ENCYCLOPÆDIA
BRITANNICA

MACROPÆDIA

The Encyclopædia Britannica
is published with the editorial advice
of the faculties of the University of Chicago;
a committee of persons holding
academic appointments at the universities
of Oxford, Cambridge, London, and Edinburgh;
a committee at the University of Toronto;
and committees drawn from members of the faculties
of the University of Tokyo
and the Australian National University.

THE UNIVERSITY OF CHICAGO

"Let knowledge grow from more to more
and thus be human life enriched."

The New
Encyclopædia
Britannica

in 30 Volumes

MACROPÆDIA
Volume 16

Knowledge in Depth

FOUNDED 1768
15TH EDITION

Encyclopædia Britannica, Inc.
William Benton, Publisher, 1943–1973
Helen Hemingway Benton, Publisher, 1973–1974
Chicago/London/Toronto/Geneva/Sydney/Tokyo/Manila/Seoul

© 1977
by Encyclopædia Britannica, Inc.
Copyright under International Copyright Union
All rights reserved under Pan American and
Universal Copyright Conventions
by Encyclopædia Britannica, Inc.

Printed in U.S.A.

Library of Congress Catalog Card Number: 75-39088
International Standard Book Number: 0-85229-315-1

No part of this work may be reproduced or utilized
in any form or by any means, electronic or mechanical,
including photocopying, recording,
or by any information storage and retrieval system,
without permission in writing from the publisher.

Rubens, Peter Paul

If the Baroque style is thought of as powerful, exuberant, sensuous, and even explosive, Peter Paul Rubens is its perfect example in painting. He was able to infuse his own astounding vitality into his religious or mythological paintings, portraits, and landscapes. Rubens was a painter of illimitable resource in invention, and he organized his complex compositions in vivid, dynamic designs. Limitations of form and contour are discounted in favour of a constant flow of movement. His voluptuous women may not be to the taste of a less vigorous age, but are related to the full and opulent forms that were the ideal of womanhood and life in general for both Rubens and the Baroque period.

By courtesy of the Kunsthistorisches Museum, Vienna

Rubens, self-portrait, oil painting, c. 1640. In the Kunsthistorisches Museum, Vienna.

One of the most prolific geniuses of painting, Rubens was a great Humanist scholar and an important diplomat, as well as an artist. Although he came to live the life of a wealthy bourgeois, his art shows strong roots in the robust life of the Flemish people. Rubens' laborious life was well ordered; the creator of so many delightful pagan mythological feasts went to mass each morning before proceeding to his studio, where he worked all day. He is one of the best examples of the well-balanced genius, who combined passion and science, ardour and reflection.

Rubens studied to emulate the works of Michelangelo, Raphael, Titian, Tintoretto, Veronese, and Correggio, as well as those of his contemporaries the Carracci and Caravaggio. All these influences were fused in his own highly personal and dramatic style. By no means all of the canvases attributed to Rubens were painted by him. He established a huge workshop employing on occasion a great number of assistants and apprentices. But the original inventive designs underlying his paintings are his own.

Although Rubens' father, Jan, was born a Roman Cath-olic, his name had appeared on a list of Calvinists as early as 1566. This accounted for the Rubens' family exile to Germany, where Peter Paul was born on June 28, 1577. Victims of the hysterical religious persecution following the decapitation in 1568 in Brussels of the freedom-seeking Counts of Egmond and Horn, the Rubens family fled the wrath of the Spanish rulers of their native Flanders. Jan Rubens became a diplomatic agent and adviser to the Protestant Princess Anna of Saxony (d. 1577), second wife of the latitudinarian Catholic William the Silent, who led the resistance to Spanish rule of the Netherlands. An unfortunate pregnancy revealed the intimate extent of the relationship between this princess of the house of Orange-Nassau and Rubens' father. She obtained clemency from her husband for Jan, but he and his family were placed under house arrest at Siegen, a Nassau stronghold in Westphalia. Here Peter Paul was born, as well as his brother Philip. The Rubens children were grounded in the classics by their exiled father, who was a doctor of both civil and canon law. Jan died in 1587, after he had been allowed to leave Siegen and go to the German city of Cologne. Rubens' mother then thought it prudent to take her four surviving children to Antwerp, where their father had been an alderman.

Early life in exile

Antwerp training. At the age of ten, Peter Paul was sent with Philip to a Latin school in Antwerp. There the future painter befriended a contemporary, Balthasar Moretus, who was to be a future patron and head of the leading Flemish publishing house, the Plantin Press. In 1590, shortage of money and the need to provide a dowry for his sister Blandina forced Rubens' mother to break off his formal education and make him a page to the Countess of Lalaing. Soon tired of courtly life, he was allowed to become a painter. He was sent first to his kinsman Tobias Verhaecht, a minor painter of Mannerist landscapes in the tradition of the more important Antwerp painter Joos de Momper. Having quickly learned the rudiments of his profession, he was apprenticed for four years to an abler master, Adam van Noort, and subsequently to Otto van Veen, one of the most distinguished of the Antwerp Romanists, a group of Flemish artists who had gone to Rome to study the art of antiquity and the Italian Renaissance. Vaenius, or Venius, as van Veen called himself, had been in Italy an active admirer of the proto-Baroque painter from Urbino, Federico Barocci, as well as of the great masters of the Florentine-Roman tradition of Renaissance art such as Michelangelo and Raphael. His culture and vision impressed Rubens, whose earliest independent works are reputed to have resembled his style.

Italian Period. In May 1600, with two years' seniority as a master in the Antwerp Guild of St. Luke, Rubens set out with Deodatus del Monte, his constant travelling companion and first pupil, for the visual and spiritual adventure of Italy. Reaching Venice in about a month, he had the good fortune to meet a gentleman in the service of Vincenzo I Gonzaga, duke of Mantua. He was offered employment in Mantua, which duchy held one of the largest and finest collections outside the Vatican of works by Italian artists. Moreover, Mantua was ideally located for sightseeing in the northern Italian provinces of Lombardy, Emilia, and the Veneto. During the eight years that Rubens was to call Vincenzo his lord, he had unmatched opportunities of fulfilling his expressed intention "to study at close quarters the works of the ancient and modern masters, and to improve himself by their example in painting." The Early Renaissance painter Andrea

Mantegna and the Mannerist architect and painter Giulio Romano were his admired predecessors in the service of the Gonzaga family. The abundant achievement in mural decoration of Giulio Romano, especially, had a lasting and highly productive effect on him.

Rubens was sent to Rome (1601–02) by the Duke to paint copies of pictures, and to live under the protection of Cardinal Montalto. There, through Flemish connections, he obtained his first public commission to paint three altarpieces for the crypt chapel of St. Helena in Sta. Croce in Gerusalemme. In Rome, the Bolognese painter Annibale Carracci and his assistants were at work in the gallery of the Palazzo Farnese. Their bold scale in drawing and working methods decidedly influenced the young Rubens. Through Annibale's example, he could apprehend the nobility and energy of design of Leonardo da Vinci, Raphael, and Michelangelo, the masters of High Renaissance painting. He assimilated Venetian colour, light and loose application of paint first through the works of Tintoretto, then through those of Veronese, long before he could penetrate the inward meaning of Titian's art. His copies, and his reworking of drawings, offer the most complete conspectus of the achievement of 16th-century Italian art in a pungently personal revision.

In 1603 he was entrusted with his first diplomatic mission, to bring Philip III and the Spanish court costly presents from Mantua. This mission gave him a first view of the royal collections in Madrid. Two paintings in the groups of copies offered to Philip's favourite, the duke of Lerma, being rainsodden beyond repair, were promptly replaced by him with a "Democritus and Heraclitus" (1603: private collection, England) of his own invention. His resource and his tact in dealing with the temperamental regular Mantuan representative to the Spanish court raised him in the Duke's estimation and helped prepare him for future diplomatic missions. His fruitful association with the banking patriciate of Genoa, of whom he was to paint many elegant portraits, began with his return voyage and his meeting with Nicolò Pallavicino, the Duke of Mantua's banker, in order to recoup the extraordinary expenses of the mission.

The only major works he executed for Mantua were the three pictures finished by Trinity Sunday 1605 for the Jesuit church of SS. Trinità ("The Baptism of Christ," Musée Royal des Beaux-Arts, Antwerp; "The Transfiguration," Musée des Beaux-Arts, Nancy, France; and "The Gonzaga Family in Adoration of the Trinity," Palazzo Ducale, Mantua). In the same year he completed the "Circumcision" for the high altar of the Jesuit church in Genoa. Only portraits of court beauties by Rubens himself were commissioned by the Duke for the Gonzaga Gallery itself, of which Rubens was curator. One of his major achievements while in this position was inducing the Duke to buy for his gallery the "Death of the Virgin" (c. 1605; Louvre, Paris), a masterpiece by Caravaggio that had been rejected for its excessive realism by the monks of Sta. Maria della Scala in Rome.

Studies in Rome   Toward the end of 1605, Rubens obtained leave from the Duke of Mantua to continue his studies in Rome. There he shared a house with his brother Philip, then librarian to Cardinal Ascanio Colonna, a member of one of Rome's most wealthy and powerful families. Daily contact with Philip, a brilliant student of the famed Flemish Humanist and Classical scholar Justus Lipsius (1547–1606), added zest to his personal discovery of the antique world. They combined their interest in the antique by collaborating to produce the book *Electorum Libri II*, published in Antwerp in 1608 by the Plantin Press. Dealing with Roman social life and customs, Philip wrote the text, and Peter Paul prepared drawings for the execution of the engraved illustrations.

During the two years he spent in Rome, Rubens was left largely undisturbed by the Duke of Mantua. In the summer of 1607, however, he was asked to accompany the Gonzaga court to the Italian seaside resort of San Pier d'Arena, where he continued to paint with splendour portraits of the Genoese aristocracy. Chronic arrears in payment of his salary, and an ambition to establish him-

self as an international, rather than just a Mantuan artist, motivated him to accept other patronage. He received the backing of the wealthy Genoese banker to the papacy, Monsignor Jacopo Serra, who was instrumental in obtaining for him the coveted commission for the painting over the high altar of the Roman church of S. Maria in Vallicella (popularly known as the Chiesa Nuova, the New Church). He concurrently painted the altarpiece of the "Adoration of the Shepherds" for another church of the Oratorian Order in Fermo. In October of 1608, his brother summoned him to their mother's deathbed in Antwerp. She died before he could reach her.

Return to Antwerp.   Soon after his mother's death Rubens was "bound with golden fetters" to the service of the Spanish Habsburg regents of Flanders. Although he was never to return to Italy, he kept up his Italian contacts. He supplied, for example, cartoons or model drawings for tapestry to Genoese patrons as late as the 1620s. He always remained an Italophile. Fluent in six languages, Italian was his favourite for correspondence. The house that he built for himself, the pride of Antwerp, was filled with paintings, statuary, cameos, coins, and jewels from Renaissance and ancient Roman Italy. He built a private pantheon to house his antiquities. His enthusiasm for Italian architecture is best expressed in his publication the *Palazzi di Genova*. Printed in Antwerp in 1622, this book of engravings illustrates the great Renaissance palaces of Genoa. He practiced the spirit of the book's preface, which extols Italian design, in the magnificent new church of the Antwerp Jesuits, St. Charles Borromeo, where he was the chief designer, along with the Flemish architect Pieter Huyssens (1577–1637), of the facade, tower, and all architectural detail. Rubens was also the master decorator, and provided oil sketches as designs for the ceiling paintings on which he was to be assisted by Anthony Van Dyck (1599–1641) and others.

Settling permanently in Flanders, he married in October 1609, Isabella, daughter of Jan Brandt, a leading Antwerp Humanist and lawyer. He became not only the court portraitist but a major religious painter. His Baroque altarpieces of the "Erection of the Cross" for St. Walburga's in Antwerp; "Descent from the Cross" for Antwerp Cathedral; and "The Miracle of St. Bavon" for the Cathedral of St. Bavon in the neighbouring city of Ghent, established Rubens as the leading painter of Flanders and one of the most important in Europe. Because of his prestige, he was allowed to live in Antwerp, rather than in Brussels, where the Flemish court was based. He was also exempt from the regulations of the Antwerp painters' guild and thus was free to engage pupils or collaborators without having them enrolled in this organization. By 1611 he wrote that he had to refuse more than 100 applicants who wished to become his pupils.

Rubens' studio

Rubens' international reputation spread not only because of the large number of works produced in his studio but because he reproduced so many of his paintings in prints, which served further to advertise his art. Many of the large-scale pictures that prolifically issued from his studio were largely painted by his students and assistants, although generally certain areas were by the hand of the master, even if it was only a retouching of the work. During the period of 1606–07 he used small wood panels prepared with gesso, a priming substance made of plaster of paris and glue, to present models to clients or to instruct engravers, sculptors, tapestry weavers, and painting assistants. These marvellous exercises in the painter's craft are often only inches high and executed in colour or in tones of grey, brown, and white. Rubens also evolved his compositions according to the Renaissance practice of doing preparatory drawings in chalk, charcoal, or pen and ink.

Diplomatic career.   In the period between 1621 and 1630, Rubens was increasingly used as a diplomat by the Spanish Habsburg rulers. His contact with the leading political and intellectual personalities of Europe, as well as his gracious manner, made him the ideal political agent. Furthermore, as a painter, he could often act as a covert diplomat or observer.

His first important diplomatic functions were in connection with the attempt of Spain and the Spanish Nether-lands to renegotiate the Twelve Years' Truce (1609–21) between the Habsburg-controlled area of Flanders and the independent Dutch Republic to the north. The regent of Flanders, the Archduke Albert, a Habsburg of the Austrian line, died in 1621, leaving the renewal of the truce to his widow, the infanta Isabella, the daughter of the Habsburg ruler of Spain, Philip II. Rubens became her adviser and tried unsuccessfully to intercede with the Dutch. The French ambassador wrote in 1624 from the Flemish capital of Brussels:

> Rubens is here to paint the likeness of the prince of Poland, by order of the infanta (Archduchess Isabella). I am persuaded he will succeed better in this than in his negotiations for the truce.

War again broke out in the Netherlands between the predominantly Protestant Dutch and the Catholic Flemish, and continued for the rest of Rubens' life.

Marie de Médicis series

Early in 1622 Rubens was summoned to Paris by Marie de Médicis, the widow of Henry IV and mother of the reigning king of France, Louis XIII. This Florentine princess, whose wedding by proxy Rubens had attended in Florence in 1600, commissioned him to paint two series of paintings for two long galleries in her newly constructed Luxembourg Palace. One cycle of 21 pictures representing episodes from Marie's life now hang in the Louvre, while the other proposed series of pictures, dealing with the life of Henry IV, was never completed. After six weeks of discussion and arrangements, Rubens returned to Antwerp, where he worked for two years on his most artistically important secular commission.

When Rubens returned to Paris in 1625 to install the Medici pictures, the political atmosphere at court had changed. Formerly friendly to Spain and the Spanish Netherlands, France had signed before 1624 treaties with the Dutch, the Danes, and the English, all hostile to the Habsburgs. This new French alliance was due to the influence of Cardinal Richelieu, the powerful adviser to young Louis XIII. Not without reason, the Cardinal suspected that Rubens was more spy and agent than artist during his second Paris visit. Further suspicions were aroused when Rubens was seen frequenting the company of the Duke of Buckingham, the favourite of Charles I of England, who was in Paris for the marriage by proxy of his master and the youngest daughter of Marie de Médicis and Henry IV, the princess Henrietta-Maria. The Duke was an avid art collector. His head was drawn by Rubens in Paris. He ordered from him an equestrian portrait (1625; formerly Osterley Park, near London); and he bought the painter's famous collection of antiquities, with some paintings. This is often considered more a diplomatic gesture on Rubens' part to stay in Buckingham's graces than an economic necessity. During their acquaintance in France, Rubens tried to persuade the Duke that England should enter into an alliance with the Spanish Netherlands and cease supporting the Dutch. Since Buckingham was currently engaged in promoting a war between England and Spain, he was uncommittal; but through his Flemish-born servant, agent, and painter, Sir Balthasar Gerbier, a hopeful secret correspondence was maintained by Rubens until the Duke's assassination in 1628. The English-Spanish war proved economically disastrous for Flanders, since its sea and land trade was cut off by its neighbours—France, the Dutch Republic, and the Palatinate of the Rhineland, who were allied with England. Rubens described Antwerp as "languishing like a consumptive body, declining little by little."

Spanish-English peace treaty

The death of Buckingham reopened the way for Rubens to attempt the negotiation of a peace treaty on behalf of the sorely tried Spanish Netherlands. Unfortunately, the minister of Spain, the count of Olivares, persuaded his master, Philip IV, to make a close pact with France to reconquer England for Catholicism. In 1628 Rubens travelled in secret haste to Madrid to plead for peace, rather than another war between Spain and England. The Papal Nuncio reported of his arrival:

> It is considered certain that Rubens, the Flemish painter, is the bearer of a negotiation, for we hear that he often confers in secret with the *conde-duque* (Count of Olivares), and in a manner very different from that which his profession permits. Since he is said to be a great friend of Buckingham, it is believed that he comes with some peace treaty between the two crowns. Others think his main object is the truce of Flanders, and that he had received this commission as one who enjoys the confidence of all that country.

During nine months in Madrid, besides pleading for a peace treaty rather than war with England, Rubens painted royal portraits. He again studied Titian's masterpieces and revisited the extensive art collection in the royal monastery of the Escorial with the gifted young Spanish painter Diego Velázquez. He eventually was deemed a suitable envoy by Philip IV and was named Secretary of the Privy Council of the Spanish Netherlands to give him sufficient status for a special peace mission to England. Rubens hastened across France, again avoiding the hostile Cardinal Richelieu, to report to the archduchess Isabella. News awaiting his arrival in Brussels made his mission even more urgent and difficult: on April 24, 1629, England had signed a treaty with France.

Charles I waived the formalities of exchanging ambassadors and sent for Rubens directly, indicating that he was most eager to meet a man with such an international reputation for intellect and artistic genius. He was not disappointed, and it is to Rubens personally that the peace treaty of 1630 between England and Spain largely can be attributed. He was knighted and given an honorary degree by Cambridge University. "Peace and War" (*c.* 1630; National Gallery, London) is Rubens' painted proclamation of success. He discussed painting with Charles I, a great connoisseur of the arts and the only prince to whom Rubens ever vouchsafed a self-portrait (*c.* 1625; Windsor Castle). The king commissioned him to decorate the ceiling of the royal Banqueting House (1619–22) designed by the court architect Inigo Jones as a part of the Whitehall Palace complex of buildings in London. Finished in 1634, the nine huge panels allegorize the reign of James I, the father of Charles I. Rubens was struck by the beauty and peacefulness of the English countryside. The "Landscape with St. George" (1630; Buckingham Palace) incorporated his view of the River Thames from his lodgings as a background to King Charles and Queen Henrietta envisaged in masquerade as the patron saint of England and the princess he reputedly rescued from a dragon.

Banqueting House at Whitehall

Late years in Flanders. On his return to Flanders in 1630, Rubens was rewarded by the Archduchess with exemption from further missions. "This favour I obtained with more difficulty than any other she ever granted me," he was to write. "Now, for three years I have found peace of mind, having given up every sort of employment outside my beloved profession." The peace Rubens had worked for nearly ten years to achieve, however, did not last, and for most of the next 20 years Europe continued to be embroiled in the Thirty Years' War. In a letter written two years before his death, Rubens explains the figures in his allegorical painting "The Horrors of War" (1637–38; Pitti Palace, Florence), which he sold to the Medici in Florence:

> that grief-stricken woman clothed in black, with torn veil, robbed of all her jewels and other ornaments, is the unfortunate Europe, who, for so many years now, has suffered plunder, outrage, and misery.

Having been a widower for four years, he married in December of 1630 the 16-year-old Hélèna Fourment, whose charms recur frequently among his later figure subjects. He bought the château (Het Steen) of Elewijt, in 1635. In his last years, he spent much time there depicting the rural life and scenery outside of Antwerp such as in "The Kermesse" (*c.* 1636–38; Louvre, Paris). His long-established interest in landscape painting, early expressed in drawings of his Roman period, reached its grandest and most emotionally romantic expression in such late works as "Landscape with a Rainbow" (*c.* 1636; Wallace Collection, London) or "Château de Steen" (*c.* 1635–37; National Gallery, London). Another long-established interest that he revived at this time was the planning of civic stagings and decorations designed to welcome a dignitary, in this case the Infante Ferdinand, who in 1635 succeeded his aunt, the Archduchess Isabella, as regent of Flanders. Thirty-seven years before, Rubens had assisted Vaenius in converting the city of Antwerp into a theatre of celebration to welcome the Archduchess Isabella as ruler of the Spanish Netherlands. Rubens' major commission during these last years, however, was to provide for the Infante's brother, King Philip IV of Spain, models for about 120 scenes from the writings of the Roman poet Ovid and other classical authors to decorate the Torre de la Parada, the royal hunting lodge near Madrid.

Rubens died at Antwerp on May 30, 1640, when gout, which had for months troubled his painting arm, reached his heart.

Achievement. Rubens is one of the most methodically assimilative, most prodigiously and variously productive of Western artists. Schooled in the confusing stylistic traditions of Mannerism in Antwerp, he educated himself to be heir of the full range of Renaissance art both north and south of the Alps. His abundant energy fired him to study and emulate the masters both of antiquity and of the 16th century in Rome, Venice, and Parma. His warmth of nature made him responsive to the artistic revolutions being worked by living artists: to the plein air study of nature and times of day in the Roman campagna by the German landscape painter Adam Elsheimer; to the colour combinations and delicate appreciation of warm and cool tones vibrant on flesh of the proto-Baroque Italian artist Federico Barocci; to the emotive exploitation of strong Tenebrism by Caravaggio; and, most profoundly and lastingly, to Annibale Carracci's impassioned yet strenuously disciplined approach to the practice of figure composition.

Robust powers of comprehension nourished his limitless resource in invention. The larger the scale of the undertaking the more congenial it was to his spirit. The success of his public performance as master of the greatest studio organization in Europe since Raphael's in Rome has obscured for many the personal intensity of his vision as evinced in such works as his oil sketch for "All Saints" (Museum Boymans-van Beuningen, Rotterdam) and in his deeply felt study for the head of St. John in the Antwerp Cathedral "Descent from the Cross," as well as in portraits of his family and friends and in his treatment of the mood and grandeur of landscape. Not only Sir Anthony Van Dyck, Jacob Jordaens, and his immediate following in Flanders but artists at almost every period have responded to the force of his genius. The architect and sculptor Gian Lorenzo Bernini, the other seminal mind of the early Baroque, developed in his Roman altarpieces figurative ideas and the dramatic handling of light parallel to Rubens' work. And in the fulfillment of the Italian Baroque, the painters Domenico Fetti (c. 1588/9–1623), Giovanni Castiglione (c. 1600?–65?), and Bernardo Strozzi (1581–1644) are in individual ways Rubensians. Antoine Watteau (1684–1721), Jean-Honoré Fragonard (1732–1806), Eugène Delacroix (1798–1863), and Pierre-Auguste Renoir (1841–1919) are only the four most distinguished in the long succession of French painters who were attracted after the late 17th century to some aspects of his art. Sir Joshua Reynolds (1723–92), Thomas Gainsborough (1727–88), and John Constable (1776–1837) are outstanding among his English admirers. He is a central figure to Western art history.

His own deepest love as a painter, consummated by his second visit to Spain, was for the poetry, the control of glowing colour, and the sheer mastery in handling of oil paint that excelled in the art of Titian. In these qualities Rubens himself became supreme, whether with the brilliant play of fine brushes over the white reflecting surface of a small panel, or with masterful gestures often more than six feet long, sweeping a richly loaded brush across some huge canvas.

MAJOR WORKS

PORTRAITS: "Rubens and His Friends at Mantua" (c. 1602; Wallraf-Richartz Museum, Cologne); "Duke of Lerma" (1603; Museo del Prado, Madrid); "Rubens with His First Wife, Isabella Brant, Amidst Honeysuckle" (c. 1609; Alte Pinakothek, Munich); "Le Chapeau de Paille" (c. 1620; National Gallery, London); "Thomas Howard, Earl of Arundel, with His Wife Alathea Talbot" (c. 1620; Alte Pinakothek, Munich); "Marie de Médicis" (c. 1622–25; Museo del Prado, Madrid); "Vladislav Sigismund IV, King of Poland" (1624; Metropolitan Museum of Art, New York); "Philip II of Spain" (c. 1628–29; Museo del Prado, Madrid); "Hélèna Fourment with Fur Cloak" (c. 1638–40; Kunsthistorisches Museum, Vienna); "Self-Portrait" (c. 1639; Kunsthistorisches Museum, Vienna).

GENRE AND LANDSCAPE PAINTINGS: "The Garden of Love" (1632–34; Museo del Prado, and Waddesdon, Buckinghamshire, England); "The Kermesse" (c. 1636–38; Louvre, Paris).

MYTHOLOGICAL AND HISTORICAL PAINTINGS: "The Toilet of Venus" (c. 1613–15; Collection of the Prince of Liechtenstein); "The Rape of the Sabines" (1635; National Gallery, London); "Venus and Adonis" (c. 1635; Metropolitan Museum of Art, New York); "The Three Graces" (c. 1638–40; Museo del Prado, Madrid); "The Judgment of Paris" (1638–39; Museo del Prado, Madrid).

PICTURE CYCLES AND DECORATIONS: "Médicis Cycle" (c. 1622; Louvre, Paris); Whitehall ceiling (c. 1634; London).

RELIGIOUS SUBJECTS: "Circumcision" (1605; S. Ambrogio, Genoa); "Adoration of the Magi" (1609; Museo del Prado, Madrid); "Deposition Triptych" (1612–14; Cathedral, Antwerp); "The Rockox Altarpiece" (1613–15; Musée Royal des Beaux-Arts, Antwerp); "The Holy Family" (c. 1615; Wallace collection, London); "The Last Judgment" (c. 1616; Alte Pinakothek, Munich); "Judith with the Head of Holofernes" (1616–18; Herzog-Anton-Ulrich-Museum, Braunschweig, Germany); "Lot Fleeing from Sodom" (1625; Louvre, Paris); "The Ildefonso Altarpiece" (1630–32; Kunsthistorisches Museum, Vienna); "Bathsheba Receiving David's Letter" (c. 1635; Gemäldegalerie, Dresden); "The Brazen Serpent" (c. 1638; National Gallery, London); "The Massacre of the Innocents" (c. 1635–39; Alte Pinakothek, Munich); "Christ on the Cross" (1635–40; Musée des Augustins, Toulouse, France).

BIBLIOGRAPHY. C.V. WEDGWOOD, *The World of Rubens, 1577–1640* (1967); and MICHAEL JAFFÉ, "Rubens," *World Encyclopedia of Art*, vol. 12, col. 590–606 (1966), are the best modern biographies. The latter contains the most useful modern bibliography, including the early Italian, Latin, German, and French sources. For illustrations and discussion of the works, the following remain the most worthwhile: R. OLDENBOURG, *Peter Paul Rubens* (1922), in German; J.S. HELD, *Rubens: Selected Drawings*, 2 vol. (1959); F. VAN DEN WIJNGAERT, *Inventaris der Rubeniaansche Prentkunst* (1940); and the exhibition catalog, E. HAVERKAMP-BEGEMANN (ed.), *Olieverfschetsen van Rubens* (1953). They supplement M. ROOSES, *L'oeuvre de P.P. Rubens*, 5 vol. (1886–92). Rubens' letters were edited by R.S. MAGURN, *Letters of Peter Paul Rubens* (1955); and his diplomacy was the subject of an exhibition catalog by F. BAUDOUIN, *Rubens diplomate* (1962).

(Ml.J.)

Rugby

Rugby is a football game played with an oval ball by two teams of 15 or 13 players each, its distinctive features being: (1) players may use their hands and catch, throw, or run with the ball (a practice introduced at Rugby School in the 1820s) in addition to manoeuvring it with their feet as in association football (soccer); and (2) the scrum, or scrummage (from "scrimmage," tussle, confused struggle), a method of putting the ball in play from a set formation in which eight men on each team—six in a 13-per-side game—form a closely packed group behind two front rows of three men each, the ball being thrown onto the ground between them and each team trying to get possession. Although the ball may be kicked or carried or passed from player to player by hand or foot, it may not be passed forward. Permitting players to run with the ball inevitably made tackling a part of the game. A tackle occurs when a player carrying the ball is sent to the ground or is held by one or more opponents so that he is unable to free himself without delay and cannot play the ball.

There are two principal types of rugby football: Rugby Union, which is the amateur game; and Rugby League, a mainly professional game; the chief differences between the two are described under *Rugby League*, below. For the background, origins, and history of these games see the article FOOTBALL, AMERICAN AND CANADIAN: *Early History*. See also ASSOCIATION FOOTBALL (SOCCER).

RUGBY UNION

History. The formation of the Rugby Football Union, the governing body of the sport in England, on Jan. 26, 1871, was closely followed by the first match between England and Scotland, at Edinburgh on March 27 of the same year, Scotland winning in front of a crowd of 4,000 spectators. At that stage there was no official central authority for the game in Scotland, but the Scottish Football Union—which changed its name to Scottish Rugby Union in 1924—was formed in 1873. The game had grown in Scotland, as in England, through the schools and especially through the numerous public schools grouped in and around Edinburgh. In Ireland too it was in academic circles that the first organized Rugby took place. A club was formed at Trinity College, Dublin, in 1865; and others soon followed as students continued to play in their home towns, both during vacations and after they had finished their university careers. The visit in 1873 of the Dingle Football Club of Liverpool to play Trinity in College Park, Dublin, prompted the formation in 1874 of the Irish Football Union. This body, however, did not embrace the whole of Ireland; and after a match in Belfast between North of Ireland Football Club and Wanderers (from Dublin), a North of Ireland Football Union was set up, also in 1874, as a rival authority. The two unions amalgamated in 1879 to form the Irish Rugby Football Union. With the formation of the Welsh Rugby Union in 1881, Rugby was established in all four divisions of the British Isles.

By this time the game had already been started in distant countries of the British Empire, sometimes through the influence of the army, sometimes by men who had travelled from Britain to the colonies, sometimes by students from different corners of the Empire who attended English educational establishments. Thus the Southern Rugby Football Union, ancestor of the Australian Rugby Football Union, was founded as early as 1875. That same year is generally accepted by the game's historians as the year in which Rugby was first played in southern Africa, at Cape Town. In 1882 a club was formed at the University of Stellenbosch, and the return of students to their homes soon led to the establishment of Rugby clubs in other areas.

The presence of British regiments led to formation of a club in King William's Town in 1878; the discovery of diamonds helped to establish the game in the Kimberley area between 1883 and 1886; and the gold rush encouraged its spread in the region of Johannesburg and Pretoria by 1888. The first provincial union was that of Western Province formed in 1883, and the South African Rugby Football Board was founded at Kimberley in 1889. Meanwhile C.J. Monro, son of the Speaker of the New Zealand House of Representatives, had returned home from England to Nelson, in the South Island of New Zealand, fired with enthusiasm for the game of Rugby, which he had got to know while at Christ's College in London, and in 1870 had organized the first Rugby match ever played in New Zealand—Nelson Football Club versus Nelson College. Monro then went to Wellington, in the North Island, and organized a game between his Nelson players and a collection of players from Wellington. A Wellington club was officially formed in 1871, and by 1890 there were approximately 700 clubs playing Rugby throughout New Zealand. These were soon organized in various unions, the first being the Canterbury Rugby Union in 1879, and the New Zealand Rugby Football Union was founded as the country's central authority in 1892. Thus was the game established in those countries that were destined to become its most formidable exponents.

Rugby soon also found its way from the British Isles into France. British businessmen, especially those engaged in the wine trade, took the game to such Channel ports as Le Havre, Nantes, and Bordeaux; and students, embassy and consular officials, and others introduced it to Paris. It has been written that British residents were playing Rugby in Paris by 1877, and certainly Rosslyn Park, the London club, played (and beat) Stade Français in Paris in 1893. In the early days the Union des Sociétés Françaises de Sports Athlétiques (USFSA), a multisports organization founded in 1887, looked after the interests of French Rugby players and set up competitions for them. In 1919 the Rugby club broke away from the USFSA and formed the Fédération Française de Rugby (FFR), to which 173 clubs affiliated. It was largely through the influence of France that the game took root in Romania. The contact was made by Romanian students who discovered the game at the university in Paris and then went home and formed clubs of their own. Romanian clubs became affiliated to a multisports organization in 1912, and the Federatia Romana de Rugby was founded in 1931. Other continental European countries took up the game, but none to the extent of France and Romania.

Before the end of the 19th century, Rugby was played in many lands outside the European area, besides New Zealand, South Africa, and Australia. Immigrants from the British Isles had established the game in Ontario by 1882; it reached Argentina in the 1880s, thanks largely to British residents in Buenos Aires and to engineers involved in constructing railways, and the Argentine Rugby Union was founded in 1899; the local police are believed to have played Rugby as early as 1880 in Fiji, and the Fiji Rugby Union dates from 1913; the game was introduced into Japan in 1899 by Ginnosuke Tanaka, who had discovered it at Cambridge University.

Although Rugby was being played in all these countries and many others by the early years of the 20th century, it remained predominantly a game of the British Empire and Commonwealth. This was reflected in the membership of the International Board (International Rugby Football Board, established 1886), which for many years was confined to the four home countries, 6 of its 12 members being English, 2 Scottish, 2 Irish, and 2 Welsh. This proportion was maintained until 1911, when England's representation was reduced from six to four. In 1948 New Zealand, South Africa, and Australia were admitted, with one member each, and England's representation was reduced from four to two to conform with the other home countries. In 1958 all seven member countries were allowed two representatives each.

At the instigation of Germany, some of the other Rugby countries held a meeting in 1933, and in January 1934 the Fédération Internationale de Rugby Amateur (FIRA) came into being. Represented at the inaugural meeting were Germany, France, The Netherlands, Italy, Portugal, Romania, Sweden, Czechoslovakia, and Catalonia. Membership has expanded since then but has not extended beyond Europe and the Mediterranean coast. The FIRA constitution requires that every match within its organization be played in accordance with International Board laws. In the 1970–71 European season, the centenary of the Rugby Football Union, the representatives of 50 countries throughout the world attended the Centenary Congress at Cambridge. At that time, England was able to report a membership of 1,600 clubs with more than 100,000 regular players. And, to give some examples from less prominent Rugby countries, Japan reported 60,000 players, Fiji 12,000, and Romania 6,500.

The progress of Rugby inside the various countries has been steady rather than spectacular. An exception to this norm occurred in France between 1960 and 1970, when the number of French clubs almost doubled—from 646 to 1,160—and the number of French players increased from 39,000 to 75,000. These increases were attributed largely to television. France was also involved in one of the two famous "splits" in the history of the game. Allegations of professionalism in the French club championship led to the breaking off of relations between the U.K. and France, from 1931 to 1939, but the Second World War prevented the resumption of fixtures until 1947. The other split directly concerned England alone, although its effects were felt throughout the Rugby world. This occurred in 1895, when 22 clubs in the North of England resigned from the RFU because they wanted payment to their players for "broken time"—*i.e.*, for loss of wages due to playing the game. The RFU would not agree to such payment, and the 22 clubs promptly set up the Northern Union, which evolved into the Rugby League game (see below *Rugby League*).

Formation of the Rugby unions

Spread to European and other countries

International organizations

Disputes over professionalism

On the other hand, the partition of Ireland in 1922 did not lead to the cancellation of any international Rugby matches; and Dublin, Belfast, Limerick, and Cork all regularly contribute players to Ireland's team for the home unions' championship.

Development of the game.   From the general free-for-all, with hacking (kicking in the shins) and tripping that existed in the early days, the game was gradually refined until it reached its present shape. When the first match between England and Scotland was played in 1871, there were 20 men on each team, and it was not agreed to reduce the number to 15 until 1877. Scotland won the 1871 game, scoring the only goal of the match. Scotland and England each achieved a try, but it was not possible to win a match in any other way than by scoring goals. A try, touching the ball down in the goal area behind the opponents' goal line, scored no points but allowed the player's team an unimpeded place kick at goal from a point on the field not further from the touchline than the try had been scored. In 1875–76 it was agreed that if the number of goals (field goals) kicked by each side was the same or if no goal was kicked, the result would be decided by the number of tries achieved. Thus was the try (in U.S. and Canadian football, a touchdown), the scoring of which was to become the chief aim of the game, for the first time brought into the reckoning. A further refinement was introduced during the 1886–87 season with the adoption of the Cheltenham College rating, which had been in force at that college for some 20 years, making three tries equal to one goal. Then in 1905 the modern scoring values were introduced, a try being worth three points, its subsequent conversion into a goal providing an additional two points. Dropped goals, at that stage worth four points, in the 1947–48 season were devalued to three. A dropped goal is scored by a dropkick from the field—*i.e.*, when a player, in play, lets the ball fall from his hands and kicks it at the first rebound as it rises so that it goes between the goal posts and above the crossbar. Three points may also be scored by a successful free kick or by penalty kick at goal awarded for an infringement of the laws by the opposition. A free kick (a place kick or dropkick at goal or a punt not at goal but to gain a territorial advantage) may be taken by a player catching while stationary a ball kicked or otherwise propelled by an opponent if he simultaneously calls "mark"; the kick is taken from behind the mark. A penalty kick is taken from a mark at the spot of the infringement.

The try in Rugby is the same as the touchdown in U.S. and Canadian football; while in Rugby a "touchdown" is the grounding of the ball behind his own goal line by a defending player, in the U.S.-Canadian game this is called a "touchback."

The two basic set pieces or formations of the game are the scrum and the line-out. A scrum is formed by the eight forwards of each side bending forward, binding one another with their arms, and pushing against the opposing eight forwards similarly bound in three ranks or rows. The ball is put into the tunnel between the two front rows, whose members use their feet to try to procure the ball for their team.

A line-out is the method of bringing the ball back into play after it has gone out over the touchline (out-of-bounds). To form a line-out, at least two forwards of each team line up in single files in a line perpendicular to the spot where the ball crossed the touchline. A gap or space is left between the two lines of players, and the ball is thrown in above this gap so that the forwards of both teams may try to grab it or otherwise obtain possession of it for their team.

While the forwards are forming a scrum or a line-out, the other players, normally divided into two halfbacks, four three-quarters (the left- and right-centre backs and left- and right-wing backs), and a fullback, take up position several yards apart in various formations between their forwards and their own goal line. For a line-out the three-quarters stay at least ten yards back, the idea being that by passing or running or kicking the ball in the open field they may find a way either of scoring a try or of dropping a goal.

Besides the scrum and the line-out there is also the loose maul or ruck. This occurs when, in the open field, the progress of the ball is temporarily checked—by a player dropping it, falling over while carrying it, or being held by an opponent while in possession of it, for instance—and two or more players gather round and struggle to procure the ball for their team. The maul or ruck is an especially profitable source of possession because the opposing defense is unlikely to be as strictly aligned as it is for a scrum or a line-out.

The game settled into the pattern of big forwards struggling for the ball so that their faster and more agile backs could pass it and run with it in the hope of scoring goals. But as players increased in pace through improved fitness, without a corresponding increase in the size of the field, the open spaces became fewer, defenses became more effective, and attacking moves were all too easily stifled.

Scrums and line-outs (margin)

Tries and goals (margin)

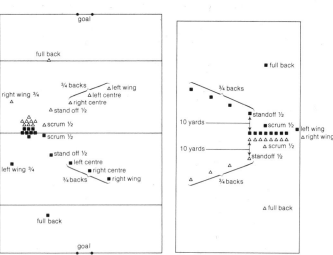

(Left) Players in position for a scrummage. (Right) Positions of players for a line-out.

Rugby playing field, showing divisions and goals.

Play began to stagnate and to become dull, both for the player and for the spectator. In order to reverse this trend and to encourage the return of flowing movement to the game, the International Board made several important changes in the laws in 1964. It was ruled that while a line-out (putting the ball back in play after it had gone out-of-bounds) was taking place, each set of three-quarters must remain at least ten yards nearer their own goal line than the point of the line-out, thus leaving a clear no-man's-land in which attacks could be developed; that backs must not advance beyond the hindmost foot of scrums until the ball was out; that forwards must not advance from a scrum until the ball was out; and that the team throwing in the ball at a line-out had the right to determine the shortness of the line-out, thus preventing opponents from straggling across the field in a defensive screen. Another change, in 1970, made it illegal for a player to kick the ball directly over the touchline or sideline except from within 25 yards of his own goal line. Thus the player retained the right to kick his way out of a desperate defensive situation but was dissuaded from seeking the safety of kicking out-of-bounds from positions in which he could attack through running and passing.

Styles of play. When it was customary to have 20 players a side, they were arranged in the formation of 13 forwards, 3 halfbacks, 1 three-quarter, and 3 fullbacks. With the reduction of a team to 15 men in 1877, the normal formation became eight forwards, two halfbacks, two three-quarters, and three fullbacks. Scotland used the innovation of three three-quarters in 1881 and was followed in this by England and Wales in 1882 and by Ireland in 1883. Wales used four three-quarters in the 1885–86 season; England, Ireland, and Scotland adopted this formation in 1893–94. At that time, the two halfbacks both played close to the scrum, and when the ball came out it was taken by whichever of them seemed the better placed to use it. The fixed positions of scrum half and standoff half were introduced in the early years of the 20th century.

Forma-
tions

Overseas the game developed slightly differently, especially in New Zealand, where they had a scrum with only two men in the front row instead of the normal three, but the International Board outlawed this formation in 1932. New Zealand also considered the first three men to handle the ball behind the scrum as a halfback and two five-eighths, whereas in the British Isles the first two were known as halfbacks. Australia kept the British conception of two halfbacks but emphasized that one of the centres would always be considered the inside centre and would always position himself next to the standoff half. Thus the Australians looked upon their centres as one inside centre and one outside centre, whereas in the British Isles the centres played left and right rather than inside and outside.

National
styles

Quite apart from their formations, different countries developed different styles of play, partly because of the differences in climate. In Scotland, where the grounds tended to be wet and muddy, the ball was more often kicked or dribbled along the ground than in other countries. While their opponents on wet days dropped the ball or slipped in trying to pass or to change direction while running with the ball, Scotland's men would put the ball on the ground and drive it up the field with their boots. Scotland's teams, of course, have tried more sophisticated methods as the game has developed over the years, but they are still best known for their hard forward play. Irish teams, too, have made a reputation for uncompromising forward play. The Welsh, on the other hand, have complemented their tough forward game with clever, elusive play at halfback. It has been their misfortune that their grounds and their weather have often been too wet for full profit to be drawn by their talented halfbacks. England, from the early days, established itself as the country of the orthodox in Rugby and has generally relied on teamwork and cooperation within well-balanced teams. New Zealand, as was to be expected from a community largely devoted to farming, developed big, strong, capable forwards. Its teams have sometimes used these tough forwards as the mainspring of their attack, and at other periods they have trusted in the hard running of their backs to make full use of the clean and regular possession provided by the forwards. When the New Zealanders visited the British Isles in 1905–06, the brilliance of their open play was much appreciated; and they won much acclaim with the same kind of attractive football when, as the New Zealand Army team, they toured Britain immediately after World War II. But for a period after that they neglected back play and sought to win matches through tight forward play and kicking. In the 1950s and 1960s they had a good deal of success with these methods and with what became known as "second-phase Rugby," in which, instead of attacking directly as soon as the ball had been obtained, they deliberately sought, by running into a tackle or by accurate kicking, to create loose play. The theory behind this style was that an attack direct from a set piece (a scrum or a line-out) was unlikely to succeed because the defense would be lined up in a set position; but if the defense could be drawn out of position by an initial thrust, which might well cause at least one defender to be pinned on the ground, then the attack had a greater chance of bearing fruit. This style of play was widely copied, but the New Zealanders then surprised everyone by reverting to all-out, flowing, open football on a tour of the British Isles in 1967, during which they remained unbeaten in 15 games. While New Zealand has led the world in these ways, South Africa has pioneered the techniques of scrummaging. While other countries settled for a scrummage formation of three men in the front row, two in the second, and three in the back row, the South Africans discovered that more efficient scrummaging could be obtained with three in the front row, four in the second, and one in the back. Their mastery of this formation was largely responsible for making them the outstanding Rugby country of the 1930s. At times, the South Africans, like the New Zealanders, have concentrated on forward play to the detriment of back play, but the solid work of their scrum pack over the years has been an eminently reliable basis from which to proceed. The game in Australia has remained almost invariably spectacular and entertaining to watch. The ball has been thrown about, and running and passing have been carried out at high speed. The hard grounds and dry climate of the country have undoubtedly contributed to Australia's emphasis on open Rugby rather than on hard forward play. Another important reason why Australian teams have played in this style over the years has been the strength of the professional Rugby League game in and around Sydney and Brisbane. In Australia, Rugby Union, an amateur game, is the poor relation of Rugby League, and it is felt that Rugby Union players must play attractive football to win and hold public support. Like the Australians, the French have become famous for their open attacking Rugby. Here again the influence of the climate has been considerable, for the game is largely confined to the southern half of the country where sunshine and dry grounds are the rule. But it was not until shortly before World War I that the French adopted the fluid style for which they were to become so admired in later years. A vital influence in the adoption of this method was exerted on the French by a Welshman, Owen Roe, who settled in the town of Bayonne and taught the local club team the intricacies of back play as he had learned them at Penarth in south Wales. In 1913 Roe's Bayonne team not only inflicted a first ever championship home defeat on the great Bordeaux club but also took their brilliant three-quarter play up to Paris and there won the final of the French club championship by 33 points to 8. Such a score immediately attracted attention, and Bayonne's style was soon copied by teams in other parts of the country. In the 1950s, France gave the Rugby world a lesson in the art of getting a scrum half and loose forwards to attack in intimate combinations close to their pack; and in 1958, in particular, they had great success with peeling, or churning, moves from the back of the line-out. The ball would be tapped down from the line-out, and other forwards, often spearheaded by Lucien Mias, would go hurtling towards their opponents' goal line. This method sometimes led directly to tries, and sometimes tries were scored from a subsequent quick ruck or scramble for the ball, rather than in the manner of the New Zealanders' second-phase attack. The most uninhibited and improvised of all Rugby played at an international level has been that of the Fiji, who drew a crowd of 42,-000 to one of their matches when they visited Australia in 1952. Their play has been the very antithesis of the

Second-
phase
Rugby

The open
styles of
Australia
and
France

orthodoxy of England. They have simply run and passed the ball at every possible opportunity, making the job of planning a defense against them an extremely difficult task.

Competition.   In most Rugby countries a need for competitions was felt at club level early in the game's development, but the club game in England, Scotland, and Wales remained largely based on friendly matches. England has had county cup competitions, confined to the clubs within individual county areas, for many years; but these were knock-out competitions rather than leagues, and it was not until the 1970s that a national club competition was set up. A national competition for county, as opposed to club, teams was started as early as 1889, however, and there was also a national competition for university teams. The club game in Scotland had its first official national competition in the 1970s, and the Scots also have a competitive interdistrict championship. Wales similarly developed a national club competition in the 1970s and also has a county championship. Ireland early developed a comprehensive pattern of league and cup competitions for clubs, although the competitions are based on the provinces rather than on the country as a whole, and many friendly matches are also played. Ireland also has a thriving interprovincial championship.

Outside the British Isles, club Rugby was almost universally based on the league system, often with cup competition as well. In New Zealand, for instance, competitive leagues were set up almost as soon as there were sufficient clubs to make this feasible, and New Zealand club Rugby has remained highly competitive with interclub leagues for 15 separate grades of players, from the 15th grade with its little boys to the top teams of senior clubs. By the 1970s New Zealand had 28 unions with competitions for 500 senior clubs and many more junior clubs. Some clubs were reporting more than 700 playing members each. New Zealand also developed a keenly contested interprovincial competition, stimulated by the presentation in 1902 of the Ranfurly Shield by the Earl of Ranfurly, Governor General of New Zealand. The competition for the Shield is run on a challenge basis, the holders retaining the Shield until beaten by a challenging provincial union. A similar pattern developed in South Africa, with local leagues for clubs and a national competition for teams representing provinces. The trophy awarded to the top province is the Currie Cup, dating from 1892 and originally presented by Sir Donald Currie, of the Castle Shipping Line, to the captain of the 1891 British team about to tour South Africa, for presentation to the South African side that put up the best performance. It was duly awarded to Griqualand West, which in turn presented it to the South African Rugby Board as a trophy for the interprovincial competition. In Australia local club leagues were established early in the game's development, but the institution of a full interprovincial competition remained impractical because Rugby of quality was largely confined to the two states of New South Wales and Queensland. The club game has been differently arranged in France, where a championship for clubs, with a trophy called the Bouclier de Brennus, has been organized on a national basis for many years. The details of this championship have been varied from time to time, but by 1970 the regular formula was a First Division divided into eight groups of clubs with eight clubs in each group. The clubs in each group played one another at home and away on a league basis; then the four leading clubs in each group went forward to form the 32 clubs needed for five knockout stages. Including this First Division, the French regularly have had 13 annual national championships at various levels as well as local and regional club competitions. Like New Zealand, the French have arranged competitions for the schoolboy teams of clubs, but they have not followed the New Zealand pattern of establishing a championship for representative provincial teams. As a result, although teams have often been chosen to represent regions, notably against touring teams from overseas, there has been no regular representative Rugby that the ambitious French player might use as a stepping stone between his club team and France's national team.

Interprovincial New Zealand competition

In Rugby, as in cricket, the highest form of competition is the Test series consisting of two or more games between representative national teams—*i.e.,* teams made up of the best players in each country. Also in Rugby, the four "Home Unions," England, Scotland, Ireland, and Wales, are considered as "countries" and their teams as national teams (teams representing the whole of the British Isles are known as the Lions). Thus the first "international" match was that between Scotland and England in 1871. A complete program of matches was established for England, Scotland, Ireland, and Wales in the season of 1883–84. This championship has continued more or less every year since, except during World Wars I and II. The regular formula has been for each "country" to play the other once a season, at home one year and away from home the next. France entered this championship in the 1909–10 season but had to wait until 1954 before managing to come out on top of the championship table. Even then, France had to share top place with England and Wales, and it was not until 1959 that a French team won it unshared for the first time. In 1970, however, France beat England 35–13, the biggest number of points ever scored against England in one match.

International competition

On the other side of the world, the first international activity occurred in 1882, when a team from New South Wales visited New Zealand. This was, in fact, the first international Rugby tour made anywhere in the world. The New South Wales side did not meet a full New Zealand team, but in 1894 such a match did take place, New South Wales winning this first Test. The Queensland state team also visited New Zealand in this period, and from 1903 onwards the Australian states combined, whenever possible, to form representative teams for international matches. Thus, in the strictest sense, the first Test match between the two countries took place in 1903. The two countries have continued playing each other more or less regularly since then. The New Zealanders have generally been the more successful, but in 1929 the Australian Wallabies beat New Zealand in three Tests played in Australia and in 1949 two Tests in New Zealand. Since 1931 the Tests have been played for the Bledisloe Cup, presented by Lord Bledisloe, Governor General of New Zealand.

South Africa's first international competition occurred when the British team toured South Africa in 1891, playing 16 matches including three Tests, all of which the visitors won. Such tours were to become a distinctive feature of Rugby Union, and other tours of South Africa by teams from the British Isles followed in 1896, 1903, and 1910. Meanwhile, a British team, in which England, Scotland, and Wales were represented, had toured New Zealand and Australia in 1888. This was the first overseas tour ever made by a team from the British Isles, and it established a precedent of tours to Australasia that has been followed at fairly regular intervals ever since.

Nor was the traffic one-way. The season of 1888–89 was enlivened by a visit by 26 New Zealanders, the first team from overseas ever to visit the British Isles, who played 74 matches in the British Isles, 16 in Australia, and 17 in New Zealand. This team, officially called the New Zealand Native Team, became known as the Maori although four of the players were in fact of European stock. They beat Ireland but lost to England and Wales. This tour was followed in the 1905–06 British season by a visit by New Zealand's fully representative team, known as the All Blacks, who won 32 of the 33 matches they played on tour and established New Zealand as one of the two most powerful Rugby countries in the world. During the following season, a fully representative team from South Africa, the Springboks, toured Britain for the first time; and they, together with their successors in 1912–13, who beat all four home countries and France, made it clear that they were to be reckoned in the same bracket as New Zealand. Since then, teams from New Zealand and South Africa have continued to make tours of the British Isles, usually including a brief visit to France, at more or less regular intervals. Australian teams, too, have made similar tours to Britain, normally, like New Zealand and South Africa, playing roughly 30 matches on each visit.

The All Blacks and the Springboks

In the 1920s, New Zealand, South Africa, and Australia settled into the routine of making tours of one another's country, the first such tour taking place in 1921, when South Africa toured New Zealand and Australia. In the middle years of the 20th century, international matches between New Zealand and South Africa became recognized as being for the unofficial world championship, and each found great difficulty in winning on the other's territory. An exception to this rule was the 1937 South African tour of New Zealand, when the South Africans won the international series 2–1 and also won all their 14 provincial matches there. The South African government's policy of apartheid (racial segregation) led to the postponement of New Zealand's scheduled 1967 tour of South Africa, the South African prime minister refusing to allow the New Zealanders to include Maori in their touring team. When the tour did finally take place in 1970, however, the New Zealanders became the first multiracial sports team ever to tour South Africa. Anti-apartheid demonstrations during South Africa's tour of the British Isles in the 1969–70 British season caused unpleasant moments for the tourists; but in general the national Rugby unions, unlike the national bodies of many other sports, held firmly to the belief that the political activities of a country's government should not be a reason for refusing to take part in a sport against players of that country.

France and international Federation competition The first international team to play in France was the 1905–06 New Zealanders, and England first met France later the same season in Paris. The French themselves did not make an overseas tour until 1958, when they went to South Africa and surprised the Rugby world by becoming the first international side to win a Test series in South Africa since the British team of 1896. In 1961 the French tried their luck in New Zealand for the first time but were defeated in all three Tests. France has also played international Rugby against Romania for many years, their first meeting having been in 1924, when France won 59–3. But by 1938 the score was no more than 11–8 to France, and in 1960 Romania beat France for the first time, the score being 11–5. France's first match against Italy was in 1937. Italy and Romania have played international matches against each other, and they have also played frequently against other Rugby countries under the jurisdiction of the Fédération Internationale de Rugby Amateur, such as Spain, Czechoslovakia, Poland, and Germany.

Other countries that have made their presence felt in international Rugby include Fiji, which regularly plays against Tonga and which has beaten Australia; Canada, which has played against major touring teams that have been on their way to or from Britain or Australasia; Argentina, which has beaten Wales, Scotland, and Ireland at Buenos Aires; and the United States, which won the Rugby competition at the Olympic Games of 1920 and 1924.

For all-time records of Rugby Union international (or Test) matches see RELATED ENTRIES under SPORTING RECORD in the *Ready Reference and Index*.

The game. Rugby is played on a rectangular field not more than 75 yards (68.6 metres) wide; the maximum distance between the goal lines is 110 yards (100 metres) and beyond each goal line the end zone, called "in goal," extends not more than 25 yards (23 metres). At the centre of the goal lines are two goal posts 18 feet 6 inches (5.6 metres) apart with a crossbar 10 feet above the ground.

The ball is oval, less pointed than the U.S. and Canadian football, and is inflated. It is 11 to 11¼ inches (28 to 29 centimetres) long, 24 to 25½ inches (61 to 65 centimetres) in circumference, and weighs 13½ to 15 ounces. The outside casing of the ball is usually of leather.

The players wear jerseys, shorts, stockings, and studded (cleated) boots. They are not allowed to wear protective harness or shoulder pads. The game is controlled by a referee assisted by two touch judges, and in international matches there are two periods of 40 minutes each.

Playing the game: tactics One of the charms of the Rugby Union game is the infinite variety of its tactics. In a basic orthodox situation, like a scrum on the right-hand side of the field, the ball may simply be passed rapidly by hand through the half-

Forwards engaged in a scrummage (Wales–France Rugby International, Paris, 1970).
Sports Illustrated photograph by Gerry Cranham, © Time Inc.

backs and the centre three-quarters to the left-wing three-quarter, each man running a few yards before parting with the ball; the wing may then be able to run past his immediate opponent by swerving or sidestepping or simply by using strength and speed; a try will probably be scored. But the attacking team may already have tried an orthodox move of this kind and may have discovered that the opposition is especially strong defensively and also possesses exceptional speed. In this case, the attacking team must depart from the orthodox and try to discover a chink in their opponents' armour elsewhere. One of the halfbacks, for instance, might discover that the defence in his particular sphere is vulnerable to a sudden change of direction. He may therefore run himself rather than pass the ball out, and he may decide, after making his initial breach, that a try is most likely to be scored if he subsequently passes the ball not outside to his three-quarters but inside to his big and heavy forwards, who may be able to barge their way over the opponents' goal line.

An attack may also be launched not into the open field but, for the sake of surprise, on the other side of the set piece. Instead of passing at all, the halfback may prefer to test the nerve of the opposing fullback by kicking the ball high into the air and instructing his teammates to bear down menacingly upon the opposing fullback as he is about to try to make the catch. A harassed fullback may drop the ball, leaving it conveniently placed for an attacker to pick up and run off with.

The weather has a big influence on the tactics adopted. If the day is very wet and the field very muddy and slippery, a team's captain may prefer to keep play confined largely to his forwards rather than to risk seeing one of his halfbacks or three-quarters let the wet ball slip from his hands in the open field. He may therefore instruct his forwards not to deliver the ball from a line-out to the scrum half but to hold on to it and try to make headway in a closely knit group. Similarly, at a scrum he may order his forwards to try to retain the ball and take it up the field at their feet.

RUGBY LEAGUE

Origin. The Rugby League game was originated by 22 Rugby Football Union clubs in the North of England who broke away from the parent body because they wanted their players to be paid for "broken time"—*i.e.*, loss of wages due to playing the game. The matter first came to a head in 1893 when the Yorkshire Rugby Union proposed "that players be allowed compensation for bonefide loss of time." The proposal was defeated, but the RFU was frequently called upon to hold inquiries into alleged acts of professionalism in the North. When the RFU therefore proposed some even stricter "laws against professionalism," in 1895, these were rejected by many of the leading clubs in the counties of Yorkshire and Lancashire, which then formed "the Northern Union Football Union," later, in the 1920s, to become the Rugby Football League.

The main difference between the Rugby League game

Differences between League and Union games

and the Rugby Union game is that Rugby League is largely professional whereas Rugby Union has remained entirely amateur. The two games are played on similar fields, and the aim in League, as in Union football, is to score tries and goals. A try in Rugby League, as in Rugby Union, is worth three points, but in the League game every successful kick at goal is worth two points only. There are only 13 men on a Rugby League team instead of 15. The two who have been dispensed with are the two wing forwards, so that a League scrum has three men in the front row, two in the second, and one in the back. There are no line-outs in Rugby League; if the ball goes out of play over the touchline, a scrum is ordered. Nor is the Union game's ruck or maul to be found in Rugby League. When a player is brought down in possession of the ball, he has to be allowed to stand up face-to-face with an opponent and attempt to tap the ball back to his own teammates with his foot.

Development of game. Although it has been played in other parts of the British Isles, such as south Wales and the London area, the Rugby League game has established a firm foothold in Britain only in the three northern counties of Yorkshire, Lancashire, and Cumberland. In those areas it is organized into numerous competitions of which the best known are the Northern Rugby League and the Rugby League Challenge Cup competition. Both these are for club teams, the former on a league basis, the latter a knockout event.

The game has also taken firm root in France, Australia, and New Zealand. Like Rugby Union, the League game in France is largely confined to the southern part of the country, and it has flourished on a strictly competitive basis. In Australia the main centres of the game are Sydney and Brisbane, though it is widely played in cities and towns throughout the country and has a larger following than has Rugby Union. In New Zealand the game is less firmly established than Rugby Union, but it is played in most cities and big towns and notably strongly in Auckland and Wellington.

As a largely professional game, requiring a steady intake of money from gate receipts, Rugby League has been ahead of Rugby Union in developing along crowd-pleasing lines. The reduction of a team from 15 to 13, with the removal of wing forwards, for instance, left the field less cluttered and so more suitable for attractive open play. Rugby League was also ahead of Rugby Union in introducing laws to curb the stagnation of repeated kicks over the touchline.

Competition. Although Rugby League has been played at strength in no more than four countries, the national teams of these four, Great Britain, France, Australia, and New Zealand, have managed to come together from time to time to play a World Cup tournament. This has provided the summit of international competition, but there have also been regular tours somewhat after the manner of Rugby Union tours, by Australia, for example, in Great Britain and France and by Great Britain in Australia and New Zealand. The French have toured Australia and New Zealand, and the New Zealanders have toured in Great Britain and France. Great Britain had an exceptionally successful tour in Australia and New Zealand in 1970, when they played 24 matches, winning 22, drawing one, and losing one, with a points record of 753 for and 288 against. They scored 165 tries.

In less far-ranging international encounters, Great Britain has settled into a pattern of playing France at home and away each season, and Australia has had more or less regular matches against New Zealand. Matches between Australia and New Zealand are for the Trans-Tasman Cup, which is retained by the one country until beaten in a Test series by the other.

A national team has also been raised, though less regularly, to represent Wales. The Welsh team is chosen chiefly from former Welsh Rugby Union players who have joined Rugby League clubs in the North of England. Such players, of course, are eligible for the Great Britain team; but during periods when there have been sufficient numbers of them, they have also formed a Welsh team to play against England or against France. In October 1969

a special triangular tournament was held in England involving the national teams of England, France, and Wales. The countries finished in that order in the final table, but later that season Wales had the satisfaction of beating France 15–11 at Perpignan, becoming the first Welsh Rugby League team to win in France since 1936.

For records of Rugby League World Cup competition and Test matches see SPORTING RECORD in the *Ready Reference and Index*.

BIBLIOGRAPHY

Histories: U.A. TITLEY and ROSS MCWHIRTER, *Illustrated History of the Rugby Football Union* (1971), the history of the Rugby Union game in England from the earliest times to 1971, including a detailed examination of the origins of the Rugby League, fully illustrated; A.C. PARKER, *The Springboks 1891–1970* (1970), a historical and statistical record of the South African Rugby Union, with a narrative section on the development of the game in South Africa from the beginnings to 1970; GORDON SLATTER, *On the Ball* (1970), a complete history of the game in New Zealand.

Instruction and coaching: GERWYN WILLIAMS, *Tackle Rugger this Way* (1968), a simple textbook explaining the basic skills and the basic moves of the game, especiallly useful for beginners; RUGBY FOOTBALL UNION, *A Guide for Coaches* (1967), a collection of pamphlets dealing with all aspects of playing the game, designed primarily for the use of coaches, but also of value to the experienced player wanting to improve his understanding of the game and the standard of his own play.

Rugby Union rules: RUGBY FOOTBALL UNION, *Laws of the Game with Instructions for Referees and Notes for Guidance of Players,* (n.d.), bylaws of the Rugby Football Union and the International Board, addresses of the governing bodies of the game, and other useful information.

Rugby League rules: RUGBY FOOTBALL LEAGUE, *The Rugby League Handbook* (annual).

(D.B.J.F.)

Rugs and Carpets

The term carpet was used until the 19th century for any cover made of a thick material, such as a table cover or wall hanging; since the introduction of machine-made products, it has been used almost exclusively for a floor covering. Both in Great Britain and in the U.S. the term rug is often used for a partial floor covering as distinguished from carpet, which is tacked down to the floor and covers it wall-to-wall. In reference to handmade carpets, however, the terms rug and carpet are used interchangeably and are so used in this article, which deals almost exclusively with handmade products. Since such carpets are not always intended for use on the floor, the article extends the term rugs and carpets to cover products intended for other uses as well.

Handmade carpets are works of art as well as functional objects. Indeed, many Oriental carpets have reached such supreme heights of artistic expression that they have always been regarded in the East as objects of exceptional beauty and luxury in the same way as masterpieces of painting have been in the West. Handmade carpets are discussed in this article in terms of their elements of design, material, technique, ornament and imagery, use, and stylistic characteristics in different periods and cultures.

This article is divided into the following sections:

ELEMENTS OF DESIGN

Field and border designs. Designs usually consist of an inner field—the pattern in the centre of the carpet—and a border. The latter serves, like the cornice on a building or the frame on a picture, to emphasize the limits, isolate the field, and sometimes control the implied movements of the interior pattern. The design of inner field and border must harmonize pleasingly, yet remain distinct.

The border consists of a minimum of three elements: a main band, which varies greatly in width according to the size of the rug and the elaborateness of the field design, and inner and outer guard stripes, decidedly subordinate bands on either side of the main band. The guard stripes may be the same on both sides of the main band or be different. The most common decoration for the field is an allover pattern, a panel composition, or a medallion system. The allover pattern may be of identical repeats (Figure 1), either juxtaposed or evenly spaced, though the latter, while common on textiles, is rare on carpets; or it may be of varied motifs in a unified system (*e.g.*, different plant forms of the same size), but even this freest type of design almost invariably includes bilaterally balanced repetitions. The varied motif type of design is found most typically in formalized representations of the parks or woods that were a feature of Persian palace grounds (see Figure 7).

Another type of allover design appears to be entirely free but is actually organized on systems of scrolling stems, notably on the east Persian carpets of the 16th and 17th centuries.

The value of panel subdivisions for controlling patterns had been discovered in a simple rectangular version by the Upper Paleolithic period (*c.* 25,000 BC), and panel systems have been a basic form of design since 4000 BC, when pottery painters were already devising varied systems. On carpets, the lattice provides the simplest division of the field, often a diagonal lattice as on an embroidered carpet found in an excavated tomb (1st century BC to 1st century AD) at Noin Ula in northern Mongolia; the diagonal scheme also appears on Sāsānian capitals and in Coptic tapestries. But a characteristic field design of the Persian court carpets of the Shāh 'Abbās period, the so-called Vase pattern, is constructed from the ogee, a motif that became prominent in Near Eastern textile design in the 14th century. Simple rectangular panelling—really a large-scale check—is typical of one style of Spanish rugs of the 15th and 16th centuries.

Types of field decoration (margin note)

Figure 2: Persian silk carpet from Kashan, Iran, late 16th century. The field is decorated with a central medallion, surrounded by a wreath of small cartouches and framed by corresponding cornerpieces. In the National Gallery of Art, Washington, D.C. 2.41 × 1.65 m.

By courtesy of the National Gallery of Art, Washington, D.C., Widener Collection; photograph, Otto E. Nelson—EB Inc.

The most frequent medallion composition consists of a more or less elaborate medallion superimposed on the centre of a patterned field and often complemented with cornerpieces, which are typical quadrants of the central medallion (Figure 2). But multiple-medallion systems also are developed: either a succession or a chain of medallions on the vertical axis; two or more forms of medallions alternating in bands, a scheme typical of the Turkish (Ushak) carpets of the 16th and 17th centuries; or systematically spotted medallions that may or may not be interconnected or that may interlock so that the scheme logically becomes an elaborate lattice.

Medallion carpets (margin note)

Persian carpets of the 15th–17th century commonly have multiple-design schemes; that is, composition systems on two or more "levels." The simplest is the medallion superimposed on an allover design, but more typical are subtler inventions such as two- or three-spiral stem systems, sometimes overlarded with large-scale cloud bands, all intertwining but each carried independently to completion. The finer Vase carpets have double or triple ogival lattices set at different intervals (staggered), each with its own centre, and tangent motifs that also serve other functions in the other systems. What at first sight appears to be a great multiplicity of independent motifs thus proves on careful examination to be ingeniously contrived and firmly controlled.

Occasionally, stripe systems are used, either vertical or diagonal; but this conception is more natural to shuttle-woven fabrics, and, when employed in the freer techniques of rug weaving, it is probably an imitation of textiles.

Design execution. Transferring the design is done in various ways. It can be transferred to the carpet directly

By courtesy of the Victoria and Albert Museum, London

Figure 1: Detail of a Persian *kilim* from Sehna (Sanandaj), Iran, 19th century. A tapestry-woven wool rug with an allover identical repeat pattern of *bōteh* (leaf with curling tip) in rows. In the Victoria and Albert Museum, London. Full size 1.65 × 1.19 m.

from the mind and hand of the craftsman or indirectly from a pattern drawn on paper. Using the latter technique, a rug can be executed directly from the pattern, or the design can be transferred first to a cartoon. The cartoon, or *talim*, is a full-size paper drawing that is squared, each square representing one knot of a particular colour. The weaver places the *talim* behind his loom and translates the design directly onto the carpet. The cartoon is used for reproduction of very intricate designs and as a master pattern for the production of more than one carpet. Many of the finest Oriental rugs, which achieve a magnificent effect through wealth of detail, are thought to have been woven from cartoons drawn by manuscript illuminators. Such methods of transfer result in unavoidable irregularities of pattern that, because they are signs of the artistic individuality of the craftsman, lend a particular charm to the handwoven carpet. The major difference between handmade and machine-made carpets is that the mechanical transfer of design in the latter creates a uniformity of pattern, obliterating signs of individual workmanship.

Natural dyes

Colour. From earliest times until the late 19th century, only natural dyes were used. Some have come from vegetables such as madder, indigo, sumac, genista, and woad; some from minerals such as ochre; and some from animals, mollusks, and insects. Most have been improved by the addition of various chemicals, such as alum, which fix colours in the fibre. Except for dark brown to black dyes, which have high iron-oxide content that often decomposes fibres, natural dyes have proved to be excellent; they have remarkable beauty and subtlety of colour, and they are durable. Much of the charm of antique carpets lies in the slightly varying hues and shades obtained with these natural dyes. In the 19th century, synthetic, aniline dyes were developed, becoming popular first in Europe and, after 1860, in the East; but their garish colours and poor durability were later thought to outweigh the advantages of brilliance and quick application, and natural dyes regained favour with many craftsmen. More recently, synthetic dyes have been improved.

MATERIALS AND TECHNIQUE

Most carpets are made of sheep's wool, which is durable, dyes readily, and handles easily. Camel or goat wool is rarely used. Too dull to make an attractive pile, cotton's strength and smooth yarn make it an ideal warp (see below); it is used in the East for the entire foundation or for the warp only.

Silk is so expensive that its use is restricted; but no other material produces such luxurious, delicate rugs, displaying subtle colour nuances of particular charm in different lights. Some of the finest 16th- and 17th-century Persian carpets are entirely of silk. It has never been used for knotting in Europe; but often since the 15th century it has augmented wool in the weft of European tapestries.

Linen was used in Egyptian carpets, hemp for the foundations of Indian carpets; and both materials are used in European carpets. Since around 1820, jute has been used in the foundation of machine-made carpets.

Knotted pile carpets, combining beauty, durability, and possibilities for infinite variety, have found greatest favour as floor coverings. Long ago, weavers first began to produce pile fabrics or fabrics with a surface made up of loops of yarn, attempting to combine the advantages of a woven textile with those of animal fleece. Knotted pile is constructed on the loom on a foundation of woven yarns, of which the horizontal yarns are called weft yarns and the vertical are called warp yarns. Coloured pile yarns, from which the pattern is obtained, are firmly knotted around two warp yarns in such a way that their free ends rise above the woven foundation to form a tufted pile or thick cushion of yarn ends covering one side of the foun-

(Centre) The Textile Museum Collection, Washington, D.C., gift of Mrs. David B. Karrick, by courtesy of (left) the Metropolitan Museum of Art, New York, gift of John D. Rockefeller, Jr., 1950, (right) the National Rug and Textile Foundation, Washington, D.C., gift of W. Russell Pickering; photographs, Otto E. Nelson—EB Inc.

Figure 3: *Techniques of rug making.*
(Top left) Detail of a Polish carpet, a gold-and-silver brocaded silk rug from Persia, 17th century. In the Metropolitan Museum of Art, New York. Full size 3.96 × 1.77 m. (Bottom left) Englarged section of above showing the contrast between silken knotted pile and areas brocaded with metal-covered yarns. (Top centre) Detail of a Shirvan wool *kilim* (tapestry-woven carpet), southeastern Caucasus (Azerbaijan S.S.R.), late 19th century. In the Textile Museum, Washington, D.C. Full size 2.59 × 1.47 m. (Bottom centre) Enlarged section of above showing slits produced where two colours meet along the vertical, the yarn of each colour having been returned on the same warp. (Top right) Detail of a wool Soumak carpet, Caucasus, 19th century. In the collection of the National Rug and Textile Foundation, Washington, D.C. Full size 2.29 × 1.75 m. (Bottom right) Enlarged section of above showing the herringbone effect created by the Soumak method of brocading.

dation weave. The knots are worked in rows between several interlocking, tautly drawn weft yarns that keep every row of knotted tufts securely in place in the foundation. When a row of knots is tied, it is beaten down against the preceding rows with a heavy mallet-like comb so that on the front the pile completely conceals both warp and weft. When a certain area has been woven, the pile ends are sheared to an even height. This varies according to the character of the rug, being short on the more aristocratic type and as much as an inch (2½ centimetres) on some shaggy nomadic rugs.

Types of knots
There are various ways of knotting the pile yarn around the warp yarn. The Turkish, or Ghiordes, knot is thought to be the oldest. It is used mainly in Asia Minor, the Caucasus, Iran (formerly Persia), and Europe. The Persian, or Sehna, knot is used principally in Iran, India, China, and Egypt. The Spanish knot, used mainly in Spain, differs from the other two types in looping around only one warp yarn. After the 18th century it became extremely rare. The kind of knot used affects the delicacy and tightness of the pile. Knotting each pile yarn by hand is comparable to setting small pebbles in a mosaic, and expert execution is vital in achieving a beautiful finished product. Angular-patterned carpets requiring only a coarsely knotted pile are easier to produce than curvilinear and finely patterned ones, which require finer material and a much more densely knotted pile for clear reproduction of their intricate designs. Some Chinese carpets have fewer than 20 knots per square inch (three per square centimetre); certain Indian ones, more than 2,400. The highest density can be achieved with the Persian, or Sehna, knot.

Brocading can be added to the pile, heightening its colourfulness. The gold and silver thread in this procedure lies flat against the woven foundation, giving the appearance of low relief (Figure 3, left). Metal threads, however, quick-wearing and with diminishing lustre, are less suitable as floor coverings than as hangings.

Many carpets do not have knotted pile. Called *kilims*, they are woven similarly to tapestries. The weft yarns of a given colour area never cross into another area, and if the weft yarns of different colour areas are hooked around adjacent warps rather than around one another or around warp yarn, small slits are created where different colours meet (Figure 3, centre). A variation is used in fully brocaded Soumak carpets in which one or two rows of coloured pattern weft alternate with an invisible functional weft. Brocading with passes of alternate rows given a differing direction, or slant, produces a herringbone effect (Figure 3, right).

Embroidery has rarely been used on floor coverings. Embroidered rugs are almost exclusively European and American, except for certain Turkmen *kilims* and Turkish *cicims* (ruglike spreads or hangings). Only relatively strong backings can be used, such as in appliqué work or embroideries done in designs of counted stitching (the cross-stitch, and the gros point and petit point of needlework) that cover the entire surface.

ORNAMENT AND IMAGERY

Individual motifs. Three main classes of motifs are used: geometrical; conventional, or stylized; and illustrative, or naturalistic. The geometrical repertoire is built up from variations and combinations of meanders, polygons, crosses, and stars. Meanders, chiefly for borders, range from the simple serration employed from earliest times to fairly complex hooked forms, characteristically the angular "running wave," or "Greek key," which is also very ancient. Little trefoil (tri-lobed) motifs are used for guard stripes in the Caucasus, central Iran, and India. Chief among the polygons employed are the lozenge and the octagon. The Maltese cross is frequently used, as is the gamma cross, or swastika. Purely geometrical stars are usually based on the cross or the octagon. Many of these motifs, which are rudimentary and very ancient, may have originated in basket weaving and the related reed-mat plaiting, for they are natural to both techniques; but in rug weaving they have survived chiefly in the work of Central Asia, Asia Minor, and the Caucasus, in both pile-knotted and flat-woven fabrics.

One of the principal stylized motifs in 16th- and 17th-century Persian carpets is the so-called arabesque, an ambiguous term that generally implies an intricate scrolling-vine system. In a common Persian ornamental scheme, two asymmetrical members cross at an acute angle, forming a lilylike blossom, and then describe curves in opposite directions, readily continuing into further scroll systems (Figure 4). This highly individual form was begun in China in the late Chou period (*c.* 600 BC), notably on a few bronze mirrors and was beautifully developed during the Han dynasty (206 BC–AD 220). It appeared in Persia in the 12th century (on pottery and architectural stucco ornament), possibly influenced by the Chinese form.

Arabesque carpets

Directly traceable to China are the cloud knot and cloud band, or ribbon—both in use by the Han period at least and with a continuous history thereafter. The cloud knot, a feature of the Persian court carpets of the time of Shāh 'Abbās, was continued to the end of the 18th century. The cloud band became important on 16th-century carpets; it was employed with especial elegance and skill by Persian designers and perhaps most beautifully in Turkish court carpets, which owed much to Persian inspiration. The cloud band and knot motifs moved from Syrian textile design into Asia Minor with the Ottoman Turkish conquest in the 15th century and became typical of one group of 16th–17th century Turkish carpets.

Palmettes, a second major class of stylized motifs dominant in a considerable range of carpet designs from Asia Minor to India, originated in Assyrian design as styliza-

By courtesy of the Metropolitan Museum of Art, New York, gift of Mrs. Harry Payne Bingham, 1959; photograph, Otto E. Nelson—EB Inc.

Figure 4: Detail of a wool Persian arabesque carpet from Kerman, Iran, late 16th century. A system of double intersecting arabesque bands covers the field. In the Metropolitan Museum of Art, New York. Full size 6.05 × 2.49 m.

Figure 5: Detail of a wool Persian carpet from Kurdistan, Iran, late 18th century. Stylized palmettes dominate the field, which also includes motifs derived from the Chinese lotus blossom. In the Metropolitan Museum of Art, New York. Full size 6.96 × 2.69 m.
By courtesy of the Metropolitan Museum of Art, New York, gift of Joseph V. McMullan; photograph, Otto E. Nelson

mask, sometimes used as the centre of a palmette; tigers; cheetahs; bears; foxes; deer of numerous species; goats, sometimes picturesquely prancing; the wild ass, a fleet prey; ferocious-looking Chinese dragons, and the gentle *ch'i-lin*, a fantastic equine also imported from China. Fish sometimes swim in pools or streams or are conventionally paired to suggest a shield, or escutcheon, in the borders of the carpet. Huntsmen, usually mounted, are the major human figures, though musicians are also depicted. Angels are occasionally present (see Figure 8).

The underlying theme of both the stylized and naturalistic vocabularies is nearly always fertility or abundance. The great Persian carpet of Ardabīl (1539–40; Victoria and Albert Museum, London), for example, embodies a huge golden stellate medallion, developed from the multiple-pointed rosette that from time immemorial symbolized the Sun. At its centre are four lotus blossoms floating on a little gray-blue pool, which represents the source of rain in the heavens. The medallion thus symbolizes the two basic vitalizing elements—Sun and water. As proof of its magical potency, a complex system of tendrils and blossoms issues from it (see Figure 12).

In Oriental carpet design, a flat surface pattern is always emphasized, even where small details are plentiful. European designs, however, tend more toward the illusionistic effects of painting, often using shading and picture-like

Oriental versus European design

tions of the palm, a symbol of vitalistic power that was often, if not always, associated with the Moon (Figure 5). Many of the almost uncountable variations that developed through the centuries continued to refer directly to the palm. As early as the 1st millennium BC, however, others derived from the lotus blossom, a complementary motif connected primarily with the fertility symbolism of the Sun. Still others involved the pomegranate, another fertility symbol, utilizing primarily the fruit, while yet another group presented the vitalistic emblem of the vine, this last design being built on the single leaf. The forms of these four main types of palmettes found in Oriental rug designs are directly descended from styles current in textile designs from the 4th century onward and are often modified by Chinese influences. The patterns in the 16th and early 17th centuries were beautifully and realistically elaborated, and blossoms such as the Chinese peony sometimes compete with the more stylized lotus. The lanceolate leaf, often associated with palmettes (especially in east Persian designs), is generally stylized. The chalice, fan, and half-palmette, all evolved from the palmette and used in Oriental rugs, were also used in 17th- and 18th-century European designs.

Naturalistic motifs

Outstanding among the more naturalistic plants are cypresses and blossoming fruit trees, symbolizing life eternal and resurrection, respectively. Willows and jasmine flowers are prominent in the Shāh 'Abbās Vase carpet and tulips in Turkish court carpets. Many minor foliate and floral forms had no specific botanical identification, though they give a realistic effect (Figure 6). Naturalistic red or pink roses, rare in Oriental rugs before the 19th century, were already widespread in European designs by the mid-16th century. Under European influence, they appeared in Oriental designs, particularly Persian, in the later 19th century.

The most important illustrative motifs, other than naturalistic plants, are those connected with the garden and the hunt: many small songbirds (in Persia, especially the nightingale); the pheasant (*feng-huang*), taken over from China and much favoured in the 16th century; occasionally the peacock; lions and a semi-conventional lion

By courtesy of the Metropolitan Museum of Art, New York; photograph, Otto E. Nelson—EB Inc.

Figure 6: Indian wool floral carpet, Mughal, 17th century. The field is decorated with an allover pattern of naturalistic flowering plants. In the Metropolitan Museum of Art, New York. 4.27 × 2.01 m.

compositions and incorporating architectural motifs (a cornice, for example) and even portraiture. This tendency is particularly evident in French carpets of the 17th and 18th centuries.

Symbolism of overall design. In addition to the symbolism inherent in individual motifs incorporated into the design of the carpet, the total design—indeed, the carpet itself—can be symbolic, as are some of the earliest Persian designs. The ultimate example is the Spring (or Winter) of Khosrow Carpet made for the audience hall of the Sāsānid palace at Ctesiphon (southeast of Baghdad) in the 6th century. The carpet has not survived, but, according to written records, it represented a formal garden with watercourses, paths, rectangular beds filled with flowers, and blossoming shrubs and fruit trees. Yellow gravel was represented by gold; and the blossoms, fruit, and birds were worked with pearls and different jewels. The outer border, representing a meadow, was solid with emeralds. Made of silk and measuring about 84 feet square (about 26 metres square), the carpet must have seemed overwhelmingly splendid when the great portal curtains of the hall were drawn back and the sun flooded the interior.

This dazzling carpet symbolized the divine role of the king, who regulated the seasons and guaranteed spring's return, renewing the earth's fertility and assuring prosperity. On another plane, it represented the Garden of Eden, a symbol of eternal paradise (the English word paradise is ultimately derived from the Persian word, which means "walled park"). With its flowers, birds, and water, it symbolized deliverance from the harsh desert and the promise of eternal happiness.

This most sumptuous of fabrics made a profound impression on everyone, especially the Persians. For centuries it bewitched Persian imagination, becoming a legend in history, poetry, and art. Vain attempts at emulation were made by Oriental craftsmen for more than a millennium; and though its realistic depiction has disappeared, the Garden of Eden concept lingers on in Oriental designs (Figure 7). The garlands, vines, flowers, trees, animals, and beasts all strive to create a landscape, picturing hunting scenes or game, lakes with water birds, and often images of supernatural or celestial beings, such as jinn, houris (maidens who are among the pleasures of the Muslim paradise), or a gathering of the blissful righteous at a banquet or dance (Figure 8). Accompanying verses support the image, lyrically extolling the carpet as a garden, for example, or a blooming meadow and comparing its beauty to that of the Garden of Eden.

USES OF RUGS AND CARPETS

Carpets originated in Central and Western Asia as coverings for beaten-earth floors. From time immemorial, carpets covered the floors of house and tent as well as mosque and palace. In the homes of wealthy Eastern families, floor coverings serve an aesthetic as well as a practical function. Rugs are often grouped in a traditional arrangement, partly to allow for simultaneous display; and the carpet's size and shape is determined by the intended place within that arrangement. There are usually four carpets. The largest, called *mīān farsh*, usually measuring some 18 feet by 8 feet (5.5 by 2.5 metres), is placed in the centre. Flanking the *mīān farsh* are two runners, or

By courtesy of the Osterreichisches Museum fur Angewandte Kunst, Vienna; photographs, Eric Lessing—Magnum

Figure 8: *Naturalistic human figure and animal motifs.*
Details of a Persian silk hunting carpet from Kashan, Iran, 16th century. In the Österreichisches Museum für Angewandte Kunst, Vienna. Full size 6.93 × 3.23 m. (Top) Winged figures from the border, possibly jinn or houris, seated amid flowering stems and birds in paradise. (Bottom) Scene from the field showing mounted huntsmen attacking a leopard.

By courtesy of the Fogg Art Museum, Harvard University, gift of Joseph V. McMullan; photograph, Otto E. Nelson

Figure 7: Detail of a wool Persian garden carpet from Kurdistan, Iran, late 18th century. The pattern, which consists of varied stylized motifs in a unified system, is based on the design of a Persian garden. In the Fogg Art Museum, Cambridge, Mass. Full size 6.9 × 2.4 m.

Figure 9: *Specialized rugs.*
(Left) Cruciform wool tabletop rug made in Cairo for export to Europe, Ottoman, 16th century.
In the Museo d'Arte Sacra, San Gimignano, Italy. 2.60 × 2.30 m. (Right) Wool prayer rug
(namāzlik) from Bursa, Turkey, Ottoman, 16th century. The field contains a *mihrāb*, or prayer
niche, with a mosque lamp hanging in the central arch. In the Metropolitan Museum of Art,
New York. 1.68 × 1.27 m.
By courtesy of (right) the Metropolitan Museum of Art, New York, gift of
J.F. Ballard; photographs, (left) SCALA, New York, (right) Otto E. Nelson—EB Inc.

*kanāreh*s, which are mainly used for walking and which measure some 18 feet by 3 feet (5.5 by 1 metre). The principal rug, or *kellegi*, averaging 12 feet by 6 feet (3.7 by 1.8 metres), is placed at one end of the arrangement of three carpets, so that its length stretches almost completely across their collective widths.

The prayer rug
The intended use sometimes determines both design and size, as in the prayer rug, or *namāzlik*. Because a Muslim must carry it everywhere, the prayer rug is relatively small (Figure 9, right). Design, naturally linked to religious imagery, is characterized by the *mihrāb*, or prayer niche (an imitation of the prayer niche in the wall of a mosque), the apex of which could be pointed toward Mecca. But other religious properties also appear, such as hanging lamps, water jugs, or "hand prints" to mark the place of the worshipper on the rug.

Until mid-17th century, Asian carpets imported into Europe were considered too precious to serve as permanent floor coverings. Placed on the floor only on church holidays or in an aristocrat's presence, they were otherwise used on the wall or to cover tables, benches, and chests; and, particularly in Italy, they were hung over balconies as decoration during festivals. Taking this European attitude into account, the Egyptian manufacturers created several unusual shapes and sizes for the European market: square, round, and cruciform carpets, obviously designed for tables rather than floors (Figure 9, left). During the 17th century, covering the entire floor with costly knotted carpets became fashionable. The mid-20th century witnessed a boom in antique-carpet prices that resulted in choicer pieces ending up back on the wall.

Table carpets

Oriental carpets frequently served many uses besides covering floors. They made handsome curtains, served as tribute money, and were frequently gifts of one state to another. They were used as blankets, canopies, coverings for tent openings, and tomb covers. They have also made excellent saddle covers and storage bags for use in tents. Such modest rugs were always close to the life of the people, who lavished care on them and into them wove

life-protecting symbols. Other, more bizarre, uses have included assisting in the demise of Baghdad's last caliph —who in 1258 was wrapped in a carpet and beaten to death—and dramatically enhancing Cleopatra's introduction to Julius Caesar, when she stepped out of an unrolled rug. In less well-documented instances, they have assumed magical properties and taken flight, transporting their owners through the air.

PERIODS AND CENTRES OF ACTIVITY

Floor coverings of plaited rushes have been used at least since the 4th or 5th millennium BC, and rush weaving in the Middle East had reached a high standard by medieval times.

Oriental carpets. Oriental carpets are those made in Western and Central Asia, North Africa, and the Caucasus region of Europe. Rug design, in Western Asia at least, had gone beyond felt and plaited mats before the 1st millennium BC. A threshold rug represented in a stone carving (now in the Louvre) from the 8th-century-BC Assyrian palace of Khorsabad (in modern Iraq) has an allover field pattern of quatrefoils (four-leafed motifs), framed by a lotus border. Other Assyrian carvings of the period also show patterns that survive in modern designers' repertories.

Excavation of royal graves, dating from the 5th to the 3rd century BC, at Pazyryk, in the Altai Mountains of Southern Siberia, has uncovered the oldest known examples of knotting. The finds include various articles of felt with appliqué patterns and a superb carpet (Figure 10) with a woollen pile, knotted with the Ghiordes, or Turkish, knot (Hermitage). The carpet, probably of Persian origin, measures 6 × 6½ feet (1.8 × 2.0 metres). The central field has a checkerboard design with a floral star pattern in each square. Of the two wide borders, the inner one shows a frieze of elk, the outer one a frieze of horsemen.

Knotting was not necessarily the only or even the most important method of carpet making. Felt carpets were

Figure 10: Detail of the wool carpet from the royal graves at Pazyryk in the Altai Mountains of Southern Siberia, 5th to 3rd century BC. Probably of Persian origin, the rug is knotted with the Ghiordes, or Turkish, knot. The central field is an allover checkerboard pattern. The two wide bands of the fivefold border contain friezes; the outer one has men mounted on stallions, the inner one grazing elk. In the Hermitage, Leningrad. 2.0 × 1,8 m.
Novosti Press Agency

used for a long time in Central and East Asia, as indicated by magnificent 1st-century-AD specimens from Noin Ula in Northern Mongolia (1st century BC to the 1st century AD; in the Hermitage) or those in the Shōsō-in (Japanese Imperial storehouse) in Nara near Osaka (before the 8th century). The costly rugs with figure motifs and gold mentioned by Greek and Arab writers may have been woven or embroidered and were probably exhibited on the wall as well as on the floor. The large carpet made in the 6th century for the Sāsānid palace in Ctesiphon (see above *Ornament and imagery: Symbolism of overall design*) is the most famous; but other Oriental courts, such as the caliphate at Baghdad (8th–13th century), also used valuable carpets.

Early Anatolian and Caucasian rugs

In the 13th, 14th, and 15th centuries, Asia Minor and the Caucasus produced coarse, vividly coloured rugs with stars, polygons, and often patterns of stylized Kūfic writing. A special group with simple, highly conventionalized animal forms was also woven; the most important of these carpets are represented by seven fragments of strong, repeating, geometric patterns in bold colours—red, yellow, and blue—found in the mosque of 'Alā' ad-Dīn at Konya in Anatolia and now in the Museum of Turkish and Islāmic Art, Istanbul. They probably date from the 13th century. In the Staatliche Museen zu Berlin and in the Nationalmuseum at Stockholm are two primitive rugs, one, a highly conventionalized dragon-and-phoenix combat (Figure 11), the other, stylized birds in a tree. Both of these rugs are probably early-15th-century Anatolian.

Later, many rugs of finer weave, more delicate patterns, and richer colour—mostly geometric and possibly from Seljuq looms in Asia Minor—appeared in Europe. They were depicted by Flemish painters, such as Hans Memling, Jan van Eyck, and Petrus Christus, with such skill that the separate knots are sometimes visible. Many of these designs are repeated in the Bergama district of Asia Minor and the Southern Caucasus today, a complication when dating work.

Persia. Little is known about Persian carpet making before the 15th century, when the art was already approaching a peak. The Mongol invasion of the 13th century had depressed Persia's artistic life, only partly restored by the renaissance under the Mongol Il-Khan dynasty (1256–1353). Although the conquests of Timur Lenk (died 1405) were in most respects disastrous to Persia, he favoured artisans and spared them to work on his great palaces in Turkistan.

Under Timur's successor, Shāh Rokh (died 1447), art flourished, particularly carpets. Their production exclusively by palace workshops and court-subsidized looms gave them unity of style; and a sensitive clientele and lavish royal support guaranteed perfect materials and the highest skill: sheep were especially bred, dye plantations were cultivated like flower gardens, and designers and weavers could win court appointments. These conditions continued under the Ṣafavīds (1501/02–1732).

In the 15th century the art of the book, which had long been considered the supreme artistic accomplishment and already had behind it centuries of superb achievement, reached a degree of elegance and sophistication unknown either before or since. The bindings, frontispieces, chapter headings, and, in the miniatures themselves, the canopies, panels, brocades, and carpets that furnished the spaces all received the richest and most elegant patterning. These beautiful designs were appropriated in various degrees by the other arts and account in no small measure for the special character of the court carpets of the period, the variety of colour, the ingenuity and imaginative range of pattern schemes, and the superlative draftsmanship that is both lucid and expressive.

Among the products inspired by book illumination were the Medallion carpets of northwest Persia, which consist of a large centre medallion connected with pendants or cartuoches on the long axis and with quarter-section designs of the medallion in the corner areas. First used on ornamental pages and bindings of Persian books, on carpets this arrangement provided an effective centre and allowed several layers of designs to overlap because the

By courtesy of the Staatliche Museen zu Berlin, Islamisches Museum

Figure 11: Wool carpet with octagons containing a stylized dragon-and-phoenix combat motif, attributed to Anatolia, *c.* early 15th century. In the Staatliche Museen zu Berlin. 172 × 90 cm.

medallions could cover multiple vine and flower patterns. The depiction of the latter motifs is more relaxed than their medieval rendering, and new motifs (inspired by painting) such as animals, humans, and landscapes began to be worked in.

A special court atelier, possibly located in Solṭānīyeh, translated the most gorgeous illuminations into carpets.

The world's most famous Persian carpets

Among the 12 or so surviving examples are the world's most famous carpets, each a masterpiece of superb design, majestic size, purity and depth of colour, and perfection of detail. The best known are two carpets from the mosque at Ardabīl in eastern Azerbaijan, Iran, dated 1539–40. The better, skillfully restored, is now in the Victoria and Albert Museum (Figure 12); the other, reduced in size, is in the Los Angeles County Museum of Art. An extremely rich, intricate system of stems and blossoms covers a velvety, glowing indigo field, the whole dominated by a complex gold-star medallion. A near rival to the Ardabīl weaving is the Anhalt Carpet (possibly 19th century), named after a previous owner, the Duke of Anhalt, and now in the Metropolitan Museum of Art, New York City. An intricate star medallion dominates a brilliant yellow field covered with scrolling arabesques and fluttering cloud bands, framed by a scarlet border. One of the most beautiful of northwest Persian rugs is the "animal" carpet, half of which is in Kraków Cathedral, Poland, and half in the Musée des Arts Décoratifs. It has the same glowing scarlet and gold as the Anhalt Carpet but with more subtle halftones (buff on yellow, gray on taupe, brown on gray) and represents paradise more pictorially. Historically more important, and in beauty a rival of any, is the great "hunting" carpet in the Museo Poldi Pezzoli in Milan (Figure 13), inscribed: "It is by the efforts of Giyath-ud-Din 'Jami that this renowned carpet was brought to such perfection in the year 1521." A scarlet and gold medallion dominates a deep blue field, covered with an angular network of blossoming stems, across which hunters dash after their prey.

These carpets, in the opinion of many, represent the supreme achievement in the whole field of carpet designing. Nonetheless, other royal workshops were also producing many beautiful rugs. Particularly costly silk carpets with figure motifs (such as the silk hunting carpet in Vienna's Österreichisches Museum für Angewandte Kunst; see Figure 8) were woven in Kashan, Persia's silk centre. Smaller silk medallion carpets were also made there during the later 16th century, their designs mostly variations of the original medallion system. The court manufacture of Kashan also produced silk carpets with a decidedly royal style.

The distinctive rugs called Vase carpets (because of the flower vases in their designs) are generally thought to be Kerman. The pattern usually consists of several lattice systems with profuse blossoms and foliage. Many of these carpets survive as fragments; but only a scant 20 are intact, the finest of which is in the Victoria and Albert Museum. The rugs were apparently not for export but for court and mosque. Woven on a solid double warp, their boardlike stiffness holds them flat to the floor. In Iran they are still called "Shāh 'Abbās" carpets after the monarch of that name. The typically Persian style widely influenced carpets in Kurdistan and the Caucasus and also Indian court carpets, as well as embroideries from Bukhara.

Later in the 17th century, increasing luxury and wealth demanded the production of so many gold- and silver-threaded carpets that soon they were available in bazaars and exported to Europe, where more than 200 have been found. Some were made in Kashan, but many of the finest came from Isfahan. With their high-keyed fresh colours and opulence, they have affinities with European Renaissance and Baroque idioms. The Polish nobility ordered many gold-threaded rugs from Kashan, for Poland and Persia had close relations in the 17th century. Because there had been a rug- and silk-weaving industry using gold thread in 18th-century Poland, these imported Persian rugs, when first exhibited at the Paris exposition in 1878, were considered Polish, especially as nothing quite like them had at the time been found in Persia itself. They

Figure 12: Wool and silk Persian medallion carpet from the mosque at Ardabīl (Iranian Azerbaijan), probably made in a workshop at Tabriz, Iran, dated 1529–40. A gold star medallion is centred on an indigo field of scrolling stems and blossoms. The medallion symbolizes the Sun; at its centre are four lotus blossoms in a pool, symbolizing the source of rain. In the Victoria and Albert Museum, London. 11.51 × 5.33 m.
By courtesy of the Victoria and Albert Museum, London

were accordingly dubbed "tapis Polonais," or Polish carpets, and the name has stuck. The type degenerated in the later 17th century, materials deteriorating, weaving coarsening, and designs muddling.

East Persian Herāt carpets, which were named after their centre of production and were characterized by their combination of a wine-red field and a border of clear emerald green with touches of golden yellow, became known in Europe as the typical Persian carpet. Many of the European artists of the period owned them, and Anthony Van Dyck and "Velvet" Brueghel (Jan the Elder), in particular, rendered them with complete fidelity in datable paintings. Indian princes also were enamoured of them and acquired them by plunder and pur-

Herāt carpets

Figure 13: Detail of a Persian wool hunting carpet probably from Tabriz, Iran, dated 1521. Hunters and their prey are positioned symmetrically on a dark blue field covered with blossoming stems. The central motif is a scarlet and gold medallion; at its centre is an inscription cartouche signed Giyath-ud-Din Jami. In the Museo Poldi Pezzoli, Milan. 5.70 × 3.65 m.
SCALA, New York

chase alike. Their popularity resulted in mass production with all its attendant deleterious effects, and the style finally expired in mediocrity.

Throughout 17th-century Persia, increasing refinement accompanied slackening inspiration. Silk carpets woven to surround the sarcophagus of Shāh ʿAbbās II (died 1666) in the shrine at Qom (in Central Iran) were the last really fine achievements in Persian weaving. Even Orientalists have mistaken their finish for velvet; the drawing is beautiful, the colour varied, clear, and harmonious. The set is dated and signed by a master artist, Ni ʿmat Allāh of Jūsheqān.

At the end of the 17th century, nomads and town dwellers were still making carpets using dyes developed over centuries, each group maintaining an unadulterated tradition. Not made for an impatient Western market, these humbler rugs of the "low school" are frequently beautifully designed and are of good material and technique. A great rug industry was developed in western Persia in the Solṭānābād district; and from individual towns come beautifully woven rugs such as Sarūks, with their ancient medallion pattern; Serabands, with their repeating patterns on a ground of silvery rose; and Ferahans, with their so-called Herāti pattern—an allover, rather dense design with a light-green border on a mordant dye that leaves the pattern in relief. The earlier Ferahans (two are known, dated to the end of the 18th century) are on fields of dark lustrous blue with a delicately drawn open pattern. Later, Ferahans degenerated in colour and material, and the pattern became clumsy and crowded. "Low school" rugs maintained their standards down to the later 19th century, when insatiable Western demand ruined their artistry; but in the 20th century fine weaving in Persia has been somewhat revived.

Turkey. After the 16th century, Turkish rugs either followed Persian designs, indeed, were possibly worked by immigrant Persians and Egyptians, or followed native traditions. The former, made on court looms, displayed exquisite cloud bands and feathery, tapering white leaves on grounds of pale rose relieved by blue and emerald green. Turkish patterns embellished stately carpets, designed for mosques or noble residences, with rich, harmonious colours and broad, static patterns. They contrast with the lively, intricate Persian designs, in which primary, secondary, and tertiary patterns often interact with one another in subtle dissonances and resolutions.

Turkish styles are best illustrated by the carpets from Uşak in Western Anatolia, in which central star medallions in gold, yellow, and dark blue lie on a field of rich red. So-called Holbein rugs, similar to Caucasian carpets (see below), have polygons on a ground of deep red, dark green, or red and green; they often have green borders and conventionalized interlacing Kūfic script. Such a carpet is depicted in a portrait of Georg Gisze by the 16th-century German painter Hans Holbein the Younger—hence the name. Similarly, a handsome carpet pattern of interlacing yellow arabesques on a ground of deep red appears so often in the paintings of the 16th-century Venetian artist Lorenzo Lotto that they are called Lotto rugs. Carpets with a muted deep-red ground of wonderful intensity, patterned with small medallions, hail, perhaps, from Bergama. In the 17th century they developed into a type known as Transylvanian, so called because so many of them, particularly prayer rugs, were found in Transylvanian churches. They are nonetheless purely Turkish, with rich, quiet colour and sturdy designs. The majority are dominated by a fine red, though a few have faded to the colour of old parchment.

In the 17th century, the "bird carpet," or White Ushak, with conventionalized floral motifs suggesting birds, developed (Figure 14). The few surviving examples are

Uşak carpets

Turkish "bird carpets"

serenely beautiful, with fields of soft ivory and various discreet colours.

Eighteenth- and 19th-century "low school" rugs from Asia Minor continued the tradition of blending sober patterns and luxurious colour. Yürük "low school" rugs, made by nomadic Anatolian peoples like the Kurds, have attracted collectors because of their wide range of rich colours and the use of simple patterns, often geometric, that are organized in bold designs, frequently having a diagonal rather than a vertical emphasis (Figure 15). But the chief creations were prayer rugs, more plentiful among the Turks than among the other faithful. Handsome pieces were woven in Anatolia at Melas, Konya, Lâdik, and Kirşehir, Lâdik's being the most brilliant, both in colour and pattern. The most famous Anatolian prayer rugs came from Ghiordes and Kula, mostly in the 18th and 19th centuries; and in the United States they became the first passion of the collector. Regions such as Smyrna (İzmir) produced a great number of utility carpets for the West.

The Caucasus.   Fine rugs were woven in the Caucasus from the earliest times. During Persia's long political and cultural dominance, the magnificent carpets produced at the Persian court furnished models for the more ambitious Caucasian rugs, such as those woven for the local nobles, or khans. But the Caucasus has its own individual character; while it borrowed motifs from other areas, it completely transformed them by a furious vigour of design unequalled in the textile world. For example, al-

Figure 15: Wool nomad carpet, either Yürük or Kurdish, from near the border between Anatolian Turkey and Iran, 19th century. The geometric pattern of hexagons and lozenges is diagonal rather than vertical. In the Textile Museum, Washington, D.C. 1.73 × 1.48 m.

The Textile Museum Collection, Washington, D.C.; photograph, Otto E. Nelson—EB Inc.

though the Dragon carpets of Kuba continue medieval Persian motifs, the beasts, recognizable in the earliest Caucasian examples, are later stylized and enclosed in repeated rhomboid designs (Figure 16). This stylization process resulted perhaps from the combination of a taste for abstract design and the poverty of the region. The dense knotting required for curvilinear, natural designs is possible only with fine material, which the Caucasians could not afford. Their rugs, therefore, were of coarse weave, the Dragon carpets often having fewer than 80 knots per square inch (12 per square centimetre).

The "low-school" rugs are among the most individual and satisfactory. Their patterns are practically all geometric, densely juxtaposed, generally without organic connection and without implied movement; but they are clear, ingenious, and entirely suitable for floor decoration. More recent examples seem a little dry in colour; but many of them, such as the rugs woven by the Kazakhs, Sarūqs, and other nomads, are sometimes of flaming brilliance; and the older rugs from Dagestan, Kuba (both west of the Caspian Sea), and Shirvan (on the borders of Iraq and Iran) are done in beautifully clear, discreet, and well-balanced tones. *(margin: Caucasian "low-school" rugs)*

Shirvan *kilims*, or tapestry rugs, with their broad horizontal stripes, have bold motifs assembled in harmonious colours.

Another type of flat-stitch carpet, brocaded with a mass of loose threads at the back, comes from the Shemakha region (in Azerbaijan). It has mistakenly been called cashmere because of its superficial resemblance to cashmere shawls. The design usually embodies large, beautifully articulated mosaic-tile patterns in rich and sober colours.

Turkistan.   The carpets of western Turkistan (wrongly called Bokhara carpets) are made by nomadic Turkmen tribes. Few extant examples are more than 100 years old, though similar rugs have almost certainly been made for centuries. Many older pieces are not intended as floor coverings. Some, called *jovāls*, are bags (about 5 by 3 feet; 1.5 by 1 metre) for storage in tents. Some are sad-

By courtesy of the Metropolitan Museum of Art, New York, gift of Joseph V. McMullan, 1963; photograph, Otto E. Nelson—EB Inc.

Figure 14: Wool "bird carpet," possibly from Uşak, Turkey, 17th century. The ivory white ground is patterned with an allover, stylized floral motif reminiscent of a bird. In the Metropolitan Museum of Art, New York. 4.44 × 2.31 m.

dlebags consisting of two squares of about 2 feet (0.6 metre), joined together. There are also long tent bands (called *kibitka*s) about 1 foot (0.3 metre) wide and perhaps 60 yards (55 metres) long, used for decorating large tents, and rugs (called Tekkes) used as hangings for tent doorways. Small, squarish rugs and larger ones of about 10 by 7 feet (3 by 2 metres) seem later and were made perhaps mainly for sale. Turkmen carpets have woollen warp, weft, and pile, two lines of weft, and either Sehna or Ghiordes knots. Except for the Baluchi, Turkmen rugs are characterized by a dark-red colouring and geometric designs. After the predominant red, the chief colours are blue, white, and a natural black wool toning pleasantly to brown. The characteristic design is the octagon, or elephant's foot, arranged in rows and columns, often with diamond-shaped figures in between. Door hangings have cross-shaped panelling, smaller pieces a rectangular diaper (allover pattern). Woven end webs and tassels are used freely as embellishments. Carpets made by Turkmen tribes are the Tekke, Yomud, Afghan, Sarūk, Ersar, Beshir, and Baluchi.

Chinese Turkistan. The oldest surviving Chinese Turkistan rugs date perhaps from the 17th century. Most have a silk pile and some metal and gilded thread, with floral, Persian-influenced patterns showing distinct Chinese treatment. Later carpets are loosely woven with the Sehna knot and have a wool or, more rarely, silk pile and a cotton warp. Eighteenth-century examples have rich, dark colouring, which became brighter in the 19th century and, at last, excessively crude. There are two main types of design. The Medallion carpet usually has three squarish medallions placed down the centre and, almost invariably, one border with a conventional Chinese pattern of foam-crested waves (Figure 17). This design is generally called Samarkand in the trade, though the rugs themselves come from Kashgar, Khotan, Yarkand (modern Su-fu, Hot'ien, So-ch'e in China's Sinkiang region). The Five-blossom carpet has a floral diaper with groups of five blossoms. The colouring is often red and orange with a little clear blue.

Egypt. Egyptian carpets used to be called Damascus carpets but are now termed Mamlūk, after the Muslim

The Textile Museum Collection, Washington,
D.C.; photograph, Otto E. Nelson—EB Inc.

Figure 16: Detail of a wool Kuba Dragon carpet, probably from Karabagh or Shirvan in southern Caucasia, 17th century. The dragon, enclosed in an ogee lattice intersected by palmettes and blossoms, is derived from Chinese motifs through medieval Persian models. In the Textile Museum, Washington, D.C. Full size 5.34 × 2.39 m.

Figure 17: Chinese Turkistan three-medallion wool carpet from Khotan (Hot'ien), Sinkiang Uigur Autonomous Region, China, 19th century. The top and centre medallions contain a pomegranate branch and vase motif. The corner filling is a Turkish form of the Chinese cloud scroll. The guard stripe has a stylized Chinese wave pattern, the centre band of the main border a swastika meander. In the collection of Voitech Blau, New York. 3.71 × 1.83 m.

In possession of Voitech Blau, New York; photograph Otto E. Nelson—EB Inc.

dynasty (1250–1517) that subsidized their manufacture, or Cairene rugs after Cairo, the city in which they were made.

Knotting was thought to have reached Egypt from Asia Minor, but early Cairene carpets differ from Anatolian ones: they are knotted with the Persian knot, and their colours are red, yellow green, and light blue, applied evenly in inner field and border. Moreover, Egyptian designs concentrate on the centre, subordinating surrounding motifs. Border designs match rectangular with square panels. Although filled with plants, the carpet designs seem geometric (Figure 18). The heyday of these rugs occurred during later Mamlūk rule, when there was extensive export.

India. Carpets are less important in India than elsewhere in Asia because the climate makes knotted floor coverings unsuitable. As an art, carpet weaving was brought from Persia by the 16th- and 17th-century Mughal emperors, who subsidized the manufacture of beautiful rugs with an almost silken sheen. Although Indian artistry was influenced by Southern and Eastern Persian carpets, it maintained a native taste for pictorial representation (Figure 19).

The carpets made for the courts of the grand Mughals were of extravagant and luxurious beauty. Expense was ignored, and a series of carpets was made with 600 to 1,200 knots per square inch (95 to 190 per square centimetre). Special carpets were of even finer weave, 2,100 knots per square inch (325 per square centimetre; Metropolitan Museum of Art). For the palace of Shāh Jahān

Characteristics of Turkmen rugs *(margin heading, left)*

Mughal carpets *(margin heading, right)*

Figure 18: Cairene wool carpet from Egypt, 16th century, Mamlūk period. The field features a star medallion centred in a geometrically designed ground, covered with stylized forms of the papyrus and other plants. In the Metropolitan Museum of Art, New York. 2.41 × 2.17 m.

By courtesy of the Metropolitan Museum of Art, New York, gift of George Blumenthal; photograph, Otto E. Nelson—EB Inc.

(died 1666) a set of rugs was made from the most precious wool, imported from Kashmir and remote Himalayan valleys. But because the sources of the art were in imitation, not in the life roots of the people, these wonderful fabrics never reached the artistic height that characterized many periods of Persian weaving. Once established, the rug industry continued, becoming a jail industry, particularly in the Punjab. Designs degenerated, and good wool was difficult to obtain. Later Indian carpets are thus mostly inferior to Persian work.

China. The rugs of China are recognizable by their characteristic Chinese ornament. Of coarse texture, they are Sehna-knotted on a cotton warp. The pile is thick, smooth-surfaced, and "sculptured" so as to form a furrow at the pattern's contours. Yellow predominates, sometimes intentionally, sometimes as the result of the fading of red and orange. Blue and white are commonly used; but true red, brown, and green are rarely seen.

Some carpets have repeating plant scrolls; others scattered flowers and various Chinese symbols. Frets, or key designs, often decorate the border.

Chinese Pillar carpets

Peculiar to China are Pillar carpets, designed so that when wrapped around a pillar the edges will fit together to form a continuous pattern, usually a coiling dragon (Figure 20). Small mats and seat covers are also common. Chinese rugs are virtually impossible to date, since they vary little with time. Many large carpets have been made for export in the 20th century.

Western carpets. *Spain.* Spain's close ties with Islām after the 8th century made it quick to accept and produce knotted carpets. Early examples of the unusual Spanish knot suggest manufacture as early as the 12th century, but not until the 15th century do enough examples remain to allow grouping of work. Many designs imitate Anatolian forms (Figure 21); others, with coats of arms or Christian emblems, indicate purely European origin. During the 16th century, Renaissance influence was prevalent. The manufacturing centres were Cuenca, Alcaraz, and possibly Almería. The knotted carpet lost ground during the 18th century; and native work, known as Al-

pujarra (after the district), is embroidered or done in uncut weft-loop technique.

France. In France, too, the stimulus for the production of knotted carpets came from the East; but the designs of the rugs were inspired by contemporary French decoration rather than Oriental carpet design. Jean Fortier and Pierre Dupont won fame knotting pieces in the Hospice de la Savonnerie at Chaillot, which was converted from a soap factory to a carpet factory in the early 17th century. "Savonnerie" became a mark of distinction in French carpets, reaching a zenith during the later 17th century with Louis XIV's immense order for Versailles. Combined since 1826 with the Gobelins factory, the firm still operates. Thick and strong, these carpets consist of a woollen pile on a mostly linen warp. During the 18th century and afterward, many tapestry-woven carpets were made at Aubusson as well as at other tapestry factories. Even though their production has not been confined to that city, they are known as Aubusson carpets.

Savonnerie and Aubusson carpets

The European concept of carpet design, as distinguished from the Oriental concept, is most explicit in the Savonnerie carpets, in which three-dimensional compositions complement architecture, and even portraits are reproduced (Figure 22). The style of such carpets is best seen in sketches of rug design made by Charles Le Brun for Louis XIV (mostly in the Mobilier National in Paris).

United Kingdom and Ireland. The growth of a native craft in the United Kingdom soon followed on the introduction of carpets from Turkey, though 16th- and 17th-century intact specimens number only about a dozen. They are characterized by a hemp warp and weft, medium-fine woollen pile, and the Ghiordes knot. The background usually is green, and there are so many shades of the other colours that the entire number of tints is greater than in Oriental carpets. The designs can be divided into two groups. In the first are typically English patterns resembling contemporary embroidery, often with heral-

By courtesy of the Museum of Fine Arts, Boston, gift of Mrs. Frederick L. Ames in the name of Frederick L. Ames

Figure 19: Indian wool pictorial carpet, Mughal, late 16th or early 17th century. The field design resembles Mughal painted miniatures, or illuminated manuscripts. In the Museum of Fine Arts, Boston. 2.4 × 1.5 m.

dic devices and dates. The oldest specimen, dated 1570, belongs to the Earl of Verulam. In the second group are many pieces of carpet knotting—called at the time "Turkey work"—imitating Oriental designs and made to cover chairs and stools. As the demand for carpets increased in the 18th century, factories were established at Paddington, Fulham, and Moorfields, near London, and at Exeter and Axminster in Devon. Axminster worked on well into the 19th century, when it merged with the Wilton Royal Carpet Factory Ltd. at Wilton, Wiltshire, which still operates. The industry dwindled and almost disappeared with the advent of mechanization until about 1880. The craft was revived by the English artist and poet William Morris. Later in the 19th century, a factory opened in Donegal, Ireland; and during the 20th century, many small rugs have been knotted by handicraft societies.

Scandinavia. Scandinavian work is similar in concept despite national differences of colour and motif. Abundant handmade products include floor coverings, coverlets, upholstery for benches, chairs, stools, and pillows. Techniques dating from the Vikings (and probably imported by them from Turkey) are continued in Swedish and Finnish rugs, called Rya rugs. Knotted work includes pieces with pile on either side, many Ghiordes on three warps, and braided and woven patchwork carpets with interwoven strips. Geometric designs, rooted in the native arts, are common, appearing, for example, in opulent "wedding carpets." Design was also influenced by Dutch tapestry flower motifs.

Eastern Europe. Knotted Mazovian rugs of East Prussia show the strongest Oriental influence, though at the same time they are deeply rooted in peasant traditions. Many other textiles untouched by west European influence, however, came from southeast Poland, the Ukraine, and southern Russia; some are characterized by ancient textile motifs (such as simple stripes) and forceful colour harmonies, others by geometric designs resembling those of the Orient. *Kilims*, or tapestry-woven carpets, are common in those areas, as they are in the Balkans. In Romania, government promotion and the interest taken by contemporary artists in folk idiom have stimulated modern production during the 20th century.

European folk carpets. Carpet making is so widespread in European folk art that it probably would have developed even without stimulus from the Orient. The most varied techniques are represented in these tradition-bound products the designs of which remained unchanged for generations. The work includes floor coverings, chest covers and bedcovers, and draperies, most of modest size (or pieced together) and many made in sets. The colour scheme is very limited, for even the raw materials were homemade. Machine-made carpets in the later 19th century quickly engulfed home products, but a conscious revival and renewal followed in the 20th century.

North America. The technique of knotting has not been used by the Indians, but many tribes have been making flat-woven floor rugs and blankets since the earliest days of their known history. Before sheep were introduced in the 16th century and wool became dominant, the principal material was cotton, together with various fibres and dog's hair. Indian designs are traditionally abstract, making much use of stripes and a zigzag, or "lightning," motif. The colours are black, white, yellow, blue, tan, and red, the latter often dominant. Among the most skillful carpet makers are the Pueblo and Navaho tribes.

Rugs were made by the colonists in a variety of techniques: knitting; crocheting; braiding thin strips of material into small squares and then sewing them together; and embroidering on a coarse-woven foundation. Hooking (drawing material through a canvas foundation) be-

Axminster carpets (margin note)

North American Indian rugs (margin note)

The Textile Museum Collection, Washington, D.C.; photograph, Otto E. Nelson—EB Inc.

Figure 20: Chinese wool Pillar carpet, late 19th century. When the rug is placed around a pillar, the dragon becomes continuous, and the animal masks at the top form a capital. Chinese cloud motifs and Buddhist symbols cover the field. At the base, a mountain rises from ocean waves. In the Textile Museum, Washington, D.C. 2.41 × 1.23 m.

The Textile Museum Collection, Washington, D.C.; photograph, Otto E. Nelson—EB Inc.

Figure 21: Wool carpet from Cuenca, Spain, 17th century, a Spanish version of the Anatolian Lotto rug. In the Textile Museum, Washington, D.C. 2.31 × 2.11 m.

Figure 22: Savonnerie wool carpet made at Chaillot, France, 17th century. A predominately floral arabesque design covers the field, at either end of which are medallions with landscape scenes. The centre motif is a Baroque cartouche. In the collection of Mr. and Mrs. Charles B. Wrightsman, 3.0 × 9.1 m.
Collection of Mr. and Mrs. Charles B. Wrightsman; photograph, the Metropolitan Museum of Art, New York

gan around the turn of the 18th century and became very popular; early examples have crude floral, geometric, or animal designs and are very colourful. No knotted carpets were manufactured by the early settlers. In 1884, however, a factory established in Milwaukee (and later moved to New York City) began to weave carpets in traditional European designs. During the 1890s a branch of the English Wilton Royal Carpet Factory made Axminsters at Elizabethport, New Jersey; and a few beautiful, flat-woven carpets in French Baroque and Neoclassical designs were produced around the turn of the century by a tapestry factory in Williams Bridge, New York. After this, machine weaving, which began in the U.S. in the late 1700s, gradually displaced hand weaving.

BIBLIOGRAPHY. For further study in this area the following important summaries are recommended: RUDOLF M. RIEFSTAHL, *A Short Bibliography for the Student of Oriental and Western Hand-knotted Rugs and Carpets* (1926); FRIEDRICH SARRE and HERMANN TRENKWALD, *Altorientalische Teppiche*, 2 vol. (1926–28; Eng. trans., *Old Oriental Carpets*, 2 vol., 1926–29), excellent large plates with exact description and technical analysis of masterpieces of Oriental rugs and carpets, including a comprehensive bibliography; KURT ERDMANN, *Der orientalische Knüpfteppich*, 3rd ed. (1965; Eng. trans., *Oriental Carpets*, 2nd ed., 1962), the most important newly revised discussion of Oriental rugs and carpets with regard to artistic development—contains the most comprehensive bibliography for all areas of the Oriental carpet, including newspaper and journal essays, and museum and auction catalogs, arranged according to subject areas; and *Siebenhundert Jahre Orientteppich* (1966; Eng. trans., *Seven Hundred Years of Oriental Carpets*, 1970), a posthumous collection of the author's articles, presenting material not found in his earlier works; WILHELM VON BODE and ERNST KUHNEL, *Vorderasiatische Knüpfteppiche aus alter Zeit*, 4th ed. (1955; Eng. trans., *Antique Rugs from the Near East*, 1958), a handbook on the scientific study of rugs and carpets; ALBERT F. KENDRICK and C.E.C. TATTERSALL, *Hand-woven Carpets, Oriental and European*, 2 vol. (1922), a monographic treatment of the individual types, including products after 1800; ARTHUR U. POPE and PHYLLIS ACKERMAN, *The Art of Carpet Making in a Survey of Persian Art from Prehistoric Times to the Present*, 7 vol. (1938–39), the most comprehensive study of the art of carpet making in Persia, richly illustrated; CORNELIA B. FARADAY, *European and American Carpets and Rugs* (1929), a comprehensive study of European and American carpet production, including native arts and machine-made carpets (very richly illustrated but without bibliography); C.E.C. TATTERSALL, *A History of British Carpets* (1934), an extensive study of carpet production in England, including machine-made carpets; M.J. MAJORCAS, *English Needlework Carpets, 16th–19th Centuries* (1963), a richly illustrated treatise; MADELEINE JARRY, *Manufacture nationale de la Savonnerie* (Eng. trans., *The Carpets of the Manufacture de la Savonnerie*, 1966) and *The Carpets of Aubusson* (1969), two recent studies of French floor coverings, with ample illustrations.

Rummy Games

Rummy refers to a family of card games whose many variants make it the best known and most widely played family of games in the United States, if not in the world. The basic principle of all Rummy (rum, rhum, romme) games is to form sets of three or four cards of the same rank (as four eights, three sixes), or sequences of three or more cards of the same suit ($\diamond$ 6–5–4–3, etc.). Some variants allow only one or the other of these combinations. In Canasta, for example, sequences are not permitted.

History. Many games of the 17th century, during which card playing became popular in Europe, included the principle of building such structures, or melds, before or during a period of play. The ancient Chinese game of Mah-Jongg (see BOARD AND TILE GAMES), played with tiles long before the invention of playing cards and based on forming matching groups of three and four, is a venerable ancestor of Rummy. The earliest modern form of Rummy, however, became popular in Mexico in the latter half of the 19th century as Conquian, from the Spanish *con quien*, "with whom," a mysterious misnomer since it was a two-hand rather than a partnership game.

Earliest modern form

Conquian, better known as Cooncan (or Coon-Can) as it spread to Texas and the southern United States early in the 20th century, used the "Spanish pack" of 40 cards—the regular 52-card pack with tens, nines, and eights removed. The modern game of Panguingue, or Pan as it is more often called in the many gaming clubs on the Pacific Coast and in southwestern United States, where it is very popular, uses eight such packs shuffled together to make it possible for the game to be played by as many as 15 players, although the usual game is for six or seven. Pan is one of the few games that still follows the principle of dealing and playing to the right instead of to the left. Pan also requires that the winner have a hand of 11 matched cards; no discard can be made on the last turn.

In the United States, Cooncan soon developed into Rum. It is not clear whether this name followed the theme of "Whiskey" in the game of Whiskey Poker or was adopted when the game was characterized by an Englishman as "Rum" ("Queer") Poker. A later variant, however, introduced as a two-hand game in 1909 in New York by Elwood Baker, was named Gin with the deliberate intention of keeping it in the alcoholic beverage family. Because it seemed desirable to remove card playing from the same sinful category as drinking, both names were soon bowdlerized, becoming Rummy and Gin Rummy. Another Rummy variant, Canasta, originated in Uruguay in the late 1940s and quickly became the most popular game in the clubs of Argentina. In the early 1950s it temporarily eclipsed Contract Bridge in popularity in the U.S., but was never more than moderately popular in Europe.

The game of Rum

Principles and procedures. There are no official rules for the basic game of Rummy, but the following procedures are generally observed.

From two to six may play, using a standard deck of 52 cards, with or without jokers. Cards rank: K (high), Q, J, 10, 9 etc., to A, low. In some variants, but not generally in the basic game, A–K–Q is allowed as a sequence. In two-hand play, ten cards are dealt to each, face down, one at a time beginning with the player on dealer's left and continuing clockwise. For three or four players, a hand is seven cards; for five or six players, six cards are dealt. The remainder of the pack, the stock, is placed face down; the top card of the stock is faced to begin the talon, or discard pile. Each player in his turn may take the top card of the discard pile or draw the top card of the stock; he may then place face up on the table any legal meld of three cards or more or add (lay off) one or more cards from his hand that match his own or any other player's exposed melds. He ends his turn by discarding one card face up on the discard pile, except that on the turn when a player goes out no discard need be made. A player goes out when he has melded all the cards in his hand. Joker may be used as any needed card.

Melding and scoring

The melds, as previously noted, may be sets of three or four cards of the same rank or sequences of three or more cards in the same suit or additions of such cards to melds previously tabled. Melding an entire hand at one turn is called going rummy and counts double.

The winner of each deal collects from each of the other players the index value of the cards each still holds in his hand, even if such cards are matched up. Face cards count 10 each; aces 1 or 11 as previously agreed; jokers, if used, count 15.

When stock is exhausted, play ends and the hand with the lowest unmatched count wins. In some games, each player is permitted an additional turn to take or refuse the top card of the talon.

A running score is kept and the game ends when any player reaches the predetermined goal (as 100 points) or after an agreed number of deals.

500 Rum

Variants. Among the most widely played Rummy games is 500 Rum, also called Pinochle Rummy, and its variants including Michigan Rum, Oklahoma, Persian Rummy, and Canasta and its many derivatives, Samba, Bolivia, and others. From two to eight may play. With five players or more, two full packs shuffled together are used. When two play, each is dealt 13 cards; with three or more, 7 cards are dealt to each.

At his turn, each player draws the top card of the stock or any card in the discard pile provided that: (1) he melds such card at once, and (2) he takes into his hand (to meld immediately or not, as he pleases) all cards lying above the one he has drawn. Melds and layoffs are the same as in the basic game of Rummy, but each player keeps his melds in front of him, and when the deal ends he receives credit for their index value minus the value of all cards remaining in his hand. Aces count 15 if left in hand or if melded as a set of aces; they count one if melded A–2–3. Game ends when any player has scored 500 or more. No bonus is given for winning the game.

Canasta

In the variant Canasta, two full packs plus four jokers are used and all jokers and deuces are wild. Each player is dealt 11 cards. If a player takes the top card of the discard pile, which he must be able to meld immediately, he must also take the entire pile. A meld of seven or more cards of the same rank (sequences cannot be melded) is a natural Canasta worth 500 points if it contains no wild card, and a mixed Canasta worth 300 points if it contains at least four natural cards and one or more wild cards. Each card is assigned a point value and there is a 100-point bonus for going out. The game ends when either side's score is 5,000 or more, the higher score winning.

Knock Rummy

In Knock Rummy any player, at his turn and after drawing and discarding, may knock (lay down his entire hand) and declare the total value of his unmatched cards. If his assumption that he has the lowest total of unmatched cards proves correct, he collects the difference in counts from each opponent. If another hand is lower, the low hand wins from all and collects an extra ten points from

the knocker. (Some play that knocker must pay double.) If a player ties for low, he collects from all but the knocker, who neither pays nor collects. If two or more other players tie for low, they divide the winnings.

Gin Rummy

At first played sporadically as a game between two players waiting for a fourth at bridge clubs, Gin Rummy became an American fad in the 1940s. Essentially a competition between two players, it is widely played with two, three, or four players on two teams. Each plays head-to-head against one adversary, but the scores made by each of the players in his individual match are combined, and the net result is entered as the score of each deal.

Each player is dealt ten cards, and the top card of the stock is turned face up. Nondealer may take it; if he refuses, dealer has the opportunity to do so. If both refuse, nondealer draws the top card of the stock. Thereafter, each player may take the other's discard or draw from stock.

Melds are as in basic Rummy. Either player in turn may knock if the total of his unmatched cards will be ten or less after he has discarded. (Some play that the rank of the first up-card determines the number for which a player may knock on that deal, a turned ace requiring completing "gin" to go out; some play that if a spade is turned the score of that deal is doubled.)

Opponent of the knocker may lay off any of his unmatched cards upon the knocker's melds, thereby reducing his count. If the knocker wins, he collects the difference between the total of his and his opponent's unmatched cards. If the opponent remains with an equal or lesser count, he has undercut the knocker and wins the difference (if any) plus a bonus of 25 points.

To score "gin"

If all of the knocker's cards are matched (after he discards), he announces "gin" and receives a bonus of 25 points in addition to the total of his opponent's unmatched cards. Some play that an opponent cannot lay off on a gin hand; others permit layoffs to reduce the loser's total, but the player who goes gin cannot be undercut and is assured of at least his 25 point bonus. Some pay an additional 25 point bonus for 11-card gin (no discard).

A deal ends with no score when only two cards remain in the stock and neither player has knocked. First to reach 100 points wins the game and receives, in addition to the difference in scores, a 25-point bonus. Each player then adds to his score 25 points for each deal he has won, called a box. If the loser failed to score, the game is a shutout, or schneider, and the winner's total score is doubled.

Some score (Hollywood system) as if three games were being played simultaneously—each player's first score is entered under game one, his second score under game one and game two, his third and subsequent scores under all three; if he does not score in game one, his first score is entered under game two, his second and subsequent scores under games two and three. Bonuses are scored for each game independently of the others.

In a four-hand or six-hand game, the winning side must reach 150 or (by agreement) 200.

BIBLIOGRAPHY. A.H. MOREHEAD, *The New Complete Hoyle* (1964); C.H. GOREN, *Go With the Odd: A Guide to Successful Gambling* (1969); R.L. FREY, *According to Hoyle* (1970).

(R.L.Fr.)

Rural Society, Contemporary

Rural societies differ from urban in many obvious ways, but it is not easy to define the differences so that they fit every case. This article will classify as rural societies those in which the predominant human activities are those which are involved in the production of foods, fibres, and raw materials. These field activities require a relatively high ratio of land per person. To the extent that a population is engaged in such field activities, it can be considered rural. A population can be considered urban, on the other hand, if it is engaged in activities by which the foods, fibres, minerals, and raw materials from the field are processed and distributed to their users. These activities are usually performed in densely settled areas. Most actual communities display a mixture of the two kinds of activities, combining rural and urban features in varying proportions. This article is divided into the following sections:

RURAL SOCIETY DELINEATED

In industrialized countries, large metropolitan areas usually consist of one or two very large centres within which are overlapping groupings of localities of various sizes. The progression from the centre of the urban area to the open country usually is uneven: minor concentrations of centre activities occur here and there between the urban heart and the rural periphery.

In nonindustrialized countries, the change from city to countryside is often more abrupt. Within the city itself, there is likely to be a considerable mixture of urban and rural elements. While the city dwellers in the nonindustrialized country will be chiefly engaged in centre pursuits, they may also carry on field activities, such as poultry and dairy production and gardening. The city itself in such societies is usually less urban than the city in an industrialized society. The nature of transportation and communication facilities in nonindustrialized societies has a profound influence on both the urban centre and the rural hinterland. When there are few such links, the transition from city to countryside becomes a cultural and social transition as well. Passage from the city to its hinterland in societies of low technological development has been described as passing from the modern world to one in which people's actions are governed largely by tradition.

A difficulty in classifying places as urban or rural is that governments do not use the same definition, a difficulty nowhere better demonstrated than by the data on rurality and urbanity supplied to the United Nations. As shown in the accompanying Table, which is based on the *Demographic Yearbook 1970* of the United Nations, definitions of urban area vary from places of 500 inhabitants to places of 30,000. The United States and Canada profess to have almost identical urban population ratios, but this similarity exists because, as shown in the footnotes of the Table, their definitions of urban area differ. Albania reports all centres with 400 or more inhabitants as urban, while Czechoslovakia requires that a town have a popula-

Varying definitions

Urban Population Ratios

key: c—census; e—estimate

continent and country*	date	total population	urban population	urban percentage	comments
Africa					
South Africa	1970 c	21,448,169	10,280,202	47.9	areas of 500 or more inhabitants and adjoining suburban areas; well-established towns of fewer than 500 but at least 100 white inhabitants and with specified urban characteristics; certain "rural" portions of districts containing metropolitan areas
Burundi	1970 e	3,429,000	120,000	3.5	commune of Bujumbura
Central African Republic	1966 e	1,437,000	392,000	27.3	20 principal centres with a population of over 3,000 inhabitants
Morocco	1971 c	15,379,259	5,403,466	35.1	117 urban centres
Asia					
Israel	1970 e	3,001,400	2,477,000	82.5	all settlements of more than 2,000 inhabitants, except those in which at least one-third of heads of households earn their living from agriculture
Nepal	1961 c	9,412,996	336,222	3.6	cities of 10,000 or more inhabitants in identifiable agglomerations with essentially urban characteristics
Syria	1970 c	6,292,000	2,740,000	43.5	cities, *muḥāfaẓah* centres, and *minṭaqat* centres
Philippines	1970 e	35,104,000	12,992,000	34.1	Baguio, Cebu, and Quezon cities; all cities and municipalities with a density of at least 1,000 persons per square kilometre (2,600 persons per square mile); administrative centres, barrios, of at least 2,000 inhabitants; others with specified numbers, density, and contiguity to larger centres
Japan	1970 c	103,720,060	74,853,337	72.2	urban municipalities usually having 30,000 or more inhabitants and that may include some rural area as well as urban cluster
Europe					
England and Wales	1971 e	48,987,700	38,425,340	78.4	areas classified as urban for local government purposes
The Netherlands	1969 e	12,953,731	10,101,897	78.0	all municipalities with at least one population cluster of 5,000 or more inhabitants and other municipalities in which not more than 20 percent of the economically active male population are engaged in agriculture
Portugal	1970 e	9,561,000	3,556,000	37.2	agglomerations of 10,000 or more inhabitants
Albania	1967 e	1,964,738	653,950	33.3	towns and other industrial centres of more than 400 inhabitants
Czechoslovakia	1970 c	14,361,557	7,981,000	55.6	large towns, usually of 5,000 or more inhabitants, having a density of more than 100 persons per hectare of built-up area and specific urban characteristics; small towns, usually of 2,500 or more inhabitants, having a density of more than 75 persons per square hectare of built-up area and specific urban characteristics
North and Central America					
Canada	1966 c	20,014,880	14,726,759	73.6	centres of 1,000 or more, including urbanized fringes of metropolitan areas, other major urban areas, and those having 10,000 or more inhabitants in the city and its urban fringe
Haiti	1971 c	4,243,926	824,186	19.4	administrative centres of communes
U.S.	1970 c	203,165,573	149,280,769	73.5	places of 2,500 or more inhabitants and densely settled urban fringes of urbanized areas
El Salvador	1970 e	3,533,628	1,350,429	38.2	administrative centres of municipal districts
Oceania					
Australia	1971 c	12,728,461	10,888,636	85.5	cities and towns of 1,000 or more inhabitants and contiguous urban developments
New Guinea	1966 e	1,578,650	74,067	4.7	centres with population of 500 or more but excluding separately located schools, hospitals, rural settlements, and rural villages regardless of population size
New Zealand	1971 c	2,862,631	2,328,876	81.4	all cities, boroughs, and town districts and designated suburban areas
South America					
Uruguay	1970 e	2,886,000	2,262,000	78.4	cities
Bolivia	1968 e	4,680,000	1,347,100	28.8	administrative centres of departments, provinces, and cantons
Colombia	1970 e	21,363,000	12,732,000	59.6	not indicated
U.S.S.R.	1970 c	241,748,000	136,003,000	56.3	cities and urban-type localities officially designated as such
of which:					
Estonian S.S.R.	…	1,357,000	882,000	65.0	cities and urban-type localities officially designated as such
Moldavian S.S.R.	…	3,572,000	1,131,000	31.7	cities and urban-type localities officially designated as such

*Countries listed include those having the highest and lowest urban population ratios in each continent; for some continents, other countries are included for comparison.
Source: United Nations *Demographic Yearbook 1970;* official country sources.

tion of at least 5,000, that there be a density of more than 100 persons per hectare (40 persons per acre), and that there be other specific urban characteristics. In Japan, which is a densely settled country, an area is classed as urban when it is a municipality having 30,000 or more inhabitants.

Rural relationships. One way of comparing the distinctive characteristics of rural and urban personalities and organizations is by means of ideal, or constructed, types. Such a type is called ideal because it is a construct embodying all of the characteristics of the thing it seeks to describe in their most concentrated state; it is not a sample drawn from reality. Probably the most generally used of these types are those untranslatable concepts of the German sociologist Ferdinand Tönnies, gemeinschaft and gesellschaft, sometimes rendered in English as community and society. The gesellschaft-like organization is one that has an all-important, functionally specific goal, such as profit making for a factory or battle winning for an army. Toward the attainment of its goal it employs all of its mean and resources, including the relationships among the human beings who compose it. Organizations possessing such qualities are sometimes called rational organizations, and those who efficiently and economically operate them are said to be rational actors. The polar opposite of the gesellschaft-like organization is a gemeinschaft-like entity. Among actual organizations the family-sized farm and small peasant community are much closer to the gemeinschaft pole than to the gesellschaft pole: they carry on farming as a way of life, viewing its relationship as ends in themselves rather than as means to an end. Such an organization is said to be natural willed; its members are rational minded only to the extent that they do not embody the gemeinschaft-like characteristics but instead take on some of the impersonal characteristics of the gesellschaft. Just as actual states and territories are neither completely rural nor completely urban but a mixture of both, so organizations and their personnel in real life are neither completely gesellschaft-like nor completely gemeinschaft-like.

Until the time of the Industrial Revolution in the 18th and 19th centuries, agricultural organizations were almost universally gemeinschaft-like; the relationships within them were either those of kinship or resembled those of kinship. Extensions of parent–child relationships were common; thus the feudal lord was a surrogate father to his vassal, who was a surrogate child to his lord. A person's rank was commonly determined by his parentage, his sex, and other inborn characteristics, whereas in gesellschaft-like organizations and societies rank is more likely to be determined by achievement. In traditional agricultural societies the resistance to change and to the adoption of improved practices is generally very great. There are many explanations for this resistance to change. A commonly accepted sociological explanation is that there is a widespread fear that change may result in starvation. In few societies in which starvation and famine are common is land treated as a commodity in a completely rational manner.

Because land is so important for the food supply, its ownership and transfer becomes hedged about by many restrictions. In some present-day peasant societies (such as those in the Yucatan Peninsula of Mexico), food crops are considered sacred and their use and movement must be accompanied by proper ritual. These crops lose their sacred nature once they are sold. Various other human and nonhuman resources come to be infused with sentiments that prevent completely rational use. The resistance to change among peasant peoples and their dislike of the ambitious individual may stem from the belief that if any individual accumulates more wealth than his associates, he must have done so at their expense. The prevalence of suspicion, distrust, and lack of faith in people in peasant societies may arise from the common belief that there is a given sum of wealth and that one person can become rich only if his associates are deprived or exploited.

Problems of transition. Some of the problems of rural societies and rural people are the result of changes that are being forced upon them. Everywhere, even in some rural areas, the old gemeinschaft relationships are giving way to gesellschaft ones. Whereas the work teams of simple rural communities have known each other well and have relationships that are fused with sentiment resulting from prolonged and intimate associations, the bureaucratic work teams of rationalized rural and urban societies know each other in very limited, segmented ways. Workers reveal to each other on the job only a small part of their total beings. Rural migrants thrust into such organizations find the rational bureaucracy emotionally sterile. Devices such as management cafeterias and executive elevators are foreign to the worker who has previously rubbed elbows with his father and others as authority figures. In Communist countries in which bureaucratic administration is applied to farming as well as to urban life, it is not uncommon for authorities in collective farms to tell their counterparts in the cities that they should come to the country to experience how difficult administration can be.

The problems of transition from the old traditional society to the new bureaucratic one are not confined to the developing countries. Only one farm boy out of every ten growing up in industrial countries, such as the United States, will have the opportunity to acquire an adequate-sized commercial farm. If he is one of the nine forced to leave the land, he must learn to conduct himself in a way totally different from the way he behaved in his old setting where he was known to everyone. He will have contacts with groups the meaning of which for him will be so segmented that he will conceal from each individual he meets far more than he will reveal. He will have to learn that the anonymity that he despises as cold and sterile is in reality the only means by which he can have freedom and privacy in the midst of a dense population. The tenth boy, who realizes his dream of operating a farm, will also have to make an adjustment. He will have to understand and use a bewildering array of new machines, chemical fertilizers, improved seeds, and new strains of livestock. If he does not master the constantly changing technology, he will not be able to stay in business. To the extent that he values the traditional aspects of farming, he will accept innovations with some reluctance.

These problems relate to what sociologists call institutionalization. Stable rural societies are usually strongly institutionalized—that is, they have certain accepted organizational structures and predictable patterns of action and interaction. In some cases they may even be described as overinstitutionalized if their norms and goals are so intensely felt by their members that deviation from the norms or failure to achieve the goals is regarded as intolerable. Such overinstitutionalization is found in rigid, traditional societies that resist social change. Thus, among the Amish in the United States, a farmer who adapts a new forbidden practice, such as use of a truck for hauling or a tractor for draft power, is subjected to the *Meidung*, a sanction requiring that none among the Amish, not even the members of the person's family, speak to him. Suicide or complete loss of memory has resulted from the application of this powerful sanction. A society may be underinstitutionalized if norms and goals are absent or so loosely structured that they fail to give direction to the activities of individuals. Underinstitutionalization is usually found in rapidly changing societies in which the old norms and goals are no longer applicable and in which new forms of organizational structure have not yet coalesced. Transient labourers, especially those without family or other similar bonds, who must work here and there for short periods in different cultures or societies or conditions, may suffer from underinstitutionalization. High rates of mental disturbance and suicide are common in such groups. In societies experiencing rapid migration from rural villages to the cities, members may suffer from both overinstitutionalization and underinstitutionalization. In many parts of India and in numerous African countries, the rural-bred migrant to the city finds little to guide him in his new surroundings. When he returns to his village, he is equally at a loss, for different reasons. Although the problem is particularly acute in developing countries, it also exists

(margin left) Gemeinschaft and gesellschaft

(margin right) Transition in industrialized countries

for the Southern sharecropper in the United States who moves to a Northern industrial city and for the large number of Puerto Ricans who have migrated to New York.

As a society becomes urbanized and industrialized, the countryside must increasingly produce food and raw materials for the urban population. It must do this with reduced manpower, because the urban areas are populated with recruits from the countryside who man the city's factories. In scarcely any developing country has agricultural production kept pace with urban growth. In the industrialized West, on the other hand, farm output has not only been sufficient to feed the farmers but has been great enough to take care of the burgeoning cities and even to supply surpluses, while at the same time the number of farm workers has decreased. In 1970 only 6.7 percent of the gainfully employed persons in the United States were engaged in agriculture, forestry, and fisheries. The typical farmer in the U.S. can produce enough to supply the needs of his household and 50 or more others. This situation contrasts strongly with that in the United States a century earlier or with the present situation in such countries as India. In India the typical farm worker produces enough for himself and for three others, two of whom are in his own household. Most countries fall between these extremes.

The countryside not only produces food and fibre for society; it also produces people. The birth rates among those engaged in rural occupations have historically been higher than among others. This demographic difference increases the difficulty of adjusting to modern society because so few children born to farm life can reasonably expect to choose farming as a career and because those who migrate to the cities not only encounter personal hardship but contribute to the overpopulation there.

RURAL PEOPLES

Settlement patterns. Most of the farm and peasant peoples of the world have lived in villages until recent times. Another common settlement pattern is the isolated holding, found in most parts of Canada and the United States. After the passage of the Northwest Ordinance of 1785, westward expansion in the U.S. followed the so-called checkerboard system in which one-mile-square sections of 640 acres (260 hectares) were homesteaded as four equal quarter sections of 160 acres (65 hectares) each. When settlers were free to build their dwellings wherever they wished, they built along roads and within reasonable distance of neighbours. When the settler followed principles dictated by economic use of energy, he might build in the middle of his square holding, but in time the pattern created by such choices gave way, in more thickly populated areas with improved highways, to string-along-the-road or line-type settlements resembling those common in France.

The typical French holding consists of narrow strips; the house is located at one end of the holding, most frequently on a road, river, or stream. In Germany, the traditional settlement, or *Gewanndorf,* was centred on a core of houses, barns, churches, and other buildings. Extending out from this core were small garden plots, then cultivated lands, then pasturelands, and finally the wastelands and wooded areas. This pattern fostered cooperation in the management of common lands and in such activities as harvesting, seeding, and pasturing. The German example influenced villages in England and New England. Spanish–Portuguese settlements, especially those developed in colonies, often centred on a plaza where the church and other community buildings were located. The extension of the square plaza resulted in straight streets and quadrangle blocks, unlike the crooked streets of the Germanic form.

The automobile and the highway have changed settlement patterns in at least four ways: (1) on the outskirts of cities, fringe areas have developed that combine rural and urban characteristics; (2) string-along-the-road developments have sprung up, inhabited by people who rely on their automobiles to carry them to the relatively distant city, resulting sometimes in tentacle-like extensions of the city into the surrounding country; (3) the expansion of the suburbs has reduced the importance of the central-city shopping areas as additional shopping areas have grown up in the outskirts; (4) a hierarchy of centres and subcentres has emerged as a working interchange between rural and urban life; these include populated places of various sizes, from regional centres to towns, villages, and hamlets, all of which exchange goods and services with the rural population.

Rural demography. Much information about rural society is to be found in demographic statistics, such as sex ratios, age structures, birth rates and death rates. The United Nations publishes demographic data of international scope in its *Demographic Yearbook,* which, together with reports of the U.S. Bureau of the Census, constitutes the basis for the following analysis.

Age composition. The age composition of rural populations tends to differ from that of urban. Rural-farm populations have higher concentrations of the young and lower proportions of those in the most productive ages. If one draws a chart showing the numbers of individuals of various ages in a particular population, with the young ages at the bottom and the old ages at the top, the chart will be roughly pyramidal in shape. Countries in which both the birth rate and the death rate are high will tend to have age pyramids that are very broad at the base because of the large numbers of children, and taper fairly rapidly and evenly to a peak because of the comparatively small number who live to old age. A quite different profile is presented by such countries as New Zealand or the United States, where relatively fewer children are born, relatively few die in infancy, and relatively many live to old age: the pyramid is not so evenly tapered, being "pushed outward" by those of working and older ages. The opposite pattern is common in Latin America and much of Africa and the Middle East, where the age pyramid has a relatively high proportion of children. In a number of industrialized countries, the pyramid bulges in the middle because of the high proportion of persons in the productive ages of life and older.

Sex composition. The sex composition of a population is usually given in terms of the number of males per hundred females. Among newborn infants the ratio is about 105. It varies in succeeding years because of differences in the death rate (usually higher among male children) and in rates of long-distance out-migration (usually higher among young males) and of short-distance out-migration (usually higher among young females). More males than females die at all ages, except in such countries as India, where the girl child receives less care. Most of the differences in sex ratios among countries can usually be attributed to different migration patterns. Males in the productive periods of their lives often leave areas of limited economic opportunity to take work elsewhere. Malaysia, an area of colonial and plantation industry, reports a higher sex ratio for the age bracket 15–64 than it does for the age bracket under 15. Frontier districts, such as Alaska, report even higher sex ratios. Sex ratios are generally low in urban areas and high among farming populations, especially where rural women can find urban employment. Marriage rates and birth rates are lower in these areas than they would be if rural women were available in sufficient numbers to rural men and urban men in sufficient numbers to urban women.

Birth rates and death rates. Traditional rural societies have very high birth rates; modern public health techniques have reduced death rates to a degree that has resulted in rapid population growth in these societies. The developing countries are now faced with the task of lowering their birth rates to a level more compatible with their economic possibilities. One difficulty in doing so is that the factors governing rural birth rates are often religious and cultural. The rural Hindu father, for example, not only wants to have enough children to carry on the farm work but also needs a male child to take him in his aging years to the sacred places.

Population is affected by numerous variables. Sex differentials, for example, have much to do with the rate of reproduction, and these, in turn, are related to the rural–

urban character of a particular area: the more urban an area, the lower the fertility of the population and, the more rural an area, the higher the fertility.

Kinship structures. Rural societies also differ from urban societies in their family structures. Rural families throughout history have generally been larger and more extended than urban families. In some cultures they include several generations of the male line (grandfather, father, son, and grandson) as well as uncles, aunts, and cousins. The family in old China and Japan sometimes extended to 200,000 or 300,000 members. Such families, known as clans, and other clanlike organizations have been important in the history of human society and still constitute the major organizational device for millions. Family and kinship relationships are closely involved with the institution of property, the institution of marriage, and basic norms of behaviour such as those governing the definition of incest. The extended family makes easier the transfer of property and with it the transfer of role responsibility from an aging farmer to a younger family member, particularly when the norms of succession have been institutionalized as is common in many peasant societies. Certain privileges and rights are accorded the retiring peasant owner-operator, and certain duties and responsibilities accompany the assumption of the role by his successor.

The extended family

In cultures in which the family is the most important organizational structure for every facet of life, including the economic, the norms supporting it are all-prevailing and are deeply felt. Marriage is typically very strictly controlled. Relatives within a clan often marry but only according to the prescriptions of accepted custom. In most Arab countries, children of two sisters or children of two brothers may marry. In old Chinese families, children of siblings of opposite sexes (brother and sister) could marry. In both cases the rationale behind the mating norms is the protection of the larger family; the definition of incest varies according to the requirements of social stability.

The kinship structure of rural societies affects the age at which men marry and determines what proportion of them must remain unmarried. If the marriage bond gives primacy to the male line and is subordinate to the filial bond, as in the family structure of old China, it is not necessary to attain economic independence before marriage within the extended family. The father or grandfather need not worry about any threat to his authority at the marriage of his son or grandson. In the families of northwestern Europe, the situation is very different. Reluctance to permit a son to marry before the father is ready to relinquish control of the farm enterprise appears to delay or prevent marriage there and to be associated with lower birth rates.

The small nuclear family of northwestern Europe is an advantageous arrangement in an industrial society, in which mobility of the labour force is more important than the rights of property in land. There are wide variations in the closeness of the relations maintained between the nuclear family and other relatives such as grandparents, sisters, brothers, uncles, and aunts. Even when these relations are intimate, the immediate family is usually considered to be the married pair and their children.

Technological and economic influences. In the developing countries, farmers tend to be self-sufficient. Only a small amount of the produce goes to market, most of it being retained to support the farmer and his household. Agriculture in highly mechanized societies produces much more than can be used by the household.

Differences in output

Increased production in agriculture requires that there be some surplus income that can be put back into the productive process in the form of tools or fertilizer or other improvements. Farmers may, instead, choose to have larger families that guarantee a larger work force. This is particularly true in traditional agricultural societies and is in part due to the fact that the life cycle of families there differs from that of families in modern agricultural and industrial societies. In the life cycle of a given family in traditional agriculture, a time will come when the ratio of the young, nonproductive family members to the

adult producers is very high. Survival then will require the adults to work harder. This situation will be followed by a period during which income will be higher and directly proportional to the number of workers available. When the people in the productive enterprise consume an amount just equal to what they produce, economic development is almost impossible because gains are literally eaten up. In societies in which, one way or another, capital has come to be invested in agriculture, production may increase without a corresponding need for manpower, and surplus labour will migrate to the city. To avoid the creation of new urban slums, many experts on agricultural development recommend practices that will increase production without displacing masses of workers; these include soil technology, improved seeds, irrigation, and drainage but not large-scale mechanization. The effects of mechanization on the use of labour can be seen in the United States, where less than 6 percent of the labour force is employed in farming. The tendency of Western industrialized countries to export their own patterns and institutions is giving way to the realization that agricultural techniques must be adapted to the particular needs of each society if they are to be accepted and put to profitable use.

Some basic agricultural patterns are set by nature. Land-use specialists can tell by looking at maps showing farm population density, along with such other variables as temperature and precipitation, what is being produced in a particular area and how. But nature cannot be taken for granted. In some parts of the world, timber and livestock are being produced with little thought for anything except short-run profit. Sustained yields of forests and grazing lands require that society take a long view, or the consequence will be erosion and despoilment.

Social rank. Karl Marx thought of farmers as capitalists exercising private and exploitative control over one of the major means of production—the land. Thomas Jefferson saw in the farmer a free yeoman who, because he was free and independent, was the mainstay of the republic. Consistent with Marx's views, the leaders of the Soviet Union have abolished most private holdings except for small household plots and have sought to model agricultural management upon that of the factory. Practice in the West and in areas under Western influence has been in the direction of breaking up large estates and creating family-sized enterprises. Under proper conditions, the family-sized farm has been efficient and progressive, yielding some of the social and civic benefits anticipated by Jefferson. To say this is not to deny that farms may be too small, as often occurs after centuries of equal land division among sons. An efficient family-sized farm may be formed by the bringing together of small pieces of land as well as by the division of large tracts.

The owner-operator of a family-sized farm is both labourer and entrepreneur. Political movements among farmers sometimes have ties with labour, sometimes with business, and sometimes they have had Socialistic tendencies.

In areas in which large holdings prevail, the social class assigned to rural workers is lower than that in which family-sized holdings are common. Thus, throughout Latin America the day labourers and sharecroppers on haciendas form a rural proletariat. The owners of the land, the managers of agricultural processing plants, and the store owners form an upper class. In between are the supervisors, teachers, and other specialists or professionals. In India and Pakistan, caste distinctions prevail even on the family-sized farm. Elsewhere, however, even where there are distinctions of rank, the categories are not rigid enough to constitute classes. The Costa Rican peasant who lives in a floorless *rancho,* covered only by a thatched roof, is ranked by his associates lower than the inhabitant of the *casa* with a metal roof and a floor; but, because they may be rather closely related and have a considerable amount of interaction, they cannot be considered members of different classes.

Distinctions among rural workers

In rural society generally, social rank—whether reflected in caste, class, or estate—is determined more by birth than is the case in urban society. In the city, symbols of differentiation in rank are omnipresent; they extend from squalid tenements to magnificent houses. The differences among the mud houses in a village in Lebanon or between the *rancho* and the *casa* in rural Costa Rica are much less obvious. One reason for the importance of class symbols in the city is that everyone in that anonymous society looks for all the clues he can find to assign some sort of identity to the strangers he encounters each day. Because the city dweller's rank is dependent upon achievement, he reveals himself to others through his dress, speech, grooming, and personal possessions. The rural dweller, on the other hand, is known to those among whom he moves, and the rank assigned to him is beyond his power to change. An interesting analogy to the striving of the individual in urban life may be seen in the process by which whole castes in India and Pakistan attempt to rise together by adopting the norms and lifestyles of those above.

Attempts have been made by governments to abolish caste and class. In India, where many hereditary privileges have been outlawed and members of lower castes have been given access to government positions, universities, and civic life, an individual's caste remains one of his most important characteristics. In the Soviet Union, the Communists set out to build a classless society; but Soviet social scientists report "intraclass differences" in the incomes and levels of living of rural workers in state farms and collective farms. Some of the differences are attributable to the income from household plots, which are larger in the collective farms than on the state farms. One of the most reliable indicators of class differences is the number of religious icons displayed in the home, the number decreasing rapidly or vanishing as the class scale is ascended.

The family-owned farm is a vital force in agriculture in many parts of the world. The rank of the rural resident largely depends on his relation to the land. The owner of land, other things being equal, has the highest rank; labourers, especially transient ones, rank lowest; and the various types of tenants rank in between. The once-independent yeoman or farm owner is everywhere becoming less independent as agriculture becomes increasingly industrialized, specialized, and regulated. The ownership of land, however, still retains its importance in rural life. Farmers' and peasants' movements seldom demand that ownership of land be abolished. Even the demands raised in the Mexican Revolution (1911–17) for communal land tenure represented in reality a demand that the *hacendados* (large landowners) return the land to those who had occupied it under a former system. Most rural uprisings demand more, not less, private ownership of property for those revolting.

Organizations. Schools, health services, and adult-training agencies in rural settings tend to be less effective than those of the city, largely because the per-capita cost is always greater in an area of low population density. Also, to the extent that effective service requires highly trained personnel, rural areas find it difficult to attract them from urban areas, where supporting agencies are more available and income greater. To the extent that tradition is hallowed and certain beliefs and procedures are considered sacred, the rural agencies may become instruments for the preservation of custom rather than means of judicious exploration and change.

Informal groups

What rural areas often lack by way of effective formal organization is partly compensated for by the vitality of their informal organizations. The division between the two is not always great. A group that begins by informally purchasing and jointly owning a grain combine may grow into a cooperative buying society. Groups organized informally against horse thievery have been known to grow into formal farmers' organizations with some political power. Work exchange and borrowing is prevalent throughout traditional rural society, and much of it serves a real function without ever becoming formally organized. Cooperative neighbourhood activity, usually work-related, often provides occasion for informal recreation: a barn raising, a harvesting bee, a quilting party are social occasions fully as much as they are work ses-

sions. Harvest celebrations are common in most countries, even in highly modernized societies.

People in traditional rural societies are not good at organizing effective bureaucracies—one of the reasons why the many hundreds of bloody peasant and farmer revolts in the past have failed to bring much improvement in the lot of the agriculturist. Only in recent times, with improved communication and better education, have farmers and peasants begun to play effective political and economic roles. Organizations of rural young people have done much to spread knowledge and social awareness in countries as diverse as Japan, Yugoslavia, and the United States. In addition to socializing and training the youth in practical affairs, these groups often help to modernize their elders.

PROBLEMS OF CHANGE

Large farms versus small. If one examines rural and urban problems from a global point of view, it appears that cities everywhere are in danger of being swamped by a flood of migrants from rural areas. Most cities find it hard to absorb all of the migrants, and the necessary services are more costly and difficult to supply in the largest centres than in the smaller ones. Some students of the problem believe that the trend toward larger and larger agricultural units, with increasingly heavy traffic between farm and city, may have to be reversed. In Japan, the highly mechanized family farm produces most of the agricultural output, as in the United States, but the average Japanese farm is only about three acres (1.2 hectares) as compared with about 400 acres in the U.S. It may be that the future of rural society will conform to the Japanese rather than the American pattern.

The need for balanced growth

In most Communist countries the Marxist predilection for large-scale agriculture has led toward the elimination of rural villages and family farms. Important exceptions are Poland and Yugoslavia, where peasant opposition and the fear of food shortages have prevented collectivization.

The role of planning. Rural and agricultural planning is carried on in most societies, in developed as well as in underdeveloped nations, in countries where agriculture is socialized and in countries where it is not. Denmark, for example, plans for specialization in agricultural exports, India maintains a national ministry for planning, and Yugoslavia plans in order to support its rural cooperatives. In the United States, much planning goes on at the national level in government agencies dealing with farm credit, soil conservation, fish life and wildlife, wood plots, irrigated lands, and rural housing. Very often the planning personnel are not the executive personnel and are not charged with the authority or responsibility for transforming the plans into action programs. For these reasons, planning is not always consistent nor is it undertaken with a sense of urgency.

In India there is great emphasis on the need to plan from the bottom upward and to make planning a two-way process so that the cultivators themselves can play a part in it. A most important Indian planning activity is the establishment between the district centre and the villages of growth centres in which educational, welfare, marketing, and other agencies may be located. This activity is seen as a means of relating the villages to governmental and marketing services. Similar institutions are evolving in many developing societies.

Communist countries make use of the cooperative, the collective, the state farm, the production brigade, and the commune as instruments of rural planning. An important factor in these countries is the power and organization of the centrally directed party apparatus, which cannot be matched in such countries as India.

BIBLIOGRAPHY. HENRI MENDRAS, *La Fin des paysans: changement et innovations dans les sociétés rurales françaises* (1970; Eng. trans., *The Vanishing Peasant: Innovation and Change in French Agriculture*, 1970), deals primarily with French peasants, but the author's concern is not confined to France. T. LYNN SMITH and PAUL E. ZOPF, JR., *Demography: Principles and Methods* (1970), is a useful source of comparative demographic data. JOEL M. HALPERN, *The Changing Village Community: The Global Problem* (1970), is about what the author calls the rural revolution, or the increasing linkage of urban and rural cultures as revealed in Mexican, Serbian, Chinese, Russian, and American community studies. CHARLES P. LOOMIS and J. ALLAN BEEGLE, *Rural Sociology: The Strategy of Change* (1957), is a general treatment. J. PAUL LEAGANS and CHARLES P. LOOMIS (eds.), *Behavioral Change in Agriculture: Concepts and Strategies for Influencing Transition* (1971), is a symposium by various authorities. CHARLES P. LOOMIS, *Social Systems: Essays on Their Persistence and Change* (1960), presents a framework for analysis of societies in general, as well as rural societies. G.V. OSIPOV (ed.), *Town, Country and People* (1969), is a book by Soviet scholars dealing with population trends, rural planning, collectives, state farms, village surveys, religion, rural social structure, and rural sociology in the U.S.S.R. The chapter by Y.V. ARUTYUNYAN on rural social structure is of particular interest. WILLIAM T. LIU (ed.), *Chinese Society Under Communism* (1967), brings together available material on Chinese rural society. D.G. GADGIL, *Planning and Economic Policy in India* (1961), describes the Indian approach to rural planning.

(C.P.L.)

Rush, Benjamin

Benjamin Rush, physician, teacher, patriot, and reformer, was one of the most versatile and influential figures among the founders of the United States. Passing his entire professional life in Philadelphia, then the largest city and the cultural and political centre of the country, Rush knew all of his great contemporaries, corresponded with many of them, and, after the death of his friend Benjamin Franklin, was recognized as the leading citizen of Philadelphia and a major figure in American science and letters. An ardent nationalist, he wrote in 1786 that although the War of Independence had come to an end, the American Revolution had just begun; and he saw it as his mission "to effect a revolution in our principles, opinions, and manners so as to accommodate them" to a truly republican government.

By courtesy of the Independence National Historical Park Collection, Philadelphia, Pa.

Rush, oil painting by Charles Willson Peale (1741–1827), after a painting by Thomas Sully (1783–1872). In the Independence National Historical Park Collection, Philadelphia, Pennsylvania.

Rush was born on December 24, 1745 (new style, January 4, 1746), in Byberry township, now part of Philadelphia, into a pious Presbyterian family. He was sent to a private academy and on to the College of New Jersey at Princeton, from which he graduated in 1760. After a medical apprenticeship of six years, he sailed for Europe. He took a medical degree at the University of Edinburgh in 1768 and then worked in London hospitals and briefly visited Paris.

Medical publications

Returning home to begin medical practice in 1769, he was appointed professor of chemistry in the College of Philadelphia, and in the following year he published his *Syllabus of a Course of Lectures on Chemistry*, the first American textbook in this field. Despite war and political upheavals, Rush's practice grew to substantial proportions, partly owing to his literary output. The standard checklist of early American medical imprints lists 65 publications under his name, not counting scores of communications to newspapers and magazines. The best known guide to world medical classics (L.T. MORTON, *Garrison and Morton's Medical Bibliography*, 2nd ed., 1954) contains seven entries for Rush, ranging in subject from military hygiene and "breakbone fever" to psychiatry. Another source of Rush's professional prestige was the large number of his private apprentices and students from all over the country. He taught some 3,000 students during his tenure, successively, as professor of chemistry, the theory and practice of medicine, and the institutes of medicine and clinical medicine in the College of Philadelphia and the University of Pennsylvania. After 1790 his lectures were among the leading cultural attractions of the city.

As a physician, Rush was a theorist, and a dogmatic one, rather than a scientific pathologist. Striving for a simple, unitary explanation of disease, he conjectured that all diseases are really one—a fever brought on by overstimulation of the blood vessels—and hence subject to a simple remedy—"depletion" by bloodletting and purges. The worse the fever, he believed, the more "heroic" the treatment it called for; and in the epidemics of yellow fever that afflicted Philadelphia in the 1790s his cures were more dreaded by some than the disease. But in some measure the equally heroic presence of the doctor himself made up for his theories. He refused to flee the city when others did and entered hundreds of sickrooms with a confident air and the reassuring words, "You have nothing but a yellow fever."

Contributions to psychiatry

In psychiatry Rush's contributions were more enduring. For many years he laboured among the insane patients at the Pennsylvania Hospital, advocating humane treatment for them on the ground that mental disorders were as subject to healing arts as physical ones; indeed, he held that insanity often proceeded from physical causes, an idea that was a long step forward from the old notion that lunatics are possessed by devils. His *Medical Inquiries and Observations upon the Diseases of the Mind* (1812) was the first and for many years the only American treatise on psychiatry.

Rush was an early and active American patriot. As a member of the radical provincial conference in June 1776, he drafted a resolution urging independence and was soon elected to the Continental Congress, signing the Declaration of Independence with other members on August 2. For a year he served in the field as surgeon general and physician general of the Middle Department of the Continental Army, but early in 1778 he resigned because he considered the military hospitals mismanaged by his superior, who was supported by General Washington. Rush went on to question Washington's military judgment, a step that he was to regret and one that clouded his reputation until recent times. He resumed the practice and teaching of medicine and in 1797, by appointment of President John Adams, took on the duties of treasurer of the U.S. Mint. He held this office until his death, of typhus, in Philadelphia on April 19, 1813.

Rush early reflected the humanitarianism of the Enlightenment by publishing antislavery tracts, and after the Revolution he issued a stream of articles and pamphlets attacking tobacco, "spirituous liquors," war, oaths, public punishment of criminals, capital punishment, and the like, while, on the other hand, he espoused free public schools, the education of girls, a national university, and life-saving societies. In later years, however, Rush lost faith in political and social reforms. He kept up his political friendships by writing charming letters, some of which show a capacity to laugh at his own follies. A late triumph of his letter writing was the reconciliation he effected between former Presidents John Adams and Thomas Jefferson. The characterization Rush furnished for himself among his sketches of the signers of the Declaration of Independence was singularly brief and appropriate: "He aimed well."

BIBLIOGRAPHY. The standard biography is NATHAN G. GOODMAN, *Benjamin Rush: Physician and Citizen, 1746–1813* (1934); more recent and very readable is CARL A. BINGER, *Revolutionary Doctor: Benjamin Rush (1746–1813)* (1966). Both contain reference notes and bibliographies. Rush's separately published works are listed in ROBERT B. AUSTIN, *Early*

American Medical Imprints: A Guide to Works Published in the United States, 1668–1820 (1961), which must be supplemented by Rush's nonmedical writings, particularly his Essays: Literary, Moral & Philosophical (1798), containing many of his educational and reform proposals. Rush's lively and invaluable Autobiography has been admirably edited, with related materials, by GEORGE W. CORNER (1948); and his Letters, touching on every aspect of his life, were edited by L.H. BUTTERFIELD, 2 vol. (1951). JOHN H. POWELL, Bring Out Your Dead (1949), is a vivid account of the yellow fever epidemic of 1793 and Rush's part therein.

(L.H.Bu.)

Ruskin, John

As a writer, critic, and artist, Ruskin more than anyone else influenced the public taste of Victorian England, and, in economic theory, he did much to inspire the opposition to the philosophy of laissez-faire, or non-interference. He was one of the first to bring the work of art into relation with its creation and with the age in which he lived and one of the first to preach with some effect that a respect for art must be a part of civilization. He inspired the artist and writer William Morris to create the Society for the Protection of Ancient Buildings and preached the necessity for a National Art Collections Fund a generation before one was founded. He included visual training in his educational schemes and made the social condition of the workman a part of the judgment of the work of art and of the products of manufacturing on a larger scale. It is easy and partly true to say that he lost the battle against the doctrines and practice of Manchester and the political economists who followed John Bright in advocating laissez-faire; yet many of his words did not fall on stony ground. No one who has read any of his more important works seriously will ever be quite free from his influence; in what he wrote there was always an element of single-minded nobility. No picture of the Victorian age can be complete without him.

By courtesy of the Royal Academy of Arts, London

Ruskin, oil painting by Sir John Everett Millais, 1853–54. In a private collection.

Life. Youth. John Ruskin was born in London on February 8, 1819. His grandfather was gifted, a spendthrift, and a little mad, and he finally killed himself. His parents recognized a dangerous precocity and an unstable genius in their child and sheltered him from contact with reality. At the same time, they checked and restrained him and allowed him little spontaneity of interest or action. The father, John James Ruskin, was a successful wine merchant. He had a liking for pictures, and, when he toured England to solicit orders, he saw the galleries in the great houses, accompanied, in time, by his son. The Ruskins moved to Herne Hill, on the southern outskirts of London, when Ruskin was four, and to nearby Denmark Hill, near Dulwich, when he was 20. His natural appetite for pictures found satisfaction in the Dulwich College Picture Gallery, and the pictures exhibited there remained the basis of his thoughts on art long after he was free to seek wider knowledge.

The Dulwich gallery, constant reading of the Bible with his mother and of the 18th-century classics with his father, and his father's encouragement of his facile talents in writing and drawing were the most valuable part of his education. His father's interest in art secured him drawing lessons from the watercolorist Copley Fielding. When he was 14 the family began a series of tours in Europe, of a conventional kind—northern France, Flanders, the Rhine, the Black Forest, and Switzerland. In the Alps he found the beauty and sublimity that his imagination needed, and he justified his love of the Alps by amateur geologizing and botanizing. Such justification of his enjoyment was made necessary largely by the intense moral preoccupations of his parents, which had left their mark on him.

When he was 17 Ruskin fell in love with Adèle Domecq, the daughter of his father's Spanish partner. The frustration of this affair seems to have been the effective cause of a permanent failure to attain emotional maturity, which left him vulnerable and incomplete.

In 1836 Ruskin went up to Christ Church, Oxford, where his studies were desultory and his social life was hampered by his mother's presence in lodgings nearby. Nonetheless, he had gotten away from the suburbs and made friends—chief among them Henry (later Sir Henry) Acland, who became regius professor of medicine—who were permanently to enrich his life. He won the Newdigate prize for poetry in 1839 and, because of a generous allowance from his father, was able to begin to collect pictures by J.M.W. Turner.

Oxford friend-ships

First visit to Italy. Ruskin's time at Oxford was interrupted suddenly in the spring of 1840, when he suffered a hemorrhage, which the doctors considered to be of consumptive origin. They advised that he should winter abroad, and the family departed for Italy. Ruskin made many sketches in the course of the long, leisurely journey, but in Rome, where he made friends with the artist George Richmond, he began to have a clearer idea of the difference between amateur and professional work. They went on to Naples, where he had another attack, but on the return journey, by Venice through Switzerland, he regained energy and hope. He found himself able to see natural beauty in all its gamut—from great mountains to minute plants—with a new vividness, and he devoted himself to describing it with artistry.

Ruskin returned to Oxford in the autumn and graduated in the spring of 1842. The Ruskins spent the summer at Chamonix-Mont-Blanc in the French Alps. There John began to plan a book in defense of Turner, whose late style had been exemplified in the pictures that he exhibited in the Royal Academy that year and that had been laughed at by the critics. Returning to a new house on Denmark Hill, he began to work seriously at the National Gallery and at Dulwich and to write the first draft of what was to become the first volume of Modern Painters. He set out to examine the "truth to Nature" of the accepted masters of landscape painting, always with the glorification of Turner in mind; and in his description of landscape in Italy and in the Alps he gave rein to his own capacity for word painting. The book appeared in May 1843, when Ruskin was just 24. It had a considerable success, though Turner himself showed nothing but embarrassment. Ruskin immediately set to work on a second volume, which had no such definite scheme as the first and contained even more of the author's sensibility—a sensibility that had by then escaped from Protestant inhibitions in the study of religious painting.

Composition of Modern Painters

Second visit to Italy; marriage. In April 1845 Ruskin set out on a journey that was to mark a new stage in his development. Together with a valet and an elderly mountaineer guide and without his parents, he set forth to explore northern Italy and found in its medieval architecture and sculpture a romantic beauty he had not known before. The sketches he made were the best he ever achieved, and the things he saw were forever imprinted on his memory; for once he was really happy.

When he returned to Denmark Hill it was to complete the second volume of *Modern Painters* in less congenial surroundings. It appeared in April 1846. A subsequent journey to Italy with his parents, to show them the beauties he had lately discovered, was an anticlimax and led to an attack of nervous depression. On their return he began to think of marriage and, with hesitant encouragement from his parents, became engaged to Euphemia Chalmers (Effie) Gray, the pretty daughter of Scottish friends of the family, whom he married in April 1848. He was completely self-centred and very gifted; she was rather demanding, a born social climber, and essentially commonplace. It is not surprising that the marriage (which was never consummated) was not a success.

Marriage to Effie Gray

After a few months in London, where Effie was determinedly social, in August they visited northern France, for Ruskin had it in mind to write a book on the essential qualities of Gothic architecture. By April *The Seven Lamps of Architecture* was finished. The book had a considerable success. It took the fruits of the labours of a generation of medievalists and gave them a generalized basis and a moral flavour; and it was extremely well written. In the autumn of 1849 the young Ruskins went to Venice for the winter. Ruskin wished to apply the general principles of *The Seven Lamps of Architecture* to Venetian architecture and to relate its rise and fall to the working of moral and spiritual forces. He worked hard; the first volume of *The Stones of Venice* duly appeared in 1851. In the course of that year Ruskin was induced to champion the Pre-Raphaelite Brotherhood, a group of young English artists founded in reaction against contemporary academic painting, less because he admired them from the first than because he thought the critics unfair to them. He befriended the painter and poet Dante Gabriel Rossetti, who disliked him; established a lasting and happy friendship with the artist Edward Burne-Jones; and cultivated the company of John Everett Millais, with the result that the artist and Effie fell in love. As soon as Millais had been elected a member of the Royal Academy, with an assured future, Effie left Ruskin. In July 1854 she secured an annulment of her marriage on the ground of her husband's impotence, and a few months later she married Millais.

Return to Denmark Hill. Ruskin was back in the old narrow circle of Denmark Hill. His only escape was to rather futile teaching at the Working Men's College (established in 1854 by the moral philosopher and Christian Socialist J.F.D. Maurice, whom he did not like) and in sitting at the feet of the historian and essayist Thomas Carlyle, who made him waste a good deal of time on causes irrelevant to his real interests. The third and fourth volumes of *Modern Painters* were written on an increasingly authoritarian note, and by the middle of 1855 he felt written out. His chief interest was in the construction of the Oxford Museum of Natural History, under the aegis of his friend Acland and according to his own principles of Gothic beauty. He offered to undertake the sorting and arrangement of the mass of drawings that Turner had left to the National Gallery, and, from February 1857 for about a year, this was his chief occupation. He gave many lectures, less on art pure and simple than on its implications. In those on *The Political Economy of Art* (1857)—later retitled *A Joy for Ever*—he entered economics, with an able and effective disquisition on economy as "the art of managing labour."

In 1858, again alone but for a valet and the old guide, he spent six weeks in Turin, Italy, and recaptured the magic of the mature Renaissance in the paintings of Paolo Veronese. The fifth volume of *Modern Painters* (1860), written in the winter of 1858–59, is largely influenced by these interests. The volume is extremely disconnected; and, indeed, Ruskin's mind was gradually declining into madness. He fell in love with a hysterical young Irish girl of good family, Rose La Touche, who, when he first knew her, was a child of ten; when she was 16 he declared himself to the parents, who were horrified. Soon after, Rose fell mentally and physically ill, and the affair dragged sadly and hectically on until her death in 1875. During these years, Ruskin became a habitué of Miss

Affair with Rose La Touche

Bell's girls' school at Winnington, Cheshire, where the company of the children provided a refuge; some of his books—notably *The Ethics of the Dust* (1866)—were developed from talks he gave to her pupils. His only important work at this time was a set of essays on the nature of wealth that he wrote in 1860. His views (based to some extent on those of the reformer and Socialist Robert Owen) included the theory of social justice and were utterly contrary to the laissez-faire doctrines of the time, which derived from the teachings of the Utilitarian philosopher Jeremy Bentham. *The Cornhill Magazine* began to publish the essays, but they roused so much opposition among its readers that, after the fourth essay, William Makepeace Thackeray, the distinguished novelist who was its editor, discontinued them. Ruskin published them as a book under the title *Unto This Last* (1862).

He was near a breakdown and retired for a time to Mornex, near Geneva. He returned in time for his father's last illness and death in March 1864 and continued to live with his aging mother at Denmark Hill. His father bequeathed Ruskin £120,000, various properties, and a fine collection of pictures; but he had neither peace of mind nor strength of purpose left. He wrote no more on art, except as a part of his social and economic theories, and when he travelled he was apt to delegate the making of sketches to artists whom he took with him.

Last years. In 1869 Ruskin was elected the first Slade professor of fine art at Oxford University, and he had a great personal success as a lecturer, though his lectures were diffuse and on many subjects other than art. He gave the university a collection of prints, photographs, and drawings for undergraduates to study, and he set up a drawing school for them. He had a need to address himself to those of another intellectual class than himself and, thus, wrote two series of letters to workingmen, *Time and Tide* (1867) and a much longer set, *Fors Clavigera* (1871–84.) The last was the organ of the Company of St. George, which he founded in 1871 and endowed with a capital of £10,000. It was intended to carry out his economic doctrines; every "companion" was to give it a tenth of his income, and for many years Ruskin did. Its activities were often ill-judged and were usually unfortunate; a museum of art at Sheffield was the most successful. Bouts of illness interrupted work at Oxford and the publication of *Fors;* after his mother's death, in 1871, Ruskin sold the house at Denmark Hill and bought Brantwood, an ugly residence beautifully situated on Coniston Water in the Lake District, where he spent much of his time, with a married cousin to keep house for him. He began to be obsessed with the idea of the "Storm-Cloud and Plague-Wind" that were everywhere defiling natural beauty, and finally in 1878 suffered some months of acute mania. Early in 1879 he resigned his professorship, giving as his excuse that the painter James McNeill Whistler had won a libel action against him for his intemperate criticism of one of the "Nocturnes."

The Company of St. George

His intellectual life was over. He showed improvement in 1880–81 and even resumed work at Oxford, with grotesque and tragic results. The years that followed were checkered by attacks of mania; yet it was in these years that he wrote the most charming of his works, the autobiography called *Praeterita* (1885–89). It offered escape from the present, and, since he had kept a diary for much of his life, he had materials to work on. It was never finished; after a sixth attack of madness, in the summer of 1889, he was incapable of writing anything but his signature. He died on January 20, 1900, and was buried at Coniston, Lancashire.

Assessment. It is usual to think of Ruskin as a typical public figure of Victorian England, the keeper of the artistic conscience of his country who upheld the preeminence of the Gothic style and demanded its employment in building and decoration. Nevertheless, acceptance of Ruskin as a prophet in art was not immediate. Though the substantive part of his pure art criticism was written before he was 35, he was considered to be something of an amateur, a rich dilettante, until after he was 50, in the 1860s. By this time, the Gothic Revival movement, with roots in the late 18th century, had already become established as a leading current style, independently of his championship of it. By the last quarter of the 19th century, Ruskin's opinions on art were regarded as almost infallible; but from the 1860s onward he himself had lost interest in art criticism for its own sake, and his creative ideas were now active in political and social economy.

Interests and character. His puritanical conscience never let him rest easy in the enjoyment of his unearned wealth: he tried at first to justify his enjoyment of beauty by theorizing about it, and later, when this no longer satisfied him, he turned to the study of economic and social questions.

Ruskin lived an inwardly difficult, lonely life, often pursued and struck at by madness. His interests were wide, embracing art, such branches of natural science as geology, mineralogy, and botany, political science, and economic and social studies. Yet the variety of interest was also symptomatic of a want of concentration that increased with time and caused him, from one hour to the next, to abandon one kind of study for another. His art criticism, too, for all its influence and its breadth, is unsystematic and established on his personal response to works of art; here his apparent limitations are partly those of his time, when art criticism and art history—to which his own writings gave a major impetus—were still only lightly cultivated fields: he had little knowledge or appreciation of French, Dutch, or Spanish art or indeed of any art outside that of Renaissance Italy and of England, and he had no sympathy with the Impressionist movement of his own day.

Style and ideas. Yet John Ruskin was a man of true originality. His literary style, though it has echoes of the King James Version of the Bible and of writers such as Richard Hooker and Dr. Samuel Johnson, is unmistakably his own; although his ideas might owe something to the Greek philosopher Plato and more still to the Bible, he shaped them in his own way. He was a completely honest and curiously innocent man. As a rich man's son, he was free to work at what he liked and generally wrote easily of what interested him. This amateur quality gives a characteristic sparkle and zest to his treatment of all his themes, and they were many. His originality and his intellectual self-indulgence were inextricably mixed with his psychological weakness. He is the archetype of the manic-depressive, swinging from elation to misery, always sensitive and always expressive. The narrow religiosity of his early upbringing, his lack of systematic education, and his mother's overanxious care did nothing to give him the poise and repose that might have helped him to keep a balance; and two frustrated love affairs and an unhappy marriage removed any hope of emotional maturity.

But, in spite of these disabilities (and sometimes because of them), he was able to perceive beauty with an infectious intensity and to express his perception in memorable prose, sometimes made even more cogent by accompanying drawings and sketches, for he was a good amateur draftsman.

What, then, are Ruskin's essential ideas on art and society, and how can they be summarized? It must be remembered first that Ruskin was a follower of the great poet William Wordsworth in his love of nature and of mountain scenery in particular. Ruskin founded his aesthetic principles upon truth to nature in landscape painting and tried to prove his point by contrasting, in *Modern Painters,* the sensitive accuracy in this respect of his hero J.M.W. Turner, the great landscape painter of the first part of the 19th century in England, with the conventional generalizations of Claude Lorrain, the great landscapist of 17th-century France. He went on to find the same truthfulness, but now united with religious feeling, in Gothic architecture. He looked with care at the natural forms of its decoration, carved with delicate reserve by a host of anonymous craftsmen. The gesticulation of the Baroque and its ornaments, such as urns, scrolls, and obelisks—forms not found in nature—seemed artificial and false to him and so, in his view, constituted bad art. His conception of good art as a storehouse of natural truth, which also was its source, led to his ideal view of the workman, whether craftsman or manual labourer, as

Limitations of Ruskin's art criticism

Ruskin's aesthetic principles

a dedicated individual who needed to find fulfillment through doing work with a valid purpose. Social justice required the provision of conditions that would allow all to share with the creative artist the opportunity for work of this kind, but such conditions were not generally to be found in the heedless economic expansion of 19th-century England. Thus, he was led from criticism and exposition of art to a concern with social welfare. Yet one comes back to the fact that he is remembered best in the world of art.

MAJOR WORKS

WRITINGS ON ART: *Modern Painters*, 5 vol. (1843–60, epilogue 1888); *The Seven Lamps of Architecture* (1849); *The Stones of Venice*, 3 vol. (1851–53).

WRITINGS ON SOCIAL AND POLITICAL ECONOMY: *Unto This Last* (1862), four articles first published in *The Cornhill Magazine*, 1860; *Time and Tide* (1867), letters in newspapers of the same year; *Fors Clavigera*, monthly publication, occasionally interrupted, of letters to workmen, 1–96 (1871–84); *Munera Pulveris* (1872), four articles in *Fraser's Magazine*, 1862–63.

OTHER WORKS: *The Two Paths* (1859) and *A Joy for Ever* (1880), both compiled from lectures given in 1856–59; *Sesame and Lilies* (1865) and *The Crown of Wild Olive* (1866), miscellaneous lectures; *The Ethics of the Dust* (1866); *Praeterita*, parts 1–28 (1885–89), an incomplete autobiography.

BIBLIOGRAPHY

Editions: Ruskin's *Works* were edited by E.T. COOK and A. WEDDERBURN, 39 vol. (1903–12). The *Diaries* were edited by JOAN EVANS and J.H. WHITEHOUSE, 3 vol. (1956–59). There are separate editions of *Letters* to various people, of which *Ruskin's Letters from Venice, 1851–1852, ed.* by J.L. BRADLEY (1955), may be noted.

Selections: JOAN EVANS (ed.), *The Lamp of Beauty* (1959), an anthology of his writings on art; also *Ruskin Today*, chosen and annotated by KENNETH CLARK (1964).

Biography and criticism: E.T. COOK, *The Life of John Ruskin*, 2 vol. (1911, reprinted 1968), a classic that now seems overdiscreet; DERRICK LEON, *Ruskin, the Great Victorian* (1949); PETER QUENNELL, *John Ruskin: The Portrait of a Prophet* (1949); JOHN D. ROSENBERG, *The Darkening Glass: A Portrait of Ruskin's Genius* (1961); and R.W. WILENSKI, *John Ruskin: An Introduction to a Further Study of His Life and Work* (1933, reprinted 1967), are good biographies.

More specialized aspects: J.T. FAIN, *Ruskin and the Economists* (1956); W.M. JAMES (ed.), *The Order of Release: The Story of John Ruskin, Effie Gray and John Everett Millais, Told for the First Time in Their Unpublished Letters* (1947); MARY LUTYENS, *Millais and the Ruskins* (1967); and (ed.), *Effie in Venice: Unpublished Letters of Mrs. John Ruskin Written Between 1849–1852* (1965); H.G. VILJOEN, *Ruskin's Scottish Heritage* (1956); J.H. WHITEHOUSE, *Vindication of Ruskin* (1950).

(J.Ev.)

Russell, Bertrand

Bertrand Russell had one of the most widely varied and persistently influential intellects of the 20th century. During most of his active life, a span of three generations, Russell had at any time more than 40 books in print ranging over philosophy, mathematics, science, ethics, sociology, education, history, religion, politics, and polemic. The extent of his influence resulted partly from his amazing efficiency in applying his intellect (he normally wrote at the rate of 3,000 largely unaltered words a day), his memory, and his aristocratic independence and partly from his deep humanitarian feeling that was the mainspring of his actions. This feeling expressed itself consistently at the frontier of social change through what he himself would have called a liberal anarchistic, left-wing, and skeptical atheist temperament. His first major undertaking in the field of logic and mathematics had a profound influence upon philosophy in the Western world. In his middle years his books on morals, politics, education, pacifism, and other subjects were an illumination and encouragement to the rebellious layman. Finally, during the last decades of his life (just as he felt himself in danger of becoming respectable by sheer weight of years), he became an inspiration to idealistic youth throughout the world in his active opposition to the manufacture of H-bombs and to the war in Vietnam.

Bertrand Russell, 1960.
By courtesy of the British
Broadcasting Corporation, London

Early years. Bertrand Arthur William Russell, 3rd Earl Russell, was born at Trelleck in Monmouthshire on May 18, 1872, the second son of Viscount Amberley and his wife Katherine, daughter of the 2nd Baron Stanley of Alderley. Lord Amberley was the third son of Lord John Russell, who was twice prime minister and became the 1st Earl Russell.

Katherine Amberley died of diphtheria in 1874, and Amberley himself died 18 months later. The Amberleys had very advanced views and had intended to place Bertrand and his brother Frank (then aged ten) under the guardianship of friends who were atheists. But the children's grandparents had no difficulty, given the feeling of the time, in upsetting the will and getting the two boys made wards in Chancery, so that they were brought up by their Russell grandmother, a strict yet politically liberal-minded Puritan with a rigid personal conscience and exacting standards. Bertrand Russell was educated privately, had little contact with other children, and developed an intense inner life, full of idealistic feeling and metaphysical profundities (partly a product, he later theorized, of sublimated sexual desires), all imbued with a passionate desire for certainty in knowledge. At the age of 11 he had already begun to have religious doubts, and, eventually, the skeptical cast of his intelligence prevailed over his upbringing. He came to disagree with his family on everything except politics, but he was also able to accept the disillusionment of finding that logical certainty was unattainable in empirical matters and to accept as well the stunning disappointment (when introduced by his brother at the age of 11 to the delightful certainties of mathematics) of being told that the axioms of geometry could not be proved but had to be taken on trust.

This situation set the pattern of Russell's philosophical career. He was determined not to be beguiled by human pretensions to knowledge or by unbacked assumptions either about the foundations of knowledge or about what may be said to exist. Henceforth, one of his primary aims was to inquire, with skeptical and parsimonious intent, "how much we can be said to know and with what degree of certainty or doubtfulness."

He entered Trinity College, Cambridge, in 1890, was at once recognized as intellectually outstanding, and soon became a member of the exclusive Society known to outsiders as "The Apostles." He was winner of first-class honours in the Mathematical Tripos (honours examination) in 1893 and then turned to philosophy, becoming for several years an Idealist under the influence of the Cambridge metaphysician J.M.E. McTaggart, and taking a first-class degree in moral sciences in 1894.

In the same year, against the wishes of his family, he married Alys Pearsall Smith, the sister of Logan Pearsall Smith (the author of *Trivia*) and a Quaker from Philadelphia with advanced views. In the next two years he lectured in the United States on non-Euclidian geometry, travelled in Germany to study economics, was introduced to Marxism by the Social Democrats there, and, as a result, was appointed first lecturer at the London School of Economics and Political Science. His first published book—written from the orthodox liberal point of view—was *German Social Democracy* (1896). He remained a liberal until he joined the Labour Party in 1914. He also won a fellowship at Trinity with a dissertation entitled "An Essay on the Foundations of Geometry."

First philosophical works. In 1898, with Trinity Fellow G.E. Moore leading the way, he rebelled against Idealism and became, broadly, an Empiricist, a Positivist, and what philosophers would call a physical Realist (though in everyday matters he was what the layman would call a Materialist) for the rest of his philosophical career.

His career may be said to have involved three main aims, with an underlying premise that the scientific view of the world is largely the correct view. The most fundamental and pervasive aim was the one already mentioned: that of paring down to a minimum and to their simplest expression the pretensions of human knowledge. This aim manifested itself in such books as *An Inquiry into Meaning and Truth* (1940) and his last major work *Human Knowledge, Its Scope and Limits* (1948), which was intended to be a definitive survey. The second aim involved the linking of logic and mathematics, as in his first major work, *The Principles of Mathematics* (1903), with the object of showing that mathematics can be deduced from a very small number of logical principles. The third aim was analytic: assuming that it is possible to infer something about the world from the language in which it is (correctly) described, Russell analyzed that language down to its minimum requirements—its atomic facts—in order to avoid unnecessarily postulating the existence of the objects denoted by descriptive phrases (such as "The present king of France"). This aim manifested itself in the so-called theory of descriptions, in the philosophy of Logical Atomism, and in such books as *The Analysis of Matter* (1927) and *The Analysis of Mind* (1921), the main thesis of which holds that mind and matter are different "structurings" of the same "neutral" elements.

After an interlude of work on Leibniz (*A Critical Exposition of the Philosophy of Leibniz* [1900]), Russell embarked upon his major work on logic and mathematics, starting with the first draft of *The Principles of Mathematics* (1903) and culminating over a decade later in the publication of the three volumes of *Principia Mathematica* (1910, 1912, and 1913), written in collaboration with his friend and former tutor, the philosopher and mathematician Alfred North Whitehead. This work, together with Russell's ancillary work on logic, was immensely influential among logicians for many years, even though the two authors agreed that they had not completely fulfilled their purpose of deriving mathematics from self-evident logical principles.

At the beginning of this decade of work—the hardest in Russell's whole life—he underwent what he called a "mystic illumination," which in five minutes transformed him into a pacifist (and a pro-Boer in England's war against the Boers of South Africa) and overwhelmed him with "semi-mystical feelings about beauty." It was in 1903 that he suddenly fell out of love with his wife Alys (though the couple did not separate until 1911), Russell in 1910 having met Lady Ottoline Morrell, a prominent literary hostess, with whom he developed a long-lasting relationship.

In 1902 there appeared the popular and, as he later felt, overwritten essay "The Free Man's Worship." In 1907 he stood unsuccessfully for Parliament, campaigning for women's suffrage and free trade. In 1908 he was elected a fellow of the Royal Society. (Russell's travels, lecture tours, professorships, degrees, and prizes, not to mention the books he wrote, are too numerous for complete listing in this article.)

Later political and philosophical works. During World War I his activities as a pacifist resulted in his being fined

Family and education

Three aims of his career

£100 in 1916, being dismissed from his lectureship at Trinity College, and being imprisoned for six months in 1918. While in prison he wrote his *Introduction to Mathematical Philosophy* (1919) and started reading for his work *The Analysis of Mind* (1921).

In 1916 he had met Lady Constance Malleson, a young and beautiful fellow pacifist. In 1919 he met Dora Black, with whom he visited China in 1920 and whom he married as his second wife in 1921. Russell visited the Soviet Union in 1920 and, the same year, published *The Practice and Theory of Bolshevism*, which was markedly critical of the regime, stressing its totalitarian nature and predicting and condemning many of the aspects of what was later to be called Stalinism.

Since the publication of *Principia Mathematica*, Russell's philosophical work had been mainly analytic and as such was one of the inspirations for the Analytic movement in philosophy, with which, however, Russell himself eventually lost sympathy. In working out his philosophy of Logical Atomism, he was influenced to some extent by his pupil Ludwig Wittgenstein, whom he had first met in 1911, and in particular by the basic doctrine of Wittgenstein's *Tractatus Logico-Philosophicus* (1922), which held that a proposition is a picture of the facts that it asserts and must have in a sense the same structure. Russell continued throughout his life to stress the importance of structure and indeed used the notion of similarity of structure in *Human Knowledge, Its Scope and Limits* (1948) as a criterion in inferring causal relationships. But he disagreed with Wittgenstein's later and influential *Philosophical Investigations* (1953).

Works for the layman During the 1920s much of his work was written for the layman; some of it was vulgarization in the respectable sense, as in *The ABC of Atoms* (1923) and *The ABC of Relativity* (1925); the rest ranged from *What I Believe* (1925) to *Marriage and Morals* (1929), *The Scientific Outlook* (1931), and *Education and the Social Order* (1932). All of these highly influential books were written with barbed wit from a politically, morally, and intellectually left-wing radical and anti-obscurantist point of view. He also wrote, at the expert's level, on ethics—mainly from a Utilitarian standpoint—and on political, social, and educational philosophy.

In 1927 he and his wife Dora started an experimental school at Telegraph House, near Petersfield, which was carried on by Dora after their divorce (in 1935) until the outbreak of war in 1939 and the permissiveness of which, though advanced for those days, was somewhat exaggerated by public gossip.

On his brother's death in 1931, Russell succeeded to the title as 3rd earl. In 1934 he published *Freedom and Organization, 1814–1914* and, in 1937, *The Amberley Papers*, both written with the help of a research assistant, Patricia Spence, whom he married in 1936.

As a pacifist, he supported British policy at Munich in 1938, though after war broke out he acknowledged that Hitler had to be defeated as "a necessary prelude to anything good." After lectureships in the United States during 1938 and 1939, his appointment to a professorship at City College in New York was annulled by the courts, one of the grounds being that he was an advocate of sexual immorality. (See the appendix to his *Why I Am Not a Christian*, 1927, edited by Paul Edwards.) Russell was temporarily saved from poverty by a five-year contract to lecture at the Barnes Foundation in Pennsylvania, but this was cancelled in 1943. He used his lectures as a basis for his *History of Western Philosophy* (1945), which became an immediate best seller both in Britain and in the United States and was his main source of revenue for many years. In the meantime, on his return to Britain in 1944, Russell had been appointed lecturer and fellow of Trinity College.

The next 15 years saw him attain rapidly increasing fame and respectability, initiated by appearances on the British Broadcasting Corporation (BBC) "Brains Trust" programs and consolidated by the delivery in 1949 of the first BBC Reith Lectures, by the receipt in 1949 of the Order of Merit, and, in 1950, of the Nobel Prize for Literature.

Political activism. When *Human Knowledge, Its Scope and Limits* was published in 1948, it received a respectful but lukewarm reception, partly because the theory of knowledge was at that time out of fashion and partly because, since the war, there had been in any case a turning away from Russell's ideas. This reception was a sharp disappointment to Russell, but he was in any case unsympathetic to the then current linguistic movement in philosophy; and (except for the writing of *My Philosophical Development* [1959] and a few reviews) he began to divert his attention from philosophy to international politics. As a result, from about 1952, when he was divorced from Patricia Spence and married Edith Finch, an American, he became progressively less respectable in the eyes of established authority and more influential in the eyes of the young and left-wing throughout the world. (During the late 1960s he would receive more than 1,000 messages and cards at Christmas, many of them from the Far East.) In 1954 he made his famous "Man's Peril" broadcast on the BBC, condemning the Bikini H-bomb tests; this led to the Russell–Einstein statement of protest by Nobel scientists, to the Pugwash Conferences of scientists from both East and West (Russell was elected president of the first conference in 1957), and, eventually, to the Campaign for Nuclear Disarmament, launched in 1958, again with Russell as president. He resigned, however, in 1960 and formed the more militant Committee of 100 with the overt aim of inciting mass civil disobedience, and he himself with Lady Russell led mass sit-downs in 1961 that brought them a two-month prison sentence, which was reduced to seven days, however, on health grounds.

Attacks on nuclear weapons

In 1962, at the age of 90, his energy and strength of purpose were still such that, during the Cuban crisis and the Sino-Indian border conflict, he intervened with heads of state and with U Thant of the United Nations. After the publication of the Warren Report, he chaired the Who Killed Kennedy Committee. In the meantime, in order to systematize his work for peace, he had established, in 1963, the Bertrand Russell Peace Foundation and the Atlantic Trust. During the remainder of the '60s, he vehemently attacked U.S. policies in Vietnam. With the help of the French Existentialist Jean-Paul Sartre, the Yugoslav historian Vladimir Dedijer, the Polish author Isaac Deutscher, and others, he convened the International War Crimes Tribunal.

The last three years of the '60s saw the publication in three volumes of one of Russell's finest works—witty, candid, absorbing, and beautifully written—his own *Autobiography*. He died on February 2, 1970, at Plas Penrhyn, near Penrhyndeudraeth in north Wales, his much-loved home for 15 years.

MAJOR WORKS

MATHEMATICS AND LOGIC: *The Principles of Mathematics* (1903); *Principia Mathematica* (in collaboration with A.N. Whitehead), 3 vol. (1910–13).

PHILOSOPHY: *A Critical Exposition of the Philosophy of Leibniz* (1900); *Philosophical Essays* (1910); *The Problems of Philosophy* (1911); *Our Knowledge of the External World* (1914); *The Philosophy of Pacifism* (1916); *Introduction to Mathematical Philosophy* (1919); *The Analysis of Mind* (1921); *The Analysis of Matter* (1927); *An Outline of Philosophy* (1927); *Why I Am Not a Christian* (1927); *The Conquest of Happiness* (1930); *An Inquiry into Meaning and Truth* (1940); *History of Western Philosophy* (1945); *Human Knowledge, Its Scope and Limits* (1948); *My Philosophical Development* (1959); *Has Man a Future?* (1961).

SOCIAL AND POLITICAL SUBJECTS: *German Social Democracy* (1896); *Principles of Social Reconstruction* (1916); *Roads to Freedom* (1918); *The Practice and Theory of Bolshevism* (1920); *On Education* (1926); *Marriage and Morals* (1929); *Education and the Social Order* (1932); *Freedom and Organization, 1814–1914* (1934); *Power: A New Social Analysis* (1938); *Authority and the Individual* (1949); *New Hopes for a Changing World* (1951); *Human Society in Ethics and Politics* (1954); *Common Sense and Nuclear Warfare* (1959); *Political Ideals* (1963).

SCIENCE: *The ABC of Atoms* (1923); *The ABC of Relativity* (1925); *The Scientific Outlook* (1931).

OTHER WORKS: *In Praise of Idleness, and Other Essays*

(1935); *The Amberley Papers* (1937), an edition of his parents' diaries and letters; *Satan in the Suburbs, and Other Stories* (1953), consisting of five imaginative short stories. The Russell Archives are at McMaster University in Canada.

BIBLIOGRAPHY. ALAN WOOD, *Bertrand Russell: The Passionate Skeptic* (1957), written by a friend and philosophical disciple, with Russell's cooperation; G.H. HARDY, *Bertrand Russell and Trinity* (1942, reprinted 1970); RUPERT CRAWSHAY-WILLIAMS, *Russell Remembered* (1970), a portrait and memoir of Russell's last 25 years; RALPH SCHOENMAN (ed.), *Bertrand Russell: Philosopher of the Century* (1967), contributions from personal friends and experts; A.J. AYER, *Russell and Moore: The Analytical Heritage* (1971); D.F. PEARS, *Bertrand Russell and the British Tradition in Philosophy* (1967), Russell's philosophy from 1905 to 1919; JOHN WATLING, *Bertrand Russell* (1971), the early philosophy of Russell, with a bibliography of books and articles; HERBERT GOTTSCHALK, *Bertrand Russell* (1962; Eng. trans., 1965), a short biography; JOHN LEWIS, *Bertrand Russell: Philosopher and Humanist* (1968), a Marxist approach; P.A. SCHILPP (ed.), *The Philosophy of Bertrand Russell* (1944).

(R.C.-W.)

Russell, Henry Norris

Henry Norris Russell, U.S. astronomer, helped lay the foundations of modern astrophysics (the study of the physics and chemistry of heavenly bodies) and stellar astronomy. In particular, he developed a graphic way of showing a relationship between a star's brightness and its spectrum that led to many ideas about the evolution of stars. Russell also devised a means of computing the distances of binary stars, which are systems of two stars revolving around each other. He exerted considerable influence on the development of 20th-century astronomy, both in the United States and abroad.

By courtesy of Princeton University

Henry Norris Russell.

Early life and works

Russell was born on October 25, 1877, in Oyster Bay, New York, the son of a Presbyterian minister. In 1882, at the age of five, Russell was shown a rare phenomenon, the transit of Venus across the Sun's disk, by his parents, and his interest in astronomy began. He was educated at home until the age of 12 and then went to Princeton, first to the preparatory school and later to the university, from which he graduated in 1897 with the highest distinction ever earned to that date by an undergraduate. Russell then entered the university's astronomy department to work under Charles Augustus Young, whom he found to be "a great teacher as well as a great astronomer." He devised a new way of determining the orbits of binary stars around each other and made some planetary studies, obtaining his Ph.D. in 1900.

Russell then left Princeton to work at the university observatories at Cambridge with Arthur Robert Hinks in determining stellar distances by photography, a technique then in its infancy. Maintaining his interest in binary

stars, he published another method of determining orbits, this time for pairs of stars that could not be directly observed as such but that from an analysis of their light by a spectroscope were known to be separate orbiting bodies, now called spectroscopic binaries. In 1905 Russell returned to Princeton as an instructor in astronomy, becoming an assistant professor three years later, when he also married. In 1911 he became professor and director of the university observatory, and from 1921 he held the additional appointment of research associate of the Mount Wilson Observatory. In 1927 his Princeton classmates of 1897 honoured him by endowing the C.A. Young Research Professorship, to which he was appointed.

Major astronomical work

At Princeton Russell continued his lifelong study of binaries, devising a means of calculating masses from their orbital behaviour and a method of using both orbits and masses for computing distances. He pioneered the study of eclipsing variables—that is, binary stars that appear to move in front of each other as they orbit, thus undergoing periodic eclipses and so displaying characteristic variation in brightness. It is a mark of his lifelong interest that his last scientific paper was on binaries, in this case those in the two small galaxies that are closest to our own and known as the Magellanic Clouds.

In his early works on stellar distances, Russell concluded that there were two main classes of stars, one much brighter than the other. The Danish astronomer Ejnar Hertzsprung, sharing this view, found the two classes to have similar spectra. By plotting luminosity and spectra in a diagram, Russell showed a definite relationship between true brightness and type of spectrum. He announced his results in December 1913, and the important Hertzsprung–Russell diagram was published the next year. This graphical demonstration of relationships stimulated Russell to work out his theory of stellar evolution by emphasizing the changes of spectrum, mass, and luminosity that stars undergo in time. In 1929 he summarized his views in his article "Stellar Evolution" in the 14th edition of the *Encyclopædia Britannica*, suggesting that stars begin as huge cool red bodies and then undergo a continual shrinkage. At first this contraction causes a rise in temperature accompanied by a change in colour from red to yellow, white, and blue; but finally they shrink to become small cool red bodies. The theory was widely accepted, but, in the light of later evidence, it was eventually replaced.

Russell performed extensive research on spectrum analysis, by which he applied laboratory techniques to the study of stellar conditions. This research led him to postulate the composition of stars—the Russell mixture, widely accepted by other astrophysicists—which took account of the great predominance of hydrogen. During World War I, Russell worked on aircraft navigation; but otherwise his professional life was concerned with astronomy, both at Princeton and as consultant to a number of American observatories. His broad interests led him to the wider philosophical problems of cosmic evolution. His *Solar System and Its Origin* (1935) proved to be a pioneering guide for later research. He took seriously the teaching of astronomy. With two colleagues he helped prepare a textbook, volume 2 of *Astronomy* (1927), that, with an extensive coverage of astrophysics and stellar astronomy, changed the whole emphasis of the way the subject was taught. He was also a successful popularizer of science and for over 40 years regularly published articles of high quality on the general progress of astronomy.

Holding to a mechanistic view of nature, Russell did not believe in life after death; but he thought science was really an ally of morals and religion, giving his views in a series of lectures, published as *Fate and Freedom* (1927). His interests ranged from archaeology to botany, from ancient history to boating and travelling. Many honours came to him from universities and academies, both at home and abroad; and he was, as a contemporary said of him, the "Dean of American astronomers." He died in Princeton, New Jersey, on February 18, 1957.

BIBLIOGRAPHY. Most of Russell's work was published in technical periodicals, especially in the *Astronomical Journal* and the *Astrophysical Journal*. The famous and readable textbook *Astronomy*, 2 vol., written in conjunction with RAYMOND SMITH DUGAN and JOHN QUINCY STEWART, appeared in 1926–27, with a suppl. to vol. 2 in 1938 and a revision of vol. 1 in 1945. In 1927, his views on science and religion were published as *Fate and Freedom*; and in 1935, his stimulating work, *The Solar System and Its Origin*. Between March 31, 1900, and August 1943, he published monthly articles on astronomy in *Scientific American* and made contributions to *Science*. An almost complete bibliography is given in *Biogr. Mem. Natn. Acad. Sci.*, 32:363–378 (1958), but this should be read in conjuction with that provided in *Biog. Mem. Fellows R. Soc.*, 3:185–191 (1957).

(C.A.R.)

Russell, John Russell, 1st Earl

Twice prime minister of Great Britain (1846–52; 1865–66), Lord John Russell was an aristocratic statesman whose liberalism was ahead of his time. As leader of the Whig Party, he pushed for liberal reforms on a broad front and led the fight for the great Reform Bill of 1832.

By courtesy of the National Portrait Gallery, London

The 1st Earl Russell, painting by F. Grant, 1853. In the National Portrait Gallery, London.

Lord John Russell was born in London on August 18, 1792, the third son of John Russell, the 6th duke of Bedford. (As the younger son of a peer, he was known for most of his life as Lord John Russell; he himself was created earl in 1861.) He thus came of a family that had long demonstrated its public spirit. The depth of his liberalism probably owed much to an untypical education. Poor health forbade the rigours of an English public school; and later, his father, who was critical of Oxford and Cambridge, sent him to the University of Edinburgh, where he drank deeply of Scottish philosophy. In 1813 he became a member of Parliament and four years later made his first important speech—characteristically, an attack on the government's suspension of the Habeas Corpus Act. In December 1819 Russell took up the cause of parliamentary reform, making it in the early 1820s not only his own cause but also that of the Whig Party. When the Whigs came to power in 1830, he joined the small ministerial committee that was to draft a reform bill, and on March 31, 1831, he presented it to the House of Commons. Overnight, he had won a national reputation.

In the 1830s and '40s, Russell remained the chief promoter of liberal reform in the Whig Party—although never again, perhaps, was this role so glorious as in the protracted but successful conflict over the passing of the first Reform Bill. As paymaster general under Charles Grey, 2nd Earl Grey, during roughly the first half of the

Work
on
parliamentary
reform

1830s, Russell championed the cause of religious freedom for both English Dissenters and Irish Catholics. Indeed, he pursued these aims so zealously that in seeking to divert some of the wealth of the established Church of Ireland (which was Protestant) to the Roman Catholics (who formed the bulk of the population) he frightened leading Whigs like Lord Stanley (later earl of Derby) out of the party. In the second half of the 1830s, as home secretary under Lord Melbourne, Russell, among other things, democratized the government of large towns (with the exception of London). He also reduced the number of criminal offenses liable to capital punishment and began the system of state inspection and support of public education.

Even out of office from 1841 to 1846, when he stood in opposition to Sir Robert Peel, Russell left his mark. For in 1845, in advance of his party, he came out in favour of total free trade, a crucial step in forcing Peel to follow him. As a result Peel split his party, the Whigs came to power, and Russell became prime minister.

This administration (1846–52) demonstrated that although Russell's penchant for advanced ideas was as strong as ever, his ability to implement them was now seriously reduced. He was able to establish the ten-hour day in factory labour (1847) and to found a national board of public health (1848). But, largely because of party disunity and weak leadership, he was unable to end the civil disabilities of the Jews, extend the franchise to the workers in the cities, or bring peace to the countryside of Ireland by guaranteeing security of tenure to its farmers.

First
administration

In the remaining years of his public career, Russell's difficulties increased. Party disunity continued and brought down his second administration (1865–66) when he made his last attempt to extend the franchise. But more significant, in the 1850s the national temper had changed. An age of reform had given way to a mood of self-complacency, even of belligerence. This was already evident in the Ecclesiastical Titles Act of 1851, which Russell's government had passed and which in effect was England's defiance of the papacy. This mood deepened, transformed, on the one hand, into an appetite for foreign war and, on the other, into boredom with social and political reform. In such an atmosphere Russell was inevitably overshadowed by the forceful and popular Lord Palmerston, who seized the forefront of the national stage in the Crimean War (1854–56). Indeed, for four years, from 1855 to 1859, Russell retired from public life and devoted more and more of his time to literature. Private life had always beckoned to him, as had the life of a littérateur. Among the English prime ministers, few wrote so copiously—biography, history, poetry—as Russell. He accepted an earldom in 1861, and he died at Pembroke Lodge, Richmond Park, May 28, 1878.

The underlying theme of Russell's career—his long tenure of liberal opinion—is frequently ignored or minimized. But his failings were less evident in the realm of ideas than in the realm of personality. He was neither a gifted administrator nor an efficient and commanding prime minister. More important, he combined in his personality elements of both rashness and timidity. Although he came to liberal ideas sooner and held them longer than did William Ewart Gladstone, he failed where Gladstone succeeded: in building up a Liberal Party firmly based on popular support. His rashness often alienated his followers, and his timidity prevented him from seeking out a massive popularity in the country at large in order to drive home his ideas. In a sense a rebel against aristocracy, he found himself constantly frustrated by the great aristocratic Whigs—remaining in the last analysis, as one historian has said, their prisoner.

Assessment

BIBLIOGRAPHY. S. WALPOLE, *The Life of Lord John Russell*, 2nd ed., 2 vol. (1889, reprinted 1968), still the definitive biography (useful but too uncritical); JOHN RUSSELL, *Recollections and Suggestions 1813–1873* (1875), autobiography written in old age; G.P. GOOCH (ed.), *The Later Correspondence of Lord John Russell, 1840–1878*, 2 vol. (1925); B. and P. RUSSELL, *The Amberley Papers*, vol. 1 (1937), scenes of Russell's family life in later years.

(D.Sp.)

Russia and the Soviet Union, History of

The term Russia properly refers only to the empire that occupied approximately the present area of the Soviet Union in the 18th, 19th, and early 20th centuries. In the title of this article, however, it is used very loosely to describe the European part of the Soviet Union from ancient times as well.

The main divisions of the article are as follows:

I. From the beginnings to c. 1700

PREHISTORY

Indo-European and Ural-Altaic peoples have occupied what is now the European territory of the Union of Soviet Socialist Republics (U.S.S.R.) since the second millennium before Christ, but little is known about their ethnic identity, institutions, and activities. In ancient times, Greek and Iranian settlements appeared in the southernmost portions of what is now the Ukrainian S.S.R. Trading empires of that era seem to have known and exploited the northern forests, particularly the Permian triangle formed by the Kama and Volga rivers, but these contacts seem to have had little lasting impact. Between the 4th and 9th centuries, the Huns, Avars, Goths, and Magyars passed briefly over the same terrain, but these transitory occupations also had little influence upon the East Slavs, who during this time were spreading south and east from an area between the Elbe River and the Pripet Marshes. For them, the period of mute prehistory extends into the 9th century, when, as a result of a dramatic penetration into the area from north and south by north European and Middle Eastern merchant adventurers, their society was exposed to new economic, cultural, and political forces.

Exploration and the rise of the Rus.   The scanty written records tell little of the processes that ensued, but archaeological evidence—notably, the Oriental coins found in eastern Europe—indicate that the development of the East Slavs passed through several stages.

From about 770 to about 830, commercial explorers began an intensive penetration of the Volga region. From early bases in the estuaries of the rivers of the eastern Baltic region, Germanic commercial–military bands, probably in search of new routes to the East, began to penetrate territory populated by Finnic and Slavic tribes, where they found amber, furs, honey, wax, and timber products, all of which provided generous rewards for the hardy and fortunate. The indigenous population, unlike that of western areas where the Vikings were becoming active, offered little resistance to their incursions, and there was no significant local authority to negotiate the balance among trade, tribute, and plunder. From the south, trading organizations based in northern Iran and North Africa, seeking the same products, particularly slaves, became active in the Lower Volga, the Don, and, to a lesser extent, in the Dnieper region. The history of the Khazar state (see below *The Khazars*) is intimately connected with these activities.

Around 830 commerce appears to have declined in the Don and Dnieper regions. There was increased activity in the north Volga, where Scandinavian traders who had previously operated from bases on Lakes Ladoga and Onega established a new centre, near Ryazan. Here, in this period, the first nominal ruler of Rus (called, like the Khazar emperor, *khaqan* or *kagan*) is mentioned in Islāmic and Western sources. This Volga Rus kaganate may be considered the first direct political antecedent of the Kievan state.

Within a few decades, these Rus, together with other Scandinavian groups operating farther west, extended their raiding activities down the main river routes toward Baghdad and Constantinople, reaching the latter in 860. The Scandinavians involved in these exploits are known as Varangians; they were adventurers of diverse origins, often led by princes of warring dynastic clans. One of these princes, Rurik of Jutland, is considered the progenitor of the dynasty that ruled in various portions of East Slavic territory until 1598. Evidences of the Varangian expansion are particularly clear in the coin hoards of 900–930. The number of Oriental coins reaching northern regions, especially Scandinavia, indicates a flourishing trade. Written records tell of Rus raids upon Constantinople and the northern Caucasus in the early 10th century.

In the period from about 930 to 1000, the region came under complete control by Varangians from Novgorod. This period saw the development of the trade route from the Baltic to the Black Sea, which established the basis of the economic life of the Kievan principality and determined its political and cultural development.

The degree to which the Varangians may be considered the founders of the Kievan state has been hotly debated since the 18th century. The debate has from the beginning borne nationalistic overtones. Recent works by Russians have generally minimized or ignored the role of the Varangians, while non-Russians have occasionally exaggerated it. Whatever the case, the lifeblood of the sprawling Kievan organism was the commerce organized by the princes. To be sure, these early princes were not "Swedes" or "Norwegians" or "Danes"; they thought in categories not of nation but of clan. But they certainly were not East Slavs. There is little reason to doubt the predominant role of the Varangian Rus in the creation of the state to which they gave their name.

The Khazars.   In the mid-7th century, the Khazars, a nomadic confederation of Turkic and Iranian tribes in the North Caucasus, rapidly expanded their power, pressing the Hunnic Bulgars northward and westward and confronting Byzantine and Arab power to the south. Khazar relations with Constantinople became very close (a son of Emperor Leo III was married to a daughter of the Khazar Kagan in 731) but could not forestall a terrible defeat by the Arabs in the Caucasus in 737, at which time the Khazar capital was destroyed. The centre of Khazar activities shifted north to a new capital at Itil on the Lower Volga, and by the end of the century the Khazars had recovered and surpassed their previous power. The Khazar state was multinational, based upon the military might of Turkic and Iranian nomadic horsemen and the skills of Iranian and Jewish traders. The Khazars seem to have retained their importance through the 9th century, in spite of competition from the Rus and the Hungarians, but were eclipsed in the 10th century.

KIEV

Rise of Kiev.   The consecutive history of the first East Slavic state begins with Prince Svyatoslav (died 972), the greatest of the Varangian princes. His victorious campaigns against other Varangian centres, the Khazars, and the Volga Bulgars and his intervention in the Byzantine–Danube Bulgar conflicts of 968–971 mark the full hegemony of his clan in Rus and the emergence of a new political force in eastern Europe, similar in some ways to the princely dynasties of the Piasts in Poland and the Árpáds in Hungary. But Svyatoslav was neither a lawgiver nor an organizer; and on his death he left, in true Varangian style, only his sword and that which had been

The Varangian expansion (margin note)

The first East Slavic state (margin note)

gained by it. The role of architect of the Kievan state fell to his son Vladimir (*c.* 980–1015), who established the dynastic seniority system of his clan as the political structure by which the scattered territories of Rus were to be ruled. He also promulgated the first code of law and invited or permitted the patriarch of Constantinople to establish an episcopal see in Rus in 988. Vladimir's reign inaugurated the golden century of Kievan life, and he has remained in later tradition a figure of heroic stature.

Vladimir extended the realm to its natural limits (the watersheds of the Don, Dnieper, Dniester, Neman, Western Dvina, and Upper Volga), destroyed or incorporated the remnants of competing Varangian organizations, and established regular relations with neighbouring dynasties. The successes of his long reign made it possible for the reign of his son Yaroslav (ruled 1019–54) to produce a flowering of cultural life. But neither Yaroslav, who gained control of Kiev only after a bitter struggle against his brother Svyatopolk (1015–19), nor his successors in Kiev, however, were able to provide lasting political stability within the enormous realm. The political history of Rus is one of clashing separatist and centralizing trends inherent in the contradiction between local settlement and colonization, on the one hand, and the hegemony of the clan elder, ruling from Kiev, on the other. As Vladimir's 12 sons and innumerable grandsons prospered in the rapidly developing territories they inherited, they and their retainers acquired settled interests that conflicted both with one another and with the interests of unity.

Adapted from *Westermann Grosser Atlas zur Weltgeschichte* Georg Westermann Verlag, Braunschweig

The Kievan Rus in the 10th and 11th centuries.

The conflicts were not confined to Slavic lands: the Turkic nomads who moved into the southern steppe in the 11th century (first the Torks, later the Kipchaks—also known as the Polovtsy or Kumans) became involved in the constant internecine rivalries, and Rurikid and Turkic princes often fought on both sides. In 1097 representatives of the leading branches of the dynasty, together with their Turkic allies, met at Liubech, north of Kiev, and agreed to divide the Kievan territory among themselves and their descendants, although, later, Vladimir Monomakh made a briefly successful attempt (1113–25) to reunite the land of Rus.

Decline of Kiev. The hegemony of the prince of Kiev depended upon the cohesion of the clan of Rurik and the relative importance of the southern trade, both of which began to decline in the late 11th century. The primary reason for this decline was a major shift of trade routes in the eastern Mediterranean, which can conveniently be associated with the First Crusade (1096–99). The re-establishment of the traditional east–west routes, together with other factors, made the route from the Baltic to the Black Sea superfluous and less profitable. Moreover, much of the trade that had followed that route now began moving over land routes through central Europe. At the same time, conflicts among the Rurikid princes acquired a more pronounced regional and separatist nature, reflecting new patterns in export trade along the northern and western periphery. Novgorod, in particular, began to gravitate toward closer relations both with the cities of the Hanseatic League, which controlled the Baltic trade, and with the rapidly developing hinterland in Suzdalia, between the Oka River and the Upper Volga. Smolensk, Polotsk, and Pskov became increasingly involved in trade along western land routes, while Galicia and Volhynia established closer links with Poland and Hungary. The princes of these areas still contested the crown of the "Grand Prince of Kiev and All of Rus," but the title became an empty one; when Andrew Bogolyubsky of Suzdal won Kiev and the title in 1169, he sacked the city and returned to the Upper Volga, apparently seeing no advantage in establishing himself in the erstwhile capital. (Roman Mstislavich of Galicia and Volhynia repeated these actions in 1203.) By the middle of the 12th century, the major principalities, thanks to the prosperity and colonization of the Kievan period, had developed into independent political and economic units, some as large as modern European nation-states.

Social and political institutions. The paucity of evidence about social and political institutions in Kievan Rus suggests that they were rudimentary. The East Slavs had no significant tradition of supratribal political organization before the coming of the Varangians, who themselves, until well into the 10th century, had little interest in institutions more elaborate than those necessary for the exploitation of their rich, new territory. Nor did the Varangians soon acquire any attachment to Rus as a second homeland: archaeology and the sagas agree in portraying the "East" as a theatre of heroic adventure and freebootery, not of colonization. The territory of Rus, moreover, was immense and sparsely settled. The scattered towns, some probably little more than trading posts, were separated by large primeval forests and swamps.

Thus, although the campaigns of Svyatoslav indicate the extent of the political vacuum that his clan filled, he construed his domains as a clan possession rather than as a territorial or national state. His successor Vladimir, however, seems to have been conscious of one political element—organized religion—that distinguished both the contemporary empires and the newly established principalities in Poland and Hungary from his own. The church provided the concepts of territorial and hierarchical organization that made states out of tribal territories; its teachings transformed a charismatic prince into a king possessing the attributes and responsibilities of a national leader, judge, and first Christian of the realm.

Once Vladimir had adopted Christianity in 988, his rule was supported by the propagation of Byzantine notions of imperial authority, and there is ample evidence that Kievan princes after him styled themselves as autocrats in the Byzantine tradition. The political traditions and conditions of Rus, however, required that the actual workings of the political system and some of its style be derived from other sources. The succession system, probably a vestige of the experience of the Rus kaganate in the Upper Volga, was based upon two principles: the indivisibility of the basic territory of Rus (the principalities of

Kiev, Chernigov, and Pereyaslavl) and the sovereignty of a whole generation. Seniority passed through an ascension by stages from elder brother to younger and from the youngest eligible uncle to the eldest eligible nephew. Such a system was admirably suited to the needs of the dynasty, because, by providing a rotating advancement of members of the clan through apprenticeships in the various territories of the realm, it assured control of the key points of the far-flung trading network by princes who were subject to traditional sanctions, and it gave them experience in lands over which they could someday expect to rule from Kiev. This system served well for a century after it was given final form by Vladimir and was revived by Monomakh (Vladimir II, ruled 1113–25), but it could not survive the decline of Kiev's importance.

Each of the princes had a retinue composed of boyars (upper nobility), who gave personal allegiance and military service to the prince in return for grants of income from specified territories. Some of these boyars were originally Scandinavians—perhaps members of dynasties defeated by the Rurikids. Others may have been leading members of local tribal units. The princes and their retinues drew their most significant revenues from the tribute or taxes collected annually in kind from the various territories and disposed of in the export trade.

Some slaves were apparently employed in princely and boyar households, but their number was not large. The main group of dependent peasants consisted of indentured freemen, while most people were apparently free peasants organized in communes, who paid tribute to the prince but not to a landlord.

Very little is known of law in this period; it may be assumed that juridical institutions had not developed on a broad scale. The earliest law code (1016), called the "Russian Law," was one of the "Barbarian" law codes common throughout Germanic Europe. It dealt primarily with princely law—that is, with the fines to be imposed by the prince or his representative in the case of specified offenses; it was later modified by the inclusion of ecclesiastical and moral law from Byzantine and Slavic sources.

Soviet scholars have adhered to a rather literal Marxist view of the nature of the Kievan state, holding that, since land was in the hands of the boyar class, who exploited the labour of slaves and peasants, Kievan society should be termed feudal. The meagre sources indicate, however, that Kiev experienced nothing like the complex and highly regulated legal and economic relationships associated with feudalism in western Europe. Kiev's political system existed primarily for and by international trade in forest products and depended upon a money economy in which the bulk of the population scarcely participated. The rich and powerful doubtless exploited the tillers of the soil. The subsistence agriculture of the forest regions, however, was not the source of Kiev's wealth, nor was it the matrix within which law and politics and history were made.

Formal culture came to Rus, along with Christianity, from the multinational Byzantine synthesis, primarily through South Slavic intermediaries. A native culture, expressed in a now lost pagan ritual folklore and traditions in the arts and crafts, existed before the Kievan period, and then persisted alongside the formal culture, but its influence on the latter is conjectural. Authorities often speak of the imitative nature of Kievan culture, especially of its literature, and of Kiev's "silence." There were no heresies or great disputes in the Kievan church; Christianity came to virgin territory, where there were no native religious or philosophical traditions vital enough to force a confrontation or synthesis such as occurred elsewhere. The Kievan achievement, however, was none the less remarkable: within a few generations, an enormous population was brought within the embrace of Western culture and introduced to the artistic, philosophical, and literary treasures of the contemporary Christian world.

No single one of the regional (or, later, national) cultures, perhaps least of all that of Muscovy, can be called the heir of Kiev, although all shared the inheritance. The strands of continuity were everywhere strained, if not

(margin left) The adoption of Christianity

(margin right) The boyars

broken, in the period after Kiev's decline. But "Golden Kiev" was always present, in lore and bookish tradition, as a source of emulation and renascence.

THE LANDS OF RUS

The decline of Kiev led to the disintegration of Rus into its component principalities. Regional developments are so striking in the subsequent period that it has often been called the Period of Feudal Partition. This is misleading: "feudal" is hardly more applicable to the widely varying institutions of this time than to those of the Kievan period. "Partition" implies a former unity for which there is no historical evidence. The distinct character and historical fortunes of each of the major East Slavic regions is clear even in the Kievan period and has persisted into the 20th century. The following is a brief coverage of the most important states.

Novgorod. The town of Novgorod arose in the 9th century as one of the earliest centres of the exploitation of the forest hinterland and remained the most important commercial centre of the Kievan period. The changes of the latter Kievan period did not diminish Novgorod's importance, for it benefitted both from the increased activity of the Hanseatic League and from the development of the Upper Volga region, for which it was a major trade outlet. Although Novgorod was the first base of the Rurikids, from which Kiev was repeatedly captured and to which Kievan princes often returned to recruit Varangian retinues during their struggles for the Kievan throne, the princely traditions characteristic of Kiev and other post-Kievan centres never developed in Novgorod. During the height of Kiev's power, Novgorod was usually ruled by a son of the grand prince rather than by a member of the "generation of brothers," who held decidedly less important towns. When Kiev declined, Novgorod soon (1136) declared its independence from princely power, and, although it accepted princely protectors from various neighbouring dynasties, it remained, until conquered by Muscovy (Moscow), a sovereign city.

During the 13th century, Novgorod's burghers easily found an accommodation with the invading Mongols. In the Mongol period, its energetic river pirates pushed farther north and east toward the Urals and even down the Volga, and Novgorod's prosperity was generally unbroken until the commercial revolution of the 16th century. Its absorption by the growing principality of Muscovy in 1478 ended its political independence and changed its social structure, but Novgorod's characteristic economic and cultural life did not end with that catastrophe.

Novgorod is notable for its sociopolitical institutions, similar in some ways to those of north European towns but almost unique in East Slavic territory. Novgorod was governed by an oligarchy of great trading boyar families who controlled the exploitation of the hinterland. They chose (from among themselves) a mayor, a military commander, and a council of aldermen, who controlled the affairs of the city and its territories. The town itself was divided into five "ends," which seem to have corresponded to the "fifths" into which the hinterland was divided. There was, in addition, a *veche* ("council"), apparently a kind of town meeting of broad but indeterminate composition, whose decisions, it would appear, were most often controlled by the oligarchy. A major role in politics was played by the archbishop, who after 1156 controlled the lands and incomes previously owned by the Kievan princes and who appears throughout Novgorod's history as a powerful, often independent figure.

The northwest. During this period, much of the territory of the principalities of Smolensk, Polotsk, Turov, and Pinsk was controlled by the grand principality of Lithuania, which was essentially an international or non-national formation, led by a foreign dynasty (of east Lithuanian pagan origins) ruling over predominantly Belorussian and Ukrainian populations. By the 15th century, the dynasty had become Slavic in culture (a version of Belorussian was the official language of the realm), and at its height under Vytautas (1392–1430) it controlled all of the old Kievan territory outside of Great Russia proper—that is, most of the present-day Lithuanian, Belorus-

The commercial centre of Novgorod

sian, Moldavian, and Ukrainian Soviet Socialist Republics. In 1385 the grand principality joined the Kingdom of Poland, and the union was sealed shortly thereafter by the marriage of Grand Prince Jogaila (Jagiełło) to Jadwiga, the Polish queen.

The northeast. The region bounded by the Oka and Volga rivers, later to be the heartland of the grand principality of Moscow, was settled before the arrival of Slavs from Novgorod and the Baltic area by a Finnic tribe with whom the Slavic newcomers intermingled. Rostov, the earliest princely centre, was from Vladimir's time included in the princely rotation system. In the 12th century, it became the patrimony of the younger branch of Vladimir Monomakh's family (who founded the new princely centre Vladimir in 1108). Under his son Yury Dolgoruky (1125–57) and grandson Andrew Bogolyubsky (1157–74), the principality reached a high political and cultural development, which it retained through much of the succeeding century. Early in the 13th century, the principality of Moscow was created as an appanage (royal grant) within the grand principality of Vladimir, and this new seat grew in importance when Michael Khorobrit, brother of Alexander Nevsky, conquered Vladimir (1248) and made himself prince of both centres. Daniel, Nevsky's son and the progenitor of all the later Rurikid princes of Moscow, had a long and successful reign (1276–1303), but at his death the principality still embraced little more than the territory of the present Moscow *oblast* (an area of 140 miles [225 kilometres] in length and width). The beginning of Moscow's rise to its later pre-eminence came in the reign of Daniel's son Ivan (1328–41), who, by cooperating with Öz Beg, khan of the Golden Horde, and also by his shrewd purchases (probably of tax-farming rights), greatly expanded the influence of his principality.

The southwest. The lands of Galicia and Volhynia were always ethnically and economically distinct from the Kievan region proper, as well as from more distant regions. Agriculture was highly developed, and trade, particularly in the valuable local salt, tended to take westward and overland routes. Galicia, already a separate principality by 1100, grew as Kiev declined. Later, Roman Mstislavich of Volhynia (ruled 1199–1205) conquered Galicia and united the two principalities. Under his son Daniel (1202–64), difficulties with the Galician landed magnates and the interference of the Hungarians weakened the principality, and it was subjugated in 1240 by the Mongol invasion. Eventually, this region came under the domination of Lithuania (Volhynia) and Poland (Galicia).

Early Moscow

THE MONGOL PERIOD

The Mongol invasion. In 1223, when the first Mongol reconnaissance into former Kievan territory led to the disastrous defeat of a Volhynian–Galician–Polovtsian army on the Kalka River, the various Rurikid principalities had for generations been intermittently at war, usually in complex alliances with equally disunited groups of Polovtsian clans. Kiev was in ruins, Novgorod was preoccupied with commerce and with its northern neighbours, Galicia was being torn internally and drawn increasingly into Polish and Hungarian dynastic affairs, and Vladimir-Suzdal, apparently the leading principality, was unable to resist the finely organized and skillful mounted bowmen of the steppe, the greatest military force of the age.

Pious tradition, born of the works of monkish annalists and court panegyrists, has exaggerated both the destructiveness of the first Mongol conquests and the strength of the resistance. The Mongols aimed to revive, under a unified political system, the trade that had traditionally crossed the central Asian steppe and vitalized the economy of the pastoral nomads. As they moved westward, they easily gained the collaboration of groups of Turkic nomads and the predominantly Iranian and Muslim traders in the towns of the old silk route; they encountered the greatest resistance in sedentary political centres and among land-owning elites. The lands of the Rus presented numerous similarities with the central Asian areas the

Impact of Mongol victories

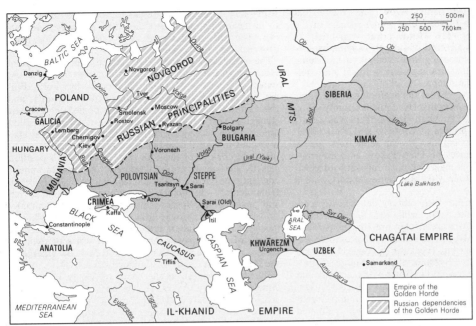

The empire of the Golden Horde at its greatest extent.
From A. Herrmann, *An Historical Atlas of China*

Mongols had already conquered. Here, too, a former commercial empire had fallen apart into an aggregation of warring principalities. Here, too, ready recruits were to be found in the Polovtsians, who controlled the lower Dnieper and Volga and Don, and in the Muslim merchants, who dealt in the towns of the Crimea and the Upper Volga. These merchants showed the way, first (1223) to the Crimea and up the Volga to the old centre of Bolgary, later (1236) to Bolgary a second time, then to Ryazan, Rostov, and the Suzdalian towns, and still later (1240) to Kiev and Galicia.

Many of the conquered cities made a striking recovery and adjustment to the new relationships. Some towns, such as Kiev, never fully recovered in Mongol times, but the cities of the Vladimir-Suzdal region clearly prospered. New centres, such as Moscow and Tver, hardly mentioned in any source before the Mongol period, arose and flourished in Mongol times.

Thus, the Mongol invasion was not everywhere a catastrophe. The local princely dynasties continued unchanged in their traditional seats; some princes resisted the new authority and were killed in battle, but no alien princes ever became established in Slavic territory. Few Mongols remained west of the Urals after the conquest; political and fiscal administration was entrusted to the same Turkic clan leaders and Islāmic merchants who had for generations operated in the area. The whole of the Novgorodian north remained outside the sphere of direct Tatar control, although the perspicacious burghers maintained correct relations with the khans.

Tatar rule. After a brief attempt to revive the ancient centres of Bolgary and the Crimea, the Jucids (the family of Jöchi, son of Genghis Khan, who inherited the western portion of his empire) established a new capital, Itil. (It was moved to "New Sarai," near present Volgograd *c.* 1260.) These towns became the commercial and administrative centres of what was later to be called the "Golden Horde" (the term is probably a Western invention). Its East Slavic territories were tributaries of an extensive empire, including, at its height, the Crimea, the Polovtsian steppe from the Danube to the Ural River, the former territories of the Bulgar empire (including the fur-rich Moldavian forests and parts of western Siberia), and in Asia the former kingdom of Khwārezm, including Urgench, the cultural capital of the Jucids. Control of the Slavic lands was exercised through the native princes, some of whom spent much of their time at the Mongol capital, and through agents charged with overseeing the activities of the princes and particularly the fiscal levies. The meagre evidence indicates that the Tatar rulers were,

for the first century at least, more interested in developing commerce than in despoiling their subjects.

This multinational commercial empire was unstable. Early in the history of the Horde, the khans of Sarai, who tended to reflect the interests of the Volga tribes, were challenged by the tribal princes of the west, whose control of the Danube, Bug, and Dnieper routes and of the access to the Crimea gave them considerable political and economic power. As early as 1260, Nokhai, one of these western chieftains, showed his independence of Sarai by establishing his own foreign policy, and toward the end of the 13th century he seized control of Sarai itself. At his death, the eastern tribes re-established their control in Sarai, but in the reign of the great Öz Beg (1314–41), the high point of Horde power, the west was again ascendant. Öz Beg based his power upon firm control of the Crimea and had extensive relations with the Genoese and Venetians, who controlled the main ports there. After the death of Öz Beg's son Jani Beg (died 1357), however, the empire began to reveal serious internal strains. The tribes of the west paid little heed to the khans who appeared in dizzying succession in Sarai; the north Russian princes fell to quarrelling and to manoeuvring for their own advantage in the internecine politics of the Horde; the Volga Bulgar region was detached by a dissident Tatar prince; and the lands of the east were drawn into the orbit of the Turkic conqueror Timur (Tamerlane).

The Horde's last cycle of integration and dismemberment was closely linked with events in Timur's domains. Tokhtamysh, son of a minor Tatar prince, had been unsuccessfully involved in the skirmishes around the throne of Sarai in the 1370s and had fled to the court of Timur, with whose aid he returned to Sarai and vanquished the tribal leaders who had opposed him. Having defeated and made peace with them, he now turned to defeat Mamai (1381), who had the previous year been defeated by Prince Dmitry Donskoy ("of the Don"; grand prince of Moscow, 1359–89). Mamai's western tribal allies went over to Tokhtamysh, and, for a brief time, the major components of the tribal structure of the Horde were reunited. Tokhtamysh successfully attacked Moscow (just as Mamai had hoped to do) and set about consolidating his gains. As his power grew, however, Tokhtamysh was drawn into a struggle with Timur, who had conquered much of Iran, the south Caucasus, and eastern Anatolia. After a number of encounters in the northern Caucasus, Timur, who apparently was intent upon diversion of east–west trade through his own Transoxanian and North Iranian territories, set out to destroy Tokhtamysh and the latter's commercial centres. In 1395 and 1396, Timur's armies sys-

The
Mongol
commercial empire

tematically annihilated Sarai, Azov, and Kaffa and marched through the Lower Volga to the borders of the Russian principalities. The Horde never recovered; its subsequent history is a record of struggles among its erstwhile subjects for supremacy and attempts to find some new *modus vivendi* that would restore political and commercial stability to the steppe.

The rise of Muscovy.   From the beginning of the Tatar period, the Rurikid princes displayed much disunity. During the reign of the Tatar khan Öz Beg there was a shift of alignments. The princes of Moscow and their allies, together with Öz Beg and his Crimean supporters, generally opposed the princes of Tver, Pskov, and, intermittently, Novgorod. The major punitive measures directed by Öz Beg against Tver with Muscovite support were a part of this pattern.

The links forged in the 14th century between Moscow and the Crimea (and Sarai, while Öz Beg controlled it) were crucial to Moscow's later pre-eminence. They not only afforded Moscow a steady and profitable export trade for its furs but (because of contacts between Crimean merchants and Byzantium) also led quite naturally to close relations between the Muscovite hierarchy and the patriarchate of Constantinople. This special relationship was but one of the reasons for the eventual rise of Moscow as leader of the Russian lands. Admirably situated in the northeast, linked with all of the major navigable river systems and with the steppe, close to the major fur-producing regions and to the most intensely settled agricultural lands, served by a succession of shrewd and long-lived princes, Moscow came naturally to a position of pre-eminence during the 14th century and was best equipped to enter the struggle for the political inheritance of the Horde that followed the destruction of its capitals by Timur.

Cultural life and the "Tatar influence."   Most traditional scholarship has accepted the notions that (1) the Mongol invasion "destroyed" Kievan culture; (2) the Tatar period was one of "stultification" and "isolation from the West"; (3) "Russian" culture was deeply influenced by Golden Horde culture, in particular by "Oriental" conceptions of despotism. These views do not accord with the evidence and should probably be discarded.

In the first place, it seems incorrect to say that Kievan culture was destroyed. In the shift of the cultural centre of gravity to the numerous regional centres, Kievan traditions were in the main continued and in some cases (*i.e.*, Galician literature, Novgorodian icon painting, Suzdalian architecture) enjoyed remarkable development.

Similarly, the notions of stultification and isolation from the West cannot be supported. The enormous Novgorodian culture sphere, the Upper Dnieper territories that eventually came under Lithuanian control, and the principalities of Volhynia and Galicia all had, if anything, closer contacts with western and central Europe than in the previous period. Each of these areas, in its own way, acted as a repository of the Kievan traditions and produced some features that later were to be incorporated into the new Muscovite culture.

As to "Tatar influence," in the areas of religion and intellectual life, it was practically nonexistent. Control of formal culture by the Orthodox clergy and Muslim divines and limited contact between the Slavic and Turkic populations prevented it. There is no evidence that any single Turkic or Islāmic text of religious, philosophical, literary or scholarly content was translated directly into Slavonic or any East Slavic vernacular during the period.

Concerning the secular culture of the court and counting house, the situation was radically different. These spheres were controlled by very pragmatic princes, merchants, and diplomats. Here, Slavs and Tatars elaborated together an international subculture whose language was Turkic and whose administrative techniques and chancellery culture were essentially those of the Golden Horde. Slavic merchants took full part in this culture, and the princes of Muscovy, in particular, developed their original court culture and chancellery practices within its context. These borrowings, however, were not of a theoretical or ideological nature, and to ascribe later despo-

Factors favouring Moscow

tism—and its theoretical basis—to "Oriental" influence is to misunderstand the development of Muscovite absolutism. The phenomenon and its justification spring from other sources (see below).

The post-Sarai period.   The collapse of the Golden Horde saw a growth in the political power of the old sedentary centres—Muscovy, Lithuania, the Volga Bulgar region (which became the khanate of Kazan), and the Crimea. This growth was accompanied by dynastic struggles. This period of recovery also saw cooperation among the emerging dynasties against their internal enemies and toward the stabilization of the steppe.

Even by the end of the 14th century, Moscow's position was by no means as dominating as the cartographers' conventions or the historians' hindsight make it seem. Other centres—Lithuania, Tver, Novgorod—were as rich and powerful as Moscow; many of the areas nominally subject to the Muscovite princes retained their own dynasties, whose members often broke away and sided with one of Moscow's rivals. Only after a series of dynastic conflicts in the early 15th century did Moscow emerge as the leader of the Great Russian territory.

The struggle began at the death of Vasily I, a son of Dmitry Donskoy, in 1425. The succession of his ten-year-old son Vasily II was challenged by his uncle Yury, prince of the important Upper Volga commercial town of Galich. Although the ensuing conflict was conducted in the name of the right succession to the grand princely throne, the underlying issues were regional and economic. After many turns of fortune, Vasily II succeeded, with the help of Lithuanian and Tatar allies, in establishing his house permanently as the rulers of Muscovy.

RURIKID MUSCOVY

Ivan III.   Ivan III (ruled 1462–1505), known to history as the Great, consolidated from a secure throne the gains his father, Vasily II, had won in the saddle. Although little is known of Ivan, an exceptional intelligence is apparent behind the consistent and brilliantly effective military and diplomatic campaigns of his time.

The "gathering of the Russian lands," as it has traditionally been known, became under Ivan a conscious and irresistible drive by Moscow to annex all East Slavic lands, both the Great Russian territories, which had traditionally had close links with Moscow, and the Belorussian and Ukrainian regions, which had developed under distinctly different historical and cultural circumstances. In 1471 Ivan mounted a simultaneous attack upon Novgorod and its Upper Volga colonies, which capitulated and accepted Moscow's commercial and political demands. The trading republic, however, retained considerable de facto independence and became involved with the Lithuanian princes in an attempt to resist Moscow. Ivan, using these dealings as a pretext, attacked again, and in 1478 Novgorod was absorbed by Moscow. A Muscovite governor was installed, and 70 Novgorodian boyar families were deported and assigned estates elsewhere to hold in service tenure, being replaced by members of the Moscow military-service class.

Tver suffered a similar fate. Ivan had agreed with Prince Michael Borisovich of Tver to conduct foreign relations in concert and by consultation, but, when the Tverite complained that Ivan was not consulting him on important matters, Ivan attacked him and annexed his lands (1485). By the end of Ivan's reign, there were no Great Russian princes who dared conduct policies unacceptable to Moscow.

The success of Ivan's expansion was determined by his skillful dealings with the Polish–Lithuanian state, which had expanded down the Dnieper Basin and into Slavic territories on the south flank of Moscow. After 1450 a competition developed for control of the numerous semi-independent principalities of the Dnieper and Upper Donets regions. In the early 1490s, some minor East Slavic princes defected from Lithuania to Moscow. The first phase of the conflict, confined to border skirmishes, ended in 1494 with a treaty ceding Vyazma to Moscow and with the marriage of Ivan's daughter Yelena to Alexander, grand duke of Lithuania. In 1500, on the initiative

The gathering of the Russian lands

of Lithuanian defectors, Ivan's armies seized a number of important border towns; this began a war that ended somewhat inconclusively in 1503 with a truce that extended Ivan's border considerably to the west.

The third major element of Ivan's foreign policy comprised his relations with the various Tatar confederations. In the 1470s, the Crimean khan Mengli Giray came into increasing conflict with Khan Ahmed of the Horde and became interested in an alliance with Moscow against Ahmed and Lithuania. Ivan, eager to dissolve the connection between Lithuania and the Crimea, but not wanting to alienate Ahmed, stalled for time. In 1481, when Ahmed died, Ivan was able to forge an alliance with the Nogais, Mengli Giray, and Kazan. The security provided by this system became the cornerstone of his later policies. Ivan was the first Muscovite prince to have an integrated foreign policy, but he did not "cast off the Tatar yoke" as he is traditionally supposed to have done. The yoke—if such it was—had long since fallen of itself.

In addition to problems of war and diplomacy, Ivan was faced with a number of challenges from within his own family and court. In 1472 his eldest brother, Yury, died childless, and Ivan appropriated his entire estate. This action antagonized the two eldest surviving brothers, Andrey and Boris, whose grievances were further increased by Ivan's refusal to give them a share of conquered Novgorod. In 1480 they rebelled, at a time when he was threatened by a Tatar invasion, and only with difficulty were they persuaded to remain loyal. A more serious conflict arose (1497–1502) in the form of an open and murderous struggle among Ivan's relatives for succession to the throne. Ivan had originally named as his heir his grandson Dmitry, son of his deceased son Ivan and the Moldavian princess Yelena, but a group close to Ivan's second wife, Sophia (Zoë) Paleologue, opposed this; her son Vasily threatened and perhaps attempted an insurrection, and Ivan was forced to accept Vasily. Historians have long pondered the causes of this struggle, in which most of the strands of Ivan's politics are brought together, but the motives and actions of the prince and his family remain obscure. For all its obvious achievement, Ivan's reign was nevertheless full of conflict and contradiction.

The entrance into Europe

Ivan made the first effort on the part of a Muscovite ruler to become involved in the diplomacy of western Europe. He and his advisors realized the need for a counterpoise to the Polish–Lithuanian power, while the diplomats of Rome and Vienna were interested in the possibility of flanking the growing empire of the Ottomans with a Muscovite–Tatar force. In the 1470s and 80s, there was an unprecedented traffic between these capitals and Moscow. It was through these channels that Ivan arranged his marriage to Sophia (Zoë) Paleologue, a niece of the last Byzantine emperor. Sophia has been credited with considerable influence over Ivan, in particular with urging him to adopt the Byzantine political style (*e.g.*, autocracy, state domination of the church, etc.), but in fact she probably had little influence over Ivan's policies. His reign ended on a note of failure, with his overtures to the west and his brief rapprochement with Lithuania both disrupted by the intractable territorial and religious conflicts of the Slavic east and by the opportunism of the local magnates. Moscow's situation was worsened after Ivan's death by the collapse of the alliance with the Crimean khan Mengli Giray upon the Khan's death in 1515, opening a new period of chaos and readjustment in the steppe.

A similar appraisal must be made of Ivan's domestic policies. Although his reign was notable for the annexation of the rich Novgorodian provinces, for the establishment of a regular bureaucracy and a land-tenure system, and for certain improvements in agriculture, these achievements created new problems for his successors. The system of land grants to military servitors led to a major struggle over monastic land owning and hastened the enserfment of the free peasantry in the central lands. His territorial annexations were to be the seeds of future administrative and political problems.

Vasily III. Ivan's son Vasily, who came to the throne in 1505, greatly strengthened the monarchy. He completed the annexation of Great Russian territories with the absorption of Pskov (1510) and Ryazan (1521) and began the advance into non-Great Russian territories (Smolensk, 1514). He also undertook to limit the scale of monastic and lay landholdings, as well as the juridical immunities attached to them. In these measures he relied upon the growing crops of bureaucrats and service gentry, rather than upon the great boyars, whose power subsequently declined.

Faced with a continuing Lithuanian war and with the breakdown of his father's Tatar policy, Vasily carefully temporized in order to avoid uniting his enemies. Once he had secured peace in the west, he was able to deal directly with the khan of the Crimean Tatars. In the end, however, much of what Vasily accomplished was undone by his failure as a procreator: divorcing his first wife for her apparent barrenness, he married Yelena Glinskaya, who bore him only two children—the congenitally retarded Yury and the sickly Ivan, who was three years old at Vasily's death, in 1533.

Ivan IV the Terrible. Vasily had been able to appoint a regency council composed of his most trusted advisors and headed by his wife Yelena. The grievances created by his limitation of landholders' immunities and his antiboyar policies soon found expression in intrigue and opposition. The bureaucracy he had relied upon could not function without firm leadership. Although Yelena continued Vasily's policies with some success, on her death, in 1538, various parties of boyars sought to gain control of the state apparatus; a decade of intrigue followed, during which affairs of state, when managed at all, went forward because of the momentum developed by the bureaucracy. Foreign policy was moribund, in spite of considerable opportunities presented by the continuing decay of the khanate of Kazan, and domestic policy vacillated so wildly that scholars cannot agree upon an appraisal of its main directions.

Toward the end of the 1540s, however, there emerged a strong coalition of bureaucrats, clergy, and old Muscovite boyars. Apparently inspired by a common awareness of the needs of the state, they ended the debilitating intrigues and embarked upon a thoroughgoing program of reform. The first important step was the re-establishment of the monarch (for the first time to be officially designated tsar), accomplished through the coronation of the 16-year-old Ivan in unprecedented solemnity and pomp. Shortly afterward, he was married to Anastasia Romanovna Zakharina, of the leading boyar family.

Power of politicians over Ivan

Although there is a voluminous literature devoted to Ivan, almost nothing is known of his personality, his political views, or his methods of rule. There is little reliable biographical information about him aside from the facts of his six marriages, his lifelong ill health, and his mercurial temper. It is not even known when he began to rule in fact or which of the policies of his reign can be considered his.

Ivan was doubtless a puppet in the hands of the leading politicians long after his coronation. The major reforms of the middle 1550s, which produced a new law code, a new military organization, a reform of local government, and severe restrictions upon the powers of hereditary landowners (including the monasteries), were probably the work of the bureaucrats and clergy, their objective being to modernize and standardize the administration of the growing state. The immediate goal was to strengthen the state and military apparatus in connection with major campaigns (the first undertaken in 1547) against the khanate of Kazan, and to prepare for the major colonization of the new lands that that conquest and others were expected to secure. Toward the end of the 1550s, Ivan seems to have gained the support of certain groups opposed to these policies and to have seized control of the government. The issue was evidently foreign policy. The planned conquest of the Volga and steppe region had been delayed in execution, and the Kazan campaigns had been enormously costly. By 1557, when the campaigns against the Crimea began, there was much opposition in the highest military circles. Ivan took the dissidents' part and for the first time emerged as an independent figure.

Ivan was a disastrously bad ruler, in part because no one had ever anticipated that he would rule. His lifelong ill health and the idiocy of his brother made it quite natural for the regency and the politicians to ignore him and to neglect his education. In his adulthood, he contracted a painful and incurable bone disease, from which he sought relief in potions provided by a succession of foreign doctors and quacks and in alcohol. Once he had acquired full power, he set about destroying those who had ruled during the interregnum, as well as the machinery of government they had built up.

Ivan's famous *oprichnina*, an aggregate of territory to be separated from the rest of the realm and put under his immediate control as crown land, established in 1564, was the device through which he expressed his hatred and misunderstanding of the established government. As his private domain, a state within the state, he took into it predominantly northern and commercial territories that had enjoyed a special prosperity in preceding decades. Specific towns and districts all over Russia were included in the *oprichnina*, their revenues being assigned to the maintenance of Ivan's new court and household. He established a new, much simplified officialdom and a court composed of sycophants and mercenaries, prone to rule through terror, accompanied by persecution of precisely those groups that had contributed so much to the modernization of the state. As trained statesmen and administrators were replaced by hirelings and cronies, the central government and military organization began to disintegrate. The destructiveness of the *oprichnina* was heightened by Ivan's involvement in the costly and ultimately disastrous Livonian Wars throughout this period (indeed, some historians have viewed the *oprichnina* as a device for the prosecution of these taxing campaigns). Even before they had ended, Ivan was forced by the utter incompetence of his special *oprichnina* army to reintegrate it (1572) with the regular army and to revert, in theory at least, to the previous institutions of government. By the time he died, in 1584, the state that he had wanted to reclaim from its makers was in ruins.

Boris Godunov.   Ivan had murdered his eldest son, Ivan, in a fit of rage in 1581, and his only legitimate heir, Fyodor, was an idiot. Power passed to those who were at Ivan's deathbed, among whom Boris Godunov, who had capped a rapid rise in court circles by the cynical marriage of his sister Irina to the pathetic Fyodor, soon emerged as the leading force. Godunov's judicious combination of chicanery, vision, and force enabled him to disarm his most dangerous enemies and to have himself proclaimed tsar after Fyodor's death in 1598. His policies during Fyodor's reign had been consistently restorative and conciliatory, and he had apparently succeeded in repairing much of the damage done to the state in Ivan's time. He conducted a cautious and generally successful foreign policy: the 20 years of his reign were, except for a short, successful war against Sweden, peaceful. In domestic policy, he returned to the modernizing and standardizing policies of the mid-century. He reorganized the land-tenure system, commerce, and taxation.

For a number of his problems Godunov could find no solution. Chief among these were the depopulation of the central Muscovite lands and the discontent among small landholders in the territories recently acquired in the south and southwest. Added to these problems was the continuing opposition of the boyars.

In spite of these difficulties and widespread famine caused by crop failures in 1601–02, Godunov remained well in control of the situation until the appearance of the so-called first False Dmitry, a defrocked monk who had appeared in Poland in 1601 claiming to be the son of Ivan IV. (The true Dmitry had died during an epileptic seizure in 1591.) The False Dmitry found some supporters in Poland—notably, Jerzy Mniszech, to whose 15-year-old daughter, Maryna, he became engaged. As the impostor moved northeast toward Muscovy, he acquired growing support among the disaffected petty gentry and Cossacks (peasants who had escaped from serfdom to a nomadic life) of the regions through which he passed, and border cities throughout the south opened their gates

The
struggle
for Ivan's
succession

to him. Godunov's troops easily defeated the ragtag force, which apparently had many secret supporters among Muscovite boyars, but a few weeks later Godunov died. The boyars staged a coup against Godunov's family and declared Dmitry tsar. The pretender entered Moscow in triumph, was crowned, and married Maryna Mniszchówna.

The Time of Troubles.   The events of 1606–13 cannot be captured in a few words. Chaos gripped most of central Muscovy; Muscovite boyars, Polish–Lithuanian–Ukrainian Cossacks, and assorted mobs of adventurers and desperate citizens were among the chief actors. In May 1606, a small-scale revolt supported by popular indignation at the foolishly insulting behaviour of Dmitry and his Polish garrison brought the overthrow and murder of the pretender. The boyars gave the crown to Prince Vasily Shuysky, a leader of the revolt against Dmitry, with the understanding that he would respect the special rights and privileges of the boyars. While the new tsar had the support of most boyars and of the northern merchants, he could not, however, end the disorders in the south or the adventures of the Polish and Swedish kings, who used Muscovy as a battlefield in their continuing conflict with each other. In 1608 a number of boyars, led by the Romanovs, went over to a second False Dmitry, who had ridden a wave of discontent and freebootery from the Cossack south into the centre of Muscovy. A kind of shadow government was formed in the village of Tushino, 14 kilometres west of Moscow, in which the boyars and bureaucrats of the Romanov circle took leading posts. It managed to gain Cossack support and to manipulate Dmitry's pretensions while dealing with the Polish king Sigismund III over terms on which his son Władysław IV might become tsar. Shuysky, in desperation, turned to Sweden for aid, promising territorial concessions along the Swedish–Muscovite border. At this, the Polish king invaded Muscovy and besieged Smolensk (September 1609). The Tushino coalition dissolved, and Dmitry withdrew to the south. The position of the Shuysky government deteriorated, and in 1610 the tsar was deserted by his army and his allies. The boyars formed a seven-man provisional government with the aim of installing a Polish tsar. This government proved unable to settle its affairs and to restore order to the country. A new insurgent army, financed by northern merchants and staffed with Swedish troops, marched on Moscow with the intention of ousting the Polish garrison and of bringing the various Cossack bands under control. It nearly gained Moscow but fell apart because its leadership could make no arrangement with the Cossack leaders. A year later, a second force, raised in the same northern cities and supported by Cossacks who had been part of the Tushino camp, was able to take possession of the Kremlin. A call was issued for the election of a new tsar.

Social and economic conditions.   In the flux of social and economic life in the 15th and 16th centuries, three interconnected processes may be observed: a steady economic growth, mainly from colonization and trade but also from the productivity of agriculture; an expansion in the power of the central government; and the encroachment of the nobility upon the lands previously held by the free peasantry, accompanied by the reduction of the bulk of the peasantry to serf status.

In the middle of the 15th century, society and the economy were still organized along traditional lines. The land was sparsely settled. Life for most of the population was simple and probably close to the subsistence level. Serfdom did not yet exist. Most of the peasantry lived on state lands and paid whatever taxes could be extracted from them by their prince or his bailiff.

A number of changes occurred in this pattern in the latter part of the 15th century. Around 1460, measures were taken to bring the peasantry under more regular control of the state and the landlord. Peasant registration appeared at this time, and also the requirement spread that peasants might renounce the tenancy of the land they were working only at the end of the agricultural cycle, in the week of St. Yury's Day (November 26). The growing

The false
Dmitrys

controls upon the peasantry received impetus from the large-scale deportations and colonizations that accompanied the annexations of Novgorod, Tver, Pskov, and Ryazan, when the old nobility were replaced with nobility owing service to the prince of Muscovy. The nationwide promulgation of the restriction on movement to St. Yury's Day was contained in the law code of 1497, which added the stipulation that peasants leaving a former situation must pay the landlord all arrears in addition to a departure fee. All of the measures, together with the expansion of the state apparatus for tax gathering and adjudication of disputes over land and peasants, were associated with the growing complexity and power of the central government.

The law code of 1550 repeated the stipulation of 1497 limiting peasant departure, but with much more specific provisions and stronger sanctions. Other reforms put an end to local administration by rotating military governors and limited monastic landholding and the juridical rights of landlords over their peasants. The events and policies of the latter half of the reign of Ivan IV destroyed many of the beneficial results of the reforms. The Livonian Wars imposed unprecedented burdens on the tax-paying population and required such long absences by the landed nobles that their estates fell into ruin. Ivan's *oprichnina* caused the breakup of the great independent boyar holdings, in which the vitality of the peasant commune had been preserved, and replaced them with smaller service estates, often too small to be operated efficiently, whose masters needed to exploit serf and indentured labour in order to meet their obligations of service to the grand prince. These burdens led to the mass flight of the peasantry from the central agricultural regions, resulting in serious economic difficulties and a sharp fiscal crisis. Godunov's government attempted to deal with the problems through remission of taxes, avoidance of war, and harsher measures to keep the peasants on the land; but the country entered the Time of Troubles weakened by decades of economic chaos.

Cultural trends. This period also saw the crystallization of that complex of forms and ideas that can, for the first time, be identified as Great Russian culture. There was a gathering and integration of the Novgorodian, Tverite, and Suzdalian cultural traditions. Moscow began to attract the artists, craftsmen, and learned monks who built the eclectic but "national" churches of Ivan III's otherwise Italianate Kremlin and who wrote the revised national, pro-Muscovite versions of the chronicles that had been kept in Rostov, Ryazan, and Novgorod. The regional traditions were not always easily reconciled. Novgorodian attitudes, in particular, clashed with those of Muscovy.

The reign of Ivan III saw a marked turning toward the West. Ivan surrounded himself with Italian and Greek diplomats and craftsmen. His palace of 1487, his Kremlin with its Latin inscription over the main gate, and his churches, the original aspect of which has been altered by successive russifying restorations, were clearly in the Italian style, as contemporary foreign visitors noted. His marriage to Sophia, the niece of the last Byzantine emperor, Constantine Palaeologus, had, in addition to its diplomatic significance, a symbolic function of bringing Ivan into the circle of Western princes. This was the time of the "Third Rome" theory, when Muscovy supposedly regarded itself as the heir of Byzantium and as the spiritual leader of the Orthodox world. It may be that the church leadership, militantly anti-Roman, thought of itself in this light. Ivan and many around him viewed the Byzantine heritage as Western, by contrast with the Ottoman and Tatar world, and were at pains to associate Muscovy with Western traditions and interprincely relations. This striving to be accepted in the Western world marked most of the changes in regalia and style of Ivan's reign, although these were later to be buried in the lore of Muscovite Byzantinism.

Three significant causes can be discerned for the evolution of Muscovite culture in the 16th century. The first was the growth and prosperity of the Great Russian population, united under a stable and increasingly centralized

monarchy, which produced the conditions for the rise of a national culture. The second was the diplomatic and cultural isolation in which Muscovy found itself, particularly in the first half of the 16th century, as a result of hostile relations with increasingly powerful Lithuania and Poland, a cause that, more than any other, brought an end to Ivan III's westward turn and to the revolutionary adjustments of the age of exploration. The third cause was the resolution of church–state relations, in the course of which the church submitted to the power of the princes in politics but gained control over the culture, style, and ideology of the dynasty, producing the peculiar amalgam of nationalistic, autocratic, and Orthodox elements that became the official culture of high Muscovy. This new synthesis was reflected in the great undertakings associated with the name of Metropolitan Makary of Moscow: St. Basil's Cathedral in the Kremlin; the encyclopedic Menolog, or calendar of months, which contained all of the literature, translated and original, permitted to be read in the churches; and the *Illustrated Codex*, a compilation of East Slavic and Greek chronicles in an official Muscovite version.

ROMANOV MUSCOVY

Michael Fyodorovich. The military drive that finally expelled the Poles from Moscow led to the election of Michael, the sickly 16-year-old son of Fyodor Romanov, as the new tsar. The composition of the coalition that elected him is not clear, but he evidently represented a compromise among the Cossacks, the boyars (especially the Tushino boyars), and the leaders of the northern army. It would be difficult to imagine circumstances less favourable for the beginning of the reign of the adolescent monarch and a new ruling coalition. The military campaigns had left much of the central and southwestern portions of the country in ruins. In many areas, populations had fled, land lay fallow, and administration was in disarray. Significant portions of the Novgorod, Smolensk, and Ryazan regions were occupied by Swedish and Polish armies and by sundry insurrectionary forces, who threatened to renew hostilities.

The Romanov government required more than a decade to establish itself politically and to restore economic and social order. Few had expected the election of a new tsar (the fourth in eight years) to bring an end to the turmoil. But the election of Michael reflected a resolution of political forces that permitted the coalition government to address itself to the problems of reconstruction. Another cause was the survival of the central bureaucracy; the civil servants in Moscow had served all successive governments without much interruption and were ready to restore administrative regularity as soon as political order was established. Fortunately, the new government refrained from involving itself in the Polish–Swedish conflicts, which reached their height at this period. This restraint was a most important element in the success of the 1613 settlement, for the international situation was, if anything, grimmer than the domestic. Polish–Swedish differences permitted Muscovite diplomats to bring the two countries to separate truces (Poland, 1618; Sweden, 1617); although these left substantial territories under the control of Poland and Sweden, they provided a needed interlude of peace. The Romanov government wisely avoided any significant participation in the Thirty Years' War, in which most European states engaged. At the death of the Polish king Sigismund III in 1632, Muscovy made an ill-advised attempt to regain Smolensk that ended in military disaster; but, in 1634, it obtained Władysław's formal abjuration of the Polish king's questionable claim to the title of tsar.

After the failure of the Smolensk campaign, the government refrained from further military involvement with Poland for nearly a generation. It concentrated instead upon the extension and fortification of its southern borders, where the incursions of Crimean Tatars were an impediment to colonization. Moscow, however, was not prepared to go to war with the Ottomans, who were the protectors of the Crimean khan; when in 1637 the Don Cossacks, Muscovy's clients, captured the critical port of

The crystallization of Great Russian culture

Establishment of the Romanovs

Azov and appealed to Moscow for aid in holding off a counterattack, a *zemsky sobor*, or national assembly (see below *Trends in the 17th century*), decided not to intervene, and the port was lost.

Alexis Mikhaylovich. The reign of Michael's son Alexis, whom later generations considered the very model of a benevolent and gentle tsar, began badly. Like his father, Alexis came to the throne a mere boy. Immediately, the boyar who controlled the government, Boris Ivanovich Morozov, embarked upon policies that brought the government to the brink of disaster. Morozov cut government salaries; he also introduced a tax on salt and a state monopoly of tobacco, the first of which caused widespread hardship and discontent, while the second brought the church's condemnation. At the same time, he alienated boyar groups close to the throne by his interference in his ward's marriage.

Morozov's actions exacerbated an already dangerous situation in the country. The city populations and service gentry, in particular, were heavily burdened by taxes and other obligations and were increasingly angry at the growing wealth and power of the ruling clique. During a riot in Moscow in May 1648, a mob surrounded the 19-year-old tsar, demanding the execution of Morozov and the leading officials. Some of the latter were thrown to the mob, and a brief protective exile was arranged for Morozov. Morozov's boyar enemies, who may have abetted the riot, took control of affairs and carried out a series of reforms. The salt tax and tobacco monopoly were ended, and a commission was established for the drafting of a new law code. Serious disorders continued in the cities of the north, particularly in Pskov and Novgorod, where force was required to reimpose authority.

In Novgorod, the principal actor in the government's interest was the metropolitan Nikon, an energetic and authoritarian monk who had made influential friends in Moscow while archimandrite at the Romanov family church and continued assiduously to cultivate the tsar and his relations while in Novgorod. In 1652 his solicitations earned him the patriarchate. Tradition has it that, before accepting the position, Nikon demanded a declaration of full obedience in religious and moral matters from the tsar. In the first years of Nikon's tenure, his relations with Alexis and the court were good; the patriarch, with official support, carried out a number of liturgical and organizational reforms; he surrounded himself with an impressive bureaucracy modelled upon the state apparatus. Relations with the tsar became strained in 1658, however, and, after he was publicly snubbed by Alexis, Nikon announced that he was abandoning the patriarchate. He later held that he had simply gone into temporary seclusion, but his effective power and influence were at an end.

The main event of Alexis' reign was the annexation of the eastern Ukraine. His government had continued the previous policy of avoiding entanglements in the West while expanding eastward but could not resist the opportunity offered, in 1654, when the leader of a Cossack revolution against Polish rule in the Ukraine appealed to Moscow for the help he had been unable to obtain from Sweden and the Turks. Moscow accepted his allegiance in return for military assistance and thus became involved in a protracted struggle with Poland and Sweden for the Ukrainian, Belorussian, and Baltic territories. At first, the war went well, but the differing objectives of the Ukrainian and Muscovite allies soon revealed themselves; when Charles X of Sweden entered the fray against Poland, Alexis made peace in 1656; he feared a strong Sweden as much as a strong Poland. Muscovite forces plunged into war with Sweden for the Estonian, Livonian, and Karelian territories along the Baltic coast. The situation in the Ukraine became increasingly confused and dangerous for Moscow, and it was necessary to end the war with Sweden in 1661, even at the cost of yielding, once again, the Baltic coast.

In the Ukraine, the war took on a new aspect when, in 1664, Peter Doroshenko, a new leader, put himself under the protection of the Ottomans. The Turks joined in a number of major military operations, alarming both Po-

land and Moscow sufficiently to bring them to a truce at Andrusovo (1667). Poland recognized Moscow's control over eastern Ukraine and Kiev, while Moscow yielded most of Belorussia and the Ukraine west of the Dnieper.

The peace did not greatly improve the government's position, for the same year saw the beginning of a threatening movement among the Don Cossacks and peasants of the Volga region, led by Stenka Razin, and a political battle within the inner circles at court, caused by the death of Alexis' wife. After two years, Alexis was married to Nataliya Naryshkina. In 1676, however, Alexis himself died, and Fyodor, a sickly son of his first wife, Mariya Miloslavskaya, succeeded him. A struggle began between the rival Naryshkin and Miloslavsky families. The Naryshkins were exiled, and the Miloslavskys, with their clients and supporters, took over. In 1682, however, Fyodor died, and the Naryshkin faction sought to place his half-brother Peter on the throne instead of Fyodor's full brother, the ailing Ivan. The elite corps of *streltsy* (a hereditary military caste) revolted and established Ivan's elder sister Sophia as regent. (For the accession and reign of Peter the Great, see below *II. The 18th century: The reign of Peter I [1689–1725]*.)

Trends in the 17th century. Economic reconstruction was slow, particularly in agriculture and in the old central lands, but it was accompanied by a growth of trade and manufacturing. The state revenues profited from the expansion eastward beyond the Urals and southward into the black-soil region. In the north, the port of Archangel handled the export of forest products and semimanufactures (naval stores, potash) to the English and Dutch, and its merchants took a leading role in the early exploitation of Siberia. The government itself became deeply involved in the development of trade and commerce, both through its monopolistic control of certain areas and commodities and by its efforts to build up such strategic industries as metallurgy. The economy grew at unprecedented speed during the 17th century. By 1700 Russia was a leading producer of pig iron and potash, and the economic base upon which Peter's military successes were to depend had been firmly established.

The political recovery of the Russian state after the Time of Troubles was due largely to the survival of the central bureaucracy and ruling oligarchy. The lines of subsequent development were determined by the growth, consolidation, and almost unimpeded self-aggrandizement of these groups in the 17th century. The expansion of the bureaucratic apparatus can be measured in various ways. In 1613 there were 22 *prikazes*, or departments; by mid-century there were 80. At the beginning of the period, the jurisdiction of the bureaucracy included primarily fiscal, juridical, and military matters; by the end of the century, it also covered industrial, religious, and cultural life. At the close of the Time of Troubles, the bureaucracy's functions were exercised by leading boyars and professional administrators; by Peter's time, the mercantile class, the whole of the nobility, and the clergy had become part of its ubiquitous network. This bureaucracy was the buttress —indeed, the substance—of an absolute monarchy whose prerogatives knew no internal bounds.

The ease with which the extension of central authority overwhelmed all other political and social forces is to be explained by the frailty of local institutions and by the absence of independent ecclesiastical or social authority. The Muscovite administration was extended first into the devastated areas, where local institutions had been swept away, and then into new territories that had no significant political institutions, until it became a standardized and centralized mechanism powered by the colossal wealth generated by its own expansion.

These processes were reflected in the great law code of 1649, the first general codification since 1550, which was to remain the basis of Russian law until 1833. Its articles make clear the realities of Muscovite political practice: the rule of the bureaucrats and the extension of the powers of the state into all spheres of human activity. It was based in large measure upon the accumulated ad hoc decisions of the officials and was intended for their guidance. It made ecclesiastical affairs a matter of state juris-

Domination of Morozov

Territorial expansion in the 17th century

The expansion of central authority

diction; it gave legal expression to the practice of serfdom; and, in an important new article, it enumerated crimes "of word and deed" against the "Sovereign"—by which were to be understood the state and all its agents.

Social development paralleled and was determined by the developments just described. The great families of hereditary princes, still rich and powerful at the turn of the century, were systematically reduced, first through direct repression by the Romanovs, who feared them, and later through fiscal and administrative measures. By the end of the century, only those families that had made new careers in the state apparatus through service as generals, ministers, and ambassadors remained at the apex of society; they were joined by numerous parvenu families that had risen in government service. Particularly striking was the prosperity of the *dyak* class of professional administrators, which had become a closed hereditary estate by a decree of 1640; this class had become a new and powerful "nobility of the seal" that was to survive into modern times.

During much of the 17th century, the government was run, for all practical purposes, by high officials in cooperation with relatives and cronies of the reigning tsar. Nineteenth-century historians, eager to find constitutional traditions in Russia's past, have stressed the role of the *zemsky sobor*—an assembly of dignitaries that from the time of Ivan IV had been called together when matters of crucial importance had to be decided. In the period after 1613, it was in almost continuous session for some years. After 1619, however, the services of these assemblies were no longer required. It is questionable whether they ever had, in law or in fact, any power beyond that of a crowd of military and administrative leaders. They were summoned by the government, and their composition was determined by the government.

Cultural life. No period of Russia's cultural history has been as full of change, turmoil, creativity, failure, and sheer destructiveness as the 17th century. Russian society emerged from the Time of Troubles shattered and unsure of itself, disoriented and impoverished. This shaken society was then subject to wrenching social and economic change and strong external influences.

The old culture, in its formal aspects, had been the culture of the monasteries. Art, literature, architecture, and music remained, until the end of the 16th century, traditional, canonical, and orthodox.

The emergence of a new elite

The 17th century produced, first among the officials and boyars, later among the merchants and middle classes, a new elite that was increasingly interested in European culture and that had mainly secular interests. Yet the government of these same officials and boyars worked to stifle native cultural development, and many of these merchants and nobles were drawn into movements opposed to westernization.

The reasons for this paradoxical development were three. First, Western culture had reached Muscovy largely through Polish and Roman Catholic mediation, which rendered it unacceptable to all but those sophisticated enough to take a very broad view of the events of the Time of Troubles. In the Ukrainian and Belorussian territories, the Polish counter-reformation had brought a national cultural revival. The books and ideas and men flowing from these lands into Muscovy in the 17th century, however, were hardly less suspect than those of Catholic Poland, and, as these "aliens" acquired a dominant position in Muscovite cultural affairs, resentment was added to suspicion.

A second reason for the character of Muscovite cultural development in the 17th century was the preponderant role of the church and, later, of the state, which took over at last the assets, liabilities, and responsibilities of the ecclesiastical establishment. From 1620, when the patriarch Philaret pronounced an anathema upon "books of Lithuanian imprint" (in effect the only secular books in print for the Russian reader) until the end of the century, when the government turned to imposing Greek and "Lithuanian" (*i.e.*, Ukrainian and Belorussian) views upon a resisting populace, the state and its ecclesiastical adjunct had a repressive and stultifying influence.

Finally, indigenous cultural forces were, for various reasons, unable to assert themselves. They were physically dispersed, socially diverse, and set at odds by cultural and political disaffection. The development of a vernacular literature, which can be seen in the synthetic "folk songs," pamphlets, tales, and imitations produced for and by the growing educated class, remained an underground phenomenon; they were unpublished because of the ecclesiastical monopoly of the press, and they were anonymous out of fear. The promising experiments of a group of noble writers who worked within the formal Slavonic tradition were ended by exile and repression. The gay and expressive architecture and painting of the northern regions, which continued certain Novgorod traditions, fell victim to official discrimination against this region and its predominantly Old Believer population.

Despite these negative influences, the court, especially in the time of Alexis, was a centre of literary and artistic innovation, and many of the leading men of the realm were considered cultured and cosmopolitan by Westerners who knew them.

The great schism. The contradictions of the age were reflected in the great schism within the Russian church. The doctrinal debate began over obscure and petty matters of ritual, but larger, unarticulated issues were at stake. Religion in the Time of Troubles had taken two directions, which were at first closely associated: the reformation of religious life, (with stress on the pastoral functions of the clergy and the simplification of the liturgy) and the correction and standardization of the canonical books (which had, over centuries of regional mutation and textual degradation, come to vary widely from the Greek originals). The government had at first supported these linked objectives, but the supporters of "Old Russian piety" fell into opposition to the reforms as they were officially promulgated. When, in the 1650s, the patriarch Nikon began to enforce the reforms in the parishes, where they had been generally ignored, the discontent developed into a massive religious and regional insurrection. Towns and parishes of the north were riven by warring "old" and "new" bishops. The Old Believers were either crushed by government force, driven to self-destruction, or reduced to silent resistance.

Enforcement of religious reforms

In the end, the Western secular culture fostered at the court and the new religious culture and education, spread by Ukrainians and Belorussians, who came to dominate church life, submerged and displaced the disparate beginnings of a modern synthesis within native matrices and cleared the way for Peter's cultural policies, which erected a Western facade over the ruins of the native culture.

(E.L.K.)

II. The 18th century

THE REIGN OF PETER I (1689–1725)

Peter's youth and early reign. The accession of Peter I ushered in and established the social, institutional, and intellectual trends that were to dominate Russia for the next two centuries. Both Russian and Western historians, whatever their evaluation of Peter's reign, have seen it as one of the most formative periods of Russia's history. The seminal nature of the reign owes much to Peter's own personality and youth. The child of his father's second marriage, Peter was pushed into the background by his half brother Fyodor and exiled from the Kremlin during the turbulent years of the regency (1682–89) of his half sister Sophia. He grew up among children of lesser birth, unfettered by court etiquette. Playing at war and organizing his young friends into an effective military force, he could manifest his energy, vitality, and curiosity almost untrammeled. He also came into close contact with the western Europeans who lived in Moscow; the association kindled his interest in navigation and the mechanical arts —at which he became a skilled practitioner—and gave him the experience of a socially freer and intellectually more stimulating atmosphere than he might otherwise have had. He resolved to introduce this more dynamic and "open" style of life into Russia, a goal he pursued after the overthrow of Sophia in 1689 and that he erected into a policy of state after he became sole ruler following the death of his mother in 1694. (His half-witted half brother, Ivan V, remained co-tsar but played no role and died in 1696.)

Peter's first political aim was to secure Muscovy's southern borders against the threat of raids by Crimean Tatars supported by the Ottoman Empire. For lack of adequate sea power, his initial attempt in 1695 failed to gain a foothold on the Sea of Azov. Undaunted, Peter built up a navy—the first Russian ruler since early Kievan times to do so—and succeeded in capturing Azov a year later. The experience convinced him of the necessity of extending his own technical knowledge and of securing tools and personnel from the West. To this end Peter travelled to western Europe, something no Muscovite tsar had ever done; he spent almost a year in Holland and England acquiring mechanical and maritime skills, hiring experts in various fields, purchasing books and scientific curiosities, and carrying on diplomatic negotiations for a crusade against the Turks. In the course of negotiations with Poland-Saxony and Denmark, an alliance was formed, not against Turkey but against Sweden. The alliance led to the Great Northern War (1700–21), which became Peter's major concern for almost the remainder of his reign.

Not only did the war absorb the country's resources and energies, but the war's requirements—defensive at first, and offensive after Peter's decisive victory over Charles XII at Poltava in 1709—determined most domestic policy measures as well. Only when victory was well in sight could Peter devote more of his attention to a systematic overhaul of Russia's institutions. The hastiness and brutality of steps taken under the stress of war had an effect on subsequent history. Historians have debated whether Peter's legislation was informed by an overall plan based on more or less clearly formulated theoretical considerations, or whether it was merely a series of ad hoc measures taken to meet emergencies as they occurred. Pragmatic elements predominated, no doubt, over theoretical principles. Yet the struggle against Sweden's modern military machine, together with the prevailing intellectual climate and administrative practices of Europe, contributed to orient Peter's thinking.

The Petrine state. Formally, Peter changed the tsardom of Muscovy into the Empire of All Russias, and he himself received the title of "emperor" from the Senate at the conclusion of the peace with Sweden (Treaty of Nystad, 1721). The title not only aimed at identifying the new Russia with European political tradition, it also bespoke the new conception of rulership and of political authority that Peter wanted to implant: that the sovereign emperor was the head of the state and its first servant, not the patrimonial owner of the land and "father" of his subjects (as the tsar had been). Peter stressed the function of his office rather than that of his person and laid the groundwork of a modern system of administration. Institutions and officials were to operate on the basis of set rules, keep regular hours and records, apply laws and regulations dispassionately, and have individual and collective responsibility for their acts. Reality, of course, fell far short of this ideal, because Muscovite traditions and conditions could not be eradicated so rapidly. Furthermore, there was a great shortage of educated and reliable persons imbued with such rationality and efficiency (a problem that bedevilled the imperial government until its end). They were mainly to be found in the military establishment, where officer and noncommissioned ranks acquired the requisite outlook, experience, and values in the army and navy established by Peter. The Russian bureaucracy thus acquired a preference for uniformity and militarism that did not foster respect or concern for the individual needs of the various regions and peoples of the far-flung empire.

In the new administration, performance was to be the major criterion for appointment and promotion. Peter wanted this principle to apply to the highest offices, starting with that of the emperor himself. As a result of his bad experience with his own son, Alexis (who fled abroad, was brought back, and died in prison), Peter decreed in 1722 that every ruler would appoint his own successor. He did not have the opportunity to avail himself of this right, however, and the matter of regular succession remained a source of conflict and instability throughout the 18th century. Peter's concern for performance lay at the basis of the Table of Ranks (1722), which served as the framework for the careers of all state servants (military, civil, court) until the second half of the 19th century. In it, the hierarchy was divided into 14 categories, or ranks; theoretically one had to begin at the bottom (14th rank) and proceed upward according to merit and seniority. Throughout the 18th century the 8th rank (1st commissioned officer grade) automatically conferred hereditary nobility on those who were not noble by birth. In a sense, therefore, the Table of Ranks opened all offices to merit and thus democratized the service class; but because service was contingent on good preparation (*i.e.*, education), it was accessible only to the few—nobility and clergy—until later in the 18th century.

The same need for qualified personnel that had brought about the Table of Ranks also determined Peter's policies toward the several social classes of his realm. The traditional obligation of members of all estates to perform service to the state, each according to his way of life (*i.e.*, the nobleman by serving in the army and administration, the peasantry and merchants by paying taxes, the clergy by prayer), was given a modern, rational form by Peter. Paradoxically, the reform helped to transform the traditional estates into caste-like groups from which—except in rare instances of clergy and rich merchants—it became impossible to escape. The nobility was most directly affected by the change, not only in Peter's lifetime but under his successors as well. The nobleman's service obligation became lifelong, regular, and permanent. The staffs of military and government institutions were no longer recruited on the basis of regional origin or family ties, but strictly according to the need of the state and the fitness of the individual for the specific task at hand. The serviceman was transferred from one assignment, branch, or locality to another as the state saw fit. The office of heraldry within the Senate kept the service rosters up to date and decided on appointments and transfers. Peter also introduced single inheritance of real estate (1714), attempting in this way to break the traditional inheritance pattern that had led to the splintering of estates. In so doing he hoped to create a professional service nobility unconnected with the land and totally devoted to the state; but the resistance the law met in its application forced its revocation in 1731. He also required the nobility to be educated as a prerequisite for service. Schooling, whether at home or in an institution, became a feature of the nobleman's way of life. Until the late 18th century, a nobleman was not considered to have attained his majority and did not have the right to marry unless he had passed a government examination in basic subjects. Schooling was a radical innovation, at first resented and resisted; but within a generation it was accepted as a matter of course and became the decisive element in the status and self-image of the nobility.

The peasantry had been enserfed during the 17th century, but the individual peasant had retained his traditional ties to the village commune and to the land that he worked. To prevent tax evasion through the formation of artificial households, Peter introduced a new unit of taxation, the "soul"—*i.e.*, a male peasant of working age—and the lords were made responsible for the collection of the tax assessed on each of their souls. The peasant thus became a mere item on the tax roll who could be moved, sold, or exchanged according to the needs and whims of his master—whether a private landlord, the church, or the state. The serf became practically indistinguishable from a slave. The noble landlord, on the other hand, was turned into an agent of the state; he stood in the path of the peasantry's traditional personal relationship with the sovereign and thereby contributed to the sense of alienation that the ordinary Russian felt toward the new, rational, but remote, Petrine state.

As befitted a secular-minded autocrat who saw his main task as enlightening and leading his people to "modernity," Peter had little regard for the church. He recognized its value only as an instrument of control and as an agent

Western influence in Russia

Peter I's new administration

Policies toward the social classes

Reform of
the church

of modern education. When the patriarch died in 1700, Peter appointed no successor; finally in 1721 he gave the church a bureaucratic organization: a Holy Synod composed of several appointed hierarchs and a lay representative of the emperor; the latter, called the chief procurator, came to play the dominant role. Ecclesiastic schools turned into closed institutions with a narrowly scholastic curriculum. Membership in the clerical estate became strictly hereditary; the priesthood was transformed into a closed caste of government religious servants cut off from the new secular culture being introduced in Russia and deprived of their traditional moral authority. One of the priests' main tasks was to assist the state in enforcing its laws, in particular those directed against the Old Believers, so that the clergy became an instrument of persecution and oppression. Both on economic and religious grounds, therefore, the reign of Peter I appeared particularly oppressive to the common people. It seemed unnatural and contrary to tradition; for many it clearly was the reign of Antichrist from which one escaped only through self-immolation (practised by some of the Old Believers), open rebellion, or flight to the borderlands of the empire.

Resistance and flight were made possible by Peter's failure, despite all his modernizing and rationalizing, to endow the government with effective means of control on the local level. The noble landlords might have acted as police agents; but Peter removed them from the local scene by forcing them into permanent and lifelong service. Regular officials were short in number and experience and could not be easily spared for local administration. Peter tried to have the officers of the regiments that were garrisoned in the provinces double as local officials; but the experiment failed because of the necessities of war and because regular officers proved incompetent to administer peasants. The attempts at copying Western models were also unsuccessful, for the Russian nobility lacked (and was not allowed to develop) a local corporate organization that could serve as the foundation for local self-government.

Peter concentrated his attention almost entirely on the central administration, an area in which his reforms provided the basic framework within which the imperial government was to operate until its fall in 1917. To prosecute the war, the Petrine state had to mobilize all the resources of the country and to supervise practically every aspect of national life. This required that the central executive apparatus be extended and organized along functional lines. Peter hoped to accomplish this by replacing the numerous haphazard *prikazy* (administrative departments) with a coherent system of functional and well-ordered colleges (their number fluctuating around 12 in the course of the century). Each college was headed by a board for more effective control; it had authority in a specific area such as foreign affairs, the army, the navy, commerce, mining, finances, justice, etc. The major problems of this form of organization proved to be the coordination, planning, and supervision of the colleges. Peter endeavoured to cope with these defects pragmatically through the creation of a Senate, which came to serve as a privy council as well as an institution of supervision and control. In addition, he set up a network of espionage agents (*fiskaly*), who acted as tax inspectors, investigators, and personal representatives of the emperor. Internal security was vested in 1689 in the chancery of the Preobrazhensky Guards, the tsar's own military group, which became a much dreaded organ of political police and repression. Under different names the police apparatus remained a permanent feature of the imperial regime. The police were also the instrument of the ruler's personal intervention, an essential function for the preservation of the autocracy as a viable political system.

Petrine
economy

The needs of war, as well as the desire to modernize Russia, led Peter to promote and expand industry, particularly mining, naval construction, foundries, glass, and textiles. The Emperor aimed at maximizing the use of all potential resources of the country to heighten its power and further its people's welfare; these goals were pursued in mercantilist fashion through discriminatory tariffs,

state subsidies, and regulation of manufactures. Peter hoped to involve the rich merchants and the nobility in economic enterprise and expansion. As a class, however, the merchants failed to follow his lead; many were Old Believers who refused to work for the Antichrist. Nor did Peter's urban legislation provide the townspeople with the incentives and freedom necessary to change them into an entrepreneurial class; as a matter of fact, the municipal reforms were simply means to collect taxes and dues in kind. As to the nobility, only a few had the necessary capital to become entrepreneurs, and their time and energies were completely taken up by their service obligations. The shortage of capital could be, and in some specific cases was, overcome by direct government grants. But the equally serious shortage of labour was not so easily resolved. Peter permitted the use of servile labour in mines and manufactures, with the result that thousands of peasants were moved and forced to work under unfamiliar conditions, in new places, at very difficult tasks. Resentment ran high and the productivity of this forced labour was very low. Most of the enterprises established in Peter's lifetime did not survive him. But the impetus he had given to Russian industrial development was not altogether lost; it revived with new vigour—under different policies—in the middle of the 18th century.

Among the important factors in Russia's economic development under Peter was the building of St. Petersburg (now Leningrad) on the then inhospitable shores of the Gulf of Finland. Its construction cost an estimated 30,000 lives (lost from disease, undernourishment, and drowning) and engulfed vast sums of public and private monies. Nobles who served in the central administration and at court were required to settle in the new city and to build townhouses.

The location of the new capital symbolized the shift in the empire's political, economic, and cultural centre of gravity toward western Europe. After two decades of war, during which the survival of Russia seemed at times to hang in the balance, Peter emerged victorious. The Treaty of Nystad gave him control of the Gulf of Finland and of the eastern shore of the Baltic Sea and put under his sceptre several provinces having Western constitutions, social structures, and cultural traditions. This acquisition was to create constitutional and administrative problems for the multinational empire; but in the meantime trade and social intercourse with western Europe became easier, and the icebound peripheral ports of what is now Murmansk and Archangel were abandoned for the more convenient harbours of Riga, Revel (now Tallinn), and the new St. Petersburg. Secure on the Baltic, Russia could now take an active part in the diplomatic and military affairs of the comity of European states, although sometimes this was to its disadvantage because it became embroiled in dynastic and political conflicts not involving its own interests. After 1721 Peter also extended the borders of the empire in the south along the Caspian Sea as a result of a successful war against Persia (Treaty of St. Petersburg, 1732).

The changes that made Peter's reign the most seminal in Russian history were not the administration reforms and the military conquests, significant as those were, but the transformation in the country's culture and style of life, at least among the service nobility. Foreign observers made much of Peter's requirement that the nobility shave off their beards, wear Western clothes, go to dances and parties, and learn to drink coffee. These were only the external marks of more profound changes that in a generation or so were to make the educated Russian nobleman a member of European polite society. The common people, especially the peasantry, were not so immediately and positively affected, although by the end of the 18th century most peasants, and all inhabitants of towns, had moved a considerable distance from the values and habits of their 16th- and 17th-century forebears.

Change in
Russia's
culture
and
life-style

Most important of all, perhaps, the reign of Peter I marked the beginning of a new period in Russian educational and cultural life. Peter was the first to introduce secular education on a significant scale and to make it compulsory for all state servants. (More significant than the limited quantitative results during Peter's lifetime was the fact that education eventually became indispensable to membership in the upper class.) First, Peter tried to use the church to establish a network of primary schools for all children of the free classes; this plan failed largely because the clergy were unable to finance and staff schools for secular learning. But the specialized technical schools Peter founded, such as the Naval Academy, struck roots and provided generations of young men with the skills necessary for leadership in a modern army and navy. Although he did not live to see its formal inauguration, Peter also organized the Academy of Sciences as an institution for scholarship, research, and instruction at the higher level. The Academy's beginnings were quite modest—German professors lectured in Latin to a handful or poorly prepared students—and its development was not free from difficulties; but at the end of the 18th century it was a leading European centre of science and enlightenment, preparing and guiding Russia's scientific and technological flowering in the 19th century.

Assessment of Peter's reign. Contemporaries as well as later historians have given first place among Peter's accomplishments to his conquest of the Baltic provinces and areas on the Caspian Sea. More important was the fact that during his reign Russia became a major European power, in regular intercourse with the major trading powers and especially with Holland and Great Britain. This status of European power, however, burdened Russia with the maintenance of a large and up-to-date military establishment, which became involved in many costly conflicts. The weakening of Poland during the Northern War with Sweden led ultimately to Poland's partitioning, which proved a heavy burden for the Russian body social. Finally, the cultural, religious, and linguistic diversity of the empire was increased by the incorporation of national and social groups that were not easily assimilated. The new institutional forms that Peter introduced helped to shape a less personal and more modern (i.e., routinized and bureaucratized) political authority. This led to an ambiguous relationship between the autocratic ruler and his noble servants and also to a sense of alienation between the common people and the ruler.

Russia as a major European power

Contemporaries and later generations alike shared the feeling that Peter's reign had been revolutionary—a radical and violent break with the centuries old traditions of Muscovy. To some extent this was the consequence of Peter's ruthless manner, his dynamism, his harsh suppression of all opposition, and his obstinate imposition of his will. From a historical perspective, Peter's reign may appear to have been only the culmination of 17th-century trends rather than a radical break with the past. But men are more conscious of changes in manners and customs than of deeper transformations that require a long time for their working out. Thus Russia's cultural Europeanization in the early 18th century produced works of literature in a new manner, using foreign styles and techniques, such as the treatises and sermons of Feofan Prokopovich, Peter's main assistant in church matters, and the satires and translations of Prince Antiokh Kantemir, the first modern Russian poet. These writers, and many anonymous ones, praised Peter's work, stressing its innovative and necessary character; and the educated elite, reared on the cultural elements introduced by Peter, perceived his reign as the birth of modern Russia. This fact in itself became the source of critical thought and raised the question of whether the break with the past was desirable or a betrayal of the genuinely national patterns of development of Russian culture. It appeared that forcible imposition of foreign elements had led to an alienation between the elite and the Russian people. This debate as to the nature and value of the reign of Peter I served as the main stimulus to a definition of Russian national culture and to the elaboration of competing political and social philosophies in the 19th century (e.g., those of the Slavophiles and the westernizers). Peter's reign has been at the centre of all debates over Russian history, since any attempt to define its periods and to assess Russia's development in modern times requires a prior judgment of the reign and work of Peter I.

PETER I'S SUCCESSORS (1725–62)

Peter's unexpected death in 1725 at the age of 52 left unresolved two major institutional problems. The first was the succession to the throne, which remained unsettled not only because Peter did not choose his own successor but also because during the remainder of the century almost any powerful individual or group could disregard the choice of the preceding ruler. The second problem was the lack of firm central direction, planning, and control of imperial policy; closely related to it was the question of who would have the determining role in shaping policy (i.e., what would be the nature of the "ruling circle" and its relationship to the autocrat). The failure to solve these problems produced a climate of instability and led to a succession of crises in St. Petersburg and Moscow that make it difficult to give unity and meaning to the period from 1725 until the accession of Catherine the Great in 1762.

Instability and crisis

Normal and peaceful succession to the throne was thwarted by a combination of biological accidents and palace coups. At Peter's death his chief collaborators, headed by Prince A.D. Menshikov and with the help of the guard regiments (the offshoots of the play regiments of Peter's youth), put on the throne Peter's widow—his second wife, Catherine I, the daughter of a Latvian peasant. Quite naturally, Menshikov ruled in her name. Soon, however, he was forced to share his power with other dignitaries of Peter's reign. A Supreme Privy Council was established as the central governing body, displacing the Senate in political influence and administrative significance. Catherine I's death in 1727 reopened the question of succession; Peter's grandson (the son of Alexis who had perished in prison) was proclaimed emperor Peter II by the Council. An immature youngster, Peter II fell under the influence of his chamberlain, Prince I. Dolgoruky, whose family obtained a dominant position in the Supreme Privy Council and brought about the disgrace and exile of Menshikov. It looked as if the Dolgorukys would rule in fact because Peter II was affianced to the chamberlain's sister; but Peter's sudden death in January 1730 crossed the plans of that ambitious family.

Anna (1730–40). Under the leadership of Prince Dmitry Golitsyn—scion of an old Muscovite boyar family and himself a prominent official under Peter I—the Supreme Privy Council elected to the throne Anna, dowager duchess of Courland and niece of Peter I (daughter of his co-tsar, Ivan V). At the same time, Golitsyn tried to circumscribe Anna's power by having her accept a set of conditions that left to the council the decisive voice in all important matters. This move toward oligarchy was foiled by top level officials (the generalitet; i.e., those with the service rank of general or its equivalent), in alliance with the rank-and-file service nobility. While the former wanted to be included in the ruling oligarchy (and Golitsyn seemed to have been ready to concede them this right), the latter opposed any limitation on the autocratic power of the sovereign. Indeed, the ordinary service nobles feared that an oligarchy, however broad its membership, would shut them off from access to the ruler and thus limit their opportunity to rise in the hierarchy of the Table of Ranks.

Anna left most of her authority to be exercised by her Baltic German favourite, Ernst Johann Biron, who acquired a reputation for corruption, cruelty, tyranny, and exploitation and who was felt to have set up a police terror that benefitted the Germans in Russia at the expense of all loyal and patriotic Russians. Recent scholarship has modified this image and shown that Biron's bad reputation rested on his inflexibility in applying the law and collecting taxes, rather than on malevolence. The Supreme Privy Council was abolished upon Anna's accession in 1730, and the functions of coordination, supervision, and policy planning were vested in a cabinet of ministers composed of three experienced high officials, all Russians.

Role of Ernst Biron

Elizabeth (1741–62). Anna was childless; she appointed as successor her infant nephew, Ivan Antonovich, under the regency of his mother, Anna Leopoldovna. Biron, who had at first retained his influence, was overthrown by Burkhard Christoph, Graf von Münnich, who had made his fortune in Russia. The continuing domination of a few favourites—many of whom were Germans—much displeased the high officials, whose position was threatened by the personal caprices of ruler or favourite, and incensed even more the rank and file of the service nobility, who could not obtain rewards or favours from the sovereign without the approval and help of the favourites. The malcontents banded together around Peter I's daughter, Elizabeth, whose easygoing and open ways had gained her many friends; she was also popular because of her Russian outlook, which she emphasized, and because she shared the aura of her great father. With the help of the guard regiments and high officers, and with the financial support of foreign diplomats (in particular the French envoy), Elizabeth overthrew the infant Ivan VI and the regent Anna Leopoldovna in 1741. Her 20-year reign saw the rise of certain trends and patterns in public life, society, and culture that were to reach their culmination under Catherine the Great. On the political plane, the most significant development was the restoration of the Senate to its earlier function of chief policy-making and supervising body. At the end of her reign Elizabeth also established a kind of permanent council or cabinet for planning and coordination—the Special Conference at the Imperial Court.

Stabilization under ElizabethDuring this period Peter's administrative reforms began to bear fruit. The Table of Ranks became the framework for a class of servicemen whose lives were devoted to the interests of the state. In principle, entry to this class of officials was open to anyone with the required ability and education, including the sons of priests and non-Russian landowners. In fact, however, promotion in the Table of Ranks was possible only if the individual's merit and performance were recognized by the ruler or, more likely, by high officials and dignitaries who had access to the ruler. The personal element, bolstered by family and marriage ties, came to play an important role in the formal system of promotion; most significantly, it determined the makeup of the very top echelon of the administrative and military hierarchies (which were interchangeable), the so-called *generalitet*. This group constituted an almost permanent ruling elite, co-opting its own membership and promoting the interests of the families most directly connected with it; in order to solidify its influence and function it aimed at bringing as many routine government operations as possible under a system of regulations that would make appeal to the ruler unnecessary. The latter's autocratic power could not be infringed however, because his authority was needed not only to settle special cases but to promote, protect, and reward members of the ruling group and their clients. The greatest threat to the system was the interference or interposition of favourites—"accidental people"—and to guard against this, the oligarchy entered into an alliance with the rank-and-file service nobles who wanted to join its ranks and could hope to do so with the help of the dignitaries' patronage; this alliance permitted successful palace coups against favourites. The system benefitted both the high and low nobility; but it worked only with the help of a strong autocracy in which the ruler could easily fend off any attempt at limiting his power, as Anna had demonstrated in 1730. The system worked well enough to allow the consolidation of Peter's reforms, some success in foreign policy, and a general increase in the power and wealth of the state, despite the low calibre of the rulers and the mismanagement of favourites.

The service noblemanThe system rested on the availability to all nobles of the minimum education necessary for entrance and promotion in service; this created a desire to go through rapidly, or omit altogether, the most arduous and tedious lower echelons of the Table of Ranks. As a consequence, cultural policy became a major concern of the government and the nobility alike; the members of the service class demanded that institutions of learning be set up to prepare the nobility for better careers, skipping the lowest ranks. The demand was fulfilled in 1731 with the creation of the Corps of Cadets. In the course of the following decades, the original corps was expanded and other special institu-

tions for training the nobility were added. General education became accessible to a large stratum of the rank-and-file nobility with the founding of the University of Moscow in 1755, although the lack of automatic preferment for its graduates kept it from being popular among the wealthier nobles until the end of the century. The Corps of Cadets and similar public and private institutions also acted as substitutes for the local and family bonds that had formerly given cohesion to the Muscovite service class but which Petrine practices had destroyed; these schools were also the seedbeds for an active intellectual life, and their students played a leading role in spreading the literature and ideas of western Europe in court circles and in the high society of the capitals.

The service nobleman was a landlord and serf owner; he was very poor for a number of reasons, chief among which were the low productivity of Russian agriculture and the continual splintering of estates through inheritance. As a rule his estates provided him only with the minimum necessary for his maintenance in service. But as long as he remained in service and away from his estates, he could do little to improve his property. He thus depended on the ruler for additional income, either in the form of a salary or as grants of land (and serfs) in reward for service. The salary was not very large, it was often in kind (furs), and it was paid out rather irregularly; lands and serfs could be obtained only from the ruler, and most went to favourites, courtiers, or high dignitaries. Service, it is true, provided the nobleman with some extras such as uniforms, sometimes lodgings, and—most important—greater accessibility to court, cultural life, and education for his children. Thus, he remained in service, took less and less direct interest in his estates and serfs, and became almost a rootless, permanent serviceman.

Shuvalov's gifts to the nobilityElizabeth's chief advisor, Pyotr Shuvalov, had the government grant exclusive privileges and monopolies to some of the nobility, hoping to involve them in the development of mining and manufacturing. Shuvalov also initiated a gradual loosening of state controls over economic life in general. He began to dismantle the system of internal tariffs, so that local trade could develop; he strengthened the landlord's control over all the resources on his estate; and he gave the nobles the right to distill alcohol.

At the same time, the landlords were obtaining still greater power over their serfs. The full weight of these powers fell on the household serfs, whose number increased because their masters used them as domestics and craftsmen in their town houses to make Western-style objects with which they surrounded themselves. When noblemen established factories or secured estates in newly conquered border areas, they transferred their serfs to them without regard for family or village ties. The operation of most estates was, in the absence of the landlord, left to the peasants. This only perpetuated the traditional patterns of agriculture and made the modernization and improvement of agricultural productivity impossible.

THE REIGN OF CATHERINE II THE GREAT (1762–96)

Elizabeth, too, was childless, and the throne passed to the heir she had selected—her nephew the Duke of Holstein, who became Peter III. Intellectually and temperamentally unfit to rule, Peter III made himself personally unpopular with St. Petersburg society; in addition, he allowed his entourage (mainly his Holstein relatives and German officers) to take control of the government. The regular hierarchy of officials—particularly the Senate—was pushed into the background; power passed into the hands of the emperor's favourites, while a modernized police, under the personal control of a general who was one of the emperor's minions, spread its net over the empire. The pro-Prussian foreign and military policy pursued by Peter III (who abruptly ended Russia's victorious involvement in the Seven Years' War) and his treatment of his wife Catherine provoked much resentment. As a result, the Emperor lost all support in society. It was easy for Catherine, with the help of the senators, high officials, and officers of the guard regiments (led by her lover

Grigory Orlov and his brothers) to overthrow Peter III on July 9 (June 28, old style), 1762. Thus began the long and important reign of Catherine II, whom her admiring contemporaries named "the Great."

The daughter of a poor German princeling, Catherine had come to Russia at the age of 15 to be the bride of the heir presumptive, Peter. She matured in an atmosphere of intrigue and struggle for power. She developed her mind by reading contemporary literature, especially the works of the French Encyclopaedists and of German jurists and cameralists. When she seized power at the age of 33 she was intellectually and experientially prepared, as the more than 30 years of her reign were to show.

Assessment of Catherine's reign

The historiography of Catherine's reign has been dominated by two main approaches: a dramatization and romanticization of her personal life, which was indeed colourful for the number and variety of her lovers; and the viewpoint of 19th-century liberalism, which took literally her self-description as a "philosophe on the throne." Marxist and Soviet historians, to the extent that they have dealt with her reign at all, see it primarily in terms of the pressures put on the state by the serf-owning nobility faced with the demands of an expanding market economy. In recent years, scholars have come to think of Catherine's government as working to further the formation of a modern civil society in which social classes and groups pursue their own interests rather than serving the needs of the state exclusively.

Even before she seized power, Catherine wrote that the task of good government was to promote the general welfare of the nation by providing for the security of person and property; to that end, government should operate in a legal and orderly fashion, furthering the interests of individual subjects and giving groups and classes as much autonomy in the pursuit of their normal activities as possible. All the same, Catherine believed that the autocratic state had important functions; she had no intention of relinquishing or limiting her authority, even though she was willing to withdraw from those areas of national life that could be safely administered by an educated elite.

Expansion of the empire. Catherine's reign was notable for imperial expansion. The expansion had been prepared by military and political efforts since the reign of Peter I; in particular, an important process of incorporating and settling empty land (especially in the south, corresponding roughly to the modern Ukraine) had been initiated in the reign of Elizabeth. This continued with the partitions of Poland, in which Catherine played a leading role, with the result that all eastern Poland and the former Grand Duchy of Lithuania came under Russian rule. A disadvantage of this was that Russia became a partner in the alliance of the three partitioning powers and had to mind its common border with Prussia. An additional source of difficulty was that the Roman Catholic Poles, proud of their cultural and political traditions and resentful of their loss of independence, proved less easy to assimilate and draw into Russian society than had the Baltic Germans. Also, the large number of Jews in the formerly Polish and Lithuanian provinces created special problems for the imperial government.

Of greater immediate importance for the empire were the securing of the northern shore of the Black Sea (Treaty of Küçük Kaynarca, 1774), the annexation of the Crimea (1783), and the expansion into the steppes beyond the Urals and along the Caspian Sea. This permitted the adequate protection of Russian agricultural settlements in the south and southeast and the establishment of trade routes through the Black Sea and up the Danube. On the other hand, these gains involved Russia more and more in the political and military struggle over the crumbling Ottoman Empire in the Balkans (the Treaty of Küçük Kaynarca, for example, allowed intervention on the pretext of protecting the Christian populations under Turkish rule). Russian sovereignty was extended over these territories through traditional means of war and diplomacy, but their incorporation into the Russian polity and their economic integration showed the hand of Catherine.

G.A. Potemkin, Catherine's favourite in the 1770s, may be considered the chief architect of her imperial policy. He promoted large-scale foreign colonization and peasant resettlement in the south—with only mediocre success so far as agricultural settlements went but with great success in the foundation and rapid growth of such towns and ports as Odessa, Kherson, Nikolayev, Taganrog, and Mariupol (now Zhdanov). Within a generation or two these became lively cultural centres and major commercial cities for all of southern Russia, contributing to the reorientation of Russia's pattern of trade with the development of agricultural exports from the Ukraine. Local society was transformed on the Russian pattern: the landlords became imperial service nobles with full control over their peasants; vast new lands were parcelled out to prominent officials and made available for purchase by wealthy Russian nobles, who also received the right to resettle their own serfs from the central regions. Thus, serfdom, along with elements of the plantation system, was extended to still more people and over whole new provinces. If this expansion benefitted the state and a small and already wealthy part of the Russian nobility, it increased the misery and exploitation of the Ukrainian and Russian peasantries. The traditional military democracies of the Cossack hosts on the Dnieper, Don, Ural, Kuban, and Volga rivers lost their autonomy and special privileges; the wealthier officers became Russian service nobles, receiving the right to own and settle serfs on their own lands, while the rank-and-file Cossacks sank to the level of state peasants with special military obligations.

Policies toward new nationalities

Integration of the new territories required the absorption of a large number of non-Russian, non-Christian, nomadic peoples. The approach of Catherine's ministers, which prevailed until the late 19th century, was based on the idea, taken from Enlightenment writings, that there is a natural progress of society from primitive hunting and fishing groups through the stage of nomadism to settled agriculture, trade, and urbanization. Accordingly, the government sought to bring the nomadic peoples up to what it considered to be the Russian peasantry's higher way of life; this policy had the advantage also of producing uniformity in administrative and legal structures. Catherine's government was quite willing to let religious, cultural, or linguistic differences stand, although it did not feel committed to protect them actively. Inevitably, however, its effort to change the ways of the nomads affected their culture and religion and, through these, their social equilibrium and sense of national identity. While Catherine's policy led some peoples to accept (more or less under duress) changes in their way of life, thus facilitating the extension of Russian agricultural settlements onto the open steppes, it also gave rise to a new national self-consciousness and to a growing sense of identity based on cultural, linguistic, and religious traditions. These nationalistic sentiments clashed with the outlook and practices of officials accustomed to thinking in universal categories. The government found it difficult to rely upon native elites to operate the institutions it imposed on the new territories. Russian officials had to be sent in, strengthening uniformity and centralization in contradiction to the professed aim of furthering autonomy in local affairs. The policy thus defeated its own aims: it handicapped the economic development of the empire's border regions (e.g., in Siberia) and worked against the social and cultural integration of the natives into the fold of the dominant Russian culture (although russification did take place on a significant scale in the case of some native elites, as in the Caucasus and the Crimea).

Government administration under Catherine. The reforms of local government carried out by Catherine also contained contradictions. The successors of Peter I had not solved the problem of local administration. St. Petersburg relied on appointed officials, too few in number and much given to abuse and corruption, and on the informal control exercised by individual landowners and village communes; but a great peasant rebellion, led by Ye.I. Pugachov in 1773–74, demonstrated the inadequacy of this system. Taking up suggestions of various officials and mindful of the information and complaints offered by the

Reforms of local government

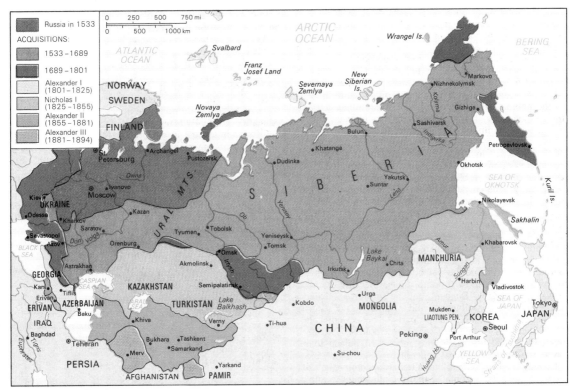

Russian expansion in Asia.

From M. Florinsky, *A Short History of Russia*, © copyright,
Michael T. Florinsky, 1964; published by the Macmillan Company

deputies to the Legislative Commission (1767–68), Catherine shaped the local administration into a structure that remained in force until the middle of the 19th century and also served as a foundation for the *zemstvos* (local elected councils), established in 1864. The basic pattern was established by the statute on the provinces of 1775 and complemented by the organization of corporate self-administration contained in the charters to the nobility and the towns (1785). Essentially, the reforms divided the empire's territory into provinces of roughly equal population, disregarding historical traditions and economic ties; each of these units (*guberniya*) was put under the supervision and responsibility of a governor or governor general acting in the name of the ruler, with the right of direct communication with him. A governor's chancery was set up along functional lines (paralleling the system of colleges) and subordinated to and supervised by the Senate. The regular provincial administration was assisted by officials who were elected from among the nobility for the countryside and from the higher ranks of townspeople for the cities; these elected officials took care of routine police matters in their jurisdictions, helped to enforce orders received from the central authorities, and assisted in the maintenance of law and the collection of taxes. Other elected personalities (marshals of the nobility and heads of city councils) protected the interests of their respective classes and helped to settle minor conflicts without recourse to regular tribunals. This delegation of some administrative functions to the local level (albeit under the strict control of St. Petersburg) not only relieved the bureaucracy of much burdensome detail and multiplied the number of its agents on the local level but also fostered a sense of responsibility among the active and cultured members of the local upper classes. On the other hand, the serfs and the lower classes in the towns found themselves without anyone to protect their interests.

The central government under Catherine Catherine made no fundamental changes in the administration of the central government. The system of colleges was retained; but the authority of the presidents increased at the expense of the boards, initiating an evolution that culminated in the establishment of monocratic ministries in 1802. The Senate supervised all branches of administration, regulating the orderly flow of business. The Senate was also involved—albeit indirectly—in coordina-

tion, mainly because its procurator general, Prince A. Vyazemsky, held the office for a quarter of a century with the full trust of the empress. At the same time, the judicial functions of the Senate as a high court of appeal and administrative review were widened.

The major institutional weakness of the Petrine system remained—namely, the lack of a body to coordinate the jurisdictions and resolve the conflicts of the colleges and to plan policies and control their implementation. A ruler as energetic, hard-working, and intelligent as Catherine could perform these tasks almost single-handedly, as had Peter I; but with the growing complexity of administration even Catherine felt the need for such a body, if only to reduce her involvement in every small detail or contested matter and to provide a wider scope for government by permanent laws and uniform regulations. Eventually, she set up a council of state as a kind of cabinet but without giving it any specific authority or jurisdiction.

A major need of the empire was an up-to-date code of laws. The last code, issued in 1649, had become largely inoperative as a result of Peter's reforms and the transformation of society. Peter and his successors had recognized this need by appointing commissions to prepare a new code; none of the several efforts having reached a successful conclusion, Catherine tried to tackle the job again, but in a different manner. In 1767 she convoked a commission of representatives elected by all classes except private serfs. For their guidance she drafted an instruction largely inspired by Western political thinkers; but, far from providing a blueprint for a liberal code, it emphasized the need for autocracy and strong central institutions. In its civil part the instruction owed much to German political philosophy and natural-law jurisprudence, putting the individual's duties before his rights emphasizing the state's responsibility for the welfare of the nation, and encouraging the pursuit of material self-interest within the established order. Although not implemented by the commission (which was dissolved in 1768), the instruction stimulated the modernization of Russian political and legal thought in the early 19th century.

In her social policy Catherine aimed at steering the nobility toward cultural interests and economic activity so as to reduce their dependence on state service. (They already had been freed from its compulsory character by

Peter III [February 18, 1762].) To this end she made a general land survey that fixed clearly and permanently the boundaries of individual estates, and she granted the nobility the exclusive right to exploit both the subsoil and surface resources of their land and to market the products of their estates and of their serfs' labour. The nobles also obtained a monopoly of ownership of inhabited estates, which, in fact, restricted ownership of agricultural serfs to the noble class. Catherine hoped to stimulate agricultural expansion and modernization by providing easy credit and by disseminating the latest techniques and achievements of Western agriculture through the Free Economic Society founded in 1765. She also fostered the nobility's corporate organization. The Charter to the Nobility, 1785, gave the corps of nobles in every province the status of a legal entity. The corporation's members gathered periodically, in the provincial and district capitals, to elect a marshal of the nobility, who represented their interests before the governor and the ruler himself; they also elected a number of officials to administer welfare institutions for the nobility (schools, orphanages, etc.), to help settle disputes, and to provide guardianships for orphans. The corporate life of the nobles did not develop as well as expected, however, and the nobility never became the class it was in Prussia or England; but the charter did foster a sense of class consciousness and afforded legal security to the members and their property. The periodic electoral meetings stimulated social intercourse, led to a livelier cultural life in the provinces, and helped to involve the nobility in local concerns.

Turning the nobility's interests toward economic activity brought the return home of many landowners to supervise the operation of their estates. Interested in obtaining greater income, they not only intensified the exploitation of serf labour but also interfered in the traditional routine of the village by attempting to introduce new agricultural techniques. In most cases this meant increased regimentation of the serfs. The secularization of the monasteries and episcopal sees in 1764 had brought a considerable amount of land into the possession of the state. To reward her favourites and to encourage the nobles to economic activity, Catherine gave away large tracts with many peasants, who now had to work for ambitious and capricious masters.

Serfdom had never been acceptable to the Russian peasant; it now became particularly burdensome and unjust, the more so since the lord's extensive police powers removed his serfs from the state's protection, and the new local officials enforced strictly the prohibition against appealing for relief to the sovereign. There were also the specific grievances of the Cossacks, whose traditional liberties had been sharply curtailed and their social organization undermined, and the discontent of the nomadic peoples forced to accept a new way of life. Peasant misery erupted in rebellion that engulfed all of eastern European Russia in 1773–74, led by the Cossack Yemelyan Pugachov. The peasant forces captured a number of towns and cities before they were finally defeated by government armies. The revolt demonstrated the inadequacy of local controls and was thus partly responsible for the reform of provincial administration mentioned above. It also brought the educated elite to a new awareness of the profound alienation of the peasantry from the culture of St. Petersburg.

The reign of Catherine II was a period of active town planning and building. The number and size of the urban centres grew slowly but steadily. Along with new cities in the south, many old towns were rebuilt and developed. The renaissance of the old provincial centres was in part due to the administrative reforms of 1775 and 1785, which brought an influx of officials and nobles. Along with them came craftsmen, artisans, and merchants. An act of Peter III, which permitted peasants to trade in neighbouring towns without passports or controls at the gates, gave impetus to the emergence of a class of small merchants from among the peasantry. This trend received support from the administrative reorganization of the towns and the limited degree of corporate self-administration granted by the Charter of 1785.

EDUCATION AND SOCIAL CHANGE IN THE 18TH CENTURY

Secular education had been actively propagated by Peter I. At first it focussed on technical subjects—those directly related to the prosecution of a war, the building of a navy, and the running of the government. This was also the original emphasis of the Academy of Sciences and the school connected with it. But as education became the prerequisite for advancement in service and as Western ways of life spread among the upper classes, the focus of education gradually broadened. A class of nobles grew up who were interested in culture for the sake of their own development, as well as for cutting a good figure in society. Beginning in the 1760s the demand for western European artistic and cultural works grew in the salons of St. Petersburg increasingly. By the 1780s the major classics of European literature had become easily available in translation to any educated person. Private boarding and day schools proliferated, as did the number of tutors hired by wealthy nobles for their children (and for less fortunate neighbours and relatives). The Academy of Sciences took its place among the major academies of Europe. The University of Moscow and the chief schools of the military, naval, and civil services had become regular institutions.

There were also ecclesiastical schools. Paradoxically, the instruction they gave was almost irrelevant for the future priest but quite useful for the future official or scholar; it emphasized the rhetorical arts and logic and gave a solid foundation in scholastic philosophy, natural-law doctrine, the classical languages, and mathematics. The seminaries and theological academies not only trained future members of the episcopate and officials of the Holy Synod but also staffed government bureaus on the middle and higher levels and produced the first native Russian academics, scholars, and scientists. Russia's lack of professional experts in such fields as jurisprudence, civil and military engineering, astronomy, and geophysics brought a great influx of foreigners. Peter I imported large numbers of engineers and technicians from Holland and England, and the practice continued on a reduced scale after his death, so that foreign scholars, scientists, and experts staffed the Academy of Sciences and the University of Moscow and supplied the requirements of the state for such purposes as geological surveys. They brought with them French and German philosophy: the metaphysics and epistemology of René Descartes and the natural-law doctrines of the German school of Gottfried Leibniz, Samuel von Pufendorf, and Christian Wolff. These emphasized social obligation and the individual's dependence on the community. Stressing his duties to the group, they laid the foundation for a critique of society. The critique was at first directed against the moral inadequacies of individuals—the vain courtier, the superficially westernized fop, the corrupt official—but it soon broadened into the view that the educated man had an obligation to help his fellowmen improve themselves. In the Russian context the class most obviously in need of improvement was the peasantry. Moral progress, it was quickly realized, was not possible without material progress, and this led quite naturally to an advocacy of practical philanthropy and social action.

German natural-law doctrines furthered the dissemination of German Pietism, with its emphasis on spiritual progress and on the need to serve man and the community. Similar tendencies underlay the most influential branch of Freemasonry; the Freemasons devoted themselves to disseminating knowledge, relieving hunger, and caring for orphans and other destitutes. The publisher Nikolay Novikov carried the Pietist and Masonic messages to the public in his satirical journals and periodicals for women and children. All would-be reformers were concerned about the serf, especially since the Pugachov revolt had shown the degree of the peasantry's alienation. The major writers of Catherine II's reign (including the empress herself, who dabbled in journalism and drama) produced satires, fables, and comedies of manners attuned to the belief that moral and spiritual progress would lead to social improvements. A similar approach was noticeable in education, which stressed the develop-

[margin: Catherine's social policy]

[margin: Town planning and building]

[margin: Western intellectual influences]

ment of moral feeling in the conviction that a good heart would guide the well-filled head in the proper direction. This was the context in which the writings of the French philosophes (*e.g.*, Jean-Jacques Rousseau, Guillaume Raynal, Claude Helvétius, Paul-Henri Holbach) struck a response in the Russian educated elite. The Russians had been prepared by natural-law teachings, Pietism, and Freemasonry for a more radical criticism of contemporary society looking to the perfectibility of man through education and social change.

Growth of national pride

All of these intellectual currents combined to awaken among educated Russians a sense of national pride and a feeling that, thanks to the impetus given by Peter I, Russia had managed to lift itself to the cultural and political level of a great European state. The educated Russian was no longer a servile and mute slave of the tsars; he had made himself into a gentleman, a man of heart and honour, a "true son of the fatherland," concerned about his fellow men. Nor was this regarded simply as imitation of the West; it was the fruit of Russian history, which was not to be scorned or neglected. A revived interest in Russian history led to the first important native works of modern Russian historiography.

The response of the empress and her entourage to these intellectual developments was ambivalent. The new sense of national pride and personal dignity enhanced the government's prestige and was in line with Catherine's own aspirations for the nobility. But the spread of these new interests and ideas was also dangerous, for the moral criticism of abuses could easily turn into criticism of Russia's social and political system. The outbreak of the French Revolution made Catherine II particularly anxious. She felt that large-scale private philanthropic and educational activities without government guidance and control were trespassing on her own prerogatives as an enlightened autocrat. By the end of the 18th century the ideal of service to the state, which had underlain the Russian nobility's value system, had been transformed into one of service to the people; this meant the elite's separation from the state, which Catherine II could not accept. A dramatic illustration of Catherine's concern occurred after the appearance in 1790 of Aleksandr Radishchev's *Journey from St. Petersburg to Moscow*. A member of the nobility, Radishchev had returned from Germany to rise to a prominent position in the government service. He depicted social conditions as he saw them, particularly the dehumanization of the serfs and the corruption of their masters, warning that these threatened not only the stability of the existing order but also Russia's survival as a nation. Incensed by the book, Catherine had Radishchev arrested and banished to Siberia. He became the first political martyr of the Russian elite; his book and his fate foreshadowed the antagonism between the intelligentsia and the government that was to dominate Russia's history in the 19th century.

THE REIGN OF PAUL I (1796–1801)

Catherine died in 1796 and was succeeded by her son Paul. A capricious, somewhat unstable individual, Paul had a passion for military order that conflicted with the basic values of the developing civil society; he felt that the nobility should again become a service class (or withdraw completely into agriculture) and help the ruler in implementing his reform program, even at the expense of its private interests. In trying to re-establish compulsory state service, he made it more rigid, harsh, and militaristic. He sought to promote the welfare of the serfs, but the manner of his approach—a decree permitting a maximum of three days of labour service a week—was clumsy and high-handed; it did nothing to help the serfs and angered their lords. Paul also made the same mistake as his father, Peter III: he wanted to govern with his own minions, disregarding both tradition and the administrative patterns that had developed during his mother's 30-year reign. Paul's hatred of the French Revolution and of everything connected with it led him to impose tight censorship on travel abroad and to prohibit foreign books, fashions, music, etc. He thereby earned the enmity of upper society in St. Petersburg. On March 23 (March 11,

O.S.), 1801, he was murdered by conspirators drawn from high officials, favourites of Catherine, his own military entourage, and officers of the guard regiments. The accession of his son, Alexander I, inaugurated a new century and a new period in the history of imperial Russia. (M.Ra.)

III. Russia from 1801 to 1917

THE REIGNS OF ALEXANDER I AND NICHOLAS I

General survey. When Alexander I came to the throne in March 1801, Russia was in a state of hostility with most of Europe, though its armies were not actually fighting; its only ally was its traditional enemy, Turkey. The new emperor quickly made peace with both France and Britain and restored normal relations with Austria. His hope that he would then be able to concentrate on internal reform was frustrated by the reopening of war with Napoleon in 1805. Defeated at Austerlitz, the Russian armies fought Napoleon in Poland in 1806 and 1807, with Prussia as an ineffective ally. After the Treaty of Tilsit (1807), there were five years of peace, ended by Napoleon's invasion of Russia in 1812. For further information see FRENCH REVOLUTIONARY AND NAPOLEONIC WARS: *The Napoleonic Wars, 1801–15*. From the westward progress of its arms in the next two years of heavy fighting, Russia emerged as Europe's greatest land power and the first among the continental victors over Napoleon. The immense prestige achieved in these campaigns was maintained until mid-century. During that period, Russian armies fought only against weaker enemies: Persia in 1826, Turkey in 1828–29, Poland in 1830–31, and the mountaineers of the Caucasus during the 1830s and 1840s. When Europe was convulsed by revolution in 1848, Russia alone among the Great Powers was unaffected; and in the summer of 1849 the Tsar sent troops to crush the Hungarians in Transylvania. Russia was not loved, but it was admired and feared. To the upper classes in central Europe, Nicholas I was the stern defender of monarchical legitimacy; to democrats all over the world, he was "the gendarme of Europe" and the chief enemy of liberty. But the Crimean War (1853–56) showed that this giant had feet of clay. The vast empire was unable to mobilize, equip, and transport enough troops to defeat the medium-sized French and English forces under very mediocre command. Nicholas died in the bitter knowledge of general failure.

Russian victories against weak enemies

Alexander I as a young man had longed to reform his empire and benefit his subjects. His hopes were disappointed, partly by the sheer inertia, backwardness, and vastness of his domains but chiefly because Napoleon's aggressive enterprises diverted Alexander's attention to diplomacy and defense. Russia's abundant manpower and scanty financial resources were both consumed in war. The early years of his reign saw two short periods of attempted reform. During the first, from 1801 to 1803, the Tsar took counsel with four intimate friends, who formed his so-called Unofficial Committee, with the intention of drafting ambitious reforms. In the period from 1807 to 1812, he had as his chief adviser the liberal Mikhail Speransky (*q.v.*). Both periods produced some valuable administrative innovations, but neither initiated any basic reform. After 1815 Alexander was mainly concerned with grandiose plans for international peace; his motivation was not merely political but also religious, for the years of war and national danger had aroused in him an interest in matters of faith to which, as a pupil of the 18th-century Enlightenment, he had previously been indifferent. While he was thus preoccupied with diplomacy and religion, Russia was ruled by conservatives, among whom the brutal but honest Gen. Aleksey Arakcheyev was outstanding. Victory in war had strengthened those who upheld the established order, serfdom and all. The mood was one of intense national pride: Holy Russia had defeated Napoleon, the Corsican Antichrist, and therefore it was not only foolish but also impious to copy foreign models. Educated young Russians, who had served in the army and seen Europe, who read and spoke French and German and knew contemporary European literature, felt otherwise. Masonic lodges and secret societies flourished in the early 1820s. From their deliberations emerged a conspiracy to overthrow the government, inspired by a variety of ideas: some men looked for a model to the United States, others to Jacobin France. The conspirators, known as the Decembrists because they tried to act in December 1825 when the news of Alexander I's death became known and there was uncertainty about his successor, were defeated and arrested; five were executed and many more sentenced to various terms of imprisonment in Siberia. Nicholas I, who succeeded after his elder brother Constantine had finally refused the throne, was deeply affected by these events and set himself against any major political change, though he did not reject the idea of administrative reform. After the revolutions of 1848 in Europe, his opposition to all change, his suspicion of even mildly liberal ideas, and his insistence on an obscurantist censorship reached their climax.

The sections that follow cover the development, under Alexander I and Nicholas I, of the machinery of government; of social classes and economic forces; of education and political ideas; of the relations between Russians and other peoples within the empire; and of Russian foreign policy.

Government. The discussions of Alexander I's Unofficial Committee were part of an ongoing debate that was to remain important until the end of the imperial regime. This may be called the debate between enlightened oligarchy and enlightened autocracy. The proponents of oligarchy looked back to a somewhat idealized model of the reign of Catherine II. They wished greater power to be placed in the hands of the aristocracy for the purpose of achieving a certain balance between the monarch and the social elite, believing that both together were capable of pursuing policies that would benefit the people as a whole. Their opponents, of whom the most talented was the young Count Pavel Stroganov, were against any limitation on the power of the tsar. Whereas the oligarchs wished to make the Senate an important centre of power and to have it elected by senior officials and country nobility, Stroganov maintained that, if this were done, the sovereign would have "his arms tied, so that he would no longer be able to carry out the plans which he had in favour of the nation." In the event, neither enlightened oligarchs nor enlightened absolutists had their way: Russia's government remained autocratic but reactionary. Alexander, however, never quite abandoned the idea of representative institutions. He encouraged Speransky to prepare in 1809 a draft constitution that included a pyramid of consultative elected bodies and a national assembly with some slight powers of legislation. In 1819 he asked Nikolay Novosiltsev, a former member of the Unofficial Committee who had made a brilliant career as a bureaucrat, to prepare another constitution, which turned out to be rather similar. Neither was ever implemented, though Alexander took some features of the first and used them out of their intended context.

In 1802 Alexander instituted eight government departments, or ministries, of which five were essentially new. The organization of the departments was substantially improved in 1811 by Speransky. In the 1820s, the ministry of the interior became responsible for public order, public health, stocks of food, and the development of industry and agriculture. Inadequate funds and personnel and the dominant position of the serf-owning nobility in the countryside greatly limited the effective power of this ministry. There was no question of a formal council of ministers, or of anything corresponding to a cabinet, and there was no prime minister. A committee of ministers coordinated to some extent the affairs of the different departments, but its importance depended on circumstances and on individuals. When the tsar was abroad, the committee was in charge of internal affairs. Aleksey Arakcheyev was for a time secretary of the committee, but he did not cease to be the strongest man in Russia under the tsar when he ceased to hold this formal office. The committee had a president, but this office did not confer any significant power or prestige.

Under Nicholas I the committee of ministers continued to operate, but the individual ministers were responsible only to the emperor. The centre of power to some extent shifted into the emperor's personal chancery, which was built up into a formidable apparatus. The Third Department of the chancery, under Count Aleksandr Benckendorff, was responsible for the security police. Its head was also chief of gendarmes, and the two offices were later formally united. The task of the security force was to obtain information on the state of political opinion and to track down and repress all political activity that might be considered dangerous to the regime. The Third Department was also considered by the tsar as an instrument of justice in a broad sense, the defender of all those unjustly treated by the powerful and rich. Some of the department's reports show that there were officials who took these duties seriously, but as a whole it showed more talent for repressing opposition and stifling opinion than for redressing the grievances of the powerless. This was the case notwithstanding the fact that the department was often on the worst of terms with other branches of the public service.

Russia under Alexander I and Nicholas I was ruled by its bureaucracy. The efforts of successive sovereigns after Peter the Great to establish a government service of the European type had had partial success. The Russian bureaucracy of 1850 combined some features of a central European bureaucracy of 1750 with some features of pre-Petrine Russia. One may speak of a "service ethos" and trace this back to 16th-century Muscovy. But the foundation of this ethos was, for the great majority of Russian officials, servile obedience to the tsar and not service to the state as that phrase was understood in a country such as Prussia. The notion of the state as something distinct from and superior to both ruler and ruled was incomprehensible to most government servants. Russian bureaucrats were obsessed with rank and status. Indeed, this was the only incentive that the government could give, as salaries were very meagre. Rank was not so much a reward for efficient service as a privilege to be grasped and jealously guarded. In order to prevent able persons, especially of humble origin, from rising too quickly, great emphasis was laid on seniority. There were exceptions, and outstandingly able, cultured, and humane men did reach the top under Nicholas I, but they were few.

The rank and file of the bureaucracy was mediocre, but its numbers steadily increased, perhaps trebling in the first half of the century. It remained poorly paid. The government's poverty was caused by the backward state of the economy, by the fact that no taxes could be asked of the nobility, and by the cost of waging wars—not only the great wars but also the long colonial campaigns in the Caucasus. Government officials were badly educated. They lacked not only precise knowledge but also the sort of basic ethical training that competent officials need. They were reluctant to make decisions: responsibility was pushed higher and higher up the hierarchy, until thousands of minor matters ended on the emperor's desk. Centralization of responsibility meant slowness of decision, and delays of many years were not unusual; death often provided the answer. There were also many antiquated, discriminatory, and contradictory laws. Large categories of the population, such as Jews and members of heretical Christian sects, suffered from various legal disabilities. Since not all of those discriminated against were poor and since many small officials were unable to support their families, bending or evasion of the law had its market price, and the needy official had a supplementary source of income. Corruption of this sort existed on a mass scale. To a certain extent it was a redeeming feature of the regime: if there had been less corruption the government would have been even slower, less efficient, and more oppressive than it was.

Social classes. No significant changes were made in the condition of the serfs in the first half of the century. Alexander I, perhaps from fear of the nobility and with the memory of his father's fate in mind, approached the problem with caution, though with a desire for reform, but first war and then diplomacy diverted him. His successor, Nicholas, disliked serfdom, but there were politi-

*The
debate
between
oligarchy
and
autocracy*

*Rule by
bureau-
cracy*

*Problems
of the
countryside*

cal hazards in eliminating it. The power of the central government extended down to the provincial governors and, more tenuously, down to the *ispravnik*, or chief official of the district, of which each province had about three or four. The *ispravnik* was elected by the local nobility. Below the level of the district, the administration virtually ceased to operate: the sole authority was the serf owner. If serfdom were to be abolished, some other authority would have to be put in its place, and the existing bureaucratic apparatus was plainly inadequate. The Decembrist conspiracy in 1825 had greatly increased the tsar's distrust of the nobility. He was determined to avoid public discussion of reform, even within the upper class.

The one important exception to the general picture of bureaucratic stagnation was the creation of the Ministry of State Domains, under Gen. Pavel Kiselev. This became an embryonic ministry of agriculture, with authority over peasants who lived on state lands. These were a little less than half the rural population: in 1858 there were 19,000,000 state peasants and 22,500,000 private serfs. Kiselev set up a system of government administration down to the village level and provided for a measure of self-government under which the mayor of the *volost* (a district grouping several villages or peasant communes) was elected by male householders. There was also to be a *volost* court for judging disputes between peasants. Kiselev planned to improve medical services, build schools, establish warehouses for stocks of food in case of crop failure, and give instruction in methods of farming. Something was done in all these fields, even if less than intended and often in a manner that provoked hostility or even violent riots; the personnel of the new ministry was no more competent than the bureaucracy as a whole.

Only minor measures were taken to benefit the serfs on private estates. Opposition to serfdom grew steadily, however, not only among persons of European outlook and independent thought, but also among high officials. It seemed not only unjust but intolerable that in a great nation men and women could be owned. Serfdom was also obviously an obstacle to economic development. Whether serfdom was contrary to the interests of serf owners is a more complex question. Those who wished to abolish it argued that it was, since their best hope of getting the nobility to accept abolition lay in convincing them that their self-interest required it. Certainly in parts of southern Russia where the soil was fertile, labour was plentiful, and potential profits in the grain trade with Europe were high, a landowner would do better if he could replace his serfs by paid agricultural labour and be rid of obligations to those peasants whom he did not need to employ. In other regions, where the population was scanty, serfdom provided the landowner with an assured labour supply; if it were abolished, he would have to pay more for his labour force or see it melt away. In large parts of northern Russia where the land was poor, many serfs made a living from various crafts—in cottage industry or even in factories—and from their wages had to pay dues to their masters. The abolition of serfdom would deprive the serf owner of this large income and leave him with only what he could make from farming and from tenants with rather poor economic prospects. On balance, it seems likely that the short-term interests of the great majority of serf owners favoured the maintenance of serfdom, and, in any case, there is no doubt that this is what most serf owners believed.

Industry and trade made slow progress during these years. In the latter part of the 18th century, Russia had been, thanks to its Urals mines, one of the main producers of pig iron. In the next 50 years, it was left far behind by Great Britain, Germany, and the United States. In cotton textiles and sugar refining, Russia was more successful. Count Ye.F. Kankrin, minister of finance from 1823 to 1844, tried to encourage Russian industry by high protective tariffs. He also set up schools and specialized institutes for the advancement of commerce, engineering, and forestry. Russia's exports of grain increased substan-

Opposition to serfdom

tially, though its share of total world trade remained about the same in 1850 as in 1800. The first railways also appeared; rail traffic between St. Petersburg (now Leningrad) and Moscow was opened in 1851. The road system remained extremely inadequate, as was demonstrated in the Crimean War.

The urban population grew significantly. There were a few prosperous merchants, well protected by the government. Some centres, such as Ivanovo, in central Russia, with its textile industry, had the beginnings of an industrial working class. The rest of the inhabitants of the cities consisted of small tradesmen and artisans, together with serfs living in town with their owners' permission as household servants or casual labourers.

Education and intellectual life. Alexander I's School Statute (1804) provided for a four-tier system of schools from the primary to the university level, intended to be open to persons of all classes. Under its provisions, several new universities were founded, and gymnasiums (pre-university schools) were established in most provincial capitals. Less was done at the lower levels, for the usual reason of inadequate funds. In the latter part of Alexander's reign, education was supervised by Prince A.N. Golitsyn, head of the ministry of education and spiritual affairs. In an effort to combat what he believed to be dangerous irreligious doctrines emanating from western Europe, Golitsyn encouraged university students to spy on their professors and on each other; those who taught unacceptable ideas were frequently dismissed or threatened with prison. Under Nicholas I there was some improvement. Count Sergey Uvarov, minister of education from 1833 to 1849, permitted a much freer intellectual atmosphere, but he also began the practice of deliberately excluding children of the lower classes from the gymnasiums and universities, which was continued under his successors.

Nevertheless, in increasing numbers the children of minor officials, small tradesmen, and especially priests, were acquiring education. Together with the already Europeanized nobility, they began to form a new cultural elite. Direct political criticism was prevented by the censorship of books and periodicals. Petty police interference made life disagreeable even for writers who were not much concerned with politics. Aleksandr Pushkin, Russia's greatest poet, got into trouble with the police for his opinions in 1824; he was also a friend of some leading Decembrists. After 1826 he lived an unhappy life in St. Petersburg, tolerated but distrusted by the authorities, producing magnificent poetry until he met his death in a duel in 1837. The writers Mikhail Lermontov and Nikolay Gogol were also objects of suspicion to the bureaucrats.

The censorship was not always efficient, and some of the censors were liberal. It became possible to express political ideas in the form of philosophical arguments and literary criticism. Thus, it was partly in intellectual periodicals and partly in discussions in the private houses of Moscow noblemen that the controversy between "westernizers" and "Slavophiles" developed. It began with the publication of a "philosophical letter" by Pyotr Chaadayev in the periodical *Teleskop* in 1836. One of the most penetrating essays ever written about Russia's historical heritage, it argued that Russia belonged neither to West nor to East, neither to Europe nor to Asia:

> Standing alone in the world, we have given nothing to the world, we have learnt nothing from the world, we have not added a single idea to the mass of human ideas; we have made no contribution to the progress of the human spirit, and everything that has come to us from that spirit, we have disfigured. . . . Today we form a gap in the intellectual order.

Nicholas declared that Chaadayev must be mad and gave orders that he should be confined to his house and regularly visited by a doctor. This humiliating but relatively mild treatment silenced him.

It is misleading to represent the westernizers as wishing slavishly to copy all things Western or the Slavophiles as repudiating Europe and rejecting reform. The chief Slavophiles—Aleksey S. Khomyakov, the brothers Ivan and Pyotr Kireyevsky, and the brothers Konstantin and Ivan

Westernizers and Slavophiles

Aksakov—were men of deep European culture and bitter opponents of serfdom. Indeed, as landowners they knew more about the problems and sufferings of the serfs than many westernizers. The leading westernizers—Aleksandr Herzen, Vissarion Belinsky, and Mikhail Bakunin—were for their part profoundly Russian. Belinsky was ill at ease with foreigners, and Herzen and Bakunin, despite many years' residence in France, Germany, England, and Italy, remained not only hostile to the world of European bourgeois liberalism and democracy but also strangely ignorant of it.

The difference between westernizers and Slavophiles was essentially that between doctrinaire radicals and empirical conservatives, a familiar theme in the history of most European nations. It was the difference between those who wished to pull the whole political structure down and replace it by a new building, according to their own admirable blueprints, and those who preferred to knock down some parts and repair and refurnish others, bit by bit. Another basic difference was that the Slavophiles were Orthodox Christians and the westernizers either atheists or, like the historian T.N. Granovsky, deists with their own personal faith. Belinsky described the Orthodox Church, in his famous "Letter to Gogol" (1847) as "the bulwark of the whip and the handmaid of despotism." He maintained that the Russian people was "by its nature a profoundly atheistic people," and that they viewed the priesthood with contempt. These were but half-truths: the church was indeed subject to the government and upheld autocracy, and priests were often unpopular; but this did not mean that the peasants and a large part of the upper and middle classes were not devoted to the Orthodox faith.

The Slavophiles idealized early Russian history. They believed that there had once been a happy partnership between tsar and people: the tsar had consulted the people through their elected spokesmen in the *zemsky sobor*. This had been changed by Peter the Great when he sought to copy foreign models and interposed an alien bureaucracy, staffed largely by Germans, between himself and his people. The Slavophiles held that Russia should return to the way from which it had strayed under Peter. They asked not for a legislative body of the Western type, still less for parliamentary government, but for a consultative assembly to advise the emperor. This was quite unacceptable to Nicholas, who was proud of Peter the Great and believed himself his political heir. To the westernizers, on the other hand, Peter the Great was a symbol of radical change, not of autocracy.

The Russian Empire.   Russia in the 19th century was both a multilingual and a multireligious empire. Only about half the population were at the same time Russian by language and Orthodox by religion. The Orthodox were to some extent privileged in comparison with other Christians; all Christians enjoyed a higher status than Muslims; and the latter were not so disadvantaged as the Jews. The basis of legitimacy was obedience to the tsar: Nicholas expected all his subjects to obey him, but he did not expect non-Russians to become Russians. Admittedly, he detested the Poles, but that was because they had been disloyal subjects and revolted against him.

The idea that Russians, as such, should have a status superior to that of other peoples of the empire was distasteful to Nicholas. Russian nationalism nevertheless received some support from Count Uvarov, who, in his famous report to the tsar in 1832, proclaimed three principles as "truly Russian": autocracy, Orthodoxy, and the national principle (*narodnost*). In 1833 Uvarov set up a new university in Kiev, to be the centre for a policy of spreading Russian language and culture through the schools in the western provinces, at the expense of the Polish. Nicholas approved of this, for the Poles had been guilty of rebellion. But when the attempt was made to russify the Germans of the Baltic provinces, he objected. The Baltic Germans were loyal subjects and provided admirable officers and officials: they must be allowed to preserve their German culture and to maintain their cultural and social domination over the Estonians and Latvians. The young Slavophile and landowning nobleman

(margin left, beside "The Russian Empire." paragraph) The multilingual and multireligious empire

Yury Samarin, a junior official in Riga, was severely reprimanded by the Emperor for his anti-German activities.

The most revolutionary of the Decembrist leaders, Pavel Pestel, had insisted that all non-Russian peoples of the empire except the Poles should "completely fuse their nationality with the nationality of the dominant people." Another group of Decembrists, however, the Society of United Slavs, believed in a federation of free Slav peoples, including some of those living under Austrian and Turkish rule. In 1846 this idea was put forward in a different form in the Brotherhood of Cyril and Methodius, in Kiev. This group, among whose members was the Ukrainian poet Taras Shevchenko, believed that a federation of Slav peoples should include the Ukrainians, whom they claimed were not a part of the Russian nation but a distinct nationality. The society was crushed by the police, and Shevchenko was sent as a private soldier to the Urals; Nicholas himself gave orders that the great poet should be forbidden to write or draw. But Ukrainian national consciousness, though still confined to an educated minority, was growing; and nothing did more to crystallize Ukrainian as a literary language than Shevchenko's poetry.

During the first half of the century Russia made substantial conquests in Asia. In the Caucasus, the kingdom of Georgia united voluntarily with Russia in 1801, and other small Georgian principalities were conquered in the next years. Persia ceded northern Azerbaijan, including the peninsula of Baku, in 1813 and the Armenian province of Erivan (Yerevan) in 1828. The mountain peoples of the northern Caucasus, however, proved more redoubtable. The Chechens, led by the Shaykh Shāmil, resisted Russian expeditions from 1834 until 1859, and the Circassians were not finally crushed until 1864. In the 1840s, Russian rule was established over the pastoral peoples of Kazakhstan. In the Far East, Russian ships explored the lower course of the Amur River and discovered the straits between Sakhalin and the mainland of Asia in 1849. The Russian-American Company, founded in 1799, controlled part of the coast and islands of Alaska.

Foreign policy.   At the beginning of the 19th century, Russian foreign policy was essentially concentrated on the three western neighbour countries with which it had been preoccupied since the 16th: Sweden, Poland, and Turkey. The policy toward these countries also determined Russian relations with France, Austria, and Great Britain.

Russo-Swedish relations were settled during the Napoleonic era. When Napoleon met with Alexander at Tilsit, he gave the latter a free hand to proceed against Sweden. After two years of war, in which the Russians did not always fare well, the Swedish government ceded Finland to the Tsar in 1809. Alexander became grand duke of Finland, but Finland was not incorporated into the Russian Empire, and its institutions were fully respected. In 1810, when Napoleon's former marshal, Bernadotte, was elected heir to the Swedish throne, he showed no hostility to Russia. In 1812 he made an agreement recognizing the Tsar's position in Finland in return for the promise of Russian support in his aim to annex Norway from Denmark. Bernadotte achieved this in the Treaty of Kiel of 1814, and thereafter the relations between Russia and Sweden, now a small and peaceful state, were not seriously troubled.

Alexander I, influenced by his Polish friend Prince Adam Czartoryski, had plans for the liberation and unity of Poland, which had ceased to exist as a state in the 18th century, when it had been partitioned among Russia, Prussia, and Austria. After his defeat by Napoleon in 1805, he abandoned those plans in favour of an alliance with Prussia. In 1807 Napoleon established a dependency called the Grand Duchy of Warsaw and in 1809 increased its territory at the expense of Austria. Alexander's attempts to win the Poles to his side in 1811 and to persuade Austria to make concessions to them failed; when Napoleon invaded Russia in 1812, he had 100,000 first-class Polish troops fighting for him. After Napoleon's defeat Alexander was not vindictive. He protected the Poles against the demands of Russian nationalists who

(margin right, top) Russian victories in Asia

(margin right, beside Poland paragraph) Defeat by Napoleon

wanted revenge, and sought once more to create a large Polish kingdom comprising the territories annexed by Russia and Prussia in the partitions of the 18th century. He was opposed at the Congress of Vienna in 1814–15 by Austria and Britain, and the ensuing kingdom of Poland, which, though nominally autonomous, was to be in permanent union with the Russian Empire, consisted of only part of the Prussian and Russian conquests. Alexander was popular in Poland for a time after 1815. But real reconciliation between Poles and Russians was made impossible by their competing claims for the borderlands, which had belonged to the former Grand Duchy of Lithuania. The majority of the population of this region was Belorussian, Ukrainian, or Lithuanian; its commercial class was Jewish; and its upper classes and culture were Polish. Neither Russians nor Poles considered Belorussians, Ukrainians, or Lithuanians to be nations, entitled to decide their own fates: the question was whether Lithuania was to be Polish or Russian. Russians could argue that most of it had been part of "the Russian land" until the 14th century, and the Poles that it had been Polish since the 16th. Alexander had some sympathy for the Polish point of view and allowed the Poles to hope that he would reunite these lands with Poland, but the effective political forces in Russia were strongly opposed to any change. The disappointment of Polish hopes for Lithuania was probably the most important single cause of the growing tension between Warsaw and St. Petersburg in the late 1820s, which culminated in the revolt of the Poles in November 1830 and the war of 1831 between Polish and Russian armies. It ended in the defeat of the Poles and the exile of thousands of political leaders and soldiers to western Europe. Poland's constitution and, thus, its autonomy were abrogated; and there began the policy of russification of Poland.

International reactions to the Russo-Polish war were of some importance. There was much public sympathy for the Poles in France and Britain, but this had no influence on Russian actions. On the other hand, the governments of Prussia and Austria strongly supported Russia. It is arguable that the cooperation among the three monarchies, which continued over the next two decades and was revived from time to time later in the century, had less to do with their eloquently proclaimed loyalty to monarchical government than with their common interest in suppressing the Poles.

Balkan problems

Turkey had long been the main object of Russian territorial expansion; through a certain inertia of tradition, the Turkish policy had become almost automatic. It was to some extent reinforced by religious motives—by the romantic desire to liberate Constantinople, the holy city of Orthodoxy—but more important in the mid-19th century was the desire to assure the exit of Russian grain exports through the Black Sea. During certain periods, Russia sought to dominate Turkey as a powerful ally: this was its policy from 1798 to 1806 and again from 1832 to 1853. When this policy was successful, Russia supported the integrity of the Ottoman Empire and made no territorial demands. When it was not successful, Russia sought to undermine Turkey by supporting rebellious Balkan peoples or, more directly, by war: this was the case from 1806 to 1812, from 1828 to 1829, and from 1853 to 1856.

The periods of cooperation were more profitable for Russia than those of conflict. In the first period, a promising foothold was established in the Ionian Islands, which had to be abandoned after the Treaty of Tilsit. In the second period, Russia achieved a great success with the 1833 Treaty of Hünkâr İskelesi, which in effect opened the Black Sea Straits to Russian warships. It achieved a more limited but more durable gain by the Straits Convention of 1841, signed by all the Great Powers and by Turkey, which forbade the passage of foreign warships through either the Dardanelles or the Bosporus as long as Turkey was at peace, thus protecting Russia's position in the Black Sea unless it was itself at war with Turkey.

In the periods of hostility between Russia and Turkey, the main object of Russian expansion was the area later known as Romania—the Danubian principalities of Moldavia and Walachia. In 1812 Moldavia was partitioned between Russia and Turkey: the eastern half, under the name of Bessarabia, was annexed to Russia. In the war of 1828–29, Russian armies marched through the principalities and afterward remained in occupation until 1834. In 1848 the Russians returned, with Turkish approval, to suppress the revolution that had broken out in Bucharest. It appeared to be only a matter of time before the two Romanian principalities were wholly annexed to Russia. This did not occur, however, because of Russia's defeat in the Crimean War.

The Crimean War (1853–56) pitted Russia against Great Britain, France, and Turkey. It arose from a series of misunderstandings and diplomatic errors among the powers in their conflict of interests in the Near East, particularly over Turkish affairs. It has been called "the unnecessary war." The fact that it was fought in the Crimea was due to Austrian diplomacy. In June 1854 the Russian government accepted the Austrian demand that Russian troops be withdrawn from the Danubian principalities, and in August Austrian troops entered. It is arguable whether, on balance, the presence of Austrian troops benefitted Russia by preventing French and British forces from marching on the Ukraine or whether it damaged Russia by preventing its troops from marching on Constantinople. The tsar resented the Austrian action as showing ingratitude toward the power that had saved Austria from the Hungarian rebels in 1849. When the British and French were unable to attack in the principalities, they decided to send an expedition to the Crimea to destroy the Russian naval base at Sevastopol. It was here that the war dragged out its course. The war showed the inefficiency of Russia's top military command and of its system of transport and supply. The Russian armies, nevertheless, won victories over the Turks in the Caucasus; and the defense of Sevastopol for nearly a year was a brilliant achievement.

FROM ALEXANDER II TO NICHOLAS II

Emancipation and reform. Defeat in the Crimea made Russia's backwardness clear, and the first step toward modernization was the abolition of serfdom. It seemed to the new tsar Alexander II (reigned 1855–81) that the dangers to public order of dismantling the existing system, which had deterred Nicholas I from action, were less than the dangers of leaving things as they were. As the Tsar said to the nobility of Moscow in March 1856, "it is better to abolish serfdom from above than to wait until the serfs begin to liberate themselves from below." The main work of reform was carried out in the ministry of the interior, where the most able officials, headed by the deputy minister Nikolay Milyutin, were resolved to get the best possible terms for the peasants. In this they were assisted by a few progressive landowners, chief among whom was the Slavophile Yury Samarin; but the bulk of the landowning class was determined, if it could not prevent abolition of serfdom, to give the freed peasants as little as possible. The settlement, proclaimed on March 3 (February 19, old style), 1861, was a compromise. Peasants were freed from servile status, and a procedure was laid down by which they could become owners of land. The government paid the landowners compensation and recovered the cost in annual "redemption payments" from the peasants. The terms were unfavourable to the peasants in many, probably most, cases. In the north, where land was poor, the price of land on which the compensation was based was unduly high: in effect this served to compensate the landowners for the loss of their serfs and also for the loss of the share that they had previously enjoyed of the peasants' earnings from nonagricultural labour. In the south, where land was more valuable, the plots given to the peasants were very small, often less than they had had for their use when they were serfs.

It is arguable that the main beneficiary of the reform was neither peasant nor landowner, but the state. A new apparatus of government was established to replace the authority of the serf owner. From the *ispravnik*, the chief official of the district, who in 1862 ceased to be elected by

The emancipation of the serfs

the nobility and became an appointed official of the ministry of the interior, the official hierachy now stretched down to the village notary, the most powerful person at this level, who was assisted by an elder elected by an assembly of householders. The lowest effective centre of power was the village commune (*obshchina*), an institution of uncertain origin but great antiquity, which had long had the power to redistribute land for the use of its members and to determine the crop cycle, but which now also became responsible for collecting taxes on behalf of the government.

Further important reforms followed the emancipation. A new system of elected assemblies at the provincial and county levels was introduced in 1864. These assemblies, known as *zemstvos*, were elected by all classes including the peasants, although the landowning nobility had a disproportionately large share of both the votes and the seats. The *zemstvos* were empowered to levy taxes and to spend their funds on schools, public health, roads, and other social services, but their scope was limited by the fact that they also had to spend money on some of the tasks of the central government. In 1864 a major judicial reform was completed. Russia received a system of law courts based on European models, with irremovable judges and a proper system of courts of appeal. Justices of the peace were instituted for minor offenses; they were elected by the county *zemstvos*. A properly organized, modern legal profession now arose, and it soon achieved very high standards. The old system of endless delays and judicial corruption rapidly disappeared. There were, however, two important gaps in the system: one was that the ministry of the interior had power, regardless of the courts, to banish persons whom it regarded as politically dangerous; the other was that the courts for settling disputes between peasants were maintained and operated on the basis of peasant custom. Their institution by Kiselev in the 1840s had been a well-intentioned reform, but their continuation after emancipation meant that the peasants were still regarded as something less than full citizens.

During the first years of Alexander II's reign there was some demand from a liberal section of the nobility for representative government at the national level—not for full parliamentary rule, still less for a democratic suffrage, but for some sort of consultative assembly in which public issues could be debated and which could put before the Emperor the views of at least the educated section of the Russian people. The tsar and his bureaucrats refused to consider this. The principle of autocracy must remain sacred. Such was the view not only of bureaucrats but of such men as Nikolay Milyutin and Yury Samarin, both of whom rested their hopes for the progressive reforms they so ardently desired on the unfettered power of the Emperor. Their attitude was essentially that of Pavel Stroganov at the beginning of the century, that the sovereign must not have "his arms tied" and so be prevented from realizing "the plans which he had in favour of the nation." The decision against a national assembly in the early 1860s was a negative event of the greatest importance: it deprived Russia of the possibility of public political education such as that which existed, for example, in contemporary Prussia, and it deprived the government of the services of hundreds of talented men.

Revolutionary activities. The emancipation was received with bitter disappointment by many peasants as well as by the radical intellectuals. The serfs' view of their relationship to the landowners had been traditionally summed up in the phrase: "We are yours, but the land is ours." Now they were being asked to pay for land that they felt was theirs by right. During the 1860s small revolutionary groups began to appear. The outstanding figure was the socialist writer N.G. Chernyshevsky; the extent of his involvement in revolutionary action remains a subject of controversy, but of his influence on generations of young Russians there can be no doubt. In 1861 and 1862 revolutionary leaflets were distributed in St. Petersburg, ranging from the demand for a constituent assembly to a passionate appeal for insurrection. The Polish uprising of 1863 strengthened the forces of repression. An unsuccessful attempt on the tsar's life in 1866

led to a certain predominance, among Alexander's advisers, of extreme conservatives. Nevertheless, there were still some valuable reforms to come. In 1870 the main cities of Russia were given elected municipal government (on a very narrow franchise), and in 1874 a series of military reforms was completed by the establishment of universal military service. This was the work of Dmitry Milyutin, the brother of Nikolay and like him a liberal, who was minister of war from 1861 to 1881.

In the 1870s revolutionary activity revived. Its centre was the university youth, who were increasingly influenced by a variety of socialist ideas derived from Europe but adapted to Russian conditions. These young people saw in the peasantry the main potential for revolutionary action. In 1873 and 1874 hundreds of the youth, including women, "went to the people," invading the countryside and seeking to rouse the peasants with their speeches. The peasants did not understand, and the police arrested the young revolutionaries. Some were sentenced to prison, and hundreds were deported to remote provinces or to Siberia. It became clear that no progress could be expected from overt action: conspiratorial action was the only hope. In 1876 a new party was founded that took the title of Land and Freedom. Some of its members favoured assassination of prominent officials in reprisal for the maltreatment of their comrades and also as a means to pressure the government in order to extract Western-type political liberties. Experience also had shown them that while the peasants were physically too scattered to be an effective force, and in any case too apathetic, the workers in the new industrial cities offered a more promising audience. This faction was opposed by others in the party who deprecated assassination, continued to pay more attention to peasants than to workers, and were indifferent to the attainment of political liberties. In 1879 the party split. The politically minded and terrorist wing took the name People's Will and made its aim the assassination of Alexander II. After several unsuccessful attempts it achieved its aim on March 13 (March 1, O.S.), 1881, when the tsar was fatally wounded by a bomb while driving through the capital. All the main leaders of the group were caught by the police, and five of them were hanged.

Shortly before his death the Tsar had been considering reforms that would have introduced a few elected representatives into the apparatus of government. His successor, Alexander III (reigned 1881–94), considered these plans. Under the influence of his former tutor, Konstantin Pobedonostsev (*q.v.*), the procurator of the Holy Synod, he decided to reject them and to reaffirm the principle of autocracy without change. In 1882 he appointed Dmitry Tolstoy minister of interior. Tolstoy and Pobedonostsev were the moving spirits of the deliberately reactionary policies that followed. Education was further restricted, the work of the *zemstvos* was hampered, and the village communes were brought under closer control in 1889 by the institution of the "land commandant" (*zemsky nachalnik*)—an official appointed by the ministry of interior, usually a former officer or a local landowner, who interfered in all aspects of peasant affairs. The office of elected justice of the peace was abolished, and the government was authorized to assume emergency powers when public order was said to be in danger. By this time Russian public officials were better paid and educated, and less addicted to crude corruption, than they had been in the reign of Nicholas I, but they retained their arrogant contempt for the public and especially for the poorer classes. The discriminatory laws against Jews and members of dissenting Christian sects remained a source of widespread injustice, hardship, and resentment.

The repressive policies of Dmitry Tolstoy worked for a time. But the economic development of the following decades created new social tensions and brought into existence new social groups, from whom active opposition once more developed. The *zemstvos* were in growing conflict with the central authorities. Even their efforts at social improvement of a quite unpolitical type met with obstruction. The ministry of the interior, once the centre of Russia's best reformers, now became a stronghold of

Introduction of the zemstvos

From reform to terrorism

Attempts at repression

resistance. In the obscurantist view of its leading officials, only the central government had the right to care for the public welfare, and *zemstvo* initiatives were undesirable usurpations of power. Better that nothing should be done at all than that it should be done through the wrong channels. This attitude was manifested in 1891, when crop failures led to widespread famine and relief work by *zemstvo* officials met with government obstruction. The revival of political activity may be dated from this year. It was accelerated by the death of Alexander III in 1894 and the succession of his son Nicholas II (reigned 1894–1917), who commanded less fear or respect but nevertheless at once antagonized the *zemstvo* liberals by publicly describing their aspirations for reforms as "senseless dreams." In the late 1890s moderate liberalism, aiming at the establishment of a consultative national assembly, was strong among elected *zemstvo* members who were largely members of the landowning class. A more radical attitude, combining elements of liberalism and socialism, was to be found in the professional classes of the cities, including many persons employed by the *zemstvos* as teachers, doctors, engineers, or statisticians. The growth of an industrial working class provided a mass basis for socialist movements, and by the end of the century some interest in politics was beginning to penetrate even to the peasantry, especially in parts of the Middle Volga Valley.

Economic and social development. Liberation from serfdom was a benefit for the peasants that should not be underrated. The decades that followed brought a growth of prosperity and self-reliance to at least a substantial minority. In 1877, when about four-fifths of the land due to be transferred to the former serfs was actually in their possession, this "allotment land" constituted about half of the arable land in 50 provinces of European Russia. A further one-third of the arable land was still owned by the nobility, and the rest belonged to a variety of individual or collective owners. In 1905 substantially more than half the arable land was in allotment land and another 10 percent belonged to individual peasants or to peasant associations; the nobility's share of arable land had fallen to a little more than 20 percent. Peasant land had increased by more than 40,000,000 hectares between 1877 and 1905, of which more than half had been obtained by purchase from landowners and the remainder by the completion of the transfer of allotment land. Peasant purchases had been assisted by loans from the Peasants' Land Bank, set up by the government in 1882. The Nobles' Land Bank, set up in 1885, made loans to landowners at more favourable rates of interests; it may have retarded, but did not prevent, the passage of land from landowners to peasants. In 1894 the rate of interest charged by the two banks was equalized.

Though many peasants improved their position, agriculture remained backward, and poverty increased more rapidly than prosperity. One of the main reasons for this was the indifference of the government to agriculture. The government's economic policy was motivated by the desire for national and military power. This required the growth of industry, and great efforts were made to encourage it. Agriculture was regarded mainly as a source of revenue to pay for industry and the armed forces. Exports of grain made possible imports of raw materials, and taxes paid by peasants filled the state's coffers. The redemption payments were a heavy charge on the peasants' resources, though a gradual fall in the value of money appreciably reduced it with the passage of years. Consumption taxes, especially on sugar, tobacco, matches, and oil, affected the peasants, and so did import duties. In 1894 the government introduced a liquor monopoly that drew enormous revenues from the peasants, to whom vodka was a principal solace in a hard life. The techniques and tools of agriculture remained extremely primitive, and farm output low; virtually nothing was done to instruct peasants in modern methods.

The second main cause of peasant poverty was overpopulation. The vast landmass of Russia was, of course, sparsely populated, but the number of persons employed in agriculture per unit of arable land, and relative to

Difficulties in agriculture

output, was extremely high as compared to western Europe. There was a vast and increasing surplus of labour in the Russian villages. Outlets were available in seasonal migration to the southern provinces, where labour was needed on the great estates that produced the grain that Russia exported; and peasants could move permanently to new land in Siberia, which at the end of the century was absorbing a yearly influx of 200,000; or they could find seasonal work in the cities or seek permanent employment in the growing industrial sector. These alternatives were not enough to absorb the growing labour surplus, which was most acute in the southern part of central Russia and in the northern Ukraine, in the provinces of Kursk and Poltava. Peasants competed with each other to lease land from the landlords' estates; this drove rents up; the existence of the large estates became more and more resented; and class feeling began to take the form of political demands for further redistribution of land.

The difficulties of agriculture were also increased by the inefficiency of the peasant commune, which had the power to redistribute holdings according to the needs of families and to dictate the rotation of crops to all members. In doing so, it tended to hamper enterprising farmers and protect the incompetent. In defense of the commune it was argued that it ensured a living to everyone and stood for values of solidarity and cooperation that were more important than mere profit and loss. Russian officials also found it useful as a means of collecting taxes and keeping the peasants in order. The 1861 settlement did provide a procedure by which peasants could leave the commune, but it was very complicated and was little used. In practice, the communal system predominated in northern and central Russia, and individual peasant ownership was widespread in the Ukraine and in the Polish borderlands. In 1898, in 50 provinces of European Russia, about 80,000,000 hectares of land were under communal tenure, and about 22,000,000 were under individual tenure.

The dispute over the peasant commune divided the ranks both of officialdom and of the government's revolutionary enemies. The ministry of the interior, which stood for paternalism and public security at all costs, favoured the commune in the belief that it was a bulwark of conservatism, of traditional Russian social values, and of loyalty to the tsar. The Socialist Revolutionaries favoured it because they took the view that the commune was, at least potentially, the natural unit of a future socialist republic. The ministry of finance, concerned to develop capitalism in town and country, objected to the commune as an obstacle to economic progress; it hoped to see a prosperous minority of individual farmers as a basis of a new and more modern type of Russian conservatism. The Social Democrats agreed that the commune must and should be replaced by capitalist ownership, but they saw this only as the next stage in the progress toward a socialist revolution led by urban workers.

The emancipation of the serfs undoubtedly helped capitalist development, though this began rather slowly. A rapid growth of railways came in the 1870s, and in the same decade the exploitation of petroleum began at Baku in Azerbaijan. There was also progress in the textile and sugar industries. Only in the 1890s did the demand for iron and steel, created by the railway program and by military needs in general, begin to be satisfied on a large scale within Russia. By the end of the century there was a massive metallurgical industry in the Ukraine, based on the iron ore of Krivoy Rog and the coal of the Donets Basin. The iron industry of the Urals, which lost a large part of its labour force when the serfs became free to leave, lagged far behind. Poland was also an important metallurgical centre. Textiles were concentrated in the central provinces of Moscow and Vladimir; by the end of the century they were drawing much of their raw cotton from the newly conquered lands of Central Asia. Baku was also booming, especially as a supplier of petroleum to the Moscow region. St. Petersburg had begun to develop important engineering and electrical industries. Count Sergey Witte (*q.v.*), minister of finance from 1892 to 1903, was able to put Russia on the gold standard in 1897 and to encourage foreign investors. French and Bel-

Industrial growth

gian capital was invested mainly in the southern metallurgical industry, British in petroleum, and German in electricity.

Industrial growth began to produce an urban working class, which seemed fated to repeat the history of workers in the early stages of industrial capitalism in Western countries. The workers were unskilled, badly paid, overworked, and miserably housed. Uprooted from the village communities in which they had at least had a recognized place, the peasants' sons who flocked into the new industrial agglomerations suffered both physical and moral privation. This was especially true of central Russia, where the surplus of labour kept wages down to the minimum. It was in St. Petersburg, where employers found it less easy to recruit workers, that the transformation of the amorphous mass of urban poor into a modern working class made the most progress. St. Petersburg employers were also less hostile to government legislation on behalf of the workers. In 1882, Finance Minister N.Kh. Bunge introduced an inspectorate of labour conditions, and limited hours of work for children. In 1897, Count Witte introduced a maximum working day of 11½ hours for all workers, male or female, and of ten hours for those engaged in any night work. Trade unions were not permitted, though several attempts were made to organize them illegally. The ministry of the interior, being more interested in public order than in businessmen's profits, occasionally showed some concern for the workers. In 1901 the head of the Moscow branch of the security police, Col. S.V. Zubatov, encouraged the formation of a workers' society intended to rally the workers behind the autocracy; but it became largely infiltrated by Social Democrats. Strikes were strictly forbidden but occurred anyway, especially in 1885, 1896, 1902, and 1903.

A Russian business class also developed rapidly under the umbrella of government policy, benefitting especially from the high protective tariffs and the very high prices paid for government purchases from the metallurgical industry. Russia's industrial progress took place under private capitalism, but it differed from classical Western capitalism in that the motivation of Russian industrial growth was political and military, and the driving force was government policy. Russian and foreign capitalists provided the resources and the organizing skill, and they were richly rewarded. The richness of their rewards accounted for a second difference from classical capitalism: Russian capitalists were completely satisfied with the political system as it was. English and French capitalists had material and ideological reasons to fight against absolute monarchs and aristocratic upper classes; Russian businessmen accepted the principle and the practice of autocracy.

Education and ideas. At the time of the first modern census in Russia, in 1897, there were 104,000 persons who had attended or were attending a university—less than 0.1 percent of the population—and 73 percent of these were children of nobles or officials. The number who had studied or were studying in any sort of secondary school was 1,072,977, or less than 1 percent of the population, and 40 percent of these were children of nobles and officials. In 1904 primary schools managed by the ministry of education had rather more than 3,000,000 pupils, and those managed by the Orthodox Church not quite 2,000,000. The combined figure represented only 27 percent of the children of school age in the empire at that time. Persistent neglect of education could no longer be explained by sheer backwardness and lack of funds: the Russian empire of 1900 could have afforded a modern school system if its rulers had thought it important.

In the last half of the 19th century the word intelligentsia came into use in Russia. This word is not precisely definable, for it described both a social group and a state of mind. Essentially the intelligentsia consisted of persons with a good modern education and a passionate preoccupation with general political and social ideas. An uneducated or stupid man could not be a member of the intelligentsia, but not all educated and intelligent men could belong to it either; for example, a brilliant scientist devoted solely to his science would not be reckoned a member

The Russian intelligentsia

of the intelligentsia. Its nucleus was to be found in the liberal professions of law, medicine, teaching, and engineering, which grew in numbers and social prestige as the economy became more complex; yet it also included individuals from outside those professions—private landowners, bureaucrats, and even army officers. The intelligentsia was by its very nature opposed to the existing political and social system, and this opposition coloured its attitude to culture in general. In particular, the value of works of literature was judged by the intelligentsia according to whether they furthered the cause of social progress. This tradition of social utilitarianism was initiated by the critic Vissarion Belinsky and carried further by N.A. Dobrolyubov in the late 1850s. Its most extreme exponent was Dmitry I. Pisarev, who held that all art was useless and that the only aim of thinking people should be "to solve forever the unavoidable question of hungry and naked people." In the last decades of the century the chief spokesman of social utilitarianism was the sociological writer Nikolay K. Mikhaylovsky, a former supporter of the terrorist group People's Will. It is hardly an exaggeration to say that Russian literature was faced with two censorships—that of the official servants of the autocracy and that of the social utilitarian radicals. Yet the great writers of this period—Leo Tolstoy, Fyodor Dostoyevsky, Aleksandr Blok, and the symbolist poets of the early 20th century—though profoundly concerned with social issues, did not conform to these criteria.

The intelligentsia did not consist of active revolutionaries, although it preferred the revolutionaries to the government; but it was from the intelligentsia that the professional revolutionaries were largely recruited. The lack of civil liberties and the prohibition of political parties made it necessary for socialists to use conspiratorial methods. Illegal parties had to have rigid centralized discipline. Yet the emergence of the professional revolutionary, imagined in romantically diabolical terms in the "Revolutionary Catechism" of Mikhail Bakunin and Sergey Nechayev in 1869 and sketched more realistically in *What Is To Be Done?* by Vladimir Ilyich Ulyanov, better known as Lenin, in 1902, was not entirely due to the circumstances of the underground political struggle. The revolutionaries were formed also by their sense of mission, by their absolute conviction that they knew best the interests of the masses. For these men and women, revolution was not just a political aim; it was also a substitute for religion. It is worth noting that a remarkably high proportion of the young revolutionaries of the late 19th century were children of Orthodox priests or persons associated with religious sects. It is also worth noting that the traditional Russian belief in autocracy, the desire for an all-powerful political saviour, and the contempt for legal formalities and processes had left its mark on them. The autocracy of Nicholas II was, of course, odious to them, but this did not mean that autocratic government should be abolished; rather, it should be replaced by the autocracy of the virtuous.

Russian revolutionary socialism at the end of the century was divided into two main streams, each of these being subdivided into a section that favoured conspiratorial tactics and one that aimed at a mass movement to be controlled by its members. The Socialist Revolutionaries (founded in 1901 from a number of groups more or less derived from People's Will) first hoped that Russia could bypass capitalism, and when it became clear that this could not be done, they aimed to limit its operation and build a socialist order based on village communes. The land was to be socialized but worked by peasants on the principle of "labour ownership." The Social Democrats (founded in 1898 from a number of illegal working-class groups) believed that the future lay with industrialization and a socialist order based on the working class. The Socialist Revolutionaries were divided between their extreme terrorist wing, the "Fighting Organization," and a broader and looser membership that at one end merged imperceptibly with radical middle-class liberalism. The Social Democrats were divided between Lenin's group, which took the name Bolshevik (derived from the Russian word for "majority," after a majority won by his

The socialists

group at one particular vote during the second congress of the party, held in Brussels and London in 1903), and a number of other groups that were by no means united but that came to be collectively known as Menshevik (derived from the word for "minority"). The personal, ideological, and programmatic issues involved in their quarrels were extremely complex, but it is a permissible oversimplification to say that Lenin favoured rigid discipline while the Mensheviks aimed at creating a mass labour movement of the west European type; that the Mensheviks were much more willing to cooperate with nonsocialist liberals than were the Bolsheviks; and that Lenin paid much more attention to the peasants as a potential revolutionary force than did the Mensheviks.

The repression of nationalities

Russification policies. After the Crimean War the Russian government made some attempt to introduce in Poland a new system acceptable to the Polish population. The leading figure on the Polish side was the nobleman Aleksander Wielopolski. His pro-Russian program proved unacceptable to the Poles. Tension increased and in January 1863 armed rebellion broke out. This was put down, being suppressed with special severity in the Lithuanian and Ukrainian borderlands. In order to punish the Polish country gentry for their part in the insurrection, the Russian authorities carried out a land reform on terms exceptionally favourable to the Polish peasants. Its authors were Nikolay Milyutin and Yury Samarin, who genuinely desired to benefit the peasants. The reform was followed, however, by a policy of russification intended to separate the Polish peasants from their own culture. In the 1880s this went so far that the language of instruction even in primary schools in areas of purely Polish population was Russian. At first, all classes of Poles passively accepted their defeat, while clinging to their language and national consciousness; but in the 1890s two strong, though of course illegal, political parties appeared—the National Democrats and the Polish Socialist Party, both fundamentally anti-Russian.

After 1863 the authorities also severely repressed all signs of Ukrainian nationalist activity. In 1876 all publications in Ukranian, other than historical documents, were prohibited. In Eastern Galicia, however, which lay just across the Austrian border and had a population of several million Ukrainians, not only the language but political activity flourished. Here the great Ukrainian historian Mikhail Hrushevsky and the socialist writer Mikhail Drahomanov published their works; Ukrainian political literature was smuggled across the border. In the 1890s small illegal groups of Ukrainian democrats and socialists existed on Russian soil.

In the 1890s the government began to adopt a general policy of russification. It was no longer enough that the subjects of the tsar should obey him loyally: they were required to become Russians. The social driving force behind this policy was the growing bureaucracy, comprised mainly of children of landowning families who no longer owned estates. The Orthodox Church played an active part, since russification and imposition of Orthodoxy went naturally together. It must be recognized that russification had considerable support among all classes of the Russian population except the intelligentsia. Part of the large-circulation conservative press in particular was intensely nationalistic.

The main victims of russification were the very peoples that had shown consistent loyalty to the empire and now found themselves rewarded by being pressed to abandon their own culture. The Germans of the Baltic provinces were deprived of their university and their ancient secondary schools were russified. The Latvians and Estonians did not object to action by the government against the Germans, whom they had reason to dislike as landowners and rich burghers; but the prospect of the German language being replaced by the Russian had no attraction for them, and they strongly resented the pressure to abandon their Lutheran faith for Orthodoxy. The attempt to absorb and russify Finland united the Finns in opposition to St. Petersburg in the 1890s. In 1904 a Finnish terrorist murdered the Russian governor-general, and passive resistance to Russian policies was almost universal. Effec-

tive and widespread passive resistance also occurred among the traditionally Russophile Armenians of the Caucasus when the Russian authorities began to interfere with the organization of the Armenian church, and to close the schools maintained from its funds.

Of the Muslim peoples of the empire, those who suffered most from russification were the most economically and culturally advanced, the Tatars of the Volga Valley. Attempts by the Orthodox Church to convert Muslims, and the rivalry between Muslims and Orthodox to convert small national groups of Finno-Ugrian speech who were still pagans, caused growing mutual hostility. The Tatars had developed a substantial merchant class by the end of the century and the beginnings of a national intelligentsia. Modern schools, maintained from merchants' funds, were creating a new Tatar educated elite that was increasingly accessible to modern democratic ideas. In Central Asia, on the other hand, modern influences had barely made themselves felt. In those newly conquered lands, Russian colonial administration was paternalistic and limited: like the methods of "indirect rule" in the British and French empires, it made no systematic attempt to change old ways. Here there was no russification.

The position of the Jews was hardest of all. As a result of their history and religious traditions, as well as of centuries of social and economic discrimination, the Jews were overwhelmingly concentrated in commercial and intellectual professions. They were thus prominent both as businessmen and as political radicals, hateful to the bureaucrats as socialists and to the lower classes as capitalists. In the 1880s legal discrimination against them became more severe both in education and in economic life. It was at this time that the police began the practice of pogroms, or officially sponsored riots that led to the destruction of Jewish shops and to physical assaults on Jews—in some cases to killings. These were deliberately used by the authorities as a means of diverting popular discontent to a convenient scapegoat in order to diminish popular hostility to the government.

Foreign policy. During the second half of the 19th century, Russian foreign policy gave about equal emphasis to the Balkans and the Far East. The friendship with Germany and Austria weakened; and in the 1890s the Triple Alliance of Germany, Austria-Hungary, and Italy stood face to face with a dual alliance of France and Russia.

The Balkans

The demilitarization of the Black Sea coast that had resulted from the Crimean War was ended by the London Conference of 1871, which allowed Russia to rebuild its naval forces. In 1876 the Serbo-Turkish War produced an outburst of Pan-Slav feeling in Russia. Partly under its influence, but mainly in pursuit of traditional strategic aims, Russia declared war on Turkey in April 1877. After overpowering heavy Turkish resistance at the fortress of Pleven in Bulgaria, the Russian forces advanced almost to Constantinople. By the Treaty of San Stefano of March 1878 the Turks accepted the creation of a large independent Bulgarian state. Fearing that this would be a Russian vassal, giving Russia mastery over all the Balkans and the straits, Britain and Austria-Hungary opposed the treaty. At the international Congress of Berlin, held in June 1878, Russia had to accept a much smaller Bulgaria. This was regarded by Russian public opinion as a bitter humiliation, for which the German chancellor Bismarck was blamed. In 1885–87 a new international crisis was caused by Russian interference in Bulgarian affairs, with Britain and Austria-Hungary once more opposing Russia. Once more, Russia suffered a political reverse. In the 1890s, despite the pro-Russian sentiment of many Serbs and Bulgarians, neither country's government was much subject to Russian influence. In the crises that arose in connection with the Turkish Armenians and over Crete and Macedonia, Russian policy was extremely cautious and on the whole tended to support the Turkish government. In 1897 an Austro-Russian agreement was made on spheres of influence in the Balkans.

The attempt of Bismarck to restore Russo-German friendship through the Reinsurance Treaty of 1887, with a view to an ultimate restoration of the alliance of Russia, Germany, and Austria, did not survive Bismarck's fall from power in 1890. The Russian government, alarmed by indications of a closer cooperation between the Triple Alliance and Britain and by some signs of a pro-Polish attitude in Berlin, reluctantly turned toward France. The French needed an ally against both Germany and Britain; the Russians needed French capital, in the form both of loans to the Russian government and of investment in Russian industry. The Franco-Russian alliance was signed in August 1891 and was supplemented by a military convention. Essentially the alliance was directed against Germany, for it was only in a war with Germany that each could help the other.

Russia established diplomatic and commercial relations with Japan by three treaties between 1855 and 1858. In 1860, by the Treaty of Peking, Russia acquired from China a long strip of Pacific coastline south of the mouth of the Amur and began to build the naval base of Vladivostok. In 1867 the Russian government sold Alaska to the United States for $7,200,000. The Treaty of St. Petersburg between Russia and Japan in 1875 gave Russia sole control over all of Sakhalin and Japan all the Kuril Islands.

The systematic Russian conquest of Turkistan, the region of settled population and ancient culture lying to the south of the Kazakh steppes, began in the 1860s. This was watched with distrust by the British authorities in India, and fear of Russian interference in Afghanistan led to the Anglo-Afghan War of 1878–80. In the 1880s, Russian expansion extended to the Turkmen lands on the east coast of the Caspian, whose people offered much stiffer military resistance. The Russian conquest of Merv in 1884 caused alarm in Calcutta, and in March 1885 a clash between Russian and Afghan troops produced a major diplomatic crisis between Britain and Russia. An agreement on frontier delimitation was reached in September 1885, and for the next decades Central Asian affairs did not have a major effect on Anglo-Russian relations.

War with Japan   Much more serious was the situation in the Far East. In 1894–95 the long-standing rivalry between the Japanese and Chinese in Korea led to a war between the two Oriental empires, which the Japanese won decisively. Russia faced the choice between collaborating with Japan (with which relations had been fairly good for some years) at the expense of China, or assuming the role of protector of China against Japan. The tsar chose the second policy, largely under the influence of Count Witte. Together with the French and German governments, the Russians demanded that the Japanese return to China the Liaotung Peninsula, which they had taken in the treaty of peace. Russia then concluded an alliance with China in 1896, which included the establishment of a Russian-owned Chinese Eastern Railway to cross northern Manchuria from west to east, linking Siberia with Vladivostok, and administered by Russian personnel and a Russian police force with extraterritorial rights. In 1898 the Russian government went still further and acquired from China the same Liaotung Peninsula of which it had deprived the Japanese three years earlier. Here the Russians built a naval base in ice-free waters at Port Arthur. They also obtained extraterritorial rights of ownership and management of a South Manchurian railroad that was to stretch from north to south, linking Port Arthur with the Chinese Eastern Railway at the junction of Harbin. When in 1900 the European powers sent armed forces to relieve their diplomatic missions in Peking, besieged by the Boxer Rebellion, the Russian government used this as an opportunity to bring substantial military units into Manchuria. All of this bitterly antagonized the Japanese. They might have been willing, nonetheless, to write off Manchuria as a Russian sphere of influence provided that Russia recognize Japanese priority in Korea, but the Russian government would not do this. It was not so much that the tsar himself wished to dominate the whole Far East; it was rather that he was beset by advisers with several rival schemes and could not bring himself to reject any of them. The British government, fearing that

Russia would be able to establish domination over the Chinese government and so interfere with the interests of Britain in other parts of China, made an alliance with Japan in January 1902. Negotiations between Russia and Japan continued, but they were insincere on both sides. On the night of February 8/9, 1904, Japanese forces made a surprise attack on Russian warships in Port Arthur, and the Russo-Japanese War began.

THE LAST YEARS OF TSARDOM

Defeat and disorder.   The Russo-Japanese War brought a series of Russian defeats on land and sea, culminating in the destruction of the Russian Baltic fleet in the Straits of Tsushima. Political discontent grew steadily at home. The efforts of the moderate *zemstvo* liberals to organize help for the war effort were discouraged by the authorities, and criticism of the government in the press and at public banquets grew bolder. On Sunday, January 22 (January 9, O.S.), 1905, a large crowd of workers, led by a priest named Georgy Gapon, who was active in one of the officially sponsored workers' societies, marched to the square in front of the Winter Palace. Troops opened fire and several hundred were killed or injured.   **Revolutionary disturbances of 1905**

Bloody Sunday was followed by disorders in gathering momentum. There were strikes, workers' demonstrations, street fighting, peasant insurrections, and mutinies in both the army and navy. The disorders were especially violent in regions inhabited by non-Russians: in Poland, Latvia, Georgia, and parts of the Ukraine. There were also numerous pogroms, not only of Ukrainians and Russians against Jews but also of Tatars in Azerbaijan against Armenians. Armed bands of townsmen of various social origin, led by men of the extreme right, in many cases by policemen or priests, formed to fight against left-wing bands. These groups, known as Black Hundreds, were a prototype of the fascist gangs of central Europe in the 1930s. The revolutionary movement of 1905 reached its climax in October with a nationwide railway strike and the formation in St. Petersburg of a Soviet (council) of Workers' Deputies. Faced by the threat of collapse, the Tsar issued a manifesto promising to convoke a national Parliament. Count Witte, who had just successfully conducted peace negotiations at Portsmouth (New Hampshire), saving for Russia the northern half of Sakhalin and the Chinese Eastern Railway but ceding Port Arthur and the South Manchurian Railway, became Russia's first prime minister. In the following weeks a series of laws established the powers of the Parliament, called the State Duma, and the procedure for its election.

The Dumas.   The election, held in April 1906 on a rather broad franchise, produced a Duma with a left-wing majority even though the Social Democrats and Socialist Revolutionaries had for the most part boycotted the election. The largest party, the Constitutional Democrats (Kadets), were the heirs to the earlier Union of Liberation (a group of nonsocialist radicals formed in 1903). The second largest, the Labour Group (Trudoviki), may be described as moderate socialists. The non-Russian peoples returned a large number of deputies, among them 40 Ukrainians and 30 Muslims. Russian conservatives were a tiny minority. Cooperation proved impossible between this assembly and the tsar's ministers, who were responsible to him only and could not be overthrown by Duma majorities. The reforms demanded by the Duma—redistribution of landowners' estates to peasants with or without compensation, amnesty for political prisoners, equal rights for Jews and for religious dissenters, autonomy for Poland—were unacceptable to the government. After two months of deadlock the tsar dissolved the Duma in July. For the next eight months the new premier, Pyotr Stolypin, ruled by decree. Peasant riots were ruthlessly suppressed, with hundreds executed by specially established courts-martial. By the beginning of 1907 the last stirrings of revolution were over; the discipline of the armed forces was restored, and the police functioned effectively. In February 1907 elections were held for a second Duma. This time the Social Democrats put up official candidates and won 65 seats, giving them the third largest representation after the Trudoviki   **Popular sentiment and the Dumas**

(101) and the Kadets (92). Conservative groups had 63 seats, and the Octobrists, heirs to the moderate *zemstvo* liberals of the 1890s, had 32. The political centre of gravity thus lay still further to the left than it had in the first Duma. Cooperation again proved impossible. In June 1907 the tsar dissolved the second Duma and Stolypin changed the electoral law, restricting the franchise in favour of the upper classes against the peasants and in favour of the Russians as against the other nationalities.

The third and fourth Dumas were accordingly more conservative in their composition; the Kadets, the Socialists, and the non-Russians had a total of about a quarter of the seats. The regime that followed from 1907 to 1914 was, however, substantially different from that before 1905. On the one hand, the principle of autocracy was officially upheld: the tsar had complete control over military affairs and over the appointment of ministers; while many bureaucrats, from provincial governors down to local police officials, continued to treat the public with contempt, and even flouted the laws that they were supposed to administer. On the other hand, political parties now existed, with public meetings and open political debate in the Duma. The press was relatively free. Workers were able to form trade unions, although strikes were illegal. The central government no longer obstructed local governments; it even made substantial money grants to them for social services. Primary education was improving in quantity and quality. The government was less positive in its attitude toward the universities, and there were massive disorders accompanied by resignations of teachers in the University of Moscow in 1911. Though conditions and prospects did improve, there was still plenty for educated men and women to resent; and the alienation of the intelligentsia from the regime was only marginally reduced.

Stolypin's reformsStolypin's main concern, apart from restoring order, was to improve agriculture. He introduced measures facilitating the dissolution of peasant communes and the formation of individual farms, with scattered strips consolidated in economically viable holdings. The events of 1905–06 had shattered the view, formerly held by ministry of interior officials, that the commune was a bulwark of conservative feeling. Since the political arguments in favour of the commune were no longer considered valid, the economic arguments against it carried more weight. The extent to which Stolypin's reforms benefitted the Russian peasants, or would have done so if the war had not come, is debatable. The Stolypin policy was, however, a recognition that it was worthwhile to put money, effort, and education into agriculture and that the countryside could no longer simply be milked for the benefit of other parts of the economy. The assassination of Stolypin in September 1911 deprived the regime of its one outstanding leader; thereafter the government reverted to the old pattern of a weak and irresolute tsar surrounded by intriguing bureaucrats and flatterers. In these years the religious adventurer Grigory Rasputin obtained great influence over the empress through his ability to check by some hypnotic power the hemophilia that afflicted her only son Aleksey.

These years also saw continued progress in industry and a marked tendency toward the formation of large concentrations of capital. In June 1912 the Duma introduced health insurance for industrial workers. In Siberia land of first quality was brought under cultivation, and a self-reliant farmer class began to grow up using modern machinery and efficient marketing cooperatives.

While the non-Russian peoples had made political and cultural gains in 1905 and 1906, these were reversed after 1907. Russification was one of the most important features of the policy of Stolypin and his successors. The Finns and the Volga Tatars suffered especially, though they resisted stubbornly. Ukrainian nationalism gained ground despite the efforts to repress it, and extended from its nucleus in the intelligentsia to embrace a growing section of both peasants and workers. In Central Asia the increasing colonization of the lands of the Turkic peoples by immigrants from European Russia caused bitter resentment.

War and the fall of the monarchy. After 1906 Russia pursued a policy of cooperation with Japan in the Far East. Conflicts with Great Britain in Persia, Afghanistan, and Tibet were mitigated by the Anglo-Russian Convention of 1907. The alliance with France was reaffirmed after massive French loans had been received in return for Russian diplomatic support to France in its conflict with Germany over Morocco. Russian policy became absorbed by Balkan affairs after the Bosnian crisis of 1908–09, in which Russia was publicly humiliated by Germany and forced to abandon its support for Serbia. In the ensuing years Russian diplomacy tried to organize an anti-Austrian block of Balkan states, including Turkey. This failed, but the organization of the Serbian–Greek–Bulgarian alliance against Turkey in 1912 was a success for Russia. The second Balkan War of 1913 again placed Bulgaria in the Austrian camp. When Austria made demands upon Serbia in the summer of 1914, Russia was faced by a terrible dilemma. If it abandoned Serbia, it would lose the whole of the Balkans, raising doubt as to its usefulness as an ally of France; in that event Russia would be likely to drift into the status of a satellite of Germany. The alternative was to escalate the Balkan conflict. By the conventional wisdom of 1914, Russia's choice of the second alternative must be considered reasonable; but it destroyed the imperial regime.

Outbreak of First World WarIn 1914 the Franco-Russian alliance proved its value. The German Army could have crushed either France or Russia alone, but not both together. The Russian invasion of East Prussia was a failure, and in two unsuccessful battles the Russians lost nearly 150,000 as prisoners. It did, however, enable the French to win the First Battle of the Marne. In Galicia the Russian armies advanced far into Austrian territory. The entry of Turkey into the war as an ally of Germany was a major disaster, since it not only created a new front in the Caucasus (where the Russian armies did rather well), but, by closing the straits, enormously reduced the amount of supplies the allies could deliver to Russia. The Russian armies were seriously short of munitions. The failure of the British and French campaign in the Dardanelles and the entry of Bulgaria into the war on the German side meant that no relief could come from the south. In May 1915 the central powers launched their offensive in Poland and made enormous gains of territory. By the autumn Russia had lost more than 1,000,000 men.

These disasters aroused bitter discontent. A demand was raised, both in the Duma and in the press, for a "government commanding the confidence of the nation." The tsar ignored the demand; he insisted on assuming the supreme command of the armies in the field and left in the capital a collection of ministers of second-rate ability that could hardly be said to constitute a government at all. Economic conditions deteriorated. The mobilization of manpower disorganized both industry and agriculture; transport was overloaded; the military authorities interfered arbitrarily with civilian needs; prices rose much faster than wages; and there were serious shortages of goods, even of food. Working class discontent grew.

Political collapseDuring 1916 the military situation improved. Gen. A.A. Brusilov advanced in Galicia and captured nearly 400,000 Austrian prisoners. Public discontent, however, increased. The official bureaucracy and the leaders of the *zemstvos* and municipalities wasted much energy in fighting each other. The ministers chosen by the tsar—in some cases probably on the advice of the empress and Rasputin—were exceptionally incompetent and unpopular. The murder of Rasputin in December 1916 probably made matters still worse by further demoralizing the emperor. In January 1917 the food supply in the capital worsened. At the beginning of March (February, O.S.) strikes, demonstrations, and food lines filled the streets with aimless crowds. Mutinies took place in some barracks—their origin remains obscure—and it became clear that the troops were not going to fire on crowds. The tsar refused for several days to appoint a "government of public confidence." In Petrograd (formerly St. Petersburg), a Soviet of Workers' and Soldiers' Deputies was formed; a standing committee was also set up by the

Duma, which the tsar had prorogued. By agreement between the Soviet and the Duma committee, a Provisional Government was formed, composed principally of Kadets and Octobrists, headed by Prince G.Ye. Lvov. On March 15 its emissaries reached Pskov, where the tsar had been held up in a vain attempt to return from military headquarters to Petrograd. Here he handed to them his abdication: the thousand-year-old Russian monarchy had come to its end. (H.S.-W.)

IV. The U.S.S.R. from 1917 to 1939

THE GOVERNMENTS OF 1917

Results of the February (March) Revolution. To fill the vacuum left by the collapse of the ancient Russian monarchy, the leaders of the recently dissolved Duma set up a Provisional Committee to maintain order and establish democratic reforms. The same day, March 12 (February 27, old style), leaders of the Petrograd workers and the rebellious garrison created the Petrograd Soviet of Workers' and Soldiers' Deputies, an unofficial but representative body elected by the factories and regiments and dominated at the outset by the Menshevik and Socialist Revolutionary parties. Similar soviets were quickly set up all over Russia on the Petrograd model. Unsure of their strength and convinced that Russia was still in the stage of the bourgeois revolution, the leaders of the soviet refrained from any claim to exercise governmental power.

Establishment of the soviets

Prodded by the potential challenge of the soviet, the Duma Committee on March 15 (March 2, O.S.) established the Provisional Government. Prince Georgy Lvov was designated prime minister; Pavel Milyukov, leader of the Constitutional Democratic Party, was foreign minister and the strong man of the Cabinet; Aleksandr Guchkov, leader of the conservative Octobrist Party, became war minister. Aleksandr Kerensky, a Duma deputy of the moderately socialist Labour Group, became minister of justice and the unofficial liaison man with the soviet.

The Provisional Government. The Provisional Government was faced with a series of difficult and controversial problems. The food shortages and worsening economic crisis that led to the fall of the tsar were no nearer solution. Russia's participation in World War I, underlying these difficulties, raised agonizing questions—whether to fight or make peace and on what terms. Above all, the circumstances of the revolutionary overthrow of the monarchy released the latent grievances and demands of every sector of a frustrated population. As the year wore on, the political mood of the masses grew more and more radical, with the increasingly insistent demands of the peasants for land, of the workers for food and for control of the factories, of the soldiers for an end to the war, and of the national minorities for independence.

The first serious crisis of the Provisional Government was occasioned by foreign policy. Foreign Minister Milyukov wanted to continue the war for the territorial gains promised by the Allies, despite growing popular sentiment for a "democratic peace without annexation or indemnities." The release of a note from Milyukov promising Russian solidarity with Britain and France precipitated the mass demonstrations of the "April Days." Milyukov and Guchkov were compelled to resign, and the Cabinet was reshuffled to strengthen its popular base. Kerensky took over the war ministry, and Mikhail Tereshchenko, a businessman of moderate persuasion, became foreign minister. Several leaders from the soviet were brought in, including the Socialist Revolutionary Viktor Chernov as minister of agriculture and the Menshevik Irakly Tsereteli as minister of posts and telegraphs.

The "April Days": demonstrations against the war

This first coalition cabinet made no more progress than its predecessor toward solving the country's fundamental problems, despite the convening in June of the First All-Russian Congress of Soviets, designed to permit the delegates from the local soviets all over the country to define their program. Major decisions were postponed until a Constituent Assembly could be elected to draft a democratic constitution for Russia. (The election was finally scheduled in September and held in November, after the Bolshevik Revolution.) Meanwhile, at the prodding of

War Minister Kerensky, the Provisional Government turned to the prosecution of the war, which had been more or less dormant on the eastern front since the outbreak of the revolution. In June, Kerensky ordered an offensive; at first, the Russians were successful, but in July they were routed by the counterattacking Germans. Russian discipline and morale then began to disintegrate rapidly, desertions mounted, and, by the time of the Bolshevik Revolution, the army was scarcely a fighting force.

The rise of the Bolsheviks and the crisis of the Provisional Government. At the time of the March Revolution, the Bolshevik Party was small (fewer than 30,000 members) and disoriented. Most of its leaders, including Lenin, were in exile abroad or in Siberia. Initially, the Bolsheviks in Petrograd were hostile to the Provisional Government; then, higher ranking leaders returning from Siberia, including Lev Kamenev and Joseph Stalin, endorsed the Soviet's conditional acceptance of the Provisional Government. Lenin, in Switzerland, denounced the Provisional Government as a bourgeois, imperialist regime, and was independently echoed by Leon Trotsky in New York (though he was not yet a member of the Bolshevik Party). Refused passage by the Allied powers, Lenin secured permission to travel across Germany (and thence, via Sweden and Finland, to Petrograd) in the famous "sealed train" (actually one car to which Lenin and his party were confined while in transit).

Lenin's return to Russia

There has been much controversy over Lenin's relations with the German government. It seems certain from the German archives that the Germans facilitated Lenin's journey in the hope that he would help undermine the war effort of the Provisional Government and that they also made funds available to the Bolsheviks and other extremist groups for the same purpose. On the other hand, the allegations that Lenin was literally a German agent, after, as well as before, the Bolshevik Revolution, are without foundation. Documents published to this effect have proved to be forgeries.

Upon his arrival in Petrograd at the Finland Station on April 16 (April 3, O.S.), 1917, Lenin issued an open call for the overthrow of the Provisional Government and "All Power to the Soviets" (his so-called April Theses). He quickly brought the Bolshevik Party around to this position and launched it on a campaign of organization and propaganda to win the allegiance of the increasingly radical Russian masses. He was joined in this by Trotsky and a number of other people formerly in the left wing of the Menshevik Party. Rank and file Bolshevik membership grew rapidly, until, on the eve of the Revolution, it stood at around 200,000. The party rapidly attracted popular support at the expense of the Mensheviks and Socialist Revolutionaries, reflected in increasing Bolshevik representation in the soviets.

The first test of strength between the Bolsheviks and the Provisional Government came in the violent mass demonstrations of the "July Days" in Petrograd. Sparked by sailors from the Kronstadt naval base, the Petrograd mob started to act on the Bolshevik appeal for a new revolution. The Bolshevik leadership drew back, however, and the Provisional Government was able to restore order with loyal troops and outlaw the Bolshevik Party. Trotsky was arrested, and Lenin went into hiding in Finland, where he composed his principal theoretical work, *The State and Revolution*. In the aftermath of this setback for the Bolsheviks, Kerensky replaced Prince Lvov as prime minister in the second coalition cabinet.

The "July Days": the abortive revolt and the new Kerensky government

The next two months witnessed a temporary swing toward the right. Conservatives, rallying around the appeal for discipline and the war effort, looked to Kerensky's chief of staff, Gen. Lavr Kornilov, as the man who could restore order and check the course of the revolution. The State Conference held by Kerensky in Moscow in August only underscored the gulf between the right and the moderate left. Finally, late in August, on the pretext of supporting the government against the soviet, General Kornilov ordered troops to march on Petrograd in what Kerensky, at least, perceived to be a right-wing plot to overthrow him. Kerensky turned at this point to the forces of the left, even relaxing the ban on the Bolsheviks. Kornilov's troops deserted him, and the attempted counter-revolutionary coup collapsed. The consequence of the attempt was to drive the country further to the left and imbue it with an acute fear of counter-revolution.

The October (November) Revolution. Following the Kornilov affair, popular support for the Provisional Government dissipated rapidly, as the country polarized toward the extremes of left and right. The revolutionary mood of the masses, accentuated by rampant inflation and worsening shortages of goods, reached the stage of direct action. Peasants, impatient with the legal delays of the government, began seizing and plundering the landlords' estates. Strikes mounted, and workers began imposing "Workers' Control" in the factories through elected factory committees. Nationalist leaders in Kiev and Helsinki made the Ukraine and Finland virtually independent. The army began to crumble as peasant troops deserted to return home and share in the land seizures. The reserve units in the cities, fearful of being sent to the front, came under increasing Bolshevik influence.

Against this setting of growing turmoil, the Bolsheviks, with their slogan "Peace, Land, and Bread," were the only party (along with their allies, The Left Socialist Revolutionaries) ready to acknowledge the most extreme popular demands. They scored a series of political victories in the soviets, winning control of the key Petrograd and Moscow soviets by mid-September. Trotsky, released from jail at the time of the Kornilov affair, was elected chairman of the Petrograd Soviet.

At this juncture, Lenin (still hiding in Finland) concluded that the time had come for the Bolshevik Party to attempt the armed seizure of power, overthrow the Kerensky government, and make the soviets the official organs of power. He so instructed the Bolshevik leaders in Petrograd, but the latter, convinced that power was coming to the party more or less democratically, at first resisted his instructions. Against Lenin's wishes, they participated in the Democratic Conference convoked by the Provisional Government to speed consideration of Russia's political future.

The conference merely registered the deepening political cleavages in Russia, between Kerensky and the moderate left, as well as among the government, the right, and the far left. To continue its work until the Constituent Assembly could be convoked, the conference authorized the establishment of a provisional parliament, the Council of the Republic, or Pre-Parliament, composed, like the Democratic Conference, of representatives nominated by the various parties and interest groups. When the Pre-Parliament convened early in October, the Bolsheviks walked out in a gesture of revolutionary defiance. The Second Congress of Soviets had been scheduled for later on in the month, and the Bolsheviks made it clear that they expected this body to resolve the question of power.

Lenin's advocacy of armed insurrection

This was not sufficient for Lenin. On October 20 (October 7, O.S.) he returned secretly to Petrograd to urge the policy of armed insurrection, and on October 23 (October 10, O.S.) the Bolshevik Central Committee voted in principle (with only Kamenev and Grigory Zinoviev in opposition) to "place armed insurrection on the agenda." Meanwhile plans by the government to move the capital to Moscow stirred up rumours that Kerensky meant to surrender Petrograd to the Germans in order to defuse the revolution. Utilizing the consequent state of panic, the Bolsheviks persuaded the soviet to assert emergency authority over the garrison through the Military Revolutionary Committee, finally activated on November 2 (October 20, O.S.). Although it is generally believed (and asserted by the official Soviet historians) that by this time the Bolsheviks were actively planning an armed uprising to coincide with the Congress of Soviets on November 7 (October 25, O.S.), there is no documentation of such planning, and the preponderance of evidence indicates that the Bolshevik leaders were concentrating on defensive measures to prevent another Kornilov-style coup and to protect the Congress of Soviets while it voted itself into

power. This was contrary to Lenin's demands, but he was sidetracked by polemics against the more openly expressed opposition of Zinoviev and Kamenev.

The actual revolution was precipitated by an abortive government crackdown. Angered by the soviets' claim to control the garrison, Kerensky sent troops on the morning of November 6 (October 24, O.S.) to close the Bolshevik newspapers. This was seen by the Bolsheviks as the opening of the expected counter-revolutionary coup. They called out sympathetic troops and the workers' Red Guards to defend the soviet, only to find that effective government forces were almost nonexistent. With most of the city in their hands by evening, the Bolshevik leaders then began a more deliberate take-over of public utilities and government buildings. It is not clear from the evidence whether this preceded or followed Lenin's midnight return from his hiding place to soviet headquarters in the Smolny Institute. On the morning of November 7 (October 25, O.S.), the Bolsheviks proclaimed the overthrow of the Provisional Government. The virtually bloodless siege and capture of the Cabinet members in the Winter Palace that night came as an anticlimax.

The Bolshevik Revolution

The circumstances of the Bolsheviks' armed insurrection turned out, in part by accident, to be close to the strategy Lenin had demanded. Retrospectively, the Bolsheviks' victory can be attributed to a combination of factors—superior organization, skillful manipulation of the mood of the masses, and Lenin's single-minded leadership—but, on balance, their success was more a matter of good fortune and of default, thanks to the dissension and mistakes on the government side.

The Bolshevik coup was quickly ratified by the Second Congress of Soviets, where the Bolsheviks and their allies, the Left Socialist Revolutionaries, had a substantial majority. The soviets were proclaimed to be the ruling organs in Russia, headed by the Soviet Central Executive Committee as a quasi-parliament and by the Council of People's Commissars as the Cabinet. Lenin was designated chairman of the Council of People's Commissars—in effect, prime minister; Trotsky took the post of commissar of foreign affairs; Stalin, in line with his Georgian origin, was made commissar of nationalities. An abortive attempt by Kerensky to return to power with loyal troops and military cadets was quickly put down, and the new Soviet government of the Bolsheviks proceeded to consolidate its hold. Kerensky went into hiding and the following year fled to England and thence to the United States.

The consolidation of the Soviet government. The revolutionary seizure of power by the Bolsheviks in Petrograd in the name of the soviet was quickly followed by similar moves on the part of the local soviets in most other parts of Russia. In Moscow alone there was serious fighting for about a week, before the Soviet forces prevailed over conservative military units. The Soviet take-over was resisted in southern Russia, where the Ukrainian nationalists and the Don Cossacks under General Kaledin established autonomous regimes. Thus, a state of civil war existed from the outset of Soviet rule. As to Finland, its independence was recognized by the Soviet regime in December 1917, in anticipation of a take-over by pro-Bolshevik Finnish revolutionaries.

The Soviet government lost no time in proclaiming its revolutionary intentions in a series of sweeping decrees. The decree on land abolished private property and ordered the distribution of the land to those who worked it, thus ratifying the peasants' land seizures. The decree on peace called for an immediate armistice and a peace "without annexations or indemnities" among all the warring powers, on pain of unleashing the forces of world revolution. These two basic steps were soon followed by decrees legitimizing workers' control in industry; nationalizing the banks; abolishing the old courts and police in favour of revolutionary tribunals and a workers' militia; removing legal class privileges and titles and abolishing inheritance; separating church and state; and establishing the legal equality of the sexes. Calendar reform was proclaimed in order to bring Russia into line with the new-style Western dates in February 1918.

The revolutionary decrees

Aside from these initial steps, there arose a basic disagreement among the Bolshevik leaders over the future shape of the regime. A hard-line faction headed by Lenin and Trotsky insisted on one-party Bolshevik rule, representing the dictatorship of the proletariat. Zinoviev and Kamenev, joined by several of the new people's commissars and seconded by the Left Socialist Revolutionaries, argued for a coalition government in order to avoid violence and defeat. Negotiations among the parties broke down, and only the Left Socialist Revolutionaries joined the Council of People's Commissars.

Suppression of opposition

Meanwhile, the Soviet government was suppressing the Constitutional Democrats and other conservative groups. In December the Cheka (All-Russian Extraordinary Commission for Combatting Counterrevolution and Sabotage—or secret police) was established to root out opposition to the government. The elections to the Constituent Assembly, held as scheduled in November, were disappointing for the Bolsheviks: they won around 25 percent of the seats against an absolute majority for the Right Socialist Revolutionaries, with the rest scattered among the other moderate socialist and conservative groups. The Soviet government allowed the Assembly to convene in January 1918 for one day only; it was then closed down as a counter-revolutionary body.

The appeal for peace by the new Soviet government was rejected by the Allied powers as a betrayal of the war effort. On the other hand, Germany and its allies quickly took advantage of the Soviet proposal, agreed to an armistice on the eastern front, and commenced peace negotiations in the city of Brest–Litovsk in Russian Poland. Confronted with a Soviet determination to turn the negotiations into a forum for revolutionary propaganda, the Germans broke off the talks and resumed their offensive in February 1918, meeting virtually no resistance. Lenin, faced with an imminent threat to his regime, called for acceptance of the German peace terms, assuming that a proletarian revolution was due soon in Germany anyway. He was bitterly resisted by the left wing of the Bolshevik Party, led by Nikolay Bukharin, and by the Left Socialist Revolutionaries, who called for guerrilla war against the Germans as an example to inspire revolutionaries elsewhere. Trotsky took the position "No war, no peace" and abstained on the final vote in the Central Committee, which backed Lenin by a narrow margin.

Treaty of Brest–Litovsk

The Soviet delegates thereupon signed the Treaty of Brest–Litovsk on March 3, surrendering the Baltic provinces, Poland, the Ukraine, Finland, and the Caucasus to German, Austrian, and Turkish occupation. At the cost of a major part of Russia's population and economic resources, Lenin had won a "breathing space" for the consolidation of his rule.

WAR COMMUNISM

The Civil War and intervention. The period of relatively peaceful consolidation for the Soviet government was ended by the outbreak of civil war in May 1918, triggered by a clash between Soviet forces and the troops of the Czechoslovak Legion who were being evacuated from Russia via the Trans-Siberian Railway. Anti-Communist Russians, called the "Whites" and led by officers of the old army, seized this opportunity to take control of most of the country from the Volga River to the Pacific Ocean. Bitter fighting ensued between White units and the Red Army, newly organized by Trotsky (as Commissar of Military Affairs since Brest–Litovsk), and a White thrust on Moscow was barely turned back in August.

Meanwhile, the Allied powers had begun to intervene militarily in Russia. With the original aim of keeping Allied munitions shipments out of German hands, British forces had landed in Murmansk in March by arrangement with the Soviet government. Following the Czech revolt, Great Britain, France, and the United States landed troops in northern Russia, while the U.S. and Japan landed forces in eastern Siberia, all in support of the Whites. The Allied motives were mixed, with Britain and France impelled by the hope both of getting Russia back into the war against Germany and of suppressing the Communist Revolution. Japan was interested in annexing Russian territory, and the United States was concerned mainly to restrain the Japanese and help rescue the Czechoslovaks.

The collapse of Germany and the end of World War I in November 1918 terminated the original excuse for intervention and, at the same time, appeared to herald the world revolution anticipated by the Communists. Intervention now assumed an avowedly counterrevolutionary aim. U.S. Pres. Woodrow Wilson proposed a peace conference on Russia to be held on the Turkish island of Prinkipo (Büyükada), but the Whites, backed by French Premier Georges Clemenceau and British War Secretary Winston Churchill, rejected the idea. The British and French landed additional forces and stepped up their logistical support of the White armies, despite sharp cleavages of opinion at home over the Russian Revolution.

Stiffened by their foreign backing, the Whites launched a series of determined offensives toward Moscow in 1919 —from Siberia under Adm. Aleksandr Kolchak, from the Don region under Gen. Anton Denikin, and from the Baltic region under Gen. Nikolay Yudenich toward Petrograd. Though militarily formidable, the White cause was weakened politically by its authoritarian tendencies, its unwillingness to leave the peasants in possession of the land, and its harsh treatment of non-Russian minorities, particularly the Jews. The Communists had the advantage of interior communications and a spirit of national resistance against foreign intervention. Allied intervention was not sufficiently massive or resolute to be decisive. One by one, the White thrusts were turned back, and, by early 1920, with the capture and execution of Kolchak, the serious challenge of counterrevolution was at an end. Acknowledging the futility of intervention, all the Allied powers, except the Japanese, now withdrew their forces.

Reoccupation of lost territories

In the course of its victories, the Red Army reoccupied much of the territory that had been lost under the Treaty of Brest–Litovsk. Where independent states had been set up under the aegis of the Central Powers—in the Ukraine and in Georgia, Armenia, and Azerbaijan in the Caucasus—local Communists were installed in power to form new soviet republics, linked to Russia by treaty. A similar republic was set up for the area of Belorussia ("White Russia," as distinguished by language, not to be confused with the White Russians in the political sense). In the Baltic region, the Communists were not able to take power; and the republics of Estonia, Latvia, and Lithuania, which had proclaimed their independence when the Armistice ended the German occupation, survived with Allied backing.

Poland, which had similarly proclaimed independence, uniting Polish-speaking territory formerly under German or Austrian rule with German-occupied Russian Poland, was soon at odds with Soviet Russia over the undefined frontier between them. The Poles rejected the Curzon Line proposed by British Foreign Secretary Lord Curzon as Poland's eastern frontier and attacked in the Ukraine in the spring of 1920. The Russians pushed back and very nearly took Warsaw, before a Polish counteroffensive with French staff and logistical support routed the Red Army. In the Treaty of Riga of March 18, 1921, the Russians accepted a frontier leaving considerable Belorussian- and Ukrainian-speaking territory under Polish rule. This region was the object of Soviet annexation in 1939 and again at the close of World War II.

The last White offensive against the Soviet regime was led by Baron Ferdinand von Wrangel from his base in the Crimea in mid-1920. The Red Army, once a settlement with the Poles was in prospect, turned its full force against Wrangel and easily drove him and his army into exile. There remained only the Japanese and White Russian forces in eastern Siberia, with which Moscow dealt through a nominally independent government known as the Far Eastern Republic. In the fall of 1922, the Japanese finally withdrew, the Whites went into exile (mainly in Manchuria), and the Far Eastern Republic was absorbed into Soviet Russia.

The Communist dictatorship. The passions and desperation of the Russian Civil War rapidly transformed the Communist regime into a terroristic one-party dictatorship. With the dissolution of the Constituent Assembly and the suppression of the conservative parties, it was clear that the Bolsheviks (renamed Communists at the Seventh Party Congress in March 1918) would brook no serious challenge to their own power. The Left Socialist Revolutionaries resigned from the Council of People's Commissars in protest against the Treaty of Brest–Litovsk, thus leaving a one-party Communist executive. For a time, along with the Mensheviks and Right Socialist Revolutionaries, they continued to function as opposition parties in the local soviets and in the Central Executive Committee (both of which were given legal sanction as the official organs of government by the first constitution of the Russian Socialist Federated Soviet Republic in July 1918). The outbreak of civil war and the sympathy of the Right Socialist Revolutionaries for the anti-Communist cause led to the prompt outlawing of that party. The Left Socialist Revolutionaries sealed their own doom by an abortive uprising against the Soviet government in July 1918 (intended mainly to provoke a resumption of war with Germany by assassinating the German ambassador). Only the Mensheviks remained, sharply curtailed despite their neutrality in the civil war, until they were finally suppressed and their leaders exiled in 1920. By this time, Lenin had made one-party rule by the Communists a cardinal principle in his doctrine of the dictatorship of the proletariat.

The Civil War and the suppression of opposition parties were accompanied by a rising tide of political violence. Socialist Revolutionaries, true to their terrorist tradition, assassinated a number of Communist leaders and wounded Lenin in August 1918. The Communists replied with **The Red Terror** an avowed campaign of Red Terror, designed to extirpate or terrorize any opposition to the regime within the territory they held. Among both Reds and Whites, the murder of hostages and prisoners and the execution of suspected enemies without trial became the rule. The number of victims probably reached a figure of 100,000 on the two sides. A far greater number of persons, perhaps 2,000,000, mainly of the educated upper and middle classes, were lost to Russia by emigration to escape Communist rule. Russian social life has never recovered the element of sophistication and westernization that these groups represented.

The suppression of opposition parties was paralleled by the development of progressively more authoritarian practices within the Communist Party itself. Though formally democratic in structure and reasonably so in practice in 1917, the party rapidly tightened its internal organization in order to wage civil war and deal with the staggering problems of the Soviet government. The leadership structure was more sharply delineated in 1919 by the creation, in addition to the Central Committee, of a political bureau (Politburo) for policy decision making, an organizational bureau (Orgburo) to supervise the party organization, and a Secretariat to superintend the assignments of individual party members. At the same time, Lenin's principle of "democratic centralism" was affirmed—that party decisions once arrived at had to be obeyed with "iron discipline" by the members and that the decisions of higher party organizations were automatically binding on the local organizations. Utilizing this authority, the party Secretariat commenced the practice of transferring dissidents out of positions of influence and of appointing the secretaries of local organizations to impose party discipline. The stage was thus set for the development of personal control over the party organization by Joseph Stalin after he became general secretary in 1922.

The experiment of War Communism. With the onset of civil war and the emergence of the one-party dictatorship in mid-1918, the Communists abandoned the relatively gradual approach that they had taken in economic and social matters since the October Revolution, an approach characterized by Lenin as "one foot in socialism." Beginning with the sweeping nationalization of large-scale industry in June 1918, an attempt was made to transform Russian society directly into the classless communist ideal. At the same time, a pattern of centralization and coercion was adopted to channel the country's efforts and resources into victory in the civil war. Economic conditions deteriorated rapidly, and by 1921, amid a crisis of opposition within the Communist Party as well as outside, the experiment of War Communism had to be admitted a failure.

Nationalization, initiated ostensibly to forestall German influence, was eventually extended to practically every enterprise of consequence, including small-scale as well as large-scale industry and trading and service enterprises. Workers' control was now rejected by Lenin as an impediment to production; instead, he pressed for one-man management by paid experts, with the tight centralization of overall administration of each industry in the *glavki* ("chief administrations") in Moscow. Nevertheless, industrial production, already declining in 1917 as a result of the disruptions of war and revolution, continued to sag. Transportation (mainly the railroads) was in a critical state, which contributed further to the paralysis of industry. Steel production, for example, fell from a level of 4,200,000 tons in 1913 to a mere 200,000 tons in 1920. Nationalization and centralization

To finance the costs of government and the Civil War, the Soviet regime relied mainly on the printing press (a practice already begun by the tsarist government during the war years), with the inevitable consequence of accelerating inflation. By 1922 the ruble was worth approximately 1/200,000 of its prewar value. Some Communists welcomed the result as a victory over the capitalist economic system, and increasingly the government relied on measures of a "natural economy," rewarding workers with rations in kind, free streetcar tickets, confiscated apartments, and so forth, in place of the depreciated currency. The breakup of the large landholdings and the propensity of the peasants to consume their produce or curtail production rather than sell it for worthless money caused a catastrophic drop in the food available for the urban sector and the army. The Soviet government responded by having grain "requisitioned" by armed detachments, aided by "committees of the Village poor." The consequence was further disruption of food production and a severe alienation of the majority of the peasants, to the point of armed insurrection against the Soviet authorities in some districts of central Russia.

The practices of War Communism—above all the centralizing trend in political life and in industry—evoked within the Communist Party a series of protests by leftwing idealists. These included the "Democratic Centralist" group led by Valerian Osinsky and the "Workers' Opposition" group led by Aleksandra Kollontay and Aleksandr Shlyapnikov (commissars of welfare and of labour, respectively, in 1917–18). With the end of the pressure of civil war in 1920, these groups temporarily made considerable headway.

Soviet Russia experienced its most severe internal crisis after the cessation of civil war. By the end of 1920, the experiment of War Communism, coupled with the wartime disruptions, had brought industry almost to a standstill. The countryside was seething with unrest over the requisitioning of food. Strikes, though outlawed by the Soviet government, erupted in the major cities.

Within the Communist Party, bitter controversy broke out in the winter of 1920–21 over the future of Soviet society, focussed on the test issue of the trade unions. In this controversy, the ultraleft groups, with a goal of democratic communism in mind, called for control of industry by the unions; Trotsky and Bukharin and their followers wanted to absorb the unions into the government and press toward communism by strict discipline and central authority; Lenin, backed by Zinoviev, Kamenev, and Stalin, took the less ambitious stand that industry should be run by qualified managers and that the function of the unions was only to protect the workers. This was a harbinger of the retreat from communism soon to be announced in the New Economic Policy (NEP).

As the delegates of the Communist Party were assembling in March 1921 to resolve their deep disagreements at the Tenth Party Congress, the Soviet regime was confronted by armed challenge in the mutiny of the sailors and garrison at the Kronstadt naval base. The Kronstadt Rebellion was bloodily put down, though it professed to represent the true goals of the revolution. Kronstadt made it clear to Lenin and most of the Communist leadership that a continuation of War Communism would endanger the existence of the Soviet regime. There was virtually no opposition when Lenin called a halt to War Communism and, as a "strategic retreat" of the revolution, introduced the New Economic Policy.

The Kronstadt mutiny

THE NEW ECONOMIC POLICY

The decisive step marking the end of War Communism and the beginning of the era of the New Economic Policy was the suspension of food requisitioning and the introduction of a tax in kind specifying the amounts that each peasant had to contribute. From this there followed a series of measures putting the government on a more legal and orderly basis, while temporarily sacrificing the collectivist and equalitarian goals of the Communist Party. In the perspective of the history of revolution, the NEP had many of the characteristics of a Thermidorean reaction on the model of France in 1794 after the overthrow of the Jacobins. Although the revolutionary party remained in power in the Soviet case, there was a marked psychological relaxation and a turning away from revolutionary extremism.

The policies of the NEP. The NEP was described frankly by Lenin as a retreat from the momentarily unattainable goal of Communism to state capitalism. The monetary system and the market economy were restored. The peasants were allowed to dispose of their produce freely after meeting their tax obligations. Most trading enterprises and much small-scale industry were denationalized, permitting the rise of a new class of small businessmen, the Nepmen. On the other hand, large-scale industry, transportation, public utilities, the financial system, and major natural resources—the so-called "commanding heights"—were kept under state ownership.

State capitalism: denationalization and decentralization

Within the state-owned sector, there were further steps back toward capitalistic economic arrangements. Individual, professional management became the rule, and profit-and-loss accounting was restored. State-owned enterprises traded with each other and sought to grow by earning profits. Wages and salaries were set to reflect effort and responsibility, an acknowledged reversion from the Marxist goal of equality. Economic planning was reduced to a modest effort at forecasting resources, rehabilitating war-torn plants, and building up the infrastructure, particularly electric power.

The NEP quickly achieved a recovery in both agricultural and industrial production, although a drought in 1921 on top of the ravages of War Communism caused a devastating famine in the Volga region in 1921–22 (the occasion of a major international relief effort headed by the U.S. relief administrator Herbert Hoover). By the mid-1920s, most branches of the economy reached prewar levels. A major issue then developed over the manner of future development—an issue between the proponents of gradual growth in the pattern of market socialism, on the one hand, and the advocates of more deliberate planning for a high tempo of industrialization, on the other. The issue was ultimately decided by the political succession struggle that characterized the years of the NEP.

The politics of succession. The leadership of the Communist Party was nominally collective, although Lenin enjoyed such personal force and prestige that his will was seldom resisted successfully by his colleagues. Lenin's illness and then his death, on January 21, 1924, which invited a contest for ultimate control of Soviet Russia, put the system of collective leadership to a test that it could not withstand. By 1928, when the period of the NEP came to an end, the Soviet Union was well on the way to the unrestricted personal dictatorship of Joseph Stalin.

A critical step toward a monolithic system of rule within the Communist party was taken at the Tenth Party Congress in 1921, when it was resolving the crisis of War Communism. At Lenin's behest, the congress condemned the ultraleft factions of the Democratic Centralists and the Workers' Opposition as "petty-bourgeois deviations" and banned any further existence of organized factions within the party. Thus, while Lenin was making economic concessions to the general public on the right and curtailing secret-police terror (the Cheka was curbed and renamed State Political Administration, or GPU), he was cracking down on idealistic sentiment within the party of the left. To underscore this shift of emphasis, the party Secretariat, composed of ideologically oriented friends of Trotsky, was replaced by a more discipline-oriented group (including Vyacheslav Molotov) under the influence of Stalin. A systematic purge of the party membership was instituted in the fall of 1921, expelling individuals guilty of such sins as corruption, incompetence, alcoholism, or opposition; the membership was cut from some 700,000 before the purge to around 400,000 in 1922. Finally, to tighten the organization further, Lenin decided to install Stalin in the new post of General Secretary of the party in April 1922.

The 1921 purge and the rise of Stalin

In May 1922, Lenin fell ill with the first of a series of cerebral hemorrhages. Although Trotsky was clearly the party's second-ranking figure in terms of prestige, he was opposed by all the other members of the Politburo and most of the Central Committee, who backed instead a temporary troika, or triumvirate, of Zinoviev, Kamenev, and Stalin. Recovering briefly in the fall of 1922, Lenin found serious fault with the leadership of the troika, particularly Stalin. In a series of articles and letters, Lenin attacked the reappearance of traditional bureaucratic habits and the lack of systematic economic policy (particularly in the foreign-trade area). He took Stalin particularly to task for his heavy-handed approach in forcing the non-Russian soviet republics to accept formal federation with the Russian Republic in the Union of Soviet Socialist Republics (established in December 1922). Finally, in his so-called "Testament" written December 23–26, 1922, Lenin recognized the personal power that Stalin was accumulating through the party Secretariat and concluded,

Stalin is too rude, and this deficiency, fully tolerable in the milieu and dealings among us Communists, becomes intolerable in the office of General Secretary. Therefore I propose to the comrades to think up a means of transferring Stalin from that position.

Felled by new attacks of arteriosclerosis in December 1922, Lenin turned to Trotsky to lead the attack on Stalin. Trotsky temporized, possibly hoping that he could enlist Stalin against Zinoviev, until then his chief personal antagonist. Stalin continued to tighten his control through the appointment of local party secretaries and the handpicking of congress delegates, and at the Twelfth Party Congress in April 1923 he had effective control of the selection of new members for the expanded Central Committee. By this time, a final stroke had rendered Lenin speechless and removed him from the political scene altogether.

In the fall of 1923, a coalition of Trotsky supporters and former Democratic Centralists launched an open attack on the leadership of the troika, charging economic mismanagement, neglect of the industrial workers, and violation of the principle of democracy within the party. In this "New Course" controversy (so termed from a pamphlet by Trotsky), the opposition was overwhelmed by the organizational machinery of the party and was condemned in January 1924 for factionalism and anti-Marxist deviation. Lenin's death a few days afterward came as an anticlimax; Stalin's leading role at the funeral was symbolic of the advantage that he had already won in the contest for power.

Death of Lenin and final triumph of Stalin

In December 1925 the succession struggle took a new turn, when Zinoviev and Kamenev, alarmed at Stalin's accretion of power, tried to unseat him at the Fourteenth Party Congress. Stalin easily turned back the challenge and removed the Zinoviev supporters from their Leningrad power base.

Early in 1926, Zinoviev and Trotsky finally joined forces in the "United Opposition," waging a desperate battle of polemics with the party leadership for a year and a half. They re-echoed the themes of party democracy and economic mismanagement, criticized the trend toward "State capitalism" and favouritism for the peasants as against the workers, and called for the institution of vigorous planned industrial development to strengthen the proletarian base of Communist rule. In foreign policy, they alleged that the leadership was abandoning the world revolution.

To defend himself from these charges, Stalin appealed to the theory of "Socialism in one country," which he had first suggested in 1924. This was the argument, based on a statement made by Lenin in 1915 and taken out of context, that the Soviet Union could build socialism by itself without waiting, as the Communists had earlier assumed, for the victory of the proletarian revolution in the more advanced countries of the West. The "Socialism in one country" issue is often interpreted to mean that Trotsky and Zinoviev believed in promoting world revolution, whereas Stalin was a Russian nationalist, but in practice there was little difference between the two groups. The significance of "Socialism in one country" lay first of all in the attempt of the opposition to argue that the Party leadership was deviating in an unsocialist direction because of the isolation of the revolution and should therefore be removed. Secondly, the controversy represented a landmark in the manipulation of party doctrine and history by Stalin, who was able to make a palpably false interpretation of Lenin and compel the party to accept this by organizational pressure. This manoeuvre established the pattern, still followed, of ideological reinterpretations imposed by the party leadership to suit the political needs of the moment, with the consequent necessity of strict control over all ideological discussion within the party.

The 1927 purge

Beginning in the fall of 1926, Trotsky, Zinoviev, and their followers were progressively stripped of their party and governmental positions, with the vacancies going to Stalin's followers. At the Fifteenth Party Congress in December 1927, the entire opposition group was expelled from the Communist Party. The Zinoviev–Kamenev group recanted and shortly afterward won temporary readmission to the party. Trotsky and his supporters were exiled, tsarist fashion, to remote parts of the country, Trotsky himself being sent to Alma Ata in Central Asia. A year later, in January 1929, Trotsky was deported from the Soviet Union altogether. After periods of residence in Turkey, France, and Norway, during which he organized the "Fourth International" of anti-Stalinist splinter groups from numerous Communist parties around the world, Trotsky settled in Mexico. He was assassinated in 1940, most probably on orders from Stalin.

Foreign policy during the NEP. Along with their relinquishment of utopian goals in internal affairs, the Soviet leaders were compelled to recognize that the forces of international revolution had subsided. By 1921 Lenin had made it clear that the survival of the Soviet state—if necessary, through accommodation with the major capitalist powers—took precedence over any momentary gains for international revolution.

In 1921 the Soviet Union concluded treaties of peace or nonaggression with its immediate neighbours Poland, the Baltic states, and the Middle Eastern tier of Turkey, Persia, and Afghanistan, where the Soviets endeavoured to align themselves with nationalist sentiment against the European powers. Also in 1921, a trade agreement with Great Britain opened the way to normalization of commercial relations with most of the world.

Treaty of Rapallo and the ally-seeking policy

On April 16, 1922, the U.S.S.R. scored a major diplomatic breakthrough by concluding the Treaty of Rapallo with the Weimar Republic of Germany, providing for diplomatic recognition and secret military collaboration, despite the fact that the German Communists were still attempting revolution. As a sequel to Rapallo the Soviet Union secured diplomatic recognition by Great Britain early in 1924 (by the first Labour government), and soon afterward by most other countries. The United States remained the major holdout—over the issue of repudiated tsarist debts and Communist propaganda—until the advent of the Franklin D. Roosevelt administration in 1933; commercial relations, including the award of business concessions to U.S. firms, nevertheless became active in the 1920s.

Following the achievement of recognition, the U.S.S.R. continued its quest for allies, particularly in the European labour movement and among Asian anti-Western nationalists. In Europe, the Communist parties were brought under tight Soviet control but were directed to curtail revolutionary activity in the interest of collaboration with reformist groups. In Asia, the Soviets vested their hopes in the Chinese Nationalist Party (Kuomintang) of Sun Yat-sen and Chiang Kai-shek, then struggling to extend its power from Canton to the whole of China. The U.S.S.R. supplied advisors, directed the small Chinese Communist Party to work within the Nationalist movement, and helped Chiang organize a Leninist-style one-party system of political controls. Nevertheless, as soon as Chiang had achieved national power in 1927, he purged the Communists from his ranks and abandoned the Soviet alliance. The end of the NEP period saw the U.S.S.R. almost as bereft of allies as the beginning of the era.

Society and culture during the NEP. As in the "Thermidorean" periods of earlier revolutions, Soviet social and intellectual life during the NEP swung back substantially toward the pre-revolutionary norm, far more so than during War Communism or after 1928. In literary and cultural matters the regime was generally content to suppress overt political opposition, allowing a variety of artistic schools to work out their ideas. The same held true for social thought—economic, educational, and philosophical—among representatives of the regime itself. No attempt was made to control the conclusions of scientists. Strictly speaking, the Soviet regime, while dictatorial, was not yet totalitarian; nonpolitical areas were not subjected to the positive and exclusive dictates of official controllers.

Experimentalism and freedom in the arts and sciences

Literature and the arts during the NEP were distinguished by the emergence of a variety of extreme leftist groups, experimenting radically in their respective media and contending for the right to represent the proletariat and the new society. Most notable were the poets Sergey A. Yesenin and Vladimir V. Mayakovsky (both suicides after official controls began to close in), the theatrical directors Konstantin Stanislavsky and Vsevolod Meyerhold (the latter purged in 1938), and the film director Sergey M. Eisenstein. The "proletarian culture" movement of Aleksandr Bogdanov was suppressed, however, in favour of the doctrine that former bourgeois artists and writers could be induced to create in the service of the proletarian state. Overall, Russia's leading role in the international artistic revolution of modernism, begun in the decade before World War I, was sustained.

In education as well as in the arts, a doctrine of service to the proletariat was combined with serious attempts at experimentation. Radical educators, encouraged by Anatoly Lunacharsky, the commissar of education, borrowed from American theories of progressive education and pressed further, in their reaction against discipline, to the doctrine of the "withering away of the school." At the same time, great strides were made in expanding the basic primary and secondary school system, creating the machinery that, by the end of the following decade, substantially wiped out illiteracy among the younger Soviet generation. In higher education, class principles required admission preference for children of workers and peasants, regardless of preparation, to the great detriment of the universities. Much was achieved, however, in the education of the working class (and of many future Soviet leaders) through the so-called rabfak, or workers' night courses.

A liberating attitude toward social mores generally prevailed. The family was regarded as a bourgeois anachronism by many Communist leaders (notably Aleksandra Kollontay, an outspoken exponent of free love). Abortion was legalized and divorce made a matter of request (the so-called postcard divorce). Children were encouraged to inform on anti-Soviet parents. The effect of social change among the mass of the population, however, was probably not as great as during the industrialization era that followed.

Religion continued to be actively discouraged, though not persecuted violently as it had been before 1922. Patriarch Tikhon of the Russian Orthodox Church, elected in 1917 when the office was restored, was arrested in 1922 and thereupon abandoned political opposition to the Soviet regime. After his death in 1925, however, the government kept the office vacant until World War II.

THE STALIN REVOLUTION

In 1928 the relatively relaxed and pluralistic character of Soviet life came abruptly to an end. Joseph Stalin, having made himself to all intents and purposes the unchallenged ruler of the Communist Party, proceeded to impose the controls of the Party on every aspect of life in the Soviet Union, and to use those controls to drive the country through an unprecedented experience of violent economic transformation.

The character and origins of Stalinism

The Stalin revolution had its origins in the circumstances of internal political struggle within the Communist Party. After Stalin had destroyed the Left Opposition of Trotsky and Zinoviev, his next concern was to isolate and discredit the people with whom he had shared the leadership during the NEP—particularly Nikolay Bukharin (editor of the official Party newspaper *Pravda* and chairman of the Comintern, or Third International of Communist parties), Aleksey Rykov (chairman of the Council of People's Commissars after Lenin's death), and Mikhail Tomsky (chairman of the trade unions). In an adroit series of political manoeuvres, Stalin shifted to leftist lines of policy that his colleagues were bound to oppose. Then he brought into play the organizational machinery of party discipline to condemn them for factionalism and deviation.

Stalin's "left turn" began early in 1928, with moves for a more militant stance by the Comintern and with pressure on the peasantry who were failing to sell their grain in the needed amounts. By virtue of Stalin's shift and his evident determination to get rid of them, Bukharin, Rykov, and Tomsky found themselves the leaders of the Right Opposition. There was an open rupture in the Central Committee in July, followed by a decisive battle in the Moscow provincial party organization in the fall, when Stalin's control of the central Secretariat proved decisive. In 1929 and 1930, after they had lost effective power, Bukharin, Rykov, and Tomsky were removed from their posts and relegated to minor jobs. Rykov yielded the chairmanship of the Council of People's Commissars to Molotov in 1930. Tomsky was replaced by Nikolay Shvernik, who served as trade union chief (with an interruption as chief of state after World War II) until 1956. Meanwhile, the policies that Stalin had adopted as a political vantage point for fighting the Right Opposition became permanent commitments, the foundations for a violent and profound transformation of Soviet society.

The Five-Year Plans. The concept of a planned economy—in particular, planned industrial development through investment of governmental funds—was not new with Stalin, though, on the other hand, there was little clear background for it in Marxist or pre-revolutionary Russian thought. Mainly it had its origins in the improvised central industrial administration of War Communism, encouraged by Lenin's admiration for the "war socialism" of German economic controls during World War I. The first substantial steps toward economic planning had been the creation of the State Commission for the Electrification of Russia (Goelro) in 1920 and the State Planning Commission (Gosplan) in 1921.

Gosplan and the growth of centralized economic controls

During the NEP, Gosplan built a highly competent staff of economists studying various planning approaches, some relying more on market mechanisms (the "geneticists") and some stressing the role of deliberate governmental action (the "teleologists"). The planning controversy became deeply involved in the factional struggle within the Communist Party, as the Trotskyists called for an aggressive industrialization drive, while the Stalin–Bukharin leadership held to the virtues of gradualness. Nevertheless, the leadership accepted the concept of comprehensive planning, and the Fifteenth Party Congress in 1927 directed Gosplan to prepare a five-year plan.

During 1928 Stalin repeatedly raised his expectations for the targets of the plan and resorted to the Supreme Economic Council under Valerian Kuibyshev to prepare a more ambitious version. Bukharin vainly supported the caution expressed in the work of Gosplan, which was purged and restaffed early in 1929. In April 1929 the Central Committee adopted the most optimistic variant of the plan, backdated to October 1928. The plan called for more than quadrupling the output of heavy industry and at the same time substantially increasing the output of agriculture and consumer-goods industries.

Implementation of the five-year plan entailed the imposition of much tighter controls over the Soviet economy. The managers of state-owned enterprises lost most of their autonomy; rather than produce for the market as they saw it, they were placed under intense pressure to fulfill specific output plans. The relative autonomy of the trade unions was brought to an end, and their function was redefined from the protection of the workers to the promotion of productivity. All small-scale industry and trade that had been left in private hands during the NEP were renationalized and subjected to the same system of central planning.

The manner in which the five-year plan was adopted precluded the practice of careful, scientific planning. The five-year plan was rather a set of politically prescribed targets, demanding maximum effort. Given the limitations of existing resources and trained manpower, the plan as a whole was unrealizable. As shortages appeared, decisions were made according to the implicit primacy of heavy industry, sacrificing consumer goods and agriculture. Although money incomes rose, particularly with the influx of peasants into industrial jobs, a very substantial inflation caused a serious net decline in consumer real income. To absorb excess purchasing power, the "Turnover" tax—actually a sales tax with high rates depending on the supply of each item—was instituted and still remains the basic Soviet governmental revenue. While the industrialization drive stimulated rapid urbanization all over the country, inadequate provision was made for housing, a chronic Soviet problem ever since.

In December 1932, Stalin proclaimed the First Five-Year Plan completed. Actually it had been in effect only three years and eight months. In the area of heavy industrial construction the results were impressive: steel output up 40 percent, electrical power up 150 percent, machinery output multiplied significantly. On the other hand, the targets for consumer goods production were far underrealized, and agricultural production was woefully inadequate, thanks to collectivization. Statistically, the achievements of the plan were exaggerated by the tabulation of new products at higher prices, a practice that has distorted Soviet economic claims ever since.

The Second Five-Year Plan

The Second Five-Year Plan, initiated in January 1933, ran full term. Consumer needs were more favourably reflected than in the actual conduct of the First Five-Year Plan, and the standard of living recovered appreciably. At the same time, many of the new plants begun in 1929–32 only now went into production, so that output of certain commodities such as steel scored their most spectacular increases during this period. With the Third Five-Year Plan, begun in 1938, the rate of increase sagged again—partly because of the shift of expenditures to armaments and partly because of the impact of the Great Purge (see below) on industrial management. Nevertheless, with all their defects, the five-year plans had accomplished their purpose of turning the Soviet Union into a first-class industrial power and providing the technological foundation for modern war.

Collectivization. The forcible reorganization of the Soviet peasantry into collective farms was the second great accomplishment of the Stalin revolution, closely related to the first, as the economic foundation on which the industrialization drive was based. Like forced-tempo industrialization, compulsory collectivization was hit upon by Stalin as a political expedient, but it answered his economic need for a guaranteed farm surplus and became a permanent commitment of his regime, regardless of cost.

Marxism offered little guidance for the organization of the peasants under socialism, having assumed that capitalism would already have converted them into proletarians or hired labourers. Non-Marxist Russian revolutionary thought stressed the maintenance of the peasant commune as well as the distribution of all land to those who tilled it. This was the program accepted by Lenin in 1917. During the NEP the Soviet peasants were fully individual proprietors, not altogether equal; the class of kulaks—those peasants with above average landholdings and hired labour—grew distinctly stronger. Only a few voluntary communal experiments and a few large-scale state-owned demonstration farms were maintained.

Until 1928 the government induced the peasantry to join cooperatives voluntarily, while meanwhile satisfying their economic needs in return for the sale of food for the urban market. This approach was inherently unsatisfactory, largely because of the propensity of the peasants to consume the produce of confiscated estates that had been the source of a major part of the marketable food supply before the Revolution. There was still enough surplus to feed the cities, but the prospects for supplying a growing industrial labour force were uncertain, and the prewar grain surplus for export and earning foreign exchange had been lost altogether. Faced with this problem, the Trotskyists called openly for exploitive taxation of the peasants to finance the "primary socialist accumulation" of capital for industrial construction.

In the course of his struggle with the Right Opposition in 1928–29, Stalin opted for a more and more ambitious program of collectivization, first couched in voluntary terms, but by the fall of 1929 implemented by force in many parts of the country. The program called for the complete socialization of the peasants' land, tools, and animals. Actual residence was not affected, since the new collective farms were generally based on the villages in which most of the peasantry were concentrated. Legally, each collective farm (*kolkhoz*) was regarded as a cooperative, using land allotted to it by the state, and in return paying taxes and meeting obligatory deliveries of food at prices favourable to the state. Peasants were to be remunerated with a share of the produce in proportion to the amount and skill of their work. Mechanization was supposed to accompany collectivization and to constitute one of its major advantages; in fact, the availability of tractors fell far short of meeting the loss in horses eaten by the peasants. Machinery was not assigned to the *kolkhozy* but was concentrated in "machine-tractor stations" (MTS), which also functioned as centres of political indoctrination and control in the countryside. For special crops and agricultural experiments, the state-owned-and-managed farms (*sovkhozy*) were retained, with labour paid on an industrial basis.

There was widespread peasant resistance to collectivization, not only among kulaks but also among "middle" (that is, self-sufficient) peasants. A significant element in the passive resistance that followed was the slaughter and consumption of livestock rather than surrendering it to the collective; in consequence, over half the national livestock resources were lost in most categories. Resistance was most severe in the major grain-surplus-producing regions (the Ukraine, the Volga region, and the North Caucasus), where the peasants were more prosperous and traditionally more independent, and where the government pushed collectivization earliest and most vigorously to get control of the grain surplus. Active resisters were branded as kulaks; kulaks were denied membership in the collectives and were subjected to "liquidation as a class," that is, deportation en masse to Siberia and central Asia. The toll is unknown, but probably some millions of lives were lost in the deportation process and in the labour camps, where many were incarcerated.

Early in 1930 Stalin criticized the excesses of collectivization and permitted partial decollectivization. The following winter, however, the drive was resumed again and pursued steadily, until by 1936 virtually 100 percent of peasant households were incorporated in some form of collective enterprise. The cost in terms of disruption to agriculture was a serious decline in production, although

at the same time the farms proved their efficacy as a tax-collecting device for the government by delivering steadily larger amounts of grain to the state. The peasants, doubly pinched, were stricken further by the disastrous drought and famine of 1932–33 in the Ukraine and Volga regions. Unlike the famine of 1921–22, the government now refused to admit the existence of the famine and allowed no disaster relief for the suffering areas. As in the dekulakization, the exact loss of life is not known, but it probably reached several million.

The famine crisis prompted the government to make certain concessions in the collective farm system. Each peasant household was allotted a small plot with the right to raise vegetables and livestock for its own use and to sell the surplus in the free *kolkhoz* markets established for this purpose. Certain chronic limitations remained in the system: investments of machinery and fertilizer were inadequate; centralized instructions were inappropriate to the local requirements of farming; and the peasants lacked incentive to work more than a minimum on the collective fields. Collective agriculture remains the weakest single aspect of the Soviet economic system, though it does represent a system of effective political control over the peasantry, and it has assured a minimum grain supply for the cities and the troops in time of war or famine.

Social and cultural policies. The Stalin revolution embodied as its third major aspect, along with industrialization and collectivization, the imposition of totalitarian regimentation in practically all realms of life. With the rise of Stalin, the Communist Party had been subjected to strict centralization of authority within its ranks; after 1928, using the party as his primary agent of control, Stalin extended this pattern to most aspects of Soviet social, cultural, and intellectual life.

The social pattern of the period of the Stalin revolution was based above all on the subordination of the individual to the collective organization. This was most apparent in the elimination of individual economic enterprise among Nepmen and peasants, but it also became the rule among writers, scholars, and scientists. At the same time, the old revolutionary impulse toward collective equality was suspended. Stalin put heavy emphasis on the development of individual responsibility, on the strengthening of the authority of organizers and managers, and on the expansion of wage and salary differentials on the basis of skill and effort. This was no longer represented as a postponement of the Marxian ideal but as a permanent aspect of it.

The educational experimentation of the 1920s was abruptly suspended in 1929 with the replacement of Lunacharsky by Aleksey Bubnov as commissar of education. The new emphasis, under the label "polytechnicism," was heavily toward practical industrial skills. In this realm, the challenge of training uneducated peasants for the tasks and responsibilities of industrial life was a monumental one, but, through a complex network of technical schools and institutes and on-the-job training, the Soviet government made a substantial breakthrough in the modernization of its population.

In 1929 the power of the party was turned on Soviet intellectual life, until then the freest aspect of the system. Beginning with crackdowns on the philosophers and historians, every academic and artistic field was subjected to the dictates of extreme Marxism and the imposition of strict party controls. Typically, the party found a leader in each particular field who represented the doctrinaire Marxist view—notably, the historian Mikhail Pokrovsky and the literary critic Leopold Averbakh—and gave them authority to impose the party line on their colleagues. "Bourgeois" (that is, nonconformist) thinkers and artists were silenced or, in many cases, imprisoned. Immediate technological or propaganda contributions to production were the overriding demand. Few artistic works of merit were produced, with the notable exception of Mikhail Sholokhov's novels. Overall, the doctrine of *partiinost*—party spirit—was stressed, entailing party judgments in every field as to the ultimate truth and the appropriateness of any piece of work. Party judgment, in turn, ultimately meant Stalin's personal judgment.

Forced collectivization: the *kolkhozy* and *sovkhozy*

Chronic problems in agriculture

Suppression of freedom in the arts and sciences

Foreign policy in the "third period." During War Communism, Soviet foreign policy had been characterized by defiance of the outside world; during the NEP it had involved a search for allies. During the period of the Stalin revolution Soviet foreign policy took still another turn in consonance with the domestic radicalism of the period. Essentially, the years 1928–34 witnessed a resumption of revolutionary rhetoric and a tendency in practice to withdraw into diplomatic isolation, although trade with the West and the solicitation of Western engineering services were pursued vigorously in support of the Five-Year Plan.

Commencing in 1928, the so-called left turn was enjoined on the parties of the Comintern, with emphasis (particularly in Germany) on hostility toward the Social Democrats and reformist governments (labelled "Social Fascism"). In consequence, the Soviet Union did nothing to prevent the rise of Hitler, hoping he would pave the way for Communist revolution in Germany. Hitler's victory and his avowed plans to expand eastward soon made it clear that the U.S.S.R. needed a new diplomatic approach.

In Soviet–Far Eastern relations much the same crisis developed even earlier. Relations with China had degenerated to the point of armed clashes in Manchuria in 1929. In 1931, with the rise of Japanese militarism and the Japanese occupation of Manchuria, a new and more serious threat emerged. By 1933, the Soviet Union was confronted with the spectre of aggressive enemies both to the West and to the East and an absence of any allies at all. The stage was thus set for the fundamental change in Soviet foreign policy characteristic of the period of collective security.

THE PURGES AND THE CONSOLIDATION OF STALINISM

The Great Purge. By 1934 the essential framework of Stalinist society had been laid down in the economic and political structure of the Soviet Union. The country was nevertheless in a state of severe tension and unrest, not only among the masses who had experienced the privations of collectivization, famine, and forced industrialization, and among the intellectuals newly subjected to severe regimentation, but within the party hierarchy as well, where misgivings about the rigours of Stalin's approach had never been entirely overcome. These were the circumstances in which Stalin launched the Great Purge, involving the arrest, exile, or liquidation of some millions of persons, mainly Communists and officials in Soviet government and industry.

Although the Right Opposition had been hopelessly defeated by 1929, occasional manifestations of opposition by small groups in the party continued, mainly over the issue of collectivization. These critics were uniformly denounced as counter-revolutionary, expelled from the party, and turned over to the police. The rank and file of the party were subjected to a purge in 1929 similar to the purge of 1921, directed officially at personal inadequacies but also at opposition sympathies. In 1933 the purge was renewed, in the course of re-issuing party cards. Meanwhile, the practice of staging show trials with elaborate confessions was begun with a series of groups accused of "wrecking" and sabotage. In all cases, the culprits—mainly managers and economists of bourgeois background—were found guilty and sentenced to long terms.

The critical event signalling the advent of the Great Purge was the assassination of Sergey Kirov, Leningrad party secretary and Politburo member, in December 1934. Kirov was thought to be Stalin's chosen second-in-command, but he had recently become associated with the protests against collectivization; he apparently figured in moves to alleviate the lot of the peasants and consumers. There is some evidence that Stalin had the secret police (absorbed into the Commissariat of Internal Affairs, or NKVD, under Genrikh Yagoda in 1934) arrange or allow the assassination of Kirov in order to eliminate a potential challenger.

In any event, Kirov's murder was taken as the pretext for a sweeping roundup of old oppositionists in Leningrad, including Zinoviev and Kamenev and most of their known sympathizers. Zinoviev and Kamenev were put on

The purges of 1929 and 1933

trial in 1935 on charges of abetting the assassination and were sentenced to long terms. The following year, in the first of the "Moscow trials," Zinoviev and Kamenev and their principal followers were tried again for conspiring to assassinate the entire Soviet leadership; they confessed to the charge, were condemned to death, and shot.

The Zinoviev–Kamenev trials opened the most familiar aspect of the purges—namely, the show trials of the old Communist oppositionists. The 1936 trial was followed early in 1937 by the trial of the principal supporters of Trotsky, including Karl Radek and Grigory Pyatakov. The charges were extended to include conspiring with Germany and Japan to partition the U.S.S.R. Again the defendants confessed and were condemned to death or long prison terms.

The third trial, in 1938, was the most bizarre. The leaders of the Right Opposition, including Bukharin and Rykov, were accused along with additional Trotskyists and physicians and with Yagoda, who as head of the NKVD had prepared the first trial. The charges included the medical murders of Maksim Gorky and others, and a plot in 1918 to depose and assassinate Lenin. All confessed again (with the exception of the former Trotskyist party secretary Nikolay Krestinsky), and most were shot.

There has been much speculation over the reasons for the uniform confessions to clearly absurd charges. Most probably it was a combination of torture, psychological pressure, and promises of leniency for the accused or their families. A number of former oppositionists were not brought to trial but simply liquidated without publicity, and it can be presumed that this was the fate of individuals who could not be induced to confess.

Alongside the spectacular liquidation of the old opposition leaders, a sweeping, though unpublicized purge of the newer, Stalinist party leaders was conducted in 1937 and 1938. The reasons are generally obscure, but, in any event, members of almost the entire party hierarchy below the rank of the Politburo and over the age of 35 were secretly arrested and executed; two members of the Politburo, five of the six candidate members, and over two-thirds of the Central Committee elected at the Seventeenth Party Congress in 1934 were liquidated. The purge was particularly severe in the non-Russian Soviet republics, where virtually the entire party and government leadership were liquidated on the charge of "bourgeois nationalism."

Purges of the newer party leaders

Simultaneously with the purge of the party hierarchy, the "Yezhovshchina" (the "Yezhov business," named for the new head of the NKVD) extended down into the government bureaucracy, industrial management, cultural circles, and the army. The chief of staff, Marshal Mikhail Tukhachevsky, and seven other Red Army commanders were brought to trial in June 1937 on charges of conspiring with Germany and were executed. Most of the upper-grade officers of the army were likewise liquidated or committed to labour camps (from which many returned in the hour of need in 1941). Numerous intellectual figures who had incurred Stalin's ire also perished, usually without mention. Altogether, in the dragnet of forced confessions and fabricated incriminations, some millions of Soviet officials, high and low, with members of their families, were caught up and executed, jailed, or exiled.

The reasons for the Great Purge remain obscure and controversial. The official charges of wrecking, espionage, and counter-revolutionary activity were repudiated by Nikita S. Khrushchev in 1956, when he "rehabilitated" all the victims except those accused in the Moscow trials. Some authorities hold that periodic mass purging is inherent in the maintenance of totalitarian personal control over the bureaucracy. Others believe that the purges of the late 1930s were a distinct aberration, as the secret police instrument got temporarily out of hand. Still others see the period as the manifestation of a psychotic state of paranoid suspicion on the part of Stalin himself. It does seem clear, in view of the damage done to Soviet administration, industry, and the army, that the purge was an irrational phenomenon, detracting from, rather than adding to, the strength of the dictatorship. No further purge of similar scale has occurred, although lesser purges of the same nature continued, particularly in the late 1940s.

The Stalin constitution. Simultaneously with the onset of the purges, Stalin took steps to improve the democratic appearances of his regime, notably by introducing the Stalin Constitution in 1936. Reportedly drafted by Bukharin shortly before he was arrested, the constitution abolished the structure of local soviets, indirectly elected and class-based, which had constituted the formal basis of government since 1917. The new soviets were directly

Establishment of a parliamentary and democratic facade

elected by universal suffrage, culminating at the top in the Supreme Soviet, a directly elected, parliamentary-style body, bicameral in composition (the Soviet of the Union and the Soviet of Nationalities). Nominally, the Council of People's Commissars was responsible to the Supreme Soviet. The chairman of the Presidium of the Supreme Soviet functioned as ceremonial chief of state (Mikhail Kalinin, from 1919 to 1946). The individual rights traditional in democracies were guaranteed, along with the right to work and other economic rights. In practice, the constitution was vitiated by the de facto power of the Communist Party, which controlled all nominations, and the practice of treating any manifestation of opposition as a criminal and anti-Soviet act.

The constitution continued the formal federal structure of the U.S.S.R. and even accorded union republics the right of secession. Five new republics had meanwhile been added, for a total of 11, by partitioning the Turkic and Iranian-speaking areas of Central Asia from the Russian Republic—the Uzbek, Turkmen, and Tadzhik republics in 1929, and the Kazakh and Kirghiz republics in 1936. On the other hand, the actual autonomy of the union republics was strictly limited by the centralized authority of the Communist Party, which subordinated all of them to Moscow. Cultural and linguistic autonomy of the non-Russian nationalities had been encouraged in the 1920s, but in the purge period it yielded to a renewed Russification effort in many regions. Accompanying this was the severe shake-up of the republic governments and Communist Party organizations in the purge itself.

New doctrine and theory resting on the permanency of the state

In line with the more conventional appearances of the Stalin constitution, Soviet legal doctrine and political theory were fundamentally revised during the later 1930s. Older revolutionary notions, expressed in the formulas, "the withering away of the state" and "the withering away of law"—conceiving government and law as essentially transitional devices to combat the remnants of capitalism—were rejected in favour of emphasizing the permanent or very long-term functions of the state and law in the development and protection of the communist society. The legal theoreticians of the old school were purged, and Andrey Vyshinsky, prosecutor at the Moscow trials, became the chief spokesman for the new "socialist law." Subsequently, a reasonably orderly legal procedure, both civil and criminal, has prevailed, except in the case of political crimes. In political theory Stalin himself made the basic pronouncements at the Eighteenth Party Congress in 1939, stressing the positive role of the state, the armed forces, and the police even after the presumed attainment of the communist society.

The culture of Stalinism. A remarkably consistent shift, analogous to Stalin's new legal and political interpretations, characterized most fields of Soviet thought and culture after 1934. Using the machinery of Communist Party control imposed on Soviet cultural life in the service of extreme Marxist doctrines during the period of the First Five-Year Plan, Stalin and his lieutenants now ordered a shift in the party line in one field after another, away from the revolutionary mode and toward traditional and conservative models, though all in the name of Marxism. Writers, artists and scholars who attempted to adhere to earlier, more obviously Marxist ideas were swept away in the purges. By 1939 Soviet cultural life was cast in the mold that has essentially contained it ever since—restrictive in form, conservative in substance, revolutionary in labels.

Control of arts and sciences

The writers were the first to feel the new strictures, beginning as early as 1932 with the manifest failure of proletarian propagandistic writing. The Russian Associa-

tion of Proletarian Writers (RAPP), which had controlled the field since 1929, was dissolved and replaced by the Union of Soviet Writers. The new line was enunciated in 1934—Socialist Realism, meaning in practice artistic work that was traditional in form, accessible to the masses, hortatory, and optimistic. Similar standards were enjoined on all other fields of artistic creation during the next few years. Modern art and literary experimentation were condemned as "bourgeois formalism," and their dissemination was altogether banned.

The sciences were affected less severely and somewhat later. Work in the physical sciences generally proceeded without interference, except when philosophical issues were involved. The theory of relativity, for example, was condemned as a bourgeois idealist doctrine. Biology, and particularly genetics, was subjected to increasingly severe political interference, as the party gave official sanction to Trofim Lysenko (*q.v.*) and his theory of acquired characteristics. The eminent Soviet geneticist Nikolay Vavilov was purged and perished in a labour camp.

In historical teaching and research, ultra-Marxism was condemned in 1934 in favour of a more conventional approach stressing nationalism and great leaders, though still couched in Marxist language. A related reversal was imposed on the behavioral sciences, dismissing modern deterministic and analytical approaches to the study of man and emphasizing the traditional model of rationality, will power, and incentives. Freudian psychology was condemned as "reactionary idealism."

Soviet educational policies shifted similarly. Beginning in 1934, traditional discipline, examinations, and the like were restored. The polytechnic approach was dropped in favour of a classical secondary school curriculum, heavily oriented toward language and science, for those who could master it. Educational preference for children of proletarians was abandoned in the late 1930s in favour of a combination of merit and political reliability.

Stalin's concern for order

Changes in the area of social policy reflected the Stalin regime's paramount concern with order and discipline. The loose family legislation of the 1920s was abolished; in 1936, new laws banned abortion and made divorce difficult and expensive. Leniency toward crimes on the part of juveniles and the insane yielded to much stricter definitions of responsibility. Labour regulations put a premium on discipline, punctuality, and incentives. In 1935 there was launched the "Stakhanovite" movement (named after a Donets coal miner, Aleksey Stakhanov, whose team had speeded up output remarkably); it rewarded "shock brigades" and "innovators" with higher pay and other privileges and dramatized the stress on individual productive effort in the service of the state. Overall, the regime acquired an aura of grim puritanism, compared by some commentators with the Protestant ethic that earlier spurred the forces of industrial revolution in the West.

Soviet foreign policy in the era of collective security. The external threats that Soviet Russia faced by 1933 as a diplomatically isolated and internally hardpressed power were sufficient to compel a basically new approach in foreign policy. The architect of this shift was Maksim Litvinov, commissar of foreign affairs from 1931 to 1939. Under Litvinov, and with Stalin's implicit backing, the Soviet Union commenced a pragmatic search for allies and supporters, in the Comintern in the form of the Popular Front and diplomatically in the policy of collective security.

The Popular Front movement

In the international Communist movement, by 1934, the ultraleft stance of the "third period" had given way to the quest for political accommodation with socialist, reformist, or nationalist groups and governments. The new strategy was formalized by the Seventh (and last) Congress of the Communist International in 1935, with the doctrine of the Popular Front allying Communists with any other anti-Fascist elements.

In 1936 the Popular Front tactic succeeded in bringing Communist-supported governments to power in France and Spain. The ensuing Spanish Civil War constituted a severe test of collective security, as the Soviets endeavoured to expand their influence in Spain while restraining the extremist revolutionaries so as not to alarm the potential allies of the Soviet Union.

Meanwhile, the Soviet Union concluded an agreement for diplomatic recognition by the United States in 1933, joined the League of Nations in 1934, and entered into defensive military alliances of the traditional type with France and Czechoslovakia in 1935. Litvinov became a familiar figure in the League of Nations, espousing disarmament and collective security against aggression. Collective security finally collapsed in 1938, however, when Britain and France came to terms with Nazi Germany at Munich. Stalin apparently interpreted the Munich agreement as a free hand for Hitler in the East. He thereupon replaced Litvinov with Molotov early in 1939 and began to explore possibilities of accommodation with the Germans.   (R.V.D.)

V. The U.S.S.R. since 1939

PRELUDE TO WAR

Military and diplomatic preparations for war

As the year 1939 opened, the storm clouds of an impending war cast their shadow over Soviet life. The rising power of Hitler's Germany posed dangers that could not be ignored. During the Second Five-Year Plan (1933–37), Soviet defense industries expanded about two and a half times as rapidly as industry as a whole. The military and naval budget rose from 1,420,700,000 rubles in 1933 to 23,200,000,000 rubles in 1938, and by 1940 it had reached 56,800,000,000 rubles. New industrial centres were erected beyond the Urals, and military industries were dispersed with the contingency of war in mind. The size of the standing army was greatly increased; the Universal Military Service Act of 1939 made service in the armed forces obligatory for all citizens of the U.S.S.R. The draft age was lowered to 19, the age limits for reservists increased from 40 to 50, and the terms of service substantially lengthened in the air force, the navy, and other branches with special technical requirements.

Despite these intensive military preparations, the state of the Soviet armed forces left much to be desired. The purge of the officer corps following the execution of Marshal Mikhail Tukhachevsky and other high-ranking generals in 1937 for alleged "treason to the Fatherland" and Stalin's decision to keep the army under the closest political supervision weakened the authority of the military command structure and deprived it of some of its most professional and experienced leadership. The damaging effects of the Great Purge were also registered in a slowing up in the rate of industrial growth and in a lag in technical innovation in weaponry. Although desperate efforts were made to modernize the military equipment of the Soviet Army during the middle and late '30s—advanced designs in tanks and aircraft were on the drawing board and in prototype—the existing stock, except for artillery, did not compare in quality or performance with the equipment the Nazis already had available in 1939.

Clearly the Soviet leaders were not ready for war, though this did not deter them from proclaiming their invincibility. Hitler, after disposing of Austria and Czechoslovakia, turned his energies eastward, hurling threats against Poland. If Poland succumbed, or joined with Germany, and if the Western powers stood aside, the Soviet Union would be left alone. The British declaration of March 31, 1939, concurred in by the French, that they would "lend the Polish government all support in their power" in the event of a Nazi attack, gave Moscow room to manoeuvre. If it joined in the British–French guarantee and concerted its military plans with the western Allies, there was the possibility that Hitler might be deterred; but there remained the great risk that Hitler would persevere in his invasion plans and that the Soviet Union would then find itself embroiled in a war in which it would receive the main brunt of Nazi military action. If, on the other hand, it held off from participation in the British–French guarantee, with its implicit commitment to join in a war against Hitler, and banked on the possibility that Hitler wished to avoid a two-front war, it might extract concessions from the Nazis as the price of Soviet neutrality. In the event, Hitler proved ready to

bargain. The result was the German–Soviet Nonaggression Pact of August 23, 1939, with its secret protocol providing for the partition of Poland between Germany and the Soviet Union, reserving Lithuania to the German sphere of influence and giving the Soviet Union a free hand in Estonia, Latvia, Finland, and Bessarabia. On September 1 the German armies marched into Poland, and two days later France and Britain declared war on Germany.

WORLD WAR II

Consolidation in eastern Europe. The outbreak of World War II seemed at first to represent a triumph of Soviet diplomacy. Vast territorial gains were achieved with virtually no effort. The expectation that Germany and the western Allies would wear each other out in a bloody and prolonged war of attrition opened up the prospect that the Soviet Union would emerge as the arbiter of Europe's destinies. But unfolding events betrayed Stalin's calculations. The quick collapse of Polish resistance and the decision of the French high command not to advance against the Germans aroused the most acute apprehensions in Moscow. Stalin undertook to ease possible friction with Germany in Poland by yielding the provinces of Lublin and Warsaw to Hitler in exchange for most of Lithuania. Meanwhile, Moscow moved swiftly to consolidate its new-found gains and improve its defensive posture. The Polish territories assigned to it were occupied by the Soviet Army and absorbed into the White Russian and Ukrainian Soviet republics. The fate of the three Baltic states was settled, first by military occupation and then, in August 1940, by annexation to the Soviet Union. Finland proved more difficult. When the Finns refused to cede territories and yield naval bases that the Soviets deemed vital to the defense of Leningrad, the Soviet Army invaded Finland. The so-called Winter War, which lasted from the end of November 1939 to March 1940, proved costly to the Russians. The Finns offered fierce resistance, attracting worldwide sympathy and support for their cause. Although the Soviet Army finally succeeded in breaching the Mannerheim line, Soviet casualties were large and the army's performance was unimpressive. Hitler concluded that the U.S.S.R. was militarily weak and that he could afford to press his aggressive designs without much concern for Soviet reactions.

The German occupation of Denmark and Norway in April 1940, and the crushing defeat of the Anglo-French armies in June, reinforced Soviet fears and apprehensions. All Europe appeared to be at Hitler's feet. The question was no longer who would win a war of attrition in western Europe but rather which way the Nazi juggernaut would turn next—against Britain or the Soviet Union. The Soviet response was fourfold. First, it accelerated its efforts to strengthen its armaments industry, modernize its military equipment, and prepare its armed forces for war. Second, it sought to expand its borders, particularly at the expense of Romania, and to limit Nazi penetration into Finland, eastern Europe, and the Balkans. Third, it undertook to protect its Far Eastern flank by concluding a neutrality and nonaggression pact with Japan. Finally, it did what it could to placate Hitler by giving trade concessions and abstaining from anti-German propaganda or other provocatory gestures.

The Soviet seizure of the Romanian territories of Bessarabia and Bukovina in late June 1940 exacerbated Nazi–Soviet relations. Hitler's reply was to move German troops into what remained of Romania. By late July, Hitler had reached a tentative decision to invade the Soviet Union, though the official directive for "Operation Barbarossa" was not signed until December 18, 1940. Other preparatory moves were made. German armed forces were granted the right of passage through Finnish territory. On September 27, 1940, Germany, Italy, and Japan concluded a Tripartite Pact proclaiming the "leadership of Germany and Italy in the establishment of a new order in Europe" and according a similar status to Japan in Greater East Asia. In November Vyacheslav M. Molotov, then head of government as well as foreign

The uneasy truce with Hitler

commissar, was invited to Berlin, where Hitler offered the Soviet Union a chance to share in the spoils of the "bankrupt" British Empire by expanding in the direction of the Indian Ocean. The Soviet reply was to accept the offer, provided German troops were withdrawn from Finland and the Soviet Union was permitted to establish military bases in Bulgaria. Hitler's response was to move troops into Bulgaria and later into Yugoslavia and Greece. His determination to consolidate his hold on the Balkans and strengthen his ties with Finland foreshadowed the coming invasion. In this increasingly ominous situation Stalin scored at least one diplomatic coup. The negotiation of the Soviet–Japanese Neutrality Pact of April 13, 1941, held out the hope that Japan would not join in a strike against the Soviet Union.

By late spring German preparations for the onslaught on the U.S.S.R. became so obvious that it seemed impossible to ignore them: German troops were massing on the Soviet frontier; German overflights of Soviet territory were virtually a daily occurrence; intelligence reports testified to Nazi intentions. Yet Stalin persisted in behaving as if war could be averted. Large-scale shipments of Soviet materials to Germany continued. The Soviet press derided the idea that there might be a war with Germany. Soviet frontiers were poorly defended. Front-line troops were ordered not to respond to Nazi provocations. There seems to have been no carefully drawn plan of defense against a surprise attack. One can only speculate that Stalin believed to the end that Hitler would not march, or that he could be appeased by concessions. Hitler made no demands. In the early dawn of June 22, 1941, the German divisions crossed the borders and advanced rapidly, meeting little resistance.

The German offensive. The first phase of the war was a Soviet disaster. The Luftwaffe dominated the air, destroying some 2,000 Soviet planes in the first two days of the war and subjecting the retreating troops to incessant bombing and machine-gunning. German tank columns contributed to the disorganization of the Soviet Army. Hundreds of thousands of Soviet soldiers were killed during the early days of the war, and many more hundreds of thousands were encircled and taken prisoner. By mid-November the German army was at the gates of Leningrad, had penetrated into the suburbs of Moscow, had captured Kiev, and was in occupation of the whole of the eastern Ukraine and most of the Crimean Peninsula.

Leningrad and stiffening of Soviet resistance

As the Germans began to outrun their supply lines, Soviet resistance stiffened. Leningrad held firm. In early December the Soviet command, with the aid of fresh troops hurriedly brought from Siberia, launched a counteroffensive on the Moscow front that pushed the Germans back as much as 200 miles in some areas. Soviet forces also recaptured the Kerch Peninsula in the Crimea.

By the end of 1941 it was already clear that the quick victory on which Hitler was counting had eluded him. Soviet losses had been huge, but German casualties were also heavy (1,250,000 in the first 12 months). The Russian winter was hard on German troops and equipment. Supplying them was becoming increasingly difficult because of long lines of communications, poor roads, shortages of railway rolling stock, and guerrilla attacks in rear areas. The Soviets had recovered from their early panic and were beginning systematically to rebuild their army, reorganize their armaments industries, and gird their forces for a long war. Over 1,500 factories, including 1,360 armaments plants, were evacuated with their workers from European U.S.S.R. to the east. During the next years they were to contribute significantly to the mounting supply of planes, tanks, and munitions; together with British and American Lend-Lease aid, they helped turn the tide of battle.

Stalingrad. After the grim winter of 1941–42 the Germans returned to the attack. In May they recaptured the Kerch Peninsula and routed three Soviet armies that sought to liberate Kharkov; in early June they completed their occupation of the Crimea by overwhelming the defenders of Sevastopol. Toward the end of June they launched a major offensive in the direction of Voronezh. Halted there, they turned south toward Stalingrad (now Volgograd), where they again met stubborn resistance. Farther to the south they scored a series of victories, occupying the rich Donets Basin, capturing Rostov, and overrunning the Kuban granary. Turning in the direction of the Caucasus, they seized the Maykop oil fields and drove toward Baku, but they were finally stopped in the mountains that stood between them and their objective. By this time the German armies were dangerously dispersed, and the Soviet high command began preparations for a new counteroffensive. Hitler's insistence that the Battle of Stalingrad be fought to a successful finish and that no retreat be tolerated provided the Russians with their opportunity. Marshalling fresh reserves, the Soviet forces under the command of Gen. Georgy Zhukov encircled the German 6th Army in Stalingrad and barred the way to German columns sent to relieve it. In Stalingrad more than 200,000 German soldiers perished. On February 2, 1943, the remaining 91,000 men of the 6th Army surrendered after their commanding general, Friedrich Paulus, and 23 other generals had been taken prisoner. The German defeat at Stalingrad marked the turning point of the war. Although many bitter battles remained to be fought, the U.S.S.R. had reason to be confident that it would emerge victorious.

Victory at Stalingrad

In the aftermath of Stalingrad the German armies began to yield ground. Fearing that their forces in the Caucasus would be cut off, they managed an orderly withdrawal, but with the Soviet Army in hot pursuit they abandoned Rostov and retreated into the Ukraine. In mid-February Soviet troops fought their way into Kharkov, but the German general Erich von Manstein staged a successful counterattack, pushing the Soviets back across the Donets River and reoccupying Kharkov on March 12, 1943. Meanwhile, however, the Germans were forced to withdraw from the Vyazma salient near Moscow; and Soviet forces in the Leningrad area broke through the blockade lines over a seven-mile front and established a precarious railway link with the rest of the U.S.S.R. Hitler's final bid for victory—the July battle for the Kursk salient, in which he hoped to trap and annihilate four Soviet armies —proved a fiasco. The Germans were thrown back with heavy losses, and the Soviet Army advanced on a wide front, recapturing Kharkov, Kiev, and Smolensk. By the end of 1943 the Soviet Army had liberated nearly two-thirds of the vast areas seized by the Nazis.

The advance into Europe. Soviet military historians describe 1944 as the "Year of the Ten Blows." The first, which came in January, freed Leningrad from encirclement. The second, struck in the Ukraine in February and March, forced a German retreat to the old Polish and Romanian borders. The third, in April and May, resulted in the recapture of the Crimea. The fourth was directed against the Karelian Isthmus and forced the Finns out of the war. The fifth, in June–July, was aimed at German Army Group Centre and resulted in the capture of 30 German divisions, the seizure of Minsk and Vilnius, and the clearing of the road to the Vistula and Warsaw. The sixth hammered German forces in Galicia and resulted in the capture of Lvov on July 25 and a march to the San and Vistula rivers and the Carpathian passes. The seventh was directed against the German and Romanian armies along the Dnestr River. It produced the unconditional surrender of Romania on August 23 and opened the road to Hungary and the Balkans. The eighth carried the Red Army to Yugoslavia and Hungary. The ninth cleared the Baltic states, cutting off a number of German divisions in Courland. The final blow was directed against the Petsamo region and northern Norway.

By January 1945, when the Soviet Army launched its final drive toward Berlin, it possessed a decisive superiority in troops, aircraft, tanks, artillery, and munitions. The Soviet advance was rapid. In the north, two army groups invaded East Prussia. In the centre, General Zhukov drove from the Vistula directly toward Berlin. To the south, I.S. Konev's armies cleared Upper Silesia. Farther south, Gen. R.Ya. Malinovsky and Gen. F.I. Tolbukhin occupied Austria and Slovakia. In early March, Soviet forces established bridgeheads across the Oder, and by April 25 Berlin was completely surrounded. On April 30

Final drive toward Berlin

The expansion of Russia, 1300—1796.

From W. Shepherd, *Historical Atlas;* Barnes & Noble Books, New York

The Principality of Moscow about 1300	Fyodor I and Boris Godunov (1584–1605)
The Grand Principality of Moscow in 1462	Michael Romanov (1613–45)
Acquisitions under	Alexis (1645–76)
Ivan III the Great (1462–1505)	Peter I the Great (1682–1725)
Vasily III (1505–33)	Anna (1730–40)
Ivan IV the Terrible (1533–84)	Elizabeth (1741–62)
	Catherine II the Great (1762–96)

Hitler committed suicide. By May 2 the last pockets of Nazi resistance in Berlin were eliminated, and a joyful Soviet nation celebrated victory.

The sacrifices of the war

The war had entailed bitter sacrifices for the Soviet people. Some 15,000,000 to 20,000,000 soldiers and civilians were killed, and many millions more were maimed, wounded, or weakened by malnutrition. The material losses were equally staggering. Officially estimated at 679,000,000,000 rubles, they spelled destruction on so vast a scale as to pose a colossal task of reconstruction. The stoicism with which the Soviet populace endured its suffering had few parallels in history. After the panic and disorganization of the first phase of the war, the will to resist stiffened. Stories of brutal treatment of Soviet prisoners of war and Nazi atrocities in occupied areas contributed to a deep hatred for the German invaders. As the armed forces drained factories and farms of manpower, the women, old men, and children who replaced them worked all the harder because they were bound to the front by the knowledge that the fate of husbands, brothers, and sons depended on them. The reservoirs of patriotic sacrifice on which the regime was able to draw helped to ensure its survival.

Stalin, in his first broadcast to the nation on July 3, 1941, was wise enough to identify himself with this patriotic upsurge and to exploit it to the full. The war became the Great Patriotic War, the Great Fatherland War, and a National War of Liberation. The cult of Stalin fused with the new patriotism. Slogans of class struggle were put aside, at least temporarily. Anti-religious propaganda was subdued, church leaders were wooed, the patriarchate was restored, and the church faithful joined in defense of their country. A new national anthem replaced the "Internationale." The Army was glorified, and patriotic slogans dominated the mass media. The nationalist revival that Stalin led was an important key to victory.

Perhaps equally significant was the ruthless determination of the Soviet leadership to gear the economy to the needs of the front. Beginning in 1942, the industries evacuated to the east and new factories and mines began to lift the tempo of production. In 1943 tank production totalled 19,500 and included such advanced models as the T-34, one of the best medium tanks used in the war. In the same year, 35,000 planes were produced, an increase of 37 percent over 1942. During the next years, production of all types of arms continued to increase. Soviet production was supplemented by a mounting flow of supplies from Britain and the United States. By the end of the war, U.S. Lend-Lease aid to the Soviet Union totalled $9,100,000,000; U.S. trucks and Jeeps had contributed significantly to the mobility of the Soviet Army.

The war alliance. The Soviet–British–U.S. alliance during the war proved a troubled partnership. Relations were poisoned by Stalin's deep-seated suspicion that the delay in opening a second front in the west represented a deliberate effort to bleed and weaken the Soviet Union. Once the tide of battle had turned and victory appeared inevitable, the conflicting interests of the Allies came more sharply into focus. The initial clashes centred on the future of Poland. For Stalin, security considerations dictated the installation of a "friendly" regime in Poland, and in his eyes the only friendly regime was a Communist-dominated one. The British and Americans pressed instead for a freely elected Polish government. The disposition of the Soviet forces at the end of the war made certain that Stalin would have his way, but at the price of the war alliance. His diplomatic moves at the conferences of Teheran, Yalta, and Potsdam, and his actions in the closing days of the war and in the immediate postwar period, revealed that he was determined to assume a dominant position in eastern Europe and to regain the Far Eastern territories lost in the Russo-Japanese War of 1904–05. But his claims extended farther. They included a military base on the Turkish straits, which would enable the Soviet Union to control access to the Black Sea; trusteeship of one of the former Italian North African colonies, which would establish the Soviet Union as a Mediterranean power; participation in control of Germany's industrial Ruhr area as well as unilateral control of the eastern occupation zone of the country; and a continued Soviet occupation of Iranian territory. These demands met increasing resistance from the United States and Britain, who became determined to contain what they regarded as Soviet expansionist tendencies.

By the end of the war the Soviet Union could justly claim that its military triumph over Germany entitled it to the status of one of the world's two great powers. To the territories it had seized during the German–Soviet pact were now added a slice of East Prussia taken from Germany, the Western Ukraine taken from Poland, the Carpatho-Ukraine taken from Czechoslovakia, and the Far Eastern outposts yielded by Japan. Soviet armies of occupation extended from Germany and Poland through Czechoslovakia and the eastern section of Austria to Hungary, Romania, and Bulgaria. But the imposing military establishment also concealed serious internal weaknesses: the economic base on which it rested had been ravaged by the war, and Soviet industry and agriculture were in a sorry condition.

POSTWAR POLICY TO STALIN'S DEATH

The
task of
rehabilita-
tion

Reconstruction. With the end of hostilities, the Soviet Union faced difficult problems of demobilization, reconversion, and reconstruction. The pattern of industrial location had shifted to the east during the war, and areas nearer the front lines had been neglected. In the war-devastated areas of European U.S.S.R., enormous tasks of rehabilitation presented themselves. As early as 1943, a special committee attached to the Council of People's Commissars was established to work on the restoration of the economy in regions liberated from the Germans. The first of the postwar five-year plans was announced early in 1946. Its proclaimed objective was to reach and surpass the prewar levels of output in industry and agriculture. Because of the deterioration of relations with the United States, Stalin could no longer count on American aid in postwar reconstruction. He exploited to the utmost such war booty and reparations as were available to him.

Table 1: Total Livestock in the Soviet Union (000,000)					
	cows	cattle (including cows)	hogs	sheep and goats	horses
1916	28.8	58.4	23.0	96.3	38.2
1928	33.2	66.8	27.7	114.6	36.1
1941	27.8	54.5	27.5	91.6	21.0
1950	24.6	58.1	22.2	93.6	12.7
1951	24.3	57.1	24.4	99.0	13.8
1952	24.9	58.8	27.1	107.6	14.7
1953	24.3	56.6	28.5	109.9	15.3

Source: Report of Khrushchev to the Plenary Session of the Central Committee, Sept. 3, 1953, *Pravda*, September 15, 1953, and *Vestnik Statistiki*, No. 5 (May 1961).

The Five-Year Plan gave priority to heavy industry, and in this area its goals were by and large reached and even exceeded. The first Soviet atomic bomb was exploded in September 1949, much sooner than many knowledgeable Western scientists had anticipated. If the progress made in heavy industry and military technology was impressive, the same could not be said of consumer goods and agriculture. In these low-priority areas even the relatively modest targets set by the plan were not met. The situation was particularly critical in agriculture. In 1946 a devastating drought in the Ukraine and other grain-producing areas resulted in a famine of major proportions. Despite Stalin's efforts to force the collective farms to increase their production, Soviet agriculture remained backward and stagnant. Inadequate incentives and meagre capital investment contributed to low agricultural productivity. The full dimensions of the agricultural crisis were not publicly revealed until after his death. Tables 1 and 2, based on official data, show how little progress agriculture had made.

Table 2: Gross Physical Output for Selected Food Items*						
year	grain	potatoes	vegetables	milk	meat (dressed weight)	eggs
1940	83.0	75.9	13.7	33.640	4.695	12.214
1950	81.4	88.6	9.3	33.311	4.867	11.697
1951	78.9	59.6	9.0	36.154	4.671	13.252
1952	92.0	68.4	11.0	35.702	5.170	14.399
1953	82.5	72.6	11.4	36.475	5.822	16.059

*All values are in millions of tons, except for eggs which are given in billions of units.
Source: Joint Economic Committee (86th Cong., 1st sess.), *Comparisons of the United States and Soviet Economies* 1959.

Stalin's
harsh
postwar
policies

The return to Stalinism. The postwar years were also marked by intensive political mobilization. During the war the party leadership had sought to broaden its appeal to the army and the nation by muting its Marxist–Leninist ideology and stressing the great unifying theme of patriotism. Early in the war, when the army was undergoing vast expansion, the party also expanded its ranks to include many members of the armed forces, particularly front-line fighters. Glorification of the army and the high command formed part of the wartime pattern, but as the war drew to a close the party reasserted its ascendancy. The organs of mass communication put increasing emphasis on the role of Stalin and the party as the major architects of victory; the heroic exploits of Soviet marshals were painted in more subdued colours. When there were signs at the end of the war that Marshal Zhukov was becoming too prominent, he was removed from the limelight and relegated to a less conspicuous military command in the Ukraine. Ideological indoctrination of the army, which had been relaxed during the war, was revived and intensified. The ranks of the party were purged.

A series of authoritative pronouncements by party leaders at the end of the war reasserted the historical perspectives of Marxism–Leninism. Stalin's election speech of February 9, 1946, restated the basic Communist analysis of capitalism and imperialism, as well as the dangers they posed for the Soviet Union. The increasingly strong Western resistance to Soviet expansion aroused an equally strong Soviet reaction. Gen. Andrey A. Zhdanov's blunt speech at the organizing conference of the Cominform in September 1947 allowed no doubt as to the Soviet position. The world, Zhdanov declared, was divided into two camps, the imperialist camp led by the United States and the anti-imperialist camp led by the Soviet Union. The Communists of the world were summoned to join in the battle against the "imperialist aggressors." All Soviet party members were called upon to alert the population to its peril and to discipline the masses for new sacrifices.

Soviet patriotism, as Stalin propounded it in the postwar years, fused Russian nationalism with an ideological commitment to Marxism–Leninism. In one of its aspects, it stressed the leading position of the Great Russian people in the Soviet family of nations. In another aspect, it proclaimed the superiority of the Soviet social and political order over capitalism.

Under the cover of Soviet patriotism, Stalin also attempted to ignite a xenophobic hatred for the capitalist world. By making "cosmopolitanism" equivalent to treason, he sought to destroy pro-Western sentiment among the people; in doing so he virtually sealed off the Soviet populace from contact with the outside world. History, literature, drama, music, and art were purged of every trace of "bourgeois objectivism" and noncommitment. *Partiynost* (devotion to the party) became the new watchword; in fact, it meant complete subservience to Stalin.

The cult of Stalin reached its apogee in the postwar period. In theory, the party ruled the state. In practice, Stalin ruled the party and through it dominated every other sector of Soviet life. His colleagues in the party's Politburo functioned as administrative henchmen and assistants on a high level; the Central Committee of the party went into a shadowy eclipse, meeting rarely; no party congress was held between 1939 and 1952. The party ranks (members and candidates) expanded from 3,876,885 in February 1941 to 6,882,145 on October 1, 1952, but as the party grew its influence diminished because of the undisputed personal authority that Stalin exercised. His method of governance was shaped to a very considerable extent by his own personality—his paranoiac suspicion, his fear of rivals, his distrust of those around him, and his insistence on holding all the strings of power in his own hands. In his drive to safeguard his own authority, he evolved a system of competing and overlapping bureaucratic hierarchies in which he depended on the party apparatus and the security police to penetrate and watch each other and made use of both to control the administrative organs of government as well as all other parts of Soviet life. The same pattern of rule was imposed on his East European Communist partners, at least as far as his power could reach. In the postwar years Poland, Czechoslovakia, Hungary, Romania, Albania, and Bulgaria were all transformed into Soviet satellites, completely subservient to Stalin's will. Only Tito's Yugoslavia managed a successful resistance; leaders elsewhere in eastern Europe who might have sought to imitate Tito were executed or purged.

The intrigues of the leaders

The system of calculated insecurity in which Stalin enveloped his henchmen carried over to the postwar years. At the end of the war the two chief rivals for Stalin's favour were Georgy M. Malenkov and Andrey A. Zhdanov. Malenkov's primary area of jurisdiction was the party apparatus. Immediately after the war his prestige suffered a temporary eclipse, and in 1946 he ceased to be listed as a party secretary. Meanwhile, Zhdanov, who had been recalled to Moscow from his post as Leningrad first party secretary, occupied the limelight as the ideological spokesman of the party and exercised his influence to promote members of his Leningrad entourage to leading party and governmental posts. If Nikita S. Khrushchev's later testimony is to be believed, Malenkov conspired with Lavrenty P. Beria, who had charge of the security police, to curb Zhdanov and to fan Stalin's distrust of the Leningraders. On July 21, 1948, the party newspaper *Pravda* revealed that Malenkov had been restored to his secretarial authority. The death of Zhdanov on August 31, 1948, was followed by a ruthless purge of his dependents in the apparatus, most of whom were executed for their alleged involvement in a conspiracy called the Leningrad Affair. According to Khrushchev, the case was fabricated from beginning to end. Among its victims were N.A. Voznesensky, a Politburo member; A.A. Kuznetsov, the Central Committee secretary who had been entrusted by Stalin himself with the supervision of state security organs; P.S. Popkov, first secretary of the Leningrad party organization; and many others. Malenkov seized the opportunity to fill many of the vacancies with his supporters, although after 1949 his own authority was somewhat diluted by Stalin's appointment of Khrushchev as Central Committee secretary with some jurisdiction over party organizational affairs. Until Khrushchev's transfer from the Ukraine to Moscow in 1949, A.A. Andreyev had served as the chief Politburo spokesman on

agricultural policy. Khrushchev replaced him in that role in the following year, when Andreyev was publicly attacked and discredited for championing the link, or small team, method of organizing agricultural production in preference to reliance on the larger brigade unit then coming into favour. Khrushchev in turn soon found himself in troubled waters because of the radical and overambitious character of his proposals for the limitation of peasants' private plots and for the resettlement of the rural population in large *agrogorods*, or rural towns. But Khrushchev, unlike Andreyev, remained a member of Stalin's inner circle.

During the last years of Stalin's life, according to Khrushchev, "Stalin became even more capricious, irritable and brutal"; his distrust extended even to his closest associates. A mass purge of the party organization in the republic of Georgia was apparently directed against Beria. The anti-Semitic campaign of the years 1948–52, which began with a sweeping denunciation of rootless cosmopolitans and culminated in the execution of several dozen Jewish writers, even extended into the Kremlin: Foreign Minister Vyacheslav Molotov's Jewish wife was sent to Siberia to live. The 19th Party Congress (1952), with its reiterated call for vigilance, suggested that there were still more purges to come. According to Khrushchev, Stalin had plans "to finish off the old members of the politburo." Andreyev was expelled from it. Marshal Kliment Ye. Voroshilov was forbidden to attend meetings, was spied upon, and was accused by Stalin of being an English agent. Molotov and Anastasy I. Mikoyan, then a deputy prime minister, were under suspicion, and the decision after the 19th Congress to create a Presidium of 25 members and 11 alternates to replace the Politburo was intended, according to Khrushchev, as a cover "for the future annihilation of the old Politburo members." The arrest of the Kremlin doctors (a majority of them Jews) for allegedly having cut short the lives of Zhdanov and Politburo member Aleksandr S. Shcherbakov and having conspired to destroy the health of leading Soviet military personnel, evoked grim memories of the earlier "doctors' plot" during the great purge of the late 1930s and seemed to portend its repetition on a mass scale. If Khrushchev's testimony is to be credited, only Stalin's death averted a blood-bath reaching into the very highest Kremlin circles. Indeed, the cloud of fear that Stalin projected cast its shadow over the whole of Soviet society.

The Cold War. The fear and tension evident inside the Soviet Union were reflected in its foreign policy. Deeply suspicious of his wartime capitalist partners, Stalin failed to utilize the goodwill that the Soviet Union had acquired in the West. Instead, he chose to pursue the most brutal policies of power, assuming that the withdrawal of U.S. military forces would leave the Soviet Union dominant in Europe. At the same time he did not overestimate his strength and sought to avoid confrontations that might lead to war. Urged by Tito to help drive the Anglo-Americans out of Trieste, he gave the Yugoslavs diplomatic support but stopped short of military action. In a revealing exchange with the Yugoslavs, he declared:

The struggle with the West

> Since all other methods were exhausted, the Soviet Union had only one other method left for gaining Trieste for Yugoslavia—to start war with the Anglo-Americans over Trieste and take it by force. The Yugoslav comrades could not fail to realize that after such a hard war the U.S.S.R. could not enter another.

Stalin did not hesitate to press hard where he thought substantial Soviet interests were at stake. The U.S. atomic monopoly in the immediate postwar years did not deter him from consolidating his position in eastern Europe. But stiffening Anglo-U.S. resistance led him to withdraw his troops from Iran in 1946, and he did not challenge the program of U.S. military and economic aid to Greece and Turkey that began in March 1947. Another barrier to the expansion of Soviet influence arose in western Europe, where the economic assistance program known as the Marshall Plan, put forward by the United States in June 1947, succeeded in restoring those countries to economic viability.

The main battlefront between the Soviets and the West

in the postwar years lay in Germany. The breakdown of cooperation over the matter of reparations, the transformation of the eastern zone of occupied Germany into a Soviet satellite, the decision of the Western powers to unify the three western zones, and their introduction of a currency reform in 1948 set the stage for the Berlin crisis of 1948–49. Berlin had been divided into sectors by the occupying powers, and it lay far within the Soviet-occupied part of Germany. The Soviet blockade of West Berlin, which appeared primarily designed to prevent a West German state from coming into being, was answered by an Anglo-U.S. airlift. The blockade was finally lifted in May 1949. Its de facto result was the division of Germany into two states: the Federal Republic of Germany, aligned with the West; and the German Democratic Republic, incorporated into the Soviet satellite system. Stalin then sought unsuccessfully to prevent or impede the rearmament of West Germany.

Difficulties in Yugoslavia and Korea

Meanwhile, Stalin was encountering problems with Tito. Not only did Tito seem to have his own expansionist plans in the Balkans, but he also insisted on running the affairs of his party and state without interference. When Tito refused to subordinate himself to Stalin's dictates and showed himself powerful enough to make his defiance effective, he and his party were expelled from the Cominform and denounced as counterrevolutionary agents of American imperialism. Facing the possibility of Soviet invasion, Tito turned to the West for aid and demonstrated that a Communist regime could survive without Moscow's support or approval. Tito's successful assertion of national independence opened the first crack in the international Communist monolith. Stalin moved to tighten his hold over the rest of eastern Europe by purging some of the leading Communists in Poland, Bulgaria, Hungary, and Czechoslovakia.

Far Eastern problems. While Stalin sought to contain Titoism in eastern Europe, a far more formidable threat was beginning to take shape in Asia. The victory of the Chinese Communists in 1949 was saluted as a great triumph for the world Communist movement, but friction between Peking and Moscow began almost at once. The Chinese leader, Mao Tse-tung, proved a hard bargainer. A treaty concluded between the Soviet Union and China on February 14, 1950, provided for the return to China of the Manchurian Railway and the Soviet-held base of Port Arthur no later than 1952. The ultimate disposition of Dairen was to be settled after the conclusion of a peace treaty with Japan; meanwhile, its administration was transferred to China.

There was also Korea. At the end of World War II Soviet troops had occupied Korea north of the 38th parallel of latitude, the area south of the parallel being occupied by U.S. forces. The withdrawal of Soviet and U.S. troops in early 1949 set the stage for conflict between the Soviet-sponsored Korean National Democratic Republic in the north and a regime established in the south with the help of the Americans. Both claimed to represent the Korean nation. Stalin, perhaps impressed by the American failure to intervene on behalf of Chiang Kai-shek on the Chinese mainland and misled by authoritative U.S. pronouncements that South Korea was outside the sphere of U.S. defense commitments, either allowed or encouraged the North Koreans to invade the south on June 25, 1950, and apparently counted on a quick victory. Operating under United Nations auspices, U.S. forces intervened to aid the South Koreans and in their march north threatened for a time to eliminate Stalin's North Korean satellite altogether. The intervention of Chinese "volunteers" drove the Americans back to the 38th parallel, where the front remained more or less stabilized. Negotiations for a truce began in July 1951, but sporadic fighting continued over the next two years, and the conclusion of an armistice had to await Stalin's death. While the Soviet Union managed to avoid direct involvement in the conflict, the Korean War set off a formidable American rearmament drive and hardened American attitudes, in Europe as well as in Asia. As a direct result of the Korean conflict, the United States concluded a peace treaty and security pact with Japan in September 1951.

Stalin's legacy. The patrimony that Stalin handed on to his successors was in many respects impressive. The territorial gains achieved as a result of World War II, and the consolidation of control in eastern Europe, testified to the Soviet Union's status as a major power. The industrialization drive launched by Stalin had made the Soviet Union second only to the United States in heavy industry and military power. To this end Stalin invested heavily in elementary and higher education; pushed the training of engineers, technicians, and scientists; reorganized the incentive system to reward skills essential to the production process; and assigned great prestige to the new industrial elite in Soviet society. But forced-draft industrialization had exacted its toll. Its cost could be measured in the millions Stalin consigned to forced-labour camps or killed in mass purges, and in the chronic shortages of food, consumer goods, and housing that resulted from the priority accorded to heavy industry.

Heavy investment in education

Stalin left a legacy of suppressed aspirations with which his successors had to reckon. First, there was a widespread desire for improvement in the standard of living. The most disadvantaged groups were the collective farmers and the unskilled and semiskilled workers, but the pressure for improvement extended well beyond these groups into the middle and even relatively privileged strata of Soviet society.

Second, there was an equally widespread yearning for greater personal security, for a life of stable expectations free from the numbing uncertainties of arbitrary arrest, police surveillance, denunciation by one's associates, or sentencing to forced labour.

Third, there was the desire for greater freedom—not necessarily freedom in the Western political sense, but freedom to use one's talents and capacities without fearing the consequences. These aspirations found their sharpest focus in the new Soviet intelligentsia. Their dreams of greater autonomy did not necessarily involve an overt challenge to the ruling ideology; many of those who harboured thoughts of greater independence and authority operated within a framework of loyalty to the Soviet system and envisaged such developments as strengthening a regime of which, after all, they were an integral part.

THE KHRUSHCHEV ERA

Stalin's successors had to deal with these aspirations. The first response of Stalin's lieutenants upon his death on March 5, 1953, was to submerge their differences. Two facts quickly became apparent: first, that none of Stalin's former colleagues had the strength immediately to assume the position of undisputed leadership that Stalin had commanded; second, that all of them were at least temporarily agreed on the necessity of presenting a united front to the nation and the world. Faced with the uncertainties of the transitional period and the necessity of stabilizing their authority, they embarked on a policy of concessions and relaxation of tensions at home and abroad. Amnesties, reductions in the prices of consumer goods, and promises to raise living standards showed a new disposition to seek popular support. The ending of the Korean War helped to ease tensions with the West.

The transition. But the issue of the succession remained to be resolved. The leading figures were Georgy M. Malenkov, who served as head of government; Lavrenty P. Beria, who had the formidable police weapon in his hands; Vyacheslav M. Molotov, who headed the foreign ministry; Nikita S. Khrushchev, who had succeeded Malenkov as the senior party secretary; and Nikolay A. Bulganin, the minister of defense. The threat posed by Beria's control of the police was eliminated with his arrest in July and execution in December 1953.

At the September 1953 session of the Central Committee, Khrushchev was elected first secretary of the party, and his star began to rise. His report on the agricultural situation contained a remarkable acknowledgment of the seriousness of the agricultural crisis and initiated a series of measures to raise production, particularly by offering the collective farmers a higher return for their efforts. His propensity for bold and daring ventures was

The rise of Khrushchev

manifest in early 1954, when he obtained Central Committee approval for his virgin lands program. This sought to bring new areas into cultivation, mainly in western Siberia and northern Kazakhstan. The hope was to obtain a vast increase in grain output with minimal capital investment, but success depended on favourable weather in areas that were climatically marginal and subject to drought. Khrushchev was gambling his political future on harvests that might not materialize. Fortune favoured him in the early years, but later there were failures that contributed to his downfall.

Except for the innovations that Khrushchev sponsored in agriculture, his first public pronouncements followed a conservative course. There was a settlement of accounts with various Beria henchman, and a number of Stalin's victims were discreetly rehabilitated. Friction with Malenkov became evident. Khrushchev's militant speech at Prague on June 12, 1954, with its boast of Soviet leadership in developing the hydrogen bomb and its declaration that a nuclear war would spell the end of capitalism, contrasted sharply with Malenkov's earlier declaration that nuclear war would mean the destruction of civilization. In a series of speeches he clearly dissociated himself from Malenkov's alleged "consumerism" and reasserted the priority of heavy industry over light industry. The denouement came on February 8, 1955, when Malenkov resigned as head of government and was replaced by Bulganin.

It is not clear whether the positions taken by Khrushchev at this time represented his deep convictions or whether they were designed to undercut Malenkov among the more conservative elements in the party. Subsequently, however, Khrushchev adopted Malenkov's formulation on the danger of nuclear warfare, wavered on the issue of heavy versus light industry, and became a strong partisan of the consumer.

Overtures toward Tito

With the downgrading of Malenkov, Khrushchev's field of manoeuvre widened and he began to place his personal stamp on foreign as well as on domestic policy. One of his most dramatic initiatives was the effort to woo Tito back into the fold by flying to Belgrade in May 1955. The expedition, undertaken against the opposition of Molotov, was apparently inspired by Khrushchev's faith that shared ideological commitments would serve to transcend all past difficulties. Although the visit did result in improved relations, Tito wrung heavy concessions from the Soviet leadership, including recognition of Yugoslavia's independence in both domestic and international affairs. The ultimate consequences for the unity of the Soviet bloc were to be less than happy.

At the same time, Khrushchev moved toward an easing of relations with the West. The conclusion of the Austrian State Treaty with the Western powers in May 1955 put an end to the occupation of Austria and neutralized that country, marking the first significant withdrawal of Soviet power in Europe. Against this background of a negotiated settlement, Khrushchev met with U.S. Pres. Dwight D. Eisenhower in July 1955 in Geneva. No agreements of substance emerged from the conference, but the very fact that the sessions took place in an atmosphere of relative cordiality raised hopes for peace throughout the world. The "spirit of Geneva," as it came to be called, provided Khrushchev with a useful theme for his peace-seeking stance.

Khrushchev also undertook to strengthen Soviet influence among the new nations of Asia and Africa. Abandoning Stalin's postwar policy of encouraging local Communists to struggle for power in these countries, Khrushchev wooed their nationalist leaders with offers of aid and trade, sought to weaken their ties with the West, and tried to influence them to adopt a policy of positive neutrality favourable to Soviet interests. The campaign began with Khrushchev's and Bulganin's trip to India toward the end of 1955. A more ominous note was struck by an agreement to supply large quantities of arms to Egypt, thus aligning the Soviet Union with the anti-Israeli and anti-Western forces of Arab nationalism.

The 20th Party Congress. While the new dynamism thus introduced into Soviet foreign policy reflected a departure from the Stalinist legacy, it remained for the 20th Congress of the party, held in February 1956, to define the content of what has since come to be described as de-Stalinization. Khrushchev made a "secret speech" to the delegates in which he combined a wide-ranging condemnation of Stalin's methods of rule with sensational disclosures of his crimes. Khrushchev's motivation in making the speech is not known, but it can be seen as a bold manoeuvre in the struggle for the succession, freeing him to pursue new policies of his own. In repudiating Stalin's terrorist excesses, he in effect offered his personal guarantee that they would not be repeated.

Khrushchev's denunciation of Stalin

The Congress also brought a number of ideological innovations designed to make Communism more attractive abroad. The doctrine that Lenin had formulated and Stalin had often reiterated—that war between the Soviet Union and the so-called imperialist states was inevitable—was now amended to read that war was not "fatalistically inevitable." This new formulation laid the groundwork for a reaffirmation of the theory of peaceful coexistence, this time without the usual qualification as to its temporary character. Khrushchev's effort to present communism in a more attractive guise was particularly evident in his theses on ways of building socialism. In defending the proposition that there were different roads to socialism, he went so far as to include the Yugoslav road in his approved list. Even more startling was his statement that the parliamentary road to power was now open to the working class "in many capitalist countries," though he added that victory would be possible only under Communist leadership and that the use or non-use of violence would depend on the resistance offered by the capitalists.

The de-Stalinization campaign and the ideological reformulations announced at the 20th Congress were intended both to broaden the appeal of the Communist movement and to strengthen Khrushchev's own position within it. In the event, they came close to destroying Khrushchev, and they released divisive forces within the Communist world that have not yet run their full course. In the Soviet Union, the ferment stirred up by Khrushchev's secret speech—which did not long remain secret—infected wide circles of the intelligentsia and the youth and inspired a protest literature that went beyond denunciation of Stalin to criticism of the Soviet system itself. The demoralization elsewhere assumed proportions serious enough to threaten the Soviet hold over eastern Europe. The gathering unrest came to a climax in October 1956, when large contingents of Soviet troops had to be rushed into Hungary to suppress a revolution in which native Communists were leading workers into battle against the Soviet Union. In Poland, direct military intervention was narrowly averted when a last-minute modus vivendi was worked out with Władysław Gomułka, who had reassumed leadership in the Polish party over Soviet objections. The bloody repression in Hungary and the reimposition of cultural curbs within the Soviet Union tarnished the image of Khrushchev as a liberalizer. In the aftermath of Hungary, his prestige declined sharply. His handling of Hungarian events also exacerbated relations with Yugoslavia. The Chinese party leaders gave him public support, but subsequent disclosures showed that they were privately highly critical of his de-Stalinization campaign, of his ideological initiatives, and above all of his failure to consult with them. Within the Soviet party leadership his opponents began to organize a cabal to unseat him, and by May 1957 they were able to mobilize a seven-to-four majority against him in the Presidium, where they confronted him with a demand for his resignation.

Decline of Khrushchev's prestige

It is a measure of the power concentrated in the office of the first secretary, as well as of Khrushchev's capacity to turn adverse developments to his own advantage, that he was able to triumph even in these circumstances. By appealing from the 11-member Presidium to the several-hundred-member Central Committee, in which his followers were strongly installed, he turned the tables on his opponents and emerged victorious. Molotov, Malenkov, and L.M. Kaganovich were expelled from both the Presidium and the Central Committee. In October of the same year he further consolidated his position by ousting his erstwhile supporter Zhukov from the Presidium and moving quickly to bring the armed forces under firm party control.

Khrushchev's position as party leader appeared unassailable. He had surmounted the crisis in eastern Europe, where the political structure seemed to have been stabilized. The world now saw a startling demonstration of Soviet accomplishments in rocketry. On August 26, 1957, the Soviet goverment announced the successful firing of an intercontinental ballistic missile. On October 4 the Soviets launched the first space satellite, Sputnik 1, followed on November 3 by Sputnik 2, with the dog Laika aboard as passenger. These dramatic developments lifted the Soviet Union's world prestige to new heights. They also enhanced the prestige of its political leadership. The space exploits had obvious military implications, and Khrushchev was not slow to claim that they marked a significant shift in the balance of power. He initiated a major drive to translate Soviet rocket superiority into diplomatic gains: he held up the Soviet pattern of rapid industrialization and scientific progress as one to be imitated in the underdeveloped world, and he also played upon a decline of confidence in U.S. leadership to widen the fissures in the Western camp. In a militant speech on November 10, 1958, he ignited a new Berlin crisis by demanding that the occupation regime in West Berlin be liquidated. Tension over Berlin persisted for several years, but Khrushchev failed to win concessions from the Western powers.

There were limits to the pressure that Moscow could apply on the West. The United States was still a formidable thermonuclear power with larger resources than the Soviet Union, and any confrontation that imperilled vital American interests might have disastrous consequences for both sides. As long as relations remained tense and difficult, they fostered an expensive arms race that diverted resources from domestic development and required continual sacrifices from the Soviet people. An easing of relations with the United States, by contrast, would offer hope of more rapid economic development and better living standards. But obstacles to even a partial détente remained formidable. There was the continuing Berlin crisis and the Soviet fear that the United States was determined to equip West Germany with nuclear weapons. There were problems in the Middle East. Khrushchev's visit to the United States in the fall of 1959 was made in the hope both of easing tensions and of winning concessions in Berlin and Germany. No concessions were forthcoming. On May 1, 1960, a U.S. high-altitude reconnaissance airplane, designated a U-2, crashed deep in Soviet territory and its pilot was captured. This was followed by the collapse of a Paris summit conference in May 1960. A further deterioration in Soviet–American relations was manifest in connection with the civil war in the Democratic Republic of the Congo in the early 1960s, the building of the Berlin Wall in 1961, and finally in the Cuban missile crisis in October 1962.

The Cuban crisis

The Cuban crisis seemed to bring the two great nuclear powers to the brink of war. Under the guise of providing Cuba with defensive weapons the Soviet government was found to be trying to establish launching sites on the island for medium- and intermediate-range missiles. The U.S. government's rapid deployment of a naval blockade around Cuba and an exchange of letters between Pres. John F. Kennedy and Khrushchev resulted in the latter's agreement to withdraw what he admitted were "aggressive" weapons.

The rift with China. Khrushchev also faced increasing difficulties in his relations with China. At the root of the Sino-Soviet dispute lay the fact that the Soviet Union and China were two great nations with different destinies. Each had its own defined set of interests; both had very different conceptions of how those interests could be promoted. Khrushchev saw his main tasks to be those of building up Soviet power, minimizing the risks of thermonuclear war, demonstrating the superiority of the Soviet system, and at the same time exploiting the vulnerabilities

of the non-Communist world within the framework of a nuclear stalemate. The Chinese leaders saw their problems in different and more urgent terms. The liquidation of the Chinese Nationalist regime in Taiwan was a prime objective; but involved with this, and going well beyond it, was the need for large-scale Soviet military and economic support in order to overcome Chinese backwardness. Operating on the assumption that American resistance would crumble like a "paper tiger" in the face of a hard, uncompromising policy, they urged a far more militant and aggressive stance that would put revolutionary action in the forefront.

Khrushchev's reluctance to challenge U.S. power, as well as his insistence on giving priority to Soviet interests, became sharply evident as the Sino-Soviet dispute developed. Faced with a choice between providing massive economic and military assistance to the Chinese or concentrating on the homeland, he chose the latter. Fearing that the Chinese might embroil him in a war with the West, he denied them nuclear weapons and gave them only token support in their campaign to win Taiwan. Concerned to maintain good relations with the neutral and nonaligned nations, he refused to back the Chinese in their border conflict with India and continued to provide India with economic and even military aid. Determined to bring the Chinese to heel, he imposed more and more severe sanctions on them, cutting down trade and military and economic assistance, withdrawing specialists, demanding the repayment of debts, and exerting pressure on the east European countries to take corresponding measures. Khrushchev sought vainly to persuade the Chinese to desist from attacks on the Soviet leadership. Faced with defiance and with Chinese efforts to mobilize support within the international Communist movement, he moved to solidify his own ranks and to expel the Chinese and their allies as heretics who had broken away from the true faith of Communist internationalism.

Growing dissension with China

For Mao and his followers, Soviet policies were suspect on every count. They charged Khrushchev with betraying his international Communist obligations, abandoning the revolutionary banner of Marxism–Leninism, and embarking on a course of "great power chauvinism." Indeed, as the bitterness of the Sino-Soviet dispute mounted and the prospects of reconciliation faded, the positions of both sides hardened to the point where they saw each other not merely as rivals for supremacy in the Communist camp but as potential national enemies.

In the wake of the Cuban missile crisis of 1962, with its sobering reminder of how close the world had come to thermonuclear extinction, Khrushchev demonstrated a renewed eagerness to improve his relations with the United States and the West. In August 1963 he signed, with the U.S. and the U.K., a treaty banning the testing of nuclear weapons; he joined in establishing better communications between Moscow and Washington; undertook in cooperation with the United States to ban missiles in orbit and to cut back the production of fissionable material; pressed restraints on the regime of Fidel Castro in Cuba; and relaxed tension over Berlin and undertook to improve relations with West Germany. All these efforts to "normalize" relations with the West were received by Peking as additional confirmations of Khrushchev's apostasy from true Marxism–Leninism. The split was rapidly becoming unbridgeable.

Economic problems. Khrushchev's decision to seize the "peace issue" even at the cost of further alienating Peking won support among Communists as well as non-Communists who feared nuclear war. But perhaps the most compelling reasons for seeking a détente with the West were domestic strains and difficulties. The efforts of the post-Stalin leadership to raise the low living standards in the U.S.S.R. had whetted the appetite of the Soviet populace but failed to satisfy it. Their deeply felt need for more and better food, clothing, and housing could not be met without a diversion of investment from armaments and heavy industry to light industry and agriculture. The situation in agriculture was particularly troublesome. The banner harvest of 1958, largely attributable to uniformly favourable weather, was followed by a series of

Domestic strains and difficulties

mediocre harvests. Disaster struck in 1963, when bad weather and widespread drought sharply curtailed output and compelled the government to purchase abroad approximately 12,000,000 tons of grain to meet consumer needs. While there were various reasons for the decline in agricultural output, one important factor was the failure to invest adequate capital in agriculture. In a belated effort to meet the problem, Khrushchev announced a large-scale program for the expansion of the chemical industry (including fertilizer production), increased output of agricultural machinery, an extension of irrigation, and other measures that required substantial new capital investment. This would mean less rapid expansion in heavy industry, as well as reduced funds in other sectors, including the military. Understandably, the proposed shift in priority met resistance in powerful quarters.

Nor were Khrushchev's problems limited to agriculture. Industrial progress also lagged. The industrial slowdown and the sharp fall in agricultural output combined to produce a dramatic decline in the overall economic growth rate in 1962–63. The promised rapid improvement in living standards was belied by food shortages. The continuing debate on allocations policy, cautiously aired in Soviet journals, revealed the usual array of vested bureaucratic interests, each seeking to defend its own special position. Khrushchev's efforts to cope with his problems by periodic reorganizations of the state and party machinery created more confusion. His division of the party organization into separate industrial and agricultural branches in November 1962 antagonized many regional party leaders and eroded his support in that section of the apparatus where he had previously commanded the strongest loyalties. His increasing disposition to announce important changes in policy without consulting his Presidum colleagues tended to antagonize them. These domestic developments, taken together with his unsuccessful efforts to dislodge the Western powers from Berlin, the rebuff he received during the Cuban missile crisis, and his inability to contain the dispute with China, helped set the stage for his removal. His Presidium associates were determined to unseat him, and this time could count on solid support in the Central Committee.

THE BREZHNEV–KOSYGIN ERA

The fall of Khrushchev

Collective leadership.   On October 16, 1964, the Soviet press announced that the Central Committee had met two days earlier and granted Khrushchev's request that he be released from his responsibilities "in view of his advanced age and deterioration in the state of his health." *Pravda* the next day charged him with:

> harebrained schemes, halfbaked conclusions and hasty decisions and actions divorced from reality; bragging and bluster; attraction to rule by fiat; unwillingness to take into account what science and practical experience have already discovered.

The new collective leadership was led by Leonid I. Brezhnev, the new first secretary of the party, and Aleksey N. Kosygin, who succeeded to the chairmanship of the Council of Ministers (head of government). Public polemics with Peking ceased. The parallel industrial and agricultural hierarchies that Khrushchev had introduced into the party and governmental structure were combined. The agronomist Trofim D. Lysenko, whom Khrushchev had supported, was exposed as a charlatan, and a campaign was initiated to break his control of Soviet agricultural research. The new leaders announced the removal of "unwarranted limitations" on the size of household plots of land in the collective farms and on private livestock holdings by collective farmers. The party apparatus was assured that it could count on stability; the industrial managers were told that more rational economic policies would be pursued; and the intellectuals were told that capricious interference in cultural affairs would be avoided.

The style of the new Brezhnev–Kosygin leadership was much less dramatic than that of Khrushchev. There was a renewed emphasis on collective leadership and bureaucratic decision making. The indiscretions and earthy expressions that had enlivened Khrushchev's speeches were not to be found in the committee-written prose of his successors. The extravagant promises of rapid industrial progress and soaring living standards were quietly discarded. His theories that the dictatorship of the proletariat would be replaced by an all-people's state, that the party of the proletariat would become the party of the whole people, and that agencies of public self-government would gradually replace those of the state were ignored although not officially disclaimed. The repudiation of Khrushchev extended in many directions. De-Stalinization was arrested, and indeed reversed, despite sharp opposition from liberal intellectual circles. Brezhnev took the lead by stressing Stalin's leadership during World War II and his achievements as an industrializer and builder of Soviet power. Khrushchev, on the other hand, vanished from the public eye; the only acknowledgment of his existence was when he was attacked indirectly for his sins of commission and omission.

Within the new collective leadership, Brezhnev became increasingly prominent. His position was strengthened when N.V. Podgorny, one of the party secretaries, was elevated to the largely ceremonial post of chairman of the Presidium of the Supreme Soviet (head of state) in place of Anastas I. Mikoyan in December 1965. Another potential rival was eliminated when A.N. Shelepin lost his post as deputy premier and Central Committee Secretary. At the 23rd Party Congress in March–April 1966 Brezhnev's title of first secretary was changed to secretary-general, a title that had last been used by Stalin. During the next years he emerged as the most authoritative spokesman on issues of domestic and foreign policy. But there were few signs that he could achieve the kind of personal authority exercised by Khrushchev in the heyday of his power.

Reforms in agriculture and industry

Unbinding the economy.   Among the economic problems inherited by Khrushchev's successors, the most serious were in agriculture. In March 1965 Brezhnev promised the collective and state farmers a new deal: higher prices for grain and livestock; stable delivery quotas; a decreased tax burden on collective farms; and a doubling of investments in farm machinery, trucks, tractors, fertilizer, and land improvement. The promises came too late to prevent a poor harvest in 1965, but 1966 saw a banner harvest and an apparent vindication of Brezhnev's initiative. That year the prices of trucks, tractors, and agricultural machinery were reduced for collective and state farms; rural electricity rates were also reduced; and retail prices in rural stores on certain consumer items were lowered to the level of retail prices in the cities. Collective farms were authorized to introduce guaranteed monthly pay for their members based on rates of corresponding categories of state farm workers.

Poor harvests in 1967 and 1969 alternated with good harvests in 1968 and 1970. But even the harvest of 1970, estimated at over 160,000,000 tons of grain, fell short of the projected goal for that year of 190,000,000–200,000,000 tons. If the overall performance of agriculture in the 1966–70 period compared favourably with that of the preceding five-year period, it was still far from satisfactory.

Khrushchev's successors also confronted difficult problems in the industrial sector. While space and weapons technology and the iron and steel industry matched the best that the West had to offer, technological progress in such new industrial fields as automation, computers, petrochemicals, industrial research, and management techniques lagged well behind that of the United States; many industries, particularly in the consumer-goods sector, were far less technologically developed than in major Western countries. The slowing of the industrial growth rate and the difficulty of resolving increasingly intricate and complex planning and management problems aroused sharp concern in the top leadership. The industrial reforms announced in September 1965 represented an effort to come to grips with the management problem by widening managerial discretion in decision making and by establishing an incentive system designed to reward the efficient use of resources. Hand in hand with these changes went a complete liquidation of Khrushchev's administrative reforms. The whole system of regional, republic, and U.S.S.R. economic councils was abolished, and the ministerial system that had prevailed before 1957 was re-established. Each ministry was made responsible for a sector of the economy, while central planning functions were concentrated in the State Planning Committee (Gosplan), and responsibility for the allocation and distribution of supplies was entrusted to a new State Committee for Material and Technical Supplies.

The 1965 industrial changes were hailed by economic reformers as a modest step in the right direction, but enterprise managers complained that they were still hemmed in by rigid supply restrictions and that their superiors in the party and government agencies still held them in petty tutelage: essentially, the economy continued to function much as it had earlier—the bureaucratic machinery resisted change and innovation. In 1968 the Central Committee initiated still another effort to spur scientific research and development and to improve the quality of management. Emphasis was placed on bringing science closer to industry and on the provision of special bonuses and awards for innovation.

The Five-Year Plan for 1966–70, which was presented at the 23rd Party Congress in April 1966, represented a considerable scaling down of the targets Khrushchev had originally set for 1970. Even the relatively modest new goals for 1970 turned out in many cases to be impossible of fulfillment. The draft directives for the 1971–75 economic plan, which were released in February 1971, called for a 37–40 percent increase in national income, a 30 percent increase in per capita real income, a 42–46 percent increase in industrial production, and a 20–22 percent increase in gross agricultural production.

Cultural controls. In cultural affairs the Brezhnev–Kosygin regime, after a brief flirtation with liberalization, became increasingly conservative and regressive. Innovations in the arts and literature had been greatly stimulated by Khrushchev's de-Stalinization program. The problem for Stalin's heirs was that of defining the limits of cultural freedom. While Khrushchev's own position wavered, his prime concern was to enlist the energies of talented writers and artists in the party cause as he understood it. But his conception of how the "cultural workers" could best serve the party differed significantly from the views of some whose talents he sought to mobilize. A man of plebeian tastes, he believed that art should minister to the needs of the masses; that paintings and sculpture should be representational; that poetry should be easily understood; and that literature should carry a social message. It was perhaps inevitable that Khrushchev should find himself increasingly out of sympathy with the bolder spirits who wanted greater freedom of expression and found his cultural outlook oppressive. Nevertheless, his experiments in controlled relaxation provided the liberals with a field of manoeuvre, and it was Khrushchev himself who authorized the publication of Aleksandr I. Solzhenitsyn's powerful concentration-camp novel, *One Day in the Life of Ivan Denisovich.*

Khrushchev's successors were less tolerant. The arrests of Andrey Sinyavsky and Yuly Daniel on September 13, 1965, for publishing abroad (under the pseudonyms Abram Terts and Nikolay Arzhak) works allegedly slandering the Soviet Union, signalled a period of increased repression. Over the next years many other dissident writers and their sympathizers were also arrested, imprisoned, or consigned to forced-labour camps. In the aftermath of the Arab defeat by Israel in the Six Day War of 1967, attacks on Israel and Zionism took on anti-Semitic overtones. The events in Czechoslovakia in 1968 (see below) also had repercussions within the Soviet Union. After the invasion of Czechoslovakia, Soviet cultural policy hardened. The treatment of Solzhenitsyn was symbolic: even before Czechoslovakia the police had seized all his unpublished manuscripts and withdrawn his few published works from circulation; in November 1969 he was expelled from the Writers' Union, and the Nobel Prize for Literature that came to him the next year only intensified the attacks on him. Even such a moderate party spokesman as Aleksandr T. Tvardovsky found himself

in deep trouble. Deprived of his seat as an alternate member of the Central Committee in 1966, he was subjected to increasing harassment as editor of the literary magazine *Novy Mir* until a purge of the staff of that journal in 1970 forced him to relinquish his editorship.

The repressive measures did not go unchallenged. After the sentencing of Sinyavsky and Daniel to seven and five years hard labour, respectively, 63 well-known Moscow writers joined in an appeal for their release. On the eve of the 23rd Party Congress, 25 distinguished figures in Soviet public life, including some leading nuclear physicists, signed an open letter to Brezhnev registering their opposition to Stalin's rehabilitation. Thus, the protest movement that began to take form in the post-Khrushchevian period ran the gamut from prominent representatives of the scientific and creative intelligentsia, who confined their activities chiefly to signing occasional statements, to groups of dedicated activists largely recruited from young students and intellectuals, who engaged in illegal public demonstrations, circulated underground literature among the intelligentsia, and constantly risked arrest and imprisonment. Their common bond was their dissatisfaction with the regime's policy and their commitment to civil rights, greater intellectual freedom, and democratization.

Foreign policy. The Brezhnev–Kosygin regime also had to contend with an array of difficult problems in the foreign policy area. The most troublesome was that of relations with China. After an initial effort to lower tensions, the quarrel flared into violence culminating in bloody border clashes along the Ussuri River in March 1969 and along the Sinkiang frontier in August. Subsequently both sides agreed to negotiate their differences, but friction persisted. The U.S.S.R. strengthened its military formations along the Chinese border in the Soviet Far East, Central Asia, and the Mongolian People's Republic. It continued to provide military aid to India as well as to Pakistan in an effort to counter Chinese influence in those countries. Indeed, even the extensive military and economic aid the U.S.S.R. supplied to North Vietnam could be viewed not only as a demonstration of its willingness to come to the assistance of a brother Communist state but also as an effort to decrease North Vietnamese dependence on China and to reinforce historic Vietnamese resistance to Chinese domination.

In eastern Europe, Khrushchev's successors were confronted with an erosion of their authority. Romania had begun to stake out an increasingly nationalist position, proceeding with plans for all-around industrialization despite Soviet insistence that Romania's economic role should be based on a division of labour with other countries in eastern Europe. Over the next years Romania continued to display independence by maintaining friendly relations with China, reorienting its foreign trade away from the Soviet bloc, concluding a trade treaty with the United States in 1964, expanding contacts with the West, opposing Soviet attempts to strengthen the Warsaw military pact in 1966, establishing diplomatic relations with West Germany in January 1967, and adopting a neutral stance in the Arab–Israeli War the following June. Despite these actions, which obviously displeased the Soviet leadership, Romania was able to avoid a direct confrontation with the U.S.S.R.

Czechoslovakia was less fortunate. The downfall of the party leader, Antonín Novotný, and his replacement by Alexander Dubček in January 1968 was followed by the "Czech Spring," a period of remarkably free political expression. Past abuses were attacked and demands were raised for the democratization of the system. Fearful that the Dubček leadership had lost control of the situation and that the challenge to party authority might spread to other Communist countries, the Soviet leaders decided on military intervention. On August 20, 1968, Soviet forces aided by token military contingents from East Germany, Poland, Hungary, and Bulgaria occupied Czechoslovakia. The invasion was justified by what later came to be called the Brezhnev doctrine: in essence, that the Soviet Union reserved the right to intervene militarily in the affairs of any of its east European Communist neighbours whenev-

The conserva-tive trend in culture

Conflicts with China and eastern Europe

er it believed that its interests or the security interests of its allies were significantly threatened. The effect of Soviet intervention was to force Czechoslovakia back on a more orthodox Communist course and to warn other Communist states in eastern Europe that there were limits to the degree of autonomy Moscow would tolerate.

Other areas of foreign policy

Soviet policy in the Middle East was oriented toward protecting the interests of its Arab clients, expanding Soviet influence, and eliminating the residual Western presence. While the failure of the Soviet Union to come to the aid of its Arab friends in the Six Day War in 1967 tarnished its prestige, the Soviet decision to rearm its Arab clients won it renewed favour. Expanded Soviet military missions were attached to the Egyptian and Syrian armies, the Soviet Mediterranean fleet was enlarged, naval bases were established in Arab ports, and Soviet airlift capacity was improved.

The primary objective of Soviet policy in western Europe continued to be to weaken U.S. influence in that area. A special relationship was cultivated with France, which had withdrawn its forces from the North Atlantic Treaty Organization. A substantial increase in trade with various west European countries served to emphasize mutual needs and dependencies. At the same time, the Soviet Union remained determined to keep Germany divided and to press for general recognition of East Germany's sovereignty. The decision of West Germany to sign the nuclear Non-Proliferation Treaty on November 28, 1969, eased tensions on the nuclear armaments issue and helped prepare the way for an effort to normalize relations. At Moscow, in August 1970, Chancellor Willy Brandt of West Germany agreed in essence to recognize the postwar German borders, but he also made clear that the treaty embodying this agreement would not be submitted for ratification by the West German parliament until satisfactory arrangements could be worked out for guaranteeing West German access to West Berlin and for improving communications between the two parts of that city.

Soviet attacks on "American imperialism" became increasingly sharp following the U.S. bombing attacks on North Vietnam in February 1965. The cooling of relations did not, however, prevent agreement on specific questions of mutual interest. In March 1966 a cultural agreement between the two countries was renewed; in September arrangements were made to exchange weather information; and in November an agreement was reached to inaugurate direct commercial air flights between New York and Moscow. On January 27, 1967, an outer space treaty was approved prohibiting the orbiting of nuclear weapons and providing, among other things, for assistance to astronauts downed in either country. The ending of the India–Pakistan war in early 1966, as a result of Kosygin's successful mediation, was supported by parallel American efforts and stemmed from a common desire to contain Chinese penetration into southern Asia. The Middle East crisis of May 1967, which culminated in the six-day Arab–Israeli war in June, brought a new clash of Soviet and U.S. interests; but both sides joined in efforts to stop the fighting in order to prevent the war from broadening into a direct Soviet–American military confrontation.

During the next year there were some signs of a thaw in Soviet–American relations with the opening of peace talks on Vietnam in Paris, the Soviet ratification on May 4, 1968, of a consular agreement negotiated four years earlier, and the signing of the nuclear Non-Proliferation Treaty on July 1. The Soviet invasion of Czechoslovakia in August, however, dimmed hopes of a détente. Its effect was to revive fear of Soviet aggression. A projected U.S.–U.S.S.R. summit meeting was cancelled; the reduction of American troops in West Germany suspended; and Washington announced a decision to deploy a light antiballistic missile system. It was not until November 17, 1969, that the long-delayed SALT (strategic arms limitation talks) negotiations began in Helsinki, and they promised to be both difficult and drawn-out. As the decade drew to a close, large and important issues continued to divide the Soviet Union and the United States in many parts of the globe. But the realization that neither could afford a nuclear conflict also impelled them to seek terms of accommodation that would enable them to coexist in a changing world.   (M.F.)

BIBLIOGRAPHY

Russia to c. 1700: The best brief survey of early Russian history in English is SERGEI F. PLATONOV, *History of Russia* (1925; orig. pub. in Russian, 1910; French trans., 1929). A readable and judicious survey is NICHOLAS V. RIASANOVSKY, *A History of Russia* (1963). An idiosyncratic but stimulating treatment is JAMES H. BILLINGTON, *The Icon and the Axe: An Interpretive History of Russian Culture* (1966). Other useful surveys are JEROME BLUM, *Lord and Peasant in Russia, from the Ninth to the Nineteenth Century* (1961); V.O. KLIUCHEVSKY, *A History of Russia*, 5 vol. (1911–31; new trans. of vol. 3–4, 1961–68; orig. pub. in Russian, 1904–10); and PAVEL N. MILIUKOV, *Outlines of Russian Culture*, 3 vol. (1942; orig. pub. in Russian, 1898–1903). On the history of Kiev, see SAMUEL H. CROSS, *The Russian Primary Chronicle* (1953); BORIS D. GREKOV, *Kiev Rus* (1959); M.W. THOMPSON, *Novgorod the Great* (1967); and GEORGE VERNADSKY, *Kievan Russia* (1966). The Mongol period is treated in BORIS GREKOV and A.I. YAKUBOVSKY, *La Horde d'Or* (1939; orig. pub. in Russian, 1937); and also in GEORGE VERNADSKY, *The Mongols and Russia* (1953). For the history of Muscovy, see JOHN L.I. FENNELL, *The Emergence of Moscow, 1304–1359* (1968) and *Ivan the Great of Moscow* (1961); V.O. KLIUCHEVSKY, *A Course in Russian History: The Seventeenth Century* (1968; orig. pub. in Russian, 1908); SERGEI F. PLATONOV, *The Time of Troubles: A Historical Study of the Internal Crises and Social Struggle in Sixteenth- and Seventeenth-Century Muscovy* (1970; orig. pub. in Russian, 1924); A.E. PRESNIAKOV, *The Formation of the Great Russian State* (1970; orig. pub. in Russian, 1918); GEORGE VERNADSKY, *Russia at the Dawn of the Modern Age* (1959) and *The Tsardom of Muscovy, 1547–1682*, 2 vol. (1969).

1700–1801: A topical interpretive synthesis, with a comprehensive bibliographical guide, is MARC RAEFF, *Imperial Russia 1682–1825: The Coming of Age of Modern Russia* (1971). For a repertory of imperial institutions, see the indispensable ERIK AMBURGER, *Geschichte der Behördenorganisation Russlands von Peter dem Grossen bis 1917* (1966), which may be used by scholars unfamiliar with the German language. For the reforms and reign of Peter the Great a very brief summary is B.H. SUMNER, *Peter the Great and the Emergence of Russia* (1950); while the only comprehensive survey is REINHARD WITTRAM, *Peter I, Czar und Kaiser*, 2 vol. (1964). Plans of reform with a general discussion of the nature of government are included in MARC RAEFF, *Plans for Political Reform in Imperial Russia, 1730–1905* (1966). The special issue of *Canadian Slavic Studies* (Winter 1970), gives many insights and descriptions of institutional problems in the reign of Catherine II as well as references to the most recent literature. The diplomatic history of the Russian Empire, as well as its territorial expansion, are best traced in general European political histories of the period. For some further considerations, and bibliographic suggestions on this little-studied problem, see MARC RAEFF, "The Style of Russia's Imperial Policy and Prince G.A. Potemkin," in G.N. GROB (ed.), *Statesmen and Statecraft of the Modern West* (1967), as well as the individual histories of frontier provinces and neighbouring states. The standard economic history of Russia is PETER I. LYASHCHENKO, *History of the National Economy of Russia to the 1917 Revolution* (1949, reprinted 1970; orig. pub. in Russian, 2 vol. 1947–48). For an introduction to a history of the nobility both as social class and matrix of the intelligentsia, see MARC RAEFF, *Origins of the Russian Intelligentsia: The Eighteenth-Century Nobility* (1966); and for the peasantry and its plight LYASHCHENKO and BLUM (*op. cit.*). For the Russian Church, in addition to the titles cited earlier, IGOR SMOLITSCH, *Geschichte der russischen Kirche 1700–1917* (1964), along topical lines; and JAMES CRACRAFT, *The Church Reform of Peter the Great* (1971), are recommended. For an insight into the dissident Old Believers, see ROBERT O. CRUMMEY, *The Old Believers and the World of Antichrist: The Vyg Community and the Russian State, 1694–1855* (1970). On education, cultural life, and the emergence of radical thought among an intelligentsia, see HAROLD B. SEGEL (comp.), *The Literature of Eighteenth-Century Russia*, 2 vol. (1967). Sources to philosophy and social thought may be found in JAMES M. EDIE, JAMES P. SCANLAN, and MARY-BARBARA ZELDIN (eds.), *Russian Philosophy*, 3 vol. (1965); and MARC RAEFF (ed.), *Russian Intellectual History: An Anthology* (1966). For a comprehensive survey of philosophical trends, see V.V. ZENKOVSKY, *A History of Russian Philosophy*, 2 vol. (1953; orig. pub. in Russian, 1948–50). On educational and scientific institutions, see A.S. VUCINICH, *Science in Russian Culture*, vol. 1, *A History to 1860* (1963). Other problems of cultural life are well treated by HANS ROGGER in *National Consciousness in Eighteenth-Century Russia* (1960); while the seminal revolt of Radishchev is discussed by ALLEN MCCONNELL in *A Russian Philosophe: Alexander Radishchev* (1964), and in Radishchev's *Journey from St. Petersburg to Moscow*, trans. and ed. by LEO WIENER and RODERICK PAGE THALER (1958). On the impact of the German enlightenment and Russia's relations with the West, see MARC RAEFF, "Les Slaves, les Allemands, et les 'Lumières,'" *Revue canadienne d'études slaves*, 1:521–551 (1967).

1801–1917: General surveys of Russian history in the 19th century include: MICHAEL T. FLORINSKY, *Russia: A History and an Interpretation*, 2 vol. (1953–54); and HUGH SETON-WATSON, *The Russian Empire, 1801–1917* (1967). The best work in English on the reign of Alexander I is MARC RAEFF, *Michael Speransky, Statesman of Imperial Russia, 1772–1839* (1957). The best work on the reign of Nicholas I is NICHOLAS V. RIASANOVSKY, *Nicholas I and Official Nationality in Russia, 1825–1855* (1959). A useful addition is JOHN S. CURTISS, *The Russian Army Under Nicholas I, 1825–1855* (1965). For the general economic development of Russia in the 19th century, see LYASHCHENKO (*op. cit.*). The economic and social problems of the peasantry in the first half of the 19th century are discussed in BLUM (*op. cit.*); for the second half of the century, see G.T. ROBINSON, *Rural Russia Under the Old Régime* (1932). The industrialization drive of the 1890s is treated in THEODORE VON LAUE, *Sergei Witte and the Industrialization of Russia* (1963). Economic and political trends at the turn of the 20th century are discussed in D.W. TREADGOLD, *The Great Siberian Migration* (1957). Two biographical studies that do much to explain the interplay of cultural and political factors in the 19th century are M. MALIA, *Alexander Herzen and the Birth of Russian Socialism, 1812–1855* (1961); and RICHARD PIPES, *Struve: Liberal on the Left*, vol. 1, *1870–1905* (1961). An outstanding survey of early Marxist groups is J.H.L. KEEP, *The Rise of Social Democracy in Russia* (1963). For the earlier revolutionary movement and the development of so-called Populism, the classical description and interpretation is FRANCO VENTURI, *Il populismo russo* (1952; Eng. trans., *Roots of Revolution*, 1960). An absolutely essential source for the history of revolutionary activity up to 1917 are of course the earlier volumes of Lenin's *Works* (available in English in many editions). Three useful books on individual non-Russian peoples in this period are MICHAEL HRUSHEVSKY, *A History of the Ukraine* (1941, reprinted 1970; orig. pub. in Russian, 1918); S.A. ZENKOVSKY, *Pan-Turkism and Islam in Russia* (1960); and GEOFFREY WHEELER, *The Modern History of Soviet Central Asia* (1964). Four studies of important moments and problems in Russian foreign policy, which thoroughly examine the Russian point of view, are MARIAN KUKIEL, *Czartoryski and European Unity, 1770–1861* (1955); MICHAEL B. PETROVICH, *The Emergence of Russian Panslavism, 1856–1870* (1956); B.H. SUMNER, *Russia and the Balkans, 1870–1880* (1937); and A. MALOZEMOFF, *Russian Far Eastern Policy, 1881–1904* (1958). On the final collapse of tsardom, MICHAEL T. FLORINSKY, *The End of the Russian Empire* (1931), remains the best general survey. It may be usefully supplemented with the minutes of the Council of Ministers in 1915, ed. by MICHAEL CHERNIAVSKY under the title *Prologue to Revolution* (1967).

1917–1939: General works on the period include: GEORG VON RAUCH, *Geschichte des bolschewistischen Russland* (1955; Eng. trans., *A History of Soviet Russia*, 5th rev. ed., 1967), a critical survey; EDWARD HALLETT CARR, *A History of Soviet Russia*, 8 vol. to date (1950–), a detailed history of the years 1917–29; LEONARD B. SCHAPIRO, *The Communist Party of the Soviet Union* (1960); RAPHAEL R. ABRAMOVITCH, *The Soviet Revolution, 1917–1939* (1962), the Menshevik viewpoint; B.N. PONOMAREV et al. (eds.), *History of the Communist Party of the Soviet Union*, 2nd rev. ed. (1963), translation of an official Soviet textbook; and MAURICE DOBB, *Soviet Economic Development Since 1917* (1948), sympathetic though critical. Biographies of the Bolshevik leaders are: ADAM B. ULAM, *The Bolsheviks* (1955), on Lenin; ISAAC DEUTSCHER, *The Prophet Armed: Trotsky 1879–1921* (1954), *The Prophet Unarmed . . . 1921–1929* (1959), and *The Prophet Outcast . . . 1929–1940* (1965); and BORIS SOUVARINE, *Stalin* (1935; Eng. trans., 1939). Among the many studies of the 1917 Revolution and subsequent developments are: W.H. CHAMBERLIN, *The Russian Revolution*, 2 vol. (1935); ROBERT V. DANIELS, *Red October* (1967) and *The Conscience of the Revolution* (1960); JOHN A. ARMSTRONG, *The Politics of Totalitarianism* (1961); ROBERT CONQUEST, *The Great Terror* (1968), an exhaustive study of the purges of the 1930s; and NICHOLAS S. TIMASHEFF, *The Great Retreat* (1946), a survey of trends in social and cultural life to World War

II. Outstanding works on Soviet foreign relations include: MAX BELOFF, *The Foreign Policy of Soviet Russia, 1929–1941*, 2 vol. (1947–49); LOUIS FISCHER, *The Soviets in World Affairs*, 2 vol. (1930); GEORGE F. KENNAN, *Russia and the West Under Lenin and Stalin* (1961), a critical analysis of the period 1917–45; and ADAM B. ULAM, *Expansion and Coexistence: The History of Soviet Foreign Policy, 1917–67* (1968).

1940 to the present: (*Domestic politics*): JOHN A. ARMSTRONG, *The Politics of Totalitarianism* (1961), a history of the Communist Party from 1934 to 1960; ABRAHAM BRUMBERG (comp.), *In Quest of Justice* (1970), commentaries and documents of protest and dissent in the U.S.S.R.; ROBERT CONQUEST, *Power and Policy in the USSR* (1961), an analysis of the party leadership in the period 1949–60; ALEXANDER DALLIN and T.B. LARSON (eds.), *Soviet Politics Since Khrushchev* (1968), an account of developments in various sectors of Soviet life after Khrushchev's removal; MERLE FAINSOD, *How Russia Is Ruled*, rev. ed. (1963); WOLFGANG LEONHARD, *Kreml ohne Stalin* (1959; Eng. trans., *The Kremlin Since Stalin*, 1962), on developments within the U.S.S.R. from Stalin's death to the 22nd Party Congress; CARL A. LINDEN, *Khrushchev and the Soviet Leadership, 1957–1964* (1966), an analysis of leadership conflicts; the RUSSIAN INSTITUTE, COLUMBIA UNIVERSITY (ed.), *The Anti-Stalin Campaign and International Communism* (1956), text of Khrushchev's secret speech at the 20th Party Congress and other related documents; LEONARD B. SHAPIRO, *The Communist Party of the Soviet Union* (1959), a study of the party's origins and development; MICHEL TATU, *Le Pouvoir en URSS* (1967; Eng. trans., *Power in the Kremlin: From Khrushchev to Kosygin*, 1969), a study of power conflicts in the leadership during the period 1960–66. (*International relations*): ZBIGNIEW K. BRZEZINSKI, *The Soviet Bloc: Unity and Conflict*, rev. ed. (1967), an analysis of Soviet-bloc politics; WILLIAM E. GRIFFITH (ed.), *Sino-Soviet Relations, 1964–65* (1967), a collection of documents with a valuable introduction by the author; M.F. HERZ, *Beginnings of the Cold War* (1966), a balanced and careful treatment of the origins of the Cold War; WALTER LAFEBER, *America, Russia, and the Cold War, 1945–1966* (1967), a revisionist view of the origins and progress of the Cold War; RAYMOND J. SONTAG and JAMES S. BEDDIE (eds.), *Nazi-Soviet Relations, 1939–1941* (1948), documents on the German-Soviet Pact from the archives of the German foreign office; ADAM B. ULAM (*op. cit.*), a lively and penetrating review of developments in Soviet foreign policy; THOMAS W. WOLFE, *Soviet Power and Europe, 1945–1970* (1970), an overall view of Soviet policies in Europe, with emphasis on the Soviet military posture; DONALD S. ZAGORIA, *The Sino-Soviet Conflict, 1956–1961* (1964), a thorough treatment of the origins of the Sino-Soviet conflict and its early manifestations. (*The economy*): JEREMY R. AZRAEL, *Managerial Power and Soviet Politics* (1966), a careful analysis of the changing role of the managerial elite in the Soviet policy-making process; ALEC NOVE, *The Soviet Economy*, rev. 3rd ed. (1968), an excellent introduction to the Soviet economy; HARRY SCHWARTZ, *The Soviet Economy Since Stalin* (1965), a history of economic developments since Stalin's death; L. VOLIN, *A Century of Russian Agriculture: From Alexander II to Khrushchev* (1970), a scholarly treatment of both pre-Soviet and Soviet agricultural policies and problems. (*Military problems*): SEWERYN BIALER, *Stalin and His Generals* (1969), extracts from Soviet military memoirs of World War II; JOHN ERICKSON, *The Soviet High Command* (1962), an extremely well-informed study of Soviet military leadership; ROMAN KOLKOWICZ, *The Soviet Military and the Communist Party* (1967), a scholarly treatment of party-military relations; ALEXANDER WERTH, *Russia at War, 1941–1945* (1964), a sympathetic treatment of its subject by a correspondent who was there. (*Biographies*): ISAAC DEUTSCHER, *Stalin*, 2nd ed. (1967), a well-written biography; EDWARD CRANKSHAW, *Khrushchev: A Career* (1966), a standard biography. (*Cultural issues*): PRISCILLA JOHNSON and LEOPOLD LABEDZ (eds.), *Khrushchev and the Arts: The Politics of Soviet Culture, 1962–1964* (1965), a very useful collection of documents on political control of the arts; HAROLD SWAYZE, *Political Control of Literature in the USSR, 1949–1959* (1962), a historical analysis of literary controls.

(E.L.K./M.Ra./H.S.-W./R.V.D./M.F.)

Russian Soviet Federated Socialist Republic

In terms of territory, population, and economic development, the Russian Soviet Federated Socialist Republic is pre-eminent among the 15 republics that make up the

Soviet Union. It covers 76 percent of that nation's area and—following it—is the second largest political unit in the world; with 6,592,800 square miles (17,075,400 square kilometres), it is almost twice the size of either China or the United States. Its population in 1975, 133,-700,000, places it fifth among the political units of the world, exceeded only by China, India, the Soviet Union itself, and the United States. The "Russian" of its title (often abbreviated R.S.F.S.R., otherwise known as the Russian Federation, or simply Russia) derives not from *russkaya*—"pertaining to the Russian nationality"—but from *rossiyskaya*—"pertaining to the country Russia," and the vast territory is in fact the home of some 60 nationalities. This situation is reflected in the republic's complex system of administrative subdivisions.

The character of the R.S.F.S.R.

Extending halfway round the northern portion of the globe and covering much of eastern and northeastern Europe and all of northern Asia, the Russian S.F.S.R. displays an enormous variety of landforms and environments. These form great bands across its territory: Arctic deserts lie to the north, giving way toward the south to the wastes of tundra and the forest that covers two-thirds of the entire republic and accounts for much of its character. In the far south, beyond belts of open steppes, portions of the land assume a subtropical and even a hot semidesert character. The republic's position, in latitudes in which evaporation can scarcely keep pace with the accumulation of moisture, engenders abundant rivers (including a number of the world's largest), lakes, and swamps.

Most of the people are found in a great triangle in the western, or European, portion of the republic, but since World War II there has been a great flow of population to the Siberian Basin of the east, where deposits of minerals are being exploited.

The republic itself was set up immediately after the October Revolution of 1917 and became a union republic on December 31, 1922, when the federal state of the Soviet Union was created. Its capital, Moscow, is also the capital of the Soviet Union.

The Russian S.F.S.R.'s maritime border, longer than the Equator, meets the Arctic and Pacific oceans. The land borders touch Norway, Finland, and Poland on the northwest and west and the People's Republic of China, the Mongolian People's Republic, and North Korea on the south. They also touch eight constituent Soviet republics: to the west Estonia, Latvia, Lithuania, and Belorussia, to the south the Ukraine, Georgia, Azerbaijan, and Kazakhstan.

Historically, the republic was the core of the expanding Russian state and suffered onslaughts ranging from that of the Mongol hordes in the 13th century to the Nazi invasion of World War II. This heritage, together with a vast area and great natural wealth, has given Russia a unique place among the Soviet republics. Its brooding landscapes and the complexities of the old society have been celebrated in prose and in music by such giants of world culture as Pushkin, Tolstoy, and Tchaikovsky, while the October Revolution and enormous transformations engendered in the Soviet period have been recorded by such people as the novelists Maksim Gorky and Mikhail Sholokhov, the poet Vladimir Mayakovsky, and the composers Dmitry Shostakovich and Sergey Prokofiev.

This article describes the land and peoples of the contemporary republic and the specific contribution it makes to the overall Soviet economy, society, and culture. For historical treatment, see RUSSIA AND THE SOVIET UNION, HISTORY OF. There are also separate articles on the major cities and physical features of the republic.

THE LAND

The natural regions. The Russian S.F.S.R. is divided basically into plains and mountains and, using these and other natural characteristics as criteria, may be subdivided into nine physical regions.

The Kola–Karelian region. The Kola–Karelian region lies in the northwest of the European Russian S.F.S.R. To the west, beyond the Finnish (and, in the north, a small portion of the Norwegian) frontier, it continues as Scandinavia. Karelia is a plateau marked by ridges and knolls and dotted with many lakes, the largest being Ladoga, Onega, Segozero, Pyaozero, Imandra, Umbozero, and Lovozero (*ozero*, "lake"). Ancient glaciation is evident everywhere, both in the scoured landscape of the glaciers' advance and in the mask of drift left on their retreat.

Karelian lakes

Taiga and swamps cover the southern part. The Kola Peninsula is mainly hills and plateaus, though Mt. Khibini rises to 3,907 feet (1,191 metres).

Despite the Arctic location, the climate here is temperate continental, averaging 12° F (—11° C) in January and 57° F (14° C) in July, with annual precipitation of 14–20 inches (350–500 millimetres). The principal rivers are the Ponoy, Vodla, Kem, and Suna. There is a narrow band of tundra in the northern Kola Peninsula and a zone of taiga forests on rocky podzolic soil in the south.

The Kola region has deposits of nickel, copper, iron, valuable types of mica, apatite, and nepheline as well as raw materials for the construction industry and peat.

Animal life depends on the character of the natural zones. The Arctic fox, northern reindeer, and snowy owl are characteristic of the tundra; elk, wolverine, brown bear, lynx, hare, and fox are found in the taiga and forest zones.

The Russian Plain. The Russian Plain, one of the great lowland areas of the world, extends east from the western border to the Ural Mountains and from the Arctic Ocean south to the Caucasus and the Caspian Sea. The topography is varied; there are elevations of up to 1,300 feet (400 metres) in the Valdai Hills west of Moscow, in central Russia stretching south of Moscow, and in the Volga Hills (just west of the Volga, southeast of Moscow), alternating with the vast lowlands of the Oka–Don and the Caspian littoral, part of which lies below sea level. The Oka–Don lowland, passing imperceptibly into the Volga Hills, ends sharply at the Volga, where the Zhiguli Mountains begin, sometimes rising to 1,200 feet.

The climate is mainly temperate continental, with January temperatures varying from 29° F (—1.5° C) in the southwest to —8° F (—22° C) in the northeast. July temperatures average 48° F (9° C) in the north and 77° F (25° C) in the southeast. Annual precipitation ranges from around 24 inches (600 millimetres) in the west to five inches (125 millimetres) in the southeast. Many great rivers flow across the plain, most of them—for instance, the Volga, Dnepr, Don, and Western Dvina—originating in the north. They are fed mainly by snow and freeze for about two months in the south and seven in the northeast. The Volga is the principal river, its basin encompassing nearly half the Russian Plain. In the north there are many lakes and swamps.

The European triangle is nearly devoid of exploitable natural resources. The soil is very thin podzol, which historically has yielded poor crops and much of which has been allowed to return to forest, where the Russians like to hunt mushrooms. The situation for the homeland of the Great Russians is desperate in regard to underground minerals, for there are none. Prior to the 18th century, iron, copper, and more precious metals had to be imported into Muscovy. The situation changed when the Russians began to exploit the Urals during the reign of Peter the Great and subsequently moved to develop Siberia, the Ukraine, and other regions outside their homeland. The absence of local natural resources explains much of Russia's geopolitics for the past quarter millennium.

Absence of natural resources

A significant part of the Russian Plain is covered with forests: taiga (spruce, fir, and Siberian spruce), mixed, and broad-leaved (oak, birch, beech, and linden). In the north of the plain are tundras; on the southeast fringes, steppes and semideserts.

Animal life varies: Arctic fox, northern reindeer, snowy owl, and willow ptarmigan are found in the tundras; white elk, brown bear, lynx, wolverine, squirrel, sable, hare, and fox in the forests. In the forest steppes and steppes are rodents—suslik (ground squirrels, genus

Spermophilus), jerboa, and marmot—and birds—bustard, eagle, and *strepet* (related to the bustard).

The Caucasus. The Russian S.F.S.R. includes the northern part of the Great Caucasus (Bolshoy Kavkaz), extending north-northwest to south-southeast from the Black Sea to the Caspian, containing the Kuban–Azov and Terek–Kuma lowlands, separated by the Stavropol Upland, about 2,300 feet high. Alpine and moderate-altitude relief prevails, and the region's climate is temperately continental; January temperatures average 21° F (−6° C) and July 76° F (24.5° C). In parts of the east the climate is arid. Maximum annual precipitation is 15.7 inches (400 millimetres). The mountaintops have permanent snow and glaciers, feeding the numerous rivers, which can flood for up to six months in warm years. Tundra vegetation and, on the lower slopes, alpine meadows are found. Pine, spruce, and fir grow to elevations of 6,500 feet (2,000 metres), and oak, hornbeam, ash, beech, and wild fruit trees are found to 5,000 feet (1,500 metres).

The foothills form sloping plateaus, sometimes intersected by spurs rising 5,000 feet. Fields, vineyards, and orchards are numerous, and in the subtropical southwest are laurel, palm, bamboo, and boxtree. The seaward slopes of the Caucasus Mountains, with their extremely fertile *zheltozem* (yellow-earth) soils, luxuriant vegetation, and subtropical climate, make good sites for health resorts, rest homes, Pioneer camps, and tourist centres.

Mountain animals of the Caucasus

Mountain animals include species from temperate forests, semideserts, and high mountains: tur (wild goat), chamois, stag (red deer), brown bear, lynx, fox, and leopard, and, among the birds, eagle, Caucasian grouse, and pheasant. (See also CAUCASUS MOUNTAINS.)

The Urals and Novaya Zemlya. The great north–south spine of the Urals and of their continuation, Novaya Zemlya (a group of islands in the Arctic Ocean), separates Europe from Asia. The Urals extend about 1,250 miles north–south and are extended an additional 600 miles into the Arctic Ocean by Novaya Zemlya; their landscapes vary from tundra to steppes. Tundra and forest tundra cover Novaya Zemlya and the Polar and Nether-Polar Urals, culminating in Mt. Narodnaya at 6,214 feet (1,894 metres). Shrubs are the commonest vegetation, but there are leaf-bearing trees in the south. The animal life is sparse, mostly reindeer, Arctic fox, willow ptarmigan, duck, and goose. An extremely harsh climate and permafrost inhibit the development of this northernmost area.

The Northern Urals and the northern part of the Central Urals form a taiga zone, rich in forests and potash minerals, predominantly carnallite and sylvite. The Central Urals and much of the Southern Urals are forest steppes and steppes, including extensively eroded massifs and high plains. The Southern Urals' highest point is 5,374 feet (1,638 metres), and it has a continental climate; coniferous, mixed, and broad-leaved forests are found on the slopes, with forest steppe and steppe in the foothills. The area's favourable climate and topography, valuable iron, copper, nickel, asbestos, gemstone, construction-stone, and petroleum deposits, and comparative proximity to areas of dense population have caused it to become highly industrialized. (See also URAL MOUNTAINS.)

The West Siberian Plain. The West Siberian Plain, between the Urals (west) and the Yenisey River (east), is a subdivision of the Siberian Basin, the taming and exploitation of which is forming what may be the greatest developing region in the world today. The area is a plain, marshy in the north and with marked differences encountered in proceeding from tundra to steppe. The climate is continental, with prolonged winter; January's temperatures average −18° F (−28° C) in the north and 3° F (−16° C) in the south, while July's average is 37° F (3° C) in the north and 73° F (23° C) in the south. Precipitation varies between about 18 inches (450 millimetres) in the taiga and about half that amount in the tundra and steppes.

The rivers belong to the Ob and Yenisey systems (both of which traverse the plain from the south to north and empty into the Kara Sea of the Arctic Ocean), and there are various lakes: Chany, Ubinka, and Kulunda. Tundra and forest tundra with peat bogs cover the north, under which vast oil and natural gas deposits have been discovered. The Urengoy natural gas deposits (some 100 miles up the Pur River, which lies about halfway between the Yenisey and Ob) are considered to be the world's largest.

Taiga prevails in the central West Siberian Plain, to the north growing spruce and cedar, in the centre cedar and pine, and to the south fir, spruce, and cedar. Precipitation is, as noted above, twice that of the tundra, and the climate is kinder. Large oil and natural gas deposits have been discovered in the Ob region, and deposits of brown iron ore lie along the Yenisey River. Great expanses are covered with peat.

Western Siberia's southern stretches include the Ishim (west of Lake Chany), Baraba, and Kulunda (south of Lake Chany) steppes. This area is one of the Russian S.F.S.R.'s most important granaries. The vegetation and animal life are meagre: fir and cedar, the large-eared hedgehog, the migratory and striped hamsters, and the chestnut and red-cheeked suslik. The Kulunda Steppe has many ill-drained lakes with high mineral content.

Central Siberia. Central Siberia is a vast territory between the Yenisey River, on the west, and the mountains of northeastern Siberia, on the east. The region includes the Byrranga and Severnaya Zemlya mountains (in the far north), the North Siberian Plain, and the Central Siberian Plateau (farther south), the peaks of which reach 5,600 feet. In the east, along the Lena and Vilyuy rivers, lies the Central Yakut Lowland. The climate is harshly continental, January temperatures dropping to −47° F (−44° C), though summer, when 68° F (20° C) may be recorded in the south, is benign. Annual precipitation is eight to 20 inches (200–500 millimetres). Permafrost is virtually ubiquitous. There is a dense river network, the largest river being the Lena, with its tributary the Vilyuy, and the Yenisey, with its tributaries the Angara, Podkamennaya Tunguska, and Nizhnyaya Tunguska.

Pine forests cover about 60 percent of the Central Siberian terrain; in the north there are Arctic deserts and mountain and plain tundras and in the south small strips of forest steppe and steppe, as in the areas around Achinsk, Krasnoyarsk, Irkutsk, and Kansk.

The Central Siberian Plateau is a high plain, marked by fracture zones along the edges and mountainous in places. The northern borders are covered by tundra and forest tundra, the southern by forest steppe. The remainder is taiga, with stone outcrops covered by mountain tundra sometimes rising to 2,600 feet (800 metres). In the taiga area are dark-coned forests below 1,300 feet and cold-resistant larch forests—the preponderant form of arboreal vegetation in Central Siberia—above.

The climate becomes increasingly continental eastward, while precipitation diminishes, with a long, cold, almost snowless winter and a short, mild summer.

The rivers are numerous, swift, and full of rapids, providing sources of energy complementing the rich deposits of lead and iron ores, nephelines, and coal. The Irkutsk and Bratsk hydroelectric power plants on the Angara River, which flows northwest from Lake Baikal, and the Ust-Ilimsk hydroelectric power plant, which, though not completed, began generating power in 1974, augur well for the future development of the Russian S.F.S.R.

Hydro-electric power of Central Siberia

To the north of the Central Siberian Plateau extends the Taymyr Depression. The Byrranga Mountains—an isolated, compact upland some 1,800 feet high—break into separate ridges near the Laptev Sea, in the east. In the southwestern Taymyr Depression are deposits of copper, nickel, and rare-earth metals.

Southern Siberia's mountains, which include the Altai, Salair, Kuznets Alatau, Sayan, and Stanovoy ranges, are part of the belt forming the southern border of the Soviet Union and average 1,100 feet. The climate is sharply continental, January temperatures averaging −13° F (−25° C), with mild summers. Intermontane basins receive about six inches in precipitation; the windward western slopes gather 60–80 inches (1,500–2,000 millimetres). The region contains the sources of the Ob, Yenisey, and Lena rivers as well as Lake Baikal, the deepest lake in the world. Soil and vegetation vary greatly: a widespread mountain-taiga belt, with subalpine and alpine meadows and mountain tundras in the high mountains, steppes in the intermontane hollows and foothills, and semideserts in the south.

The greatest elevations are in the Tsentralny Alatau (Central Alatau), particularly the southern chain, formed by the Katun and Yuzhno-Chuysky (South Chuya) ranges, where Mt. Belukha, the highest point in the entire Asiatic Russian S.F.S.R., rises 14,783 feet (4,506 metres). Snow and glaciers cover the peaks—numbering more than 1,000—all year.

In the intermontane hollows are steppes: Uymon, Abay, and Kansk, the highest of which, at around 6,000 feet, are reminiscent of the deserts of neighbouring Mongolia. The soil, vegetation, and animal life differ with altitude, though mountain taiga vegetation predominates.

The Altai Mountains (*q.v.*) are crossed by rivers that, with their rapids, are large reserves of energy. Near Mt. Belukha is the source of the Katun River, which joins the Biya to form the Ob. There are more than 3,500 mountain lakes, the principal being Lake Telets.

To the east of the Altai stretch the Zapadny Sayan (West Sayan) Mountains, well broken up, and on the border with the Mongolian People's Republic are the broad Tannu-Ola Mountains. Between them is the Tuva Trough, at about 2,000 to 3,000 feet above sea level. The climate here is harshly continental—severe winters with little snow, and hot, dry summers. To the northwest of the Altai and Sayan mountains extend three nearly parallel ranges: the Salair Ridge, Vostochny Sayan (Eastern Sayan), and Kuznets Alatau. In the west of this latter chain is the Kuznetsk Basin, or Kuzbass, where high-quality coal is mined. In the east is the Minusinsk Basin, an important agricultural region. The Sayan-Shushenskoye hydropower station, one of the world's largest, is being developed there, along with a number of power-consuming industrial plants. By the end of the 1970s the region is expected to be well developed industrially and agriculturally.

The Baikal area. The Cisbaikalia area, west of Lake Baikal, and Transbaikalia, east of it, lie between Southern Siberia's mountains and the Central Siberian Plateau on the west and the Yakutsk Basin on the north. The climate is harshly continental—hot, dry summers and severe, almost snowless winters. Annual precipitation is only eight to 12 inches (200–300 millimetres), occurring chiefly in short spring cloudbursts.

Through the Yakutsk Basin, surrounded by mountains, pass the Middle Lena as well as the Lower Vilyuy and Aldan rivers. Again the climate is harshly continental, with winter temperatures reaching −76° F (−60° C) and a short, dry, hot summer. Annual precipitation is less than 16 inches (400 millimetres).

Northeastern Siberia. Northeastern Siberia is the area east of the Lena River and west of the Kolyma Mountains. Moderately high mountain ranges alternate with vast plateaus, such as the Alazeya and Yukagir, and swampy lowlands, such as those of Yana–Indigirka and Kolyma. The highest ranges—the Verkhoyansk, Chersky, Sarychev, and Suntar-Khayata—reach more than 10,000 feet (3,000 metres).

The climate of the region is, once more, harshly continental, January's temperature sometimes sinking to −94° F (−70° C). The summer is moderately warm, except in maritime and extremely mountainous parts, with an average July temperature of 63° F (17° C) in the south. The Yana, Indigirka, and Kolyma rivers belong to the Arctic Basin.

Lichen tundra, forest tundra, and thin forests predominate in the north, sparse mountain-taiga larch forests in the south.

The swampy, lake-studded East Siberian Lowland extends along the shores of the East Siberian and Laptev seas. The Anadyr Plain, extending in a broadening path to the Bering Sea, never rises above 660 feet. The extreme

(margin left) Extreme climate of the Tuva Trough

eastern part is occupied by the Chukchi Highlands, covered with mountain tundra and cedar.

Northeastern Siberia has an extremely severe climate, wide expanses of mountain tundra, and extreme permafrost (up to 2,000 feet deep); possesses large deposits of gold and tin; and is still remarkably little settled. Its indigenous peoples, like those of much of the less developed regions of Siberia, retain a vigorous folk culture with roots deep in antiquity.

The Far East. The Far East, traditionally regarded as a distinctive region, extends from the Chukchi Peninsula in the north to Vladivostok in the south, including the Kamchatka Peninsula and the Commander, Kuril, and Sakhalin islands. It is of medium elevation, the highest ranges being the Dzhugdzhur, Stanovoy, Burein, and Sikhote-Alin in the southwest and the Koryak Mountains and the Sredny (Central) and Vostochny (Eastern) ranges on Kamchatka in the northeast.

The region has many active volcanoes, and severe earthquakes are common. There are more than 250 volcanoes on Kamchatka and the Kuril Islands, of which 67 are active, including Klyuchevskaya Sopka (15,584 feet [4,750 metres]). There are small lowlands—the Anadyr, Central Amur, Lower Amur, and Khanka lowlands. The climate is monsoonal, with cold, fairly snow-free winters and moderately warm, wet summers. Precipitation ranges from eight inches in the north to 30–40 inches (760–1,000 millimetres) in the Primorye (the southeasterly mainland coast) and southwest Kamchatka.

(margin right) Monsoonal climate of the Far East

The northern Far East consists mainly of plains and mountain tundras, while in the forest zone are stony birches and Dahurian larches (*Larix gmelini*) on Kamchatka and spruce and firs around the Sea of Okhotsk. In the south grow Dahurian larch, Sayan spruce (*Picea ajanensis*), stony birch, oak, hornbeam, ash, maple, Korean cedar, Manchurian nut (*Juglans mandshurica*), and fir, with some relict vegetation, such as Amur cork and the vine *Actinidia*.

The Lower Amur Basin has a dry winter and rainy summer; 85–96 percent of the annual precipitation falls from mid-April to September, causing many floods.

The Primorye area, with its Sikhote-Alin mountain complex parallel to the coast and its intermontane and coastal plains, is economically well developed. The deeply indented coast provides many convenient inlets.

Sakhalin Island, lying between the Tatar Strait and the Sea of Okhotsk, is the largest island in the east Russian S.F.S.R. Its north is lowland, with tundra vegetation; the remainder is forest. The climate is fairly warm in the intermontane plains of the south and on the coast, the soil is fertile, and there are waterpower and timber resources. In the forests are many furbearing animals and medicinal plants. Iron, tin, molybdenum, antimony, polymetallic ores, gold, coal, and oil have been discovered there, and Siberian salmon, humpback (Pacific) salmon, carp, and bream are found in the sea and river waters.

The Kamchatka–Kuril Ridge is made up of young folded mountains, covered by Arctic tundra on the Koryak Mountains (north of the Kamchatka Peninsula) and by tundra–taiga vegetation on the Kamchatka Peninsula, where turf–podzolic soil predominates. The southern islands of the archipelago are washed by the warm Soi Current. Coal, oil, gold, copper, and sulfur have been discovered in the Kamchatka–Kuril Ridge, but only coal is mined in the Kamchatka Peninsula. It was there that Soviet engineers first harnessed the hot subterranean waters for electric power and heating.

The sealing industry is important, as is fishing for Pacific herring, cod, *Eleginus navaga*, Pacific and Siberian salmon, smelt, and crab.

Rivers and drainage. The Russian S.F.S.R. contains some of the world's largest rivers: the Ob–Irtysh system (3,362 miles, or 5,410 kilometres), Amur (1,755 miles), Lena (2,650 miles), and Yenisey (2,543 miles). There are about 100,000 rivers more than six miles long. They flow into the Arctic Ocean—such as the Northern Dvina, Pechora, Ob, Yenisey, Lena, Indigirka, and Kolyma; to the Pacific Ocean—such as the Amur, Anadyr, and Kamchatka Peninsula rivers; and to the Atlantic Ocean, by way of the Baltic and Black seas—such as the Neva, Don, Dnepr, and Kuban. The Volga and Ural rivers flow into the Caspian Sea. Most rivers are fed by snow and rain, while ice lasts from a month in the south of the European section to nine months in Northern Siberia. There are more than 200,000 lakes, particularly in the Kola–Karelian region. Large artificial reservoirs include Rybinsk, Gorky, Kuybyshev, and Volgograd on the Volga, Kama on the Kama, Tsimlyansk on the Don, and Ob on the Ob.

Reclaimed land
Russia has the largest amount of artificially drained land in the Soviet Union, mostly in the European part. Such drainage is also widespread in the Baraba Steppe beyond the Urals and along the Upper Angara, the Lower Selenga, and the Amur. Artificial irrigation occurs in the Northern Caucasus, in the Middle and Lower Volga region, in the Oka River Basin around Moscow, in the Tuva Trough, east of Lake Baikal, and near Yakutsk.

The 10th Five-Year Plan (1976–80) envisages that land improvement will be continued on a large scale. Almost 10,000,000 acres (4,000,000 hectares) of irrigated land are to be commissioned at state expense, 11,600,000 acres to be drained, and 92,800,000 acres of pastures in desert areas to be watered.

THE PEOPLE

National origins, linguistic groups, and ethnic composition. The ancient group of peoples known as the Slavs developed in eastern Europe between the 3rd and 8th centuries AD, and the first Slav state, Kievan Rus, arose in the later 9th century, laying the foundation of three related nationalities: Russian (the national backbone of the Russian S.F.S.R.), Ukrainian, and Belorussian.

The Russia that emerged from this historic nucleus has since had to ward off the Pechenegs (a Turkic people from an area north of the Black Sea) and Polovtsy (or Kipchak; a tribe from the steppe north of the Black Sea) in the 10th–12th centuries, Mongol hordes in the 13th–15th centuries, Teutonic Knights and Swedes in the 13th century, Poles and Swedes in the 17th, Napoleon's army in the 19th, the intervention of 14 governments from 1918 to 1920, and Nazi Germany from 1941 to 1945. This heritage has strongly molded the national character.

The multiplicity of peoples
The multiplicity of peoples in the contemporary republic is reflected in 16 Autonomous Soviet Socialist republics (A.S.S.R.'s) within the Russian S.F.S.R., as well as the five autonomous regions and the 10 national districts (see Table). The rest of the republic is administratively divided into six *kraya* (territories) and 49 *oblasti* (regions).

The population of the Russian S.F.S.R. was 133,700,000 on January 1, 1975, including Russians (82.8 percent), Tatars (3.7), Ukrainians (2.6), Chuvash (1.3), Bashkirs (0.9), Mordvins (0.9), Dagestani nationalities (0.9), Belorussians (0.7), Jews (0.6), Germans (0.6), Udmurts (0.5), Chechens (0.4), Kazakhs (0.4), Cheremis (or Mari; 0.4), and many others, more than 60 in all. Most of the nationalities have deep historical roots, and communities speaking different languages have long-established economic and cultural ties, facilitating communication among them.

Linguistically, the people of the Russian S.F.S.R. can be divided into the Indo-European group, comprising East Slavic- and Iranian-speakers; the Altaic group, including Turkic, Mongolian, and Manchu-Tungus; the Uralic group, with the Finno-Ugric and Samoyedic; and the Caucasian group, comprising Abkhazo-Adyghian and Nakho-Dagestanian.

Main language groups

The Slavic group. The Russian language, together with Ukrainian and Belorussian, constitutes the East Slavic group of the Indo-European languages. Despite the fact that the Russians cover an expanse from the Baltic Sea to the Pacific Ocean, the Russian language's main features are homogeneous.

The Altaic group. Another major group of languages, the Altaic, includes the Turkic-speaking people of the Altai–Sayan foothills, the Altaics, Khakass, Shors, Tuvinians, and Tofalars (or Karagasy). Various groups of Siberian Tatars live in the forest steppe regions of Western Siberia and on the Upper Ob, while many Yakuts have settled in the basin of the Lena River and Dolgans in the northern Krasnoyarsk area. The Bashkirs live in the Southern Urals.

The Turkic cluster also includes the Chuvash and Tatars living along the Middle Volga, and there are Turkic peoples in the Northern Caucasus, among them the Kumyks, Nogay, Karachay, and Balkars. The Evenks and Evens speak Manchu-Tungus languages and the Buryats and Kalmyks Mongolian tongues.

The Uralic group. The Uralic-speaking group, widely disseminated along the Eurasian forest and tundra zone, has complex origins. Finnic people inhabit the European part of the Russian S.F.S.R.: Mordvins, Cheremis (or Mari), Udmurts (or Votyaks), and Komi (or Zyryans) and the closely related Komi-Permyaks are found along the Volga and in the Urals, while Estonians, Karelians, Finns, and Veps inhabit the northwest. The Mansi (or Vogul) and Ostyak (or Khant) peoples, few in number and living beyond the Urals and in the Ob Basin, belong to the Ob-Ugric group.

The Samoyedic group likewise has few members but is dispersed over a vast territory: the Selkups on the Middle Ob and on the Taz; the Nenets in the forest tundra and tundra from the Yenisey to the Yamal Peninsula and from the Urals to the Kola Peninsula; the Enets (Entsy) along the Lower Yenisey; and the Nganasans mainly on the Taymyr Peninsula.

The Caucasian group. The Caucasian-speaking aggregate, which includes people of the Abkhazo-Adyghian, Nakh, and Dagestani groups, is remarkable in its complexity. In the Northern Caucasus, the Abkhaz, Abaza, Kabardian (or Circassian), and Adyghian languages are similar to each other but differ sharply from the languages of the Nakh group (Chechen and Ingush) and of the Dagestani group (Avar, Lezgian, Dargin, Lakk, Tabasaran, Andi, Tzez, Archi, and about 20 others).

Other groups. There are in Siberia a few Paleo-Asiatic peoples, having much of their way of life and culture in common but differing in origin and also, largely, linguistically. Some of these peoples are nevertheless related by language, so that the Chukchi, Koryaks, and Kamchadals (Itelmens) belong to a group known as Luorawetlan, while the Eskimos and Aleuts belong to the Eskimo-Aleut group. The languages of the Gilyaks (or Nivkhs) on the Lower Amur and Sakhalin Island and the Yukaghirs of the Kolyma area are quite isolated, while the language of the Kets, a small population living along the Middle Yenisey, is likewise unique.

Minority peoples

(See further ALTAIC LANGUAGES; CAUCASIAN LANGUAGES; PALEOSIBERIAN LANGUAGES; SLAVIC LANGUAGES; URALIC LANGUAGES.)

Population distribution and demographic trends. The distribution of population in the republic is not uniform, depending both on the opportunities offered or denied by the environment and on the equally varied potential of various eras of history. Regions in the central band of European Russia are of long settlement

Minority Republics, Regions, and Districts of the Russian S.F.S.R.	
Autonomous Soviet Socialist republics	autonomous *oblasti* (regions)
Bashkir (Bashkiriya)	Adygey
Buryat (Buryatiya)	Gorno-Altay
Chechen-Ingush (Chechen-Ingushetiya)	Karachay-Cherkess
Chuvash	Khakass
Dagestan	Yevreyskaya (Jewish)
Kabardino-Balkar (Kabardino-Balkariya)	national *okruga* (districts)
Kalmyk (Kalmykiya)	Agin-Buryat
Karelian (Karelia)	Chukchi
Komi	Evenk
Mari	Khanty-Mansi
Mordvinian (Mordviniya)	Komi-Permyak
Severo-Ossetian (Severo-Ossetiya)	Koryak
Tatar (Tatariya)	Nenets
Tuvinian	Taymyr
Udmurt (Udmurtiya)	Ust-Ordynsky Buryat
Yakut (Yakutiya)	Yamalo-Nenets

and economically well developed. Here the population density varies from 135 to 200 persons per square mile (52 to 77 per square kilometre), sometimes rising to 676 (261). Elsewhere, mainly in the tundra and taiga zone, the density is well under one person per square mile.

In European Russia, the population is densest in an area between a line linking Leningrad–Cherepovets–Vologda–Kirov in the north and the Caucasus Mountains in the south. In the Urals region the people live mainly between Sverdlovsk and Chelyabinsk, the population tailing off to the east. The Trans-Siberian Railroad forms an axis along which Siberia's agricultural colonization has proceeded since the mid-19th century. The narrow population belt widens around Novosibirsk (because of the Kuznets Basin and its coalfield) and along the Yenisey to the south of Krasnoyarsk (around the Minusinsk Basin). To the east of Lake Baikal the population band narrows further, stretching along the railway to the Pacific Ocean and terminating in the Suyfun-Khanka Plain near Vladivostok.

Migration from the crowded central portion of European Russia is traditional. Immigrants traversed the Urals with the first caravans as the Russian government extended its boundaries. The Soviet period has seen rapid economic development of the eastern Russian S.F.S.R., stimulating the flow of population there. Migration has not been solely across the Urals but also to other union republics, as economic development accelerated, natural resources were exploited, and capital was invested in industry and urban construction.

Urbanization Rapid urbanization has been an important factor in Soviet demography. The Russian S.F.S.R.'s urban population was 14 percent of the total in 1920, 52 percent in 1959, and 67 percent in 1974. Seven of the 12 Soviet cities with more than 1,000,000 inhabitants were in the Russian S.F.S.R., as were 47 of the 74 cities with populations of more than 300,000 in 1974. There are many large, rapidly growing cities in the republic, such as Tolyatti, which from 1959 to 1974 increased 460 percent, Bratsk (328), Volzhsky (166), Cheboksary (141), and Cherepovets (140).

The population's natural growth shows a moderate birth rate, of about 15 per 1,000 annually; the death rate, around 9 per 1,000, is low. A slightly declining birth rate reflects rapid urbanization and increasing employment of women. An equally slight growth in the death rate reflects an increasing proportion of old people. The natural increase in population is slightly less than 6 per 1,000 (0.59 percent) annually.

THE ECONOMY

The Russian S.F.S.R. since World War II has been transformed into a powerful, highly developed, industrial–agrarian republic. Natural resources have undoubtedly been significant in this development. Hundreds of deposits of mineral wealth have been discovered: more than 70 percent of Soviet coal reserves are concentrated in the Russian S.F.S.R., exceptionally large deposits, estimated at 6,000,000,000,000 tons, having been discovered in Eastern Siberia and the Far East. There are also large deposits of iron ore as well as copper, zinc, lead, nickel, aluminum, tin, molybdenum, gold, platinum, and other nonferrous metals. The world's largest petroleum and natural gas reserves are located in the republic, in the northern part of Western Siberia, and the petroleum reserves have been estimated as second only to those of the Persian Gulf region.

The republic can be divided into 10 economic regions: Northwest, Central, Volga-Vyatka, Central-Chernozem, Volga, Northern Caucasus, Urals, Western Siberia, Eastern Siberia, and Far East. Industry is the principal component of the republic's economy, its structure hardly differing from that of the industry of the Soviet Union as a whole. Food and light industries account for about 12 percent of industrial production.

Heavy industry. Heavy industry plays a decisive role in the Russian S.F.S.R.'s economy, particularly the fuel and power sectors.

Fuel. More than half the fuel sector is engaged in the processing of petroleum; a third produces coal; and the remainder exploits natural gas. In 1974 the Russian Federation extracted 419,000,000 tons of petroleum, 410,000,000 tons of coal, and about 3,530,000,000,000 cubic feet of gas.

Petroleum and natural gas Directives of the 25th Congress of the Communist Party of the Soviet Union in 1976 called for increasing the output of natural gas to 15,400,000,000,000 cubic feet (436,000,000,000 cubic metres) and petroleum to 695,-000,000 tons by 1980. Western Siberia has become the largest petroleum centre in the country. Expansion of the oil refinery at Komsomolsk-na-Amure's (in the Far East) was completed during the previous Five-Year Plan (1971–75), and new factories were set up in the Far East and in the Arkhangelsk region (around the White Sea, an inlet of the Arctic Ocean).

Pipelines from the oil and gas areas in Western Siberia were extended to the Central region via the Urals and across Siberia to the Far East, and underground gas reservoirs were significantly enlarged in European Russia near the main industrial centres. A centre for gas extraction and processing was built near Orenburg.

Power. Electrical energy occupies a special place in the complex fuel and power economy of the Russian S.F.S.R. Power plants generated 605,000,000,000 kilowatt-hours in 1974, thermal power plants supplying about 80 percent of the total electric energy.

During the Five-Year Plan covering the years 1966–70, construction work on 40 large thermal power plants was undertaken: Kostroma (completed in 1973), Karmanovo (first stage completed in 1973), Reft (first stage completed in 1972, enlarged in 1975), and Novocherkassk (completed in 1972). The Konakovo thermal power plant was operating at a full capacity of 6,000,000 kilowatts early in the 1970s.

Thermal power plants During 1971–75 the Russian S.F.S.R.'s electric energy capacity was expanded with the construction of thermal power plants having power units of 300,000–800,000 kilowatts' capacity. The Kirishi power plant on the Volkhov River, near Leningrad, was enlarged, and the Ryazan power plant was commissioned (1973). New power units were also installed at the Iriklinsky and Reft power plants in the industrial parts of the Urals (1974), while the Surgut power plant, on the Ob River (inaugurated in 1972), and the Primorskaya, near Vladivostok, also began functioning.

Construction of hydroelectric power plants, providing generating power, with simultaneous provision of water supply and water for irrigation and development of river navigation and fishing, was also being pressed forward. The main centres of activity were on the Volga and Kama and the rivers of the Northern Caucasus. The Krasnoyarsk hydroelectric power plant, with a capacity of 6,000,000 kilowatts, was completed in 1971. Work was started or continued on the Kolyma (in Eastern Siberia), Ust-Ilimsk (first power delivered in 1974), Zeya, and Sayan plants during the mid-1970s.

Atomic power plants with unit capacity of 1,000,000 kilowatts and more were also increasing in number. Plants in operation by late 1973 included the Leningrad and Kola (near Murmansk). The Kursk and Novovoronezhsky plants were to be the next, and the construction of the Smolensk and Dūkštas (Lithuania) plants was continuing in the mid-1970s.

The total amount of electrical energy generated during the 10th Five-Year Plan (1976–80) by all types of power plants was expected to show an increase to 830,000,000,-000 kilowatt-hours.

Metallurgy. About half the ferrous metallurgy plants existed before the Revolution, and they have since been fundamentally reconstructed. A large proportion of the products of ferrous metallurgy is supplied by plants built after the Revolution. The latter include the complexes at Magnitogorsk (in the Southern Urals) and Kuznetsk (in Western Siberia) and the plants at Novotulsky, Novylipetsk, Tagil, and Petrov-Transbaikalia. The Amurstal, Komsomolsk-na-Amure, and Chelyabinsk metallurgical plants and the Orsk-Khalilovo and Cherepovets complexes began production during World War II. The first unit of the large West Siberian Iron and Steel Works, near Novokuznetsk, was constructed during 1966–70. The Russian S.F.S.R. contributes 50 percent of the cast iron and 55 percent of the steel and rolled iron to the national economy.

Extension of iron mining was planned for 1971–75. In particular, the annual output of magnetite ore from the Kursk region was expected to increase to about 40,000,000 tons and that of rolled iron to 59,000,000 tons. The leading place in the production of rolled iron was to be occupied by cold-rolled sheets, curved and shaped profiles, high-precision profiles, and various types of pipes and implements.

Nonferrous metallurgy

Most of the nonferrous metallurgical plants have been installed under the Soviet administration, whether in the Northern Caucasus (at Nalchik and Ordzhonikidze) or in the subpolar region (at Monchegorsk, Kandalaksha, and Norilsk). The Urals, Western Siberia, and the Far East are the centres of nonferrous metallurgy. The industry developed rapidly in the Russian S.F.S.R.'s eastern regions during 1966–70. The production of alumina from the Belogorsk (Western Siberia) nepheline was started at Achinsk, and the output of the Bratsk, Krasnoyarsk, and Irkutsk aluminum plants has increased. The Norilsk (in Northern Siberia) copper and nickel plant and the Khrustalny (in the Far East) complex for dressing tin ores have expanded, and construction of the Gay (in the Urals) and the Solnechny (in the Far East) ore-dressing plants has been completed. The tungsten reserves in the Primorye region are also being exploited.

The base of raw materials for nonferrous metallurgy was expected to widen significantly by 1975 with the exploitation of deposits in the eastern part of the republic. Technological innovations to improve the use of raw materials were in process. The construction of a large aluminum plant and enterprises for processing nonferrous metals in the Sayan complex of Southern Siberia during the Ninth Five-Year Plan was contemplated, and the Zhireken complex for dressing molybdenum ores in the Chita *oblast* was to be constructed.

In addition, development of a northern Onega bauxite mine, the largest in the country, was under way by the mid-1970s.

Machine building. The Russian S.F.S.R.'s machine-building industry provides 96 percent of the Soviet Union's total requirements for steam boilers, 100 percent of its grain-harvesting combines, 81 percent of its automobiles, 75 percent of its main-line electric locomotives, 53 percent of its metal-cutting machine tools, and more than 60 percent of various types of instruments, means of automation, and spare parts.

Automobile manufacturing

There are important automobile factories in Moscow, notably the Likhachyov plant and the MZMA (Moscow low-powered car works), and in Gorky, Miass, Yaroslavl, Ulyanovsk, and Izhevsk (in the Udmurt A.S.S.R.). A factory at Tolyatti (near Kuybyshev) manufacturing the Zhiguli car was completed and a heavy-truck factory was being built in the same period in Naberezhnye Chelny, in the Tatar A.S.S.R. Major automobile-trailer factories were also being constructed in Stavropol and Orsk and near Krasnoyarsk.

There was a dramatic increase between 1965 and 1973 in the production of automobiles (from 160,600 to 810,000), trucks (from 334,900 to 533,800), and buses (from 27,400 to 41,500).

The Russian S.F.S.R. manufactures high-power hydraulic and steam turbines and electrical generators with unit capacity of 500,000 and 800,000 kilowatts.

By 1975 a factory manufacturing bearings at Vologda was to be built, and machine-tool factories manufacturing transfer lines were to be set up in Sukhinichi and Sasovo, while it was hoped that the Chuvash A.S.S.R. would become a tractor supplier. A railroad-car factory and electrotechnical industries were planned for Sayan. The production of instruments, means of automation, agricultural machinery, and construction and land-reclamation equipment was to be expanded as much as possible.

Chemicals. The chemical industry was developing even more rapidly by the 1970s than manufacturing, with coal, wood, and foodstuffs providing raw materials for most of its branches. Accordingly, synthetic-rubber factories had been set up at Yaroslavl, Yefremov, and Voronezh, in the potato-growing centres; sulfuric acid factories at Krasnouralsk, Kirovograd, Karabash, Mednogorsk, Chelyabinsk, and Ordzhonikidze, where nonferrous metallurgy was developed; and potassium and phosphorus fertilizer plants at Solikamsk, Berezniki, Perm, Voskresensk, Bryansk, and Krasnouralsk, near deposits of potassium salts and phosphorites.

At the end of the 1950s the chemical industry was able to make use of new natural and by-product gas and by-products of the petroleum industry and therefore no longer needed to appropriate to itself valuable raw materials that could be used for food processing instead. The result was an immediate shift in the location of newly erected chemical enterprises, which gravitated toward the Urals–Volga zone and the Northern Caucasus. Siberia, too, offers favourable conditions for chemistry involving large amounts of electrical energy. Factories manufacturing synthetic rubber, nitrogenous fertilizers, automobile parts and accessories, and various plastic goods are already in operation there.

The Russian S.F.S.R. supplies 80 percent of the Soviet Union's automobile tires, more than 70 percent of its chemical fibres and chemical insecticides, and more than 50 percent of its mineral fertilizers and sulfuric acid.

The enlargement of the Novgorod chemical complex (completed in 1975) and the starting of the second Berezniki potassium complex (first stage completed in 1973) and the Uvarovo disuperphosphate factory (completed in 1973) took place under the Eighth Five-Year Plan (1966–70), while the output of mineral fertilizers increased at the Voskresensk, Novomoskovsky, and Nevinnomyssk chemical complexes.

Fertilizer production

Output of fertilizers in the Russian S.F.S.R. by 1973 had climbed to 37,000,000 tons, and by 1980 chemical plants were expected to produce 74,000,000 tons of mineral fertilizers, almost half the national total. New construction under the Ninth Five-Year Plan (1971–75) included a fertilizer factory in the Tula region; the third Berezniki and Solikamsk potassium fertilizer plants were already under way at the beginning of the 1970s. The Primorye chemical and mining complex was expanded; construction of the Zimino electrochemical complex in the Irkutsk region had been started; a synthetic-fibre factory was being built in the Altai region; and several petrochemical complexes in the European Russian S.F.S.R. and one at Achinsk in Siberia, based on Siberian crude, were under construction. The Five-Year Plan also looked forward to the construction of petrochemical complexes around Tobolsk and Tomsk.

Forestry and wood pulp. The forest, paper, and wood industries are important, since more than 90 percent of Soviet wood resources are in the Russian S.F.S.R.; indeed, the republic has the largest forest reserves in the world. More than 43 percent of the Russian S.F.S.R. is forest, amounting to 2,773,000,000,000 cubic feet (78,500,000,000 cubic metres). Most of this is matured and over-matured trees, which are of the greatest value.

Coniferous trees, including pine, are important, and the Russian S.F.S.R. is the world's richest area in this valuable species, though other coniferous trees, such as spruce, cedar, and especially larch, are equally important.

The principal forestry enterprises are concentrated in the northwest and the Urals, supplying almost half the republic's total volume (more than 12,670,000,000 cubic feet in 1973), around 35 percent of the lumber, and about 64 percent of the paper.

Within the Soviet period the forest industry has extended even to the trans-Urals forests. Eastern Siberia has overtaken the Urals in terms of timber output, and the tempo is increasing in Western Siberia and the Far East: extensive complexes were under construction in Tavda, the Verkhnaya Konda, Asino, Yeniseysk, Chuna, and Amursk in the 1970s, while Bratsk, where the first stage of a large forestry complex was completed, had become the country's foremost chemical processor of wood. In the Far East the Komsomolsk cellulose and cardboard complex was not far behind Bratsk.

The Eighth Five-Year Plan saw the start of construction of new workshops in the Novo-Maklakovo sawmill and woodworking complex. In 1973 the Russian S.F.S.R. supplied 9,994,000,000 cubic feet (283,000,000 cubic metres) of commercial wood, 4,503,000 tons of paper, almost the same amount of lumber, and 6,250,000 tons of cellulose. Further developments would be concentrated in Siberia, the Far East, and the northern regions of the European Russian S.F.S.R.

The construction of the Bratsk timber industry complex was expected to be completed by 1975, and work on the new Ust-Ilimsk complex was to have begun.

Construction materials. During the Soviet period, rapid growth in the production of structural materials has taken place. For the Ninth Five-Year Plan, the structural-materials industry was called on to produce materials and implements ready for the factory, to widen the assortment of finished materials and sanitary equipment, and to increase production of ceramic drainage and irrigation pipes.

The industry was to be helped by utilizing intermediate products from other branches of industry, such as slag and cinders.

Light and food industries. Light industry, which is concentrated in the Central region, provides 82 percent of the nation's cotton fabric, 75 percent of the linen, more than 70 percent of the silk and woollen fabrics, 51 percent of the knitted wear, and 53 percent of leather footwear.

During 1966–70, 14 textile, 13 knitting, 19 sewing, and nine leather footwear enterprises were erected in other parts of the Russian S.F.S.R. The republic was expected to produce 81,000,000,000 to 85,000,000,000 square feet (7,500,000,000 to 7,900,000,000 square metres) of textiles and 413,000,000 pairs of footwear by 1975.

The republic accounts for 70 percent of the Soviet Union's total catch of fish, whales, and seals and its utilization of other sea products. In addition, it produces 62 percent of all sausage and ham products, as well as soap, 62 percent of all whole milk, around 58 percent of the candy, 50 percent of the meat, 51 percent of all animal oil, more than 40 percent of the canned food, 34 percent of the vegetable oil, and about 28 percent of the sugar.

The Eighth Five-Year Plan (1966–70) for the food industry led to the creation of many enterprises producing cheese, whole milk, yogurt, sour milk, curds, and sour cream, while more than 700 other plants producing dairy and meat products were built or reconstructed. Six new modern sugar refineries were built, and the capacity of the canned-food industry increased by 300,000,000 containers. The construction of the largest chocolate factory in the Soviet Union was undertaken at Kuybyshev, on the Volga.

The Russian S.F.S.R.'s food output by 1975 was forecast at 5,200,000 tons of meat products, 15,400,000 tons of whole-milk products, and a wide assortment of other foods.

Agriculture. The Russian S.F.S.R. accounts for half the total agricultural production of the Soviet Union, there having been about 13,300 *kolkhozy* (collective farms) and about 10,300 *sovkhozy* (state farms) in the republic in 1974.

Agricultural land covers about 14 percent of the Russian S.F.S.R. and represents more than 36 percent of the total agricultural land of the Soviet Union. In addition, there is great potential for substantial increase through drainage and clearance. Mechanization and technological innovation are proceeding: in 1973 alone, 156,000 new tractors, 97,000 combines, 100,000 automobiles, and more than 500,000 pieces of other agricultural equipment were manufactured. Additionally, 29,000,000 tons of mineral fertilizers and more than 28,900,000,000 kilowatt-hours of electric energy were consumed in the republic.

Cereals, vegetables, and fruits. The main product of farming in the Russian S.F.S.R. has always been grain,

and 60 percent of the farmlands are devoted to wheat, rye, barley, oats, and groat (hulled) crops. Fodder crops come second, grown on 30 percent of the arable land and including about 19 percent annual and perennial grasses and almost 9 percent maize (corn). The Volga area, the Urals, the Northern Caucasus, the Central and Central-Chernozem regions, and Western Siberia are the main grain producers of the Russian S.F.S.R., supplying 87 percent of the total grain yield and about 88 percent of the wheat. In 1973 the republic harvested 142,000,000 tons of grain, including around 64,000,000 tons of wheat. In 1975, however, grain production fell to only 85,000,000 tons. European Russia has always been the leading producer of the main commercial crops, such as sunflower seeds, sugar beets, and flax fibre, which together take up more than 5 percent of the farmland; another 4.5 percent goes to potatoes, vegetables, and melons. The output of principal commercial crops in 1973 approached 34,000,000 tons of sugar beets, 189,000 tons of flax fibre, 4,100,000 tons of sunflower seeds, 68,200,000 tons of potatoes, and 13,100,000 tons of vegetables.

Livestock. Livestock breeding is the second main agricultural feature. The livestock population at the end of 1974 was 54,747,000 cattle (including 21,415,000 dairy cows), 34,981,000 pigs, and 67,304,000 sheep and goats. Animal products in the mid-1970s amounted annually to around 7,450,000 tons of meat, 47,000,000 tons of milk, 29,650,000,000 eggs, and 230,000 tons of wool.

European and Asiatic Russia differ in livestock breeding. Intensive processes such as raising of beef and dairy cattle take place in the European part; raising of distant pasture sheep takes place in Asia. About 2,300,000 reindeer graze on moss and lichens in the north.

Land reclamation projects. The Ninth Five-Year Plan anticipated that, by 1975, 3,000,000 acres (1,200,000 hectares) of irrigated lands would be available, 4,400,000 acres (1,800,000 hectares) of pasture land would be drained, and at least 1,600,000 acres (650,000 hectares) of highly productive meadows and pastures would be created.

In the Volga region and the Northern Caucasus are the main regions for irrigation, such areas having increased by 140,000 acres (57,000 hectares) in the Volga region and by about 930,000 acres (375,000 hectares) in the Northern Caucasus.

By 1975 the Bolshoy Stavropolsky Kanal (Great Stavropol Canal) was scheduled to be built in the Northern Caucasus, and the expansion of the Donskoy Magistralny Kanal (Don Main-Line Canal) was to begin. Work started in 1974 on the West Siberian Irrigation Canal. In the Volga region attention was to be concentrated on vegetable and melon cultivation, and in the Volga–Akhtuba floodlands rice was to be emphasized.

The area of irrigated lands in the Far East was to increase by almost 124,000 acres, and 800,000 acres of waterlogged lands were to be drained. Further, there were plans to increase the production of soybeans and rice in this region.

Transportation. Some 48,000 miles (77,000 kilometres) of railroad tracks form the base of the Russian S.F.S.R.'s transportation system. There are also more than 77,000 miles (124,000 kilometres) of navigable internal water routes and about 161,000 miles (260,000 kilometres) of surfaced motor roads; 81,000 miles (130,000 kilometres) of oil and natural gas pipelines; and more than 250,000 miles (400,000 kilometres) of air routes; long-distance and coastal sea routes supplement them.

Railroads. The railroads, the most widely used form of transport, are responsible for about three-quarters of the freight turnover in the republic, accounting for more than 1,420,000,000,000 ton-miles (2,070,000,000,000 metric ton-kilometres) and carrying 2,070,000,000 tons of goods. The density of the modern railroad network is by no means uniform, ranging from 39 to 49 miles of track per 1,000 square miles in the Central and Central-Chernozem regions to 2.5 to 6.5 in Western Siberia and to a mile or less in Eastern Siberia and the Far East.

Marginal notes:

Textiles and footwear

Grain and subsidiary crops

Electrification of railways

More than 30 percent of the railroads were electrified by 1971; not only individual sections around principal industrial centres but also entire trunk lines, such as the Moscow–Chita (running east of Lake Baikal), Leningrad–Yerevan, and Barnaul–Zheleznogorsk lines, are electrified.

Inland waterways. River navigation plays an important role in regions in which there are no other means of communication. Freight turnover by river transport in the Russian S.F.S.R. during 1973 amounted to 121,300,-000,000 ton-miles, with a total of 396,000,000 tons of goods being transported. Thanks to the realignment of natural water routes, the creation of new types of craft, the mechanization of ports, and the improvement of navigational services, the speed of river transportation has increased substantially.

Almost 45 percent of the freight travelling by water is minerals and construction materials. Timber, wool, grain, and salt constitute one-third, though grain freight, taken by itself, has decreased to 2 percent from its 14 percent in pre-Revolution times. Oil and coal take up 15 percent. Passenger travel has increased, more than 114,500,000 passengers being transported in 1973. The river passenger fleet includes numerous high-speed hydrofoils and Hovercraft.

Roads. Motor transportation accounted for 104,460,-000,000 ton-miles of freight turnover, and trucks carried 11,120,000,000 tons of goods in 1973, a contribution of more than 5 percent to the republic's annual turnover.

Pipelines. Pipelines for petroleum, petroleum products, and gas are carrying 395,000,000 tons of petroleum and products each year. The Grozny–Tuapse pipeline exceeds 380 miles and the Tuymazy–Omsk pipeline 810 miles in length. Others include the Almetyevsk–Gorky pipeline, with branches extending to Yaroslavl and to the Ryazan–Moscow line. The Druzhba ("Friendship") is the longest pipeline—2,900 miles (4,700 kilometres)—beginning on the shores of the Volga and ending in the socialist countries of central Europe. In the early 1970s lines were built to transport gas to Italy and West Germany.

Shipping. The merchant fleet plays a great role in establishing ties within the republic, especially between regions on the Arctic seaboard, despite the seasonal nature of Arctic shipping. The port of Murmansk is open 365 days a year, partly by means of icebreakers; Arkhangelsk is open 175 days and Nizhnyekolymsk 110 days. Merchant shipping is also very important in foreign trade.

Air. Air transport is widely used for bulk goods. In 1973 more than 53,000,000 passengers and more than 1,-900,000 tons of goods were carried by air. Aviation is important in the extreme north, in parts of Siberia, and in the Far East, being nonseasonal and the only means of long-distance transport to some areas.

The outlook for transportation. Under the Ninth Five-Year Plan (1971–75) the railroad networks with the heaviest freight traffic (particularly those of the Kuznets Basin–Urals and the Urals–Central region) were strengthened by second tracks. The Tyumen–Tobol–Surgut railway was completed (1974), and electrification continued, along with the construction of new routes to ensure a growing system of transportation to serve the new industrial regions.

Waterway-expansion plans

Freight turnover by river transport was expected to increase by about 24 percent; the traffic capacity of river ports and landings was increasing, and the water-communication routes were improving, especially in the east. The construction of the Tobol and Surgut river ports was expected to be completed by 1975, and the reconstruction and widening of important seaports in the Far East was undertaken. New oil and gas pipelines were extended from Western Siberia to the oil refineries and to the areas of the Russian S.F.S.R. lacking in fuel.

ADMINISTRATION AND SOCIAL CONDITIONS

The constitutional background. The Russian Soviet Federated Socialist Republic is, according to its current constitution, a sovereign socialist state, the power of which derives from workers and peasants. The socialist economic system and the socialist ownership of tools and means of production form the economic basis of the republic. Even before the Russian S.F.S.R. had been formed, the Second All-Russian Congress of Soviets had created the Soviet government and promulgated decrees on peace and on land, which ultimately took Russia out of World War I and transferred land to the peasants.

Creation of the R.S.F.S.R.

The Third All-Russian Congress of Soviets, which sat from January 23 to 31, 1918, announced the creation of the Russian S.F.S.R., and the republic's first constitution dates from the fifth congress, which assembled in July 1918. During and after the Civil War (1918–20) the Russian S.F.S.R. was organized to include Autonomous Soviet Socialist republics, the first of which was the Bashkir A.S.S.R., on March 23, 1919.

The Russian S.F.S.R. entered the Soviet Union, then being formed, in 1922.

The Soviet dictator Joseph Stalin, during the purges of the 1930s, advanced a new constitution, established by the Extraordinary 17th All-Russian Congress of Soviets on January 21, 1937.

As described above (see *The people*), the Russian S.F.S.R. is composed of A.S.S.R.'s, autonomous *oblasti*, and national *okruga* for the larger non-Russian nationalities, as well as administrative *oblasti* and *kraya* (territories), the latter incorporating such national administrative subdivisions as autonomous *oblasti*.

Autonomous republics. The autonomous republics enjoy a form of political independence; each has its own constitution, higher organs of state power, legislature, and higher judicial bodies. Each autonomous republic, being a federated part of the Russian S.F.S.R., is represented in the Presidium of the Supreme Soviet of the Russian S.F.S.R. by a vice chairman of the Presidium.

Autonomous regions and districts. Another administrative form of autonomy—the autonomous *oblast* and national *okrug*—extends only to self-government in internal affairs. While non-Russians participate extensively in the administration of both units, the needs of the Russian Communist Party to control the given nationality are always paramount.

Autonomous *oblasti* and national *okruga* send deputies directly to the Soviet of Nationalities of the Supreme Soviet of the U.S.S.R.

Legislative and executive bodies. The Soviet Union since the October Revolution of 1917 has been ruled by the Communist Party. While there are semi-autonomous administrative bodies corresponding to various geographic levels (republics, autonomous regions and *oblasti*, and so forth; see below), there is only one Communist Party. While local first secretaries of the Communist Party in non-Russian areas of the Russian Federation as well as in the other 14 republics are often non-Russians, the second secretary is almost invariably a Russian, thus assuring direct control from Moscow.

The Communist Party structure is pyramidal. At the apex is the secretary general, himself one of the 16 full members of the Politburo. The Politburo, which also has six alternate members, is the central policy-making body of the Soviet Union. Below the Politburo is the Central Committee, with 287 full members and 139 candidate (nonvoting) members. In theory, the Central Committee controls the Politburo, but in reality it serves as a forum for the preliminary testing of policies and supports the Politburo. Next is the party congress, which meets every five years to ratify the current five-year plan and to elect unanimously the Central Committee.

Supreme Soviet

The highest organ of state power is the unicameral Supreme Soviet of the Russian S.F.S.R. Between sessions the Presidium of the Supreme Soviet of the Russian S.F.S.R. is the highest organ of state power, embodying all the rights accorded to the Russian S.F.S.R. by the constitution. It is elected by the Supreme Soviet of the Russian S.F.S.R. and includes a chairman, 16 vice chairmen (one for each autonomous republic), a secretary, and 13 members.

The Presidium in all its activity is subordinate to the Supreme Soviet. The latter confirms the border and regional division of the autonomous republics, autonomous *oblasti*, territories (or *kraya*), and regions; confirms the economic plan and state budget of the Russian S.F.S.R.; reports on its implementation; and chooses the government of the republic—the Council of Ministers of the Russian S.F.S.R.

The Council of Ministers is the highest executive and administrative organ of state power. It coordinates and directs the work of the ministries of the republic and other bodies subordinate to it, adopts measures to carry out the economic planning and state and local budgets of the Russian S.F.S.R., ensures social order while defending the interests of the state and protecting the rights of citizens, directs and inspects the work of the councils of ministers of the autonomous republics, and supervises and inspects the work of the executive committees of the territorial and regional soviets of workers' deputies.

A unicameral Supreme Soviet with its Presidium is the highest organ of state power in each autonomous republic. The Supreme Soviet of the autonomous republic chooses the governing body of the republic—the Council of Ministers.

The local bodies of state power in the *oblasti*, autonomous *oblasti*, national *okruga*, *kraya*, *rayony*, cities, and other localities are the corresponding soviets of workers' deputies.

Electoral procedure. The Supreme Soviet of the Russian S.F.S.R. is elected, from a single list of candidates, by the citizens of the Russian S.F.S.R. for a term of four years; the Supreme Soviet of an autonomous republic is elected by the citizens of that republic only, also for a term of four years.

The Soviet of Workers' Deputies of an autonomous *oblast* is elected, also from a single slate, by its citizens for a two-year term. The regional and territorial soviets of workers' deputies, soviets of workers' deputies of national *okruga*, towns, the regions of large cities, settlements, villages, farmsteads, and *auly* (North Caucasian villages) are elected (under the same circumstances as other elections) for a term of two years. In 1975, of 904 deputies, including 317 women, elected to the Supreme Soviet of the Russian S.F.S.R., 34.8 percent were workers and 15.4 percent collective farmers.

Franchise qualifications

Any citizen of the Russian S.F.S.R. over the age of 21 may be elected a deputy to the republic's Supreme Soviet or to that of an autonomous republic, regardless of racial and national affiliation, sex, religion, educational attainments, social origin, place of settlement, property holdings, or past activity. Citizens over the age of 18 may be elected to local organs of power.

Judiciary. The Supreme Court of the republic, chosen by the Supreme Soviet for a five-year term, is the highest judicial body of the Russian S.F.S.R., supervising the activities of all other judicial bodies. The main task of the supreme courts of the autonomous republics and courts of territories, provinces, autonomous *oblasti*, and national *okruga* lies in controlling the activities of the people's courts.

Judicial proceedings in the Russian S.F.S.R. are carried on either in Russian or in the language of the prevailing nationality; persons not knowing the language of the court, however, have full access to an interpreter and the right to testify in their native language.

According to the constitution enacted under Stalin, justice in the courts is based on the equality of citizens before the law and the court and in exact accordance with the law. Judges are independent and subordinate only to the law. Trials are open, and the accused is guaranteed a defense. The public procurator of the Russian S.F.S.R., who, like the procurators of the lesser jurisdictions, holds his appointment in five-year terms, has the ultimate responsibility for upholding the law.

These ideals, however, have been violated in the extreme since their promulgation. In the 1930s millions suffered from official illegality, in the 1970s thousands. The unconstitutional use of psychiatric institutions and drugs as coercive and control instruments has remained part of the Soviet judicial process since Stalin's time.

Major organizations. *The Communist Party.* The organizations of the Communist Party of the Soviet Union (CPSU) direct political life. They are guided by the Central Committee of the Communist Party and by its regional and territorial committees.

The republic's Komsomol (Young Communist League) organizations accomplish political and educational work with people between 14 and 25 years of age.

Labour organization. Trade unions in the Russian S.F.S.R., with about 62,750,900 members in 1975, were charged with looking after labour protection, industrial safety, labour legislation, and social-insurance funds. They were also prominent in business efficiency and investment and were part of an effort to enhance the popularity of socialist competition and the Communist-labour movement.

Developing production and public services require a larger labour force. The number of workers and serving personnel increased from 39,500,000 in 1960 to 58,240,000 in 1973. Women, who played an active role, accounted for 53 percent of the workers and serving personnel, 76 percent of those engaged in educational work, and 87 percent of those in health care.

The social milieu. The national income of the Russian S.F.S.R. in 1973 was more than nine times that of 1940. The average monthly wages of workers and serving personnel in the early 1970s were considerably enhanced by benefits from public-welfare funds. Wages depend on the type, chiefly the heaviness, of the work, working conditions, and importance of the branch of industry. In 1973 the average wage was 141 rubles per month. Wages higher than average are paid to labour engaged in construction work, transportation, and mining. Collective farm wages are paid after all other commitments (taxes, compulsory investments, seed reserves) have been met.

Wages

Public-welfare funds from the state budget, enterprises, and trade unions are used substantially to improve the condition of workers in the Russian S.F.S.R., both materially and socially. A major portion of public-welfare funds goes for free medical service, training, pensions, and scholarships.

Approximately 24,600,000 persons were receiving pensions in 1974, and expenditure on pensions had increased by 90 percent over the previous eight years. In addition, more than 700,000 mothers with four or more children were receiving a monthly state allowance.

Health. Health care has attained a high level. In 1974 there were almost 2,000,000 medical workers, of whom about 433,000 were doctors of all types and about 1,337,000 were subsidiary medical personnel. There were 119 hospital beds for every 10,000 inhabitants as well as 19,200 outpatient clinics, more than 11,000 maternity and pediatric consultation clinics, more than 1,200 sanatoriums, about 620 rest homes, and 875 homes for the aged and invalid. Preventive-medicine facilities are provided directly in plants, institutions, and collective and state farms.

Housing. During 1918–73, around 17,855,000,000 square feet of living space were constructed or restored and put into use, of which more than 8,012,000,000 square feet were built during 1961–73. Some 6,500,000 persons moved into newly built housing in 1973. Towns are now planned and constructed by creating self-contained residential areas, rather than mere living quarters, as before. This ensures more comfortable living conditions for residents, since day nurseries and kindergartens, schools, stores, dining halls, studios, and repair shops are located nearby.

New housing construction

Education. The Russian S.F.S.R.'s educational system encompasses ages from preschool onward. The main links in the educational system are the general-education schools, specialized secondary schools, and institutions of higher education, with about 43,000,000 persons involved in some form of training. Ten-year compulsory education is effective throughout the republic.

The number of general-education schools of all types was approximately 86,900, with about 24,255,000 pupils at the beginning of the academic year 1973–74. The general-education school, as in all of the union republics, is officially based on principles of full secularism, respect for the individual child, humanism, and democracy. The national schools carry on instruction in their native language (there are in all 42 languages of instruction). School personnel are trained in 107 institutes, of which each autonomous republic has one for its nationals. A large amount of instructional and educational work with students is carried out through extracurricular activities; there are Young Pioneer and student palaces and houses, young-technician and young-naturalist stations, excursion and tourist centres, athletic schools, and children's parks and stadiums.

The specialized secondary schools, of which there were 2,472 in the 1973–74 academic year, prepare specialists with technical training for various branches of the economy, including industry and construction, culture, health care, and education. Highly qualified specialists are trained in 474 institutions of higher education, most of which also have evening and correspondence classes. In 1974 there were 2,700,000 students studying in institutions of higher education and 2,600,000 in the specialized secondary schools. Vocational training schools graduated about 650,000 students annually in the early 1970s. There are higher education institutions in all the territories, regions, and autonomous republics of the R.S.F.S.R.

In 1974 there were 2,952 scientific institutions, including 1,646 scientific-research institutes and their subsidiaries and divisions. The Academy of Sciences of the U.S.S.R. and its branches function in the autonomous republics and major cities. With headquarters in Moscow, the Academy of Sciences is one of the great research institutions of the world. Founded by Peter the Great in 1725, the academy and its various divisions investigate nearly every branch of knowledge and have made many valuable contributions.

The Siberian branch of the Academy of Sciences of the U.S.S.R., in Novosibirsk, is a major scientific centre focussed on Akademgorodok, where 50 academicians and associate members of the Academy of Sciences, 100 doctors of sciences, and about 2,000 candidates of sciences are employed. In the early 1970s similar centres were being established in the Urals, Western Siberia, and the Far East.

There was a total of about 760,000 scientific workers at the end of 1973, more than 207,000 with the degree of doctor or candidate of sciences.

A significant part of the public-welfare funds is spent on the very young, the system of preschool institutions having been widely developed: there were 6,100,000 children in day nurseries and kindergartens in 1974. Some 15–25 percent of the average annual expenditure on the support of children in preschool institutions is covered by contributions from parents, with the state making up the remainder.

Preschool education

Standard of living. With free and universal education, the rise in the workers' cultural and technological level, and mechanization and automation, distinctions between intellectual and physical labour are being reduced, and material and cultural differences between population groups are, it is hoped, disappearing.

All workers and professionals in the Russian S.F.S.R. receive paid vacations of up to one month. Advances in health care and material well-being have led to a sharp decline in mortality, especially among children, the disappearance of the more dangerous infectious diseases, and an increase in the average life-span. The mortality rate among children under the age of one year decreased from 205 per 1,000 in 1940 to 22 in 1973. By the early 1970s the average life-span in the republic exceeded 70 years, 1.6 times that of 1926–27.

CULTURE AND RECREATION

The cultural background. The Russians' modern culture differs markedly from that of the non-Slavic nations in the Russian S.F.S.R. After the October Revolution, village planning, the peasant household, dress, national cuisine, holidays, and folklore underwent substantial changes as a result of the complete reorganization of individual agriculture, cultural innovation, and the availability of medical aid in the villages, as well as of other factors that the republic shared with the rest of the world: development of various rapid modes of transport, radio, and television. Particularly great changes came about in dress and the arts, while several holidays, although closely related to Russian traditions, took on a new colour, such as New Year's Day, End of the Russian Winter, and Harvest Festival. The centuries-old culture, with its regional variations, nonetheless still finds wide, colourful, and vigorous expression.

Innovations have also come about in the case of non-Slavic people living in the Russian S.F.S.R., though individuality is preserved and reflected in architecture, interior decoration, festivals, and folklore. The peoples of the Northern Caucasus, for example, have adopted urban attire without completely abandoning their traditional dress: Circassian coat (*cherkeska*) with cartridge belt, quilted jacket (*beshmet*), sheepskin hat (*papakha*), felt cloak (*burka*), with silver-ornamented belts, shirt (*rubakha*), and long, wide trousers (*sharovary*) for men and, for women, a dress fitting loosely at the waist, high headdress, and shawl and ornamented belt. There are also many unique features in the headdress and in the style, colours, and ornaments of clothing of the nationalities along the Volga, such as the Tatars, Chuvash, Mari (Cheremis), Kalmyks, and Mordvins.

Traditional costumes

Significant changes, too, have occurred in the customs of the Siberian people, especially in the far north. The nomadic life that prevailed before the Revolution has been replaced by a settled one; now only reindeer herders and hunters are nomadic. The log house has remained, but urban dress has replaced traditional clothing, except among the reindeer herders, who still prefer clothing made of warm reindeer skins, the most comfortable for their occupation. The ancient art of the Siberian people is preserved and encouraged, as in the case of the masterly bone carving of the Chukchi, the birch-bark carving of the Khants (Ostyaks), and the colourful fur appliqué work of the Nenets.

Cultural institutions. In the mid-1970s the Russian S.F.S.R. had about 62,000 libraries housing about 820,-000,000 volumes; 77,000 clubs; and about 93,000 motion-picture projectors (79,100 in rural areas); while, each year, about 70,000,000 visits were made to the theatre and 2,700,000,000 to motion pictures. There are about 6,000,000 persons engaged in clubs, studios, and various other creative activities. Drama is one of Russia's leading cultural pursuits, and there are 312 theatres, including 31 national theatres, presenting plays in all 22 languages of the autonomous republics.

Theatres in Russia that are of world renown include, in Moscow, the Bolshoi Theatre, Moscow Art Theatre, Maly (Small) Theatre, Vakhtangov Theatre, and State Central Puppet Theatre; in Leningrad, the Kirov State Academic Theatre of Opera and Ballet and the Leningrad Bolshoi Dramatic Theatre; and in Novosibirsk, the Novosibirsk Theatre of Opera and Ballet. Creative artists from the theatre belong to the All-Russian Theatrical Society in Moscow.

Dance and theatre

Music has always flourished in Russia; the symphonic and chamber works, oratorios, and songs of Dmitry Shostakovich, Sergey Prokofiev, V.P. Solovyov-Sedoy, and Georgy Sviridov are performed throughout the world, while the Pyantnitsky, Voronezh, and Northern chorus troupes, the Siberian Omsk Folk Choir, the Aleksandrov Song and Dance Troupe of the Soviet Army, and the State Academic Folk Dance Ensemble are also popular.

Authors are united in a collective, the Union of Writers of the Russian S.F.S.R. Artists and sculptors belong to the Union of Artists of the Russian S.F.S.R., architects to the Union of Architects of the Russian S.F.S.R.

Among recent sculptural and architectural monuments, the best known are the Piskarevskoye Memorial Cemetery to those who died during the siege of Leningrad in World War II, the memorial to the soldiers who perished at Stalingrad, and the Tsiolkovsky State Museum of Cosmonautical History in Kaluga.

Russian achievements in science, literature, music, and fine arts have received international recognition. Mikhail

Lomonosov, Dmitry Mendeleyev, Klement Timiryazev, Ivan Michurin, Konstantin Tsiolkovsky, Ivan Sechenov, and Ivan Pavlov are famous in Russian science; Aleksandr Pushkin, Mikhail Lermontov, Leo Tolstoy, Anton Chekhov, and Maksim Gorky in literature; Ilya Repin and Vasily Surikov in art; and Mikhail Glinka and Peter Ilich Tchaikovsky in music.

In Soviet times their successors in various fields have included Gleb Krzhizhanovsky, Igor Kurchatov, Nikolay Semyonov, Sergey Korolyov, Boris Petrovsky, Vladimir Mayakovsky, Boris Pasternak, Mikhail Sholokhov, Aleksandr Solzhenitsyn, Aleksandr Tvardovsky, Isaak Brodsky, and Tikhon Khrennikov.

There are more than 600 museums in the republic, some of them world renowned: the Central Lenin Museum, the Central Museum of the Revolution, the State Historical Museum, and the State Tretyakov Gallery in Moscow; the Hermitage and the State Museum of Russian Art in Leningrad; the museum-estate of Leo Tolstoy, Yasnaya Polyana, near Tula; and the Mikhaylovskoye A.S. Pushkin Museum in Pushkin. More than 72,000,000 visits are made to the museums annually.

Publish-
ing
The Russian S.F.S.R. leads the Soviet Union in book, newspaper, and journal publication. Almost 55,000 different books and pamphlets are published annually in the republic, amounting to some 1,369,200,000 copies, including more than 1,287,900,000 in Russian. The Sovetskaya Rossiya (Moscow), Tatarskoye Izdatelstvo (Kazan), Bashkirskoye Izdatelstvo (Ufa), and Lenizdat (Leningrad) are the leading publishing houses. The universities of Moscow, Leningrad, Voronezh, Rostov, Saratov, and Tomsk also have their own presses.

More than 5,100 journals are published in the republic. The literary journals Novy Mir ("New World"; Moscow), Neva (Leningrad), Ural (Sverdlovsk), and Sibirskiye Ogni ("Siberian Lights"; Novosibirsk) are the most widely read.

The Russian S.F.S.R. publishes more than 4,400 newspapers, Sovetskaya Rossiya ("Soviet Russia") being the most widely read. There are also newspapers published in the native languages of the autonomous republics, autonomous regions, and national districts. More than 2,200 newspapers are published directly by industrial enterprises, schools, and large collective and state farms.

Sports. The Russian S.F.S.R. also encourages sports. New stadiums, playing fields, and sporting camps and centres are built each year, the largest being the Lenin Central Stadium in Moscow and the Kirov Stadium in Leningrad. There are more than 1,600 stadiums, 20,000 volleyball and basketball courts, 50,000 soccer fields, 560 tourist centres and mountaineering camps, and many other sporting facilities. Large physical-fitness organizations, with 30,000,000 members in 100,000 physical-fitness collectives, have grown up in factories, plants, schools, and collective and state farms. The Russian S.F.S.R. national athletic games are held every four years.

THE OUTLOOK

Since the Russian S.F.S.R. became a union republic in 1922, it has seen the growth of thousands of major industrial enterprises, high-voltage power-transmission lines, railway and highway networks, pipelines, and agricultural technology.

The directives of the Communist Party of the Soviet Union provide for continued increase in industrial output, to be accomplished by accelerating the growth of the manufacturing, gas, petroleum, atomic energy, and chemical industries, as well as increasing labour productivity and automation.

Plans have been drawn for the further development of agriculture and for increases in the annual yield of grain crops and tonnages of meat, milk, and wool. It is expected that the continuing development of the Siberian portion of the republic will further tend to spread settlement out from the old European Russian economic and demographic base.

This process, together with added emphasis on consumer goods, social services, and science and technology, will further transform the way of life in this large political unit. In doing so it will undoubtedly have a very significant effect upon life in the entire Soviet Union.

(S.A.V./R.He.)

BIBLIOGRAPHY. The best available sources for the Russian S.F.S.R. are usually those devoted to the entire Soviet Union. For bibliographic guides to available sources the reader may consult CHAUNCY D. HARRIS, Guide to Geographical Bibliographies and Reference Works in Russian or on the Soviet Union (1975), arranged both topically and regionally and extensively annotated; or, in Russian, the annual Bibliografiya sovyetskoy bibliografy ("Bibliography of Soviet Bibliographies"). A comprehensive work in Russian is the 23-vol. Sovetskii Soyuz: Geograficheskoye opisaniye, ed. by S.V. KALESNIK et al. (1967–72), of which 7 vol. are on the Russian S.F.S.R. For general topical reference, the 3rd ed. of A.M. PROKHOROV (ed.), Bolshaya Sovetskaya entsiklopediya (1969–   ), and its English translation, Great Soviet Encyclopedia (1973–   ), are the fullest sources. Dated though still valuable is ROBERT MAXWELL, Information U.S.S.R. (1962), with extensive and well-indexed coverage of topics related to the Russian S.F.S.R. The best general English-language geographies are JAMES S. GREGORY, Russian Land—Soviet People (1968), and, for historical perspective, WILLIAM H. PARKER, An Historical Geography of Russia (1968); for coverage of human geography the 2-vol. study by THOMAS FITZSIMMONS (ed.), R.S.F.S.R., Russian Soviet Federated Socialist Republic (1957), is still valuable. Statistical data given in the 800-page annual statistical abstract for the Soviet Union, Narodnoye khozyaystvo SSSR ("National Economy of the U.S.S.R."; 1956 ff.), are usually broken down by republic, while annual data for the R.S.F.S.R. alone can be found in the smaller Narodnoye khozyaystvo RSFSR ("National Economy of the R.S.F.S.R."; 1960 ff.).

(Ed.)

Russian Steppe

The Russian steppes are vast, open, treeless expanses of predominantly grassy, drought-resistant vegetation on rich chernozem (black earth) and chestnut-brown soils. They extend across Eurasia in a vast wedge, running over the south of the Soviet Union from the southernmost part of the Moldavian S.S.R. across the southern Ukraine, the Don Basin, northern Caucasia, the Volga Basin below the Kama confluence, the lowlands north of the Caspian Sea, and northern Kazakhstan into southwestern Siberia, beyond which—east of the Altai—they break up among the mountains. Covering an area of about 1,400,000 square miles (3,500,000 square kilometres), they have been of immense importance in the historical and economic development of a huge area and have been a constant theme in Russian literature and art. (For related information see SOVIET UNION.)

General environmental characteristics. Those parts of the steppe that escaped glaciation during the early Quaternary Period of the Cenozoic Era (2,500,000 years before present [BP]) are mostly covered with loose carbonaceous rock loesses (soft porous rocks of a pale yellowish or buff colour) and loesslike loam. These deposits, together with the absence of forests and the presence of occasional torrential rain, have contributed to the formation of a water-eroded relief. Within the river valleys, which are wide and asymmetrical, some two to four terraces may often form, of which the lowest are usually of sand.

The plateaus between the rivers are also asymmetrical and are interrupted by ravines through which water flows only during the spring thaw and summer storms. In many places the steep sides of both valleys and ravines are scoured by recent gullies, the majority of which occur in the highlands rising successively west of the Dnepr, west of the Don, and west of the Volga. (In order to limit the spread of gullies, which reduce the economically exploitable potential of the steppe lands, trees have been planted and grass has been sown on them; grazing has been restricted, and surface water has been drained.)

Shallow interfluvial areas are spotted with round depressions, or "steppe saucers"; caused by subterranean collapse, they rarely exceed six feet in depth but are generally more than five times (and sometimes even 50 or more times) this measure in diameter. In the Ukrainian steppes nearest to the Black Sea, larger depressions, pody, are found. Between the depressions the country is

Relief

**Topo-
graphic
saucers
and
mounds**

drained by long, winding channels with shallowly slanting sides—the products of superficial erosion. Sometimes
the uniformity of the interfluvial area's relief is broken by
mounds—barrows or lookout points that reach a height
of from 16 to 20 feet—or by erosion–denudation residual
outcrops. Rather less conspicuous are the little mounds
thrown up by burrowing marmots.

Climate. The climate is continental, with warm, sunny
summers, fairly cold winters in the east, and milder winters in the west, with a stable but shallow covering of
snow. Temperatures for July are about 70° F and 75° F
(21° C and 24° C), while those of January are wider
,ranging, −22° F (−30° C) in the east, 28° F (−2°
C) in the west. Most precipitation takes the form of
snow. Toward the end of winter the snow cover of the
Ukrainian steppe and that of northern Caucasia is from
four to eight inches deep—though it may reach from
eight to 16 inches or even 19 inches elsewhere—and
drops sharply over the trans-Baikalian steppe. Rainfall is
comparatively sparse, with 18–24 inches of rain in the
northwest and ten to 12 inches in the southwest. It is
heaviest at the end of spring and at the beginning of
summer. The degree of humidity varies. Every third year
is arid, with strong dry winds blowing in spring and summer, and dust storms.

Vegetation. Among the turf grasses, of which the
steppe is mainly composed, bunchgrass (*Stipa*), fescue
(*Festuca*), bluegrass (*Poa*), and agropyron (*Agropy-
rum*) are most characteristic. Mixed perennial grasses
include sage (*Salvia*), pinks (*Dianthus*), vetch (*Astrala-
gus*), bedstraw (*Galium*), and yarrow (*Achillea*). Mosses are often found among the turf grasses, with lichens
and blue-green algae also in the south. Annual and perennial plants with a short vegetational period occur—
particularly in the south. Grassy plants of various species,
collectively known to the Soviet people as *perekati-pole*,
take on a spherical brushwood shape with their seasonal
maturing; then, breaking off easily in the wind, they roll
along the steppe to mass along the edges of the forests
and ravines. Thick clumps of shrubs and bushes—including karageny, steppe cherry, blackthorn, dwarf almond,
and spirea—occur in the steppes of the east European
plain and in the foothills of the Urals and of the Altai.

Interrelation of forest and steppe. Though to the north
of the steppe a dry climate, saline soils, and proliferation of various grasses, and the uninterrupted relief discourage forests, they do sometimes occur on interfluvial plateaus and in complicated relation to expanses

**The
advancing
forest**

of meadow and grass. Most paleo-botanists and paleo-zo-
ologists agree that the forest was advancing over the
steppe before the advent of man and cite as evidence
those studies that show that in postglacial times the
boundary between forest and steppe was little changed
and that their natural interrelation was disturbed by man,
who, with axe, fire, and grazing cattle, was responsible for
the destruction of many forested areas.

Animal life. The absence of natural shelter on the
steppe conditions the kind of animals that inhabit it. Typical rodents include various types of marmot and other
such burrowing animals and various species of mouse.
The skunk, fox, and wolf are common—as was the tar-
pan (or small wild horse) until the second half of the
19th century. Antelopes are found in the south. The commonest birds are bustards, steppe eagles, steppe kestrels,
larks, and gray partridges. Insects are many and various.

River flow. The rivers are fed mostly by snow. They
overflow their banks during the spring thaw and in summer become very shallow. A high rate of evaporation
reduces river flow to insignificance. The network of rivers
is not dense, and those belonging properly to the steppe
(as distinct from those rising outside, such as the Volga
and the Ob) are shallow; the Don, with a length of 1,160
miles and a catchment area of 163,000 square miles, has
an average discharge of only 33,000 cubic feet per second
at low water.

Types of steppe. The amount of moisture in the soil
conditions both the composition and the structure of the
steppe, so that, from north to south, marked changes in
vegetation and soil occur.

Mixed grass-and-meadow steppe. This northern region of the steppe is humid and is characterized by a thick
vegetation, mainly of thick grasses, and a solid or almost
solid ground cover of soil. Forty or 50 different species
of plants may be found in every 10-foot square. As the
alternate masses of mixed grass bloom, the steppe repeatedly changes colour. In spring and early summer it begins
to shade from lilac to golden yellow, then to pale blue,
and finally to white. In late summer the burned-out
steppe takes on a buff-coloured hue.

**Steppe
coloration**

Tracts of forest break up the grass–meadow steppe along
the floodplains and depressions, occurring also on the
sandy areas and on outcrops of close-grained bedrock
between the rivers. Under the grass meadows lie granular
chernozems—soils rich in humus and in ash and very
fertile. Around the saucer-like depressions de-alkalized,
less fertile clays (de-alkalized solonetz) have formed by
draining and leaching their silty upper layers. Meadow
chernozem soils occur near underground water.

Grass steppe. A drought-resistant variety in which
clumps of grass or turf predominate, the grass steppe is
characterized by feather grass (*stipa*), fescue, *Koeleria*, the
perennial oat, and wheat grass. Ground cover is not continuous, and bare soil is visible between the clumps of
grass. In the interfluvial areas, forests are extremely rare.
(Tidal forests tend to proliferate in flood-river valleys or
to spring up on the slopes and tops of gullies in times of
flood.)

Sage-and-grass steppe. This most southern variety of
steppe, ending in desert, abounds in drought-resistant
shrubs and such herb species as *Artemisia, Kochia,* and
Matricaria. Various species of bluegrass are also present,
as are tulips. In general, vegetation is mainly sporadic,
and various combinations of different species occur according to accidents of relief and soil (including irregular
salinity). Chestnut-coloured soils, in which solonetz soils
and meadow-chestnut soils are interspersed, predominate.
(Their fertility is considerably lower than that of the
chernozem and dark-chestnut soils.)

Regional differences. The nature of the steppe changes
significantly from west to east. In the west, the East
European Plain is characterized by an uninterrupted
relief, a relatively mild climate, and little of the sage-
and-grass vegetation common to the east. Feather grass
and fescues predominate in the grass steppe, and oaks
and broad-leaved species of tree dominate the forest. Soils
are chernozems. Many species of animals and plants common to western Europe occur.

The steppe of eastern Kazakhstan and Western Siberia
has a more complicated relief—flat lowlands typical of
Western Siberia in the north, and in the south, low,
rounded, isolated hills common to Kazakhstan—and a
more continental climate. The vegetation, in general, resembles that of the East European Plain, but local Kazakh species of feather grass may also occur. Broad-
leaved trees appear less frequently than in the east, and
island birch forests predominate. The proportion of
rocky and alkaline soil increases, and the chernozems,
though rich in humus, are shallow and unstable.

In Central and Eastern Siberia the Russian steppe gravi-
tates toward the steppes of Mongolia. The climate is
harsh, with winters in which little snow falls but which
are characterized by sharp frosts that may last for several
months. Average temperatures in January are about −22°
F (−30° C). *Diplachne* and *Stipa capillata* are typical
grasses, and in trans-Baikalia *Stipa capillata* and tansey
also occur.

Steppe resources and conservation. Mixed grass-and-
meadow steppe and grass steppe have long served as the
country's granary, for they produce most of the wheat,
sugar beets, sunflowers, corn, millet, and cucurbitaceous
(cucumber family) cultures, and to the west they support
both horticulture and viticulture. Agricultural products
include cattle, sheep, and poultry, and there is also horse
breeding. To the west some 70 or 80 percent of the steppe
has been tilled, and in Kazakhstan and Siberia all suitable
land has been put to the plow. On sage-and-grass steppe
less soil is tilled, but cattle and sheep are raised, horses
are bred, and agriculture is pursued with the help of

**Agricul-
tural
products**

artificial irrigation. Windbreaks and strips of forest have been planted over wide areas to prevent soil erosion—particularly on the banks at the Don, Volga, and Ural rivers and on several interfluvial plateaus. Ponds and reservoirs have been built in ravines, and small river valleys and dams have been constructed across many rivers.

Few natural expanses of mixed grass-and-meadow and grass steppe remain, save in the state national forests (the most important of which is the V.V. Alekhin Central Chernozem National Forest, south of Kursk) and on the shores of the Black Sea, where certain rare species of animals are also preserved. (F.N.M.)

Rutales

The large flowering plant order Rutales consists of 12 families, about 324 genera, and 4,000 species. Meliaceae is the largest family in the group with about 50 genera and 1,400 species. Some families, such as Aitoniaceae and Coriariaceae, among others, consist of only a single genus. The largest genera in the order are *Trichilia* (300 species, distributed in tropical America and Africa), *Aglaia* (about 300 species in China, Indo-Malaysia, and tropical Australia), *Fagara* (250 species in the tropics generally), *Dysoxylum* (200 species in Indo-Malaysia), and *Commiphora* (185 species in North Africa). Some genera, such as *Blepharocarya* (family Anacardiaceae), *Nymania* (Aitoniaceae), *Toddalia* (Rutaceae), *Limonia* (Rutaceae), and others, are monotypic; *i.e.*, they consist of only a single species each.

The order is possibly of greater importance as a source of hardwood timber than any other in the plant kingdom. It also includes some of the best known tropical and subtropical fruits—the cashew nut (*Anacardium occidentale*), one of the first West Indian fruit trees to be distributed throughout the tropical world by early Spanish and Portuguese adventurers, and the Indian mango (*Mangifera indica*), often called the queen of all tropical fruits; it has delightfully aromatic flesh. The mango has long been cultivated in the Indo-Malaysian regions and has recently been introduced into other parts of the world. The myrrh (*Balsamodendron*) and frankincense (*Boswellia carteri*) of biblical fame also belong to this order.

GENERAL FEATURES

Size range and diversity of structure. The order Rutales consists predominantly of woody shrubs and trees. Herbs are, as a rule, absent, although some are present in the families Rutaceae and Podoaceae. A few, such as the genera *Naregamia* and *Dictamnus*, are undershrubs. Rhizomatous (creeping) tuberous-rooted perennials are found in the family Podoaceae. The order has only few climbers, but poison ivy (*Rhus radicans*) is one well-known example. A great many beautiful forest trees, some of which are reckoned among the most elegant on earth because of their feathery foliage and magnificent fruits, belong to this order. Several trees, such as *Campnosperma auriculata*, *Mangifera lagenifera*, *Buchanania lucida*, and others, attain a height of 33 metres (108 feet). Trees like *Irvingia malayana* may even reach a magnificent height of 66 metres (216 feet). Many have buttresses, which may be thin and steep as in *Irvingia*, spreading as in *Pentaspadon*, or thick and prominent as in *Gluta*, *Parishia*, *Canarium*, and others. Several growth forms occur among the trees of the order. Many, such as *Mangifera lagenifera*, have a dense and almost hemispherical crown with a tall columnar trunk. *Dracantomelon mangiferum* has a conical crown when young, becoming dense and rounded at maturity. *Campnosperma auriculata* has a flat-topped crown. There are several thorny trees in the family Rutaceae, among them the genera *Aegle*, *Citrus*, *Limonia*, and others. *Canarium* has aerial roots, especially on the side to which it leans. These roots may arise from a height above the ground of four metres (13 feet) or even more.

Distribution and abundance. The order Rutales is dominantly pantropical in distribution, with a few genera

Trees of the order

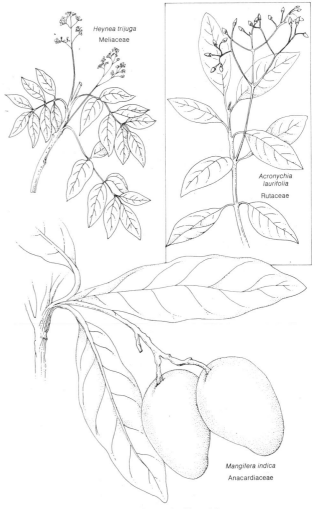

Heynea trijuga
Meliaceae

Acronychia laurifolia
Rutaceae

Mangifera indica
Anacardiaceae

Figure 1: Representative plants of three families of the order Rutales.

extending to temperate regions of both hemispheres. The chief centres of distribution are tropical America, South Africa, *Cneorum* in the Mediterranean region and the Some genera show restricted distribution; *e.g.*, *Kirkia* in tropical and southern Africa, *Nymania* in southern Africa, *Naregamia* on the west coast of India and in eastern Africa, *Cneorum* in the Mediterranean region and the Canary Islands, *Melosma* in California, and *Stylobasium* in southwest Australia.

Economic importance. The group is important in several respects. It includes many fruit trees, such as the Indian mango and cashew nut. The axis under the nut in the latter swells into a pearlike body that is also edible and is used for distilling wine. This false fruit, known as cashew apple, is fragrant. In many varieties of cashew apple the juice causes a slight irritation in the throat. Other varieties are known chiefly from tropical America, where the pulpy portion is extensively consumed. The shell of the cashew nut contains an irritant skin poison that produces blisters and dermatitis. The shell liquid is salvaged and used as a lubricant in electrical insulations in airplanes. The cashew kernel is generally removed and eaten after roasting the nut.

Mango is one of the earliest fruit trees known to mankind. The representation of this tree in the Buddhist *stūpas* bears testimony to its antiquity in India. The tree is inextricably connected with Indian life and religious ceremonies. Sanskrit literature is replete with delineations of its qualities. Every part of the tree, from root to the top, is used by man in one form or another. The fruit itself, in all stages of development, is used in India and neighbouring countries. Raw fruits are used for extraction of tannin and other astringent products, for chutnies and in pickles, and for cool drinks. Squashes, syrups, marmalades, jams,

Skin poisons

jellies, and candies are made from the ripe fruits. The kernel, rich in carbohydrates, calcium, and fat, is used as a stock feed for pigs. When dried and ground into flour, it is used as food by people in some parts of Southeast Asia.

Pistachio nuts are obtained from *Pistacia vera* of the Mediterranean countries and west Asia. Lemons (*Citrus medica* variety *limonum*), oranges (*C. aurantium*), limes (*C. medica* variety *acida*), and other citrus fruits are well-known. Originally, *Citrus* was a fruit of the Orient, where it has been in cultivation for thousands of years. The oldest Oriental literature includes stories about *Citrus*. The United States is now a principal grower of the fruit. Citrus fruits are among the best sources of vitamin C.

Kumquat (*Fortunella*), hog plum (*Spondias*), and bael (*Aegle*) are some of the other common fruits of the Rutales order. *Lansium domesticum* is cultivated for its fruit, known as langsat or lansa, in the Malayan region. The fruits of *Canarium album* are eaten like olives. The brown pulp of wood apple (*Feronia limonia*) mixed with sugar is eaten after straining through a sieve to remove the seeds. Santol (*Sandoricum koetjape*) is a favourite fruit in the Philippines.

Timber from trees of the Rutales order is often excellent. Some of the well-known timber trees are mahogany (*Swietenia mahogani*) of tropical America and the West Indies, Guiana crab tree (*Carapa guianensis*), African cedar (*Khaya senegalensis*) of West Africa, Indian redwood (*Soymida febrifuga*), Chittagong wood (*Chikrassia tabularis*) of the Indo-Burma region, toon (*Toona ciliata*) of India, satinwood (*Chloroxylon swietenia*) of the Indo-Malayan region, yellow wood (*Flindersia oxleyana*) of east Australia, and sneeze-wood, or cape mahogany (*Ptaeroxylon utile*). The important gaboon mahogany, or okoume of commerce (*Aucoumea klaineana*), is used for veneers and plywood. Sapele mahogany (*Entandrophragma*), Colorado wood (*Quebrachia lorentzii*), Spanish cedar (*Cedrela*), and African walnut (*Lovoa*), though less important, are known the world over. The best known timbers are typically reddish in colour, lustrous, easy to work, and unusually free of tendencies to warp under changing conditions of moisture and other atmospheric factors. Such characteristics make these woods eminently suited for cabinetmaking.

Tannin-yielding plants are known in the group—e.g., *Carapa* species (Indo-Malaysia), *Schinopsis* species (South America), *Coriaria myrtifolia* (Mediterranean).

Many barks are medicinal. The bark of *Guarea rusbyi*, known to pharmacologists as cocillana, has properties similar to those of ipecacuanha (*i.e.*, *Cephaelis ipecacuanha*, the dried roots of which contain alkaloids such as emetine, cephaeline, and psychotrine). The tropical South American casparia bark is obtained from *Galipea officinalis*. The extract of Surinam quassia wood (*Quassia amara*) is a tonic. Bitters are prepared from the bitter principles present in the barks of several species, such as cedron (*Simaba cedron*) of Central America, simaruba bark (*Simarouba amara*) of tropical America, and quassia wood (*Picrasma excelsa*) of the West Indies. The bitter fruits of *Brucea amarissima* are used in Malayan and Chinese medicines, particularly to treat dysentery. Among the medicinal plants are neem, or margosa (*Azadirachta indica*), and bael, both of India.

The art of lacquering had its origin in China centuries before the beginning of the Christian Era and reached its climax of development there during the time of the Ming rulers, AD 1368–1644. The lacquers used for this were obtained from the varnish tree (*Rhus vernicifera*). The exudation, a milky liquid, darkens and thickens rapidly on exposure to air. Lacquer, when applied as a varnish, affords remarkable protection, as it is unchanged by acids, alkalies, alcohol, or heat up to 160° F (70° C). *Melanorrhoea usitata* is the Burmese lacquer tree.

Members of the family Burseraceae have an abundance of fragrant balsams (aromatic substances that exude from plants spontaneously or by incision) and resins in their bark. Myrrh and frankincense, both in the family Burseraceae, contain the fragrant substances. Resins and balsams are oxidation products of various essential oils and are very complex and varied in their chemical constitution. The resins, secreted in definite passages or cavities, exude from the bark and harden on exposure to air into lumps. Tapping usually is necessary for commercial exploitation. Other important resins are the carana gum (from *Protium carana*) of South America and balm of Gilead (from *Commiphora opobalsamum*). *Bursera gummifera* is the turpentine tree, which furnishes the resin known as American elemi, cachibou, or gomart. From the elephant tree (*Bursera*) of Mexico is obtained a copal (a type of resin), which is used as a cement and varnish. Chian turpentine is obtained from *Pistacia terebinthus*. *Amyris elemifera* gives African elemi. *Canarium commune* furnishes the resin Manila elemi, and its nuts are edible (Java almond). *C. strictum* of Kerala (India) is the source of black dammar. Fruits of *Canarium* are also valued for their kernels, which are processed to produce a cooking oil. Fat from the seeds of *Carapa* is used for making soap and as an illuminant. Rue (*Ruta graveolens*) is a narcotic and stimulant. Its leaves are used as savory in Mediterranean regions, and oil of rue is also distilled from it. Leaves of *Murraya koenigii* are used for flavouring curries in Indo-Malayan regions. Dyes from the fruits of *Coriaria* have been used to prepare indelible inks. *Khaya*, *Feronia*, and other genera give gums that can be used in place of gum arabic. *Anacardium humile*, *A. occidentale*, and *A. nanum* provide cashew or acajou gum, which is not only a reasonably good adhesive but also contains a small amount of cashew oil, which acts as an insect repellent. *Pistacia lentiscus* of Greece furnishes mastic. Fruits of *Semecarpus anacardium* are known as marking nuts. The young fruits yield a black resin insoluble in water and useful as a marking ink in Southeast Asia.

A few, like the tree of heaven (*Ailanthus altissima*), Persian lilac (*Melia azedarach*), cork tree (*Phellodendron*), and orange jasmine (*Murraya*), are grown in parks and gardens. Orange flowers are used widely in perfumery in France. Because of the pleasantly fragrant aroma, citrus flowers are used throughout the world as decorations in special celebrations. Various kinds of citrus oils are extracted from the rinds (peel) of fruits. These oils develop in sacs or vesicles, which are ductless and without communication with surrounding cells or the exterior.

The fruits of Persian lilac are poisonous to rabbits, poultry, pigs, sheep, and cattle. *Dysoxylum angustifolium* has a preference for riversides, and, during fruiting season, the fruits often fall into the water, where they are eaten by fishes. The flesh of such fishes becomes poisonous to men and animals. The foliage and fruits of *Coriaria* are reported to be very poisonous, and the fruits are used as a dog poison in Mexico. The poison ivy of North America, which is a pest in some of the southern states, is *Rhus radicans*.

NATURAL HISTORY

Life cycle. Members of the order are perennials. The trees in the group play a dominant role in the formation of tropical forests. Many are quick growing and evergreen, as in *Campnosperma auriculata*, *Buchanania lucida*, *Melanorrhoea wallichian*, and *Mangifera indica,* or deciduous, as in *Lannea*, *Juliania*, *Pentaspadon*, and *Rhus*.

Gluta is remarkable in having intensely violet young leaves. The young leaves of *Mangifera* may be brown, reddish brown, or violet. The leaves of *Campnosperma macrophylla* wither red. The deciduous trees usually flower when leafless. Some trees, such as *Samadera indica* (Indo-Malayan), are reported to flower only once in three years. *Mangifera lagenifera* flowers only at long intervals of many years, sometimes as long as 20 years.

The flowers are mostly suited for pollination by insects. The coloured corolla (petals) and sometimes stamens (male reproductive structure) render some flowers conspicuous. Fragrance makes others attractive. The disc (a fleshy structure inside the flower) secretes an abundance of easily accessible honey. Cross-pollination appears to

Timber characteristics

Miscellaneous products from fruits, seeds, and leaves

Unusual leaf colours

be favoured by the proterandry (*i.e.*, the maturing of the stamens before the female parts of the same flower) in many flowers. In rue (*Ruta*) the stamens rise in the centre of the flower, shed pollen successively, fall back, and wither. The stigma (part of the female reproductive structure) ripens only after all the stamens have fallen back. Some of the stamens, though fallen back, may not wither, and they often retain some pollen. If by chance no insect visitor comes, the unwithered stamens may rise up again and shed the pollen grains on the stigma, effecting self-pollination. Here is a remarkable instance in which seed setting is ensured by self-pollination if necessary, but cross-pollination is sought until the last possible moment. The usual visitors are small flies and bees. Many species are also vegetatively propagated.

Ecology.   Members of the family Rutaceae are adapted to various conditions. Some are xerophytes (adapted to dry habitats), frequently of heathlike habit (low dense shrubs)—*e.g.*, the South African *Diosma*. Some members have short shoots whose leaves are reduced to spines. Generally, the members of the order do not prefer open land. Many have a liking for riverside flood zones, as in the Malaysian *Aglaia salicifolia* and *Dysoxylum angustifolium*. Some species of *Aglaia* and *Amoora* grow in swamps. *Xylocarpus obovatus* and *Amoora cucullata* are found in mangrove forests. *Suriana maritima* is coastal in distribution. Plants of tidal stretches include *Gluta velutina*, but species of *Balsamodendron*, *Boswellia*, and others have a preference for dry hills. Mango does best where the climate has strongly marked seasons and rain is scarce at fruiting time. A shower at the time of flowering is inimical to the development of fruits.

FORM AND FUNCTION

Distinguishing characteristics.   Members of the families Anacardiaceae, Julianiaceae, and Burseraceae have resinous bark. Leaves are generally alternately arranged along a stem and are only rarely opposite or whorled. The leaves are mostly pinnately compound (leaves with small leaflets along both sides of a central axis) and rarely simple. An interesting form of leaf is found in *Citrus*, in which the simple blade is separated from the wedge-shaped petiole (leaf stalk) by a joint. Because this type of leaf occurs in genera with compound leaves, it is believed that this is a reduced form. Reduction goes still further in *Citrus*, in which the first one or two leaves of an axillary bud (a bud located in an axil or upper angle between a stem and a branch or leaf) are reduced to spines. Leaves of *Chisocheton* (family Meliaceae) show continued growth at their tips. Members of the family Rutaceae have gland-dotted aromatic leaves. Stipules, small leaflike appendages at the base of petioles, are usually absent, and if present, obscure. In *Ailanthus* (family Simaroubaceae) abscission layers (zones of weakness) form at the base of the leaflets as well as in the petiole; the leaflets usually drop first.

Flowering habits   The flowers may be single in the axils of leaves, as in *Naregamia*, or they may be arranged in racemes (spikelike flower dusters), cymose spikes (clusters that bloom from the top downward), or panicles (many-branched flower clusters). They may be bisexual, unisexual, or polygamous (bearing unisexual and bisexual flowers on the same plant). In *Juliania* the flowers are not only dioecious (*i.e.*, the male and female flowers are on separate plants), but the male flowers are in racemose panicles (panicles that bloom from the bottom upward), and females are crowded in an involucre (a cuplike whorl of green leaflike bracts). Generally, both calyx (sepals) and corolla (petals) are present, but in some the corolla may be lacking. In *Juliania*, which lacks petals, the male flowers have a three- to nine-lobed calyx; the females have none. The calyx in other members is generally three- to five-parted, as in the corolla. A conspicuous disc, which may be annular (ring-shaped), cushion-like, cuplike, or tubular, is present in most of the members.

Stamens are usually double the number of petals, but in some they are equal to the number of petals or sometimes indefinitely numerous. Filaments (the stalks of the stamens) are usually free, but in most of the members of

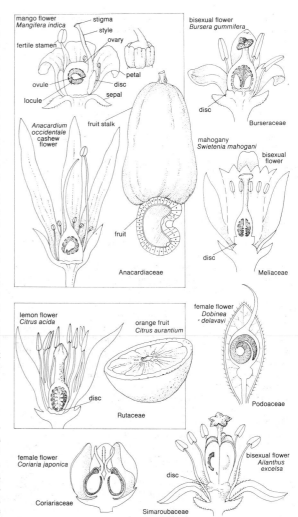

Figure 2: Representative flowers and fruits of seven families of the order Rutales.
Drawing by M. Pahl based on (Podoaceae) J. Hutchinson, *Families of Flowering Plants*, the Clarendon Press, Oxford; (Coriariaceae) G.H.M. Lawrence, *Taxonomy of Vascular Plants*, the Macmillan Company

the family Meliaceae the stamens are united into a tube at the tip of which are borne the anthers, on the inside. Some species in the family Rutaceae also have filaments united at the base. When the flowers are unisexual, staminodes (sterile stamens) are usually present in the female flowers, and pistillodes (sterile pistils—female structures) in the male flowers, but not in *Juliania*, however. Anthers, the saclike, pollen-producing parts of the stamens, are two locular (chambered) and open lengthwise. The gynoecium (female complex) may be composed of one to 20 carpels, structures of the ovary wall. It may be unilocular (*Coriaria*), multilocular at the base and unilocular above (several members of the family Meliaceae), multilocular throughout (some members of the family Rutaceae), or the carpels may be separate, as in *Ailanthus*, *Brucea*, *Samadera*, and others of the family Simaroubaceae. Styles, the upper parts of the pistil, may be three, as in the family Julianiaceae, or they may be united, as in some members of the families Rutaceae and Meliaceae. Each carpel has a single ovule (seed precursor) in some members of the families Anacardiaceae, Simaroubaceae, and others; two ovules, as in the family Burseraceae and some members of the Meliaceae; or several ovules, as in some of the Rutaceae. In the family Julianiaceae the funiculus, the stalk attaching the ovule to the ovary wall, or placenta, is unusual in being cuplike; and the nucellus, the central part of the ovule, is generally massive. An outgrowth from the base of the funiculus called the obturator is present in several genera. These obturators aid in conducting pollen tubes to the ovules. The genus *Rhus* is exceptional in that the pollen tube enters the ovule through the chalaza, the end of the ovule opposite from where the funiculus attaches, in a process known as chalazogamy.

The fruit may be a drupe (stony-seeded—*e.g.*, *Mangifera*), a capsule (*Swietenia*), winged (*Ailanthus*), a berry (some *Burseraceae*), a berry with a woody rind (*Aegle*), or a hesperidium, a three-layered berrylike fruit derived from a multilocular ovary, as in lemons, oranges, and others of the genus *Citrus*. In *Coriaria* the petals enlarge and protect the fruits. *Juliania* has fruits enclosed in enlarged involucres. In some the fruits develop from an ovary with only partially united carpels, as in *Dictamnus*, and the carpels become isolated in fruit and dehisce (open) along the ventral suture. *Citrus* has a smooth endocarp (inner layer of a fruit) or encloses a fleshy part consisting of juicy emergences from the inner walls of the many-chambered fruit that fills the cavity.

Cedrela, Swietenia, and others have winged seeds. The seeds may be with or without endosperm, the starchy nutrient tissue for the developing embryo. The embryo in the family Burseraceae is sometimes rolled (contortuplicate). Cotyledons (seed leaves) are usually fleshy. Some genera like *Zanthoxylum, Citrus,* and *Mangifera* have many embryos in the seed. The embryos may come from different parts of the ovule. Apomixis, the development of unfertilized seed, is known in *Citrus*.

Physical and biochemical characteristics. It is known that the genus *Canarium* synthesizes a large series of turpenes, naturally occurring hydrocarbons of great variety, an example being turpentine, which is a mixture of turpenes. The oil obtained from various *Canarium* species contains paracymol, an aromatic hydrocarbon widely distributed in the essential oils of flowering plants. Trees with resinous sap are usually irritating and poisonous. Notable among these are some species of *Mangifera, Holigarna,* and the rengas trees of Malaya. Because of the irritant sap, the wood of several species, though excellent, is seldom used because no method is known to remove the annoying agent. It is known that the poison in these is a volatile and aromatic substance that gradually disappears from the sap after it has been drawn. It is doubtful whether this poison has any effect on animals such as monkeys and squirrels, which are known to eat the fruits of these trees, and insects, which feed on the sap. The irritant present in cashew nut shells has been studied in detail and has been found to contain cardol, anacardol, and anacardic acid. *Coriaria* is one of the very few non-leguminous (leguminous plants belong to the family Leguminosae, sometimes called Fabaceae) plants that fix atmospheric nitrogen in root nodules.

EVOLUTION

The order Rutales appears to be fairly old, as is evidenced by the available fossil records. *Anacardites amissus, A. antiquus, Rhus membranacea,* and others are known from Cretaceous Period (beginning about 136,000,000 years ago) rocks. Tertiary (beginning about 65,000,000 years ago) deposits are abundant in fossils of *Rhus, Pistacia, Cedrela, Evodia, Ailanthus,* and *Bursera.* Some families, such as Simaroubaceae, are not known from deposits older than the Tertiary.

Certain lines of specialization can be traced within the group. These include changes from spiral arrangement of leaves to opposite arrangement; reduction from two whorls of perianth (sepals and petals considered together) to one whorl and from two whorls of stamens to one whorl; gradual adnation (fusion) and cohesion of stamens to form a staminal tube; changes from bisexuality to unisexuality; changes from apocarpy (single, free carpels) to syncarpy (fused carpels); reduction in the number of carpels from several-carpelled ovaries to single-carpelled ovaries; and reduction in the number of ovules from many to one for each carpel.

As presented here, the order is derived from the order Saxifragales. Affinities with the orders Sapindales and Dilleniales cannot, however, be ignored.

CLASSIFICATION

Distinguishing taxonomic features. There are several characters, combinations of which are used by taxonomists to set the limits of the order Rutales, that may be used to assess the relationships among the various families included within the group and to determine connections with other groups. The characters used are, chiefly, woody habit, presence or absence of oil glands in the leaves, presence or absence of resinous bark, presence of a conspicuous disc within the stamens, nature of the staminal whorl, nature of the ovary, number and attachment of the ovules in the ovary, number of styles, and features of the seed and embryo.

Annotated classification. The arrangement of the families adopted in the following section is a recent one of rather wide acceptance.

ORDER RUTALES

Mainly trees or shrubs, herbs extremely rare; bark resinous or not; leaves mostly alternate or opposite, mostly compound, sometimes simple, often gland-dotted; stipules very rare; flowers hypogynous (*i.e.*, sepals, petals, and stamens arise at the base of the ovary) to slightly perigynous (sepals, petals, and stamens partly enclose the ovary), mostly bisexual, sometimes unisexual; sepals mostly imbricate (overlapping), rarely valvate (meeting at the edges without overlapping); petals mostly present, contorted, imbricate or valvate, usually free; stamens mostly equal to or twice the number of petals, often in two whorls; disc mostly conspicuous; ovary superior (hypogynous), syncarpous (of fused carpels), or subapocarpous (of partly free carpels), 1- to 20-carpelled; styles free or united; ovules 1 or 2, rarely more; fruit various; seeds with thin (or without) endosperm, straight, curved, or rolled embryo, and usually fleshy cotyledons.

Family Anacardiaceae (Mango family)
Evergreen or deciduous trees with resin ducts in bark, leaves odd-pinnate (compound, with leaflets alternately arranged on either side of the central axis) or simple, without stipules or very obscurely stipulate, often polygamous flowers in panicles; sepals 3 to 7; petals 3 to 7 or absent; stamens usually twice or rarely equal to the number of petals; ovary usually 1-locular, rarely 2- to 5-locular; ovules solitary, pendulous; fruit mostly drupes; seeds with little or no endosperm. About 73 genera and 600 species found mainly in the tropics, though some are temperate.

Family Julianiaceae
Resinous trees or shrubs; leaves deciduous, alternate, pinnate compound, without stipules; flowers dioecious, without petals, males in racemes, females crowded in involucres; calyx of male 3- to 9-lobed, absent in female; stamens equal to calyx lobes; ovary 1-locular, 1-ovuled; style 3-parted; fruits enclosed in enlarged involucres; seeds without endosperm. Two genera and 5 species distributed in Mexico and Peru.

Family Podoaceae
Shrubs or perennial rhizomatous (creeping) herbs; leaves alternate or opposite, long-petioled, without stipules; flowers unisexual, in panicles, some bracts of male spikes large, coloured and membranous with a reticulate pattern; calyx 4-toothed; petals 4, free, clawed; stamens 8; anthers extrorse (opening away from the central axis of the flower); disc only in female flowers; ovary 1-locular, 1-ovuled; style undivided. Two genera and 3 species distributed in eastern Asia.

Family Burseraceae (Myrrh family)
Resinous trees or shrubs; leaves alternate and compound; flowers unisexual or bisexual, solitary or in panicles; sepals and petals 3 to 5 each, imbricate or valvate; disc present; stamens twice the number of petals, free; ovary 2- to 5-locular; ovules 2 or 1 in each locule; fruit a drupe; embryo rolled or straight. Sixteen genera and 500 species distributed chiefly in tropical America with some in Africa and Asia.

Family Simaroubaceae (Tree of Heaven family)
Trees with bitter bark, no oil glands; leaves pinnate compound; flowers bisexual or polygamous, in panicles; calyx and corolla 3- to 7-parted; disc present; stamens equal to or double the number of petals, sometimes with basal scales; ovary 2- to 5-lobed or carpels free; ovule 1 for each carpel; fruit often winged. Thirty genera and 200 species distributed mainly throughout the tropics.

Family Stylobasiaceae
Small shrubs; leaves simple, alternate, coriaceous (leathery); flowers bisexual or polygamous; calyx campanulate (bell-shaped), 5-lobed; petals absent; disc absent; stamens 10, anthers extrorse; ovary 1-carpelled; ovules 2; fruit surrounded by enlarged calyx. One genus with 2 species distributed in southwest Australia.

Family Rutaceae (Orange family)
Shrubs, trees, or rarely herbs; leaves simple or compound with pellucid (clear, almost transparent) glands; sepals and petals 4 or 5, free or connate (fused) at the base; disc present;

stamens usually twice the number of petals, often in 2 whorls; ovary 4- or 5-celled, sometimes up to 20-chambered; ovules usually 2 in each cell; seeds with or without endosperm; fruit various. About 150 genera and 900 species distributed throughout temperate and subtropical regions.

Family Cneoraceae

Leaves alternate, simple, entire; leathery, exstipulate, with oil glands; flowers solitary or in corymbs, 3- or 4-merous (parts present in 3s or 4s), bisexual; disc bolster-like; stamens 3 or 4; ovary 3- or 4-lobed with 2 ovules in each; style 1; fruit a drupe; seeds with endosperm. Two genera and 3 species distributed in the Mediterranean region, the Canary Islands, and Cuba.

Family Meliaceae (Mahogany family)

Trees and shrubs without resin or oil glands; leaves mostly pinnate compound, alternate; flowers usually bisexual, in panicles or rarely solitary; sepals and petals 4- or 5-parted; stamens united into a tube or rarely free; disc conspicuous; ovary 1- to 5-celled; usually 2 ovules in each carpel; style undivided; fruit a drupe, capsule, or berry; seeds often winged. Fifty genera and 1,400 species distributed generally throughout the tropics and subtropics.

Family Aitoniaceae

Woody plants; twigs angular; leaves simple and alternate, coriaceous; flowers solitary, axillary, and bisexual; sepals and petals 4 each, imbricate; stamens twice the number of petals; disc fleshy; ovary 4-carpelled and lobed; ovules 2 in each carpel; style filiform (thin—thread-like); fruit a capsule; seeds nonendospermous. One genus (*Nymania*, formerly *Aitonia*) with a single species distributed in South Africa.

Family Kirkiaceae

Trees or shrubs; leaves pinnate compound, without stipules; flowers polygamous in axillary cymes; sepals and petals 4 to 5, imbricate; stamens equal to or double the number of petals; disc present; ovary 2- to 5-carpelled; styles free; fruit a capsule; embryo straight. One genus (*Kirkia*) and 8 species in tropical and southern Africa.

Family Coriariaceae

Shrubs; leaves opposite or whorled, parallel-veined; without stipules; flowers bisexual or unisexual in racemes, protogynous (the pistil matures before the stamens of the same flower); sepals 5, imbricate; petals 5, valvate; stamens in 2 whorls of 5 each; ovary 5- to 10-carpelled; ovules 1 in each carpel; petals become fleshy and enclose carpels in fruit. One genus and 15 species distributed from the Mediterranean to Japan, in New Zealand, and from Mexico to Chile.

Critical appraisal. There is no unanimity of opinion among taxonomists with regard to the systematic positions of the families included in the order Rutales. While most of them agree that there is close relationship among the families Rutaceae, Meliaceae, Simaroubaceae, and Burseraceae, some treat the family Meliaceae in a separate order, Meliales. The above four families are placed in the order Geraniales in the majority of earlier classification systems. These families are included in the order Rutales by several important authorities who, however, also include other families not presented here. The families Julianiaceae, Coriariaceae, Cneoraceae, and Anacardiaceae have been placed in other orders or have been elevated to ordinal status by themselves in several different classification schemes. To this list have been added Podoaceae, Stylobasiaceae, Aitoniaceae, and Kirkiaceae in the classification presented here. The affinities of Aitoniaceae, Kirkiaceae, and Coriariaceae are, however, obscure. On anatomical grounds there is strong evidence for considering the families Rutaceae, Simaroubaceae, Meliaceae, Sapindaceae, Burseraceae, and Anacardiaceae as forming a natural group, with Rutaceae standing somewhat apart, showing the closest resemblance to the family Simaroubaceae. It has been stated that pollen grains in the families Anacardiaceae, Burseraceae, Meliaceae, Rutaceae, and Simaroubaceae show similarities. Totality of evidence indeed suggests that these families are related. The genus *Blepharocarya* has been segregated from Anacardiaceae to an independent family Blepharocaryaceae by some authorities who feel that the female inflorescence (flower cluster) of *Blepharocarya* is apparently almost exactly homologous to the cupule (*i.e.*, the structure forming the cup in an acorn) of the family Fagaceae (oaks and beeches). The genus *Rhabdodendron* has been removed from the family Rutaceae and referred to the family Phytolaccaceae on anatomical

Doubtful affinities of some families

grounds by some authorities. *Rhabdodendron* has also been raised to family status, and this view has been endorsed by many. Sometimes the genera *Suriana*, *Irvingia*, and *Picrodendron* of the family Simaroubaceae are treated as independent families, based on anatomical characters. *Irvingia* is sometimes placed in the family Ixonanthaceae (order Geraniales; *q.v.*). It has been suggested that the tribes Melieae, Cedreleae, and Swieteneae should be raised to the status of families. This is not supported by wood anatomy, palynology (pollen morphology), or floral anatomy. The family Podoaceae was included under the family Sapindaceae by some early workers and with Anacardiaceae by others. It has also been suggested that it could be raised to a family in its own right; this has been accepted by many authorities and is so presented here. Palynology supports such a contention. The genus *Kirkia* was formerly included in the family Simaroubaceae by early authorities. Sometimes it is referred to the family Ptaeroxylaceae, with which it has, however, fewer similarities than differences.

Differing opinions on status of some groups

BIBLIOGRAPHY. C. DE CANDOLLE, "Meliaceae," in ALPHONSE DE CANDOLLE, *Monographiae phanerogamerum . . .*, vol. 1 (1878); and A. ENGLER, "Anacardiaceae," *ibid.*, vol. 4 (1883), monographic treatments of these two families; A. ENGLER, "Coriariaceae" and "Anacardiaceae," in A. ENGLER and K. PRANTL (eds.), *Die natürlichen Pflanzenfamilien III*, 5 (1897), general and taxonomic accounts of these families; "Burseraceae, Simaroubaceae, and Rutaceae," *ibid.*, 2nd ed., vol. 19a (1931); and H. HARMS, "Meliaceae," *ibid.*, vol. 19b (1940), general accounts of these families; J. HUTCHINSON, *The Families of Flowering Plants*, vol. 1, *Dicotyledons* (1959), a general account of families of dicotyledons; G.H.M. LAWRENCE, *Taxonomy of Vascular Plants* (1951), a general account of families of vascular plants; A. TAKHTAJAN, *Flowering Plants: Origin and Dispersal* (1969; Eng. trans. from the 2nd Russian ed., 1961), a treatment of the classification and phylogeny of families; J.C. WILLIS, *A Dictionary of the Flowering Plants and Ferns*, 7th ed. rev. by H.K. AIRY SHAW (1966), general information, affinities, and economic importance of genera and families.

(N.C.N.)

Rutherford, Lord

Ernest Rutherford, nuclear physicist and Nobel prize winner, is to be ranked in fame with Sir Isaac Newton and Michael Faraday. Indeed, just as Faraday is called the "father of electricity" so a similar description might be applied to Rutherford in relation to nuclear energy. He contributed substantially to the understanding of the disintegration and transmutation of the radioactive elements; discovered and named the particles expelled from radium; identified the alpha particle as a helium atom and with its aid he evolved the nuclear theory of atomic structure, and he used that particle to produce the first artificial disintegration of elements. In the universities of McGill, Manchester, and Cambridge he led and inspired two generations of physicists who—to use his own words—"turned out the facts of Nature," and in the Cavendish Laboratory his 'boys' discovered the neutron and artificial disintegration by accelerated particles.

Rutherford was born in Spring Grove, New Zealand, on August 30, 1871, the fourth of the 12 children of James, a wheelwright at Brightwater near Nelson on South Island, and Martha Rutherford. His parents, who had emigrated from Great Britain, denied themselves many comforts so that their children might be well educated. In 1887 Ernest won a scholarship to Nelson College, a secondary school —similar to a public (private) school in England— where he was a popular boy, clever with his hands, a keen footballer, and won prizes in history, languages as well as mathematics. Another scholarship allowed him to enroll in Canterbury College, Christchurch, from where he graduated with the B.A. in 1892 and the M.A. in 1893 with first class honours in mathematics and physics. Financing himself by part-time teaching, he stayed for a fifth year to do research in physics, studying the properties of iron in high-frequency alternating magnetic fields. He found that he could detect the electromagnetic waves—wireless waves—newly discov-

Education in New Zealand

Rutherford, oil painting by J. Dunn, 1932. In the National Portrait Gallery, London.
By courtesy of the National Portrait Gallery, London

ered by the German physicist Heinrich Hertz, even after they had passed through brick walls. Two substantial scientific papers on this work won for him an "1851 Exhibition" scholarship, which provided for further education in England.

Before leaving New Zealand he became unofficially engaged to Mary Newton, a daughter of his landlady in Christchurch. Mary preserved his letters from England, as did his mother, who lived to age 92. Thus, a wealth of material is available that sheds much light on the non-scientific aspects of his fascinating personality.

On his arrival in Cambridge in 1895, Rutherford began to work under J.J. Thomson, professor of experimental physics at the university's Cavendish Laboratory. Continuing his work on the detection of Hertzian waves over a distance of two miles, he gave an experimental lecture on his results before the Cambridge Physical Society and was delighted when his paper was published in the *Philosophical Transactions* of the Royal Society of London, a signal honour for so young an investigator.

Rutherford made a great impression on colleagues in the Cavendish Laboratory, but also aroused jealousies in the more conservative members of the Cavendish fraternity, as is clear from his letters to Mary; and Thomson held him in high esteem. In December 1895, when Röntgen discovered X-rays, Thomson asked Rutherford to join him in a study of the effects of passing a beam of X-rays through a gas. They discovered that the X-rays produced large quantities of electrically charged particles, or carriers of positive and negative electricity, and that these carriers, or ionized atoms, recombined to form neutral molecules. Working on his own, Rutherford then devised a technique for measuring the velocity and rate of recombination of these positive and negative ions. The published papers on this subject remain classics to the present day.

In 1896 the French physicist Henri Becquerel discovered that uranium emitted rays that could fog a photographic plate as did X-rays. Rutherford soon showed that they also ionized air but that they were different from X-rays, consisting of two distinct types of radiation. He named them alpha rays, highly powerful in producing ionization but easily absorbed, and beta rays, which produced less radiation but had more penetrating ability. He thought they must be extremely minute particles of matter.

In 1898 Rutherford was appointed to the chair of physics at McGill University in Montreal. To Mary he wrote, "the salary is only 500 pounds but enough for you and me to start on." In the summer of 1900 he travelled to New Zealand to visit his parents and get married. When his daughter Eileen, their only child, was born the next year, he wrote his mother "it is suggested that I call her 'Ione' after my respect for ions in gases."

Toward the end of the 19th century, many scientists thought that no new advances in physics remained to be made. Yet within three years Rutherford succeeded in marking out an entirely new branch of physics called radioactivity. He soon discovered that thorium or its compounds disintegrated into a gas that in turn disintegrated into an unknown 'active deposit,' likewise radioactive. Rutherford and a young chemist, Frederick Soddy, then investigated three groups of radioactive elements—radium, thorium, and actinium. They concluded in 1902 that radioactivity was a process in which atoms of one element spontaneously disintegrated into atoms of an entirely different element, which also remained radioactive. This interpretation was opposed by many chemists who held firmly to the concept of the indestructibility of matter; the suggestion that some atoms could tear themselves apart to form entirely different kinds of matter was to them a remnant of medieval alchemy.

Nevertheless, Rutherford's outstanding work won him recognition by the Royal Society, which elected him a fellow in 1903 and awarded him the Rumford medal in 1904. In his book *Radio-activity* he summarized in 1904 the results of research in that subject. The evidence he marshalled for radioactivity was that it is unaffected by external conditions, such as temperature and chemical change; that more heat is produced than in an ordinary chemical reaction; that new types of matter are produced at a rate in equilibrium with the rate of decay; and that the new products possess distinct chemical properties.

Rutherford, a prodigious worker with tremendous powers of concentration, continued to make a succession of brilliant discoveries—and with remarkably simple apparatus. For example, he showed (1903) that alpha rays can be deflected by electric and magnetic fields, the direction of the deflection proving that the rays are particles of positive charge; he determined their velocity and the ratio of their charge (E) to their mass (M). These results were obtained by passing such particles between thin metal plates stacked closely together, the size of a matchbox, each plate charged oppositely to its neighbour in one experiment; and in another experiment putting the assembly in a strong magnetic field; and in each experiment he measured the strengths of the fields which just sufficed to prevent the particles from emerging from the stack.

Rutherford wrote 80 scientific papers during his seven years at McGill, made many public appearances, among them the Silliman Memorial Lectures at Yale University in 1905, and received offers of Chairs at other universities until 1907, when he returned to England to accept a Chair at the University of Manchester, where he continued his research on the alpha particle. With the ingenious apparatus that he and his research assistant, Hans Geiger, had invented they counted the particles as they were emitted one by one from a known amount of radium; and they also measured the total charge collected from which the charge on each particle could be detected. Combining this result with the rate of production of helium from radium, determined by Rutherford and the American chemist, Bertram Borden Boltwood, Rutherford was able to deduce Avogadro's number (the constant number of molecules in the molecular weight in grams of any substance) in the most direct manner conceivable. With his student, Thomas D. Royds, he proved in 1908 that the alpha particle really is a helium atom by allowing alpha particles to escape through the thin glass wall of a containing vessel into an evacuated outer glass tube and showing that the spectrum of the collected gas was that of helium. Almost immediately, in 1908, came the Nobel Prize—but for Chemistry, for his investigations concerning the disintegration of elements.

In 1911 Rutherford made his greatest contribution to science with his nuclear theory of the atom. He had observed in Montreal that fast-moving alpha particles, on passing through thin plates of mica produced diffuse images on photographic plates, whereas a sharp image was produced when there was no obstruction to the passage of the rays. He considered that the particles

Arrival at the Cavendish Laboratory

The nuclear theory of the atom

must be deflected through small angles as they passed close to atoms of the mica, but calculation showed that to deflect such particles travelling at 20,000 kilometres per second, an electric field of 100,000,000 volts per centimetre was necessary, a most astonishing conclusion. This phenomenon of scattering was found in the counting experiments with Geiger; Rutherford suggested to Geiger and another student, Ernest Marsden, that it would be of interest to examine whether any particles were scattered backward, i.e., deflected through an angle of more than 90 degrees. To their astonishment, a few particles in every 10,000 were indeed so scattered, emerging from the same side of a gold foil as that on which they had entered. After a number of calculations Rutherford came to the conclusion that the requisite intense electric field to cause such a large deflection could only occur if all the positive charge in the atom, and therefore almost all the mass, were concentrated on a very small central nucleus some 10,000 times smaller in diameter than that of the entire atom. The positive charge on the nucleus would therefore be balanced by an equal charge on all the electrons distributed somehow around the nucleus.

Although Hantaro Nagaoka, a Japanese physicist, in 1904 had proposed an atomic model with electrons rotating in rings about a central nucleus, it was not taken seriously because, according to classical electrodynamics, electrons in orbit would have a centripetal acceleration toward the centre of rotation and would thus radiate away their energy, falling into the central nucleus almost immediately. This idea is in marked contrast with the view developed by J.J. Thomson (q.v.) in 1910; he envisaged all the electrons distributed inside a uniformly charged positive sphere of atomic diameter, in which the negative "corpuscles" (electrons) are imbedded. It was not until 1913 that Niels Bohr, a Danish physicist, postulated that electrons, contrary to classical electrodynamics, do not radiate energy during rotation, and do indeed move in orbits about a central nucleus, thus upholding the convictions of Nagaoka and Rutherford. A knighthood conferred in 1914 further marked the public recognition of Rutherford's services to science.

During World War I he worked on the practical problem of submarine detection by underwater acoustics. He produced the first artificial disintegration of an element in 1919, when he found that on collision with an alpha particle an atom of nitrogen was converted into an atom of oxygen and an atom of hydrogen. Thus began the search that ultimately ushered in the age of nuclear energy. The same year he succeeded Thomson as Cavendish professor. Although his experimental contributions henceforth were not as numerous as in earlier years, his influence on research students was enormous. In the second Bakerian lecture he gave to the Royal Society in 1920, he speculated upon the existence of the neutron and of isotopes of hydrogen and helium; three of them were eventually discovered by workers in the Cavendish Laboratory.

His service as president of the Royal Society (1925–30), and, as chairman of the Academic Assistance Council, which helped almost 1,000 university refugees from Germany, increased the claims upon his time. But whenever possible he worked in the Cavendish Laboratory, where he encouraged and admonished students, always probed for the facts, and always sought an explanation in simple terms. When in 1934 Enrico Fermi in Rome successfully disintegrated many different elements with neutrons, Rutherford wrote to congratulate him "for escaping from theoretical physics."

Rutherford read widely, enjoyed good health, the game of golf, his home life, and hard work. He could listen to the views of others, his judgments were fair, and from his many students he earned affection and esteem. In 1931 he was made Baron Rutherford of Nelson, but this honour was marred by the death of his daughter. He died in Cambridge on October 19, 1937, following a short illness, and was buried in Westminster Abbey.

BIBLIOGRAPHY. A.S. EVE, Rutherford (1939), the official biography sanctioned by Lady Rutherford; A.S. EVE and SIR JAMES CHADWICK, Obit. Not. R. Soc. Lond. (1938); SIR E. MARSDEN, Obit. Not. R. Soc. New Zealand, vol. 68 (1938–39); J.B. BIRKS (ed.), Rutherford in Manchester (1962), a discussion of his work at the university there; SIR JAMES CHADWICK, The Collected Papers of Lord Rutherford of Nelson, 4 vol. (1962); NORMAN FEATHER, Lord Rutherford (1940), a discussion of his research work at Cambridge University; E.N. DA C. ANDRADE, Rutherford and the Nature of the Atom (1964), a biographical treatment which emphasizes the development of Rutherford's ideas; LAWRENCE BADASH (comp.), Rutherford and Boltwood (1969), contains the correspondence between the two scientists concerning the question of radioactivity.

(T.E.A.)

Rwanda

The Republic of Rwanda lies at an altitude of more than 5,000 feet (1,500 metres) in the mountains of east central Africa. Rwanda and Burundi, to the south, are the most densely populated countries on the African continent. Roughly rectangular in shape, Rwanda has an area of 10,169 square miles (26,338 square kilometres) and a population of about 3,736,000. Its average population density is about 386 persons per square mile. The capital is Kigali (population about 59,000).

Physically, Rwanda is bounded on the west by Lake Kivu and the Ruzizi River; on the south by the Luhwa and Akanyaru rivers; on the east by the Kagera River; and on the northwest by a chain of volcanoes, almost all extinct, whose heights range up to just under 15,000 feet. Politically its neighbours are Uganda to the north, Burundi to the south, Tanzania to the east, and Zaire (formerly Congo [Kinshasa]) located on the west and northwest.

Although Rwanda was the more important of the two, Rwanda and its southern neighbour Burundi were for centuries twin kingdoms—first as autonomous realms, then as parts of German East Africa, and then as Belgian administered territories. Rwanda became a definitive territorial unit at the end of the 19th century, as a result of the German colonial occupation, which put an end to the conquests of its ancient line of kings, dating back to the 14th century. The ruling Tutsi (Tussi, Batusi, Watusi) feudal monarchy ended, however, as a result of a social revolution on the part of the previously subject Hutu (Bahutu, Wakhutu) people, which began in 1959. The country obtained its independence on July 1, 1962. (For a detailed discussion of associated physical features, see EAST AFRICAN LAKES; EAST AFRICAN MOUNTAINS; and VIRUNGA MOUNTAINS. For a consideration of historical aspects, see EAST AFRICA, HISTORY OF.)

The natural environment. The mountain system of Rwanda is dominated in the west by a crest that separates the basin of the Nile from that of the Congo. At the western foot of this ridge lies Lake Kivu, which guards riches as yet latent. To the east, Rwanda takes the form of a high plateau, which slopes gently downward to the low marshy plains of the Kagera River. The plateau has an average altitude of about 5,600 feet (1,700 metres) in the centre, and about 4,200 feet (1,300 metres) in the plains. The extreme southeast of the country forms a great bowl-

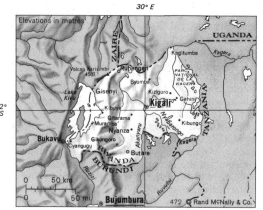

RWANDA

shaped depression, in which numerous small lakes are scattered.

Drainage The hydrographic network of Rwanda is principally situated firstly to the east of the Ruzizi, through which the waters of Lake Kivu empty into Lake Tanganyika, and secondly in the interior of the country, where numerous small rivers flow through deep, steeply embanked valleys to feed the two principal tributaries of the Kagera, the Nyabarongo in the centre, and the Akanyaru in the south. These two tributaries, together with the Ruvubu in Burundi, form the remote sources of the Nile; the Ruvubu is the more southerly, and the Nyabarongo has a more copious flow. The hydrographic network as a whole is dense; the consistent volume of its outflow is exceptional.

The subsoil of Rwanda in part belongs to an ancient geological system known as the Rusizi, which is composed of crystalline schist (flaky metamorphic rock, which splits into thin sheets), gneiss (a coarse-grained metamorphic rock, imperfectly foliated) and micaschist (a metamorphic rock, composed essentially of mica and quartz), and in part to the system called the Burundi, which is composed of dark schists, with or without quartzite (a granular metamorphic rock consisting of quartz in interlocking grains). Formations of secondary age, such as soft schist, or argillites (clay stone), as well as some recent volcanic lavas and sedimentary deposits, are also found. Except for areas of volcanic and of alluvial origin, the soil of Rwanda is generally poor. A multiplicity of unfavourable factors, such as erosion and the incidence of brush fires, have created and progressively aggravated the problem of soil sterility.

Climate. Rwanda has a varied rainfall regime and a generally mild climate with temperatures averaging 66° F (19° C). The region of the Congo–Nile divide has an inclement climate with frequent rain, which is often accompanied by an abrupt fall in temperature. The central plateaus, however, while experiencing abundant rainfall, enjoy a temperate climate. The region of volcanoes, to the northwest, receives much more rain. To the east, the East African type of climate, which is tropical rather than Equatorial, already makes itself felt. The mean annual rainfall is about 45 inches (1,143 millimetres) in the centre of the country and increases with altitude. Rwanda has two wet and two dry seasons per year. These are the short rainy season, which lasts from October to December; the short dry season, lasting from January to February; the long rainy season, from March to May; and the long dry season, from June through September.

Vegetation. The chain of mountains in the west is the only natural region in which the primeval forest still survives. Savannas (a grassland region), with scattered thorn trees and euphorbias (cactus-type growths containing a milky juice and having flowers with no petals), are to be found in the northeast, where the Kagera National Park is located. In the east, enormous papyrus swamps, whose topography is constantly shifting, are to be found. Grassy savanna, often broken for agriculture or left lying fallow for pasturage, occupies the centre of the country. From the altitude of 6,500 feet (2,000 metres) upward, notably in the immediate vicinity of the volcanoes, bamboo forests are found.

Animal life. Rwanda possesses an exceptionally rich and varied animal life. In the primeval-forest zone, as well as sometimes in the bushy or grassy savanna regions, are found elephants, lions, gorillas, chimpanzees, buffaloes, zebras, various antelopes, and warthogs. Kagera National Park and the adjacent Mutura Hunting Reserve contain many rare species, including the giant pangolin (a kind of anteater). Game birds include guinea fowl, partridge, ducks, and various species of geese.

The landscape under human settlement. The first impression given by the Rwandan landscape is that it resembles an immense green park dominated by banana plantations. The eye does not at first clearly distinguish the habitations standing on small hills and submerged in a sea **Village** of vegetation. Dwellings in Rwanda are not clustered **dwellings** together in compact villages but instead are disposed in familial groups, for which a hill serves as the basic unit.

Each place of habitation is circled by an enclosure formed by a hedge, or palisade, of growing plants; this enclosure extends rearward in circular sections, each of which shelters—according to the social importance of the family head—one or more houses, likewise circular. Livestock are also kept in the enclosure.

The house itself, in former days, was a hut several yards in diameter, made of an interlaced frame supported inside by wooden posts and covered with straw. Its rooms were separated from each other by panels of basketwork, often ornamented with geometric designs. The entrance to the house, a low opening in the framework, faced the opening to the hedge enclosure. This type of house has now been replaced by the rectangular house built of mixed clay and straw or of baked brick, with a roof of tiles or of sheet iron.

The people. The population of Rwanda (3,735,585) is the most dense in Africa and among the most prolific in the world. The annual rate of population growth is between 3 and 3.6 percent. Assuming a rate of 3.2 percent and excluding the possibility of emigration, the population of Rwanda could reach 4,500,000 by 1976 and over 6,000,000 by 1986.

Rwanda, Area and Population			
	area		population
	sq mi	sq km	1970 census
Prefectures			
Butare	707	1,830	530,000
Byumba	1,925	4,987	370,000
Cyangugu	859	2,226	284,000
Gikongoro	846	2,192	329,000
Gisenyi	925	2,395	385,000
Gitarama	865	2,241	487,000
Kibungo	1,596	4,134	249,000
Kibuye	510	1,320	235,000
Kigali	1,255	3,251	390,000
Ruhengeri	680	1,762	477,000
Total Rwanda	10,169	26,338*	3,736,000

*Converted area figures do not add to total because of rounding.
Source: Official government figures.

The inhabitants of Rwanda are divided into three distinct ethnic groups: the Hutu, classified anthropologically as Bantu, form the bulk of Rwandan society, constituting 90 percent of the total population; the Twa (Batwa), who are Pygmies, form only a tiny minority, constituting less than 1 percent; and the Tutsi of Ethiopic or Nilotic origin represent just under 10 percent. These groups are distinguished not only by physical characteristics but also by their occupations and their mode of life. Some Twa are potters, while others are hunters; the Hutu are primarily farmers; and the Tutsi are by preference raisers of long-horned cattle. Watusi, Watousi, and Watutsi are all Swahili corruptions of the original and true name of this people, which is Abatutsi.

Language. The official languages are Kinyarwanda and French. The Swahili that is spoken in Arab or Arab-influenced town districts is only a lingua franca that diverges from the pure Swahili of the East African coast.

Kinyarwanda is a tonal Bantu language of considerable complexity. While associated with the cultural system of the interlake region, it may be classified as a dialect of a language group that also includes the languages of Burundi, as well as the Buha language of Tanzania.

The Kinyarwanda linguistic area covers all the national territory. It is spoken in nearly the same manner by all Rwandans and contributes to their cultural unity.

Religion. Traditionally, Rwandans believe in a supreme being called Imana. There is also a belief in the **Tradi-** survival of the spirits of the dead, who are said to inhabit **tional** the lower world; as they are thought to be capable of **beliefs** harming the living, rites of propitiation are consecrated to them by diviners. A public initiation rite is sacred to the hero Ryangombe, king of the *imandwa* (a group of 30 powerful spirits who are joined by the spirits of humans who have been initiated before they die). The equivalent of Ryangombe in the north is Nyabingi, the spirit of a woman.

Christianity has established itself, overlaying these traditional beliefs without being able to destroy them. Nearly 45 percent of the population is Roman Catholic, 9 percent is Protestants, 1 percent is Muslim, and 45 percent is Imanists.

The national economy. As Rwanda is a landlocked country in the heart of the great lake region, having a mountainous and broken terrain, geography does not favour its economic development. As its natural resources are insufficient, the economic level of the country is low; per capita income averages only about $70 a year. Production is based primarily upon agriculture and livestock raising. Since, however, the peasant producer owns on the average only about one hectare (about two and a half acres) of arable land and uses only rudimentary tools, such as a hoe and a cutless, the increase in food production lags behind the increase in population. Rwanda thus is confronted with the necessity of moving from a simple subsistence economy to a market economy. At present such traditional crops as beans, peas, and sweet potatoes are grown for internal consumption. Such cash crops as coffee, tea, pyrethrum, cotton, barley, and rice accounted for over 60 percent of all exports in 1970.

Although not as important as agriculture, livestock raising is also economically significant. Dairy products constitute about 7 percent of the gross domestic product, and of this about half is consumed by the producers themselves. Mining production is also significant; in 1970 it represented 30 percent of the value of all exports, although representing only 2 percent of the gross domestic product. The principal resources are cassiterite (a tin ore), tungsten, beryl, and tantalite (a mineral containing manganese and columbium). Two other resources as yet virtually unexploited are the methane gas of Lake Kivu, which is estimated to amount to 200,000,000,000 cubic feet, and peat, estimated at 10,000,000,000 cubic feet. Deposits of limestone, clay, kaolin (china clay), and glass sand are also found.

> Mining

The hydroelectric energy potential is more than 2,000,000,000 kilowatt hours per year; present energy resources amount to 90,000,000 kilowatt hours a year. The small industrial economy that began to develop after the country became independent consists of the processing of coffee and tea, brewing, flour milling, butchering, cigar making, soapmaking, building, and printing.

Hunting and fishing remain the monopoly of the forest Twa and of the lakeshore inhabitants. Such crafts as basketry, coopering, and pottery are practiced by a few specialists.

> Finance

To develop its export capacity, Rwanda requires certain imports that, in turn, must be paid for in either domestic or foreign currency or by a combination of the two. The national investment program amounts to an average of 1,000,000,000 Rwanda francs a year. (One Rwanda franc equals U.S. $0.01, and 4/10 of a new penny sterling.) The share of public investment is estimated at 46 percent, that of private investment at 39 percent, and that of small savings at about 15 percent. The investment itself is directed as follows: 48 percent is invested in production, 10 percent in the economic infrastructure (roads, water supplies, etc.), and 40 percent in the social and administrative infrastructure. To accelerate the rate of investment, the domestic product would have to grow by about 5 percent a year, and exports by about 70 percent. The development of tourism, it is hoped, may constitute another source of revenue. Yet external aid, whether bilateral or multilateral, would, it seems, be required to transform the prevailing pattern.

Transport. To overcome its geographical isolation, Rwanda is faced with the necessity of improving its road system, particularly the routes linking it to neighbouring countries. At the moment, internal transport is provided by a bus service. There is an international airport at Kanombe (a suburb of Kigali), and a smaller one at Kamembe; smaller airfields link the various prefectures and also provide services to neighbouring countries.

Administration and social conditions. Three supreme institutions are empowered with the exercise of public authority. These are the presidency and the government, which exercise executive power; the National Assembly, which, concurrently with the president, exercises legislative power; and the Supreme Court, which supervises the judiciary.

The country is divided into 10 prefectures, which are subdivided into 141 communes. Each prefecture takes the name of its chief town and is directed by a prefect who also supervises the administration of the communes. Each commune is directed by a burgomaster (a Belgian term, equivalent to mayor) and by an elected communal council.

Kigali is the principal town of the prefecture; more importantly, it is the administrative, political, and economic capital of the country. Until its independence in 1962, Rwanda was a province of Ruanda-Urundi, the capital of which was Bujumbura, now in Burundi. Hence Kigali's role as a capital is a new one.

In social affairs particular effort is being devoted to improving working conditions, as well as rural living conditions. Social centres have been opened to promote the welfare of young women and girls.

Education and health. In the early 1970s about 420,-000 children were receiving primary education, and about 10,000 secondary education. The National University of Rwanda (UNR), opened in 1963, has faculties of medicine, letters, sciences, and social and economic sciences. The National Institute for Scientific Research (INRS) conducts research in the human and natural sciences, and the Rwandan Institute of Agronomic Sciences (ISAR) is concerned with the improvement of agriculture and of livestock.

Malaria is endemic in certain parts of the country, and pulmonary diseases are common. There is a shortage of doctors (1 to 60,000 inhabitants).

Cultural life and institutions. National policy encourages activities associated with art and folklore. As a result, a period of lethargy is being followed by a revival in which much spontaneity is evident. Folk songs and dances are exhibiting a new vigour, which is further stimulated by the demand for them from abroad. The museums of the country are encouraging such crafts as basketwork, coopering, ceramics, and ironwork.

There is a local press as well as a national radio broadcasting service, Kigali Radio, which broadcasts in French, Kinyarwanda, English, and Swahili and conducts a radio university.

Prospects for the future. Originally one of the more powerful of the states in the interlake region, Rwanda has a strong national tradition upon which to build. The conflicts between the Tutsi and Hutu peoples that broke out immediately before and shortly after independence was obtained in 1962 have now subsided. Geographic isolation, which has permitted the development of a marked national character, has, however, hindered economic development. External aid, whether bilateral or multilateral, is required to make available the investment needed to transform the present subsistence economy into a market economy.

BIBLIOGRAPHY. M. WALRAET, *Les sciences au Rwanda: Bibliographie (1894-1965)* (1966), is a systematic bibliography covering all fields of research. Access to the rich oral literature, including historical traditions, is provided by A. COUPEZ and T. KAMANZI, *Récits historiques Rwanda* (1962), *Littérature de cour au Rwanda* (1970); M. D'HERTEFELT and A. COUPEZ (eds.), *La royauté sacrée de l'ancien Rwanda* (1964); and A. KAGAME, *Introduction aux grands genres lyriques de l'ancien Rwanda* (1969), all of them editing the Rwandan texts with a French translation, notes, and interpretations. A. KAGAME, *L'histoire des armées-bovines dans l'ancien Rwanda* (1961), and *Les Milices du Rwanda précolonial* (1963), are minimal elaborations of the historical traditions relating to cattle herds and armies. L. DE LACGER, *Ruanda* (1961); A. KAGAME, *La notion de génération appliquée à la généalogie dynastique et à l'histoire du Rwanda des Xe-XIe siècles à nos jours* (1959); J. VANSINA, *L'évolution du royaume Rwanda des origines à 1900* (1962); and L. DE HEUSCH, *Le Rwanda et la civilisation interlacustre* (1966), provide conflicting interpretations of Rwanda history. Aspects of these are critically examined by M. D'HERTEFELT, *Les clans du Rwanda ancien: Elements d'ethnosociologie et d'ethnohistoire* (1971). M. D'HERTEFELT, "The Rwanda," in J.L. GIBBS (ed.), *Peoples of Africa*, pp. 405–440

(1965), gives a factual account of Rwandan society and culture; J.J. MAQUET, *Le Système des relations sociales dans le Ruanda ancien* (1954; Eng. trans., *The Premise of Inequality*, 1961), is an interpretation of the traditional political system. This has been criticized by H. CODERE, "Power in Ruanda," *Anthropologica, n.s.*, 4:45–85 (1962). R. LEMARCHAND, *Rwanda and Burundi* (1970), contrasts recent political developments in Rwanda and neighbouring Burundi. J.J. MAQUET, *Ruanda: Essai photographique sur une société africaine en transition* (1957), is a magnificent pre-independence collection of pictures of Rwandan life.

(T.Ka.)

Sa'adia ben Joseph

The versatile medieval Jewish exegete and philosopher Sa'adia ben Joseph (Sa'īd ibn Yūsuf al-Fayyūmī) was a keen polemicist and a brilliant stylist, both in Hebrew and in Arabic, with a deep sensitivity to the spiritual needs of his time. Sa'adia ushered in a new epoch in almost every field of Jewish literary and communal activities. He is one of the foremost figures in the history of Diaspora Judaism.

He was born in 882 at Dilaz in al-Fayyūm, Egypt. Little is known of his early years. When he departed from Egypt, at the age of about 23, he left behind, besides his wife and two sons, a distinguished group of devoted students. By that time he had already composed a Hebrew–Arabic dictionary, later expanded and issued under the name *ha-Egron*. For unknown reasons he migrated to Palestine. There he found a growing community of Karaites, a heretical Jewish sect that rejected the Talmud (the authoritative rabbinic compendium of law, lore, and commentary); this group enjoyed the support of the local Muslim authorities.

Apparently disappointed with the standards of learning in Palestine, he left for Babylonia. There he was confronted with not only the Karaitic schism but also a gnostic trend (derived from an ancient dualistic, theosophical movement), which rejected the foundations of all monotheistic religions. Books such as that of the Persian Jewish heretic Ḥiwi ad-Balkhī, which denied the omnipotence, omniscience, and justice of the biblical God and pointed to biblical inconsistencies, were then popular. In the face of such challenges, Sa'adia marshalled his great talents in the defense of religion in general and Jewish tradition in particular. Employing the same manner as Ḥiwi, Sa'adia composed his refutation of him in a somewhat complicated rhymed Hebrew. Then, too, he wrote his *Kitāb ar-radd 'alā 'Anān* ("Refutation of Anan," the founder of Karaism), a lost work that has been identified with Sa'adia's partially extant polemical poem *Essa meshali*.

In 921 Sa'adia, who by then had attained scholarly prominence, headed the Babylonian Jewish scholars in their conflict with the Palestinian scholar Aaron ben Meir, who had promulgated a far-reaching change in the Jewish calendrical computation. The conflict ended with no definite victory for either side. Yet, Sa'adia's participation in it demonstrated his indomitable courage and his importance for the Jewish community in Babylonia. Throughout this period he continued his literary polemics against the Karaites. In 928 he completed his *Kitāb at-tamyīz* ("Book of Discernment"), a defense of the traditional Rabbanite calendar.

On May 22 of the same year he was appointed by the exilarch (head of Babylonian Jewry) David ben Zakkai as the gaon (head) of the academy of Sura, which had been transferred to Baghdad. Upon assuming this office, he recognized the need to systematize Talmudic law and canonize it by subject. Toward this end he produced *Kitāb al-mawārīth* ("Book on the Laws of Inheritance"); *Aḥkam al-wadī'ah* ("The Laws on Deposits"); *Kitāb ash-shahādah wa al-wathā'iq* ("Book Concerning Testimony and Documents"); *Kitāb aṭ-ṭerefot* ("Book Concerning Forbidden Meats"); *Siddur*, a complete arrangement of the prayers and the laws pertaining to them; and some other minor works. In the *Siddur* he included his original religious poems. These works clearly show the Greco-Arabic methods of classification and composition.

His accomplishments intensified his sense of chosenness

Scholar and gaon in Babylonia

and made him more unyielding and less compromising. As it seems, these attitudes alienated some of his friends and provoked the envy of the Exilarch. In 932, when Sa'adia refused to endorse a decision issued by the Exilarch in a litigation, an open breach ensued between the two leaders. The Exilarch excommunicated Sa'adia and the latter retaliated by excommunicating the Exilarch. After three years of embittered struggle, in which each side enjoyed the support of some rich and politically influential Jews of Baghdad, Ben Zakkai succeeded in having the Muslim ruler al-Qāhir remove Sa'adia from his office. The Gaon went into seclusion. The years that followed turned out to be the brightest in Sa'adia's literary career. During these years he composed his major philosophical work, *Kitāb al-amānāt wa al-i'tiqādāt* ("The Book of Beliefs and Opinions"). The objective of this work was the harmonization of revelation and reason. In structure and content it displays a definite influence of Greek philosophy and of the theology of the Mu'tazilites, the rationalist sect of Islām. The introduction refutes skepticism and establishes the foundations of human knowledge. Chapter one seeks to establish *creatio ex nihilo* (creation out of nothing) in order to ascertain the existence of a Creator-God. Sa'adia then discusses God's uniqueness, justice, revelation, free will, and other doctrines accepted both by Judaism and by the Mu'tazilah (a great Islāmic sect of speculative theology, which emphasized the doctrines of God's uniqueness and absolute justice). The second part of the book deals with the essence of the soul and eschatological problems and presents guidelines for ethical living.

In 937 a reconciliation between the Gaon and the Exilarch occurred, and Sa'adia was reinstated as gaon. In 940 Ben Zakkai died and seven months later his son died, leaving behind a young child. Sa'adia took the orphan into his home and treated him like his own. Sa'adia himself died in September 942.

Exact chronology for many of Sa'adia's works cannot be definitely determined. The most important of these in philology is: *Kutub al-lughah* ("Books on Grammar"), fragments of which were published by Solomon Skoss, and *Tafsīr as-sab 'īn lafẓah* ("The Explanation of the Seventy Hapaxlegomina"), fragments of which were edited by N. Alony.

Sa'adia's opus magnum was on exegesis. He prepared an Arabic translation of the whole Pentateuch (published by Joseph Derenbourg) and a translation with an extensive commentary on Genesis 1–28, Exodus, and Leviticus. Only a few fragments of this extensive commentary have been published. His translation and commentaries on Isaiah, Proverbs, Job, and Psalms are extant in their entirety. Fragments of his commentaries on Daniel and Canticles, Esther, and Lamentations are preserved in the Geniza collection (fragments of medieval texts found in an old synagogue in Cairo and transferred to various libraries). In his biblical commentaries the Gaon formulated new principles of interpretation modelled on the rules of Greco-Arabic rhetoric.

His anti-Karaite works include *Kitāb ar-radd 'alā Ibn Sākawayhī* ("Refutation of Ibn Sākawayhī") and *Kitāb taḥsīl ash-sharā'i' as-samā'īyah* ("Book Concerning the Sources of the Irrational Laws"). In the latter work the Gaon contends that matters pertaining to the irrational commandments of the Mosaic Law may never be decided by means of analogy but only by the regulations transmitted through oral tradition. Talmudic tradition is therefore, he argues, indispensable. Another anti-Karaite work is the *Maqālah fī sirāj as-sabt* ("Treatise on the Lights of Sabbath"). It refutes the Karaite injunction forbidding the preparation of light for the sabbath.

In philosophy he wrote a philosophical commentary on the mystical book *Sefer yetzira*. In contrast to his "Book on Beliefs and Opinions," this volume does not show any influence of *kalām* (Islāmic scholastic theology).

Sa'adia's works

BIBLIOGRAPHY. NECHEMIAH ALONI, *Ha-Egron* (1969), an edition (in Hebrew) with extensive annotations; ISRAEL DAVIDSON (ed.), *Saadiah's Polemic Against Hiwi al-Balkhi* (1915), and *The Book of the Wars of the Lord* (1934), polemics against Sa'adia by Solomon ben Yeruhim (Hebrew edition with English translation)—the introductions to both editions require revision in light of new Genizah fragments; JOSEPH DERENBOURG, *Oeuvres complètes de R. Saadia Ben Iosef al-Fayyoûmî*, vol. 3, *Version arabe d'Isaïe* (1896), and vol. 6, *Version arabe des Proverbes* (1894), Sa'adia's Arabic version of Isaiah and his version of the Proverbes—the Isaiah translation is accompanied by fragments of Sa'adia's lost commentary; Z. DIESENDRUCK, "Saadya's Formulation of the Argument for Creation," in *Jewish Studies in Memory of George A. Kohut, 1874–1933* (1953), a profound article; JAKOB GUTTMANN, *Die Religionsphilosophie des Saadia* (1882), traces the Greek and Arabic sources of Sa'adia's philosophy (the Arabic sources are not fully exhausted); HENRY MALTER, *Saadia Gaon: His Life and Works* (1921), the most comprehensive study on Sa'adia, although many aspects need to be revised in light of later studies; JACOB MANN, "A Fihrist of Sa'adia's Works," *Jewish Quarterly Review*, New Series, 11:423–428 (1921); MOISE VENTURA, *La Philosophie de Saadia Gaon* (1934), a doctoral dissertation with some merit; HARRY A. WOLFSON, "Saadia on the Trinity and Incarnation," *Studies and Essays in Honor of Abraham A. Neuman* (1962), a very exhaustive study; collections of articles of Sa'adia in the *Jewish Quarterly Review*, New Series, vol. 33 (1942–43); Sa'adia anniversary volume, *Proceedings of the American Academy for Jewish Research* (1943); ERWIN I.J. ROSENTHAL (ed.), *Saadya Studies* (1943); MOSES ZUCKER, *Rav Saadya Gaon's Translation of the Torah* (in Hebrew, with English summary; 1959), and *A Critique Against the Writings of R. Saadya Gaon by R. Mubashshir* (1955), an edition important for restoration of Sa'adianic material as well as for the study of the relationship of some of Sa'adia's contemporaries to his literary work.

(M.Z.)

Saarinen, Eero

A gifted American architect who died at the height of his career, Eero Saarinen largely initiated a trend toward exploration and experiment in design—a trend that departed from the doctrinaire rectangular prisms that were characteristic of the earlier phase of modern architecture. He was born in Kirkkonummi, Finland, on August 20, 1910, the son of a great architect, Eliel Saarinen, and Loja Gesellius, a sculptor. The Saarinen family of four, including a sister, Eva-Lisa, came to the United States in 1923. Eero attended public schools in Michigan. In 1929 he studied sculpture at the Académie de la Grande Chaumière in Paris but, as he recounted years later, "it never occurred to me to do anything but follow in my father's footsteps." Between 1931 and 1934 he studied architecture at Yale University, where the curriculum was untouched by modern theories. His father's architecture in Finland had focussed on a free adaptation of medieval Scandinavian forms, and in the U.S. he designed various private school buildings from 1925 to 1941, including Cranbrook Academy of Art in Bloomfield Hills, Michigan, following this loose, romantic style. At Yale, young Saarinen won a travelling fellowship that made possible a leisurely European visit in 1934–35. He stayed an additional year in Helsinki working with the architect Jarl Eklund.

Eero Saarinen's professional work in the United States began in 1936 with research on housing and city planning with the Flint Institute of Research and Planning in Flint, Michigan. He joined his father's practice in Bloomfield Hills in 1938, and their collaboration was marked by the winning of first prize in the Smithsonian Institution Gallery of Art competition (1939), a tranquil yet monumental design for the mall in Washington, D.C. Unfortunately, it was never built.

In 1939 Saarinen married Lillian Swann, a sculptor, and they had two children, Eric and Susan. This marriage ended in divorce in 1953, and Saarinen was remarried the following year to Aline Bernstein Loucheim, an art critic. A son, Eames, was born later that year.

In 1940 Eero and his father designed Crow Island School in Winnetka, Illinois, which influenced postwar school design, being a one-story structure, generously extended in plan, and suitably scaled for primary-grade children. Also in 1940 he became a naturalized citizen of the United States. In 1945 Eero joined a partnership with Eliel Saarinen and J. Robert F. Swanson that had been organized in 1939. This partnership was dissolved in 1947 and a new partnership of Saarinen, Saarinen and Asso-

Collaboration with Eliel Saarinen

Saarinen seated in one of his chair designs; photograph by Arnold Newman, 1948.
© Arnold Newman

ciates was then formed that lasted until the elder Saarinen's death in 1950.

In the eleven years that he survived his father, Saarinen's own work included a series of dramatically different designs that displayed a richer and more diverse vocabulary. In questioning the presuppositions of early modern architecture, he introduced sculptural forms that were rich in architectural character and visual drama unknown in earlier years. The exciting results were welcomed by many who were bored by the uniformity and austerity of the International Style of modern architecture.

Saarinen's first independent work, one that brought immediate renown, was the vast General Motors Technical Center in Warren, Michigan (1948–56). Here Saarinen arranged five major building complexes, each for a different research study, around a 22-acre (nine-hectare) reflecting pool. Strips of planted forest rimmed the 320-acre (130-hectare) site. The precision and modular rhythm of the low buildings recalls the design of the German-American architect Ludwig Mies van der Rohe, as well as the early automobile factories of the U.S. architect Albert Kahn. Saarinen's technical solution of the curtain wall (metal panels and glass set in aluminum frames) was widely copied. The scale and visual splendour of the centre suggests a 20th-century Versailles.

First independent work

In 1953 Saarinen began to design the Kresge Auditorium and chapel of the Massachusetts Institute of Technology, choosing the basic forms of an eighth of a sphere for the auditorium and a cylinder for the chapel. The partial sphere is a "handkerchief" dome resting on three points. The auditorium is arranged entirely within this dramatically simple form. The small chapel is a stark, red-brick cylinder, lighted only from above. Both were completed in 1955. While some critics felt that the solutions were forced and arbitrary, these buildings indicated the search Saarinen had begun for significant and identifying character in public buildings.

Although Saarinen continued to use rectilinear forms on occasion, such as the United States Embassy in London (1955–60) and the Law School at the University of Chicago (1956–60), it was his freely sculptural designs that achieved greater attention. In 1956 two such works were initiated that can be considered representative: Ingalls Hockey Rink at Yale University in New Haven, Connecticut (1958) and the Trans World Airlines terminal at John F. Kennedy International Airport, New York City (1956–62). For the Yale rink, Saarinen, avoiding the typical field house, achieved a unique and sympathetic sports building. From a lengthwise curved spine in reinforced concrete, he suspended cables to anchors on the oval periphery. This tent-like form suggests an almost Oriental shrine for the game of hockey, a blending of the structural, emotional, and aesthetic that Saarinen himself was proud of. For the design of the TWA terminal, Saarinen continued exploration of interior–exterior sculptural effects. Based on a symmetrical plan, two major cantilevered concrete shells extend dramatically outward, suggesting wings, and on the inside sculptural supports and curving stairways evoke a feeling of movement. In this distinctive and memorable building, Saarinen presented a symbol of flight. While to some it proclaimed virtuosity over logic, Saarinen believed "we must have an emotional reason as well as a logical end for everything we do." Later, Saarinen designed the Dulles International Airport at Chantilly, Virginia, outside Washington, D.C. (1958–62), with a hanging roof suspended from diagonal supports.

Saarinen's effort was primarily concerned with institutional buildings for education and industry. He built only one skyscraper, the CBS Headquarters in New York (1960–64), and one house in the midwest. His 1948 prizewinning Jefferson National Expansion Memorial design for St. Louis was completed in 1964. It is a graceful and spectacular arch of stainless steel, with a span and height of 630 feet (190 metres). It conveys a sense of ceremony and special place yet also one of delight and ease, qualities that are present in all Saarinen's works, whatever their function.

Furniture
design

Like many contemporary architects, Saarinen was challenged by furniture design, especially the chair, which presents aesthetical and structural problems that are particularly difficult to solve. In 1941 he and the designer-architect Charles Eames won a national furniture award for a chair design in molded plywood. In 1948 Saarinen created a womblike chair using a glass fibre shell upholstered in foam rubber and fabric. His last furniture designs comprised a series of pedestal-based chairs and tables (1957) that combined a sculptural aluminum base with plastic shells for the chairs and discs of marble or plastic for the table tops. The curvilinear forms of his furniture designs paralleled his growing interest in sculptural architectural forms.

As a person, Saarinen was outwardly a stocky, calm man of informal manner and puckish humour, but underneath he was intensely serious about architecture and seemed compulsively competitive with his own most recent designs. His wish that a building make an expressive statement established new horizons for modern architecture. He was exploratory in his thinking and committed to research on every level. His buildings were created with meticulous care, from the original analysis of a client's problem to the final execution, and were sympathetically received by both the general public and his fellow architects.

Saarinen died of a brain tumour in Ann Arbor, Michigan, on September 1, 1961, leaving numerous projects to be completed by his associates. Always immersed in architecture, Saarinen had no other real interest. He never wrote a book and commented only occasionally on his buildings and architectural philosophy.

MAJOR WORKS

General Motors Technical Center, Warren, Michigan (1948–56); Jefferson National Expansion Memorial, St. Louis, Missouri (1948–64); Milwaukee County War Memorial, Milwaukee, Wisconsin (1953–57); Concordia Senior College, Fort Wayne, Indiana (1953–58); Kresge Auditorium and chapel, MIT, Cambridge, Massachusetts (1955); U.S. Embassy, Oslo, Norway (1955–59); U.S. Embassy, London (1955–60); Law School, University of Chicago, Chicago, Illinois (1956–60); Trans World Airlines terminal, John F. Kennedy Airport, New York (1956–62); Thomas J. Watson Research Centre, IBM, Yorktown, New York (1957–61); Deere & Company, Moline, Illinois (1957–63); Ingalls Hockey Rink, Yale University, New Haven, Connecticut (1958); Dulles International Airport, Chantilly, Virginia,

serving Washington, D.C. (1958–62); North Christian Church, Columbus, Indiana (1959–63); Ezra Stiles and Morse College, Yale University, New Haven, Connecticut (1962); Vivian Beaumont Theatre, Lincoln Center, New York (1962–63); CBS Headquarters, New York (completed 1964).

BIBLIOGRAPHY. There are only two books devoted entirely to Saarinen's work. *Eero Saarinen on His Work,* ed. by his wife, ALINE SAARINEN (1962), contains Saarinen's own comments but no supplementary evaluation. It includes a listing of the architect's buildings and is handsomely illustrated. ALLAN TEMKO, *Eero Saarinen* (1962), is an informative, well-illustrated, brief account with evaluation. Details on individual buildings have been reported and illustrated in professional architectural journals.

(H.F.K.)

Saarland

Its population makes the Saar one of the smallest of the ten states, or *Länder,* that make up the Federal Republic of Germany. The Saar is probably best known for its extensive deposits of coal and for its steel production, which have been sources of both wealth and political contention for over a thousand years. The state has alternated between French and German control with bewildering frequency over the centuries, and its contemporary culture contains a heritage from both nations. It is the youngest of the modern West German states, and its economy was still closely linked to that of France as late as the 1960s. By the early 1970s, however, extensive changes were taking place in the local economy, and the diversification and redirection of Saar industry in particular marked a distinct shift toward the German sphere of influence.

The *Land* is bounded by France on the south, Luxembourg on the west, and the *Land* of Rheinland-Pfalz on the north and east. It covers an area of 991 square miles (2,568 square kilometres) and supports a population that exceeded 1,100,000 at the beginning of the 1970s. The administrative capital is at Saarbrücken. (For further details see FRANCE, HISTORY OF; GERMANY, HISTORY OF; GERMANY, FEDERAL REPUBLIC OF.)

History. The Celts and Germanic Franks were the first inhabitants of the area. In AD 843 the Treaty of Verdun divided the Carolingian Empire into three realms, and the lands bordering the Saar and Mosel rivers were included in the central kingdom, which was ruled by Lothair I. In 870, however, the region was transferred to the eastern Frankish Empire, where German was spoken. The boundaries of the district (Landkreis) of Saarbrücken took shape during the 11th century at the intersection of the significant transportation routes from the upper Rhine to Flanders and from Metz to Mainz. The French Province de la Sarre was created by the Truce of Regensburg in 1684, and the area, with its centre at Saarlouis, was added to the empire of Louis XIV. In 1697, however, France was forced to return all territories except Saarlouis at the Treaty of Rijswijk. In 1792, in the aftermath of the French Revolution, French troops again occupied the Saar, along with territory on the east bank of the Rhine. With the final defeat of Napoleon in 1815, the eastern boundary of Lorraine was established, and most of the Saar was ceded to Prussia. When Alsace-Lorraine was added to the German Empire in 1871, the Saar ceased to be a boundary state and experienced rapid economic development based on the coal and iron deposits of Lorraine.

French
and
German
origins

After World War I, the Saar mines were awarded to France, and Saarland was placed under the administration of the League of Nations for 15 years. In the plebiscite of 1935, however, more than 90 percent of the inhabitants of the Saar voted for its return to Germany.

In 1945, the French military forces occupied the Saar following World War II, and two years later the first state Parliament adopted a constitution that called for total independence from Germany. France and the Federal Republic of Germany agreed, in 1954, to a statute that provided for the Saar's autonomy under a European commissioner. The new status was to be approved by a referendum, but 68 percent of the voters rejected the statute and, by implication, the separation of the Saar from Germany. The French subsequently agreed to the return of the Saar to West Germany, and, on June 7, 1959, it finally achieved its present status as the tenth *Land* of the Federal Republic.

The land and the people. *Topography.* The state's low, heavily forested hills are crossed by a series of brooks and three small rivers—the Saar in the west, the Prims in the north, and the Blies in the south. The highest elevation, of 2,280 feet (695 metres), is attained by the Weisskircher Heights. The climate is largely continental in character, but the maritime influence is quite evident, and the annual average temperature is 50° F (10° C). The warmest month is July, with an average temperature of 64° F (18° C), and the coldest is January, at 34° F (1° C). The annual precipitation amounts to about 31 inches (800 millimetres); winters are mild, and strong frosts seldom occur.

Vegetation and animal life. The animal and plant life of the Saar does not differ essentially from that of other similar densely settled European regions. Free-living animals—particularly mammals, birds, and fish—have lost several species and have been greatly decreased in number because of human settlements. The state program of wildlife conservation seeks to prevent the extinction of other species. Among the animals that have been hunted in the Saar are wild boars, deer, foxes, badgers, martens, hares, wild rabbits, pheasants, partridges and wild ducks.

Settlement. Most of the *Land* is settled in small, agricultural towns, and the only area with a pronounced industrial character is a nine-mile strip between Brebach, a suburb of Saarbrücken, and Völklingen, where three of the *Land*'s large smelting works are located. The greatest population density is in the state's southwestern corner, in a triangle linking Saarbrücken, Dillingen, and Neunkirchen. In addition to functioning as the state capital, Saarbrücken (population 131,000) is the largest city; other urban areas include Neunkirchen (44,000), Völklingen (40,000), and Saarlouis (36,000).

Population. By the early 1970s, the Saar had a population of approximately 1,130,000, or about 2 percent of the national total, although the average density of 439 inhabitants per square mile was almost double the national average. About 70 percent of its citizens are Roman Catholic; the remainder belong to the Evangelical and Protestant churches. The official language is German, but French is also spoken. The population has quadrupled during the last century, while the mining and iron-producing industries were becoming major economic activities. During the 19th century, the Saar's mines attracted workers from Hundsruck, the Palatinate, the Harz Mountains, Thuringia, Saxony, Bohemia, and Alsace-Lorraine. In later decades, migrations were essentially internal and were detrimental to lesser developed German regions. Population concentrations vary considerably, and Saarbrücken in the early 1970s had the highest density of over 6,400 inhabitants per square mile. In the early 1970s there were 100 males for every 111 females. There are about 14 live births for every 1,000 inhabitants, and the infant-mortality rate averages about 28 per 1,000.

The economy. The Saar is dominated by its highly developed industrial activity. Over 58 percent of the gross domestic product is contributed by industry and mining, 24 percent is derived from services, 16 percent results from trade and transportation, and the remaining 2 percent is contributed by agriculture. Of the state's 157,000 industrial workers, almost 18 percent are engaged in coal mining, and 33 percent are employed by the iron, investment, and manufacturing industries.

Coal mining. The coal seams stretch for a distance of about 20 miles from Saarlouis and Völklingen in the west to Neunkirchen in the east. The reserves of 2,800,000,000 tons of workable coal are located at depths of up to 4,000 feet. In the early 1970s, about 11,100,000 tons of bituminous coal were mined annually, and the industry employed over 28,000 workers.

The iron industry. The extraction of coke from bituminous coal and the smelting of iron ore rich in phosphorous have been the bases assisting the growth of the iron industry since the 19th century. In the early 1970s iron-

producing firms employed approximately 38,000 workers. Annual production amounted to 3,900,000 tons of pig iron and 4,400,000 tons of raw steel.

The iron- and metal-processing industries include the production of steel and the construction of machinery and motors. The approximately 60,000 persons employed in the early 1970s represented 38 percent of all industrial workers.

Other industries. Other important industries include the manufacture of ceramics and textiles and food processing. Small businesses and the trades—of which construction is the most important—employ approximately 60,000 persons. Commerce, credit unions, and insurance companies serve the needs of the Saar without assuming any significance outside the region.

Agriculture. Agriculture is relatively insignificant. The major products are grains, potatoes, vegetables, fruit, dairy products, and livestock. Production is oriented toward the need of the Saar's urban population, but small quantities of dairy produce are exported to the other *Länder* and meat, cattle, and bread are sold abroad.

Foreign trade. France is the most important trading partner of the Saar, receiving approximately 70 percent of all exports. About half of the Saar's industrial products —excluding mining and electrical-engineering equipment —are sold to the other *Länder*. Primary exports to France include bar and cast iron, sheet metal, tools, wire, coal, coke, and ceramics. Among the imports from France are meat and meat products, motor vehicles, sheet metal, and iron ore.

Transportation. The Saar has a well-developed road network. A superhighway connects the Saar with the Rhine–Main area, and other roads link the state with Paris, Luxembourg, Karlsruhe, and Cologne.

The railways are equally favourable, and the main lines have been electrified. The railways cover a total distance of 250 miles; there are several multiple-railed stretches. Water transport along the canalized portion of the Saar River can accommodate ships as large as 270 tons, carrying 519,000 tons of goods annually. This is inadequate, however, and the federal government plans to equip the Saar with an efficient canal system to connect to the Rhine River through the neighbouring state of Rheinland-Pfalz. An airport at Saarbrücken-Ensheim handles both domestic and international traffic.

Administration, social services, and cultural life. The state Parliament is composed of 50 members who are elected every five years. The prime minister is assisted by a six-member Cabinet.

A well-developed educational system includes a series of technical high schools and the University of the Saarland at Saarbrücken. Public health services are adequate; in the early 1970s there were 11 hospital beds for every 1,000 inhabitants. The legal system and social welfare legislation conform to national standards.

Cultural institutions—including the City Theatre, Radio Saarland, and the Modern Gallery of Saarbrücken— draw their support from both Germany and France. In 1970 there were 12 museums and galleries, and a large number of singing, music, and theatrical groups. Of the two large daily newspapers, the *Saarbrücker Zeitung* has the greater circulation. A number of magazines are also published in the state.

The future. The future of the Saar depends both on the success of its industry and on the development of the Common Market. The federal government supports the diversification of industry and is promoting the relocation of businesses to its second least populated state. It is also possible that the Saar will be merged with another, larger state—a step that may prove necessary if current economic policy should prove unsuccessful.

BIBLIOGRAPHY. F. KLOEVEKORN and A.G. HOFER (eds.), *Das Saargebiet, seine Struktur, seine Probleme* (1929), a voluminous text on all of the essential aspects of the history, economy, culture, and politics of the Saar district; K. ALTMEYER et al., *Das Saarland: Ein Beitrag zur Entwicklung des jüngsten Bundeslandes in Politik, Kultur und Wirtschaft* (1958), a book with detailed information on politics, culture, and economy in the Saar district; *Die Saar-wirtschaft, Industrie-und Handelskammer des Saarlandes,* annual reports

Three main rivers

Demographic expansion

The industrial base

of the chamber of industry and commerce of the Saar district that include detailed views on actual aspects of the economy of the Saar district and a presentation of the activity of the chamber in that year. See also the over 300 annual reports of the statistical office of the Saar district.

(He.K.)

Sacrament

The Latin word *sacramentum*, which etymologically is an ambiguous theological term, was used in Roman law to describe a legal sanction in which a man placed his life or property in the hands of the supernatural powers that upheld justice and honoured solemn contracts. It later became an oath of allegiance taken by soldiers to their commander when embarking on a new campaign, sworn in a sacred place and using a formula having a religious connotation.

NATURE AND SIGNIFICANCE

When *sacramentum* was adopted as an ordinance by the early Christian Church in the 3rd century, the Latin word *sacer* ("holy") was brought into conjunction with the Greek word *mystērion* ("secret rite"). *Sacramentum* was thus given a sacred mysterious significance that indicated a spiritual potency. The power was transmitted through material instruments and vehicles viewed as channels of divine grace and as benefits in ritual observances instituted by Christ. St. Augustine defined sacrament as "the visible form of an invisible grace" or "a sign of a sacred thing." Similarly, St. Thomas Aquinas wrote that anything that is called sacred may be called *sacramentum*. It is made efficacious by virtue of its divine institution by Christ in order to establish a bond of union between God and man. In the Anglican catechism it is defined as "an outward and visible sign of an inward and spiritual grace."

The term sacrament has become a convenient expression for a sign or symbol of a sacred thing, occasion, or event imparting spiritual benefits to participants; and such signs or symbols have been associated with eating, drinking, lustration (ceremonial purification), nuptial intercourse, or ritual techniques regarded as "means of grace" and pledges of a covenant relationship with the sacred order. In this way the material aspects have become the forms of the embodied spiritual reality.

TYPES AND VARIATIONS

Types. The several types of sacraments (*i.e.*, initiatory, purificatory, renewal, communion, healing, cultic elevation) are well exemplified in Christianity, though they also may be found in other Western religions, the Eastern religions, and preliterate religions. In the 12th century the several sacraments of the Western Christian Church were narrowed by Peter Lombard (12th-century theologian and bishop) to seven rites, viz., Baptism, confirmation, the Eucharist (the Lord's Supper), penance, holy orders, matrimony, and extreme unction. This enumeration was accepted by St. Thomas Aquinas, the Council of Florence in 1439, and subsequently by the Council of Trent (1545–63). All these rites were thus affirmed by the Roman Catholic Church as being sacraments instituted by Christ. The number, however, has been modified by modern theologians since the precise origins of some of the seven sacraments are uncertain. Protestant Reformers of the 16th century accepted two or three sacraments as valid: Baptism, the Lord's Supper, and, in some fashion, penance. Both Roman Catholicism and Eastern Orthodoxy accept the sevenfold enumeration. In addition to these, any ceremonial actions and objects related to sacraments that endow a person or thing with a sacred character have been designated "sacramental," though they are differentiated from those of dominical (*i.e.*, Christ's) institution in conveying divine grace *ex opere operato* (it works by itself) or in conferring an indelible character on the recipient, such as Baptism, confirmation, and holy orders. Sacramentals include the use of holy water, incense, vestments, candles, exorcisms, anointing and making the sign of the cross, fasting, abstinence, and almsgiving.

The word sacrament, in its broadest sense as a sign or symbol conveying something "hidden," mysterious, and efficacious, has a wider application and cosmic signif-

Christian sacraments (margin)

"Sacramentals" (margin)

icance than that used in Christianity. For example, the evolutionary process is viewed by some as a graded series in which the lower stratum provides a basis for the one next above it. The lower, indeed, seems to be necessary to the growth of the higher. This view has introduced concepts of new powers and potentialities in organic evolution culminating in the human synthesis of mind transcending the process. The entire universe, therefore, can be said to have a sacramental significance in which the "inward" (or spiritual) and the "outward" (or material) elements meet in a higher unity that guarantees for the latter its full validity. Thus, the sacred meal has been at once a sacramental communion and a sacrificial offering (*e.g.*, wine, bread, or animal as a sign or symbol of a divine death and resurrection for the benefit of man) in which the two fundamental and complementary rites have been closely combined throughout their long and varied histories.

Variations. *Sacramental ideas and practices in preliterate societies.* In preliterate society everyday events have been given sacramental interpretations by being invested with supernatural meanings in relation to their ultimate sources in the unseen divine or sacred powers. The well-being of primitive society, in fact, demands the recognition of a hierarchy of values in which the lower is always dependent on the higher and in which the highest is regarded as the transcendental source of values outside and above mankind and the natural order. To partake of the flesh of a sacrificial victim or of the god himself or to consume the cereal image of a vegetation deity (as was done among the Aztecs in ancient Mexico), makes the eater a recipient of divine life and its qualities. Similarly, portions of the dead may be imbibed in mortuary sacramental rites to obtain the attributes of the deceased or to ensure their reincarnation. To give the dead new life beyond the grave, mourners may allow life-giving blood to fall upon the corpse sacramentally. In this cycle of sacramental ideas and practices, the giving, conservation, and promotion of life, together with the establishment of a bond of union with the sacred order, are fundamental. In Paleolithic hunting communities this sacramental idea appears to have been manifested in the sacramental rites performed to control the fortunes of the chase, to promote the propagation of the species on which the food supply depended, and to maintain right relations with the transcendental source of the means of subsistence, as exemplified in paintings—discovered in the caves at Altamira, Lascaux, Les Trois Frères, Font-de-Gaume and elsewhere in France and Spain—that show men with animal masks (illustrating a ritual or mystical communion of men and animals that were sources of food).

Mortuary sacramental rites (margin)

Sacramental ideas and practices in the ancient Near East. When agriculture and herding became the basic type of food production, sacramental concepts and techniques were centred mainly in the fertility of the soil, its products, and in the succession of the seasons. This centralization was most apparent in the ancient Near East in and after the 4th millennium BC. A death and resurrection sacred drama arose around the fertility motif, in which a perpetual dying and rebirth in nature and humanity was enacted. In this sequence birth, maturity, death, and rebirth were ritually repeated and renewed through sacramental transitional acts, such as passage rites, ceremonies ensuring passage from one status to another. In passage rites the king often was the principal actor in the promotion of the growth of the crops and the propagation of man and beast and in the promotion of the reproductive forces in nature in general at the turn of the year.

Fertility motifs (margin)

Sacramental ideas and practices in the Greco-Roman world. In the Greco-Oriental mystery cults the sacramental ritual based on the fertility motif was less prominent than in the Egyptian and Mesopotamian religions. It did, nevertheless, occur in the Eleusinia, a Greek agricultural festival celebrated in honour of the goddess Demeter and her daughter Kore. The things spoken and done in this great event have remained undisclosed, though some light has been thrown upon them by the contents of the museum at Eleusis, such as the vase paintings, and by later untrustworthy references in the writings of the early

Church Fathers (*e.g.*, Clement of Alexandria) and some Gnostics (early Christian heretics who held that matter was evil and the spirit good). The drinking of the *kykeōn* —a gruel of meal and water—can hardly be regarded as a sacramental beverage since it was consumed during the preparation for the initiation rather than at its climax. There is nothing to suggest that a ritual rebirth was effected by a sacramental lustration, or sacred meal, at any point in the Eleusinian ritual. What is indicated is that the neophytes (*mystae*) emerged from their profound experience with an assurance of having attained newness of life and the hope of a blessed immortality. From the character of the ritual, the mystery would seem to have been connected with the seasonal drama in which originally a sacred marriage may have been an important feature, centred in Demeter, the corn mother, and Kore (Persephone), the corn maiden.

In the 6th century BC, or perhaps very much earlier, the orgiastic religion of the god Dionysus, probably originating in Thrace and Phrygia, was established in Greece. In the Dionysiac rites the Maenads (female attendants) became possessed by the spirit of Dionysus by means of tumultuous music and dancing, the free use of wine, and an orgiastic meal (the tearing to pieces and devouring of animals embodying Dionysus Zagreus with their bare hands as the central act of the Bacchanalia). Though not necessarily sacramental, these rites enabled the Maenads to surmount the barrier that separated them from the supernatural world and to surrender themselves unconditionally to the mighty powers that transcended time and space, thus carrying them into the realm of the eternal. Ecstatic rites of this nature did not commend themselves to the Greeks of the unemotional nonsacramental Homeric tradition; such rites did appeal, however, to many, some of whom had come under the influences of the Orphic mysteries in which it was possible for them to rise to a higher level in its *thiasoi* (brotherhoods). The purpose of the Orphic ritual was to confer divine life sacramentally on its initiates so that they might attain immortality through regeneration and reincarnation, thereby freeing the soul from its fleshly bondage.

Sacramental ideas and practices in the Indo-Iranian world. To what extent, if at all, metempsychosis (the passing of the soul at death into another body) was introduced into Greece from India can be only conjectural in the absence of conclusive evidence. Though belief in rebirth and the transmigration of souls has been widespread, however, especially in preliterate religions, it was in India and Greece that the two concepts attained their highest development. In post-Vedic (the period after the formulation of the Hindu sacred scriptures, the Veda) India, belief in the transmigration of souls became a characteristic doctrine in Hinduism, and the priestly caste (*i.e.*, the Brahmins) reached their zenith as the sole immolators of the sacrificial offerings; but sacramentalism was not a feature in the *Brāhmaṇas*, the ritual texts compiled by the Brahmins. In the earlier Vedic conception of *soma*, the personification of the fermented juice of a plant, comparable to that of *ambros* in Greece, kava in Polynesia, and especially *haoma* in Iran, the sacramental view is most apparent (see HINDUISM).

In Zoroastrianism *haoma* (Sanskrit *soma*, from the root *su* or *bu*, "to squeeze" or "pound") is the name given to the yellow plant, from which a juice was extracted and consumed in the *Yasna* ceremony, the general sacrifice in honour of all the deities. The liturgy of the *Yasna* was a remarkable anticipation of the mass in Christianity. Haoma was regarded by Zoroaster as the son of the Wise Lord and Creator (Ahura Mazdā) and the chief priest of the *Yasna* cult. He was believed to be incarnate in the sacred plant that was pounded to death in order to extract its life-giving juice so that those who consumed it might be given immortality. He was regarded as both victim and priest in a sacrificial-sacramental offering in worship. As the intermediary between God and man, Haoma acquired a place and sacramental significance in the worship of Mithra (an Indo-Iranian god of light) in his capacity as the immaculate priest of Ahura Mazdā with whom he was coequal. The Mithraic sacramental banquet was derived

Margin: Rebirth

Margin: Incarnation of Haoma

from the *Yasna* ceremony, wine taking the place of the *haoma* and Mithra that of Ahura Mazdā. In the Mithraic initiation rites, it was not until one attained the status of the initiatory degree known as "Lion" that the neophyte could partake of the oblation of bread, wine, and water, which was the earthly counterpart of the celestial mystical sacramental banquet. The sacred wine gave vigour to the body, prosperity, wisdom, and the power to combat malignant spirits and to obtain immortality.

The early Christian leaders noticed the resemblances between the Mithraic meal, the Zoroastrian *haoma* ceremony, and the Christian Eucharist; and between Mithraism and Christianity, to some extent, there was mutual influence and borrowing of respective beliefs and practices. But Mithraism's antecedents were different, being Iranian and Mesopotamian with a Vedic background before it became part of the Hellenistic and Christian world (*c.* 67 BC to about AD 385).

Sacramental ideas and practices of pre-Columbian America. The recurrent and widespread practice of holding sacred meals in the sacramental system, in addition to being well documented in the Greco-Roman world, also occurred in the pre-Columbian Mexican calendrical ritual in association with human sacrifice on a grand scale. In the May Festival in honour of the war god Huitzilopochtli, an image of the deity was fashioned from a dough containing beet seed, maize, and honey; then the image was covered with a rich garment, placed on a litter; and carried in a procession to a pyramid-temple. There pieces of paste similarly compounded and in the form of large bones were transformed by rites of consecration into Huitzilopochtli's flesh and bones. A number of human victims were then offered to him, and the image was broken into small fragments and consumed sacramentally by the worshippers with tears, fears, and reverence, a strict fast being observed until the ceremonies were over and the sick had been given their communion with the particles. This ceremony was repeated at the winter solstice when the dough was fortified with the blood of children, and similar images were venerated and eaten by families in their houses. The main purpose of the sacrament was to secure a good maize harvest and a renewal of the crops, as well as human health and strength. In Peru at the Festival of the Sun, after three days of fasting, llamas, the sacred animals, were sacrificed as a burnt offering, and the flesh was eaten sacramentally at a banquet by the lord of the Incas and his nobles. It was then distributed to the rest of the community with sacred maize cakes. Dogs, regarded as divine incarnations, also were slain and parts of their flesh solemnly eaten by the worshippers.

Similar rites were celebrated in North America by Indians at the Feast of Grain among the Natchez of Mississippi and Louisiana and among the Creeks in the Mississippi Valley when the corn was ripe. Among the Plains Indians sacrificial blood was employed sacramentally to make the earth fruitful by the fructifying power of the sun.

Margin: Mexican sacramental rites

THEOLOGY AND PRACTICE OF SACRAMENTS IN CHRISTIANITY

Though the widespread conception of the sacramental principle is an ancient heritage, in all probability going back before the dawn of civilization, it acquired in Christianity a unique significance. There it became the fundamental system and institution for the perpetuation of the union of God and man in the person of Jesus Christ through the visible organization and constitution of the church, which was viewed as the mystical body of Christ.

Baptism. Baptism, as the initial rite, took the place of circumcision in Judaism in which this ancient and primitive custom was the covenant sign and a legal injunction rather than a sacramental ordinance. Baptismal immersion in water was practiced in Judaism for some time before the fall of Jerusalem in AD 70, and it was adopted by John the Baptist (a Jewish prophet and cousin of Jesus Christ) as the principal sacrament in his messianic movement.

The purificatory lustration of John the Baptist, however, was transformed into the prototype of the Christian sacrament by the baptism of Jesus in the river Jordan and by

Margin: Significance of the sacramental principle in Christianity the imagery of this event combined with the imagery of his death and resurrection. A distinction was made, however, between the water baptism of John and the Christian Spirit Baptism in the apostolic church. Under the influence of the missionary Apostle St. Paul, the Christian rite was given an interpretation in the terms of the mystery religions, and the catechumen (initiate instructed in the secrets of the faith) was identified with the death and Resurrection of Christ (Rom. 6:3–5; Gal. 3:12). The bestowal of the new life constituted a sacramental rebirth in the church in union with the risen Lord as its divine head.

Confirmation. With the development of infant Baptism, the regenerative initial sacrament was coupled with the charismatic apostolic laying on of hands as the seal of the Spirit in the rite of confirmation (Acts 8:14–17). By the 4th century, confirmation became a separate "unction" (rite using oil) administered by a bishop or, earlier and in the Eastern Church, by a priest to complete the sacramental baptismal grace already bestowed at birth or on some other previous occasion. At first, especially in the East, a threefold rite was performed consisting of Baptism, confirmation, and first communion; but in the West, where the consecration of the oil and the laying on of hands were confined to the episcopate, confirmation tended to become a separate event with the growth in the size of dioceses. It was not, however, until the 16th century that Baptism and confirmation were permanently separated. In England Queen Elizabeth I was confirmed when she was only three days old; and infant confirmation is still sometimes practiced in Spain. But the normal custom in Western Christendom has been for confirmation to be administered at or after the age of reason and to be the occasion for instruction in the faith, as in the case of the *mystae* in the Mysteries of Eleusis. But whether or not confirmation conveys a new gift of the Spirit or is the sealing of the same grace bestowed in Baptism, which is still debated, it has come to be regarded in some churches as conferring an indelible quality on the soul. Therefore, it cannot be repeated when it has once been validly performed as a sacrament.

The Eucharist. Together with Baptism the greatest importance has been given to the Eucharist, both of which institutions are singled out in the Gospels as dominical (instituted by Christ) in origin, with a special status and rank. Under a variety of titles (Eucharist from the Greek *eucharistia*, "thanksgiving"; the Latin mass; the Holy Communion; the Lord's Supper; and the breaking of the bread) it has been the central act of worship ever since the night of the betrayal of Christ on the Thursday preceding his crucifixion. It was then that the elements of bread and wine were identified with the body and blood of Christ in his institution of the Eucharist with his disciples and with the sacrifice he was about to offer in order to establish and seal the new covenant. This "real presence" has been variously interpreted in actual, figurative, or symbolical senses; but the sacramental sense, as the *anamnesis*, or memorial before God, of the sacrificial offering on the cross once and for all, has always been accepted.

Along these lines a eucharistic theology gradually took shape in the apostolic and early church without much controversy or formulation. In the New Testament, in addition to the three accounts of the institution of the Eucharist in the first three "books" of the New Testament known as Synoptic Gospels because they have a common viewpoint and common sources (Matt. 26:26ff.; Mark 14:22ff.; Luke 22:17–20), St. Paul's earliest record of the ordinance in I Cor. 11:17–29, written about AD 55, suggests that some abuses had arisen in conjunction with the common meal, or *agapē*, with which it was combined. Like the Iranian *haoma* ceremony, it had become an occasion of drunkenness and gluttony. To rectify this, St. Paul recalled and re-established the original institution and its purpose and interpretation as a sacrificial-sacramental rite. Fellowship meals continued in association with the postapostolic Eucharist, as is shown in the *Didachē* (a Christian document concerned with worship and church discipline written *c.* 100–*c.* 140) and in the doctrinal and liturgical development described in the writings of the Early Church Fathers little was changed. Not until

the beginning of the Middle Ages did controversial issues arise that found expression in the definition of the doctrine of transubstantiation at the fourth Lateran Council in 1215. This definition opened the way for the scholastic interpretation of the eucharistic Presence of Christ and of the sacramental principle, in Aristotelian terms. Thus, St. Thomas Aquinas maintained that a complete change occurred in the "substance" of each of the species, while the "accidents," or outward appearances, remained the same. During the Reformation, though the medieval doctrine was denied by the continental Reformers, it was reaffirmed by the Council of Trent in 1551. Holy Communion was retained as a sacrament by most of the Protestant groups, except the Society of Friends, the Salvation Army, and some of the Adventist groups, which abandoned the sacramental principle altogether.

Repentence. In its formulation, the Christian doctrine of conciliation, which, as St. Paul contended, required a change of status in the penitent, had to be made sacramentally effective in the individual and in redeemed humanity as a whole. In the Gospel According to Matthew (16:13–20, 18:18) the power to "bind and loose" was conferred on St. Peter and the other Apostles. Lapses into paganism and infidelity in the Roman world by the 3rd century had demanded penitential exercises. These included fasting, wearing sackcloth, lying in ashes and other forms of mortification, almsgiving, and the threat of temporary excommunication. Details of the sins committed were confessed in secret to a priest, who then pronounced absolution and imposed an appropriate penance. In 1215 the sacrament of penance received the authorization of the fourth Lateran Council and was made obligatory at least once a year at Easter on all mature Christians in Western Christendom. When pilgrimages to the Holy Land, to Santiago de Compestela in Spain, or going on a Crusade could be imposed as penitential exercises, commutation by means of payment of money led to abuses and traffic in indulgences and the treasury of merits, a superabundance of merits attributed to Christ and his saints that could be transferred to sinful believers. The abuses opened the way for the Lutheran revolt against the penitential system, before they were abolished by the Council of Trent. The power of absolution was retained in the Anglican ordinal and conferred upon priests at their ordination and in the Order of the Visitation of the Sick. The sacrament of penance, however, ceased to be of obligation in the Anglican Communion, though it was commended and practiced by John Whitgift, Richard Hooker, and, after the Restoration in 1660 by the Nonjurors (Anglican clergy who refused to take oaths of allegiance to William III and Mary II in 1689) and revived by the Tractarians (Anglo-Catholic advocates of High Church ideals) after 1833, who encountered some Protestant opposition notwithstanding its entrenchment in canon law and in *The Book of Common Prayer.*

Ordination. The church has claimed that the ministry of bishops, priests, and deacons derives its authority and sacramental efficacy from Christ through his Apostles. In the Roman Catholic Church it has been maintained that a special charismatic sacramental endowment conveying an indelible "character" has been conferred on those who receive valid ordination by the laying on of hands on their heads by bishops (who thus transfer to them the "power of orders"), prayer, and a right intention. In Protestant churches the ministry is interpreted as a function rather than as a status. Just as the sacramental power to ordain, confirm, absolve, bless, and consecrate the Eucharist can be given, so also it can be taken away or suspended for sufficient reason.

Marriage. In the Roman Catholic Church the institution of holy matrimony was raised to the level of a sacrament because it was assigned a divine origin and made an indissoluble union typifying the union of Christ with his church as his mystical body (Matt. 5:27–32; Mark 10:2–12; Luke 16:18; I Cor. 7:2, 10; Eph. 5:23ff.). The adherence of Jesus to a rigorist position in regard to divorce and remarriage (Matt. 19:9; *i.e.,* unchastity the only cause for divorce), similar to that adopted by the rabbinical school headed by the conservative teacher Shammai in

The Eucharist as the central act of Christian worship

Penitential exercises

Roman Catholic and Protestant views

Judaism, was made the basis of the nuptial union as taught by St. Paul, except in regard to the dissolution of a marriage contracted between a Christian and a pagan who refused to live with his or her partner (I Cor. 7:2ff., 15ff.).

Apart from this deviation, known as the "Pauline Privilege," which was recognized in canon law in the 13th century, a marriage validly contracted in the presence of a priest, blessed by him, and duly consummated has been regarded as a sacramental ordinance by virtue of the grace given to render the union indissoluble. In Protestant churches, marriage is regarded as a rite, not a sacrament; views about divorce, however, vary, and many traditional concepts regarding marriage and divorce are now being debated.

Healing of the sick. The anointing of the sick, an initiatory rite, conforms to the general pattern of the sacramental principle and is comparable to the other rites of passage, such as those concerned with birth and death, seed time and harvest, and with the securing of supernatural power and spiritual grace against the forces of evil that are looked upon as rampant at these critical junctures.

In Christianity anointing of the sick was widely practiced from apostolic times as a sacramental rite in association with the ceremony of the imposition of hands to convey a blessing, recovery from illness, or with the last communion to fortify the believer safely on his new career in the fuller life of the eternal world. Not until the 8th and 9th centuries, however, did extreme unction, another term for the final anointing of the sick, become one of the seven sacraments. In Eastern Christendom, it has never been confined to those *in extremis* (near death) nor has the blessing of the oil by a bishop been required; the administration of the sacrament by seven, five, or three priests was for the recovery of health rather than administered exclusively as a mortuary rite. Extreme unction is also coupled with exorcism for the restraint of the powers of evil—a practice taken over from Judaism by the early church and still retained by the Orthodox Eastern Church for mental diseases.

CONCLUSION

The ecumenical movement in the 20th century has initiated reforms in liturgical worship and in private devotions within Christianity. Such reforms, involving the celebration of sacraments (primarily the Eucharist), have done much to promote the recovery of a unity among Christians that transcends differences in beliefs and ritual practices. The second Vatican Council (1962–65) has played a significant part in the process of recovery of unity and of renewal.

BIBLIOGRAPHY

Sacramental principle: The standard pioneer work on the wider pre-Christian occurrence and interpetations is W.R. SMITH, *Lectures on the Religion of the Semites*, 3rd ed. (1927), laying stress on sacramental communion with the deity. A. GARDNER, *History of Sacrament in Relation to Thought and Progress* (1921), applied the sacramental principle to various aspects of life and belief; R.R. MARETT, *Sacraments of Simple Folk* (1933), wrote on sacraments among peoples in a primitive state of culture. In his *Dawn and Twilight of Zoroastrianism* (1961), R.C. ZAEHNER discussed the anticipation of the Christian eucharistic sacramental rite in the *Yasna* ceremony in the Avestian liturgy. The basic sacramental beliefs and cultus throughout the ages are examined and discussed anthropologically with bibliographies in E.O. JAMES, *Sacrifice and Sacrament* (1962).

Christian doctrine of sacraments: A good general study is P.T. FORSYTH, *Lectures on the Church and the Sacraments* (1917); O.C. QUICK, *The Christian Sacraments* (1927, reprinted continually to 1952), is one of the most comprehensive surveys. The positions of various religious bodies are presented in: A.J. TAIT, *Nature and Functions of the Sacraments* (1917), the evangelical viewpoint; B. LEEMING, *The Principles of Sacramental Theology*, new ed. (1960), the Roman Catholic viewpoint; D.M. BAILLIE, *The Theology of the Sacraments and Other Papers* (1957), the Protestant viewpoint; and A. SCHMEMANN, *Sacraments and Orthodoxy* (1965), the Orthodox viewpoint. J.H. SRAWLEY, *Liturgical Movement: Its Origin and Growth* (1954), gives an account of the development of sacramental worship with special reference to the participation of the laity.

(E.O.J.)

Sacred Kingship

Sacred kingship, a religio-political concept that sees a ruler as an incarnation, manifestation, mediator, or agent of the sacred or holy (the transcendent or supernatural realm), traces its origins to prehistoric times and, at the same time, exerts a recognizable influence in the modern world. At one time, when religion was totally connected with the whole existence of the individual as well as that of the community and when kingdoms were in varying degrees connected with religious powers or religious institutions, there could be no kingdom that was not in some sense sacral.

Among the many possible kinds of sacral kingdoms, there was a special type in which the king was regarded and revered as a god—the god-kingdom, a polity of which there were three forms: preliminary, primary, and secondary.

Forms of the god-kingdom

The preliminary form exists in primitive cultures in which the chieftain is regarded as divine. The primary form was the god-kingdom of the large empires of the ancient Near and Far East, of ancient Iran, and of pre-Columbian Meso-America and South America. The secondary form occurred in the Persian, Hellenistic (Greco-Roman cultural), and European empires. Between these three forms there are many transitional types (see also SACRED OR HOLY).

The principal schools of interpretation. The phenomenon of sacred kingship was known and described in ancient times by various travellers (*e.g.*, Aristotle, in the 4th century BC, and the 1st-century BC Greek geographers and historians Strabo and Diodorus Siculus). In more recent times, Sir James Frazer, a British anthropologist, introduced the study of sacred kingship in *The Golden Bough* (1890–1915). Taking his comprehensive material from ethnological reports and studies, Frazer concentrated on the preliminary stage. With the discovery of texts in cuneiform writing in Mesopotamia and Asia Minor, however, a new stage of research began. Called Pan-Babylonism by some scholars, the theories based on the results of these discoveries placed the god-kingdom of the ancient Near East in the foreground.

Building on the thesis of Pan-Babylonism that a homogeneous Near Eastern culture existed and on the theories of cult as a ritual drama, the so-called British and Scandinavian cult-historical schools maintained that the king, as the personified god, played the main role in the overall cultural pattern. The English branch of this school (the "Myth and Ritual School") concentrated on anthropological and folklore studies. The Scandinavian branch (the "Uppsala School") concentrated on Semitic philological, cultural, and history-of-religions studies. It is represented in the latter part of the 20th century by Swedish historians of religion who have theorized that, for the entire ancient Near East, certain cult patterns existed and that behind those cult patterns lay the sacred-king ideology.

The "Myth and Ritual" and "Uppsala" schools

Rejecting the cult-historical school theory of an unchanging cult pattern and an unchanging sacred-king ideology, many scholars in the latter part of the 20th century have tended to emphasize individual research of case histories. The fundamental differences between the kingdom ideology in Egypt and that in Mesopotamia have been investigated by historians and questions concerning sacred kingship in the Old Testament by Old Testament scholars. One result of such scholarly research is that the theory and practice of sacred kingship—in a history extending over thousands of years—has undergone immense changes and that, because of these widespread and extensive differences, all generalizations and categorizations are difficult to maintain. Though there may be an amazing correspondence among numerous individual phenomena, each individual sacral form of government can be explained only in its own historical, social, and religious context (see also RITUAL; MYTH AND MYTHOLOGY).

The sacred status of kings, leaders, and chieftains. Basic to an understanding of sacred kingship is a recognition that the exercise of power of one person over other persons or over a community (local, regional, or imperial) in early times was general and not divided. Power could be exercised only by one person—one who simultaneously had the necessary physical (individual and corporate) and spiritual (psychic) strength and influence—over both people and objects. As ruler over a community, the king's power extended to everything pertaining to the life of the community. Only gradually did a division of these powers develop.

The sacral status of the ruler differs in form and origins. Three main forms can be distinguished: (1) the possessor of supernatural power, (2) the divine or semidivine king, or (3) the agent of the sacred.

The possessor of supernatural power. The ruler may be viewed as the possessor of supernatural power—both beneficial as well as malevolent—needed to maintain the welfare and order of the community and to avert danger and damage. In primitive, or preliterate, societies, he represents the life-force of the tribe, in which worldly and spiritual or political and religious spheres are not distinguished. Concentrated in the chief is the common inheritance of the magical power of the community, and his authority is based solely on the possession and exercise of this supernatural power. The impact and comprehensiveness of such power wielded by a chief, for example, reaches into all areas of life of the tribe: provision of food, fertility, weather, all forms of communal life, and protection against enemies and misfortune. Because the supernatural (magical) power of the chief is identical with his own life-force, the chief (or king) of such a society is not allowed to have any physical defects. With the dwindling of his own physical powers (illness, graying of hair, and loss of teeth), his own power to maintain and secure the common welfare and his own ability to rule are believed to be correspondingly diminished.

This form of sacral status is found mainly among rulers over one tribe (or several) in primitive cultures—he may be a chief, medicine man, shaman (a religious personage who has healing and psychic transformation powers), or king (as, for example, a rainmaker-king in Africa)—in which a fixed definition or limitation of such functions is not possible.

The divine or semidivine king. In some societies, especially in ancient kingdoms or empires, the king was regarded as a god or identified with some god. In early Egypt he was identified with the sky-god (Horus) and with the sun-god (Re, Amon, or Aton). Similar identifications were made in early China and early Erech in Mesopotamia. In the Turin Papyrus (a list of kings written *c.* 13th–12th centuries BC), the sun-god Ra is viewed as the first king of Egypt and the prototype of the pharaoh (the god-king). The symbol of the sun circle, one of the most prevalent artistic representations of the sacred king, and the practice of addressing the king as "my sun" are well depicted in rock reliefs and inscriptions in areas ruled by the Hittite kings. The Persian king was regarded as the incarnation of the sun-god or of the moon-god. In addition to sky or sun deities, the sacred king has also been identified with other gods: the town-god (Mesopotamia), the gods of the country, the god of the storm, and the weather-god. Generally, however, the king was not identified with a specific god but rather was regarded as himself a god. As the incarnation of all that is divine, the Egyptian pharaoh was addressed simultaneously in inscriptions as Aton, Horus, and Re (sun deities). Significant for Egyptian royal theology was the doctrine of the god-kingdom spanning two generations; each king ruled as King Horus and became Osiris (the father of Horus, a fertility god and later god of the dead) after his death.

A broader foundation for the divinity of the king is the view of the king as the son of a god, which can take on different forms. The first king has been regarded as a god and his successors as sons of the god in a number of societies—in Africa, Polynesia, Japan (where the emper-

or, until the end of World War II, was revered as a descendant of the sun goddess), Peru (where the inca, or ruler, was believed to be a descendant of the sun-god), Egypt, Mesopotamia, and Canaan. Because he personifies the divine national hero (as among the Shilluk in Africa), the king can demand divine status, a practice that was taken up in the Greco-Roman world by Alexander III the Great and by the Roman emperors. When a king who has been sired by a god or when a god who takes on the external form of the living king approaches his queen, he begets the future king—the queen is thus called the mother of God. An essentially different foundation is the king's divine sonship through adoption, as, for example, in the legend of King Sargon of Akkad in ancient Mesopotamia. The adoption of the crown prince by a god is often part of the coronation ritual, especially in Mesopotamia: the god declares the king as his son when he ascends the throne.

An especially frequent expression of the relationship of the king to divinity, in Egypt and Mesopotamia, was that of the king as a god's image. In Egypt, the king—addressed by the god as "my living image on earth"—is shown in the likeness of Re, Aton, Amon, or Horus. In Mesopotamia, this kind of description was rare.

The myth of divine birth, such as that of Romulus, the legendary founder of Rome, in many places served to legitimatize the claims of the king. Unusual natural phenomena, such as an especially bright star, are sometimes connected with the birth of a divine king.

The conception and practice of making a king divine after his death are very old and widespread. Probably connected with ancestor worship, deification is practiced most often when the living king, although connected with gods, is not regarded as a god in the fullest sense. Only after his death does he become god. Among the Hittites, for example, the expression "the king becomes a god" means that the king has died.

The king as the principal agent of the sacred. In addition to the conception of a king as the incarnation of supernatural power and the possible equality of the king with the divinity, there is also a widespread belief that the king is the executive agent of a god. As the servant of a god, he carries out the work of the god on Earth. The divine character of this form of sacred kingship is connected not so much with the individual king as with the institution of kingship. In this emphasis on the institution of kingship lies the difference between kingship in Mesopotamia and Egypt and in India and China. The institution was emphasized in Mesopotamia and China. Sharp distinctions cannot be drawn between the different conceptions of the relationship of a god to kingship. Despite all the different expressions of kingship in the history of Mesopotamia (especially among the empires of Sumer, Babylon, and Assyria), there nevertheless was a continuous theme: the real lord of the city, the country, or the state remains the god, and the king remains in a subservient relationship to him. Even when the king possessed or disposed divine power and had sacral character and sacral duties, he remained subordinate to the god who selected him and put him into his regal position. The king had a mediating position between the gods and man, especially in his significance for the cult (thus, Sargon of Akkad is first described in inscriptions as deputy of Ishtar). The king also had a similar status as agent in Mongolia, where it was believed that the king came from heaven and was enthroned by God to carry out his will.

Functions of the sacred king: the king as the source of cosmic power, order, and control. *The king as bringer of blessed power.* The usual function of a sacred king is to bring blessings to his people and area of control. Because he has a supernatural power over the life and welfare of the tribe, the chief or king is believed to influence the fertility of the soil, cattle, and man but mostly the coming of rain. He has power over the forces of nature. Where rain is vitally necessary for the welfare and continuity of a people, the king can be described primarily in terms of this special function. Protection against evil of all sorts also is important for the welfare of the country. If the tribe or the country is beset by misfortune, epidem-

Marginal notes:

The basis of authority in tribal communities

The king as a god's image

The king's influence over men and nature

ic, starvation, bad harvests, or floods, the king can be held responsible. Sometimes the king is believed to have the power to heal sickness by means of touch or contact with his garment.

The function of the king as bringer of good fortune is prevalent in primitive cultures. Especially prevalent in Africa, it also has been observed in Polynesia, Scandinavia, and in ancient Greece. This power to bring good fortune is also an aspect of sacral kingship in advanced cultures, such as in India, Iran, China, Japan, pre-Columbian Meso-America, Egypt, Mesopotamia, and Canaan. The difference between Egypt and Mesopotamia is significant; in Egypt the pharaoh is the direct dispenser of all good fortune in the country, whereas in Mesopotamia the king mediates for good fortune through cultic speeches and actions.

The function of the king as dispenser of good fortune has had an amazingly long influence: the English king was believed to have had healing power over a special disease (the king's evil) until the time of the Stuarts in the 17th century, and until the 20th century a folklore belief persisted in Germany that the ruler has influence over the weather ("emperor weather"). Words sometimes used to symbolize the king as the wielder of beneficial influence are gardener, fisherman, and shepherd.

The king as shepherd. An Egyptian pharaoh once said of himself: "He made me the shepherd of this country." In Mesopotamia the description of the king as a shepherd was quite frequent; in the 3rd millennium BC, the term was applied to Sumerian city princes (*e.g.,* Lugalbanda in the 1st Dynasty of Uruk [Erech]). The function of the king as shepherd also has been noted in India. The image of the shepherd expresses the most important functions of the king—he provides his people with food; he leads them and protects them from dangers and, at the same time, shows his superiority over them. Christ's description of himself in the New Testament as the "good shepherd" is, in a sense, a description of his official position in the Christian Church, which also describes him as king, prince of peace, and Lord.

The king as judge. From earliest times, in addition to other functions, the chief was the judge of his tribe; he personified the protection that the community provided for the individual. Providing for a balance of power in the community, mediating quarrels, and protecting individual rights, the chief or king was the lawgiver and the highest administrator for all community affairs. The *ensi,* the lawgiver and the highest judicial authority in the Sumerian city-state, was responsible for order. In Egypt the king was the highest judge, the guarantor of all public order, the lord over life and death. Early Egypt and India developed a high degree of justice that described the activities of the king as *ma'at* in Egypt and *dharma* in India. Both conceptions may be expressed as "justice" or "order" but actually are more comprehensive. Because the king preserves the god-given world order, the task to be just has been viewed as one of his fundamental functions. The pharaoh of Egypt and the emperor of China were believed to be responsible for the maintenance of cosmic as well as social order.

The king as warlord. Belief in the supernatural power of the ruler caused him to be viewed as the protector of his tribe or his people from enemies. On the one hand, he was the chief warlord and decided on questions of war and peace (as in ancient Sumer). The Egyptian pharaoh was represented, in his divine capacity as warrior, in larger-than-life dimensions. He alone was regarded as the one who triumphed over the enemy. On the other hand, there was the concept that the king, because of his sacral character, should not personally take part in war. These concepts existed, for example, among the Persian kings.

The king as priest and seer. Religious duties quite often are connected with the office of chieftain, who is also priest or seer and rainmaker—all in one. Correspondingly, in nontribal societies, cultic functions belong to the office of the king. In the 3rd Dynasty of Uruk, Lugalzaggisi is described as king of the country, priest of the god Anu (the god of the heavens), and prophet of Nisaba (goddess of grasses and writing).

When a division of functions evolved, the intrinsically royal priestly and other cultic functions were transferred to priests, seers, and other servants of the cult; the old concept of the king as priest, however, survived in some fashion for thousands of years. The Egyptian king was the chief priest of the land and the superior of all priests and other cult functionaries. In many images he is portrayed as presiding over the great festivals and bringing offerings to the gods. Later, priests carried out their functions as his representative. In Mesopotamia, the king was viewed as the cultic mediator between god and man. As head of all of the priests of the country, he had important cultic functions at the New Years' festival. In critical situations, the king might issue an oracle of blessing; through him the land would be promised salvation, which was often accompanied by the words, "Fear not!" The Persian king performed the sacrifice at the horse offering and was also the "guardian of the fire." In all questions of religion he was the highest authority; he was also the most cultivated of the magicians. The king in Ugarit (in Canaan) also carried out priestly functions and as prophet was the receiver of revelations. Like other ancient Near Eastern monarchs, the Hittite king was the chief priest.

The relationship between sacred kingship and priestly cultic functions has extended over widespread geographical areas and historical eras: East Asia, China, Japan, India, Europe (among the Germanic and Scandinavian kings), Africa (in the great empires), and Madagascar. Sometimes, the division of functions brought about a transfer of the royal title to those who carried out cultic functions. In Africa, from the earliest times, there was a type of king who was called lord of the earth; he originally combined political and cultic functions but, with changing times, retained only the cultic ones. The strict separation of the priestly office from that of the king, as in India, where king and priest belong to different castes —Kṣatriya and Brāhman, respectively—is an unusual exception, however.

The king may be the recipient of a direct revelation of the will of a god. Thus, in Egypt the pharaoh received a divine oracle through dreams in the temple (a practice known as incubation). In Mesopotamia, the duty of the king to ascertain the will of the gods was more strongly emphasized; a directive of the gods could result from omens, dreams, or reading the entrails of offerings. All major undertakings of the king were dependent on directives of the god, who was to be consulted in advance. A direct divine revelation to a king is related in the Old Testament I Kings, chapter 3, which tells of a dream of the 10th-century-BC Israelite Solomon in which he received the promise of the gift of wisdom. Likewise, in the Old Testament (in Genesis, chapter 41), Yahweh, god of the Hebrews, gives the pharaoh a directive in a dream (see also PRIESTHOOD; DIVINATION).

The king as the centre of ruler cults. Although a pharaonic cult occasionally existed in Egypt, the ruler cult differs entirely from sacred kingship, because it came into being from political impulses. The ruler cult, generally developed in a country or empire with many peoples and many religions, was one of the ruler's means of power. Syncretism, the fusing of various beliefs and practices, often succeeded in bringing together completely different religious and nonreligious motives. Alexander the Great (who established an empire of many peoples and religions), for example, revealed a conscious effort at continuity with the Egyptian kingdom, inasmuch as the oracle of the Egyptian god Amon at Sīwah designated him as the son of Amon and thus the successor of the pharaohs. Among the *diadochoi* (successors to Alexander) of the first generation, the ruler cult remained limited, but, under Ptolemy II Philadelphus of Egypt (reigned 285–246 BC), it became an established institution that was connected with the deified Alexander. When the ruler cult was carried over to Rome, the emperor Augustus (reigned 27 BC–AD 14) allowed it to be practiced only in the east in connection with the worship of the goddess Roma—though he allowed it to be pursued with fewer restrictions in the newly conquered western provinces; the adaptation of honouring the divine Caesar (or emper-

Side margin notes:

Relationship of kings to ritual and divination

The king as the personification of protection

The difference between ruler cults and sacred kingship

or of Rome) soon became, however, an important expression of the unity of the empire. Serious resistance to the imperial cult was encountered only among the two radical monotheistic religions: Judaism (*e.g.*, against Antiochus IV Epiphanes of Syria in the mid-2nd century BC) and Christianity. The Hellenistic and Roman ruler cults never generated a strong religious movement. The sacrifices brought to the king (emperor) go back to the custom of bringing tribute to the king (or chief) of primitive cultures. From this practice, the custom of bringing offerings to the deceased king developed.

Regal ceremonies. *Modes of selection and succession.* Succession to rulership was not in the beginning necessarily connected with the sacral kingship; the sacral king could also be elected or, through a power struggle, could also receive a divine, magical, or supernatural anointment. If the first-born son of the king was not stipulated to succeed him or if the king left no children, severe struggles for the succession often occurred, generally resulting in a change of dynasty. The death of a king often was kept secret until the succession was assured, because of potential danger to the people and country. To counteract problems of succession, there were rituals to secure the continuity of the sacral power. In primitive cultures the successor of the dead chief was brought into physical connection with his predecessor, his utensils, or clothing —he had to stay, for example, in the home of the dead chief and use his utensils. The funeral of the dead king took place after the new king was established in his office or just before his coronation (as in Egypt). Efforts to secure the succession show high regulatory standards; in Egypt a complicated succession theology linked the new and old king as Osiris and Horus. During the lifetime of his father, the crown prince could be designated as co-regent. The designation of the successor often came through an oracle, a sign, or some other manifestation of the word of the god; Thutmose III of Egypt (reigned 1504–1450 BC), for example, reported how he was designated to the succession through the oracle of the god Amon. In ancient Iran, after an interregnum, the election of the king took place through an omen. The king was chosen by the god; sometimes he was described as divinely predestined in the womb of his mother as the ruler.

Forms and types of sacred legitimation of kings. The coronation or ascent to the throne by a king is an official act that most clearly shows the sacral character of the kingdom. Until the 20th century two characteristics in the coronations of kings and emperors remained: through ascent to the throne, the king is placed higher than other men, and the act of accession is connected with supernatural powers. With this action a new era begins. This was expressed in Egypt and Mesopotamia in two acts that marked the beginning of the government of the new ruler. First, with the death of the old ruler, the crown prince took control of the government and soon thereafter established his accession in a festive celebration. The coronation, however, generally had to coincide with a new beginning in nature, such as the New Years' festival. The coronation also was viewed as a cosmic new beginning. The most important initial actions of sacred kingship— the ascent to the throne and coronation with proper insignia and king's robes—have remained the same in primitive cultures in ancient and modern times, as well as in the high cultures of the present. The throne, crown, headdress, garment (as sign of dignity), and sceptre (the staff through which the rule is carried out) were originally believed to contain the power through which the king ruled. The star garment of the Persian king symbolized his world rulership, similar to the feather mantle of the kings of Hawaii. In many higher cultures the throne, the crown, and the sceptre are viewed as divine and identified with gods and goddesses. This view was especially expressed in the Egyptian royal theology: in the hymnal prayer during coronations, the crowns of Upper and Lower Egypt were addressed as goddesses of the red and white crown by the king. In India the throne personified the kingdom. Sometimes, the throne that a new king ascends is viewed as the throne of the god. For example, Hatshepsut, an Egyptian queen (reigned 1503–1482 BC),

was announced by Horus: "You have appeared on the throne of Horus." On many Egyptian images the king sits on the throne, and the god is at his side holding a hand over the king. In becoming someone else (a god), the king receives a new name, a throne name. Throne names are known in Africa, Mesopotamia, and Egypt (where the five throne names comprise the whole king theology: birth name, royal name, hawk name, serpent name, and a name that designates the king as heir of the power of the gods of the stars). In Iran, for example, the king is proclaimed by his royal name as world ruler. Immediately upon the proclamation of the new status of the king and his royal name, the subject people generally evoke a jubilant shout, such as "Long live the king." An African variety of a response to the proclamation is "He is our corn and our shield," which shows the importance of the king for his people. Another response to the proclamation is a prayer for the king: African and Polynesian prayers; Egyptian, Mesopotamian, and Israelite psalms; and hymns, such as the British hymn "God Save the King."

The act of adoration of a king is based on the throne rite, which is known only in areas having national kings. Though ascent to the throne and coronation with investiture are worldwide, there are many other rituals connected with sacred kingship. Among these are the anointment of the kings in Israel, India, and Iran, which originally was a ritual that gave strength to the recipient—as noted in primitive cultures (*e.g.*, rubbing with the fat of a lion); pseudo-fights (sham battles), from which the king emerges as victor; ritual cleansing; and ritual meals. The survival of elements of the sacred kingship in the Christian West is especially depicted in coronation rites. In early Christian art, Christ is shown as kingly ruler on his throne with a royal court; he is emperor and universal ruler. Sacred kingship also survived in the papacy, as well as in the Holy Roman Empire (until the words Holy Roman were dropped in 1806). In the papacy, for example, the court ceremonies employ forms of address that go back to the imperial language of ancient sacred kingdoms: "Holy Father" or "Holiness."

Ritual roles prescribed for kings in public or state functions. Many and various rituals express the concept that in the chief or king is concentrated the well-being of the country. At the order of a god, a Mesopotamian king might become involved in war; thus, his loot was placed before the god in the temple. If the king made a decision as judge, it was because of his unique wisdom as king. If he mediated a quarrel, the parties recognized his supreme power. The king acted to protect his land against the enemy; after his accession, in some areas, the king shot four arrows to the cardinal directions of the compass. In Africa and Egypt, for example, he then said: "I am shooting down the nations, to overcome them." He acted to insure fertility and to distribute growth power when he started sowing corn, the seed of the tribe. He also was regarded as the guardian of the hearth fire (*e.g.*, Africa and Rome).

The king exercised an important function through his participation in the great festivals, which were of utmost importance to the life of his people. In such festivals, various functions were differentiated: (1) priestly, as when the king presided over the sacrifices, said prayers, and gave the benediction; and (2) cultic participation, as when the king took part in the cult drama. The origin of the cult drama as a spontaneous event is known in primitive cultures (*e.g.*, the Ashanti in Africa), but it had its fullest expression in Mesopotamia and Egypt. In the Sed festival (in Egypt), the king, as ruler, renewed his rulership over the whole world. In the New Years' festival his ascent to the throne was renewed; and at the festival of Min, the god of life-force and reproduction, the king played a significant role.

In Mesopotamia, festivals, originating in cultic drama had great importance, especially the Babylonian New Years' festival. The events of the epic *Enuma elish,* which describes the sun god Marduk's victory over the powers of chaos and the resulting creation of the universe, were re-created in the cultic drama of the New Years' festival,

Regulatory standards of succession

Symbols of sacred kingship

Ascent, coronation, and other rituals

The king's participation in great festivals

in which the king represented Marduk, the victor and creator. Another cult drama represented the death and resurrection of the god of vegetation, in which the participants in mourning processions searched for the vanished god (represented by the king) and rejoiced at this triumphant return. Another Mesopotamian cult drama was the sacred marriage that the god Dumuzi celebrated with the goddess Innana. In the "holy wedding" the king and a priestess represented the god and the goddess and through this sexual union the forces of growth and fertility in nature were renewed. These cult dramas originated in early prehistory, when gods were identified with the forces of nature and the cultic actions were understood as exerting direct influences on nature. At the Persian New Years' festival the king appeared as a killer of the dragon, whose rule was identified with the dry season.

The theory of the kingship in which the king occupied the position of mediator between people and gods also implies that the king may have to atone and suffer for the people of the cult. Under such a theory the absolution and reinstatement of the king meant the renewal of land and people. Perhaps behind this theory was a ritual similar to that found among African coronations of prehistory (as, for example, among the Ashanti) in which the king was beaten by priests before his installation.

Private ritual forms peculiar to kings and their families. The special status of the sacral king necessarily also influences his private life. In order to keep the supernatural force dwelling within him, the king had to observe a number of regulations and taboos in the details of his daily life. To this belongs temporary separation—in some cases, the king lived completely separated (*e.g.*, in Africa). The king often appeared only for audiences, on great festivals, or special occasions—sometimes veiled (as in Iran) or with a mask. There also have been special food taboos: he was not allowed to eat certain foods or may have had to drink only from a certain well. The custom of the king taking his meals alone is widespread. The isolation—separation theme in sacred kingship also appears in court ceremonials: the king must be addressed only from a certain measured distance; a person is only allowed to approach the king kneeling; if the king is encountered the head of the subject must be covered with the hands (as in Iran); he must not be touched; and the king must not touch the ground. Inasmuch as the king is filled with supernatural power, everything he touches can take on some of that power (as in Tahiti). Such proscriptions and taboos for the private life of the king are especially evident in Africa but also occur in Polynesia and Micronesia, East Asia, and the ancient Near East. The divine or superhuman character pertained not only to the king but also, in lesser measure, to his family. The king's consecration could involve ritual incest. The participation of the family in the sacral status of the king was evidenced in several places (*e.g.*, Egypt), where, upon the death of the king or queen, members of the royal family and the court were killed or buried with them. Brother–sister marriages in some areas give evidence to this kind of royal ideology.

When a king began to grow old, it was said in Africa: "The grass is fading." To preserve the growth and well-being of the land, the aging king had to be killed and his power transferred to his successor. The compulsory killing of the king was widespread among the Hamitic and Nilotic peoples in northern Africa; and among some peoples the killing of the king occurred after a specified period of time and was integrated into the cosmic ritualistic rhythm. The real meaning of the killing of the king showed itself in rituals in which the blood of the murdered king is mixed with the seed corn, which then became especially fertile.

Conclusion. With the increasing secularization of all areas of life, sacred kingship will of necessity disappear everywhere. Where monarchies are still retained, the sacred features will most likely diminish or vanish altogether. Only in the great regal ceremonies—especially coronations—are traces of sacred kingship still retained in the 20th century.

Certain elements of sacred kingship, however, are still

Personal regulations for a king's daily life

encountered in modern life: in state ceremonies (*e.g.*, the red carpet at formal receptions), in governmental and ecclesiastical titles, and in the honour and respect given to particular personalities in different walks of life, such as in politics, art, and sports, in which the title king is often used to designate the secular veneration of an individual in the modern cult of personalities.

BIBLIOGRAPHY. SIR JAMES FRAZER, *The Golden Bough*, 3rd ed., 12 vol. (1911–15; abridged ed., 1922 and 1959), is the fundamental and classical work. Also significant is ARTHUR M. HOCART, *Kingship* (1927), which considers the apotheosis of the king for the oldest religions of mankind. (*The English school*): SAMUEL H. HOOKE (ed.), *Myth and Ritual* (1933), *The Labyrinth* (1935), *Myth, Ritual and Kingship* (1958). (*The Scandinavian school*): IVAN ENGNELL, *Studies in Divine Kingship in the Ancient Near East*, 2nd ed. (1967); AAGE BENTZEN, *Messias-Moses Redivivus-Menschensohn* (1948; Eng. trans., *King and Messiah*, 1955); GEO WIDENGREN, *Sakrales Königtum im Alten Testament und im Judentum* (1955); SIGMUND MOWINCKEL, *He That Cometh*, pp. 21–95 (1956). (*On particular areas*): HENRI FRANKFORT, *Kingship and the Gods* (1948), ushers in the new epoch of research. (*On Egypt*): ALEXANDRE MORET, *Du Caractère religieux de la royauté pharaonique* (1902). (*Mesopotamia*): RENE LABAT, *Le Caractère religieux de la royauté assyro-babylonienne* (1939); THORKILD JACOBSEN, *Toward the Image of Tammuz and Other Essays on Mesopotamian History and Culture* (1970). (*Canaan*): JOHN GRAY, "Canaanite Kingship in Theory and Practice," *Vetus Testamentum*, 2:193–220 (1952). (*Africa*): LEO FROBENIUS, *Erythräa Länder und Zeiten des heiligen Königsmordes* (1931); DIEDRICH WESTERMANN, *Geschichte Afrikas*, pp. 20–46 (1952). (*Israel*): MARTIN NOTH, "Gott, König, Volk im Alten Testament," in *Gesammelte Studien zum Alten Testament*, 2nd ed. (1960; Eng. trans., "God, King, and Nation in the Old Testament," in *The Laws in the Pentateuch, and Other Studies*, 1966); AUBREY R. JOHNSON, *The Sacral Kingship in Ancient Israel*, 2nd ed. (1967); HELMER RINGGREN, *La regalità sacra* (1959); JEAN DE FRAINE, *L'Aspect religieux de la royauté israélite* (1954); KARL H. BERNHARDT, *Das Problem der altorientalischen Königsideologie im Alten Testament* (1961); HAROLD H. ROWLEY, *Worship in Ancient Israel*, pp. 186–202 (1967); J.A. SOGGIN, *Das Königtum in Israel* (1967). (*Rome*): L. ROSS TAYLOR, *The Divinity of the Roman Emperor* (1931). (*General views*): GERARDUS VAN DER LEEUW, *Phänomenologie der Religion*, 2nd ed., 2 vol. (1956; Eng. trans., *Religion in Essence and Manifestation: A Study in Phenomenology*, 2nd ed., 2 vol., 1963); GEO WIDENGREN, "Das sakrales Königtum," in *Religionsphänomenologie*, 2nd ed. (1969), with bibliography. (*Anthropological views*): R.H. LOWIE "Chiefs and Kings," in *Social Organization* (1948); a view of the present position of research is given in the omnibus volume *The Sacral Kingship: Contributions to the Central Theme of the VIIIth International Congress for the History of Religions* (1959).

(C.W.)

Sacred or Holy

The sacred (or holy) is the power, being, or realm understood by religious persons to be at the core of existence and to have a transformative effect on their lives and destinies. Other terms, such as divine, transcendent, ultimate being (or reality), mystery, and perfection (or purity) have been used for this domain. "Sacred" is also an important technical term in the scholarly study and interpretation of religions.

THE EMERGENCE OF THE CONCEPT OF THE SACRED IN THE STUDY OF RELIGION

It was during the first quarter of the 20th century that the concept of the sacred (or holy) became dominant in the comparative study of religions. Nathan Söderblom, an eminent Swedish churchman and historian of religions, asserted in 1913 that the central notion of religion was "holiness" and that the distinction between sacred and profane was basic to all "real" religious life. In 1917 Rudolf Otto's *Heilige* (Eng. trans., *The Idea of the Holy*, 1923) appeared and exercised a great influence on the study of religion through its description of religious man's experience of the "numinous" (a mysterious, majestic presence inspiring dread and fascination), which Otto, a German theologian and historian of religions, claimed, could not be derived from anything other than an a

Otto's Idea of the Holy

priori sacred reality. Other scholars who used the notion of sacred as an important interpretive term during this period included the sociologist Émile Durkheim in France, and the psychologist-philosopher Max Scheler in Germany. For Durkheim, sacredness referred to those things in society that were forbidden or set apart; and since these sacred things were set apart by society, the sacred force, he concluded, was society itself. In contrast to this understanding of the nature of the sacred, Scheler argued that the sacred (or infinite) was not limited to the experience of a finite object. While Scheler did not agree with Otto's claim that the holy is experienced through a radically different kind of awareness, he did agree with Otto that the awareness of the sacred is not simply the result of conditioning social and psychological forces. Though he criticized Friedrich Schleiermacher, an early 19th-century Protestant theologian, for being too subjective in his definition of religion as "the consciousness of being absolutely dependent on God," Otto was indebted to him in working out the idea of the holy. Söderblom recorded his dependence on the scholarship of the history of religions (*Religionswissenschaft*), which had been a growing discipline in European universities for about half a century; Durkheim had access to two decades of scholarship on nonliterate peoples, some of which was an account of actual fieldwork. Scheler combined the interests of an empirical scientist with a philosophical effort that followed in the tradition of 19th-century attempts to relate human experiences to the concept of a reality (essence) that underlies human thoughts and activities.

Since the first quarter of the 20th century many historians of religions have accepted the notion of the sacred and of sacred events, places, people, and acts as being central in religious life if not indeed the essential reality in religious life. For example, Dutch phenomenologists of religion (students of the basic patterns and meanings of religious phenomena) such as Gerardus van der Leeuw and W. Brede Kristensen have considered the sacred (holy) as central and have organized the material in their systematic works around the (transcendent) object and (human) subject of sacred (cultic) activity, together with a consideration of the forms and symbols of the sacred. Such German historians of religions as Friedrich Heiler and Gustav Mensching organized their material according to the nature of the sacred, its forms and structural types. Significant contributions to the analysis and elaboration of the sacred have been made by Roger Caillois, a French sociologist, and by Mircea Eliade, an eminent Romanian-American historian of religions.

BASIC CHARACTERISTICS OF THE SACRED

Sacred–profane and other dichotomies. The term sacred has been used from a wide variety of perspectives and given varying descriptive and evaluative connotations by scholars seeking to interpret the materials provided by anthropology and the history of religions. In these different interpretations, however, common characteristics were recognized in the sacred, as it is understood by participant individuals and groups: it is separated from the common (profane) world; it expresses the ultimate total value and meaning of life; and it is the eternal reality, which is recognized to have been before it was known and to be known in a way different from that through which common things are known.

Sacer and numen

The term sacred comes from Latin *sacer* ("set off, restricted"). A person or thing was designated as sacred when it was unique or extraordinary. Closely related to *sacer* is *numen* ("mysterious power, god"). The term numinous is used at present as a description of the sacred to indicate its power, before which man trembles. Various terms from different traditions have been recognized as correlates of *sacer*: Greek *hagios*, Hebrew *qadosh*, Polynesian *tapu*, Arabic *ḥaram*; correlates of *numen* include the Melanesian *mana*, the Sioux *wakanda*, the old German *haminja* (luck), and Sanskrit *Brahman*.

Besides the dichotomy of sacred–profane the sacred includes basic dichotomies of pure–unpure and pollutant–"free." In ancient Rome the word *sacer* could mean that which would pollute someone or something that came

into contact with it, as well as that which was restricted for divine use. Similarly, the Polynesian *tapu* ("tabu") designated something as not "free" for common use. It might be someone or something specially blessed because it was full of power, or it might be something accursed, as a corpse. Whatever was tabu had special restrictions around it, for it was full of extraordinary energy that could destroy anyone unprotected with special power himself. In this case the sacred is whatever is uncommon and may include both generating and polluting forces. On the other hand there is the pure–impure dichotomy, in which the sacred is identified with the pure and the profane is identified with the impure. The pure state is that which produces health, vigour, luck, fortune, and long life. The impure state is that characterized by weakness, illness, misfortune, and death. To acquire purity means to enter the sacred realm, which could be done through purification rituals or through the fasting, continence, and meditation of ascetic life. When a person became pure he entered the realm of the divine and left the profane, impure, decaying world. Such a transition was often marked by a ritual act of rebirth.

Ambivalence in man's response to the sacred. Because the sacred contains notions both of a positive, creative power and a danger that requires stringent prohibitions, the common human reaction is both fear and fascination. Otto elaborated his understanding of the holy from this basic ambiguity. Only the sacred can fulfill man's deepest needs and hopes; thus, the reverence that man shows to the sacred is composed both of trust and terror. On the one hand, the sacred is the limit of human effort both in the sense of that which meets human frailty and that which prohibits human activity; on the other hand, it is the unlimited possibility that draws mankind beyond the limiting temporal–spacial structures that are constituents of human existence.

The elements of fear and fascination

Not only is there an ambivalence in the individual's reaction to the numinous quality of the sacred but the restrictions, the tabus, can be expressive of the creative power of the sacred. Caillois has described at length the social mechanism of nonliterate societies, in which the group is divided into two complementary subgroups (moieties), and has interpreted the tabus and the necessary interrelationship of the moieties as expressions of sacredness. Whatever is sacred and restricted for one group is "free" for the other group. In a number of respects, *e.g.*, in supplying certain goods, food, and wives, each group is dependent on the other for elemental needs. Here the sacred is seen to be manifested in the order of the social-physical universe, in which these tribal members live. To disrupt this order, this natural harmony, would be sacrilege, and the culprit would be severely punished. In this understanding of the sacred, a person is, by nature, one of a pair; he is never complete as a single unit. Reality is experienced as one of prescribed relationships, some of these being vertical, hierarchical relationships and others being horizontal, corresponding relationships.

Another significant ambiguity is that the sacred manifests itself in concrete forms that are also profane. The transcendent mystery is recognized in a specific concrete symbol, act, idea, image, person, or community. The unconditioned reality is manifested in conditioned form. Eliade has elucidated this "dialectic of the sacred," in which the sacred may be seen in virtually any sort of form in religious history: a stone, an animal, or the sea. The ambiguity of the sacred taking on profane forms also means that even though every system of sacred thought and action differentiates between those things it regards as sacred or as profane, not all people find the sacred manifested in the same form; and what is profane for some is sacred for others.

Manifestations of the sacred. The sacred appears in myths, sounds, ritual activity, people, and natural objects. Through retelling the myth the divine action that was done "in the beginning" is repeated. The repetition of the sacred action symbolically duplicates the structure and power that established the world originally. Thus, it is important to know and preserve the eternal structure

Sacred
sounds

through which man has life, for it is the model and source of power in the present.

The recognition of sacred power in the myth is related to the notion that sound itself has creative power—in particular special, sacred sounds. Sometimes these sounds are words, such as the name of god, divine myth, a prayer, or hymn; but sometimes the most sacred sounds are those that do not have a common meaning, for example, the Hindu *om*, the Buddhist *oṃ maṇi padme hūṃ*, or the Jewish and Christian "Hallelujah."

Closely connected with verbal expressions of sacred power are activities done in worship, in sacraments, sacrifices, and festivals. Part of the importance of religious ritual is that in the realm of the sacred all things have their place. In order for human existence to prosper (or even continue) it must correspond as closely as possible to the divine pattern (destiny, or will). Different religious traditions have different theological and philosophical formulations of the meaning of sacraments. In Roman Catholic Christianity, a sacrament is "an outward and visible sign of an inward and invisible grace." In Brahmanic Hinduism a *saṃskāra* (sacrament) is a sacred act that perfects a person and that culminates at the end of a series of *saṃskāras* in a spiritual rebirth, a symbolic "second birth." In both of these cases, the sacred action establishes the relation between the divine and human worlds.

Initiation,
sacrifice,
and
festival

Other sacred activity includes initiation, sacrifice, and festival. Initiation rites among nonliterate societies both expose and establish the world view of the participants. The initiate learns the eternal order of life as proclaimed in the myth. Life is viewed essentially as the work of supernatural beings, and the initiate in this ritual is taught this secret of life and how to gain access to divine benefits. The initiate learns the tabus and is often given a sacred mark, *e.g.*, circumcision, tattoo, or incisions, to express physically that he is part of the sacred (original) community. In other religions, such as Christianity, Buddhism, and Hinduism, an initiate to a special holy (often monastic) community within the larger religious community is designated by a change in name and wearing apparel, denoting his special relation to the sacred.

In festivals and sacrifices two religious functions are often combined: (1) to provide new power (energy, life) for the world, and (2) to purify the corrupted, defiled existence. Religious festivals are a return to sacred time, that time prior to the structured existence that most people commonly experience (profane time). Sacred calendars provide the opportunity for the profane time to be rejuvenated periodically in the festivals. These occasions symbolically repeat the primordial chaos before the beginning of the world; and just as the world was created "in the beginning," so in the repetition of that time the present world is regenerated (see also *Dimensions of the sacred*, below). The use of masks and the suspension of normal tabus express the unstructured, unconditioned nature of the sacred. Dancing, running, singing, and processions are all techniques for re-creation, for stimulating the original power of life. Ritual activity moves power in two directions: (1) it concentrates it in one place, time, and occasion, and (2) it releases power into the everyday stream of events through its self-abundance—the primal vibration reverberates throughout existence. The new energy dispels the old, depleted, polluted energy; it cleanses the constricted, clogged, hardened channels of life.

One of the most important forms in which man has access to the sacred is in the sacrifice. The central procedure in all sacrifices is the use of a victim or substitute to serve as a mediator between the sacred and profane worlds. The sacrifice (Latin *sacri-ficium*, "making sacred") is a consecration of an offering through which the profane world has access to the sacred without being destroyed by the sacred. Instead, the sacrificial object (victim) is destroyed in serving as a unique, extraordinary channel between these two realms. In sacrificial rites it is important to duplicate the original (divine) act; and because creation is variously conceived in different religious traditions, different forms are preserved: the burning or crushing of the "corn mother," the crushing of

the *soma* stalks, the slaughter of the lamb without blemish, the blood spilling of a sacred person, such as the firstborn.

Sacredness is manifested in sacred officials, such as priests and kings; in specially designated sacred places, such as temples and images; and in natural objects, such as rivers, the sun, mountains, or trees. The priest is a special agent in the religious cult, his ritual actions represent the divine action. Similarly, the king or emperor is a special mediator between heaven and earth and has been called by such names as the "son of heaven," or an "arm of god."

Just as certain persons are consecrated, so specific places are designated as the "gate of heaven." Temples and shrines are recognized by devotees as places where special attitudes and restrictions prevail because they are the abode of the sacred. Likewise, certain images of God (and sacred books) are held to be uniquely powerful and true (pure) expressions of divine reality. The image and the temple are, in traditional societies, not simply productions by individual artists and architects; they are reflections of the sacred essence of life, and their measurements and forms are specified through sacred communication from the divine sphere. In this same context, natural objects can be imbued with sacred power. The sun, for example, is the embodiment of the power of life, the source of all human consciousness, the central pivot for the eternal rhythm and order of existence. Or, a river, such as the Nile for the ancient Egyptians and the Ganges for the Hindu, gave witness to the power of life incarnated in geography. Sacred mountains (*e.g.*, Sinai for Jews, Kailāsa for Hindus, Fujiyama for Japanese) were particular loci of divine power, law, and truth.

Dimensions of the sacred. The sacred, by definition, pervades all dimensions of life. Within the kind of religious apprehension that is expressed in sacred myth and ritual, however, there is a special focus on time, place (cosmos), and active agents (heroes, ancestors, divinities). When existence is seen in terms of the dichotomy of sacred and profane—which assumes that the sacred is wholly other than, yet necessary for, everyday existence —it is very important to know and to get in contact with the sacred. In periodic festivals men celebrate sacred time; a sacred calendar marks off the intervals of man's life, and these sacred festivals provide the pattern for productive and joyous living.

Sacred
time and
place

Seasonal sacred calendars are especially important in predominantly agricultural societies. In the very order of nature, people see that different seasons have their distinct values. These differences are celebrated with spring festivals (when the world is re-created through ritual expressions of generation) and harvest festivals (of thanksgiving and of protecting the life force in seeds for the next spring). Here time is regarded as cyclical, and one's life is marked by those rituals in which one continually returns to the divine source.

Similarly, the myths and rituals mark off the world (cosmos) into places that have special sacred significance. The territory in which one lives is real insofar as it is in contact with the divine reality. Within this territory is life; outside it is chaos, danger, and demons. Throughout most of history the "sacred world" was coextensive with a certain territory, and one could speak literally of Christian lands, the Jewish homeland, the Muslim world, the place of the noble people (*Āryāvarta*, Hindu), or the central kingdom (China). Consecrating one's possession of land with certain rituals was equal to establishing an order with divine sanction. In Vedic ritual, for example, the erection of a fire altar (in which the god Agni—fire —was present) was the establishment of a cosmos on a microcosmic scale. Once a cosmos is established, there are certain places that are especially sacred. Certain rivers, mountains, groves of trees, caves, or human constructions such as temples, shrines, or cities provide the "gate," "ladder," "navel," or "pole" between heaven and earth. This sacred place is that which both allows the sacred power to flow into existence and gives order and stability to life.

Another dimension of the sacred is divine or heroic

Divine
or
heroic
activity
and social
relations

activity: the decisive action done by creative or protective agents. One's spiritual ancestors need not be biologically defined ancestors; they may not even be human. They are the essential forces on which survival depends and can be embodied in animal skills (longevity, rebirth, magical skills), in the "ways of the ancients," or through a special hero who has provided present existence with material and spiritual benefits. If the notion of sacred manifestation is extended to include the social relationships (especially tabus) in a community, then communal relations can be viewed as a dimension through which the sacred is manifested. Here human values are sacralized by social restraints that prescribe, *e.g.*, with whom one can eat or whom one can marry or kill. The establishment of a community requires forming certain relationships; and these relationships are sacred when they bear the power of ultimate, eternal, cosmic force. For example, the consecration of a king or emperor in traditional agricultural societies was the establishment of a system of allegiance and order for society.

By extending the notion of "sacralization" to include human reorganization of experience within the context of any absolute norm, the sacred can be seen in such dimensions of life as history, self-consciousness, aesthetics, and philosophical reflection (conceptualization). Each of these modes of human experience can become the creative force whereby some people have "become real" and gained the most profound understanding of themselves.

CRITICAL PROBLEMS

Phenomenologists of religion who use the concept "sacred" as a universal term for the basis of religion differ in their estimation of the nature of the sacred manifestation. Otto and van der Leeuw hold (in different formulations) that the sacred is a reality that transcends the apprehension of the sacred in symbols or rituals. The forms (ideograms) through which the sacred is expressed are secondary and are simply reactions to the "wholly other." Kristensen and Eliade, on the other hand, regard the sacred reality to be available through the particular symbols or ways of apprehending the sacred. Thus, Kristensen places emphasis on how the sacred is apprehended, and Eliade describes different modalities of the sacred, while Otto looks beyond the forms toward a meta-empirical source.

Nonuniversalist
views of
the sacred

A second problem is the continuing question of whether or not the sacred is a universal category. There are religious expressions from various parts of the world that clearly manifest the kind of structure of religious awareness characterized above. It is especially apropos of some aspects in the religion of nonliterate societies, the ancient Near East, and some popular devotional aspects of Hinduism. There is, however, a serious question regarding the usefulness of this structure in interpreting a large part of Chinese religion, the social relationships (*dharma*) in Hinduism, the effort to achieve superconscious awareness in Hinduism (Yoga), Jainism, Buddhism (Zen), some forms of Taoism, and some contemporary (modern) options of total commitment that, nevertheless, reject the notion of an absolute source and goal essentially different from human existence. If one takes the notion of sacred as something above (beyond, different from) the religious structure dominated by divine or transcendent activity (described above), then this suggests that the notion of sacredness should not be limited to that structure. Thus, some scholars have found it confusing to use the notion of sacred as a universal religious quality, for it has been accepted by many religious people and by scholars of religion as referring to only one (though important) type of religious consciousness.

The 20th-century discussion of the nature and manifestation of the sacred includes other approaches than those of scholars in the comparative study of religions. For example, Sri Aurobindo, a Hindu mystic-philosopher, speaks of the supreme reality as the "Consciousness-Force"; and Nishida Kitaro, a Japanese philosopher, expresses his apprehension of universal reality as that of "absolute Nothingness." Martin Heidegger, a German philosopher, speaks of "the holy" as that dimension of

existence through which there is the illumination of the things that are, though it is no absolute Being prior to existence; rather it is a creative act at the point of engaging the Nothing (*Nichts*). In contrast, the Protestant theologian Karl Barth rejects philosophical reflection or mystical insight for apprehending the sacred, and insists that personal acceptance of God's self-revelation in a particular historical form, Jesus Christ, is the place to begin any awareness of what philosophers call "ultimate."

Sociologists who study religion have, since Durkheim, usually identified the sacred with social values that claim a supernatural basis. Nevertheless, the sacred has been identified predominantly as found in the social occasions (festivals) that disrupt the common social order (by Caillois), or as the reinforcing of social activities that secure a given social structure (by Howard Becker). During the 1960s, however, the usual definition of religion as those sacred activities which claimed a transcendent source was questioned by some empirical scholars. For example, Thomas Luckmann, a German-American sociologist, described the sacred in modern society as that "strata of significance to which everyday life is ultimately referred"; and this definition includes such themes as "the autonomous individual" and "the mobility ethos."

THE SACRED TODAY

The problems of defining and investigating religion mentioned above are already expressive of the shifts in modern consciousness regarding the sacred. Both the physical and social sciences have given modern man a new image of himself and techniques for improving his present life. The acceptance of rational and critical perspectives for judging the claims of religious authorities in Europe since the 18th century, plus the development of historical criticism and a sense of historical relativism, has contributed to the affirmation of man as basically a secular person. The once absolute authorities in the West (the Bible, priest, rabbi) are no longer the prime sources for one's self-identity. To a growing extent the cultures in the East are also experiencing a loss of their traditional authorities. Some attempts have been made to resacralize contemporary cosmology, history, and personal experience by (1) extending the scope of religious concerns to "secular" areas such as politics, economics, personality development, and art; and (2) modifying theological positions, ethical norms, and liturgical forms to incorporate new modes of expression and to experiment with new styles of living.

An important 20th-century development in religious life has been the easy flow of information between religious communities on different continents. This has provided an opportunity for experimenting with religious forms from outside the traditionally acceptable forms in a culture. During the 1950s and 1960s, for example, Yoga and Zen meditation were serious religious options for some Westerners and a form of experimentation for large numbers. The concern to experiment with personal experience and with styles of living during the 1960s in the West has itself been considered an important religious expression by some commentators. These years saw considerable exploration in exotic experience with psychedelic drugs, many attempts to set up new communities for group living (communes)—though few lasted more than a year —and a shift in the values of middle class youth from a concern for personal economic security to social and experiential concerns. These recent activities may be viewed as attempts to recapture the experience of the sacred.

Throughout the past hundred years a number of philosophers and social scientists have asserted the disappearance of the sacred and predicted the demise of religion. A study of the history of religions shows that religious forms change and that there has never been unanimity on the nature and expression of religion. Whether or not man is now in a new situation for developing structures of ultimate values radically different from those provided in the traditionally affirmed awareness of the sacred is a vital question. The suggestion that a radically different

Assertions
of the
end of
the sacred

kind of reality is possible is, of course, nonsense for those to whom the sacred already has been manifested once and for all in a particular form.

BIBLIOGRAPHY. The socio-anthropological analyses written near the beginning of the 20th century that are still useful for their interpretations of the sacred in preliterate societies include HENRI HUBERT and MARCEL MAUSS, *Essai sur la nature et le fonction du sacrifice* (1899; Eng. trans., *Sacrifice: Its Nature and Function*, 1964); and EMILE DURKHEIM, *Les Formes élémentaires de la vie religieuse, le système totémique en Australie* (1912; Eng. trans., *The Elementary Forms of the Religious Life*, 1954; paperback 1961). More recently, in the same vein, are E.O. JAMES, *Sacrifice and Sacrament* (1962), a comparative analysis of sacred ritual from many different religious traditions; and ROGER CAILLOIS, *L'Homme et le sacré* (1939; Eng. trans., *Man and the Sacred*, 1960), a general reflective interpretation of various social expressions of the sacred. From a position combining philosophical and theological concerns are the following: RUDOLF OTTO, *Das Heilige*, 9th ed. (1922; Eng. trans., *The Idea of the Holy*, 2nd ed. 1950, reprinted 1966), originally published in 1917, appealed to an a priori preconceptual knowledge of the holy; MAX F. SCHELER, *Vom Ewigen im Menschen*, 2nd ed. (1923; Eng. trans., *On the Eternal in Man*, 1960), an expression of an intuitive philosopher who insisted on the eternal reality of the sacred prior to man's awareness or social expression of it; NATHAN SODERBLOM's long article "Holiness," in the *Encyclopedia of Religion and Ethics*, vol. 6, which stressed the quality of holiness in all religion four years prior to Otto's more famous statement, and his *Living God: Basal Forms of Personal Religion* (1933), which is a comparative study of religion organized according to various ways through which man encounters God; and JOACHIM WACH, *The Comparative Study of Religions*, ed. by J.M. KITAGAWA (1958), a systematic analysis of the modes (thought, action, fellowship) used to express the religious experience. Two Dutch phenomenologists of religion who have made notable contributions to the interpretation of forms that express man's relation to the sacred are GERARDUS VAN DER LEEUW, *Phänomenologie der Religion* (1933; Eng. trans., *Religion in Essence and Manifestation*, 1963), which organizes a wide spectrum of data into three foci: the object of religion, the subject of religion, and their reciprocal relation; and W. BREDE KRISTENSEN, *The Meaning of Religion* (1960), a series of lectures given during the 1930s that elucidates the sacredness of man's cosmological, anthropological, and cultic awareness as expressed in the preliterate cultures and those of the ancient Mediterranean area. The most extensive analysis of the forms and modes in which the sacred is recognized is found at present in the writings of MIRCEA ELIADE. Four of his works that deal with the nature and meaning of the sacred in different types of expression are: *Le Mythe de l'éternel retour* (1949; Eng. trans., *The Myth of the Eternal Return*, 1954; rev. ed., 1965); *Myth and Reality* (1963); *Traité d'histoire des religions* (Eng. trans., *Patterns in Comparative Religion*, 1958); and *The Sacred and the Profane: The Nature of Religion* (1959). For Eliade, the apprehension of the sacred is a unique kind of experience in which the creative power(s) of life appear(s) in particular symbols, myths, and rites.

(F.J.S.)

Sacred Scriptures

Sacred scriptures, the revered texts, or Holy Writ, of the world's religions, comprise a large part of the literature of the world. They vary greatly in form, volume, age, and degree of sacredness; but their common attribute is that their words are regarded by the devout as sacred.

Nature and significance. Sacred words differ from ordinary words in that they are believed either to possess and convey spiritual and magical powers, or to be the means through which a divine being or other sacred reality is revealed to men in phrases and sentences full of power and truth.

Religious rituals and myths provide both ancient and modern instances of the way in which sacred words are believed to possess and convey power; examples of such instances are when, with the aid of sacred words, one experiences a sacred reality in everyday life (the function of ritual), or when one, with the use of the traditional and correct words, establishes beyond question the fact of such a reality (the function of myth). When men first began to use words, they most likely tended to regard the names for persons and things as possessing a subtle, even organic, tie with the objects that these words desig-

nated, and therefore believed that an inherent power imparted a magical potency to phrases and sentences containing them. (There is still a tendency to find hidden power in swear words, curses, and holy names.) But with the fuller development of language, men in all parts of the world attributed sacred power not to words used in ordinary senses but rather to words that had proved to be magically or religiously effectual in securing certain desired relations with the sacred realities in the world around them—realities that seemed to wield power and appeared to exist in a superior and changeless condition, in contrast to mankind's changeful and relatively powerless condition. Such words and sentences were principally the province of revered old men, leaders of the community, magicians, and priests; and they were spoken not only to impart sacred truths or to establish the existence of transcendent, eternal realities but also to bring dynamic, eternal realities to bear on human existence. From very early times, myths and rituals throughout the world arose from such origins and were orally transmitted until they were eventually written down and became sacred scripture.

A later, and very important, source of sacred scripture has been the experience of revelation. Revelation is believed to occur when a divine being or sacred reality is revealed in a crucial event, a supernatural manifestation, or, more immediately, in an auditory experience of a group or an individual receiving an oral communication from a divine being (see also REVELATION).

Oral tradition and sacred texts. Most sacred scriptures were originally oral, and were passed down through memorization from generation to generation until they were finally committed to writing. A few are still preserved orally, such as the hymns of the American Indians (only now being recorded by anthropologists). Many bear the unmistakable marks of their oral origin and can best be understood when recited aloud; in fact, it is still held by many Hindus and Buddhists that their scriptures lack, when read silently, the meaning and significance they have when recited aloud, for the human voice is believed to add to the recited texts dimensions of truth and power not readily grasped by the solitary reader. A further instance of Hindu and Buddhist recognition of the oral nature of their scriptures is their use of certain portions (stanzas, syllables) as *mantras*—formulas having a magical and spiritual efficacy, when recited with the correct gestures (*mudrās*) or used in connection with the correct magical symbol (*yantra*). By pronouncing a *mantra* in the correct manner it is believed that one may induce or even coerce the gods to bestow upon the devotee magical and spiritual powers not available to him otherwise (see also BUDDHISM).

Most oral compositions that were effectual in securing the flow of magical and spiritual powers were everywhere considered as possessed of a sacred authority of their own and in no need of the sanction or authorization of rulers and priests.

Types of sacred and semisacred writings. Not all scriptures, however, were originally oral, nor were they in all parts directly effectual in rituals that sought the granting of magical and spiritual powers. The greater part of recorded scripture has either a narrative or expository character. The types of sacred and semisacred texts are, in fact, many and varied. Besides magical runes (ancient Germanic alphabet characters) and spells from primitive and ancient sources, they include hymns, prayers, chants, myths, stories about gods and heroes, epics, fables, sacred laws, directions for the conduct of rituals, the original teachings of major religious figures, expositions of these teachings, moral anecdotes, dialogues of seers and sages, and philosophical discussions; in fact, they include every form of literature capable of expressing religious feeling or conviction.

Canonical texts of superior authority. Types of sacred literature vary in authority and degree of sacredness. The centrally important and most holy of the sacred texts have in many instances been gathered into canons (standard works of the faith), which, after being determined either by general agreement or by official religious bodies, be-

[margin note left: Importance of the sacred word]

[margin note right: Significance of oral recitation]

come fixed—*i.e.*, limited to certain works that are alone viewed as fully authoritative and truly beyond all further change or alteration. The works not admitted to the canons (those of a semisacred or semicanonical character) may still be quite valuable as supplementary texts.

Distinction between canonical and semicanonical scriptures

A striking instance of making a distinction between canonical and semicanonical scriptures occurs in Hinduism. The Hindu sacred literature is voluminous and varied; it contains ancient elements and every type of religious literature that has been listed, except historical details on the lives of the seers and sages who produced it. Its earliest portions, namely, the four ancient Vedas (hymns) seem to have been provided by Indo-Aryan families in northwest India in the 2nd millennium BC. These and the supplements to them composed after 1000 BC, the *Brāhmaṇas* (commentaries and instruction in ritual), the *Āraṇyakas* (forest books of ascetics), and the *Upaniṣads* (philosophical treatises), are considered more sacred than any later writings. They are collectively referred to as *Śruti* ("heard"; *i.e.*, communicated by revelation); whereas the later writings are labelled *Smṛti* ("remembered"; *i.e.*, recollected and reinterpreted at some distance in time from the original revelations). The former are canonical and completed, not to be added to nor altered, but the latter are semicanonical and semisacred. Sects like the Vaiṣṇavites (followers of the god Viṣṇu) and Śaivites (followers of the god Śiva) prefer texts in the *Smṛti* category (*e.g.*, their own *Tantras*, or treatises on esoteric practices) even to the *Śruti* (see also HINDU SACRED LITERATURE).

Where a literature clusters about a single founding figure, as in the cases of Christianity and Buddhism, it bases itself on recollections and interpretations of the founder's life and original teaching. Buddhist sacred literature recollects Gautama Buddha's life and teaching in the 6th century BC, and first appeared in the dialect called Pāli, allied to the Māgadhī that he spoke. As time passed, and his movement spread beyond India, Buddhism adopted as its medium Sanskrit, the Indian classical language that was widely used in the ancient Orient. A distinction arose between the Theravāda (or "Way of the Elders"), preserved in Pāli and regarded as canonical, and the vast number of works written in Sanskrit within the more widely dispersed Buddhism called by its adherents Mahāyāna (the "Greater Vehicle"). The Mahāyāna works were later translated and further expanded in Tibetan, Chinese, and Japanese. Depending on the school (or sect) of Mahāyāna Buddhism making the judgment, selected works—in effect a canon in relation to the whole body of scriptures—are preferred as more inspired—*i.e.*, believed to be closer to the ultimate truth, and thus to the centres of spiritual power (see also BUDDHIST SACRED LITERATURE).

Whether the basic texts of indigenous Chinese religion should be called sacred, in the sense of Holy Writ, is open to question. Neither classical Taoism nor Confucianism can be said to have been based on revelation; the texts of these faiths were originally viewed as human wisdom, books written by men for men. They acquired authority, actually a canonical status, however, that caused them to be regarded with profound reverence and thus, in effect, as sacred. This certainly was true of the Taoist revered book, the *Tao-te Ching* ("Classic of the Way of Power"), and of the *Wu Ching* ("Five Classics") and the *Ssu Shu* (*Four Books*) of Confucianism. The present government of China, however, seeks to deprive these books of whatever sacredness they once possessed (see also TAOIST LITERATURE; CONFUCIAN TEXTS, CLASSICAL).

The Jewish and Christian canons

The most precisely fixed canons are those that have been defined by official religious bodies. The Jewish canon, known to Christians as the Old Testament, was fixed by a synod of rabbis (religious leaders and teachers) held at Yavneh, Palestine, about AD 90. The semisacred books that were excluded were labelled by Christians the Apocrypha (which means in Greek "hidden away"). Roman Catholicism later included them in its canon. Jesus, the founder of Christianity, left nothing in writing, but he so inspired his followers that they preserved his sayings and biographical details about him in oral form until they were written down in the four Gospels. To these were added the letters of St. Paul and others, and the Book of Revelation to John, the whole forming a sacred canon called the New Testament, which was ecclesiastically sanctioned by the end of the 4th century AD. There was also a New Testament Apocrypha, but it did not achieve canonical status because of numerous spurious details (see also BIBLICAL LITERATURE).

Where no religious body has provided sanction or authorization, scriptures have had to stand on their own authority. Muslims believe that the Qur'ān does this easily. The Qur'ān, their only sacred canon or standard of faith, authenticates itself, they believe, by its internal self-evidencing power, for it is composed of the very words of God communicated to Muḥammad and recited by him without addition or subtraction. This faith of Muslims in the Qur'ān is similar to that of Fundamentalist Christians who believe that the Bible, as God's word, is verbally inspired from beginning to end.

Secondary sacred literature with semicanonical authority. There exists a large body of literature that possesses less of the aura of true scripture than the works just noted. They are interpretations about divine truth and divine commands, or stories that illustrate how persons, exalted or lowly, have acted (with or without awareness) in response to a divine stimulus. They are, in effect, supportive of true scripture.

An outstanding instance is the Talmud, a compendium of law, lore, and commentary that to many Jews has very nearly the authority of the Mosaic Torah (the Law, or the Pentateuch). Indeed, in the postbiblical rabbinical writings it was generally considered a second Torah, complementing the Written Law of Moses (see also TALMUD AND MIDRASH). Another instance is provided by the Christian Church. Its major creeds have, at one time or another, been regarded as infallible statements, to depart from which would be heresy. This is particularly true of the Apostles' Creed and the three "ecumenical creeds" of Nicaea (325), Constantinople (381), and Chalcedon (451). Roman Catholics add to these the papal decrees summarizing in credal form the conclusions of the councils of the Roman Catholic Church concerning the sacraments, transubstantiation (the changing of the substance of the bread and wine in the mass into the body and blood of Christ), confession, the immaculate conception of the Virgin Mary, papal infallibility, and the assumption of the body and soul of the Virgin Mary to heaven. More or less binding for Protestants are their distinctive statements of faith: the Augsburg Confession of 1530 (Lutheran), the Heidelberg Catechism of 1563 (Reformed), the Westminster Confession of 1646 and Shorter Westminster Catechism of 1647 (Presbyterian), and others.

Epics, myths, and other writings

An exceedingly large body of literature, accorded a more or less sacred character by millions of people, especially in the Orient, comprises the epics, myths, legends, folk tales, and allegories of mankind. This type of literature has proliferated in every part of the world and has amazing staying power, being composed of unforgettable stories of the origin of the world and man's exciting life in it. In ancient Europe, such literature determined the structure of Greek and Roman religious and civic rituals (see also GREEK RELIGION; GREEK MYTHOLOGY; ROMAN RELIGION). The lives of Egyptians and Mesopotamians were deeply affected by their mythologies and books dealing with death (see also EGYPTIAN RELIGION; MESOPOTAMIAN RELIGIONS). Of equal significance were the myths, epics, and sagas of the ancient Germans, the Slavs, the Scandinavians, and the Celts (see also GERMANIC RELIGION AND MYTHOLOGY; SLAVIC RELIGION; CELTIC RELIGION; FINNO-UGRIC RELIGION).

India and the Far East have their corresponding semisacred traditions. The great religious and cultural epics of India (the *Mahābhārata* and the *Rāmāyaṇa*), the 18 *Purāṇas* (ancient legendary histories) so important to the followers of Śiva and Viṣṇu, and the esoteric *Tantras* central to Śāktism (a system of Hindu cults and philosophical schools devoted to the supreme energy personified in the mother-goddess), all attest to the power of religion in India. The many Chinese myths are difficult to locate in the remaining literature, but the Shintō myths are very significant in Japanese literature and were given the status of true scripture during the nationalistic period in Japan prior to World War II (see HINDU MYTHOLOGY; CHINESE MYTHOLOGY; JAPANESE MYTHOLOGY; SHINTO).

During the last seven centuries in the West, some religious writings have attained a semisacred, if not a fully sacred, status: *Imitatio Christi* of Thomas à Kempis (1379/80–1471); John Bunyan's (1628–88) *Pilgrim's Progress*; Mary Baker Eddy's (1821–1910) *Science and Health with a Key to the Scriptures*; and the reputed discovery of Joseph Smith (1805–44), the *Book of Mormon*.

The cultural role of sacred writings. That sacred writings perform the public function of shaping an emerging culture or stabilizing an established one is demonstrable in nearly every national history. In this process the private reading and study of scripture is less important than their public recitation and their ritualization and use in public ceremonies; but their effect on private life and domestic ceremony is cumulatively important.

Sacred scriptures are a rich source for symbols and themes in the arts. They provide images and imagery for sculpture, painting, architectural ornamentation, stories that are acted out in drama and dancing, and the inspiration for and thematic content of much music, poetry, and secular literature.

The impact of sacred scriptures on education, oratory, nationalism, wars, religious sects and denominations, international missionary efforts, ecumenical movements, peace crusades, and other aspects of culture is very noticeable throughout human history.

BIBLIOGRAPHY

Translations: The following are selections from a vast literature. For further titles, see CHARLES J. ADAMS (ed.), *A Reader's Guide to the Great Religions* (1965). F. MAX MUELLER (ed.), *Sacred Books of the East*, 50 vol. (1879–1910); *The Sacred Books of the Hindus*, 32 vol. (1909–37); *The Upanishads*, ed. and trans. by SWAMI NIKHILANANDA (1963); *Bhagavad Gītā*, trans. by FRANKLIN EDGERTON, 2 vol. (1944); *Sacred Books of the Buddhists*, 23 vol., trans. by the PALI TEXT SOCIETY (1895); EDWARD CONZE (ed.), *Buddhist Texts Through the Ages* (1954); E.A. BURTT (ed.), *The Teachings of the Compassionate Buddha* (1955); *The Chinese Classics*, 5 vol., trans. by JAMES LEGGE (1893–95, reprinted 1960); *The Way and Its Power: A Study of the Tao Tê Ching*, trans. by ARTHUR WALEY (1934); "*Ko-ji-ki*," or "Records of Ancient Matters," trans. by B.H. CHAMBERLAIN (1883); *Nihongi: Chronicles of Japan from the Earliest Times to A.D. 697*, trans. by W.G. ASTON (1956); *Selections from the Sacred Writings of the Sikhs*, trans. by TRILOCHAN SINGH *et. al.* (1960); *Ancient Near Eastern Texts Relating to the Old Testament*, 3rd ed. by J.B. PRITCHARD (1969); I. MENDELSOHN (ed.), *Religions of the Ancient Near East: Sumero-Akkadian Religious Texts and Ugaritic Epics* (1955); *The Babylonian Talmud*, 34 vol., translation ed. by I. EPSTEIN (1935–48).

General anthologies: Especially useful are ROBERT O. BALLOU (ed.), *The Bible of the World* (1940); LIN YUTANG (ed.), *The Wisdom of China and India* (1944); LEWIS BROWNE (ed.), THE WORLD'S GREAT SCRIPTURES (1946).

Mythologies: S.N. KRAMER (ed.), *Mythologies of the Ancient World* (1961); L.H. GRAY and GEORGE FOOT MOORE (eds.), *The Mythology of All Races*, 13 vol. (1916–32).

Literary histories and general surveys: MORIZ WINTERNITZ, *A History of Indian Literature*, 3 vol. (1927–63); J.M. FARQUHAR, *An Outline of the Religious Literature of India* (1920), an old, but still indispensable guide; FUNG YU-LAN, *A History of Chinese Philosophy*, 2 vol., trans. by DERK BODDE (1952); R.H. PFEIFFER, *Introduction to the Old Testament* (1941); E. KAUFMAN, *The Religion of Israel, from Its Beginnings to the Babylonian Exile*, trans. and abridged by M. GREENBERG (1960); B.F. WESTCOTT, *A General Survey of the History of the Canon of the New Testament*, 5th ed. (1881), still the standard authority on the subject.

(J.B.N.)

Sacrifice

Sacrifice is a religious rite in which an object is offered to a divinity in order to establish, maintain, or restore a right relationship of man to the sacred order. It is a complex phenomenon that has been found in the earliest known forms of worship and in all parts of the world. The present article will treat the nature of sacrifice and will survey the theories about its origin. It will then analyze sacrifice in terms of its constituent elements, such as the material of the offering, the time and place of the sacrifice, and the motive or intention of the rite. Finally, it will briefly consider sacrifice in the religions of the world.

NATURE AND ORIGINS

Nature of sacrifice. The term sacrifice derives from the Latin *sacrificium*, which is a combination of the words *sacer*, meaning something set apart from the secular or profane for the use of supernatural powers, and *facere*, meaning "to make." The term has acquired a popular and frequently secular use to describe some sort of renunciation or giving up of something valuable in order that something more valuable might be obtained; *e.g.*, parents make sacrifices for their children, one sacrifices a limb for one's country. But the original use of the term was peculiarly religious, referring to a cultic act in which objects were set apart or consecrated and offered to a god or some other supernatural power; thus, sacrifice should be understood within a religious, cultic context.

Religion is man's relation to that which he regards as sacred or holy. This relationship may be conceived in a variety of forms. Although moral conduct, right belief, and participation in religious institutions are commonly constituent elements of the religious life, cult or worship is generally accepted as the most basic and universal element. Worship is man's reaction to his experience of the sacred power; it is a response in action, a giving of self, especially by devotion and service, to the transcendent reality upon which man feels himself dependent. Sacrifice and prayer—man's personal attempt to communicate with the transcendent reality in word or in thought —are the fundamental acts of worship.

In a sense, what is always offered in sacrifice is, in one form or another, life itself. Sacrifice is a celebration of life, a recognition of its divine and imperishable nature. In the sacrifice the consecrated life of an offering is liberated as a sacred potency that establishes a bond between the sacrificer and the sacred power. Through sacrifice, life is returned to its divine source, regenerating the power or life of that source; life is fed by life. Thus, the word of the Roman sacrificer to his god: "Be thou increased (*macte*) by this offering." It is, however, an increase of sacred power that is ultimately beneficial to the sacrificer. In a sense, sacrifice is the impetus and guarantee of the reciprocal flow of the divine life-force between its source and its manifestations.

Often the act of sacrifice involves the destruction of the offering, but this destruction—whether by burning, slaughter, or whatever means—is not in itself the sacrifice. The killing of an animal is the means by which its consecrated life is "liberated" and thus made available to the deity, and the destruction of a food offering in an altar's fire is the means by which the deity receives the offering. Sacrifice as such, however, is the total act of offering and not merely the method in which it is performed.

Although the fundamental meaning of sacrificial rites is that of effecting a necessary and efficacious relationship with the sacred power and of establishing man and his world in the sacred order, the rites have assumed a multitude of forms and intentions. The basic forms of sacrifice, however, seem to be some type of either sacrificial gift or sacramental meal. Sacrifice as a gift may refer either to a gift that should be followed by a return gift (because of the intimate relationship that gift giving establishes) or to a gift that is offered in homage to a god without expectation of a return. Sacrifice as a sacramental communal meal may involve the idea of the god as a participant in the meal or as identical with the food consumed; it may also involve the idea of a ritual meal at which either some primordial event such as creation is repeated or the sanctification of the world is symbolically renewed.

Theories of the origin of sacrifice. Since the rise of the comparative or historical study of religions in the latter part of the 19th century, attempts have been made to discover the origins of sacrifice. These attempts, though helpful for a greater understanding of sacrifice, have not been conclusive.

Theories of Tylor, Smith, and Frazer

In 1871 Sir Edward Burnett Tylor, a British anthropologist, proposed his theory that sacrifice was originally a gift to the gods to secure their favour or to minimize their hostility. In the course of time the primary motive for offering sacrificial gifts developed into homage, in which the sacrificer no longer expressed any hope for a return, and from homage into abnegation and renunciation, in which the sacrificer more fully offered himself. Even though Tylor's gift theory entered into later interpretations of sacrifice, it left unexplained such phenomena as sacrificial offerings wholly or partly eaten by worshippers.

William Robertson Smith, a Scottish Semitic scholar and encyclopaedist, marked a new departure with his theory that the original motive of sacrifice was an effort toward communion among the members of a group, on the one hand, and between them and their god, on the other. Communion was brought about through a sacrificial meal. Smith began with totemism, according to which an animal or plant is intimately associated in a "blood relationship" with a social group or clan as its sacred ally. In general, the totem animal is taboo for the members of its clan, but on certain sacred occasions the animal is eaten in a sacramental meal that ensures the unity of the clan and totem and thus the well-being of the clan. For Smith an animal sacrifice was essentially a communion through the flesh and blood of the sacred animal, which he called the "theanthropic animal"—an intermediary in which the sacred and the profane realms were joined. The later forms of sacrifice retained some sacramental character: people commune with the god through sacrifice, and this communion occurs because the people share food and drink in which the god is immanent. From the communion sacrifice Smith derived the expiatory or propitiatory forms of sacrifice, which he termed *piaculum*, and the gift sacrifice. There were great difficulties with this theory: it made the totem a sacrificial victim rather than a supernatural ally; it postulated the universality of totemism; and, further, it did not adequately account for holocaust sacrifices in which the offering is consumed by fire and there is no communal eating. Nevertheless, many of Smith's ideas concerning sacrifice as sacramental communion have exerted tremendous influence.

Sir James George Frazer, a British anthropologist and folklorist, author of *The Golden Bough*, saw sacrifice as originating from magical practices in which the ritual slaying of a god was performed as a means of rejuvenating the god. The king or chief of a tribe was held to be sacred because he possessed mana, or sacred power, which assured the tribe's well-being. When he became old and weak, his mana weakened, and the tribe was in danger of decline. The king was thus slain and replaced with a vigorous successor. In this way the god was slain to save him from decay and to facilitate his rejuvenation. The old god appeared to carry away with him various weaknesses and fulfilled the role of an expiatory victim and scapegoat.

Theories of Hubert and Mauss, and van der Leeuw

Henri Hubert and Marcel Mauss, French sociologists, concentrated their investigations on Hindu and Hebrew sacrifice, arriving at the conclusion that "sacrifice is a religious act which, through the consecration of a victim, modifies the condition of the moral person who accomplishes it or that of certain objects with which he is concerned." Like Smith, they believed that a sacrifice establishes a relationship between the realms of the sacred and the profane. This occurs through the mediation of the ritually slain victim, which acts as a buffer between the two realms, eliminating the need for direct contact, and through participation in a sacred meal. The rituals chosen by Hubert and Mauss for analysis, however, are not those of preliterate societies.

Another study by Mauss helped to broaden the notion of sacrifice as gift. It was an old idea that man makes a gift to the god but expects a gift in return. The Latin formula *do ut des* ("I give that you may give") was formulated in classical times. In the Vedic religion, the oldest stratum of religion known to have existed in India, one of the Brāhmaṇas (commentaries on the Vedas, or sacred hymns, that were used in ritual sacrifices) expressed the same principle: "Here is the butter; where are your gifts?" But, according to Mauss, in giving it is not merely an object that is passed on but a part of the giver, so that a firm bond is forged. The owner's mana is conveyed to the object, and, when the object is given away, the new owner shares in this mana and is in the power of the giver. The gift thus creates a bond. Even more, however, it makes power flow both ways to connect the giver and the receiver; it invites a gift in return.

Gerardus van der Leeuw, a Dutch historian of religion, developed this notion of gift in the context of sacrifice. In sacrifice a gift is given to the god, and thus man releases a flow between himself and the god. For him sacrifice as gift is "no longer a mere matter of bartering with gods corresponding to that carried on with men, and no longer homage to the god such as is offered to princes: it is an opening of a blessed source of gifts." His interpretation thus melded the gift and communion theories, but it also involved a magical flavour, for he asserted that the central power of the sacrificial act is neither god nor giver but is always the gift itself.

Theories of Jensen and Freud

German anthropologists have emphasized the idea of culture history, in which the entire history of mankind is seen as a system of coherent and articulated phases and strata, with certain cultural phenomena appearing at specific levels of culture. Leo Frobenius, the originator of the theory that later became known as the *Kulturkreislehre*, distinguished the creative or expressive phase of a culture, in which a new insight assumes its specific form, and the phase of application, in which the original significance of the new insight degenerates. Working within this context, Adolf E. Jensen attempted to explain why men have resorted to the incomprehensible act of killing other men or animals and eating them for the glorification of a god or many gods. Blood sacrifice is linked not with the cultures of the hunter–gatherers but with those of the cultivators; its origin is in the ritual killing of the archaic cultivator cultures, which, in turn, is grounded in myth. For Jensen the early cultivators all knew the idea of a mythic primal past in which not men but Dema lived on the Earth and prominent among them were the Dema-deities. The central element of the myth is the slaying of a Dema-deity, an event that inaugurated human history and gave shape to the human lot. The Dema became men, subject to birth and death, whose self-preservation depends upon the destruction of life. The deity became in some way associated with the realm of the dead; and, from the body of the slain deity, crop plants originated, so that the eating of the plants is an eating of the deity. Ritual killing, whether of animals or men, is a cultic re-enactment of the mythological event. Strictly speaking, the action is not a sacrifice because there is no offering to a god; rather, it is a way to keep alive the memory of primeval events. Blood sacrifice as found in the later higher cultures is a persistence of the ritual killing in a degenerated form. Because the victim is identified with the deity, later expiatory sacrifices also become intelligible: sin is an offense against the moral order established at the beginning of human history; the killing of the victim is an intensified act restoring that order.

Another interpretation of some historical interest is that of Sigmund Freud in his work *Totem und Tabu* (1913; Eng. trans., *Totem and Taboo*, 1918). Freud's theory was based on the assumption that the Oedipus complex is innate and universal. It is normal for a child to wish to have a sexual relationship with its mother and to will the death of its father; this is often achieved symbolically. In the primal horde, although the sons did slay their father, they never consummated a sexual union with their mother; in fact, they set up specific taboos against such sexual relations. According to Freud, the ritual slaughter of an animal was instituted to re-enact the primeval act of parricide. The rite, however, reflected an ambivalent attitude. After the primal father had been slain, the sons felt some remorse for their act, and, thus, the sacrificial ritual expressed the desire not only for the death of the father but also for reconciliation and communion with him through the substitute victim. Freud claimed that his reconstruction of the rise of sacrifice was historical, but this hardly seems probable.

Mid-20th-
century
theories
In 1963 Raymond Firth, a New Zealand-born anthropologist, addressed himself to the question of the influence that a people's ideas about the control of their economic resources have on their ideology of sacrifice. He noted that the time and frequency of sacrifice and the type and quality of victim are affected by economic considerations; that the procedure of collective sacrifice involves not only the symbol of group unity but also a lightening of the economic burden or any one participant; that the use of surrogate victims and the reservation of the sacrificial food for consumption are possibly ways of meeting the problem of resources. Firth concluded that sacrifice is ultimately a personal act in which the self is symbolically given, but it is an act that is often conditioned by economic rationality and prudent calculation.

Most social anthropologists and historians of religion in the mid-20th century, however, concentrated less on worldwide typologies or evolutionary sequences and more on investigations of specific historically related societies. Consequently, since World War II there have been few formulations of general theories about the origin of sacrifice, but there have been important studies of sacrifice within particular cultures. For example, E.E. Evans-Pritchard, a social anthropologist at Oxford University, concluded after his study of the religion of the Nuer, a people in the southern Sudan, that for them sacrifice is a gift intended "to get rid of some danger of misfortune, usually sickness." They establish communication with the god not to create a fellowship with him but only to keep him away. Evans-Pritchard acknowledged, however, that the Nuer have many kinds of sacrifice and that no single formula adequately explains all types. Furthermore, he did not maintain that his interpretations of his materials were of universal applicability. Many scholars would agree that, though it is easy to make a long list of many kinds of sacrifice, it is difficult, if not impossible, to find a satisfactory system in which all forms of sacrifice may be assigned a suitable place.

ANALYSIS OF THE RITE OF SACRIFICE

It is possible to analyze the rite of sacrifice in terms of six different elements: the sacrificer, the material of the offering, the time and place of the rite, the method of sacrificing, the recipient of the sacrifice, and the motive or intention of the rite. These categories are not of equal importance and often overlap.

Sacrificer. In general, it may be said that the one who makes sacrifices is man, either an individual or a collective group—a family, a clan, a tribe, a nation, a secret society. Frequently, special acts must be performed by the sacrificer before and sometimes also after the sacrifice. In the Vedic cult, the sacrificer and his wife were required to undergo an initiation (*dīkṣā*) involving ritual bathing, seclusion, fasting, and prayer, the purpose of which was to remove them from the profane world and to purify them for contact with the sacred world. At the termination of the sacrifice came a rite of "desacralization" (*avabhṛta*) in which they bathed in order to remove any sacred potencies that might have attached themselves during the sacrifice.

There are sacrifices in which there are no participants other than the individual or collective sacrificer. Usually, however, one does not venture to approach sacred things directly and alone; they are too lofty and serious a matter. An intermediary—certain persons or groups who fulfill particular requirements or qualifications—is necessary. In many cases, sacrificing by unauthorized persons is expressly forbidden and may be severely punished; *e.g.*, in the book of Leviticus, Korah and his followers, who revolted against Moses and his brother Aaron and arrogated the priestly office of offering incense, were con-

The role
of the
inter-
mediary

sumed by fire. The qualified person—whether the head of a household, the old man of a tribe, the king, or the priest—acts as the appointed representative on behalf of a community.

The head of the household as sacrificer is a familiar figure in the Old Testament, particularly in the stories of the patriarchs; *e.g.*, Abraham and Jacob. Generally, in cattle-keeping tribes with patriarchal organization, the *paterfamilias* long remained the person who carried out sacrifices, and it was only at a late date that a separate caste of priests developed among these peoples. In ancient China, too, sacrifices were not presided over by a professional priesthood but by the head of the family or, in the case of state sacrifices, by the ruler.

The old man or the elders of the tribe are in charge of sacrifices among several African peoples. Among the Ila, a people of Zambia, for instance, when hunters have no success, the oldest member of the band leads the others in praying for the god's aid; when the hunters are successful in killing, the old man leads them in offering portions of the meat to the god. Similarly, among peoples in Australia the leading role in all sacrificial acts is filled by the old men as bearers of tradition and authority. In cases in which there is a matriarchal organization, as in some parts of West Africa, the oldest woman of the family acts as priestess.

The king has played an important role as the person active in sacrificing, particularly in those cultures in which he not only has temporal authority but also fulfills a religious function. The fact that the king is the primary sacrificer may stem from two roots. It may be that the most important gods of the state were originally family gods of the rulers, and, thus, the king is simply continuing the task of *paterfamilias*, only now on behalf of the whole community. The second root lies in the notion of sacred kingship, according to which the royal office is sacred and the king set apart from ordinary people is the intercessor with the supernatural world. These two concepts often go together. Thus, in ancient Egypt the pharaoh was divine because he descended from the sun god Re. The pharaoh stood for Horus, the son of Re. The concepts of the god as family ancestor and of sacred kingship were combined. Although worship in ancient Egypt was controlled by a powerful priesthood, officially all sacrifices were made by the pharaoh.

Most frequently, the intermediary between the community and the god, between the profane and the sacred realms, is the priest. As a rule, not everyone can become a priest; there are requirements of different kinds to be satisfied. Usually, the priest must follow some training, which may be long and severe, There is always some form of consecration he has to undergo. For communities in which a priest functions, he is the obvious person to make sacrifices.

Gods as
sacrificers
The sacrificer is not always man, however; at times gods also make sacrifices. Examples of this are found chiefly in India and are set down particularly in the *Brāhmaṇa* texts; *e.g.*, it is said in the *Taittirīya Brāhmaṇa*: "By sacrifice the gods obtained heaven." The idea of gods making sacrifice, however, is found in the older Ṛgveda-Saṃhitā, a collection of sacred Vedic hymns: "With offerings the gods offered up sacrifice." In this conception man makes sacrifices in imitation of a divine model inaugurated by the gods themselves. Another instance is the Iranian primordial god Zurvān (Time), who offered sacrifice for 1,000 years in order to obtain a son to create the world.

Material of the oblation. Any form under which life manifests itself in the world or in which life can be symbolized may be a sacrificial oblation. In fact, there are few things that have not, at some time or in some place, served as an offering. Any attempt to categorize the material of sacrifice will group together heterogeneous phenomena; thus, the category human sacrifice includes several fundamentally different sacrificial rites. Nevertheless, for convenience sake, the variety of sacrificial offerings will be treated as (1) blood offerings (animal and human), (2) bloodless offerings (libations and vegetation), and (3) a special category, divine offerings.

Blood offerings. Basic to both animal and human sacrifice is the recognition of blood as the sacred life-force in man and beast. Through the sacrifice—through the return of the sacred life revealed in the victim—the god lives, and, therefore, man and nature live. The great potency of blood has been utilized through sacrifice for a number of purposes; *e.g.,* earth fertility, purification, and expiation. The letting of blood, however, was neither the only end nor the only mode of human and animal sacrifice.

A wide variety of animals have served as sacrificial offerings. In ancient Greece and India, for example, oblations included a number of important domestic animals, such as the goat, ram, bull, ox, and horse. Moreover, in Greek religion all edible birds, wild animals of the hunt, and fish were used. In ancient Judaism the kind and number of animals for the various sacrifices was carefully stipulated so that the offering might be acceptable and thus fully effective. This sort of regulation is generally found in sacrificial cults; the offering must be appropriate either to the deity to whom or to the intention for which it is to be presented. Very often the sacrificial species (animal or vegetable) was closely associated with the deity to whom it was offered as the deity's symbolic representation or even its incarnation. Thus, in the Vedic ritual the goddesses of night and morning received the milk of a black cow having a white calf; the "bull of heaven," Indra, was offered a bull, and Sūrya, the sun god, a white, male goat. Similarly, the ancient Greeks sacrificed black animals to the deities of the dark underworld; swift horses to the sun god Helios; pregnant sows to the Earth mother Demeter; and the dog, guardian of the dead, to Hecate, goddess of darkness. The Syrians sacrificed fish, regarded as the lord of the sea and guardian of the realm of the dead, to the goddess Atargatis and ate the consecrated offering in a communion meal with the deity, sharing in the divine power. An especially prominent sacrificial animal was the bull (or its counterparts, the boar and the ram), which, as the representation and embodiment of the cosmic powers of fertility, was sacrificed to numerous fertility gods (*e.g.,* the Norse god Freyr; the Greek "bull of the Earth," Zeus Chthonios; and the Indian "bull of heaven," Indra).

Human sacrifice

The occurrence of human sacrifice appears to have been widespread and its intentions various, ranging from communion with a god and participation in his divine life to expiation and the promotion of the Earth's fertility. It seems to have been adopted by agricultural rather than by hunting or pastoral peoples. Of all the worldly manifestations of the life-force, the human undoubtedly impressed men as the most valuable and thus the most potent and efficacious as an oblation. Thus, in Mexico the belief that the sun needed human nourishment led to sacrifices in which as many as 20,000 victims perished annually in the Aztec and Nahua calendrical maize ritual in the 14th century AD. Bloodless human sacrifices also developed and assumed greatly different forms: *e.g.,* a Celtic ritual

By courtesy of the National Museum, Copenhagen

Celtic sacrifice by immersion, detail of the Gundestrup Cauldron, *c.* 1st century BC. In the Nationalmuseet, Copenhagen.

involved the sacrifice of a woman by immersion, and among the Maya in Mexico young maidens were drowned in sacred wells; in Peru women were strangled; in ancient China the king's retinue was commonly buried

with him, and such internments continued intermittently until the 17th century.

In many societies human victims gave place to animal substitutes or to effigies made of dough, wood, or other materials. Thus, in India, with the advent of British rule, human sacrifices to the Dravidian village goddesses (*grāma-devīs*) were replaced by animal sacrifices. In Tibet, under the influence of Buddhism, which prohibits all blood sacrifice, human sacrifice to the pre-Buddhist Bon deities was replaced by the offering of dough images or reduced to pantomime. Moreover, in some cults both human and animal oblations could be "ransomed"—*i.e.,* replaced by offerings or money or other inanimate valuables.

Bloodless offerings. Among the many life-giving substances that have been used as libations are milk, honey, vegetable and animal oils, beer, wine, and water. Of these, the last two have been especially prominent. Wine is the "blood of the grape" and thus the "blood of the earth," a spiritual beverage that invigorates gods and men. Water is always the sacred "water of life," the primordial source of existence and the bearer of the life of plants, animals, human beings, and even the gods. Because of its great potency, water, like blood, has been widely used in purificatory and expiatory rites to wash away defilements and restore spiritual life. It has also, along with wine, been an important offering to the dead as a revivifying force.

Vegetable offerings have included not only the edible herbaceous plants but also grains, fruits, and flowers. In both Hinduism and Jainism, flowers, fruits, and grains (cooked and uncooked) are included in the daily temple offerings. In some agricultural societies (*e.g.,* those of West Africa) yams and other tuber plants have been important in planting and harvest sacrifices and in other rites concerned with the fertility and fecundity of the soil. These plants have been regarded as especially embodying the life-force of the deified earth and are frequently buried or plowed into the soil to replenish and reactivate its energies.

Divine offerings. One further conception must be briefly mentioned: a god himself may be sacrificed. This notion was elaborated in many mythologies; it is fundamental in some sacrificial rituals. In early sacrifice the victim has something of the god in itself, but in the sacrifice of a god the victim is identified with the god. At the festival of the ancient Mexican sun god Huitzilopochtli, the statue of the god, which was made from beetroot paste and kneaded in human blood and which was identified with the god, was divided into pieces, shared out among the devotees, and eaten. In the Hindu soma ritual (related to the *haoma* ritual of ancient Persia), the soma plant, which is identified with the god Soma, is pressed for its intoxicating juice, which is then ritually consumed. The Eucharist, as understood in many of the Christian churches, contains similar elements. In short, Jesus is really present in the bread and wine that are ritually offered and then consumed. According to the traditional eucharistic doctrine of Roman Catholicism, the elements of bread and wine are "transubstantiated" into the body and blood of Christ: *i.e.,* their whole substance is converted into the whole substance of the body and blood, although the outward appearances of the elements, their "accidents," remain.

Gods as victims

Time and place of sacrifice. In many cults, sacrifices are distinguished by frequency of performance into two types, regular and special. Regular sacrifices may be daily, weekly, monthly, or seasonal (as at planting, harvest, and New Year). Also often included are sacrifices made at specific times in each man's life—birth, puberty, marriage, and death. Offerings made on special occasions and for special intentions have included, for example, sacrifices in times of danger, sickness, or crop failure and those performed at the construction of a building, for success in battle, or in thanksgiving for a divine favour.

In the Vedic cult the regular sacrifices were daily, monthly, and seasonal. The daily rites included fire offerings to the gods and libations and food offerings to the ancestors and the Earth divinities and spirits. The monthly sacrifices, conducted at the time of New and Full Moons, were of cakes or cooked oblations to sundry deities, especially the storm god Indra. Some daily and monthly sacrifices could be celebrated in the home by a householder, but only the official priesthood could perform the complex seasonal sacrifices, offered three times a year—at the beginning of spring, of the rainy season, and of the cool weather—for the purpose of expiation and of abundance. Of the occasional sacrifices, which could be celebrated at any time, especially important were those associated with kingship, such as the royal consecration and the great "horse sacrifice" performed for the increase of the king's power and domain.

In ancient Judaism the regular or periodic sacrifices included the twice daily burnt offerings, the weekly sabbath sacrifices, the monthly offering at the New Moon, and annual celebrations such as *Pesah* (Passover), Yom Kippur (Day of Atonement), and Sukkot (Feast of Tabernacles). Special sacrifices were usually of a personal nature, such as thank and votive offerings and "guilt offerings."

The common place of sacrifice in most cults is an altar. The table type of altar is uncommon; more often it is only a pillar, a mound of earth, a stone, or a pile of stones. Among the Hebrews in early times and other Semitic peoples the altar of the god was frequently an upright stone (*matztzeva*) established at a place in which the deity had manifested itself. It was *bet el*, the "house of God."

Frequently, the altar is regarded as the centre or the image of the universe. For the ancient Greeks the grave marker (a mound of earth or a stone) was the earth altar upon which sacrifices to the dead were made and, like other earth altars, it was called the omphalos, "the navel" of the Earth—*i.e.*, the central point from which terrestrial life originated. In Vedic India the altar was regarded as a microcosm, its parts representing the various parts of the universe and its construction being interpreted as a repetition of the creation of the cosmos.

Method of sacrifice. Along with libation and the sacrificial effusion of blood, one of the commonest means of making an oblation available to sacred beings is to burn it. In both ancient Judaism and Greek religion the major offering was the burnt or fire offering. Through the medium of the fire, the oblation was conveyed to the divine recipient. In ancient Greece the generic term for sacrifice (*thysia*) was derived from a root meaning to burn or to smoke. In Judaism the important sacrifices (*'ola* and *zevah*) involved the ritual burning, either entirely or in part, of the oblation, be it animal or vegetation. For the Babylonians, also, fire was essential to sacrifice, and all oblations were conveyed to the gods by the fire god Girru-Nusku, whose presence as intermediary between the gods and men was indispensable. In the Vedic cult the god of fire, Agni, received the offerings of men and brought them into the presence of the gods.

As burning is often the appropriate mode for sacrifice to celestial deities, so burial is often the appropriate mode for sacrifice of Earth deities. In Greece, for example, sacrifices to the chthonic or underworld powers were frequently buried rather than burned or, if burned, burned near the ground or even in a trench. In Vedic India the blood and entrails of animals sacrificed on the fire altar to the sky gods were put upon the ground for the Earth deities, including the ghosts and malevolent spirits. In West Africa yams and fowls sacrificed to promote the fertility of the Earth are planted in the soil.

In sacrifice by burning and by burial, as also in the effusion of blood, the prior death of the human or animal victim, even if ritually performed, is in a sense incidental to the sacrificial action. There are, however, sacrifices (including live burial and burning) in which the ritual killing is itself the means by which the offering is effected. Illustrative of this method was the practice in ancient Greek and Indian cults of making sacrifices to water gods by drowning the oblations in sacred lakes or rivers. Similarly, the Norse cast human and animal victims over cliffs and into wells and waterfalls as offerings to the divinities dwelling therein. In the Aztec sacrifice of human beings

Margin note: Burning, burying, and ritual killing

to the creator god Xipe Totec, the victim was lashed to a scaffold and shot to death with bow and arrow.

There are also sacrifices that do not involve the death or destruction of the oblation. Such were the sacrifices in ancient Greece of fruits and vegetables at the "pure" (*katharos*) altar of Apollo at Delos, at the shrine of Athena at Lindus, and at the altar of Zeus in Athens. These "fireless oblations" (*apura hiera*) were especially appropriate for the deities of vegetation and fertility; *e.g.*, Demeter and Dionysus. In Egypt bloodless offerings of food and drink were simply laid before the god on mats or a table in a daily ceremony called "performing the presentation of the divine oblations." In both Greek and Egyptian cults such offerings were never to be eaten by the worshippers, but they were probably surreptitiously consumed by the priests or temple attendants. In ancient Israel, on the other hand, the food offerings of the "table of the shewbread" (the "bread of the presence" of God) were regarded as available to the priests and could be given by them to the laity. In Hinduism the daily offering of cooked rice and vegetable, after its consecration, is distributed by the priests to the worshippers as the deity's "grace" (*prasāda*). In some cases the sacrificial gifts are put out to be eaten by an animal representative of the deity. In Dahomey wandering dogs consume, on behalf of the trickster deity Eshu (Elegba), the consecrated food oblations presented to the god each morning at his shrines.

Margin note: "Fireless oblations"

Recipient of the sacrifice. Sacrifices may be offered to beings who can be the object of religious veneration or worship. They will not be made to human beings unless they have first been deified in some way. In some cases sacrifice is made only to the god or gods; in others it is made to the deity, the spirits, and the departed; in others it is made only to the spirits and the departed, who are considered intermediaries between the deity and men. The Nkole people of Uganda, for example, are said to make no sacrifices to God, thinking he does not expect any. But, on the third day following the New Moon, they make offerings to the guardian spirits (*emandwa*), and they also make offerings at the shrines of ancestors (*emizimu*) of up to three generations back. Worship of spirits and of ancestors, often including the offering of sacrifices, occurs in widely distributed cultures; in fact, according to some scholars, probably the major recipients of sacrifice in non-Western traditions are the ancestors (see ANCESTOR WORSHIP).

Intentions. Sacrifices have been offered for a multiplicity of intentions, and it is possible to list only some of the most prominent. In any one sacrificial rite a number of intentions may be expressed, and the ultimate goal of all sacrifice is to establish a beneficial relationship with the sacred order, to make the sacred power present and efficacious.

Propitiation and expiation. Serious illness, drought, pestilence, epidemic, famine, and other misfortune and calamity have universally been regarded as the workings of supernatural forces. Often they have been understood as the effects of offenses against the sacred order committed by individuals or communities, deliberately or unintentionally. Such offenses break the relationship with the sacred order or impede the flow of divine life. Thus, it has been considered necessary in times of crisis, individual or communal, to offer sacrifices to propitiate sacred powers and to wipe out offenses (or at least neutralize their effects) and restore the relationship.

Among the Yoruba of West Africa, blood sacrifice must be made to the gods, especially the Earth deities, who, as elsewhere in Africa, are regarded as the divine punishers of sin. For the individual the oblation may be a fowl or a goat; for an entire community it may be hundreds of animals (in former days, the principal oblation was human). Once consecrated and ritually slain, the oblations are buried, burnt, or left exposed but never shared by the sacrificer.

In ancient Judaism the *hatta't*, or "sin offering," was an important ritual for the expiation of certain, especially unwittingly committed, defilements. The guilty laid their hands upon the head of the sacrificial animal (an unblem-

Atonement
in Judaism
and
Christianity

ished bullock or goat), thereby identifying themselves with the victim, making it their representative (but not their substitute, for their sins were not transferred to the victim). After the priest killed the beast, blood was sprinkled upon the altar and elsewhere in the sacred precincts. The point of the ritual was to purify the guilty and to re-establish the holy bond with God through the blood of the consecrated victim. It was as such an expiatory sacrifice that early Christianity regarded the life and death of Christ. By the shedding of his blood, the sin of mankind was wiped out and a new relationship of life—eternal life —was effected between God and man. Like the innocent and "spotless" victim of the *ḥaṭṭa't*, Christ died for men —*i.e.*, on behalf of but not in place of them. Also, like the *ḥaṭṭa't*, the point of his death was not the appeasement of divine wrath but the shedding of his blood for the wiping out of sin. The major differences between the sacrifice of Christ and that of the *ḥaṭṭa't* animal are that (1) Christ's was regarded as a voluntary and effective sacrifice for all men and (2) his was considered the perfect sacrifice, made once in time and space but perpetuated in eternity by the risen Lord.

There are sacrifices, however, in which the victim does serve as a substitute for the guilty. In some West African cults a person believed to be under death penalty by the gods offers an animal substitute to which he transfers his sins. The animal, which is then ritually killed, is buried with complete funeral rites as though it were the human person. Thus the guilty person is dead, and it is an innocent man who is free to begin a new life.

Finally, some propitiatory sacrifices are clearly prophylactic, intended to avert possible misfortune and calamity, and as such they are really bribes offered to the gods. Thus, in Dahomey libations and animal and food offerings are frequently made to a variety of Earth spirits to ensure their good favour in preventing any adversary from befalling the one making the offering.

Gift sacrifices. Although all sacrifice involves the giving of something, there are some sacrificial rites in which the oblation is regarded as a gift made to a deity either in expectation of a return gift or as the result of a promise upon the fulfillment of a requested divine favour. Gift sacrifices have been treated above. Here, it can be briefly noted that numerous instances of the votive offering are recorded. In ancient Greece sacrifices were vowed to Athena, Zeus, Artemis, and other gods in return for victory in battle. The solemnity and irrevocability of the votive offering is seen in the Old Testament account of the judge Jephthah's sacrifice of his only child in fulfillment of a vow to Yahweh.

Thank offerings. One form of thank offering is the offering of the first fruits in agricultural societies. Until the first fruits of the harvest have been presented with homage and thanks (and often with animal sacrifices) to the deity of the harvest (sometimes regarded as embodied in the crop), the whole crop is considered sacred and thus taboo and may not be used as food. The first-fruits sacrifice has the effect of "desacralizing" the crops and making them available for profane consumption. It is a recognition of the divine source and ownership of the harvest and the means by which man is reconciled with the vegetational, chthonic powers from whom he takes it.

Fertility. Another distinctive feature of the first-fruits offering is that it serves to replenish the sacred potencies of the earth depleted by the harvest and to ensure thereby the continued regeneration of the crop. Thus, it is one of many sacrificial rites that have as their intention the seasonal renewal and reactivation of the fertility of the earth. Fertility rites usually involve some form of blood sacrifice—in former days especially human sacrifice. In some human sacrifices the victim represented a deity who "in the beginning" allowed himself to be killed so that from his body edible vegetation might grow. The ritual slaying of the human victim amounted to a repetition of the primordial act of creation and thus a renewal of vegetational life (see above *Theories of Jensen and Freud*). In other human sacrifices the victim was regarded as representing a vegetation spirit that annually died at harvest time so that it might be reborn in a new crop. In still other

Offerings
of the
first fruits
of harvest

sacrifices at planting time or in time of famine, the blood of the victim—animal or human—was let upon the ground and its flesh buried in the soil to fertilize the earth and recharge its potencies.

Building sacrifices. Numerous instances are known of animal and human sacrifices made in the course of the construction of houses, shrines, and other buildings, and in the laying out of villages and towns. Their purpose has been to consecrate the ground by establishing the beneficent presence of the sacred order and by repelling or rendering harmless the demonical powers of the place. In some West African cults, for example, before the central pole of a shrine or a house is installed, an animal is ritually slain, its blood being poured around the foundations and its body being put into the posthole. On the one hand, this sacrifice is made to the Earth deities and the supernatural powers of the place—the real owners—so that the human owner may take possession and be ensured against malevolent interferences with the construction of the building and its later occupation and use. On the other hand, the sacrifice is offered to the cult deity to establish its benevolent presence in the building.

Mortuary sacrifice. Throughout the history of man's religions, the dead have been the recipients of offerings from the living. In ancient Greece an entire group of offerings (*enagismata*) was consecrated to the dead; these were libations of milk, honey, water, wine, and oil poured onto the grave. In India water and balls of cooked rice were sacrificed to the spirits of the departed. In West Africa, offerings of cooked grain, yams, and animals are made to the ancestors residing in the Earth. The point of such offerings is not that the dead get hungry and thirsty, nor are they merely propitiatory offerings. Their fundamental intention seems to be that of increasing the power of life of the departed. The dead partake of the life of the gods (usually the chthonic deities), and sacrifices to the dead are in effect sacrifices to the gods who bestow never-ending life. In Hittite funeral rites, for example, sacrifices were made to the sun god and other celestial deities—transcendent sources of life—as well as to the divinities of Earth.

Communion sacrifices. Communion in the sense of a bond between the worshipper and the sacred power is fundamental to all sacrifice. Certain sacrifices, however, promote this communion by means of a sacramental meal. The meal may be one in which the sacrificial oblation is simply shared by the deity and the worshippers. Of this sort were the Greek *thysia* and the Jewish *zevaḥ* sacrifices in which one portion of the oblation was burned upon the altar and the remainder eaten by the worshippers. Among the African Yoruba special meals are offered to the deity; if the deity accepts the oblation (as divination will disclose), a portion of the food is placed before his shrine while the remainder is joyfully eaten as a sacred communion by the worshippers. The communion sacrifice may be one in which the deity somehow indwells the oblation so that the worshippers actually consume the divine; *e.g.*, the Hindu *soma* ritual. The Aztecs twice yearly made dough images of the sun god Huitzilopochtli that were consecrated to the god and thereby transubstantiated into his flesh to be eaten with fear and reverence by the worshippers.

The
sacra-
mental
meal

SACRIFICE IN THE RELIGIONS OF THE WORLD

The constituent elements of sacrifice have been incorporated into the particular religions and cultures of the world in various and often complex ways. A few brief observations that may illustrate this variety and complexity are given here.

Religions of India. Speculations regarding sacrifice and prescribed rituals seem to have been worked out more fully in the Vedic and later Hindu religion in India than anywhere else. These rites, laid down in a complicated system known mainly from the *Brāhmaṇa* texts, included obligatory sacrifices following the course of the year or the important moments in the life of an individual and optional sacrifices occasioned by the special wishes of a sacrificer. Yet cultic sacrifice has not developed in Buddhism, another religion that arose in India. Ritual sacri-

The Eucharist as sacrifice: "La Ultima Cena," oil painting by Juan de Juanes (c. 1523–79).
In the Prado, Madrid.
Archivo Mas, Barcelona

fice was judged to be ineffective and in some of its forms to involve cruelty and to run counter to the law of *ahiṃsā*, or non-injury. There are, however, in the *Jātaka* stories of the Buddha's previous births accounts of his self-sacrifices. Furthermore, Buddhism emphasizes the notion of ethical sacrifices, acts of self-discipline; and there are instances of devotional offerings, such as burnt incense, to the Buddha.

Religions of China. In China sacrifice, like other aspects of religion, has existed at a number of different levels. The essential feature of Imperial worship in ancient China was the elaborate sacrifices offered by the emperor himself to Heaven and Earth. There are also records of sacrifice, including human sacrifice, associated with the death of a ruler because it was thought proper for him to be accompanied in death with those who served him during life. But, because the common people were excluded from participation in Imperial sacrifices, they had lesser gods—some universal, some local—to whom sacrifices were made. Furthermore, ancestor worship has been the most universal form of religion throughout China's long history; it was the responsibility of the head of a household to see to it that sacrificial offerings to the dead were renewed constantly. The blending of these elements with such established religions as Buddhism and Taoism influenced the great diversification of sacrificial rites in China.

Religions of Japan. In ancient Japan offering occupied a particularly important place in religion because the relationship of the people to their gods seems frequently to have had the character of a bargain rather than of adoration. It is probable that the offerings were originally individual, but they gradually became collective, especially as all powers, including religious, were concentrated in the hands of the emperor, who officiated in the name of all his people. Human sacrifice to natural deities and at burials was once common but seems generally to have been abandoned in the early Middle Ages. Besides human sacrifices and their more modern substitutes, the Japanese offered to the gods all the things that man regards as necessary (*e.g.*, food, clothing, shelter) or merely useful and pleasing (*e.g.*, means of transportation, tools, weapons, objects of entertainment) for life. These practices, which were found in the traditional religion known as Shintō, were modified when Confucianism and Buddhism were introduced into Japan during the 5th and 6th centuries AD.

Ancient Greece. The Homeric poems contain the most complete descriptions of sacrificial rites in ancient Greece. These rites, which were maintained almost without change for more than 10 centuries, were of two types: rites (*thysia*) addressed to the Olympian deities, which

included burning part of a victim and then participating in a joyful meal offered to the gods during the daytime primarily to serve and establish communion with the gods; and rites (*sphagia*) addressed to the infernal or chthonic deities, which involved the total burning or burying of a victim in a sombre nocturnal ceremony to placate or avert the malevolent chthonic powers. Besides the official or quasi-official rites, the popular religion, already in Homer, comprised sacrifices of all kinds of animals and of vegetables, fruits, cheese, and honey offered as expiation, supplication, or thanksgiving by worshippers belonging to all classes of society. Furthermore, the secret worship of what are known as the mysteries—cults normally promising immortality or some form of personal relationship with a god—became widespread. This practice became especially prominent during the Hellenistic period.

Judaism. The destruction of the Second Temple in AD 70 marked a profound change in the worship of the Jewish people. Before that event, sacrifice was the central act of Israelite worship; and there were many categories of sacrificial rites that had evolved through the history of the Jews into a minutely detailed system found in that part of the Torah (Law; the first five books of the Hebrew Bible) that is ascribed by biblical scholars to the Priestly Code, which became established following the Babylonian Exile (586–538). The sacrificial system ceased, however, with the destruction of the Temple, and prayer took the place of sacrifices. In modern Judaism the Orthodox prayer books still contain prayers for the reinstitution of the sacrificial cult in the rebuilt Temple. Reform Judaism, however, has abolished or modified these prayers in keeping with the conception of sacrifice as a once adequate but now outmoded form of worship, and some Conservative congregations have also rephrased references to sacrifices so that they indicate solely past events without implying any hope for the future restoration of the rite.

Christianity. The notion of sacrifice emerged in the early Christian communities in several different contexts. The death of Christ upon the cross preceded by the Last Supper was narrated in the Gospels in sacrificial terms; the life of Christ, culminating in his Passion and death, was seen as the perfect sacrifice, and his Resurrection and glorification were seen as God the Father's seal of approval on that life. The notion that members of the church are vitally linked to Christ and that their lives must be sacrificial was also elaborated, especially in the letters of St. Paul. Moreover, from the first decades of the church's existence, the celebration of the eucharistic meal was connected with the sacrifice of Jesus; it was a "memorial" (*anamnēsis*)—a term denoting some sort of identity

Thysia
and
sphagia
rites

between the thing so described and that to which it referred—of that sacrifice.

The Eucharist as sacrifice

The interpretation of sacrifice and particularly of the Eucharist as sacrifice has varied greatly within the different Christian traditions, partly because the sacrificial terminology in which the Eucharist was originally described became foreign to Christian thinkers. In short, during the Middle Ages, the Eastern Church viewed the Eucharist principally as a life-giving encounter with Christ the Resurrected; the Roman Church, however, saw it primarily as a bloodless repetition of the bloody sacrifice of Christ on the cross. For the Protestant Reformers in the 16th century, the sacrifice of Christ was unique and all sufficing, so that the idea of repeating it in cult became unnecessary. Sacrifice was separated from liturgy and was associated, especially in Calvinist Protestantism, with the personal ethical acts that should be made by a Christian believer. The ecumenical movement of the 20th century, bolstered by modern biblical scholarship, has led some of the Christian churches—*e.g.*, the Roman Catholic and Lutheran churches—to realize that they are not so far apart in their understanding of the Eucharist as sacrifice as was formerly thought and that they hold many elements of belief in common.

Islām. Sacrifice has little place in orthodox Islām. Faint shadows of sacrifice as it was practiced by the pre-Islāmic Arabs have influenced Muslims, so that they consider every slaughter of an animal an act of religion. They also celebrate feasts in fulfillment of a vow or in thanksgiving for good fortune, but there is no sacrificial ritual connected with these festive meals. On the last day of the annual pilgrimage to Mecca, animals are sacrificed; nevertheless, it is not the sacrificial rite that is important to the Muslims, but rather their visit to the sacred city.

Conclusion. The organization of sacrificial rites in the different cultures and religions has undoubtedly been influenced by a number of factors. Economic considerations, for example, certainly have had some impact upon primitive peoples in the selection of the victim and the time of sacrifice and in the determination of whether the victim is consumed or totally destroyed and whether the sacrificer is an individual or a collective group. The importance of such factors is an aspect of sacrifice that deserves increased investigation. Nevertheless, sacrifice is not a phenomenon that can be reduced to rational terms; it is fundamentally a religious act that has been of profound significance to individuals and social groups throughout history, a symbolic act that establishes a relationship between man and the sacred order. For many peoples of the world, throughout time, sacrifice has been the very heart of their religious life.

BIBLIOGRAPHY

General treatments of sacrifice: Classic formulations of theories of the origin and nature of sacrifice are found in: EDWARD B. TYLOR, *Primitive Culture*, 2 vol. (1871, reprinted 1958), a presentation of the gift theory of sacrifice; W. ROBERTSON SMITH, *Lectures on the Religion of the Semites*, 3rd ed. (1927), the clearest formulation of the author's theory of communion through a sacrificial meal; JAMES G. FRAZER, *The Golden Bough*, 3rd ed., 12 vol. (1907–15; abridged ed., *The New Golden Bough*, 1964), a famous and influential treatise on ancient religion that advanced the notion of sacrifice as a means for rejuvenating a god; HENRI HUBERT and MARCEL MAUSS, "Essai sur la nature et la fonction du sacrifice," *L'Année sociologique* (1898; Eng. trans., *Sacrifice: Its Nature and Function*, 1964), a sociological approach that explained the sacrificial victim as a buffer between man and the god. More recent formulations include: GERARDUS VAN DER LEEUW, *Phänomenologie der Religion* (1933; Eng. trans., *Religion in Essence and Manifestation*, 1938), an expansion of the notion of the sacrificial gift by a phenomenologist of religion; ADOLF E. JENSEN, *Mythos und Kult bei Naturvölkern*, rev. ed. (1960; Eng. trans., *Myth and Cult Among Primitive Peoples*, 1963), which correlates types of cultures and their sacrifice; RAYMOND FIRTH, "Offering and Sacrifice: Problems of Organization," in W.A. LESSA and E.Z. VOGT, (eds.), *Reader in Comparative Religion*, 3rd ed., pp. 185–194 (1971), an economic interpretation of sacrifice; and E.O. JAMES, *Sacrifice and Sacrament* (1962), a good survey.

Treatments of sacrifice in particular religions and civilizations: Brief articles on several religions are found in "Sacrifice," in JAMES HASTINGS (ed.), *Encyclopaedia of Religion and Ethics*, vol. 11, pp. 1–39 (1928, reprinted 1955). On Vedic religion, A.B. KEITH, *The Religion and Philosophy of the Veda and Upanishads*, 2 vol. (1925), is still a standard work; LOUIS RENOU, *Religions of Ancient India* (1953), offers a brief survey. On Chinese sacrificial rites, see C.K. YANG, *Religion in Chinese Society* (1961); on ancient Egypt, J.H. BREASTED, *The Elder Development of Religion and Thought in Ancient Egypt* (1912); and on ancient Greek and Roman religions, R.K. YERKES, *Sacrifice in Greek and Roman Religions and Early Judaism* (1952), a clearly written, well-documented work; M.P. NILSSON, *Geschichte der griechischen Religion*, 2nd ed., 2 vol. (1941–50; Eng. trans., *A History of Greek Religion*, 2nd ed., 1963), the best handbook on the whole subject of Greek religion. On sacrificial rites in Judaism there is extensive literature, including the article "Sacrifice" in the *Encyclopedia Judaica*, vol. 14, pp. 599–615 (1971), which offers a good survey with a bibliography; ROLAND DE VAUX, *Les Sacrifices de l'Ancien Testament* (1964; Eng. trans., *Studies in Old Testament Sacrifice*, 1964); and YERKES (above). On ancient Scandinavian rites, see E.O.G. TURVILLE-PETRIE, *Myth and Religion of the North* (1964); on the rites of the ancient civilizations of the American continents, WALTER KRICKEBERG et al., *Die Religionen des Alten Amerika* (1961; Eng. trans., *Pre-Columbian American Religions*, 1968). On the religions of the peoples of Africa, JOHN S. MBITI, *Concepts of God in Africa* (1970), is an introduction with extensive bibliography. Important specific studies include: MELVILLE HERSKOVITS, *Dahomey*, 2 vol. (1938); E.E. EVANS-PRITCHARD, *Nuer Religion* (1956); E.B. IDOWU, *Olódùmarè: God in Yoruba Belief* (1962); and GEOFFREY PARRINDER, *West African Religion*, 2nd ed. rev. (1961).

(R.F.)

Sade, Marquis de

Count Donatien-Alphonse-François de Sade, better known as the Marquis de Sade, was the author of erotic and licentious writings from which developed the concept of "sadism," meaning a sexual compulsion to achieve gratification by inflicting pain on others. In the course of a life that scandalized his contemporaries, he lived out many examples of his compulsion. His writings are still officially banned by the French courts. As an author, Sade is to some an incarnation of absolute evil who advocates the unleashing of instincts even to the point of crime. Others have looked upon him as a champion of man's total liberation through the satisfaction of his desires in all forms. Sade's works were widely read (mostly "underground") in the 19th century, especially by writers and artists. At the outset of the 20th century the French poet Guillaume Apollinaire helped to establish Sade's status in the domain of culture. Today Sade's writings belong to the history of ideas and mark an important moment in the history of literature—with Sade figuring as the first of the modern *écrivains maudits* (the "damned writers").

Related to the royal house of Condé, the Sade family numbered among its ancestors Laure de Noves, whom the 14th-century Italian poet Petrarch immortalized in verse. When the Marquis was born on June 2, 1740, at the Condé mansion, his father was on a diplomatic mission at the court of the Elector of Cologne; his mother, Marie Elénore Maillé de Carman, was lady-in-waiting to the Princess de Condé. He inherited estates in France from the seigneury of Saumane, La Coste, and from the co-seigneury of Mazan, as well as domains in the provinces of Bugey, Valromey, and Gex.

Heritage and youth

After early schooling with his uncle, Abbé de Sade of Ébreuil, he continued his studies at the Lycée Louis-le-Grand in Paris. His aristocratic background entitled him to various ranks in the king's regiments, and in 1754 he began a military career, which he abandoned in 1763 at the end of the Seven Years' War. In that year he married the daughter of a high-ranking bourgeois family *de robe* (of the magistracy), the Montreuils. His wife's father was president of the Parisian Parlement, a judicial and legislative body under the monarch. By her he had two sons, Louis-Marie and Donatien-Claude-Armand, and one daughter, Madeleine-Laure.

In the very first months of his marriage he began an

affair with an actress, La Beauvoisin, who had had numerous previous protectors. He invited prostitutes to his "little house" at Arcueil and subjected them to various sexual abuses. For this he was imprisoned, on orders of the King, in the fortress of Vincennes. Freed several

By courtesy of the trustees of the British Museum; photograph, J.R. Freeman & Co. Ltd.

Sade, engraving by H. Biberstein.

First
public
scandal

weeks later, he resumed his life of debauchery and went deeply into debt. In 1768 the first public scandal erupted: the Rose Keller affair.

Rose Keller was a young prostitute he had met on Easter Sunday in Paris. He took her to his house in Arcueil, where he locked her up and abused her sexually. She escaped and related the unnatural acts and brutality to persons in the neighbourhood, as well as showing them her wounds. Sade was sentenced to the fortress of Pierre-Encise, near Lyons.

After his release he retired to his château of La Coste. In June 1772 he went to Marseilles to get some much-needed money. There he engaged his male servant Latour to find him some prostitutes, upon whom the Marquis committed his usual sexual excesses. (Meanwhile, at his bidding, Latour engaged in sodomy with him.) The young women helped themselves liberally to the Marquis' pill-box filled with candies that contained the aphrodisiac Spanish fly. When soon thereafter they suffered upset stomachs, they feared they had been poisoned. Sade and Latour fled to the estates of the King of Sardinia, who had them arrested. The Parlement at Aix sentenced them to death by default and, on September 12, 1772, executed them "in effigy." After escaping from the fortress of Miolans, Sade took refuge in his château at La Coste, rejoining his wife. She became his accomplice and shared his pleasures, until the parents of the neighbourhood boys and girls he had abducted complained to the crown prosecutor. Sade fled to Italy accompanied by his sister-in-law, the Canoness of Launay, who had become his mistress. He returned to La Coste on November 4, 1776. One incident followed another in an atmosphere of continual scandal, and, on his return to Paris, the Marquis was arrested and sent to the dungeon of Vincennes on February 13, 1777.

Detention
at
Vincennes

Conditions in this prison were harsh. During his detention Sade quarrelled with his jailer, with the prison director, and with a fellow prisoner, Victor Riqueti, the Marquis de Mirabeau, whom he had insulted. He tried to incite the other prisoners to revolt. Visits from his wife, who was eventually allowed to see him, were banned after an episode in which he fell into a fit of jealous rage precipitated by his suspicion that she was about to leave him and was plotting against him. The Marquise retired to a convent.

Sade overcame his boredom and anger in prison by writing sexually graphic novels and plays. In July 1782 he finished his *Dialogue entre un prêtre et un moribond* (*Dialogue Between a Priest and a Dying Man*), in which he declared himself an atheist. His letters to his lawyer as well as to his wife combine incisive wit with an implacable spirit of revolt. On February 27, 1784, he was transferred to the Bastille in Paris. On a roll of paper some 12 metres (39 feet) long, he wrote *Les 120 Journées de Sodome* (*One Hundred and Twenty Days of Sodom*), in which he graphically describes numerous varieties of sexual perversion. In 1787 he wrote his most famous work, *Les Infortunes de la vertu* ("The Adversities of Virtue"), and, in 1788, the novellas, tales, and short stories later published in the volume entitled *Les Crimes de l'amour* (*Crimes of Passion*).

A few days before the French Revolutionaries stormed the Bastille on July 14, 1789, Sade had shouted through a window, "They are massacring the prisoners; you must come and free them." He was transferred to the insane asylum at Charenton, where he remained until April 2, 1790.

On his release, Sade offered several plays to the Comédie-Française as well as to other theatres. Though five of them were accepted, not all of them were performed. Separated from his wife, he lived now with a young actress, the Widow Quesnet, and wrote his novels *Justine, ou les malheurs de la vertu* (*Justine; or, the Misfortunes of Virtue*) and *Juliette*. In 1792 he became secretary of the Revolutionary Section of Les Piques in Paris, was one of the delegates appointed to visit hospitals in Paris, and wrote several patriotic addresses. During the Reign of Terror he saved the life of his father-in-law, Montreuil, and that of the latter's wife, even though they had been responsible for his various imprisonments. He gave speeches on behalf of the Revolution, but was nevertheless accused of *modérantisme* ("moderatism") and mistakenly inscribed on the list of émigrés. He escaped the guillotine by chance, the day before the Revolutionary leader Robespierre was overthrown. At the time he was living with the Widow Quesnet in conditions of abject poverty.

On March 6, 1801, he was arrested at his publisher's where copies of *Justine* and *Juliette* were found with notes in his hand and several handwritten manuscripts. Again he was sent to Charenton, where he caused new scandals. His repeated protests had no effect on Napoleon, who saw to it personally that Sade was deprived of all freedom of movement. Nevertheless he succeeded in having his plays put on at Charenton, with the inmates themselves as the actors. He began work on an ambitious ten-volume novel, at least two volumes of which were written: *Les Journées de Florbelle ou la nature dévoilée* ("The Days of Florbelle or Nature Unveiled"). After his death on December 2, 1814, his elder son burned these writings, together with other manuscripts.

His remains were scattered. There is no portrait of him. In his will, drawn up in 1806, he asked that "the traces of my grave disappear from the face of the earth, as I flatter myself that my memory will be effaced from the mind of men."

Composition of
Justine and
Juliette

MAJOR WORKS

Justine, ou les malheurs de la vertu (1791; *Justine; or, The Misfortunes of Virtue,* new trans. by Helen Weaver, 1966); *Les Infortunes de la vertu,* another version of *Justine* (1930 and 1946); *La Nouvelle Justine . . . suivie de l'histoire de Juliette sa soeur* (1797; *The Complete Justine, Philosophy in the Bedroom, and Other Writings,* comp. and trans. by Richard Seaver and Austryn Wainhouse, 1966); *Juliette, ou la suite de Justine* (published in the last 6 vol. of the 1797 *Nouvelle Justine* edition; Eng. trans. by Austryn Wainhouse, 1 vol., 1968); *Aline et Valcour, ou le roman philosophique. Écrit à la Bastille, un an avant la Révolution de France* (1793); *La Philosophie dans le boudoir* (1795; see Seaver-Wainhouse above); *Les Crimes de l'amour, nouvelles héroïques et tragiques, précédées d'une idée sur les romans* (Year VIII, 1800; *Crimes of Passion,* ed. and trans. by Wade Baskin, 1965); *Historiettes, contes et fabliaux* (1926–27); *Les 120 Journées de Sodome, ou l'école du libertinage,* 3 vol. (1931–35; *The 120 Days of Sodom, and Other Writings,* comp. and trans. by Austryn Wainhouse and Richard Seaver, 1966); *Dialogue entre un prêtre et un moribond* (1926; *Dialogue Between a Priest and a Dying Man,* 1927); *Oxtiern, ou les malheurs du libertinage* (Year VIII, 1800); *Correspondance inédite du marquis de Sade*, ed. by Paul Bourdin (1929); *Lettres choisies*, ed. by Gilbert Lély (1963; *Selected Letters*, trans. by W.J. Strachan, ed. by Margaret Crosland, 1966).

BIBLIOGRAPHY. The *Oeuvres complètes* of the Marquis de Sade have been in the course of publication since 1962. Numerous recent editions of the major works of the Marquis exist, certain of which are tolerated by censorship, others whose publication always falls within the provisions of law. One man, above all, had linked his name to these publications —MAURICE HEINE, who died in 1940. He published the first version of *Justine*, under the title *Les Infortunes de la vertu* (1930); collected the stories which make up the volume *Historiettes, contes et fabliaux* (1926–27); published the manuscript of *Les 120 Journées de Sodome, ou l'école du libertinage*, 3 vol. (1931–35); revealed the existence of the *Dialogue entre un prêtre et un moribond* (1926); put together an anthology under the title *Oeuvres choisies et pages magistrales du Marquis de Sade* (1933); and undertook a biography that remained unfinished, and was published in 1950 under the title *Le Marquis de Sade*. Other biographical studies are GILBERT LELY, *La Vie du Marquis de Sade*, 2 vol. (1952–57; Eng. trans., 1961; paperback edition, 1970); and GEOFFREY GORER, *The Life and Ideas of the Marquis de Sade* (1963).

The works of Sade have provoked studies and commentaries by several contemporary French writers. The most remarkable of these studies come as prefaces to the publication of the works: that of GEORGES BATAILLE for *Justine, ou les malheurs de la vertu* (1930); that of JEAN PAULHAN for *Les Infortunes de la vertu* (1946); and that of MAURICE NADEAU for the most complete anthology to date: Marquis de Sade, *Oeuvres* (1948). The philosophical exegesis of Sade's work was undertaken by PIERRE KLOSSOWSKI in a fundamental, though debatable, work—*Sade, mon prochain* (1947); while MAURICE BLANCHOT expressed the most pertinent views in *Lautréamont et Sade* (1949). See also SIMONE DE BEAUVOIR, *The Marquis de Sade* (Eng. trans. 1962), with selections from his writings. ROLAND BARTHES has studied Sade from a point of view that owes a great deal to structuralism and to the science of language: *Sade, Fourier, Loyola* (1972).

(M.Na.)

Safety Engineering

Safety engineering is that profession concerned with the scientific analysis of the causes of accidental deaths and injuries in a given environment and their elimination or reduction. In the industrialized areas of the world, accidents now cause more deaths than all infectious diseases and more than any single illness, except those related to cancer and heart disease. In 1967, some 459,000 accidental deaths occurred in 50 countries reporting to the World Health Organization. Of this number, 175,000 or 38 percent occurred in motor vehicle accidents. On a worldwide basis, motor vehicle accidents tend to be the primary cause of accidental deaths, followed by those in industry and in the home. Nonfatal injuries are far more frequent than deaths, but the pattern of frequency changes. In the United States, for example, each year about six times as many persons receive nonfatal injuries in accidents at home as in motor vehicle accidents, and about twice as many at home as in industrial accidents.

The most striking advances in safety during the last 40 or 50 years have been made in industry. Safety engineering has played an important role in this development. Between 1926 and 1961, the frequency rate for disabling injuries dropped from approximately 32 to 6 in the United States. After that year, however, there was no significant improvement. During the same period, both the number of accidental deaths and total disabilities, in relation to the man-hours worked declined by almost 80 percent. The reduction in accident rates was the result of the cooperation of management and trained specialists in the fields of safety engineering, industrial hygiene, and industrial medicine in (1) reducing the hazards inherent in the equipment and working methods and (2) in educating employees in the basic principles of accident prevention. In many companies, the time lost from injuries that occur off the job constitutes a greater problem than that lost from accidents while at work.

An especially productive area for safety engineering has been that involving relatively stable industrial situations, repetitive in nature, in which there are common accident factors that can be identified and controlled. The great majority of highway and nonoccupational accidents, on the other hand, are not homogeneous in regard to common variables. In addition, most such accidents have multiple causes, making it more difficult to introduce preventive measures. Consequently, in these areas the impact of safety engineering has not yet been so great.

DEVELOPMENT OF THE INDUSTRIAL SAFETY MOVEMENT

The initial stimulus for the industrial safety movement came from the largest industries, in which severe injuries and loss of life were common occurrences. Public opinion based on humanitarian motives was aroused in both Europe and the U.S., but the most significant advances did not occur until management became fully aware that accidents interrupted production, raised operating costs, and formed the basis for future injuries and loss of equipment.

In the 19th century, the safety of an employee was generally considered to be his own responsibility. The liability of the employer for accidental injuries depended on certain common-law doctrines that operated against the employee. The "fellow-servant" doctrine, for example, held that the employer was not responsible for employee injuries resulting from the action of a fellow worker. The "assumption of risk" doctrine stated that by accepting employment, the worker assumed any risks connected with it. Finally, the doctrine of "contributory negligence" absolved the employer from responsibility for injuries resulting from accidents if the employee had contributed to the cause in any degree. *[Early common-law liability doctrines]*

An important segment of progressive industrial management saw the fallacies in these concepts and felt that management should do more for the safety of the workers. The social progress of the times was reflected in the development of the safety movement which was given impetus by workmen's compensation laws enacted in most of the industrial countries in the late 19th and early 20th centuries. A new concept was inherent in these laws, namely that the employer should accept primary responsibility for injuries incurred at work, even though they could not be attributed to any one person or cause. Industry became legally liable for injuries to its workers and became obligated to provide benefits during time lost from work, medical and surgical care, and death benefits to dependents.

Once it was recognized that disablement represented a part of the cost of industrial production and had to be incorporated in the price of the product, management had a strong economic incentive for preventing accidents. At the same time, workmen's compensation laws led to the rapid growth of casualty insurance as a means of furnishing protection to the employer. The insurance companies collaborated with industry in playing a major role in accident-prevention programs, developing methods of evaluating risks, and aiding employers in taking preventive action.

The three specialized skills—safety engineering, industrial hygiene, and industrial medicine—were developed as methods of preventing injury to the worker and of reducing costs. The first two aim at reducing the number of work injuries and disabilities in the occupational setting by removing their causes, and the third is concerned with minimizing the consequences of injury and disease and with restoring disabled workers to useful employment. The initial emphasis in safety engineering was on the installation of guards and protective devices; this led to a sudden, sharp decline in machine accidents, and today the rates for accidents involving machine hazards are only about half those of about 40 years ago. Industrial hygiene has concentrated on controlling environmental hazards: *i.e.*, the inhalation of toxic gases, fumes, and other harmful exposures. More recently there has been a growing emphasis on personal factors, including recognition of the role mental and emotional adjustment may play in accidents.

From an emphasis on mechanical guarding and education of workers in safety, experience tended to shift the focus to an application of basic safety engineering principles in the design of machinery, plant layout, and working methods. More emphasis was placed on the role of supervisory personnel, and safety was recognized as an integral part of normal operating procedure. The role of personal errors and accident proneness has been dealt with by analysis of jobs and of the functional capacities of workers. Variables relating to the health of the worker have been stressed, and working methods have been modified to ensure an optimum working environment as far as employee health is concerned.

These developments were paralleled by a growing participation of various states in setting up supervisory and enforcement agencies. In addition, organizations such as the United States Bureau of Mines, the United States Department of Labor, the National Safety Council (NSC), the American National Standards Institute, the Underwriters' Laboratories, and various professional societies were formed in the United States and elsewhere. The Bureau of Mines, which was organized in 1912, has led in research and education pertaining to hazardous agents and their control; it sets the pattern for the mining industry. The NSC is the organization around which the general industrial safety movement evolves; it is a focal point of leadership in the safety movement. The other organizations have performed specialized and important functions. Safety principles have been incorporated into engineering courses, and departments of safety engineering have been established in various graduate and technical schools. The most important directing force for accident prevention, however, remains within industry itself. Although many outside agencies may contribute, the direct and immediate responsibility for the application of safety engineering principles, employee education, and on-the-job enforcement rests upon the individual employer. In most instances, laws represent only minimal requirements and are below the goal of ultimate objectives.

Accident frequency and severity rates. Most statistical analyses of accidents are based on either frequency or severity. Of the many systems devised, one—used by the American National Standards Institute—provides a substantial degree of standardization for comparative purposes. In this system, the standard frequency rate represents the number of disabling injuries per 1,000,000 man-hours of exposure. The standard severity rate is the total time charged as a result of lost-time injuries per 1,000,000 man-hours of exposure. The time charges include both actual days lost and certain standardized charges for permanent disabilities and deaths. The greatest penalties are imposed for death or permanent total disability, for each of which the time charges are arbitrarily set at 6,000 days per case. Various permanent partial-disability charges range from 35 to 4,500 days, in accordance with a prescribed schedule.

The frequency rate indicates how many injuries are occurring in relation to the number of man-hours worked, and the severity rate indicates how serious those injuries are in terms of days lost in relation to hours of exposure. The former has been most widely used and can be most quickly and easily computed. It does not, however, indicate the seriousness of an accident, since it merely gives the rate at which accidents are occurring. The severity rate was developed to meet this need and to give an expression of the total time lost per million man-hours of exposure. Other composite indexes usually involve weighted averages of some type, obtained by multiplying the severity rate by ten and adding the frequency rate.

The safety engineer is concerned with reducing both the frequency with which accidents occur and the frequency with which they threaten. He wants to know why a man fell off a ladder even if no serious injury resulted. The severity rate, which takes into account the extent and seriousness of the injuries, is also closely associated with the efficiency of the safety program. If an employee receives lacerations and abrasions in falling from a ladder,

Standard frequency rate

prompt and adequate medical care will limit this to a first-aid case, whereas inadequate care may permit infection to occur.

Frequency and severity rates vary widely from one industry to another. Certain industries, such as communications, have low-frequency and low-severity rates; mining and lumbering are at the opposite extreme. These differences reflect not only the inherent dangers in an industry but also many other factors, including the efficiency of the safety program. In the electrical-equipment industry, hazards are limited and most injuries minor. In the steel industry, the frequency rates have been kept down by extensive accident-control programs, but the hazards are such that most of the accidents that do occur result in serious disabling injuries. In mining and lumbering, the men work more or less independently over a large area and direct supervision is quite difficult. Permanent safeguards are not widely applicable because the work location is constantly changing. The worker is very frequently his own protector from a mining machine, explosives, or axes.

Methods of evaluating safety programs. Various attempts have been made to obtain more useful and accurate indexes of the effectiveness of safety programs than the frequency and severity rates. One method is to obtain an estimate of the total direct and indirect costs of accidents. Another method is to find the "loss ratio," an index based on the amount paid for insurance compensation in terms of what might be expected on the basis of averages in a similar industry. A third method is to apply the techniques of statistical quality control to the accident record. This procedure gives an accurate index of whether the frequency of accidents is becoming excessive, or improving, in relation to past experience. Although none of these indexes give information as to what is wrong in the work situation, they alert management and safety directors. All are sufficiently quantitative to indicate the extent to which accidents can be reduced if effective efforts are applied.

The currently recommended approach is to define the total costs of work injuries and accidents as the sum of "insured" and "uninsured" costs. The former are simply the amount paid for compensation and medical insurance premiums. For the ascertainment of "uninsured" costs, methods and recording procedures have been developed to provide more reliable quantitative data. This involves the calculation of specific categories of uninsured costs for each of four classes of accidents: lost-time cases; injuries requiring the attention of a physician, but not loss of a day's work; first-aid cases; and accidents involving property damage and disruption of work.

Cost of accidents

Statistical control shows when increases or decreases in rates should be considered excessive and indicates other than chance variations in the work situation. The changes may reflect the introduction of new machines in which adequate safety features are not incorporated; the influx of new personnel without adequate training in safety practices; an increasing laxity in the supervision of employees by the foreman; or many other sources of trouble.

In summary, if the criteria of direct and indirect costs, loss ratio, or quality control are applied in evaluating the accident-injury rates of a plant, they will indicate to the safety engineer, medical officer, or management whether their accident rates are acceptable. An evaluation should include items relating to plant layout, housekeeping, maintenance, protective equipment, safety organization, medical facilities, and employee training. The degree of cooperation achieved between the safety engineer, the shop foremen, and medical officers is critical. Employee safety education is of paramount importance, especially if a relatively high proportion of the injuries are occurring in new and untrained workers. Finally, the effectiveness achieved will reflect the active participation of management at the higher executive levels.

Safety engineering as a profession. The field of safety engineering has not developed as a unified, specific discipline, and its practitioners have operated under a wide variety of position titles, job descriptions, responsibilities, and reporting levels in industry and the loss-prevention activities of insurance companies. There has also been little uniformity in the development of educational programs in engineering schools and universities for the specialized training needed for this field.

The most recent trends include increased emphasis on prevention by the anticipation of hazard potentials; changing legal concepts concerning product liability and negligent design or manufacture, and the developing emphasis on consumer protection; and the development of national and international legislation and controls, not only in the areas of transportation safety, product safety, and consumer protection, but also in occupational health and environmental control.

Safety engineer's functions

Four general areas that have been identified as the major functions carried out by the professional safety engineer or safety professional are: (1) identification and appraisal of accident-producing conditions and practices and evaluation of the severity of the accident problem; (2) development of accident and loss-control methods, procedures, and programs; (3) communication of accident and loss-control information to those directly involved; and (4) measurement and evaluation of the accident and loss-control systems, and the modifications needed to obtain optimum results. Some of the more specific techniques developed and utilized in these functional areas will be subsequently outlined.

The basis for specific safety procedures. The safety engineer contributes to the prevention of accidents by using his specialized knowledge of accident causation and control by (1) seeking to eliminate hazards and causation factors, (2) designing machines and procedures to reduce the hazards, and (3) minimizing their effects by prescribing specialized equipment to prevent injury or reduce the severity.

The control of abnormal exchanges of energy. In studies of accidents, the "agent" of injury has often been identified as the environmental object; *e.g.*, loose floor board, or motor vehicle. A more comprehensive and more useful approach appears to be the understanding that all injuries (and damage to inanimate objects) result from abnormal exchanges of energy between persons and the environment (or objects and the environment). Thus, accidental injuries are considered to result from (1) the application of various forms of energy to the human body in amounts exceeding the tolerance thresholds of its various parts, or (2) interference with the normal exchanges of energy between the body and the environment (as in drowning). The forms of energy producing accidental injuries of all types would logically include thermal, electrical, radiant, mechanical, and chemical.

The concept of energy as the cause of injury presents a close analogy to the agent in the causation of disease. Each form of energy produces specific kinds of injury. Thermal energy impinging on the body, for example, may produce inflammation, coagulation, charring, and incineration at all body levels; *i.e.*,· first-, second-, and third-degree burns. The specific result will depend on the location and manner in which the energy is dissipated. The energy that impinges on the body is delivered by various means, usually inanimate objects. Wires carry electricity, moving objects carry mechanical or kinetic energy, poisonous plants carry toxins. The modification of the carriers of injurious energy thus affords an important means of preventing injury.

Resistance to injury

Another parallel to disease is the variation in natural or acquired resistance to injury, corresponding to resistance to infection. Increased susceptibility to mechanical injuries characterizes such conditions as hemophilia. Shifts in resistance with age and sex also occur. Thus, postmenopausal women, compared with men of comparable ages, more frequently suffer fractures in falls. One study has shown a positive correlation between the incidence of fractures and osteoporosis (wasting away of bone tissue). Thus, postmenopausal women suffer more fractures and osteoporosis than men of comparable age. Lower death rates from falls have been found in areas with naturally high fluorides in the water. Physical conditioning and training for contact sports increases the resistance to injury. Repeated or continuous exposure to moderately high

altitudes produces some tolerance to oxygen deficiency.

The prevention of abnormal exchanges of energy between the body and the environment can be achieved through interference in the early stages leading to the transfer event, or by directly blocking or attenuating the exchange. Four initial levels of prevention are: (1) elimination of the source of hazardous energy (*e.g.*, by prohibiting the manufacture of fireworks or of flammable blankets and clothing); (2) prevention or modification of its release (*e.g.*, by grounding of electrical appliances); (3) separation of the energy and the persons in time or space (*e.g.*, by unplugging the power cord of the television set before replacing a part); and (4) interposition of a barrier that blocks or attenuates the energy transfer between the energy source and the person (*e.g.*, providing a guard on a power saw, crash padding on dashboards, helmets for motorcyclists, and insulation on electrical appliances).

Engineering and medical collaboration. Two considerations are essential in devising barrier measures to prevent or attenuate injurious energy exchanges that result: the identification of the carriers or "vectors" of energy, which then may be modified; and a knowledge of injury thresholds of the human body in relation to the magnitude of the forces encountered in accident situations. These are of particular importance for the prevention of injury in motor-vehicle crashes, but little precise information has been available until recently. Information is being obtained from on-the-site medical-engineering analyses of accidents, experimental crashes of instrumented cars, and laboratory studies on injury thresholds using cadavers or animals.

Sources of data

Classification of injuries and accidents. One of the most important functions of the safety engineer is to identify hazards in the working area and to evaluate the loss-producing aspects of a given method or operational system. In the past, a great deal of attention has been devoted to analyzing the existing hazards and products, while the newer methods involve not only learning from accidents that have occurred but also emphasizing the advance analysis of accident potentials and the prevention of accidents prior to their occurrence.

One widely used analysis of the circumstances of accidents includes the following: (1) identification and location of the materials, machines, and tools most frequently involved in accidents and the jobs most likely to produce injuries; (2) location of the departments and occupations involved; (3) disclosure of the unsafe practices, which may necessitate retraining or shifting of employees; (4) study of the role of supervisors, and provision of information about the principal hazards.

Significant factors include the type of physical injury incurred; the source of the injury in relation to the object, substance, or motion that inflicted it; the specific part of the material or agency that was hazardous; and finally, the unsafe act that took place, presumably in violation of commonly accepted safety practices. Other aspects include age, sex, occupation, and type of work being performed.

Advance analysis and critical incident technique. All possible faults in equipment and in the work areas in industry or in transport vehicles, as well as the capacities

---

Table 1: Advance Analysis of Equipment

Operational job analysis:	requirements of task
	working area
	displays
	controls
Blueprint phase:	analysis of task
	prediction of efficiency
	prediction of errors
	human limitations
Mock-up stage:	task performance
	physical size of operators
	age of operators
	skill levels
	accessory equipment
	interfering structures or motions
	physiological changes
	errors
	"near accidents"

of the operator, should be subjected to an advance analysis designed to prevent accidents. If defects are present, it is only a matter of time before some operator "fails" and has an accident.

Advance analysis assumes the following: (1) an operational job analysis that should include a survey of the nature of the task, the work surroundings, the location of controls and instruments, and the way the operator performs his duties (Table 1); (2) a "functional concept of accidents" (that is, anticipation of the errors that may occur while the operator is working at the machine). The repetition or recurrence of near or real accidents clearly indicates a need for redesign (Table 2); (3) an assumption of human limitations.

Table 2: Typical Human Errors in Equipment Operation

type of error	possible causal factors
Failure to detect signal	input overload: too many significant signals input underload: too little variety of signals too few signals adverse noise conditions: poor contrast high intensity of distraction stimuli
Incorrect identification of signal	code form or typology unclear lack of differential cues conflicting cues
Error of commission	correct tool or control not available action-control relationship not understood action feedback unavailable or delayed

A wide margin of safety should be provided to eliminate any possible situation that places the operator near his maximum ability with regard to aptitude or effort, especially when adverse factors, such as fatigue, are present.

Operational job analysis. One of the first steps in insuring safety on the job is an analysis of what is required of the individual worker, focussing on the hazardous features. Techniques involving "near accidents" are often revealing. Studies have been made of near accidents during routine bus operations at night and during the day to discover the number of variables involved in emergencies; how drivers reacted; the variety and frequency of critical situations; and the relations between near and real accidents.

The study revealed that as a rule critical situations develop rapidly and are of short duration. Of the 66 near accidents observed, 53 or 80 percent were closely related to the three most common types of accidents that actually occur on the highway, namely, sideswipe, rear-end, and head-on collisions.

The most important variables contributing to the critical situations were as follows: (1) following too closely; (2) following too closely while approaching to pass (cornering); (3) operator inattention—*i.e.,* dozing at the wheel; (4) vehicle running off the road; (5) errors at intersection; (6) errors in passing; (7) operating in wrong lane of traffic; (8) leaving and entering the roadway; and (9) pedestrian errors.

It is possible that some of the near accidents are related to the personality and aptitude of the drivers or that certain drivers have a tendency to become involved in the same type of situation repeatedly. Observations thus far indicate a characteristic failure of most drivers to take defensive action at an early stage of a developing hazardous situation. This is found to have occurred in 95 percent of the 66 incidents observed. The implications are clear that studies of near accidents offer an unusual opportunity for training the driver to anticipate hazardous situations and to avoid them.

The critical-incident technique. One method of identifying unsafe conditions involves selecting a random sample of workers from various portions of the plant or population, exposed to various hazards. An interviewer questions the workers, asking them to describe near-miss safety errors they have made in the past, or unsafe conditions they have observed. The data are classified into hazard categories to illuminate factors which have contributed to an actual or potential loss-producing event. In

The "near-accident" technique

one large manufacturing plant 187 different unsafe acts or conditions were identified by an analysis of "near-misses." It was also found that 52 percent more unsafe acts and conditions were revealed by the critical-incident technique than had been identified from accident records compiled during the previous two-year period.

Systems safety engineering. In recent years, a great deal of attention has been devoted to "systems safety engineering." In brief, the primary objective of systems safety engineering is the reduction or elimination of all hazardous consequences of equipment operation in an industrial plant or similar large man-machine complex. It characteristically involves a systematic application of special analytical techniques, derived criteria, evaluation methodology, and management skills. Since it emphasizes prevention rather than correction of problems, particular attention is placed upon early engineering design and procedural analysis. It is broadly conceived to take into consideration all aspects of the planning, design, development, fabrication, test, installation, maintenance, operation, and overall evaluation of man-machine systems.

Until recently, when a new aircraft was developed, it first was designed, then an experimental model was constructed and test flown to determine its capabilities and faults. From this came information to make necessary design changes, and the process was repeated until the performance specifications were achieved. Present aircraft and missiles are too complex and costly for this procedure. Now the defects must be located and corrected as far as possible in the design stage, using the analytic techniques of systems analysis and the systems approach to safety. These procedures are applicable for all complex equipment and man-machine combinations.

Accidents result from deficiencies in human operation, defects in tools and mechanical equipment, and a variety of environmental influences. Usually failures are compound. An accident may include mechanical or electrical failure, defective materials, and such environmental conditions as extreme heat or noise levels inhibiting intercommunication. Human failure may derive from such factors as distraction, fatigue, worry, improper attitude, lack of skill, and taking chances.

One of the principal methods of analyzing potential failure of equipment is to trace through the system and detect the ultimate effect on the task being performed, such as a switch being jammed in the "on" position. The "failure mode and effect analysis" is straightforward, providing that the analyst is well informed. It has the drawback, however, of analyzing only one failure in the system at a time, and, thus, other possibilities may be overlooked.

In recent years, especially in the aircraft industry, the "fault-tree" method has been developed. In this plan, an undesired event is selected, and all of the possible happenings that can contribute to the event are diagrammed in the form of a tree. The branches of the tree are continued until independent events are reached. Mathematical probabilities for the independent events are determined and both the probability of the undesired event and the most likely chain of events leading to it can be computed.

One of the most difficult problems in analyzing the effectiveness of systems is to evaluate quantitatively the role of human errors in the degradation of the quality or effectiveness of a product. One of the newer methods of predicting errors in quantitative terms depends upon the calculation of rates at which errors occur in various operations.

The value of the systems-analysis approach for the safety engineer is to widen or enlarge his point of view. In visualizing the interrelationships of the various components that enter into accidents, it helps to change safety engineering from an art to a science by codifying much of the knowledge that has been derived, especially before or in advance of the occurrence of damaging events.

Design failures and human limitations. The concept of design failure appears to be promising. In many instances failures in the designing of equipment are so subtle that those responsible for analyzing and reporting accidents are not aware of them. Often because the designers of

"Fault-tree" method

Table 3: Limits for Variables Influencing Comfort and Safety

variable	desirable	maximum or minimum value for comfort
Ventilation	sufficient additional fresh or recirculated odour-free air to remove all odours	20 cubic feet (0.6 cubic metres) per minute of fresh air
Air temperature	ambient temperature adjusted to give effective temperature of 63–71° F (20–22° C) (winter) or 66–75° F (21–24° C) (summer)	70–72° F or 22° C
Air velocity	adjusted to ambient temperature to give appropriate cooling power without drafts	40–60 feet (12–18 metres) per minute
Humidity	adjusted to air temperature and velocity to maintain comfort	25–50 percent relative humidity
Carbon dioxide	not a requirement as long as ventilating requirements for removal of odours are met	0.5–1.0 percent
Carbon monoxide	none	0.003 percent
Noise	reduced to permit conversation at least 3 feet (900 millimetres) with no extra effort	80–85 decibels overall and 50–60 decibels in 1200–2400 hertz band
Vibration	reduced to below threshold of perception	0.002 inches (0.05 millimetres) at 20 hertz or more

equipment are unaware of human limitations no attempts are made to build the apparatus or working areas in relation to the wide range of human capabilities, differences, and limitations. This applies particularly to such problems as variations in body size of the working population, design and arrangement of controls and displays, and the influence of environmental factors on safety. Some of the basic principles in each of these areas are outlined below (see also HUMAN-FACTORS ENGINEERING).

Layout of working areas and human-sizing problems. In order to improve the ease, efficiency, and safety of operating all types of equipment in shops and hangars, consideration has to be given to the application of physical anthropometric data to design and to its use in a dynamic setting. In many instances, an engineer is given instructions to design the equipment and the operator's area in such a way as to "prevent reaching beyond range of vision," to "avoid off-balance positions," and to "provide adequate head room and clearance." He is rarely supplied with quantitative descriptions to meet these requirements. On the other hand, if quantitative measurements are provided, the "average value" fallacy is often committed. Although such values can be applied to special cases in the design of equipment, arrangements based on averages would be unsuitable for 50 percent of the operators in a normally distributed group. Provision should be made for 90 or 95 percent or any other predetermined percentage of the potential operators. If this is not done for such a requirement as arm reach required to operate manual controls, many of those who exceed or are below the average values are handicapped. Mannequins are often used in mock-ups of proposed machines to see if the controls are within reach and if sufficient clearance is provided. Standard sources of anthropometric data relating to body measurements are available.

Many other illustrations could be given for the use of standard body measurements in an industrial setting. Requirements for standing and sitting heights should be such that controls that must be used often and smoothly are not placed at shoulder height or below the waistline. Splash guards and machine aprons should be so designed that work is within easy reach of the operator. Control pressures relating to arm, hand, and leg strength should be within the limits of the weakest persons who are expected to run the machines. Unless all these conditions are fulfilled, unnecessary fatigue, irregular operation, and injuries will occur.

Dynamic body measurements of the worker while operating his machine are also valuable. Among desirable criteria are a stable standing or sitting posture with an adequate base support, an unobstructed view of all operations, and readily accessible controls designed for operating at an advantage with respect to muscular activity. In regard to moving equipment, such as trucks, boats, and other vehicles, either adequate distances for deceleration or restraining or protective devices are needed.

Design of controls and displays. In the design of controls, safety is enhanced by the shape and colour-coding of knobs, the radius of knobs and winding handles, the gear ratio, and the amount of friction and inertia.

Among important factors relating to the operation of controls are convenient location, efficient direction of movement, and appropriate speed in relation both to rotary and wrist movements and to movement from point to point. Unless controls are designed carefully, placed properly, and identified easily, they may be operated inadvertently. Design criteria for many of these variables have been determined experimentally for aircraft, and similar techniques are now being used in studying automotive and industrial equipment.

A fundamental principle is to make the various switches and dials of different sizes and shapes to eliminate errors of identification. Accidents may occur if an operator does not clearly perceive the location or movement of indicators, meters, or dials. Clear and unambiguous information is especially important if several tasks must be performed successively or simultaneously for long periods.

The following factors have a significant effect on ease of seeing: size and spacing of critical detail, especially in instrument markings and figures; contrast between object and background; amount of illumination, including the use of colour; and contrast between the objects to be seen and their surroundings.

Auditory signals should be recognizable against the background of the sound pattern, and attempts should be made to use a range in which the ear is most sensitive with respect to frequency, intensity, and duration.

Environmental factors influencing safety. Additional factors influencing the efficiency and safety of workers relate to the physical variables in the environment. These may be broken down into temperature, humidity, ventilation, noise, and vibration. Extremes of any of the factors result in discomfort, lowered efficiency, and increased accident risk.

A summary of the various stimuli influencing worker comfort and safety in terms of desirable and maximum values is presented in Table 3. The highest degree of comfort would be achieved by conforming to the comments listed in the "desirable" column. Discomfort might be expected to arise if the maximum values given in the last column are exceeded.

The values indicated in the table cannot always be considered as rigid standards because of the interdependence of one variable with others.

HAZARDS AND THEIR PREVENTION

Safeguarding machinery and working areas. The automation of devices to move and handle materials for machine operations has greatly reduced exposure to mechanical and handling hazards. The basic principles of safeguarding continue to be of great importance, however, in many industrial operations. The primary purpose of machine guarding is to prevent injury from direct contact with moving parts, from features of the work in progress (*e.g.*, chips from metal, splashing of chemicals, kickback from a saw), from mechanical or electrical failures in the equipment, and from predictable human errors or failures.

In general, machine guards relate to hazards in the transmission of power to the working areas such as belts, gears, rotating shafts, and sliding parts, and to the area in

Manne-
quins in
mock-ups

Machine
guards

which the operator performs his functions. Injuries result when loose clothing or hair is caught by rotating mechanisms; when fingers and hands are caught in pinch points such as rollers, meshing gear teeth, belts, and chain drives; and when moving parts supply cutting, shearing, or crushing forces. In the modern machine lathe, for example, external shafts, pulleys, and belts are eliminated, and the motor and gear train are completely enclosed. When fixed guards cannot be used, automatic interlocking guards can be designed to prevent operation of a machine unless a guard is in position at the danger point. Another type of guard that automatically comes into position while the machine is in operation prevents the operator from coming in contact with the dangerous part through a barrier, through devices which push his hands away, or by using sensor devices to stop the machine when hands are put into danger zones.

The principles of guarding are also important in relation to plant layout and the movement of men and materials. Railings and toe boards around floor openings or on elevated platforms, for example, prevent workers and rolling objects from falling. Guards may be needed on forklifts and motorized dollies to protect the operators. Piping conveying hot or hazardous substances may be identified by appropriate colour-coding.

Safety principles in materials handling.   In the industrial countries a steady trend toward mechanization of materials handling has long been discernible. Yet in the 1970s a vast amount of manual lifting and carrying remained indispensable in industry and agriculture, especially in the underdeveloped regions of the world. Prevention of unsafe work practices, such as improper lifting, carrying too heavy a load, incorrect gripping or failing to observe proper foot or hand clearances, is still an important safety function. Many injuries can be avoided by proper design of the work station or of the physical activities involved. One of the most commonly reported injuries is to the back and spinal column. Manual handling of materials is the cause of a large percent of all fatal injuries and of permanent and temporary disabilities.

Factors in lifting   In lifting, the most important determinant of the force exertable is the distance of the feet from the point at which the object is grasped. Lifting force is greatest when the weight lifted is in the same vertical plane as the body, and decreases sharply as the weight moves away from the body plane. The best height for lifting, as in vertical pull, is at or slightly above the level of the middle fingertip of a person standing erect with arms hanging at his sides. Above this height, lifting power decreases very rapidly; below it, more slowly. With a load near the floor, lifting force is about ¾ to ⅘ that at the best height.

In general, "leg lift," with back vertical and legs bent, affords a slightly stronger vertical pull than "back lift," with legs straight and back bent, and entails much less risk of back injury.

Women, when measured by their ability to lift a weight, demonstrate about 55 to 65 percent as much strength as do men.

Relatively little research has been done on carrying, though it is established that a "normal" man can move about 200 metric tons (220 tons) a day through a horizontal distance of one metre (3.3 feet), or 50 metric tons (55 tons) through a vertical distance of one metre. For loads of 20 to 60 pounds (nine to 27 kilograms) a yoke has been found to be most efficient (though this may sometimes be impractical), with the hand carry, one load in each hand, the next best. For heavy weights, it is less physically tiring to carry one load a given distance than to carry two loads, each weighing half as much, the same distance in two trips.

In general, the more compact the container the more easily it can be carried. For bulky equipment the centre of gravity should be not more than 20 inches (51 centimetres) from the carrier's body, and when such articles are as big as 30 inches (76 centimetres) to a side, their weight should not exceed 20 pounds (nine kilograms).

While the above statements on lifting and carrying are by no means as definitive and comprehensive as could be wished, they represent a synthesis of the currently available data, and they illustrate the kind of potential contribution that the study of human-body mechanics can make to industrial safety.

Electrical hazards.   It is now generally recognized that electricity is less hazardous in many ways than steam or other sources of energy. The fire and explosion hazards of steam boilers and other systems involving vapours under pressure have led to many specific standards for performance and safety features required to prevent accidents, as well as strict inspection programs in most countries. Yet in spite of the advances in the control of electrical hazards, many injuries and fatalities result from causes that are preventable. The severity of electric shock is a function of the rate of current flow through the body. In general, a 60-cycle commercial-voltage, alternating current of 100 milliamperes (0.1 ampere) may result in fatal injury if it passes through the vital organs. The average values of current at which a person can still free himself from an object held by the hand ranges from about eight milliamperes to 16, depending on a number of factors.

The body's resistance to electric current is chiefly supplied by the skin, and is greatest when the skin is dry. The resistance of moist or wet skin is 100 to 600 times less than that of dry skin. The longer the current continues to flow through the body, the more serious the result is likely to be, and with high-voltage sources, only very short exposures can be survived. The effects of electric currents on the body may involve interference with breathing through contraction of chest muscles or paralysis of the respiratory nerve centres; interference with or blocking of the rhythm and muscular action of the heart; or destruction of tissues, nerves, and muscles from the heat due to heavy current. Burns from electrical flashes and arcs are deep and slow to heal.

Protection against electrical injuries   In many respects, the general principle of machine guarding can be applied to electrical equipment (*e.g.*, barriers and enclosures) with consideration also given to the conductivity of materials used and the necessity for proper insulation and grounding of all electrical fixtures and equipment. Many accidents are caused by use of switches and items improperly selected for the specific purpose, or without interlock or fail-safe features. Modern circuit breakers and ground-fault circuits interrupters (devices that cut off electrical current if the machine is improperly grounded) are important protective devices; and the significance of control of such factors as dirt, stray oil, and moisture for the safe operation of electric motors is well recognized. Air-tight and explosion-proof switching equipment (that will not release sparks into the atmosphere) has been developed for locations in which flammable gases, vapours, and ducts are present. Sparks and arcs in electrical equipment are frequently the cause of fires and explosions, and explosion-proof equipment has been developed for use against specific hazards of different types. In most countries, independent testing laboratories test and approve electrical equipment for use in industry and in the home. Such laboratories test for shock and fire hazards and may also evaluate radiation and heat hazards.

Protection against chemicals.   Many common industrial chemicals involve toxic and fire hazards. New chemicals are constantly being introduced, and safety experts generally consult the most up-to-date references for each chemical substance.

Modern chemical plants are designed and constructed to provide protection from specific hazards and for control of the effects of all possible mishaps. Personnel are protected by a high degree of safeguarding and by automatic control of processes at all stages in the flow from entry of the raw materials through packaging of the final product. This degree of automation and control is less prevalent, however, in many manufacturing processes in which chemicals in solid, gaseous, or liquid form are used for a variety of purposes. These substances may be poisonous or harmful, corrosive, or combustible and explosive.

Chemical hazards, in general, are described in terms of their biological effects (*i.e.*, their toxicity and such physical characteristics as ignition temperatures, corrosive actions, chemical reactions with other agents, and decomposition under heat). The safety engineer is concerned with the identification of exposures to chemical agents and how exposure can be prevented; and the industrial toxicologist the application of information on the biological and potential toxicity of substances. In industry, toxic materials are most commonly absorbed either through the respiratory system, from breathing dusts and atmospheric contaminants, or through the skin, or through the gastro-intestinal tract. Effects may be local, as in the case of burns and tissue damage from splashes of caustic liquids or acids or transient dermatitis (inflammation of the skin) from irritants. Systemic reactions result when poisons are carried to organs of the body where they exert their effects, such as the liver, kidneys, and bones. All organic solvents, with sufficient exposure, involve a paralysis of the central nervous system; *e.g.*, inhaling cleaning fluids has resulted in many accidental deaths. Asphyxiation may result from excessive carbon monoxide exposure.

Recommended practices have been developed for the storage, transport, and handling of hazardous and flammable materials. Exhaust hoods; air-filtering and air-monitoring systems to protect against gases, vapours, and air-borne hazards; individual respiratory devices; protective clothing to guard against splashes and spillage; and safety showers and eye-wash stands illustrate some of the devices used to prevent or minimize injuries.

Control of radiation hazards. Both very subtle and extreme effects derive from overexposure to radiation. Radiation is emitted from either the atom's unstable nucleus or its unstable orbital area and is divided into two general types, particulate and electromagnetic. Particulate (also called corpuscular) radiation is the motion of small particles that have mass and usually electric charge and that transfer energy from one part to another. Electromagnetic radiation (radio waves, light waves, X-rays) has both particulate and wavelike aspects. In its particulate phase, electromagnetic radiation is described as small bundles of energy called photons or quanta. The energy of a photon depends on the frequency or wavelength of the electromagnetic radiation associated with it. Measurement of radiation is indirect, by the ionization (production of electrically charged atoms) produced in the passage of the radiation through a medium. Cosmic radiation may be a hazard to humans during space flights, but few of these particles reach the earth's surface because the earth's atmosphere acts as a protective shield.

The problem of greatest concern to the safety specialist concerns alterations in the cells of the body induced by radioactive exposure. The serious aspects of these effects is that they can occur in any of the cells of the body, since all of the body tissue may be vulnerable. Extensive research work has been concerned with determining the lowest dose at which injurious effects can occur. The safest biological assumption is that at any level of exposure, no matter how small, it can be assumed that when a large number of people suffer the exposure, at least a few individuals will suffer damage.

Protection against radiation

While keeping as closely as possible to the principle that all ionizing radiation may be harmful, protection programs include detection and measurement, shielding, and monitoring of personnel to limit exposure to the accepted minimum level.

Radioactive sources increasingly are being used in production processes. Potential applications in industry are almost limitless. Irradiated tools, for example, can measure the wear of cutting tools, pistons, and dies; gauges can measure and control the thickness of steel, paint, or other processed products; tracers can follow fluid flow in process lines; and radiation as low-intensity light sources may power exit signs or traffic-lane markers.

A number of instruments have been developed to make surveys of radiation. The devices most widely employed are designed to determine contamination, dosage, and dosage rate. These operate variously on the basis of the capacity of certain materials to absorb radiation at a known rate, the measurement of ionization (*e.g.*, by the Geiger counter), and on the rates at which certain materials emit flashes of light when struck by radiation. Monitoring systems measure the radiation exposure of personnel and of work areas. The film badge, which indicates degree of exposure by means of photographic film worn by the person; hand and foot counters; and pocket dosimeters for continuously monitoring the total radiation, or "dose," received by the wearer, all devised for determining exposure to specific radiation such as X-rays and gamma rays, are examples of devices worn by personnel. Preplacement physical examinations are important in safeguarding the health of employees. Attempts are made in the medical examinations to learn whether or not a new worker has a family history of cataracts, deformity, anemia, retarded blood clotting, or leukemia, because these data may offer clues relating to the individual's sensitivity to radiation.

Importance of physical examinations

The safety specialist in cooperation with the company medical department is also concerned with protection in the handling and storage of radioactive materials, the disposal of residue and wastes, and the proper shielding of new installations. Comprehensive regulations covering such activities have been developed in each country.

Personal protective equipment. Protection through engineering and equipment design is generally more reliable than through methods dependent on human behaviour. The use of personal protective equipment becomes imperative, however, when hazards, revealed by advance analysis or from analyses of injuries by type or part of the body involved, are impossible to control through engineering revision. In construction work, for example, it would be extremely difficult to design the job processes to eliminate the possibility of a dropped hand tool, bolt, or a wind-blown piece of debris or building material from falling from an elevated level. Thus, protective headgear for construction workers is essential in minimizing injuries from falling objects.

If many injuries involve the eyes, safety goggles may be required, or if they are already provided, their use may be enforced when working at such jobs as grinding, chipping, or hammering. Flying particles or chips frequently occur when such work is being done. It must be emphasized, however, that the development of protective devices does not represent a basic solution of an accident hazard. More satisfactory corrective measures are those that are incorporated in the design of the equipment or the plant layout, preferably in the original planning.

The nature of injuries and parts of the body involved in first-aid cases often furnishes additional information on the type of accident hazards to which workers are being subjected. For example, the daily records of first-aid treatments in an air-transport maintenance unit for a two-year period were analyzed at half-year intervals in terms of nature of injury and area of the body involved. Lacerations and abrasions and foreign bodies in the eye were the most frequent type of injury. Most of the lacerations and abrasions occurred to hands and fingers. An inspection of the records indicated that most of the injuries resulted from misuse of hand tools—*e.g.*, the slipping of a poorly fitting screwdriver or wrench resulting in cut fingers or scraped knuckles. In addition, an important factor was the necessity for working in close quarters or around very compact assemblies. The puncture wounds were attributed almost entirely to the use of safety wire, cotter pins, screwdrivers, and steel wool. Flying particles associated with the machining or grinding of parts, the slipstream of a propeller, or the use of compressed air for dislodging dirt also constituted hazards for which protective goggles were either not available or their use not enforced.

A wide variety of devices have been developed for protection of relevant parts of the body against many specific hazards. Performance standards have been formulated for some categories, such as safety belts, devices to protect the eyes from impact and harmful radiations, rubber insulating gloves, and safety shoes. Factors determining the selection—or development—of a particular protective device include both the amount of protection provided under the various conditions of use, its ease of use,

Metal
helmets

and acceptability by workers. A few examples of other devices follow.

The familiar "hard hat" helmet worn by construction workers is designed to absorb the energy of falling objects and spread it over a wider surface through its inner suspension. In addition to impact resistance, helmets may also, for certain purposes, be constructed of material that protects against electric shocks and be fire resistant; for example, for electric linemen and fire fighters. Lightweight plastic "bump caps" are frequently used in industrial situations involving working in close quarters and with low overhead clearances. Special caps have been developed for use in general factory work to reduce the hazard of hair being caught by moving machine parts or lifted into them by static electricity. The welder's helmet with face shield is an example of protection against a combination of hazards—infrared heating from the process, impact from flying molten metal particles, electric shock, and injury to the eye from the ultraviolet rays of the electric arcs. Other types of face shields have also been developed to protect the face and neck from flying particles, chemical mists and sprays, and splashes from hot liquids or molten metals. For some operations, such as in the handling of acids or where there are high concentrations of acid fumes, it has been necessary to design combined face shields and hoods to envelop the head and shoulders, which may also be equipped with devices to provide the worker with breathing air and ventilation.

The need for eye protection in many industrial operations has long been recognized, and many types of safety glasses or goggles have been devised. These range from nonbreakable lenses for general use by those normally wearing glasses, through special designs for the specific hazards of particular jobs. For example, flying dust and small particles occur in woodworking, stone dressing, and metallurgical and other grinding operations. Some goggles are especially designed to protect against chemical splashes and fumes, and others are essentially optical filters to screen out intense light or harmful rays. One of the most recent applications is in relation to the increasing use of laser devices. Lenses in these spectacles or goggles are designed to attenuate (cut down) the intensity of light at the specific wavelength of the laser beam involved by factors of 10, 100, or 1,000.

Injuries to the fingers, hands, and arms comprise about a third of the disabling injuries in work accidents and are responsible for about a quarter of the compensation paid for injuries. The most frequently used protective device is some adaptation of the glove, but sometimes extending from fingertips to shoulder. For handling rough or abrasive materials or using edged tools, gloves of leather, or leather reinforced with metal stitching, are often used. Asbestos and wool protect against heat. Rubber gloves extending above the wrist are common in handling chemicals, but synthetic rubbers are necessary in gloves if petroleum products are involved. Specially designed rubber gloves are required by linemen and others working on high-voltage electrical equipment, and these are usually worn with an outer leather glove to protect the integrity of the insulation from cuts and abrasions. For gloves, headgear, and other items of personal equipment, proper fitting is important, and the wide ranges of individual differences in size must be considered. Also, for the operation of recessed knobs, or the grasp of lifting handles, it is necessary to take into account the increase in clearances necessitated by the thickness of protective clothing.

Safety
shoes

Safety shoes have been developed for protection in a wide variety of situations. A common form is one in which the toes and front part of the foot are covered by a steel cap, guarding against objects dropped or bumped into. Insulated soles are provided for electrical workers, and demolition workers wear shoes with additional metal shields over the instep and steel innersoles to prevent penetration by nails and sharp objects.

Some of the most complex personal protective equipment is illustrated by the items developed for firefighting and emergency rescue workers, where extremes of heat, flame, atmospheric contamination, and other forms of destructive energy may be encountered. The space-walks

and lunar excursions of the cosmonauts and astronauts have involved very advanced equipment to protect against the hostile environmental factors of space, and to provide a personal atmosphere adequate for sustaining human life and performance (see also LIFE-SUPPORT SYSTEMS).

SAFETY ENGINEERING IN NONINDUSTRIAL AREAS

Impact injuries from abrupt decelerative forces. One of the most important functions of the safety engineer is to prevent injuries resulting from the exchanges of energy beyond human limitations. As indicated previously, helmets are recommended for construction workers and athletes, and susceptible humans have been protected from many different sources of energy to prevent damage. In the field of medicine, once immunization procedures are developed and applied, the need for active participation on the part of human subjects is eliminated. If it becomes necessary to rely on voluntary participation, it is well known that safety measures are often not applied. Thus it is necessary for the safety engineer to identify the sources of energy and to reduce injury through designs that control the forces that are encountered in accident situations. This principle is of particular importance for the prevention of injury in motor-vehicle crashes.

It would be desirable, of course, to prevent crashes from occurring, and the engineer aids in this respect by providing good handling and operating qualities, fail-safe braking systems, good vehicular stability, adequate vision both day and night, controls that are easily identified and operated, and designs for highways that eliminate collision hazards. The record thus far, however, does not lead to anticipation of substantial reductions in the frequency of crashes and protection of vehicle occupants against the very high decelerative forces involved has become of great importance.

In automobile crashes these forces are dissipated in two phases, the first—the initial collision—producing vehicle damage; and the second, the collision of the occupants with the interior of the vehicle or, if ejected, with the environment. The effects of the high-impact forces on the body can be greatly minimized by restraining devices and, also, if certain well-established principles of crashworthiness are carried out. These principles have been proved to be very effective in aviation. The rigidity of the structures determines the abruptness and seriousness of the forces for both the car and the occupants. Bumper heights, protective characteristics of roofs, and strength of door locks are important, as is the padding of interior surfaces—such as dashboards, visors, and door handles. The role of the steering wheel and column in inflicting head and chest injuries is well documented, and this control has now been redesigned to absorb some of the energy on impact. Penetration-resistant windshields significantly reduce injuries to the head and face. Numerous studies have shown that multiple injuries result in most automobile crashes, but the head appears to be most vulnerable and may be seriously affected in 70–80 percent of the severe crashes.

Penetration-resistant windshields

Insofar as protective devices are concerned, the combined lap belt and shoulder strap gives the greatest amount of protection if properly adjusted and worn. According to a recent Swedish study, fatalities were reduced by approximately 85–90 percent when a three-point belt was used, in comparison to crashes in which protective equipment was not worn. In fact, no belted occupant was killed in any accident at speeds below 60 miles (97 kilometres) per hour, whereas fatalities occurred among unbelted occupants at speeds as low as 12 miles (19 kilometres) per hour. In spite of the convincing evidence for the proper use of restraining devices, it has been found that only a fraction of persons in automobiles use them when they are available. Current efforts are being directed toward developing devices or systems that do not depend on voluntary use, such as the automatically inflating airbag.

Product safety engineering. In recent years an increasing amount of attention has been given to the safe design of all types of products.

While legal responsibilities fixed by laws and courts vary, a trend was apparent in the early 1960s toward increasing the liability of the manufacturer for all the hazards associated with his product and its use or reasonably foreseeable misuse.

Defects in products may involve faulty materials, manufacturing, and packaging, and may be aggravated or brought into play by human errors in product use. Thus, the design engineer must avoid features that enhance the probability of errors or misuse. It is only logical to believe that the future will see considerably greater attention paid by the safety engineer to product safety at the stage of original design.

Educational programs in safety engineering. In the past many safety engineers have had their academic training in courses of industrial or management engineering. Graduate courses are also offered in some universities in such areas as industrial safety and accident prevention, safety engineering, safety management and administration, fire protection, driver and traffic safety, and in more general areas of safety and accident prevention. Only a small proportion of colleges and universities (about one in five in the U.S. and Canada) offer courses in safety and related subjects. The 1970s and '80s are certain to see a substantial increase in such courses and in the licensing of safety engineers.

The development of a uniform curriculum for the safety-engineering profession has been subject to considerable disagreement and debate. In part this is the result of the variety of scientific disciplines applied in safety procedures and the varied importance of different sciences and specialties in different industries, work situations, and work processes.

BIBLIOGRAPHY. Sources for statistical information regarding accidents include the *Annual Statistical Reports* of the International Labour Office of the United Nations; *Annual Global Data on Mortality*, published each year by the World Health Organization of the United Nations; and reports published by various national governments. R.H. SIMONDS and J.V. GRIMALDI, *Safety Management: Accident Cost and Control*, rev. ed. (1963), is one of the more detailed textbooks giving comprehensive coverage of safety management and basic principles governing the prevention and control of work accidents in both large and small industrial organizations. The NATIONAL SAFETY COUNCIL in Chicago publishes the *Accident Prevention Manual for Industrial Operations*, 6th ed. (1969), which is the most comprehensive manual for accident prevention in industrial organizations. Specific details are clearly presented for the safety engineering of a wide variety of hazards, such as mechanical, chemical, electrical, principles of guarding, and fire protection, with extensive bibliographies at the end of each chapter. A. DAMON *et al.*, *The Human Body in Equipment Design* (1966), contains extensive data on anthropometric measurements of the working population, and includes a discussion of working activities from the point of view of human body mechanics. The *International Labour Office Bibliography on Safety Engineering* (1970) contains extensive listings of international sources of information on safety engineering.

(R.A.McF.)

Saga

In medieval Iceland the literary term saga denoted any kind of story or history in prose, irrespective of the kind or nature of the narrative or the purposes for which it was written. Used in this general sense, the term applies to a wide range of literary works, including those of hagiography (biography of saints), historiography, and secular fiction in a variety of modes. Lives of the saints and other stories for edification are entitled sagas, as are the Norse versions of French romances and the Icelandic adaptations of various Latin histories. Chronicles and other factual records of the history of Scandinavia and Iceland down to the 14th century are also included under the blanket term saga literature. In a stricter sense, however, the term saga is confined to legendary and historical fictions, in which the author has attempted an imaginative reconstruction of the past and organized the subject matter according to certain aesthetic principles. Using the distinctive features of the hero as principal guideline, medieval Icelandic narrative fiction can be classified as:

(1) kings' sagas, (2) legendary sagas, and (3) sagas of Icelanders.

The origin and evolution of saga writing in Iceland are largely matters for speculation. A common pastime on Icelandic farms, from the 12th century down to modern times, was the reading aloud of stories to entertain the household, known as *sagnaskemmtun* ("saga entertainment"). It seems to have replaced the traditional art of storytelling. All kinds of written narratives were used in *sagnaskemmtun*: secular, sacred, historical, and legendary. The Icelandic church took a sympathetic view of the writing and reading of sagas, and many of the authors whose identity is still known were monks or priests.

NONFICTIONAL SAGA LITERATURE

Translations. A good many European narratives were known in Iceland in the 12th and 13th centuries, and these undoubtedly served as models for Icelandic writers when they set out to form a coherent picture of early Scandinavian history. Translations of lives of the saints and the apostles and accounts of the Holy Virgin testify to the skill of Icelandic prose writers in handling the vernacular for narrative purposes from the 12th century onward. Histories were also adapted and translated from Latin, based on those of the 7th- and 8th-century Anglo-Saxon writer Bede, the 7th-century Spanish historian Isidore of Seville, and other authorities; on fictitious accounts of the Trojan wars, notably, one of the 5th century attributed to Dares Phrygius and one of the 4th century attributed to Dictys Cretensis; on the 12th-century British chronicler Geoffrey of Monmouth; and on the 1st-century Roman historians Sallust and Lucan. In the 13th century, Abbot Brandr Jónsson wrote a history of the Jews based on the Vulgate, on the 10th-century biblical scholar Peter Comestor, and on other sources.

In the 13th century, saga literature was also enriched by a number of Norwegian prose translations of French romance literature. These soon found their way into Iceland, where they became immensely popular and were quite a strong influence on native storywriting. Probably the earliest, *Tristrams saga* (the story of Tristan and Iseult), was translated in 1226. Most of the themes of French romance appear in Icelandic versions; *e.g.*, *Karlamagnús saga* was based on Charlemagne legends.

Native historical accounts. Icelandic historians seem to have started writing about their country's past toward the end of the 11th century. Saemundr Sigfússon, trained as a priest in France, wrote a Latin history of the kings of Norway, now lost but referred to by later authors. The first Icelander to use the vernacular for historical accounts was Ari Thorgilsson, whose *Íslendingabók* (or *Libellus Islandorum* [*The Book of the Icelanders*]) survives. It is a concise description of the course of Icelandic history from the beginning of the settlement (*c.* 870) to 1118. Ari seems to have written this book about 1125, but before that date he may already have compiled (in collaboration with Kolskeggr Ásbjarnarson) the so-called *Landnámabók* ("Book of Settlements"), which lists the names and land claims of about 400 settlers. Because this work survives only in 13th- and 14th-century versions, it is impossible to tell how much of it is Ari's. Both books gave the Icelanders a clear picture of the beginning of their society; both works served to stimulate public interest in the period during which events recounted in the sagas of Icelanders (see below) are supposed to have taken place. Other factual accounts of the history of Iceland followed later: *Kristni saga* describes Iceland's conversion to Christianity about the end of the 10th century and the emergence of a national church. *Hungrvaka* ("The Appetizer") contains accounts of the lives of the first five bishops of Skálholt, from the mid-11th to the third quarter of the 12th century; the biographies of other prominent bishops are in the *Biskupa sögur*. Though some of these have a strong hagiographical flavour, others are soberly written and of great historical value. The period *c.* 1100–1264 is also dealt with in several secular histories, known collectively as *Sturlunga saga*, the most important of which is the *Íslendinga saga* ("The Icelanders' Saga") of Sturla Thórdarson, who describes

Themes of French romance literature

in memorable detail the bitter personal and political feuds that marked the final episode in the history of the Icelandic commonwealth (c. 1200–64).

LEGENDARY AND HISTORICAL FICTION

Kings' sagas. After Saemundr Sigfússon, Icelandic and Norwegian authors continued to explore the history of Scandinavia in terms of rulers and royal families, some of them writing in Latin and others in the vernacular. Broadly speaking, the kings' sagas fall into two distinct groups: contemporary (or near contemporary) biographies and histories of remoter periods. To the first group belonged a now-lost work, written in about 1170 by an Icelander called Eiríkr Oddsson, dealing with several 12th-century kings of Norway. *Sverris saga* describes the life of King Sverrir (reigned 1184–1202). The first part was written by Abbot Karl Jónsson under the supervision of the King himself, but it was completed (probably by the Abbot) in Iceland after Sverrir's death. Sturla Thórdarson wrote two royal biographies: *Hákonar saga* on King Haakon Haakonsson (c. 1204–63) and *Magnús saga* on his son and successor, Magnus VI Lawmender (Lagabøter; reigned 1263–80); of the latter only fragments survive. In writing these sagas Sturla used written documents as source material and, like Abbot Karl before him, he also relied on the accounts of eyewitnesses. Works on the history of the earlier kings of Norway include two Latin chronicles of Norwegian provenance, one of which was compiled c. 1180, and two vernacular histories, also written in Norway, the so-called *Ágrip* (c. 1190) and *Fagrskinna* (c. 1230). The Icelandic *Morkinskinna* (c. 1220) deals with the kings of Norway from 1047–1177; an outstanding feature of it is that it tells some brilliant stories of Icelandic poets and adventurers who visited the royal courts of Scandinavia.

The kings' sagas reached their zenith in the *Heimskringla*, or *Noregs konunga sögur* ("History of the Kings of Norway"), of Snorri Sturluson, which describes the history of the royal house of Norway from legendary times down to 1177. Snorri was a leading 13th-century Icelandic poet, who used as sources all the court poetry from the 9th century onward that was available to him. He also used many earlier histories of the kings of Norway and other written sources. *Heimskringla* is a supreme literary achievement that ranks Snorri Sturluson with the great writers of medieval Europe. He interpreted history in terms of personalities rather than politics, and many of his character portrayals are superbly drawn. Two of the early kings of Norway, Olaf Tryggvason (reigned 995–1000) and Olaf Haraldsson (Olaf the Saint; reigned 1015–30), received special attention from Icelandic antiquarians and authors. Only fragments of a 12th-century *Ólafs saga helga* ("St. Olaf's Saga") survive; a 13th-century biography of the same king by Styrmir Kárason is also largely lost. (Snorri Sturluson wrote a brilliant saga of St. Olaf, rejecting some of the grosser hagiographical elements in his sources; this work forms the central part of his *Heimskringla*.) About 1190 a Benedictine monk, Oddr Snorrason, wrote a Latin life of Olaf Tryggvason, of which an Icelandic version still survives. A brother in the same monastery, Gunnlaugr Leifsson, expanded this biography, and his work was incorporated into later versions of *Ólafs saga Tryggvasonar*. Closely related to the lives of the kings of Norway are *Færeyinga saga*, describing the resistance of Faeroese leaders to Norwegian interference during the first part of the 11th century, and *Orkneyinga saga*, dealing with the rulers of the earldom of Orkney from about 900 to the end of the 12th century. These two works were probably written about 1200. The history of the kings of Denmark from c. 940 to 1187 is told in *Knýtlinga saga*.

Legendary sagas. The learned men of medieval Iceland took great pride in their pagan past and copied traditional poems on mythological and legendary themes. In due course some of these narrative poems served as the basis for sagas in prose. In his *Edda* (probably written c. 1225), Snorri Sturluson tells several memorable stories, based on ancient mythological poems, about the old gods of the North, including such masterpieces as the tragic death of Balder and the comic tale of Thor's journey to giantland. Snorri's book also contains a summary of the legendary Nibelungen cycle. (A much fuller treatment of the same theme is to be found in *Völsunga saga* and *Thidriks saga*, the latter composed in Norway and based on German sources.) Other Icelandic stories based on early poetic tradition include *Heidreks saga; Hrólfs saga kraka*, which has a certain affinity with the Old English poem *Beowulf; Hálfs saga ok Hálfsrekka; Gautreks saga;* and *Ásmundar saga kappabana*, which tells the same story as the Old High German *Hildebrandslied*. The term legendary sagas also covers a number of stories the antecedents and models of which are not exclusively native. These sagas are set in what might be called the legendary heroic age at one level and also vaguely in the more recent Viking age at the other, the action taking place in Scandinavia and other parts of the Viking world, from Russia to Ireland, but occasionally also in the world of myth and fantasy. It is mostly through valour and heroic exploits that the typical hero's personality is realized. He is, however, often a composite character, for some of his features are borrowed from a later and more refined ethos than that of early Scandinavia. He is in fact the synthesis of Viking ideals on the one hand and of codes of courtly chivalry on the other. Of individual stories the following are notable: *Egils saga ok Ásmundar*, which skillfully employs the flashback device; *Bósa saga ok Herrauds*, exceptional for its erotic elements; *Fridthjófs saga*, a romantic love story; *Hrólfs saga Gautrekssonar; Göngu-Hrólfs saga;* and *Halfdanar saga Eysteinssonar*. There are many more. The legendary sagas are essentially romantic literature, offering an idealized picture of the remote past, and many of them are strongly influenced by French romance literature. In these sagas the main emphasis is on a lively narrative, entertainment being their primary aim and function. Some of the themes in the legendary sagas are also treated in the *Gesta Danorum* of the 12th-century Danish historian Saxo Grammaticus, who states that some of his informants for the legendary history of Denmark were Icelanders.

Sagas of Icelanders. In the late 12th century, Icelandic authors began to fictionalize the early part of their history (c. 900–1050), and a new literary genre was born: the sagas of Icelanders. Whereas the ethos of the kings' sagas and of the legendary sagas is aristocratic and their principal heroes warlike leaders, the sagas of Icelanders describe characters who are essentially farmers or farmers' sons or at least people who were socially not far above the author's public, and their conduct and motivation are measurable in terms of the author's own ethos. These authors constantly aimed at geographic, social, and cultural verisimilitude; they made it their business to depict life in Iceland as they had experienced it or as they imagined it had actually been in the past. Though a good deal of the subject matter was evidently derived from oral tradition and thus of historical value for the period described, some of the best sagas are largely fictional; their relevance to the authors' own times mattered perhaps no less than their incidental information about the past. An important aim of this literature was to encourage people to attain a better understanding of their social environment and a truer knowledge of themselves through studying the real and imagined fates of their forbears. A spirit of humanism, sometimes coloured by a fatalistic heroic outlook, pervades the narrative. The edificatory role, however, was never allowed to get out of hand or dominate the literary art; giving aesthetic pleasure remained the saga writer's primary aim and duty.

Nothing is known of the authorship of the sagas of Icelanders, and it has proved impossible to assign a definite date to many of them. It seems improbable that in their present form any of them could have been written before c. 1200. The period c. 1230–90 has been described as the golden age of saga writing because such masterpieces as *Egils saga, Víga-Glúms saga, Gísla saga, Eyrbyggja saga, Hrafnkels saga Freysgoda, Bandamanna saga, Haensa-thóris saga*, and *Njáls saga* appear to have been written during that time. Although a number of

Contemporary writings of remoter periods

Sagas in prose

Aim of the sagas of Icelanders

sagas date from the 14th century, only one, *Grettis saga*, can stand with the classical ones.

The sagas of Icelanders can be subdivided into several categories according to the social and ethical status of the principal heroes. In some, the hero is a poet who sets out from the rural society of his native land in search of fame and adventure to become the retainer of the king of Norway or some other foreign ruler. Another feature of these stories is that the hero is also a lover. To this group belong some of the early-13th-century sagas, including *Kormáks saga*, *Hallfredar saga*, and *Bjarnar saga Hítdaelakappa*. In *Gunnlaugs saga ormstungu*, which may have been written after the middle of the 13th century, the love theme is treated more romantically than in the others. *Fostbraeda saga* ("The Blood-Brothers' Saga") describes two contrasting heroes: one a poet and lover, the other a ruthless killer. *Egils saga* offers a brilliant study of a complex personality—a ruthless Viking who is also a sensitive poet, a rebel against authority from early childhood who ends his life as a defenseless, blind old man. In several sagas the hero becomes an outlaw fighting a hopeless battle against the social forces that have rejected him. To this group belong *Hardar saga ok Hólmverja* and *Droplaugarsona saga;* but the greatest of the outlaw sagas are *Gísla saga*, describing a man who murders his own brother-in-law and whose sister reveals his dark secret; and *Grettis saga*, which deals with a hero of great talents and courage who is constantly fighting against heavy odds and is treacherously slain by an unscrupulous enemy.

Most of the sagas of Icelanders, however, are concerned with people who are fully integrated members of society, either as ordinary farmers or as farmers who also act as chieftains. *Hrafnkels saga* describes a chieftain who murders his shepherd, is then tortured and humiliated for his crime, and finally takes cruel revenge on one of his tormentors. The hero who gives his name to *Hænsa-thoris saga* is a man of humble background who makes money as a peddler and becomes a wealthy but unpopular landowner. His egotism creates trouble in the neighbourhood, and after he has set fire to one of the farmsteads, killing the farmer and the entire household, he is prosecuted and later put to death. *Ölkofra tháttr* (the term *tháttr* is often used for· a short story) and *Bandamanna saga* ("The Confederates' Saga") satirize chieftains who fail in their duty to guard the integrity of the law and try to turn other people's mistakes into profit for themselves. The central plot in *Laxdœla saga* is a love triangle, in which the jealous heroine forces her husband to kill his best friend. *Eyrbyggja saga* describes a complex series of feuds between several interrelated families; *Hávardar saga* is about an old farmer who takes revenge on his son's killer, the local chieftain; *Víga-Glúms saga* tells of a ruthless chieftain who commits several killings and swears an ambiguous oath in order to cover his guilt; while *Vatnsdœla saga* is the story of a noble chieftain whose last act is to help his killer escape.

In the sagas of Icelanders justice, rather than courage, is often the primary virtue, as might be expected in a literature that places the success of an individual below the welfare of society at large. This theme is an underlying one in *Njáls saga*, the greatest of all the sagas. It is a story of great complexity and richness, with a host of brilliantly executed character portrayals and a profound understanding of human strengths and weaknesses. Its structure is highly complex, but at its core is the tragedy of an influential farmer and sage who devotes his life to a hopeless struggle against the destructive forces of society but ends it inexorably when his enemies set fire to his house, killing his wife and sons with him.

Theme of Njáls saga

BIBLIOGRAPHY. The best guide to current research is the annual *Bibliography of Old Norse-Icelandic Studies* (1964–); for earlier works on the sagas, see *Islandica* (1908–). Standard editions of important texts include *Íslenzk fornrit* (1933–); *Altnordische Saga-Bibliothek*, ed. by G. CEDERSCHIOLD *et al.*, 18 vol. (1892–1929); *Editiones Arnamagnaeanae* (1958–); *Fornaldar Sögur Nordurlanda*, 4 vol. (1950); *Sturlunga saga*, 2 vol. (1946); and *Nelson's Icelandic Texts* (1957–), with English translations. Useful general surveys of the sagas are PETER HALLBERG, *Den Isländska Sa-*

gan (1956; Eng. trans., *The Icelandic Saga*, 1962); S. NORDAL, *Sagalitteraturen* (1953); and KURT SCHIER, *Sagaliteratur* (1969). Conflicting theories of the origin of this literature are discussed by WALTER BAETKE, *Über die Entstehung der Isländersagas* (1956); THEODORE M. ANDERSSON, *The Problem of Icelandic Saga Origins* (1964); and GABRIEL TURVILLE-PETRE, *Origins of Icelandic Literature* (1953). For literary interpretations of the sagas of the Icelanders, see THEODORE M. ANDERSSON, *The Icelandic Family Saga: An Analytic Reading* (1967); HERMANN PALSSON, *Art and Ethics in Hrafnkel's Saga* (1971); and EINAR O. SVEINSSON, *Á Njálsbúd, bok um mikid listaverk* (1943; Eng. trans., *Njáls Saga: A Literary Masterpiece*, 1971). For the background of the legendary sagas, see GABRIEL TURVILLE-PETRE, *The Heroic Age of Scandinavia* (1951) and *Myth and Religion of the North* (1964). Their literary qualities are discussed in HERMANN PALSSON and PAUL EDWARDS, *Legendary Fiction in Medieval Iceland* (1970). The outstanding works on the Romances are MARGARET SCHLAUCH, *Romance in Iceland* (1934); and E.F. HALVORSEN, *The Norse Version of the Chanson de Roland* (1959). Of translations into English, the following may be mentioned: L.M. HOLLANDER (ed. and trans.), *Heimskringla: History of the Kings of Norway* (1964) and *The Sagas of Kormák and the Sworn Brothers* (1949); GWYN JONES (ed. and trans.), *The Vatnsdalers' Saga* (1944), *Egil's Saga* (1960), and *Eirik the Red, and Other Icelandic Sagas* (1961); GEORGE JOHNSTON (ed. and trans.), *The Saga of Gisli* (1963); HERMANN PALSSON (ed. and trans.), *Hrafnkel's Saga and Other Icelandic Stories* (1971); PAUL EDWARDS and HERMANN PALSSON (eds. and trans.), *Arrow-Odd: A Medieval Novel* (1970), *Gautrek's Saga, and Other Medieval Tales* (1968), *Hrolf Gautreksson: A Viking Romance* (1972), and *Eyrbyggja Saga* (1973); MAGNUS MAGNUSSON and HERMANN PALSSON (eds. and trans.), *Njal's Saga* (1960), *The Vinland Sagas* (1965), *King Harald's Saga* (1966), and *Laxdaela Saga* (1969); M.H. SCARGILL and MARGARET SCHLAUCH (eds. and trans.), *Three Icelandic Sagas* (1950); J.I. YOUNG (ed. and trans.), *The Prose Edda of Snorri Sturluson: Tales from Norse Mythology* (1964); J.H. McGREW (ed. and trans.), *Sturlunga Saga*, vol. 1 (1970) DENTON FOX and HERMANN PALSSON (eds. and trans.), *Grettir's Saga* (1973).

(He.P.)

Sahara (Desert)

The Sahara is the largest tropical and climatic desert in the world. With an area of 3,320,000 square miles (8,600,000 square kilometres), it fills almost all of the east–west oriented northern part of the African continent and constitutes the western end of the Afro-Asian desert zone. It is bordered by the Mediterranean Sea and the Atlas Mountains to the north, the Atlantic Ocean to the west, and the Red Sea (an arm of the Indian Ocean) to the east; in all, the Sahara has a 3,200-mile coastline. Its main topographical features include plains lying at from 600 to 1,200 feet (180 to 360 metres) above sea level, lowlands and depressions (the largest of these being the Qattara Depression, with its deepest point 436 feet [133 metres] below sea level), and two mountain chains—the Ahaggar (Hoggar) mountains, which rise to a height of 9,852 feet (3,003 metres), and the Tibesti mountains, which rise to 11,204 feet (3,415 metres) in Emi Koussi, the highest point in the Sahara. Only about 20 percent of the desert is sand; the remainder of the region is covered by rubble or smooth rock.

Sharp borderlines in the north and south cannot be drawn. Rather, the concept of a 60-mile border zone, in each instance, is useful. The northern zone is defined (to the east and west) by a band of salt savanna receiving seven inches of precipitation annually and stretching from the Atlantic Ocean to the Atlas Mountains, the southern slope of the Atlas Saharien (Saharan Atlas), and the Mediterranean coast. The southern border (the *sahel* in Arabic) is composed of a belt of vegetation covering "dead" (fossil) sand dunes and receiving an annual rainfall of six inches. This region contains "critical zones," where the desert is slowly encroaching.

Definition of its major zones

The name Sahara derives from the Arabic noun *ṣaḥrā'*, meaning desert, and its plural, *ṣaḥārā'*. It is also related to the adjective *aṣḥar*, meaning desert-like, and carrying a strong connotation of the reddish colour of the vegetationless plains. There are also indigenous names for particular areas—such as Tanezrouft (a region of southwestern Algeria) and Ténéré, or Land of Fear (central Niger),

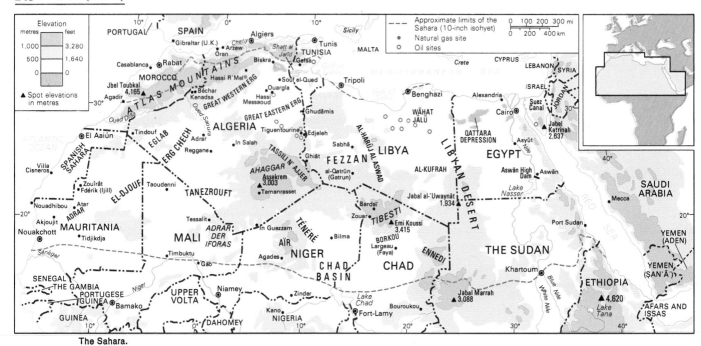

The Sahara.

in the eastern Sahara—which are often of Berber origin.

The desert is divided up within the boundaries of 11 countries. The Spanish Sahara, Morocco, Algeria, Tunisia, Libya, and Egypt contain its northern reaches, while Mauritania, Mali, Niger, Chad, and The Sudan comprise the southern section. According to their proportion of arid area, Libya (which is 99 percent arid), and Egypt (98 percent) are strictly Saharan states. (For associated physical features, see ATLAS MOUNTAINS; NIGER RIVER; and NILE RIVER).

LANDSCAPE AND ENVIRONMENT

General description and relief. The Sahara's topography is dominated by the monotony of its plains. The lack of any plant cover, the uniform covering of gravel or sand, the slight undulation, and the empty horizons evoke —even more than in the dune regions—the notion of the boundless "ocean of the sands." Even the escarpments, stretching for long distances, provide only slight variety. Wide areas, regardless of variations in the type of surface stone, are uniformly covered with a brown to black "stone skin"—the fatty, glossy "desert varnish" resulting from physio-chemical processes.

The most prominent feature of the desert is the Mid-Sahara Rise, a series of peneplains (erosion surfaces of considerable extent and slight relief) and plateaus. These form a vast semicircle, extending from west to north to east—from the Adrar des Iforas, to the Ahaggar, Tibesti, and Ennedi mountains. The rise encloses a depression, separated by the Aïr massif into two expanses of unequal size—the Jadal and Talak regions in the west, and the larger Ténéré region in the east.

Drainage and soils. Networks of valleys, originating in past wet periods, extend over the mountains and plains. An individual valley is called a wadi (oued), *kori, enneri,* or *karkur.* Many of them are so narrow as to be canyonlike, being plugged with boulder detritus in their pitch-dark depths, while those with high groundwater tables may hide thick acacia forests. The valley sands retain water that can be obtained from springs, ephemeral lakes, and water holes.

Except for absolutely smooth rock surfaces (sometimes called billiard-table deserts), the plains are covered with angular stone fragments of boulders (hamada; found in al-Ḥamrā' in Libya), gravel (known as reg in the west and as serir in the east), and sand (erg, *edeyin,* or *ramlah*). Dust and gypsum deserts also occur north of the Tibesti, their powder-fine earth being known as *fesch-fesch.* Salt soils (*sabkhah*) and salt lakes (*chotts* or *shaṭṭs,*) are very common, while salt-free depressions (*daya*s) are located

in the northwest. Structured soils of reticular pattern, similar to those of the Arctic tundras, also occur.

Although they cover only about 20 percent of the Saharan surface, the ergs (areas of continuous sands) were long considered to be a typical feature of the desert. The dunes are mainly oriented in a southwesterly direction but also acquire a southerly direction in the east and a varying orientation in the south. Their rotating movement in the north and west and their long "tails" in the lee of mountains reflect the formative influence of ground-surface configuration and of air movements near the ground. Long, narrow dunes are called *sif* and half-moon-shaped dunes, barchan. Many reach heights of from 325 to 750 feet. Within the ergs, pyramid-shaped dunes are formed. The ergs store water, therefore sometimes having grassy surfaces. In the wind, the sand "smokes" and a drumming is heard, called the Spirit of Raoul, the drummer of death.

Erosional forces have produced fantastic rock formations. In the sandstone regions, "ghost castles," grotesque "mountains," and forests of stone pillars seem tossed about in confusion. On the plains, petrified trees are found, half buried in the sand.

The movement of the ergs and the formation of transverse dunes have not yet been adequately studied. It is known, however, that wandering sand masses threaten settlements and that sandstorms and dust clouds hinder travel. Almost all ergs are rich in relics of the Stone Age, containing fishhooks on old lake bottoms, artifacts, pottery, and tombs.

Climate. Recent studies of the Sahara's climatic history reveal a series of pluvial and arid periods. In a wet stage of the Tertiary Period (from 2,500,000 to 65,000,-000 years ago), also characterized by a strongly marked annual dry season, the monsoon front lay more than 750 miles farther north of its modern line, as is revealed by the fossil soils of tropical red earth in the Ahaggar mountains. An arid period in the early part of the Pleistocene Epoch (from 10,000 to 2,500,000 years ago) was followed in the middle Pleistocene by a cool, wet stage characterized by brown loam soils. Another arid period at the end of the Pleistocene was followed by the short wet stage that occurred within the past 10,000 years, producing a growth of Atlas cedar, sycamore, ash, linden, and willow.

The transition to the present arid period took place about 3000 BC, and—except for temporary minor fluctuations—the Saharan climate has since remained uniform. Desiccation effects are cumulative and are hastened by overgrazing and wood-gathering—activities that prevent a

The ergs

natural regeneration of plant cover originating from the desert's edge.

The Sahara exhibits climatic extremes. It has the highest evaporation rates in the world—more than 304 inches (7,720 millimetres) per year at Bouroukou, in Chad—and contains the largest areas (about 770,000 square miles [2,000,000 square kilometres]) receiving no precipitation for years at a time. During the summer months, in the north where there are high wind velocities or elsewhere on mountain heights, the relative humidity (with a mean value of 30 percent) can fall to the life-endangering value of 2.5 percent, the world's lowest. Also, the highest degree of aridity—that of the hyperarid "extreme" desert—was found at Sebhah, Libya, where isolation (the amount of solar radiation received at ground level) is measured at 3,285 hours per year.

The temperatures may also reach extremes: the highest value of the annual amplitude of the ground temperature at Tamanrasset, Algeria, at an altitude of 4,513 feet (1,376 metres) was 183° F (84° C). The warmest months are July and August in the north and May and June in the south. The latter is generally hotter, while frost and ice formation can occur in the north and at high altitudes. In the Tibesti mountains, at 8,200 feet, temperatures fall as low as 5° F (−15° C). Areas covered with bushes as well as ravines register lower temperatures than the bare surface, and oases, usually located in low areas close to the groundwater level, constitute microclimatic areas.

Prevailing winds The Saharan climate is controlled by the north–south shifting of the trade-wind belt. The dry northeast wind (called the *alizés*) is directed toward the Equator, in opposition to the flow of the southwest wind (the monsoon). During the summer months, their common front stretches in a line west to east through Taoudenni, Mali, around the southern end of the Ahaggar mountains, and on through Bilma, Niger. This front shifts southward in the winter, from the bend of the Niger River to the northern margins of Lake Chad.

The winds blow continuously during the day, often laden with sand and dust. The town of Salah, Algeria, experiences 55 sand-wind days, while Bouroukou, Chad, receives a maximum of 70. The dry, desiccating south winds, moving walls of dust that darken everything, are known by various Arabic names, such as *ghibli*, simoom or *samūn*, khamsin, haboob, and *irifi*.

Atmospheric pressure changes with the winds. During the summer months, low pressure over the desert attracts the moist wind from the southwest, and rain falls on the central mountains, in a decreasing degree to the north. In the winter, high pressure over the Ahaggar mountains attracts the eastward-moving polar front from near the Mediterranean coast, bringing rain and snow to the Atlas Mountains and the northern oases. In the southern Sahara during October, the dry, easterly wind called the harmattan reaches upper Senegal.

The climate is only slightly affected by the surrounding oceans. In the west, the cool ocean current moves southward and parallel to the coast, bringing little moisture inland. In the north, however, cloud banks, fog, and dew have some effect as far as 155 miles into the semi-savanna region.

Climatic data is incomplete because the few research stations are situated in unfavourable locations, as much as 600 miles apart; moreover, most of them, in the early 1970s, had been in operation for less than 25 years. Little is known about the climatic effects of the high-altitude winds (the jetstream) or of the infrared heat rays given off by the dust particles in the dry fog of the southern interior.

Rainfall patterns occur in three distinct zones—a northern zone with rain in the winter; the tropic region, where, except in the mountains, a succession of years without rain is possible; and a southern area, with fairly regular precipitation in the summer. Thunderstorms have sharp regional boundaries and last for several hours. They cause shock waves as well as tremendous flash floods that rush into areas where no precipitation has fallen. Continuous rain also occurs and may last for several weeks, with the raindrops evaporating over the hot-air strata lying next to the ground. Dew is not infrequent, while cloud formation decreases toward the east.

Vegetation and animal life. The Sahara's natural vegetation may be divided into two groupings—that of the northern and central regions, which belongs to the Holarctic region (the biogeographic realm of the world that includes the northern parts of both the Old and New Worlds), and that of the southern region, which belongs to the Paleotropical realm (which includes the Oriental and Ethiopian regions). About 25 percent of the plant species occurring in the north are still of Mediterranean origin. Over large areas, great poverty of species prevails; in some areas there are as few as 150 to 230 species every 4,000 square miles (10,000 square kilometres), as compared to 1,500 species in Europe. The drier eastern half of the Sahara is particularly poor in species. Among the endemic species found in the higher parts of the mountains is *Pentzia monodiana* (a member of the sunflower family). Evidence of earlier wet periods is furnished by the presence of figs, olives, myrtles, and cypresses.

Plant species

The most frequently found plants include grasses, Fabaceae (members of the pea family), and species belonging to the goosefoot and sunflower families; the briefly flourishing rain vegetation of the *acheb* (a group of plants that flower for a few days) is composed of these. Adaptive plant characteristics occurring in the desert climate include expanded root systems and salt tolerance. The most frequently occurring trees are date palms in the north, doum palms in the centre, and various species of tamarisk and acacia. Huge pistachio trees grow in the depressions, and Mediterranean types of vegetation are found in the mountains between about 4,000 and 5,000 feet.

Near the high humidity of the west coast, the trees are covered with lichens, and there are also succulents. On the east coast, where very high temperatures occur, accompanied by high humidity, there is only a narrow strip of vegetation with salt marshes; mangroves are also found. In the southern part there are fog oases (where the vegetation derives sustenance from the fog) in the mountains. Deep in the interior, in valleys with high groundwater tables, one may be startled to find forests with thousands of acacias.

Most of the Saharan animals belong to the Paleoarctic region, and the desert offers them few means of existence. Their characteristic traits are dull colours, moderate water requirements, and a subterranean mode of life. Insects and mouselike rodents are the most common, and some reptilian species inhabit the interior. The characteristic animal of the plateaus is the gazelle, while in the mountain regions the waddan (*Ammotragus lervia*) is the most typical animal. Other animals occur only sporadically, or in specialized locations. The Mendes antelope, the maned sheep, and the coney (a rabbit) are found in the north and east, while monkeys and guinea fowl occur in the Tibesti region, crocodiles and one species of parrot in the Ennedi area, and bustards in the south. Foxes and fennec (small African foxes) inhabit the islands of vegetation, and fish, toads, and frogs are found in the water holes. *Gambusia* (the mosquito fish) have been introduced to oasis ponds to combat mosquitoes. Domestic animals include camels, sheep, goats, donkeys, and chickens. The interior regions are traversed by migrating species of locusts, butterflies, and birds.

(H.Sc.)

THE HUMAN FACTOR

The inhabitants. Although as large as the United States, the Sahara is estimated to contain barely 2,000,000 inhabitants. Huge areas are wholly empty; but wherever meagre vegetation can support grazing animals or reliable water sources occur, scattered clusters of inhabitants have survived in fragile ecological balance with one of the harshest environments on earth.

Long before recorded history, the Sahara was evidently more widely occupied. Stone artifacts and rock pictures, widely scattered through regions now far too dry for occupation, reveal the former presence of man, together with big game animals including buffalo, giraffe, ele-

Early human occupation

phant, and even hippopotamus. Hunters of the early Paleolithic Period (the second period of the Stone Age, characterized by the use of rough or chipped stone implements) of perhaps 50,000 to 100,000 years ago ultimately gave way to cattle herders of the Neolithic Period (the latest period of the Stone Age, characterized by polished stone implements, the domestication of animals, some agriculture, and the invention of the wheel) during the last 10,000 years, while horsemen appear in the petroglyphs (rock inscriptions) before the camel and the present aridity—the camel appearing in the last few centuries BC. Although discovered skeletal remains are few, indications suggest these early peoples had Negroid affinities; but by the 1st millennium BC, with aridity well-established, racial migrations (presumably from the east and north) had established the Hamitic-to-Semitic-speaking Eurasian ancestors of the present populations—the dominant Berber element. The historic invasions of the Arabs introduced Islām and Arabic speech but probably did not significantly alter the racial composition. Southward, increasing elements of darker peoples occur and are found in pockets in the Fezzan and in Mauritania—and in the Ḥarāṭīn a depressed class found in most oases (possibly an element of an earlier population or descendants of slaves); and, in the south, the Teda group.

The modern peoples of the Sahara are usually divided into four main groups: the Arabo-Berber peoples in the north; the less Arabized Moors of the west; the distinctive Tuareg of the south central mountains; and the Teda (also Toubou) of Tibesti and areas south. Ethnically, all are predominantly Berber, although the Teda show a Negroid intermixture.

Despite much diversity in culture, speech, and linkage, primary differences among Saharan peoples stem from the dominant modes of subsistence—whether characterized by pastoralism or by sedentary cultivation. Pastoralism, always nomadic in some degree, occurs where sufficient scanty pasturage exists, as in the marginal areas, on the mountain borders, and in the slightly moister west. Cattle appear along the southern borders with the *sahel*, but sheep, goats, and camels are the mainstays in the desert. Major pastoral groups include the Regeibat of Mauritania and the Chaamba of the northern Algerian Sahara. Hierarchical in structure, the larger pastoral groups formerly dominated the desert, owning the oases (which supplied dates and grain) and controlling the caravan trade and all movement. Warfare and raiding (razzias) were endemic, and in drought periods wide migrations in search of pasture took place, with heavy loss of animals. The Tuareg were renowned for their warlike qualities and fierce independence, their men wearing the blue litham—a strip of cloth worn around the head, covering all but the eyes—hence their name: "People of the Veil." Although Islāmic, they retain a matriarchal organization and an unusual degree of female freedom. The Moorish groups to the west formerly possessed powerful tribal confederations and warred with both Moroccans and with black-skinned peoples to the south. The Teda, isolated and less advanced, are mainly camel herders, renowned for their endurance.

In the desert proper, sedentary occupation is confined to the oases, where irrigation permits limited cultivation of the date palm (the mainstay), millet, barley and wheat, fruits (apricot and others), and vegetables. Cultivation is in small "gardens," maintained by a great expenditure of hand labour. Irrigation utilizes ephemeral streams in mountain areas, *gueltas* (permanent pools), *foggaras* (inclined underground tunnels dug to tap dispersed groundwater in the beds of oueds), springs ('*ayn*), and wells (*bi'r*). Some shallow groundwaters are artesian, but generally water has to be lifted from wells by devices such as the shadoof (a pivoted pole and bucket), worked by hand or animal. To a limited extent diesel pumps are now replacing these ancient means in more accessible oases. Water availability strictly limits oasis expansion, and in some, overuse of water has produced a serious fall in the water level, as in the Oued R'Hir (Algeria). Salinization of the soil by the fierce evaporation as well as

burial by encroaching sand are further dangers; the latter, as in the Souf oases (Algeria), necessitates constant hand labour in clearing. Overcrowding, moisture, and elementary sanitation tend to produce much ill health.

History and exploration. Classical accounts describe the Sahara much as it is today—a vast and formidable barrier. The Egyptians controlled only their neighbouring oases and, occasionally, lands to the south; the Carthaginians confined their settlements to the coast. Although attempting a few recorded desert penetrations and one possible crossing, the Romans also confined the limits of their occupation to the desert margins. The Arab invasions (dating from AD 642 to that of the Banū Hilāl in the mid-11th century) swept along the northern coastlands but met powerful Berber confederations inland; the Almoravids of northwest Africa, who ruled in the 11th and 12th centuries, drove them back and conquered Morocco. Islām steadily spread, and Arab traders penetrated to the Sudan (the area stretching east to west across Africa between the Sahara and the rainy tropics). European penetration of the Sahara did not begin until the end of the 18th century.

Attempts to solve the mystery of the course of the Niger River took J. Ritchie and G.F. Lyon to the Fezzan area in 1819, and in 1822 the British explorers Dixon Denham, Hugh Clapperton, and Walter Oudney succeeded in crossing the desert and discovering Lake Chad. The Scottish explorer Maj. Alexander Gordon Laing crossed the Sahara and reached the fabled city of Timbuktu in 1825, but he was killed there. The French explorer René Caillié, disguised as an Arab, returned from his visit to Timbuktu by crossing the Sahara from south to north in 1828.

European explorers

The French military conquest of North Africa had begun in 1830, and by 1850 the French stood on the edge of the desert. Their advance south was slow and was preceded by the penetrations of a series of European explorers, of which the most notable were those by the German geographer Heinrich Barth from 1849 to 1855, the French explorer Henri Duveyrier in the 1850s, and the German explorers Gustav Nachtigal (1869 to 1874) and Gerhard Rohlfs (1862 to 1878). The discoveries of these men and those of others revealed the main features of the western and central Sahara. After a period marked by "pacification" and military occupation by the various European colonial powers in the desert—in which Gen. François Henry Laperrine was pre-eminent—more detailed exploration took place. Radio, the motorcar, and light aircraft facilitated further investigation of the desert. While by the early 1970s prospecting and scientific exploration had greatly increased knowledge of the Sahara, vast tracts remained remote, little known, and difficult of access.

ECONOMIC DEVELOPMENT

Mineral resources. The century of colonial dominion over the Sahara, which lasted from the mid-19th to the mid-20th century, witnessed little fundamental change, except for military pacification; colonial powers were little interested in the economic development of this unpromising region. After World War II, however, France began a major program of Saharan assessment; the discovery of oil, in particular, attracted international interest and investment. Within a few years major discoveries had been made, particularly in mineral resources.

In metallic minerals, major iron-ore reserves have been found, particularly at Gara-Djebilet, Algeria, southeast of Tindouf, Algeria, where reserves are estimated to approach 1,500,000,000 metric tons, and at Kediet Ijill in western Mauritania, where reserves are also substantial. Smaller iron-ore reserves have been found elsewhere. Near Akjoujt, in southwest Mauritania, lie an estimated 27,000,000 tons of copper ore; extensive manganese deposits occur at Djebel Guettara, south of Béchar, in Algeria; and in the older crystalline rocks of the Ahaggar, Aïr, Tibesti, and Eglab regions have been found a long list of metals, including tin, nickel, chromium, zinc, lead, cobalt, silver, gold, platinum, molybde-

Oil and
gas
reserves

num (a metallic element used in strengthening steel), wolfram (used as a source of tungsten), thorium (a radioactive metallic element), and uranium. Inaccessibility, however, delays exploitation.

In fuels, no significant coal reserves have been found to supplement the small and poor-quality field at Kenadsa, near Béchar, but the discovery of major oil and gas resources followed the first strikes in 1954 near In Salah, Algeria; estimated reserves amount to some 1,000,000,000 tons. Algerian resources so far discovered are mainly near the Tunisian border (at Tiguentourine, Zarzaitine, Edjeleh, and other places) and around Hassi Messaoud, east of Ouargla. There is also a major natural-gas field at Hassi R'Mel, with estimated reserves of 1,000,000,000,000 cubic yards (800,000,000,000 cubic metres). In Libya, minor oil strikes in the extreme west led to major oil discoveries in the region south of the Khalīj Surt; estimated Libyan reserves amount to about 4,000,000,000 tons. Some smaller fields have been found in the Tunisian and Egyptian (el-Alamein) sectors of the Sahara.

As a result of geological and oil prospecting, vast underground reserves of water have also been found in at least seven sedimentary basins, mainly within sandstone formations. Some recoverable water is also present in surface sand formations.

Resource exploitation. While the iron-ore deposits at Gara-Djebilet await exploitation, those at Kediet Ijill have been linked by rail to Nouadhibou on the Atlantic coast of Mauritania since 1962; in 1971 alone, some 6,000,000 tons of high-grade hematite (red-coloured) iron ore was exported. Pipelines collect oil from the Algerian fields and convey it to outlets on the coast. In 1971, Algerian oil production totalled some 38,000,000 tons. A pipeline from the Hassi R'Mel field delivers gas to Arzew, near Oran, where it is used both for export and for local industry. In Libya, in 1971, some 30 oil centres were in production, which were connected by pipeline to coastal outlets. Total Libyan production in 1971 was some 150,000,000 tons.

Economic development of the desert, however, offers enormous difficulties and has not yet changed the traditional Sahara. Oil and ore extraction bring modern technology and improved communications to scattered locations but provide limited opportunities for local employment. While the oil revenues offer the means for desert development, the more immediate and attractive returns possible in inhabited coastal regions tend to take priority. The underground water offers possibilities for major developments in both agriculture and industry, but exploitation on a large scale would be expensive; some aquifers are heavily mineralized. Heavy exploitation would also result in progressive depletion, and hydrological changes might also increase the threat of locust plagues, such as those that have occurred in Niger.

Currently, the desert peoples have benefited little from mineral exploitation—perhaps indeed the reverse. The decline in pastoralism, started by pacification, has been accelerated by changing economic conditions and official settlement policies (for nomads are administratively inconvenient). Archaic methods and excessive animal numbers have produced ecological deterioration, increasing the drift of people to oases and towns, with resultant overcrowding and poverty. High wages in the oil fields attract labour but disrupt traditional life, and the jobs are relatively few and impermanent. Of the traditional desert products—animal skins and wool, surplus fruits, salt—only dates (particularly the *daglet nour* of the northern oases) retain much commercial importance. Salt, although still extracted and sent south to The Sudan, now competes with cheap imported salt. Industrial occupations to relieve growing unemployment have as yet made little progress. In the long-term future, as pressures build up in the advanced and overcrowded Western countries, the high costs of Saharan development may become more acceptable. Nuclear energy and more efficient solar energy convertors could be utilized to raise deep-seated water (and, if necessary, to remove the salt) for new settlements and to provide power for industries needing space and a dry sunny climate. Tourism, already beginning to grow, also has potentialities if handled with imagination. But the high costs of transport, of provision of acceptable artificial living conditions, and of technology seem likely to prevent any rapid changes.

Travel and transport. Traditionally, travel in the Sahara was by camel caravan and was slow, arduous, and dangerous. To the hazards of losing the way, excessive heat, stifling sandstorms, and death by starvation—or more probably thirst—were added those of attack by raiders. Despite all this, trans-Saharan trade along caravan routes linking oases has persisted from very early times. The principal routes were (in sequence from west to east): the "Mauritanian Way" (Senegal–Atar–Ijill–Agadir); Gao–Tessalit–Reggane–Adrar–Béchar; Gao–Tessalit–In Salah–Laghouat–Algiers; (or In Salah–Ouargla–Biskra); Zinder (or Tahoua)–Agades–In Guezzam–Tamanrasset–In Salah; Agades (or Chad)–Bilma–Gatrun–Fezzan–Tripoli; and Faya–Zouar–Gatrun–Tripoli. East of Tibesti, oases are too few, but the *darb al-arbaʿīn* ("road of the forty" [days]), west of the Nile, was a former slave route. Gold, ivory, slaves, and salt were major items of trade in the old days, but today camel caravans have almost ceased, except for a residual trade in salt (from Bilma, Niger, and Taoudenni, Mali). The main routes remain in use, however, by especially equipped motor trucks, often travelling in convoys. Year by year newly made roads extend along them and their feeders; by 1971 good modern roads extended south to Tindouf, Adrar (Saoura), In Salah, Ouargla, the Polignac oil fields, and the Fezzan oases. Beyond these limits, two main routes continue across the desert that are usable by ordinary cars. The French initiated a trans-Saharan bus service, but it has been terminated. Off the main routes a network of recognized tracks are motorable, with care; but in the open desert four-wheel drive is virtually essential, with at least two vehicles, ample spares, and large emergency supplies of fuel, food, and water—particularly in summer, when special regulations apply to all travellers. In large areas maps are inadequate, and navigational methods may be necessary.

The
caravan
routes

To supplement ground travel, numerous international air services cross the Sahara on scheduled flights, while local services link the main inhabited centres. Railways, with the abandonment of the "Trans-Saharan" at Abadla (near Béchar, Algeria), have been little developed except for the new mineral line in Mauritania. Future mineral developments may, however, justify extensions.

Prospects for the future. The Sahara, the Earth's largest desert, remains a challenge. Traditional solutions to the problems of living in it are becoming obsolete, but, although technology now offers technically possible alternatives, high costs for limited returns seem likely to delay their serious adoption for a long time. Proposals to alter natural conditions on a large scale have often been made, as by cutting canals to admit the sea to the below-sea-level Tunisian *chott*s and the Qattara Depression, but the resultant climatic benefits are at best doubtful. Greater benefit might result from a suggested scheme (were it feasible) of diverting central African rivers north into the lower areas, but the engineering problems and costs would be colossal. Suggestions for progressive reclamation by planting trees seem to have very limited application (apart from the vast scale required), for, although overgrazing and reckless cutting of trees and shrubs for firewood have undoubtedly extended the desert margins through history, the basic causes of Saharan aridity are climatic and far beyond man's power to alter. Significantly increased and varied uses of this and other major deserts seem likely to await extreme pressure on areas elsewhere, which will render the economic returns greater and more certain.   (R.F.Pe.)

BIBLIOGRAPHY

General works: ROBERT CAPOT-REY, *L'Afrique blanche française,* vol. 2, *Le Sahara français* (1953), remains the standard work, listing over 800 references. It does not, however, cover the eastern areas. Earlier standard works include: E.F. GAUTIER, *Le Sahara* (1923; rev. Eng. trans., *Sahara: The Great Desert,* 1935); AUGUSTIN BERNARD, *Afrique septentrio-*

nale et occidentale, vol. 11, pt. 2, in P. VIDAL DE LA BLACHE and L. GALLOIS (eds.), *Géographie Universelle* (1939). More modern general works include: HEINRICH SCHIFFERS-DAVRING-HAUSEN, *Die Sahara und die Syrtenländer* (1950) and *Die Sahara* (1972); JACQUES BRITSCH, *Perspectives Sahariennes* (1956); RAYMOND FURON, *Le Sahara* (1957); BRUNO VERLET, *Le Sahara*, 3rd ed. rev. (1960); FRANCOIS VERGNAUD, *Sahara* (1959), in French; GEORG GERSTER, *Sahara* (1959; Eng. trans., 1960); ROBERT CAPOT-REY, *Borkou et Ounianga* (1961); RENE GARDI, *Sahara* (1967; Eng. trans., 1970), with colour plates. Numerous research papers, reports, and monographs may be found in *Travaux de l'Institut de Recherches Sahariennes* (1942–   ).

Prehistory, early history, and ethnography: HENRIETTE ALI-MEN, *Préhistoire de l'Afrique* (1955; Eng. trans., 1957); CREIGHTON GABLE, "African Prehistory," *Biennial Review of Anthropology*, 4:40–83 (1965); K.W. BUTZER, *Environment and Archaeology* (1964); J.M. COLES and E.S. HIGGS, *The Archaeology of Early Man* (1969); HENRI LHOTE, *À la decouverte des fresques du Tassili* (1958; Eng. trans., *The Search for the Tassili Frescoes*, 1959); HENRI DUVEYRIER, *Exploration du Sahara: les Touareg du Nord* (1864); F.J. REN-NELL RODD, *People of the Veil* (1926); R.F. PEEL, "The Tibu Peoples and the Libyan Desert," *Geogrl. J.*, 100:73–87 (1942); LLOYD CABOT BRIGGS, *Tribes of the Sahara* (1960); CLAUDE BATAILLON (ed.), *Nomades et nomadisme au Sahara* (UNESCO, 1963).

Exploration: DIXON DENHAM, HUGH CLAPPERTON, and WAL-TER OUDNEY, *Narrative of Travels and Discoveries in Northern and Central Africa, in the Years 1822, 1823, 1824* (1826); RENE CAILLIE, *Journal d'un voyage à Tembouctou et à Jenné dans l'Afrique centrale*, 3 vol. (1830; Eng. trans., *Travels Through Central Africa to Timbuctoo, and Across the Great Desert to Morocco, Performed in the Years 1824–1828*, 2 vol., 1830, reprinted 1968); JAMES RICHARDSON, *Travels in the Great Desert of Sahara, in 1845 and 1846*, 2 vol. (1848); HEINRICH BARTH, *Reisen und Entdeckungen in Nord- und Central-Afrika in den Jahren 1849 bis 1856*, 2 vol. (1859–60); Eng. trans., *Travels and Discoveries in North and Central Africa in the Years 1849 to 1856*); GUSTAV NACHTIGAL, *Sáhará und Sûdân*, 3 vol. (1879–89), reprinted 1967); FRIEDRICH GER-HARD ROHLFS, *Quer durch Afrika: Reise von Mittelmeer nach den Tchad see und zum Golf von Guinea*, 2 vol. (1874); THEODORE MONOD, "Travels in the Western Sahara, 1934–35," *Geogrl. J.*, 87:534–539 (1936), and "A New Journey to the Western Sahara, 1935–1936," *ibid.*, 89:152–155 (1937); E.F. GAUTIER, *La Conquête du Sahara*, 5th ed. rev. (1935); H.P. EYDOUX, *L'Éxploration du Sahara* (1938).

Economic resources and development: CLAUDE TREYER, *Sahara 1956–1962* (1967); J.I. CLARKE, "Economic and Political Changes in the Sahara," *Geography*, 46:102–119 (1961); R.P. AMBROGGI, "Water Under the Sahara," *Scient. Am.*, 214:21–29 (1966); J. DRESCH, "Utilization and Human Geography of the Deserts," *Trans. Inst. Brt. Geogr.*, 40:1–10 (1966); R.J. HARRISON CHURCH, "Problems and Development of the Dry Zone of West Africa," *Geogrl. J.*, 127:187–204 (1961); J. DESPOIS, "Le Sahara et l'écologie humaine," *Annls. Géogr.*, 70:577–584 (1961); H.T. NORRIS, "The Wind of Change in the Western Sahara," *Geogrl. J.*, 130:1–14 (1964).

Transport: E.W. BOVILL, *The Golden Trade of the Moors* 2nd ed. rev. (1968); B.E. THOMAS, *Trade Routes of Algeria and the Sahara* (1957), and "Modern Trans-Saharan Routes," *Geogr. Rev.*, 42:267–282 (1952).

(H.Sc./R.F.Pe.)

Saʿīd ibn Sulṭān

Saʿīd ibn Sulṭān, Āl Bū Saʿīd, sayyid (ruler) of Muscat and Oman and of Zanzibar, was one of the most remarkable of 19th-century Arab rulers. He made Oman stable and organized a prosperous East African commercial empire, stretching from Mogadishu to the Ruvuma River and inland to the great lakes.

Born in 1791, he succeeded his father jointly with his brother Salīm in 1804, but their cousin Badr immediately usurped the throne. In 1806 Saʿīd assassinated Badr and became virtual sole ruler, though Salīm, a non-entity, had titular status until his death in 1821. Although Europeans frequently called him *imām* and *sulṭān*, Saʿīd himself used the style sayyid. He was never elected to the purely religious office of *imām* that all his predecessors held.

His earlier years were complicated by family and tribal quarrels, by Anglo-French rivalry in the Indian Ocean, by the expansion of the Wahhābī Muslim puritan move-

Early years

ment in Arabia, and by the incessant depredations of the Qawāsim pirates. He developed a small army and a fleet that also served mercantile purposes. His pilgrimage to Mecca in 1824 was in the nature of a triumph: it demonstrated that he had overcome both internal and external enemies and could risk absence from his own land.

At this time the eastern African coast was divided into numerous small states owing allegiance to Oman because Oman had expelled the Portuguese from them in 1698. At Saʿīd's accession Omani weakness made this allegiance little more than nominal, for at Mombasa the Mazar'i family had set up a virtually independent dynasty. In 1822 Saʿīd sent an expedition that drove them from Pemba Island. A British naval force occupied Mombasa irregularly from 1824 to 1826, when the action was repudiated by the British government. In 1827 Saʿīd went to assert his authority in person: one effect was greatly to increase the revenues remitted. There ensued a struggle between Saʿīd and the Mazar'i for Mombasa that ended only in 1837 when, by a ruse, he took some 30 of the enemy captive. All were deported and some were killed. If he preferred peaceable settlements, Saʿīd could show himself as ruthless as any Mamlūk.

Saʿīd first visited Zanzibar in 1828: he shortly acquired the only two properties on which cloves were then grown. He lived to make the islands of Zanzibar and Pemba the largest clove producers in the world. By 1834 it was believed that he intended to transfer his capital from Muscat to Zanzibar, but, until the 1840s, he divided his time more or less equally between them. His interest in East Africa was not simply to gain increased tax revenue: it was primarily commercial. From the 1820s caravans from Zanzibar reversed the immemorial system of trade by which African products had been brought to the coast by African caravans. Now the Zanzibar caravans, Saʿīd's among them at latest by 1839, actively sought ivory, slaves, and other products, and a wholly new commercial system was created reaching beyond Lake Tanganyika and into modern Uganda. At a formal level the transfer of his court and other changes are marked by the establishment in Zanzibar of foreign consulates: United States (1837), Britain (1841), France (1844). These countries, with Germany, became the principal buyers, but Saʿīd also exported goods in his own ships to Arabia and India and, occasionally, to Europe and to the United States. By the 1840s he had made Zanzibar the principal power in eastern Africa and the commercial capital of the western Indian Ocean. There was no mock modesty in his remark, "I am nothing but a merchant." Trade was his predominant interest.

Development of East Africa's coast

Throughout his reign he was under British pressure to end the slave trade. He told a captain of the Royal Navy that "to put down the slave trade with the Muslims, that is a stone too heavy for me to lift without some strong hand to help me." By a treaty of collaboration with Britain concluded in 1822, he agreed to forbid his subjects to sell slaves to the subjects of Christian powers. By 1842 the average annual import of slaves was reported as some 15,000, some doubtless necessitated by the development of the clove plantations. In 1845 he signed a further treaty with Britain, prohibiting both the export and import of slaves from or into his African dominions. His domestic slaves may have numbered over 1,000. On his death, his will freed them but not his plantation slaves.

His commercial empire had no developed system of administration. His government was essentially personal and patriarchal. He sat daily in public to settle cases and complaints. He depended heavily in his commercial ventures on Indian merchants, whose immigration he encouraged. His naval force was commanded by officers who also traded on his behalf. He belonged to the Ibāḍī sect of Islām, which, if puritanical, is notably tolerant of others. A majority of his subjects were Sunnī (orthodox), and for them he appointed a special judge. His daughter Salamah's *Memoirs of an Arabian Princess* (1886) gives an intimate portrait of his private life. He left no children by his legal wives. He maintained some 70 *suria*s, or concubines, chiefly Circassians or Ethiopians, by whom he had 25 sons and an unknown number of daughters.

Assessment

Strict in his habits, lavish in his generosity, he was an affectionate father, taking great pleasure in elaborate family gatherings. He had a patriarchal relationship with his many slaves, whose weddings he sometimes attended. He was a keen horseman and practical seaman. He died at sea in 1856 and was greatly mourned by his subjects. His will divided his dominions between his sons Mājid, who became ruler of Zanzibar, and Thuwayn, who received Muscat and Oman. Saʿīd, wrote the British consul, was "most truly every man's friend: he wishes to do good to all."

BIBLIOGRAPHY. J.M. GRAY, *History of Zanzibar, from the Middle Ages to 1856* (1962), gives a very detailed account of Saʿīd's reign in Zanzibar; for the earlier part of his reign it is superseded by J.B. KELLY, *Britain and the Persian Gulf, 1795-1880* (1968), based on a most exhaustive study of the available archives. E. SAID-RUETE (the married name of Saʿīd's daughter Salamah), *Memoirs of an Arabian Princess* (Eng. trans. 1888), gives an intimate portrait of his court, and is one of the very few descriptions of a *ḥarīm* written by a woman.

(G.S.P.F.-G.)

Saigon

The capital and chief port of South Vietnam (Republic of Vietnam), Saigon lies on the Saigon River (Song Sai Gon) immediately to the west of the delta of the Mekong and about 60 miles west of the South China Sea. The city proper (Saigon municipality [*thi-xa*], of which Cho Lon, a former town, has been part since 1932) is the centre of an urban area that also includes the northern suburb of Gia Dinh. In the early 1970s the municipality had an area of 27 square miles (70 square kilometres) and a population of about 1,845,000. The entire urban area had a population of about 3,150,000. Saigon is South Vietnam's largest city, as well as its economic, commercial, and administrative centre.

History. Vietnamese first occupied the Saigon area in the 1670s, spreading down the coast from the north, where they had been present for some 15 centuries. In the 18th century the Saigon area was the scene of bitter conflict between three rival houses—the Trinh, the Nguyen, and the Tay Son; in 1773 the latter invaded Bien Hoa, a city to the northeast of Saigon, and large numbers of Chinese traders from Bien Hoa fled to the present site of Cho Lon, modern Saigon's predominantly Chinese area. They called their new settlement Ta Ngon, which, pronounced by Vietnamese, sounded like "Saigon." As a result of this influx of Chinese the city flourished as a market centre but was not free from strife, changing hands frequently and in 1782 suffering a massacre of some 2,000 of its residents at the hands of the Tay Son. The latter were eventually driven out (1789) by Nguyen

Anh, who was able to reunify the entire country, ruling from the city of Hue as Emperor Gia Long (1802–20). Gia Long had been aided by the French, whose traders and proselytizing Catholics became present in ever-increasing numbers during the early part of the 19th century. The French assisted in the construction of Saigon's citadel or fortress, an extensive structure with eight gates and encircled by a road and a moat, providing security.

After 1789 ensued 70 years of peace and prosperity for the Chinese and Vietnamese inhabitants of Cho Lon and Saigon, a peace that was interrupted when the French, in 1859, captured the city and destroyed the citadel. Progress henceforth was even more rapid as the city became the capital of the province of Cochinchina and later of all French Indochina. Port and transport facilities and public utilities were developed, and Saigon–Cho Lon emerged as the leading trade centre of the colony.

The era of French administration

From 1941 to 1945 Saigon was administered by a pro-Vichy French colonial administration under the guns of the Japanese, who were in military control of Indochina. Following the withdrawal of the Japanese in 1945, a Communist Viet Minh administration was somewhat prematurely proclaimed in the city, soon to be ousted by British forces in the area. As the most important city in the southern part of Vietnam, Saigon naturally became the capital of the Republic of Vietnam following the division of Vietnam during the contest for power between the Viet Minh and the anti-Communist forces backed by the United States.

The contemporary city. With its boulevards, gardens, tree-lined squares, and fine public buildings—especially the Romanesque-style cathedral—modern Saigon is still clearly stamped with its French heritage. Since the departure of the French, however, the city has changed greatly due to the impact of the Indochina war and the massive influx of population from the countryside. The population has quintupled over the decade 1960–70 to about 3,150,000 persons for the greater Saigon–Gia Dinh area. It consequently has one of the world's highest population densities—approaching 13,000 persons per square mile in the most crowded areas. The Cho Lon area and the peripheral areas of Saigon have absorbed most of the newcomers. Chinese constitute some 30 percent of the population but there are also several thousand Laotians, Cambodians, Europeans, and Americans.

The climate is tropical—hot and humid—and debilitating to those used to more northerly latitudes. The average temperature in the coolest months (December and January) is about 78° F (26° C), and in May, the warmest month, it is about 86° F (30° C). Annual rainfall is heavy, amounting to an average of 78 inches per year, 67 inches of which fall from May to October in heavy afternoon downpours.

Climate

Van Bucher—Photo Researchers

Pool at the end of Hai Ba Trung, a main street in downtown Saigon.

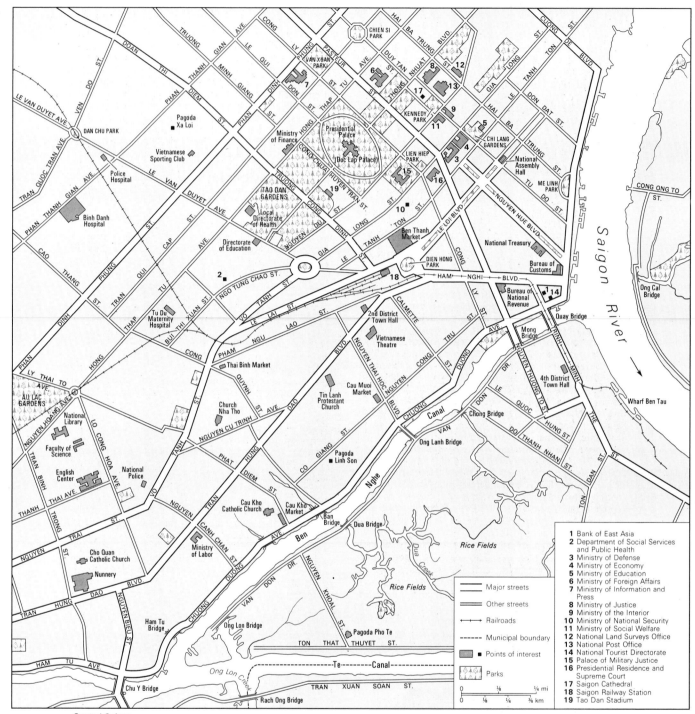

Central Saigon.

1 Bank of East Asia
2 Department of Social Services and Public Health
3 Ministry of Defense
4 Ministry of Economy
5 Ministry of Education
6 Ministry of Foreign Affairs
7 Ministry of Information and Press
8 Ministry of Justice
9 Ministry of the Interior
10 Ministry of National Security
11 Ministry of Social Welfare
12 National Land Surveys Office
13 National Post Office
14 National Tourist Directorate
15 Palace of Military Justice
16 Presidential Residence and Supreme Court
17 Saigon Cathedral
18 Saigon Railway Station
19 Tao Dan Stadium

Despite its situation as a beleaguered city, Saigon has experienced a building boom since the mid-1960s: streets have been widened, 15-story buildings erected, and large supermarkets constructed. Immediately west of the river and north of the National Assembly Hall (the old Opera House) is a region of spacious, tree-lined streets laid out in neat rectangles and containing foreign embassies and large, well-maintained residences, as well as the government palace and gardens. The riverfront is largely commercial, although a few pleasant spots and two or three remaining floating restaurants are to be found where the northern city area meets the river.

The character of the city changes abruptly as one proceeds southwest from the National Assembly Hall, down Tran Hung Dao Boulevard, toward the Cho Lon area. The streets become narrow and haphazard and the buildings a mixture of small shops, dwelling houses, and small factories. This area degenerates into a shantytown in many areas bordering the drainage and navigation canals that flow east into the Saigon River. There, wooden shacks crowd the edge of the murky, sewage-contaminated water in which children swim and women wash clothes.

The streets of the southern downtown area bustle with activity and are frequently choked with the thousands of small motor bicycles that provide the main form of transportation: public transport is almost nonexistent. Thousands of people earn a precarious living from street vending, selling a large variety of items from soap and film to delicacies such as *banh bo* (rice cake) and *hot vin lon* (half-hatched duck eggs, hard boiled).

Saigon is the major manufacturing and distribution centre of South Vietnam. Its rich hinterland produces large quantities of rice, as well as substantial amounts of rubber and sugarcane. The port is accessible to vessels of up to 30-foot draft, and the three miles of quays along the Transport river proved to be capable of handling even the massive flow of war material until the peace of 1973. Junks and other shallow-draft vessels bring in rice and other crops from the Mekong Delta.

Arterial roads connect the city with Hue, the Laotian Mekong, and Phnom Penh, Cambodia. Severed road and rail links with Hanoi also exist. The international Tan Son Nhut airport to the northwest of the city provides connections with Bangkok, Manila, Singapore, and Guam. Manufacturing establishments include shipyards, railroad repair shops, forges and foundry shops, food-processing plants, distilleries, and textile factories.

The economy of the Saigon area, however, was completely altered by the war effort and the influx of material and money from the United States. Its swollen population can, in fact, only be supported in the postwar period by continuing large scale aid.

The war-generated prosperity, evidenced most obviously by the abundance of consumer durables, such as motor bicycles and radio and television sets, will inevitably decline. Those who worked at the former United States bases and other facilities can no longer earn inflated wages that enabled them to achieve an artificially high standard of living and a spending power that enabled large numbers of indigent to survive by offering whatever services they could. Black markets in foreign currency, drugs, and stolen war supplies continued to flourish in the post-1973 period of uneasy peace.

Despite the essentially pathological condition of the economy and the American cultural impact, everyday life in Saigon continues with a surprising degree of normalcy. The city is administered by a prefect appointed by the government and an elected consultative council. Local services, such as buses and garbage collection, however, frequently break down or have to be suspended due to lack of funds or equipment.

There are two universities, the larger of which has some 40,000 students, as well as a technical institute with 400 students. Other educational and cultural institutions include a major museum situated in a fine botanical garden, the Société des Études Indochinoises (Society of Indochinese Studies), and the Archaeological Research Institute. There are 10 public high schools and numerous private schools.

Public gardens and squares, cinemas, and open-air theatrical troupes provide the city's main relaxations.

BIBLIOGRAPHY. HILDA ARNOLD, *Promenades dans Saigon* (1948), presents some particularities of Saigon and its boroughs. J.C. BAURAC, *La Cochinchine et ses habitants*, 2 vol. (1894–99), is an ethnographic and geographic study of Saigon and the western part of the Mekong Delta. See also JEAN BOUCHOT, "Saigon sous le domination Cambodgienne et Annamite," *Bulletin de la Société des Études Indochinoises*, 1:3–31 (1926), a short commentary on Saigon before the French occupation; J.M. DE KERMADEC, *Cholon, ville chinoise* (1956), a study of the "Chinatown" of Saigon, its wealth and mystery; P.J.B. TRUONG-VINH-KY, *Souvenirs historiques sur Saigon et ses environs* (1885), a presentation of Saigon in the 19th century from a Vietnamese point of view; and for statistics, the Vietnam *Statistical Yearbook* (annual).

(Q.-T.-T.)

Saigō Takamori

Saigō Takamori, a Japanese soldier-hero, was one of the leaders of the movement that overthrew the Tokugawa shogunate, which had ruled Japan since 1603, and restored power to the emperor. He had already become a legendary hero when, mortified by the relegation to impotence of his own samurai class, which he had helped to bring about in promoting the Restoration, as the final act of his life, he rose in rebellion against the Imperial government.

Saigō was born on January 23, 1828, at Kagoshima, in Kyushu. His family were samurai of a low but honourable rank whose traditional responsibility was that of serving in the feudal lord's bodyguard.

From boyhood, Saigō was distinguished by his unusual size and physique; as an adult he was almost six feet tall, weighing some 200 pounds. A giant among his contemporaries, he appeared frightening at first glance with his

Saigō Takamori, crayon on paper by Edoardo Chiossone, 1883. In a private collection, Tokyo.
By courtesy of the International Society for Educational Information, Tokyo, Inc.

large piercing eyes and bushy eyebrows, but he was friendly and unassuming in manner. With all the samurai virtues—brave, generous, and an excellent swordsman—he attracted friends and followers in great numbers. He was impatient with details, making decisions quickly, and preferring action over argument; his natural disposition was probably reinforced by his education, which included training in both Zen thought and that of the Chinese philosopher Wang Yang-ming, who espoused sincere convictions and forthright action. Saigō's personal motto was *Kei-ten; ai-jin* ("Revere Heaven; love man").

Role in Meiji Restoration. Before reaching the age of 40, Saigō had achieved prominence as commander of Satsuma forces in Kyōto, the Imperial capital. One of the inner group of decision makers in his own *han* (feudal domain), he also had wide contacts among the Imperial loyalist element throughout the country that was soon to overthrow the shogunate government. He was experienced in the complicated internal diplomacy of the time, having arranged the surrender of the fief of Chōshū to the shogunate in 1864–65 and was one of the small group who negotiated a secret Satsuma-Chōshū alliance in 1866. He also worked under cover to force the Shogun's resignation, which occurred November 8, 1867.

But the events that made Saigō a national hero began immediately after this, when the loyalists, dissatisfied with the administrative stalemate resulting from the Shogun's resignation, plotted the coup d'état that was to become known as the Meiji Restoration. Before dawn on January 3, 1868, troops under Saigō's command seized control of the palace gates. A council of notables was summoned to which the young Emperor read the Imperial rescript that was to inaugurate a new era for Japan.

A brief war ensued between the shogunate and troops, now called the Imperial forces, supplied mainly by the fiefs of Satsuma and Chōshū. Saigō as chief of staff successfully arranged for the surrender of Edo (the shogunal administrative centre; modern Tokyo) in May; he then directed a campaign against holdouts in the north that lasted until November 1868.

Saigō had completed the task as he saw it: that of insuring the supremacy of the Imperial court over the nation. Now, instead of participating in the difficult problems of organizing a new administration or even merely basking in the adoration of his countrymen, Saigō entered into retirement in Satsuma. In 1869, when the Emperor awarded honours to those who had brought about the Restoration, Saigō's were the highest granted; but he still refused to take any part in the new government.

In 1871 Saigō was at last persuaded to join the government and was given command of the newly created Imperial Guard, consisting of some 10,000 troops. With a reliable military force under their control for the first time, the leaders of the Restoration were able to take a vital step, which they considered the most daring taken

Commander of the Imperial Guard

so far: the abolition of the *han* (see above) and their replacement by prefectures. To further strengthen the government at this juncture, Saigō was appointed to the Council of State (*Dajōkan*) and assumed joint responsibility (with Kido Takayoshi) for carrying out the new program. The change went smoothly and was followed by the disbandment of all *han* troops. Thus, by the end of 1871, the government had eliminated all potential military opposition, and, in the summer of 1872, Saigō was promoted to the new rank of full general.

During this period, however, serious differences were developing over the question of introducing conscription. Some members of the government, influenced by a study of European army organization, insisted that universal military training was a necessity. Others felt that it was unwise to deprive the samurai class of their ancient monopoly on warfare. While the debate raged, Saigō, the leading military figure in the nation, declined to commit himself publicly. It is known that he privately supported the plan, and there is general agreement that without his encouragement, conscription probably would not have been adopted by the government. The question remains, however, as to why he could not bring himself to support it openly. Saigō's inability to take a stand on conscription was perhaps an indication of a deeper malaise: fearful that Japan was losing the samurai spirit, he was beginning to regret his part in having started an apparently irreversible process. During the summer 1873, these emotions boiled over in connection with the problem of Korea.

This "Hermit Kingdom" had refused to recognize the Meiji government, and it rebuffed three successive missions from Japan. Like many others, Saigō felt Korea's attitude was insulting and that Korea deserved chastisement. From his particular viewpoint, a war would also have the advantage of reinvigorating the samurai, many of whom were sulking or rebellious over the trend toward modernization that had set in with the Restoration, but who felt especially aggrieved by the conscription act.

In order to realize these objectives, Saigō argued in the Council of State for a unique plan: he would go to Korea as a special envoy, ostensibly to settle outstanding issues. While there he would contrive to behave in such a way as to provoke his own murder, thus affording Japan unquestionable justification for a declaration of war. Saigō replied to all objections that offering up his life for his country was his dearest desire. After continued entreaties, he succeeded in having his proposal approved by the Emperor on August 18, shortly before government leaders returned from a lengthy foreign trip. Appalled at the decision, these men argued the priority of internal development over foreign adventure and were eventually able to have the plan cancelled.

Furious at this reversal, Saigō resigned as state councillor and commander of the Imperial Guard and returned once more to his old home; several other high-ranking officials tendered their resignations also, while at a lower level, over 100 officers of the Imperial Guard shared Saigō's retirement. Thus, his intransigence had irreparably split the leadership of the nation. That Saigō felt impelled to take such a drastic step indicates the depth of his feeling.

A few months after returning to Kagoshima, Saigō opened his own private school, with emphasis on military science and physical training. Disaffected former samurai from all parts of Japan flocked to study under him. It was estimated that by 1877 the students numbered about 20,000. To Saigō, this was a simple private school that trained young men for public service. To the government in Tokyo, however, it was a cause for concern: the administration of the prefecture from the governor down was in the hands of Saigō's supporters, and graduates of his school were being preferred for new appointments. With samurai rebellions occurring in other parts of the country during 1876, there was real fear that Kagoshima might become the centre of a serious insurrection. In an attempt to assert authority, the government took some ill-advised steps that only inflamed the already tense atmosphere, and on January 29, 1877, a group of Saigō's disciples attacked the Kagoshima arsenal and navy yard.

The fight over conscription

Saigō's Korean plan

Rebellion against Imperial government. Saigō, who was in the mountains on a hunting trip, hastily returned. By the time he reached Kagoshima his supporters were operating the arsenal themselves to provide supplies for further military action, and Saigō reluctantly agreed to become the leader of their rebellion.

Plans were made to march on Tokyo with the vague idea of presenting grievances to the government, and on February 15, Saigō's army started out. Government forces blocked his advance at Kumamoto, and full-scale war ensued for the next six months. Saigō's old friend Yamagata Aritomo (1838–1922), now minister of war, became the field commander against him. By May, Saigō was on the defensive; during the summer he suffered a series of disastrous defeats, and by September the situation was hopeless. With a few hundred men, he returned to Kagoshima to make his last stand on a hill overlooking the city. On September 24, 1877, the government troops launched the final attack; Saigō was critically wounded and as previously had been arranged one of his faithful lieutenants took his life by beheading him. Of the 40,000 troops he had captained in February, only some 200 remained to surrender to the government. Losses on both sides were estimated at about 12,000 dead and 20,000 wounded.

Last stand at Kagoshima

In the narrow sense, the failure of Saigō's rebellion meant the end of what he had lived for. The conscript army had defeated the samurai; never again would the government fear local uprisings or samurai threats. If the great Saigō could not win, no one else would be foolhardy enough to try. But in a broader sense, Saigō probably emerged the victor. To the Japanese people, he became the apotheosis of the national character, one more exemplification of the *giri-ninjō* conflict ("duty" versus "sentiment," or "compassion") that is such a well-loved theme of Japanese tale and drama. He became a legend: as late as the 1890s, some still believed that he had not really died but was in retirement waiting to emerge once more at the proper time.

Assessment. Such a complex character must necessarily have had detractors as well as admirers. His critics have called him changeable, because he joined a government he did not believe in and then left it; insincere, because he proposed offering negotiation to Korea although he was hoping for war; undignified, in seriously proposing to have himself murdered by the Koreans. Possibly the most serious criticism is that if Saigō had truly regarded the rebellion as unwise, he could certainly have prevented it. Yet there are few who would call him a rebel: the government itself gave him a posthumous pardon and raised his son, Toratarō, to the nobility. His contemporary Fukuzawa Yukichi, Japan's great modernizer and one of its most independent thinkers, in a detailed analysis of the rebellion pointed out that Saigō could not be called a rebel against the Emperor, since there was never the slightest doubt of his loyalty, and that the government with its increasing authoritarianism, suppression of criticism, and lack of interest in consulting public opinion, was as much at fault as Saigō.

In attempting to summarize this argument objectively, it is probably fair to say that Saigō's real weakness lay in his inability to think things through logically to their conclusion; that he was ruled more by intuition than by reason. To say this is to say that he was a tragic figure, possessed of undeniable talent, who, although he had had much to do with bringing a new age to birth, could not make a complete adjustment to it in his own mind, and finally sought escape in the only way that seemed honourable to him: self-destruction.

BIBLIOGRAPHY. Of the many Japanese-language biographies of Saigō, MUSHAKOJI SANEATSU, *Great Saigō* (1942), is the only one translated and published in English. Not completely satisfactory in every way, it is nevertheless distinguished by its interpretation of Saigō's attitudes and motivations. Also useful are: FURUKAWA TESSHI, "Saigō Takamori," *Philosophical Studies of Japan*, 8:1–17 (1967); W.G. BEASLEY, *Modern History of Japan* (1963); and JOHN K. FAIRBANK, EDWIN O. REISCHAUER, and ALBERT M. CRAIG, *East Asia: The Modern Transformation* (1965).

(D.M.Ea.)

Sails and Sailing Ships

One of man's earliest inventions, the sail, which utilizes the power of the wind, was the most important means of propelling boats and ships for most of maritime history. Not until the second half of the 19th century was the sail seriously challenged by steam, and, as it faded out in the competition for commercial cargo, it found a growing role in recreation. The following article treats both the history of the sailing ship, from the earliest known beginnings up to the present day, as well as the sport-sailboat industry. For the history of the sport and the classes of boats, racing competition, and the techniques of sailing, see BOATING AND YACHTING.

HISTORY

Developments to the 14th century. *Early sails and sailboats.* The boat, either as a single log or a raft, may be nearly as old as man, and sailing craft can be traced back almost to the beginning of recorded history. Boats with sails appear in predynastic (*c.* 3300 BC) Egyptian rock carvings in Wadi Hammamat in the Nile Valley, on a scrap of Egyptian linen now in a Turin museum, and on Egyptian vases currently housed in the British Museum. Egyptian vessels altered little in basic character during the next thousand years, except for their increasing size and seaworthiness. In the earliest craft, which were made of reeds, the mast was a bipod, composed of two spars joined together at the top to form a triangle. The mast, supported by lines from the masthead to various parts of the vessel, carried a square sail, of papyrus or cotton, laced at the head to a long, heavy horizontal spar called a yard. The halyards (lines for hoisting and lowering sails) were led aft from the masthead toward the stern of the ship to act as additional support for the mast. A crew of strong rowers served as an alternative motive force, and the vessel was steered by a large oar or with two or three oars in parallel, slung over each quarter (the side of the boat near the stern).

By about 2000 BC a pole mast had replaced the bipod, and the foot of the sail, like the head, was spread on a horizontal spar. The multiple steering oars gave way to two ponderous oars hinged behind the helmsman and pivoted on the quarter. Each steering oar was worked by a tiller that projected downward from the high top of the oar. A curious feature was the hogging truss, a stout rope stretching from bow to stern above the heads of the crew, strained taut to prevent the high ends of the narrow craft from sagging and causing it to arch up, or hog, in the middle.

Egyptian seamen had habitually traded with Crete during the time Cretans dominated the eastern Mediterranean (about 1500 BC). Though the Cretans also sailed cargoes to Egypt, only cryptic scratches on stone remain to tell of their ships. The later, far-ranging Phoenicians, master seafarers of antiquity, left more explicit records in bas-reliefs, cylinder seals, on coins, and even through a crude ship model of terra-cotta, made sometime between 1580 and 1200 BC at Byblos, on the coast of Lebanon. The Phoenicians may even have sailed through the Strait of Gibraltar on trading voyages to Britain, and it is possible that they sailed around the coasts of Africa. They were able to stand clear of the coast and to sail by night, using tables of distances and navigating by the stars.

As ships developed in size from small fishing or trading craft, used perhaps in sporadic raids, they diverged into two distinct types: merchantmen and warships. This divergence was true of the vessels of Assyria, which closely resembled the Phoenician ships.

Those of the Etruscans, of pre-Roman Italy, are represented by a unique wall painting of a merchant vessel, discovered in an Etruscan tomb in 1968 and now exhibited in the Tarquinia museum, north of Rome. This vessel, which dates from about 475–450 BC, has a short mast, carrying a sail of some size, stepped forward of her mainmast. In common with later ships, her bulwarks (sides above the upper deck) are latticed and her hull deep, appearing to disprove theories that no Mediterranean craft had more than one mast until well into the 2nd century BC.

The Greeks succeeded the Phoenicians as the leading sea power and built a war galley very similar to that of the Phoenicians, with a fierce ram, a wide sail, and two tiers of oars of different lengths, rowed by men on two different levels. Roman shipbuilders took over this long, low warship, changing its general design little.

The Greco-Roman merchantman, however, was essentially a sailing vessel, not a galley, even though it could be rowed when the wind failed. The mainmast stood in the centre of the ship and carried two small triangular topsails in addition to the mainsail; a strong spar, the artemon, was canted upward at a steep angle in the bow to carry a small square sail, which made the ship easier to steer. Also typical of the merchantman was the way her curving sternpost was brought up through the deck, its end becoming a large carving of a swan facing aft. Both warship and merchant ship had two features in common adopted from Egypt: the sail halyards served as extra backstays for the masts, and precautions were taken against hogging. In these ships, however, there was a thick belt of planking along the ships' sides instead of the hogging truss. From these times until the Middle Ages, the galley, fast and manoeuvrable independent of wind, was used primarily for war; the larger, rounder sailing and oar ship carried cargo. A ship raised from the bottom of the Thames River in 1962, believed to have been built by native craftsmen in the 2nd century AD and the oldest vessel yet discovered in northwest Europe, was a Romano-British sailing barge designed for river navigation. A coin from the reign of the emperor Domitian still lay in the mast step, placed there as part of the age-old rite of ensuring good fortune to a ship.

The Viking ships. By at least the 7th century AD a new phase of ship design was opening in northern Europe, a phase that can be traced by the remains of large, open rowboats, such as the Nydam boat found near Flensburg in Schleswig (1863) and others like it discovered elsewhere in Scandinavia. These boats had only a rudimentary keel and resembled the 7th-century Saxon vessel, found buried with a hoard of treasure in a mound at Sutton Hoo in England. In the 8th century, as a series of carvings on the Swedish island of Gotland attest, the sail grew from a scrap of cloth into the full square sail that, striped red and blue or plain bloodred, became a flamboyant warning on many a coast. This sail was loose-footed; that is, it was not attached to a spar at the foot.

The true Viking ship, which was raiding the coast of Europe by the end of the 8th century, was of similar shape and construction to the Nydam boat but immensely improved. Evidence for this comes from two ships found in Norway, one at Gokstad in 1880 and the other at Oseberg in 1903, after being buried for 1,000 years. The 70-foot- (21-metre-) long Oseberg galley with shallow draft and intricate carving may well have been a pleasure craft for sheltered waters. The 78-foot (24-metre) Gokstad ship, however, was a typical war vessel and may have taken part in raids on the British coast in the 9th century.

The Gokstad ship was clinker-built—that is, with overlapping 16-inch- (41-centimetre-) wide oak planks (strakes). Because the lower eight strakes were lashed in place, rather than bolted to the ribs, they had elasticity and give in a seaway. The mast was stepped, nearly in the centre, in a solid block shaped like a fish. Like all Viking craft it was double ended with bow and stern rearing up in a graceful sweep to a high stem or sternpost and probably to a figurehead of a fierce snake or dragon, which could be removed when necessary to avoid risk of damage. The ship was rather flat bottomed for easy landing on a beach, even though the Norsemen had by now evolved a definite keel. A long, massive rudder had its pivot on the starboard or "steer-board" quarter (right-hand side) and was swung by a short tiller, placed at a right angle to the oar. The holes for 16 oars, cut below the gunwale (upper edge of the ship's side) along each side, were ingeniously shaped like keyholes and could be closed by shutters when under sail. Outboard of the gunwale was a rack in which the crew's round shields were

Egyptian sailing vessels

Merchantmen and warships

The Gokstad ship

placed for a harbour display of overlapping black and yellow. In time the Vikings devised the bowline, a line leading forward to pull the weather edge of the sail around to enable the ship to sail off the wind.

The discovery, at the entrance to Roskilde Fjord, north of Copenhagen, of five double-ended ships has greatly increased our knowledge of these craft. The five ships had been filled with stones and skillfully sunk to block the narrow channel against some invader, probably in the 10th century. Although all were built roughly in the same pattern, no two of the five vessels were exactly alike in size, type, or age. The largest of the five, built more for sailing than rowing, is thought to have been a 10th-century troop transport. Smaller vessels probably sailed with marauding fleets up the Thames and the Seine to plunder London and Paris or up the Tagus to Lisbon or even into the Mediterranean. One stout ship was deep, with high sides and an open hold. Had she been manned from Norway instead of Denmark, she might have made the ocean voyages to the Faeroe Islands, Iceland, Greenland, and perhaps to the mainland of North America.

Medieval developments. The ships that carried William the Conqueror's army to England in 1066, as shown in the more or less contemporary Bayeux tapestry, are hardly distinguishable from Viking vessels of two centuries earlier. In northern European waters, ships continued to be clinker-built and double ended, with a single, central mast, for another 300 years. Some improvements were introduced, however, in the form of "castles," or fighting towers, at either end, at first temporary (for war only) and later permanent. Also a "fighting top," a square box from which men could fire or drop missiles on an enemy craft, was added to the mast. Its weight, together with the pull of the large square sail, made it necessary to add extra stays and shrouds to the standing rigging. At the start of the 13th century, or perhaps earlier, northern ships received a bowsprit, a large spar projecting over the stem (the timber to which the ship's sides are joined at the bow) to hold the bowline farther out and give the sail greater effect. Even so, the outsize oars, known as sweeps, were retained by every vessel as a standby precaution.

In the Mediterranean, where commerce was far ahead of that in northern regions, ships were better built and much larger in size. Instead of the overlapping clinker construction, Mediterranean ships, both Arab and European, had their planks fitted together edge to edge (carvel construction), nailed to the ribs, and caulked with pitch. By the mid-12th century, Genoese ships had two decks, three-deckers appearing in the late 13th century. Two masts were used, the forward, taller and slightly heavier and carrying three lateen-rigged, triangular fore-and-aft sails to two for the aftermast. The best sails, made of strong cotton or linen canvas, were of Genoese or Marseilles manufacture. Often, instead of a single castle at the stern, Italian ships had two castles, one atop the other. A combination galley and sailing ship, the *tarida*, was widely used throughout the high Middle Ages. One reason for the continued survival of the galley, in the face of competition from the sail, was that the large crew of a galley made it formidable in the event of attack by pirates.

Yet a significant advance in ship design, the stern rudder, first appeared not in the Mediterranean but in the north. The earliest picture of a stern rudder with the gudgeons (metal eyes or sockets attached to the sternpost to receive the rudder pintles, or pins) to form a hinge appears on an English civic seal dated 1200. At first the new rudder had to be curved to conform to the curving sternpost; later, ships were built with straight rudders. Despite the spread of the innovation in the north (a German seal shows a stern rudder in 1242), it did not appear in the Mediterranean until the 14th century. Possibly the larger Mediterranean ships, some of which were over 100 feet long in the mid-13th century, could be handled better with the existing technique of a pair of lateral rudders, one on either side, near the stern. In all other respects the Mediterranean shipbuilders remained in the vanguard of the world, their only serious competition being the Chinese junks, which Marco Polo admired.

Sailboat development (15th–17th century). At the start of the 15th century, three-masted ships were common in the Mediterranean, while in northern European waters the single mast remained the rule. But during the course of this century, the three-master became universal, with a short foremast forward of the tall mainmast and a mizzenmast aft. The foremast at first carried a single lateen sail; later, a square spritsail was rigged under a pole extending from the ship's bow, which made it practicable to move the foremast farther aft and increase its height. The additional shrouds (lines fixed to the sides of the ship to brace the mast) that were necessary found a secondary use: ratlines (short horizontal lines secured between shrouds) provided rope ladders, which replaced the wooden ladders used to climb the mast.

At this time a new fashion was being set by the carracks, the deep, broad vessels of Venice, Genoa, and Spain. These carracks had a high poop (stern) and a still higher forecastle thrusting out over the bow. Competing with the Italian and Spanish carracks, as the century progressed, were the simpler and lighter Portuguese caravels. Originally a fishing vessel, the caravel was not so deep and broad as a carrack. Named for the carvel method of construction, the caravel helped to popularize the fore-and-aft, lateen-rigged sail, which permitted a ship to take advantage of a beam wind. The two types of sails were often used in combination in an effort to allow for changing winds, but opinions varied on how the two sails should be mixed. One favoured rig had square sails on foremast and mainmast, possibly with a square topsail above the mainsail and the high, pointed lateen on the mizzen. Another class of caravels, however, kept to a complete lateen rig.

A few of the larger ships could carry three sails on the mainmast: from bottom to top, the course, the topsail, and the topgallant. Four-masters were also built, with square sails on the foremast and lateens on the other three masts.

There was now a standard method of shortening sail. A square sail was no longer reduced in area by reefing (folding and tying). Instead, a length of sailcloth called a bonnet, which had been added to its foot, could be unlaced and taken off. For increasing the sail area in light winds, there was a narrower strip called the drabbler, which could be laced to the bonnet. Both bonnet and drabbler remained in use until the 18th century.

Along with revolutions in the design, size, and rigging of ships came improvements in navigational equipment, notably the cross-staff, a 16th-century device that virtually replaced the astrolabe as a means of finding the altitude of a star or the sun and therefore the latitude of the ship. The mariner's compass had long been known in various forms. As early as AD 868 Norsemen are reputed to have used a lodestone (magnetic iron ore) compass during a voyage to Iceland. In the 13th century a lodestone that floated on a circular piece of wood in a bronze bowl was used in Scandinavian waters. Meantime, the instrument had arrived in the Mediterranean in the 12th century. In the latter part of the 15th century, the Portuguese sailed their caravels southward down the African coast and around the Cape of Good Hope, while Columbus sailed similar Spanish ships across the Atlantic.

Guns, galleons, and galleasses. The 16th century ushered in the era of the large carrack, which was followed by the galleon. In the early part of the century, there was an outburst of rivalry among six countries in the building of big carrack-type ships, with their triangular, overhanging forecastles. The "Santa Anna" of the Knights of Malta, the "São João" of Portugal, the "Great Michael" of Scotland, the French "Grand François," the Swedish "Stora Karfvel," and the English "Henri Grâce à Dieu" were all launched within a few years of one another.

The "Great Michael," built by James IV and launched in 1511, was 200 feet (61 metres) in length and 36 feet (11 metres) in beam. Its building exhausted the timber of Fifeshire, and extra lumber was brought from Denmark. Its canvas and cables came from France and its anchors from Spain. Its sides were protected along the waterline by a stout belt of timber five feet (1.5 metres) in thick-

---

Marginal notes:

"Castles," or fighting towers

Three-masted ships

Improvements in navigational equipment

ness, an odd predecessor of the blisters that were added to the sides of British warships in World War I. Its crew is said to have included 300 mariners, 120 gunners, and 1,000 men-at-arms. After brief service at sea, when the king was killed in 1513, it was sold to the French.

Iron guns, sometimes lethal to their crews when they exploded, had been carried on board ships as early as the 14th century and were later placed in the forecastle and sterncastle. In the early 1500s an abrupt and universal change occurred. The clumsy iron guns gave way to heavy brass or bronze cannons, and these were mounted along the side to fire through holes cut in the ship's sides. The development of gunports is traditionally ascribed to a French shipbuilder in about 1501, and the idea was adopted in the "Great Michael," the builders of which lined its gunports with leather as precaution against fire.

Henry VIII laid down his "Henri Grâce à Dieu," known as the "Great Harry," in 1512. The first four-masted ship to be launched in England, it set square sails on the foremast and mainmast and lateen sails on the mizzen and bonaventure (the two masts aft of the mainmast). It had topsails on all of its masts and topgallants on the first three masts. After a major refit in 1540, it took gun mounting a step further by arranging some of its guns in two tiers, firing through ports in the side.

In the Mediterranean, oared galleys, with lateen sails as auxiliaries, continued to be used; but these were never a success in the rough, northern waters, although the English navy retained a few into the 16th century. The Spanish Armada (1588) included no galleys, but there were four galleasses, a hybrid type. More seaworthy than the galley, the galleasse supplemented a crew of rowers with two or three high-peaked lateen sails.

The galleon The galleon, which seems to have originated in Spain, was slimmer than the carrack that it was built to replace. Decked in a series of steps at each end and mounting high at the stern, it had a long, projecting beakhead, which was largely composed of open gratings instead of the carrack's overhanging forecastle. It may have looked top-heavy with the towering stern; and, though its weaknesses became apparent to the Spaniards after the defeat of the Armada, it did much ocean voyaging. In the 16th and early 17th centuries the Spaniards, identifiable from afar by the large pictures of saints on their sails, as were the Portuguese by their huge crosses, brought gold and silver from the New World in "plate fleets" composed of such vessels. The whipstaff, a vertical lever that was pivoted through the poop deck, was invented to control the tiller. Though a clumsy contrivance by later standards, it greatly facilitated steering and lasted until early in the 18th century.

Another idea, originated by the English captain John Hawkins, was more effective. He had the topmast made separate from its lower mast, secured with a cap and supported by trestletrees (two horizontal timber cross-pieces fixed fore and aft of the mast to support the crosstrees, which spread the shrouds at the upper section of a mast and the top, a platform at the lower crosstrees). Now topmasts could be struck and sent down on deck in threatening weather, making taller masts and more sails feasible. A Swedish warship of this era, the "Wasa" of 1627, which sank on first hoisting sail, was salvaged in astonishingly good state from the mud of Stockholm Harbour in 1962. It is now on view as a unique example of a 17th-century ship.

By the 17th century all English warships were rigged with square topsails on the mizzen. In addition to the regular spritsail under the bowsprit, a spritsail topsail was rigged on a small mast at the end of the bowsprit. A different kind of spritsail, one supported by a diagonal spar called a sprit and rigged as a fore-and-aft sail on the mainmast—in addition to the regular square sail—appeared on some coastal vessels. At the opposite extreme was the rigging of the huge "Sovereign of the Seas" of Charles I of England in 1637. Some idea of its size can be gathered from the fact that six men could stand upright inside the great lantern at its stern. The "Sovereign of the Seas" had three masts instead of the usual four. In order to spread something like the same amount of canvas on

one less mast, she was rigged for a new sail above her topgallants on foremast and mainmast. This new sail was called a royal, possibly because it was set where the flagstaff for the royal standard had previously been placed. But royals were not seen again until they reappeared as fair-weather sails in men-of-war at the end of the century.

The junk *Sailing ships of the East.* The Chinese junk, unwieldy and strange as it appears to Western eyes, is one of the most efficient vessels under sail; it has been said that it represents the ultimate in aerodynamic efficiency. Nobody knows how long junks have sailed the Far Eastern seas, but they were making prosperous voyages to India in the 9th century and for a time controlled the Indian Ocean. Through the Middle Ages Chinese merchantmen sailed regularly to Indonesia, Ceylon, India, the east coast of Africa, and even to Aden (Yemen). A good demonstration of the junk's seaworthiness was an 1848 voyage from China all the way to Boston, New York, and London.

There are, or were, upward of 70 different types of junks, oceangoing and riverine, varying in hull form and other respects. The number of masts vary from one to five (five-masters are uncommon, however); all share the same general characteristics. Usually, junks are high-sterned, with outthrust bows. There is no keel, but the massive rudder, often mounted in a slot so that it can be raised and lowered, is deep enough to act as a centreboard to reduce drifting to leeward. The unique feature of the junk was the watertight compartment. The junks of the Huang Ho were built with four of these compartments, but the idea was not adopted in the West for centuries. A curiosity is the square lugsail. It is composed of a series of panels, of matting or linen, each panel stiffened and kept flat by a bamboo batten, which extends all the way across the sail. Each panel has its own parrel, or collar, around the mast and its own sheet leading to the mainsheet. Thus, all parts of the sail, from foot to head, can be close-hauled, enabling the junk to sail very close to the wind. These bamboo battens also act on the principle of a Venetian blind. When the halyard is let go, the panels fold up on top of one another, so that shortening sail is a matter of minutes for a practiced hand. Between one-third and one-sixth of each sail is forward of its mast. The mast itself is unsupported, having no stays or shrouds.

Invention of the compass The Chinese invented the lodestone compass long before the 11th century, but by 1085 they were using the floating needle. This was described by the author Shen Kua in his book of that year on the magnetic compass. The dry compass (with pivoting needle) was also devised in China, during the 13th century, but was not in general use until it was reintroduced in the 16th century by the Portuguese and the Dutch.

The Japanese junk, now rapidly passing from the sea, is different from the Chinese in nearly every respect. There is only one type, squat and heavy. The sails, made of matting or cloth, have no bamboo panels but are loose-footed and square. The rudder, while it can also be raised or lowered, is not enclosed but works in a well, open to the sea. Strangely enough, the Japanese junk has more than a hint of the old Roman artemon in the short foremast canted up in the bows to take the square sail.

To the south and southwest of Japan, in the Pacific and Indian oceans, there were and are myriad types of craft, each built to suit local conditions, and a host of varied rigs. There are mixtures of lateen and square sails, sails in parallelograms, sails like lobster's claws or leaves, and sails in inverted triangles. Outstanding among these craft for their ocean sailing were the big canoes of the Polynesians, who made voyages of several days' duration to other islands 200 to 300 miles (300 to 500 kilometres) distant. They are credited with having a corps of pilots trained in weather lore and the courses of the heavenly bodies for their own mysterious kind of navigation. Remarkable as these craft were, all that the West has borrowed from them—and that only recently—has been the modern catamaran and trimaran.

18th-century and later developments. *East Indiamen and frigates.* During the 17th and 18th centuries the

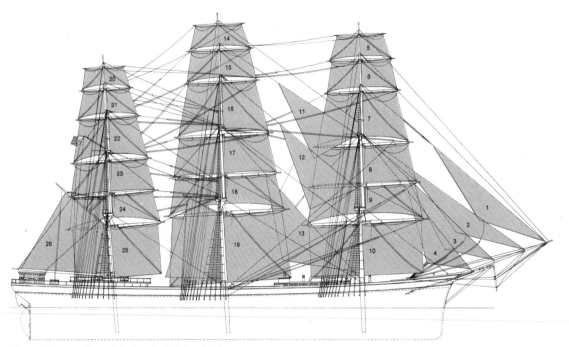

Figure 1: *Spars, sails, and rigging of a full-rigged ship.*
(1) Flying jib. (2) Outer jib. (3) Inner jib. (4) Jib. (5) Fore skysail. (6) Fore royal. (7) Fore topgallant sail. (8) Fore upper topsail. (9) Fore lower topsail. (10) Foresail. (11) Main royal staysail. (12) Main topgallant staysail. (13) Main topmast staysail. (14) Main skysail. (15) Main royal. (16) Main topgallant sail. (17) Main upper topsail. (18) Main lower topsail. (19) Mainsail. (20) Mizzen skysail. (21) Mizzen royal. (22) Mizzen topgallant sail. (23) Mizzen upper topsail. (24) Mizzen ower topsail. (25) Crossjack. (26) Spanker or driver.

finest merchantmen of six European countries—Portugal, France, the Netherlands, England, Denmark, and Sweden—traded in rivalry in India and the East Indies. Ships of the Dutch and British East India companies, similar in appearance, were built like men-of-war, apart from the fuller lines for their cargo carrying, which made them the "fat East Indiamen." They were well armed; English ships, for example, had more than 20 guns. These were used to cope with the normal hazards of Algerian and Malabar corsairs as well as rival European ships. The Dutch Indiaman "Amsterdam" (1749), found in the sand on an English south coast beach in 1970, was 150 feet (46 metres) in length and carried 56 guns.

Though the East Indiamen gave good service, they were not very speedy; the swiftest sailer of the era was a new class of warship, the frigate, designed for scouting, escort duty against privateers, and commerce raiding. Smaller, lighter, speedier than the massive ships of the line, frigates originated with the Spanish Navy; they were copied and redesigned by the French, and these French frigates were in turn copied by the British and U.S. navies. The first U.S. frigates were built during the Revolutionary War. A later class, which included the renowned "Constitution," still in existence at Boston, came into service in 1797. They were intended for the protection of American merchant ships in the Mediterranean against the piratical xebecs (or chebecs) of the Bey of Algiers and later of Tunis. The xebecs were very swift craft of shallow draft with high, triple lateen sails.

Refinements of hull and rigging. From 1765 to 1812, within the span of the active life of Nelson's flagship, "Victory," large British men-of-war underwent a number of changes, which were copied in other navies. Forecastle and quarter deck had been linked by temporary gangways above the main deck guns; these gangways were gradually widened into a permanent decking, all but covering the waist of the ship. Bulwarks were added, low at first but heightened later. Instead of the old, beaklike prow, ships were given round bows, which allowed more guns to be brought forward and also helped to reduce the amount of water coming on board in a heavy sea. The square shape of the stern was altered to a curve, which allowed guns to be fired from each quarter, and, later, the curve became an ellipse. The stern gallery (balconies across the stern and around the quarters) returned after vanishing in Elizabethan times. The elaborate decorations of the 17th century nearly disappeared; only some gilding around the figurehead and fancy scrollwork at the stern remained. A method was found, at last, to protect the ship's bottom from the teredo worm by sheathing it below the waterline with copper, fastened by copper nails. The sheathing also had the effect of reducing marine growths on the bottom and so gave the ship more speed. This practice proved so successful that it was speedily adopted by merchant ships in the tropics.

Sails were undergoing a transformation that had begun in the 16th century, when the jib, a triangular headsail, was first used in some light craft. The staysail, also triangular and set on a stay (a line led forward and down from the upper part of a mast—to pull against the backstay to help support the mast—and set between masts) appeared in Dutch and then in British vessels late in the next century. Jibs began to be rigged on a jibboom (a spar extending from the bowsprit to which the foot of the jib was secured), at first on smaller ships, later by the big three-deckers. The jib's advantage over the old spritsail was that it was much easier to handle in heavy weather, and also it is a fore-and-aft sail. The pull of jib and fore-staysail on the bowsprit was countered by a line or chain, the bobstay, leading from the tip of the bowsprit down to the ship's stem at the waterline. Another step was an overdue alteration to the lateen mizzen. Because the part of the sail forward of the mast had little effect, it was cut off. Eventually the cumbersome lateen yard was replaced with a gaff, and the sail, increased in length over the stern, was set on a boom to become the spanker or, as it was named in men-of-war, the driver.

For more than a century, ships had reefed or shortened sail by the use of reef points. These short, light lines, hanging down across both sides of the head of the sail (or across the foot, if a fore-and-aft sail), reefed it to smaller size by tying it up to its yard (or down to its boom, if fore-and-aft). In time, in place of the bonnet, reef points were added to the courses, the lowest sails. In 1805, however, a British naval captain maintained that if sails were reefed at the foot instead of, or as well as, at the head, it would save time and labour and would lessen risks to men's lives. Sails made to his specifications and

New kinds of sail

tested in a dozen naval and merchant ships brought enthusiastic reports but failed to convince the Admiralty. Later, however, reef points were lowered among Western shipping.

In the 19th century the square-rigged ship had reached maturity. The mizzen had been lengthened, by addition of a mast, to take a topgallant sail, and in light winds royals were set above the topgallants. A pair of the light, additional studding sails (stuns'ls), extending wide of the mainsails on either side could be set on foremast and mainmast in a man-of-war. Merchant captains were even more ambitious. The mass of canvas they might spread when the wind served could verge on insanity. The most extravagant ever was probably the East Indiaman "Essex," with its capability of setting 63 sails. Taking only the mainmast and starting with the lowest sail, it could set eight sails: the course or mainsail, topsail, topgallant, royal, skysail, cloudscraper, moonraker, and stargazer; in addition, each of these, up to the skysail, could be extended on each side with studding sails. By 1880, however, stuns'ls had gone out of fashion, along with several of the topmost sails.

Schooners, clippers, and Cape Horners. Though the forerunners of the schooner were probably Dutch craft of the 17th century, the type was developed by American shipbuilders into a vessel designed for speed. The fame of these slim, fast schooners, called Baltimore clippers because the Baltimore yards specialized in them, spread quickly. As freighters down the American east coast, as light naval cruisers, as privateers, as fishing vessels on the Grand Banks, or as smugglers or slavers, they soon came into their own. Most of these Baltimore clippers had two masts and were rigged as topsail schooners, having two jibs, gaff-rigged foresails and mainsails, a square foretopsail, and a gaff main-topsail. Others were rigged as brigs, brigantines, and hermaphrodite brigs—all of which are square-rigged on the foremast, with varying combinations of square or fore-and-aft sails, or both, on the mainmast (see Figures 1 and 2).

Soon shipbuilders, notably at Boston, turned to designing larger ships with more speed. These were the three-masted, ship-rigged American clippers that came into service in time for the California gold rush of 1849. Ship after ship was crowded with those who preferred the sea passage round Cape Horn to a hazardous overland jour-

ney. Two years later (1851) gold was discovered in Australia. The demand for shipping rocketed to such heights that British shipowners placed orders with yards in the United States.

One eventual result was the tea clipper, first American-and then British-built. The British tea clippers were rather smaller than the American clippers and had a narrower beam; their registered tonnage was in most cases a little more than half that of the American ships. But they were just as fast and, in some cases, faster. Since the first consignment of the yearly crop of tea gained high prices and a rich bonus on the London market, speed was more important than the amount of cargo. The captains drove the ships hard. Their additional canvas in suitable weather went far beyond the normal style of stuns'ls, with such oddities as new-style bonnets, water sails, save-alls, and jib o' jibs. They made astonishingly good passages. The "Ariel," "Taiping," and "Serica," in their remarkable race of 1866, took 98 days from Foochow to London, while the "Fiery Cross" and "Taitsing," which had started later, took 101 days. The first three ships were in the English Channel together, and they sailed up the Thames at 13 knots (nautical miles per hour) to dock on the same tide. The "Fiery Cross," however, had made the fastest day's run of all five, logging 328 nautical miles in a single 24 hours. The most famous of all clipper ships, the "Cutty Sark," is now permanently in dock at Greenwich, England.

But the brief day of the great American clipper ship was over and was fading fast for the smaller English tea clippers. These were indeed the last days of sail, for improved steamships and the opening of the Suez Canal in 1869 drove the clipper from the China tea trade in the 1870s. Instead, a number began carrying wool from Australia, even though the trade was already flourishing with large, iron-hulled ships that had been specially built for the purpose. Although these iron ships were fast, they were straight stemmed and less graceful than the clippers. They had greater length and were able to carry huge cargoes but were slim enough to move easily through the water. Although they carried about the same square footage of sail as a clipper, modern improvements enabled them to get along with much smaller crews. Later vessels were still longer and rigged as four-masted ships or, as in the case of the typical Australian grain ship, a bark, with a fore-and-aft rig on the aftermast or jiggermast.

When wool cargoes dwindled after 1890, many ships were altered and others built to bring Chilean nitrate around Cape Horn. Others fetched guano from Peru, which, as there were no loading facilities, meant backbreaking work for their crews. At the height of the nitrate trade, the harbours of Iquique, Chile, and Callao, Peru, each held a mass of ships—German, British, American, and French. Prominent among these were the fine ships of the Flying P line of Hamburg, such as the "Padua" and "Pamir," which ran a regular service with nitrate cargoes to Europe, each ship making three round voyages every two years. The opening of the Panama Canal in 1914 and the invention of artificial fertilizers killed the nitrate and guano trade for sailing vessels, and World War II finally swept away all but the last stragglers, which served in the Australian wheat trade for a few more years.

Novel developments. Throughout the last century of commercial sail, steam's ever-growing threat forced shipowners to simplify the work in big ships. Topsails and topgallants were split into upper and lower sections for easier handling, and the old chain slings holding the lower yards were replaced by new patent trusses, which allowed the yard to be braced farther aft so that the ship could sail nearer the wind without the yards fouling the shrouds. Bulky, short-lived manila hemp gave way to steel wire for stays and shrouds; iron replaced wood for the ships' hulls and, in its turn, was replaced by steel. The greatest gain, however, came from steam itself. Steam power was adopted for the capstan, for raising and lowering the sails, for weighing anchor, and for assisting the steering gear.

The largest of all sailing vessels that had no form of propulsion other than her sails was the great steel, full-

The tea clipper

Simplifying the big sailing ships

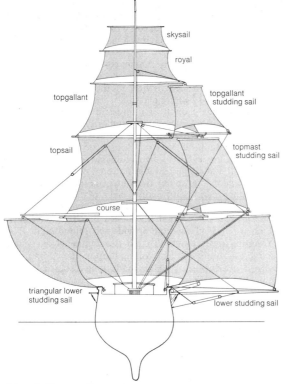

skysail

royal

topgallant

topgallant studding sail

topsail

topmast studding sail

course

triangular lower studding sail

lower studding sail

Figure 2: *Square sails.*
Studding sails shown astern with rigging.

rigged ship "Preussen" of Hamburg, launched in 1902. It used steam power solely for working cargo and weighing anchor. Its five steel masts were three feet (91 centimetres) in diameter, and its main yard was 100 feet (30 metres) long. The ship itself was 433 feet (132 metres) in length, with a beam of 54 feet (16 metres).

Among wooden sailing vessels the largest was the American "Great Republic" of 1853, with four decks. The first to use steam winches to hoist its yards and the first to have double topsails, it was built as a four-masted bark for the Australian trade but was gutted by fire on the eve of its maiden voyage. Partly rebuilt and drastically cut down in size and rig, it went into service carrying gold rush passengers around Cape Horn; later, after taking part in the guano trade, it returned to passenger carrying.

The "Great Britain," largest ship afloat when it was launched in 1844, was the first passenger vessel with a screw propellor to cross the Atlantic. It had a length of 322 feet (98 metres), a beam of 51 feet (16 metres), and draft of 32 feet (ten metres) with its 3,720 tonnage. It relied heavily on the schooner-rigged sails on its six masts. Three of the masts were removed later, but it continued as a mixed steam–sail vessel through a long career. It was too large for its time and a commercial failure, though for a time it was usefully employed in laying an undersea telegraph cable across the Atlantic Ocean. It ended as a coal hulk in the Falkland Islands, but in 1970 it was towed back the 7,500 miles to England to be refitted and preserved.

Far more than twice its size was the "Great Eastern," launched in 1858. Its length was 692 feet (211 metres), beam 82 feet (25 metres), and draft 30 feet (nine metres), though it was of 18,914 tons. Also rigged as a schooner, it had both a propellor and paddle wheels, but it was sold, to end as a floating fair.

The big steel-hulled American schooner "Thomas W. Lawson," of 5,218 tons, built in 1902, had seven masts, each 195 feet (59 metres) high. In spite of its size, it had a crew of only 16, with steam winches used for sail handling. It was in service only five years when it capsized off the Scilly Isles, southwest of England.

Flettner's rotor ship

In 1924 a wholly new kind of sailing vessel, the rotor ship, was extensively tested. Its German inventor, Anton Flettner, based his idea on the discovery that the wind pressure on a revolving cylinder was considerably greater than on a conventional sail. Flettner began by installing in a small freighter two cylinders 50 feet (15 metres) high, which were spun by an electric motor. Steering by controlling the spinning of the rotors, he reached a speed of nine and a half knots. He made further tests with three cylinders 60 feet (18 metres) high in a larger ship but found he could obtain satisfactory results only when all conditions were favourable. The idea was not pursued, and there seems to have been no other invention using wind power in such a radical way.

The end of an era. In 1775 the first successful trial of a boat driven by steam, on the Seine by Jacques Périer, foreshadowed the end of the age of sail. The sailing vessel fought long and hard, not admitting defeat for 100 years and more. One of the last rearguard actions was the struggle of a diehard Finnish skipper, Capt. Gustaf Ericson, who in the 1920s and 1930s built up a fleet of 16 sailing ships, ran them uninsured, except for their cargoes, and manned them with boys in training. The pride of Ericson's fleet, the four-masted bark "Herzogin Cecile," was finally wrecked on the rocks off the coast of Cornwall in 1936, and he died shortly afterward.

Yet there are plenty of schooners and similar fore-and aft-rigged vessels trading or pleasure cruising about the world today. Of the big square-riggers there are more than 80 sailing the seas. One or two serve as yachts or commercial pleasure ships, but nearly all the others are used to train youngsters for the navy or the mercantile marine of 18 different nations. The U.S.S.R. has the largest fleet, with the United States next but some way behind. The Scandinavian countries have quite a number, and Indonesia has a four-masted bark. Several have been launched since World War II, notably the German bark "Georg Foch," built in West Germany in 1958 in the

same yard and of the same design as four others (two of which are now Russian, one Portuguese, and another the training cutter of the U.S. Coast Guard). Britain has only two large schooners, owned by a private and highly successful sail-training association, and a brig built for sea scouts.

Two of the European barks have been tragically lost. In 1928–29 the five-masted "Kjøbenhavn," with 40 cadets in its crew, vanished mysteriously while at sea on passage. Then, in 1958, the four-masted German "Pamir" was overwhelmed in heavy weather, leaving only six survivors of its 35-man crew and 51 cadets. Yet in both Denmark and West Germany new vessels were soon built to replace them. Despite occasional losses of a lesser kind, large and small craft, ketches, schooners, and even a square-rigged ship or two are being launched in many parts of the world to carry on the long tradition of sea and sail.

The training ships may be the last of the utilitarian sailing vessels, but a whole new and rapidly growing fleet has meantime emerged for sport and recreation. Mostly small craft, designed for coastal and inland waters, small boats are being constructed by the thousands in many parts of the world, in a variety of types and of many different materials.

Classes of boats. Sailing craft designed primarily for pleasure are yachts, other than small open boats known as dinghies. The yachts are fully or partially decked and have open cockpits. Lesser differences include a fixed keel or a centreboard that can be raised and lowered. Another difference is that many decked-over boats have a self-bailing cockpit and built-in ballast. Small vessels may be rigged as single-masted catboats, sloops, or cutters or as two-masted yawls or ketches. For small craft the rig is largely a matter of personal choice. Opinions differ on the advantages or disadvantages of various rigs in their seaworthiness, handiness, and weatherly qualities and in their performance in light airs and a strong breeze.

The Marconi, or Bermuda, rig, with its lofty fore-and aft triangular mainsail, has now triumphed over the gaff rig, with its more or less rectangular fore and aft mainsail, for most yachts and racing dinghies. In northern European waters small boats also have a choice between the simplicity of the balanced lugsail and the standing lugsail (a four-sided sail bent to a yard that hangs obliquely on a mast and is hoisted and lowered with the sail). There is also the sliding gunter (a simple triangular sail), which has some of the efficiency of the Marconi and can be shortened without leaving a useless length of mast above it.

The old J-class sloops, which competed in the early races for the America's Cup (see BOATING AND YACHTING), were superseded, owing to their increasing cost, by the so-called 12-metre class.

The worldwide growth of interest in sailing is perhaps most evident in the increasing popularity of the multihull catamarans and trimarans. Borrowed from the Polynesians, the catamaran was developed for sport sailing in England in the 1950s by two builders, working independently, and quickly gained international popularity.

Catamarans and trimarans

The British trimaran has two outrigger floats, the one to the weather side, flying mainly clear of the water, while the leeward one acts as a stabilizer. A type of trimaran developed in the United States has much larger floats, which are bridged over and provide accommodation.

Yachting owes much to such developments as roller-reefing (shortening sail by rolling it up on the boom) and the self-steering gear, which made long-distance, single-handed sailing practical and led to the round-the-world voyages of the 1960s.

The sailboat industry. The introduction of man-made materials has had an increasing impact year by year on the sailboat industry. Boats in the early 1970s were being built mainly of glass fibre (glass-reinforced plastic), ferrocement, and steel.

Glass fibre. Glass-fibre hulls are light, strong, free of rust, and need little maintenance. The manufacturing process consists of bolting together the two halves of a wooden mold, polishing it to a glassy surface, and then, at a fixed temperature, building it up layer by layer with successive mixtures of synthetic resin, glass-fibre matting, and a catalyst. The percentage of boats built with glass fibre advanced from 4 percent in 1955 to 69.6 percent in 1970. Some spars, and even masts, were being made of glass fibre in the early 1970s.

Metal. The percentage of boats built with metal hulls, taking steel and aluminum together, fluctuated in the late 1960s, but the average of 3.4 percent rose with an increased proportion of steel hulls pioneered by the Dutch and increasingly built by the British.

Stainless- and galvanized-steel masts are proving satisfactory. So also are aluminum masts, which, in addition to their light weight and strength, are more versatile than spruce or pine. Laboratory experiments are being made in Britain with an alloy of aluminum and carbon fibre as a possible new material for masts.

Ferrocement. In ferrocement hull construction, a frame of light steel pipe, steel reinforcing rods, and chicken wire is built. Cement is then forced through the frame, filling the spaces and forming a smooth hull. The ferrocement varies in thickness from ⅝ to ⅞ inch (16 to 22 millimetres), according to the length of the vessel, but it is immensely strong and, unlike unreinforced cement, is not brittle. Its resistance to shock and explosion is high. No maintenance is needed, and it is immune from rot or rust.

Timber. In the 1960s manufacture of timber hulls, except for luxury yachts, fell off sharply, declining from 82.4 percent to 13.6 percent in four years.

Synthetics. Ninety percent of all sails are now made of Dacron, known in Britain as Terylene. Dacron stretches a little when new, just the right amount, and has the virtue of keeping its shape.

In rope or cord it is preferred to nylon for sheets and halyards but, as with all man-made fibres, it is liable to stretch under a steady strain. Nylon, being slightly stronger than Dacron in ropes over ¼ inch (six millimetres) in diameter, is widely used. It is resistant to oil and alkalis, though not to all acids, whereas Dacron resists acids but is vulnerable to alkalis. As with all man-made fibres, they are free from rot and mildew.

Polystyrene (Styrofoam) is used in a variety of ways to add buoyancy, such as being packed under the deck or molded to fit inside a mast. It is liable, however, to disintegrate when in contact with petroleum products, and only a rubberized adhesive may be used.

New developments in boat-building materials and techniques are continuous, and current methods may well be superseded in the not far-distant future.

BIBLIOGRAPHY

General: R. and R.C. ANDERSON, *The Sailing Ship* (1926), particularly good on rigging; B.W. BATHE et al., *The Great Age of Sail* (1967), authoritative and finely produced; B. LANDSTROM, *Skepped* (Eng. trans., *The Ship*, 1969), a magnificent work where the story of sail is told and illustrated in much detail; R.C. LESLIE, *Old Sea Wings, Ways and Words in the Days of Oak and Hemp* (1930), a fascinating old nautical classic; "TRE TRYCKARE," *The Lore of Ships* (1964), outstanding both in text and illustrations.

Works dealing with specific periods in history: W.L. ROGERS, *Greek and Roman Naval Warfare* (1937), very useful within the limits of its subject; C. TORR, *Ancient Ships* (1894); L. CASSON, "New Light on Ancient Rigging and Boatbuilding," AMERICAN NEPTUNE, 24:81–94 (1964); J. BROENSTED, *The Vikings* (1960), a sound, comprehensive survey; "The Skuldelev Ships," *Acta Archaeologica,* 29:161–175 (1958) and 38:73–174 (1967), only English translation from Danish giving full account of the Roskilde find; S. FLIEDNER et al., *Die Bremer Hanse Kogge* (1967), salvage of cog of Hanseatic League, profusely illustrated; S. SVENSSON, *Sails Through the Centuries* (1965), of value here for its earlier period; C.M. CIPOLLA, *Guns and Sail in the Early Phase of European Expansion, 1400–1700* (1965; U.S. title, *Guns, Sails and Empires,* 1966), comprehensive work; P. COWBURN, *The Warship in History* (1966), particularly recommended for its chapters on the 17th and 18th centuries; A. SHARP, *Ancient Voyagers in the Pacific* (1956), interesting facts and theories on ocean navigation and migrations, but rather dogmatic; G.R.G. WORCESTER, *Sail and Sweep in China* (1966), for clear and full descriptions of Chinese junks; M.K.E. WILBUR, *The East India Company and the British Empire in the Far East* (1945), includes excellent chapters on the role of the ships; G.P.B. NAISH, *The Wasa: Her Place in History* (1968), the only detailed account in English of the raising and reconditioning of the 17th-century Swedish warship; H.I. CHAPELLE, *The History of American Sailing Ships* (1936), useful diagrams of hull and line drawings; H.A. UNDERHILL, *Sailing Ships' Rigs and Rigging* (1955), helpful both in text and illustrations; D.R. MACGREGOR, *The Tea Clippers* (1962), satisfyingly written; S. ROGERS, *Freak Ships* (1936), limited in scope but the chosen subjects are well handled; O. SCHAEUFFELEN, *Great Sailing Ships* (Eng. trans. 1969), splendidly illustrated collection of 150 ships and large vessels still in existence. See also *The Mariner's Mirror* (1911–   ).

(D.P.C.)

Saint

The phenomenon of saintliness (*i.e.*, the quality of holiness, involving a special relationship to the sacred sphere as well as moral perfection or exceptional teaching abilities) is widespread in the religions of the world, both ancient and contemporary. Various types of religious personages have been recognized as saints, both by popular acclaim and official pronouncement, and their influence on the religious masses (the broad spectrum of those holding various wide-ranging religious beliefs) has been, and is, of considerable significance.

NATURE AND SIGNIFICANCE

Saints are persons believed to be connected in a special manner with what is viewed as sacred reality—gods, spiritual powers, mythical realms, and other aspects of the sacred or holy. The existence of such persons has been a widespread phenomenon throughout the religions of the world. The religious person may have various relationships with the sacred: as seer, prophet, saviour, monk, nun, priest, priestess, or other such personage. In the case of each of these, however, a specific kind of relationship to the holy is involved. Seers, for example, have an inspirational vision of the future; prophets proclaim a revelation; saviours are entrusted with effecting redemption, liberation, or other salvatory conditions; monks and nuns lead religious lives in accordance with ascetic regulations that they generally observe as long as they live. Every one of these religious personages may simultaneously be, or become, a saint, but there is no necessary connection. Sainthood thus implies a special type of relationship to the holy, a relationship that is not automatically obtained by other religious personages through their performance of religious duties or offices. *(margin: Relationships with the sacred or holy)*

The significance of saintly personages is generally based upon real or alleged deeds and qualities that became apparent during their lifetimes and continue to exert influence after their deaths. The special character of their feats and qualities of living is believed to arise from an especially close association with a deity or sacred power. In addition to such a relationship, sainthood also requires the existence of a sacral institution that can grant such recognition, or of a popular cult that acknowledges and posits a belief in the saint's special qualities. In institutionalized religions, such as Roman Catholicism, there is a regularized process (called canonization) by which saints are officially recognized. Canonization requires, among other things, proof that the person in question wrought miracles during his or her lifetime. On the other hand, folk belief often recognizes the saintly powers of a living or dead person long before the institutional religion acknowledges him as a saint. Nor does the lack of official recognition discourage continued veneration.

The special relationship of the saint to the divine, sacred, or numinous (spiritual) powers is often enhanced by ascetic self-realization and self-negation. It does not necessarily follow, however, that the saint is an ethical example to others, though the saintliness often manifests itself in ethically outstanding deeds or qualities.

SAINTS IN EASTERN RELIGIONS

Confucianism and Taoism. Confucianism, the Chinese religion named after its 6th-century-BC founder, Confu-

The importance of right conduct

cius (K'ung Fu-tzu, or Master Kung), but containing many elements of pre-Confucian times, is in the main, ethically oriented. Confucius taught that right conduct was a means of acquiring ideal harmony with the Way (Tao) of Heaven and that the "holy rulers of primal times" were representative examples of such ideal conduct. In the oldest known Chinese historical work, the *Shu Ching* ("Classic of History"), such a ruler, King T'ang (11th century BC), is described as one who "possessed the highest degree of virtue, and so it came to be that he acquired the bright authority of Heaven." Thus, in Confucianism, the saintliness of its holy men lay in ethical perfection, and through the practice of ethical ideals a contact with Heaven (T'ien) was established. Confucius himself serves as an example of a man who was first regarded as a saint because of his deep wisdom and conscientious observance of ethical precepts and was even considered to be "more than human." During the Han dynasty (206 BC–AD 220) Confucius was elevated to a new status: Emperor Kao Tsu offered sacrifice at the Confucian temple, and Emperor Wu proclaimed Confucianism the official ideology of China. The titles duke (AD 1) and king (739) were further tributes to "the perfect sage." During the T'ang dynasty (618–907) sacrifices were regularly offered in Confucian temples, and in 1906 Confucius was declared equal to the Lord of Heaven.

Taoism, founded by the 6th-century-BC sage Lao-tzu (Master Lao) and the second major religion native to China, is oriented toward another kind of sanctity: the attainment of a passionless unity with the Absolute. Chuang-tzu (died *c.* 300 BC), a mystical Taoist sage, speaks of the "pure men of early times" in his work, the *Chuang-tzu*, and characterizes them by saying that

> they did not forget where they had come from, they did not care about where they should pass to; readily, they accepted what was allotted to them, peacefully they awaited their decease. It is this that is called "not resisting the Tao" (the divine Absolute). (Tschuangtse, *Reden und Gleichnisse.* [Deutsche Auswahl], ed. Martin Buber. 1920. p. 27.)

Later, popular Taoism also incorporated into its pantheon saints who were called "true men" (*chen jen*). The "true men" were usually recluses who were close to nature and who exhibited a passive acceptance of the Way (Tao) of nature.

Shintō. Shintō, the native Japanese religion, is concerned with the veneration of nature and with ancestor worship; it does not have saints according to the standards of ethical perfection or of exceptionally meritorious performance. According to Shintō belief, every person after his death becomes a *kami*, a supernatural being who continues to have a part in the life of the community, nation, and family. Good men become good and beneficial *kami*s, bad men become pernicious ones. Being elevated to the status of a divine being is not a privilege peculiar to those with saintly qualities, for evil men also become *kami*s. There are in Shintō, however, venerated mythical saints—such as Ōkuni-nushi (Master of the Great Land) and Sukuma-Bikona (a dwarf deity)—who are considered to be the discoverers and patrons of medicine, magic, and the art of brewing rice.

Buddhism. Founded by Siddhārta Gautama (*c.* 560 BC), the Buddha (or Enlightened One), Buddhism developed into three major forms in the course of its more than 2,500-year history: Theravāda ("Way of the Elders"), also called in derogation Hīnayāna ("Lesser Vehicle"); Mahāyāna ("Greater Vehicle"), and, stemming from it, Vajrayāna ("Vehicle of the Thunderbolt"). A belief in saints prevails in all three groups.

Differing concepts of saints in Buddhism

Theravāda Buddhism, claiming strict adherence to the teachings of the Buddha, recognizes as saints (*arhat*s) those who have attained Nirvāṇa (the state of bliss) and hence salvation from *saṃsāra* (the compulsory circle of rebirth) by their own efforts. The Buddha himself—having obtained Nirvāṇa ("the destruction of greed, . . . hate, . . . and illusion")—is viewed as the first Buddhist saint; he says of himself,

> I am the holy One in this world, I am the highest teacher, I alone am the completely enlightened One; I have gained peacefulness and have obtained Nirvāṇa.

Disciples of the Buddha who reached Nirvāṇa after him are also considered holy men: his apostles Śāriputra and Moggalāna, converts from Brahmanism (a form of Hinduism); Ānanda, the Buddha's cousin and beloved disciple; Rāhula, the Buddha's son; Nāgasena, an erudite monk; and Angulimāla, a former thief and murderer who turned to Buddhism and reached Nirvāṇa. Furthermore, in early Buddhism, there were also women regarded as holy, including Prajāpatī, the Buddha's aunt and stepmother—whose repeated requests finally caused the Buddha to permit women to enter his order—and his wife Yaśodharā.

Mahāyāna saints

Mahāyāna Buddhism, originating about the beginning of the Christian Era, rejected the Theravāda belief that only monks may attain salvation. In Mahāyāna belief, there is a path to redemption for all people, irrespective of their social standing. Salvation and the way to redemption are conceived in terms more liberal than those of Theravāda. Mahāyāna Buddhists believe in an otherworldly paradise that allows for personal existence and in which dwell heavenly Buddhas (those who have attained Nirvāṇa in previous worlds), and *bodhisattva*s ("Buddhas-to-be"). The heavenly Buddhas and *bodhisattva*s are believed to grant grace to sentient beings, so that salvation is no longer acquired by fleeing from the world and giving up worldly professions, but rather by faith (in the sense of trust) in the promise of a saviour deity. Thus, in Mahāyāna Buddhism, the Buddhas and *bodhisattva*s are viewed as the holy ones, the saints, who in compassion, attempt to aid others struggling for salvation. This concept is in striking contrast to the *arhat*s of Theravāda Buddhism, who follow the dying Buddha's last words, "Seek *your own* salvation with diligence." The basic altruistic concept of Mahāyāna then is that of the helping *bodhisattva*. Everyone should strive for this ideal in order to save as many fellowmen as possible as a *bodhisattva*, and to bring them into the "Greater Vehicle" (Mahāyāna). Hence, the idea of faith in benevolent saints gains prominence in Mahāyāna Buddhism as a theistic religion of salvation. In Japanese Mahāyāna there are patron saints, such as Shōtoku Taishi, the regent who supported the introduction and development of Buddhism in his country in around AD 600, after it had been introduced in AD 552. Shōtoku Taishi posthumously became the patron saint of carpenters. Other saints are Nomi No Sukume, the patron saint of businessmen, and Daruma, the patron of tobacco dealers. Nichiren, the founder of the nationalistic Japanese Mahāyāna sect named after him, is considered to be the incarnation of the *bodhisattva* Viśiṣṭacāritra. The ashes of this saint are kept in a pagoda-like reliquary.

Vajrayāna Buddhism, embodying, among other views, Tantrism (a system of magical and esoteric practices), is mainly represented by Lamaism (the Buddhism of Tibet). In addition to the innumerable saints of Mahāyāna Buddhism, Lamaism also accepts as living saints those who are regarded as incarnations (*tulku*s) of saints, scholars of the past, deities, or demons. The Dalai Lamas, heads of the Tibetan hierarchy, are viewed as reincarnations of Chen-re-zi (the *bodhisattva* of Mercy, Avalokiteśvara).

Jainism. The Jain religion is named after the 6th-century-BC Indian religious leader Mahāvīra (Great Hero) Vardhamāna, the Jina, or "Victor," over the bondage of life and death. Both of his honorary titles—Jina and Mahāvīra—indicate that he was regarded as an ascetic saint. According to Jain teaching, there were 23 Tīrthaṅkaras (saintly prophets or proclaimers of salvation) before Mahāvīra; today they are venerated as saints in temples containing their images. Veneration of the Holy Tīrthaṅkaras is viewed in terms of purifying the devotee morally, since these saints are but examples for the Jainas, and not actually objects of a cult.

Hinduism. Hinduism, the predominant religion of India, in a wider sense encompasses Brahmanism, a belief in the Universal Soul, Brahman; in a narrower sense it comprises the post-Buddhist, caste-ordered religious and cultural world of India. The Indian religions are by and large mystical in character; hence, even in early Hinduism ascetics were highly honoured. Mysticism generally starts with ascetic practices as a means of eliminating a desire for worldly existence. Thus, Yājñavalkya, a sage and mystic of the *Upaniṣads* (philosophical commentaries on Vedic concepts) is addressed as a holy one, and he himself describes the nature of a redeemed person with these words, "If a man is without desires, free of desires, his vital spirits will not depart; Brahman he is and into Brahman he goes."

In later Hinduism, when the ascetics continued to be revered by the masses as *sādhu*s (saints, or "good ones") and *yogi*s (ascetic practitioners), the concept of the *avatāra* (the idea of the incarnation of a divine being in human form) served to interpret the existence of holy men. By means of this concept it was, and still is, possible to consider living and dead saints as incarnations of a deity, and also to incorporate saints of other religions into the Hindu world of belief. Thus Jesus Christ, for instance, is regarded as an *avatāra* of the god Viṣṇu (Vishnu), and the great Hindu saint Rāmakrishna is considered to be an *avatāra* of the god Śiva.

SAINTS IN WESTERN RELIGIONS

Ancient Greek religion. The ancient heroes of Greek religion may be regarded as saints. One basis for belief in heroes and the hero cult was the idea that the mighty dead continued to live and to be active as spiritual powers from the sites of their graves. Another source of the cult of heroes was the conception that gods were often lowered to the status of heroes. One of the best known heroes is Heracles, who became famous through his mighty deeds. In Greek religion, the numinous (spiritual) qualities of a person lay in such heroic deeds. Those persons killed in war might become heroes according to ancient Greek belief, and the mythical progenitor of a genetic stock also was regarded as a hero. The 3rd-century philosopher Philostratus pictures Apollonius of Tyana (1st century AD) as a philosophical saint endowed with supernatural powers and hence capable of performing miracles, such as raising the dead; he was often contrasted with Jesus as a miracle worker (see also HERO WORSHIP).

Zoroastrianism and Parsiism. Zoroastrianism, the religion founded by the 6th-century-BC Iranian prophet Zoroaster, and its modern Indian variety (Parsiism), includes the veneration of Fravashis—*i.e.*, preexistent souls that are good by nature, gods and goddesses of individual families and clans, and physical elements. According to Zoroastrian belief, man is caught up in a great cosmic struggle between the forces of good, led by Ahura Mazdā (Wise Lord), and the forces of evil, led by Angra Mainyu, or Ahriman, the Evil Spirit. In the battle between Asha (Truth) and Druj (Lie), the Fravashis may correspond to the saints of Roman Catholicism, who can be called upon for aid in times of trouble. In the liturgical hymns called *Yasht*s are sections devoted to more than 300 Fravashis, both male and female. Among the female saints is Hvōvī, Zoroaster's wife; among the male saints are Gayōmart, the primal man; Saoshyans, the eschatological (last times) saviour; and (in later writings) Artāy Virāf, the saint who journeyed through hell to paradise.

Judaism. The cult of saints in terms of veneration was not a part of the monotheistic religion of Israel. Saintliness, however, was an ideal which many hoped to exhibit. The model of a pious person is depicted in the righteous one of Psalm 5, "his delight is in the law of the Lord, and on his law he meditates day and night." In the Hellenistic period (*c.* 300 BC—*c.* AD 300), when many Jews were susceptible to foreign religious influences, the Ḥasidim (the "pious" ones), segregated themselves from the others, holding fast to the faith of their fathers.

The concept of the Ḥasidim gained new significance in the 18th century when Israel ben Eliezer called Ba'al Shem Ṭov, or "Master of the Good Name," started the modern movement called Ḥasidism. As opposed to the Orthodox Israelite religion with its emphasis on rationalism, cultic piety, and legalism, Ba'al Shem Ṭov stood for a more mystically oriented form of Judaism. He emphasized the love of God filling the world and stated that this love should find its correspondence in man, thus helping

to restore harmony between God and the world. The leaders of this movement were called the tzaddiqim ("righteous ones") and many edifying legends were told about these saints.

Christianity. Jesus and his disciples did not speak of saints; but during the period (1st to early 4th century) in which they were persecuted, Christians began to venerate the martyrs as saints. They believed that the martyrs, being sufferers "unto death" for Christ, were received directly into heaven and could therefore be effective as intercessors for the living. By the 3rd century, the veneration of martyr saints was already common.

In the Nicene Creed (AD 325), the early church called itself the "communion of saints." Here, however, the word "saint" has the broader meaning of "believer" rather than being applied strictly to a holy person or numinous personality worthy of veneration. In the 10th century, a procedure of canonization (official recognition of a public cult of a saint) was initiated by Pope John XV. Gradually, a fixed process was developed for canonization by the pope, requiring that the person must have led a life of heroic sanctity and performed at least two miracles.

Saints in the Roman Catholic Church are venerated— but not worshipped—because of their spiritual and religious significance, and are believed to be the bearers of special powers. Because of a belief in the powers of the saints, their relics are regarded as efficacious. The relics of St. Polycarp, the 2nd-century AD martyr-bishop of Smyrna in Asia Minor, are described as more precious than gems and more costly than gold. In the early church every new Christian congregation sought for relics of saints to be placed in their altars. Since the 6th century, side altars have been built in honour of particular saints. In the Eastern Orthodox Church saints also are venerated, but the process of canonization is less juridical and not always ecumenical. In some Protestant churches (Lutheran and Anglican) saints are recognized, but not venerated as in the Roman Catholic and Orthodox.

Islām. Islām is a rigorously monotheistic religion, strictly prohibiting any kind of "conjunction" (*i.e.*, affiliation, or consortship) to Allāh. Thus the concept of sainthood was rejected. Yet even here a variegated belief in holy men arose because of the demands of popular religion. Over against the one distant God, whose almighty power and whose role as a strict judge was emphasized repeatedly, there emerged a desire for intercessors. Such were seen in saintly men who were believed to be endowed with charismatic powers (*karāmāt*), allowing them to go miraculously from one place to another far away; to wield authority over animals, plants, and clouds; and to bridge the gap between life and death. The Prophet Muḥammad (died AD 632) had negated the existence of saints, but the piety of the masses "canonized" holy men while they were still living. After they died, cults of devotion arose at the sites of their graves, and pilgrimages to such sites were believed to aid the believer in acquiring help and blessing. Miraculous deeds were believed to be wrought by these "friends" (*walī*) of God, and as a result of this belief Islām differentiates between the wonders that Allāh performs and those of his true messengers in making opponents realize their own helplessness. The Prophet performs such miracles whereas the mere saint, the *walī*, is incapable of doing them.

In Islāmic mysticism, or Ṣūfism, the concept of the saint, or *walī*, is not defined in terms of extensive miracles, but rather in terms of the relationship of the person concerned to God. Men who live a life of service and obedience to Allāh are viewed as living saints, and the world is believed to owe its preservation to their intercession. Concerning such holy men, the Ṣūfī al-Hujwīrī (died between 1072 and 1077) stated,

> God has saints [*awlīyā*'] whom he had distinguished especially through his friendship, and whom he has chosen to represent his kingship; He has granted them the special gift of bringing His deeds to light, He has especially favored them with [being able to do] manifold miracles [*karāmāt*], He has purified them from the corruptions of nature and freed them from servitude over against their souls which incline toward the evil, and over against their souls' desires.

In Islām it is believed that the saint should be remembered for his deeds rather than for his person. Thus, biographies of Islāmic saints tend to omit personal details.

MODES OF RECOGNITION

The bases of recognition. The basic motive for the belief in and veneration of saints is, primarily, the recognition by people of religious persons whom they view as holy. In order for a religious personage (*e.g.*, prophet) to be recognized as a saint, it is necessary that other people see in him the aura of holiness. The holiness recognized in him may be an impersonal sacred or spiritual power—which is often perceived in quite insignificant persons—and is believed to be present even in the bones and other material relics of a recognized holy person after his death. Religious personalities are also believed to possess a personal holiness, either bestowed upon them by divine grace or acquired through asceticism and moral discipline. Such sanctity reveals itself in the power to perform miracles.

The highest form of holiness in a holy person is reflected in the interpretation of that person as an incarnation of divine reality or as the possessor of godly nature. Divine qualities are perceived in such a person, and through him, such as the Logos (divine Word, or Reason) in Jesus.

Popular recognition. Popular recognition of saints arises out of a predilection of the religious masses (those who maintain popular belief, or folk belief, along with beliefs officially promulgated) to grasp the supernatural in that which is believed to be unusual and uncommon—*i.e.*, in the miraculous event. Thus, the religious masses long for men who can perform wonders that are awe awakening and satisfy their desire for the miraculous and mysterious. When saints perform miracles, they satisfy one of the basic religious needs of the people.

Besides the desire for miracles, there is another basic requirement of the masses, especially within monotheistic religions: the yearning for a superhuman being in human form. The one abstract God who is believed to be present everywhere and capable of helping everybody and everything is too unperceptual and remote for the average religious person. There is a tendency among the religious masses to split up the deity into many numinous beings that fulfill the desires of the people. The religious masses often have polytheistic tendencies. The term "dear saints," as the holy ones are called in Roman Catholicism, expresses an emotional relationship to those near, benevolent, heavenly, or spiritual powers that are the heirs to the ancient ethnic and patron deities of pre-Christian times. Peter and Paul, for instance, are patron saints of Rome, John is patron saint of Ephesus, and Ambrose of Milan. St. George (reduced to commemoration in 1961 and dropped from the liturgical calendar in 1969) is regarded as patron of warriors, and St. Barbara (dropped from the liturgical calendar in 1969) as patroness of miners, artillerymen, and firemen.

In the course of their histories, and as they expand, the great universal religions (*e.g.*, Christianity, Buddhism, and others) incorporate ever more people with their particular folk beliefs. As their numbers grow and their influence increases in the religious communities, the indigenous peoples retaining many earlier folk beliefs form the majority and their inclinations prevail. Since their behaviour patterns generally remain constant, their religious forms are preserved. Occasionally, religious reform movements arise within the organized mass religions. Such movements attempt to restore what is believed to be the original form of the respective religions and often turn against a belief in and veneration of saints, regarding such forms of religiosity as degenerate. This was the case in the 16th-century Protestant Reformation, and also in the Wahhābīyah movement, an 18th-century reform movement in Islām.

Theological interpretations of popular recognition. In monotheistic religions, the belief in saints in its popular form generally contradicts orthodox teaching. Such religiosity is usually opposed and rejected or else reinterpreted in view of its ineradicability. If the latter is the case, the orthodox interpretation given the cult of saints in order to justify it is a theological construction. In Roman Catholicism, for instance, church doctrine makes a distinction between veneration (*veneratio, douleia*) and adoration (*adoratio, latreia*). Veneration is defined as a proper attitude toward saints, whereas adoration is applicable only in connection with God. The veneration of images as practiced especially in the Eastern Orthodox Church is explained similarly. The Roman Catholic Church also teaches that the saints are representatives of God's grace on earth and that they are completely subject to his will. The vestigial remains of polytheistic beliefs and practices connected with the veneration of saints are thus theologically, though not popularly, eliminated.

Similar interpretations have been made in regard to the cult of relics in Buddhism. In Ceylon, for instance, the tooth of the Buddha is venerated. Since this practice contradicts the original teaching of the "Elders," the worship of the relic is explained as pertaining to the Buddha himself, who is the actual and true object of veneration.

A similar situation prevails in Islām. Islāmic theology acknowledged the miracles of the saints, but tried to differentiate them from the *mu'jizāt* ("miracles") of the Prophet. The miraculous deeds of the saints and the prophets are viewed similarly in that God alone bestows supernatural power in each case. But in the Muslim orthodox view, the miracles of the saints are viewed as the results of a prayer that has been answered and also as a power granted by God to perform such deeds. The miracles of the prophets, on the other hand, lie in the creation of something new, or in the transformation of the substance of a thing.

All these and similar interpretations of the belief in saints in a monotheistic religion serve to justify an existing cult. The people themselves are hardly influenced by such interpretations, however. According to many scholars, the differentiation between *douleia* (veneration) and *latreia* (worship), or between *veneratio* (veneration) and *adoratio* (adoration), has little meaning for the masses. In practice, they observe their cult of saints quite in accordance with polytheistic devotion toward gods. The supplications actually directed to the saints in the various religions can hardly be distinguished from prayers to deities, even though the saints are theologically regarded as mere intercessors having special access to God, and the answer to prayer is considered as coming from God alone. From the perspective of scholars of comparative religion, however, beings to whom prayers are dedicated are gods.

Forms of cults. The form of a cult of saints can be categorized as either *indirect* or *direct*. An indirect cult form involves the veneration of objects that stand in a magical relationship to the respective saint. In this connection there can be a veneration of the saint's relics. Such religious practices are to be understood in terms of spiritual power. Numinous power is viewed as issuing from the saint; and it is believed to be acquired by veneration or, in practice, mainly by touching (or kissing) the object itself. Another indirect cult form is the veneration of the image of the saint. According to primitive belief, there is a magical connection between the image and the original, which is itself holy. A common and widespread custom is the depositing of votive offerings, dedicated to certain saints, at holy places—temples, churches, shrines, or chapels where the supplicant can be certain of their direct presence and aid. This custom is of ancient origin —*e.g.*, the votive offerings dedicated to the healing god Asclepius in the museum of Epidaurus (Greece). This practice is still to be found in present-day popular belief in Greece or at Roman Catholic places of pilgrimage.

In these forms of indirect cult, then, saints are venerated through the medium of concrete objects. In direct veneration, on the other hand, the saint himself is addressed in invocation and praise. According to popular belief, such direct worship is most effective at the place of the predominant presence of the respective saint. This belief in the localization of the numinous, a typical element of folk belief, is to be found throughout history, from earliest times to the present. For instance, Absalom (the son of the Israelite King David) went to pay his vow to

"Yahweh of Hebron" (II Samuel) at the place of his special presence. The idea of pilgrimage is always based upon such a belief in the localized presence of numinous power.

TYPES AND FUNCTIONS OF SAINTS

Saints as moral examples. A classical illustration of the saint who is distinguished by his virtue is St. Francis of Assisi. Giving up a life of extravagance, he began in 1209, together with several friends, to actualize his ideal of the imitation of Christ by leading a life of poverty. For St. Francis, three virtues constituted the preconditions of true divine vision: poverty, ascetic chastity, and humility.

An example of a similar kind of saintliness is reflected in the person of the Indian leader and reformer, Mahatma Gandhi (1869–1948). In his life, devoted to the acquiring of freedom for India, he also lived according to three ideals. The first was *satyāgraha*, holding fast to the truth with all the powers of the spirit. Gandhi's second basic principle was *ahiṃsā*, which is to be understood not only in the negative sense of "not killing" but also positively as a renunciation of the self and an indulgence in "kind actions" toward all beings. His third ideal was *brahmacarya*, which often is rendered too narrowly as chastity; it is the ascetic way of life that Gandhi followed as a saint and as a statesman, hence receiving boundless veneration by the masses.

By living their lives as moral examples, saints influence the personal lives of the religious masses who attempt to emulate saintly ideals in everyday life.

Saints as prophets and reformers. Many prophets and prophetic reformers form a second group of saints. One prophet in early Christianity was Paul, who is honoured as a saint by Roman Catholics, Eastern Orthodox, and Protestants. He was a most powerful spiritual personality, decisively and significantly involved in the development of Christianity from a Jewish sect to a world religion.

The Tibetan reformer Tsong-kha-pa belonged to a completely different world from that of St. Paul. Originally, he did not want to be an innovator, but only a renewer of old religious patterns. He was mainly concerned with the restoration of the discipline and the development of the Lamaistic cult. His fame grew, and due to his activity, many monasteries were founded. The "Yellow Hat" sect was established by him. According to legend, Tsong-kha-pa was taken up to heaven before the eyes of the people. This accounts for the veneration he received, and still receives, by the Tibetan people.

Reforming, mystical, and intellectual ideals
Through their reforming ideals, prophetic reformers provide goals toward which the religious masses aim, both personally and socially (or in terms of cult).

Saints as mystics. There are also saints among the great number of mystics—*e.g.*, Bernard of Clairvaux, Gertrude the Great of Helfta, and Teresa of Avila.

At the little nunnery of Helfta near Eisleben in Germany, a centre of mysticism in the 13th century, the mystic Gertrude the Great lived. She said that Christ had appeared to her on January 27, 1281, and that though her physical condition deteriorated, her spiritual life grew. Because of her physical condition, she was all the more devoted to the work of spreading her view of the spiritual life through her writings (such as the *Messenger of Divine Love*), which reflect a life filled with the love of God and deepest thankfulness for the gift of grace granted to her. Since 1606 she has been venerated as a saint, and in 1738 her cult was permitted throughout the Roman Catholic Church.

By their devotion to the spiritual life, mystical saints point out new and contemplative directions of religious thought to the religious masses, who seldom are capable of following such a life.

Theological teachers as saints. Often numbered among the saints are certain religious personalities whose significance lies in their work as illuminating interpreters of religious tradition or as proponents of a new view of the divine or the eternal. An example from Indian religions is the great teacher (*ācārya*) Śaṅkara, the representative of Advaita (the teaching of the nonduality of divine reality). When he died at the age of 32, a short and outwardly uneventful life lay behind him. Yet even today the personality and work of Śaṅkara continue to determine the intellectual and religious life of India. Equally significant in the Christian West, and specifically in the Roman Catholic Church, is Thomas Aquinas, a Dominican scholar. Although first disputed, his work finally received general recognition, and he became recognized as the *doctor communis* ("general teacher") of the Roman Catholic Church. His significance lies in his encompassing and methodically clear theological and philosophical system, in which he reconciled the views of the ancient Greek philosopher Plato with those of his student Aristotle, antiquity with Christianity, knowledge with faith, and nature with grace. He was proclaimed a saint in 1323.

Local saints. The cults of some holy persons (local saints) are restricted to a particular locality. Though there are innumerable examples, only one will be used to illustrate this type. Brother Conrad of Parzham (in Germany), who died in 1894, was proclaimed a saint by the Roman Catholic Church in 1934 and his relics are buried in the Church of the Capuchin order at Altötting in Upper Bavaria (Germany). The veneration of this holy personality began in 1930, and today Brother Conrad is one of the most popular saints of Bavaria. The cult at his grave at times almost supplanted the cult of the wonder-working image of Maria of Altötting, whose shrine has been famous for centuries. The veneration of St. Conrad, a former gatekeeper at the Capuchin monastery of Altötting, led to a special form of invocation practiced today. Devout Catholics write detailed letters to St. Conrad as though he were still living, then place the letters in envelopes and address them to him. In the house where the saint was born, in the so-called Venushof von Parzham (Venus Court of Parzham), the cult of St. Conrad has also established itself. The room where he lived as a farm servant has been prepared as a memorial place with a little domestic altar. Local enterprise seeks to make this cult serviceable to its interests by producing lemonade made from water from a spring on the farmstead. It is sold in bottles with a picture of the saint attached.

Brother Conrad

Mythic saints. There is also a group of holy personages that can be termed mythic saints. These are holy ones who are believed to have lived on earth during mythic times and who are yet venerated. Examples of this type are the Indian saints *Kṛṣṇa* (Krishna) and Rāma. They are regarded as incarnations (*avatāras*) of the god Viṣṇu. Kṛṣṇa was perhaps a hero in early times, or a shepherd god who was associated with Viṣṇu as his human embodiment at a later period. However that may be, the saintly figure of Kṛṣṇa is mythic in character. In the *Purāṇas* (ancient Hindu writings), Kṛṣṇa's life is narrated to peasants in the style of myth and legend. In the *Mahābhārata* (ancient Indian epic), it is told to warriors in terms of their concepts of honour and caste. Here Kṛṣṇa is the vassal of Prince Arjuna; in the *Bhagavadgītā* (the "Song of God," part of the *Mahābhārata*) he teaches a religio-ethical way of salvation. Rāma also is viewed as an incarnation of Viṣṇu. An account of his life is to be found in the *Rāmāyaṇa* (ancient Indian epic) in which there is an account of his killing the giant king Rāvaṇa who had abducted his wife Sītā.

Conclusion. As long as the religious masses demonstrate a desire or need for saintly figures—whatever their functions are conceived to be—veneration of such holy personages will continue to be practiced and will exert a religious influence even in the modern world, which has been described as oriented toward a secular, or nonreligious, value system.

BIBLIOGRAPHY. P.D. CHANTEPIE DE LA SAUSSAYE, *Lehrbuch der Religions-Geschichte*, 4th ed., 2 vol. (1925), gives information, under the key-word "Heiligenverehrung" (veneration of saints), on the significance of saints in the religions of the world. Similar, though less detailed, is H. RINGGREN and A.V. STROM, *Die Religionen der Völker* (1959; Eng. trans. from the 3rd Swedish ed., *Religions of Mankind Today and Yesterday*, 1967). The cult of saints is dealt with in connection with the phenomenology of religion by G. MENSCHING in his *Die*

Religion (1959), as well as his *Soziologie der Religion*, 2nd ed. (1968). The miraculous deeds of saints are discusssed in the same author's *Das Wunder im Glauben und Aberglauben der Völker* (1957). See also W.J. BURGHARDT, *Saints and Sanctity* (1965). The characteristics and the actions of holy men in non-Christian religions are treated in the following works: R.A. NICHOLSON, *The Mystics of Islam* (1914, reprinted 1963); H.A. GILES, *Chuang Tzŭ, Mystic, Moralist and Social Reformer* (1926); YU-LAN FUNG (trans.), *Chuang Tzŭ, A New Selected Translation with an Exposition of the Philosophy of Kuo Hsiang* (1931); W.T. DE BARY *et al.* (comps.), *Sources of Chinese Tradition* (1960); W. FILCHNER, *Kumbum Dschamba Ling* (1933); G. VON GRUNEBAUM, *Medieval Islam*, 2nd ed. (1953). In the realm of Christianity, F. HEILER, *Der Katholizismus*, 3rd ed. (1970); and P. MOLINARI, *I Santi e il loro culto* (1962; Eng. trans., *Saints: Their Place in the Church*, 1965), give information concerning the veneration of saints in folk piety. The veneration of saints in the Eastern Church is canvassed, among other works, by E. BENZ and L.A. ZANDER (eds.), *Evangelisches und orthodoxes Christentum in Begegnung und Auseinandersetzung* (1952); and by D. ATTWATER, *Saints of the East* (1963). An article summing up the various aspects of the Christian veneration of saints is R. KLAUSER, "Christliche Heiligenverehrung," in *Religion in Geschichte und Gegenwart*, 3rd ed., vol. 3 (1959). A treatment of saints in the early church may be found in B. KOTTING, *Der frühchristliche Reliquienkult und die Besattung im Kirchengebäude* (1965). R. KRISS and H. KRISS-HEINRICH have reviewed the Greek cult of saints in their book *Peregrinatio Neohellenika* (1955), as well as the manifold forms of the Bavarian-German veneration of holy ones in R. KRISS, *Die Volkskunde der altbayrischen Gnadenstätten,* 2nd ed., 3 vol. (1953–56). S. BEISSEL, in his work *Die Verehrung der Heiligen und ihrer Reliquien in Deutschland bis zum Beginne des 13. Jahrhunderts* (1890), deals with the historical development of the veneration of saints in Germany. A catalog of the saints of the Roman Catholic Church and of their functions was edited by J.E. STADLER and F.G. HEIM, *Vollständiges Heiligen-Lexikon,* 5 vol. (1858–82).

(G.Me.)

Sainte-Beuve, Charles-Augustin

One of France's most prominent and influential literary critics of the 19th century, Charles-Augustin Sainte-Beuve owes much of his reputation to his unequalled sensitivity in applying historical frames of reference to the evaluation of contemporary writing.

By courtesy of the Musee des Beaux-Arts et d'Archeologie, de Boulogne-sur-Mer; photograph, H. Devos

Sainte-Beuve, oil painting by Barthelemy-Eugene Demarquay (b. 1818). In the Musée des Beaux-Arts et d'Archéologie, Boulogne-sur-Mer, France.

Romantic period.   Sainte-Beuve was born at Boulogne on December 23, 1804, the posthumous only child of a tax collector. After a sheltered childhood, he completed his classical education in Paris and began to study medicine, which, however, he abandoned after a year. A talented but in no way brilliant youth, he continued his general education at his own pace, attending the University of Paris and extension institutions, and in 1825 was drawn into journalism by his former teacher, Paul Du-

bois, editor of a new liberal periodical, *Le Globe.* In its pages he wrote his first essays on the poetry of Victor Hugo and soon became a member of his literary circle of Romantic writers and poets. In his first book, *Tableau historique et critique de la poésie française et du théâtre français au XVIᵉ siècle* (1828), he discovered, perhaps naturally, a Renaissance ancestry for Hugo and others of his new friends. A brief visit to England in 1828 strengthened his taste for the poetry of Wordsworth and Coleridge, both of whom were then little known in continental Europe. His visit to England may also account for the appearance of elements of the style of William Cowper and George Crabbe in volumes of his own poetry, *Vie, poésies et pensées de Joseph Delorme* (1829) and *Les Consolations* (1830), which on their publication attracted some attention—not least because of their deliberate flatness and apparent uncouthness, much in contrast to the grander manner of his new friends Hugo and the poet Alfred de Vigny.

He had meanwhile developed a taste for social speculation and a concern for problems of religious experience. His social concerns first crystallized in a passing attachment to the group of reformers assembled around the doctrines of Count Claude-Henri de Saint-Simon. According to Saint-Simon's disciples, the feudal and military systems were to be replaced by one controlled by industrial managers, and scientists rather than the church were to become the spiritual directors of society. When this group in 1830 took over management of *Le Globe,* Sainte-Beuve was entrusted with drafting two manifestos, or "professions of faith"; and, although he was soon to be repelled by the sentimental excesses and intemperance of its leaders, he retained for 30 years a lingering sympathy for its vision of a technocratic society founded on the brotherhood of man. Almost simultaneously, Sainte-Beuve came under the powerful spell of a religious reformer and polemist, Félicité Robert de Lamennais, to whom for a time he looked for religious guidance. Lamennais was then the spiritual adviser of the wife of Victor Hugo, with whom Sainte-Beuve in 1831 struck up a lasting but seemingly platonic relationship of great intensity. Many of the details of this shadowy affair are more or less accurately related in the critic's privately printed volume of lyrics, *Livre d'amour,* which was, however, not published in the lifetime of either of them.

Social and religious concerns

In the 1830s, in his "portraits" of contemporaries, he developed a kind of critique, novel and much applauded at the time, of studying a well-known living writer in the round and entering into considerable research to understand the mental attitudes of his subject.

By 1832 Sainte-Beuve was writing regularly for leading Parisian literary periodicals but was much hampered by his dislike for the newly established regime of King Louis-Philippe, which had aroused his anger mainly by its brutal handling of the riots of 1832. He accordingly refused several educational posts that would have relieved his poverty, fearing that they might compromise his freedom of judgment.

In 1834 he tried his hand at novel writing and published *Volupté,* an intensely introspective and troubling study of frustration, guilt, religious striving, and "renunciation" of the flesh and the devil. Like so much that he wrote —poetry, criticism, fiction—*Volupté* represented a breach with the flamboyance of current taste and won the minority approval mainly of those friends—Lamennais, the novelist George Sand, and the poet and dramatist Alfred de Musset—who recognized its subtlety or approved of its literary transmutation of his feelings for Adèle Hugo.

While continuing to chronicle the intellectual "portraits" of his literary contemporaries—*Critiques et portraits littéraires* (1836–39); *Portraits contemporains* (1846)—friends or former friends, he became a member of the circle presided over by Mme Récamier, the famous hostess, and the writer and politician François-René de Chateaubriand. Sainte-Beuve celebrated the appearance of Chateaubriand's memoirs with enthusiasm, though a decade and a half later he was to write an extensive and far more detached study, *Chateaubriand et son groupe littéraire sous l'Empire.*

Break with Romanticism. A softening of Sainte-Beuve's attitude toward Louis-Philippe's regime coincided in 1836 with an invitation from François Guizot, then minister of education, to accept a one-year appointment as secretary of a government commission studying the nation's literary heritage. Guizot's suggestion at that time that Sainte-Beuve demonstrate his eminence as a scholar by producing a major work led to *Port-Royal*, his most famous piece of writing.

The history of Port-Royal

In 1837 this essentially Parisian critic accepted a year's visiting professorship at Lausanne to lecture on Port Royal, the convent famous in the 17th century for advancing a highly controversial view of the doctrine of grace, loosely called Jansenism. For his lectures he produced the first version of the history of *Port-Royal*, which he published and revised over the next two decades. This monumental assemblage of scholarship, insights, and historical acumen—unique of its kind—reflects most of the varied intellectual adventures through which Sainte-Beuve had passed in the preceding ten years. Its theme ends by comprising nothing less than the study of religious and literary history of the great age of French culture, the 17th century, perceived through the lens of Jansenism.

Appointment as conservateur. On completing his year in Lausanne, Sainte-Beuve returned to Paris. Following his last major journey, to Naples and Rome, he was appointed in 1840 to a post in the French Institute's Mazarine Library, which he held until 1848. In addition to a regular gossip column that he undertook for anonymous publication by his friends in Lausanne, he continued regular essay writing. The first two volumes of *Port-Royal* had also been published when he was elected to the French Academy in 1844. By then he had already broken his earlier close links with the Romantics and was highly critical of what now appeared to him as the undisciplined excesses of that movement. He had also taken a strong stand against what he called industrial literature—the flood of popular fiction addressed (especially in serial form) to the growing readership of undistinguished reviews and newspapers of that time.

After the overthrow in 1848 of Louis-Philippe, Sainte-Beuve was not impressed by what he saw of Revolutionary democracy. Unfairly accused in the republican press of accepting secret government funds for the repair of a chimney in his apartment, he resigned his library appointment in a fit of pique, considered emigrating to London, and finally settled for a year at Liège (Belgium) as visiting professor. Here he wrote his definitive—but unfinished—study of Chateaubriand and the birth of literary romanticism and carried out research on medieval French literature.

"Causeries du lundi." Returning to Paris again in 1849, he contracted with the review *Le Constitutionnel* to furnish a weekly essay; this was the start of the famous collection of studies that he named *Causeries du lundi* ("Monday Chats"), after the review's day of publication. With few interruptions he maintained a prodigious level of literary production and research until his death 20 years later; the *Lundis* fill 15 volumes in the definitive 3rd edition and are followed by a further 13 volumes of *Nouveaux lundis.*

Concept of culture

In these essays he tried, first, to reformulate his concept of culture, a concept based on a strong sense of tradition, stability, and decorum. To him, the highest manifestation of French culture was the world of the salons of Mme du Deffand, in pre-Revolutionary France, or Mme Récamier in his own time; but he expanded his survey to suit the larger horizons of the 19th century, also giving some attention to the contribution of other European and Oriental cultures. Not surprisingly, he welcomed the rise of Napoleon III's more dictatorial and orderly regime. In due course, his sympathy was rewarded by appointment to the chair of Latin at the Collège de France, a well-paid but largely nominal post. In his own case it remained entirely nominal, since his first lectures were interrupted by demonstrations of radical students, and he resigned his duties and salary, retaining only the title. The intended lectures were published as a full-length study of Virgil.

In 1858 Sainte-Beuve received a temporary teaching appointment in literature at the École Normale Supérieure, where he drew upon his 1848 researches to deliver a course on medieval French literature; but otherwise his whole later career was based upon free-lance essay writing.

Critical essays during the Second Empire. Under the Second French Empire, which survived him by less than a year, many of Sainte-Beuve's earlier acquaintances, now dead or in retirement, were replaced by other writers: Gustave Flaubert, Ernest Renan, the Goncourt brothers, Prosper Mérimée, Ivan Turgenev, Alexandre Dumas, Matthew Arnold, and a large number of scholars, historians, and academicians. He frequented the salon of the Emperor's cousin, the princess Mathilde, somewhat of a literary centre itself, though less formal in style than had been the salon of Mme Récamier until 1848. At the restaurant Magny he relaxed from time to time with his literary friends. He regularly attended the theatre once a week. And he continued to see old friends from time to time—including Adèle Hugo, who occasionally visited him in Paris.

Nevertheless, the crushing task of researching, writing, correcting, and proofreading a 3,000-word essay for publication every Monday in effect largely prevented Sainte-Beuve from exploring in the same leisurely way as in his youth the many new trends being developed by young writers.

In religious matters, he retained (like his young friend and admirer Renan) a lively sensibility and curiosity but essayed no further commitment whatever. He was uninterested in the debates on evolution. Living a sheltered, almost monastic, bachelor existence, he paid little attention to the rise of industrialism or the economic controversies of the empire. On the other hand, his social conscience remained extremely acute. He welcomed the influence of earlier Saint-Simonian friends at the new court, and his sympathy for the underdog was reflected not only in his charitable activities but also in his support for popular education and self-help.

Defense of intellectual liberty

Politically, also, he retained a very decided independence even vis-à-vis his imperial patrons and protectors. Although in 1865 he was made a senator, he took little or no part in the formal proceedings of the upper legislative house except on one occasion. When, under heavy pressure from the church, the government banned the works of Ernest Renan from the public libraries as being subversive of good morals and religion, he prepared and attempted to deliver a withering denunciation of this violation of intellectual liberty. This brought down upon him the wrath of the princess Mathilde and the indignation of many officials and friends, but Sainte-Beuve was unrepentant. In fact, he transferred his weekly essay to an independent review.

Sainte-Beuve died on October 13, 1869, in Paris after unsuccessful bladder stone operations. For the last year of his life he had suffered considerable pain, borne courageously.

Reputation and influence. His writings were not only voluminous but also enormously influential in the world of French literature, and they continue to be consulted and used. For the study of French literature from the Renaissance to the mid-19th century, they constitute a vast and unequalled repository of information, much of it well indexed. A portion of his scholarly research has, with time, become old-fashioned, but within limits the precision of his documentation is almost always impeccable, even over details on which it has been challenged by literary opponents. This precision is due to a lifetime's habit of extreme care in documentation as well as to his fanatical respect for historical accuracy. In one of the commonplace books in which he recorded his thoughts as they came to him, he wrote:

> The *Good*, the *True*, and the *Beautiful* make a fine motto, and a specious one. It has been adopted by M. Cousin for his well-known book: but dare I say it, it is not my motto. If I had a motto it would be *"Truth* and *Truth* alone." And let the *Good* and the *Beautiful* look after themselves as best they may.

Concept of criticism

This attitude lies back of a somewhat unfavourable aura that surrounds the critic's reputation as a judge. From his earliest review articles on Hugo, Sainte-Beuve was never afraid to introduce specific reservations into his most enthusiastic eulogies; and it was this liberty that in his own eyes justified his claim to uncompromising independence but also earned him the reputation of being an unreliable, or even perfidious, critic of friends. In the first years of his career the then fashionable romantic doctrine of inspiration made no provision for the role of the critic as adviser, sounding board, or judge, and it was partly the recognition of this fact that caused Sainte-Beuve to move away from Lamartine, Hugo, Vigny, George Sand, and others in the years 1834–37 and to resist the charm of these romantic spellbinders. His essay "Critical Genius" (1835) postulates a critical activity that is inquisitive, untrammelled, independent, and a contributory element in the formation of public opinion and private taste; and to this liberal conception he adhered throughout his working life.

It is sometimes claimed that Sainte-Beuve made, or wished to make, of criticism a form of comparative psychology, a botany of minds, as he himself said. This claim is based on several famous passages in *Port-Royal*. Unquestionably, he detected in the Jansenists of Port-Royal a number of family characteristics, due to common religious beliefs, shared experiences, and common values; but this was for him only one of many ways of critical study—along with textual analysis, biographical inquiry, historical contextualization, etc. Sainte-Beuve, in fact, escapes simple definition not only by the mass but also by the variety of his criticism.

MAJOR WORKS

VERSE: *Vie, poésies, et pensées de Joseph Delorme* (1829); *Les Consolations* (1830); *Pensées d'août* (1837); *Livre d'amour* (1843).

NOVEL: *Volupté* (1834).

CRITICISM: *Tableau historique et critique de la poésie française et du théâtre français au XVIe siècle* (1828); *Port-Royal*, 3 vol. (1840–48); *Critiques et portraits littéraires* (1836–39); *Portraits de femmes* (1844); *Portraits contemporains* (1846); *Causeries du lundi*, 15 vol. (1851–62); *Étude sur Virgile* (1857); *Chateaubriand et son groupe littéraire sous l'Empire* (1861); *Nouveaux lundis*, 13 vol. (1863–70); *Premiers lundis*, 3 vol. (1874–75).

TRANSLATIONS: Not all of Sainte-Beuve's works are available in English, but some useful collections include *Causeries du lundi* (selected and ed. by G. Saintsbury, 1885; Eng. trans. with introduction and notes by E.J. Trechmann, 8 vol., 1909–11; 2 vol. also by Trechmann, 1933); *Essays by Sainte-Beuve*, ed. by A. Tilley (1918); and *Sainte-Beuve: Selected Essays,* ed. by F. Steegmuller and N. Guterman (1963).

BIBLIOGRAPHY. J. BONNEROT, *Bibliographie de l'oeuvre de Sainte-Beuve*, 3 vol. (1937–52), covers the huge range of textual and critical problems and also attempts to itemize what Sainte-Beuve actually read in his long career. The principal collection of manuscripts, with the bulk of the critic's notes and notebooks and many letters, is the Collection Spoelberch de Lovenjoul, Bibliothèque de l'Institut, Chantilly, France. The best editions containing the critic's last revisions are as follows: *Causeries du lundi*, 3rd ed., 15 vol. (1857–72); *Chateaubriand et son groupe littéraire sous l'Empire*, new ed., 2 pt. (1948), with useful notes by M. ALLEM; *Étude sur Virgile* (1857); *Le Clou d'or* (1881, reprinted 1920), several minor short stories; *Livre d'amour* (1904, first edition to be strictly speaking published); *Nouveaux lundis*, 13 vol. (1863–70); *Poésies complètes*, 2 pt. (1861–63); *Portraits contemporains*, new ed., 5 vol. (1869–71); *Portraits de femmes*, new ed. (1870); *Portraits littéraires*—the best edition is that of the "Pléiade Series," 2 vol. (1949 and 1951); *Port-Royal*, 3rd ed., 6 vol. (1866–67, "Pléiade"); *Premiers lundis*, 3 vol. (1874–75, "Pléiade"); *Tableau historique et critique de la poésie française et du théâtre français au XVIe siècle*, 2nd ed. rev. (1843), with many changes from the first edition; and *Volupté*, 8th ed. (1874). The *Correspondance générale*, ed. by J. BONNEROT, 16 vol. to date (1934–70), is the most fully annotated and comprehensive collection of Sainte-Beuve's letters. A.G. LEHMANN, *Sainte-Beuve: A Portrait of the Critic, 1804–1842* (1962), based on recent research, is a study of the critic in the world of ideas and letters of his time; A. BILLY, *Sainte-Beuve: sa vie et son temps*, 2 vol. (1952–62), contains many anecdotes.

(A.G.L.)

Saint-Just, Louis de

Famous as one of the most zealous advocates of the Reign of Terror during the French Revolution, Louis de Saint-Just played a prominent, although brief, role in the National Convention and the Committee of Public Safety, as well as serving as commissioner to the armies. Many of his contemporaries acknowledged his ability but considered him a monster of pride and cruelty. Others, particularly in later generations, have viewed him as an incorruptible patriot who paid with his life for his allegiance to democracy. Some have seen in him the prototype of the rebel. These contradictions arise in part from Saint-Just's complex character and in part from an imperfect knowledge of his childhood and adolescence.

Early years

Louis-Antoine-Léon de Saint-Just was born on August 25, 1767, at Decize in central France, the son of a cavalry captain. His mother, the daughter of a wealthy local notary and a woman of egalitarian notions, wished to reduce the nobility to the level of the middle class. The family eventually moved to Blérancourt, a rural town in Picardy, the native province of his father, who died there in 1777.

After attending the College of the Oratorians in nearby Soissons, he returned to Blérancourt, a small town offering few distractions. In 1785 Saint-Just became attached to the daughter of one of the town's notaries. Her forced marriage to the son of the other notary in July 1786 marked the beginning of a crisis for Saint-Just. Hurt and angry, he fled to Paris one night in September, taking with him a few family valuables. Lodging near the Palais Royal, then the centre of a brilliant and dissolute society, he soon ran out of money. His adventure came to a sudden end when his mother, advised of the situation, had him put into a reformatory. He remained there from October 1786 to April 1787. Sobered by his experience, he decided, like so many young men of the middle class, to establish himself and enter upon a career. He became a clerk to the public prosecutor of Soissons, studied at Reims, and took his law degree in April 1788.

France at that time was shaken by the effects of a poor harvest and a hard winter, which coincided with pre-Revolutionary tremors. In 1789, Saint-Just anonymously published his first book, an epic poem, *Organt*. It was ignored by the public. A long satirical and licentious poem strewn with political allusions, it was reminiscent of Voltaire's "La Pucelle" ("The Maiden"), but it lacked the force and spirit needed for public acclaim. Perhaps Saint-Just was trying to set his own mind free rather than to achieve fame. *Organt* sometimes suggests the misadventures of Saint-Just, with his violent enthusiasms and resentments; but the eroticism is heavy, and few of the

By courtesy of the Bibliotheque Nationale, Paris

Saint-Just, portrait by an unknown artist after a red chalk drawing by Christophe Guérin, 1793.

themes of his later work appear. Saint-Just's friends scarcely mentioned it, and his enemies derided it. The book was seized by the authorities in June 1789, and, although it had been issued anonymously, Saint-Just was prudent enough to hide at a friend's home in Paris.

In the midst of the Revolutionary upheaval, Saint-Just, eager to participate, found himself ignored. Neither a Parisian nor a popular orator nor a leader of men, he was also not inclined to approve of slaughter. He did not speak of the storming of the Bastille, which he had witnessed, until a year later, when his attitude seemed reminiscent of that of the British politician Edmund Burke, who opposed the French Revolution. Saint-Just returned to his home town at the end of July. The provinces, like Paris, were in full revolt. Militia or national guard units were spontaneously forming everywhere, and Saint-Just became commander of the second unit organized in Blérancourt.

But first he had to overcome the handicap of his youth and the opposition of local cliques. As a militia commander he went to Paris for the Fête de la Fédération on July 14, 1790. He did not linger there and later spoke of it in tones of disillusionment.

Saint-Just realized that he could play the role to which he aspired in the Revolution only by election to a key post as an administrator or, preferably, as a deputy. He had, however, not reached the legally required age of 25. For most men the political clubs provided the necessary stepping-stone but not for Saint-Just, who was never a club man, doubtless because he was too overbearing. Instead, he became the municipal corporation counsel of Blérancourt, championed communal welfare and free trade, and set himself up as a spokesman for the voters. At the same time, however, he resumed his friendship with the girl whom he had been unable to marry and, in defiance of gossip, met her publicly.

He succeeded in establishing his reputation beyond Blérancourt in the district, where he was considered an energetic and able candidate for the next National Assembly. To further his candidacy, he wrote letters to politicians shamelessly flattering their self-esteem and even managed to receive the congratulations of the National Assembly after publicly burning a counter revolutionary pamphlet.

Though he was driven by ambition, his ambition was to serve the cause of the poor and the peasants, and, if he turned toward Robespierre, the most pitiless of the Revolutionaries, it was from conviction. Saint-Just now proposed directing the Revolution beyond benevolent and patriotic activity toward the making of a new society. In

Publication of Esprit de la Révolution

1791 he finally published *Esprit de la Révolution et de la Constitution de France*. The exposition was bold, vigorous, and lofty. The brief, forceful, and elliptical formulations characterized the author. According to him, the constitution framed by the Assembly was acceptable as a first step, but the French were not yet free. Nor were they sovereign, but sovereignty of the people was acceptable only if the people were just and rational. "Law should yield nothing to opinion and everything to ethics," Saint-Just maintained. He confided to his publisher that the boldness of his exposition attracted readers and rightly added that his work, because it was based on less extensive reading than he might have wished, had the originality of a solitary thinker.

At that time Saint-Just believed himself to be on the eve of a political career, and his elimination from the Assembly as a result of his age provoked a serious crisis. "I am a slave of my adolescence!" he cried revealingly.

He then continued his reflections on the great task of building a society based on nature in which men would live together rather than merely side by side. Taking his region as a model, he observed the village communal traditions. This sojourn in the provinces directed his thinking while straining his energies.

Elected to the Convention

His election to the National Convention in September 1792, shortly after he became 25, finally gave him a task cut to his measure. The new Assembly had to untangle the crisis created by the fall of the King and the invasion of France and to undertake the vast task of reconstruction. "The people have looked only for oracles and for

their happiness," he said. He was the oracle, self-assured and bold, personifying the uncompromising republican virtues. With unshakable authority he tackled financial and economic problems and, finally, military questions. His thought and style made him, with Robespierre, one of the leaders of the extreme left.

When sent on a mission to the armies, he revealed himself also as a man of action. His dreaded decisiveness was accompanied by a solicitude for the soldiers: "True happiness is found only in the comforting of the unhappy." A terror to the generals, he exercised his role of benificent dispenser of justice throughout a series of missions to the armies that gave rise to the romanticized concept of Saint-Just.

He rose by degrees in the Convention, and beginning in May 1793 he joined the Committee of Public Safety, the small group that governed France. After playing a considerable part in eliminating both left and right deviationists, he finally supplanted the less audacious Robespierre.

The year II of the French Republican calendar (1793–94), in which Saint-Just, elected president of the Convention, passed the Ventôse (March) decrees and led the victorious attack against the Austrians at Fleurus in the Austrian Netherlands (modern Belgium) on June 26, 1794, marked the high point of his career. The Ventôse laws, by which the property of enemies of the Revolution was confiscated for the benefit of poverty-stricken patriots, were the most revolutionary act of the French Revolution, because they expropriated from one class for the benefit of another. During the same period Saint-Just drafted *Fragmens sur les institutions républicaines*, far more radical proposals than the constitutions he had helped to frame; this work laid the theoretical groundwork for a communal and egalitarian society.

But his rise to power had wrought a remarkable change in Saint-Just's public personality. He became a cold, almost inhuman fanatic, bloodthirsty as even his "god" Robespierre, a man of many human weaknesses, was not. "The vessel of the Revolution can arrive in port only on a sea reddened with torrents of blood," Saint-Just once declared to the Convention. He, rather than Robespierre, showed himself to be the forerunner of the totalitarian rulers of the 20th century when he said on another occasion, "We must not only punish traitors, but all people who are not enthusiastic. There are only two kinds of citizens: the good and the bad. The Republic owes to the good its protection. To the bad it owes only death."

Dreaded, almost totally isolated, and detested, he was arrested on 9 Thermidor (July 27, 1794). Like Robespierre, he did not try to incite the Parisian sans-culottes to rise against the Convention in his defense and was guillotined the next day.

Assessment

Saint-Just has, by turns, been lauded as the archangel of the Revolution or abhorred as the terrorist par excellence. Recent scholarly research has made it possible to draw the line between man and myth. Undoubtedly the Revolution changed the unruly, self-indulgent youth into a principled and decisive, though ruthless, leader. To friends he was also kind, helping them in securing positions. Yet, it is doubtful whether he had friends in the true sense, for those whom he helped attached themselves to him without becoming his equals.

Women admired his attractive appearance, and he could be very engaging when he wished. Nonetheless, he had to make notes on the conduct required "to be fortunate with women." He measured out doses of eagerness and indifference, affection and restraint, so as to make a love affair last. Yet, he could be genuinely affectionate and display real family feeling. This other Saint-Just appears in the famous portraits of Jean-Baptiste Greuze, Jacques-Louis David, and other painters.

BIBLIOGRAPHY. E.N. CURTIS, *Saint-Just, Colleague of Robespierre* (1935), a thorough study of the manuscripts and publications of the period, with bibliography; ALBERT OLLIVIER, *Saint-Just et la force de choses* (1954), André Malraux's preface emphasizes the orientation: Saint-Just is the prototype of the rebel—the interpretation is more engaging than truly historical, although it is provided with references, bibliography, and critical discussions; ALBERT

SOBOUL, *Proceedings de Saint-Just symposium* (1968), authoritative contributions to the historical understanding of Saint-Just, with an exhaustive bibliography of his works.

(M.Re.)

Saint Lawrence, Gulf of

The Gulf of St. Lawrence, in southeast Canada, fringes the shores of half the provinces of that country and is a gateway to the interior of the entire North American continent. Its name is not entirely accurate, for in a hydrological context the gulf has to be considered more as a sea bordering the North American continent than as a simple river mouth. Its area is approximately 60,000 square miles (155,000 square kilometres), a little less than half that of the Baltic Sea. Its boundaries, which have always been a subject for discussion among geographers, may be taken as the maritime estuary at the mouth of the St. Lawrence River, in the vicinity of Anticosti Island, on the west; the narrow Strait of Belle Isle between Newfoundland and the mainland, to the north; and the Cabot Strait, separating Newfoundland from the Nova Scotian peninsula, on the south.

The gulf is also a relief phenomenon, for the underlying topography is in fact made up of submerged portions of the northern end of the Appalachian mountain range, as well as of the southern periphery of the vast, ancient rock mass known as the Canadian Shield. The topography of the floor of the gulf can be subdivided into several sections. First of all, there are the deepest zones: the St. Lawrence Channel and the Mingan Passage, whose orientation is toward the southeast, and the Eskimo Channel running to the southwest. Together, these channels occupy approximately one-quarter of the total area of the gulf. Then there are the submarine platforms, often less than 165 feet (50 metres) in depth, of which the most important, known as the Acadian Platform, occupies a large semicircle between the Gaspé Peninsula and Cape

Submarine relief

Breton. The relief of this area is not at all uniform because it includes such depressions as the Chaleurs Trough, shelves like the Banc de Bradelle, the Northumberland Strait, and above-water sections such as Prince Edward Island. On the far side of the axial St. Lawrence Trough are three northern elongated platforms: the Anticosti Platform, near to the island of the same name; one which skirts the low northern coast of the gulf; and finally, one lying between the Eskimo Channel and Newfoundland. The reefs on these surfaces, coupled with the hazards of fog and ice, have caused a large number of shipwrecks among the numerous vessels plying the region.

The body of water constituting the gulf is replenished not only by the local rainfall (35.5 inches [902 millimetres] annually at Cap-aux-Meules in the Magdalen Islands) but also from three great "gateways." The first of these, the maritime estuary, pours in approximately 495,000 cubic feet (14,000 cubic metres) per second of cool, soft water, and at ebb tide, a considerably larger volume of sea water, together with a formidable quantity of ice in the winter months. In the Strait of Belle Isle, which forms the second entry, the oceanographic situation is very complex. No less than seven types of water have been distinguished there, with temperatures varying from 29.1° F (−1.6° C) to 51.8° F (11° C), and a salinity fluctuating from 27.2 to 34.5 parts per thousand. The third gateway, Cabot Strait, is by far the most important; through it the Atlantic and Arctic waters enter (having already passed Newfoundland to the east), and it is through here that the major proportion of water and ice leaves the gulf.

The principal current consists of a peripheral counterclockwise circulation, which hugs the platforms of the northeast and then enters the estuary. This penetrates as far inland as the Pointe des Monts and even reaches as far as the entry of the Saguenay River into the St. Lawrence just over a hundred miles from the city of Quebec. This current continues under the name of the Gaspé Current, having three branches between the Honguedo and Cabot straits.

This circulation, as well as a weak tide, tends to mix the waters of the gulf, but they remain stratified. In the centre of the gulf are three superimposed levels: the deep stratum (38.3° F [3.5° C] and 33.5 parts per thousand salinity), the intermediate stratum with a depth of 50 metres (165 feet) (33° F [0.5° C] and 32.5 parts per thousand salinity), and the surface stratum, which is less salty and undergoes strong seasonal thermal variations.

Ice

Ice floes constitute one of the most prominent characteristics of the gulf. Ice formation is delayed because of the salinity, the latent heat of the mass of water, and the slow passage of upstream ice; thus ice is not abundant in the gulf before mid-February. The thaw, often late, permits the Cabot Strait to have normal maritime traffic at least a month before the Strait of Belle Isle. At the end of May, the sheltered water surface between Prince Edward Island and Nova Scotia, into which the north wind drives the ice, is the last section of the gulf to be ice-free.

The life of the gulf is a function of various general conditions: light, temperature, salinity, available food, ice, etc. In addition to such organisms as the phytobenthos and zoobenthos of the coastline and of the depths, fish such as cod and mammals such as the white whale may be distinguished. The banks and the islands of the gulf include numerous nesting places of birds, notably the Bassan gannet (see also SAINT LAWRENCE RIVER; SAINT LAWRENCE SEAWAY).

BIBLIOGRAPHY. CANADA, DEPARTMENT OF TRANSPORT, *Ice Summary and Analysis: Eastern Canadian Seaboard* (annual), a series of maps showing floating ice concentration in the gulf of St. Lawrence and its relationship to climate and navigation; CANADA, FISHERIES RESEARCH BOARD, *Report of the Atlantic Herring Investigation Committee*, Bull. No. 111 (1957), a series of scientific articles on the waters of the gulf and the biological conditions of fishing, principally herring fishing; CANADA, HYDROGRAPHIC SERVICE, *Gulf of St. Lawrence Pilot* (rev. annually), an official publication containing precise surveys of bathymetry and navigation; *Cahiers de géographie de Québec*, a special issue devoted to the St. Lawrence, No. 23 (1967), a series of multidisciplinary studies (in English and French), with an important bibliography; L.E. HAMELIN, *Sables et mer aux Iles-de-la-Madeleine* (1959), a study of the physical and general geography of the archipelago of the Madeleine Islands and of the surrounding waters of the St. Lawrence; W.H. TWENHOFEL, *The Geology of Anticosti Island* (1927), a geological study of the large island situated between the estuary and the gulf of St. Lawrence.

(L.-E.H.)

Saint Lawrence River

The great hydrographic system connecting the source of the St. Louis River, in the U.S. state of Minnesota, with Cabot Strait, leading into the Atlantic Ocean from the extreme east of Canada, the St. Lawrence River crosses the interior of the North American continent for almost 2,500 miles (4,023 kilometres), and is of vital geographic and economic importance. It can be divided into three broad sectors. Upstream lies the Great Lakes region, with narrow riverlike sections linking the broad expanses of the lakes themselves. In the centre, from the eastern outflow of Lake Ontario, near the town of Kingston, to the Île d'Orléans, just downstream from the city of Quebec, the system passes through a more normal watercourse. From the Île d'Orléans to the Cabot Strait, between Newfoundland and Nova Scotia, the system broadens out again, first as the St. Lawrence estuary, and then, passing the island of Anticosti, as the oval shaped marine region known as the Gulf of St. Lawrence.

The article GREAT LAKES covers the first of the regions described above, and the article SAINT LAWRENCE, GULF OF treats of the marine section from Anticosti Island to Cabot Strait. The article entitled SAINT LAWRENCE SEAWAY considers the engineering, economic, and political aspects of the vast man-made improvements to the system as a whole, and the present article concentrates on the course of the St. Lawrence River from Kingston to Anticosti Island (that is, on the riverlike and estuarine portions of the system). This region, passing through the heartland of the Canadian nation, has abundant scientific documentation relating to it.

The St. Lawrence River occupies a geologically old depression that involves three great geologic regions of

Origin

North America: the Canadian Shield, the Appalachian Mountains, and the intervening sedimentary rock platform. This ancient setting has been broken up by earth movements along several zones of structural weakness and has also been worn down by a number of separate cycles of erosion. Toward the end of the geologically recent Quaternary Period, the Ice Age glaciers that had occupied the depression were replaced by the Champlain Sea, which flooded the floor of the depression from about 11,400 to 9,500 years ago. The subsequent slight uplifting of the continent was enough to expel this arm of the ocean and, about 6,000 years ago, a residual riverlike watercourse was established, and the St. Lawrence—a young watercourse as rivers go—was born.

In terms of both climate and hydrology, the St. Lawrence system as a whole has several regional zones. First, in the movement downstream from the upper part of the system, some of the associated boreal character is lost; in its path from the northern streams tributary to Lake Superior down to Lake Erie, the system passes from a sub-Arctic to a more temperate southern zone. In a similar, but reverse, fashion, the eastern half of the system increases in northern character downstream; that is, from the Detroit–Windsor metropolitan area at the western end of Lake Erie to the northern coast of the St. Lawrence estuary, the climate deteriorates again to a semi-Arctic level. This basic division brings out the regional contrasts in the hydrology of the central section of the river. Lake Erie, for example, loses much water through summer evaporation, whereas the affluents feeding the estuary of the St. Lawrence are heavily influenced by snowfall characteristics. At Montreal a good part of the river flow comes from the Great Lakes; hence its remarkable regularity. At the mouth of the estuary, on the other hand, the volume of ocean water coming in at high tide is 12 times the volume of river water flowing down at low tide; and here the St. Lawrence is profoundly marine, rather than lacustrine, in character. These basic regional hydrographic traits are accentuated also by a large seasonal variation in water temperature.

Regional divisions. The regional division of the St. Lawrence raises difficult problems, and despite several works on the subject, the debate among scientists remains open. The following division has been based on such overall criteria as longitudinal gradient of the riverbed, tidal characteristics, salinity, the width of the river bottom, human geography, and animal life. Threshold zones, a dozen miles or so in length, mark the transition from one region to the next.

The St. Lawrence of the international rapids. This forms a clearly defined region extending from Kingston to above Montreal, where the presence of sudden breaks of gradient in the riverbed, the necessity of a navigable route between Montreal and southern Ontario, and the regional needs for power have led to the creation of hydroelectric stations, canals, and, of course, a significant part of the St. Lawrence Seaway. The flow volume of this section of the St. Lawrence, as measured at Cornwall, is 218,000 cubic feet per second (6,104 cubic metres per second).

Quebec Basses Terres. This region is made up of a short section with a calm and nonreversible flow. Situated for the most part in the Quebec Basses Terres area, this portion of the river course is characterized by the inflow of the system's principal tributary, the Rivière des Outaouais, by the presence of numerous islands (the Hochelaga Archipelago upstream, the Cent Îles downstream), by the development of the Greater Montreal conurbation, and also, unfortunately, by a certain degree of pollution. The development of the port of Montreal has depended upon, among other factors, the deepening of the river channel—downstream through dredging and upstream by canalization—by means of engineering projects that were begun in the 19th century. During the winter months, a thick crust of ice connects the two banks of the river, and icebreakers must open a channel in order for even a limited number of ships to reach Montreal. In earlier years, the possibilities of ice jams were great, with notable ice catastrophes occurring in 1642, 1838, and 1896.

The upper estuary. This extends from Lake Saint-Pierre to below the Île d'Orléans at Quebec. Here, the current of a freshwater tide begins to be reversible. During the winter months, the ice covering recalls the conditions at Montreal, but it also anticipates those of the middle estuary (see below), where a distinction is necessary between banked, or reef, ice, which is solid and fissured, and conglomerate ice, which moves past offshore. Topographical conditions at the river littoral, which had great military value, led to the foundation of the city of Quebec in this region, in 1608. The immediately adjacent area has been the historical cradle of the distinctive French-speaking population of Canada.

The middle estuary. From the eastern end of the Île d'Orléans to the upstream side of the confluence with its major tributary, the Saguenay, the St. Lawrence broadens but remains relatively shallow. Progressively, the water ceases to be fresh and becomes brackish, and with an east wind one may, for the first time, catch a whiff of seaweed. Tides, thrust into a narrowing channel, attain maximum height in this section. Breakaway reef ice from this area constitutes one of the major sources of ice in the downstream parts of the estuary.

The lower estuary. One of the greatest topographic alterations in the entire course of the St. Lawrence is found near the Saguenay confluence, at right angles to a submarine furrow. In this region, the river bottom exhibits a brutal break of gradient: within ten miles, all in the vicinity of the confluence, the depth of the water increases from 82 feet (25 metres) to 1,148 feet (350 metres). It is by way of this drowned valley that the cold, salt waters from downstream, classed as Arctic, enter the region. In spite of the width of the watercourse, a number of ferries connect the two banks. In contrast to the thinly settled northern bank, behind which lie the inhospitable, rugged landscapes of the ancient rock region known as the Canadian Shield, the southern frontage of the lower estuary is largely open toward its hinterland, and major roads, including the Trans-Canada Highway, lead inland toward the province of New Brunswick.

The maritime estuary. The limits of this region are, upstream, the promontory of the Pointe des Monts, and, leading to the Gulf of St. Lawrence, the island of Anticosti. (The latter, by reason of its size and its own circular currents, is an entity in its own right and cannot be considered as an element of the estuary.) Below the Pointe des Monts, the submarine valley mentioned above doubles in width, to over 50 miles. A major arm of the counter-clockwise current stemming from the Gulf of St. Lawrence, after entering the northern portion of this region, turns back to the east. The salinity found here discourages ice formation, and, on the northern shore, the port of Sept Îles—although situated much farther north than Montreal—is in fact more open to navigation. The north frontage, with a hinterland rich in iron ore and electricity-generating potential and running at right angles to this portion of the estuary, seems to have greater capacity for development.

River life. In spite of centuries of human influence, the biological world of the St. Lawrence continues to reflect natural conditions. Some clear regional distinctions must be made between not only the upper and lower sections of the system but also between the depths and the surface of the water and between the banks and the centre of the river course. Scientists have not, as yet, succeeded in identifying fully the basic life-producing conditions, the identity of the various eutrophic, or nutrition-generating, water levels, or the migrations of food supply, all of which go to make up the biomass, or life system, associated with the river. Animal life comprises fish (including the sturgeon, the smelt, and the herring), mammals (including an "Arctic" species, the beluga [white whale], and mollusks (including the mussel [mye]). A noted phenomenon, which is characteristic of all regions of the river, is the massive migration of ducks, bustards, and geese, which utilize the sandy shores or river reefs as seasonal food sources. The vegetation associated with the river undoubtedly reflects the great shrubby zones that extend from Lake Erie to the northeast of the Gulf of St. Lawrence, made up of deciduous forest, mixed forest, coniferous forest, and open taiga. In addition, however, it exhibits such specifically river-linked characteristics as the sandbank grasses of the freshwater section, and the plants with a high tolerance of salt found from the middle estuary onward.

Conclusion. The St. Lawrence is a mighty, unique river, estuarine over much of its course; bedded in an ancient geological depression, it drains the heart of a continent. It is at once an international, an intra-Quebec, and a multiprovincial system. An axis of regional population, it is also a routeway linking Canada, the United States, western Europe, and a large part of the rest of the world. The frontages of the six regions of the St. Lawrence River described above are not equally developed and do not maintain the same types of relationship with their hinterlands and with the outside world. Throughout its length, nevertheless, the St. Lawrence is a river retaining a great natural beauty, with landscapes beloved by all who live on its banks or make the long passage along its course.

BIBLIOGRAPHY. CANADA, HYDROGRAPHIC SERVICE, *St. Lawrence Pilot* (rev. annually), an official publication of the Canadian government containing data relative to bathymetry, the shores, and navigation; "Bibliographie choisie sur L'océanographie de l'estuaire du Saint-Laurent" and "Les grandes divisions du Saint-Laurent," *La Revue de géographie de Montréal*, 24:277–303 (1970), expositions of various points of view on the definition and boundaries of the regions of the St. Lawrence (particularly noteworthy are the contributions of P. Brunel and C. Laverdière); *Cahiers de géographie de Québec*, a special issue devoted to the St. Lawrence, no. 23 (1967), a series of multidisciplinary studies, with a large classified bibliography (the article by Jacques Rousseau is particularly useful).

(L.–E.H.)

Saint Lawrence Seaway

A massive $466,000,000 Canadian–United States navigational project opened North America's industrial and agricultural heartlands to deep-draft ocean vessels in April of 1959. It forged the final link in a 2,342-mile waterway from Duluth, Minn., to the Atlantic by clearing a way through a 182-mile stretch of the St. Lawrence River (*q.v.*) between Montreal and Lake Ontario. The entire Great Lakes–St. Lawrence system, with 9,500 miles (15,300 kilometres) of navigable waterways, has come to be known as the St. Lawrence Seaway and has created a "fourth coast line" for the United States and Canada.

Efforts to sail into the heart of the continent date from 1535, when the French explorer Jacques Cartier, seeking a northwest passage to the Orient, found his path blocked by the Lachine Rapids, west of what is now Montreal. The digging of shallow St. Lawrence canals for bateaux (long, tapering boats with flat bottoms) in 1783, the construction of the Erie Canal from Buffalo, N.Y., to the Hudson River from 1817 to 1825, the opening of the first canal around Niagara Falls in 1829, and the completion of the first lock, at Sault Ste. Marie, in 1855, all fostered the dream. But the United States proved a reluctant partner in a venture, pursued by Canada from 1913 onward, to open the Great Lakes to sea traffic. The U.S. Senate rejected the Seaway Treaty of 1932 and allowed a second treaty, signed in 1941, to remain unratified for eight years. Faced with the likelihood that Canada would proceed alone, the U.S. Congress approved participation in the project in May of 1954, and construction began just three months later.

Technology. The seaway project is considered one of man's greatest engineering feats. Locks in the seaway and Canada's Welland Canal raise and lower large ships 557 feet, the world's greatest waterway lifting operation. It takes only about 7 minutes for 22,000,000 gallons of water to pour in or out of a seaway lock, but the average locking takes about 33 minutes. The total seaway system overcomes a 602-foot drop from Lake Superior to the sea. To overcome the navigational hazard of the swift-flowing 226-foot fall of the St. Lawrence River between Lake Ontario and Montreal, and to develop its power potential, re-

quired an investment of more than $1,000,000,000. It employed 22,000 workers and utilized $70,000,000 of construction equipment, enough cement to build a 1,000-mile highway and enough steel to girdle the earth. Communities containing 6,500 people had to be relocated, bridges raised, and tunnels, dikes, and roads constructed.

Construction

The navigation portion of the project included a $332,-500,000 expenditure by the Canadian government to build two canals and five locks around Soulanges and Lachine Rapids and three seaway dams, and $133,-500,000 spent by the U.S. government to build two locks, a ten-mile canal around the International Rapids, and two seaway dams, and to clear shoals from the Thousand Islands section of the river. This series of operations created a 27-foot-deep waterway, replacing six canals and 22 locks limited to 14-foot depth. Opening of the seaway required many other projects as well. The U.S. Army Corps of Engineers spent about $200,000,000 to deepen the Straits of Mackinac, between Lake Michigan and Lake Huron; the St. Marys River, between Lake Superior and Lake Huron; the Detroit River, Lake St. Clair, and the St. Clair River, between Lake Erie and Lake Huron; and many Great Lakes harbours. Between 1913 and 1932, Canada had spent $132,000,000 to build seven lift locks of seaway dimensions in the Welland Canal, which overcomes the 326-foot plunge of the Niagara River and Falls, between Lake Erie and Lake Ontario.

To tap the energy of the St. Lawrence River's tumbling waters, the seaway project included a power dam containing 32 hydroelectric turbine generators and two related dams to control and direct the full force of the river through the power dam. The $600,000,000 cost and 1,600,000 kilowatts of generating capacity were shared equally by the Hydro-Electric Power Commission of Ontario and the Power Authority of the State of New York. The dams created a 30-mile lake. Generation of hydroelectric power began in July 1958.

Economic significance. Over its first decade of operation, the St. Lawrence Seaway carried more than 500,-000,000 tons of cargo, worth about $22,000,000,000, at estimated transportation savings of about $500,000,000. By 1970, annual combined traffic through the Seaway–Welland Canal locks totalled nearly 9,000 cargo-carrying vessels, loaded with over 65,000,000 tons of freight, of which approximately 16,000,000 tons were destined for, or arriving from, overseas ports. The total tonnage was more than triple that in the seaway's first year, 1959, and foreign trade (non-U.S. and Canadian) was about seven times greater. The overall value of cargo carried approached $5,000,000,000. As the price of approving seaway legislation, the U.S. Congress required that the project be self-liquidating, and Canada too adopted this as a national policy. Tolls were to be assessed at a rate sufficient to pay back cost of the project in 50 years, to pay annual interest on the funds borrowed to build it, and to pay all operating costs. The two nations jointly established a system of tolls, which were criticized as too high by shippers and as too low by competing ports. By the early 1970s, vessels were charged 40 cents a ton for bulk cargo, or 90 cents a ton for general cargo, to use locks between Montreal and Lake Ontario, plus 4 cents per gross registered ton of the vessel itself. There was a minimum charge of $14 for pleasure craft and $28 for other vessels, plus a $3.50 charge per passenger. Each nation collects tolls in its own currency, on facilities in its territory, resulting in a split of about 73 percent of the revenue to Canada and 27 percent to the U.S. There are no tolls on the Welland Canal, but a charge per lock is made. By the mid-1970s, this was expected to amount to $100 for cargo and passenger vessels, $3 for pleasure craft, and $5 for other vessels. Seaway revenue, in the first two decades of its operation, consistently fell far short of annual interest and operating costs, putting the seaway deeper in debt. By the opening of the decade of the 1970s the St. Lawrence Seaway Authority, which runs Canada's installations, had accumulated operating losses in excess of $65,000,000, excluding over $70,000,000 in losses, since 1959, by the Welland Canal, the latter covered by Parliamentary appropriations. The Authority had also ac-

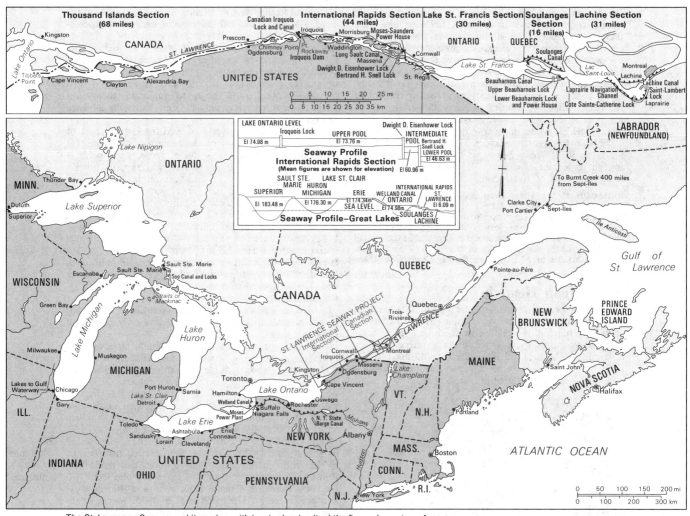

The St. Lawrence Seaway and its region, with insets showing (top) the five main sectors of
the project and (centre) cross sections of the lock and canal system.
By courtesy of The St. Lawrence Seaway Development Corp.

Financial
problems

cumulated a debt of nearly $70,000,000 in unpaid inter-
est. This boosted its total debt to over $400,000,000. The
Saint Lawrence Seaway Development Corporation,
which runs U.S. operations, had an accumulated deficit of
almost $40,000,000 at the end of the 1960s. This, together
with some $23,000,000 of unpaid interest, had raised its
overall debt to nearly $160,000,000.

Financial problems have not prevented the seaway from
having a major economic impact on the U.S. and Canada.
A major reason for its construction was the discovery, in
Quebec and Labrador, of vast iron ore deposits needed by
U.S. steel mills. Canada, an importer of U.S. iron ore
before the seaway, exported ore to the U.S. at an annual
rate of 15,000,000 tons by the end of the 1960s—about
one-fourth of all seaway volume. The second largest commodity moved was feed grains, with about 14,000,000 tons
from farms on Canada's prairies and in the U.S. Midwest,
shipped through the seaway at savings of six to eight cents
a bushel. Major users of the seaway are vessels known as
lakers, which are designed to the maximum limits of the
seaway locks in order to facilitate an ideal two-way trade.
A laker picks up over 1,000,000 bushels of grain in the
western Great Lakes, destined for world markets, and will
return with 27,000 tons of Canadian iron ore, loaded in
the lower St. Lawrence. The third-largest seaway commodity is coal. About 11,000,000 tons were moved annually by the 1970s, chiefly from U.S. mines to Canadian
steel mills and power plants.

Bulk commodities made up well over 80 percent of annual cargo tonnage, but vessels of more than 30 nations
also used the seaway to deliver or pick up general cargoes.
U.S. Midwestern manufacturers can often realize major
savings on export shipments by using the seaway. For

Traffic

example, a cargo of 3,784 pounds of auto parts made in
Cincinnati was shipped to Stockholm from Toledo by way
of the seaway at 31.2 percent less cost than if it had been
shipped from New York. Through the seaway, Chicago is
just 4,807 miles from London.

Problems and prospects. The Great Lakes–St. Lawrence River system is often characterized as a vast inland
sea, comparable to the Mediterranean. But it suffers from
difficult access and a severe winter climate that shortens
the shipping season to about eight months. When constructed, the seaway would admit about 80 percent of the
world's ships to this inland waterway. But its limitations
of 25-foot-9-inch draft, 730-foot length, and 75-foot-6-
inch beam restrict use to vessels carrying no more than
about 27,000 tons of cargo, which is becoming small by
world trade standards. To deepen the seaway to 35 feet
would cost as much as $5,000,000,000, and such a proj-
ect would face stiff opposition from competing regions of
the U.S. and Canada. Seaway tolls were subject to review early in the 1970s, but it was feared that any sharp
increase would hurt traffic, leaving the seaway's revenue
problems unsolved. Proposals were being considered to
eliminate seaway interest payments, but the effort could
falter on a broader debate as to whether charges should
be made for use of all other inland waterways. Railroads
are accused of hurting the seaway by charging discriminatory rates to Great Lakes ports, and the seaway faces
competition from unit trains (handling fixed, equal quantities of cargo per car) and saltwater containership ports
handling huge, standardized metal containers. Great
Lakes ports also are installing containership facilities,
but, since their initial expenditures of some $65,000,000
on new ports when the seaway opened, cities have been

faced with many urban problems of a higher priority than harbour facilities. In the early 1970s, studies were underway to extend the shipping season, but costs could prove prohibitive. Traffic experts predicted that seaway use would continue to grow but probably at a reduced rate. Iron ore and grain shipments also were expected to climb. The seaway could gain a major new commodity, as air pollution control regulations on sulfur content of fuels bring about substitution of heavy industrial fuel oils for coal in Midwest power plants and factories. This heavy fuel oil would have to come primarily from the Caribbean through the seaway. Despite a host of problems, the St. Lawrence Seaway is likely to continue playing an important economic role in an area containing about one-third of North America's population.

BIBLIOGRAPHY. There is no good overall survey of the Seaway. Information may be found in the annual financial reports of the Saint Lawrence Seaway Development Corp., and of the St. Lawrence Seaway Authority; in the annual traffic reports of the St. Lawrence Seaway; and in the annual reports of the Power Authority of the State of New York. Excellent articles may be found in *Seaway Review Magazine*.

(R.W.B.)

Saint-Simon, Henri de

A French social reformer of the early 19th century, Claude-Henri de Rouvroy, comte de Saint-Simon, founded a religion of socialism in which he tried to combine the teachings of Jesus with ideas of science and industrialism. He attracted little attention during his lifetime, but after his death his disciples acquired considerable influence among European intellectuals.

Radio Times Hulton Picture Library

Henri de Saint-Simon, lithograph by L. Deymaru, 19th century.

Early life Saint-Simon was born in Paris on October 17, 1760, of an impoverished aristocratic family. His grandfather's cousin had been the duc de Saint-Simon, famous for his memoirs of the court of Louis XIV. Henri was fond of claiming descent from Charlemagne. After an irregular education by private tutors, he entered military service at 17. He was in the regiments sent by France to aid the American colonies in their war of independence against England and served as a captain of artillery at Yorktown in 1781.

During the French Revolution he remained in France, where he bought up newly nationalized land with funds advanced by a friend. He was imprisoned in the Palais de Luxembourg during the Reign of Terror and emerged to find himself enormously rich because of the depreciation of the Revolutionary currency. He proceeded to live a life of splendour and license, entertaining prominent people from all walks of life at his glittering salons. Within several years he had brought himself close to bankruptcy.

He turned to the study of science, attending courses at the École Polytechnique and entertaining distinguished scientists.

In his first published work, *Lettres d'un habitant de Genève à ses contemporains* (1803), Saint-Simon proposed that scientists take the place of priests in the social order. He argued that the property owners who held political power could hope to maintain themselves against the propertyless only by subsidizing the advance of knowledge.

By 1805 he was impoverished, and the last 20 years of his life were lived mainly on the generosity of friends. He devoted himself to a long series of projects and publications through which he sought to win support for his social ideas. As a thinker, Saint-Simon was deficient in system, clearness, and coherence; but in the main his ideas represented a reaction against the bloodletting of the French Revolution and the militarism of Napoleon. He foresaw the further industrialization of the world, believing that science and technology would solve most social problems. He also proposed that the states of Europe form an association to suppress war. He had a profound influence on the social philosopher Auguste Comte (*q.v.*), who worked with him for a time, until, eventually, they quarrelled.

In 1823, in a fit of despondency, Saint-Simon attempted to kill himself with a pistol, succeeding only in putting out one eye.

In his last writings he sought to embody his ideas in a religion. In *Nouveau Christianisme* (1825), he argued that religion "should guide the community toward the great aim of improving as quickly as possible the conditions of the poorest class." He called upon the kings of Europe to abandon their militarism and their preoccupation with maintaining themselves in power and to return to true Christianity with its concern for the poor.

His movement and its influence

Saint-Simon died in Paris on May 19, 1825, surrounded by friends and by his disciples, who carried his message to the world in the years that followed and made him famous. The most important of these disciples were two bankers, Benjamin-Olinde Rodrigues and Barthélemy-Prosper Enfantin. Their first step, in 1825, was to establish a journal called *Le Producteur,* but it was discontinued in 1826. The movement had begun to grow, however, and before the end of 1828 was holding meetings not only in Paris but in many provincial towns. In 1828 Amand Bazard began a "complete exposition of the Saint-Simonian faith" in a long course of lectures in Paris lasting until 1830; they were well attended and won more adherents. In July 1830, revolution brought new opportunities to the Saint-Simonians. They issued a proclamation demanding the ownership of goods in common, the abolition of the right of inheritance, and the enfranchisement of women. In the following year they obtained control of the important newspaper *Le Globe.* The sect now included some of the ablest and most promising young men of France.

The Saint-Simonians formed themselves into an association arranged in three grades and constituting a society or family living together in a house in the Rue Monsigny. Before long, however, they were split by dissensions between Bazard, a man of logical and stolid temperament, and Enfantin, who wished to establish a fantastic sacredotalism with much freedom between the sexes. After a time Bazard seceded, with many of the strongest supporters of the school. A series of extravagant entertainments given by the society during the winter of 1832 reduced its financial resources and discredited it. The Saint-Simonians finally moved to a large estate belonging to Enfantin in the suburb of Ménilmontant, where they lived in a communistic society practicing chastity and poverty and wearing blue tunics and red berets. Shortly after, the chiefs were tried and condemned for offenses against the public order and morality. The movement broke up, its leaders turning to practical affairs.

The ideas of the Saint-Simonians had a pervasive influence on the intellectual life of 19th-century Europe. John Stuart Mill and Thomas Carlyle in England, Heinrich Heine in Germany, Russian literary men such as Aleksandr Herzen and Vissarion Belinsky, and a U.S. Socialist, Albert Brisbane, were among those influenced in one way or another by the ideas of Saint-Simon or his followers. Friedrich Engels, who, like his friend and collaborator Karl Marx, had little use for most of the French Socialists, found in Saint-Simon "the breadth of view of a genius," containing in embryo most of the ideas of the later Socialists. Felix Markham has said that Saint-Simon's ideas have a peculiar relevance to the latter part of the 20th century, when Socialist ideologies have taken the place of traditional religion among the political institutions of many countries.

BIBLIOGRAPHY

Works by Saint-Simon: Among his important works are *Lettres d'un habitant de Genève à ses contemporains* (1803), *De la Réorganisation de la société européenne* (1814), *Du Système industriel* (1820–21), *Catéchisme des industriels* (1823–24), and *Nouveau Christianisme* (1825). The standard and most complete edition of all his works is *Oeuvres de Saint-Simon et d'Enfantin,* 47 vol. (1865–78). Useful selections are *Textes choisis,* ed. by C. BOUGLE (1925); *Textes choisis,* ed. by JEAN DAUTRY (1951); and, in English, *Social Organization, the Science of Man and Other Writings,* ed. by FELIX MARKHAM (1964), which contains nearly all of *New Christianity.*

Biography and criticism: H.R. D'ALLEMAGNE, *Les Saint-Simoniens, 1827–1837* (1930); A.J. BOOTH, *Saint-Simon and Saint-Simonism* (1971); E.M. BUTLER, *The Saint-Simonian Religion in Germany* (1926); SEBASTIEN CHARLETY, *Histoire du Saint-Simonisme (1825–1864),* rev. ed. (1931); M.M. DONDO, *The French Faust: Henri de Saint-Simon* (1955); M.G. HUBBARD, *Saint-Simon, sa vie et ses travaux* (1857); MAXIME LEROY, *La Vie véritable du Comte Henri de Saint-Simon (1760–1825)* (1925); F.E. MANUEL, *The New World of Henri de Saint-Simon* (1956) and *The Prophets of Paris* (1962). See also the relevant chapters in D.G. CHARLTON, *Secular Religions in France, 1815–1870* (1963); EMILE DURKHEIM, *Le Socialisme* (1928; Eng. trans., *Socialism and Saint-Simon,* 1959); and ALEXANDER GRAY, *The Socialist Tradition,* rev. ed. (1963).

Saladin

Saladin, medieval sultan of Egypt, Syria, Yemen, and Palestine and founder of the Ayyūbid dynasty, was perhaps the most famous Muslim hero of all time. Both in the East, where he has become a symbol of the wise ruler and consummate military commander, and in the West, where he has attained legendary stature as a paragon of the chivalrous enemy during the Third Crusade, Saladin's fame has outstripped the authentic, though not undramatic, facts of his life.

Early career

He was born in 1137 or 1138 into a prominent Kurdish family then at Takrīt in Mesopotamia. On the night of his birth, his father, Najm ad-Dīn Ayyūb, gathered his family and moved to Aleppo, there entering the service of 'Imad ad-Dīn Zangī ibn Aq Sonqur, the powerful Turkish governor in northern Syria. Growing up in Ba'lbek and Damascus, Saladin, whose full Arabic name was Şalāḥ ad-Dīn, Yūsuf ibn Ayyūb (Righteousness of the Faith, Joseph, son of Job), was apparently an undistinguished youth, with a greater taste for religious studies than military training.

His formal career began when he joined the staff of his uncle Asad ad-Dīn Shīrkūh, an important military commander under the emir Nureddin, son and successor of Zangī. During three military expeditions led by Shīrkūh into Egypt to prevent its falling to the Latin–Christian (Frankish) rulers of the states established by the First Crusade, a complex, three-way struggle developed between Amalric I, the Latin king of Jerusalem, Shāwar, the powerful vizier of the Egyptian Fāṭimid caliph, and Shīrkūh. After Shīrkūh's death and after ordering Shāwar's assassination, Saladin, in 1169 at the age of 31, was appointed both commander of the Syrian troops and vizier of Egypt. His relatively quick rise to power must be attributed not only to the clannish nepotism of his Kurdish family but also to his own emerging talents. As vizier of Egypt, he received the title king (*malik*), although he was generally known as the sultan.

Vizier of Egypt

Saladin's position was further enhanced when, in 1171,

he abolished the Shī'ī Fāṭimid caliphate, proclaimed a return to Sunnism in Egypt, and consequently became its sole ruler. Although he remained for a time theoretically a vassal of Nureddin, that relationship ended with the Syrian emir's death in 1174. Using his rich agricultural possessions in Egypt as a financial base, Saladin soon moved into Syria with a small but strictly disciplined army to claim the regency on behalf of the young son of his former suzerain. Soon, however, he abandoned this claim, and from 1174 until 1186 he zealously pursued a goal of uniting, under his own standard, all the Muslim territories of Syria, northern Mesopotamia, Palestine, and Egypt. This he accomplished by skillful diplomacy backed when necessary by the swift and resolute use of military force. Gradually, his reputation grew as a generous and virtuous but firm ruler, devoid of pretense, licentiousness, and cruelty. In contrast to the bitter dissension and intense rivalry that had up to then hampered the Muslims in their resistance to the crusaders, Saladin's singleness of purpose induced them to rearm both physically and spiritually.

Saladin's every act was inspired by an intense and unwavering devotion to the idea of *jihād*—the Muslim equivalent of the Christian crusade. It was an essential part of his policy to encourage the growth and spread of Muslim religious institutions. He courted its scholars and preachers, founded colleges and mosques for their use, and commissioned them to write edifying works especially on the *jihād* itself. Through moral regeneration, which was a genuine part of his own way of life, he tried to re-create in his own realm some of the same zeal and enthusiasm that had proved so valuable to the first generations of Muslims when, five centuries before, they had conquered half the known world.

Saladin also succeeded in turning the military balance of power in his favour—more by uniting and disciplining a great number of unruly forces than by employing new or improved military techniques. When at last, in 1187, he was able to throw his full strength into the struggle with the Latin crusader kingdoms, his armies were their equals. On July 4, 1187, aided by his own military good sense and by a phenomenal lack of it on the part of his enemy, Saladin trapped and destroyed in one blow an exhausted and thirst-crazed army of crusaders at Ḥaṭṭin, near Tiberias in northern Palestine. So great were the losses in the ranks of the crusaders in this one battle that the Muslims were quickly able to overrun nearly the entire Kingdom of Jerusalem. Acre, Toron, Beirut, Sidon, Nazareth, Caesarea, Nābulus, Jaffa (Yafo), and Ascalon (Ashqelon) fell within three months. But Saladin's crowning achievement and the most disastrous blow to the whole crusading movement came on October 2, 1187, when Jerusalem, holy to both Muslim and Christian alike, surrendered to the Sultan's army after 88 years in the hands of the Franks. In stark contrast to the city's conquest by the Christians, when blood flowed freely during the barbaric slaughter of its inhabitants, the Muslim reconquest was marked by the civilized good faith and courteous behaviour of Saladin and his troops.

Rout of the crusaders

His sudden success, which in 1189 saw the crusaders reduced to the occupation of only three cities, was, however, marred by his failure to capture Tyre, an almost impregnable coastal fortress to which the scattered Christian survivors of the recent battles flocked. It was to be the rallying point of the Latin counterattack. Most probably, Saladin did not anticipate the European reaction to his capture of Jerusalem, an event that deeply shocked the West and to which it responded with a new call for a crusade. In addition to many great nobles and famous knights, this crusade, the third, brought the kings of three countries into the struggle. The magnitude of the Christian effort and the lasting impression it made on contemporaries gave the name of Saladin, as their gallant and chivalrous enemy, an added lustre that his military victories alone could never confer on him.

The Crusade itself was long and exhausting, and, despite the obvious, though at times impulsive, military genius of Richard I the Lion-Heart, it achieved almost nothing. Therein lies the greatest—but often unrecognized—

achievement of Saladin. With tired and unwilling feudal levies, committed to fight only a limited season each year, his indomitable will enabled him to fight the greatest champions of Christendom to a draw. The crusaders retained little more than a precarious foothold on the Levantine coast, and when King Richard set sail from the Orient in October 1192, the battle was over. Saladin withdrew to his capital at Damascus. Soon, the long campaigning seasons and the endless hours in the saddle caught up with him, and on March 4, 1193, he died. While his relatives were already scrambling for pieces of the empire, his friends found that the most powerful and most generous ruler in the Muslim world had not left enough money to pay for his grave.

BIBLIOGRAPHY. On the sources, see H.A.R. GIBB, "The Arabic Sources for the Life of Saladin," *Speculum*, 25:58–72 (1950). C.W. WILSON's English translation, *The Life of Saladin* (1897), of one of the most important Arabic works has recently been reprinted (1971). The best biography to date is STANLEY LANE-POOLE, *Saladin and the Fall of the Kingdom of Jerusalem*, new ed. (1926, reprinted 1964), although it does not take account of all the sources. See also H.A.R. GIBB, "The Achievement of Saladin," *Bull. John Rylands Library*, 35:44–60 (1952), and "The Rise of Saladin," in KENNETH M. SETTON (ed.), *A History of the Crusades* (1958).

(P.W.)

Sales and Excise Taxes

Sales taxes are taxes imposed upon the sale of goods and services. A sales tax levied on the manufacture, purchase, sale, or consumption of a specific type of commodity is known as an excise tax. Sales taxes are commonly classified according to the levels of business activity at which they are imposed—at the level of production or at the wholesale or retail level. Very often tax rates applied to commodities will vary according to whether the commodities are considered essential or nonessential. If the intention behind a tax is to place a burden on particular goods or to curtail consumption of such goods, it is called a sumptuary excise or a luxury tax. Many countries impose sumptuary taxes on such products as automobiles, gasoline, tobacco, alcoholic beverages, coffee, and sugar. Luxury taxes are less common because, although they are politically popular, luxury consumption is difficult to define for tax purposes and such taxes raise complex administrative problems.

Multiple sales taxes, imposed at more than one level of production and distribution, are sometimes called turnover taxes. For reasons of administration and simplicity such taxes are based on gross receipts; consequently, the taxable value at each stage includes the taxes already paid at previous stages. In order to avoid such pyramiding of taxes, some governments employ a value-added tax. This is a modified sales tax based on the net value added at each stage rather than on gross receipts. Roughly speaking, an enterprise's net value added within a given period is equal to output minus input, calculated as its total sales minus expenditure on goods and services purchased from other enterprises.

History.   Excise taxes were well known in the ancient world. It is said that the Roman emperor Vespasian when asked for the justification of a new excise on public urinals answered, "Pecunia non olet" ("money does not smell"). Excises of various kinds were important sources of public revenue in medieval Europe. In the United States, customs duties were the primary source of federal government revenue before World War I. General sales taxes are a comparatively recent innovation. Modern multistage turnover taxes were developed during and after World War I in Europe. The large-scale use of value-added taxation began when France adopted it in 1954; it was subsequently taken up in other European countries. The importance of sales and excise taxes in four countries is shown in the accompanying Table.

Sales and excise taxes in various countries.   In western Europe value-added taxes existed in 1971 in Belgium, Denmark, France, Luxembourg, the Netherlands, Norway, Sweden, and the Federal Republic of Germany. Normal tax rates in those countries ranged from 10 to 23 percent. Italy and Austria introduced value-added taxes in January 1973 in place of their multistage turnover taxes. Spain had a multistage turnover tax, and Switzerland, a single-stage turnover tax. Great Britain had a purchase tax, levied at the wholesale stage upon all commodities not otherwise taxed by special excises. In most western European countries, excises on automobiles, mineral fuels, tobacco, and alcoholic beverages are among the major types of excises. A wide variety of other special excises are in use, such as taxes on coffee, sugar, salt, vinegar, matches, and amusements. In the Soviet Union and other Communist countries, general turnover taxes are among the most important sources of revenue.

Value-added taxes in western Europe

In the United States, single-stage sales taxes exist in more than 40 states. Only two states have made use of multistage turnover taxes (as of 1971). Many local governments are also financed by taxes at retail level. The federal government does not levy a general sales tax; it imposes special excises on liquor, tobacco, motor fuels, automobiles, and other items. In Canada, retail sales taxes are levied in nearly all provinces; the federal government also collects a manufacturer's sales tax.

Most Latin American countries rely heavily on excises and on either turnover or sales taxes. Brazil has a manufacturer's tax and a value-added tax. Excises on tobacco, alcoholic beverages, automobiles, gasoline, and other items are the rule not only in most Latin American countries but in Africa, Asia, Australia, and New Zealand. The last two also make vigorous use of sales taxes.

In general, excise and turnover taxes have been more important in Latin countries and in the less developed world than in Scandinavia or in Anglo-Saxon countries. The latter rely comparatively more on direct taxes (income taxes) than do the Latin countries, where resistance to such direct taxation has traditionally been strong. The fact that excise and turnover taxes are easier to administer and enforce may be another reason why they are preferred in some countries. The recent adoption of value-added taxes in European countries may stem from a desire to harmonize tax systems, and perhaps also from a reaction against the rather excessive use of income taxation during World War II.

Importance of Excise and Sales Taxes in Four Countries
(1969, except where otherwise noted)

	France	Germany	Great Britain*	United States
Taxes† as percentage of gross national product	36.7	33.8	35.3	31.1
Tax receipts† in national currency (000,000,000)	167.0	145.3	12.8	235.9
Turnover‡	72.6	34.1	1.0	14.2§
Mineral fuels	11.4	10.6	1.1	3.1§
Tobacco	4.2	6.2	1.1	8.7§
Alcoholic beverages	2.8	3.5	0.8	8.7§
Other excises	5.8	6.4	0.5	10.5§

*1968–69.   †Including social security taxes.   ‡Including sales taxes and purchase taxes.   §1968.
Source: Ministry of Finance, Federal Republic of Germany, *Informationsdienst zur Finanzpolitik des Auslandes*.

The burden of sales and excise taxes. It is generally assumed that sales and excise taxes are borne by the consumer. To facilitate easy collection, most such taxes are levied at the manufacturing, wholesale, or retail level. The tax burden is expected to be shifted to the last buyer in the form of a higher price. Whether the burden is shifted entirely or partly depends on market conditions. If consumers insist on having a commodity, the tax burden can be shifted to them more completely than if they are sensitive to price rises. For goods the prices of which are not much affected by quantities sold, the tax may be added to the price to a greater extent than for goods the prices of which are sensitive to the quantity factor. Usually both the supplier and the consumer share the tax burden in terms of lower profits or higher prices.

[margin: Conditions under which tax burden can be shifted]

Sales and excise taxes also affect the way in which goods are allocated to different uses. Higher prices resulting from taxation may decrease the quantities produced and sold; manufacturers and sellers may have to reduce production or sales of heavily taxed commodities. In time of war or other stringency, excises and sales taxes can therefore be used as a means of reducing the production and consumption of goods that are not considered essential. It has been argued that excises interfere with the natural functioning of prices and distribution and therefore have a distorting effect on the economy. Such a conclusion, however, depends on certain assumptions as to how the economy would perform in the absence of such taxes.

More general types of taxes, such as turnover or value-added taxes, are thought to be less distorting in their effects. Single-stage sales taxes, as well as taxes on value added, if applied each at the same rate on total turnover, are assumed not to affect price relations to any marked degree.

Arguments for and against excises. Certain arguments can be advanced in favour of excise taxes. Since they are levied on specific goods, they allow the consumer to avoid them by purchasing substitutes and other nontaxed commodities. They place the burden of taxation on luxuries or nonessential goods rather than on necessities. They can also be allocated in such a way that the tax burden falls on those who receive the benefits of the tax expenditures, as the taxes on motor fuel that are used to build and maintain roads. Excise taxes, unlike taxes on income, are not thought to weaken the taxpayer's incentive to earn more. Finally, they are relatively easy to administer; the costs of collection are low.

Other arguments have been advanced against excise taxes. As mentioned above, they affect the allocation of resources in purely arbitrary ways. Also, the burden they impose is not related to the taxpayer's ability to pay. They discriminate against persons engaged in the production of the specific goods taxed.

Generally, excises are regressive in that the percentage of income spent on goods liable to taxation is higher among low-income groups. Regressiveness is often increased by the practice of applying the same tax to cheaper brands as to more expensive ones. Excises, unlike other taxes, cannot be used flexibly as a weapon for fighting inflation and maintaining economic stability.

[margin: Sales taxes and excises compared]

Some of the inconveniences mentioned in connection with excises do not apply to sales taxes, but some of the advantages do not apply either. Nonselective, single-stage sales taxes do not discriminate between goods if a single flat rate is applied. On the other hand, if all goods are taxed, there is no longer a tax-influenced choice for the consumer. Sales taxes are generally more regressive than excises. Unlike excises, they cannot be related to benefits received. Multistage turnover taxes pose more serious disadvantages. Here, the amount of the tax depends on the number of turnover stages at which it is applied. Products that pass through relatively few hands on their way to the market will be taxed less than those that pass through many stages of production or distribution.

Some of the inconveniences of sales and excise taxes can be avoided by value-added taxation, in which the number of stages of turnover does not matter. The value-added tax affects neither the allocation of resources nor the price structure so long as a single tax rate is applied. It is,

however, more difficult and expensive to administer. Techniques may be simplified by using receipts that show the amount of tax at each step; each seller adds the tax to the price and acknowledges this on his bill. Each enterprise's net tax liability will be equal to the sum of all taxes it collects on goods it sells minus the sum of all the taxes it has paid on goods it has bought, the difference representing the tax on the value added by that enterprise.

BIBLIOGRAPHY. *On sales and excise taxes in general*: *Report of the Committee on Turnover Taxation* (Great Britain) (1964); JOHN F. DUE, *Sales Taxation* (1957); ROLF GRABOWER, DETLEF HERTING, and GOTTFRIED SCHWARZ, *Die Umsatzsteuer*, 2nd ed. (1962); GUNTHER SCHMÖLDERS, "Die Umsatzstevern," in WILHELM GERLOFF and FRITZ NEUMARK (eds.), *Handbuch der Finanzwissenschaft*, vol. 3 (1956); NED SHILLING, *Excise Taxation of Monopoly* (1969). *On valued-added taxation*: RICHARD W. LINDHOLM, "The Value Added Tax: A Short Review of the Literature," *J. Econ. Lit.*, 8:1178–1189 (1970); NATIONAL ECONOMIC DEVELOPMENT OFFICE (Great Britain), *Value Added Tax* (1969); CLARA K. SULLIVAN, *The Tax on Value Added* (1965).

(K.Hä.)

Salicales

The willows and poplars together form a single, coherent family—the Salicaceae—of the distinctive order of flowering plants, the Salicales. Many grow in moist habitats, such as along riverbanks or on floodplains. The willow and the aspen have been used since the time of early man as a febrifuge (fever-controlling drug) and as basket material. Many wild animal species depend on the twigs and buds of Salicaceae species as food; others use the thickets formed by certain species as protective cover. Ecologically, members of the order are aggressive pioneers —plants that appear first in newly created habitats such as burned-over areas.

General features. *Size range and diversity of structure.* The aspens and poplars are trees ranging from small to very large; although some willows are medium-sized trees, often with clustered stems, most are shrubs that form thickets.

The giant of the poplars is the black cottonwood (*Populus trichocarpa*), which, in the virgin forests of the Pacific Northwest in North America, reaches a height of nearly 200 feet (60 metres) and a diameter of seven or eight feet (up to two and one-half metres). No other hardwood tree in that region reaches this size. The eastern cottonwood (*P. deltoides*) becomes nearly as large. Other species of large poplars also occur in the Northern Hemisphere, often achieving heights of 100 feet (30 metres) or more, such as the white poplar (*P. alba*) of Europe, Central Asia, and Western Siberia; the swamp cottonwood (*P. heterophylla*) of the southeastern U.S.; *P. suaveolens* from Soviet Central Asia to the Korean Peninsula; and *P. maximowiczii* of Japan, the Korean Peninsula, and Manchuria (Northeast Provinces). In addition to the great poplars and cottonwoods, the aspen group is also included in the genus *Populus*. Although exceptional individuals of the trembling aspen (*P. tremuloides*) are recorded as having reached a height of 100 feet and a diameter of three feet, they are characteristically small trees of 60 to 70 feet (about 20 metres) in height and 18 to 20 inches (46 to 51 centimetres) in diameter. A few of the willows become quite large trees, as much as 90 feet high—e.g., the crack willow (*Salix fragilis*) of Europe and western Asia. Many, such as the common osier (*S. viminalis*) or the weeping willow (*S. babylonica* and similar species), may become 15 to 30 feet high, but most willows are shrubs. Larger shrubs such as the shining willow (*S. lucida*), become 15 to 20 feet (five to six metres) high. But the great mass of willow species either form low thickets or sprawl on the surface.

[margin: The largest poplar]

Geographic distribution. The members of the Salicales are widely distributed in cool temperate areas of the Northern Hemisphere, with only a few extending into the tropics. Most of the species are relatively widespread; endemics, species restricted to a relatively small area, are virtually nonexistent. The species are prominent in the communities and habitats where they occur and, in the case of the poplars, at times form forests of great extent.

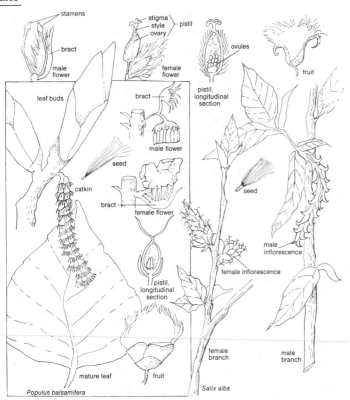

Representative plants and structures from the two genera of
the willow family and order.
Drawing by R. Findahl based on (*Populus* flowers) G.H.M. Lawrence,
Taxonomy of Vascular Plants (1957); the Macmillan Company

The two genera—*Populus* and *Salix*—are widespread in
their distribution today; both are circumpolar, so that
species of each have invaded the areas left by the retreating ice of the last glaciation. Thus, the balsam poplar
(*P. balsamifera*), although a tree up to 90 feet (30 metres) high under favourable conditions in the central
part of its range, forms low thickets at the northern
limit of its range. The shrubby willows in great numbers
of species and individuals have likewise moved into the
Arctic and sub-Arctic upon the retreat of the ice, where
they now form a prominent part of the flora. The various
members of the genus *Populus* are found from the sub-
Arctic tree line near the Arctic Circle southward in North
America to northern Mexico and Baja California, and
southward in the Old World to northern Africa and the
southern slopes of the Himalayas and from sea to sea
in both North America and Eurasia. Of the 35 or more
species, about ten occur in North America. Two of these,
the quaking aspen and the balsam poplar, extend from
the Atlantic to the Pacific oceans. The other poplars of
North America are more limited in occurrence; the black
cottonwood, for instance, occurs only on the west coast
from Baja California to Alaska and inland to the Rocky
Mountains. The eastern cottonwood extends from the
Great Lakes to the Gulf of Mexico and from the Central
Plains to the East Coast, with but limited occurrence in
the region of the Appalachian Mountains. The plains cottonwood (*P. deltoides* variety *occidentalis*), however, extends the range of the eastern cottonwood west to the
Rocky Mountains.

Two basic distribution patterns of *Populus* occur in
North America, the one transcontinental in formerly glaciated regions, with southward extensions predominantly
in the Rockies, the other roughly from the southern limits
of glaciation to the Gulf of Mexico, with the east–west
boundaries of the various species set by the Atlantic
Ocean, the Pacific Ocean, the north–south Rockies and
Appalachians, and the Great Plains, each of which is a
barrier to migration.

In the Old World there are similar wide-ranging species,
such as the European aspen (*P. tremula*), which extends
from Europe and North Africa to western Asia and Siberia. Other species, such as *P. koreana* of the Korean

Peninsula or *P. szechuanica* of western China, are more
restricted in their occurrence.

The willows occur in such a multitude of species (300 or
more) that distributional patterns are relatively obscure.
There seem to be four centres of distribution in the North
Temperate Zone. One is the area centring on the Bering
Sea; another is central Europe; a third is the Himalayas;
and a fourth is Pacific North America. In addition, there
are limited occurrences of the genus in the Philippines,
Madagascar, and in South America as far south as Chile.
Isolated occurrences in mountains south of its region of
continuous distribution are interpreted as survivals of
Salix populations from an earlier period of colder climates, when many Arctic species grew much farther
south. Another interesting type of distributional pattern
is represented by very similar species pairs, or vicariads,
one member of which occurs in eastern North America
(such as *Salix discolor*), the other in the west (in this
case, *S. scouleriana*). Some species are pronounced examples of disruption in range, such as *S. brachycarpa*,
which occurs in the Rocky Mountains and then again
only in the Gaspé, Anticosti, and Hudson Bay areas.

Such diverse distributional patterns are difficult to explain. The failure of active migration by members of a
species after the retreat of the continental ice could have
resulted in disrupted ranges. Similar disruption of the
range of a single species, by ice or some other cataclysmic
phenomenon, followed by genetic change in these separated populations could have produced the vicariads.

Economic importance. The outstanding and major
usefulness of the members of the willow family lies in the
use of the wood of the North American large-toothed
aspen (*Populus grandidentata*) and the trembling aspen for
high quality paper pulp. Many species of willow provide
twigs for basketwork of all kinds throughout the Northern Hemisphere. On the other hand, the wood of poplars,
such as the aspen of Europe (*P. tremula*), is now used
more for matchsticks and matchboxes than for construction.

The wood of some willows is still much used. The
British prefer the wood of *Salix alba* variety *caerulea* for
the manufacture of cricket bats. The American *Salix nigra* (as well as other species) is used to produce charcoal

Willow centres of distribution

for black-powder manufacture. *Salix nigra* wood is also used for artificial limbs because of its light weight and its ability to dent without splintering. No doubt it is these qualities that make the wood useful for the soles of clogs and for the manufacture of wooden shoes and a multitude of other small domestic objects.

The tough, stringy bark obtained by stripping willow twigs is an excellent material for tying objects. It was once so important in commercial vineyards for tying up grapevines that grape growers were encouraged to grow one acre of willows for every 25 acres of vineyard. One early writer sounded the note of caution that the farmer who could not grow his own willows and reeds had better stay out of the vineyard business.

Many primitive peoples in the Northern Hemisphere discovered that the inner bark of the poplars served as a crude substitute for flour, which they used in time of famine. They also used willow leaves and bark for tanning leather.

The most important folk use of willow (and even poplar) bark—as a febrifuge—was discovered by virtually all the peoples living in the distributional range of the genus *Salix*. It was not until 1827 that the active bitter component salicin was first isolated. In 1838 salicylic acid was prepared from intermediate products obtained from salicin. Salicylic acid has a pronounced antifever and pain-controlling action. The important household medicine aspirin is a derivative of salicylic acid.

Shade tree and ornamental uses Both willows and poplars are widely used for shade trees and landscaping. The weeping willow (*Salix babylonica* and its relatives) is much used for ornamental plantings because of its gracefully drooping and generally handsome form. Another decorative tree is the Lombardy poplar (*Populus nigra* variety *italica*). The austere, columnar growth habit of the male tree made it a tremendous favourite after its introduction into Europe before 1750 and into North America in 1784. It has become a familiar roadside tree and is still much used in long row plantings as a screen.

The uses of Salicaceae to wildlife have long been recognized by the conservationist. Deer find the young shoots of aspen excellent for browsing. In fact, in the United States a deer population in excess of 15 to 20 per square mile will seriously interfere with the reproduction of the aspen crop. Aspen is also an important source of food for beaver. *Salix* and *Populus* buds form an important food source for various game birds, which also use willow brush for cover.

Natural history. *Life cycle.* The life cycle of poplars and willows follows the usual pattern in the flowering plants, although there are a few peculiarities. There is segregation of the sexes; male and female flowers occur on separate trees. There are, however, authenticated cases of sex reversal and also of hermaphroditism (both sexes in one individual), so that the normal unisexuality is not a constant feature, at least in some species. Furthermore, the maturation of the ovule (seed precursor) is later than that of the pollen grain; as a result, a considerable interval of time elapses between pollination and fertilization.

After the fertilized ovule has developed and the fruit, a capsule, has formed, it splits open, releasing the seeds, which float away on a parachute of silky hairs. One to 12 seeds are produced per capsule, and there are about 150 capsules per catkin (flower cluster) in *Populus tremula;* the number of catkins varies with the size of the tree, so that from 8,000 to 54,000,000 seeds may be produced by a single tree. The seeds are minute, there being about 3,500,000 per pound (after removal of the silky hairs) in *P. tremula*. A female tree thus produces millions of the seeds, which accumulate in windrows on the ground or float in masses on the water. They become attached by their silken parachutes to all sorts of rough surfaces, often clogging window screens, air conditioners, and other similar items.

Seed germination, which under natural conditions is prompt—usually in one or two days—is facilitated by the presence in the mature seed of mucilaginous hairs on a raised girdle around the base of the embryo and on the tip of the root. Growth in the seedlings is very rapid, and

reproductive maturity is often achieved in only a few years. The male and female plants then produce their flowers. The yellow and red aggregations of anthers associated with nectar-producing glands in the male flowers attract bees and other insects, which accidentally pick up the slightly rough pollen of certain species and transfer it to the flowers on the female plants. In some *Populus* species the transfer of the smooth pollen is by wind.

Ecology. The willows and poplars are generally plants of very moist habitats—riverbanks and stream banks and floodplains. The soil may be light or heavy, ranging from sandy to clay; loamy soils where the water table is a few feet below the surface are best for rapid growth. Some species, such as the swamp cottonwood (*P. heterophylla*) of the southeastern United States, thrive in swamps and sloughs where the water table is at the soil surface. Many willows grow where the soil is below water level, as along riverbanks. In apparent contrast is the Arctic tundra, in which a large number of species of shrubby willows occur; soil moisture, however, is always abundant in those places.

It is seldom that the willows or poplars form pure stands. They are more commonly associated with birches and alders, or otherwise grow as part of the understory among other larger trees.

In North America only two species of willow (*Salix nigra* and *S. atropurpurea*) and about six of poplar (*Populus balsamifera*, *P. grandidentata*, *P. trichocarpa*, *P. deltoides*, *P. tremuloides*, *P. heterophylla*) are important forest trees. The balance consists of small trees or shrubs. As shrubs, willows grow everywhere in the Arctic tundra. Some species occur in openings in various forest types, along the margins of woods, in open fields, in recently burned-over regions, in the moist and wet places of the treeless prairies, and along watercourses generally. Little detailed and experimental evidence is available, but circumstantial evidence for most of these shrubby species indicates a "demand" for light or, conversely, an intolerance of shade. The forest species as a group are among the most shade-intolerant of forest trees. Some of them, such as the balsam poplar or the black cottonwood, cannot grow in competition with other species but must be dominant, thrusting their crowns out of the canopy formed by the crowns of their associates. The large-tooth aspen of the Great Lakes region of the United States cannot reproduce in its own shade. The intolerance of competition and demand for light make these trees valuable as pioneer species, which occupy with vigour and aggressiveness areas cleared by lumbering, burning, windthrow, and other catastrophes.

In some instances, tree species, such as the aspens, form pure stands, but more frequently they are associated with other trees of the region that have similar preferences as to site. Thus the balsam poplar may be associated with birch or white spruce in the west and balsam fir and other species in the east. The large-tooth aspen may occur with a quaking aspen and balsam poplar, or to a lesser extent with jack pine, balsam fir, and gray and paper birches. The black cottonwood of the west occurs commonly with willow, white spruce, and red alder. The eastern cottonwood is often associated with American elm, burr oak, and sweet gum.

The Arctic and sub-Arctic shrubby willows form an integral part of the characteristic low, matlike vegetation of the region; occur in stream valleys, forming thickets; or grow as individuals in the lee of a rock. They are, depending on the species, virtually ubiquitous. Similarly, the various species that grow above the tree line on mountains tend to find similar habitats. Some prefer limy soil, others acid. The basic requirements are moisture during the growing season and light. The few willows that occur in the tropics, such as *Salix tetrasperma* of tropical and subtropical Asia, also are found along watercourses and on the banks of pools and lakes. The basic ecological requirements seem to be much the same as for the temperate and Arctic members of the genus. Basic requirements for willow growth

Form and function. The outstanding anomaly in this group of plants is the simplicity of the flowers in the willows, which are specialized for insect pollination. No other group of flowering plants has simpler flowers and yet is insect pollinated. It has been assumed that such simplicity is intimately interrelated with wind pollination, as it is in many of the other members of the "Amentiferae," or "catkin bearers," a group of plants that includes the birches, hop hornbeams, alders, oaks, chestnuts, walnuts, and poplars. The willows, however, are so thoroughly converted to insect pollination that they have become adapted or specialized to some species of *Andrena* (solitary bees). The appearance of these bees in the spring coincides with the opening of willow catkins. Many other kinds of bees, butterflies, and flies also visit willow catkins. It is sometimes assumed that the ancestors of the willows, like the poplars today, were wind-pollinated, but that both evolved from bisexual, insect-pollinated ancestors. If so, there has been a reversion to a more primitive function by the willows.

The growth habit of the willows is woody, which in general demands a high degree of efficiency in the retention of moisture in the living cells when the leafless stems and branches are above ground during the winter. The willows and poplars have an effective waterproofing system composed of cork cells on the exposed stems. Furthermore, the winter buds are covered with one (in willow) or more (in poplar) modified leaves in the form of bud scales, often covered by a balsam-like, resinous waterproofing material. The most extreme shrubs of the exposed tundra or mountain tops supplement their waterproofing devices by sprawling close to the ground. They are often protected from desiccation and windblown ice crystals by a covering of snow. The most extreme of all sprawling willows is *Salix herbacea*, which often grows only tall enough for its buds to come to the surface of the tundra; the thin, little branches remain safely submerged the year around.

An adaptation of great value to many members of the group is the unusual facility with which the roots produce adventitious (unusual in origin) "sucker" shoots. Following the destruction of an aspen stand by fire, sprouts come up in vast numbers from the roots of the burned trees. This type of regeneration permits the aspen to continue to occupy territory from which it would otherwise become eliminated because of its intolerance to shade. A similar characteristic of many of the willows, such as the sandbar willow, permits the plants to thrive on the unstable sites provided by sandy and gravelly, often inundated, islands in rivers and shorelines of rivers and lakes.

One of the peculiar vegetative characteristics of many of the willows and poplars is the readiness with which the branchlets are abscised (cut off by specialized cells). Such branchlets, which may be carried considerable distances by water currents, provide excellent means of vegetative propagation. This is because of the readiness with which adventitious roots form on twigs of this group of plants, a phenomenon well appreciated by housewives who obtain starts of pussy willows by putting twigs in water until roots grow.

Some of the aspens possess the interesting property of having much chlorophyll—the green pigment of photosynthesis—in the bark of their trunks. As a result, photosynthesis occurs before the leaves come out in the spring and even during part of the winter. It has been suggested that, in the colder, short-season part of the range of the aspen, this property may account for its ability to thrive in what is otherwise mainly an evergreen conifer environment.

Evolution. As in the rest of the flowering plants, fossil evidence for determining the real evolutionary origins of the order Salicales is absent or, alternatively, has not been properly interpreted. *Salix* and *Populus* were already present in Europe and North America during the Cretaceous Period (from 65,000,000 to 136,000,000 years ago). The presence of *Populus* and *Salix* in the rich flora of the Tertiary (beginning 65,000,000 years ago) of Greenland and Spitsbergen, then, from the upper Oligocene (some 26,000,000 years ago) onward in central and northern Europe, suggests a southward migration. Some authorities see a similarity between the Tertiary species of *Salix*

and the species that survive today in the tropics; this suggests that the latter are primitive.

Close study of the living poplars and willows discloses a wide range of variation in some structural features and marked uniformity in others. The total of characteristics suggests a moderately advanced group of plants, which in some respects has become very highly modified. The wood is quite specialized and is far removed in its characteristics from the primitive magnolias and their tropical relatives. The leaves similarly are somewhat advanced. The woody habit rather than a herbaceous one, however, is a less specialized character.

Evolutionarily advanced structural features

The unisexual flowers are very small and crowded in great numbers into highly condensed spikes (*Salix*) or dangling catkins (*Populus*)—all very advanced features, as is their individual structure. The interpretation of the large number of stamens (male reproductive structures that produce pollen)—up to 50 or 60—which are spirally arranged in some poplars, is puzzling, the more so because the stamens are attached well out on a curious cuplike structure. The cup is provided with a vascular supply that is suggestive of a highly modified perianth (petals and sepals). This is interpreted to be a single flower with few to many stamens. But a quite different interpretation suggests that each stamen is a separate flower. A similar cup occurs in one of the tropical willows, but in most of them the cup found in the poplar is represented by one or more isolated nectar-producing glands, associated with few or even but a single stamen—an extreme reduction from the poplar state. In the female flowers similar cups occur in the poplars and glands in the willows, inserted in each type of flower below the pistil (female structure containing the ovules)—a primitive location for the perianth, if it is indeed a perianth. The pistil is crowned with styles (the elongated upper part of the pistil), which not infrequently have dichotomously branched—two-forked—stigmas (sticky pollen-receiving areas), another primitive feature.

The pollen also is quite advanced, especially in *Populus*, which is wind-pollinated. It has lost its superficial sculpturing, some evidence of which still remains in the insect-pollinated willows. Chalazogamy occurs in some species—*i.e.*, the pollen tube approaches the embryo sac by penetrating the base of the ovule rather than entering by the normal pathway, an opening called the micropyle. This is a rare phenomenon in flowering plants, and its significance is difficult to assess.

In one characteristic after another, therefore, varying degrees of advancement are evident that require interpretation of the order Salicales as being well along the path of specialization. But its ancestors and close relatives are a puzzle. Various suggestions have been made, such as a relationship with the families Tamaricaceae or Flacourtiaceae or, again, with the orders Caryophyllales or Papaverales or with the Betulales—Fagales order complex by way of the Hamamelidales. None can be supported with strong, positive evidence, and most of the proposals can be dismissed by pointing out a pronounced lack of consistent similarity with any of these plants. One thing is certain: the Salicales cannot be lumped with other catkin-bearing trees and shrubs to become a member of that artificial group, the "Amentiferae."

Classification. *Annotated classification.*

ORDER SALICALES

Woody trees or shrubs with simple, spirally arranged, tooth-margined, usually deciduous (falling) leaves that have stipules, small leaflike appendages at the base of the leafstalk. Flowers unisexual, male and female usually on separate plants. Male flowers with 1 to many stamens, vestigial pistils absent. Female flowers with a single pistil unaccompanied by vestigial stamens. Pistil composed of 4, 3, or, most often, of 2 carpels (ovule-bearing segments). Ovary superior (positioned above the other flower parts), with a single chamber and several to many ovules. Style present or absent, the number of stigmas equal to or double the number of carpels. Inflorescence (flower cluster) a characteristic cylindrical spike (a catkin or ament) that is erect (in *Salix*) or pendulous (in *Populus*). Pollination in the spring by wind (*Populus*) or insects (*Salix*). Maturation of the fruit and shedding of seed occurs in the spring. Fruit a somewhat leathery-walled capsule, splitting into as many segments as there are carpels to release the minute seed, each with a tuft of cottony hair attached at the base. Seeds with a small, straight embryo, lacking endosperm, and with a thin seed coat.

Family Salicaceae

The only family of the order; it has the characters of the order. Two genera—*Populus* (poplars, aspen), with about 30 species, and *Salix* (willows) with about 320 species.

Critical appraisal. The Salicales has consistently been recognized to contain a single family, the Salicaceae. The two genera, *Populus* and *Salix*, are sufficiently similar in flowers, wood, and reproductive structures that they cannot be put into separate tribes or subfamilies. The genus *Chosenia* has been recognized by some authorities as a third genus but has few characters that distinguish it from *Salix*, in which genus it is here included.

BIBLIOGRAPHY. GEORGE H.M. LAWRENCE, *Taxonomy of Vascular Plants* (1951), an excellent introduction to the morphology and taxonomy of the Salicales; A. REHDER, *Manual of Cultivated Trees and Shrubs Hardy in North America, Exclusive of the Subtropical and Warmer Temperate Regions*, 2nd ed. rev. (1940, reprinted 1962), the authoritative treatment of those species hardy in North America; S.A. GRAHAM, ROBERT P. HARRISON, JR., and CASEY E. WESTELL, JR., *Aspens, Phoenix Trees of the Great Lakes Region* (1963), an account of the spectacular increase in importance of this "Cinderella" tree in the forest economy of the North Central United States; T.J. CROVELLO, *A Numerical Taxonomic Study of the Genus Salix, Section Sitchenses* (1968), a fine example of a very technical application of numerical taxonomy; M.J. FISHER, "The Morphology and Anatomy of the Flowers of the Salicaceae," *Am. J. Bot.*, 15:307–326, 372–394 (1928), the most complete, although technical, account of floral anatomy for this group; H. HJELMQVIST, "Studies on the Floral Morphology and Phylogeny of the Amentiferae," *Bot. Notiser, Suppl.*, 2:147–163 (1948), a different (from M.J. Fisher) point of view about floral morphology in the willow order and related groups; C. PICKERING, *Chronological History of Plants* (1879), a classic book answering the interesting question of when various members of the Salicales were first mentioned in man's history.

(E.C.A.)

Salisbury, Robert Cecil, 3rd marquess of

A British Conservative statesman, a three-time prime minister, and a four-time foreign secretary, Robert Arthur Talbot Gascoyne-Cecil, the 3rd marquess of Salisbury, was, with Gladstone and Disraeli, one of the towering political figures of the last quarter of the 19th century. Salisbury's fame rests on his successful handling of Britain's foreign affairs during a time of almost continuous crisis caused by international rivalries in Europe, Africa, and Asia. He maintained Britain's worldwide interests, always working for general peace, which among the then great powers (Germany, Britain, Russia, France, Italy, Austria-Hungary, and later Japan and the United States) remained unbroken throughout his years of office.

At home, as Conservative prime minister, he supported practical reforms on particular questions, such as housing the poor, rather than policies designed to bring about social change. Throughout his life he remained opposed to arguments in favour of democracy, believing that it was better to have a balance of "classes." He opposed Gladstone's policy of Home Rule for Ireland; instead, he followed a firm policy of maintaining law and order there while introducing some constructive reforms. This cautious reforming spirit, with its stress on the strict limitations of government, won solid electoral support and gave the Conservatives long periods in office (1886–1892; 1895–1905).

Salisbury was born at Hatfield in Hertfordshire, England, on February 3, 1830, the second surviving son of the 2nd marquess of Salisbury, who had married Frances Gascoyne, an heiress to large landed estates. His elder brother suffered from a debilitating illness all his life and died in 1865, and thus Lord Robert Cecil became heir to the estates and on the death of his father the 3rd marquess of Salisbury, in 1868. His family background allowed him easy entry into any profession but only merit and ability could ensure high office.

Robert Cecil's childhood was unhappy and lonely. He

Domestic policy (margin note)

Salisbury.
Radio Times Hulton Picture Library—Globe

was exceptionally clever but not especially strong, and he hated games. His father was conscientious but lacking in warmth. His mother, by all accounts sociable and vivacious, died when he was only ten. He was sent to Eton, where he was perpetually bullied. He was by nature pessimistic, withdrawn, and shy, but his courtesy, modesty, and fair-minded tolerance combined to make an attractive personality. Taken from school when he was 15, he was tutored privately. His love for scholarship was deep. At 18 he entered Christ Church, Oxford, but his stay was cut short by a breakdown in health. In accordance with the advice of his doctors, he set out on a long sea voyage to Australia and New Zealand. He was absent from England for almost two years. During this time his character matured. He regained his health and acquired self-confidence. He was still uncertain as to his future career; both the church and politics attracted him. When he was offered a seat in Parliament for Stamford in 1853, he chose politics and was elected to the House of Commons.

He fell in love with Georgina Alderson, but his father objected to the marriage, regarding her lack of social standing and wealth as an impediment to an alliance with the Cecil family. Nonetheless, the marriage took place in 1857. They had five sons and two surviving daughters. Salisbury was a man of strong religious faith and enjoyed a happy home life. Lady Salisbury was intelligent and sociable, and all the Cecils came to regard Hatfield as their home. Hatfield also became one of the great houses in which distinguished visitors were entertained.

During the years from 1853 to 1874, Salisbury was only briefly a government minister (secretary of state for India, July 1866 to March 1867) but resigned office in disagreement over the Conservative government's espousal of parliamentary reform. He became deeply suspicious of the new Conservative leader, Disraeli. Out of the government he was active as a member of the House of Commons and as a writer; he frequently contributed political articles to the *Saturday Review* and *The Quarterly Review*. He also interested himself in science, especially in botany and in electricity and magnetism; later he had his own laboratory built at Hatfield.

In February 1874 Salisbury was persuaded to join Disraeli's ministry and once more became secretary of state for India. During their seven years together in and out of office, Salisbury, overcoming his earlier prejudice, came to regard Disraeli with admiration and affection.

Succeeding the inept Lord Derby as foreign secretary, Salisbury first became responsible for Britain's foreign relations in April 1878, at a time of great crisis in the Balkans. It seemed probable that war might break out between Britain and Russia over the control of Constantinople. By masterly diplomacy Salisbury ensured that the

Appointment as foreign secretary (margin note)

Russians came to the conference table at the Congress of Berlin (June–July 1878). Disraeli occupied the limelight, but Salisbury's careful and patient diplomacy secured the essential compromises. For their success Disraeli and Salisbury were granted the Order of the Garter, the highest decoration Queen Victoria could bestow.

After Disraeli's death (1881), Salisbury was the obvious successor and led the Conservative opposition in the House of Lords. He became prime minister during the brief Conservative administration from June 1885 to January 1886. Ireland and imperial problems were the chief issues of the time. Salisbury opposed Gladstone on the question of Home Rule for Ireland and three times won the electoral support necessary to become prime minister (1886–92, 1895–1900, and 1900–02). During the greater part of these years, Salisbury combined the offices of prime minister and foreign secretary. He was not autocratic but left wide discretion to individual ministers. Weak control by the government as a whole sometimes had harmful results. This was one of the causes of the South African War (1899–1902), which occurred when Joseph Chamberlain was colonial secretary. But at the Foreign Office, Salisbury succeeded in avoiding serious conflict with the great European powers despite major crises and rivalries.

The partition of Africa largely preoccupied Salisbury's second ministry (1886–92) and remained a source of serious Anglo-French conflict until 1898, when France accepted British dominance on the Nile after the Fashoda

Attitude toward empire

Crisis. Salisbury was an imperialist: he believed a phase of European, preferably British, rule indispensable for the advancement of the "backward" races and had no hesitation in imposing this rule by force, as he did in the Sudan (1896–99). His foreign policy was directed toward the defense and enlargement of the British Empire. He had no sympathy for older empires, such as the Ottoman, whose rulers he regarded as corrupt oppressors. Salisbury attempted but failed to gain the cooperation of the European powers to intervene against Turkey to bring to a halt the Armenian "massacres" (1895–96). He refused to be frightened either by American threats over Venezuela (1895) or by the Kaiser's Kruger telegram sent in January 1896, after the unsuccessful Jameson raid into the Transvaal in South Africa.

During the last decade of the 19th century, when the principal powers grouped themselves into alliances, Salisbury maintained a free hand for Britain. He was opposed to alliance commitments, fearing that when the time came a democratic electorate might refuse to go to war; he also regarded alliances for Britain as unnecessary and dangerous. He did not back Chamberlain's unsuccessful efforts to conclude an alliance with Germany (1898–1901).

Recent scholarship has re-evaluated Salisbury's contribution and acquitted him of the charge of "secret diplomacy"; nor was Salisbury an "isolationist," since his diplomacy was active wherever Britain's interests extended. During the last two years of his ministry, from the autumn of 1900 until the summer of 1902, old age and ill health forced him to give up the Foreign Office, though he continued as prime minister. With Lord Lansdowne as the new foreign secretary, he saw his principles of diplomacy partially abandoned when Britain concluded an alliance with Japan in January 1902. Later that year, in July, Salisbury retired. He died on August 22, 1903.

Salisbury was the last aristocratic statesman to head a British government while in the House of Lords and not the elected Commons. He represented a tradition that passed away with him. His contemporaries recognized his greatness as a statesman. He combined a realism and clarity of view with a fundamentally ethical approach to diplomacy, which sought to conciliate and pacify while maintaining important national interests.

BIBLIOGRAPHY. The most important biography is LADY GWENDOLEN CECIL, *Life of Robert, Marquis of Salisbury*, 4 vol. (1921–32), but a projected fifth volume was never published. More recent assessments are A.L. KENNEDY, *Salisbury, 1830–1903: Portrait of a Statesman* (1953); J.A.S. GRENVILLE, *Lord Salisbury and Foreign Policy: The Close of the Nineteenth*

Century (1964); and L.P. CURTIS, *Coercion and Conciliation in Ireland, 1880–1892: A Study in Conservative Unionism* (1963).

(J.A.S.G.)

Sallust

A Roman politician and historian, Sallust made a unique contribution to historiography with his development of the monograph. His vivid and dramatic narratives describing Roman politics in the 2nd and 1st centuries BC and his fascination with the personalities of the leading political figures of his time influenced the great Roman historian Tacitus, among others.

Sallust (Gaius Sallustius Crispus) was born at Amiternum (now San Vittorino, near L'Aquila) in central Italy, probably in 86 BC; a late source gives his birth date as October 1. His family probably belonged to the local aristocracy, but Sallust was the only member known to have served in the Roman Senate. Thus he embarked on a political career as a *novus homo* ("new man"); that is, he was not born into the ruling class, which was an accident that influenced both the content and tone of his historical judgments. Nothing is known of his early career, but he probably gained some military experience, perhaps in the east in the years from 70 to 60 BC. His first political office, which he held in 52, was that of a tribune of the plebs. The office, designed originally to represent the lower classes, by Sallust's time had developed into one of the most powerful magistracies. The evidence that Sallust held a quaestorship, an administrative office in finance, sometimes dated about 55, is unreliable.

Early political life

Because of electoral disturbances in 53, there were no regular government officials other than the tribunes, and the next year opened in violence that led to the murder of Clodius, a notorious demagogue and candidate for the praetorship (a magistracy ranking below that of consul), by a gang led by Milo. The latter was a candidate for consul. In the trial that followed, Cicero defended Milo, while Sallust and his fellow tribunes harangued the people in speeches attacking Cicero. While these events were not of lasting significance, though they did result in Pompey's appointment as sole consul, Sallust's experience of the political strife of that year provided a major theme for his writings.

In 50 Sallust was expelled from the Senate for alleged immorality on the initiative of Appius Claudius, who had close connections with Pompey and with whom Sallust had probably quarrelled. The following year Sallust sought refuge with Caesar, and, when the civil war between Caesar and Pompey broke out in that year, he was

Association with Caesar

placed in command of one of Caesar's legions. His only recorded action was unsuccessful. Two years later, designated praetor, he was sent to quell a mutiny among Caesar's troops, again without success. In 46 he took part in Caesar's African campaign (with modest success), and when Africa Nova was formed from Numidian territory (modern Algeria), Sallust became its first governor. He remained in office until 45 or early 44.

Upon returning to Rome, Sallust was accused of extortion and of plundering his province, but through Caesar's intervention he was never brought to trial. The evidence is suspect: it contains few details and is in part of doubtful authenticity. It also draws moralizing contrasts between Sallust's behaviour and his censorious writings and suggests a source for the ill-gotten wealth that created the splendid Sallustian Gardens (Horti Sallustiani). Maladministration was common enough and Sallust may have been guilty. Yet the tradition about his morals seems to have originated in scurrilous gossip and by a confusion between the historian and his adopted son, Augustus' minister Sallustius Crispus, a man of great wealth and luxurious tastes who may have created the gardens. The remains of the palace where they were located—the gardens became an imperial possession—may still be seen in the Piazza Sallustio.

Sallust's political career ended soon after his return to Rome. His retirement may have been voluntary, as he himself maintains, or forced upon him by the withdrawal of Caesar's favour or even by Caesar's assassination. Cae-

Writings

sar seems not to have considered him for the consulship, nor did the Triumvirate of Antony, Octavian, and Lepidus, Caesar's heirs. Sallust may have begun to write even before the Triumvirate was formed late in 43.

Sallust was born in a time of civil war. As he grew to maturity, foreign war and political strife were commonplace; thus it is not surprising that his writings are preoccupied with violence. His first monograph, *Bellum Catilinae* (43–42 BC; *Catiline's War*), deals with corruption in Roman politics by tracing the conspiracy of Catiline, a ruthlessly ambitious patrician who had attempted to seize power in 63 BC after suspicions of his fellow nobles and the growing mistrust of the people prevented him from attaining it legally. He was supported by certain members of the upper classes who were prompted either by ambition or by the hope of solving their financial problems by Catiline's accession to power. But he also had the backing of Italy's dissatisfied veterans, impoverished peasants, and overburdened debtors. In Sallust's view, Catiline's crime and the danger he presented were unprecedented. Indeed, alarmed contemporaries may have exaggerated the significance of the incident; yet had the government not acted as firmly as it did, a catastrophe could have occurred. Sallust describes the course of the conspiracy and the measures taken by the Senate and Cicero, who was then consul. He brings his narrative to a climax in a senatorial debate concerning the fate of the conspirators, which took place on December 5, 63. In Sallust's eyes, Caesar and Cato represented civic virtue and were the significant speakers in the debate; he regarded the deaths of these men as marking the end of an epoch in the history of the republic. A digression in this work indicates that he considered party strife as the principal factor in the republic's disintegration.

In his second monograph, *Bellum Jugurthinum* (41–40 BC; *The Jugurthine War*), he explored in greater detail the origins of party struggles that arose in Rome when war broke out against Jugurtha, the king of Numidia, who rebelled against Rome at the close of the 2nd century BC. This war provided the opportunity for the rise to the consulship of Gaius Marius, who, like Sallust and Cicero, was a "new man." His accession to power represented a successful attack on the traditionally exclusive Roman political elite, but it caused the kind of political conflict that, in Sallust's view, resulted in war and ruin. Sallust considered Rome's initial mismanagement of the war the fault of the "powerful few" who sacrificed the common interest to their own avarice and exclusiveness. Political turmoil in Rome during the late republic had social and economic causes (not overlooked by Sallust), but essentially it took the form of a power struggle between the aristocratic group in control of the Senate and those senators who enlisted popular support to challenge the oligarchy. This is the underlying framework of Sallust's schematic analysis of the events of that time—the clash between nobility, or Senate, and people, or plebs. The *Histories*, of which only fragments remain, describes the history of Rome from 78 to 67 BC. Here Sallust deals with a wider range of subject matter, but party conflict and attacks on the politically powerful remain a central concern. Hints of hostility to the Triumvirate may be detected in both *Bellum Jugurthinum* and the *Histories*.

Two "Letters to Caesar" and an "Invective Against Cicero," Sallustian in style, have often been credited, although probably incorrectly, to Sallust. A report that he wrote a speech, now lost, for Ventidius, a victorious general, in 38 BC would indicate that Sallust enjoyed a high reputation, for Ventidius would be likely to approach a currently esteemed writer. His influence pervades later Roman historiography, whether men reacted against him, as Livy (59 BC–AD 17) did, or exploited and refined his manner and views, as Tacitus (*c*. 56–*c*. 120) did. His narratives were enlivened with speeches, character sketches, and digressions; and, by skillfully blending archaism and innovation, he created a style of classic status. And to the delight of moralists he revealed that Roman politics were not all that official rhetoric depicted them to be.

Sallust is not an entirely admirable historian; his work shows many instances of anachronisms, inaccuracies, and prejudice; the geography of the *Bellum Jugurthinum* scarcely reveals personal acquaintance with North Africa; he treats the destruction of Carthage in 146 BC as the beginning of the Roman crisis, whereas symptoms were clearly visible before that date. Nor is he a deep thinker, being content to operate with philosophical commonplaces. He makes no attack on the structure of the Roman state; his moral and political values are traditional; they commemorate the past to castigate the present. But his own experiences in politics imbued his analysis and his idiom with an energy and passion that compel the attention of readers.

Sallust died in 35 or 34 BC; a late source adds a date, May 13.

BIBLIOGRAPHY. The standard editions of the text of Sallust's works are C. SALLUSTIUS CRISPUS, *Catilina, Iugurtha, Fragmenta ampliora,* ed. by A.W. AHLBERG and A. KURFESS (1968); and *Historiarium reliquiae,* ed. by B. MAURENBRECHER, 2 fasc. (1891–93, reprinted 1967). A serviceable bibliography, though not complete, is A.D. LEEMAN, *A Systematical Bibliography of Sallust, 1879–1964,* rev. ed. (1965); it may be supplemented for works after 1964 by the successive volumes of *L'Année philologique.* D.C. EARL, *The Political Thought of Sallust* (1961), is the only substantial treatment of this subject in English. See also R. SYME, *Sallust* (1964), a comprehensive work with a useful bibliography.

(G.M.P.)

Salmoniformes

The order Salmoniformes is a diverse and complex group of fishes consisting of about 1,000 species in the fresh waters and oceans of the world. Included are the familiar trout, salmon, and pike, as well as most of the bizarre forms of fishes inhabiting the middepths of the oceans.

The framework of the order Salmoniformes in the discussion below should not be considered as a definitive taxonomic category but rather as an assemblage of diverse fishes possessing several primitive anatomical features representative of an early stage in the evolution of modern bony fishes (teleostean fishes).

GENERAL FEATURES

Evolutionary importance of the order. The significance of the order Salmoniformes as presently classified—a major departure from early schemes of fish classification—is in the evolutionary position of the group; the Salmoniformes are now considered a basal stock in the mainstream of modern bony-fish evolution. The present classification implies that the ancestors of salmoniform fishes developed several evolutionary trends in the Late Mesozoic Era, about 100,000,000 years ago, providing the necessary source of evolutionary raw material to initiate several successful evolutionary lineages, ultimately leading to most of the modern bony fishes.

The order Salmoniformes, as treated here, is based on the combined work of a British ichthyologist and several American ichthyologists, who have divided the order into eight suborders and 37 families. Constructed in this way, the order Salmoniformes brings together many extremely diverse groups. Several major alterations have recently been proposed for the classification of salmoniform fishes; thus the classification used in this article is provisional and may be subject to extensive changes when more precise information is available. The order Salmoniformes can be considered more as an evolutionary grade in the phylogeny of teleostean fishes than a well-defined taxonomic category. No single character or group of characters can distinguish all salmoniform fishes from all other fishes.

Divisions of the order

Reasons for interest in the order. The trouts, salmons, chars, whitefishes, and graylings of the family Salmonidae are the most widely known and intensively studied family of fishes. Their famed sporting qualities and excellent taste ensure their economic importance. At the other extreme, some deep-sea families of salmoniform fishes are known only to a few ichthyologists, and often only on the basis of a few imperfectly preserved specimens. The bulk of salmoniform species are fishes of the middepths (mesopelagic and bathypelagic zones) of the open

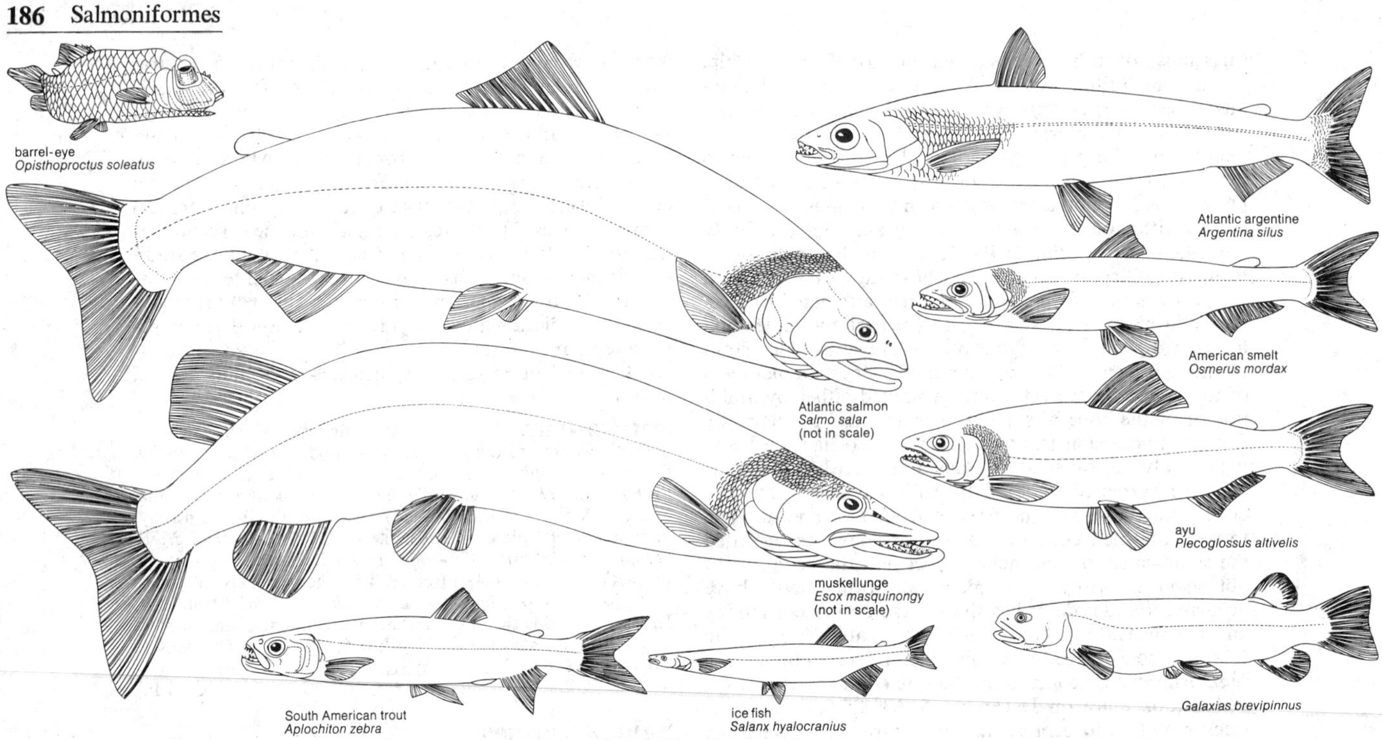

barrel-eye
Opisthoproctus soleatus

Atlantic argentine
Argentina silus

American smelt
Osmerus mordax

ayu
Plecoglossus altivelis

Atlantic salmon
Salmo salar
(not in scale)

muskellunge
Esox masquinongy
(not in scale)

Galaxias brevipinnus

South American trout
Aplochiton zebra

ice fish
Salanx hyalocranius

Figure 1: Body plans of salmoniform fishes of the suborders Salmonoidei, Galaxioidei, Argentinoidei, and Esocoidei.

oceans. The deep-sea salmoniforms have evolved unusual body forms and structures—such as luminous organs, telescopic eyes, complex appendages, and enormous and well-developed jaws and teeth—to cope with existence in the twilight and dark zones of the ocean and are of great interest in the study of evolutionary and developmental biology. Some of the anatomical structures evolved by the deep-sea salmoniforms are among the most striking and strange ones found in the animal kingdom.

Size range. The largest of the salmoniform fishes are members of the salmonidae and include the Pacific king salmon (*Onchorhynchus tshawytscha*) and the Danube and Siberian huchen (*Hucho hucho*), which are known to attain a weight of 50 kilograms (110 pounds) or more. The North American muskellunge (*Esox masquinongy*), of the pike family, approaches this size. The majority of the salmoniform species, however, are small. Most of the deep-sea species do not exceed 150 millimetres (six inches) in length, and many at maturity are 25 to 50 millimetres (one to two inches) long. The largest of the marine salmoniforms is one of the lancet fishes (family Alepisauridae), which may reach a maximum length of 2.1 metres (6.9 feet). The lancet fish has an elongated body with tremendously enlarged, dagger-like teeth, a fragile sail-like dorsal fin, and a soft, flaccid body. Occasionally a lancet fish migrates from the depths to the surface and may be caught by a fisherman or found washed up on a beach. Lancet fishes, like other deep-sea salmoniforms, are so highly modified that the relationships to trout and salmon are not obvious. A basic salmoniform feature, however, the small, fleshy adipose (fatty) fin situated between the dorsal fin and the tail, is found on both trouts and lancet fishes and has been inherited from a very ancient, but common, ancestor.

Most salmoniform species, including the smaller forms, are predacious fishes. Many peculiar modifications have been evolved by the small species of marine salmoniforms to allow them to capture and consume prey sometimes as large as themselves. Some of these lilliputian monsters appear to be mostly head and jaws, all out of proportion to the soft, gelatin-like body. The lack of a neck in fishes limits the mobility of the head and jaws; remarkable adaptations increase the flexibility of the head and allow a great enlargement of the mouth opening to engulf prey quickly. Several deep-sea salmoniforms lack bone on the anterior portion of the vertebral column, increasing the flexibility of the head and jaws.

Distribution and abundance. Salmoniform fishes are found in fresh water on all continents and in all of the oceans of the world. Various representatives of the trout, pike, and smelt families are indigenous to the cooler fresh waters of the Northern Hemisphere. Species of the family Salmonidae inhabit the colder waters of North America, from tributaries of the Arctic Ocean to tributaries of the Gulf of California in northwestern Mexico; in Europe and Asia, a comparable distribution is found, from the Arctic Ocean to the Atlas Mountains in North Africa and to the island of Taiwan. The Arctic char (*Salvelinus alpinus*) is the most northerly occurring of any freshwater fish. The development of an anadromous life cycle—spawning in fresh water but migrating to the sea for feeding and maturation—has allowed species of trout and salmon to extend their range greatly, particularly into fresh waters of glaciated regions after the glaciers recede and waters become inhabitable. The use of marine invasion routes allows a rapid expansion in the distribution of a species into new areas, often inaccessible to other species completely restricted to a freshwater life cycle. Species of the family Salmonidae are clearly the dominant fishes of the recently glaciated fresh waters of the Northern Hemisphere.

The pike and its allies (family Esocidae) have a distribution somewhat similar to the Salmonidae but extending neither so far north nor so far south. The pikes are completely restricted to fresh water throughout their life cycle; however, the distribution of the northern pike (*Esox lucius*) in Europe, Asia, and North America is one of the broadest distributional patterns of any fish species. Such a distribution must have been achieved when direct freshwater connections existed between the present major drainage basins and between Asia and North America. The smelts of the family Osmeridae are small fishes of Europe, Asia, and North America. Some smelts are permanent freshwater inhabitants, but the distribution of freshwater smelts is associated with relatively recent geological events; most smelts are anadromous or marine. No smelt species has penetrated far enough inland to establish a broad distribution in fresh water comparable to that of the salmonid fishes. The other salmoniform fishes with anadromous and freshwater species in the Northern Hemisphere are members of the Far Eastern families Plecoglossidae and Salangidae. In the Southern Hemisphere, salmoniform fishes ecologically similar to the trouts and smelts are encountered in the fresh waters of southern Africa, southern South America, Australia,

The anadromous life cycle

New Zealand, and Tasmania. These fishes are classified in the families Galaxiidae, Retropinnidae, Aplochitonidae, and Prototroctidae (of the suborder Galaxioidei). The galaxioid fishes are typically small (100 to 300 millimetres [four to 12 inches]) marine and freshwater fishes. The family Galaxiidae contains the most species (about 35) and has the broadest distribution—in Africa, South America, Australia, New Zealand, and Tasmania. The smeltlike fishes of the family Retropinnidae comprise about six species native to Australia, New Zealand, and Tasmania. The family Aplochitonidae consists of three species in southern South America and a larva-like (neotenic) species in Tasmania. The Prototroctidae has two, troutlike species in Australia and New Zealand. Various species of Salmonidae, particularly the North American rainbow trout (*Salmo gairdneri*) and the European brown trout (*S. trutta*), have been widely introduced and successfully established in suitable waters in Africa, South America, Australia and New Zealand. When introduced into lakes with abundant food fishes but previously lacking large predator fishes, the introduced trout flourish, growing rapidly to a large size. In certain lakes in Australia and New Zealand, famed for their trophy-sized trout, the trout feed avidly on their distant relatives, species of the Retropinnidae and Galaxiidae.

The remaining 25 or more families of Salmoniformes, with about 800 species, are entirely marine, typically middepth and deep-sea fishes. Representatives are found in all oceans and all depths, but in temperate and tropical waters major concentrations occur at depths of 200 to 2,000 metres (about 650 to 6,500 feet). The tremendous abundance attained by some populations of these marine salmoniforms has become evident only with the advent of modern sonar equipment, which has detected aggregations many square kilometres in extent.

IMPORTANCE TO MAN

The economic significance of the trouts and salmons as sporting fishes and as commercial products is well-known. Governments invest heavily to maintain and increase the production of trout and salmon; hundreds of millions of trout and salmon are hatched, reared, and stocked each year for sport and commerce. A large private industry has developed, particularly in Denmark, Japan, and the United States to supply trout to markets and restaurants. With the problems of increased human population and the demands made on rivers by industry and agriculture, the challenge of perpetuating and increasing the abundance of salmon and trout has become a serious one.

The demand for trout as a sport fish far exceeds the supply in heavily populated regions. This situation, particularly in the United States, has resulted in a massive program by state and federal agencies to raise trout to acceptable size and to stock them in heavily fished waters. Such an artificial abundance, however, is a poor substitute for natural trout fishing.

Except for the pikes, the remaining freshwater salmoniforms are too small or too rare to be significant sport fish, but most are considered excellent food fish. The oceanic salmoniforms have little direct importance to man; because of their tremendous abundance, however, they form a vital link in the food chain of the oceans, providing forage for valuable predator species such as the tuna. Many of the deep-sea salmoniforms undertake daily vertical migrations, rising toward the surface layer of the ocean at night for feeding. This vertical migration exposes them to predation by larger fishes and functions in the recycling of energy in the ocean by elevating energy accumulated in the lower depths (in the bodies of the small salmoniforms) and making it available to large predators in the upper zones.

NATURAL HISTORY

Life cycle and reproduction. Virtually every type of life cycle and mode of reproduction known for fishes is exhibited by some salmoniform fishes. These life cycles range from passage of the entire life-span in the confines of a small pond or stream to migrations encompassing thousands of kilometres from a stream to the ocean and

back to the stream. Some species have a direct development stage from the egg, hatching as miniature adults, ready to fend for themselves. Most deep-sea marine species have larval stages, drastically different from the adult. Some larvae have eyes attached to long stalks from the head. Most salmoniform species consist of males and females, but several deep-sea groups are hermaphrodites, a single individual having functional testes and ovaries. Evidently, in the darkness of the ocean depths, it is advantageous for an individual to function both as male and female.

The life cycles of salmons and trouts have been intensively studied because of the economic importance of salmonid fishes. Factual information of the life cycle and reproduction is used to settle disputes between nations regarding the origin of salmon caught in the open ocean and for the intelligent management of the resource.

The life cycle and reproduction of the deep-sea salmoniforms, however, are little known except for interpretations gained from examination of a few specimens and collection of eggs and larvae. Eggs and larvae of many of the marine species have not yet been found.

Among the salmoniform fishes, only the pike family (Esocidae) and the mudminnow family (Umbridae) are completely restricted to fresh water throughout their life cycle. All other families that have freshwater representatives contain some species that enter the marine environment for growth and maturation, returning to fresh water to spawn. One species of the family Galaxiidae has a catadromous life cycle—spawning takes place in a marine environment, and the young migrate to fresh water to mature. All of the oceanic salmoniforms are completely marine throughout their life cycle.

The families Salmonidae and Osmeridae demonstrate a transition between freshwater and marine life cycles. All species of salmonids spawn in fresh water, but the Pacific pink salmon (*Onchorhynchus gorbuscha*) has reduced the freshwater stage to the spawning migration and incubation of the eggs. As soon as the eggs hatch and the yolk sac is absorbed, pink salmon fry migrate to sea. Some pink salmon may spawn in the intertidal zone at the mouths of small streams, virtually eliminating the freshwater stage in the life cycle. Other species of Salmonidae, such as the lake char, or lake trout (*Salvelinus namaycush*), the graylings (*Thymallus*), and many of the whitefishes (*Coregonus*), have completely freshwater life cycles. Life cycles may differ among closely related species or even between populations of the same species; for example, rainbow trout that go to sea and return as large, silvery individuals are called steelhead trout. A single river system may contain local resident populations of small rainbow trout—maturing, spawning, and completing a life cycle within 100 metres (about 300 feet) of the site of their birth—as well as anadromous steelhead rainbow trout returning from the ocean after a two- or three-year journey spanning several thousand kilometres. Evidently the heritable differences that govern the type of life cycle in trouts—anadromous or freshwater—are slight. Offspring from anadromous parents can be used to establish populations in completely landlocked environments, and the progeny of nonanadromous parents may go to sea if given the opportunity.

Reproductive behaviour, the type and size of the eggs laid, and the amount of parental care have been developed in each species by the process of natural selection. In an evolutionary sense, spawning success is ultimately judged by the number of mature adults resulting from any spawning act. If the eggs and larvae are exposed to a harsh and perilous environment, there is a selective advantage for a female to produce fewer but larger eggs and to provide some extra measure of protection for the developing embryos. Cold, swift rivers with sparse food, typically utilized by salmons and trouts for spawning, undoubtedly have been a major selective force in the evolution of large eggs (four to eight millimetres [0.15–0.3 inch] in diameter) and of nest-building behaviour in the trouts and salmons.

A large egg with a large yolk to supply food to the developing embryo allows for direct development—that

The catadromous life cycle

National programs assisting sport fishing

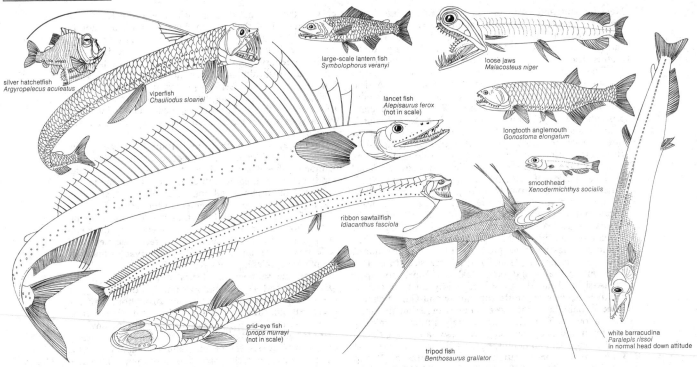

silver hatchetfish
Argyropelecus aculeatus

viperfish
Chauliodus sloanei

large-scale lantern fish
Symbolophorus veranyi

loose jaws
Malacosteus niger

lancet fish
Alepisaurus ferox
(not in scale)

longtooth anglemouth
Gonostoma elongatum

smoothhead
Xenodermichthys socialis

ribbon sawtailfish
Idiacanthus fasciola

grid-eye fish
Ipnops murrayi
(not in scale)

tripod fish
Benthosaurus grallator

white barracudina
Paralepis rissoi
in normal head down attitude

Figure 2: Body plans of salmoniform fishes of the suborders Stomiatoidei, Alepocephaloidei, and Myctophoidei.

is, the young hatch in an advanced stage, resembling a miniature adult. In more benign environments, such as lakes and the ocean, most salmoniform fishes produce smaller but more numerous eggs, and hatching takes place when the larvae are only partially developed. In many species the larvae are quite unlike the adult form and undergo a rather striking transformation (metamorphosis). Eggs of all freshwater spawning salmoniform fishes are heavier than water (demersal eggs) and develop on or in the bottom of a stream or lake. Marine species typically have pelagic (free drifting) eggs and larvae; the eggs are of neutral buoyancy and thus drift with the currents in the surface layer of the ocean. The eggs and larvae of many deep-sea salmoniforms have not yet been described, and in some species the eggs and larvae may be associated with the ocean bottom.

As far as known, all salmoniform fishes lay eggs and have external fertilization (oviparous fishes). In several of the deep-sea salmoniform families, in which hermaphroditism is common, it is not known if the species are self-fertilizing.

Some of the deep-sea salmoniforms have luminescent organs, one of the functions of which probably is sexual recognition. In the lantern fishes (Myctophoidei), the light organs are arranged in distinctive patterns that distinguish males and females of a species.

Behaviour and locomotion. Only the freshwater salmoniform fishes can be studied in any detail by direct observation. Most of what is known about the deep-sea species is based on preserved specimens, and, for most species, behaviour and locomotion can only be surmised from an examination of the morphology and anatomy.

The generalized body form of trout and salmon is characteristic of active, swift-moving fishes. A trim, fusiform body, powerful caudal (tail) muscles, and a well-developed tail combine to propel the fish against strong currents with a minimum of resistance and to give it the ability to leap barrier falls as high as three metres (ten feet) or more.

Adaptations of predators

Predatory fishes that dart out to grasp their prey are exemplified by the pike, in which the dorsal fin is situated posteriorly on the body to act more as a rudder than a keel. The pikelike body form has been evolved independently many times among predatory fishes such as the barracuda (*Sphyraena sphyraena*, of the order Perciformes). Among the deep-sea salmoniforms, however, certain predatory species are sedentary and have only

weak swimming ability. Such fish remain immobile until unsuspecting prey ventures close enough to be grasped. Some evidently use a luminous lure to attract their prey.

A peculiar type of locomotion is encountered among the barracudinas (family Paralepididae), marine salmoniforms of the suborder Myctophoidei. The barracudina swims in a vertical plane, darting up and down with the head oriented downward.

The behaviour of a fish toward other members of its species can be highly variable. Often, predator species are territorial and aggressive, whereas plankton-feeding species typically form schools and do not function normally unless they are close to other members of their species. Although behaviour patterns are largely innate and species-specific, striking differences occur between closely related species. Pink salmon fry, on hatching, seek each other and form schools prior to seaward migration. The young of the coho, or silver salmon (*Onchorhynchus kisutch*), however, establish territories and aggressively attack other young cohos that invade their territory. This difference in aggressive behaviour is associated with the longer period of freshwater life and limited food supply experienced by the coho salmon.

Homing by trout and salmon

One fascinating aspect of the behaviour of trout and salmon is their homing instinct—*i.e.*, the ability to return to the stream of their birth after migrating thousands of kilometres in the ocean for one to three years. Homing to the site of birth for reproduction is apparently a rather universal trait among the Salmonidae. Trout, char, and whitefishes in lakes segregate into discrete populations during the spawning season, each at a specific site.

It is now generally accepted that the sense of smell plays the major role in guiding an anadromous trout or salmon to its precise natal stream once it enters a river drainage from the ocean. How it finds the mouth of the river system leading to the natal stream from the open ocean is not yet understood; celestial navigation and detection of fields of gravity by some unknown means have been hypothesized. Several senses besides smell may be used to locate the natal stream. Cutthroat trout (*Salmo clarki*) in Yellowstone Lake, Wyoming, have been found to be able to return to their spawning stream after experimental blocking of the senses of smell and sight.

Homing behaviour has allowed the development of discrete populations among anadromous species of salmon and trout. Different life-history characteristics can be maintained because different populations segregate for spawning, and individuals of a population spawn only with each other, perpetuating hereditary traits. In major river systems such as the Columbia and Fraser in North America, one species may include several distinct races, each having different life cycles; such a situation greatly complicates the management of a species.

Ecology. As with other aspects of the biology of salmoniform fishes, the ecology of species of the family Salmonidae is best known. All species of salmonid fishes evolved in clear, cold water, and they thus require pure, well-oxygenated, cold water; for this reason salmonid fishes are the first species to suffer when water quality is degraded. Other freshwater salmoniforms, although not quite so sensitive to water quality as the salmonid fishes, are also susceptible to the inimical effects of man-induced environmental degradation.

Most salmoniform fishes are predators, feeding on other fish and large invertebrates. The process of evolution, however, works to modify and adapt species for certain ecological specializations in order to exploit a variety of food resources. In the lakes of the Northern Hemisphere, several whitefish species (*Coregonus*) are comparable, ecologically, to the herrings in the ocean. Such whitefishes, which are often called freshwater herrings, cruise the open water of lakes, filtering out minute organisms by straining the water through a fine mesh of gill rakers—minute bony elements attached to the gill arches. The sheefish, or inconnu (*Stenodus leucichthys*), a large, predatory whitefish of the Arctic, demonstrates that evolution for ecological adaptation is occasionally reversible: the adults feed on other fish and have evolved a pikelike body shape and large, powerful jaws, the development of teeth taking precedence over that of the gill rakers; the sheefish is quite unlike the typical whitefish from which it has evolved.

There probably has been strong selection for freshwater salmoniforms to utilize the marine environment for feeding. All groups except the esocoid fishes (pike family and related groups) have species that migrate to the ocean for feeding. This presents a problem of osmotic regulation in waters of different salinities. The physiology of most fishes is fixed for life in fresh water or in the sea, but most of the freshwater salmoniforms are able to live in the sea because they can excrete excess salts through cells in the gills. They also possess well-developed kidneys, which, in the freshwater environment, handle the excess of water that diffuses into their blood via the gills.

Little is known of the ecology of the wholly marine salmoniforms. They may be ecologically grouped by the depths that they inhabit and by their feeding preference. Those found in the twilight zone of the ocean (200–1,000 metres [650–3,300 feet]) consist of plankton feeders and predators. The plankton feeders typically are more active and have a more fully developed and functional swim bladder than is typical of the predatory forms.

Abundance of deep-sea species Because virtually all primary food production in the oceans takes place in the upper, sunlit layer, the deep-sea fishes live in a food-poor environment. At first, it may seem contradictory that they are able to maintain such numerical abundance; certain features of the biology of the deep-sea salmoniforms, however, allow them to attain great numbers. The body of the typical oceanic salmoniform is feebly developed, appearing to consist of little more than gelatinous material. The skeleton and muscles are reduced, so that little energy is needed to maintain the body. Many of the deep-sea species make nightly migrations to the food-rich surface zone for feeding. The species inhabiting the deepest parts of the ocean must depend on a food supply that filters down from above. This food is concentrated in a narrow bottom layer (the benthic zone), with the result that the benthic species may attain a relatively high abundance.

FORM AND FUNCTION

Features of the generalized salmoniform. *External characteristics.* The tremendous range of structural diversity found in salmoniform fishes has already been mentioned. Comparisons of some of the extreme morphological and physiological modifications with a generalized,

standard type can be useful in understanding the evolutionary trends leading to certain specializations. A trout of the genus *Salmo*, such as a rainbow trout or brown trout, can serve as a "standard" for the form and function of salmoniform fishes. The nonspecialized morphology and physiology of a typical trout species allow it to utilize diverse ecological niches during its life. A trout's diet consists of a variety of organisms, and its habitat may vary from small streams, large rivers, or lakes to the ocean. The body and fins are streamlined and symmetrical; the body is covered with small, smooth (cycloid) scales; the fins are formed from soft supporting rays, without spines. A small, fleshy adipose fin is located between the dorsal fin and the tail. The dorsal fin is located midway along the body on the dorsal surface. On the ventral surface, the paired pectoral fins are directly posterior to the head, the paired pelvic (or ventral) fins are directly beneath the dorsal fin, and the single anal fin is positioned beneath the adipose fin. The well-developed tail (caudal fin) connotes a powerful swimming ability. The presence, absence, rearrangement in position, and modifications in size, shape, and function of the various fins are characteristic of the numerous families of Salmoniformes.

Digestive system. The structures associated with feeding and digestion denote the diversity in a trout's diet. The mouth is fairly large with moderate development of nonspecialized teeth on the jaws and on several bones within the mouth. An adult trout can capture and consume a fish about one-quarter its own length without undue difficulty. Feeding on invertebrate organisms, as small as a few millimetres (perhaps 0.2 inch) in length, is facilitated by the gill rakers on the surface of the gill arches; they strain small organisms from a stream of water passing over the gills and funnel them to the esophagus. The well-defined muscular stomach opens by a valve into the intestine. A series of fingerlike appendages opens off of the intestine immediately posterior to the stomach. These appendages, called pyloric ceca, secrete enzymes and provide additional digestive areas to the intestine. Among closely related species of the family Salmonidae, there is a tendency for the more predacious species to have more numerous pyloric ceca. Generalizations relating pyloric cecal development to diet cannot be extended, however, to other fishes. The highly predacious pikes of the genus *Esox* completely lack pyloric ceca, whereas the algae-eating ayu (*Plecoglossus altivelis*, family Plecoglossidae) probably has more numerous ceca than any other fish, up to 400 or more.

Sense organs. Because vision is important in the life of a trout, the eyes are well developed; the retina possesses both rods (for vision in dim light) and cones (for perceiving more acute images and for colour vision). The sense of smell is also highly developed.

The lateral line nervous system functions as a pressure receptor and a direction finder for objects that move, such as another fish. The lateral line might be considered as a remote sense of touch; it does not, however, function in hearing low-frequency sound waves as was once believed. It has been demonstrated that sound waves are well below the threshold necessary to stimulate the lateral line cells. In trout, the lateral line consists of a series of connected sensory cells (neuromasts) with tiny, hairlike projections. These cells are embedded under the scales along the midline of the body and open to the surface through pores in the scales. An extension of the lateral line system on the head consists of a ramification of sensory canals. In some deep-sea salmoniforms living in the absence of the effects of sunlight, other senses are needed to compensate for vision in perceiving the environment, and the neuromast sensory cells may be exposed on raised papillae, thus increasing their sensitivity. The lateral line system

The swim bladder (or air bladder) has a hydrostatic function, adjusting internal pressure to maintain a weightless condition of neutral buoyancy at various depths. The trouts have a primitive type of swim bladder with a connecting duct from the bladder to the esophagus. The duct is an evolutionary holdover from an ancestor in which the swim bladder was mainly an accessory respiratory organ. Many salmoniform fishes lack the duct, and several deep-sea marine species lack a swim bladder altogether.

Departures from the generalized body plan. From the primitive body plan exemplified by the trouts, it is possible to derive all of the specialized body types of other salmoniform fishes by the elimination of some structures and by the modification, exaggeration, and rearrangement of others.

The pike is an example of a specialized predator whose diet, after the first year of life, consists almost entirely of other fishes. Its success depends on how effectively it captures and consumes other fishes, and its whole morphology and physiology are directed toward this end. A pike has an elongated body with a large head and large, powerful jaws. Its mouth is armed with large, canine-like teeth that can handle large prey. Patches of teeth on the gill arches replace the typical gill rakers. Vision is the primary sense used by pike to detect and capture prey. The visual centre of the brain (optic lobe) is more highly developed than are the centres of smell (olfactory lobes). The eyes have a high proportion of cones to rods in their retinas and are positioned to provide partial binocular vision (*i.e.*, the eyes are aimed in the same direction), sighting down grooves on the snout to aim at moving prey. The body form and position of the fins are specialized for swift, darting movements. The dorsal fin is placed posteriorly, over the anal fin, and, as is typical of other salmoniform fishes with posteriorly oriented dorsal fins, the adipose fin is absent.

The most extraordinary modifications in the basic salmoniform body plan are found among the marine species of the middepths and great depths of the ocean. The more striking adaptations include luminous organs, eyes specialized to function in dim light, feeding adaptations allowing some predatory species to kill and eat a fish as large as themselves, and drastic departures in body shape and fin development.

Bioluminescence, the production of chemical light by living organisms, is widespread in nature. Among vertebrate animals, only marine fishes have light organs. Light organs (or photophores) are encountered in many diverse groups of fish. These structures apparently have been evolved independently several times in different groups of fish. It is believed that light organs of fish have evolved from mucous cells of the skin. Salmoniform fishes, particularly species in the suborders Stomiatoidei and Myctophoidei, have developed some elaborate and highly complex light-producing systems. Some structures have lenses, reflectors, and eyelid-like shades. In addition to light cells on the sides of the body, luminous tissue may be found on the head, around the eyes, on fin rays and barbels, and on the ventral surface; in the myctophoid family Paralepididae, an internal duct makes the whole fish glow. The great diversity in the type and position of light organs suggests that they must serve different functions in the groups possessing them. In the family Searsiidae (suborder Alepocephaloidei), a large sac on the shoulder emits a display resembling a shower of sparks when the fish is disturbed. Such a structure probably is a defensive mechanism. Light organs on the head may help in locating food, and those on elongated dorsal fin rays or chin barbels may lure prey. Sexual recognition and territorial behaviour are other suggested functions. Although not all marine salmoniform fishes have light organs, the latter are typically found in species that spend most of their life in the lower twilight and upper dark zones of the ocean. The effects of sunlight essentially disappear at about 700 metres (2,300 feet); the maximum abundance of luminous fishes occurs at about 800 metres (2,600 feet).

There are some parallels in the development of eyes and light organs in fishes correlated with the depth at which the species lives. Perhaps the most sensitive of all vertebrate eyes is found in fishes inhabiting the dim twilight zone of the ocean; the eyes, specialized to function at very low light intensity, may be greatly enlarged. The retina typically consists entirely of rods with golden pigment to increase sensitivity to blue light of the light spec-

trum (the last part of the visual light spectrum to be filtered out in water). Another adaptation found in some marine salmoniforms for concentrating weak light is tubular eyes. Fish with tubular eyes appear to be wearing exaggerated goggles. Tubular eyes are aimed in the same direction (binocular vision) and may be directed straight ahead or directly upward. Two sets of retinas are associated with tubular eyes, one on the side of the shaft and one in the normal position at the base. The two sets of retinas function to enlarge the field of vision. A most unusual modification of the eyes is found in the myctophoid genus *Ipnops* (family Ipnopidae), which appears to be eyeless; however, a thin, transparent bony plate on top of the head covers a mass of retinal cells. Evidently such an eye functions to perceive faint luminescence at great depths. Larval stages of a few salmoniforms have eyes extended out from the body on stalks, which are resorbed when the eyes assume a normal position during metamorphosis.

Some grotesque fishes are found among the predatory stomiatoids and myctophoids. The teeth may be developed into tremendously enlarged fangs, which may be likened to daggers, spears, or sabres. The gape of the jaws is sufficiently large to engulf a prey as large as the predator. Stomiatoid predators have a peculiar modification of the anterior vertebral column, which remains unossified, resulting in a flexible jointlike mechanism allowing the head to snap back and enlarge the gape. To allow the swallowing of large prey, the body is soft, distensible, and usually lacks scales; the stomach is highly elastic.

EVOLUTION AND CLASSIFICATION

Evolutionarily important taxonomic characters. Studies of the skeletal system (osteology) and comparative anatomy have produced most of the information used in the classification of salmoniform fishes. At present, however, the taxonomy of Salmoniformes is not well defined because no character or group of characters is exclusive to salmoniform fishes, and little consistent difference in characters occurs among the suborders.

The fishes grouped in Salmoniformes possess a mosaic of primitive characters from which it is possible to derive most of the more advanced orders of teleostean fishes. Both evaluation of the hypothetical evolutionary branching sequences to denote relationships and judgment concerning the primitive or derived (advanced) state of a character are based on an evolutionary principle that a structure lost or highly modified during evolution will never be re-evolved in its original condition; for example, the adipose fin, the mesocoracoid bone of the pectoral skeleton, and teeth on the maxillary bone of the jaw are considered to be primitive salmoniform characters. The absence of these characters represents an advancement; evolutionary lines that have lost these features therefore could not have been ancestral to fishes that possess one or more of these characters. No family of Salmoniformes has all of the primitive characters, but the families Salmonidae and Osmeridae have most of them.

The primitive dentition pattern of the ancestral salmoniform would be with teeth on the premaxilla and maxilla (bones of the upper jaw) and on the dentary bone of the lower jaw, with the maxilla clearly dominant over the premaxilla in forming the gape of the upper jaw. Inside the mouth, on the upper surface, teeth would be on palatine and pterygoid bones on each side and on the median vomerine bone. On the lower surface of the mouth, teeth would cover the tongue and occur on a plate overlying the basibranchial bones (between the gill arches). Many separate lines of salmoniforms show evolutionary advancement for the loss of teeth and the dominance of the premaxilla over the maxilla, with loss of teeth on the maxilla.

The primitive structure of the pectoral girdle, associated with the ventral position of the pectoral fin, consists of an additional supporting bone—the mesocoracoid. The advanced condition, related to a more dorsally positioned pectoral fin, is the loss of the mesocoracoid.

The primitive salmoniform condition of the caudal skeleton has three separate vertebral centra (the centrum

*Lumines-
cent
organs*

*Eye
adapta-
tions in
deep-sea
forms*

*Skeletal
features*

is the main body of the vertebra) and associated bony elements functioning in support of the bony plates (hypural plates), which form the base of the tail. Such a structure is a vestige of the upturned tail (heterocercal tail) characteristic of a more primitive stage of fish evolution. Other such vestiges found in some salmoniform fishes include abdominal pores (minute ducts from the body cavity to the exterior), remnants of a preteleostean type of intestine (spiral valve), and the absence of oviducts in females. Evolution in several salmoniform lines has reduced by fusion the three supporting caudal vertebrae to two or, more commonly, one. The primitive type of salmoniform swim bladder is connected to the esophagus by a duct. The absence of the duct or absence of the swim bladder is the advanced state. The primitive salmoniform had pyloric ceca on the intestine—a variable trait among living species. The light organs of some marine salmoniforms are an advanced character and are considered to be derived from mucous cells.

Annotated classification.   The classification presented here is based on that of P.H. Greenwood *et al.*, with some modifications incorporated from more recent publications. These alterations consist of transferring the family Salangidae from the suborder Galaxioidei to the suborder Salmonoidei, placing the family Bathylaconidae in the suborder Alepocephaloidei (eliminating the suborder Bathylaconoidei), and the recognition of two additional families: Prototroctidae (in the suborder Galaxioidei) and Searsiidae (in the suborder Alepocephaloidei).

ORDER SALMONIFORMES
A diverse group of fishes with a mosaic of primitive characters. Typically fusiform or elongated predatory fishes. Adipose fin usually present; dorsal fin and pelvic fins typically placed midway along body; fin rays without true spines; pectoral fin generally in ventral position. Scales, if present, typically smooth (cycloid). Light organs present in several marine families. Caudal skeleton with 1 to 3 vertebral centra functioning in support of tail. Fossils from Cretaceous.

Suborder Salmonoidei
About 100 species; 10–150 cm long: freshwater, anadromous, or marine; Northern Hemisphere. Adipose present in all species; swim bladder with open duct; maxilla dominant over premaxilla in upper jaw; no light organs; intestine with pyloric ceca (except Salangidae); tail support on 3 distinct vertebral centra in Salmonidae, fused into single element in other families. Suborder includes the families Salmonidae (including Coregonidae and Thymallidae), salmons, trouts, chars; Osmeridae, smelts; Plecoglossidae, ayu; and Salangidae, ice fishes.

Suborder Galaxioidei
About 50 species; 7.5–40 cm long; freshwater, anadromous, or catadromous; Southern Hemisphere. Adipose fin absent in Galaxiidae, present in other families; swim bladder with or without duct; relationship of maxilla and premaxilla variable between genera. Light organs absent. Pyloric ceca present or absent. Tail support on 1 or 2 vertebral centra; mesocoracoid bone of pectoral girdle absent; teeth present on mesopterygoid bone in roof of mouth. Suborder contains the families Galaxiidae, no group name; Retropinnidae, New Zealand smelts; Aplochitonidae, South American trouts; and Prototroctidae, New Zealand "grayling."

Suborder Esocoidei
Ten species; 5–150 cm long; freshwater; Northern Hemisphere. Adipose fin lacking; swim bladder with open duct; maxilla without teeth; pyloric ceca lacking; pectoral girdle without mesocoracoid; tail support on 3 separate vertebral centra; 2 sets of paired ethmoid bones on snout region of skull. Suborder includes the families Esocidae, pikes; and Umbridae (including Dalliidae), mudminnows.

Suborder Argentinoidei
About 50 species; 3–40 cm; marine; worldwide. Adipose fin present on most species; swim bladder without duct or absent entirely; maxilla and premaxilla reduced, without teeth; light organs present in several species; tail support on 2 vertebral centra. Suborder includes the families Argentinidae (including Xenophthalmichthidae and Microstomatidae), argentines; Bathylagidae, deep-sea smelts; and Opisthoproctidae (including Dolichopterygidae, Macropinnidae, Winteridae), barrel-eyes.

Suborder Stomiatoidei
About 350 species; 2.5–45 cm; marine; worldwide. Adipose fin present or absent, some species with both a dorsal and a ventral adipose fin; swim bladder without duct or absent entirely; maxilla the dominant bone of the upper jaw; some species with greatly enlarged, depressable teeth; anterior vertebrae sometimes unossified; light organs present in most families; members of some families with chin barbel, which may be a highly elaborate structure; tail support on single vertebral centrum. Suborder includes families Stomiatidae, scaly dragonfishes; Gonostomatidae, bristlemouths; Sternoptychidae, hatchetfishes; Astronesthidae, snaggletoothed fishes; Melanostomiatidae, scaleless dragonfishes; Chauliodontidae, viperfishes; and Idiacanthidae, black dragonfishes.

Suborder Alepocephaloidei
About 120 species; 3–700 cm; marine, deep-sea; worldwide. Adipose fin lacking; swim bladder lacking; teeth small; intestine with pyloric ceca. Light organs present in some species (on raised papillae). Tail supported by 3 vertebral centra. Suborder contains the families Alepocephalidae, smoothheads; Bathylaconidae, bony throats; Searsiidae, tubeshoulders; and Bathyprionidae.

Suborder Myctophoidei
About 470 species; 2.5–200 cm; marine; worldwide. Adipose fin usually present; swim bladder, if present, with duct. Premaxilla dominant over maxilla in upper jaw; no mesocoracoid bone in pectoral girdle. Light organs present in all species of family Myctophidae, but absent in species of most other families; tail support on single vertebral centrum. Suborder includes the following 15 families: Myctophidae, lantern fishes; Aulopodidae, thread-sail fishes; Synodontidae, lizard fishes; Harpadontidae, bombay duck; Chlorophthalmidae, green-eyes; Bathypteroidae, spider fishes; Ipnopidae, grid-eye fishes; Paralepididae, barracudinas; Omosudidae, hammerjaw; Alepisauridae, lancet fishes; Anotopteridae, javelin fish; Evermannellidae, sabre-toothed fishes; Scopelosauridae, paperbones; Neoscopelidae, blackchin; Scopelarchidae, pearleyes.

Critical appraisal.   Previous schemes of fish classification have been based mainly on the work of the British ichthyologist C.T. Regan and the Soviet ichthyologist L.S. Berg. Both Regan and Berg grouped most of the generally primitive fishes with soft fin rays and smooth scales in an order with the herring family, Clupeidae. Regan called this order Isospondyli, and Berg used the name Clupeiformes. Such a classification considered Isospondyli or Clupeiformes as the most primitive of the teleostean fishes and as ancestral to all other advanced orders of Teleostei. The work of Greenwood and his colleagues clearly demonstrated that the classifications of Regan and Berg were without evolutionary reality, that the fishes classified as Clupeiformes or Isospondyli, as formerly arranged, were not all derived from a common ancestor but consisted of several unrelated groups. The true herrings (family Clupeidae and their direct derivatives) possess some unique characters, such as the structures involved with the connection of the swim bladder to the inner ear, not found in any other teleostean fishes; the herrings thus are not very likely to have been the progenitors of all other modern teleosts. The order Salmoniformes was created to remove several diverse groups of dubious relationships from the order Clupeiformes; these groups are thus considered as the basal stocks in the evolutionary radiation of teleostean fishes. The order Iniomi of Regan (Scopeliformes of Berg) was placed as a suborder, Myctophoidei, in Salmoniformes. It should be emphasized, however, that this taxonomic revision has added little new knowledge concerning the relationships among the various suborders grouped in Salmoniformes. At present no coherent picture of evolutionary affinities between the suborders and with other orders has emerged. Undoubtedly the present interpretation of Salmoniformes will undergo major revisions in the future both in structure and in its implications regarding the evolutionary links leading to other teleostean orders. Publications by D.E. Rosen and by the British ichthyologist Colin Patterson consider new evidence and a more critical interpretation of previous data; they have separated the suborder Myctophoidei from the Salmoniformes into the order Myctophiformes and have suggested that the suborder Giganturoidei of the order Cetomimiformes should be placed in Salmoniformes. The myctophoid fishes are well separated from other salmoniforms, having undergone their own independent evolution at least since Cretaceous times (about 100,000,000 years ago)—fossil records of four families are known from Cretaceous depos-

Alternate views on the nearest relatives of the salmoniforms

its—and recognition of the order Myctophiformes seems justified.

Hopefully, new evidence will be forthcoming from future studies providing new insights into the evolutionary events that transpired from 50,000,000 to 100,000,000 years ago and resulted in the evolution of the various families and suborders of Salmoniformes. From such evidence, a better understanding of the ancient divergences leading to the bulk of the present teleostean fishes should follow. Ichthyologists may have exploited anatomical characters to the limit of potential information yield, but it is to be expected that new fossil finds of extinct, intermediate groups will yield valuable information.

New techniques for examining chromosomes and comparing their number, size, shape, and content and for comparing the structure of certain evolutionarily stable protein molecules are promising approaches for the interpretation of evolution.

BIBLIOGRAPHY. J.W. JONES, *The Salmon* (1959); W.E. FROST and M.E. BROWN, *The Trout* (1967), two works with general information on Salmoniformes; J.E. FITCH and R.J. LAVENBERG, *Deep-Water Teleostean Fishes of California* (1968), a book designed for the interested layman, covering many deep-sea Salmoniformes; P.H. GREENWOOD et al., "Phyletic Studies of Teleostean Fishes with a Provisional Classification of Living Forms," *Bull. Am. Mus. Nat. Hist.*, 131: 339–455 (1966), created the order Salmoniformes; S.H. WEITZMAN, "The Origin of the Stomiatoid Fishes with Comments on the Classification of Salmoniform Fishes," *Copeia*, pp. 507–540 (1967), created a new suborder Osmeroidei and modified the classification of GREENWOOD et al. (above); R.M. MCDOWALL, "Relationships of Galaxioid Fishes with A Further Discussion of Salmoniform Classification," *Copeia*, pp. 796–824 (1969), suggested further modifications in the classification of Salmoniformes; D.E. ROSEN and C. PATTERSON, "The Structure and Relationships of the Paracanthopterygian Fishes," *Bull. Am. Mus. Nat. Hist.*, 141:357–474 (1969), a revision of Salmoniformes with new information on early teleostean evolution; C. PATTERSON, "Two Upper Cretaceous Salmoniform Fishes from the Lebanon," *Bull. Br. Mus. Nat. Hist.*, *Geol.*, 19:207–296 (1970), provides new information and suggested relationships of primitive salmoniforms; W.A. GOSLINE, "The Morphology and Systematic Position of the Alepocephaloid Fishes," *Bull. Br. Mus. Nat. Hist.*, *Zool.*, 18:183–218 (1969), a review of suborder Alepocephaloidei; J.G. NIELSEN and V. LARSEN, "Synopsis of the Bathylaconidae (Pisces, Isospondyli) with a New Eastern Pacific Species," *Galathea Rep.*, 9:221–238 (1968), revises the suborder Bathylaconoidei, family Bathylaconidae in suborder Alepocephaloidei; N.B. MARSHALL, "*Bathyorion danae*, a New Genus and Species of Alepocephaliform Fishes," *Dana Rep.*, 68:1–10 (1966), a technical paper on the suborder Alepocephaloidei; G.J. NELSON, "Gill Arches of Some Teleostean Fishes of the Families Salangidae and Argentinidae," *Jap. J. Ichthyol.*, 17:61–66 (1970), another technical article revising the order Salmoniformes; R.J. BEHNKE, "A New Subgenus and Species of Trout, *Salmo (Platysalmo) platycephalus*, from Subcentral Turkey, with Comments on the Classification of the Subfamily Salmoninae," *Mitt. Hamb. Zool. Mus. Inst.*, 66:1–15 (1968), classification of trouts and salmons, and "The Application of Cytogenic and Biochemical Systematics to Phylogenetic Problems in the Family Salmonidae," *Trans. Am. Fish Soc.*, 99:237–248 (1970), classification of whitefishes, subfamily Coregoninae.

(R.J.B.)

Salt and Salt Production

Salt, sodium chloride (symbol, NaCl), is a mineral substance of great importance to man. The mineral form, halite or rock salt, is sometimes called common salt to distinguish it from a class of chemical compounds called salts.

Uses of salt

Salt is essential to the health of men and animals. Table salt, used universally as a seasoning, is fine-grained and of high purity. To ensure that this hygroscopic substance will remain free-flowing when exposed to the atmosphere, small quantities of sodium aluminosilicate, tricalcium phosphate, or magnesium silicate are added. Iodized salt —that is, salt to which small quantities of potassium iodide have been added—is widely used in areas where iodine is lacking from diet, a situation which can cause swelling of the thyroid gland, commonly called goitre. Livestock also require salt; it is often made available in solid blocks.

Table 1: Properties of Salt

Chemical formula	NaCl (sodium chloride)
Physical form at room temperature	colourless, transparent, or translucent cubic crystals
Hygroscopicity	salt is hygroscopic; *i.e.*, it absorbs atmospheric moisture and in pure form will lump together unless countermeasures are taken
Density	2.165 times as heavy as water at 0° C (32° F)
Melting point	800° C (1,472° F)
Solubility	100 parts by weight of water dissolve 36.0 parts of salt at 20° C (68° F); 39.1 parts at 100° C (212° F); and 39.7 parts at 107° C (222° F), the boiling point of a saturated solution; salt is also soluble in glycerin, slightly soluble in alcohol or liquid ammonia, and insoluble in concentrated hydrochloric acid
Sodium chloride hydrate	if a saturated solution of salt in water is cooled below 0.10° C (32.18° F), a crystalline hydrate (NaCl·2H$_2$O) separates
Electrolysis of salt	under the influence of an electric current, molten salt decomposes to form metallic sodium and chlorine; its aqueous solutions form caustic soda and chlorine

The meat-packing, sausage-making, fish-curing, and food-processing industries use salt as a preservative or seasoning or both (see also FOOD PRESERVATION). It is employed for curing and preserving hides, and as a brine for refrigeration.

In the chemical industry, salt is required in the manufacture of sodium bicarbonate (baking soda), sodium hydroxide (caustic soda), hydrochloric acid, chlorine, and many other chemicals. Salt is also employed in soap, glaze, and porcelain enamel manufacture and enters into metallurgical processes as a flux (a substance promoting fusing of metals).

When applied to snow or ice, salt lowers the melting point of the mixture. Thus, large amounts are used in northern climates to help rid thoroughfares of accumulated snow and ice. Salt is used in water-softening equipment that removes calcium and magnesium compounds from water.

HISTORY

In some parts of the Western Hemisphere and in India, salt was introduced by Europeans. In parts of central Africa it is still a luxury available only to the rich. Where men live mainly on milk and raw or roasted meat (so that its natural salts are not lost), sodium chloride supplements are unnecessary; nomads with their flocks of sheep or herds of cattle, for example, never eat salt with their food. On the other hand, peoples with largely cereal, vegetable, or boiled meat diets require supplements of salt.

The habitual use of salt is intimately connected with the advance from nomadic to agricultural life, a step in civilization that influenced the rituals and cults of almost all ancient nations. The gods were worshipped as the givers of the kindly fruits of the earth, and salt was usually included in offerings consisting wholly or partly of cereal elements. Such offerings were prevalent among the Greeks and Romans and among a number of the Semitic peoples.

Covenants were ordinarily made over a sacrificial meal, in which salt was a necessary element. The preservative qualities of salt made it a peculiarly fitting symbol of an enduring compact, sealing it with an obligation to fidelity. The word salt thus acquired connotations of high esteem and honour in ancient and modern languages. Examples include the Arab avowal "There is salt between us," and the Hebrew expression "to eat the salt of the palace," and the modern Persian phrase *namak ḥarām*, "untrue to salt" (*i.e.*, disloyal or ungrateful). In English the term "salt of the earth" describes a person held in high esteem.

Salt contributes greatly to our knowledge of the ancient highways of commerce. One of the oldest roads in Italy is the Via Salaria (Salt Route) over which Roman salt from Ostia was carried into other parts of Italy. Herodotus tells of a caravan route that united the salt oases of the Libyan Desert. The ancient trade between the Aegean and the Black Sea coasts of southern Russia was largely

The Salt Route

Table 2: Composition of Some Concentrated Natural Brines (percentage)

item	Droitwich, England	Winsford, England	Syracuse, N.Y.	St. Charles, Mich.	Artern, German Dem. Rep.	Friedrichshall, Germany, Fed. Rep. of
Sodium chloride	24.97	25.46	21.71	22.84	25.27	25.49
Sodium sulfate	0.26	...	...	...	...	...
Potassium chloride	...	...	...	...	...	...
Potassium sulfate	...	...	...	...	0.12	...
Magnesium bromide	...	...	...	0.26	0.29	...
Magnesium chloride	0.05	0.21	0.14	4.03	0.42	...
Calcium sulfate	0.37	0.45	0.50	0.20	0.40	0.01
Calcium chloride	...	...	0.19	0.77	...	0.44
Total solids	25.65	26.12	22.54	28.10	26.50	25.94

dependent on the salt pans (ponds for evaporating seawater to obtain salt) at the mouth of the Dnepr (Dnieper) River, and on the salt fish brought from this district.

The economic importance of salt is further indicated by the prevalence, even down to the present, of taxes on salt and government salt monopolies. In Oriental systems of taxation high, oppressive imposts on salt are customary, with the result that salt usually reaches the consumer in an impure state largely mixed with earth.

Cakes of salt have been used as money in Ethiopia and elsewhere in Africa, and in Tibet. In the Roman army an allowance of salt was made to officers and men; in imperial times, this *salarium* (from which the English word "salary" is derived) was converted into an allowance of money for salt.

(F.O.W.)

OCCURRENCE

Seawater. Though the material which gives seawater its salty flavour is comprised of many substances, sodium chloride, or common salt, is by far the predominant compound. On the assumption that each gallon (about four litres) of seawater contains 0.231 pound (about 105 grams) of salt and that on the average rock salt is 2.24 times as dense as water, it has been estimated that if the oceans of the world were completely dried up they would yield at least 4,500,000 cubic miles of rock salt, or about 14½ times the bulk of the entire continent of Europe above high-water mark.

Seawater contains on the average about 3 percent salt, the actual concentration varying from about 1 percent (in the polar seas) to 5 percent. Enclosed seas such as the Mediterranean and Red seas contain a higher proportion of salt than does the open ocean at the same latitude. Irrespective of the source of the seawater, salt obtained by evaporation of seawater has the following composition: sodium chloride 77.76 percent; magnesium chloride 10.88 percent; magnesium sulfate 4.74 percent; calcium sulfate 3.60 percent; potassium chloride 2.46 percent; magnesium bromide 0.22 percent; and calcium carbonate 0.34 percent.

Natural brines. Brine is water containing a high concentration of salt. Natural brines of commercial importance are found in the Dead Sea, Austria, France, Germany, India, the United States, and Great Britain. Salt in brines is nearly always accompanied by chlorides and sulfates of potassium, calcium, and magnesium; carbonates and the element bromine are often present as well.

Table 2 gives the composition of some concentrated natural brines used for salt production.

The Dead Sea, which covers an area of 393 square miles (1,020 square kilometres), contains approximately 12,650,000,000 tons of salt. The Jordan River, which contains only 35 parts of salt per 100,000 parts of water, adds 850,000 tons of salt to this total each year. The composition of Dead Sea water is given in Table 3.

The concentration of salts in the Dead Sea varies from 270 to 300 parts per thousand to a depth of 130 feet (40 metres); it increases gradually from 130 to 330 feet, and remains a fairly constant 332 parts per thousand below 330 feet. Dead Sea water is relatively free from sulfates and has a high proportion of potassium and bromine. Because atmospheric conditions are favourable to evaporation by means of sunlight (solar evaporation) for about eight months of the year, the production of salt, potassium, and bromine is feasible in the Dead Sea area. The

process used for recovery of salt and potash is similar to that described below under *Salt Manufacture*. The Indian brines at Khārāghoda resemble seawater in the character of their dissolved salts, but are much more concentrated and in some cases virtually saturated; that is, they have dissolved all the salt they can.

Table 3: Composition of Dead Sea Water

item	surface water	deep water (250 ft)
Specific gravity	1.1651	1.2356
Sodium chloride	6.11%	7.20%
Potassium chloride	0.85%	1.25%
Magnesium bromide	0.38%	0.61%
Magnesium chloride	9.46%	13.73%
Calcium chloride	2.63%	3.82%
Calcium sulfate	0.11%	0.05%
Total solids	19.54%	26.66%

Certain natural brines occurring in England and the United States are of special interest because they contain special salts, such as the chlorides of barium and strontium, not usually found in brines. Special processing methods are required to produce salt from such brines. In Great Britain, these unusual brines are found at great depths during test drillings for petroleum, while in the United States, they occur in deep wells in several places.

Special natural brines

(F.O.W./R.H.Ra.)

Table 4: Natural Brines Containing Unusual Salts

item	Renishaw, England	West Calder, Scotland	Pomeroy, Ohio	Malden, W. Virginia
Depth (feet)	3,198	3,910	...	...
Specific gravity	1.127	1.063	1.075	1.063
Sodium chloride	10.28%	6.26%	7.92%	6.01%
Potassium chloride	0.03%	0.04%	0.04%	0.06%
Magnesium bromide	0.11%	0.07%	...	...
Magnesium chloride	0.84%	0.55%	0.57%	0.50%
Calcium chloride	4.23%	1.34%	1.36%	1.49%
Strontium chloride	0.12%	0.16%	0.03%	0.02%
Barium chloride	0.14%	0.07%	0.04%	0.07%
Total solids	15.75%	8.49%	9.96%	8.15%

Rock salt. Rock salt is crystalline sodium chloride, called halite by mineralogists. It occurs widely in the form of rock masses and beds and is abundant in rocks from all geological periods. Because of its great solubility in water, it occurs under extremely thick cover in humid regions, but lies close to the surface in arid regions.

All major rock-salt deposits originated from the evaporation of seawater at some time during the geologic past. Seventy-eight percent of the mineral matter in normal seawater is sodium chloride. Upon evaporation of about nine-tenths of the volume of seawater, rock salt is precipitated. Calcium sulfate (gypsum and anhydrite) and potassium and magnesium salts are also precipitated. Deposits are found in beds from a few feet to many hundreds of feet thick. The ages of these beds range through much of geologic time. Because evaporation of a large quantity of seawater leaves only a small amount of salt, it is theorized that many extremely thick rock-salt beds were deposited in partly enclosed arms of the seas in which evaporation was greater than the inflow of salt water. A barrier on the sea floor at the entrance to the basin prevented the outflow of the concentrated saline water.

Such bedded salt deposits occur in the Punjab Salt Range in Pakistan and in Iran, but are little exploited. Similar deposits in the United States and in Canada are extensively worked for industrial and domestic use. Other important salt deposits, usually classified by the age of the surrounding rock, exist in Germany, Nova Scotia, the sub-Carpathian region extending from Poland through Hungary and Romania, the Soviet Union, the United States, and the province of Szechwan, China, where salt wells have been in existence for more than 2,000 years.

Salt domes   Another economically important type of rock-salt deposit is the salt domes (q.v.), which were formed when earth pressure forced up plugs of rock salt measuring approximately a mile across. The domes appear to result from pressure, which pushes the salt up through the rocks from depths as great as 50,000 feet (15,000 metres). Many domes occur at shallow depths, and are extensively mined. Domes in the sub-Carpathian region of Europe have been worked since ancient times. The North German Plain has many domes, extensively mined, which are thought to have originated below 6,000 feet (1,830 metres); domes are also abundant along the U.S. Gulf Coast. Rock salt may be obtained from domes by the usual mining methods or by drilling wells into the salt strata and pumping water down to dissolve the salt; the brine is then returned to the surface where it is processed like natural brine.   (F.O.W./J.M.Hi./R.H.Ra.)

SALT MANUFACTURE

At one time almost all the salt used in commerce was produced from the evaporation of seawater, and sea salt still is a staple commodity in many maritime countries, especially where the climate is dry and the summer of long duration. Commercial salt is manufactured from rock salt, and from seawater and other natural and artificial brines. Most of the artificial brines are obtained by pumping water into underground salt beds. A considerable amount of brine itself is used directly in industrial countries.

Manufacture from rock salt.   The beds of rock salt are mined or quarried by the usual excavation methods, depending upon the depths and thicknesses of the deposits and upon local conditions. The mined rock salt sometimes is dissolved and the salt manufactured by treatment of the brine, as described below. The method affords opportunities for purification of the salt. When the rock salt is of a high degree of purity, as in Poland and the United States, the salt may be ground, screened, and marketed without further processing. The salt is mined in large lumps which are first crushed, then more finely ground and screened by size into various grades; the salt is then bulk-loaded into trucks, hopper cars, or barges, or loaded into bags for further handling. Bulk handling has been greatly facilitated by the use of anticaking agents which allow the salt to be stored uncovered and outdoors without becoming a hard mass again.

Manufacture from seawater and brines.   Only a certain quantity of salt will dissolve in water at any given temperature. Once the solution contains as much salt as it can hold, it is said to be saturated; any further additions of salt will not dissolve.

Evaporation is the reverse of this process. When an aqueous solution of several salts (seawater, for example) is evaporated, each of the salts precipitates as it reaches its point of saturation in the solution. Thus the different salts in seawater will precipitate at different times, forming layers on the bottom of the evaporating pond. For seawater and many brines, the order of deposition is calcium carbonate, calcium sulfate, sodium chloride, magnesium sulfate, potassium magnesium chloride, and magnesium chloride.

Solar evaporation.   In maritime countries where there is a negative evaporation rate—i.e., the amount of water evaporating exceeds the amount of rainfall by at least 30 inches (about 75 centimetres)—salt is produced by solar evaporation from seawater. The processes used are similar in general principle from country to country, but details of equipment vary from sophisticated in the United States, the Bahamas, France, and Africa to quite primitive in India and most of the developing nations. There is no solar salt production in Canada, Great Britain, Germany, and Iceland.

A preliminary concentration is usually accomplished by allowing the seawater to flow through a series of gates constructed of wood or a combination of wood and concrete into a series of shallow ponds separated by dikes. In these ponds, the solution is concentrated to a specific gravity of about 1.22; this means that a given volume of brine is 1.22 times as dense as a given volume of pure water. At this stage, suspended impurities such as sand, clay, and the less soluble salts such as calcium carbonate, or chalk, and calcium sulfate are removed. Solar evaporation of the Dead Sea water is hastened by adding dye to the water. The dye permits more heat to be absorbed from sunlight in thinner layers of brine so that shallow ponds may be used and the penetration of brine into the ground is reduced.

Once it has been concentrated, the brine is run through a series of crystallizing pans, usually four in number, where the salt is deposited. In the first crystallizing pan, the brine is concentrated to a specific gravity of 1.23 and remains partly contaminated with calcium sulfate. The specific gravity of the solution in the pan increases slowly during crystallization of the salt, reaching 1.24 in the second pan. In the third pan, the specific gravity of the solution reaches 1.25; the salt deposited there contains small amounts of magnesium sulfate as an impurity. The final solution, termed bitterns, has a specific gravity of 1.25–1.26 and is used in some countries (United States and Israel) in the manufacture of potash, bromine, epsom salts (magnesium sulfate), and magnesium chloride.

In developing countries, the salt in each crystallizing pan is raked into rows and allowed to drain for several days, after which it is collected into heaps, drained again, lifted from the pans, and finally dried. In the industrial countries, the salt is harvested mechanically, washed with saturated brine, dewatered, washed with fresh water, then stored for further processing or direct sale.

Use of artificial heat.   In areas where bedded deposits can be solution mined, evaporated salt is recovered from these solutions with artificial heat. Some evaporated salt is also made from natural brine or solar salt. Formerly, brine was concentrated in open pans over fire. More recently, steam-jacketed vessels have been used. The largest amount of salt produced in the colder climates is rock salt. The largest amount of evaporated salt is produced by multiple-effect vacuum evaporators, and an important quantity is made in so-called open crystallizers or grainers that produce a type of crystal preferred for use in some of the food industries. The brine, natural or artificial, is first pumped into settling tanks, where calcium and magnesium compounds may be removed by chemical treatment. In grainer operations the settled and filtered brine is delivered to the grainer, a long open trough heated with steam coils. The brine is fed into the grainer at approximately the same rate that evaporation is taking place and at a temperature only slightly below that of the brine in the grainer. The residue of brine, or bitterns, may be removed continuously, once a day, or less often. Evaporation occurs at the surface of the liquid and the crystals originate there. They remain at the surface, held up by the surface tension of the brine. The crystal grows at the top edges, becoming a small inverted hollow pyramid, or hopper. Eventually the hopper sinks and ceases to grow. When the crystals are recovered, the salt is largely in the form of flakes, hence the name flake   Flake
salt.   salt

When multiple-effect evaporators are used, the vacuum in each vessel is adjusted so that the vapour from the first vessel is hot enough to boil the brine in the second; the vapour from the second supplying the heat to operate the third vessel or effect. The brine is usually sent through the stages or effects in succession, although in the case of salt manufacture, fresh brine may be fed to each stage if desired. With open pans, 10,000 to 12,000 pounds (4,500 to 5,400 kilograms) of steam are required to produce one ton (900 kilograms) of salt. With triple-effect evaporation, 1,400 pounds (630 kilograms) of steam produce one ton of salt.

The Alberger process

The Alberger process is partially a vacuum-pan and partially a grainer operation in which cubic crystals are formed in the solution fed to the grainer pans by a partial vacuum-pan evaporation. These seed crystals in the grainer produce a salt that is a mixture of the grainer-type flake and the flake grown on seed crystals. About 3,000 pounds (1,350 kilograms) of steam are required to produce one ton of salt. Salt from the Alberger process is centrifuged (spun) from the brine and then dried. Table salt may have small amounts of aluminum calcium silicate, calcium silicate, magnesium silicate, tricalcium silicate, magnesium carbonate, or tricalcium phosphate added to it to keep it free-flowing. Iodized salt has potassium iodide added. In some countries yellow prussiate of soda, to prevent caking, is added in minute amounts as regulated by the government. (F.O.W./R.H.Ra.)

PRODUCTION STATISTICS

Salt production is one of the world's most widely distributed mineral industries. Outputs vary with the population and industrial activity of each country. The major part of the production of heavily populated countries such as India and China is for food uses. The United States, on the other hand, uses several times as much salt for industry as it does for food. The leading producing countries are China, France, India, Italy, the Soviet Union, the United Kingdom, the United States, and West Germany.

World production of salt increased 67 percent in the ten years up to 1970, when it reached 156,365,000 tons. Of that total, the United States produced 44,804,000 tons, or about 29 percent. Solar evaporation of seawater accounted for 45 percent of world production. (F.O.W.)

BIBLIOGRAPHY. A general reference on this subject is G.L. ESKEW, *Salt, the Fifth Element: The Story of a Basic American Industry* (1948). A more technical reference is D.W. KAUFMANN (ed.), *Sodium Chloride: The Production and Properties of Salt and Brine* (1968). Highly technical references on salt geology, geochemistry, mining, rock mechanics, solution mining, and underground storage are given in the proceedings of the *Symposium on Salt*, ed. by A.C. BERSTICKER (1963). Later volumes in the "Salt Symposium Series" with the same scope as the first are JON L. RAU (ed.), *Second Symposium on Salt*, 2 vol. (1966); and JON L. RAU and LOUIS F. ELLWIG (eds.), *Third Symposium on Salt*, 2 vol. (1970). A factual survey of salt deposits of the world by countries is given in STANLEY LaFOND, *Handbook of World Salt Resources* (1969). The authoritative work in English on the deposition and geologic history of salt deposits is H. BORCHERT and R.O. MUIR, *Salt Deposits* (1964). The best source for statistics on salt production and markets is the U.S. BUREAU OF MINES, "Salt," in the *Minerals Yearbook* (1970).

(R.H.Ra./J.M.Hi./F.O.W.)

Salt Domes

A salt dome is a largely subsurface geologic structure that consists of a vertical cylinder of salt (including halite and other evaporites) a kilometre or more in diameter, embedded in horizontal or inclined strata. In the broadest sense, the term includes both the core of salt and the strata that surround and are "domed" by the core. Similar geologic structures in which salt is the main component are salt pillows and salt walls, which are related genetically to salt domes, and salt anticlines, which are essentially folded rocks pierced by upward migrating salt. Other material, such as gypsum and shale, form the cores of similar geologic structures, and all such structures, including salt domes, are known as diapiric structures, or diapirs, from the Greek word *diapeirein*, "to pierce." The embedded material in all instances appears to have pierced surrounding rocks. Upward flow is believed to have been caused by the following: gravity forces, in situations where relatively light rocks are overlain by relatively heavy rocks and the light rocks rise like cream to the surface; tectonic (earth-deformation) forces, in situations where mobile material (not necessarily lighter) is literally

squeezed by lateral stress through less mobile material; or a combination of both gravity and tectonic forces.

Salt domes are one of a number of kinds of salt structures whose interrelationships are shown diagramatically in Figure 1. "Classic" salt domes develop directly from

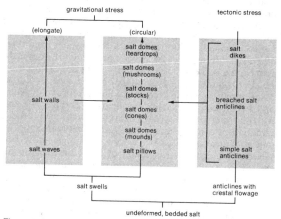

Figure 1: Interrelationships of salt structures (see text).

bedded salt by gravitational stress alone. Salt domes also may develop from salt walls and salt anticlines, however. In the latter case, the development of the domes results from superposition of gravitational stress on salt masses that initially developed due to tectonic stress. Salt domes can exist in any sedimentary basin that contains thick salt buried beneath a thick sequence of sedimentary rocks or subject to tectonic stress or both. In some areas, salt domes are valuable as sources of oil, natural gas, sulfur, salt, and potash.

This article treats the characteristics, mode of origin, and world distribution of salt domes. For further information on the origin of the salts involved, see EVAPORITES; and for the economic and geological significance of these structures, see PETROLEUM; NATURAL GAS; SALT AND SALT PRODUCTION; SULFUR PRODUCTS AND PRODUCTION; and ROCK DEFORMATION. The latter article presents a discussion of the various types of folds and faults that are relevant to salt domes as well as more detail on the tectonic and gravitational stresses involved in salt dome formation.

PHYSICAL CHARACTERISTICS OF SALT DOMES

A salt dome consists of a core of salt and an envelope of surrounding strata. In some areas, the core may contain "cap rock" and "sheath" in addition to salt.

The size of domes

The size of typical salt domes (including cap rock and sheath) varies considerably. In most cases, the diameter is a kilometre or more and may range up to more than ten kilometres. The typical salt dome is at least two kilometres high (in the subsurface), and some are known to be higher than ten kilometres. Many individual salt domes actually are salt spires that are connected to much larger massifs of salt at depth. Four domes in the Caillou Island–Bay Marchand area of coastal Louisiana rise from a salt massif that measures 43 by 20 kilometres at a depth of 6 kilometres. This massif contains over 1,000 cubic kilometres of salt above 6 kilometres and, depending upon the depth to the base and shape of the bottom of the massif, possibly over 5,000 cubic kilometres of salt in total. Many of the salt walls of the North German–North Sea area are 3 to 5 kilometres wide, 2 kilometres high, and over 50 kilometres long.

Mineral content

The salt core. The cores of salt domes of the North American Gulf Coast consist virtually of pure halite (sodium chloride) with minor amounts of anhydrite (calcium sulfate) and traces of other minerals. Layers of white pure halite are interbedded with layers of black halite and anhydrite. German salt dome cores contain halite, sylvite, and other potash minerals. In Iranian salt domes, halite is mixed with anhydrite and marl (argillaceous limestone) and large blocks of limestone and igneous rock.

The interbedded salt–anhydrite and salt–potash layers are complexly folded; folds are vertical and more complex at the outer edge of the salt. In German domes, when relative age of the internal layers can be deciphered, older material is generally in the centre of the salt mass and younger at the edges. Study of halite grains in some Gulf Coast salt domes indicates a complex pattern of orientation that varies both vertically and horizontally in the domes. Mineral grains in the centre of a Caspian salt dome are vertical; those at its edge are horizontal.

Cap rock. Cap rock is a cap of limestone–anhydrite, characteristically 100 metres thick but ranging from 0 to 300 metres. In many cases, particularly on Gulf Coast salt domes, the cap can be divided into three zones, more or less horizontally, namely, an upper calcite zone, a middle transitional zone characterized by the presence of gypsum and sulfur, and a lower anhydrite zone. These zones are irregular and generally are gradational with each other, although in some instances the contact between gypsum and anhydrite is quite abrupt. Cap rock is generally believed to develop from solution of salt from the top of the salt core; this leaves a residue of insoluble anhydrite that is later altered to gypsum, calcite, and sulfur. Presumably, solution takes place in the circulating (shallow) water zone; deeply buried domes with cap rock must have been shallow at some former time and subsequently buried.

Shale sheath. Shale sheath is a feature that is common to many Gulf Coast salt domes. In shape, it may completely encase the salt (like a sheath), or it may be limited

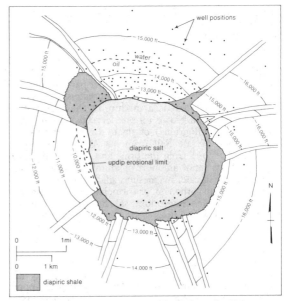

Figure 3: Plan view of the Weeks Island salt dome. Contours represent the elevations of an overlying sandstone formation.
From Atwater and Forman, *American Association of Petroleum Geologists Bulletin* (1959)

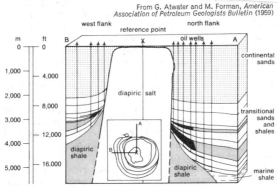

From G. Atwater and M. Forman, *American Association of Petroleum Geologists Bulletin* (1959)

Figure 2: North and west flanks of Weeks Island salt dome in Iberia Parish, Louisiana, showing relationship of the shale sheath to the dome.

to the lower portions of the salt. It is most common on the deeper portions of salt domes whose tops are near the surface or on deeply buried salt domes. The fluid pressure within the shale is significantly greater than that within the surrounding rocks, and the stratification (bedding planes) of the shale is distorted. Fossils in the shale are older than in surrounding sediments, indicating that the shale came from an older, and therefore deeper, layer.

Surrounding sediments. The strata around salt cores can be affected in three ways: they can be uplifted, they can be lowered, or they can be left unaffected while surrounding strata subside relatively. Uplifted strata have the structural features of domes or anticlines; characteristically they are domed over or around (or both) the core (including cap and sheath if present) and dip down into the surrounding synclines. The domed strata are generally broken by faults that radiate out from the salt on circular domes but which may be more linear on elongate domes or anticlines with one fault or set of faults predominant. Lowered strata develop into synclines, and a circular depression called a rim syncline may encircle or nearly encircle the domal uplift. Unaffected strata develop into highs surrounded by low areas. These highs, called remnant highs or turtleback highs, do not have as much vertical relief as the salt domes among which they are interspersed. Present-day structure of strata around salt domes may not in every instance coincide with the present-day position of the salt. This offset relationship suggests that late uplift of the salt dome shifted its centre compared with early uplift.

Geophysical properties. Salt domes have some unique properties, compared to their surrounding rocks, and for

Domed strata, rim synclines, and other structures

this reason they can be detected by geophysical methods. Salt has a specific gravity of 2.2, whereas sedimentary rocks, such as sandstone and compacted shale, have a density of 2.5. Because gravitational attraction is related directly to mass, the forces of gravity are weaker in the vicinity of a salt dome; thus they provide a negative gravity anomaly when compared with gravity values of the surrounding terrain. Shock waves are propagated through salt faster than through sandstone and shale; this serves as another means of detecting salt bodies. Because seismic waves are partially reflected at the interface between low-velocity and high-velocity material, a salt dome will reflect shock waves. High-velocity sandstone that becomes uplifted around a salt dome will also reflect shock waves and thus suggest the existence of the dome.

ORIGIN OF SALT DOMES

The number of theories proposed by geologists to explain the origin of salt domes has been even larger than the number of types of salt domes observed in nature. In general, salt structures associated with folds have been linked with the same forces that caused the folding. Salt structures in areas without any apparent folding, however, puzzled early geologists and gave rise to a bewildering series of hypotheses. In the late 19th century, the volcanic theory held sway as a hypothesis of origin for Gulf Coast salt domes. This was followed by a group of theories that in some way were associated with deposition from solution. From 1912 to 1934 there followed a period during which flow of salt was generally accepted as a factor in structural development, but the motivating force behind salt flow was the centre of considerable geologic debate. It was suggested in Sweden that the upward movement of salt was caused by the buoyancy of the salt itself, but a number of German scientists proposed that salt domes developed as the result of tectonic forces. An American geophysicist, L.L. Nettleton, revised the buoyancy concept in 1934, formulated the fluid mechanics theory, and demonstrated that upward movement can result from density differences alone. It is now generally agreed that salt structures (and diapiric or piercement structures in general) develop as the result of gravitational forces, tectonic forces, or some combination of these forces, at the same time or with one force following the other. Whatever the precise circumstance, development of diapiric structures requires a rock that flows.

Theories of folding and buoyancy

Flowage of rocks. Although rock flow is difficult to visualize because of slow rates of movement, its results can be clearly seen: stonework that sags, mine and tunnel openings that flow shut, and glaciers of rock salt that move down mountainsides with all the features of glaciers of ice. Given very long periods of time and the relatively high temperature and pressure due to depth of burial, considerable movement of a relatively plastic material such as salt can result. A movement of one millimetre a year, for example, over a period of 1,000,000 years (a short period geologically) would produce a net movement of 1,000 metres. The most common rocks that flow are halite, sylvite, gypsum, and high-pressure shale. These rocks also have densities that are lower than consolidated rock such as sandstone, and if buried by sandstone they would be gravitationally unstable. All of them are deposited by normal processes of sedimentation (see SEDIMENTARY ROCKS) and are widespread in sedimentary strata. Thick salt is especially common and has been found in rocks from Precambrian to Holocene (the last 10,000 years, approximately) in age; great thicknesses of it are, in fact, now being deposited.

Mechanics of growth. Study of models and natural salt structures have led to a reconstruction of the sequence of events in the development of salt domes, as shown in Figure 4. First, thick salt is deposited and buried by dens-

After L.L. Nettleton in M. Halbouty, *Salt Domes—Gulf Region*, U.S. and Mexico. Copyright 1967 by Gulf Publishing Company, Houston, Texas. Used with permission

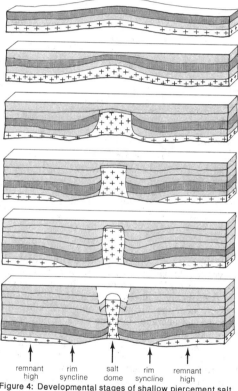

remnant high — rim syncline — salt dome — rim syncline — remnant high

Figure 4: Developmental stages of shallow piercement salt dome. Initial stage is shown at top.

er sedimentary strata. The salt and overlying strata become unstable and salt begins to flow from an undeformed bed to a rounded salt pillow. Flow continues into the centre of the pillow, doming the overlying strata; at the same time the area from which the salt flowed subsides, forming a rim syncline. The strata overlying the salt, because they are literally spread apart, are subject to tension, and fractures (faults) develop. Eventually, the salt breaks through the centre of the domed area, giving rise to a plug-shaped salt mass in the centre of domed, upturned, pierced strata. Upward growth of the salt continues apace with deposition of additional strata, and the salt mass tends to maintain its position at or near the surface. If the salt supply to the growing dome is exhausted during growth, development ceases at whatever stage the dome has reached, and the dome is buried. In models, as in nature, movement of the light material does not take place until it has been covered by some critical thickness of heavy material. This amount appears to depend upon the density contrast between the two materials and their

relative mobility. In nature, as in models, some discontinuity in the overburden appears necessary to localize movement; such discontinuities may be faults, folds, or stratigraphic variations.

WORLD DISTRIBUTION

Salt structures develop in any sedimentary basin in which thick salt deposits were later covered with thick sedimentary strata or tectonically deformed or both. With the exception of the shield areas, salt structures are widespread; Figure 5 shows the world distribution of salt structures. By their very nature, the classic salt domes generated by gravitational instability alone are limited to areas that have not been subject to significant tectonic stress. Some salt domes do, however, occur in regions that were subject to tectonic stress. Three of the many areas of salt structures in the world are representative of all; these are the Gulf of Mexico region of North America, the North German–North Sea area of Europe, and the Iraq–Iran–Arabian Peninsula of the Middle East.

Gulf of Mexico region. The Gulf of Mexico region contains more than 500 known salt structures in a circle of land and water 1,000 miles in diameter; this circle consists of eight sub-basins around its outer portion and two in its central portion. Starting in Mississippi and moving counterclockwise around the Gulf, the rimming basins are the East Central Basin, the North Louisiana Basin, the East Texas Basin, the Rio Grande Basin, the Sabinas Basin of northeastern Mexico, the Veracruz and Tabasco–Campeche basins of southern Mexico, and the Cuban Basin. The two central basins are the Texas–Louisiana Coastal Basin, which extends from the coastal lowlands to beyond the continental shelf, and the Sigsbee Basin, which is the deepest portion of the Gulf of Mexico. In all the basins, Cretaceous–Tertiary sediments (from about 136,000,000 to 4,500,000 years in age) are thick; they may be ten kilometres or thicker in the Coastal Basin. In all of the basins except the Sabinas and the Cuban basins, evidence of tectonic activity is lacking. In all of the basins, the salt is probably Triassic–Jurassic (from 225,000,000 to 136,000,000 years ago) in age and may have been part of one large saline basin. Salt structures on the outermost rim of the Gulf region, where the salt was originally thin, are generally salt swells or salt anticlines. Salt structures toward the centre of the region are generally cylindrical or spire-shaped salt domes.

The salt domes of the Coastal Basin, despite their possible connection at depth to a massif or to bedded salt, can be classified according to the relationship that they bear to the encasing sedimentary strata. For the purposes of classification, the sedimentary rock is divided into three zones: an upper zone of sandstone, approximately 1,500 metres thick; a middle zone of interbedded sandstone and shale, 2,000 metres thick, which is the primary reservoir zone for oil and gas; and a lower zone of shale, extending from a depth of 3,500 to 10,000 metres.

Salt domes that do not reach above the lower shales are called deep or nonpiercement types because they do not pierce the interbedded sandstone and shale of the middle zone. These salt domes may be plug or spire-shaped at depth, but they produce only simple, relatively unfaulted domes in the middle zone. They have no cap rock but generally have some sheath above and on the side of the salt. Oil and gas are found above the salt.

Salt domes that penetrate the middle sandstone and shale zone but not the upper sandstone zone are called intermediate or semipiercement domes. The strata of the middle zone are domed above the salt and are pierced and dragged up by it. The strata around the salt core have a complex radial fault pattern, and those above it have a complex network of faults like a pane of shattered glass. Cap rock is rare, but sheath is present in many instances both above and beside the salt. Oil and gas are found both above and beside the salt.

Salt domes that pierce the middle zone and extend into or through the upper zone are called shallow or piercement salt domes. The strata of the middle zone are dragged up around the cores and have a typical radial fault pattern. Cap rock is common on the top of these

Side notes (left margin): Conditions and rates of salt flow

Side notes (right margin): Occurrence of domes in relation to regional tectonics; Classification of domes; piercement and nonpiercement types

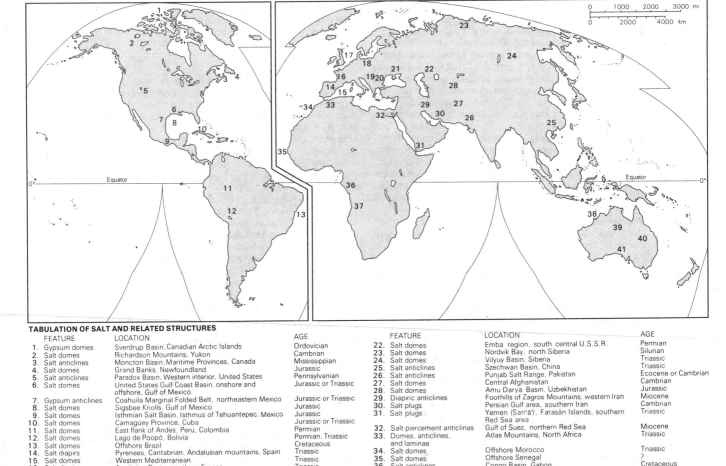

TABULATION OF SALT AND RELATED STRUCTURES

	FEATURE	LOCATION	AGE
1.	Gypsum domes	Sverdrup Basin, Canadian Arctic Islands	Ordovician
2.	Salt domes	Richardson Mountains, Yukon	Cambrian
3.	Salt anticlines	Moncton Basin, Maritime Provinces, Canada	Mississippian
4.	Salt domes	Grand Banks, Newfoundland	Jurassic
5.	Salt anticlines	Paradox Basin, Western interior, United States	Pennsylvanian
6.	Salt domes	United States Gulf Coast Basin, onshore and offshore, Gulf of Mexico	Jurassic or Triassic
7.	Gypsum anticlines	Coahuila Marginal Folded Belt, northeastern Mexico	Jurassic or Triassic
8.	Salt domes	Sigsbee Knolls, Gulf of Mexico	Jurassic
9.	Salt domes	Isthmian Salt Basin, Isthmus of Tehuantepec, Mexico	Jurassic
10.	Salt domes	Camagüey Province, Cuba	Jurassic or Triassic
11.	Salt domes	East flank of Andes, Peru, Colombia	Permian
12.	Salt domes	Lago de Poopó, Bolivia	Permian, Triassic
13.	Salt domes	Offshore Brazil	Cretaceous
14.	Salt diapirs	Pyrenees, Cantabrian, Andalusian mountains, Spain	Triassic
15.	Salt diapirs	Western Mediterranean	Triassic
16.	Salt diapirs	Aquitaine Basin, southern France	Triassic
17.	Salt domes	North Sea	Permian
18.	Salt domes	Hannover Basin, northern Germany	Permian
19.	Salt domes	Transylvanian Basin, Romania	Miocene
20.	Salt diapirs	Carpathian Mountains, Romania	Miocene
21.	Salt domes	Dneper—Donets Basin, southeastern U.S.S.R.	Devonian

	FEATURE	LOCATION	AGE
22.	Salt domes	Emba region, south central U.S.S.R.	Permian
23.	Salt domes	Nordvik Bay, north Siberia	Silurian
24.	Salt domes	Vilyuy Basin, Siberia	Triassic
25.	Salt anticlines	Szechwan Basin, China	Triassic
26.	Salt anticlines	Punjab Salt Range, Pakistan	Eococene or Cambrian
27.	Salt domes	Central Afghanistan	Cambrian
28.	Salt domes	Amu Darya Basin, Uzbekhistan	Jurassic
29.	Diapiric anticlines	Foothills of Zagros Mountains, western Iran	Miocene
30.	Salt plugs	Persian Gulf area, southern Iran	Cambrian
31.	Salt plugs	Yemen (Ṣanʿāʾ), Farasān Islands, southern Red Sea area	Triassic
32.	Salt piercement anticlines	Gulf of Suez, northern Red Sea	Miocene
33.	Domes, anticlines, and laminae	Atlas Mountains, North Africa	Triassic
34.	Salt domes	Offshore Morocco	Triassic
35.	Salt domes	Offshore Senegal	?
36.	Salt anticlines	Congo Basin, Gabon	Cretaceous
37.	Salt anticlines	Cuanza Basin, Angola	Cretaceous
38.	Salt domes	Timor Sea, offshore Australia	Devonian, Silurian
39.	Salt diapirs	Amadeus Basin, Northern Territory, Australia	Precambrian
40.	Salt domes	Adavale Basin, Queensland	Devonian
41.	Salt domes	South Australia	Devonian

Figure 5: World distribution of diapiric structures.
Adapted from Gerald D. O'Brien, "Survey of Diapirs and Diapirism," American Association of Petroleum Geologists *Memoir 8*, pp. 1–9 (1968)

Salt pillows, walls, and domes

domes, but sheath is limited to the deep flanks of the core. This type of dome traps oil and gas on the sides of the core and in the cap rock; some domes that reach the surface are mined for salt. In the coastal swamps and on the floor of the Gulf of Mexico, shallow salt domes cause circular uplifts. These uplifts form round "islands" or areas of high ground a kilometre in diameter in the swamps—hence the "islands" of Louisiana such as Weeks Island and Avery Island.

North German–North Sea area. The North German-North Sea area contains more than 300 salt structures beneath the North Sea and the land areas of Denmark, Germany, and the Netherlands. Three types of salt structure are present: salt pillows, salt walls, and salt domes.

The salt walls and salt domes rise from depths of 2,500 to 4,000 metres and pierce Triassic to Recent strata. The salt, mostly Permian (225,000,000 to 280,000,000 years ago) in age, is thought to have had an original thickness of up to 1,200 metres. Movement of the salt appears to have taken place from Triassic time onward. Two views have been expressed on the origin of these salt structures. Some believe that the structures are due to gravitational forces alone, whereas others claim that the structures owe their characteristics, position, and development to presalt structural trends and postsalt tectonic deformation. Recent geophysical surveys indicate that the strata below the salt of many salt structures are undeformed; this suggests that at least some of the structures are not of tectonic origin. The alignment of salt features with structural trends, however, suggests that regional tectonics did play some role in the origin of many of the structures present.

A particularly interesting feature of many of the German salt domes is an upward bulging of the salt. This overhang of the salt (also present on some Gulf Coast salt domes) gives the domes an appearance of a mushroom, and in some cases oil is trapped beneath it. The origin of overhangs is probably connected with a decrease in confining pressure near the surface, which would allow the salt mass to spread laterally. In some cases, it may represent a fossil salt glacier. Oil and gas are trapped in sands and limestone associated with German and North Sea salt domes in many ways: above the salt, beside the salt, under the salt overhangs, in stratigraphic traps away from the salt, and in turtleback highs between salt domes. Salt pillows predominate in English parts of the North Sea, whereas salt walls predominate in northern Germany, and salt domes in southern Germany and in the North Sea between England and Norway.

The Middle East. Salt structures exist in four principal areas in the Middle East. Circular and elongate salt masses of tectonic origin occur in northern and central Iran near Tehran and in southwest Iran in the foothills of the Zagros Mountains; and circular, gravity-induced salt domes occur in southern Iran and the Persian Gulf and in Yemen and the Red Sea.

More than 150 salt domes have been mapped in southern Iran and the Persian Gulf. They consist of a core of Cambrian salt (500,000,000 to 570,000,000 years old), are in a basin with a thick sequence of sedimentary rock, and appear to have been unaffected by tectonic forces. The salt core has penetrated more than 5,000 metres of sedimentary strata, largely Cretaceous and younger in age. In the Persian Gulf, these domes form spectacular, multicoloured islands, the best known of which is Hormuz Island. Some of the domes on land form mountains of salt that are 1,000 metres high and salt glaciers that flow from the

Salt mountains and salt glaciers

mountaintops to the valleys. Most of the salt cores are about three kilometres in diameter, but, due to flow of salt away from the centre, salt may cover an area of more than 60 square kilometres. The southern Iran and Persian Gulf salt domes contain blocks of limestone, gypsum, and igneous rocks; many of these blocks exceed 100 metres in diameter. No oil or gas are found on these salt domes.

ECONOMIC SIGNIFICANCE OF SALT DOMES

Salt domes make excellent traps for hydrocarbons because surrounding sedimentary strata are domed upward and blocked off. Major accumulations of oil and natural gas are associated with domes in the United States, Mexico, the North Sea, Germany, Romania, and the U.S.S.R. In the Gulf Coastal Plain of Texas and Louisiana, salt domes have produced 6,000,000,000 barrels of oil and will be a major source of hydrocarbons for many years to come. Huge new supplies of oil have recently been found in salt dome areas off the coast of Louisiana. Some individual salt domes in this region are believed to have reserves of over 500,000,000 barrels of oil. Salt domes in northern Germany have produced oil for many years. Exploration for salt dome oil in the North Sea is extending production offshore, and it is possible that salt domes in the North Sea may ultimately supply Europe's oil and gas needs.

The cap rock of shallow salt domes in the Gulf Coast contains major quantities of elemental sulfur. By the early 1970s, 170,000,000 tons had been produced by the Frasch process (the sulfur is melted by injecting hot water in wells and is then pumped to the surface), and 70,000,000 additional tons were known to exist; exploration is continuing. Salt domes are major sources of salt and potash in the Gulf Coast and Germany; halite and sylvite are extracted from domes by underground mining and by brine recovery.

Salt domes have recently been utilized for underground storage of liquefied propane gas. Storage "bottles" are made by drilling into the salt and then forming a cavity by subsequent solution. Such cavities, because of their impermeability, also have been considered as sites for disposal of radioactive wastes. In 1962 an atomic device was successfully detonated inside the Tatum salt dome of Mississippi, suggesting the potential use of domes for this purpose.

BIBLIOGRAPHY. J. BRAUNSTEIN and G.D. O'BRIEN (eds.), *Diapirism and Diapirs* (1968), a symposium on the principles and examples of diapirism, containing detailed information on salt domes; R.B. MATTOX *et al.* (eds.), *Saline Deposits* (1968), a symposium on all aspects of salt, from deposition to structural features; M.T. HALBOUTY, *Salt Domes: Gulf Region—United States and Mexico* (1967), a detailed text on Gulf Coast salt domes. All three works have extensive bibliographies.

(G.D.O'B.)

Salt Range

The Salt Range is a range of hills and low mountains between the valleys of the Indus and Jhelum rivers in the northern part of the Punjab region of Pakistan. It derives its name from extensive deposits of rock salt that form one of the richest salt fields in the world. The range is approximately 186 miles (300 kilometres) long from east to west, and its width, in the central and eastern parts, is from five to 19 miles. Its average height is 2,200 feet, and its highest altitude, at Sakesar mountain, is 4,992 feet (1,522 metres). In addition to the salt deposits, mined from ancient times, the Salt Range contains coal, gypsum, and other minerals.

Physiography. The landform is that of a range of low mountains from which the top strata have been removed by erosion. Forming the southern terrace of the Potwar Plateau (1,700 feet), southwest of Rāwalpindi, it consists of two unsymmetrical, parallel ridges divided by a longitudinal valley. The southern slopes of both ridges are steep; the northern slopes are slanting. The northern ridge (a cuesta—*i.e.*, a sloping plain, culminating at the upper end at the crest of a cliff), with an average height of from 2,300 to 2,600 feet and with very steep southern

Relief and structure

slopes, is the lower. In the west and east, the Range divides into separate mountain masses, or massifs. West of Sakesar the course of the Range swings to the northwest, with low, longitudinal ranges. The Indus River breaks through the ranges at Kālābāgh, flowing between vertical cliffs inaccessible to communication. The summits of the Salt Range are slanting, hilly, and plateau-like. The highest peaks are Sakesar, in the west, and the massif Chel (Chail), 3,700 feet (1,128 metres), in the east. On the northern slope, a system of deep ravines (badlands) has developed.

Structurally, the Salt Range is a highly upheaved block of the northwestern part of the Indian Platform, or Shield, raised to a significant height along the southern fracture, with the sedimentary strata sloping uniformly to the north. The incline of the strata in the central part is around 10°, and in the western, eastern, and northern parts it is up to 45°.

The structural characteristics are well expressed in the topography: the course of the range follows the trend of basic structural elements, the steepness of the southern slopes reflects the fracture and uplift of the block, and the slanting surface corresponds to the slant of the strata. At the time of the upheaval of the Salt Range, beginning in the mid-Tertiary Period (about 26,000,000 years ago), the ancient river system was dislocated. The present main watershed does not coincide with the axis of the largest upheavals of the southern ridge but follows the lower crest of the northern slope. During the upheaval of the Salt Range, lateral cutoffs arose in the longitudinal valley in connection with which the valley lost its sharp, continuous course. The depth of the valley is 600–1,000 feet; the transverse section is sharper in the valleys cut through limestones and dolomites (the narrow ones up to 15–30 feet at the bottom) than in those cut through the sandstones and clay slates (150 or more feet). The foot of the southern ridge is marked by a sloping (1°–2°) zone of loose slope wash (alluvial) taluses with a width of a mile or more. The water of the temporary rivers and streams is absorbed by this debris. The rivers of the northern slope belong to the Sokan River Basin on the Potwar Plateau. There are small lakes of karstic (sinkholes formed by underground erosion) or eolian (wind-formed basins) origin without external drainage, including the beautiful salt lake, Kallar Kahār. The water level of Lake Nammal is maintained by a dam. The Nammal River does not reach the Indus River but disappears into the Indus alluvial plain. In the east, only the Bhura River has a constant flow into the Jhelum River. The undercurrent of the river has cut a wide trough on exit from the ravine.

Stratigraphy. The sedimentary mantle in the northwestern part of the Indian Platform in the region of the Salt Range is represented by thick deposits of Late Precambrian, Paleozoic, and Mesozoic times (*i.e.*, from more than 65,000,000 to 570,000,000 years ago). In the eastern part there are layers of Late Precambrian, Cambrian (from 570,000,000 years ago), and Permian (280,000,000 years ago) deposits, and in the western part there are Mesozoic (65,000,000 to 225,000,000 years ago) and Early Tertiary (25,000,000 to 65,000,000 years ago) deposits. The Precambrian deposits are represented by the widely known salt-bearing strata cropping out along the southern slope of the range, which have an overall thickness of more than 1,600 feet. In the lower part they contain marl, gypsum, and bituminous argillite (a slaty shale). In the central part are located the main strata of salt. The upper part of the strata includes dolomites (magnesium-rich limestones), gypsum, and bituminous argillites. The Precambrian layer is topped by obliquely laminated sandstones up to 650 feet thick. One school of geologists has held that the saline deposits are of Tertiary age on the basis of their superior position in relation to other deposits in the western part of the range, interpreting their underlying position in the central part as resulting from an overthrust of the older sandstones.

Deposits of the Lower Cambrian (thickness around 700 feet) are represented by argillites with interlayers of dolomites and limestones, dolomitic sandstones, and bright red argillites with interlayers of sandstones. With the high stratigraphical variance above are located rubbly con-

Reconstruction of drainage system

The salt-bearing strata

glomerates appearing as deposits of the Permian (225,-000,000 to 280,000,000 years ago) glaciers. The conglomerates are overlapped by argillites and sandstones (thickness from 65 to 650 feet) and a layer (around 1,000 feet) of limestone and marl with abundant fauna. Triassic (190,000,000 to 225,000,000 years ago) deposits in the lower part are represented by a stratum of limestones, marls, and sandstones of a thickness of 160–260 feet. In the central part, thin-layer dolomites and sandstones from 80 to 400 feet thick are located. In the eastern parts of the range, red laterites (porous, claylike, iron-rich rocks) are characteristic for the Upper Triassic deposits. Limestone layers in the eastern parts of the range contain more clay, and the overall thickness of the Triassic in this direction diminishes. Jurassic (136,-000,000 to 190,000,000 years ago) deposits with a thickness of 500 to 600 feet are represented by varicoloured terrestrial rocks in the lower part and limestones and dolomites in the upper part. Cretaceous (65,000,000 to 136,000,000 years ago) deposits have developed only in the western part of the range and are represented by argillites and sandstones up to 500 feet thick. Clays, limestones, and sandstones of the Early Tertiary with layers of coal, widely developed on the northern slope of the range, occur with more ancient deposits. Overall thickness of the Early Tertiary is from 500 to 1,800 feet.

Along the northern edge of the range a thick (up to several thousand feet) stratum of varicoloured continental deposits of Miocene (from 26,000,000 years ago) to Recent (10,000 years ago) age consisting of conglomerates, coarse stones, sandstones, and clays developed.

Climate. The climate of the Salt Range is continental and arid, changing from tropic to subtropic. Tropical air prevails during all seasons of the year, except the cold winter months, when the relatively cool polar air penetrates at the tail end of high-pressure systems (cyclones). This is a cold, damp season. During summer, precipitations are connected with the equatorial, moist, southwestern (Indian) monsoon, which reaches the limits of its occurrence in West Punjab but brings the largest amounts of precipitation (more than 50 percent annually).

Average temperature in June is 77°–81° F (25°–27° C); in January it is 54° F (12° C) (at the highest peaks it is 63°–66° F [17°–19° C] and 41°–43° F [5°–6° C]). On the average, annual amounts of precipitation in the east are from 20 to 24 inches; in the west they are from 14 to 18 inches. The ultimate maximum of precipitation occurs in summer, during the second half of July and in August. Annual evaporation is more than 80 inches. Evaporation exceeds precipitation even during rainy seasons. Weather during winter is unstable. Warm, dry days alternate with cold, rainy days with northwestern winds (from December through February); frosts and snowfalls occur. The spring is dry and warm. Strong winds are not infrequent, giving rise to dust storms. Mist clings for several days. The dustiness of the air falls abruptly with the first monsoon rains in the second part of the summer. In years of intensive distribution of monsoons, the number of rainy days during the two moist months is more than 20; in years of slight distribution it is less than ten. In September the rains cease, and the temperature gradually falls toward the beginning of October. In the end of October and November, nights may be cold (down to 41° F). Northwestern winds become stronger, accompanied by dust winds and mist, as in the dry months of spring.

Soil. Soil-forming rocks appear as residual mantles (weathering crusts). Insufficient moisture leads to the formation of rocky crusts, usually rubble. Primitive soils are widely distributed; in the outcrop of bedrock there is lithosol (skeletal soils), and, on the continually restored taluses and alluvial fans of the plain at the foot of the southern mountains, there is soft and imperfectly consolidated soil washed down from the slopes (regosol). The soils of the Salt Range belong to the cinnamonic, or cinnamon-coloured, soil type with claying at a depth from 8 to 16 inches, which is characteristic for the types. At upper levels, claying is reduced because of the drying out of the soil in nonrainy seasons. The contents of humus, which penetrates deeply down the cross section, is around

Effects of dryness

2 percent. At high humidity the calcareous layer is found at some depth; at lower humidity, calcareousness is seen beginning with the surface. Water-soluble salts are few. The soils of the Salt Range are not saline, a condition that is connected with good drainage. The exception is a narrow strip of alluvial fans with effloresences of salt at the foot of the southern spur, where there is active erosion of salt-bearing strata. Occurrences of alluvial soils are not large, being confined to the longitudinal valley between the northern and southern ridge and to the small sections of terraces in the river valleys of the northern slope. Destruction of vegetation and excessive pasturing of cattle have led to an increase of areas of eroded soils and badlands.

The use of land for agriculture is limited because of a lack of water for irrigation. Small sections on the slopes and in the longitudinal valleys are being terraced for cultivation of irrigated crops using the water of lakes and springs. In the valleys dry farming prevails.

Vegetation. In the flora of the Salt Range there are both African–Arabian and Mediterranean elements. Before the loss of the natural vegetation, the area was covered in the south by xerophyte (drought-resisting) thin forests and in the north chiefly by savannas. At present a small mass of thin forest has been preserved by conservation on the southeast of the Salt Range. Among the forest trees are acacia, pine, wild olive, and others. The trees are low (up to 33 feet) with deciduous leaves. Other characteristic vegetation includes spurge (*Euphorbia*) and camel thorn and other scrubs and brushwood. The grasses burn out in April or May.

Mineral resources. On the southern slope of the Salt Range are located the largest deposits of rock salt in Pakistan, at Khewra, Warcha, and Kālābāgh. Salt deposits smaller in importance occur at Jatta, Bahādur Khel, and Kharak. Coal deposits are found at Dandot, Pidh, and Makarwāl Kheji. Traces of petroleum content are associated with limestone and sandstone deposits in the western part of the Salt Range. In the salt-bearing series in the eastern part of the Salt Range, layers of bituminous shales and dolomites are found. In the eastern parts, too, occur beds of bauxite (aluminum-bearing laterite).

Rock salt and coal deposits

Large deposits of high-grade gypsum and anhydrite, an important calcium mineral, are traced from Jalalpur Kālābāgh and the district of Khewra-Dawdot. Economically, the salt and coal mines and limestone quarries are the most important.

Human resources and prospects. The only population centre of any size associated with the Salt Range is Jhelum, headquarters of the district of that name that encompasses the range and stretches north to Rāwalpindi. Most of the towns in the range itself serve the mines and quarries. The Salt Range divides the district of Gujrāt, to the southeast, from the districts of Jhelum, Attock, and Rāwalpindi, the four districts together making up the Rāwalpindi Division, which occupies the north of Pakistan.

The main ethnic groups of the region are the Pandzhabt, Dzhat, and Aran peoples, who speak Indian languages (mainly Lakhrda). While there is marginal farming in the valleys and on the few terraces and some animal husbandry on the overgrazed hillsides, the principal occupation is salt mining.

Farming, animal husbandry, and mining

Although the Salt Range has been a barrier to travel and communication, its modest peaks have never presented a challenge to explorers or mountain climbers.

The future economic and social development of the Salt Range appears to depend on the future development of the Rāwalpindi Division, and especially on the development of the Jhelum District.

BIBLIOGRAPHY. Two standard works—M.B. PITHAWALLA, *An Introduction to Pakistan: Its Resources and Potentialities* (1948); and O.N.K. SPATE, *India and Pakistan*, 2nd ed. (1957) —contain some information on the Salt Range. K.S. AHMAD, *A Geography of Pakistan* (1964), is a popular work that mentions some characteristics of the range. The geology of the range is covered by AUGUST GANSSER in *Geology of the Himalayas* (1964).

(N.V.A./V.I.Sl.)

Salvation

Salvation is the deliverance or redemption of man from such fundamentally negative or disabling conditions as suffering, evil, finitude, and death. In some religious beliefs it also entails the restoration or raising up of the natural world to a higher realm or state. The idea of salvation is a characteristic religious notion related to an issue of profound human concern.

NATURE AND SIGNIFICANCE

It could be argued reasonably that the primary purpose of all religions is to provide salvation for their adherents, and the existence of many different religions indicates that there is a great variety of opinion about what constitutes salvation and the means of achieving it. That the term salvation can be meaningfully used in connection with so many religions, however, shows that it distinguishes a notion common to men and women of a wide range of cultural traditions.

The fundamental idea contained in the English word salvation, and the Latin *salvatio* and Greek *sōtēria* from which it derives, is that of saving or delivering from some dire situation. The term soteriology denotes beliefs and doctrines concerning salvation in any specific religion, as well as the study of the subject. The idea of saving or delivering from some dire situation logically implies that mankind, as a whole or in part, is in such a situation. This premise, in turn, involves a series of related assumptions about human nature and destiny.

Objects and goals. The creation myths of many religions express the beliefs that have been held concerning the original state of mankind in the divine ordering of the universe. Many of these myths envisage a kind of Golden Age at the beginning of the world, when the first human beings lived, serene and happy, untouched by disease, aging, or death and in harmony with a divine Creator. Myths of this kind usually involve the shattering of the ideal state by some mischance, with wickedness, disease, and death entering into the world as the result. The Adam and Eve myth is particularly notable for tracing the origin of death, the pain of childbirth, and the hard toil of agriculture, to man's disobedience of his maker. It expresses the belief that sin is the cause of evil in the world, and implies that salvation must come through man's repentance and God's forgiveness and restoration.

In ancient Iran, a different cosmic situation was contemplated, one in which the world was seen as a battleground of two opposing forces: good and evil, light and darkness, life and death. In this cosmic struggle, mankind was inevitably involved, and the quality of human life was conditioned by this involvement. Zoroaster, the founder of Zoroastrianism, called upon men to align themselves with the good, personified in the god Ahura Mazdā, because their ultimate salvation lay in the triumph of the cosmic principle of good over evil, personified in Ahriman. This salvation involved the restoration of all that had been corrupted or injured by Ahriman at the time of his final defeat and destruction. Thus the Zoroastrian concept of salvation was really a return to a Golden Age of the primordial perfection of all things, including man. Some ancient Christian theologians (*e.g.*, Origen) also conceived of a final "restoration" in which even devils, as well as men, would be saved; this idea, called universalism, was condemned by the church as heresy.

In those religions that regard man as essentially a psychophysical organism (*e.g.*, Judaism, Christianity, Zoroastrianism, Islām), salvation involves the restoration of both the body and soul. Such religions therefore teach doctrines of a resurrection of the dead body and its reunion with the soul, preparatory to ultimate salvation or damnation. In contrast, some religions have taught that the body is a corrupting substance in which the soul is imprisoned (*e.g.*, Orphism, an ancient Greek mystical cult; Hinduism; and Manichaeism, an ancient dualistic religion of Iranian origin). In this dualistic view of human nature, salvation has meant essentially the emancipation of the soul from its physical prison or tomb and its return to its ethereal home. Such religions generally explain the incarceration of the soul in the body in terms

that imply the intrinsic evil of physical matter. Where such views of human nature were held, salvation therefore meant the eternal beatitude of the disembodied soul.

Christian soteriology contains a very complex eschatological program (regarding the final end of man and the world), which includes the fate of both individual persons and the existing cosmic order. The return of Christ will be heralded by the destruction of the heaven and earth and the resurrection of the dead. The Last Judgment, which will then take place, will result in the eternal beatitude of the just, whose souls have been purified in purgatory, and the everlasting damnation of the wicked. The saved, reconstituted by the reunion of soul and body, will forever enjoy the Beatific Vision; the damned, similarly reconstituted, will suffer forever in hell, together with the devil and the fallen angels. Some schemes of eschatological imagery, used by both Christians and Jews, envisage the creation of a new heaven and earth, with a New Jerusalem at its centre.

Means. The hope of salvation has naturally involved ideas about how it might be achieved. These ideas have varied according to the form of salvation envisaged; but the means employed can be divided into three significant categories: (1) the most primitive is based on belief in the efficacy of ritual magic—initiation ceremonies, such as those of the ancient mystery religions, afford notable examples; (2) salvation by self-effort, usually through the acquisition of esoteric knowledge, ascetic discipline, or heroic death, has been variously promised in certain religions—Orphism, Hinduism, Islām, for example; and (3) salvation by divine aid, which has usually entailed the concept of a divine saviour who achieves what man cannot do for himself—as in Christianity, Judaism, Islām.

BASIC CONTEXT

The cosmic situation. *Time.* Study of the relevant evidence shows the menace of death as the basic cause of soteriological concern and action. Salvation from disease or misfortune, which also figures in religion, is of a comparatively lesser significance, though it is often expressive of more immediate concerns. But the menace of death is of another order, and it affects man more profoundly because of personal awareness of the temporal categories of past, present, and future. This time-consciousness is possessed by no other species with such insistent clarity. It enables man to draw upon past experience in the present and to plan for future contingencies. This faculty, however, has another effect: it causes man to be aware that he is subject to a process that brings change, aging, decay, and ultimately death to all living things. Man, thus, knows what no other animal apparently knows about itself, namely, that he is mortal. He can project himself mentally into the future and anticipate his own decease. Man's burial customs grimly attest to his preoccupation with death from the very dawn of human culture in the Paleolithic Period. Significantly, the burial of the dead is practiced by no other species.

The menace of death is thus inextricably bound up with man's consciousness of time. In seeking salvation from death, man has been led on to a deeper analysis of his situation, in which he has seen in his subjection to time the true cause of the evil that besets him. The quest for salvation from death, accordingly, becomes transformed into one for deliverance from subjugation to the destructive flux of time. How such deliverance might be effected has been conceived in varying ways, corresponding to the terms in which the temporal process is imagined. The earliest known examples occur in ancient Egyptian religious texts. In the so-called Pyramid Texts (*c.* 2400 BC), the dead pharaoh seeks to fly up to heaven and join the sun-god Re on his unceasing journey across the sky, incorporated, thus, in a mode of existence beyond change and decay. A passage in the later Book of the Dead (1200 BC) represents the deceased, who has been ritually identified with Osiris, declaring that he comprehends the whole range of time in himself, thus asserting his superiority to it.

The recognition that mankind is subject to the inexorable law of decay and death has produced other later

Original and ultimate states of man and the world

Resurrection and immortality

Man's awareness of time and death

Man's deliverance from time and death

attempts to explain its domination by time and to offer release from it. Such attempts are generally based on the idea that the temporal process is cyclical, not linear, in its movement. Into this concept, a belief in metempsychosis transmigration of souls can be conveniently fitted. For the idea that souls pass through a series of incarnations becomes more intelligible if the process is seen as being cyclical and in accordance with the pattern of time that apparently governs all the forms of being in this world. The conception has been elaborated in various ways in both Eastern and Western religions. In Hinduism and Buddhism, elegantly imaginative chronological systems have been worked out, comprising *mahāyugas*, or periods of 12,000 years, each year of which represented 360 human years. In turn, 1,000 *mahāyugas* made up one *kalpa*, or one day in the life of Brahmā, and spanned the duration of a world from its creation to its destruction. After a period of quiescence, the world would be re-created by Brahmā for another *kalpa*. The purpose of this immense chronological scheme was to emphasize how the unenlightened soul was doomed to suffer an infinite series of incarnations, with all of their attendant pain of successive births and deaths. In the Orphic texts of ancient Greece, man's destiny to endure successive incarnations is significantly described as "the sorrowful weary Wheel," from which the Orphic initiate hoped to escape through the secret knowledge imparted to him.

Nature. As an alternative interpretation to this view of man's fatal involvement with time, the tragedy of the human situation has also been explained in terms of the soul's involvement with the physical universe. In some systems of thought (*e.g.*, Hinduism and Buddhism), the two interpretations are synthesized; and in such systems it is taught that, by accepting the physical world as reality, the soul becomes subject to the process of time.

Man's deliverance from the body and the natural world

Concentration on the soul's involvement with matter as being the cause of the misery of human life has generally stemmed from a dualistic view of human nature. The drawing of a sharp distinction between spirit and matter has been invariably motivated by a value judgment: namely, that spirit (or soul) is intrinsically good and of transcendent origin, whereas matter is essentially evil and corrupting. Through his body, man is seen to be part of the world of nature, sharing in its processes of generation, growth, decay, and death. How his soul came to be incarcerated in his corruptible body has been a problem that many myths seek to explain. Such explanations usually involve some idea of the descent of the soul or its divine progenitor from the highest heaven and their fatal infatuation with the physical world. The phenomenon of sexual intercourse has often supplied the imagery used to account for the involvement of the soul in matter and the origin of its corruption. Salvation has thus been conceived in this context as emancipation from both the body and the natural world. In Gnosticism and Hermeticism—esoteric theosophical and mystical movements in the Greco-Roman world—and the teaching of St. Paul deliverance was sought primarily from the planetary powers that were believed to control human destiny in the sublunar world.

Man's responsibility. The idea that man is in some dire situation, from which he seeks to be saved, necessarily involves explaining the cause of his predicament. The explanations provided in the various religions divide into two kinds: those that attribute the cause to some primordial mischance and those that hold man to be himself responsible. Some explanations that make man directly responsible represent him also as the victim of the deceit of a malevolent deity or demon.

Because death has been universally feared but rarely accepted as a natural necessity, the mythologies of many peoples represent the primeval ancestors of mankind as having accidentally lost, in some way, their original immortality. One Sumerian myth, however, accounts for disease and old age as resulting from the sport of the gods when they created mankind. In contrast, the Hebrew story of Adam and Eve finds the origin of death in their act of disobedience in eating of the tree of knowledge of good and evil, forbidden to them by their maker. This

Moral and intellectual defects

causal connection between sin and death was elaborated by St. Paul in his soteriology, outlined in his letter to the Romans, and formed the basis of the Christian doctrine of original sin. According to this doctrine, through seminal identity with Adam, every human being must partake of the guilt of Adam's sin, and even at birth, a child is already deserving of God's wrath for its share in the original sin of mankind and before it acquires the guilt of its own actual sin. Moreover, because each individual inherits the nature of fallen humanity, he has an innate predisposition to sin. This doctrine of man means that no person can, by his volition and effort, save himself but depends absolutely upon the saving grace of Christ.

Wherever a dualistic view of human nature has been held, it has been necessary to explain how ethereal souls first became imprisoned in physical bodies. Generally, the cause has been found in the supposition of some primordial ignorance or error rather than in a sinful act of disobedience or revolt—*i.e.*, in an intellectual rather than a moral defect. According to the Hindu philosophical system known as Advaita Vedānta, a primordial ignorance (*avidyā*) originally caused souls to mistake the empirical world for reality and so become incarnated in it. By continuing in this illusion, they are subjected to an unceasing process of death and rebirth (*saṃsāra*) and all of its consequent suffering and degradation. Similarly, in Buddhism, a primordial ignorance (*avijjā*) also started the "chain of causation" (*paṭiccasamuppāda*) that produces the infinite misery of unending rebirth in the empirical world.

METHODS AND TECHNIQUES

Ritual. The means by which salvation might be achieved has been closely related to the manner in which salvation has been conceived and to what has been deemed to be the cause of man's need of it. Thus in ancient Egypt, where salvation was from the physical consequences of death, a technique of ritual embalmment was employed. Ritual magic has also been used in those religions that require their devotees to be initiated by ceremonies of rebirth (*e.g.*, Baptism in water in Christianity, in bull's blood in rites of Cybele) and by symbolic communion with a deity through a ritual meal in the Eleusinian Mysteries, Mithraism, and Christianity (communion).

Knowledge. Religions that trace the ills of man's present condition to some form of primordial error, or ignorance, offer knowledge that will ensure salvation. Such knowledge is of an esoteric kind and is usually presented as divine revelation and imparted secretly to specially prepared candidates. In some instances (*e.g.*, Buddhism and Yoga), the knowledge imparted includes instruction in mystical techniques designed to achieve spiritual deliverance.

Devotion and service. Whenever mankind has been deemed to need divine aid for salvation, there has been an emphasis on a personal relationship with the saviour-god concerned. Such relationship usually connotes faith in and loving devotion and service toward the deity, and such service may involve moral and social obligations. Judaism, Christianity, Islām, and the *bhakti* cults of India afford notable examples. Christianity adds a further requirement in this context: because human nature is basically corrupted by sin, God's prevenient (antecedent, activating) grace is needed before man's will can be disposed even to desire salvation.

VARIETIES OF SALVATION IN WORLD RELIGIONS

Ancient Eygpt. The Pyramid Texts of ancient Egypt provide the earliest evidence of man's quest for salvation. They reveal that by about 2400 BC a complex soteriology connected with the divine kingship of the pharaohs had been established in Egypt. This soteriology was gradually developed in concept and ritual practice and was popularized; *i.e.*, the original royal privilege was gradually extended to all of the classes of society, until by about 1400 BC it had become an elaborate mortuary cult through which all who could afford its cost could hope to partake of the salvation it offered. This salvation con-

Post-mortem salvation through Osiris

cerned three aspects of postmortem existence, as imagined by the ancient Egyptians, and, in the concept of Osiris, it involved the earliest instance of a saviour-god. An elaborate ritual of embalmment was designed to save the corpse from decomposition and restore its faculties so that it could live in a well-equipped tomb. This ritual imitated the acts that were believed to have been performed by the gods to preserve the body of Osiris, with whom the deceased was ritually assimilated. The next concern was to resurrect the embalmed body of the dead person, as Osiris had been resurrected to a new life after death. Having thus been saved from the consequences of death, the revivified dead had to undergo a judgment (presided over by Osiris) on the moral quality of his life on earth. In this ordeal, the deceased could be saved from an awful second death only by personal integrity. If he safely passed the test, he was declared *maa kheru* ("true of voice") and was admitted to the beatitude of the realm over which Osiris reigned.

This Osirian mortuary cult, with its promise of postmortem salvation, was practiced from about 2400 BC until its suppression in the Christian Era. In some respects, it constitutes a prototype of Christianity as a salvation religion.

Hinduism. Running through the great complex of beliefs and ritual practices that constitute Hinduism is the conviction that the soul or self (*ātman*) is subject to *saṃsāra*—*i.e.*, the transmigration through many forms of incarnation. Held together with this belief is another, *karman*—*i.e.*, that the soul carries with it the burden of its past actions—which conditions the forms of its future incarnations. As long as the soul mistakes this phenomenal world for reality and clings to existence in it, it is doomed to suffer endless births and deaths. The various Indian cults and philosophical systems offer ways in which *mokṣa* or *mukti* ("release"; "liberation") from the misery of subjection to the inexorable process of cosmic time may be attained. Basically, this liberation consists in the soul's effective apprehension of its essential unity with Brahman, the supreme *Ātman* or essence of reality, and its merging with it. Most of the ways by which this goal may be attained require self-effort in mastering meditation techniques and living an ascetic life. But in the devotional (*bhakti*) cults associated with Viṣṇu (Vishnu) and Śiva (Shiva), an intense personal devotion to the deity concerned is believed to earn divine aid to salvation.

Buddhism. Buddhism accepts the principles of *saṃsāra* and *karman* (Pāli, *kamma*) but it differs in one important respect from the Hindu conception of man. Instead of believing that an *ātman*, or soul, passes through endless series of incarnations, Buddhism teaches that there is no such pre-existent immortal soul that migrates from body to body. According to it, each individual consists of a number of physical and psychical elements (*khandhas*) that combine to create the sense of personal individuality. But this combination is only temporary, and is irreparably shattered by death, leaving no element that can be identified as the soul or self. By a subtle metaphysical argument, however, it is maintained that the craving for personal existence generated by the *khandhas* causes the birth of another such personalized combination, which inherits the *karma* of a sequence of previous combinations of *khandhas*.

Salvation through Enlightenment or *bodhisattvas*

The Enlightenment won by Gautama Buddha was essentially about the cause of existence in the phenomenal world, from which suffering inevitably stemmed. Buddhist teaching and practice have, accordingly, been designed to acquaint men with their true nature and situation and enable them to free themselves from craving for existence in the space–time world and so achieve Nirvāna. Traditionally, this goal has been presented in negative terms—as the extinction of desire, attachment, ignorance, or suffering—creating the impression that Buddhist salvation means the complete obliteration of individual consciousness. In one sense this is so; but in terms of Buddhist metaphysics, ultimate reality transcends all the terms of reference relevant to existence in this world.

Theoretically, the Buddhist initiate should, by his own effort in seeking to eradicate desire for continued existence in the empirical world, achieve his own salvation. But as Buddhism developed into a popular religion in its Mahāyāna ("Greater Vehicle") form, provision was made for the natural human desire for assurance of divine aid. Consequently, belief in many saviours, known as *bodhisattvas* ("Buddhas-to-be") developed, together with elaborate eschatologies concerning human destiny. According to these, before the ultimate achievement of Nirvāna, the faithful could expect to pass through series of heavens or hells, according to their merits or demerits and the intensity of their devotion to a *bodhisattva*.

Judaism. Because Judaism is by origin and nature an ethnic religion, salvation has been primarily conceived in terms of the destiny of Israel as the elect people of Yahweh, the God of Israel. It was not until the 2nd century BC that there arose a belief in an afterlife, for which the dead would be resurrected and undergo divine judgment. Before that time, the individual had to be content that his posterity continued within the holy nation. But even after the emergence of belief in the resurrection of the dead, the essentially ethnic character of Judaism still decisively influenced soteriological thinking. The apocalyptic faith, which became so fervent as Israel moved toward its fateful overthrow by the Romans in AD 70, conceived of salvation as the miraculous intervention of Yahweh or his Messiah in world affairs. This saving act would culminate in the Last Judgment delivered on the nations that oppressed Israel and Israel's glorious vindication as the people of God. From the end of the national state in the Holy Land in AD 70, Jewish religion, despite the increasing recognition of personal significance, has remained characterized by its essential ethnic concern. Thus, the Exodus from Egypt has ever provided the typal imagery in terms of which divine salvation has been conceived, its memory being impressively perpetuated each year by the ritual of the Passover. The restoration of the holy nation, moreover, always has been linked with its Holy Land; and Hebrew literature, both in biblical and later forms, has lovingly described the establishment of a New Jerusalem and a new Temple of Yahweh ("the Lord"), whether it be in this world or in some new cosmic order. Into this new order, the rest of mankind, repentant and purified, will be incorporated; for the original promise made to the patriarch Abraham included all of the men within the divine blessing. In the Book of Zechariah, the ultimate salvation of mankind is graphically envisaged: the Gentiles, in company with the Jews, will return to serve God in an ideal Jerusalem.

Salvation through Yahweh's action and power

Christianity. Christianity has been described as the salvation religion *par excellence*. Its primary premise is that the incarnation and sacrificial death of its founder, Jesus Christ, formed the climax of a divine plan for mankind's salvation. This plan was conceived by God consequent on the Fall of Adam, the progenitor of the human race, and it would be completed at the Last Judgment, when the Second Coming of Christ would mark the catastrophic end of the world. This soteriological evaluation of history finds expression in the Christian division of time into two periods: before Christ (BC) and Anno Domini (AD)—*i.e.*, the years of the Lord.

Salvation through Christ

The evolution of the Christian doctrine of salvation was a complicated process essentially linked with the gradual definition of belief in the divinity of Jesus of Nazareth. In Christian theology, therefore, soteriology is an integral part of what is termed Christology. Whereas the divinity of Jesus Christ has been the subject of careful metaphysical definition in the creeds, the exact nature and mode of salvation through Christ has not been so precisely defined. The church has been content to state, in its creeds, that Christ was incarnated, crucified, died, and rose again "for us men, and for our salvation."

The basic tenets of Christian soteriology may be summarized as follows: man is deserving of damnation by God for the original sin, which he inherits by descent from Adam, and for his own actual sin. But because sin is regarded as also putting man in the power of the devil, Christ's work of salvation has been interpreted along two different lines. Thus his crucifixion may be evaluated as a vicarious sacrifice offered to God as propitiation or atonement for human sin. Alternatively, it may be seen as the price paid to redeem man from the devil. These two ways of interpreting the death of Christ have provided the major themes of soteriological theory and speculation in Christian theology. Despite this fluidity of interpretation, belief in the saving power of Christ is fundamental to Christianity and finds expression in every aspect of its faith and practice.

Islām. Muḥammad regarded himself as "a warner clear," and as the last and greatest of a line of prophets whom Allāh had sent to warn his people of impending doom. Although the word *najāt* ("salvation") is used only once in the Qur'ān, the basic aim of Islām is salvation in the sense of escaping future punishment, which will be pronounced on sinners at the Last Judgment. Muḥammad did teach that Allāh had predestined some men to heaven and others to hell; but the whole logic of his message is that submission to Allāh is the means to salvation, for Allāh is merciful. Indeed, faithful submission is the quintessence of Islām (Arabic "submission") as the name itself signifies. Although in his own estimation Muḥammad was the prophet of Allāh, in later Muslim devotion he came to be venerated as the mediator between God and man, whose intercession was decisive.

Zoroastrianism and Parsiism. According to Zoroaster, a good and evil force struggled for mastery in the universe. Man had to decide on which side to align himself in this fateful contest. This dualism was greatly elaborated in later Zoroastrianism and Parsiism, which derived from it. Good, personified as the god Ormazd, and evil, as the demonic Ahriman, would contend for 12,000 years with varying fortune. At last Ormazd would triumph, and Saoshyans, his agent, would resurrect the dead for judgment. The righteous would pass to their reward in heaven, and the wicked be cast into hell. But this situation was of temporary duration. A meteor would later strike the earth, causing a flood of molten metal. Through this flood all would have to pass as an ordeal of purgation. The sensitivity of each to the anguish would be determined by the degree of his guilt. After the ordeal, all men would become immortal, and all that Ahriman had harmed or corrupted would be renewed. Salvation thus took the form of deliverance from postmortem suffering; for ultimate restoration was assured to all after suffering the degree of purgation that the nature of their earthly lives entailed.

BIBLIOGRAPHY. For recent and comprehensive studies of the subject, s.g.f. BRANDON, *Man and His Destiny in the Great Religions* (1962), provides extensive documentation and bibliographies; important aspects of salvation are specially dealt with in his *History, Time and Deity* (1965) and *The Judgment of the Dead* (1967), also well-documented and including bibliographies. s.g.f. BRANDON (ed.), *The Saviour God* (1963), comprises 15 essays by specialists in the major religions; c.j. BLEEKER (ed.), *Anthropologie religieuse* (1955), also contains 15 specialized essays (in English, French, and German) that relate to salvation in various religions. J. HASTINGS (ed.), *The Encyclopaedia of Religion and Ethics*, vol. 11 (1921), provides a series of articles on salvation in various religions; these articles are valuable, but are necessarily dated in both material and approach. The German encyclopaedia *Die Religion in Geschichte und Gegenwart*, 3rd ed., vol. 2, col. 576–600 (1958), gives a useful survey under "Erlöser" and "Erlösung," but attention is heavily concentrated on the Christian theological issues. A valuable and well-documented study of the subject in Hebrew, Greco-Roman religions, and early Christianity may be found in T. KLAUSER (ed.), *Reallexikon für Antike und Christentum*, vol. 5, col. 54–219 (1964). ADOLF VON HARNACK's monumental *Lehrbuch der Dogmengeschichte*, 3rd ed., 3 vol. (1893; Eng. trans., *History of Dogma*, 7 vol., 1900, reprinted 1961), traces the development of Christian soteriology; g. AULEN, *Christus Victor* (1931), deals particularly with early classical interpretation of Christ's soteriological role; L.W. GRENSTED, *A Short History of the Doctrine of the Atonement* (1920, reprinted 1962), is a reliable concise guide. Aspects of salvation in the religions concerned are treated in the following books: R.C. ZAEHNER, *Hinduism*, 2nd ed. (1966) and *The Dawn and Twilight of Zoroastrianism* (1961); E.J. THOMAS, *The History of Buddhist Thought*, 2nd ed. (1951); and A.J. WENSINCK, *The Muslim Creed* (1932).

(S.G.F.B.)

Samarkand

Samarkand, a town and *oblast* (province) centre in the Uzbek Soviet Socialist Republic, U.S.S.R., was one of the great cities of Central Asia during the Middle Ages. It lies at an altitude of about 2,330 feet (710 metres) in the valley of the Zeravshan River, 168 miles (270 kilometres) southwest of Tashkent by rail and about 155 miles (249 kilometres) north of the Afghanistan frontier (population of the city, 1970 census [prelim.] 267,000).

History. Samarkand is one of the oldest cities of Central Asia. In the 4th century BC, then known as Maracanda, it was the capital of Sogdiana and was captured (329) by Alexander the Great. In the 6th century AD it was part of a Turkish kingdom. At the beginning of the 8th century it was conquered by the Arabs, and in the 9th and 10th centuries it was ruled by the Sāmānids of Persia. From the 11th century to the Mongol invasions, Samarkand was ruled by various Turkic peoples. In the 11th century it was conquered by the Qarakhanids (Karakhanids) and later by the Seljuq Turks; in the 12th century by the Karakitai; and in the 13th century it was annexed to the kingdom of Khwārezm (Khorezm). In 1220 it was captured and destroyed by Genghis Khan. In 1365 the city revolted against the Mongol emirs, and at the end of the 14th and the beginning of the 15th centuries, it was the capital of the empire of Timur. During this period Samarkand was the most important economic and cultural centre of Central Asia. In 1500 it was conquered by the Uzbeks, the Muslim people of the Golden Horde, and came under the dominion of the Shaybānid dynasty, who in the middle of the 16th century transferred their capital to Bukhara. Samarkand later became part of the khanate of Bukhara. During the 17th and 18th centuries, as a result of attacks by nomad tribes and by the Iranians, Samarkand underwent a serious economic crisis, and from the 1720s until the 1770s it was uninhabited. In 1868 it was occupied by Russian troops and became a part of the Russian empire as capital of the Zeravshan District, which in 1887 became the Samarkand Province. When the Uzbek S.S.R. was constituted in 1924, Samarkand became its capital until 1930.

Major features. The old city of Samarkand, as opposed to the "new town" built after the Russian conquest of 1868, took shape in the Middle Ages. Its plan consisted of streets converging toward the centre from six gates in the five-mile-long, 11th-century walls. The walls and gates were destroyed after the capture of the town by the Russians, but the plan of the medieval period is still preserved. Here are to be found monuments of Central Asian architecture in which the developments of six centuries can be observed. The earliest of these are the five small 14th-century edifices (in the collection of mausoleums known as the Shāh-e Zendah) and the Rūḥābād mausoleum dating from the middle of the 14th century. In the time of Timur (Tamerlane), the congregational mosque of Bībī-Khānom (his Chinese wife) and the mausoleum of Timur himself, known as the Gūr-e Amīr, were built. To the second half of the 15th century belongs the Ak Saray tomb with a superb fresco of the interior. A fine example of the town-planning culture of Central Asia is Rīgestān Square with its group of monumental buildings: the *madrasahs* (Muslim schools) of Ulūgh Beg (1417–20), Shirdar (1619 to 1635/36), and Tilakari (mid-17th century), which border the square on three sides. In the environs of Samarkand are the tomb of 'Abd-e Darūn (15th century), the mausoleum of Chopān-Aṭā (mid-15th century), the mausoleum of 'Eshrat Khān, the ruins of a 16th-century aqueduct leading to the Zeravshan River, the mosque of Namāzgāh (17th century), the *madrasah* at the tomb of Khoja Ahrār (built 1630–36 by a Samarkand architect Dūst Moḥammad), and the *khānegāh* (cloister) at the tomb of 'Abd-e Bīrūn (1633–34). The main features of the 15th- to 17th-century monuments are the splendid portals, the vast coloured domes, and the remarkable exterior decoration in majolica, mosaic, marble, and gold. The new town, construction of which began in 1871, has expanded considerably during the Soviet period; and public buildings, houses, and parks have been built. There are Uzbek and Russian theatres, a uni-

Conquest by the Golden Horde

The Gūr-e Amīr (mausoleum of Timur), Samarkand, 1405.
By courtesy of the Society for Cultural Relations with the U.S.S.R., London

versity (established 1933), and higher educational institutions for agriculture, medicine, and trade.

Commercial importance

Samarkand's commercial importance, which in ancient and medieval times derived from its location at the junction of trade routes from China (the "silk road") and India, declined during the 17th and 18th centuries but greatly increased with the coming of the railway in 1896. Samarkand then became an important centre for the export of wine, dried and fresh fruits, cotton, rice, silk, and leather. Under the Soviet regime, industry has been expanded and, although mainly based on agriculture (*e.g.*, cotton ginning; silk spinning and weaving; fruit canning; production of wine, clothing, leather and footwear, and tobacco), also includes the manufacture of tractor and automobile parts and cinema apparatus.

Samarkandskaya (Samarkand) oblast. The *oblast,* formed in 1938, is divided into 16 *rayony* (districts). Its area is 11,270 square miles (29,200 square kilometres), and its population mainly Uzbek but includes Tadzhiks, Russians, and Ukrainians. More than one-quarter of the population lives in the three towns of Samarkand, Katta-Kurgan, and Dzhizak. The *oblast* is drained by the Zeravshan River and includes the Nuratau and Ak-Tau mountain ranges in the north. In the southwest is the Karnabchul Steppe. The geological structure includes marble, granite, limestone, gypsum, and other valuable building materials and minerals. The climate is continental and is noted for the amount of sunshine and the absence of cloud cover. There is no frost during 200 days in the year. The economy, mainly agricultural, includes cotton and fruit growing and sericulture in the Zeravshan Valley; elsewhere there is dry wheat farming. Karakul sheep and goats are bred. Extensive irrigation systems have been developed. The *oblast* is traversed by the Krasnovodsk–Tashkent railway to an extent of 200 miles and there are about 5,000 miles of motor roads.

BIBLIOGRAPHY. *Istoriya Samarkanda,* 2 vol. (1969), a complete history of Samarkand; EUGENE SCHUYLER, *Turkistan,* 2 vol. (1876, reissued 1966), a description of the city as it was in 1873; CENTRAL ASIAN RESEARCH CENTRE, *Cities of Central Asia* (1961), with sketch map.

(G.E.Wh.)

Samoa

The Samoa Islands, situated in the eastern Pacific Ocean about 1,600 miles northeast of New Zealand, 2,700 miles east of Australia, and 2,200 miles southwest of the Hawaiian Islands, are among the westernmost islands of Polynesia. The archipelago is divided administratively into two parts—American Samoa and Western Samoa. American Samoa, a dependency of the United States, consists of the six islands east of the 171° W meridian. Western Samoa, a self-governing nation that until 1962 was a United Nations trust territory administered by New Zealand, consists of the nine islands west of that meridian.

American Samoa, with a total land area of 76 square miles (197 square kilometres), includes the inhabited islands of Tutuila, Tau, Olosega, Ofu, and Aunuu and two uninhabited coral atolls named Rose Island. Swains Island (inhabited), a coral atoll 210 miles northwest of Tutuila and geographically not a part of the archipelago, was made a part of American Samoa in 1925. Western Samoa, with a total land area of 1,097 square miles (2,841 square kilometres), includes the inhabited islands of Upolu, Savai'i, Manono, and Apolima, and the uninhabited islands of Fanuatapu, Namua, Nuutele, Nuulua, and Nuusafee. The capital of American Samoa is Pago Pago, on Tutuila; the capital of Western Samoa is Apia, on Upolu.

The landscape. *Relief features.* Except for the coral atolls, the islands are rocky and were formed by volcanic activity that progressed from east to west within the past 7,000,000 years. The islands of American Samoa are thus the oldest geologically. The main island of Tutuila, with an area of 53 square miles, rises steeply above deep inlets, of which the most notable is Pago Pago Harbour, which almost divides the island in two. Its highest peak is Matafao (2,142 feet [653 metres]).

The largest island of Western Samoa is Savai'i (662 square miles); its highest peak is Silisili (6,096 feet [1,858 metres]). There have been two eruptions from Savai'i volcanoes in historic times, the most recent in 1905. The other large island is Upolu (433 square miles), which has five uninhabited, offshore islets. Manono and Apolima lie between the two main islands.

Apart from cliffs formed by recent lava flows, all of the islands are ringed by coral reefs and shallow lagoons. The volcanic soils are easily exhausted by farming but support a lush natural vegetation which varies from plantations of taro, coconut, breadfruit, and other food crops on the coast to rain forest and mountain rain (or mist) forest further inland.

Climate. Rainfall varies from over 100 inches on the coasts to 300 inches inland, but porous soils and rocks make water supplies unreliable. Hence, coastal wells are the only water source for almost half the rural population. Temperatures are unusually constant, the monthly mean varying only 1.2° F (0.7° C) from an average of 79° F (26° C). The southeast trade winds prevail, varying occasionally to northerlies during the wet season, from November to March. Hurricanes are liable to occur between May and November.

Animal life. The islands are not rich in animal life. Nevertheless, of the 53 species of birds, at least 16 are unique, including a rare tooth-billed pigeon. The only native mammals are the flying fox and smaller bats. There are several lizards and two harmless snakes of the boa family. Rats, wild cattle, and pigs have been introduced. There are centipedes and millipedes, scorpions, spiders, and a rich insect life. A United Nations-South Pacific Commission project has been studying methods to control the rhinoceros beetle, which attacks the copra crop.

People and population. The Samoan people are of eastern Polynesian stock. Their language, believed to be the oldest of the Polynesian tongues, is closely related to the Maori, Tahitian, Hawaiian, and Tongan languages. Within the villages, close kinship ties have traditionally bound individuals into a sternly collectivist society. Elected family leaders called *matai* (titled chiefs or orators) form village or district councils to administer group affairs. Extended blood ties linked family or village groups; beyond the social framework of well-regulated village life a network of allegiances arose, with the major families striving for supremacy and regularly plunging

Village life and culture

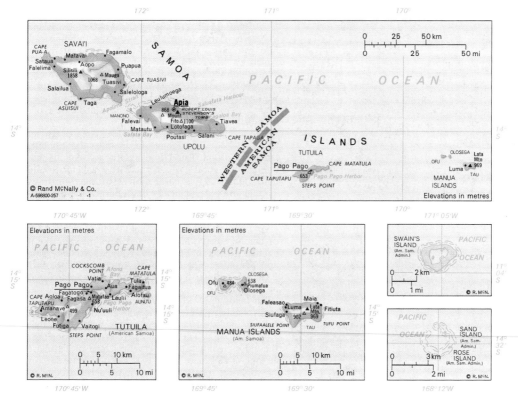

AMERICAN AND WESTERN SAMOA

the islands into warfare. The material culture was utilitarian, and most artifacts are unadorned. There appears to have been no dominant priestly class; family elders performed the rituals of a pantheistic religion.

While European contact and the introduction of a cash economy have produced some changes in values and traditional authority, preservation of the culture has become a shibboleth amongst Samoan leaders, particularly in Western Samoa; many outward features of rural life have thus remained virtually unchanged. The Christian churches were easily absorbed into the village social structure; sanctuaries of cathedral proportions made of coral cement dot the most remote settlements. The Congregational Christian Church (formerly the London Missionary Society) is predominant, followed by the Methodist and the Roman Catholic faiths, and the Church of Jesus Christ of Latter-day Saints mission.

The population of American Samoa in 1970 was over 27,000; of these 4,000 lived in Pago Pago and Fagatoga, and 21,000 on Tutuila Island. It was estimated that an additional 20,000 American Samoans were living in Hawaii and in California. Out of the total population of Western Samoa of 149,000, one-fifth lived in Apia and three-quarters on Upolu Island. Many Western Samoans lived overseas, perhaps as many as 20,000 of them in New Zealand.

The economy. *American Samoa.* The United States administration, with about 3,000 employees, is the main employer. Tuna canning (by American-owned canneries) and tourism are major industries, in addition to those in the retail business sector. The canneries are supplied by a fleet of about 150 oriental vessels and employ about 1,000 Samoans to process the catch. Tourists in 1971 totalled nearly 30,000. A major hotel is owned by a corporation, whose shareholders are mostly Samoan. One other hotel is in operation, and more are planned, and the government has formed a development bank to encourage the establishment of light industry.

Apart from the cultivation of copra on the outlying islands, agriculture is not widely practiced, although family gardens provide subsistence crops to supplement cash wages. Fewer than 200 acres are under commercial cultivation, mostly vegetable gardens for local markets.

Social legislation ties American Samoa more closely to U.S. costs of living than its South Pacific neighbours.

Samoa, Area and Population				
	area		population	
	sq mi	sq km	1960 census	1968 estimate
Territory of American Samoa				
Districts				
Eastern* (Eastern Tutuila)	25	65	11,000	16,000
Manua†	22	57	3,000	2,000
Swains Island	1	3	100	70
Western (Western Tutuila)	28	73	6,000	9,000
Total American Samoa	76	197‡	20,000§	27,000§

	area		population	
	sq mi	sq km	1966 census	1969 estimate
Western Samoa				
Islands				
Savai'i	662	1,715	36,000§	39,000
Political districts				
Fa'aseleleaga	...	...	10,000	11,000
Gaga'emauga	...	...	4,000	4,000
Gaga'ifomauga	...	...	5,000	5,000
Palauli	...	...	8,000	8,000
Satupa'itea	...	...	4,000	5,000
Vaisigano	...	...	6,000	6,000
Upolu	433	1,121	95,000	109,000§
Political districts				
A'ana	...	...	18,000	21,000
Aiga-i-le-Tai	...	...	4,000	4,000
Atua	...	...	18,000	20,000
Gaga'emauga	...	...	2,000	3,000
Tuamasaga	...	...	51,000	59,000
Va'a-o-Fonoti	...	...	2,000	2,000
Total Western Samoa	1,097‖	2,841‡‖	131,000	149,000

*Including Aunuu Island.   †Including Ofu, Olosega, and Tau islands.
‡Converted area figures do not add to total given because of rounding.
§Figures do not add to total given because of rounding.   ‖Area of island totals may include, and county total does include areas of small outlying islands.   Source: Official government figures.

Western Samoa. Fish and timber are the only exploitable large-scale natural resources. A United States company opened a large veneer and lumber operation on Savai'i in 1971; and fisheries research and promotion is in progress. The growing of cash crops for local sale or export has been difficult; individual commercial enterprise is not suited to the communal way of life. Despite this, such export crops as copra, cocoa, and bananas, nevertheless provide strong support for the economy.

The balance of payments position is favourable, assisted by a growing tourist industry, now second in economic importance only to copra, and to the receipt of remittances from family members overseas, particularly in New Zealand.

Tourism was increasing in the early 1970s. To encourage the industry, a new airstrip and a road from the airport to Apia have been built with the aid of an Asian Development Bank Loan, and more hotel projects are planned in addition to those now operating.

Increase in tourism

Transport. Regular shipping services link the islands with ports abroad; international airlines operate flights to and from the United States, New Zealand, and Fiji. The principal trade and transport links are with Hawaii and California to the north, and Fiji, New Zealand, and Australia to the south.

Administration and social conditions. *American Samoa.* American Samoa is an unincorporated, unorganized territory, the people of which are United States nationals but not citizens. The territory is administered by the United States Department of the Interior, which appoints the governor.

Under the islands' second constitution, adopted in 1966, the Fono (bicameral legislature) is autonomous in its disposition of local revenues. The 21 members of the House of Representatives are elected by universal suffrage; the minimum voting age is 18. The 18 senators are chosen by councils of chiefs, in accordance with Samoan custom. The 1970 Commission on Future Political Status recommended that the present status be retained but that the governor and senate be elected. An unofficial delegate to the Congress of the United States was elected in 1970. Apart from Swains Island, the islands are divided into three administrative districts (each with an appointed district governor), which are subdivided into a total of 14 counties. Chiefs representing each family form village and district councils. This autonomous village control is linked with the central government through three district governors appointed by the governor. Each village has a Samoan magistrate with authority to adjudicate on minor misdemeanours.

Administration: Western Samoa. In 1962 Western Samoa became the first independent Polynesian state, and in 1970 it joined the Commonwealth of Nations. The constitution provides for parliamentary government. There were originally two heads of state, with the provision that when one died the other would continue as sole head of state for life, after which the head of state would be elected by the Parliament for a five-year term. The present surviving head of state is Malietoa Tanumafili II. The prime minister is elected by the Parliament and appoints a cabinet of eight other ministers from elected members.

The parliament has 45 Samoan members, and two representing the Individual Voters, who are mixed blood or non-Samoan citizens claiming European status and enjoying universal suffrage. In the 41 Samoan electorates, only chiefs are eligible as candidates or voters, but they in their turn have been chosen by consensus of their entire family. In each village, chiefs form a council to run their own affairs, and there is little contact with the central government.

Education. Education is compulsory between the ages of six and 18 in American Samoa; 36 percent of the population is of school age. Televised instruction over six channels, given mostly by teachers and technicians from the United States, is available to local schools. In Western Samoa more than half the population is under the age of 15; although education is not yet free or compulsory, most children receive a primary education. Selected pupils are sent to government or mission high schools.

Prospects for the future: Western Samoa. There is a need to diversify the economy to support the fast-growing population—expanding at a rate of 2.9 percent a year. To meet this need research is being pursued with help from the United Nations Development Program, from New Zealand, and other sources. Some secondary industries have already been established. These, along with beef farming, food processing, canning, tourism, and

the cultivation of export crops will form the mainstay of the economy in the foreseeable future. At the same time a family-planning campaign is being instituted to prevent a booming population from lowering the standard of living.

A major aim of Samoan leaders is to create jobs in order to lessen the emigration of young people to Hawaii and the United States mainland. Such growth in industry would also enable the territory to provide more of its own revenue, and thus diminish reliance on the United States subsidies, thus tying living costs less closely to those in the United States. The retention of Samoan control over land is the main bulwark against radical changes in the life-style of both the Samoas.

BIBLIOGRAPHY. The traditional way of life in the Samoas is described most definitively in A.F. KRAMER, *Die Samoa-Inseln,* 2 vol. (1902–03); and SIR PETER H. BUCK, *Samoan Material Culture* (1930). The customs of the people are discussed in MARGARET MEAD, *Coming of Age in Samoa* (1928, reprinted many times); and F.M. and M.M. KEESING, *Elite Communication of Samoa: A Study of Leadership* (1956). For historical reference, see R.P. GILSON, *Samoa 1830 to 1900: The Politics of a Multi-Cultural Community* (1970); and J.A.C. GRAY, *Amerika Samoa: A History of American Samoa and Its United States Naval Administration* (1960); and for political development in Western Samoa, J.W. DAVIDSON, *Samoa mo Samoa* (1967). Geographical publications are JAMES W. FOX and KENNETH B. CUMBERLAND (eds.), *Western Samoa: Land, Life, and Agriculture in Tropical Polynesia* (1962); and MYRTLE J. ASHMOLE, *Guide to the Birds of Samoa* (1963), practically the only reference for natural history. Modern development in the islands is dealt with in F.M. KEESING, *The South Seas in the Modern World,* rev. ed. (1945); and D. PITT, *Tradition and Economic Progress in Samoa* (1970); the WOLF MANAGEMENT SERVICES, *Economic Development Plan for American Samoa* (1967); and the DEPARTMENT OF ECONOMIC DEVELOPMENT, APIA, *Western Samoa: Second Five-Year Development Plan* (1970).

(P.R.C.)

Samuel

Samuel, the most outstanding religious hero in the history of Israel between Moses and David, is represented in the Old Testament in every role of leadership open to a Jewish man of his day—seer, priest, judge, prophet, and military leader; his greatest distinction,. however, was his role in the establishment of the monarchy. Although no exact dates can be given for him, he was a contemporary of Saul, the first king of Israel, who is placed by historians roughly in the period 1050–1010 BC.

Information about Samuel is contained in the First Book of Samuel. The ancient designation of the two books of Samuel does not indicate that he is the author (in fact, his death is related in I Sam. 25) or the hero of the books; indeed, it is difficult to deduce what the title was intended to mean.

Samuel, the son of Elkanah (of Ephraim) and Hannah, was born in answer to the prayer of his previously childless mother. In gratitude she dedicated him to the service of the chief sanctuary of Shiloh, in the charge of the priest Eli; as a boy Samuel received a divine oracle in which the fall of the house of Eli was predicted (I Sam. 1–3). When he became an adult, Samuel inspired Israel to a great victory over the Philistines at Ebenezer (chapter 7). The proposal of the elders of Israel to install a king was indignantly rejected by Samuel as infidelity to Yahweh, the God of Israel (chapter 8). By the revelation of Yahweh, however, he anointed Saul king and installed him before all Israel (chapters 9–10). Saul was vindicated as king by his leadership of Israel in a campaign against the Ammonites (chapter 11); after this, Samuel retired from the leadership of Israel (chapter 12). He reappeared, however, to announce the oracle of Yahweh rejecting Saul as king, once for arrogating to himself the right of sacrifice (chapter 13) and a second time for failing to carry out the law of the ban—a primitive institution by which persons or objects were devoted to the deity, normally by destruction—against the Amalekites (chapter 15). By the oracle of Yahweh, Samuel secretly anointed David as king (chapter 16). He then faded into the background, appearing at the sanctuary

Samuel's priestly leadership

of Naioth (chapter 19). He died, and his ghost was evoked by a necromancer, or sorceress, at the request of Saul; he then announced a third time the rejection of Saul (chapter 28).

Samuel thus appears as a leader in all Israel; his leadership is exercised in war and law, but his authority is basically religious, mostly prophetic, although with some features of priestly authority. He appears at first as being hostile to the monarchy and then as being favourable to it. He is the spokesman of Yahweh in the election both of Saul and of David. Yet, the picture is not entirely straightforward, and a close examination of the material, as conducted by a large number of critical historians, reveals inconsistencies that raise questions about both the history of Samuel and the sources in which this history has been preserved. The same examination reveals that none of the material in its present form was contemporary with the events; if one source is taken as controlling, then the other materials lose all historical value.

The "pro-monarchic" and "anti-monarchic" sources

The two major divergences lie in those passages that critics call the "pro-monarchic" source (I Sam. 9:1–10:16) and the "anti-monarchic" source (I Sam. 8 and 10:17–27). The word source here means tradition rather than a hypothetical document that can be reconstructed. In the pro-monarchic account of the rise of Saul, Samuel is an obscure village seer (with distinct evidence of occult practices). The institution of the monarchy and the election of the King occur according to the will of Yahweh as revealed to Samuel. The story of the anointing, however, has no story of accession to complete it; instead, there is the account of Saul's victory over the Ammonites. Examination discloses that this is still another account of Saul's rise without an anointing story; Saul is chosen king as the judges—the leaders of the Israelites during their conquest of the land of Canaan—were chosen, by a charismatic display of military courage and leadership. Samuel was very probably intruded into this narrative.

The anti-monarchic account presents a different kingship, a different Saul, and a different Samuel. Samuel is a figure known through "all Israel" (a term of uncertain meaning at this period); his authority rests on his position as judge. The institution of kingship comes not from divine revelation but from the request of the elders of Israel, and this request is treated by Samuel as rebellion against Yahweh. The king is chosen not by divine election but by lot, implying that no special qualities were required, and the bashful candidate has to be summoned from a hiding place. This story is related to the account of Samuel as judge in chapters 7 and 12, and he is clearly presented as the last of the judges; it is indicated that the system of the judges was rejected by the Israelites not because of its failure but because of their worldliness. This tradition has two questionable features: Samuel is the only judge who is a permanent magistrate as well as a military leader, and his victory over the Philistines in chapter 7 cannot be historical.

The story of the birth and vocation of Samuel is regarded by critics as legendary because of a number of obviously unhistorical features. The narrative is the major piece in establishing the role of Samuel as a prophet, but it is questionable whether the "prophet" as a distinct religious figure had emerged at this early date. The story is also at the root of the priestly role imposed on Samuel at a later date in I Chron. 6; but this is an effort to explain in terms of the later priesthood the sacred functions performed by Samuel.

There are also two traditions in the account of the rejection of Saul by Samuel. The first story (chapter 13) is motivated by Saul's assumption of the prerogatives of the priesthood. It is quite unlikely that either the powers of the king or the prerogatives of the priest were as closely defined as this in the early period. The second story (chapter 15) is motivated by the failure of Saul to observe the ethic of the holy war. This story does not exhibit the same improbability. It seems that there was a firm tradition of a split between the two men but an inexact memory of the details of the incident.

There must have been some reason why Samuel was important enough to be remembered for a major role in the establishment of the monarchy. Yet, his roles as prophet, seer, and judge are all incredible in certain respects, apart from the fact that each of them is considerable. The problem may be resolved by identifying a role for Samuel that receives only passing mention because it no longer existed when this material was written. This is his leadership of the sons of the prophets, a group of young men organized for ecstatic worship. Indications are that they were a group of fanatical religious and national conservatives. That they were young and active gave Samuel a base of power that was physical as well as moral. As conservatives, they must have been torn between the threat to Israel by the Philistines and the promise that the new political system, alien to religious and national traditions, offered against this threat. This internal division in Israel is reflected in the person of Samuel, who stood with most Israelites on both sides of the question.

Samuel's importance

BIBLIOGRAPHY. Two recent histories of Israel, JOHN BRIGHT, *A History of Israel*, pp. 163–172 (1959); and MARTIN NOTH, *Geschichte Israels*, 3rd ed. (1956; Eng. trans., *The History of Israel*, 2nd ed., pp. 168–176, 1960), represent the two dominant schools of thought in Israelite historiography. H.W. HERTZBERG, *Die Samuelbücher*, 2nd ed. (1960; Eng. trans., *I & II Samuel: A Commentary*, 1964), is the most recent thorough study of the texts on which the history depends, and deals with both criticism and exegesis.

(J.L.McK.)

Sand Sheets and Sand Dunes

A dune is a mound of windblown sand. The smallest dunes are about a metre (three feet) high and cover about ten square metres (107 square feet); the largest may be over 400 metres (1,300 feet) high and cover several square kilometres. Large areas of gently undulating sandy surfaces with low local relief are called sand sheets. Because aerial photography shows these to have dunelike patterns and other evidence shows them to be windblown, it is appropriate to describe them with dunes.

True sand dunes are found in very arid areas and are the result of the movement of sand grains by the wind under the influence of gravity. They are comparable to other forms that appear when a fluid moves over a loose bed, such as subaqueous "dunes" on the beds of rivers and tidal estuaries and sand waves on the continental shelves beneath shallow seas and are known as "bedforms." True dunes must be distinguished from dunes formed in conjunction with vegetation. The latter cover relatively small areas on quite humid coastlands and also occur on the semi-arid margins of deserts. True dunes cover much more extensive areas, primarily in the great sand seas (ergs), some of which are as big as France or Texas, but they also occur as small isolated dunes on hard desert surfaces. Sand sheets are poorly mapped, but some are probably almost as extensive as some of the great sand seas.

In the last 2,000,000 years or so the areas of very low rainfall in which true dunes form expanded once or twice into areas that are now more humid. The best evidence for these changes is the presence of sand seas that are now immobilized by vegetation. Dunes were not uncommon in the geological past, and at certain times there were deserts as extensive as modern ones. Rocks formed by the solidification of ancient sand seas occur, for example, in the walls of the Grand Canyon, Arizona; in the west Midlands of England; and in southern Brazil.

This article treats dune formation, fixed and mobile dunes and their patterns, and the basic characteristics of sand sheets and sandy terrains. For further information on the arid environment in general, see DESERTS. See also WIND ACTION; PLAYAS, PANS, AND SALINE FLATS for discussions of deflation or erosion by the wind.

DUNE FORMATION

An understanding of sand dunes requires a basic knowledge of their sands, the winds, and the interactions of these main elements; these factors will be treated in turn.

Sands. Dunes are almost invariably built of particles of sand size. Clay particles are not usually picked up by the wind because of their mutual coherence, and if they are picked up they tend to be lifted high into the air. Only where clays are aggregated into particles of sand size, as on the Gulf Coast of Texas, will they be formed into dunes. Silt is more easily picked up by the wind but is carried away faster than sand, and there are few signs of dunelike bed forms where silt is deposited, for instance as sheets of loess (*q.v*). Particles coarser than sands, such as small pebbles, only form dunelike features when there are strong and persistent winds, as on top of some sea cliffs in Peru. Even larger particles, such as small boulders, can only be moved by the wind on such slippery surfaces as ice or wet saline mud and never form into dunes.

Common dune sands have median grain diameters between 0.02 and 0.04 centimetres (0.008 and 0.016 inches). The maximum common range is between 0.01 and 0.07 centimetres. Most dune sands are well sorted, and a sample of sand from a dune will usually have particles of very similar size. The sand on sand sheets, however, is poorly sorted and often bimodal; that is, it is a mixture of coarse sands, often about 0.06 centimetres in diameter, and much finer sands, with few particles of intermediate size. Windblown (eolian) sands, especially the coarser particles, are often rounded and minutely pitted, the latter giving the grains a frosted appearance when seen under a microscope.

Minerals in windblown sand

Most windblown sand is composed of quartz. Quartz exists in large quantities in many igneous and metamorphic rocks in crystals of sand size. It tends to accumulate when these rocks are weathered away because quartz resists chemical breakdown better than most minerals, which are taken away in solution. Most of the great sand seas occur in continental interiors that have been losing soluble material for millions of years; as a consequence, quartzose sandstones are common. These sandstones are eroded by rainwash and stream runoff, processes that are spasmodic but violent in deserts. The eroded products are transported to great interior basins where they are deposited. These alluvial deposits are the sources of most windblown sand. Quartz also predominates in most coastal dune sands, but there usually are considerable mixtures of other minerals in such dunes.

Dune sands not composed of quartz are rarer but not unknown. Near volcanic eruptions in Tanzania, for example, dunes are built of volcanic dust. In many arid areas, gypsum crystals of sand size are deposited on the floors of ephemeral lakes as the water dries out; they are then blown like sand to form dunes. Gypsum dunes occur in New Mexico, northern Algeria, and southwestern Australia. Some coastal dunes are built of broken shells, as in the western Isles of Scotland, or of broken coral, as in the West Indies. These carbonate sands are sometimes recemented after deposition to become hard and rocklike. In desert and coastal dunes, heavy minerals are often sorted out and may occur in commercial concentrations, as does rutile on the southeastern Australian coast.

Winds. Winds have three sources of variation that are important, namely, direction, velocity, and turbulence. Most of the great deserts are found in the subtropical areas of high atmospheric pressure, where the winds circulate in a clockwise direction in the Northern Hemisphere and a counterclockwise direction in the Southern Hemisphere. The high-pressure systems tend to dip down to the east so that winds are stronger there, a pattern mirrored by the dunes. Poleward of these circulation systems are the zones of eastward moving depressions in which there are generally westerly winds that mold the dunes of the North American and Central Asian deserts and of the northwest Sahara. The boundaries between these two circulation systems migrate back and forth seasonally so that complicated dune patterns are found in the zones of overlap. Only a few deserts, such as the Thar Desert of India, are affected by monsoonal wind systems. Some dunes are built by local winds, as in coastal Peru. Coastal dunes in the temperate latitudes may sometimes be built by local winds, but in general they are built to greater heights on west coasts by the westerly winds.

The direction of the wind at any one place in the desert is affected by a number of local factors. Winds are particularly channelled around topographical features, such as the Tibesti Massif in the Sahara, so that dunes are affected by different winds on different sides of the obstruction.

The pattern of wind velocity also is important. Like many natural phenomena, wind velocities have a log-normal distribution: there is a large number of moderate breezes, and a diminishing number of increasingly more violent winds. The greatest volumes of sand are probably moved by winds somewhat in excess of the median wind velocities. Strong winds often blow from a particular direction, as in the southern Sahara, where the strong winds of the sandstorms come predominantly from one direction and are responsible for the undulations of the sand sheets because they alone can move coarse sands. Lighter winds blow from several different directions, and the dunes, being of finer sand, are therefore affected by several winds.

Wind velocity patterns

The wind is retarded near the surface by friction. Above the ground the wind velocity increases rapidly. The near-surface velocity must rise above a certain threshold value before sand will be picked up, the value of this depending on the size of the sand grains; for example, a wind of 12 kilometres per hour (7 miles per hour) measured at a height of 10 metres (33 feet) is required to move sands 0.02 centimetre (0.8 inch) in diameter, and a 21-kilometre-per-hour (13-mile-per-hour) wind is required to move 0.06 centimetre (0.24 inch) sands. Once sand movement has been initiated by such a wind it can be maintained by lower wind speeds. Because instantaneous wind speeds in eddies can rise well above the average velocity, turbulence also is important, but it is difficult to measure. The amount of sand moved by a wind is a power function (exponential factor) of the windspeed; for example, a 10-kilometre-per-hour (6-mile-per-hour) wind carries 13 grams per hour (0.39 ounce per hour), a 20-kilometre-per-hour (12-mile-per-hour) wind carries 274 grams per hour (8 ounces per hour), and a 30-kilometre-per-hour (18-mile-per-hour) wind carries 1,179 grams per hour (35 ounces per hour). A wind of a particular velocity will move fewer larger than smaller grains.

Growth of a dune. The dune-forming process is complex, but an introductory account can be given based on the example of a single dune on a hard desert surface.

Three quarters of the sand carried by the wind moves as a mass of jumping (saltating) grains; the remaining quarter moves slowly along the surface as creep, kept in motion by the bombardment of the saltating grains. Saltating sand bounces more easily off hard surfaces than off soft ones so that more sand can be moved over a pebbly desert surface than over a smooth or soft one. Slight hollows or smoother patches will reduce the amount of sand that the wind can carry, and a small sand patch will be initiated. If it is large enough, this patch will attract more sand.

The wind adjusts its velocity gradient on reaching the sand patch; winds above a certain speed decrease their near-surface velocity and deposit sand on the patch. This adjustment takes place over several metres, the sand being deposited over this distance, and a dune is built up. The growth of this dune cannot continue indefinitely; the windward slope is eventually adjusted so that there is an increase in the near-surface velocity up its face to compensate for the drag imposed by the sandy surface. When this happens, the dune stops growing and there is no net gain or loss of sand.

As the dune grows, the smooth leeward slope steepens until the wind cannot be deflected down sharply enough to follow it; the wind then separates from the surface leaving a "dead zone" in the lee into which falls the sand brought up the windward slope. When this depositional slope is steepened to the angle of repose of dry sand (about 32°), this angle is maintained and the added sand slips down the slope or slip face. When this happens, the dune form is stabilized, and the dune moves forward as a whole, sand being eroded from the windward side and deposited on the lee.

Angle of repose and the slip face

If, from meteorological measurements the regional rate of sand flow can be calculated, and if it is assumed that the dune has a simple cross section that migrates forward without change of form, a formula for the rate of movement of a dune that agrees with actual measurements can be derived. In Peru dunes have been observed to move at 30 metres per year (100 feet per year), and in California rates of 25 metres per year (82 feet per year) have been measured.

Dune patterns. Thus far it has been assumed that the wind is a homogeneous stream of air blowing from one constant direction. If this were so, long straight dunes oriented at right angles to the wind would result. But most dunes are neither straight nor at right angles to the wind, and this indicates that the winds are not a uniform stream or that they blow from different directions.

Barchan dunes (small crescent-shaped sand bodies) occur in areas where the regional wind blows consistently from one direction. Their crescentic shape must be due to spatial variations in wind velocity and the regular repetition of dune shapes and spacings when they are close together indicate that the variations in the wind are also regular. This is a property common to all bed forms. It is thought that flow of a fluid (air or water) arranges itself in long spiral vortices parallel to the direction of flow, which, with zones of faster and slower velocities arranged transverse to the flow, gives a regular sinuous pattern on the bed.

Where there is a continuous sand cover, a varied dune pattern results from the pattern of flow. The main forms are transverse ridges composed of alternating crescentic elements, like barchans, facing downwind, and other crescentic elements facing upwind. These enclose between them a regular pattern of small hollows. Superimposed on this are small straight ridges parallel with the flow. These elements form a network pattern that is extremely common in the great sand seas. The slip faces reach a maximum height of about 10 metres (33 feet), and the dunes are about 100 metres (330 feet) apart.

An important feature of sandy terrains is that their forms occur at a number of distinct sizes. Large features are covered with smaller ones, and the smaller ones are covered with ripples. Between these size groupings there are no features of intermediate size. This is an example of bed-form hierarchy; the two most important groups in this particular hierarchy are the dunes, which are seldom higher than about 20 metres (66 feet) or more than about 200 metres (660 feet) apart, and *draa* (a north Saharan term for large sand features), which can be over 200 metres high and are usually over one kilometre (0.6 mile) apart. In the larger sand seas there is usually a massive skeleton of *draa* sometimes arranged parallel to the apparent flow, in long ridges, and sometimes transverse to it in great sand waves. The *draa* are usually covered with a dune pattern. Within each of the size groups of the hierarchy (ripples, dunes, or *draa*) there are variations in size depending on grain size and wind velocity; for example, whereas most ripples are

Sand dunes in irregular patches that rise as high as 600 feet from the ground, Libyan Desert.
Aero Service Corporation, Division of Litton Industries

spaced only a few centimetres apart, "mega-ripples," built in very coarse sand, are spaced almost as far apart as small dunes; and whereas most dunes are about 100 metres apart, the low undulations of coarse sand on sand sheets are up to 500 metres apart.

Other dune forms can be related to variations in the overall wind direction, usually on a seasonal cycle. There is some evidence for example, that the linear *seif* dune, which has steep slopes on either side and a sharp sinuous summit, occurs in areas where two or more sand-carrying winds blow at an acute angle to each other, the alignment of the *seif* being that of the resultant of these winds. *Seif*, however, can have very puzzling patterns, such as two crossing directions, and meanders, which must be explained in other ways. Most *seif* occur in open desert resting on a coarse sand sheet.

Seif, reversing and other patterns

In some areas, winds from opposed directions blow at different seasons. In the San Luis Valley in Colorado, for example, westerly winds bring sand from the west for most of the year, but on the eastern side of the valley the sands meet easterly winds at some seasons, so that "reversing dunes" are formed, in which the slip faces face first in one direction and then in the other.

In the northwestern Sahara, the sand seas have a complex pattern of intersecting *draa* ridges, probably built by consistent seasonal combinations of winds, blowing over thousands of years. Where these patterns are particularly complex, they break up into regularly spaced pyramidal dunes of great size.

Distinct dunes are formed around topographic obstructions. Sheltered zones are found on the lee of small hills into which the sand migrates from the wind to form one or two trailing *seif*-like dunes, depending on the width of the hill. If the wind meets a high scarp or large hill massif, an "echo dune" is deposited on the upwind side separated from the scarp by a rolling eddy of air that keeps a corridor free of sand. Many oases and routeways are found in this kind of corridor. Echo dunes are the largest dunes in the desert, sometimes reaching a height of more than 400 metres (1,300 feet).

Most sand sheets (known in the Sahara as *serir*) have coarse bimodal sands and low undulating dune forms. Where there are large amounts of coarse sand, the *serir* may be almost completely flat. Some thin drifts of sand are found where the desert floor is too rough to allow dunes to form.

By courtesy of the Servicio Aerofotografico Nacional, Lima, Peru

Mega-barchan dune, Virú Valley, Peru.

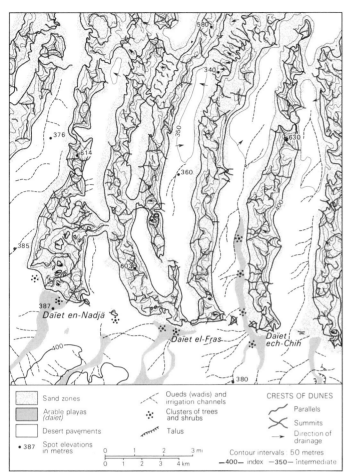

					CRESTS OF DUNES
▨	Sand zones	⟋⟍	Oueds (wadis) and irrigation channels		
▨	Arable playas *(daiet)*	⋰	Clusters of trees and shrubs	∿	Parallels
☐	Desert pavements	⏜	Talus	⤬	Summits
• 387	Spot elevations in metres			→	Direction of drainage

```
0    1    2    3 mi
0  1  2  3  4 km
```

Contour intervals : 50 metres
—400— index —350— intermediate

Sand ridges in the Great Eastern Erg, Algeria.

The role of vegetation. Dunes on coasts and in semi-arid areas have distinctive forms of two kinds: those built up around vegetation and those formed when the plant cover is destroyed. Winds blowing off a beach carry sand inland where the stems and fronds of plants slow it down so that the sand builds up a shore dune parallel to the beach. Some plants are adapted to live in these conditions, and in fact thrive on the continued supply of nutrients; marram grass (*Ammophila arenaria*), a native of northwestern Europe, is one of the best known of these dune-adapted plants and has been introduced to many coasts expressly to stabilize the dunes. On coasts where it did not exist before introduction, such as in the northwestern United States or on desert or wet tropical coasts where sand-fixing plants do not thrive, there are no typical shore dunes.

The supply of sand for dune formation is renewed on the beach by longshore drift in the sea. A wide tidal range, exposing a wide foreshore, encourages dunes, but on lakes such as Lake Michigan, the role of tides can be played by fluctuations in lake levels. Some shore dunes, for instance, in southwestern France, can grow to very great heights; but as with desert dunes, there is a stable height beyond which growth stops. On shores that are themselves being built out by the sea, a series of dunes parallel to the shore often forms. Dunes also form around plants in the desert where these are fed by subterranean water. The usual dune forms in such instances are isolated mounds around each plant and are known as coppice dunes or *nebkha*.

Shore dunes, even when vegetated, are very unstable. Breaches in the plant cover are enlarged by the wind into blowouts facing the wind. These are then further enlarged by erosion, often down to a hard bed or the water table; the sand blown out of them covers and kills the plants downwind so that a free dune may form, which then moves downwind, leaving trailing edges of sand on either side to form a U-shaped, or parabolic dune, eventu-

ally stabilized again with vegetation. A series of these dunes moving downwind may form "nested parabolics."

In semi-arid areas, hollows may be eroded by the wind in a similar way, and the eroded material then forms a U-shaped lunette on the downwind side. If the hollow is filled with water draining off the land, salt crystals, deposited when the water dries up, loosen the other deposits of the lake bed. Clay, silt, sand, and salt are then blown onto the lunette, which is later stabilized by recrystalization of the salts or by plants. Lunettes are found in west Texas, northern Algeria, and southern Australia.

Extensive as the active sand seas are, there are areas of dunes fixed by vegetation that are nearly as extensive. They serve as undeniable evidence that the areas in which they are found were once more arid and are interesting because they indicate the nature of former climatic changes and because they are of much more use to man than free dunes.

Fixed dunes

Fixed dunes occur in cool temperate climates such as North America or northern and eastern Europe, where they were formed beyond the edges of the ice during the last glaciation, when conditions were evidently cool and dry and when winds were intensified around the ice sheets. They also occur on the edges of the tropical and subtropical deserts, where they formed when the deserts expanded during the Pleistocene Epoch (10,000 to 2,500,000 years ago), and on the edges of the Soviet and Chinese deserts. On the North American high plains, in Hungary, and in Mongolia, the fixed sands have a cover of rich grassland. In Poland they are covered with coniferous forest. On the southern edges of the Sahara the grassland of the desert margins merges into a zone in which the gum arabic tree (*Acacia senegal*) is dominant and then into zones of thick impenetrable bush with broadleaved species in which the rainfall may reach 1,000 millimetres (40 inches) a year. Patterns of vegetation that are similar to those in the southern Sahara are found on the edges of the Kalahari, Indian, and Australian deserts.

The dune patterns on these fixed sands bear a close resemblance to those in active sand seas, except that their forms are rounded and subdued. Because relationships between the winds and forms of the active sands can only be assumed, conclusions about the changes in wind patterns since the fixed sands were formed must be tentative. In The Sudan, for example, it seems likely that the wind and rainfall belts were both some 450 kilometres (270 miles) south of their present positions at the height of the dune-building period. In Poland at the turn of the century, there were lengthy arguments between those who believed that the fixed dunes were barchans formed by strong easterly winds and those who, it now seems correctly, saw the accumulations as parabolic dunes formed by westerly winds.

Some coastal dunes also yield evidence of formerly different conditions. Ancient lake shores are shown to have existed in North Dakota, to the south of modern Lake Chad, and to the west of the lower White Nile by a series of fixed shore dunes. On the coasts of California, the modern dunes are formed on top of ancient dunes, which were connected with a different sea level in the recent past. In the Bahamas, carbonate dunes were built when the sea level was lower, and they since have been cemented and flooded by the sea to form the bases of many islands. In southeastern Australia, a whole series of ancient ridges is visible evidence for a progressive retreat of the sea.

SAND TERRAINS

Characteristics. The firm, gently undulating sand sheets that are ideal for motor transport contrast with the variable topography and treacherous surfaces of dunes; the latter are difficult to traverse even on camel. Dune surfaces have great contrasts in firmness due mainly to the way in which the sand is laid down. Most of the body of a dune consists of sand laid down on the slip face, for as the dune moves foreward this sand is constantly being re-exposed on the windward slope. These beds are very soft, in contrast to the flatbedded sands laid down on top of the dune and in the intervening hollows.

In few of the great sand seas are there extensive continuous areas of dunes. There are usually many corridors of firm sand sheet or desert floor on which travel is easy and routes often follow these in a tortuous pattern.

The surfaces of coastal and fixed dunes need to be treated with caution; the plant cover is usually fragile, and when it is destroyed by the passage of a few hooves or wheels, the sand beneath becomes a loose and difficult surface.

One valuable property of windblown sands is that they are highly permeable to water. The actual infiltration rate depends on several things: water penetrates more quickly into the slip-face-bedded sands than into flatbedded sands and into well sorted better than poorly sorted sands (since fine particles fill up the spaces between the coarse ones in the latter); and some humus substances can reduce the wettability of the soils if they coat the sand particles. Most sandy soils imbibe water easily, however, and the high air content of the upper soil insulates the water from evaporation. Plants, too, can remove water more easily from sandy than from heavier soils, and thus sandy soils often support the densest plant cover in arid and semi-arid areas. Sandy terrains have virtually no surface drainage.

Coastal dunes in temperate climates provide poor dry soils, but their permeability means that they can be used as storage reservoirs for domestic and industrial water supplies, as they are, to great advantage, in The Netherlands.

Economic importance. Although many desert sand seas are relatively unexplored, it is probable that they are of little agricultural or industrial value. They occur in areas of extreme aridity, most of which have been arid for millions of years, and their lack of vegetation cannot be attributed to depredation by man. Even if water became readily available, their poorly permeable soils would make them difficult to cultivate. They are unlikely to contain many mineable concentrations of minerals. Although gypsum sands are mined at present, they are of very limited extent; quartz for use as building sand and in glass manufacture occurs in vast quantities, but it is remotely situated, and foreseeable demands are quite likely to be minute when compared to the vastness of the sands.

Sand seas will probably be opened up in other ways. Many of the rocks beneath the barren sands do have valuable deposits of oil or minerals, and many are being opened up for the first time by prospecting and mining. As the world's population expands and as some of it becomes more affluent and claustrophobic, sand seas will probably become vast recreation parks as they are already in the United States. Dunes have many advantages for recreation: they have variety; they can absorb many people in relative privacy; they are virtually indestructible; they can be exciting for such sports as racing or exploring with especially equipped vehicles such as "dune buggies"; and they are dry and absorbent and for that reason are hygienic.

Agriculture on fixed dunes

Fixed dunes, on the other hand, support very dense agricultural populations, as in northern Nigeria and Senegal, where they produce huge amounts of groundnuts (peanuts). In Nebraska, pasture lands on fixed sands produce some of the world's finest cattle. Settled systems of agriculture, however, are less common on fixed sands than seminomadic cattle herding, although cattle grazing has its dangers on these soils. In recent years cattle numbers have grown very rapidly, and although deep wells have opened up new areas, overgrazing around the wells has meant that the vegetation cover has often been completely removed and consequently the sands have started to move again. Local customs have made it difficult to find the best plan for the wise use of these lands, but properly managed they provide a rich potential source of protein.

Temperate coastal dunes are seldom of use agriculturally, being more used for forestry or recreation. Too many human feet, however, like too many cattle hooves, can destroy the plant cover and so lead to blowouts and the loss of nearby agricultural land in the subsequent burial by moving sand. In The Netherlands, for example, this has to be watched very carefully because the dunes provide an essential protection from the sea for the farmland and cities behind. Coastal dunes occur near many large cities and are therefore convenient, if not ideal, building land. Parts of Liverpool, Ostend, The Hague, Durban, and much of San Francisco are built on coastal dunes. In some places the higher dunes are used as a convenient water reservoir for such cities.

BIBLIOGRAPHY

Desert dunes: R.A. BAGNOLD *The Physics of Blown Sand and Desert Dunes* (1941, reprinted 1960); Maps of the Sahara produced by the Institut Géographique National, Paris; A. WARREN, "A Bibliography of Desert Dunes and Associated Phenomena," in W.G. MCGINNIES and B.J. GOLDMAN (eds.), *Arid Lands in Perspective*, pp. 75–99 (1969); I.G. WILSON, "Aeolian Bedforms—Their Developments and Origins," *Sedimentology*, 19:173–210 (1972).

Fixed dunes: A.T. GROVE and A. WARREN, "Quaternary Landforms and Climate on the South Side of the Sahara," *Geogrl. J.*, 134:194–208 (1968).

Coastal dunes: W.S. COOPER, "The Coastal Sand Dunes of Oregon and Washington," *Mem. Geol. Soc. Am. 72* (1958), "Coastal Dunes of California," *ibid. 104* (1967).

(A.Wa.)

Sandstones

The weathering of rocks into their constituent mineral grains yields great quantities of sand-sized particles. This material is carried down rivers to the coast where it accumulates as dunes on beaches and as submarine bars, deltas, and other offshore deposits. Gradual consolidation converts such sand deposits into sandstone, which is one of the sedimentary rocks (*q.v.*).

Sandstones generally are defined as consisting mainly of grains between 0.06 and 2 millimetres (0.00234 and 0.078 inch) in diameter; they grade on the one hand into conglomerates (*q.v.*) and breccias and on the other into siltstones and shales (*q.v.*). When the proportion of shell fragments, oolites, and other biogenic material increases, they also grade into limestones.

Most sandstones are resistant to erosion, and they form about one-fourth of the sedimentary rocks of the earth's crust and thus create the backbone of many mountain ranges, such as the Appalachians, Carpathians, Pennines, and Appenines. Sandstone beds that are gently folded or nearly horizontal tend to form plains and uplands on which poor soils develop.

Sandstone components and colour

There are three basic components of sandstones. These are (1) detrital grains, mainly transported, sand-sized minerals such as quartz and feldspar; (2) a detrital matrix of clay or mud, which is absent in "clean" sandstones; and (3) a cement that is chemically precipitated in crystalline form from solution and that serves to fill up original pore spaces. The conversion of any sediment to rock is called diagenesis. Most diagenesis is caused by cementation, but some occurs by the recrystallization of clay minerals (*q.v.*). Some sandstones that have no cement and little or no clay matrix are loose enough to be crushed with the fingers. Sandstones bonded with calcite or iron oxide cements are moderately hard. The hardest of all sandstones are those in which the pore spaces have been completely filled with chemically precipitated quartz cement, particularly if this quartz is in crystallographic continuity with detrital quartz grains. In this event, the quartz has the strength that would be attributable to a single mass. The original, detrital quartz grain is separated from the overgrowth by a thin line of water bubbles, clay, or hematite (iron oxide). These thoroughly cemented, quartz-rich rocks, or quartzites, form some of the hardest, most resistant rocks in the earth's crust. The Tuscarora Quartzite of Silurian (395,000,000 to 420,000,000 years ago) age, for example, makes the high ridges in most of the Appalachian Mountains.

Other minerals that may occur as cement in sandstones include feldspar, gypsum, barite, dolomite, opal, pyrite, and chert, among others. Deep burial of sandstones may produce more unusual cements, such as zeolites (*q.v.*) or chlorite, and the original clay matrix may be recrystallized to micas (*q.v.*). Electron luminescence examination of thin sections of such formations can reveal special features of cementation that are not visible by any other means. For the identification of very fine-grained or complex minerals such as clays or zeolites, X-ray diffraction may be necessary.

The colour of a sandstone depends upon its detrital grains and bonding material. An abundance of potassium feldspar often gives a pink colour; this is true of many arkoses, which are feldspar-rich sandstones. Fine-grained, dark-coloured rock fragments, such as pieces of slate, chert, or andesite, however, give a salt-and-pepper appearance to a sandstone. Iron oxide cement imparts tones of yellow, orange, brown, or red, whereas calcite cement imparts a gray colour. A sandstone consisting almost wholly of quartz grains cemented by quartz may be glassy and white. A chloritic clay matrix gives a greenish-black colour and extreme hardness; such rocks are called gray-wackes (*q.v.*).

Formation of sandstones today

Sandstones occur in strata of all geologic ages. Much of man's understanding of the depositional environment of ancient sandstones comes from detailed study of sand bodies forming today. One of the clues to the origin is the overall shape of the entire sand deposit. Inland desert sands today cover vast areas as a uniform blanket; some ancient sandstones in beds a few hundred feet thick but 1,000 or more miles in lateral extent, such as the Mesozoic Nubian Sandstone of North Africa, also may have formed as blankets of desert sand. Deposits from alluvial fans (*q.v.*) form thick, fault-bounded prisms. River sands today form "shoestring-shaped" bodies, tens of feet thick, a few hundred feet wide, up to 100 or more miles long, and usually oriented perpendicularly to the shoreline. In meandering back and forth, a river may construct a wide swath of sand deposits, mostly accumulating on meander-point bars. Beaches, coastal dunes, and barrier bars also form "shoestring" sands, but these are parallel to the shore. Deltaic sands show a fanlike pattern of radial, thick, finger-shaped sand bodies interbedded with muddy sediments. Submarine sand bodies are diverse, reflecting the complexities of underwater topography and currents. They may form great ribbons parallel with the current; huge submarine "dunes" or "sand waves" aligned perpendicularly to the current; or irregular shoals, bars, and sheets. Some sands are deposited in deep water by the action of density currents (*q.v.*), which flow down submarine slopes by reason of their high sediment concentrations and, hence, are called turbidity currents. These characteristically form thin beds interbedded with shales; sandstone beds often are graded from coarse grains at the base to fine grains at the top of the bed and commonly have a clay matrix.

BEDDING STRUCTURE

One of the most fruitful methods of deciphering the environment of deposition and direction of transport of ancient sandstones is detailed field study of the sedimentary structures.

Bedding-plane markings and cross-bedding

Bedding in sandstones may be tens of feet thick, but it can range downward to paper-thin laminations, expressed by layers of clays, micas, heavy minerals, pebbles, or fossils. Flagstone breaks in very smooth, even layers a few inches thick and is used in paving. Thin, nearly horizontal lamination is characteristic of many ancient beach sandstones. Bedding surfaces of sandstones may be marked by ripples (almost always of subaqueous origin), by tracks and trails of organisms, and by elongated grains that are oriented by current flow (fossils, plant fragments, or even elongated sand grains). Sand grain orientation tends to parallel direction of the current; river-channel trends in fluvial sediments, wave-backwash direction in beach sands, and wind direction in aeolian sediments are examples of such orientation.

A great variety of markings, such as flutes and scour and fill grooves, can be found on the undersides of some sandstone beds. These markings are caused by swift currents during deposition; they are particularly abundant in sandstones deposited by turbidity currents.

Within the major beds, cross-bedding is common. This structure is developed by the migration of small ripples, sand waves, tidal-channel large-scale ripples, or dunes and consists of sets of beds that are inclined to the main horizontal bedding planes. Almost all sedimentary environments produce characteristic types of cross-beds; as one example, the lee faces of sand dunes (side not facing the wind) may bear cross-beds as much as 100 feet (35 metres) high and dipping 35°. This structure can be seen in modern desert dunes and in ancient dune sandstones such as the Jurassic Navajo Sandstone of the western United States. Cross-bedding that forms in river sands is generally six inches to three feet (0.174 to 1.04 metres) high and dips at angles of about 20°. Careful regional mapping of such cross-beds has contributed enormously to understanding of the directions of old shorelines, location of ancient landmasses, flow of river systems, and former wind belts.

Graded beds, slump structures, and fossils

Some sandstones contain series of graded beds. The grains at the base of a graded bed are coarse and gradually become finer upward, at which point there is a sharp change to the coarse basal layer of the overlying bed. Among the many mechanisms that can cause these changes in grain size are turbidity currents, but in general they can be caused by any cyclically repeated waning current.

After the sand is deposited, it may slide downslope or subside into soft underlying clays. This shifting gives rise to contorted or slumped bedding on a scale of inches to many tens of feet. Generally these are characteristic of unstable areas of rapid deposition.

Local cementation may result in concretions of calcite, pyrite, barite, and other minerals. These can range from sand crystals or barite roses to spheroidal or discoidal concretions tens of feet across.

The fossil content also is a useful guide to the depositional environment of sandstones. Desert sandstones usually lack fossils. River-channel and deltaic sandstones may contain fossil wood, plant fragments, fossil footprints, or vertebrate remains. Beach and shallow marine sands contain mollusks, arthropods, crinoids, and other marine creatures, though marine sandstones are much less fossiliferous than marine limestones. Deep-water sands are frequently devoid of skeletal fossils, although tracks and trails may be common. The fossils are not actually structures, of course, but the living organisms are able to produce these. Burrowing by organisms, for example, may cause small-scale structures, such as eyes and pods or tubules of sand.

TEXTURES

The texture of a sandstone is the sum of such attributes as the clay matrix, the size and sorting of the detrital grains, and the roundness of these particles. To evaluate this

Textural maturity and mineralogical composition of sandstones from various environments.

property, a scale of textural maturity that involved four textural stages was devised in 1951. These stages are described as follows.

Immature sandstones contain a clay matrix, and the sand-sized grains are usually angular and poorly sorted. This means that a wide range of sand sizes is present. Such sandstones are characteristic of environments in which sediment is dumped and is not thereafter worked upon by waves or currents. These environments include stagnant areas of sluggish currents such as lagoons (*q.v.*) or bay bottoms or undisturbed sea floor below the zone of wave or current action. Immature sands also form where sediments are rapidly deposited in subaerial environments, such as river floodplains, swamps, alluvial fans, or glacial margins. Submature sandstones are created by the removal of the clay matrix by current action. The sand grains are, however, still poorly sorted in these rocks. Submature sandstones are common as river-channel sands, tidal-channel sands, and shallow submarine sands swept by unidirectional currents. Mature sandstones are clay free, and the sand grains are subangular; but they are well sorted, that is, of nearly uniform particle size. Typically, these sandstones form in environments of current reversal and continual washing, such as on beaches (*q.v.*). Supermature sandstones are those that are clay free; well sorted; and, in addition, those in which the grains are well rounded. These sandstones probably formed mostly as desert dunes, where intense aeolian abrasion over a very long period of time may abrade sand grains to nearly spherical shapes.

More detailed study of texture, first accomplished in 1898, involved grain-size analysis, and the establishment of the following grain-size terms: 1–2 mm (0.039–0.078 in.), very coarse sand; 0.5–1.0 mm (0.019–0.039 in.), coarse sand; 0.25–0.5 mm (0.009–0.019 in.), medium sand; 0.125–0.25 mm (0.0045–0.009 in.), fine sand; and 0.062–0.125 mm (0.0022–0.0045 in.), very fine sand. For purposes of analysis, the cement is removed chemically, and the sandstone is carefully broken down into its constituent detrital grains. These grains are then filtered through a stack of sieves with fixed, decreasing mesh size. Size can also be measured by allowing the grains to settle in a water column (the larger grains settle more rapidly). From these analyses a size frequency distribution showing the weight of grains in each size class can be constructed. Often an analysis of a beach or river sand will show a typical Gaussian curve or bell-shaped size distribution. A logarithmic transformation (the φ scale) invented in 1934 greatly facilitates statistical analysis. The main parameters it measures are mean size, standard deviation (a measure of sorting), skewness (symmetry of the frequency distribution), and kurtosis (peakedness).

Such information is useful in identifying depositional environments. For example, dune sands in all parts of the world tend to be in the 0.12–0.25 millimetre (0.0022–0.0045 inch) mean size range, because sand of that size is easiest to move by winds. Desert floor sediments tend to be bimodal or polymodal, with two (or more) abundant sizes of grains with a gap in between. Dune and beach sands exhibit the best sorting, and river and shallow marine sands are less well sorted. Such sediments as glacial tills, river-floodplain deposits, and submarine sands in areas of sluggish currents have much poorer sorting. Skewness serves to separate beach sands, which are often negatively skewed (with a tail of coarse grains), from dune and river sands, which tend to be positively skewed (with a tail of fine grains). Kurtosis is valuable in identifying sediments that have come from a mixture of two materials, such as beach sands blown into a muddy lagoon.

Careful analysis of grain roundness and grain shape also can aid in distinguishing the high-abrasion environments of beach and especially dune sands from those of fluvial or marine sands. Rounding takes place much more rapidly in sands subjected to wind action (*q.v.*) than in water-laid sands. In general, coarser sand grains are better rounded than finer grains because the coarser ones hit bottom more frequently and also hit with greater impact during transport. Sand grains may also have polished, frosted,

pitted, or otherwise characteristic surfaces. These depend on the grain size, the agent of transport, and the amount of chemical attack. For example, polish can occur on medium-grained beach sands and fine-grained desert sands and can also be produced chemically by weathering processes.

MINERAL COMPOSITION

Mineralogical study of sandstones has proceeded along two distinct lines. One method involves cutting a thin section (0.03 millimetre [0.0012 inch] thick) from the rock for examination of the mineralogy, cementation, texture, and structures with a petrographic microscope. This thin section approach was first used in the 1870s. Another method is to disaggregate the sand and place the grains in a heavy liquid such as bromoform (density about 2.8). This concentrates the heavy minerals that are present in minute amounts (0.01 to 1 or 2 percent of the rock) for detailed microscopic study. These methods offer valuable clues to source area composition.

Although sandstones may be composed of any mineral, the most common mineral is quartz (SiO_2), which comprises about 80 percent of the average sandstone; a few sandstones, however, lack quartz entirely, whereas others contain more than 99 percent quartz. Microscopic study reveals a great many types of quartz, recognizable by their appearance in polarized light and by inclusions of gas or liquid bubbles or other substances. Volcanic quartz, various types of metamorphic quartz, hydrothermal quartz, and other varieties are known. Other detrital minerals of common occurrence are the feldspars and micas. The abundance of these chemically less resistant silicates has been used as a climatic indicator. Sand-sized fragments of older fine-grained rocks (*e.g.*, chert, slate, basalt) are common in many sandstones. Clay matrix, if present, may consist of the minerals illite, kaolinite, montmorillonite, or clay-sized micas. Some marine sandstones contain an abundance of pellets of glauconite (greensands) or phosphates in the form of bones, teeth, scales, or chemical precipitates. These sands are useful as fertilizers.

CLASSIFICATION OF SANDSTONES

There are many different systems of mineralogic classification of sandstones. The system presented here is that

By courtesy of R.L. Folk

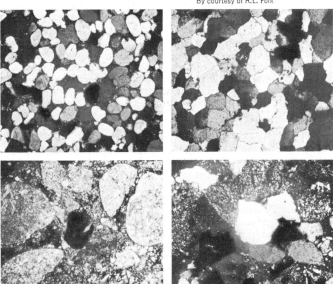

(Top left) Cambrian quartzarenite, cemented with calcite and typical of those formed originally as dune sands. (Top right) Silurian Tuscarora quartzite, a former beach sand. Quartz sand grains are well rounded and are completely cemented by quartz overgrowths visible as clear rims around the "dusty" detrital nuclei. (Bottom left) Submature calclithite of the Ordovician Marathon Formation. (Bottom right) Chert-arenite consisting of about 50 percent quartz and 50 percent chert (finely speckled). It probably is a channel sandstone derived from older sedimentary rocks. (All photographs magnified about 50 ×.)

of R.L. Folk (1966), based upon the concepts of P.D. Krynine, an American sedimentologist, and others. In it sandstones are divided into three main groups based on percentages of quartz, feldspar, and rock fragments. Clays are considered only in the textural part of the name (*e.g.*, clayey fine sandstone), and cements and accessory minerals are handled by descriptive adjectives. Rocks whose sand grains consist of more than 95 percent quartz are termed quartzarenites. If the sand grains consist of more than 25 percent feldspar, the rock is termed arkose; if the feldspar content is between 5 and 25 percent it is "subarkose." Sandstones with more than 25 percent rock fragments are called litharenites and are further subdivided according to the nature of the rock fragments (see below). "Sublitharenite" contains 5 to 25 percent rock fragments.

By courtesy of R.L. Folk

(Top left) Immature Devonian quartzarenite with clay matrix. This rock originated from turbidity-current deposition in a deepwater marine basin. (Top right) Precambrian submature arkose with angular and poorly sorted grains. (Bottom left) Devonian phyllarenite consisting of about 50 percent quartz and 50 percent metamorphic rock fragments (speckled grains). (Bottom right) Carboniferous volcanic arenite with clay matrix and poorly sorted grains of volcanic rock fragments containing tiny feldspar laths. This sandstone was deposited in an island arc area. (All photographs magnified about 50 ×.)

Quartz-arenites

Quartzarenites are usually white but may be any other colour; cementation by hematite, for example, makes them red. They are usually well sorted and well rounded (supermature) and often represent ancient dune, beach, or shallow marine deposits. Characteristically, they are ripple marked or cross-bedded and occur as very widespread thin blanket sands. On chemical analysis, some of these are found to contain more than 99 percent SiO_2 (silicon dioxide, or silica). Most commonly they are cemented with quartz, but calcite and iron oxide are also common cements.

This type of sandstone is widespread in stable areas of continents surrounding the craton (a stable area), such as central North America (St. Peter Sandstone, Ordovician), central Australia, or the Russian Platform, and are particularly common in Paleozoic strata. Quartzarenites have formed in the past when large areas of subcontinental dimensions were tectonically stable (not subject to uplift or deformation) and of low relief, so that extensive weathering (*q.v.*) could take place, accompanied by prolonged abrasion and sorting. This process eliminated all the unstable or readily decomposed minerals such as feldspar or rock fragments and concentrated pure quartz together with trace amounts of such resistant heavy minerals as zircon and tourmaline. Occasionally, deeply subsiding basins adjoining stable cratons were filled with many thousands of feet of quartzarenite. Quartzarenites also form in geosynclines (large

depositional troughs that are loci of mountain building) if the source area is sufficiently stable to permit beach abrasion and chemical weathering to remove rock fragments and feldspars. Apparently this was the origin of the Tuscarora Quartzite (Silurian) of the Appalachians.

Arkosic sandstones are of two types. The most common of these is a mixture of quartz, potash feldspar, and granitic rock fragments. Chemically, these rocks are 60–70 percent SiO_2 and 10–15 percent aluminum oxide (Al_2O_3), with significant amounts of potassium (K), sodium (Na), and other elements. This type of arkosic sandstone, or arkose, can form wherever block faulting of granitic rocks occurs, given rates of uplift, erosion, and deposition that are so great that chemical weathering is outweighed and feldspar can survive in a relatively unaltered state. These rocks are usually reddish, generally immature, very poorly sorted, and frequently interbedded with arkose conglomerate; alluvial fans or fluvial aprons are the main depositional environments. The Triassic Newark Group of Connecticut is a classic example of this type of arkosic sandstone.

Arkosic sandstones

Arkoses also form under desert (or rarely Arctic) conditions in which the rate of chemical decomposition of the parent granite or gneiss is very slow. These arkoses generally are well sorted and rounded (supermature) and show other desert features, such as aeolian cross-beds (of wind origin), associated gypsum, and other evaporitic minerals. The Precambrian Torridonian Arkose of Britain is thought to be of desert origin. Basal Sands deposited on a granitic-gneissic craton (stable continental interior) are also usually arkosic. Subarkose sandstones (*e.g.*, Millstone Grit, Carboniferous of England) have a feldspar content that is diminished by more extensive weathering or abrasion or by dilution from nonigneous source rocks.

Less commonly, arkoses may contain plagioclase feldspar (sodic to calcic types) as the dominant variety. These generally result from volcanic activity and are frequently associated with volcanic rock fragments and a chlorite matrix.

Litharenites occur in several subvarieties, but they are normally gray or of salt-and-pepper appearance because of the inclusion of dark-coloured rock fragments. Most commonly, fragments of metamorphic rocks such as slate, phyllite, or schist predominate; this dominance produces the phyllarenite variety of sandstone. If volcanic rock fragments such as andesite and basalt are most abundant, the rock is a volcanic arenite. It is termed a vitric arenite if glass predominates. These sandstones are transitional to tuffs (derived from volcanic dust and ash). Finally, if chert or carbonate rock fragments prevail, the rock is a chert arenite or calclithite. Texturally immature litharenites of Paleozoic age (225,000,000 to 570,000,000 years ago), if deposited in flysch sequences (rapidly deposited sands in Alpine zones) and involved in tectonic activity, may become extremely hard and have a dark greenish-black colour. These rocks are further described and discussed in the article GRAYWACKES.

Litharenites and graywackes

Litharenites are a diverse family of rocks that in general were formed by rapid deposition under unstable tectonic conditions. Among the subvarieties, the phyllarenite is most common. It is a typical sandstone of geosynclines in which a low-rank (low temperatures and pressures of origin) metamorphic source of fold mountains with slates and phyllites has been exposed. These sandstones are usually rich in mica and texturally immature; the SiO_2 content is 60–70 percent; Al_2O_3 is 15 percent; and potassium, sodium, iron, calcium, and magnesium are present in lesser amounts. Most examples are deposited as fluvial apron, deltaic, coastal-plain, and shallow marine sandstones, interbedded with great thicknesses of shale and frequently with beds of coal or limestone. If laid down in an oxidizing environment, such as a well-drained river system, they are reddish (*e.g.*, Devonian Catskill Formation of New York or the Devonian Old Red Sandstone of England). Many sandstones of the Appalachians are phyllarenites, and they are common in the Carpathians and many other mountain chains. Heightened abrasion in the beach environment eliminates the soft rock fragments, and the rock may pass into a subphyllarenite; these are often good oil reservoirs, such as the Devonian Bradford Sand of Pennsylvania.

Volcanic arenites occur mainly in unstable, island-arc volcanic regions, such as the Paleozoic Tasman Geosyncline of Australia, and they also are deposited as continental beds derived from the erosion of volcanic terranes. Chert arenites and calclithites result from rapid erosion of uplifted chert and carbonate mountain tracts, respectively. Many of these are alluvial fan deposits that front areas of intense faulting. Calclithites are common among the younger sandstones of the Alps and Slovak Carpathians.

The study of heavy minerals reveals many details about changes in source area and climate and aids in the correlation of sandstones. Quartzarenites contain only the most durable and chemically stable heavy minerals, such as tourmaline, zircon, and magnetite; yet these minerals may be present in a great number of varieties based upon colour, shape, and inclusions. Arkose and litharenite specimens often have upward of 20 species of heavy minerals, such as rutile, pyroxene, epidote, amphibole, kyanite, staurolite, and monazite. More than 100 heavy minerals are known to occur in sandstones, and in some places (Florida, Brazil, Queensland) they form black sand beaches from which the minerals can be commercially mined. In sea-bottom sediment, heavy minerals occur in distinct geographic provinces, indicating derivation from diverse source areas and revealing the direction of marine currents.

Special types of sandstones

Certain types of sandstones are defined by special features; they may have any mineral composition and form in a wide range of environments. Flysch was originally a European term for thick sequences of rhythmically interbedded sandstone and shale in beds a fraction of an inch to several feet thick. Most workers in geology believe that the sands have been deposited by turbidity currents; the beds are thought to fill deep-water marine geosynclines with rapid sediment influx fed by rising mountain chains.

Molasse is also a European term. It refers to sandstones that are deposited on top of flysch. They are coarser grained than flysch; tend to be shallow marine, fluvial, or alluvial fan deposits; and are thought by workers to represent the peak of the mountain-building, when mountains are at their maximum height. In theory, as a mountain chain rises, the resulting deposits should grade from deep-water dark shales into flysch sands and shales, and finally into continental, molasse sands and conglomerates. Redbed is a general term referring to red shales, sandstones, and conglomerates. The problem of the significance and origin of the red colour has intrigued geologists for more than 100 years. Doubtless this type of sediment can originate in many ways, the only requisite being survival of the red hematite (iron oxide) pigment in an oxidizing environment. Redbeds form in many environments, from alluvial fans to fluvial, deltaic, and shallow marine areas. Some geologists think that redbeds are the result of hot desert climates, whereas other scientists believe that hot humid climates with seasonal rainfall are responsible for them; still other investigators think that they are caused by postdepositional alteration not necessarily related to climate.

USES OF SANDSTONES

Sandstone reservoirs

The most valuable aspect of sandstone depends on its natural storage capacity for underground fluids: water, oil, and natural gas. Many sandstones contain an interconnected spongelike network of tiny pores. Porosity is a measure of the total volume of holes in the rock and may range up to 35 percent for some sandstones, although an average oil sand has 10–20 percent porosity. Permeability is a measure of the rate at which a fluid may pass through a rock and is greater if the pores are large and well interconnected. Both permeability and porosity are at a maximum in coarser sands that are well sorted and lack both clay matrix and chemical cement. Many sandstones are so tightly bonded with clay or cement that they are for practical purposes devoid of useful porosity and are use-

less as fluid reservoirs (see also PETROLEUM; GROUND-WATER).

Approximately half the world's oil comes from sandstone strata. A typical porous sandstone is folded and faulted by tectonic movements. One common site of occurrence of oil is in anticlines (arch-shaped folds), wherein the three fluids arrange themselves in order of density, with water filling the pores at greatest depths, then oil, and finally gas on top. Early oil prospectors concentrated on searching for oil in anticlines. Another type of oil trap is one in which a sandstone gradually decreases in porosity in a lateral direction, and the migration of oil is stopped at the porosity–permeability barrier where an oil pool may accumulate. Most good oil sands are of deltaic, beach, or shallow marine origin.

Sandstones provide a very valuable reservoir of water. The Dakota Sandstone in the western United States provides artesian-well water for a widespread area of the Great Plains. After the water falls as rain in the Rocky Mountains and percolates into the surface outcrop of the Dakota Sandstone there, then it travels through the sandstone underground for 1,000 miles (1,600 kilometres) to the east, where (through deep wells) it is brought to the surface for use in irrigation. Sandstone aquifers (water-bearing strata) are of great importance in most developed countries.

Building stone and glass sands

An important use of sandstones is in the construction industry. Relatively clay-free, little-cemented sands or sandstones are crushed and sieved for use in concrete, plaster, or as fill in the manufacture of bricks, asphalt paving, etc. Such sandstones should be free of soft constituents such as slate fragments and reactive minerals such as pyrite or opal. Sandstones that are readily split (such as flagstones) and of attractive colour are used as building stone (e.g., Triassic arkose "brownstone" of New York) or paving stones. Such sandstones should be resistant to weathering and should have easy workability combined with high crushing strength. A former use was as millstones and grindstones (Millstone Grit of England; Berea Sandstone of Ohio).

Glass sand requires easily crushable, medium-grained quartzarenite sandstones of the highest purity, often over 99 percent SiO_2 and particularly low in iron oxides and aluminum (under 0.1 percent and 0.2 percent, respectively). The Devonian Oriskany Sandstone of West Virginia and Pennsylvania supports an important glass industry. Ganister is a tough, quartz-cemented sandstone used as firebrick in industrial furnaces.

Certain sandstones are used as a source of commercially valuable heavy minerals (titanium, zirconium, rare earths), and some sandstones in the American Southwest are cemented with uranium minerals and form a valuable ore of this element.

BIBLIOGRAPHY. F.J. PETTIJOHN, *Sedimentary Rocks*, 2nd ed. (1957), the most thorough general work on sedimentary rocks; F.H. HATCH and R.H. RASTALL, *Petrology of the Sedimentary Rocks*, 4th ed. rev. by J. TREVOR GREENSMITH (1965), a concise summary of sandstones; A.V. CAROZZI, *Microscopic Sedimentary Petrography* (1960), on the study of sedimentary rocks in thin section; R.L. FOLK, *Petrology of Sedimentary Rocks* (1968), a general work in analytical techniques and sandstone genesis; P.D. KRYNINE, "The Megascopic Study and Field Classification of Sedimentary Rocks," *J. Geol.*, 56:130–165 (March 1948), the most important early sandstone classification, relating their properties to tectonics.

(R.L.F.)

San Francisco

San Francisco holds a secure place in the United States' romantic dream of itself—a cool, elegant, handsome, worldly seaport whose steep streets offer breathtaking views of one of the world's great bays. San Franciscans, according to the dream, are sophisticates whose lives hold full measures of such civilized diversions as music, art, and good food. Their city is a magic place, almost an island, saved by its location and its history from the overpowering ugliness that allegedly afflicts so much of the rest of urban California.

Flavour of the city

For all the truth there may be in this picture, there is, of course, also another San Francisco in which the per capi-

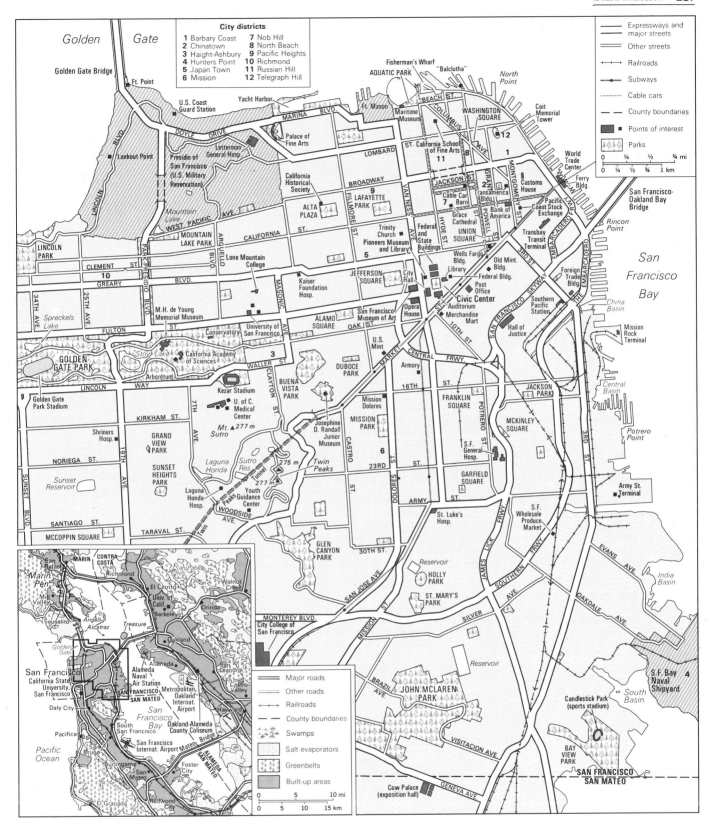

Central San Francisco and (inset) its metropolitan area.

ta consumption of alcohol is the highest of any U.S. city, the suicide rate is twice the national average, and the divorce rate is several times that of New York City. San Francisco is clearly a city in which the tensions between the dream and the reality have, from its beginnings, demanded a high price.

Furthermore, since World War II, San Francisco has had to come to grips with the common urban problems of the latter half of the 20th century: pollution of both the air and the water; the uglification that comes from ram-

pant building, violence, and vandalism; and the decay of the inner city. San Francisco has been shrinking as families, mainly white, mainly middle class, have moved to its suburbs, leaving the city to a population that, viewed statistically, tends to be older, less married, more probably less white than the stereotype has it. Every third San Franciscan is, in the sterile term of the census taker, "nonwhite"—black, Oriental, Filipino, Samoan, or American Indian. Many others are immigrants from Spanish America. Their dreams increasingly demand a realization that has little to do with the romantic dream of San Francisco.

But both the dreams and the realities are important, for they are interwoven in the fabric of the city that might be called Paradox-by-the-Bay.

THE GROWTH OF THE METROPOLIS

The explorers and early settlers. It is extraordinary that the site of San Francisco should have been discovered by land instead of from the sea, for San Francisco Bay is one of the most splendid natural harbours of the world, and great captains and explorers sailed unheeding past the entrance—Juan Rodríguez Cabrillo (1542–43), Sir Francis Drake (1578), Sebastián Vizcaíno (1602). In 1769 a scouting party from an expedition led by the Spanish explorer Gaspar de Portolá looked down from a hilltop onto a broad body of water, the first white men known to have seen San Francisco Bay. It was not until August 5, 1775, that the first Spanish ship, the "San Carlos," commanded by Lieut. Juan Manuel de Ayala, turned eastward between the headlands, breasted the ebbing tide, and dropped anchor just inside the harbour mouth. (Though it is possible that Drake may have entered the bay, most evidence is against it.)

Settlers from Monterey, under Lieut. José Joaquin Moraga and the reverend Francisco Palóu, established themselves at the tip of the San Francisco peninsula the next year. The military post (which remains in service as the Presidio of San Francisco, a major U.S. Army installation) was founded September 17, 1776, and the Mission San Francisco de Asis (later renamed the Mission Dolores) heard its first mass on October 9.

Almost half a century later, a village sprang up on the shore of Yerba Buena Cove, two miles east of the mission. The pioneer settler was an Englishman, Capt. William Anthony Richardson, who in 1835 cleared a plot of land and erected San Francisco's first dwelling—a tent made of four pieces of redwood and a ship's foresail. In the same year, the United States tried unsuccessfully to buy San Francisco Bay from the Mexican government, having heard reports from whalers and captains in the hide-and-tallow trade that the great harbour held bright commercial possibilities. Richard Henry Dana, whose ship entered the bay in 1835, recalled in *Two Years Before the Mast* (1840) that "If California ever becomes a prosperous country, this bay will be the centre of its prosperity."

The Americans had to wait only another 11 years. After fighting began along the Rio Grande, Capt. John B. Montgomery sailed the sloop of war "Portsmouth" into the bay on July 10, 1846, anchored in Yerba Buena Cove, and went ashore with a party of sailors and marines to raise the U.S. flag in the plaza. On January 30, 1847, Yerba Buena was renamed San Francisco, which was regarded as a more propitious name for the town's future development.

The white population of Yerba Buena had been reported as 25 to 30 in 1844. In 1846, the school board counted 700 whites (half of them American) and 150 Indians, Negroes, and Hawaiians. Two years later, just before the discovery of gold on the American River, the town had grown to about 200 shacks and adobes inhabited by about 800 white people.

The city of the '49ers. With the discovery of gold, the history of San Francisco picks up pace and direction. The modest village was at first almost entirely deserted as its population scrambled inland to the Mother Lode, and then it exploded into one of the most extraordinary cities ever constructed. Some 40,000 gold hunters arrived by sea, another 30,000 plodded across the Great Basin, and still another 9,000 moved north from Mexico. By 1851, more than 800 ships rode at anchor in the cove, deserted by their crews.

Everybody except the miners got rich. Eggs sold for $1 apiece, and downtown real estate claimed prices that would almost hold their own in the inflation of the 1970s. Until the bubble burst in the Panic of 1857, 50,000 San Franciscans became rich and went bankrupt, cheated and swindled one another, and took to the pistol and knife all

too readily. As *The Sacramento Union* noted in 1856, there had been "some fourteen hundred murders in San Francisco in six years, and only three of the murderers hung, and one of these was a friendless Mexican." Two vigilance committees (1851 and 1856) responded to the challenge with crude and extralegal justice, hanging four men apiece as an example to the others.

In 1859 silver was discovered in the Nevada Territory. The exploitation of the Comstock Lode, which eventually yielded $300,000,000, turned San Francisco from a frontier boomtown into a metropolis whose leading citizens were bankers, speculators, and lawyers who dressed their ladies in Paris gowns and ate and drank in splendid restaurants and great hotels.

San Francisco then was by all accounts an intoxicating city whose many charms moved the historian-moralist B.E. Lloyd to advise parents in 1876

to look closer to their daughters, for they know not the many dangers to which they are exposed . . . and to mildly counsel their sons, for when upon the streets of this gay city they are wandering among many temptations.

The 1860s and 1870s saw the birth of the modern San Francisco, which has for 100 years laid claim with some justice to being the Athens, Paris, and New York of the West but which never completely lost the mark of its wild beginning. As Rudyard Kipling was to observe after he visited the city in the 1890s, "San Francisco is a mad city, inhabited for the most part by perfectly insane people whose women are of remarkable beauty."

San Francisco's growth in the first half of the 20th century was shaped by two cataclysmic events. The first of these was the great earthquake and fire of 1906, which destroyed the central business district. Between 1906 and 1910, however, the city rebuilt atop its ashes. The other cataclysm was World War II, during which hundreds of thousands of servicemen passed through San Francisco on their way to the war in the Pacific, and some 500,000 war workers settled temporarily in the cities around the bay. This was the beginning of the great postwar surge in the area's permanent population, which saw San Francisco become the centre of a metropolitan area of nine counties and more than 4,000,000 people.

THE CONTEMPORARY CITY

Physical characteristics. *Layout of city and bay.* Hilly, roughly square, and 44.6 square miles (116 square kilometres) in area, San Francisco occupies the northern tip of a peninsula. To its south are the bedroom suburbs of San Mateo County; to the east and northeast is the bay; to the west and northwest lies the Pacific Ocean.

The most prominent of San Francisco's famous hills are Twin Peaks, Mt. Davidson, and Mt. Sutro, all over 900 feet (270 metres) in height. The best known are Nob Hill, where the wealthy "nobs" built extravagant mansions in the 1870s, and Telegraph Hill, which once looked down on the Barbary Coast, a neighbourhood alive with gaudy wickedness. Thanks to the pioneer planners' prejudice in favour of a squared-off grid, the downtown streets march intrepidly up precipitous slopes, terrifying newly arrived drivers, making the cable cars something more than sentimental anachronisms, and providing splendid views of the bay. *The hills and dizzying streets*

San Francisco Bay is a drowned river valley, submerged during the melting of the last glacial ice sheet. Enthusiastic and profitable filling of the tidelands has reduced its area from about 700 square miles in 1880 to a mere 435 square miles at mean high tide. More than half of the bay is still fillable, but in 1965 the state legislature created the Bay Conservation and Development Commission to control further landfill projects. At its widest point, the bay measures 13 miles and, at its deepest, in the Golden Gate channel, 357 feet. The maximum daily flow of water through the Golden Gate into the Pacific is seven times the flow of the Mississippi River at its mouth.

Within the 93.1 square miles of water lying inside the city limits are the natural islands of Alcatraz and Yerba Buena and man-made Treasure Island, created for a world's fair in 1939 and soon turned into a naval base. Alcatraz (Spanish: "pelican") was from 1934 until 1962

The San Francisco Bay Area. At upper right is the San Francisco–Oakland Bay Bridge, which tunnels through Yerba Buena Island.
George Hunter

the most notorious maximum-security, "escape-proof" prison in the United States. In 1970, after the decaying cell blocks had been given up by the Federal Bureau of Prisons, the island was invaded by a multi-tribal force of Indians who asserted their rights to abandoned federal property until they were forcibly evicted in 1971.

Climate. Winter in San Francisco is rainy and mild, the spring sunny and mild, the summer foggy and cool, and the fall sunny and warm. The average mean minimum temperature is 51° F (11° C), the average mean maximum, 63° F (17° C). The mean rainfall, almost all of which occurs between November and April, is about 21 inches (790 millimetres). The sun shines during two-thirds of the possible daylight hours. The most characteristic feature of the weather, however, is the summer fog, which lies low over the city until midday, creating consternation among the tourists shivering in seersuckers and cotton prints. This fog is a phenomenon of temperature contrasts created when warm, moist ocean air comes in contact with cold water welling up from the ocean bottom along the coast.

Building and nature's demolition. The central business district, the financial district, North Beach, and Chinatown occupy the site of the Gold Rush city, expanded by progressive fillings along the waterfront. The bones of many a ship deserted in 1849 now lie under business buildings several blocks inland. To the west, at the approach to the Golden Gate Bridge, lies the Presidio, green and parklike although it is still a military garrison. South of the Presidio are the 1,017 acres of Golden Gate Park, reclaimed from a onetime sandy desert. The rest of San Francisco is largely comprised of the neighbourhoods, from Pacific Heights, in which the old, monied families live, to Hunter's Point, which is 86 percent black.

In the late 1960s and early 1970s, a great change, which has been described as the Manhattanization of San Francisco, became apparent and has been both welcomed and excoriated. The financial district in particular has seen one tall building after another rise in a city in which, for generations, few buildings were higher than 20 stories. Among the new skyscrapers are the Bank of America building (52 stories) and the Transamerica Corporation building (48 stories and a 212-foot spire), which rises to a point like a fantastically elongated pyramid. Between 1967 and 1969 the total valuation of authorized high-rise projects in the Bay Area rose from $18,500,000 to $226,100,000. As the architect Frank Lloyd Wright once noted: "Only San Francisco could survive what you people are doing to it."

Concern has also arisen from the experience that San Francisco shares with no other U.S. city—destruction by earthquake. Severe quakes had been felt in 1864, 1898, and 1900, but it was not until 5:13 AM of April 18, 1906, that the rocky masses of the San Andreas Fault, the greatest fracture anywhere on the Earth's crust, heaved violently and doomed San Francisco as it then existed. The quake was followed by a fire that destroyed the centre of town and burned on until April 21, when the ashes were wetted down by rain. Four square miles, making up 512 blocks in the centre of town, were gone, along with 28,000 buildings and a total property value of about $500,000,000. Perhaps 700 people died; 250,000 were left homeless. Survivors camped in Golden Gate Park. An Eastern newspaperman, celebrating the survival of a local distillery, composed the verse, "If, as they say, God struck the town/ For being over-frisky,/ Why did He burn the churches down/ But spare Hotaling's whisky?"

The lore of the earthquake and fire has become overlaid with much sentiment, but in recent years seismologists and structural engineers have been reminding San Franciscans that it could happen again. There have been charges that the new office towers could not withstand another quake like the one in 1906 and that the next great rumbling of the San Andreas Fault may take a vastly greater toll.

The people. The 1970 census counted some 716,000 San Franciscans, less than the 740,000 of 1960 and the 775,000 of 1950. By ethnic group, the 1970 population included 511,000 whites, 96,000 blacks, 59,000 Chinese, 25,000 Filipinos, 12,000 Japanese, 2,900 American Indians, and 10,000 people of other origins. Among the

The great earthquake and fire of 1906

whites were 51,602 people with Spanish surnames, most of them comparatively recent immigrants. The original settlers—the Spanish and Mexican families who held land grants on the shores of the bay—disappeared into the mists of history, done out of their holdings by aggressive and land-hungry Americanos.

Americans and Europeans. The pattern of immigration into San Francisco during the latter half of the 19th century was significantly different from that of anywhere else in the United States. The waves of newcomers included not only native-born Americans moving west but also Europeans arriving directly by ship without previous Americanization along the Eastern Seaboard. The demography of the Gold Rush city was summed up concisely by a real-estate firm that advertised that it could "transact business in the English, French, German, Spanish and Italian languages."

San Francisco remains one of the two most European of American cities—New Orleans is the other—and surely the most Mediterranean. The Italians are still the dominant European minority, with 41,000 Italian-born San Franciscans reported in 1970, followed by Germans, Irish, and British.

The blacks. Before World War II about 20,000 blacks lived in the entire Bay Area, about 4,000 of them in San Francisco. The 24-fold increase during the next 30 years was set in motion by the war, which brought at least 500,000 war workers to the Bay Area's shipyards and other industries. Among them were tens of thousands from the South, who settled mainly in San Francisco, Oakland, and Richmond. In San Francisco they moved into the old "carpenter gothic" houses in the blocks around Fillmore Street, vacated when the Japanese were driven into wartime internment camps. The Fillmore district and the Hunter's Point housing project are decaying slums afflicted with the full gamut of social problems that come from poverty, inadequate education, unemployment, official neglect, and all the frustrations that grow out of desperate conditions of life. An increasing number of black men and women have become prominent in the city's life, however—a state assemblyman, a county supervisor, the president of the school board, a newspaper publisher, and numerous clergymen, educators, physicians, and civil servants.

The Chinese. Chinatown, which is said to be the largest Chinese community outside of Asia, is also probably the least understood minority community in the city. The colourful shops and restaurants of Grant Avenue mask a slum of crowded tenements and sweatshops that has the highest population density in an already densely populated city. Increasingly, those Chinese who can escape do so, into North Beach, hitherto predominantly Italian, onto the nearby slopes of Russian Hill, or into the Richmond district north of Golden Gate Park. Those who cannot move include many recent immigrants from Hong Kong, trapped by their ignorance of English.

The Japanese. Never as large as Chinatown, the Japanese community of San Francisco was wiped out at a single stroke by the infamous Executive Order 9066 of 1942, which sent them, foreign-born and native alike, into "relocation centers" that were, in all but name, concentration camps. The present centre of the Japanese community is Japan Town (Nihonmachi), a few blocks east of Fillmore Street. There, an ambitious new trade and cultural centre has risen, with restaurants, a hotel, shops, and business establishments. Though the rising generation of Japanese-Americans go to Japan Town as visitors, bound for a birthday dinner or to buy imported goods, their own roots are elsewhere.

The Spanish-speaking. Few visitors see the Mission district, which is a great irony, because the historic origins of the city extend to Spain and Mexico and the Spanish-speaking population rivals the Chinese as the second-greatest ethnic minority.

Before World War II the Mission district, named for the Mission Dolores, was principally blue collar and Irish. The Irish have largely been replaced by Spanish-speaking immigrants, mainly from Central America and Mexico. Living among them are pockets of American Indians and Samoans. Hampered by language and cultural difficulties, the Spanish-speaking San Franciscans are found in service occupations such as restaurants and hotels, from which they are struggling to escape.

The Filipinos. The Filipino community, despite its size, is virtually invisible, for, unlike the minorities who live in clearly defined neighborhoods, the Filipinos impinge on the visible city only in the form of a few blocks of modest shops on the edge of Chinatown. Culturally and educationally handicapped in a world in which the power lies with English-speaking whites, they have yet to assert themselves.

Economic life. The Gold Rush and the Comstock madness established San Francisco as the premier city of the West, known from the Oregon border to the pueblo of Los Angeles simply as the City. It is still a great port, the financial and administrative capital of the West, and a substantial centre for commerce and manufacturing.

In 1970, San Francsico employed more people in the service occupations (over 110,000) than in any other officially reported category. This reflects, among other things, the importance of tourism in the city's economy. Wholesale and retail trade followed and then governmental employment; finance, insurance, and real estate; transportation, communications, and utilities; manufacturing and construction. The total figure came to some 535,000 employed workers. The total personal income of San Franciscans in 1969 represented an increase of about 68 percent over that of 1960.

From its beginnings as a port of call in the hide-and-tallow trade and, later, as the home port of the Pacific whale fishery, San Francisco has always been acutely conscious of the importance of shipping. A century ago, ships sailed around Cape Horn or from the Isthmus of Panama, and "steamer day" was a civic institution; after 1914, cargo and passenger vessels arrived from the East by way of the Panama Canal. In 1867, the Pacific Mail Steamship Company opened the first transpacific service, sailing from San Francisco to Yokohama and Hong Kong.

Imports and exports passing through the San Francisco Customs District in 1969 made the combined ports of San Francisco Bay—San Francisco, Oakland, Alameda, Sacramento, and Stockton—the eighth most active international port in the country. As in the case of other material things, however, San Francisco has fallen behind Los Angeles, which ranks even higher. The chief source of imports was Japan, holding a giant 33 percent of the trade, followed by West Germany. In 1969 the greatest number of ships arriving flew the U.S. flag, followed by vessels of Norwegian and Japanese registry.

Manufacturing is the main source of wage and salary income in the Bay Area. In San Francisco, in which manufacturing is a lesser source of income, the principal industries are food processing and printing and publishing, while the aerospace and electronics industries are strong in the cities of the peninsula.

A financial centre since the first pinch of gold dust was exchanged for hard cash, San Francisco is the seat of the Pacific Coast Stock Exchange—which opens at 7:00 AM in order to keep pace with New York City's Wall Street —as well as the headquarters of such banks as the Bank of America, the largest in the country. In banking activity, San Francisco ranks second only to New York.

San Francisco has, rightly, the reputation of being a strong union town. Older union members still remember Bloody Thursday, July 5, 1934, when two strikers were killed in a pitched battle with police along the waterfront. The strike spread from the longshoremen and seamen until 127,000 union workers walked off their jobs in a general strike. The settlement brought the longshoremen their first union hiring hall. Continuing union strength was evident in the prolonged dock strike of 1971–72.

Transportation and services. Los Angeles long ago surrendered unconditionally to the automobile; San Francisco has on occasion rebelled and found it possible to oppose "progress." A monument to this revolt is the elevated Embarcadero Freeway, which stops dead as if sliced off by a guillotine. Again, angry citizens in 1964 defeated the state highway commission when it threatened to run a freeway through the "panhandle" of Golden Gate Park.

Among the serious problems that remain is periodic smog, produced mainly by the more than 2,000,000 cars in the area. (An air-pollution-control district was formed in 1955.) Another is that access to San Francisco from its commuter towns is largely by a network of freeways that are anything but free at rush hours. Travel from the East Bay cities of Oakland and Berkeley and from Marin County to the north is over two great but overburdened bridges. Completed in 1936, the 4¼-mile-long San Francisco-Oakland Bay Bridge consists of two silver spans, one suspension and one cantilever, that meet at Yerba Buena Island and that on an average day in 1970 carried about 165,000 cars. The orange-red Golden Gate Bridge, leading north to Marin County, followed in 1937. On an average day in 1970 it carried 90,000 cars. A pure suspension bridge, its 4,200-foot centre span was, until recently, the longest such span in the world.

The once-busy ferries

Until the ferries were doomed by the bridges, San Francisco was served by a great network of ferry routes whose splendid vessels were said to deliver more passengers, about 50,000,000 a year, to the Ferry Building at the foot of Market Street than arrived at any other transportation depot except Charing Cross in London. Only after the bridges began to choke with traffic did San Franciscans realize what they had lost, and the ferries are now returning, on a smaller scale, between San Francisco and Marin County.

A much greater undertaking is the 75-mile-long inter-urban rapid-transit system known as BART (Bay Area Rapid Transit), beginning operations in the summer of 1972. Operating between San Francisco and the East Bay through a four-mile underwater tube, BART is the first system of its sort, part subway and part elevated, to be built in half a century, but it does not resemble the older systems in all respects. Comfortable, computerized automatic trains running at speeds up to 80 miles an hour are a major feature.

Situated at the head of a peninsula, San Francisco has always been a dead-end for rail traffic, with the transcontinental trains (the first westbound train arrived over the tracks of the Central Pacific on September 6, 1869) discharging their passengers in Oakland, whence they were carried to San Francisco by ferry and, in recent times, by bus. As in the rest of the country, the railroad's importance has been declining since World War II. For carrying goods, trucking has largely taken over.

Owned and operated by the municipal government, San Francisco International Airport is located seven miles south of the city–county limits, on a filled site on the southwestern shore of the bay. In 1970, the combined Bay Area airports ranked fourth in passenger traffic among the metropolitan areas of the United States. Since 1934 San Francisco's principal source of water has been the Hetch Hetchy Reservoir, 167 miles away, in the High Sierra. Other sources are the Calaveras Reservoir in Alameda County and reservoirs in San Mateo County to the south. The Hetch Hetchy project required the damming of a valley almost as splendid as that of Yosemite National Park and the construction of tunnels, one 25 miles long, through the Coast Range. In 1902 the first high-voltage line transmitting hydroelectric power was completed between a powerhouse on the Mokelumne River and San Francisco, some 180 miles away. Since then, the Bay Area has developed a network of hydroelectric plants on the rivers of the interior as well as a steam-powered plant on Monterey Bay.

Government and politics. Unlike any other California city, San Francisco (incorporated 1850) has a consolidated city–county government. The 1932 freeholders' charter, under which the city–county still operates, provides the mayor with strong executive powers but delegates substantial authority to a chief executive officer (appointed by the mayor) and a controller. The legislative authority is lodged with an elected board of supervisors. The other key officials are the superintendent of schools and the manager of utilities, both appointed.

Within recent memory, the government of San Francisco has been reasonably efficient and reasonably honest. It was not always so. Survivors of the earthquake can still recall the scandal that erupted in 1906 when it was discovered in the course of planning the rebuilding of the city that the mayor, a handsome violinist named Eugene Schmitz (the "hero of the hour" after the disaster), had become the creature of a political boss named Abe Ruef and both were indicted for extortion, Ruef eventually doing penance in San Quentin Prison.

The civic present and past

Present-day civic issues are concerned less with the possibility of corruption than with the implications of the high-rise building boom and with the certainty that the minority groups have been given seats farther down the banquet table than their white neighbours. Although the city has yet to elect a black, Chinese, or Spanish-speaking mayor, advances have been made on the board of supervisors and the school board and, increasingly, in other civic bodies.

Along with their pro-labour sentiments, San Franciscans have traditionally leaned toward the Democratic Party.

Cultural life. *Higher education.* Although strictly speaking they cannot be counted as San Francisco institutions, the greatest universities in the Bay Area are the University of California, located across the bay in Berkeley, and Stanford University, down the peninsula in Palo Alto. Within San Francisco, the most noted institution of higher education is California State University, San Francisco (formerly San Francisco State College), which was founded as a normal school in 1899 but has achieved national prominence for its academic excellence and for a prolonged campus strike that came close to destroying it as a functioning institution in 1968–69. Other colleges are the University of San Francisco (Jesuit), Lone Mountain College (also Catholic), City College (a two-year public college), and the California School of Fine Arts.

Music and theatre. San Francisco is the home of two major musical organizations. Since World War II the San Francisco Symphony has been conducted by a Frenchman, Pierre Monteux, a Spaniard, Enrique Jorda, an Austrian, Josef Krips, and a Japanese, Seiji Ozawa whose spirited style is widely admired. The San Francisco Opera enjoys an early season so that its leading singers may fulfill their commitments at New York's Metropolitan Opera. With the exception of the American Conservatory Theatre (ACT), a resident repertory group, the professional theatre is virtually nonexistent. The surviving downtown theatres are occupied largely by the touring casts of Broadway successes.

The visual arts. One of the amiable illusions held by San Franciscans is that theirs is a great city for artists. But no matter how many painters and sculptors live and work in the city, few are visible from beyond its boundaries. It has been cruelly observed that if San Francisco's three museums were to be combined, the city would then have one good second-rate museum. A possible exception to the asserted mediocrity is the collection of Far Eastern art at the M.H. de Young Museum in Golden Gate Park.

Literature. The greatest writer to make San Francisco his home was the young man who arrived as Samuel L. Clemens in 1861 and, after working as a newspaper reporter, left town as Mark Twain in 1864. Other notables of the past century have included Frank Norris, Ambrose Bierce, Bret Harte, Jack London, and Robert Louis Stevenson, who lived in great poverty in a boarding house. The current population of writers includes many reputable practitioners, a number of whom are affiliated with the creative writing program on the San Francisco campus of California State University.

Popular culture. A most vital part of San Francisco culture from the beginning has been found in its restaurants, hotels, and drinking places. To this must be added the popular culture of the ethnic enclaves—Chinatown, the Italian community of North Beach, the black culture of the Fillmore, Japan Town, the Russian colony along Clement Street, and the Spanish-speaking Mission district.

San Francisco's greatest contribution to the nation's life in recent years, however, had nothing to do with either its ethnic cultures or with its officially anointed institutions —or, indeed, as has been suggested, with the emergence of the "topless" dancer in a North Beach nightclub in 1964. Instead, it was the unheralded appearance in 1967 of the "flower children," a generation of youngsters, long of hair and usually grubby in appearance, who declared themselves in headlong flight from the Great Society and preached the saving graces of peace and love. Unhappily, as the 1960s turned into the 1970s, the main street of their capital, the Haight-Ashbury district, turned into an ugly and dangerous marketplace for drugs.

San Francisco also emerged, for a period in the late 1960s, as the capital of rock music, which achieved national prominence for the San Francisco sound of such groups as the Jefferson Airplane, the Grateful Dead, and the Quicksilver Messenger Service, as well as such individual performers as Janis Joplin.

Problems and prospects. As it progressed through the 1970s, San Francisco faced a critical period that, in the popular phrase, could be described as an identity crisis. In the general low opinion in which San Franciscans held Los Angeles could be detected not only a dislike for the ugliness and brashness of the city to the south but also envy and perhaps even fear of its vitality. San Francisco itself was still handsome, elegant, and worldly, but all too often its admiration was turned to its own past, while a perceptible apathy could be sensed when it faced the future. Middle class white residents and commuters tended to share the beguiling dream that San Francisco was "everybody's favourite city," and that it was still, as it had been to the muckraking newspaperman Will Irwin in the early 1900s, "the gayest, lightest-hearted, most pleasure-loving city of the Western continent." The hard reality of San Francisco in the 1970s was still in the process of being defined.

Crisis of the civic image

BIBLIOGRAPHY. For accounts of the early history of San Francisco, the serious reader should not be discouraged by the voluminousness and variousness of the works of the historians HUBERT HOWE BANCROFT and THEODORE H. HITTELL, the latter of whom is particularly readable. FRANK SOULE, JOHN H. GIHON, and JAMES NISBET, *The Annals of San Francisco* (1854), is invaluable; while B.E. LLOYD, *Lights and Shades of San Francisco* (1876), is both vivid and divertingly moralistic. HERBERT ASBURY, *The Barbary Coast* (1934, reprinted 1968), is the classic account of the underworld; while JULIA COOLEY ALTROCCHI, *The Spectacular San Franciscans* (1949), is a useful social history. Of the many books about the earthquake and fire of 1906, WILLIAM BRONSON, *The Earth Shook, the Sky Burned* (1959), is a first-rate work of historical reconstruction. The FEDERAL WRITERS' PROJECT, *San Francisco: The Bay and Its Cities* (1940), although out of date, remains a useful starting point. MEL SCOTT, *The San Francisco Bay Area: A Metropolis in Perspective* (1959), is the best systematic description of the area, with particular emphasis on planning. Of the many books that celebrate the distinctive flavours of San Francisco life, ROBERT O'BRIEN, *This Is San Francisco* (1948); and HERB CAEN, *Only in San Francisco* (1960), are recommended. *San Francisco Bay* (1957), by the naturalist-conservationist HAROLD GILLIAM, is both authoritative and evocative. JOHN HASKELL KEMBLE, *San Francisco Bay: A Pictorial Maritime History* (1957), contains a splendid collection of drawings and photographs from the earliest days to the present.

(K.La.)

Sankara

Śaṅkara, medieval Indian philosopher and exegete, Hindu theologian and religious leader, was the most famous exponent of the school of the Indian religious philosophy known as Vedānta. He affirmed that there is only one true reality (Brahman), an eternal principle that is the source of all things, and that all differentiations, plurality, and change are illusory. This school of thought has exercised a deep and wide influence upon religion, philosophy, and culture in India for many centuries.

There are at least 11 works that profess to be biographies of Śaṅkara. All of them were composed several centuries later than the time of Śaṅkara and are filled with legendary stories and incredible anecdotes, some of which are mutually conflicting. Today there are no materials with which to reconstruct his life with certainty.

His date of birth is naturally a controversial problem. It has been customary to assign him the birth and death dates of 788–820. But the dates 700–750, grounded on a recent study, are more acceptable at present.

According to one tradition, Śaṅkara was born into a pious Nambūdiri Brahmin family in a quiet village called Kālaḍi on the banks of the Cūrṇā (or Pūrṇā, Periyār) River, Kerala, southern India. He is said to have lost his father, Śivaguru, early in his life. He renounced the world and became a *sannyāsin* (ascetic) against his mother's will. He studied under Govinda, who was a pupil of Gauḍapāda. Nothing certain is known about Govinda, but Gauḍapāda is notable as the author of an important Vedānta work, *Māṇḍūkya-kārikā*, in which the influence of Mahāyāna Buddhism— a form of Buddhism aiming at the salvation of all beings and tending toward nondualistic or monistic thought—is evident and even extreme, especially in its last chapter.

A tradition says that Śiva, one of the principal gods in Hinduism, was Śaṅkara's family deity and that he was, by birth, a Śākta, or worshipper of Śakti, the consort of Śiva and female personification of divine energy. Later he came to be regarded as a worshipper of Śiva or even as incarnation of Śiva himself. His doctrine, however, is far removed from Śaivism and Śāktism. It is ascertained from his works that he had some faith in, or was favourable to, Vaiṣṇavism, the worship of the god Viṣṇu. It is highly possible that he was familiar with Yoga (one of the classical systems of Indian philosophy, as well as a technique to achieve salvation). A recent study has suggested that in the beginning he was an adherent of Yoga and later became an Advaitin ("advocate of nondualism").

Biographers narrate that Śaṅkara first went to Kāśī (Vārāṇasī), a city celebrated for learning and spirituality, and then travelled all over India, holding discussions with philosophers of different creeds. His heated debate with Maṇḍana Miśra, a philosopher of the Mīmāṃsā ("investigation") school, whose wife served as an umpire, is perhaps the most interesting episode in his biography and may reflect a historical fact; that is, keen conflict between Śaṅkara, who regarded the knowledge of Brahman as the only means to final release, and followers of the Mīmāṃsā school, which emphasized the performance of ordained duty and the Vedic rituals.

Śaṅkara was active in a politically chaotic age. He would not teach his doctrine to city dwellers. The power of Buddhism was still strong in the cities, though already declining, and Jainism, a nontheistic ascetic faith, prevailed among the merchants and manufacturers. Popular Hinduism occupied the minds of ordinary people, while city-dwellers pursued ease and pleasure. There were also epicureans in cities. It was difficult for Śaṅkara to communicate Vedānta philosophy to these people. Consequently, Śaṅkara propagated his teachings chiefly to *sannyāsin*s and intellectuals in the villages, and he gradually won the respect of Brahmins and feudal lords. He enthusiastically endeavoured to restore the orthodox Brahmanical tradition without paying attention to the *bhakti* (devotional) movement, which had made a deep impression on ordinary Hindus in his age.

It is very likely that Śaṅkara had many pupils, but today only four are known (from their writings): Padmapāda, Sureśvara, Toṭaka (or Troṭaka), and Hastāmalaka. Śaṅkara is said to have founded four monasteries, at Śṛṅgeri (south), Purī (east), Dvārakā (west), and Badarīnātha (north), probably following the Buddhist monastery (*vihāra*) system. Their foundation was one of the most significant factors in the development of his teachings into the leading philosophy of India.

More than 300 works—commentative, expository, and poetical—written in the Sanskrit language, are attributed to him. Most of them, however, cannot be regarded as authentic. His masterpiece is the *Brahma-sūtra-bhāṣya*, the commentary on the *Brahma-sūtra*, which is a fundamental text of the Vedānta school. He also wrote commentaries on the principal *Upaniṣads*, which are certainly all genuine, with the possible exception of the commentary on the *Śvetāśvatara Upaniṣad*. The commentary on the *Māṇḍūkya-kārikā* was also composed by Śaṅkara himself. It is very probable that he is the author of the *Yoga-sūtra-bhāṣya-vivaraṇa,* the exposition of Vyāsa's commentary on the *Yoga-sūtra,* a fundamental text of the Yoga school. The *Upadeśasāhasrī,* which is a good introduction to Śaṅkara's philosophy, is the only non-commentative work that is certainly authentic.

Śaṅkara's style of writing is lucid and profound. Penetrating insight and analytical skill characterize his works. His approach to truth is psychological and religious rather than logical. He was a prominent religious teacher rather than a philosopher. His works reveal that he was not only versed in the orthodox Brahmanical traditions but also was well acquainted with Mahāyāna Buddhism. He is often criticized as a "Buddhist in disguise" by his opponents because of the similarity between his doctrine and Buddhism. Despite this criticism, it should be noted that he made full use of his knowledge of Buddhism to attack Buddhist doctrines severely or to transmute them into his own Vedāntic nondualism, and he tried with great effort to "vedanticize" the Vedānta philosophy, which had been made extremely Buddhistic by his predecessors. The basic structure of his philosophy is more akin to Sāṅkya, a philosophic system of nontheistic dualism, and the Yoga school than to Buddhism.

It is said that Śaṅkara died at Kedārnātha in the Himalayas. The Advaita Vedānta school founded by him has always been pre-eminent in the learned circle of India. His doctrine has been the source from which the main currents of modern Indian thought are derived.

BIBLIOGRAPHY. Among the biographies of Śaṅkara written in Sanskrit, VIDYARANYA, *Śankaradigvijaya* (14th century) in verse, is best known, though legendary. T.M.P. MAHADEVAN, *Homage to S'ankara* (1959), gives a short account of Śaṅkara's life based upon the traditions. S. RADHAKRISHNAN, *Indian Philosophy,* vol. 2 (1958), contains a brief but fairly critical biography and a detailed account of his works and philosophy.

(Se.M.)

San Marino

Situated on the slopes of Monte Titano, on the Adriatic side of central Italy between the Romagna and the Marche regions, the Republic of San Marino is surrounded on all sides by the Republic of Italy. It centres on the capital of the same name. The republic's area of 23.5 square miles (61 square kilometres) makes it the smallest independent state in Europe after Vatican City and Monaco and the smallest republic in the world. It is linked with the Italian Republic by a treaty of friendship and a customs union.   C.Bo.

History. The Republic of San Marino traces its origin to the early 4th century AD when, according to tradition, St. Marinus and a group of Christians settled there to escape persecution. By the 12th century San Marino had developed into a commune ruled by its own statutes and consuls. The commune was able to remain independent despite encroachments by neighbouring bishops and lords, largely because of its isolation and its mountain fortresses. Against the attacks of the Malatesta family, who ruled the nearby seaport of Rimini, San Marino enjoyed the protection of the rival family of Montefeltro, who ruled Urbino. By the middle of the 15th century it was a republic ruled by a Grand Council—60 men taken from the Arengo, or assembly of families. Warding off serious attacks in the 16th century (including an occupation by Cesare Borgia), San Marino survived the Renaissance, a relic of the self-governing Italian city-states. Rule by an oligarchy and attempts to annex it to the Papal States in the 18th century mark the history of the decline of the republic.

When Napoleon invaded Italy he respected the independence of the republic and even offered to extend its territory (1797). The Congress of Vienna (1815), at the end of the Napoleonic Wars, also recognized its independent status. During the 19th-century movement for Italian unification, San Marino offered asylum to revolutionaries, among them Giuseppe Garibaldi. After Italy became a national state, a series of treaties (the first in 1862) confirmed its independence.   (Ed.)

Landscape. The territory has an irregular rectangular form with a maximum length of eight miles, northeast to southwest; it is crossed by the Marano and Ausa (Aussa) streams, which flow into the Adriatic Sea, and by the stream of San Marino, which falls into the Marecchia River. The landscape is dominated by the huge, central limestone mass of Monte Titano (2,424 feet [739 metres]); hills spread out from it on the southwest, whereas the northeast part gently slopes down toward the Romagna plain and the Adriatic coast. The silhouette of Monte Titano, with its three summits crowned by ancient triple fortifications, may be seen from many miles away. Correspondingly, the panorama from the top of Titano is superb and enchanting: on one side the azure Adriatic, as far as the Yugoslav coastline on clear days, and on the other, the green hills of Montefeltro and the serried ranges of the Apennines.

Monte Titano

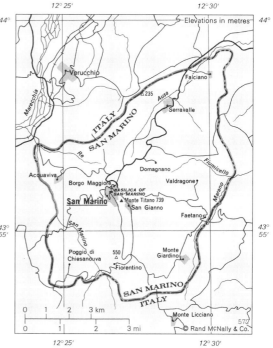

SAN MARINO

The climate is mild and temperate, with maximum temperatures of 79° F (26° C) in summer and 19° F (−7° C) in winter. Annual rainfall ranges between about 22 inches (560 millimetres) and 32 inches (810 millimetres). Vegetation is typical of the Mediterranean zone, with variations due to altitude, and includes olive, pine, oak, vine, ash, poplar, fir, and elm and many kinds of grasses and flowers. Besides domestic and farmyard animals, moles, hedgehogs, foxes, badgers, martens, weasels, and hares are found. Indigenous birds and birds of passage are plentiful.

The capital, San Marino, is set, like an eyrie, high on the western side of Monte Titano, beneath the fortress crowning one of its summits, and is encircled by triple walls. It has about 4,000 inhabitants and is the goal of many tourists.

Borgo Maggiore, lower down the slope, was for centuries San Marino's commercial centre, and Serravalle, beneath its castle of the Malatesta family, is agricultural and industrial. Most of the nine districts (*castelli*) remain agricultural, but industrial concerns are beginning to intrude on the centuries-old forms of agricultural life. In Borgo Maggiore and San Marino, new construction is spreading and penetrates the ancient centre.

Population. Although traces of human presence from both prehistoric and Roman times exist in the territory, Monte Titano and its slopes are known to have been populated, with certainty, only after the Dalmatian stone-cutter St. Marinus, traditional founder of the San Marino state (AD 301), came to the Titano to escape the emperor Diocletian's persecution of Christians. San Marino's population (7,080 in the first census [1864]) is now about 19,000, of whom more than 3,000 are non-San Marino citizens and, in a strong majority, Italian citizens. More than 20,000 San Marino citizens, or Sammarinesi, are resident abroad, principally in Italy, the United States, France, and Argentina. The increase in the population is due not only to births but also to the re-entry of citizens from abroad. The average birthrate at the beginning of the 1970s was 16.9 percent, the death rate, 8.5 percent.

Almost all the people are Catholics. The official language is Italian. A widely spoken dialect has been defined as Celto-Gallic, akin to the Piedmont and Lombardy dialects as well as to that of Romagna. A characteristic of the San Marino dialect, as compared with the others of the same origin, is its singular homogeneity, due to long isolation.

Economy. The territory has no mineral resources, for the centuries-long quarrying of Monte Titano stone and the craft that depended upon it have become exhausted. The republic's economy, therefore, relies entirely upon its inhabitants' enterprise. Its principal resources are, in order of importance, industry, tourism, commerce, agriculture, and crafts.

Industry, only recently set up, employs nearly 3,000 people and produces principally building materials, paints and varnishes, paper, metalwork, textiles, clothing, furniture, rubber and leather footware, ceramics, china, food and confectionery products, liqueurs, cosmetics, and sanitary articles.

Importance of tourism

Tourism is the sector that has seen the greatest expansion, with more than 2,400,000 visitors in 1969, mostly on day trips, from April to October; and it makes a major contribution to the inhabitants' resources. Alongside this form of excursion tourism, a convention-type tourism, based on the recently opened, modern Congress Palace, and, although still on a modest level, a residential tourism are developing.

Commerce flourishes on account of the high standard of living and in conjunction with the tourist trade. It is also encouraged by free trade agreements, which form, in fact, a customs union between the republic and Italy.

Agriculture, although no longer the principal economic resource in San Marino, has not shown any major decrease in production: wheat, maize (corn), and barley are the chief crops; dairying and livestock also are important.

Industry includes characteristic and interesting handicraft articles in ceramics and wrought iron, modern and reproduction furniture, and fine printing. The issue of new postage stamps is a useful source of revenue.

Transport. The San Marino road network totals 137 miles. The territory is connected with Italy by three main roads and by a dual-carriageway highway to nearby Rimini. Motorcoach services connect San Marino with its districts and with Rimini and, in summer, directly with other centres on the Adriatic coast. In summer, too, a helicopter service operates from Rimini to Borgo Maggiore. The capital is reached from Borgo Maggiore by means of a funicular.

The state. The San Marino constitution, originating from the Statutes of 1600, provides for the following instruments of government: the Great and General Council (Parliament), the captains regent (*capitani reggenti,* heads of state and of the administration and presidents of the parliamentary assembly), the Council of Twelve (appellate judicial body), and the Congress of State (a council of ministers). The Great and General Council has 60 members, elected every five years by all adult citizens. It has legislative and administrative powers and nominates every six months the two captains regent, who hold office for that period and may not be elected again until three years have elapsed. The Congress of State is composed of ten members, elected by the Great and General Council from among its members, and constitutes the central organ of executive power. Each member has charge of a ministerial department.

Judicial power is entrusted to judges who must not be San Marino citizens. One judge, called a commissioner of the law, attends to civil cases; an additional commissioner of the law acts in preliminary hearings of criminal cases and lesser criminal cases. The first-grade penal judge presides over criminal cases involving heavier penalties. Appeal lies, in the first instance, with civil and criminal appeals judges.

San Marino has no army but a military corps (the Great and General Council Guard, the Uniformed Militia, the Fort Guard), who today serve on parade during ceremonies at the republic's national festivities. Public order is maintained by the gendarmerie.

Social organization. San Marino can boast of provisions for social security. The state finds employment for those who cannot find work with private concerns; when this is not possible (during winter or a slack period), workers receive unemployment pay equal to 60 percent of their salary. Against a social security contribution, all citizens receive free, comprehensive medical care, assistance in sickness, accident, and old-age, as well as family allowances. The state aids home ownership through its buildings schemes. Education is free up to 14 years of age. For higher level schooling, the state grants aid to students attending universities and institutions outside San Marino. Children up to the age of 12 are guaranteed an annual seaside holiday; and two private mountain establishments, subsidized by the state, welcome young people and adults during the summer.

High level of social security

Cultural life. Tangible signs of life in centuries past live on in San Marino: from the three "fortresses" that surmount Titano's three summits to the triple wall that encircles the city of San Marino, a reminder of the long, hard struggle to defend its freedom; from the public and private buildings with their simple, austere lines to the narrow, winding streets; from the captains regent's costumes to the many-coloured uniforms of the Uniformed Corps; from the folklore shows, such as the Crossbowmen's Contest, to the country fetes.

The State Archives, Government Library, State Art Gallery, St. Francis' Church and Convent, and the Museum of Antique Weapons possess precious relics of the life and history of the republic and evidence of art and culture.

The outlook. San Marino is a tiny state with 17 centuries of history, known more to collectors of its magnificent stamps than for Abraham Lincoln's words "Your country is one of the most honoured in all history." It maintains with jealous pride some medieval institutions in its administration, but it is neither a museum nor a lifeless relic left by history but a community awake to the needs of the present-day world, aware of the new demands being made, and seeking a clear-cut answer in spite of its scanty resources to the human, civil, and social problems that today challenge every state.

BIBLIOGRAPHY. NEVIO MATTEINI, *Republica di San Marino, guida storia artistica* (1966), is a useful guide. There is no work devoted specifically to the geography of San Marino. For geology, see GIULIANO RUGGIERI, "Geologia di San Marino," in *Studi Sanmarinesi,* pp. 3–9 (1960). On the flora, the monograph by R. PAMPANINI, *Flora della Republica di San Marino* (1930), is a fundamental work. The following cover the history of the state: GINO ZANI, *Il territorio e il castello di San Marino attraverso i secoli* (1963); PAUL AEBISCHER, *Essai sur l'histoire de Saint Marin des origines à l'an mille* (1962); and MARINO FATTORI, *Ricordi storici della Republica di San Marino,* 8th ed. (1956). On art, CARLA NICOLINI, *Pittura e scultura à San Marino* (1965), should be consulted. Descriptive works in English include: VIRGINIA WALES JOHNSON, *Two Quaint Republics, Andorra and San Marino* (1913); GILES PLAYFAIR and CONSTANTINE FitzGIBBON, *The Little Tour: Andorra, Monaco, Liechtenstein, San Marino* (1954); CHARLES L. SHERMAN, *The Five Little Countries of Europe: Luxembourg, Monaco, Andorra, San Marino, Liechtenstein* (1958); and C. NEVILLE PACKETT, *Guide to the Republic of San Marino* (1964).

(C.Bo.)

San Martín, José de

South American soldier and statesman and national hero of Argentina, José de San Martín led rebel troops in freeing Chile and Peru of Spanish domination. Together

San Martín, portrait by F. Bouchot (1800–42). In the West Point Museum, New York.
By courtesy of the West Point Museum Collection, United States Military Academy

with Simón Bolívar, he was the major architect of South American independence.

San Martín is believed to have been born on February 25, 1778, at Yapeyú, formerly a Jesuit mission station in Guaraní Indian territory, on the northern frontier of Argentina. There his father, Juan de San Martín, a professional soldier, was administrator. His mother, Gregoria Matorras, was also Spanish. The family returned to Spain when José was six. From 1785 to 1789 he was educated at the Seminario de Nobles in Madrid, leaving there to begin his military career as a cadet in the Murcia infantry regiment. For the next 20 years he was a loyal officer of the Spanish monarch, fighting against the Moors in Oran (1791); against the British (1798), who held him captive for over a year; and against the Portuguese in the War of the Oranges (1801). He was made captain in 1804.

The turning point in San Martín's career came in 1808, following Napoleon's occupation of Spain and the subsequent patriotic uprising against the French. For two years he served the Seville junta that was conducting the war on behalf of the imprisoned Spanish king Ferdinand VII. He was promoted to the rank of lieutenant colonel for his conduct in the Battle of Bailén (1808) and was elevated to command of the Sagunto Dragoons after the Battle of Albuera (1811). Instead of taking up his new post, he sought permission to go to Lima, the capital of the viceroyalty of Peru, but travelled by way of London to Buenos Aires, which was the principal centre of resistance in South America to the Seville junta. There, in the year 1812, San Martín was given the task of organizing a corps of grenadiers against the Spanish royalists centred in Peru who threatened the revolutionary government in Argentina.

Change of allegiance One explanation for this startling change of allegiance on the part of a soldier who had sworn a fealty to Spain is that it was prompted by British sympathizers with the independence movement in Spanish America and that San Martín was recruited through the agency of James Duff, 4th earl of Fife, who had fought in Spain (and who caused San Martín to be made a freeman of Banff, Scotland). In later years, San Martín averred that he had sacrificed his career in Spain because he had responded to the call of his native land, and this is the view taken by Argentinian historians. Undoubtedly, peninsular Spanish prejudice against anyone born in the Indies must have rankled throughout his career in Spain and caused him to identify himself with the criollo (creole) revolutionaries.

In the service of the Buenos Aires government, San Martín distinguished himself as a trainer and leader of soldiers, and, after winning a skirmish against loyalist forces at San Lorenzo, on the right bank of the Paraná (February 3, 1813), he was sent to Tucumán to reinforce, and ultimately replace, General Belgrano, who was being hard pressed by forces of the Viceroy of Peru. San Martín realized that the Río de la Plata provinces would never be secure so long as the royalists held Lima, but he perceived the military impossibility of reaching the centre of viceregal power by way of the conventional overland route through Upper Peru (modern Bolivia). He therefore quietly prepared the masterstroke that was his supreme contribution to the liberation of southern South America. First, he disciplined and trained the army around Tucumán so that, with the assistance of gaucho *guerrilleros*, they would be capable of a holding operation. Then, on the pretense of ill health, he got himself appointed governor intendant of the province of Cuyo, the capital of which was Mendoza, the key to the routes across the Andes. There, he set about creating an army that would link up with the soldiers of the patriotic government in Chile and then proceed by sea to attack Peru. To his disappointment, when the first stage of this plan was nearing completion, loyalist forces recaptured Chile (although the Chilean liberator, Bernardo O'Higgins, was able to escape to Mendoza). This made it necessary for San Martín to fight his way across the formidable barrier of the Andes. This was accomplished between January 18 and February 8, 1817, partly by a double bluff, which caused the Spanish commander to divide his forces in order to guard all possible routes, and more especially by careful generalship that ensured the maximum concentration of force at the enemy's weakest point, backed by adequate supplies. San Martín's skill in leading his men through the defiles, chasms, and passes—often 10,000 to 12,000 feet (3,000 to 4,000 metres) above sea level—of four Andean *cordilleras* has caused him to be ranked with Hannibal and Napoleon. On February 12, he surprised and defeated the royalists at Casas de Chacabuco and took Santiago, where he refused the offer of the governorship of Chile in favour of Bernardo O'Higgins (who became supreme director) because he did not wish to be diverted from his main objective, the capture of Lima. Nevertheless, it took him over a year to clear the country of royalist troops. He finally routed the remaining 5,300 on April 5, 1818, at the Battle of Maipú.

Campaign across the Andes

The next stage of San Martín's plan involved the creation of the Chilean Navy and the accumulation of troop ships. This was accomplished, despite shortage of funds, by August 1820, when the rather shoddy fleet, consisting mainly of armed merchant ships, under the command of Thomas Cochrane (later 10th earl of Dundonald), left Valparaíso for the Peruvian coast. Cochrane, whom San Martín found a cantankerous colleague, had failed the year before to take the chief port, Callao, which was well-defended. The port was therefore blockaded, and the troops landed to the south near Pisco; from this point they could threaten Lima from the landward side. True to his cautious nature, San Martín resisted the temptation to assault the capital, which was defended by a superior force, and waited for almost a year, until the royalists, despairing of assistance from Ferdinand VII (who had since been restored to the Spanish throne), withdrew to the mountains. San Martín then entered Lima, the independence of Peru was proclaimed on July 28, 1821, and the victorious commander was made protector.

Capture of Lima

San Martín's position was nevertheless insecure. He had broken with his supporters in Buenos Aires when, against their wishes, he insisted on pressing on to Lima; he was unsure of the loyalty of the Peruvian people and of the backing of some of his officers, many of whom suspected him of dictatorial or monarchical ambitions; and he lacked the forces to subdue the royalist remnants in the interior. Moreover, Simón Bolívar, who had liberated the northern provinces of South America, had annexed Guayaquil, a port and province that San Martín had hoped would opt for incorporation in Peru. He therefore decided to confront Bolívar. The two victorious generals met, ostensibly on equal terms, on July 26, 1822, at Guayaquil. What passed between them in their secret discussions is unknown, but what is clear is that San Martín hurried back to Lima, a disappointed man. There, seriously ill, faced by recriminations and overt disaffection, he resigned the protectorship on September 20. The rest of his life was spent in exile with his daughter, in Brussels, Paris, and Boulogne-sur-Mer, wisely avoiding any further

Meeting with Bolívar

involvement in the anarchic situations that marred the early history of the newly independent nations. He died in Boulogne-sur-Mer on August 17, 1850.

San Martín's abiding contribution to the cause of independence in the Río de la Plata, Chile, and Peru was the military skill that he had acquired in his long career in the Spanish Army. He knew how to train and inspire soldiers, how to lead them, and how to avoid involvement with the enemy until he was sure of superiority on every count. Above all, the boldness of his plan to attack the viceroyalty of Lima by crossing the Andes to Chile and going on by sea, and the patience and determination with which he executed it, was undoubtedly the decisive factor in the defeat of Spanish power in southern South America. Whether at Guayaquil he consciously made a great renunciation of personal ambition so that Bolívar, and with him the cause of independence, might triumph, or whether he went into voluntary exile because Bolívar made it clear that he was not prepared to help Peru so long as San Martín remained in control, remains an unresolved historical problem.

BIBLIOGRAPHY. The basic documents on San Martín's career will be found in Documentos del archivo de San Martín, 12 vol. (1910–11). The classic biography is BARTOLOME MITRE, Historia de San Martín y la emancipación sudamericana, 2nd ed., 4 vol. (1890 and later reprints), of which WILLIAM PILLING, The Emancipation of South America (1893), is an abridged translation. RICARDO LEVENE, El genio político de San Martín (1950), summarizes the known facts. The controversial meeting that occurred between Simón Bolívar and San Martín at Guayaquil is examined in two articles in the Hispanic American Historical Review: GERHARD MASUR, "The Conference of Guayaquil," 31:189–229 (1951), and VICENTE LECUNA, "Bolívar and San Martín at Guayaquil," 31:369–393 (1951).

(J.C.J.M.)

Santa Catarina

Santa Catarina, one of the 22 states of Brazil, is situated in the southern part of the country. It is bounded on the north by the state of Paraná, on the south by the state of Rio Grande do Sul, on the east by the Atlantic Ocean, and on the west by Misiones territory of Argentina. One of the smaller Brazilian states, it has an area of 37,060 square miles (95,985 square kilometres) and a population, in 1970, of more than 2,900,000. The capital is Florianópolis, located on coastal Santa Catarina Island. The region was given various names by early Spanish and Portuguese cartographers; the name Santa Catarina is said to have been given in honour of St. Catherine of Alexandria by the Italian navigator Sebastian Cabot, when he was in the service of Spain.

History. Santa Catarina was part of a larger hereditary captaincy (district administered by a captain) established by the Portuguese crown in 1532, although the first Portuguese settlement, at what is today the port of São Francisco do Sul near the Paraná border, was not made until 1648. Interior highland prairies were used for cattle raising, and early in the 18th century trading posts were opened along the cattle trails leading across the plateaus toward the coastal towns and the northern markets.

The captaincy of Santa Catarina was created in 1738 to serve as an outpost in the Portuguese–Spanish territorial wars. It was governed from Rio de Janeiro by the military until 1822, when Brazil became an empire independent of Portugal. A revolution that spread northward from Rio Grande do Sul in 1839 created the short-lived Republic of Santa Catarina. One of the participants was Giuseppe Garibaldi (q.v.), who married a Brazilian, Anna Maria Ribeiro da Silva, and in later decades led the battles that unified his native Italy.

During the 19th century a considerable immigration of non-Portuguese peoples occurred. Germans arrived as early as 1829 and came in great numbers during the 1850s, settling along the coastal valleys and founding the cities of Blumenau, Joinvile, and Brusque. Many Italians immigrated after 1875, and Poles, Ukrainians, and Russians arrived in the 1880s. African slaves comprised about 10 percent of the population in the 1870s; they were emancipated in 1888. Santa Catarina became a state

of Brazil when, in 1889, a republic was proclaimed to replace the empire; Florianópolis was designated as the capital.

The physical environment. Behind the seacoast a great escarpment rises like a mountain wall; the state has little level ground. Its highest point is Campo do Padres, at 6,000 feet (1,800 metres) in altitude, located in the southeast part of the state. There are two principal river systems, one formed by the coastal rivers flowing eastward to the coast, the other flowing south to the Uruguay River, which forms part of the state's southern border.

Rainfall is heavy, ranging from 47 to 97 inches annually; temperatures range from a summer high of about 69° F (21° C) to a winter low of about 48° F (9° C). Although much of the original forest cover, which consists of mixed tropical and subtropical vegetation, has been cleared, there are extensive reforestation programs that are now being pursued.

Santa Catarina is among the less developed Brazilian states, and the rugged aspect of its land is a handicap to diversification of the economy and modernization of rural life.

The people. About 95 percent of the population of more than 2,900,000 are white, the remainder predominantly Negro and Indian. The Portuguese spoken by the majority has also influenced the languages spoken by the descendants of the various immigrant groups. More than 70 percent of the people are Roman Catholic; there are also several Protestant sects, and spiritualism has much influence, principally in urban areas.

Administration. The administration of the state is centralized, in accordance with Brazil's 1967 constitution, in a governor, who is assisted by several secretaries of state. There is a 35-member assembly representing the various regions of the state. There is also a tribunal of justice. The 197 municipalities are administered by local governors, or *prefeitos*, who are either elected or nominated. Each municipality also has a municipal chamber that is composed of seven to 15 members, who are known as *vereadores*.

Social conditions. There have been elementary schools in Santa Catarina for centuries, but secondary education became prevalent in the interior only in the 20th century. Higher education was introduced in 1919, and a number of universities are located in the major cities, the most prominent being the Federal University of Santa Catarina, in Florianópolis.

A prominent feature of state welfare is the public housing program. There are about 150 hospitals throughout the state, and about 700 doctors and an additional 1,000 medical personnel serve the population.

Economy. The manufacture of wood products forms a major part of Santa Catarina's industry; these products include processed wood, furniture, and charcoal. Brazil's best coal is mined about 70 miles northwest and southwest of Tubarão on the southern coast. Fishing and fish processing are important, as also are cattle raising and other forms of food production and processing. There is rather low productivity, however, which is caused by a scarcity of skilled labour and a lack of knowledge of modern marketing techniques.

Transportation. The road system dates from the colonial era but has been modernized during the mid-20th century. Two national highways cross the state from north to south and one from east to west. Secondary roads from the main producing areas are linked to these highways. A railway line crosses the centre of the state from south to north but is no longer of major significance; there are also some minor branch lines. River and sea transport is poorly developed. The principal ports are São Francisco do Sul, Itajaí, Florianópolis, Imbituba, and Laguna. The local airports are at Florianópolis, Joinvile, Joaçaba, Cricúma, Caçador, Chapecó, and Navegantes. An international airport is under construction at Navegantes.

Cultural life and institutions. The theatre is popular in Florianópolis and Blumenau; there are 12 museums and more than 300 libraries in the state. There are nine daily newspapers, two television stations, and 61 radio sta-

Margin notes:

Administrative changes and immigration

Education

tions. The state Institute of History and Geography has been in existence since 1896 and the Academy of Letters since 1920. Traditional folk dancing is a favourite activity, and folk arts and crafts are widely practiced. Public festivals celebrate a number of Catholic saints. When religious processions are held, it is a common practice to cover the roads with carpets of flowers.

(W.F.P.)

Santalales

The Santalales, or sandalwood order of flowering plants, consists chiefly of members either partially or entirely parasitic on other plants. The order is of interest from several points of view. The true sandalwood (*Santalum album*) and some of its near relatives play an important role in the practices of various religious groups in the Orient. The oil distilled from its wood continues to be of commercial importance and is used as a body ointment and a constituent of many soaps and perfumes. The European mistletoe (*Viscum album*) is thought to have had special ritual significance in Druidical ceremonies and lives in folklore today, its special status as the Christmas mistletoe having come from Anglo-Saxon times. *Phoradendron serotinum*, somewhat similar to its European counterpart, is an acceptable substitute in North America.

GENERAL FEATURES

The order contains trees up to 60 feet (18 metres) high and many shrubs and perennials, but no shorter lived annuals or biennials. The smallest member of the order is the dwarf mistletoe (*Arceuthobium minutissimum*), one of the smallest of all vascular plants, its flowering stems extending from the host plant for no more than about three millimetres (about ⅛ inch).

Distribution and abundance. The great majority of species in the order are tropical and subtropical, but a number of genera, especially in the families Santalaceae and Loranthaceae, have temperate representatives. There are no truly Arctic species, although *Geocaulon* (Santalaceae) occurs north to the shores of Hudson Bay and to north of Inuvik in Canada. Of the mistletoe genera only *Arceuthobium* of the Northern Hemisphere is present in both the Old and New Worlds. In other large families in the order, such as the following, geographic distribution is more limited: Erythropalaceae (Southeast Asia); Cardiopteridaceae (Indo-Malayan); Dipentodontaceae (Southeast Asia); Medusandraceae (tropical West Africa); Myzodendraceae (southern tip of South America); and Cynomoriaceae (Mediterranean). Many of the parasitic forms are restricted in occurrence, but some of the smaller species may be extremely abundant and widespread, as in *Arceuthobium*, *Phoradendron*, and *Comandra*.

Importance. The economic importance of the order focusses on the sale of mistletoe, the use of sandalwood products, and the destructive effects of various parasitic mistletoes.

Mistletoe branches are gathered in rural areas of many central and western European countries and shipped to larger cities, to reach the market during the week before Christmas. In North America most of the commercially important mistletoe is harvested in Texas, New Mexico, and Oklahoma.

The use of sandalwood products is varied and goes back to the dawn of history. Sandalwood was known as long ago as 1700 BC (Egypt), and its use in the Far East is probably older. It is used as a ceremonial burning material during religious rites (especially burials) of Hindus, Buddhists, Parsis, and Moslems in Southeast Asia. The wood is also of excellent quality for wood carvings. The famous sandal oil is slowly distilled from the wood, that of older roots being especially high in oil content. Used for centuries as a body ointment, it has more recently been found to be extremely useful in fixing such delicate and quickly vanishing fragrances as jasmine. Both the United States and France import significant amounts of sandal oil from Australia and India, respectively, for use in the manufacture of perfumes and soaps. Because of the high cost of sandalwood, various substitutes are offered locally, some from closely related members of the fami-

Sandal oil

lies Santalaceae or Olacaceae in the sandalwood order (as in the Australian *Eucarya spicata* and the Indian genus *Ximenia*); others from quite unrelated families of other orders (as in *Erythroxylum* of the family Erythroxylaceae in India and the Venezuelan genus *Amyris* in the family Rutaceae). The best sandal oil is derived from the wood of *Santalum album*, a tree extensively planted in Southeast Asia. The most important industry is centred in the Indian state of Mysore where it has been a state monopoly for many years. In Hawaii, the rise of King Kamehameha in the 19th century has been credited to the income from local sandalwood, which was exported to the Orient.

Although the great majority of species in the sandalwood order are parasitic upon other vascular plants, only the mistletoes cause serious damage to economically important plants. Primitive agricultural practices in many tropical areas frequently take little account of the occasionally very great populations of mistletoes on cacao, rubber, citrus, and many other trees, especially fruit. The genus *Dendropthoe* in the Indian region, and *Struthanthus* in tropical America can be especially bothersome. *Viscum album*, the Christmas season mistletoe, malforms ornamental trees in many European countries, thus decreasing their value. The dwarf mistletoes, *Arceuthobium americanum, A. douglasii, A. campylopodum* and *A. vaginatum*, in western North America are among the most serious forest pathogens (causes of diseases) because they attack most of the conifers in the region to varying degrees. Numerous *Phoradendron* species in the United States are also important pathogens of several trees, including walnut, oak, and some conifers.

NATURAL HISTORY

Predominance of parasitism. By far the most interesting evolutionary development in the order is the phenomenon of parasitism. More than half of the species in the order are parasitic, including all known members of the following families: Santalaceae, Loranthaceae, Viscaceae, Eremolepidaceae, Myzodendraceae, Cynomoriaceae, and Balanophoraceae. In addition, the genera *Cansjera* (Opiliaceae), *Olax*, *Ptychopetalum*, and *Ximenia* (Olacaceae) are known to be parasitic.

The most obvious evidence of parasitism lies in the occurrence of the haustorium, a specialized absorbing organ that penetrates into living host tissues and functions to transfer various materials from the host into the parasite.

In certain advanced species an extensive invasion of host tissues takes place. The intrusive organ becomes fragmented and branches out through the softer tissues of the host. This development is especially noteworthy in most members of the family Viscaceae, and probably in the genus *Phacellaria* (Santalaceae). In certain species of dwarf mistletoe (*Arceuthobium*) parasitic on conifers, a threadlike system develops internally and may reach into the growing point of the host. The host tree responds to such an all-pervasive parasite attack by developing a striking abnormal bushy growth at its top, known as a witches' broom.

Witches' broom response of host plants

The degree to which the parasitic species is dependent on the host is poorly understood but is probably high for most species, even obligatory under natural conditions. Chlorophyll is present in all species except those of the families Cynomoriaceae and Balanophoraceae, which are completely dependent on parasitism for nutrition. Studies with radioactive isotopes indicate that the more reduced forms, such as *Arceuthobium*, have a greater dependence on the host compared with greener and more leafy parasites such as *Phoradendron*.

Dispersal. In the treelike or shrubby species of the order, the nutlike or drupelike fruits are probably spread by birds or other animals. It has been known since Roman times, however, that a rather special relationship exists between mistletoes and birds. The fleshy, one-seeded berries of mistletoes are eaten by a great variety of birds. The extremely viscous seeds pass through the digestive tract unharmed and, when voided on a suitable object, will sometimes germinate and become established on

Birds as agents of dispersal

a new host tree. Outside the mistletoe families, *Phacellaria*, and possibly some other santalacean, tree-inhabiting genera have evolved a similar dependence upon bird dispersal. In most mistletoes, the degree of dependence on this partnership is complete.

Several mistletoes, however, are not dependent upon birds. The Australian treelike mistletoe *Nuytsia floribunda* has winged, dry nuts, which hold no interest for birds. The minute fruits of the family Myzodendraceae bear long, hairy structures that attach themselves to leaves and branches of the host tree. These seeds are probably wind dispersed. In the dwarf mistletoe genus *Arceuthobium* (Viscaceae), the fruit is explosive, and the sticky bullet-shaped seed may travel up to 15 metres (49 feet) with astonishing velocity (initially, 24 metres per second [79 feet per second]) before adhering to a new host branch.

FORM AND FUNCTION

Vegetative characters. One of the most remarkable vegetative characters of the sandalwood order is the haustorium, a specialized absorbing organ that attaches to other plants and provides a means by which the parasite obtains water and nutrients from the victimized host plant. The typical young haustorium is a small bell-like or even clamplike organ, which attaches by its lower surface to a suitable host. From the central tissues of the anatomically complex haustorium a small intrusive, wedgelike organ grows out toward and into the host tissues, where it undergoes further development. The mature haustorial organ is characterized by a partial fusion of the xylem, or water conducting tissues, of host and parasite. The bell-like shape of the original haustorium soon disappears during expansion of the host–parasite contact zone. The size of the haustorium ranges from about one millimetre in most species up to one foot in diameter in the exceptionally large, mature *Psittacanthus* haustorium. The *rosas de palo*, or *flores de palo*, sold as curiosities in Mexico, consist of the abnormally developed wood of the host tree where these large haustoria were once attached.

Few generalizations can be made about other vegetative characters. Nearly all species have simple leaves lacking stipules, and only a few bear surface hairs on the leaves or stems. In many parasites of the order, including, among others, all members of the family Balanophoraceae, leaves are reduced to scalelike organs. Even among species with well-developed leaves, including the temperate-climate woody species the evergreen habit predominates and leaf fall in autumn is rare.

Flower and fruit characters. The flower may have both petals and sepals as in any typical flower, or, as is common in many members of the order, one or both of these sets of flower structures may be entirely lacking. The male parts of the flower, the stamens, usually occur in numbers equalling the number of petals and are positioned directly opposite the lobes of the petals rather than between adjacent ones. The female structure, the ovary, is positioned in the flower embedded in tissues below the region where the petals and sepals are attached, or it may be positioned higher up in such a way that the sepals and petals are located at its base. The first condition, termed inferior ovary is the type that predominates in the order. Inside the ovary, two to several ovules, or developing seeds, are present. Sometimes these ovules lack the tissues that are destined to become seed coats in later development.

Variations in fruit The fruit ranges from rather large nuts in many members of the Olacaceae family to exceedingly minute fruits in the Balanophoraceae family. Almost invariably, the seed is solitary and contains special nutrient tissue, the endosperm. In especially the parasitic groups a trend toward reduction of seed coats and embryos is evident, resulting in a propagative unit that in some groups is different from a typical seed. In most mistletoes a portion of the ovary wall supplies the viscous layer of this "seed."

Evolution and paleontology. There is no significant fossil record for the order Santalales, and evolutionary considerations must therefore be based upon contemporary members.

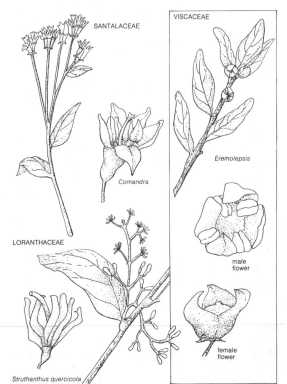

Floral characteristics in representative families of the sandalwood order.
Drawing by R. Findahl

CLASSIFICATION

Distinguishing taxonomic features. The order Santalales as defined by most authorities consists of an apparently unnatural (*i.e.*, unrelated by descent from a common ancestor) association of the Santalales core families with various other small families, the number and assortment of which depend upon the authority consulted. It is, therefore, virtually impossible to describe meaningful characteristics held in common by all members of the order. In the restricted conception of the order the primitive olacacean complex (families Olacaceae, Opiliaceae, Schoepfiaceae) plus the families Loranthaceae and Santalaceae predominantly contains species with bisexual flowers; all other derived (*i.e.*, related by descent from primitive complex) families have unisexual flowers only (families Viscaceae, Myzodendraceae, Eremolepidaceae). Leaves are without stipules except in the families Dipentodontaceae and Medusandraceae. Leaves are simple in all families except Cardiopteraceae, in which palmately lobed leaves occur. In more advanced parasites, the leaves are often reduced to small scales. Ovules are few, frequently only one or two, and their attachment to the ovary tends to be on a central column unsupported except at its base. Seeds of nearly all have nutritive tissues called endosperm for the use of the developing young plant at germination.

Annotated classification. The extremely variable composition of this order and the apparently unnatural assemblage of families, even in many recently proposed systems, makes an acceptable grouping of families by relationship impossible. The following annotated classification, therefore, consists of two parts: (1) Santalales, in the restricted sense, including all families of some indisputable relationship to Santalaceae, and (2) an alphabetical list of various other families placed at some time in Santalales by one or more responsible authorities.

ORDER SANTALALES

Woody plants ranging from a few millimetres to 15 m (49 ft) or more in height, mostly parasitic on the branches of trees or on the roots of perennial plants. Leaves simple, entire, and without stipules (small leaflike appendages at the base of the leaf stalk) alternate or opposite. Corolla (petals) and calyx (sepals) usually 5- or 4-parted (*i.e.*, the number of petals and/or sepals is either 5 or 4) but the calyx greatly reduced in some families and completely absent in others. Stamens as many as the perianth (sepals and petals) members or petals, in the latter case mostly opposite the petals. Ovary superior or (more commonly) inferior, ovules or embryo sacs few and basal, ovules frequently greatly reduced.

Family Aptandraceae
A small family of trees with the general characters of Olacaceae and usually included in that family. The calyx enlarges after fertilization to enclose the entire fruit; filaments are fused to form a tube surrounding the style. Equatorial America, Africa, and southwest Asia.

Family Eremolepidaceae
A small neotropical family of mistletoes parasitic on various tree species. Leaves alternate; in 1 genus (*Eubrachion*) reduced to scales. Inflorescences spikelike or catkin-like, flowers small and drab, unisexual. Fruit a 1-seeded berry. Three genera and about 10 species. Only recently revived, the family in the past has been part of Viscaceae or Loranthaceae.

Family Loranthaceae   (in the broad sense)
Trees or shrubs parasitic on branches of trees, rarely on roots of smaller vascular plants. Leaves usually opposite and evergreen. Flowers unisexual (subfamily Viscoideae) or bisexual (most of subfamily Loranthoideae). Stamens opposite petals, ovary inferior, giving rise to a (usually) viscous single seed disseminated by birds. Corolla 2- to 7-parted (*i.e.*, there are 2 to 7 petals), calyx absent (subfamily Viscoideae) or reduced to rimlike outgrowth (subfamily Loranthoideae). Embryo sacs embedded in ovarian papilla representing joined, reduced ovules. Seed with endosperm in nearly all species. A largely tropical family, only some genera being established in temperate zones, especially of the Northern Hemisphere (*Arceuthobium*, *Viscum*, and *Phoradendron* in particular). The family has been regarded as a single family through most of its history, commonly known as the mistletoe family. Two clear subfamilies have been recognized, Loranthoideae and Viscoideae. Recent authors agree in separate familial status for each, the 3 genera *Eremolepis*, *Antidaphne*, and *Eubrachion* sometimes being removed from Viscoideae to form the family Eremolepidaceae. Loranthaceae in the broad sense contains about 75 genera and 1,300 species.

Family Loranthaceae   (in the restricted sense)
A nearly exclusively tropical family of mistletoes parasitic mostly on branches of trees. Some are, or can be, terrestrial trees up to 10 m high, parasitic on roots of even small herbaceous plants (*e.g.*, *Nuytsia* from Western Australia, *Gaiadendron* from tropical America). Leaves usually evergreen and opposite. Flowers mostly bisexual, calyx reduced to a rimlike structure called a calyculus, corolla usually 4-, 5-, or 6-parted (*i.e.*, there are 4, 5, or 6 petals), each petal bearing a basally attached stamen. Ovary inferior, ovules reduced to a knoblike basal placenta, or embryo sacs originating in receptacular tissue. Fruit a 1-seeded berry (except *Nuytsia*) disseminated by birds. Some 65 genera and 850 species, the most important centre of distribution being from tropical Asia to New Guinea and Australia.

Family Myzodendraceae
Mistletoe-like plants parasitic on *Nothofagus* (false beech) in southern South America. Leaves small and deciduous or squamate, inflorescences catkin-like. Flowers reduced to 2 or 3 stamens or a minute ovary, perianth virtually absent. Fruit a small achene (a small, dry, 1-seeded, nonsplitting fruit with a tight, thin seed coat) with 3 long, feathery modified stamens. One genus and about 10 species.

Family Octoknemaceae
A problematic family maintained in several systems. One of the 2 constituent genera (*Octoknema*) has recently been placed in the Olacaceae family, the other (*Okoubaka*) with Santalaceae.

Family Olacaceae
A tropical and subtropical family of trees and shrubs 3 of which (*Olax*, *Ximenia*, and *Ptychopetalum*) are known to be parasitic on roots of other plants. Leaves simple, alternate. Inflorescence usually a raceme (a simple elongate flower cluster having flowers on stalks, the lowermost flowers maturing first), sometimes catkin-like, and flowers bisexual. Calyx reduced to calyculus, frequently expanding greatly in fruit. Corolla 3- to 6-parted. Stamens 1 to 3 times as many as petals and opposite them, or more numerous and in varying positions, surrounded by a disklike rim or nectary. Ovary inferior to superior, with a central stalk from which 3 ovules are suspended. Fruit a 1-seeded drupe or nut. The family contains 25 genera and 250 species unless it is united with the related Opiliaceae, making then a total of 33 genera and 310 species.

Family Opiliaceae
A family sharing most characters with Olacaceae, but distinguished from it by the usual absence of the calyculus or calyx,

and by an apparent fragmentation of the nectary-like disk into frequently staminode-like units. Petals 4 to 5, each with an opposite stamen. One genus (*Cansjera*) is known to be parasitic. Opiliaceae is perhaps more properly added to Olacaceae to which, in any case, it is very closely related. Eight genera and 60 species.

Family Santalaceae   (sandalwood family)
Named after the true sandalwood, *Santalum album*. Small parasitic herbs, shrubs, or trees with mostly alternate leaves. Inflorescence variable, flowers mostly bisexual. Perianth of 1 whorl of 3 to 5 stamen-bearing members. Ovary mostly inferior, containing 1 to 3 ovules suspended on a twisted basal stalk, or embedded in an ovarian papilla as in mistletoes. Fruit a 1-seeded drupe or nut. About 30 genera and 400 species, mostly tropical or subtropical.

Family Schoepfiaceae
An infrequently recognized family containing the single genus *Schoepfia*, more commonly placed in Olacaceae. Separation as a family has been justified on the basis of the apparent absence of a calyculus and the inferior position of the ovary. *Schoepfia* has perhaps 25 species, mostly tropical.

Family Viscaceae
A mistletoe family parasitic on branches of trees. Leaves mostly opposite, in many species reduced to scales. Flowers unisexual; perianth of 1 whorl of 2 to 5 members, each bearing a stamen, the latter reduced to a sessile anther (anther having no stalk) in some genera. Ovary inferior, with ovarian papilla containing 2 embryo sacs. Fruit a 1-seeded berry with viscous seed, the endosperm often containing chlorophyll. Including Eremolepidaceae, the family contains 11 genera and about 450 species, mostly tropical. The European mistletoe, *Viscum album*, is the best known member of the family.

FAMILIES FREQUENTLY PLACED IN SANTALALES BUT OF UNCERTAIN AFFINITIES

Family Balanophoraceae
Mushroomlike parasites on the roots of trees or shrubs. Chlorophyll absent; leaves reduced to fleshy scales or absent. Inflorescence usually unbranched, fleshy, bearing many minute, unisexual flowers. All species in tropical areas except the Mediterranean *Cynomorium coccineum* (the Maltese fungus of the Crusaders), which is sometimes placed in a separate family, Cynomoriaceae. Probably not related to the family Santalaceae. About 100 species in 16 genera.

Family Cardiopteridaceae
(or Cardiopterygaceae or Peripterygiaceae)
Green climbing plants with small bisexual flowers, superior ovary, and winged fruits. A single genus (*Peripterygium*) with 3 species. Southeast Asia to Queensland.

Family Cynomoriaceae
See under Family Balanophoraceae.

Family Cytinaceae
Two genera (*Cytinus* and *Bdallophyton*) of wholly parasitic species, normally included in family Rafflesiaceae.

Family Dipentodontaceae
A single genus and species of deciduous small trees, native to southwestern China and adjacent India. Little in common with Santalales, and probably related to the family Flacourtiaceae in the order Violales.

Family Erythropalaceae
Liana-like shrubs with simple leaves and slender divided inflorescences of bisexual flowers. Fruit nutlike, with a long stripe, and completely enclosed by a persistent calyx. One genus, with perhaps 2 species; tropical Asia. The family is not satisfactorily placed in Santalales and shows similarities with the families Icacinaceae and Celestraceae, both in the order Celestrales. Included in Olacaceae in earlier works.

Family Grubbiaceae
A South African family of shrubs at one time regarded as santalalean but now believed to belong to the orders Ericales, Pittosporales, or some other group. Two genera, 5 species.

Family Hydnoraceae
A small family of 2 genera with 2 species each, in arid South America and eastern Africa. Leafless parasites on roots of various plants. Only individual fleshy flowers emerge from the soil. The fruit is a pulpy mass with numerous minute seeds. The family is related to the family Rafflesiaceae but probably not to Santalales.

Family Medusandraceae
Trees with simple alternate leaves and catkin-like inflorescences of bisexual flowers. A single genus and species of obscure affinities. West Equatorial Africa.

Family Peripterygiaceae
See under Family Dipentodontaceae.

Family Rafflesiaceae

A small family of about 50 species of mostly tropical, chlorophyll-less parasites in most cases reduced to no more than (sometimes very large) flowers that emerge from a mycelium-like absorptive organ embedded within host tissues. In older systematic treatments Rafflesiaceae (and the related Hydnoraceae) were commonly placed in Santalales, but recent authors have realized the artificiality of this position and now place it in the order Rafflesiales.

Critical appraisal. The order Santalales, in the broad sense, is clearly a miscellaneous collection of families many of which are of uncertain affinity. Following detailed analysis, some of these families may eventually be placed in different orders related to but outside the order Santalales. Others (Cynomoriaceae, Balanophoraceae) seem to be included mainly because of their parasitism and extreme reduction and are not likely to remain in the vicinity of Santalales. Other parasitic families (Hydnoraceae, Rafflesiaceae) were at one time placed in the order for similar reasons. When stripped to families of undoubted relationship there remain five to nine families, depending on taxonomic judgment. The olacacean complex (families Olacaceae and Opiliaceae, including Aptandraceae and Schoepfiaceae) is very inadequately known. Nearly all authors agree that other families in the order are traceable to Olacaceae-like ancestors, although the exact lineages are not completely agreed upon. The more common concept visualizes a descent of all mistletoe-like plants (Loranthaceae, Viscaceae, Myzodendraceae, Eremolepidaceae) from Olacaceae, via Santalaceae. This particular evolutionary pathway has logical obstacles, except for Viscaceae. Separate evolutionary lines from the olacacean complex to each of Eremolepidaceae, Myzodendraceae, Santalaceae, and Loranthaceae is perhaps a more accurate concept of descent. Viscaceae as a separate family might be derived from ancestral members of the Santalaceae family.

BIBLIOGRAPHY. J. KUIJT, "Mutual Affinities of Santalalean Families," *Brittonia*, 20:136–147 (1968), a historical resumé of the composition of Santalales, with an exposition of newly conceived evolutionary relationships, *The Biology of Parasitic Flowering Plants* (1969), a worldwide treatment of all parasitic groups of angiosperms, with special sections on history, folklore, haustorium, physiology, evolution, and each parasitic group; B.A. BARLOW, "Classification of the Loranthaceae and Viscaceae," *Proc. Linn. Soc. N.S.W.*, 87:51–61 (1969), a formal recognition of two mistletoe families, and natural grouping within each; A. TAKHTAJAN, *Flowering Plants: Origin and Dispersal* (1969; Eng. trans. from the 2nd Russian ed., 1961), a recent book treating plant relationships at the level of families and orders; J. HUTCHINSON, *The Families of Flowering Plants*, vol. 1, *Dicotyledons*, 2nd ed. (1959); A. ENGLER and K. PRANTL, *Die natürlichen Pflanzenfamilien*, 2nd ed., vol. 16b (1935), the only recent, detailed coverage of the plant kingdom. Vol. 16b contains chapters, written by various specialists, on all important santalalean families, including Balanophoraceae, Hydnoraceae, and Rafflesiaceae.

(J.Ku.)

Santayana, George

George Santayana was an early-20th-century philosopher, novelist, and man of letters, the speculative naturalism and critical Realism of whose thought was expressed in prose of great formal beauty. At once a Skeptic and a humanist, Santayana gave a rich and perceptive account of human experience—ethical, social, religious, and artistic—skillfully interweaving themes that modern technical philosophy keeps apart.

Career at Harvard and in England. George Santayana was born of Spanish parents on December 16, 1863, in Madrid. He never relinquished his Spanish citizenship, and, although he was to write in English with subtlety and poise, he did not begin to learn that language until taken to join his mother in Boston in 1872. Santayana was to reside in New England for most of the ensuing 40 years. He went through the Boston Latin School and Harvard College, graduating summa cum laude in 1886. He then spent two years studying philosophy at the University of Berlin before returning to Harvard to complete his doctoral thesis under the Pragmatist William

Santayana.

James. He joined the faculty of philosophy in 1889, forming with James and the Idealist Josiah Royce a brilliant triumvirate of philosophers. Yet his attachment to Europe was strong. He spent his summers in Spain with his father, visited England, and spent his sabbatical leaves abroad: at Cambridge, in Italy and the East, and at the Sorbonne.

At Harvard he began to write. *The Sense of Beauty* (1896) was an important contribution to aesthetics. The essay is concerned with the nature and elements of man's aesthetic feelings and holds that to judge that anything is beautiful is "virtually to establish an ideal"; and the understanding of why something is thought to be beautiful enables one to distinguish transitory ideals from those that, springing from more fundamental feelings, are "comparatively permanent and universal." The vital affinity between such aesthetic faculties and man's moral faculties is illustrated in Santayana's next book, *Interpretations of Poetry and Religion* (1900), particularly in the discussion of the poetry of Robert Browning, which is a model of its kind.

The Life of Reason (1905–06) was a major theoretical work consisting of five volumes. Conceived in his student days after a reading of Hegel's *Phenomenology of Spirit*, it was described by Santayana as "a presumptive biography of the human intellect." The life of reason, for Santayana as for Hegel, is not restricted to purely intellectual activities, for reason in all of its manifestations is a union of impulse and ideation. It is instinct become reflective and enlightened. The theory is given practical illustration in a series of essays, gathered into two volumes: *Three Philosophical Poets: Lucretius, Dante, and Goethe* (1910); and *Winds of Doctrine* (1913), in which the poetry of Percy Bysshe Shelley and the philosophies of Henri Bergson, a French evolutionary philosopher, and of Bertrand Russell are discussed.

Santayana was appointed a full Harvard professor in 1907. In 1912, however, while he was in Europe, his mother died, and he sent in his resignation from there. He never returned to America, although several attractive offers were made by Harvard in an attempt to draw him back.

Santayana's resignation astonished his colleagues, for it came at the height of his career. All of his books were admired and influential, and there seemed to be an intimate connection between them and his teaching. Clearly, he was a gifted teacher: interested in his students, devoid of pedantry, and with a superb capacity for analyzing philosophies and related poetry with lucid sympathy while judging them by standards that remained rational and humane. His resignation, nevertheless, can be seen as inevitable: he disliked the academic straitjacket; he wished to devote himself exclusively to his writing; and he was ill at ease in America. His Latin heritage and allegiance gave to his thinking a striking range and perspective, but the net result was to make him want "to say plausibly in English as many un-English things as possible." From the strain of doing this, he was thankful to escape.

Early writings

When World War I began, Santayana was in Oxford, and he settled there for the duration. Though he enjoyed the friendship of several eminent people, the war saddened him, and he led a secluded life. *Egotism in German Philosophy* appeared in 1916, making clear his strong allegiance to the Allied cause; he also wrote a number of popular essays centring on the English character and countryside. At the end of the war he was offered a life membership in Corpus Christi College, Oxford, but he declined.

Career in Rome. In 1924 he settled permanently in Rome. The atmosphere was congenial to a native-born Catholic who, though evolving into a philosophical materialist for whom the world of spirit was wholly ideal and nonexistent, had always admired the Catholic and classical traditions. Three new books consolidated his reputation as a humanist critic and man of letters, and this side was brought to perfect expression in a novel, *The Last Puritan* (1935).

The bulk of his energies in the interwar years, however, went into speculative philosophy. *Scepticism and Animal Faith* (1923) marks an important departure from his earlier philosophy and serves as "a critical introduction" to and résumé of his new system developed in the four-volume *Realms of Being* (1928, 1930, 1937, 1940), an ontological (nature of being) treatise of great concentration and finish. In these later works Santayana enhanced his stature as a philosopher by achieving greater theoretical precision, depth, and coherence. *Scepticism and Animal Faith* conveys better than any other volume the essential import of his philosophy. It formulates his theory of immediately apprehended essences and describes the role played by "animal faith" in various forms of knowledge.

In *Realms of Being* extraordinarily complex points are elucidated with luminous succinctness, although the general reader is deterred by their technicality and by the aestheticism inherent in a view of Truth as simply "that segment of the realm of essence which happens to be illustrated in existence." "The realm of essence," in Santayana's system, is that of the mind's certain and indubitable knowledge. Essences are universals that have being or reality but do not exist. They include colours, tastes, and odours as well as the ideal objects of thought and imagination. "The realm of matter" is the world of natural objects; belief in it rests—as does all belief concerning existence—on animal faith. Naturalism, the dominant theme of his entire philosophy, appears in his insistence that matter is prior to the other realms.

Such a philosophy enabled Santayana to accept imperturbably another onset of war. He took rooms in a Catholic nursing home and began a three-volume autobiography, *Persons and Places* (1944, 1945, 1953). When Rome was liberated in 1944, the 80-year-old author found himself visited by an "avalanche" of American admirers. By now he was immersed in *Dominations and Powers* (1951), an analysis of man in society; and then with heroic tenacity—for he was nearly deaf and half blind—he gave himself to translating Lorenzo de' Medici's love poem, "Ambra," during which he was overtaken by his last illness. He died on September 26, 1952, a few months before his 89th birthday, and was buried, as he had wished, in the Catholic cemetery of Rome in a plot reserved for Spanish nationals.

New system of philosophy

Last years

MAJOR WORKS

PHILOSOPHY: *The Sense of Beauty* (1896); *The Life of Reason; or the Phases of Human Progress* (1905–06), five volumes consisting of *Reason in Common Sense, Reason in Society, Reason in Religion, Reason in Art,* and *Reason in Science; Scepticism and Animal Faith* (1923); *Realms of Being* (1927–40), four volumes consisting of *The Realm of Essence, The Realm of Matter, The Realm of Truth,* and *The Realm of Spirit; Dominations and Powers* (1951).

CRITICAL WRITINGS: *Interpretations of Poetry and Religion* (1900); *Three Philosophical Poets: Lucretius, Dante, and Goethe* (1910); *Winds of Doctrine* (1913); *Egotism in German Philosophy* (1916); *Philosophical Opinion in America* (1918); *Character and Opinion in the United States* (1920); *Platonism and the Spiritual Life* (1927); *Some Turns of Thought in Modern Philosophy* (1933); *The Idea of Christ in the Gospels* (1946).

OTHER WORKS: *The Last Puritan* (1935), a novel; *Persons and Places,* 3 vol. (1944–53), autobiography.

BIBLIOGRAPHY. There is no full-length biography of Santayana, but GEORGE W. HOWGATE, *George Santayana* (1938), and DANIEL CORY, *Santayana: The Later Years* (1963), together provide a detailed portrait that may be supplemented by DANIEL CORY (ed.), *The Letters of George Santayana* (1955), and by Santayana's three-volume autobiography, *Persons and Places* (1944–53). A comprehensive study of Santayana's philosophy, and in particular of his later ontology, has still to be written, but of special interest among book-length studies of his moral philosophy are: WILLARD E. ARNETT, *Santayana and the Sense of Beauty* (1955); MILTON K. MUNITZ, *The Moral Philosophy of Santayana* (1939); and JACQUES DURON, *La Pensée de George Santayana: Santayana en Amérique* (1950), which contains a detailed list of book reviews and articles on Santayana up to 1950. Two volumes bring together most of the shorter critiques of Santayana's philosophy: P.A. SCHILPP (ed.), *The Philosophy of George Santayana* (1940); and JOHN LACHS (ed.), *Animal Faith and Spiritual Life* (1967). The contents are of uneven quality, but there are informative essays by Bertrand Russell, Justus Buchler, and several others. An admirably detailed article on Santayana's critique of Idealism and Pragmatism is TIMOTHY L.S. SPRIGGE, "Santayana and Verificationism," *Inquiry,* 12: 265–286 (1969). Editorial introductions to the following collections of Santayana's work provide interesting appraisals of his achievement as humanist and social and literary critic: NORMAN HENFREY (ed.), *Selected Critical Writings of George Santayana* (1968); RICHARD COLTON LYON (ed.), *Santayana on America* (1968); and DOUGLAS L. WILSON (ed.), *The Genteel Tradition* (1967), in which is traced the historical influence of that phrase as coined and given conceptual currency by Santayana in 1911.

(N.V.He.)

Santiago

Santiago is the capital and major city of the Republic of Chile. It is also the capital of Santiago province and the country's largest industrial centre. Located in north central Chile, the city has grown rapidly during the 20th century and has developed into the sprawling urban complex known as Greater Santiago, which covers an area of 132 square miles (342 square kilometres) with a complex of residential areas, industrial zones, and slums. Its national importance is reflected in its metropolitan population of about 2,780,000—almost one-third of the nation's inhabitants.

Santiago is plagued by the urban problems of overcrowding, air and water pollution, lack of services, and the economic and social consequences of the migration of city residents to the ever-expanding suburbs. It is also the object of rivalry from other Chilean cities that desire more development for themselves. It has always been Chile's principal city, however, and its continued position as the major economic and cultural centre of the country seems assured.

History. The city was founded as Santiago del Nuevo Extremo (Santiago of the New Frontier) in 1541 by the Spanish conquistador Pedro de Valdivia. The area was inhabited by the Picunche Indians; who were placed under the rule of the Spanish settlers who formed the city. The original city site was limited by the two surrounding arms of the Mapocho River and by Huelén (renamed Santa Lucía) Hill to the east, which served as a lookout.

The city's origin

Santiago was the original headquarters of the Spanish governor of Chile and has been the nation's capital throughout its history. As they were created, various governmental, military, ecclesiastic, and cultural institutions were established there. These included the Town Council (founded 1541), the archbishopric (1561), the Royal Court (1609)—a subsidiary of the Spanish Royal Court, the University of San Felipe (1747), the Mint (1743), and the Court of the Consulate (1795), which served both commercial and judicial functions.

During the period of Spanish domination, growth was slow. In 1700, the city covered one and a half square miles and had a population of 10,000. A century later it had expanded to almost three square miles and had 25,000 residents. Its checkerboard outline was maintained until the early 1800s, when it grew to the north, to the south, and especially to the west. The south shore of the

Expansion in the 18th century

Cerro Santa Lucía with downtown Santiago, Chile, to the upper right.
Carl Frank

Mapocho River was drained and converted into a public promenade, now the Alameda Bernardo O'Higgins. The more densely inhabited neighbourhoods formed a suburban area to the north of the river called La Chimba.

At the beginning of the struggle for independence in 1810, the city covered nearly four square miles and had 35,000 inhabitants. It suffered little during the War of Independence (1810–18), since the decisive Battle of Maipú took place outside the city limits. Santiago was named the republic's capital in 1818; it became the seat of the National Congress, the Supreme Court of Justice, the University of Chile, the ministries, and the municipal theatre. Thus, during the remainder of the 19th century, the wealth of the nation flowed into Santiago.

Prosperous saltpeter, copper, and coal magnates and absentee landlords moved to the capital, living in upper income neighbourhoods such as Cousiño Park. Middle income areas also developed. By 1900 the city's population had reached 250,000, with its area extended over 11 square miles.

During the 20th century, Santiago has grown rapidly and in an unplanned fashion. The absorption of nearby villages and towns has caused enormous increases in expenditure and has resulted in a sharpening of economic and cultural differences between the capital and other Chilean cities. By 1960, Greater Santiago covered 132 square miles and housed nearly 2,000,000 inhabitants.

The contemporary city. *The city site.* Santiago lies in a depression formed by the coastal mountain range, the Cordillera Occidental to the west, the Chacabuco Ridge to the north, and the towering Andes to the east. Its elevation is about 1,700 feet (520 metres) above sea level. The city centre covers an area of 21 square miles. It is triangular in shape, with Santa Lucía Hill forming the eastern tip of the triangle, the Mapocho River forming its northern border, and the Avenida Bernardo O'Higgins —or the Alameda—forming its southern boundary. Together with its surrounding suburbs, Greater Santiago spreads out in all directions over the Mapocho River's alluvial plains, but is confined on the east by the Andes. By 1970, the metropolitan area extended to the towns of Colina to the north, Buin to the south, Melipilla to the west, and Cajón del Maipo to the east.

Climate. The climate resembles that of the Mediterranean. Summer occurs between October and March; it is warm and dry with an average January temperature of 68° F (20° C). The annual average rainfall of 15 inches occurs mainly in winter, when high humidity and low temperatures result in penetrating cold; the average July temperature is 46° F. Fog is common in winter.

Vegetation and animal life. The original vegetation consisted of grasses and brambles. It has largely disappeared within the city but can be found at the edges of the suburbs, especially to the east in the Andean foothills. Remnants of the original forests of peumus (a laureceous plant bearing edible fruit) and litre (a hardwood tree with poisonous leaves) are found at Manquehue to the northeast and Peñalolén to the east.

In addition to the sparrows and pigeons introduced from Europe, there are indigenous birds such as the fieldfare, gold finch, *tiuque* (a bird of prey), and turtle dove. Rodents such as the rat and spiney mouse occur in the surrounding rural area.

The city layout. Greater Santiago includes 18 different *comunas* (districts). They are Santiago, Conchalí, Renca, Quilicura, Providencia, Las Condes, Nuñoa, La Reina, San Miguel, La Florida, La Granja, La Cisterna, Puente Alto, San Bernardo, Pirque, Quinta Normal, Maipú, and Las Barrancas. Until 1960 each community enjoyed complete autonomy, but since then the degree of autonomy has been reduced with the introduction of the Intercommunity Regulating Plan of Santiago, which harmonizes city development. The suburbs have nevertheless continued to expand, and the outlying districts are not under the plan's control. *(margin: Neighbourhood districts)*

Santiago's checkerboard plan of rectangular city blocks has spread monotonously over the flat valley and has partly climbed up the Andean piedmont and the spur of the coast mountains. Apart from the basic triangular shape of the city, the city map resembles a misshapen star, whose five points correspond to the main highways, along which homes have been built.

The *centro*, or downtown area, the city's original nucleus, is centred on the Plaza de Armas and the Barrio Cívico, which contain a concentration of high-rise buildings primarily intended for administrative and commercial use and only secondarily for residences. The *barrio alto*, or high district, includes the upper-income communities of Providencia (6,658 feet), Las Condes (2,719 feet), and La Reina (1,827 feet), which are located on the elevated ground of the Andes foothills. The altitude of the area is a symbolic socioeconomic segregating barrier. Its occupants are largely managers, high-level professionals, and members of the business community. *(margin: Social stratification)*

Social stratification in the rest of the city is complex. The middle-income group is predominant in Santiago proper and in Nuñoa. The lower income group is crowded into the peripheral northern, western, and southern communities.

Transportation. Santiago's urban interests have largely conditioned the development of Chile's transportation system. The city is the focus of the nation's internal communications. Because of the configuration of the country, most transportation routes are established to the north and south of Santiago, where the northern and southern sections of the Pan-American Highway meet. The state railroads also run north and south from Santiago. There are eight city railroad stations, the most important of which are Alameda and Mapocho. Highways and roads connect the city with the ports of San Antonio to the west and Valparaíso to the northwest, thus providing an outlet to the Pacific Ocean. To the east, there are only short roads leading to winter resorts.

Air communications are provided by the international airport at Pudahuel and the airport at Los Cerrillos, which handles domestic flights. There are also two smaller civil airports—Lo Castillo and Tobalaba—as well as El Bosque, a military airport.

The internal road system in Greater Santiago does not meet the increasing traffic needs, especially during the rush hour. Construction of a north–south highway through the city and an avenue encircling it are scheduled for the early 1970s. A subway is to be completed by 1976.

Demography. In 1970 the population of Greater Santiago was approximately 2,780,000. Its rapid growth, as mentioned, is due mainly to an influx of migrants from rural areas and small towns. The Santiago metropolitan area contains 29 percent of the nation's inhabitants.

There is a noticeable movement from the old city to the suburbs. Between 1960 and 1970, the population of Santiago proper dropped from more than 646,000 to about 510,000. Each of the suburbs, however, has gained in population. Some areas have densities of over 52,000 inhabitants per square mile, especially in low-income districts. The upper-income suburbs in the east have much lower densities.

Housing. Houses are built in a wide variety of architectural styles. The one-floor family house prevails, although large apartment buildings for workmen and other employees have been built. A large percentage of the population is inadequately housed in the central slum tenements, called *conventillos*, as well as in the marginal shanty towns, or *callampas*. The inevitable social pressures have been accumulating in these districts.

Building types. Architectural remnants of the colonial era include the Palace of the Governors, the Metropolitan Cathedral, the Mint, the Consulate Tribunal, and the churches of San Francisco, Santo Domingo, the Recoleta Franciscana, and the Church of Mercy. The Cousiño Palace is an example of 19th-century architecture, while early-20th-century styles are expressed in the Fine Arts Palace, the National Library, and the Union Club. Modern architectural achievements are represented by residences at Vitacura, San Luis Hill, and Lo Curro.

Industry. Greater Santiago contains Chile's greatest concentration of industry and produces about 50 percent of the nation's total industrial output. There are over 13,000 industries, employing more than 227,000 people —almost half the nation's industrial work force. The main products are foodstuffs, textiles, shoes, and clothes; metallurgy is also important. The preferred industrial locations are in Santiago proper and in the southern suburbs of San Miguel, Nuñoa, and Maipú. Important copper deposits are mined in Las Barrancas and Las Condes.

Principal products

Commerce and services. Most of the labour force is engaged in providing services, but commercial activities are also of great importance. The city has an active financial sector, as well, including a stock exchange, 20 major banks with hundreds of branches, and many insurance companies. These activities were traditionally concentrated downtown, but, by the 1970s, other centres were forming, such as those in Nuñoa and Providencia.

Political institutions. Most of the governmental and public institutions are located near the Mint, near the residence of the president of the republic, and along Bulnes Avenue, an area known as the Civic District. Santiago, as noted, is the seat of the National Congress and the Supreme Court of Justice.

Public utilities. Santiago's accelerated growth has outstripped the effective capacity of public services. The provision of drinking water, sewage disposal, lighting, gas, telephones, and sanitation is reliable in the downtown area and the high-income district, while such services have deteriorated in the less wealthy neighbourhoods. Drinking water is supplied from Laguna Negra (Black Lagoon), situated approximately 30 miles eastsoutheast of Santiago, the Yeso Dam in the Andes, and the Vizcachas and Vizcachitas filtration plants east of Puente Alto. Electricity is provided by the Chilean Electricity Company from hydroelectric stations in the Andes, a coal-powered thermal plant in Renca, and the facilities of the National Electricity Enterprise.

Health and safety. There are over two dozen public hospitals and several first-aid stations. Public medical assistance is available for private homes, and there are also about 30 private clinics.

Police services are provided by a force of *carabiñeros*, or armed policemen, who are organized into precincts and subprecincts; there are also radio-patrol services. Fire protection is efficient and is provided by a nonprofit institution called the Firemen of Chile, consisting of about 50 units.

Education. Public education facilities include primary schools, vocational schools, and private high schools. Advanced educational institutions include the University of Chile, the Catholic University, and the State Technical University.

Cultural life. The city's cultural life is cosmopolitan, its native institutions exhibiting European and North American influences. There is a strong resurgence of mestizo artisanship, especially in the fields of music, theatre, painting, and literature.

The city contains about nine libraries and the National Archives. Museums include the National Museum of Natural History, which contains objects from Easter Island; the Museum of Maipú, containing colonial furniture and religious art; the National Historical Museum; the San Francisco Museum, with exhibits of colonial art; the Contemporary Art Museum; the Fine Arts Museum; and the Popular Arts Museum housing pieces of Chilean folk art.

There are almost a dozen newspapers, with a combined daily circulation of 400,000 copies. There are also 20 radio stations and three television channels that broadcast in Spanish.

Recreational facilities

The most prominent recreation areas are the public parks of Santa Lucía Hill; San Cristóbal Hill, with its zoo and camping grounds; Forestal; Cousiño; Quinta Normal; and La Quintrala. There are also more than 60 swimming pools, almost all of which belong to private institutions, and two circuses.

The National Stadium has a seating capacity of 80,000 people and is used for soccer games and gymnastic events. Many private and public sports clubs, as well as stadiums, offer varied facilities. There are ski slopes in Farellones and excellent transportation to the nearby seaside resorts spread along the coast between Algarrobo and Santo Domingo.

The popularity of drama and motion pictures is evidenced by Santiago's eight legitimate theatres and 90 movie houses.

BIBLIOGRAPHY. DEPARTAMENTO DE EXTENSION CULTURAL DE LA UNIVERSIDAD DE CHILE, *Seminario del Gran Santiago*, 2 vol. (1957–58), a fundamental collection of essays on the urban problems of Greater Santiago; KARL BRUNNER, *Santiago de Chile, su estado actual y su futura formación* (1932), a classic work necessary for an understanding of urban development; CHILE, OFICINA DE PLANIFICACION NATIONAL, *Política de desarrollo nacional: Directivas nacionales y regionales* (1968), contains a chapter on the city's effect on the national economy; CHILE, MINISTERIO OBRAS PUBLICAS, PROGRAMA CHILE-CALIFORNIA, *Encuesta de origin y destino del movimiento de* *personas en el Gran Santiago* (1966), a valuable demographic study; CENTRO INTERDISCIPLINARIO DE DESARROLLO URBANO Y REGIONAL, *Santiago Oriente: Acción 1969–1990* (1968), contains notes of interest on the development of the communities of Providencia, Las Condes, and La Reina.

(P.Cl.)

Santo Domingo

Santo Domingo, the capital of the Dominican Republic and the oldest surviving city established by Europeans in the Western Hemisphere, is situated on the southeast coast of the island of Hispaniola, on the west bank of the Ozama River. It was founded in 1496 by Bartolomeo Columbus, brother of Christopher, as the capital of the first Spanish colony in the New World. The Distrito Nacional (federal district) of the Dominican Republic includes the capital city and bears the same name. Its area is 570 square miles, with a population of about 800,000, of which about 670,000 live in the city proper.

History.   From its beginnings in 1496, Santo Domingo was the seat of many of the New World's earliest important institutions: the first bishopric, 1504; the first Spanish viceroyship, 1509; the first Royal High Court of Justice, 1511; the first cathedral, 1521; and the first university (the Royal and Pontifical University of Saint Thomas Aquinas, now Santo Domingo University), 1538.

Some scholars believe that the city was named after Domenico (or Domingo) Columbus, father of Bartolomeo and Christopher, whereas others think it was named in honour of the Spanish Saint Dominic (Domingo de Guzmán).

The original city   The original city was located on the left (east) bank of the Ozama River and was called Nueva Isabela in honour of Queen Isabella. It was destroyed by a hurricane, however, and was rebuilt in 1502 at its present location on the right bank of the river. It became the starting point of most of the expeditions of exploration and conquest of the other West Indian islands and the adjacent mainland. The colony prospered as the seat of government of the Spanish possessions in the Americas until the conquest of Mexico and Peru, after which its importance declined.

In 1586, Sir Francis Drake, the famous English buccaneer, sacked the city and even cannonaded the cathedral, retiring only after he had been paid a ransom of 25,000 gold ducats. In 1655 its inhabitants defeated a British force that had been sent to seize the city.

For a few years, from 1795 to 1809, Santo Domingo was under French domination, and then, after a brief Spanish period, it was conquered by invaders from Haiti. Independence was proclaimed in 1844, and Santo Domingo became the capital of the new Dominican Republic until the republic's annexation to Spain in 1861–1865. It has been the Dominican capital since the restoration of independence in 1865. The city's name, officially changed to Ciudad Trujillo in honour of the dictator Rafael L. Trujillo Molina, who governed the republic from 1930 to 1961, was restored after his assassination in 1961.

The contemporary city.   *Districts and landmarks.*   Like many other Hispano-American cities, Santo Domingo was built on a geometric pattern. After a period of rapid growth since World War II, there are now two distinct districts: the old colonial city and the modern new city, or garden city. In addition there are some colourless, styleless buildings that are remnants of the 19th and early 20th centuries and some dilapidated slum areas that are being replaced by apartment complexes. These belong neither to the old city nor to the new.

The Distrito Nacional, as distinguished from the capital city, includes rural areas as well as suburbs, such as Boca Chica, San Lorenzo de los Minas, Guerra, La Victoria, and Los Alcarrizos, all of which are within an average of about 12 miles of the capital's centre.

Reconstruction of the colonial city   Much of the colonial city has been painstakingly reconstructed. The old section near the Ozama River continues south along the coast of the Caribbean and rises to the west and north until it reaches what is called the barrio (quarter or district) of San Carlos de Tenerife, where at one time the city fortifications ended. Within this area are almost all the buildings in the colonial style, including churches, convents, palaces, civic buildings, and forts. The two most prominent colonial monuments are the cathedral, containing the reputed remains of Christopher Columbus, and the palace (or alcazar) of Diego Columbus. Other edifices of the colonial period include the San Diego Gate; the impressive ruins of the church of San Francisco; the church of the Society of Jesus, now the National Pantheon; the Count's Gate; and the Gate of Mercy, three Carmelite churches, and the church and fort of Santa Barbara, part of the old city's defense system. Among the secular remains are the Ozama Fortress, with what is called the Tower of Homage; the Sun Clock in front of the old Palace of the Generals; the House of the Cordon; the Arsenal; and the House of the Roasting (Casa del Tostado).

To the west of the old city the new city stretches along the coast and inland. Growing continuously toward the west, it includes thousands of middle-class and well-to-do homes. Broad front gardens and flowering interior patios present an orgy of colours and tropical plants, with geraniums, carnations, poinsettias, rose bushes, gladiolas, climbing plants, and trees such as the almond, mahogany, and palm in abundance. The homes are of many different styles, including colonial, modern, Bermudian, and Mediterranian. The government has built well-designed duplex and multifamily dwellings for working families. The architecture of privately owned suburban development is also attractive. This building boom, however, is resulting in the overexpansion of the city.

Climate.   Santo Domingo enjoys a tropical climate. Tropical cyclones and hurricanes have usually missed the urban area, except for the one that destroyed the original city in 1502 and a hurricane that devasted the city of wooden houses in 1930. The average annual temperature has been 78° F (about 26° C), with a maximum of 91° F (33° C) in the summer and a minimum of 66° F (19° C) in the winter. The annual average rainfall is about 50 inches.

Transportation.   Three principal roads connect the capital with the rest of the republic: the Duarte expressway to the north, the Mella road to the east, and the Sánchez road to the west. There are no railway lines from the capital, except those of the nearby sugar refineries. The port of Santo Domingo handles heavy passenger and freight traffic between Santo Domingo and the United States, Japan, and Europe. The Airport of the Americas, 18 miles from the city, is one of the most modern in the Americas. In 1969 a new air-conditioned terminal and a 270,000-square-foot airplane park were built.

Economic activity.   Santo Domingo is the industrial and commercial centre of the country and is the location of a central bank for issuing currency and of the Dominican State Reserve Bank, as well as of branches of the most important United States and Canadian banks. The government has enacted an industrial-incentive law, exempting businesses in the city from heavy duties, and has ceded 2,000 acres for the Herrera industrial zone, which is four and a half miles from the capital and is supplied with all the basic urban services. Santo Domingo's progress, especially its industrial development, has been greatly influenced by the construction of two hydroelectric dams. The country's most important industries, such as metallurgy, refrigerators, automobile batteries, petrochemicals and plastics, cement, construction, furniture, textiles, shoes, perfumes, brewing, and food processing, are located in Santo Domingo.   *Industrial development*

The city's health services are advanced, and malaria, which had been a serious problem throughout the republic, has been eliminated. In early 1969 there were about 90 public and private health establishments of all types in the capital, with a total of about 5,000 beds.

Education, cultural life, and recreation.   There are two universities, one public—the autonomous University of Santo Domingo—and the other private—the Pedro Henríquez Ureña National University—founded in 1966. In addition to primary schools, there are numerous private lycées and secondary schools (*colegios*) with religious affiliations, both Roman Catholic and other.

Santo Domingo's cultural institutions include the Na-

The Armed Forces building in Santo Domingo. A statue to Trujillo Molina stands at right foreground.
Photo Research International

tional Institute of Dominican Culture, the Higher Education Institute, the Higher School of Fine Arts, the National Theatre-School of Art, the Music Conservatory and the National Symphony Orchestra, the National Museum—important for its pre-Columbian collection—and various public and private libraries, especially the great National Library.

In the early 1970s three daily newspapers were published—two in the morning and one in the evening—plus several weeklies and magazines. There are 22 radio transmitters and two television stations; one, Dominican Radiotelevision, is the government station, and the other, Rahintel, is privately owned.

In addition to its zoo, Santo Domingo has also a beautiful green area, Mirador Sur Avenue, featuring small parks, illuminated fountains, and statues. There are also numerous plazas and parks.

For sports there are numerous volleyball fields and basketball courts in the schools and barrios, a magnificent baseball stadium capable of holding 16,000 spectators for the professional championship, and the Juan Pablo Duarte Olympic Centre for track and field events. Work has begun on the stadium in which the Central American Olympic Games will be held in 1974. There are five first-class international hotels, one of which has a polo field and golf course.

BIBLIOGRAPHY. For a general picture, HOWARD J. WIARDA, *The Dominican Republic* (1969), has much material on Santo Domingo. For the historical and political background, see V.T. ROJAS, *This Is the Dominican Republic* (1954); and the *Santo Domingo Year Book*, 1950–54 (1954).

(M.G.A.)

São Francisco River

One of the greatest rivers in South America, the São Francisco is the third largest river system of Brazil and the largest river wholly within the country. It is regarded as "the river of national unity" because it has long served as a 1,800-mile (2,900-kilometre) line of communication between Brazil's maritime and western regions and between the north and the south. The river is named for the 16th-century Jesuit leader, St. Francis Borgia (São Francisco de Borja). It is an important source of hydroelectric power for northeastern Brazil and is a potential source of irrigation water for the country's dry interior plain. (For related articles, see BRAZIL and articles on the states of ALAGOAS; BAHIA; MINAS GERAIS; PERNAMBUCO; and SERGIPE.)

The river's course. The São Francisco rises at about 2,400 feet above sea level on the eastern slope of the Serra da Canastra (Canastra Mountains) in southwestern Minas Gerais state (*estado*), some distance south of the Brazilian capital of Brasília (*q.v.*). It flows for more than

The upper course

1,000 miles northward across the State of Bahia to the twin cities of Juàzeiro and Petrolina. In this stretch the river receives the main left-bank tributaries—the Paracatu, Urucuia, Corrente, and Grande rivers—and the right-bank tributaries—the Verde-Grande, Paramirim, and Jacaré.

About 100 miles above Petrolina, the river begins a great curve to the northeast and enters a 300-mile-long stretch of rapids and falls. In this section the São Francisco forms the border between the states of Bahia to the south and Pernambuco to the north. The upper rapids are navigable during periods of high water, but below Petrolina the river is impassable. The broken course—during which the São Francisco receives the San Pedro, Cocheira, and Pajehú rivers—culminates in the great Paulo Affonso Cachoeira (Paulo Affonso Falls). At the top of the falls, the river divides suddenly and violently and cuts three successive falls through the granite rocks for a total drop of about 250 feet. Below the falls, the river flows about 150 miles to its one mile-wide mouth on the Atlantic Ocean, about 60 miles north of Aracaju. In its lower section it is joined by the Rio Moxotó and forms the border between the states of Sergipe to the south and Alagoas to the north.

The environment. The São Francisco Valley includes a total area of 243,681 square miles (631,133 square kilometres). The upper river valley is an area of *caatinga*, or thorny forest, vegetation. Important plants include the caroá, used for its fibres, and the mamona, which yields castor oil. There are trees, such as the oil, carnauba, and date palms; the cajú (cashew), which yields edible fruits; the palma, a spineless cactus with a high water content; and rubber trees. The upper middle valley, extending to the falls zone, is less dry and is covered with grassland (*campos cerrados*) and forests of semi-deciduous trees. Hardwoods include the jacaranda, Brazilian cedar (*cedro*), and vinhatico, and cochineal cactus, aloes, and vanilla plants also grow here.

The falls zone passes through the dry Brazilian interior, known as the *sertão*. The small amount of rainfall in the area permits the growth of only drought-resistant brush and grasses. The dry forests of the hilly uplands support carnauba and babassu palms and such plants as the cactus, the rock rose, and the rhododendron. Underground water in the region is too saline for irrigation or drinking.

The Lower São Francisco flows through a floodplain of fine silt soils. Most of the original tropical semi-deciduous forest that grew along the river has been cleared for agriculture.

The river's fish are an important source of food. They include robalo, sardines, pocomó, and sarapó. The river mouth supports meru (squalas), manatees (sea cows), and sharks.

The climate of most of the river basin is hot and dry. The average maximum temperature for the region is 97° F (36° C) and the average minimum 66° F (19° C). The highest temperature recorded is 107° F (42° C). The prevailing winds are from the southeast, east, and northeast. Rainfall is deficient over most of the area and drought is frequent. Average annual precipitation measures 20 to 40 inches in the middle basin and 40 to 80 inches at the river mouth; about 8 percent of the basin receives only ten inches of rain annually. Precipitation occurs during the summer months, from December to March, while the rest of the year—the winter season—is dry.

Human ecology.   Except for the blacks who live along the coast, the people of the São Francisco Basin are of mixed Portuguese and Indian descent. The upper middle valley is an agricultural region in which cotton, rice, and maize (corn) are grown. The region also produces pineapples, barley, potatoes, rye, maté (tea), melons, sugarcane, beans, coffee, castor and cottonseed oils, and rum. Its major urban centre is Pirapora.

Pastoralism and *vazante* agriculture

The dry *sertão* is used largely for the grazing of cattle, goats, sheep, and donkeys. Along the river banks *vazante* agriculture is practiced: during the rainy season, shallow waterbeds (*vassantes*) are enclosed by bars of river sediment, and support the cultivation of manioc (cassava), water beans, and melons. Truck crops are grown on the river banks, and carnauba, caroá, and rubber are collected. The major town is the market centre of Salvador. Most of the lower river valley is dry and suitable to pastoral activities. Along the coast, wetland rice is grown.

Hydrology, navigation, and river crossings.   Because the river flows through the driest region of Brazil, it is subject to seasonal changes in water level of up to 30 feet (ten metres). All of its tributaries run dry during the winter; above Juàzeiro, the riverbed varies from a narrow channel during drought periods to several miles in width during the rainy season.

The river is navigable for small steamers for more than 1,000 miles from Pirapora, Minas Gerais, to Várzea Redonda, Bahia, upstream of Petrolina. Sandbars at the river's mouth prevent the entry of deep-draft ocean vessels. There is a railway bridge across the river at Pirapora, and another bridge connects the cities of Petrolina and Juàzeiro. Although river transport is slow and difficult, the São Francisco is an important link between the mining district of Minas Gerais and roads that radiate north and east from Juàzeiro.

The river's hydro-electric potential

Resources and their development.   The river's hydroelectric potential is its most important resource. The main centre of power for northeastern Brazil is the Paulo Afonso Cachoeira, where the Três Marias Dam, completed in 1960, has a total installed capacity of 520,000 kilowatts. Further construction will provide another 900,000 kilowatts by the mid-1970s. There are also hydroelectric possibilities of providing electricity to the coastal cities of Salvador, Aracaju, and Recife with dams on the upper and lower stretches of the river, the total hydroelectric power potential of the river is estimated at 520,000,000 kilowatts.

The river basin is also important as a source of irrigation water. The largest storage dam is at Quixadá, Ceará state. There are large reservoirs at Cachoeira and Pedra d'água, and there are plans for a reservoir on the Jaguaribe and a 300-mile-long irrigation canal to join the São Francisco at Petrolina to branches in eastern Pernambuco, Paraiba, and eastern Ceará states.

The river basin contains deposits of agate, gold, iron, diamonds, opals, antimony, galena (the principal ore of lead), mercury, copper, arsenic, manganese, cobalt, and pyrites. There are also deposits of salt, sulfur, alum, marble, limestone, and clay.   (C.E.Ca.)

São Paulo (State)

One of the 22 states of Brazil, São Paulo comprises the richest and most populous region of the country. With a total area of 95,714 square miles (247,898 square kilo-

metres) and a population that in 1970 numbered about 18,000,000, it produces nearly two-thirds of the nation's manufactures and about a third of its leading crop—coffee.

São Paulo is bordered by the states of Paraná to the south and Mato Grosso to the west and north, by Minas Gerais to the north and east, by Rio de Janeiro to the east, and by a 386-mile Atlantic coastline to the southeast. About 80 percent of its population is urban and suburban. The state capital, São Paulo, is the largest city in Brazil. (See city article SAO PAULO; for an associated physical feature, see PARANA RIVER.)

History.   The area that was to become São Paulo was settled in 1532 by the Portuguese under the explorer Martim Afonso de Souza, who established a flourishing settlement at São Vicente, now a resort town near Santos, as well as the village of Piratininga on the plateau. When Brazil was divided into captaincies, or hereditary fiefs, the captaincy of São Vicente, comprising the whole of Brazil south of Rio de Janeiro, was granted to Souza (1534). By the middle of the 16th century, the captaincy had a population of about 5,000, including the growing port of Santos and the town of São Paulo (founded 1554). The Vicentinos (inhabitants of São Vicente) had begun to explore the hinterlands, and new villages began to appear on the coastline (Iguape, Cananéia) and on the plateau (Paraíba, Mogi das Cruzes, Taubaté, and others), which became the main region of inland settlement. In 1681 the captaincy was renamed São Paulo, and the town of that name was designated the capital.

Early Portuguese settlement

Throughout the 17th century, roaming bands of armed pioneers (*bandeirantes*) explored the interior in search of Indian slaves and precious metals. Their enslavement of the Indians brought the settlers into conflict with the Jesuit mission—a conflict that continued intermittently until after the introduction of slaves from Africa.

In the 18th century the Portuguese inhabitants of the captaincy (called Paulistas or Paulistanos) continued to penetrate the west, north, and south. But before the end of the century the regions conquered and peopled by the pioneers—Minas Gerais, Mato Grosso, Goiás, Santa Catarina, and Rio Grande do Sul—were separated from the captaincy, leaving it impoverished and in decline. São Paulo existed on its commerce, sugar growing, and diversified agriculture until the introduction of coffee planting in the 19th century opened a new economic era.

The national independence of Brazil was proclaimed in São Paulo in 1822, at which time the captaincy became a province of the Brazilian Empire. São Paulo became a state when the republic was formed in 1889. Political importance grew with the economy. The nation's first three civilian presidents after the downfall of the empire in 1889 were Paulistas. The state provided leadership for the frustrated military uprising against Pres. Arthur Benardes in 1924 and for the abortive revolution against Pres. Getúlio Vargas in 1932. Paulistas, who first served as mayors of the capital city, as governors, or as local political or industrial leaders, have occupied the presidency, cabinet, and other federal positions with significant regularity in the 20th century.

The natural environment.   São Paulo's narrow coastal zone is broken by lagoons, tidal channels, and mountain spurs. It is bordered by the well-wooded slopes of the Serra do Mar (Mountains of the Sea), which lead up to the Great Escarpment, behind which is an extensive plateau with wide grassy plains, about 1,500 to 3,000 feet above sea level. The most productive land occurs in streaks of *terra roxa* ("red-purple earth"), a deep, porous soil containing humus. Isolated ranges of low elevation break the surface in places, but in general the undulating tableland slopes toward the Rio Paraná (Paraná River), the state's western boundary.

The Paraná—and its tributaries, the Paranapanema, Tieté (which traverses the whole state), Pardo, Canoas, Inferno, Anhanguera, Turvo, and Dourados—flows westward into the estuary of the Río de la Plata. The extreme eastern part of the tableland, however, slopes to the east, and, from a little east of the city of São Paulo, the Rio Paraíba do Sul turns northeastward and flows parallel to

The rivers

the coast, meandering across a wide floodplain used for the production of rice. The state has no lakes of importance, but has several sizeable artificial weirs (such as Cjuarapìranga, and Billings). On the coast the average temperature is about 68° F (20° C), and the annual rainfall is about 79 inches; on the plateau the average temperature varies between about 64° and 68° F (18° and 20° C), and in the mountainous areas annual rainfall reaches 59 inches.

The lower third of the state is crossed by the Tropic of Capricorn. The weather in general is mild and healthy and in some places—such as Campos do Jordão and Cunha—comparable to southern Europe. The coastal zone has a hot climate and heavy rainfall. On the plateau rainfall is ample, but the air is drier and more bracing, daytime temperatures being high and the nights cool.

The evergreen forests are reminiscent of the wealth of vegetation in Brazil in days gone by. The vegetation is greatly diversified and includes several kinds of hardwoods, wild fruits, and plants that are used for medicinal and ornamental purposes or for making textiles. The hardwoods have furnished the rosewood and other cabinet woods for which Brazil is famous.

The Paulist animal life is rich and diverse. Mammals include the jaguar, cougar, tapir, capybara (an edible rodent related to the guinea pig), squirrel, and howling monkey. Birds range from the parrot and macaw to such songbirds as the sabia and red grackle. Reptiles include the alligator, the rattlesnake, freshwater turtles, and lizards. The rivers abound with fish and there are many kinds of insects.

Population. Before the arrival of the Portuguese, the region was inhabited by Indians of various tongues and cultures. The two principal tribes were the Tupí-Guaraní, who lived on the coast and on the plateau, and the Tapuia, who lived farther inland. Remnants of these tribes either escaped to other regions, were killed off by disease or war, or were enslaved by the conquerors. Portuguese men, however, formed unions with some of the women, which resulted in the creation of a new ethnic group called *mamelucos* ("Mamelukes," since they were thought to resemble the Mamlūks of Egypt, a military class originally consisting of a group of Caucasian slaves) or *mestiços* (mestizos). With the introduction of black Africans during the 17th century and after, a new element was added to the population. Further ethnic intermixing between Portuguese and Africans resulted in the appearance of mulattos, while intermixing between Africans and *mamelucos* resulted in a group called *cabures*. Those descended from all three stocks were called mestizos.

With the absorption of the Indian element and with further European immigration, from the end of the 19th century onward, the population of the state was reduced to three elements—white, black, and mulatto. Subsequently, however, a small number of Japanese immigrants arrived. In the early 1970s the population of the state was composed of 62 percent white, 11 percent black, 26 percent mulatto, and about 1 percent of either Asian or unidentified origin. Of the 3,000,000 immigrants who have been admitted to São Paulo since 1885, more than 1,000,000 have been Italian, about 600,000 Portuguese, 500,000 Spanish, and almost 300,000 Japanese.

The population of São Paulo, as mentioned, is predominantly urban. In addition to the capital, other principal cities of more than 200,000 population are Santo André, Campinas, Santos, Osasco and Guarulhos. Ribeirão Prêto, São Bernardo do Campo, Sorocaba and Jundiaí have populations of about 150,000 and several other cities have more than 100,000 inhabitants.

While Portuguese is the language in general use, the idiom has some semantic differences from the Portuguese spoken in Portugal. English is also relatively widely spoken and is more in use than such other European languages as French, Spanish, Italian, and German.

São Paulo is predominantly Roman Catholic, though other Christian religions are relatively widely practiced by various Protestant and Orthodox sects.

Administration and education. The state administration consists of independent executive, legislative, and judiciary branches. The executive function is carried out by a governor (who serves for a term of four years), with the assistance of 13 undersecretaries of state. The legislature consists of the Assembly of Deputies, composed of men and women, all aged over 21, elected in secret ballot by men and women voters who must be more than 18 years old and literate. The judiciary power is exercised by tribunals and judge advocates, with the members chosen by the governor.

Under federal law all citizens are entitled to primary education, which is free and compulsory. The cities have the best educational facilities, but more primary as well as secondary schools have been built outside the cities, and the numbers of pupils have increased.

Institutions of higher learning include the Universidade de São Pauló (University of São Paulo, with its constituent colleges and affiliated institutes), Mackenzie University, Pontifícia Universidade Católica de São Paulo (Pontifical Catholic University, and the Polytechnic School of Engineering)—all of which are in the city of São Paulo—and Luis de Queiroz' Higher School of Agriculture in Piracicaba.

Economy and transport. The economy of the state is based on agriculture and industry. Agriculture is largely mechanized; it owes its modernization largely to the Luis de Queiroz school and to the Instituto Agronômico de Campinas (Institute of Agronomy of Campinas).

Coffee was formerly the main source of wealth of the state and still accounts for a considerable portion of the total value of its products, although industry is surpassing it in importance. Besides coffee, other crops are sugarcane, cotton, corn (maize), rice, beans, Indian or Paraguay tea (maté), potatoes, and such fruits as bananas and oranges.

Cattle raising has begun to transform the old coffee lands into stock-raising areas and pastures. The local horses are renowned, and there are vast herds of cattle. Hog, sheep, and goat raising are actively pursued. Most of the industry is centred in the city of São Paulo and its environs.

The state has an extensive network of highways and of federal, state, and private railroads of varying gauges. Santos is the nation's busiest port and the largest coffee-shipping port in the world. The ports of São Sebastião, Iguape, Ubatuba, and Cananéia, which are considerably smaller, serve the coastal trade; Iguape and Cannéia are known especially for the rice grown in their vicinity. In addition to a large international airport at São Paulo, there are about 50 other airports in the state.

Cultural life. The most important cultural institutions are concentrated in the capital. Many of the other cities and towns, however, have their own press, literary associations, public libraries, cinemas, theatres, and sports and recreation clubs and associations. Among the more important institutions in São Paulo (in addition to those named in the São Paulo city article) are the Academia Paulista de Letras (São Paulo Academy of Letters), Museu do Ipiranga (Museum of Ipiranga), the Biblioteca Municipal Mário de Andrade (Mário de Andrade Municipal Library), the Museum of Sacred Art, the Brazilian Union of Writers, the Museum of Archaeology, and the Association of Medical History.

BIBLIOGRAPHY. For a comprehensive bibliography of writings about São Paulo, see AURELIANO LEITE, *História da Civilização Paulista* (1954). General works include: CINCINATO BRAGA, *Magnos Problemas Economicos de São Paulo*, 3rd ed. (1948), a comparative study including financial and economic statistics for the state and the country; PEDRO CALMON, *História do Brasil*, 7 vol. (1959), a recent history of Brazil containing a large number of illustrations; AFFONSO DE FREITAS, *Geografia do Estado de São Paulo* (1906), contains geographic, demographic, political, and statistical reports; INSTITUTO BRASILEIRO DE GEOGRAFIA E ESTATISTICA, *Boletims* (annual), a statistical report of the state; PIERRE MONBEIG, *Pionniers et planteurs de São Paulo* (1952), a history of the coffee plantations in São Paulo and Paraná; SALVATORE PISANI, *Lo stato di San Paolo* (1937), contains a study of the work of the Italians in building the state; EGON SHADEN, *Primeiros Habitantes de São Paulo* (1954), discusses the Indians in São Paulo before discovery; ROBERTO SIMONSEN, *História Economica do Brasil, 1500–1820*, 2 vol. (1937), a

Higher education

The transport network

The complexity of the ethnic composition

study of economic progress in São Paulo; ROBERT SOUTHEY, *History of Brazil*, 3 vol. (1817–22, reprinted 1969), written from a large number of documents and manuscripts, condemns the colonizers and gives the highest credit to the achievements of the Jesuits; OCTAVIO TARQUINIO DE SOUSA, *José Bonifácio, 1763–1838* (1945), a biography of a hero of independence who was born in São Paulo; AFFONSO DE TAUNAY, *História Geral das Bandeiras Paulistas*, 11 vol. (1948–50), a classic work about the *bandierantes*, the epic inland explorers; PADRE VASCONCELLOS, *Atlas Geográfico* (1944), concerned with São Paulo; PADRE ANTONIO VIEIRA, *Cartas*, 3 vol. (1925–28), a study by an author who does not agree with the methods of the *bandierantes* concerning the Indians, but praises them in matters of war.

(A.Le.)

São Paulo (City)

The largest city of Brazil and the dynamic capital of the state of the same name, São Paulo is the foremost industrial centre in Latin America. With a metropolitan area population of about 6,000,000, it is one of the five most populous cities in the Western Hemisphere. Located in the hills of the Serra do Mar (Mountains of the Sea) on the edge of Brazil's Great Escarpment 30 miles inland from its port of Santos, it is 220 miles southwest along the Atlantic coast from Rio de Janeiro. The city obtained its name from a religious settlement founded by the Jesuits in 1554, on the anniversary of the conversion of St. Paul.

History. São Paulo began as a small Indian settlement founded on January 25, 1554, around a modest house that was at the same time a school, church, and residence for Portuguese Jesuits under Manuel da Nóbrega, assisted, among others, by the saintly José de Anchieta, to whom is attributed the prophecy that the little village would become the metropolis of Brazil.

São Paulo became a township in 1560, at which time it had a city council that could enact and enforce laws. In 1683 it succeeded São Vincente as capital of the captaincy, or hereditary fief; the inhabitants thereafter became known as Paulistanos or Paulistas. Throughout the 17th century São Paulo was a base for expeditions (*bandeiras*) of armed pioneers (*bandeirantes*) who penetrated the remote hinterlands in search of Indian slaves, gold, silver, and diamonds. It was raised to the status of a city in 1711.

During the 18th century the importance of the captaincy, and thus of its capital city, declined as successive parts of its vast territory were cut off to form other captaincies in southern Brazil. In the early 19th century, São Paulo—for a time without its own government—remained an agrarian town.

Development- / ment in the / 19th / century

In 1822 Emperor Pedro I proclaimed Brazil's independence in São Paulo at a site marked by the museum and monument of Ipiranga. Nevertheless, São Paulo continued to retain its colonial aspect until the latter part of the 19th century. The spread of coffee planting to the province opened a new source of wealth that, after 1880, stimulated the city's sudden growth. Immigrants arrived in large numbers, including Italians (who for a time outnumbered native Brazilians), Portuguese, Spaniards, Germans, east Europeans, Syrians, Lebanese, and Japanese. An era that was to transform São Paulo into a modern city had begun.

The contemporary city. Located at an altitude of 2,400 feet, the terrain on which the city stands consists of open country, valleys, and foothills. The higher parts, as in the district of Sumaré (2,600 feet), constitute the preferred residential areas; the lower parts are on alluvial land on the banks of three rivers—the Tietê, the Pinheiros, and the Tamanduateí. The area of the city proper is 627 square miles (1,624 square kilometres), while Greater São Paulo covers an area of about 884 square miles. Suburban communities include São Bernardo do Campo, Santo André, São Caetano do Sul, Osasco, Guarulhos, Mairiporã, Barueri, Santana de Parnaíba, and Franco da Rocha. Open spaces nearby, which are clayey with sandy deposits, are extensively used for market gardening. The nearby Jaragua Hills, the Serra da Cantareira (maximum altitude 3,900 feet)—where there is a forest reserve of about 39 square miles—and the beaches at Santos and Guarujá provide pleasant resort areas.

Climate. Although just within the tropics, the city enjoys a temperate climate because of its elevation; the temperature occasionally reaches freezing point in winter and on rare occasions rises to 86° F (30° C) in summer. The air, brought by the gentle wind that blows from the Serra da Cantareira, would be excellent if it were not for pollution by automobile exhaust fumes and dust from the demolition and reconstruction of buildings.

City plan. São Paulo had no city plan until 1889; it was only with the astonishingly rapid development of the metropolis that thought was given to the matter. Formerly a capital city of colonial aspect—its narrow streets unpaved, and its buildings shabby, with here and there old churches and convents in Jesuit and Franciscan styles—its urban growth in general was swift and uncontrolled.

Successive city administrations since then have attempted to stimulate more rational urban growth and to modernize the city's transportation system. Projects have included the straightening and rechanneling of the Tietê and Tamanduateí rivers, the widening and relocation of streets and avenues, and the construction of bridges, overhead roads, subterranean passages, and new parks and lakes, as well as the beginning of construction of a 40-mile subway network, due for completion in the mid-1970s.

The residential districts of the well-to-do are attractively laid out, the more recent—influenced by English town planning—contrasting sharply with the crowded sections of the industrial districts.

Transportation. In addition to improved transport within the city, São Paulo is served by good highways connecting it with the inland cities and with Rio de Janeiro, Minas Gerais, and almost all the other states of Brazil. The city is also a key junction for three of the country's important railroads. It is connected with the Atlantic at Santos by a cable railway and a four-lane highway, both of which cross the steep escarpment. Its airport is one of the busiest in the world.

Population. The city is divided into three regions—urban, suburban, and rural. The population of the metropolitan area is 5,921,796, that of the city proper 5,186,752 and that of Greater São Paulo approximately 8,000,000. The proportions of the various racial, religious, and ethnic groups in the population approximate those of the state as a whole—that is to say, about 62 percent white, 11 percent black, 26 percent mulatto, and 1 percent miscellaneous.

Economic life. Industrial development, beginning in the late 19th century, transformed São Paulo with its neighbouring municipalities—notably Santo André—into the foremost industrial centre of Latin America. (It has been called the "Chicago of South America.") Leading industries produce textiles, mechanical and electrical appliances, building and furniture, foodstuffs, and chemical and pharmaceutical products. There are also heavy metallurgical plants at Taubaté and oil refineries at Cubatão (which has the largest refinery in Brazil) and Capuava; there are also plants manufacturing motor vehicles and farm machinery at various places. Altogether, about 3,000 industrial establishments employ almost 2,000,000 workmen. Power for the industries is supplied by hydroelectric stations. The demand for electricity outstrips local hydroelectric resources, however, so that extra power is brought from the gigantic complex at Salto do Urubupungá, nearly 400 miles to the northwest.

Industrial / development

Both wholesale and retail commerce are strongly developed, being spread over the city in zones, each according to its own speciality. The banks, although centralized in the old part of the city (the Triângulo), maintain agencies and branches in almost every district. In addition to important local, state, and national banks, there are banking institutions representing interests in North and South America, Europe, Asia, and Africa. Savings banks are operated by the federal government and by the state.

Government and services. The city is governed by a mayor and council. It is also the seat of the state government, the headquarters of which is at the Palácio dos Bandeirantes (Bandeirantes Palace) in the district of Mo-

Downtown São Paulo.
Manchete—Pictorial Parade

rumbi. In addition to the state offices and departments that have headquarters in the capital, there are more than 50 consulates representing the countries of all the Americas excepting Cuba and many of the countries of Europe, Asia, and Africa.

The city has a plentiful piped supply of drinking water of good quality. In order to ensure a sufficient supply for a population of 12,000,000 projected by the year 2000, the government has undertaken to divert the flow of some rivers toward the city by tunnelling through hills for many miles. The drainage system, as well as the water supply service, are both entrusted to the Sanesp (from Saneamento do Estado de São Paulo—literally, sanitation of São Paulo state). Municipal electricity services have been provided since 1900 by an enterprise of Canadian origin, the Brazilian Traction, Light, and Power Company.

Health facilities

No epidemics have been registered in the city since extensive sanitation measures were undertaken at the beginning of the 20th century. Public and private hospitals and nursing homes are plentiful; hospitals include the Santa Casa de Misericórdia, the General Clinics Hospital, and the Beneficiência Portuguêsa, as well as hospitals for civil servants, maternity hospitals, and hospitals specializing in cancer, tuberculosis, and other diseases.

Education. São Paulo has a well-developed system of primary and secondary schools and a variety of vocational schools. Under Brazilian law, primary education for all up to the age of 14 is free and compulsory.

Among the institutions of higher learning the most esteemed is the state-supported Universidade de São Paulo (University of São Paulo), established in 1934, which incorporated the historic Faculdade de Direito (College of Law) in the old São Francisco Square and pre-existing polytechnical schools, as well as schools of pharmacy and dentistry, agriculture, and medicine; faculties of economics, architecture, and engineering were added later. Affiliated institutions include the School of Sociology and Politics, founded in 1933, and the Instituto Butantã (Butantã Institute), a world-famous research centre for the study of snakes and the production of antitoxins and antivenins. The Pontifícia Universidade Católica de São Paulo (Pontifical Catholic University of São Paulo) was established in 1946, and Universidade Mackenzie (Mackenzie University) in 1952.

Cultural life and institutions. São Paulo early became a prominent cultural and intellectual centre, largely because of the opening in 1827 of the College of Law—one of the first two in Brazil—where many of the nation's most eminent men ware educated. Its Instituto Histórico e Geográfico de São Paulo (São Paulo Historical and Geographical Institute), founded in 1894, is one of the oldest cultural associations in the state. It is also a leading centre for libraries (which include a skyscraper municipal library), publishing houses, and theatres. In 1922, São Paulo's Modern Art Week—celebrated by a group of young writers, artists, and musicians in the Teatro Municipal (Municipal Theatre)—introduced modernism in the arts of Brazil, and in 1951 the city's Museu de Arte Moderna (Museum of Modern Art) organized the first biennial exhibition in the Americas.

The city is also a focal point for news media and is the location for several of the largest and most important newspapers, television stations, and radio networks in Latin America. Its great dailies, *O Estado de São Paulo* and *Diário Popular*, are both nearly 100 years old.

Sports facilities

The Paulistas are enthusiastic followers of sports, particularly soccer, and its association football clubs, especially Santos, are world renowned. Facilities include a stadium seating 10,000 spectators, the Jockey Club, and one of the world's largest car-racing tracks. The permanent fairgrounds, erected for the city's fourth centennial (1954), are distinguished for their modern architecture.

BIBLIOGRAPHY. JORGE AMERICANO, *São Paulo Naquele Tempo 1895–1915* (1957), *São Paulo Nesse Tempo, 1915–1935* (1962), and *São Paulo Atual, 1935–1962* (1963), cover the customs, social life, and literary and traditional culture of the city in different epochs; LEONARDO ARROYO, *Igrejas de São Paulo*, 2nd ed. (1966), a description of the city's churches; SILVA BRUNO, *História e Tradições da Cidade de São Paulo*, 3 vol. (1954), a valuable historical work; DONALD PIERSON, *Negroes in Brazil* (1942), a social, anthropological, and statistical work about Negroes in the city; AFFONSO DE TAUNAY, *História de Cidade de São Paulo*, 2 vol. (1949) and *Velho São Paulo*, 3 vol. 1953–54), by the acknowledged specialist on the early history of the city.

(A.Le.)

Sapindales

The plant order Sapindales consists of perhaps 2,300 species in 168 genera and nine families. Although not a very large group compared to many other natural orders of flowering plants, the Sapindales attract much attention because most species are trees or shrubs, many of which are favoured ornamental, shade, or timber trees of both tropical and temperate regions. Several of the tropical trees produce fruits with distinctive flavours. Some of the widely disjunct distribution patterns possessed by several genera are of interest to biogeographers.

GENERAL FEATURES

Growth habit and size range. Centred around the largest family, Sapindaceae, the order is basically a tropical to warm-temperate group, relatively nonspecialized in habit of growth. Most members of the order are small to moderate sized trees, large shrubs, or woody climbers.

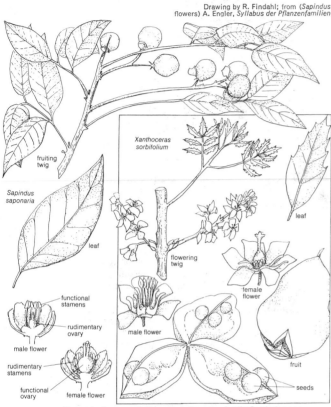

Drawing by R. Findahl; from (*Sapindus* flowers) A. Engler, *Syllabus der Pflanzenfamilien*

Figure 1: Representative plants from the family Sapindaceae, the largest family of the order Sapindales.

There are no small annual herbs, desert succulents, or aquatic species. Even in the forests none has evolved into an epiphyte (plant that grows upon tree branches), a saprophyte (nongreen plant that absorbs nutrients from dead organic matter), or a parasite. The most specialized growth forms are rather strange, unbranched, palm-like trees (such as *Pseudima* and *Talisia*), woody climbers (*Paullinia*, *Serjania*, *Urvillea*, and *Sabia*), subshrubs or perennial herbs with woody basal parts (*Diplopeltis* and *Melianthus*), and one annual vine (*Cardiospermum halicacabum*, balloon vine).

The largest trees of the order are in the family Sapindaceae; they include *Schleichera oleosa* (to 60 metres, or 200 feet, in Burma), *Pometia pinnata* (to 40–50 metres, or 130–160 feet, in the Malesian region), and *Tristiropsis canarioides* (to 45 metres, or 145 feet, in New Guinea).

Distribution. Although the family Sapindaceae is mostly distributed in the tropics and subtropics, it does have some temperate representatives. In temperate North America these include, among others: *Sapindus* (soapberries) with two species that extend north as far as Georgia, Missouri, Kansas, and Colorado; *Ungnadia speciosa* (Mexican-buckeye) of Texas, New Mexico, and Mexico; the circumtropical *Dodonaea viscosa* (hopbush) reaching into Arizona and temperate Florida; and several members of the climbing, tropical genera *Cardiospermum, Serjania,* and *Urvillea,* all represented in Texas. The herbaceous vine *Cardiospermum halicacabum* (balloon vine), which presumably has escaped from cultiva-

tion, is occasionally found as far north as Missouri, Illinois, and New Jersey.

Other warm, temperate areas of the world also have a few representatives of the family Sapindaceae. China, for example, has, among others, the decorative *Koelreuteria paniculata* (goldenrain tree) and *Xanthoceras sorbifolium.* Chile has several shrubs or small trees, as does the Republic of South Africa. Temperate Australia has numerous shrubby species of *Dodonaea* (varnish leaf), subshrubs or even prostrate herbs of *Diplopeltis,* and small trees of such genera as *Atalaya* and *Heterodendron.*

The order Sapindales presents many examples of the widely discontinuous patterns of distribution that are of interest to biogeographers. Among the more striking disjunctions are the following: (1) the essentially temperate North American–Eurasian (represented by the genera *Acer, Aesculus,* and *Staphylea*); (2) the largely tropical Asiatic–American (*Meliosma, Sapindus,* and *Turpinia*); (3) the tropical American–African–Madagascan (*Paullinia*); (4) the Mascarene Islands–Fiji–New Caledonia (*Cossinia*); (5) the African–Asian–Malesian region (*Aphania, Filicium,* and *Ganophyllum*); and (6) the tropical African–Asian–Australian–American (*Allophylus, Cardiospermum,* and *Dodonaea*). On the other hand, many genera are restricted to single continents or portions thereof, archipelagos, or single islands. **Economic importance.** Because of the large number of trees, the principal economic importance of the order is for wood products. Undoubtedly the best known timber tree is *Acer saccharum* (sugar, hard, rock, or black maple), which has been described as the most valuable hardwood tree of North America. The figured wood (curly and bird's-eye maple) is valued for cabinet work; the plain wood for construction, flooring, interior finish, and furniture. The species also provides choice firewood and abundant maple syrup and sugar from the sap. The hard, strong, heavy, close-grained wood is often beautifully patterned. The sugar maple, too, is a splendid ornamental, shade, and street tree because of its thick, shapely crown and the bright yellows and reds of its autumnal coloration. Other American maples are of lesser importance as timber, paper-pulp, sugar, and ornamental trees.

Next to the maples, the buckeyes probably have the most economic significance in temperate areas. The Balkan *Aesculus hippocastanum* (horse-chestnut), the American *A. glabra* (Ohio buckeye), and *A. octandra* (yellow, or sweet, buckeye) have light, soft, tough, fine-grained wood; although once used for artificial limbs, splints, and various kinds of woodenware, the wood is now more important as a source of paper pulp. Selected varieties and hybrids of these species are frequently cultivated as ornamentals or as shade or street trees.

Economically valuable species of the order in the tropics belong mostly to the family Sapindaceae. Some of the larger tree species, such as *Pometia pinnata* of the Malesian region and *Blighia sapida* of tropical Africa, are useful for their timber. *Pometia pinnata* has been described as one of the most important timber trees in New Guinea, where its wood is useful for general construction, furniture, mouldings, veneer, floors, interior finish, and boats. *Blighia sapida* (akee) wood in tropical West Africa is used for furniture, boxes, oars, punting poles, and charcoal. It is light, hard, close-grained, durable, and apparently resistant to termites. In tropical America, none of the family is of more than local importance for timber or fuel because of scarcity or low resistance to decay. Some woods of this order are not durable if exposed to weather; they are not resistant to termites or borers, are somewhat saponiferous (*i.e.,* they produce a soapy lather), are cross-grained and hard to work, require very careful seasoning, and have heartwood difficult to impregnate with preservatives.

As with the temperate maples, some species of the family Sapindaceae are much esteemed as ornamentals or shade trees. Among the more desirable of these are *Koelreuteria paniculata* (goldenrain tree), *Ungnadia speciosa* (Mexican-buckeye), *Blighia sapida* (akee), various species of *Sapindus* (soapberries), and *Dodonaea viscosa* (hopbush, varnish leaf).

Discontinuous distribution patterns

Ornamental and shade trees

The plants of the family Sapindaceae are better known in the tropics for their fruit than for their wood. Most popular for the fleshy pulp or succulent seed coats are *Litchi chinensis* (lychee), *Nephelium lappaceum* (rambutan), *Euphoria longana* (longan), *Blighia sapida* (akee), *Melicoccus bijugus* (Spanish lime), and *Aphania senegalensis* (Senegal cherry).

Saponins—chemical substances that produce soapy lathers—are present in the fruits, seeds, and other tissues of many members of the family Sapindaceae; genera such as *Sapindus, Aphania,* and *Paullinia* are used in tropical countries as soap substitutes. Crushed materials from some species of *Paullinia, Serjania,* and related genera stupefy fish when thrown into pools or small streams. The seeds of the Brazilian *Paullinia cupana* (guarana) contain much caffeine, and the roasted seeds are used to prepare a stimulating beverage. The bark of *P. yoco* (yoco) is similarly used as a caffeine source.

NATURAL HISTORY

Pollination agents.   Although little is known about pollination in the Sapindales, most species are thought to be pollinated by insects. This assumption is based on the usual presence of petals, the strong tendency toward bilateral symmetry in the flowers, and the presence in the flowers of a glandular nectar-secreting disc. The small size of the flowers of the families Sapindaceae, Aceraceae, and Sabiaceae indicates small flies or bees as the pollinating insects. The larger flowers of *Aesculus,* often supplied with coloured honey guides, which are patterns on the flowers that indicate the location of nectar glands, are visited extensively by bumblebees. The white-flowered *A. parviflora* (bottlebrush buckeye) is probably pollinated by moths. The brilliant red flowers of *A. pavia* (firecracker plant; red, or scarlet, buckeye) and *Billia hippocastanum* closely match the colour and shape of known hummingbird flowers, and in the South African *Melianthus* (honey bush) the sturdy, dark purplish flowers with their abundance of nectar probably attract the nectar-eating sugarbirds and sunbirds.

Wind pollination in maples

The maples (*Acer*) demonstrate marked evolution toward wind pollination. Some species, which retain both petals and well-developed, ring-shaped, nectar-producing discs, are mainly visited by bees. Others, particularly the hard maples, retain the disc but have lost the petals. *Acer saccharinum* (silver maple) has lost both petals and disc, and its flowers form headlike yellow or reddish clusters; pollination may occur by both insects and wind. *Acer negundo* (box-elder) has lost both petals and disc and is functionally and anatomically dioecious—the male and female flowers occur on separate plants. The male flowers produce an abundance of pollen in large anthers from densely clustered and pendulous flowers. The female flowers are in drooping clusters and have long, narrow stigmas. This is a characteristic group of features that points to complete reliance on wind pollination and to the highly specialized position of the species.

Dispersal.   The wide variety of fruit types in the Sapindales indicates adaptations to an equally wide variety of dispersing agents. Among the kinds of fruits are capsules (in *Aesculus, Cupania, Dodonaea,* and *Melianthus*); drupes, which are fleshy fruits with a single-seeded, stony pit (*Exothea, Melicoccus,* and *Meliosma*); berries (*Allophylus, Aphania,* and *Hypelate*); and samaroid schizocarps, fruits that break up into winged segments (*Acer, Dipteronia,* and *Thouinia*). Possibly the most primitive fruit type is the simple, readily opening capsule containing seeds with fleshy outer seed coats (sarcotesta). During the evolution of the order this became reduced to the arillode, or partial sarcotesta. Later, through transference of function, the fleshiness of the seed was replaced by the fleshy pulp of the fruit, the fleshy, outer fruit wall (drupe), or the entirely fleshy fruit (berry). All these fruit types are especially attractive to birds, and some also attract small mammals. The fruits of several genera, including *Sapindus, Melicocca, Nephelium,* and *Xerospermum,* are thought to be dispersed by fruit-eating bats.

Throughout the order there is a rather marked evolution toward bladdery or winged fruits designed for transportation by wind. Because of their wide occurrence on oceanic islands and tropical shores, the polymorphic *Dodonaea viscosa* (hopbush) and some *Sapindus* (soapberry) species are thought to be transported by ocean currents.

Ecology.   Most species in the order are found in tropical or subtropical rain forests, mostly below elevations of 2,000 metres (6,600 feet). A few of the larger tree species, as *Pometia pinnata* in the Malesian regions, are important constituents of the canopy layer of lowland rain forest. Most members of the order, however, are smaller trees and thus are common members of the lower rainforest strata. In tropical Australia and in New Caledonia, they are frequent components of drier, more seasonal types of tropical forest and woodland. *Dodonaea viscosa* (hopbush) is a common pioneer species not only on beaches and lava flows but also on landslides and other disturbed areas inland. *Jagera* also has rather weedy tendencies. *Meliosma, Billia,* and *Turpinia* are, in Mexico, frequent components of high-elevation oak forests. *Acer* and *Aesculus* are important components of the temperate deciduous forests, with *Acer saccharum* and *Aesculus octandra* often among the dominant trees of the richest deciduous forests of eastern North America.

FORM AND FUNCTION

Distinguishing vegetative characteristics.   The order of Sapindales is overwhelmingly composed of woody plants, mostly trees, large shrubs, or woody climbers. Small subshrubs and herbaceous vines are rare. Most species have compound leaves, usually pinnately divided (*i.e.,* with the leaflets of each compound leaf arranged along both sides of a central axis). The leaves are alternate on the branches and are without stipules, the small leaflike appendages at the base of leaf stalks. Some genera, however, have

Leaves

Drawing by R. Findahl based on G.H.M. Lawrence,
Taxonomy of Vascular Plants (1951); The Macmillan Company.

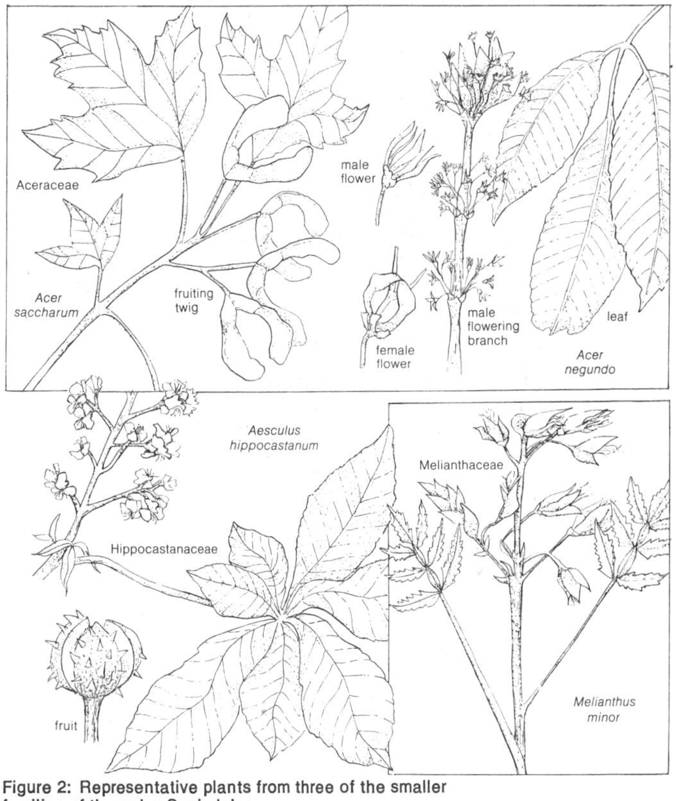

Figure 2: Representative plants from three of the smaller families of the order Sapindales.

simple or palmately divided leaves (compound leaves with leaflets radiating from one point) that are either alternate or opposite in arrangement on the branches and may have very small or large stipules attached to the leaf stalks. Stomates, microscopic pores in the leaf surfaces, are mostly restricted to the lower surfaces of the leaves and are anomocytic (surrounded by ordinary epidermal cells). Most leaves have mucilage cells or secretory cells or sacs or both. The vascularization of the petiole (leaf stalk) appears in cross section either as a circular strand or as a ring, sometimes dorsally flattened, of separate vascular bundles.

Flower and fruit characteristics. Throughout the order there is a strong tendency toward obligate crossbreeding through progressive decrease in bisexuality, culminating in dioecism, a condition in which there are species with male and female flowers borne on separate plants. Most species in the order appear to be polygamous—having bisexual and unisexual flowers on the same plant—thus presumably combining the advantages of maximum fertility through inbreeding with increased variability through outcrossing. Some species are polygamomonoecious—*i.e.*, with bisexual flowers and both male and female flowers on the same plant. Most are apparently polygamodioecious, with male and female plants each bearing a few bisexual flowers. Many structurally bisexual flowers, however, as in many maples, are functionally unisexual, for either the stamens (male organs) produce no fertile pollen or the stigmas (sticky pollen-receiving areas of the female flower parts) are not receptive. Even in species with functionally bisexual flowers, cross-pollination is assured through proterogyny or proterandry; *i.e.*, the female or the male organs, respectively, mature before the structures of the other sex in the same flower. Some species—*e.g.*, *Acer platanoides, A. spicatum,* and *A. saccharinum*—are self-sterile. Most unisexual flowers in the order have become that way through abortion, in which either the male or the female structures fail to develop, for the flowers often retain rudimentary structures of the nonfunctional sex. Only a few species, such as *Acer negundo* (box-elder), have unisexual flowers with usually no vestige at all of the organs of the other sex. Thus, though most species of the Sapindales have insured outbreeding by one technique or another, most have not achieved complete anatomical dioecism.

The anatomically bisexual flower is either radially or bilaterally symmetrical and is typically small, except in a few genera. The male flowers often have a nonfunctional pistil (the female structure consisting of stigma, style, and ovary), called a pistillode, and female flowers similarly have sterile stamens.

Fruit characteristics

The fruit is basically a capsule that splits open between the partitions but is often modified into many other types, such as fleshy, berrylike, stony-pitted, or dry and bladdery or winged. In the seed, endosperm (the starchy nutrient tissue for the developing embryo) is usually absent or scanty, and the embryo is often curved, folded, or contorted.

EVOLUTION

Fossil record. The fossil record, the many present-day relict endemics (species of restricted range that are remnants of an earlier widespread flora), and the widely disjunct distribution patterns, often relict, attest to the ancientness of this group. Because of the easily preserved and recognizable leaves, flowers, and fruits, the fossil record is rather good for *Acer, Dipteronia, Aesculus, Cupania-Cupaniopsis, Dodonaea,* and *Sapindus,* among other genera. Fossil evidence indicates that the distributions of these genera in former times exceeded their present ranges, especially in North Temperate areas.

The earliest fossils attributed to this order, believed to represent early ancestors of the genus *Sapindus* (soapberries), are two species of the fossil genus *Sapindopsis* from late Lower Cretaceous time (the Cretaceous Period extended from 136,000,000 to 65,000,000 years ago) of Crook County, Wyoming. *Sapindophyllum* is also from Cretaceous deposits. *Sapindus oregonianus,* one of several early Tertiary Period (beginning 65,000,000 years ago) fossils of the modern genus, is known from the Miocene Epoch (26,000,000 to 7,000,000 years ago) of Idaho, Oregon, and Nevada and approaches most closely still living Asiatic species. Two fossil *Cupania* species, resembling living South American species, are known from the Goshen and Chalk Bluff floras of the upper Eocene–lower Oligocene boundary (about 38,000,000 years ago) of central Oregon. Several species of the fossil *Cupanites* are represented by leaves and fruits in Europe-

an Tertiary deposits and by leaves in the Eocene (54,000,000 to 38,000,000 years ago) of the southeastern United States. Tertiary leaves and fruits have been described from 15 fossil species of *Dodonaea* from western Europe, the southeastern United States, Colorado, California, Bolivia, and Brazil. *Dipteronia,* now restricted to China, was represented in western North America during the Tertiary by *D. insignis.*

The genus *Acer* has the most extensive Tertiary fossil record, consisting of fruits, inflorescences, and leaves, throughout the North Temperate and Boreal zones north to Iceland and Spitsbergen. The red maples, now restricted to Japan and eastern North America, were once found in Eurasia and North America north to Greenland. As late as Miocene time they were represented in Oregon by *A. chaneyi;* in northern Italy they were present until the Pliocene (7,000,000 to 2,500,000 years ago) and Quaternary Period (beginning 2,500,000 years ago). Other groups of maples, now absent from Europe, were present there in the Tertiary. Fossil species of *Aesculus* ranged farther north in the Tertiary in Europe, eastern Asia, and North America than they do today.

Phylogeny. Most authorities are convinced that the two groups of families here called the orders Sapindales and Rutales are closely related (see also RUTALES). Within the Sapindales, the family Sapindaceae is the large, varied, and central group. Very closely related to the Sapindaceae are the families Aceraceae, Hippocastanaceae, and the monotypic (single-species) relicts *Akania* and *Bretschneidera*. Less closely but still rather obviously related to this family complex are the Asiatic–American family Sabiaceae (at least the *Meliosma* group) and the African family Melianthaceae.

CLASSIFICATION

Distinguishing taxonomic features. Within the order the families are usually distinguished from one another by combinations of characteristics or by the level or degree of advance along certain evolutionary trends. Regarded as especially critical in the group's classification have been placement and division of the leaves; presence, size, and position of stipules; kind of inflorescence; symmetry, size, and sexuality of the flowers; number and position of stamens; presence, shape, and position of the nectar-producing disc; number of locules (chambers) in the ovary; kind of fruit; abundance or absence of endosperm; and the alignment of the embryo.

Criteria used to determine classification

Within the larger families, classification depends largely upon such characteristics as the number and position of ovules in each locule, habit of growth, presence of a terminal leaflet in compound leaves, shape and position of the disc, and number of fertile stamens.

Annotated classification. The classification, as outlined below, is generally accepted for the first seven families, both in relationship to one another and in family content. The last two families, Greyiaceae and Staphyleaceae, however, are no longer widely accepted as members of the Sapindales. Totality of evidence indicates that they really belong with the order Saxifragales (Rosales, suborders Saxifragineae and Cunoniineae of traditional classifications). They are retained here because of long association with the true members of the order.

ORDER SAPINDALES

Trees, shrubs, or lianas, rarely herbs. Leaves mostly alternate, pinnately compound, and without stipules. Inflorescences mostly thyrses (compact panicles like clusters of grapes), panicles (many-branched loose clusters), racemes (clusters with flowers on short stalks arising from a central axis, the lower flowers maturing first), or corymbs (flat-topped flower clusters maturing from edge to centre). Species mostly polygamous (bisexual and unisexual flowers both present) but functionally monoecious (male and female flowers on the same plant) or dioecious (separately sexed flowers on different plants). Flowers mostly small, with sepals, petals, and stamens attached at the base of the ovary (hypogynous), radially or bilaterally symmetrical, usually unisexual but with rudimentary organs of the opposite sex retained. Sepals 3 to 5, overlapping in the bud (imbricate), separate or basally joined (connate). Petals 3 to 5, imbricate, usually clawed, separate, rarely absent. Nectar-producing disc present. Stamens mostly 8 but sometimes 10, in

2 whorls, distinct or connate at the base; anthers 2-chambered, opening longitudinally. Pollen mostly with 3 germination furrows, subspheroidal in shape with a reticulate (net-patterned) or striate surface. Ovary of 2 to 5 but mostly 3 fused carpels (simple ovaries or segments of compound ovaries) with a similar number of locules (chambers). One or 2 ovules in each locule, attached along central axis of ovary (axile placentation), variously oriented, with 2 integuments (outer tissue layers). Fruits various but basically capsules; seeds mostly with no or scanty endosperm and a well-developed, curved, plicate (pleated, fanlike) or contorted embryo, less commonly with abundant endosperm and a straight embryo. Nine families, 168 genera, and about 2,300 species, primarily of tropical to warm-temperate forests of the world.

Family Sapindaceae (soapberry family)

Trees, shrubs, or tendril-climbing lianas, rarely perennial herbs. Tissues often rich in saponines. Leaves mostly alternate, even-pinnate (compound, without a terminal leaflet) to decompound (with many leaflets), rarely simple. Stipules absent or rarely present. Flowers mostly in thyrses or panicles, small, hypogynous, radially or more commonly bilaterally symmetrical, usually unisexual by abortion but sometimes also bisexual. Sepals mostly 5 or 4, distinct, unequal, and imbricate. Petals mostly 5 to 3, distinct, imbricate, clawed, with a petal-like appendage above the claw inside, rarely absent. Nectar-producing disc mostly extrastaminal (positioned outside the whorl of stamens), annular or unilateral. Stamens mostly 8 or 7 (but from 6 to 12 occasionally), distinct. Gynoecium (ovary) 2- to 6- but mostly 3-locular; stigmas simple, lobed, or 3 on single style. Fruit a capsule, often inflated or winged, or a drupe, berry, or schizocarp (a fruit that breaks into 1-seeded pieces). Seed with fleshy to bony coat; endosperm scanty or absent; embryo usually curved. About 150 genera and 1,500 to 2,000 species in all tropical areas of the world, especially tropical America. A few genera extend into warm-temperate regions, and a few are wholly extratropical.

Family Akaniaceae (akania family)

Small trees with alternate, leathery, odd-pinnate (with a terminal leaflet) leaves without stipules. Flowers in panicles, bisexual, radially symmetrical. Sepals 5, imbricate, separate. Petals 5, separate, contorted. Disc lacking. Stamens usually 8, separate, with outer 5 opposite the sepals. Gynoecium 3-locular with 2 anatropous (inverted and straight), pendulous ovules in each locule; style simple and stigma 3-lobed. Fruit a loculicidal (splitting dorsally into cavity of locules) capsule. Seed with straight embryo in abundant, fleshy endosperm. One genus and species (*Akania lucens*) of the eastern Australian subtropical rain forests in southeastern Queensland and adjacent New South Wales.

Family Bretschneideraceae (bretschneidera family)

Trees with alternate, compound leaves with terminal leaflets and without stipules; with myrosin cells (secretory cells producing the enzyme myrosin) in bark of branches and in inflorescences. Flowers in terminal racemes, large, pale rose, bilaterally symmetrical; calyx (the whorl of sepals) 5-lobed, open bell-shaped. Petals 5, clawed, somewhat unequal, imbricate, arising from a position on the inner surface of the calyx tube; disc lacking. Stamens 8 in 2 whorls. Gynoecium 3-locular with 2 pendulous ovules in each locule; style long and curved with small capitate stigma. Fruit an obovate (approximately oval but more swollen at end opposite stem), thick-walled, 3-valved capsule; seeds red, lacking endosperm. One genus and species (*Bretschneidera sinensis*) in the low mountain forests of southwestern China.

Family Hippocastanaceae (horse-chestnut family)

Trees and shrubs with stout twigs and opposite, 3- to 11-parted, palmately compound (divided into leaflets that attach at a single point and radiate like fingers on a hand) leaves. Flowers large, showy, bilaterally symmetrical, in terminal thyrses. Calyx of 5 sepals, separate or fused to half or more of their length. Petals 5 or 4, unequal, clawed, often slightly crested at top of claw inside. Stamens separate, 8 to 5, in 2 whorls. Nectar-producing disc extrastaminal, eccentric, one-sided or, rarely, annular. Gynoecium 3- (rarely 2- or 4-) locular; style and stigma 1; ovules 2 in each locule, amphitropous (half-inverted and straight). Fruit a loculicidal, leathery capsule with smooth to spiny surface. Seeds 1 to 3 (rarely 4 to 6), large, with smooth, shining, dark testa with pale hilum (scar where developing seed attached to ovary wall), endosperm lacking and embryo large with thick, unequal, incurved cotyledons (seed leaves). Two genera, *Billia*, with 2 polymorphic species in tropical forests from southern Mexico to northern South America, and *Aesculus*, with 13 species in the temperate, deciduous forests of North America, southeastern Europe, and southeastern Asia from India to Japan.

Family Aceraceae (maple family)

Trees or shrubs with opposite, simple, entire (smooth mar-gined) or palmately lobed or pinnately compound, 3- to 7-foliolate leaves mostly without stipules, often with milky sap. Inflorescences mostly terminal corymbs, racemes, thyrses, or umbellate fascicles (clusters radiating from one point). Flowers small, radially symmetrical, bisexual to usually unisexual. Sepals 5 or 4, distinct or basally connate, imbricate. Petals 5 or 4, distinct, imbricate, rarely lacking. Disc thick, annular, lobed, exterior to or interior to stamens, rarely lacking. Stamens 4 to 10 but mostly 8, distinct. Stigmas 2, spreading on a single style. Ovary mostly 2- (rarely 3- to 8-) locular, much compressed at right angle to partition; ovules 2 in each locule. Fruit a schizocarp, separating at maturity into 2 samara-like mericarps (segments), winged on one side or all around. Seeds with no endosperm and embryo conduplicate or coiled. Two genera, *Dipteronia*, with two species in central and western China, and *Acer*, with about 150 species throughout the North Temperate Zone.

Family Sabiaceae (sabia family)

Trees, shrubs, or lianas; leaves alternate, pinnately compound with a terminal leaflet or simple, without stipules. Flowers in panicles, racemes, or cymes (similar to racemes but with flowers maturing from the top down), small, usually bisexual, bilaterally symmetrical. Sepals 3 to 5, distinct or basally connate, open or overlapping. Petals sometimes 6, usually 4 or 5, distinct or basally connate. Disc small, annular, cup-shaped, with serrations. Stamens sometimes 6, usually 3 to 5, distinct, opposite the petals, free from or attached to them, all but 2 sometimes reduced to staminodes (sterile stamens); anthers with thick connective. Gynoecium 3- or 2-locular; ovules 2 or 1 in each locule, horizontal or pendulous. Stigmas 2 on joined or separate styles. Fruit of 2 1-seeded drupes or dry; seed with scanty or no endosperm and large, plicate cotyledons and bent or folded hypocotyl (the part of the embryo below the cotyledons—the root-end). Four genera (*Sabia, Meliosma, Phoxanthus*, and *Ophiocaryon*) with about 90 species in tropical and subtropical continental and island regions of the world.

Family Melianthaceae (honey bush family)

Trees, shrubs, or, rarely, suffrutescent (woody at the base) herbs. Leaves alternate, pinnately compound with a terminal leaflet, with large, intrapetiolar stipules. Flowers in racemes, bisexual or unisexual (species then polygamodioecious); bilaterally symmetrical, twisted on pedicels (stalks) 180°. Sepals 4 or 5, distinct or basally connate, unequal, imbricate. Petals 4 or 5, distinct, unequal, clawed, imbricate. Disc extrastaminal, unilateral, crescent-shaped. Stamens 4 or 5, separate or united at base, often bent or curved downward. Gynoecium 4- or 5-locular with 1 to 4 basal or axile ovules in each locule; ovules erect or pendulous, anatropous; stigma 4- or 5-lobed on a single style. Fruit a woody or papery capsule, seed with straight embryo in abundant endosperm. Two genera, *Bersama* with 2 polymorphic species of tropical and southern Africa, and *Melianthus* with 6 species of South Africa.

Family Greyiaceae (greyia family)

Small trees or shrubs with soft wood. Leaves alternate, simple, with shallow marginal lobes bearing smaller rounded teeth, without stipules but with base of petiole (leaf stalk) sheathing the stem, deciduous. Flowers in a terminal raceme, bisexual, slightly bilaterally symmetrical, showy, with stamens maturing before pistil of the same flower. Sepals 5, small, imbricate, shortly connate at base. Petals 5, scarlet, imbricate. Disc fleshy, extrastaminal, cupular, crowned with 10 glands. Stamens 10 in 2 whorls, extending beyond petals. Gynoecium deeply 5-lobed, 5-locular; ovules numerous; style simple, slender with small, mostly 5-lobed stigma. Fruit a septicidal (opening through the partitions and between the locules) capsule; seeds with straight small embryo in abundant endosperm. One genus *Greyia* with 3 species in South Africa.

Family Staphyleaceae (bladdernut family)

Trees or shrubs. Leaves alternate or opposite, pinnately compound with a terminal leaflet, trifoliate (with 3 leaflets), or rarely with a single leaf blade. Flowers in panicles or racemes, bisexual or unisexual, radially symmetrical. Sepals 3 to 5, imbricate, distinct or connate. Petals 3 to 5, imbricate, distinct. Stamens 5, distinct, inserted outside the large, cup-shaped disc, or disc small or absent. Gynoecium with 2 to 4 carpels, separate or connate; ovules few to 1 in each locule, anatropous, mostly ascending; styles as many as carpels and mostly distinct, some connate. Fruit free follicles (single carpels that split open by a ventral suture), membranous, inflated capsules, berries, or drupes; seeds few, with straight embryo in abundant, fleshy or horny endosperm. Five genera (*Euscaphis, Tapisica, Huertea, Turpinia*, and *Staphylea*) and about 60 species of the North Temperate Zone but reaching into tropical southeastern Asia and tropical America.

Critical appraisal. The major problems related to the classification of the Sapindales are how to circumscribe

Alternate
classifi-
cation
systems

the order and whether the order is distinct from or better treated as a suborder of the Rutales. The families included here are those of a recent classification system. Other recent attempts at phylogenetic classification treat the order differently. One treatment, for example, includes eight of the above families along with ten others, primarily from the Rutales, and a few from the Rosales and Geraniales. The family Sabiaceae is placed in the order Ranunculales. Another recent treatment includes seven of the above families in the suborder Sapindineae, coordinate with the suborders Rutineae and Juglandineae, in the order Rutales. The families Greyiaceae and Staphyleaceae are transferred to the order Rosales of that system. Several other classification systems also exist and if any consensus can be drawn from recent classifications, it might be that seven of the families are indeed closely related, *Bretschneidera* perhaps too close to the family Sapindaceae for independent recognition as a family; that the sapindalean group is too close to the rutalean group to treat the two as separate orders; and that the families Greyiaceae and Staphyleaceae do not belong with the Sapindales but probably in the vicinity of the Saxifragaceae and Cunoniaceae.

General agreement in the treatment of the families described here must await more research and accumulation of data. Especially profitable areas of research not yet sufficiently investigated are paleobotany, leaf and stem anatomy, comparative biochemistry, embryology, palynological (pollen) fine structure, and the natural history of sexuality, pollination, and seed dispersal. Such important living relicts as *Akania* and *Bretschneidera* need definitive study; *Sabia*, *Greyia*, and some of the little-known genera of the family Staphyleaceae require monographic treatment. Whether the families Aceraceae and Hippocastanaceae are truly distinct on the family level from the Sapindaceae also needs careful examination.

BIBLIOGRAPHY. G.K. BRIZICKY, "The Genera of Sapindales in the Southeastern United States," *J. Arnold Arbor.*, 44:462–501 (1963), a thorough discussion of the Sapindaceae, Aceraceae, and Hippocastanaceae of the Southeastern United States, with good descriptions, drawings, and bibliographies; A. ENGLER, *Syllabus der Pflanzenfamilien*, vol. 2 of 12th ed. by H. MELCHIOR (1964), an authoritative, abbreviated compendium (in German) of taxonomic information about angiosperms, with excellent drawings and floral diagrams, good bibliographies, and a conservative classification; G. ERDTMAN, *Pollen Morphology and Plant Taxonomy: Angiosperms* (1952), descriptions, with numerous drawings, of the pollen grains of 327 angiosperm families, treated alphabetically; J.W. HARDIN, "A Revision of the American Hippocastanaceae," *Brittonia*, 9:145–171, 173–195 (1957), an authoritative treatment of *Billia* and the American species of *Aesculus*, with discussion of morphology and anatomy, inter- and intra-familial relationships, and evolution in the family, as well as taxonomic revision of the American species; F.R. IRVINE, *Woody Plants of Ghana, with Special Reference to Their Uses* (1961), many sapindaceous trees and *Bersama* described and illustrated and their economic and folk uses discussed; L. VAN DER PIJL, "On the Arilloids of *Nephelium*, *Euphoria*, *Litchi* and *Aesculus*, and the Seeds of Sapindaceae in General," *Acta Bot. Neerl.*, 6: 618–641 (1957), an important discussion of evolution in the seeds and fruits of Sapindaceae and *Aesculus* as related to their dispersal; S.J. RECORD and R.W. HESS, *Timbers of the New World* (1943), descriptions and discussions of distributions, uses, and xylem characteristics of the larger American woody plants; C.S. SARGENT, *Manual of the Trees of North America (Exclusive of Mexico)*, 2nd ed. (1922), descriptions, illustrations, and ranges of American trees, including those of Sapindales.

(R.F.Th.)

Sardinia

Character
and
location

One of the largest islands in the western Mediterranean, second only in size to Sicily, Sardinia (Italian Sardegna) was for centuries ravaged by invaders, malaria ridden, backward, and poverty stricken. Almost ignored by the modern world until the 1950s, this autonomous region within the Italian republic was, by the early 1970s, included in one of the most ambitious industrial development schemes in Europe. It was also rapidly becoming an important tourist centre.

Ichnusa or Sandaliotis, the names given to the island by

the Greeks, derived from its shape, which resembles a sandal or foot, the later name, Sardinia, stemming from Latin.

Divided into the three provinces of Sassari (in the north), Nuoro (covering most of the centre), and Cagliari (in the south), Sardinia measures some 150 miles (240 kilometres) from north to south and about 75 miles (120 kilometres) at its widest point, with a surface area of 9,194 square miles (23,813 square kilometres). It lies 112 sea miles from the Italian mainland and 120 from Africa, which is just visible on a clear winter's day from Sardinia's most southerly point, Capo Teulada. Its island neighbour, Corsica, lies 7½ miles to the north, across the Strait of Bonifacio. By the early 1970s, Sardinia was the home of about 1,500,000 people. For related information see ITALY AND SICILY, HISTORY OF; MEDITERRANEAN FOLK CULTURES, WESTERN.

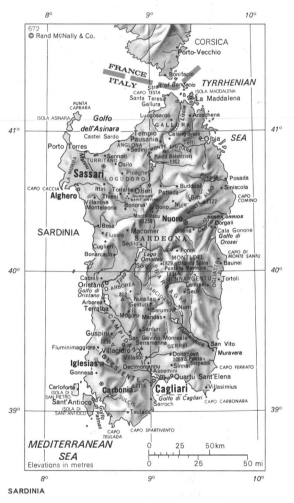

SARDINIA

History. *Ancient origins and the classical period.* The dominating feature of the island (7,000 examples are said to exist) is the nuraghi: strange, truncated cone structures of huge blocks of basalt taken from extinct volcanoes, built without any bonding. Most are quite small, a few obviously fortresses, with wells and other defensive measures; two of these latter, Sant'Antine at Torralba and Su Nuraxi at Barumini, are three stories, and about 50 feet, high. One nuraghe is always within sight of another, the greatest concentrations being in the northwest and south centre. There is also an important nuraghic village at Serra Orrios, near Dorgali, with traces of nearly 80 buildings identified, including temples, wells, and a theatre. The rock-cut tombs of Anghelu Ruju, the Dolmen, Thombe dei Giganti (Tombs of the Giants, for mass burial), and Domus de Janas (Witches' Homes) are also yielding much interesting information to archeologists.

But though modern science has helped to identify and approximately date weapons, jewelry, utensils, and votive objects of metal, pottery, obsidian, and other stones, almost nothing is known of the nuraghic people themselves. The expression "*il vero Sardo*" (the true Sard), referring to a certain type of man or woman, rarely met with, obviously different, may hint at an ethnic survival, and there are a few place names that have no origin in Greek, Punic, or Latin tongues. Expert opinion now gives the dates of the nuraghi from about 1500 to 400 BC, but the mystery remains how such a people, well organized, with remarkable engineering skill and an equal talent in the creation of the beautiful and often witty bronzes to be seen in the Cagliari and Sassari museums, apparently left no trace of a written word.

Phoeni-
cian,
Roman,
and
Vandal
imprint
Phoenicians were the island's first recorded settlers, at about 800 BC. They traded in metals and founded colonies in the south at Nora, Sulcis, Bithia, Tharros, and Karalis (or Cagliari). The Greeks soon raided the north and sacked the town of Olbia, to be followed in turn by the Carthaginians, against whom the Sards revolted repeatedly. In 238 BC the long and brutal Roman occupation began. It was to last nearly 700 years, with Sardinia becoming the first Roman province and Cagliari a port for the Roman fleet in AD 46.

The medieval and modern period.   After the Romans there were the Vandals, about AD 477, followed briefly by the Romans again, then Byzantines, and later still the Saracens, who in 711 sacked and occupied Cagliari, forcing the luckless Sards to pay heavy ransom.

Ninth-century records mention the *giúdice* (governing judge) for the first time, and at the beginning of the 11th century the four divisions of the island are described: that of Cagliari (for the south), Arborea (the centre), Logudoro (Torres), and Gallura (northeast), each with its own *giúdice*. By this time the Italian cities of Pisa and Genoa, with papal support, were struggling against each other and the Sards for domination of the islands. Vatican influence shifted, however, to Alfonso IV of Aragon, who in 1326 defeated the Pisans, taking Cagliari by force. Later in the same century, the famous warrior queen Eleanor of Arborea unsuccessfully rallied the island against the invaders. Her outstanding work, the codifying of the laws begun by her father, was nevertheless completed, and in 1421, after her death, her Carta de Logu was accepted by the Sard Parliament as valid for the whole island and remained so until the Treaty of Utrecht in 1713. In the 15th century, meanwhile, under Spanish occupation, Sardinia was raised to the status of a dominion, with its own viceroy. In 1720 Victor Amadeus II of Savoy was proclaimed first king of all Sardinia, and in 1861 the accession of Victor Emmanuel II finally united Sardinia with Italy, although it was not until 1948 that Sardinia was given a degree of autonomous government.

The land.   Among the natural features of the island, the mountains are outstanding, particularly the Gennargentu in Nuoro, the Limbara heights in Gallura, and the famous *macchia*, the grasslands mingled with scrub of cistus, lentisk, myrtle, prickly pear, and dwarf oaks, which covers most of the uncultivated countryside. Yet man, too, has left an impressive imprint: among a notable range of architectural monuments, generally Romanesque or Pisan in style, the Paleo-Christian Church of San Gavino at Porto Torres is exemplary. Rising, like many of its kind, among solitary, rolling hills, the beautiful Pisan Saccargia di Santa Trinità (located near Sassari), of alternate limestone and basalt, lends its own character to the landscape, as do the ancient citadel walls rising high above the modern city of Cagliari.

Topographically, a pattern of rolling uplands predominates. It leads in the eastern centre to the Gennargentu, with La Marmora (6,017 feet [1,834 metres]), the highest point in Sardinia, just above Bruncu Spina (6,001 feet). The Punta Balesteri (4,468 feet) tops the granite range of the Limbara, surrounded by ancient cork forests. Only in the extreme northwest and in the west coast near Oristano are there large areas of low-lying land. The plain of the Campidano, 60 miles long, running diagonally from Cagliari to Oristano, is an exception. Today, its fertile soil produces much of the island's corn, as well as fruit and vegetables.

With some nine months each year of sunshine, Sardinia has a predominantly mild climate; there are only slight variations of temperature—between 43° and 55° F (6° and 13° C) in winter and from 61° to 79° F (16° to 26° C) in summer, except in the mountains, where snow may lie on the topmost peaks for as long as six months. The name Gennargentu—"the silver gate"—refers to the spectacular effect of the sun on the gleaming snow crystals. There is generally a breeze, the prevailing wind being the *maestrale*, from the northwest; the *greco* is from the east, and only when the *sirocco* blows from the southeast is the air damp and oppressive. Climatic
patterns

Rainfall is low, the mean in Cagliari being only 18.9 inches (480 millimetres), in Sassari, 23.1 inches (587 millimetres), though this increases in the higher lands. The longest rivers, the Tirso (93 miles) and the Flumendosa (79 miles), both rise in Nuoro, fed by innumerable mountain streams that dry up in summer, but for months from the end of January onward the island is a paradise of fruit blossoms and of wild flowers that yield their fragrance and colour to the thyme and other herbs mingling in the *macchia*. Oleander blooms abound in every shade from white to vivid reds. In addition to cork oaks, ilex, chestnuts, and pines throng the forests.

Cattle, goats, and pigs are allowed to wander freely in the uplands, with only sheep being herded as protection against foxes and other predators. In early summer the shepherds lead their flocks to the highlands, the men taking only a little wine and their *carta da musica* (wafer-thin bread), finding meat and water as they need it, milking their ewes and making *peccorino* cheese.

Donkeys abound; the only albinos in the world are found in Asinara, and at Castel Sardo there is a diminutive breed hardly larger than a big dog. The Sard's horse is prized above all, and its well-being was protected by laws in medieval times. In the heart of the island, in the plain of Gesturi, there is still a breed of wild horse, swift and beautiful, of unknown origin, also protected by law. Conservation measures also apply to the mufflon (horned sheep), the rare red and fallow deer, and, in the marshes of Cagliari, a species of heron and also the fleeting spring flocks of flamingos. Other wild birds include eagles, quail, and woodcock. Wild-boar hunting is allowed only at certain seasons, and there are no poisonous snakes.

The 500 miles of coastline, fringed with small bays and endless white sands lapped by translucent seas, are riddled with deep caves, many unexplored. The two most famous are the Grotto di Nettuno (Cave of Neptune), among the coral beds of Alghero, and the Grotta del Bue Marino (the Grotto of the Sea Ox), stretching more than two miles long at Cala Gonone on the east coast. Here, stalactites and stalagmites of unbelievable hue and texture, of metal as well as quartz and other stone, share hidden beauty with white-fronted seals, the only ones left in the Mediterranean.

Sardinia has also three first-class natural harbours: at Cagliari; at Asinara on the northwest; and, on the extreme northeast, among an archipelago of seven small islands, the harbour of La Maddalena, where Lord Nelson held his fleet for nine months before setting out on the voyage that led to Trafalgar. He declared it to be the finest harbour in the Mediterranean and—unavailingly—besought his country to take it.

The people.   A people whose origin remained unknown in the early 1970s, the Sards (and their similarly mysterious language) have inevitably been influenced by the successive nations that occupied the island. Some of the linguistic results are not without humour: at Alghero, half the people speak Catalan but the others Sardo, so communication has to be in Italian. Similarly, the islanders of San Pietro still speak Genoese, inherited from refugees from Tabarca who settled there in the 18th century; on the adjacent San'Antioco, Sardo is the language, so once more Italian must be used. In general, Tuscan has a definite sphere of influence north of a line from Olbia, through Tempio, to Castel Sardo; Genoese predominates around Sassari, with the exception of Alghero, Spanish, and Arab in the south; and the purest native strains, both of people and of language, are found in the isolated Linguistic
complexi-
ties

mountains of the Gennargentu. The strongest foreign associations are Spanish, contacts with the Iberian Peninsula having been dated from as early as the 2nd millennium BC. The legendary foundation of Nora by an Iberian chief, Norax, from Tartessus, before the Phoenician arrival, is perhaps associated with this link. Certainly, modern Sardo includes many Spanish words.

The Sardinians are a devout Catholic people. The population has increased in recent years, in spite of considerable migration, and reached about 1,500,000 by the early 1970s. Distribution was uneven, the only considerable concentrations being in Cagliari and Sassari, and then, much further down the scale, at Nuoro, Iglesias, and Oristano. By the early 1970s annual death and live-birth rates were given as 8.1 and 19.2 per thousand population, respectively.

Profound material and psychological changes are besetting contemporary Sard life. All serious observers agree that the Sards are a dignified, brave, and loyal people, whose backward, almost tribal way of life, especially in isolated villages and mountain areas, is suddenly being catapulted, as it were, from the flint to the jet age, without the centuries of gradual transformation experienced on the mainland of Europe.

In the past, robbery or violence among the Sards arose generally from either hunger or vendetta, the former often tempered by generosity from others hardly better off and from which stems, in part, the fiercely held tradition of hospitality to the stranger. Loyalty to friend or family has, for centuries, facilitated survival in the face of savage butchery. It is a natural habit as ingrained as sleeping and eating, the results of failure to observe it in the past often being so dire that only blood could wash away the stain. It is said, with pride, that if a Sard is your friend he is your friend for life and that no Sard will ever betray another to a "foreigner." That includes Italians, who, after all, were invaders, too.

The economy. The two most important developments in the economy in recent years have been the inclusion of Sardinia in the Italian government-sponsored scheme of aid for the developing areas of southern Italy, Sardinia, and Sicily and the extermination of the malaria mosquito. Known as the Cassa per il Mezzogiorno (Fund for the South), the former project involves giving financial help and technical advice toward the establishment of new businesses, assistance in the training of workers, remission of taxes for ten years, and other incentives. The plan is based on the idea that in the scheduled areas lies a potentially enormous supply of untapped labour that could help to give Italy an important lead in export markets and increase its value within the European Economic Community. Petrochemical plants in Sardinia at Porto Torres and at Sarroch near Cagliari are being extended, and other far-reaching plans involve foreign as well as Italian investors.

The campaign against the mosquito

The extermination of the malaria mosquito, begun in 1943 by the United Nations Relief and Rehabilitation Administration, UNRRA, with a pilot scheme at Oristano, was followed in 1947 by a campaign that covered the whole island and that was financed by the Rockefeller Foundation of the U.S. For centuries the ubiquitous disease, known as *intemperie*, was thought to be caused by the climate, and its elimination, apart from the obvious improvement in health of the people, helped to treble the number of foreign tourists over the 1950s and 1960s. An outstanding example of tourist development was the construction, over a short period in the 1960s, of a luxury resort, the Costa Smeralda, at Arzachena, by an international consortium headed by the Agha Khan.

Sardinian mining for gold, silver, lead, copper, and other ores has been known since ancient times, and the island is the most important source of fluorspar in Europe. Poor-quality coal is mined at Carbonia and is mainland Italy's only source of natural supply, as is the sea salt from the lagoons of Carloforte and Cagliari. The centuries-old cork forests of Gallura produce 80 percent of Italy's total output. Other industries include the making of *peccorino* cheese, and the processing of such wines as

the *vernaccia* and *Malvasia*, from the Ogliastra, and the celebrated red wine of Olbia.

At Stintino, on the Golfo dell' Asinara (Gulf of Asinara), and also at Carloforte, fishing for *tonno* (tunny) is skilled, well organized, and profitable for all. It is financed by Genoese. The only difficulty with this industry is that the course of these great fish, storming their way through to spawning grounds in the Black Sea, remains uncertain until the last moment.

The building of good motor roads linking the main centres of Sardinia and improvements of lesser routes, in conjunction with considerable government concessions to tourists bringing cars to the island, probably doubled motor traffic over the 1960s. Rail communications between the main centres are now fairly good, but other services are slow and limited. The two international airports at Cagliari and Alghero were joined in the early 1970s by a third, at Olbia. A private airline connects the Costa Smeralda with the mainland. In the peak season there are scheduled daily flights to main Italian and Sicilian cities and to Nice and twice weekly a direct service to London. In 1970 alone, there were 300 charter flights bringing passengers from all over Europe. Maritime services are good and include car ferries. Connections are frequent between the Sardinian towns of Cagliari, Olbia, Golfo degli Aranci, and Porto Torres and the mainland towns of Civitavecchia, Genoa, Naples, Palermo, Toulon, and Tunis.

Administration and social conditions. Article 1 of the special statute for Sardinia, dated February 26, 1948, states: "Sardinia and its islands shall be considered an autonomous region with its own legal status, within a united Republic of Italy." Government is administered by a small executive body, the *giunta,* appointed from among members of the Regional Council, themselves elected on the basis of proportional representation in the ratio of one councillor for every 20,000 inhabitants. Members of the Council elect a president from among themselves; he has the right to be present at Cabinet meetings in Rome when matters concerning Sardinia are involved. Only in rare cases—usually where expert knowledge is required—are other than regional councillors appointed to administrative posts within the *giunta.*

The constitutional background

Elections are held every four years. Every citizen reaching the age of 21 has the right to vote but cannot become a councillor until the age of 25. There are no postal votes; although, in theory, absentee voters abroad can claim free second-class transport "to the border," this privilege is not much exercised.

The wide legislative powers held by the *giunta* affect nearly all spheres of life: social services, labour, industrial conditions, hotel and tourist trade, and public works, including building and urban planning. The region retains 90 percent of the income collected from the many tax sources, as well as from a state tobacco monopoly. The central government nevertheless retains control of customs and excise, the armed forces, the *carabinieri* and the finance police (who watch the entry of goods and may examine corporate records in tax matters), the urban and rural police having only limited functions. The railways are also state property, but other means of transport within the island, as well as local sea and air traffic, are the responsibility of the *giunta.* Two years of military service are compulsory, as on the mainland.

Under Italian law every citizen has the right to free education, and in Sardinia "subscription" is available to assist talented children from poor families to attend universities. Taxes include contributions toward medical care and pensions, the latter being payable at the age of 55 for women and 65 for men.

Within the framework of the Regional Council the three provinces have considerable administrative powers over their domestic affairs, all of which are jealously guarded. Isolation of small villages is one of the problems but is, to a growing extent, being overcome by the organization of communes (numbering about 300), whereby two or more communities join for mutual benefit and protection. Each commune has at least one policeman, while in other, solitary villages, the local mayor has authority to enlist up to 15 volunteers, known as *baracelli*, whose powers are limited but who perform a useful function. The origin of this force goes back to the days of the Spanish vigilantes.

Cultural life and institutions. As might be expected in an island with so long and varied a history, folklore and craftwork abound in Sardinia, in many cases the origins and inspiration for both going back to forgotten centuries and pagan beginnings. Witchcraft and both black and white magic are still part of life. No one realized this better than the Nuorese authoress Grazia Deledda, who was given the Nobel Prize for literature in 1926 for her understanding portrayal of the power and passions of life in the primitive communities around her.

Every town and village has its own festival, but the most important is the Sagra di Sant'Efisio at Cagliari in early May, which commemorates the martyrdom of a Roman general who was converted to Christianity. All Sardinia flocks to the capital for this spectacle, which affords an opportunity to witness the exquisitely embroidered (and often valuable) costumes of the women. The men's national costume includes, together with the stocking cap seen on the nuraghic bronzes, a tunic said to be similar to that worn under their armour by Roman soldiers.

Most of the festivals involve feats of horsemanship, as at the Sartiglia of Oristano, the dangerous Ardia at Sedilo, and the Cavalcata at Sassari, where there is also a Feast of the Candles. At Mamoiada, in Nuoro, a remarkable feature is the Feast of the Mamuthones, where men, wearing masks and sheepskins on their backs loaded with bells, perform a ritual dance, ending with a symbolic "killing" of the scapegoat. The variety of songs and dances is endless; they are often performed to the accompaniment of the *launeddas*, ancient triple pipes.

Much of the craftwork, still unspoiled by the intrusion of modernity, is skilled and beautifully made, some being decorated with designs based on Punic and even earlier symbolic patterns. Gold filigree, often allied to coral, is always worn on special occasions. Woodcarving exhibits a great variety and includes the making and decorating of the cassapanca, the bridal chest. Other examples include leatherwork from Dorgali, basket making of palm or asphodel from Castel Sardo or Flussio, as well as finely woven carpets from Nule and Ploaghe, filet lace from Bosa, ceramics and terra-cotta from, among other places, Tortoli, Assemini, and Oristano, and the finely woven *arazzi*, or wall hangings, made in Mogoro, some of which show Arab influence.

The outlook. The success of the development of Sardinia is likely to hinge on the skill and understanding with which new ideas, new standards of living, and new industries are welded on to the existing strata of life and how well the tourist trade is extended. Experienced observers who both know and appreciate the basic qualities of the Sards do not expect the transition to be an easy one. Much will depend on access to education and on the manner whereby a man is enabled to earn a better living for his family, yet still call his soul his own.

BIBLIOGRAPHY. MARGARET GUIDO, *Sardinia* (1963), is a scholarly book on Sardinian prehistory, with important illustrations. The section on Sardinia by the ECONOMIST INTELLIGENCE UNIT in *The Mezzogiorno: Investment Prospects for the Seventies* (1971), deals with economics but is rather technical. T. and B. HOLME and B. GHIRADELLI, *Travellers' Guide to Sardinia* (1967), is a short guide for the interested tourist covering a wide range of subjects; MARY DELANE, *Sardinia: The Undefeated Island* (1968), an account of a journey, includes descriptions of terrain, as well as history and folklore. JOHN WARRE TYNDALE, *The Island of Sardinia*, 3 vol. (1849), is a survey by a barrister dealing in great detail with the history and customs of Sardinians at that time, as does LA MARMORA, *Voyage en Sardaigne*, 3 pt. (1839–60), D.H. LAWRENCE, *Sea and Sardinia* (1921), is a highly personalized report of people encountered on a brief visit. MARCELLO SERRA, *Mal di Sardegna* (1955), is considered as something of a classic in its analysis of the effects of history and the conditions of life on the island. G.M. TREVELYAN, *Garibaldi and the Thousand* (1909), is of special note for the description of the island of Caprera where Garibaldi lived and is buried, his tomb guarded always by a sailor. GRAZIA DELEDDA, *Canne al Vento* (1958), is a novel demonstrating the continuing belief in witchcraft, as well as a remarkable understanding of the attitudes of the Sards to each other; the author received the Nobel Prize for Literature in 1926 for her descriptions of Sardinian life.

(M.De.)

Sargon of Akkad

One of the great rulers of the ancient Near East, Sargon of Akkad (*c.* 2334–2279 BC) wrested the hegemony of the Mesopotamian city-states from the Sumerians and established a Semitic dynasty in the area. That dynasty, though it lasted little more than a century, left a permanent imprint on Mesopotamian society and culture.

Sargon is known almost entirely from the legends and tales that followed his reputation through 2,000 years of cuneiform Mesopotamian history, and not from documents that were written during his lifetime. The lack of contemporary record is explained by the fact that the capital city of Agade, which he built, has never been located and excavated. It was destroyed at the end of the dynasty that Sargon founded and was never again inhabited, at least under the name of Agade.

Hirmer Fotoarchiv, Munchen

Bronze head from Nineveh believed to be Sargon of Akkad, 2nd half of the 3rd millennium BC. In the Iraq Museum, Baghdad.

According to a folktale, Sargon was a self-made man of humble origins; a gardener, having found him as a baby floating in a basket on the river, brought him up in his own calling. His father is unknown; his own name during his childhood is also unknown; his mother is said to have been a priestess in a town on the middle Euphrates. Rising, therefore, without the help of influential relations, he attained the post of cupbearer to the ruler of the city Kish, in the north of the ancient land of Sumer. The event that brought him to supremacy was the defeat of Lugalzaggisi of Uruk (biblical Erech, in central Sumer). Lugalzaggisi had already united the city-states of Sumer by defeating each in turn and claimed to rule the lands not only of the Sumerian city-states but also those as far west as the Mediterranean. Thus Sargon became king over all of southern Mesopotamia, the first great ruler for whom, rather than Sumerian, the Semitic tongue known as Akkadian was natural from birth, although some earlier kings with Semitic names are recorded in the Sumerian king list. Victory was ensured, however, only by numerous battles, since each city hoped to regain its independence from Lugalzaggisi without submitting to the new overlord. It may have been before these exploits, when he was gathering followers and an army, that Sargon named himself Sharru-kin (Rightful King) in support of an accession not achieved in an old-established city through

Legendary origins

Magical survivals

hereditary succession. Historical records are still so meagre, however, that there is a complete gap in information relating to this period.

Military campaigns Not content with dominating this area, his wish to secure favourable trade with Agade throughout the known world, together with an energetic temperament, led Sargon to defeat cities along the middle Euphrates to northern Syria and the silver-rich mountains of southern Anatolia. He also dominated Susa, capital city of the Elamites, in the Zagros Mountains of western Iran, where the only truly contemporary record of his reign has been uncovered. Such was his fame that some merchants in an Anatolian city, probably in central Turkey, begged him to intervene in a local trouble and, according to the legend, Sargon, with a band of warriors, made a fabulous journey to the still-unlocated city of Burushanda (Purshahanda), at the end of which little more than his appearance was needed to settle the dispute.

As the result of Sargon's military prowess and ability to organize, as well as of the legacy of the Sumerian city-states that he had inherited by conquest, and also of previously existing trade of the old Sumerian city-states with other countries, commercial connections flourished with the Indus Valley, with the coast of Oman, with the islands and shores of the Persian Gulf, with the lapis lazuli mines of Badakhshān, with the cedars of Lebanon, with the silver-rich Taurus Mountains, with Cappadocia, with Crete, and perhaps even with Greece.

During Sargon's rule Akkadian became adapted to the script that previously had been used in the Sumerian language, and the new spirit of calligraphy that is visible upon the clay tablets of this dynasty is also clearly seen on contemporary cylinder seals, with their beautifully arranged and executed scenes of mythology and festive life. Even if this new artistic feeling is not necessarily to be attributed directly to the personal influence of Sargon, it shows that, in his new capital, military and economic values alone were not important.

Because contemporary record is lacking, no sequence can be given for the events of his reign. Neither the number of years during which he lived nor the point in time at which he ruled can be fixed exactly; 2334 BC is now given as a date on which to hang the beginning of the dynasty of Agade, and, according to the Sumerian king list, he was king for 56 years.

Difficulties in his last years The latter part of his reign was troubled with rebellions, which later literature ascribes, predictably enough, to sacrilegious acts that he is supposed to have committed; but this can be discounted as the standard cause assigned to all disasters by Sumerians and Akkadians alike. The troubles, in fact, were probably caused by the inability of one man, however energetic, to control so vast an empire without a developed and well-tried administration. There is no evidence to suggest that he was particularly harsh, nor that the Sumerians disliked him for being a Semite. The empire did not collapse totally, for Sargon's successors were able to control their legacy, and later generations thought of him as being perhaps the greatest name in their history.

Attributing his success to the patronage of the goddess Ishtar, in whose honour Agade was erected, Sargon of Akkad became the first great empire builder. Two later Assyrian kings were named in his honour. Although the briefly recorded information of his predecessor Lugalzaggisi shows that expansion beyond the Sumerian homeland had already begun, later Mesopotamians looked to Sargon as the founder of the military tradition that runs through the history of their people.

BIBLIOGRAPHY. C.J. GADD, "The Dynasty of Agade and the Gutian Invasion," in the *Cambridge Ancient History*, rev. ed., vol. 1, ch. 19 (1963), contains both general and particular bibliographies.

(S.M.D.)

Sargon II of Assyria

Sargon II, one of the most outstanding rulers of Assyria, during his reign (721–705 BC) consolidated Assyrian predominance over an area that was to remain the mainstay of the Assyrian empire for a century.

Sargon II, detail of a relief from the palace at Khorsabad. In the Louvre, Paris.
By courtesy of the Musee du Louvre, Paris; photograph, Maurice Chuzeville

Sargon is the Hebrew rendering (Isaiah 20:1) of Assyrian Sharru-kin, a throne name meaning the King is Legitimate. The name was undoubtedly chosen in reminiscence of two former kings of Assyria, particularly in commemoration of Sargon of Akkad (flourished 2300 BC).

Early career Although Sargon's ancestry is partly veiled in mystery, he was probably a younger son of Tiglath-pileser III and consequently a brother of his predecessor Shalmaneser V, who may have died ignominiously or may have been deposed. It was for Sargon to resume the conquests and to improve the administration of the empire his father had begun to assemble.

Upon his accession to the throne, he was faced immediately with three major problems: dealing with the Chaldean and Aramaean chieftainships in the southern parts of Babylonia, with the kingdom of Urartu and the peoples to the north in the Armenian highlands, and with Syria and Palestine. By and large, these were the conquests made by Tiglath-pileser III. Sargon's problem was not only to maintain the *status quo* but to make further conquests to prove the might of the god Ashur, the national god of the Assyrian empire.

When Sargon succeeded to the Assyrian throne, Marduk-apal-iddina II (Merodach-Baladan of the Old Testament), a dissident chieftain of the Chaldean tribes in the marshes of southern Babylonia, committed the description of his victory over the invading Assyrian armies (720 BC) to writing on a clay cylinder, which he deposited in the city of Uruk (biblical Erech; modern Tall al-Warkā). The presence of this record obviously did not suit Sargon. After having discharged other commitments, he uncovered Marduk-apal-iddina's record and removed it to his own residence, then at Kalakh (modern Nimrūd), substituting what has been described as an "improved" version that was more to his liking.

At the beginning of his reign, Sargon had limited time to concentrate his efforts on the building of his palace at Khorsabad, and indeed the palace was not dedicated until the year 706 BC, less than a year before he met his death.

The extant texts reveal little about Sargon himself. With few exceptions, ancient Mesopotamian rulers have left no documents from which to write an actual biography. No personal documents have survived from Sargon's reign; but it seems fair to assume that phraseologies uncommon in the inscriptions of other Assyrian kings, found in his texts, must have met with his approval, even though it is uncertain whether such phrases—sometimes turning into what is obviously poetry—were in fact conceived by Sargon himself or ascribed to him by his historiographers. The discovery, at Nimrūd, of series of texts of omens written in cuneiform on beeswax encased in ivory and walnut boards and marked as being the property of the palace of Sargon perhaps also throws some light on Sargon the man. Although he may not have been the one to introduce cuneiform texts written on wax, this novel method of committing texts to writing apparently took his fancy. This assumption tallies well with the interest he took in the engineering projects undertaken in cities he conquered. Sargon's palace at Khorsabad was dedicated in 706 BC, less than a year before he died.

The Letter to Ashur — An unparalleled record of Sargon's eighth campaign (714 BC)—in the form of a letter to the god Ashur—has been recovered. According to this letter, Sargon, in 714, led the Assyrian armies from Kalakh, which at the time was still his residence, into the areas around modern as-Sulaimānīyah in Iraqi Kurdistan and into the highlands of the Zagros Range beyond. His purpose was to come to the aid of allies of the Assyrian realm who were threatened by Rusas I, a king of Urartu and a bitter enemy of Assyria. During the progress of this campaign, the author of the account visualized, or anticipated, the reactions of his adversary as, from a mountain, he watched the approach of the Assyrian armies. The passage, like many others in this unique text, constitutes an ingenious stylistic device unparalleled in Assyrian historical literature. The phraseology employed by the author is original by Mesopotamian standards as they are known today: inventive, resourceful, testifying to a fertile mind, and clearly deviating from the commonplace platitudes that mostly characterize the standard accounts of Assyrian kings. Whether or not Sargon himself is responsible for the wording of this narrative, it is to his credit that an account of this nature emerged from his chancery, with his approval and endorsement. Sargon is assumed to have died in battle in 705.

BIBLIOGRAPHY. A.G. LIE, *The Inscriptions of Sargon II., King of Assyria* (1929), is still the only acceptable edition of Sargon's various inscriptions other than his account of the eighth campaign. FRANCOIS THUREAU-DANGIN, *Une Relation de la huitième campagne de Sargon* (*714 avant Jésus-Christ*) (1912), remains a standard edition of a unique document. It was left for A. LEO OPPENHEIM, in his article "The City of Assur in 714 B.C.," *Journal of Near Eastern Studies*, 19: 133–147 (1960), to expound ingenious and stylistically sophisticated analyses of this unparalleled example of a first account of an Assyrian campaign into a foreign territory. A rendering, in translation, of the entirety of this text may be found in D.D. LUCKENBILL, *Ancient Records of Assyria and Babylonia*, 2 vol. (1927, reprinted 1969), as well as translations of various texts laid down by Assyrian monarchs. With its small shortcomings, owing to subsequent research and corrections of some readings of cuneiform configurations, Luckenbill's two volumes remain a standard work of reference. A.T. OLMSTEAD, *History of Assyria* (1923, reprinted 1960), athough old, seems to be the only comprehensive history of Assyria so far available. SIR MAX MALLOWAN, *Nimrud and Its Remains*, 2 vol. (1966), contains a full account of the excavations of Nimrūd (ancient Kalakh) that were continued from 1949 for more than a decade.

(Jo.La.)

Sarmatians

The Sarmatians were a people who, during the 4th century BC–4th century AD, occupied much of southern European Russia and penetrated into the eastern Balkans beyond.

Sarmatian studies were in their infancy in the early 20th century; but excavations conducted in the U.S.S.R. since the 1920s have provided much information. The earliest accounts of the Sarmatians are those of Herodotus and other ancient Greek historians who stated that the Sarmatians, or Sauromatians, were an association of tribes. As with the Scythians and the Cimmerians before them, the most vital element in their political group came from central Asia. Its members were of Iranian stock and language; their tongue closely resembled that of the Scythians (Herodotus, Book IV, 117). Like the Scythians they were nomadic, excelling in horsemanship and displaying the same skill in warfare. They also had a keen political sense and administrative ability and followed their conquest of the western Eurasian plain by obtaining full political control over what is now southern European Russia. In consequence their name acquired generic significance; it quickly came to represent a large group of kindred and allied tribes that remained thenceforth attached to the smaller Sarmatian core. The Alani and Roxolani were the most important of these secondary tribes, yet, even when acting independently, all retained their place in the Sarmatian community. All of them accepted the culture favoured by the Sarmatians, practicing and disseminating it with such vigour and enthusiasm that Sarmatian taste and influence were felt even on the shores of the Black Sea and in the west.

History. It is evident now that the Sarmatians advanced from central Asia to invade and conquer the Scythians (q.v.) and did not, as stated by Diodorus Siculus (Book II, 43), rise against them from within their own territory. It has become possible to divide Sarmatian history into four periods. The first extends from the 6th to the 4th century BC, during which the Sarmatians migrated from Asia and penetrated to the western foothills of the Urals. Toward the end of this period the Roxolani pushed on toward the Volga River and the Alani settled in the Kuban Valley. For the most part they remained till they were dislodged in the period of the great migration, when some of the latter infiltrated into Ossetia, surviving there as a community till about the 9th century AD.

The Sarmatians followed closely in the steps of these tribes, and by the 5th century BC they had already made themselves masters of the plain that stretches between the Urals and the Don River. This success encouraged them to intensify their pressure on the Scythians, and in the 4th century BC they crossed the Don and entered Scythia proper. This rapid advance may well have coincided with a decline in Scythian might, resulting from the death of their aged king, Ateas, in battle against Philip II of Macedon in 339 BC; if so, this would help to account for its speed. — Invasion of Scythia

The incursion serves to herald the second (Early Sarmatian) period in Sarmatian history, from the 4th to the 2nd century BC, often called the Prokhorov Period after the important burials of that name with which it is associated. During this period the Sarmatians partially overcame the Scythians and gradually succeeded them as rulers over most of southern Russia. The Roxolani had begun by joining with the Sarmatians in attacking the Scythians, advancing upon them from the south. Toward the end of this period, when the Sarmatians had strengthened their hold over the territory of the Royal Scyths, the Roxolani changed their allegiance, joining forces with the Scythians to attack the Greek Black Sea cities.

In the third (Middle Sarmatian) period, between the 1st century BC and the 1st century AD, the Sarmatians conquered all but the Crimean Scythians, bringing the assaults on the Greek cities to an end. Having consolidated their hold over the captured areas, the Sarmatians did not attempt to annex any of these cities; instead, early in Nero's reign, they invaded the Roman province of Lower Moesia (Bulgaria). Although the Roman general Plautius Silvanus Aelianus ejected them in AD 62–63, the Sarmatians and some Germanic tribes they had joined were thenceforth a menace to the Romans in the west, as were the Alani in the Caucasian area. Vespasian, Trajan, and Marcus Aurelius were forced to adopt such defensive measures as to attempt to transform the vassal Bosporan kingdom into a buffer state. Hadrian had to build a network of fortresses manned with Roman troops along the borders of Lower Moesia and Cappadocia.

In the last phase of their history, spanning the 2nd to 4th centuries AD, the Sarmatians and their Germanic allies entered Dacia (Romania) and began raiding the lower reaches of the Danube, but in the 3rd century the Gothic invasion put an end to their independence. Many Sarmatians nevertheless retained their position and influence under the Goths; others joined them to sweep into western Europe, fighting at their sides. Soon after AD 370, however, waves of migrating Huns effectively ended the very existence of Sarmatia; the majority of the Sarmatians who remained in southern Russia perished at the hands of these Asian invaders. Some of the survivors were assimilated by their new masters and others by the Slavs of the lower Dnieper, but most fled westward to join their neighbours in harassing the Huns and the remaining Goths. Their descendants continued to do so until the 6th century, when they finally disappeared from history.

Social structure and way of life. Very little was known till the 1960s about the social structure or way of life developed by the Sarmatians. Basically both at first followed closely those established by the Scythians, largely as the result of a common Central Asian origin and heritage. Nevertheless, several fundamental differences serve to distinguish the two peoples. Scythians venerated nature deities, while the Sarmatians were fire worshippers who sacrificed horses to their god. Scythian women were relegated to a life of semiseclusion; Sarmatian women, at least in the earlier periods, however, were expected to fight in time of war, and could not marry until they had killed an enemy in battle. After marriage, however, women were obliged to abandon warfare and to devote themselves entirely to their homes and families. Greek tales about Amazons may have been based on exploits of early Sarmatian women, many of whom were buried with their weapons.

Amazons

When the Sarmatians penetrated into southeastern Europe, they were already accomplished horsemen. They followed a nomadic way of life, devoting themselves to hunting and to pastoral occupations; most of them adhered to this form of existence to the end. There is evidence that some of them practiced an elementary form of husbandry, but few settlements of Sarmatian origin have as yet been studied. In the earlier periods their customs, clothes, and many other possessions resembled those of the Scythians, but their society was matriarchal in character. Gradually, as a prosperous class began to form, the tribe entered a transitional phase during which tribal chieftains tended to replace women as rulers; eventually, kings seem to have predominated.

The rise of a male monarchy may have been stimulated by the formation of a male corps of heavy cavalry, facilitated by the probably Sarmatian invention of a metal stirrup, soon followed by that of the spur. The methods of warfare thus made possible were largely responsible for Sarmatia's military supremacy. The Romans noted and gradually adopted certain of their tactics. During the 3rd century they went so far as to incorporate Sarmatian units in some Roman regiments, equipping them with their traditional weapons and encouraging them to fight in their own manner. From early times onward Sarmatian military accoutrements included conically shaped helmets worn with scale, ring, or plate armour of iron that often protected horses as well as riders. Unlike the Scythians, the Sarmatians did not excel at archery; they relied on long lances or spears and long, sharply pointed swords.

The Sarmatians were excellent craftsmen. Perhaps artistically less inventive than the Scythians, they were nevertheless equally proficient metalworkers, better potters, and no less adept at curing hides; they were thus able to maintain the important trade in furs, grain (levied from local settlers), honey, fish, and metal that the Scythians had established with the Greek cities on the northern shores of the Black Sea. The Sarmatians also developed commercial contact with the Syr-Darya region, the borderlands of China, and the kingdom of Khwārezm (Chorasmia).

Until disrupted by the Huns, Sarmatian culture presented a uniform and all-embracing character, even though it altered with each period in its history. Its evolution is reflected in burials that distinguish each of the four periods. Thus, no large mounds are associated with the earliest phase when objects were seldom included in the graves, though the occasional presence of articles points to the beginnings of a class society. Burials of the second period often display considerable wealth; those of the third phase also reflect the growth of a more complex way of life, stemming in part from the Sarmatian subjugation of alien tribes and assimilation of many of their customs. It also was a result of the flourishing trade the Sarmatians had established. During these periods the truly typical Sarmatian culture evolved and was imposed on the entire region. In the last phase Germanic influence led to the introduction of fibulae (brooches or clasps like safety pins), with resulting changes in costume.

Tombs and their contents. The richest Sarmatian burials have been found in the Kuban area, and on the edges of the great riverbeds of the southern Russian S.F.S.R. and the Ukraine, where many have been subjected to regular seasonal flooding. Hundreds of other graves are to be found throughout the area the Sarmatians once occupied. Many of these were excavated in the second half of the 19th and in the first half of the 20th centuries, and sufficient material has become available to permit an overall picture to be outlined.

Except in the Kuban, where they are generally oval in shape, the mounds the Sarmatians constructed are similar to those of the Scythians; but the tombs beneath them are different from the elaborate Scythian mortuary chambers. For the most part Sarmatian graves consist of simple square, circular, or oval holes (sometimes pocketed trenches); very occasionally, tombs are found lined with rushes. No coffins were used; the body was usually wrapped in a leather or fur rug and laid on the bare earth, though sometimes on a rush mat. In the vicinity of Kerch, paintings survive on the walls of some graves of late date, some showing Sarmatians wearing cloaks held in place by fibulae; some contain traces of what may be the beginnings of an alphabet.

Burial rites

Diagonal and crouched burials and cremations occur side by side; thus although Sarmatian culture prevailed, local habits evidently persisted. In the last phase the influence of the Huns is reflected in the practice of cranial deformation. In the graves of earlier periods Scythian influence is often apparent throughout; horses are associated with most burials, their trappings being generally placed in the graves. In richer burials, such as those of Starobelsk and Yanchokarski, their hooves and skulls were often included, but not, as was customary in Scythian times, the rest of their bodies. Most of the tombs also contained caldrons of the Scythian type as well as utensils for inhaling hemp, bronze vessels, and mirrors of Oriental form in silver alloy. Tiny gold plaques designed as trimmings for clothes are also common but, in contrast to similar gold plaques of Scythian date, which were generally decorated with an animal design, these are usually geometric in character. Among articles of personal adornment, fibulae make their first appearance in graves of Sarmatian date; little gold bottles set with jewels are especially characteristic of the period, and various types of glass are numerous. The locally made pottery is of a higher quality than the pottery that is typical of the Scythian age.

Sarmatian horse trappings differ from those used by the Scythians, as do some of their arms. The iron Sarmatian bits had rings to hold the leather and had fewer animal terminals and decorations than those of Scythian date; hard saddles with a high frontal arch were also new to the Black Sea region. The saddles were often covered with gold leaf, studded with bosses and adorned with coloured glass or precious stones; trappings tended to be less ornate than those of the Scythians, although often of silver or silver gilt. The long swords peculiar to the Sarmatians were set into wooden hilts surmounted by a knob of precious stone (*e.g.,* agate or onyx) or in wood laced with gold; the handguards were generally cut from a single large stone. Spears were longer and sharper than the Scythian, but the variety of knives and daggers was equally great.

Metalwork and the polychrome style. Whereas the Scythian was an animal art, the Sarmatian, though it retained many animal forms, was primarily geometric and was largely in polychrome (many colours). The Sarmatians apparently delighted in glass inlay, gold-wire granulations, and embossed effects achieved by repoussé or inset stones and jewels; the taste was basically Asian, the designs primarily geometric and floral, though frequently also of an animal character. Jewellers produced diadems, torques, bracelets, rings, fibulae, gold plaques, buckles, buttons, and mounts of various sorts. Hoards that have been found and objects acquired from the more important tombs form an important collection of jewelry and fine metalwork. The Pashkov group of burials in the Kuban, excavated during 1929–37 and 1946–49, are among the earliest known. They are associated with a Meteo-Sarmatian tribe and date in the main from the 5th to the 3rd

Jewelry

century BC, though one mound contained jewelry and vessels assigned to the 3rd century AD. In the earlier instances the men were buried with spears, swords, and arrows; the women were adorned with beads and with bronze bracelets of local manufacture. The Prokhorov burials lie near Sharlyk in Orenburg *oblast* (province), Russian S.F.S.R., and were excavated by the Russian archaeologist S.I. Rudenko in 1916. The largest belonged to a chieftain who had been buried in an iron chain-mail coat with gold torque and bronze bracelets; a sword and gold-handled knives were placed within easy reach of his hands, and two magnificent silver vessels of Persian workmanship stood close to him. One of these was inscribed in Aramaic with the words "the cup of Atromitra." The richest burial so far known belonged to the Novocherkassk group and is to be dated to the 2nd century BC. Discovered in 1864, it produced objects of such value that it seems probable the tomb was for a queen. In addition to a magnificent crown the woman wore a gold necklace and gold bracelets. A small agate bottle mounted in gold and adorned with animal designs and several gold cups and silver vessels lay beside her. All these were of Sarmatian workmanship but placed with them was a terra-cotta statuette of Eros, of Greek origin, and two Greek-inscribed silver dishes; these testify to the links that the Sarmatians maintained with their Greek neighbours. Another burial in the same region produced a gold vessel, dating from between the 2nd century BC and the 1st century AD, signed in Greek letters with the name of its Sarmatian maker, Tarulla.

BIBLIOGRAPHY. M.I. ROSTOVTSEV, *Iranians and Greeks in South Russia* (1922), remains essential reading for all serious study in this field, although much new information has come to light since its publication. T. SULIMIRSKI, "The Forgotten Sarmatians," in E. BACON (ed.), *Vanished Civilisations* (1963), is a convenient introduction to the subject; the same author's *The Sarmatians* (1970), a careful and detailed summary of all available archaeological evidence and analysis of the tribes and their movements.

(T.T.R.)

Sarpi, Paolo

Paolo Sarpi, Venetian patriot, polemicist, and scholar, was the theological adviser to the Republic of Venice during its struggle in the 17th century with Pope Paul V, author of an influential work attacking papal absolutism, and, among Italians, a pioneer advocate of the separation of church and state.

Thomas-Photos, Oxford

Sarpi, portrait by an unknown artist. In the Bodleian Library, Oxford, Eng. (The black spot on his face covers the scar from an unsuccessful attempt on his life in 1607.)

Sarpi was born in Venice on August 14, 1552, the son of Francesco Sarpi, an unsuccessful businessman, and Isabella Morelli, of a prominent but not noble Venetian family. His father died when Sarpi was a child and he was brought up in poor circumstances by his pious mother and his maternal uncle Ambrogio, a priest. Delicate, studious, and clever, at 14 Sarpi joined the Servite Order and

at 20 became court theologian to the Duke of Mantua, a post which gave him leisure to study Greek, Hebrew, mathematics, anatomy, and botany. Young Sarpi was known as La Sposa—"the bride"—because of his modesty and moral seriousness. Of medium height, with a large brow, long nose, black eyes, and thin beard, he lived simply and suffered from poor health. He is reported to have possessed a photographic memory and to have been a most persistent scholar.

Personal characteristics

At 27 Sarpi was appointed provincial of his order and won a reputation as a firm but sensible ruler. He visited Rome several times and became friendly with Pope Sixtus V and the great theologian Robert Bellarmine. Continuing his anatomical studies, he discovered the valves of the veins that facilitate the circulation of the blood, and he was the first to demonstrate that the pupil of the eye dilates under the action of light. His many friends included Galileo, who thought no one in Europe could surpass Sarpi in mathematics, while Sarpi said of the astronomer's condemnation by Rome, "The day will come, I am almost sure, when men, better versed in these matters, will deplore the disgrace of Galileo and the injustice dealt so great a man."

Venice, with its cosmopolitan population, had long followed a liberal religious policy, resisting any intrusion by Rome into its internal affairs. In 1606 Paul V demanded that Venice repeal a law restricting church building and hand over to him two priests, one charged with murder, whom the Venetian government intended to try before civil courts. When Venice refused, Paul excommunicated the senate and the doge (the Venetian head of state) and put the republic under an interdict, meaning that all priests were debarred from their functions.

Sarpi, having been appointed consultor to the government, wrote powerfully in support of the Venetian case. He argued that the Pope was infallible only in matters of faith and that his interdict was invalid. Sarpi's basic tenet was that "princes have their authority from God, and are accountable to none but him for the government of their people." It was in the public interest, he said, to fix limits on church building in a small city like Venice, for ecclesiastical property—already extensive—paid no taxes to the state. As for the two priests, while the church had every right to try them for crimes committed as priests, for crimes such as murder and adultery the state courts must be responsible. Sarpi concluded that Venetians were not bound to observe the interdict, and his advice was followed.

Defense of Venice against the papacy

Sarpi's works were influential because he wrote in a clear, witty style and argued not from legal textbooks but from the evident facts of history. He constantly argued, for example, that the pope's power should not exceed that of St. Peter. Sarpi's writings played an important part in sustaining Venetian morale and in winning sympathy abroad. Paul V had a powerful ally in Spain, then dominant in Italy, and when he threatened recourse to arms, Venice secured the support of France and even threatened to call on Protestant countries. Finally the Pope, fearing Venice would become Protestant, agreed to a settlement. The interdict was ended, and Venice handed over the two priests, reserving, however, her right to try churchmen before civil courts. "The Republic," said Sarpi, "has given a shake to papal claims. For whoever heard till now of a papal interdict, published with all solemnity, ending in smoke?"

Sarpi refused to answer a summons to appear before the Roman Inquisition. On October 5, 1607, he was stabbed during an attack on him in the street. He blamed the Roman Curia but the charge has never been proved.

Between 1610 and 1618 Sarpi wrote the first full history of the Council of Trent (1545–63), using Venetian archives and private papers, notably those of Arnauld du Ferrier, French ambassador to the council. Sarpi strongly criticized the council for not giving bishops more autonomy, for hardening differences with the Protestants, and for increasing the Curia's absolutism. The only one of Sarpi's writings to be printed in his lifetime, the *History of the Council of Trent*, appeared in London in 1619, under the pseudonym Pietro Soave Polano. Though put

Writings

on Rome's *Index* of prohibited books, it went through several editions and five translations in ten years.

The *History*, like most of Sarpi's writings, is a partisan work, written with one eye on the Protestants whom Sarpi saw as Venice's potential allies against Rome and Spain. Similarly, in his extensive correspondence, Sarpi sought the friendship of all who took an independent line toward Rome, including French Huguenots and German Protestants; but there is no evidence to suggest that he himself was, in doctrine, anything but an orthodox Roman Catholic. Sarpi's quarrel was never with the Roman Church but—as he saw it—with an interfering Roman Curia.

In his later life Sarpi was something of a hero to the Venetians and was sought out by foreign visitors. He continued to live frugally and, though excommunicated, he celebrated mass to the end. He died on January 14, 1623, and his last words—"Esto perpetua" ("May she endure")—were, characteristically, a reference to Venice.

BIBLIOGRAPHY. PAOLO SARPI, *Opere* (1761–68), is the first collected, and still the most complete, edition of Sarpi's writings, though it will eventually be superseded by the critical edition of individual works in course of publication by LATERZA OF BARI. The *Lettere* (1863), throw light on Sarpi's character and his relations with a wide variety of Italian and foreign thinkers. *Istoria del Concilio Tridentino* (1935), is a critical edition by G. GAMBARINI of Sarpi's largest and most influential work, based on the manuscript by one of Sarpi's copyists in the Biblioteca Marciana, Venice. There is still no adequate balanced biography of Sarpi; the best existing biography is the uncritical and laudatory *Vita del padre Paolo dell'ordine de' servi*, by FULGENZIO MICANZIO (1646).

(V.C.)

Sarraceniales

The Sarraceniales, or pitcher-plant order, consists of the single family Sarraceniaceae, a small group of low perennial herbs of bogs and wet savannas with pitcher-like leaves specialized for trapping insects and other tiny animals. The Sarraceniaceae is confined to the New World, where it ranges from the tropics to the southern rim of the Arctic; but it has a counterpart in the Old World pitcher-plant family, Nepenthaceae (see NEPENTHALES). The approximately 15 species, despite their relative homogeneity, constitute three distinct genera, which are endemic (native) to three widely separated regions.

Sarracenia, the largest genus (eight or nine species), occurs in the Atlantic coastal regions of North America. The South American pitcher plants, genus *Heliamphora*, number four to six species and are known only from isolated mountains of the Guiana Highlands of northern South America. The genus *Darlingtonia* includes only *D. californica*. This distinctive pitcher plant is endemic to Pacific North America, where it is highly localized in montane (mountain) meadows in northern California and adjacent Oregon.

FEATURES OF THE ORDER

General description. The pitcher plants are totally unlike any other plants in the Western Hemisphere. As a group, they take their common name from their hollow tubular leaves, which are shaped like urns, trumpets, or small pitchers. Some species have hooded pitchers. In *Darlingtonia californica*, for example, the overarching hood gives to the tall, upright, tubular leaf the appearance of a cobra raised in striking position, hence its local name, cobra lily, or cobra plant. The curious landing ramp protruding from the mouth even suggests a snake's tongue.

Entrapment of insects

The hollow leaves of pitcher plants are carefully constructed pitfalls that entrap insects or other tiny prey lured to the mouth of the leaf by glistening surfaces or unusual light-transmitting patches. Downward-pointing (retrorse) hairs in the throat of the pitcher and other devices prevent escape, and the exhausted prey fall into the digestive liquor at the bottom. The liquor is a mixture of digestive enzymes (biological catalysts) and other secretions involved in digestion, rainwater (in hoodless species), and decomposing bacteria. In all species the trapping mechanism is of this passive, pitfall type.

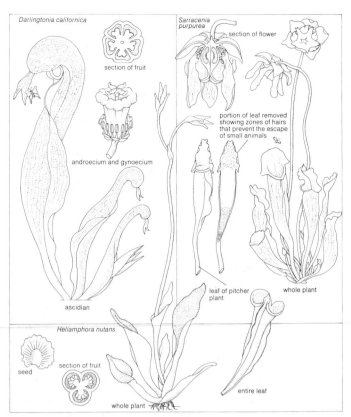

Representative plants from each of the three genera in the family Sarraceniaceae.

Drawing by M. Pahl based on (*Darlingtonia californica* section of fruit, androecium and gynoecium; *Sarracenia purpurea* section of flower; *Heliamphora nutans* seed, section of fruit, entire leaf) Wunschmann, Warburg, and Hegi in A. Engler, *Syllabus der Pflanzenfamilien* vol. II (1964); Gebruder Borntraeger

Distribution and abundance. Excepting *Sarracenia purpurea*, species of the genus *Sarracenia* are confined to the southeastern part of the United States, where they occur mainly on the Coastal Plain and adjacent Piedmont from southern Virginia to eastern Texas. The green pitcher plant, *S. oreophila*, the only species whose geographic distribution is completely isolated from the other species, occurs in the Appalachian Mountains of northeastern Alabama and extreme west central Georgia. The greatest concentration of species, populations, and individuals is in the region from southern Georgia and northern Florida to the southern half of Alabama.

Sarracenia purpurea is the most widespread species, ranging from the sub-Arctic to the subtropics, from Labrador to Great Bear Lake, near the Arctic Circle in northwest Canada, southeastward over central and eastern North America to Georgia, Florida, Alabama, Mississippi, and possibly Louisiana on the Coastal Plain. The yellow pitcher plant, *S. flava*, probably the most common species of the genus in terms of numbers of individuals, ranges from southern Virginia to northern Florida and southern Alabama on the Coastal Plain and Piedmont. The hooded pitcher plant, *S. minor*, is relatively common on the Coastal Plain from South Carolina to southern Florida (east coast). The other species of *Sarracenia* all have very restricted distributions.

Darlingtonia occurs from the central Oregon coast through the southwest Oregon mountains southward to Nevada County in the Sierra Nevada Range of northern California. It is abundant in the Mt. Shasta region, where it may be found in at least 30 to 40 localities within a 15- to 20-mile (25- to 30-kilometre) radius. Thus, despite its localized distribution, the California pitcher plant is by no means rare. Distribution of South American pitcher plants is still poorly known, but they exist in Guyana and Venezuela.

Economic importance. The pitcher-plant order is of minor economic importance, even though species of *Sarracenia* have been cultivated as curiosities for many years. The species most commonly cultivated are *Sarra-*

cenia flava, S. purpurea, and *S. rubra.* The common pitcher plant was introduced into culture in England at least as early as 1640. Since their discovery, both *Darlingtonia* and *Heliamphora* have been grown in cultivation but on a much more limited basis; the latter is grown only rarely, however, because of the inaccessibility of its native habitats. *Darlingtonia* is extremely difficult to grow and seldom survives long under artificial conditions, although it has done well when transplanted to New England bogs.

Medicinal properties

It is not unusual that such bizarre plants as the sarracenias would draw the attention of the American Indians and early explorers and settlers in North America as possible sources of medicines and drugs. For a time the roots were reputed to have various medicinal properties, including efficacy in treating smallpox. Indians in Newfoundland used the root to treat smallpox, and the treatment enjoyed a short-lived popularity in England, beginning about 1865. Neither the root nor any other part of the plant has ever been proved to have real medicinal value.

Common names and lore. Pitcher plants have received many fanciful vernacular names through the years, some of which allude to a specific feature of the plant. The first English settlers in North America called the common pitcher plant (*S. purpurea*) the sidesaddle flower, apparently in reference to the peculiar umbrella-like expansion of the style (a portion of the female structure). This wide-ranging species has been called by a host of other interesting names: huntsman's-cup, Adam's cup, whippoorwill's-boots, devil's boots, flytrap, northern pitcher plant, forefather's-cup; and, in Quebec, petits cochons and herbe-crapaud. Some of the common names given to other species are huntsman's-horn, flycatchers, trumpets, trumpet-leaf, biscuit flower, fiddler's trumpet, white-top pitcher plant, sweet pitcher plant, parrot pitcher plant, and calf's head.

Fantastic claims have often been made about pitcher plants—for example, that they will catch all the flies in a house—and the layman may find it difficult to separate fact from fiction. Carnivorous plants have excited the imagination of many popular writers; most stories involving so-called man-eating plants seem to be inspired by a vague knowledge of the tiny, harmless Venus's-flytrap (*Dionaea;* see NEPENTHALES) or of some other carnivorous species with an active trapping mechanism. There is no scientific fact to substantiate such stories.

NATURAL HISTORY

Life cycle. The pitcher plants are herbaceous perennials (*i.e.,* nonwoody plants that live several years) with a round, horizontal, underground stem (rhizome or rootstock). An upright, above-ground stem is lacking, with the occasional exception of *Heliamphora.* The mature rhizome, which is three to 12 inches (eight to 30 centimetres) long and of a typical form for each species, grows for 10 to 15 years (*Darlingtonia*) or as many as 20 to 30 years (*Sarracenia*). It forms new nodes (stem regions that give rise to leaves or other structures) at intervals. The nodes usually remain compacted and give rise to adventitious roots, rosettes of leaves, and flowering stalks. The interior of the rhizome is white from the abundant store of starch. During the life of the plant, the older end of the rhizome slowly decays; the middle part is covered with leaf scars and decaying roots; and the growing end (perhaps half of total length of rhizome) has functional roots and leaves, as well as older leaves in various stages of decay. A new set of roots forms and develops to maturity every season; the older roots continue to function as storage organs for six or seven years. During the years of rhizome growth, lateral underground buds may occasionally form; the buds develop into separate plants by forming new roots and leaf rosettes, after which the parent rhizome decays. In *Darlingtonia* but rarely in *Sarracenia,* the internodes (stem regions between nodes) elongate slightly, spacing out the new plants that are formed. This gives rise to gradual vegetative spreading in pitcher-plant colonies, particularly of *D. californica.* Thus, once established, pitcher-plant species slowly propagate themselves vegetatively.

Leaf forms. Two and sometimes three types of leaves are formed each year in *Sarracenia.* A crop of pitchered, insect-catching leaves is produced in the spring, and a second crop, differing markedly in shape, may be produced in the fall. Half or all of the autumn leaves, depending on the species, may be swordlike and tubeless (phyllodia); phyllodia overwinter in the green condition. They may also develop in the summer in cool, shady places. The pitchered leaves are evergreen in species in which they lie close to the ground (*S. psittacina* and *S. purpurea*) but tend to die back in the fall in the upright species (*e.g., S. flava*). In addition, all species produce small, scalelike leaves.

Seasonal variation of leaves

The pitchered leaves clearly seem to be adapted to function like flowers in attracting the insects they trap. The leaves are flower-like in their striking colour patterns and shapes, which are distinctive for each species, and may be easily mistaken for true flowers. During May and June, the active period of the leaves, glands over the surfaces of the flower-like leaves exude nectar drops containing fruit sugar, which permeates the air with a fruity or honey-like fragrance. By early June the entire outer surface of the pitcher below the mouth in some species may glisten with almost continuous secretion. Heavy feeding activity by ants, wasps, bees, butterflies, moths, and other insects indicates the great attraction of the nectar and its sweet scent.

Flowering and seed germination. The flowers of all pitcher-plant species are showy and have a more or less agreeable scent. Most of the sarracenias produce their flowering scapes (leafless stalks) in the spring before the new leaves appear, but the common pitcher plant flowers after new leaves have begun to mature. Only a minority of the plants in a given population seem to produce flowers in any one year. Flower buds form the previous year in August and September and remain concealed in the leaf bases until March or April. In the southern states the sarracenias begin to bloom in March or April, continuing for a month or two or throughout the summer until August or September, depending on the species. *Sarracenia purpurea,* which has a wide latitudinal distribution, begins flowering during the first week of April in Florida but not until about the second week of August in Labrador. The petals of a sarracenia flower wither after two or three weeks; the rest of the flower remains green until the capsule and seeds mature in four to five months.

The flowers, at first pendulous, may in some species become erect after pollination. The anthers (male reproductive organs) begin to shed pollen copiously as soon as the flower opens, and in *Sarracenia* the inverted umbrella-like style (a portion of the female structure) catches the pollen and holds it where insect visitors can find it readily. The nectar-scented flowers attract ants, bees, pollen-eating beetles, and other insects but especially bees, which seem to be the primary pollinators and tend, in the course of their nectar-feeding activities, to carry the pollen of younger flowers to the stigmas (female pollen-receiving areas) of older flowers. Glands on the ovary, sepals, or accessory leaves (*Heliamphora*) secrete the nectar that attracts insects, and the scent is more or less specific to each species. Cross pollination seems to be essential in *Darlingtonia* and *Sarracenia,* both of which have protandrous flowers—*i.e.,* flowers in which the pollen is ripe before the stigmas are receptive.

Pollination

Heliamphora pollination is poorly known. The floral structure suggests that insects, which are attracted by the nectar secreted by the sepals and ovary walls, effect pollination.

Seeds are shed from July to September, and in the warmer southern states germination may take place in three to five weeks; a recognizable seedling may form before winter dormancy sets in. Germination may be delayed until the following spring in the colder latitudes. The wide and sporadic distribution of some species suggests that migrating birds, by picking up seeds on their feet, may play a role in dispersing the seeds.

Hybridization and chromosome number. Species of the *Sarracenia* have been known to hybridize freely, both in cultivation and in nature. Perhaps the most common natural hybrid is the cross between *Sarracenia purpurea* and *S. flava*, two species with overlapping ranges.

The chromosomes, which carry the hereditary material, have been counted in all species of *Sarracenia*, and the number has been found to be the same (26) throughout the genus. It is not surprising, therefore, that the species hybridize freely. The reproductive barriers between species are weak. Geographic separation and separation of flowering time seem to be the chief means by which a species are isolated. Bees, the most common pollinators, visit different plants or species indiscriminately. Four to seven years are required for a *Sarracenia* hybrid to reach flowering stage.

The chromosome number of *Darlingtonia* is 30. There are no known reports of attempts to hybridize this genus with *Sarracenia*.

Carnivorous adaptations.   *Trapping mechanism.* Insects are trapped in basically the same way by the various species of *Sarracenia*. They are attracted to the mouth of the pitcher by a trail of nectar-secreting glands on the leaf extending downward from the lip along the outside. The lip is provided with stiff, downward-pointing (retrorse) hairs; below the lip, in the steepest part of the throat, is the highly polished area without hairs, from which digestive enzymes are secreted. Insects attempting to garner nectar around the lip almost invariably fall into the pitcher. Like a greased slide, the polished zone sends them tumbling into the liquor below, where they quickly become submersed and drown. Escape is prevented by the retrorse hairs at the mouth, which are too dense for the insects to crawl between and too stiff and downward directed for them to climb over.

Several species of *Sarracenia* have specialized luring devices that resemble those of the cobra lily, *Darlingtonia*. The cobra lily has a landing ramp from which insects can enter the pitcher. Because of the domelike hood, insects must enter from the side. The presence of the hood darkens the pitcher; this would discourage insects from entering if numerous translucent "windows" that permit light to penetrate were not present. The windows also serve to attract insects that have already entered the pitcher toward a point other than the true opening; they waste their energy trying to crawl through or fly against the translucent tissue, eventually tire, and drop into the liquid below. Retrorse hairs and a polished secretory zone are also present in this species.

The trapping mechanism of *Heliamphora* differs only in details from that of *Sarracenia*.

The quantity of debris—the undigested remains of the plant's victims—in any mature pitcher, especially in the fall, when the pitcher of some species may be half full of remains, illustrates the effectiveness of the pitcher-plant leaf as an insect-trapping mechanism. Ants are especially common prey, but flies, wasps, spiders, crickets, and other tiny animals often fall victim.

Digestive mechanism. *Sarracenia* species secrete digestive enzymes that accumulate in the bottom of the pitcher, where they become diluted with rainwater in species in which the leaves are not entirely closed off at the mouth by a hood or lid (*e.g.*, *S. purpurea*). The liquid in the pitchers usually includes bacteria, and digestion is accomplished by the combined action of enzymes and bacteria. The insect that falls into this digestive broth is attacked almost immediately, and odours of decay are often evident. The end products, including nitrogen compounds, are absorbed by the leaves; the indigestible outer skeletons of the insects accumulate at the bottom of the leaf until it dies.

In *Darlingtonia* and *Heliamphora*, enzymatic glands are lacking, and apparently only bacterial digestion occurs.

Evidence suggests that the carnivorous habit is not essential to the survival of the pitcher plants but that they grow better and probably flower more profusely when provided with an animal diet. In the long run, young plants benefit more directly from an animal diet than mature ones, but carnivory helps the latter to produce more leaves and flowers.

Animals that exploit pitcher plants.   Some   animals, apart from the pollinators, have evolved methods of elud-

Contents of pitcher fluid [margin note]

ing the trap and using the pitcher plant for food, for shelter, or as a host for part of their life cycle. Certain insects parasitize the plant tissue; others rob the pitchers by parasitizing insects trapped there. In fact, some of these insects have lost the ability to survive under any other conditions. Birds often slit the pitchers to get at the insects inside, and tree frogs—which sometimes take shelter by day in the mouth of the pitcher by clinging to the inside walls with the suction pads of their feet—probably eat some of the insects visiting the traps.

Several moth species lay eggs in the pitchers, in which the caterpillars hatch and feed before they spin a cocoon and overwinter. The pitcher-plant moth (*Exyra* species) even passes its adult phase sitting inside the pitcher by day. Other moths parasitize the flowers and seed capsules and then spin a cocoon or tunnel into the stem to pupate; one moth larva is a root borer in sarracenias.

Flies of the genus *Sarcophaga* deposit larvae (maggots) within the pitcher's mouth; the larvae prey on flies captured by the plant and then bore through the pitcher wall to pupate in the soil. These larvae apparently do not have any structural adaptation for this dangerous habitat, but they do secrete an anti-enzyme that protects them from the otherwise destructive digestive enzymes produced by the plant. Like the pitcher-plant moth, the flies are able to go in and out of the pitcher without falling victim to it. Wrigglers (larvae and pupae) of the pitcher-plant mosquito, *Wyeomyia smithii*, thrive in the pitchers of *Sarracenia purpurea* and overwinter in them, emerging as adults in the spring. This northern species of mosquito, which belongs to an otherwise tropical group of mosquitoes, is rarely absent from a colony of the common pitcher plant, even at its northern limits of distribution in Canada.

Larvae of the minute gnat, *Metriocnemus edwardsi*, are found in the pitchers of *Darlingtonia*, where they hatch and feed in great numbers.

Ecology.   The pitcher plants are hydrophytes—water plants—that commonly inhabit bogs, swamps, wet, sandy meadows, or savannas where the soils are water saturated, moderately to intensely acidic, and deficient in nitrates and phosphates. Some species can tolerate standing water, and a few may even thrive underwater for a time (*e.g.*, *S. psittacina*). The montane species, *S. oreophila*, occurs in sands and gravels on stream banks rather than in bogs or swamps, and other pitcher plants may be able to tolerate moderately well-drained acidic soils. On the Atlantic coastal plain, the pitcher plants characteristically inhabit wet, sandy areas in the pinelands, often over extensive areas. Frequently, several species occur together, and there may also be other carnivorous plants (*e.g.*, sundews and flytraps—see NEPENTHALES). The most common plant associated with pitcher plants is sphagnum or peat moss. In Alabama, in both the bogs of the uplands and the boggy marshes of the coastal plain, sarracenias form characteristic hydrophytic associations with sundews, pipeworts, orchids, and dichromenas. In the pine barrens of New Jersey, the common pitcher plant, sunken in the peat moss, helps to make the bogs and white-cedar swamps attractive. The sarracenias usually demand full or partial sunlight, but at least one species (*S. rubra*) can grow in dense shade.

Characteristic habitats of pitcher plants [margin note]

Grass fires often burn *Sarracenia* colonies to the ground during the summer months, but these plants are remarkably fire-resistant and usually can survive underground and make a comeback.

The California pitcher plant occurs in marshy or boggy habitats from near sea level to 6,000 feet (2,000 metres), ranging from the redwood forest zone to the red-fir forest zone. The soils in these regions are very acid, and the temperature never goes above about 65° F (18° C).

Heliamphora grows under extremely humid and wet conditions; it occurs from the lower slopes to the exposed crests and cliffs of Mt. Roraima (British Guyana, now Guyana) and Cerro Duida (Venezuela), two mountains about 400 miles (600 kilometres) apart at the eastern and western ends of the Pakaraima Mountains of the Guiana Highlands, which constitutes the known distributional range of the genus. On Mt. Roraima it reaches its full size and best development on the ledges of the cliff of Roraima. On Cerro Duida it occurs in association with various other plants, as part of the dense undergrowth in the forested valleys of the plateau, and as a cushiony growth in patches on practically all the adjoining ridge crests. In swampy depressions it mingles with sphagnum.

FORM AND STRUCTURE

Most of the pitcher plants are herbaceous, stemless (acaulescent) perennials consisting of a basal cluster (rosette) of leaves arising from a short, creeping rhizome. The hollow, tubular leaves curve outward and upward with their basal portion resting on the ground (*e.g., Sarracenia purpurea*) or are erect (*e.g., S. flava*), with sheathing bases; the leaves widen gradually into pitchers. A prominent wing runs along the outer surface of the leaf from bottom to top on the side facing the centre (adaxial, or ventral, side) of the plant. At the top the wing forms a lip. On the back (dorsal) side a bladelike expansion forms a lid or hood over the mouth of the pitcher, in some cases effectively closing the opening to light and rain. The leaves of *S. purpurea* and of all the species of *Heliamphora* are open at the mouth and collect rainwater. The strikingly coloured leaves vary from yellow green to dark green suffused with red to deep red, the intensity of red depending in part on the amount of sunlight in the habitat. One species is white with red and green reticulations (netlike patterns); other species have translucent-spotted leaves.

The height of the plant usually is determined by the height of the leaves, which in most species average one to two, but may reach four feet (120 centimetres). By contrast with the North American pitcher plants, three of the six described species of *Heliamphora* are stemmed (caulescent), branched, almost shrubby perennials, which attain a height of four feet. Their pitchers vary from eight to 20 inches (20 to 50 centimetres) in length.

Flowering structures

The inflorescence (flower cluster) of *Sarracenia* and *Darlingtonia* consists of a tall, leafless stalk (scape) with a solitary, nodding flower. The flowering scapes generally average about a foot in height but may vary from a few inches to four feet. Typically, the flowering scape more or less equals the length of the longest leaves, although in *Darlingtonia* and *Heliamphora* species the scape may be as much as twice the length of the leaves (to four feet in *Darlingtonia*). In *Heliamphora*, the inflorescence is several-flowered and one to two feet long; the flowers lack differentiated petals, the sepals being white to pink or rose purple and showy. The large flower (several inches across) of the North American species has five yellow, greenish-yellow, or pink to wine-coloured petals and five firm, green sepals, which persist long after the petals have fallen. The petals may be short or long and showy, as in *S. flava*, in which they hang down like a hound's ears. The sarracenias have a unique, umbrella-like style, which has tiny stigmas on its five points.

EVOLUTION AND CLASSIFICATION

Evolution. No fossils have been reported for the pitcher-plant order. Phylogenetic relationships must be inferred from the morphological and biological relationships of the modern species, and such considerations, not surprisingly, have led to diverse views. Most authorities now agree that the carnivorous flowering plants form a more heterogeneous group than was traditionally thought and that, therefore, carnivory must have arisen independently in several more or less unrelated evolutionary lines. No two authorities agree, however, on the number or relationships of the lines, some assigning these plants to as many as six different orders. Furthermore, different authorities place the same carnivorous species in different orders.

On the basis of floral morphology, phylogenists at present have quite different views about the origin of the order Sarraceniales. Some regard the Sarraceniales as a very specialized order that has retained some primitive features that place it near the order Ranunculales (Ranales), from which it and the order Papaverales are derived. Others place the pitcher-plant order next to the order Violales and derive both orders from the Theales

(Guttiferales). Still others propose different origins and alliances within the framework of their own phylogenetic systems.

Classification. *Distinguishing taxonomic features.* The Sarraceniales is distinguished from other orders chiefly by its distinctive, highly modified leaves and to a lesser extent by features of the inflorescence and flowers. The more important distinguishing features used to separate the three genera within the single family are presence or absence of above-ground stem, form of leaves, number and arrangement of flowers, presence or absence of petals, coloration of sepals, number of carpels (simple ovaries or sections of a compound ovary), and form of style.

Annotated classification. The order Sarraceniales, as presented here, is defined in the strictest sense and includes only the family Sarraceniaceae.

ORDER SARRACENIALES

Perennial, rhizomatous, acaulescent (stemless) or caulescent-branched, insectivorous herbs, with usually basal rosettes of tubular or pitcher-like, often winged leaves specialized for luring and trapping insects and other tiny animals. Flowers solitary, on a leafless stalk or in loose, stalked, axillary racemes (clusters arising from the angle between stem and leaf), radially symmetrical, bisexual. Perianth (sepals and petals) with 1 or 2 series; the sepals commonly 5, overlapping, often coloured and showy, persistent; the petals commonly 5 or absent, free, yellow to purple. Stamens (pollen-bearing organs) many, free; the anthers (male reproductive organs) 2-celled, opening before stigmas are receptive. Pistil (female parts—ovary, style, and stigma) 1, with 3 or 5 fused carpels, the ovary superior (positioned above the attachment point of sepals, petals, and stamens), 3- or 5-loculed (chambered). Ovules numerous. Style simple, cylindrical, with simple, slightly lobed stigma or apex expanded into large umbrella-like structure with as many lobes as carpels, each with a minute stigma beneath. Fruit a capsule, with as many locules as carpels. Seeds minute, numerous.

Family Sarraceniaceae (pitcher-plant family)

The only family, it has the characteristics of the order. Distribution disjunct in the New World in bogs, seepages, swamps, and wet savannas. Three genera (*Darlingtonia, Heliamphora,* and *Sarracenia*) and 13 to 16 species.

Critical appraisal. Unquestionably, the three genera named above belong in the same family. So similar is the California pitcher plant to some of the eastern species that *Darlingtonia* probably could not be defended as a separate genus if it were not for its great geographic isolation from the eastern species. The chief taxonomic problems of the family arise at two levels. First, there is no agreement about the relationship of the Sarraceniaceae to the families Droseraceae and Nepenthaceae of the order Nepenthales. Some authorities continue to hold to the older view that the three distinct families form a natural order. This view rests on the theory that the leaves of the three families represent modifications from a common type. Authors have gone so far as to propose that the families Nepenthaceae and the Sarraceniaceae should be merged into a single family because *Heliamphora* seems to bridge the gap. Other authorities place greater weight on floral and pollen morphology, both of which suggest that the Sarraceniaceae stands apart from the other two families. Increasingly, evidence indicates that these families belong in two or three perhaps widely separated orders.

Relationships of carnivorous plants disputed

Second, within the family Sarraceniaceae there has never been agreement about the number of species in the genus *Sarracenia*, even though the group has been known for 400 years. Furthermore, there is reason to suspect that a similar problem of delineating species exists in *Heliamphora*, although knowledge of this genus is scant. The most useful taxonomic features in *Sarracenia* pertain to the form and habit of the pitchered leaves. The overall shape of the pitcher is generally constant and represents the single most useful feature, but colour and marking are important in some cases. Leaf size is quite variable within species and of itself is not useful. In combination, other characteristics (*e.g.,* colour and shape of petals, odour, curvature of sepals, and presence and number of sword-like leaves) may be diagnostic. As with family relationships, specific relationships cannot be known any more definitively than they are without new lines of evidence.

BIBLIOGRAPHY. FRANCIS ERNEST LLOYD, *The Carnivorous Plants* (1942), the definitive treatment of all groups of carnivorous plants on a worldwide basis; CLYDE RITCHIE BELL, "A Cytotaxonomic Study of the Sarraceniaceae of North America," *J. Elisha Mitchell Scient. Soc.*, 65:137–166 (1949), the authoritative cytological study and the most exhaustive recent taxonomic and evolutionary study of the family; "Natural Hybrids in the Genus *Sarracenia*," *ibid.*, 68:55–80 (1952), the only comprehensive scientific study of natural hybridization in the genus; CARROLL E. WOOD, JR., "The Genera of Sarraceniaceae and Droseraceae in the Southeastern United States," *J. Arnold Arbor.*, 41:152–163 (1960), an excellent synoptical review of the salient features of the family Sarraceniaceae; WILLIAM R. WEST, "Carnivorous Plants," pt. 1, 4, *Carolina Tips*, 28:31–32, 29:1–2 (1965–66), brief general articles on pitcher plants and the culturing of carnivorous plants; GAYTHER L. PLUMMER, "Foliar Absorption in Carnivorous Plants," pt. 1–2, *Carolina Tips*, 29:25–26, 29–30 (1966), readable general account of the digestive mechanism of *Sarracenia*; STANWYN G. SHETLER and FLORENCE MONTGOMERY, "Insectivorous Plants," *Smithson. Inf. Leafl.*, no. 447 (1965), a brief popular account of the major groups of carnivorous plants in the world; MARY VAUX WALCOTT, *Illustrations of North American Pitcherplants,* with "Descriptions and Notes on Distribution," by EDGAR T. WHERRY, and "Notes on Insect Associates," by FRANK MORTON JONES (1935), watercolour illustrations of all North American species, popular descriptions, and the best source of information on insect associates; SOPHIA PRIOR, "Carnivorous Plants and 'The Man-Eating Tree,' " *Chicago Nat. Hist. Mus. Bot. Leafl.*, no. 23 (1939), a brief account of popular lore on carnivorous plants.

(S.G.S.)

Sartre, Jean-Paul

Jean-Paul Sartre, a French philosopher, playwright, and novelist and an internationally known figure in contemporary intellectual life, is the leading French exponent of Existentialism, a philosophical attitude that emphasizes the freedom and importance of individual human beings. With Sartre, the power of the subject—the self-conscious individual—comes to the fore, an emphasis that has influenced recent generations of writers all over the world; for he, more than any other philosopher, has drawn attention to individual freedom and creativity. In the eyes of some critics it may appear that the foremost Existentialist has been less cogent in his philosophy of the group and of the intersubjective themes stressed in his later work.

Gisele Freund

Sartre, photograph by Gisèle Freund, 1968.

Early life and writings. Sartre was born in Paris on June 21, 1905. Having lost his father at an early age, Sartre grew up in the home of his maternal grandfather, Carl Schweitzer, uncle of the medical missionary Albert Schweitzer and himself professor of German at the Sorbonne. The boy, who wandered in the Luxembourg Gardens of Paris in search of playmates, was small in stature and cross-eyed. His brilliant autobiography, *Les Mots*, (Eng. trans., *The Words*), narrates the adventures of the mother and child in the park as they went from group to group—in the vain hope of being accepted—then finally retreated to the sixth floor of their apartment "on the heights where (the) dreams dwell." "The words" saved the child, and his interminable pages of writing were the escape from a world that had rejected him but that he would proceed to rebuild in his own fancy.

Sartre went to the Lycée Henri IV in Paris and, later on, after the remarriage of his mother, to the lycée in La Rochelle. From there he went to the prestigious École Normal Supérieure, from which he graduated in 1929. Sartre resisted what he called "bourgeois marriage," but while still a student he formed with Simone de Beauvoir a union that has remained a settled partnership in life. Simone de Beauvoir's memoirs, *Mémoires d'une jeune fille rangée* (1958; Eng. trans., *Memoirs of a Dutiful Daughter*, 1959) and *La Force de l'âge* (1960; Eng. trans., *The Prime of Life*, 1962), provide an intimate account of Sartre's life from student years until his middle 50s. It was also at the École Normale Supérieure and at the Sorbonne that he met several persons who were destined to be writers of great fame; among these were Raymond Aron, Maurice Merleau-Ponty, Simone Weil, Emmanuel Mounier, Jean Hippolyte, and Claude Lévi-Strauss. From 1931 until 1945 Sartre taught in the lycées of Le Havre, Laon, and, finally, Paris. Twice this career was interrupted, once by a year of study in Berlin and the second time when Sartre was drafted in 1939 to serve in World War II. He was made prisoner in 1940 and released a year later.

During his years of teaching in Le Havre, Sartre published *La Nausée* (1938; Eng. trans., *Nausea*), his first claim to fame. This novel, written in the form of a diary, narrates the feeling of revulsion that a certain Roquentin undergoes when confronted with the world of matter—not merely the world of other people but the very awareness of his own body. According to some critics, *La Nausée* must be viewed as a pathological case, a form of neurotic escape. Most probably it must be appreciated also as a most original, fiercely individualistic, antisocial piece of work, containing in its pages many of the philosophical themes that Sartre later developed.

Sartre took over the phenomenological method, which proposes careful, unprejudiced description rather than deduction, from the German philosopher Edmund Husserl and used it with great skill in three successive publications: *L'Imagination* (1936; Eng. trans., *Imagination: A Psychological Critique*), *Esquisse d'une théorie des émotions* (1939; Eng. trans., *Sketch for a Theory of the Emotions*), and *L'Imaginaire: Psychologie phénoménologique de l'imagination* (1940; Eng. trans., *The Psychology of Imagination*). But it was above all in *L'Être et le néant* (1943; Eng. trans., *Being and Nothingness*) that Sartre revealed himself as a master of outstanding talent. Sartre places human consciousness, or no-thingness (*néant*), in opposition to being, or thingness (*être*). Consciousness is not-matter and by the same token escapes all determinism. The message, with all the implications it contains, is a hopeful one; yet the incessant reminder that human endeavour is and remains useless makes the book tragic as well.

Post-World War II work. Having written his defense of individual freedom and human dignity, Sartre turned his attention to the concept of social responsibility. For many years he had shown great concern for the poor and the disinherited of all kinds. While a teacher, he had refused to wear a tie, as if he could shed his social class with his tie and thus come closer to the worker. Freedom itself, which at times in his previous writings appeared to be a gratuitous activity that needed no particular aim or purpose to be of value, became a tool for human struggle in his brochure *L'Existentialisme est un humanisme* (1946; Eng. trans., *Existentialism and Humanism*). Freedom now implied social responsibility. In his novels and plays Sartre began to bring his ethical message to the world at large. He started a four-volume novel in 1945 under the title *Les Chemins de la liberté*, of which three were eventually written: *L'Âge de raison* (1945; Eng. trans., *The Age of Reason*), *Le Sursis* (1945; Eng. trans., *The Reprieve*, 1947), and *La Mort dans l'âme*

Marginal notes: Education · Influence of Husserl · Novels and plays

(1949; Eng. trans., *Iron in the Soul*; U.S. title, *Troubled Sleep*). After the publication of the third volume, Sartre changed his mind concerning the usefulness of the novel as a medium of communication and turned back to plays.

What a writer must attempt, said Sartre, is to show man as he is. Nowhere is man more man than when he is in action, and this is exactly what drama portrays. He had already written in this medium during the war, and now one play followed another: *Les Mouches* (produced 1943; Eng. trans., *The Flies*), *Huis-clos* (1944; Eng. trans., *In Camera;* U.S. title, *No Exit*), *Les Mains sales* (1948; Eng. trans., *Crime passionel;* U.S. title, *Dirty Hands;* acting version, *Red Gloves*), *Le Diable et le bon dieu* (1951; Eng. trans., *Lucifer and the Lord*), *Nekrassov* (1955), and *Les Séquestrés d'Altona* (1959; Eng. trans., *The Condemned of Altona*). All of the plays, in their emphasis upon the raw hostility of man toward man, seem to be predominantly pessimistic; yet, according to Sartre's own confession, their content does not exclude the possibility of a morality of salvation. Other publications of the same period include a book, *Baudelaire* (1947), a vaguely ethical study on the French writer and poet Jean Genet entitled *Saint Genet, comédien et martyr* (1952; Eng. trans., *Saint Genet, Actor and Martyr*), and innumerable articles that were published in *Les Temps Modernes*, the monthly review that Sartre and Simone de Beauvoir founded and edited. These articles were later collected in several volumes under the title *Situations*.

Political activities   After World War II, Sartre took an active interest in French political movements, and his leanings to the left became more pronounced. He became an outspoken admirer of the Soviet Union, although he did not become a member of the Communist Party. In 1954 he visited the U.S.S.R., Scandinavia, Africa, the United States, and Cuba. With the entry of the Soviet tanks into Budapest in 1956, however, Sartre's hopes in Communism were sadly crushed. He wrote in *Les Temps Modernes* a long article, "Le Fantôme de Staline," that condemned both the Soviet intervention and the submission of the French Communist Party to the dictates of Moscow. Over the years this critical attitude opened the way to a form of "Sartrian Socialism" that would find its expression in a new major work, *Critique de la raison dialectique* (1960; Eng. trans., of the introduction only, under the title *The Problem of Method*, U.S. title, *Search for a Method*). Sartre set out to examine critically the Marxist dialectic and discovered that it was not livable in the Soviet form. Although he still believed that Marxism is the only philosophy for the current times, he conceded that it has become ossified and that, instead of adapting itself to particular situations, it compels the particular to fit a predetermined universal. Whatever its fundamental, general principles, Marxism must learn to recognize the existential concrete circumstances that differ from one collectivity to another and to respect the individual freedom of man. The *Critique*, somewhat marred by poor construction, is in fact an impressive and beautiful book, deserving of more attention than it has gained so far. A projected second volume was abandoned. Instead, Sartre prepared for publication *Les Mots*, for which he was awarded the 1964 Nobel Prize for Literature, an offer that was refused.

The biography of Flaubert   From 1960 until 1971 most of Sartre's attention went into the writing of a four-volume study called *Flaubert*. Two volumes with a total of some 2,130 pages appeared in the spring of 1971. This huge enterprise aimed at presenting the reader with a "total biography" of Gustave Flaubert, famous French novelist, through the use of a double tool: on the one hand, Karl Marx's concept of history and class and, on the other, Sigmund Freud's illuminations of the dark recesses of the human soul through explorations into his childhood and family relations. Athough at times Sartre's genius comes through and his fecundity is truly unbelievable, the sheer volume of the work and the minutely detailed analysis of even the slightest Flaubertian dictum hamper full enjoyment. As if he himself were saturated by the prodigal abundance of his writings, Sartre moved away from his desk during

1971 and did very little writing. Under the motto that "commitment is an act, not a word," Sartre often went into the streets to participate in rioting, in the sale of left-wing literature, and in other activities that in his opinion were the way to promote "the revolution."

Paradoxically enough, this same radical socialist published in 1972 the third volume of the work on Flaubert, *L'Idiot de la famille*, another book of such density that only the bourgeois intellectual can read it. But still this volume does not match the commentary on *Madame Bovary* in this respect and, in spite of its intricate structure and detail, it is much more readable than the two previous ones. It is also reminiscent of his autobiography *Les Mots*, and in the eyes of some critics appears as the work of a man who willy-nilly discovers himself in Flaubert and Flaubert in himself.

MAJOR WORKS

PHILOSOPHY: *L'Imagination* (1936; *Imagination: A Psychological Critique*, trans. by Forest Williams, 1962); *Esquisse d'une théorie des émotions* (1939; *Sketch for a Theory of the Emotions*, trans. by Philip Mairet, 1962); *L'Imaginaire: Psychologie phénoménologique de l'imagination* (1940; *The Psychology of Imagination*, 1950); *L'Être et le néant* (1943; *Being and Nothingness*, trans. by Hazel E. Barnes 1956); *L'Existentialisme est un humanisme* (1946; *Existentialism and Humanism*, trans. by Philip Mairet, 1948); *Question de méthode* (1960; *The Problem of Method*, trans. by Hazel E. Barnes, 1963; U.S. title, *Search for a Method*); *Critique de la raison dialectique* (1960).

NOVELS: *La Nausée* (1938; Eng. trans. by Lloyd Alexander, 1949); *L'Âge de raison* (1945; *The Age of Reason*, trans. by Eric Sutton, 1947); *Le Sursis* (1945; *The Reprieve*, trans. by Eric Sutton, 1947); *La Mort dans l'âme* (1949; *Iron in the Soul*, trans. by G. Hopkins, 1950; U.S. title, *Troubled Sleep*, 1950); and *Drôle d'amitié* (1949, unfinished). The novels are collectively known as *Les Chemins de la liberté*.

PLAYS: *Les Mouches* (first performed 1943; *The Flies*, trans. by Stuart Gilbert, 1946); *Huis-clos* (1944; *In Camera*, trans. by Stuart Gilbert, 1946; U.S. title, *No Exit*, 1946); *La Putain respecteuse* (1946; *The Respectful Prostitute*, 1949); *Les Mains sales* (1948; *Crime passionel*, trans. by Kitty Black, 1949; U.S. title, *Dirty Hands*; acting version *Red Gloves*, 1949); *Le Diable et le bon dieu* (1951; *Lucifer and the Lord*, trans. by Kitty Black, 1953); *Nekrassov* (1955; Eng. trans. by S. and G. Leeson, 1956); *Les Séquestrés d'Altona* (1959; *Loser Wins*, trans. by S. and G. Leeson, 1960; U.S. title, *The Condemned of Altona*, 1961).

OTHER WORKS: *Le Mur* (1939; *Intimacy*, trans. by Lloyd Alexander, 1956), short stories; *Les Jeux sont faits* (1947; *The Chips Are Down*, 1949), film script; *Qu'est-ce que la littérature?* (1947; *What is Literature?*, trans. by Bernard Frechtman, 1949); *Baudelaire* (1947; Eng. trans. by Martin Turnell, 1949); and *Saint Genet, comédien et martyr* (1952; *Saint Genet, Actor and Martyr*, trans. by Bernard Frechtman, 1963), all essays; *Les Mots* (1963; *Words,* trans. by I. Clephane, 1964), autobiography; *L'idiot de la famille: Gustave Flaubert, 1821–1857,* vol. 3 (1972).

BIBLIOGRAPHY. FRANCIS JEANSON, *Le Problème moral et la pensée de Sartre* (1947), a discussion of the moral implications of Sartre's thought, and *Sartre par lui-même* (1955), considerations on Sartre taken from his own writings or from personal communication; IRIS MURDOCH, *Sartre: Romantic Rationalist* (1953), valuable insights on Sartre's philosophy; WILFRID DESAN, *The Tragic Finale; An Essay on the Philosophy of Jean-Paul Sartre* (1960), a commentary on *Being and Nothingness*, and *The Marxism of Jean-Paul Sartre* (1965), a commentary on the *Critique de la Raison Dialectique*; MAURICE N. CRANSTON, *Sartre* (1965), a survey of Sartre's work with emphasis on earlier production; NORMAN N. GREENE, *Jean-Paul Sartre: The Existentialist Ethic* (1960), an examination of the ethical implications in the earlier Sartre; RONALD O. LAING and DAVID G. COOPER, *Reason and Violence: A Decade of Sartre's Philosophy, 1950–1960* (1964), a comment on the *Critique* and other works in Sartre's own, and at times involved, semantics; PHILIP THODY, *Jean-Paul Sartre: A Literary and Political Study* (1960); MARY WARNOCK, *The Philosophy of Sartre* (1967), an abbreviated but sound survey of Sartre's philosophy; ROBERT DENOON CUMMING, *The Philosophy of Jean-Paul Sartre* (1965), an anthology with a valuable introduction; JOSEPH H. MCMAHON, *Humans Being: The World of Jean-Paul Sartre* (1971), a general yet sound study, on Sartre, mostly in his literary works; ALLEN J. BELKIND (comp.), *Jean-Paul Sartre, Sartre and Existentialism in English: A Bibliographical Guide* (1970).

(W.De.)

Saskatchewan

Saskatchewan is one of only two Canadian provinces without a saltwater coast, and the only one whose boundaries are wholly artificial. It lies between the 49th and 60th parallels of latitude and is bounded on the west by longitude 110 degrees west of Greenwich, and its eastern limit, with minor adjustments, is longitude 102. Its southern half is largely an extension of the Great Plains of central North America, rarely rising 2,000 feet above sea level, and its northern half, most of which lies in the ancient rock mass of the Precambrian Shield, is sparsely populated bush country with many lakes and tundra. Its area is 251,700 square miles (651,900 square kilometres), of which 31,518 are water; and it measures 760 miles from south to north, tapering from a width of 393 miles where it abuts Montana and North Dakota, to 277 where it meets the Northwest Territories. In areas, Saskatchewan is Canada's fifth largest province, and in population, its sixth. Economically, the province has always been heavily dependent on the exportation of its agricultural and mineral products, and is thus peculiarly sensitive to fluctuations in world markets beyond its own or even Canada's control.

HISTORY

Since Saskatchewan became a full member of the Canadian federation only in 1905, much of the area's historical interest depends on events vastly older than the province. Dinosaur and mammoth finds have been common. The first known human inhabitants were Indians of several linguistic groups who were present at least 5,000 years ago, and possibly much before that; they were mainly hunters, particularly of the buffalo. With the coming of the white man, they became trappers involved in the fur trade. The first white man known to see the Saskatchewan River was Henry Kelsey, who in 1691 explored part of the plains for his employer, the Hudson's Bay Company, which received its charter in 1670 and is still extant. Fur traders and buffalo hunters, variously Indian, Métis (of mixed racial origin), French, British, and explorers and missionaries, comprised the bulk of the area's inhabitants until the second half of the 19th century.

The area from which Saskatchewan is carved was first granted to the Hudson's Bay Company and then, in 1868, surrendered by the Rupert's Land Act back to the British crown, in order that it could be turned over to the newly formed Dominion of Canada, which was done in 1870. Canada administered its newly acquired western territories almost as if they were colonies, and, in 1873, created the North West Mounted Police to maintain law and order. In 1885 the national authorities sent out troops to quell the second Riel Rebellion, an uprising in which a large number of Métis, by now deprived of their main sustenance, the buffalo, sought to establish their rights to western lands in the face of growing settlement. Constitutionally, the territories in 1875 were granted an executive council with a promise of an elected assembly, and by 1897 they had won responsible parliamentary government on the British model.

Saskatchewan, created by the Saskatchewan Act (a Canadian statute) in 1905, entered confederation with its present boundaries and the status of a province equal to the others except that, as with its sister province Alberta, the federal government retained control of its natural resources, paying a subsidy in place of the revenues the resources might have yielded. (The resources were assigned to the province in 1930.) The new provincial government, after a good deal of rivalry among the towns, chose Regina, the former territorial capital, as its centre of operations, and the first premier appointed was Walter Scott (1867–1938), a believer in partisan politics, as opposed to those who favoured a continuation of the kind of cooperative effort that had led up to the creation of Saskatchewan as a separate province. A member of the party in federal power at the time, the Liberal Scott was the first of several able politicians who have kept the party in power in Saskatchewan except in 1929–34 and 1944–64, and after 1971. The 1944–64 period was unique in North American history: during it the Cooperative Commonwealth Federation (CCF), successively led by T.C. Douglas (1904–) and Woodrow Lloyd (1913–), established the first avowedly Socialist government on the continent, and the party won international attention in 1962 when it implemented the continent's first compulsory medical care program, accompanied by a doctors' strike.

Regardless of which political party has been in power at any given time, the Saskatchewan environment has always demanded much governmental intervention in the economy. The provincial telephone company and the power and gas utility, for example, are publicly owned, but neither was created by a Socialist government. The cooperative movement has been encouraged by all parties and has been influential in a wide range of service, retail, and wholesale activities that include large credit unions and an oil refinery. In the handling of grains, the backbone of the province's economy, the Saskatchewan Wheat Pool, also a cooperative, has been a dominant influence. The co-ops helped many individuals survive the desperate drought and depression of the 1930s, when Saskatchewan society, according to an official investigation, sustained setbacks as severe as any to which comparable communities were exposed during that time. In the decades following World War II, the province attained a major development in mineral exploitation and industrial growth, and its diversified base, combined with new farming techniques, made a repetition of the 1930s appear unlikely.

THE NATURAL AND HUMAN LANDSCAPE

Although familiarly known as one of the "prairie provinces," Saskatchewan has little true prairie; a large proportion of its productive acreage (barely half the province) is rolling ranch and parkland, both of which offer immense vistas from their higher points. There is not a single mountain in the province, although the term is loosely used to identify several landmarks. The Cypress Hills, in the southwest corner of Saskatchewan, include the provincial summit: 4,567 feet (1,392 metres) above sea level. The Hills are unique in that they constitute the only part of the area to escape glaciation and contain unique plant and animal life. Wood Mountain (3,275 feet [998 metres]) and the Vermilion Hills (2,500 feet [760 metres]) are the province's other major departures from the rolling plains topography. Cut into the plains are many spectacular river valleys, the most notable being those of North and South Saskatchewan and the Qu'Appelle.

Saskatchewan drains from west to east, its great rivers (which provided the first transportation routes) rising in the Rocky Mountains and emptying ultimately into Hudson Bay. The soils through which the rivers flow are predominantly chernozemic (dark-coloured grassland) and podzolic (light-coloured forest) with extensive deposits of poorly drained mineral and peat soils in the north. The climate alone keeps much land out of production. Only in the southern half of the province are there even as few as from 80 to 100 frost free days annually. Temperature variations are extreme; January temperatures have exceeded −65° F (−53° C) in settled parts, and in July temperatures upward of 105° F (41° C) have often been recorded. The normal mean daily reading for the arable regions ranges from −5° F (−21° C) to 10° F (−12° C) in January, and from 55° F (13° C) to 65° F (18° C) in July. Precipitation generally is not high, averaging from ten to 20 inches each year; snowfall ranges from 30 inches in the southwest to over 60 inches in the northeast.

The vast unsettled parts of Saskatchewan support a large wildlife population of great variety. Grizzly bear and mountain lion are now rare, but brown bear, moose, deer, and antelope are common, together with enormous numbers of smaller mammals. Coyote, fox, and lynx, together with the gophers, rabbits, and other creatures they prey on, are abundant, and the northern portion of the province still supports a considerable amount of trapping. Saskatchewan is on the main western flyway of waterfowl, songbirds, hawks, and owls, many of which nest in the

Early exploration

Climatic factors

province. The extensive water resources maintain both commercial and game fish in quantity. Northern Saskatchewan, particularly, is one of the world's last frontiers for the hunter and angler.

The lack of heavy industry and of metropolitan areas keeps Saskatchewan relatively free of the kinds of pollution associated with high population density and manufacturing, but the extensive agricultural development subjects it to those connected with weed killers and insecticides. Significant amounts of mercury have been found in fish and birds, and continuing research suggests that the amount of contamination in wildlife may be larger than had been apparent. The sources of the major rivers also subject Saskatchewan to upstream pollutants from areas over which it has no control; but prevailing winds do not come from heavily polluted regions, and the air is generally clean, though an occasional northern forest fire casts a pall over thousands of square miles to the south.

Saskatchewan's landscape makes its inhabitants conscious of the sky; and the changing patterns of light and shadow on clouds, which commonly offer magnificent sunrises and sunsets, are as much a part of the scenery as any contour of the earth. All of Saskatchewan is further north than any of the most densely populated parts of Canada, and the province's own north is largely inaccessible except by air, with the result that few citizens are familiar with it. The provincial university, at its Saskatoon campus, maintains an Institute for Northern Studies and an Institute of Space and Atmospheric Studies that has done extensive research on the aurora borealis. When a

Regional divisions

resident thinks of Saskatchewan's chief regions, he is less likely to think of the north than of the province's main agricultural and recreational areas: the wheat belt, the ranching country, the Qu'Appelle Valley, the Cypress Hills, Waskesiu Lake; or, if he is historically minded, of the old fur-trading routes and trails, and their inevitable forts, or the sites of Saskatchewan's few battles. To the untrained eye the relative uniformity of the rolling plains is not conducive to thinking in terms of regions as such. Nor is Saskatchewan dominated by any metropolitan centres. Unlike many Canadian provinces, Saskatchewan has in effect two capitals: Regina, the official capital, in the central south, and Saskatoon 160 miles to the north, both of them among the most rapidly growing cities in North America, with populations exceeding 140,000 and 125,000 respectively, by the start of the 1970s. The next largest cities were Moose Jaw (32,000) and Prince Albert (28,000). Each city (there were three others above 10,000) has its "constituency," the surrounding area for which it provides goods and services, but although the seven largest communities contain well over one-third of the population, none is typical of the most obvious settlements. The most striking man-made feature of the landscape is the grain elevator, and the typical town is a cluster of houses around three or four elevators, surrounded by enormous fields. The towns are rarely more than a dozen miles apart on the railways and highways, and their original locations were settled largely by the amount of track that a railway maintenance crew could cover with a hand-propelled "jigger" cart. Technological development having reduced the necessity for many of them, Saskatchewan's rural and small town population was, by the 1970s, generally in a state of decline.

THE PEOPLE

In numbers, the people of Saskatchewan have remained much the same for over 40 years: the population was 921,785 in 1931, and up to 926,242 in 1971, having dipped to a low of 831,728 in 1951. In almost every other way, however, the population has changed markedly during the area's history. It was originally exclusively Indian, to which French and British elements were added early. Then other European groups—German, Austrian, Ukrainian, Scandinavian, Russian, and Polish, among others—were attracted, some by generous homestead grants, and some in part by a desire to avoid compulsory military service in their own countries. The period of heaviest immigration was before 1920, when the population rose suddenly from less than 100,000 in 1901 to

Ethnic origins

nearly 700,000. The population of British origin was, by the 1970s, less than 40 percent. Many of these groups, including the British, settled in separate communities where they could use their own language and continue their own religion and customs, and Saskatchewan contains many settlements readily identifiable as Ukrainian, French Canadian, German, etc. Provincial law permits the use of languages other than English in schools for specific purposes, and widespread advantage has been taken of the law. Ethnic variety is matched by that found in religious affiliation: although individual communities may be predominantly of one persuasion, in the provinces as a whole the largest church, the United Church of Canada, had, by the 1970s, only 30% of the population as adherents, followed by the Roman Catholic (26%), Lutheran (10%), Anglican (10%), Ukrainian Catholic (4%), Greek Orthodox (3.5%), Mennonite (3%), Presbyterian (3%), Baptist (2%), and a host of others.

The birth rate in Saskatchewan has, since 1950, been close to the national average, and like it has declined sharply: it was 27.5 per 1,000 population for the years 1951–5, and by 1970 was 19.0, ranking sixth among the provinces. The death rate during the same periods has remained stable, rising from 7.6 to 7.8. The whole population grows slowly, when it does, because of the high emigration rate, which exceeds immigration by over five to one: the net migration loss between the censuses of 1961 and 1966 was 45,528, and this is attributed to increases in the efficiency of Saskatchewan's basic industries, which can steadily produce more with less manpower. Internally, the province, although still one of the least urbanized, has one of the highest rates of urbanization in Canada, the growth coming chiefly from the movement of rural dwellers into urban areas. Rural and urban populations were of virtually equal size by the census of 1966.

Demographic trends

THE PROVINCE'S ECONOMY

Saskatchewan has since its beginning been based economically on extractive industries: furs, agriculture, oil and gas, and potash, in almost all cases the products being consumed outside the province, and generally outside Canada, a fact that makes the province one of the most economically vulnerable areas in the world. The grain belt (predominantly wheat, but also including large acreages of barley, oats, rape, flax, and rye) lies between the southern border and the 54th parallel of latitude; over 540,000,000 bushels of wheat were harvested annually by the decade of the 1970s and the barley and oats crops were each nearly 100,000,000. Potash is found in a narrower band running diagonally across the province from west to east, its northernmost point being west of Saskatoon. Oil and gas lie in the southernmost quarter of the province, while there are rich uranium deposits in the far north. Other significant minerals include salt, sodium sulfite, and a variety of clays. In terms of employment, manufacturing has always played a relatively minor role in the provincial economy and is characterized by several hundred small establishments, few of which have over 100 employees. The trade union movement is correspondingly small, its total membership rarely exceeding 50,000. The gross farm value of the principal field crops, by 1970, was almost $1,000,000,000; of mineral production, $370,000,000, of which $225,000,000 was fuel; of all manufacturing $514,000,000. By the start of the 1970s, Saskatchewan generated nearly 4,000,000,000 kilowatt hours electrical energy, all of it consumed domestically.

The Saskatchewan economy, always dependent on external markets, has internally required a variety of governmental supports; and as a result the province has never had a truly free-enterprise system, while public enterprise, and mixed public and private ventures, have characterized the development of the economy from the beginning. The Canadian protective tariff, long criticized by prairie dwellers because it made them pay more for goods of all kinds, appears to be the mainstay of the secondary industries developing in the province. The first waves of settlers, attracted to Saskatchewan by federal government policies, were carried on railways built with federal assistance. Saskatchewan grain moves to federal terminal ele-

Government support

vators at controlled freight rates. Within the province, political parties in power, regardless of ideology, have sponsored and maintained publicly owned utilities, a bus company, an insurance company, and public hospitalization and medical care. Although ostensibly a free-enterprise party, the Liberal Party, when elected in 1964, kept intact, for the remainder of the decade, many of the major policies of its allegedly Socialist predecessor.

TRANSPORTATION

Modern Saskatchewan was originally the creation of transcontinental railroads, which carried settlers and supplies in, and grain out. Though freight remains an important rail component, passenger carriage has declined to such an extent that the major railways have for years been seeking permission to curtail and even abandon services, so far with modest success. The province is now crisscrossed with highways, the main routes among which have been paved only since 1945. The system of land division in the rural areas makes provision for "road allowances," strips of territory a mile or two apart, and while most of these are simple dirt, they are, as long as they are dry, firm passable roads, widely used for local travel.

Except for recreation, water transportation is all but obsolete in Saskatchewan; small shallow-draft steamers formerly sailed the main rivers, but since the rivers are shallow with shifting sandbars, they have not been significant transportation routes since before World War I. Airlines, by contrast, have developed dramatically in Saskatchewan, where approximately half the province is accessible only by air. The small plane serves the north for both commerical and recreational purposes, and all major centres are on scheduled airlines.

ADMINISTRATIVE AND SOCIAL CONDITIONS

Saskatchewan's constitution, based on custom and the Saskatchewan Act (of admission) of 1905, in essence provides for a British parliamentary system, in which the life of the executive depends on the support of a majority in the legislature. By law (1972) the legislature has 60 to 65 members. A general election must be held every five years; short of that period, the premier may advise the holding of an election at any time, and most assemblies last only four years. As in all the provinces, the lieutenant governor is appointed (for a term) and paid by the Dominion government and has become by custom and judicial decision the counterpart of a constitutional monarch, with powers whose exercise is almost wholly formal. At Ottawa, Saskatchewan is represented by six senators (all appointed by the Dominion government) and thirteen MPs in the House of Commons, scheduled to become 12 after the census of 1971. The administration of justice is under provincial jurisdiction, but all judges above the rank of magistrate are appointed by the Dominion government. Saskatchewan's larger centres have their own local police, but in the province as a whole the law is enforced by the Royal Canadian Mounted Police under a contract between federal and provincial authorities.

Unlike Canada's other prairie provinces, the Saskatchewan legislature has a long tradition of strong vocal opposition in the assembly, with the Liberals and the New Democratic Party (formerly the CCF) providing what is in effect a two-party system ideologically divided into free enterprise versus democratic socialism; there are other parties, but they have been of negligible significance for nearly 40 years. The Liberal Party draws its greatest strength from rural ridings; the New Democrats have a stronger urban base. Whichever party is in power is vigorously opposed by the other, with the Liberals generally espousing development of the province by business and corporate devices and the NDP as strongly urging the use of public and cooperative enterprise.

The great proportion of the province's annual budget, which by the 1970s exceeded $450,000,000, goes to education, health and welfare, and highways, in that order. (Saskatchewan, averaging from three to five persons per square mile in its rural areas, has one of the highest per capita road mileages in the world.) The province is divided into a multiplicity of local administrations including

The constitution

Political parties

hospital districts and school districts, all constitutionally under provincial jurisdiction, but all having considerable local responsibility. Municipal government in Saskatchewan is based on the American model, with a mayor elected separately from the council, and a number of boards and commissions operating largely independently of either.

For most of its history the province has qualified for the kinds of federal aid available to those whose economy operates below the national average. The province's reliance on federal subsidies as a percentage of total revenues, though it varies with crop conditions, is generally above the national average. Saskatchewan's wage levels for both industry and agriculture are never among the lowest for the provinces, but are never among the highest, either. The province's "middle" position carries over into its internal affairs: it is socially and economically (except for its Indian and Métis peoples) one of the least stratified areas in Canada, having little of great individual or corporate wealth on the one hand, and little general destitution on the other.

CULTURAL LIFE AND INSTITUTIONS

Lacking great metropolitan centres, Saskatchewan has been unable as yet either to develop large permanent art collections, and theatre and opera companies, or to retain within the province its own leading professional artists. The province has, nonetheless, contributed a number of outstanding performers to the world at large, in both popular and classical fields of musical endeavour. The Saskatchewan writer most sensitively attuned to the prairie is Edward McCourt, who has written both fiction and descriptive works. The province has many competent painters who exhibit widely, and both Saskatoon and Regina have small but excellent galleries. Both cities have civic auditoriums capable of staging any known theatrical or operatic work, resident symphony orchestras, and Regina has a fine provincial museum of natural history and a professional theatrical company.

Saskatoon has a Western Development Museum whose chief exhibits consist of outmoded farm machinery and automobiles, many of which are annually refurbished in a celebration of pioneer days. The machinery museum serves to remind the observer that culture in Saskatchewan is not, for most citizens, associated with the values of an intellectual middle class. It centres, instead, around the curling and hockey rinks, the small radio and television stations serving their immediate localities, and the daily and weekly newspapers. The splendid services of the Canadian Broadcasting Corporation's radio network reach most of settled Saskatchewan, but it is the local stations that have the mass audiences. Apart from the CBC, the province supports 18 radio stations (two broadcasting in French) and 24 television outlets, four daily newspapers, and over 100 weeklies (six in French). None of these (again except for the CBC) attempts to qualify as a national institution. Each serves one local constituency, and many of them do it very well. A central focus is given to many of them part of each year when the province's only major league athletic team, the Saskatchewan Roughriders football club, which has won the Canadian championship, is playing. Though the province has produced many famous hockey players, it has no major team.

The province's oldest recognizable cultural institution is the University of Saskatchewan, established in 1907 and, with remarkable foresight, given a huge campus at Saskatoon, and later a second campus in Regina. It has a total student body of 16,000. The university has produced much fundamental research relevant to Saskatchewan and has also a tradition of extension services on and off campus. It has sent forth a steady stream of distinguished workers in a variety of fields, from acting to nuclear physics. As a result of the limited opportunities offered, not many of these have been able to remain in the province.

PROBLEMS AND PROSPECTS

Saskatchewan, since shortly after World War II, has been slowly progressing toward a state of modest affluence. A whole generation exists that has no recollection of the drought and depression of the 1930s, a fact that occasionally gives rise to interesting confrontations with those who do remember. For several consecutive years in the 1950s and 1960s, almost every economic indicator showed continuing development, and in 1966 the province failed for the first time to qualify, as a "have-not" province, for important federal subsidies. Since then, thanks in part to crops so large that the world market has been unable to absorb them, the province has hovered on the brink of being a "have" province.

It is clear that Saskatchewan's future will continue to rest on external markets, for there is no way it can consume its own chief products. It is equally clear that Canadian population patterns will make the province an increasingly smaller fraction of the Dominion, with its representation in Parliament dwindling accordingly. Both these facts suggest that Saskatchewan will remain indefinitely an area acutely sensitive to influences beyond its borders. It has, on the other hand, one immense and almost untapped resource: fresh and relatively clean water. If water users can be induced to move to the province, Saskatchewan's political and economic history could undergo a dramatic change of direction; but if the established pattern is followed, the water will move to those who need it.

BIBLIOGRAPHY. The most comprehensive source book is J.H. RICHARDS and K.I. FUNG (eds.), *Atlas of Saskatchewan* (1969). Other invaluable aids are the two annuals: *Canada Year Book*, and J.T. SAYWELL (ed.), *Canadian Annual Review*. A brilliant survey of the land and its peoples is E.A. MCCOURT, *Saskatchewan* (1968); the main political developments are in N. WARD and D. SPAFFORD (eds.), *Politics in Saskatchewan* (1968); and S.M. LIPSET, *Agrarian Socialism* (1968). There is no recent history of the province. J.H. ARCHER and A.M. DERBY, *The Story of a Province* (1955), is a readable introduction; an excellent economic history is V.C. FOWKE, *The National Policy and the Wheat Economy* (1957).

(N.W.)

Satellite Communication

Satellite communication, the use of man-made satellites travelling in Earth orbits to provide communication links between various points on Earth, is man's most important nonmilitary exploitation of space technology. Communication satellites permit an interchange of live television programs and news events between nations and continents. International telephone service is carried out through Earth stations located in over 50 countries. Basically, the technique involves transmitting the desired signals from an Earth station to an orbiting satellite. The equipment aboard the satellite receives these signals, amplifies them, and rebroadcasts them to another Earth station, thus providing the desired communication link.

In the early 1970s, an organization known as the International Telecommunications Satellite Consortium, usually referred to as Intelsat, was responsible for all non-Soviet international nonmilitary satellite communications. A U.S. government-regulated private corporation known as the Communications Satellite Corporation (Comsat) acts as manager for Intelsat and operates its satellites. Total operating revenues for this corporation were $47,000,-000 in 1969, not including the income of many of the Earth stations located outside the U.S.

The practical utility of unmanned space vehicles has been appreciated only since World War II and the German V-2 rocket, used in the air assault on London. Man first travelled to the Moon in fiction in the 2nd century AD. Rockets were first seriously considered as a means for sending man through space by the Russian Konstantin E. Tsiolkovsky and the American Robert H. Goddard early in the 20th century. Though early satellite communication proposals envisioned manned satellites, the great success of satellite communication has been achieved by the use of highly reliable unmanned satellites.

Communication satellites are used to provide high-capacity communication circuits via microwaves (explained below) between widely separated locations. To transmit television signals and thousands of telephone signals between centres of population requires high-capacity circuits. Over land, such circuits can be provided in many ways, including pairs of wires, coaxial cables, waveguides, and microwave radio relay systems. Improved

submarine cables can now carry hundreds of telephone signals across oceans, but satellites can provide even greater capacity in many cases at less cost per channel.

Microwaves are very short radio waves, of wavelength ranging from ten centimetres to one centimetre (four to 0.4 inches). This range corresponds to a frequency range from three gigahertz to 30 gigahertz (a gigahertz [GHz] is 1,000,000,000 [10^9] cycles per second, or hertz). Microwaves are launched from or received by parabolic (bowl shaped) reflectors of considerable area, or from especially designed horn-shaped antennas. The waves travel in straight lines in narrow beams; therefore, microwave repeaters or amplifiers must be located within line of sight of one another. On land, this can be achieved by using towers and hilltop locations, but transoceanic microwave systems were impossible until the stationing of satellites in the sky.

HISTORY

The theoretical stage. *Science fiction.* The idea of radio transmission of voice and picture signals through space is at least as old as the U.S. science fiction pioneer Hugo Gernsback's space novel, *Ralph 124C41+* (1911). Yet, the idea of a radio repeater located in space was slow to come. In October 1942, the U.S. science fiction writer George O. Smith published a story "QRM Interplanetary" in the magazine *Astounding Science-Fiction.* Smith's "Venus Equilateral" radio repeater, in a position equidistant from Venus and the Sun, was used to relay signals between Venus and Earth.

Early proposals. In 1945 the British author-scientist Arthur C. Clarke proposed the use of an Earth satellite for radio communication between (and radio broadcast to) points widely removed on the surface of Earth. Clarke assumed a manned space station with living quarters for a crew, built of materials flown up by rockets. The station was to be at an altitude of about 22,300 miles (36,000 kilometres) so that its period of revolution about Earth would be the same as the period of Earth's rotation. This synchronous satellite, which would always appear in the same place in the sky, could be provided with receiving and transmitting equipment and directional antennas to beam signals to all or parts of the visible portion of Earth. Clarke suggested the use of solar power, either a steam engine operated by solar heat, or photoelectric devices. Three such space stations could provide broadcast to or communication among all locations on Earth except the most remote arctic regions.

Early plan for a manned space station

In a paper published in April 1955, the U.S. engineer-scientist J.R. Pierce analyzed various sorts of unmanned communication satellites. These included passive devices, such as metallized balloons and plane reflectors and corner reflectors, that would merely reflect back to Earth part of the energy directed to them. Active satellites, incorporating radio receivers and transmitters, were also considered. Pierce discussed satellites at synchronous altitudes, satellites at lower altitudes, and the use of Earth's gravity to control the altitude or orientation of a satellite.

These two early papers laid the groundwork for satellite communication development by showing that very modest powers would suffice for transoceanic communication.

Early satellites. *Project SCORE.* The first satellite communication experiment was the U.S. government's Project SCORE (Signal Communication by Orbiting Relay Equipment), which launched a satellite on December 18, 1958. The orbit had a 112-mile (180-kilometre) perigee, or closest point to Earth, and an apogee, or greatest distance from Earth, of 926 miles (1,490 kilometres); the extreme latitudes of the orbit were 30° north and south. The satellite transmitted at 132 megahertz (132,000,000 cycles per second, or hertz) with a power of eight watts and received at 150 megahertz. The audio bandwidths used were 3,000 and 5,000 hertz. The satellite operated in a real-time (immediate) and a delayed-repeater mode, in which messages were recorded in the satellite on magnetic tape and retransmitted on receiving a command signal from the ground station. Earth stations were located in California, Arizona, Texas, and Georgia.

Military
potential
of SCORE

SCORE operated until December 30, 1958, when its battery power was exhausted. During its active life SCORE transmitted the equivalent of 140,000 words in the delayed mode.

The military potential of this approach was of interest: by using a low-altitude orbit, as in SCORE, a military message could be sent to a satellite out of sight, range, and jamming capability of an enemy, recorded in the satellite, and, when commanded to do so by a ground station, read out at some distant point, again out of range of the enemy.

Project Courier. The U.S. Army Signal Corps's Courier project, started in the fall of 1958, was a further development of the SCORE approach. Courier was designed primarily to handle teletypewriter data at 55,000 bits (individual pieces of information) per second and secondarily to handle voice and facsimile (photographs and drawings) traffic, both delayed and real time.

Courier was powered by storage batteries that were kept charged by solar cells, devices that convert the Sun's energy directly into electricity. It was spherical in shape, 52 inches (132 centimetres) in diameter, and weighed 500 pounds (227 kilograms). It transmitted at a frequency of 1.8 to 1.9 gigahertz with a power of four watts (one-tenth the power consumption of a 40-watt light bulb) and received on a frequency 1.7 to 1.8 gigahertz. Earth stations were in Puerto Rico and Fort Monmouth, New Jersey. A successful launch on October 4, 1960, placed the satellite in an orbit of 600 miles perigee, 748 miles apogee, and a 28° inclination to the plane of the Equator. A number of successful tests were carried out.

Project Echo. Echo I, a balloon 100 feet (30 metres) in diameter, made of a plastic material called Mylar and coated with a thin layer of aluminum, was launched after SCORE but before Courier. The satellite was placed in an almost exactly circular orbit at an altitude of 1,000 miles, with an inclination of 47.3°.

Echo stemmed from two sources: John R. Pierce's 1955 article concerning passive satellites, and the construction by the U.S. engineer William J. O'Sullivan of a 100-foot Mylar balloon intended as a means for measuring the atmospheric density in a 1,000-mile orbit. Echo was launched by the U.S. National Aeronautics and Space Administration (NASA). An east-coast terminal was built by the American Telephone & Telegraph's Bell Telephone Laboratories; NASA paid for its use. NASA's Jet Propulsion Laboratory provided a west-coast terminal at Goldstone, California. To avoid possible interference the frequencies of transmission selected were 2.39 gigahertz west to east and 0.96 gigahertz east to west.

Communications tests carried out by reflecting radio signals from Echo's surface were completely successful. The satellite was used for experimental telephone, facsimile, and data transmission. Signals from Echo were detected in Europe, but no messages were transmitted across the ocean.

Project Telstar. Echo stimulated interest in the development of active communications satellites. The first of these, built and launched at the expense of the American Telephone & Telegraph Company, was given the name Telstar. Telstar was powered by solar cells and chargeable batteries and provided an output transmitter power of about two watts. Upward transmission was at 6.39 gigahertz; downward transmission was at 4.17 gigahertz. Telstar was spherical, with a diameter of 32 inches (81 centimetres); it weighed about 172 pounds (78 kilograms). Launched on July 10, 1962, Telstar had an orbit with a perigee of 568 miles (914 kilometres), an apogee of 3,378 miles (5,435 kilometres), and orbital inclination of 44.8°.

Telstar's
trans-
oceanic
tele-
vision
trans-
mission

On Telstar's pass over an Earth station at Andover, Maine, demonstrations were made of speech and television transmissions; these were received at Andover, at the Echo Earth station at Crawford Hill, New Jersey, and at a station built by the French at Pleumeur-Bodou in Brittany. On the next day, a British Post Office station in Cornwall received signals. Numerous demonstrations of transatlantic telephony and television transmission followed.

Project Relay. NASA's Relay, the next step in communications satellite development, was launched on December 13, 1962. Built for NASA by the Radio Corporation of America, Relay was an elongated, eight-sided satellite 33 inches (84 centimetres) high with a maximum breadth of 29 inches (74 centimetres), and weighed 172 pounds (78 kilograms). Powered by solar cells and rechargeable batteries, it provided a transmitter power of ten watts. Upward transmission was at 1.725 gigahertz; downward transmission at 4.17 gigahertz. The orbit achieved on launch had a perigee of 817 miles (1,315 kilometres), an apogee of 4,611 miles (7,419 kilometres), and an inclination of 47.4°. Relay was successfully employed in a number of communication experiments.

Syncom. Syncom II, the first synchronous communication satellite, was conceived by Harold J. Rosen of Hughes Aircraft Company. It was launched by NASA on July 26, 1963. As a synchronous satellite Syncom was in the Earth's shadow only 1 percent of the time; consequently it could be powered by solar batteries, and storage batteries could be omitted to save weight. An ingenious system of only two jets was used for fine adjustments of the orbit and attitude of the satellite after launch. The whole satellite, less fuel, weighed only 79 pounds (36 kilograms).

Syncom II was cylindrical in shape, 28 inches (71 centimetres) in diameter, and 28 inches in total length; it housed the motor used for final injection in orbit (apogee motor), and the length, including this motor, was 46 inches (117 centimetres). It had a transmitted power of two watts; the up frequency was 7.4 gigahertz and the down frequency 1.82 gigahertz. Syncom III, launched August 19, 1964, relayed the first sustained transpacific television picture during the Olympic Games held in Japan.

Other early experiments. In the early days, it was not clear what techniques of satellite communication would prove practical or useful, with the result that many different techniques were proposed and tested.

Reflections from the Moon. The very earliest communication by means of a satellite made use of signals reflected from the Moon. As early as 1954, the U.S. Naval Research Laboratory transmitted a voice message by such reflections. By 1960 the U.S. Navy had established the first operational communications link involving the Moon between Washington, D.C., and Hawaii. The Moon reflects back to Earth about as much power as Echo I did, but the signal is poor and variable because of the Moon's uneven terrain.

Satellites as
protection
against
jamming

Military communications experts have always been concerned with the reliability of communications in the face of enemy interference or jamming. The use of low altitude satellites out of view of the enemy for a portion of their orbit, such as Courier, was one approach. Passive satellites reflect a wide range of frequencies so that some protection against jamming can be achieved by changing the frequency of operation rapidly according to a prearranged plan.

Project West Ford. Project West Ford, originated in 1958, was an ingenious passive scheme. The proposal was to launch in orbit around Earth a dispersed ring of wires about half a wavelength long; such wires, or dipoles, strongly reflect radio waves. Communication could be established both by pointing transmitting and receiving antennas toward any portion of the ring. Astronomers objected to such a cluttering of space because of the possibility of interference with radio telescopic observations. To overcome this objection, it was proposed that wires be made of some substance that would gradually disintegrate in space.

In May of 1963, 20 kilograms of eight-gigahertz copper dipoles were launched into a 3,000-kilometre-altitude orbit above the north and south poles. The dipoles dispersed into a ring as had been predicted, and radar reflections from the belt had the expected strength. Several communication experiments were carried out; the West Ford proposal, however, was not pursued further, chiefly because of the success and rapid progress of active communication satellites.

Other forms of passive reflector were proposed, including planar reflectors, caps of spheres, corner reflectors, and open structures of wire, but none was tested.

Evolution of attitude control. Telstar and Relay were launched in elliptical orbits at a comparatively low altitude because the available launching vehicle could not put them higher. Subsequently, communication systems using a number of low-altitude satellites were seriously considered, because the time required for a signal to reach a low-altitude satellite and return to Earth is less than that using a synchronous satellite. (The effect of transmission time will be discussed later.) The disadvantages of tracking low-altitude satellites, however, and the relative inefficiency and complexity of low-altitude systems, outweighed any advantages.

Before attitude control (control of the satellite's orientation in space) had proved effective, consideration was given to installing electronically steerable antenna systems on board the satellites. By using a pilot beam from the ground as a control, signals fed to a large number of small nondirective antennas on a randomly oriented satellite could be so phased as to produce a transmitted beam aimed at the source of the pilot beam. Effective attitude control, however, proved to be simpler than such a system.

It is desirable to control the attitude of a satellite so that the transmitting and receiving antennas will always be pointed toward the Earth. Before the remarkable success of active attitude-control systems in Syncom and later satellites, a great deal of analysis and inventiveness were devoted to an attitude-control system known as gravity-gradient control, in which the fact that the gravitational force decreases with increasing altitude was exploited to maintain the satellite's orientation. Indeed, NASA's ATS-5 satellite, launched on August 12, 1969, included a gravity-gradient attitude-control experiment; this could not be tried, however, because the satellite tumbled end over end in orbit. Because of the effectiveness of other techniques of attitude control, there has been little sustained interest in the gravity-gradient technique.

In the early days of communication satellites, it was not universally accepted that solar cells could reliably produce the large amount of power necessary to keep the communications equipment aboard a satellite functioning properly. A good deal of effort was therefore spent on other power sources, chiefly, nuclear. Although experimental communication satellites built by Lincoln Laboratory of MIT (Massachusetts Institute of Technology) have used nuclear power sources, it seems unlikely that they will displace the solar cell because of the latter's simplicity, reliability, and relative cost advantage.

DEVELOPMENT OF TECHNOLOGY

Successful communication satellites, complicated as they now seem, represent a gradual evolution from comparatively simple satellites such as Telstar and Syncom. The importance and the art of staying within the limitations of a rapidly advancing technology were not universally appreciated in the early days of satellite communication. Studies begun as early as 1958 led to the inauguration in 1960 of Project Advent. Advent was to have been an operational active synchronous satellite, not an experiment. It was heavy, weighing 1,250 pounds (567 kilograms), and elaborate, with built-in attitude-control capabilities. But no vehicle then existing could have launched Advent had it been built, and in May 1962, the project was abandoned.

Space technology. Satellite communication has been made possible by both space technology and communication technology, drawing on many aspects of both. In part, the technology important to satellite communication is common to many space projects involving vehicles and the Earth facilities used in launching.

Launching and guidance. A variety of reliable launch vehicles, or boosters, has been most important to satellite communication. The vehicles that have proved useful have all been boosters originally built for military purposes equipped with various upper stages. A guidance system is included in the booster, usually in the second stage. This system is tracked and interrogated by Earth

radar, computations are made, and guidance commands are given to the vehicle.

In a typical launch the booster motors put the satellite in an elliptical orbit whose apogee lies at the correct synchronous altitude (about 22,300 miles or 35,900 kilometres). The satellite is then started spinning and tracked while it completes four to 12 orbits. It is so aligned that the thrust of the final, or apogee, motor (fired at apogee) will both place the satellite in a circular orbit and move the plane of the orbit to the plane of Earth's Equator. The axis of spin is then adjusted to be parallel to Earth's axis. Further orbital corrections can be made by pulsing the jets provided for attitude control and station keeping (maintaining the desired position above Earth). The position and attitude of the satellite are determined by radio observations from Earth and from information transmitted to Earth from solar and Earth sensors on the satellite.

Attitude control and station keeping. Development of vehicles and of guidance and launching techniques are space technologies necessary to all space projects. (Other techniques that have been crucial to the success of communication satellites are noted below.)

A spinning body can maintain a nearly constant direction of axis of spin despite small disturbing forces, while a nonspinning body can be turned appreciably by such forces and thus lose its desirable orientation. For this reason, all useful communication satellites, except the Soviet Molniya satellites, have used spin as a means for attitude control.

In Telstar; Relay; Syncom; and Intelsats I, II, and III (the name given a series of communications satellites sponsored by the International Telecommunications Satellite Consortium), the satellite was designed so that the axis of maximum moment of inertia (the axis of greatest angular momentum) was the spin axis of the vehicle. These satellites were equipped with internal dampers to prevent undesired motions such as nutation (wobble).

Intelsat IV has a massive despun antenna (an antenna mechanically isolated from the satellite that does not spin with it) and a communication system driven so as to have a fixed orientation with respect to Earth while the main body of the satellite spins.

In a satellite with a despun antenna, some sort of bearing must be provided between the antenna portion and the spinning portion of the satellite. Because metals tend not to slide freely on one another in space, the problem of designing space bearings proved difficult. It was solved successfully in the U.S. orbiting solar observatory satellite (OSO) by a technique involving deposition of specially developed thin films containing molybdenum disulfide and certain organic compounds on the bearing surfaces in vacuum.

A satellite in synchronous orbit tends to wander from position, chiefly because Earth and its gravitational field are not symmetrical, but also because of gravitational effects of the Sun and Moon. This wandering necessitates corrections in position, and corrections in attitude must be made as well.

Syncom made use of an extremely simple attitude-control and station-keeping mechanism consisting of two jets. One, the lateral motor, acts normal (perpendicular) to the spin axis, with its thrust through the satellite's centre of mass. Thus, this motor can move the spinning satellite in a direction perpendicular to its axis, without changing the axis of rotation. The axial motor provides a thrust parallel to the axis of rotation, but is as far as practical to one side of the centre of mass. This motor can be used either to change motion in the axial direction or to change the axis of rotation.

In station keeping and attitude control the motors are turned on briefly, or pulsed, at appropriate times by signals from the ground station. The axial control motor acts perpendicular to the plane of the orbit, so its operation will tilt the plane of the orbit. Operation 12 hours later will tilt the orbital plane in an opposite direction. A brief series of short pulses from the axial motor will also shift the axis of rotation slightly.

When the satellite is properly oriented, the lateral motor produces a thrust in the plane of the orbit. Depending on

Margin notes:

Gravity-gradient attitude control

Boosters

Attitude control by pulsed jets

the time of pulsing, this thrust can be used to increase or reduce orbital speed and hence to change the shape and period of the orbit.

Thus, a pair of pulsed jets allows all functions of attitude control and station keeping. This system has been used in all Intelsat satellites. For reasons of reliability, two axial and two radial jets are provided, and in Intelsat IV two additional jets are added to provide the spinning motion of the satellite.

These control jets must function reliably throughout the life of the satellite. Further, station and attitude can be maintained only for a period dependent on the amount and efficiency of the fuel used. Fuels have been improved considerably: Syncom II used compressed gas and hydrogen peroxide with a platinum catalyst; Syncom III, Intelsat I, and Intelsat II used hydrogen peroxide; Intelsat III and Intelsat IV used hydrazine, a liquid chemical fuel, and a special catalyst; this combination has proved to be very satisfactory.

Electronic technology. Communication satellites also draw widely on the electronic art. The electronic communication circuits in a communication satellite are essentially the same as those in an Earth-based microwave radio repeater. Certain electronic devices, however, are particularly vital to the success of communication satellites.

Power supply. One of these devices is the solar cell, developed around 1954 as a possible source of energy for telephone systems far removed from conventional, reliable power sources. Solar cells, which convert light directly into electrical energy, consist of thin wafers of silicon in which the electrical properties of the surface are changed by exposure, while heated, to a suitable gas. Early solar cells were of a type known as P-on-N (acceptor on donor atoms device) and were subject to damage from radiation in space; shortly before the design of Telstar it was found that a structure known as N-on-P (donor on acceptor atoms device) was more resistant to damage by radiation in space; Telstar and subsequent satellites have used N-on-P solar cells (see also SEMI-CONDUCTOR DEVICES).

Nickel-cadmium storage batteries used by satellites for standby power are suitable because they can be sealed hermetically; no gas is evolved during normal operation.

Other components. Transistors and other solid-state and semiconductor devices because of their small size are essential for the long-life, low-power operation required in satellites. In the early 1970s, one electron tube had not been displaced by solid-state and semiconductor devices from satellites: that was the travelling-wave tube used to amplify the microwave signal sent back to Earth. In this tube, the microwave signal travels in a spiral through the tube and is amplified by interacting with a beam of electrons travelling through the centre of the spiral. Travelling-wave tubes for satellite use are very small, light, efficient, and long lived. A typical tube requires about 12 watts of input power and provides an output power of four watts, giving an efficiency of 35 percent. It is about 9.3 inches (23 centimetres) long and 1.6 inches (four centimetres) in largest transverse dimension when packaged, and weighs less than a pound (0.4 kilogram), complete with a permanent magnet system for focussing the electron beam. The expected life is five years or more.

OPERATIONAL CONSIDERATIONS

The radio signal. Suggestions have been made that communications satellites might pass messages from one to another. This possibility does not appear to offer important practical advantages, and it is unlikely to be done in the near future. A communication satellite is simply a means for obtaining two line-of-sight radio paths, one from Earth to the satellite and the other from the satellite back to Earth.

Atmospheric attenuation. In travelling between Earth and a satellite, electromagnetic (radio) waves must pass through the atmosphere. The atmosphere will not permit electromagnetic waves of all frequencies to pass through it. Figure 1 shows how a wave is reduced in intensity (attenuated) between Earth and space as a function of

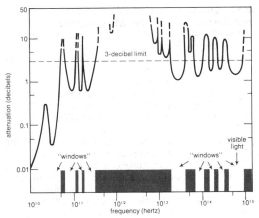

Figure 1: The attenuation of radio waves by the Earth's atmosphere as a function of frequency for an Earth-to-space signal. The chart assumes that the waves originate in clear weather at a high and dry location on the Earth and are directed upward toward space within 45° of vertical (see text).

frequency. A three-decibel (db) attenuation means that half the power is lost. (A decibel is a measure of power ratio; it is equal to ten times the logarithm of the ratio of power levels at two different points in the system.) "Windows" are regions in the frequency range where attenuation is small; for frequencies in the windows the attenuation is less than 3 decibels.

There is a window in the frequency range of visible light, but it cannot be used for efficient and reliable communication between Earth and space because of the frequent presence of clouds, haze, and other obstructions.

The atmosphere is quite transparent (introduces little attenuation) to radio waves for frequencies below 50 gigahertz. The ionosphere (an ionized layer of air high above the atmosphere) affects transmission severely below ten megahertz. At frequencies above 100 megahertz the ionosphere has some effect on the speed of propagation and the polarization (direction of vibration of the electric and magnetic fields) of radio waves. These effects decrease continually as the frequency is increased.

Frequencies above ten gigahertz are appreciably attenuated during heavy rain. Extensive measurements of space-to-Earth attenuation at 16 and 30 gigahertz have been made using the Sun as a microwave source. It has been found that at 16 gigahertz the attenuation due to rainfall is greater than 9 decibels, the acceptable upper limit, about 0.05 percent of the time, or about four hours per year. Attenuations above 9 decibels occur very infrequently; these can last, however, for ten minutes or longer. Failure of commercial telephone service for such periods has been judged unacceptable for modern systems. Thus, if frequencies of 16 gigahertz or higher were used, alternative receiver sites some miles apart would be required. With high probability, one would remain operational if the other were rained out.

There are various technical reasons for choosing particular ranges of frequencies for satellite communication. Clearly, as demand for satellite-communications facilities increases, a broader range of frequencies will be required. This increase must ultimately involve the use of higher and higher frequencies. Ionospheric effects (those from 25 to 250 miles [40–400 kilometres] or more) decrease with increasing frequency; rain attenuation increases with increasing frequency. In addition to technical considerations, there are regulatory considerations that involve the assignment of bands of frequencies to various uses, both civilian and military.

Regulatory considerations. Frequency allocations for various uses are determined at various international meetings and approved by the International Telecommunication Union (ITU) World Administrative Radio Conference. National administrations make further, more detailed, allocations within the international allocations and control the use of radio frequencies in the areas under their jurisdiction.

In the early 1970s, commercial satellite communications

"Windows" in the sky

Frequency
allocations

systems operated in frequency allocations shared by ground microwave radio relay systems. This circumstance means that satellite Earth stations must be located far from terrestrial microwave terminals, and hence far from cities. Two bands of frequencies, each 500 megahertz wide, are used; 3.7 to 4.2 gigahertz for space-to-Earth, and 5.925 to 6.425 gigahertz for Earth-to-space. The lower frequency is chosen for the space-to-Earth path to favour the low-power satellite transmitter in case of rain in the signal path.

Some 500 megahertz of bandwidth might be available around 12 gigahertz. Much larger bandwidth allocations, perhaps 3,500 megahertz, could be made in the vicinity of 20 and 30 gigahertz. While a substantial increase in satellite communication can be realized within the present allocations, it is apparent that large domestic requirements can be met only by going to the 20 and 30 gigahertz ranges. This extension would also allow Earth stations to be put near cities, for cities do not use frequencies in this range for communications purposes.

Radio transmission considerations. The power reflected from the passive Echo satellite was distributed almost equally in all directions much as light reflected from a round object. The power transmitted from the Telstar satellite also went out almost uniformly in all directions. Syncom was made to rotate on an axis parallel to the axis of Earth. Power went out equally in all directions perpendicular to its axis, so as to reach Earth at all times as the satellite spun, but little power was radiated to the north or south. Intelsat III and Intelsat IV radiate narrow conical microwave beams, similar to a searchlight beam, which are largely intercepted by Earth.

The antenna of a satellite Earth station is about 90 feet in diameter. The diameter of Earth is about 8,000 miles or 42,000,000 feet. The ratio of areas of the antenna and the cross section of Earth as seen from a synchronous satellite is thus about 1 to 200,000,000,000. Thus, if the signal transmitted from a satellite covered Earth uniformly, a 90-foot antenna would receive only about one part in 200,000,000,000 of the power intercepted by Earth. Clearly, only a very small fraction of the power sent to Earth by the Syncom satellite is received by the Earth station. Intelsat IV will send a larger fraction of its power to an Earth station, because its antennas produce two narrow beams that cover only part of Earth's surface; *e.g.*, Europe and North America.

Parabolic
reflector
antennas

The antennas used in Earth stations and those used in Intelsat III and Intelsat IV make use of parabolic reflectors. When such a reflector is used in transmitting, the power from the transmitter is directed by an antenna feed (perhaps a small horn) toward the reflector. The reflector focusses this power into a narrow conical beam. When a similar antenna is used in receiving, the parabolic reflector collects the signal energy that strikes it and directs this energy toward the feed, whence it goes to the microwave radio receiver. The received power is proportional to the product of the areas of the transmitting and receiving antennas. If, using the same pair of antennas at the same locations, the transmitter and receiver are interchanged, the fraction of the transmitted power that is received remains the same.

In communication satellites, the same Earth and satellite antennas are used for Earth-to-space and space-to-Earth transmission, even though the two directions of transmission are at slightly different frequencies. The satellite transmitter power for a given channel is less than ten watts; the Earth power may be as high as 1,000 to 10,000 watts. Thus, the signal the satellite receiver receives is much stronger than the signal the ground receiver receives.

Power on Earth is cheap. By using a high-power ground transmitter, it is possible to avoid system failure (outages) or degradation caused by an insufficient signal reaching the satellite, or caused by degradation in the performance of the receiver in the satellite. High Earth power also allows the use in the satellite of a receiver that has a lower performance (is less sensitive, or requires a stronger signal for proper operation) than the Earth receiver but is more simple and rugged.

If a beam of specified width (one that will cover a certain area on Earth, for example) is desired from a satellite, it is necessary to use a larger antenna at lower frequencies than at higher frequencies. Hence, at the higher frequencies it is easier to cover a small part of Earth's surface with a satellite antenna of moderate size. If a satellite transmitted at a frequency of 20 gigahertz, an antenna ten feet (three metres) in diameter would cover a circular area about 110 miles (177 kilometres) in diameter on Earth's surface. Thus, by using frequencies around 20 gigahertz and antennas of feasible size, the same band of frequencies could be reused to provide independent communication paths linking a large number of different Earth stations as long as the different Earth stations were located a few hundred miles apart. Such high frequencies could be used to provide a great deal of communication capabilities among carefully located ground stations.

The equipment. *Earth-station antennas.* The problems of constructing an Earth-station antenna and aiming it at a satellite are considerable. The power an antenna receives increases as its area increases. Its beam width (sharpness of the conical beam) decreases when either the diameter or the frequency, or both, are increased. Hence, the required accuracy of pointing of Earth-station antennas increases with frequency. Further, the mechanical tolerances within which an antenna must be fabricated are more severe as the frequency is increased. The surface of an antenna's parabolic reflector should be accurate to within a small fraction of a wavelength.

The efficient exploitation of communication satellites requires the use of large Earth antennas. Antennas for use with nonsynchronous satellites such as Echo, Telstar, and Relay were required to track the satellite as it crossed the sky; this is no longer necessary with synchronous satellites.

All Earth antennas make use of a parabolic reflector. In transmitting, the parabolic reflector focusses the microwaves from a feed that illuminates the reflector into a nearly parallel beam of microwaves. In a common type of antenna, the feed illuminates a circular parabolic reflector, as indicated in Figure 2A. In such an antenna,

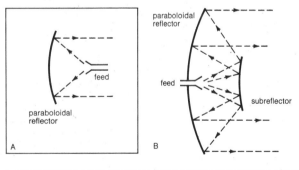

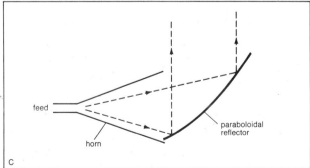

Figure 2: *Three types of antenna configurations used in Earth stations.*
(A) Parabolic reflector; (B) Cassegrainian; and (C) horn-reflector antenna (see text).

either the illumination is low near the edges of the reflector, which is wasteful, or some microwave energy spills over past the edge of the reflector. In the case of an antenna transmitting to a satellite, such energy goes to-

Use of
Casse-
grainian
antenna to
reduce
spillover

ward Earth and can interfere with terrestrial microwave systems operating at the same frequency. When such an antenna is used as a receiving antenna, spillover can result in reception of interfering signals from terrestrial sources, including radiation from Earth generated by Earth's temperature.

The disadvantages of spillover can be reduced by using a Cassegrainian antenna, illustrated in Figure 2B. The feed is located near the vertex (peak height) of the paraboloidal reflector and points away from it. The energy from the feed is reflected back toward the paraboloid by a subreflector. Spillover is largely around the edges of the subreflector, in the general direction of the sky, toward which the antenna is pointed. Thus, spillover tends to result in transmission of signals toward or reception of signals from space rather than Earth. Many Earth stations use Cassegrainian antennas.

In Echo and Telstar Earth stations, spillover was avoided through the use of horn-reflector antennas. Figure 2C illustrates such an antenna. The microwaves are guided from the feed to the reflector by a metal horn. The beam reflected by the reflector emerges from a hole in one side of the horn. The performance of horn-reflector antennas is very good, but they are bulky and costly. Some satellite Earth terminals make use of a modified form of Cassegrainian antenna, called a near-field Cassegrainian antenna, to reduce spillover.

Receiver and signal considerations. All bodies, solid, liquid, or gaseous, emit electromagnetic radiation or noise, the amount of such radiation depending on the temperature of the body.

In actual reception, some noise comes from outer space, which has a temperature around $3°$ K ($-270°$ C); some noise can come from rain, which has a temperature around $293°$ K ($20°$ C) but is partially transparent; some noise can come from Earth because the receiving antenna has some response to signal sources at which it is not pointed; and some noise is generated in the receiver itself. It is convenient to specify the strength of these sources of noise by a noise temperature, T_N, a measurement of the overall noisiness of the receiver. The higher the T_N, the noisier, and the poorer, the receiver. A noise temperature T_N may be given for a receiver alone or for the whole receiving system, including the antenna. It is this system T_N that is of practical importance.

The Echo satellite Earth terminal had a system noise temperature of $24°$ K. This low value was attained through the use of a microwave amplifier called a maser, an acronym for microwave amplification by stimulated emission of radiation. The maser amplifier was cooled by liquid helium (see LASER AND MASER).

The advantage of going to a noise temperature as low as $24°$ K is not great; for example, the signal from a satellite is weakest during heavy rain, and at such times, the rain alone can produce a noise temperature approaching $293°$ K. Most satellite Earth terminals make use of a special type of microwave amplifier called a parametric amplifier cooled to a temperature of around $4°$ K. The system noise temperature attained with such an amplifier is around $65°$ K.

Noise figure is an alternative way of specifying receiver noise. It is measured in decibels and is related to noise temperature. The simple receivers on a satellite commonly have a noise figure of around 6 decibels, corresponding to a noise temperature of $879°$ K.

The ratio of the received radio power to the noise power of a receiver is called the carrier-to-noise ratio. The ratio of signal to noise in the television or telephone signal after it has been separated from the carrier is called signal-to-noise ratio. Most satellite systems use frequency modulation (FM), a system in which the frequency of the carrier is varied by the modulating signal, as opposed to amplitude modulation, in which the amplitude of the carrier is varied. By means of this system a signal-to-noise ratio considerably higher than the carrier-to-noise ratio can be attained if the radio bandwidth is sufficiently large. If the carrier-to-noise ratio becomes too low, however, the FM receiver does not operate properly and the demodulated television or telephone signal becomes very noisy. A

carrier-to-noise ratio of around 20 times (13 decibels) is required for satisfactory communication. An additional fading margin of around ten times (10 decibels) is tolerated to permit operation during rain and to allow for other possible degradations in performance.

The foregoing indicates that the allowable bandwidth increases with power radiated from the satellite and with the size or sharpness of the beam of the satellite and Earth antennas. The overall performance of a satellite can best be measured in terms of the number of television or telephone signals of adequate quality that it can transmit.

Transponders. The communication portion of a satellite is a transmitter-receiver system called a transponder. The received signal is converted into a signal of lower or intermediate frequency and then amplified at this lower frequency by an intermediate-frequency amplifier. The amplified signal is then converted to the output frequency, and this output-frequency signal is amplified by a power amplifier to a power of a few watts.

Early satellites, including Telstar, Syncom, and Intelsats I and II, had a single transponder. Intelsat III has two transponders and Intelsat IV has 12 transponders. Multiple transponders allow more output power, as well as giving more total bandwidth.

SATELLITE SYSTEMS

The Intelsat satellites. The Intelsat satellites, which provide transoceanic telephone and television transmission, illustrate successive advances in the art of satellite communication. All the Intelsat satellites transmit up in the 6-gigahertz band and down in the 4-gigahertz band.

Intelsat I, also called Early Bird, weighs 85 pounds (38 kilograms) and gives a power output of 6 watts. It provides 240 two-way voice circuits or one television channel. It was launched on April 6, 1965, and for many years has been kept on reserve status over the Atlantic. The antenna of Intelsat I was pointed toward the Northern Hemisphere and thus the signal covers only a part of Earth.

Intelsat II weighs 192 pounds (87 kilograms) and provides a maximum power output of 24 watts, needed in part to cover the Southern as well as the Northern Hemisphere. Intelsat II provides about the same number of circuits and channels as Intelsat I. Three Intelsat II satellites were successfully launched in 1967; the second and third are still in use over the Atlantic and Pacific.

Intelsat III weighs 350 pounds (159 kilograms) and incorporates two repeaters that operate simultaneously. Each has a power output of 16 watts and can handle 1,200 voice channels or two television channels; this gives a capacity of 1,200 two-way voice channels or four one-way television channels. Intelsat III is the first communication satellite to have a mechanically despun antenna (an antenna mechanically isolated from the spinning satellite) capable of producing a narrow beam just covering Earth. Four Intelsat III satellites were launched in 1968 and 1970, and other launchings were planned.

Intelsat IV was launched in January 1971. It weighs 1,544 pounds (700 kilograms), and each channel has a six-watt output. The despun antenna system provides two steerable spot beam antennas for communication between areas of maximum service; *e.g.*, United States and Europe; two Earth-coverage transmit antennas; and two Earth-coverage receive antennas. The satellite provides 12 one-way television channels or about 3,000 to 9,000 two-way telephone channels.

The U.S. military program. In June of 1965 the U.S. Department of Defense directed the U.S. Air Force to plan for launching simple satellites into near-synchronous orbits in the Equatorial plane. While it would be necessary to track the slow motions of near-synchronous satellites, studies had shown that if a number of satellites were placed in orbits some 1,000 miles below synchronous orbit, at least one satellite would be in view from two locations almost all of the time. Satellites built for this program weigh 97 pounds (44 kilograms) each and are spin stabilized without active stabilization control. Operating frequencies are eight gigahertz Earth-to-satellite and 7.8 gigahertz satellite-to-Earth. The power output of each is 3.3 watts. With 40-foot ground antennas, a single satellite provides two two-way voice channels.

Multiple launches from a single booster placed seven of these satellites in orbit on June 16, 1966, and eight in January of 1967. Three more satellites were added in July of 1967 and eight in June of 1968, giving a total of 26. The system has provided reliable voice, teletypewriter, and data communication and has been used to transmit photographic information.

Other programs. *NATO and Skynet.* A North Atlantic Treaty Organization (NATO) communication satellite was successfully launched on March 20, 1970. Skynet is a British defense satellite system; two satellites have been launched, one in 1969 and a second in 1970.

The NATO and Skynet satellites are almost identical. They are synchronous satellites and are provided with station-keeping capabilities. Each has two transponders, a despun antenna, and weighs 285 pounds (129 kilograms).

Soviet Molniya. The Soviet Union has not developed truly synchronous satellites for use within the U.S.S.R., partly because such an Equatorial satellite would be difficult to launch from within its territory, and partly because it would not satisfactorily cover the far northern reaches of the country. The territory of the U.S.S.R. extends to 80° north latitude, where a synchronous satellite would be only 1.3° above the horizon. The Soviet Molniya communications satellites have been launched in elliptical orbits with an inclination of 65°. At this inclination the perigee moves very slowly and the apogee remains in the Northern Hemisphere. Under suitable conditions, the angular velocity near apogee roughly matches the angular velocity of Earth, and the satellite is visible over the U.S.S.R. every other revolution for a period of about eight hours; that is, the satellite is visible about a third of the time. Such an orbit can be stabilized more or less over the centre of the land mass of the U.S.S.R.

The first Molniya satellite was launched on April 23, 1965; the thirteenth on February 19, 1970. Of these satellites, at least eight were stabilized or partially stabilized.

The Molniya satellites are large and complicated. They are not spun. A Soviet description and sketch of the first shows that six large panels of solar cells unfold; the satellite is turned so that these continually face the Sun. Two parabolic antennas are provided. One is a spare; the other tracks Earth during operation. The satellite is hermetically sealed.

The Molniya satellites have been used for transmission of colour television. On November 30, 1965, an experimental Moscow-to-Paris television transmission was conducted, using the first Molniya satellite. Some Molniya satellites include a television camera and have transmitted pictures of Earth. Molniya satellites have also been used for telephonic transmission. Little more information is publicly available concerning them.

Tascat. On February 9, 1969, the largest communication satellite ever built was launched by the U.S. from Cape Kennedy, Florida. This 1,600-pound experimental Tascat (tactical communications satellite) was designed for use by the U.S. Army, Navy, and Air Force in communicating with mobile field units, aircraft, and ships. Signals from the satellite can be picked up by antennas as small as one foot in diameter. This synchronous, spin-stabilized satellite is 17.6 feet (5.4 metres) in total height and eight feet (2.4 metres) in diameter. The satellite uses ultrahigh frequency (UHF) signals in the hundreds of megahertz range for air-ground communication and signals around eight gigahertz for communication between fixed terminals.

OSCAR. OSCAR (Orbiting Satellites Carrying Amateur Radio) is a low-budget U.S. program using small satellites for scientific and communications applications. The program is oriented toward small terminals, such as amateur radio stations. Five satellites have been launched. OSCAR I and II contained low-power beacons that transmitted in the amateur two-metre (150-megahertz) band. OSCAR III contained a repeater for receiving, amplifying, and rebroadcasting signals in the two-metre band. OSCAR

IV received signals in the two-metre band and transmitted them in the 70-centimetre (430-megahertz) band. OSCAR V carried beacons in the two- and ten-metre bands. OSCAR I weighed ten pounds; OSCAR V, 39 pounds. The OSCAR satellites have been orbited as an additional part of the payload of other launches of satellites and space vehicles.

Proposed satellite systems. *Canadian Telesat.* The Canadian Parliament has given the Telesat Corporation, which was established by the Canadian government, authority to contract for communication satellites. When complete, the system will make use of a satellite very similar in capacity to Intelsat IV but weighing only 40 percent as much. The system is particularly aimed at communication with the Northwest Territories.

ESRO/CEPT. The ESRO (European Space Research Organization)/CEPT (European Conference of Postal and Telecommunications Administrations) communication satellite program is aimed at setting up a European operational satellite system about the period of 1978–80, to meet the requirements expressed by CEPT, including EBU (European Broadcasting Union). The satellite would handle around 10,000 telephone circuits and perhaps two colour television channels. The satellite would cover continental Europe, the lands situated on the southern and eastern shores of the Mediterranean, Iceland, and the Canary Islands. The use of frequencies from 11 to 13 gigahertz is envisaged. The satellite weight would be of the order of 1,500 pounds.

Symphonie. The cooperative French and German government Symphonie program envisages a satellite for communication with Europe, the northern part of Africa, South America, and part of North America. The satellite would weigh about 440 pounds.

Launch considerations. The ESRO/CEPT and Symphonie programs raise a particular question of launching communication satellites. Despite a considerable European expenditure toward space vehicles, the U.S. and the U.S.S.R. have the only vehicles capable of launching large, effective communication satellites. The present policy of the U.S. with respect to other countries is to launch strictly defense or strictly national satellites, such as Skynet, the NATO satellite, or those of the Canadian Telesat Corporation, but not to launch any satellites for international or regional use, except under Intelsat.

Political considerations. Technologically, communication satellites are the result of many advances and many programs. The vehicles used to launch them were originally developed for military purposes, as were their guidance systems. NASA has adapted these vehicles and provided tracking and guidance facilities suitable for launching communication satellites, and has launched all nonmilitary satellites. It has also supported the construction and launching of a number of satellites, including Relay and Syncom. The art that has gone into the design and construction of communication satellites has been the general art acquired by and common to the communication and aerospace industries.

The U.S. Communications Satellite Act of 1962 provided that the sole right of U.S. ownership of satellites for international communication rest in a single private corporation, Comsat (the Communications Satellite Corporation), which was incorporated in 1963. In order to deal with Comsat the European common carriers banded together into a consortium. The eventual outcome was the establishment on August 20, 1964, of Intelsat (International Telecommunications Satellite Consortium), an international corporation for the construction, launching, ownership, and operation of communication satellites. Most of the Earth stations are owned and operated by the common carriers of the nations they serve, but in the U.S. they are owned by Comsat. Membership in Intelsat rose to 75 countries in 1970. Intelsat satellites provide communication among over 50 countries.

Establishment of Intelsat

Potentialities and problems. Initially, satellite communication was conceived of as a means for providing reliable, broad-band circuits across oceans, where no such circuits existed. As the space art has provided large, reliable boosters and adequate means for attitude control, and as the electronic art has provided highly reliable solid-state circuitry, the cost of satellite communication circuits has approached that of land-based communication circuits.

Domestic traffic. While international communication traffic grows faster than domestic traffic, domestic traffic is far the larger and presumably will remain so. At some point in their development, satellites may be expected to compete economically for domestic traffic, and thereafter they might carry an increasing share of such traffic, especially over long distances. Partly, the future will be determined by who is allowed to establish domestic satellite systems, and of what kind. Economy of scale would seem to argue for one or a few systems.

To attain an economy of scale, satellites must provide a great many circuits. It seems unlikely that sufficient circuits can be provided in the long run using present common carrier frequencies. The potentialities of frequencies above 10 gigahertz for large capacity satellite systems has been pointed out. There is some indication that large frequency assignments may be made near 20 and 30 gigahertz.

While frequencies in this range have the disadvantage of large attenuation during heavy rain, they have the advantage that antennas of feasible size can produce very narrow microwave beams. Thus, it is possible that a satellite could use the same frequency in sending signals to two Earth stations 100 miles or more apart, and that an Earth station could use the same frequency in sending signals to two satellites only 1° apart. In this way, a number of satellites could provide hundreds of millions of telephone circuits or hundreds of thousands of television circuits connecting various cities—a number of circuits far exceeding the demands of the near future.

The realization of a large capacity system of this sort would require larger satellites and more accurate attitude control than present Intelsat satellites have. The requirements do not appear unreasonable in view of the present state and rate of progress in the space art.

Delay and echo problems. The future of satellite communication for telephony as opposed to one-way uses, such as the transmission of television programs, may hinge on the problem of echo in long-distance telephone circuits. In any practical telephone system, some of the energy directed toward a telephone is reflected back to the talker. When the talker hears this reflected speech delayed by a tenth of a second or more, as it will be on long circuits, it has an intolerably unpleasant and upsetting effect. To help overcome this effect, echo suppressors are inserted at the ends of circuits that are longer than 1,500 miles. These devices turn off the outward path when a signal is present on the inward path. Provisions are made for breaking in by talking very loudly.

Echo suppressors are tolerable for delays encountered in continental telephony and even for transoceanic telephony by means of submarine cable. For conversations employing a synchronous satellite, however, the echo may be delayed as much as 0.6 second. Many studies have been made in an effort to determine the effects of this delay on telephone users.

Careful studies show that only about 10 percent of users rate intercontinental cable calls fair or poor rather than good, while about 20 percent rate satellite calls as fair or poor. The poorer rating of satellite circuits is caused by the interaction of the transmission delay with the action of the echo suppressor. The difficulties experienced depend on the users and the conversation. Occasionally, a talker, receiving no reply to his queries, will repeatedly speak again at such a time as to cut off the reply made by the person with whom he is conversing. The effect of delay and echo suppressors has not been great enough to cause widespread complaint among users. This situation might be otherwise in domestic communication, however, where users are different and have a higher standard of comparison.

While all echo suppressors that have been tried give about the same results, it has been shown experimentally that self-adjusting circuits can be used to cancel the echo, so that the circuit can be made available to both talkers at all times. The degree of cancellation and the economic feasibility of this approach have not been determined.

Direct television broadcasting. Beginning in 1945, there have been numerous suggestions that satellites be used to broadcast television directly to homes. The chief arguments against this in highly industrialized countries are that the number of channels would be small, especially in comparison with cable television, that large geographical areas would receive the same program at the same time, without local news, weather, or advertising, that the antennas and equipment needed to receive the signals would be bulky and costly, and that industrialized countries have television already.

But some countries do not have television. NASA's Applications Technology Satellite (ATS) F and G will broadcast television signals experimentally by means of a 30-foot diameter antenna that can be directed at a limited geographical area. ATS-F is scheduled for launch in early 1973 and ATS-G in 1975. The Department of Atomic Energy in India signed an agreement on September 18, 1969, to provide for the use of ATS-F for community instructional telecasts to receivers in several thousand villages in India. This experiment should help to ascertain the value of direct satellite broadcasting.

BIBLIOGRAPHY. R.B. MARSTEN (ed.), *Communication Satellite Systems Technology* (1966), the best available compendium on satellites; MEMBERS OF BELL TELEPHONE LABORATORIES TECHNICAL STAFF, *Transmission Systems for Communications*, 4th ed. (1970), a comprehensive treatment applicable to all communication systems; COMMUNICATION SATELLITE CORPORATION, *Report to the President and Congress* (1970), a report on the present state of COMSAT and INTELSAT; J.R. PIERCE, *The Beginnings of Satellite Communications* (1968), reprints of both Arthur C. Clarke's 1945 paper ("Extra-terrestrial Relays") and J.R. Pierce's 1955 paper ("Orbital Radio Relays"), now of historical interest.

(J.R.P.)

Satire

"Satire" is a protean term. Together with its derivatives, it is one of the most heavily worked literary designations and one of the most imprecise. The great English lexicographer Samuel Johnson defined satire as "a poem in which wickedness or folly is censured," and more elaborate definitions are rarely more satisfactory. No strict definition can encompass the complexity of a word that signifies, on one hand, a kind of literature—as when one speaks of the satires of the Roman poet Horace or calls the American novelist Nathanael West's *A Cool Million* a satire—and, on the other, a mocking spirit or tone that manifests itself in many literary genres but can also enter into almost any kind of human communication. Wherever wit is employed to expose something foolish or vicious to criticism, there satire exists, whether it be in song or sermon, in painting or political debate, on television or in the movies. In this sense satire is everywhere. Although this article deals primarily with satire as a literary phenomenon, it records its manifestations in a number of other areas of human activity.

THE NATURE OF SATIRE

Historical definitions of satire. The terminological difficulty is pointed up by a phrase of the Roman rhetorician Quintilian: "satire is wholly our own" ("satura tota nostra est"). Quintilian seems to be claiming satire as a Roman phenomenon, although he had read the Greek dramatist Aristophanes and was familiar with a number of Greek forms that one would call satiric. But the Greeks had no specific word for satire; and by *satura* (which meant originally something like "medley" or "miscellany" and from which comes the English "satire") Quintilian intended to specify that kind of poem "invented" by Lucilius, written in hexameters on certain appropriate themes, and characterized by a Lucilian–Horatian tone. *Satura* referred, in short, to a poetic form, established and fixed by Roman practice. (Quintilian mentions also an even older kind of satire written in prose by Marcus Terentius Varro and, one might add, by Menippus and his followers Lucian and Petronius.) After Quintilian's day *satura* began to be used metaphorically to

Echo suppressors

designate works that were "satirical" in tone but not in form. As soon as a noun enters the domain of metaphor, as one modern scholar has pointed out, it clamours for extension; and *satura* (which had had no verbal, adverbial, or adjectival forms) was immediately broadened by appropriation from the Greek word for "satyr" (*satyros*) and its derivatives. The odd result is that the English "satire" comes from the Latin *satura;* but "satirize," "satiric," etc., are of Greek origin. By about the 4th century AD the writer of satires came to be known as *satyricus;* St. Jerome, for example, was called by one of his enemies "a satirist in prose" ("satyricus scriptor in prosa"). Subsequent orthographic modifications obscured the Latin origin of the word satire: *satura* becomes *satyra,* and in England, by the 16th century, it was written "satyre."

Satire and satyr
Elizabethan writers, anxious to follow Classical models but misled by a false etymology, believed that "satyre" derived from the Greek satyr play: satyrs being notoriously rude, unmannerly creatures, it seemed to follow that "satyre" should be harsh, coarse, rough. The English author Joseph Hall wrote:

> The Satyre should be like the Porcupine,
> That shoots sharpe quils out in each angry line,
> And wounds the blushing cheeke, and fiery eye,
> Of him that heares, and readeth guiltily.
>
> *(Virgidemiarum,* V, 3, 1–4.)

The false etymology that derives satire from satyrs was finally exposed in the 17th century by the Classical scholar Isaac Casaubon; but the old tradition has aesthetic if not etymological appropriateness and has remained strong.

In the prologue to his book, Hall makes a claim that has caused confusion like that following from Quintilian's remark on Roman satire. Hall boasts:

> I first adventure: follow me who list,
> And be the second English Satyrist.

But Hall knew the satirical poems of Geoffrey Chaucer and John Skelton, among other predecessors, and probably meant that he was the first to imitate systematically the formal satirists of Rome.

Influence of the satires of Horace and Juvenal. By their practice, the great Roman poets Horace and Juvenal set indelibly the lineaments of the genre known as the formal verse satire and, in so doing, exerted pervasive, if often indirect, influence on all subsequent literary satire. They gave laws to the form they established, but it must be said that the laws were very loose indeed. Consider, for example, style. In three of his Satires (I, iv; I, x; II, i) Horace discusses the tone appropriate to the satirist who out of a moral concern attacks the vice and folly he sees around him. As opposed to the harshness of Lucilius, Horace opts for mild mockery and playful wit as the means most effective for his ends. Although I portray examples of folly, he says, I am not a prosecutor and I do not like to give pain; if I laugh at the nonsense I see about me, I am not motivated by malice. The satirist's verse, he implies, should reflect this attitude: it should be easy and unpretentious, sharp when necessary, but flexible enough to vary from grave to gay. In short, the character of the satirist as projected by Horace is that of an urbane man of the world, concerned about folly, which he sees everywhere, but moved to laughter rather than rage.

Horace's concept of the satirist
Juvenal, over a century later, conceives the satirist's role differently. His most characteristic posture is that of the upright man who looks with horror on the corruptions of his time, his heart consumed with anger and frustration. Why does he write satire? Because tragedy and epic are irrelevant to his age. Viciousness and corruption so dominate Roman life that for an honest man it is difficult *not* to write satire. He looks about him, and his heart burns dry with rage; never has vice been more triumphant. How can he be silent (*Satires,* I)? Juvenal's declamatory manner, the amplification and luxuriousness of his invective, are wholly out of keeping with the stylistic prescriptions set by Horace. At the end of the scabrous sixth satire, a long, pervervid invective against women, Juvenal flaunts his innovation: in this poem, he says, satire has gone beyond the limits established by his predecessors; it has taken to itself the lofty tone of tragedy.

The results of Juvenal's innovation have been highly confusing for literary history. What *is* satire if the two poets universally acknowledged to be supreme masters of the form differ so completely in their work as to be almost incommensurable? The formulation of the English poet John Dryden has been widely accepted. Roman satire has two kinds, he says: comical satire and tragical satire, each with its own kind of legitimacy. These denominations have come to mark the boundaries of the satiric spectrum, whether reference is to poetry or prose or to some form of satiric expression in another medium. At the Horatian end of the spectrum, satire merges imperceptibly into comedy, which has an abiding interest in the follies of men but has not satire's reforming intent. The distinction between the two modes, rarely clear, is marked by the intensity with which folly is pursued: fops and fools and pedants appear in both, but only satire tries to mend men through them. And, although the great engine of both comedy and satire is irony, in satire, as the 20th-century critic Northrop Frye has said, irony is militant.

Comical satire and tragical satire
Boileau, Dryden, and Alexander Pope, writing in the 17th and 18th centuries—the modern age of satire—catch beautifully, when they like, the deft Horatian tone; however, satire's wit can also be sombre, deeply probing, and prophetic, as it explores the ranges of the Juvenalian end of the satiric spectrum, where satire merges with tragedy, melodrama, and nightmare. Pope's *Dunciad* ends with these lines:

> Lo! thy dread Empire, CHAOS! is restor'd;
> Light dies before thy uncreating word:
> Thy hand, great Anarch! lets the curtain fall;
> And Universal Darkness buries All.

It is the same darkness that falls on Book IV of Jonathan Swift's *Gulliver's Travels,* on some of Mark Twain's satire—*The Mysterious Stranger, To The Person Sitting in Darkness*—and on George Orwell's *1984.*

Structure of verse satire. Roman satire is hardly more determinate in its structure than in its style; the poems are so haphazardly organized, so randomly individual, that there seems little justification for speaking of them as a literary kind at all. Beneath the surface complexity of the poems, however, there exists, as one modern scholar has pointed out, a structural principle common to the satires of the Roman poets and their French and English followers. These poems have a bipartite structure: a thesis part, in which some vice or folly is examined critically from many different angles and points of view, and an antithesis part, in which an opposing virtue is recommended. The two parts are disproportionate in length and in importance, for satirists have always been more disposed to castigate wickedness than to exhort virtue.

Most verse satires are enclosed by a "frame." Just as a novel by the early-20th-century writer Joseph Conrad may be framed by a situation in which his narrator sits on a veranda in the tropics, telling his tale, stimulated into elaboration by the queries of his listeners, so the satire will be framed by a conflict of sorts between the satirist (or, more reasonably, his persona, a fictive counterpart, the "I" of the poem) and an adversary. Usually the adversary has a minor role, serving only to prod the speaker into extended comment on the issue (vice or folly) at hand; he may be sketchily defined, or he may be as effectively projected as Horace's Trebatius (*Satires,* II, i) or his awful bore (I, vi) or his slave Davus, who turns the tables on his master (II, vii). Similarly, the background against which the two talk may be barely suggested, or it may form an integral part of the poem, as in Horace's "Journey to Brundisium" (I, v) or in Juvenal's description of the valley of Egeria, where Umbricius unforgettably pictures the turbulence and decadence of Rome (*Satires,* III). In any event, the frame is usually there, providing a semidramatic situation in which vice and folly may reasonably be dissected.

The satirist has at his disposal an immense variety of literary and rhetorical devices: he may use beast fables, dramatic incidents, fictional experiences, imaginary voyages, character sketches, anecdotes, proverbs, homilies;

Literary and rhetorical devices

he may employ invective, sarcasm, burlesque, irony, mockery, raillery, parody, exaggeration, understatement —wit in any of its forms—anything to make the object of attack abhorrent or ridiculous. Amid all this confusing variety, however, there is pressure toward order—internally, from the arraignment of vice and appeal to virtue, and externally, from the often shadowy dramatic situation that frames the poem.

The satiric spirit. Thus, although the formal verse satire of Rome is quantitatively a small body of work, it contains most of the elements later literary satirists employ. When satire is spoken of today, however, there is usually no sense of formal specification whatever; one has in mind a work imbued with the satiric spirit—a spirit that appears (whether as mockery, raillery, ridicule, or formalized invective) in the literature or folklore of all peoples, early and late, preliterate and civilized. According to Aristotle (*Poetics*, IV, 1448b–1449a), Greek Old Comedy developed out of ritualistic ridicule and invective—out of satiric utterances, that is, improvised and hurled at individuals by the leaders of the phallic songs. The function of these "iambic" utterances, it has been shown, was magical; they were thought to drive away evil influences so that the positive fertility magic of the phallus might be operative. This early connection of primitive "satire" with magic has a remarkably widespread history.

Power of ancient satire

In the 7th century BC, the poet Archilochus, said to be the "first" Greek literary satirist, composed verses of such potency against his prospective father-in-law, Lycambes, that he and his daughter hanged themselves. In the next century the sculptors Bupalus and Athenis "knit their necks in halters," it is said, as a result of the "bitter rimes and biting libels" of the satirical poet Hipponax. Similar tales exist in other cultures. The chief function of the ancient Arabic poet was to compose satire (*hijā'*) against the tribal enemy. The satires were thought always to be fatal, and the poet led his people into battle, hurling his verses as he would hurl a spear. Old Irish literature is laced with accounts of the extraordinary power of the poets, whose satires brought disgrace and death to their victims:

> . . . saith [King] Lugh to his poet, "what power can *you* wield in battle?"
> "Not hard to say," quoth Carpre. . . . "I will satirize them, so that through the spell of my art they will not resist warriors."
>
> ("The Second Battle of Maytura," trans. by W. Stokes, *Revue Celtique*, XII [1891], 52–130.)

According to saga, when the Irish poet uttered a satire against his victim, three blisters would appear on the victim's cheek, and he would die of shame. One story will serve as illustration: after Deirdriu of the Sorrows came to her unhappy end, King Conchobar fell in love again—this time with the lovely Luaine. They were to be married; but, when the great poet Aithirne the Importunate and his two sons (also poets) saw Luaine, they were overcome with desire for her. They went to Luaine and asked her to sleep with them. She refused. The poets threatened to satirize her. And the story says:

> The damsel refused to lie with them. So then they made three satires on her, which left three blotches on her cheeks, to wit, Shame and Blemish and Disgrace. . . . Thereafter the damsel died of shame . . . .
>
> ("The Wooing of Luaine . . . ," trans. by W. Stokes, *Revue Celtique*, XXIV [1903], 273–85.)

An eminent 20th-century authority on these matters adduces linguistic, thematic, and other evidence to show a functional relation between primitive "satire," such as that of Carpre and Aithirne, and the "real" satire of more sophisticated times. Today, among various preliterate peoples the power of personal satire and ridicule is appalling; among the Ashanti of West Africa, for example, ridicule is (or was recently) feared more than almost any other humanly inflicted punishment, and suicide is frequently resorted to as an escape from its terrors. Primitive satire such as that described above can hardly be spoken of in literary terms; its affiliations are rather with the magical incantation and the curse.

SATIRICAL MEDIA

Literature. When the satiric utterance breaks loose from its background in ritual and magic, as in ancient Greece (when it is free, that is, to develop in response to literary stimuli rather than the "practical" impulsions of magic), it is found embodied in an indefinite number of literary forms that profess to convey moral instruction by means of laughter, ridicule, mockery; the satiric spirit proliferates everywhere, adapting itself to whatever mode (verse or prose) seems congenial. Its targets range from one of Pope's dunces to the entire race of man, as in *Satyr against Mankind* (1675), by John Wilmot, the earl of Rochester, from Erasmus' attack on corruptions in the church to Swift's excoriation of all civilized institutions in *Gulliver's Travels*. Its forms are as varied as its victims: from an anonymous medieval invective against social injustice to the superb wit of Chaucer and the laughter of Rabelais; from the burlesque of Luigi Pulci to the scurrilities of Pietro Aretino and the "black humour" of Lenny Bruce; from the flailings of John Marston and the mordancies of Francisco Gómez de Quevedo y Villegas to the bite of Jean de La Fontaine and the great dramatic structures of Ben Jonson and Molière; from an epigram of Martial to the fictions of Nikolay Gogol and of Günter Grass and the satirical utopias of Yevgeny Zamyatin, Aldous Huxley, and Orwell.

It is easy to see how the satiric spirit would combine readily with those forms of prose fiction that deal with the ugly realities of the world but that satire should find congenial a genre such as the fictional utopia seems odd. From the publication of Thomas More's eponymous *Utopia* (1516), however, satire has been an important ingredient of utopian fiction. More drew heavily on the satire of Horace, Juvenal, and Lucian in composing his great work. For example, like a poem by Horace, *Utopia* is framed by a dialogue between "Thomas More" (the historical man a character in his own fiction) and a seafaring philosopher named Raphael Hythloday. The two talk throughout a long and memorable day in a garden in Antwerp. "More's" function is to draw Hythloday out and to oppose him on certain issues, notably his defense of the communism he found in the land of Utopia. "More" is the adversary. Hythloday's role is to expound on the institutions of Utopia but also to expose the corruption of contemporary society. Thus he functions as a satirist. Here Hythloday explains why Englishmen, forced off their land to make way for sheep, become thieves:

Use of satire in fictional utopias

> Forsooth . . . your sheep that were wont to be so meek and tame and so small eaters, now as I hear say, be become so great devourers and so wild, that they eat up and swallow down the very men themselves. They consume, destroy, and devour whole fields, houses, and cities. For look in what parts of the realm doth grow the finest and therefore dearest wool, there noblemen and gentlemen, yea and certain abbots, holy men no doubt, not contenting themselves with the yearly revenues and profits that were wont to grow to their forefathers and predecessors of their lands, nor being content that they live in rest and pleasure nothing profiting, yea, much annoying the weal-public, leave no ground for tillage. They enclose all into pastures; they throw down houses; they pluck down towns and leave nothing standing but only the church to be made a sheep-house.
>
> (More's *Utopia*, Everyman edition, 1951.)

Here are characteristic devices of the satirist, dazzlingly exploited: the beast fable compressed into the grotesque metaphor of the voracious sheep; the reality-destroying language that metamorphoses gentlemen and abbots into earthquakes and a church into a sheep barn; the irony coldly encompassing the passion of the scene. Few satirists of any time could improve on this.

Just as satire is a necessary element of the work that gave the literary form utopia its name, so the utopias of Lilliput, Brobdingnag, and Houyhnhnmland are essential to the satire of More's great follower Jonathan Swift. He sent Gulliver to different lands from those Hythloday discovered, but Gulliver found the same follies and the same vices, and he employed a good many of the same rhetorical techniques his predecessor had used to expose them. *Gulliver's Travels*, as one scholar points out, is a salute across the centuries to Thomas More. With this kind of precedent, it is not surprising that in the 20th century, when utopia turns against itself, as in Aldous Huxley's *Brave New World* (1932), the result is satire unrelieved.

Aristophanes' use of satire

Drama. The drama has provided a favourable environment for satire ever since it was cultivated by Aristophanes, working under the extraordinarily open political conditions of 5th-century Athens. In a whole series of plays—*The Clouds, The Frogs, Lysistrata,* and many others—Aristophanes lampoons the demagogue Cleon by name, violently attacks Athenian war policy, derides the audience of his plays for their gullible complacency, pokes fun at Socrates as representative of the new philosophical teaching, stages a brilliantly parodic poetic competition between the dramatists Aeschylus and Euripedes in Hades, and in general lashes out at contemporary evils with an uninhibited and unrivalled inventiveness. But the theatre has rarely enjoyed the political freedom Aristophanes had—one reason, perhaps, that satire more often appears in drama episodically or in small doses than in the full-blown Aristophanic manner. In Elizabethan England, Ben Jonson wrote plays that he called "comicall satyres" —*Every Man Out of His Humour, Poetaster*—and there are substantial elements of satire in Shakespeare's plays —some in the comedies, but more impressively a dark and bitter satire in *Timon of Athens, Troilus and Cressida, Hamlet,* and *King Lear.* The 17th-century comedy of Molière sometimes deepens into satire, as with the exposure of religious hypocrisy in *Tartuffe* or the railing against social hypocrisy by Alceste in *The Misanthrope.* George Bernard Shaw considered himself a satirist. He once compared his country's morals to decayed teeth and himself to a dentist, obliged by his profession to give pain in the interests of better health. Yet, as inventive and witty as Shaw is, compared to the 20th-century German playwright Bertolt Brecht, whose anatomizing of social injustice cuts deep, Shaw is a gentle practitioner indeed.

Motion pictures and television. The movies have sometimes done better by satire than the theatre, and it is in the movies that an ancient doctrine having to do with principles of decorum in the use of satire and ridicule has been exploded. The English novelist Henry Fielding was reflecting centuries of tradition when, in the preface to *Joseph Andrews* (1742), he spoke of the inappropriateness of ridicule applied to black villainy or dire calamity. "What could exceed the absurdity of an Author, who should write *the Comedy of* Nero, *with the merry Incident of ripping up his Mother's Belly?*" Given this point of view, Hitler seems an unlikely target for satire; yet in *The Great Dictator* (1940) Charlie Chaplin managed a successful, if risky, burlesque. Chaplin has written, however, that, determined as he was to ridicule the Nazi notions of a superrace, if he had known of the horrors of the concentration camps, he could not have made the film. Stanley Kubrick's *Dr. Strangelove; or, How I Learned to Stop Worrying and Love the Bomb* (1964) denies all limitation; through some alchemy Kubrick created an immensely funny, savagely satirical film about the annihilation of the world. A combination of farce and nightmare, *Dr. Strangelove* satirizes military men, scientists, statesmen—the whole ethos of the technological age —in the most mordant terms; it shows the doomsday blast, yet leaves audiences laughing. "You can't fight in here," says the president of the United States as doom nears, "this is the War Room." The film's tone is less didactic than in most powerful satire—the mushroom cloud carries its own moral—yet satire's full force is there.

Television has not proved a notably receptive medium. *That Was the Week That Was,* a weekly satirical review started in England in 1962, had remarkable success for a time but succumbed to a variety of pressures, some of them political; when a version of the program was attempted in the United States, it was emasculated by restrictions imposed by sponsors fearful of offending customers and by program lawyers wary of libel suits. Jonathan Swift said that he wrote to vex the world rather than divert it; it is not an attitude calculated to sell soap.

Festivals. Yet satire does much more than vex, and even in Swift's work there is a kind of gaiety that is found in many nonliterary manifestations of the satirical spirit. Satire always accompanies certain festivals, for example, particularly saturnalian festivals. Many different cultures set aside a holiday period in which customary social restraints are abandoned, distinctions of rank and status are turned upside down, and institutions normally sacrosanct are subjected to ridicule, mockery, burlesque. The Romans had their Saturnalia, the Middle Ages its Feast of Fools; and in the 20th century many countries still have annual carnivals (Fasching in Austria, the Schnitzelbank in Basel, Switzerland, for example) at which, amid other kinds of abandon, an extraordinary freedom of satirical utterance is permitted. Even in Africa among the Ashanti, for whom ridicule has such terrors, there is a festival during which the sacred chief himself is satirized. "Wait until Friday," said the chief to the enquiring anthropologist, "when the people really begin to abuse me, and if you will come and do so too it will please me." Festivals such as these provide sanctioned release from social inhibition and repression, and, in these circumstances, satire directed at men in power or at taboo institutions acts as a safety valve for pent-up frustrations.

The gaiety of satire

Satire may often function this way. A story is told that the 16th-century pope Adrian VI was highly offended at satirical verses written against him and affixed to Pasquino's statue (a famous repository for lampoons in Rome), but he became a willing target once he realized that his enemies vented otherwise dangerous hostility in this relatively harmless manner. Similar mechanisms operate today when, at a nightclub or theatre, audiences listen to satirical attacks on political figures or on issues such as racial discrimination, identify with the satirist, laugh at his wit, and thereby discharge their own aggressive feelings. Satire of this order is a far cry, of course, from that written by a Swift or Voltaire, whose work can be said to have a revolutionary effect.

Visual arts. The critique of satire may be conveyed even more potently in the visual arts than by way of the spoken or written word. In caricature and in what came to be known as the cartoon, artists since the Renaissance have left a wealth of startlingly vivid commentary on the men and events of their time. The names alone evoke their achievement: in England, William Hogarth, Thomas Rowlandson, Sir John Tenniel, Max Beerbohm; in France, Charles Philipon (whose slow-motion metamorphosis of King Louis-Philippe into a *poire*—that is, "fathead," or "fool"—is classic) and Honoré Daumier; in Spain, Francisco Goya—out of Spain, Pablo Picasso; among recent political cartoonists, Sir David Low, Vicky (Victor Welsz), Herblock (Herbert Block), Conrad. The favourite medium of these men is the black-and-white print in which the satirical attack is pointed up by a brief verbal caption. The social impact of their art is incalculable. Dictators know this, and in times of social tension political cartoonists are among the first victims of the censor.

Caricature and cartoon

THE SATIRIST, THE LAW, AND SOCIETY

Indeed, the relations of satirists to the law have always been delicate and complex. Both Horace and Juvenal took extraordinary pains to avoid entanglements with authority—Juvenal ends his first satire with the self-protective announcement that he will write only of the dead. In England in 1599 the Archbishop of Canterbury and the Bishop of London issued an order prohibiting the printing of any satires whatever and requiring that the published satires of Hall, John Marston, Thomas Nashe, and others be burned. Today, the satirist attacks individuals only at the risk of severe financial loss to himself and his publisher. In totalitarian countries he risks imprisonment or death. Under extreme conditions satire against the reigning order is out of the question: so canonical is this rule that political analysts use the amount and character of satire permitted in the U.S.S.R. as a gauge of political pressure at any given time. Whereas the poet Osip Mandelstam was sent to a concentration camp and his death for composing a satirical poem on Stalin, today Isaac Deutscher can interpret as a favourable sign the increasing amount of Soviet satire against internal abuses.

Repressions of satire

One creative response the satirist makes to social and legal pressures is to try by rhetorical means to approach his target indirectly; that is, a prohibition of direct attack fosters the manoeuvres of indirection that will make the attack palatable: irony, innuendo, burlesque, parody, allegory, etc. It is a nice complication that the devices that render satire acceptable to society at the same time sharpen its point. "Abuse is not so dangerous," said Dr. Johnson, "when there is no vehicle of wit or delicacy, no subtle conveyance." The conveyances are born out of prohibition.

Anthony Cooper, 3rd earl of Shaftesbury, writing in the 18th century, recognized the "creative" significance of legal and other repressions on the writing of satire. "The greater the weight [of constraint] is, the bitterer will be the satire. The higher the slavery, the more exquisite the buffoonery." Shaftesbury's insight requires the qualification made above. Under a massively efficient tyranny, satire of the forms, institutions, or personalities of that tyranny is impossible. But, under the more relaxed authoritarianism of an easier going day, remarkable things could be done. Max Radin, a Prussian-born Armenian author, writes of how satirical journals in Germany before World War I, even in the face of a severe law, vied with each other to see how close they could come to caricatures of the Kaiser without actually producing them. "Satire which the censor understands," said the Austrian satirist Karl Kraus, "deserves to be banned." The 20th-century critic Kenneth Burke sums up this paradoxical aspect of satire's relation with the law by suggesting that the most inventive satire is produced when the satirist knowingly takes serious risks and is not sure whether he will be acclaimed or punished. The whole career of Voltaire is an excellent case in point. Bigots and tyrants may have turned pale at his name, as a famous hyperbole has it; but Voltaire's satire was sharpened and his life rendered painfully complicated as he sought to avoid the penalties of the law and the wrath of those he had angered. Men such as Voltaire and Kraus and the Russian Zamyatin attack evil in high places, pitting their wit and moral authority against cruder forms of power. In this engagement there is often something of the heroic.

Readers have an excellent opportunity to examine the satirist's claim to social approval by reason of the literary convention that decrees that he must justify his problematic art. Nearly all satirists write apologies, and nearly all the apologies project an image of the satirist as a plain, honest man, wishing harm to no worthy person but appalled at the evil he sees around him and forced by his conscience to write satire. Pope's claim is the most extravagant:

> Yes, I am proud; I must be proud to see
> Men not afraid of God, afraid of me:
> Safe from the Bar, the Pulpit, and the Throne,
> Yet touch'd and sham'd by *Ridicule* alone.
> O sacred Weapon! left for Truth's defence,
> Sole Dread of Folly, Vice, and Insolence!
>
> (*Epilogue to the Satires*, II, 208–13.)

Relationship between the satirist and his audience

After the great age of satire, which Pope brought to a close, such pretensions would have been wholly anachronistic. Ridicule depends on shared assumptions against which the deviant stands in naked relief. The satirist must have an audience that shares with him commitment to certain intellectual and moral standards that validate his attacks on aberration. The greatest satire has been written in periods when ethical and rational norms were sufficiently powerful to attract widespread assent yet not so powerful as to compel absolute conformity—those periods when the satirist could be of his society and yet apart, could exercise a double vision. Neoclassic writers had available to them as an implicit metaphor the towering standard of the classical past; for the 19th and 20th centuries no such metaphors have been available. It is odd, however, that whereas the 19th century in general disliked and distrusted satire (there are obvious exceptions), our own age, bereft of unifying symbols, scorning traditional rituals, searching for beliefs, still finds satire a congenial mode in almost any medium. Although much

of today's satire is self-serving and trivial, there are notable achievements. Joseph Heller's novel *Catch-22* (1961) once again employs farce as the agent of the most probing criticism: Who is sane, the book asks, in a world whose major energies are devoted to blowing itself up? Beneath a surface of hilariously grotesque fantasy, in which characters from Marx-brothers comedy carry out lethal assignments, there is exposed a dehumanized world of hypocrisy, greed, and cant. Heller is a satirist in the great tradition. If he can no longer, like Pope, tell men with confidence what they should be for, he is splendid at showing them what they must be against. The reader laughs at the mad logic of *Catch-22*, and as he laughs he learns. This is the way satire has worked from the beginning.

BIBLIOGRAPHY. DAVID WORCESTER, *The Art of Satire* (1940), a study of rhetorical techniques available to the satirist; JAMES R. SUTHERLAND, *English Satire* (1958), a sound scholarly history; ALVIN B. KERNAN, *The Cankered Muse: Satire of the English Renaissance* (1959), valuable theory and criticism; ROBERT C. ELLIOTT, *The Power of Satire: Magic, Ritual, Art* (1960), on the margins of satire in magic and its development into an art; RONALD PAULSON, *The Fictions of Satire* (1967), a study of satire in fiction from Lucian to Swift, and (ed.), *Satire: Modern Essays in Criticism* (1971), an authoritative and indispensable collection; MATTHEW J.C. HODGART, *Satire* (1969), a well-illustrated, readable survey of satire in many forms and in many countries.

(R.C.E.)

Saturn

Saturn, symbol in astronomy ♄, is the outermost of the planets known in ancient times. The earliest known observations, by the Babylonians, can be reliably dated to the mid-7th century BC, but it may have been noticed earlier, as it is brighter than most stars. To the naked eye it appears yellowish; it moves slowly against the background of stars. The Greeks named it after Cronus, the original ruler of Olympus, whose Roman equivalent is the god Saturn.

Physical properties

The sixth planet in order of distance from the Sun, Saturn can never approach the Earth closer than about 740,000,000 miles. Its brightness is due to its large size, inferior only to that of Jupiter. The equatorial diameter is 75,100 miles, but the globe is appreciably flattened and the polar diameter is only 67,200 miles. The mass of Saturn is 95.14 times that of the Earth, or $1/3,500$ of that of the Sun; the volume is 743.7 times that of the Earth, and the escape velocity—the speed which, once attained, will allow a spacecraft or other body to coast out of Saturn's gravitational domain—is 22 miles per second, more than three times that of Earth. The density is surprisingly low —only 0.7 that of water—and the surface gravity is 1.16 times as great as that of the Earth. Saturn is made up of gas, at least in its outer layers, and is a world quite unlike man's own.

Saturn's ring system makes it unique in the solar system. The rings cannot be seen with the naked eye but a telescope of moderate power will show them excellently, and there can be no doubt that Saturn is one of the most beautiful objects in the entire sky. Data for Saturn are given in Table 1.

Table 1: Planetary Data for Saturn

Mean distance from Sun	9.54 a.u.
Eccentricity of orbit	0.056
Inclination of orbit to ecliptic	2°29'22"
Sidereal period of revolution	29.46 years
Rotation period	10 hours 14 minutes at equator
Mean synodic period	378.1 days
Mean orbital velocity	6 miles/sec.
Inclination of equator to orbit	26°44'
Mass (Earth = 1)	95.14
Diameter (equatorial, including atmosphere)	75,100 miles
Density (water = 1)	0.7
Satellites	10

Early telescopic observations. The first telescopic observations of Saturn are thought to have been made by

Galileo in July 1610. He saw the disk of the planet clearly, but his telescope gave a magnification of only 32 diameters and was not good enough to show the ring system in recognizable form; moreover, conditions were unfavourable because the rings were seen almost edgewise. Galileo thought that Saturn must be a triple planet, and wrote that "Saturn is not one alone, but is composed of three, which almost touch one another." Two years later, he found to his surprise that the "companions" had vanished, so that Saturn appeared as a single body. The ring system was then edge on to the Earth, so that it could not be seen at all in Galileo's telescope. The original aspect was again seen in the years following 1613, but Galileo never was able to interpret it correctly. Subsequently, various strange theories were proposed to explain the planet's unusual form; Hevelius of Danzig, for instance, believed that Saturn must be elliptical in shape, with two appendages attached to the surface.

The problem was solved by the Dutch astronomer Christiaan Huygens, who began his observations in 1655. The telescopes that he used were much more powerful than Galileo's, and gave sharper definition, so that by 1659 he was satisfied that "Saturn is surrounded by a thin, flat ring which nowhere touches the body" of the planet. His theory, published originally in anagram form, met with a surprising amount of opposition, but by 1665 it had been universally accepted even though the nature of the ring system was not established until the late 19th century.

By courtesy of the Hale Observatories, California

Saturn and ring system in blue light, November 24, 1943, 9:38 Universal Time lantern slide, no filter; taken at the Cassegrain focus of the 100-inch telescope with a scale of 5 inches per millimetre.

The orbit of Saturn. Among planetary orbits, Saturn's is of fairly low eccentricity (0.056). Saturn's mean distance from the Sun is 886,100,000 miles, or 9.539 times that of Earth. The perihelion distance of Saturn, its closest approach to the Sun, is 834,600,000 miles, and its farthest retreat from the Sun, or aphelion, is at 937,-600,000 miles. The distance between Saturn and the Earth can thus be as great as 1,032 million miles or as little as 740 million miles. The revolution period is 29.46 years (10,759.2 days). Because Saturn is so far from the Sun and the Earth, phase effects for the disk are negligible; that is, it always appears to be full, or nearly so, in the sense of the full moon.

Synodic period · The mean synodic period, the interval between successive oppositions, when Earth passes approximately between Saturn and the Sun, is 378.1 days, so that Saturn is well placed for observation during several months in each year. Opposition dates up to 1975 are November 11, 1970; November 25, 1971; December 8, 1972; December 22, 1973; and January 6, 1975.

Like all the superior planets, that is, those outward from the Earth, Saturn moves for the greater part of the year eastward against the stars; its average rate is about one degree in eight days. As it approaches opposition, however, its motion slows down, and stops altogether about 70 days before the opposition date. For a period that may be as little as 133 days or as great as 141 days, it then moves in a retrograde, or westward, direction before reaching another stationary point and resuming its eastward movement. This behaviour does not, of course indicate any real alteration in motion. The regression is due to the fact that the Earth, moving in a much smaller orbit at a greater velocity (average 18.5 miles per second as against only six miles per second for Saturn), is catching up with Saturn and passing it.

When at conjunction, on the far side of the Sun, Saturn cannot be observed, as it is too close to the Sun in the sky; it is therefore out of view for part of each year. The inclination of the orbit to the ecliptic is 2° 29′ 22″. During its synodic period of 378 days, Saturn advances for nearly eight months and retrogrades slowly for about 4½ months, so that on balance it progresses eastward along its path by about 12 degrees per year. During the 1970s it will be well placed in the northern sky for observers in Europe and the United States.

The surface of Saturn. The colour is yellowish; darker belts, parallel with the equator, are permanent features. These belts are not nearly so conspicuous as those on Jupiter, nor do they show so much fine detail or variation. Saturn's greater distance makes it less easy to observe than Jupiter, but there can be no doubt that the surface activity really is considerably less. The beauty of the ring system tends to divert attention from the disk of Saturn, particularly because when the rings are wide open they hide a considerable part of the globe.

Saturn's albedo (the proportion of incident sunlight it reflects) is 0.42, but the planet's apparent magnitude depends largely on the angle at which the ring system is displayed, because the rings are more reflective than the disk. When the rings are wide open, as they were in 1972–73, the magnitude attains −0.3, so that, of the stars, only Sirius and Canopus are brighter than Saturn. At oppositions when the rings are edge on, as in 1966, the magnitude is as faint as +0.8, though even at these times Saturn is still a very prominent object.

Polar and equatorial zones · The brightest part of the disk, the equatorial zone, is creamy, sometimes almost white. The polar regions are less brilliant, and photographs taken through colour filters confirm that they have a slightly greenish cast with variations in colour and intensity from one opposition to another. The belts do not show any perceptible colour in a telescope, but filter photographs indicate that they are somewhat orange. As with Jupiter, the two most prominent belts flank the equatorial zone; the other belts are much less conspicuous. Unless the rings are at a narrow angle, one or other of the equatorial belts will be covered up. During the early 1970s, for instance, the north equatorial belt is hidden by the rings.

Well-defined spots on Saturn are rare. The most prominent example known during the present century was discovered on August 3, 1933, by an English amateur, W.T. Hay, using a six-inch refractor. It took the form of a large, white, oval patch on the equatorial zone, about one-fifth of the planet's diameter in length, and with both ends well defined. During the next few weeks, it lengthened rapidly, until by mid-September it had spread out so much that it could no longer be called a spot. W.H. Wright, who studied it with the 36-inch refractor at the Lick Observatory, considered that it must be of an eruptive nature, with material being sent up from below the visible surface of Saturn. Other white spots, presumably of the same type, have been seen since, but these have been short-lived and much less striking.

The lack of well-defined local features means that it is not easy to determine the planet's rotation period by visual observation. Nevertheless, careful studies of such features as have been seen over many years have indicated an equatorial-zone rotation of 10 hours 14 minutes; at latitude 60°, the period is 10 hours 40 minutes. Another useful method depends upon the Doppler effect. As Saturn spins, one limb is approaching Earth, and the spectral lines will be shifted toward the blue or shortwave end of the spectrum; the other limb is receding and yields a red shift. The displacements are small but measurable, and from them the speed of rotation can be found. The derived equatorial-rotation period agrees well with the visual results, but knowledge of the behaviour at high latitudes is not as complete as might be desired.

A theory that Saturn might be faintly self-luminous as

the result of internal heat has long since been disproved; the surface temperature has been measured at -290 degrees Fahrenheit, 60 degrees colder than that of Jupiter. This may well explain the more sluggish character of the cloud formations and the lack of complex details. Infrared determinations lead to much the same result. Unlike Jupiter, Saturn is not a strong source of radio waves; at radio frequencies it emits only what might be expected from any body its size having a low temperature.

Mass, density, and composition. The mass of Saturn has been measured (1) by its gravitational interaction with other planets, particularly Jupiter, resulting in small changes in orbits; and (2) by observations of its satellites. Individual satellite masses may be neglected, except in the case of the largest satellite, Titan. The results of all the investigations are in good accord; and the best value of the mass is 95.1 times that of the Earth. Measuring the diameter of the planet then leads to a value for the density.

Saturn is the only planet that is less dense than water. The mass must be highly concentrated toward the centre, where there must be considerable heat. Theoretical investigations indicate that Saturn may contain about 63 percent of hydrogen by mass.

Hydrogen compounds may be directly studied in the visible layer at the top of the planet's atmosphere. Spectral evidence shows that both methane and ammonia are plentiful and that there are large quantities of molecular hydrogen; helium is presumably abundant. There is more methane and less ammonia than on Jupiter, presumably because more of the ammonia has been frozen out of the planet's atmosphere.

The core It is not known whether Saturn has a definite core. One proposed model suggests a 35 percent, rocky core, a 20 percent ice layer, and a 45 percent hydrogen-rich atmosphere; but according to other models there is no sharp lower boundary to the atmosphere, and there may well be a core made up of compressed hydrogen in a metallic state. Despite the low overall density, the central pressure is likely to be about 5,000,000 atmospheres.

Present knowledge of the internal composition of Saturn is far from complete. More information may be obtained from unmanned probes, possibly during the 1970s.

The rings. The rings of Saturn, unique in the solar system, have been studied since the days of Galileo. The ring plane remains in an almost fixed position with reference to the stars, but as seen from the Earth and the Sun, the tilt of the rings is continually changing. Twice in each Saturnian revolution, at alternate intervals of 13 years 9 months and 15 years 9 months, the plane of the rings passes through the Sun. A few months before and after each such occasion, the ring plane must pass through the Earth, which is near the Sun as viewed from Saturn. During the shorter interval, the south pole of Saturn is tilted toward the Sun, so that the southern aspect of the rings is illuminated and the northern hemisphere of the planet is partly obscured; also, Saturn passes through perihelion. While the northern ring face is displayed, and the southern hemisphere of the globe partly obscured, Saturn passes through aphelion; it is then moving more slowly in its orbit, which explains why the two intervals between successive edgewise presentations are unequal.

The ring system almost vanishes when edge on because it is extremely thin. Though the overall diameter of the rings is 169,000 miles, the thickness is no more than 10 miles. When the Sun is in the ring plane, there is very little illumination of the rings, and for some months they appear as nothing more than a thin, delicate line of light. Powerful telescopes will almost always show traces of them, but in small instruments or those of moderate size they disappear completely.

Two of the three rings, A (outer) and B, are bright. In 1675 G.D. Cassini, at the Paris Observatory, discovered the gap between them, now known as Cassini's Division. The "ring" seen by Huygens was a combination of the two; his telescope was not good enough to show the division. The two rings are not alike because B is much the brighter of the two. The width of the Cassini Division amounts to 1,700 miles.

In 1850 a dusky inner ring was discovered by W.C. Bond

and G.P. Bond at Harvard, and independently by W.R. Dawes in England, whose friend W. Lassell named it the Crêpe Ring—a term still used, though the official designation is Ring C. It is 10,000 miles wide, and extends to within 9,000 miles of the surface of the planet. Unlike A and B, it is transparent, and where the rings cross the disk the Crêpe Ring may be seen as a hazy darkish band outlining their inner edge. A fourth dusky ring still closer to the planet has been reported, but awaits definite confirmation.

Table 2 shows the dimensions of the three well-authenticated rings.

Table 2: Dimensions of Saturn's Ring System (in kilometres)

ring	exterior diameter	breadth of ring
A	139,300	16,300
B	117,200	27,900
C	89,300	17,300

Source: A. Dollfus, *Surface and Interiors of Planets and Satellites*, 1970.

Cassini's Division is due to the gravitational effects of the inner satellites of Saturn. A particle moving in the Division would have a revolution period equal to about one-half that of the Saturnian satellite Mimas, one-third that of Enceladus, and one-quarter that of Tethys—slightly over 11 hours—so that it would be perturbed through resonance and forced into a different orbit. The satellites thus keep the region of Cassini's Division "swept clear" of ring particles.

In 1837, J.F. Encke, at Berlin, discovered a less prominent division in Ring A, now known by his name. This, too, is due to satellite perturbations, but is much less noticeable than Cassini's Division. Other divisions in both Rings A and B have been reported from time to time, but seem to be mere ripples rather than true gaps.

An extra dusky ring, outside Ring A, was announced in 1907 by French observers. Further reports of it have been made occasionally, but its reality must be regarded as highly dubious.

The rings cannot be solid or liquid sheets, for they lie within the volume of space in which a solid ring would be disrupted by the planet's powerful gravity. In 1895, it was established spectroscopically that the inner sections of the rings rotate more rapidly than the outer parts, so that the whole system must be made up of swarms of particles that are too small to be seen independently. The composition of these particles is not certainly known, but the high albedo and the negligible mass of the ring system indicate that they are made of ice. They may be debris from an old satellite that approached Saturn too closely and was broken up. *Composition of the rings*

The satellites. Saturn has ten satellites. The brightest, Titan, was discovered by Huygens in 1655; Janus, the most elusive and closest to the planet, was found by A. Dollfus in 1966. Data are given in Table 3.

Mimas, Enceladus, and Tethys are of low density—about the same as that of water—and have been described as "snowballs," a term that may be quite appropriate. Ice, frozen ammonia, and other light materials must presumably be present in them. Dione, which is no brighter than Tethys, is much more massive and is probably about as dense as Earth's Moon. Rhea is appreciably larger and brighter, and is easily visible in modest telescopes. Its density is less than that of Dione, but greater than for the rest of the inner satellites (possibly excluding Janus, about which very little is known as yet).

Titan, the largest of the satellites, is about the same size as the planet Mercury, though considerably less dense and massive. Its escape velocity is 1.73 miles per second, and it is the only satellite in the solar system known to possess an atmosphere; in 1943–44 methane bands were photographed in its spectrum, and it was determined that its atmosphere contains about half as much methane as the atmospheres of Jupiter and Saturn. It is able to retain an atmosphere because it is so cold; if the temperature were raised by as little as 100° F, the atmosphere would es-

Table 3: Saturn Satellites

satellite		discoverer, date	mean distance from centre of Saturn (miles)	revolution period (days, hours, minutes)			orbital eccentricity	orbital inclination to Saturn's equator (degrees)	diameter* (miles)	mean opposition magnitude
X	Janus	Dollfus, 1966	98,000	00	17	59	0.0	0.0	190	14
I	Mimas	Herschel, 1789	115,000	00	22	37	0.0202	1.5	300	12.1
II	Enceladus	Herschel, 1789	148,000	01	08	53	0.0045	0.0	350	11.8
III	Tethys	Cassini, 1684	183,000	01	21	19	0.0	1.1	600	10.3
IV	Dione	Cassini, 1684	234,000	02	17	41	0.0022	0.0	600	10.4
V	Rhea	Cassini, 1672	327,000	04	12	25	0.0010	0.3	800	9.8
VI	Titan	Huygens, 1655	758,000	15	22	41	0.0292	0.3	3,000	8.4
VII	Hyperion	Bond, 1848	919,000	21	06	38	0.1042	0.6	300	14.2
VIII	Iapetus	Cassini, 1671	2,210,000	79	07	56	0.0283	14.7	1,100?	var.
IX	Phoebe	Pickering, 1898	8,040,000	550	10		0.1633	150	130	16

*The diameters of the satellites are uncertain, particularly the smaller ones.

scape. Large telescopes can show a certain amount of surface detail on Titan, but the observations are difficult, and nothing can be made out except for a few shadings. The general colour of Titan is distinctly yellowish.

Hyperion, another small body, has no remarkable characteristics, but the eighth satellite, Iapetus, is particularly interesting. It is variable in light and is six times brighter when west of Saturn than when to the east; at its brightest it may surpass Rhea. If its rotation period is equal to its revolution period, as seems probable, it must either be irregular in shape or else have one hemisphere much more reflective than the other. Estimates of its diameter vary between 700 miles and over 1,200 miles.

Phoebe is extremely remote from Saturn and moves in a retrograde direction; its orbit is also highly inclined. The suggestion that it may be a captured asteroid rather than a genuine satellite appears reasonable.

Janus

In December 1966, when the ring system was edge on and the opportunities for observing the inner satellites were particularly good, A. Dollfus at the Pic du Midi Observatory photographed a very faint object that seems to be a new satellite. It has been named Janus. The closeness to Saturn makes it a difficult object, though it was recorded several times during the autumn of 1966 without being recognized as a satellite. As it is visible only during the edgewise presentation of the rings, it will not be seen again until 1980. There is a slight fading of the rings at a position corresponding to a revolution period two-thirds that of Janus.

The satellites can pass in transit across the face of Saturn and can also undergo eclipses and occultations, but these phenomena are difficult to observe except in the case of Titan. On one occasion Rhea was seen in eclipse by the shadow of Titan. Valuable data about ring transparency have also been obtained when Iapetus has been occulted by the ring system. Apart from Iapetus and Phoebe, all the satellites move in almost circular orbits practically in the plane of Saturn's equator. Other faint satellites may exist, but they will be very hard to detect. Even Phoebe, the smallest of Saturn's outer satellites, is very much brighter than the six faint outer satellites of Jupiter.

BIBLIOGRAPHY. The only modern book devoted entirely to the planet is A.F.O'D. ALEXANDER, *The Planet Saturn: A History of Observation, Theory and Discovery* (1962). This work contains a list of all important papers published up to 1962. An account of the discovery of Janus, the tenth satellite of Saturn, may be found in *Sky and Telescope*, 34:136–137 (1967).

(P.Mo.)

Saudi Arabia

Saudi Arabia is a kingdom in southwestern Asia. Its total area is 865,000 square miles (2,240,000 square kilometres), and it occupies some four-fifths of the Arabian Peninsula. The capital is Riyadh. The population, about half of which is nomadic, is estimated by various agencies as between 5,074,000 and 7,740,000. On the east it is bounded by the Persian Gulf (Arabian Gulf) and the Gulf of Oman and on the west by the Red Sea. Fringing the kingdom in a clockwise direction, starting from the east, are Qatar, the United Arab Emirates, Oman, Yemen (Aden), and Yemen (Ṣanʿāʾ) and to the north—Jordan, Iraq, and Kuwait. The northern boundaries are established, as is the boundary with Qatar. The boundary on the northern side of Yemen (Ṣanʿāʾ) was defined by the 1934 Treaty of aṭ-Ṭaʾif, but during the Yemeni civil war of the 1960's, Yemen (Ṣanʿāʾ) renounced the treaty, challenged the boundary, and made claim to Qīzān and Najrān. The border between Saudi Arabia and Kuwait was formerly a neutral zone, until the zone was partitioned and the frontier demarcated in 1969. Other borders are in dispute. Saudi Arabia claims 12 miles of territorial waters, plus the seabed, and jurisdiction over the subsoil beyond this limit. Offshore boundaries have been established with Bahrain (1958) and Iran (1968).

Position in the world

Saudi Arabia is a Muslim state and an Arab state. These two attributes have been a fundamental influence upon the country's foreign relations. It is a member of the Arab League and has made attempts to form an Islāmic Congress that would transcend the limits of the Arab world. At the same time, its foreign policy, like that of other states, is based primarily on self-interest and sometimes reflects the caprices and paradoxes of international affairs. In the mid-1960s, for instance, Saudi Arabia and the United Arab Republic supported opposite sides in the civil war in Yemen (Ṣanʿāʾ); yet after the Arab–Israeli Six Day War in June 1967, Saudi Arabia contributed money to compensate for the United Arab Republic's loss of revenue because of the closing of the Suez Canal. Nevertheless, the kingdom continues to be isolationist rather than otherwise. A person can secure a visa to visit it only if invited by an individual or an organization within the country. Once inside, a visitor encounters a pervading sense of independence and pride.

Yet change has not bypassed Saudi Arabia. The possession of Mecca and Medina, the two holiest cities of Islām, has always provided the country with outside contacts, and such contacts have been hastened by innovations in transportation technology and organization. More recently, the oil era has wrought irreversible domestic changes—educational and social, as well as economic. The 10,000 Saudi Arabs employed by Aramco (the Arabian American Oil Company) are exposed to modern industrial skills, technology, and methods of organization. This influence cannot help affecting, in turn, the rest of society. Television is increasingly becoming a medium for education and entertainment and a force for social change. Highways, airways, and a railroad are replacing traditional means of movement, notably the camel caravan. Thus, whereas to the outside world Saudi Arabia appears secluded behind a wall of traditionalism, from within the country there is now access, as it were, to windows that offer an outside perspective (see the city article MECCA). An associated physical feature can be found in ARABIAN DESERT and historical aspects in ARABIA, HISTORY OF.

THE LANDSCAPE

Physiography. *Relief.* The Arabian Peninsula is dominated by a plateau that rises abruptly from the Red Sea and dips gently towards the Persian Gulf. In the north, the western highlands are upward of 5,000 feet above sea level, decreasing slightly to 4,000 feet in the vicinity of Medina, and increasing southeastward to over 10,000 feet. The watershed of the peninsula is only 25 miles from the Red Sea in the north, receding to 80 miles near the Yemen (Ṣanʿāʾ) border. The coastal plain, known as Tihāmah, is virtually nonexistent in the north, except for occasional wadi (water courses, which may remain dry for several years) deltas, and widens slightly towards the south. Water courses flowing to the Red Sea are short and steep, with one unusually long inland extension made by Wādī al-Ḥamḍ, which rises near Medina. The imposing scarp, running parallel to the Red Sea, is somewhat interrupted by a gap northeast of Mecca but becomes more clearly continuous southward.

Toward the interior, the surface gradually descends into a broad plateau covered with extensive lava flows and volcanic debris as well as with occasional sand accumulations; its average elevation is about 4,000 feet. Here the drainage is more clearly dendritic (patterned like the branches of a tree) and is much more extensive than that flowing toward the Red Sea. To the east, this region is bounded by a series of cuestas (long, low ridges, with steep slopes on one side, and gentle slopes on the other) 750 miles long and curving eastward from north to south, with west-facing escarpments. The most prominent of these cuestas is Jabal Ṭuwayq, some 2,800 feet above sea level, which rises to more than 3,500 feet southwest of Riyadh, overlooking the surface to the west by 800 feet and more.

The
Empty
Quarter

The interior of the Arabian Peninsula contains extensive sand surfaces. Among them is the world's largest continuous sand area—Rubʿ al-Khali (or Empty Quarter), which dominates the southern part of the kingdom and covers 250,000 square miles. It slopes from above 3,400 feet near the Yemen (Ṣanʿāʾ) border northeastward down almost to sea level on the Trucial Coast; individual sand mountains rise to 800 feet. A smaller sand area of about 22,000 square miles, called an-Nafūd, is in the north central part of the country at about the latitude of the Gulf of Aqaba. A great arc of sand, almost 900 miles long and only about 30 miles wide, joins an-Nafūd with Rubʿ al-Khali; this is ad-Dahnāʾ. Eastward, as the plateau surface slopes very gradually down to the gulf, there are numerous salt flats (sabkhahs) and marshes. The coastline of the gulf is irregular, and the coastal waters are very shallow.

Geology. Geologically, the country may be divided into two regions—one composed of rocks that are crystalline and metamorphic (changed in structure by heat and pressure) and the other of sedimentary rocks. The crystalline-metamorphic series is of Precambrian age (from 4,600,000,000 to 570,000,000 years old) and occupies the western third of the country. Volcanic flows and cinder cones that are probably about 2,500,000 years old or less, are present here, and occasionally intrude and overlie the Tertiary sediments (from 65,000,000 to 7,000,000 years old) in the north. The sedimentary rocks surrounding the Precambrian rocks on the northwest, east, and southwest, range in age from Cambrian-Ordovician (from 570,000,000 to 430,000,000 years old) to Tertiary. They dip gently toward the Persian Gulf, where they exceed 20,000 feet in thickness. Saudi Arabia's vast petroleum reserves occur in rocks of Cretaceous and Jurassic age (*i.e.*, from 190,000,000 to 65,000,000 years old).

Drainage. There are no permanent surface streams in the country, but wadis are numerous. Those leading to the Red Sea are short and deep, but those draining eastward are longer and are more developed, except in the enormous sand regions of an-Nafūd and Rubʿ al-Khali. Soils are poorly developed and reflect in composition the rocks from which they were formed, such as the volcanic rocks in the west. Large areas are covered with pebbles of different sizes. Alluvial deposits are found in wadis, basins, and oases. Salt flats are especially common in the east.

Climate. Climatically, the kingdom is almost entirely a desert. In winter, cyclone systems (large-scale atmospheric wind and pressure systems, with low pressure at the centre and characterized by a circular counterclockwise, wind motion in the Northern Hemisphere) skirt the Arabian Peninsula, moving from the Eastern Mediterranean region to the Tigris-Euphrates region. Some cyclones move southward along the Red Sea trough and provide some winter precipitation as far south as Mecca, and apparently even as far as Yemen (Ṣanʿāʾ). In March and April some rain falls, normally torrential. In summer the highlands of Asir, to the southeast of Mecca, receive enough rain from the monsoonal winds from the west and southwest to result in a strip of steppe conditions (more than 10 inches of rainfall annually), tapering northward from Yemen (Ṣanʿāʾ).

Winters, from December to February in Saudi Arabia are cool, and frost and snow occur in the southern highlands. Average temperatures for the coolest months of January and February are 74° F (23° C) at Jidda, 58° F (14° C) at Riyadh, and 63° F (17° C) at ad-Dammām. Summers, from June to August, are hot, with daytime shade temperatures exceeding 100° F (38° C) in almost all of the country, and frequently reaching 120° F (49° C). Humidity is low, except along the coasts, where it can be very oppressive. Average temperatures for the warmest months are 90° F (32° C) at Jidda, 93° F (34° C) at Riyadh, and 94° F at ad-Dammām. Precipitation is low throughout the country, amounting to about two and a half inches at Jidda, a little over three inches at Riyadh, and three inches at ad-Dammām; these figures, however, represent mean precipitation, and large variations are normal. In the highlands of Asir more than 15 inches a year are received, falling during the summer when the monsoon winds prevail. In Rubʿ al-Khali, a decade may pass with no rain whatsoever.

There are three climatic zones: (a) desert almost everywhere, (b) steppe (an extensive treeless plain) along the western highlands, forming a strip less than 100 miles in the north but becoming almost 300 miles wide at the latitude of Mecca, and (c) a very small area of humid mesothermal conditions (medium ranges of temperature and pressure), with long summers, located in the highlands just north of Yemen (Ṣanʿāʾ).

Three
climate
zones

Vegetation and animal life. Saudi Arabia's vegetation belongs to the North African and Indian desert floristic region, and is characterized by a small number of species; there are only about 370 species in the country. The plants are xerophytic (adapted to dry conditions), and are mostly small herbs and shrubs that are valuable as forage. Animal life includes wolves, hyenas, foxes, honey badgers, mongooses, porcupines, hedgehogs, hares, sand rats, and jerboas. Such larger animals as the gazelles, oryxes, leopards, ostriches, and mountain sheep seem to have been relatively numerous until quite recently. Birds include eagles, hawks, falcons, vultures, owls, ravens, flamingos, egrets, pelicans, doves, and quail, as well as sandgrouse and bulbuls (a species of songbird). Five species of harmless snakes have been identified. Domesticated animals include camels, fat-tailed sheep, long-eared goats, saluki hounds, donkeys, and chickens. The Arabian horse is now bred by a few rich individuals and by the Ministry of Agriculture and used for special occasions such as shows and parades.

The landscape under human settlement. *Traditional regions.* Four traditional regions stand out—the Hejaz, the Asir, the Najd, and al-Hasa. The Hejaz is in the northern part of western Saudi Arabia. It contains the two holiest cities of Islām, Mecca and Medina, as well as the kingdom's primary port and diplomatic centre, Jidda. Asir is the highland region south of Hejaz. Its capital, Abhā, is at an elevation of about 8,000 feet. Subregions in Asir are formed by the oasis cluster of Najrān, a highland area east of the Yemen (Ṣanʿāʾ), and by the coastal plain of Tihāmah. Najd occupies a large part of the interior, which includes the capital of Riyadh. Al-Hasa, now known as the Eastern Province, is in the east along the Persian Gulf; it includes the principal petroleum producing areas as well as parts of Rubʿ al-Khali.

The cultural landscape. Saudi Arabia is dominantly pastoral: over one third of the total area is pastureland and about half of the population is engaged in herding. Less than one percent of the area is under crops, although almost a quarter of the population are cultiva-

Pastoral-
ism

tors. Amongst the pastoralists, less than half (about 20 percent of the total population) are nomadic camel herders, and the number is decreasing. The rest are seminomads who raise sheep and goats for meat and wool. Agriculture is acquiring increasing importance because of governmental land reclamation programs of irrigation and the planting of vegetation to alter the ecology, especially in the Eastern Province. Pastoral nomadism is widespread, from the Eastern Province through the Najd to the northern Hejaz. Seminomadism is more clearly associated with the better watered pastures, such as occur in the southern Hejaz and in the Asir. More areas are under cultivation in the Asir than elsewhere because of the more plentiful and more reliable water supply there; the narrow Tihāmah Plain along the Red Sea is especially fertile. The Eastern Province contains the country's largest concentration of oases, which are centred on al-Hufūf and supplied by an extensive artesian-well system. The principal crops cultivated are wheat, alfalfa, millet, maize, fruit, and dates. With increasing prosperity and attendant dietary changes, dates are giving way to vegetables, melons, market-garden crops, and such fodders as alfalfa.

The larger towns are cosmopolitan in character. Some are associated with definite functions: Mecca and Medina are religious; Riyadh is political and administrative; and Jidda is commercial and financial.

PEOPLE AND POPULATION

Language. Arabic is a Semitic language, and its home is Saudi Arabia. It is here that the language is presumed to be the "purest." Classical Arabic is standard throughout the Arab world, while spoken Arabic varies considerably. Such colloquial variations are evident even within Saudi Arabia—in part because of the strength of traditional group allegiances that limit intermixture, and in part because of different external influences, which are prevalent in different parts of the kingdom. These differences, however, should not be overemphasized. English is gradually becoming understood, especially in the Eastern Province, where the oil industry is located, as well as in the commercial and diplomatic centre of Jidda.

Ethnic groups. Considerable ethnic uniformity is also evident. Saudi nomads are "pure" Arabs, or at least descendants therefrom. As in the case of language, variations have developed because of a long history of regionalism and of tribal autonomy. At the same time, some localities have been subjected to important outside influences. Thus, the influence of black Africa is evident along the Red Sea littoral and influences from Iran, Pakistan, and India can be noticed in the east. Blacks from Africa, intermixed with Semitic stock, live along the Red Sea coast; they appear to have the lowest social status. Two other groups, numerically small but economically important are the non-Saudi Arabs, and the Americans and Europeans, both resident aliens and both associated with the recent boom in the oil industry and various associated activities. The non-Saudi Arabs tend to be Palestinians, Jordanians, Lebanese, and Syrians. There are more Americans than Europeans; most are employed by Aramco. The annual influx of pilgrims, presently numbering half a million a year, must also be noted. The pilgrims come from as far away as the shores of the Atlantic and Pacific; they stay mostly in the vicinity of Jidda and Mecca.

Religion. Saudi Arabia is the home of Islām, and its population is almost entirely Sunnī Muslim. (*i.e.*, adhering to the chief branch of Islām, called traditionalist or orthodox). The Sunnī Muslims recognize four orthodox schools of classical law—the Ḥanbalī (the most rigid), the Ḥanafī (the most liberal), the Shāfi'ī, and the Mālikī. The puritan Wahhābī sect, which was founded in the 18th century in the Najd and represents the Ḥanbalī school of thought, is dominant. Wahhābism is also well represented in the Eastern Province, the Hejaz, and the Asir, where it is especially strong in the towns. The Ḥanafī school is represented in the areas that reflect Turkish influence—the Eastern Province and the Hejaz. Also in the Eastern Province are Mālikīs, while Shāfi'īs live in the Hejaz and the Asir. In the Asir the strict Idrīsid sect is also found. There are some 100,000 Shī'ites (a

Margin note: Ethnic uniformity

Muslim sect who recognize 'Ali to have been the legitimate caliph after the death of the Prophet), particularly Ja'farīs, in al-Hasa and al-Qaṭīf oases in the east. Other Shī'ite groups are the Makramīs, once established in Najrān in southern Asir near Yemen (Ṣan'ā') and the Zaydīs, represented near Mecca. Christianity is limited to noncitizens, chiefly the oil industry employees.

Demography. A census of population was taken in 1962–63, but the results have not been made public, nor has the total figure been released. United Nations and United States data use a total population figure ranging from 5,074,000 to 7,740,000, although some scholars and other informed persons use lower estimates. About three-fourths of the population is rural and one-fourth urban. Major cities and estimated populations are: Riyadh 300,-000; Mecca 250,000; Jidda 300,000; Medina 72,000; and aṭ-Ṭā'if 54,000. Vital statistics can only be speculated about, but conventional demographic methodology suggests that both birth rates and death rates are high, with an estimated annual rate of population growth of 2.8 percent. This rate, if maintained, would double the population before the end of the century. The migration factor is small but includes those pilgrims who remain in the country and students abroad who elect not to return. Three areas of relatively high population density are noticeable: (1) along the east coast, especially in the settlements of al-Hasa oasis and the oil industry; (2) in the interior, especially northwestward from Riyadh, and where settlements are frequently associated with springs and wadis in the escarpment zone; and (3) along the west coast and highlands, mostly south of the latitude of Medina, especially in the Asir.

THE NATIONAL ECONOMY

Resources. The economy of Saudi Arabia is dominated by oil and its associated industries. The country's known reserves, amounting to an estimated 150,000,-000,000 barrels, comprise one quarter of the total proved reserves in the world, ranking the kingdom first in the world in the volume of known deposits. The amount of reserves is likely to continue to be revised upward for many years. Saudi Arabia's production of about 1,740,-000,000 barrels a year ranks it third in output in the world, after the United States and the Soviet Union.

Oil deposits are in the east. They are located southward from Iraq and Kuwait into Rub' al-Khali, and along and under the Persian Gulf. Half of the reserves are in the giant Ghawār field of Eastern Province. Numerous other mineral resources are known to exist; among these are gold, silver, iron, copper, zinc, manganese, tungsten,

Margin note: The dominance of oil

Saudi Arabia, Area and Population			
	area*		population†
Provinces (*manāṭiq ĭdārīyah*)	sq mi	sq km	1970 estimate
'Afīf	20,000	50,000	...
al-Jawf	75,000	200,000	...
al-Khāṣirah	10,000	25,000	...
al-Madīnah	55,000	140,000	...
al-Maṭaqah ash-Sharqīyah	220,000	570,000	...
al-Qaṣīm	35,000	95,000	...
al-Qurayyāt	5,000	15,000	...
ar-Riyāḍ	165,000	425,000	...
'Asīr (Asir)	25,000	70,000	...
Baljarshī	10,000	20,000	
Bīshah	15,000	40,000	...
Ḥā'il	75,000	195,000	
Makkah	50,000	135,000	...
Minṭaqat al-Ḥudūd ash-Shamālīyah	55,000	140,000	...
Najrān	30,000	80,000	...
Qīzān	5,000	20,000	...
Ranyah	10,000	30,000	...
Total Saudi Arabia	865,000‡	2,240,000‡	7,740,000§

*Areas approximate. †No complete census of individuals has ever been conducted by Saudi Arabia. ‡Area figures do not add to total given because of rounding. §United Nations estimate. Other estimates range downward to about 5,000,000. No breakdown by province available.
Source: Official government figures; UN.

lead, sulfur, phosphate, soapstone, asbestos, and feldspar. They are scattered in the highlands of Hejaz and of Asir and in the central and western Najd, but their extent is largely unknown, and production is virtually nil. As mentioned earlier, vegetation and animal resources are very limited. Not surprisingly, until recently hydroelectric power has been totally absent. The Jidda desalination plant has a daily production of 5,000,000 gallons of fresh water and produces 50,000 kilowatt hours of electricity. Coal is not known to exist in usable quantities.

Sources of national income. Oil accounts for about 85 percent of the government's revenues. In 1965 the rate of increase in oil production was about 16 percent, and in 1966 about 18 percent more than in preceding years. But the 1967 war in the Middle East, with the concomitant closure of the Suez Canal and the subsequent interruption of the oil flow along Tapline (the Trans-Arabian Pipeline), resulted in a lowering of the rate of increase in the years that followed. In the early 1970s indications were that the rate of production had again begun to increase. Of Saudi Arabia's production, about 93 percent is accounted for by Aramco. Oil's crucial role in the kingdom's economy is expected to continue for many years.

Prospecting continues for other mineral resources. An offshore natural gas field has been discovered some 20 miles southeast of the entrance to the Gulf of Aqaba. Potentially productive copper, zinc, and iron ore deposits have been discovered in the Arabian Shield, which comprises the central and western provinces.

The fertilizer industry

Manufacturing. Manufacturing activity, other than petroleum refining, includes a nascent fertilizer industry; in 1970, the first consignment of fertilizer was exported to Iran from the plant at ad-Dammām harbour. The plant's daily capacity is 1,100 tons of urea (a compound used as a fertilizer), 600 tons of ammonia, and as many as 50 tons of liquid sulfur. A steel rolling mill in Jidda opened in 1967, producing reinforced bars; annual capacity is being expanded from 45,000 to 70,000 tons, and it is also intended that the mill be made capable of smelting iron ore and producing steel ingots by the mid-1970s. An oil refinery was completed at Jidda in 1968, with a planned capacity of 33,000 barrels a day, and another in Riyadh, with a daily capacity of 15,000 barrels, due for completion in the early 1970s. A new petroleum products plant in Jidda was completed in 1971, with an initial annual capacity of 75,000 barrels. Cement plants are located at Jidda, Riyadh, and al-Hufūf.

Foreign trade. During the decade preceding the 1967 Middle East war, Saudi Arabia's imports increased annually at a little over 11 percent. An erratic period ensued, but by 1969 import figures suggested a resumption of the prewar rate of increase. Three quarters of the imports come from nine industrial countries, with the United States alone contributing about 20 percent. Others are Japan (about 10 percent), Lebanon (10 percent), the United Kingdom (9 percent), and West Germany (8 percent). Almost 30 percent of the imports are foodstuffs, 15 percent motor vehicles, 13 percent machinery and appliances, and 13 percent building materials. Of Saudi Arabia's exports, which are overwhelmingly dominated by petroleum products, about 45 percent go to Western Europe (more than half of which is to Common Market countries), 30 percent to Asia (Japan alone accounts for over 20 percent), and less than 5 percent to North America. Exports to Europe and Asia have doubled from 1965 to 1970.

Transportation. Saudi Arabia is a large country with a sparse, widely dispersed population. Nowhere in the kingdom is there anything approaching a transportation network. Modern means of transport are a very recent phenomenon, although domestic air travel is being developed fairly rapidly. This sector of the economy has been accorded a high priority: in 1970 transportation and communications were allocated more than a quarter of the development budget, and this amount is six times that allocated only eight years earlier.

Road routes

In 1951 Saudi Arabia had fewer than 30 miles of paved roads. In 1971 there were 7,767 miles with 1,560 miles under construction and almost 4,000 miles more projected. There are also more than 1,500 miles of rural roads. The first coast to coast connection, from ad-Dammām on the Persian Gulf to Jidda on the Red Sea, by way of Riyadh, was opened in 1967; it includes a spectacular descent of the western escarpment from aṭ-Ṭā'if to Mecca. Another trans-peninsular connection is from the Eastern Province to Jordan, with the road running parallel to the Tapline. Other important connections recently built or due to be completed in the early 1970s are (1) from Riyadh northwestward into the Najd, (2) between the central Najd and Medina, (3) from Medina northwestward into the interior of the Hejaz and southwestward to the Red Sea, (4) from aṭ-Ṭā'if southeastward along the plateau edge into the Asir, and (5) from the Najrān region in the southern Asir northeastward to Riyadh.

The country's only railroad, ad-Dammān-Riyadh line, passes through al-Hufūf, Ḥaraḍ, and the al-Kharj Oasis. This 357-mile railroad was completed in 1951. The Saudi and Jordanian governments are planning the reconstruction of the section of the "Hejaz Railway," abandoned during World War I, that ran between Ma'ān in southern Jordan and Medina.

Major ports

The country's three main ports are Jidda, ad-Dammām, and Yanbu'; they currently handle about 2,000 ships a year and almost 2,000,000 tons of cargo. Yanbu' (also called Yanbu' al-Bahr) is easing some of the pressure on Jidda, and facilities for handling increasing numbers of pilgrims are being constructed there. Qīzān is a small port on the Red Sea, at the border with Yemen (Ṣan'ā'). Al-Qaṭīf, 12 miles north of ad-Dammām, is being developed for maintenance operations, and at al-Jubayl, 40 miles further north, fishing facilities are being developed.

The Saudi Arabian Airlines, initially attached to the

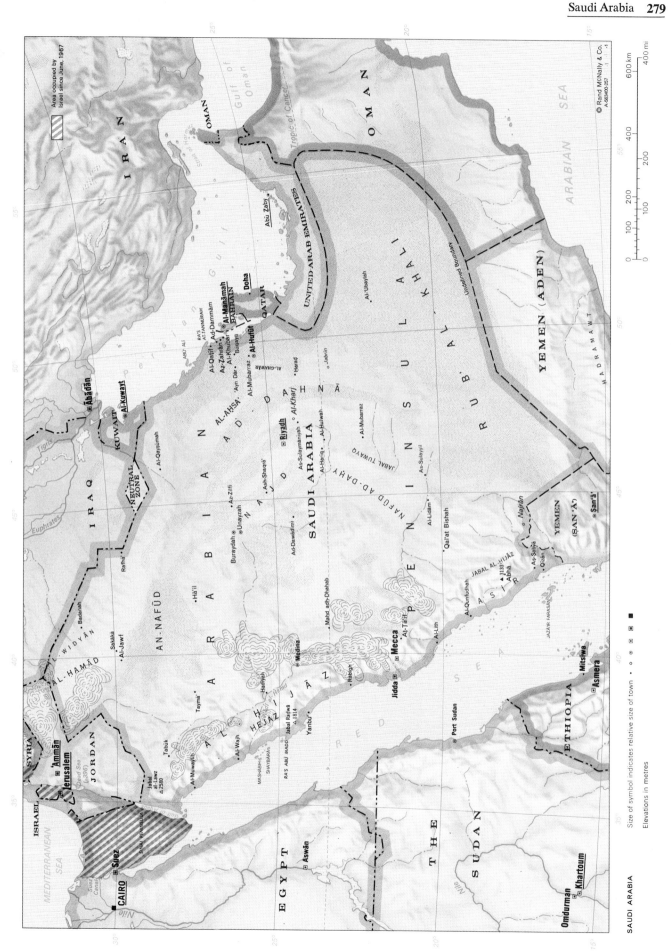

SAUDI ARABIA

Size of symbol indicates relative size of town · ○ ⊙ ◉ ◙ ■

Elevations in metres

Area occupied by
Israel since June, 1967

© Rand McNally & Co.
A-563400257 -1

0   100   200   400   600 km
0   100   200   400 mi

ISRAEL
JORDAN
SYRIA
'Amman
Jerusalem
Suez
CAIRO
EGYPT
Aswân
SINAI PENINSULA
Suez Canal
Nile
MEDITERRANEAN SEA
Dead Sea (-396)
Jabal al-Lawz △2580
Tabūk
Al-Muwajib
Al-Wajh
SHAYBĀRA
RAS ABU MADD
MASHĀBIH
Tayma'
Yanbu'
Jabal Radwā △1814
Madīnah
Hadīyah
Rābigh
Jidda
Mecca
Al-Tā'if
Al-Lith
Mahd adh-Dhahab
Al-Quntudhah
Al-Lidām
Qal'at Bishah
Abha △3133
As-Sabyā
Qizān
JAZA'IR FARASĀN
Najrān
YEMEN (SAN'Ā')
San'ā'
YEMEN (ADEN)
HADRAMAWT
ARABIAN SEA
ETHIOPIA
Asmera
Mitsiwa
THE SUDAN
Omdurman
Khartoum
Port Sudan
RED SEA
AL HIJĀZ
JABAL AL-HIJĀZ
ASIR
AD-DAHY
NAFŪD AD-DAHY
Rafhā'
Badanah
AL-HAMĀD
WIDYĀN
Sakākā
Al-Jawf
AN NAFŪD
Hā'il
Burāydah
Unayzah
Ad-Dawādimi
Ash-Shaqrā'
Az-Zilfi
Al-Qaysūmah
KUWAIT
Al-Kuwayt
Ābādān
NEUTRAL ZONE
IRAQ
Tigris
Euphrates
IRAN
Gulf of Oman
Strait of Hormuz
OMAN
RA'S AL-TANNŪRAH
Ad-Dammām
Al-Khubar
Az-Zahrān
Al-Qatīf
ABU 'ALĪ
Buqayq
'Ayn Dār
Al-Mubarraz
Al-Hufūf
AL-AHSA
AL-GHAWĀR
Harad
Jabrīn
Al-Manāmah
BAHRAIN
Doha
QATAR
UNITED ARAB EMIRATES
Abu Zaby
Al-'Ubaylah
AR RUB' AL KHĀLĪ
Undefined Boundary
Tropic of Cancer
ARABIAN PENINSULA
AD DAHNĀ
JABAL TUWAYQ
Riyadh
As-Sulaymānīyah
Al-Khari
Al-Hariq
Al-Huwaiah
Al-Mubarraz
As-Sulayyil
SAUDI ARABIA

© Rand McNally & Co.
A-563400257 -1

Ministry of Defense, became a semi-autonomous corporation in 1963. It has a technical and management arrangement with Trans World Airlines of the United States. There are international airports at Dhahran, Riyadh, and Jidda, and several domestic airports in various parts of the country. The airline's headquarters and training centre are at Jidda.

ADMINISTRATION AND SOCIAL CONDITIONS

The structure of government. Saudi Arabia's constitutional basis is the law of Islām, or the Sharī'ah, based on Muḥammad's pronouncements and on the traditions of Islām's first adherents. Muslim law prescribes civil as well as religious rights, duties, obligations, and responsibilities, insofar as these apply to both ruler and ruled. Law is revealed and not created, and it is interpreted by the 'ulamā', or learned religious men. A reserve of power resides in the monarch, acting through his Council of Ministers.

The monarchy The person of the king (Faisal) combines legislative, executive, and judicial functions. The Council of Ministers is a legislative body, although it is also responsible for such executive and administrative matters as foreign and domestic policy, defense, finance, health, and education. Appointment to the Council is a royal prerogative, as is dismissal; prospective members must first swear allegiance to the king. The king has veto power over Council decisions unless he fails to act within 30 days. The Council has considerable authority for the supervision of regional and local government. The kingdom is administratively divided into 17 *manāṭiq idārīyah* (provinces), and local officials of the central government report directly to the ministries in Riyadh. Provincial governors are responsible for such functions as finance, health, education, agriculture, and municipalities. The consultative principle operates at all levels of government, including the government of villages and tribes.

Justice. The Sharī'ah law is the basis of justice. Judgment is according to the Ḥanbalī tradition of Islām; the law thus tends to be conservative and the punishment severe. Rapid changes of the last two or three decades have produced circumstances—such as traffic violations and industrial accidents—not encompassed by the traditional law, and these have been handled by the issuance of royal decrees, which, in turn, have evolved into a body of administrative laws. Avenues of appeal are available, and the monarch is both the final court of appeal and the dispenser of pardon.

The White Army **The armed forces.** The Saudi armed forces consist of the regular army and the national guard, the latter popularly known as the White Army. The regular army numbers 35,000 and the White Army 30,000. Both are sources of employment and education; the White Army is the more prestigious. It is a highly mobile, lightly armed force that can move quickly to restore internal order. The air force, which has a strength of 5,000, has been extensively re-equipped since 1966, mostly with British and some United States equipment. There are some 100 aircraft (including supersonic fighters, strike aircraft, transports, helicopters, and trainers), plus surface to air missiles. The navy numbers 1,000 men.

Education. Education is free at all levels and is receiving increasing emphasis and attention. In the five years after 1965, budget allocations for education increased 47 percent. During this period more than 600 new schools were opened—about 400 for boys and amost 200 for girls. There has been a relatively rapid increase in education for girls in recent years. There are also 600 adult education schools. It was expected that universal primary education for boys would be achieved by the mid-1970s, and for girls, by 1980. The government also grants scholarships for the education of Saudi students overseas, of whom, by 1970, there were some 2,000.

There are three universities that specialize in Islāmic studies. The University of Riyadh was founded in 1957 and has 3,500 students; the Islāmic University at Medina, founded in 1961, has 1,000 students; the King 'Abd al-'Azīz Private University in Jidda, founded in 1967, has 440 students. Other institutes include the

Higher Institute of Technology, the Higher Juridical Institute, the King 'Abd al-'Azīz Military Academy, the College for the Arabic Language, the Technical Institute, and the College of Islāmic Jurisprudence, all at Riyadh; the College of Petroleum and Minerals at Dhahran; School of Ḥadīth (narrative traditions), the Sharī'ah College of Islāmic Jurisprudence and the Saudi Arabian Institute for Higher Education, all at Mecca; the School of Applied Arts and the Teacher Training Centre (both at Medina); and schools of industrial education at Riyadh, Jidda, Medina, and ad-Dammām. Institutes for religious teaching are located in at least 20 cities and towns.

Health. Health and medical services are satisfactory in terms of equipment, but the local staffing is still inadequate. There are almost 90 hospitals, 200 dispensaries, 300 health centres, and almost 800 doctors. Medical treatment is still limited to the larger towns, however, and folk practitioners abound. The Jidda Quarantine Centre, built for Muslim pilgrims, forms a large complex that can house 2,400 patients.

Social and economic divisions. Traditionally, social and economic divisions may be thought of as occurring in an ecological trinity composed of the nomads, the villagers, and the townsmen. Pervading this trinity, however, is the patrilineal kinship principle, and superimposed on all is the administrative organization. The kinship principle is most pronounced among the nomads, who are organized along tribal and subtribal lines. Villages constitute local service centres and usually contain representatives from more than one tribe, though one family will be dominant. Towns are not tribally organized, though local affairs still tend to be dominated and administered by a few families. Social stratification is much more clearly developed in the towns than elsewhere. Before the impact of oil on the economy, status was a matter of lineage and occupation rather than of wealth, but with the development of the oil industry, wealth and material position have acquired social value. The new technology and industry have produced a growing middle income economic group that is increasingly aware of the widening gap between the ruling elite and the rest of the population. Thus, the traditional links between the upper and lower levels of Saudi society are being disrupted, and substitutes have not yet evolved. *Nomads, villagers and townsmen*

CULTURAL LIFE AND INSTITUTIONS

The cultural milieu. The cultural setting is Arab and Muslim. For a thousand years artistic expression usually consisted of perpetuating ancient forms. From the 18th century onward the strict Wahhābī religious outlook discouraged intellectual deviations from accepted purist positions, and the nomadic life greatly limited the development of nonportable art forms. The theatre and public cinema do not exist. With the oil industry came exposure to outside influences, such as housing styles, furnishings, and clothes, and at the same time local craftsmen found themselves in competition with imported goods.

Intellectual activity is dominated by religious studies, though influences from other Arab countries are filtering in, and Saudi students who study abroad are exposed to radically different milieus. Poetry and formal prose, including speech, have been among the highest of arts since pre-Islāmic days, and poets and peripatetic storytellers abound today. Literary works now appear in newspapers and periodicals, though the nomad and the illiterate villager still have their own body of folk literature consisting of stories and proverbs in prose and verse. Music and dance have always been part of Saudi everyday life, though the strict Wahhābī code forbids their public expression. Music traditionally consists of ballads. The themes are those of traditional poetry—war, love, bravery, virtues, animals, and religion. Dance is associated with folk music. It is usually performed not by individuals and certainly not by couples but by groups at festive occasions such as holidays, weddings, and circumcisions. Visual arts are limited to geometric, floral, and abstract designs and to ornate calligraphy; these can be very intricate indeed. Saudi Arabia's decorative art has, nevertheless, not developed as much as elsewhere in the Arab and *Traditional arts*

Muslim world. Architecture also has been simple, with designs on doors and windows, and with a tendency to build crenelated walls. There are variations in the construction material, such as mud bricks, limestone, coral rock, and reinforced cement. The recent wave of change has influenced architectural styles, so that "modern" stark, linear motifs are becoming common in office and residential buildings, as well as at airports and tourist hotels. Crafts are limited to such products as textiles, brass ware, copper ware, jewelry, wooden articles, pottery, baskets, mats, leatherwork, and weaving.

Press and broadcasting. There are five Arabic daily newspapers (three in Jidda, and one each in Riyadh and Mecca) with a combined circulation exceeding 50,000. There are 13 weeklies in Arabic (four in Mecca, four in Riyadh, two in ad-Dammām, and one each in Jidda, al-Khubar, and Dhahran and three in English (published in Jidda, Mecca, and by Aramco). There are five Arabic monthly periodicals (two in Riyadh, two in Jidda, and one in Mecca). One monthly periodical (*New Eve*) is a women's magazine.

There are two radio and two television services, one of each operated by the Ministry of Information and by Aramco. The content of programs is frequently religious and literary.

PROSPECTS FOR THE FUTURE

During the past two decades Saudi Arabia experienced enormously greater and more rapid changes than it had encountered for several centuries. The traditional tribal behaviour patterns—for long decentralized into mobile clusters—are today being exposed to alien cultures and technologies, which are making irreversible impacts, both on the cultural landscape and on mental perspectives. Such influences are spatially uneven, and the direction of their diffusion is not always clear. Eastern Province, where the oil industry is located, comes first to mind, and the changes that have been wrought there are certainly phenomenal. Dhahran is a pleasant suburban community in the American style, with wide roads, lawns, and trees. It seems out of place, for in the whole country there is nothing else like it. There is even a golf course, though the "greens" are black, consisting of hardened crude oil, which has been spread over a smoothed desert surface. Ad-Dammām, al-Khubar, al-Qaṭīf, Abqaiq, and other places are all secondary diffusion centres for new influences, and together with such other cities as Jidda and Riyadh are exerting a magnetic effect on the people of the desert. Bedouins come to the towns, perhaps first as individuals, but soon as families: almost invariably the movement is one way. Tribal ties tend to loosen, no matter how much the affiliation may still be felt and despite the fact that tribal members certainly remain alien to urban life. The Bedouins, therefore, witness the evolving social and economic rifts between their earlier world and the new, while finding it difficult to blend into the new milieu. Their lot is not so different from that of other migrants: they become rootless, often frustrated.

Saudi Arabia's historic isolation is now at an end. Change is clearly the norm. The powerful traditional religious mores and convictions remain, and are all-pervading. But the pull of new ideas and new material values is also strong and is increasing. A shot fired in Palestine reverberates to the fringes of Rubʿ al-Khali. A speech given in Cairo causes a stir in the heart of the Najd. Saudis are caught in the political cross-currents, both as individuals and as groups. More and more the physical horizon is the beginning, and not the end, of their curiosity. Dislocations and disruptions will continue —social, economic, ideological, and moral. What remains problematical is the way Saudi Arabia will be affected by the strain.

BIBLIOGRAPHY. ARABIAN AMERICAN OIL COMPANY, *Aramco Handbook: Oil and the Middle East,* rev. ed. (1968), historical surveys of the Middle East and of the oil industry, with emphasis on the government, people, land, and customs of Saudi Arabia, and on Aramco; GEORGE A. LIPSKY, *Saudi Arabia: Its People, Its Society, Its Culture* (1959), a standard reference work, extensive and balanced; "Saudi Ara-

bia," in *The Middle East and North Africa* (annual), a survey containing statistical tables, and information on government, press, finance, economy, and education; *Emergent Nations,* vol. 2, no 2 (Summer 1966), an issue devoted to Saudi Arabia; *Aramco World Magazine* (monthly), emphasis on Saudi Arabia, oil, the Arab world, and Islām (wide ranging, but excludes politics); *Middle East Journal* (quarterly), regular features include a chronology of events, and a bibliography of periodical literature; OXFORD REGIONAL ECONOMIC ATLAS, *The Middle East and North Africa* (1960), topical and regional maps, with supplementary notes and tables; KINGDOM OF SAUDI ARABIA, SAUDI ARABIAN MONETARY AGENCY, *Annual Report,* emphasis on economic developments; KINGDOM OF SAUDI ARABIA, MINISTRY OF PETROLEUM AND MINERAL RESOURCES, *Economic Geographic Map of the Arabian Peninsula,* 1:4,000,000 (1970); YUSIF A. SAYIGH, "Problems and Prospects of Development in the Arabian Peninsula," *International Journal of Middle East Studies,* 2:40–58 (1971), an appraisal of the economy, with special reference to oil.

(B.K.N.)

Saul

The first king of Israel (*c.* 1020–1000 BC), Saul instituted the Israelites' experiment with monarchy that culminated in the illustrious kingdom of David.

The account of Saul's life comes from the Old Testament book of I Samuel (9–31; there is also an account of his death in I Chron. 10). The son of Kish, a well-to-do member of the tribe of Benjamin, he was made king by the league of 12 Israelite tribes in a desperate effort to strengthen Hebrew resistance to the growing Philistine threat. (The Philistines were a people of Aegean origin who settled in the coastal region and contended with the Israelites for control of Palestine.) For roughly two centuries, since the days of Joshua, the successor of Moses as leader of Israel, Israel had existed as a loose confederation of tribes, dependent for their unity upon bonds of religious faith and covenant that were renewed periodically in cultic ceremonies at the central shrine at Shiloh. The Book of Judges attests to the effectiveness of these religious ties in uniting the tribes behind charismatic leaders (judges) in time of enemy attack. By Saul's day, however, the tribal rallies were no match for the superior iron weapons and chariots of the Philistines, who, no longer confined to the southern Palestinian coast, were pressing ever deeper into the central highlands.

Two literary strands are discernible in the accounts in I Samuel involving Saul. One of these (9:1–10:16), reflecting a favourable attitude toward the monarchy, relates how the tall, handsome son of Kish was initially selected by Samuel the seer in a private encounter between the two men. From this same circle of tradition (ch. 11) comes the account of Saul's heroic deliverance of the town of Jabesh-gilead from oppression by the Ammonites (a Semitic people in the Transjordan region), which brought him to the attention of all Israel and resulted in his acclamation as king in a public ceremony at Gilgal. A second body of tradition (I Sam. 8, 10:17–27, 12) is at pains to record Samuel's misgivings about the kingship. Although in this account he anoints Saul as a concession to popular pressure, Samuel warns of the loss of personal and tribal freedom that will follow and interprets the action as tantamount to a rejection of God. This latter tradition may reflect Israel's subsequent disappointments with the monarchy, but it doubtless preserves an authentic memory of the suspicion with which some Israelites viewed monarchal rule from the beginning.

In many respects, Saul's reign bears a closer resemblance to the judges who preceded him than to the succession of kings that followed. His chief service to Israel, like that of the judges, lay in the sphere of military defense. Together with his stalwart son Jonathan and an army constituted largely of volunteers, he won significant victories over the Philistines and succeeded in driving them out of the central hills. A successful campaign against the Amalekites in the south is also recorded (I Sam. 15). There is no evidence, however, that Saul made any appreciable changes in the nation's internal structures. There appears to have been no reordering of the old tribal territories into governmental districts and, accordingly, no formal programs of taxation or military

Assumption of kingship

conscription. The only royal official named in the accounts is the military commander Abner, Saul's cousin. In effect, Saul's reign was marked by few of the trappings of the typical eastern monarchies, with no court bureaucracy, splendid palace, or harem. His capital at Gibeah is revealed by archaeology as a simple, rustic fortress.

Influence of Samuel and David

The two men who significantly influenced Saul's career were Samuel and David. Even as Samuel's endorsement proved crucial in assuring Saul the kingship, probably nothing contributed so much to the King's subsequent disintegration as his break with the powerful and respected Samuel. Separate accounts attributed this to Saul's failure in religious duties: presumption in offering unauthorized sacrifice before battle and a reluctance to devote Amalek to destruction according to the principle of holy war. Samuel's rejection of Saul, which was complete and irrevocable, withdrew from the King the religious sanctions essential for popular support and Saul's own mental well-being.

David, who came into Saul's court because of either his military prowess or his skill as a harpist, according to varying accounts in I Samuel, is named both as the one who soothed the King with his sweet music and as the object of a fierce jealousy resulting from the young warrior's successes in battle. When secret attempts to take David's life proved no more successful than the King's efforts to turn the hearts of his daughter Michal (David's wife) and his son Jonathan away from their winsome husband and friend, Saul declared openly his intention to slay David. Only David's flight to Philistia, which was beyond Saul's reach, saved him from the King's unprovoked and manic attacks. These accounts, though written from a perspective favourable to David, portray dramatically and convincingly the mental deterioration of Saul. Nothing is more revealing of the extent of the King's derangement than the story of his senseless slaughter of the 85 priests at Nob in I Sam. 22.

Saul's deterioration, defeat, and death

Adding to the problems of Saul's final days, the Philistines mounted new attacks on the Israelite heartland. At no time strong enough to deliver a final knockout blow to the persistent enemy, Saul gathered his forces at Mount Gilboa in an effort to cut off their drive into the Valley of Jezreel. A vivid story in I Sam. 28 relates how, on the eve of the fateful battle, Saul sought, through a necromancer at Endor, some word of encouragement from the dead Samuel. The oracle of Samuel's ghost, however, could only foretell the doom awaiting on the following day: the defeat of the Israelite forces and the death of Saul and his sons. The Israelites, once again confronted by the desperate conditions prevailing at Saul's accession to the throne, had to look to a new deliverer. The man best fitted for the job was David.

Any fair evaluation of Saul's stormy career must look beyond the antimonarchal tendencies of his biographers and the implicit comparisons with the more successful David. Best described as a tragic hero, Saul displayed a strength in battle and an ability to inspire his followers that place him high in the ranks of the military great. If unable finally to solve the Philistine problem, he nevertheless prevented their complete subjugation of the land. So enduring was the devotion of the men of Jabesh-gilead that they risked their lives to remove Saul's exposed body from the Philistine fortress at Beth-shan and give it proper burial (I Sam. 31:11–13). The finest tribute paid the fallen leader is found in the immortal words of David's magnificent elegy in II Sam. 1, which begins, "Thy glory, O Israel, is slain upon thy high places! How are the mighty fallen!"

BIBLIOGRAPHY. MARTIN NOTH, Geschichte Israels (1950; Eng. trans., The History of Israel, 2nd ed., pp. 164–178, 1960); and JOHN BRIGHT, A History of Israel, pp. 163–174 (1959), provide the best historical assessments of Saul's reign. A somewhat romanticized but provocative personality study is in FLEMING JAMES, Personalities of the Old Testament, pp. 96–116 (1939).

(J.K.W.)

Sauria

Lizards (suborder Sauria) are familiar scaly-skinned reptiles, closely allied to snakes but usually distinguished by the possession of legs, movable eyelids, and external ear openings. Most of the 3,000 species of lizards inhabit warm regions, but some species of lizards are found nearly to the Arctic Circle in Eurasia and others to the southern tip of South America. The lizards are usually considered part of the reptilian order Squamata. The "worm lizards," or amphisbaenians, included in this article for convenience of comparison with lizards, are placed in their own suborder, Amphisbaenia, by many modern taxonomists. For a further discussion of this problem, see the article REPTILIA.

Distribution

GENERAL FEATURES

Lizards are by far the most diverse group of modern reptiles in body shape and size. They range in total length from geckos of 3 cm to monitor lizards of 3 m, and in adult weight from less than a gram to more than 150 kg. The popular conception of a lizard as a scampering reptile with head and body about 15 cm long and a slender tail of about equal length may be applied accurately to only a small number of species. Representatives of several families are limbless, resembling snakes; others have elongate hind legs and can run bipedally. A variety of ornaments is found, including extensible throat fans, tail crests, horns or casques on the head, and spines and frills around the throat.

Lizards occupy diverse habitats: underground, on the surface, and in elevated vegetation. Some are slow-moving, relying on cryptic coloration for protection; others can run swiftly across desert sands. The mosasaurs, an extinct family, were strictly marine. Some were giants, attaining lengths of 10 m (30 ft), with an elongate head, short neck, and long thin body and tail. One living lizard, the marine iguana of the Galápagos Islands, feeds on algae in the sea. No other extant species is marine, but several are partially aquatic, feeding on freshwater organisms.

Modern lizards do not play a major role in human ecology. Some large species (iguanas) are eaten, and others are used for leather goods. Predators, such as the tegu, can be pests around chicken farms, but the vast majority are primarily insectivorous or consume undesirable rodents. Small species such as geckos, which tend to live around houses, are often welcomed because of their efficiency in destroying insects; they may transmit *Salmonella* bacteria, however. In general though, lizards are not disease vectors.

Importance to man

Only two species, the Gila monster of the southwestern United States (*Heloderma*) and a close relative in Mexico, are venomous. They bite man only when provoked and fatalities are very rare. Unfortunately, diabolical powers attributed to lizards have made them objects of fear in many countries. Lizards are valued as subjects for biological research: the varied modes of reproduction and ability to regulate body temperatures are only two of many areas studied by comparative physiologists; the great abundance and easy observability of numerous species make them ideal subjects for ecologists and ethologists; the ability of some species to regenerate broken tails has led to their use by developmental biologists. In addition, because they are clean and easy to keep, lizards are quite popular as house pets.

NATURAL HISTORY

Life cycle. Most lizards reproduce by laying eggs. In some small species the number of eggs is rather uniform for each laying or clutch. For example, all anoles lay but a single egg at a time; many geckos lay one or two eggs (depending upon the species), and some skinks have fixed clutches of two eggs. A more general rule is that clutch size varies with size, age, and condition of the mother. A clutch of four to eight eggs may be considered typical, but large species such as iguanas may lay 50 or more eggs at one time. Lizard eggs are usually leathery shelled and porous and can expand by absorption of moisture as the embryos grow. An exception occurs in the majority of egg-laying geckos, whose eggs have shells that harden soon after deposition and then show no further change in size or shape.

Figure 1: *Variation in body form among lizards.*
(A) Old World chameleon *(Chamaeleo)*. (B) Flying lizard *(Draco)*. (C) Wall lizard *(Lacerta)*.
(D) Basilisk *(Basiliscus)*. (E) Horned lizard *(Phrynosoma)*. (F) Gecko *(Gekko)*. (G) Glass snake
(Ophisaurus). (H) Worm lizard *(Amphisbaena)*. (I) Gila monster *(Heloderma)*. (J) Cylindrical
skink *(Chalcides)*.

Some lizards bear live young. In the family Scincidae this is true for about one-third of the species, many of which are tropical. In most other families that have live-bearing representatives, the species that are exposed to cold—either at high altitude or at extreme latitude—generally are the live bearers. For example, all New Zealand geckos have live young, yet all other geckos lay eggs. Live bearers are divided into two categories. Ovoviviparous forms essentially retain eggs in the oviduct with no definite shell laid down, whereas truly viviparous forms have a chorio-allantoic placenta. Whether there is an actual exchange of nutrients across this placenta, as in mammals, is currently under study.

Sex in lizards is genetically and rigidly determined; a hatchling normally has either only male or female reproductive structures. In representatives of at least three diverse families (Iguanidae, Teiidae, Pygopodidae), the males have dissimilar sex chromosomes. This is similar to the sex-chromosome system of most mammals but differs from snakes, in which sex-chromosome differences, when present, are found in the female.

Most lizard populations are evenly divided between females and males. Deviations from this pattern are found in parthenogenetic (all female) species, in which the young are produced from unfertilized eggs. In the Caucasus all-female races of *Lacerta* and in the southwestern United States and parts of Mexico all-female species of whiptailed lizards *(Cnemidophorus)* have interesting parallels. They appear to live in areas ecologically marginal for representatives of their genera. In the case of *Cnemidophorus*, there is convincing evidence that parthenogenetic forms arose through hybridization between two bisexual species.

Parental care among lizards tends to be minimal following egg deposition. Many species dig holes in which the eggs are placed; others bury them under leaf litter or utilize a cranny in a tree or cave. Some species, however, notably the five-lined skink *(Eumeces fasciatus)* of the United States, remain with their eggs throughout incubation time (about six weeks), leaving only infrequently to feed. These skinks turn the eggs regularly and, if the eggs are experimentally scattered, will return them to the nest cavity. As soon as the young disperse, family ties are severed.

Certain lizards, particularly some geckos, are known to be communal egg-layers, many females depositing their

Partheno-
genesis

eggs at the same site. Whether this is due to social interaction or simply to ideal site conditions has not been determined.

Juvenile lizards are essentially miniature adults; they do not go through any larval phase nor any stage of depen-

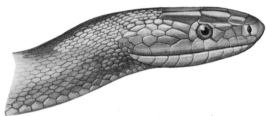

Figure 2: *Comparison of heads of a typical lizard and a typical snake.*
(Top) Legless lizard *(Ophisaurus)*. (Bottom) Green rat snake *(Elaphe triaspis)*.

dence upon adults. They often differ from the adult in colour or pattern and in certain body proportions. For example, heads of hatchling lizards of some species tend to be proportionally larger than those of adults. Certain ornamental structures, such as the throat fan of the male American chameleon *(Anolis)* or the horns of some true chameleons, develop as the lizards become sexually mature.

Some of the smaller lizards mature very quickly, and population turnover is essentially an annual event. The small, side-blotched lizards of the iguanid genus *Uta* of western North America have this type of population dynamics. The young hatch in July and reach sexual maturity that autumn. At this time males undergo spermatogenesis and mating takes place. Females accumulate large quantities of fat, which appears to be utilized in the production of eggs the following spring. Losses of 90 percent or more adults per year may come from predation, inclement weather, or other environmental variables. A single species living under a variety of environmental conditions may have very different population dynamics in different regions. For example, in areas with long winters there are periods of hibernation, coupled with greater longevity and slower population turnover.

Large lizards may take several years to reach sexual maturity. Unfortunately, there is little information on the dynamics of natural populations of most lizard species. In captivity many species are long-lived. There is a report of a male slowworm *(Anguis fragilis)* 46 years old mating with a female 20 years old. Gila monsters *(Heloderma)* have been kept in captivity for more than 25 years, and even some small geckos have been kept for as long as 20 years.

Ecology. The most important environmental variable to a lizard is almost certainly temperature. Like fish and amphibians, lizards are ectothermic ("cold-blooded"); they tend to assume the temperature of their surroundings. Yet all temperatures are not equally acceptable to lizards. Most species seek out relatively specific body temperatures, called "preferred temperatures," mostly ranging from 28° to 38° C. Although metabolic energy is not utilized to control body temperature, considerable thermo regulation can be accomplished largely through behavioral means, if the lizard has a choice. Typically, a diurnal lizard will emerge early in the morning and will sun itself, orienting the body to maximize exposure to the sun, until the preferred temperature is approached. The ability to absorb heat from solar radiation may permit the lizard to warm itself well above air temperatures. For example, *Liolaemus multiformis*, a small iguanid that lives high in the Andes, has the ability to raise its body

temperature to 35° C, while air temperatures are at 10° C or lower.

The preferred body temperature plays a critical physiological role in the life of a lizard. It has been demonstrated in the laboratory that animals kept without the opportunity to achieve the preferred temperature may be unable to attain the normal reproductive condition or may become sterilized. There is also evidence that enzymes catalyze reactions most efficiently at or near the preferred body temperature.

A lizard living in the tropics often will find the immediate environmental temperatures within its preferred range. To be successful in other habitats, a species must be able either to function at less than optimal temperature or, at least, to have less time at the optimal temperature and spend more time attaining this temperature. Thus it is not surprising that diversity of lizard species decreases with increasing latitude or with high altitude within the tropics.

Water is less of a problem to lizards than is temperature. All reptiles excrete uric acid and hence do not need great amounts of liquid to get rid of nitrogenous wastes. Many lizards have salt glands for active excretion of mineral salts. Deserts, therefore, do not pose severe problems to lizards and actually serve as a major habitat for the group. Lizards form a conspicuous portion of the fauna of oceanic islands, where amphibian and mammalian species' diversity is generally low. The ability of lizards to withstand desiccation may well account for their success at colonizing oceanic islands. They are believed to arrive on mats of floating vegetation washed up on the island shore. Hard-shelled gecko eggs seem to be particularly equipped for such journeys.

Other variables that affect lizards are day length (photoperiod) and rainfall. Lizards living far from the equator experience marked variation in photoperiod, with short winter days and long summer days. Certain species are adapted to respond to such cues. *Anolis carolinensis* of the southeastern United States ceases reproduction in the late summer and fattens up for winter hibernation. This change occurs while the days are still warm and appears to be triggered by decreasing day length. It is adaptive for the species because eggs laid in September would essentially be wasted, the young hatching in November when food is not readily available and temperatures are too low to permit efficient, rapid growth. Some tropical species respond to alternations between rainy and dry seasons, and egg-laying may cease during the driest months of the year. This may be adaptive for a variety of interrelated reasons. When food abundance is low, it is of direct advantage to the parent not to channel energy into production of eggs. Additionally, eggs might be less viable because of desiccation.

Lizards provide valuable models for the study of competition between species. On some Caribbean islands as many as ten species of *Anolis* may live in a single restricted area. For so many species to be accommodated, each must be specialized for a rather precise niche. The species come in a variety of sizes, feed on different sizes of prey, and have different preferences for structural and climatic niches. Some live in tree crowns others on trunks, others in grass; some live in open sun, others in "filtered" sun, and still others in deep shade. Thus, with ten anoles in a single area, each species has its own characteristic microhabitat.

Behaviour. Most lizards are active during daylight hours, when acute binocular vision is necessary for most nonburrowing species. The family Gekkonidae, however, is comprised predominantly of species that are most active from dusk to dawn. In conjunction with night activity, geckos are highly vocal and communicate by sound, whereas most other lizards are essentially mute.

Lizards spend considerable time obtaining food, usually insects. Iguanids and agamids tend to perch motionless at familiar sites and wait for prey. They are attracted by motion and dart suddenly for the capture. The true chameleons move slowly, carefully observant, each eye moving independently, and capture their prey by shooting out the sticky tongue. Lizards of other groups actively search

Marginal notes:
Population turnover

Temperature regulation

Hibernation

for prey by probing and digging, using scent as well as visual cues. Plants are eaten by many of the largest lizards, such as the iguanas and the spiny-tailed agamid (*Uromastix*).

Defense

Lizards themselves are food for many birds, mammals, and reptiles, and they have many defensive mechanisms. The chuckwallas (*Sauromalus*) remain close to rock piles. When danger threatens, they move into crevices and puff themselves up so that extrication is most difficult. A number of spiny-tailed forms also move into crevices and expose only the formidable tail. Perhaps the highest development of this sort of defense is found in the African armadillo lizard (*Cordylus*), which holds its tail in its mouth with the forefeet and presents a totally spiny appearance to an attacker. To intimidate intruders on its territory, the frilled lizard of Australia (*Chlamydosaurus*) extends a throat frill almost as wide as the lizard is long. The tails of many lizards break off (autotomize) easily. The broken-off section wriggles rapidly, distracting the predator as the tailless lizard scurries for cover.

Social interactions among lizards are best understood for the species that respond to visual stimuli. Many lizards defend certain areas against intruders of the same or closely related species. Territorial defense does not al-

ways involve actual combat. Elaborate, ritualized displays have evolved, presumably to avoid physical harm. The displays often involve erection of crests along the back and neck, increasing apparent size; showing bright colours, either by extending a throat fan or exposing a coloured patch of skin; and stereotyped movements such as push-ups, head bobbing, and tail waving. Impressive ornamentation is often restricted to males, but females of many species defend territories by stereotyped movements similar to those of males. Energy is expended in territorial defense, and a displaying male is very conspicuous and vulnerable to predation; but territoriality is evidently advantageous and has evolved through natural selection. Successful defense of a territory increases the chances of obtaining the necessary amount of food and at the same time increases the probability of a successful mating with any females living within the defended area. Thus a successful territorial male has a higher probability of reproductive success than one living in a marginal area. The displays used by males in establishing territories also may function to "advertise" their presence to females; in species that breed seasonally, territoriality diminishes during the nonbreeding season. In iguanids, actual courtship displays differ from territorial displays in that males approach females with pulsating, jerky movements. In addition to visual cues used for bringing the sexes together, there are undoubtedly chemical stimuli, but these have not been well studied. Numerous lizard species have femoral pores, small blind tubes along the inner surface of the thighs, whose function may be to secrete chemical attractants and territorial markers.

Courtship

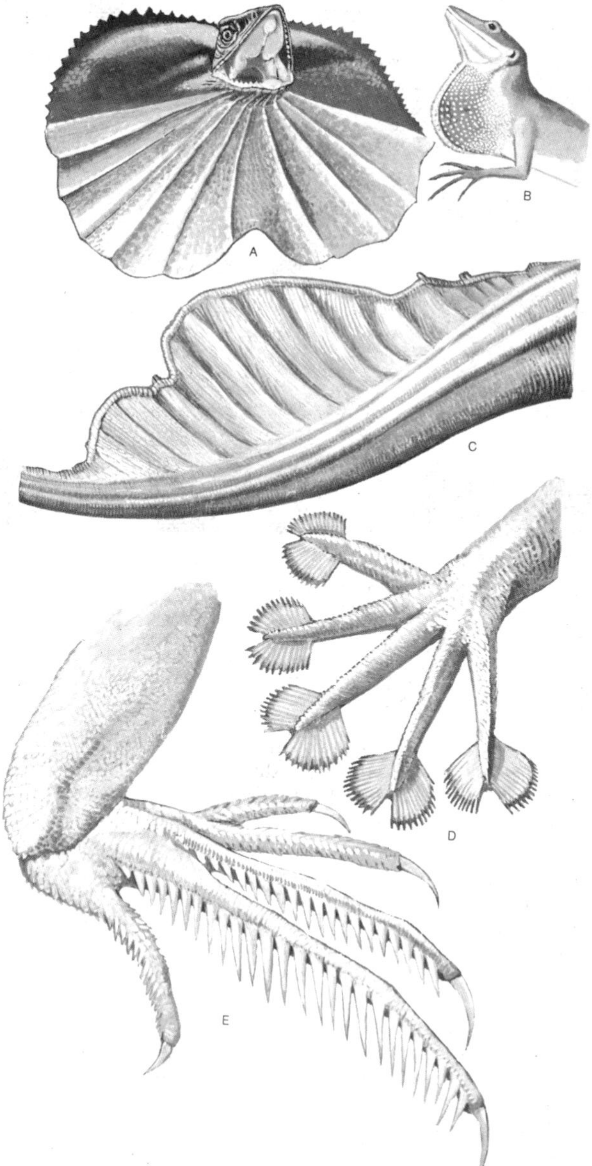

Copulation follows a common pattern. The male grasps the female by the skin, often of the neck or side of the head, places the fore and rear legs on the near side over the female, pushes his tail beneath hers, and twists his body to bring the cloacae together. One hemipenis is then everted and inserted into the cloaca of the female. Depending upon the species, copulation may last from seconds to 15 minutes or more.

FORM AND FUNCTION

Rather than present a detailed anatomical report of a lizard, this section discusses certain structures either characteristic of lizards in general or specializations of certain groups.

Skull and jaws. The skull is derived from the primitive diapsid condition; but the lower bar leading back to the quadrate bone is absent, giving greater flexibility to the jaw. In some burrowers, for example *Anniella* and the amphisbaenians, as well as some surface-living forms including the geckos, the upper as well as lower temporal bar has been lost. The small burrowers have thick, tightly bound skulls, with braincases well protected by bony walls. In most lizards the front of the braincase is made up of thin cartilage and membrane. The eyes are separated by a thin vertical interorbital septum. In burrowing forms with degenerate eyes, the septum is reduced, adding to the compactness of the skull. Most lizard skulls are kinetic; *i.e.*, the upper jaw can move in relation to the rest of the cranium. Since the anterior part of the braincase is cartilaginous and elastic, the entire front end of the skull can move as a single segment on the back part, which is solidly ossified. This increases the gape of the jaws and probably assists in pulling struggling prey into the mouth.

Teeth. Most lizards are insectivores (insect eaters), with sharp, tricuspid teeth adapted for grabbing and holding. Some herbivorous (plant-eating) species, for example iguanas, have tooth crowns expanded to a leaf shape with serrated cutting edges. The teeth of some large predators are conical and slightly recurved. Mollusk and crustacean feeders, such as the caiman lizard (*Dracaena*), may have blunt, rounded teeth in the back of the jaw designed for crushing. The venomous lizards (*Heloderma*) have a longitudinal groove or fold on the inner side of each mandibular tooth. These grooves conduct the venom. In most lizards, teeth are present along the jaw margin (on the maxilla, premaxilla, and dentary bones) and, in some forms, on the palate. In the embryo, an egg-tooth develops on the premaxilla and projects forward from the

The egg-tooth

Figure 3: *Specialized structures of some lizards.*
(A) Frill of the frilled lizard (*Chlamydosaurus*). (B) Dewlap of the anole (*Anolis*). (C) Fin of the water lizard (*Hydrosaurus*).
(D) Toe fans of the fan-footed gecko (*Ptyodctylus*). (E) Toes of the fringe-toed lizard (*Uma*).

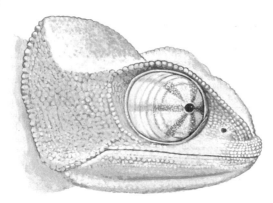

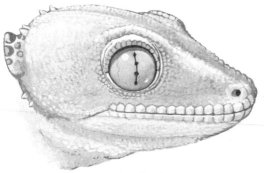

Figure 4: *Specialized eyes of two lizards.*
(Top) Turreted eye of chameleon *(Chamaeleo)*. (Bottom) Slit pupil of gecko *(Gekko)*.

The true chameleons (Chamaeleontidae), a predominantly arboreal family, have a different type of highly specialized limb. The digits on each foot are divided into two groups by webs of skin. On the hind limb, three of the

Joseph F. Gennaro, Jr.

Figure 5: *Fine structure of gecko foot.*
(Top left) Foot of gecko *(Gekko gecko)* showing chevron-shaped ridges or lamellae (about life size). White rectangle indicates the area covered by the photograph at the next larger magnification. (Top right) More detailed view of six of the lamellae (magnified 25 ×). (Bottom left) Part of lamella revealing its surface, covered by setae (magnified 220 ×). (Bottom right) Seta with attached suction cups visible at fringe terminals (magnified 2,550 ×).

snout. It aids in piercing the shell and is lost soon after hatching. This is a true tooth, unlike the horny epidermal point in turtles and crocodilians.

The common mode of tooth implantation is pleurodonty, in which the teeth are fused to the inner side of the labial wall. In the other mode, acrodonty, teeth are fused to the tooth-bearing bone, often to the crest of the bone. Acrodont teeth are rarely replaced, once a certain growth stage is reached. The dentition of the Agamidae is usually described as acrodont, but most species have several pleurodont teeth at the front of the upper and lower jaws.

Locomotion and limb adaptations. The majority of lizards are quadrupedal, with powerful limb musculature. They are capable of rapid acceleration and possess great ability to change direction of motion rapidly. The racerunners (*Cnemidophorus*) can attain speeds of 15 mph, which, in terms of their own body length, puts them in a class with fast terrestrial mammals. A tendency toward elongation of the body is found in some families, often accompanied by reduction of limb length and, not infrequently, complete loss of limbs. Such lizards propel themselves entirely by lateral undulations emanating from highly complicated ventral abdominal musculature. Limbless lizards that move quickly on the surface or through sand tend to have elongate tails (*Ophisaurus*, the glass "snake"), whereas the burrowers have extremely reduced tails (amphisbaenians). The burrowers (amphisbaenians in particular) dig by ramming the head into the substrate, then rotating the head around the head joint, compacting the substrate.

Many modifications of the toes are to be seen in lizards. Some desert geckos, the iguanid *Uma*, and the lacertid *Acanthodactylus* have fringes on the toes that provide increased surface area and prevent sinking into loose desert sand. Arboreal geckos and anoles have lamellae (fine plates) on the undersides of the toes. Each lamella is made up of brushlike setae, each double; and the tips divide several times, the final strand less than .25 μm (1/100,000 in) in diameter. These fine hairlike processes greatly enhance the clinging ability of the lizards, as they are able to find purchase in the smallest irregularities of the substrate. Geckos and anoles can easily climb vertical panes of glass.

toes are on the outside, two on the inside (a form of zygodactyl); on the forelimb the pattern is reversed. Each foot is thus divided into an outer and an inner portion, which can be opposed as the branch is gripped. In addition, these and some other lizards have prehensile tails, which aid in grasping branches.

Several terrestrial iguanids and agamids are able to run bipedally. Basilisks are actually able to run across water for short distances. During bipedal locomotion the tail is held out backward and upward and acts as a counterweight.

Some lizards are able to parachute or glide through the air and make soft landings. The most highly adapted of these are the agamid lizards called flying lizards (*Draco*), which have extensible lateral expansions of the skin, supported by elongate ribs.

Skin and colour change. Except for openings of nostrils, mouth, eyes, and cloaca, most lizards are completely covered in scales, which vary among species and on different parts of the body of the individual. Scales may be smooth and overlapping, form a mosaic of flat plates, or have keels or tubercles. Osteoderms, bony plates that de-

Bipedal
locomotion

velop in the dermis, underlie head and body scales of some lizards. The outer parts of the scales are composed of dead horny tissue made up largely of the protein keratin. The dead layer is shed at intervals and is replaced by proliferating cells in the deep part of the epidermis. Certain lizards have scale organs, with a stiff projecting seta emerging from the serrated edge of the scale and presumably responsive to tactile stimuli.

Many lizards can show some colour change. Two groups, the chameleons and the anoles, are particularly noteworthy in this ability. They can change from bright green to deep, chocolate brown, and patterns such as lines and bars may appear and disappear. The pigment cells that permit colour change are melanophores. Within these cells, pigment granules are able to migrate. In general, the animal is light when pigment is concentrated and dark when it is dispersed throughout the cells. The actual colour state, complexly controlled, is not simply matching of background but seems to be controlled by an interaction of hormones, temperature, and the nervous system.

PALEONTOLOGY

Lizards belong to the diapsid reptiles, a group characterized by the presence of an opening in the temporal bone of the skull, both above and below a bar formed by the postorbital and squamosal bones. The diapsids comprise two subclasses of reptiles: the Archosauria (crocodiles, pterosaurs, dinosaurs) and the more primitive Lepidosauria (lizards, snakes, eosuchians, and rhynchocephalians). The earliest known Lepidosaurian order (Eosuchia) appeared in the Late Permian (about 230,000,000 years ago) and almost undoubtedly was ancestral to lizards. Modern lizards differ from their ancestors in several skeletal features, the most diagnostic differences being in the construction of the upper temporal and quadrate regions of the skull. A.S. Romer divides true lizards from their ancestors on the basis of the quadrate region. Among true lizards the quadrate articulates flexibly with the squamosal above it. This occurred through loss of the lower temporal arch and reduction of squamosal development. The oldest fossil true lizards appeared in the Late Triassic (200,000,000 years ago). These were not primitive but highly specialized, having ribs that could be projected outward to provide a gliding ability. Thus it is possible that even older lizards will be found. Representatives of many modern lizard families have been found in Cretaceous deposits (from 136,000,000 to 65,000,000 years ago); and representatives of modern genera, virtually indistinguishable from living forms, were common from the Oligocene (38,000,000 to 26,000,000 years ago) on.

CLASSIFICATION

Distinguishing taxonomic features. Lizards differ from other reptilian groups in several anatomical characters, including the possession of not more than a single bony arch across the temple and paired reversible copulatory organs, the hemipenes.

G. Underwood (1967) summarized the differences between snakes and lizards. Lizards have the eyes separated by a thin vertical interorbital septum, whereas in snakes this septum is absent and the entire width of the bony braincase separates the orbits. Other features that distinguish lizards from snakes include: (1) the pectoral (shoulder) girdle, absent even as a trace in all snakes, present in all lizards; (2) the histological structure of the adrenal glands; (3) the placement of the thymus bodies. M.R. Miller (1968) found that the internal ear of snakes is considerably different from and more primitive than that of any lizard. The families of lizards are defined primarily by osteology and dentition, as well as presence or absence of the rectus superficialis muscle. When this muscle is absent in a group, there is not the slightest tendency for limb reduction and serpentine locomotion. The limits of the families seem to be agreed upon by most systematists; although relationships among the families are not always so clear.

Annotated classification. The classification presented here is adapted from Underwood (1957), which is an updating of C.L. Camp (1923). Definitions of taxa follow Camp where feasible. The classification of the Gekkonidae follows A.G. Kluge (1967). The dates of earliest fossils are from R. Hoffstetter (1962).

SUBORDER SAURIA

Reptiles with a single temporal opening lying above the bar formed by postorbital and squamosal bones. Pectoral girdle and interorbital septum always present. About 3,000 species.

Infraorder Ascalabota

Rectus superficialis rarely present; usually more than four transverse rows of ventral scales over each body segment; body covered by scales that overlap by wide margin ("deciduous").

Superfamily Gekkonoidea

Family Gekkonidae (geckos). No supratemporal arch; well defined limbs. Jurassic to present. Eighty-two genera, 650 species. Virtually worldwide in subtropical and tropical regions. Adult total length from slightly under 4 cm to 35 cm. Most with soft, granular skin, easily autotomized tails, no movable eyelids, and toes with fine setae.

Family Pygopodidae (flap-footed lizards). Australia and New Guinea. Some burrowers, others surface dwelling; hind limbs represented by scaly flaps. Eight genera, 15 species.

Family Dibamidae. Philippines and Viet Nam, to New Guinea. Burrowers; females limbless, males with flaplike hind limbs. One genus, 3 species.

Family Anelytropsidae. Eastern Mexico. Limbless; one species.

Superfamily Iguanioidea

Family Iguanidae. Dentition pleurodont. Teeth replaced when lost. Well-developed limbs. Movable eyelids. Oligocene, possibly late Eocene to present. Dominant family of North, Central, and South America, West Indies, and Galápagos Islands. One genus on Fiji and Tonga, two genera on Madagascar, no others in Eastern Hemisphere. Adult lengths from 10 cm (*Uta*) to 2 m (*Iguana*). A family of diverse forms including short, spiny desert dwellers (*Phrynosoma*), slender arboreal species (*Anolis*), and sea-going iguanas (*Amblyrhynchus*). Fifty genera, 600 species (200 in one genus, *Anolis*).

Family Agamidae. Most teeth acrodont. Many examples of convergent evolution with iguanids, but tooth difference absolute. Late Cretaceous to present. Old World tropics and subtropics, except Madagascar. Thirty-three genera, 300 species (60 in genus *Agama*).

Superfamily Rhiptoglossoidea

Family Chamaeleontidae (Old World chameleons). Feet zygodactylous, grasping. Dentition acrodont. Tongue long, slender, extensile. Two genera, *Brookesia* 16 species, *Chamaeleo* 68 species. About half restricted to Madagascar, remainder primarily African, two species in western Asia, one in India, one reaching Mediterranean region. Most are insectivores 17–25 cm (7–10 in); the largest, reaching 60 cm, will eat birds.

Infraorder Autarchoglossa

Superfamily Scincomorphoidea

Family Scincidae (skinks). Skull arches present, osteoderms (dermal bone) present. Late Cretaceous to present. Worldwide (except in polar and subpolar regions), greatest diversity in Old World tropics. Typically with conical heads, cylindrical bodies, tapering tails. Less variable than the other large families. Primarily ground dwelling or burrowing, some arboreal with prehensile tails. Limb reduction common. Majority below 12 cm, largest reaches 60 cm. About 50 genera, 800 species.

Family Cordylidae (girdle-tailed lizards). Femoral pores and osteoderms present. Supratemporal fossa roofed over. Late Jurassic to present. Southern Africa and Madagascar. 20–60 cm (8–24 in). About ten genera, 50 species.

Family Lacertidae. Osteoderms absent, supratemporal fossa roofed over. Eocene (possibly Cretaceous) to present, Europe, Asia, and Africa. Morphologically uniform, conical heads, scaly bodies, movable eyelids, well developed limbs and tail. Length 15–60 cm. Approximately 20 genera, 150 species.

Family Teiidae. Osteoderms absent, supratemporal fossa open. Late Cretaceous to present. New World only, primarily in tropics and subtropics. Great variation in the family, including large terrestrial predators (*Tupinambis*), large semiaquatic snail eaters (*Dracaena*), lacertid-like "racerunners" (*Cnemidophorus*), and small burrowers. Size range 7–120 cm. Forty genera, 200 species.

Superfamily Anguinomorphoidea

Family Anguidae. Skull arches, osteoderms present. Six mandibular bones. Late Cretaceous to present. Most in Americas, a few Eurasian. Glass lizards (*Ophisaurus*) are limbless "grass swimmers" reaching 120 cm. Alligator lizards (*Gherrhonotus*) and galliwasps (*Diploglossus*) have four limbs, somewhat elongate bodies, and reach 37 cm. Seven genera, 67 species.

Family Anniellidae (California legless lizards). Limbless burrowers. No skull arches. Length 11–25 cm. California and Baja California. One genus, two species.

Family Xenosauridae. Shape of interclavicle bone and presence of tubercles in the osteoderms distinguishes the family. Late Cretaceous from North America. Presently, two genera, one in Mexico, one in China; four species.

Family Helodermatidae (gila monster and beaded lizard). Venomous; grooved hollow fangs in lower jaw; heavy-bodied. Skin texture "beaded." Oligocene to present; southwest United States and Mexico. Adult length to 50 cm in Gila monster, 80 cm in beaded lizard. One genus, two species.

Family Varanidae (monitor lizards). Osteoderms reduced, seven cervical vertebrae, postorbital arch incomplete. Restricted to Old World tropics and subtropics. Fossils from Cretaceous of North America. Smallest species is adult at 20 cm, largest exceeds 3 m. General uniformity of appearance with elongate head and neck, relatively heavy body, long tail, well developed limbs. One genus, 30 species.

Family Lanthanotidae (earless monitor lizard). Fossils from Recent only. No external ear. Restricted to Borneo; rare and little known. Length to 40 cm. One genus and species.

Family Xantusiidae (night lizards). Vertebrae procoelous, supratemporal arch present. No movable eyelid. Relationships to other lizards unclear, even as to assignment within suborder. Share some features with gekkonids, others with skinks. Four genera, 12 species, California through Central America, and Cuba. All moderately small; bodies covered with small scales; ventral surfaces and head with larger platelike scales.

SUBORDER AMPHISBAENIA

Family Amphisbaenidae (amphisbaenians or worm lizards). Long cylindrical bodies with shallow grooves. No external ears, no readily visible eyes. Burrowers. Eocene to present. Primarily tropical, one species reaches Florida, and one reaches Spain. All genera lack hind limbs, and all but three lack forelimbs. Fifteen genera, about 100 species.

Critical appraisal. The boundaries of most lizard families have been stable for the past half-century, with several exceptions. The most important involves Gekkonidae, which Underwood (1954) divided into three families but which Kluge (1967) reunited into a single family with four subfamilies. C. Gans (1960) considers the Amphisbaenia so distinct that he raised them to ordinal status, equivalent in rank to lizards and snakes, and raised the two amphisbaenid subfamilies to family status. Studies by M.R. Miller (1966, 1968) on the internal ear, and A.E. Greer (1970) on cranial osteology clarify the relationships of some of the obscure burrowers and demonstrate that members of the so-called family Feylinidae are merely specialized skinks and are not closely related to the superficially similar Anelytropsidae. Perhaps of greatest significance is the finding that the cochlear duct of all snakes is more primitive than that of any lizard. This throws doubt on the theory that snakes are derived from highly advanced lizards (varanid relatives).

BIBLIOGRAPHY. General surveys of the species of lizards and their life histories, with many photographs, are found in K.P. SCHMIDT and R.F. INGER, *Living Reptiles of the World* (1957); A.F. CARR, *The Reptiles* (1963); and R. MERTENS, *La vie des amphibiens et reptiles* (1959; Eng. trans., *The World of Amphibians and Reptiles*, (1960).

Anatomy, paleontology and biology: A. BELLAIRS, *Reptiles,* 2nd ed. (1968), is a concise and well written introduction to all aspects of reptilian biology, with references to original scientific papers. V.A. HARRIS, *The Anatomy of the Rainbow Lizard* (1963), provides a dissection manual for students, moderately technical but very readable. Of a more technical nature are two works by A.S. ROMER: *Osteology of the Reptiles* (1956) and *Vertebrate Paleontology*, 3rd ed. (1966).

Behaviour and ecology: V.A. HARRIS, *The Life of the Rainbow Lizard* (1964); W.W. MILSTEAD (ed.), *Lizard Ecology*; *A Symposium* (1967), contains summaries of current research in population ecology, physiological ecology, and social behaviour, with panel discussions of the reports; an excellent source for understanding trends in current research.

Important taxonomic books and papers, not easily read by the layman, but fundamental to an understanding of the classification are: C.L. CAMP, "Classification of the Lizards," *Bull. Am. Mus. Nat. Hist.*, 48:289–480 (1923); R. HOFFSTETTER, "Revue des récentes acquisitions concernant l'histoire et la systématique des squamates," in *Problèms actuels de paléontologie (évolutions des vertébrés)*, pp. 243–279 (1962); A.G. KLUGE, "Higher Taxonomic Categories of Gekkonid Lizards, and Their Evolution," *Bull. Am. Mus. Nat. Hist.*, 135:1–59 (1967); S.B. MCDOWELL and C.M. BOGERT, "The Systematic Position of *Lanthanotus* and the Affinities of the Anguinomorphan Lizards," *ibid.*, 105:1–142 (1954); M.R. MILLER, "The Cochlear Duct of Lizards," *Proc. Calif. Acad. Sci., 4th series*, 33:255–359 (1966), and "The Cochlear Duct of Snakes," *ibid.*, 35:425–476 (1968); G. UNDERWOOD, "On the Classification and Evolution of Geckoes," *Proc. Zool. Soc., Lond.*, 124:469–492 (1954), "On Lizards of the Family Pygopodidae, a Contribution to the Morphology and Phylogeny of the Squamata," *J. Morph.*, 100:207–268 (1957), and "A Contribution to the Classification of Snakes," *Publs. Br. Mus. Nat. Hist.*, no. 635 (1967); A.E. GREER, "A Subfamilial Classification of Scincid Lizards," *Bull. Mus. Comp. Zool. Harv.*, 139:151–183 (1970).

(G.C.G.)

Savigny, Friedrich Karl von

Friedrich Karl von Savigny was the most influential figure in 19th-century German jurisprudence. He was the founder of a modern system of German civil law and of a general theory of private law. He became internationally known for his system of private international law.

Deutsche Fotothek Dresden

Savigny, lithograph by E. Winterhalder (b. 1879) after a chalk drawing by Louise Claude Henry (1798–1839).

Savigny was born on February 21, 1779, in Frankfurt am Main, a descendant of landed nobility who had emigrated to Germany from Lorraine. He studied at the universities of Göttingen and Marburg, where he received his degree in 1800 and at once took up his teaching career. His wealth and social position enabled him to devote all of his considerable talents to scholarly work. In 1803 he established his reputation with *Das Recht des Besitzes* (Eng. trans., *Treatise on Possession; or, the Jus Possessionis of the Civil Law*, 6th ed., 1848), a book that was the beginning of the 19th-century scholarly monograph in jurisprudence.

In 1804 he married Kunigunde Brentano of the famous and artistic Frankfurt family. Through his wife's brother and sister (Clemens Brentano the poet, and Bettina Brentano, the writer, who married the poet Achim von Arnim) he came in close contact with the Heidelberg group of Romantic writers.

In 1808 Savigny went to the University of Landshut in Bavaria as a professor of Roman law, and in 1810 he was invited to the new University of Berlin, where he soon became one of the most famous and influential members of the faculty. He taught there for the rest of his career.

The German Romanticism of the early 19th century had a strong influence on Savigny's philosophy of law. In 1814 the wave of nationalism inspired by the war of liberation against Napoleon led the law professor A.F.J.

Education and early career

Legal
philosophy

Thibaut to demand a unified civil code for all the German states. Savigny replied in a famous pamphlet, "Vom Beruf unserer Zeit für Gesetzgebung und Rechtswissenschaft" (Eng. trans. "Of the Vocation of Our Age for Legislation and Jurisprudence," 1831), that started juristic thought along a new path. To him, the lesson of history was the futility of hasty codification. The essential prerequisite was a deep and far-reaching appreciation of the genius of the particular community. The prescriptive content of the law must accord with the spirit of the people, the *Volksgeist*. A law that was not in conformity with this was doomed. Custom becomes the chief manifestation of law, although as law grows more technical a specialist body of experts, known as lawyers, emerges, whose function is to reflect the *Volksgeist* in technical matters. In the current age, Savigny argued, few had the requisite skill or vocation to codify German law. In his classic words, law

> is first developed by custom and popular faith, next by judicial decisions—everywhere, therefore, by internal silently operating powers, not by the arbitrary will of a law-giver.

He was not, it should be emphasized, opposed to legal reform and codification; he sought rather to uncover the content of existing law through historical research.

In 1815, shortly after the appearance of this epochal pamphlet, he founded, together with K.F. Eichorn and J.F.L. Göschen, the *Zeitschrift für geschichtliche Rechtswissenschaft*, which became the organ of the new historical school of jurisprudence. In the same year he began publishing his seven-volume work on the history of the Roman law in the Middle Ages, *Geschichte des römischen Rechts im Mittelalter* (1815–31). This was the foundation of the modern study of medieval law.

Savigny strove to establish a German science of civil law. His approach to legal methodology was first put forward in a lecture at Marburg in the academic year 1802–03 (published in 1951 as *Juristische Methodenlehre, nach der Ausarbeitung des Jakob Grimm*). He held that legal science should be both historical and systematic, meaning that it should endeavour to show the inner coherence of the material handed down in the historical sources of Roman law. For all his emphasis on history, Savigny was by no means an exponent of natural law theory. Instead he accepted the view of the philosopher Immanuel Kant, who held that law and morality were not identical; law, according to Kant, is the complex totality of conditions under which maximum freedom is provided for all. One might characterize Savigny's system of private law based on the Kantian approach as a system of the rights of private freedom of individuals who organize their legal relations mainly by independent contracts. This conception obviously harmonized well with the rising capitalism of the second half of the 19th century.

Later
works

Savigny gave embodiment to his systematic approach in his eight-volume treatise on modern Roman law, *System des heutigen römischen Rechts* (1840–49). The eighth volume, which contained his system of international private law, showed the influence of the U.S. lawyer and Supreme Court justice Joseph Story.

In 1817 Savigny was made a member of the Prussian Privy Council. In 1819 he was appointed to the Berlin Court of Appeal and Cassation for the Rhine Provinces. In 1826 he became a member of the commission for revising the Prussian code, and in 1842 he gave up his teaching position to accept a ministerial post as head of the newly founded department for revision of statutes. The revolution of 1848 ended his governmental career.

In 1850 he published a collection of his monographs, *Vermischte Schriften*, and in 1851–53 a two-volume work on the law of contracts, *Das Obligationenrecht*, a supplement to his work on modern Roman law. He died in Berlin on October 25, 1861.

Judgments of Savigny have varied. His famous essay of 1814 caused him to be regarded for a long time as a leader of the romantic branch of the historical school of law. Only recently has he been seen more accurately as a thinker in the line of the rationalist jurisprudence of the 18th century, basing his system on Kant's critical philosophy.

BIBLIOGRAPHY. There is no definitive biography of Savigny. Much material about his life, with many letters, is contained in ADOLF STOLL, *Friedrich Karl v. Savigny*, 3 vol. (1927–39). A well-balanced description of his life and work is in ERIK WOLF, *Grosse Rechtsdenker der deutschen Geistesgeschichte*, 4th ed., pp. 467–542 (1963). Fundamental background is contained in FRANZ WIEACKER, *Privatrechtsgeschiichte der Neuzeit*, 2nd ed., pp. 348–399 (1967). See also JULIUS STONE, *The Province and Function of Law*, pp. 421–448 (1946).

(H.Kie.)

Savonarola, Girolamo

The famous 15th-century Italian preacher, reformer, and martyr Girolamo Savonarola was born at Ferrara on Sept. 21, 1452, the son of Niccolò Savonarola and of Elena Bonaccorsi. He was educated by his paternal grandfather, Michele, a celebrated doctor and a man of rigid moral and religious principles. From this elderly scholar, whose own education was of the 14th century, Savonarola may have received certain medieval influences. In his early poetry and other adolescent writings the main characteristics of the future reformer are seen. Even at that early date, as he wrote in a letter to his father, he could not suffer "the blind wickedness of the peoples of Italy." He found unbearable the humanistic paganism that corrupted manners, art, poetry, and religion itself. He saw as the cause of this spreading corruption a clergy vicious even in the highest levels of the church hierarchy.

Alinari—Art Reference Bureau

Savonarola, painting by Fra Bartolommeo.
In the Museé di S. Marco, Florence.

On April 24, 1475, he left his father's house and his medical studies, on which he had embarked after taking a degree in the liberal arts, to enter the Dominican Order at Bologna. Returning to Ferrara four years later he taught Scripture in the Convento degli Angeli. Scripture, together with the works of Thomas Aquinas, had always been his great passion.

Career in Florence. In 1482 Savonarola was sent to Florence to take up the post of lecturer in the convent of San Marco, where he gained a great reputation for his learning and asceticism. As a preacher he was unsuccessful until a sudden revelation inspired him to begin his prophetic sermons. At San Gimignano in Lent 1485 and 1486, he put forward his famous propositions: the church needed reforming; it would be scourged and then renewed.

The following year (1487) he left Florence to become master of studies in the school of general studies at Bologna. After the year of his appointment was over, he was sent to preach in various cities until Lorenzo de' Medici used his influence to have Savonarola sent back to Florence, thus opening the doors there to the bitterest enemy of Medici rule. Having returned to the city of his destiny (1490), Savonarola preached boldly against the tyrannical abuses of the government. Too late Lorenzo tried to dam the dangerous eloquence with threats and flattery, but his own life was drawing to a close, while popular enthusiasm

Attack on
Medici rule

for Savonarola's preaching constantly increased. Soon afterward Savonarola gave his blessing to the dying Lorenzo. The legend that he refused Lorenzo absolution is disproved by documentary evidence.

Medici rule did not long survive Lorenzo and was overthrown by the invasion of Charles VIII (1494). Two years before, Savonarola had predicted his coming and his easy victory. These authenticated prophecies, the part he had played in negotiations with the King and in moderating the hatred of the factions after the change of government, enormously increased his authority. Once the Medici had been driven out, Florence had no other master than Savonarola's terrible voice. He introduced a democratic government, the best the city ever had. He has been accused, but unjustly, of interfering in politics. He was not ambitious or an intriguer. He wanted to found his city of God in Florence, heart of Italy, as a well-organized Christian republic that might initiate the reform of Italy and of the church. This was the object of all his actions. The results he obtained were amazing: the splendid but corrupt Renaissance capital, thus miraculously transformed, seemed to a contemporary to be a foretaste of paradise.

Savona-
rola's
enemies Savonarola's triumph was too great and too sudden not to give rise to jealousy and suspicion. A Florentine party was formed in opposition to him called the Arrabbiati. These internal enemies formed an alliance with powerful foreign forces, foremost of which were the Duke of Milan and the Pope, who had joined in the Holy League against the King of France and saw in Savonarola the main obstacle to Florence's joining them. It was then, after a firm rejection of the league by Florence, that the Pope sent to Savonarola the brief of July 21, 1495, in which he praised the miraculous fruits of Savonarola's work and called him to Rome to pronounce his prophecies from his own lips. As that pope was the corrupt Alexander VI, the trap was too obvious. Savonarola asked to be allowed to put off his journey, offering illness as his excuse.

The Pope appeared to be satisfied, but on September 8, under pressure from his political friends and Savonarola's enemies, he sent him a second brief in which praises turned into vituperation. He ordered him to go to Bologna under pain of excommunication. Savonarola replied to this strange document with respectful firmness, pointing out no fewer than 18 mistakes in it. The brief was replaced by another of October 16, in which he was forbidden to preach. As the Pope himself frankly confessed, it was the Holy League that insisted. After a few months, as Lent 1496 drew near, Alexander VI, while refusing the Florentine ambassadors a formal revocation of the ban, conceded this verbally. Thus Savonarola was able to give his sermons on Amos, which are among his finest and most forceful, and in which he attacked the Roman Court with renewed vigour. He also appeared to refer to the Pope's scandalous private life, and the latter took offense at this. A college of theologians found nothing to criticize in what the friar had said, so that after Lent he was able to begin without further remonstrances from Rome, the sermons on Ruth and Micah.

At that time, as Savonarola's authority grew, the Pope tried to win him over by offering him a cardinal's hat. He replied: "A red hat? I want a hat of blood." Then Alexander VI, pressed by the League and Arrabbiati, mounted a fresh attack. In a brief of Nov. 7, 1496, he incorporated the Congregation of San Marco, of which Savonarola was vicar, with another in which he would have lost all his authority. If he obeyed, his reforms would be lost. If he disobeyed, he would be excommunicated. Savonarola, however, while protesting vigorously, did not disobey, because no one came forward to put the brief into force. He therefore went on unperturbed in Advent 1496 and Lent 1497 with his series of sermons on Ezekiel. During the carnival season that year his authority received a symbolic tribute in the "burning of the vanities," when personal ornaments, lewd pictures, cards, and gaming tables were burned. Destruction of books and works of art was negligible. Events in Italy now turned against Savonarola, however, and even in Florence his power was lessened by unfavourable political and economic developments. A government of Arrabbiati forced him to stop preaching

and incited sacrilegious riots against him on Ascension Day. The Arrabbiati obtained from the Roman Court, for a financial consideration, the desired bull of excommunication against their enemy. In effect the excommunication, besides being surreptitious, was full of such obvious errors of form and substance as to render it null and void, and the pope himself had to disown it. The Florentine government, however, sought in vain to obtain its formal withdrawal; wider political issues were involved. Absorbed in study and prayer, Savonarola was silent. Only when Rome proposed an unworthy arrangement, which made withdrawal of the censure dependent on Florence's entry into the league, did he again go into the pulpit (Lent 1498) to give those sermons on Exodus that marked his own departure from the pulpit and from life. He was soon silenced by the interdict with which the city was threatened. He had no other way out but an appeal to a church council, and he began a move in this direction but then burned the letters to the princes that he had already written, in order not to cause dissension within the church. Once this road was closed the only remaining one led to martyrdom.

Martyrdom. The imprudence of the most impassioned of his followers, Fra Domenico da Pescia, brought events to a head. Fra Domenico took at his word a Franciscan who had challenged to ordeal by fire anyone who maintained the invalidity of Savonarola's excommunication. The Signoria and the whole population of the most civilized city in Italy greedily encouraged that barbarous experiment, as it alone seemed to promise a solution of an insuperable problem. Only Savonarola was dissatisfied. The decree, which assigned to the ordeal Fra Domenico himself and a Franciscan, declared the loser whichever might withdraw or even vacillate. In fact the Franciscan failed to appear and so the ordeal did not take place. Savonarola, victorious by the terms of the decree, was blamed for not having achieved a miracle. The following day the rabble led by the Arrabbiati rioted, marched to San Marco, and overcame the defenders. Savonarola was taken like a common criminal together with Fra Domenico and another follower. After examination by a commission of his worst enemies and after savage torture, it was yet necessary to falsify the record of the inquiry if he were to be charged with any crimes. But his fate was settled. The papal commissioners came from Rome "with the verdict in their bosom," as one of them said. After the ecclesiastical trial, which was even more perfunctory, he was handed over to the secular arm, with his two companions, to be hanged and burned. The sentence was carried out on May 23, 1498, and the account of his last hours is like a page from the lives of the Church Fathers. Before mounting the scaffold he piously received the Pope's absolution and plenary indulgence.

Trial and
execution

Assessment. In fact Savonarola's quarrel was with the corruption of the clergy of whom Alexander VI was merely the most scandalous example, not with the Roman pontiff, for whom he always professed obedience and respect. He was a reformer, but Catholic and Thomist to the marrow; his faith is borne out in his many works, the greatest of which is the *Triumphus crucis*, a clear exposition of Christian apologetics. His *Compendium revelationum*, an account of visions and prophecies that came true, went through many editions in several countries. Of his sermons, some exist in a version taken down verbatim.

After Savonarola's death a cult was dedicated to him, which had a long history. Saints canonized by the church, such as Philip Neri and Catherine de' Ricci, venerated him as a saint; an office was said for him, and miracles he had performed were recorded. He was portrayed in paintings and medals with the title of *beatus*. In the *Acta sanctorum* he was included among the *praetermissi*. When the 500th anniversary of his birth came around in 1952, there was again talk of his canonization.

BIBLIOGRAPHY. The most modern and up-to-date biography is that of ROBERTO RIDOLFI, *Vita di Girolamo Savonarola,* 2 vol. (1952; Eng. trans., 1959). JOSEPH SCHNITZER, *Savonarola,* 2 vol. (1924; Eng. trans., 1931), is a fundamental and irreplaceable work because of the enormous quantity of systematic notes. PASQUALE VILLARI, *La storia di Fra Girolamo*

Savonarola e de'suoi tempi (1859–61), 2 vol. (1887; new ed., 1927; Eng. trans., *The Life and Times of Girolamo Savonarola*, 2nd ed., 1889, reprinted 1969), is an old book but a classic. Fourteen volumes of the Italian national edition of Savonarola's works (1953–   ) have been published to date. *Le Lettere*, ed. by ROBERTO RIDOLFI (1933), is the only critical edition of his letters. PASQUALE VILLARI, *Scelta di prediche e scritti* (1898), is the best anthology of the writings of Savonarola. For a bibliography of the ancient editions of his works, see LUCIA GIOVANNOZZI, *Contributo alla bibliografia delle opere del Savonarola* (1953); MARIO FERRARA, *Bibliografia savonaroliana* (1958), is a complete bibliography of the published writings about Savonarola from 1801 to 1956.

(Ro.Ri.)

Saxifragales

Saxifragales is a large and diverse order of flowering plants containing 28 families and over 3,000 species. They may be large forest trees, shrubs, stout woody vines, or delicate herbs. Plants belonging to this order are distributed throughout the world; they grow on all continents and on many islands in the Pacific Ocean. Their distribution ranges from cold temperate regions to the tropics and from sea level to the high mountains, and they grow in habitats as diverse as deserts and tropical rain forests. Some species produce medicinal products; a few produce edible fruits; and one genus is an alternate host for a serious disease-causing organism that attacks pines. Certain groups of the order Saxifragales are reputed to capture and utilize the bodies of insects as a source of nitrogen. Flowers and fruits are borne directly on the leaf blades in one small group of trees and shrubs. Exceedingly fleshy, thick, and succulent leaves characterize hundreds of species in one section of the order.

ECONOMIC IMPORTANCE

Ornamental plants. Brexias (family Brexiaceae) are trees from Madagascar that are sometimes grown as specimen plants in greenhouses or outdoors in the subtropics or tropics. Indoors, brexias seldom become trees but grow to the size of tall shrubs. Both greenhouse specimens and those grown outdoors produce characteristic greenish or white, waxy-petalled flowers.

Species of several genera of the family Bruniaceae are widely grown as horticultural plants. Among them are *Berzelia*, *Brunia*, *Raspalia*, *Staavia*, and *Thamnea*. These plants are all natives of southern Africa and reflect the characteristic bushy, evergreen, heathlike nature of all members of the family Bruniaceae. In cooler temperate climates they must be grown under glass.

Among the most important and familiar perennial garden plants of temperate, subtropical, and tropical regions are members of the family Crassulaceae (stonecrop or orpine family). Many are grown as pot plants, especially in cooler climates, and a few are favoured for rock gardens and open border plantings in climatically suitable regions. The family Crassulaceae is native in many parts of the world, but the plants are often characteristic of arid and semi-arid regions and rocky places, particularly in southern Africa. They are typically fleshy-leaved plants, often with handsome, prevailingly red or yellow flowers. The genera *Rochea*, *Crassula*, *Cotyledon*, *Bryophyllum*, *Kalanchoë*, *Pachyphytum*, *Urbinia*, and *Echeveria* are frequently grown under glass or in the home in temperate or cold climates. *Sedum* (stonecrop), however, is used as an outdoor plant for rock gardens in temperate lands. Generally, flowers of plants in the family Crassulaceae are small, but the clusters are particularly showy, especially in *Sempervivum* (houseleek), *Gormania*, *Graptopetalum*, and *Oliveranthus elegans*. Other garden genera are *Monanthes*, from Morocco and the Canary Islands, and *Byrnesia weinbergii*, which is Mexican.

The Crassulaceae, although easily propagated from seeds, also root readily from stem and leaf cuttings. Some species regularly produce offsets from the bases of parent rosettes. In *Kalanchoë* and *Bryophyllum* young plants appear in notches around the margins of leaves still attached to the parent plant; these plantlets either drop off naturally and become established below the main plant, or they can be removed from the parent leaf and planted.

Geissois racemosa (of the family Cunoniaceae) of New Caledonia is a handsome tree with leathery leaves and showy, crimson flowers borne in elongated clusters. Strictly tropical, it is grown only in greenhouses in temperate climates. *Cunonia capensis* of southern Africa is a small tree or large shrub with leathery leaves and dense clusters of small, white flowers. It is occasionally grown as a greenhouse plant.

Davidsonia pruriens (of the family Davidsoniaceae), the Queensland itch tree, is sometimes grown in greenhouses for its two-foot- (60-centimetre-) long leaves, which are covered with bright-red, pungent hairs when young and for its long-stalked clusters of flowers. It is native in northeastern Australia.

Although several genera of the family Escalloniaceae have been introduced into ornamental horticulture—*e.g.*, *Abrophyllum ornans* of New South Wales, Australia; *Anopterus glandulosus* of Tasmania; *Carpodetus serratus*, the putaputaweta of New Zealand; *Corokia cotoneaster* of New Zealand; the New Zealand species *Quintinia acutifolia* and *Q. serrata*, tawhewheo; and *Valdivia gayana* of Chile—none has achieved the importance or interest of the various species and cultivated varieties of *Escallonia*. Escallonias are mainly shiny-leaved, evergreen shrubs or small trees native only to South America, where they are found mostly in the Andes mountains and eastern Brazil. White, pink, or red flowers are frequently present in large clusters; sometimes they are pleasantly aromatic. In the United States these handsome shrubs are very popular in California, where their late-autumn or winter bloom is most welcome.

Eucryphia (of the family Eucryphiaceae) is a small genus of glossy-leaved, evergreen trees and shrubs native in the Southern Hemisphere. *Eucryphia pinnatifolia*, a small tree of Chile, is grown outdoors in parts of England and Scotland—*e.g.*, the Royal Botanic Garden, Edinburgh. The flowers, which are produced in late summer and early fall, are large and white-petalled, with a central cluster of conspicuous yellow stamens giving the whole the appearance of camellia flowers.

Francoa (of the family Francoaceae) is a genus, native in Chile, of several perennial herbs with horizontal underground stems (rhizomes). The plants bear deeply cut, hairy leaves and long-stalked clusters of pure-white, pink, or deep-rose-coloured flowers.

Although the gooseberries and currants (genus *Ribes*, of the family Grossulariaceae) are known chiefly for the edible fruits produced by some species, a number of strikingly handsome, sometimes thorny shrubs are available for the ornamental garden. Species of *Ribes* abound, particularly in western North America and in temperate Eurasia and South America. Among those most attractive as flowering plants are *R. odoratum* and *R. aureum*, both of which have fragrant, yellow flowers; *R. sanguineum* with white or reddish flowers; *R. viscossissimum* with sticky, greenish-white or pinkish, aromatic flowers; and *R. lobbii* with velvety, purple-red flowers. Often the fruits are attractive, some species having translucent scarlet or deep-red fruits and others bearing powder-blue fruits. *Ribes roezlii*, of central and Southern California, has both handsome flowers, which are purple and white, and attractive reddish-purple fruits, which are clothed with reddish, bristly spines.

Probably the most important family of woody ornamental plants in the Saxifragales is Hydrangeaceae. The family is widely distributed in nature, and representatives occur in all parts of the world except Africa, Australia, New Zealand, and the coldest parts of both the Northern and Southern Hemispheres. Species of the family Hydrangeaceae are trees, shrubs, or woody vines, and at least one genus is composed of rhizomatous herbs (*i.e.*, nonwoody plants with underground stems, or rhizomes). Among the plants that have been introduced into ornamental horticulture in greenhouses, gardens, and homes, are the following: *Cardiandra* from China and Japan; *Carpenteria californica*, a native shrub from California; *Decumaria*, a woody climber with two species, one of which occurs in southeastern United States and the other in central China; *Deutzia*, a genus of mostly Asiatic shrubs; *Di-*

*Orna-
mental
stonecrops*

*Goose-
berries and
currants*

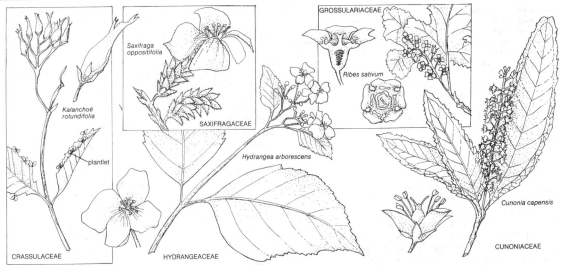

Representative plants from five of the largest families in the order Saxifragales.
Drawing by R. Findahl; *(Ribes sativum)* based on G.H.M. Lawrence,
Taxonomy of Vascular Plants; copyright © by Macmillan Company (1966)

chroa febrifuga of the Himalayas, Malaysia, and China; *Fendlera,* a genus of western American shrubs; *Hydrangea,* a genus of trees, shrubs and woody vines of North and South America, the Himalayas, and central and eastern Asia; *Jamesia americana* (waxflower, wild mock orange), a shrub of semi-arid and mountainous parts of west central United States; *Kirengeshoma palmata,* a perennial herb of Japan; *Philadelphus,* a genus of shrubs of northern Asia and Japan, western America, the southern Atlantic Coast of the United States, and Mexico; *Pileostegia,* a genus of climbing or prostrate evergreen shrubs of the Himalayas and eastern Asia; *Platycrater arguta,* a prostrate shrub of Japan; *Schizophragma,* a genus of climbing shrubs of Japan and China; and *Whipplea,* a genus of low, barely shrubby plants endemic (native) in Oregon, California, Utah, and Colorado. Of the horticulturally important members of the family Hydrangeaceae, the most widely planted and best known to gardeners are species of *Philadelphus, Hydrangea,* and *Deutzia.*

Philadelphus (mock orange, sweet syringa) species are shrubs with solid, white pith and often flaky bark. The flowers are showy and usually white-petalled, with clumps of bright-yellow stamens. These shrubs and their many cultivated varieties, which are widely planted in shrubbery borders, bloom late in spring.

Hydrangeas are known to most gardeners as shrubs, although some are woody vines—*e.g., Hydrangea petiolaris,* climbing hydrangea—and others are small trees, such as *H. arborescens* (mountain hydrangea, sevenbark). *Hydrangea macrophylla* (hortensia), the common hydrangea of florists, is sold as a pot plant for household adornment in many northern cities in the early spring. *Hydrangea paniculata* and its varieties, particularly *grandiflora,* comprise the most commonly grown group. Variety *grandiflora,* a treelike shrub, is probably the best all-around hardy (cold-resistant) hydrangea now in cultivation. Many garden hydrangeas are not entirely hardy in the north, and the aerial stems may die partially or completely to the ground each winter, new flowering stems being produced at the beginning of the next growing season. Hydrangea flowers, white, blue, or pink in colour, are produced in large, showy clusters. Flower clusters of *H. paniculata* often remain on plants for long periods of time, providing colour during midsummer in temperate regions when other garden plants are not flowering. In some species of *Hydrangea,* flower colour seems to be related to soil acidity. The pink-flowered hortensias, for example, show a tendency to turn blue when iron filings or alum are added to the soil to increase acidity. Flowers of *H. paniculata* are white when young, later changing to pink and purple.

Deutzias are shrubs that bear white flowers mostly in terminal clusters. Blooms in some horticultural forms are "double flowered"; that is, they have more than the usual

Hydrangea flowers

single whorl of petals. Like the mock oranges, deutzias often have shreddy bark, but the stem is hollow and does not have the white pith of the mock oranges. Deutzias are very easy to cultivate and provide a fine floral display, mostly in the spring, even on small shrubs 12 inches (30 centimetres) tall. The best known, *Deutzia gracilis,* is a rather bushy shrub that produces numerous white flowers in loose clusters.

Virginian willow (*Itea virginica*) is one of several species of the genus *Itea.* Most species occur in tropical and subtropical Asia. *I. virginica,* the only American species, occurs southward from Pennsylvania and New Jersey to Florida and Louisiana. It is a slender-leaved, deciduous (*i.e.,* the leaves fall in winter), low shrub, two to three feet tall. The white, fragrant flowers, which individually are tiny and not particularly showy, occur in terminal clusters. In autumn, the foliage becomes brilliant red. *Itea yunnanensis* is a large, stout shrub, nine or ten feet (about three metres) tall.

The family Parnassiaceae contains two genera, only one of which, *Parnassia* (grass-of-Parnassus), has any horticultural interest. The low-growing plants are moisture-loving, hardy, perennial herbs of tufted growth habit. The flowers, usually white, greenish white, or yellow, appear between June and September. Species of *Parnassia* occur throughout the Northern Hemisphere, but *P. palustris* is the only one common in Europe.

Penthorum sedoides, the Virginian stonecrop (Penthoraceae), is one member of a small family of plants native in North America and eastern Asia. The leaves of the Virginian stonecrop, which is a branched perennial herb that attains heights of two feet (60 centimetres), are pale green, becoming bright orange with age. These hardy plants, which are used for waterside or shallow-water planting, have flowers that are pale greenish yellow.

Species of several genera of the family Pittosporaceae have achieved horticultural importance; namely, *Billardiera, Marianthus, Sollya,* and *Pittosporum.* The first three genera consist of low sub-shrubs (shrubby forms that are woody only at the base or also very small shrubs) with rather slender, twining or climbing branches. *Pittosporum* is a genus of stout, evergreen shrubs and small trees. All species of the Pittosporaceae are natives of the Old World: *Billardiera* and *Sollya* occur in Australia; *Marianthus* in Australia and Tasmania; and *Pittosporum* chiefly in Australia but also in tropical and subtropical Africa, Asia, New Zealand, and the Pacific Ocean islands. A number of endemic species occur on the Hawaiian Islands. Greatest horticultural interest is centred in *Pittosporum,* certain species of which are hardy or half-hardy plants frequently grown outdoors in California and Florida. Several species, including *P. tobira* (tobira) of China and Japan, are excellent hedge plants. Tobira is also used to decorate the lobbies of hotels and office buildings. Most species of *Pittosporum* have fragrant flowers that may be white, red, yellow, purple, or greenish. *Pittosporum crassifolium* (karo) of New Zealand is a tall shrub or small tree sometimes reaching heights of 30 feet (ten metres). Planted in rows, it is suitable as a windbreak or shelter near the sea because it is resistant to strong winds and salt spray.

The saxifrage family

Among the herbaceous families of the Saxifragales, Saxifragaceae, perhaps with the exception of Crassulaceae, is the most important horticulturally. The genus *Saxifraga* (saxifrage, or rockfoil) has the largest number of species in cultivation. They occur in temperate (principally alpine) and boreal regions. They are rare in Asia, few in South America, and totally absent in southern Africa and the islands of the Pacific Ocean. Other genera with species of more or less horticultural importance include *Astilbe, Bergenia, Bolandra, Boykinia, Heuchera* (alumroot), *Leptarrhena, Lithophragma, Mitella* (bishop's-cap, mitrewort), *Oresitrophe rupifraga, Peltiphyllum peltatum* (umbrella plant), *Rodgersia, Suksdorfia violacea, Sullivantia, Tanakaea radicans, Tellima, Tiarella* (false mitrewort), *Tolmiea menziesii* (pickaback plant), and *Zahlbruckneria paradoxa*.

Practically all Saxifragaceae species are perennial except for a few species in the genus *Saxifraga*. Saxifragaceous plants of ornamental value have a variety of uses in the garden. *Heuchera, Astilbe,* and *Rodgersia,* for example, are best suited to the open garden. Wild garden genera include *Boykinia, Heuchera, Mitella, Tellima,* and *Tiarella. Saxifraga, Tolmiea,* and *Lithophragma* do well in rock gardens. Species of *Bergenia* are often utilized in garden borders because of their ornamental foliage and very early blooming pink or white flowers.

Flowers in the Saxifragaceae range from greenish to white and yellow and from pink and red to purple. Leaves are often thick, almost leathery, shining, and evergreen.

Medicinal and folk uses. A number of saxifragalean plants are used in native medicine and ceremony in different parts of the world. Although several remedies have been ascribed to these plants, it is doubtful that more than a few are of therapeutic value.

Kalanchoë laciniata is used as an external medicine in India. *K. paniculata* is said to have occult uses in Africa. *K. laciniata* is used by the Malays to attract good spirits; twigs of the plant are placed in houses to summon the return of good spirits after a death. The same process is used to drive away evil spirits and to ward them off during serious illnesses such as cholera and smallpox. Children are bathed in water containing leaves of the plant. Leaves are also used to make a poultice for application to the chest of persons with coughs or colds. A compound lotion made of the leaves of *K. laciniata, Costus speciosus, Stachyphrynium* species, *Drymoglossum heterophyllum,* and *Psophocarpus tetragonolobus* is used to treat smallpox. Pulped leaves of *K. laciniata* are used in the Philippines to treat chronic ulcers, sores, and headaches.

Bryophyllum pinnatum is widely used in Malaya; lifegiving properties are attributed to it because of the production of plantlets by the leaves. It is used medicinally by the natives of India, Malaysia, and the Pacific islands. Poultices are prepared from the crushed leaves to relieve headache, coughs, and chest pains. Poultices are used to treat sore eyes in Java, and in Singapore the leaves are sometimes pounded in water, the resulting infusion being drunk to reduce fevers. As a ceremonial plant *B. pinnatum* is employed in connection with fishing—its twigs make up the besom (a brush made of bundled twigs) that is used to sprinkle yellow gruel during incantations designed to improve fishing. Leaves of this species are also used in Malaya during the ceremonial washing of newborn infants.

Ceremonial uses of *Bryophyllum*

It has been reported in South Africa that the fresh juice of *Cotyledon orbiculata* is occasionally used beneficially to treat epilepsy even though the plant is considered toxic. Various species of *Sedum* are also employed medicinally: *S. acre* is sometimes used as a laxative; the juice of *S. dendroideum* is employed in Mexico as an astringent to harden the gums and to relieve hemorrhoidal discomfort.

Leaves of *Sempervivum tectorum* are chewed in parts of Europe as a home remedy for toothache and to relieve the pain of bee stings. A decoction (extract produced by boiling) of the leaves is employed to cure intestinal worms.

The bark of *Weinmannia pinnata* is considered astringent; the same plant secretes a gum that is used in some parts of Cuba as an adulterant of quinine. Similarly, the bark of *W. selloi* is a strong astringent and is used in parts of Brazil to treat wounds. The bitter bark of *Belangera tomentosa* is used as a tonic in some parts of Brazil.

Wood of the Javanese *Polyosma longipes* is said to be useful in treating epidermal scaling (scurf), and the steam produced by boiling the leaves of this species is employed to relieve sore eyes. An extract from the leaves of *Corokia buddleioides* is used in some parts of New Zealand to treat stomachache.

A decoction of the shoots and bark of *Dichroa febrifuga* is taken in the Himalayas as an antipyretic (fever-controlling agent). In Indochina, a decoction of the leaves is used for the same purpose. In Java, the leaves are pounded finely and taken without cooking, together with certain other substances, for fever. In one prescription, the powdered leaves are taken with wormwood (*Artemisia absinthium* and other species of *Artemisia*) as an anthelminthic (intestinal-worm treatment). In another prescription, the powdered leaves are used externally, apparently for intestinal difficulties following childbirth. Fresh leaf and root juices cause vomiting; after the leaves and roots have been soaked in wine and boiled, however, the juice no longer causes vomiting but becomes a gentle purgative.

The dried rhizomes (horizontal underground stems) and roots of *Hydrangea arborescens* of northeastern United States are used medicinally as a diaphoretic (a substance that promotes perspiring) and diuretic. The active principle, hydrangin, is an organic compound known as a cyanogenic glucoside; apparently hydrangin is present in all species of *Hydrangea*. Hydrangin occurs in rhizomes, roots, leaves, and buds. Accidental ingestion of any plant part, under certain conditions, may cause nausea, vomiting, and diarrhea. Treatment consists of washing out the stomach or inducing vomiting.

Poisonous properties of hydrangeas

Penthorum sedoides is employed medicinally in a variety of ways, some of which are quite contradictory—*e.g.,* as a demulcent (a medicine used to soothe irritated mucous membranes) and astringent (a substance that contracts tissues); as a laxative and to treat diarrhea. It reportedly has been used to treat hemorrhoids and gastric ailments.

Phyllonoma laticuspis is known as *hierba de la viruela* (smallpox weed) in parts of Oaxaca, Mexico. It is administered with sugar as a syrup prepared from the green leaves.

An aromatic decoction brewed from the leaves of *Pittosporum pentandrum* in the Philippines is used by women in their baths following childbirth. The powdered bark is employed in small doses to reduce fever. If taken in larger dosages, it is considered a general antidote. It is also effective in relieving bronchitis. The Malays use poultices of both leaves and roots of *P. ferrugineum* to treat malaria. The leaves and fruit are used as a fish poison in Malaysia; the toxic action is probably related to the presence of such complex compounds as saponins, tannins, and alkaloids.

Leaves of *Astilbe philippinensis* are used in northern Luzon, Philippines, for smoking. Sometimes a little tobacco is mixed with the leaves. The rhizome of *Bergenia purpurascens* is used in Chinese medicine to stop bleeding and as a tonic. *Tiarella cordifolia* of North America is considered useful as a diuretic and tonic; in particular, it is said to be beneficial in relieving cases of urinary-bladder stones and other urinary complaints. *Saxifraga sarmentosa,* a native of China and Japan, is used in Java to treat earache. In Tonkin (North Vietnam) and in various parts of China it is also used for complaints of the ear. It is also employed in China for attacks of cholera and to treat hemorrhoids. To treat the former, administration is internal; to treat the latter, application is by steaming.

Timber and other forest products. Timber from trees of *Brunellia* is only of limited importance in tropical

America. The light wood is rather soft, finely textured, easy to work, and perishable when in contact with the ground. The hard, durable wood of *Crypteronia paniculata* trees is used extensively for house building in Malaysia and the Philippines. It is also used for fuel. The sapwood is white, the heartwood reddish brown.

Several trees of the family Cunoniaceae produce timber and other forest products. The bark of *Belangera* of southern Brazil, Paraguay, and Argentina, is used in tanning. The light-pinkish-brown wood is easily worked. The principal use of *Caldcluvia paniculata*, a small tree of southern Chile, is as fuel.

Timber trees of the family Cunoniaceae

Trees of several species of *Weinmannia* occur in both Old and New World tropics. The bark is rich in tannins, and the timber is suitable for furniture and for interior construction. Timber of *W. blumei* from Malaysia is fairly hard but easy to work; red and lustrous, it is moderately resistant to decay. *W. benthami*, the brush mahogany of Australia, produces a timber that is useful in construction and is occasionally used for cabinet work, handles of small utensils, brush backs, and veneer and plywood. *W. lachnocarpa* (rose marara of Australia) is noted for its straight-grained, hard timber, which is employed for turnery, machinery bearings, chisel handles, mallets, and printer's blocks. Timber of *W. racemosa* finds limited use in New Zealand for cabinet work, interior trim, fencing and mine timbers. Wood of *W. descendens* (encinillo) is imported into the United States from northern South America. The timber, light brown to pinkish and reddish brown, is of medium luster, moderately heavy, and fine textured; it is employed for general construction, furniture, cabinets, joinery, turnery (such as brushes, broom handles, dowels, shoe heels, bobbins), and sporting goods.

Tanning substances are extracted from the bark of *W. racemosa* of New Zealand, *W. luzoniensis* of the Philippines, and *W. tinctoria* of Mauritius. Bark of the last named imparts to animal skins a red hue, hence *tinctoria*, which means "used in dyeing."

Ceratopetalum apetalum, the coachwood, or rose mahogany, of Australia, is sometimes imported into the United States, where it is used for the same purposes as *Weinmannia descendens*. Red els, or red alder, *Cunonia capensis* of southern Africa, produces a light, soft timber that is durable underwater. It is suitable for furniture, wagon building, and for construction. Species of *Pancheria* of New Caledonia produce wood that is locally important for cabinetwork and turnery. The wood of *Spiraeanthemum samoense* has been used by natives of the Samoa Islands for canoe construction and war clubs.

The timber of *Escallonia* apparently has no commercial possibilities, owing mostly to the small size of the trees. Locally, however, where trees of sufficient size occur, the wood is utilized for building purposes. The moderately hard and heavy wood is easy to cut, tough to split, and appears to be fairly resistant to decay. Fresh wood of *Escallonia floribunda* has a peculiar odour, and, in certain localities in the Venezuelan Andes, it is called *cochinito* or *puerquito*, both of which mean "little pig."

Eucryphia lucida, Tasmanian leatherwood, produces a fine-textured, tough, durable, brownish wood that is not in general use but is suitable for tool handles, furniture, and heavy construction. *E. moorei* of Australia is sometimes called coachwood because it has been used for frames and bodies of wooden vehicles. Ulmo trees, *Eucryphia cordifolia* of Chile, produce fine-textured timber with good working qualities but not very resistant to decay. The lustrous heartwood is brown and variable. In Chile, ulmo wood makes excellent flooring, and, in the nitrate-mining areas, it is used for railway crossties and for poles that support power lines. Other uses of ulmo are for furniture manufacture, vehicle parts, oars, and pilings. An extract of the bark, which contains about 15 percent tannins, is used in commercial tanning.

Woods of the hydrangea family

The fine-textured, whitish wood of *Deutzia scabra* is used in Japan for marquetry (delicate inlaywork) and for wooden nails. *Hydrangea paniculata* produces a hard, fine-textured wood prized in Japan for walking sticks, umbrella handles, tobacco pipes, and wooden nails; the bark is used to manufacture paper. The wood of *Itea nutans* is attractive and is used in Malaysia for small articles of turnery.

Pittosporum crassifolium of New Zealand furnishes a very tough, whitish wood favoured for marquetry. In the Philippines, fruits of *P. resiniferum* are known as "petroleum nuts" because of the fancied resemblance of the odour of the oil to that of petroleum and because even the green, fresh fruits burn brilliantly. The oil contains two organic compounds, a dihydroterpene and considerable quantities of heptane. The white, fine-textured wood of *P. resiniferum* is not durable; it is sometimes used in Malaysia for house rafters and for firewood.

Fruits, seasonings, and other edible products.   *Sedum album* is sometimes used as an herb in salads; leaves of *S. reflexum* are occasionally consumed in salads or soups; and the leaves of *S. roseum* are eaten fresh, soured, or in oil by Eskimos in Alaska. Young shoots of *Crypteronia paniculata* are eaten as flavouring with rice in Indonesia. Flowers of *Eucryphia cordifolia* of Chile are rich in nectar and are prized as a source of honey.

Many species of *Ribes* bear edible fruits of considerable commercial importance. Among the important fruit-producing species is the European gooseberry (*R. grossularia*), which is used in desserts, in pies, and in jams and wines. The European black currant (*R. nigrum*) is eaten fresh or in jams or puddings. *R. rubrum* produces both red and white currants that are used for desserts, pastries, and wine. *R. vulgare*, an American currant, is eaten fresh or in desserts and pies. Other species of less importance for their edible fruits include the buffalo, or Missouri, currant (*R. odoratum*) and some American gooseberries, such as *R. hirtellum, R. cynosbati, R. oxyacanthoides, R. setosum,* and *R. inerme*. The most important fruit-bearing species of *Ribes* are available in many improved and selected varieties.

Young leaves of *Hydrangea thunbergii* from Japan are gathered, steamed, rolled between the hands, dried, and used as a substitute for tea; the preparation is called amacha, or ama-tsja (tea-of-heaven).

Edible saxifrages

Plants of *Saxifraga erosa*, mountain lettuce, or deertongue, are used in salads by mountain people in southern Pennsylvania. The thick, fleshy leafstalks of *S. peltata* (Indian rhubarb) were peeled and eaten raw or boiled by Indians of the west coast of North America. Succulent leaves of *S. punctata* (dotted saxifrage) are consumed by Eskimos either raw or after being kept in oil. *Chrysosplenium alternifolium* (golden saxifrage), a perennial herb of Eurasia and North America, is occasionally used in salad and as an emergency food in the Vosges mountains (France). The leaves of *Bergenia crassifolia* (badan) are used by the Mongols as a substitute for tea called tschager tea.

Role in white-pine blister rust disease.   Among the most serious and widespread diseases of forest trees is the white-pine blister rust. This disease is caused by a parasitic fungus, *Cronartium ribicola*, which spends part of its life cycle as a parasite of a susceptible five-needled pine and the other part on certain species of *Ribes* (currants and gooseberries of the family Grossulariaceae). *Ribes nigrum* is the most susceptible species.

The fungus overwinters as a mycelium (filamentous vegetative body) in the stems of *Ribes;* spores (reproductive bodies) are produced by the first week in April, depending upon climatic conditions. The wind-borne spores may be carried several miles. They germinate on moist leaves of *Ribes* plants, and the fungal germination tube enters the leaves through stomates (pores) on the lower surface. Following growth of the fungus in the tissues of the leaves, pustules form on the leaves; from them, other wind-borne spores are released that carry the disease to the pines. The spores germinate on the pine needles, entering through stomates. Eventually, the rapidly growing fungus enters the water and food conducting system of the pine and then moves into the bark, on which externally visible cankers form. After about two years, pustules appear on the surfaces of these cankers. Wind-borne spores from the pustules can infect only species of *Ribes*, not pines. Thus, both *Ribes* and pines must be present together within a favourable environment in order to perpetuate the fungus. When control measures proved insufficient to halt the spread of the disease after its introduction from Europe in the early 1900s, programs for the systematic eradication of *Ribes* plants, including wild, nursery, and crop plants, were begun in regions in which white pines are of commercial and economic importance. Thus today, in many places in the United States where *Ribes* was once native, wild plants are very difficult to find in nature.

NATURAL HISTORY

Insect-trapping plants. The families Cephalotaceae, Byblidaceae, and Roridulaceae have been reported to be insectivorous. Insectivorous implies the ability of plants to "eat" insects, which, of course, they do not; rather, by a series of mechanisms, insectivorous plants trap insects and externally digest parts of them. Although insectivorous plants doubtless receive some nutrition from the bodies of insects, most can exist quite well without an insect diet. Insectivorous plants usually grow in soils that are deficient in nitrogen salts, which are used by plants in the manufacture of amino acids and proteins. Therefore they require a supplementary source of nitrogen, which they obtain by digesting the proteins in captured insect bodies.

Of the three families of Saxifragales noted above, only Cephalotaceae and Byblidaceae are truly insectivorous in the sense that they both capture and digest insects. Plants of the Roridulaceae, a family restricted to southwestern Africa, are known to trap insects in the resinous secretions of their leaves, but there is no evidence that any form of digestion takes place or that the plants benefit from these accidentally ensnared insects.

Roridula dentata, for example, is known not to digest the insects, which, by incidentally coming into contact with the leaves, become stuck on the plants. Even though these insects apparently do not benefit the plant, they are used as food by a spider of the genus *Synaema*. This spider, which has become adapted to life on *Roridula* plants, is immune to the sticky secretions and is thus able to move without difficulty. The spiders generally hide among the dried leaves or in nests that they build there, awaiting the vibration of a twig, indicating the presence of an ensnared insect, which the spider kills. There thus appears to be a symbiotic relationship between the spider and the plant; clearly the spider benefits from the relationship, but whether the plant is benefitted or not is unknown.

The insectivorous nature of plants of Byblidaceae and Cephalotaceae is more firmly established; apparently, a true capture-and-digest system exists. Byblidaceae consists of one genus, *Byblis,* and two species in western Australia. Plants of *B. gigantea* are shrublets, attaining heights of 50 centimetres (20 inches) and consisting of a woody rhizome bearing in any one season the dying parts of the previous growing season and the growing parts of the present season. These parts consist usually of a main stem, which is sparsely branched near the base. The long, linear, yellow-green leaves of the stems are covered with numerous mucilage glands, which give the leaf a glistening surface. Plants of *B. linifolia* are more delicate than those of *B. gigantea,* and the annual stem and its branches arise from a slender rhizome. These parts are also clothed with mucilage-secreting glands.

The glands are of two kinds, stalked and unstalked. Experiments have shown that minute cubes of coagulated egg albumen—a proteinaceous material such as might be found in insect bodies—placed in contact with the unstalked glands completely disappear after a period of from two to eight days. When this same proteinaceous material is placed in contact with the stalked glands, there is no evidence of digestion.

In other observations, when trapped insects came in contact with unstalked glands, the latter produced a secretion that was much less viscous than that of the stalked glands. The actual mode of digestion of insects by these plants is still not completely known.

Plants of *Byblis* are sometimes infested with a small

Spider immune to insect-trapping secretions

(Top left) *Byblis gigantea* (Byblidaceae), showing glandular, haired leaves and flowers. (Top right) *Cephalotus follicularis* (Cephalotaceae), showing complete plant with both normal and pitcher leaves. (Bottom left) *Brexia madagascariensis* (Brexiaceae) twig with fruits, flowers, and buds. (Bottom right) *Ribes roezlii* (Grossulariaceae) twig with flowers, showing reflexed sepals, two-lobed stigma, and hairy ovary; base of thorn can be seen at upper right.

(Top left, top right, bottom right) Sherwin Carlquist, Rancho Santa Ana Botanic Garden, Claremont, California; (bottom left) William Louis Stern

wingless capsid (members of a family of the insect order Heteroptera). Although other small insects are ensnared in the mucilage, capsids appear to be able to move unhindered over the surface of *Byblis* leaves.

The family Cephalotaceae consists of one species, *Cephalotus follicularis,* the west Australian pitcher plant, which occurs only in the southwestern corner of Australia. The plant has an underground rootstock from which two kinds of leaves are produced, foliage leaves and pitcher leaves. Foliage leaves and pitcher leaves are produced in a seasonal rhythm: the foliage leaves develop in the autumn, reaching full size and abundance in spring; pitchers grow in winter and spring and are fully formed and functional in summer when the insects they capture are most plentiful.

Foliage leaves attain a maximum length of 13 or 14 centimetres (about five inches); the blade is ovate and pointed at the apex and is equally as long as the petiole (leafstalk). The thick, leathery, and smooth foliage leaves are studded with nectar glands. Pitcher leaves are about five centimetres or more long when fully mature. They measure about two centimetres (about one inch) across and are somewhat compressed front to back. There is an oval opening, wider crosswise than from back to front. The petiole, or leafstalk, is approximately at right angles to the axis of the pitcher; it is attached dorsally below the "hinge" of the lid at about the level of the opening. The mouth of the pitcher is surrounded by a thickened corrugated rim, each ridge of which forms a clawlike tooth that extends into and is directed downward toward the base of the pitcher. Each pitcher has a lid that overhangs the opening and is more or less open, depending upon the age of the leaf. The lid is traversed radially by narrow patches of green tissue between which are clear patches devoid of chlorophyll. The clear patches have the appearance of window-like areas framed in green. To entrapped insects, the clear patches probably appear to be open spaces, and they attempt to escape through them until, eventually exhausted, they fall into the depths of the pitcher.

The interior of the pitcher has two zones. The upper

Pitcher-shaped, insect-trapping leaves

zone forms a ridge around the mouth of the pitcher and arches over the internal cavity. The epidermis (surface) of the upper zone is studded with downward pointing hairs, as is the inside of the lid. A smooth, glassy surface characterizes the interior zone of the pitcher, which has a glandular surface. The flask-shaped glands have been reported to be digestive in function. Within the pitcher a shelflike bolster projects inwardly but is not apparent externally; it contains glands, among which are many "water pores," or hydathode-like (water-secreting) structures. The water pores resemble stomates, but the orifice between the guard cells is continuously open. Presumably, the fluid that fills the pitcher is produced from these pores. This action, however, has not yet been proven conclusively.

Some botanists have demonstrated that fluid taken from virgin, or unopened, pitchers can digest animal substances. Others, however, have not been able to find any fluid in unopened pitchers and have reported the presence of fluid only in opened pitchers. In any event, it has repeatedly been observed that pitchers do capture insects, notably ants. Small pitchers catch small insects. That soft parts of these insects undergo dissolution of some sort is evident. There is some question, however, as to whether this dissolution is the result of digestive enzymes secreted by the pitcher glands, by extraneous micro-organisms, or both.

Although pitcher fluid, sterilized to kill any micro-organisms, will digest proteinaceous material in the laboratory, it still cannot be concluded that this digestive process actually takes place in pitchers under normal circumstances. It is presumed, nevertheless, that digestion by pitcher fluid may take place very slowly in the pitchers; available evidence indicates that both the secretions of the pitchers and the actions of micro-organisms contribute to the digestion of insect proteins. Plants grown under laboratory conditions without the presence of insects thrive and flower. The question, therefore, remains concerning the usefulness or necessity of insect protein to insectivorous plants.

Reproductive biology. *Epiphyllous flowers.* Flowers that are borne on or produced from leaves are termed epiphyllous flowers. Flowers and fruits of plants in the genus *Phyllonoma* are borne directly on the upper surface of leaf blades. In *P. ruscifolia,* all stages of flower and fruit development may be found on one plant at any time. The cluster of flowers is produced from the midvein well toward the tip of the mature leaf. From the point of attachment of the cluster of flowers, the leaf narrows rapidly toward the pointed apex. Not all leaves bear flower clusters. There has been some question about the morphological nature of the flower-bearing green leaves. Some botanists have thought them to be expanded stems (cladodes) modified for both photosynthesis and reproduction; others have proposed that the leafstalk and flower stalk represent fused structures. Studies of the minute structure of the leaf indicate, however, that they are true leaves and that a separate flower stalk is not fused to midvein of the leaf.

Pollination processes. Before fertilization can take place in flowering plants, it is necessary for viable pollen to be transferred from stamens (male reproductive organs) and deposited on receptive pistils (female structures). If this transfer takes place within the same flower, it is called self-pollination. Self-pollination, however, is not always accompanied by fertilization and the setting, or producing, of seed, because some plants are not self-compatible; that is, some plants do not have the genetic capacity to produce seed even when the style (the narrow upper portion of the pistil) is dusted with pollen from the same flower. When seed is produced as a result of fertilization by pollen from the same flower, the term self-compatible is used. Cross-pollination refers to the transfer of pollen from flowers of one plant to the pistils in flowers of another plant of the same species in order to effect pollination and subsequently fertilization and the setting of seed.

Species of the family Saxifragaceae apparently have mechanisms that prevent self-pollination. Dichogamy,

for example, is a condition that involves the separate maturing, in terms of time, of stamens and pistils in the same flower. It results when the anthers do not release their pollen at the same time the stigmas (pollen-receptive surfaces of the pistil) are receptive. There are two variations of this arrangement, protandry and protogyny. In protandry, the anthers are ready to liberate their pollen before the stigma of the same flower is structurally and physiologically receptive; in protogyny, the stigma matures before the anthers of the same flower are ready to shed pollen. In the Saxifragaceae that have been studied, protandry is predominant. This condition has also been reported for *Parnassia*, of the family Parnassiaceae. As with many groups of plants, biological phenomena of this kind have not been studied in detail in most families of the order Saxifragales.

Heterostyly is another reproductive phenomenon that has been observed in members of the Saxifragaceae. Heterostylous plants have bisexual flowers of two or three different kinds. They are distinguished from each other by the size and behaviour of the reproductive structures; for example, *Jepsonia heterandra*, a very locally distributed native plant of California, has distylous flowers. Some plants produce long-styled (called pin) flowers, and others produce short-styled (thrum) flowers. Pin flowers also have large stigmas and short stamens that produce many small pollen grains. Thrum flowers have small stigmas and long stamens that produce fewer but larger pollen grains.

Heterostyly is one of the most extraordinary reproductive devices by which cross fertilization is insured in higher plants. Even though a heterostylous flower contains complete and functional structures of both sexes, the plants, because they contain a genetic factor that inhibits self-fertilization, must be cross-pollinated. Although the flowers are bisexual, functionally they are either male or female, and cross-pollination is as obligatory as in species with separate male and female flowers.

Pollination agents. Pollination in saxifragalean families is usually by insects. The following account of pollinators in *Jepsonia heterandra* is typical of other species with similar breeding systems. Soon after the opening of anthers in the morning, flowers of *J. heterandra* are visited by flies, especially by several genera of syrphids, as well as by small bees, especially the species *Dialictus ornduffi*. The male insects visit flowers to obtain nectar (but not pollen) and to mate with females. In the course of these activities, pollen occasionally adheres to the bodies of the bees and is consequently available for transfer to other flowers. The females, which visit flowers to gather both pollen and nectar, collect abundant quantities of *Jepsonia* pollen on the posterior pair of legs.

Syrphid flies drink nectar from *Jepsonia* flowers but do not crawl into the flowers as do female *Dialictus ornduffi*; rather, the flies remain at the entrance to the floral axis and on the styles. From this position the proboscis (elongated mouthparts) is extended down to the nectaries at the base of the petals. When this happens, pollen from the anthers is transferred to the underside of the fly's head, and the proboscis also becomes coated with pollen. During grooming activities, pollen from the head and proboscis is transferred to the forelegs. Flies visiting other flowers transfer the pollen to them, effecting cross-pollination.

Other pollinators of saxifragalean plants have been recorded, and flies have been observed transferring pollen of certain species of the family Crassulaceae and *Parnassia*. Most flowers of *Parnassia* have conspicuous nectar-secreting staminodia (sterile, or aborted, stamens), which act as glands and secrete glistening droplets of nectar; flies feeding on this nectar may become dusted with pollen. Pollination in *Roridula* appears to be carried out by small Heteroptera. When the sensitive anthers in *Roridula* are touched by a suitable visitor, they suddenly spring upright, scattering pollen over the insect. The brightly coloured tubular flowers of some Crassulaceae —e.g., *Bryophyllum*—are pollinated by birds. Pollination of *Escallonia* has not been observed in the wild, but the abundant nectar makes insect pollination very likely.

Flowers growing from leaf surfaces

Cross-pollination ensured by flower structure

Flowers of *E. rubra* growing in England have been observed to be visited both by honeybees and bumblebees, the latter even biting their way into closed flowers to secure the nectar (see POLLINATION for additional information about the mechanisms involved in the process).

Ecology. Plants belonging to the order Saxifragales inhabit almost the complete range of environmental conditions on earth. They are to be found growing in deserts and semideserts, under mesic (moist) conditions, and in water; they occur at sea level and in the mountains above the tree line; they grow in humid and dry tropical atmospheres, in the cold of the Arctic and Antarctic, and in the snowy reaches of the European Alps, the Andes, and the Himalayas.

Escallonias growing at high elevations

Escallonia, the largest in numbers (60 species) of the seven genera of the family Escalloniaceae, is confined to South America except for one species that reaches Costa Rica. The genus is found predominantly in mountainous regions, but in the southernmost portion of its range in South America, it grows in a temperate climate near the sea. In the cordilleras of Bolivia, Peru, Ecuador, and Colombia, plants of *Escallonia* grow as low shrubs at an elevation in excess of 4,000 metres (13,000 feet), extending above the tree line. The Valdivian rain forests of Chile contain several species of *Escallonia*. In the dry scrub vegetation of central Chile, *Escallonia* grows in company with *Araucaria* (monkey-puzzle tree), *Alnus* (alder), and sclerophyllous shrubs—typically leathery-leaved plants of dry habitats. In such dry areas of Chile, and from Argentina to Venezuela, *Escallonia* species occur at the bases of valleys near sources of underground water. In southeast Brazil, Uruguay, and portions of adjacent Argentina, *Escallonia* occurs in the forest. In other regions of Chile and Brazil, some species of *Escallonia* grow in flooded areas and swamps, but they are rarely found in the shrub-covered *campos* (level, grassy plains areas with scattered trees or shrubs). In the high cordilleras from northwestern Argentina to Peru, *Escallonia* plants are not scarce on the upper cloud forest border, and further north in Colombia, they penetrate the *páramos* (high, treeless plains). The highest cloud forest sites that support the growth of *Escallonia* occur in parts of the southeastern Brazilian coastal ranges and in Costa Rica, where species live in sub-alpine meadows together with numerous members of the family Ericaceae (heaths).

Brunelliaceae, consisting of the single genus *Brunellia*, is another strictly tropical American group of plants. It is distributed along the western side of America from about 23° north latitude in Mexico and the Greater Antilles south to 18° in Bolivia. Like *Escallonia*, most species of *Brunellia* grow in mountain forests, from elevations of about 600 metres (2,000 feet) to 3,800 metres (12,500 feet). One group of *Brunellia* species occurs at low elevations, from 600 to 2,000 metres (2,000 to 6,500 feet). Another group inhabits cold regions and is usually found between 2,800 and 3,200 metres (9,200 and 10,500 feet) elevation. In contrast, *B. hygrothermica* is part of the sea-level vegetation, where temperatures range between 30° and 39° C (86° and 102° F) and the rainfall amounts to 8,000 millimetres (320 inches).

The family Crassulaceae is of cosmopolitan distribution, but species are particularly concentrated in the dry regions of southern Africa, the Macronesian islands (Azores, Canary Islands), and in western North America. Most plants of the Crassulaceae are characterized by their moderate to extreme succulence—thick, fleshy stem and leaf growth—and most members of the family are remarkable for their dry-habitat-adapted structure, particularly mucilaginous water-storage tissues in the leaf and stem. Some species are believed capable of absorbing water directly from the air through special hairs, surface cells, or aerial roots. Bladder hairs of *Crassula falcata*, for example, can take up moisture from the atmosphere. Many plants of the family are of the rosette growth habit. Their crowded, basically disposed leaves are able to retain moisture in the form of dew; absorption of this moisture may take place directly through the leaves or through special hairs. The viviparous habit (*i.e.*, the production of plantlets directly from leaves of the parent plant) of *Bryophyllum* species may be an adaptation to arid conditions; the plantlets are ready to grow in the presence of the slightest moisture.

The family Saxifragaceae illustrates the entire range of adaptation to differing moisture conditions found in the order. *Saxifraga nutans* is a true aquatic plant, *S. pennsylvanicum* is a bog plant, and *S. micranthidifolia* grows in cold mountain streams and on wet rocks. Other species are more or less adapted to dry conditions (*i.e.*, they are xerophilous), among them *S. tridactyloides*, which stores moisture in small bulblike bodies on the stem (bulbils). Similarly, *S. trifurcata* has a strongly cuticularized (wax-coated) epidermis, *S. globulifera* produces membranous bud scales and hairy stipules, and *S. aspera* stores moisture in its fleshy, heavily cuticularized, long-persistent leaves; all are examples of adaptations to dry habitats. In some saxifrages, leaf rosettes are produced. The bases of the lower leaves in the rosettes are only weakly cuticularized, so that dew accumulating there may be absorbed by the leaves in sufficient quantity to enable the flowering shoot to develop.

Saxifrages growing on rocks

Species of the genus *Saxifraga* are known for their tenacious ability to grow and thrive on exposed rocky crags and in fissures of rocks. The name *Saxifraga* literally means "rock breaker." Thus saxifrages grow high in the Alpine regions of the mountains of Europe, in places that are covered with snow and ice for long periods of the year. The plants have tough, wiry root systems and deeply penetrating taproots. In the same harsh environments, some saxifrages (*e.g.*, *S. hirculus*) develop as cushion plants. This involves a considerable reduction in leaf surface (that is, a diminution of the evaporating surface) and a foreshortened shoot. These low cushion plants are also often adaptable to bog conditions.

Most Saxifragaceae species, however, grow in moist, shaded woodlands. Among these are species of *Saxifraga*, *Astilbe*, *Rodgersia*, *Astilboides*, *Peltiphyllum*, and *Boykinia*.

FORM AND FUNCTION

The several families that make up the order Saxifragales are held together by a pattern of overlapping similarities, rather than by characteristics held in common by all families. Perhaps the order is best described by its internal heterogeneity instead of by its homogeneity. Practically all growth forms of plants are found, including trees, shrubs, and woody climbers among the woody types; and annual and perennial herbs among the herbaceous types. Leaves are alternate or opposite, with or without stipules (basal appendages). Sometimes the flowers contain elements of both sexes—that is, stamens (male) and pistils (female)—but in some groups the flowers may be either entirely male or female. The flowers are almost always radially symmetrical. Generally the petals are free; that is, separate and not fused to each other. Stamens vary from few in each flower to many and indefinite in number. The ovule-bearing segments of the pistil (carpels) may be separate, but more often they are fused to each other. All conditions of ovary insertion are present, ranging from ovaries positioned above the other flower parts (superior ovaries) to those wholly enclosed by the fused bases of the sepals, petals, and stamens (inferior ovaries) as well as various intermediate conditions. Seeds usually have abundant nutrient tissues for the developing embryos (endosperm). More homogeneity exists among the anatomical features. The pollen grains, for example, are usually tricolporate, which means they have three germinal pores. Among the woody families, vessel elements (water-conducting cells) have end openings predominantly with ladderlike cross-bars (scalariform perforations), whereas among the herbaceous families, the vessel elements usually have simple perforations.

Several of the families are very distinctive in certain features. The family Phyllonomaceae is characterized by flowers borne directly on the leaves. The family Crassulaceae is well known for its extreme succulence and the presence of crassulacean acid metabolism. Byblidaceae is insectivorous, and Cephalotaceae is distinguished by its remarkable urn-shaped leaves and its insectivorous nutrition. The family Francoaceae is distinctive in having a diacytic stomatal apparatus (*i.e.*, stomates, pores in leaf surfaces, with two epidermal cells enclosing the pore so that their common wall is at right angles to the long axis of the stomate). The family Davidsoniaceae is characterized by its irritant hairs. In addition to normal phloem external to the water-conducting xylem, the family Crypteroniaceae also has internal phloem; *i.e.*, food-conducting tissues located within the stem interior, between the pith and the inner surface of the xylem. The families Roridulaceae and Byblidaceae are characterized by the circinate vernation of their leaves; the leaves are rolled lengthwise in the bud, like those of ferns. Pittosporaceae has secretory canals in the axis.

EVOLUTION

Fossil record. Although many species of fossils have been described and assigned saxifragalean names and relationships, it is impossible in many cases to establish with any degree of certainty the veracity of these assignments as far as the real relationships of the fossil plant material is concerned; thus the following examples should be viewed with an understanding of this qualification.

The family Saxifragaceae is represented in the fossil record by *Saxifraga,* found in many European localities in deposits as old as the Tertiary Period (65,000,000 to 2,500,000 years ago), but most have come from the Pleistocene Epoch (which began about 2,500,000 years ago) and more recent deposits. Various fruits and leaves from England, Czechoslovakia, and Germany in Eocene (54,-000,000 to 38,000,000 years ago) and more recent deposits, and *Chrysosplenium* from the middle Pliocene of England, are also known from the Saxifragaceae. The family Hydrangeaceae is represented by *Philadelphus,* known from Canada in deposits as old as the Upper Cretaceous; and by *Deutzia, Schizophragma, Decumaria,* and *Hydrangea* from many European, Central Soviet Union, Japanese, Alaskan, and North American localities of Tertiary age. *Ixerba* of the family Brexiaceae has been found in the Pliocene of New Zealand. *Itea* of the family Iteaceae occurs in Tertiary deposits of Italy. The family Escalloniaceae is known from the Pliocene of New Zealand and Bolivia (*Quintinia* and *Escallonia,* respectively) and is also known from the Pleistocene of New Zealand (*Carpodetus*).

The family Grossulariaceae is known in fossil form by *Ribes,* found in European and North American Tertiary deposits, and by *Riboidoxylon* (wood) from the Upper Cretaceous in California. The family Cunoniaceae is represented by the fossil genus *Cunonioxylon* (wood) from Upper Oligocene deposits in the eastern Alps of Europe. Leaf and stem fossils of the family Crassulaceae are known from France and The Netherlands in Tertiary deposits. A flower of *Billardierites* of the family Pittosporaceae has been found in amber of Miocene age (26,000,000 to 7,000,000 years ago) from the Smaland Peninsula of the Baltic coast.

Several conclusions can be drawn from the above data. Members of the Saxifragales have been present at least since the beginning of the Tertiary Period—that is, from the Paleocene Epoch (which began about 65,000,000 years ago)—and probably even earlier. There are several reports of saxifragalean plants from earlier strata (*e.g.*, *Philadelphus* and *Ribes* from Upper Cretaceous sediments). The occurrence of the wood of *Ribes,* represented by the form genus *Riboidoxylon,* is well dated and based on modern methods. It can probably be accepted as the earliest documented discovery of a saxifragalean plant. The Late Upper Cretaceous deposits of the Panoche Formation, in which *Riboidoxylon* occurs, are dated at between 70,000,000 and 80,000,000 years ago.

A comparison of the geographic distribution of fossil forms with modern representatives of the same genera is instructive. Modern species of *Philadelphus* grow in southern Europe, Asia, and North and Central America. The fossil occurrence of *Philadelphus* in what is today northern Germany is thought to indicate a recent contraction of an originally broader range for the genus.

Fossils of the hydrangea family

Today, species of *Hydrangea* occur from India to Japan, in the Malay Archipelago, in North and Central America, and in western South America. The fossil range of *Hydrangea* in northern, central, and southern Europe provides evidence that the genus was more widely distributed in geologically earlier times than it is now.

More difficult to explain are the occurrences of other fossil saxifragalean plants in northern latitudes, for example, the *Cunonia*-like wood in the eastern European Alps and the *Billardiera*-like flower in the Baltic region of present-day Germany. The family Cunoniaceae is mostly southern in distribution today and the Pittosporaceae, to which family *Billardiera* belongs, is fundamentally Australian, eight of its nine genera being found on that continent.

These outstanding disjunctive distributions must be viewed with considerable prudence pending other forms of corroborative evidence such as a re-examination of the identifications and a search for other southern plant forms in the beds containing these reputed saxifragalean ancestors. Overall, however, the conclusion that is drawn from presently available data and observations is that present-day distributions of saxifragalean plants are remarkably similar to those that existed as long ago as the Upper Cretaceous Period.

Phylogeny. The fossil record of the order Saxifragales is too fragmentary to enable any conclusions to be drawn concerning its early origins and relationships. All that can be stated with any assurance is that saxifragalean plants appeared in Late Upper Cretaceous times contemporaneously with representatives of many other families of flowering plants. Doubtless, the actual progenitors of plants with saxifragalean relationships were in the process of evolving long before Saxifragales are recorded in fossil-bearing strata. Nothing is known about the real relationships of these ancient plants of saxifragalean alliance nor from which plants they may have evolved.

Information from comparative studies of present-day Saxifragales species seems to point to an origin from ancestors of the order Dilleniales. The order Saxifragales is closely related to the order Rosales, and perhaps its nearest affinities are with members of this group. Although the anatomy of the wood of several families in the Saxifragales is more primitive than that of the most primitive representatives of the Rosales, floral structure in some saxifragalean families reaches a higher level of specialization than that found in any rosalean families. It appears, then, that both the Rosales and Saxifragales owe their origins to forebears of the Dilleniales, perhaps to ancient plants of magnolialean (*i.e.*, the order Magnoliales and its relatives) alliance.

Ancestry of the order Saxifragales

CLASSIFICATION

Distinguishing taxonomic features. In flowering plants, floral characteristics provide the major bases for family delineations. To a lesser extent, vegetative features are used—*i.e.*, the morphology of leaves and twigs, growth habit of the plant, texture of the bark, and sometimes microscopic structure and chemical constituents. Some plant families have unique or almost unique properties, such as insectivorousness or epiphyllous flowers, which enable the plant taxonomist to characterize the family. Usually, however, this is not the case, and families are established on a combination of characteristics; it is this combination of characteristics that sets the family apart from other closely related families.

The generalizations above hold true for the families that comprise the order Saxifragales. Some families have evolved very specialized structural innovations, but most owe their distinctiveness to a combination of characters rather than to any single character. Because the elements that make up the order Saxifragales can be interpreted in various ways, plant taxonomists over the years have assembled different schemes of arrangement; usually the schemes are influenced by their creators' ideas of the features that are the most reliable indicators of relationship and whether larger or smaller groups of plants are more reflective of natural conditions. Nevertheless, the several schemes of arrangement are more or less based on the same data and raw materials. The manner in which these are employed and weighted gives rise to some of the differences in systems of arrangement of saxifragalean families.

Among the useful characters employed to subdivide the order Saxifragales into families is the predominant habit (growth form) and duration of the plants—that is, whether the plants are woody or herbaceous, and, if herbaceous, if they are annual or perennial. Using these criteria, the order is divided into two main groups of families, those with mostly woody, perennial plants and those made up mostly of herbaceous species. Herbaceous Saxifragales are usually perennials, but annual plants predominate in a few families. Useful characteristics of the leaves concern phyllotaxy—that is, whether the leaves are alternate, opposite, or whorled on the stem. All three dispositions occur in different parts of the order. The presence or absence of stipules (basal appendages on leafstalks) and of simple or compound leaves have been useful in separating families. Fusion of sepals and petals, and of the carpels (the ovule-bearing segments of the ovary), are pertinent criteria in distinguishing among the families. The number of stamens, whether they are definite or indefinite in number, is also a meaningful character for delineating saxifragalean families. Position of other floral parts in relation to the pistil (female organ)—that is, whether sepals, petals, and stamens are attached below, at, or above the attachment to the floral axis of the ovary—is an important means of segregating families in this order. The kind of fruit produced is indicative of familial cohesiveness, as is the number of coats on the seeds.

Annotated classification. The classification of the order Saxifragales into families as presented here incorporates both traditional information from floral structure and vegetative morphology, and ancillary data on the microscopic anatomy of plant parts. This classification, in its broader aspects, conforms to others published in recent years. Unlike some systems, however, which separate the families Philadelphaceae and Hydrangeaceae, these two are united here, and the combined group is considered under the name Hydrangeaceae. Because of the many overlapping characters between the two groups, relationships are better preserved and expressed by joining rather than by separating them.

Basis of the classification system

The family Paracryphiaceae (with *Paracryphia* as the only genus) is included provisionally within the order, but the relationship is not wholly certain. *Lepuropetalon*, considered as the basis of a separate family (Lepuropetalaceae) by some plant taxonomists, is tentatively included within the family Parnassiaceae (which has two genera, *Parnassia* and *Lepuropetalon*). Unlike the situation with *Paracryphia*, *Lepuropetalon* has long been included in the family Saxifragaceae, and it seems to be related to this general alliance of plants. Its inclusion as a second genus of Parnassiaceae, however, is a departure from traditional treatments.

A number of the taxa here considered as families are assigned merely to generic status by some taxonomists. In treatments by other taxonomists, all or some of the families included here in the order Saxifragales are put into different orders along with another variety of families. Such dispositions reflect valuation and weighting by different taxonomists and are not to be considered "wrong" on this basis alone; rather, they are legitimate expressions of personal predilections. The classification system presented below is based on that of the Soviet botanist Armen Takhtajan (1969).

ORDER SAXIFRAGALES

Trees, shrubs, lianas (vines), and perennial and annual herbs bearing alternate or opposite, entire or lobed, simple or compound leaves, with or without stipules (basal appendages). Flowers mainly bisexual, sometimes unisexual, radially symmetrical (actinomorphic) or rarely weakly bilaterally symmetrical (zygomorphic), usually both sepals and petals present. Petals free or rarely more or less joined (connate). Stamens (male reproductive organs) few, the same in number as the sepals, twice as many, or numerous. Gynoecium (female flower parts) of separate free carpels (ovule-bearing structures) or more often of fused carpels. Ovary is positioned above the

insertion point of the sepals, petals, and stamens (superior), half-inferior, or inferior (*i.e.*, below the attachment point of the other flower parts). Ovules with 2 outer tissue layers (integuments, or seed coats) or more rarely with only 1 integument. Seeds usually with abundant endosperm (nutrient tissue for developing embryo) and a small embryo. Twenty-eight families, 165 genera, and about 3,340 species with worldwide distribution. Major centres of distribution include New Guinea and Australasia; Australia; Japan, Taiwan, and the Philippines; southern Africa; and tropical and temperate America.

Family Cunoniaceae

Shrubs and trees with opposite or whorled, often pinnately (with leaflets on both sides of a central axis) or trifoliolately (with 3 leaflets) compound leathery leaves, frequently with marginal serrations (notches or teeth) that bear glands. Stipules present, often united in pairs. Flowers small, usually bisexual in compound inflorescences (clusters); receptacle (expanded stem tip bearing the flower parts) usually flat. Sepals 4 or 5. Petals 4 or 5, usually smaller than sepals, often lacking. Stamens 8 to 10, many, or 4 or 5; disc (tissue region from which stamens arise) often annular. Ovary superior, usually of 2 fused carpels, 2-chambered; rarely 2 separate carpels; generally with many to 2 ovules in 2 rows in each chamber; styles (upper narrow part of pistil) free. Fruit usually a capsule, rarely a drupe (single-seeded, bony-pitted, fleshy fruit) or nut. Endosperm usually copious. Twenty-six genera and 250 species, chiefly distributed between 13° and 35° south latitude; most numerous in New Guinea, Australia, and Australasia, but a few north to the Philippines, southern Mexico, and the Caribbean islands; also found in New Caledonia, the Polynesian islands, Fiji, southern Africa, and South America. The largest genera include *Weinmannia* (about 170 species), *Pancheria* (25 species), *Spiraeanthemum* (20 species), *Geissois* (20 species), *Schizomeria* (18 species), *Cunonia* (17 species), and *Lamanonia* (10 species).

Family Davidsoniaceae

Small slender trees bearing irritant hairs. Leaves alternate, pinnately compound, elongated, with large kidney-shaped stipules. Inflorescence a large, lax, stalked panicle (many-branched cluster) or a dense, stalked spike. Bracts (leaflike structures on stem, below flowers or inflorescences) large, clasping the stem. Flowers bisexual. Sepals 4, fused, disposed edge-to-edge, thick. Petals absent. Stamens 10, plus 10 nectar-producing scales inserted on the disc. Ovary superior, of 2 fused carpels, 2-chambered, with 2 free threadlike styles abruptly bent (kneelike) above, and about 7 ovules per ovary chamber. Fruit a large 2-pyrened (pitted) drupe, velvety red when young, covered with a powdery bloom when mature. Seeds 2, large, pendulous, and lacking endosperm. One genus and 1 species (*Davidsonia pruriens*), northeastern Australia.

Family Eucryphiaceae

Trees or shrubs with evergreen, opposite, simple, or pinnately compound leaves and small stipules. Flowers solitary, located in the upper angles between leaves and stems (axillary), regular, bisexual, conspicuous. Sepals 4, rigid, overlapping, cohering at the apex and becoming detached as a caplike unit. Petals 4, large, white, overlapping, sometimes asymmetrical. Stamens numerous in many series (whorls) on a thin disc. Ovary superior, of 4 to 14 fused carpels, 4- to 14-chambered and grooved or furrowed lengthwise, each chamber with pendulous ovules. Styles and mature carpels free but joined by threads to the axis. Fruit a leathery or woody capsule. Seeds few, compressed, winged, fleshy. Endosperm present. One genus (*Eucryphia*) with 5 species, distributed in southeastern Australia, Tasmania, Patagonian Argentina, and southern Chile.

Family Paracryphiaceae

Shrubs or small trees with simple, tooth-margined leaves lacking stipules and in an arrangement on the stem resembling true whorls. Flowers bisexual and separately male, sessile (without a stalk), with 1 bract and 2 early-falling bracteoles (secondary bracts borne on an axis above the main bracts) in terminal rusty-pubescent (hairy) panicles or compound spikes. Sepals and petals absent. Stamens 8 to 11. Ovary superior, with 12 to 15 fused carpels, with few ovules per locule, and 12 to 15 sessile, shortly recurved stigmas (pollen-receptive surfaces at tips of styles). Fruit a 12- to 15-chambered capsule, the segments of which separate from the central axis except at the apex. Seeds unknown. One genus, *Paracryphia*, and 2 species, from New Caledonia.

Family Crypteroniaceae

Trees with 4-angled (more or less square in cross section) branches and opposite, entire, simple, leathery leaves that lack stipules. Inflorescence a true panicle with white- or green-coloured, small, short-stalked, radially symmetrical flowers. Flowers bisexual and unisexual, both occurring on the same plant (*i.e.*, plants polygamodioecious). Sepals fused, forming a broadly bell-shaped, 4- to 5-lobed calyx. Petals absent. Stamens 4 to 5, alternate with the sepals. Disc absent. Ovary superior, carpels 2, chambers 2, style simple, stigma slightly 2-lobed. Ovules numerous. Fruit a capsule separating into 2 parts that usually remain connected by the style. Seeds many, small, elongated, sometimes winged; embryo cylindrical, endosperm absent. One genus (*Crypteronia*) and 4 species distributed in tropical Asia from northeastern India (Assam) to southeastern Asia, Malaysia, and the Philippines.

Family Brunelliaceae

Tall trees, sometimes spiny, usually tomentose (covered with dense, wooly hairs) throughout. Leaves opposite or whorled, simple, trifoliolate or pinnately compound, often with toothed margins, and with small early-falling stipules. Flowers small, regular, with separate male and female flowers on separate plants (*i.e.*, plants dioecious), borne in panicles. Sepals 4 or 5, disposed edge-to-edge, shortly joined below. Petals lacking. Disc cup-shaped, fused to the sepals, 8- to 10-lobed. Stamens 8 to 10 inserted at the base of the disc, with filiform, pubescent filaments. Sterile stamens (staminodia) present in female flowers. Ovary superior, with 5, 4, or 2 free carpels, each gradually tapering into long, awl-shaped, recurved styles and dotlike stigmas. Ovules 2 per ovary chamber. A small, rudimentary female structure (pistillode) present in male flowers. Fruit of 5 to 2 dehiscent follicles (1-carpel, podlike structures that open along one suture or line). Seed 1 or 2 per follicle, with mealy endosperm. One genus (*Brunellia*) and 45 species, distributed in tropical America from Mexico to Peru and on the Caribbean islands.

Family Escalloniaceae

Trees or shrubs with alternate or opposite, simple, evergreen leaves. Leaves often toothed, lobed with small, forward-pointing teeth along lobes, with gland-bearing marginal teeth or with gland-dotted surfaces. Stipules absent. Flowers bisexual, rarely unisexual. Sepals 4 or 5, or calyx of 4 or 5 fused segments. Petals free, 4 or 5, overlapped or edge-to-edge, sometimes clawed. Stamens 4 or 5, sometimes with 4 or 5 sterile stamens. Disc present, the lobes alternating with the stamens. Ovary superior or inferior with 1 to 6 fused carpels, sometimes 1-chambered, with 1 to 6 free styles and many ovules. Fruit a capsule, rarely a drupe or berry. Endosperm copious. Seven genera and about 170 species, distributed in the tropics and southern temperate zone, mostly in South America and Australasia; also Australia, Philippines, New Caledonia, New Zealand, and eastern Himalayas. Genera include *Quintinia* (20 species), *Polyosma* (60 species), *Escallonia* (60 species), *Carpodetus* (10 species), *Argophyllum* (11 species), *Abrophyllum* (2 species), and *Corokia* (6 species).

Family Tribelaceae

Prostrate shrublets with robust flexible stems that produce short, ascending, densely leafy branches. Leaves alternate, simple, sessile (without a leafstalk), partly clasping the stem, smooth-margined but with apex bearing minute teeth, thickish, smooth, more or less covered with a powdery bloom above, lacking stipules. Flowers small, regular, bisexual, solitary at apex of branchlets. Sepals 5, small, shortly fused below, overlapping, persistent. Petals 5, relatively large, elliptical, thickish, slightly clawed, contorted. Stamens 5 alternating with the petals. Disc lacking. Ovary superior, of 3 united carpels with short, simple style and capitate (headlike), 3-lobed stigma. Ovules numerous. Fruit a small, many-seeded, 3-grooved capsule. Seeds shiny, black, remaining attached to floral axis long after capsule opens, with fleshy or oily endosperm. One genus and 1 species (*Tribeles australis*), distributed in temperate South America in southern Chile and Tierra del Fuego.

Family Tetracarpaeaceae

Low shrubs with alternate, simple, doubly toothed, evergreen, strongly incised (deeply slashed around margins) and prominently veined leaves that lack stipules. Flowers regular; bisexual; in erect, persistent, bract-bearing racemes (elongated clusters). Sepals 4 or 5, overlapping, very shortly fused, small. Petals 4, overlapping, round, erose (as though chewed), clawed, falling early. Stamens 8, in 2 whorls of 4 each. Ovary superior, of 4 free carpels. Ovules numerous. Fruit of 4 spindle-shaped follicles. Seeds numerous, with fleshy endosperm. One genus and 1 species (*Tetracarpaea tasmanica*), Tasmania.

Family Iteaceae

Shrubs or trees with simple, toothed or spiny-margined, alternate leaves with stipules. Flowers small, regular, bisexual, or polygamous, with bisexual and unisexual flowers in the same plant. Inflorescence terminal or axillary, densely elongated and raceme-like or short and cymose (more or less flat-topped with central flowers blooming first). Sepals 5, touching at edges or open. Petals 5, disposed edge-to-edge. Stamens 5. Disc annular. Ovary of 2 fused carpels, semi-inferior, often elongated, with few to many ovules; styles 2, joined but becoming free above, though sometimes united by the capitate stigma. Fruit a narrow or ovoid capsule with few to many oblong or sawdust-like seeds. Embryo large in sparse, fleshy endosperm. Two genera (*Itea* and *Choristylis*) and 17 species, in eastern and northwestern Himalayas to southeastern Asia and the Philippines; also in eastern North America and tropical and southern Africa.

Family Brexiaceae

Shrubs or small trees. Leaves simple, alternate, rarely almost opposite or whorled; smooth-margined, finely toothed, spiny-toothed, or coarsely toothed; leathery. Stipules present in *Brexia*, absent in *Roussea* and *Ixerba*. Flowers large, solitary or in axillary, few-flowered cymes (flower clusters that mature from top or centre flowers downward). Sepals 4 to 6, overlapping or touching at the edges, deciduous or persistent. Petals 4 to 6, free and overlapping, clawed, or fused and valvate; deciduous or persistent. Stamens 4 to 6 with large anthers. Disc annular or 5-lobed. Ovary superior, of fused carpels, with 4 to 7 chambers, each with 2 to many ovules. Style solitary, with a capitate, lobed, or dotted stigma. Fruit a capsule, drupe, or berry. Three genera and about 11 species, distributed in eastern Africa, Madagascar, the Mascarene and Seychelles islands, and New Zealand.

Family Phyllonomaceae (Dulongiaceae)

Trees or shrubs. Leaves alternate, simple, smooth-margined or toothed; with a long, sharp tip; and with small, fringed or glandular, early-falling stipules. Flowers small, green, borne on the leaves in bundle-like inflorescences. Sepals 5 or 4, open, toothed, persistent. Petals 5 or 4, touching at the margins. Stamens 5 or 4. Disc large, cushion-shaped, positioned within the whorl of stamens and surrounding the ovary. Ovary inferior, of 2 fused carpels, with 1 chamber and many ovules. Styles 2, very short, widely spreading, with small stigmas. Fruit a small, incompletely 2-chambered, 3- to 6-seeded berry. Seeds wrinkled, with endosperm. One genus (*Phyllonoma*) with 8 species, distributed from Mexico to Colombia, Peru, and Bolivia.

Family Pterostemonaceae

Much-branched shrubs with alternate, simple, tooth-margined leaves. Leaves shining, sticky, and resin-producing above; softly pubescent (hairy) below. Stipules small, deciduous. Flowers in few-flowered clusters, regular, bisexual. Sepals 5, touching edge-to-edge. Petals 5, overlapping, conspicuous, pubescent, more or less persistent. Stamens in two whorls of 5 each, the outer whorl fertile, the inner sterile and lacking anthers. Disc absent. Ovary inferior, with 5 fused carpels, 5 chambers, and a shortly 5-lobed style. Ovules 4 to 6 per chamber. Fruit a woody capsule. Seeds few, with tough, gristly outer coats, and without endosperm. One genus (*Pterostemon*) and 2 species, Mexico.

Family Grossulariaceae

Shrubs, sometimes spiny, with alternate, simple, variously lobed leaves, often with resin-producing glands. Stipules absent or connected to the petiole (leafstalk). Flowers regular, bisexual, or male and female and borne on separate plants. Sepals 4 or 5, fused, overlapping or somewhat disposed edge-to-edge, forming a calyx tube, sometimes petallike or coloured, persistent. Petals 5, small, scalelike. Stamens 5, alternate with the petals. Petals and stamens joined to the calyx tube. Disc absent. Ovary inferior, consisting of 2 fused carpels with a single chamber. Styles 2, somewhat connected, with simple stigmas. Ovules few to many. Fruit a juicy berry crowned by the persistent calyx. Seeds many, with endosperm. One genus (*Ribes*, currents and gooseberries) with 150 species, distributed in temperate Eurasia, northwestern Africa, North and Central America, and Pacific South America to Tierra del Fuego.

Family Hydrangeaceae

Small trees, shrubs, lianas (vines), or herbs with horizontal, underground stems (rhizomes). Leaves usually opposite, rarely whorled, simple, and lacking stipules. Flowers usually conspicuous, regular, bisexual, or plants are polygamodioecious —with both unisexual and bisexual flowers on the same plant. Outer flowers of inflorescence sometimes sterile and bilaterally symmetrical with noticeably enlarged petallike sepals. Sepals 4 or 5, occasionally up to 10, fused, or rarely separate. Petals 4 or 5, occasionally up to 10, separate, touching edge-to-edge, overlapping, or contorted. Stamens 4 or 5, or, more often, 8 to 10 to numerous. Ovary superior to partially or wholly inferior, consisting of sometimes 2 but usually 3 to 5 (or more rarely 10) carpels with 1 to usually many ovules in each chamber. Styles free, short, or becoming joined. Stigmas thick. Fruit a capsule or rarely a berry. Seeds with a straight embryo and fleshy endosperm. Nineteen genera and about 260 species, distributed in north temperate regions, the tropics, and the subtropics from Mexico and the Andes to southern Chile, and from southern Europe to eastern Asia, the Philippines, Japan, and Taiwan. Representative genera include *Kirengeshoma* (1 species), *Cardiandra* (5 species), *Philadelphus* (75 species), *Hydrangea* (80 species), *Dichroa* (13 species),

Broussaisia (2 species), *Deinanthe* (2 species), *Deutzia* (50 species), *Decumaria* (2 species), *Schizophragma* (8 species), *Carpenteria* (1 species), and *Fendlera* (4 species).

Family Montiniaceae

Shrubs or small trees with opposite, subopposite, or alternate, smooth-margined leaves without stipules. Flowers male and female on separate plants (dioecious). Male flowers: sepals 3 to 5, fused, calyx tube cuplike or flattened with smooth or lobed margins; petals 3 to 5, overlapping, slightly fleshy, deciduous; stamens 3 to 5, alternate with the petals; disc flat, discoid. Female flowers: Sepals 4 or 5, fused together and joined to the ovary, forming a short tubular structure with a smooth or minutely toothed margin; petals 4 or 5, overlapping, fleshy, deciduous; sterile stamens present, 4 or 5; disc surrounding ovary, fleshy, 4- or 5-angled. Ovary inferior, consisting of 2 fused carpels and bearing a short, thick, persistent style with 2 large stigmas. Ovules in 1 or 2 series in each chamber. Fruit a capsule. Seeds compressed and winged or more or less globose. Endosperm copious or absent. Two genera (*Montinia* and *Grevea*) and 4 species, distributed in southwestern and tropical eastern Africa and Madagascar.

Family Roridulaceae

Questionably insectivorous shrublets with glands of various lengths on stems, leaves, and sepals. Leaves alternate, elongated, lance-shaped, smooth-margined or with incised lateral margins, rolled lengthwise (circinate) in the bud, without stipules. Flowers regular, bisexual, solitary. Sepals 5, fused at the base, overlapping, persistent. Petals 5, overlapping, broadly elliptical, sharp-tipped. Stamens 5, alternating with the petals. Ovary superior, composed of 3 fused carpels, with short simple style and small, headed stigma. Ovules 1 to several per ovary chamber. Fruit a 3-sectioned capsule. Seeds large, with crustlike outer coat and copious fleshy endosperm. One genus (*Roridula*) and 2 species, southwestern Africa.

Family Pittosporaceae

Trees, shrubs, or twiners (vinelike forms) with elongated, leathery, evergreen, usually smooth-margined leaves that lack stipules. Resin present in large quantities in ducts in outer stem tissue layers. Flowers bisexual, regular, white, blue, yellow, or rarely reddish. Sepals, petals, and stamens 5 each. Petals often with erect claws. Stamens inserted below the ovary, alternating with the petals, free. Ovary of 2, sometimes 3 to 5, fused carpels with 1 to several chambers. Ovules many, arranged in 2 ranks. Style simple. Fruit a capsule or berry. Seeds with endosperm often black, shining, and embedded in a pulp. Nine genera and 200 species, distributed from tropical Africa to the Pacific Islands; in Madeira and Tenerife, Sri Lanka (Ceylon), Japan, and Tasmania; 8 of the 9 genera are endemic (native and restricted) to Australia. Representative genera include *Pittosporum* (150 species), *Marianthus* (16 species), *Billardiera* (9 species), and *Sollya* (2 species).

Family Byblidaceae

Insectivorous herbs or shrublets. Leaves alternate, elongated and linear, round in cross section, crowded, rolled lengthwise in the bud (circinate), bearing both stalked and unstalked capitate glands. Stipules absent. Flowers blue, regular, bisexual, solitary, on long stalks without bracts. Sepals 5, overlapping, fused at the base, persistent. Petals 5, contorted, broadly wedge-shaped, with the narrow end at the point of attachment, the outer edge fringed. Stamens 5, alternating with the petals, sometimes unequal or bent. Ovary superior, with 2 fused carpels, 2 chambers. Style elongated, threadlike, with headlike stigma. Ovules numerous. Fruit a 2-chambered, 2- to 4-sectioned, many-seeded capsule. Seeds with a coarsely warty or nodule-covered coat; endosperm present. One genus (*Byblis*) and 2 species, western Australia.

Family Bruniaceae

Heathlike shrubs and sub-shrubs with clustered, erect, slender branchlets and small, smooth-margined, alternate leaves that lack stipules. Flowers bisexual, small, usually regular, solitary or occurring in dense spikelike or headlike inflorescences. Calyx tube more or less joined to the ovary, with 4 or 5 overlapping segments, persistent. Petals 4 or 5, free, rarely joined below, overlapping, often persistent. Stamens 4 or 5, free or rarely inserted on the corolla (petals) forming a tube, often persistent. Disc rarely present. Ovary mostly half-inferior, rarely completely inferior, of 1 to 3 fused carpels and 1 to 3 chambers, with 2 to 4 pendulous ovules, or 1-chambered with one ovule. Style simple, 2-forked. Fruit a capsule with 2 seeds or a nut with 1 seed. Seeds with fleshy appendages (arils). Endosperm copious, fleshy. Twelve genera and 75 species, distributed in the Cape Region of southern Africa. Representative genera include *Brunia* (7 species), *Lonchostoma* (4 species), *Audouinia* (1 species), *Berzelia* (11 species), *Thamnea* (7 species), *Raspalia* (16 species), and *Staavia* (10 species).

Family Penthoraceae

Perennial herbs with underground stems (rhizomes) and alternate, simple, toothed leaves that lack stipules. Flowers small, regular, bisexual, in one-sided cymes (flower clusters that mature from top or centre flowers downward) at the branch tips. Sepals 5, touching edge-to-edge, persistent. Petals 5 and inconspicuous or, more often, absent. Stamens in 2 whorls of 5 each. Ovary superior with 5 to 8 more or less separate carpels united half their length and slightly sunken in the receptacle, recurved, each with a short style and headlike stigma. Ovules many. Fruit more or less flattened lengthwise, of 5 follicles opening by a line around the middle (lidlike) above their union, containing many sawdust-like seeds with pimple-like projections on their surfaces. One genus (*Penthorum*) and 3 species, distributed in eastern Asia and eastern North America.

Family Crassulaceae

Perennial herbs or sub-shrubs (shrubby in form but woody only at the base or a very low shrub) inhabiting dry, often rocky places and exhibiting structural adaptations to dry habitats. Leaves opposite or alternate, without stipules. Flowers usually in cymes, bisexual or rarely unisexual, very regular. Sepals free or united into a tube, often 4 or 5. Petals of the same number as the sepals, free or variously joined, inserted below the ovary. Stamens as many as or twice as many as the petals. Ovary superior, composed of carpels equal in number to the petals; carpels free or united at the base, 1-chambered. Ovules many or rarely few. Fruit a membranous or leathery follicle. Seeds usually with fleshy endosperm. Thirty-five genera and 1,500 species of cosmopolitan distribution, but mainly in warm, dry regions; especially abundant in southern Africa and Macronesia. Representative genera include *Crassula* (300 species), *Sempervivum* (25 species), *Cotyledon* (40 species), *Kalanchoë* (200 species), *Diamorpha* (2 species), *Pagella* (1 species), *Monanthes* (12 species), and *Bryophyllum* (20 species).

Family Cephalotaceae

Perennial herbs produced from a short, woody rhizome. Lower leaves form stalked, lidded, insect-trapping pitchers; upper leaves flat, elliptical, smooth-margined, and green. Flowers bisexual, regular. Sepals 6, disposed edge-to-edge, coloured. Petals absent. Stamens in 2 whorls of 6 each, those in 1 whorl longer than the others. Disc broad, thick, green, covered with pimple-like projections. Ovary superior, hairy, consisting of 6 free or more or less united carpels, each carpel with 1 ovule. Styles short, recurved, awl-shaped, with simple stigmas. Fruits 1-seeded follicles. Seeds with fleshy endosperm. One genus and 1 species (*Cephalotus follicularis*), distributed in the southwestern corner of Australia.

Family Saxifragaceae

Perennial, rarely annual, herbs with usually alternate leaves that lack stipules. Flowers usually bisexual, regular, 5-parted exclusive of carpels, with male parts usually maturing first (protandrous). Receptacle (expanded axis tip bearing flower parts) flat or hollowed to various depths making stamen and petal positions relative to ovary range from surrounding it (perigynous) to upon it (epigynous). Sepals usually 5, overlapping or touching at the edges and sometimes fused, or absent. Stamens usually in 2 alternating whorls of 5 each, those of the outer whorl opposite the petals (obdiplostemonous). Carpels rarely free, rarely as many as the petals, usually fewer and joined below, often 2. Ovules many, in several rows. Styles free, as many as the carpels. Fruit a capsule. Seed with abundant endosperm. Thirty genera and 580 species, mainly of northern cold and temperate regions, the Andes mountains, and alpine regions generally. A few are found in south temperate regions and Antarctic South America. Representative genera include *Saxifraga* (370 species), *Mitella* (15 species), *Astilbe* (25 species), *Heuchera* (50 species), and *Chrysosplenium* (55 species).

Family Vahliaceae

Erect, branched, sometimes glandular, annual or biennial herbs with opposite, simple, smooth-margined leaves that lack stipules. Flowers regular, bisexual, paired. Sepals 5, touching along the margins. Petals 5, overlapping or open. Stamens 5, alternating with the petals. Disc at upper end of ovary, inconspicuous. Ovary inferior, with 2 or 3 fused carpels, 1 chamber, and many ovules. Styles 2 or 3, thick, widely spreading, with capitate stigmas. Fruit a more or less globular capsule with many minute, appendaged seeds. One genus (*Bistella*) and 5 species, ranging from tropical and southern Africa to northwestern India.

Family Francoaceae

Perennial herbs with hairy surfaces, arising from rhizomes. Leaves crowded or arising from the base of the plant, alternate, without stipules. Flowers in racemes or panicles. Sepals 4, touching along margins, persistent. Petals 4 or 2, overlapping or contorted, sometimes clawed. Stamens 8 or 4, alternating with 8 or 4 sterile stamens. Ovary superior, composed of 4 fused carpels, with 4 chambers, with many ovules and 4 sessile (unstalked), globose or flattened stigmas. Fruit a capsule, oblong, membranous, erect, 4-lobed, 4-chambered, many-seeded. Seeds very small, with a thin coat and with fleshy endosperm. Two genera (*Francoa* and *Tetilla*) and 2 species, in temperate Chile.

Family Eremosynaceae

Small, annual, hairy herbs, much branched from the base. Leaves alternate, sessile (without stalks), smooth-margined to incised along the sides without stipules. Flowers very small, in terminal 2-forked cymes. Calyx of 5 fused, narrow sepals, deeply lobed. Petals 5, free, narrowly elliptical, spreading. Stamens 5, alternate with the petals, free. Ovary about three-quarters superior, of 2 fused carpels, joined to the calyx at the base, with 1 ovule per chamber and 2 free, slender, divergent styles. Fruit a 2-chambered capsule. Seeds with copious endosperm. One genus and 1 species (*Eremosyne pectinata*), in southwestern Australia.

Family Parnassiaceae

Perennial (*Parnassia*) or very small annual (*Lepuropetalon*) herbs with basally clustered or alternate simple leaves that lack stipules. Flowers solitary, conspicuous or small, bisexual, radially symmetrical. Sepals 5, free or joined together in the lower part, overlapping. Petals 5, overlapping, sometimes fringed, longer than the sepals, minute, or absent. Stamens 5, alternating with 5 sterile stamens. Ovary of 3 or 4 fused carpels, superior, half-inferior, or inferior, 1-chambered, with numerous ovules. Styles 1, 3, or 4, very short, or absent, with 3 or 4 mutually touching stigmas. Fruit a capsule. Seeds with cylindrical embryo and very little or no endosperm. Two genera (*Parnassia* and *Lepuropetalon*) and more than 56 species distributed throughout temperate and subtropical areas of the Northern Hemisphere (*Parnassia*). *Lepuropetalon,* with 1 species, occurs in America from the southeastern United States to Mexico and Chile.

Critical appraisal. In older taxonomic systems, the family Saxifragaceae is placed in the order Rosales along with other families traditionally placed there, such as Hamamelidaceae, Rosaceae, Platanaceae, Crassulaceae, Cunoniaceae, and others. More recent authorities have placed the plant groups included in the traditional Saxifragaceae in different categories and have given different taxonomic importance to the categories themselves.

Other classification systems

Among recent systems of classification the older Saxifragaceae (treated as a family in the order Rosales) is, in one system, placed in two different orders: Saxifragales, consisting of the families Crassulaceae, Cephalotaceae, Saxifragaceae, Eremosynaceae, Vahliaceae, Francoaceae, Donatiaceae, Parnassiaceae, and Adoxaceae; and Cunoniales, containing the families Pterostemonaceae, Cunoniaceae, Philadelphaceae, Hydrangeaceae, Grossulariaceae, Oliniaceae, Greyiaceae, Escalloniaceae, Baueraceae, and Crypteroniaceae. Another recent system treats the older saxifragaceous groups under the order Saxifragales, consisting of the families presented in the annotated classification section above. In still another recently proposed system, the saxifragaceous groups of traditional classification systems are all included in the order Rosales under four families: Hydrangeaceae, Grossulariaceae, Cunoniaceae, and Saxifragaceae. Woody taxa are concentrated in the first three families, the majority falling into Grossulariaceae. The order Rosales in that system contains 17 families and nearly 20,000 species.

Thus, among the several recently proposed systems of classification, there is considerable diversity of opinion as to the taxonomic values and the composition of the groups comprising the Saxifragales.

All of the recombinations, re-evaluations, and reinterpretations appear to be based on little more than a reworking and re-sorting of presently available evidence. Such activities are not productive; a better approach would be taxonomies based on new evidence, thus reducing or even eliminating conjectural aspects. New data can come from intensive studies in plant anatomy, from comparative plant chemistry and cytotaxonomic studies, intensified paleobotanical investigations, and other nontraditional means.

BIBLIOGRAPHY. L.H. BAILEY, *The Standard Cyclopedia of Horticulture,* 6 vol. (1914–17), a well-illustrated, semitechnical dictionary of ornamental and edible plants with descriptions and cultural notes; ALWIN BERGER, "A Taxonomic Review of Currants and Gooseberries," *Tech. Bull. N.Y. St. Agric. Exp. Stn.,* no. 109 (1924), a technical publication on the edible fruit-producing species and varieties of the genus *Ribes* with special reference to those grown in the United States; W.H. BROWN, *Useful Plants of the Philippines,* 3 vol. (1951–58), a profusely illustrated semitechnical series on the edible, drug-, textile-, timber-, and oil-producing plants of the Philippines and adjacent regions of southeastern Asia; I.H. BURKILL, *A Dictionary of the Economic Products of the Malay Peninsula,* 2 vol. (1935), a semitechnical publication concerning all kinds of useful plants of the southeastern Asia area, the most complete and reputable source for the area; F.J. CHITTENDEN (ed.), *Dictionary of Gardening,* 2nd ed. by PATRICK M. SYNGE, 4 vol. (1956 and suppl. 1969), an outstanding illustrated, semitechnical compilation of ornamental and edible plants with cultural instructions and plant descriptions; U.P. HEDRICK (ed.), *Sturtevant's Notes on Edible Plants* (1919), a semitechnical dictionary of wild and cultivated edible plants of worldwide application, old but still useful; F.E. LLOYD, *The Carnivorous Plants* (1942), a technical, well-illustrated work, but very difficult to read, which considers all kinds of insectivorous plants on a worldwide basis—the only compendium of its kind to date; S.J. RECORD and R.W. HESS, *Timbers of the New World* (1943), a technical to semitechnical book on woody plants of the Western Hemisphere, poorly illustrated but with excellent technical descriptions of the gross structure and microscopic structure of timber, lists of vernacular names, uses, properties of wood, working qualities of timbers, sources of supply, and minor forest products—the only book of its kind for the area covered; A. TAKHTAJAN, *Flowering Plants, Origin and Dispersal* (1969; Eng. trans. from the 2nd Russian ed. of 1961), a technical work containing discussions of the origin and evolution of the flowering plants, their paleogeography, the dispersal of plants throughout the world, and a classification of flowering plant families and higher categories; NORMAN TAYLOR (ed.), *Taylor's Encyclopedia of Gardening, Horticulture, and Landscape Design,* 4th ed. rev. (1961), a semitechnical, highly useful book covering cultural and descriptive aspects of home gardening (well illustrated); J.C.T. UPHOF, *Dictionary of Economic Plants,* 2nd ed. rev. (1968), a nontechnical list with short descriptions of useful plants, worldwide coverage; J.C. WILLIS, *A Dictionary of the Flowering Plants and Ferns,* 7th ed. rev. by H.K. AIRY SHAW (1966), a technical reference to all genera and families of flowering plants and ferns containing brief descriptions, numbers of species and genera, geographic distribution, and notes on relationships.

(W.L.St.)

Scales, Musical

Theoretical descriptions of the pitch relationships that exist in music are called musical scales. The specific selection of different tones in any piece of music generally reveals a pattern of relationships among its pitches that can be expressed as a series of fixed distances (intervals) from one pitch to another within the span of an octave. The interval relationships among pitches of a scale are its essential feature, and a particular pattern of intervals defines every scale. Other aspects of pitch usage in music, such as range (distance from the highest pitch used to the lowest), emphasis placed on certain pitches, or the simultaneous (harmonic) and successive (melodic) occurrence of tones, do not alter the identity of the scale, although they may be essential in describing its function.

Although the number of different scales that can be formulated is theoretically nearly infinite, particular scales tend to become conventionalized within any given culture or musical tradition. The scale of a single piece of music may therefore be characteristic of the tone system of a whole culture. In general, the simplest scales can be found in very old music and in the music of nonliterate cultures, while the most complex scales occur in the world's most advanced cultures.

Scale and melody. Scales have proven to be important in the analysis of folk music and the music of nonliterate cultures, but scholars have been obliged to deduce the scales through a study of the actual music, since the creators of the music were not cognizant of scales as theoretical concepts. By contrast, music of the most highly developed cultures (variously described as classical music, art music, cultivated music, and high-culture music) is created in full awareness of rules or conventions pertaining to scale usage.

Nonexplicit scales

In view of the wide range of possibilities, a surprisingly small number of scale types predominate throughout the world. The intervals found in non-Western music often approximate rather closely the basic whole-step and half-step intervals that are used in Western music. Variations from Western intervals are often expressed as measurements in cents (100 cents = one half step in equal temperament, the pattern of 12 equal half steps used in Western music; cf. TUNING AND TEMPERAMENT, MUSICAL). The task of identifying scales in non-Western music is complicated further by the occasional appearance of highly variable intervals or by singing techniques that produce sounds whose pitches cannot be specified accurately through conventional notation, like the "tumbling strains" (falling melodies) described by musicologist Curt Sachs in the singing of Aboriginal Australians.

Although music performed only on one pitch does exist, the study of scales properly begins with the occurrence of at least two different pitches. Scales consisting of only one or two intervals (i.e., two or three pitches) can be found throughout the world in monophonic music (that consisting of a single unharmonized melodic line), though they are perhaps most numerous in Ceylon, eastern Siberia, California Indian cultures, and in regions near the Ural Mountains. Such scales commonly display a narrow range in which the pitches are separated by a half step, a whole step, or a minor third (one and one-half steps, as, C–E♭). Larger skips in two- and three-note scales do occur but are less frequent. Some simple scales have probably acquired additional pitches through a tendency to fill in large skips with intervening pitches. Another process by which scales may have expanded is the transposition within a single melody of one characteristic melodic motive (identifiable fragment) to a different pitch level, thus creating additional scale degrees, as in the melody of the Makurap Indians shown below.

From F. Blume (ed.), *Die Musik in Geschichte und Gegenwart*; Barenreiter-Verlag Kassel, Basel

Occasionally, primitive melodies apparently generated by motivic transposition also contain evidence of emphasis on particular pitches. As an example, the skips in the following Osage Indian melody are arranged so that the pitches G and C are consistently reiterated.

From F. Blume (ed.), *Die Musik in Geschichte und Gegenwart*; Barenreiter-Verlag Kassel, Basel

The melodic "weight" given to those two pitches could not have been achieved by the simple transposition of motives. Further, weighted scales may also give prominence to certain pitches by using them as range limits or by placing a particular pitch at the ends of sections or the end of a piece.

Explicit scale systems

Scales function somewhat differently in the art-music traditions of highly sophisticated cultures, since they are not only a means of description and analysis but are also pre-existent assumptions for the composer or performer. Within those cultures, knowledge of the characteristics and requirements of various scales is often perpetuated by written treatises on music theory as well as by oral communication from generation to generation. The existence of professional composers and performers also encourages continuity in musical knowledge, even though some cultures, like those of the Western world, advocate continuous change in musical practices within acceptable limits. Through gradual evolutionary processes, the nature of scales and their functions may change radically over a period of several centuries.

Highly developed, complex systems governing the use of scales exist in a variety of cultures, principally in the Far East, India, Iran, the Muslim world, and the West. The differences in musical styles among those cultures are indeed great, yet there are some similarities in the manner in which scales function in each instance. Each culture has a number of basic scales (interval patterns), called *grāma* in India, *dastgah* in Iran, *maqām* in Muslim cultures. Generally, a basic scale is used to produce a number of different modes, or bases for melodic construction, in which the intervallic structure of the scale remains intact while primary and secondary melodic importance is attached to different pitch degrees (see MODES, MUSICAL). This hierarchy in which modes are generated by basic scale types consequently produces a greater number of modes than there are basic scales. The terms *maqām* and *dastgah* also are used to refer to such modes; the corresponding Indian term is *jāti*. In some art-music traditions the modes serve as the basis for an even larger number of specific melody types, which may again be elaborated further by improvisation in performance. In India the basic melodies are called *rāgas*; in Iran they are *gūsheh*. Although Western art music has a system of scales and modes, the melody types are not used as systematically or as consciously as they are in some of the non-Western traditions.

Common scale types. Pentatonic (five-note) scales are used more widely than any other scale formation. In fact, Western art music is one of the few traditions in which pentatonic scales do not predominate. Their frequency is especially notable in the Far East and in European folk music. The most common varieties of pentatonic scales use major seconds and minor thirds, with no half steps (anhemitonic). A representative type could be spelled C–D–E–G–A, for example. The pentatonic scale is so pervasive that melodies exhibiting tetratonic (four-note) scales often appear to be pentatonic with one pitch omitted. Hexatonic (six-note) scales appear rather rarely in folk music and nonliterate cultures. Examples that are known often seem to be fragments of the seven-note Western diatonic scale.

Heptatonic scales are especially prominent in the world's art-music traditions. The tone systems of India, Iran, and the West are entirely heptatonic, and seven-note scales are also present in the art music of some cultures that do not use such scales exclusively (e.g., the *ritsu* scale in Japan and the *pelog* scale in Java).

With some exceptions in both the distant and the recent past, Western art music has been based largely on one heptatonic scale, known as the diatonic scale. The origins of this scale can be traced to ancient Greece, and it has been formulated to some extent according to acoustical principles (see HARMONY). Since the octave in Western music is normally divided into 12 equal half steps, the characteristic intervals of the diatonic scale can be constructed upon any one of the 12 pitches. Such transpositions of the scale are known as keys.

The diatonic scale

Before the 17th century, as many as 12 different mode permutations of the diatonic scale were in common use, but only two modes—now called major and minor—have been in general use during most of the past 300 years. The diatonic scale itself consists of five whole steps (W) and two half steps (H), with the half steps dividing the whole steps into groups of two or three. The major scale uses the sequence W–W–H–W–W–W–H, as shown in the first of the following examples, while the intervals in the minor scale are W–H–W–W–H–W–W, as in the second.

In actual music the minor scale is usually altered in one of two ways to create greater emphasis on particular pitches. In the harmonic minor scale (the third example shown) the seventh note is raised one half step, and in the melodic minor scale (the fourth example) both the sixth and seventh notes are raised by one half step in ascending patterns while they are left unaltered in descending patterns (the fifth example).

In the 19th and 20th centuries, composers have made increasing use of pitches lying outside the diatonic scale, and that tendency has stimulated a variety of novel scale systems, developed as alternatives to the diatonic scale. Principles for composition within the chromatic scale (consisting of all of the 12 half steps within the octave) were first articulated by the Austrian-born composer Arnold Schoenberg early in this century. Other scales have also been employed on an experimental basis. The whole-tone scale (comprising six whole steps) was used prominently by the French composer Claude Debussy and others, especially in France and England. Microtonal scales requiring intervals smaller than the conventional half step have also appeared sporadically in this century. Among microtonal structures the most important, perhaps, have been scales calling for quarter tones (equal to half the distance of a half step).

Chromatic, whole-tone, and microtonal scales

Other uses of the term scale. The term scale is sometimes used to describe musical passages consisting of a succession of consecutive scale degrees in ascending or descending patterns. It is also used to describe scalelike exercises that are practiced for the development of technical proficiency on a musical instrument. "Scale" can refer in rare instances to the ordering of some musical element other than pitch. An example is the term *Klangfarbenmelodie* used in some recent music to denote a carefully arranged succession of different tone colours.

BIBLIOGRAPHY. CURT SACHS, *The Wellsprings of Music*, ed. by JAAP KUNST (1965), a systematic study of rudimentary scale types throughout the world and their evolution; BRUNO NETTL, *Music in Primitive Culture* (1956), a concise and authoritative introduction to scale types and their geographical distribution; WILLIAM P. MALM, *Music Cultures of the Pacific, the Near East, and Asia* (1967), lucid summaries of scale systems in non-Western art-music traditions; JOHN L. DUNK, *The Structure of the Musical Scale* (1940), a thorough description of the diatonic scale; ANTOINE AUDA, *Les Gammes musicales* (1947), a classic, comprehensive study of the history of scales in Western art music.

(J.C.Gr.)

Scandinavia, History of

The history of Scandinavia involves five independent nations—Norway, Denmark, Sweden, Finland, and Iceland —with a population in the 1970s of about 20,000,000, tied together by geography, language, and culture. For more than 1,000 years these nations have been bound to each other in political unions of various combinations, but they have also been separated by divergent strategic, economic, and political interests, often resulting in wars and conflicts between them. Yet the common ties outweigh the differences, and it is possible to speak of a common "history of Scandinavia."

From the first appearance of the Scandinavians in European history, as the Vikings, cooperation among them has made them a unit in the eyes of the world. All the Scandinavian countries were politically united only during the period of the Kalmar Union (1397–1523), but in later times Scandinavians have often acted together in the face of external pressure.

Scandinavia has had two periods of profound impact on European history: the Viking Age and the Swedish Age of Greatness. During the Viking Age, the Norsemen ravaged much of Christendom, built a European settlement that extended to the distant North Atlantic islands, and, for a brief moment, touched the shore of North America. During the 17th century, Sweden held the balance of power in Europe and built an empire that stretched deep into Germany. Denmark and Norway too have had periods of empire in the 13th century: Denmark's domain covered the south coast of the Baltic from the Elbe to the Oder and included a base in Estonia, while Norway ruled over Iceland, Greenland, and the Faeroe, Shetland, Orkney, and Hebrides Islands.

For most of its history, however, Scandinavia has been more influenced by the outside world than a power within it. Most developments were late in reaching Scandinavia: the area was the last in western Europe to be Christianized, for example, and industrialization did not begin until the second half of the 19th century. Yet in the last half of the 20th century, the Scandinavian countries have taken their place among the leaders of the modern world.

I. Scandinavia to 1523

THE VIKING AGE: SETTLEMENT ABROAD

Prehistoric Scandinavia. Prehistoric Scandinavia lasted until the 9th century AD, when writing began to be used in the Nordic lands, at the same time as the inhabitants began to exert an influence on world history through the Viking excursions and the world, in turn, sent emissaries into Scandinavia to introduce Christianity and Western civilization. Written evidence of dwellers in Scandinavia before this time appears only in brief and sometimes controversial mentions in classical sources such as Pytheas, Pliny the Elder, and Tacitus and in runic inscriptions found within Scandinavia that date from the Roman Iron Age (*c.* AD 1–*c.* 400). Other information comes from archaeological finds, on the basis of which an approximate division into periods can be made.

It appears that the first inhabitants arrived in Scandinavia before the last ice had receded. Finds in Denmark point to possible Neanderthalic hunters in the area (*c.* 45,000 BC), and two cultures (the Komsa and Fosna) seem to have existed on the northern and western coasts of Norway during the last Ice Age. These groups were apparently isolated phenomena, and links between their members and the Stone Age inhabitants of the area have not been determined. The direction from which the permanent settlers of Scandinavia appeared is generally accepted to have been south and southeast, but their origin is unknown. Some of them seem to have migrated from European Russia over the land bridge between the Gulf of Bothnia and the Arctic Ocean, others through present-day Denmark.

During the Stone Age (Paleolithic, *c.* 10,000 BC–*c.* 3000 BC; Neolithic, *c.* 3000 BC–*c.* 1500 BC), the population of Scandinavia progressed from existence as hunters and fishers to a more stationary life as agriculturalists, with the help of improved tools and weapons, influenced by and sometimes imported from the lands to the south. It is speculated that major changes of tools, weapons, and burial styles were introduced by new groups of settlers rather than by the innovations of established residents, but controversy on this point continues. Among the more interesting cultures uncovered by archaeologists are the kitchen-midden people (*køkkenmødding*) in Denmark (*c.* 5000 BC–*c.* 3000 BC), whose waste heaps attest to the spread of their culture over what is now Denmark, the southern coast of Norway, and the eastern Baltic.

The kitchen-midden culture

During the Bronze Age (*c.* 1500 BC–*c.* 500 BC), most tools were still made of stone, especially flint, with bronze used largely for luxury items. Because copper and tin for the making of bronze had to be imported, trade relations

Viking expansion, 7th to 10th centuries.
From *Grosser Historischer Weltatlas*, vol. II, *Mittelalter* (1970); Bayerischer Schulbuch-Verlag, Munich

between Scandinavia and Europe became lively; amber was the principal export. At this time, drawings were made on rocks, especially on the Scandinavian Peninsula, depicting people, tools, ships, animals, and suns, apparently signifying a sun or fertility religion. The former burial methods (in mass and single graves) were replaced by burial above ground in mounds and by funeral pyres.

In the early stages of the Iron Age (pre-Roman, or Celtic, Iron Age, *c*. 400 BC–*c*. AD 1; Roman Iron Age, *c*. AD 1–*c*. 400; and Germanic Iron Age, *c*. 400–*c*. 800), iron ore was imported, until it was discovered that the native bog iron could be exploited. The dominance of the Celts in Europe cut the Scandinavians off from the Mediterranean, until the German tribes and Julius Caesar pushed back the Celts. Exports from Rome flowed into Germany and on to Scandinavia along the rivers to the Baltic and North seas. Gotland became an important trading centre, as attested by hoards of Roman coins that have been found there. (Roman coins have been unearthed throughout Scandinavia, even on Iceland.) Exports from the North were primarily amber, furs, horses, and slaves. During the final stage of the Iron Age, the Swedes established colonies, which were apparently for trading, along the southeast coast of the Baltic at the mouth of the Vistula and in Latvia, as evidenced by building patterns and graves. Hedeby, on the Schlei, attracted traders from as far away as the Arab world. The disruptions of the 4th- and 5th-century migrations of barbarian peoples across Europe and the fall of the Roman Empire were reflected in Scandinavia by internal warfare, shown in the building of fortifications and hoarding of valuables in underground caches and immortalized in the epic of

Beowulf. Place-names indicate much new settlement during the last two centuries of the Iron Age, indicating a return to more peaceful and prosperous conditions, while finds in Sweden indicate contacts with the south Germans and in Norway with Merovingian France.

The Vikings. When the Viking Age began (*c*. 800), Scandinavia was by no means an isolated, unknown corner of Europe. Trading contacts with other people had existed for centuries, and colonization abroad had been started by the Swedes in one of the directions the Vikings would later take. The cause of the explosion of the Vikings into the world is a matter of much controversy. Obviously, the urge for adventure and desire for loot motivated some of the Vikings, but deeper explanations vary. Some historians posit overpopulation in Scandinavia, while others point to a deteriorating climate that made agriculture less profitable and more difficult. On the other hand, new land was broken at home throughout the age, and a limit to new cultivation was apparently not reached. The deterioration of the Mediterranean trade, caused by conflicts between Muslims and Christians, undoubtedly played a role, with the northern route from east to west becoming an important alternative. Other factors were the lack of organized resistance to the Norse raiders and the superior shipbuilding techniques of the Scandinavians, which made possible the Viking ship, shallow, pointed at both ends, easily manoeuvrable in rivers and bays, and powered by sail and oars. The word Viking is itself controversial: some linguists trace it to the Old Norse *vig* ("battle," "fight"), while a more common theory derives it from *vik* ("bay," "gulf"), making a Viking a person who is tied to bays (with the further meaning of attacking passing ships from the bays).

Cause of Viking expansion

Origin of the word Viking

The western route. *The British Isles.* The Viking expeditions went in two general directions—west and east—with the Danes and Norwegians more prevalent in the former and the Swedes in the latter. The Scandinavian states were loose confederations at the beginning of the Viking Age, and the identity of the Vikings as Danes, Norwegians, and Swedes is only approximate. The Viking Age is generally accepted as having begun in 793 with the raid on the English cloister, at Lindisfarne (Holy Island, off northern Britain). Monasteries—isolated, wealthy, and inadequately defensed—provided an attractive target for these early Vikings, who were interested in easily won booty and travelled singly or in small groups of ships. After several decades, however, the raiders began to assemble large fleets and to winter abroad. They established camps at strategic places in the British Isles and, later, in France, from which they could make raids into the interior areas; settlements by the Norsemen followed soon after. By 842 half of Ireland was subject to the Vikings, and 11 years later, Olaf the White was the overking of the land where the kingdoms of Dublin and Waterford were established. The Vikings first wintered in England in 851, and in 865 their armies began the overthrow of the Anglo-Saxon kingdoms of Northumbria, Mercia, and East Anglia. In 878 Alfred the Great ceded the territory north and east of a line from London to the northern edge of Wales (about three-fourths of England) to the invaders. This area of Viking settlement was given the name Danelaw; the Danes were predominant in the southern and northeastern parts of the territory, and the Norwegians in the northwest. For more than a century, the Vikings apparently devoted themselves to peaceful settlement and trading in the areas they had won; but around 1000, a new series of raids began, led by the Danish king Sweyn Forkbeard (Svend Tveskæg), and the English were forced to pay tribute (Danegeld) in the hope of avoiding attacks and plundering. In 1013 the attacks reached a peak; all of England submitted, and Denmark and England were joined in one kingdom. But the distance between the two countries and the lack of unifying interests worked to prevent a real unification; when Sweyn died in 1014, it was only through the efforts of his son Canute (Knud) that England remained in the Danish sphere. Canute succeeded his older brother on the Danish throne in 1018, reuniting the kingdoms, and later efforts led to the inclusion of Norway and the Swedish territory of Västergötland in the Danish Empire. Canute devoted most of his attention to England but also sent English missionaries to Christianize Denmark. With the death of Canute's son and successor, Hardecanute (Hardeknud; ruled 1035–42), the Danish empire dissolved. An attempt by the Norwegian king Harald Hardraade (Norw. Hårdråde; 1047–66) to reconquer England in 1066 failed but facilitated the conquest of the island by William I the Conqueror, whose Norman kingdom had been formed out of another wave of Nordic expansion.

The Islands. While Vikings from Norway and Denmark were raiding and, later, settling the British Isles, where they soon became assimilated with the native population, the Norwegians were also travelling to the uninhabited or sparsely inhabited islands west of the Scandinavian peninsula: the Shetland, Hebrides, Orkney, and Faeroe islands; Iceland; Greenland; and, finally, North America. The Shetlands were visited quite early: with a favourable wind, the Vikings could reach them from the Norwegian coast in one day. With the Shetlands as a base, settlers moved on to the Hebrides, Orkneys, and Faeroes and to Iceland, where the few residents, Irish monks, were driven out beginning in 874. Expeditions proceeded to Greenland in *c.* 986, and around the year 1000, a few Vikings reached Vinland (Wineland) on the North American coast; no settlements were made there, however.

Of these settlements, Iceland is the best known because of medieval Icelandic documents and histories. A West Norwegian chieftain, Ingólfur Arnarson, moved to Iceland in 874 and was followed by settlers, mainly chieftains and their retinues. By 1100 the population was between 70,000 and 80,000. Early local government by the

The Danish Empire of Canute

chieftains led to the establishment of the Icelandic commonwealth in 930, with a national parliament.

The Continent. While some of the Vikings concentrated on the islands and England, others raided the Continent. By the end of the 9th century, Frisia was controlled by the invaders, mainly Danes, and there were attacks on Paris in 845 and 885–887. The lower Loire was also ravaged during the 9th century. Around 900 the Vikings attacked the northern coast of France, and in 911 the French king ceded land on both sides of the mouth of the Seine to the chieftain Rollo and his followers, who in turn promised to prevent attacks by other Norsemen. The territory ruled by the Danes received the name Normandy, and settlers moved in along with the warriors. The attacks, beginning in the 9th century, in Germany, northern Spain, the North African coast, and Italy were more sporadic, and their permanent effects were negligible.

The eastern route. The primary attraction of the eastern route, followed primarily by Swedish Vikings, was the riches of the East, brought to Byzantium and Baghdad along the major East–West trade routes; and because these riches were found in well-established, well-defended states, the primary activity of the Vikings here was trade. Early in the 9th century the Swedes had begun to penetrate into Russia, via the Dnieper River to the Black Sea and Constantinople and via the Volga River to the Caspian Sea and Baghdad; and in the later part of the 9th century, kingdoms (most prominently Kiev and Novgorod) were established by the Swedes in Russia. The native Slavs and Finns in the area were easily conquered; the Swedish settlers were quickly assimilated. The export of Russian and Swedish products (furs, slaves, and weapons) and the import of metals and spices from the Orient brought great wealth to Sweden, and the town of Birka, on an island in Lake Mälaren, became an important trading centre during the 9th and 10th centuries; the town disappeared during the 11th century, when the Viking Age was waning. In an attempt to monopolize the northern trade route, the Swedes captured Hedeby (in southern Jutland) in *c.* 900, which remained in Swedish hands for about 30 years.

The decline of the Vikings. By the mid-11th century, the Viking Age was over; the last eruption was Harald Hardraade's unsuccessful attempt to win back England in 1066. In the west, the weak states of the 9th century had been replaced by powers no longer defenseless; in the east, the entrance of the Turks produced unease, and the goods of the Orient no longer flowed into Russia as they had a century earlier. Around 1050 the political connections between Sweden and Russia ceased. At the end of the century, the Mediterranean was reopened to the Orient trade by the First Crusade, and the northern route was no longer necessary or attractive. At the same time, Christianity had been established in the Scandinavian countries, and its teachings were inimical to the bold Viking life-style and to the trade of slaves, a prime export. The rise of primitive national states in Scandinavia during the Viking Age also provided an outlet for talents formerly used in trading, settling abroad, or raiding.

Russian settlements

Decline of the northern route

THE VIKING AGE: SCANDINAVIA

Denmark. The early centres of Denmark were Roskilde (on the island of Zealand) and Hedeby and Jelling (in southern and northern Jutland, respectively). At the beginning of the Viking Age, the most important seems to have been Hedeby, which served as an outpost against the Frankish empire of Charlemagne; and, after the successes of the Danish kings Godfred (or Gudfred; died 810) and Hemming (died 812) against the Franks, the Eider River became the established southern frontier. To protect the border area and the town of Hedeby (also called Slesvig), the Danevirke, a great rampart south and west of the town, was built, but it proved to be more of a symbol than an adequate defense structure. Louis the Pious, the son of Charlemagne, attempted to Christianize the Danes. He sent a monk, Ansgar, to Hedeby in 826, where his message was resisted. Four years later, the monk visited the Swedish town of Birka, where he met with greater temporary success; the following year he was made archbishop of Hamburg (later of Bremen, when the Vikings burned the former town), with all of Scandinavia his see. After Ansgar's death, in 865, his successor, Rimbert, wrote a hagiography of him, which is the most important source for 9th-century Danish history.

During the 10th century, after internal struggles between rival kings, the centre of power moved to Jelling, where Gorm became king of Jutland (*c.* 940). His son, Harald Bluetooth (Blåtand), attributed to himself the unification of all Denmark, the conquest of Norway, and the Christianization of the Danes. It is possible that he agreed to become a Christian (*c.* 960) in order to avoid German meddling in Denmark, although he was later forced to protect the southern border from a German attack. Under the King's protection, the new bishops of Jutland proceeded with the Christianization of the kingdom, and the gravesite of Harald's pagan parents was made into a Christian shrine. Harald's conquest of Norway was short-lived, and his son Sweyn Forkbeard and grandson Canute were each forced to rewin the country. Sweyn, as noted above, also conquered England and formed an Anglo-Danish empire, which his son and grandson continued until the latter's death in 1042. English missionaries were sent into Denmark, to counteract the power of the Hamburg archbishops, but Denmark never left the orbit of the German prelates. Norway elected a native king in 1035, who also ruled in Denmark from 1042 to 1047, when Denmark elected Canute's nephew Sweyn Estridson, who battled with the Norwegian king Harold Hardraade for reunification, with the result that each recognized the other's sovereignty.

Norway. The early local kings and chieftains of Norway ruled over distinct areas, usually with a local assembly or *thing*. The area around the Oslo fjord was closely tied to Denmark, while the inland areas in southeastern Norway, with the Eidsvating at Eidsvold, were more influenced by Sweden. The Gulating on the Sogne fjord was the centre for an aristocratic confederation in the southwestern part of the country, and the Øreting at Trondheim was the meeting place for the leaders in the Trondheim fjord area. Farthest north, the earls (*jarls*) of Lade ruled an ancient monarchy and added the Trondheim area to their territory in the 9th century.

At the end of the 9th century, Harald Fairhair (Hårfagre) united most of western Norway after the Battle of Hafrsfjord (872, sometimes dated 892). His son and successor, Erik Bloodaxe (Blódøx, so-called because of his murder of seven of his eight brothers) ruled *c.* 930–935 and was replaced by his only surviving brother, Haakon, who had been reared in England. Haakon was Norway's first missionary king, but his efforts failed; he died in a battle and was followed by Erik's son Harald II Graycloak (Gråfell). Harald II killed two of the kings in the Oslo region and the Earl of Lade, and became unpopular because of his prohibition of the public worship of the pagan gods. He was killed *c.* 970 in a battle against Haakon, son of the Earl of Lade.

Haakon allied himself with Denmark and took over the Gulating area as a Danish fief while the Danish king, Harald Bluetooth, annexed southeastern Norway. Haakon refused to assist in the Christianization of the country and revolted against Harald, becoming sovereign in western and northern Norway until his death during a peasant rebellion in 995. In the same year, Olaf Tryggvason, a descendant of Harald Fairhair, returned from England, where he had led a Viking invasion in 991 and had been baptized. Olaf was acknowledged as king along the Norwegian coast; he Christianized those areas, by peaceful means if possible and by force if necessary; he also sent missionaries to Iceland, where the new religion was adopted by the parliament (*Althingi*) in 1000. When Olaf encroached upon Danish territory in Norway, he was challenged by a group of enemies (Sweyn Forkbeard, the Swedish king Olof Skötkonung, and a son of Earl Haakon) and killed in the Battle of Svolder (*c.* 1000). The Earl of Lade now took power in those parts of Norway not held by Denmark, but when he went to England with Canute (1015), another descendant of Harold Fairhair, Olaf Haraldsson, who had returned from England,

was acknowledged as king throughout Norway, including the inland areas. Olaf worked to increase royal power and to complete the Christianization of the country. In so doing, he alienated the former chieftains, who called on Canute, now ruler of England, for help. Olaf was killed in battle with the Danes and peasant leaders at Stiklestad in 1030. His popularity with the people and the church led to a demand for his canonization; one year after his death, he became St. Olaf, patron saint of Norway.

Canute's rule proved unpopular with the chieftains, and at his death, in 1035, the Norwegians elected Olaf's young son Magnus as king. In 1042, when Hardecanute died, Magnus also became king of Denmark, where he held off an invasion of Wends in Jutland. He died in battle in 1047 and was succeeded in Norway by his uncle, Harald Hardraade, with whom he had shared the kingdom since 1046. Denmark chose Canute's nephew, Sweyn Estridson, and after several years of battle between Sweyn and Harald for the rule of Denmark, the two acknowledged each other as king. In 1066 Harald was killed during a vain attempt to conquer England.

Sweden. Several centuries before the Viking Age, the area of Uppland became the most important in Sweden (*c.* 500). Large grave mounds were raised near the present city of Uppsala over local kings. Political conditions in Sweden before *c.* 1000 are little known, however, and it is only with the reign of Olof Skötkonung (*c.* 994–*c.* 1022) that the political history of Sweden begins.

The first attempt to Christianize Sweden was made by the Frankish monk Ansgar in 830. He was allowed to preach and set up a church in Birka, but the Swedes were little interested. A second Frankish missionary was forced to flee. In the 930s another archbishop of Hamburg, Unni, undertook a new mission with as little success. A heathen temple at Uppsala provided a centre for pagan resistance, and it was not until the temple was pulled down at the end of the 11th century that Sweden was successfully Christianized.

The struggle between the old and new religions strongly affected the political life of Sweden in the 11th century. Olof Skötkonung, ruler of all Sweden, was baptized and supported the new religion, as did his sons Anund Jakob (reigned *c.* 1022–*c.* 1050) and Edmund (*c.* 1050–60). The missionaries from Norway, Denmark, and even Russia and France, as well as from Hamburg, won converts, especially in Götaland, the area where the royal dynasty made its home and where early English missionaries had prepared the ground. Many pagans refused to abandon their old faith, however, and civil wars and feuds continued. Claimants vied for the throne until the mid-13th century, when a stable monarchy was finally achieved.

Scandinavian society. During the Viking Age, the most important unit of Scandinavian society was the family, and blood feuds were legal and quite common. It appears that the rise of villages was tied to the family, which included the dead. The great majority of people were farmers, and a wide gulf existed between the free men, equal before the law, and the thralls (or slaves), who had extremely limited rights. The chieftains arose from the class of free men by virtue of their wealth and power, and they often combined religious power with secular, serving as local pagan priests. The early kings were chosen by the *thing*s (parliaments), comprised of the free men in an area, who also made laws and carried out justice; before the acceptance of Christianity, these kings seem to have been considered holy. The local *thing*s became provincial *thing*s for the *land*s (provinces) of Denmark and Sweden and the *fylker* (provinces) of Norway. When a single king won control of each country, he became the link between the provinces, each of which voted on his candidacy; his power in peacetime seems to have been small, but during wars he served as the leader. The three states were electoral monarchies, and the kings were usually chosen from the established royal families.

Already during the Viking Age, the geographic areas of concern and influence of the Scandinavian countries began to emerge. The Norwegians went primarily west, to the British Isles, Iceland, and Greenland; the Danes

Margin notes:

Unification under Harald Bluetooth

Christianization

Uppland

southwest, to England, France, and northern Germany; the Swedes, east, to Finland and Russia. During the following centuries, Norway continued to concentrate on the west, receiving cultural influences and establishing trade connections with England. Denmark remained the Scandinavian country most closely tied to the Continent and, in its period of empire, concentrated on the south Baltic coast. Sweden's empire began in the Gulf of Finland, and its sovereignty over Finland, which had begun with the trade contacts during the Viking Age, extended from the 13th century to the beginning of the 19th. These early spheres of influence developed into conflicts of interest, especially between Sweden and Denmark, that lasted until the end of the 18th century.

FROM 1050 TO THE UNION OF KALMAR

Denmark. The unification of Denmark had begun in the mid-10th century with Harald Bluetooth and continued under his son Sweyn Forkbeard and grandson Canute, who briefly extended Danish rule to England and Norway. Canute's nephew Sweyn Estridson succeeded in ending the short-lived Norwegian rule of Denmark (1042–47) and, working together with the church, he strengthened royal power. The country was divided into eight bishoprics: Slesvig, Ribe, Århus, Viborg, Vendyssel, Odense, Roskilde, and Lund. The royal succession re-

11th-century kings

mained in the hands of the provincial *things*. Five of Sweyn's sons succeeded each other on the throne—Harald Hén (1074–80), Knud (1080–86), Oluf (1086–95), Erik Ejegod (1095–1103), Niels (1104–34); and their reigns were marked by battles between the king, the people, and the church over the extent of royal power. Knud (the Holy) was anxious to strengthen royal power, and his bailiffs were ruthless in their treatment of the peasants. A general rebellion in Vendyssel forced the King to flee to Odense, where he was killed in St. Alban's Church. The peasants supported the election of Olaf, but Knud's closest supporter among his brothers, Erik Ejegod, was elected king. Under Erik Scandinavia was recognized as an archbishopric with the seat in Lund (1104).

In order to defend the southern border, Niels made Erik Ejegod's son Knud Lavard duke in South Jutland. Knud's successes against the Wends won him great popularity but cost him the increasing ill will of the King and his supporters, chief among whom was Niels's son Magnus the Strong. In 1131 Magnus killed Knud, precipitating a civil war in which Knud's brother Erik Emune took up the fight against Magnus. In 1134 Erik's army defeated that of Magnus, who was killed along with five bishops and 60 priests. Shortly after the battle, Niels visited Slesvig, a centre of Knud Lavard's support, and was killed by the townspeople; his successsor was Erik Emune (1134–37). The civil war continued, and by 1146 the kingdom was divided between the sons of Erik Emune, Magnus the Strong, and Knud Lavard. After continued struggles, Knud's son Valdemar was acknowledged as the single king in 1157.

The Wends continued to be troublesome through attacks on the Baltic trade and the Danish coast; when the Ger-

The reign of Valdemar

mans began their expansion eastward across the Elbe, Valdemar allied himself with the Saxon prince Henry the Lion against the Wends and acknowledged the Hohenstaufen emperor Frederick Barbarossa as his overlord. With the blessing of the church, represented by Absalon, the bishop of Roskilde (later archbishop of Lund), Valdemar undertook repeated crusades against the Wends; in 1169 he captured Rügen and placed it under Danish rule, beginning the Danish medieval empire. The cooperation of King and church resulted in the crowning of Valdemar's oldest legitimate son, Knud, as king in 1170 by the archbishop, 12 years before Valdemar's death.

At the beginning of the 1180s, north Germany was split among petty counts, and Absalon, who ruled Denmark after Valdemar's death in 1182 during Knud's minority, abandoned Valdemar's subjection to Barbarossa, attacked Pomerania, and annexed it along with part of Mecklenburg to the Danish realm (1184). Knud's brother Valdemar, count of South Jutland, defeated the Count of Holstein, adding the duchy to his own territory.

When Valdemar Sejr became king (1202), the land between the Elbe and the Eider, including Lübeck, was brought under the Danish crown. The empire then extended from the Elbe to the Oder-Vistula. Valdemar began crusades to Estonia in 1219 and established the fortress at Reval (Tallinn), marking the culmination of the Danish empire. In 1223 Valdemar was taken prisoner by one of his north German vassals, bringing the Danish advance to a standstill. Valdemar bought his freedom in 1225, promising to give up all the conquered areas except Estonia and Rügen. A final attempt to win back the lost areas led to his decisive defeat in 1227.

Valdemar's son Erik was crowned during his father's lifetime (1232), and Valdemar made his sons Abel and Christopher dukes: Abel was given South Jutland and Christopher received Lolland-Falster. Soon after Valdemar's death (1241), a struggle broke out between Erik and Abel; Erik was captured and killed in 1250 by his brother's men. Abel succeeded him but was himself killed during an attack on the Frisians in 1252; Christopher became king, and Abel's eldest son became duke of South Jutland, which was soon acknowledged as the only hereditary duchy in Denmark.

Under Christopher I, the former cooperation between church and king ended. The archbishop, Jakob Erlandsen, demanded the full extension of canon law but was opposed by both the King and the peasants. The King had Erlandsen imprisoned, and Denmark was placed under interdict. Erlandsen found support among the South Jutland dukes, the Count of Holstein, and particularly the Prince of Rügen, who attacked Denmark; during the ensuing war Christopher died (1259). The regents for his young son Erik Glipping released the Archbishop, who left the kingdom; after several years, Erlandsen compromised and died on his way back to Denmark.

During Valdemar Sejr's reign, the institution of the *hof* began. As a check against the royal misuse of power, the king was prevailed upon to call together the *hof* composed of the secular leaders and prelates. After the first *hof*s were called under Valdemar, it became the custom for the *hof* to meet at short intervals. When Valdemar's grandson Erik Glipping came of age, a meeting of the *hof* (1282) forced him to sign a coronation charter, in which he agreed to call the *hof* each year, to have no one imprisoned purely on suspicion, and to hold "King Valdemar's law." This charter is the first written constitution of Denmark. The provincial *things* lost their old power to elect kings, although they retained legislative approval. The *hof* also functioned as the highest court in the kingdom.

Development of the hof

In 1286 Erik Glipping was murdered, and the *hof* that elected his 12-year-old son Erik Menved as king (1286–1319) without a charter also appointed a commission to investigate the murder, resulting in the expulsion of a group of leading magnates. The remaining magnates in the *hof* were supporters of the royal policy, and the *hof* decreased in importance. At the same time, the archbishop, Jens Grand, took up his predecessor's policies. The King threw him into prison, and Denmark was again placed under interdict. In 1303 Erik Menved reached a compromise with the Pope in which the King would pay a fine and Jens Grand would be transferred to another see. Erik Menved also tried to take advantage of the weakness of the north German states but was unable to maintain his early gains because of the inability of Denmark's finances to support a mercenary army. At the King's death in 1319, the national finances were chaotic.

The childless Erik was succeeded by his brother Christopher II, who was forced to sign a strict charter. Christopher was the first king who accepted the *hof* as a permanent organ independent of his personal supporters; but he did not abide by the charter, and after a battle with the Danish magnates and the Count of Holstein, he was driven from the kingdom. For a time (1326–30), the young Duke Valdemar of Slesvig ruled under the regency of the Count of Holstein; after Christopher returned, the country was split by a peasant uprising, church struggles, and battle with the Holsteiners. The Holstein counts had received almost all of the kingdom in pawn, and even be-

Holstein rule

fore Christopher's death in 1332, Skåne rebelled against its Holstein count and joined the Swedish king, Magnus Eriksson, who bought it from its Holstein owner.

For the next eight years (1332–40), Denmark had no king, and the counts of Holstein ruled. In 1340 one of the counts was murdered during a visit to Jutland; several weeks later, Christopher's son Valdemar was chosen as king. After negotiations with the sons of the dead count, it was agreed that Valdemar would be the Danish king, would buy back the pawned areas, and would marry the sister of the South Jutland duke, who for her dowry would present her husband with the northern quarter of North Jutland, which was thus the only kingdom Valdemar began his reign with. He made the reunion of Denmark his first priority: by selling Estonia (1346) and collecting extra taxes, he reclaimed some of the pawned areas, and he brought others back into the kingdom through negotiations or through force of arms. In 1360 he won back the provinces on the east side of the Sound, and Denmark was reunited.

Valdemar also took up the strengthening of the royal power. At a *hof* in 1360, a "great national peace" was agreed between the King and his people. Valdemar was also faced with major economic problems: after the Black Death (1349–50), he confiscated the ownerless estates and seized the royal estates that had been lost during the interregnum. The army was also reorganized: the king's estates became the backbone, and the *lensmænd* (royal representatives), who led civil and military administration from the estates, together with their armed men, became the core of the army. The *hof* was replaced by the Rigsråde, a national council of the highest civil servants, bishops, and chiefs at the main castles, and the king's *retterting* (court of law) became the supreme court.

Valdemar Atterdag's downfall was caused primarily by his foreign policy. In 1361 he attacked Gotland and forced Visby under his rule. Gotland was loosely tied to Sweden and the Hanse cities, and the Hanse declared war on Denmark. Sweden's king, Magnus Eriksson, agreed to the marriage of his son, the Norwegian king Haakon VI, to Valdemar's daughter Margaret and was soon overthrown by the Swedish magnates and replaced by his nephew Albert of Mecklenburg (1363). By 1367 Valdemar, faced with a coalition of the Hanse cities, Sweden, the north German princes, and the Jutland magnates, was forced to flee. Three years later, the council signed the Treaty of Stralsund, which gave the Hanse trading rights in Denmark and pawned western Skåne to them for 15 years. Valdemar returned home and died in 1375.

The royal Danish male line died with Valdemar, and the magnates elected Olaf, the five-year-old son of Margaret and Haakon, on the condition that he sign a charter. When Haakon died, in 1380, Olaf became king of Norway. Margaret served as regent for her son and gained the confidence of Norwegians and Danes, so that when Olaf died in 1387, she became ruler of the two kingdoms.

Norway. At the end of the Viking Age, Norway was an independent kingdom with the right to elect the monarch resting in the *lagtings*, four district assemblies of the peasants. All royal sons, legitimate or illegitimate, were considered to have equal claims on the crown if they were accepted by a *lagting*. During the 11th and early 12th centuries, it was not unusual for Norway to have two or more joint kings ruling without conflict. Thus Harald III Hardraade's son Olaf III reigned together with his brother Magnus II until the latter died in 1069. Olaf ruled from 1066 to 1093 without being involved in a war; by giving the dioceses (Nidaros, Bergen, Stavanger, and Oslo) permanent areas, he inspired the first Norwegian towns. Olaf's son, Magnus III Barefoot (Barfot) ruled for ten years, during which he undertook three expeditions to Scotland to establish Norwegian sovereignty over the Orkneys and the Hebrides. He was succeeded by his three sons Olaf IV (1103–15), Eystein I (1103–22), and Sigurd I Jerusalemfarer (Jorsalafarer; 1103–30), who ruled jointly and imposed tithes, founded the first Norwegian monasteries, built cathedrals, and incorporated the clergy on the Scottish Isles into the church of Norway.

Following the rule of Magnus III's sons, the increasing power of the church and the monarch contributed to the century of civil war. During the early 12th century, the kings expanded their power over the various provinces, and the family aristocracy in Norway grew discontented. After 1130 interest groups within Norwegian society supported pretenders, and the church was successful in exploiting civil unrest to win independence. Civil war

In 1152–53, the English cardinal Nicholas Breakspear (later Pope Adrian IV) visited Norway, resulting in the establishment of an archbishopric in Nidaros (Trondheim). The clergy was exempted from military service. In 1163 the church supported the claims of a pretender, `Magnus V, in return for his obedience to the Pope, guarantees for the reforms of 1152, and the issuance of a letter of privileges for the church. Magnus' coronation was the first at which the archbishop presided. The first written law of succession, dating from this coronation, established primogeniture in principle and the prior right of legitimate royal sons to the crown. Instead of election by the *things*, a representation, dominated by the church, served as the electoral body. The law was never applied, and Magnus was succeeded by Sverrir Sigurdsson, a priest from the Faeroe Islands, who represented himself as a grandson of the first pretender king. After seven years of fighting, Sverrir was acknowledged in 1184 as king of all Norway and set out to bring ·the church under royal control. He refused to recognize the reforms and privileges made since 1152, and the Archbishop and most of the bishops went into exile; Sverrir was excommunicated. The exiles in Denmark established a rebellious party and allied themselves with the secular enemies of the King, who were opposed to the King's administrative reforms, which included the establishment of the *hird* as a new aristocracy composed of court officials and the heads of estates. This opposition party won control of the Oslo area and the inland areas and threatened Sverrir's rule until his death in 1202.

Civil war continued until 1217, when Sverrir's grandson Haakon IV became king, beginning the "Golden Age" of Norway. Haakon modernized the administration by creating the chancellor's office and the royal council. He prohibited blood feuds, and a new law of succession was passed by a national assembly (1260) that established the indivisibility of the kingdom, primogeniture, the prior claim of the legitimate royal sons, and, most importantly, the hereditary right of the king's eldest legitimate son to the crown; no election was to be held unless the royal line died out. During Haakon's reign, the northern boundary was regulated by a treaty with Russia. Greenland and Iceland agreed voluntarily to personal unions with the Norwegian king in 1261 and 1262, marking the greatest extent of the Norwegian empire, which included the Faeroes and the Scottish isles. Haakon died during an unsuccessful expedition to the Hebrides in 1263, and in 1266 his successor ceded the Hebrides and the Isle of Man to Scotland in return for recognition of the Norwegian claim to the Orkney and Shetland islands. The "Golden Age" of Norway

Haakon's son and successor, Magnus VI, earned the epithet Lawmender (Lagabøter) for his work on Norway's legislation. During his reign (1263–80), a common national law (1274) replaced the earlier provincial laws; Haakon's law of succession was confirmed; and a hereditary nobility, exempted from taxes in return for military service, was established. The king took over the legislative functions, while the *things* became courts. The towns also received new laws, and the privileges of the church were extended.

Magnus was succeeded by his young son Erik II (1280–99). Erik's regency was led by secular magnates who controlled central power throughout Erik's reign. The rivalry between secular and church leaders caused the regency to negate the political position and the privileges that the church had gained under Magnus' rule. They also tried to limit the rights of the German merchants in Norway but were answered by a blockade from the Hanse cities and were forced to agree to the German demands. Erik was succeeded by his brother Haakon V (1299–1319), who determined to renew the royal power.

He built a series of fortresses, including Akershus in Oslo, marking the shift of political power from the west coast to the Oslo area. Haakon was unable to restore royal power to the extent he wished, however.

Haakon's successor was Magnus, the young son of his daughter Ingeborg and Duke Erik, son of Magnus Ladulås of Sweden. The child was also elected to the Swedish crown in 1319, creating a personal union between the two countries that lasted until 1355. The countries were to be governed during the King's minority by the two national councils with the King's mother as a member of both regencies. The regency in Norway failed to prevent the increasing power of the magnates, and after the King came of age, he was forced to recognize his younger son Haakon as king of Norway (1343) and to abdicate in his favour when he reached his majority (1355). Magnus'
The impact of the Black Death elder son Erik was designated king of Sweden. The Black Death struck Norway in 1349–50 and killed nearly half the population. The upper classes were particularly hard hit: only one of the bishops survived, and many noble families were reduced to the peasantry by the death of their workers and the decrease of their incomes.

Haakon VI's rule (1355–80) reduced the power of the aristocracy, but his royal power was also limited. The casualties of the Black Death among the high civil servants and clergy were replaced by Danes and Swedes. The central government as a whole lost control over the kingdom, and the local areas began to conduct their own affairs.

Haakon VI married Margaret, the daughter of Valdemar Atterdag of Denmark, and their son Olaf was elected king of Denmark in 1375. Olaf also became king of Norway at his father's death (1380), but he died in 1387 at the age of 17, and his mother, who had served as regent in both kingdoms for him, now became the ruler.

Sweden. At the end of the Viking Age, Sweden remained a loose federation of provinces. The old family of kings died out in 1060; after the death of the last of these kings' son-in-law, Stenkil, in 1066, a civil war broke out. Around 1080 Stenkil's sons, Ingi and Halsten, ruled, but Ingi was overthrown by his pagan brother-in-law Blotsven, who then held the kingship for three years before Ingi regained power. Around 1130, Sverker, a member of a magnate family from Östergötland, was acknowledged as king, and this province now became the political centre of Sweden. Sverker sided with the church and established several cloisters staffed by French monks; he was murdered c. 1156. During the later years of Sverker's reign, a pretender named Erik Jedvardsson was proclaimed king in Svealand; little is known about Erik, but according to legend he undertook a crusade to Finland, died violently c. 1160, and was later canonized as the patron saint of Sweden.

The reforms of Knut Erik's son Knut killed Sverker's son (1167) and was accepted as king of the entire country. Knut organized the currency system, worked for the organization of the church, and established a fortress on the site of Stockholm. After his death in 1196, members of the families of Erik and Sverker succeeded each other on the throne for half a century. While the families were battling for the throne, the country received its own archbishopric at Uppsala (1164), the country was organized into five bishoprics (Linköping, Skara, Strängnäs, Västerås, and Växjö, joined later by Åbo in Finland), and cloisters were founded. The church received the right to administer justice according to canon law and a separate system of taxation, protected by royal privileges, and the pretenders sought the church's sanction for their candidacies. The first known coronation by the archbishop was that of Erik Knutsson in 1210. The church also gave its sanction to the "crusades" against Finland and the eastern Baltic coast, which combined an attempt at Christianization with an attempt at conquering the areas.

By the mid-13th century, the civil wars were drawing to an end. The most important figure in Sweden at that time
Birger Jarl was Birger Jarl, a magnate of the Folkung family. The *jarl*s organized the military affairs of the eastern provinces and commanded the expeditions abroad. Birger was appointed *jarl* in 1248 by Erik Eriksson, the last member

of the family of St. Erik, to whose sister he was married. Birger's eldest son, Valdemar, was elected king when Erik died (1250). After Birger defeated the rebellious magnates, he assisted his son in the government of the country and gave fiefs to his younger sons. Birger improved the inheritance rights of women, made laws ordering the peace of the home, women, church, and *thing*, and began the building of Stockholm. The Hanse merchants in Sweden received privileges, and the establishment of towns blossomed.

Birger died in 1266; in 1275 Valdemar was overthrown by his brother Magnus Ladulås with the help of a Danish army. Two years later, Valdemar agreed to abandon his claims on the crown and in return received parts of Götaland, which he lost in 1279. In 1280 a law was accepted establishing freedom from taxes for magnates who served as members of the king's cavalry, creating a hereditary nobility; the following year, Magnus Ladulås exempted the property of the church from all taxes. Under Magnus' reign, the position of *jarl* disappeared and was replaced by the *drots* (a kind of vice king) and the *marsk* (marshall), together with the established *kansler* (chancellor). The export of silver, copper, and iron from Sweden increased trade relations with Europe, especially with the Hanse cities.

Magnus died in 1290 and was succeeded by his ten-year-old son Birger. The regency was dominated by the magnates, especially by the *marsk*, Torgils Knutsson; even after Birger's coronation in 1302, Torgils retained much of his power. The King's younger brothers Erik and Valdemar, who were made dukes, attempted to establish their own policies and were forced to flee to Norway (1304), where they received support from the Norwegian king; the following year, the three brothers were reconciled. A new political faction was created by the leaders of the church, whom Torgils had repressed, together with a group of nobles and the dukes, and in 1306, the *marsk* was executed. Birger then issued a new letter of privileges for the church, but his brothers captured and imprisoned him. Two years later the kings of Denmark and Norway attacked Sweden on his behalf. Birger was again recognized king of Sweden in 1310, and transferred half of the kingdom to his brothers as fiefs. Erik's territory, together with his earlier acquisitions, then consisted of western Sweden, northern Halland, southern Bohuslän, and the area around Kalmar and stretched across the borders of the three Scandinavian kingdoms. In 1312 the dukes married two Norwegian princesses, increasing their power and dynastic position; but in December of 1317 the dukes were imprisoned by their brother following a family dinner, and they died in prison. The nobility rebelled against Revolt Birger, who was forced to flee to Denmark in 1318, and of the the King's son was executed. magnates

The magnates now seized control of Sweden and reasserted their power to elect a king. They chose Magnus, three-year-old son of Duke Erik, who had shortly before inherited the crown of Norway. In connection with the election, the privileges of the church and the nobility were confirmed, and the King was not to be allowed to raise taxes without the approval of the council and the provincial assemblies. The magnates now revised the laws of Svealand and by the Treaty of Nöteborg (1323) established the Finnish border with Russia. The Danish province of Skåne was bought and put under the Swedish king; by 1335 Magnus ruled over Sweden, Finland, Blekinge, and Norway, to which he soon added Halland. During Magnus' reign, a national law code was established (c. 1350), providing for the election of the king, preferably from among the royal sons, and a new town law code was written that gave the German merchants considerable privileges. In 1344 Magnus' elder son Erik was elected heir to the Swedish throne, one year after his younger brother Haakon received the crown of Norway. Erik made common cause with the nobility and his uncle, Albert of Mecklenburg, against his father; and in 1356, Magnus was forced to share the kingdom with his son, who received Finland and Götaland. Two years later, Erik died and the kingdom was again united under Magnus' rule.

In his struggles with the nobles, Magnus received the support of the Danish king, Valdemar Atterdag, and in 1359 Magnus' son Haakon of Norway was engaged to Valdemar's daughter Margaret. The following year, Valdemar attacked Skåne, and Magnus relinquished Skåne, Blekinge, and Halland in return for Valdemar's promise of help against Magnus' Swedish enemies. In 1361 Valdemar attacked Götaland and captured Visby, an important Baltic trading centre. Haakon, who had been made king of Sweden in 1362, and Margaret were married in 1363. Magnus' opponents among the nobility went to Mecklenburg and persuaded Duke Albert's son, also named Albert, to attack Sweden; Magnus was forced to flee to Haakon's territory in western Sweden. In 1364 the Folkung dynasty was replaced by Albert of Mecklenburg. Albert joined in a coalition of Sweden, Mecklenburg, and Holstein against Denmark, and succeeded in forcing Valdemar Atterdag from his throne for several years. Albert was not as weak as the nobles had hoped, and they forced him to sign two royal charters stripping him of his powers (1371, 1383). At the end of the 1380s, Albert had plans to reassert his power, primarily by recalling the royal lands that had been given to the nobles; and in 1388 the Swedish nobles called upon Margaret, now regent of Denmark and Norway, for help. In 1389 her troops defeated and captured Albert, and she was hailed as Sweden's ruler. Albert's allies harried the Baltic and continued to hold out in Stockholm, and it was only in 1398 that Margaret finally won the Swedish capital. In 1396 her great-nephew Erik of Pomerania was hailed as king of Sweden, and in 1397 he was crowned king of Sweden, Denmark, and Norway, marking the beginning of the Kalmar Union.

Expansion. *Finland.* Finland has been populated since the end of the Stone Age; in the 1st millennium AD, Finnish tribes entered the area and pushed the aboriginal Lapps northward. Even before the beginning of the Viking Age, Swedes had settled on the southwestern coast. During the Viking Age, Finland lay along the northern boundary of the trade routes to Russia, and the inhabitants of the area served as suppliers of furs. The Finns apparently did not take part in the Viking expeditions. The end of the Viking Age was a time of unrest in Finland, and Swedish raids were made on the area. No permanent Swedish colonies were established in Finland, and the trading colonies of Swedes, Russians, and Germans were assimilated or returned to their own countries when trade declined.

From the 12th century, Finland became a battle ground between Russia and Sweden. The economic rivalry of the powers in the Baltic was turned into a religious rivalry, and the Swedish expeditions took on the character of crusades. Finland is mentioned together with Estonia in a list of Swedish provinces drawn up for the Pope in 1120, apparently as a Swedish missionary area. The First Crusade, according to tradition, was undertaken *c.* 1157 by King Erik, who was accompanied by an English bishop named Henry. Henry remained in Finland to organize the affairs of the church and was murdered by a Finnish yeoman; by the end of the 12th century, he was revered as a saint, and he later became Finland's patron. In a papal bull (*c.* 1172), the Swedes are advised to force the Finns into submission by permanently manning the Finnish fortresses in order to protect the Christianization effort from attacks from the east.

By the end of the 12th century, competition for influence in the Gulf of Finland intensified: German traders had regular contacts with Novgorod via Gotland, and Denmark tried to establish bases on the gulf. The Danes reportedly invaded Finland in 1191 and 1202; in 1209 the Pope authorized the Archbishop of Lund to appoint a minister stationed in Finland. The Swedish king counterattacked, and in 1216 he received confirmation from the Pope of his title to the lands won by himself and his predecessors from the heathens. He was also authorized to establish a seat for one or two bishops in the Finnish missionary territory. In eastern Finland the Russian church attempted to win converts, and in 1227 Duke Jaroslav undertook a program of forced baptisms, de-

signed to tie Karelia closer to Novgorod. In response the Pope placed Finland under apostolic protection and invoked a commercial blockade against Russia (1229). A large force, led by a Swedish *jarl*, including Swedes, Finns, and crusaders from various countries, was defeated in 1240 by a duke of Novgorod, and the advance of Western Christendom into Russia was halted, while the religious division of Finland was sealed, with the Karelians in the Eastern sphere. The bishop of Finland, Thomas, resigned in 1245, and the mission territory was left without leadership until 1249, when the Dominicans founded a monastery in Turku (Åbo).

Birger Jarl now decided that a full effort was necessary in order to bring Finland into the Swedish sphere; in 1249 he led an expedition to Tavastia, an area already Christianized. Birger built a fortress in Tavastia and some fortifications along the northern coast of the Gulf of Finland, where Swedish settlement on a mass scale began. Swedes also moved to the eastern coast of the Gulf of Bothnia; in both areas, the native population was sparse, and relations between the Swedes and the Finns were peaceful. In 1293 Torgils Knutsson launched an expedition in an attempt to conquer all of Karelia, and built a fortress near the present city of Leningrad. The war lasted until 1323, when the Treaty of Nöteborg drew the boundary between the Russian and Swedish spheres of influence in a vague line from the eastern part of the Gulf of Finland through the middle of Karelia northwest to the Gulf of Bothnia, and the Crusades were ended, with Finland a part of the Swedish realm.

The Swedes now began to set up the administration of Finland in accordance with Swedish traditions. Castles were built and taxes were collected, mainly in furs and, later, in grain and money. During the early Middle Ages, Finland was often given to members of the royal family as a duchy. Two new estates, the clergy and the nobility, evolved, with the nobility increased by transplantation from Sweden and the clergy containing a large native element. The first native bishop was appointed in 1291. In 1362 King Haakon of Sweden established the right of the Finns to participate in royal elections and the equal status of Finland with the other parts of the kingdom. Several years later, Haakon was overthrown and Albert of Mecklenburg was crowned. Albert was unpopular with the Finns, and by 1374 a Swedish nobleman, Bo Jonsson Grip, had gained title to all of Finland. Grip died in 1386, and Finland soon after became part of the Kalmar Union.

Iceland. The Norsemen, settling in Iceland between 874 and 930, created an aristocratic commonwealth with all power resting in the local chieftains (*goar*), who also served as pagan priests. The national parliament (Althingi), established in 930, was preceded by local assemblies through which the chieftains directed law and order for their districts. After the Althingi was founded, the chieftains and their advisers constituted the *lögrétta* (legislature) of the country, and they also held the judicial power. There was no national executive power.

Christian missionaries were sent to Iceland by Olaf Tryggvason at the end of the 10th century, and in the year 1000 the new religion was accepted by the Althingi to stop the civil disputes that threatened to tear the country apart. The chieftains retained their religious power: many of them received clerical educations, and the early bishops were ordained chieftains. Most of the churches were also owned or run by the chieftains. The first Icelandic bishop was installed in 1056, and, after 1106, Iceland had two bishoprics. Tithe laws were passed in 1096, and slavery was abolished before 1100. After the Trondheim archbishopric was established in 1152, the Icelandic church belonged to its jurisdiction.

Family feuds broke out *c.* 1200, and some families were completely destroyed. The economy stagnated, with sheep farming, the major industry, having reached its peak under the methods then followed, and the climate deteriorated. Trade increasingly came under the control of Norwegian merchants, and Icelandic shipbuilding declined because of the lack of native wood and iron. In 1262 the Icelandic commonwealth voluntarily agreed to a

(margin notes)

Albert's attack on Sweden

Russo-Swedish competition

Birger Jarl's conquest

Christianization of Iceland

personal union with Norway, and the Norwegian king promised to provide regularly for the shipping of important goods to Iceland in return for taxes. The church was given full independence, the chieftains were replaced in administration by the king's officials, and a new set of laws replaced the old. In 1380 the government of Iceland passed to Denmark. The fishing industry progressed, and, when English and German traders and fishermen arrived around 1400, fish became the chief export. In 1402–04, the Black Death ravaged the island.

Greenland. The first Nordic settlers on Greenland reached the island in 985 under the leadership of Erik the Red. Two colonies were established on the western coast, one near Godthåb and one near Julianehåb, where a few thousand Norsemen engaged in cattle breeding, fishing, and sealing. The most important export was walrus tooth. A bishopric and two cloisters were organized on Greenland. The Greenlanders lacked wood and iron for shipbuilding and could not support communications with Europe; in 1261 they submitted to the Norwegian king, to whom they would pay taxes in return for his acceptance of responsibility for the island's provision through a yearly voyage. After the Crusades, ivory replaced walrus tooth on the European market, and relations with Europe diminished. A worsening of the climate occurred around this time, resulting in a decline in agriculture and livestock breeding, and plagues ravaged the populace: the Black Death alone (mid-14th century) is estimated to have halved the population. When Norway, with Greenland and Iceland, became subject to the Danish king, conditions worsened; the only ships that now sailed to Greenland belonged to pirates. Around 1350 the Godthåb settlement was apparently destroyed by the Eskimo, and in 1379 the Julianehåb area was attacked. The last certain notice of Norsemen on Greenland came in 1410. Sometime during the following 150 years, the Norsemen on Greenland disappeared. It was not until the beginning of the 17th century that Greenland again came into the Danish sphere.

Social and economic conditions. During the Middle Ages, Scandinavia moved from a family society toward a society of estates. Through the production of national law codes and the establishment of royal privileges for various groups in society, the estates were given legal rights and duties. The growth of the church provided an estate of clergymen, while the rise of towns created professional traders and craftsmen. The exemption of the clergy from military service and, later, from taxes was a matter of conflict between the monarch and the church throughout the Middle Ages. The exemption of the nobility from taxes was established in Denmark in the 1240s and in Sweden and Norway in the 1270s. Only Norway had a hereditary monarchy (from *c.* 1260); Sweden and Denmark remained a blend of elective and hereditary kingdoms, with the national leaders usually electing a king from among the royal sons. Agriculture remained the basis for Scandinavian society throughout the period, and the dominant feature from the Viking Age to the 13th century was new cultivation in connection with the increasing population. Norway could not meet the continually rising native demand for grain, and, from the mid-13th century, imports were drawn from the Baltic area. The usual form of settlement in Denmark was the village, while in Sweden and Norway the single farm predominated. The raising of livestock was common in all three countries and was most important in Norway, where it served in place of grain cultivation as the major source of livelihood. Slavery died out in Denmark and Norway in the early 13th century and in Sweden about a century later. An agrarian crisis occurred in the 14th century, due to the decline in population caused by the Black Death, and many farms were abandoned. Fishing served as an additional source of income for many peasants. The herring catches from the Sound contributed to the expansion of the markets in Skåne, and cod was already main Norwegian export in the 12th century.

Throughout the 12th century, the Scandinavians were the leading traders in the Baltic area. After 1200, however, the Germans began to appear more frequently in

Agriculture and fishing

Towns and trade

the Baltic, and the city of Lübeck, founded in 1158, competed with Slesvig for the trade from the Baltic to the North Sea. A number of new German cities were founded on the Baltic coast in the 13th century. In the Scandinavian countries, a large number of towns were established at the same time, including Stockholm, and Copenhagen and Bergen grew into important centres of trade. By 1300 the establishment of towns in Scandinavia declined; at the same time the German traders were winning privileges in the existing towns. The Germans were especially interested in fish, and the Skåne towns and Bergen were their main bases, while the ore from the Swedish mines was also exported through the German towns. Norway became most dependent on the Hanse for imports of grain, and the Germans dominated Norwegian trade. Bergen became the site of a German colony, and the merchants there won considerable political influence on the affairs of the kingdom. The battle against the influence of the Hanse continued throughout the Middle Ages.

The primary organ for government in medieval Scandinavia was the assembly of magnates, called the Hof in Denmark, the Hovingmöte or Riksmöte (assembly of chieftains or national assembly) in Norway, and the Herredag (diet) in Sweden. After the beginning of the 14th century, the functions of these assemblies were taken over by the national council in each country, and the councils in Sweden and Denmark became powerful organs, while in Norway political conditions stunted the council's development. The councils were composed of the bishops and the leaders of the aristocracy and were designed to assist the king's administration, whereby they protected the interests of the aristocracy. A main source of political power was control of the highest local administrative positions, tied to the possession of the royal castles, and the right of the native aristocracy to hold these positions was a source of conflict between the nobles and the kings in each country throughout the Middle Ages. Meetings of the four estates did not win influence until the 15th century.

Administration

THE KALMAR UNION

The formation of the union. The Kalmar Union, which from 1397 to 1523 comprised Denmark, Norway, and Sweden, grew out of the dynastic ties between the three countries. In 1319 Magnus Eriksson, son of Duke Erik of Sweden and Princess Ingeborg of Norway, inherited the Norwegian crown and was elected king of Sweden. The Norwegians selected his younger son Haakon as their king (1343), while Magnus' eldest son Erik was elected king in Sweden (1344), thus breaking the personal union of Sweden and Norway when Haakon came of age (1355). After a rebellion of the nobles in Sweden, Haakon and his father ruled that country jointly (1362–63); and in 1363 Haakon married Margaret, daughter of Valdemar Atterdag of Denmark. Shortly afterward, Haakon and Magnus were driven from Sweden, and Albert of Mecklenburg, son of Magnus' sister, was elected king.

When Valdemar Atterdag died in 1375, Olaf, the son of Margaret and Haakon, was elected king of Denmark; and five years later, Olaf succeeded his father to the crown of Norway. Margaret, who served as regent of both Denmark and Norway during her only son's minority, worked to win the crown of Sweden for Olaf, but he died (1387) before she could be successful. After Olaf's death, she was acknowledged as regent in both his kingdoms; and in 1388 rebellious Swedish nobles, unhappy with Albert of Mecklenburg's rule, hailed her as regent in Sweden. The following year, her troops defeated Albert's army and the King was captured; the war continued until 1398, when Stockholm was finally turned over to Margaret.

In order to assure the continuance of the union, Margaret set out to secure the royal succession. In 1389 her sister's grandson, Erik of Pomerania, was acknowledged as king of Norway, and in 1396 the Danes and the Swedes accepted him. The following year, he was crowned king at a meeting in Kalmar, where two documents of union were presented. The first, a letter of homage, contained a declaration of fidelity to Margaret and Erik. The second, a letter of union, concerned the conditions for the union, with a common king to be chosen from the sons of the late king and with a common foreign policy, while the internal matters of each country would be determined by the national laws administered by natives. The letter of union is among the most controversial documents in Scandinavian history; present opinion holds that the existing document is a draft and that the provisions contained in it were never accepted.

German gains in the Baltic

Along with the dynastic background of the Kalmar Union, an important reason for its formation was the geographical position of the Scandinavian states and the growing influence of the Germans in the Baltic. The north German trading centres had joined in the Hanseatic League in the mid-14th century, and these cities engaged in wars, bribes, and financial speculations to defend their markets from competition. The Treaty of Stralsund (1370), with Denmark, gave the Hanse the right of free passage through the Sound, control of the fortresses dominating the herring fisheries, and two-thirds of the revenues of Skåne for 15 years. Norwegian trade was completely under the control of the Hanse, which established an office in Bergen; Sweden was ruled by a German king from 1363 to 1389. Throughout Scandinavia, Germans were given important positions and castles. The individual Scandinavian countries were not strong enough to combat the increasing power of the Germans, and it was hoped that a union would enable the Scandinavians to build a common front against the Mecklenburgers, Hanse cities, and Holsteiners.

Scandinavia under the Union. The primary objective of Margaret, who ruled the Kalmar Union until her death, in 1412, was to strengthen royal power. In Denmark she avoided calling the national council, left high posts unoccupied, and reduced the privileges of the nobles. The church was a major supporter of the Queen, and she was extremely generous to it in return. The Swedish council had agreed in 1396 to return the royal property it had received since 1363, and Margaret called back much of this property. She placed her supporters in control of castles throughout the kingdoms but managed to win over opinion so that this intrusion in Sweden and Norway did not evoke serious protests. Margaret's foreign policy was based on a desire to keep peace without yielding unnecessarily to the Germans.

Margaret was succeeded by Erik of Pomerania in 1412. The most successful area of Erik's reign was his economic policy: Erik promoted national trade in Denmark through the founding of towns, especially in the Sound area, and began the Sound toll (1429) to replace the lost revenue from the Skåne market. Erik also gave the Danish towns a monopoly on trade and crafts. He increased the number of Danes appointed to offices in Sweden and Norway, arousing the anger of the native aristocracies, and his effort to control church appointments irritated the clergy. Most aggravating was his foreign policy, however, which consumed great sums of money and great numbers of men. In 1413 he had the Danish *hof* recall the fiefs of the Holsteiners, which started a long war, and in 1426 Lübeck and its allies began a war with Erik over trade privileges. The Hanse cities began a trade blockade of the Scandinavian countries, which especially affected the mining districts of Sweden; in 1434 a rebellion broke out in Bergslagen and Dalarna under the leadership of Engelbrekt Engelbrektsson. After a march through Sweden, Engelbrekt forced the Swedish council to renounce its allegiance to Erik. The Swedish rebellion roused Erik's enemies in Denmark and Norway, and in 1438 Erik went into exile on Gotland. The Danish council renounced its allegiance to Erik in 1438, followed in 1439 by his deposition by the Swedish council and in 1442 by the Norwegian.

Eric of Pomerania and economic reform

Erik's nephew, Christopher of Bavaria, was called by the Danish council to become king in 1440. Christopher was accepted by Sweden (1440) and Norway (1442) after he promised to keep the administrations of the countries separate and to appoint only natives to positions. The power was now in the hands of the national council in each country. When Christopher died without heirs (1448), the union was temporarily dissolved: Sweden elected Karl Knutsson as Charles VIII and hoped that the other Scandinavian countries would accept him as king, while the Danish council elected Count Christian of Oldenburg. Norway joined with Sweden (1449) but in the following year was forced to accept Christian I as king.

With Christian I began the revival of the coronation charter for Danish kings, which now included a guarantee for the national council's participation in foreign policy, legislation, taxation, and justice. According to the charters, if the king failed to keep his guarantees, his subjects had the right to renounce him, but this did not prevent the early Oldenburgs from ignoring their charters. Christian attempted to circumvent the position of the council by calling a meeting of the four estates (1468), a practice followed by his successors. After the death of the last male heir to the Holstein counts, Christian reached an agreement with the family making him count of Slesvig and duke of Holstein (1460), with the two areas to be "eternally undivided" and ruled by a royal heir chosen by the local nobility. In paying off a number of princes who had claims on the areas, Christian went into considerable debt, which, together with the costs of the war with Sweden, forced him to pawn the Norwegian Shetland and Orkney islands to the Scottish king in order to provide a dowry for his daughter.

Christian I and the coronation charter

One of the major concerns of the first Oldenburgs was the re-establishment of the union. Danish opinion held that Denmark's position of power depended on the union, and many Swedish nobles desired a union if their influence on Swedish affairs could be maintained. In 1450 a meeting of the Swedish and Danish councils agreed to a renewal of the union under the surviving king, Charles VIII or Christian I, or under a new king when both had died. Charles was not amenable to this agreement, and the Danes attacked Sweden in 1451. The war continued until 1457, when rebellious Swedish nobles drove Charles from the kingdom and hailed Christian as king. In 1464 a new rebellion broke out that Christian's troops failed to conquer, and Karl Knutsson again became the Swedish king (1464). Christian's attempt in 1471 to force the Swedes back into the union was unsuccessful.

Renewal of the union

Christian died in 1481 and was succeeded by his son Hans (1481–1513), who wanted to reduce the power of the nobility and the Hanse and to create a strong Nordic monarchy with support from the peasants and burghers. Many of Denmark's administrative posts were given to non-nobles, and the King signed trade agreements with the Dutch and English. Hans was acknowledged as Swedish king in 1483, but he was not crowned until 1497, after a war between Sweden and Denmark. Hans ruled in Sweden from 1497 to 1501, when rebellious Swedish nobles called back Sten Sture, who had served as regent from 1470 to 1497. Another war between Denmark and Sweden lasted from 1506 to 1513, and from 1510 to 1512 Hans was also involved in a successful war with Lübeck.

Hans' successor was his son Christian II (1513–23). A struggle broke out in Sweden between the Sture party (now led by Sten Sture the Younger) and a union party (led by Archbishop Gustaf Trolle); in 1520, after Trolle had been captured by the Stures, a Danish army attacked Sweden and defeated the Sture army. Christian II was crowned hereditary king of Sweden, and 82 people were executed in the "Stockholm Bloodbath." Christian returned to Denmark and left the Swedish government in the hands of the Archbishop and his allies, who were soon met by a rebellion led by Gustav Vasa (*q.v.*). After battles between the Danish army and the Swedish rebels, Vasa was chosen regent of Sweden (1521). In Denmark, Christian attempted to increase the royal power by ignoring the nobles and replacing them with men from the burgher class; he also interfered with the affairs of the church. The opposition to the King grew, and in 1523 the members of the council from Jutland renounced allegiance to him and joined his enemies: Lübeck and Christian's uncle, Frederik of Holstein-Gottorp. The burghers and peasants, pressed by high taxes, joined the rebellion. In 1523 Christian abdicated in favour of his uncle Fred-

The "Stockholm Bloodbath"

erik, who, as Frederick I, was hailed as king of Denmark and Norway. Sweden elected Gustav Vasa, and the Kalmar Union was permanently dissolved.

Denmark. The major political conflict during the Kalmar Union in Denmark took place between the monarchs and the nobility, both of which were anxious to increase their power. Under Margaret and Erik, the influence of the nobility was diminished by the absolutist policies of the monarchs. Margaret forbade private wars, tore down noble fortresses, and convinced the nobles to promise not to buy taxable peasant land, while Erik favoured the burghers over the nobles. From 1439 the national council reasserted the position of the nobles and took over the government of the kingdom, demanding coronation charters from the kings after 1448. These charters provided for the right of the council to dethrone the monarchs if the power of the council was not respected. Christian I tried to evade the council by calling representatives of the four estates, which later kings used to greater effect. Hans began a policy of appointing non-nobles to important posts in the kingdom, a practice that was increased by Christian II and that together with other misuses of power, led the council to overthrow him.

The peasantry suffered a decline under the Kalmar Union. The towns enticed the young people from the farms, which, together with the loss of the labour force from the plague, led to an increase in abandoned farms. In order to stop this process, landlords in Zealand and Lolland-Falster began the *vornedskabe*, which bound the descendants of tenured peasants to the land and gave the owner the right to recall a dead peasant's heirs to take over the land. By the 16th century, those tenured peasants who lived near the manor worked off a portion of their taxes by service in the manor's fields.

Under the Kalmar Union, Danish towns prospered and the influence of the burghers grew. By 1500 there were approximately 80 towns in the country, most of them fortified. Copenhagen had at most 10,000 inhabitants. The monopoly on internal trade given to the Danish towns by Erik of Pomerania improved the economic position of the burghers, and many German merchants took out citizenship in the towns in order to compete.

Reappearance of the *hof*

During the Kalmar Union, the old *hof* disappeared and the participation of the provincial *things* in legislation and royal elections ceased, while the people were represented by the estates, which remained unimportant during the period. The national council, composed of the bishops and nobles chosen by the king, including the highest civil servants (the *hofmester*, or master of the court, in charge of finances; the *kansler*, or chancellor; the *marsk*, or marshall, in charge of justice; and the *riksamiral*, or admiral), held the power of legislation and taxation together with the king. The Council's consent was necessary for declarations of war, and, together with the king, it served as the highest court. The entire council was seldom called, and its influence on the daily affairs of administration was negligible. The fiefs were controlled by the king's representatives, who collected taxes and upheld the law, and were never made hereditary.

Norway. Under the Kalmar Union, Norway became an increasingly unimportant part of Scandinavia, politically, and it remained in a union (ultimately as a province) with Denmark until 1814. Margaret and Erik of Pomerania left vacant the highest Norwegian administrative position and governed Norway from Copenhagen. Most appointments made in Norway were given to Danes and Germans. Whereas in Denmark and Sweden national councils took over the government, in Norway the council was unable to assert itself. After the accession of Christian I, Norwegian government was again centred in Copenhagen. The lower estates were also essentially powerless against the Danes, and isolated peasant uprisings had neither good leadership nor clear political goals. In 1448 Norway accepted the Swedish candidate for king, Karl Knutsson, but was forced to acknowledge Christian I of Oldenburg and remain in the union with Denmark. In 1468 Christian pawned the Orkney and Shetland islands to the Scottish king to provide a dowry for his daughter, and the islands were never reclaimed.

The cause of this political impotence in Norway has been a subject of considerable debate. According to one theory, the conscious policy of the kings since the 12th century of crushing the local family aristocracy to strengthen royal power deprived the country of a counterpart to the strong and often rebellious Danish and Swedish aristocracies. A second theory holds that geography was responsible for the absence of a strong aristocracy: the poorness of the soil prevented economic expansion through the creation of large estates. The most accepted theory, however, attributes the Norwegian decline to the Black Death, which affected Norway more than it did the rest of Scandinavia. Approximately half of the population was lost, and the aristocracy, along with losing many members, was deprived of much of its labour force, which led to the abandonment of farms and the decline of many nobles into the peasant class.

Sweden. Sweden entered the Kalmar Union on the initiative of the noble opponents of Sweden's German king, Albert of Mecklenburg (1363–89). The nobility, many of whom held estates over the national borders, called on Margaret for help; and after a war with the Germans, Margaret was hailed as the regent of Sweden (1389), with her great-nephew Erik of Pomerania as her successor (1396). The national council announced its willingness to return those royal estates that had been given to its members during Albert's reign, and Margaret succeeded in carrying out the recall of this property. She remained popular with the Swedes throughout her reign, but her successor, Erik, appointed a number of Danes and Germans to administrative posts and interfered in the affairs of the church. His bellicose foreign policy caused him to extract taxes and soldiers from Sweden, arousing the peasants' anger. His war with Holstein resulted in a Hanse blockade of the Scandinavian states in 1426, cutting off the import of salt and other necessities and the export of ore from Sweden, and led to a revolt by Bergslagen peasants and miners in 1434. The leader, Engelbrekt Engelbrektsson, formed a coalition with the national council; in 1435 a national meeting in Arboga named Engelbrekt captain of the realm. Erik agreed to change his policies and was again acknowledged as king of Sweden by the council. Erik's agreement was not fulfilled to the Swedes' satisfaction, however, and in 1436 a new meeting at Arboga renounced allegiance to Erik and made the nobleman Karl Knutsson captain of the realm along with Engelbrekt. Soon after, Engelbrekt was murdered by a nobleman; Karl Knutsson became the Swedish regent, and in 1438 the Danish council deposed Erik, followed in 1439 by the Swedish council.

The Danish council elected Christopher of Bavaria as king in 1440, and Karl Knutsson gave up his regency receiving, in return, Finland as a fief, whereupon the Swedish council also accepted Christopher. He died in 1448 without heirs, and Karl Knutsson was elected king (Charles VIII) of Sweden. It was hoped that he would be accepted as the union king, but the Danes elected Christian of Oldenburg. The Norwegians chose Charles as king, but a meeting of the Danish and Swedish councils in 1450 agreed to give up Charles's claims on Norway, while the councils agreed that the survivor of Charles and Christian would become the union king or, if this was unacceptable, that a new joint king would be elected when both were dead. Karl refused to accept this compromise, and war broke out between the two countries. In 1457 the noble opposition, led by Archbishop Jöns Bengtsson Oxenstierna, rebelled against Charles, who fled to Danzig. Oxenstierna and Erik Axelsson Tott, a Danish noble, became the regents, and Christian was hailed as king of Sweden. Christian increased taxes, and in 1463 the peasants in Uppland refused to pay and were supported by Oxenstierna, whom Christian then imprisoned. The Bishop of Linköping, a member of the Vasa family, led a rebellion to free the Archbishop, and Christian's army was defeated. Karl Knutsson was recalled from Danzig and again became king, but within six months difficulties between him and the nobles, especially Oxenstierna and Vasa, forced him to leave the kingdom. Oxenstierna served as regent from 1465 to 1466 and was succeeded by

Tott; and the battles between the two families led to the recall of Karl Knutsson, who ruled from 1467 to his death, in 1470.

The period of Charles VIII's reigns was marked by the rivalry of two native parties in Sweden: one, led by the Oxenstiernas and Vasas, contained the old landowning class in central Sweden, including the church and the nobility, who preferred the rule of the council to a strong monarch and felt that a distant union monarch was best; the other, led by the Totts and Karl Knutsson and comprised of representatives for the growing commercial interests who were interested in uninterrupted trade with Lübeck, saw a national monarchy as the best safeguard for their interests. The new leading family in the 1470s, the Stures, represented the anti-union party.

After Karl's death, Sten Sture the Elder was elected regent by the council; and his army, including the Totts and their sympathizers, burghers, and men from Bergslagen, defeated Christian's troops in the Battle of Brunkeberg on the outskirts of Stockholm (1471). During Sten's rule, the University of Uppsala was founded (1477). When Christian I died, in 1481, the matter of the union again arose, and in 1483 Hans was accepted as king of Sweden; but Sten managed to delay his coronation until 1497. In 1493 a new element entered Nordic affairs: Hans formed an alliance with the Muscovite Ivan III Vasilyevich directed against Sweden, which led to an unsuccessful Russian attack on Finland in 1495. The council became discontented with Sten's acquisition of power and, in 1497, called on Hans, whose army defeated Sture's. Hans was crowned and Sture returned to Finland. By 1501 Hans's supporters were discontented with his rule, and Sten Sture was recalled as regent. He died in 1503 and Svante Nilsson Sture became regent. In 1506, a new war with Denmark began, in which Lübeck supported the Swedes. Svante died in 1512, and the council now attempted a reconciliation with Denmark under the regency of Erik Trolle, whose family supported the union. Svante's son, Sten Sture the Younger, led a coup, however, and was elected regent. Peace with Denmark was concluded in 1513.

Last years of the Kalmar Union

The final years of the Kalmar Union were marked in Sweden by the struggle between the archbishop, Gustav Trolle (inaugurated 1516), and Sten Sture the Younger. The Archbishop was head of the council, and he took over the leadership of the pro-union party. A civil war broke out, and in 1517 a meeting of the estates in Stockholm declared Trolle removed from his position. Despite military assistance from Christian II, Trolle was imprisoned. After a defeat by the Swedes, Christian began negotiations and took six noblemen, among them Gustav Vasa, to Denmark as hostages. The Swedish treatment of Trolle brought a papal interdict of Sweden, and Christian could now act as executor. In 1520 the Danish army of mercenaries attacked Sweden, and Sten Sture was mortally wounded in a battle won by the Danes. No leader came forward to replace the regent, and the noblemen and clergy sought a compromise. Christian was acknowledged as king in return for a promise of mercy and constitutional government. The peasants, led by Sten's widow, refused to abandon the war, however, and it was several months before Stockholm capitulated. Christian was then crowned by the Archbishop as hereditary monarch, breaking his promises to the council; and despite promises of amnesty, 82 people, noblemen and clergy who had supported the Stures, were executed for heresy in the Stockholm Bloodbath. The responsibility for this execution has aroused considerable discussion among Swedish and Danish historians; the large part played by Gustav Trolle is now generally accepted.

Christian II now appeared to have Sweden under his control, but not all his opponents were dead or in prison. The nephew of Sten's widow, Gustav Vasa, had escaped from his Danish prison and returned to Sweden in 1520. After the Bloodbath, he went to Dalarna, where the Stures had their staunchest support, and soon a rebellion there was underway, followed by others around the country. By the spring of 1521, the army of men from Dalarna had won its first battle with the Danes, and soon noble-

men were allying themselves with Gustav, who was chosen regent in August. In 1522 he persuaded Lübeck to aid the Swedish rebels; in 1523 the Danish nobility forced Christian to give up the Danish throne and elected Frederik of Holstein-Gottorp as king. Three months later Gustav Vasa was elected Sweden's king by a meeting of the estates, and the Kalmar Union was dissolved.

The balance of power in Sweden shifted during the union from the monarchy to the nobility, who took over the government of the country while the union kings were resident in the other kingdoms. The monarchs' attempts to control the administration by appointing their own supporters from Denmark aroused protests and rebellion from the Swedes. During the later half of the union, a split developed within the nobility between a pro-union and an anti-union faction. The pro-unionists generally owned estates in Denmark or Norway as well as in Sweden and believed that a union monarch would enable the nobility to exercise greater influence; the anti-union nobles preferred a strong national monarchy supported by a strong national nobility. The king and regents elected in Sweden during the union period came from within the ranks of the anti-union nobility.

An important new class in society was composed of the commercial men and miners from Bergslagen, who were interested in the unimpeded export of Sweden's iron and copper. When the Danish interests conflicted with their own, most notably during the wars with the Germans, these men rebelled and supported a strong national monarchy, as did the burghers, who were also interested in the growth of trade. The church, on the other hand, preferred a weak monarch and supported the union.

The great majority of Swedes continued to be peasants, and cultivation was expanded into areas of Norrland and the Finnish wilderness. The major surplus product was butter; from the mid-14th century, a fourth of Sweden's export consisted of this product. As the lands exempt from taxation owned by the nobility and the clergy increased, the burden of taxation on the peasants grew; from the Engelbrekt rebellion in the 1430s through the remaining decades of the union, the peasants fought on the side of the anti-union forces.

(H.En.)

II. The 16th and 17th centuries

SEPARATION OF SWEDEN FROM DENMARK–NORWAY

Political and dynastic causes of separation. Until 1523, Denmark, or the Scandinavian Union, was the only important power in northern Europe. The secession of Sweden started a process of disunion lasting for more than 400 years.

The events in the 1520s finally weighed the balance toward Swedish independence. After the Bloodbath of Stockholm in 1520, Sweden in 1521 was moved to revolt against Christian. The King went back to Denmark, only to see another revolt there in 1523, upon which he chose to retire to the Netherlands and the protection of his mighty brother-in-law, the Holy Roman emperor Charles V. But there was no hope for Christian to reconquer Sweden. Although the Swedish bishops had as a rule favoured the union, no Swedish bishop after the Bloodbath could possibly dream of an alliance with Christian —the "tyrant" in the propaganda of Gustav I Vasa, who became king in 1523. The victorious independence faction was an alliance between Swedish high nobility, the farmer-miners of the Dalarna region, and Lübeck, the old enemy of a Scandinavian Union. Gustav, in fact, liberated Stockholm in 1523 with the economic and military help of the Hansa. In his next step toward complete independence, however, Gustav convinced the Diet of Västerås in 1527 to transfer the major part of church property to the crown in order to rid Sweden of Hanseatic influence.

Swedish independence

Subsequent wars between Sweden and Denmark. For more than a century thereafter, an aim of Danish foreign policy was to re-establish the union. The real issue, however, was the competition for mastery of the Baltic Sea (*Dominium Maris Baltici*). In the 16th and 17th centuries the Baltic region was far more important than either the Mediterranean or the Atlantic, providing Europe's main source of grain, iron, copper, timber, tar, hemp, and furs. Thus the mastery of the Baltic, in addition to being an internal Scandinavian problem, was vital to the western European powers, which needed free access to the Baltic commodities. These powers, and later Russia, on its ascendancy, wanted a divided but evenly balanced north.

In this perspective, the wars between Denmark and Sweden might be divided into the following periods: (1) the Swedish buildup, 1520–1628; (2) Swedish predominance, 1628–1709; (3) the annihilation of Sweden as a great power (1709–21).

The Swedish buildup. Because of Swedish measures against Lübeck after 1523, which aided the Danes, Denmark had no interest in waging war against dissident Sweden. Further, Denmark had to look to the empire and the Emperor, whose nieces claimed the Danish throne. Thus there was peace in Scandinavia until 1560. Perhaps this was due to the wisdom of the Reformation kings— Christian III of Denmark and Gustav Vasa of Sweden. Russians, from the principality of Moscow, advanced toward the part of the Baltic coast east of Poland in the 1550s. Denmark, since 1360 in possession of Gotland off the eastern coast of Sweden, now also bought the island of Ösel, in the northeastern Baltic. In 1560 Sweden decided on the ominous project of crossing the Gulf of Finland from Finland, hoping to annex the harbour of Reval (in northern Estonia; now Talinn). This established the Swedish strategy for the following 150 years (*i.e.*, to conquer the important Baltic harbours and to control sufficient parts of the hinterland to dominate and tax the Baltic trade). Denmark, with Zealand (Sjaelland) and Skåne and the fortifications of Helsingør (Elsinore) and Helsingborg, controlled the Sound; but its offensive strategy was to gain maritime hegemony of the Baltic Sea and to destroy any Swedish harbour in the west. From this point of view, the importance of the Nordic Seven Years' War (1563–70) is that Denmark failed in its aspirations to Baltic hegemony and that the greater part of its navy was sunk off Gotland. Thus Sweden could henceforth transport its armies quite freely in the Baltic area and could not be invaded. This situation remained unchanged until the early 18th century, when Tsar Peter the Great of Russia built Kronstadt, at the eastern end of the Gulf of Finland, and a Baltic fleet.

With its growing mastery of the Baltic area, Sweden needed free access to the Atlantic in order not to depend entirely on the passage through the Sound. Its brief occupation in 1564 of Trondheim, Norway, is an indication of this need, as are Swedish claims to the entire northern half of the Nordic peninsula. These also show that Sweden wanted a harbour in the north, to compete with the Russian harbour of Murmansk. Faced with these pretensions, Denmark decided on a war against Sweden (the Kalmar War, 1611–13), with the ultimate aim of restoring the union. The Danes forced Sweden to accept the occupation of what later became Göteborg harbour until Sweden had paid a huge war tribute, and to give up its pretensions in the north. In four years Sweden had paid the war tribute, chiefly by selling copper on the bourse of Amsterdam. With Dutch support, the harbour of Göteborg grew, thus assuring Swedish access to the Atlantic in case Denmark blocked the Sound.

Swedish predominance. The Thirty Years' War (*q.v.*; 1618–48) and its aftermath brought a different strategic situation. Denmark tried, not very wisely, to stop the Habsburg advance toward the north in 1625–29. Sweden, suddenly seeing its position in the Baltic threatened by the Emperor, concluded the Truce of Altmark (1629) with Poland, gaining possession of much of Livland. Then Sweden went to war against the Emperor, with the blessing and support of France and of Poland. Denmark was now faced with Swedish armies in the south. Sweden attacked through Jutland in 1645, and at the Peace of Brömsebro Denmark lost the islands of Ösel and Gotland in the Baltic and even the old Norwegian provinces of Jämtland and Herjedalen. For the Danes, worse was to follow. At the Peace of Westphalia (1648), ending the Thirty Years' War, Sweden annexed the bishoprics of

Breman and Verden and established conditions for friendly relations and dynastic alliances with part of the ducal family of the duchies (Holstein–Gottorp). Sweden thus acquired a permanent base south of Denmark.

With things seeming to go badly for Swedish armies in Poland, Denmark desperately tried for revenge in 1657. The effort resulted in a catastrophe. Swedish armies repeated the attack of 1645 through Jutland. In the late winter 1658 the Straits froze—an extraordinary occurrence—so that Charles X Gustavus could lead his armies from Jutland over Fyn to Zealand and toward Copenhagen. In the Peace of Roskilde (1658) Denmark lost all its provinces east of the Sound (notably Skåne), and in addition Norway lost Bohuslän and the county of Trondheim. Still the king of Sweden wanted more. He declared another war late in 1658 to take the rest of the kingdom of Denmark–Norway. Perhaps Sweden could have managed, even with heavy resistance, but the Swedish policy was contrary to the interests of the European powers, notably Holland, which went to the aid of Denmark. The county of Trondheim was recaptured, but Sweden retained Skåne and Bohuslän. The Peace of Copenhagen (1660) thus settled the frontiers between Sweden, Denmark, and Norway at their present boundaries.

The annihilation of Sweden as a great power. It suited European powers that Denmark and Sweden should each have its side of the Sound. Denmark got no support when it tried several times to reconquer the very rich province of Skåne. Nor did the Skånians themselves welcome these attempts. In the Great Northern War (1700–21) Sweden was annihilated as a great power. After the defeat of Charles XII any Swedish hope to rule the Baltic Sea was an illusion. Poland was crumbling. Russia had suddenly made its appearance on the Nordic stage, and Prussia was lurking offstage.

DENMARK–NORWAY

Denmark. The Danish high nobility never accepted Christian II's strong monarchy, and its members were his most bitter enemies. His uncle and successor Frederick I (ruled 1523–33) adopted a careful, nonprovocative policy toward the interests of both the nobility and the peasants, and he tried to reconcile the Danish, Dutch, and Hanseatic merchants; thus when Christian II tried to regain his power by invading Norway in 1531–32, there was no national rising. On accession to the throne, Frederick had promised the bishops to fight heresy. Actually, he invited Lutheran preachers to the country, most probably to expand the royal power at the expense of the church.

On the death of Frederick this balance exploded in Denmark's last civil war (the so-called Count's War, 1533–36), over the succession to the throne. The victor was Christian III (ruled 1534–59), Frederick's Lutheran son and ruler of the Duchies. Although Christian had been unacceptable to the bishops and to the Danish and Hanseatic merchants, he was supported by the nobility of the Duchies and by part of the Danish nobility. He was also supported by Gustav Vasa of Sweden because the merchants of Lübeck, Christian II, and the Emperor himself were their common enemies.

Growth of the monarchy. The Danish monarchy was decisively and lastingly strengthened by the civil war, primarily by the confiscation of church property. The nobility no longer had much to gain as an independent political body, and they chose to take part in the politics of the strengthened monarchy. A noble could participate in the council of the realm (Rigsråde), govern a county on behalf of the king and the council, or simply cultivate his domain to profit from rising prices on grain and cattle. The merchants of Copenhagen and Malmö had fought Christian III, but they favoured a strong monarchy that would protect their interests in the Baltic trade. Thus the monarchy got the opportunity to build a strong public administration in Copenhagen (Chancery, Rent Chamber), and even in far-off Norway. The real foundations of Danish absolutism were laid during Christian's peaceful reign.

Margin notes:

Swedish and Danish strategy

Swedish gains in the Thirty Years' War

Denmark's last civil war

The strain on the public finances during the reign (1559–88) of Frederick II, resulting from the war with Sweden, was met with stronger taxation on Danish and Norwegian farmers. But the main income came from a duty in the Sound on the constantly increasing trade in the Baltic. Originally a fixed duty per ship, it was changed into a duty on tonnage; it was at the king's own disposal, out of reach of the council. The Sound was considered Danish national waters; this fiction and the Sound duty remained until the 1840s.

These favourable political and economic conditions served as background to the ambitious policies of Christian IV (ruled 1588–1648). As noted above, his foreign policy, perhaps except for the Kalmar War, was a failure. His national policy, however, strengthened the public administration and jurisdiction, and the state actively promoted business and new industries. But the military catastrophes weakened the position of the monarchy, so that the high nobility decided to curtail the powers of his successor, Frederick III (ruled 1648–70).

Introduction of absolutism. Absolutism was nevertheless introduced during Frederick's reign. The nobility proved unable to handle a central government. After the military debacles in 1658–60 the nobles even refused to pay any taxes. The situation in 1660 could thus be exploited by the King's councillors, who drafted a new constitution that eliminated special political privileges of the nobility. The King was proclaimed absolute sovereign. This constitution (and a secret "King's Law" of 1665, which is said to be most absolutist of all European theories of absolutism) lasted until 1848 with only minor modifications.

Actually, after 1660 Denmark was governed by a quite efficient bureaucracy, but the political leaders came from the class of the great privileged landowners. After 1660 wealth, not noble birth, gave access to this class. The government in Copenhagen consisted of "colleges." There were five as a rule—namely the old Chancery, the Rent Chamber, and the new colleges for commerce, war, and navy—and they had their name from a collegiate body, which organized the work of each college. Top decisions were taken by a secret council, in which leaders of the colleges could easily influence the king. Local administration was not much changed after 1660, but the government took pains to see that the new county governors (*amtmænd*) never had any military powers. The absolutist kings, very unlike their Swedish colleagues, were rather anonymous, in part because of their feeble mental powers.

After 1660 the crown reduced its properties, so much increased by the Reformation, by massive sales to its bourgeois creditors (who thus made their way to the class of great landowners). The state compensated for loss of income by increasing taxes on the soil, according to the value of the holding that each peasant used. The new assessments made in the period from 1660 to the 1680s served as the bases of taxation in both Denmark and Norway until the 19th century. Until 1660 the king and the council had acted as supreme court; in 1661 the Danish supreme court was created, and appeals could be made to it from the whole kingdom. The last law codifications of Denmark were made in 1683, of Norway in 1687.

Norway. After 1523 the Norwegian council tried to obtain some independence for Norway within the union. But because the bishops dominated the council, they became the losers in the Norwegian parallel to the 1533–36 civil war, which brought about the council's abolition. Nor could the bishops hope for help from Sweden, which did not want to provoke Denmark and whose king was himself leaning toward Lutheranism. Olaf Engelbrektsson, the last Norwegian archbishop and head of the council, left Norway in early 1537 for the Netherlands and the Emperor, taking with him the shrine of St. Olaf.

In Norwegian political history, the year 1536 is a nadir —in Copenhagen, Norway was proclaimed a Danish province forever. Norwegian topography and society, however, were very different from those of Denmark. Thus Norway was allowed to keep most of its ancient

institutions and laws, and new institutions and laws had to be given in a special Norwegian version. From 1550 Norway's natural resources, including fish, timber, iron, and copper—commodities from outside the Baltic area and most useful to all western Europe—were increasingly exploited. Consequently, a new Norwegian bourgeoisie became a political factor. After 1560, Denmark had a constant fear of Swedish plans to occupy Norway. Therefore it was important that the Norwegians should not feel oppressed by the Danish rule. All this may explain the special attention the Danish government had to give to Norway.

Most representative of this attitude was Christian IV, who visited Norway often and founded several towns (Kristiansand, with the plan to control the Skagerak; Kongsberg, with its silver mines; Christiania, after a destructive fire in Oslo, 1624). He even went on an Arctic tour to Vardø in 1596, proclaiming the Arctic waters to be the "King's streams." This was part of his reaction to Swedish pretensions.

A certain separatist policy has been attributed to Hannibal Sehested, the King's son-in-law and in the 1640s governor of Norway. He actually created an army (by conscription of peasants) and a separate financial administration, but he may have wanted a platform against the Danish nobility, to work for absolutism. There were no signs of secession in the Norwegian population. When he was deposed in 1651, the financial administration was ruled from Copenhagen.

For almost a generation after 1664, Ulrik Frederik Gyldenløve, the illegitimate son of Frederick III, was governor of Norway. He courted the Norwegian peasants and at the same time gave monopolies on trade and on timber exports to restricted numbers of merchants. By applying such principles the government in Copenhagen and the Danish public servants managed to rule Norway after the Swedish annexations of Skåne and Bohuslän.

SWEDEN

The early Vasa kings, 1521–1611. In the Bloodbath of Stockholm in November 1520 some 80 leading opponents to the Scandinavian Union were put to death or murdered by Christian II and leaders of the Swedish unionist faction. This event became (or was made) a landmark in Swedish history because it compromised the unionist cause beyond recovery. Gustav Eriksson Vasa had lost his father in Stockholm. The next year he began inciting resistance in Dalarna, a mining district north of Lake Mälar. A rising against Christian "the tyrant" spread from Dalarna to all parts of Sweden. Gustav Vasa was elected protector of the realm in the autumn of 1521. With help from Lübeck, Stockholm and Kalmar were liberated from Christian's rule. In 1523 Gustav I Vasa (ruled 1523–60) was elected king of Sweden.

Gustav Vasa devoted the major part of his reign to the construction of the Swedish state. He convinced the Diet of Västerås (1527) to seize the properties of the church. This, with other annexations, gave the crown direct possession of about 60 percent of Swedish soil before Gustav Vasa died. He has been compared to a landowner in his behaviour toward the crown properties and the state incomes. He personally took part in developing their administration, and he personally and continuously inspected the crown servants. He nominated county governors himself and reserved the most important charges for members of his own family. Money economy had barely come to Sweden, and many state incomes were therefore paid in kind; some of these were used directly to feed and clothe public servants and soldiers, others were sold to foreign merchants. Gustav took great pleasure in literally filling the treasury, in which condition it was handed over to his son. The nobility was allowed no part in state affairs, and the Diet was convened only for royal propaganda, in which Gustav was a master. The fundamental traits of his reign resemble those of Christian III in Denmark. But Gustav was much rougher than Christian. In the 1530s and 1540s the farmers grumbled over taxes and the clergymen complained about interference in church matters. Gustav met opposition from his former friends

(margin notes:)

Rise of the Norwegian bourgeoisie

Denmark's governing bureaucracy

Construction of the Swedish state

—*e.g.*, the farmer-miners of Dalarna—with the same ruthlessness as that from other dissenters. Gustav led a careful foreign policy; nevertheless, a considerable army and a strong navy were created during his reign.

Three of Gustav's sons became kings of Sweden—Erik XIV (ruled 1560–68), John III (1568–92), and Charles IX (1599–1611). Erik XIV was an ambitious and warlike politician. He proposed to Queen Elizabeth of England with much ardour and a portrait of himself, which still exists. In addition to his wars with Denmark and expansion south of the Gulf of Finland, he tried to oust his brothers from their positions. He emptied the royal treasury in a few years and murdered some noblemen. Charged with lunacy (perhaps wrongly) in 1568, he was deposed. It has been demonstrated that his death was due to arsenic.

His brother John acceded to the throne with the help of the high nobility. John married a Polish princess and interfered in Polish affairs. Their son Sigismund was elected king of Poland before inheriting the throne of Sweden in 1592. John was a Catholic; this fact was exploited by his uncle Charles, who organized all conceivable Swedish opposition against the recognition of Sigismund. By doing so, Charles made the Diet (and of course the clergy) a political force against the high nobility. The final outcome was the resignation of Sigismund in 1599.

Charles IX was an administrator very much like his father. His foreign policy aimed at dominating the Russian trade routes toward the Kola Peninsula and the White Sea and to grasp as much as possible of the territory (Russian and other) south of the Gulf of Finland. Sweden thus was exposed to Danish attack in 1611; but Charles did not live to experience the defeat in 1613.

From D. Maland, *Europe in the Seventeenth Century;* Macmillan London Ltd.

The Swedish Empire in 1660.

The Age of Greatness. The early Vasa kings created the Swedish state. Its chief characteristic was a strong monarchy in a rather rustic and backward economy (with the mining industry as a very noteworthy exception). Its chief weaknesses were opposition from the high nobility and a thirst for revenge from Denmark. In the following decades Sweden relegated Denmark to second place in the north and became a most aggressive great power.

The reign of Gustavus II Adolphus. Gustavus II Adolphus (*q.v.*; ruled 1611–32) was only 16 years old when his father, Charles IX, died; so the actual leadership passed to the aristocrat Axel Oxenstierna (*q.v.*) and the council. After the Kalmar War the King joined in orga-

nizing the Swedes for the next war. Civil servants and officers were selected exclusively from among the nobility. A standing army was organized. The infantry was conscripted among the peasants and regularly trained by officers who lived on the King's farms among their soldiers; only the cavalry and the navy were professional. Swedish copper and iron were made into the best firearms of the period. The Swedish field artillery proved especially mobile and effective. The army's central administration was professionalized and became a model of efficiency; directing it were members of the high nobility, working together in collegiate bodies.

Swedish society under Gustavus II Adolphus

This war potential was not defensive: it could be used only abroad. It was first directed against the Baltic countries, then against the Emperor himself from 1629. The truce with Poland in 1629 gave Sweden the unique chance to keep most of the coast north of Danzig (Gdánsk) and at the same time secure Polish and French support on the German scene. At Breitenfeld, in 1631, a disciplined and mobile Swedish army practically annihilated the imperial army under Graf von Tilly of Bavaria. A year later Gustavus himself fell on the battlefield of Lützen, against imperial forces led by Albrecht von Wallenstein.

Axel Oxenstierna and the Swedish high nobility decided to carry on the war, even though the danger from the Emperor had passed. The enormous cost and debts of the war could be covered only by domination of the Baltic harbours, by French subsidies, and by a continued involvement in Germany. To retire from Germany now would cause the whole Swedish empire to crumble. The tangible results of the peace treaties of the 1640s were Sweden's grip on Denmark and its domination of most of the Baltic harbours.

Reduction of noble possessions. A generation of continuous war had had a profound impact on Swedish society. The Swedish nobility had gained about two-thirds of Swedish and Finnish soil through the transfer of crown property and of royal ground taxes. The nobles wanted to perpetuate this and to introduce the same feudal structure that they had seen and used in their annexations in the Baltic area.

This danger to Swedish and Finnish peasants was not finally averted until the 1680s, when the noble possessions were greatly reduced. The process of reduction had started in the 1650s because of serious financial problems that the peace in Europe brought to Sweden. Comparatively more of the public expenses now had to be met with taxation, but the nobles refused to pay taxes from their enormous possessions. The royalty could then resort to using the non-noble part of the Diet, in which even the peasants had a representation, to obtain consent to reductions. Faced with this threat, the high nobility agreed to pay, and even to minor reductions in their possessions. There then followed, in 1654–60, wars with Poland and with Denmark–Norway and rule by a regency of aristocrats while Charles XI was still a minor during the 1660s. The high nobles were thus able to retain possession of their advantages for yet another generation.

With the reduction of the holdings of the nobility in the 1680s Sweden returned to the political structure of the early Vasa kings. The income of public properties recaptured from the nobility was permanently allotted to public servants, officers, and soldiers. This system, which remained in force throughout the 18th century and far into the 19th, made the crown less dependent on the Diet in matters of finance. The nobles after all made a good deal during the reductions because they were able to rearrange their remaining holdings, thereby creating large contingent domains. The years 1680–1700 were a period of consolidation. It has been called the Carolingian absolutism because it occurred during the reign of Charles XI (ruled 1672–97). But because of the precariousness of the Swedish annexations in the Baltic, the Carolingian absolutism involved a continuous preparation for war.

Sweden's Carolingian absolutism

The successors of Gustavus Adolphus. One of the most fascinating of all the Swedish monarchs was Queen Christina (*q.v.*), the daughter of Gustavus Adolphus. Count Oxenstierna and the high nobility governed the realm and made war when she was a child. During her reign (1644–54) the transfer of crown property to the nobility continued on an increasing scale. She proved to have a remarkably independent will. She refused to marry. She used the Diet and threat of reductions to get her proposed husband, Charles Gustavus of the Palatinate, recognized as heir to the throne. Then Christina, daughter of the "saviour of Protestantism," abdicated, converted publicly to Catholicism, and went to Rome.

Charles X Gustav (ruled 1654–60) seems to have pursued the abortive idea of uniting Scandinavia under his scepter. His sudden death permitted another government by the high nobility until 1672, during the minority of his son. Charles XI acceded to the throne in 1672 at the age of 17. The Swedish, or Carolingian, absolutism, named after him, was exploited by his son, the most famous of all Scandinavian Kings, Charles XII (ruled 1697–1718).

The reign of Charles XII. Charles XII acceded to the throne at age 15 at a time when, in the hinterland of the Baltic coast, dominated by the Swedes, new states were being formed. Brandenburg and Russia, together with such older states as Denmark and Poland, were natural enemies of Sweden. Denmark, Poland, and Russia made a treaty in 1699, while Prussia preferred to wait and see. War started in 1700, with an overwhelming Swedish victory at Narva. Charles then turned toward Poland (1702–06). In so doing, he gave Peter the Great sufficient time to found St. Petersburg (now Leningrad) and a Baltic fleet and to reorganize the Russian army. Charles XII began his Russian offensive in 1707. The Russians for the first time used a scorched-earth strategy, thus diverting the Swedish armies from Moscow to the Ukraine, where the Swedes suffered a crushing defeat at Poltava in June 1709.

Charles spent the next five years in Bender (now Bendery, Moldavian S.S.R.), then under Turkish rule, trying in vain to convince the Turks to attack Russia. The Sultan clearly had no reason to do so, because Peter had turned his attention toward the Baltic. In the years following Poltava, Russia occupied all the Swedish annexations on the Baltic coast and even Finland; Hannover occupied Bremen and Verden; Denmark took Holstein–Gottorp; and Prussia lay waiting for the Swedish part of Pomerania.

Astonishingly, Charles governed Sweden from his residence in Bender during this catastrophe. In 1715 he returned to Sweden (he had left in 1700). He then decided to attack Norway in order to obtain a western alliance against the Baltic powers. On November 30, 1718, during a siege of the fortress of Fredriksten east of the Oslo fjord, Charles was killed by a bullet of either Norwegian or Swedish origin. His death ended the so-called Age of Greatness. By the Peace of Nystad (1721) Sweden formally resigned the Baltic provinces, part of Karelia, and the city of Vyborg (near St. Petersburg) to Russia.

Finland. Under Swedish sovereignty the Finnish tribes gradually developed a sense of unity, which was encouraged by the bishops of Turku. Study in universities brought Finnish scholars into direct touch with the cultural centres of Europe, and Mikael Agricola, the creator of the Finnish literary language, brought the Lutheran faith from Germany. As part of medieval Sweden, Finland had enjoyed, in effect, a semi-independent status, which had been underlined since 1581, when King John III raised the country to the dignity of a grand duchy. In the course of the administrative reforms (1611–32) of Gustavus II Adolphus, Finland became an integral part of the kingdom, and the educated classes thereafter came increasingly to speak Swedish.

On its eastern frontier Finland was harassed by constant warfare, and the danger became more serious when Novgorod, at the end of the medieval period, was succeeded by a more powerful neighbour, the grand duchy of Moscow. In 1595, however, by the Peace of Teusina, the existing de facto boundary, to the Arctic Ocean, was officially recognized by the Russians. By the Peace of Stolbova (1617), Russia ceded Ingermanland and part of Karelia to the kingdom of Sweden–Finland. The population of the ceded territories was of the Greek Orthodox faith, and when the Swedish government began

their forceful conversion to Lutheranism many fled to Russia and were replaced by Lutheran Finns. Though Finnish conscripts played their part in making Sweden a great power, the role of Finland in the kingdom steadily decreased in importance. As a result of the Great Northern War the Finns lost their faith in Sweden's capacity to defend Finland, and the years of hostile Russian occupation during the war gave them a permanent feeling of insecurity.

THE PROTESTANT REFORMATION

As noted above, the last Scandinavian bishops all had tied their fate to losing causes: the Swedish bishops to a union with Denmark, the Danish bishops to Christian II and the Emperor, the Norwegian bishops to Norwegian sovereignty. Rome could give very little moral or political help, if any. The winning cause, as everywhere else in Europe, was the national monarchies.

In Swedish and Danish towns (though not in Norway) some serious attempts were made by preachers in the 1520s to reform the church. These attempts received royal support. At the Diet of Västerås in Sweden (1527), Gustav Vasa convinced the Estates to surrender most of the church territories or properties to the crown and to support the preaching of the "pure gospel." The monasteries were suppressed, but the organization of the Swedish Church remained intact. Only in the 1540s was the church reorganized by royal intervention. But the Lutheran Confession of Augsburg was not adopted in Sweden until 1593, and then only as a reaction against a dynastic alliance with Poland and attempts to re-Catholicize Sweden. The Swedish clergy remained one of the four estates in the Diet until 1866.

In Denmark and Norway the civil war of 1533–36 offered a unique chance for the King to arrange church affairs as it suited him or the state. The old bishops were arrested and the properties of the church were confiscated. The state took over the religious tasks of the church, and the clergy became a body of civil servants. The clergy had no political power of their own, even though new Lutheran bishops were appointed. After 1536–37 there was no archbishop in Denmark or Norway. A special law, the Church Ordinance of 1537–39, regulated the religious activity and the affairs of the clergy. In retrospect from the 19th century, the system was named a "state church." But because it had no independent institutions of its own, it would be more appropriate from an institutional point of view to call it a confessional state.

Because the Reformation enabled the Scandinavian monarchies to increase their powers enormously, Lutheran orthodoxy became a political necessity in the following centuries. This explains the still existing religious homogeneity in the Scandinavian countries and the existence of "the public religion of the state" (first paragraph of the Norwegian constitution).

SOCIAL AND ECONOMIC CONDITIONS

As in most of Europe, agriculture was the main preoccupation in the Scandinavian countries in the 16th and 17th centuries. But rising economic activity in these centuries stimulated a more specialized and commercial exploitation of their natural resources.

Because of the growing demand for cereals and meat in western Europe, Denmark underwent the same change as did the countries east of the Elbe—the domanial system was introduced for commercial agriculture and cattle raising. Sweden and Norway had other resources. Their forests were still virgin, thus providing the indispensable raw materials for European shipbuilding and overseas expansion. Because the trees grew slowly, the wood became hard and well suited also for furniture and tools.

The mining industry in Sweden was founded in the 13th century. In the 16th and 17th centuries copper and iron were the most important exports from Sweden. But Sweden also had its own metallurgical industry, producing weapons especially. The mining industry of Norway was less important, but it supplied Denmark with necessary strategical commodities and with silver from the mines of Kongsberg.

The margin notes:
Swedish defeat at Poltava (1709)

Decline of the Scandinavian clergy

The age-old export of western Norway was stockfish, or dried cod. It now had to compete with cod from Newfoundland in North America. All the North Sea countries joined in the herring fisheries.

The Scandinavian countries had very little active foreign trade of their own. Only Dutch and British and to a certain extent German merchants had sufficient capital and foreign relations to organize the export.

The social consequences of these economic changes were profound. In Denmark the free peasant practically disappeared during these centuries. The Danish county population came to consist of serfs and crofters. Correspondingly, the masters of Danish economic and social life were the landlords. But the state was strong enough to assure a public jurisdiction. In contrast to the Swedish nobility, the Danish landlords had more to gain by exploiting their estates than by waging war; the Danish policy of revenge against Sweden was primarily the affair of the crown. Copenhagen was the political and the economic centre of Denmark–Norway; its name means "harbour of merchants," and it was Danish policy to control and profit by the enormous transit through the Sound.

The natural resources of Norway and Sweden gave no economic basis for landlordship. In Norway the peasants remained free. After 1660 most of the crown properties were sold. Although in Denmark they passed over to the landlord class, in Norway the peasants themselves came to buy the farms they used. Characteristic of Norwegian farming was a combination with other activities—farming and fishing along the coast, farming and forestry in the eastern valleys. This latter combination gave rise to a group of most well-to-do farmers, with crofters dependent on them. The naturalization of foreign merchants was also important in these centuries. Thus Norway for the first time in its history got a native bourgeoisie.

The landlordship in Sweden sprang less from economic than from political causes. The Swedish nobility had a vested interest in lifting Sweden from its underdog position of the 16th century. As noted, the nobles acquired strong positions as commanders and administrators in the conquered areas. Thus, in Sweden, they were able to introduce the domanial system on the soil transferred to them during the Age of Greatness. But, in great contrast to Denmark or the conquered areas, serfdom never came to Sweden; the Swedish farmers remained free. Sweden was the only European country in which peasants formed the Fourth Estate in the Diet. Since the Middle Ages royal propaganda had been designed to influence the opinion of the peasants in political matters.

Peasant
involve-
ment in
Swedish
politics

Because Swedish industry was adapted to Sweden's aggressive foreign policy and because exports were in foreign hands, there was little room for an independent bourgeoisie in this period. Social mobility was primarily influenced by the state. Individual careers and personal fortunes could best be made as soldiers, purveyors to the crown, officers, and public servants. In the 16th and 17th centuries the social structure of Sweden also spread to the formerly completely agrarian Finland.

Swedish society had a considerable capacity for assimilation. Although Denmark–Norway did not until 1720 give up hope of recapturing the provinces that had been lost to Sweden around the middle of the 17th century, it could not count on active support from the populations of these provinces.

III. The 18th century

DENMARK–NORWAY

Denmark. The Great Northern War demonstrated that even with alliances Denmark had no hope for recapturing the territories it had lost to Sweden during the preceding century. On the other hand, Sweden no longer had the strength to invade Denmark from the south (Gottorp). Thus, Denmark decided on a careful foreign policy to keep a balance in the north and to safeguard communications between Denmark and Norway. For guarantees, this implied alliances with Russia and the Netherlands and, from time to time, with France. This policy succeeded for the rest of the 18th century, proba-

bly because of the common European need for free access to the Baltic.

Only once in the century did Denmark experience a political nightmare. In January 1762 the lunatic Duke of Gottorp became tsar of Russia as Peter III. He immediately concluded peace with Prussia (thus really saving its King Frederick II in the Seven Years' War) and declared war on Denmark. But with the murder of the Tsar in July and the accession of Catherine to the Russian throne, the clouds disappeared. In the 1770s Denmark managed to bring Gottorp under the Danish throne.

During the 18th century Denmark–Norway acquired an important merchant marine and a navy as well. Freedom of the seas had become a vital issue and a difficult problem, complicated especially by the Norwegian timber export to England. During wars in the middle of the century (1740–63) Denmark–Norway had to bow to the British claim of ruling the seas. But during the U.S. War of Independence (1775–83) the Danish foreign minister A.P. Bernstorff in 1780 organized an armed neutrality treaty with Russia, Sweden, and Holland. Because of a war between England and France, Denmark and Sweden concluded a similar treaty in 1794, which Russia and Prussia joined in 1800. Norwegian export interests would have been threatened, however, if England considered these treaties hostile acts, so in 1780 Bernstorff also concluded a special treaty with England, much to the annoyance of Russia. Such a policy of balance proved to be impossible after 1800.

The
importance
of freedom
of the seas

Denmark, poor in natural resources except for its soil, made no important economic gains in the 18th century. No important industry developed. Following mercantilist theory the government supported trade, to the benefit of Copenhagen merchants. But Denmark had not the political strength to exploit the strategic position of Copenhagen; imports dominated its trade. Except for oxen and meat, Denmark had very little to export. Eastern Norway was made an outlet for Danish grain in the 1730s, but the grain was inferior and normally could not compete with Baltic grain on the western European markets.

The principal reason for Denmark's stagnant economy was the backward state of Danish agriculture in the 18th century. A body of some 300 Danish landlords owned about 90 percent of the Danish soil, grouped in 800–900 estates. The landlords were the real rulers of the country, because their social position gave them privileged positions in filling the leading posts in the administration, the chanceries, and the Rent Chamber.

A price depression beginning in the 1720s enabled the landlords to use their position to impose very strict laws and regulations on the Danish peasants, who lived in villages, renting their farms from landlords whose demesne lands alone covered about 10 percent of the land. To get cheap labour, a compulsory requirement that one live in the village of his birth was extended to all Denmark for all people between four and 40 years of age. When the system was coupled with conscription for military service, the landlord could threaten a young peasant with at least six years of army service if he did not rent a farm. Every tenant had to perform labour on the landlord's domain for an average of three days a week. This work was considered to be the rent of the peasant's holding. A tenant had no right to demand a contract when he took over a holding, nor could he demand payment for improvements he might make on the holding when the lease expired or was lifted by the landlord. Each landlord also had the right of petty jurisdiction on his estate. Even if the landlords got cheap labour and the army received sufficient manpower by this system, Danish agriculture suffered from incredibly low productivity. The farmers performed poorly on the domains of the landlords; they had too little time to cultivate their own holdings; and they had no reason whatsoever to improve them.

Until the 1780s, Danish society seemed stagnant. A financial crisis in the 1760s, after the Russian threats during the Seven Years' War, was solved by a lasting poll tax. But apparently, for economic reasons, no further tax increase was possible. In 1770 a German doctor, Johann Friedrich Struensee, depending on palace intrigues and

Danish
society

the queen's bed, gained control of the government through the half-mad king Christian VII (ruled 1766–1808). For a year and a half, freedom of the press and intense reform activity reigned, but mostly on paper. Struensee had no popular support, and he naturally provoked resistance and fury among the landlord class. He was arrested for crime against the majesty and, in April 1772, was tortured to death. His short reign has been classified as another failure of the enlightened despotism of the 18th century. The old men who came back to power led an even more reactionary policy than before, one lasting until a bloodless coup d'etat in 1784.

The years between 1784 and 1797 have been called the happiest period in all Danish history. Danish politics of those years were led by A.P. Bernstorff, Ditlev Reventlow, and E.H. Schimmelmann, all from the landlord class, by the benevolent crown prince Frederick (Frederick VI, 1808–39), and by the Norwegian jurist Christian Colbjørnsen. Notable reforms included liberal custom tariffs (1797) and the abolition of the Danish grain monopoly in Norway. But above all, the time was an age of land reforms, beginning in 1786 and lasting until the state suffered financial bankruptcy in 1813. Sixty percent of the Danish peasants became landowners. Compulsory residence, compulsory labour on the domains of landlords, and private jurisdiction were abolished, and the land was redistributed and made into independent farms. The army had to get soldiers by ordinary conscription. Landlords were compensated for the rights they lost, and together with the new landowning farmers they were assured stable labour by strict legislation on the landless crofters. The land reforms were possible because of a continuous rise in grain prices between 1750 and 1815 and because the new men of 1784 had carried out successful reforms on their own estates. As responsible politicians they had an insight into the benefits of a mild inflation and a liberal allocation of state credit, with which they guided the transition to peasant landownership. No doubt the Revolution in France, beginning in 1789, influenced this evolution. The example of the independent French farmers after 1789 hindered an evolution like that in England, with great domains and a numerous class of rural workers. From the land reforms, and from the school act of 1814, which introduced compulsory schooling for all children between ages seven and 14, there stemmed a high standard of Danish agriculture.

The Danish land reforms are remarkable also as the only successful feat of European enlightened despotism.

Norway. Among the common population of Norway there were few signs of unrest during the 18th century. Taxation was reasonable because the Norwegian topography and the status of the free Norwegian peasants made tax collection impossible. For defense against Sweden the Danish government had to rely on the Norwegian peasants themselves, with their own arms, rather than on a professional army. The public servants would not have been able to perform their work surrounded by a hostile population. On the contrary, because Norwegian society was so different, the public servants in Norway could influence Danish decisions regarding Norway by local information and advice. Moreover, Norwegian peasants traditionally complained to "the king in Copenhagen" if the laws were violated by the public servants. This habit was useful for central supervision of the local administration in a thinly populated and distant country.

Real opposition to Danish rule came from the timber merchants and exporters in eastern Norway. For their business, peaceful relations with England were a prerequisite, and banking institutions in Christiania were highly desirable. The first need was met until war with England in 1807–14. The second need was never accepted, however, because of the centralizing economic policy of the government and the interests of the Copenhagen bourgeoisie. The Norwegian exports assured Copenhagen of an important influx of foreign currency and helped to pay the imports to the capital. As long as peace was kept with England, however, the Norwegian and Danish economies were to a large extent complementary, and opposition was only regional.

Norwegian opposition to Danish rule

Romanticists of the later 18th century idealized the Norwegian rural society, with its free peasants in a wild landscape. Certainly, their situation contrasted favourably with that of the Danish tenants; the landowning farmers in eastern Norway, especially, earned sizable incomes from their timber forests. In the east, therefore, and in the region of Trøndelag, the countryside was characterized by a class of rich farmers and a large rural proletariat. Elsewhere in the countryside, social conditions were more nearly equal. The Norwegian population consisted almost exclusively of peasants and fishermen; no city or urban agglomeration exceeded 15,000 inhabitants.

Malthus was the first demographer to see the exceptional possibilities for population studies in the Scandinavian countries, where civic registers were kept by parsons. In 1799, the year following his publication of *An Essay on the Principle of Population*, Malthus went to Norway to confirm his theories about checks on population growth. He found a late marital age, which he ascribed incorrectly to military service and a numerous servant class. In fact, early marriages were hindered by poverty and lack of land. Moreover, Norwegian population statistics of the 18th century indicate years of famine and epidemics, as do Swedish and Danish statistics. Malthus was correct, however, in discerning that demographic evolution in nonindustrialized countries could be studied better in Scandinavia than anywhere else in the world.

Revival of settlement in Greenland. How and why a Norse community in Greenland perished at the end of the Middle Ages is an unsolved and fascinating problem. In the beginning of the 18th century there still was hope of finding Norse descendants among the Eskimos in Greenland. A Norwegian clergyman, Hans Egede, having managed to convince the authorities that such people should be converted to the Lutheran confession, arrived in the Godthåb Fjord (in the southwest), finding only Eskimos, to begin a new European settlement in Greenland. Later in the century another colony was founded at Julianehåb (almost at the southern tip of the island).

Two factors are visible in this activity. First, the Pietist movement, which had a considerable influence in Denmark, demanded religious conversion and stressed an obligation to bring the gospel to the heathens. A Ministry of Missions, founded in 1714, supported Egede in Greenland as it supported missionary activity among the Lapps in northern Norway and among Indians at Tranquebar on the Coromandel Coast.

Factors in the new European settlement in Greenland

Second, missionary activity became possible because of a close alliance with commercial interests. Egede himself founded a company in Bergen for trade with Greenland. The trade later passed to the Royal Greenland Trading Company of Copenhagen. The trade with Finnmark (now the northernmost part of Norway) was reserved, in principle, for merchants of Copenhagen as well. Since the 17th century the East India Company (later the Asiatic Company) had been in charge of the trade with the Far East, with a principal port at Tranquebar.

Missionary activity was not extended to Africans. From the end of the 17th century Denmark–Norway had fortifications on the Guinea Coast (Christiansborg at Accra is very well known) to participate in the slave trade. In the 18th century the West India Company bought some sugar-producing islands in the Caribbean Sea (notably St. Croix) and then organized a three-way trade between Africa, the West Indies, and Copenhagen.

The missionary and commercial activities were manifestations of mercantilism. Lasting results were the settlements in Greenland and the Danish trade to the Far East. The Danish islands in the West Indies were sold to the United States in 1916.

SWEDEN

Growth of parliamentary government. Charles XII had no successor. In 1718 his sister Ulrika Eleonora had to convene the Diet in order to be elected. In 1720 she abdicated in favour of her husband, Frederick of Hessen (ruled 1720–51).

This period saw a transition from absolutism to a parliamentary form of government. The real reason for the change was the complete failure of the policy of "greatness" connected with the Carolingian absolutism. According to the constitutional laws of 1720–23 the power now rested with the estates. The estates met regularly in the Diet, which designated the council. There the king was accorded a double vote but had no right to make decisions. In the Diet, decision making took place in the "Secret Committee," from which the peasants, or the Fourth Estate, were excluded. The public sessions of the estates in the Diet were reserved for speeches and debates. The three upper estates consisted mainly of state servants. Thus the so-called Age of Freedom until 1772 also was an age of bureaucracy.

Adoption of the dual party system in Sweden

During this period, a dual party system evolved; the parties were known by the nicknames "Nightcaps" (or "Caps") and "Hats." Both parties were mercantilist, but the Nightcaps were the more prudent. Up to 1738 the Nightcaps were in power. They led a most careful foreign policy so as not to provoke Russia. From 1738 to 1765 power passed to the Hats, who made treaties with France in order to obtain subsidies and support against Russia. War with Russia in 1741–43 led to a temporary Russian occupation of Finland and to a further loss of Finnish provinces northwest of St. Petersburg. A war with Prussia in 1757–62 was very expensive. The Hats attempted to make Sweden a great economic power; but their economic policy and the war costs led to inflation and financial collapse, and their regime came to an end in 1765.

For some years political confusion reigned in Sweden. The Nightcaps received subsidies from Russia, and their negotiations with Prussia and Denmark intensified party struggle in Sweden. Economic chaos, territorial losses, foreign infiltration, and famine in the countryside undermined the parliamentary system. Historians have sometimes stressed these failures too strongly, however, in glorifying the past Carolingian age and the future Gustavian epoch.

Absolutism of Gustav III. At the death of Adolf Frederick (ruled 1751–71), Gustav III (ruled 1771–92), visiting in Paris, acceded to the throne. Before returning he concluded another treaty with France. In 1772 he used the royal guard and officers of the Finnish army to seize control of the government from the parliament in a bloodless coup d'etat. Gustav tried to exploit the Vasa and Carolingian traditions of personal royal power. He could rely on no class of the Swedish society nor on the political institutions of the 18th century, so he had to make the most of royal propaganda to the public. In this he was not without success; the traditional picture of Gustav is that of "King Charming," the promoter of the arts and sciences.

But Gustav's politics were unstable. Until 1786 he put into effect social reforms that belonged to enlightened despotism, thus enmeshing himself in its traditional dilemma: alienating the "haves" without satisfying the "have nots." Even his solution to the dilemma was a traditional one—war. After Turkey attacked Russia in 1787, Gustav went to war against Russia in 1788 to recapture the Finnish provinces. One reason the Swedish attack failed was a conspiracy by noble Swedish officers —the Anjala association—who, during the war, sent a letter to Catherine II of Russia, proposing negotiations.

Conspiracy by the Anjala association

Gustav used the treason of the Anjala association to provoke an outburst of genuine patriotism in Sweden, hoping to channel popular opinion through the Diet, which he convened in 1789. This Diet, however, against his will, abolished practically all the privileges of the nobility (e.g., the nobility no longer had special rights to any posts in the administration nor to any category of Swedish land). In March 1792 the King was mortally wounded by a nobleman and former officer of the royal guards. The last years of the King and especially the days between the assassination attempt and his death (March 29) made him a martyr in the minds of his people, perhaps undeservedly.

The one notable feat in the Swedish economy during the 18th century was a growth in iron production. With growing competition from Russia, Sweden was a main supplier of iron to the European market. Royal manufactures were a failure, however, and there were no Swedish economic innovations during the century.

In the rural population a social change took place. Most of the peasants during the 18th century came to own their farms. This development coincided with the growth of a large rural proletariat, mainly different types of tenants who served as soldiers or labourers to landlords and peasants. The nobility became less exclusive, and money became more useful for social climbing. But noble birth still helped greatly.

Finland. In the course of the Russo-Swedish War of 1741–43, the Russian empress Elizabeth declared her intention of making Finland a separate state under Russian suzerainty. She failed to follow up the idea, however, and at the peace settlement of Turku (Åbo) in 1743 contented herself with annexing a piece of Finland. Meanwhile, her original idea had found favour with some Finns, not so much as a tempting possibility but as a last resort against merging with Russia. During the next Russo-Swedish war (1788–90), a number of Finnish officers involved themselves in the activities of G.M. Sprengtporten, a Finnish colonel who had fled to Russia and wanted to detach Finland from Sweden; but this movement won little support.

IV. Era of revolution

DENMARK–NORWAY

Denmark. The Napoleonic Wars of the early 19th century tore Denmark–Norway out of a peaceful period that had lasted since 1720. The armed neutrality treaty of 1794 between Denmark and Sweden, to which Russia and Prussia adhered in 1800, was considered a hostile act by England. In 1801 a detachment of the English navy entered the Sound and destroyed much of the Danish fleet in a battle in the harbour of Copenhagen. When the English fleet next proceeded to threaten the Swedish naval port of Karlskrona, Russia started negotiations with England. The result was a compromise, which Sweden was forced to adopt in 1802. The neutrality treaty had fallen in ruins. Denmark–Norway, nevertheless, managed to keep outside the wars and to profit from them until 1807.

The Treaty of Tilsit (1807) between France and Russia worsened the situation. In 1805 France had lost its fleet to the English at Trafalgar. England feared that the continental powers might force Denmark to join them so that the Danish navy could be used to invade England. To eliminate this threat, England resorted not to diplomacy but to force. In September English troops occupied Zealand and an English fleet bombarded Copenhagen. Denmark had no choice but to capitulate to the English demands. On October 20 the English commander sailed away with the whole Danish fleet. The "fleet robbery" was severely criticized, even in the British House of Commons. For fear of a French or Russian occupation, Denmark chose what seemed to be the lesser evil and joined the continental alliance against England on October 31. This step also meant war with Sweden. Denmark might have reacted differently if England had used diplomacy, but the events of September had been too much of an affront to the Danish government and especially to the crown prince Frederick (later Frederick VI, ruled 1808–39). An alliance with England was no longer possible.

English humiliation of Denmark

Norway. The continental blockade of England, which was against Danish interests, was a catastrophe to Norway. Fish and timber exports were stopped, as well as grain imports from Denmark. The consequences were isolation, economic crisis, and hunger. In 1810–13 England consented to some relaxation of its counterblockade against Norway. As a whole, however, the years 1807–14 convinced leading groups in Norway that they needed a political representation of their own.

Swedish foreign policy was erratic during those years (see below), but Denmark–Norway remained an ally of Napoleon until 1814. After Napoleon's defeat at the Battle of Leipzig (1813), Sweden repeated its 17th-century strategy by attacking Denmark from the south. At the Peace of Kiel (January 14, 1814), Denmark gave up all its rights to Norway (but not to the old Norwegian dependencies of Iceland, the Faeroes, and Greenland) to Sweden.

The Danes did not intend this agreement to end their union with Norway. Officially very loyal to the Treaty of Kiel, the Danish government worked for the eventual return of Norway. This probably is why the crown prince Christian Frederick, governor of Norway, in collusion with the Danish king, organized a rising against the Treaty of Kiel. In doing so he needed support in Norway, and he thus came to rely on two political forces, each with regionalist aims. The larger faction consisted of public servants and peasants, with traditional opposition to the centralizing policy of Copenhagen. The other was the small but important group of timber merchants in eastern Norway, who wanted independence from Copenhagen for their trade with western Europe. Since 1809 they even had conspired for a union between Sweden and Norway.

This was the main background of a constituent assembly, called by Christian Frederick to meet at Eidsvoll, 40 miles north of Christiania. It drew up a constitution on May 17, 1814 (which still exists), and elected Christian Frederick to the throne of Norway.

Norwegian independence got no support from the great powers, and Sweden attacked Norway in July 1814. After a fake war of 14 days, Christian Frederick resigned. Jean Bernadotte, the Swedish crown prince, accepted the fait accompli of the Norwegian constitution, and in so doing could no longer argue on the basis of the Treaty of Kiel. This was of the greatest political importance to the Norwegians. As a constitutional monarchy, Norway entered the union with Sweden in November 1814; only minor modifications were made in its constitution—the king and the foreign policy would be common; the king would be commander in chief of Norway's armed forces, which could not be used outside Norway without Norwegian consent; a government in Christiania (with a section in Stockholm) and the Storting (Norwegian parliament) would take care of national affairs.

SWEDEN

Royalist reaction. A fear of influences from revolutionary France dominated the Swedish government during the last decade of the 18th century and the first of the 19th. These fears were reflected in major economies in public finances, the legislation of land reforms, and the censoring of French literature. Gustav IV (ruled 1792–1809), unlike his father, Gustav III, was pious and superstitious. He considered events in France to be insults to moral order. A deep aversion toward the revolutionaries and Napoleon characterized his foreign policy. Of decisive importance was his resolution in 1805 to join the coalition against France. When France and Russia signed the Treaty of Tilsit in 1807, Gustav stubbornly accepted war, even with Russia. Denmark, which had sided with France in October 1807, declared war against Sweden in 1808. England, at the moment busy in Spain, could offer little help. Sweden thus became politically isolated, with enemies in the east, south, and west. The Swedish army defended Finland poorly, reaching its nadir when the strong fortress of Sveaborg near Helsingfors was handed over to the Russians by treason. The Russians advanced as far as Umeå in Sweden. Finally, in 1809, a bitter peace was made at Frederikshavn, in which Sweden surrendered Finland and the Åland Islands (northeast of Stockholm) to Russia.

Surrender of Finland to Russia

In March 1809 Gustav IV was deposed by a group of high officials and officers. More than anything, a widespread longing for a quick and cheap peace brought the men of 1809 to power, but they were unable to save Finland. A new constitution was made, embodying the principle of separation of powers. The division of the Diet in four estates remained. Charles XIII (ruled 1809–18), the uncle of Gustav IV, was elected king. That he was senile and childless opened the question of succession to the throne.

With the consent of Denmark, the commander in chief of the Norwegian army, Christian August (at the moment waging war against Sweden), was elected crown prince, and took the name Charles August. Behind this decision were thoughts of a Scandinavian confederation. This solution was cherished by Denmark and even by Napoleon.

In 1810 Charles August died, and the question of the succession to the throne was reopened. A Swedish lieutenant, Baron Carl Otto Mörner, was sent to Paris to explain the situation to Napoleon. At the same time he worked for his own plans—to pick one of Napoleon's commanders for the throne of Sweden. The choice fell on the prince of Pontecorvo, the marshal Jean-Baptiste Bernadotte. This choice pleased Napoleon, though he may have preferred the Swedish throne to be taken over by his ally King Frederick VI of Denmark–Norway. Meanwhile the French consul in Göteborg and the francophile Swedish foreign minister, Engeström, managed to persuade the Diet to set aside the Danish alternative and to name Bernadotte as crown prince of Sweden in August 1810.

Bernadotte. From his arrival in Sweden in October 1810, Bernadotte, who took the name Charles John, became the real leader of Swedish politics. In designating him for the crown, the Swedes hoped that he would somehow reconquer Finland and the Åland Islands. When Napoleon attacked Russia in 1812, Charles John personally negotiated with Tsar Alexander, offering help against Napoleon if the Tsar would permit Sweden to occupy Finland or even only Åland. The Tsar declined. Quite soon Russia needed no foreign help against Napoleon.

Charles John then turned to the West. In March 1813 he negotiated a treaty with England by which, for participating in the final offensive against Napoleon, Charles John was to obtain Norway. Thus Charles John became commander in chief of the northern allied army, consisting of Prussian, Russian, and Swedish soldiers. He used this army sparingly, especially the Swedish contingent, even at the Battle of Leipzig in October 1813, because he cherished a hope of succeeding Napoleon and also because he needed troops to attack Denmark. After Leipzig, Charles John refused to cross the Rhine; instead he led the northern army against Denmark. The result was the Peace of Kiel, whereby Norway was surrendered.

Charles John's ambitions

By accepting a constitution in Norway, Charles John became heir, peacefully, to his second throne in four years and consequently gained a more independent position in Sweden. He hoped, moreover, to impress favourably liberal circles in France.

The cession of Finland to Russia. In the words of Swedish historian, Sten Carlsson, in 1969, "The loss of Finland was the price of the long and still unbroken period of peace that was to begin in 1814." The statement implies that the possession of Finland in the past centuries forcibly brought Sweden in collision with other powers in the Baltic area. When Peter the Great founded the new Russian capital at St. Petersburg and the harbour of Kronstadt at the bottom of the Gulf of Finland in the first decade of the 18th century, the danger became much more serious. It is significant that Russia acquired wide Finnish areas around St. Petersburg in 1721 and in 1743.

As a part of the Swedish monarchy, Finland had been accorded practically no institutions of its own, but from the middle of the 18th century the majority of officials and intellectuals were of Finnish origin. In those circles there was a growing feeling that Finland had to bear the cost of Swedish extravagances in foreign policy. The feeling was not unfounded. Swedish strategical directives of 1785 implied that in case of Russian attack, Swedish forces should retire from the frontier, leaving Finnish detachments behind, and that under extreme danger the whole of Finland should be evacuated. This strategy was put into effect in 1807–09. Even the treachery of the Anjala association in 1788 was repeated in 1808, when Sveaborg near Helsingfors capitulated to the Russians. The feeling that the Finns could trust nobody other than themselves was born in the end of the 18th century. In 1809 the Finns themselves had to carry the responsibility of coming to terms with Russia. Tsar Alexander offered to recognize constitutional developments in Finland and to give it autonomy as a grand duchy under his throne.

When Sweden surrendered Finland in 1809, it even had to give up the Åland Islands northeast of Stockholm. "Russia would not take a trunk (Finland) without the keys."
(G.Sa.)

V. The 19th century

DENMARK

Economic development and the liberal reform movement. *Economic consequences of the war.* The Napoleonic Wars had proved a national catastrophe for Denmark, both economically and politically. The policy of armed neutrality had failed, and the fleet had been destroyed or surrendered. Copenhagen, the capital, which was the country's commercial and administrative centre, had been devastated by the bombardment of 1807, while Norway had been lost at the Treaty of Kiel in 1814. Trade had been hard-hit by the blockade, and the widespread overseas connections that formerly had played so large a part in the economic life of Denmark could not be resumed. Copenhagen's role as an international financial and trading centre was taken over by Hamburg, and even a considerable part of Danish home trade was controlled from there. Inflation further contributed to the crisis. The state was forced to make a formal declaration of bankruptcy, and not until an independent national bank with sole rights to issue banknotes was established in 1818 was economic stability slowly re-established. It was 20 years, however, before the coinage rose to parity with the silver standard, and banknotes were first redeemable in 1845.

The economic crisis was worsened by low corn prices. The loss of Norway and the high import duties on corn that Great Britain imposed at this time meant that Denmark was deprived of its surest markets for its corn export. The period from 1818 to 1828 was characterized by an agricultural crisis that resulted in the compulsory auctioning of many estates and farms, forcing the agrarian reform to a complete standstill.

In about 1830 economic life took a turn for the better with, among other things, more stable prices for agricultural products, increased trade, and the first signs of industrialization.

The liberal movement. Denmark's government under Frederick VI (ruled 1808–39) could be described as a patriarchal autocracy. In the Privy Council, which was regularly convened after 1814, Poul Christian Stemann became the leading figure and was responsible for the government's strongly conservative policies until 1848. His close colleague, Anders Sandøe Ørsted, pleaded for a somewhat more liberal policy, at least on economic questions. After the July Revolution in France, a demand was made in Denmark for a liberal constitution. The government was forced to make concessions, and in 1834 four provincial consultative diets (or assemblies) were created, two in the kingdom itself, one in Schleswig (Slesvig), and one in Holstein. These had merely an advisory function, but both the eligibility and the right to vote were fairly extensive. Simultaneously, the liberal movement grew in strength, especially in the academic world and among the middle classes. The liberal press whose leading journal was *Faedrelandet* ("The Fatherland," established in 1834), subjected the absolute monarchy and its conservative administration to severe criticism. When Frederick VI, the popular monarch, died in 1839 the liberals had great hopes of his successor Christian VIII (ruled 1839–48), who, during his youth as regent in Norway, had appeared as the spokesman for a liberal government. Over the years, however, he had become much more conservative and as king of Denmark did not consider the time ripe to dissolve the absolute monarchy. He confined himself, therefore, to modernizing the administration, especially in establishing local government by municipal laws between 1837 and 1841, granting some independence to parishes and counties. Parallel with the liberal movement ran the farmers' movement. This started as a religious movement but soon became dominated by social and political ideas, with agitators such as Jens Anderson Hansen leading the way. When the government intervened, the liberals and farmers joined forces against the common adversary. In 1846 the farmers' case received support when a group of liberal reformers led by Anton Frederik Tscherning founded the Bondevenneselskabit (Society of the Friends of the Peasant), which developed into the Venstre (the liberal farmer's party).

The 1849 constitution. After the death of Christian VIII in January 1848 and under the influence of the February Revolution in Paris and the March Revolution in Germany, the new king Frederick VII (ruled 1848–63) installed the March Cabinet, in which the National Liberal leaders Orla Lehmann and Ditlev Gothard Monrad were given seats. After a constituent assembly had been summoned, the absolute monarchy was abolished and was replaced by the June constitution of 1849. Together with the king and his ministers there was now also a Parliament with two chambers, the Folketing and the Landsting, both elected by popular vote but with a property-owning qualification as a prerequisite for a seat in the Landsting. Parliament, together with the king and government, shared legislative power while the courts independently exercised judicial power. The constitution also secured the freedom of the press, religious freedom, and the right to hold meetings and form associations.

From W. Carr, *Schleswig-Holstein, 1815–1848;* Manchester University Press

Language distribution in Schleswig-Holstein, 1849.

The National Liberals and the Schleswig-Holstein question. Nationalism was, together with liberalism, the most important movement in the 19th century. In Denmark, national feelings were inflamed by the conflict with Germany on the Schleswig-Holstein question. After the loss of Norway, the Danish monarchy consisted of three main parts: the kingdom of Denmark and the duchies of Schleswig and Holstein, the last of which was a member of the German Confederation. Whereas Holstein was German, Schleswig was linguistically and culturally divided between a Danish and a German population. When the liberal German-speaking population in Schleswig opposed autocratic rule and demanded a free constitution and affiliation to Holstein and the German Confederation, a Danish National Liberal movement emerged and demanded that Schleswig be incorporated in Denmark (the Eider Policy, named for the Eider River, which formed the southern boundary of Schleswig). When the

The Eider Policy

National Liberal Government officially adopted this policy in 1848, the Schleswig-Holsteiners resorted to arms. As the rebellion received military aid from Prussia, the Danish Army could not suppress it. The war, which lasted three years, ended in the agreements of 1851 and 1852 in which Denmark pledged to take no measures to tie Schleswig any closer to itself than to Holstein. The Eider Policy was thus abandoned, and the June constitution of 1849 applied only to Denmark. The National Liberal government was succeeded in 1852 by a Conservative government under Christian Albrecht Bluhme.

Under the influence of the Pan-Scandinavian movement and the German Confederation's constant interference in constitutional matters in Schleswig and Holstein, the Eider Policy again won ground, and the Conservative government was replaced in 1857 by a moderate National Liberal government led by Carl Christian Hall. This government introduced a number of reforms of which the most important was a law of freedom of enterprise in trade and industry. In 1863, in the belief that Prussia was preoccupied with the Polish rebellion against Russia and in expectation of support from Sweden, the government separated Holstein from the rest of the state and conferred a joint constitution on the kingdom and Schleswig. This "November constitution" meant that Schleswig was annexed to Denmark, in contravention of the agreements of 1851 and 1852.

Prussia, however, under the leadership of Otto von Bismarck, reacted immediately, and in February 1864 war broke out between Denmark on the one side and Prussia and Austria on the other. After the Danish defeat at Dybbøl and the consequent occupation of the whole of Jutland, Denmark was forced by the Treaty of Vienna to surrender the whole of Schleswig and Holstein to Prussia and Austria.

The conservative regime. *Realignment of political factions.* The defeat in 1864 led to the fall of the National Liberal government. Under Christian IX (ruled 1863–1906) a Conservative government was appointed, and in 1866 a new constitution followed that introduced electoral rules giving the Landsting a distinct conservative leaning, with great landowners and civil servants as the dominating elements. The National Liberal Party was swallowed up by the Conservative Party. As a counterweight, the various groups that represented the farmers combined together in 1870 to form The United Left, (Det forenede Venstre), which in 1872 secured a majority in the Folketing. Venstre demanded that the 1849 June constitution be reintroduced together with a number of other reforms. With Jacob Brønnum Scavenius Estrup, a great landowner, as prime minister (1875–94), however, a strictly conservative policy was pursued. Despite the opposing parliamentary majority, the government forced its policy through by means of provisory law and with support from the king. The result was that all reforms came to a standstill. Not until the "compromise" of 1894 was the crisis solved, at which time Estrup himself left the government. The demand for parliamentary democracy was not granted, however, until the 1901 election, when Venstre came to power, and what has become known in Denmark as the "Change of System" was introduced.

Social and economic change. The progress of Venstre and the formation of the Social Democratic Party in the 1870s must be viewed against the background of the great economic and social changes. During the 1850s and 1860s a network of railroads was created, industrialization began, agrarian reforms were introduced, and a number of technical improvements in corn production were effected. In the years between 1870 and 1901 the urban population increased from 25 percent to 44 percent of the total population. The rapid development of harbours, ships, and foreign trade meant that the shortage of raw materials, such as iron and coal, did not hinder the development of industry to any essential degree. There was a steady stream of foreign capital to Denmark. Trade unions and employers' federations were established at this time and spread nationwide by 1899. The fall in the world market price of corn after 1875 resulted in an increased production of butter and bacon. England became even more the main market for agricultural products. Even the smallest farm arranged its production with exports in mind, while at the same time foodstuffs were imported. Standardization of butter and bacon and their export was arranged by the farmers themselves on a cooperative basis and with a view to the existing struggle with townsmen and the great landowners. The cooperative movement won ground in rural areas. Culturally, the farmers gathered around the folk high schools, educational institutions with a mainly liberal arts program, inspired the ideas of N.F.S. Grundtvig, the writer, educationist, and theologian.

SWEDEN

Population, agriculture, and industry. The population of Sweden, which in 1815 was barely 2,500,000 reached 3,500,000 by 1850 and 5,100,000 by 1900. During the period 1815 to 1900, therefore, the country's population had more than doubled, despite a loss of 850,000 emigrants (mainly to North America) during the period 1840 to 1900.

Until the last quarter of the 19th century, Sweden was a predominantly agricultural country. In 1850, 90 percent of the population lived off the land. By 1900 the figure was still as high as 75 percent. At the beginning of the 19th century, rural dwellings were clustered together in the villages, and the fields were cultivated under an old open-field system. The basis for an agricultural modernization was laid down by a statute of 1827 on enclosures (Laga skifte), which stated that when possible the fields of the individual farm should be assembled together in a compact area. Enclosures of lands, which took place throughout the 19th century, changed the face of the countryside. Villages were split up, and scattered farms became the predominant type of dwelling in Sweden. The move away from the village system brought about a widespread reclamation of wasteland and the modernization of agriculture, which accounted in part for the increase in population.

During the first half of the 19th century, trade and industry were still restricted by regulations and guild rules. The middle of the 19th century saw the beginning of industrial organization, primarily in the timber trade, and in the last quarter of the 19th century the industrial revolution began in earnest with the advent of new methods in iron and steel production and the birth of a number of specialized industries, such as those of machines and machine tools. During the greater part of the 19th century, however, Sweden was a poor and overpopulated country.

The Conservative Era (1815–40). At the conclusion of the Napoleonic Wars, Sweden was hard-hit by an economic slump that lasted until 1830, characterized by abortive attempts to reestablish the value of the currency. After devaluation in 1834, the currency was finally stabilized. Crown Prince Charles John (Carl Johan), who was king under the name of Charles XIV John (ruled 1818–44), pursued a strictly conservative policy. The king's power, invested in him by the constitution, was exploited to the limit; and the ministers were recruited from his henchmen without regard to the wishes of Parliament. In the 1820s the liberal opposition steadily increased its demands for reforms, and 1830 was the year in which liberal opinion made a breakthrough. In Sweden this was indicated by the establishing of a newspaper, *Aftonbladet*, which with Lars Johan Hierta as editor, became the leading journal of the liberal opposition. Simultaneously, the king's one-man-rule, which was exercised through his powerful favourite Magnus Brahe, became even more emphatic. The struggle against the growing liberal opposition, which reached its climax at the end of the 1830s, was characterized by actions against the freedom of the press and indictments of high treason and countered by the liberals with sharp criticism, demonstrations, and street riots.

The liberal reform period. The pressure of the opposition, however, at last forced the king to yield, and the 1840 Parliament, in which the liberal opposition had the

The United Left

Enclosures

The growth of the liberal opposition

majority, forced through the "departmental reform," which meant that the ministers actually became the heads of their own ministries. Another reform of great significance was the introduction in 1842 of compulsory school education. When Charles XIV John died in 1844 and was succeeded by his son Oscar I (ruled 1844–59), the liberal reform period had already gained momentum.

Principal reforms. Among the most important of the reforms was the introduction of free enterprise in 1846, which meant the abolition of the guilds. They were now replaced by free industrial and trade associations. Simultaneously, the monopoly of trade that the towns had held since the Middle Ages was also abolished. Finally, by the introduction of a statute in 1864, complete freedom of enterprise became a reality. The lifting of almost all bans on exports and imports in 1847, together with a reduction in customs duties, was the first step toward free trade. A number of other liberal reforms were introduced: equal rights of inheritance for men and women (1845), unmarried women's rights (1858), a more humane penal code through a number of reforms (1855–64), religious freedom (1860), and local self-government (1862). Another significant step was the decision in 1854 that the state should be responsible for the building and management of main-line railroads.

Parliamentary reform. Oscar I, who took the initiative himself in many of these reforms, became more conservative after the disturbances in Stockholm in 1848. When he was succeeded by his son, Charles XV (ruled 1859–72), the power had in reality gradually passed into the hands of the Privy Council, which, under the leadership of the minister of finance, Baron Johan August Gripenstedt, and the minister of justice, Baron Louis De Geer, completed the reforms. From the beginning of the 19th century the most important of the liberal demands had been for a reform of the system of representation. It was not until 1865–66 that agreement was reached to replace the old Riksdag with its four Estates of nobility, clergy, burghers, and peasantry with a parliament consisting of two chambers with equal rights. The members of the first were chosen by indirect vote and with such a high eligibility qualification that it bore the stamp of an upper chamber representing great landowners and commercial and industrial entrepreneurs. The members of the second were chosen by direct popular vote, which was limited, however, by a property qualification and therefore gave the farmers an advantage.

Introduction of a two-chamber Riksdag

Political stagnation (1866–1900). The reform of the representative system marks the end of the liberal reform period. During the following 20 years, Swedish politics were dominated by two issues: the demand for an abolition of ground tax, which had been levied from ancient times, and the defense question, where the demand was for an abolition of the military system of *indelningsverket* (that is to say, an army organization in which the soldiers were given small holdings to live on). The defense system was to be modernized by an increase in conscription. The First Chamber's demand for rearmament, however, was impossible in view of the Second Chamber's demand for the abolition of the ground tax. As these issues had been linked together in the 1873 compromise, they were not resolved until 1892, when it was decided to abolish the ground tax and replace the old army organization with a larger and better trained conscripted army. The latter was completed through the defense reform of 1901, which introduced a conscripted army with a 240-day period of service.

The heavily falling prices of corn on the world market in the 1880s gave rise to a serious agricultural crisis. In 1888 a moderate tariff was introduced that was gradually raised in the following years. The Second Chamber, which, since the electoral reform had been dominated by the farmers' party, was at this time split into a protectionist faction and a free-trade faction. With the appearance of the Social Democrats in 1889, the Liberal factions in the Riksdag merging into the Liberal union in 1900, and the Conservative groups forming a united election organization in 1904, there came into being the parties that still dominate Swedish politics today.

Foreign policy. Until the end of the 19th century, foreign policy was still regarded as the monarch's personal province. Already, as crown prince, Charles John had concluded an alliance with Russia against almost unanimous opposition and by so doing initiated the Russia-oriented policy that characterized the whole of his reign. The succession of Oscar I to the throne in 1844 brought no immediate alteration. The only deviation was in his somewhat carefully demonstrated sympathy for the growing Pan-Scandinavian movement. When the German nationals rebelled against the Danish king in 1848, Oscar I aligned himself with Frederick VII and contributed, together with the tsar, to a cease-fire and armistice.

Change in alliance policy. During the negotiations on Schleswig-Holstein, Oscar I was still on the side of Tsar Nicholas I of Russia, aligned more or less against the radical nationalism in Germany. But in reality he endeavoured to extricate Sweden from the conservative Russia-orientated policy that Charles John had initiated in 1812. The opportunity came during the Crimean War (1853–56), when Oscar I adopted a friendly attitude to the Western powers and, among other things, opened Swedish harbours to English and French warships, and tried to induce the Western powers, with the help of Swedish troops, to attack St. Petersburg. With this intention, he signed the November Treaty with the Western powers in 1855. The peace treaty that was concluded in Paris shortly afterward, however, ended the hopes cherished in Sweden of winning Finland, or at least Åland, back again. All that was gained was the Åland Convention, which forbade Russia to build fortifications or have other military installations on Åland.

Pan-Scandinavianism. During the 1840s and 1850s the idea of a united Scandinavia had won great support among students and intellectuals. Crown Prince Charles had spoken out enthusiastically in favour of this ideal, and, after his succession to the throne in 1859, he assured the Danish king of Sweden's solidarity with Denmark, promising Swedish support in 1863 to defend the frontier at the Eider—the southern boundary of Schleswig. Encouraged by these promises, Denmark embarked upon the policy that led to the Danish-Prussian War of 1864. In the event, the Swedish government reluctantly refused to honour the king's pledge. Scandinavian unity therefore suffered a decisive defeat and ceased to be the guiding light of Swedish foreign policy.

Promise of cooperation with Denmark

Neutrality and friendship with Germany. In the wars between Prussia and Austria in 1866 and between Germany and France in 1870–71, Sweden was officially neutral, even if in the latter the king's personal sympathies were with France. Oscar II (ruled in Sweden 1872–1907) reorientated the country's foreign policy. The new German Empire under the leadership of Otto von Bismarck excited his admiration and sympathy. At the same time, connections with Germany became much closer, and from the mid-1870s Swedish politics were influenced by a close friendship with Germany that was even more emphasized during the last years of the 19th century by the growing fear of Russia.

The Swedish-Norwegian Union. From the Swedish viewpoint the union with Norway was a disappointment. Instead of an alliance of the two countries, the incompatibilities grew, and the union remained a personal one, on the whole confined to a joint monarch and foreign policy. One of the few positive results of the union was an 1825 statute that abolished or greatly reduced tariffs between the countries. The union also had an important influence on Sweden's domestic affairs, and Norway served as a model for Swedish radicals who demanded parliamentary democracy.

As crown prince in the 1850s, Charles XV had promised the Norwegians that on his succession to the throne he would abolish the post of governor general, which in Norway was regarded as a sign of the country's subordinate position in the union. In reality, this question was relatively unimportant, as the post of governor general had not been occupied by a Swede since 1829 and had been vacant since 1855. When Charles XV succeeded to the throne, however, and tried to honour his pledge to

The governor-general question

abolish the post, the Swedish Parliament and the government headed by the powerful minister of finance, Baron J.A. Gripenstedt, opposed the resolution. Charles XV was forced to give way and withdraw his support for the abolition of the post. The government, with support from Parliament, had thus strengthened its position over the king. The governor-general question marked the beginning of the struggle for power between king and Parliament that characterized Sweden's internal politics for the latter part of the 19th century. In 1905 the union question again influenced Swedish domestic affairs. With the dissolution of the union, the king's power was usurped, and a government chosen by the majority parties in Parliament and headed by the right-wing leader Christian Lundeberg was appointed to negotiate with Norway. Thus the dissolution of the union led to the first real parliamentary government in Sweden.

NORWAY

For Norway the Treaty of Kiel (1814) meant seccession from Denmark and the forming of its own separate state with complete internal self-government. The history of Norway during the 19th century is marked by the struggle to assert its independence of Sweden within the union and its attempts to emancipate itself from Danish cultural influences.

Population, trade, and industry. *Population.* Norway's population grew more rapidly during the 19th century than in any other period of its history. The population rose from 883,000 in 1801 to 2,240,000 in 1900. Whereas the urban population was only 8.8 percent in 1800, it had reached 28 percent by 1900. After Ireland, Norway had the highest relative emigration of all European countries in the 19th century. From 1840 to 1914 about 750,000 people emigrated.

Economic conditions. Norway was also severely hit by the economic crisis that followed the Napoleonic Wars. Norway's exports consisted mainly of wooden goods to Great Britain and, to a certain extent, of glass and iron products. After the war, when the British introduced preferential tariffs on articles of wood from Canada, Norwegian forest owners and sawmills and export firms were badly hit. Iron and glass exports also met with marketing difficulties. Fish, which after timber was the country's most important export commodity, was only lightly hit by the slump; and by the 1820s the herring fisheries on the west coast enjoyed a period of vigorous expansion. From the 1850s on, agriculture developed rapidly. Modern methods were adopted and an emphasis was laid on cattle breeding. Simultaneously, the building of railroads began ending the isolation of the small communities and opening the way for the sale of agricultural products. It was, however, above all the great expansion of merchant shipping (especially between 1850 and 1880) that gave the most powerful boost to the country's economy. Norway's percentage of world tonnage rose from 3.6 percent to 6.1 percent; and at the end of the century Norway possessed, after the United Kingdom and the United States, the largest merchant navy in the world. The economic resources that merchant shipping brought to the country laid the basis for industrialization. From 1860 Norway's industry expanded rapidly, especially in the timber trade and in engineering. Socially and economically this expansion was a springboard for shipowners, manufacturers, and businessmen, all of whom began to play a much greater role in politics toward the end of the 19th century.

The age of bureaucracy (1814–59). The economic development in the decades immediately after the Napoleonic Wars meant a reduction in the power of the big business concerns and great estates. The decision to abolish the nobility in 1821 was indicative of the greatly reduced social and economic circumstances of the upper classes. At the same time, the position of the bureaucrats was strengthened, and from then until the latter part of the 19th century they controlled the political power of the country. Apart from the bureaucrats, there were only two other political factors of any importance in Norway at this time: the farmers and the monarch.

Parliamentary authority. The Eidsvoll constitution of 1814 gave Parliament greater authority than parliamentary bodies had in any other country except the United States. The king retained executive power and chose his own ministers, but legislation and the imposition of taxes required the participation of the Storting (Parliament). The Storting had the power to initiate legislation, and the king had only a suspension veto. When the union's monarch Charles XIV John (ruled 1818–44) demanded the right of absolute veto, the Storting categorically refused, despite the King's attempt to intimidate them with shows of military strength. Faced with this unanimous resistance, the King was forced to abandon his struggle, and the Storting's dominant position became the firm defense against Swedish attempts to unite the two countries. As a national demonstration, Norway began in the 1820s to celebrate May 17, the date of the Eidsvoll constitution, as a national day. The King's attempt to outlaw the celebration resulted in violent demonstrations, and during the 1830s he conceded this point also.

Monetary problems. Norway had at the same time many major problems to resolve on the domestic front. The war, which had been to a great extent financed by an increased issue of banknotes, had brought about a reduction of the riksdaler to one-fifteenth of its original value. To ward off inflation, a severe sterling tax was imposed, and in 1816 a new bank of Norway was established that had the monopoly of issuing banknotes. In spite of strong precautionary measures, however, it was not until the currency reform of 1842 that finances were stabilized. From an economic point of view, the bureaucratic rulers were decidedly liberal, and the guild system and old trade regulations were abolished during the 1840s and 1850s. By 1842 it was decided to reduce tariffs, a decision that gradually made Norway a free-trade country.

Political change. The influence that the vote gave to the farmers was not exploited at first, and they continued to elect bureaucrats as their parliamentary representatives. About 1830, however, a demand was raised for a decrease in expenditure, and under the leadership of Ole Gabriel Ueland, a more deliberate "class" policy began to be conducted in the Storting. The farmer's policy, which led to sharp conflicts with influential groups of bureaucrats, became a struggle for political power, resulting in the passing of a bill on local government in 1837. Under pressure from both a radical labour movement, which arose after 1848 under the leadership of Marcus Möller Thrane, and the later mounting tension in the relationship with Sweden, the farmers allied themselves in the 1850s and 1860s with the Venstre Party, which had been founded during the 1850s by the middle classes and minor civil servants. The party's intensely nationalistic attitude was expressed in its attempts to strengthen national culture and language. The struggle for the introduction of the vernacular as the official language instead of the bureaucrats' Danish influenced tongue became an important item of the party's policy.

The union conflict (1859–1905). As the union's king usually resided in Sweden, he was represented in Norway by a governor general. This gave rise to the governor-general conflict, which was not resolved until 1873, when Sweden yielded to Norway's main demands. The result was that in Norway the king was regarded as purely Swedish, and his right to nominate the government in Norway was considered a danger to the country's autonomy. The conflict revolved around the question of the Storting's confidence in the government. During the reign of Oscar II (ruled in Norway 1872–1905), matters came to a head when a Conservative government refused to pass a bill that the Storting had three times accepted. After a trial before the court of impeachment (Riksretten) the government was forced to resign. The Storting and not the king had thus acquired the decisive influence on the government, and Norway became the first country in Scandinavia to be governed by parliamentary means. Although Norway had won full self-government on the domestic front, the union was still represented externally by the Swedish-Norwegian king, and the country's foreign policy was conducted by the Swedish foreign minis-

(margin left) Merchant shipping

(margin right) Resignation of the government

ter. From the 1880s, therefore, there was an increasing demand for an independent Norwegian foreign minister. In 1891, Venstre won an impressive majority at the polls with the Foreign Minister question, among other things, on its program. In spite of this, the Venstre government headed by Johannes Steen, which the King had appointed after the election, did not take up the foreign minister question but raised instead a more limited demand for a Norwegian consular service. Even this was flatly refused by Sweden in 1892. When the Norwegian Parliament attempted to carry out this reform independently, it was forced under threat of military action to negotiate with Sweden on a revision of the whole question of the union. Though Sweden soon showed its readiness to be most compliant, the incompatibilities had become so marked that there was no real chance of a compromise. The negotiations collapsed in 1898, and Norway at the same time demonstrated its independence by abolishing the union emblem on its merchant flag, despite the king's veto. New negotiations were opened in an attempt to solve the more limited demand for an independent consular service, but when these negotiations also failed Norway took the matter into its own hands, and the Storting passed a bill establishing Norway's own consular service. When the king refused to sanction the bill, the coalition government, under the leadership of Christian Michelsen, resigned. As, under the circumstances, it was impossible for the king to form a new Norwegian government, the Storting declared "the Union with Sweden dissolved as a result of the King ceasing to function as Norwegian King," on June 7, 1905. The Swedish Parliament refused, however, to accept this unilateral Norwegian decision. Under threat of military action and partial mobilization in both countries, Norway was forced to submit and enter into negotiations on the conditions for the dissolution of the union. A settlement was reached in Karlstad in September 1905, which embodied concessions from both sides. The Swedish-Norwegian union was thus legally dissolved, and shortly afterward Prince Charles of Denmark was chosen as Norway's king and came to the throne under the name of Haakon VII.

Margin note: Dissolution of the union

FINLAND

Authoritarian government (1809–63). On its separation from Sweden in accordance with the Treaty of Fredrikshamn (Hamina, 1809) Finland had a population of over 900,000. As elsewhere in Scandinavia, population growth was rapid, and by 1908 the figure had exceeded 2,000,000. The bulk of the population lived off the land. Manufacture of wooden articles, export of timber, shipbuilding, and merchant shipping were practiced to a certain extent in the small coastal towns.

Political organization. The political framework was laid down by the Porvoo (Borgå) Diet (Valtiapäivät) in 1809, at which time the Russian tsar Alexander I promised to respect the religion and fundamental laws of Finland, as well as the privileges and rights of the inhabitants (that is to say, the Swedish constitution of 1772 as amended in 1789 by which the regent alone had the executive power, while the consent of the Diet "Lantdag" was required for legislation and the imposition of new taxes). The grand duke (the tsar) was not obliged to convene the Lantdag at regular intervals, and the result was that it did not meet until 1863. From 1809 to 1863 Finland was ruled by a bureaucracy chosen by the tsar, though, with the exception of the governor-general, this was solely Finnish. The highest administrative organ during the period was the Senate, which consisted of a judicial department and an economic department. The former was the country's supreme court, while the latter became a sort of ministry. A ministerial state secretary in St. Petersburg represented Finnish affairs to the tsar.

Russian reforms and repression. Despite the strongly authoritarian form of government, a number of important reforms were implemented. In 1812 the tsar was induced to restore those areas of Finnish territory that Sweden had ceded to Russia by the treaties of Nystad (Uusikaupunki) 1721 and Åbo (Turku) 1743. Furthermore, in 1812 the town of Helsingfors (Helsinki) was

chosen as the capital, and the monumental buildings in its centre stem from this period. The vast rural population and purely agrarian structure prevented the spread of liberal and national ideas to any great extent during the first part of the 19th century. The reaction reached its climax with the Finnish language ordinance of 1850, which forbade the publication in Finnish of books other than those that aimed at religious edification or economic benefit. Since Finnish was the only language understood by the majority of the population, the ordinance smacked of an attempt to maintain class differences and was well suited to preserve the existing bureaucracy.

Margin note: The Finnish language ordinance

Language controversy and political reforms. *The language problem.* As late as the mid-19th century, Swedish was the only language allowed within the Finnish administration. There was an almost total lack of literature in Finnish, and teaching at both the secondary and university levels was in Swedish. The division between the two languages became not only of national and cultural significance but also a social distinction. This is one of the reasons why the language controversy in Finland created such bitterness. To begin with, the advocates of a Finnish-speaking Finland, or Fennomans, were successful. By recording folksongs and writings, a Finnish literature was developed during the latter part of the 19th century. The first purely Finnish-speaking grammar school appeared in 1858. In 1863 Alexander II (ruled 1855–81) issued a decree stating that after a 20-year interim period, Finnish was to be placed on an equal footing with Swedish in the administration and in the law courts, as far as their relations with the public were concerned. Swedish, however, remained the language of internal administration, and it was not until 1902 that Swedish and Finnish were placed on an equal footing as official languages.

Reform of the Diet. During the reign of Alexander II other reforms were begun. The most important was his convening of the Diet (Lantdag) in 1863, and the promulgation of a new act in 1869 providing that the Diet thereafter should be convened regularly. The next great reform period came after the Russian defeat in the war against Japan (1904–05). The most important action was the Parliamentary reform of 1906, which replaced the old Diet of the Four Estates by a one-chamber Eduskunta (Riksdag) elected by universal and equal franchise for both men and women. Thus, from having one of Europe's most unrepresentative political systems, Finland had, at one stroke, acquired the most modern. The Parliamentary reform polarized the political factions, and the ground was laid for the modern party system. The introduction of universal and equal suffrage meant that the farmers and workers potentially commanded a great majority. Social and economic problems came to the fore. The breakthrough in democracy, made possible by this reform, was an important prerequisite for Finland's success in winning its independence in 1917–18.

Margin note: Adoption of the universal and equal franchise

Relations with Russia. Until the 1890s, Russia respected Finland's special position within the Russian Empire in all essentials. During the reign of Alexander II (ruled 1855–81), the country's independent position was strengthened still further. In addition to the Lantdag ordinance of 1869, the country acquired its own monetary system (1865), and a law on conscription, which laid the foundations for the Finnish Army, was passed in 1878.

Russian expansion. Pan-Slavism's pressure for a Russian expansionist policy and the sharpening clashes between the great powers, brought about a change in Russia's policy toward Finland. During the 1890s an attempt was made to "russianize" Finland, with, for example, the introduction of Russian postal, toll, and monetary systems. The appointment of Nicolay Bobrikov as governor general in 1898 signified an acute intensification of Russian policy. In the February Manifesto of 1899 it was decreed that all legislation would be instituted by the Russian authorities. In 1901 a new law was passed dissolving the Finnish national army and making it possible to conscript Finnish nationals to serve in Russian units. In Finland a fierce independence movement grew in reaction to Russian policy, and in 1904 Governor General Bobrikov was assassinated. The Russo-Japanese War saved Finland from an immediate Russian reaction and led instead to the 1906 reform. After a few years, however, "russianization" was resumed in earnest. In 1910 it was decreed that all important laws should be passed by the Russian Duma (Parliament). By late autumn 1914 a program for Finland's annexation to Russia was announced.

The struggle for independence. During World War I the Finnish liberation movement sought support from Germany, and a number of young volunteers received military training and formed the Jägar Battalion. After the Russian Revolution in March 1917, Finland obtained its autonomy again, and a Senate, or coalition government, took over the ruling of the country. By a law of July 1917 it was decided that all the authority previously wielded by the tsar (apart from defense and foreign policy) should be exercised by the Finnish Diet. After Russia was taken over by the Bolsheviks in November 1917 the Diet issued a declaration of independence for Finland on December 6, 1917.

Effect of the Russian Revolution

ICELAND

The Treaty of Kiel (1814). By the Treaty of Kiel in 1814, when Denmark ceded Norway to Sweden, it was explicitly decided that Iceland, Greenland, and the Faeroe Islands, which belonged to the united Danish-Norwegian kingdom, should remain under the Danish crown. As these outlying lands, especially Greenland, were formerly considered as belonging to Norway, Norway protested against the decision. The Treaty of Kiel did not change the status of Iceland. The country remained under the king of Denmark and was ruled by a landsfoged (governor) nominated by him. When Denmark introduced provincial consultative diets in 1834, Iceland was represented by two members in the Roskilde Diet. In 1838, however, a separate council of higher civil servants was established in Reykjavík, and in 1843 a separate provincial advisory body, which took the old Icelandic name Althing, was set up.

Demands for self-government. Under the influence of the National Liberal movement in the 1830s and 1840s, a nationalistic Icelandic movement arose and, under the leadership of Jón Sigurdsson, demanded a much more independent position for Iceland. During the drawing up of the 1849 Danish constitution, Iceland demanded complete internal self-government and a union consisting only of a joint monarchy and a common foreign policy. In 1851 an Icelandic national meeting was held to discuss the question of the country's relations with Denmark, but no positive result was reached. After long-drawn-out negotiations, Denmark resolved in 1871 to implement a provisional solution by which Iceland was declared an integral part of the Danish kingdom but with special internal rights. Iceland refused to accept this decision and continued to press for complete internal self-government.

Granting of home rule

This policy was shortly afterward crowned with success. When Christian IX visited Iceland in 1874, on the occasion of the country's 1,000-year jubilee, he granted Iceland its own constitution, which in all essentials fulfilled the demand for home rule. Icelandic affairs still continued under the supervision of a special minister in the Danish government, however, and this led to repeated conflicts during the 1880s and 1890s between the Althing and the Danish government.

It was not until 1903, two years after the "Change of System" (the year when parliamentary democracy made its breakthrough in Denmark) that Iceland was granted its own national government by the establishment of a separate ministry for Iceland in Reykjavík. Under the leadership of Hannes Hafstein a number of social and economic reforms were carried out during the years preceding World War I. These included the modernization of the fishing fleet, which was implemented during the 1890s and the first decade of the 20th century. The old farming community began to be replaced by an organized industrial way of life. The demand for complete internal self-government was not realized, however, before the Act of Union of 1918, which made Iceland a completely independent state, united with Denmark solely by the monarchy and a common foreign policy.

VI. The 20th century

DENMARK

Liberal rule. The Venstre government that came to power under the "Change of System" in 1901 went swiftly to work on a number of reforms. A free-trade law that corresponded to the agricultural export interests was passed; in conformity with the ideas of the 18th-century theologian N.F.S. Grundtvig, the state church was transformed into a folk church with parochial church councils; the educational system was democratized; and changes in the system of taxation were effected so that income and not land was the main criterion for taxation. After the victory over the Conservatives (*Højre*) it became apparent that it was impossible for Venstre, led by J.C. Christensen, to remain united. In 1905, therefore, the radical faction broke away to become the Radical-Liberal Party (Det Radikale Venshe), the most important members of which were Peter Munch and Ove Rode. Between 1913 and 1920 the Radicals, supported by the Social Democrats, were in power. In 1915 the constitution was revised, and the privileged franchise to the Landsting was revoked, although the electoral qualifying age of 35 was retained. At the same time, the franchise to both the Folketing and the Landsting was extended to women, servants, and farm hands. The right-wing majority in the Landsting agreed to the constitutional reform on condition that the single-member constituency be replaced by proportional representation. There followed a number of reforms, including a judicial reform introducing trial by jury and a land reform bill that aimed to redistribute land from the large estates to increase the size of smallholders' farms.

Formation of the Radical Party

Foreign policy and World War I. After the Franco-German War (1870–71), Danish foreign policy was developed along strictly neutral lines. There were strong differences of opinion between Højre and Venstre on the way in which this should be carried out. Højre demanded a strong defense policy and J.B.S. Estrup carried through by provisory law the fortification of Copenhagen. Within Venstre itself there was disagreement on the lines the neutrality should take. The most radical viewpoint was held by Viggo Hørup, who wanted complete disarmament. After the split within Venstre in 1905, the Radical Liberal Party continued Hørup's ideas. In the years before 1914, it became increasingly important to define Germany's intended attitude to Denmark in the event of a European conflict. The Germans were well aware that the Schleswig affair had left a good many Danes with a loathing for everything German, while the constant friction between the Danish minority and the German administration in Schleswig added fuel to the flames. Successive Danish governments after 1901 made persistent efforts to assure Germany of Denmark's benevolent neutrality, but there was wide disagreement between the parties on the means Denmark should employ to maintain its neutrality. At the outbreak of war, Germany forced Denmark to lay mines in the Store Baelt in August 1914, and as the British fleet made no serious attempts to break through, neutrality was maintained.

World War I gave Denmark, together with a number of other neutral countries, an extremely good export market to the belligerent countries but an inevitable shortage of supplies. With a widespread overseas trade, the country's economic life was exceedingly vulnerable and became especially so after Germany opted for unrestricted submarine warfare from 1917 on. Denmark's exports to Great Britain were, to a certain extent, reoriented to Germany. There was a shortage of raw materials in both agriculture and industry, and the government rationed a number of consumer goods and controlled the country's economic life to a certain extent.

The interwar period. By the Treaty of Versailles it was decided that part of Schleswig should revert to Denmark in accordance with the principle of self-determination. The boundary was determined by a plebiscite in 1920. The discontent that arose as a consequence of the drawing of the boundary, coupled with labour unrest and dissatisfaction with remaining wartime restrictions, led to the fall of the government in the same year. It was succeeded by a Venstre government supported by the Conservatives. From 1924 to 1926 the Social Democrats, under the leadership of Thorvald Stauning and supported by the Radicals, were in power. The years 1926 to 1929 saw Venstre in power again, supported by the Conservatives. The recurring problem for the governments of the 1920s was the critical economic conditions that followed World War I. The gold convertibility of the Danish krone had been suspended for the duration of the war and was only restored to par in 1926. The economic life of the country proved extraordinarily sensitive to international markets and fluctuating currency policies. In 1922, the country's largest private bank, Landmandsbanken, failed. At times unemployment reached a very high level. The Social Democrats scored a great victory at the polls in 1929, and a coalition government was formed with the Radical Party under the leadership of the Social Democrat Stauning, with Peter Munch as foreign minister.

Economic crisis. The Depression during the early 1930s led to unemployment, which in 1933 affected 40 percent of the organized industrial workers. When Great Britain went off the gold standard in 1931, Denmark followed suit. The greatest blow to the Danish economy, however, was the system of preferential Commonwealth tariffs established in 1932. To cope with the crisis, the government subjected foreign trade to stringent control by the establishment of a "currency centre." The falling prices of agricultural products, together with the greatly reduced volume of exports, led to the demand by Venstre (which of all parties represented agricultural interests) for a devaluation of the krone. At the same time, at the beginning of 1933 employers pressed for a reduction in the wages of industrial workers and threatened a lockout. In this state of affairs, Stauning won the support of Venstre in the "Kanslergade compromise," by which it was agreed to devalue the krone and to freeze existing wage agreements by law. In addition, Venstre supported social reforms that included old-age pensions and health, unemployment, and accident insurance. A number of measures were also adopted in support of agriculture; for example, production was to be regulated and restricted in order to stabilize prices. The general election of 1935 returned the Social Democrats again, and after the elections to the Landsting in 1936 the government coalition of Social Democrats and Radicals held the majority in both the Folketing and the Landsting. At the same time, trade conditions improved, and during the late 1930s industry again began to expand.

Foreign policy. Denmark had joined the League of Nations in 1920 and had worked for a peaceful solution to international problems during the whole of the interwar period. When Adolf Hitler came to power and Germany began to rearm, Denmark's position was again very vulnerable. Although Germany had never recognized the alteration in its boundary as laid down by the Treaty of Versailles, Hitler did not raise the matter. Under foreign minister Munch's leadership, Denmark tried in vain during the 1930s to obtain recognition of the boundary, and at the same time it avoided all measures that might possibly offend its powerful neighbour. When in the spring of 1939 Hitler offered nonaggression pacts to those countries that might feel threatened by Germany's expansionist policy, Denmark, in contrast to the other Scandinavian countries, accepted the offer.

Denmark during World War II. On the outbreak of war in 1939 Denmark, in common with the other Nordic countries, issued a declaration of neutrality. On April 9, 1940, German troops crossed the border, and after token resistance the Danish government submitted to a military occupation of the country. Formally, however, Denmark remained a sovereign state until August 29, 1943, and in this its position differed from the other occupied countries of Europe. A coalition government was formed by the major parties, with Thorvald Stauning as leader, and in July 1940 Erik Scavenius became foreign minister. Although the Danish government was forced to work closely with the Germans, a proposal for common currency and customs with Germany was rejected. The Danish Nazis' demand to take power

was also rejected, though the threat implicit in this was exploited on many occasions by the Germans to induce the Danish government to make still more concessions. Thus, in the autumn of 1940, the Germans ordered Conservative minister John Christmas Møller to leave the government. In 1942 he fled to London, where, as head of the Danish council, he became one of the leaders in the Danish resistance. When Germany attacked the Soviet Union, the Danish government was forced to allow the formation of a Danish volunteer corps and at the same time to forbid all Communist activity in the country. In November 1941, Denmark signed the Anti-Comintern Pact. Stauning died suddenly in May 1942, and was succeeded by Vilhelm Buhl, who was forced to resign in November of the same year under pressure from the Germans. He was succeeded by Erik Scavenius. The 1943 elections proved to be a great national demonstration that showed that the people were united in support of the four old democratic parties and the fight against Nazism. At the same time, the resistance movement was organized, and Germany's military defeats paved the way for demands for an open breach with the powers of occupation. Dissatisfaction caused by consumer shortages and inflation, combined with the growing opposition against German occupation, led to a series of strikes in the summer of 1943 that in August culminated in actions aimed directly at the Germans. When the Danish government refused to introduce the death penalty for sabotage, allow persecution of Jews, or use force against the strikers, the Germans declared a state of emergency. The Danish government ceased to function and the German *Reichskommissioner* assumed political control. The Danish army and navy were disbanded but not before many of the ships were scuttled by their own crews. In September 1943 Denmark's Freedom Council was formed, and under its leadership the resistance movement was organized, mainly in the form of illegal newspapers, a comprehensive intelligence service, and numerous acts of sabotage. During the last year of the war, closer cooperation began between the Freedom Council and leading politicians. When the Germans surrendered, on May 5, 1945, a government was formed consisting of half of representatives of the Freedom Council and half of politicians from the old political parties. After elections in the autumn of 1945, a Venstre government came to power, led by Knud Kristensen.

The postwar period. The first task after the liberation was to take legal proceedings against German collaborators. By a retroactive law these persons were brought to trial and sentenced to death or given long-term prison sentences. Another consequence of the war was that the Schleswig question arose once more. The Nazi dictatorship and the great numbers of refugees fleeing from eastern Germany to South Schleswig caused a reaction that won the Danish faction strong support among the local population. In Denmark there were divided opinions, but when the United Kingdom in the autumn of 1946 made enquiries about Denmark's opinion on the boundary, all the parties agreed in the October Note of 1946 to reject any alteration to the boundary. After the 1947 elections, when Knud Kristensen's government was replaced by a Social Democratic minority government led by Hans Hedtoft, all plans to pursue an active policy concerning the boundary question were abandoned.

Defense policy. When the tensions between the great powers grew in 1948, the question of a neutral policy or affiliation to a defense alliance became an urgent concern. Sweden took the initiative in proposing the formation of a Nordic defense union. Denmark, under the leadership of Hedtoft, was favourably disposed toward the proposition, but because of differences between Sweden and Norway it came to nothing. Denmark thus became a member of the North Atlantic Treaty Organization (NATO) in April 1949. Denmark's military defense has since been considerably strengthened by statutes in 1950 and 1951, and has been further complemented by armament supplies from the United States. Denmark nevertheless rejected a request by the United States to establish air bases on Danish territory. With the Federal Republic of Germany's admission to NATO, Denmark succeeded in obtaining guarantees—confirmed in the Bonn Protocol of 1955 —for the rights of the Danish minority group in South Schleswig.

Domestic policy. On the domestic front, the scene was dominated during the early 1950s by economic difficulties resulting from inflation. The 1950 coalition government of Venstre and the Conservatives, under the leadership of Erik Eriksen, fought the crisis with greatly increased taxation and various forms of compulsory savings. The constitution was revised in 1953, abolishing the Landsting. This meant that Parliament would in future consist of only one chamber, the Folketing, the membership of which was at the same time increased to 179. King Frederick IX, who had succeeded Christian X in 1947, signed the new constitution on June 5, 1953.

After the election of 1953, the Radicals declined to support the government, which was replaced by the Social Democrats led by Hans Hedtoft and, after his death in 1955, by H.C. Hansen. The election of 1957 resulted in a very complicated parliamentary situation, as no single party was able to form a government. After a prolonged crisis, a coalition of Social Democrats, Radicals, and the small Georgist, or Single Tax, Party (Retsforbund) was formed. The Georgist Party left the government in 1960 and the Radicals in 1964, but the Social Democrats remained in power under Jens Otto Krag. The 1968 election resulted in a coalition of the Venstre, Conservatives, and Radicals. After the 1971 elections Krag formed a new Social Democratic government. Krag resigned in October 1972 and was replaced by Anker Jorgensen. Frederick IX died in 1972 and was succeeded by his daughter, Margrethe II.

Economic issues. Among the main issues in Danish politics during the 1950s and 1960s were the frequently negative balance of payments, the labour market, and the country's trade policy. During the early 1950s, the Danish economy suffered a large deficit in the trade balance. The adverse situation improved during the later 1950s as the result of lower import prices for raw materials, a considerable increase in industrial production, and the stabilization of prices of agricultural export products. The period 1957 to 1965 was marked by steeply rising prosperity. During the 1960s, however, the balance of payments deficit became larger, and the government was forced to intervene in an attempt to control rising consumption. This was done by a purchase tax in 1962, by compulsory savings, by intervention in labour conflicts, and by the regulation of wages and prices. Denmark's commercial policy during the whole of the post-World War II period has been to liberalize trade and create a larger market for Danish products. Within the framework of the Organization for European Economic Cooperation (OEEC) Denmark, during the 1950s, abolished most of the regulations that had restricted its foreign trade. Denmark was one of the countries that became a member of the European Free Trade Association (EFTA) on its formation in 1959. Together with Sweden, Denmark took the initiative in negotiations for a Scandinavian customs union, Nordek, which aimed at far-reaching economic integration. When Finland was unable to sanction the plan, however, the negotiations failed. Negotiations on Denmark's membership in the European Economic Community (EEC), or Common Market, were conducted in 1961–63 and 1970–72. Denmark was offered, and it accepted, EEC membership in 1972, effective January 1, 1973.

(margin) Trade deficits

SWEDEN

The introduction of parliamentary democracy. The economic expansion that started in the early 19th century laid the foundations for internal developments in Sweden during the 20th century. The turning point came during and immediately after World War I. There was suddenly a worldwide demand for Swedish commodities such as steel and pulp, matches and ball-bearings, telephones and vacuum cleaners. The composition of the population underwent a decisive change, and Sweden was transformed from an agricultural to a modern industrial country.

Political reform. Politically, the economic development meant that a universal and equal franchise was more and more vociferously demanded. The issue was solved in 1909 by a compromise submitted by a Conservative government under the leadership of Arvid Lindman. The motion granted a universal and equal franchise for the Second Chamber, a certain democratization of the First Chamber, and proportional representation for elections to both chambers of Parliament. The elections to the Second Chamber in 1909 produced a landslide victory for the Liberal Party (Liberala Samlingspartiet) and Gustav V (ruled 1907–50) was forced to ask Karl Staaff to form a Liberal government.

Defense policy. One of the most important points of Liberal policy in 1911 was a decrease in military expenditure. The realization of this demand led to sharp conflicts between Gustav V and Staaff. When the tension between the great powers grew at this time, a farmers' rally was organized, and 30,000 farmers from all over the country sought out the King and demanded a strengthening of the country's defenses. In his reply—Borggårdstalet (the Courtyard Speech) Gustav V promised to reinforce the military defenses. As the King had given this pledge without having consulted the government, it resigned, and the King appointed a Conservative government with Hjalmar Hammarskjöld as prime minister. The outbreak of World War I in the summer of 1914 saved the King from having to defend his action before Parliament, and Hammarskjöld's Conservative government remained in power despite its not having a parliamentary majority.

(margin) The minority Conservative government

Policy during World War I. During World War I, Sweden attempted to remain neutral and to assert its right to trade with the belligerent countries. For Great Britain, the blockade was an important weapon, and Sweden's demand to import freely favoured Germany exclusively. As a result, the Allies stopped a large percentage of Sweden's trade. This, however, hit not only Sweden's exports to Germany but from 1916 caused a severe shortage of food supplies. The situation was worsened by unrestricted submarine warfare and by the entry of the U.S. into the war in 1917. Hammarskjöld was forced to resign; he was followed by a Conservative government and shortly afterward by a Liberal one, both of which conducted a more diplomatic trading policy with the Allies. In May 1918 an agreement was reached with Great Britain and the U.S. that allowed Sweden again to import produce from the West, on condition that exports to Germany be limited and that a large part of Sweden's merchant fleet be put at the Allies disposal.

The Social Democrat-Liberal coalition. In the general election of 1917, the left-wing parties (the Social Democrats and Liberals) secured a further increase in their majority in the Second Chamber. As a consequence, the King was obliged to choose a government based upon the majority of the Second Chamber. With the Liberal-Social Democratic government of Nils Edén, parliamentary democracy had obtained definite recognition in Sweden. One of the first measures of the new government was to amend the constitution. The main issues were female suffrage and the introduction of a universal and equal franchise for elections to the First Chamber and in local elections. The resulting constitutional reform was introduced between 1918 and 1920.

Domestic policy (1918–45). *Party politics.* It was the demand for parliamentary democracy that had above all constituted the basis for cooperation between the Liberal and the Social Democratic parties. When these demands had been realized, the two parties went their separate ways. From 1920 onward, a line was drawn between the Socialist parties on one side and the Liberals and Conservatives on the other. The regrouping of the parties in Swedish politics did not produce any dynamic changes. From 1920 to 1932 the parties held power alternately, but no government—whether Social Democratic, Liberal, or Conservative—had any chance of gaining firm support for its policy in the Riksdag. From a political viewpoint the 1920s were a period of stagnation.

The economic climate. From an economic point of view, however, the picture was quite different. The 1920s were marked by steadily improving trade conditions, and in this period Sweden was one of the countries that prospered significantly from the boom.

The Depression

Like other countries, Sweden suffered severely during the Depression of the early 1930s. Unemployment rose, and reductions in wages caused a series of harsh labour conflicts. The 1932 election marked a considerable advance for the Social Democratic Party, and to some extent for the Farmers' Party as well and led to a Social Democratic administration under the leadership of Per Albin Hansson. It offered a comprehensive policy to fight the crisis, including extensive public works and various moves in support of agriculture. This policy was subjected to scathing criticism by the right-wing parties, but an agreement was reached with the Farmers' Party in 1933, making it possible to implement the program. The economic crisis of the 1930s was overcome more rapidly in Sweden than in most other countries. As early as 1936 wages had reached their old level, and by the end of the decade unemployment had become insignificant.

From a political point of view, the 1930s were in fact a time of preparation, when a series of bills for radical reforms were worked out. The whole program could be summarized in the term *folkhemmet*, in which society is viewed as a "home" for the people, taking care of their needs in unemployment, sickness, and old age.

The planned economy. During the 1930s only a few rather moderate reforms were realized, and with the advent of World War II in 1939, reforms were postponed because of rising military expenditure and supply difficulties. In the meantime, food rationing and the detailed planning of the use of the country's resources meant that the government obtained practically complete control over trade and industry. The planned economy, which had constantly eluded the Social Democrats during the 1930s, was thus implemented during World War II with the support of all parties.

Foreign policy (1918–45). When World War I ended, Russia and Germany were among the defeated nations, and Sweden thus found itself in an unusually good position regarding external security. In 1925, military expenditure was considerably reduced. Problems regarding foreign policy were confined to Sweden's application for membership in the newly formed League of Nations, which was granted in 1920, and to its relationship with Finland.

The Åland question

When the Civil War in Finland ended, the problem of Åland re-emerged. The inhabitants of the Åland Islands were purely Swedish-speaking, and a plebiscite revealed that almost all were in favour of affiliation to Sweden. The League of Nations, however, decided in 1921 to award Finland the sovereignty of the islands, though with certain conditions pertaining to internal self-government and limiting the right to fortify or otherwise utilize the islands for military purposes.

Hitler's rise to power resulted in a re-examination of Sweden's defense policy, which in 1936 was amended to strengthen the country's defenses. Sweden followed a strictly neutral course, in close collaboration with the other Scandinavian countries, and The Netherlands, Belgium, and Switzerland. As a consequence, Hitler's proposal in the spring of 1939 for a nonaggression pact was rejected. Sweden's attempt to form a Nordic defense union or, if that could not be achieved, a Swedish-Finnish defense alliance, led to a negative result in both cases, primarily because the Soviet Union objected.

On the outbreak of war in 1939 Sweden declared itself neutral. When the Soviet Union shortly afterward launched an attack on Finland, Sweden gave Finland aid in the form of vast material supplies and a volunteer corps organized with the support and consent of the authorities. On the other hand, Sweden, in common with Norway, refused the request made by the Allies to march through Sweden in order to intervene in the war. After the German occupation of Denmark and Norway in 1940, however, Sweden was forced by Germany's military superiority to allow the transit of German troops through Sweden to Norway. Many Norwegians and Danes sought refuge in Sweden, the majority of them with the intention

of fleeing to England. When Germany attacked the Soviet Union in June 1941, transit facilities were demanded for a division of German troops from Norway to Finland, and Sweden acquiesced under threat of military reprisals. In 1943 the agreement concerning the transit of German troops was revoked. Toward the end of the war, Norwegian and Danish police were trained and equipped in Sweden. Immediately after the end of the war, Sweden sought and was granted membership in the United Nations, without having relinquished its principally neutral foreign policy.

The welfare state. The coalition government that was formed in 1939 was replaced shortly after the end of the war in 1945 by a Social Democratic government under the leadership of Per Albin Hansson. After his death in 1946, Tage Erlander became prime minister, a post that he held until his resignation in 1969 both as leader of the Social Democratic Party and as prime minister. He was succeeded by Olof Palme, who took over the leadership of the government without any other changes being made in its composition.

The period of social reform. The period 1946 to 1950 may justly be called the great period of reform, during which new, comprehensive laws were adopted concerning old-age pensions, child allowances, health insurance, rent allowances, educational reforms, and the expansion of universities and other institutions of higher education and research. Those parts of the Social Democrats' postwar program that aimed at nationalization of industry were not, however, carried through. The Social Democratic government contented itself with preserving a good deal of the control over manufacturing and service industries that had been obtained during World War II. By tax reorganization they tried at the same time to achieve wider distribution of wealth. The early 1950s were marked by the absence of proposals for really important reforms. All available resources were exploited to create the material basis of the reforms, adopted in the period 1946 to 1950. In addition, the favourable trade conditions changed for the worse in the early 1950s.

Surprisingly, the years after World War II had been marked by stable trading conditions and a scarcity of labour. During the Korean War (1950–53), the boom reached its climax, entailing large price rises and rapid inflation. A recession followed at the end of 1951. In Sweden this meant that the upward movement of prices and incomes was interrupted, and for the first time since World War II there was a rise in unemployment. Even though the crisis of 1951–52 was neither a serious nor a long one, it drew attention to the problems of economic stability. The Social Democrats now became primarily preoccupied with securing the advances already achieved. They began to collaborate with the Farmers' Party, and in the autumn of 1951 the Social Democratic government was replaced by a coalition government consisting of Social Democrats and Farmers, which lasted until 1957.

The retirement pension controversy

In the late 1950s the question of a compulsory pension for all employees became a principal political issue. The opposition fought it energetically, mainly because of the enormous expenditure that it would entail. In Conservative and Liberal quarters it was feared that control of the pension fund would create a latent risk of complete Socialism; the government finally enacted the bill in 1959.

By 1960 the fluctuating trade conditions of the 1950s had stabilized, but the increase in economic resources was used primarily for revising, and in certain cases, improving, the actual value of the personal social services whose purchasing power had been reduced by the inflation of the 1950s. But at the same time problems other than the social ones began to attract attention.

Reform of Parliament. In 1955 a committee to review the 1809 constitution was appointed. On its recommendations, the old two-chamber Parliament was replaced in 1971 by a one-chamber Parliament comprising 350 members elected by proportional representation. In the 1970 election, which was the first to be held under the new system, the Social Democrats lost the absolute majority they had held since 1968 but formed the government with the support of the Communists.

Foreign policy. Sweden's foreign policy since 1945 has remained strictly neutral. When the international situation became tense in 1948 after the coup in Czechoslovakia and during the Berlin blockade, the Swedish government took the initiative in negotiations on a defense alliance between Sweden, Norway, and Denmark. Sweden insisted that the alliance should be truly independent of the great powers, while Norway wanted cooperation with the Western powers, and so negotiations fell through. In accordance with its policy of neutrality, Sweden has not applied to join the European Economic Community (EEC). Trading policy has been aimed at liberalizing trade, and this has been pursued in close connection with the United Kingdom, with whom Sweden participated in the establishment of the European Free Trade Association (EFTA) in 1959. Although the Nordic defense alliance was not achieved, Scandinavian collaboration has been intensified by the Nordic Council, formally inaugurated in 1952. Important results of the Council's work are that passports are not required between the countries, a free labour market has been created, and a far-reaching coordination of economic and social legislation has taken place. Conversely, the plans for a Scandinavian customs union, which had been discussed during the 1960s, led to no result.

NORWAY

Economic and industrial growth. The period 1905 to 1914 was characterized by rapid economic expansion. The development of the merchant fleet, which had begun during the second half of the 19th century, continued, though at a somewhat slower pace. The capacity and effectiveness of merchant shipping, however, increased to a marked degree after the transition from sail to steam, which in turn resulted in a concentration of the smaller firms into larger shipping companies. At the outbreak of World War I, Norway's merchant navy was the fourth largest in the world.

Expansion of waterpower

From about the turn of the century, Norway's immense resources of waterpower were the basis for great industrial expansion. The capital for this expansion came largely from abroad, especially from Sweden and France. The large number of waterfalls bought by various companies gave rise to grave concern that the country's natural resources were falling into foreign hands or becoming monopolized by a small number of capitalists. In 1906 three-quarters of all developed waterpower in Norway was owned by foreign concerns. Venstre and the growing Labour Party pressed for legislation to protect the natural resources of the country. The proposed bill on concessions (later known as the Concession Laws) played a dominating role in Norwegian politics from 1905 to 1914. It led to a split in the Venstre Party, but the majority of Venstre supported the bill, which was passed by the Storting in 1909 and remained in force despite continued criticism.

Rapid industrialization resulted in increasing demands from the working classes for political rights. In 1887 the Norwegian Labour party was founded, and universal suffrage was one of the principal points in the party program. In the 1890s Venstre likewise adopted this policy, and in 1898 universal male suffrage was introduced. By new reforms in 1907 and 1913 the vote was extended to women. One consequence of industrialization and the introduction of universal suffrage was the growing influence of the Labour Party. A number of social reforms were enacted: a factory act, which included protection for women and children, accident insurance for seafaring men, health insurance, and in 1915 a law on a ten-hour working day.

Norway in World War I and the interwar years. *World War I.* With the outbreak of war in 1914, Norway, like Sweden and Denmark, issued a declaration of neutrality. Norway was badly hit by the war at sea, and about one-half of Norwegian merchant shipping was lost, reducing the merchant fleet from the fourth to the sixth largest in the world. Norway's greatest risk of being drawn into the war was rooted in its dependence on foreign trade, above all on the import of foodstuffs. As the Allied powers

could almost totally control Norway's foreign trade, they forced it to break off exports of fish to Germany, and at the same time they forbade exports of sulfur pyrites and copper, which were important commodities for the German war industry. Because of the many casualties caused by submarine warfare, public feeling in Norway was strongly anti-German. The government, however, under the leadership of Venstre politician Gunnar Knudsen, insisted upon maintaining the appearance of neutrality. The war brought a distinct boom to Norway, although the prosperity was unevenly distributed. The steeply rising prices imposed hardships on the working classes and the lower income groups of civil servants. Within the Labour Party, the left wing formed the majority in 1918, and in 1919 the Norwegian Labour Party, unlike all the other Social Democratic parties in Western and Central Europe, joined the Comintern (Third International). The Labour Party, however, was unwilling in the event to submit to the centralization that Moscow demanded, and in 1923 it withdrew.

Dependence on foreign trade

The Depression. During the interwar years politics in Norway were dominated by economic issues. In the years up to 1935 the various governments—formed alternately by the Conservatives, the Liberals, and the Farmers' Party—pursued, by and large, a liberal economic policy. After the inflation caused by World War I and the postwar years, the main aim during the 1920s was to guide its currency (the krone) back to its former value. Norway received only an insignificant share in improved world-market conditions, and by 1927 the unemployment figures were as high as 20 percent of the organized labour force. The Depression in the early 1930s increased unemployment still further, and by 1933 at least 33 percent of the work force, including many civil servants, were unemployed. The government, led by the Farmers' Party (1931–33) and Venstre (1933–35), tried to combat the crisis with extensive reductions in governmental expenditure, but refused to consider an expansionist financial policy or the emergency relief measures that the Labour Party demanded. The Labour Party thus enjoyed great success in the 1933 elections, although failing to gain a majority in the Storting. When the Labour Party formed the government in 1935, with Johan Nygaardsvold as prime minister, they needed the support of at least one other party. By a compromise with the Farmers' Party, which included a number of measures in support of agriculture, the Labour Party received support for a social program that included old-age pension reform, revision of the factory act, statutory holidays, and (some years later) unemployment insurance financed by increased taxation. State investments were also greatly increased. Although the situation was improved, unemployment in Norway was still as high as 20 percent of the organized labour force in 1938.

Social reforms

Economic recovery. Despite economic difficulties, the high rate of unemployment, and the many labour conflicts, the interwar years were a period of vigorous expansion within certain sections of trade and industry. This was especially true of the metal and electrical industries. Merchant shipping also increased rapidly and soon retrieved its position as the fourth largest in the world. Other industries also expanded considerably, including fishing and whaling. Agriculture was rationalized, enabling Norway during the 1930s to export animal products. On the whole, the country's industrial production was increased by 75 percent during the years 1913 to 1938.

Foreign policy. Norway's security between the wars was good, with land boundaries only to Sweden and Finland and a sea boundary that was protected by the United Kingdom. In the League of Nations, Norway aligned itself with the other neutral countries, and like these attempted to reduce the commitments imposed by the League on its members. During the 1920s, Norway acquired Svalbard and Jan Mayen. At the same time, Norwegian hunters and fishermen occupied an area on the east coast of Greenland. Denmark's demand for sovereignty of the area led to a conflict that was settled in the Permanent Court of International Justice in The Hague in 1933 in Denmark's favour. As the League of Nations in

1936 had proved ineffective at keeping the peace, Norway's foreign minister, Halvdan Koht, made strenuous efforts within the framework of the League to coordinate the policy of the smaller states in an effort to preserve peace. Norway continued to pursue a strictly neutral policy and declined Germany's invitation to a nonaggression pact in 1939.

Norway during World War II. With the outbreak of hostilities in 1939 Norway declared itself neutral. Despite Norway's strong pro-Finnish sympathies, permission was refused to the Western powers (just as it was by Sweden) to march through Norwegian territory in February 1940. It was feared that the intention was first and foremost to win control over Narvik, and by this to hinder export of iron ore from northern Sweden. The Allies also tried to stop German sea traffic in Norwegian coastal waters and on April 8, 1940, they laid mines in Norwegian territorial waters. On April 9, 1940, German troops invaded Norway and occupied Oslo, Bergen, Trondheim, and Narvik. In contrast to Denmark, the Norwegian government rejected the German ultimatum regarding immediate capitulation. The king, the government, and Parliament succeeded in fleeing from Oslo. The Norwegian Army, which received help from an Allied expeditionary force, was unable to resist the superior German troops, however. After three weeks the war was abandoned in southern Norway. The Norwegian and Allied forces succeeded in recapturing Narvik but withdrew again on June 7, when the Allied troops were needed in France. Some days later the Norwegian troops in northern Norway capitulated, and the king and the government fled to London. The Norwegians in London were augmented considerably by the Norwegian merchant navy—directed from the Norwegian Shipping and Trade Mission (Nortraship) in London—which played an important part during the war. The war, however, caused the loss of half of the merchant fleet.

In Norway, Vidkun Quisling, leader of the small Norwegian National Socialist party, Nasjonal Samling, proclaimed on April 9 his intention of forming a national government. This aroused such strong resistance, however, that the Germans thrust him aside and organized an administrative council instead, consisting of apolitical civil servants. Political power was wielded by the German commissioner, Josef Terboven. In September 1940 the administrative council was replaced by a number of "commissarial counsellors" who in 1942 formed a Nazi government under the leadership of Quisling. The "nazification" attempt aroused strong resistance. To begin with, this took the form of passive resistance and general strikes, which the Germans countered with martial law and death sentences. At the same time, the resistance movement became more firmly organized and undertook large-scale industrial sabotage, of which the most important was that against the production of heavy water in Rjukan, southern Norway.

At the end of the war, the German troops in Norway capitulated without offering resistance. Only the most northerly part of the country was ravaged by the German retreat from Finland in the winter of 1944 to 1945.

The postwar period. The liberation was followed by trials of collaborators, and 24 Norwegians, including Quisling (whose name has gone down in history as a byword for a traitor), were sentenced to death and executed, and 19,000 received prison sentences. By a strict policy that gave priority to the reconstruction of productive capacity in preference to consumer goods, Norway quickly succeeded in repairing the ravages left by the war. By 1949 the merchant fleet had attained its prewar size, and the figures for both industrial production and housing were greater than in the 1930s. During the whole of the postwar period Norway has enjoyed full employment and a swiftly rising standard of living.

Political and social change. After the liberation in 1945, a coalition government was formed under the leadership of Einar Gerhardsen. The general election in the autumn of 1945 gave the Labour Party a decisive majority and a purely Labour government was formed with Gerhardsen as prime minister. The Labour Party gov-

erned from 1945 to 1965 with the exception of a few weeks in 1963 when a right-wing government came to power. The 1965 election, however, resulted in a clear majority for the four right-wing parties—Høyre, Venstre, Senterpartiet, and Kristelig Folkeparti, who formed a coalition government under the leadership of Per Borten. In the spring of 1971 there was a split within the coalition government, and the Labour Party again came to power, headed by Trygve Bratteli. During the postwar period the various governments have continued the social policies initiated in the 1930s. A law on a general retirement pension was passed in 1956 and a law on social welfare, which replaced the former "poor law," in 1964.

Postwar foreign policy. Norway's foreign policy has also undergone a change. When the antagonisms between the great powers came to a head in 1948, Norway took part in the negotiations set in motion by Sweden on a Nordic defense union. Norway, however, was not willing to participate unless a clear guarantee of help from the Western powers was obtained, while Sweden stood firm on a neutral policy. In 1949 Norway and Denmark joined the newly formed North Atlantic Treaty Organization (NATO). Within the framework of NATO, Norway's defense system has been drastically reinforced, but NATO has not been allowed to establish airfields or to stockpile atomic weapons on Norwegian territory.

Another aspect of foreign policy is the question of Norway's proposed membership in the European Economic Community. Since 1959 Norway, together with Denmark and Sweden, has been a member of the European Free Trade Association (EFTA). Norway has also favoured increased Nordic economic cooperation in the form of a customs union, unsuccessful negotiations on which were carried out in 1969–70. Norway continued to work for closer Nordic cooperation concerning, for example, legislation and a common labour market; in 1972 it rejected an opportunity to join the EEC.

FINLAND

Between the wars. *The Civil War.* With its declaration of independence, Finland was recognized as an independent state in 1918. Although the liberation from Russia occurred peacefully, Finland was unable to avert a violent internal conflict. After the revolutionaries had won control of the Social Democratic Party, they went into action and on January 28, 1918, seized Helsinki and the larger industrial towns in southern Finland. The right-wing government led by the Conservative Pehr Evind Svinhufvud fled to the western part of the country, where a counterattack was organized under the leadership of Gen. Carl Gustaf Mannerheim. At the beginning of April the White Army under his command won the Battle of Tampere (Tammerfors). German troops also came to the aid of the government and by May the rebellion had been suppressed. It was followed by trials in which harsh sentences were passed.

Political change. When the Civil War ended, it was decided, during the summer of 1918, to make Finland a monarchy, and in October the German prince, Frederick Charles of Hessen, was chosen as the coming king of Finland. With Germany's defeat in the war, however, General Mannerheim was designated regent, with the task of submitting a proposal for a new constitution. As it was obvious that Finland was to be a republic, the struggle now concerned presidential power. The liberal parties wanted power to be invested in the Parliament, while the Conservatives wanted the president to have powers independent of Parliament. The strong position held by the Conservatives after the Civil War enabled them to force through their motion that the president should be chosen by popularly elected representatives, independent of Parliament, and also that he should possess a great deal more authority, especially regarding foreign policy, than was usual for a head of state. After the new constitution had been confirmed on July 17, 1919, Kaarlo Juho Ståhlberg, a member of the National Progressive Party, was elected first president of Finland.

Agrarian reform. During the interwar years Finland was, to a much greater extent than the rest of Scandina-

The German invasion

The Labour Government

The new constitution

via, an agrarian country. In 1918, 70 percent of the population were employed in agriculture and forestry, and by 1940 the figure was still as high as 57 percent. Paper and wooden articles were Finland's most important export commodities. Before World War I, the independent farmer accounted for only one-third of the rural population, one-sixth of whom were tenant farmers, while about one-half were landless farm labourers. By the Smallholdings Law of 1918 and by a land reform in 1922, which allowed the expropriation of estates of more than 495 acres (200 hectares), an attempt was made to give tenant farmers and landless labourers their own smallholdings. More than 90,000 smallholdings were created, and since then the independent smallholders, who form the majority of the Agrarian Party (now the Centre Party or Keskustapuolue), have been one of the most important factors in Finnish politics.

Political parties. During K.J. Ståhlberg's period as president (1919–25), the right-wing parties and the Agrarian Party held power by means of various coalitions. During this period the president tried determinedly to minimize the recriminations of the Civil War, and in the course of time granted amnesties to those who had received long terms of imprisonment. At the same time, the Social Democratic Party was reorganized under the leadership of Väinö Tanner with an exclusively reformist program. When he formed a Social Democratic minority government in 1926, which granted a general amnesty, the old differences from the Civil War had been almost eliminated. Lauri Kristian Relander, the Agrarian Party's candidate, was elected president in 1925.

The
Lapua
Movement As a reaction to the growing Finnish Communist Party, the Lapua (Lappo) Movement emerged, which, in the years 1929 to 1932, attempted to force its demands through by actions against Communist newspapers, acts of terrorism against individual citizens, and by mass demonstrations. These actions, which were supported by the Conservatives and many members of the Agrarian Party, were at first successful. After the election of 1930, an anti-Communist law was forced through that resulted in the banning of the Communist Party's public activity. In 1931 the Conservative P.E. Svinhufvud was elected president with the help of the Lapua Movement. When the Lapua Movement shortly afterward turned its activities against the Social Democrats, too, and tried to seize power by force in the Mäntsälä Rebellion in 1932, the president intervened and crushed the rebellion. Another failure at this time was the law on the total prohibition of alcohol, introduced in 1919. As in the United States, the law resulted in a sharp increase in organized crime and smuggling, and after a referendum in 1932 it was repealed.

The language question. The 1919 constitution provided that both Finnish and Swedish should be the national languages. A younger radical generation now raised the demand for the supremacy of Finnish. The language controversy, which, during the interwar period was a very bitterly fought issue, caused the position of the Swedish language to be progressively weakened toward the end of the 1930s. During World War II, however, the differences were ironed out; and after the war the laws governing language were revised, first in 1947 and again in 1961. They now embody certain guarantees for the Swedish language.

Foreign policy. After the recognition of Finland as a sovereign state there were two problems to be faced. The first was in connection with the eastern boundary, where influential groups wished to annex East Karelia. By the Treaty of Tartu (Dorpat) in 1920, however, the boundary was unchanged except in the north, where Finland acquired a route to the Arctic Ocean and the harbour of Petsamo. The other problem concerned the Åland Islands. The demands of the population of Åland to be united with Sweden were firmly rejected. The League of Nations settled the question in 1921 in accordance with Finland's wishes. Finland's main security problems resulted from the threat from the Soviet Union. An attempt to solve this by a defense alliance with Estonia, Latvia, and Poland in 1922 failed when Parliament refused to

ratify the agreement, and in 1932 a Finnish-Russian non-aggression pact was signed. During the second half of the 1930s a Finnish-Swedish defense association was planned that, among other things, would have brought about the rearming of Åland. But since the Soviet Union objected to these plans they could not be realized.

Finland during World War II. *Defeat by the Soviet Union.* After Poland's defeat in the autumn of 1939, the Soviet Union, wishing to safeguard Leningrad, demanded, from Finland, a minor part of the Karelian Isthmus and some islands deep in the Gulf of Finland. When Finland rejected the demand, the Soviet Union launched an attack on November 30, 1939. Immediately after the attack a coalition government was formed under Risto Ryti. Despite courageous resistance and a number of successful defense actions, the Finnish Army was eventually defeated. When the defense of the Karelian Isthmus broke down, Finland initiated peace negotiations. By the Treaty of Moscow of March 12, 1940, Finland surrendered a large area of southeastern Finland including the city of Viipuri (Viborg), and leased the peninsula of Hanko (Hangö) to the Soviet Union for 30 years. The
Treaty
of Moscow

Cooperation with Germany. After the Treaty of Moscow the plan for a Nordic defense union was resumed. The Soviet Union objected, however, and the plan was thus abandoned. In December 1940 President Kyösti Kallio resigned, and Risto Ryti was elected in his place. When the tension between Germany and the Soviet Union grew in spring 1941, Finland approached Germany but did not conclude a formal agreement. Nevertheless, Finland, like Sweden after Norway's capitulation, allowed the transit of German troops. When Germany attacked the Soviet Union on June 22, 1941, therefore, German troops were already on Finnish territory; and after a few days Finland was drawn into the war. The "War of Continuation" (1941–44) began with a successful Finnish offensive that led to the capture of large areas of East Karelia. From the winter of 1942–43, however, Germany's defeats gave rise to a growing demand for peace in Finland. After the breakthrough of the Soviet Army on the Karelian Isthmus in June 1944, President Ryti resigned on August 1, 1944. He was succeeded by Marshal Gustaf Mannerheim, who immediately demanded the evacuation of the German troops and began negotiations for an armistice. This was signed on September 19, 1944, on condition that Finland recognize the Treaty of Moscow of 1940. A pledge was given, moreover, to cede Petsamo, lease out an area near Porkkala, southwest of Helsinki, for a period of 50 years (in place of Hanko) and within six years to pay the equivalent of $300,-000,000 in goods for war reparations. In the meantime, however, the German Army refused to leave the country, and in a series of clashes that followed, it devastated great areas of northern Finland in its retreat. The final peace treaty that was signed in Paris on February 10, 1947, reiterated the conditions of the armistice agreement.

The postwar period. After the armistice in 1944 a coalition government was formed under the leadership of Juho Kusti Paasikivi. When conditions had been stabilized, Gustaf Mannerheim resigned, and Paasikivi was elected president in his place in 1946. In 1956 the leader of the Agrarian Party, Urho Kekkonen, who acted as prime minister a number of times during the period 1950 to 1956, was elected president. He was subsequently reelected twice, most recently in 1968.

Foreign policy. Under the leadership of Paasikivi and Kekkonen, relationships with the Soviet Union were stabilized by a consistently friendly policy on the part of Finland. A concrete expression of the new foreign policy —which has been designated the Paasikivi-Kekkonen line —was the Agreement of Friendship, Cooperation, and Mutual Assistance concluded between Finland and the Soviet Union in the spring of 1948. After war reparations had been paid in full, trade with the Soviet Union continued, rising to more than 20 percent of the country's total. Further signs of the détente showed when the Soviet Union returned its base at Porkkala in 1955, did not protest at Finland's associating with EFTA in 1961, and opened the Saimaan Kanava (Canal) in 1968.

Relationship with the Soviet Union

Relationships with the Soviet Union, however, have not been entirely without complications. After the 1958 elections a coalition government under the leadership of the Social Democrat Karl August Fagerholm was formed, in which certain members considered anti-Soviet were included. The Soviet Union responded by recalling its ambassador and cancelling credits and orders in Finland. When the Finnish government was reconstructed, relationships were again stabilized. During the autumn of 1961, when international relationships were severely strained because of the Berlin crisis, the Soviet Union requested consultations in accordance with the Agreement of Friendship, Cooperation, and Mutual Assistance. President Kekkonen succeeded—during a personal meeting with the Soviet leader Nikita Sergeyevich Khrushchev—in inducing the Soviet Union to abandon its request.

Finland has participated in the work of the Nordic Council since 1955. The proposal for a Nordic customs union, introduced in 1969–70, failed because of Finland's last-minute refusal to take part.

Domestic policy. During the postwar period, Finland's domestic affairs have been marked by economic difficulties. After World War II Finland was left with the dual task of having to absorb about 300,000 refugees from the areas ceded to the Soviet Union, at the same time paying war reparations. Despite these obstacles, Finland quickly recovered. The war reparations brought about rapid expansion in the metal and shipbuilding industries, and the timber trade soon resumed exporting and quickly exceeded its prewar level. The rebuilding and colonization required to resettle the refugees, however, was such a drain on the country's economic resources that inflation could not be avoided; as a result Finland has had to devalue its currency on a number of occasions.

In the government that was formed after the armistice, the new Communist Party held a strong position, which it retained in the following government. When in the spring of 1948 it was revealed that the party had planned a coup Parliament forced the Communist minister of the interior to resign from the government. After the parliamentary elections in the autumn of 1948, a Social Democratic government came to power under the leadership of K.A. Fagerholm. During the 1950s the governments changed rapidly and consisted of various party coalitions, usually under the leadership of the Agrarian Party or the Social Democrats. During this period, however, both the Conservative National Coalition Party and the Communist People's Democratic League (SKDL) were excluded from the government. In 1962 a Conservative-led government was formed; and after a left-wing victory in 1966, a new government included the Agrarian Party, the Social Democrats, and the Communist Party. The Conservatives won a victory in 1970, and in 1971 the Communists were removed from the Cabinet.

ICELAND

The union (1918–43). The modernization of Iceland's trade and industry continued during the interwar period. The trawl was introduced in the fishing trade, the communications system was improved, and the country acquired its own merchant fleet.

The Icelandic Parliament

After 1918 the government in Reykjavík consisted of a ministry headed by three elected members, while legislative power lay jointly with the king and the Althing (Parliament). The Althing was composed of three major parties: the Progressive Party (a liberal party that had evolved from the old Farmers' Party), the Independence Party (a conservative right-wing party), and the Social Democrats. The Progressive Party was in power for most of the interwar years, and, supported by the Social Democrats, effected a number of economic and social reforms.

When the Germans occupied Denmark in 1940, connections between Iceland and Denmark were broken off, and the Icelandic government took over all governmental functions, including foreign policy, which had previously been conducted by the king and the foreign office in Copenhagen. In May 1940, Iceland was occupied by British troops, who were later replaced by Americans. During the whole of World War II, Iceland was used as a strategic air base in the blockade against Germany and as an intermediate station between the United Kingdom and the United States. In 1941 Sveinn Björnsson was elected regent and assumed all the authority that had formerly been the king's prerogative. In February 1944 the Althing decided unanimously that the Act of Union with Denmark was no longer valid, and in March of the same year a constitution approving Iceland's status as a republic was accepted. Both of these decisions were confirmed by an overwhelming majority in a plebiscite in May 1944. On June 17, 1944, Iceland was proclaimed a republic, and Sveinn Björnsson was elected its first president.

The republic of Iceland. World War II brought severe inflation, which caused great political unrest in Iceland. Shortly after the country became a republic, the bureaucratic government that had functioned since 1942 was replaced by a coalition consisting of the Socialist parties and the right-wing Independence Party, whose leader, Ólafur Thors, became prime minister. During the postwar period, power has been held by one of the three major parties, often in the form of a coalition between two of them. Sveinn Björnsson was re-elected president in 1945 and remained in power until his death in 1952. Ásgeir Ásgeirsson was his successor in 1952–68. Kristjan Eldjarn was elected in 1968 and again in 1972.

Immediately after World War II there was a period of vigorous economic expansion characterized by large investments in the modernization of the agricultural and fishing industries and a comprehensive building program. As a consequence of shrinking prices and smaller catches in the fishing industry, however, Iceland was again faced with great economic problems, and, as a result, the Icelandic krona has been repeatedly devalued.

The question of United States air bases in Iceland became the dominating issue in postwar foreign policy. After lengthy negotiations, an agreement was reached in 1946 that entailed the withdrawal of the American troops in Iceland within six months. Permission was granted, however, to use the air base at Keflavík for a further five-year period, especially in respect of flights to the Federal Republic of Germany. In 1949 Iceland became a member of the North Atlantic Treaty Organization (NATO). In 1951, in the East-West crisis, it was agreed that U.S. troops should be stationed in Keflavík. Since then, opinion has changed in favour of U.S. withdrawal.

Controversy over fishing limits

The other great political issue has concerned the right to fish in Icelandic waters. When Iceland extended its territorial waters from a three- to a four-mile limit in 1952, the United Kingdom and other countries protested. In 1958 the fishing limit was extended from four to 12 miles. The United Kingdom refused to recognize Iceland's decision, and when Iceland announced its intention of confiscating British trawlers that fished within the 12-mile limit, the United Kingdom responded by sending gunboats to protect the fishing vessels. A series of minor incidents followed between Icelandic coastguard cutters and British trawlers and frigates. In 1972 Iceland again unilaterally extended its fisheries limit—this time to 50 miles. This provoked strong protests from other nations, particularly Britain and West Germany, and led to increased tension in the so-called "cod war" involving the British navy.

(Jo.We.)

BIBLIOGRAPHY

Scandinavia to 1523: For a good general history of Scandinavia, see PIERRE JEANNIN, *Histoire des pays scandinaves* (1956). The following are general histories of the individual countries: INGVAR ANDERSSON, *Sveriges historia*, 7th ed. (1969; Eng. trans. of 1st ed., *A History of Sweden*, 1956); JOHN DANSTRUP, *A History of Denmark*, 2nd ed. (1948); SKULI JOHNSON (ed.), *Iceland's Thousand Years: A Series of Popular Lectures on the History and Literature of Iceland* (1945); EINO JUTIKKALA, *A History of Finland* (1962); KAREN LARSEN, *A History of Norway* (1948). (*The Viking Age and before*): JOHANNES BRONSTED, *The Vikings* (1960), an extensive description of the Viking Age; PETER V. GLOB, *Mosefolket* (1966; Eng. trans., *The Bog People*, 1969), about findings in Denmark of well-preserved bodies from the early Iron Age; ARCHIBALD R. LEWIS, *The Northern Seas: Shipping and Com-*

merce in Northern Europe, A.D. 300–1100 (1958), an extensive analysis of trade routes and the European trade during the period; HAAKON SHETELIG (ed.), *The Viking Antiquities in Great Britain and Ireland*, 3 vol. (1940–54), an extensive investigation of Viking raids, settlements, and society; E.O.G. TURVILLE-PETRE, *Myth and Religion of the North* (1964), deals with pre-Christian religious beliefs in Scandinavia. Some of the sagas and the old Norse poetry—*e.g.*, the *Poetic Edda* and the *Prose Edda* are translated into English. (*The later Middle Ages*): JOHN A. GADE, *Hanseatic Control of Norwegian Commerce During the Late Middle Ages* (1951), a dissertation making extensive use of primary material describing the German control of Scandinavian trade; ERIK LONNROTH, *Sverige och Kalmarunionen, 1397–1457* (1934), a dissertation dealing with the much-debated Union of Kalmar, mainly concentrated on Swedish aspects but also an interpretation of the document in a Scandinavian concept; S.U.P. PALME, *Kristendomens genombrott i Sverige* (1959), a detailed study of the Christianization of Sweden and the previous pagan cults; LAURITZ WEIBULL, *Kritiska undersökningar i Nordens historia omkring år 1000* (1911), a classic work dealing with Scandinavian legends and myths but also sorting out what little reliable source material there is from the end of the 10th century; GUNNAR T. WESTIN, *Maktkamp i senmedeltidens Sverige* (1971), analytical studies about the power conflict between the church and the crown and Swedish–Danish conflicts in the beginning of the 16th century.

1523–c. 1815: English readers should consult the relevant chapters of INGVAR ANDERSSON, JOHN DANSTRUP, EINO JUTIKKALA, and THOMAS K. DERRY in *A Short History of Norway*, 2nd ed. (1968). PIERRE JEANNIN, *L'Europe du Nord-Ouest et du Nord aux XVIIe et XVIIIe siècles* (1969), puts 16th- and 17th-century Scandinavia in its European setting. The *Scandinavian Economic History Review* (semi-annual), publishes historical research on Scandinavian subjects. Two outstanding works specifically on this period in English are R.M. HATTON, *Charles XII of Sweden* (1968); and MICHAEL DRAKE, *Population and Society in Norway, 1735–1865* (1969).

Modern Scandinavia: RAYMOND E. LINDGREN, *Norway-Sweden* (1959), deals with the Swedish–Norwegian Union from its inception in 1814 to its dissolution in 1905, together with an account of the cooperation between the Scandinavian countries during the 20th century. (*Denmark*): See the relevant chapters of JOHN DANSTRUP, *Winding, Kjeld: Danmarks historie*, 3rd ed. (1967). (*Norway*): ARNE BERGSGARD, *Fra 17. mai til 9. april. Norsk historie 1814–1940* (1958), a summary of modern Norwegian history based on the results of recent historical research and emphasizing political development; SVERRE STEEN, *Det frie Norge*, 6 vol. (1951–71), covers Norway's history from 1814 to 1836; when complete, this series will constitute the standard history of 19th- and 20th-century Norway. (*Sweden*): STEN CARLSSON, *Svensk historia*, vol. 2, *Tiden efter 1718* (1962), the generally accepted standard work on the history of Sweden, gives a detailed account of political events; each chapter concludes with a detailed bibliography that gives an excellent starting point for further study. *Den Svenska utrikespolitikens historia*, 10 vol. (1951–59), gives a detailed account of Swedish foreign policy and is written by the country's leading historians and based on extensive research. Each volume concludes with a short bibliography of sources and literature on Sweden's foreign policy. (*Finland*): LAURI PUNTILA, *Finlands politiska historia 1809–1955* (1964), a good survey of Finland's political history after 1809, incorporating results of modern historical research—also provides good coverage of the post-1918 period. KRISTER WAHLBACK, *Från Mannerheim till Kekkonen. Huvudlinjer i finländsk politik 1917–1967* (1967), a sober and clear account of Finland's political history from the declaration of independence in 1917 to 1967. The appendixes give a survey of presidents, governments and government members, political parties, and election returns from both the presidential and parliamentary elections during the period 1918–66. (*Iceland*): WILLIAM C. CHAMBERLIN, *Economic Development of Iceland Through World War II* (1947), a detailed and well-documented account of the economic development of Iceland from the beginning of the 20th century to the end of World War II—coverage is broader than indicated by the title; DONALD E. NUECHTERLEIN, *Iceland, Reluctant Ally* (1961), describes the development of relations between Iceland and the United States, 1940–60.

(H.En./G.Sa./Jo.We.)

Scarlatti, Domenico

One of the major keyboard composers of all times, Domenico Scarlatti, in his 555 sonatas for harpsichord,

dazzlingly expanded the technique of the keyboard, and his innovations in harmony and form enhance one of the most strikingly original styles of the 18th century.

Son of the famous vocal composer Alessandro Scarlatti,

Domenico Scarlatti, engraving by an unknown artist.
Ziolo

Giuseppe Domenico was born in Naples on October 26, 1685, in the same year as Bach and Handel. Domenico Scarlatti's career demonstrates aspects both of precocity and of delayed maturity. More than the entire first half of his life was devoted to the composition of vocal music that seldom shows any independence from the all-pervading influence of his father. But nearly all those keyboard works in which he developed his own almost totally unprecedented style appear to date from the period subsequent to his father's death and to his own departure from his native Italy. In fact, the majority of them appear to date from the very last years of his life.

Early life and vocal works: Italy. Scarlatti began the first half of his career at the age of 16 with the production in Naples in 1703 of his first operas, *Ottavia restituita al trono and Il Giustino*. The librettos and part of the music still survive. In 1705 his father sent him away from Naples, reputedly to study with the then famous opera composer and pedagogue Francesco Gasparini, musical director at the Ospedale della Pietà in Venice, where the composer Antonio Vivaldi also served.

First operas

While in Venice, Domenico met with a young Irishman, Thomas Roseingrave, who later became the founder of an English Scarlatti cult that lasted throughout the century. Many years later he described Domenico's harpsichord playing to the English musicologist Charles Burney as sounding as if "ten hundred d....s had been at the instrument; he had never heard such passages of execution and effect before." At about the same time, Domenico formed a friendship with Handel, who was only a few months older than himself. Although they never again met after Domenico's establishment in Rome and Handel's departure from Italy in 1709, they spoke of each other for the rest of their lives with affection and admiration.

By the spring of 1709 Domenico had taken over his father's position in Rome as musical director and composer to the exiled Queen Maria Casimira of Poland. Until her departure in 1714, he composed a series of operas and occasional pieces, all of them on texts by the Queen's secretary, Carlo Sigismondo Capeci. Many of these had set designs by the young Filippo Juvarra, one of the last of the great Italian Baroque architects. Their grandiose perspectives, as shown in surviving drawings, quite belied the size of the Queen's tiny theatre in the Palazzo Zuccari. Some of the music has survived, but, were it not for the reflected glory cast upon it by the later harpsichord sonatas, this music would inspire little interest today.

By 1713 at least, Domenico had established relations

Musical
director at
St. Peter's

with the Vatican, and from 1714 to 1719 he held the position of musical director at St. Peter's. Of the surviving church music that appears to date from this time, only the ten-voice *Stabat Mater* gives a hint of the genius that was to find its long-delayed flowering in the harpsichord sonatas.

During these years Domenico brought to an end his apparently never-too-successful career as an opera composer with *Ambleto* (1715); it had an intermezzo, *La Dirindina*, which, because of the liberties of its text, was withdrawn from performance in Rome. His endeavours also produced *Berenice, regina di Egitto* (1718), with music by both Scarlatti and Nicola Porpora. More promising for the future were his relations with the Portuguese embassy, for which in 1714 he composed a cantata in honour of the birth of a crown prince of Portugal.

In September 1719 Domenico abandoned his post at the Vatican, and the records indicate a departure for England, but no substantiating evidence of a visit to the British Isles has ever been discovered. By the end of 1720, if not earlier, he was in Lisbon, and his serenata the *Contesa delle Stagione* (of which half the music survives) was performed at the royal palace in Lisbon on September 6. He had become musical director to that flamboyant and extravagant monarch John V of Portugal, as well as music master to the King's younger brother Don Antonio and to the Princess Maria Bárbara de Bragança, who was to remain his patroness and for whom most of the harpsichord sonatas were later written. The production of serenades and church music continued, most of it adequate but hardly distinguished, if judged by surviving pieces. But a major change was taking place in Scarlatti's life. In 1725 his father died; in 1728 he made his last visit to Italy to marry at the unusually late age of 43 a young Roman, Maria Catalina Gentili, by whom before her death in 1739 he was to have five children (four more were born to his second marriage, with the Spanish Anastasia Maxarti Ximenes); and in 1729 his pupil Maria Barbara married the Spanish crown prince, the future Ferdinand VI, and Scarlatti followed the royal pair to Spain.

Later life and keyboard works: Spain. There he was to spend his remaining years, first in Seville, perhaps already listening to Spanish popular music and imitating, as Burney tells us, "the melody of tunes sung by carriers, muleteers, and common people," and after 1733 in the royal residences of Madrid and at the nearby palaces of La Granja, Escorial, and Aranjuez. Many links with the past seem to have been cut, and an emancipation seems to have taken place that permitted the extraordinary stylistic development of the harpsichord sonatas. Scarlatti virtually disappears as a composer of vocal music, and there is no evidence of his participation in the extravagant opera productions directed by his friend the castrato singer Farinelli, whose singing in 1737 had so charmed the half-mad Philip V that he rose to a position of unparalleled eminence and power at the Spanish court.

The
harpsi-
chord
sonatas

Scarlatti is seldom mentioned, and the fullest surviving record of his life and character is to be found in the series of harpsichord sonatas that begins with the sumptuous publication of the *Essercizi per gravicembalo* (*Exercises*) in 1738, preceded by a dedication to his former patron John V of Portugal, doubtless in acknowledgement of the knighthood in the Order of Santiago that he had received from him earlier that year. The series of harpsichord sonatas continues brilliantly with manuscript volumes copied out for Maria Barbara in 1742 and 1749. She became queen of Spain in 1746, and the musical activities of the Spanish court became more lavish than ever, always under the direction of Farinelli. But the principal evidence of Scarlatti's own activity continues to reside in the final great series of harpsichord sonatas copied out for the Queen from 1752 to 1757, the year of Scarlatti's death.

This music ranges from the courtly to the savage, from an almost saccharine urbanity to an acrid violence. Its gaiety is all the more intense for an undertone of tragedy. Its moments of meditative melancholy are at times overwhelmed by a surge of extrovert operatic passion. Most particularly he has expressed that part of his life which

was lived in Spain. There is hardly an aspect of Spanish life, of Spanish popular music and dance, that has not found itself a place in the microcosm that Scarlatti created with his sonatas. No Spanish composer, not even Manuel de Falla in the 20th century, has expressed the essence of his native land as completely as did the foreigner Scarlatti. He has captured the click of castanets, the strumming of guitars, the thud of muffled drums, the harsh bitter wail of gypsy lament, the overwhelming gaiety of the village band, and above all the wiry tension of the Spanish dance. (R. K.: *Domenico Scarlatti*)

There are also abundant echoes of the festivities of the Spanish court, of the wind instruments and drums of state processions, of the horns and oboes of the royal hunt, of fireworks and artillery salvos, and of the music from the royal barges that floated over the waters of the Tagus during the summer embarcations at Aranjuez.

All of this does not find expression merely in loosely knit impressionistic program music, but is assimilated and distilled with all the rigour that Scarlatti had learned from his 16th century ecclesiastical masters, and is given forth again in a pure musical language that extends far beyond the domain of mere harpsichord virtuosity. All is assimilated into an unfailing sense of the larger context. In those last five years as he wrote sonata after sonata Scarlatti was reliving his entire life, living it more intensely than ever before, bringing it to fruition. (*Ibid.*)

A consistent development is perceptible in Scarlatti's harpsichord music, essentially characterized by an expansion of simple binary dance form through elaborations of thematic organization and extensions of tonal range. Spectacular innovations in keyboard virtuosity are often accompanied by audacious dissonances, unconventional voice leading, and far-flung modulations. The predominance of fast movements in the earlier sonatas gives way to a greater frequency of slow movements in the middle period, to a wider range of lyricism, and in the later sonatas to a leaner, more concentrated style.

Organiza-
tion of
the
sonatas

Beginning with the Queen's volume of 1749, an increasing number of sonatas are arranged in pairs, contrasting slow movements with fast, coupling complementary fast movements, or extending the total tonal range of a pair conceived as a unit. Nearly 400 of the later sonatas appear arranged in pairs, and there are at least a dozen sonatas arranged in triptychs. A general absence of recognition of this organization of Scarlatti sonatas into a larger context has provided a serious obstacle to the appreciation of their true stature.

The instrument for which most of the late sonatas were composed appears to have been a one-manual harpsichord of the traditional Mediterranean kind, in cedar and cypress, with an extended compass of five octaves and with two eight-foot registers. Queen Maria Barbara was supplied with such instruments in each of the three principal royal residences, Buen Retiro (in Madrid), Aranjuez, and Escorial. On a background of such simplicity and seeming limitation of resources, Scarlatti imposed the variety and contrasts of sonorities and textures that elevate his writing for the harpsichord to a level comparable to that of Chopin and Liszt for the piano.

Shortly before his death, Scarlatti returned at least once more to vocal music, with a *Salve Regina* for soprano and strings, perhaps the most beautiful of his vocal compositions and one of the few meriting survival. He died at Madrid on July 23, 1757.

Personal verbal utterances of Scarlatti have survived only in his preface and dedication of the *Essercizi*, in a letter to the Duke of Alba (1752), and indirectly in a few legal documents. Known samples of his handwriting are less than a dozen, and no autographs of the harpsichord sonatas have been found. A handsome portrait by Domingo Antonio de Velasco was in the possession of Scarlatti descendants until 1912 and is now in the municipal museum of Alpiarça, Portugal.

Except for 18th-century English publications, mainly of his earlier sonatas, and for a few continental reprints, the bulk of Scarlatti's keyboard music was hardly known beyond his immediate circle and can have exercised very little direct influence on his Italian successors (with the exception of one of his editors, the composer Muzio Clementi), or on those German and Austrian composers such as C.P.E. Bach, Haydn, Mozart, and Beethoven, many of whose stylistic features it anticipates.

It was not until the edition prepared by the Italian pianist Alessandro Longo (began in 1906) that virtually all the harpsichord sonatas became available, and, even then, serious flaws in this and other editions prior to 1953 severely hampered any serious understanding of their stylistic development and coherence. Only with the respective complete editions of Ralph Kirkpatrick and Kenneth Gilbert, which maintain the chronological order and pairwise arrangement of sources, can an unobstructed view of Scarlatti's keyboard work at last generally be obtained.

MAJOR WORKS

HARPSICHORD MUSIC: The main body of Scarlatti's work consists for the most part of one-movement sonatas for the harpsichord. There are 555, of which the majority are grouped in pairs.

OPERAS: Scarlatti wrote over a dozen operas. These include: *Tolomeo et Alessandro, overo La corona disprezzata* (1711); *Tetide in Sciro* (1712); *Amor d'un ombra, e gelosia d'un aura* (1714, produced in London in 1720, under the title *Narciso); and Ambleto* (1715).

OTHER WORKS: The rest of his output comprises cantatas and church music, including a mass, two settings of Salve Regina, and a Stabat Mater.

BIBLIOGRAPHY. The definitive biographical and critical study, including the most complete existing catalog of compositions, a comprehensive bibliography, and an account of sources, is RALPH KIRKPATRICK, *Domenico Scarlatti* (1953; paperback edition, 1968). It is supplemented by DOMENICO SCARLATTI, *Sixty Sonatas . . .,* ed. with a preface by RALPH KIRKPATRICK, 2 vol. (1953) and also recorded by him. Superseding all previous editions are DOMENICO SCARLATTI, *Complete Keyboard Works in Facsimile from the Manuscript and Printed Sources,* ed. by RALPH KIRKPATRICK, 18 vol. (1971); and *Complete Keyboard Works,* ed. by KENNETH GILBERT, 9 vol. 1971–   ).

(R.Ki.)

Schelling, Friedrich

Friedrich Wilhelm Joseph von Schelling was one of the three towering figures whose works, in the period following the death of Immanuel Kant (early 19th century), comprised the movement that marks the climax of classical German philosophy—that of German Idealism. The other two figures were Johann Fichte, an ethical, subjective Idealist, and G.W.F. Hegel, a dialectical, absolute Idealist. Schelling himself was an aesthetic, objective Idealist: for, spurning Fichte's starting point in the human ego, Schelling grounded his metaphysics (on the nature of being) instead in objective nature, which he reconciled with mind through the aesthetic creativity that they both share. Schelling's philosophy of nature, which was intensely Romantic, and his philosophy of man, which discerned the darker, irrational recesses of man's being, foreshadowed the 19th-century reaction against the shallow confidences of the Enlightenment and has even been seen by some as a harbinger of 20th-century Existentialism.

Early life and career. Schelling was born on January 27, 1775, in Leonberg, a small town in the Württemberg, where his father was a Lutheran minister. In 1777 his father became a professor of Oriental languages at the theological seminary in Bebenhausen, near Tübingen. It was there that Schelling received his elementary education. He was a highly gifted child, and he had already learned the classical languages at the age of eight. On the basis of his rapid intellectual development, he was admitted, at the age of 15, to the theological seminary in Tübingen, a famous finishing school for ministers of the Württemberg area, where he lived from 1790 to 1795. Among his fellow students were G.W.F. Hegel, later to become the foremost philosopher of the 19th century, and J.C.F. Hölderlin, later to become one of the greatest German poets. The youth at Tübingen were inspired by the ideas of the French Revolution and, spurning tradition, turned away from doctrinal theology to philosophy. The young Schelling was inspired, however, by the

Schelling, oil painting by Joseph Karl Stieler (1781–1858). In the Bayerische Staatsgemäldesammlungen, Munich.
By courtesy of the Bayerisches Nationalmuseum, Munich

thought of Immanuel Kant, who had raised philosophy to a higher critical level, and by the Idealist system of Fichte, as well as by the pantheism of Benedict de Spinoza, a 17th-century Rationalist. When he was 19 years old Schelling wrote his first philosophical work, *Über die Möglichkeit einer Form der Philosophie überhaupt* (1795; "On the Possibility and Form of Philosophy in General"), which he sent to Fichte, who expressed strong approval. This work was followed in 1795 by *Vom Ich als Prinzip der Philosophie* ("Of the Ego as Principle of Philosophy") and by an article, "Philosophische Briefe über Dogmatismus and Kritizismus" (1796; "Philosophical Letters on Dogmatism and Criticism"). One basic theme governs all of these works—the Absolute. This Absolute cannot be defined, however, as a God who stands over the world; each person is himself the Absolute as the Absolute ego. This ego, eternal and timeless, is apprehended in a direct intuition, which, in contrast to sensory intuition, can be characterized as intellectual.

Early works on the Absolute

From 1795 to 1797 Schelling acted as a private tutor for a noble family, who had placed its sons under his care during their studies in Leipzig. The time spent in Leipzig marked a decisive turning point in the thought of Schelling. He attended lectures in physics, chemistry, and medicine. He acknowledged that Fichte, whom he had previously revered as his philosophical model, had not taken adequate notice of nature in his philosophical system, inasmuch as Fichte had always viewed nature only as an object in its subordination to man. Schelling, in contrast, wanted to show that nature, seen in itself, shows an active development toward the spirit. This interpretation becomes especially obvious in the organic forms of nature: a plant, according to Schelling, is an interlacing tendency of soul. This philosophy of nature, the first independent philosophical accomplishment of Schelling, made him known in the circles of the Romanticists and won the approval of the famous writer Johann Wolfgang von Goethe.

Period of intense productivity. In 1798 Schelling was called to a professorship at the University of Jena, the academic centre of Germany at the time.

Career at Jena. The foremost intellects of the time —Goethe, the writer Friedrich Schiller, the Romanticists Friedrich and August Wilhelm Schlegel, the writer and critic Ludwig Tieck, and, from 1801, Hegel—were all together at Jena. During this period Schelling was extremely productive: he developed his philosophy of nature through lectures and books; and between 1797 and 1800 he published in rapid succession several works on the philosophy of nature, notably *Ideen zu einer Philosophie der Natur* (1797; "Ideas Toward a Philosophy of Nature") and *Von der Weltseele, eine Hypothese der höheren Physik zur Erklärung des allgemeinen Organismus* (1798; "On the World Soul, a Hypothesis of Advanced Physics for the Interpretation of the General

Organism"). It was Schelling's desire, as attested by his famous work *System des transzendentalen Idealismus* (1800; "System of Transcendental Idealism"), to unite his concept of nature with Fichte's philosophy, which took the ego as the point of departure. Schelling saw that this unity of the natural and the spiritual spheres was given by art. Art mediates between these spheres insofar as, in artistic creation, the natural (or unconscious) and the spiritual (or conscious) productions are united. In this work it became evident that Schelling had drawn up a pantheism of historical development. Naturalness and spirituality are explained as emerging from an original state of indifference, in which they were submerged in the yet-undeveloped Absolute, and as rising through a succession of steps of ever-higher order. Schelling explicates this statement especially in an article, "Darstellung meines Systems der Philosophie" (1801; "An Exposition of My System of Philosophy").

Fichte did not acknowledge this concept, however, and the two writers attacked each other most sharply in an intensive correspondence from the years around 1800. Fichte reproached Schelling for not acknowledging in his speculations the only sure foothold of philosophy, the certitude of the ego; and Schelling, in his turn, asserted that Fichte had never risen to the true origin of all philosophy, the Absolute, which comprehends both nature and spirit. Their correspondence ended without result in 1802.

Marriage to Caroline Schlegel

The time spent in Jena was important for Schelling also in a personal respect: there he became acquainted with Caroline Schlegel, who was among the most gifted women in German Romanticism. Caroline was born in 1763, the daughter of a professor in Göttingen, and she married a physician, Wilhelm Böhmer, at the age of 21. After his death she lived in Mainz in the house of a librarian, Georg Forster, who was a partisan of the French Revolution. There she met a French officer, to whom she bore a child. In 1796 she married August Wilhelm von Schlegel, a poetical translator and a leader of the new Romantic criticism, and moved with him to Jena. There she met Schelling and was immediately enthusiastic about him both as a person and as a thinker. Thus they soon came to love one another. The death, in 1800, of Auguste, Caroline's daughter (from her marriage with Böhmer), whom Schelling had treated in her last illness, drew Schelling and Caroline even closer together. Through Goethe's intervention, Caroline obtained a divorce from Schlegel in May 1803 and married Schelling in the same year. The unpleasant intrigues that accompanied this marriage reached their climax when Schelling was held responsible for the death of Auguste. It was rumoured that Schelling had treated her according to Brunonian theories, which regarded all disease as due to either deficient or excessive stimulation. Such personal difficulties and the dispute with Fichte caused Schelling to leave Jena, and he accepted an appointment at the University of Würzburg in 1803.

Career at Würzburg and Munich. At first, Schelling lectured at Würzburg on the philosophy of identity, conceived in his last years in Jena, in which he tried to show that, in all beings, the Absolute expresses itself directly as the unity of the subjective and the objective. It was just on this point that Hegel initiated his criticism of Schelling.

Hegel's criticisms

As attested in Hegel's work *Differenz des Fichte'schen und Schelling'schen Systems der Philosophie* (1801; "Difference Between the Philosophical Systems of Fichte and Schelling"), Hegel had at first taken Schelling's side in the disagreement between Schelling and Fichte. A complete unanimity seemed to exist between Hegel and Schelling, and in 1802 the *Kritisches Journal der Philosophie* ("Critical Journal of Philosophy") appeared in Jena, with Hegel and Schelling as coeditors. In the following years, however, Hegel's philosophical thought began to move significantly away from Schelling's. Hegel's famous work *Phänomenologie des Geistes* (1807; Eng. trans., *The Phenomenology of Mind,* 1910) contained strong charges against Schelling's system, without, however, mentioning his name. To Schelling's definition of the Absolute as an indiscriminate unity of the subjective and

the objective, Hegel replied that such an Absolute is comparable to the night, "in which all cows are black." Besides, Schelling had never explicitly shown how one could ascend to the Absolute; he had begun with this Absolute as though it were "shot out of a pistol."

This criticism struck Schelling a heavy blow. The friendship with Hegel that had existed since their time together at the seminary in Tübingen broke up. Schelling, who had been regarded as the leading philosopher of the time until the publication of Hegel's *Phänomenologie*, was pushed into the background by Hegel, whose philosophy was now generally regarded as the authoritative system.

This situation caused Schelling to retreat from public life. From 1806 to 1841 he lived in Munich, where, in 1806, he was appointed as general secretary of the Academy of Plastic Arts. He lectured from 1820 to 1827 in Erlangen. Caroline died on September 7, 1809. This sad event, which dealt a heavy blow to Schelling, led him to write a philosophical work on immortality. The text on Caroline's gravestone, which Schelling himself wrote, ends with the words "Every sensitive being stands with devotion here, where the husk that once enclosed the most noble heart and beautiful spirit slumbers." In 1812 Schelling married Pauline Gotter, a friend of Caroline. In a letter to Pauline, written shortly after Caroline's death, Schelling declared that, if the dead had any awareness of the sorrows of the survivors, Caroline would thank Pauline Gotter for everything she would do for Schelling. The marriage was calm and harmonious, but the great passion that Schelling had felt for Caroline was unrepeatable.

Consolidation of his philosophy

During the years in Munich, Schelling tried to consolidate his philosophical work in a new way, producing a revision that was instigated by Hegel's criticism of his philosophy of identity. Schelling questioned all Idealistic speculations built on the assumption that the world presents itself as a rational cosmos. Were there not also irrational things, he asked, and was not evil the predominant power in the world? In his *Philosophische Untersuchungen über das Wesen der menschlichen Freiheit* (1809; Eng. trans., *Of Human Freedom,* 1936), Schelling attempted to explore this question. In this important work he declared that the freedom of man is a real freedom only if it is freedom for good and evil. The possibility of this freedom is founded on two principles that are active in every living thing: one, a dark primal foundation that manifests itself in carnal desire and impulse; the other, a clearheaded sensibleness that governs as a formative power. Man, however, has placed the dark stratum of impulse, which was meant only to serve the intellect as a source of power, above the intellect and has thus subordinated the intellect to the impulses, which now rule over him. This reversal of the right order is the occurrence known in the Bible as the Fall from grace, through which evil came into the world. But this perversion of man is revoked by God, who becomes man in Christ and thus re-establishes the original order. In addition to Schelling's obvious use of Christian dogma in this work, the influence of Jakob Böhme, a theosophical thinker, can also be seen. Schelling adopted Böhme's thought that God must give birth to himself by raising himself from the dark ground of nature into the light.

Period of the later, unpublished philosophy. The position developed in the work on freedom forms the basis of Schelling's later philosophy, covering the time from 1810 until his death, which is known only through a draft of the unpublished work *Die Weltalter* (written in 1811; partial Eng. trans., *The Ages of the World,* 1942) and through the manuscripts of his later lectures. In *Die Weltalter* Schelling wanted to relate the history of God. God, who originally is absorbed in a quiet longing, comes to himself by glimpsing in himself ideas through which he becomes conscious of himself. This self-consciousness, which is identical to freedom, enables God to project these ideas from himself—*i.e.,* to create the world.

The Ages of the World

This conception was adopted and, at the same time, significantly extended in the "Vorlesungen zur Philosophie der Mythologie und der Offenbarung" ("Lectures on the Philosophy of Mythology and of Revelation"), a series that Schelling repeated several times. Through them he hoped to develop a great public interest once more, as he had done during his time in Jena. His appointment to the University of Berlin in 1841 gave him this opportunity. It had been brought to the attention of the Prussian king of that time, Frederick William IV, that Schelling had deviated from Idealistic thought and turned to the primary Christian truths—*i.e.,* to the doctrines of the defection of man from God and the reconciliation of man with God through Christ. The King hoped that Schelling would combat the so-called dragon's seed of Hegelianism in Berlin, where Hegel had been working until his death in 1831. Schelling's first lecture in Berlin manifested his self-consciousness. Schelling declared that in his youth he had opened a new page in the history of philosophy and that now in his maturity he wanted to turn this page and start yet a newer one. Such notables as Friedrich Engels, the Marxist theoretician, Søren Kierkegaard, a Danish religious thinker, Jakob Burckhardt, a German historian, and Mikhail Bakunin, a Russian revolutionary agitator, were in his audience. Schelling, however, was denied any great success in his appearance in Berlin. Moreover, he was embittered when his lectures were plagiarized in a publication by one of his opponents, H.E.G. Paulus, who wanted to submit the positive philosophy of Schelling, now finally disclosed in these lectures, to the public for examination. Schelling initiated a legal suit but lost the case. Resigned, he discontinued lecturing.

The content of these lectures, however, represented the definitive climax of Schelling's creative activity. Schelling now divided philosophy into a *negative* philosophy, which developed the idea of God by means of reason alone, and, in contrast, a *positive* philosophy, which showed the reality of this idea by reasoning a posteriori from the fact of the world to God as its creator. Schelling then explained (referring to his work on freedom) that man, who wanted to be equal to God, stood up against God in his Fall into sin. But God was soon elevated again as the principle. During the era of mythology, God appeared as a dark power. During the era of revelation, however, God emerged in history as manifestly real in the figure of Christ. Thus, the complete history of religion should be conveyed through philosophical thought.

In 1854 Schelling travelled to Switzerland to recover from a cold in Bad Ragaz, where on August 20, he died. The king of Bavaria, Maximilian II, erected a gravestone there for him as the foremost thinker of Germany.

Personality and significance. Schelling is described as a man of thickset build, and, according to favourable reports, his high forehead and sparkling eyes were impressive. Opponents of his philosophy, however, such as Karl Rosenkranz, a disciple of Hegel, spoke of a sharp and piercing look. His character was unbalanced. Schelling has been described as nervous, unpredictable, and deeply sensitive in his proud fashion. Particularly striking was his unwavering consciousness that it was his mission to bring philosophy to a definite completion.

In order to understand Schelling's life, two periods must be clearly discerned: the first, from his philosophical beginnings to 1809 (his composition of the work on freedom); the second, from 1809 until his death. During the first period Schelling stood in the limelight. He knew personally the most important people of his time and was recognized by them as a genius. Stimulated by his fame, Schelling was able to achieve, especially during the time at Jena, a productivity that was truly amazing. In the works of this time, however, Schelling quickly changed his philosophical concepts; thus, in the earlier Schelling studies he is spoken of as the Proteus of Idealism—an infinitely changing being.

The second period was of a completely different character. It was introduced by certain occurrences: Caroline's death and Hegel's criticism. Schelling no longer published any extensive works, even though he repeatedly announced new books. Evidently, he was convinced that, due to the influence of Hegelianism, his philosophy would not receive proper consideration. This belief was decisively strengthened when his appearance in Berlin, which he had hoped would enhance the evaluation of his

(margin left) Negative and positive philosophy

(margin left) The two periods of Schelling's thought

thinking, was a failure. His feeling for life was significantly changed in comparison with the first period of his life, for he now declared that melancholy and sadness are the true moods to which man inevitably is exposed. He attempted, however, to overcome this pessimistic view of life by drafting a metaphysics that was defined by recourse to the personal God of the Christian revelation. At the end of his "Vorlesungen zur Philosophie der Offenbarung," he declared that: "The highest is, indeed, to acknowledge and worship God in spirit; but in order that this might happen in truth as Christ demands, it is also true that what we worship must be the real God as revealed by deeds, and not some abstract Idol." For Schelling, recourse to the God of revelation meant that despair cannot be the last word.

Great philosophical influence was denied to Schelling. The philosophical situation at the time was determined not by the few disciples of Schelling but by the Hegelians. The right-wing Hegelians occupied all of the philosophical professorial chairs and handed down the tradition of Hegel's system. The left-wing Hegelians explained that, even to suspend Hegel's system, an analysis of Hegel's philosophy was necessary. Thus, in tracing the development of German Idealism, the early and middle Schelling—that is, the Schelling who drew up the philosophy of nature and the philosophy of identity—has been placed between the Idealism of Fichte, who started from the ego, and Hegel's system of the Absolute spirit.

The independence of Schelling and his importance for philosophy are only now being recognized, and that in connection with Existential philosophy and philosophical anthropology, which conceive themselves as counteracting the philosophy of absolute reason. The later Schelling now turns out to have been the first thinker to illuminate Hegel's philosophy critically. In particular, Schelling's insight that man is determined not only by reason but also by dark natural impulses is now valued as a positive attempt to understand the reality of man on a level more profound than that attained by Hegel.

BIBLIOGRAPHY

Works: Schelling's works have been published by his son, K.F.A. SCHELLING (ed.), *Sämtliche Werke,* 14 vol. (1856–61; reprinted unchanged as the "Münchner Jubiläumsdruck," entitled *Werke,* ed. by MANFRED SCHROETER, 12 vol. (1927–54). The Schelling-Kommission, which existed for a time at the Bayerischen Akademie der Wissenschaften in Munich, prepared a critical new edition of his works that includes the unpublished manuscripts. His instructive and often intimate correspondence with influential men and women was edited by GUSTAV L. PLITT, *Aus Schellings Leben: In Briefen,* 3 vol. (1869–70). Because this edition is out of date, HORST FUHRMANS has planned a new collection of the letters, with detailed commentaries, of which only one volume had appeared by the early 1970s: *Schelling: Briefe und Dokumente* (1962). Important for the change in Schelling's thought is his correspondence with Johann Gottlieb Fichte: WALTER SCHULZ (ed.), *Fichte-Schelling: Briefwechsel* (1968), which presents the philosophical development that characterized his position in German Idealism.

Studies: For an older classical work see KUNO FISCHER, *Geschichte der neuern Philosophie,* 4th ed., vol. 7 (1923), which details Schellings's life and interprets his individual writings. KARL JASPERS, *Schelling: Grösse und Verhängnis* (1955), is an important work that achieves a critical understanding of Schelling from the standpoint of Existentialism. Two works by HORST FUHRMANS, *Schellings letzte Philosophie* (1940) and *Schellings Philosophie der Weltalter* (1954), provide guidance on the salient problem of whether Schelling changed from the building of a system of Idealism to espousing a philosophy of freedom that also recognizes the irrational. See also WALTER SCHULZ, *Die Vollendung des deutschen Idealismus in der Spätphilosophie Schellings* (1955). From the standpoint of art, which played an essential role in his philosophy, DIETER JAEHNIG, *Schelling: Die Kunst in der Philosophie,* 2 vol. (1966–69), is important. The entire Schelling literature is cited in the two bibliographies: GUIDO SCHNEEBERGER, *Friedrich Wilhelm Joseph von Schelling* (1954), listing publications from 1797 to 1953; and HANS-JORG SANDKUEHLER, *Friedrich Wilhelm Joseph Schelling* (1970), which brings it up to 1969.

(W.Sc.)

Schiller, Friedrich

One of the greatest German dramatists, poets, and literary theorists, Johann Christoph Friedrich von Schiller (ennobled in 1802) exemplifies in his life and work the triumph of man's spirit over adverse circumstance. In one of his last letters (April 2, 1805) he said to his friend Wilhelm von Humboldt: "After all, we are both idealists, and should be ashamed to have it said that the material world formed us, instead of being formed by us." The pursuit of beauty was to him a matter of greatest moment in human affairs; his devotion to his literary work was his personal religion. Thomas Carlyle recognized this when he wrote: "As Schiller viewed it, genuine Literature includes the essence of philosophy, religion, art; whatever speaks to the immortal part of man."

By courtesy of the Staatliche Museen, Berlin

Schiller, chalk drawing by F.G. Weitsch, 1804.
In the Staatliche Museen, Berlin.

Schiller was born at Marbach on the River Neckar on November 10, 1759, the second child of Lieutenant Johann Kaspar Schiller and his wife, Dorothea. His father saw much strenuous service in Bavarian, French, and Swabian regiments; when his campaigning days were over, he devoted himself to horticulture and was appointed superintendent of the gardens and plantations at Ludwigsburg, the residence of Duke Karl Eugen of Württemberg. Johann Kaspar gave his only son what he himself had been denied, a sound grammar school education until the age of 13 when, in deference to what amounted to a command from his despotic sovereign, he reluctantly agreed to send his boy to the Military Academy (the Karlsschule), an institution founded and personally supervised by the Duke. Against the wishes of the parents, who had hoped to have their son trained for the ministry, the Duke decreed that young Friedrich was to prepare for the study of law; later, however, he was allowed to transfer to medicine. Having endured the irksome regimentation at the academy for eight years—during which period he was virtually cut off from his family and the outside world—Schiller left to take up an appointment as an assistant medical officer (noncommissioned) to a Stuttgart regiment, a post that brought him no prestige and very little pay.

Early drama. His adolescence under the rule of a petty tyrant confronted Schiller with the problem of the use and abuse of power, a theme that recurs in most of his plays. His resentment found expression in some of his early poems (published in the *Anthologie auf das Jahr 1782*) and especially in his first play, *Die Räuber* (*The Robbers*, printed at his own expense and with borrowed money in 1781), a stirring protest against stifling convention and corruption in high places. The hero, Karl Moor, a young man of fiery spirit and abundant vitality, has led a somewhat disorderly life at the university. His villainous younger brother Franz (modelled on Shakespeare's Iago, Edmund, and Richard III) poisons their

Success of Die Räuber

aged father's mind against the prodigal elder son. When the old Count Moor disowns Karl, the young man turns brigand and defies all established authority at the head of a band of outlaws, until, before long, he discovers that however corrupt the existing order may be, violence and anarchy do not offer a workable alternative and society cannot be reformed by terrorism and crime. He decides to give himself up to justice, thus submitting to the law that he had flouted. Schiller could therefore claim to have written in defense of law and morality. At the same time, Karl Moor is represented as a "sublime criminal," and the play is a scathing indictment of a society that could drive so fundamentally noble a character to a career of crime.

In order to have the play accepted, Schiller had to prepare a stage version in which the rebellious ardour of his original text was toned down. Nevertheless, the first performance (January 13, 1782) at the National Theatre at Mannheim in the neighbouring state of the Palatinate created a sensation; it was a milestone in the history of the German theatre and, incidentally, in the career of August Wilhelm Iffland, who appeared in the role of Franz Moor and who was destined to become the leading German actor of his time. Schiller travelled to Mannheim without the Duke's permission in order to be present on the first night. When the Duke heard of this and of a subsequent secret visit, he sentenced the poet to a fortnight's detention and forbade him to write any more plays. To escape from this intolerable situation, Schiller decided to cut himself adrift. It meant giving up his livelihood, such as it was, his home ties, and the prospect of a reasonably secure future; but he was determined to follow his literary bent, whatever the cost. In the company of a loyal friend, the musician Andreas Streicher, he fled from Stuttgart at night, crossed the frontier that separated Duke Karl Eugen's territory from the neighbouring state, and set out for Mannheim, in the hope of receiving help from Heribert Baron von Dalberg, the director of the theatre that had launched his first play. He brought with him the manuscript of a new work, *Die Verschwörung des Fiesko zu Genua* (*Fiesco; or, the Genoese Conspiracy*), subtitled "a republican tragedy": the drama of the rise and fall of a would-be dictator, set in 16th-century Genoa, picturing, in Schiller's own phrase, "ambition in action, and ultimately defeated."

The new play proved an ill-starred venture. It was rejected, and when Schiller prepared a revised version for the Mannheim stage, with a different ending, this was rejected, too. Baron Dalberg, not anxious to provoke a diplomatic incident by sheltering a deserter, kept the embarrassing visitor at arm's length. For some tense weeks Schiller led the hand-to-mouth life of a refugee, until he found a temporary home with Henriette von Wolzogen, whose sons had been fellow students of his and who invited him to stay at her house at Bauerbach in Thuringia. There he finished his third tragedy, *Kabale und Liebe*, and started work on *Don Carlos*.

As the title suggests, *Kabale und Liebe* is a tragedy of love thwarted by intrigue. In this play about the love of a young aristocrat for a girl of humble background, Schiller's innate sense of drama is seen at its best. The appeal of its theme—the revolt of elemental human feeling against the artificialities of convention—the vigour of its social criticism, the vitality of dialogue and characters, and the shapeliness of its structure all combine to make *Kabale und Liebe* great theatre.

About six months after Schiller's flight from Stuttgart, Dalberg judged it safe to re-establish contact with his former protégé. He eventually offered Schiller an appointment as resident playwright with the Mannheim theatre. Schiller accepted and had the satisfaction of seeing *Kabale und Liebe* score a resounding success; but his hopes of clearing his debts and gaining a measure of financial security were doomed to disappointment. There were other worries as well, chief among them a serious illness that attacked him soon after he had arrived in Mannheim. Applying in his own case the rather violent methods that had made him notorious among his patients in his Stuttgart days, he tried to control successive bouts of fever by taking vast quantities of quinine. After several

Resident playwright of the Mannheim theatre

relapses, the trouble finally abated; but the damage done to his health at that time probably prepared the way for the illness that was to be the constant companion of his later life. When his contract expired after a year, it was not renewed; and once again Schiller needed the help of friends to extricate him, from both his financial predicament and from an emotional crisis caused by his attachment to a married woman, the charming but unstable Charlotte von Kalb. Four unknown admirers wrote to him from Leipzig and finally invited him to join them there. One of them, Christian Gottfried Körner, became his close and lifelong friend; being a man of some substance, he was able to support Schiller during his two years' stay in Saxony, toward the end of which *Don Carlos*, his first major poetic drama, was published in book form (parts had appeared in his journal *Thalia*).

Classical drama. *Don Carlos* marks a turning point in Schiller's development as a dramatist. The first sketch had been in prose; this was recast in verse, and what had originally been conceived as "a domestic drama in a royal house" (as Schiller put it in 1784) evolved into a play about large political issues. The domestic drama concerns the relations between the aging King Philip II of Spain, his third consort, Elizabeth of Valois, and his son by his first marriage, Don Carlos, who is in love with his stepmother. The conflict between father and son is not confined to their private lives; it has political implications as well. The change of focus from the domestic to the political sphere produced a play of inordinate length (the original version runs to 6,280 lines) and a tortuous plot. But there are positive qualities to compensate for these faults: a wealth of exciting and moving scenes and a wide range of sharply individualized characters, the most memorable being the complex, brooding, and tragic figure of King Philip. The characteristically resonant note of Schiller's Schiller's blank verse blank verse is heard here for the first time. Blank verse had been used by German playwrights before, notably Gotthold Lessing in *Nathan der Weise* (published 1779), but it was Schiller's *Don Carlos*, together with Goethe's *Iphigenie auf Tauris* (both published after extensive revision in 1787), that definitely established it as the recognized medium of German poetic drama.

Schiller had accepted Körner's generous offer of hospitality and financial help in the spirit in which it was made. In the congenial circle of his new friends he experienced a sense of contentment and joyous confidence such as he had not known before. He gave jubilant expression to this mood in his hymn "An die Freude," which Beethoven was to use for the choral movement of his *Ninth Symphony*. He could not stay with Körner indefinitely, however, and the moment came when he felt he had to make another bid for independence. In July 1787 he set out for Weimar, in the hope of meeting some of the men who had made Weimar the literary capital of Germany. He soon established friendly relations with Johann Gottfried Herder and especially with Christoph Martin Wieland, in whose journal *Der teutsche Merkur* he published the long poem "Die Künstler" ("The Artists"), a meditation on the role of the arts as the great civilizing force in human evolution. Goethe, who was in Italy at the time, returned to Weimar in the following year. At first Friendship with Goethe Goethe's studied aloofness prevented any close personal contact, but in the long run the older man could not resist the magnetism of Schiller's personality. A chance meeting in 1794 and the ensuing exchange of letters mark the beginning of their friendship, a union of opposites that forms an inspiring chapter in the history of German letters. Their fascinating correspondence is a worthy memorial to a momentous literary partnership.

Historical studies. In spite of his initial antipathy, Goethe had recommended Schiller for appointment to a professorship of history at the University of Jena, Schiller having presented the requisite credentials in his history of the revolt of the Netherlands (*Geschichte des Abfalls der vereinigten Niederlande von der spanischen Regierung*, 1788). His history of the Thirty Years' War (*Geschichte des dreissigjährigen Krieges*, 1791–93) further enhanced his prestige as a historian; it also provided him with the material for his greatest drama, *Wallenstein*,

published in 1800 and brilliantly translated into English by Samuel Taylor Coleridge, who thought it "not unlike Shakespeare's historical plays—a species by itself." While Schiller does not rank with such later masters as Theodor Mommsen and Leopold von Ranke, his contribution to German historiography is not to be underrated. He wrote at a time when modern methods of historical research had not yet been perfected, but he applied a critical mind to the sources accessible to him; he had a dramatist's eye for character and motive, and he handled his subjects with literary skill. What he offered to his readers was history seen through the medium of his own individuality, presented with all the verve and eloquence of his distinctive prose style.

Although Schiller's academic post was unremunerative, he felt sufficiently confident about his prospects to embark upon matrimony: in 1790 he married Charlotte von Lengefeld, a cultured young woman of good family, who bore him two sons and two daughters. Schiller was an affectionate husband and father, and Charlotte proved her devotion in all the trials that lay ahead. In the second year of their married life, Schiller's health gave way under the strain of perpetual overwork. For a time he lay critically ill, and although he rallied after several relapses, he never fully recovered. He was under no illusions. With the scientific detachment of the medical man, he analyzed his own condition, a combination of chest trouble and digestive disorder, which, as he suspected, proved intractable. He commented, in a letter to Körner, "My mind, by the way, is serene, and I shall not be found lacking in courage, even though the worst may befall." The rest of his life was a losing battle, fought with superb fortitude, against the inexorable advance of disease.

Philosophical studies. Calamitous as his illness was, it produced a piece of great good luck. To give him time to recuperate at leisure, without worrying about publishers' contracts or tradesmen's bills, two Danish patrons—Prince Friedrich Christian of Schleswig-Holstein-Augustenburg and Heinrich Ernst, Count Schimmelmann—granted him a generous pension for three years. Schiller decided to devote part of this time to studying the philosophy of Immanuel Kant—a project he had had in mind ever since his arrival in Weimar. As he proceeded to assimilate Kant's views, he soon felt the urge to formulate his own. The encounter with Kant's philosophy thus produced between 1793 and 1801 a series of essays in which Schiller sought to define the character of aesthetic activity, its function in society, and its relation to moral experience: his essays on moral grace and dignity, "Über Anmut und Würde," and on the sublime, "Über das Erhabene," as well as the celebrated essay on the distinction between two types of poetic creativity, "Über naive und sentimentalische Dichtung." The latter, like his letters on the aesthetic education of man, "Briefe über die ästhetische Erziehung des Menschen," first appeared in *Die Horen*, an ambitious but short-lived literary periodical edited by Schiller and published by Johann Friedrich Cotta, one of Germany's leading publishers, whom Schiller had met during a visit to his native Swabia in 1793–94. Cotta became a personal friend and a trusted adviser. This period of critical stocktaking also produced some exquisite reflective poems: "Das Ideal und das Leben") Reflective poetry "Life and the Ideal"), "Der Spaziergang" ("The Walk"), "Die Macht des Gesanges" ("The Power of Song"). These are "philosophical lyrics" in the true sense: not versified philosophy, but poetic utterance inspired by an intellectual experience. They contain the quintessence of Schiller's philosophical and critical thinking, and they are among his best poems, but they are poems for the few. On the other hand, the ballads written in 1797 (including "Der Handschuh" ["The Glove"], "Der Taucher" ["The Diver"], and "Die Kraniche des Ibykus" ["The Cranes of Ibycus"]) are among his most popular productions. In these poems and in the famous "Lied von der Glocke" ("The Song of the Bell") Schiller shows how to make poetry accessible to the man in the street without debasing it. Popularity, he insists in his review of Gottfried August Bürger's poems, need not and should not mean pandering to vulgar taste.

Historical drama. In the *Wallenstein* cycle—a work on the grand scale, consisting of a prefatory poem, a dramatic prologue, and two five-act plays—Schiller reached the height of his powers as a dramatist. Against the sombre background of the Thirty Years' War there rises the sinister figure of the emperor Ferdinand II's commander in chief, who in his secret heart is meditating high treason: by joining forces with the enemy, he hopes to make himself the arbiter of the empire. Wallenstein sees himself as a privileged being, a superman beyond good and evil, the man of destiny. While these traits repel, his bearing in the hour of crisis compels admiration and even wins a measure of sympathy. His portrayal is a profound study of the lure and the perils of power.

Working against time, Schiller produced four more plays in quick succession (apart from his adaptations of *Macbeth* and of the Italian dramatist Carlo Gozzi's *Turandot* for the German stage and his fine translation from the French of Jean Racine's *Phèdre*): *Maria Stuart* (first performed in 1800); *Die Jungfrau von Orleans* (1801; a "romantic tragedy" on the subject of Joan of Arc, in which the heroine dies in a blaze of glory after a victorious battle, rather than at the stake like her historical prototype, who was burned to death in 1431 as a witch and a heretic); *Die Braut von Messina* (1803; *The Bride of Messina*, written in emulation of Greek drama, with its important preface, Schiller's last critical pronouncement); and *Wilhelm Tell* (1804; probably Schiller's most popular play; picturing the revolt of the Swiss forest cantons against Habsburg rule and the assassination of a tyrannous Austrian governor by the hero, it deals with the justifiability of violence in political action). Each one of these later plays has its own distinctive merit, but as a piece of dramatic craftsmanship *Maria Stuart* is superior to the rest. The action is compressed into the last three days in the life of Mary, queen of Scots, before her execution at Fotheringhay; all the antecedents—her French marriage, her brief and troubled Scottish reign, her long and increasingly strait imprisonment in England—emerge by means of retrospective analysis: a striking example of what Schiller called "the Euripidean method." Although Schiller treated his subject with the freedom of the artist, repeatedly diverging from the recorded facts, his play is anything but a travesty of history; on the contrary, it shows a profound grasp of the historical situation. It offers a disturbing analysis of the problems that arise whenever political expediency masquerades as justice and judges are subjected to the pressures of power politics or ideological conflict. Schiller's heroine turns outward disaster into inward triumph by accepting the verdict of the English tribunal—which she regards as both unjust and ultra vires—in expiation of sins committed in former days; by giving to the decree of her judges a meaning that they had not intended, she rises superior to their jurisdiction, a sinner redeemed and transfigured. This conforms to Schiller's theory of tragedy, which turns on the hero's moral rebirth through an act of voluntary self-abnegation.

Death overtook Schiller at Weimar (May 9, 1805) while he was working at a new play on a Russian theme, *Demetrius*. Judging by the noble fragments that remain, it might well have developed into a masterpiece.

Correspondence. In any account of Schiller's life and works, his letters deserve special attention, whether read as an autobiography, as a running commentary on his plays and poems, as a supplement to his critical writings, or as reflections on German intellectual life in the second half of the 18th century. They are as rich in self-revelation as they are in portraits of contemporaries; they show the author's personality from all angles: free and easy with intimates, ceremonious when the occasion demands it, clear and precise in matters of business, affectionate to his wife, coolly incisive when provoked, with a touch of humour even in adversity. As one would expect, literary and philosophical topics predominate, but not to the exclusion of other matters; Schiller's letters reflect the whole range of his interests, from the most important to the most trivial: the future of German drama and the price of tobacco, society gossip and the French Revolu-

Dramatic craftsmanship of Maria Stuart

tion, the philosophy of Immanuel Kant and his children's teething troubles. When Goethe was editing his correspondence with Schiller for publication, he described the letters Schiller had addressed to him as "perhaps the greatest treasure he possessed."

Assessment. In one of the first of those letters the writer, then 34 years old, sized up his prospects:

> Now that I have begun to know and to employ my spiritual powers properly, an illness unfortunately threatens to undermine my physical ones. . . . However, I shall do what I can, and when in the end the edifice comes crashing down, I shall perhaps have salvaged what was worth preserving.

He was as good as his word. "The idea of freedom," Goethe said to his young friend Johann Peter Eckermann, "assumed a different form as Schiller advanced in his own development and became a different man. In his youth it was physical freedom that preoccupied him and found its way into his works; in later life it was spiritual freedom." Schiller's early tragedies are attacks upon political oppression and the tyranny of social convention; his later plays are concerned with the inward freedom of the soul that enables a man to rise superior to the frailties of the flesh and to the pressure of material conditions; they show the hero torn between the claims of this world and the demands of an eternal moral order, striving to keep his integrity in the conflict. In his reflective poems and in his treatises, Schiller sets out to show how art can help man to attain this inner harmony and how, through the "aesthetic education" of the individual citizen, a happier, more humane social order may develop. His reflections on aesthetics thus link up with his political and historical thinking.

Schiller's thought has sometimes been called escapist, a retreat into an ivory tower; and yet he has also been charged with trying to press art into the service of morality or social reform. Both criticisms are unjust. Nowhere does Schiller advocate an ascetic or cowardly withdrawal from ordinary experience; on the contrary, he boldly faces the problems of modern life: the disintegration of the human personality in a highly mechanized civilization, the loss of individual freedom under forms of government that put a premium on conformity. Nor does he deny the autonomy of art: far from postulating any direct influence of art on private morals or public affairs, he insists that its effect can only be a mediate and long-term one.

Schiller's thought

One of the most striking features of Schiller's *oeuvre* is its modernity, its startling relevance to the life of the 20th century. Although for a time he fell out of favour with the German intelligentsia, the enduring value of his work is not likely to be obscured by fashions in criticism.

MAJOR WORKS

PLAYS: *Die Räuber* (1781; *The Robbers*, trans. by A.F. Tytler, Lord Woodhouselee, 1792; and the Rev. W. Render, 1799); *Die Verschwörung des Fiesko zu Genua* (1783; *Fiesco; or The Genoese Conspiracy*, trans. by G.H. Noehden and J. Stoddart, 1796); *Kabale und Liebe* (1784; first trans. as *Cabal and Love*, 1795; *The Minister*, trans. by M.G. Lewis, 1798); *Don Carlos, Infant von Spanien* (1787; first trans. 1798; also trans. by J. Kirkup in *The Classic Theatre*, vol. 2, 1959); *Wallenstein, ein dramatisches Gedicht* (1800; trans. by C.E. Passage, and in *Schiller's Tragedies: The Piccolomini and the Death of Wallenstein*, trans. by S.T. Coleridge, 1840); *Maria Stuart* (1801; first trans. 1801; also by L.A. Rhoades, 1894; and *Mary Stuart*, trans. by S. Spender, 1959); *Die Jungfrau von Orleans* (1801; *The Maid of Orleans*, first trans. 1835; also trans. by L. Filmore, 1882); *Die Braut von Messina oder die feindlichen Brüder* (1803; *The Bride of Messina*, first trans. 1837; also trans. by A. Lodge, 1841, and, in English verse, by E. Allfrey, 1876); *Wilhelm Tell* (1804; first trans. 1829; rev. trans. by W. Peter, 1968); *Demetrius* (unfinished) (1805; trans., together with part of *The Bride of Messina* by C. Hodges, 1836).

VERSE: *Anthologie auf das Jahr 1782* (1782); *Xenien*, with Goethe (1796; both trans. in the *Complete Works*, trans. by S.T. Coleridge *et al.*, with careful revision and new translation, C.J. Hempel, 2 vol., 1870); *Gedichte*, 2 vol. (1800–03). Many of Schiller's poems are collected in *The Poems of Schiller*, trans. by E.P. Arnold Forster (1901), and *The Ballads and Shorter Poems of Frederick v. Schiller*, trans. by G. Clarke (1901), as well as in the *Complete Works*.

NOVELS: *Der Verbrecher aus Infamie* (1786, later pub. as *Der Verbrecher aus verlorener Ehre*, 1802; *The Criminal from Lost Honour*, trans. by J. Oxenford and C.A. Feiling, 1844); *Der Geisterseher* (1789; *The Apparitionist*, trans. by T. Roscoe in *The German Novelists*, vol. 3, 1826).

HISTORICAL: *Geschichte des Abfalls der vereinigten Niederlande von der Spanischen Regierung* (1788; *The History of the Defection of the United Netherlands from the Spanish Empire*, trans. by E.B. Eastwick, 1844); *Geschichte des dreissigjährigen Krieges*, 2 vol. (1791–93; *The History of the Thirty Years War in Germany*, trans. by Capt. Blaquière, 1799); *Belagerung von Antwerpen* (1794; trans. in the *Complete Works*).

PHILOSOPHICAL: "Über den Grund des Vergnügens an tragischen Gegenständen" (1792); "Über die tragische Kunst" (1792); "Über Anmut und Würde" (1793); "Über das Pathetische" (1793); all trans. in the *Complete Works*; "Briefe über die ästhetische Erziehung des Menschen" (1795; "On the Aesthetic Education of Man," trans. by E.M. Wilkinson and L.A. Willoughby, 1967); "Über naive und sentimentalische Dichtung" (1795–96); "Über das Erhabene" (1801); "Über den Gebrauch des Chors in der Tragödie" (1803); all trans. in the *Complete Works*.

BIBLIOGRAPHY. For detailed bibliographical information, see WOLFGANG VULPIUS, *Schiller-Bibliographie, 1893–1958* (1959); and R. PICK (comp.), "Schiller in England, 1787–1960: A Bibliography," *Publications of the English Goethe Society*, vol. 30 (1961). The largest collection of Schilleriana is housed in the Schiller-Nationalmuseum at Marbach. The *Jahrbuch der Deutschen Schillergesellschaft* is mainly devoted to the study of Schiller.

Two of the principal modern editions of Schiller's works are the centenary edition, the *Säkular-Ausgabe*, ed. by EDUARD VON DER HELLEN, 16 vol. (1904–05); and the *Horenausgabe*, ed. by C. SCHUDDEKOPF and C. HOFER, 22 vol. (1910–26), which presents Schiller's *oeuvre*, including most of his letters, in chronological order. The letters were edited by F. JONAS, 7 vol. (1892–96). Supplementary material that has since come to light is incorporated in the comprehensive *Nationalausgabe*, ed. by JULIUS PETERSEN *et al.* (1943–), a major critical edition designed to consist of about 40 volumes.

Schiller's style does not readily lend itself to translation into English; most of the existing English versions of his works do not rise above mediocrity. *Wallenstein* is the outstanding exception: *Die Piccolomini* and *Wallensteins Tod* were translated by Coleridge, at a time (December 1799–April 1800) when the poet, who had just returned from his visit to Germany, was still at the height of his powers. Among later contributions, a translation of the letters *On the Aesthetic Education of Man* by E.M. WILKINSON and L.A. WILLOUGHBY (1967, with elaborate commentary), deserves to be specially mentioned.

Of the many critical biographies, see THOMAS CARLYLE, *Life of Friedrich Schiller* (1825), the earliest monograph on Schiller of any lasting value; JAKOB MINOR, *Schiller*, 2 vol. (1890); OTTO HARNACK, *Schiller* (1898); EUGEN KUHNEMANN, *Schiller* (1905); KARL BERGER, *Schiller*, 2 vol. (1905–09); HERBERT CYSARZ, *Schiller* (1934); WILLIAM WITTE, *Schiller* (1949); MELITTA GERHARD, *Schiller* (1950); REINHARD BUCHWALD, *Schiller*, 2 vol., rev. ed. (1953–54); BERNHARD ZELLER, *Schiller, eine Bildbiographie* (1958), richly illustrated; GERHARD STORZ, *Der Dichter Friedrich Schiller* (1959); BENNO VON WIESE, *Schiller* (1959); EMIL STAIGER, *Friedrich Schiller* (1967). The biographies by Carlyle and Witte are in English; all others are in German.

Various special aspects of Schiller's work and personality are treated in the following: LUDWIG BELLERMANN, *Schillers Dramen*, 2 vol. (1888–91); HEINRICH DUNTZER, *Schillers lyrische Gedichte*, 3rd rev. ed. (1893); *Schillers Gespräche*, ed. by JULIUS PETERSEN (1911); MAX HECKER, *Schillers Tod und Bestattung* (1935); E.L. STAHL, *Friedrich Schiller's Drama: Theory and Practice* (1954); THOMAS MANN, *Versuch über Schiller* (1955); W.F. MAINLAND, *Schiller and the Changing Past* (1957); WILLIAM WITTE, *Schiller and Burns, and Other Essays* (1959); *Schiller Bicentenary Lectures*, ed. by FREDERICK NORMAN (1960). The reception of Schiller's works and the history of his posthumous fame up to his first centenary are richly documented in *Schiller: Zeitgenosse aller Epochen*, pt. 1, ed. by NORBERT OELLERS (1970).

(W.Wi.)

Schleiermacher, Friedrich

Friedrich Schleiermacher, widely known during his lifetime as theologian, preacher, classical philologist, and shaper of Prussian church life and culture, is generally recognized as the founder of modern Protestant theology and the most influential Protestant theologian of the 19th century. His best known work, *The Christian Faith*, is a Christian dogmatics expounding the Christian religion as an individual formation of the "feeling of absolute dependence," the original unity of knowledge and action. Through this dogmatics and other works on theology, ethics, philosophy, and art, Schleiermacher has continued to contribute to the discussion of particular problems in theology and philosophy and to present a vision of the unity of religion and culture.

By courtesy of the Staatsbibliothek, Berlin

Schleiermacher, engraving by F. Lehmann, middle of the 19th century.

He was born November 21, 1768, in Breslau, Lower Silesia (now Wrocław, Poland), the son of Gottlieb and Katharina-Maria (*née* Stubenrauch) Schleiermacher. His father, a Reformed (Calvinist) military chaplain, and his mother both came from families of clergymen. He had an older sister, Charlotte, and a younger brother, Carl.

Childhood and education

From 1783 to 1785 he attended a school of the Moravian Brethren (Herrnhuters), an influential Pietistic group, at Niesky. In this milieu, individualized study was combined with a piety based on the joy of salvation and a vividly imaginative relation with Jesus as Saviour, rather than (as in the Pietism centred in Halle) on a struggle to feel sorrow and repentance. Here Schleiermacher developed his lifelong interest in the Greek and Latin classics and his distinctive sense of the religious life. Later he called himself a Herrnhuter "of a higher order."

Yet the lifeless and dogmatic narrowness of the Moravian seminary at Barby, which he attended from 1785 to 1787, conflicted with his increasingly critical and inquiring spirit. He left in 1787 with the reluctant permission of his father, who had at first harshly rebuked him for his worldliness and accused him of hypocrisy; and at Easter he matriculated at the University of Halle. There he lived with his maternal uncle, Samuel Stubenrauch, a professor of theology, who could understand his restlessness and skepticism.

A diligent and independent student, Schleiermacher began, along with his theological studies, an intensive study of Immanuel Kant's philosophy. In his epistemology (theory of knowledge), though not in his ethics and religion, he remained a Kantian throughout his life. After two years he moved to Drossen (Ośno), near Frankfurt an der Oder, where his uncle had assumed a pastorate, and began preparing for his first theological examinations. Though he read more in ethics than in theology, he took his examinations in Reformed theology in 1790, achieving marks of "very good" or "excellent" in all fields except dogmatics, the one in which he was later to make his most original contribution.

Schleiermacher then took a position as tutor for the family of the Graf (Count) zu Dohna in Schlobitten, East Prussia. Besides tutoring, he preached regularly,

Early career

chiefly on ethical themes, and continued his philosophical study, particularly of the question of human freedom. After taking his second theological examinations in 1794, the same year in which his father died, Schleiermacher became assistant pastor in Landsberg and then, in 1796, pastor of the Charité, a hospital and home for the aged just outside Berlin. In that city he found his way into the circle of the German Romantic writers through the creator of early Romanticism, Friedrich von Schlegel, with whom he shared an apartment for a time, began a translation of Plato's works, and became acquainted with the new Berlin society.

In *Über die Religion. Reden an die Gebilden unter ihren Verächtern* (*On Religion: Speeches to Its Cultured Despisers*), written in 1799 as a kind of literary confession, Schleiermacher addressed the Romantics with the message that they were not as far from religion as they thought; for religion is the "feeling and intuition of the universe" or "the sense of the Infinite in the finite," and Christianity is one individual shaping of that feeling. This work, perennially attractive for its view of a living union of religion and culture, greatly impressed the young theologians of the time. The *Monologen* (1800; *Soliloquies*), written in a somewhat artificial rhythmic prose, presented a parallel to religion in the view of ethics as the intuition and action of the self in its individuality. The individuality of each human being is here seen as a unique "organ and symbol" of the Infinite itself.

A six-year courtship of Eleonore Grunow, unhappily married to a pastor in Berlin, ended in 1802, when Schleiermacher accepted a call to a small Reformed congregation in Stolp, Pomerania (now Słupsk, Poland), and she decided to remain with her husband; but until 1805 he continued to hope she might still consent to become his wife. In this pastorate he became aware of the deep cleavage between a church preacher and a modern man, but at the same time he came to acquire a great fondness for preaching.

Years at Halle and Berlin

In 1804 he accepted a call to be university preacher and extraordinary professor of theology at the University of Halle. As the first Reformed theologian on that Lutheran theological faculty and as a spokesman for Romantic Idealism, he met a cool reception. But the situation changed, and after a year he was made ordinary professor of theology.

In *Die Weihnachtsfeier* (1805; *Christmas Celebration*), written in the style of a Platonic dialogue, Schleiermacher adopted the definition of religion he later incorporated into *The Christian Faith.* Instead of speaking of religion as "feeling and intuition," he now called it simply "feeling"—namely, the immediate feeling that God lives and works in us as finite human beings.

Napoleon's invasion of Prussia forced Schleiermacher to leave Halle in 1807. He moved to Berlin, giving lectures on his own and travelling about to encourage national resistance; he also assisted Wilhelm von Humboldt in laying plans for the new university to be founded in Berlin. He married Henriette von Willich, the widow of a close friend of his, in 1809. In that same year he became pastor of Dreifaltigkeitskirche (Trinity Church) in Berlin and, in 1810, professor of theology at the new university, this latter position one that he retained to the end of his life.

His activities in the years following were many and varied. He lectured on theology and philosophy; he preached in Dreifaltigkeitskirche almost every Sunday until the end of his life; he was a member (from 1800) and permanent secretary of the Berlin Academy of Sciences; he carried on an extensive correspondence; and he was active in promoting the Prussian Union, which brought Lutheran and Calvinist churches into one body. His major publications during this period were the *Kurze Darstellung des theologischen Studiums* (1811; *Brief Outline of the Study of Theology*), presenting a curriculum in which the function of theology is to shape and direct the church as a religious community, and *Der christliche Glaube* (1821-22; 2nd ed. 1831; *The Christian Faith*), an original and impressively systematic treatment of Christian dogmatics.

His relations with the Prussian king were tense until 1831, partly because of differences of view concerning the Prussian constitution and the relation between church and state, and partly because of machinations of his personal rivals. At one stage, an edict of banishment was issued against him, but it was not carried out.

He preached his last sermon on February 2 and gave his last lecture on February 6, 1834. On February 12 he died from inflammation of the lungs. His death stirred the populace of the whole city; Leopold von Ranke, a famous historian, estimated that there were from 20,000 to 30,000 people in the long funeral procession through the streets of Berlin. He was buried in the cemetery of Trinity Church.

Influence

Schleiermacher's thought continued to influence theology throughout the 19th century and the early part of the 20th. Between about 1925 and 1955 it was under severe attack by followers of the "kerygmatic" theology of the Word of God (founded by Karl Barth and Emil Brunner) as leading away from the gospel toward a religion based on human culture. Since then, however, there has been a renewed study and appreciation of Schleiermacher's contributions, partly because the critique was one-sided, and partly because of a new interest in 19th-century theology.

BIBLIOGRAPHY. Schleiermacher's works, *Sämtliche Werke,* have been published in 30 volumes in three parts: 1. *Theologie,* 2. *Predigten* (sermons), 3. *Philosophie* (1835–1864). The best available study of his life and thought is MARTIN REDEKER, *Friedrich Schleiermacher* (1968), a thorough and readable work (in German) based on meticulous research. A brief and charmingly personal biography is that of MARY F. WILSON, "Biographical Sketch," in *Selected Sermons of Schleiermacher,* pp. 1–37 (1890). HUGH ROSS MACKINTOSCH, *Types of Modern Theology,* pp. 31–100 (1937), contains a critical study of Schleiermacher's thought ("The Theology of Feeling") from the point of view of a "kerygmatic" theology of the Word. TERENCE TICE, *Schleiermacher Bibliography* (1966), includes over 1900 items with introductions and annotations.

(R.P.S.)

Schleswig-Holstein

The most northerly *Land* (state) of the Federal Republic of Germany, Schleswig-Holstein has an area of 6,052 square miles (15,676 square kilometres), which constitutes 6.3 percent of the whole country. The *Land* was the home of about 2,500,000 people by the early 1970s. Less than half were urbanized and just over a quarter were of refugee origin; both factors help shape the personality of the contemporary *Land,* which is also the most Protestant in the republic. Extending from the lower course of the Elbe River and the *Land* of Freie und Hansestadt Hamburg northward to Denmark, Schleswig-Holstein occupies the southern half of the Jutland Peninsula. Its eastern coast is on the Baltic Sea and its western coast on the North Sea; on the mainland it is bounded on the east by the German Democratic Republic. This northerly location has also lent considerable character to the region. Throughout much of European history, Schleswig-Holstein has straddled strategically vital routes between Scandinavia and the south of Europe, and also those running east–west across the great expanses of the continent's northern plain. The important Kiel Canal, linking the Baltic and North seas, and the associated modern four-lane highway reflect a continuation of this role. The *Land* also includes Fehmarn, the island in the Baltic; and, in the North Sea, the islands of Sylt, Föhr, Amrum, Pellworm, Nordstrand, Helgoland, and lesser islets known as Halligen, all of the North Frisian group. The capital is at Kiel. For related information, see the articles GERMANY, HISTORY OF; BALTIC SEA; and GERMANY, FEDERAL REPUBLIC OF.

The character of the *Land*

History. The history of the area is well-known for its complexity. The two areas of Schleswig and Holstein, without much in the way of natural resources except some arable land, have at times been subject to the claims and counterclaims of Denmark, Sweden, the Holy Roman Empire, Prussia, and Austria. Internally, with Danish minorities in predominately German areas and German minorities surrounded by Danes, Schleswig-Holstein's history has been one of internal conflicts and, more recently, accommodations.

It took centuries for the two areas, separated by the Eider River, to grow together and become a unified and independent entity. Jutish, Frisian, and Saxon legal traditions existed side by side, a situation that, to some extent, continued up to 1900. This resulted in complicated social and political problems in a land confusedly divided between different forms of government but having a typically European social and constitutional structure, in which princes, the Church, nobility, towns, and peasantry all played parts of varying importance.

The histories of Schleswig and Denmark were closely connected; in the 12th century Schleswig became a dukedom and remained a fief associated (but not without dispute) with Denmark until 1864. Holstein, on the other hand, developed more independently, belonging first as a county, and then (from 1474) as a dukedom, to the Holy Roman Empire. After 1815, Holstein was incorporated in the newly formed German Federation.

The Peace of Prague (1866)

During the 1840s, issues relating to the rights of the various national minorities, to the succession rights of the Danish royal family, and to Denmark's interests in the two duchies resulted in their political future becoming involved in larger questions of European politics, particularly the rivalry between Austria and Prussia for the leadership of Germany. The result was that both the duchies were incorporated into Prussia as a single province by the Peace of Prague (1866). The incorporation was not exactly trouble free, because many Schleswig-Holstein people had hoped to set up a German state of their own. The Danish population of North Schleswig was equally discontent under Prussian rule. At the turn of the century the nationality quarrels in North Schleswig reflected similar struggles throughout Europe. The conflict lasted past World War I, until, in 1920, a plebiscite, fixed by the Treaty of Versailles, led to the establishment of borders corresponding very nearly to differences of nationality. An area of North Schleswig voted for incorporation into Denmark. The German minority in this area was consequently a cause of much unrest during the interwar years.

After World War II, Schleswig-Holstein was organized as a *Land*. The first Landtag, or Diet (legislative assembly), was elected in 1947, and a Social-Democratic government was formed. After 1950 there followed different coalitions led by the Christian Democratic Union.

Landscape. The surface features of Schleswig-Holstein were largely formed by the deposition of glacial drift as a result of the southern advance of Scandinavian ice sheets during the Pleistocene Ice Age some 2,000,000 years ago. Glacial moraines (small hills of ice-carried debris) and outwash plains with stretches of alluvium and sea marshes characterize the landscape. A rough division into eastern, central, and western regions is nevertheless possible. The hilly eastern countryside, a young moraine landscape, is rich in lakes. The loamy soil in this area brings one of the best wheat harvests in Germany. Along the Baltic coast are sheer cliffs, indented by fjords.

The three topographic zones

In the middle of the state lie the uplands, an old moraine area. The soil is so poor in this area that only in the last two centuries has it been cultivated.

In the west is flat, marshy, treeless land, which can only be partly cultivated. It is known for its numerous ditches, dikes, and ponds. West of the marshes are shallows and flats, which are exposed to the tides, creating a hazard for shipping. Some tidal flats and marshes have been reclaimed, planted to grass, and used for livestock grazing. The east coast, however, is always losing land through exposure to wind, tide, surf, and storm.

Climatically, Schleswig-Holstein lies in an area affected by the Gulf Stream. It has mild winters and temperate summers (yearly average temperature 46° F [8° C]). A high degree of humidity and high rainfall (yearly average 30 inches) make for strong vegetation growth. Strong winds, however, lead to a drying out and drifting of the upland soil.

The people. Schleswig-Holstein has about 2,500,000 inhabitants (412 per square mile [159 per square kilometre]). Thirty percent of the population is urbanized, being concentrated in Kiel (272,000), the main town and the administrative and industrial centre; and also in Lübeck, Neumünster, and Flensburg. The end of World War II brought difficult social problems as retreating army units and more than 1,000,000 evacuees and refugees (many from the east) raised the population about 50 percent above the pre-war level. Unemployment at one time reached 21 percent, but reconstruction programs and aid from the federal government have helped overcome major economic problems. There is a tendency for young workers to migrate away from the state, particularly to Hamburg.

The composition of the population has been greatly altered since World War II through the residual effects of the influx of people from Mecklenburg, East Prussia, and similar areas. This has led to a decline of dialects, although *Holsteiner Platt* (or Plattdeutsch [Low German]) is still spoken. In the north of the state, there is still a small Danish-speaking minority with its own schools. In the border districts, however, nationalistic tendencies seem to have been relaxed as an awareness of the necessity for a united western Europe has gained ground.

Schleswig-Holstein contains the highest proportion of Protestants in the German Republic—over 86 percent; Roman Catholics make up only 6 percent of the population.

The economy. Agriculture accounts for less than 10 percent of the state's net economic output, but Schleswig-Holstein still uses almost 75 percent of its total area (which is not, as a whole, well endowed by nature) for agricultural purposes. The farms of the area have been forced to rationalize their structure, partly as a result of foreign competition, and much land reform and crop specialization has taken place since 1945. Wheat, sugar beets, and potatoes are among the more common arable crops. Livestock provides a far higher proportion of farm incomes, however: a third of farm sales are derived from milk and milk products; nearly a half from pigs; and 16 percent from cattle breeding. The integration of farms, food-processing plants, and marketing concerns in one organization is increasingly characteristic of the agricultural system. Although the state is low in forest reserves, its importance as a supplier of nursery plants for the forests of other regions has caused it to be called "the cradle of German forests."

Industries are increasingly important to the *Land*'s economy. Major branches include shipbuilding, machine construction, and electrical engineering—all important in Kiel—as well as paper, textile, and clothing industries. Recently, there has been a large increase in tourism, notably from the various urban and industrialized regions in the south.

Main industries

Its long coastline and strategic location have, for centuries, made the area a focus of sea traffic. The Baltic fjords contain the large harbours of Lübeck, Kiel, and Flensburg, and the Kiel Canal, traversing Schleswig-Holstein to connect the North Sea and the Baltic, is the most heavily used in the world. About 80,000 ships pass through it annually.

Air traffic is less important, but a large airport is planned at Kaltenkirchen, near Hamburg, to meet the needs of supersonic air travel.

Administration and education. Since the 1960s there have been problems of area planning and of adjustment to the European Economic Community, of which Germany is a member. Schleswig-Holstein has begun a number of administrative reforms, including reform of its legal system. Under a 1970 reform, the number of *Landkreise* (rural districts) was reduced to 12 and that of municipalities to just under 1,300. As a result, Schleswig-Holstein has, on the average, counties with the largest area within the Federal Republic. Constitutionally, and within the federal framework, the state is headed by a chief minister, assisted by ministers who are responsible to the 73-seat legislative assembly.

The *Land* is noted for a high standard of education. The centre of the system is the historic University of Kiel, founded in 1665; a Medical Academy, in Lübeck, was added in 1964. There are also two teacher-training colleges and a number of other specialized institutions of higher learning. At a lower level, cooperative secondary schools have been built to serve the needs of scattered villages.

Cultural life and institutions. As elsewhere in the republic, the state offers generous support to several theatres and orchestras. There are also about 50 significant museums primarily concerned with local and state history. Adult education and libraries enjoy a special tradition and promotion. The Institute for World Economies at Kiel is one of the oldest economic research institutes in Europe and has a very large special library for political economy.

BIBLIOGRAPHY. CHRISTIAN DEGN and UWE MUUSS (eds.), *Topographischer Atlas Schleswig-Holstein*, 3rd ed. (1966), an excellent historical-geographical work with comprehensive bibliography; and *Luftbildatlas Schleswig-Holstein*, 2 pt. (1965–68), a readable work with economic, geographical, and historical notes and a valuable bibliography; KLAUS THIEDE (ed.), *Schleswig-Holstein: Landschaft und wirkende Kräfte* (1962), a comprehensive, illustrated survey; OLAF KLOSE (ed.), *Handbuch der historischen Stätten Deutschlands*, 2nd ed., vol. 1, *Schleswig-Holstein und Hamburg* (1964), a handy reference work; and *Geschichte Schleswig-Holsteins*, 3 vol. to date (1757–60, in progress), a standard treatment of the history of Schleswig-Holstein; OTTO BRANDT, *Geschichte Schleswig-Holsteins*, 6th ed. rev. by W. KLUVER (1966), the best introductory historical survey with extensive bibliography; *Die Wirtschaft Schleswig-Holsteins in der europäischen Integration: Ein Arbeitsprogramm der Landesregierung* (1963), a recent survey of political-economic problems; *Schleswig-Holstein* (1967), informative promotional literature with synopses in English, issued by the Ministerium für Wirtschaft und Verkehr; SCHLESWIG-HOLSTEIN STATISTICAL OFFICE, *Statistisches Jahrbuch Schleswig-Holstein* (annual), useful for contemporary statistical data.

(M.-E.V.)

Schliemann, Heinrich

Fascinated from childhood by Greek history and Homeric epics, the German businessman and archaeologist Heinrich Schliemann retired at a relatively early age, after making a fortune in international trade, in order to devote himself to the archaeology of Greece and Turkey. He discovered the sites of the ancient cities of Troy and Mycenae, and his excavations there revealed Bronze Age civilizations hitherto entirely unknown. A pioneer of Greek prehistoric archaeology, he was one of the first excavators on a major scale and one of the first to make the results of his findings widely known to the general public.

By courtesy of the Deutsche Staatsbibliothek, Berlin

Schliemann, engraving by A. Weger, after a photograph.

Born on January 6, 1822, at Neubukow, in Mecklenburg-Schwerin (now in East Germany), Schliemann was the son of a poor pastor. A picture of Troy in flames in a history book his father had given him when he was seven years old remained in his memory throughout his life and sustained his fervent belief in the historical foundations of the Homeric poems. At the age of 14 he was apprenticed to a grocer, and it was in the grocer's shop that he heard Homer declaimed in the original Greek. After several years in the shop, ill health forced him to leave, and he became a cabin boy on a ship bound from Hamburg to Venezuela. After the vessel was wrecked off the Dutch coast, he became office boy and then bookkeeper for a trading firm in Amsterdam. He had a passion and a flair for languages, as well as a remarkable memory; these factors, combined with great energy and determination, enabled him to learn to read and write fluently between eight and 13 languages—accounts vary, but his competence certainly included Russian and both ancient and modern Greek. **Business career**

In 1846 his firm sent him to St. Petersburg as an agent. There he founded a business on his own and embarked, among other things, on the indigo trade. In 1852 he married Ekaterina Lyschin. He made a fortune at the time of the Crimean War, mainly as a military contractor. In the 1850s he was in the United States and became a U.S. citizen, retaining this nationality for the rest of his life. Returning to Russia he retired from business at the age of 36 and began to devote his energies and money to the study of prehistoric archaeology, particularly the problem of identifying the site of Homeric Troy. To train himself, he travelled extensively in Greece, Italy, Scandinavia, Germany, and Syria and then went around the world, visiting India, China, and Japan (he wrote a book about the last two countries). He also studied archaeology in Paris.

In 1868 Schliemann took his large fortune to Greece, visiting Homeric sites there and in Asia Minor, and the following year he published his first book, *Ithaka, der Peloponnes und Troja* ("Ithaca, the Peloponnese, and Troy"). In this work he argued that Hisarlık, in Asia Minor, and not Bunarbashi, a short distance south of it, was the site of Troy and that the graves of the Greek commander Agamemnon and his wife, Clytemnestra, at Mycenae, described by the Greek geographer Pausanias, were not the *tholoi* (vaulted tombs) outside the citadel walls but lay inside the citadel. He was able to prove both theories by excavation in the course of the next few years. He had divorced his Russian wife, Ekaterina, and married in 1869 a young Greek schoolgirl named Sophia Engastromenos, whom he had selected through a marriage bureau.

Although some isolated discoveries had been made before he began digging, Schliemann has rightly been called "the creator of prehistoric Greek archaeology." The French geologist Ferdinand Fouqué dug at Santorin in 1862 and found fresco-covered walls of houses and painted pottery beneath 26 feet (eight metres) of pumice, the result of the great eruption that divided the original island into Thera (modern Thira) and Therasis (modern Thirasia). Geologists at that time dated the Santorin eruption to 2000 BC, which suggested a great antiquity for Fouqué's finds and the existence of prehistoric cultures hitherto unknown in the Aegean. The English archaeologist Frederick Calvert had dug at Hisarlık, and in 1871 Schliemann took up his work at this large man-made mound. He believed that the Homeric Troy must be in the lowest level of the mound, and he dug uncritically through the upper levels. In 1873 he uncovered fortifications and the remains of a city of great antiquity, and he discovered a treasure of gold jewelry, which he smuggled out of Turkey. He believed the city he had found was Homeric Troy and identified the treasure as that of Priam. His discoveries and theories, first published in *Trojanische Altertümer* (1874), were received skeptically by many scholars, but others, including the prime minister of England, William Ewart Gladstone, himself a classical scholar, and a wide public, accepted his identification. **Discovery of Homeric Troy**

When he proposed to resume work at Hisarlık in February 1874, he was delayed by a lawsuit with the Ottoman government about the division of his spoils, particularly the gold treasure, and it was not until April 1876 that he obtained permission to resume work. In 1874–76 Schliemann dug instead at the site of the Treasury of Minyas, at Orchomenus in Boeotia, but found little except the remains of a beautiful ceiling. During this delay he also published *Troja und seine Ruinen*, (1875) and began excavation at Mycenae. In August 1876, he began work in the *tholoi*, digging by the Lion Gate and then inside the citadel walls, where he found a double ring of slabs and, within that ring, five shaft graves (a sixth was found immediately after his departure). Buried with 16 bodies in this circle of shaft graves was a large treasure of gold, silver, bronze, and ivory objects. Schliemann had hoped to find—and believed he had found—the tombs of Agamemnon and Clytemnestra, and he published his finds in his *Mykenä* (1878).

After an unsuccessful excavation in Ithaca in 1878, he resumed work at Hisarlık the same year. He conducted a third excavation at Troy in 1882–83 and a fourth from 1888 until his death. In his first season he had worked alone with his wife, Sophia. In 1879 he was assisted by Emile Burnouf, a classical archaeologist, and by Rudolf Virchow, the famous German pathologist, who was also the founder of the German Society for Anthropology, Ethnology, and Prehistory. In his last two seasons Schliemann had the expert assistance of Wilhelm Dörpfeld, who was a practical architect and had worked at the German excavations at Olympia. Dörpfeld brought to Troy the new system and efficiency of the German classical archaeologists working in Greece, and he was able to expose the stratigraphy at Troy more clearly than before and to revolutionize Schliemann's techniques. In 1884, Schliemann, together with Dörpfeld, excavated the great fortified site of Tiryns near Mycenae.

Toward the end of his life, Schliemann suffered greatly with ear trouble and travelled in Europe, visiting specialists and hoping for a cure. None was forthcoming. In great pain and alone, on December 25, 1890, while walking across a square in Naples, he collapsed; he died the next day, December 26.

Assessment Schliemann's work of discovery in archaeology is easy to assess. He discovered Homeric Troy as well as a city that existed long before Homer—a prehistoric Bronze Age civilization in Turkey; this was also what he discovered at Mycenae. Hitherto, ancient historians had thought of four empires: Greece, Rome, Egypt, and Babylon-Assyria; Schliemann discovered two new civilizations and enormously lengthened the perspective of history. He nearly discovered a third, namely that of prehistoric Crete.

He had long thought that there must have existed in the Mediterranean a civilization earlier than Mycenae and Bronze Age Hisarlık, and he guessed that it might be in Crete. At one time he contemplated excavation in Crete, but he could not agree to the price asked for the land; thus, the discovery of the pre-Mycenean civilization of Minoan Crete was left to Sir Arthur Evans ten years after Schliemann's death.

Schliemann was one of the first popularizers of archaeology. His books and his dispatches to *The Times*, the *Daily Telegraph*, and other papers kept the world informed and excited by his archaeological discoveries as no one previously had been able to do. It has been said that "every person of culture and education lived through the drama of discovering Troy." Schliemann became a symbol not only of the new archaeological scholarship of the second half of the 19th century but also of the romance and excitement of archaeology. Scholars and the public were inspired by him, and, when he died, Sir John Myres, Camden Professor of Ancient History at the University of Oxford, said that to many it seemed that "the spring had gone out of the year."

When Schliemann began excavating, no corpus of accepted practice existed for archaeological fieldwork. Like Sir Flinders Petrie and Augustus Pitt-Rivers, he was a pioneer. Stratigraphy had been observed and understood in the Danish peat bogs, the Jutland barrows, and the prehistoric Swiss lake dwellings, but Hisarlık was the first large dry-land man-made mound to be dug. It is not surprising that Schliemann was at first puzzled by what he found, but, eventually, with the assistance of Dörpfeld, he was able to untangle the stratigraphy. There is a wide variation in the assessment of his technique as an excavator. He did extremely well for someone starting to dig in the 1870s, yet he is often unfairly criticized by those who are excavating similar mounds in the Near East 100 years later.

BIBLIOGRAPHY. Schliemann's own books, *Ilios* (1880) and *Troy and Its Remains* (1875), deserve reading not only for their account of his own reconnaissances and excavations but also for the autobiographical material contained. CARL SCHUCHHARDT, *Schliemanns Ausgrabungen im Lichte der heutigen Wissenschaft* (1889; Eng. trans., *Schliemann's Excavations and Archaeological and Historical Studies*, 1891), is a contemporary assessment of his role in the development of archaeology. STANLEY CASSON, *The Discovery of Man* (1939); JOHN MYRES, *The Cretan Labyrinth: A Retrospect of Aegean Research* (1933); and GLYN DANIEL, *A Hundred Years of Archaeology* (1950), give more recent assessments of his work. EMIL LUDWIG, *Schliemann of Troy: The Story of a Gold-Seeker* (1931); and ROBERT PAYNE, *The Gold of Troy* (1958), are popular and slightly sensationalized biographies. For a more balanced picture, containing much new information, see LYNN and GRAY POOLE, *One Passion, Two Loves: The Story of Heinrich and Sophia Schliemann, Discoverers of Troy* (1966).

(G.E.D.)

Schoenberg, Arnold

"Whether right or left, whether forward or backward—one must always go on without asking what lies before or behind one. That should be hidden; you ought to—nay, *must*—forget it, in order to fulfill your task." These words, spoken by the Angel Gabriel in Arnold Schoenberg's *Jakobsleiter* (*Jacob's Ladder*), might well describe the composer's entire career. Of himself he said, "I am a conservative who was forced to become a radical." Beginning as an imitator of Johannes Brahms and, even more, of Richard Wagner, he discovered and developed a principle—the method of composition with 12 tones related only to one another—that changed the course of 20th-century music.

Pictorial Parade

Schoenberg.

Schoenberg was born on September 13, 1874, in Vienna. His father, Samuel, owned a small shoe shop in the Second, then predominantly Jewish, district. Neither Samuel nor his wife Pauline (*née* Nachod) was particularly musical, although, like most Austrians of their generation, they enjoyed music. There were, however, two professional singers in the family—Heinrich Schoenberg, the composer's brother, and Hans Nachod, his cousin. Nachod, a gifted tenor, was the first to sing the role of Waldemar in Schoenberg's *Gurrelieder*.

Before he was nine years old, Schoenberg began composing little pieces for two violins, which he played with

Childhood
composi-
tions

his teacher or with a cousin. A little later, when he acquired a viola-playing classmate, he advanced to the writing of string trios for two violins and viola. His meeting
with Oskar Adler (later the famed astrologer and author
of *Das Testament der Astrologie*) was a decisive one.
Adler encouraged him to learn the cello so that a group
of friends could play string quartets. Schoenberg promptly began composing quartets, although he had to wait for
the "S" volume of *Meyers Grosses Konversations-Lexi-
kon* (an encyclopaedia that his family was buying on the
installment plan) to find out how to construct the sona-
ta-form first movement of such works. Until about his
18th year he had no models for composition other than
violin duets, opera potpourris, and band music played in
parks and beer gardens.

Schoenberg's father died in 1890. To help the family
finances, the young man worked as a bank clerk from
1891 to 1895. During this time he came to know Alexander von Zemlinsky (1872–1942), a rising young composer and conductor of the amateur orchestra Polyhym-
nia in which Schoenberg played cello. The two became
close friends, and Zemlinsky gave Schoenberg instruction
in harmony, counterpoint, and composition. This resulted in Schoenberg's first publicly performed work, the
String Quartet in D Major (1897). Highly influenced by
the style of Brahms, the quartet was well received by
Viennese audiences during the 1897–98 and 1898–99 concert seasons.

First major works.   A great step forward took place in
1899, when Schoenberg composed the string sextet *Verklärte Nacht* (*Transfigured Night*), a highly romantic
piece of program music (unified by a nonmusical story or
image). Based on a poem of the same name by Richard
Dehmel (1863–1920), it was the first piece of program
music to be written for such an ensemble. Its programmatic nature and its harmonies, surpassing even the harmonic extremes of Wagner, outraged conservative program committees. Consequently, it was not performed
until 1903, when it was violently rejected by the public.
Since then it has become one of Schoenberg's most popular compositions, both in its original form and in Schoenberg's later versions for string orchestra.

First
move to
Berlin

In 1901 Schoenberg decided to move to Berlin, hoping
to better his financial position. He married Mathilde von
Zemlinsky, his friend's sister, and began working as musical director at the Überbrettl, an intimate artistic cabaret.
He wrote many songs for this group, among them, *Nacht-
wandler* (*Sleepwalker*) for soprano, piccolo, trumpet,
snare drum, and piano (published 1969). Schoenberg did
not find this position sufficiently rewarding, either artistically or materially. The German composer Richard
Strauss (1864–1949) helped him to get a job as composition teacher at the Stern Conservatory and used his influence to secure him the Liszt stipend awarded by the All-
gemeiner Deutscher Musikverein, or Society for German
Music. With the encouragement of Strauss, Schoenberg
composed his only symphonic poem for large orchestra,
Pelleas und Melisande (1902–03), after the drama by the
Belgian writer Maurice Maeterlinck (1862–1949).

Back in Vienna in 1903, Schoenberg became acquainted with the Austrian composer Gustav Mahler (1860–
1911), who became one of his strongest supporters.
Schoenberg and Zemlinsky induced Mahler to become
the honorary president of their Verein Schaffender Ton-
künstler, or Society of Creative Musicians, founded in
March 1904. Although the society lasted but one season, it gave a number of important concerts, including
the first performance of *Pelleas und Melisande* under the
composer's direction. In a sense, this organization was a
precursor of the Society for Private Musical Performances, founded by Schoenberg in Vienna after World
War I.

Schoenberg's next major work was the *String Quartet
No. 1 in D Minor*, Opus 7 (1904). The composition's
high density of musical texture and its unusual form (the
conventional four movements of a "classic" string quartet
blended into one vast structure played without interruption for nearly 50 minutes) caused difficulties in comprehension at the work's premiere in 1907. A similar form

was used in the more concise *Chamber Symphony in E
Major* (1906), a work novel in its choice of instrumental
ensemble. Turning away from the "monster" post-Romantic orchestra, Schoenberg wrote for a chamber-like
group of 15 instruments: flute, oboe, English horn, three
clarinets, bassoon, contrabassoon, two horns, and string
quintet.

Impor-
tance as a
teacher

During these years, Schoenberg's activity as a teacher
became increasingly important. The young Austrian
composers Alban Berg (1885–1935) and Anton Webern
(1883–1945) began studying with him in 1904; both
gained from him the impetus to their notable careers. As
Webern wrote in 1912:

> People think Schoenberg teaches his own style and forces
> the pupil to adopt it. That is quite untrue—Schoenberg
> teaches no style of any kind; he preaches the use neither
> of old artistic resources nor of new ones. . . . Schoenberg
> does in fact educate his student as a creator. With the ut-
> most energy, he tracks down the pupil's personality, seeking
> to deepen it, to help it break through—in short, to give the
> pupil the courage and the strength to find an attitude to
> things which will make everything he looks at into an ex-
> ceptional case, because of the *way* he looks at it. It is an
> education in utter truthfulness with oneself. (From Willi
> Reich, *Schoenberg: A Critical Biography*; ©English trans-
> lation 1971, Longman Group Limited.)

In turn, Schoenberg benefitted greatly from the intellectual stimulation of his loyal disciples. He stated at the
beginning of his *Harmonielehre* ("Theory of Harmony";
1911), "This book I have learned from my pupils." His
great gifts as teacher are manifest in this work as well as
in his textbooks—most of them, unfortunately, published
only after his death: *Models for Beginners in Composition* (1942), *Structural Functions of Harmony* (1954),
Preliminary Exercises in Counterpoint (1963), and *Fundamentals of Musical Composition* (1967).

Evolution away from tonality.   Until this period all of
Schoenberg's works had been strictly tonal; that is, each
of them had been in a specific key, centred upon a specific
tone. However, as his harmonies and melodies became
more complex, tonality became of lesser importance. The
process of "transcending" tonality can be observed at the
beginning of the last movement of his *Second String
Quartet* (1907–08). This work is innovative in another
respect, too: it is the first string quartet to include a vocal
part (soprano; texts of last two movements by Schoenberg's contemporary, the poet Stefan George). The opening words of the Finale, "Ich fühle Luft von anderen
Planeten" ("I feel air from another planet"), have often
been symbolically interpreted in the light of Schoenberg's
breakthrough to a new world of sound.

Atonal
composi-
tions

On February 19, 1909, Schoenberg finished his piano
piece Opus 11, No. 1, the first composition ever to dispense completely with "tonal" means of organization.
Such pieces, in which no one tonal centre exists and in
which any harmonic or melodic combination of tones
may be sounded without restrictions of any kind, are
usually called "atonal." Schoenberg himself disliked
this negative-sounding term, preferring "pantonal"; but
"atonal" is still more widely used. Atonal instrumental
compositions are usually quite short; in longer vocal
compositions, the text serves as a means of unification.
Schoenberg's most important atonal compositions include *Five Orchestral Pieces*, Opus 16 (1909); the monodrama *Erwartung* (*Expectation*), a stage work for soprano and orchestra, Opus 17 (1924); *Pierrot Lunaire*,
21 recitations ("melodramas") with chamber accompaniment, Opus 21 (1912); *Die glückliche Hand* (*The
Hand of Fate*), drama with music, Opus 18 (1924); and
the unfinished oratorio *Die Jakobsleiter* (begun, 1917).

Schoenberg was aware that his new style would not be
understood. As he wrote in the program notes for the first
performance of his piano pieces Opus 11 and songs Opus
15, on January 14, 1910:

> Now that I have set out along this path once and for all,
> I am conscious of having broken through every restriction
> of a bygone aesthetic; and though the goal toward which
> I am striving appears to me a certain one, I am, nonetheless,
> already feeling the resistance I shall have to overcome; I
> feel how hotly even the least of temperaments will rise in re-
> volt, and suspect that even those who have so far believed

in me will not want to acknowledge the necessary nature of this development. . . . I am being forced in this direction not because my invention or technique is inadequate, nor because I am uninformed about all the other things the prevailing aesthetics demand, but because I am obeying an inner compulsion, one stronger than any upbringing: that I am obeying the formative process which, being the one natural to me, is stronger than my artistic education. (Also from *Schoenberg: A Critical Biography*.)

Schoenberg's earlier music was by this time beginning to find recognition. On February 23, 1913, his *Gurrelieder* (begun in 1900, orchestration completed in 1911) was first performed in Vienna. This gigantic cantata calls for unusually large vocal and orchestral forces: six solo singers (soprano, mezzo-soprano or contralto, two tenors, bass, and speaker), three four-part men's choirs, one eight-part mixed choir, and a huge orchestra of 25 woodwinds, 25 brasses, 16 percussion (including several large iron chains), and 84 strings. Along with Mahler's *Eighth Symphony* (*Symphony of a Thousand*), the *Gurrelieder* represents the peak of the post-Romantic monumental style. This music was received with wild enthusiasm by the audience, but the embittered Schoenberg could no longer appreciate or acknowledge their response.

In 1911, unable to make a decent living in Vienna, he had moved to Berlin. He remained there until 1915, when, because of wartime emergency, he had to report to Vienna for military service. He spent brief periods in the Austrian Army in 1916 and 1917, until he was finally discharged on medical grounds. During the war years he did little composing, partly because of the demands of army service and partly because he was meditating on how to solve the vast structural problems that had been caused by his move away from tonality. He wanted to find a new principle of unification that would help him to control the rich harmonic and melodic resources now at his disposal. Near the end of July 1921, Schoenberg told a pupil, "Today I have discovered something which will assure the supremacy of German music for the next 100 years." This was the method of composition with 12 tones related only to one another. Schoenberg had just begun working on his *Piano Suite*, Opus 25, the first 12-tone piece.

In the 12-tone method, each composition is formed from a special row or series of 12 different tones. This row may be played in its original form, inverted (played upside down), played backward, or played backward *and* inverted. It may also be transposed up or down to any pitch level. All of it, or any part of it, may be sounded successively as a melody or simultaneously as a harmony. In fact, all harmonies and melodies in the piece must be drawn from this row.

Although such a method might seem extremely restrictive, this did not prove to be the case. Using this technique, Schoenberg composed what many consider his greatest work, the opera *Moses und Aron* (music begun in 1930, second act finished in 1932; music for third act never composed). Music and text vividly contrast the personalities of Moses, possessed of a vision yet powerless to communicate it to his people, and Aaron, glib and fluent, who manipulates and misrepresents Moses' ideas for his own ends. Some writers have seen in this an allegory of Schoenberg and his disciples, although Schoenberg was never inarticulate.

For the rest of his life, Schoenberg continued to use the 12-tone method. Occasionally he returned to traditional tonality, for, as he liked to say, "There is still much good music to be written in C major." Among these later tonal works are the *Suite for String Orchestra* (1934); the *Variations on a Recitative for Organ*, Opus 40 (1940); and the *Theme and Variations for Band*, Opus 43A (orchestral version, Opus 43B; 1943). Schoenberg thought of school groups when writing the *Suite* and *Band Variations*, but their difficulty and sophistication make them accessible to only the best of these.

After World War I Schoenberg's music won increasing acclaim, although his invention of the 12-tone method aroused considerable opposition. Tragedy came in 1923, when his wife Mathilde died after a long illness. A year later he married Gertrud Kolisch, the sister of the violin-

Twelve-tone method

ist Rudolf Kolisch (1896–   ). His success as a teacher continued to grow. In 1925 he was invited to direct the master class in musical composition at the Prussian Academy of Arts in Berlin. The Viennese, who began to feel that they had been neglecting Schoenberg, deplored his departure. But he desired no publicity, for, as he wrote to a journalist who wanted to interview him, "My most pressing need is to depart from Vienna as unnoticed as I have always been while I was here."

It seemed that Schoenberg had reached the peak of his career. His teaching was well received, and he was writing important works: the *Third String Quartet*, Opus 30; the opera *Von Heute auf Morgen* (*From Today to Tomorrow*), Opus 32 (1928–29, first performed in 1930); the *Accompaniment to a Film Scene*, Opus 34 (1929–30); the *Cello Concerto after G.M. Monn* (1932–33); and the *Concerto for String Quartet and Orchestra after Handel* (1933). But political events proved his undoing. The rise of National Socialism in Germany in 1933 led to the extirpation of Jewish influence in all spheres of life. Schoenberg was dismissed from his post at the academy. He emigrated to the United States via Paris, where he formally returned to the Jewish faith, which he had abandoned in his youth. In November 1933 he took a position at the Malkin Conservatory in Boston, Massachusetts. Although he had talented pupils there, he was disappointed in the smallness of the institution, and the northern climate was detrimental to his health. In 1934 he moved to California, where he spent the rest of his life, taking U.S. citizenship in 1941. He held major teaching positions at the University of Southern California (1935–36) and at the University of California at Los Angeles (1936–44).

Emigration to the United States

Schoenberg's major American works show ever-increasing mastery and freedom in the handling of the 12-tone method. Some of the outstanding compositions of his American period are the *Violin Concerto*, Opus 36 (1934–36); the *Fourth String Quartet*, Opus 37 (1936); the *Piano Concerto*, Opus 42 (1942); and the *Fantasia* for violin with piano accompaniment, Opus 47 (1949). He wrote a number of works of particular Jewish interest: *Kol Nidre* for mixed chorus, speaker, and orchestra, Opus 39 (1938); *Prelude to the Genesis Suite* for orchestra and mixed chorus, Opus 44 (1945); *A Survivor from Warsaw* for speaker, male chorus, and orchestra, Opus 46 (1947); *Dreimal tausend Jahre* (*Thrice a Thousand Years*), for mixed chorus a cappella, Opus 50A (1949); and *De Profundis* (Psalm 130, set in Hebrew), also for mixed chorus a cappella, Opus 50B (1950). It was a deep disappointment to him that, because of ill health and other problems, he was unable to complete either *Die Jakobsleiter* or *Moses und Aron*.

During the last years of his life Schoenberg wrote a series of texts called "Modern Psalms." There are 16 of them, dealing with various religious and ethical problems faced by modern man. Schoenberg was able to compose only part of one of the Psalms. The unfinished work was published as *Modern Psalm*, Opus 50C.

On July 2, 1951, Hermann Scherchen, the eminent conductor of 20th-century music, conducted the "Dance Around the Gold Calf" from *Moses und Aron* at Darmstadt, West Germany, as part of the program of the Summer School for New Music. The telegram telling of the great success of this performance was one of the last things to bring Schoenberg pleasure before his death. Eleven days later, he died at his home in Los Angeles.

In 1912 Schoenberg had prophesied concerning his own work: "The second half of this century will spoil by overestimation whatever the first half's underestimation left unspoilt." Certainly, no overestimation occurred after Schoenberg's death. Rather, there was a more just appraisal of the historic importance of his music and teaching. He did not live to see the revolution in electronic music, yet it could not have taken place without his horizon-expanding activities. To him can be applied (as did his pupil Alban Berg) the words of the German musical historian Hugo Riemann on J.S. Bach:

One of the greatest masters of all times, one of those who cannot be surpassed because in them is embodied the musical feeling and thinking of an entire epoch. He gains a special importance, an unexampled greatness because in him the styles of two different ages reached their peak, so that he stands between them like a towering landmark.

MAJOR WORKS

Orchestral music

Pelleas und Melisande, symphonic poem, op. 5 (1902–03); *First Chamber Symphony*, op. 9 (1906); *Second Chamber Symphony*, op. 38 (1906–39); *Five Orchestral Pieces*, op. 16 (1909); *Variations for Orchestra*, op. 31 (1928); *Suite for String Orchestra* (1934); *Violin Concerto*, op. 36 (1934–36); *Piano Concerto*, op. 42 (1942).

Chamber music

STRING SEXTET: *Verklärte Nacht*, op. 4 (1899).
STRING QUARTETS: *Quartet in D Major* (1897); *No. 1 in D Minor*, op. 7 (1905); *No. 2 in F Sharp Minor*, op. 10 (1907–08), with soprano voice in the last movement; *No. 3*, op. 30 (1927); *No. 4*, op. 37 (1936).
STRING TRIO: op. 45 (1946).
CHAMBER ENSEMBLE: *Wind Quintet*, op. 26 (1923–24); *Suite for Seven Instruments*, op. 29 (1925).
VIOLIN AND PIANO: *Fantasia*, op. 47 (1949).
PIANO SOLO: *Three Piano Pieces*, op. 11 (1909); *Five Piano Pieces*, op. 23 (1920–23); *Piano Suite*, op. 25 (1921–23).

Vocal music

STAGE WORKS: *Erwartung*, monodrama, op. 17 (1924); *Die glückliche Hand*, drama with music, op. 18 (1924); *Von Heute auf Morgen*, opera in one act, op. 32 (1930); *Moses und Aron*, opera (unfinished; begun 1930).
VOICE AND ORCHESTRA: *Gurrelieder* (1900–11); *Pierrot Lunaire*, op. 21 (1912); *Die Jakobsleiter*, oratorio (unfinished; 1917); *Kol Nidre*, for speaker, mixed chorus, and orchestra, op. 39 (1938); *A Survivor from Warsaw*, for speaker, chorus, and orchestra, op. 46 (1947).
VOICE AND INSTRUMENTS: *Das Buch der hängenden Gärten*, for voice and piano (on poems by S. George), op. 15 (1908–09); *Herzgewächse*, for soprano, celesta, harmonium, and harp, op. 20 (1911); *Serenade*, for bass voice and seven instruments, op. 24 (1923); *Ode to Napoleon Buonaparte*, for speaker, string quartet, and piano, op. 41 (1942).
CHOIR: *Four Pieces for Mixed Chorus*, op. 27 (1925); *Three Satires for Mixed Chorus*, op. 28 (1925); *Six Pieces for Male Chorus*, op. 35 (1930).
SONGS: *Four Songs*, op. 2 (1898–1900), including "Erhebung," no. 3; *Six Songs*, op. 3 (1898–1900), including "Warnung," no. 3; "Hochzeitslied," no. 4; and "Geübtes Herz," no. 5; *Eight Songs*, op. 6 (1905), including "Mädchenlied," no. 3; "Verlassen," no. 4; and "Ghasel," no. 5.

Literary works

Harmonielehre (1911; *The Theory of Harmony*, 1947); "Compositions with Twelve Tones" in *Style and Idea*, ed. by DIKA NEWLIN (1941); *Models for Beginners in Composition* (1942); *Structural Functions of Harmony* (1954); *Preliminary Exercises in Counterpoint* (1963); *Fundamentals of Musical Composition* (1967).

BIBLIOGRAPHY. JOSEF RUFER, *Das Werk Arnold Schönbergs* (1959; Eng. trans., *The Works of Arnold Schoenberg*, 1962), a catalog of Schoenberg's compositions, writings, and paintings, lists both published and unpublished materials. Schoenberg bequeathed many manuscripts and letters to the Library of Congress, Washington, D.C. Among them is the original manuscript of his *Quartet in D Major*. The North Texas State University, Denton, Texas, holds the Schoenberg-Nachod Collection, which comprises correspondence between Schoenberg and his cousin Hans Nachod, as well as many early manuscript compositions. A partial description of the collection is found in DIKA NEWLIN, "The Schoenberg-Nachod Collection: A Preliminary Report," *The Musical Quarterly*, 54:34–41 (1968).

Correspondence: ERWIN STEIN (ed.), *Arnold Schönberg: Ausgewählte Briefe* (1958; Eng. trans., *Letters*, 1964), provides a good selection of the correspondence.

Biographical and critical studies: DIKA NEWLIN, *Bruckner-Mahler-Schoenberg* (1947), a standard work, is the first study in English of the relationship among these composers. EGON WELLESZ, *Arnold Schönberg* (1921; Eng. trans., 1925, reprinted 1969), the first biography of the composer, covers his works through 1923 (the first 12-tone compositions). This version must be used with caution because of many mistakes in translation. H.H. STUCKENSCHMIDT, *Arnold Schönberg* (1951; Eng. trans., *Arnold Schoenberg*, 1959), is sketchy, but the first biography to cover Schoenberg's entire life. WILLI REICH, *Arnold Schönberg* (1968; Eng. trans., *Schoenberg: A Critical Biography*, 1971), has no musical examples, but is especially rich in citations of contemporary documents. RENE LEIBOWITZ, *Schoenberg et son école* (1947; Eng. trans.,

Schoenberg and His School, 1949, reprinted 1970), introduced French readers to the music of the Neo-Viennese School. KARL H. WORNER, *Gotteswort und Magie, die Oper "Moses und Aron" von Arnold Schönberg* (1959; Eng. trans., *Schoenberg's "Moses and Aaron,"* 1963), is a thorough study of both the musical and philosophical-theological aspects. MERLE ARMITAGE (ed.), *Schoenberg: A Symposium* (1937), contains essays varying greatly in quality, but provides some interesting insights into the composer. ARNOLD SCHOENBERG, *Style and Idea*, trans. and ed. by DIKA NEWLIN (1950), comprises essays from many periods of Schoenberg's life, including "Composition with Twelve Tones," which has not been surpassed as a lucid and economical presentation of its subject.

(D.N.)

Scholasticism

From the time of the Renaissance until at least the beginning of the 19th century, the term "Scholasticism," not unlike the name "Middle Ages," was used as an expression of blame and contempt. The medieval period was widely viewed as an insignificant intermezzo between Greco-Roman antiquity and modern times, and Scholasticism was normally taken to describe a philosophy busied with sterile subtleties, written in bad Latin, and above all subservient to the theology of popery. Even the German Idealist Hegel, in his *Vorlesungen über die Geschichte der Philosophie* (1833–36; Eng. trans., *Lectures on the History of Philosophy*, 1892–96), declared that he would "put on seven-league boots" in order to skip over the thousand years between the 6th and 17th centuries; and having at last arrived at Descartes, said that now he could "cry land like the sailor." In those same first decades of the 19th century, on the other hand, the Romanticists swung the pendulum sharply to the opposite side, to an indiscriminate overestimation of everything medieval.

Today, scholars seem better able to confront the medieval epoch, as well as Scholasticism—*i.e.*, its philosophy (and theology)—without prejudgments. One reason for this state of affairs is the voluminous research which has been devoted to this era and which has revealed its true nature, not only as a respectable continuation of the genuinely philosophical tradition but also as a period of exemplary personalities quite able to stand comparison with any of the great philosophers of antiquity or of modern times.

NATURE AND SIGNIFICANCE

Scholasticism is so much a many-sided phenomenon that, in spite of intensive research, scholars still differ considerably in their definition of the term and in the emphases that they place on individual aspects of the phenomenon. Some historians, seeming almost to capitulate to the complexity of the subject, confine themselves to the general point that Scholasticism can only be defined denotatively as that kind of philosophy that during the European Middle Ages was taught in the Christian schools. The question of its connotation, however, remains, viz., What kind of philosophy was it?

The answer that Scholasticism was "school" philosophy and, in fact, "Christian" school philosophy can be understood only by examining the historical exigencies that created the need for schools. The search thus leads the inquirer back to the transition from antiquity to the Middle Ages—a point which, according to Hegel, was marked by the symbolic date AD 529, when a decree of the Christian emperor Justinian closed the Platonic Academy in Athens and sealed "the downfall of the physical establishments of pagan philosophy." In that same year, however, still another event occurred, which points much less to the past than to the coming age and, especially, to the rise of Scholasticism, viz., the foundation of Monte Cassino, the first Benedictine abbey, above one of the highways of the great folk migrations. This highly symbolic fact suggests not only the initial shift of the scene of the intellectual life from places like the Platonic Academy to the cloisters of Christian monasteries, but it marks even more a change in the dramatis personae. New nations were about to overrun the Roman Empire and its Hellenistic culture with long-range effects: when, centuries lat-

Barbarians' need for school learning

er, for example, one of the great Scholastics, Thomas Aquinas, was born, though he was rightly a southern Italian, his mother was of Norman stock, and his Sicilian birthplace was under central European (Hohenstaufen) control.

It was a decisive and astonishing fact that the so-called barbarian peoples who penetrated from the north into the ancient world often became Christians and set out to master the body of tradition that they found, including the rich harvest of patristic theology as well as the philosophical ideas of the Greeks and the political wisdom of the Romans. This learning could be accomplished only in the conquered empire's language (*i.e.*, in Latin), which therefore had to be learned first. In fact, the incorporation of both a foreign vocabulary and a different mode of thinking and the assimilation of a tremendous amount of predeveloped thought was the chief problem that confronted medieval philosophy at its beginnings. And it is only in the light of this fact that one of the decisive traits of medieval Scholasticism becomes understandable: Scholasticism above all was an unprecedented process of learning, literally a vast "scholastic" enterprise that continued for several centuries. Since the existing material had to be ordered and made accessible to learning and teaching, the very prosaic labour and "schoolwork" of organizing, sorting, and classifying materials inevitably acquired an unprecedented importance. Consequently, the writings of medieval Scholasticism quite naturally lack the magic of personal immediacy, for schoolbooks leave little room for originality. It is therefore misleading, though understandable, that certain polemicists have wrongly characterized Scholasticism as involving no more than the use of special didactic methods or a narrow adherence to traditional teachings.

First of all, if the major historical task of that epoch was really to learn, to acquire, and to preserve the riches of tradition, a certain degree of "scholasticity" was not only inevitable but essential. It is not at all certain that today's historians would have direct intellectual access to Plato, Aristotle, and Augustine had the Scholastics not done **Desirability** their patient spadework. Besides, the progress from the **of** stage of mere collection of given sentences and their in- **Scholasti-** terpretation (*expositio, catena, lectio*), to the systematic **cism** discussion of texts and problems (*quaestio, disputatio*), and finally to the grand attempts to give a comprehensive view of the whole of attainable truth (*Summa*) was necessarily at the same time a clear progression toward intellectual autonomy and independence, which in order to culminate, as it did in the 13th century, in the great works of Scholasticism's Golden Age, required in addition the powers of genius, of men like Albertus Magnus and Thomas Aquinas.

On the other hand, the moment had to come when the prevalent preoccupation with existing knowledge would give way to new questions, which demanded consideration and answers that could emerge only from direct experience. By the later Middle Ages, procedures for exploiting and discussing antecedent stocks of insight had been largely institutionalized, and it was an obvious temptation to perpetuate the dominion of those procedures—which could lead only to total sterility. It is widely agreed that this is almost exactly what did happen in the 14th century in what is called the "decline" and disintegration of Scholasticism.

HISTORY AND ISSUES

Roots of Scholasticism. From the beginning of medieval Scholasticism the natural aim of all philosophical endeavour to achieve the "whole of attainable truth" was clearly meant to include also the teachings of Christian faith, an inclusion which, in the very concept of Scholasticism, was perhaps its most characteristic and distinguishing element. Although the idea of including faith was expressed already by Augustine and the early church fathers, the principle was explicitly formulated by **Boethius** pivotal, early 6th-century scholar Boethius. Born in **and** Rome and educated in Athens, Boethius was one of the **Cassio-** great mediators and translators, living on the narrow **dorus** no-man's-land that divided the epochs. His famous book,

The Consolation of Philosophy, was written while he, indicted for treachery and imprisoned by King Theodoric the Goth, awaited his own execution. It is true that the book is said to be, aside from the Bible, one of the most translated, most commented upon, and most printed books in world history; and that Boethius made (unfinished) plans to translate and to comment upon, as he said, "every book of Aristotle and all the dialogues of Plato." But the epithet that he won as "one of the founders of Scholasticism" refers to quite another side of his work. Strictly speaking, it refers to the last sentence of a very short tractate on the Holy Trinity, which reads, "As far as you are able, join faith to reason"—an injunction which in fact was to become, for centuries, the formal foundation of Scholasticism. Instead of "faith," such concepts as revelation, authority, or tradition could be (and, indeed, have been) cited; and "reason," though unambiguously meant to designate the natural powers of human cognition, could also be granted (and, in fact, has been granted) very different meanings. In any case, the connection between faith and reason postulated in this principle was from the beginning and by its very nature a highly explosive compound.

Boethius himself already carried out his program in a rather extraordinary way: though his *Opuscula sacra* ("Sacred Works") dealt almost exclusively with theological subjects, there was not a single Bible quotation in them: logic and analysis was all.

Though called the "first Scholastic," Boethius was at the same time destined to be for almost a millennium the last layman in the field of European philosophy. His friend Cassiodorus, author of the *Institutiones*, an unoriginal catalog of definitions and subdivisions, which (in spite of their dryness) became a source book and mine of information for the following centuries, who, like Boethius, occupied a position of high influence at the court of Theodoric and was also deeply concerned with the preservation of the intellectual heritage, decided in his later years to quit his political career and to live with his enormous library in a monastery. This fact again is highly characteristic of the development of medieval Scholasticism: intellectual life needs not only teachers and students and not only a stock of knowledge to be handed down; there is needed a certain guaranteed free area within human society as well, a kind of sheltered enclosure, within which the concern for "nothing but truth" can exist and unfold. The Platonic Academy, as well as (for a limited time) the court of Theodoric, had been enclosures of this kind; but in the politically unsettled epoch to come "no plant would thrive except one that germinated and grew in the cloister."

The principle of the conjunction of faith and reason, which Boethius had proclaimed, and the way in which he himself carried it out were both based on a profound and explicit confidence in man's natural intellectual capacity—a confidence that could possibly lead one day to the rationalistic conviction that there cannot be anything that exceeds the power of human reason to comprehend, not even the mysteries of divine revelation. To be sure, the great thinkers of Scholasticism, in spite of their emphatic affirmation of faith and reason, consistently rejected any such rationalistic claim. But it must nonetheless be admitted that Scholasticism on the whole, and by virtue of its basic approach, contained within itself the danger of an overestimation of rationality, which recurrently emerged throughout its history.

On the other hand, there had been built in, from the beginning, a corrective and warning, which in fact kept the internal peril of Rationalism within bounds, viz., the **The** corrective exercised by the "negative theology" of the **Pseudo-** so-called Pseudo-Dionysius, around whose writings re- **Dionysius** volved some of the strangest events in the history of Western culture. The true name of this protagonist is, in spite of intensive research, unknown. Probably it will remain forever an enigma why the author of several Greek writings (among them *On the Divine Names*, "On the Celestial Hierarchy," and *The Mystical Theology*) called himself "Dionysius the Presbyter" and, to say the least, suggested that he was actually Denis the Areopagite, a disciple of Paul the Apostle (Acts). In reality, almost all historians agree that "Pseudo-Dionysius," as he came to be called, was probably a Syrian Neoplatonist, a contemporary of Boethius. Whatever the truth of the matter may be, his writings exerted an inestimable influence for more than 1,000 years by virtue of the somewhat surreptitious quasi-canonical authority of their author, whose books were venerated, as has been said, "almost like the Bible itself." A 7th-century Greek theologian, Maximus the Confessor, wrote the first commentaries on these writings, which were followed over the centuries by a long succession of commentators, among them Albertus Magnus and Thomas Aquinas. The main fact is that the unparalleled influence of the Areopagite writings preserved in the Latin West an idea, which otherwise could have been repressed and lost (since it cannot easily be coordinated with rationality)—that of a negative theology or philosophy that could act as a counterpoise against Rationalism. It could be called an Eastern idea present and effective in the Occident. But after the Great Schism, which erected a wall between East and West that lasted for centuries, Denis the Areopagite, having become himself (through translations and commentaries) a Westerner "by adoption," was the only one among all of the important Greco-Byzantine thinkers who penetrated into the schools of Western Christendom. Thus negative theology was brought to medieval Scholasticism, as it were, through the back door.

The most important book of Denis, which dealt with the names that can be applied to God, exemplified his negative theology. It maintained first of all the decidedly biblical thesis that no appropriate name can be given to God at all unless he himself reveals it. But then Denis showed that even the revealed names, since they must be comprehensible to man's finite understanding, cannot possibly reach or express the nature of God; and that in consequence, every affirmative statement about God requires at once the corrective of the coordinate negation. The theologian cannot even call God "real" or "being," because he derives these concepts from the things to which God has given reality; and the Creator cannot possibly be of the same nature as that which he has created. Thus, *The Mystical Theology* concluded by finally relativizing also the negations, because God surpasses anything that man may possibly say of him, whether it be affirmative or negative.

Scholasticism certainly could have learned all of this also from Augustine, who repeatedly warned that "Whatever you understand cannot be God." But probably an authority of even greater weight than Augustine was needed to counteract a reason that was tending to overrate its own powers; and this authority was attributed, although falsely, to the works of Denis the Areopagite. This impact could, of course, not be restricted to the idea of God; it necessarily concerned and changed man's whole conception of the world and of existence. The influence of Denis is reflected in the noteworthy fact that Thomas Aquinas, for instance, not only employed more than 1,700 quotations from Denis the Areopagite but also appealed almost regularly to his work whenever he spoke, as he often did (and in astonishingly strong terms), of the inexhaustible mystery of being. Thomas Aquinas, however, who also wrote a remarkable commentary on Denis' book *On the Divine Names,* is mentioned here only as an example, albeit a most telling example.

At the very end of the medieval era of Scholasticism, the Areopagite emerged once more in the work of a 15th-century cardinal, Nicholas of Cusa, also known as a mathematician and advocate of experimental knowledge, in whose library there are preserved several translations of the Areopagite writings—replete, moreover, with marginal notes in the Cardinal's handwriting. But even without this concrete evidence, it would be quite plain that Cusanus' doctrine of "knowing nonknowing" is closely linked to the Areopagite's conviction that all of reality is unfathomable.

Erigena's translation The translation into Latin of the *Corpus Areopagiticum,* which was made in the 9th century—*i.e.,* some 400 years after the death of its author—by John Scotus Erigena, is itself worthy of mention, especially because the translator was one of the most remarkable figures of early medieval philosophy. After generations of brave and efficient collectors, organizers, and schoolmasters had come and gone, Erigena, in his *De divisione natura* ("On the Division of Nature"), developed the Dionysian Neoplatonism on his own and tried to construct a systematic conception of the universe, a more or less pantheistic world view, which (as Gilson says) for a moment offered the Latin West the opportunity—or the temptation—to choose the way of the East once and for all. The church, though not until centuries later, condemned the book, apparently convinced that any counterpoise to its own position can become dangerous in itself.

Early Scholastic period. If there was any philosophical-theological thinker of importance during the Middle Ages who remained untouched by the spirit of the Areopagite, it was the 11th-century Benedictine Anselm of Canterbury, a highly cultivated Franco-Italian theologian who for years was prior and abbot of the abbey Le Bec in Normandy and then became, somewhat violently, the archbishop of Canterbury. In Anselm's entire work there is not a single quotation from Denis; not even the name is mentioned. Consequently, Anselm's thinking, thus freed from the corrective embodied in the Areopagite's negative theology, displayed a practically unlimited confidence in the power of human reason to illuminate even the mysteries of Christian faith; he thus frequently approached a kind of Rationalism, which did not shrink from the attempt to demonstrate, on compelling rational grounds, that salvation (for example) through God incarnate was philosophically necessary. To be sure, a theologian such as Anselm certainly would never have subscribed to the extreme thesis that nothing exists that is beyond the power of human reason to comprehend: the two famous phrases, coined by him and expressing again, in a grandiose formulation, the principle of Boethius, "faith seeking to be understood" and "I believe in order to understand," clearly proclaim his faith in the mysteries of revelation as comprising the very basis of all reasoning. Nevertheless, in the case of Anselm, the very peculiar conjunction of faith and reason was accomplished not so much through any clear intellectual coordination as through the religious energy and saintliness of an unusual personality. It was accomplished, so to speak, rather as an act of violence, which could not possibly last. The conjunction was bound to break up, with the emphasis falling either on some kind of Rationalism or on a hazardous irrationalization of faith.

Anselm's belief in human reason

That this split did actually happen can be read to some extent in the fate of the "Anselmic argument," which Kant, 700 years later, was to reject as the "ontological proof of God"—connecting it, however, not with the name of Anselm but with that of Descartes, the earliest modern philosopher. It is, in fact, significant that Descartes, in his proof of the existence of God, imagined that he was saying the same thing as Anselm, and that, on the other hand, Anselm would scarcely have recognized his own argument had he encountered it in the context of Descartes's *Discours de la méthode* (1637; *Discourse on Method,* 1950), which claims to be "pure" philosophy based upon an explicit severance from the concept of God held by faith. But given Anselm's merely theoretical starting point, that severance was not only to be expected; it was almost inevitable.

But, also within the framework of medieval Scholasticism, a dispute was always brewing between the dialecticians, who emphasized or overemphasized reason, and those who stressed the suprarational purity of faith. Berengar of Tours, an 11th-century logician, metaphysician, and theologian, who was fond of surprising formulations, maintained the pre-eminence of thinking over any authority holding, in particular, that the real Presence of Christ in the Eucharist was logically impossible. His contemporary the Italian Hermit-monk and cardinal Peter Damian, however—who was apparently the first to use the ill-famed characterization of philosophy as the "handmaid of theology"—replied that, if God's omnipotence

Bernard
and
Abelard

acts against the principle of contradiction, then so much the worse for the science of logic. Quite analogous to the foregoing controversy, though pitched on a much higher intellectual level, was the bitter fight that broke out almost one century later between a Cistercian reformer, Bernard of Clairvaux, and a logician and theologian, Peter Abelard. Bernard, a vigorous and ambivalent personality, was in the first place a man of religious practice and mystical contemplation, who, at the end of his dramatic life, characterized his odyssey as that of *anima quaerens Verbum,* "a soul in search of the Word." Although he by no means rejected philosophy on principle, he looked with deep suspicion upon the primarily logical approach to theology espoused by Abelard. "This man," said Bernard, "presumes to be able to comprehend by human reason the entirety of God."

Logic was at that time, as a matter of fact, the main battleground of all Scholastic disputations. "Of all philosophy, logic most appealed to me," said Abelard, who by "logic" understood primarily a discipline not unlike certain present-day approaches, the "critical analysis of thought on the basis of linguistic expression." From this viewpoint (of linguistic logic), Abelard also discussed with penetrating sharpness the so-called "problem of universals," which asks, Is there an "outside" and objective reality standing, for example, not only for the name "Socrates" but also for such common names as "man," "canineness," and the like? Or do common concepts ("universals") possess only the reality of subjective thought or perhaps merely that of the sound of the word? As is well known, it has been asserted that this was the principal, or even the only, subject of concern in medieval Scholasticism—a charge that is misleading, although the problem did greatly occupy philosophers from the time of Boethius. Their main concern from the beginning was the whole of reality and existence.

Hugh's
summa
and
Lombard's
Sentences

The advance of medieval thought to a highly creative level was foreshadowed, in those very same years before Peter Abelard died, by Hugh of Saint-Victor (an Augustinian monk of German descent), when he wrote *De sacramentis Christianae fidei* ("On the Sacraments of the Christian Faith"), the first book in the Middle Ages that could rightly be called a *summa;* in its introduction, in fact, the term itself is used as meaning a comprehensive view of all that exists (*brevis quaedam summa omnium*). To be sure, its author stands wholly in the tradition of Augustine and the Areopagite; yet he is also the first medieval theologian who proclaims an explicit openness toward the natural world. Knowledge of reality is, in his understanding, the prerequisite for contemplation; each of the seven liberal arts aims "to restore God's image in us." "Learn everything," he urged; "later you will see that nothing is superfluous."

It was on this basic that the university—which was not the least of the achievements of medieval Scholasticism—was to take shape. And it was the University of Paris, in particular, that for some centuries was to be the most representative university of the West. Though there are usually a variety of reasons and causes for such a development, in this case the importance of the university—unlike that of Bologna and also of Oxford—lay mainly in the fact that it was founded in the most radical way upon those branches of knowledge that are "universal" by their very nature: upon theology and philosophy. It is, thus, remarkable, though not altogether surprising, that there seems to have existed not a single *summa* of the Middle Ages that did not, in some way or other, derive from the University of Paris.

Strangely enough, the classical theological-philosophical textbook used in the following centuries at the universities of the West was not the first *summa,* composed by Hugh of Saint-Victor, but was instead a work by Peter Lombard, a theologian who probably attended Abelard's lectures and who became *magister* at the cathedral school of Notre-Dame and, two decades later, bishop of Paris. Lombard's famous *Four Books of Sentences,* which, though written one or two decades later than Hugh's *summa,* belonged to an earlier historical species, contained about 1,000 texts from the works of Augustine,

which comprise nearly four-fifths of the whole. Much more important than the book itself, however, were the nearly 250 commentaries on it, by which—into the 16th century—every master of theology had to begin his career as a teacher. In view of this wide usage, it is not astonishing that Lombard's book underwent some transformations, at the hands, for instance, of its most ingenious commentator, Thomas Aquinas, but also (and even more so) at the hands of Duns Scotus in his *Opus Oxoniense,* which, in spite of being a work of extremely personal cast, was outwardly framed as a commentary on the "Master of Sentences."

Maturity of Scholasticism. Clearly, the world view of Western Christendom, on the whole Augustinian and Platonic in inspiration and founded upon Lombard's "Augustine breviary," was beginning to be rounded out into a system and to be institutionalized in the universities. At the very moment of its consolidation, however, an upheaval was brewing that would shake this novel conception to its foundations: the main works of Aristotle, hitherto unknown in the West, were being translated into Latin—among them his *Metaphysics,* the *Physics,* the *Nichomachean Ethics,* and the books *On the Soul.* These writings were not merely an addition of something new to the existing stock; they involved an enormous challenge. Suddenly, a new, rounded, coherent view of the world was pitted against another more-or-less coherent traditional view; and because this challenge bore the name of Aristotle, it could not possibly be ignored, for Aristotle's books on logic, translated and equipped with commentaries by Boethius, had for centuries been accepted as one of the foundations of all culture. During the lifetime of Abelard the full challenge of the Aristotelian work had not yet been presented, though it had been developing quietly along several paths, some of which were indeed rather fantastic. For instance, most of the medieval Latin translations of Aristotle stem not from the original Greek but from earlier Arabic translations.

The
renascence
of
Aristotle

Within the Western Christendom of the 2nd millennium, a wholly new readiness to open the mind to the concrete reality of the world had arisen, a view of the universe and life that resembled the Aristotelian viewpoint. The tremendous eagerness with which this new philosophy was embraced was balanced, however, by a deep concern lest the continuity of tradition and the totality of truth be shattered by the violence of its assimilation. And this danger was enhanced by the fact that Aristotle's works did not come alone; they came, in fact, accompanied by the work of Arabic commentators and their heterodox interpretations.

The most influential Arabic commentators were an 11th-century polymath, Avicenna, a Persian by birth, and a 12th-century philosopher, Averroës, born in Spain. Avicenna, personal physician to sovereigns, but also a philosopher and theologian, read—according to his own account—Aristotle's *Metaphysics* 40 times without understanding it, until he learned the text by heart. F.C. Copleston has called him "the real creator of a Scholastic system in the Islāmic world." In the view of Averroës, who was not only a philosopher but also a jurist and a doctor, Aristotle's philosophy represented simply the perfection of human knowledge; and to the West, he himself was to become *the* commentator. A third great commentator was a 12th-century orthodox Jewish philosopher, Moses Maimonides, also born in Spain, who wrote his main works in Arabic. Maimonides was at the same time a vigorous adherent of the Aristotelian world view and was, thus, confronted by the same unending task that preoccupied the great teachers of medieval Christendom. At first sight it appears strange that none of these three thinkers had any appreciable influence within his own world (neither Islām nor Judaism knew of any such thing as a "discovery" of Aristotle), whereas on almost every page of the 13th-century Christian *summae* the names of Avicenna, Averroës, and Maimonides are found.

The first theologian of the Middle Ages who boldly accepted the challenge of the new Aristotelianism was a 13th-century Dominican, Albertus Magnus, an encyclo-

Albertus
Magnus
and
Aristote-
lianism

pedic scholar. Although he knew no Greek, he conceived a plan of making accessible to the Latin West the complete works of Aristotle, by way of commentaries and paraphrases; and, unlike Boethius, he did carry out this resolve. He also penetrated and commented upon the works of the Areopagite; he was likewise acquainted with those of the Arabs, especially Avicenna; and he knew Augustine. Nevertheless, he was in no wise primarily a man of bookish scholarship; his strongest point, in fact, was the direct observation of nature and experimentation. After having taught for some years at the University of Paris, he travelled, as a Dominican superior, through almost all of Europe. Not only was he continually asking questions of fisherman, hunters, beekeepers, and birdcatchers but he himself also bent his sight to the things of the visible world. But amidst the most palpable descriptions of bees, spiders, and apples, recorded in two voluminous books on plants and animals, Albertus formulated completely new, and even revolutionary, methodological principles: for instance, "There can be no philosophy about concrete things," or, "in such matters only experience can provide certainty."

With Albertus, the problem of the conjunction of faith and reason had suddenly become much more difficult, because reason itself had acquired a somewhat new meaning. "Reason" implied, in his view, not only the capacity for formally correct thinking, for finding adequate creatural analogies to the truths of revelation, but it implied, above all, the capacity to grasp the reality that man encounters. Henceforth, the Boethian principle of "joining faith with reason" would entail the never-ending task of bringing belief into a meaningful coordination with the incessantly multiplying stock of natural knowledge of man and the universe. Since Albertus' nature, however, was given more to conquest than to the establishment of order, the business of integrating all of these new and naturally divergent elements into a somewhat consistent intellectual structure waited for another man, for his pupil Thomas Aquinas.

Thomas
Aquinas

To epitomize the intellectual task that Aquinas set for himself, the image of Odysseus' bow, which was so difficult to bend that an almost superhuman strength was needed, is fitting. As a young student at the University of Naples, he had met in the purest possible form both extremes, which, though they seemed inevitably to be pulling away from one another, it was nevertheless his life's task to join: one of these extremes was the dynamic, voluntary poverty movement whose key word was "the Bible"; and the second phenomenon was the Aristotelian writings and outlook, which at that time could have been encountered nowhere else in so intensive a form. And "Aristotle" meant to Thomas not so much an individual author as a specific world view, viz., the affirmation of natural reality as a whole, including man's body and his natural cognitive powers. To be sure, the resulting *Summa theologiae* (which Thomas himself chose to leave incomplete) was a magnificent intellectual structure; but it was never intended to be a closed system of definitive knowledge. Thomas could no longer possess the magnificent naïveté of Boethius, who had considered it possible to discuss the Trinitarian God without resorting to the Bible, nor could he share Anselm's conviction that Christian faith so completely concurred with natural reason that it could be proved on compelling rational grounds.

In the meanwhile, the poles of the controversy—the biblical impulses, on the one hand, and the philosophical and secular ones, on the other—had begun to move vigorously apart, and partisans moving in both directions found some encouragement in Thomas himself. But in his later years he realized that the essential compatibility as well as the relative autonomy of these polar positions and the necessity for their conjunction had to be clarified anew by going back to a deeper root of both; that is, to a more consistent understanding of the concepts of creation and createdness. At Paris, he had to defend his own idea of "a theologically based worldliness and a theology open to the world" not only against the secularistic "philosophism" of Siger of Brabant, a stormy member of the faculty of arts, and against an aggressive group of heterodox Aristotelians around him, but also (and even more) against the traditional (Augustinian) objection that by advocating the rights of all natural things Thomas would encroach upon the rights of God, and that, besides, the theologian needs to know only that part of creation that is pertinent to his theological subject. The latter idea was supported also by the Italian mystical theologian Bonaventura, who, in his earlier days as a colleague of Thomas at the university, had likewise been enamoured of Aristotle, but later, alarmed by the secularism that was growing in the midst of Christendom, became more mistrustful of the capacities of natural reason. Thomas answered this objection in somewhat the following way: The benefit that the theologian may derive from an investigation of natural reality cannot be determined in advance, but, in general, faith presupposes and therefore needs natural knowledge of the world; at times, an error concerning the creation leads men astray also from the truth of faith. This may sound like an optimistic Rationalism; but the corrective of negative theology and philosophy was always present in the mind of Thomas, as well. Not only, as he argued in his treatise on God, does man not know what God is, but he does not know the essences of things either.

Late Scholastic period. Thomas did not succeed in bridging the faith–reason gulf. When he left Paris (1272) and after his death (1274), the gulf became much more radical; and on March 7, 1277, the Archbishop of Paris, in fact, formally condemned a list of sentences, some of them close to what Thomas himself had allegedly or really taught. This ecclesiastical act, questionable though it may have been in its methods and personal motivations, was not only understandable; it was unavoidable, since it was directed against what, after all, amounted in principle to an antitheological, rationalistic secularism. Quite another matter, however, were the factual effects of the edict, which were rather disastrous. Above all, two of the effects were pernicious: instead of free disputes among individuals, organized blocks (or "schools") now began to form; and the cooperative dialogue between theology and philosophy turned into mutual indifference or distrust. Nonetheless, the basic principle itself ("join faith with reason") had not yet been explicitly repudiated. This was to happen in the next generation.

Duns
Scotus
and
William
of Ockham

The negative element, as formulated in the theology of the Areopagite, proved to be insufficient as a corrective to counter the overemphasis of reason, for reason seemed to imply the idea of necessity; Anselm's asserted "compelling grounds" for revealed truths, for example, were akin to such a necessitarianism. A second corrective was therefore demanded and this took the name of "freedom"—which indeed was the battle cry of an important Franciscan, Duns Scotus, known as the "subtle doctor," who lived at the turn of the 14th century. Scotus used "freedom" primarily with reference to God; consequently, since redemption, grace, and salvation as well as all of creation were the work of God's groundless, absolute freedom, there could be no "necessary reasons," if indeed any reasons at all, for anything. It was therefore futile to attempt to coordinate faith with speculative reason. Clearly, Scotus' theological starting point made the conjunction of what man believes with what he knows every bit as difficult as it had been in Siger of Brabant's secularistic "philosophism." From both positions there was only one step to the doctrine of a "double truth"—a step that in fact was taken in the 14th century by the Nominalist William of Ockham, also a Franciscan, to whom singular facts alone are "real," and their coherence is not; this mere factuality, he held, can neither be calculated nor deduced, but only experienced; reason therefore means nothing but the power to encounter concrete reality. And upon such soil only a consistently "positive" theology could thrive. Any collaboration with speculative reason must be rejected as untheological. Faith is one thing and knowledge an altogether different matter; and a conjunction of the two is neither meaningfully possible nor even desirable. Inexorably, and justified by reasons on both sides, a divorce was taking place between faith and reason—to the connection of which the energies of almost a thousand years had been devoted. What was occurring was the demise of medieval Scholasticism.

ENDURING FEATURES

But not all of Scholasticism is specifically medieval and therefore definitively belonging to the dead past; there are perennial elements that are meant for every age, the present one included, three of which may be here distinguished. First, not only has Scholasticism held true to the normal historical rule that ideas, once thought and expressed, remain present and significant in the following time; but the medieval intellectual accomplishments have surpassed the rule and exerted, though more or less anonymously, a quite exceptional influence even on philosophers who consciously revolted against Scholasticism. New historical investigations clearly show that the classical modern philosophers Descartes, Locke, Spinoza, and Leibniz owe much to medieval ideas. Of Descartes, for instance, it has been said, contrary to the usual view, that he could quite well have been "included with the later Scholastics"; and even Charles Sanders Peirce, the originator of 20th-century American Pragmatism, refers not too rarely to Scholastic maxims. Secondly, there have been explicit attempts to go back to Scholastic thinkers and inspire a renascence of their basic ideas. Two chief movements of this kind were the Scholasticism of the Renaissance (called *Barockscholastik*) and the Neoscholasticism of the 19th and 20th centuries, both of which were primarily interested in the work of Thomas Aquinas.

Renaissance Scholasticism received its first impulses from the Reformation. One of its leading figures, a Dominican, Cardinal Thomas de Vio (16th century), commonly known as Cajetan, had some famous disputations with Martin Luther. Cajetan's great commentary on Thomas Aquinas, published again in a late edition of the *Summa theologiae* (1888–1906), exerted for at least three centuries an enormous influence on the formation of Catholic theology. He was much more than a commentator, however; his original treatise on the "Analogy of names," for example, can even pass as a prelude to modern linguistic philosophy. The so-called Silver Age of Scholastic thought, which occurred in the 16th century, is represented by two Spaniards: Francisco de Vitoria of the first half and Francisco Suárez of the last half of the century were both deeply engaged in what has been called the "Counter-Reformation." Though likewise commentators on the works of Thomas Aquinas, the Renaissance Scholastics were much less concerned with looking back to the past than with the problems of their own epoch, such as those of international law, colonialism, resistance to an unjust government, and world community. Though Suarez was for more than a hundred years among the most esteemed authors, even in Protestant universities, Renaissance Scholasticism was eradicated by Enlightenment philosophy and German Idealism. This, in turn, gave rise in due time to the Neoscholasticism of the 19th century, one of the most effective promoters of which was a German Jesuit, Joseph Kleutgen, who published a voluminous scholarly apology of patristic and Scholastic theology and philosophy, and was also responsible for the outline of the papal encyclical *Aeterni Patris* of Leo XIII (1879), which explicitly proclaimed the "instauration of Christian philosophy according to St. Thomas." The result, fed of course from many different sources, was that all over the world new centres of Scholastic research and higher learning (universities) arose—some more traditionalistic, some from the start engaged in the dialogue with modern philosophy and science, and some primarily devoted to historical studies and the preparation of critical editions of the great medieval Scholastics—and that a multitude of periodicals and systematic textbooks were produced. It is too early for a competent judgment on this enterprise to be made. Its immeasurable educational benefit for several generations of students, however, is as undeniable as the unique contributions of some Neoscholastic thinkers to current intellectual life. A weak point, on the other hand, seems to be a somewhat "unhistorical" approach to reality and existence. In any case, it is scarcely a matter of mere chance that, after World War

Renaissance and Neoscholasticism

II, the impact of Existentialism and Marxism caused a noticeable decline in Neoscholasticism and that the positions of "Scholastic" authors active in the 1970s is already beyond Neoscholasticism.

The third and most important aspect of the enduring significance of the Scholastic movement implies the acceptance of the following fundamental tenets: that there exist truths that man knows, and also revealed truths of faith; that these two kinds of truth are not simply reducible to one another; that faith and theology do not, by means of symbols and sensuous images, merely say the same as what reason and science say more clearly by conceptual argumentation (Averroës, Hegel); that, on the other hand, reason is not a "prostitute" (Luther), but is man's natural capacity to grasp the real world; that since reality and truth, though essentially inexhaustible, are basically one, faith and reason cannot ultimately contradict one another. Those who hold these convictions appear quite unable to refrain from trying to coordinate what they know with what they believe. Any epoch that addresses itself to this interminable task can ill afford to ignore the demanding and multiform paradigm of Scholasticism; but to the problems posed it will have to find its own answer.

Perennial tenets of Scholasticism

BIBLIOGRAPHY. For the latest and most detailed bibliography, see W. TOTOK, *Handbuch der Geschichte der Philosophie*, vol. 2, *Mittelalter und frühe Neuzeit* (1970). Among the most reliable, best-grounded presentations of the whole period are: E. GILSON, *History of Christian Philosophy in the Middle Ages* (1955); F. COPLESTON, *A History of Philosophy*, vol. 2, *Mediaeval Philosophy*, vol. 3, *Late Mediaeval and Renaissance Philosophy* (1950, 1953; paperback edition, 1962, 1963); M. DE WULF, *Histoire de la philosophie médiévale*, 6th ed., 3 vol. (1934–47; Eng. trans. of vol. 1, 1951); and E. BRÉHIER, *La Philosophie du moyen âge*, 2nd ed. (1949). Still indispensable, though obsolete in some details is: F. UEBERWEG, *Grundriss der Geschichte der Philosophie*, vol. 2, B. GEYER, *Die patristische und scholastische Philosophie*, 11th ed. (1928). Lucidly arranged and divided is the 13th volume of FLICHE-MARTIN, *Histoire de l'Église: Le Mouvement doctrinal de XIᵉ au XIVᵉ siècle* (1951), which includes contributions by A. Forest, F. van Steenberghen, and M. de Gandillac. M. GRABMANN's masterpiece, *Die Geschichte der scholastischen Methode*, 2 vol. (1909–11, reprinted 1956), covers only the time until the first years of the 13th century. For a first introduction for the general reader, see J. PIEPER, *Scholastik* (1960; Eng. trans., *Scholasticism*, 1960). Special problems concerning the continuing influence of medieval Scholasticism are treated in the following monographs: A. KOYRE, *Descartes und die Scholastik* (1923); A. TELLKAMP, *Das Verhältnis John Locke's zur Scholastik* (1927); and J.O. FLECKENSTEIN, *Scholastik, Barock, exakte Wissenschaften* (1949). The following are sources on Neoscholasticism: J.P. GOLINAS, *La Restauration du Thomisme sous Leon XIII et les philosophies nouvelles* (1959); GIOVANNI ROSSI, *Le origini del Neotomismo nell'ambiente di studio del Collegio Alberoni* (1957); A. VIEL, "Le Mouvement thomiste au XIXᵉ siècle," *Revue Thomiste* (1909–10); E. BETTONI, *La Situation actuelle de la philosophie parmi les catholiques dans les divers pays* (1948), a survey of centres of study, institutes, and publications; and J.S. ZYBURA (ed.), *Present-Day Thinkers and the New Scholasticism: An International Symposium* (1926).

(Jf.Pi.)

Schopenhauer, Arthur

Arthur Schopenhauer, called "the philosopher of pessimism," was a discoverer of the irrational impulses of life arising from the will, an opponent of the absolute Idealism of G.W.F. Hegel and of the rationally determined awareness of progress and of the present in the 19th and 20th centuries, and a pioneer of the new "life" philosophy.

Early life and education. Schopenhauer was born on February 22, 1788, the son of a wealthy Danzig merchant, Heinrich Floris Schopenhauer, and his wife Johanna, who later became famous for her novels, essays, and travelogues. In 1793, when Danzig came under Prussian sovereignty, they moved to the free city of Hamburg.

Young Arthur enjoyed a gentlemanly, urbane education. He spent two years (1798–1800) in the home of one of his father's business friends in Le Havre, France, in order to learn the French language. After his return, he

Preparatory studies

Schopenhauer, 1855.
Archiv fur Kunst und Geschichte, Berlin

attended a private business school, where he became acquainted with the spirit of the Enlightenment and was exposed to a Pietistic attitude sensitive to the plight of man. During this time, the Pietistic phrase that characterized life as a "vale of tears" became as familiar to him as did the writings of the German lyric poet Matthias Claudius, known as the Wandsbeck Messenger. In 1803 he accompanied his parents for a year on an extensive journey through Belgium, England, France, Switzerland, and Austria. Again, predominantly negative impressions prevailed: the sight of such want and misery as that at the Bagno (prison) in Toulon, France, with its 6,000 galley slaves, reinforced his tendency toward a pessimistic outlook on life. According to the wishes of his father, he reluctantly entered a business apprenticeship in 1805.

The sudden death of his father in April 1805, however, precipitated a decisive change in his life. His mother and his young sister Adele moved to Weimar, where his mother succeeded in joining the social circle of the poets Goethe and Christoph Martin Wieland (often called the German Voltaire). Arthur himself had to remain in Hamburg for more than a year, yet with more freedom to engage in the arts and sciences. *Phantasien über die Kunst* (1799; "Reveries on Art"), a work by Wilhelm Wackenroder, known for his writings on old German art and music, provided the young man with a significant initiation into literature. Here music was depicted as the liberating counterbalance to man's base existence, and it was from this fundamental mood that Schopenhauer's philosophy of music later arose. In May 1807 he was finally able to leave Hamburg. During the next two years, spent in Gotha and Weimar, he acquired the necessary academic preparation for attendance at a university.

University studies   In the fall of 1809 he matriculated as a student of medicine at the University of Göttingen and mainly attended lectures on the natural sciences. As early as his second semester, however, he transferred to the humanities. On the advice of the famous author of the *Aenesidemus*, Gottlob Ernst Schulze, a critic of Kantianism, Schopenhauer concentrated first on the study of Plato and Kant. This course proved to be of great consequence to his intellectual growth, for it caused him to reject the post-Kantian development, as expounded by the Idealists J.G. Fichte, F.W.J. von Schelling, and G.W.F. Hegel, that was to be the predominant philosophical current for a long time to come. In the fall of 1811, Schopenhauer went to the University of Berlin. For one semester he attended the lectures of Fichte, at first with appreciation, later with mocking indignation. The philosopher Friedrich Schleiermacher, one of the fathers of modern theology, could likewise offer him little. What the professors of philosophy were lacking—results that were clarifying and, in their lucidity, convincing—he found instead in the representatives of classical philology (Friedrich August Wolf and August Böckh) and in a long series of lectures on the natural sciences. The war situation eventually constrained him to leave Berlin. In Rudolstadt, during the summer of 1813, he finished his dissertation, *Über die vierfache Wurzel des Satzes vom zureichenden Grunde* (Eng. trans., *On the Fourfold Root of the Principle of Sufficient Reason*, 1889), which earned him the doctor of philosophy degree from the University of Jena.

Active maturity. The following winter (1813–14) he spent in Weimar, in intimate association with Goethe, who invited his assistance with some problems concerning his *Farbenlehre* ("theory of colours"). Schopenhauer was able to "profit immensely" from his conversations with the poet, which covered the most varied philosophical topics. In that same winter, however, the Orientalist Friedrich Majer, a disciple of Johann Gottfried Herder, introduced him to the teachings of Indian antiquity—the philosophy of Vedānta and the mysticism of the Vedas (Hindu scriptures). Later, Schopenhauer considered that the *Upaniṣads* (philosophic Vedas), together with Plato and Kant, comprised the foundation on which he erected his own philosophical system.

In May 1814 he left his beloved Weimar after a quarrel with his mother, whose frivolous way of life he disapproved of. He then lived in Dresden until 1818, associating occasionally with a group of writers for the *Dresdener Abendzeitung* ("Dresden Evening Newspaper"). For some time he kept in close contact with the panentheist philosopher K.C.F. Krause, proponent of a "league of mankind," with whom he shared a love for Indian antiquity. Schopenhauer finished his treatise *Über das Sehn und die Farben* (1816; "On Vision and Colours"), supporting Goethe against Newton; yet he did not receive the poet's approbation.

His next three years were dedicated exclusively to the preparation and composition of his main work, *Die Welt als Wille und Vorstellung* (1819; Eng. trans., *The World as Will and Idea*, 1883–86). The fundamental idea of this work—which is condensed into a short formula in the title itself—is developed in four books comprising two comprehensive series of reflections that include successively the theory of knowledge, the philosophy of nature, aesthetics, and ethics. The first book begins with Kant. The world is my representation, says Schopenhauer. It is only comprehensible with the aid of the constructs of man's intellect: space, time, and causality. But these constructs show the world only as appearance, as a multiplicity of things next to and following one another—not as the thing in itself, which Kant considered to be unknowable. The second book advances to a consideration of the essences of the concepts presented. Of all the things in the world, only one is presented to a person in two ways, viz., the person himself: he knows himself externally as body, as appearance and, internally, directly as part of the primary essence of all things, as will—in the general sense that Schopenhauer gave to the concept. The will is the thing in itself; it is unitary, unfathomable, unchangeable, beyond space and time, without causes and purposes. In the world of appearances, it is reflected in an ascending series of realizations. From the blind impulses in the forces of inorganic nature, through organic nature (plants and animals) to the rationally guided actions of men, an enormous chain of restless desires, agitations, and drives stretch forth—a continual struggle of the higher forms against the lower, an eternally aimless and insatiable striving, inseparably united with misery and misfortune. At the end, however, stands death, the great reproof that the will-to-live receives, posing the question to each single person: Have you had enough?

Whereas the first two books present the will in an affirmative mode, the last two, dealing with aesthetics and ethics, surpass them by pointing to the negation of the will as a possible liberation. Evoking as their leading figures the genius and the saint, who illustrate this negation, these books present the "pessimistic" world view that values non-being more highly than being. The arts summon man to a will-less way of viewing things, in which

Work on *The World as Will and Idea*

the play of the passions ceases. To the succession of levels achieved by the realizations of the will corresponds a gradation of levels in the arts—from the lowest—the art of building (architecture)—through the art of poetry to the highest—music. But the arts liberate a person only momentarily from the service of the will. A genuine liberation results only from breaking through the bounds of individuality imposed by the ego. Whoever feels acts of compassion, of selflessness, of human kindness, and the suffering of other beings as his own is on the way to the abnegation of the will to life, achieved by the saints of all peoples and times in asceticism. Schopenhauer's anthropology and sociology do not, in the manner of Hegel, commence with the state or with the community; they focus upon man—patient, suffering man who toils by himself—and show him certain possibilities of standing his ground and of living together with others, possibilities with which modern sociology has yet to become thoroughly and fruitfully conversant.

The book, published in December of 1818, marked the summit of Schopenhauer's thought. In the many years thereafter, no further development of his philosophy occurred, no inner struggles or changes, no critical reorganization of basic thoughts. From then onward, his work consisted merely of more detailed exposition, clarification, and affirmation.

Schopenhauer then embarked on his first journey through Italy; indeed, he was one of the last such travellers to perceive the monuments of classical antiquity with a sensitivity comparable to that of Johann Joachim Winckelmann, author of an epoch-making history of ancient architecture.

University teaching

In March 1820, after a triumphant dispute with Hegel, he qualified to lecture at the University of Berlin. Though he remained a member of the university for 24 semesters, only his first lecture was actually held; for he had scheduled (and continued to schedule) his lectures at the same hour when Hegel lectured to a large and ever-growing audience. Clearly, he could not successfully challenge a persistently advancing philosophy. Even his book received scant attention. For a second time Schopenhauer went on a year-long trip (1822–23) to Italy, and this was followed by a year of illness in Munich. In May 1825 he made one last attempt in Berlin, but in vain. He now occupied himself with secondary works: a translation of *El oráculo manual* (1647; Eng. trans., *The Oracle*, 1953) by the Spanish Jesuit Baltasar Gracián, which appeared only posthumously; plans (which were never realized) for translations of Hume into German and Kant into English; and a rendering of his treatise on colours into Latin (*Theoria Colorum Physiologica;* 1830).

Scholarly retirement in Frankfurt. During his remaining 28 years (after 1833), he lived in Frankfurt, which he felt to be free from the threat of cholera, and left the city only for brief interludes. He had finally renounced his career as a university professor and lived henceforth as a recluse, totally absorbed in his studies and writings.

Pursuit of cultural interests. The natural-science collections of the city afforded him the opportunity to observe and inform himself of progress in the empirical sciences, and he attended plays and concerts; but he took little interest in what he considered the trivial events of everyday life. The classical authors Plato, Aristotle, Horace, and Seneca; the major writers of more recent times, such as Shakespeare and the Spaniard Calderón de la Barca; the leading spirits of mysticism; the French moralists and psychologists; and the influential exponents of the Enlightenment—these were his familiar companions. Thus, he progressively lost contact with his former connections, and his social life was restricted almost exclusively to conversations with fellow patrons at the dinner table.

His life now took on the shape that posterity first came to know: the measured uniformity of the days; the strict, ascetic life-style modelled after Kant; the old-fashioned attire; the tendency to gesticulative soliloquy; the brisk walks with an accompanying poodle. Brief excursions to nearby locations and to the Rhine and occasional re-

unions with early friends were for a long time the only diversions in a life of continued robust health and mental alacrity.

Publication and continuing obscurity. His leisure was not idle. Despite the disappointments engendered by his indifferent contemporaries, he relied on the eventual triumph of truth, as presented by his life's accomplishments: "The truth can wait," he wrote, "for it lives a long time." Thus, in 1836, after 19 years of "silent indignation," he published his short treatise *Über den Willen in der Natur* (Eng. trans., *On the Will in Nature*, 1889), which skillfully employed the queries and findings of the rapidly expanding natural sciences in support of his theory of the will. The preface for the first time openly expressed his devastating verdict on the "charlatan" Hegel and his clique. During the years from 1837 to 1839, he entered two academic competitions sponsored by the Norwegian and Danish societies of the sciences. The treatise *Über die Freiheit des menschlichen Willens* (submitted 1839; Eng. trans., *On the Freedom of the Will*, 1960) won him a first prize, whereas the treatise *Über das Fundament der Moral* (submitted 1840; *On the Basis of Morality*, 1903) did not—a fact that Schopenhauer expressly noted on the title page of a volume that included both essays under the title *Die beiden Grundprobleme der Ethik* (1841; "The Two Main Problems of Ethics").

Treatises on will and morality

The treatise *On the Will in Nature* and the *Ethics* were intended as supplements to the second and fourth books of *The World as Will and Idea*, with which they were to share, for the time being, the fate of remaining unnoticed. Even the second edition of his main work (1844), which included an additional volume of great significance, failed to break what he called "the resistance of a dull world"—despite the fact that, by then, Schopenhauer's first disciples, whom he jokingly called "apostles" and "evangelists," had gathered. Notable among these followers was a convert from Hegelianism, Julius Frauenstädt, who later became his literary executor. The little weight that Schopenhauer's name carried became evident when three publishers rejected his latest work. It was Frauenstädt who in the end persuaded a rather obscure Berlin bookseller to accept the manuscript without remuneration.

In this book Schopenhauer turned to significant topics hitherto not treated individually within the framework of his writings: the work of six years yielded the essays and comments compiled in two volumes under the title *Parerga und Paralipomena* (1851; selective Eng. trans., *Essays from . . .* , 1951). The *Parerga* ("Minor Works") include fragments concerning the history of philosophy; the famous treatise "Über die Universitäts-Philosophie"; the enigmatically profound "Transzendente Spekulation über die anscheinende Absichtlichkeit im Schicksale des Einzelnen" ("Transcendent Speculation on the Apparent Premeditation in Personal Fate"); the "Versuch über das Geistersehn und was damit zusammenhängt" ("Essay on Ghost-seeing and its Related Aspects")—the first investigation, classification, and critical reflection concerning parapsychology; and the "Aphorismen zur Lebensweisheit" ("Aphorisms on Practical Wisdom"), a serene and brilliant account garnered from his long life. The *Paralipomena* ("Remnants"), or as Schopenhauer called them ". . . separate, yet systematically ordered thoughts on various subjects," included essays on writing and style, on women, on education, on noise and sound, and on numerous other topics.

Minor works and remnants

Worldwide recognition. After the stormy events of the Revolution of 1848 had subsided (condemned by Schopenhauer as an eruption of man's primitive nature), the *Parerga und Paralipomena* brought the beginning of worldwide recognition. In April 1853 John Oxenford, an English critic, writing in *The Westminster Review*, broke the ice with an influential attack on Hegelian philosophizing, entitled "Iconoclasm in German Philosophy." Reviews, essays, and more extensive treatises on Schopenhauer and his theory followed in rapid succession. Already in 1857, in Bonn and in Breslau, the first lectures on his philosophy were given; the University of Leipzig proposed the first scholarly competition on his teachings; initial translations and eulogies appeared in French; Italy's foremost critic, Francesco de Sanctis, in a dialogue written with Neapolitan verve, drew a parallel between Schopenhauer and Italy's own poet of pessimism, Count Giacomo Leopardi. Suddenly, the hermit of Frankfurt drew admiration and visitors. Richard Wagner sent him (in 1854) *The Ring of the Nibelung*, bearing a dedication "in veneration and gratitude." He was visited by the later founder of characterology, Julius Bahnsen (1856); by the dramatist Friedrich Hebbel (1857); and by the French statesman Foucher de Careil. Other, mostly younger, academicians sought his acquaintance at the dinner table of the "Englischer Hof." Famous artists arrived to preserve his features on canvas for posterity. "The Nile has reached Cairo," he came to say.

During the last years of his life, he added the finishing touches to most of his works. Even a third edition of his main work, containing an exultant preface, appeared in 1859 and, in 1860, a second edition of his *Ethics*. On the morning of September 21, 1860, he succumbed to a sudden and painless death.

Soon thereafter, Julius Frauenstädt published new and enlarged editions, with many handwritten additions, of the *Parerga and Paralipomena* (1862), the *Fourfold Root* (1864), the essay *On the Will in Nature* (1867), the treatise on colours (1870), and finally even a fourth edition of his main work (1873). Later that same year Frauenstädt published the first complete edition of his works in six volumes.

Influence. During this time, the actual impact and influence of Schopenhauer began to spread. By turning away from spirit and reason to the powers of intuition, creativity, and the irrational, his thought has affected—partly via Nietzsche—the ideas and methods of vitalism, of life philosophy (Dilthey, Bergson), of Existential philosophy, and of anthropology. Through his disciple Julius Bahnsen and through Eduard von Hartmann's philosophy of the unconscious, the connection to modern psychology and to Sigmund Freud and his school can be established. The philosophy of history of Jacob Burckhardt, a Swiss cultural historian, also proceeds from Schopenhauer. Within the German cultural realm, Schopenhauer's influence on music and literature brings to mind such names as the opera composers Richard Wagner and Hans Pfitzner; Wilhelm Busch, a humorous artist and poet; the dramatists Gerhart Hauptmann and Frank Wedekind; and Thomas Mann, the greatest of modern German novelists. Since 1911, the Schopenhauer Society in Frankfurt am Main has been dedicated to the study, exposition, and dissemination of Schopenhauer's philosophy.

MAJOR WORKS
Über die vierfache Wurzel des Satzes vom zureichenden Grunde (1813, reissued 1847; *On the Fourfold Root of the Principle of Sufficient Reason*, 1889); *Über das Sehn und die Farben* (1816, rev. 1854 after Latin adaptation, *Commentatio Exponens Theoriam Colorum Physiologicam, Eandemque primariam*, 1830); *Die Welt als Wille und Vorstellung: vier Bücher, nebst einem Anhange der die Kritik der Kantischen Philosophie enthält* (1819; augmented editions 1844 and 1859; *The World As Will and Idea*, 3 vol., 1883–86; *The World As Will and Representation*, 2 vol., 1958); *Über die Freiheit des menschlichen Willens* and *Über das Fundament der Moral*, published together as *Die beiden Grundprobleme der Ethik* (1841; *The Basis of Morality*, 1903, 1965; first section, *On the Freedom of the Will*, 1960); *Parerga und Paralipomena*, 2 vol. (1851; selections trans. as *Religion: A Dialogue*, 1889; *The Wisdom of Life*, 1890; *Counsels and Maxims*, 1890; *Studies in Pessimism*, 1891; *The Art of Literature*, 1891; *Essays from the Parerga and Paralipomena*, 1951). *Der handschriftlicher Nachlass* ("Manuscript Remains"), selections 1864 and 1891–93, critical edition (vol. 1–3, 5, 1966–70; vol. 4 in prep.), the first complete edition of the *Nachlass* manuscripts, including the marginal inscriptions in Schopenhauer's private library; trans. *Baltasar Gracians Hand-Orakel und Kunst der Weltklugheit* (many German editions).

BIBLIOGRAPHY
Editions: Collections of Schopenhauer's *Werke* are numerous; the edition by JULIUS FRAUENSTAEDT, 6 vol. (1873–74), has been re-edited several times; it is, like the one by EDUARD GRISEBACH, 6 vol. (1891), now out of date. PAUL DEUSSEN (ed.), *Sämtliche Werke*, 16 vol. (1911–42, unfinished), contains Schopenhauer's correspondence, ed. by ARTHUR HUEBSCHER (vol. 14–16). ARTHUR HUEBSCHER (ed.), *Sämtliche Werke*, 2nd ed., 7 vol. (1946–50; 3rd ed., 1972–), is the standard edition based on new research.

Biographies: ARTHUR HUEBSCHER, *Arthur Schopenhauer: Ein Lebensbild*, 2nd ed. (1949), a comprehensive evaluation of research results up to its date of publication; and *Schopenhauer: Gespräche* (1971), an authentic source for his life and work history; WILHELM VON GWINNER, *Arthur Schopenhauer aus persönlichem Umgange dargestellt*, 3rd ed. (1910, reprinted 1963), a description of a personal acquaintance with Schopenhauer; PATRICK GARDINER, *Schopenhauer* (1963), an English-language biography.

Studies: KUNO FISCHER, *Geschichte der neuern Philosophie*, vol. 8, *Arthur Schopenhauer*, 4th ed. (1934), a biassed account; JOHANNES VOLKELT, *Arthur Schopenhauer*, 5th ed. (1923); and HEINRICH HASSE, *Schopenhauer* (1926), both thorough descriptions in German; ARTHUR HUEBSCHER, *Schopenhauer: Gestern-Heute-Morgen* (1973), on his importance and influence.

(Ar.Hü.)

Schrödinger, Erwin

Erwin Schrödinger, with the physicists Albert Einstein, Niels Bohr, Max Born, Werner Heisenberg, Wolfgang Pauli, Louis de Broglie, and P.A.M. Dirac, developed quantum mechanics in the late 1920s and shared the Nobel Prize in Physics with Dirac in 1933. In 1926 Schrödinger discovered the partial differential equation that is the basic equation of quantum mechanics and bears the same relation to the mechanics of the atom as Newton's equations of motion bear to planetary astronomy. Adopting a proposal made by de Broglie in 1924 that particles of matter have a dual nature and in some situations act like waves, Schrödinger introduced a theory describing the behaviour of such a system by a wave equation. The solutions to Schrödinger's equation, unlike the solutions to Newton's equations, are wave functions that can only be related to the probable occurrence of physical events. The definite and readily visualized sequence of events of the planetary orbits of Newton is, in quantum mechanics, replaced by the more abstract notion of probability. This aspect of the quantum theory made Schrödinger and several other physicists, including Einstein, profoundly unhappy, and Schrödinger devoted much of his later life to formulating philosophical objections to the generally accepted interpretation of the theory that he had done so much to create.

Schrödinger was born in Vienna on August 12, 1887. An only child, he was brought up in a family devoted to scientific and cultural activity. He was privately tutored until the age of 11, when he entered a Gymnasium. Schrödinger received a broad classical education that served as the basis for his lifelong interest in languages, philosophy, and literature. *Early work in Vienna*

Schrödinger entered the University of Vienna in 1906 and remained there, with brief interruptions, until 1920; he saw military service in World War I. His work in physics during this period was distinguished, but hardly of the calibre of his later discoveries in atomic wave mechanics. Indeed, late in his life, he wrote that in 1918 he had more or less decided to abandon theoretical physics for philosophy, when it appeared that he would get an academic post in Czernowitz, Romania, now Chernovtsy, Ukrainian S.S.R. Czernowitz was taken from Austria after the war, and instead Schrödinger went to Zürich in 1921, where he remained for the next six years. There, in a six-month period in 1926, at the age of 39, a remarkably late age for original work by theoretical physicists, he produced the papers that gave the foundations of quantum wave mechanics. In 1927 he accepted an invitation to succeed Max Planck, the inventor of the quantum hypothesis, at the University in Berlin, and he joined an extremely distinguished faculty that included Einstein. There he remained until 1933 when, although of Catholic background, he decided that he could no longer live in a country in which the persecution of Jews had become a

Schrödinger.
Foto IWAN

national policy. He then began a seven-year odyssey that took him to Austria, Great Britain, the Pontifical Academy of Science in Rome, and—finally in 1940—to the Dublin Institute for Advanced Studies, founded under the influence of Premier Eamon de Valera, who had been a mathematician before turning to politics. Schrödinger remained in Ireland for the next 15 years, doing both research in physics and in the philosophy and history of science. During this period he wrote *What Is Life?*, an attempt to show how quantum physics can be used to explain the stability of genetic structure. Although much of what Schrödinger had to say in this book has been modified and amplified by later developments in molecular biology, his book remains one of the most useful and profound introductions to the subject. In 1956 Schrödinger retired and returned to Vienna as professor emeritus at the University. He died on January 4, 1961.

Of all of the physicists of his generation, Schrödinger stands out because of his extraordinary intellectual versatility. He was at home in the philosophy and literature of all of the Western languages, and his popular scientific writing in English, which he had learned as a child, is among the best of its kind. His study of ancient Greek science and philosophy, summarized in his *Nature and the Greeks* (1954), gave him both an admiration for the Greek invention of the scientific view of the world and a skepticism toward the relevance of science as a unique tool with which to unravel the ultimate mysteries of human existence. Schrödinger's own metaphysical outlook, as expressed in his last book, *Meine Weltansicht* (1961; *My View of the World*, 1964), closely paralleled the mysticism of the Vedānta.

Because of his exceptional gifts, Schrödinger was able in the course of his life to make significant contributions to nearly all branches of science and philosophy, an almost unique accomplishment at a time when the trend was toward increasing technical specialization in these disciplines.

BIBLIOGRAPHY. WILLIAM T. SCOTT, *Erwin Schrödinger: An Introduction to His Writings* (1967), is a good critical study of Schrödinger and his works.

(J.Be)

Schubert, Franz

One of the principal Austrian composers of the early 19th century, Franz Peter Schubert stands between the worlds of Classical and Romantic music and is noted particularly for the extraordinary melodic and harmonic gifts he displayed in his numerous songs and chamber works.

Early life and career. Schubert was born on January 31, 1797, in Himmelpfortgrund (modern Alsergrund), then a suburb of Vienna. His father, Franz Theodor Schubert, was a schoolmaster; his mother, Elisabeth,

whose maiden name was Vietz, was in domestic service at the time of her marriage. Franz was their fourth surviving son. His elder brothers were Ignaz, Karl, and Ferdinand, and there was a younger sister, Maria Theresa. The elder Franz Schubert was a man of character who had established a flourishing school. The family was musical and cultivated string quartet playing in the home, the boy Franz playing the viola. He received the foundations of his musical education from his father and his brother Ignaz, continuing later with organ playing and musical theory under the instruction of the parish church organist. In 1808 he won a scholarship that earned him a place in the imperial court chapel choir and an education at the Stadtkonvikt, the principal boarding school for commoners in Vienna, where his tutors were Wenzel Ruzicka, the imperial court organist, and, later, the composer Antonio Salieri, then at the height of his fame. Schubert played the violin in the students' orchestra, was quickly promoted to leader, and in Ruzicka's absence conducted. He also attended choir practice and, with his fellow pupils, cultivated chamber music and piano playing.

From the evidence of his school friends, Schubert was inclined to be shy and was reluctant to show his first compositions. His earliest works included a long *Fantasia for Piano Duet*, written in 1811–12, D. 1 (*i.e.*, no. 1 in Otto Erich Deutsch's *Schubert: Thematic Catalogue of All His Works in Chronological Order*, 1951); his first song (1811); several orchestral overtures; various pieces of chamber music; and, in 1811, three string quartets. An unfinished operetta on a text by August von Kotzebue, *Der Spiegelritter* (*The Looking-glass Knight*), also belongs to those years. The interest and encouragement of his friends overcame his shyness and eventually brought his work to the notice of Salieri.

In 1812 Schubert's voice broke; he left the college but continued his studies privately with Salieri for at least another three years. During this time he entered a teachers' training college in Vienna and in the autumn of 1814 became assistant in his father's school. Rejected for military service because of his short stature, he continued as a schoolmaster until 1818.

The numerous compositions written between 1813 and 1815 are remarkable for their variety and intrinsic worth. They are the products of young genius, still short of maturity but displaying style, originality, and imagination. Besides five string quartets, including those in E flat major and G minor, there were three full-scale masses and three symphonies. The third of these symphonies, in D major, a charming example of Schubert's youthful lyricism and high spirits, was finished in 1815. His first full-length opera, *Des Teufels Lustschloss* (*The Devil's Palace of Desire*), was finished in 1814 while he was at the training college. But at this period song composition was his chief, all-absorbing interest. On October 19, 1814, he first set to music a poem by Goethe, "Gretchen am Spinnrade" ("Gretchen at the Spinning

By courtesy of the Historisches Museum der Stadt Wien

Schubert, watercolour by W.A. Rieder, 1825. In the Historisches Museum der Stadt Wien.

Creation
of the lied

Wheel"), from *Faust*; it was his 30th song and in this masterpiece he created at one stroke the German lied (art song). The following year, 1815, brought the composition of more than 140 songs.

The many unfinished fragments and sketches of songs left by Schubert provide some insight into the working of his creative mind. Clearly, the primary stimulus was melodic. The words of a poem engendered a tune. Harmony (chordal structure of a composition) and modulation (change of key) were then suggested by the contours of the melody. But the external details of the poet's scene—natural, domestic, or mythical—prompted such wonderfully graphic images in the accompaniments as the spinning wheel, the ripple of water, or the "shimmering robe" of spring. These features were fully present in the songs of 1815. The years that followed deepened and enriched but did not revolutionize these novel departures in song. During 1815 Schubert also continued to be preoccupied with his ill-fated operas: between May and December he wrote *Der vierjährige Posten* (*A Sentry for Four Years*), *Fernando*, *Claudine von Villa Bella*, and *Die Freunde von Salamanka* (*The Friends of Salamanca*).

At this time Schubert's outward life was uneventful. Friends of his college days were faithful, particularly Josef von Spaun, who in 1814 introduced him to the poet Johann Mayrhofer. He also induced the young and brilliant Franz von Schober to visit Schubert. Late in 1815 Schober went to the schoolhouse in the Säulengasse, found Schubert in front of a class with his manuscripts piled about him, and inflamed the young composer, a willing listener, with a desire to break free from his duties. In the spring of 1816 Schubert applied for the post of music director in a college at Laibach (now Ljubljana, Yugoslavia) but was unsuccessful. His friends tried to interest Goethe in the songs and in April 1816 sent a volume of 16 settings to the poet at Weimar. It produced no result. At length, in December 1816, Schober persuaded Schubert to apply for leave of absence. Despite his father's reluctance, he obtained the leave of absence and subsequently spent eight months with Schober, living in the home of his friend's widowed mother and paying for his keep whenever he could.

Early in 1817 Schober brought the baritone Johann Michael Vogl to his home to meet Schubert. As a result of this meeting, Vogl's singing of Schubert's songs became the rage of the Viennese drawing rooms. His friendships with the Huttenbrenner brothers, Anselm, a composer, and Josef, an amateur musician, and with Josef von Gahy, a pianist with whom he played duets, date from these days. But this period of freedom did not last, and in the autumn of 1817 Schubert returned to his teaching duties. He wrote to his friends of himself as a *verdorbener* ("frustrated") musician. The two earlier years had been particularly fruitful. Songs of this period include "Ganymed" (the song which had captivated Vogl at their first meeting), "Der Wanderer," and the *Harper's Songs* from Goethe's novel *Wilhelm Meister*. Smaller but equally remarkable songs are "An die Musik" ("To Music"), "Der Tod und das Mädchen" ("Death and the Maiden"), and "Die Forelle" ("The Trout"). There were two more symphonies: *No. 4 in C Minor*, which Schubert himself named the *Tragic* (1816), and the popular *No. 5 in B Flat Major* (1816). A fourth mass, in C major, was composed in 1816. The year 1817 is notable for the beginning of his masterly series of piano sonatas. Six were composed at Schober's home, the finest being *No. 7 in E Flat Major* and *No. 11 in B Major*; both were published posthumously.

First
public
perfor-
mance of
Schubert's
work

Schubert's years of uncongenial schoolmastering ended in the summer of 1818. His frustrated period in the spring had produced only one substantial work, the *Symphony No. 6 in C Major*. But in the meantime his reputation was growing, and the first public performance of one of his works, the *Italian Overture in C Major*, took place on March 1, 1818, in Vienna. In June he left the city to take up the post of music master to the two daughters, Marie and Karoline, of Johann, Count Esterházy, in the family's summer residence at Zseliz, Hungary. Letters to his friends show him in exuberant spirits, and the summer months were marked by a fresh creative outburst. The piano duets *Variations on a French Song* in E minor and the *Sonata in B Flat Major*, sets of dances, songs, and the *Deutsche Trauermesse* (*German Requiem*) were all composed at Zseliz.

Maturity. On his return to Vienna he shared lodgings with Mayrhofer and during the winter months composed the operetta *Die Zwillingsbrüder* (*The Twin Brothers*). Although sponsored by Vogl, the production of the work was postponed, and in June 1819 Schubert and Vogl set off for a protracted holiday in the singer's native district of upper Austria. The composer delighted in the beauty of the countryside and was touched by the enthusiastic reception given everywhere to his music. At Steyr he composed the first of his widely known instrumental compositions, the *Piano Sonata in A Major*, D. 664, and the celebrated *Trout Quintet* for piano and strings. The close of 1819 saw him engrossed in songs to poems by his friend Mayrhofer and by Goethe, who inspired the masterly *Prometheus*. A fifth mass, in A flat major, was started but laid aside. Another sacred work, begun in 1820 but left unfinished, was the cantata *Lazarus*, anticipating, by its fusion of lyrical and declamatory styles, the style of Richard Wagner.

In June 1820 *Die Zwillingsbrüder* was performed with moderate success in Vienna, Vogl doubling in the parts of the twin brothers. It was followed by the performance of incidental music for the play *Die Zauberharfe* (*The Magic Harp*), given in August of the same year. The lovely, melodious overture became famous as the *Rosamunde* overture. Schubert was achieving renown in wider social circles than the restricted spheres of friend and patron. The wealthy and influential Sonnleithner family was interested in his development; their son Leopold became a great friend and supporter. At the close of the year 1820, Schubert composed the *Quartettsatz* (*Quartet-Movement*) in C minor, heralding the great string quartets of the middle 1820s, and another popular piece, the motet for female voices on the text of Psalm XXIII. In December 1820 he began the choral setting of Goethe's *Gesang der Geister über den Wassern* (*Song of the Spirits over the Water*) for male-voice octet with accompaniment for bass strings, D. 714, completed in February 1821.

All of Schubert's efforts to publish his own work were fruitless. Early in 1821, however, a few friends offered his song "Erlkönig" ("Erl King") on a subscription basis. The response was so successful that enough money was raised for the printing of "Gretchen am Spinnrade" also. "Erlkönig" appeared as Schubert's opus 1 on April 2, 1821, and "Gretchen" as opus 2 on April 30, 1821. From then on songs, part-songs, dances, and pianoforte duets were published. Eighteen months later, opus 12 had been reached.

Publication
of first
works

In Vienna the popularity of Schubert's songs and dance music became so great that concert parties were entirely devoted to them. These parties, called *Schubertiaden*, were frequently given in the homes of wealthy merchants and civil servants. But the wider worlds of opera and public concerts still eluded him. He worked during August 1821 on a seventh symphony in E minor and major, but this, too, was put aside, along with many other unfinished works of the period. His determination to establish himself in opera led him in September and October to spend a short holiday with Schober at St. Pölten, west of Vienna, where the friends devoted their energies to the production of a three-act opera, *Alfonso und Estrella*. It was completed in February 1822 but was never performed. While spending a few days at Atzenbrugg in July 1822, with Schober and other friends, he produced the document called *Mein Traum* ("My Dream"), describing a quarrel between a music-loving youth and his father. Fanciful biographical interpretations of this document have little, if any, factual foundation. The autumn of 1822 saw the beginning of yet another unfinished composition—not, this time, destined to obscurity: the *Symphony in B Minor* (*Unfinished*), which speaks from Schubert's very heart. Two movements were completed in October and November 1822, the abandoned work including also a half-finished scherzo. In November of the same year Schubert composed a piano fantasia in which the variations are on a theme from his song "Der Wanderer." The *Mass in A Flat Major* was also completed in this month.

At the close of 1822 Schubert contracted a venereal disease, probably syphilis, and the following year was one of illness and retirement. He continued to write almost incessantly. In February 1823, he wrote the *Piano Sonata in A Minor*, and in April he made another attempt to gain success in Viennese theatres with the one-act operetta *Die Verschworenen (The Conspirators)*, the title being changed later (because of political censorship) to *Der häusliche Krieg (Domestic Warfare)*. The famous work of the year, however, was the song cycle *Die schöne Müllerin (The Miller's Beautiful Daughter)*, representing the epitome of Schubert's lyrical art. Other songs of this period are "Auf dem Wasser zu singen" ("Singing on the Water") and "Du bist die Ruh" ("You are Peace"). Schubert spent part of the summer in the hospital and probably started work—while still a patient —on his most ambitious opera, *Fierrabras*. The work was rejected by the directorate of the prestigious Kärntnerthor Theatre in Vienna. The year 1823 closed with Schubert's composition of the music for the play *Rosamunde*, performed at Vienna in December. This production failed. The text of the play is lost, and the music was subsequently heard only in the concert hall.

Illness, poverty, and depression

The early months of 1824 were again unhappy. Schubert was ill, penniless, and plagued by a sense of failure. Yet during these months he composed three masterly chamber works: The *String Quartet in A Minor*, a second string quartet in D minor containing variations on his song "Der Tod und das Mädchen," and the *Octet in F Major* for strings and wind instruments. His dejection is manifest in a letter of March 31, 1824, to his friend Leopold Kupelwieser, the painter, in which he speaks of himself as "the most unfortunate, the most miserable being in the world." In desperate need of money, he returned in the summer to his teaching post with the Esterházy family and in May 1824 went again to Zseliz. Once more his health and spirits revived. The period was marked by some magnificent piano duets, the *Piano Sonata in C Major (Grand Duo)*, the *Variations on an Original Theme in A Flat Major,* and the *Divertissement à la hongroise (Hungarian Divertissement)*. The first work was published posthumously, the other two in Schubert's lifetime, in 1825 and 1826.

Although his operas remained unperformed, there were frequent public performances of his songs and part-songs in Vienna during these and the following years. Publication proceeded rapidly, and his financial position, though still strained, was at any rate eased. In 1825 he spent another holiday in upper Austria, with Vogl, visiting Linz, Gmunden, and Badgastein and finding a warm welcome for himself and his music wherever he went. This is the period of the *Lady of the Lake* songs (to words of Sir Walter Scott, translated by P.A. Storck), including the once popular but later neglected "Ave Maria." Instrumental compositions are the piano sonatas in A minor and in D major, the latter composed at Badgastein. He sketched a symphony during the summer holiday (in all probability the beginnings of the *Symphony in C Major* [*Great*], completed in 1828). The spring of 1825 had seen the composition of two well-known songs, "Im Abendrot" ("At Sunset") and "Die junge Nonne" ("The Young Nun"); they were followed in the late summer by "Die Allmacht" ("The Almighty") and "Das Heimweh" ("Homesickness"), two of his greatest songs inspired by nature. New friends, Moritz von Schwind, a young painter, and Eduard Bauernfeld, a dramatist, were almost continuously in his company during this period. Schwind left pictorial records of Schubert; Bauernfeld, reminiscences.

Last years. The resignation of Salieri as imperial *Kapellmeister* (musical director) in 1824 had led to the promotion of his deputy, Josef Eybler. In 1826 Schubert applied for the vacant post of deputy *Kapellmeister*, but in spite of strong support by several influential people he was unsuccessful. From then until his death two years later he seems to have let matters drift. Neither by appli-

cation for professional posts nor submission of operatic work did he seek to establish himself. It can hardly be believed that Schubert was unaware of his exceptional powers; yet, together with an awareness of genius and the realization that it opened doors into cultivated society went the knowledge of his humble birth and upbringing and also of his somewhat uncouth bearing. This self-consciousness made him diffident, reserved, and hesitant. His life was almost entirely devoted to composition, and he derived his livelihood from publishers' fees and occasional teaching. The songs of 1826 include the settings of Shakespeare's "Hark! Hark! the lark!" and "Who is Silvia?" written during a brief stay in the village of Währing. Three fine instrumental works of this summer and autumn are the last *String Quartet in G Major*, the *Piano Sonata in G Major*, and the beginning of the *Piano Trio in B Flat Major*.

In 1827 he composed the first 12 songs of the cycle *Winterreise (Winter Journey)*, a return to the poems of Wilhelm Müller, author of *Die schöne Müllerin (The Miller's Beautiful Daughter)*. Beethoven's death in 1827 undoubtedly had a profound effect on Schubert, for there is no denying that a more profound, more intellectual quality appears in his last instrumental works. Some of them, especially the *Piano Trio in E Flat Major* (1827) and the *Piano Sonata in C Minor* (1828), suggest the authority of Beethoven, yet his own strong individuality is never submerged.

In September 1827 Schubert spent a short holiday in Graz. On his return he composed the *Piano Trio in E Flat Major* and resumed work on Part II of the *Winterreise*; the 13th song, "Die Post," was written in October 1827. This is the period of his piano solos, the *Impromptus* and *Moments musicaux*.

Final compositions

A succession of masterpieces marks the last year of his life. Early in the year he composed the greatest of his piano duets, the *Fantasy in F Minor*. The *Great Symphony* was concluded in March, as was also the cantata *Miriams Siegesgesang (Miriam's Victory Song)*. In June he worked at his sixth mass—in E flat major. A return to songwriting in August produced the series published together as the *Schwanengesang (Swan Song)*. In September and early October the succession was concluded by the last three piano sonatas, in C minor, A major, and B flat major, and the great *String Quintet in C Major*—the swan song of the Classical era in music.

The only public concert Schubert gave took place on March 26, 1828. It was both artistically and financially a success, and the impecunious composer, it is recorded, was at last able to buy himself a piano. At the end of August he moved into lodgings with his brother Ferdinand, then living in a suburb of Vienna. Schubert's health, broken by the illness of 1823, had deteriorated, and his ceaseless work had exhausted him. In October he developed typhoid fever as a result of drinking tainted water. His last days were spent in the company of his brother and several close friends. He died in Vienna on November 19, 1828. On his tomb in the Währingerstrasse Cemetery was engraved the epitaph of the Austrian dramatist Franz Grillparzer: "The Art of Music has here entombed a rich treasure, but yet far fairer hopes."

Although it has been said that Schubert's place in the history of music is equivocal, he is, however, the last of the great Classical composers. His music, subjectively emotional in the Romantic manner, poetically conceived, and revolutionary in language, is nevertheless cast in the formal molds of the Classical school—with the result that in the 20th century it has become increasingly apparent that Schubert more truly belongs to the age of Haydn, Beethoven, and Mozart than to that of Schumann, Chopin, and Wagner.

MAJOR WORKS

OPERAS AND OPERETTAS (dates given are years of writing): Nine completed and existing, which include *Des Teufels Lustschloss* (1813–14), *Claudine von Villa Bella* (1815), *Die Zwillingsbrüder* (1818–19), *Alfonso und Estrella* (1821–22), *Fierrabras* (1823), *Die Verschworenen*, later changed to *Der häusliche Krieg* (1823).

CHORAL MUSIC: Seven masses, including *Mass in A Flat*

Major (1819–22) and *Mass in E Flat Major* (1828); various other settings of religious texts; 3 cantatas; *Gesang der Geister über den Wassern* (*Song of the Spirits over the Water*) for male voices and strings (1820–21); various songs with piano, including "Gott im Ungewitter" ("God in the Storms," *c.* 1815), "Hymne an den Unendlichen" ("Hymn to Infinity," 1815), "Gott in der Natur" ("God in Nature," 1822), "Gebet" ("Prayer," 1824), "Der Gondelfahrer" ("The Gondolier," 1824); "Nachthelle" ("Night's Brightness," 1826), "Miriams Siegesgesang" ("Miriam's Victory Song," 1828); various unaccompanied songs.

ORCHESTRAL WORKS: Nine symphonies, including *No. 4 in C Minor* (*Tragic*, 1816), *No. 5 in B flat Major* (1816), *Symphony in B Minor* (*Unfinished*, 1822), *Symphony in C Major* (*The Great*, 1828).

CHAMBER MUSIC: Two string trios; 4 piano trios for strings and piano, including *Trio in B Flat Major* (1827) and *Trio in E Flat Major* (1827); 22 string quartets, including quartets in B flat major, D. 112 (1814), in A minor, D. 804 (1824), in D minor, D. 810 ("Death and the Maiden"; 1824), in G major, D. 887 (1826); *String Quintet in C Major* (1828); *Piano Quintet in A Major* (*Trout*, 1819); *Octet in F Major* for wind and strings (1824); 3 sonatas for violin and piano; *Sonata in A Minor* for arpeggione (now played on cello, 1824).

PIANO WORKS: 21 sonatas; two sets of impromptus; 6 *Moments musicaux*; various waltzes and marches; *Fantasy in C Major* (*Wanderer*, 1822); *Fantasy in F Minor* for piano duet.

SONGS: More than 500, including the song cycles *Die schöne Müllerin* (*The Miller's Beautiful Daughter*, 1823), *Winterreise* (*Winter Journey*, 1827), *Schwanengesang* (*Swan Song*, 1828), and many well-known individual songs.

BIBLIOGRAPHY. OTTO E. DEUTSCH, *Franz Schubert: Die Dokumente seines Lebens und Schaffens*, 2 vol. (1913–14; Eng. trans., *Schubert: A Documentary Biography*, 1946, reprinted 1965; U.S. title, *The Schubert Reader*, 1947); *Schubert: Thematic Catalogue of All His Works in Chronological Order* (1951), the universal source of the D. numbers for Schubert's works, particularly useful in identifying works with similar titles; and *Schubert: Die Erinnerungen seiner Freunde* (1957; Eng. trans., *Schubert: Memoirs by His Friends*, 1958), a collection of obituaries and reminiscences of people who knew Schubert that were published in various journals at odd times during the 19th century—care should be exercised in the use since these reminiscences often contain romantic—*i.e.*, fictional—anecdotes; ALFRED EINSTEIN, *Schubert* (1951), a lively appreciation by a scholar who was not primarily a Schubert specialist; RICHARD CAPELL, *Schubert's Songs*, 2nd ed. (1957), a beautifully written and penetrating study of the songs; MAURICE J.E. BROWN, *Schubert: A Critical Biography* (1958), a standard life, with a study of Schubert as artist; and *Essays on Schubert* (1966), essays on manuscripts and editions, with a study of the sources for a complete edition of the sonatas; HEINRICH KREISSLE VON HELLBORN, *Franz Schubert: Eine biografische Skizze* (1861; Eng. trans., *Franz Schubert*, 1865), the first biography of the composer, by now unreliable factually but still invaluable as giving a picture of the attitude of the mid-19th century to Schubert; SIR DONALD F. TOVEY, "Franz Schubert, 1797–1828," in HUBERT J. FOSS (ed.), *Heritage of Music*, vol. 1 (1927), an important essay that marks the start of the 20th century's realization of Schubert's greatness.

(M.J.E.B.)

Schumann, Robert

One of the leading German composers of the early 19th century, Robert Schumann was first and foremost a miniaturist, known particularly for his short piano pieces and songs, two genres in his case so closely connected as to be hardly more than two facets of the same thing. In larger fields, his touch was less certain, although some of his orchestral works, such as the *Symphony No. 4 in D Minor*, the *Piano Concerto in A Minor*, and the *Manfred* overture, show him successfully overcoming his difficulties with more ambitious composition. In his day he was rightly considered a very advanced composer, and his influence on his contemporaries and successors was considerable.

Schumann was born at Zwickau, Saxony, on June 8, 1810. His father was a bookseller and publisher. After four years at a private school, the boy entered the Zwickau *Gymnasium* (high school) in 1820 and remained there for eight years. He began his musical education at the age of six and in 1822 produced his earliest known composition, a setting of Psalm 150. At the same time he began to show at least equal literary ability, embarking

Robert and Clara Schumann, lithograph by J. Hofelich.
The Bettmann Archive

on plays (a comedy and two "horror dramas") and poems, including some translations of Horatian odes, which have been preserved. In 1827 he came under the musical influence of the Austrian composer Franz Schubert and the literary influence of the German poet Jean Paul Richter, both of which proved deep and enduring; in the same year he composed some songs (all of which have since been published).

In 1828 Schumann left school and, under pressure from his mother and his guardian (his father having died), entered the University of Leipzig as a law student. At Leipzig his time was devoted not to the law but to song composition, improvisation at the piano, and attempts to write autobiographical novels in the manner of Richter. For a few months he studied the piano seriously with a celebrated teacher, Friedrich Wieck, and thus got to know Wieck's nine-year-old daughter Clara, a brilliant pianist who was just then beginning a successful concert career.

In the summer of 1829 he left Leipzig for Heidelberg where one of the law professors, Anton Friedrich Justus Thibaut, was known as a writer on musical aesthetics, and under Thibaut's influence Schumann made the acquaintance of a great deal of early choral music. He composed waltzes in the style of Franz Schubert, afterward used in his piano cycle *Papillons* (1832), and practiced industriously with a view to abandoning law and becoming a virtuoso pianist—with the result that his mother agreed to allow him to return to Leipzig in October 1830 to study for a trial period with Wieck, who thought highly of his talent but doubted his stability and capacity for hard work.

His Opus 1, also a set of variations, was published in 1831. An accident to one of the fingers of his right hand, which put an end to his hopes of a career as a virtuoso, was perhaps not an unmitigated misfortune, since it confined him to composition. For Schumann, this was a period prolific in piano pieces, which were published either at once or, in revised forms, later.

Two important piano works arose from a love affair with another of Wieck's pupils, Ernestine von Fricken: first, the cycle *Carnaval* (1835), based on the letters (and notes) A, S (Es, *i.e.*, E♭), C, H (B♮ in German), which spelled the town, Asch, where she lived and also were contained in his own name; and, second, the *Études symphoniques* (*Symphonic Studies*, 1834), variations on a theme by her father. The affair lasted for more than a year, but long before the engagement was formally broken off (January 1, 1836) Schumann had fallen in love with the then 16-year-old Clara Wieck. Clara returned his kisses but obeyed her father when he ordered her to break off the relationship. Schumann found himself aban-

Early career

Romance with Clara Wieck

doned for 16 months, during which he expressed his alternate despair and resignation in the great *Fantasy in C Major* for piano, drank wildly, sought consolation with other girls, and even published a bitter, veiled lampoon on Clara in the *Neue Zeitschrift für Musik* (*New Journal for Music*, a periodical that he had helped to found in 1834 and of which he had been editor and principal proprietor since the beginning of 1835). Clara herself made the first move toward a reconciliation, and on September 13, 1837—her 18th birthday—Schumann formally asked her father's permission to marry her; the request was at first evaded rather than refused.

Schumann now entered upon one of his most fertile creative periods, producing a series of imaginative works for piano. Even this was not a time of unalloyed happiness, for Clara refused to marry without financial security, and her father still withheld his consent. A formal statement by Clara on June 15, 1839, initiated legal proceedings for the setting aside of that condition. The affair dragged on for more than a year; it was taken to a court of appeal, which still upheld one of Wieck's objections, that Schumann was a heavy drinker, and then to a yet higher court, which ruled that Wieck must produce proof of habitual drunkenness. This he failed to do, and on September 12, 1840, the marriage took place. Early that year Schumann returned to a field he had neglected for nearly 12 years, that of the solo song; in the space of 11 months (February–December 1840) he composed nearly all the songs on which so much of his reputation rests: the cycles *Myrthen* (*Myrtle*), the two *Liederkreise* (*Song-Cycles*) on texts by Heinrich Heine and Joseph Eichendorff, *Dichterliebe* (*Poet's Love*), *Frauenliebe und Leben* (*Woman's Love and Life*), and many separate songs.

The larger works

Clara had been pressing him to widen his scope, to launch out in other media—above all, the orchestra. He had in earlier days made at least five unsuccessful attempts at works for piano and orchestra; even the *Symphony in G Minor* was never finished. Now in January–February 1841 he composed the *Symphony No. 1 in B Flat Major*, which was at once (March 31) performed under the German composer Felix Mendelssohn at Leipzig; an *Overture, Scherzo, and Finale* (April–May); a *Phantasie* for piano and orchestra (May) which was expanded into the famous *Piano Concerto in A Minor* by the addition of two more movements in 1845; another symphony, in D minor (June–September); and the sketches for yet a third symphony, in C minor, of which only one movement, the scherzo, survives as a piano piece, in *Bunte Blätter*, Opus 99, No. 13. The orchestral impulse was temporarily spent.

Between June 1842 and January 1843 he wrote several chamber works, a new departure for him. The year 1843 was marked by Schumann's most ambitious work so far, a "secular oratorio" (originally conceived as an opera), *Das Paradies und die Peri* (*Paradise and the Peri*), on Thomas Moore's *Lalla Rookh*. He made his debut as a conductor—a role in which he was invariably ineffective —with its first performance (December 4).

During his work on *The Peri* the Staatliche Hochschule für Musik, Leipzig, had been opened with Mendelssohn as director and Schumann as professor of "piano playing, composition, and playing from score"; again he had embarked on activities for which he was unsuited. The first few months of 1844 were spent on a concert tour of Russia with Clara, which depressed Schumann by making him conscious of his inferior role. On returning to Leipzig he resigned the editorship of the *Neue Zeitschrift*. In August he composed some numbers for an opera on Goethe's *Faust*, but work was interrupted by a serious nervous collapse, which led to the Schumanns' leaving Leipzig. From December 1844 to September 1850 he and Clara lived in Dresden, where his health was gradually restored. In December 1845 he began another symphony, *No. 2 in C Major*; but because of aural nerve trouble nearly ten months passed before the score was finished.

Last years

Attempts to get posts in Leipzig and Vienna had also been abortive. In the end, for want of anything better, Schumann accepted the appointment of municipal director of music at Düsseldorf. At first things went tolerably well; in 1850–51 he composed the *Cello Concerto in A Minor* and the *Symphony No. 3 in E Flat Major* (the *Rhenish*) and drastically rewrote the ten-year-old *Symphony in D Minor*, ultimately published as *No. 4*. He also conducted eight subscription concerts, but temperamental differences soon showed themselves, and Schumann's shortcomings as a conductor became obvious. There were a number of painful scenes and chaotic rehearsals; in December 1852 he was asked to resign but declined, and in October 1853 the choir's refusal to sing Mendelssohn's *Die erste Walpurgisnacht* under him brought the final break.

On February 10, 1854, Schumann complained of a "very strong and painful" attack of the ear malady that had troubled him before; this was followed by aural illusions, such as the dictation by angels of a theme (actually a reminiscence of his violin concerto) on which he proceeded to write some variations for piano. On February 26 he asked to be taken to a lunatic asylum and the next day attempted suicide by drowning. (He had contemplated suicide on at least three occasions during the 1830s.) On March 4 he was removed to a private asylum at Endenich, near Bonn, where he lived for nearly two and a half years, able to correspond for a time with Clara and his friends. One or two visits by Brahms or the young violinist Joseph Joachim agitated him terribly, and Clara was kept from him until July 27, 1856, when it was realized that the end was near. He seemed to recognize her but was unable to speak intelligibly. On July 29, 1856, he died.

MAJOR WORKS
Orchestral works

SYMPHONIES: Four complete symphonies, *No. 1 in B Flat Major*, op. 38 (*Spring Symphony;* 1841); *No. 2 in C Major*, op. 61 (1846); *No. 3 in E Flat Major*, op. 97 (*Rhenish Symphony;* 1850); *No. 4 in D Minor*, op. 120 (1841; rewritten 1851).

OVERTURES: Overture to Byron's *Manfred*, op. 115 (1848–49).

CONCERTOS: *Piano Concerto in A Minor*, op. 54 (1841–45); *Cello Concerto in A Minor*, op. 129 (1850).

Chamber music

Three string quartets; three piano trios; three violin sonatas; *Piano Quintet in E Flat Major*, op. 44 (1842); *Piano Quartet in E Flat Major*, op. 47 (1842).

Vocal music

SONGS: Numerous sets of solo songs with piano, including the song-cycles *Liederkreis* (on a text by Heine), op. 24 (1840); *Liederkreis* (on a text by Eichendorff), op. 39 (1840); *Frauenliebe und Leben*, op. 42 (1840); *Dichterliebe*, op. 48 (1840).

OPERA: *Genoveva*, op. 81 (1847–50).

CHORAL WORKS WITH ORCHESTRA: *Das Paradies und die Peri*, op. 50 (1841–43).

Piano music

Theme and Variations on the Name of Abegg, op. 1 (1830); *Papillons*, op. 2 (1832); *Études symphoniques*, op. 13 (1834); *Carnaval*, op. 9 (1834–35); *Davidsbündlertänze*, op. 6 (1837); *Fantasiestücke*, op. 12 (1837); *Kinderszenen*, op. 15 (1838); *Kreisleriana*, op. 16 (1838); *Fantasy in C Major*, op. 17 (1836); three piano sonatas.

BIBLIOGRAPHY. GERALD ABRAHAM (ed.), *Schumann: A Symposium* (1952), authoritative essays on all the works; WOLFGANG BOETTICHER, *Robert Schumann: Einführung in Persönlichkeit und Werk* (1941), a monumental study of various aspects of the personality and works, based on fresh sources; JOAN CHISSELL, *Schumann*, rev. ed. (1967), a succinct general biography and study of the works; *Schumann's Keyboard Works* (1972), an introduction to the piano music; HENRY PLEASANTS (ed. and trans.), *The Musical World of Robert Schumann: A Selection from His Own Writings* (1965), a recent translation of Schumann's letters; LEON PLANTINGA, *Schumann as Critic* (1967), a valuable study of the prose writings; ERIC SAMS, *The Songs of Robert Schumann* (1969), an exhaustive study of the songs; STEPHEN WALSH, *The Lieder of Robert Schumann* (1971), a shorter, more general, and very perceptive study of the songs; GEORG EISMANN (ed.), *Robert Schumann: Tagebücher*, vol. 1, *1827–1838* (1972), the private diaries published in full for the first time.

(G.E.H.A.)

Science, History of

Until recently, the history of science was a story of success. The triumphs of science represented a cumulative process of increasing knowledge and a sequence of victories over ignorance and superstition; and from science flowed a stream of inventions for the improvement of human life. The recent realization of deep moral problems within science, of external forces and constraints on its development, and of dangers in uncontrolled technological change has challenged historians to a critical reassessment of this earlier simple faith.

The historian soon recognizes that the idea of science that he acquired during his education is only one of many and that it is a product of temporary circumstances. The latter include the presence of nearly autonomous centres of research in universities; large-scale application of scientific results by technologists; and the independence of scientific research from politics and religion. In the 19th century there was a blurring of these present distinctions between science, industry, and philosophy, and three or four centuries earlier, the historian finds that the study of nature was conducted within a framework of assumptions about the world that are now rejected as magical or superstitious. Also, the deeper that historians penetrate into the roots of modern European science, the more difficult it is to separate the "scientific" attitudes, and the "factual" results, from those that appear to be their opposites. Earlier historians treated these mixtures as anomalies; they are now used as clues to reveal conceptions of the natural world, and man's way of knowing it, that had vitality and meaning in their own time. Thus the history of science demands and fosters an enhanced imagination: the ability to see oneself and one's science as one phase in a continuing evolution. In a period when relevance is demanded of scholarly studies, the history of science provides this just as much in its exploration of the distant and strange structures of inquiry into the natural world as in its critical analysis of the immediate sources of contemporary conceptions and practices.

Aims of the history of science

This account will be organized around the natural science created by modern European civilization, for this is the form of science that has brought the world to its present condition and that, it seems, must be understood and controlled if mankind is to survive. The roots of this science lie deep in the human past and in many civilizations. Here, they can be mentioned only in passing, but at the outset it must be pointed out that the present way of comprehending the natural world is a very recent development. It was possible for great civilizations of the past to achieve highly developed technologies and religious and legal systems in the complete absence of a conception of science as it is now understood. Such were the civilizations of ancient Egypt, Mesopotamia, India, and the Western Hemisphere. Even the Hebrews, people whose religion forms a large part of the basis of European civilization, were indifferent to science. Although some two and a half millennia ago the Greeks created a system of thought that was similar to the scientific, in succeeding centuries there was little progress beyond their achievement and little comprehension of it. In Europe, science has enjoyed continuous progress for some 500 years, even though for most of that period it was of minor interest among a cultural elite. The lives of ordinary people were affected only in the most indirect ways by the thoughts of scientists and the application of their results. The great power of science and its pervasive influence on all aspects of life are thus very recent developments. Although knowledge of the world is independent of the particular circumstances of its first discovery and can be transmitted between nations and cultures, the human endeavour whereby that knowledge is achieved is a product of its everchanging human environment.

In this article, only a broad and general survey can be made. For details in the history of any particular subject, see the historical section in the article on that subject.

SCIENCE IN ANCIENT AND MEDIEVAL WESTERN CIVILIZATION

Science in Greek civilization. The dawn of European science has traditionally been located among the philosophers of the Greek city-states on the coast and islands of the eastern Mediterranean, in the later 6th and 5th centuries BC. Their work is known only through fragments, references, and brief quotations made by authors who came later, perhaps by hundreds of years. By selection of fragments they can be made to appear more rational and scientific than is justified. For example, the famous saying of the earliest known philosopher, Thales, "All is water," is in its fragment actually followed by "and the world is full of gods." It does appear likely, however, that the early Greek philosophers were concerned with explaining the phenomena of the perceptual world rather than offering recipes for practice and that they did so by invoking causes rather than personal agents, even if these causes were themselves derived by analogy with handicraft experience and human behaviour (thus the cosmic principles of "love and strife" of Empedocles). In this break from the mythological explanations of their own culture and of the ancient civilizations from which they probably borrowed much of their detailed knowledge, the Greeks are precursors of the modern European scientific attitude. One very important tradition, that of the Pythagoreans, was explicitly religious. Their founder attempted to find the key to universal harmony, both natural and social, and the personality of numbers, which were seen as shaped arrays of dots, was an important clue. Somewhat later appeared the Eleatics, Zeno and Parmenides, using a sophisticated conceptual analysis to support the philosophical position that asserted the unchanging unity of existence. Zeno's paradoxes of aggregation and motion presented a challenge that is still alive.

Basic principles of the Greek view

Although by the later 5th century this inquiry became quite sophisticated, it was still speculative explanation of commonsense phenomena rather than highly technical argument about controlled artificial experiences; the latter emerges only with Aristotle. Also, although this philosophy flourished among the elite in the so-called golden age when Pericles ruled Athens, the common sense of the time was still mythical and magical, as can be seen from the list of crafts in Aeschylus' *Prometheus Bound*. In the troubled times of the later 5th century, the suspicion of irreligion among the philosophers became strong and is implicit in the condemnation of Anaxagoras and in the attacks on Socrates in *The Clouds* of Aristophanes.

The two learned arts in which there was an approach to maturity by this time were, first, medicine, the practice of which was at least attempting to apply disciplined method in observation and inference, and, second, geometry, which was accumulating a body of results about relations between particular constructed figures and was approaching the problems of logical structure (in successive editions of *Elements*, precursors of Euclid) and of definition (as with the irrational ratios, as $\sqrt{2}$).

Plato, early 4th century BC, is the earliest philosopher whose writings are extant. He was a powerful propagandist for mathematics. In the *Republic* he argued that geometry prepares the mind for the discourse of dialectic about the real ideas, of which perceptible things are but images, and thence to wisdom and illumination. His *Timaeus* was in earlier times a more influential work; in this he sketches a cosmogony along Pythagorean lines, including a theory of music in terms of simple ratios and a survey of accepted theories of physics and physiology. He befriended geometers, including Eudoxus, who probably founded the mathematical cartography of the spherical Earth, and also gave a profound treatment of irrational quantities.

Aristotle, also in the 4th century BC, was one of the world's first, and greatest, scholars. His interests ranged over the entire natural and human world, including ethics and metaphysics. Through accurate observations and disciplined theorizing, he created a biological science and a taxonomy much like those in use today. Later scholars have identified mistakes in his descriptions, but there are classic cases where his apparently false reports were checked and confirmed (on rare, local species) less than a century ago. He also organized cooperative research for large-scale studies, as in the comparative study of the constitutions of the Greek city-states. He was a master of scholarly method; in each study he would define the area and its problems, dialogue critically with his predecessors (usually showing they were naïve in some important respect), and then proceed by experience and reason to develop his argument. To him are owed most of the basic divisions of learning and also the articulation of the principles of method and of the different sorts of knowledge attainable by the use of reason.

The root of the philosophy of nature

Aristotle started his career as a disciple of Plato but eventually came to disagree with him on fundamentals. In particular, he considered mathematics as an abstraction from natural reality, which for him was a complex, self-regulating living system. Indeed, all subsequent philosophy of nature is a dialogue between Plato and Aristotle, for whom the deepest philosophical problems were related to life. His biological studies culminated in the problem of generation, the transmission of form between separate bodies. He tried also to explain the workings of the first cause of all physical phenomena, through the realization of its purposes in the celestial cycles. He had little sympathy with enchantments; for him, dreams were a result of subconscious thoughts and bodily discomfort rather than messages from a spirit. His principles of explanation were in terms of perceptible qualities (*e.g.*, hot or cold, wet or dry) and a series of causes (matter, agent, plan, and purpose, in ascending order) on the analogy of craftwork by the principle "art imitates nature."

For some years he was tutor to the prince who later became Alexander the Great, and, though later this caused him difficulties at Athens, his influence passed on to the Museum of Alexandria. His writings were the basis of natural philosophy wherever it was practiced up to the 17th century, but he was inevitably misunderstood, and his writings were used for the framing of sterile dogmas. Aristotle was centuries ahead of his times and is still a source of insight and instruction today.

In the empire created by Alexander the Great (late 4th century BC) Greek culture flourished. The great cities competed for famous scholars and classical texts, and some of them established centres of learning such as the Museum at the planned city of Alexandria. Independent of the religious temples, these had large libraries, provided employment for scientists and scholars, and by preserving records and instruments lent continuity to research work. Although this Hellenistic Age (roughly 323 to 30 BC) did not reach the heights of genius of the earlier one, it produced some great mathematicians (Euclid, Archimedes, and Appolonius) and astronomers (Hipparchus). Studies in medicine and physiology also advanced, and, during this period, the origins of European alchemy were developed by Egyptian chemists attempting to rationalize chemical change by Aristotelian theories.

Science in Rome. Toward the close of the pre-Christian period, the Roman Empire achieved dominance over the entire Mediterranean world. Rome presents a paradox to historians of science. This civilization, so sophisticated and apparently modern in its politics and personalities, very strong in the learned discipline of the law, very progressive in the state technologies of warfare and public hygiene, with direct access to the corpus of Greek science, nonetheless failed to produce a single scientist. Two very great scientists lived during the reign of Marcus Aurelius in the 2nd century AD, but they were both Greek: Galen of Pergamon, who synthesized and advanced the study of medicine, anatomy, and physiology; and Ptolemy of Alexandria, who brought mathematical astronomy near to a classic perfection and also tried to bring the mathematical, scientific approach to the earliest empirical social science, astrological prediction. The Romans themselves considered science as fit only for casual speculation, on the one hand, and practical techniques, on the other. Their encyclopaedia literature is a cautionary tale of the corruptions of knowledge in the absence of critical standards. Scientific matters were discussed seriously among the Romans only in connection with basically ethical philosophies. The two leading schools were the Stoics and Epicureans, and the messages offered by them to the wise man were, respectively, dignified resignation

and the pursuit of happiness. The latter school, however, produced a masterpiece of speculative science, *De rerum natura* (*On the Nature of Things*), by Lucretius (1st century BC). The message of his atomistic explanations of phenomena was that immaterial spirits are only fictions whose function is to instill fear and obedience among the superstitious masses.

Causes of Roman failure in science

To explain the Romans' utter failing in science, historians have speculated on whether slavery, by stifling the drive for industrial innovation, was the cause; but this seems too simple. Perhaps the social structure of Rome, combined with its long adherence to gross forms of magic, left no place for an appreciation of that peculiar commitment to the hard and hazardous road to knowledge and wisdom that lies through disciplined inquiry into isolated aspects of the natural world. Indeed, when one considers how few have been the cultures in which science has flourished, one may reverse the question and consider Rome as the normal and classical Greece as the surprising phenomenon to be explained.

Medieval science. The Greco-Roman civilization went through its full cycle in about 1,000 years. The next half millennium in Europe, up to the year 1000, is often called the Dark Ages. Literate culture in western Europe, ruled by Rome, was barely kept alive in the monasteries, with occasional attempts at revival by great kings such as Alfred and Charlemagne. By contrast, in the Eastern Empire ruled by Constantinople a civilized society continued, although in all its own 1,000-year history Byzantium produced little new science of note. As a new, ruder form of society took shape in the West, there was great pioneering work in the clearing of forests and swamps for settlement, and some crucial inventions (horse collar, stirrup, heavy plow, windwheels, and waterwheels) were either invented or borrowed. In the early 11th century, most learned men knew and understood only a few tattered fragments of ancient science, but thereafter progress was rapid. The 12th century enjoyed a renaissance brought about partly by contact with the superior Islāmic civilization in Spain and Palestine, partly by the development of towns with literate upper classes. From this period come the first speculative treatises on natural philosophy. The 13th century saw the founding of the universities and the great age of scholastic learning. To this age belong the great theologian St. Thomas Aquinas and the experimentally minded Roger Bacon. In the 1350s, however, Europe was struck by economic and social disaster in the form of a general financial collapse and the Black Death (the bubonic plague). Although philosophical debate, including interesting mathematical speculation, still took place, scientifically this later period was sterile.

Opinions on medieval science have oscillated wildly. Earlier historians saw it as unrelieved dogmatism and superstition, while others have tried to show that many essential facts and principles of modern science were discovered then. The problem becomes clearer when it is realized that learned men were not at all trying to do scientific research as it is understood now. Natural philosophy and particular facts were studied mainly in connection with problems relating to religion, either for the elucidation of biblical texts (literally and figuratively) or for debate with adherents of pagan philosophies (notably Aristotle as interpreted by the Muslim philosopher Averroës) or in the development of a mystical Neoplatonic cosmology in which light was studied as the clue to reality that can be grasped by the senses and described geometrically. The distinction between technique, theoretical magic, and folk magic was not at all clear to anyone. Hence in modern terms, even Roger Bacon was the gullible victim of superstition. Thus in Europe in a formative period of the present civilization, there is something that could be called science but that requires anthropological imagination to understand.

SCIENCE IN OTHER CIVILIZATIONS

Description of the scientific achievements of the other great civilizations of the world is brief in this article because of the considerably lesser contributions they made to science as it is presently understood.

Islām. Islāmic culture is the most relevant to European science. Not only is the religion itself closely related to Judaism and Christianity, but there was active cultural contact between Arabic-speaking lands and Latin Europe at crucial periods. Ironically, the great age of Islām coincided with the low point of culture in western Europe. Conquests by the Prophet's followers began in the 7th century, and, by the 10th, Arabic was the literate language of nations stretching from Persia to Spain. Arabic conquerors generally brought peace and prosperity to the countries they settled. For example, the library of Córdoba in Spain apparently had more than 500,000 books at a time when scarcely 5,000 survived north of the Pyrenees. Also, the Muslims were tolerant of the other monotheistic faiths, so that Jews rose to high position in Islāmic lands at a time when they were scarcely permitted survival in Europe. Drawing on the traditions of Greek science through Christian scholars of Syria, the early Arabic rulers of Baghdad in the 9th century had the bulk of the corpus of Greek science translated, and, soon after, their own scholars advanced further, particularly in mathematics, astronomy, optics, chemistry, and medicine. The social base of science, however, was thin. In a theocratic society, medicine alone among the pagan sciences was considered acceptable. Hence no single centre of scientific culture flourished for much more than a century, and, although materials were transmitted between them, the loss of continuity prevented a sustained development. Also, the style of scholarship was for a single man to try to encompass the whole world of learning for the achievement of secular wisdom, perhaps as a way toward illumination. The very greatest men could make creative advances, but cooperative scholarship, necessary for making lesser men effective, was rare.

Islāmic Spain

Contact between Islām and Latin Europe came mainly through Spain, where Christians and Jews could act as intermediaries and translators. The 12th century saw a heroic program of translation of works from Arabic to Latin, at first in astrology and magic, then in medicine, and finally in philosophy and science. A lesser route was through southern Italy, where commercial contacts existed with Tunisia. It is significant that the earliest medical school in Europe was at Salerno and that it was later rivalled by Montpellier, also close to Arabic and Jewish sources. Despite its leadership, however, even by the time of the translations, the Islāmic civilization was under pressure from barbarians all along its periphery, and it soon went into decline. In addition to its enormous service to Western civilization in preserving and then transmitting the Greek heritage, Arabic has also contributed to modern science a number of words, mainly of plants and foods, but also such words as alcohol and algebra.

India. The Indian civilization is about the oldest still alive, and it achieved a high level of technology at an early stage. European contacts with it come mainly through Arabic sources, and historical research is not yet sufficiently advanced to distinguish priorities and lines of transmission. It does appear that Indian mathematics, with a highly developed system of numeration and reckoning, influenced Arabic algebra; it also provided the principal arabic numerals (*i.e.*, the nine digits and a zero in a place-value system). But the characteristic science of this civilization is that of the higher consciousness, and, in this, European thought has been so deficient that it becomes aware of its lack only occasionally. Hence the achievements of Europe and India cannot be compared strictly but must be recognized as being complementary.

China and Japan. China presents more of a challenge to the historian of European science. Its basic common sense is this-worldly, although it is based on interpersonal harmonies rather than abstract regularities. In spite of the distances between them and their totally different languages, there has been more or less continuous contact between Europe and China since classical Greek times. Usually the connection was indirect and restricted to trade in luxury goods, but even in classical times there were curious synchronisms in philosophical movements in Europe and China, and in the 13th century there was considerable personal contact, of which that of Marco

Polo is but the most famous instance. Also, Chinese technology until the Renaissance was consistently more advanced than European, and, in his monumental work, the British historian of science Joseph Needham has shown the patterns of transmission of a series of important inventions from China westward. Indeed, the three great inventions that 16th-century writers and, later, Francis Bacon saw as crucial for the transformation of European society all came from China: the magnetic compass, gunpowder, and the printing press. Yet Europe never recognized its debt to China, while, more important, the Chinese never achieved the breakthrough to modern science of the European sort. China's crucial inventions

The ignorance of the debt of the West to China is easily explained. In the period when technical devices were imported or copied, they were of little concern to the learned, and so their ultimate origins were never questioned. When the Jesuit missionaries arrived in China in the late 16th century, bringing the fruits of Western science and technology as proofs of the superiority of Christianity, it was at a time when these pursuits were at a low ebb in China, so that many native achievements had been forgotten. The failure of China to make the breakthrough may be considered in relation to the two phases of the creation of European science discussed below. Chinese society was always stable, ruled by a nonhereditary civil service with a governing philosophy that was one of practical accommodation rather than of abstract principles. Merchants were a distrusted class, and technical innovation had to be accomplished within the bureaucracy. Thus, the features of European Renaissance society that impelled the practical arts forward at a rapid pace were never present in China. Moreover, the Chinese philosophy of nature was also based on organic analogies and relations of harmony. It never could have accommodated the picture of dead matter moving in accordance with mathematical laws, on which Galilean science was based. Related to this is the technical fact that only the Greeks had produced an abstract, logical mathematics that could function as the language of science. Chinese mathematics consisted of reckoning rules, and, in spite of their great sophistication, these could be applied only to the detailed calculations for which they had been designed. Thus, China failed to become Europe. It is likely, however, that with the new appreciation in the West of the need for the establishment of a subtle harmony between the individual self and nature, scientific society may yet have something to learn from the ancient Chinese way.

Finally, there is the fascinating case of Japan. For centuries a cultural colony of China, it had a brief exposure to Western science and religion before its rulers decided early in the 17th century to close the door on such dangerous influences. In the latter part of the 19th century, the Japanese decided to assimilate with the rest of the world and then did so with a vengeance. Their own native religion was sufficiently vague to accommodate any assertions of Western science, and the Japanese scientists, technologists, and ordinary folk now manage to live partly in a hyper-modern world and partly still in one of ancient, rigid social tradition.

CREATION OF EUROPEAN SCIENCE

The "science" of which histories are written is European. Although other civilizations made essential contributions toward it, and though now all nations participate in research, natural science is a distinctive creation of Europe and its cultural colonies. Its roots in thought and society are the same as those of European technology and of its acquisitive spirit; hence science is an important part of the process that achieved domination for this small and, until recently, barbarous corner of the world. The creation of European science has two phases, one of technical development in the 16th century, the other of philosophical revolution in the 17th century. Out of these came the idea of science that is current to this day.

Rebirth of science in the Renaissance. The word science and its ancestors in Greek and Latin is an old one, with continuously changing meanings. In the period now

Liberal
and
mechanical
arts

being considered, it was restricted to the fields providing knowledge: theology and philosophy. For the rest, the term was art or technique. Some arts were called liberal and were taught in Latin at schools and universities. They were language, logic, rhetoric, mathematics, and the learned, or professional, arts of medicine and law. The other arts were mechanical and generally involved unpleasant work for low pay. The ruling conception of knowledge was still radically different from that of the present day. It was universally accepted that there had been a golden age when all things were known (in the Garden of Eden and perhaps again in some age of sages or in classical times). The rediscovery of these truths was not merely a matter of gathering facts; for their first provision and subsequent loss had been events with religious significance. As the perceptible world was strongly influenced by divine, demonic, and magical agencies, so too the penetration of its secrets was more than a secular task. Since the modern conception of science has some of its roots in the conflict against this world view, it is difficult to imagine how a scientific point of view could have existed within it. Until the historian comes to terms with it, however, he remains imprisoned in his own temporary categories, unable to understand the larger world outside.

A convenient starting date for the period of European expansion is 1413, the year of the first raid by Europeans on the African coast, just a half millennium before World War I began the breakup of the European empires. In the early 15th century the cultural scene in Europe was generally bleak: the universities were in decay, the church was disintegrating, and the economy still suffered from effects of the Black Death; the subjects now called science barely existed except when studied in connection with some practical art; even then, materials were scarce, competence low, and social organization rudimentary.

Roots of
the rebirth

The roots of the rebirth of science can be located in three main centres. The first and most famous root is something that can be called the discovery of man and nature, a product of the artistic Renaissance of 15th-century Italy. The inspiration for this was the discovery of classical antiquity and the fact that the Humanist scholars edited and published Latin and Greek texts and translations in all fields, including science. The visual arts, loosely grouped as architecture, were raised in social esteem and given a classical pedigree in a book by the Roman author Vitruvius. The great artists became men of wide interests and culture, whom the nobility sought to patronize; the career of Leonardo da Vinci in the later 15th century exemplifies this exalted position and many-sided activity.

At the same time, the mountainous region in southern Germany, with end points at Nuremberg and Cracow, enjoyed a rapid growth in mining, metallurgy, and trade. Practical mathematics and the theory and practice of metalworking were developed there. The Rhine linked this region with the prosperous weaving centres of Flanders, and it was on this trade route that printing was invented by Gutenberg. This was a highly sophisticated and expensive venture in what might be called research and development, the problem being to find alloy metals of the correct properties for molds in which to cast replaceable bits of type. Once invented, the process spread rapidly. By the end of the century every major city had its press, and the availability of cheap books worked its transformation on learning and culture.

During the century, the Spanish and Portuguese began their explorations. The Portuguese worked down and around the coast of Africa, perhaps using Brazil for a landfall, looking for gold and for the legendary Prester John in Ethiopia. Instead, they found the sea route to India, thus bypassing the Middle East route for spices (then defined as anything purchased from the technically superior Eastern nations, including flavourings, condiments, and drugs). Joining the search late, the Spanish financed Columbus, and their conquistadores then opened up the New World. Transoceanic navigation created new demands on astronomy and on mathematical techniques and instruments, and the earliest research establishments were those of Spain and Portugal, specifically for hydrographic techniques. The New World introduced new plants, animals, diseases, and civilizations to Europe; the excitement and unsettling effects of its discovery lasted for generations.

The printed books of the 16th century provide (in their modern reproductions) a convenient source of evidence for the state of science. At the beginning of the century, knowledge was still rudimentary and largely dependent on confused digests of ancient and Arabic sources. By midcentury there appeared works that surpassed the best of their predecessors. In astronomy, there was the *De revolutionibus* (1543) of the Polish Nicolaus Copernicus, a technical masterpiece as well as a revolutionary treatise on cosmology. In anatomy, the Belgian Andreas Vesalius created a new approach to anatomical research and teaching in his *De fabrica* (1543). In mathematics, the Italian Gerolamo Cardano advanced algebra (providing the general solution of the cubic equation) in his *Ars magna* (1545).

During this century the Protestant Reformation touched off a series of wars for which gentlemen officers needed certain new mathematical skills associated with fortification and gunnery, which also called for new classes of practitioners, such as military surgeons and engineers. Although some of the theoretical fields tended to be speculative, there was in general an enormous improvement in all these arts. By the end of the century, the applied mathematical arts were a standard part of the education of a gentleman on the Continent. The French mathematician-philosopher René Descartes learned them at his Jesuit school and the Italian Galileo taught them at the University of Padua. In this way there came a temporary lowering of the barriers of class snobbery against such arts. This was crucial for the formation of the new philosophy and its acceptance by the liberally educated audience to which it was directed.

The new
philosophy
of the
late 16th
century

The new philosophy, however, was not a prerequisite for successful science. Around the turn of the century, and later, there appeared great works of science containing particular discoveries that are still accepted as facts to this day, but the scientists who achieved them were still working within the world view that was shortly to be rejected by the new philosophy. Thus William Gilbert (1600) in England explained the compass needle in terms of the Earth's being a giant, very weak magnet, but he did this in the course of proving that the world soul is embodied in the magnet. In Prague, Johannes Kepler shortly afterward (1609) discovered the true orbits of the planets as ellipses around the sun, and he never ceased his search for the harmonies of the cosmos. Later (1628), William Harvey in England established the circulation of the blood, but for him it was more a microcosmic image of the circulations of the world than it was a purely mechanical system. The strangest mixture, by modern standards, is to be found in the chemistry of Paracelsus and his followers of the 16th and 17th centuries. They combined elements of metallurgical crafts, folk medicine, alchemy, mystical religion, and social reform, and yet they were successful as chemists.

Revolution in natural philosophy. In the 17th century, there occurred a radical recasting of the objects, methods, and functions of natural knowledge. The new objects were regular phenomena in a world devoid of human and spiritual properties; the methods were of disciplined, cooperative research; and the functions were the combination of scholarly knowledge and industrial power. Although this is frequently called the scientific revolution, it was a revolution about science rather than in it. In most fields of inquiry, progress was continuous through both centuries, nor did the external social environment of science change drastically. For a leading cause of the inception and rapid diffusion of this philosophy, the radical change in educated common sense about the world must be examined; briefly stated, the change was from the notion of a living cosmos of earlier times to that of a dead universe.

The main target of attack by the revolutionaries was the traditional higher education that was called Scholastic. Scholasticism assumed a living world, created and guided by God quite simply for man's benefit, and its study was largely accomplished by citing authorities, either philosophical or scriptural. The function of this knowledge was to rationalize sense experience in harmony with revealed religion. By contrast, the ancient and honourable sciences of astrology and alchemy, and their relations, were usually dismissed by the new philosophers with a passing sneer because, in their common sense, these were so ridiculous as to require no refutation. Thus, in 1600 an educated man knew that the Earth was in the centre of the cosmos, the seat of change, decay, and Christian redemption, while above it circled the planets and stars, themselves pure and unchanging but moved by some sort of intelligent or divine spirits and also signalling and influencing human events by their locations and aspects. One hundred years later, his equally Christian descendant knew (unless he lived in a church-controlled Catholic country) that the Earth was but one of the planets moving through unimaginable distances in empty space and that God could still operate. Similarly, the earlier man, as a reasonable person, would accept the overwhelming evidence for the working of enchantments and the prevalence of witches; while the later one, with equal certainty, would dismiss all those stories as the effects of charlatanry, in the one case, and torture, in the other.

The prophets of revolution in the 17th century

The prophets of this 17th-century revolution were Francis Bacon in England, born 1561, René Descartes in France, born 1596, and Galileo Galilei in Italy, born 1564. Each of them was committed to a great mission, over and above particular facts and theories, and each in his way tasted tragic defeat. Bacon, professionally in the law and politics, borrowed themes from earlier pietistic philosophers and saw himself as inaugurating a reform of knowledge, so that the material redemption of mankind could go with spiritual salvation in preparation for the millennium. He hoped to effect this program through royal patronage and was shattered when his public career came to an end suddenly in an unjust disgrace. Descartes believed that he had rescued truth and religion from the corrosive criticism of the skeptics, by a method based on the example of geometry. By its means he would be the new Aristotle, constructing a complete philosophy, starting with mechanics and reaching medicine. Thus he would inaugurate a new epoch of longevity and wisdom, realizing the program of the Rosicrucian mystical fraternity with whose ideals he had become identified. But his work became bogged down in complexities of every sort, and, by the end of his short life, he knew that he was only a great metaphysician and mathematician. Galileo was less exalted in his ideals and more thorough in practice. He only wanted to destroy the Scholastic conception of philosophy and substitute his own, one of free exploration of an impersonal mathematical universe. For him, the Copernican system was a very beautiful fact in its own right and also a weapon against the professorial simpletons. He was insufficiently sensitive to the religious and ideological consequences of what he thought was his little revolution in its time and place, and so he blundered disastrously into a conflict with his former friend and protector Pope Urban VIII. Although under house arrest, ill, and going blind, he maintained an invigorating hate for his enemies and, at the age of 74, published his masterpiece on mechanics, the *Two New Sciences*. Bacon's contribution to science was nil, but he provided an inspiring ideal and also shrewd judgments on the social activity of science. Descartes created a new metaphysics, a radically improved algebra and geometry, and some viable results in physics (explanation of the rainbow). Galileo's vast labours for Copernicus had only an indirect effect, and that a mixed one; but by his mechanics he brought relative clarity to the science of motion and laid firm foundations for future work.

In spite of their differences in style and contribution, these three prophets shared a common commitment about the natural world and its study. Nature itself was seen by them as devoid of spiritual and human properties. There could be no dialogue with it, whether using mystical illumination or inspired authority. Rather, it had to be investigated soberly and impersonally, using sense experience and reason. Strange and prodigious phenomena, such as earthquakes, wonder cures, and monstrous births, which had been important subjects of speculation over the ages, were seen to be of less significance than regular, repeatable observations. Care and self-discipline were necessary in observation as well as theorizing, and cooperative work was important for the steady accumulation and testing of results.

The goals of inquiry still retained an influence from magic in that the traditional philosopher's ideal of contemplative wisdom was replaced by that of domination over nature for human benefit. But the loss of belief in magical powers entailed changes in methods and also in responsibilities. In the absence of potent enchantments and elixirs, knowledge of nature was either beneficial when applied to marginal improvements of industry and medicine or was innocent. The moral optimism of modern European science was thus built into its foundations and became unquestioned common sense, until the hour when atomic bombs were dropped on the civilians of Hiroshima and Nagasaki.

The scientific societies

The establishment of scientific societies was a direct result of the new conception of natural knowledge and the methods of its pursuit. From the outset it was recognized that such societies, and their journals, must achieve a harmony between the needs of the community for rapid diffusion of results and the needs of scientists for the protection of their private property in their hard-won results. The Royal Society in London, proclaiming its adherence to the ideals of Francis Bacon and suppressing its connections with reformers on the parliamentary side, was chartered in 1662 by the newly restored king, Charles II. The French followed suit in a few years' time, and somewhat later other continental monarchs did the same. National styles asserted themselves even this early. The Royal Society, for example, was a private club with little more than moral support from the crown, while the continental academies were established by the state and the members gained an income though they lost their independence.

As regards the constitution and workings of the natural world, the new philosophers (with the exception of Bacon) assumed that all visible phenomena are the result of interactions of invisibly small particles of matter. These have neither intelligence nor purpose, and thus the paradigm reaction is the collision of balls. Hence the perceptible qualities of things (on which Aristotelian science was based) are only secondary, mere effects in our minds. The primary qualities are those capable of mathematical description. Although this view had many disputed variations (Newton in particular adding force as a real agent), there was an unusually sharp demarcation between its adherents and those of its rival views, Aristotelianism and alchemy.

In some fields the new philosophy was appropriate for progress at that stage, and the fields were transformed. Such were cosmology, mechanics, and pneumatics. Elsewhere in science its distinctive achievements were modest. Optics had received its modern start from Kepler and electricity and magnetism from Gilbert. Chemical theory was not significantly advanced; the corpuscular explanations of Robert Boyle in England (middle 17th century) only rationalized existing ideas. In biology and medicine, although there was a premature attempt at reduction to a physical model, this did not show results for another two centuries. The direct impact on technology was restricted to the rationalization of simple machines and the development of vacuum techniques. Thus the new philosophy was not a generalization from the success of a new science. Rather, it was a prior metaphysical commitment that, eventually, over later generations, proved its fruitfulness in all fields.

Under these circumstances, it is not surprising that many scientists, particularly those in chemistry and medicine, rejected the corpuscular philosophy as a useless revival of an ancient atheistic system, since, if the corpuscles had no intelligence or purpose, their collisions were random, accidental, and the whole universe was without purpose. Chemistry was not yet a study of controlled processes involving pure reagents but was still tied to craft-industrial practice and to Paracelsian medicine. In England during the Civil War, there occurred a debate on the nature and social functions of science and education, in which the mathematically oriented scholars found themselves on the conservative side. The issue, raised in 1654 by a chemist, John Webster, was whether or not the universities should replace their antiquated, sterile curriculum by studies of honest, hardworking, practical crafts based on Paracelsian chemistry. The defenders of the status quo (including the future founders of the Royal Society) argued that genuine scientific teaching was available to those who wanted it; but at last they had to admit that they accepted the universities' role as finishing schools for the elite and for that reason would not trouble the students with compulsory new subjects.

Achievements of Sir Isaac Newton

The career of Sir Isaac Newton at the end of the 17th century illustrates the complexities that persisted even when the revolution had been successful. One of the greatest scientists and mathematicians of all time, he brought the heavens and Earth together in one impersonal law of attraction, the law of gravity, and also brought a new rigour to methods of quantitative experimental investigation. Although he advocated the utmost caution in theorizing, he still believed it possible and proper to induce from the phenomena of nature to a discussion of the deity. When he came to the foundations of his physics and discussed space, time, gravity, and force, he found theology of direct relevance. He also used astronomical methods for an improvement of ancient and biblical chronology and firmly believed that a study of the Old Testament prophecies would produce a true interpretation, thus providing guidance in the politico-religious affairs of the time. His masterpiece, the *Principia* (1687), was in many ways the culmination of the scientific revolution. By the time it appeared, however, the impetus had slackened, and no new recruits of the same calibre were coming forward. Indeed, by the end of the 17th century, interest in natural philosophy had ebbed so much that the Royal Society was nearly defunct. It was revived by Newton himself from 1704, to become a club for gentlemen who enjoyed hearing about experiments and collections. Nevertheless, the main work of the revolution in philosophy had been accomplished, and European literate culture, including science, was firmly set on the path to complete secularization.

The image of Newton dominated science in the 18th century, just as that of his friend John Locke dominated philosophy. The early 18th century was a complacent age. Europe was recovering from two centuries of turmoil. Outside the sphere of the Enlightenment, there were no great philosophical struggles, and the science that was practiced was mainly consolidation. A handful of great mathematicians (the Bernoulli family and Leonhard Euler, all of Switzerland) developed the differential and integral calculus invented by the German philosopher Gottfried Leibniz to the form in which it is now taught. Natural history developed steadily, receiving social organization and an intellectual synthesis from the Swedish botanist Carolus Linnaeus. "Experimental philosophy" was cultivated by gentlemen, and a successful theory of static electricity was established by the American scientist and diplomat Benjamin Franklin. Although these achievements did not comprise a great advance, they firmly established a certain style of science—that advocated by the prophets of the new philosophy, although, of course, without their revolutionary inspiration.

Nature of European science. The special character of European science can be explained by the circumstances in which scientists in these two successive phases worked on their inherited materials. These included the basic principle of knowing the natural world through demonstrative argument, a principle first achieved in Greek culture, then picked up by Islāmic civilization but not by any other. Although, at the beginning of the Renaissance, European science and technology were derived from older traditions and were generally inferior, certain features of European society of the time enabled it to make exceptionally rapid progress. Even though society was still largely agrarian, undemocratic, and stratified by inherited social position, there were several areas in which the style of social life was more fluid and individualistic than anywhere else. There was a freedom to invent and to exploit one's inventions for private gain unhindered by state suppression. In other civilizations (the Far East and medieval Europe), technical innovation was monitored and suppressed if it threatened political or social stability. In the relatively fluid society of Europe, individuals had a motive for innovation in that they could advance themselves thereby. Also, the barriers between different fields of activity appropriate to different classes were relaxed, permitting the educated man to dabble in invention, using his knowledge and literate skills. Invention could be in devices or in knowledge; men could move freely from one to another and back again. The context in which this destabilizing activity was fostered was one of aggressive commercial and political expansion, of states pitted against each other, and of Europe against the world. This society has been called early capitalism, and, although its political structures tended to the principle of the absolute state, even these were liberal in comparison with the totalitarian societies of earlier and more recent times. And it was in the focal points of commercial and manufacturing development (Italy, south Germany) that the technical arts first made their most rapid progress.

Nature of Renaissance society

Although, by the end of the 16th century, European science surpassed that of its sources and rivals, its products were still not qualitatively different from theirs. Then there came the revolution in philosophy that transformed European science into something unique. There had been earlier periods when an atomistic philosophy of matter had been advocated, but it had always been a philosophical speculation. This time it was injected into a flourishing scientific endeavour. Slowly at first, but at an accelerating pace, the synthesis created a new sort of science. Most important was the new style of the social activity of research, in which the secrecy and ruthless competition characteristic of private inventors were tempered and disciplined by the commitment to cooperative work for the common good. The roots of this lie partly in the loss of belief in magical powers, so that none could hope to unlock the secrets of the universe by solitary endeavour. Also, the idealism of the prophets of the new philosophy called for a new cooperative ethic of research, and, even as this inspiration waned, its effects were maintained by an adaptation of the code of honour of gentlemen scholars. Thus the mutual stimulus of theory and practice, maintained from the earlier period, was channelled into a cumulative and self-correcting process of winning reliable facts about the natural world. The successes of the new philosophy and its methods were patent by the end of the 17th century, and, even though the pace of advance slackened during the next century, the earlier achievements in knowledge and in methods were never lost. Hence a maturing European science was available for its next phase of interaction with practice, in the Industrial Revolution and beyond, and from this came the matured science of the epoch immediately preceding the present one. Also, the philosophy of dead matter turned out in the long run to be a fruitful strategy for scientific advance in that, although it suffered from many false starts, the sciences of chemical combination and of life could make their eventual triumphs in the 19th century only on the basis of this reductionist conception of the natural world.

In summary, therefore, European science owes its past successes and its special character to its sharing, in its metaphysics and methods, the basic features of European society: aggressive individualism tempered by a principle of cooperation for a common good.

SCIENCE IN THE AGE OF MODERN REVOLUTIONS

Toward the end of the 18th century, there began an industrial revolution that transformed Europe from an agrarian to an urban society; at the end of the century occurred the French Revolution, in which modern political ideas were first realized in practice. The activity of science experienced analogous changes. It was in this time

The urbanization of Europe

that social and institutional foundations were laid for the maturing of science in the 19th century. Simultaneously there occurred a romantic reaction in literature and the arts that had important repercussions in science itself.

At the beginning of this period, science was a very small-scale activity, mainly pursued by gentlemen of means or by trained professionals, such as physicians and engineers, in their spare time.

Only a very few universities (for example, Edinburgh and Leiden) provided effective instruction in science. The mathematical sciences (mathematics, astronomy, mechanics, optics) were well developed, but physics was still a scattering of experiments with qualitative and mainly speculative theories, chemistry was nearly entirely empirical, and the life sciences were concerned mainly with collectors' activities. By the end of the period there were successful examples of organized scientific work, and the foundations had been laid for coherent and effective theories in most areas of science.

Science during the Industrial Revolution.   In the gradual but deep transformation of European industry, the direct contribution of science was at first small. Most of the early progress came through the rationalization of craft techniques and the invention of simple machines to replace manual operations. Even there, elementary materials and an experimental approach, derived from the study of popular textbooks, were of great importance. Power technology was the first to be influenced by the applications of advanced science. The English Newcomen steam-vacuum engine (1711) came from 17th-century pneumatics, and the improvements made by the English engineer James Watt from 1763 onward were intimately related to developments in the theory of heat. Industrial chemistry was similarly assisted through the organization of chemical knowledge achieved by the great Dutch medical teacher Hermann Boerhaave and his followers.

The contribution of the Industrial Revolution to science was at first similarly indirect. In the industrializing regions of Britain (Lowlands Scotland, the Midlands, and Cornwall), there developed an audience for scientific results. Philosopher-manufacturers such as Josiah Wedgwood, the potter and social reformer, combined with physicians to pursue research, to form local societies, and to patronize scientists. By the end of the century, not only free-lance lecturing but also the publication of journals for the specialist became economically feasible. On the Continent, the more progressive monarchs established specialized colleges of engineering, either industrial, civil, or military; these provided a training for potential recruits and also jobs. In Britain, in spite of its early start and broad interest, advanced training remained rudimentary, and locally sponsored institutions for artisans' education were the rule through this period and the following. Although most of the problems that emerged in industrial practice and in medicine were beyond the reach of the existing scientific theories of the time, there is no doubt that engagement in solving them provided a stimulus and audience for research and so led indirectly to scientific progress.

Effects of the Industrial Revolution

Intellectual origins of revolution.   Starting somewhat earlier than the Industrial Revolution was a movement centred in France that first brought science into the realm of politics. Called the Enlightenment, it had as its program the struggle against church dogma and popular superstition, and it used the facts of science and its rational methods as the main weapon. It was started in the 1730s by Voltaire in a wave of anglophilia, who used the image of Newton to ridicule the officially imposed orthodoxy of Descartes's cosmology and physics. The Philosophes operated in the sophisticated environment of Paris salons and encouraged a growing readership for popular science books; for example, *Newtonianism for the Ladies* was a best seller. By midcentury the movement had matured. The Encyclopédiste Denis Diderot and the mathematician Jean d'Alembert edited the huge *Encyclopédie*, in which the democracy of knowledge was displayed by the alphabetical ordering of articles, and craft techniques were given equal dignity with metaphysical and scientific discussions. Aided by a hatred of a stupid and eventually

demoralized censorship, the Philosophes soon recruited all the best minds of France. They consciously considered themselves as carrying on the work of Bacon in advancing practical knowledge, but they did so in the style of Descartes, subjecting all things, social as well as philosophical, to the criticism of reason. The movement soon split into factions: the mathematician-rationalists, d'Alembert and his disciple Marie-Jean-Antoine Condorcet (who was a victim of the Terror during the Revolution); the romantics, Denis Diderot and Jean-Jacques Rousseau; and the atheist materialists, led by Paul-Henri Holbach. Nevertheless, they all agreed that their main enemy was the church. For all of them, natural science was philosophically committed, which was the opposite of being neutral and positive. From the ideas of these men came the slogans of the French Revolution, and their conflicts were eventually fought out in the realm of power politics.

The organization of science in the French Revolution.
Natural science was deeply involved in the French Revolution. From the Enlightenment the revolutionaries inherited a faith in science and its methods that permitted the greatest scientists to devote themselves to the organization of war industry for the defense of the republic in its hour of need. During and after the Revolution, there appeared a state-supported system of education, with scholarships for talented boys, jobs in teaching and examining, subsidies for research, and rewards for inventions. The centre of the system was the École Polytechnique of Paris, mainly serving to train army engineers, but the greatest scientists taught there, and there they found their most promising students.

The dominant style of this Revolutionary science was mathematical. In applications, its method was rationalization, one lasting product of which is the metric system, which was intended to produce a coherent system of measures based on natural units and the decimal. At the time of the Revolution, France already had distinguished mathematicians (Pierre-Simon Laplace, Joseph-Louis Lagrange, and Gaspard Monge); and their pupils and successors (Jean-Baptiste-Joseph Fourier, Siméon-Denis Poisson, and Augustin-Louis Cauchy) maintained their excellence. Even in chemistry, the reform of nomenclature achieved by Antoine Lavoisier and his colleagues was mathematical and abstract in style. Chemical compounds were to be described by a regular scheme of combination of the names of their constituent elements, and all traditional names were to be discarded.

At the height of the Revolution there emerged a countermovement in science that condemned the mathematical approach as sterile and elitist. Drawing inspiration from the democratic and romantic ideas of Rousseau and led by the former physician and journalist, the Revolutionary Jean-Paul Marat, this movement called for "science for the people," open to the self-educated artisans and based on practical chemistry and natural history. They achieved the dissolution of the Academy of Sciences, while promoting the more popular Museum of Natural History. The ideological struggle over the nature of chemistry was probably a factor in the execution of Lavoisier (1794) during the Terror, but, with the collapse and destruction in late 1794 of the Jacobins (a political club that was extremely effective in supporting the democratic radical movements within the Revolution and of which Marat was the leader for a while), the populist conception of chemistry was suppressed and the rationalistic, meritocratic style of French science was established in force.

Under Napoleon, the surviving grand old men and their first generation of disciples enjoyed patronage and prestige, but the "school of Laplace" went into eclipse after the restoration of the monarchy in 1815. A new group of distinguished scientists took over, but somehow the impetus was soon lost. Although Paris was the mecca of the scientific world in the 1820s, stagnation was setting in. One clue to this is the exclusion, almost certainly for political grounds in both cases, of two young men of outstanding genius: Sadi Carnot, who established the basic principles of thermodynamics, and Évariste Galois,

The role of mathematics in France

the creator of group theory in abstract algebra. After 1830, the scientific scene in Paris, which had always drained talent from the provinces, was dominated by careerism, and the great achievements of 19th-century science were made elsewhere. Historians of science now appreciate that this decline was not an accident but a significant problem requiring explanation.

Romantic reaction and science. At the same time as the Revolution in France, *Naturphilosophie* flourished in Germany. Its devotees, led by the poet Goethe and the philosopher Schelling, denounced the dry, soulless mathematical and experimental science of the Newtonian tradition. Instead, they proposed a philosophy of nature in which hand and eye, mind and spirit would all be united. Goethe unsuccessfully attacked Newton's theory of colours, but he gave inspiration to biological speculation on the organizing and unifying principles behind the structure of vertebrate animals. His followers, like other German thinkers of the time, attempted grand speculative physical and spiritual syntheses of all the world.

In England, the effects of *Naturphilosophie* are seen most clearly in the Romantic poets. Samuel Taylor Coleridge had studied it and shared his vision with William Wordsworth. Independently William Blake had drawn on the same mystical sources as *Naturphilosophie*, and he denounced "The Atoms of Democritus and Newton's Particles of Light" as part of the blind and dehumanized culture of his age.

The lasting scientific achievements of the adherents of *Naturphilosophie* are few, although many more may be recognized when more sympathetic historical research is done. For example, the discovery of electromagnetism (1820) by the Danish physicist Hans Christian Ørsted is now known to be the outcome of a search, conducted over many years, for effects to display the unity and polarity of the forces of nature. Similarly, the earliest announcement of the notion of conservation of energy was made in 1841 by a physician, Julius Robert von Mayer, who had the same sort of program. The common pattern was for a young man to be captured by the vision of such a unified wisdom while at a university and then to spend his life trying to rescue as much of it as possible by dedicated research. This sort of career is well illustrated by that of Hermann Ludwig Helmholtz, a German physiologist and physicist.

Triumph of *Naturphilosophie* Eventually *Naturphilosophie* became an orthodoxy taught by university professors. The founders of experimental science in Germany in the 1830s and 1840s found their way blocked by them, and bitter struggles ensued. Though the scientists won, they were haunted for generations by the ghost of *Naturphilosophie*, and they reacted by curbing all speculative tendencies most severely, reinforcing the dry, inhuman style of science that the poets had found abhorrent.

AGE OF MATURE SCIENCE

During the 19th century, the industrially advanced nations of Europe assimilated the consequences of the Industrial and French revolutions. Modern urban society developed in one nation after another with a constantly improving industrial base, elaborated state bureaucracies for regulation of trade and welfare, and increasing participation of the mass of people in social and political life. In one scientific discipline after another, there was a similar steady progress in the achievement of coherent systems and in the creation of institutions for the development of scientific activity. Science as a whole shared the general optimism of the age, receiving credit for its supposed contribution to industrial progress.

Science in the 19th century. In retrospect, the 19th century appears as a golden age. Science expanded successfully into new fields of inquiry, including a combination of mathematics and experiment in physics, the application of theory to experiment in chemistry, and controlled experimentation in biology. This was greatly aided by the establishment of new and reformed universities in which research was fostered, as well as teaching, and of communication through specialist journals and societies. National and international meetings, for both general science and specialists, became common by the end of the century. The principle of socially organized research, rather than inquiries by isolated individuals, became effective. In all fields of learning there was increased rigour of methods and depth of scholarship. The end-of-century editions of the *Encyclopædia Britannica* with their long historical accounts of each science are a monument to this period and remain a valuable source of information for the student.

The rise of organized research

Differences in styles of research. There were still striking differences among the leading nations regarding the circumstances and styles of research. In Britain, there was a marked absence of institutions providing jobs for researchers, and so the tradition of the gentleman-amateur lasted longer than elsewhere (for example, Charles Babbage the mathematician, James Joule, the physicist, and the biologist Charles Darwin). This made British science thin in comparison with German, especially in applied fields such as chemistry; but the scope for individual style and eccentricity compensated for the quantitative deficiencies. In Germany, the natural sciences shared in the rise in size and prestige of the university system. There, research and teaching were joined, and genuine laboratory research training was established for the first time, notably by the German chemist Justus von Liebig and his school. With this institutional base and a highly developed scholarly apparatus of handbooks and journals, German science rose in the half century from 1830 to a position of leadership in most fields. During this same period, French science declined from what had previously been its commanding position during the Revolutionary and Napoleonic periods. On the edge of Europe, Russia had a strong Academy and several progressive universities amid generally backward conditions, and a tradition of scientific excellence (set by men like Nikolay Lobachevsky and Dmitry Mendeleyev) was available for helping the rapid modernization that followed the Revolution of 1917. Through the 19th century the United States remained a cultural colony of Europe, except to some extent in the field sciences. Its larger universities were oriented toward utility, giving little social support to pure research. Around the end of the century, American scientists went to Germany in large numbers and on returning established strong traditions, but the attainment of qualitative leadership by the U.S. required the influx of refugee scholars from Nazi Germany in the 1930s.

The commitment to so-called pure science could flourish best within the German university system. In Britain, men of science freely engaged in both philosophical debates and in industrial application, a notable instance being Lord Kelvin in physics; the issue was not the scholar's remoteness from the world but the gentleman's independence of action. Also, the dominance of mathematical and experimental sciences over field sciences grew very slowly through the period. Early in the century, geology was the leading science. It had both a philosophical side in its speculations on the history of the Earth and a practical side in the utilization of resources. Natural history, inherited from the 18th century, served the squire and also the free-lance explorer and collector, such as Thomas Henry Huxley in biology. Only in the latter part of the century was there a marked trend toward dominance of the specialized professional research man, with the abstract experimental scientists as the leaders. An indication of the gradualness of this change in England can be seen in the resistance to the two terms scientist and physicist. Although suggested for general use in the 1830s, they were condemned by men of science as well as by natural philosophers until the beginning of the 20th century.

The relationship of science to its applications had an equally gradual change; in spite of claims to the contrary, the direct transition of processes from laboratory to factory became effective only toward the end of the century. At the beginning of the period, the most successfully applied sciences were those traditional ones that were descriptive techniques of interest to the state. These were either the abstract disciplines of mathematical cartogra-

Slow growth of relationship between science and industry

phy and fortification or the very detailed natural-history studies. Later physics was directly involved in qualitatively new processes, such as improved steam-power generation and electrical telecommunications. Chemistry contributed at first to the rationalization of industrial processes and also to effective theories of agriculture and nutrition. The invasion of medicine by applied science came very late, with the germ theory of disease; and it is worth remembering that the improvement in life and longevity owed more through the century to soap and sewers—that is, to sanitary reform and economic improvement—than to medical science. Synthetic dyestuffs were the first example of a laboratory discovery turned directly to profit, and this was a German achievement. Actually, the invention was made in 1856 by an Englishman, William Henry Perkin; but he was a pupil of the German chemist August Wilhelm von Hofman, and the Germans soon took a commanding lead in this industry thanks to their system of higher technical education for industrial scientists. By the end of the century they dominated all of industrial chemistry, as well as the heavy electrical equipment industry. Only the Americans, with their combination of a large market and independent inventors, could compete effectively. The French had long since lost the early lead they had gained with their rational approach to engineering, and the British rested on their early prestige as the workshop of the world. World War II found the Germans capable of synthesizing ammonia for nitrate explosives from the air (the Haber process), while the British depended for their explosives on nitrates from Chile.

Progress in physics. During the 19th century, each of the major branches of experimental science made such great progress that in retrospect its earlier state seemed to be rudimentary. Physics achieved that close union of precise experimentation with abstract mathematical theory that brought unprecedented depth of knowledge and power in application of that knowledge. Different fields were brought under control and then successively unified by the concept of energy. Thermodynamics united the sciences of heat and work and then enabled a theory of chemical change to develop. The roots of this lay in the work done by physicists in power engineering pioneered by Sadi Carnot of France and James Joule of England, in a variety of experimental fields pioneered by the German Herman Helmholtz, and in the speculative search for the single agency of physical change. Electricity and magnetism were united, first experimentally and then theoretically, by the Dane Hans Christian Ørsted and the Englishmen Michael Faraday and Kelvin; and a fundamental constant in the theory of electromagnetic measurement, determined by the German Wilhelm Weber, was observed to be equal to the astronomically determined velocity of light by the Englishman James Clerk Maxwell. Thus, the general properties of matter were successively mastered and made coherent. Later physicists justly called the century the classical age.

Progress in chemistry. Chemistry built on the theoretical foundations of Lavoisier's nomenclature and Dalton's atomic theory and spent decades on the heroic task of classifying substances into elements and compounds. The decade from 1858 saw three great victories. In Italy, Stanislao Cannizzaro solved the twin riddles of atomic weight and chemical composition by the synthesis of neglected earlier ideas (specifically Avogadro's hypothesis) and new experimental results and heuristic principles developed in teaching. At last the composition of water, as H_2O and not HO, was known. Shortly afterward, Friedrich Kekulé in Germany uncovered the true structure of organic compounds, with the alternate bonds of the benzene ring. Then Lothar Meyer in Germany and Dmitry Mendeleyev in Russia mastered the structure of the periodic table of the elements and could predict the properties of unknown elements. Thereafter chemistry could move toward a closer unity with physics and an increasing power in industrial application.

Progress in biology. In biology, the experimental approach was first successfully developed in physiology, mainly by the school of Johannes Müller in Germany in a complex reaction with *Naturphilosophie.* Philosophical considerations similarly conditioned the enunciation of the cell theory by Theodor Schwann. These Germans were generally reductionist. The French, who tended to believe in the special character of vital forces, advanced the more synthetic aspects of physiology (Claude Bernard) and medicine (Louis Pasteur). Through the field sciences came perhaps the most important conceptual achievement of the century: the time dimension in nature, both as one of very long duration and as the framework of qualitative change. The geological record showed evidence of such complex series of transformations of structure and so many successions of life-forms that the attempts to reconcile this history with that sketched in the Bible became increasingly implausible. The battle between those whose explanations were ruthlessly naturalistic and those who tried to reconcile Genesis and geology had started in the 18th century, and it continued into the 19th century on new issues. With a long time scale universally accepted, the appearance of human artifacts and remains in sealed old layers raised even more troubling problems, and the evidence was rather neglected for more than a quarter of a century. The crucial sector of advance turned out to be natural history, in the problem of the differentiation of natural varieties, a process whose results appeared quite similar to that of selective breeding of domesticated plants and animals. In England, disinterested in supernatural explanations and given insights by a political essay on population control by the political scientist Thomas Malthus, the naturalists Charles Darwin and Alfred Russell Wallace conceived of natural selection by the Victorian principle of survival of the fittest. The doctrine of evolution (1859) then unified all these historical disciplines and, through the extension of the principle to man himself, collided with religious orthodoxy. It also provided powerful explanatory principles for the nascent social sciences (supplementing the evolutionary principles of the English social philosopher Herbert Spencer); and naturally it was a source of slogans for political movements ranging from Marxist Socialism to "robber baron" capitalism. This Victorian episode shows that the neutrality of science with respect to politics and ideology, either in its inspiration or in its effects, is a very recent and probably temporary phenomenon.

The theme of this age was progress, and science received credit for much of the real progress that occurred and also shared in the general optimism of the times. Three factors were present in the general praise of science. First came the ancient tradition of respect for learning as a contribution to civilization, independently of its applications. A more popular appeal was based on the applications, first to industry and later to medicine. A third factor, intermittent in its appearance, was inherited from the Enlightenment: natural science as a weapon against religious dogma and popular superstition, both in its facts and in its methods. The memory of the trial of Galileo stayed fresh in the folklore of science, so that the debate over Darwinism in England gave new impetus to this ideological struggle, in which liberal Christians sided with agnostics against the orthodox. Taken together, these three beliefs performed many of the functions of a religion and remained a strong inspiration for science until very recently. Their discrediting in the present period presents serious problems for the future of science.

Early 20th century. Certain tendencies within 19th-century science became heightened during the succeeding period. At this time, science was professional in its social organization, reductionist in style, and positive in spirit.

Science was then conceived as essentially the work of pure research, with teaching as a lesser, ancillary activity and industrial application a task for other workers in other institutions. Almost all research was done by highly trained experts, employed wholly or mainly for this work within special institutions. Communities of scientists, organized by discipline and by nationality, enjoyed a high degree of autonomy in the setting of goals and standards of research and in the certification, employment, and rewarding of their members. Individual scientists tended

The effects of the geological record on the notion of time

The ideal of pure research

to be forced by competition to become very specialized research workers. Correspondingly, undergraduate teaching in science tended increasingly to become a specialized pregraduate program designed for the minority who would proceed to research. As the costs of research increased beyond the means of individuals, science depended on grants from large agencies, either charitable foundations (as the Rockefeller) or departments of national states. These also set up their own laboratories, usually for applied research, the best of which paralleled the university system. The tensions in this system of external support remained latent. Similarly, there was no systematic recognition that the majority of science graduates were employed outside professional science, either as teachers or as employees in technological establishments.

The dominant style of work in this period was reductionist: investigations were concentrated on the artificially pure, stable, and controllable processes achieved in the laboratory; and the favourite theories were those involving the simplest physical causes, using heavily mathematical arguments. Almost all the philosophy of science in this period assumed that a real science is one modelled on theoretical physics. The prestige of this style is shown by the many attempts to extend it to the human sciences. Its limitations, as now seen, were centred in a dangerous ignorance of the facts and principles of the behaviour of the natural environment.

The positive spirit of this science was shown by its increasing separation from philosophical reflection. Einstein's theories of relativity (1905 and 1916) and the German physicist Werner Heisenberg's "uncertainty principle" in quantum theory (1927) raised vigorous philosophical discussions among scientists and laymen alike. But these were exceptional; afterward, the only major instances of philosophical concerns, by a lay public, with scientific research were disastrous. The Nazis attacked both theories and scientists on racial grounds; the Soviet state attacked genetics and persecuted leading scientists, with the excuse of the Marxist pseudo-genetics of T.D. Lysenko. As a result, it seemed to many scientists that both the progress of science and the preservation of the values of a liberal society required an affirmation of the ideological neutrality of science and an insistence on the complete autonomy of research. For them, pure science was not a retreat but a positive commitment.

The universal advance in science in the 20th century The scientific achievements of the earlier 20th century are too immense even to be cataloged. There is, however, a common pattern of advance. In each major field, progress was based on the successful descriptive work of the 19th century. It went first to a finer analysis of constituents and their mechanisms and then to syntheses that straddled the inherited names of disciplines, producing vigorous hybrids such as biochemistry and biophysics. In physics, the classical theories of the main physical forces (heat, electricity, magnetism) had been unified at their foundations by thermodynamics; and the early part of the century saw the discovery of totally new effects (X-rays, radioactivity), the penetration into the structure of matter (atomic theory, isotopes); these required a recasting of the fundamental laws of physics and some of their metaphysical presuppositions (relativity, quantum theory). Chemical methods of analysis were necessary for much of this work in physics. Conversely, the new physical theories were sufficiently powerful to provide effective explanations for a wide variety of chemical phenomena. On this basis, the chemical industry could produce an enormous range of totally synthetic substances (fibres, plastics). In the life sciences, chemical and physical methods brought discovery and explanation of subtle agencies (vitamins, hormones) and the reconstruction of the complex cycles of chemical transformations whereby matter lives. Medical science could build on bacteriology, and, through the discovery of specific and general drugs (first Salvarsan against syphilis, then sulfonamides and penicillin), it nearly eliminated both the classic epidemic diseases and also the cruel diseases of childhood. It is little wonder that the triumphs of science seemed to promise knowledge and power in superabundance. Few men could foresee the problems that these very successes would bring to their social and natural environment on their being applied in an aggressive spirit unchanged over five centuries of European expansion.

Problems and prospects. In the perspective of this long history, it can be seen that the moral, political, and environmental difficulties facing science and technology today are not totally new. Rather, they are a return to problems that had been forgotten, first with the decline of belief in magic and then with the coming of matured science. From this were inherited an ideology of pure science, a technology in which all problems were successfully solved, and a sheltered community of scholars. But even then there could occur stagnation within a scientific community and conflict between science and society. At the present time, the intimate connection of science with industry, defense, and politics has rendered the ideal of pure science obsolete and has confronted society with the need for a working conception of the natural world different from the reductionist model of the physicist.

Yet, although historians cannot be content with the simple story of continuous success told by earlier generations, they see that modern European science is an integral part of civilization. Its faults as well as its virtues derive from aspects of Europe that are deep in the Western way of life. The survival of science and the survival of the civilization go together. To reject the intellectual and spiritual triumphs and the material benefits that European science and technology have achieved would involve a mutilation. What transformations the future will bring and whether civilization can manage to achieve the harmony with nature that is necessary for survival cannot be guaranteed. To define the problem is to go a long way toward its solution. The problem is only partly technical. It is, equally, one of the character of natural science in European civilization as it has developed over the centuries.

BIBLIOGRAPHY. For introductions to the general history of science, the following may be recommended. CHARLES SINGER, *A Short History of Scientific Ideas to 1900* (1959), is clear and comprehensible, but now somewhat obsolete. J.D. BERNAL, *Science in History*, 3rd ed., 4 vol. (1971), is well written and well illustrated but marred by the author's certainty that all important scientific discovery had a simple relation to economic and social forces of its time. S.F. MASON, *Main Currents of Scientific Thought: A History of the Sciences* (1953; British title, *A History of the Sciences: Main Currents of Scientific Thought*, 1953; rev. ed., 1962), is more of a speculative essay on science in society and has many valuable insights; RENE TATON (ed.), *Histoire générale des sciences*, 4 vol. (1957–64; 2nd ed., 1966–   ; Eng. trans., *A General History of the Sciences*, 1966–   ), is the best English-language collection of essays leading into more specialized studies. For ancient and medieval science, a scholarly introduction is E.J. DIJKSTERHUIS, *De mechanisering van het wereldbeeld* (1950; Eng. trans., *The Mechanization of the World Picture*, 1961). On China, the standard work is JOSEPH NEEDHAM, *Science and Civilization in China*, 7 vol. (1954–   ). For the creation of European science, a well-organized introduction is provided by HUGH F. KEARNEY, *Science and Change, 1500–1700* (1971). The social and institutional aspects of modern science are thoroughly explored in JOSEPH BEN-DAVID, *The Scientist's Role in Society: A Comparative Study* (1971). There is now in progress a multivolume *Dictionary of Scientific Biography*, ed. by C.C. GILLISPIE (1970–   ), which will provide reliable information on the lives and works of many scientists. For the parallel histories of medicine and technology, good introductions are R.H. SHRYOCK, *The Development of Modern Medicine: An Interpretation of the Social and Scientific Factors Involved* (1936, reprinted 1969); and FREDRICK KLEMM, *Technik: Eine Geschichte ihrer Probleme* (1954; Eng. trans., *A History of Western Technology*, 1959).

(J.R.R.)

Science, Philosophy of

Taken in a broad sense—*i.e.*, as the progressive improvement of man's understanding of nature—the intellectual enterprise of science originally formed an integral part of philosophy, and the two areas of inquiry have never finally separated. Little more than a hundred years ago, theoretical physics—concerned with the fundamental debate about physical nature—was still described as "natural philosophy," as distinguished from the two other chief divisions of abstract discussion, viz., moral philosophy and metaphysical philosophy—the latter comprising the study of the deepest nature of reality or being, also called ontology. In fact it was only during the 20th century, following on the professionalization and specialization of the natural sciences themselves, that the philosophy of science has become recognized as a separate discipline.

Methodological and epistemological issues—*i.e.*, issues regarding the investigator's manner of approach to nature—are treated in the present article. On the other hand, issues regarding the substantive character of nature as so revealed—*i.e.*, as it is in and of itself—are treated in NATURE, PHILOSOPHY OF. The present article is arranged under the following headings:

I. General approach to the philosophy of science
    Nature, scope, and relations of the subject
    Historical development of the subject
II. Conceptualization and methodology of science
    Elements of the scientific enterprise
    Movements of scientific thought
III. Deeper issues and broader involvements of science
    Philosophical status of scientific theory
    Interrelationships of science and culture

I. General approach to the philosophy of science

NATURE, SCOPE, AND RELATIONS OF THE SUBJECT

As a discipline, the philosophy of science attempts, first, to elucidate the elements involved in the process of scientific inquiry—observational procedures, patterns of argument, methods of representation and calculation, metaphysical presuppositions, and so on—and then to evaluate the grounds of their validity from the points of view of formal logic, practical methodology, and metaphysics. In its contemporary form, the philosophy of science is thus a topic for explicit analysis and discussion in the same sense as are other subdivisions of philosophy: ethics, logic, and epistemology (the theory of knowledge). At the same time, the boundaries between these subdivisions are, at certain points, still somewhat arbitrary; it is not easy, for example, to separate completely the philosophical validation of scientific hypotheses from the formal study of inductive logic (which reasons from facts to general principles), or the debate about theory and observation in philosophy of science from that in epistemology.

Ontal versus epistemic concern

Throughout the development of philosophy, the preoccupations of those who, if living today, would be called philosophers of science have been of two main kinds: ontological, or ontal, and epistemological, or epistemic. This division reflects a long-standing distinction between object and subject; *i.e.*, between nature, regarded as that about which man sets out to acquire scientific knowledge, and man himself, regarded as the creator, and either discoverer or possessor of that knowledge. Since 1920 new directions within physics itself—particularly in quantum mechanics—have discredited any hard-and-fast distinction between the knower and the known or between the observer and his observation. Nevertheless, the distinction remains relevant on an everyday, or working, level and can be cautiously retained for the purposes of initial exposition.

The ontal preoccupations of philosophers of science (*i.e.*, their concerns with being) have frequently overlapped into the substantive areas of the sciences themselves. For they have been concerned with the general problem,

What kinds of entities and elements or theoretical terms can properly figure in man's scientific theories? And what sort of existence, or other objective status, do such things possess?

As applied to particular cases, this general problem has inevitably raised questions of substance as well as of intellectual method. An early 20th-century debate between two Austrian physicists, Ernst Mach and Ludwig Boltzmann, and a German physical chemist, Wilhelm Ostwald, about the existence and reality of atoms, for instance, involved both substantive issues of physics and chemistry and philosophical issues of a more strictly analytical kind. Similar overlaps have been unavoidable, also, in the biological and social sciences; *e.g.*, over the existence and status of distinctively vital and social agencies or entities.

Until recently the epistemic concerns of the subject have been more purely philosophical in character, though this autonomy is now being challenged by developments in psychology that explore and experiment with cognitive processes and others in sociology that study the conditioning of cognition through interpersonal and group relationships. Epistemologically, philosophers of science have analyzed and evaluated the concepts and methods employed in studying natural phenomena and human behaviour, whether individual or collective; and this analysis has covered both the general concepts and methods characteristic of all scientific inquiries and also the more particular ones that distinguish the subject matters and problems of different special sciences. In treating the epistemic issues that arise about science and scientific procedures, the emphasis in this article is placed upon their consideration in general terms; the concepts and methods peculiar, say, to sociology, physiology, or quantum physics are discussed elsewhere.

Diverse approaches

Given the vast range of its concerns, the philosophy of science has attracted the attention of men with very different professional backgrounds and interests. At one extreme, as in the writings of Ernest Haeckel, the German Darwinian evolutionist, it has merged into a sweeping kind of popular science; at an opposite extreme, as in 20th-century Logical Positivism or Logical Empiricism (see below), a leading school that holds that knowledge is only what is scientifically verifiable, it has been treated as an extension of formal logic and conceptual analysis. And between these extremes it has drawn in such working scientists as the British astrophysicist Arthur Eddington and the German quantum physicist Werner Heisenberg, whose work has taken them to the frontiers of the subjects and confronted them directly with problems about the existence, status, and validity of the theoretical entities and concepts with which they were dealing.

Correspondingly, different men have approached the philosophy of science in very diverse spirits, ranging from the highly abstract and mathematical to the concrete and historical and from the severely positivistic to the frankly theological. From René Descartes, the first important modern philosopher in the 17th century, to the Logical Positivist Otto Neurath in the 20th, the success of pure mathematics and logic has inspired the mathematically minded to cast the whole of natural science into a single formal system after the pattern of geometry. From John Locke, an 18th-century British Empiricist, to N.R. Hanson, a recent U.S. philosopher of science, their opponents, on the other hand, have sought the proper basis of man's intellectual confidence within the nature of scientific investigation regarded as a human activity. Equally, Positivists such as Hans Reichenbach, a 20th-century German-American philosopher, have looked to philosophy for proof that scientific inquiries alone can provide knowledge worthy of the name; while theists such as Pierre Duhem, a French theoretical physicist, have appealed to it, rather, to demonstrate that the claims of science are inherently limited and so leave room for other, more embracing varieties of metaphysical and religious truth.

Relations with other disciplines

This diversity of concerns and approaches has affected the relations between the philosophy of science and other neighbouring disciplines. On a practical plane, for instance, different philosophical interpretations have implied different procedures for testing and assessing the strength of rival concepts and hypotheses. Thus, no clear dividing line can be drawn between the philosophical analysis of scientific theories and the statistical analysis of scientific procedures and experiments nor between the philosophy of science and the history of scientific ideas. Recent debates about the historiography of science—*i.e.*, about the problems and methods that throw light on its history—indicate that the particular questions that a historian of science brings to his analysis of scientific change inescapably depend on his philosophical attitudes and commitments.

On a more general and abstract level, the philosophy of science has never been definitively separated from metaphysics and epistemology. There are, indeed, some 20th-century philosophers—for instance, the U.S. philosophical logician Willard V. Quine—who effectively restrict the legitimate areas of metaphysics and epistemology to what have here been called the ontal and epistemic aspects of the philosophy of science. In Quine's view, the traditional ontological problem of what there is in the world as man knows it must be attacked by a logical analysis of the claims about what kinds of things exist that are implicit in alternative theoretical systems. Meanwhile, the work of such cognitive psychologists as Switzerland's Jean Piaget, who explore the processes involved in the genesis of knowledge, is eroding the barriers between the logical analysis of conceptual systems, the psychological investigation of thought processes, and the epistemological validation of intellectual procedures. Piaget, for instance, bases his investigations into the acquisition of concepts on a philosophy akin to that of Kant, who held that all knowledge bears the imprint of the mind's own structure; and, though a psychologist himself, Piaget even refers to certain aspects of his work by the name of "genetic epistemology," a philosophical designation.

The present survey of the philosophy of science, therefore, contains no effort to prejudge the central question whether the methods of logical analysis alone are legitimate or whether at certain points the subject legitimately overlaps into such neighbouring subjects as cognitive psychology, the history of science, and epistemology. About this question philosophers of science themselves have been sharply divided, some rejecting any alliance except with logic, others cultivating its wider historical and behavioral connections; and both points of view must thus be taken into account.

HISTORICAL DEVELOPMENT OF THE SUBJECT

The Pre-Socratics

Classical and medieval periods: the beginnings of a philosophy of nature. At the outset the problems of science were as much those of method as of substance and were inseparable from those of what has long been called natural philosophy. The first attempts to move beyond traditional mythologies to a rational account of nature, beginning with the Ionian and south Italian philosophers around 600 BC, involved the sorts of elements or entities that any such account should comprise. Detailed empirical, or observational, considerations favouring one or another of the rival accounts were premature. Were, for example, the diverse phenomena of nature manifestations of one single enduring form of matter or of several elementary substances mixed together, and was the fundamental substance continuous and fluid-like, or discrete and atomic? Alternatively, others asked whether the observed forms of phenomena were evidence, rather, of some universal, underlying mind or of a variety of coexisting kinds of spirit responsible for phenomena having different orders of complexity.

The various Pre-Socratics based their answers at least as much on epistemic grounds—by considering what type of account would be genuinely intelligible—as on ontal or empirical ones by considering what sorts of enduring entities could possibly have, or be found in experience to have, the required kind of existence. Their answers ranged from one extreme, the ontal Realism of Parmenides, foremost philosopher of Eleaticism (q.v.), a school of southern Italy—according to which all changes are transitory appearances concealing the mutual relations of deeper, unchanging realities—to the critical skepticism of Heraclitus, the Ephesian philosopher of change, at the other extreme, according to which nothing in nature as man knows it can ever have this Parmenidean reality, and everything empirical is in flux.

Plato and Aristotle

Though Plato and Aristotle displayed more precise concern for actual cases, their philosophies of science still rested on the same mixture of ontological, epistemological, and empirical considerations. Questions about nature discussed in Plato's *Timaeus* and Aristotle's *Physics*, for instance, were neither purely metaphysical nor purely empirical in character though they had a methodological aspect akin to that of modern philosophy of science. Moreover, Plato's construction of the fundamental theories of science around concepts and patterns borrowed from geometry have had a profound influence in the modern period—upon René Descartes, for example, in the 17th century and upon the founder of modern logic, the German mathematician Gottlob Frege, in the 1880s and after.

Mathematical entities alone, Plato argued, have the sort of enduring intelligibility that Parmenides had rightly demanded of the ultimate constituents in a rational science of nature. Thus, only a physical theory built on a numerical and geometrical framework will reveal the truly permanent structures and relationships behind the evident flux of phenomena. Within such a theory, all inferences will be self-evidently valid at all times and so exempt from the mutability of empirical events; and, correspondingly, the numbers and figures of formal mathematics will have an immutability denied to familiar physical objects. Planetary astronomy and the theory of matter were, in Plato's view, scientific fields within which this mathematical methodology showed immediate promise; the movements of the planets must be explained by constructions drawn from three-dimensional geometry, and the physics of matter seemingly involved atoms with shapes reflecting the geometry of the five regular solids (the tetrahedron, dodecahedron, etc.). In either case, however, the mathematical theories themselves would alone be fully exact and intelligible, whereas empirical objects and processes could be no more than transitory and approximate illustrations of the enduring entities and theoretical relations underlying them.

Given Aristotle's very different scientific preoccupations—which were centred on marine biology rather than planetary movements—he quite naturally developed a very different scientific methodology. In his view, mathematical entities and relations were too completely general and too remote from actual experience to explain the qualitative details of empirical entities. So the ultimate elements of nature must be not Plato's entirely general and abstract mathematical forms—which supposedly existed quite apart from actual phenomena—but rather certain more specific entities, recognizable within the familiar sequences of empirical experience. Instances of such basic essences could be discovered by studying the typical life cycles of different creatures; thus, the morphogenesis of a seed exemplifies the "coming into being" of the corresponding type of animal or plant, of which the mature specific form—as defined by its essence—is the natural destination of its development.

Having recognized the natural destinations toward which natural processes of different kinds were directed, it was then possible to construct a comprehensive classification of essences in terms of which the whole natural world would, in principle, be intelligible. Explanations within such an all-embracing natural history might not be self-evidently general and immutable, as were those of Plato's geometry; but the theoretical inferences involved would be no less deductive or necessary, and it would have the added merit of accounting directly for the specific qualitative characters of different observed objects and processes.

Atomists and Stoics

Throughout the subsequent philosophy of science, the themes stated by Plato and Aristotle have recurred repeatedly and are represented even today by two rival approaches to the subject—one (Platonic) based in logic, the other (Aristotelian) based in the history of science. Between them they dominated the subject during the later period of Greek antiquity, which was otherwise notable for only one further debate—that between the Atomist successors of Democritus and Epicurus and the Stoic philosophers, led by Zeno of Citium. This debate provided the first profound analysis of the strengths and weaknesses of atomistic explanation. Epicureans, on the one hand, argued for a purely corpuscular view in which the individual units of matter moved quite independently, except when they were in actual contact. For the Stoics, on the other hand, the empirical world was intelligible only in terms of interactions and stable patterns maintained by harmonies operative at a distance.

These two debates—between Platonists and Aristotelians and between Stoics and Epicureans—presented clearly and for the first time the chief alternative modes of explanation available to science and analyzed their possibilities and limitations in general terms. More than 2,000 years before the rise of modern thermodynamics and field theory, for instance, Aristotle had already recognized the difficulties of explaining changes in physical state (*e.g.*, melting and evaporation) within a purely atomistic theory of matter; whereas, even earlier, Plato had demonstrated the possibility of a unified mathematical explanation of the differences between different kinds of material substance. Indeed, the theoretical physicist Werner Heisenberg was quite ready in the 20th century to cite pre-Socratic arguments regarding the ultimate constitution of nature as relevant to contemporary problems.

Hellenistic through medieval times

By contrast with the period before Euclid the geometer (*i.e.*, to 300 BC), the ensuing Hellenistic, Islāmic, and medieval periods added little to the understanding of scientific methology and explanation. From the Alexandrian astronomer Ptolemy, who detailed the geocentric theory, most natural philosophers deliberately restricted their intellectual claims in an instrumentalist manner; *i.e.*, by endeavouring merely to "save the phenomena" by devising successful mathematical procedures for predicting, for example, lunar eclipses and planetary motions. In this way they disregarded the mechanisms responsible for those phenomena, thus preserving the computational techniques of the sciences from the risk of conflict with theology for the following 1,250 years, until the time of Copernicus.

In the High Middle Ages, accordingly, the possibility that man could make himself the intellectual master of nature was largely neglected. Human understanding was dependent on God's illumination. The guarantees of scientific knowledge lay not in the merits of its methodology but in the divine grace, which assured its reliability. On this interpretation, man had no direct line of access to nature; the only road to knowledge was through the divine mind. Thus, all of the central questions in the philosophy of science were restated as theological issues, as questions about the relationship between God's omniscience and the more limited knowledge of man. In this context the metaphor of "illumination" was taken so seriously in the 13th century that the very subject of optics was cultivated by a distinguished Oxford scholar as much for its theological implications as for its physical content.

The 17th and 18th centuries: from manifesto to critique. Although the intellectual Renaissance of the 16th and 17th centuries was accompanied by a secularization of learning, which shifted the centre of philosophical and scientific debate from monasteries to universities—and even to salons—the link between philosophy and theology was not abruptly snapped. Descartes, Newton, and Leibniz, the leading scholars of the time, were all concerned to demonstrate that their positions were compatible with sound theology; and medieval controversies about human knowledge and divine grace found an echo in such arguments as Descartes's assertion that the rational methods of inquiry can be relied on only provided that God does not deliberately deceive us. Two new factors, however, combined to give the 17th-century debate about scientific methodology a new autonomy: in the first place, philosophy now posed the central questions in the philosophy of science—both those about the origins and functions of scientific concepts and those about the structure and validity of scientific arguments—and faced them directly, instead of only as refracted through a theological prism. And, in the second place, these questions were acquiring an immediate relevance and significance, simply because men were then launching new, empirically based theories of nature with a seriousness unknown for some 1,200 years.

Francis Bacon and Descartes

Between 1600 and 1800 the debate in the philosophy of science was barely separable from that within science itself. From Bacon and Galileo by way of Descartes and Leibniz to Laplace and Kant, all of the major partici-

pants in the philosophical debate played significant roles on the scientific stage as well. Thus, Francis Bacon, author of the method of exhaustive induction (see below), and René Descartes both conceived the same intellectual goal, that of formulating explicitly a new method for the improvement of the intellect; *i.e.*, codifying the rational procedures of science in a way that would free them from arbitrary and unfounded or superstitious assumptions (Bacon's idols) and ground them in a logically impregnable manner on the properties of "clear and distinct," or self-evidently valid, concepts (as distinguished by Descartes).

To be sure, the two men offered different recipes for a rational science and described the outcome of a properly conducted scientific inquiry in quite different terms. On the one hand, Bacon was preoccupied with empirically observed facts as the starting point for all science and relied on theories only insofar as they were derived from those facts. Ideally, he held that the scientist should provide an exhaustive enumeration of all examples of the empirical phenomenon under investigation as a preliminary to identifying the natural "form" of which they were the manifestation. Though Bacon remained unclear about the exact character of the abstraction involved, he is commonly assumed to have claimed that theoretical propositions in science are justified only if they have been deduced formally from such an enumeration.

In contrast to such so-called "Baconian induction," Descartes focussed upon the problem of constructing self-consistent and coherent deductive systems of theory, within which argument would proceed with the formal security familiar in Euclidean geometry. Whereas Bacon had reacted against the Scholastic reliance on Aristotle's authority by calling for a return to firsthand experience, Descartes reacted against the Skepticism of 16th-century humanists by pointing to mathematics as the pattern to which all genuinely certain knowledge about nature could aspire. Inasmuch as Euclid's axioms, definitions, and postulates had captured the intrinsic characteristics of spatial relations and provided a theoretical starting point from which the whole of geometry could be deductively inferred, the task for 17th-century physics was to extend Euclid's intellectual structure by adding further, equally self-evident axioms, definitions, and postulates. Only in this way could the theories of motion, magnetism, and heat—eventually those of physiology and cosmology, too—achieve the same necessary deductive authority. Descartes set out to show, in the four volumes of his *Principia Philosophiae* ("Principles of Philosophy"), how all of the familiar phenomena of physics could be accounted for by a single, fully comprehensive system of mathematical theory, based on Euclidean foundations and conforming to his own deductivist principles. The very possibility of so interpreting nature was so impressive to Descartes that it lent a "moral certainty" to his conclusions.

Newton's hypo-thetico–deductive method

The arguments of Bacon and Descartes were really manifestos; both offered intellectual programs for a natural science yet to be built, and, while it is true that during the next 150 years, Galileo, Newton, and many others actually constructed the new physical science for which the philosophers had been calling, it is also true that the form of the resulting theories was, nonetheless, not exactly what either man had foreseen. On the one hand, there was little Baconian induction in Newton's intellectual procedures. Those 17th-century scientists, such as Robert Boyle—one of the founders of modern chemistry—who seriously attempted to apply Bacon's maxims found his pedestrian advice to be more of a hindrance than a help in the formulation of illuminating theoretical concepts. (It was said, somewhat unkindly, that Bacon "philosophized like a Lord Chancellor.") On the other hand, though Newton was powerfully influenced by Descartes's mathematical example, he followed his methodological maxims only up to a point. Granted that the theory of motion and gravitation of Newton's *Principia* did indeed conform to Descartes's recipe—adding further dynamical axioms, definitions, and postulates to those of Euclid's geometry—Newton nonetheless made no pretense of proving, in advance of empirical evidence, that these additional assumptions were uniquely self-evident and valid. Instead, he treated them as working assumptions to be accepted hypothetically for just so long as their consequences threw light, in exact detail, on hitherto-unexplained phenomena. Inevitably, the epistemic claims to be made on behalf of such explanations fell short of Descartes's full "deductivist" ambitions. Newton knew of no phenomena, for instance, that evinced the mechanisms of gravitational attraction and saw no point in "feigning hypotheses" about them.

In this way, Newton devised in practice—almost inadvertently—what philosophers of science have since labelled the hypothetico-deductive method, in which, as theorized by Descartes, the proper form of a theory is seen as a mathematical system in which particular empirical phenomena are explained by relating them back deductively to a small number of general principles and definitions. The method, however, abandons the Cartesian claim that those principles and definitions can themselves be established, finally and conclusively, before inquiring what light their consequences throw on actual scientific problems and phenomena.

Empiricists, Rationalists, and Kant

From 1700 on, the terrain of debate in the philosophy of science shifted. At first, attacks on Newton's methods and assumptions by Leibniz, Berkeley, and the remaining Cartesians continued, from different points of view. But by 1740 the time for both manifestos and objections was past; the basic scientific soundness of Newton's concepts was no longer in doubt, and the philosophical question thus became retrospective, viz., How had Newton done it? Over this new question, 18th-century philosophers were divided into three camps: Empiricism, Rationalism, and Kantianism (*qq.v.*). There were those who believed, like the Scottish Skeptic David Hume, that Newton's philosophy conformed to the Empiricist maxims of Francis Bacon and John Locke. Again, there were those—like the Swiss mathematician Leonhard Euler, one of the founders of modern analysis, and Immanuel Kant in his younger days—who assumed that Newton's physical principles would eventually be put on a fully demonstrative or self-evident basis as required by Cartesian Rationalism. Neither of these positions proved entirely successful, as Kant himself came to recognize: the Empiricists failed to do justice to the deductive rigour of Newton's theoretical arguments; and the Rationalists could not rigorously demonstrate the mathematical uniqueness of Newton's system. As was already known, even Euclidean geometry, which involves the axiom of parallels (according to which one, and only one, line can be drawn through a given point parallel to another line) could no longer claim a formal uniqueness. It has been shown, in 1733 and again in 1766, that alternative geometrical systems can consistently be developed in which the axiom of parallels is replaced by other mathematically acceptable alternatives. Clearly, the authority claimed for Newton's concepts and methodology could no longer be sustained in the old Rationalist way; thus a third alternative, that of Kantianism, arose.

One of the prime goals of Kant's so-called critical philosophy, with its famous so-called transcendental method, in which knowledge reflects the categorial structure of the mind, was to provide an alternative philosophical justification of Newton's results. The system of concepts used in Euclidean geometry and Newtonian physics is uniquely relevant to man's actual experience, Kant argued, not because the empirical applicability of their principles is self-evident—no such self-evidence can tell the inquirer anything about external nature. Still less is it because their inductive support is so strong—no Baconian argument can yield the required kind of certainty. Rather, it is because the scientist can arrive at a coherent, rational system of empirically applicable explanations only by constructing his theories around just those (Euclidean and Newtonian) concepts. He could, in fact, go even further. Euclidean axioms are required, Kant claimed, not merely for science alone; they specify explicitly cognitive structures (of the mind) that are implicitly involved also—as so-called forms of intuition (specif-

ically of space and time)—in the prescientific rational organization of sensory experience into a coherent, intelligible world of substantial objects seen as interacting by causal processes. A grasp of Kant's transcendental method would then enable a thinker to recognize (or so Kant hoped) how and in what respects the use of his established system of rational forms and categories is indispensable alike for any coherent understanding or even for any experience.

Through World War I: philosophy of classical physics. Kant's ambitious philosophical enterprise took a long time to digest. A century later, in the 1880s, philosophers of science as different in other ways as the Austrian phenomenalist Ernst Mach and Heinrich Hertz, pioneer in electromagnetic wave theory, were both pursuing questions opened up by Kant; and some of their implications were still being explored in the 1970s, as, for example, in cognitive psychology. In general terms, Kant's central thesis—*i.e.*, that man confers a structure on his knowledge through the concepts and categories that he brings to the formation and interpretation of experience—has proved extremely fertile: it has helped in the analysis of theory construction, and it has suggested in sensory psychology that man's very capacity for perception can yield effective knowledge only to the extent that his sensory inputs themselves have a cognitive or conceptual structure.

The assimilation of Kant

In one respect, to be sure, Kant seems in retrospect to have attempted too much. Including in man's framework of sensory and intellectual organization all of Euclidean geometry and of fundamental Newtonian physics and the prescientific notions of substance and cause, Kant set out to demonstrate a priori that man's actual current framework is the one and only effective framework—a proof which, as is known today, was misguided, for its thesis is simply not the case. This is so, not merely because alternative systems of geometry and dynamics can be developed consistently in mathematical terms (for Kant himself was aware of that fact); rather, it is so because 20th-century astrophysics and quantum mechanics have succeeded in giving non-Euclidean and post-Newtonian concepts an entirely coherent empirical application in the scientific explanation of natural phenomena—and this was something that Kant was not prepared to contemplate. Pure mathematics aside, indeed, Kant and most of his immediate successors were convinced that Euclid and Newton between them had somehow hit on a uniquely adequate system of geometry and physics—if not on the final mathematical truth about nature.

For about 100 years, then, the epistemic foundations and ontal commitments of this so-called classical science were largely taken for granted. The 19th-century debate in philosophy of science, accordingly, concentrated on peripheral topics and skirted all issues that might have called into question the ascendency of Euclid and Newton. The validity of the classical system having been assumed, the questions remaining for debate involved only its interpretation and implications; and the resulting positions can be classified, with slight oversimplification, under the headings of mechanistic (or Materialist) and Idealist doctrines, respectively.

The Idealists took to heart Kant's thesis that the cognitive structure of experience is imposed upon nature rather than discovered in it and sought to explore its broader consequences. The psychology of sensory perception, for example, previously barred from direct scientific study by Descartes's absolute separation of mind from matter, was now opened up for exploration; thus, by the mid-19th century, Hermann von Helmholtz, pioneer in a broad range of scientific studies, embarked on the remarkable investigations into the production of man's sensory experiences or ideas set out in his monumental *Handbuch der physiologischen Optik* (1856–67; Eng. trans., *Physiological Optics*, 1921–25).

Idealism versus mechanistic Materialism

For most of Kant's successors, however, the Idealist road led away from philosophy of science into other areas—particularly, into political ideology, philosophy of history, and sociology. Thus, it was not until well into the 20th century that the distinguished joint relativity-quantum theorist Sir Arthur Eddington, in his *Fundamental Theory* (1946), once again took up seriously the basic task of Kantian Idealism, viz., that of demonstrating, on a priori epistemological principles, that man's physical interpretation of nature embodies certain necessary structures imposed on physics by the character of his theoretical procedures themselves.

Meanwhile, the 19th-century mechanistic Materialists were disregarding Kant's central insights and concentrating instead on the apparent implications of the Newtonian system for other branches of science. A vigorous philosophical debate resulted, particularly in those fields that were just developing effective explanatory methods and theoretical concepts of their own. One good example of such a field was physiology, in which the work of a pioneering experimental physiologist, Claude Bernard, with its striking theoretical analysis of the vasomotor system and other regulatory mechanisms in the body, which anticipated 20th-century ideas about feedback systems, finally broke a long-standing deadlock between two opposed groups of scientists—the extreme mechanists, who recognized no difference at all between organic or physiological processes and the physicochemical phenomena of the inorganic world, and the outright vitalists, who insisted that the two kinds of phenomena were absolutely different. The debate also encouraged an epiphenomenal view of experience—as a kind of subjective mental froth without causal influence on the underlying physical mechanisms—and so sharpened the apparent threat to all claims about human "free will." Today it seems, indeed, that the sweeping conclusions of such scientific popularizers as the German evolutionist Ernst Haeckel, who wedded the ideas of classical physics with the new Darwinian history of nature to form a comprehensive Materialistic cosmology, or "anti-theology," carried more weight at the time than they seem in retrospect to have deserved.

There was one promising exchange about the central epistemic issues in the philosophy of science in mid-century, that which took place between William Whewell, a British philosopher and historian of science noted for his work on the theory of induction, and the political essayist, John Stuart Mill; but this was abortive. The debate ended in cross-purposes, largely on account of differences in temperament and preoccupations. Whewell's knowledge—not merely of contemporary physical science but of its whole historical background—was both broad and detailed. The mathematical necessity of arguments such as those in Newtonian dynamics impressed him quite as much as it had impressed Kant; but he gave a less grandiose account of the reasons for this necessity. Whewell's philosophy, a Kantian variation on Newton's hypothetico-deductive method, was historicized: it was only by a progressive approach that physicists arrived at the most coherent and comprehensive systems of what Whewell called "consilient" hypotheses—or separately derived, yet concordant, sets of laws—that were compatible with the empirical knowledge then at their disposal. Mill, on the other hand, principally concerned with the methodology of the social sciences, concentrated on the observational basis of science to the neglect of its theoretical organization and so emphasized the contingent, or unnecessitated, nature of all genuine empirical knowledge. In due course, certain of his doctrines, such as his account of arithmetical formulas as being a variety of empirical generalization, exposed him to some ridicule; but, for the time being, while the sheer bulk and learning of Whewell's writings muffled the force of his arguments, Mill's more fluent and less technical style of exposition captured the popular attention.

In consequence, it was not until the 1890s and early 1900s that serious doubts grew up about the finality of the Newtonian synthesis; and the writings of Ernst Mach, Heinrich Hertz, the eminent German physicist Max Planck, Pierre Duhem, and others inaugurated the new phase of far-reaching critical reanalysis characteristic of 20th-century philosophy of science. In one way or another, all of these men stood back and looked at the Euclidean and Newtonian systems with fresh and less committed eyes. They had learned Kant's lesson about the constructive character of formal theories, without sharing his belief in the unique rationality of the classical synthesis; and, as a result, the central topics of their discussions turned on the best ways of restating the Kantian problem. Granting that the intellectual activity of theory construction has the effect of building a physical necessity into man's theoretical arguments, they asked, what then follows, ontologically, about the reality or conventionality of the resulting atoms, forces, electrons, etc., and what can be said, epistemologically, about the cognitive status and logical validity of its theoretical principles?

At one extreme, an Austrian physicist and philosopher Ernst Mach, and Richard Avenarius, the author of a philosophy known as empiriocriticism, expounded a sensationalist form of Empiricism reminiscent of David Hume, who had insisted that all ideas be traceable to "impressions" (sensations). On their view, theoretical concepts are intellectual fictions, introduced to achieve economy in the intellectual organization of sensory impressions, or observations, for which alone ontal primacy can be claimed. Correspondingly, all claims to scientific knowledge had epistemic validity for them only insofar as they could be grounded in such sense impressions. As against this instrumentalist or reductionist position, Max Planck, author of the quantum theory, defended a qualified Realism, which, at the least, expressed the ideal toward which all conceptual development in physics proceeds; for, without a belief in the enduring reality of external nature, he argued, all motive for theoretical improvement in science would vanish. Between these two extremes, Henri Poincaré, equally distinguished in mathematics and the philosophy of science, and Pierre Duhem, a French theoretical physicist, occupied a range of intermediate so-called conventionalist positions, which attempted to do justice to the arbitrary elements in theory construction while avoiding the sort of radical doubt about the ontal status of theoretical entities that led Mach into lifelong Skepticism about the reality of atoms.

The 20th-century debate: Positivists versus historians. In the mid-20th century, debate in the philosophy of science became notably detailed, elaborate, and critical; those 50 years, in fact, have seen the subject finally achieving the status of a well-established professional discipline. Not least among the causes of this development have been the profound changes that have taken place since 1900 within theoretical physics and other fundamental branches of natural science. So long as the classical synthesis of Euclid and Newton retained its unquestioned authority, there had been little occasion to probe its ontological and epistemological bases at all deeply; but relativity theory—which qualified earlier geometries and laws in terms of new insights into the tie-ins between space and time—and quantum mechanics—which qualified them in terms of a statistical and indeterministic formulation—posed a frontal challenge to that synthesis and inevitably provoked critical and philosophical questions about the validity of the methods and assumptions on which it had relied. Consequently, between 1920 and 1940 there arose a renewed interaction between theoretical physicists and philosophers of science—especially between the Viennese Positivists and the authors of the new quantum mechanics.

The main themes of the subsequent debate were largely those introduced into discussion in the period around 1900. Mach's critical reductionism, based on his *Beiträge zur Analyse der Empfindungen* (1886; Eng. trans., *The Analysis of Sensations . . . ,* 1959), in which he tried to reduce all knowledge to statements about sensations, was a prime source both of the Positivism and Logical Empiricism (*q.v.*) of the Vienna Circle—a group of eminent philosophers and scientists that met regularly in Vienna during the 1920s and 1930s—and also of the epistemological theories about sense-data and logical constructions developed in Britain about the same time by Bertrand Russell, perhaps the foremost logician and philosopher then in England; by G.E. Moore, a meticulous pioneer in Linguistic Analysis; and by others. Meanwhile, the qualified Realism of Planck and Hertz was

Whewell versus J.S. Mill

Empiriocriticism; Realism; conventionalism

Relativity and quantum mechanics

carried further by such men as Norman Campbell, an English physicist known for his sharpening of the distinction between laws and theories, and Karl Popper, an Austro-English philosopher recognized for his theory of falsifiability, both of whose views reflect the explicit methodology of many working scientists today. A notable exception would be the Positivistic followers of Niels Bohr in the Copenhagen school of theoretical physics. Finally, there has continued to be substantial support for intermediate, conventionalist compromises, with Kantian overtones, along the general lines developed by Poincaré and Duhem.

Logical Positivism versus Neo-Kantianism

From the rich complexity of recent philosophy of science, two main strands may be selected for special mention here. The first is the strand of neo-Humean Positivism, which first developed in the Vienna Circle and has flourished more recently in the United States and has been fundamentally preoccupied with epistemological issues. While largely abandoning Mach's belief that sensations are the sole ultimate ground of knowledge, its proponents have continued, with Mach, to regard theoretical entities as fictions or logical constructs, the validity of which depends entirely on the capacity to give them a basis in empirical observations. This neo-Humean position has derived much encouragement, if not formal confirmation, both from Einstein's emphasis on the essential role of the observer in relativity physics and from the attack from the side of quantum theory made by the German physicist Werner Heisenberg on any sharp distinction, at the subatomic level, between the observer, his observation, and the system observed (see NATURE, PHILOSOPHY OF).

The Logical Positivists and Empiricists harnessed to these epistemic arguments a formal apparatus taken over from the philosophy of mathematics—specifically, from Russell and Whitehead's *Principia Mathematica* (1910–13). In their view, the activity of theory construction is logically equivalent to the creation of propositional systems, in which groups of propositions are ideally set out in axiomatic form. So interpreted, the hypothetico-deductive method becomes a recipe for devising a succession of progressively more comprehensive axiom systems, based on alternative sets of general postulates (or primitive propositions) posited without proof, from which particular, empirical propositions can be inferred. As in the case of the special theory of relativity, these particular propositions—for instance, that the axis of Mercury's orbital ellipse will precess (or turn) at a certain rate—can then be used to validate the general postulates by comparing them with actual experience thus—directly or indirectly—substantiating the more general primitive propositions as well. The subsequent debate within the Viennese school has been concerned, very largely, with the exact character and force of this substantiation—whether it be verification, confirmation, or corroboration and/or falsification. At its most ambitious extreme, the Viennese school aimed at constructing a single system of unified science, by which the entire corpus of positive knowledge would be embraced in a single, all-embracing axiom system to be constructed around Russell's abstract symbolic logic. According to this program, all truly scientific knowledge must, first of all, be validated by appeal to neutral empirical observations, on pain of being dismissed as meaningless; and it must then be incorporated into the larger scheme of unified science.

The strongest opposition to this Empiricist or Positivist strand has come, correspondingly, from a Neo-Kantian school that has questioned the very possibility of identifying the pool of theoretically neutral observations necessary for substantiating or discrediting alternative theories in a strictly logical manner. This Neo-Kantian strand in 20th-century philosophy of science was inaugurated by the pioneering thinkers Heinrich Hertz (in electromagnetic wave theory) and Ludwig Wittgenstein (in philosophy of language). Rejecting Mach's central epistemological questions about sensations and ideas, these men have started instead from Kantian questions about the use of representations or models in the explanation of phenomena. Hertz's treatise on *The Principles of Mechanics*

(1894), for instance, expounded Newtonian dynamics as a formal representation that logically entailed empirical conclusions only insofar as the phenomena concerned were already describable in terms drawn from the theory itself; and Wittgenstein's *Tractatus Logico-Philosophicus* (1922) extended Hertz's analysis to provide a general philosophical theory of language as an instrument for the representation of facts. The implications of this approach for the philosophical analysis and methodology of science have been explored further by some of Wittgenstein's pupils and successors, who have shifted the focus of discussion away from the verification of scientific propositions to the establishment of scientific concepts and theories; by highlighting the problem of conceptual change, they have revived interest in the philosophical significance of the history of scientific ideas. For, from this point of view, logical questions about the structure of propositional systems must be joined by other, equally fundamental rational questions about the manner in which different theoretical systems come to succeed one another (see below: *Conceptual change and the development of science*).

Controversy among scientists

During this same period, the remarkable changes taking place within such sciences as theoretical physics, biochemistry, and psychology have been provoking philosophical discussions among scientists themselves. For instance, the displacement of classical Newtonian physics by Heisenberg's quantum mechanics has stimulated a new round of arguments about causality and determinism, with some people hailing Heisenberg's Principle of Indeterminacy—which holds that the location of a particle is intrinsically imprecise in the measure that its momentum is precise (and vice versa)—as giving human free will the toehold that rigorous 19th-century determinism did not seem to allow. Progress in cellular and subcellular physiology, moreover, has given rise to further rounds of debate in the philosophy of biology. Claude Bernard, the foremost experimentalist of 19th-century medicine, had never managed to extend his analysis of regulatory mechanisms, such as those of the nerves that control the size of blood vessels, to cover the processes of embryology and morphogenesis (development of organic forms); and, on this finer level, there had been a renewed deadlock, around the years 1900–20, between the vitalism of Hans Driesch, which posited an almost "soul-like" reality that guides development, and the mechanism of Jacques Loeb, both experimental biologists with philosophical concerns. Once again, supporters of neither extreme position could make out their case entirely; instead, biologists have tended toward the mediating systemic conceptions first introduced by Paul A. Weiss, a distinguished developmental biologist, in the mid-1920s, and subsequently developed in detail as applications of the new theories of cybernetics and feedback, which conduct comparative studies of automatic control systems in the nervous system and in electromechanical engineering. More recently still, the development of molecular biology has compelled scientists to reformulate the problem of morphogenesis yet again—this time as the problem of seeing how the structural patterns of nucleic acid macromolecules in the hereditary genetical material find a structural expression in the developing body as a result of interacting with the environment. At present, this question is still very largely unanswered.

Controversy in the behavioral sciences

Methodologically, since 1940 one new centre of philosophical debate has developed, this time in the behavioral sciences. Ever since Descartes and Hobbes, there has been sharp disagreement about the legitimacy of extending the methods and categories of physical science to the sphere of the higher, distinctively human mental processes; and, even in the 1970s, theoretical psychologists were still far from agreed in their explanations of human behaviour. Some psychologists insist that human actions are subject to laws and mechanisms of the same kind as physical processes; others deny that any direct analogy exists between rules of conduct and laws of nature. Currently, this dispute is most lively in the psychology of language. Behaviorists follow B.F. Skinner, an American psychologist, in rejecting any distinctive class of mental laws and processes, whereas cognitive psychologists and generative grammarians, led by Noam Chomsky, argue that linguistic activities are creative and rule conforming in respects that no behaviorist can explain. In sociology and anthropology, equally, the 20th century has been a period of methodological controversy. Here the unresolved conflict has to do with the significance of history in the explanation of collective human behaviour. On one side, there is, in sociology, a school of so-called structuralists or functionalists that follows another American scholar, Talcott Parsons; or, in anthropology, there are the British ethnologist Arnold Radcliff-Brown and Bronisław Malinowski, a student of primitive mentality and behaviour, who regard all of the cultural practices and social institutions that function within a given community at any time as related together systematically within an overall structure: to explain any one of those practices or institutions, they hold, it is enough to show how it connects up with all of the other contemporaneous aspects of the culture. On the other side, a more historically minded school, notably the German "critical Marxists" (such as Jürgen Haberman), emphasizes the dynamic, developing character of social structures and relationships. Here again, the methodological debate is still in progress, and its eventual outcome cannot yet be clearly foreseen.

II. Conceptualization and methodology of science

It is appropriate at this point to define the recurrent problems that have played a central part in the philosophical debate about science and the crucial elements that any adequate philosophy of science must include in its account. From the beginning, scientists themselves have been interested not merely in cataloging and describing the world of nature as they find it but in making the workings of nature intelligible with the help of compact and organized theories. Correspondingly, philosophers of science are obliged to consider not merely nature in isolation—as a mere assemblage of empirical facts, mutely waiting to be discovered by man—but also the manner in which man himself perceives and interprets those facts when bringing them within the grasp of an intelligible theory and the respects in which the validity of the resulting theoretical ideas (or concepts) is affected by that processing of the empirical data.

Historically speaking, the problems posed by this interaction of man and nature have been complex and confused. Though philosophers of science face, even today, many of the same questions that were already being debated in classical Athens, the range and relevance of those questions has been greatly clarified in the meanwhile. For instance, when philosophers in the 17th century analyzed the nature and possible scope of a mathematical and experimental account of nature, they helped to clear the ground for Newton to develop the intellectual program and methodology of modern theoretical physics; while the subsequent philosophical debate about natural and artificial classification similarly cleared the ground for the scientific taxonomy of the Swedish systematist Carolus Linnaeus and the theory of natural selection of Charles Darwin. Methodological clarification in the philosophy of science has, in this way, repeatedly led to creative advance in science itself and so given rise, in turn, to new experience on which philosophers can draw in taking their methodological analyses further.

ELEMENTS OF THE SCIENTIFIC ENTERPRISE

It is easy enough to list the chief elements that must find a place in any philosophy of science, but problems arise in mapping the relations between them.

Empirical data and their theoretical interpretation.
Empirical elements
First are the empirical elements. The task of science is to explain actual events, processes, or phenomena in nature; and no system of theoretical ideas, technical terms, and mathematical procedures—or mathematical procedures alone—qualifies as scientific unless it comes to grips with those empirical facts at some point and in some way and helps to make them more intelligible. On the one hand, the facts in question may be discovered by using observational methods—i.e., by recording them as and when they

occur naturally, without employing any special contrivances affecting their occurrence. This situation is, of course, the normal case in astronomy, in which the objects of study cannot be influenced or controlled. Alternatively, they may be discovered by using experimental methods—i.e., by devising special equipment or apparatus with the help of which those processes or phenomena are caused to occur on demand and under specially controlled conditions. In that case, the scientist can attack scientific problems—to use Kant's vivid metaphor—by "putting Nature to the question," as in much of physics and fundamental biology. Either way, a philosophical difficulty at once arises about the results of the scientist's empirical studies: for he must ask how such raw empirical facts can be sifted, stated, and described in a way that throws light on the scientist's own theoretical problems. Do all empirical facts whatever serve as raw material for science? Or is this true only of those that have been preselected for their theoretical relevance—or even, to some extent, reshaped to ensure it? Is a scientist concerned with every particular empirical event, as such, or only with general phenomena or regularities recognizable in those events? Different schools of philosophers treat this raw material in very different ways.

In the second place, there are conceptual elements. Conceptual and formal elements Every science employs its own characteristic abstractions, terminology, and techniques of interpretation and explanation, which can be of very different kinds. They may be ideal types, as in gas theory and parts of sociology; conservation principles, as in dynamics and energetics; taxa, as in biological systematics; particles or constituents, as in genetics and subatomic physics; models or flow diagrams, as in econometric analysis. Such conceptual elements are the intellectual keys by which phenomena are made intelligible, and a most active philosophical debate has turned around the part they play in the interpretation of phenomena. If, for instance, the idea of particles or ultimate constituents of matter is regarded as a concept created by scientists for the purpose of their own theoretical analysis, can an independent existence then be claimed for such theoretical entities in the world of nature itself? Or must all such ideas be regarded as fictions or constructs for which the claim to reality goes no further than the paper on which the scientific explanations are written? Similarly, if the theoretical descriptions of nature arrived at in science are unavoidably idealized and abstract, does this imply that the necessity attaching to arguments in, say, theoretical physics is itself only an artifact, or by-product, of scientists' own procedures for interpreting phenomena? Or can one, after all, speak of natural events themselves as happening "of necessity"?

Finally, every natural science includes also formal and mathematical elements or mathematical elements alone. These may be mathematical algorithms, or procedures of calculation, like those used in computational astronomy since Babylonian days, or like the computer programs that are their 20th-century counterparts; or geometrical constructions, as in certain branches of optics; or methods of graphical analysis, such as those used in handling statistical data; or the axiomatic systems by which, from classical times on, geometry and physics have been organized into formal schemata of propositions bound together by logical relations. Philosophers in the Platonic tradition give such formal elements special consideration, viewing as authentically intelligible only those theories the content of which can be presented explicitly in formal, and preferably in mathematical, systems of propositions. Theories of this kind alone are capable—as the seminal German logician Gottlob Frege expressed it—of employing "concepts in their pure form." Thus, 20th-century philosophers of science have devoted much time and effort to the question: How far, and on what conditions, can other branches of natural science (e.g., quantum mechanics or genetics) be cast in the same definitive, axiomatic form as classical mechanics and electrical theory? Or is this formal construction itself merely a human convenience, adopted to simplify the handling of the empirical data, which reveals nothing more about the underlying structure of nature itself?

Each of these three groups of elements poses problems about which philosophers of science are still in deep disagreement; and these differences of view can usefully be illustrated by indicating the various approaches adopted by members of rival schools when discussing each of the groups. At one extreme can be cited philosophers of a radically Empiricist frame of mind, who regard it as important, above all, to emphasize the empirical foundations of scientific knowledge; for them, the raw facts of experience are primary and entitled to absolute respect. On this view, general theoretical principles have authentic scientific content only when interpreted as empirical generalizations about directly grasped empirical data; and, correspondingly, abstract theoretical entities must be understood as logical constructions from more fundamental elements that can be directly identified in empirical experience. (This belief, of course, was the basis of Mach's conclusion that submicroscopic atoms were merely intellectual fictions and derived their scientific meaning entirely from the macroscopic sense experiences that they were used to explain.)

At the other extreme, philosophers of a fully Rationalist, or Cartesian, bent can be cited who reject the idea that raw empirical facts, in and of themselves, display any intelligible or law-governed relationships whatsoever —and still less any necessary ones. For them, as for Plato, the scientist's bare experience of nature is a disorganized aggregate, or flux, unless and until he is able to discover some rational structure or principles relating these disconnected facts to a larger, more intelligible whole. Rather than allow equal significance and authority to every passing occurrence, the scientist, on this view, must be highly selective in the observations to which he pays attention; indeed, the very function of a well-designed experiment is now to create phenomena that can illustrate the intelligible relationships that are the true concern of science and so deserve the status of scientifically authenticated facts.

Both of these approaches, the Empiricist and the Rationalist, emphasize valid and important points; but, in their extreme forms, they give rise to difficulties that are probably insuperable. As to the Empiricist approach, the credentials of any scientific concept or theory certainly depend to a substantial extent on its basis in empirical experience. Indeed, much has been learned about statistics, the calculus of probabilities, and the design of scientific experiments from careful analysis of the procedures by which empirical data are actually handled, even before questions of theoretical interpretation were directly raised. Yet it is questionable whether sense impressions alone could ever serve as evidence for any scientific position, as Mach and the sense-data philosophers assumed. All genuine scientific observations, as Kant expressed it, have the form of judgments—*i.e.*, are expressed in statements answering questions formulated beforehand. It is probably an exaggeration to insist that all legitimate theoretical statements in science must be related in a strictly deductive manner to the everyday empirical observations that they are used to explain; and it is a caricature to treat the explanatory power of theoretical laws and principles, as for example in physics, as no different in kind from that of such an elementary generalization as "All robins' eggs are greenish blue."

As to the Rationalist approach, one of the chief tasks for philosophers of science is certainly to account for the rational interconnections that give scientific explanations their characteristic intelligibility. In this respect, such men as Descartes, Kant, and Hertz have deepened the philosopher's understanding of the scientific enterprise by obliging him to recognize the ways in which the intellectual organization of scientific theories rests on the scientist's own constructive activities, rather than on the specific facts. Yet, it would again be misleading to use this fact as an excuse for regarding physical theories—to echo a phrase of Einstein's—as entirely "free creations of the human mind." While the step from observations to theories does not rest on formal entailments alone, it would be an equally serious counter-exaggeration to suggest that theory construction is totally arbitrary or uncon-

strained by the imperative demands of the specific problems to be solved.

The outstanding task for most philosophers of science is, accordingly, to find an acceptable middle way between the Rationalist and Empiricist extremes and thus to do justice both to the empirical foundations of theories and to their internal organization. The different emphases of philosophers commonly reflect, at most, differences in their substantive preoccupations. Those who are interested (as was Mill) in possible methods for developing the human or social sciences naturally place most stress on the empirical basis of scientific knowledge. Those who are familiar (as was Whewell) with the actual outcome of theory construction in established sciences, such as physics, naturally underscore the systematic coherence and structure of scientific understanding. Those who are concerned with the nature and validity of historical understanding (as Giambattista Vico was) likewise end by giving a very different account of certainty and necessity from those (like Descartes) whose ideal of scientific knowledge is a formal, mathematical one.

If the philosopher comes to grips with the full complexity of the scientific enterprise, this approach can lead him to a more exact understanding of the varied intellectual problems of the natural and human sciences. Once it is recognized how different are the kinds of questions arising within such diverse fields as quantum electrodynamics and developmental biology, clinical neurology and historical sociology, the goal of formulating a single scientific method—with a universally applicable set of procedures and criteria for judging new theories or ideas in all fields of science—may come to appear a mirage. Yet the philosopher's legitimate insistence on generality has already helped to promote important extensions and integrations of man's scientific understanding. So again, he must now avoid taking too dogmatic a stand, either for or against complete generality, bearing in mind Kant's warning that the reason can hope to map its own proper boundaries only at the price of occasionally overstepping them.

The empirical procedures of science. Along with the three groups of elements already discussed, each phase in the scientific enterprise—empirical, formal, and conceptual, or interpretative—involves its own characteristic procedures. On the level of empirical observation and description, three topics may be briefly touched upon, all of which are discussed at greater length in other articles (see MEASUREMENT, THEORY OF; CLASSIFICATION THEORY; and articles on the basic sciences).

First, there are the procedures of measurement through which scientists arrive at quantitative estimates of the variables and magnitudes considered in their theories. By now, there is a well-developed body of knowledge upon which scholars are agreed about many of the techniques and precautions to be employed in practice in the measurement of empirical quantities, in the calculation of probable errors or significant deviations, and so on. About the deeper significance of measuring procedures and their outcomes, however, there are still unresolved philosophical disputes. These disagreements reflect the same differences of approach already noted. Thus, some philosophers regard any scientific theory concerned with measurable (or quantifiable) magnitudes as intrinsically superior to a qualitative (or, as they would say, an impressionistic) one, however rich and well organized the latter may be. Others, by contrast, would argue that any insistence on employing numerical measures at all costs, even in such a science as, for example, systematic biology, can only lead the investigator to misconceive the true nature of the problems involved. Again, philosophers of an extremely Empiricist or Positivist persuasion have sometimes interpreted the experimental procedures for measuring theoretical magnitudes in, for example, physics as providing implicit definitions of the associated technical terms—the so-called operational definitions—and have thus felt able to claim that the logical entailments that the scientist is seeking between observations and theories are established by linguistic fiat (see below *Status of scientific propositions and concepts or entities*).

Secondly, there are statistical analytical procedures for the design of scientific experiments. The mathematical techniques employed for this purpose are, in fact, closely related to those involved in the theories of measurement, probable error, statistical significance, and others. In this area, the connection between philosophical discussions of inductive logic and the practical procedures of working scientists is at its closest. Whereas a religious scientist (Blaise Pascal), a Nonconformist minister (Thomas Bayes), and an astronomer (Pierre, marquis de Laplace), all mathematicians as well, analyzed the philosophical foundations of the modern calculus of probabilities in the 17th and 18th centuries, 20th-century mathematicians and inductive logicians have similarly explored the intellectual basis for the design and interpretation of significant experiments; and, by now, the relevant procedures form a full-fledged branch of mathematical statistics with many valuable applications, particularly in fields such as sociology and economics, in which large numbers of variables are involved.

Problems of experimental design, however, can be stated clearly and unambiguously only in situations in which questions of fundamental theoretical interpretations are not actively at issue; *e.g.*, in experiments to determine which of two antibiotics is the more effective against a given infection or to learn whether significant correlation exists between two known physical variables. As soon as more fundamental questions of theory arise, however, the problems of experimental design go beyond the scope of any purely statistical analysis. Moreover, the same is true of computer-programming procedures: the numerical data obtained from a straightforward scientific experiment can in many cases be fed into a computer programmed to select the graph or formula in best statistical accord with the data from among those hypotheses conforming to a predetermined set of conceptual or interpretative requirements; thus, in this sense, a computer can be used to perform inductive inferences. Devising brand-new styles of conceptual or theoretical interpretation, by contrast, involves extending or modifying present explanatory procedures to satisfy novel intellectual requirements; and these tasks call for something more than formal statistical or programming techniques.

Finally, the initial handling of the scientist's empirical data requires him to employ procedures of systematic classification. The nature and validity of scientific classification procedures and of the species, genera, families, and so on into which scientists divide their empirical subject matter have been the subject of a long and contentious debate, which is dealt with at greater length in the article CLASSIFICATION THEORY. A long-standing philosophical deadlock between supporters of natural and artificial classification systems was largely broken—in zoological taxonomy, at any rate—through the success of Darwin's theory of natural selection. As Darwin showed, the species to which organic evolution gives rise are neither eternally unchanging natural entities nor mere fictions of the zoologist's arbitrary creation; considered as coherent, self-isolating populations, they have a genuine though temporary reality that is preserved by the contrary processes of variation and selection perpetuation. In some other areas of thought, however, the preliminary identification and classification of the empirical material still raises contentious philosophical questions. When the sociologist theorizes about social groups or systems in the human sciences, for instance, he has to decide what collections of men and institutions do, or do not, fall under those general headings. Can objective tests be found for identifying natural units of sociological analysis? Or, is this choice of units merely set up for the sociologist's own convenience? This uncertainty about the very subject matter of sociology is itself an obstacle to the creation of an agreed-upon body of social theory; and comparable difficulties can arise in anthropology, linguistics, and psychology as well. It is, therefore, not surprising that some critics have even questioned whether these disciplines can truly be called sciences.

The character of these continuing difficulties underscores one point of general significance about the relation of empirical evidence to scientific theories: though philosophers may find it necessary to distinguish the empirical phases, elements, and procedures of science from the theoretical ones analytically, it does not follow that they can be kept wholly separate in actual practice. Satisfactory measuring procedures, experimental designs, and systematic classification principles are, no doubt, necessary preconditions for effective theorizing; but they themselves are subject, in turn, to revision and refinement in the light of subsequent theoretical considerations. In arriving at his dynamical theories, for example, Newton had to begin by relying on older commonsensical notions of effort, weight, and amount of movement; but he soon replaced these by the more exact, theoretically defined concepts of force, mass, and momentum, and this change reacted back onto the empirical procedures of physics also. Likewise in other fields of science, the decision as to whether or not the outcome of any empirical procedure is scientifically relevant or significant soon ceases to be a purely empirical question, as theoretical changes react back onto those empirical procedures and compel the scientist to modify his manner of collecting and describing the supposedly raw data of science. In this way, the empirical evidence by which his scientific conclusions are justified rapidly loses its pure and theoretically neutral character.

The formal structures of science. In this section and the next, those aspects of the scientific enterprise will be considered that have dominated recent debate in the philosophy of science, viz., the formal structures of scientific theory and the processes of conceptual change. It will soon be clear that the philosophical problems to which these two aspects, respectively, give rise are correlative and complementary—the one being static, the other being dynamic.

Since 1920, most analytical philosophers of science have explicitly based their program on a presupposition inherited from Descartes and Plato, viz., that the intellectual content of any natural science can be expressed in a formal propositonal system, having a definite, essential logical structure—what a leading American philosopher of science, Ernest Nagel, concisely called "the structure of science" in his book of that title (1961). One immediate inspiration of this program was the work of David Hilbert, a late-19th-century mathematician. To make the methods of mathematical proof more explicit and more perspicuous and thus more rigorous, Hilbert employed the techniques of formalization, a reduction to relations while disregarding the nature of the relata, and axiomatization, a tracing of entailments back to accepted axioms.

The same techniques were taken over into the philosophy of mathematics by a pioneer German logician, Gottlob Frege, and into symbolic logic by Bertrand Russell and his collaborator Alfred North Whitehead; and, from 1920 on, the Viennese Positivists and their successors attempted to employ them in the philosophy of science also, hoping to demonstrate the validity of formal patterns of scientific inference by the straightforward extension of methods already familiar in deductive logic.

According to the resulting program, the primary task for the philosophy of science was to repeat in quite general terms the kind of analysis by which, in the science of mechanics, Heinrich Hertz, the formulator of electromagnetic wave theory, had already sorted out the formal aspects of science from its empirical aspects. The program was founded on the expectation that it would be possible, first, to demonstrate the existence of formal structures that were essential to any science, properly so-called, and second, to identify the nature of scientific laws, principles, hypotheses, and observations by their characteristic logical functions. Once this had been done, rigorous formal definitions could then be given of validity, probability, degree of confirmation, and all of the other evidential relations involved in the judgment of scientific arguments.

The actual working out of this program has involved complex and highly technical investigations, in the course of which great ingenuity has been displayed—as, for instance, by an outstanding philosophical semanticist and analyst, Rudolf Carnap, in his system of inductive logic, for the criticism of arguments in support of empirical generalizations, and by Hans Reichenbach, an eminent German-American Positivist, in his analysis of probabilistic arguments. So far, however, the program has yielded substantial results only as applied to arguments expressed in an idealized formal symbolism modelled on the lower functional calculus of mathematical logic. By contrast, little has been done to show how one might extend the resulting formal procedures to arguments expressed in the practical terminologies of working science. That extension, in fact, raises difficulties and ambiguities that are

Problem of generalizations versus laws

so far unresolved and may prove unresolvable. The goal of a purely formal analysis of scientific inference has generated difficulties, for instance, by tempting logicians to play down important differences between mere descriptive generalizations about natural phenomena and the explanatory theories (laws, principles, etc.) that a scientist develops to make those phenomena intelligible; and succumbing to this temptation creates problems both within inductive logic and in its applications.

One distinguished supporter of this program, Carl Hempel, originally a member of the Berlin group (allied with the Vienna Circle), has discussed what he calls the theoretician's dilemma: if the task of explaining natural phenomena requires a proof that the character of those phenomena is formally entailed by the conditions of their occurrence, taken together with certain straightforward generalizations based on previous empirical experience, and if those empirical generalizations include references to hypothetical entities, then the theorist is faced with an invidious choice: for, in that case, either his generalizations (his laws) do in fact provide a logical link between the conditions of the phenomena and their actual occurrence and the assumption of hypothetical entities is formally superfluous; or else they do not succeed in doing so, and that assumption will not have strictly explained the phenomena. Clearly, this dilemma can be evaded only by challenging the identification of laws with generalizations and insisting that any appeal to laws of nature always involves the scientist in reinterpreting natural phenomena, not in merely generalizing about them.

Looking beyond the internal structure of inductive logic, the dubious equation of scientific laws with empirical generalizations has also been criticized on the ground that it treats the content of those laws as matters of happenstance, far more accidental or contingent than those expressed in any genuine law of nature. In the opposing view, the explanatory force of, say, the physicist's law of inertia is totally different from that of such a generalizing statement as "All swans are white"; and one can learn nothing about the validity of actual physical arguments unless his philosophical analysis respects that crucial difference. It has not proved easy, however, to analyze the formal structure of the sciences in any less abstract manner than that of the Viennese Positivists or to give a true representation of the working language and arguments of science. In his *Essay on Metaphysics* (1940), R.G. Collingwood, a British philosopher and historian, made one striking attempt, in which the formal structure of intellectual systems was explained in terms not of direct entailments between more or less universal propositions but rather of mutual presuppositions between more or less general concepts. In this account, the principle of inertia was not the most universally true assertion in dynamics but was, rather, the most generally applicable presupposition, or principle of interpretation. Such an account has the merit of explaining why, within a particular science, certain formal patterns of argument carry the apparent necessity that they do; but at the same time it lays itself open to the charge of yielding too much to relativism and so of destroying the objectivity of scientific knowledge by giving the impression that the conceptual structures of science are imposed on phenomena by the arbitrary choice of the scientific theorist himself.

Doubts about formalization

The late 1960s, accordingly, saw a renewal of questioning about the original assumption, viz., that the entire intellectual content of a science can be captured in a propositional or presuppositional system. Certain of the doubts about this thesis revive criticisms put forward at

the turn of the century by a U.S. Pragmatist, Charles Sanders Peirce, who argued that the logical status of the theoretical terms and statements in a science is—in the nature of the case—subject to historical change as the conceptual organization of the science develops. (This same insight has been explored more recently by a U.S. logician, Willard Quine, who rejects any attempt to classify statements within scientific theories using the traditional hard-and-fast dichotomies—contingent–necessary and synthetic–analytic—as fallacious and dogmatic.) Other criticisms of the thesis go deeper. By focussing his philosophical attention exclusively on the static formal structure of propositional systems and, so, on the intellectual content of the sciences at particular temporal cross sections in their development—they point out—the philosopher is distracted from the complementary questions about the manner in which the conceptual organization of a science changes and, so, from the traditional claims of natural science to be a rational as well as a logical enterprise. At this point in the debate, therefore, the spotlight shifts away from the static problem of analyzing a science in static logical terms to the historical problem of analyzing the dynamic processes of intellectual and conceptual change.

Conceptual change and the development of science. The problem of conceptual change has recently come back to the fore. The crucial question it poses is: "What is a concept?" In the heyday of Logical Empiricism, that question had largely been disregarded. Following the example of Frege, the Viennese Positivists had condemned any tendency to regard the philosophy of science as concerned with scientific thinking—which was in their view a matter for psychologists—and had restricted themselves to the formal analysis of scientific arguments. This preoccupation with logic was also reflected in their view of concepts. To interpret a concept such as force as referring either to a feeling of effort or to a mental image could lead, they argued, only to confusion. Instead, the philosopher must equate concepts with the terms and variables appearing in the propositional systems of science and define them, in part by reference to their roles in the formal structures of those propositional systems—thus fixing their systematic import—and in part by reference to the specific events and phenomena they are used to explain—thus fixing their empirical import. In the 1920s and 1930s, accordingly, all substantive philosophical questions about the concepts of science were dealt with summarily: they were simply translated into logical or linguistic questions about the formal roles and empirical references of technical terms and mathematical variables.

Styles of explanatory procedure

Once the philosophy of science is approached more historically, however, those substantive questions must be faced afresh in their own right. Rival scientific theories will now be distinguished not merely as so many alternative formal systems, based on different primitive terms and axioms, but also as alternative ways of organizing the knowledge of nature, based on different explanatory techniques and modes of representation. The distinctive features of different scientific concepts will lie, as a result, not in their respective formal roles and empirical references but in the styles of explanatory procedure involved in their application. Those procedures may be of many different kinds: *e.g.*, physical conservation calculations, optical-ray diagrams, functional analyses, taxonomic classifications, historico-evolutionary reconstructions, or dynamical axiom systems. Correspondingly, they provide occasions for employing mathematical formulas, or intuitively intelligible models, or genealogical trees, or other styles of representation. In each case, however, the philosopher can describe the conceptual organization of the resulting explanations in terms neither of intuitive models nor of mathematical formulas and variables taken alone: what he must now consider is the entire pattern of theoretical interpretation—models, mathematics, and all.

Viewed from this alternative standpoint, the philosophy of science will begin by identifying the different styles of explanation characteristic of different sciences or of different stages in a given science and will recognize how those differences in explanatory style reflect the characteristic problems of different scientific fields and periods. So considered, empirical generalizations and descriptive classifications will serve to organize the empirical data of science in a preliminary way; but serious theoretical interpretation can begin only after that point. The central philosophical task now is to analyze, clearly and explicitly, (1) the standards by appeal to which scientists have to decide whether or not some interpretation is legitimate, justified, and conclusively established and (2) the considerations that justify giving up one currently accepted interpretation in favour of an alternative, novel one.

The first of these questions is one that the Logical Empiricists set out to answer in their own manner. They treated the empirical data and the theoretical principles of science as being connected by purely logical relations and attempted to define the required standards in terms of a formal theory of confirmation, corroboration, or falsification. The second question is one that they never seriously tackled. Instead, they assumed that one could, first, work out a quantitative index of acceptability for individual theories taken separately and, afterward, use this as a scale for measuring and comparing the merits of rival theoretical interpretations. By now, however, it is evident that, when biophysicists, say, abandon one theoretical approach in favour of another—as being more fruitful from the standpoint of biophysics—the considerations that lead them to do so are by no means analyzable in formal terms alone. On the contrary, the ability of a biochemist, say, to judge whether or not such a change in approach will effectively help to solve his theoretical problems is one of the most severe assessments of his substantive grasp of what biochemistry is about.

Reinterpretation of concepts and principles

In this way, the shift of attention from the propositions of science to its concepts is making philosophers more aware of the extent to which theoretical understanding involves the reinterpretation of empirical results, not merely their formal transformation. Similarly, the problem of conceptual change is raising questions about the processes by which theoretical interpretations succeed one another and about the procedures of conceptual judgment that are applied in the rational development of a science. These questions are currently under active discussion, and several lines of attack are being considered, none of which has finally established itself.

At one extreme, there are some who still regard theoretical concepts and principles as organized into compact, logical systems and who attempt to define the alternative standpoints of different sciences as the consequences of different basic premises or presuppositions. Having adopted this systematic approach, the investigator then discovers that conceptual change at a fundamental level finds adequate scope only through the replacement of one complete formal system by another, distinct and separate successor system. As a result, fundamental theoretical change is, in this view, intelligible only as the outcome of thoroughgoing intellectual revolutions, in which one entire theoretical system—axioms, principles, criteria of relevance, standards of judgment, and all—is swept aside in favour of another.

Alternatively, there are those who distinguish two different kinds of fundamental principles in a science—marking off the basic theoretical assertions such as "Matter consists of atoms combining into molecules" from its methodological maxims and standards of judgment, such as "All physical phenomena are to be explained in mechanical terms"—and who recognize fundamental conceptual changes in the science as legitimate, just so long as they respect the methodological maxims that are definitive of the science in question. In this second view, conceptual changes of any depth in the intellectual substance of a science will continue to be intelligible, provided only that the new views are still governed by the established program and framework concepts of the science in question. There will then be revolutions in science only when some entire intellectual approach is discredited—e.g., that of 16th- and 17th-century iatrochemistry, which studied chemistry as a means of treating disease—

or when some entirely new science is created, with its own complete system of interpretation—e.g., molecular biology.

At the other extreme, there are some who doubt whether any sharp distinction can be drawn between substantive theoretical assertions and maxims of methodological procedure and who argue that all aspects of a natural science are alike open to historical reconsideration and modification. The more specific the theoretical doctrines and concepts being considered, the more risky they will be, and the more readily they will be modified or abandoned or both. From this third point of view, however, it is questionable whether any change, however drastic—even the hybridization of crystallography, viral genetics, and biochemistry, which led to the inauguration of molecular biology—is ever as discontinuous or revolutionary as the two former views imply. Instead, the attempt may be made to account for the procedures and processes involved in the historical development of scientific concepts by using the same general form of theory on every level —explaining innovation as requiring a selective choice between intellectual variants of different kinds; and, in this way, the theory of conceptual development can be brought into line with other historically based theories of natural and cultural change.

Whichever alternative is adopted, one point must be kept in mind: the moment that problems about the changing theoretical organization of science begin to be treated in an authentically developmental manner, philosophical inquiries are given a quite new direction. This step compels one to view all questions about the logical structure and propositional systems of science against a broader historical background. In this new context the natural sciences are seen not as static formal structures but as rational enterprises characterized by certain typical intellectual procedures or movements. These basic procedures of intellectual development in science are the topic to which attention is directed in the next section.

Developmental nature of science

MOVEMENTS OF SCIENTIFIC THOUGHT

Discovery and rationality. In analyzing the natural sciences for philosophical purposes as historically developing enterprises, the question "What is it that makes the sciences rational?" is raised in a new form: do the intellectual procedures that scientists actually employ to investigate and explain natural phenomena have definite and objective intellectual merits that make their adoption rationally prudent, wise, and obligatory? In answering this question, philosophical opinion has tended to polarize in recent years toward two extreme positions: on the one hand, a formalist or positivist extreme, on the other, a romantic or irrationalist one.

Given their mathematical inspiration and preoccupations, both the Viennese Empiricists and their successors in Britain and the United States have interpreted the rationality of scientific procedures as depending solely on the formal validity, or logicality, of scientific arguments. In their view, questions of rationality can be raised about the scientist's work only at the final stage in his inquiries —i.e., when he sets out, as the final outcome of his work, the explicit explanatory arguments in support of his novel theories or interpretations—only then, they declare, will there be anything about science that is capable of being criticized in logical or philosophical terms.

It is therefore a commonplace of recent Empiricist analysis in the philosophy of science that one must distinguish at the very outset between discovery and justification. The term discovery refers to all the stages in a scientific inquiry preceding the formulation of the new explanatory arguments that are its final outcome. The term justification refers, by contrast, to the demonstration that the formal validity or explanatory power of those arguments justifies the scientist in accepting their conclusions as scientifically validated or established. In this view, the rational concerns of the philosopher of science are restricted solely to this final phase of justification. All questions about the earlier stages—i.e., about discovery—are matters of mere psychology, not of serious philosophy. As one widely accepted epigram ex-

Formalist versus irrationalist

presses it, "There is no logic of discovery"; and this distinction—given the equation of rationality within logicality—seemingly invalidates all questions about the rationality of the preliminary steps by which a scientist arrives at a discovery.

At the opposite extreme, there are those, such as Michael Polanyi, a Hungarian-born scientist and philosopher, and Arthur Koestler, a novelist and journalist, who emphasize the parts played by intuition, guesswork, and chance in scientific investigation, citing these as evidence that theoretical achievement calls into play an intellectual creativity superior to mere rationality. According to this anti-Positivist argument, the modern scientist is a sleepwalker whose creative insight guides him to intellectual destinations that he could never clearly see or state beforehand: any excessive preoccupation with the rationality of scientific procedures, by contrast, springs from a pedestrian desire to clip the wings of imagination and to confine the scientist to stereotyped procedures, thus destroying the creative fertility of science. Rather than subjecting scientific intuition to the barren intellectual accountancy of the Positivists, the conclusion runs, one should embrace a romantic anti-rationalism.

In each of these extreme cases, however, the initial equation of rationality with logicality demands closer examination. Certainly, the activity of investigation and discovery can be examined with advantage from a psychological point of view as it has been, in fact, by a French mathematician, Jacques Hadamard, as well as from a philosophical point of view. Yet the possibility of such psychological inquiries does not obviously prove, entirely by itself, that procedures of intellectual investigation in science and mathematics are essentially nonrational. Chance, for instance, may help to bring relevant material to a scientist's attention. But chance—as has often been remarked—favours the prepared mind, and it is fair to ask how far the scientist acted rationally, after all, in picking out the items he did as being relevant to his particular problems. Similarly, in the case of creative intuition and the rest: once again, the man with the best trained mind can afford to give the freest rein to his intellectual imagination because he will be best qualified to appraise the rational context of his current problems and to recognize significant clues, promising new lines of analysis, or possible answers to his questions, as they come to mind.

Problematics of scientific inquiry

Neither denigrating the early phases of scientific inquiry as of merely psychological interest nor overpraising them as exercises of creative imagination disposes therefore of the philosophical problem that is here involved, viz., that of showing what makes certain procedures of investigation more rational than others. To find a middle way between formalism and irrationalism, it is necessary to look more closely at the nature of the problems of scientific inquiry. If the improvement of scientific concepts and theories depends on the development of more powerful explanatory procedures, the philosophical analysis of discovery then requires that one show what is essentially involved in devising such procedures, testing them out, and determining the range of their application. This problem must be dealt with, furthermore, not by a formal analysis of the resulting arguments alone but first and foremost by establishing what tasks any novel explanatory procedure in science can be required to perform, what demands its performance can properly be asked to satisfy, and so what intellectual goals a scientist is expected to be aiming at in all the phases of his investigations. Posed in these alternative terms, the problem of scientific rationality becomes a problem of showing how conceptual changes in science result in the introduction of novel ideas, which are—in a phrase coined by Mach as early as 1910—"better adapted, both to the facts and to one another." It is rational for older scientific theories to be displaced by newer ones that are functionally superior; and the task for philosophers of science is to demonstrate explicitly in what such functional adaptedness consists.

At the present time, many younger philosophers of science are actively analyzing the nature of the problems of science in these terms. Significantly, most of these men have had their own primary training within the natural sciences proper rather than in formal logic or pure mathematics, for the task requires a much more detailed analysis of the processes of intellectual innovation than has been customary hitherto. In place of the simple dichotomy between discovery and justification, for instance, it calls for a subdivision of the innovation process into a more complex sequence of distinct stages; and at each stage both rational and causal considerations are relevant. Thus, at the initial stage in any inquiry, a scientist must decide which among all of the philosophically conceivable variants from the current repertory of explanatory methods are to be taken seriously at all; which, that is, are genuine possibilities. This preliminary sorting of initially plausible from implausible innovations must be dealt with—and dealt with in the most rational manner possible—long before any question of justification arises.

This initial sorting procedure is one about which scientists themselves also speak cogently and eloquently. Far from deciding what novel suggestions are genuinely possible or plausible on a purely psychological basis or by the exercise of some mysterious, nonrational intuition, scientists will commonly explain their reasons for accepting one set of conceptual variants rather than another as deserving serious consideration. At the same time, such micro-analyses of scientific innovation must certainly leave room for causal as well as rational questions. During certain periods in the historical development of science, for instance, scientists have notoriously disregarded novel possibilities that later turned out to hold a key to the solution of crucial theoretical difficulties. Looking back at such periods, it is possible to reconstruct with care the rational considerations that might have been advanced at the time to explain this neglect; but even so, one is occasionally forced to conclude that the men involved were prejudiced against those possibilities by factors external to their sciences; *e.g.*, by influences originating in the wider social, cultural, or political framework of their time. Thus, Newton was particularly afraid that his theory of material particles might be accused of supporting Epicureanism, whereas Darwin concealed his private speculations about the cerebral basis of mental activities because of public objections to Materialism.

Diverse approaches in different fields

In analyzing the microstructure of scientific problem solving, it is necessary, accordingly, to resist any temptation to generalize prematurely. Scientific investigators working in different fields, or at different times, apparently face theoretical difficulties of quite different kinds. One must therefore begin by studying the specific needs and tasks of each particular science, at one or another stage in its evolution, separately—seeking to recognize, in each individual case, the particular intellectual demands to be met by any new concept or theory if it is to be successful. Eventually, the accumulated results of specific micro-analyses may bring the investigator to a point at which he can again afford to generalize about all of the assorted theoretical problems confronting, say, physics and about the broader intellectual demands to be met by successful theoretical changes in a variety of scientific situations. At the present stage, however, though philosophers of science still cannot afford to beg these questions, they are compelled to conduct their analyses in a more piecemeal way—building up their picture of scientific innovation and discovery by considering a wide range of sample cases and working their way only gradually toward a more comprehensive account of the problematics of the scientific enterprise.

Validation and justification. If this situation is true of the earlier stages in discovery, it is no less true in the case of justification itself. Here again, from 1920 on, the debate in the philosophy of science focussed predominantly on two sharply opposed positions, both of which appear in retrospect to be excessively narrow. On the one hand, Empiricist philosophers argued for a view that made prediction the crucial test of scientific validity; on the other hand, philosophers of a more Rationalist temperament saw coherence and scope as the crucial requirements.

Empiricist versus constructivist positions

For Empiricists, the fundamental presupposition is that the facts justifying changes in scientific ideas are both intellectually prior to the theories that are, in due course, developed to explain them and also capable of being recognized independently and in advance of all theory construction. Given this presupposition, they regard prediction and validation as the crucial and distinctive steps in scientific procedure, arguing that, to establish the validity of any general scientific proposition, it is necessary to show that the theoretical generalization of which the validity is in question entails particular factual statements that are borne out by independent empirical observations. This validation process then involves two essential steps: (1) the formal step of inferring novel predictions from the theory and (2) the empirical step of comparing those predictions with the facts and so confirming the theory or proving it false.

On closer inspection, both steps in the received Empiricist procedure face serious difficulties, and these have lent strength—by reaction—to the alternative, constructivist position. As to step (1), there appears to be no objection to the idea of deducing particular factual predictions directly from theoretical hypotheses, so long as one accepts the Empiricist interpretation of laws of nature as universal empirical assertions on the same logical level as "All polar bears are white." Once that interpretation is questioned, however, it is less clear that direct deductive inferences from theory to fact are always practicable. On the contrary, if theoretical laws and purely empirical reports are, in the nature of the case, framed in terms of distinct and diverse sets of concepts, no general procedure can be available for passing deductively from one to the other. For the theory will then be a reinterpretation of the facts, not a mere generalization from them. Similarly, with step (2), an empirical confrontation of theories and facts gives rise to a more complex range of choices than those implied by the Empiricist account. When faced with discrepancies between prediction and observation, scientists certainly have to modify their theoretical explanations; but this modification can normally be made in any of several alternative ways. For instance, the theoretical relevance of a particular observation may be questioned; or some alternative theoretical interpretation may be put forward; or further refinements may be made within the structure of the theory concerned—and all of this can be done before any question arises of a direct and necessary conflict between the discordant observation and the general theoretical doctrine under investigation.

The rival, constructivist position derives its attractions from such objections as these. This position follows lines of thought already sketched by the French theoretical physicist Pierre Duhem at the turn of the century. On this account, the essential test of a science is that it should provide coherent, consistent, and wide-ranging theoretical organizations. Empirical facts will then be recognized as scientifically relevant only to the extent that they exemplify these interpretations and make them more discriminating. Thus, no single factual observation can ever serve as a logically crucial experiment and confirm or refute any one specific doctrine conclusively, taken apart from a whole complex of theory and interpretation. What is at risk in any experiment or observation, therefore, is the whole body of the theory, together with the current conventions governing its empirical application; and the more comprehensive a theory is, the more are scientists free to vary the details of their specific applications of it, rather than to accept any single counter-example as a challenge to its general validity.

Comple-
mentarity
of the
modes of
justifica-
tion If these two philosophical approaches are reconsidered today against a broader and more historical background, however, they no longer appear to be either as exhaustive or as contradictory as they did in the 1920s and 1930s. By choosing suitable illustrations, of course, one can make each position highly attractive and plausible since, in one situation or another, the rational considerations that carry genuine weight in the actual justification of novel scientific theories include both predictive success and conceptual coherence. But the "Book of Nature," as Galileo called it, is like Holy Scripture: it offers texts to suit all occasions and purposes. And, on second thought, it can be argued that both Empiricist and constructivist philosophers oversimplify the justification process in

science and the criteria by which scientists judge the validity of novel concepts and theories. Far from there being any single or simple test of validity, the question whether predictive success or coherence, simplicity, historical authenticity, or mechanical intelligibility is the key consideration—and in what sense of each ambiguous phrase—must be considered afresh from case to case, with an eye to the specific demands of each new scientific problem situation.

Within the historically developing enterprise of science, intellectual problems arise of many different types, depending both upon the kinds of subject matter under investigation and upon the stage of development of the science concerned. In one science and at one stage, particular weight may attach to a single unexpectedly successful prediction: as when the wave theory of light led to the totally unexpected discovery that a perfectly circular obstacle placed in front of a point source of light produces a circular shadow having a bright spot at its centre. In another science or at another time, however, it may be neither practicable nor relevant to infer such specific predictions, and new theories and concepts may be validated by considerations of quite other kinds. Even within a single science such as physics, indeed, scientists are not faced at every stage by problems and judgments of a single, uniform type. Instead, the historical evolution of physics—down the centuries from Nicole Oresme, Galileo, and Newton to Maxwell, Rutherford, and Heisenberg—has generated an entire genealogy of varied problems; and the considerations bearing on the theoretical difficulties facing physicists at different stages have themselves changed, quite legitimately, along with the substantive concepts and theories of the science. So, within the more complex framework of a developing rational enterprise, the philosopher's task is no longer to impose any single or simple criterion of intellectual choice upon scientific judgments of all kinds. Rather, his task is to recognize how the rational considerations and criteria of validity relevant to particular judgments vary with the theoretical problem situations that provide their historical contexts.

Unification, pluralism, and reductionism. As one notable illustration of the tug-of-war between logical and pragmatic issues in the philosophy of science, the Unity of Science movement may be cited. Under the vigorous leadership of Otto Neurath, a polymath sociologist and philosopher, this movement represented the high point in the ambitions of Viennese Positivism between World Wars I and II; for the general philosophical aims that motivated the search for a unified science are in striking contrast with the specific problem-solving considerations that lead working physicists to unify or integrate their theoretical concepts and explanatory procedures in actual scientific practice. The Unity
of Science
philosophy

Aside from the primary test of predictive success, the Positivists of the Vienna Circle also did allow—on their own terms—for the further theoretical virtues of coherence and comprehensiveness. Their logico-mathematical approach to the propositional structure of scientific theories, however, led them to interpret this demand for coherent and comprehensive theories in a formal sense. On their interpretation, a totally unified body of scientific ideas would be a comprehensive, quasi-Euclidean system of scientific theorems, based on a single set of general axioms, postulates, and primitive propositions and applicable to natural phenomena of all kinds. Given sufficiently all-embracing empirical generalizations as the starting points of such a unified science, it would then be possible, in their view, to deduce particular statements about all the phenomena covered by the varied special sciences unified within its axiomatic scope. Taking the symbolic logic of Russell and Whitehead as their formal core, philosophical advocates of the unity of science then set out to construct, on a single axiomatic pattern, a fully comprehensive account of nature capable of explaining (i.e., entailing) all natural phenomena whatsoever.

At first glance, this ambition seemed laudable and legitimate, but once again the Empiricist program subsequently encountered unforeseen entanglements. The reasons for this situation were not merely the discovery that the theoretical ideas employed within different branches of a science (*e.g.*, of mathematical physics) are more resistent to conceptual integration than had originally been hoped (the task of constructing a self-consistent relativistic theory of quantum electrodynamics, for instance, is one that still defeats the physicists); but, what is worse, it has now become apparent that several well-founded and properly respected branches of scientific theory do not lend themselves to exposition in a formal mathematical manner at all. Any satisfactory theory of organic evolution, for instance, has an irreducibly historical dimension; and there is no possibility of putting historical zoology on the sort of predictive basis that Empiricists have demanded, still less of incorporating it into Neurath's larger unified axiom system. Faced with this particular example, indeed, one distinguished Empiricist philosopher, Carl Hempel, has drawn a somewhat extreme conclusion, viz., that the theory of natural selection is not really an explanation of organic evolution at all—not even a bad one—but is merely an elaborate redescription of the historical episodes concerned. Yet this is simply a roundabout way of conceding that neither the historical problems nor the theoretical ambitions of evolutionary zoologists conform to the quasi-mathematical pattern that the Logical Empiricists have set out to impose on all of the natural sciences alike in the interests of a longer term axiomatic unification.

Unification in scientific praxis: reductionismIf, on the other hand, the demand for integration or unification is considered as a practical problem of methodology, it will then be found that the scientists are facing problems of a different and more pragmatic kind. The science of physiology poses an interesting example because, within this field, the problem of reductionism—*i.e.*, of whether all phenomena whatsoever can be reduced to physico-chemical terms alone—has repeatedly drawn active debate. Since the time of Antoine Lavoisier, who first explained correctly the process of combustion—*i.e.*, since the late 18th century and even before—there has been a methodological division of opinion, involving, on the one hand, those chemists and physiologists who dreamed of equating physiological functions with chemical reactions and planned their program for biochemistry around that ambition and, on the other hand, those clinical scientists and functionally minded physiologists who questioned the legitimacy of this so-called physicalist program and insisted that physiological phenomena displayed certain features or aspects inexplicable in physiochemical terms alone. The scientific issues in debate in this case have never been concerned with formal matters of axiomatization and logical integration alone: once again, they have involved substantive questions of interpretation. Correspondingly, the provisional resolution of this dispute, accomplished by Claude Bernard in the mid-19th century, was not arrived at by constructing a single, unified axiom system of biochemistry-cum-physiology. Rather, Bernard distinguished the proper questions and concerns of the two sciences and demonstrated the substantive character—and limits—of their mutual relevance.

Regarded as specific, localizable processes within the main organs of the body, he argued, all physiological phenomena do, indeed, come within the scope of the same general physico-chemical laws and concepts as govern similar processes in inorganic systems. Within the special micro-environments of the body, however, those same general types of phenomena serve certain unique physiological functions, having no inorganic counterparts; and, to this extent, special problems and questions arise within physiology that cannot be exhaustively translated into the language of inorganic physics and chemistry. Though biochemistry and physiology in no sense conflict, there accordingly remains an essential plurality in the explanatory aims of the two sciences; and this plurality gives rise, in turn, to a corresponding plurality of methods and concepts.

Yet even this example does not yield conclusions from which one can safely generalize. Though in certain respects the explanatory aims of physiology and biochemis-

try will, most probably, always be distinct and separate, in other cases matters have gone the other way. When, in 1873, the Scottish physicist James Clerk Maxwell, for instance, integrated the previously independent sciences of electricity, magnetism, and optics into the unified physics of electromagnetism, there was no comparable division of opinion and no such methodological peace treaty was needed. In this case it remained possible, after Maxwell's work as before, to distinguish between straightforwardly electrical, magnetic, and optical phenomena on the empirical level; but on a more general, theoretical level such distinctions lost their earlier significance, and it ceased to be necessary to keep the problems, methods, and explanatory categories of the three earlier sciences separated.

To sum up: in the methodological drive toward the Limited scope of unification unification of the sciences, as in the earlier phases of discovery and validation, the intellectual temptation to generalize prematurely exposes the philosopher to certain real dangers. In practice, the case for unifying the theories and concepts of two or more sciences has to be considered afresh in every instance, and it can rarely be decided in advance whether or not such a unification will achieve anything useful for the sciences. Instead, one has to analyze the practical demands of the current problems in the different fields and see how far those requirements can be met by developing a unified explanatory treatment for all of the special sciences in question. The integration of theoretical concepts achieved in the process will not consist solely in the formal running together of different propositional systems: more typically, it will require the development of a whole new pattern of theoretical interpretation. And, though it may be possible, in certain cases, to expound the resulting theory in axiomatic form, it must be established, in each case separately, whether or not this can be done. In this sense, conceptual and methodological unification represents a genuine movement in the development of scientific thought; but the logical form of the unified science towards which the philosopher is working is not something that he can lay down definitively before the event.

III. Deeper issues and broader involvements of science

PHILOSOPHICAL STATUS OF SCIENTIFIC THEORY

Status of scientific propositions and concepts or entities. The section of this article entitled *Conceptualization and methodology of science* examined, first, the raw material (or elements) with which scientists have to work in developing their theories about the operations of the natural world and, second, the intellectual steps (or movements) by which they arrive at a scientific understanding of nature. By way of summary, it is appropriate to consider finally the main points of view about the intellectual status of the scientific concepts and doctrines embodying the understanding of nature that have emerged from the philosophical debate about science. Beginning with the epistemic status of theoretical propositions in science, it is well to consider the different claims that are made about the objectivity of their applications or their truth or both. Then, turning to the ontal status of the scientific concepts or entities, it is likewise necessary to consider the claims that are made about the objectivity of their reference or of their meaning or both. In either case, the purpose of a philosophical critique of science is to establish just how far the content and reference of scientific knowledge can be regarded as a true report about the actual structure and operations of nature and just how far they represent, on the contrary, intellectual constructs or artifacts in terms of which men have chanced, chosen, or found it desirable to organize their thoughts about the structure and operations of nature.

Starting with the epistemic status of scientific theories, Epistemic aspects three main views can be distinguished: At one extreme is a strict Realist position, which underscores the factual basis of all scientific knowledge and emphasizes the logical contingency that this basis implies for all substantive propositions in science. In this view, all but the most purely formal statements in science make assertions about how the world of nature is constituted and operates in fact—as contrasted with all of those alternative states of affairs that are clearly intelligible and so possible but which turn out not to be true of the actual world. Seen from this Realist standpoint, every proposition in science, from the most particular observational report to the most general theoretical principle, simply reports a more or less comprehensive empirical set of facts about nature and aspires to be an accurate, objective mirror of the more or less universal facts about which it speaks.

At the opposite extreme, there is a strict conventionalist position, which underscores the constructive role of the scientist's own theory articulation and emphasizes the logical necessity that is thereby built into the resulting conceptual structure. In this view, all but the most purely observational statements in science reflect the patterns by which the scientist shapes his conceptual picture of the world of nature—the patterns in terms of which all states of affairs clearly conceivable on the basis of current ideas have necessarily to be formulated. Seen from this conventionalist standpoint, theoretical thermodynamics, say, determines the character of all possible worlds consistent with the principles of energy conservation and entropy (or randomness) increase: a world to which thermodynamics is not applicable will then be not so much factually false as inconceivable in present terms.

Finally, a wide range of intermediate views seeks to evade the central opposition between Realists and conventionalists. One representative view of this kind, first made popular by Mach toward the end of the 19th century, invoked Kant's attack on things-in-themselves, viewing the attack as providing grounds for dismissing all debates about reality and objectivity as inescapably barren and empty. In its most developed form, this so-called operationalist position encourages the philosopher to regard theoretical propositions in science as meaningful only insofar as scientific practice includes specific operations—either manual measuring operations, or computational pencil-and-paper operations—in terms of which those propositions are given operational meaning. Nothing is then to be read into scientific knowledge beyond its operational meaning; in particular, scientists are not to be understood as claiming or disclaiming anything about the reality or conventionality of the states of affairs that they report. The idea of nature as a thing-in-itself is thus eliminated, as being an intellectual superstition and an obstacle to better scientific understanding, which survives from an earlier metaphysical era.

Ontal
aspects The primary discussions of the ontological implications of scientific theory are in the articles METAPHYSICS and NATURE, PHILOSOPHY OF. It is, nonetheless, appropriate here to distinguish the three main views. The central question is, now, whether the nouns and noun phrases used as technical terms in the theoretical propositions of science rely for meaning on any claim that they refer to objective, external entities; and current approaches to this question parallel existing views about the epistemological issues, viz., whether the propositions themselves rely for their truth on a claim to be mirroring or reporting objective, external facts. Here, too, the Realist interprets all of the chief technical terms of scientific theory as the names of objective entities existing in nature independently of all human theories and interpretations. In this view, entropy, say—a measure of the increase in randomness that every total system undergoes—is a genuine, objective magnitude that has, at all times, played a crucial part in the operations of nature even though physicists have only recently had the wit to discover it; and it just happens, correspondingly, to be the case—in those parts of the cosmos that can be observed—that the total entropy of an isolated system nowhere decreases.

The instrumentalist, for his part, regards all theoretical notions such as entropy as intellectual fictions or artifacts created by the scientist's own theory construction and quite distinct from the natural world of objects, systems, and phenomena that scientific theories have to explain. No doubt, scientific theory and the external reality of nature do come into contact on the everyday or empirical level of tables and chairs, rocks and flowers. Given the

intellectual tasks of scientific theorizing, however, the resulting concepts are essentially abstract; and any grasping after real entities, as the objective external reference of the theoretical terms, reflects a plain misunderstanding of this theoretical enterprise.

Meanwhile, the phenomenalist repeats, in the case of the technical terms of science, the same agnostic criticism as that offered by the operationalist in the case of its theoretical propositions. In this view, it is simply a meaningless waste of time for scientists to debate the existence of enduring theoretical entities, regarded as external, objective things-in-themselves; just as it is similarly wasteful for them to interpret scientific theories as making, or denying, similar claims about the existence of objective, external states of affairs. Instead, the terms and concepts of science are all to be understood as the product of so many logical, or semantic, operations or constructions, and questions about their real existence are to be swept aside as damaging metaphysical superstitions.

Philosophical analysis and scientific practice. The arguments about these rival ontological and epistemological views cannot be safely left or judged without first looking more closely at the complex relationship between the general analytical interests of philosophers and the more specific intellectual concerns of working scientists themselves. For the degree to which each view about the reality of scientific entities and facts can carry conviction depends substantially on what branches of science are at issue. As the focus of philosophical attention has shifted historically from one scientific terrain to another, so, too, have the relative degrees of plausibility of these rival positions varied.

Since the 1920s, for instance, there has been a marked revival of philosophical discussion among scientists working in several specialized fields—particularly, among physicists concerned with the structure and development of quantum mechanics. In epistemic terms, the statistical character of quantum-mechanical explanations has prompted some fundamental questions about the status and limitations of human knowledge. Clearly, the extent and accuracy of human knowledge about nature are limited by the modes of operation of scientific instruments. Is it not also possible, however, that the significance of this statistical character lies at a deeper level? Perhaps the relevant objective relationships and states of affairs in nature itself are governed intrinsically by a merely probabilistic causality and so are essentially indeterminate. Or is there a point to be reached on the microphysical level at which any such distinction between subjective human knowledge and the objective state of affairs has finally broken down? The ontal implications of quantum mechanics have been as puzzling as the epistemic. Is an electron, say, a discrete particle that just happens to elude man's exact observation; is it an essentially blurred wave bundle having no precise dynamical characteristics; is it a concentration of probability, a mere theoretical symbol, or what? Or must one set all these ontological questions aside as lacking any significance for physics and as standing in the way of the physicist's proper task, that of extending the direct explanatory power of quantum-mechanical explanation itself? (See NATURE, PHILOSOPHY OF. Also because these questions have played a significant part not merely in the philosophy of science but also in theoretical physics itself, they are discussed from the scientific standpoint in such articles as MECHANICS, QUANTUM; ELECTRON; CONSERVATION LAWS AND SYMMETRY; and RELATIVITY.)

Elsewhere, the philosophical debate about science has taken on other specific forms. Just as in Aristotle's natural philosophy the metaphysical controversy about Ideas and essences was reflected in Aristotle's own methodological approach to biology and to the study of the natural relations and classification of organisms, so once again 20th-century reappraisals of traditional taxonomy —in the light of evolution theory, genetics, and population dynamics—have been an occasion for renewed philosophical debate. As a result, earlier disagreements about natural and artificial classifications have been reformulated and have generated a new dispute, about the possibility

Quantum
mechanics;
taxonomy;
perception

of basing taxonomy on a mathematical science of phenetics—in which the defining properties of different species, genera, etc. are all given quantitative numbers or measures—and so harnessing the technical resources of modern computers to its purposes.

Similarly, in the psychology of perception and related fields, the extension of understanding in recent years at last has permitted the framing of authentically empirical questions about perception and cognition, which lend themselves to direct investigation instead of being restricted to general a priori speculations. The result has been a theoretical debate, the final outcome of which will have profound effects on both philosophical epistemology and natural science. In areas of this debate where even Mach was content to pose entirely general questions, in the philosophical tradition of David Hume, about the role of sense impressions as the raw material of all cognition and perception whatsoever, it is now clear that many preliminary differences and complexities must be unravelled before one can hope to recognize the truly operative questions in this field. Far from all modes of knowledge and perception conforming to a single common pattern, man's sensory and practical dealings with the world call into play a variety of perceptual systems of which the operations justify no simple epistemological formula about impressions and ideas, sense-data and logical constructions, or intuitions and schemata. Thus, at the present time, the investigations of some physiologists, psychologists, and cyberneticists are bringing man's sensory and cognitive activities within the scope of natural science while at the same time preserving a feeling for the more general philosophical problems and insights of such philosophers as Locke and Leibniz, Hume and Kant, Helmholtz and Mach.

Pluralism and complementarity

At this point, the alliance between science and philosophy is simply carrying over into fields of science that are areas of methodological perplexity today the same interactions that were fruitful in earlier centuries within sciences having methods by now well understood. These interactions are unlikely to vindicate finally any one of the rival positions in the philosophy of science, whether ontological (Realist, instrumentalist, or phenomenalist) or epistemological (Realist, conventionalist, or operationalist). Probably such a vindication was, in any event, too much to expect. For in all the different special sciences—both natural and social—historical development eventually brings the investigator to a point at which he is ready to operate with a variety of technical terms or entities having very different logical characters and functions and at which his most general theoretical propositions or principles display corresponding differences in their logical status and implications.

So long as philosophical discussion is confined within the limits of an artificial, ideal language or propositional system, it is possible, perhaps, to continue posing purely abstract, general dilemmas about, say, theoretical entities or confirmation theory. But the bearing of such formal dilemmas on the actual content of contemporary scientific thought is becoming increasingly unclear. In debating the ontal status of theoretical entities, for instance, the question must at some stage be faced whether that phrase is intended to cover such notions as gene or pi-meson, species or cold front, momentum or superego, social class or economic market. (Certainly, not all of these terms have identical characters and functions.) In debating the epistemic status of scientific theories, likewise, it must be made clear whether one has in mind, say, the mathematical schema of quantum-mechanical field theory, the populational analysis of natural selection, the microstructures and mechanisms of molecular biology, the developmental sequences of cognitive psychology, the labour theory of economic value, the general regularities of terrestrial meteorology, or what. (Once again, not all of these theories have identical kinds of status or implications.)

Philosophical doctrines and approaches that carry great conviction when applied to the theories and ideas of one science may—not surprisingly—lose all of their plausibility when extended to other fields. Thus, an Empiricist analysis may apply quite straightforwardly to meteorology, yet entirely misrepresent the structure and implications of electromagnetic theory; while, in return, a Neo-Kantian account of theoretical physics may lack any direct relevance, say, to ideas about animal behaviour. Today as in classical Athens, analytical clarification in the philosophy of science goes, in this respect, hand in hand with methodological refinements in the sciences themselves. In retrospect, the methodological insights of Aristotle the marine biologist and of Plato the theoretical astrophysicist can be seen to have been complementary, rather than incompatible. Similarly, today, the philosopher must look at rival positions in the philosophy of science not merely as contradictory answers to technical questions within philosophy itself but equally as complementary contributions to the methodological improvement of theoretical understanding over the whole varied range of different scientific fields.

INTERRELATIONSHIPS OF SCIENCE AND CULTURE

Turn to broader human concerns

This survey has been concerned, almost exclusively, with philosophical problems and arguments about the sciences regarded as sources of theoretical knowledge. In pitting Realism against instrumentalism, mechanistic ideas against organicist ones, divine knowledge against human fallibility, or Platonic Ideas against Aristotelian essences, the philosopher is in each case concerned with the intellectual status, implications, and validity of certain general scientific concepts, methods, or entities. To confine oneself entirely to these intellectual aspects, however, would mean accepting a total abstraction of theory from practice and of scientific ideas from their behavioral expression. Thus, along with the present-day shift of emphasis from the physical to the human and social sciences, one finds that all such abstract approaches are coming once again under criticism, as over-intellectualizing the nature and implications of science.

Some of these attacks come from the neo-Marxist direction and reflect a traditional Marxian insistence on the unity of theory and action. (It was not for nothing that Lenin picked on Ernst Mach as a special target for scorn.) Analogous criticisms, however, are also coming from men with very different intellectual loyalties—*e.g.*, from the urban sociologist Lewis Mumford and from many contemporary Existentialists. In conclusion, therefore, a concise discussion is here given of some of the views about the relations between science and the rest of culture; *i.e.*, about the relevance of scientific knowledge to other spheres of experience and concern and, conversely, about the significance of broader, practical considerations for man's understanding of scientific theory itself.

The variety of these views has always been very great. Their exponents have ranged all the way from those who, like the energeticist Wilhelm Ostwald and the evolutionist Julian Huxley—both of whom rooted ethics in nature—present scientific ideas and procedures as rational panaceas for intellectual and practical problems of all kinds to those who, like Pierre Duhem and Carl von Weizsäcker, physicist and philosopher of nature, both of whom are theists, deliberately limit the claims of science so as to preserve a freedom of manoeuvre for ethics, for example, or theology. At each stage, most advocates of extreme claims for science have been ontological Realists; and, in strengthening their ontal and epistemic claims, they have also staked a claim to overriding intellectual priority on behalf of scientific knowledge, in contrast to other forms of experience. Similarly, those who would restrict the broader cultural claims of science have tended to be phenomenalists; and, in weakening their philosophical claims, they have also attempted to limit the authority of science to its own intellectual concerns as narrowly defined.

Science, technology, and ethical values

Whatever one's general philosophical position with respect to the reality of scientific knowledge and entities may be, however, there are other more practical questions to be faced, questions about the specific implications of different scientific ideas and beliefs for parallel fields of human action and experience. On this point, one particular theme unites a wide range of radical critics of science, including both Lewis Mumford, U.S. social critic, and the Existentialists. Just as the Christian Dane Søren Kierkegaard, an early and seminal figure of Existentialism, condemned Kant's universalized system of ethics for ignoring the individuality of actual ethical problems and decisions, so today there is a widespread reaction against any tendency to treat social or practical decisions as technical matters, which can be left to the judgment of scientific or technological experts. The general methods of technology may, indeed, represent practical applications of the theoretical understanding arrived at by science; but all individual decisions about putting those general techniques to use—*e.g.*, in constructing an airport or power station—must be made not by appealing to any general formula or rule of thumb but by balancing a whole range of diverse considerations—economic and aesthetic, environmental and human, as well as merely technical.

According to another contemporary critique, the theoretical points of view adopted in natural science are general and abstract, but the practical demands of sociopolitical action and, *a fortiori*, of individual action, are concrete and particular; and, by itself, this contrast places an immediate restriction on the existential relevance of scientific ideas and engineering techniques. Such scholars as Thomas Huxley, a versatile scientist and defender of evolution, or Wilhelm Ostwald, a pioneer in electrochemistry, who viewed reality as essentially energy, might argue in general, abstract terms for interpreting ethical principles in evolutionary or thermodynamical terms if they pleased (so the critics continue); but such abstract speculative arguments have no bearing on the actual tasks of ethical decision and action. Here again, every ethical choice involves a unique constellation of considerations and demands; and this problem cannot be dealt with by appealing to any universal rule but must be appraised on an individual basis, as and when it arises.

Others take a more positive approach toward the contribution of science to an understanding of human values. Without necessarily claiming to transform ethics itself into a "science," they at any rate argue that the personal attitudes needed for effective work in science—adventurous skepticism and critical open-mindedness—have a wider relevance also to human conduct and social affairs. Supposing only that social and political discussion were conducted in this same tentative and critical spirit (they claim), its typical and deplorable passion and confusion could be replaced by the more rational consideration of the means required in order to achieve explicitly stated ends. While specific scientific ideas and doctrines may not be enough to direct social and political action by themselves, the scientific attitude may, nonetheless, have a profound significance for social policy and individual ethics alike.

Social signifi-cance of science

This contrast, between existentially minded critics of the claim that science is all-embracing and socially minded believers in the scientific attitude, may be epitomized by referring to contemporary discussions about the social significance of science itself. On the one hand, there has recently been a revival of explicitly anti-scientific views, which had been more or less dormant since the time of Blake, Johann Wolfgang von Goethe, and their successors in the Romantic movement. Supporters of this anti-science position point to the central role of military technology in the financial support of 20th-century scientific research and dismiss the average scientist's plea that he is not responsible for the uses to which his ethically neutral discoveries are put, as pallid and insincere. On the contrary (they argue), there is a long-standing and unholy alliance linking the collective institutions of the scientific and technological professions to the economic, industrial, and political powers that be. Faced with the fruits of this historical union (they conclude), it is time that scientists acknowledged their social responsibilities; and, failing better institutional controls, the outcome of this moral self-scrutiny may well prove to be a moratorium on further scientific research. Perhaps man already knows too much for his own good and needs to digest the significance of his existing stock of knowledge much further before adding to it and so widening yet again the gulf between theoretical knowledge and practical wisdom.

On the other hand, there are those who recognize science as playing a crucial role in modern society, but who go on to draw the opposite conclusion. Rather than putting a stop to science (these men would argue), its scope should be broadened; that is, scholars should be studying and understanding better the manner in which science serves as an element in the larger social order—perhaps by developing more adequate analyses of the social structure or perhaps by a large-scale extension of the methods of operations research. Aside from anything else (they point out), a moratorium on science is as impracticable as a moratorium on sin. It could be enforced only if political unanimity prevailed to an unimaginable degree among scientists. In the absence of such enforcement, liberal-minded countries will merely put themselves at a needless disadvantage—both economic and military—as compared with totalitarian states. Instead of pursuing this will-o'-the-wisp, scholars should put more effort into the task of understanding both the social preconditions of effective scientific development and the economic and political priorities involved in the practical application of scientific research.

Science and religion

As compared with the controversies of earlier centuries, the debate between science and religion is curiously muted today. There seems little room nowadays for the theological passions that engulfed the discussion of Copernicus' new planetary theory, James Hutton's history of the Earth, or Darwin's theory of natural selection; and one would hesitate to speak any longer, as so many of our forefathers did, of warfare between science and religion as unavoidable. It is true that a few partisan writers can still find it a perplexing problem to decide such issues as whether the existence of life on other worlds would require a re-enactment there of the Christian fall and redemption or can insist—conversely—that the results of astronautical exploration refute any religious belief that God is an Old Man up in the sky. For most people, however, such questions have so far lost their earlier bite that they appear, by now, quite naïve.

What is the reason for this change? In earlier times, the term cosmology embraced not only the structure of the astronomical cosmos and the origins of the human species but also the religious significance of man's place in nature. Contemporary theologians, by contrast, see physics and biology as having much less bearing on man's religious attitudes and preoccupations than their predecessors had supposed that they had. As a result, men's earlier ambition to construct a single, comprehensive world view, embracing the essential truths of both science and religion, no longer plays the active part in intellectual life that it formerly did. The only branches of science still capable of provoking vigorous theological debate, even now, are the human, rather than the natural sciences. The implications of Freudian psychology for the doctrine of grace and the use of psychedelic drugs for inducing quasi-mystical experiences are topics for live discussion today, in a way that evolution, astrophysics, and historical geology no longer are.

Limita-tions of science

This change of focus has been accompanied by a change in ideas about the intrinsic limits of science. It was formerly assumed that the boundaries between science and other aspects of human experience could be defined by marking off certain types of subject matter as essentially closed to scientific investigation. To one generation, the heart of this forbidden territory was the mind; to another, it was life; to a third, the creation. In this view, something in the essential nature of mental or vital activities, or in the origins of the present order of nature, made it impossible to treat these as phenomena open to study and explanation by the rational methods and intellectual procedures available to science. In fact, this view always had defects, from both the scientific and the theological points of view. To scientists, it seemed to impose an arbitrary restriction on their sphere of operations and so acted as a standing challenge and irritation. For theologians, it had the disadvantage of placing the essential claims of religion, so to speak, on a sandbank, where they risked being submerged in time by the rising tide of scientific knowledge. So, by tacit consent, the essential limits of science are now defined in quite different terms. These limits are now identified by recognizing that the character of scientific procedures themselves places restrictions on the relevance of their results. A scholar may choose to study whatever objects, systems, or processes he may please, but only certain of the questions that he asks about them will be answerable in the general, theoretical terms characteristic of science.

This change of approach may not have made the substantive problem—that of delimiting the frontiers of science exactly at all points—very much easier to deal with than it was before, but it has one genuine merit: it respects the crucial fact, to which attention has been drawn at several points in this present survey, that the distinctive features of science lie not in the types of object and event to which the scientist has access but in the intellectual procedures that his investigations employ and so in the kinds of problem that lend themselves to a scientific solution.

BIBLIOGRAPHY. ERNEST NAGEL, *The Structure of Science* (1961); and M.W. WARTOFSKY, *Conceptual Foundations of Scientific Thought* (1968), together cover the main approaches to the philosophy of science as a general field of study; whereas ARTHUR DANTO and SIDNEY MORGENBESSER (eds.), *Philosophy of Science* (1962), provides a useful anthology of classic papers on the subject; and SAMUEL B. RAPPORT and HELEN WRIGHT (eds.), *Science: Method and Meaning* (1964), is a stimulating anthology of nontechnical papers. The origins and development of natural science and the attitudes of philosophers toward scientific explanation in antiquity and the Middle Ages are well treated in SAMUEL SAMBURSKY, *The Physical World of the Greeks*, 2nd ed. (1962; orig. pub. in Hebrew, 1954); and *The Physical World of Late Antiquity* (1962); JOHN H. RANDALL, JR., *Aristotle* (1960); and in ALISTAIR C. CROMBIE, *Medieval and Early Modern Science*, 2nd ed., 2 vol. (1963). For the 17th and 18th centuries, see EDWIN A. BURTT, *The Metaphysical Foundations of Modern Physical Science*, 2nd ed. (1932); ALEXANDRE KOYRE, *Newtonian Studies* (1965); HERBERT BUTTERFIELD, *The Origins of Modern Science: 1300–1800*, rev. ed. (1965); I. BERNARD COHEN, *Franklin and Newton* (1956); and GOTTFRIED MARTIN, *Immanuel Kant: Ontologie und Wissenschaftstheorie* (1951; Eng. trans., *Kant's Metaphysics and Theory of Science*, 1955). For the 19th century, the most significant contributions have come from scientists writing as philosophers: CLAUDE BERNARD, *Introduction à l'étude de la médecine expérimentale* (1865; Eng. trans., *An Introduction to the Study of Experimental Medicine*, 1927, reprinted 1961); HERMANN VON HELMHOLTZ, *Popular Scientific Lectures* (1962; reprint of a selection of lectures from *Popular Lectures on Scientific Subjects*, 1st and 2nd series, 1881); T.H. HUXLEY, *Science and Culture, and Other Essays* (1882); and WILLIAM WHEWELL, *The Philosophy of the Inductive Sciences, Founded upon Their History*, 2nd ed. (1847, reprinted 1966). The background to the 20th-century debate in the philosophy of science, as it developed between 1890 and 1920, can be reconstructed from ERNST MACH, *Die Mechanik in ihrer Entwicklung historisch-kritisch Dargestellt*, 9th ed. (1933; Eng. trans., *The Science of Mechanics*, 1960); and *Die Analyse der Empfindungen und das Verhältnis des Physischen zum Psychischen*, 5th ed. (1906; Eng. trans., *The Analysis of Sensations and the Relation of the Physical to the Psychical*, 1959); KARL PEARSON, *The Grammar of Science*, 3rd ed. (1960); PIERRE DUHEM, *La Théorie physique: son objet et sa structure* (1906; Eng. trans., *The Aim and Structure of Physical Theory*, 1954); HENRI POINCARE, *La Science et l'hypothèse* (1903; Eng. trans., *Science and Hypothesis*, 1905); and HEINRICH HERTZ, *Die Prinzipien der Mechanik* (1895; Eng. trans., *The Principles of Mechanics*, 1889, reprinted 1956), especially the Introduction. The subsequent course of the debate, between 1920 and 1960, is illustrated in CARL G. HEMPEL, *Aspects of Scientific Explanation, and Other Essays in the Philosophy of Science* (1965); RUDOLF CARNAP, *Logical Foundations of Probability*, 2nd ed. (1962); KARL R. POPPER, *Logik der Forschung* (1935; 2nd ed., 1966; Eng. trans., *The Logic of Scientific Discovery*, 1959); ROBIN G. COLLINGWOOD, *An Essay on Metaphysics* (1940); NORMAN R. CAMPBELL, *What Is Science?* (1921); and WILLIAM H. WATSON, *On Understanding Physics* (1959). Two significant side-views of the debate from very different formal standpoints may be found in WILLIAM V.

QUINE, *From a Logical Point of View*, 2nd ed. rev. (1961); and RONALD A. FISHER, *Statistical Methods for Research Workers*, 14th ed. (1970). PETER ACHINSTEIN and STEPHEN F. BARKER (eds.), *The Legacy of Logical Positivism* (1969), is a first attempt at an historical appraisal of the period. The current debates about conceptual change and the rationale of discovery in science are central topics in KARL R. POPPER, *Conjectures and Refutations*, 2nd rev. ed. (1965); NORWOOD R. HANSON, *Patterns of Discovery* (1958); STEPHEN TOULMIN, *Human Understanding*, vol. 1 (1972); THOMAS S. KUHN, *The Structure of Scientific Revolutions*, 2nd ed. rev. (1970); IMRE LAKATOS and ALAN MUSGRAVE, *Criticism and the Growth of Knowledge* (1970); and MICHAEL POLANYI, *Personal Knowledge* (1958). For broader cultural aspects of the contemporary debate about science, see C.H. WADDINGTON, *The Scientific Attitude*, new ed. (1968); JACOB BRONOWSKI, *Science and Human Values*, rev. ed. (1965); THEODORE ROSZAK, *The Making of a Counter Culture* (1969); and LEWIS MUMFORD, *The Myth of the Machine* (1967).

(S.E.T.)

Scipio Aemilianus

Publius Cornelius Scipio Aemilianus—surnamed Africanus (the Younger) and Numantinus, by adoption the grandson of Scipio Africanus (*q.v.*) who ended the Second Punic War by his defeat of Hannibal—was famed for ending the Third Punic War (149–146 BC) by his destruction of Carthage and for his interest in the cultural developments of his day.

Background and early life. Scipio was born in 185 or 184 BC, the second son of Lucius Aemilius Paullus, son of the consul who fell at the Battle of Cannae in 216. Paullus himself was an outstanding Roman leader who combined traditional Roman virtues with a keen interest in Greek culture. Paullus was twice consul (182 and 168) and was censor in 164; he brought the Third Macedonian War to a conclusion by his victory at Pydna (168). Soon after Scipio's birth, Paullus divorced his wife Papiria and remarried (the name of the new wife is not known); he had two sons by the later marriage, but both these half brothers of Scipio died in 167. It was probably after the father's remarriage that Scipio and his elder brother, Quintus Fabius Maximus Aemilianus, were adopted into other families. While the elder brother was adopted by a grandson, or possibly a son, of Quintus Fabius Maximus Cunctator, the famous general of the Second Punic War, Scipio himself was adopted by Publius Scipio, the son of the elder Scipio Africanus, whose ill health prevented him from following a public career. Thus Scipio succeeded to the family tradition of two of Rome's greatest generals—the conqueror of Hannibal and the conqueror of Perseus of Macedonia.

The ramifications of Scipio's family are somewhat complicated (see illustration) but important, since family ties were very strong in Roman society, while links with other families, by either marriage or adoption, provided a Roman noble with extended political influence. Scipio's adoptive father was, in fact, also his cousin by blood. This came about because Africanus' wife Aemilia was a sister of Aemilius Paullus' father; she was thus Scipio's aunt by blood (as well as being his grandmother by adoption). Africanus had two daughters (as well as his son Publius Scipio), who were also Scipio's blood cousins and adopted aunts; the elder of these Corneliae married Publius Cornelius Scipio Nasica Corculum (consul in 162 and 155); the younger married Tiberius Sempronius Gracchus (consul 177 and 163) and became the mother of the two Gracchi, Tiberius and Gaius (tribunes in 133 and 123, respectively), and of a Sempronia. This tightly knit group was linked still closer when Scipio himself married Sempronia. One final connection must be mentioned: Aemilius Paullus, Scipio's natural father, also had two daughters, one of whom married Cato the Censor's son, Marcus Porcius Cato; the other married Quintus Aelius Tubero. Thus Scipio's contacts were extremely wide.

Scipio's upbringing is described in a passage of Plutarch's biography of his father Aemilius Paullus, who

brought up his sons in accordance with the traditional native type of education, as he himself had been brought up, but also, and more keenly, on the Greek pattern. For

Family connection (margin note)

The Family of Scipio Aemilianus

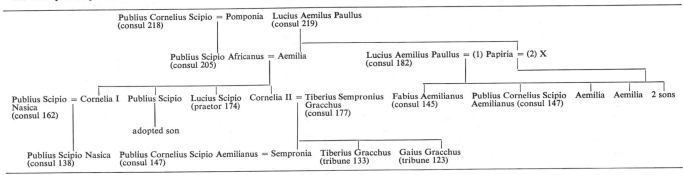

the young men were surrounded not only by Greek teachers, scholars, and rhetoricians, but also by Greek sculptors, painters, overseers of horses and hounds, and instructors in hunting.

This education, based on a combination of Greek and Roman culture, set the direction of Scipio's further interests. He was introduced to military life in 168, when he and his brother served under their father Paullus in the Third Macedonian War. At the decisive Battle of Pydna he followed up the routed enemy with such dash that he was reported missing and was feared killed. After the battle, his father put him in charge of the Macedonian royal game preserves in order to develop his strength and courage. Scipio thus acquired a permanent taste for hunting, and after his return to Rome he spent much time in that pursuit when other young nobles were devoting themselves to legal and social business. Another legacy from Macedonia was the permission he received from his father to take what books he liked from the Macedonian royal library. He also went with his father on a tour of Greece and, on his return to Rome, took part in his father's triumph (November 167), a period that was overshadowed for Paullus by the death of his two younger sons.

Friendship with Polybius

The most significant influence on Scipio's development occurred when he became friendly with the Greek historian Polybius, one of the thousand Achaean leaders who had been deported and detained without trial in Italy. Polybius records that their acquaintance originated "in the loan of some books and conversation about them." Friendship quickly followed, and Scipio and his brother persuaded the authorities to allow Polybius to remain in Rome, where he became a close friend and mentor of the two young men. Polybius tells how one day Scipio asked him why he seemed to neglect him and to speak to his elder brother: was it because Polybius shared the common opinion of Scipio as "quiet and lazy, far removed from the character and ways of a Roman, because he did not care for pleading cases in the law-courts?" Polybius promptly reassured the young man and promised to help him "speak and act in a manner worthy of his ancestors." From that moment a relationship like that of a father and son developed, and Scipio found a counsellor to help him overcome his innate diffidence. No doubt he was oppressed by the thought of the responsibility that he would have on becoming the head of the great house of the Scipios (it is uncertain when his adoptive father Publius Scipio died) as well as in representing the Aemilii. He was now determined to prove a worthy representative and to pursue the normal aims of a Roman noble: honour, glory, and military success. The ambition of a naturally quiet man was now kindled.

Polybius emphasized two aspects of Scipio's character, his personal morality and his generosity. Of the former, he tells how Scipio sought to excel all his contemporaries in his reputation for temperance at a time when morals were generally declining and young men were becoming increasingly corrupt, partly because they had "caught the dissoluteness of Greek customs" and partly because of the great influx of public and private wealth as a result of the Macedonian War; "in about five years Scipio secured a general recognition of his character for goodness and purity." Of Scipio's generosity Polybius cites several examples: he gave great wealth from the estate of Africanus to his divorced mother Papiria and to his sisters, the Aemiliae; to the two Corneliae, daughters of Africanus; and over 45 talents in all to his own brother Fabius. Polybius' comment is illuminating:

this would be thought honourable anywhere, but at Rome it was quite astonishing; for there no one ever thinks of giving any of his private property to any one if he can help it.

Polybius, however, does not draw attention to an element of cruelty in Scipio's character that is noticeable in several episodes of his life; it may generally have had a deterrent purpose and not been an unusual trait in the Roman character, but not every Roman general celebrated a victory by throwing deserters to the wild beasts.

Military and political achievements.   Scipio's early political apathy was soon cast aside; by 152 he had probably been elected quaestor, the first rung of an official career, and had entered the Senate. But at the same time he was pursuing his cultural interests: he was among the young nobles who were attracted by the lectures of three visiting Athenian philosophers whose views on political morality shocked more old-fashioned Romans, such as Cato. Scipio achieved public acclaim in 151. A series of disasters to Roman armies in Spain resulted in such reluctance to undertake military service in the peninsula that, in a dispute over the levy, the consuls who were responsible for it were even temporarily imprisoned by the tribunes who opposed the levy. In the crisis, Scipio, who had been assigned to Macedonia, inspired confidence by volunteering to serve in Spain instead: his example was at once followed by other officers and men. Serving as military tribune to Lucius Lucullus, Scipio displayed great personal courage in the Spanish campaigns; in 151 he killed a Spanish chieftain who had challenged him to single combat, and at Intercatia he won the mural crown (*corona muralis*), which was awarded to the first man to mount the walls of an enemy town. In 150 he was sent by Lucullus to Africa to obtain some elephants from the Numidian king Masinissa, the friend of his grandfather Africanus. While there he witnessed a great but indecisive battle between Masinissa and the Carthaginians: the latter then asked him to arrange a settlement, but in the event negotiations broke down. Scipio then left Africa, but he was soon to return not as a peacemaker but as a conqueror. When back in Rome, at Polybius' request, he managed to gain the somewhat grudging support of old Cato (whose son had married Scipio's sister Aemilia) for a proposal to release the 300 Achaean internees who still survived without trial. Thus a great blot on Rome's good name was at length partially removed.

Expedition to Spain

In 150, war with Carthage was in the air: it was passionately advocated by Cato and opposed by Scipio Nasica. With both these men Scipio had family links: his own attitude is unknown, but his policy is likely to have approximated closer to Cato's than to Nasica's, though, in fact, he was probably too young to have taken any effective part in the senatorial debates. At any rate, when war came in the following year, he returned to Africa with the Roman army, serving again as military tribune, and his service was very effective. The two consuls besieged Carthage by land and sea, but later in the year, after one had returned to Rome, the Carthaginians launched a night attack upon the camp of the isolated Manilius, a situation that was retrieved only by the skill of Scipio. During the winter Scipio again displayed conspicuous ability when Manilius led two unsuccessful expeditions against the Carthaginian forces in the interior. Again he came into the limelight when the aged Masinissa, on the point of death, asked that the grandson of his friend Africanus should arrange the future of his kingdom. Scipio decided to divide Numidia between the King's three sons and thereby avoided any danger that a united Numidia might have presented. As the war against Carthage dragged on without decisive result, Scipio resolved to return to Rome in 148 to stand for the curule aedileship, but such was his military record and the general disappointment with the conduct of the war that the Roman people wanted to see him in command. Since he was at least five years under the legal minimum age for the consulship and had not been praetor, his election as consul for 147 was remarkable. When a tribune, voicing the popular enthusiasm, threatened to veto the consular elections unless Scipio was accepted as a candidate, the Senate gave way and allowed the tribunes to introduce a bill to exempt Scipio from the legal restrictions: he was thus elected consul and given the African command. Once back in Africa, he determined to starve out Carthage with a blockade by land and sea: gradually the cordon was drawn tighter around the beleaguered city, and in the spring of 146 it

Destruction of Carthage fell to his final assault: after six days of street fighting the citadel was captured and Carthage was destroyed. As Scipio surveyed the burning city and meditated on the fall of great nations, he wept and, grasping the hand of Polybius (the historian himself records the incident), said: "it is glorious, but I have a dread foreboding that some time the same doom will be pronounced upon my own country." After arranging for the organization of Carthaginian territory as the new Roman province of Africa, Scipio returned to Rome for a triumph and to be hailed as the second Africanus.

Thus before the age of 40, Scipio had gained Rome's final victory over Carthage and had become a popular hero, but he still had many opponents in the Senate. He soon reached the crown of a noble's career by his election to the censorship of 142, though the other censor Lucius Mummius, who had brought peace to Greece by his sack of Corinth, was not a welcome colleague. Scipio carried out his censorial duties with sternness, in the spirit of the censorship of Cato, who had lived just long enough to express approval of Scipio's African command. In general he aimed at a return to the *mos majorum,* the traditional habits of Roman life, in face of declining moral standards. In 140 he headed a tour of inspection to Egypt and the East, taking as a companion the philosopher Panaetius. During this period many of his political opponents (*inimici*) reached high office. In 137 he gained popularity, though not in the Senate, when he supported a measure to establish the secret ballot in most trials before the people (two years earlier the secret ballot had been introduced for elections).

The background of the next phase of Scipio's life was again Spain, where for years Rome had been engaged in war with the Celtiberians and had suffered a series of defeats and humiliating setbacks. One such scandal concerned the Senate's repudiation of a truce arranged by the commander Gaius Hostilius Mancinus and his young quaestor Tiberius Gracchus, which had saved a Roman army from destruction. The story cannot be repeated here, but, while Mancinus was shamefully condemned for his conduct, Gracchus was spared, thanks to his popularity at Rome for having rescued a trapped army. Scipio helped in Gracchus' escape, possibly because of their family relationship: Gracchus was his cousin and also his brother-in-law, though in fact Scipio's marriage to Sempronia had been a private failure. Scipio also urged the adoption of a more effective policy in Spain. This led to his own election to a second consulship for 134 and the command of the Celtiberian war; special legislation was

needed, because a second consulship was unconstitutional. Scipio took with him to Spain a number of volunteers and a corps of 500 friends and dependents as a kind of bodyguard (an embryonic praetorian cohort): these were perhaps all the more necessary because his first task was to rediscipline the Roman troops in Spain, who were in a shocking state. His main objective was to reduce the Celtiberian capital, the hill town of Numantia, which could not be stormed but had to be blockaded and starved out. Around the town he built seven camps, linked by a strong wall (traces of these works still survive), and, with overwhelming forces after an eight month siege, he finally forced the 4,000 besieged to capitulate (133). The town was burned. Thus Rome's dominion in Spain was established beyond question, and Scipio returned to Rome for a second triumph in 132.

Political crisis In the meanwhile, Rome had been shaken by a constitutional crisis. The tribune Tiberius Gracchus introduced a bill for the distribution of public lands among the poor of the city. His disregard of constitutional procedure and custom in forcing his bill through had provoked the Senate to use force to crush him and his supporters and thus initiated a period of increasing political upheaval and revolution (133). Absent in Spain during the crisis, Scipio was spared the necessity for actively taking sides. In view of his friend Laelius' earlier attempted land law, it may be conjectured that he would not have opposed the bill as such. But surely he did not approve of Tiberius' methods; when forced to give a public opinion he quoted Homer's line, "So perish all who do the like again," and he admitted that Tiberius "had been killed justly." By his anti-Gracchan attitude Scipio lost much popularity, the more so when he helped to defeat a bill to legalize re-election to the tribunate. He then took up the cause of the Italian allies of Rome, who were discontented with the effects of Gracchus' land bill; he took some action to modify its working, at least as far as it concerned the allies. Then suddenly one morning, when he was due to make a speech on the Italian question, he was found dead in his bedroom (129 BC). His death remained an unsolved mystery. Various eminent people were suspected at the time or later (*e.g.,* Gaius Gracchus or even Sempronia or Cornelia), but murder is not likely: suicide is possible, but a natural death is more probable.

Assessment. As a soldier Scipio contributed much to the maintenance and extension of Rome's power in the world. For some 20 years he was an outstanding figure, but he had many political enemies and his leadership was seldom unchallenged. His political aims and ideals have been variously assessed. Stern, upright, and conservative, he sought to maintain Rome's traditional virtues, which he felt were being undermined. But, though a traditionalist in regard to standards of public and private morality, he was a man of culture who gathered around himself a so-called Scipionic circle. This, though not a compact and permanent group, included friends such as Laelius and Polybius. They had close contacts in early days with the poet Terence and later with the satirist Lucilius and the Stoic philosopher Panaetius. Thus Scipio through his patronage exerted much influence on the development of Latin literature and also upon the blending of Greek and Roman thought, not least in the adapting of Stoic ideas to Roman needs. To many later Romans, especially to Cicero, he appeared as an ideal statesman, personifying the golden days of the republic provided by the balance of a mixed constitution and by aristocratic moderation.

BIBLIOGRAPHY. The main ancient sources for Scipio Aemilianus are POLYBIUS xxxi-xxxix, APPIAN, *Punica* 98ff., and *Hispanica* 84ff. For fragments of Scipio's speeches, see H. MALCOVATI, *Oratorum Romanorum Fragmenta*, 2nd ed. (1955). The standard work is A.E. ASTIN, *Scipio Aemilianus* (1967). See also for Scipio's politics, H.H. SCULLARD, "Scipio Aemilianus and Roman Politics," *Journal of Roman Studies*, 50:59–74 (1960).

(H.H.S.)

Scipio Africanus

Publius Cornelius Scipio, surnamed Africanus (the Elder), was one of the outstanding figures in the history of the Roman Republic: his greatest achievement was the defeat of Hannibal, by which he brought the Second Punic War to a successful conclusion.

Silver coin from New Carthage, believed to be a portrait of Scipio. In the Royal Collection of Coins and Medals, National Museum, Copenhagen.
By courtesy of the Nationalmuseet, Copenhagen

Family back-ground

Publius Scipio was born in 236 BC into one of the great patrician families in Rome; his father, grandfather, and great-grandfather had all been consuls in their day. In 218 BC Scipio's father, also named Publius, held the consulship in one of the most critical years of Rome's history: the city's very existence was threatened by Hannibal's coming invasion. The father was sent to southern Gaul to prevent Hannibal's advance into Italy but arrived too late; he then doubled back to Italy, sending his army on to Spain under his brother Gnaeus in order to cut off Hannibal from the Carthaginian forces that were still there. Back in northern Italy with a fresh army, he tried to hold up Hannibal by using the tributaries of the River Po to fight delaying actions. At the first of these, a cavalry engagement on the Ticinus, his son made his first appearance in history: young Scipio, seeing his father wounded and cut off by the enemy, charged forward and saved him. This anecdote is recorded by the historian Polybius on the authority of Scipio's friend Laelius, and it may well be true. Of Scipio's mother, Pomponia, little is known beyond a story that when Publius and his younger brother Lucius were standing for the aedileship (a city magistracy), she visited temples and sacrificed to the gods for their success; this may have been no more than normal practice (though if so, it would perhaps have been hardly worth recording), but it could suggest that she was an unusually pious woman from whom her son Publius inherited a religious outlook such as some ancient authorities attribute to him.

Of Scipio's birth something is said below, but of his boyhood or the date of his marriage to Aemilia, daughter of Aemilius Paullus, consul of 216 who fell at Cannae, nothing is known. He had two sons: Publius, who was debarred by ill health from a public career and who adopted Scipio Aemilianus; and Lucius, who became praetor in 174. More famous than the sons was one of the daughters, namely, Cornelia, who became a lady of great culture and the mother of the Gracchi. Scipio's physical appearance is shown on some coins minted at New Carthage—which almost certainly bear his portrait—and also probably on a signet ring found near Naples.

Military and political achievements. Such was the impact that Scipio made upon the Romans that even during his lifetime legends began to cluster around him: he was regarded as favoured by Fortune or even divinely inspired. Not only did many believe that he had received a promise of help from Neptune in a dream on the night before his assault on New Carthage (see below) but that he also had a close connection with Jupiter. He used to visit Jupiter's temple on the Capitol at night in order to commune with the god, while later the story circulated

Con-nection with Jupiter

that he was even a son of the god who had appeared in his mother's bed in the form of a snake. Although stories of the latter kind must be dismissed, his link with Jupiter seems authentic, and at some time (probably after his death) his portrait bust was placed in the Capitoline Temple (such *imagines* were usually kept by Roman nobles on display in their private houses). The historian Polybius thought that this popular view of Scipio was mistaken and argued that Scipio always acted only as the result of reasoned foresight and worked on men's superstitions in a calculating manner. But Polybius himself was a rationalist and has probably underestimated a streak of religious confidence, if not of mysticism, in Scipio's character that impressed so many of his contemporaries with its magnanimity and generosity. Thus, although Polybius had an intense admiration for Scipio, whom he called "almost the most famous man of all time," the existence of the legend, a unique phenomenon in Rome's history, indicates that Polybius' portrait is too one-sided.

Scipio served as a military tribune at the disastrous Battle of Cannae in 216. He escaped after the defeat to Canusium, where some 4,000 survivors rallied; there he boldly thwarted a plot of some fainthearts to desert Rome. Then in 213 he returned to a civilian career by winning the curule aedileship; the story is told that when the tribunes objected to his candidature because he was under the legal age he replied "If all the Roman people want to make me aedile, I am old enough." Soon family and national disaster followed: his father and uncle were defeated and killed in Spain, where the Carthaginians swept forward to the line of the Ebro (211). In 210 the Romans decided to send reinforcements to Spain, but it is said that no senior general would undertake the task and that young Scipio offered himself as a candidate; at any rate, the Roman people decided to invest him with a command there, although he was technically a *privatus* (not a magistrate). This grant by the people, to a man who had not been praetor or consul, of a military command outside Italy, created an important constitutional precedent. Thus Scipio was given the chance to avenge his father's death in Spain, where he hoped not merely to hold the Carthaginian armies at bay and prevent them sending reinforcements to Hannibal in Italy but to resume his father's offensive policy, to turn back the tide of war, and to drive the enemy out of the peninsula. Such a task must have seemed fantastic in 210, but Scipio had the confidence and ability: it was achieved in the next four years.

From his headquarters at Tarraco (Tarragona) in 209, Scipio suddenly launched a combined military and naval assault on the enemy's headquarters at New Carthage (Cartagena), knowing that all three enemy armies in Spain were at least ten days distant from the city. Helped by a lowering of the water in a lagoon, which exposed the northern wall, he successfully stormed the city. This tidal phenomenon, attributed to the help of Neptune, was perhaps caused by a sudden wind; at any rate it increased the troops' belief in their commander's divine support. In New Carthage he gained stores and supplies, Spanish hostages, the local silver mines, a splendid harbour, and a base for an advance farther south. After training his army in new tactics, he defeated the Carthaginian commander Hasdrubal Barca at Baecula (Bailen) in Baetica (208); whereas normally the two rear ranks of a Roman Army closely supported the front line, Scipio in this battle, under a screen of light troops, divided his main forces, which fell upon the enemy's flanks. When Hasdrubal broke away, ultimately to join his brother Hannibal in Italy, Scipio wisely declined the impossible task of trying to stop him and decided rather to accomplish his mission in Spain—the defeat of the other two Carthaginian armies still there. This he brilliantly achieved in 206 at the Battle of Ilipa (Alcalá del Río, near Seville), where he held the enemy's main forces while the wings outflanked them. He then secured Gades (Cádiz), thus making Roman control of Spain complete.

Victory in Spain

Elected consul for 205, Scipio boldly determined to disregard Hannibal in Italy and to strike at Africa. Having beaten down political opposition in the Senate, he crossed to Sicily with an army consisting partly of volunteers.

While preparing his troops, he boldly snatched Locri in the toe of Italy from Hannibal's grasp, though the subsequent misconduct of Pleminius, the man he left in command of the town, gave Scipio's political opponents cause to criticize him. In 204 he landed with perhaps 35,000 men in Africa, where he besieged Utica. Early in 203 he burned the camps of Hasdrubal (son of Gisgo) and his Numidian ally Syphax. Then, sweeping down on the forces that the enemy was trying to muster at the Great Plains on the upper Bagradas (modern Sūq al Khamīs, on the Majardah in Tunisia), he smashed that army by a double outflanking movement.

After his capture of Tunis, the Carthaginians sought peace terms, but Hannibal's subsequent return to Africa led to their renewing the war in 202. Scipio advanced southwestward to join the Numidian prince Masinissa, who was bringing his invaluable cavalry to his support.

Battle of Zama Then he turned eastward to face Hannibal at the Battle of Zama; his outflanking tactics failed against the master from whom he had learned them, but the issue was decided when the Roman and Numidian cavalry, having broken off their pursuit of the Punic horsemen, fell on the rear of Hannibal's army. Victory was complete, and the long war ended; Scipio granted comparatively lenient terms to Carthage. In honour of his victory he was named Africanus (see also PUNIC WARS).

In 199 Scipio was censor and became *princeps Senatus* (the titular head of the Senate). Though he vigorously supported a philhellenic policy, he argued during his second consulship (194) against a complete Roman evacuation of Greece after the ejection of Philip V of Macedonia, fearing that Antiochus III of Syria would invade it; his fear was premature but not unfounded. In 193 he served on an embassy to Africa and perhaps also to the East. After Antiochus had advanced into Greece and had been thrown out by a Roman army, Scipio's brother Lucius was given the command against him, Publius serving as his legate (190); together the brothers crossed to Asia, but Publius was too ill to take a personal part in Lucius' victory over Antiochus at Magnesia (for which Lucius took the name Asiagenus).

Meantime, in Rome, Scipio's political opponents, led by the elder Cato, launched a series of attacks on the Scipios and their friends. Lucius' command was not prolonged; the generous peace terms that Africanus proposed for Antiochus were harshly modified; the "trials of the Scipios" followed. On the trials the ancient evidence is confusing: in 187 an attack on Lucius for refusing to account for 500 talents received from Antiochus (as war indemnity or personal booty?) was parried; and Africanus himself may have been accused but not condemned in 184. In any case, his influence was shaken, and he withdrew from Rome to Liternum in Campania where he lived simply, cultivating the fields with his own hands and living on a country farm (*villa*) of modest size: Seneca later contrasted its small and cold bathroom with the luxurious baths of his own day. He had not long to live, however; embittered and ill he died in 184 or 183, a virtual exile from his country. He is said to have ordered his burial at Liternum and not in the ungrateful city of Rome, where his family tomb lay outside, on the Appian Way.

Significance and influence. A man of wide sympathies, cultured and magnanimous, Scipio easily won the friendship of such men as Philip, king of Macedonia, and the native princes of Spain and Africa, while he secured the devotion of his own troops. Though essentially a man of action, he may also have been something of a mystic in whom at any rate contemporary legend saw a favourite of Jupiter as well as a spiritual descendant of Alexander the Great. One of the greatest soldiers of the ancient world, by his tactical reforms and strategic insight he created an army that defeated even Hannibal and asserted Rome's supremacy in Spain, Africa, and the Hellenistic east. He had a great appreciation of Greek culture and enjoyed relaxing in the congenial atmosphere of the Greek cities of Sicily, conduct that provoked the anger of old-fashioned Romans such as Cato. Indeed, he was outstanding among those Roman nobles of the day who welcomed the civilizing influences of Greek culture that

Assessment

were beginning to permeate Roman society. His Greek sympathies led him to champion Rome's mission in the world as protector of Greek culture; he preferred to establish Roman protection rather than direct conquest and annexation. For ten years (210–201) he commanded a devoted army at the people's wish. His position might seem almost kingly; he had been hailed as king by Spanish tribes, and he may have been the first Roman general to be acclaimed as imperator by his troops; but, though convinced of his own powers, he offered no challenge to the dominance of the Roman nobility ensconced in the Senate except by normal political methods (in which he showed no outstanding ability). Reaction against his generous foreign policy and against his encouragement of Greek culture in Roman life led to his downfall amid personal and political rivalries; but his career had shown that Rome's destiny was to be a Mediterranean, not merely an Italian, power.

Scipio's influence outlived the Roman world. Great interest was shown in his life during the early Renaissance, and it helped the early humanists to build a bridge between the classical world and Christendom. He became an idealized perfect hero who was seen to have served the ends of Providence. Petrarch glorified him in a Latin epic, the *Africa*, which secured his own coronation as poet laureate in 1341 on the Capitol where, some 1,500 years earlier, the historical Scipio used to commune in the temple of Jupiter.

BIBLIOGRAPHY. The chief ancient sources for Scipio are POLYBIUS and LIVY; the *Life* of Scipio by PLUTARCH does not survive. H.H. SCULLARD, *Scipio Africanus: Soldier and Politician* (1970), is a general study. For a more detailed review of Scipio's military career, see H.H. SCULLARD, *Scipio Africanus in the Second Punic War* (1930); and for details of his political activities, *Roman Politics, 220–150 B.C.* (1951). See also R.M. HAYWOOD, *Studies on Scipio Africanus* (1933); and a more popular work, B.H. LIDDELL HART, *A Greater Than Napoleon: Scipio Africanus* (1926).

(H.H.S.)

Scorpaeniformes

The scorpaeniform, or mail-cheeked fishes, are widespread throughout the oceans of the world. The group is believed to have originated in warm marine waters but has invaded temperate and even Arctic and Antarctic seas as well as freshwaters of the Northern Hemisphere. The mail-cheeked fishes are a highly successful biological group, occurring in the sea from the midlittoral (coastal) zone down to depths of at least 4,000 metres (about 13,000 feet). They inhabit some deep freshwater lakes but are more abundant in cold streams and rivers. The order is often divided into six suborders, only two of which have more than one family; these are the Scorpaenoidei (three families) and the Cottoidei (seven families). The best known groups are the scorpion fishes and rockfishes (family Scorpaenidae), gurnards or sea robins (Triglidae), flatheads (Platycephalidae), and sculpins (Cottidae). The flying gurnards (Dactylopteridae), considered by some authorities to belong in this order but more often separated in the order Dactylopteriformes, are treated here for convenience.

Many members are locally important commercial fish. Thus the redfishes of the genera *Sebastes* and *Sebastodes* of the North Atlantic and Pacific have considerable value to the fishing industries of Europe, the U.S.S.R., and North America; the flatheads are exploited in a wide area of the Indo-Pacific region, and greenlings (Hexagrammidae) are of commercial importance in the northwestern Pacific. In general, the fishery value of the group as a whole has a greater potential than is shown by the present actual utilization by man.

Members of the order Scorpaeniformes are not large fishes. Some of the deepwater species, such as the redfishes, grow to a length of 90 centimetres (three feet), but the majority attain a maximum length of around 30 centimetres (one foot). Externally, scorpaeniforms vary greatly; most are like the Perciformes in general appearance—*i.e.*, they are typical, scaled, spiny-rayed fishes—but the lumpfishes (Cyclopteridae) among them are obese,

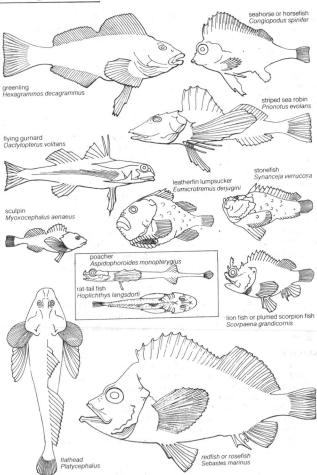

Figure 1: Body plans of representative Scorpaeniformes.
From (*Hexagrammos,Platycephalus*) Yaichiro Okada, *Fishes of Japan;* (*Congiopodus*) J.L.B. Smith, *Sea Fishes of Southern Africa;* (*Prionotus, Dactylopterus,Aspidophoroides,Scorpaena,Sebastes*) D.S. Jordan, *A Guide to the Study of Fishes,* Copyright 1905 by Holt, Rinehart and Winston, Inc., reprinted by permission of Holt, Rinehart and Winston, Inc.; (*Eumicrotremus*) adapted from original drawing by D.R. Harriott in A.H. Leim and W.B. Scott, *Fishes of the Atlantic Coast of Canada,* Fisheries Research Board of Canada Bulletin 155; (*Myoxocephalus*) reprinted by permission of G.P. Putnam's Sons from *Field Book of Marine Fishes of the Atlantic Coast* by Charles M. Breder, Jr., Copyright © 1929 by Charles M. Breder, Jr., renewed 1957 by Charles M. Breder, Jr.

often jellylike, usually scaleless, and lack sharp fin spines. Body armour is often well developed, however, and most scorpaeniforms are well equipped with spines.

NATURAL HISTORY

Ecology. The greatest diversity of scorpaeniform fishes, especially among members of the family Scorpaenidae, is found in warm tropical seas. The order is particularly well represented in the shallow waters of the continental shelf. In the tropics many scorpaenids are found in association with coral; elsewhere most are found on rocky or rough bottoms. In both cases they are highly camouflaged to match their backgrounds. The sculpins, flatheads, and scorpaenids, although not fast or powerful swimmers, feed on many more active smaller fishes and crustaceans, usually capturing prey by a swift pounce using the large pectoral fins as auxiliary power units.

Cryptic (concealing) coloration is probably best exemplified by the stonefishes (*Synanceja*), inhabitants of shallow waters, including estuaries, mud flats, coral reefs, and coral sand pools of much of the tropical Indo-Pacific. Looking like a lump of eroded coral or rock, its body concealed by the cragginess of its outline and its coloration exactly matching the background, a stonefish is perfectly hidden and makes no movement until prodded with a stick or, more often, stepped on, at which time it erects its dorsal fin spines. Each spine has a pair of large gray-brown fusiform venom glands, one on each side. The spines inflict puncture wounds into which a considerable quantity of venom is injected through a channel on each side of the spine. Intense pain at the site of the puncture is instantaneous and radiates within minutes to involve

The dangerously venomous stonefishes

the whole of the affected limb. Death occasionally occurs, and secondary infections are common.

Many other scorpaeniforms can inflict severe wounds with their fin spines or head spines, but relatively few species are equipped with venom glands. One group of venomous species includes the turkey fishes (*Pterois* and related genera), also known as lion fishes or fire-fishes. Widespread in tropical Indo-Pacific waters, they are beautifully and boldly coloured, with patterns of contrasting stripes on the head and body that are specific for individual species and extremely long dorsal and pectoral fins. All of these fishes have long, needlelike dorsal spines with glandular venom-producing tissue and shallow channels capable of inflicting very painful but rarely fatal punctures. The bold and distinctive colouring of the turkey fish is clearly a warning, for, unlike most scorpaenids, it does not hide, but boldly swims in open water around the coral heads. If disturbed, the turkey fish displays by spreading its fins to their fullest extent, rotating until it assumes a position, often head down, with its dorsal spines pointing towards the intruder. If an attacker is not intimidated by this display, the turkey fish moves toward the attacker with its dorsal spines erect.

The flatheads (Platycephalidae) are found in the same oceans as the scorpaenids, but mainly in sandy, muddy or estuarine areas. Their greatly flattened bodies are clearly an adaptation to bottom life; indeed, they bury themselves on the bottom, leaving only the eyes exposed. Many species feed mainly on small fishes, but others, like the dusky flathead (*Platycephalus fuscus*), the largest and commercially most valuable of the Australian flatheads, have a varied diet of fishes, mollusks, crustaceans, and marine worms.

The sea robins (Triglidae) are bottom-living fishes of wide distribution. The lower two or three pectoral fin rays, which are long, thickened, and detached from the remainder of the fin, form organs of taste and touch and are used for locomotion. These rays are very mobile, and an active sea robin can move slowly along the bottom apparently supported on the rays, which continuously explore the ground ahead and on either side. The diet of most of these fish consists of crustaceans, mollusks, and other fishes, many of which burrow in the sea bed.

Adaptations for bottom living in sea robins

The most abundant littoral (shore) scorpaeniforms are the sculpins (Cottidae), significantly the only group found in freshwater, other than the closely related families Cottocomephoridae and Comephoridae. Some members of the families Scorpaenidae and Cyclopteridae are also littoral fishes. The littoral sculpins are generally small, inhabiting densely weeded pools or crevices in rocks. Both the sculpins and cyclopterids found along the shore are strongly thigmotactic (attracted to surfaces), pressing as much of their bodies to the surface as possible. The cyclopterids have well-developed sucker disks, which are derived from the pelvic fin complex. The suck-

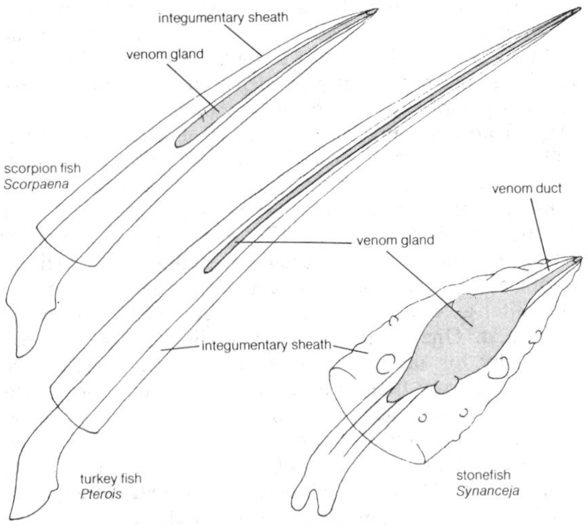

Figure 2: Basic types of venom apparatus of three scorpaeniform fishes.
From B.W. Halsted, *Poisonous and Venomous Marine Animals of the World*

ers, which are effective in resisting wave action, are capable of exerting considerable force; in one instance, a force of 13.3 kilograms (29.3 pounds) was required to break the hold of an adult lumpsucker (*Cyclopterus lumpus*). The European littoral sea snail (*Liparis montagui*) can vary the suction exerted by its sucker as necessary to adjust for the speed of passing water currents.

The cyclopterids have adopted a wide variety of life styles in addition to the littoral habit. The genus *Nectoliparis* is pelagic (*i.e.*, inhabiting open water); members of the genera *Paraliparis* and *Rhodichthys*, of the North Pacific and Arctic Oceans, are bathypelagic (*i.e.*, in deep midwaters), at least for a large part of their lives. In fishes found at depths of 2,400 metres (7,900 feet), the pelvic sucker disk is completely absent. In the semitransparent but beautifully pink-tinged species of the genus *Careproctus*, found in deep, cold polar waters, the pelvic sucker is greatly reduced in size and presumably in efficiency.

In contrast to the cyclopterids, the greenlings are pelagic fishes that adopt a benthic (bottom) life only during the spawning season. One of the best known members, the Atka mackerel (*Pleurogrammus monopterygius*), which is common in the North Pacific and has considerable sporting and commercial fishing value, spends the major part of its life in the open sea. The related yellow-fish (*P. azonus*) has been observed in the upper layers of the ocean in calm weather and is usually captured in purse seines. At night it descends to the bottom.

The scorpaeniforms have adapted particularly well to freshwater. The members of the sculpin family (Cottidae) are widely distributed in the Northern Hemisphere, reaching their greatest diversity in North America and decreasing in numbers westwards through the Eurasian landmass. In extreme western Europe there is only one species, the miller's thumb (*Cottus gobio*). Two endemic forms, *C. kneri* and *C. kessleri*, both of some commercial importance, are found in Lake Baikal, U.S.S.R., and its tributary rivers. These species share Lake Baikal with a number of other species belonging to the related families Cottocomephoridae and Comephoridae. The sculpins in Lake Baikal have become adapted to exploit all of the living space offered by this inland sea. The family Cottocomephoridae is divided into eight genera and numerous species. Although many of the benthic species are restricted to a particular type of bottom and are found only within a certain depth range, most migrate into coastal waters in the spring and remain there during the warm season. Some species, however, remain in deep water all year; others, which are primarily pelagic fishes, use the bottom only to spawn.

The two members of the family Comephoridae, called Baikal cods (*Comephorus baicalensis* and *C. dybowskii*), are pelagic fishes, the latter living at depths to 1,000 metres (more than 3,000 feet). The feeding habits of these Baikal cottoid fishes all exploit potential food resources; the pelagic species feed mainly on various pelagic crustaceans and make daily vertical migrations accompanying their prey, and the benthic forms feed chiefly on certain species of benthic copepod crustaceans. The diet of one inshore species, *Batrachocottus nikolskii*, however, is mainly chironomid and caddisfly larvae.

Reproduction. The mail-cheeked fishes are highly variable in their mode of reproduction. Some of the methods used by them to reproduce are noted below. In the Comephoridae there is a remarkable imbalance between the numbers of each sex, the proportion of males in the total population being as low as 3 or 4 percent. The biological basis for this imbalance is unknown. Members of this family are viviparous (live-bearing). The females come near the surface to give birth to their young; the males remain at their normal depths. By contrast, the remaining cottoids are oviparous (egg laying), including the Cottocomephoridae of Lake Baikal. The females of most of the latter family deposit their eggs in shallow coastal water, then leave the males to guard them until they hatch. This is also the general rule among the sculpins, in which the males guard the eggs. In some species the eggs are shed loosely and adhere to the bottom, but

little reliable evidence is available concerning the breeding habits of most cottoid fishes. The northern Atlantic short-horned sculpin, or bullrout (*Myoxocephalus scorpius*), is known to build a rudimentary nest guarded by the male, as does the freshwater European miller's thumb. The males of these and other cottids have a well-developed structure called a urogenital papilla, which some authorities have suggested is used to introduce sperm into the female. Many cottoid species develop pronounced breeding coloration with sexual differences that apparently aid in recognition between the sexes and in territorial behaviour.

Some members of the family Cyclopteridae build nests that are guarded by the male. The familiar lumpsucker, or sea hen (*Cyclopterus lumpus*), common on both sides of the North Atlantic, spawns along the coast in the winter. At least some of the inshore species, such as the striped sea snail (*Liparis liparis*), which has a distribution similar to that of the lump fish, deposit their spawn in clumps on hydroids (*e.g.*, anemones) and seaweeds, but there is no evidence of parental care. The females of some North Pacific cyclopterids (*e.g.*, *Careproctus sinensis*) have a long specialized structure (ovipositor) by which they lay their eggs under the shell of the Kamchatka crab. In general, however, little is known about the breeding biology of these fish.

In contrast to the rather specialized reproductive behaviour of the sculpins and the sea snails, the sea robins produce eggs that are simply shed in batches in the open sea. So far as is known, no special breeding behaviour accompanies spawning except that these noisy fishes become increasingly loquacious during the spawning season. The members of the family Hexagrammidae (the Atka mackerel, for example) deposit one clump of eggs, often on algae in shallow water on stony bottoms; some species, however, like the lingcod (*Ophiodon elongatus*) care for their egg masses during incubation. The sea poachers, or pogges (Agonidae), lay relatively few eggs, often hiding them away in crevices. The eggs are relatively large, 1.5–1.9 millimetres (0.06–0.07 inch) in diameter in *Agonus decagonus*, a species found in the extreme North Atlantic. The European hook-nose (*Agonus cataphractus*) lays up to 2,400 eggs inside the hollow rhizoid ("stalk") of the kelp *Laminaria* in a compact, membrane-covered mass. Incubation is prolonged, possibly as long as 12 months.

Scorpion fishes of the family Aploactinidae similarly shed their eggs in the open sea. Members of the scorpaenid subfamily Scorpaeninae extrude eggs in gelatinous balloon-shaped masses; those in the subfamily Sebastinae have internal fertilization and are viviparous. The three groups represent the principal evolutionary stem groups of the scorpion fishes. In the North Atlantic redfish (*Sebastes marinus*) fertilization is internal, and the eggs develop within the oviduct of the mother. Fertilization usually takes place during February, after which the females form shoals and migrate to spots where warm bottom currents pass. The female can be said to be a living incubator; in such fishes, which live in cold northern seas, it is clearly advantageous to carry the developing young to an area in which more favourable conditions prevail. The young at birth are very immature, nevertheless, and brood size in the redfish is relatively large (up to 360,000); the larvae must survive a lengthy planktonic life. A smaller, shallower water redfish, the Norway haddock (*Sebastes viviparus*) produces much smaller broods, with brood sizes ranging from 12,000 to 30,000 young. The scorpaeniforms are distinguishable among viviparous teleosts (advanced bony fishes) by their comparatively high fecundity; comparison with many other marine fishes, single individuals of which produce millions of freely shed eggs, however, illustrates the relative advantage, at least in numbers, of bearing living young over laying eggs.

The North Pacific redfishes or rockfishes (*e.g.*, *Sebastodes*, *Sebastiscus*, and *Hosukius*) closely resemble the North Atlantic sebastine species in their reproductive biology; all species studied have been found to have relatively large brood sizes. The sebastine rosefishes (*Helico-*

Diversity of sculpins in Lake Baikal

Differences in numbers of offspring

lenus), found in both the northern Atlantic and Pacific Oceans, have morphological affinities with the subfamily Scorpaeninae. Studies of their reproductive biology have shown that the sebastine rosefishes have intra-ovarian embryos embedded in a gelatinous matrix, and they thus appear to combine sebastine viviparity with scorpaenine egg masses.

Sound production. Since the time of Aristotle, the sea robins have been known as sound-producing fishes, and their sonic performances and mechanisms are well-known. They have a large swim bladder loosely attached to the dorsal wall of the body cavity; the swim bladder is vibrated by lateral muscles in which the striated fibres run at right angles to the muscles' length. The sea robin of the North American Atlantic coast (*Prionotus carolinus*) produces single vibrant barks and growls, and series of rapid clucks with very little provocation. Some of the sculpins (Cottidae) produce dull groans and growls; it is believed that these sounds are mechanical in origin, arising from contractions of the muscles that produce periodic movements of the pectoral girdle. Flying gurnards (Dactylopteridae) are similar to the triglids in their sonic mechanism and sound production capacity.

FORM AND FUNCTION

General features. Many mail-cheeked fishes, such as the rockfishes, have simple fusiform (spindle-shaped) body plans, but others, such as some sea poachers, are extremely slender. Most scorpaenids, triglids, and cottids have two dorsal fins (sometimes joined), the forward one supported by stiff spines. In general, the dorsal, anal, and pectoral fins are large, sometimes strikingly so, but in some groups (*e.g.*, cyclopterids) the spinous dorsal fin is reduced or absent.

The uniting feature of the order

The one feature diagnostic of the order is the presence of a bony bar, or stay, beneath the eye, an extension of the second infra-orbital bone. It is small and inconspicuous in some primitive scorpaeniforms and secondarily reduced in some specialized forms; in others, however, it is readily evident. Often it has become externally prominent, bearing protrusions or spines, or has expanded and fused other cranial bones to form a hard armour.

Camouflage and coloration. Many scorpaeniform fishes, such as scorpion fishes, rockfishes, and sculpins, which live on coral or rocky bottoms, possess a remarkable degree of cryptic (concealing) coloration and shape. Numerous fleshy lappets adorn the head, fin membranes, and body scales, rendering the fish virtually invisible against a background of rocks covered with marine organisms. The effectiveness of this camouflage cannot be appreciated unless the fish is viewed in its natural habitat.

Some members of the order, such as the sea robins, are notable for brilliant colours, especially reds. The large pectoral fins are often strikingly coloured; in the European tub gurnard (*Trigla lucerna*) they have spots of bright green and peacock blue. The spots on the pectorals of the flying gurnards resemble eyes, and apparently function to startle and frighten potential predators when the fins are suddenly spread. The brightly coloured fins of some sea robins may function in a similar manner.

CLASSIFICATION

Annotated classification. The following classification is modified from that suggested by British ichthyologist P.H. Greenwood and the Americans S.H. Weitzman, D.E. Rosen, and G.S. Myers.

ORDER SCORPAENIFORMES (mail-cheeked fishes)
Spiny-finned fishes generally with stout bodies. Second infra-orbital bone united with the preopercular to form a rigid stay across the cheek. Pelvic fins thoracic in location (sometimes modified into sucker disks), the bones directly attached to cleithra (bones like the collarbones of higher vertebrates).
Suborder Scorpaenoidei
Moderate-sized fishes with 24 to 40 vertebrae. Anterior ribs absent or sessile (rigidly attached). Numerous species.
Family Scorpaenidae (scorpion fishes and redfishes)
Paleocene to present. Marine fishes widely distributed in tropical, temperate, and northern seas. Perchlike appearance, dorsal fin spines long and numerous; head spiny, body scaly.

Locally important food fishes, some with venom glands on fin spines. Size to around 100 cm (39 in.).
Family Triglidae (gurnards and sea robins)
Upper Eocene to present. Marine fishes of warm and temperate seas. Characterized by rather slender form, body with small scales or bony plates; head heavily armoured. Lower pectoral fin rays separate, forming a tactile organ. Locally exploited by man as food. Size to around 70 cm (28 in.).
Family Synancejidae (stonefish)
Tropical Indo-Pacific. Scaleless, body covered with warty tubercles. Venom glands on fin spines; dangerously venomous. Size to around 60 cm (24 in.).
Families Aploactinidae, Pataecidae, and Caracanthidae
Tropical Pacific, often in coral. Small scaleless fishes (except Caracanthidae, which have dense dermal papillae). Size to about 25 cm (10 in.).
Suborder Hexagrammoidei
Moderate-sized, slender-bodied fishes. Vertebrae 42–64. Ribs attached to strong parapophyses (projections of vertebrae). Few species, midwater and benthic.
Families Hexagrammidae (greenlings), *Anoplopomatidae* (skilfish), *and Zaniolepididae* (comb fishes)
Northern Pacific. Small scales, long dorsal fins, spines on the head few, powerful teeth in jaws. Locally important food fishes, some with sporting value. Size of most to about 45 cm (18 in.), some longer.
Suborder Platycephaloidei
Moderate-sized with head and anterior part of body strongly flattened. Vertebrae about 27. No air bladder.
Family Platycephalidae (flatheads)
Head and body flattened anteriorly. Marine; usually buried in soft bottom, some forms on coral; Indo-Pacific and tropical eastern Atlantic. Important commercial fishes in Southeast Asia, tropical Australia, and elsewhere. Size to 130 cm (52 in.) and 15 kilograms (33 pounds).
Suborder Hoplichthyoidei
Small fishes, with very depressed bodies. Scaleless, but body with bony plates. Head with heavy spiny ridges.
Family Hoplichthyidae
Found in moderately deep water in Indo-Pacific region. Size to 25 cm (10 in.).
Suborder Congiopodoidei
Moderate-sized fishes with angular bodies and well-developed dorsal fin spines. Scaleless, but sometimes rough skins.
Family Congiopodidae (horse fishes)
In moderately deep cold waters of Southern Hemisphere, off South America, Australia, and South Africa. Size to 75 cm (30 in.).
Suborder Cottoidei
Small to moderate fishes. Marine, from temperate to polar seas, and freshwater in Northern Hemisphere. Mostly scaleless; many with spiny skins, others with bony plates. Many species.
Family Cottidae (sculpins and bullheads)
Oligocene to present. Generally large headed, with well-developed head spines. Marine and freshwater of the Northern Hemisphere (one genus said to occur in the Tasman Sea). Mostly small, some up to 60 cm (24 in.).
Families Cottocomephoridae and Comephoridae
Similar to cottids but post-cleithral bones absent or rudimentary. Freshwater, endemic to Lake Baikal, U.S.S.R. Size to about 16 cm (6 in.).
Family Icelidae (two-horn sculpins)
Head large, laterally compressed, and with small spines. Lateral line and dorsal fin base with scutes (plates). Small benthic fishes mainly of North Pacific, a few in the North Atlantic. Size to 25 cm (10 in.).
Family Normanichthyidae
Head and body with ctenoid (fringed) scales; head without spines. Two well-separated dorsal fins, soft fin rays branched. Marine waters off Chile. Size to 11 cm (4 in.). Probably does not belong in order Scorpaeniformes.
Family Cottunculidae
Body covered in loose skin covered with bony tubercles. Head large, lacking spines. Deep waters of the Arctic and North Atlantic oceans, Indian Ocean off South Africa, and Flores Sea, Indonesia. Size to 20 cm (8 in.).
Family Agonidae (poachers and pogges)
Eocene to present. Body covered in hard armour of large scutes. One or two dorsal fins. Teeth minute. Small, benthic,

coastal fishes of northern Pacific, Atlantic, Arctic oceans, and Antarctic waters. Size to 30 cm (12 in.).

Family Cyclopteridae (lumpfishes and sea snails)

Body short, thick, tadpole-shaped. Skin thick, naked or with bony tubercles or small thorns. Two dorsal fins, the first often minute or modified. Pelvic fins forming a sucker disk or absent. Marine, from littoral to abyssal depths (4,000 metres) in northern Atlantic and Pacific oceans, Arctic and Antarctic waters. Size to 60 cm (24 in.); 5.5 kg (12 lb).

ORDER DACTYLOPTERIFORMES

Resemble Triglidae. Head covered by bony plates expanded into huge shields. First infra-orbital bone connected to preoperculum. Pectoral rays long, numerous, and brightly coloured.

Family Dactylopteridae (flying gurnards)

Tropical and warm-temperate regions of Atlantic and Indo-Pacific oceans. Few species. Size to 50 cm (20 in.).

Critical appraisal. The classification of the scorpaeniforms cannot be said to have approached a final synthesis. It has been suggested that they are an aggregation of three distinct evolutionary lines, the two dominant elements being the scorpaenid and cottid-hexagrammid lines, the third, and minor group being the anoplopomatids. On the other hand, British ichthyologist P.H. Greenwood and colleagues have pointed out that all members of the order, as recognized here, share a distinctive type of caudal (tail) skeleton. The order Scorpaeniformes is clearly related to Perciformes within a superorder Acanthopterygii.

The systematic positions of some groups remain open to doubt. The flying gurnards have been placed by some workers in the Scorpaeniformes, and, indeed, the morphological and biological resemblance of the flying gurnards to members of the Triglidae suggests that such placement best expresses their phyletic affinities.

BIBLIOGRAPHY. Most of the information on the scorpaeniform fishes is found in short technical articles in scientific journals. The following works are broad in nature but contain substantial information on members of this order. E.S. HERALD, *Living Fishes of the World* (1961), is a well-illustrated book for the general reader; N.B. MARSHALL, *The Life of Fishes* (1965), contains some sections on the biology of scorpaeniforms; G.V. NIKOLSKII, *Special Ichthyology*, 2nd rev. ed. (1961; trans. of the 2nd Russian ed. of 1954), deals especially with species commercially important in the Soviet Union; B.W. HALSTEAD, *Poisonous and Venomous Marine Animals of the World*, vol. 3 (1970), provides information on the venom of these fishes and its effects. P.H. GREENWOOD *et al.*, "Phyletic Studies of Teleostean Fishes, with a Provisional Classification of Living Forms," *Bull. Am. Mus. Nat. Hist.*, 131: 339–455 (1966); and C.T. REGAN, "The Osteology and Classification of the Teleostean Fishes of the Order Scleroparei," *Ann. Mag. Nat. Hist.*, Series 8, 11:169–184 (1913), are rather technical, but important, contributions to the study of the scorpaeniforms.

(A.Wh.)

Scorpionida

Scorpions (order Scorpionida or Scorpiones), feared by man since ancient times, often play the role of evildoers in fables and legends; Greek respect for scorpions prompted the naming of the constellation Scorpio, a sign of the zodiac. A long, curved tail tipped with venomous stinger in back, and grasping fingerlike appendages in front, are typical scorpion features; in some areas of the world (*e.g.*, Mexico), venomous scorpions cause serious medical problems. Predators that have little in common with such other arthropods as insects and crustaceans, scorpions are arachnids and thus are closely related to spiders, harvestmen, and mites.

General features. The order Scorpionida comprises about 800 species, which are limited largely to tropical, subtropical, and warm temperate parts of the world. Although often thought of as desert animals, scorpions also are represented by a rich and varied fauna both in forests and in tropical jungles. Most species from deserts and other arid regions are yellowish or light brown in colour; those from moist or higher mountain habitats, however, are brown or black. Scorpions live at altitudes that range from sea level to 2,000 metres (6,000 feet) in the Alps,

Distribution

3,000 metres (10,000 feet) in the mountains of southwestern North America, and 4,000 to 5,000 metres (13,000 to 16,000 feet) in the Andes. One species is known as far north as southern Germany, but none is found in Scandinavia or the British Isles. In North America, *Vejovis boreus* is found in regions of climatic extremes as far as the western provinces of Canada.

Scorpions are relatively large arachnids with an average size of about six centimetres (about 2½ inches). Giants among scorpions are the black species from tropical Africa—*Pandinus imperator* of Guinea attains a body length of 20 centimetres (eight inches). The length of one of the smallest scorpions, *Microbuthus pusillus*, is about 1.3 centimetres (about ½ inch). Although many were of average size, a few precursors of modern scorpions were comparative giants; *Gigantoscorpio* measured about 40 centimetres, and a still undescribed species is estimated to have had a length of about 90 centimetres (almost 36 inches).

Scorpions, often called living fossils because they are the most primitive of all land arachnids, have changed little in external appearance since Silurian times (about 400,000,000 years ago). Scorpions are believed to have become truly terrestrial in the Upper Devonian Period (about 345,000,000 years ago).

Natural history. *Reproduction and life cycle.* Scorpions exhibit few sexual differences, although males usually are more slender and have longer tails than females. In both sexes the genital opening is found between genital coverings, or opercula, located at the base of the abdomen. In order to survive on land, scorpions evolved a structure and mating procedures that prevent eggs and spermatozoa from drying out. The structure, called a spermatophore, is a hard ball of spermatozoa held together by a supporting structure and transferred to the female during mating by an injecting mechanism.

Mating in scorpions, a remarkable process paralleled in only a few other groups, is preceded by a complicated, and often extended, courtship; it is initiated by the male, who faces and grasps the female by appendages called pedipalps. Abdomens pressed to the ground and tails held high and continually entwined and disengaged in a manoeuvre commonly known as an *abre droit*, the pair, directed by the male, moves sideways and backward in a dancelike motion called *promenade à deux*. Many of these actions actually result from the efforts of the pair to find a smooth surface on which the male can extrude and attach the spermatophore by its stalk; his manoeuvres also serve to bring the spermatophore near the open genital opercula of the female. After contact has been made, spermatozoa are ejected into the genital opening (gonopore) of the female. Males that remain near females after mating sometimes are killed and eaten by them.

Once fertilized, eggs are retained in the female's body for periods varying from several months to a year before the young are born alive (viviparity). A young scorpion, white in colour, is still enveloped in a membrane, or chorion, at birth; after freeing itself, the immature scorpion crawls onto the mother's back, rests for several days, and sheds its cuticle (molts) for the first time. During this period, young scorpions utilize food reserves in their bodies; after they leave the female's back, however, the young must find their own food. Scorpions undergo seven or eight molts before they attain sexual maturity. Although development is slow, they may live several years.

Behaviour. Scorpions, exclusively carnivorous, eat living insects and small invertebrates; occasionally they also feed on mice and other small vertebrates. Capable of enduring long periods without food, some scorpions apparently do not drink water. Their methods for capturing and feeding on prey, generally common among arachnids, are necessitated by limited capabilities. Scorpions wait patiently to detect prey but lack pursuit ability if a potential victim escapes the first attack. Prey is perceived by receptors on sensory hairs and comblike projections (pectines) on the appendages that together provide a kind of combined sense of touch and smell; it is then captured and firmly held by pinching fingers on appendages near the front of the body (pedipalps). At the same

Feeding

time, the long tail, swung over the back, is positioned to sting and paralyze the victim if necessary (see figure 1).

Scorpions lack conventional jaws, and their feeding hab-

After M. Vachon, ''Quelques aspects de la biologie des Scorpions,'' *Endeavour* 12:46 (April 1853) in A. Kaestner, *Invertebrate Zoology*, vol. 2 (1970); John Wiley & Sons, Inc.

Scorpion *Androctonus australis* killing prey.

its are unusual; a pair of toothed pincerlike appendages (chelicerae) and sharp edges of adjacent jawlike structures (maxillae and coxae) macerate the prey, as quantities of digestive fluids secreted from the small intestine pour over it. The victim's soft parts are broken down, liquefied, and sucked into the scorpion's stomach by a pumping action. The victim is gradually reduced to a ball of indigestible material, which is cast aside. Eating is a slow process, often taking many hours; after a large meal, a scorpion can live for long periods without food.

Respiration is accomplished by means of four pairs of book lungs (or book tracheae), so-called because they are arranged like the pages of a book, enclosed in body segments of the preabdominal region (mesosoma); each opens through a hole, or spiracle. Air enters the small spiracles and is expelled by slight movements of their covers. This is an adequate system, for these animals need little air and are only slightly affected even if most of their spiracles are artificially sealed.

Enemies

Although powerfully armed for defense, scorpions are attacked by a variety of animals; vertebrates (*e.g.*, birds, lizards, monkeys, and other mammals), predatory insects (*e.g.*, ants, ground beetles, and mantids), and some of the larger spiders eat them, sometimes first tearing off the stinger. The cannibalistic habits of scorpions are well known, and they kill many of their own kind; scorpions do not commit suicide by stinging themselves, however, even though under certain circumstances, a scorpion may accidentally strike its own body. Some African and Oriental species produce buzzing and clicking sounds, which may be intended to frighten predators.

Ecology. Scorpions are solitary nocturnal animals that live together in loosely knit colonies only during times of mating or when climatic extremes are best met by communal protection.

Scorpions usually live under rocks or other ground debris, crawling into soil crevices or beneath bark. A few live close to man and invade his buildings; a dangerous Mexican species, *Centuroides limpidus*, migrates into trees and infests native huts at the beginning of the summer rainy season. Others actually burrow into the soil; vejovid scorpions, for example, may create special retreats by digging: in the Colorado River desert, *Paruroctonus mesaensis* digs into the loose sand and buries itself during the day; in Arizona, species of *Hadrurus* dig deep into gravel banks or under imbedded rocks and remain for long periods; in California, *Anuroctonus phaeodacty-*

lus digs deep burrows in the banks of arroyos and stands at the entrance awaiting prey. Some desert scorpions have adaptations for flinging sand—*e.g.*, widened distal leg segments (tarsi), combs of stiff hairs. A thick, relatively waterproof covering, or integument, enhances their ability to retain body fluids during prolonged periods of drought. Although nocturnal and burrowing habits largely insulate them from climatic extremes, they cannot tolerate high temperatures, even for a short time.

Most scorpions shun water, but a few species live among plants near the sea, move about in the intertidal area, and are able to remain submerged under tidal waters for short periods. Although scorpions readily enter caves, few of them have adapted completely to this habitat; Mexican species of *Typhlochactas*, however, which lack both eyes and dark pigmentation, are obligate cave dwellers. One slender, spotted species, *Isometrus maculatus*, has been transported by commerce into new regions and is now widespread in tropical and subtropical climates.

Form and functions. The scorpion body is divided into two principal parts, the cephalothorax (head plus thorax) and abdomen, to which a variety of names have been applied. The cephalothorax is covered with a hardened structure (carapace) bearing a pair of median eyes and usually a cluster of two to five small lateral eyes on each side. Eyes play a small role in the lives of scorpions, probably only enabling them to distinguish night from day. The cephalothorax bears several pairs of appendages, including chelicerae, pedipalps, and four pairs of walking legs (figure 1). Chelicerae, small, pincerlike appendages in front of the mouth, are used during feeding; immediately behind the chelicerae are large pedipalps, which have the last two segments enlarged to form strong pincers for capturing prey. The walking legs are provided with tarsal claws.

The abdomen, which is broadly joined to the cephalothorax (also called prosoma), consists of 12 distinct segments, seven of which comprise a broad, flattened region (preabdomen); the remaining five narrow rings form a flexible postabdomen, or tail. Hard plates, or tergites, beneath the preabdomen have several specialized structures; the genital opercula lie just behind the ventral surface, or sternum, of the first abdominal segment; a pair of sensory appendages (pectines) on the second segment, found only in scorpions, react to tactile and vibratory stimuli; paired holes (spiracles) that open into book lungs are found on the third to the sixth segments. The postabdomen, often keel-shaped and ornamented, bears at its distal end the stinger.

The venom apparatus of the scorpion consists of a bulbous vesicle drawn out to a sharp, curved stinger. The venom, produced by a pair of glands and ejected by strong muscular contractions through an opening near the tip of the stinger, contains various proteins (including enzymes) and other elements. Some proteins carry nerve toxins capable of producing severe symptoms in warm-blooded animals, including man. Although the stings of common chactid and vejovid scorpions of southern Europe and the United States cause only trivial and transitory pain, some buthid scorpions of the Mediterranean region and the Sonoran Zone of Mexico inflict painful stings, which are followed by temporary local paralysis, fever, and general systemic effects that last a day or two. Certain dangerous buthids found in the Middle East, Brazil, western Mexico, and Arizona in the U.S. are capable of causing death within a few hours; their venom paralyzes the respiratory muscles and causes cardiac failure. Antiscorpionic serums are effective if administered in time.

Venom apparatus

Evolution and paleontology. That scorpions evolved from a now extinct group, the eurypterids, or giant water scorpions, is well established. Silurian scorpions lived in water 400,000,000 years ago, as did eurypterids, and the two groups had several common features—*e.g.*, external gill books, large compound eyes, and similar chewing structures on the first segments (coxae) of the first pair of appendages. Evolution of external gills into enclosed book lungs made possible the migration of scorpions from water to land. Until the Upper Devonian, 345,000,000 years ago, most scorpions were aquatic in habit. About 30 fossil species are known, most of which have been found in Carboniferous rocks (about 325,000,000 years old) in Europe and North America; all these latter fossils found thus far were air-breathing land animals.

Classification. *Distinguishing taxonomic features.* Six families and about two dozen subfamilies are identified by a limited number of characters, including shape and subdivision of the sternum; presence of spurs on the legs; number of lateral eyes; size and modification of the comblike appendages (pectines); and details of the granular rows on the fingers of the pedipalps.

Annotated classification. The following classification was established in 1899, and there have been few challenges to its basic features.

ORDER SCORPIONIDA (SCORPIONES) (scorpions)
Chelicerate arachnids with single carapace over cephalothorax; 2 3-jointed chelicerae, large chelate pdipalps; 4 pairs of walking legs; comblike pectines; 4 pairs of book lungs; tropics to warm temperate zone; about 800 extant and fossil species.

Family Buthidae (buthids)
Extant except for 1 Baltic amber (38,000,000 to 54,000,000 years ago in the Oligocene and Eocene Epochs) species; in tropics to warm temperate zones; triangular sternum; often with spine under stinger; about 300 species, including those most dangerously venomous.

Family Scorpionidae (scorpionids)
Extant; 1 Miocene species (about 20,000,000 years old); mostly in tropics and subtropics of Eastern Hemisphere; pentagonal sternum; single spur at base of tarsus; about 150 species; *Pandinus* of Africa and *Heterometrus* of Asia have largest known species.

Family Diplocentridae (diplocentrids)
Extant; warm regions of Middle East, Mexico, and the Antilles; pentagonal sternum, single tarsal spur, and tubercular spine under stinger; about 30 species.

Family Chactidae (chactids)
Extant; tropical to warm temperate zones, mostly in South America; a few species in Australia, Mexico, and Mediterranean region; pentagonal sternum and 2 lateral eyes on each side; about 70 species.

Family Vejovidae (vejovids)
Extant; mostly in warm temperate region of western North and South America, Middle East to eastern Asia; sternum with nearly parallel sides; 3 lateral eyes; about 125 species.

Family Bothriuridae (bothriurids)
Extant; tropical and subtropical South America; 1 Australian genus; broad, inconspicuous sternum consists of 2 narrow, transverse plates; 3 lateral eyes on each side; about 70 species.

BIBLIOGRAPHY. J.L. CLOUDSLEY-THOMPSON, *Spiders, Scorpions, Centipedes and Mites*, new ed., pp. 85–106 (1969), a general account of natural history and ecology; J.H. FABRE, *The Life of the Scorpion*, pp. 1–180 (Eng. trans. 1923), a classic literary work by a naturalist; A. KAESTNER, "Order Scorpiones," in *Invertebrate Zoology*, vol. 2, pp. 101–114 (Eng. trans. 1968), a general review at college level; J. MILLOT and M. VACHON, "Ordre des Scorpions," in P.P. GRASSE (ed.), *Traité de zoologie*, vol. 6, pp. 386–436 (1949), an excellent review, in French, of morphology and biology; C. PARRISH, "The Biology of Scorpions," *Pacif. Discovery*, 19:2–11 (1966), a well-illustrated, popular account; M. VACHON, "The Biology of Scorpions," *Endeavor*, 12:80–89 (1953), many handsome colour illustrations.

(W.J.G.)

Scotia Sea

The Scotia Sea, a marine region about 350,000 square miles (over 900,000 square kilometres) in area, lies in a complex and tectonically active marine basin enclosed on the north, east, and south by the island-dotted Scotia Ridge. The ridge forms a west-opening submarine loop about 2,700 miles long, connecting the Tierra del Fuego of South America with northern Palmer Land of the Antarctic Peninsula. The western limit of the sea is formed by a discontinuous northwest-trending rise that separates the basin from the Drake Passage (*q.v.*). The Scotia Ridge, with an active volcanic arc-trench system at its eastern end, compares in form and geologic record to the similar Northern Antilles volcanic chain in the eastern Caribbean Sea. The Scotia Ridge region was thus given the name Southern Antilles by the early geologists Eduard Suess and Otto Nordenskjöld.

Exploration. Named after the Scottish National Antarctic Expedition (1902–1904) vessel "Scotia," under command of William S. Bruce, the Scotia Sea has a lengthy record of exploration dating back to the 17th century. Through the 18th and 19th centuries exploration was encouraged by a relentless search for new and ever richer whaling and sealing grounds. Semipermanent and permanent settlements were established, particularly on South Georgia and the Falkland Islands. By the mid-20th century, sealing and whaling declined, and further exploration was largely scientific. During and since the International Geophysical Year (1957–59), the Scotia Sea region has been extensively explored, mainly by Chilean, Argentine, British, and American scientific teams.

Geology and physiography. The Scotia Sea is separated into two smaller basins, West Scotia Basin (the larger) and East Scotia Basin, by a slight rise connecting South Georgia with the South Orkney Islands. Water depths generally range between 10,000 and 13,000 feet, but to the east, across the volcanic arc of the South Sandwich Islands, depths exceed 26,000 feet in Meteor Deep of the South Sandwich Trench. Water of the Southern Seas in its unimpeded clockwise race around the Antarctic continent, is funnelled through the 600-mile-wide Drake Passage and the Scotia Sea, pouring through several main passes of the Scotia Ridge. Most escapes through the broad saddle between Burdwood Bank and South Georgia, into the Argentine Basin, and the rest through saddles between the South Sandwich Islands and South Georgia to the north and the South Orkney Islands to the south.

Reconnaissance mapping of magnetic anomaly patterns in the Scotia Sea, and their comparison to dated patterns elsewhere, suggests that the crust in this region is geologically young, perhaps no more than about 40,000,000 years old. Preliminary studies also suggest that a new South Sandwich crustal plate, growing at a rate of about 1.1 inches per year, may be overriding a southern Atlantic crustal plate. Reconnaissance seismic studies indicate that the Scotia Sea crust is in places thicker than typical oceanic crust and is probably of structure intermediate between oceanic and continental. The Eltanin Fracture Zone, which offsets the East Pacific Rise (Albatross Cordillera) in the central southern Pacific, extends southeastward, possibly meeting the northern arm of the Scotia Ridge. It is doubtless somehow related to the opening of the Scotia Sea basins.

Coring and dredge sampling indicate that the sea floor is largely covered with clayey silt, and with carbonate ooze locally along the northern margin and siliceous ooze along the eastern. Ferromanganese concretionary nodules, though occurring widely, are concentrated particularly beneath the Antarctic Convergence (of cold Antarctic water and slightly warmer Atlantic water) in a belt passing along the northern Scotia Sea and through the saddle between Burdwood Bank and South Georgia. Most of the sediments are derived from nearby volcanic terranes, having been deposited on the ocean floor by ice movements and by ocean currents. *The sea bottom*

The origin of the Scotia Sea is intimately tied to that of the Scotia Ridge. Thick sequences of highly deformed, almost unfossiliferous graywacke and shale occur in most of the islands, including South Georgia, Livingston Island in the South Shetland Islands, and the South Orkney Islands. In South Georgia, the beds are overlain by tuffaceous (volcanic detritus) graywacke, at least in part of Cretaceous age (from 65,000,000 to 136,000,000 years old). These sequences are believed to partly correlate with earlier (late Paleozoic) sequences in South America and in the Antarctic Peninsula, but the correlation is highly uncertain in the absence of dateable fossils. It has been postulated that the Andean Scotia Ridge is the remnant of a former direct connection between South America and Antarctica, a connection that in the Tertiary (2,500,000 to 65,000,000 years ago) was disrupted and bent by the eastward protrusion of the Pacific crust into the Atlantic.

Animal life and vegetation. The northern arm of the Scotia Ridge, including South Georgia, lies in the sub-

Antarctic climatic zone, and the southern arm, south of the Antarctic Convergence, lies in the cold Antarctic zone. The biota varies accordingly. South Georgia supports a rich tundra-like flora with at least 50 species of vascular plants, whereas islands in the Antarctic zone, including the South Orkneys and South Shetlands, can maintain only primitive communities of mainly seedless plants, such as lichens, mosses, and algae. Only a few species of grasses can grow in protected locales in this southern zone. Many species of birds, mostly sea and a few shore birds and land birds, including petrels, penguins, gulls, terns, skuas, and sheathbills, inhabit these regions. Other sea life south of the Convergence includes nearly 100 species of fish and several species of whale and seal. Sea lions are unknown south of the Falkland Islands. Man has seriously reduced the sea-mammal population, some species almost to the point of extinction. Accidental introduction of cats, dogs, mice, and rats threatens bird nesting grounds on some islands, and the natural tundra ecosystem is severely threatened on a few sub-Antarctic islands that have been overgrazed by introduced sheep and rabbits. Articles of the Antarctic Treaty, signed by 12 nations (see ANTARCTICA) are aimed at protecting and restoring this valuable natural habitat.

BIBLIOGRAPHY. For general information, see R. PRIESTLEY, R.J. ADIE, and G. DE Q. ROBIN (eds.), *Antarctic Research* (1964). Selective sources on geology are reports in R.J. ADIE (ed.), *Antarctic Geology* (1964); and the *Symposium on Antarctic Geology: Proceedings* (1970). Selective sources on oceanography are reports in J.L. REID (ed.), *Antarctic Oceanology*, vol. 1 (1971).

(A.B.Fo.)

Scotland

Scotland, the most northerly of the four parts of the United Kingdom—England, Scotland, Wales, and Northern Ireland—is a generally cool, hilly, and, in the west, wet country that occupies about one-third of the island of Great Britain (England, Scotland, and Wales). It is bounded by England in the south and on the other three sides by sea: by the Atlantic on the west and north and by the North Sea on the east. Its area is 29,796 square miles (77,169 square kilometres) or, including inhabited islands, 30,414 square miles (78,772 square kilometres). It is fringed by numerous islands on the west coast, and the island clusters of the Orkneys and the Shetlands lie to the north; but the east coast has only a few islands, and those are insignificant. At its greatest length, from Cape Wrath to the Mull of Galloway, the mainland extends to 274 miles, while the maximum breadth from Applecross, in western Ross, to Buchan Ness, in Aberdeenshire, is 154 miles. But, owing to the deep penetration of the sea in the fjords, or narrow, deep inlets, of the west coast and in the estuaries of the Tay and Forth rivers in the east, most places are within 40–50 miles of the sea, and only 30 miles separate the Firth of Clyde and the Firth of Forth, the two great estuarine inlets on the west and east respectively.

The country was originally known as Caledonia. The name Scotland originated in the 11th century, when the name Scotia was given to the southwestern tract settled by the tribe of Scots who had migrated from Ireland. After being independent until 1707, Scotland became an integral part of the United Kingdom, though something of a political curiosity. It has no separate legislature, executive, or political power, and, constitutionally, it is less than a state or province in a federal union. Yet it retains vestiges of ancient sovereignty in its own legal and educational systems, a national church, and a separate administration. Its economy is integrated with that of Britain, and it has no diplomatic or consular representation in other countries, but it has managed, nevertheless, to preserve its identity in the international scene by export trade and by cultural exchanges. Some of its products, especially whisky, tartan, and tweeds, are internationally known, and generations of emigrant Scots have spread the awareness of a distinctively Scottish culture. The image cherished by foreigners is often odd, but even

romantic notions of stern and wild Caledonia, of Mary, queen of Scots, and of Bonnie Prince Charlie (Charles Edward Stuart) prevent Scotland from being eclipsed in the comity of nations. (For related information see BRITAIN AND IRELAND, HISTORY OF; UNITED KINGDOM; and EDINBURGH.)

THE LAND

Natural features. Scotland is traditionally divided into three regions, the Highlands, the Lowlands, and the Southern Uplands. The coastal plain, stretching from the Buchan district of Aberdeenshire round the Moray Firth to the flat expanse of Caithness, is distinctive enough, however, to constitute a separate Northeast region. The Highlands are bisected by the fault line of the Great Glen (Glen More nan Albin), which is occupied by a series of lochs (lakes), the largest of which is Loch Ness, famous for its probably mythical monster. North of the Great Glen is an ancient plateau, which, through long erosion, has been cut into a series of peaks of fairly uniform height separated by glens (valleys) carved out by glaciers. The northwest fringe of the mainland is particularly barren, the granulated and layered rocks having been worn down by severe glaciation to produce a hummocky landscape, dotted by small lochs and rocks protruding from thin, acidic soil. Farther inland are spectacular sandstone mountains, weathered into sheer cliffs, rock terraces, and pinnacles. South of the Great Glen, the Grampian Mountains were also formed by continuous denudation and glaciation of metamorphic rocks, though there are intrusions of granitic masses in the Cairngorm Mountains. The Grampians are less rugged and rocky than the mountains of the northwest, being rounded and grassy, with more of the appearance of a plateau. There are large basins between mountain groups, the most striking being the moor of Rannoch, a bleak expanse of bogs and granitic rocks, with narrow, deep lochs, such as Loch Rannoch and Loch Ericht. The boundary of the Highland region is clearly marked by a fault (the Caledonian trend) running southwest to northeast from Helensburgh, on the River Clyde, to Stonehaven, on the east coast. The southern boundary of the Lowlands is not such a continuous escarpment, but the fault beginning in the northeast with the Lammermuir and Moorfoot hills and extending to Glen App, in the southwest, is a distinct dividing line. In some ways the label Lowlands is a misnomer, for, although the central region is low by comparison with adjoining areas, it is by no means flat. The landscape is varied by series of hills such as the Sidlaws, the Ochils, the Campsies, and the Pentlands, composed of igneous rocks rising as high as 2,363 feet and following the Caledonian trend. Most of the region is above 400 feet, but the lowlands of the Lothians and Fife in the east, the rich plain of Strathmore in the northeast, and the Clyde Valley in the west are Scotland's best areas for arable farming. The Southern Uplands are not so high and fractured as the Highlands. Glaciation has resulted in narrow, flat valleys separating table mountains. To the east of the Nith Valley in the border counties, the hills are rounded, gently sloping, and grass covered, providing excellent grazing for sheep. To the west of the Nith the landscape is rougher, with granitic intrusions around Loch Doon, and the soil more peaty and wet. The high moorlands and hills, of which Merrick (2,764 feet [842 metres]) is the highest, are also suitable for sheep farming. Toward the southeast the uplands open out into the Tweed Valley, which broadens into rich farming land, and to the southwest they slope toward the Galloway Peninsula.

Soil and drainage. With Scotland's diversity in geological structure, relief, and weather, the character of the soil varies greatly. In the northwest, the Hebrides, and the Shetlands, where the geological substratum is ancient rock, resistant to weather, the soil is poor, and cultivation is possible only at river mouths, glens, and coastal strips. On the west coast of some Hebridean islands, however, there are plains of calcareous sand (the machair) suitable for farming. On moors and hills between 1,000 and 2,500 feet, a peat covering is widespread because of high rain-

The Great Glen

Peat

fall and poor drainage. Peat is estimated to cover over 2,600 square miles. It occurs also on lower ground, and Caithness has large peat deposits. Where there is good soil for arable farming, as in the Orkneys, Caithness, the northeast coastal plain, and the Lowlands, it has been derived from old red sandstone and younger rocks. Though the sea lochs, or fjords, of the west are supposed to be remnants of a river system submerged by the Minch Channel, the present drainage system runs toward the east. In the northern Highlands the watershed runs from north to south, close to the west coast, so that rivers running to the west are very short and those to the east longer and less rapid. In the central Highlands the rivers meander more, but the longest, the Spey, Don, and Dee, drain the area toward the east, as do the Tay and the Forth in the Lowlands. The Clyde and the Tweed both rise in the Southern Uplands, the one flowing to the west and the other to the east coast, while the Nith and a few other small rivers run south into the Solway Firth. Lochs are useful for drainage, for reservoirs, and as sources of power. They are numerous in the Highlands, ranging from moraine-dammed lochans (pools) in mountain corries (hollows) to large and deep lochs filling rock basins. Many of the bigger lochs have been dammed and enlarged to provide a flow of water to generate electricity in stations at lower levels. In the Lowlands and Southern Uplands, lochs are shallower and less numerous, though some, notably Loch Lomond, are extensive.

Climate. Scotland has a temperate oceanic climate, milder than might be expected from its latitude. Despite its small area, there are considerable variations in climate. Rainfall is greatest in the mountainous areas of the west, as prevailing winds blow from the southwest and come laden with moisture from the Atlantic. East winds are common only in winter and spring, when cold, dry continental air masses envelop the east coast. Hence, the west tends to be milder in winter, with less frost and with snow seldom lying long, but it is damper and cloudier than the east in summer. Tyree (Tiree), in the Hebrides off the west coast, has a mean temperature in winter of 41° F (5° C) in the coldest month (as high as southeast England), whereas Dundee, on the east coast, has 37° F (2.8° C). Dundee's mean temperature in the warmest month is 59° F (15° C) and Tyree's 57° F (13.9° C). There is a smaller range of temperature over the year in Scotland than in southern England. Rainfall varies remarkably. In the flat Outer Hebrides it does not exceed 40 inches (102 centimetres) a year, the average rainfall in Britain. Some two-thirds of the surface of Scotland, however, has more than 40 inches. In the mountains of Inverness and Western Ross, rainfall exceeds 100 inches (250 centimetres). Most of the east coast has below-average rainfall, less than 25 inches (64 centimetres) in the Moray Firth lowlands and 27 inches (69 centimetres) in Dundee. Sunshine averages 3½ hours per day over the year.

Rainfall

Vegetation. Lower ground, up to about 1,500 feet, was once covered with natural forests, which have been cleared in the course of centuries and replaced by introduced trees, plants, and crops. Survivals of the original forest are found in the pinewoods of Rothiemurchus, in Inverness County. Grass and heather cover most of the Grampians and Southern Uplands, where the soil is not so wet and dank as in the northwest Highlands. On boggy soil, shrubs such as bearberry, crowberry, and blueberry grow, as well as bog cotton. Alpine and Arctic species flourish on the highest slopes and plateaus of the Grampians, including saxifrages, creeping azalea, and dwarf willows. Ben Lawers is noted for the wealth of its mountain flora.

Animal life. For its size, Scotland is rich in animal life. Herds of red deer graze in the corries and remote glens, and their population is estimated at nearly 500,000. Lower down in wooded country the more elusive roe deer are found. Foxes and badgers are widespread, and the number of wildcats is thought to be increasing. Rabbits were decimated but not eliminated by the disease of myxomatosis. Pine marten, otters, and mountain and brown hares are among other wild animals. A few ospreys nest in Scotland, and golden eagles, buzzards, and kestrels are the most notable of resident birds of prey. Capercaillie (a species of grouse) have been successfully reintroduced. Seabirds, such as gannets, fulmars, and guillemots, and many types of gull abound on cliffs and the isolated rocks known as stacks around the magnificent coasts. The largest mammal in Scottish waters is the Atlantic gray seal, which breeds on the island of North Rona, off the west coast; the common seal is also numerous.

The human imprint. In early times, mountains, rivers, and seas divided the people into self-sufficient communities, which developed a strong sense of identity. This sense has been eroded by social mobility and by modern transport, broadcasting, and other standardizing influences. Yet vestiges of regional consciousness linger. The Shetland islanders speak of Scotland with detachment. Galloway, cut off by hills from the rest of the country, has a vigorous regional patriotism. The Gaelic-speaking people of the Hebrides and west Highlands find their language a bond of community. A distinct dialect may differentiate some communities from others, as in the case of Aberdeenshire. Borderers celebrate their local festivals with fervour. This feeling of community survives to a varying degree in many areas, but it has no economic basis now and tends, like clan loyalty, to be a sentimental bond rather than a force of social cohesion. The most thickly populated rural areas are those with the best farming land, such as the Lothians and the Northeast. The Highlands nourished a large population before sheep farming led to continuous emigration. Now settlements in the Highlands are mostly crofting townships; that is, small farms of a few acres grouped together in an irregular manner. The old pattern of crofting was one of communities practicing a kind of cooperative farming, with strips of common land allotted annually to individuals. Examples of the old system survive, but now crofters have their own arable land fenced in, while they share the common grazing land. In the Lothians and other areas of high farming, the communal farm has long been replaced by single farms with steadings (farmsteads) and workers' houses. Scotland is noticeably lacking in those old villages that evolved in England from medieval hamlets of joint tenants. Some planned villages were built by enterprising landowners in the 18th century. Burghs, often little bigger than villages, were mostly set up as trading centres, ports, or river crossings or to command entrances to mountain passes. Around the east and northeast coast, there are many surviving small towns that were once obliged to be self-contained in consumer industries and burghal institutions because of poor land transport. Some coastal towns have preserved a dual character, the fishing community being grouped around the harbour, while other inhabitants occupy the higher ground. Growth of industry and transport has produced urbanization. Edinburgh, Dundee, and Aberdeen are centres of administration, commerce, and industry for their regions, but only Glasgow, with its satellite burghs, is large enough to deserve the official title of conurbation, with a population of more than 1,700,000. Depopulation of city centres is occurring in Scotland, as elsewhere: the population of all four cities had fallen according to the 1971 census, while that of surrounding counties had risen. In Glasgow the reduction was due to a planned overspill program, but elsewhere the trend was due to the growth in commuting.

Crofting

THE PEOPLE

Despite their diverse origins, including Celts, Angles, and Normans, the Scots in time have been fused into a fairly homogeneous population. In the 19th century there was heavy Irish immigration, which some feared would form an alien element, with different social and educational standards and religion. The Irish have settled, however, without provoking marked social conflict.

Religion. Scotland is remarkably free from racial and religious strife. The Church of Scotland is the established religion and largest communion, with more than 1,150,000 members by the early 1970s, though membership has been steadily declining. It is presbyterian in

Church of Scotland

structure and evangelical in doctrine. Its well-articulated organization begins with the parish church or congregation, governed by a kirk session composed of minister and elders. The kirk session sends representatives to the presbytery (a group of parishes), and the presbyteries in turn are represented in the synod, which has declined in status. At the apex is the General Assembly, to which presbyteries send clerical and lay commissioners in equal numbers and which is the supreme court and legislature of the church. It meets annually and reviews the reports of numerous committees. It is perhaps the most representative body in Scotland and makes its voice heard on current moral, social, and international issues. The Roman Catholic Church, organized into two archdioceses and six bishoprics, has a membership of about 820,000. The Episcopal Church in Scotland has about 50,000 members, and there are congregations of other denominations, such as the Free Church of Scotland, Baptists, Congregationalists, and Methodists. The ecumenical spirit and perhaps growing indifference have taken bitterness out of religious differences, though little progress has been made with church unity. The Roman Catholics have their own schools, built and staffed from public funds on the same terms as the state schools.

Demography. Scotland, according to the 1971 census, was the home of almost 5,230,000 people. Between 1961 and 1971 the population increased by nearly 50,000, the smallest increase recorded since 1801 except for 1921–31, when there was a decrease of almost 40,000. Natural increase would have resulted in a much bigger population had it not been for heavy losses from emigration. In the period 1931 to 1951 the natural increase was over 500,000, but the actual increase was only half this figure. Between 1951 and 1961 the corresponding figures were 337,000 and 83,000. The drain of emigration has continued for two centuries. In the first half of the 20th century the net loss was 1,133,000. From 1951 to 1961 it was 254,000, and the estimated figure for 1961 to 1971 was 325,000. The flow of emigration overseas and to the rest of the U.K. deprives Scotland of many of its young, skilled, and educated. Emigration rises and falls, and, although there was some decline in the early 1970s, adverse trends inevitably recur when economic conditions deteriorate. The birth rate in 1970 was 16.8 per 1,000, the lowest since 1945. In 1962 it was 20.1, after which it declined slightly. The death rate in 1970 was 12.2, and between 1961 and 1971 it varied between 11.5 and 12.6. Irish immigration has fallen steadily from the peak of 205,064 recorded in the 1901 census. By 1961 it had dropped to 80,533, and the great majority of the Irish-born were resident in Glasgow (about 30,000) and the surrounding counties, while Edinburgh had about 5,000. By contrast, the number of English- and Welsh-born people living in Scotland had risen considerably in the past century, from 56,000 in 1861 to 247,000 in 1961. Of these, 36,182 lived in Edinburgh and 33,788 in Glasgow. In Glasgow there are Pakistani and Indian communities, but immigration has been small and without the stresses that have occurred in parts of England.

Physical and economic factors explain the concentration of three-quarters of the population in the central Lowlands, which occupy only one-seventh of the country's area. The average density of population is about 170 per square mile, but in the central region it is 900. By contrast, the Highlands have had continuous depopulation —by 11 percent between 1851 and 1901, by 18.8 percent between 1901 and 1951, and by 2.8 percent between 1951 and 1961. But the decline may have been arrested. In 1971 there was an increase of 6,443 in the population of the seven crofting counties. Though declines continued in the Shetlands, the Orkneys, and Sutherland, there were increases in Caithness, Inverness County, Argyll, and Ross and Cromarty (where a big aluminum smelter started production). In all four cities there was a decline reflected in the 1971 census. Glasgow's population of 897,848 was 159,831 fewer than in 1961; Edinburgh's was 448,895 (18,775 fewer); Dundee's was 182,467 (1,015 fewer); and Aberdeen's was 178,441 (5,083 fewer). Depopulation has also taken place in the Border

(margin note) Depopulation in the Highlands

counties and Southwest region, though less markedly than in the Highlands. Between 1961 and 1969 the Borders lost 4,300 people and the Southwest 4,200. It was forecast that Scotland's population would rise to 5,344,000 by 1981, to 5,590,000 by 1991, and to 5,891,000 by 2001. These projections assumed that the net emigration loss would be about 20,000 a year for the rest of the century.

THE SCOTTISH ECONOMY

Scotland's economy compares unfavourably with that of European countries of similar size except Ireland. Scotland's growth is slower, unemployment higher, and per capita gross domestic product lower than other nations. Even in the context of the United Kingdom it is economically backward. Its unemployment rate in postwar years was almost consistently twice that of Britain as a whole. Fewer people were employed in 1970 than in 1960, though the number of women at work rose steadily. Male unemployment was one of the most disquieting features of the economy in the 1960s. Apart from Edinburgh, the whole of Scotland is scheduled as a development area, eligible for special state incentives to attract new enterprises. Scotland's gross domestic product (GDP) in 1970 was estimated at £3,609,000,000, or 8.5 percent of the U.K.'s product, while the Scottish GDP per capita was only 91.3 percent of the U.K.'s.

Natural resources. *Mineral resources.* Coal is Scotland's chief mineral resource, but the Lanark County coalfields are almost exhausted, and the main mining areas are now in the Lothians, Fife, and Ayr County. The industry reached its peak production of 43,000,000 tons in 1913 and has since been declining. Between 1959 and 1970, output fell from 18,500,000 to 11,300,000 tons. Many uneconomic collieries have been closed, and production has been concentrated on about 35 large, mechanized pits. Manpower had fallen from 82,000 in 1951 to some 29,000 in 1971. Though the industry has generally contracted, its productivity has risen from 287 tons per man year in 1951 to 381 tons in 1971. The colliery that supplies the huge electricity station at Longannet, Fife, has an output of 10,000 tons a day, with computer control of the volume and quality of production. Other minerals that have been worked intermittently include gold, silver, lead, chromite, diatomite, and dolomite, but none has been successfully exploited. At Muirshiels, in Renfrew County, and Gass Water, in Ayr County, 30,000 tons of barite (barium sulfate, used in paint manufacture), one-third of the U.K. output, is produced each year. Though peat is available to a depth of two feet or more over some 1,700,000 acres, its economic value is limited. Some communities in the Highlands still burn it for fuel, but the time and labour involved in cutting and drying peat in an uncertain climate have led to declining use. Experiments in using peat as fuel for generating electricity proved it uneconomical.

Power resources. Water is a valuable resource, especially for generating electricity. The North of Scotland Hydro-Electric Board (NSHEB) was set up in 1943 to build dams and power stations. By 1970 it had completed 54 hydroelectric stations, with a total capacity of 1,052 megawatts, and developed pumped storage schemes by which electricity generated in off-peak periods may be used to pump water to a higher dam, from which it descends at peak periods to operate the turbogenerators. One such scheme, at Cruachan, in Argyll, operates at a capacity of 400 megawatts and another, at Foyers, on Loch Ness, is under construction. The NSHEB has also coal- and oil-fired stations and plans a large nuclear power station for Banff County. The board's obligation to provide power to consumers in remote areas entails a financial loss, but the board was set up with a definite social responsibility. The South of Scotland Electricity Board relies mainly on coal-fired stations; those at Cockenzie, Kincardine, and Longannet are new and efficient. There are nuclear power stations at Chapelcross, in Dumfries County, and Hunterston, in Ayr County. A nuclear-research establishment, run by the Atomic Energy Authority, is located at Dounreay, in Caithness,

(margin note) Hydroelectric power

where a prototype of a commercial fast reactor has been built. Natural gas from the North Sea wells off the English coast will replace manufactured gas in Scotland. Oil from Scottish waters may become a major source of power; oil has been struck about 100 miles off Peterhead and has been found in substantial quantities in the seabed off the northeast coast and Shetland.

Agriculture, forestry, and fishing. As an economic resource wild animals, birds, and river fishes are of minor importance, though deer stalking, grouse shooting, and fishing provide employment in parts of the Highlands in which other activities are hardly possible. Venison is exported to the European mainland, and game birds, salmon, and trout are delicacies, as well as objects of sport.

Fishing. Sea fishing, however, is thriving, and although the Scottish fishing fleet is contracting, it is better equipped and more efficient. In 1961 there were over 3,000 vessels and in 1971 only 2,600; manpower fell from almost 11,000 to just over 9,000. The inshore fleet has been modernized, and boats have been equipped for both netting herring and catching whitefish by seine nets. Trawlers from Aberdeen and Granton (near Edinburgh) operate in more distant waters near the Faeroe Islands. Aberdeen and the Moray Firth ports are the busiest centres of whitefishing, but Lerwick, in the Shetland Islands, and Ullapool, Mallaig, and Stornoway, on the western side, are also important for landing and processing fish. Catches naturally fluctuate from year to year, and in 1970 landings at Scottish ports amounted to 8,836,000 tons, valued at nearly £19,000,000. Herring fishing that year resulted in landings worth £4,250,000. Shellfish, a booming section of the industry, brought in almost £4,000,000.

Agriculture. Agriculture's development is toward greater efficiency through mechanization. The labour force fell from 68,000 in 1960 to 46,000 in 1970. Output in 1970–71 was valued at £263,500,000. Since 1945 agriculture has been supported by a complex system of deficiency payments and production grants for improving buildings and land. Subsidies for hill cattle and hill sheep help farmers working in difficult conditions. There are nearly 22,000 full-time farms in Scotland, of which roughly a half are rented and half owner occupied. In the Southern Uplands and the Highlands there are 5,000 hill sheep farms, while in the Northeast livestock rearing combined with crops for animal feeding predominates. In the Southwest, dairy farming suits the damp, mild climate, and the Glasgow conurbation is a convenient market. Wheat and barley are grown in the Lothians, Fife, and Berwick County. Specialized kinds of farming flourish in certain areas, such as market gardens in East Lothian, raspberry growing in Strathmore, and tomato growing under glass in the upper Clyde Valley. Early potatoes are a specialty of Ayr and Wigtown counties. Barley is now the leading crop; there were 775,000 acres under barley in 1971. The next largest crops are oats, potatoes, and wheat. The animal population in 1971 was: beef cattle, 1,646,000; dairy cattle, 638,000; sheep, 7,454,000; and pigs, 663,000. Poultry for producing eggs numbered 7,643,000, and broilers numbered 5,522,000. Over the past 30 years the cattle population has risen by over 1,000,000. Crofting is a special section of the agricultural scene. It has to be supplemented by other work, such as forestry, road work, catering for tourists, and weaving. Though there are some 19,000 crofts in the northern counties, many of them are not cultivated. The Crofters Commission gives crofters advice, and it channels grants to them for the improvement of land and houses.

Principal crops

Forestry. Forestry is an expanding industry, which has helped retain the population in rural areas. It is managed by the Forestry Commission, a public body, and by private landowners. The commission has forests extending to 861,000 acres, while privately owned forests cover 545,000 acres. In 1969–70 the commission planted 39,000 acres, and private owners planted 28,535 acres. In 1970 the number directly employed in forestry was 5,800. Although the Forestry Commission plants throughout the country, it plays a particularly important role in Highland development. The trees it grows are conifers, including Scotch pine, Norway spruce, European larch, Sitka spruce, and Douglas fir.

Industry. Scotland's reputation as an industrial country has rested principally on shipbuilding and heavy engineering, but employment has declined in these sectors, as well as in marine engineering, agriculture, coal, and the railways. Shipbuilding employed 47,900 workers in 1966 and 44,400 in 1970. The decline of traditional industries and the failure to replace them with sufficient science-based, expanding enterprises constitutes the crucial problem of Scottish industry. As a result of the Geddes Report investigating the industry, there has been a process of mergers among shipyards. The Upper Clyde Shipbuilders, formed by a union of five shipyards, had a brief and troubled existence and went bankrupt in 1971; but it was subsequently reorganized and kept afloat by heavy government grants. The Lithgow-Scott Group, on the lower reaches of the Clyde, is a strong and versatile firm, however, capable of building anything from oil tankers to submarines. Smaller firms in Leith, Dundee, and Aberdeen build trawlers and cargo vessels.

There is a wide range of manufacturing industries in Scotland. The electronics industry has expanded remarkably in recent years, especially in Fife, the Lothians, and Lanark County. In 1960 electronics companies employed 7,000, and by 1970 the total had risen to almost 40,000, working for 80 companies, most of them branches of United States and English undertakings. Manufacture of clocks, watches, cash registers, earth-moving machinery, precision instruments, and other modern products has been introduced since World War II and diversified the industrial structure. Old, established industries such as textiles in the Border towns of Hawick, Galashiels, Selkirk, and Peebles have retained their vitality. Carpet making flourishes in Glasgow and Ayr. Dundee's characteristic jute industry has been contracted and modernized and turned to the production of other fibres as well. Automobile manufacture, though carried on in Glasgow by Albion Motors for many years, came to Scotland on a considerable scale in the early 1960s; the industry now also turns out tractors and trucks and employs over 20,000. The steel industry, concentrated in Lanark and Ayr counties, employs around 30,000. Some steel works are obsolescent, and in the early 1970s it was feared that unemployment would be inevitable, though a large strip steel mill at Ravenscraig was being enlarged at a cost of £35,000,000. An iron-ore terminal at Hunterston, in Ayr, where the water is deep enough to accommodate the largest vessels, and a huge steel plant nearby were proposed in order to ensure the future of steelmaking in Scotland.

Steel industry

Printing and brewing are well-established industries in Edinburgh and Glasgow. The 120 distilleries in the Highlands and the Northeast produce the whisky for which Scotland is internationally famous. Despite heavy taxation on home consumption, whisky sales have continued to expand dramatically. In 1970 home sales exceeded 10,000,000 gallons for the first time. Whisky exports amounted to 62,000,000 gallons in 1970 and earned £194,000,000 in foreign currency. Separate records of Scotland's exports are not available, but its contribution to the U.K.'s overseas trade is substantial. Whisky is the largest factor, but the textile industries of the Borders and the Harris tweed industry of the Hebrides also have a large export business. Mechanical- and electrical-engineering industries, with a total production valued at £395,500,000 in 1970, also export much of their output.

Finance. Scotland had eight joint-stock banks until the 1950s, but, as a result of mergers, the number was reduced to three: the Bank of Scotland, the Royal Bank of Scotland, and the Clydesdale Bank. The Scottish banks have their own notes, they have introduced computers and new accounting methods, and they have moved into hire purchase (installment purchase), merchant banking, and insurance broking. Scotland has been conspicuously lacking in merchant-bank facilities, but two native merchant banks have been established, in addition to branches of London banks. Investment trusts are among the most distinctive of Scottish financial institutions. One-third of Britain's investment trusts are managed in Edinburgh, Glasgow, and Dundee. They have large investments in North America and specialized knowledge of conditions there. Unit trusts are represented in Edinburgh, where some leading British insurance companies also have their headquarters. The Scottish stock exchange was opened in Glasgow in 1971 to provide a single market for all Scottish stockbrokers.

Economic prospects. Scotland's economic problems have arisen partly from the decline of traditional, long-established industries, but they have also been aggravated by the economic policy of successive British governments, which has been geared to the needs of the prosperous regions of southeast England and the Midlands. Credit restrictions and other measures applied to curb inflation in the south and to correct the balance of payments deficit have been damaging to the Scottish economy, which required the reverse. Scotland tends to be slow to feel the benefits of a period of expansion and the first to suffer from credit squeezes. The handicaps of distance from large markets and of high transport costs are recognized in government policy for development areas. To persuade industrialists to set up business where labour is available, building grants and loans are offered, with special depreciation allowances and subsidies for training workers. These incentives have brought large undertakings to Scotland, such as automobile plants, an aluminum smelter at Invergordon, and a pulp mill at Fort William. Special development areas (those hit by mine closures or exceptionally high unemployment) can entice manufacturers by still higher grants, a five-year rent rebate, and a payroll subsidy of 30 percent for three years. A large part of western Scotland has been put in this category.

Incentives for development

TRANSPORTATION

Most public transport in Scotland is owned by state companies or local authorities. There is a certain amount of coordination; in 1968, for example, the Scottish Transport Group was created to bring under common control steamer services in the Clyde and the Western Isles and omnibus services throughout the country. Other forms of transport—rail, road haulage, and airlines—retain their own structure. Proliferation of automobiles has made it difficult for omnibus companies to maintain economic services in rural areas, where they are being either subsidized by local authorities and the government or withdrawn. The pattern of steamship services has greatly altered. Services from mainland ports to island towns have been curtailed and replaced by car ferries using short crossings, such as Oban to Craignure, in Mull, and Uig, in Skye, to Tarbert, in Harris.

Roads and railways. The road system extends to more than 29,000 miles. Despite gradual improvement, much of it, especially many miles of single-track roads in the Highlands, is inadequate for rapidly growing traffic. Since 1964 the Forth Road Bridge, the Tay Road Bridge, and the Kingston and Erskine bridges over the Clyde have been opened. Main roads, such as Carlisle–Glasgow, Edinburgh–Glasgow, Glasgow–Stirling, and Edinburgh–Perth, have been or are being reconstructed as motorways or dual carriageways. In 1971, 220 miles of such roads had been built, and by 1975 the total is expected to be 308 miles.

Railway services have been severely reduced since 1948, when more than 3,000 miles of track were open to passenger and freight traffic. Many branch lines and stations have been closed, so that by 1970 the route mileage had shrunk to 1,974. Diesel engines have replaced steam locomotives, and suburban lines from Glasgow on both sides of the Clyde and to Airdie in the east have been electrified. Electrification of the main line from Crewe to Glasgow was also in progress. Railway employees numbered under 25,000 in 1970, against well over 30,000 in 1966.

Shipping and air transport. Scottish ports handle many more imports than exports, a large proportion of which are sent abroad via English ports. In 1970 the volume of imports was 22,230,000 tons and of exports, 6,211,000 tons. Glasgow, the largest port, is under the administration of the Clyde Port Authority. The Forth ports, including Grangemouth and Leith, are grouped under the Forth Ports Authority, while Dundee and Aberdeen are independent. Greenock and Grangemouth are equipped for container traffic, and extensive improvement schemes have been carried out at Leith and other ports. Projects are under consideration to exploit deep water at Hunterston, in Ayr County, for an iron-ore and general-traffic port. Coastal trade has dwindled because of the competition of motor transport, and inland waterways have never been a commercial success. The Forth and Clyde Canal is closed, and the Caledonian Ship Canal is used only by small craft.

Major ports

Air transport is expanding steadily. The major airports are Abbotsinch (Glasgow), owned by Glasgow Corporation, and Prestwick and Edinburgh, both operated by the British Airports Authority. Transatlantic services fly from Prestwick, on the west coast, which is remarkably fog free, and Abbotsinch and Edinburgh are used for domestic services in the U.K. and to a lesser extent for flights to European cities. The Highlands and Islands have eight airfields, but the services to them from Edinburgh and Abbotsinch are unprofitable and are operated by British European Airways for social reasons. Freight traffic is developing at Prestwick, where cargo valued at £105,000,000 was carried in 1970.

ADMINISTRATION AND SOCIAL CONDITIONS

Government. Scotland is represented in the United Kingdom Parliament by just over 70 members, and since the election of 1964 all Scottish peers have been entitled to sit in the House of Lords. The secretary of state for Scotland is responsible to Parliament for departments under his jurisdiction. These consist of the Home and Health Department, the Education Department, the Department of Agriculture and Fisheries, and the Development Department. In his multifarious functions the secretary of state is assisted by a minister of state and three parliamentary undersecretaries. In the House of Commons, bills relating solely to Scotland are referred to the Scottish Grand Committee, which consists of all Scottish MP's, plus a number of English MP's, so that the committee reflects the political balance of the House. The Grand Committee has a general debate on the bill and usually sends it for detailed examination to the Scottish Standing Committee, a smaller body of some 30 Scottish MP's, reinforced as necessary by non-Scottish members. The Grand Committee also spends eight days in each session discussing the Scottish estimates (proposals for expenditure).

Political parties. The two major parties, Labour and Conservative, have separate organizations in Scotland, hold annual conferences, and take notice of Scottish grievances and problems. They have no distinctive Scottish policy but rather adapt general proposals to Scottish purposes. The Conservatives have a devolutionary plan for a Scottish convention, an elected body that would sit in Scotland and deal with preliminary stages of legislation. In the 1955 general election the Conservatives won 36 and Labour 34 of the 71 Scottish seats. Afterward, the Conservatives lost ground, holding only 20 seats in the 1966 election and 23 in 1970. Labour returned 46 MP's in 1966 and 44 in 1970, becoming clearly established as the dominant party in Scotland. Their strength lies in industrial areas, chiefly Glasgow, Lanark County, Dundee, Falkirk, and the large Fife burghs. The Conservatives are entrenched in rural constituencies, such as Galloway, East Fife, and Banff County. The Scottish Liberal Party, which stands for federal home rule for Scotland, also holds rural seats. Full self-government, including control of defense and foreign policy, is advocated by the Scottish National Party (SNP). Its support grew in the early 1960s, and its success in a parliamentary by-election in 1967, winning the apparently impregnable Labour seat at Hamilton, near Glasgow, led to a surge of nationalism. The party enrolled a large membership and won over 100 seats in the 1968 municipal elections, but the wave subsided as rapidly as it rose, and in 1971 the SNP lost nearly all its municipal gains. There is a widespread, vague desire

Move to self-government

for Scottish control of domestic affairs, but it has never been successfully organized to challenge the power of established parties. Nearly a third of the members of the British Communist Party are in Scotland, but their political influence is negligible; the party had no MP's in the early 1970s, and its vote in the Scottish Parliamentary election was usually below 1 percent. A few Communists, however, are prominent trade union leaders.

Local government. The local government structure of Scotland consists of four cities and 33 counties (formerly shires), which are all-purpose authorities. Large burghs, with a population of 30,000 or more, control all functions except education and valuation of property. Small burghs deal with housing, cleansing, and water supply, and district councils in rural areas have minor responsibilities for local amenities. Some services, such as police and fire, are organized on a regional basis and administered by joint committees of the local authorities concerned. The feeling that local units are too small and that better services can be provided more economically by larger authorities has led to proposals for a reorganization of local government. As a result of the report in 1969 of a Royal Commission on local government, the government published its proposals for reform in 1971. The country would be divided into eight regions and 49 districts, while the Orkney and Shetland islands would retain their present status. Local authorities are financed partly by government grants and partly by the yield of local taxes levied on householders, commercial properties, and industrial subjects, the last paying only 50 percent of the tax. In 1968–69 the government met nearly 57 percent of local expenditures; grants amounted to £207,629,000 and the revenue from taxes to £157,440,000.

Justice. In law Scotland has preserved its own system and courts. The Lord Advocate and the Solicitor General for Scotland are the ministers responsible for justice; they advise the government on legal affairs and help to draft legislation. The Lord Advocate is responsible for criminal prosecutions in all courts except burgh courts, which are composed of magistrates who, like justices of the peace, deal with minor offenses. More serious offenses may be tried in sheriff courts. The country is divided into 12 sheriffdoms, each with a sheriff principal and a varying number of sheriffs substitute. Offenses triable by jury

High
Court
of
Justiciary

are reserved for the High Court of Justiciary, the supreme court for criminal cases. The judges are the same as those of the Court of Session, the supreme court for civil cases. An appeal may be directed to the House of Lords from the Court of Session, but not from the High Court of Justiciary. The Court of Session, consisting of the Lord President, the Lord Justice Clerk, and 16 other judges, sits in Edinburgh and is divided into Inner and Outer houses. The Outer House judges hear cases at first instance. The Inner House, of which there are two divisions, each of four judges, hears appeals from the Outer House and from inferior courts. The sheriff courts have a wide jurisdiction in civil cases, but certain actions, such as divorce, are reserved for the Court of Session. The police investigate cases of crime discovered by or made known to them, but the decision whether or not to prosecute is made by the Lord Advocate in the High Court, by procurator fiscals in the sheriff courts, and by burgh prosecutors in the burgh courts.

Military services. Scotsmen serve in the Royal Navy and the Royal Air Force (RAF). There is a naval base at Rosyth, in Fife, which services nuclear submarines, a NATO base on the Clyde, and an RAF station at Kinloss, in Moray. But Scotland's defense associations are primarily with the army. The infantry regiments, especially the Highland regiments, the Queen's Own Highlanders, the Black Watch, the Gordon Highlanders, and the Argyll and Sutherland Highlanders, with their colourful uniforms and pipe bands, embody the military traditions of the country. The Royal Scots are proud of being the oldest infantry regiment in the British Army.

The social milieu. *Education.* In Scotland, education is supervised by the Education Department and administered by education committees of local authorities. Unlike the English system, fee-charging, independent "pub-

lic schools" play only a minor role in Scottish education. In 1969–70 the school population was almost 1,000,000, but only 22,600 attended direct-grant schools (schools, mostly in Edinburgh and Glasgow, that get a government grant to supplement the fees paid by pupils). Though education authorities were informed in 1971 that they were no longer required to organize secondary education on comprehensive lines (*i.e.*, in comprehensive schools providing several types of secondary education —academic, vocational, technical—in one building), this system has been widely adopted, especially in urban areas. A shortage of teachers has been a constant problem in postwar years, though their numbers have risen steadily. By the early 1970s there were over 46,000 qualified teachers employed full-time.

Health and welfare services. Health and welfare services and housing are the joint responsibility of government departments and local authorities. The health service is administered on the same lines as in the rest of the U.K., and local authorities make provision for the welfare of mothers, children, and the aged. Standards of health are rising; tuberculosis has almost disappeared, and by 1970 infant mortality had been reduced to 19.6 per 1,000, the lowest rate ever recorded. Cancer and heart disease are now the major causes of mortality. Cancer caused nearly 20 percent of all deaths and heart diseases almost 35 percent of the total in 1970. Incomes rise continuously, more because of inflation than real increases, but they are lower in Scotland than in the U.K. as a whole. Average weekly earnings of manual workers doubled between 1960 and 1970, but the Scottish average in 1970 was 96.4 percent of that for the U.K., though the gap narrowed from 1960. Incomes from profits and professional services are also below the U.K. levels, and there are more people in the lower income groups and fewer in the higher ones than in the U.K. as a whole. Only in investment income is Scotland almost on equal terms.

Income
differentials

Housing. No social problem causes more concern in Scotland than housing. Since 1919 well over 1,000,000 houses have been built, but that has not been enough to eradicate the legacy of substandard, overcrowded houses, lacking proper conveniences, bequeathed by the Industrial Revolution in the 18th century. Despite much demolition and rebuilding, nearly a quarter of Glasgow's 315,000 houses are below statutory tolerable standards. Scotland differs from England in that far more houses are built by local authorities than by private enterprise for sale. In 1970 a record total of 44,537 houses were finished, of which only 18.5 percent were erected by private builders, compared with 47.9 percent in the U.K. Because most new houses are owned by local authorities, the cost in subsidies from the exchequer and from taxes is high and Scottish local authorities are commonly criticized for charging unduly low rents. In order to lessen the demand on public funds, the government has introduced a scheme for raising the rents of local-authority houses, with rent rebates for tenants unable to pay the higher charges.

Police forces. Since the secretary of state has a general responsibility for law and order, he shares control of the police forces with local authorities. The police committees provide the buildings and equipment needed by the forces. The secretary of state, assisted by the chief inspector of constabulary, is concerned with efficiency and discipline; he approves the appointment of chief constables and can make regulations on conditions of service.

CULTURAL LIFE AND INSTITUTIONS

The cultural milieu. Scotland's culture is in an indeterminate state. It could be argued that there is not a national culture but only a regional variation of a wider British culture. Scottish culture does have stirrings of independence. Although it is perhaps dominated by the intellectual and artistic influences of London, its cultural institutions and achievements transcend the provincial level. The Edinburgh International Festival of Music and Drama in scale and quality is an outstanding event in the cultural calendar. Scotland's own contribution to it is modest but creditable, and it has probably had a good effect in raising the standards of artistic performance. The Scottish National Orchestra has a higher reputation than it has ever had; the Scottish Opera has earned glowing praise in its short career, and the Scottish Ballet promises to reach the same standard of excellence. These and other enterprises are subsidized by the Scottish Arts Council, which disbursed £932,000 in 1970–71 in supporting theatres, concerts, and exhibitions, besides giving grants or scholarships to individual artists. Scottish writers have the choice of three languages: Gaelic, Lallans (or Scots vernacular), and English. Gaelic is understood by only a small minority (180,978 Gaelic speakers, mostly in western Ross, the Hebrides, and Glasgow, were recorded in the 1961 census), but at least two Gaelic poets, Sorely Maclean and George Campbell Hay, are highly esteemed. Hugh MacDiarmid, the poet, nationalist, and Marxist, the most prominent exponent of Lallans, achieved an international reputation, but the Lallans revival has faded. English is the tongue of most poets, such as Norman MacCaig, and of popular novelists and dramatists. Scottish painting and sculpture are flourishing, as the annual exhibition of the Royal Scottish Academy proves. Folk songs and music are popular and are collected by the School of Scottish Studies, which is attached to the University of Edinburgh; it is also responsible for two great works of scholarship, *A Dictionary of the Older Scottish Tongue* and *The Scottish National Dictionary*, which are nearing completion. Edinburgh houses cultural institutions of notable prominence, such as the National Library of Scotland, which has a statutory right to receive copies of all books published in Britain. It has about 2,000,000 printed books and a large collection of manuscripts. The National Gallery of Scotland has paintings by many famous European artists in addition to works by Allan Ramsay, Sir Henry Raeburn, and other Scottish painters. The National Portrait Gallery portrays the principal personages in Scotland's history, and the Scottish National Gallery of Modern Art has works by contemporary European painters and sculptors, as well as those of native artists. The National Museum of Antiquities contains archaeological and later evidence for the development of the material and domestic aspects of Scottish society. The Royal Scottish Museum, perhaps the most popular of all, has extensive collections in its departments of art and archaeology, natural history, technology, and geology. The galleries and museums are the responsibility of the secretary of state and are maintained by public funds.

Universities, too, may be included among Scotland's cultural institutions, though their main object is research and the training of students. They give increasing attention to the study of Scottish history, literature, and politics, though the extent varies from university to university. There are now eight universities; in 1960 there were only four. The University of Strathclyde in Glasgow and the Heriot-Watt University in Edinburgh, formerly technological colleges, were upgraded to universities, retaining their scientific and technological emphasis. The University of Dundee was separated from the University of St. Andrews, which had some departments in Dundee. The University of Stirling, the only completely new foundation, was opened in 1967 on an estate near Stirling. All the other universities are growing in numbers and in the scope of the curriculum. The new universities do not teach law and divinity but place most emphasis on science and technology and have close links with science-based industries in their neighbourhood. Edinburgh, famous for its medical school, is the largest of the universities, with a student population of over 10,000. Though the constitutions of the universities vary, nearly all have rectors, elected by the students, and student representative councils.

The media. *The press.* The Scottish press has tended to shrink in size because of rising costs and competition, but newspapers survive in sufficient variety of quality and popular appeal. There are Scottish editions printed in Glasgow of London's *Daily Express* and the *Sunday Express*, and northern editions of other London newspapers are imported. Among indigenous newspapers, *The*

Scotsman and the *Glasgow Herald* rank highest in antiquity and influence, giving a sound coverage of Scottish and international news and well-informed explanations and comment. Glasgow has also the *Daily Record*, a Scottish version of the London *Daily Mirror*, while Dundee and Aberdeen have well-established morning papers. There are two evening papers in Glasgow and one each in the other three major cities. The *Sunday Post*, read by more than 1,000,000, is something of an institution, owing to its individual features, especially cartoons, and its somewhat conservative views. The 155 weekly newspapers have a local range, but the venerable *People's Journal* has many local editions and circulates throughout the country. In the illustrated periodical class, four monthly magazines—*Scottish Field, Scotland's Magazine, Scots Magazine,* and *Scotland*—vividly display Scotland's scenic beauty and provide a wealth of interest for outdoor enthusiasts.

Television and radio. Television and radio are probably more influential media than the press. The British Broadcasting Corporation (BBC) broadcasts Gaelic news, music, and church services, perhaps more than the number of Gaelic-speakers would warrant. There is a good deal of Scottish dance music, songs, gardening talks, sport, and religious services on the radio and Scottish news, sport, and occasional features on television. The BBC is well disposed toward Scottish culture, but its Scottish material hardly does more than flavour programs supplied for the greater part from London. Scottish Television Ltd., a commercial company, scarcely ventures beyond sport and discussions in its specifically Scottish program content, and its contribution to Scottish culture is minimal.

Sport and recreation. Sport plays a large part in the life of Scotland. Though support is dwindling, football is still the national game. It is dominated by the Glasgow clubs, Celtic and Rangers; their rivalry is sharpened by religion, Roman Catholics supporting Celtic and Protestants supporting Rangers. Their encounters are sometimes marred by hooliganism, but the number of incidents among crowds of 100,000 or so is small. Most spectators have no interest in the religious feud, which is largely a matter of tradition. Internationally, Scotland's football prestige is tested in the World Cup contests. Rugby Union football, still a pastime for amateurs, is played by former pupils of the Edinburgh and Glasgow private schools, but in the Border towns it is one of the most popular games. Rugby internationals played at Murrayfield, in Edinburgh, attract large crowds. Hockey, tennis, and swimming are common pastimes; and athletics are enjoyed at Edinburgh's splendid sports stadium. Golf, however, is a more popular game and is within the reach of all, not only the affluent, as in many other countries. There are many municipal courses, as well as private clubs, most of which have moderate subscriptions. The Old Course at St. Andrews, Fife, is the most famous of the excellent seaside courses that abound in Scotland, especially on the links of Ayr County. As a result, Scottish golfers play creditably in international competitions, though they seldom win the top awards. For hill walking, rock climbing, and sailing Scotland has natural advantages, as for golf. Skiing has been developed in the Cairngorms; the necessary accommodations and equipment are there, but snow conditions are not as dependable as they are in countries with higher altitudes. Summer sports, many unique to Scotland, are provided by the Highland Games. Strong men toss the caber (a heavy pole) and perform other feats of strength; pipers play, and agile men and girls do Highland dances. The colour of the tartan and the panache of kilted pipe bands fascinate tourists, and the Braemar Gathering, in Aberdeen County, always attended by a royal party from Balmoral Castle, is the culmination of these displays. Many Scots find these games and other traditions, such as Burns suppers (after Robert Burns, the 18th-century national poet) and eating haggis (a delicacy consisting of offal boiled in a sheep's stomach), a self-conscious parade of legendary characteristics that have little to do with ordinary Scottish life—a show put on, like national costumes, to gratify the expectations of tourists. This objection can hardly be levelled against the National Mod, a musical festival run annually by An Comunn Gaidhealach, a society that hopes to keep Gaelic alive by competition among choirs and soloists in singing Gaelic songs and by bards in composing Gaelic verses.

THE OUTLOOK

By the early 1970s the Scottish economy was at a low ebb. Unemployment, more than 150,000, was higher than it has been since before World War II. Recovery was anticipated, however, and some Scots hoped that entry into the European Economic Community might work an economic miracle. But no decisions of any importance, political or economic, are made in Edinburgh or Glasgow. Few sizeable firms now remain in Scottish hands: most are subsidiaries of English or U.S. companies. Economic as well as political independence is lost, and able, ambitious Scots are attracted by the greater opportunities and rewards of London. Economic growth may or may not be achieved, but excessive centralization in the U.K., along with cosmopolitan and Anglicizing influences, are gradually effacing the traces of Scottish nationality. Unless there is a vigorous and unexpected revival, Scotland may become no more than a geographical expression.

BIBLIOGRAPHY. The *Reader's Guide to Scotland*, a bibliography published by the NATIONAL BOOK LEAGUE (1968), provides annotated lists of works on history, education, administration, law, the economy, sport, and other subjects. A similar bibliography for *The Highlands and Islands of Scotland* was produced by the NATIONAL BOOK LEAGUE in 1967. Excellent articles on the geography of Scottish regions appear in J.G. MITCHELL (ed.), *Great Britain: Geographical Essays* (1962). Among innumerable books on topography, MORAY MCLAREN, *The Shell Guide to Scotland* (1965), an informative gazetteer; CALUM MACLEAN, *The Highlands* (1959), written by a Gaelic-speaking Highlander; and W.H. MURRAY, *The Hebrides* (1966), are notable for text and illustrations. The "County Books Series" and the "Queen's Scotland Series" are sound introductions to counties and regions. Political history since 1870 is surveyed in J.G. KELLAS, *Modern Scotland* (1968). H.J. PATON, *The Claim of Scotland* (1968), puts a philosopher's case for self-government; and H.J. HANHAM, *Scottish Nationalism* (1969), gives the movement's history, while the title of W.H. MARWICK, *A Short History of Labour in Scotland* (1967), is self-explanatory. The most recent study of the economy is T.L. JOHNSTON, N.K. BUXTON, and D. MAIR, *Structure and Growth of the Scottish Economy* (1971), a useful textbook. G. MCCRONE, *Scotland's Economic Progress, 1951–1960* (1965), covers the 1950s; the same author's *Scotland's Future: The Economics of Nationalism* (1969), deals with the financial controversies about self-government. *Scottish Administration: A Handbook*, rev. ed. (HMSO 1967), succinctly describes the work of government departments in Scotland and the courts of law. SIR DAVID MILNE, *The Scottish Office and Other Scottish Government Departments* (1958), deals with the same subject more fully. The *Report of the Royal Commission on Local Government* (HMSO 1969) and the *White Paper on Reform of Local Government in Scotland* (HMSO 1971) review the present system of local administration and proposals for reorganizing it. On family history, R.W. MUNRO, *Kinsmen and Clansmen* (1971), is a handy reference book; and ROBERT BAIN, *The Clans and Tartans of Scotland*, rev. ed. (1964), is a standard work. J. TELFER DUNBAR, *The History of Highland Dress* (1962), is an authoritative guide. J.B. KIRKWOOD, *The Regiments of Scotland* (1949), is a general account, and there are histories of individual regiments, including the series on "Famous Regiments" published by Hamish Hamilton. On the arts, IAN FINLAY, *Scottish Crafts* (1948); and S. CURSITER, *Scottish Art to the Close of the Nineteenth Century* (1949), are concise introductions; FRANCIS COLLINSON, *The Traditional and National Music of Scotland* (1966); and D. GLEN, *Hugh MacDiarmid (Christopher Murray Grieve) and the Scottish Renaissance* (1964), give more extensive treatment of their subjects. Census reports and the annual reports of the Registrar General for Scotland, of the Departments of Education, Agriculture, Home and Health, and Development, and the Electricity Boards, Coal Boards, and other state industries are valuable sources of information, as is the *Digest of Scottish Statistics* published twice yearly from 1953 to 1971 and now replaced by the twice-yearly *Scottish Economic Bulletin and the annual Scottish Abstract of Statistics*.

(Ma.J.M.)

Scott, Sir Walter

The life and achievement of Sir Walter Scott, as well as his reputation, form a mass of contrasts and paradoxes. He was, at one and the same time, a sensible 18th-century Edinburgh intellectual and a pioneer of the Romantic movement; a conservative who celebrated the greatness of beggars, outcasts, and madmen; a rationalist constantly fascinated by superstitions, omens, and prophecies; an "incorrigible Jacobite" (a supporter of the House of Stuart's claim to the throne of England and Scotland against those of the ruling House of Hanover) who acted as master of ceremonies for George IV's Scottish coronation tour; an immensely successful writer, earning vast sums, who went bankrupt; a man of simple tastes and of reckless extravagances.

By courtesy of the National Portrait Gallery, London

Scott, oil painting by Sir Edwin Henry Landseer, 1824. In the National Portrait Gallery, London.

Perhaps Scott's greatest achievement as a novelist and his most important contribution to the study of history lay in his idea of the clash of cultures. While the Augustan writers of 18th-century England tended to assume that human nature was everywhere the same and that there was only one kind of civilization, the Greco-Roman, to which the alternative was barbarism, Scott demonstrated in his novels that there are many different kinds of civilization, and his favourite device of plot is to place his hero between two cultures, feeling the pull of a double loyalty. For Scott this involved much more than a simple moral problem. It involved completely contrasted ways of living, thinking, and feeling. So it is that the dilemma of the hero of *Waverley*, between the Jacobite and the Hanoverian cause, or of the hero of *Old Mortality*, torn between loyalty to the rebels of the Scottish lowlands and loyalty to the English king, takes on a wide historical significance; as many later historians have testified, these personal dilemmas bring to life the essential history of the times with which they deal.

The clash of cultures theme in Scott's novels

Scott was born in Edinburgh on August 15, 1771. His father was a lawyer, descended from a long line of country gentry, and his mother was the daughter of a physician. From his earliest years, Scott was fond of listening to his elderly relatives on both sides of the family, and he derived much historical material from these accounts and stories. Though bookish and in his way a distinguished scholar, Scott always preferred to rely for his historical impressions upon oral tradition. That is one reason why, though he wrote about many different centuries and often used a medieval setting, all his best books deal with Scotland and with times within a century and a half of his own.

Like many other famous Scots writers, he was educated at the high school at Edinburgh and also for a time at the grammar school at Kelso. He was then apprenticed to his father as writer to the signet, a Scots equivalent of the English solicitor (attorney). His study and practice of law were somewhat desultory, for his immense youthful energy was never directed into a single channel. He

Study and practice of law

became a traveller, a volunteer cavalryman (the Napoleonic wars were fought during most of his youth and early middle age), an antiquary, and a voracious reader in several languages—Italian, Spanish, French, German, and Latin. After a very deeply felt early disappointment in love, he married on December 24, 1797, Charlotte Carpenter, of a French royalist family, with whom he lived happily until her death in 1826. His antiquarian studies bore fruit in 1802–03 with *Minstrelsy of the Scottish Border*. In this work, Scott was playing a part in a wider movement of recovery of ancient British poetry in which the 18th-century English scholar Bishop Thomas Percy and others had preceded him. He also began to develop his work as a journalist, contributing to the very influential *Edinburgh Review*, and as a poet, publishing in 1805 *The Lay of the Last Minstrel*. At this time he was the intimate friend of several eminent English writers, notably William Wordsworth and Robert Southey; and he was later to become the trusted friend of Lord Byron. To be liked by both Wordsworth and Byron and to admire the work of both was unusual but also characteristic. It was natural to Scott to like people and to relish the strangeness of eccentric characters. His hospitable nature and thorough enjoyment of many forms of society helped to make him one of the best loved men of his time.

In the next years his popularity as a poet continued to advance. He wrote in verse with great ease and fluency, and his work showed a power of lively description and honest pathos. Nevertheless, he is essentially a minor poet, a fact he knew very well. Scott even warned his daughter against reading his poetry because it was so bad. More signifiant in some ways than his verse was his 1808 edition of the poetic works of John Dryden. It was typical of his balance and independence that he never subscribed to the fashionable Romantic denigration of the great Augustans such as Dryden.

Turning point in his literary career

The turning point of his literary career came in the early summer of 1814, when, with extraordinary speed, he wrote almost the whole of his novel *Waverley*. It was one of the rare and happy cases in literary history when something original and powerful was immediately recognized and enjoyed by a large public. A story of the Jacobite rebellion of 1745, it reinterpreted and presented with living force the manners and loyalties of a lost Highland civilization. The book was published anonymously, as were all its many successors down to 1827. The reason for anonymity has been difficult to ascertain. Some knew and many guessed that Scott was the author, but he boldly denied it and seemed to enjoy the prolonged cat-and-mouse game with the public, which his position as the "Great Unknown" entailed. After *Waverley*, there followed a rapid series of distinguished books; and much of his best work—including *Guy Mannering, Old Mortality*, and *The Heart of Midlothian*—was published in the next four or five years. It was Scott's habit to do most of his writing very early in the morning while the rest of the household was asleep. So there is the odd paradox that, while he was writing with a speed and expense of energy that did permanent damage to his health, he always seemed to have most of the day to spare for his friends and for his personal interests.

Scott's immense earnings in those years contributed to his financial downfall. Eager to own an estate and to act the part of a bountiful laird (lord), he anticipated his income and involved himself in exceedingly complicated and ultimately disastrous financial agreements with publishers. The great financial collapse of 1826, one of the worst of the century, found him defenseless, and he spent the rest of his life under the stigma of bankruptcy. Everyone, including his creditors, paid tribute to the selfless honesty with which he set himself to work to pay all his huge debts. Unfortunately, though, the corollary was reckless haste in the production of all his later works. After the notable recreation of the end of the Jacobite era in *Redgauntlet* (1824), he produced nothing equal to his best early work, though his rapidity and ease of writing remained largely unimpaired, as did his popularity. In his later years he began writing a journal, and the picture it

gives of his life after 1825 is a sad one, in which bereavement, ill health, financial disgrace, and gloom about public affairs all combine to darken the picture. However, there were consolations. His creditors were not hard with him, everyone believed in his honesty, and he was generally revered as the grand old man of English letters. His courage, his humour, and his modesty show attractively in these last personal writings.

On February 23, 1827, the authorship of the "Waverley" novels was finally made public. Characteristically, Scott said that he had now ceased to be the "Great Unknown" and became the "Small Known." In 1831 his health deteriorated sharply, and he tried a Continental tour with a long stay at Naples to aid recovery. But, while abroad, he had a further attack of apoplexy. He was taken home and died on September 21, 1832. His biographer J.G. Lockhart records that "Almost every newspaper that announced this event in Scotland, and many in England, had the signs of mourning usual on the demise of a king."

MAJOR WORKS

POETRY: *The Lay of the Last Minstrel* (1805); *Ballads and Lyrical Pieces* (1806); *Marmion: A Tale of Flodden Field* (1808); *The Lady of the Lake* (1810); *The Vision of Don Roderick* (1811); *Rokeby* (1813); *The Bridal of Triermain* (1813); *The Lord of the Isles* (1815); *Harold the Dauntless* (1817).

NOVELS: *Waverley* (1814); *Guy Mannering* (1815); *The Antiquary* (1816); *The Black Dwarf* and *Old Mortality* (*Tales of My Landlord*, first series; 1816); *Rob Roy* (1818); *The Heart of Midlothian* (*Tales of My Landlord*, second series; 1818); *The Bride of Lammermoor* and *A Legend of Montrose* (*Tales of My Landlord*, third series; 1819); *Ivanhoe* (1819); *The Monastery* (1820); *The Abbot* (1820); *Kenilworth* (1821); *The Pirate* (1822); *The Fortunes of Nigel* (1822); *Peveril of the Peak* (1822); *Quentin Durward* (1823); *St. Ronan's Well* (1824); *Redgauntlet* (1824); *The Betrothed* and *The Talisman* (*Tales of the Crusaders*; 1825); *Woodstock* (1826); *The Highland Widow, The Two Drovers,* and *The Surgeon's Daughter* (*Chronicles of the Canongate*, first series; 1827); *St. Valentine's Day; or, The Fair Maid of Perth* (*Chronicles of the Canongate*, second series; 1828); *Anne of Geierstein* (1829); *Count Robert of Paris* and *Castle Dangerous* (*Tales of My Landlord*, fourth series; 1832).

PLAYS: *Halidon Hill* (1822); *Macduff's Cross* (1823); *The Doom of Devorgoil, a Melodrama* (1830); *Auchindrane; or, The Ayrshire Tragedy* (1830).

OTHER PROSE: Essays on "Chivalry" (1818), "The Drama" (1819), and "Romance" (1824), contributed to the *Encyclopædia Britannica; Paul's Letters to His Kinsfolk* (1816); *Description of the Regalia of Scotland* (1819); "Lives of the Novelists" in *Ballantyne's Novelists' Library* (1821–24); *Provincial Antiquities of Scotland* (1826); *The Life of Napoleon Buonaparte* (1827); *Tales of a Grandfather: Being Stories Taken from Scottish History*, 4 vol. (1828–30); *History of Scotland* (1829–30); *Letters on Demonology and Witchcraft* (1830); *Essays on Ballad Poetry* (1830).

BIBLIOGRAPHY

Editions: The Waverley Novels, 25 vol. (Centenary Edition, 1870–71); *The Letters of Sir Walter Scott*, ed. by H.J.C. GRIERSON (1932); *Miscellaneous Prose Works of Sir Walter Scott, Bart.*, 28 vol. (1834–36); *The Journal of Sir Walter Scott, 1825–32*, ed. by J.G. TAIT, 3 vol. (1939–46; reprinted in one vol., 1950).

Biography and criticism: J.G. LOCKHART, *Memoirs of the Life of Sir Walter Scott*, 7 vol. (1837), is a full, intimate, and fascinating biography by Scott's son-in-law; H.J.C. GRIERSON, *Sir Walter Scott* (1932), criticizes and corrects Lockhart at various points. EDWIN MUIR, *Scott and Scotland* (1936), is a very acute analysis of Scott's relation to Scottish literature and of his use of the English and Scots languages. DONALD DAVIE, *The Heyday of Sir Walter Scott* (1961), analyzes Scott's debt to Maria Edgeworth and others and gives critical studies of some of the novels. See also EDGAR JOHNSON, *Sir Walter Scott: The Great Unknown*, 2 vol. (1970), a very full and detailed piece of research; and A.O.J. COCKSHUT, *The Achievement of Walter Scott* (1969).

(A.O.J.C.)

Scrophulariales

Economically, Scrophulariales, an order of flowering plants, is prominent for the many ornamentals it contains; for important food plants (*e.g.*, potato, tomato); for well-known drugs (atropine, scopolamine, digitalis);

for certain agriculturally significant parasitic weeds (broomrapes, witchweeds); and for tobacco. The order contains 18 families, about 870 genera, and about 11,800 species. In variety of form and colour, some flowers of the order rival the orchids.

GENERAL FEATURES

Members of the order Scrophulariales occur on most of the landmasses of the Earth, with the exception of Antarctica. About two-thirds of the species are found in the tropics, one-third in temperate regions. About 50 species occur in the Arctic; of these, only a few species of lousewort (*Pedicularis*) reach the most northern lands.

In life-span, members of the order range from short-lived desert herbs to long-lived tropical trees. Many are annuals; *i.e.*, plants that complete a life cycle from seed to seed in a single growing season and withstand unfavourable seasons in seed form. A few are biennials, plants that produce flowers and fruit the second year and then die. Most, however, are perennials, plants that live several years and withstand adverse seasons by means of underground parts (*e.g.*, the herbaceous perennials) or by means of long-lived above ground parts (*e.g.*, woody perennials). Of the perennials, most are polycarpic (*i.e.*, they come into flower year after year). A few are monocarpic and live for several years—15 to 20 in certain cases (*e.g.*, *Boea*)—before flowering and then die after flowering once.

Drawing by M. Pahl

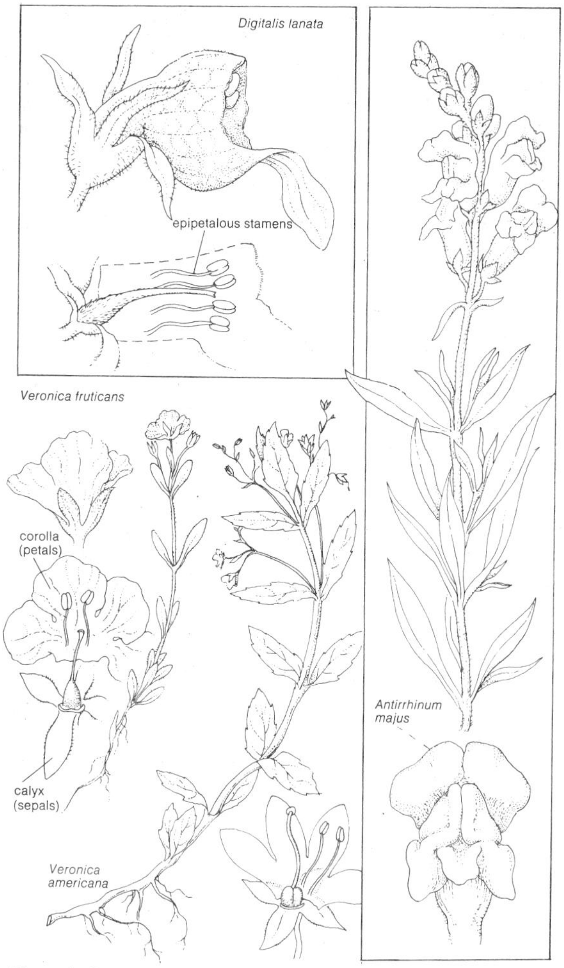

Figure 1: Some representative members of the family Scrophulariaceae, the largest family in the order Scrophulariales.

Size range and diversity of structure. The plants range in size from the diminutive aquatic bladderwort, *Utricularia olivacea*, one of the smallest in bulk of all flowering plants, with threadlike stems to about four inches (ten centimetres) in length with a very few minute leaves, to large trees, of which the largest may be the guayacan (*Tabebuia guayacan*), which reaches about 164 feet (50 metres) in height and 6.5 feet (two metres) in trunk diameter.

Flower size is also diverse. The smallest flowers are perhaps those of the aquatic *Micranthemum umbrosum*, about 0.06 inch (1.5 millimetres) in length. The largest are those of the tree daturas (*Datura*) and the related *Methysticodendron amesianum*, whose trumpet-shaped flowers grow to about 11 inches (28 centimetres) long and four to five (ten to 13 centimetres) wide.

Fruits of the order range from the minute globose capsules of *Micranthemum*, less than $\frac{1}{16}$ inch long (about one millimetre), to the elongated pods of the midnight horror, or Indian trumpet flower (*Oroxylum indicum*), two to four feet (60 to 120 centimetres) long but only about three inches (eight centimetres) wide, and the sausage-shaped fruits of the sausage tree (*Kigelia pinnata*), which attain three feet (90 centimetres) in length and sometimes exceed 15 pounds (seven kilograms) in weight.

About two-thirds of the species in the order are herbaceous—*i.e.*, nonwoody. Most of the woody species are shrubs. There are few woody vines except in the bignonia family (Bignoniaceae). Trees are few and most, except for some in the bignonia family, are small (40 feet or less in height).

Especially well known among the aquatic plants of the order are the bladderworts (*Utricularia*), which are among the few "carnivorous" plants and the only ones that capture their prey underwater. Most bladderworts produce, on their leaves, small, pear-shaped bladders provided with a trap door. These bladders trap micro-organisms, such as protozoans, crustaceans, worms, and even newly hatched fish. Within the bladders, the animals are digested, but whether this occurs by bacterial action or through the action of enzymes secreted by the plant is not certain. Nitrogenous end-products of the digestion are presumably absorbed by cells in the walls of the bladder and provide a nutritional supplement to the plant.

Parasitic species are known in 14 families of flowering plants. Two of these families, the broomrape family (Orobanchaceae) and the figwort family (Scrophulariaceae), are in the order Scrophulariales and contain all of the world's agriculturally important root parasites—*i.e.*, their roots are attached to the roots of their hosts by means of haustoria ("suckers"). Plants of the broomrape family are holoparasitic; *i.e.*, because they lack chlorophyll and are unable to carry on photosynthesis, they depend entirely upon their host for organic food materials. The broomrapes (*Orobanche*) are serious pests on various crop plants—tobacco, tomato, eggplant, hemp, and sunflowers—and on various fodder plants. *Aeginetia* attacks sugarcane in Asia. In the Philippines, sugarcane is parasitized also by *Christisonia*.

In the figwort family, parasitism is known in 26 genera. Among these, all degrees of parasitism exist, ranging from holoparasitism (*Harveya, Hyobanche*) to semiparasitism—in which the parasite, being green, can carry on photosynthesis but relies in greater or lesser degree upon the host for at least water and minerals. The most important of the parasites in the figwort family are the semiparasitic witchweeds (*Striga, Alectra*), which attack many grasses, including corn, sugarcane, rice, and sorghum, and certain broad-leaved plants, including peanuts, soybeans, and tobacco. An Old World native, the mealie witchweed (*Striga asiatica*) has appeared in the United States, where, starting in 1956, it was reported on corn in the Carolinas (see DISEASES OF PLANTS). Other well-known parasitic members of the figwort family are Indian paintbrushes (*Castilleja*), gerardias (*Agalinis, Aureolaria*), eyebrights (*Euphrasia*), bartsia (*Bartsia*), and yellow rattles (*Rhinanthus*), all semiparasitic.

All members of the broomrape family, so far as is known, and the witchweeds of the figwort family produce seeds that germinate only when close to a host root. They are stimulated to do so by substances secreted by the root. The emerging root of the parasite grows toward the host root and eventually may establish a haustorial union.

Marginal notes:

Life-span categories

Parasitic species

Epiphytes, plants that grow upon other plants for support, are infrequent in the order except in the family Gesneriaceae, which also includes species that grow on rocks. Many of these plants have tubers (thickened storage stems, such as potatoes) that function apparently as water-storage organs.

Drawing by M. Pahl

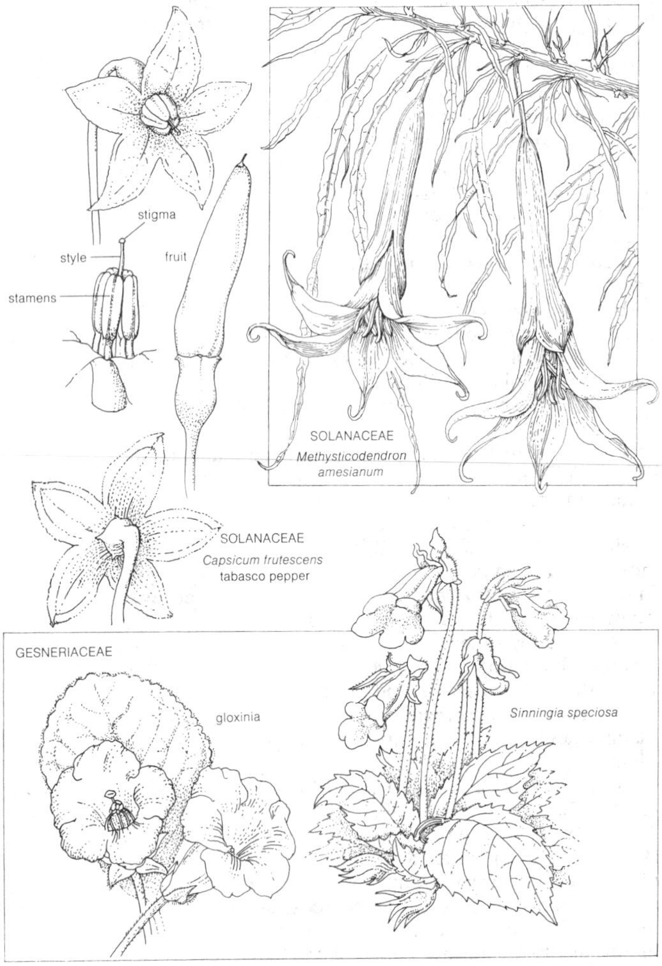

stigma

style   fruit

stamens

SOLANACEAE
Methysticodendron
amesianum

SOLANACEAE
Capsicum frutescens
tabasco pepper

GESNERIACEAE

gloxinia

Sinningia speciosa

Figure 2: Representative plants from two of the large families of the order Scrophulariales.

Economic importance. *Ornamentals.* Ornamental herbaceous plants (annuals, biennials, and perennials), shrubs, trees, and vines are well represented in the order Scrophulariales. Among the best known herbaceous garden and greenhouse plants are flowering tobacco (*Nicotiana*), datura (*Datura*), butterfly flower (*Schizanthus*), petunia (*Petunia*), apple of Peru (*Nicandra*), salpiglossis (*Salpiglossis*), calceolaria (*Calceolaria*), veronica (*Veronica*), mullein (*Verbascum*), penstemon (*Penstemon*), foxglove (*Digitalis*), snapdragon (*Antirrhinum*), torenia (*Torenia*), monkey flower (*Mimulus*), nemesia (*Nemesia*), African violet (*Saintpaulia*), gloxinia (*Sinningia*), and bear's-breech (*Acanthus*).

Ornamental shrubs of the order include: matrimony vine (*Lycium*), *Cestrum*, angel's-trumpet (*Datura*), *Hebe, Leucophyllum*, Cape fuchsia (*Phygelius*), desert willow (*Chilopsis*), caricature plant (*Graptophyllum*), and shrimp plant (*Beleperone*).

Members of the Scrophulariales are among the showiest of tropical ornamental trees. Among them are the jacaranda (*Jacaranda mimosifolia*), widely used as a street tree for its blue flowers and lovely foliage; the white-flowered Indian cork tree (*Millingtonia hortensia*), once described as the handsomest of India's flowering trees; the African tulip tree (*Spathodea campanulata*), with scarlet flowers; and the New World trumpet trees (*Tabebuia*), with white, pink, lavender, purple, red, or yellow flowers. In temperate regions the catalpas (*Catalpa*),

Orna-
mental
tree
species

with their white flowers and large leaves, and the princess tree (*Paulownia tomentosa*), with blue flowers, are well-known.

Both herbaceous and woody vines are frequent in the order. Some rank with the world's most beautiful flowering vines; including sky flower (*Thunbergia grandiflora*), with an abundance of sky-blue flowers; cat's-claw vine (*Doxantha unguis-cati*), golden yellow; flame vine (*Pyrostegia venusta*), orange; golden chalice (*Solandra maxima*), yellow; and Costa Rican nightshade (*Solanum wendlandii*), lilac blue and yellow. Woody vines are especially common in the bignonia family. Most of the vines in the order Scrophulariales are tropical but in the United States the native cross vine (*Bignonia capreolata*) and trumpet creeper (*Campsis radicans*) are well-known. Vines in the order support themselves by several means: by prickles on the stem (*Lycium*) or spines on the leaves (*Solanum*); by tendrils (*Bignonia*); by aerial clinging roots (*Campsis*); or simply by leaning on other plants.

Food plants. Food plants of the order include potato, tomato, eggplant, capsicum pepper, and sesame. The most important, and a basic food for millions of humans, is the potato (*Solanum tuberosum*). A potato is a tuber—*i.e*, a swollen portion of an underground stem. The potato was introduced into Europe from South America in the late 1500s and into the United States in the early 1620s. By the 19th century it had become a staple crop the world over, except in tropical lowlands.

The tomato (*Lycopersicon esculentum*), another New World contribution, was brought to southern Europe in the early 1500s and utilized there long before other Europeans accepted it. It was once even considered to be poisonous and was grown as a curiosity or an ornamental. By the end of the 19th century it had become a major vegetable crop.

The eggplant (*Solanum melongena*), native to India, is grown throughout warm regions for its purple, white, or yellow fruits, which are used as vegetables. The name eggplant refers to the egglike appearance of the fruits of certain white-fruited varieties, which were the first ones known to northern Europeans.

The only spice produced by a member of the order Scrophulariales is capsicum, or red pepper, derived from fruits of the genus *Capsicum,* native to tropical America. The many varieties differ in size, shape, colour, and pungency of the fruits. The fruits of some are used as a spice (*e.g.,* tabasco and paprika); those of others, the sweet, or green, peppers, are used as food.

Spice and
oil species

Cultivated for its edible, oil-rich seeds since antiquity, the sesame plant (*Sesamum orientale*), native to the Old World, is now grown in many warm regions. The oil is used largely in cooking; the seeds, in confections and as a garnish on baked goods.

Drug and narcotic plants. The order contains only a few drug plants, but they are important. In the potato family are the belladonna plant (*Atropa belladonna*), source of belladonna; henbane (*Hyoscyamus niger*), source of hyoscyamus; and jimsonweed (*Datura stramonium*), source of stramonium. Atropine, extracted from belladonna, and scopolamine, extracted from hyoscyamus, are much used in medicine. In the figwort family, the foxglove (*Digitalis purpurea*) is a source of digitalis.

Several members of the order have narcotic properties. These plants are members of the potato family. Best known are species of *Datura*, including jimsonweed and the tree daturas. Also narcotic is a relative of the tree daturas, *Methysticodendron amesianum*, unknown outside of one mountain valley in Colombia until the 1940s. The Aborigines of Australia utilized pituri, leaves of shrubs of the genus *Duboisia*, as a narcotic.

Tobacco, made from the cured leaves of *Nicotiana tabacum* (and to a much lesser extent, *N. rustica*), belongs to the potato family and is the world's most important material used for smoking. The tobacco plant, native to tropical America, is widely grown in temperate and tropical regions.

The order contains a number of poisonous plants.

Among the best known are the jimsonweeds (*Datura*), belladonna (*Atropa*), henbane (*Hyoscyamus*), tobaccos (*Nicotiana*), nightshades (*Solanum*), and foxglove (*Digitalis*). Even tomato and potato leaves are dangerous if fed to animals. Potato tubers that are turning green also contain poisons.

NATURAL HISTORY

Pollination. Pollination mechanisms in the order are varied. In addition to normally opening (chasmogamous) flowers, a few species regularly produce cleistogamous flowers; *i.e.*, flowers that never open but nonetheless develop viable seeds because they are self-pollinated in the bud. Such flowers characteristically are smaller and somewhat different in structure from chasmogamous flowers of the same species. In most members of the order Scrophulariales, the flowers open normally and then depend upon various agents for pollination. None is known to rely on water. A few species are wind-pollinated—*e.g.*, the plantains (*Plantago*), some of which are considered a cause of hayfever because they shed considerable pollen.

Insect pollination

Most members of the order rely on animals for pollination, especially insects, including bees, flies, moths, and butterflies. Some are pollinated by hummingbirds. A few are pollinated by bats; outstanding among these are the sausage tree (*Kigelia pinnata*) and the midnight horror (*Oroxylum indicum*).

Seed dispersal. The range of seed-dispersal mechanisms is great. In the family Acanthaceae seeds are thrown for short distances by the sudden—"explosive"—opening of the seed capsule. Most other plants of the order, however, rely upon external agents, such as wind, water, or animals, for dispersal. Those that are wind dispersed may have dustlike seeds or seeds with wings or netlike coats that increase their buoyancy. Those that are spread by water include some beach plants (*Nolana*), whose seeds owe their dispersal to sea drift. The seeds of animal-dispersed species are carried on or in animals. Small-seeded water plants are dispersed in the mud clinging to the feet of waterfowl. Fruits of species of the sesamum family (Pedaliaceae) and the family Martyniaceae may hook onto the feet and legs of grazing animals. Seeds of many species are eaten by birds and mammals and are voided undigested in the feces. Dispersal in this way is especially important for species that produce juicy, brightly coloured berries (*e.g.*, the nightshade, *Solanum dulcamara*). Seeds of a few members of the family Scrophulariaceae (*e.g.*, *Veronica*, *Melampyrum*, *Pedicularis*) are dispersed by ants, which seek the seeds for food. A portion of the seed, the "elaiosome," is white, oily, and edible. Such seeds are not only dispersed by the ants but can be planted by them as well—the ants carry them underground.

FORM AND FUNCTION

Vegetative characteristics. The leaves of most members of the order are simple. In few species—*e.g.*, in some louseworts (*Pedicularis*) and in tomato—they are pinnately compound (*i.e.*, each leaf has smaller leaflets arranged along both sides of a central axis). Leaf arrangement on the stem varies, being alternate, opposite, or, rarely, whorled or in rosettes. In certain members, the mature plant possesses but one leaf, up to 30 inches (76 centimetres) long and 22 inches (56 centimetres) wide, which has developed from growth of one of the two cotyledons, or "seed leaves"; the other cotyledon aborts early. This single-leaf condition is seen in several genera of the family Gesneriaceae (*e.g.*, *Streptocarpus*) in which the flowers develop on the leaf, at the base and on the midrib. Other, related species may produce a rosette of three or more leaves, the largest of which has developed from the one cotyledon.

The sesamum family and martynia family possess unique glandular ("mucilage") hairs, which secrete a mucilage responsible for the sticky feel of these plants.

Floral and fruiting characteristics. In arrangement of the flowers—*i.e.*, in the inflorescence type—the plants of the order are exceedingly diverse. The flowers of some are solitary and are borne in the axils of leaves, the upper angles between the stem and the leafstalks, as in the monkey flowers (*Mimulus*). Other solitary flowers are borne on long leafless stalks (scapes) that arise from a rosette of leaves, as in African violets (*Saintpaulia*) and butterworts (*Pinguicula*). In the majority, however, the flowers are grouped into clusters of various kinds.

Inflorescence types

Flowers. The flowers are almost always complete; *i.e.*, they have sepals (leafy parts), petals, stamens (male reproductive structures), and carpels (simple ovaries or segments of a compound ovary—the ovary and its upper portions, the style and stigma, form the female reproductive unit called the pistil). Flowers of the family Hydrostachyaceae, however, have either only one stamen or one pistil. In most members of the order the flowers are perfect (bisexual); *i.e.*, they contain both stamens and carpels. Imperfect (unisexual) flowers occur in the family Hydrostachyaceae and in *Littorella* of the plantain family (Plantaginaceae). The plants with imperfect flowers may be monoecious (flowers of both sexes occur on each plant—*e.g.*, *Littorella*) or dioecious (flowers of one sex only occur on each plant—*e.g.*, *Hydrostachys*). Flowers of the order Scrophulariales are generally irregular in shape, sometimes strikingly so. In plantains (*Plantago*), in many members of the potato family (Solanaceae), and in some members of the family Gesneriaceae, however, regular, or radially symmetrical, flowers occur. Most members of the order are hypogynous; *i.e.*, the flowers have superior ovaries. In such flowers, the sepals, petals, and stamens originate at a position at the base of the ovary. The families Trapellaceae, Columelliaceae, and some members of the Gesneriaceae, however, are epigynous; *i.e.*, the flowers have inferior ovaries—the ovaries are enclosed within the basal portions of the other flower parts, which appear to arise at the upper end of the ovary. The calyx, or collection of sepals, is regular to highly irregular. Typically it is composed of five free to variously united sepals. In some species, suppression of one or more sepals may occur, as in many veronicas (*Veronica*), in which the upper sepal is absent. In bladderworts (*Utricularia*), the calyx is strongly two lipped, the upper lip being formed from the union of three sepals and the lower lip from the union of two sepals; the whole suggests a calyx of only two parts. In the plantain family there are only four sepals.

The corolla (the collection of petals) is regular in the plantain family, nolana family (Nolanaceae), many species of the potato family, and in a few species of the gesneria family; in the rest of the order it is irregular, sometimes highly so. Typically it is composed of five united petals. The union ranges from little—only at the base, so that the five-petalled condition is evident—to complete—so that the five-petalled condition is obscure. The corolla, when composed of completely fused petals, is more or less trumpet- or funnel-shaped as in jimsonweed (*Datura*). In some of the highly irregular flowers of the order, the five-petalled condition is also obscure. The lowermost petals may, as in some linarias (*Linaria*) and in all bladderworts, bear a backwardly projecting spur. In many species the corolla is more or less two lipped; the upper lip is composed of two petals, the lower of three. The lips may be the same size, or one or the other may be larger, sometimes markedly so. An upward bulge, the palate, in the central portion of the lower lip may be pronounced in some species, such as the snapdragon (*Antirrhinum majus*), in which it closes the corolla throat. In some species (*e.g.*, *Veronica*) the corolla appears to be composed of four petals; in these, however, the upper "petal" is really two completely united petals. The plantains have only four petals.

Corolla structure and form

In some members of the order, the full complement of five stamens is present, as in many species of the family Solanaceae. Typically, however, one or more stamens is missing. Species having four stamens (an upper pair and a lower pair) lack only the uppermost stamen. Other species lack the uppermost stamen and, in addition, either the upper or the lower pair; thus they have only two stamens. Any of the "lost" stamens may be represented by a staminode, or sterile stamen, borne in place of a normal stamen but not producing pollen. A staminode may range, depending on the species, from a minute projection on the inner surface of the corolla to an elongated filament-like structure equal in size and conspicuousness to the normal stamens. Throughout the order the stamens are epipetalous; *i.e.*, their filaments are united with the petals. The union ranges from slight to considerably over one-half the length of the stamen. The stamens are alternate with the lobes of the corolla; *i.e.*, they are attached between the petals. In some highly irregular flowers, the alternate arrangement is difficult to see. The anthers (in which pollen develops) of all members of the order are tetrasporangiate; *i.e.*, they have four pollen sacs. Pollen grains are shed singly except in the family Hydrostachyaceae, in which they remain in groups of four. Pollen morphology (form and structure) is exceedingly diverse. One family of the order, the acanthus family is alleged to show a wider range of pollen morphological features than does any other plant family.

Female flower parts

The carpels of the order Scrophulariales are united into a compound gynoecium, or female structure. In the family Nolanaceae, there are five carpels. In other members of the order, almost without exception, there are two. The locule, or ovary chamber, number is usually two; the most notable exceptions are the one-locular broomrape family (Orobanchaceae) and gesneria family. In most species of the order, placentation, or ovule attachment, is axile—*i.e.*, along the central axis of the ovary. In some, however, notably the broomrape family and the gesneria family, it is parietal—to the ovary walls. The bladderwort family is characterized by free-central placentation, in which the ovules are borne on a central stalk that is attached only at one end of the ovary. In the family Globulariaceae, the solitary ovule is pendulous from the apex of the locule. In *Littorella* of the plantain family, the ovule arises from the base of the locule. In most members of the order, the septum partitioning the ovary into two chambers is horizontal. In the potato family, in contrast, the septum is oblique; its plane is about 45° from the horizontal.

Depending on the species, the ovule number may range from one to about 70,000 (in *Aeginetia*) per ovary. The ovules have one integument (covering) and are mostly anatropous (inverted and straight with the micropyle, or opening in the integument, next to the hilum, or point of attachment) or hemianatropous (similar to anatropous, but less pronounced). Less often the ovules are campylotropous (curved with the base and apex nearly together) or amphitropous (half-inverted and straight, the hilum lateral).

Fruits and seeds. Most Scrophulariales species are characterized by a capsular fruit. The capsule may open by splits or pores in its wall; in some species, the capsule top comes off like a lid. Another fruit type of the order is a berry, well illustrated by the tomato. Fruits of the nolana family typically consist of one ring of five sections or two or three such rings, one on top of another. Each section contains one to seven seeds and separates from the others at maturity.

Although most Scrophulariales species produce several to many seeds per fruit, a few produce only one (*Globularia, Littorella*). Perhaps the record for seed production in the order goes to *Boschniakia rossica* (broomrape family), an average plant of which is said to mature over 333,000 seeds. In size, the seeds of the order range from those of some members of the bignonia family, which may be several inches long, though thin and light, to the dustlike seeds of broomrapes (*Orobanche*), which are about 1/80 of an inch (about 0.3 millimetre) long.

EVOLUTION AND CLASSIFICATION

Evolution. *Fossil record.* Families of the order Scrophulariales are poorly represented in the fossil record and do not appear until the Tertiary Period (beginning about 65,000,000 years ago). These families, known from remains of leaves, pollen, fruits, and seeds, are the potato, figwort, bignonia, and acanthus families.

Relationships. The order Scrophulariales is closely related to the order Polemoniales and shares with it a common origin from the order Gentianales.

Within the order, the figwort, bignonia, sesamum, martynia, gesneria, broomrape, bladderwort, and acanthus families are clearly related to each other. The boundaries between some families are not clearly defined and thus are subject to individual interpretation.

The relationships of several families in the order are controversial; for example, the family Columelliaceae is variously considered to belong in the Scrophulariales or in the order Rosales. The family Buddlejaceae is sometimes placed in the order Gentianales. The families Solanaceae and Nolanaceae are thought by some to belong in the order Polemoniales. These differences of opinion have not yet been settled; the answers to them depend on individual—and varying—interpretations.

Controversial position of some families

Classification. *Distinguishing taxonomic features.* The order Scrophulariales comprises somewhat more than 50 percent of the families included in the order Tubiflorae of older systems. Major characteristics helpful for delineating the families within the order include: symmetry of the flowers; carpel number; locule number; ovary position; placentation type; fruit type; presence or absence of endosperm; parasitic or nonparasitic habit; and collateral or bicollateral vascular bundles.

Annotated classification.

ORDER SCROPHULARIALES

Trees, shrubs, vines, or herbs, sometimes parasitic. Leaves simple or rarely compound, alternate or opposite, rarely whorled or rosulate. Inflorescence (arrangement of flowers) various, or the flowers solitary. Flowers complete (with sepals, petals, stamens, and pistil) or rarely incomplete, perfect (with both sexes) or rarely imperfect, actinomorphic (radially symmetrical) to zygomorphic (bilaterally symmetrical), hypogynous (superior ovary) or rarely epigynous (inferior ovary). Calyx usually of 4 to 6 sepals; corolla usually of 4 to 6 united petals. Androecium (male complex) usually of 5, 4, or 2 stamens that are joined to the inner side of the corolla tube (epipetalous) and are alternate in position with the corolla lobes. Gynoecium (female complex) of 2 or rarely 5 united carpels, with usually 1 or 2 locules (chambers); with ovule attachment usually axile, (along the central axis) or parietal (to the ovary wall). Ovules 1 to many, with a single integument (outer covering). Fruit usually a capsule or a berry, rarely a schizocarp (a fruit that splits into several 1-seeded pieces), nut, or drupe (stone-seeded fruit); seeds with or without endosperm (nutrient tissue for the developing embryo).

Family Solanaceae (potato family)

Herbs, shrubs, or trees, with bicollateral vascular bundles. Leaves alternate, fascicled (clustered), or some opposite; simple or rarely compound. Inflorescences cymose (in clusters that mature from the central flower or top downward) or of solitary flowers. Flowers complete, actinomorphic to zygomorphic, hypogynous; calyx of 4 to 6 united sepals; corolla of 4 to 6 united petals. Androecium of 5, 4, or 2 epipetalous alternate stamens, the stamens frequently unequal, staminodia (sterile stamens) sometimes present. Gynoecium of 2 united carpels; ovary superior, usually 2-locular, rarely 1-locular or, by false septation, 3- to 5-locular, the septum oblique; placentae axile, the ovules many, seldom few to 1. Fruit a berry or a capsule; seeds with endosperm. Eighty-five genera and about 2,300 species widely distributed in tropical, subtropical, and temperate regions, especially of the New World.

Family Nolanaceae (nolana family)

Herbs or small shrubs, with bicollateral vascular bundles. Leaves alternate, simple, usually fleshy. Inflorescences racemose (in clusters that mature from the bottom upward) or of solitary flowers. Flowers complete, actinomorphic, hypogynous; calyx of 5 united sepals; corolla of 5 united petals. Androecium of 5 epipetalous alternate stamens. Gynoecium of 5 united carpels; ovary superior, divided longitudinally or transversely into 5 to 30 sections; placentae axile, the ovules 1 to 7 in each section of the ovary. Fruit of 5 to 30 mericarps (sections), these in 1 series or in 2 or 3 superposed series, each mericarp 1- to 7-seeded; seeds with endosperm. Two genera and 83 species distributed in western South America.

Family Buddlejaceae (buddleja family)

Trees or shrubs. Leaves opposite, alternate, or whorled; simple; with stipules (appendages at the base of the leafstalk). Inflorescence racemose, paniculate (many-branched), cymose, or capitate (headed). Flowers complete, actinomorphic to somewhat zygomorphic, hypogynous; calyx of 4 or 5 united sepals; corolla of 4 or 5 united petals. Androecium of 4 epipetalous alternate stamens, a staminodium sometimes also present. Gynoecium of 2 united carpels; ovary superior,

2-locular, rarely 4-locular by false septation; placentae axile, the ovules many. Fruit a capsule or berrylike; seeds with endosperm. Nineteen genera and 160 species widely distributed in tropical and subtropical regions, especially in southern Africa and Madagascar.

Family Retziaceae (retzia family)

Shrubs. Leaves whorled, simple. Inflorescence cymose; flowers complete, actinomorphic, hypogynous; calyx of 5 united sepals; corolla of 5 to 7 united petals. Androecium of 5 to 7 epipetalous alternate stamens. Gynoecium of 2 united carpels; ovary superior, incompletely 2-locular; placentae axile, the ovules 4 to 6. Fruit a capsule; seeds with endosperm. One genus and species (*Retzia*) distributed in southern Africa.

Family Scrophulariaceae (figwort family)

Herbs, shrubs, or trees, sometimes parasitic. Leaves alternate, opposite, whorled, or rosulate; simple or very rarely compound. Inflorescence racemose, spicate, paniculate, cymose, or of solitary flowers. Flowers complete, zygomorphic, hypogynous; calyx of 4 or 5 united sepals; corolla of 5 united petals. Androecium of 2, 4, or 5 epipetalous alternate stamens; staminodia sometimes present. Gynoecium of 2 united carpels; ovary superior, 2-locular or rarely 1-locular; placentae axile or rarely parietal (in 1-locular ovaries), the ovules 2 to many. Fruit a capsule or rarely a berry or a schizocarp; seeds with endosperm. About 200 genera and 3,000 species with worldwide distribution.

Family Bignoniaceae (bignonia family)

Trees, shrubs, vines, or rarely herbs. Leaves opposite or rarely alternate, simple or compound. Inflorescence racemose, paniculate, or cymose. Flowers complete, zygomorphic, hypogynous; calyx of 5 united sepals; corolla of 5 united petals. Androecium of 5, 2, or 4 epipetalous alternate stamens; staminodia often present. Gynoecium of 2 united carpels; ovary superior, 1- or 2-locular; placentae axile or parietal, ovules many. Fruit a capsule or sometimes fleshy and indehiscent (not splitting open); seeds without endosperm. The family contains 120 genera and about 800 species, which are widely distributed in tropical and subtropical regions, especially in South America; only a few genera occur in temperate regions.

Family Pedaliaceae (sesamum family)

Herbs, or rarely shrubs, with characteristic glandular ("mucilage") hairs. Leaves opposite or alternate; simple. Inflorescence cymose or racemose or of solitary flowers. Flowers complete, zygomorphic, hypogynous; calyx of 4 or 5 united sepals; corolla of 5 united petals. Androecium of 4 or rarely 2 epipetalous alternate stamens; staminodia usually present. Gynoecium of 2 united carpels; ovary superior, 2- to 4-locular, the locules frequently divided by false septation; placentae axile, the ovules 2 to many. Fruit a capsule or a nut; seeds with scant endosperm. The family contain 16 genera and 55 species with distributions in tropical and subtropical regions of the Old World.

Family Trapellaceae (trapella family)

Herbs of aquatic habitats. Leaves opposite, simple. Inflorescence of solitary flowers. Flowers complete, zygomorphic, epigynous; calyx of 5 united sepals; corolla of 5 united petals. Androecium of 2 epipetalous alternate stamens; 2 staminodia present. Gynoecium of 2 united carpels; ovary inferior, 2-locular, 1 locule reduced and sterile; placenta apical; ovules 2. Fruit 1-seeded, nutlike; seeds with thin endosperm. One genus (*Trapella*) with 2 species distributed in eastern Asia.

Family Martyniaceae (martynia family)

Herbs, with characteristic glandular ("mucilage") hairs. Leaves opposite or alternate; simple. Inflorescence racemose. Flowers complete, zygomorphic, hypogynous; calyx of 5 free or united sepals; corolla of 5 united petals. Androecium of 2 or 4 epipetalous alternate stamens; staminodia present. Gynoecium of 2 united carpels; ovary superior, 1-locular; placentae parietal, sometimes cohering to form false septa; ovules few to many. Fruit a capsule; seeds without endosperm. The family contains 5 genera and 16 species distributed in temperate to tropical regions of the New World.

Family Gesneriaceae (gesneria family)

Herbs, shrubs, vines, or trees. Leaves opposite, whorled, or rosulate; simple; 1 of a pair sometimes much reduced. Inflorescence cymose or of solitary flowers. Flowers complete, actinomorphic to zygomorphic, hypogynous or epigynous; calyx of 5 free or united sepals; corolla of 5 united petals. Androecium of 4, 2, or rarely 5 epipetalous alternate stamens; 1 to 3 staminodia sometimes present. Gynoecium of 2 united carpels; ovary superior or inferior, 1-locular; placentae parietal; ovules many. Fruit a capsule or a berry; seeds with or without endosperm. The family contains 140 genera and 1,800 species distributed mostly in tropical and subtropical regions of both hemispheres.

Family Columelliaceae (columellia family)

Shrubs or small trees. Leaves opposite, simple. Inflorescence cymose. Flowers complete, slightly zygomorphic, epigynous; calyx of 5 united sepals; corolla of 5 united petals. Androecium of 2 epipetalous alternate stamens. Gynoecium of 2 united carpels; ovary inferior, incompletely 2-locular; placentae parietal; ovules many. Fruit a capsule; seeds with endosperm. One genus (*Columellia*) with 4 species distributed in the Andes mountains of South America.

Family Orobanchaceae (broomrape family)

Root-parasitic herbs. Leaves reduced to scales, alternate. Inflorescence racemose or spicate or rarely of solitary flowers. Flowers complete, zygomorphic, hypogynous; calyx typically of 4 or 5 united sepals; corolla of 5 united petals. Androecium of 4 epipetalous alternate stamens. Gynoecium of 2 or 3 united carpels; ovary superior, usually 1-locular; placentae parietal; ovules many. Fruit a capsule; seeds with endosperm. The family contains 13 genera and 150 species widely distributed in temperate and warm regions, especially of the Old World and the Northern Hemisphere.

Family Lentibulariaceae (bladderwort family)

Herbs of aquatic and wet habitats. Leaves alternate or rosulate, modified for the capture of minute animals. Inflorescence racemose or of solitary flowers. Flowers complete, zygomorphic, hypogynous; calyx of 5 united sepals; corolla of 5 united petals. Androecium of 2 epipetalous alternate stamens; 2 staminodia sometimes present. Gynoecium of 2 united carpels; ovary superior, 1-locular; placentae free-central; ovules 2 or many. Fruit a capsule; seeds without endosperm. The family contains 5 genera and 300 species with wide distribution throughout the world.

Family Myoporaceae (myoporum family)

Shrubs or small trees. Leaves alternate or opposite; simple. Inflorescence cymose or of solitary flowers. Flowers complete, actinomorphic to zygomorphic, hypogynous; calyx of 5 united sepals; corolla of 5 or 6 united petals. Androecium of 4 or 5 epipetalous alternate stamens. Gynoecium of 2 united carpels; ovary superior, 2-locular, or 3- to 10-locular by false septation; placentae axile; ovules 4 to 14. Fruit a drupe; seeds with scant or no endosperm. The family contains 5 genera and 180 species distributed in tropical and subtropical regions mostly of the Old World, especially Australia.

Family Globulariaceae (globularia family)

Herbs or small shrubs. Leaves alternate, simple. Inflorescence capitate or spicate. Flowers complete, zygomorphic, hypogynous; calyx of 5 united sepals; corolla of 5 united petals. Androecium of 4 epipetalous alternate stamens. Gynoecium of 2 united carpels, which have the appearance of a single carpel (*i.e.* they are pseudomonomerous); ovary superior, 1-locular; placenta apical; ovule solitary. Fruit nutlike; seeds with endosperm. There are 2 genera and 27 species distributed in the Old World, especially the Mediterranean area.

Family Acanthaceae (acanthus family)

Herbs, shrubs, vines, or trees. Leaves opposite, simple. Inflorescence cymose, racemose, or of solitary flowers. Flowers complete, zygomorphic, hypogynous; calyx of 5 united sepals; corolla of 5 united petals. Androecium of 4, 2, or rarely 5 epipetalous alternate stamens. Gynoecium of 2 united carpels; ovary superior, 2-locular; placentae axile; ovules 2 to many. Fruit a capsule or a drupe; seeds usually without endosperm, typically supported by an indurated (hardened) funiculus. There are 250 genera and 2,600 species widely distributed in the tropics and subtropics, with limited representation in temperate areas.

Family Plantaginaceae (plantain family)

Herbs or shrubs. Leaves alternate, rosulate, or rarely opposite; simple. Inflorescence spicate. Flowers complete or rarely incomplete, perfect or rarely imperfect, actinomorphic, hypogynous; calyx of 3 or 4 united sepals; corolla of 3 or 4 united petals. Androecium of 4 or rarely 3, 2, or 1 epipetalous alternate stamens. Gynoecium of 2 united carpels, sometimes pseudomonomerous; ovary superior, 2-locular or rarely 3- or 4-locular by false septation; placentae axile, rarely basal or free-central; ovules 1 to many. Fruit a capsule or a 1-seeded nut; seeds with endosperm. There are 3 genera and 265 species with worldwide distribution.

Family Hydrostachyaceae (hydrostachys family)

Herbs of aquatic habitats. Stems tuber-like. Leaves simple or 1 to 3 times pinnatisect (deeply divided). Inflorescence spicate. Flowers imperfect, the plants dioecious· (separately sexed flowers are on separate plants) or rarely monoecious (both sexes on one plant); calyx lacking; corolla lacking; staminate (male) flowers consist of a single stamen; carpellate (female) flowers of a single pistil. Gynoecium of 2 united carpels; placentae parietal; ovules many. Fruit a capsule; seeds without endosperm. The family contains 1 genus (*Hydrostachys*) and 30 species distributed in Madagascar and tropical and southern Africa.

Critical appraisal. The families included in the order Tubiflorae of older taxonomic systems have been variously grouped, the groupings depending upon the characteristics emphasized. Some authorities recognize one large order. Others group the families of the Tubiflorae into three to seven smaller orders, of which the order Scrophulariales, as presented here, is one of three. The evidence is not overwhelmingly in favour of any of these views. It is largely a matter of personal preference how these families are divided into orders if the large group Tubiflorae is considered too unwieldy as a single order.

Because phylogenists subdivide the old group Tubiflorae differently, it is difficult to find the equivalent of the Scrophulariales, as presented here, among the orders recognized by other authorities. In older classification systems there is simply no order comparable to it. It is most closely equivalent to the suborder Solanineae of the order Tubiflorae, but it differs mainly by the inclusion of the plantain family and the myoporum family. A major distinctive feature of the order Scrophulariales, as presented here, is the inclusion of the potato family, which most other phylogenists place in an order separate from the figwort family and its allies. Thus the order Scrophulariales as defined here is not the same grouping of families as the order of that name as recognized by many other authorities. The classification presented here is, nevertheless, a recent one of wide acceptance with as much claim to authoritativeness as other widely known systems.

BIBLIOGRAPHY. CHARLES B. HEISER, JR., *Nightshades: The Paradoxical Plants* (1969), a fine popular account of the best known members of the potato family, including the potato, red peppers, tomato, tobacco, eggplant, and others; JOB KUIJT, *The Biology of Parasitic Flowering Plants* (1969), a well-illustrated account, including the broomrape family and the parasitic members of the figwort family; FRANCIS ERNEST LLOYD, *The Carnivorous Plants* (1942), includes much data on the bladderwort family; EDWIN A. MENNINGER, *Flowering Trees of the World for Tropics and Warm Climates* (1926), discussions of flowering trees, including those of the Scrophulariales (well illustrated, with many colour plates); *Flowering Vines of the World* (1970), discussions of flowering vines, including those of the Scrophulariales (well illustrated, with many colour plates); C.D. SCULTHORPE, *The Biology of Aquatic Vascular Plants* (1967), data on the structure, biology, and ecology of aquatic plants, including those of the Scrophulariales; STANWYN G. SHETLER and FLORENCE MONTGOMERY, *Insectivorous Plants* (1965), considers, among others, the carnivorous members of the Scrophulariales—the bladderwort family—and includes references for further reading, both popular and technical; R.N. SALAMAN, *The History and Social Influence of the Potato* (1949), a long and detailed account of the impact of this basic food plant on man.

(J.W.Th.)

Scrublands

Scrublands are areas where low, evergreen, leathery leaved, and often aromatic shrubs (or scrubs) dominate the vegetation. Mostly they are confined to a Mediterranean type of climate—dry, hot summers and cool, wet winters—and therefore are often called the Mediterranean vegetation. This type of climate is found most often near seacoasts, and it commonly occurs in a latitudinal zone between 30 and 40 degrees both north and south of the Equator. Scrublands merge into monsoon forests and evergreen forests toward regions of wetter climate and into thorn-shrub vegetation and steppes (dry prairies) toward regions of decreasing precipitation.

Scrubland characteristics. During the dry summer months, the temperature differential between day and night in scrublands is much greater than during winter, and during the wet winter months the night temperatures are usually between 50° and 60° F, which is optimal for the growth of scrub vegetation. The night temperature is most important in the control of plant growth.

The high summer temperatures make the small amount of precipitation insufficient for growth of scrubland plants, and most of them become dormant. Scrub plants flower and produce fruit before the onset of the hot, dry summer, the scrublands bursting into colourful display during spring. In California, for example, sage (*Salvia*), mountain lilac (*Ceanothus*), tree poppy (*Dendrome-*

con), and *Fremontia* bloom at this time. In Australia *Grevillea, Acacia, Callistemon,* and *Dryandra* are the principal genera of spring flowering plants. In the Cape scrublands of South Africa various members of the family Proteaceae and heath (*Erica*) colour the hillsides with spectacular displays of flowers. This same feature of the climate also conditions the dominance in the scrubland vegetation of winter annuals; *i.e.,* plants that complete their life cycle in a single growing season, in this case during the wet winter months. The summer drought makes it impossible for shallow-rooted herbs to survive, leaving most of the space between shrubs bare. Thus, at the beginning of the autumn rains, the seeds of annual plants are able to germinate on the bare ground.

The shrubs of the scrublands are adapted to growing in winters that combine low temperatures with adequate moisture. Typical desert plants that grow only at high temperatures, such as the creosote bush or jarillo (*Larrea*), cannot live in the scrublands nor can shrubs native to areas with summer rains and winter drought (*e.g.,* in western Texas or the Transvaal).

The dry climate of the hot summer months predisposes scrublands to fires, and most of them can be described as being a fire-maintained vegetation. The shrubs are adapted to fires in being able to sprout from their root crown. Since most trees are unable to form new shoots from the base of their trunk, a scrubland vegetation is kept free from invading trees through frequent fires.

Many of the scrubland plants have seeds whose germination is stimulated by high temperature treatment. This is known, for example, for the chamise (*Adenostoma fasciculatum*), whose seeds do not germinate until very old unless they are subjected to dry heat near 200° F or else are treated by being placed near charcoal or by being leached for a long time in water.

Scrublands are not usually browsed by animals; although deer may live nearby, they normally do not eat the frequently aromatic or toxic shrubs. Another reason why the scrublands in general are not grazed or browsed by the larger mammals is their impassable, dense growth. Although not as forbidding as the thorn-shrub vegetation, scrublands are accessible to larger animals only with difficulty. In Australia, the wallabies and even the so-called scrub wallabies use the scrub vegetation only for resting during daytime, feeding in open grasslands during night. Scrublands also are impassable to the Australian flightless birds.

While not inhabited by larger mammals, scrublands are frequented by small seed eaters. Typical of these seed eaters are small rodents, such as pocket mice and kangaroo rats, and quail. None of these animals is restricted to scrublands, however, and most prefer a more open vegetation.

Insects and insect-eating birds and reptiles are common in scrublands but not more so than in other types of vegetation. Because it is impossible to characterize scrublands by any typical animals, botanical criteria are relied upon exclusively.

Scrubland distribution. The accompanying map shows the distribution of the most important scrublands over the world. A description of each of them follows.

The Californian chaparral. The scrubland vegetation of the Californian chaparral occurs everywhere on the lower slopes (generally below 1,000 metres or 3,000 feet) of the coastal and inland mountains of southwestern North America, wherever the yearly rainfall ranges from ten to 20 inches (about 200 to 500 millimetres) per year, with a pronounced dry summer. At higher altitudes with increasing precipitation, the vegetation gradually changes into fir and pine forests, and in the interior the scrubland flora is replaced by a steppe vegetation dominated by the sagebrush (*Artemisia tridentata*).

Along the coast and in the higher rainfall areas, the dominant shrubs of the chaparral are sages (*Salvia mellifera* and *S. apiana*), mountain-lilacs (*Ceanothus* species), *Rhus* species, *Eriogonum fasciculatum,* and the scrub oak (*Quercus dumosa*). In drier localities and on poorer soil, chamise (*Adenostoma fasciculatum*), or ribbon-wood (*Adenostoma sparsifolium*), becomes domi-

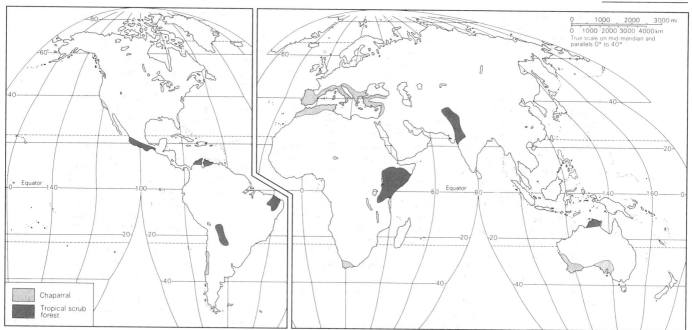

World distribution of the most important scrubland vegetation areas.

Adapted from *Biological Sciences Curriculum Study Green Version High School Biology*, 2nd ed.; Chicago: Rand McNally & Co., 1968

nant. If left undisturbed, live oaks (*Quercus agrifolia*) and big-cone fir (*Pseudotsuga macrocarpa*) invade the chaparral on the better sites of north slopes, gradually transforming them into forests. Only in exceptional localities does the chaparral remain undisturbed; normally it burns over once every ten to 40 years. After a fire the shrubs resprout from the root crown, and many germinate from seed, together with many herbaceous plants.

The Mediterranean macchie (maquis). Although human activities have removed much of the Mediterranean macchie, in Spain, southern France, Greece, Lebanon, coastal Israel, Tunisia, and Algeria a shrub vegetation still covers the lower slopes of the mountains bordering the Mediterranean Sea. This vegetation consists of many aromatic shrubs such as *Satureia* and other members of the mint family (Lamiaceae), *Cistus*, laurel, myrtle (*Myrtus*), and different brooms (*Genista*), with olives, *Ceratonia*, figs, and other semitrees transforming the scrublands into forests in the absence of human interference.

Where the soils are poorer and rockier, the macchie is more open, sometimes with shrub palms (*Chamaerops*); in the French Mediterranean this type of vegetation is called garrigue.

Many of the plants of these Mediterranean scrublands are well known, such as the laurel and the olive. The myrtle, and innumerable spices, such as rosemary, thyme, and marjoram, are also familiar members of this vegetation.

Northward, toward central Europe, summer rainfall increases, and a forest climate replaces the Mediterranean climate, whereas south and eastward the climate becomes drier and changes into a steppe and desert climate. This occurs along the Mediterranean shores in Libya and Egypt, where a semidesert vegetation replaces the macchie because of an absence of moisture.

A vegetation similar to the Mediterranean scrublands extends from Turkey along the lower mountain ranges of Asia Minor. This is a reflection of the climate, with the rainfall decreasing eastward but increasing at higher altitudes. It is at the borders of the Mediterranean scrubland climate where the first successful attempts at agriculture occurred in Asia Minor, about 10,000 years ago.

With the unprecedented increase in population since Roman times, most of the original macchie vegetation has been transformed by man into cultivated areas. River valleys are irrigated, and profitable crops now replace the macchie. On mountain slopes olive orchards now grow in areas formerly occupied by a varied macchie vegetation.

The Australian scrublands. Australia has probably the most extensive and richest scrubland vegetation. In Western Australia rainfall ranges from ten inches (about 250 millimetres) in the interior to 60 inches (about 1,500 mm) along the southwest coast. There are extensive *Eucalyptus* forests in the high rainfall area, but in areas having between 15 inches (about 380 mm) and 40 inches (about 1,000 mm) of precipitation, varied scrub vegetation covers the land except near the roads, where extensive clearings have removed the shrubs. There are about 1,000 shrub species living in southwestern Australia, many of them with spiny branches and leaves and with brightly coloured flowers ranging from deep blue, lilac, yellow, and brown to red. Most of these shrubs belong to a few families, such as the pea family (Fabaceae), especially the genus *Acacia*), the myrtle family (Myrtaceae), Proteaceae, and Rutaceae.

Eastward, past the desert of the Nullarbor Plain, another scrubland is found, commonly named mallee, where shrubby *Eucalyptus*, *Acacia*, *Banksia*, and other members of the Proteaceae family reign supreme in South Australia.

The Chilean scrublands. Also in the Southern Hemisphere are the scrublands of central Chile, where *Acacia cavenia*, *Baccharis*, and tall cacti grow on the Pacific slopes of the Andes. On the lower part of the eastern slope of the Andes in Argentina, desert shrubs are encountered, which are replaced further eastward by chaco, a thornshrub vegetation that merges into campos cerrados (scattered trees in dense grasslands) in central Brazil and into caatinga (stunted, sparse forests, leafless during the hot dry season) in eastern Brazil.

The Cape flora. The Cape flora is a very restricted shrub vegetation in South Africa, comprised chiefly of heath (*Erica*) and members of the Proteaceae family. This flora is remarkable in that it occupies an area of not more than 200 square miles, yet it is exceedingly rich in species, having more than are present on a several thousand times larger area of the central United States or of central Europe. It differs totally in its composition from the surrounding evergreen forest, karroo, veld, and desert vegetation, most of which occurs in a climate with winter drought and summer rains.

Scrubland growth and development. *Floristic comparisons between scrublands.* All of the scrubland floras have developed locally and are not related to each other, except for a few genera they have in common. In the five main regions with scrubland vegetation, all major floral constituents are unique for each of them, yet there are

The world's richest and most extensive scrublands

certain plant genera or families that have representatives in more than one of the five areas. The scrublands of the Northern Hemisphere, for example, have a number of genera in common and so have those in the Southern Hemisphere. The scrublands on the same continental masses (Chile and California, Cape and Mediterranean) also have a number of related plant species. The Australian scrubland, however, has no relationship with either North American or European scrublands, nor has the South American scrubland any relationship with the European.

Seasonal aspects of scrublands. Scrublands in general do not change much in the course of a year. The shrubs are evergreen, and they change colour only slightly during the dry season, when the bright green foliage turns an olive green. After the first rains in late autumn, lush, new, green foliage appears and remains green into early summer.

The Mediterranean climate has mild winters, and most of the scrubland species are only mildly frost resistant. In the chaparral, *Rhus laurina* is probably the least frost resistant, and after an exceptionally cold winter a number of shrubs of this species may be killed through freezing.

Temperature and precipitation effects on scrubland composition

After an exceptional series of drought years, mortality among the less drought-resistant chaparral plants is greater than normal, and many *Salvia* shrubs die during such periods. The more resistant species, such as chamise and *Eriogonum fasciculatum*, survive even after drought periods. Thus these latter drought-resistant shrubs spread into the desert shrub vegetation. It is, therefore, not in the years with average winter temperature and average winter rainfall that selection in the chaparral occurs. It is in the exceptional years that the composition of the scrubland flora is determined.

The most pronounced seasonal changes in the flora of scrublands are provided by annual plants. Their seeds germinate within a few days after the first extensive autumn or winter rain, and the plants continue to grow slowly during winter. In spring, flowers are produced in response to the lengthening of the days. Fruit is set and ripens before the long summer drought. Many of these annual plants occur both in the chaparral and in the desert. The major difference between these two habitats is the frequency of winters having rainfall sufficient for germination of the annual plants. Since annual plants require one inch of rainfall to germinate, they develop only when enough water has fallen to complete their life cycles.

Annuals occurring both in chaparral and desert are goldfields (*Baeria chrysostoma*), which can produce spectacular displays in March and April, when whole acres become golden yellow with the flowers of this tiny composite, *Emmenanthe penduliflora*, several poppy (*Eschscholzia*) species, fiddle necks (*Amsinckia*), and different kinds of forget-me-nots (*Cryptantha*).

In Western Australia the displays of annuals in the scrublands during September are just as spectacular, with the deep blue of *Leschenaultia* and *Dampiera* and the pinks of *Stylidium* and sundew (*Drosera*). Perennial herbs such as *Conostylis* and many orchids add to the flower displays in the underbrush. In the scrublands of the Mediterranean, the mustards of the Brassicaceae family, legumes, and bulbous plants such as grape hyacinths (*Muscari*) lend special colour to the spring annual flora.

Evolution of scrublands. The scrublands vegetation provides many interesting evolutionary problems. In the southwestern United States, all scrub areas are relatively young in an evolutionary sense. Until 10,000 years ago the area now occupied by chaparral in southern California had a much denser forest vegetation in which sabertooth tigers, giant sloths, and camel-like animals lived. This oak woodland, which also occupied extensive areas in the Great Basin (now the semi-deserts of Nevada), gradually retreated against the onslaught of drought, which caused the disappearance of the great inland lakes —Bonneville and Lahontan—and which caused the extension of incipient deserts.

In the Mediterranean, the climate probably was drier to start with and the vegetation did not change as rapidly as it did in the southwestern United States.

And in Australia the flora and fauna, like the continent itself, are very old. Consequently the mallee has not had invasions of exotic elements, and most of the shrubs growing in it have evolved in their present sites and long ago. They have evolved in directions different from other scrublands. The proportion of shrubs with spiny leaves, for example, is very great in Western Australia, as is the number of shrubs with spectacular flowers.

Fires in scrublands. Scrublands form dense stands of vegetation that become tinder dry towards the end of summers without precipitation and are particularly susceptible to fires. Not only the shrubs themselves but also the dry annuals and litter accumulation underneath provide plenty of fuel for very extensive fires, which burn up into the forests bordering the scrublands at higher elevations. But they stop at the transition to the more arid regions where the vegetation becomes widely spaced. Not all scrublands are equally susceptible to fire. There are fewer and less extensive fires in the Mediterranean maquis than in the Californian chaparral or the Australian mallee.

All plants consist of combustible organic matter, but there are considerable differences in their flammability. There are two major factors that influence the ease with which a plant catches fire. One is obviously its water content, and thus water-filled cacti and succulents will not burn. The other is the quantity of aromatic flammable compounds contained in the plant and the ease with which they are released. The aromatic sage (*Salvia*) plants burn easily, whereas the Mediterranean rock rose (*Cistus*) is definitely fire retardant.

Factors influencing the occurrence of fires in scrublands

Economically, scrublands are unimportant. Growth of the scrubs is rather slow, because their development is restricted to the rainy period, which occurs in winter when temperatures are too low for rapid growth. They occur predominantly on slopes, which are costly to cultivate. In central California it has been practical to replace the chaparral vegetation with a grass cover, allowing the slopes to be grazed. In the lower rainfall areas of southern California, however, a grass cover is hard to maintain, and the main effort is to maintain the shrub vegetation in its most vigorous form to counteract erosion. A shrub fire is usually followed the next winter by destructive floods. For this reason attempts are made to re-establish as quickly as possible burned-over scrub vegetation. This is done by seeding a burned area with fast growing annual plants. But since these plants—ryegrass and mustard—take some time before they produce a protective cover, and also because they need a good rain before they germinate, such seeding does not provide protection against the first rains after summer or autumn fire; moreover, a vegetation of annual plants needs to be renewed every year. The ideal solution, therefore, is to get as quickly as possible a renewal of the permanent perennial shrub vegetation. This is the natural sequence of events anyway. Whereas a climax forest vegetation usually does not directly regenerate itself and passes through one or several different successional stages before it becomes re-established after destruction by man or fire, chaparral regenerates rather easily. The old stumps of the burned shrubs often resprout and usually do so before advent of the first rains. Secondly, the seeds of many chaparral plants are stimulated to germinate by the fire. Unfortunately, there usually are not enough seeds of chaparral plants present to get a good stand in the first year after the fire. Therefore a compromise is reached: as soon as possible after the fire, the slopes are seeded thinly with some annual plant that does not interfere with the re-establishment of the natural vegetation. The second year after the fire, the natural vegetation may have grown sufficiently to provide a fairly effective protection against erosion, which it does by shielding the soil against falling raindrops with foliage and litter.

BIBLIOGRAPHY. Detailed descriptions of the scrubland vegetation of various areas are: M.L. EMBERGER, "La végétation de la région Méditerraneénne," *Rev. Gén. Bot.*, 42: 705–721 (1930), and M.A. RIKLI, *Das Pflanzenkleid der Mittelmeerländer*, vol. 1 (1943), of the Mediterranean region; C.A. GARDNER, "The Vegetation of Western Australia, with Special Reference to the Climate and Soils," *Jl. R. Soc. West.*

Aust., 28:11–87 (1942), of Australia; J. HUTCHINSON, *A Botanist in Southern Africa* (1946), of South Africa; and P.A. MUNZ and D.D. KECK, *A California Flora* (1968), of southern California; A.F.W. SCHIMPER, *Pflanzen-geographie* (1898; Eng. trans., *Plant Geography Upon a Physiological Basis*, 1903) is the fundamental work on the regional distribution of vegetation types over the world; H. WALTER, *Die Vegetation der Erde in ökophysiologischer Betrachtung*, vol. 2 (1968), a modern much-expanded, and outstanding version of A.F.W. Schimper's work. A discussion of the climatology of the scrubland areas may be found in P. MEIGS, *Geography of Coastal Deserts* (1966).

(F.W.We.)

Sculpture, Art of

Sculpture is not a fixed term that applies to a permanently circumscribed category of objects or sets of activities. It is, rather, the name of an art that grows and changes and is continually extending the range of its activities and evolving new kinds of objects. The scope of the term is much wider in the second half of the 20th century than it was only two or three decades ago, and in the present fluid state of the visual arts nobody can predict what its future extensions are likely to be.

Certain features, which in previous centuries were considered essential to the art of sculpture, are not present in a great deal of modern sculpture and can no longer form part of its definition. One of the most important of these is representation. Before the 20th century, sculpture was considered a representational art; but its scope has now been extended to include nonrepresentational forms. It has long been accepted that the forms of such functional three-dimensional objects as furniture, pots, and buildings may be expressive and beautiful without being in any way representational; but it is only in the 20th century that nonfunctional, nonrepresentational, three-dimensional works of art have been produced.

Again, before the 20th century, sculpture was considered primarily an art of solid form, or mass. It is true that the negative elements of sculpture—the voids and hollows within and between its solid forms—have always been to some extent an integral part of its design, but their role has been a secondary one. In a great deal of modern sculpture, however, the focus of attention has shifted, and the spatial aspects have become dominant. Spatial sculpture is now a generally accepted branch of the art of sculpture.

It was also taken for granted in the sculpture of the past that its components were of a constant shape and size and did not move. With the recent development of kinetic sculpture, however, neither the immobility nor immutability of its form can any longer be considered essential to the art of sculpture.

Finally, 20th-century sculpture is not confined to the two traditional forming processes of carving and modelling or to such traditional natural materials as stone, metal, wood, ivory, bone, and clay. Because present-day sculptors use any materials and methods of manufacture that will serve their purposes, the art of sculpture can no longer be identified with any special materials or techniques.

Through all of these changes there is probably only one thing that has remained constant in the art of sculpture, and it is this that emerges as the central and abiding concern of sculptors: The art of sculpture is the branch of the visual arts that is especially concerned with the creation of expressive form in three dimensions.

Definition of sculpture

Sculpture may be either in the round or in relief. A sculpture in the round is a separate, detached object in its own right, leading the same kind of independent existence in space as a human body or a chair. A relief does not have this kind of independence. It projects from and is attached to or is an integral part of something else that serves either as a background against which it is set or a matrix from which it emerges.

The actual three-dimensionality of sculpture in the round limits its scope in certain respects in comparison with the scope of painting. Sculpture cannot conjure up the illusion of space by purely optical means or invest its forms with atmosphere and light as painting can. It does have a kind of reality, however, that a vivid physical presence that is denied to the pictorial arts. The forms of sculpture are tangible as well as visible, and they can appeal strongly and directly to both tactual and visual sensibilities. Blind people, even those who are congenitally blind, can produce and appreciate certain kinds of sculpture. It has, in fact, been argued by the 20th-century art critic Sir Herbert Read that sculpture should be regarded as primarily an art of touch and that the roots of sculptural sensibility can be traced to the pleasure one experiences in fondling things.

All three-dimensional forms are perceived as having an expressive character as well as purely geometric properties. They strike the observer as delicate, aggressive, flowing, taut, relaxed, dynamic, soft, and so on. By exploiting the expressive qualities of form, a sculptor is able to create images in which subject matter and expressiveness of form are mutually reinforcing. Such images go beyond the mere presentation of fact and communicate a wide range of subtle and powerful feelings.

The aesthetic raw material of sculpture is, so to speak, the whole realm of expressive three-dimensional form. It may draw upon what already exists in the endless variety of natural and man-made form, or it may be an art of pure invention. It has been used to express a vast range of human emotions and feelings from the most tender and delicate to the most violent and ecstatic.

All human beings, intimately involved from birth with the world of three-dimensional form, learn something of its structural and expressive properties and develop emotional responses to them. This combination of understanding and sensitive response, which constitutes what is often called a sense of form, can be cultivated and refined. It is to this sense of form that the art of sculpture primarily appeals.

This article deals with the following aspects of sculpture: elements and principles of design; materials; methods and techniques; the forms of sculpture, including sculpture in the round and various types of relief; subject matter and imagery; symbolism; and uses.

ELEMENTS AND PRINCIPLES OF SCULPTURAL DESIGN

Elements of design. *Mass and space.* The two most important elements of sculpture—mass and space—are, of course, separable only in thought. All sculpture is made of a material substance that has mass and exists in three-dimensional space. The mass of sculpture is thus the solid, material, space-occupying bulk that is contained within its surfaces. Space enters into the design of sculpture in three main ways: the material components of the sculpture extend into or move through space; they may enclose or enfold space, thus creating hollows and voids within the sculpture; and they may relate one to another across space.

Ways in which space enters into the design of sculpture

The amount of importance attached to either mass or space in the design of sculpture varies considerably. In Egyptian sculpture and in most of the sculpture of the 20th-century artist Constantin Brancusi, for example, mass is paramount, and most of the sculptor's thought has been devoted to shaping a lump of solid material. In 20th-century works by Antoine Pevsner or Naum Gabo, on the other hand, mass is reduced to a minimum, consisting only of transparent sheets of plastic or thin metal rods. The solid form of the components themselves is of little importance; their main function is to create movement through space and to enclose space. In works by such 20th-century sculptors as Henry Moore and Barbara Hepworth, the elements of space and mass are treated as more or less equal partners.

Volume. It is not possible to see the whole of a fully three-dimensional form at once. The observer can only see the whole of it if he turns it around or goes around it himself. For this reason it is sometimes mistakenly assumed that sculpture must be designed primarily to present a series of satisfactory projective views and that this multiplicity of views constitutes the main difference between sculpture and the pictorial arts, which present only one view of their subject. Such an attitude toward sculpture ignores the fact that it is possible to apprehend solid

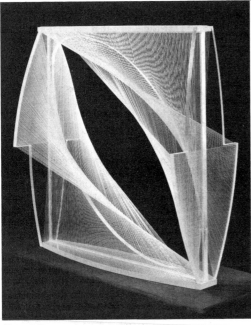

Mass and space.
(Left) "Linear Construction #1, Variation," Perspex plastic and nylon thread sculpture by Naum Gabo, 1942–43. In the Miriam Gabo Collection, Middlebury, Connecticut. 62 cm. × 62 cm.
(Right) "Torso of a Young Girl," onyx on a stone base by Constantin Brancusi, 1922. In the Philadelphia Museum of Art. Onyx height 34.9 cm.; base height 17.1 cm.
By courtesy of (left) Miriam Gabo, Middlebury, Connecticut,
(right) Philadelphia Museum of Art, the A.E. Gallatin Collection

forms as volumes, to conceive an idea of them in the round from any one aspect. A great deal of sculpture is designed to be apprehended primarily as volume.

A single volume is the fundamental unit of three-dimensional solid form that can be conceived in the round. Some sculptures consist of only one volume, others are configurations of a number of volumes. The human figure is often treated by sculptors as a configuration of volumes each of which corresponds to a major part of the body, such as the head, neck, thorax, and thigh.

Holes and cavities in sculpture, which are as carefully shaped as the solid forms and are of equal importance to the overall design, are sometimes referred to as negative volumes.

Surfaces. The surfaces of sculpture are in fact all that one actually sees. It is from their inflections that one makes inferences about the internal structure of the sculpture. A surface has, so to speak, two aspects: it contains and defines the internal structure of the masses of the sculpture, and it is the part of the sculpture that enters into relations with external space.

The expressive character of different kinds of surfaces is of the utmost importance in sculpture. Double-curved convex surfaces suggest fullness, containment, enclosure, the outward pressure of internal forces. In the aesthetics of Indian sculpture such surfaces have a special metaphysical significance. Representing the encroachment of space into the mass of the sculpture, concave surfaces suggest the action of external forces and are often indicative of collapse or erosion. Flat surfaces tend to convey a feeling of material hardness and rigidity; they are unbending or unyielding, unaffected by either internal or external pressures. Surfaces that are convex in one curvature and concave in the other can suggest the operation of internal pressures and at the same time a receptivity to the influence of external forces. They are associated with growth, with expansion into space.

Light and shade. The sculptor cannot, like the painter, create his own lighting effects within the work itself. The distribution of light and shade over the forms of his work depends upon the direction and intensity of light from external sources. Nevertheless, to some extent he can determine the kinds of effect this external light will have. If he knows where the work is to be sited he can adapt it to the kind of light it is likely to receive. The brilliant overhead sunlight of Egypt and India demands a differ-

ent treatment from the dim interior light of a northern medieval cathedral. Then again, it is possible to create effects of light and shade, or chiaroscuro, by cutting or modelling deep, shadow-catching hollows and prominent, highlighted ridges. Many late Gothic sculptors used light and shade as a powerful expressive feature of their work, aiming at a mysterious obscurity, with forms broken by shadow emerging from a dark background. Greek, Indian, and most Italian Renaissance sculptors shaped the forms of their work to receive light in a way that makes the whole work radiantly clear.

Colour. The colouring of sculpture may be either natural or applied. In the recent past, sculptors became more aware than ever before of the inherent beauty of sculptural materials. Under the slogan of "truth to materials" many of them worked their materials in ways that exploited their natural properties, including colour and texture. More recently, however, there has been a growing tendency to use bright artificial colouring as an important element in the design of sculpture.

In the ancient world and during the Middle Ages almost all sculpture was artificially coloured, usually in a bold and decorative rather than a naturalistic manner. The sculptured portal of a cathedral, for example, would be coloured and gilded with all the brilliance of a contemporary illuminated manuscript.

Combinations of differently coloured materials, such as the ivory and gold of some Greek sculpture, were not unknown before the 17th century; but the early Baroque sculptor Gian Lorenzo Bernini greatly extended the practice by combining variously coloured marbles with white marble and gilt bronze.

Principles of design. It is doubtful whether any principles of design are universal in the art of sculpture; for the principles that govern the organization of the elements of sculpture into expressive compositions differ from style to style. In fact, distinctions made among the major styles of sculpture are largely based on a recognition of differences in the principles of design that underlie them. Thus, the art historian Erwin Panofsky was attempting to define a difference of principle in the design of Romanesque and Gothic sculpture when he stated that the forms of Romanesque were conceived as projections from a plane outside themselves, while those of Gothic were conceived as being centred on an axis within themselves. The "principle of axiality" was considered by

Chiaroscuro effects

Panofsky to be "the essential principle of classical statuary," which Gothic had rediscovered.

The principles of sculptural design govern the approaches of sculptors to such fundamental matters as orientation, proportion, scale, articulation, and balance.

Orientation. For conceiving and describing the orientation of the forms of sculpture in relation to each other, to a spectator, and to their surroundings, some kind of spatial scheme of reference is required. This is provided by a system of axes and planes of reference.

An axis is an imaginary centre line through a symmetrical or near symmetrical volume or group of volumes. Thus, all the main components of the human body have axes of their own, while an upright figure has a single vertical axis running through its entire length. Volumes may rotate or tilt on their axes.

Planes of reference are imaginary planes to which the movements, positions, and directions of volumes, axes, and surfaces may be referred. The principal planes of reference are the frontal, the horizontal, and the two profile planes.

The principles that govern the characteristic poses and spatial compositions of upright figures in different styles of sculpture are formulated with reference to axes and the four cardinal planes: for example, the principle of axiality already referred to; the principle of frontality, which governs the design of Archaic sculpture; the characteristic contrapposto (pose in which parts of the body, such as upper and lower, are twisted in opposite directions) of Michelangelo's figures; and in standing Greek sculpture of the Classical period the frequently used balanced "chiastic" pose (stance in which the body weight is taken principally on one leg, thereby creating a contrast of tension and relaxation between the opposite sides of a figure).

Proportion. Proportional relations exist among linear dimensions, areas, and volumes and masses. All three types of proportion coexist and interact in sculpture, contributing to its expressiveness and beauty. Attitudes toward proportion differ considerably among sculptors. Some sculptors, both abstract and figurative, use mathematical systems of proportion; for example, the refinement and idealization of natural human proportions was a major preoccupation of Greek sculptors. Indian sculptors employed iconometric canons, or systems of carefully related proportions, that determined the proportions of all significant dimensions of the human figure. African and other tribal sculptors base the proportions of their figures on the subjective importance of the parts of the body. Unnatural proportions may be used for expressive purposes or to accommodate a sculpture to its surroundings. The elongation of the figures on the Portail Royal ("Royal Portal") of Chartres Cathedral does both: it enhances their otherworldliness and also integrates them with the columnar architecture.

Sometimes it is necessary to adapt the proportions of sculpture to suit its position in relation to a viewer. A figure sited high on a building, for example, is usually made larger in its upper parts in order to counteract the effects of foreshortening. This should be allowed for when a sculpture intended for such a position is exhibited on eye level in a museum.

Scale. The scale of sculpture must sometimes be considered in relation to the scale of its surroundings. When it is one element in a larger complex, such as the facade of a building, it must be in scale with the rest. Another important consideration that sculptors must take into account when designing outdoor sculpture is the tendency of sculpture in the open air—particularly when viewed against the sky—to appear less massive than it does in a studio.

Because one tends to relate the scale of sculpture to one's own human physical dimensions, the emotional impact of a colossal figure and a small figurine are quite different.

In ancient and medieval sculpture the relative scale of the figures in a composition is often determined by their importance; *e.g.*, slaves are much smaller than kings or nobles. This is sometimes known as hierarchic scale.

Use of unnatural proportions

Proportion.
Four figures possibly of the royal family of Judah, stone, 1145–50. Portail Royal of Chartres Cathedral, France. Height approximately 2.50 m.
ND photo

Articulation. The joining of one form to another may be accomplished in a variety of ways. In much of the work of the 19th-century French sculptor Auguste Rodin, there are no clear boundaries, and one form is merged with another in an impressionistic manner to create a continuously flowing surface. In works by the Greek sculptor Praxiteles, the forms are softly and subtly blended by means of smooth, blurred transitions. The volumes of Indian sculpture and the surface anatomy of male figures in the style of the Greek sculptor Polyclitus are sharply defined and clearly articulated. One of the main distinctions between the work of Italian and northern Renaissance sculptors lies in the Italians' preference for compositions made up of clearly articulated, distinct units of form and the tendency of the northern Europeans to subordinate the individual parts to the all-over flow of the composition.

Balance. The balance, or equilibrium, of freestanding sculpture has three aspects. First, the sculpture must have

Articulation.
(Left) Flowing surface exemplified by "St. John the Baptist Preaching," bronze sculpture by Auguste Rodin, 1878. In the Museum of Modern Art, New York. Height 2 m. (Right) Delineated surface exemplified by "L'Idolino" bronze, Roman copy of a Greek sculpture in the style of Polyclitus, c. 440 BC. In the Museo Archeologico, Florence.
(Left) Collection, the Museum of Modern Art, New York, Mrs. Simon Guggenheim Fund; (right) Alinari

actual physical stability. This can be achieved by natural balance—that is, by making the sculpture stable enough in itself to stand firmly—which is easy enough to do with a four-legged animal or a reclining figure but not with a standing figure or a tall, thin sculpture, which must be secured to a base. The second aspect of balance is compositional. The interaction of forces and the distribution of weight within a composition may produce a state of either dynamic or static equilibrium. The third aspect of balance applies only to sculpture that represents a living figure. A live human figure balances on two feet by making constant movements and muscular adjustments. An effect of this "living balance" can be achieved in sculpture by subtle displacements of form and suggestions of tension and relaxation.

Design relationships between sculpture and the other visual arts. Sculpture has always been closely related to architecture through its role as architectural decoration and also at the level of design. Architecture, like sculpture, is concerned with three-dimensional form; and, although the central problem in the design of buildings is the organization of space rather than mass, there are styles of architecture that are effective largely through the quality and organization of their solid forms. Ancient styles of stone architecture, particularly Egyptian, Greek, and Mexican, tend to treat their components in a sculptural manner. Moreover, most buildings viewed from the outside are compositions of masses. The growth of spatial sculpture during the 20th century is so intimately related to the opening up and lightening of architecture, which the development of modern building technology has made possible, that many contemporary sculptors can be said to treat their work in an architectural manner.

Some forms of relief sculpture approach very closely the pictorial arts of painting, drawing, engraving, and so on. And sculptures in the round that make use of chiaroscuro and that are conceived primarily as pictorial views rather than as compositions in the round are said to be "painterly"; for example, Bernini's "Ecstasy of St. Teresa" (Sta. Maria della Vittoria, Rome).

The borderlines between sculpture and pottery and the

Sculpture and the pictorial arts

metalworking arts are not clear-cut, and many pottery and metal artifacts have every claim to be considered as sculpture. Today there is a growing affinity between the work of industrial designers and sculptors.

The close relationships that exist between sculpture and the other visual arts are attested by the number of artists who have readily turned from one art to another; for example, Michelangelo, Bernini, Antonio Pisanello, Edgar Degas, and Pablo Picasso.

MATERIALS

Any material that can be shaped in three dimensions can be used sculpturally. Certain materials, however, by virtue of their structural and aesthetic properties and their availability, have proved especially suitable. The most important of these are stone, wood, metal, clay, ivory, and plaster. There are also a number of materials of secondary importance and many that have only recently come into use.

Stone. Throughout history, stone has been the principal material of monumental sculpture. There are practical reasons for this: many types of stone are highly resistant to the weather and therefore suitable for external use; stone is available in all parts of the world and can be obtained in large blocks; many stones have a fairly homogeneous texture and a uniform hardness that make them suitable for carving; stone has been the chief material used for the monumental architecture with which so much sculpture has been associated.

Igneous, sedimentary, and metamorphic rocks. Stones belonging to all three main categories of rock formation have been used in sculpture. Igneous rocks, which are formed by the cooling of molten masses of mineral as they approach the Earth's surface, include granite, diorite, basalt, and obsidian. These are some of the hardest stones used for sculpture. Sedimentary rocks, which include sandstones and limestones, are formed from accumulated deposits of mineral and organic substances. Sandstones are agglomerations of particles of eroded stone held together by a cementing substance. Limestones are formed chiefly from the calcareous remains of organisms. Alabaster (gypsum), also a sedimentary rock, is a chemical deposit. Many varieties of sandstone and limestone, which vary greatly in quality and suitability for carving, are used for sculpture. Because of their method of formation, many sedimentary rocks have pronounced strata and are rich in fossils.

Metamorphic rocks result from changes brought about in the structure of sedimentary and igneous rocks by extreme pressure or heat. The most well-known metamorphic rocks used in sculpture are the marbles, which are re-crystallized limestones. Italian Carrara marble, the best known, was used by Roman and Renaissance sculptors, especially Michelangelo, and is still widely used. The best known varieties used by Greek sculptors, with whom marble was more popular than any other stone, are Pentelic—from which the Parthenon and its sculpture are made—and Parian.

Because stone is extremely heavy and lacks tensile strength, it is easily fractured if carved too thinly and not properly supported. A massive treatment without vulnerable projections, as in Egyptian and pre-Columbian American Indian sculpture, is therefore usually preferred. Some stones, however, can be treated more freely and openly; marble in particular has been treated by some European sculptors with almost the same freedom as bronze, but such displays of virtuosity are achieved by overcoming rather than submitting to the properties of the material itself.

The colours and textures of stone are among its most delightful properties. Some stones are fine-grained and can be carved with delicate detail and finished with a high polish; others are coarse-grained and demand a broader treatment. Pure white Carrara marble, which has a translucent quality, seems to glow and responds to light in a delicate, subtle manner. (These properties of marble were brilliantly exploited by 15th-century Italian sculptors such as Donatello and Desiderio da Settignano.) The colouring of granite is not uniform but has a salt-and-

Colours and textures of stone

pepper quality and may glint with mica and quartz crystals. It may be predominantly black or white or a variety of grays, pinks, and reds. Sandstones vary in texture and are often warmly coloured in a range of buffs, pinks, and reds. Limestones vary greatly in colour, and the presence of fossils may add to the interest of their surfaces. A number of stones are richly variegated in colour by the irregular veining that runs through them.

Hardstones. Hardstones, or semiprecious stones, constitute a special group, which includes some of the most beautiful and decorative of all substances. The working of these stones, along with the working of more precious gemstones, is usually considered as part of the glyptic (gem carving or engraving), or lapidary, arts, but many artifacts produced from them can be considered small-scale sculpture. They are often harder to work than steel. First among the hardstones used for sculpture is jade, which was venerated by the ancient Chinese, who worked it, together with other hardstones, with extreme skill. It was also used sculpturally by Mayan and Mexican artists. Other important hardstones are rock crystal, rose quartz, amethyst, agate, and jasper.

Wood. The principal material of tribal sculpture in Africa, Oceania, and North America, wood has also been used by every great civilization; it was used extensively during the Middle Ages, for example, especially in Germany and central Europe. Among modern sculptors who have used wood for important works are Ernst Barlach, Ossip Zadkine, and Henry Moore.

Characteristics of woodBoth hardwoods and softwoods are used for sculpture. Some are close-grained, and they cut like cheese; others are open-grained and stringy. The fibrous structure of wood gives it considerable tensile strength, so that it may be carved thinly and with greater freedom than stone. For large or complex open compositions, a number of pieces of wood may be jointed. Wood is used mainly for indoor sculpture, for it is not as tough or durable as stone; changes of humidity and temperature may cause it to split, and it is subject to attack by insects and fungus. The grain of wood is one of its most attractive features, giving variety of pattern and texture to its surfaces. Its colours, too, are subtle and varied. In general, wood has a warmth that stone does not have, but it lacks the massive dignity and weight of stone.

The principal woods for sculpture are oak, mahogany, limewood, walnut, elm, pine, cedar, boxwood, pear, and ebony; but many others are also used. The sizes of wood available are limited by the sizes of trees; North American Indians, for example, could carve gigantic totem poles in pine, but boxwood is available only in small pieces.

In the 20th century, wood was being used by many sculptors as a medium for construction as well as for carving. Laminated timbers, chipboards, and timber in block and plank form can be glued, jointed, screwed, or bolted together, and given a variety of finishes.

Metal. Wherever metal technologies have been developed, metals have been used for sculpture. The amount of metal sculpture that has survived from the ancient world does not properly reflect the extent to which it was used, for vast quantities have been plundered and melted down. Countless Far Eastern and Greek metal sculptures have been lost in this way, as has almost all the goldwork of pre-Columbian American Indians.

The metal most used for sculpture is bronze, which is basically an alloy of copper and tin; but gold, silver, aluminum, copper, brass, lead, and iron have also been widely used. Most metals are extremely strong, hard, and durable, with a tensile strength that permits a much greater freedom of design than is possible in either stone or wood. A life-size bronze figure that is firmly attached Advantages of bronzeto a base needs no support other than its own feet and may even be poised on one foot. Considerable attenuation of form is also possible without risk of fracture.

The colour, brilliant lustre, and reflectivity of metal surfaces have been highly valued and made full use of in sculpture although, since the Renaissance, artificial patinas have generally been preferred as finishes for bronze.

Metals can be worked in a variety of ways in order to produce sculpture. They can be cast—that is, melted and poured into molds; squeezed under pressure into dies, as in coin making; or worked directly—for example, by hammering, bending, cutting, welding, and repoussé (hammered or pressed in relief). Each method produces a different effect.

Important traditions of bronze sculpture are Greek, Roman, Indian (especially Cōḻa), African (Bini and Yoruba), Italian Renaissance, and Chinese. Gold was used to great effect for small-scale works in pre-Columbian America and medieval Europe. A fairly recent discovery, aluminum has been used a great deal by modern sculptors. Iron has not been used much as a casting material, but in recent years it has become a popular material for direct working by techniques similar to those of the blacksmith. Sheet metal is one of the principal materials used nowadays for constructional sculpture. Stainless steel in sheet form has been used effectively by the American sculptor David Smith.

Clay. Clay is one of the most common and easily obtainable of all materials. Used for modelling animal and human figures long before men discovered how to fire pots, it has been one of the sculptor's chief materials ever since.

Clay has four properties that account for its widespread use: when moist, it is one of the most plastic of all substances, easily modelled and capable of registering the most detailed impressions; when partially dried out to a leather-hard state or completely dried, it can be carved and scraped; when mixed with enough water, it becomes a creamy liquid known as slip, which may be poured into molds and allowed to dry; when fired to temperatures of between 700°–1,400° C (1,300°–2,600° F), it undergoes irreversible structural changes that make it permanently hard and extremely durable.

Sculptors use clay as a material for working out ideas; for preliminary models that are subsequently cast in such Uses of claymaterials as plaster, metal, and concrete or carved in stone; and for pottery sculpture.

Depending on the nature of the clay body itself and the temperature at which it is fired, a finished pottery product is said to be earthenware, which is opaque, relatively soft, and porous; stoneware, which is hard, nonporous, and more or less vitrified; or porcelain, which is fine-textured, vitrified, and translucent. All three types of pottery are used for sculpture. Sculpture made in low-fired clays, particularly buff and red clays, is known as terra-cotta (baked earth). This term is used inconsistently, however, and is often extended to cover all forms of pottery sculpture.

Unglazed clay bodies can be smooth or coarse in texture and may be coloured white, gray, buff, brown, pink, or red. Pottery sculpture can be decorated with any of the techniques invented by potters and coated with a variety of beautiful glazes.

Paleolithic sculptors produced relief and in-the-round work in unfired clay. The ancient Chinese, particularly during the T'ang (618–907) and Sung (960–1279) dynasties, made superb pottery sculpture, including large-scale human figures. The best known Greek works are the intimate small-scale figures and groups from Tanagra. Mexican and Mayan sculptor-potters produced vigorous, directly modelled figures. During the Renaissance, pottery was used in Italy for major sculptural projects, including the large-scale glazed and coloured sculptures of Luca Della Robbia and his family, which are among the finest works in the medium. One of the most popular uses of the pottery medium has been for the manufacture of figurines—at Staffordshire, Meissen, and Sèvres, for example.

Ivory. The main source of ivory is elephant tusks; but Sources of ivorywalrus, hippopotamus, narwhal (an Arctic aquatic animal), and, in Paleolithic times, mammoth tusks also were used for sculpture. Ivory is dense, hard, and difficult to work. Its colour is creamy white, which usually yellows with age; and it will take a high polish. A tusk may be sawed into panels for relief carving or into blocks for carving in the round; or the shape of the tusk itself may be used. The physical properties of the material invite the most delicate, detailed carving, and displays of virtuosity are common.

Ivory was used extensively in antiquity in the Near and Far East and the Mediterranean. An almost unbroken Christian tradition of ivory carving reaches from Rome and Byzantium to the end of the Middle Ages. Throughout this time, ivory was used mainly in relief, often in conjunction with precious metals, enamels, and precious stones to produce the most splendid effects. Some of its main sculptural uses were for devotional diptychs, portable altars, book covers, retables (a raised shelf above the altar), caskets, and crucifixes. The Baroque period, too, is rich in ivories, especially in Germany. A fine tradition of ivory carving also existed in Benin, a former kingdom of West Africa.

Related to ivory, horn and bone have been used since Paleolithic times for small-scale sculpture. Reindeer horn and walrus tusks were two of the Eskimo carver's most important materials. One of the finest of all medieval "ivories" is a carving in whalebone of "The Adoration of the Magi" (Victoria and Albert Museum, London).

By courtesy of Victoria and Albert Museum, London

Bone carving.
"The Adoration of the Magi," whalebone, English, 11th–12th century. In the Victoria and Albert Museum, London. Height 37 cm.

Plaster. Plaster of Paris (sulfate of lime) is especially useful for the production of molds, casts, and preliminary models. It was used by Egyptian and Greek sculptors as a casting medium and is today the most versatile material in the sculptor's workshop.

When mixed with water, plaster will in a short time recrystallize, or "set"—that is, become hard and inert—and its volume will increase slightly. When set, it is relatively fragile and lacking in character and is therefore of limited use for finished work. Plaster can be poured as a liquid, modelled directly when of a suitable consistency, or easily carved after it has set. Other materials can be added to it in order to retard its setting, to increase its hardness or resistance to heat, to change its colour, or to reinforce it.

The main sculptural use of plaster in the past was for molding and casting clay models as a stage in the production of cast metal sculpture. Many sculptors today omit the clay-modelling stage and model directly in plaster. As a mold material in the casting of concrete and fibre-glass sculpture, plaster is widely used. It has great value as a material for reproducing existing sculpture; many museums, for example, use plaster casts of distinguished works for study purposes.

Concrete. Basically, concrete is a mixture of an aggregate (usually sand and small pieces of stone) bound together by cement. A variety of stones, such as crushed marble, granite chips, and gravel, can be used, each giving a different effect of colour and texture. Commercial cement is gray, white, or black; but it can be coloured by additives. The cement most widely used by sculptors is *ciment fondu*, which is extremely hard and quick setting. A recent invention—at least, in appropriate forms for sculpture—concrete is rapidly replacing stone for certain types of work. Because it is cheap, hard, tough, and durable, it is particularly suitable for large outdoor projects, especially decorative wall surfaces. With proper reinforcement it permits great freedom of design. And by using techniques similar to those of the building industry, sculptors are able to create works in concrete on a gigantic scale.

Advantages of concrete

Fibre glass. When synthetic resins, especially polyesters, are reinforced with laminations of glass fibre, the result is a lightweight shell that is extremely strong, hard, and durable. It is usually known simply as fibre glass. After having been successfully used for car bodies, boat hulls, and the like, it has developed recently into an important material for sculpture. Since the material is visually unattractive, it is usually coloured by means of fillers and pigments. It was first used in sculpture in conjunction with powdered metal fillers in order to produce cheap "cold-cast" substitutes for bronze and aluminum, but with the recent tendency to use bright colours in sculpture it is now often coloured either by pigmenting the material itself or by painting.

It is possible to model fibre glass, but more usually it is cast as a laminated shell. Its possibilities for sculpture have not yet been fully exploited.

Wax. Various formulas for modelling wax have been used in the past, but these have been generally replaced by synthetic waxes. The main uses of wax in sculpture have been as a preliminary modelling material for metal casting by the lost-wax, or *cire perdu*, process (see *Methods and techniques*, below), and for making sketches. It is not durable enough for use as a material in its own right, although it has been used for small works, such as wax fruit, that can be kept under a glass dome.

Paper. Papier-mâché (pulped paper bonded with glue) has been used for sculpture, especially in the Far East. Mainly used for decorative work, especially masks, it can have considerable strength; the Japanese, for example, made armour from it. Sculpture made of sheet paper is a limited art form used only for ephemeral and usually trivial work.

Other materials. Numerous other permanent materials, such as shells, amber, and brick, and ephemeral ones, such as feathers, baker's dough, ice and snow, and cake icing, have been used for fashioning three-dimensional images.

In view of recent trends in sculpture it is no longer possible to speak of "the materials of sculpture." Modern sculpture has no special materials. Any material, natural or man-made, is likely to be used, including inflated polythene, foam rubber, expanded polystyrene, fabrics, and neon tubes; the materials for a mid-20th century sculpture by Claes Oldenburg, for example, are listed as canvas, cloth, Dacron, metal, foam rubber, and Plexiglas. Real objects, too, may be incorporated in sculpture, as in the mixed-medium compositions of Edward Kienholz; even junk has its devotees, who fashion "junk" sculpture.

METHODS AND TECHNIQUES

Sculpture and the decorative arts. Although a sculptor may specialize in, say, stone carving or direct metalwork,

Unconventional materials of modern sculpture.
"Giant Hamburger," painted sailcloth stuffed with foam rubber, by Claes Oldenburg, 1962. In the Art Gallery of Ontario. 132 × 213 cm.
By courtesy of the Art Gallery of Ontario

the art of sculpture is not identifiable with any particular craft or set of crafts. It presses into its service whatever crafts suit its purposes. Technologies developed for more utilitarian purposes are often easily adapted for sculpture; in fact, useful artifacts and sculptured images have often been produced in the same workshop, sometimes by the same craftsman. The methods and techniques employed in producing a pot, a bronze harness trapping, a decorative stone molding or column, a carved wooden newel post, or even a fibre-glass car body are essentially the same as those used in sculpture. For example, the techniques of repoussé, metal casting, blacksmithing, sheet-metal work, and welding, which are used for the production of functional artifacts and decorative metalwork, are also used in metal sculpture; and the preparation, forming, glazing, decoration, and firing of clay are basically the same in both utilitarian pottery and pottery sculpture. The new techniques used by sculptors today are closely related to new techniques applied in building and industrial manufacture.

The sculptor as designer and as craftsman. The conception of an artifact or a work of art—its form, imaginative content, and expressiveness—is the concern of a designer, and it should be distinguished from the execution of the work in a particular technique and material, which is the task of a craftsman. A sculptor usually functions as both designer and craftsman, but these two aspects of sculpture may be separated.

Certain types of sculpture depend considerably for their aesthetic effect on the way in which their material has been directly manipulated by the artist himself. The direct, expressive handling of clay in a model by Rodin, or the use of the chisel in the stiacciato (very low) reliefs of the 15th-century Florentine sculptor Donatello could no more have been delegated to a craftsman than could the brushwork of Rembrandt. The actual physical process of working materials is for many sculptors an integral part of the art of sculpture, and their response to the working qualities of the material—such as its plasticity, hardness, and texture—is evident in the finished work. Design and craftsmanship are intimately fused in such a work, which is a highly personal expression.

Even when the direct handling of material is not as vital as this to the expressiveness of the work, it still may be impossible to separate the roles of the artist as designer and craftsman. The qualities and interrelationships of forms may be so subtle and complex that they cannot be adequately specified and communicated to a craftsman. Moreover, many aspects of the design may actually be contributed during the process of working. Michelangelo's way of working, for example, enabled him to change his mind about important aspects of composition as the work proceeded.

A complete fusion of design and craftsmanship may not be possible if a project is a large one or if the sculptor is too old or too weak to do all of the work himself. The sheer physical labour of making a large sculpture can be considerable, and sculptors from Phidias in the 5th century BC to Henry Moore in the 20th century have employed pupils and assistants to help with it. Usually the sculptor delegates the time-consuming first stages of the work or some of its less important parts to his assistants and executes the final stages or the most important parts himself.

On occasion, a sculptor may function like an architect or industrial designer. He may do no direct work at all on the finished sculpture, his contribution being to supply exhaustive specifications in the form of drawings and perhaps scale models for a work that is to be entirely fabricated by craftsmen. Obviously, such a procedure excludes the possibility of direct, personal expression through the handling of the materials; thus, works of this kind usually have the same anonymous, impersonal quality as architecture and industrial design. An impersonal approach to sculpture was favoured by many sculptors of the 1960s such as William Tucker, Donald Judd, and William Turnbull. They used the skilled anonymous workmanship of industrial fabrications to make their large scale, extremely precise, simple sculptural forms that are called "primary structures."

General methods. Broadly speaking, the stages in the production of a major work of sculpture conform to the following pattern: the commission; the preparation, submission, and acceptance of the design; the selection and preparation of materials; the forming of materials; surface finishing; installation or presentation.

Stages in the production of a major work

Almost all of the sculpture of the past and some present-day sculpture originates in a demand made upon the sculptor from outside, usually in the form of a direct commission or through a competition. If the commission is for a portrait or a private sculpture, the client may only require to see examples of the artist's previous work; but if it is a public commission, the sculptor is usually expected to submit drawings and maquettes (small-scale, three-dimensional sketch models) that give an idea of the nature of the finished work and its relation to the site. He may be free to choose his own subject matter or theme, or it may be more or less strictly prescribed. A medieval master sculptor, for example, received the program for a complex scheme of church sculpture from theological advisers, and Renaissance contracts for sculpture were often extremely specified and detailed. Today a great deal of sculpture is not commissioned. It arises out of the sculptor's private concern with form and imagery, and he works primarily to satisfy himself. When the work is finished he may exhibit and attempt to sell it in an art gallery.

Most of the materials used by 20th-century sculptors are readily available in a usable form from builders' or sculptors' suppliers, but certain kinds of sculpture may involve a good deal of preparatory work on the materials. A sculptor may visit a stone quarry in order to select the material for a large project and to have it cut into blocks of the right size and shape. And since stone is costly to transport and best carved when freshly quarried, he may decide to do all of his work at the quarry. Because stone is extremely heavy, the sculptor must have the special equipment required for manoeuvring even small blocks into position for carving. A wood carver requires a supply of well-seasoned timber and may keep a quantity of logs and blocks in store. A modeller needs a good supply of clay of the right kind. For large terra-cottas he may require a specially made up clay body, or he may work at a brickworks, using the local clay and firing in the brick kilns.

The main part of the sculptor's work, the shaping of the material itself by modelling, carving, or constructional techniques, may be a long and arduous process, perhaps extending over a number of years and requiring assistants. Much of the work, especially architectural decoration, may be carried out at the site, or *in situ*.

To improve its weathering qualities, to bring out the characteristics of its material to the best advantage, or to make it more decorative or realistic, sculpture is usually given a special surface finish. It may be rubbed down and polished, patinated, metal plated, gilded, painted, inlaid with other materials, and so on.

Finally, the installation of sculpture may be a complex and important part of the work. The positioning and fixing of large architectural sculpture may involve cooperation with builders and engineers; fountains may involve elaborate plumbing; the design and placing of outdoor bases, or plinths, in relation to the site and the spectator may require careful thought. The choice of the materials, shape, and proportions of the base even for a small work requires a considerable amount of care.

Carving. *Direct carving.* Whatever material is used, the essential features of the direct method of carving are the same; the sculptor starts with a solid mass of material and reduces it systematically to the desired form. After he has blocked out the main masses and planes that define the outer limits of the forms, he works progressively over the whole sculpture, first carving the larger containing forms and planes and then the smaller ones until eventually the surface details are reached. Then he gives the surface whatever finish is required. Even with a preliminary model as a guide, the sculptor's concept constantly evolves and clarifies as the work proceeds; thus, as he adapts his design to the nature of the carving process and the material, his work develops as an organic whole.

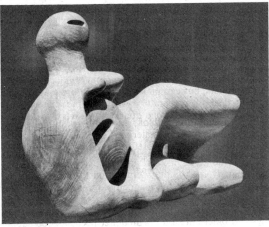

Direct carving.
(Top) "Reclining Figure" in progress, elmwood sculpture by Henry Moore, 1945–46. (Bottom) "Reclining Figure." Length 1.90 m.

The process of direct carving imposes a characteristic order on the forms of sculpture. The faces of the original block, slab, or cylinder of material can usually still be sensed, existing around the finished work as a kind of implied spatial envelope limiting the extension of the forms in space and connecting their highest points across space. In a similar way, throughout the whole carving, smaller forms and planes can be seen as contained within implied larger ones. Thus, an ordered sequence of containing forms and planes, from the largest to the smallest, gives unity to the work.

Indirect carving. All of the great sculptural traditions of the past used the direct method of carving, but in

Western civilization during the 19th and early 20th centuries it became customary for stone and, to a lesser extent, wood sculpture to be produced by the indirect method. This required the production of a finished clay model that was subsequently cast in plaster and then reproduced in stone or wood in a more or less mechanical way by means of a pointing machine (see *Reproduction techniques: pointing,* below). Usually, the carving was not done by the sculptor himself. At its worst, this procedure results in a carved copy of a design that was conceived in terms of clay modelling. Although indirect carving does not achieve aesthetic qualities that are typical of carved sculpture, it does not necessarily result in bad sculpture. Rodin's marble sculptures, for example, are generally considered great works of art even by those who object to the indirect methods by which they were produced. The indirect method has been steadily losing ground since the revival of direct carving in the early part of the 20th century, and today it is in general disrepute among carvers.

Carving tools and techniques. The tools used for carving differ with the material to be carved. Stone is carved mostly with steel tools that resemble cold chisels. To knock off the corners and angles of a block, a tool called a pitcher is driven into the surface with a heavy iron hammer. The pitcher is a thick, chisel-like tool with a wide bevelled edge that breaks rather than cuts the stone. The heavy point then does the main roughing out, followed by the fine point, which may be used to within a short distance of the final surface. These pointed tools are hammered into the surface at an angle that causes the stone to break off in chips of varying sizes. Claw chisels, which have toothed edges, may then be worked in all directions over the surface, removing the stone in granule form and thus refining the surface forms. Flat chisels are used for finishing the surface carving and for cutting sharp detail.

There are many other special tools, including stone gouges, drills, toothed hammers (known as bushhammers or bouchardes), and, often used today, power-driven pneumatic tools, for pounding away the surface of the stone.

Because medieval carvers worked mostly in softer stones and made great use of flat chisels, their work tends to have an edgy, cut quality and to be freely and deeply carved. In contrast is the work done in hard stones by people who lacked metal tools hard enough to cut the stone. Egyptian granite sculpture, for example, was produced mainly by abrasion; that is, by pounding the surface and rubbing it down with abrasive materials. The result is a compact sculpture, not deeply hollowed out, with softened edges and flowing surfaces. It usually has a high degree of tactile appeal.

Although the process of carving is fundamentally the same for wood or stone, the physical structure of wood demands tools of a different type. For the first blocking out of a wood carving a sculptor may use saws and axes, but his principal tools are a wide range of wood-carver's gouges. The sharp, curved edge of a gouge cuts easily through the bundles of fibre and when used properly will not split the wood. Flat chisels are also used, especially for carving sharp details. Wood rasps, or coarse files, and sandpaper can be used to give the surface a smooth finish, or, if preferred, it can be left with a faceted, chiselled appearance. Wood-carving tools have hardwood handles and are struck with round, wooden mallets. African wood sculptors use a variety of adzes rather than gouges and mallets.

Ivory is carved with an assortment of saws, knives, rasps, files, chisels, drills, and scrapers.

Modelling. In contrast to the reductive process of carving, modelling is essentially a building-up process in which the sculpture grows organically from the inside. Numerous plastic materials are used for modelling. The main ones are clay, plaster, and wax; but concrete, synthetic resins, plastic wood, stucco, and even molten metal can also be modelled. A design modelled in plastic materials may be intended for reproduction by casting in more permanent and rigid materials, such as metal, plaster,

Clay models

concrete, and fibre glass, or it may itself be made rigid and more permanent through the self-setting properties of its materials (for example, plaster) or by firing.

Modelling for casting. The material most widely used for making positive models for casting is clay. A small, compact design or a low relief can be modelled solidly in clay without any internal support; but a large clay model must be formed over a strong armature made of wood and metal. Since the armature may be very elaborate and can only be altered slightly, if at all, once work has started, the modeller must have a fairly clear idea from his drawings and maquettes of the arrangement of the main shapes of the finished model. The underlying main masses of the sculpture are built up firmly over the armature and then the smaller forms, surface modelling, and details are modelled over them. The modeller's chief tools are his fingers, but for fine work he may use a variety of wooden modelling tools to apply the clay and wire loop tools to cut it away. Reliefs are modelled on a vertical or nearly vertical board. The clay is keyed, or secured, onto the board with galvanized nails or wood laths. The amount of armature required depends on the height of the relief and the weight of clay involved.

To make a cast in metal, a foundry requires from the sculptor a model made of a rigid material, usually plaster. The sculptor can produce this either by modelling in clay and then casting in plaster from the clay model or by modelling directly in plaster. For direct plaster modelling, a strong armature is required because the material is brittle. The main forms may be built up roughly over the armature in expanded wire and then covered in plaster-soaked scrim (a loosely woven sacking). This provides a hollow base for the final modelling, which is done by applying plaster with metal spatulas and by scraping and cutting down with rasps and chisels.

Fibre-glass and concrete sculptures are cast in plaster molds taken from the sculptor's original model. The model is usually clay rather than plaster because if the forms of the sculpture are at all complex it is easier to remove a plaster mold from a soft clay model than from a model in a rigid material, such as plaster.

A great deal of the metal sculpture of the past, including Nigerian, Indian, and many Renaissance bronzes, was produced by the direct lost-wax process, which involves a special modelling technique (see *Reproduction techniques: casting and modelling*, below). The design is first

Eliot Elisofon

Lost-wax process bronze sculpture.
"Male Portrait Head," bronze from Ife, Nigeria, 12th century.
In the Museum of Ife Antiquities. Height 34 cm.

modelled in some refractory material to within a fraction of an inch of the final surface, and then the final modelling is done in a layer of wax, using the fingers and also metal tools, which can be heated to make the wax more pliable. Medallions are often produced from wax originals, but because of their small size they do not require a core.

Modelling for pottery sculpture. In order to withstand the stresses of firing, a large pottery sculpture must be hollow and of an even thickness. There are two main ways of achieving this. In the process of hollow modelling, which is typical of the potter's approach to form, the main forms of the clay model are built up directly as hollow forms with walls of a roughly even thickness. The methods of building are similar to those employed for making hand-built pottery—coiling, pinching, and slabbing. The smaller forms and details are then added, and the finished work is allowed to dry out slowly and thoroughly before firing. The process of solid modelling is more typical of the sculptor's traditional approach to form. The sculpture is modelled in solid clay, sometimes over a carefully considered armature, by the sculptor's usual methods of clay modelling. Then it is cut open and hollowed out, and the armature, if there is one, is removed. The pieces are then rejoined and the work is dried out and fired.

General characteristics of modelled sculpture. The process of modelling affects the design of sculpture in three important ways. First, the forms of the sculpture tend to be ordered from the inside. There are no external containing forms and planes, as in carved sculpture. The overall design of the work—its main volumes, proportions, and axial arrangement—is determined by the underlying forms; and the smaller forms, surface modelling, and decorative details are all formed around and sustained by this underlying structure. Second, because its extension into space is not limited by the dimensions of a block of material, modelled sculpture tends to be much freer and more expansive in its spatial design than carved sculpture. If the tensile strength of metal is to be exploited in the finished work, there is almost unlimited freedom; designs for brittle materials such as concrete or plaster, however, are more limited. Third, the plasticity of clay and wax encourages a fluent, immediate kind of manipulation, and many sculptors, such as Auguste Rodin, Giacomo Manzù, and Sir Jacob Epstein, like to preserve this record of their direct handling of the medium in their finished work. Their approach contrasts with that of the Benin and Indian bronze sculptors, who refined the surfaces of their work to remove all traces of personal "handwriting."

Effects of modelling on the design of sculpture

Constructing and assembling. A constructed or assembled sculpture is made by joining preformed pieces of material. It differs radically in principle from carved and modelled sculpture, both of which are fabricated out of a homogeneous mass of material. Constructed sculpture is made out of such basic preformed components as metal tubes, rods, plates, bars, and sheets; wooden laths, planks, dowels, and blocks; laminated timbers and chipboards; sheets of Perspex (used for acrylic plastic), Formica, and glass; fabrics; and wires and threads. These are cut to various sizes and may be either shaped before they are assembled or used as they are. The term assemblage is usually reserved for constructed sculpture that incorporates any of a vast array of ready-made, so-called found objects, such as old boilers, typewriters, engine components, mirrors, chairs, and table legs and other bits of old furniture.

Numerous techniques are employed for joining these components, most of them derived from crafts other than traditional sculptural ones; for example, metal welding and brazing, wood joinery, bolting, screwing, rivetting, nailing, and bonding with new powerful adhesives.

The use of constructional techniques for the production of sculpture is the major technical development of the art of sculpture in recent years. Among the reasons for its popularity are that it lends itself readily to an emphasis on the spatial aspects of sculpture that have preoccupied so many 20th-century artists; it is quicker than carving

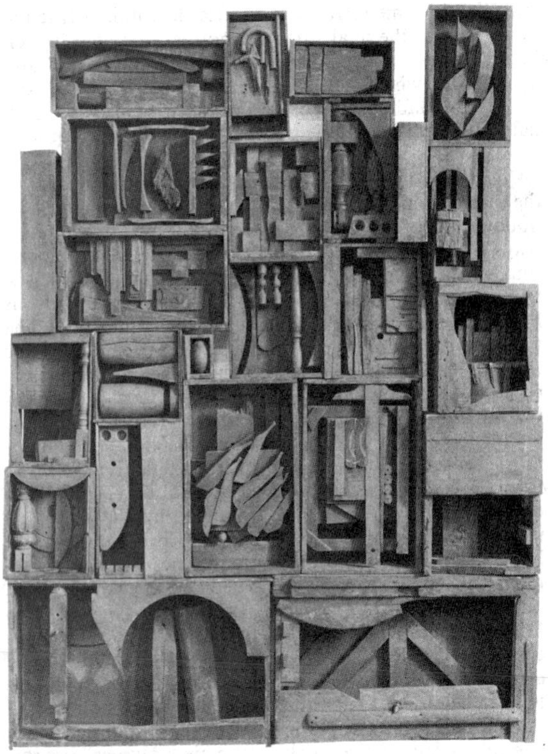

Assemblage.
"Black Wall," wood sculpture by Louise Nevelson, 1959. In the Tate Gallery, London. 2.84 × 2.16 × 0.65 m.
By courtesy of the trustees of the Tate Gallery, London

and modelling; it is considered by many sculptors and critics to be especially appropriate to a technological civilization; it is opening up new fields of imagery and new types of symbolism and form.

For constructed "gallery" sculpture, almost any materials and techniques are likely to be used, and the products are often extremely ephemeral. But architectural sculpture, outdoor sculpture, and indeed any sculpture that is actually used must be constructed in a safe and at least reasonably permanent manner. The materials and techniques employed are therefore somewhat restricted. Metal sculpture constructed by rivetting, bolting, and, above all, welding and brazing is best for outdoor use.

Direct metal sculpture. The introduction of the oxyacetylene welding torch as a sculptor's tool has revolutionized metal sculpture in recent years. A combination of welding and forging techniques was pioneered by the Spanish sculptor Julio González around 1930; and during the 1940s and 1950s it became a major sculptural technique, particularly in Britain and in the United States, where its greatest exponent was David Smith. In the 1960s and early 1970s, more sophisticated electric welding processes were replacing flame welding.

Welding and forging

Welding equipment can be used for joining and cutting metal. A welded joint is made by melting and fusing together the surfaces of two pieces of metal, usually with the addition of a small quantity of the same metal as a filler. The metal most widely used for welded sculpture is mild steel, but other metals can be welded. In a brazed joint, the parent metals are not actually fused together but are joined by an alloy that melts at a lower temperature than the parent metals. Brazing is particularly useful for making joints between different kinds of metal, which cannot be done by welding, and for joining nonferrous metals. Forging is the direct shaping of metal by bending, hammering, and cutting.

Direct metalworking techniques have opened up whole new ranges of form to the sculptor—open skeletal structures, linear and highly extended forms, and complex, curved sheet forms. Constructed metal sculpture may be precise and clean, as that of Minimalist sculptors Donald Judd and Phillip King, or it may exploit the textural effects of molten metal in a free, "romantic" manner.

Reproduction techniques: casting and molding. Casting and molding processes are used in sculpture either for making copies of existing sculpture or as essential stages in the production of a finished work. Numerous materials are used for making molds and casts, and some of the methods are complex and highly skilled. Only a broad outline of the principal methods can be given here.

Plaster waste molds. These are used for producing a single cast from a soft, plastic original, usually clay. They are especially useful for producing master casts for subsequent reproduction in metal. The basic procedure is as follows. First, the mold is built up in liquid plaster over the original clay model; for casting reliefs, a one-piece mold may be sufficient, but for sculpture in the round a mold in at least two sections is required. Second, when the plaster is set, the mold is divided and removed from the clay model. Third, the mold is cleaned, reassembled, and filled with a self-setting material such as plaster, concrete, or fibre-glass-reinforced resin. Fourth, the mold is carefully chipped away from the cast. This involves the destruction of the mold—hence the term "waste" mold. The order of reassembling and filling the mold may be reversed; fibre glass and resin, for example, are "layed-up" in the mold pieces before they are reassembled.

Plaster piece molds. Plaster piece molds are used for producing more than one cast from a soft or rigid original and are especially good for reproducing existing sculpture and for slip casting (see below). Before the invention of flexible molds (see below), piece molds were used for producing wax casts for metal casting by the lost-wax process. A piece mold is built up in sections that can be withdrawn from the original model without damaging it. The number of sections depends on the complexity of the form and on the amount of undercutting; tens, or even hundreds, of pieces may be required for really large, complex works. The mold sections are carefully keyed together and supported by a plaster case. When the mold has been filled, it can be removed section by section from the cast and then reassembled and used again. Piece molding is a highly skilled and laborious process.

Flexible molds. Made of such materials as gelatin, vinyl, and rubber, flexible molds are used for producing more than one cast; they offer a much simpler alternative to piece molding when the original model is a rigid one with complex forms and undercuts. The material is melted and poured around the original positive in sections, if necessary. Being flexible, the mold easily pulls away from a rigid surface without causing damage. While it is being filled (with wax, plaster, concrete, and fibre-glass-reinforced resins), the mold must be surrounded by a plaster case to prevent distortion.

The lost-wax (cire perdu) process. The lost-wax process is the traditional method of casting metal sculpture. It requires a positive, which consists of a core made of a refractory material and an outer layer of wax. The positive can be produced either by direct modelling in wax over a prepared core, in which case the process is known as direct lost-wax casting, or by casting in a piece mold or flexible mold taken from a master cast. The wax positive is invested with a mold made of refractory materials and is then heated to a temperature that will drive off all moisture and melt out all the wax, leaving a narrow cavity between the core and the investment. Molten metal is then poured into this cavity. When the metal has cooled down and solidified, the investment is broken away, and the core is removed from inside the cast. The process is, of course, much more complex than this simple outline suggests. Care has to be taken to suspend the core within the mold by means of metal pins, and a structure of channels must be made in the mold that will enable the metal to reach all parts of the cavity and permit the mold gases to escape. A considerable amount of filing and chasing of the cast is usually required after casting is completed.

The traditional method of casting metal sculpture

Sand casting. While the lost-wax process is used for producing complex, refined metal castings, sand molding is more suitable for simpler types of form and for sculpture in which a certain roughness of surface does not matter. Recent improvements in the quality of sand cast-

Diverse materials and techniques

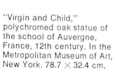

Jade horse head, Chinese, Han dynasty (206 BC–AD 220). In the Victoria and Albert Museum, London. Height 19 cm.

Jaina pottery figurine, late classic Maya style, from the state of Campeche, Mexico. In the collection of Dumbarton Oaks, Washington, D.C. Height 15.5 cm.

"Virgin and Child," polychromed oak statue of the school of Auvergne, France, 12th century. In the Metropolitan Museum of Art, New York. 78.7 × 32.4 cm.

"Isaac, Jacob, and Esau," gilded bronze relief panel from the east doors ("Gates of Paradise") of the baptistery in Florence, by Lorenzo Ghiberti, 1425–52. 79.4 cm square.

"The Ecstasy of St. Teresa," marble and gilded bronze niche sculpture by Gian Lorenzo Bernini, 1645–52. In the Coronaro Chapel, Sta. Maria della Vittoria, Rome. Lifesize.

Plate 1: By courtesy of (top left) the Victoria and Albert Museum, London, (centre) Dumbarton Oaks, Washington, D.C., (top right) The Metropolitan Museum of Art, New York, gift of J. Pierpont Morgan, 1916, (bottom left and right) SCALA, N.Y.

Plate 2   Sculpture, Art of

Painted wood male figure standing on a fish, fantastic cult image from Northern New Ireland, Melanesia. In a private collection. Height 1.53 m.

Diverse kinds of representational and nonrepresentational sculpture

"Development of a Bottle in Space," nonrepresentational sculpture by Umberto Boccioni, silvered bronze, 1912. In the Museum of Modern Art, New York. 38.1 × 32.7 × 59.7 cm.

"Cubi XVII," non-objective sculpture by David Smith, stainless steel, 1963. In the Dallas Museum of Fine Arts, Texas. Height 2.74 m.

"The Diner," representational environmental sculpture by George Segal, mixed media (plaster, wood, chrome, masonite, and formica), 1964–66. In the Walker Art Center, Minneapolis. 2.59 × 2.74 × 2.13 m.

Plate 2: By courtesy of (centre) The Museum of Modern Art, New York, Aristide Maillol Fund, (top right) Dallas Museum of Fine Arts, the Eugene and Margaret McDermott Fund; (bottom) Collection Walker Art Center, Minneapolis; photograph, (top left) H. Heinrich

ings and the invention of the "lost-pattern" process (see below) have resulted in a much wider use of sand casting as a means of producing sculpture. A sand mold, made of special sand held together by a binder, is built up around a rigid positive, usually in a number of sections held together in metal boxes. For a hollow casting, a core is required that will fit inside the negative mold, leaving a narrow cavity as in the lost-wax process. The molten metal is poured into this cavity.

The lost-pattern process. The lost-pattern process is used for the production by sand molding of single casts in metal. After a positive made of expanded polystyrene is firmly embedded in casting sand, molten metal is poured into the mold straight onto the expanded foam original. The heat of the metal causes the foam to pass off into vapour and disappear, leaving a negative mold to be filled by the metal. Channels for the metal to run in and for the gases to escape are made in the mold, as in the lost-wax process. The method is used mainly for producing solid castings in aluminum that can be welded or rivetted together to make the finished sculpture.

Slip casting. Slip casting is primarily a potter's technique that can be used for repetition casting of small pottery sculptures. Liquid clay, or slip, is poured into a plaster piece mold. Some of the water in the slip is absorbed by the plaster and a layer of stiffened clay collects on the surface of the mold. When this layer is thick enough to form a cast, the excess slip is poured off and the mold is removed. The hollow clay cast is then dried and fired.

Pressing. Simple casts for pottery sculpture—mainly tiles and low reliefs—can be prepared by pressing clay into a rigid mold. More complex forms can be built up from a number of separately press-cast pieces. Simple terra-cotta molds can be made by pressing clay around a rigid positive form. After firing, these press molds can be used for press casting.

Reproduction techniques: pointing. A sculpture can be reproduced by transposing measurements taken all over its surface to a copy. The process is made accurate and thorough by the use of a pointing machine, which is an arrangement of adjustable metal arms and pointers that are set to the position of any point on the surface of a three-dimensional form and then used to locate the corresponding point on the surface of a copy. If the copy is a stone one, the block is drilled to the depth measured by the pointing machine. When a number of points have been fixed by drilling, the stone is cut away to the required depth. For accurate pointing, a vast number of points have to be taken, and the final surface is approached gradually. The main use of pointing has been for the indirect method of carving.

Enlarged and reduced copies of sculpture can also be produced with the aid of mechanical devices. A sophisticated reducing machine that works on the principle of the pantograph (an instrument for copying on any predetermined scale, consisting of four light, rigid bars jointed in parallelogram form) is used in minting for scaling down the sculptor's original model to coin size.

Techniques of surface finishing. Surface finishes for sculpture can be either natural—bringing the material of the sculpture itself to a finish—or applied. Almost all applied surface finishes preserve as well as decorate.

Smoothing and polishing. Many sculptural materials have a natural beauty of colour and texture that can be brought out by smoothing and polishing. Stone carvings are smoothed by rubbing down with a graded series of coarse and fine abrasives, such as carborundum, sandstone, emery, pumice, and whiting, all used while the stone is wet. Some stones, such as marble and granite, will take a high gloss; others are too coarse-grained to be polished and can only be smoothed to a granular finish. Wax is sometimes used to give stone a final polish.

The natural beauty of wood is brought out by sandpapering or scraping and then waxing or oiling. Beeswax and linseed oil are the traditional materials, but a wide range of waxes and oils are currently available.

Ivory is polished with gentle abrasives such as pumice and whiting, applied with a damp cloth.

Concrete can be rubbed down, like stone, with water and abrasives, which both smooths the surface and exposes the aggregate. Some concretes can be polished.

Metals are rubbed down manually with steel wool and emery paper and polished with various metal polishes. A high-gloss polish can be given to metals by means of power driven buffing wheels used in conjunction with abrasives and polishes. Clear lacquers are applied to preserve the polish.

Painting. Stone, wood, terra-cotta, metal, fibre glass, and plaster can all be painted in a reasonably durable manner provided that the surfaces are properly prepared and suitable primings and paints are used. In the past, stone and wood carvings were often finished with a coating of gesso (plaster of Paris or gypsum prepared with glue) that served both as a final modelling material for delicate surface detail and as a priming for painting. Historically, the painting and gilding of sculpture were usually left to specialists. In Greek relief sculpture, actual details of the composition were often omitted at the carving stage and left for the painter to insert. In the 15th century, the great Flemish painter Rogier van der Weyden undertook the painting of sculpture as part of his work. — Polychrome sculpture

Modern paint technology has made an enormous range of materials available. Constructed sculptures are often finished with mechanical grinders and sanders and then sprayed with high-quality cellulose paints.

Gilding. The surfaces of wood, stone, and plaster sculpture can be decorated with gold, silver, and other metals that are applied in leaf or powder form over a suitable priming. Metals, especially bronze, were often fire-gilded; that is, treated with an amalgam of gold and mercury that was heated to drive off the mercury. The panels of the "Gates of Paradise" in Florence, by the 15th-century sculptor Lorenzo Ghiberti, are a well-known example of gilded bronze.

Patination. Patinas on metals are caused by the corrosive action of chemicals. Sculpture that is exposed to different kinds of atmosphere or buried in soil or immersed in seawater for some time acquires a patina that can be extremely attractive. Similar effects can be achieved artificially by applying various chemicals to the metal surface. This is a particularly effective treatment for bronze, which can be given a wide variety of attractive green, brown, blue, and black patinas. Iron is sometimes allowed to rust until it acquires a satisfactory colour, and then the process is arrested by lacquering. — Patinas achieved artificially

Electroplating. The surfaces of metal sculpture or of specially prepared nonmetal sculpture can be coated with such metals as chrome, silver, gold, copper, and nickel by the familiar industrial process of electroplating. The related technique of anodizing can be used to prevent the corrosion of aluminum sculpture and to dye its surface.

Other finishes. The surfaces of metal sculpture can be decorated by means of numerous metalsmithing techniques—etching, engraving, metal inlaying, enamelling, and so on. Pottery sculpture can be decorated with coloured slips, oxides, and enamels; glazed with a variety of shiny or mat glazes; and brought to a dull polish by burnishing.

Other materials have often been added to the surface of sculpture. The eyes of ancient figure sculpture, for example, were sometimes inlaid with stones. Occasionally—as in Mexican mosaic work—the whole surface of a sculpture is inlaid with mother-of-pearl, turquoise, coral, and many other substances.

FORMS OF SCULPTURE

Sculpture in the round. *Freestanding sculpture.* A great deal of sculpture is designed to be placed in public squares, gardens, parks, and similar open places or in interior positions where it is isolated in space and can be viewed from all directions. The opportunities for free spatial design that such freestanding sculpture presents are not always fully exploited. The work may be designed, like many Archaic sculptures, to be viewed from only one or two fixed positions, or it may in effect be little more than a four-sided relief that hardly changes the three-dimensional form of the block at all. Sixteenth-century Mannerist sculptors, on the other hand, made a special point of exploiting the all-around visibility of freestanding sculpture. Giambologna's "Rape of the Sabines," for example, compels the viewer to walk all

Alinari

Sculpture in the round.
The changing appearance of freestanding sculpture observed when walking around a statue is suggested by these two views of "Rape of the Sabines," marble sculpture by Giambologna, 1583. In the Loggia dei Lanzi, Florence. Height 411 cm.

around it in order to grasp its spatial design. It has no principal views; its forms move around the central axis of the composition, and their serpentine movement unfolds itself gradually as the spectator moves around to follow them. Much of the sculpture of Henry Moore and other 20th-century sculptors is not concerned with movement of this kind, nor is it designed to be viewed from any fixed positions. Rather, it is a freely designed structure of multidirectional forms that is opened up, pierced, and extended in space in such a way that the viewer is made aware of its all-around design largely by seeing through the sculpture. The majority of constructed sculptures are disposed in space with complete freedom and invite viewing from all directions. In many instances the spectator can actually walk under and through them.

The way in which a freestanding sculpture makes contact with the ground or with its base is a matter of considerable importance. A reclining figure, for example, may in effect be a horizontal relief. It may blend with the ground plane and appear to be rooted in the ground like an outcrop of rock. Other sculptures, including some reclining figures, may be designed in such a way that they seem to rest on the ground and to be independent of their base. Others are supported in space above the ground. The most completely freestanding sculptures are those that have no base and may be picked up, turned in the hands, and literally viewed all around like a netsuke (a small toggle of wood, ivory, or metal used to fasten a small pouch or purse to a kimono sash). Of course, a large sculpture cannot actually be picked up in this way,

but it can be designed so as to invite the viewer to think of it as a detached, independent object that has no fixed base and is designed all around.

Wall and niche sculpture.   Sculpture designed to stand against a wall or similar background or in a niche may be in the round and freestanding in the sense that it is not attached to its background like a relief; but it does not have the spatial independence of completely freestanding sculpture, and it is not designed to be viewed all around. It must be designed so that its formal structure and the nature and meaning of its subject matter can be clearly apprehended from a limited range of frontal views. The forms of the sculpture, therefore, are usually spread out mainly in a lateral direction rather than in depth. Greek pedimental sculpture illustrates this approach superbly: the composition is spread out in a plane perpendicular to the viewer's line of sight and is made completely intelligible from the front. Seventeenth-century Baroque sculptors, especially Bernini, adopted a rather different approach. There may be considerable recession and foreshortening in their compositions, but the forms are carefully arranged so that they present a coherent and intelligible whole from one special frontal viewpoint.

Difference between wall and niche and freestanding sculpture

The frontal composition of wall and niche sculpture does not necessarily imply any lack of three-dimensionality in the forms themselves; it is only the arrangement of the forms that is limited. Classical pedimental sculpture, Indian temple sculpture such as that at Khajurāho, Gothic niche sculpture, and Michelangelo's Medici tomb figures are all designed to be placed against a background, but their forms are conceived with a complete fullness of volume.

Relief sculpture.   Relief is a complex art form that combines many features of the two-dimensional pictorial arts and the three-dimensional sculptural arts. On the one hand, a relief, like a picture, is dependent on a supporting surface, and its composition must be extended in a plane in order to be visible. On the other hand, its three-dimensional properties are not merely represented pictorially but are in some degree actual, like those of fully developed sculpture.

Among the various types of relief are some that approach very closely the condition of the pictorial arts. The reliefs of Donatello, Ghiberti, and other early Renaissance artists make full use of perspective, which is a pictorial method of representing three-dimensional spatial relationships realistically on a two-dimensional surface. Egyptian and most pre-Columbian American low reliefs are also extremely pictorial but in a different way. Using a system of graphic conventions, they translate the three-dimensional world into a two-dimensional one. The relief image is essentially one of plane surfaces and could not possibly exist in three dimensions. Its only sculptural aspects are its slight degree of actual projection from a surface and its frequently subtle surface modelling.

Other types of relief—for example, Classical Greek and most Indian—are conceived primarily in sculptural terms. The figures inhabit a space that is defined by the solid forms of the figures themselves and is limited by the background plane. This back plane is treated as a finite, impenetrable barrier in front of which the figures exist. It is not conceived as a receding perspective space or environment within which the figures are placed nor as a flat surface upon which they are placed. The reliefs, so to speak, are more like contracted sculpture than expanded pictures.

The central problem of relief sculpture is to contract or condense three-dimensional solid form and spatial relations into a limited depth space. The extent to which the forms actually project varies considerably, and reliefs are classified on this basis as low reliefs (bas-reliefs) or high reliefs. There are types of reliefs that form a continuous series from the almost completely pictorial to the almost fully in the round.

One of the relief sculptor's most difficult tasks is to represent the relations between forms in depth within the limited space available to him. He does this mainly by giving careful attention to the planes of the relief. In a carved relief the highest, or front, plane is defined by the

Representation of forms in depth

surface of the slab of wood or stone in which the relief is carved; and the back plane is the surface from which the forms project. The space between these two planes can be thought of as divided into a series of planes, one behind the other. The relations of forms in depth can then be thought of as relations between forms lying in different planes.

Sunken relief. Sunken relief is also known as incised, coelanaglyphic, and intaglio relief. It is almost exclusively an ancient Egyptian art form, but some beautiful small-scale Indian examples in ivory have been found at Bagrām in Afghanistan. In a sunken relief, the outline of the design is first incised all around. The relief is then carved inside the incised outline, leaving the surrounding

By courtesy of the trustees of the British Museum

Sunken relief.
Egyptian woman carrying food for the dead, detail of an Old Kingdom limestone relief originally from the tomb of Thetha at Thebes, *c.* 2300 BC. In the British Museum. Figure height 43 cm.

surface untouched. Thus, the finished relief is sunk below the level of the surrounding surface and is contained within a sharp, vertical-walled contour line. This approach to relief preserves the continuity of the original surface and creates no projection from it. The outline shows up as a powerful line of light and shade around the whole design.

Low relief. Figurative low relief is generally regarded by sculptors as an extremely difficult art form. To give a convincing impression of three-dimensional structure and surface modelling with only a minimal degree of projection demands a fusion of draftsmanship and carving or modelling skill of a high order. The sculptor has to proceed empirically, constantly changing the direction of his light and testing the optical effect of his work. He cannot follow any fixed rules or represent things in depth by simply scaling down measurements mathematically, so that, say, one inch of relief space represents one foot.

The forms of low relief usually make contact with the

background all around their contours. If there is a slight amount of undercutting, its purpose is to give emphasis, by means of cast shadow, to a contour rather than to give any impression that the forms are independent of their background. Low relief includes figures that project up to about half their natural circumference.

Technically, the simplest kind of low relief is the two-plane relief. For this, the sculptor draws an outline on a surface and then cuts away the surrounding surface, leaving the figure raised as a flat silhouette above the background plane. This procedure is often used for the first stages of a full relief carving, in which case the sculptor will proceed to carve into the raised silhouette, rounding the forms and giving an impression of three-dimensional structure. In a two-plane relief, however, the silhouette is left flat and substantially unaltered except for the addition of surface detail. Pre-Columbian sculptors used this method of relief carving to create bold figurative and abstract reliefs.

Stiacciato relief is an extremely subtle type of flat, low relief carving that is especially associated with the 15th-century sculptors Donatello and Desiderio da Settignano. The design is partly drawn with finely engraved chisel lines and partly carved in relief. The stiacciato technique depends largely for its effect on the way in which pale materials, such as white marble, respond to light and show up the most delicate lines and subtle changes of surface. **Stiacciato relief**

High relief. The forms of high relief project far enough to be in some degree independent of their background. As they approach the fullness of sculpture in the round, they become of necessity considerably undercut. In many high reliefs, where parts of the composition are completely detached from their background and fully in the round, it is often impossible to tell from the front whether or not a figure is actually attached to its background.

Many different degrees of projection are often combined in one relief composition. Figures in the foreground may be completely detached and fully in the round, while those in the middle distance are in about half relief and those in the background in low relief. Such effects are common in late Gothic, Renaissance, and Baroque sculpture.

Modern forms of sculpture. Since the 1950s, many new combined forms of art have been developed that do not fit readily into any of the traditional categories. Two of the most important of these, environments and kinetics, are closely enough connected with sculpture to be regarded by many artists and critics as branches or offshoots of sculpture. It is likely, however, that the persistence of the terms environmental sculpture and kinetic sculpture is a result of the failure of language to keep pace with events; for the practice is already growing of referring simply to environments and kinetics, as one might refer to painting, sculpture, and engraving, as art forms in their own right.

Kinetic sculpture. Traditional sculptures in relief and in the round are static, fixed objects or images. Their immobility and immutability are part of the permanence traditionally associated with the art of sculpture, especially monumental sculpture. What one refers to as movement in, say, a Baroque or Greek sculpture is not actual physical motion but a movement that is either directly represented in the subject matter (galloping horses) or expressed through the dynamic character of its form (spirals, undulating curves). In recent years, however, the use of actual movement, kineticism, has become an important aspect of sculpture. Naum Gabo, Marcel Duchamp, László Moholy-Nagy, and Alexander Calder were pioneers of kinetic sculpture in modern times, but many kinetic artists see a connection between their work and such forms as the moving toys, dolls, and clocks of previous ages.

There are now types of sculpture in which the components are moved by air currents, as in the well-known mobiles of Calder; by water; by magnetism, the speciality of Nicholus Takis; by a variety of electromechanical devices; or by the participation of the spectator himself. The

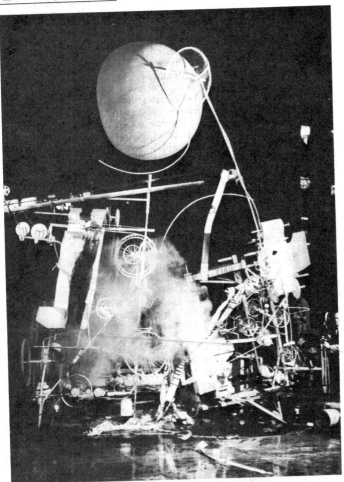

Kinetic sculpture.
"Homage to New York," a self-constructing and self-destroying
work of art by Jean Tinguely, 1960. Small pieces now in the
Museum of Modern Art, New York.
By courtesy of the Museum of Modern Art, New York; photograph, David Gahr

neo-Dada satire quality of the kinetic sculpture created
during the 1960s is exemplified by the works of Jean
Tinguely. His self-destructing "Homage to New York"
perfected the concept of a sculpture being both an object and an event, or "happening."

The aim of most kinetic sculptors is to make movement
itself an integral part of the design of the sculpture and
not merely to impart movement to an already complete
static object. Calder's mobiles, for example, depend for
their aesthetic effect on constantly changing patterns of
relationship taking place through space and time. When
liquids and gases are used as components, the shapes and
dimensions of the sculpture may undergo continual transformations. The movement of smoke; the diffusion and
flow of coloured water, mercury, oil, and so on; pneumatic inflation and deflation; and the movement of masses of
bubbles have all served as media for kinetic sculpture. In
the complex, electronically controlled "spatio-dynamic"
and "lumino-dynamic" constructions of Nicolas Schöffer,
the projection of changing patterns of light into space is a
major feature.

Environmental sculpture. The environmental sculptor
creates new spatial contexts that differ from anything
developed by traditional sculpture. The work no longer
confronts the spectator as an object but surrounds him so
that he moves within it as he might within a stage set, a
garden, or an interior. The most common type of environment is the "room," which may have specially shaped
and surfaced walls, special lighting effects, and many different kinds of contents. Kurt Schwitters' *Merzbau* (destroyed in 1943) was the first of these rooms, which now
include the nightmare fantasy of Edward Kienholz's ta-
bleaux, such as "Roxy's" (1961) or "The Illegal Operation"; (1962) George Segal's compositions, in which

casts of clothed human figures in frozen, casual attitudes are placed in interiors; and rooms built of mirrors, such as Kusama Yayoi's "Endless Love Room" and
Lucas Samaras' "Mirrored Room," in both of which the
spectator himself, endlessly reflected, becomes part of the
total effect.

Environmental art, in common with collage and assemblage, has tended toward greater concreteness not by
making a more realistic representation, as naturalistic art
does, but by including more of reality itself in the work;
for example, by using casts taken from the actual human
body, real clothes, actual objects and casts of objects,
actual lighting effects, and real items of furniture. Plastic
elements may be combined with music and sound effects,
dance, theatrical spectacles, and film to create so-called
happenings, in which real figures are constituents of the
"artwork" and operations are performed not on "artistic"
materials but are performed on real objects and on the
actual environment. Ideas such as these go far beyond
anything that has ever before been associated with the
term sculpture.

Use of real objects in environmental art

SUBJECT MATTER AND IMAGERY

Representational sculpture. Sculpture in the round is
much more restricted than relief in the range of its subject matter. The representation of, say, a battle scene or a
cavalcade in the round would require a space that corresponded in scale in every direction with that occupied by
an actual battle or cavalcade. No such problems arise in
relief because the treatment of scale and relations in
depth is to some extent notional, or theoretical, like that
of pictures. Then again, because a relief is attached to a
background, problems of weight and physical balance
and support do not arise. Figures can be represented as
floating in space and can be arranged vertically as well as
horizontally. Thus, in general, sculpture in the round is
concerned with single figures and limited groups, while
reliefs deal with more complex "pictorial" subjects in-

Albright-Knox Art Gallery, Buffalo, gift of Seymour H. Knox;
photograph, by courtesy of the Pace Gallery, New York

Environmental sculpture.
"Mirrored Room," mirror on wood by Lucas Samaras, 1966.
In the Albright-Knox Art Gallery, Buffalo. 305 × 244 cm.

volving crowds, landscape, architectural backgrounds, and so on.

The human figure. The principal subject of sculpture has always been the human figure. Next in importance are animals and fantastic creatures based on human and animal forms. Other subjects—for example, landscape, plants, still life, and architecture—have served primarily as accessories to figure sculpture, not as subjects in their own right. The overwhelming predominance of the human figure is due: first, to its immense emotional importance as an object of desire, love, fear, respect, and, in the case of anthropomorphic gods, worship; and, second, to its inexhaustible subtlety and variety of form and expression. The nude or almost nude figure played a prominent role in Egyptian, Indian, Greek, and African sculpture, while in medieval European and ancient Chinese sculpture the figure is almost invariably clothed. The interplay of the linear and modelled forms of free draperies with the solid volumes of the human body was of great interest to Classical sculptors and later became one of the principal themes of Renaissance and post-Renaissance sculpture. The human figure continues to be of central importance in modern sculpture in spite of the growth of nonfigurative art; but the optimistic, idealized, or naturalistic images of man prevalent in previous ages have been largely replaced by images of despair, horror, deformation, and satire.

GEKS

Narrative sculpture.
Lower portion of Trajan's Column, marble, Rome, c. AD 106–113. Height of one relief band about 127 cm.

Devotional images and narrative sculpture. The production of devotional images has been one of the sculptor's main tasks, and many of the world's greatest sculptures are of this kind. They include images of Buddha and the Hindu gods; of Christ, the Virgin, and the Christian saints; of Athena, Aphrodite, Zeus, and other Greek gods; and of all the various gods, spirits, and mythical beings of Rome, the ancient Near East, pre-Columbian America, Black Africa, and the Pacific Islands.

Closely connected with devotional images are all of the narrative sculptures in which legends, heroic deeds, and religious stories are depicted for the delight and instruction of peoples who lived when books and literacy were rare. The Buddhist, Hindu, and Christian traditions are especially rich in narrative sculpture. Stories of the incarnations of Buddha—*Jātaka*—and of the Hindu gods abounded in the temple sculpture of India and Southeast

Asia; for example, at Sānchī, Amarāvatī, Borobuḍur, and Angkor. Sculpture illustrating the stories of the Bible is so abundant in medieval churches that the churches have been called "Bibles in stone." Sculpture recounting the heroic deeds of kings and generals are common, especially in Assyria and Rome. The Romans made use of a form known as continuous narrative, the best known example of which is the spiral, or helical, band of relief sculpture that surrounds Trajan's Column (*c.* AD 106–113) and tells the story of the Emperor's Dacian Wars. The episodes in the narrative are not separated into a series of framed compositions but are linked to form a continuous band of unbroken relief.

Portraiture. Portraiture was practiced by the Egyptians but was comparatively rare in the ancient world until the Romans made portrait sculpture one of their major artistic achievements. The features of many famous people are known to modern man only through the work of Roman sculptors on coins and medals, portrait busts, and full-length portraits. Portraiture has been an important aspect of Western sculpture from the Renaissance to the present day. Some of the best known modern portrait sculptors are Rodin, Charles Despiau, Marino Marini, and Jacob Epstein.

Modern portrait sculptors

Scenes of everyday life. Scenes of everyday life have been represented in sculpture mainly on a small scale in minor works. The sculptures that are closest in spirit to the quiet dignity of the great 17th- and 18th-century genre paintings of Jan Vermeer and Jean-Baptiste-Siméon Chardin are perhaps certain Greek tombstones, such as that of the Stele of Hegeso, which represents a quiet, absorbed moment when a seated young woman and her maidservant are looking at a necklace they have just removed from a casket. Intimate scenes of the people and their activities in everyday rural life are often portrayed in medieval and Egyptian reliefs as part of larger compositions.

Animals. Animals have always been important subjects for sculpture. Paleolithic man produced some extraordinarily sensitive animal sculptures both in relief and in the round. Representations of horses and lions are among the finest works of Assyrian sculpture. Egyptian sculptors produced sensitive naturalistic representations of cattle, donkeys, hippopotamuses, apes, and a wide variety of birds and fish. Ancient Chinese sculptors made superb small-scale animal sculptures in bronze and pottery. Animals were the main subject matter for the sculpture of the nomadic tribes of Eurasia and northern Europe, for whom they became the basis for elaborate zoomorphic fantasies. This animal art contributed to the rich tradition of animal sculpture in medieval art. Animals also served as a basis for semi-abstract fantasy in Mexican, Mayan, North American Indian, and Oceanic sculpture. The horse has always occupied an important place in Western sculpture, but other animals have also figured in the work of such sculptors as Giambologna, in the 16th century, and Antoine-Louis Barye, in the 19th, as well as numerous sculptors of garden and fountain pieces. Among modern sculptors who have made extensive use of animals or animal-like forms are Brancusi, Picasso, Gerhard Marcks, Germaine Richier, François Pompon, Pino Pascali, and François-Xavier-Maxime Lalanne.

Fantasy. In their attempts to imagine gods and mythical beings, sculptors have invented fantastic images based on the combination and metamorphosis of animal and human forms. A centaur, the Minotaur, and animal-headed gods of the ancient world are straightforward combinations. More imaginative fantasies were produced by Mexican and Mayan sculptors and by tribal sculptors in many parts of the world. Fantastic creatures abound in the sculpture produced in northern Europe during the early Middle Ages and the Romanesque period. Fantasy of a playful kind is often found in garden sculpture and fountains.

In the period following World War I, fantasy was a dominant element in representational sculpture. Among its many forms are images derived from dreams, the technological fantasy of science fiction, erotic fantasies, and a whole host of monsters and automata. The Surrealists have made a major contribution to this aspect of modern sculpture.

Other subjects. Architectural backgrounds in sculpture range from the simplified baldacchinos (ornamental structures resembling canopies used especially over altars) of early medieval reliefs to the 17th- and 18th-century virtuoso perspective townscapes of Grinling Gibbons. Architectural accessories such as plinths, entablatures, pilasters, columns, and moldings have played a prominent role both in Greek and Roman sarcophagi, in medieval altarpieces and screens, and in Renaissance wall tombs.

Outside the field of ornament, botanical forms have played only a minor role in sculpture. Trees and stylized lotuses are especially common in Indian sculpture because of their great symbolic significance. Trees are also present in many Renaissance reliefs and in some medieval reliefs.

Landscape, which was an important background feature in many Renaissance reliefs (notably those of Ghiberti) and, as sculptured rocks, appeared in a number of Baroque fountains, entered into sculpture in a new way when Henry Moore combined the forms of caves, rocks, hills, and cliffs with the human form in a series of large reclining figures.

There is nothing in sculpture comparable with the tradition of still-life painting. When objects are represented, it is almost always as part of a figure composition. A few modern sculptors, however, notably Giacomo Manzù and Oldenburg, have used still-life subjects.

Nonrepresentational sculpture. There are two main kinds of nonrepresentational sculpture. One kind uses nature not as subject matter to be represented but as a source of formal ideas. For sculptors who work in this way, the forms that are observed in nature serve as a starting point for a kind of creative play, the end products of which may bear little or no resemblance either to their original source or to any other natural object. Many works by Brancusi, Raymond Duchamp-Villon, Jacques Lipchitz, Henri Laurens, Umberto Boccioni, and other pioneer modern sculptors have this character. The transformation of natural forms to a point where they are no longer recognizable is also common in many styles of primitive and ornamental art.

The other main kind of nonrepresentational sculpture, often known as nonobjective sculpture, is a more completely nonrepresentational form that does not even have a starting point in nature. It arises from a constructive manipulation of the sculptor's generalized, abstract ideas of spatial relations, volume, line, colour, texture, and so on. The approach of the nonobjective sculptor has been likened to that of the composer of music, who manipulates the elements of his art in a similar manner. The inclusion of purely invented, three-dimensional artifacts under the heading of sculpture is a 20th-century innovation.

Some nonobjective sculptors prefer forms that have the complex curvilinearity of surface typical of living organisms; others prefer more regular, simple geometric forms. The whole realm of three-dimensional form is open to nonobjective sculptors, but these sculptors often restrict themselves to a narrow range of preferred types of form. A recent kind of nonobjective sculpture, for example, consists of extremely stark, so-called primary forms. These are highly finished, usually coloured constructions that are often large in scale and made up entirely of plane or single-curved surfaces. Prominent among the older nonobjective sculptors are Jean Arp, Antoine Pevsner, Naum Gabo, Barbara Hepworth, Max Bill, and David Smith. Younger artists who have worked in this particular manner include Robert Morris, Donald Judd, and Phillip King.

Decorative sculpture. The devices and motifs of ornamental sculpture fall into three main categories; abstract, zoomorphic, and botanical.

Abstract shapes, which can easily be made to fit into any framework, are a widespread form of decoration. Outstanding examples of abstract relief ornament are found on Islāmic, Mexican, and Mayan buildings and on small Celtic metal artifacts. The character of the work varies from the large-scale rectilinear two-plane reliefs of the buildings of Mitla in Mexico, to the small-scale curvilinear plastic decoration of a Celtic shield or body ornament.

(Top) Henri Lehmann

Decorative sculpture.
(Top) Detail of the patio of the Palace of the Columns, Mitla, Oaxaca state, Mexico, Mixtec culture, 9th–16th century. (Bottom) Norse wood carving, late 11th century, detail of doorway of Urnes stave church, Norway. Doorway 3.90 × 2.80 m.

Zoomorphic relief decoration, derived from a vast range of animal forms, is common on primitive artifacts and on Romanesque churches, especially the wooden stave churches of Scandinavia.

Botanical forms lend themselves readily to decorative purposes because their growth patterns are variable and their components—leaf, tendril, bud, flower, and fruit—are infinitely repeatable. The acanthus and anthemion motifs of Classical relief and the lotuses of Indian relief are splendid examples of stylized plant ornament. The naturalistic leaf ornament of Southwell Minster, Reims Cathedral, and other Gothic churches transcend the merely decorative and become superbly plastic sculptures in their own right.

SYMBOLISM

Sculptural images may be symbolic on a number of levels. Apart from conventional symbols, such as those of heraldry and other insignia, the simplest and most straightforward kind of sculptural symbol is that in which an abstract idea is represented by means of allegory and personification. A few common examples are figures that personify the cardinal virtues (prudence, justice, temperance, fortitude), the theological virtues (faith, hope, and charity), the arts, the church, victory, the seasons of the year, industry, and agriculture. These figures are often provided with symbolic objects that serve to identify them; for example, the hammer of industry, the sickle of agriculture, the hourglass of time, the scales of justice. Such personifications abound in medieval and Renaissance sculpture and were until recently the stock in trade of public sculpture the world over. Animals are also frequently used in the same way; for example, the owl

Kinds of nonrepresentational sculpture [margin note]

Allegory and personification [margin note]

(as the emblem of Athens and the symbol of wisdom), the British lion, and the American eagle.

Beyond this straightforward level of symbolism, the images of sculpture may serve as broader, more abstruse religious, mythical, and civic symbols expressing some of mankind's deepest spiritual insights, beliefs, and feelings. The great tympanums (the space above the lintel of a door that is enclosed by the doorway arch) of Autun, Moissac, and other medieval churches symbolize some of the most profound Christian doctrines concerning the ends of human life and man's relations with the divine. The Hindu image of the dance of Śiva is symbolic in every detail, and the whole image expresses in one concentrated symbol some of the complex cosmological ideas of the Hindu religion. The Buddhist temple of Borobuḍur, in Java, is one of the most complex and integrated of all religious symbols. It is designed as a holy mountain whose structure symbolizes the structure of the spiritual universe. Each of the nine levels of the temple has a different kind of sculptural symbolism, progressing from symbols of hell and the world of desire at the lowest level to austere symbols of the higher spiritual mysteries at its uppermost levels.

In more individualistic societies, works of sculpture may be symbolic on a personal, private level. Michelangelo's "Slaves" have been interpreted as allegories of the human soul struggling to free itself from the bondage of the body, its "earthly prison," or, more directly, as symbols of the struggle of intelligible form against mere matter. But there is no doubt that, in ways difficult to formulate precisely, they are also disturbing symbols of Michelangelo's personal attitudes, emotions, and psychological conflicts. If it is an expression of his unconscious mind, the sculptor himself may be unaware of this aspect of the design of his work.

Many modern sculptors disclaim any attempt at symbolism in their work. When symbolic images do play a part in modern sculpture, they are either derived from obsolete classical, medieval, and other historical sources or they are private. Because there has been little socially recognized symbolism for the modern sculptor to use in his work, symbols consciously invented by individual artists or deriving from the image-producing function of the individual unconscious mind have been paramount. Many of these are entirely personal symbols expressing the artist's private attitudes, beliefs, obsessions, and emotions. They are often more symptomatic than symbolic. Henry Moore is outstanding among modern sculptors for having created a world of personal symbols that also have a universal quality; and Naum Gabo has sought images that would symbolize in a general way modern man's attitudes to the world picture provided by science and technology.

Symbolism of sculptural sites
Examples of sculpture of which the positioning, or siting, as well as the imagery is symbolic are the carved boundary stones of the ancient world; memorials sited on battlegrounds or at places where religious and political martyrs have been killed; the Statue of Liberty and similar civic symbols situated at harbours, town gates, bridges, and so on; and the scenes of the Last Judgment placed over the entrances to cathedrals, where they could serve as an admonition to the congregation.

The choice of symbolism suitable to the function of a sculpture is an important aspect of design. Fonts, pulpits, lecterns, triumphal arches, war memorials, tombstones, and the like all require a symbolism appropriate to their function. In a somewhat different way, the tomb sculptures of Egypt, intended to serve a magical function in the afterlife of the tomb's inhabitants, had to be images suitable for their purpose. These, however, are more in the nature of magical substitutes than symbols.

USES OF SCULPTURE

The vast majority of sculptures are not entirely autonomous but are integrated or linked in some way with other works of art in other mediums. Relief, in particular, has served as a form of decoration for an immense range of domestic, personal, civic, and sacred artifacts, from the spear throwers of Paleolithic man and the cosmetic palettes of earliest Egyptian civilization to the latest mass-produced plastic reproduction of a Jacobean linenfold panel (a carved or molded panel representing a fold, or scroll, of linen).

The main use of large-scale sculpture has been in conjunction with architecture. It has either formed part of the interior or exterior fabric of the building itself or has been placed against or near the building as an adjunct to it. The role of sculpture in relation to buildings as part of a townscape is also of considerable importance. Traditionally, it has been used to provide a focal point at the meeting of streets, and in marketplaces, town squares, and other open places—a tradition that many town planners today are continuing.

Sculpture has been widely used as part of the total decorative scheme for a garden or park. Garden sculpture is usually intended primarily for enjoyment, helping to create the right kind of environment for meditation, relaxation, and delight. Because the aim is to create a lighthearted arcadian or ideal paradisal atmosphere, disturbing or serious subjects are usually avoided. The sculpture may be set among trees and foliage where it can surprise and delight the viewer or sited in the open to provide a focal point for a vista.

Fountains, too, are intended primarily to give enjoyment to the senses. There is nothing to compare with the interplay of light, movement, sound, and sculptural imagery in great fountains, which combine the movement and sound of sheets, jets, and cataracts of water with richly imaginative sculpture, water plants and foliage, darting fish, reflections, and changing lights. They are the prototypes of all 20th-century "mixed medium" kinetic sculptures.

The durability of sculpture makes it an ideal medium for commemorative purposes, and much of the world's greatest sculpture has been created in order to perpetuate the memory of persons and events. Commemorative sculpture includes tombs, tombstones, statues, plaques, sarcophagi, memorial columns, and triumphal arches. Portraiture, too, often serves a memorial function.

Sculptural coins and medals
One of the most familiar and widespread uses of sculpture is for coins. Produced for more than 2,500 years, these miniature works of art contain a historically invaluable and often artistically excellent range of portrait heads and symbolic devices. Medals, too, in spite of their small scale, may be vehicles for plastic art of the highest quality. The 15th-century medals of the Italian artist Antonio Pisanello and the coins of ancient Greece are generally considered the supreme achievements in these miniature fields of sculpture.

Also on a small scale are the sculptural products of the glyptic arts—that is, the arts of carving gems and hardstones. Superb and varied work, often done in conjunction with precious metalwork, has been produced in many countries.

Finally, sculpture has been widely used for ceremonial and ritualistic objects such as bishop's croziers, censers, reliquaries, chalices, tabernacles, sacred book covers, ancient Chinese bronzes, the paraphernalia of primitive tribal rituals, the special equipment worn by participants in the sacred ball game of ancient Mexico, processional images, masks and headdresses, and modern trophies and awards.

BIBLIOGRAPHY. EDWARD LANTERI, *Modelling and Sculpture: A Guide for Artists and Students*, 3 vol. (1965; previously pub. under the title, *Modelling*, 3 vol., 1902–11), still an outstanding work on traditional methods; J.C. RICH, *The Materials and Methods of Sculpture* (1947), comprehensive coverage of all except the most recent methods and materials; GEOFFREY CLARKE and STROUD CORNOCK, *A Sculptor's Manual* (1967), intended primarily for the practicing sculptor, this work contains information on the latest methods and materials; JOHN W. MILLS, *The Technique of Casting for Sculpture* (1967) and *Sculpture in Concrete* (1968), two useful technical handbooks; N.C. HALE, *Welded Sculpture* (1968), explains and illustrates a number of ways in which welding may be used in sculpture; UDO KULTERMANN, *Neue Dimensionen der Plastik* (1967; Eng. trans., *The New Sculpture: Environments and Assemblages*, 1968), a comprehensive account of these two recently developed forms of sculpture.

(L.R.R.)

Scythians

The Scythians were a people who during the 8th–7th centuries BC moved from Central Asia to southern Russia, where they founded an empire that survived until they were gradually overcome and supplanted by the Sarmatians during the 4th century BC–2nd century AD.

Until the 20th century most of the information concerning the Scythians, as the Greeks called them, or the Śakas, as the Persians termed them, was based on the knowledge that Herodotus acquired when he visited Olbia, a Greek city founded *c.* 645 BC at the confluence of the Bug and Ingul rivers. He incorporated all that he had learned about them into the fourth book of his history. In modern times the work carried out in Siberia by Soviet scholars and archaeologists produced so much new information that the word Scythian is often extended to include the nomadic kinsmen of the Scythians who remained in Central Asia when the latter moved into Europe.

In its exact context the term Scythian should, however, be applied only to the tribes that settled in what is now southern U.S.S.R. The excavations begun in 1929 at Pazyryk in the Altai by M.P. Gryaznov and resumed in 1947 by S.I. Rudenko proved that the culture, art, and way of life of the tribesmen who continued to live in western Siberia and the Altai when the bulk of the Scythians marched into Iran and southern Russia remained closely akin to that of the migrants, the entire community being of Iranian origin and sharing a common language. Herodotus attempted to distinguish between the various tribes that settled in what later became Russia; and he was able to name among others the Callipidae, the Alazones, the Aroteres, the Neuri, the Androphagi, and the Melanchlaeni, defining the areas that each inhabited. These western Scythians seem to have maintained contact with those who had remained in Central Asia.

History. In the 9th century BC the Scythian and kindred tribes were probably concentrated somewhat to the east of the Altai, but it was not until the Chinese ruler Hsüan Wang (827–781 BC) decided to send an armed force to curb the fierce Hsiung-nu, who had begun to make a practice of raiding China's western boundaries, that the Scythian nomads became restless. When the Hsiung-nu were forced back from the Chinese frontier and, in retreating, dislodged the Massagetae, who occupied the grazing grounds to the north of the Oxus (Amu Darya) River, and when the latter in their turn assaulted their immediate neighbours, the Scythians, a wide-scale nomadic migration was set in motion. There is reason for thinking that the struggle for grazing land was rendered more acute by a severe drought and that this factor may well have decided the Scythians to move westward instead of remaining to fight for their traditional rights.

The Scythians were accomplished horsemen, among the earliest people to master the art of riding. Their mobility gave them a great advantage over their neighbours, so that when they eventually advanced westward across the Oxus they moved so fast that both Herodotus and contemporary Persian sources refer to the remarkable suddenness of their appearance on Iran's northeastern border. Their advance brought the Scythians into fierce conflict with the Cimmerians who had for centuries enjoyed possession of the Caucasus and the plain lying to the north of the Black Sea. But the Cimmerians still fought on foot and the Scythian cavalry quickly gained the upper hand. Some Cimmerians retreated through the Daryal (Dariel) Pass and were pursued across the Volga, where the Scythians were able to destroy and supplant them.

Meanwhile another Scythian force chased the rest of the Cimmerian Army across Urartu (Armenia), while a third entered the Derbent defile and reached Lake Urmia some time during the reign of King Sargon of Assyria (722–705 BC), linking up there with the second contingent to continue the fight against the Cimmerians. Thus strengthened, the Scythian troops were able to force the Cimmerians into a steady retreat that lasted for about 30 years, ending only when both combatants had reached the borders of Assyria. Then the Scythians formed an alliance with King Esarhaddon of Assyria (reigned 680–669 BC), but they soon abandoned this and concentrated on destroying the Cimmerians, giving the latter no respite until they had forced them back across Phrygia into Lydia, where they were finally wiped out.

This astonishing series of victories brought great fame to the Scythians. Their chieftain Partatua (Bartatua) and his son Madyes were quick to take advantage of it by setting themselves up as rulers of west Persian lands stretching to the Halys (Kizil Irmak) River, establishing their capital at Saqqez. They invaded Syria and Judaea *c.* 625 BC. Later they reached the borders of Egypt, but Psamtik I (663–610 BC) wisely decided to check any further advance by purchasing peace terms from them.

Meanwhile the Medes had become masters of Persia. They considered the Scythians' increasing might a real threat to their own security, and they decided to concentrate their efforts in launching a decisive attack against the tribesmen. Their better disciplined troops eventually contrived to push the Scythians northward, whence they had first appeared, some retreating through Urartu. Although the nomads thereby lost the control they had wielded during the previous 28 years over most of Anatolia, their lands still stretched from the Persian border through the Kuban into most of southern Russia. When forced by the Medes to retreat, some of them likewise settled between the Caspian and Aral seas, where they intermingled with their Dahae kinsmen to produce the

Destruction of the Cimmerians

Scythian settlements and burial grounds.

people who, some three centuries later, were to become known as the Parthians, while others penetrated into India and established kingdoms there.

The Scythians in southern Russia

The Scythians who settled in the Kuban and southern Russia quickly attained a position of importance. Many of them became extremely prosperous. Graves of the 7th–6th centuries BC situated in the Kuban abound in objects of gold and other precious materials, and although a form of patriarchal rule remained in force, it is clear that a class of wealthy chieftains or nobles was beginning to come into being there. In the 6th–5th century BC the richest burials were in southern Russia and the Crimea. These are associated with a relatively small number of Scythians who, as the Royal Scyths, established themselves as rulers of the area. Isolated groups of their tribesmen penetrated as far as what became Hungary and East Prussia. The kingdom of the Royal Scyths developed into a community that was to enjoy considerable economic power until about the 1st century BC. Its political importance was established when it was able to resist Darius on his invasion of Scythian territory about 513 BC; the Scythians resorted to a scorched-earth policy, which enabled them to avoid a large-scale battle and obliged Darius to beat a hasty retreat in order to preserve his army. His consequent withdrawal from the plain lying to the northwest of the Black Sea left the Scythians in control of it; some of the Greek cities of the Pontus even had to pay the Scythians an annual tribute in order to preserve their security. Scythian power remained paramount there until the 4th century BC, when the Sarmatians appeared on the Don. Thenceforth the new invaders began steadily to increase their pressure on the Scythians until, in the 2nd century BC, they managed to confine them within the Crimean area, gradually supplanting them as rulers of the plain until, in the 2nd century AD, they finally succeeded in destroying the last remnants of this once powerful community.

The Royal Scyths. Though the patriarchal order and the nomadic way of life remained general, the Royal Scyths were ruled by a sovereign whose powers were transmitted to his son. He was surrounded by a group of wealthy nobles who were virtually his courtiers. The dynasty claimed descent from Targitaos, the founder of the house of Phalatae; but Targitaos was probably a legendary figure, and it is more likely that Colaxis was the first of the royal line. He was succeeded by Spargapeithes, who handed the crown to his son Lycus, who in turn passed it to his son Gnurus at about the time when Partatua and his son Madyes had established themselves as co-rulers in Transcaucasia (c. 630 BC). In 589 Saulius reigned over the Royal Scyths. His brother Anacharsis (whose existence is doubted by certain authorities) went to Greece as his ambassador and became so much respected there that the Greeks spoke of him as "the Scythian eloquence." The throne then passed to Idanthyrsus, who, with his brothers Taxacis and Scopasia, expelled Darius. Ariapeithes, the son of Idanthyrsus, came to the throne next, marrying in turn a Greek woman, a Scythian, and a daughter of a Thracian chieftain. He was succeeded by his son Scyles, who was murdered shortly before the time of Herodotus by his brother Ostomasades because of his fondness for Greek manners, dress, and religious observances. The murderer succeeded his victim on the throne. His successor, Arianthus, is remarkable for having organized a census of his people. The next known ruler, Aristagorus, reigned c. 495 BC. A descendant, Ateas, was killed in 339 BC at the age of 90 while fighting against Philip II of Macedonia. King Agarus' reign likewise ended with his death in battle (310 BC). Nothing is known of the kings who followed him until Scylurus established himself at 110 BC at Neapolis (in the Crimea) and struck Scythia's first coins at Olbia. He was succeeded by his son Palakus, the last Scythian sovereign whose name has been preserved in history.

Hippocrates described the Scythians as inclined to laziness, fatness, and gaiety, likening their appearance to that of eunuchs and commenting on their sexual impotence; but his statement is corroborated neither by the events in their history nor by the appearance of those Scythians whose features have been preserved on contemporary Greek metalworks. Scythian women lived in subservience and semiseclusion.

Administration. For administrative purposes the Royal Scyths divided their kingdom into four districts, each of which was controlled by a governor provided with a paid military bodyguard. The governor dispensed justice and levied taxes from the settlers and tribute from certain of the Greek Pontic cities. The tribal way of life remained in force; communities were governed by their elders or chieftains, these dignitaries being periodically summoned to attend a general assembly held in the presence either of the governor or of the sovereign. These assemblies differed from the gatherings held by the sovereign in the spring of each year in order to inspect and feast his army. In times of war the country was divided for purposes of recruitment into three sections, the enrolled men being later grouped into units, each one of which was commanded by its own officer.

The army. The army consisted entirely of freemen; i.e., Scythian tribesmen; they were fed and clothed but paid no wage, though those of them who could produce the head of a soldier killed in battle were entitled to share in the day's booty. According to Herodotus, the Scythians scalped their victims, fashioning their skulls into cups that they wore attached to their belts, using them to pledge an oath in a mixture of blood and water. Such cups mounted in delicately worked gold have been found in several tombs.

Taking of scalps

Many Royal Scyths wore bronze helmets and chain-mail jerkins of the Greek type lined with red felt. Their shields were generally round and made of leather, wood, or iron and were often decorated with a central gold ornament in the form of an animal, but other tribesmen carried square or rectangular ones. All used a double-curved bow, shooting over the horse's left shoulder; arrows had trefoil-shaped heads made, according to date, of bronze, iron, or bone. Arrows and bow were carried in a *gōrytos* (bow case) slung from the left side of the belt. Their swords were generally of the Persian type, with a heart-shaped or triangular crosspiece intricately ornamented. According to date, the blades were of bronze or iron; in southern Russia, the sheaths were often encased in gold worked into embossed designs and offset with paste or ivory inlay and gems. Their knives were of various shapes and lengths, some being curved in the Chinese manner. They wore the dagger attached to the left leg by straps, and many carried spears or standards surmounted by bronze terminals depicting real or imaginary beasts.

Horses. Every Scythian owned at least one gelding to serve as a riding horse, but the wealthy possessed a great many mounts; most Scythians also owned oxen or rough ponies, which served as beasts of burden. The finest riding horses were of the Fergana breed, but the majority were Mongolian ponies. The Scythians devoted much time and attention to their horses and ornamented all their trappings. Bridles were provided with metal cheekpieces in the shape of animals, and the leather straps were adorned with embossed, cutout, or appliqué designs, which also often represented animals. Saddles consisted of two felt cushions mounted on wooden frames bound with yellow or red and sometimes embellished with gold plaques; the felt saddle cloths were adorned, as were the seats of the saddles, with appliqué designs. Metal stirrups were not known to the Scythians, but there is reason to believe that they rested their feet in felt or leather supports. Women travelled with their children in covered wagons with solid wheels and a central shaft along which mules or oxen could be yoked in pairs.

Possessions. The frozen tombs of Pazyryk (see below *Tombs*) contained many well-preserved articles of clothing, all of which were profusely trimmed with complicated embroidered and appliqué designs; the clothes of the wealthy in southern Russia were covered with tiny gold-embossed plaques, sewn to the garments. At Pazyryk, felt appliqué wall hangings were found, some displaying religious scenes featuring the Great Goddess or anthropomorphic beasts, others with geometric or animal motifs. Even the embalmed body of a man was covered with

Contacts with the Greeks

Artifacts preserved in the tombs of the Scythians.
(Left) Horse's burial mask of felt, leather, gilded hair, and copper in shape of stag's head,
5th century BC, from Pazyryk. (Centre) Section of felt appliqué wall hanging showing
geometric pattern, 5th century BC, from Pazyryk. (Right) Bronze caldron, 4th century BC,
from Chertomlyk; height 100 cm. In the Hermitage, Leningrad.
By courtesy of the Hermitage, Leningrad

tattooed designs of real and mythical beasts executed with great spirit and delicacy. Felt rugs were found, as well as a knotted, woollen pile carpet of Persian origin, from the 5th century BC, displaying figures of riders, elks, and stars. Felt cushions and mattresses; wooden tables with carved or turned legs and detachable, slightly hollowed, traylike tops; and wooden blocks serving as stools or head rests were customary.

The tombs of the Eurasian plain as a whole produced a mass of tools and domestic utensils, many of them made of precious materials. Rich jewelry and arms of great value and beauty are frequently found in the burials belonging to the western section. In addition, each burial throughout the entire area contained a cast bronze caldron of the distinctive Scythian shape. These caldrons vary in size from quite small examples to others weighing as much as 75 pounds; an overwhelming majority have a solid base, shaped like a truncated cone, around which the fire was heaped. The upper section is a semispherical bowl provided not with a loop handle but with handles (shaped like animals) fixed to the rim opposite each other. The finest caldron, found at Chertomlyk in the Dnepr (Dnieper) district, has six handles. At Pazyryk, small caldrons filled with stones and hempseeds were found standing beneath leather or felt tentlets with three or six supports.

Hemp smoking

Herodotus referred to what he termed a Scythian purification rite that, he noted, consisted in inhaling the fumes of hempseeds thrown onto hot stones; the passage was well-nigh incomprehensible until archaeologists discovered that a smoking outfit of this sort had been provided for each person buried at Pazyryk, making it clear that hemp fumes were inhaled for pleasure and not, as Herodotus assumed, as part of a religious observance.

Occupations and beliefs. The Scythians were keen huntsmen and fishermen; they were skilled at curing hides; they excelled at working metals; and the settlers were good agriculturalists. Though they had neither an alphabet nor, until later times, a coinage, they carried on a lively trade not only with the inhabitants of Central Asia but also with the Greeks of the Pontic cities, often exchanging surplus goods and furs for Greek luxuries such as fine ceramic wares.

The Scythians worshipped the elements but they were not a devout people and never felt the need for temples. Their deepest feelings were centred on the Great Goddess, Tabiti-Hestia, the patroness of the fire and beasts, and she alone of all their deities figures in art. They also worshipped Papeus-Zeus, god of the air; Apia-Gaea, goddess of the earth; Oetosyrus-Apollo, god of the sun; Artimpasa (Aphrodite Urania), goddess of the moon; Thagimasadas (Poseidon), god of water; and, in time of war, possibly also Ares and Heracles. They do not appear to have had any priests, but they had a class of magicians and soothsayers, the Enaries, who spoke in high-pitched voices and dressed as women. The Scythians believed that these feminine characteristics had been inflicted upon them by the Great Goddess as a punishment for desecrating her shrine at Ashkelon; they were probably eunuchs and may well have been the men Hippocrates had in mind when describing the appearance of the Scythians.

Burial customs. The Scythians venerated the graves of their ancestors, sparing neither wealth nor labour in providing vast tombs richly furnished and equipped. Their funerary rite was elaborate and as costly in lives as in material. In the Altai, interment took place only in the spring and autumn weeks, and embalming was therefore essential. The Scythians of southern Russia also resorted to it, adopting the process Herodotus ascribed to them. Once the corpse had been prepared, it was customarily placed on a cart. Then the mourners (in the case of a chieftain, the entire tribe; for a lesser person, the family and friends), having cropped their hair, wailing, and tearing their clothes, would conduct the dead man during 40 days through the lands that had once belonged to him or, if he had none, would escort him on visits to his relatives and friends.

On the 40th day the body was carried to the tomb and, while one of the dead man's wives, his principal servants such as his cupbearer and groom, and a substantial number of his riding horses were being put to death, his body was lowered into the main burial chamber; the dead man's newly killed companions and servants were then laid in the graves that had been prepared for them. The bodies of the horses were also placed within the mound, the tombs of the Scythian and kindred nomads all taking the form of horse burials.

Human and animal sacrifice

All the dead wore their finest jewelry and clothes and the best of their arms and accoutrements, and they also took with them the objects considered necessary for their future life, only the best of their possessions being chosen for the tomb. The horses were harnessed in their finest trappings; at Pazyryk some were even provided with elaborate masks made of felt and leather touched up with gold, some in the shape of a stag's head, complete with

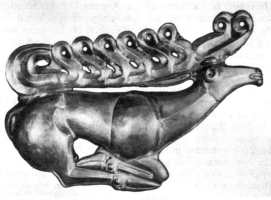 

Scythian animal art.
(Left) Semirecumbent gold stag, probably central ornament from a shield, 6th century BC, from Kostromskaya Stanitsa; length 33.4 cm. (Right) Gold belt plate showing battle between two animals, 4th–3rd century BC, from Siberia; length 12.3 cm. In the Hermitage, Leningrad.
By courtesy of the Hermitage, Leningrad

antlers, some surmounted with figures of birds. The number of horses varied with the period and the region, in some cases running into hundreds.

Finally, according to Herodotus, the Scythians marked the first anniversary of a chieftain's death by choosing 50 men from his bodyguard, all of them freeborn tribesmen, and putting them to death, together with their mounts; the men were then seated on their horses and the bodies impaled together on stakes set in a circle around the tomb so that the faithful dead might forevermore guard it from desecration. It is unfortunate that this method of protection, so costly to human and animal lives, failed to achieve its purpose; almost every Scythian grave opened by archaeologists has been found to have been rifled in antiquity.

Tombs. Tombs of the Scythian and kindred tribes are found from the Altai to eastern Europe. In the Altai the method of construction sometimes led to the formation of a layer of ice above the grave and to the preservation of the tomb contents as efficiently as in a modern deep freeze. As a result, many of the materials that perished in the western burials have been preserved in the Asiatic tombs. The frozen burials of Pazyryk date from the 5th to the 2nd century BC. There the size of the mounds is measured by their circumference rather than by their height, for all are low, being topped only with a covering of boulders. It was this boulder cover that caused the formation of a layer of ice when the rainwater that seeped through it to the earth filling beneath became frozen. The richest Scythian tombs are situated in the Soviet Union, primarily in the Kuban region and in the kingdom of the Royal Scyths (*i.e.*, on the Dnepr (Dnieper) and in the Panticapaeum region in the eastern Crimea), though poorer burials are found over a much larger area. The tombs of the chieftains are extremely elaborate, the larger having as many as five chambers, each measuring some 9 feet by 15 feet and 7 feet in height; they often lie as much as 40 feet below virgin soil, while the mounds erected on them vary from 400 to 1,200 feet in diameter.

In southern Russia, at a chieftain's death a sloping trench was first dug; at its further extremity a shaft was sunk into virgin soil to form the main burial chamber; subsidiary graves, as many as five in number, were prepared for the chieftain's companions. Next the trench had to be transformed into a corridor, and then the graves had to be made to resemble the rooms or tents in which the dead had spent their terrestrial existence. This was accomplished by smoothing the sides of the excavated areas and facing them, according to the region, with tree trunks, matting, birch bark, thatch, or even fabrics. In the Crimea painted decorations were often preferred, while at Pazyryk wall hangings were customary. Hooks were fixed into the walls and spare clothing hung on them; shelves were built around the sides to hold provisions. The ceilings of the subsidiary graves were treated in much the same manner as the walls, but four posts often were sunk into the main grave to support either a canopy placed above the corpse or a roof; floors often were covered with gravel or

rushes. The dead were oriented toward the east, laid on mattresses, often set on biers; in the Altai, however, the bodies were laid in coffins made of hollowed-out tree trunks.

In southern Russia the chieftain's body occupied the main chamber; his wife's was placed in the next best; and his retainers were laid in the others, the grooms always being given preferential treatment. No special graves were provided for the horses, their bodies being laid around the tomb in as orderly a manner as possible; but when a large number of horses were sacrificed the corpses were often piled one upon the other in a heap. At Pazyryk, on the other hand, the horses were ordinarily buried in a separate but adjoining chamber decorated in much the same manner as the section of the tomb reserved for the chieftain and his companions.

In Hungary the burials of Zöldhalompuszta and Tápiószentmárton are among the most important because of the magnificent gold plaques in the shape of stags found there; in eastern Germany the Vettersfeld find is of particular interest on account of the gold figure of a fish of remarkable design discovered in it, together with interesting items of military equipment.

Art. Nothing that has so far been found in the Altai has proved of the same intrinsic value as the objects discovered in the western burials; but they show that similar work was produced by the artists of the entire Eurasian area, whether they worked in wood, leather, bone, appliqué felts, and metals such as bronze and newly discovered iron, or whether they used more precious materials such as silver, gold, or electrum. The artists and craftsmen of the Scythian age were fascinated by the animals they saw or imagined, and though numerous objects were decorated with geometric forms, many of them symbolic or magical, the art of the period is essentially an animal art. Combat scenes between two or more animals are numerous, as are single animal figures. Many real or mythical beasts are represented, the majority of the types having roots in deep antiquity, but the Scythians fashioned them in a manner that was new and characteristically their own. As is to be expected with nomads who were constantly on the move, the objects they produced are generally small in size, but many are made of precious materials and practically all are of superb workmanship.

The gold figures of semirecumbent stags, measuring some 12 inches in length, are outstanding; they were probably used as the central ornaments for the round shields carried by many Royal Scythian fighters. In pre-Scythian times the stag was used as a totem by the tribesmen of Siberia, but in the Scythian period the emblem had lost much of its religious significance. Perhaps the loveliest of the gold stags is the 6th-century-BC example from the burial of Kostromskaya Stanitsa in the Kuban, but versions of the 5th century BC from Tápiószentmárton in Hungary and of the 4th century BC from Kul Oba in the Crimea are scarcely less beautiful. Certain scholars ascribe the former to Thracian and the latter to Ionian

Frozen tombs

The golden stags

craftsmen, yet all conform wholly to Eurasian traditions, and much more concrete evidence is necessary before the former of these attributions can be accepted as final. In the three the stag is shown in a recumbent position, with its legs tucked beneath its body, but with its head raised and its muscles taut so that it gives an impression of rapid motion. The stag also figures prominently in the art of the Pazyryk people, whether as leather or felt cutouts or as carved, wooden terminals.

The Scythians' artistic idiom is one of great compression as well as of synthesis; contrasting positions of the body are combined with astonishing skill to depict every possible aspect of the animal when visualized during all its diverse activities, zoomorphic junctures of astonishing intricacy helping to evoke the animal kingdom in its abundant multiformity. Thus, though the art is basically representational in character, it is at the same time impressionistic in spirit, while it also often verges on the abstract in conception; yet, however complex its elements, they are fused in the finished work into a single entity of compelling force and beauty.

BIBLIOGRAPHY. E.H. MINNS, *Scythians and Greeks* (1913), and M.I. ROSTOVTSEV, *Skythien und der Bosporus* (1931), although to some extent outdated by more recent excavations, remain essential standard works. G.I. BOROVKA, *Scythian Art* (1928), is a useful handbook, although the author's dating does not always accord with that held by certain contemporary scholars. See also V. PARVAN, *Dacia* (1928), dealing with the Scythians in Dacia; B.N. GRAKOV, *Skify* (1947), a useful and authoritative contribution; S.I. RUDENKO, *Frozen Tombs of Siberia: The Pazyryk Burials of Iron Age Horsemen* (1970; orig. pub. in Russian, 1953), an authoritative, detailed, and exciting study of a group of Altaian nomads practicing a Scythian type of art; M.I. ARTAMONOV, *Treasures from Scythian Tombs* (1969; orig. pub. in Czech, 1966), a lavishly illustrated historico-archaeological survey of Russia's Scythian burials; K. JETTMAR, *Art of the Steppes* (1967), a lucid, scholarly, and helpful survey; T. TALBOT RICE, *The Scythians* (1957), an introduction to the subject; and T.A.H. POTRATZ, *Die Scythen in Südrussland* (1963), which provides conclusions strictly based on archaeological evidence.

(T.T.R.)

Seaborg, Glenn Theodore

Glenn Theodore Seaborg, Nobel laureate in chemistry, is best known for his work on the discovery and detailed study of the synthetic elements that lie beyond uranium in the periodic chart of the elements. During World War II he played a key role in the preparation of plutonium for use in nuclear explosives. As chairman of the United States Atomic Energy Commission he encouraged the rapid growth of the nuclear-power industry.

By courtesy of the U.S. Atomic Energy Commission; photograph, Westcott

Seaborg, 1968.

Seaborg was born of immigrant Swedish stock in Ishpeming, Michigan, on April 19, 1912, the son of a machinist. When he was ten, the family moved to the Los Angeles area, where he graduated from high school (1929) with a strongly developed interest in physics and chemistry. After undergraduate study in chemistry at the University of California at Los Angeles (1934), Seaborg studied chemistry at the University of California at Berkeley under the direction of Gilbert N. Lewis, receiving his Ph.D. in 1937, and then spent two years as a research associate of Lewis. Appointed instructor at Berkeley in 1939 he worked on the radiochemical identification of radioactive isotopes produced by bombardment of common elements in Ernest Lawrence's cyclotron and discovered many important isotopes later widely used in medicine and industry.

In 1941 Seaborg and a group of collaborators first identified an isotope of plutonium (element 94) in uranium targets bombarded in the cyclotron and first demonstrated the high susceptibility of the plutonium-239 isotope to nuclear fission. These discoveries resulted in the secret Plutonium Project (organized 1942). At the age of 30, Seaborg organized a chemistry group at the University of Chicago, which he led in developing a chemical process for the extraction of plutonium from uranium, irradiated in nuclear reactors built at Hanford, Washington. The plutonium was used in the first test of a nuclear explosive device, code-named "Trinity," near Alamogordo, New Mexico, on July 16, 1945, and in the weapon exploded at Nagasaki, Japan, on August 9, 1945. *The Plutonium Project*

After World War II, Seaborg returned in 1946 to Berkeley as professor of chemistry to continue his pioneering development of nuclear transmutations. Of the 13 synthetic transuranium elements known in the early 1970s, Seaborg played an important role in the identification of the nine with atomic numbers 94 through 102, namely: plutonium, americium, curium, berkelium, californium, einsteinium, fermium, mendelevium, and nobelium. The prediction of the chemical properties and placement of these and many heavier elements in the periodic table of the elements was helped greatly by an important organizing principle enunciated by Seaborg in 1944 and known as the actinide concept; according to this concept, the 14 elements heavier than actinium belong in a separate group in the periodic table. In 1951 he was awarded the Nobel Prize with Edwin M. McMillan for discoveries in the chemistry of the transuranium elements. *The transuranium elements*

Seaborg served as Chancellor of the Berkeley campus from August 1958 until his appointment in January 1961 as chairman of the U.S. Atomic Energy Commission, a post he held for an unprecedented ten-year span during the administrations of Presidents Kennedy, Johnson, and Nixon. Rapid development of the nuclear-power industry occurred in this period, and plutonium emerged as the key nuclear fuel for breeder reactors, a virtually unlimited source of electrical energy. In 1971 he returned to Berkeley as university professor and as associate director of the Lawrence Berkeley Laboratory.

Seaborg is author of many scientific papers, co-author of many books on chemistry and the chemical elements, and editor of several comprehensive scientific treatises. During his period in government service Seaborg served each year as the United States Representative to the General Conference of the International Atomic Energy Agency.

BIBLIOGRAPHY. No full-scale biography exists, but data on his life and work are in the Nuclear Chemistry Division of the Lawrence Berkeley Laboratory, Berkeley, California. His work is also discussed by HERBERT CHILDS in *An American Genius: The Life of Ernest Orlando Lawrence* (1968). RICHARD G. HEWLETT and OSCAR E. ANDERSON, JR., *The New World, 1939–1946*, vol. 1 of *A History of the United States Atomic Energy Commission* (1962), is authoritative and readable on the World War II development of the atomic bomb. GLENN T. SEABORG and WILLIAM R. CORLISS, *Man and Atom* (1971), is a popular description of the use of plutonium for nuclear power.

(E.K.H.)

Sea-Floor Spreading

The 1960s witnessed a revolution within the earth sciences as a result of rapid developments in the knowledge and understanding of the structure and age of the deep ocean basins. The concept of continental drift (*q.v.*) was formulated in considerable detail in 1912 by the German meteorologist Alfred Wegener, but most scientists rejected the

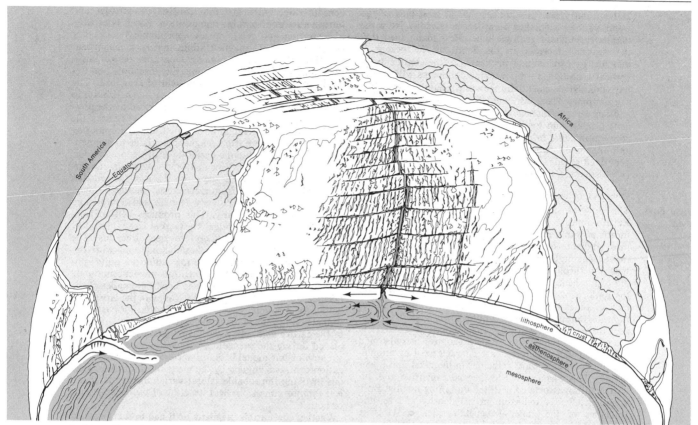

Earth's mantle and crust showing addition of crustal material at midoceanic ridge and
destruction in trench systems (as at South American margin) due to system of convection
currents at depths (see text).
By courtesy of *Fortune Magazine*. By Max Gschwind based on the work of Bruce C. Heezen and Marie Tharp

idea because there was insufficient evidence and no plausible mechanism to support it. In 1960, however, H.H. Hess, U.S. geologist, formulated a hypothesis now termed sea-floor spreading. Although unknown to Hess at that time, his ideas were very similar to a concept put forward 30 years earlier in a little-known paper by Arthur Holmes, the Scottish earth scientist.

Hess had been impressed by two fundamental discoveries about the deep ocean floor, which were made in the 1950s. A seismic refraction technique, involving the transmission of seismic waves through and along layered rocks in the Earth, was adapted for use at sea. It revealed that seismic velocities characteristic of the Earth's upper mantle are invariably encountered only 12 kilometres (7.4 miles) below sea level beneath the deep ocean basins. This implies that the crustal thickness is only 7 km in oceanic areas (because the water is about 5 km deep), which contrasts with a typical, although highly variable, thickness of 35 km of crust beneath the continents. The second discovery was that oceanic ridges (*q.v.*) are characteristic features of all the major ocean basins, with the exception of the northwest Pacific. The ridge crests can be traced on the basis of bathymetry (bottom topography) and earthquake data. In the Atlantic the ridge crest is also characterized by a median rift valley and active volcanism, both of which are developed subaerially (above water) on Iceland, which is situated astride the ridge crest.

Convection currents and rates of spreading
Hess postulated that the continents have been drifted apart by convection currents in the Earth's mantle, the zone between the Earth's crust and core, and that the midocean ridges are situated over the rising parts of such currents. Thus, the oceanic crust was considered to be no more than a surface expression of the mantle, derived from it by simple chemical modification, and continuously created at ridge crests. From consideration of the earlier ideas on continental drift (with respect to the date of initiation of drift in the Atlantic area, for example), Hess suggested that currents in the mantle move at a rate of approximately one centimetre per year (1 inch equals

2.5 centimetres). This would mean that oceanic crust is formed at twice this rate because mantle-derived material spreads laterally away from ridge crests at this rate. Thus, the rate of opening for the Atlantic basin would be 2 cm/yr because material moves away from ridge crests on both flanks. A simple calculation shows that if spreading about ridge crests has gone on continuously at a rate of a few cm/yr in the past, then all of the present deep ocean floor would have been formed within the past 200 million years or so. The first implication of the sea-floor spreading hypothesis then is that two-thirds of the present surface of the Earth has been formed within the most recent 5 percent of geologic time. Having postulated the formation of so large a proportion of the Earth's crust within so short and recent a period of earth history, Hess was faced essentially with two alternatives: either the Earth's volume expanded during this time, with a resulting increase in its surface area, or pre-existing crust is destroyed at the same rate that new crust is generated at ridge crests. Finding the implications and possible causes of large-scale Earth expansion highly implausible, Hess suggested that the island arcs (*q.v.*) and trench systems of the Pacific hemisphere, arcuate zones in which earthquakes and volcanism are prevalent, are sites of downward moving mantle-wide convection currents, and that in these areas oceanic crust is destroyed, essentially by restoration into the mantle.

An integral part of the original hypothesis was that the oceanic crust formed at ridge crests is hydrated mantle material. It was thought that the required water is derived from the mantle itself, and that the hydration reaction is limited to shallow depths by the fact that it is only possible at temperatures below 500° C. With the reversion of the crust to mantle beneath the trench systems, water would find its way into the hydrosphere, principally the oceans, and oceanic sediments that accumulated on the crust during its passage from ridge crest to trench system would be accreted to the continents. Thus, bearing in mind that previous episodes of drift and spreading may have preceded that which has occurred within the past

200 million years, this implies that at least part of the water of the oceans has been derived steadily from the mantle throughout geologic time. Hess maintained that the resulting increase in the depth of the oceans is matched by concomitant thickening of the continents by vertical accretion. In this way the continents will always have maintained essentially the same relation to sea level.

In summary, Hess postulated that despite their great age and apparent permanency continents have been passively drifted apart and together on the backs of mantle-wide convection cells. In contrast the ocean floors are young and ephemeral features, which are constantly being regenerated at ridge crests and destroyed in trench systems (see also OCEANS, DEVELOPMENT OF).

EVIDENCE OF SEA-FLOOR SPREADING

Heat-flow data

The flow of heat through the ocean floor from the Earth's interior was first determined in the 1950s by means of a thermal probe, which measured the temperature gradient (change with depth) in the bottom sediments. The preliminary results obtained revealed that the heat flow through the ocean floor is, in general, comparable to the heat flow through the continents, except over the midocean ridges, where in some localities it is three or four times the normal value (see EARTH, HEAT FLOW IN). Hess argued that these anomalously high values reflect the emplacement of hot mantle-derived material in the vicinity of ridge crests. Marine geophysicists also had discovered that ridge crests are characterized by anomalously low seismic-wave velocities in the crust and upper mantle. This was ascribed to thermal expansion and microfracturing associated with the upwelling mantle. Both would produce a reduction in the density and seismic velocities of the material beneath ridge crests. The concept of less dense material in the upper mantle as a result of enhanced geothermal gradients beneath midocean ridges was to prove an important one because no significant disturbance in the Earth's gravitational field is observed across a ridge. The mass excess of the ridge itself must, therefore, be compensated for by a corresponding mass deficiency at depth; that is, thermal expansion and probably a small degree of partial melting within the uppermost mantle give rise to the topographic expression of an oceanic ridge, and the whole system is in isostatic equilibrium or balance.

Magnetic data

Although there is no disturbance in the Earth's gravity field over ridges, by 1960 it was realized that there is, typically, a disturbance in the Earth's magnetic field. By that time magnetometers had been towed at sea by oceanographic research vessels and two surprising and enigmatic observations had been made. In the North Atlantic a pronounced enhancement of the magnetic field was observed over the median rift valley at the ridge crest. This is the reverse of what one would expect from a deficiency of magnetic material; that is, in the valley. In the northeast Pacific, and not obviously related to a ridge crest, remarkably linear disturbances were mapped; these trended approximately north-south and were bounded by steep magnetic gradients between highs and lows. The first detailed magnetic survey of an oceanic area therefore revealed anomalies unlike any known in continental areas. Moreover, the oceanic anomalies bore no obvious relation to the topography or structure of the underlying sea floor. F.J. Vine and D.H. Matthews, British geophysicists, discussed these magnetic anomalies with respect to seafloor spreading in 1963 and substantially modified the hypothesis.

The Vine and Matthews hypothesis

Hess had considered the oceanic crust to be hydrated mantle, but an alternative hypothesis maintains that it is partly or entirely derived from the mantle by partial melting. The low-melting-point fraction of the mantle is thought to be basalt, and despite the fact that both basalt and serpentinite (hydrated mantle) are dredged from the ocean floor, Hess only considered partial fusion to be important in the construction of seamounts, atolls, and guyots (flat-topped volcanic peaks). Vine and Matthews accepted the concept of sea-floor spreading but maintained that at least the uppermost part, if not the entire oceanic crust, is derived by partial fusion of the mantle

beneath ridge crests and thus consists of extrusive and intrusive rocks of basaltic composition. Basalt is capable of acquiring and retaining an appreciable intensity of permanent (fossil) magnetization; that is, a magnetization that is acquired on cooling soon after its solidification, and presumably reflecting the direction and intensity of the ambient magnetic field at that time. The intensity of this remanent (permanent) magnetization in basalts is invariably greater than that induced by the present earth's field (see ROCK MAGNETISM). Hence, the fossil magnetization might be all-important in considering disturbances in the Earth's magnetic field due to magnetization contrasts within the basalt layer of the ocean floor. To complete their idea, Vine and Matthews made one further assumption: that as new sea floor is formed and spreads laterally away from ridge crests, the Earth's magnetic field reverses its polarity (North and South magnetic poles) intermittently. This produces belts of material parallel to the ridge crests that are alternately magnetized in the normal and reverse directions. The contrasts produced between basaltic material with opposing directions of magnetization would be quite suitable to account for both the central magnetic anomaly observed over ridge crests and the linear anomalies of the northeast Pacific. The median rift valley in the North Atlantic, for example, is presumably floored by basalt extruded and intruded during the current (normal) polarity of the earth's field, but it will be flanked by material emplaced during the preceding, reversed, epoch. The great strength of this model is that it accounts for the magnetization contrasts implied by the magnetic anomalies without invoking improbable lateral variations in the chemical composition or physical structure of the oceanic crust or both.

Geomagnetic reversals

Whether the Earth's magnetic field had in fact reversed was considered debatable in 1963, and even those who believed that it had could not suggest a detailed timetable for reversals. At about this time improvements in the potassium-argon radiometric dating technique made it possible to date with accuracy basaltic lava flows that had been extruded within the past few million years. Samples whose orientation within terrestrial flows were known were dated and their direction of magnetization measured. It was found that all flows of a particular age, irrespective of their geographic locations, indicate the same polarity for the Earth's magnetic field. By studying a great number of flows, from many parts of the world, it was possible in 1966 to suggest a geomagnetic reversal time scale for the past three and a half million years, during which time the Earth's magnetic field appears to have reversed its polarity at least nine times. Simultaneously, the fossil magnetization of deep-sea sediments also was studied. Where the top few metres of sediment recovered by corers consist of a complete record of pelagic (deep sea) sedimentation for the past few million years it was found that the same sequence of reversals was represented by the remanent magnetization of the sediments. These totally independent data provided striking confirmation of the reversal time scale that had been derived from the study of subaerial lava flows.

Rates of sea-floor spreading

Armed with a magnetic reversal time scale and additional marine magnetic data it was possible to re-examine the Vine-Matthews hypothesis. Assuming that the reversal time scale, constant rates of spreading of a few centimetres per year, and the Vine-Matthews hypothesis were all applicable for the past few million years, the observed magnetic anomalies can be reproduced for almost all ridge crests for which magnetic data are available. Moreover, by obtaining a best fit between the observed and predicted anomalies, a precise rate of spreading can be deduced. Such rates vary from one centimetre per year per ridge flank in the vicinity of Iceland to more than 6 cm/yr/ridge flank in the equatorial Pacific. Two exceptions occur in the Eurasian basin of the Arctic and to the southeast of South Africa, where central anomalies are not recorded over the ridge crests. In these areas it is assumed that the ridges either are dormant or are spreading at a very slow rate. Additional profiles and surveys of the Earth's magnetic field over the oceans showed that the

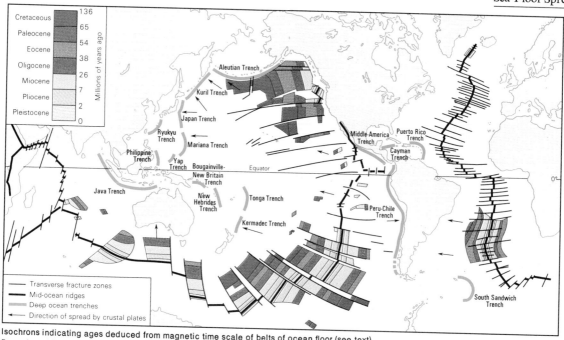

Isochrons indicating ages deduced from magnetic time scale of belts of ocean floor (see text).
By courtesy of *Fortune Magazine*. By Max Gschwind based on the work of Bruce C. Heezen and Marie Tharp

Linear
magnetic
anomalies

anomalies about ridge crests do show a symmetry and correlation with the reversal time scale as the Vine-Matthews hypothesis predicted. This is more evident in the Pacific, however, where spreading rates are high (typically greater than 3 cm/yr/ridge flank), than in the North Atlantic and northwest Indian oceans, where most of the early work was done. The spreading rates are low in these areas, ranging from 1 to 2 cm/yr/ridge flank.

Unfortunately, the technicalities of both methods for determining the age of geomagnetic reversals are such that neither could extend the time scale back beyond 4,-000,000 years very readily or precisely. Although it was possible to provide compelling evidence for spreading at ridge crests during the past few million years, the question of whether spreading had gone on for hundreds of millions of years, and formed the whole of the ridges and ocean basins, remained open. Fortunately, other tests of the hypothesis were possible. If the Earth's magnetic field has reversed its polarity throughout the past 200,000,000 years as it has recently, then spreading should be recorded in the form of linear magnetic anomalies paralleling ridge crests and symmetrically disposed about them. Moreover, if spreading has been continuous about all ridges, then the same sequence of anomalies should be reproduced across all ridge flanks. Since 1966 it has been possible to investigate this implication, and, indeed, the same sequence of anomalies is observed across ridge flanks in all the ocean basins. The distinctive linear anomalies of the northeast Pacific, which were first documented in the late 1950s, are the part of this sequence associated with the west flank of the East Pacific Rise, the crest of which has interacted with the west coast of North America since their formation. The same anomalies can be recognized on either side of the East Pacific Rise and Pacific-Antarctic Ridge in the South Pacific, to the south of Australia, and on both sides of the ridges in the South Atlantic and southeast Indian oceans. They can be recognized, to some extent, in the North Atlantic and northwest Indian oceans, but the slow spreading rates in these areas make correlations difficult without a detailed survey.

The worldwide correlation and symmetry of magnetic anomalies about ridge crests provide compelling evidence for sea-floor spreading and for reversals of the Earth's magnetic field throughout the time interval represented by these anomalies. The determination of this time interval is therefore of great interest. With the possible exception of the northwest Indian Ocean and the extreme North Atlantic, the anomaly sequence is complete in all areas. Thus, short of worldwide stoppages, spreading has

been continuous, but not necessarily at a constant rate. In fact, if one assumes a constant rate in any one area, one can deduce the implied variations in rate in all other areas. In order to provide a working hypothesis, ages were assigned to the anomalies, and hence to the oceanic crust and geomagnetic reversals, by assuming a constant rate of spreading in the South Atlantic, because this implied the least variation in rates elsewhere. The rate assumed was 2 centimetres per year per ridge flank, which was that deduced from the central anomalies. The results of this method suggested that the oldest correlative anomaly was approximately 75,000,000 years of age.

The vindication of the Vine-Matthews modification of Hess's sea-floor spreading hypothesis led to specific predictions about the age and history of the ocean basins (q.v.). In 1960 Hess claimed that no oceanic sediment or crust recovered by coring and dredging was more than 100,000,000 years in age. Many thought that it was possible to make this statement only because of the paucity of available data. Ten years later, however, after extensive coring, dredging, and, more recently, deep-sea drilling, the oldest material recovered still is only 160,000,000 years old. Hess had also maintained that the blanket of sediment in the ocean basins was 10 or 20 times thinner than one would predict if sedimentation rates in the past were similar to those of today and if the ocean basins were permanent and as old as the continents. Today, despite much more detailed and extensive determinations of the sediment thickness by seismic-reflection profiling, and more accurate determinations of sedimentation rates by use of magnetic reversal stratigraphy and new radiometric dating techniques, this conclusion remains valid.

The development of seismic-reflection profilers (low-frequency echo sounders) yielded details of the structures within the sediments and of the topography of the crust beneath them. Judicious use of profilers in conjunction with corers has facilitated sampling of deep reflecting horizons where they outcrop in erosional channels or on fault scarps. In this way, relatively old horizons have been dated and mapped. In all cases their distribution has been found to be consistent with predictions based on the distribution of the linear magnetic anomalies. Radiometric dating of basalt, serpentinite, and related rocks from the deep sea floor is fraught with difficulties, but the reliable dates obtained are consistent with the sea-floor spreading hypothesis. The results obtained from fission-track dating (which utilizes the amount of radiation damage from the fission of radioactive elements) thus far also have confirmed the ages assigned to the magnetic anomalies.

Age and
distribution
of marine
sediments

In 1969 the preliminary results of the Joint Oceanographic Institutions Deep Earth Sampling Program (JOIDES) brought final and consummate proof of the sea-floor spreading hypothesis and the geomagnetic reversal time scale. At many sampling sites in the Atlantic and Pacific oceans the whole of the sedimentary column was penetrated and basalt was recovered. In no case did the age of the sediments conflict with that predicted by the sea-floor spreading hypothesis. In the southern Atlantic Ocean, holes were drilled across the Mid-Atlantic Ridge at 30° S, beneath the previously dated magnetic anomalies. The data obtained confirmed the geomagnetic reversal time scale in a remarkable way. The age of the oldest sediment encountered in each hole—that is, the sediment immediately overlying the basalt basement—was directly proportional to the distance of the hole from the ridge axis. Moreover, the implied rate of sea-floor spreading is two centimetres per year per ridge flank; this is precisely the rate assumed in calibrating the magnetic anomaly sequence.

THE CAUSE OF SEA-FLOOR SPREADING

The concept of giant belts of material that are driven by mantle-wide convection is now thought to be somewhat misleading, in terms of the mechanics and causes of sea-floor spreading. Current ideas on the nature and cause of the spreading process have been derived from more detailed consideration of the geometry of spreading and the seismicity (earthquake activity) of the Earth.

Transform faults

In 1965 J. Tuzo Wilson noted the occurrence of an entirely new class of fractures in the Earth's crust. He named these great fractures, whose active lengths terminate at oceanic ridge crests or trench systems, transform faults. Because ridge crests are considered to be the loci of the creation of oceanic crust, and trench systems the sites of its destruction, it is possible to predict the sense (directions) of movement on such faults. Terrestrial exposures of postulated transform faults in California and New Zealand were found to vindicate the implied sense of movement, but the many transform faults on the ocean floor required sophisticated analysis of earthquake activity along them before the sense of movement could be determined.

The simplest type of transform fault is that which traverses midocean ridges at right angles to the ridge crest. These faults offset the ridges by tens, or occasionally hundreds, of kilometres. The traditional explanation of such a geometry, assuming conservation of crust, was that the ridge crests on either side of the fracture originally matched and subsequently were offset by shearing; that is, that lateral translation occurred along the intervening fracture. Wilson pointed out that the nonconservative process of spreading implies that the offset might be original and unchanging with time. If this is the case the fault will be seismically active only between the offset points on the ridge crest, and the sense of movement along this active length of the fracture will be the opposite to that predicted by the classical analysis (see also ROCK DEFORMATION).

The establishment of the World-Wide Standardized Seismograph Network (WWSSN) in the 1960s enabled seismologists to determine the foci and epicentres (points on the Earth's surface above the foci) of earthquakes with great precision. In 1966, L.R. Sykes was able to show that the distribution of earthquake epicentres along midocean ridge crests and the focal mechanisms deduced for some of the larger earthquakes occurring on the transverse fractures confirm Wilson's predictions. Focal-mechanism solutions provide an indication of the sense of movement on faults and are obtained from the analysis of the first ground motion at many seismograph stations throughout the world.

The confirmation of transform faulting on the ocean floor provided further support for the concept of sea-floor spreading, but it also raised questions and sowed the seed for modification of the hypothesis. If sea-floor spreading and continental drift are caused by mantle convection, then how could both rising and descending limbs of convection cells be abruptly terminated and offset along transform faults? Mechanically this seems quite unreasonable.

When earthquake epicentres obtained from the WWSSN were plotted on a world map it was seen that the seismicity of the Earth defines with great precision the three structural elements of the sea-floor spreading model, namely, ridge crests, trench systems, and transform faults. Furthermore, the maximum depths at which earthquakes occur beneath trench and mountain systems were very much greater than those beneath ridge crests. Earthquakes on ridge crests appear to be restricted to depths of less than 10 or 20 kilometres, whereas earthquakes beneath trench and mountain systems occur at all depths up to several hundred kilometres and, exceptionally, 700 kilometres. The seismicity of the Earth therefore is largely restricted to active ridge crests, transform faults, trenches, and young fold mountain systems. These narrow zones outline essentially aseismic areas of the Earth's crust that appear to behave as quasi-rigid plates, and the plates do not exhibit major internal deformation.

Plate tectonics

In 1967, W. Jason Morgan analyzed the geometry of sea-floor spreading in terms of relative movements between rigid crustal plates bounded by ridge crests, transform faults, and trench systems on the surface of a sphere. His success was remarkable, and it appears that much of the Earth's seismicity is clearly related to relative movements between quasi-rigid plates. Consequently, this new modification of sea-floor spreading is termed plate tectonics. The terms continental drift and sea-floor spreading are now deemed somewhat inappropriate because individual plates typically include both continental and oceanic crust. The Earth's outermost skin, or lithosphere, exhibits appreciable strength and rigidity and extends well beneath both continental and oceanic crusts to depths of 50 or even 100 kilometres. At ridge crests, the lithospheric plates are thinned by the elevation of the geotherms (temperature of the Earth's interior) due to mantle upwelling and emplacement. Beneath the trench systems the oceanic plate plunges downward, typically at an angle of about 45° to the adjacent plate as reflected in the deep focus seismicity. The processes of creation and destruction of oceanic plates display an intriguing symmetry and asymmetry, respectively.

It is clear that the most detailed and quantitative evidence for the sea-floor spreading hypotheses relates to the midocean ridges. The nature of the trench systems is an equally important aspect of the hypothesis but it is more equivocal. Many surficial structures in island arcs (q.v.) and trench systems suggest extension of the Earth's crust, as though the cold, descending lithosphere is pulling down the plates above; indeed this may be the case. Flat-lying sediments in some trenches, and the absence of buckled sediments in virtually all, have led some to doubt this aspect of the spreading hypothesis; however, the degree of buckling in sediment beneath the landward or inner wall of a trench and the extent of slumping of sediments off this wall are still unknown. The most compelling evidence for the underthrusting of island arcs and Andean-type continental margins by oceanic lithosphere comes from studies of deep-focus earthquakes.

Global analysis of the geometry of plate movements permits prediction of the direction and rate of underthrusting in trench systems because the direction and rate of spreading at ridge crests can be deduced from the transform faults and magnetic anomalies. The directions predicted in this way correspond to directions of underthrusting derived from focal-mechanism solutions for some of the larger shallow-focus earthquakes landward of trenches, and the rates deduced are directly proportional to the maximum depths at which earthquake foci occur. Presumably the latter reflect a thermal relaxation effect as the cold lithospheric slab is thrust down into the hotter upper mantle; in this case one would expect these maximum depths to depend on the rate of underthrusting. Studies of the variation in the velocity and attenuation of seismic shear waves for various ray paths beneath trench systems also confirm the picture of an underthrusting slab of cold lithosphere.

Hess's concept of convection to the surface was seen to

be improbable because of transform faults; his postulate of mantle-wide convection also seems improbable now for an equally simple geometric reason. A fixed geometry of mantle-wide convection cells, in which the rising limbs are correlated with ridge crests and descending limbs with trench systems, is incompatible with the concept of plate tectonics. The geometry of plate movements is such that only one plate, or one boundary between two plates, can be fixed with respect to some frame of reference such as the Earth's geographical coordinates. All other plates and boundaries then move with respect to each other and to the frame of reference. Consideration of the plates that incorporate Africa and Antarctica provides a simple example of this point. Both Africa and Antarctica are surrounded on at least three sides by ridge crests but by no trench systems. Therefore, if either continent is regarded as being fixed, the surrounding ridge crests must clearly migrate away from it as spreading occurs.

Despite the vast accumulation of near surface evidence favouring the hypothesis of sea-floor spreading, man is little nearer to an understanding of the process or processes deep within the Earth by which it is initiated and maintained. Many consider that thermal convection in some form is the only known process capable of supplying the energy requirements, but it now seems probable that there is no simple relationship between mantle convection currents and surface features. Convection in this context should be interpreted in its broadest terms; that is, the generation of horizontal temperature gradients that result in gravitational instabilities and, hence, in the vertical transport of hot and cold material. In this regard the cold descending slab of oceanic lithosphere landward of the trench systems is clearly a source of gravitational energy. That such a sinker exists and is an important driving force is reflected in the tensile nature of intermediate depth earthquakes beneath the trenches, and by the observation that the only systematic correlation between surface features and broad-scale gravity anomalies is that between regional gravity highs and the trench systems.

Present knowledge of the physical properties of the Earth's mantle is less than perfect, particularly with regard to temperature and viscosity, two all-important parameters. It now seems probable, however, that convection, if it occurs at all, is only possible in that part of the upper mantle that is near its melting point, probably at depths between 50 to 100 kilometres and 200 to 300 kilometres. Convection in this shell will produce two effects, namely a net viscous drag on the lithospheric plates above and, as a result of thermal convection at ridge crests and the resultant elevation of ridges, a downhill pull on the flanking plates that are situated in gravity potential gradients.

BIBLIOGRAPHY. "The Ocean," *Scient. Am.*, vol. 221, entire issue (September 1969), also published in book form (1969). The articles by E. BULLARD, "The Origin of the Oceans" and H.W. MENARD, "The Deep-Ocean Floor," in particular, cover marine geology and geophysics. H. TAKEUCHI, S. UYEDA, and H. KANAMORI, *Debate About the Earth* (1967), excellent readable background material on continental drift, paleomagnetism, and geomagnetism; O.M. PHILLIPS, *The Heart of the Earth* (1968), a slightly more quantitative introduction to the physics of the earth; R.A. PHINNEY (ed.), *The History of the Earth's Crust* (1968), a collection of pertinent research papers.

(F.J.V.)

Securities Trading

Securities are written evidences of ownership giving their holders the right to demand and receive property not in their possession. The most common types of securities are stocks and bonds, of which there are many particular kinds designed to meet specialized needs. This article deals mainly with the buying and selling of securities issued by private corporations. (The securities issued by governments are discussed in the article PUBLIC DEBT.)

SECURITIES ISSUED BY CORPORATIONS

Corporations create two kinds of securities: bonds, representing debt, and stocks, representing ownership or equity interest in their operations. (In Great Britain, the term stock ordinarily refers to a loan, whereas the equity segment is called a share.)

Bonds. The bond, as a debt instrument, represents the promise of a corporation to pay a fixed sum at a specified maturity date, and interest at regular intervals until then. Bonds may be registered in the names of designated parties, as payees, though more often, in order to facilitate handling, they are made payable to the "bearer." The bondholder usually receives his interest by redeeming attached coupons.

Since it could be difficult for a corporation to pay all of its bonds at one time, it is common practice to pay them gradually through serial maturity dates or through a sinking fund, under which arrangement a specified portion of earnings is regularly set aside and applied to the retirement of the bonds. In addition, bonds frequently may be "called" at the option of the company, so that the corporation can take advantage of declining interest rates by selling new bonds at more favourable terms and using these funds to eliminate older outstanding issues. In order to guarantee the earnings of investors, however, bonds may be noncallable for a specified period, perhaps for five or ten years, and their redemption price may be made equal to the face amount plus a "premium" amount that declines as the bond approaches its maturity date.

The principal type of bond is a mortgage bond, which represents a claim on specified real property. This protection ordinarily results in the holders' receiving priority treatment in the event that financial difficulties lead to a reorganization. Another type is a collateral trust bond, in which the security consists of intangible property, usually stocks and bonds owned by the corporation. Railroads and other transportation companies sometimes finance the purchase of rolling stock with equipment obligations, in which the security is the rolling stock itself.

Although in the United States the term debentures ordinarily refers to relatively long-term unsecured obligations, in other countries it is used to describe any type of corporate obligation, and "bond" more often refers to loans issued by public authorities.

Corporations have developed hybrid obligations to meet varying circumstances. One of the most important of these is the convertible bond, which can be exchanged for common shares at specified prices that may gradually rise over time. Such a bond may be used as a financing device to obtain funds at a low interest rate during the initial stages of a project, when income is likely to be low, and encourage conversion of the debt to stock as earnings rise. A convertible bond may also prove appealing during periods of market uncertainty, when investors obtain the price protection afforded by the bond segment without materially sacrificing possible gains provided by the stock feature; if the price of such a bond momentarily falls below its common-stock equivalent, persons who seek to profit by differentials in equivalent securities will buy the undervalued bond and sell the overvalued stock, effecting delivery on the stock by borrowing the required number of shares (selling short) and eventually converting the bonds in order to obtain the shares to return to the lender.

Another of the hybrid types is the income bond, which has a fixed maturity but on which interest is paid only if it is earned. These bonds developed in the United States out of railroad reorganizations, when investors holding defaulted bonds were willing to accept an income obligation in exchange for their own securities because of its bond form; the issuer for his part was less vulnerable to the danger of another bankruptcy because interest on the new income bonds was contingent on earnings.

Still another hybrid form is the linked bond, in which the value of the principal, and sometimes the amount of interest as well, is linked to some standard of value such as commodity prices, a cost of living index, a foreign currency, or a combination of these. Although the principle of linkage is old, bonds of this sort received their major impetus during the inflationary periods after World Wars I and II. In recent years they have had the most use in countries in which the pressures of inflation have been sufficiently strong to deter investors from buying fixed-income obligations.

Thermal convection in the mantle

Stock. Those who provide the risk capital for a corporate venture are given stock, representing their ownership interest in the enterprise. The holder of stock has certain rights that are defined by the charter and bylaws of the corporation as well as by the laws of the country or state in which it is chartered. Typically these include the right to share in dividends and other distributions, to vote for directors and fundamental corporate changes, and to inspect the books of the corporation, and, less frequently, the "pre-emptive right" to subscribe to any new issue of stock. The stockholder's interest is divided into units of participation, called shares.

A stock certificate ordinarily is given as documentary evidence of share ownership. Originally this was its primary function; but as interest in securities grew and the capital market evolved, the role of the certificate gradually changed until it became, as it is now, an important instrument for the transfer of title. In some European countries the stock certificate is commonly held in bearer form and is negotiable without endorsement. To avoid loss, the certificates are likely to be entrusted to commercial banks or a clearing agency that is able to handle much of the transfer function through offsetting transactions and bookkeeping entries. In the United States, certificates usually are registered in the name of the owner or in a "street name"—the name of the owner's broker or bank; the bank may for legal reasons use the name of another person, known as a "nominee." When a certificate is held in the name of a broker or bank nominee, the institution is able to make delivery more readily and the transfer process is facilitated. Investors, for legal or personal reasons, may prefer to keep the certificates in their own names.

A corporation may endow different kinds or classes of stock with different rights. Preferred stock has priority with respect to dividends and, if the corporation is dissolved, to the division of assets. Dividends on preferred stock usually are paid at a fixed rate and are often cumulated in the event the corporation finds it necessary to omit a distribution. In the latter circumstance the full deficiency must be cleared before payments may be made on the common shares. Participating preferred stock, in addition to stipulated dividends, receives a share of whatever earnings are paid to the common stock. Participation is usually resorted to as an inducement to investors when the corporation is financially weak. Although a preferred issue has no maturity date, it may be given redemption terms much like those of a bond, including a conversion privilege and a sinking fund. Preferred stockholders may or may not be allowed to vote equally with common stockholders on some or all propositions or more characteristically may vote only upon the occurrence of some prescribed condition, such as the default of a specified number of dividend payments.

Common stock, in some countries called ordinary shares, represents a residual interest in the earnings and assets of a corporation. Whereas distributions to bonds or preferred stock are ordinarily fixed, dividends paid on common stock are set at the time of payment by the directors and tend to vary with earnings. The market price of common stock is likely to move in a relatively wide range, depending on investors' expectations of earnings in the future.

Options. An option contract is an agreement enabling the holder to buy a security at a fixed price for a limited period of time. One form of option contract is the stock purchase warrant, which entitles the owner to buy shares of common stock at designated prices and according to a prescribed ratio. Warrants are often used to enhance the salability of a senior security, and sometimes as part of the compensation paid to bankers who market new issues.

Another use of the option contract is the employee stock option. This is used to compensate key executives and other employees; it is normally subject to a variety of restrictions and is generally nontransferrable. Stock rights, like warrants, are transferrable privileges permitting stockholders to buy another security or a portion thereof at a specified price for an indicated period of time. The stock right allows stockholders to subscribe to additional shares of stock in proportion to their present holdings. Stock rights usually have a shorter life-span than warrants, and their subscription price is below, rather than above, the market price of the common stock.

THE MARKETING OF NEW ISSUES

The marketing of securities is an essential link in the mechanism that transfers capital funds from savers to users. The transfer may involve intermediaries such as savings banks, insurance companies, or investment trusts. The ultimate user of the funds may be a corporation or any of the various levels of government from municipalities to national states.

The growth of public debt throughout the world has made governments increasingly important participants in the markets for new securities. They have had to develop financing techniques with careful attention to their influence on the markets for nongovernmental securities. The treasuries must carefully study interest rates, yield patterns, terms of financing, and the distribution of holdings among investors.

Local governments are usually subject to various statutory restrictions that must be carefully observed when offering a new issue for sale. Local government bonds are distributed through investment bankers who buy them and reoffer them to the public at higher prices and correspondingly lower yields. Sometimes the terms of the offer are negotiated. In the United States, however, a more prevalent means of selling state and local bonds is through competitive bidding, in which the issuer announces a contemplated offering of bonds for a designated amount, with specified maturity dates, and for certain purposes. Syndicates of investment bankers are formed to bid on the issue, and the award is made to the group providing the most favourable terms. The winning syndicate then reoffers the bonds to the public at prices carefully tailored to be competitive with comparable obligations already on the market and to provide a suitable profit margin.

The financial manager of a company requiring additional funds has a number of alternative courses of action open to him. He may do all of his financing through commercial banks by means of loans and revolving credit arrangements that, in essence, are formalized lines of credit. Or, he may prefer to raise capital through the sale of securities. If he chooses to do the latter, he may undertake a private sale with an institutional investor such as an insurance company, permitting him to avoid both the complicated procedures of a public distribution and the risks of unsettled market conditions. On the other hand, a private placement of this sort deprives the issuer of the favourable publicity flowing from a successful public offering; it may not afford sufficient resources for very large firms with continuing demands for capital; and it involves rather restrictive legal requirements.

A company that elects to float its securities publicly in the capital market will ordinarily utilize the services of an investment banker. The investment banker may buy the securities from the issuer and seek a profit by selling them at a higher price to the public, thereby assuming the market risks. If the issue is large, the originating investment banker may invite other houses to join with him in purchasing the issue from the company, while to facilitate disposal he may form a selling group to take over the issue from the buying firms for resale to the public. In lieu of buying the securities from the issuer, the investment banker may act as an agent and receive a commission on the amount sold. If the issuer negotiates the selection of an investment banker, the banker will serve as financial counsel and offer advice on the timing and terms of the new issue. If the selection is by competitive bidding, the relationship is likely to be more impersonal.

An accepted principle of modern finance is that investors are entitled to knowledge about the issuer in order to appraise the quality of the securities offered. A number of countries now require issuers to file registration statements and provide written prospectuses.

The security markets of Europe do not have the aggressive investment-banking machinery developed in the

Marketing
corporation
securities

United States. European commercial banks, on the other hand, play a much more important role in financing the needs of industry than do commercial banks in the United States and Great Britain.

In the 1960s, a number of industrial nations faced increasing difficulties in meeting their financing needs through local capital markets. Several issuers began to float securities that were payable in any of 17 different European currencies. This marked what might be called the beginning of an "international securities" market. Efforts were also made to issue bonds on a parallel basis in different countries with each portion denominated in the currency of the country in which it was sold. For various legal and technical reasons, these methods did not attract a wide following.

Another factor that hastened the growth of a European securities market was the balance of payments problem confronting the United States in the 1960s. Certain legislative enactments substantially shut the capital market of the U.S. to foreign issuers; and other restraints were imposed on foreign lending by United States financial institutions and on direct foreign investment by United States corporations. As a result, a number of multinational corporations headquartered in the United States were forced to seek financing in overseas securities markets for the expanding business of their foreign subsidiaries. United States and foreign investment bankers joined in syndicates to float these securities. The process was facilitated by the growth of an international market in Eurodollars, representing claims on dollars deposited in European banks. The bulk of the new bonds offered abroad were denominated in Eurodollars.

During the period 1957–65, when this new European market came into being, the volume of foreign bonds issued publicly rose from $492,600,000 to $1,489,500,-000. The principal and most consistent borrowers were in Canada, Australia, Japan, Norway, Israel, Denmark, and New Zealand. In all of these countries, the major borrower was the national government, except in Canada, where the political subdivisions were the major borrowers. In West Germany, Great Britain, and the United States, the only borrowers in international markets were private units.

THE MACHINERY OF SECURITIES TRADING

Organized securities markets and stock exchanges are a product of economic development. In the early years of economic growth, most of a country's industrial units are small and their capital requirements relatively modest. The rate of saving is low, and institutions for channelling private savings into investment are generally lacking. As the economy progresses and national income grows, new institutions enter the financial picture to direct the mounting volume of savings into productive outlets. The appearance of growing numbers of individual and institutional investors creates a need for trading markets to speed up transactions and enable stockholders swiftly and easily to convert their holdings to cash.

At this stage of development, corporations usually meet less of their financing needs through direct sales of securities in the new issue market and obtain a larger percentage through reinvesting their own earnings. This plowing back of earnings is not insensitive to the judgment of investors: if the prospects of a company are good, investors bid up the price of its shares in the trading market and show a willingness to forego dividends for the possibility of long-term capital gains achieved through internal growth. Thus, when a company is able to finance its expansion by means of reinvested earnings rather than by new stock issues, the trading segment becomes the more important aspect of the capital market.

The development of stock exchanges

History. Stock exchanges grew out of early trading activities in agricultural and other commodities. Traders in European fairs in the Middle Ages found it convenient to use credit, which required the supporting documents of drafts, notes, and bills of exchange. The French stock exchange may be traced as far back as the 12th century, when trading occurred in commercial bills of exchange. To regulate these incipient markets, Philip the Fair

(1268–1314) created the profession of *courratier de change*, the forerunner of the modern French stock-broker, or *agent de change*. At about the same period in Bruges, then a prosperous centre of the Low Countries, merchants took to gathering in front of the house of the Van der Buerse family to engage in trading. From this custom, the name of the family became identified with trading, and eventually "bourse" came to signify a stock exchange. From similar roots in trade and commerce, the institutional beginnings of stock exchanges appeared during the 16th and 17th centuries in other great trading centres throughout the world—Amsterdam, Great Britain, Denmark, Germany.

The growth of trade created a need for banks and insurance companies. Political developments caused governments to seek new sources of funds. This combination of expanding activity and intermittent capital shortages stimulated the early issuers of securities—governments, banks, insurance companies, and some joint-stock enterprises, particularly the great trading companies. From the existing exchanges for commercial bills and notes, it was an easy and logical transition to the establishment of stock exchanges for securities. By the early 1600s, shares of the Dutch East India Company were being traded in Amsterdam; in 1773, London stock dealers who had previously been meeting in coffeehouses moved into their own building; and by the 19th century, trading in securities on a formal basis was common in the industrialized nations.

The evolution of stock exchanges continued. In Great Britain, progress has for the most part been internal and voluntary; the London Stock Exchange has regulated its own activities. The French stock exchanges, in contrast, are directly subject to law, and the operations of the *agents de change* have been affected by national decrees. At one time, there were three markets for securities in Paris: an official market called the Parquet (the "floor"); a semiofficial market, the Coulisse (the "wing"); and the Hors Côté (the "outside"), an unregulated market in unlisted securities. In 1929, the Hors Côté was subjected to official regulation and in the following decade its activities were absorbed into the Coulisse, which in turn was combined with the Parquet in a reorganization in 1961. In Belgium the exchanges have had a mixed history. Strict governmental controls were imposed in 1801 and not removed until 1867. Following the economic crisis of 1929–34, the pendulum swung the other way and the exchanges were once more placed under the control of central authority. In Switzerland, the exchanges have been governed by cantonal (state) law.

Historical events have left their mark upon the development of stock exchanges in some countries. Mining, rather than trade and commerce, was the impelling influence in the establishment of stock exchanges in South Africa and Canada. In Germany, the Berlin Stock Exchange lost its dominant role after World War II, and its position was assumed by exchanges in Frankfurt and Düsseldorf. The Japanese securities markets were revolutionized following World War II, when a new securities law was enacted patterned after the U.S. model. A campaign to distribute stock formerly held by the large *zaibatsu* (family-owned combines) and semigovernment corporations greatly increased public stock ownership, which in turn contributed to the considerable growth of trading on the nine Japanese exchanges. Another post-World War II development was the interest of the governments of developing countries in the use of stock exchanges to facilitate external financing.

Securities markets in the United States began with speculative trading in issues of the new government. In 1791, the country's first stock exchange was established in Philadelphia, then the leading city in domestic and foreign trade. An exchange in New York was set up in 1792, when 24 merchants and brokers decided to charge commissions while acting as agents for other persons and to give preference to each other in their negotiations. They did much of their trading under a tree at 68 Wall Street. Government securities formed the basis of the early trading. Stocks of banks and insurance companies added to the volume of transactions. The building of roads and canals brought more securities to the market. In 1817 the New York brokers decided to organize formally as the New York Stock and Exchange Board. Thereafter, the stock market grew with the industrialization of the country. In 1863, the New York Stock Exchange adopted its present name. During the Civil War additional exchanges were organized, one of them the forerunner of the present American Stock Exchange, the second largest stock market in the country.

Organization. All stock exchanges perform similar functions with respect to the listing, trading, and clearing of securities. They differ in their administrative machinery for handling these functions.

The London Stock Exchange, the largest in the world in terms of the number and variety of domestic and international securities traded, is an independent institution not subject to governmental regulation. It resembles a private club with its own constitution and operating rules, administered by a council that, except for the government broker who is an ex officio nonvoting member, is elected by the membership. Operating responsibility is vested in the secretary and his staff.

In the United States, as in Great Britain, the government does not participate directly in the operations of the exchanges. Since 1933, however, Congress has enacted half a dozen measures that in one way or another affect the securities market. The most important are the Securities Act of 1933, which is primarily concerned with the new-issue market, and the Securities Exchange Act of 1934, which is directed toward the trading market. The latter requires that every stock exchange register with the Securities and Exchange Commission (SEC) as a national securities exchange, unless it is exempted because of the limited volume of its transactions, and that it conform to certain rules in its trading practices. This relationship between the stock exchanges and the SEC is peculiar to the United States; it involves a sort of administrative partnership between the exchanges as private associations—but functioning as quasi-public institutions—and the government. The exchanges generally may adopt policies and issue regulations governing their own operations but are subject to SEC intercession in the event that the Commission believes modifications are required in the public interest.

Most European exchanges are also subject to some form of governmental regulation. The Amsterdam Stock Exchange is a private organization, relatively free to regulate the activities of the market, but the Minister of Finance exercises some supervision under existing legislation. The Zürich exchange is governed by a board of elected members that determines general policy and coordinates the work of the exchange's committees. Of these, the Zürich Cantonal Committee, which directs dealings on the floor of the exchange, is chaired by the head of the Finance Department of the State of Zürich. Although the Frankfurt Stock Exchange is under the direct administration of a Board of Governors elected by its own members, the rules of the exchange must be approved by the authorities of the state of Hesse; and the official specialists, each responsible for the trading in certain securities, are appointed by the Minister of Finance in the state of Hesse. In Brussels the Ministry of Finance is involved in the appointment of members to major committees, while a governmental representative is attached to each exchange to supervise the observance of all rules and laws; in addition, the Banking Commission that is nominated by the government has substantial powers over the admission of securities to public trading. The policy-making Exchange Commission of the Paris bourse is headed by the Governor of the Banque de France, while the regular members are chosen by the Ministry of Finance; the *agents de change* who supervise the trading process are semigovernmental officials. New members of the Italian stock exchanges are appointed by the government from a list of candidates as a result of competitive examinations, and therefore have some public status.

Since 1953, membership in the New York Stock Exchange has been limited to 1,366. Only individuals may be members, but they may be partners or stockholders of organizations that do business with the public. Their organizations in such cases are known as member firms. The exchange supervises and regulates member firms in what it considers to be the public interest: a majority of the owners must be engaged primarily in the business of brokers or dealers in securities; exchange approval is required of any shareholder with a 5 percent interest in a member corporation; and all principal officers and directors who are active in the firm must be members or allied members of the exchange. An allied member is subject to the rules of the exchange but does not have the right to engage in transactions on the floor.

To become a member, an individual must acquire, with the approval of the board of governors, a "seat" from a present member or from the estate of a deceased one. Before granting approval, the exchange will investigate such matters as the applicant's past record and financial standing; he will also have to pass an examination demonstrating his knowledge of the securities field.

There are several kinds of brokers on the floor of the exchange. They include the commission broker who executes customer orders placed at or near the current market price; the specialist in one or more issues who, as a broker, executes limited orders for other members and, as a dealer, buys and sells securities for his own account; floor brokers, or "two-dollar" brokers, who execute orders for other brokers at a commission but have no contact with the public; brokers associated with odd-lot firms, who undertake to buy or sell in quantities other than the standard 100-share lot; and "registered traders" who buy and sell for their own account.

To become a member of the London Stock Exchange, an individual must acquire a "nomination" from a retiring member at a price that varies with demand and supply. Every applicant must be approved by at least three-quarters of the stock exchange council. A member may be a broker, dealing as an agent of the public, or a jobber, dealing for his own account with other brokers or jobbers.

Membership in the Paris stock exchange is limited to 85 *agents de change* who supervise activity while the actual work of trading and executing orders is done by their employees and those of the exchange. To become an *agent de change*, an applicant must meet prescribed standards of education and experience as well as pass a written examination. He must be nominated by a retiring member or the heirs of a deceased member and make a deposit guaranty. He is formally appointed by the Minister of Finance.

Other European exchanges set eligibility requirements of character, experience, and financial standing, and some have educational requirements as well. In Brussels, in addition to the completion of six consecutive years in a broker's office, a candidate must have a degree in commercial science or economics and pass a professional examination. In Germany, Switzerland, and Sweden, the brokerage business is dominated by banks.

Members of Japanese exchanges must be corporations doing a business in securities. There are two kinds of members: regular members, who buy and sell for customers or for their own accounts, and *saitori*, who act principally as intermediaries for regular members.

Trading procedures. Most stock exchanges are auction markets, in which prices are determined by competitive bidding. In very large, active markets, the auction is continuous, occurring throughout the day's trading session and for any security in which there is buying and selling interest. In smaller markets the names of the listed stocks may be submitted in some form of rotation, with the auction occurring at that time; this process is described as a "call market."

Trading methods on all the exchanges in the United States are similar. In a typical transaction for a security listed on the New York Stock Exchange, a customer gives an order to an employee in a branch or correspondent office of a member firm, who transmits it either indirectly through the firm's New York office or, as is becoming increasingly common, directly to a receiving clerk on the floor of the exchange. The receiving clerk summons the

Membership requirements of stock exchanges

firm's floor broker who takes the order, goes to the post where the stock is traded, and participates in an auction procedure as either buyer or seller. If the order is not a market order calling for immediate action, the broker turns it over to an appropriate specialist who will execute it when an indicated price is reached.

As in any auction market, securities are sold to the broker bidding the highest price and bought from the broker offering the lowest price. Since the market is continuous, buyers and sellers are constantly competing with each other. In the New York Stock Exchange, the specialist plays an important role. As a principal, he has the responsibility of buying and selling for his own account, thereby providing a stabilizing influence; as an agent, he represents other brokers on both sides of the market when they have orders at prices that cannot be readily executed.

With the growing demand for stocks on the part of institutions such as insurance companies, mutual funds, pension funds, and so forth, the size of orders consummated on the New York Stock Exchange has grown. In 1970, for example, 17,217 trades of blocks of 10,000 shares or more were completed on the exchange, representing 15.4 percent of reported volume, compared with 2,171 such transactions in 1965, representing 3.1 percent of reported volume. The common way of handling these big blocks on the floor of the exchange has been to break them into smaller orders executed over a period of time. Another method is to assemble matching orders in advance and then "cross" them, executing the purchase or sale at current prices in accordance with prescribed rules; since the broker initially may have obtained the matching orders off the floor, this procedure assumes some of the aspects of a negotiated rather than a pure auction transaction. It is only a step from this to so-called block positioning, in which the broker functions as a principal and actually buys the block from the seller and distributes the securities over a period of time on the floor of the exchange.

When none of these methods appears feasible, the exchange permits certain special procedures. A *secondary distribution* of stock resembles the underwriting of a new issue, the block being handled by a selling group or syndicate off the floor after trading hours, at a price regulated by the exchange. In an *exchange distribution* a member firm accumulates the necessary buy orders and then crosses them on the floor. This is distinguished from an ordinary "cross" because the selling broker may provide extra compensation to his own registered representatives and to other participating firms. A *special offering* is the offering of a block through the facilities of the exchange at a price not in excess of the last sale or the current offer, whichever is lower, but not below the current bid unless special permission is obtained. The terms of the offer are flashed on the tape. The offerer agrees to pay a special commission. A *specialist block purchase* permits the specialist to buy a block outside the regular market procedure, at a price that is somewhat below the current bid.

Trading on the London Stock Exchange is carried on through a unique system of brokers and jobbers. A broker acts as an agent for his customers; a jobber, or dealer, transacts business on the floor of the exchange but does not deal with the public. A customer gives an order to a brokerage house, which relays it to the floor for execution. The receiving broker goes to the area where the security is traded and seeks a jobber stationed in the vicinity who specializes in the particular issue. The jobber serves only in the capacity of a principal, buying and selling for his own account and dealing only with brokers or other jobbers. The broker asks the jobber's current prices without revealing whether he is interested in buying or selling. The broker may seek to narrow the spread between the bid and ask quotations or he may approach another jobber handling the same issue and undertake the same bargaining process. Eventually, when satisfied that he has obtained the best possible price for his client, the broker will complete the bargain.

A broker is compensated by the commission received from the customer. The jobber seeks to maximize his profitable business by adjusting his buying and selling prices. As the ultimate dealer in the London market, the jobber's activities provide a stabilizing factor, but unlike the specialist on the New York Stock Exchange, the jobber is under no obligation to help support prices. The growing importance of institutional customers has increased the size of transactions in the London market as it has in the U.S., and therefore the jobber has been compelled to risk larger sums. To offset this risk, arrangements for a particularly large order may be negotiated beforehand and the transaction put through the floor as a matter of procedure, with the jobber accepting a minimum "turn." Although the jobbing system provides a continuous market, it does not employ the auction bidding of the New York exchange.

The trading procedures of other major exchanges throughout the world employ the principles that have been described above, although they vary in their application of them. In the exchanges of Paris, Brussels, Copenhagen, Stockholm, and Zürich, some form of auction system is employed: prices are established through bids and offers made on specific securities at particular periods of time. In Tokyo, trading is continuous and orders are consummated through the *saitori* members, who keep order sheets on all transactions. Unlike the specialist on the New York exchange or the jobber in London, however, the *saitori* does not trade for his own account but serves only as an intermediary between regular members. In Amsterdam, trading in active securities is done directly between members during designated trading periods; specialists function as intermediaries between buyers and sellers.

Types of orders. The simplest method of buying stock is through the *market order*. This is an order to buy or sell a stated amount of a security at the most advantageous price obtainable after the order reaches the trading floor. A *limit* (or *limited*) *order* is an order to buy or sell a stated amount of a security when it reaches a specified price or a better one if it is obtainable after the order comes to the trading floor. In the Amsterdam market, the device of the "middle price" is used: an investor who gives a limit order before the opening will have it executed at the day's median level, or at a price that is better than the limit, whichever is found to be more advantageous to the client.

There are other more specialized types of orders. A *stop order* or *stop-loss order* is an order to purchase or sell a security after a designated price is reached or passed, when it then becomes a market order. It differs from the limit order in that it is designed to protect the customer from market reversals; the stop price is not necessarily the price at which the order will be executed, particularly if the market is changing rapidly. This type of order does not lend itself to the London jobbing system.

An important method of trading in stock is through the buying and selling of options. The most common option contracts are puts and calls. A *put* is a contract that permits the holder to deliver to the purchaser a specified number of shares of stock at a fixed price within a designated period of time, say six months; a *call* entitles him to buy shares from the seller within a given period. For example, a person who buys a stock hoping to sell it later at a higher price may also buy a put as a hedge against a fall in price. The put enables him to sell the stock at the price for which he bought it. If the stock rises he need not use the option and loses only the price of its purchase. Option trading is common in Brussels, Paris, London, and the United States.

In the early days of securities trading, stocks and bonds were often bought at private banking houses in the same way that commodities might be purchased over the counter of a general store. This was the origin of the term "over-the-counter." It is used today to mean all securities transactions that are handled outside the exchanges. Increasingly, this market is being subjected to regulation. The extent and nature of the over-the-counter market varies throughout the world. In the United Kingdom, there is no over-the-counter market as such. In the Netherlands, transactions are illegal if they do not involve a member of the Amsterdam exchange or one of its provin-

Unorganized, or over-the-counter, markets

cial branches as an intermediary, except with the permission of the Ministry of Finance. On the Paris bourse, one post is provided for trading in unlisted issues. In Belgium, the stock exchange committee organizes, at least once a month, public sales of stocks that are not officially quoted. In Japan a second security section has been introduced into the major exchanges to provide more effective trading procedures for over-the-counter transactions.

In the United States, the over-the-counter market includes most federal, state, and municipal issues as well as a large variety of corporate stocks and bonds. The National Quotation Bureau, which compiles over-the-counter prices, has furnished quotations on approximately 26,000 over-the-counter stocks. In early 1971, a major development occurred with the introduction of current, computerized quotations on a number of active stocks.

Transactions in the over-the-counter market are executed through a large number of broker-dealers with a complex network of private wires and telephone lines. Their operations are subject to the rules of the National Association of Securities Dealers, Inc., a self-regulating body created in 1939. In 1964 the Congress extended to the larger over-the-counter companies the same requirements as to periodic reporting, proxy solicitation, and insider trading that are applied to dealers in listed stocks.

The over-the-counter market is a negotiated market, as distinguished from the auction markets for listed securities. An investor desiring to trade an over-the-counter security gives his order to a broker functioning as a retailer, who ordinarily shops among various firms to obtain the best possible price.

Because of the difficulty that institutions often experience in disposing of large blocks of listed securities on the exchanges, nonmember firms have set up over-the-counter markets in these issues—principally in those listed on the New York Stock Exchange. Although such transactions are conducted within the framework of the over-the-counter market, their prices are tied to those on the Exchange. Accordingly, this form of trading has been labelled the "third market." In 1970 the dollar volume of third-market transactions was 7.8 percent of total volume on the New York Stock Exchange. There is now also a "fourth market," consisting of direct transactions between investors without an intermediary. This market also had its origins in the need of the institutions to find ways of executing large transactions. Impetus to such direct dealings has been given by the development of computerized systems to bring together large traders.

THE STRUCTURE OF DEMAND FOR SECURITIES

The distribution of stock ownership

Interest in the ownership of securities has increased greatly in recent decades. Inflationary tendencies have directed attention to stocks as a means of offsetting rising prices. Stock exchanges have cultivated investors through public relations programs. Government regulation has strengthened public confidence in stock trading procedures. Many governments have given support to the capital markets in order to facilitate business financing.

In the United States, according to an estimate of the New York Stock Exchange, 30,850,000 individuals, or about 15 percent of the population, had shares of publicly held corporations during early 1970. This represented an increase of about 10,700,000 since 1965 and of more than 24,000,000 since 1952, when the Exchange made its first detailed census of shareowners. Many others own shares indirectly through institutions that are large holders of stock, such as investment companies and pension funds. It is difficult to obtain strictly comparable figures for other countries. It is estimated, however, that in Japan about 6 percent of the population owned stock in March 1969 and the same proportion in the United Kingdom in 1965. In Europe, where most of the other leading stock exchanges are located, the percentages vary; in recent years the percentage was around 8 in Finland, 4 in France, 6 in Germany, 15 in the Netherlands, and 2.7 in Sweden. A major problem of developing countries has been the absence of investors able and willing to buy shares. Many investors in these countries have preferred to place their funds in tangible assets such as land.

Institutions such as insurance companies, mutual funds, pension funds, foundations, and universities have grown very important in the security markets of the United States. Because of their financial responsibilities to others, these institutions have characteristically followed conservative investment policies stressing the purchase of fixed-income securities. The long-term trend toward inflation, along with mounting stock prices, has led the institutions to look more favourably upon common stocks. At the end of 1969, as a result, the major financial institutions held 25.4 percent of the market value of all the New York Stock Exchange listed stocks, compared with 12.7 percent in 1949. In 1969, institutions also accounted for 61.9 percent of all public dollar volume on the New York Stock Exchange compared with only 39.8 percent in 1960.

Whereas purchases of shares by institutions have been important in the United Kingdom, they have been of minor significance in Belgium, Germany, Norway, and Italy. In Japan on the other hand, the proportion of shares held by individuals in March 1969 was only 41 percent; much of the remainder was held by banks and insurance companies.

Among the most rapidly growing institutions are the mutual funds. Technically, these are known as open-end investment companies because the number of their shares outstanding constantly changes as new shares are sold to investors and old ones redeemed. Indicative of their growth, between 1941 and 1969 the mutual-fund industry in the United States realized $54,200,000,000 from the sale of its shares and expended $25,500,000,000 to redeem shares, resulting in a net money flow available for the purchase of securities of $28,700,000,000 over the 29-year period.

DYNAMICS OF THE SECURITIES MARKETS

Long-term and short-term movements of stock prices

Over a long-term period, the movements of stock prices and of general business indicators tend to parallel each other. In studies of business cycles, it has been found that stock prices tend to reach their cyclical peaks and troughs somewhat ahead of general business indicators, and these are therefore generally classified as "leading indicators."

The price of a stock reflects the present value of expected future earnings, and the profits of a firm are strongly influenced by the general level of economic activity. The tendency of stocks to lead business may be attributable to investors' preoccupation with the future. Over the years, the trend of stock prices has been upward; since World War II the upward cycles has tended to be of longer duration, while declines have been relatively shorter. Within the generally expansionary movement, changes in share values of specific companies have been mixed, some showing striking long-term gains while others have suffered losses.

Dramatic events sometimes have a special influence on the psychology of investors, driving stock prices down despite improving business conditions. For example, between the fall of 1940 and the spring of 1942, the period immediately prior to and after the entry of the United States into World War II, U.S. stock prices dropped swiftly despite a continued revival of economic activity. In other cases the reasons for a fall in stock prices are not easy to discover.

Stock prices also experience daily changes of substantial size. Technical market analysts attempt to predict these changes by studying patterns in stock prices. Many theorists, however, claim that in a highly competitive market, prices fluctuate primarily as a result of new information that is not likely to appear in any organized fashion; they maintain that successive price movements are independent of each other and take place in a random fashion.

As investors' expectations change over time, their attitudes toward different types of stock change. Buoyant investors lean toward growth stocks, the value of which is expected to increase rapidly; when uncertainty prevails, the preference is for more conservative issues with stable records of earnings. Within any given period, investors' choices of particular stocks vary with their judgments of the related companies.

BIBLIOGRAPHY. W.J. BAUMOL, *The Stock Market and Economic Efficiency* (1965), an interesting effort to apply economic theory to the modern securities market; J.I. BOGEN (ed.), *The Financial Handbook*, 4th ed. (1968), a comprehensive compilation of all aspects of finance with good sections on securities trading; H. BULLOCK, *The Story of Investment Companies* (1959), an account of the development of mutual funds; W.L. CARY, *Cases and Materials on Corporations*, 4th ed. (1969), an excellent work on the law of corporations; V.P. CAROSSO, *Investment Banking in America* (1970), a relatively thorough history of investment banking; J.F. CHILDS, *Long Term Financing* (1961), a standard work providing the corporate manager with the essentials necessary to make long-range financing decisions; J.B. COHEN and E.D. ZINBARG, *Investment Analysis and Portfolio Management* (1967), a comprehensive investment text covering some of the more recent advances in the management of investments; A.S. DEWING, *Financial Policy of Corporations*, 2 vol., 5th ed. (1953), a classic treatise on financial policy, particularly useful for historical and statistical purposes; W.J. and D.K. EITEMAN, *Leading World Stock Exchanges* (1964), a survey of the practices of some of the major stock exchanges in the world; I. FRIEND *et al.*, *Investment Banking and the New Issues Market* (1967), a review of all aspects of the investment banking business with particular attention to current problems; B. GRAHAM, D.L. DODD, and S. COTTLE, *Security Analysis*, 4th ed. (1962), a classic work that led to the development of the field of security analysis; J.W. HAZARD and M. CHRISTIE, *The Investment Business* (1964), a readable abridgement of the landmark U.S. Securities and Exchange Commission's Special Study of the Securities Markets; INVESTMENT BANKERS ASSOCIATION OF AMERICA, *Fundamentals of Municipal Bonds*, 7th ed. (1969), a basic introduction to the field of municipal bonds; R.W. JENNINGS and H. MARSH (eds.), *Securities Regulation*, 2nd ed. (1968), a leading textbook on the legal background of securities regulation; G.L. LEFFLER and L.C. FARWELL, *The Stock Market*, 3rd ed. (1963), a good reference book; L. LOSS, *Securities Regulation*, 2nd ed., 3 vol. (1961), 3 vol. suppl. (1969), a classic work on all aspects of the U.S. federal regulation of securities and securities markets; H.G. MANNE (ed.), *Economic Policy and the Regulation of Corporate Securities* (1969), a compilation of articles by economists and other specialists on various aspects of the securities markets; S.M. ROBBINS, *The Securities Markets: Operations and Issues* (1966), an analysis of the current problems affecting the securities market; H.C. SAUVAIN, *Investment Management*, 3rd ed. (1967), a standard investment text; I.O. SCOTT, *The Government Securities Market* (1965), a recent general review of this market; D.E. SPRAY (ed.), *The Principal Stock Exchanges of the World* (1964), a good general survey of world stock exchanges; R. SOBEL, *The Big Board* (1965), a readable history of the New York Stock Exchange; F. ZARB and G. KEREKES (eds.), *The Stock Market Handbook* (1970), a relatively complete reference manual on the securities industry.

(S.M.R.)

Security and Protection Systems

Security and protection systems guard persons and property against a broad range of hazards, including crime; fire and attendant risks, such as explosion; accidents; disasters; espionage; sabotage; subversion; civil disturbances; bombings (both actual and threatened); and, in some systems, attack by external enemies. Most security and protection systems emphasize certain hazards more than others. In a retail store, for example, the principal security concerns are shoplifting and employee dishonesty (*e.g.*, pilferage, embezzlement, and fraud). A typical set of categories to be protected includes the personal safety of people in the organization, such as employees, customers, or residents; tangible property, such as the plant, equipment, finished products, cash, and securities; and intangible property, such as highly classified national security information or "proprietary" information (*e.g.*, trade secrets) of private organizations. An important distinction between a security and protection system and public services such as police and fire departments is that the former employs means that emphasize passive and preventive measures.

Security systems are found in a variety of organizations, such as government agencies, industrial plants, commercial establishments, hotels, apartment buildings, hospitals, and schools and universities. Sufficiently large organizations may have their own proprietary security systems or may purchase security services by contract from specialized security organizations.

Role of security systems

History and development of security systems. The origins of security systems are obscure, but techniques for protecting the household, such as the use of locks and barred windows, are very ancient. As civilizations developed, the distinction between passive and active security was recognized, and responsibility for active security measures was vested in police and fire-fighting agencies and similar public services. The inability of community police and fire departments to provide all of the security desired by some individuals and organizations led to supplemental efforts by private groups.

By the middle of the 19th century, private organizations such as those of Philip Sorensen in Sweden and Allan Pinkerton in the United States had begun to build efficient large-scale security services. Pinkerton's organization offered intelligence, counterintelligence, internal security, investigative, and law enforcement services to private business and government. Until the advent of collective bargaining, strikebreaking was a prime concern. The Sorensen organization, in contrast, moved toward a loss control service for industry. It provided personnel trained to deal with losses from crime, fire, accident, flood, and waste, and it established the pattern for security services in the United Kingdom and western Europe.

World Wars I and II, particularly World War II, brought an increased awareness of security systems as a means of protection against military espionage, sabotage, and subversion; such programs in effect became part of a country's national security system. After World War II much of this apparatus was retained as a result of international tensions and defense-production programs and became part of an increasingly professionalized complex of security functions. The post-World War II period also brought an increase in the business espionage hazard and a corresponding emphasis on safeguarding proprietary information. During the 1950s and 1960s, increases in theft brought more emphasis on theft-control programs.

The development and diffusion of security systems and hardware in various parts of the world has been an uneven process. In relatively underdeveloped countries, or the underdeveloped parts of recently industrializing countries, security technology generally exists in rudimentary form, such as barred windows, locks, and elementary personnel security measures. In many such regions, however, facilities of large international corporations and sensitive government installations employ sophisticated equipment and techniques purchased from abroad or produced indigenously as part of a national defense effort. Though little public information is available concerning security systems in China, the Soviet Union, and other Communist countries, key defense, atomic, and space-exploration facilities are known to be protected by sophisticated security systems. These probably have rigorous personnel security criteria, with more limited consideration for due process, privacy, and freedoms of speech, press, and assembly than in countries subscribing to Western democratic values.

Security in the Communist countries

Security systems are carried to new areas by the proprietary security organizations of international corporations; international defense agreements whereby the signatory countries and companies engaged in production of military items agree to abide by specified security standards; the international growth of the larger contract security agencies, particularly those with headquarters in the United States, United Kingdom, and Sweden, as they acquire or organize foreign affiliates; organization in the less developed countries of indigenous contract security companies that borrow and import security systems through various channels; and international security conferences that attract professionals in the field from all over the world.

TYPES OF SECURITY SYSTEMS

Security systems can be classified by type of production enterprise—*e.g.*, industrial, retail (commercial), governmental, government contractor, hospital; by type of organization—contract security or proprietary; by type of security process—*e.g.*, personnel or physical security; by type of security function or emphasis—for example, plant protection (variously defined), theft control, fire protection, accident prevention, protection of sensitive (national security or business proprietary) information. Some of these categories overlap. Terminologies are not consistent.

Security for small businesses constitutes a special situation. Because small firms cannot afford specialized proprietary security staffs, measures must be incorporated into regular routines and staff training or be purchased from outside organizations. Theft, both internal and external, is a prime concern.

Resi-
dential
securityResidential security constitutes another special category. Sizable housing or apartment complexes, especially if under one management, can employ sophisticated security measures, including, for example, closed-circuit television monitoring of elevators and hallways, and trained security guards. Relatively simple equipment for houses or small apartment buildings, such as exterior lighting and alarms, is increasingly used. Some neighbourhoods of large cities cooperatively employ patrol services or organize resident volunteer patrols.

Physical security. Some of the most effective advances in security technologies during the past few decades have been in the realm of physical security—*i.e.*, protection by tangible means. Physical security has two main components: building architecture and appurtenances, and equipment and devices.

A building can be designed for security, for example, by such means as planning and limiting the number and location of entrances and by careful attention to exits, traffic patterns, and loading docks.

Equipment and devices may be classified in various categories depending on the criteria used. If the criterion is purpose, some of the principal categories are record containers, including safes and files; communications, such as two-way radios and scrambler telephones; identification, including badges and automatic access-control systems requiring the use of a code; investigation and detection (*e.g.*, lie detectors) and intrusion-detection devices, such as photoelectric cells and ultrasonic-wave-propagating equipment; observation and surveillance including listening and recording devices, cameras, closed-circuit television, and one-way mirrors; countermeasures for observation and surveillance, such as equipment designed to detect electronic surveillance devices; and fire protection.

A classification system based on process results in another set of categories. Examples include perimeter barriers (fences, walls) and locks to prevent or control access; and lighting systems to aid surveillance and to deter illegal entry.

For reasons of economy, security-equipment systems frequently include, or are operated in conjunction with, production-process-control systems—for example, shutdown controls and gauges to measure heat and pressure.

Research and development "breakthroughs" in security equipment are numerous. Some of the more noteworthy examples include sensor devices that report unauthorized removal of items; personal-identification and access-control systems that directly "read" unique personal characteristics such as voice quality and fingerprints; surveillance devices, such as closed-circuit television, that can scan premises at night (see illustration); and devices that permit surveillance at considerable distances, making entry to the premises unnecessary.

Security-equipment technology faces a number of problems, one of the more important being false alarms in intrusion-detection systems. Some of these devices are so sensitive that a piece of wastepaper blown into a protected area at night will trigger an alarm. In consequence, police in some jurisdictions have refused direct connections of alarm devices to the departments or have curtailed police responses. Another problem involves equipment inadequately tested, installed, or maintained. Finally, potential purchasers need careful, objective evaluation of the many devices on the market. (For more information on surveillance and intrusion detection systems, see POLICE TECHNOLOGY.)

Security guards at a closed-circuit television console.
By courtesy of the First National Bank of Chicago

Personnel-administration technology. An important component of security programs consists of measures designed to recruit and effectively use trustworthy personnel. "Personnel security" is a term frequently used to include measures designed to select only those people for whom there is a good prognosis for trustworthiness, on the premise that losses from employee untrustworthiness are more frequent and usually larger than losses from outside the system (*e.g.*, burglary, robbery, shoplifting, espionage) and that one of the best predictors of future behaviour is past behaviour.

Employee
screeningCommon synonyms are "screening" and (in Britain) "vetting." The most common technique is the background investigation, which involves obtaining all relevant available data about a person's past education, employment, and personal behaviour and making judgments concerning the individual's likely future loyalty and honesty. Thus, the dossier and computerized national data banks exemplify a response by a society in which great geographic mobility necessitates record keeping as a basis for judgments. Another technique is the polygraph, or lie detector, examination. Research has also been directed to the possible capabilities and limitations of pencil-and-paper psychological tests and stress interviews. In addition to selection techniques there are other measures designed to keep personnel trustworthy after they have been brought into the system—for example, employee indoctrination programs and vulnerability testing (discussed more fully below).

These methods are powerful tools for the attainment of security goals because screening out bad risks can do much to determine the difference between effective and ineffective security systems. Such methods, however, if used in clumsy or unsophisticated fashion, can result in a repressive social climate. Even if administered selectively and knowledgeably, they raise important questions in a democratic system, such as the possibility of unwarranted invasions of privacy, due process, and an inhibiting effect on the exercise of liberties of expression. Therefore in most countries such methods are controversial.

Systems and procedures constitute another area of the personnel-administration approach to security. It is possible to devise work methods and management controls in such a way that security is one of the values sought along with maximizing productivity and minimizing cost. Examples include the use of cash registers and other automated record-keeping systems; forms and reports periodically checked against physical inventories; and the principle of dual responsibility, whereby work is so subdivided that the work of one employee checks the accuracy of the work of another.

Because control systems are not self-administering, they must be periodically tested and policed. A typical procedure is the vulnerability test or "created-error" check, in which an error or breach, such as an erroneous invoice, is deliberately planted in the system to see if it is detected and reported. Undercover investigators, such as hired "shoppers" who check on the honesty of sales personnel, also play a role in monitoring the operation of control systems. Vulner-
ability
test

Guard force training, supervision, and motivation are other important aspects of the personnel-administration approach to security. Much of the effectiveness of an organization's security posture depends on the effectiveness of its guards and watchmen; yet such positions are not highly paid and involve special problems such as monotony, absenteeism, and temptation to ignore, or be in collusion with, wrongdoers. Thus a considerable premium is placed on the knowledgeability with which standard personnel-administration measures are adapted and applied to people with such responsibilities.

Use of operational personnel to attain security objectives is another important approach to security. Examples include engineers, production workers, and clerical staff applying government security regulations for the safeguarding of classified information, and sales people cooperating with security staff in the detection of shoplifters. The cooperation of operational personnel to attain security objectives along with production objectives demands an interplay between knowledgeable training and communication programs, supervision, employee motivation, and management example.

The personnel relations approach implicit in much of the above recognizes that the attitudes of rank and file employees and the social climate they create can either be conducive to security or its greatest enemy. Therefore, if security programs are to be successful they must be carried out in a context of considerable understanding and cooperation of virtually the entire work force. The security program is apt to be only as good as the overall pattern and climate of social relations and loyalties of workers and executives of all ranks.

TRENDS IN THE SECURITY INDUSTRY

The evolution of security systems in industrialized countries exhibits recent and probable future trends important for an understanding of the field. The following generalizations are based primarily on information concerning the United States, with some limited comparable information from the United Kingdom. Developments in other industrialized or industrializing countries tend to follow in somewhat similar patterns if allowances are made for variations in cultural and business habits and for the unevenness in the pattern of diffusion discussed above.

During the 1960s and 1970s, crime-related security systems have grown especially rapidly in most countries. Among contributing factors have been the increase in number of security-sensitive businesses; development of new security functions, such as protection of proprietary information; increasing computerization of sensitive information subject to unique vulnerabilities; improved reporting of crime and consequent wider awareness; the need for security of enlarged or new governmental programs (defense, atomic research, space exploration); need in many countries for security against violent demonstrations, bombings, and hijackings; and simply the growing availability of security equipment and knowledge.

Security systems are becoming increasingly automated, particularly with respect to sensing and communicating hazards and vulnerabilities and, to a lesser but still considerable extent, with respect to response and action. This situation is true in both crime-related applications, such as intrusion-detection devices, and fire-protection alarm and response (extinguishing) systems. Advances in miniaturization and electronics are reflected in security equipment that is smaller, more reliable, and more easily installed and maintained.

The systems approach

Professional security managers increasingly tend to take a "systems approach," in which building architecture, equipment, and personnel systems are consciously and explicitly related in order to maximize security and to minimize costs.

Although many security systems are maintained in private or semipublic institutions, there is some tendency by security administrators to try to achieve better relationships between nongovernmental security managements and governmental police and other agencies in several important ways. Both sets of managers are becoming increasingly aware that well-conceived security programs have important preventive and deterrent effects in law enforcement and crime prevention, an assumption long accepted in the fire-protection and safety fields. This perception results in a tendency, observable in the developed countries, for government to set crime-related security standards that nongovernment enterprises must meet as a condition for action by government, such as a business license, police response to alarms, or government insurance. Standards set by insurance companies with premium discounts as the incentive have somewhat the same effect. There is also an observable trend toward government regulation of nongovernmental security managements. A related phenomenon is reflected in efforts at self-regulation, with contract security organizations in the United Kingdom a prime example.

Despite the conscious search for better articulation of governmental and nongovernmental security programs, many nongovernmental enterprises still operate essentially private criminal justice systems in which offenders, especially those charged with the less dramatic forms of theft, such as pilferage, shoplifting, and embezzlement, are apprehended and adjudicated by confession and discharge without report to the public authorities. In such instances the criterion for disposition is usually the interest of the organization as perceived by the organization rather than the welfare of the individual or the community.

BIBLIOGRAPHY. Introductory and general treatments include JOHN R. DAVIS, *Industrial Plant Protection* (1957); PETER HAMILTON, *Espionage and Subversion in an Industrial Society* (1967); RICHARD J. HEALY, *Design for Security* (1968); the NATIONAL INDUSTRIAL CONFERENCE BOARD, *Industrial Security*, vol. 1, *Combating Subversion and Sabotage* (1952); RAYMOND M. MOMBOISSE, *Industrial Security for Strikes, Riots and Disasters* (1968); ERIC OLIVER and JOHN WILSON, *Practical Security in Commerce and Industry* (1968); RICHARD S. POST and ARTHUR A. KINGSBURY, *Security Administration* (1970). The first and only definitive empirical study of the security "industry" as a whole was published in 1971 by the Rand Corporation for the United States Department of Justice: vol. 1, *Private Police in the United States: Findings and Recommendations*, vol. 2, *The Private Police Industry: Its Nature and Extent*, vol. 3, *Current Regulation of Private Police: Regulatory Agency Experience and Views*, vol. 4, *The Law and Private Police*, and vol. 5, *Special-Purpose Public Police*. Treatments oriented to business, industrial, and institutional situations, with particular reference to theft in its various forms, include S.J. CURTIS, *Modern Retail Security* (1960); the NATIONAL INDUSTRIAL CONFERENCE BOARD, *Industrial Security*, vol. 3, *Theft Control Procedures* (1954); NORMAN JASPAN and HILLEL BLACK, *The Thief in the White Collar* (1960); LESTER A. PRATT, *Embezzlement Controls for Business Enterprises* (1956). The principal general works on personnel security are RALPH S. BROWN, JR., *Loyalty and Security* (1958); HAROLD W. CHASE, *Security and Liberty: The Problem of Native Communists, 1947–1955* (1955); LEON WEAVER, "Character Assessment in Personnel Selection," in J.J. DONOVAN (ed.), *Recruitment and Selection in the Public Service* (1968); LEON WEAVER (ed.), *Industrial Personnel Security: Cases and Materials* (1964). Physical security systems and procedures are discussed in RICHARD B. COLE, *The Application of Security Systems and Hardware* (1970); S.A. YEVSKY (ed.), *Law Enforcement Science and Technology* (1967); Army Field Manual FM 19–30, *Physical Seeurity* (1965); DEFENSE MOBILIZATION OFFICE (U.S.), *Standards for Physical Security of Industrial and Governmental Facilities* (1958). Guard force administration is treated in the NATIONAL INDUSTRIAL CONFERENCE BOARD, *Industrial Security*, vol. 2, *Plant Guard Handbook* (1953); JOHN DONALD PEEL, *Fundamentals of Training for Security Officers* (1970); E.A. SCHURMAN, *Plant Protection* (1942). See also BOB CURTIS, *Security Control: External Theft* (1971); RICHARD J. HEALY and TIMOTHY WALSH, *Industrial Security Management: A Cost Effective Approach* (1971); and CHARLES F. HEMPHILL, *Security for Business and Industry* (1971). The principal periodicals in the field are *Industrial Security*, the *Security Gazette*, and *Security World*. Other important sources of current information are the *Security Systems Digest*, a newsletter; and the BUREAU OF NATIONAL AFFAIRS, *Government Security and Loyalty: A Manual of Laws, Regulations, and Procedures*, 2 vol. (1955–   ), a reference service.

(L.H.W.)

Sedative–Hypnotic Drugs

Sedative–hypnotic drugs act to reduce tension or to induce sleep, depending upon the dosage used. They belong to a wide spectrum of drugs that depress the central nervous system. Sedative–hypnotic drugs may exert a sedative (quieting or calming) effect in small doses and a hypnotic (sleep-inducing) effect in large doses. When sedative–hypnotic drugs are used in full dosage at the end of the day to produce sleep, the effect is hypnotic; when they are used in moderate dosage throughout the day to overcome anxiety or nervousness, the effect is sedative (an effect that also may enable a patient to sleep better). The barbiturates and the minor tranquillizers are the most widely used sedative–hypnotic drugs; other drugs with sedative–hypnotic effects include chloral hydrate, paraldehyde, and bromide compounds.

General properties. The degree to which sedative–hypnotic drugs relieve anxiety, induce sleep, or elicit other depressive effects (e.g., anticonvulsive action) varies from one drug to another, as do the effective dose, the distribution in the body, the route of metabolic degradation, and the elimination rate. In addition, the chemical nature of a drug does not necessarily govern its pharmacological effects. Sedative–hypnotic drugs have properties in common with other depressive drugs; e.g., narcotic analgesics, such as morphine, and major tranquillizers, such as chlorpromazine, both have calming effects, as do moderate doses of sedative–hypnotic drugs; and anesthetics produce unconsciousness, as do sedative–hypnotic drugs in excessively high doses. Detailed descriptions of these drugs are found in NARCOTIC; TRANQUILLIZER; and ANESTHETIC.

Historical background. For centuries opium and alcohol were the only drugs available with sedative-hypnotic effects. Chloral hydrate, a chlorinated derivative of ethyl alcohol, was introduced in 1869 as the first synthetic sedative–hypnotic drug, and its widespread usage within a few years stimulated further development of drug preparations with similar action. Before 1900, paraldehyde, amylene hydrate, and sulfonmethane had been introduced, and, in 1903, barbital was synthesized. Phenobarbital became available in 1912 and was followed, during the next 20 years, by a long series of other barbiturates. In the mid-1950s new types of sedative-hypnotic drugs, different in chemical structure from the barbiturates, were synthesized. These anti-anxiety drugs, called minor tranquillizers (e.g., meprobamate, chlordiazepoxide), began to replace many of the drugs then used to treat anxiety. By the 1970s, 50 to 100 different drugs with sedative–hypnotic effects had become available throughout the world.

The biological disposition of sedative–hypnotic drugs. *Metabolism and excretion.* Sedative–hypnotic drugs are readily absorbed from the intestinal tract into the bloodstream. With the exception of several barbiturates and a group of minor tranquillizers (the benzodiazepines) the drugs become evenly distributed throughout the body, so that their concentration in the blood equals that in other body tissues and organs. Benzodiazepines, on the other hand, are bound to specific tissues; e.g., kidney, liver, and brain. After absorption from the intestinal tract, sedative–hypnotic drugs may undergo chemical transformations—mainly in the liver—into metabolic products called metabolites. Either the unchanged drugs or their metabolites are excreted in the urine.

Half-life as a measure of elimination rate. With the exception of ethyl alcohol, for any quantity of a drug a constant percentage is eliminated from the body over a given time interval. The rate of elimination is measured in terms of the half-life of a drug, defined as the amount of time required to eliminate half of it from the body. Values for the half-life vary considerably among the sedative-hypnotic drugs. Phenobarbital and barbital, for example, have a half-life of about 48 hours and 24 hours, respectively, and are commonly known as long-acting barbiturates. Amobarbital and butabarbital, each with a half-life of about 12 hours, are known as medium- to short-acting barbiturates, as is pentobarbital (half-life five to six hours).

Two minor tranquillizers, meprobamate and tybamate, as well as chloral hydrate and glutethimide, each have a half-life of from four to eight hours. Hexobarbital is eliminated at an even faster rate and is called a barbiturate of ultra-short action. The half-life of the benzodiazepine tranquillizers, on the other hand, is relatively long; e.g., several days for diazepam.

The duration of action of a barbiturate is associated with its structure insofar as structural changes—for example, the substitution of sulfur for oxygen at a specific position on the molecule—influence lipid (fat) solubility; i.e., an increase in lipid solubility is associated with a decrease in the duration of action, with increases in the onset of activity and metabolic degradation and, sometimes, with an increase in hypnotic potency.

Effects on the nervous system. Although the actions of sedative–hypnotic drugs on isolated nerve cells have been studied, the actual mechanism of action has not yet been established with certainty. Sedative–hypnotic drugs depress metabolic reactions that are important for normal function of nerve cells. Other substances, however, induce the same metabolic effects. Sedative–hypnotic drugs also delay the transmission of nerve impulses through long sequences of nerve cells.

Sedative–hypnotic drugs probably induce sleep by acting on brain centres that regulate normal sleep; in this sense, sleep is defined as a state of unconsciousness that, in contrast to coma or anesthesia, can be interrupted and reversed easily and rapidly to normal wakefulness. Proper doses of these drugs facilitate the onset and maintenance of normal sleep; the wavelike pattern in the electric potential from the surface of the brain reveals, however, a reduced amount of lighter sleep, which is characterized by frequent body shifts and also by rapid eye movements (hence, the name REM sleep). The significance of such a change is not yet clear; this drug-induced sleep cannot be distinguished from regular sleep in any other way than by the observation of brain-wave patterns. After the effect of the drugs has passed, later brain-wave patterns show that REM sleep continues for a longer period than normal. The hypnotic effect of a sedative–hypnotic drug is supported by the sleep rhythm; i.e., a dose that induces sleep late in the evening may not do so in the morning.

The sedative-hypnotic drugs may cause euphoria—an artificially induced feeling of intense well-being—in 3 to 10 percent of the persons who take them; development of a euphoric state varies with the drug, the dosage, and the patient. The barbiturates, especially pentobarbital, are most likely to cause euphoria, but nonbarbiturates, such as chloral hydrate, also may induce it. Euphoria may lead to drug addiction in susceptible individuals. Most persons, however, feel only drowsiness after taking a prescribed dose of a sedative–hypnotic drug.

Depressant effects. Sedative–hypnotic drugs exert various depressant effects on the body, depending on the dosage. A dose in excess of that needed as a sedative or a hypnotic, for example, causes an increase in reaction time and an impairment of muscular coordination similar to that observed after excessive consumption of alcohol. Although certain sedative–hypnotic drugs inhibit convulsions, they usually are effective only in the large doses that produce a state of unconsciousness; a few, especially phenobarbital, are effective in small doses.

The level of consciousness may be depressed by sedative–hypnotic drugs. Doses several times greater than those necessary to induce normal sleep cause a drowsiness that is difficult to overcome; higher dosage induces a state of anesthesia, which may end with a complete coma (state of deep unconsciousness). Loss of consciousness is caused by inhibition of the transmission of nerve impulses in a region of the midbrain called the ascending reticular formation, which receives sensory impulses and transforms them into general impulses that are relayed throughout the anterior brain region, where voluntary movements are controlled and mental actions coordinated. It has not yet been established with certainty, however, that the induction of normal sleep results in part from a mild inhibition of the function of the ascending reticular formation. Deep anesthesia results from the loss of function of a number of cerebral centres.

A very large dose of a sedative–hypnotic drug may cause the respiratory centre in the brain to cease functioning, and death may occur within a few hours. In some cases, a coma may be induced without affecting respiration, and the patient may remain unconscious for several days before dying—usually either from pneumonia or impairment of a brain centre that controls the cardiovascular system.

Uses and abuses of sedative–hypnotic drugs. *Sleeplessness and anxiety.* Sedative–hypnotic drugs, including the minor tranquillizers, are used extensively. These drugs compete with antibiotics in numbers of prescriptions per year. The principal medical indications for prescribing such drugs are sleeplessness and anxiety; they usually are given to surgical patients on the night preceding surgery. Normal individuals also may have periods of sleeplessness stemming from a variety of causes—unfamiliar surroundings, sustained mental activity, excitement—and a suitable sedative–hypnotic drug is useful in such circumstances if sleep cannot be induced by other means. During acute illnesses sedative–hypnotic drugs are administered to give patients a calm sleep, but such drugs cannot eliminate pain. Insomnia, restlessness, and excitation in old people may be alleviated by periodic use of certain sedative–hypnotic drugs, chosen according to the types of sleeplessness; inability to fall asleep calls for a short-acting, rapidly eliminated barbiturate such as pentobarbital, but wakefulness during the night requires a longer acting drug.

Sedative–hypnotic drugs also are commonly prescribed as a supporting, or the sole, treatment for mild anxiety neuroses. They are helpful in overcoming sleeplessness caused by anxiety about real or imaginary worries, but their effect is symptomatic only; *i.e.*, they can relieve disturbing mental manifestations but have no lasting effect on eliminating the causes of severe neuroses. To avoid misuse or addiction, a person should not use these drugs continuously over long periods of time and should shun self-medication.

Because of their anticonvulsive effect, some sedative–hypnotic drugs are administered to treat convulsions that may result from drug overdose or from epilepsy, a disease of the nervous system. Phenobarbital was widely used in the treatment of epilepsy until it was replaced by other drugs with fewer side effects. Some short-acting sedative–hypnotic drugs, especially the thiobarbiturates, are used before surgery, either alone or in combination with other anesthetics, to produce anesthesia.

Sedative–hypnotic drugs cannot cure true psychotic states such as schizophrenia and delusions. In large doses, however, they are effective in treating the withdrawal symptoms and delirium tremens typical of alcoholism and in treating the psychotic state provoked by hallucinogens such as LSD (lysergic acid diethylamide).

In recommended doses, sedative–hypnotic drugs produce few side effects. Signs of overdosage, such as lack of muscular coordination, may occur in a few hypersensitive individuals who take a normal dose. Other individuals, especially elderly ones, may become excited instead of calmed after taking a normal dose. Some of these drugs, especially the long-acting ones, may cause drowsiness or slight headache (barbiturate hangover) the morning following their use. Allergic reactions, such as skin rashes, sometimes occur; persons who develop an allergy for one type of drug, however, usually are unaffected by a different type.

Intoxication and addiction. A chronic intoxication caused by sedative–hypnotic drugs, especially the barbiturates, is relatively common among persons who continue to take a drug after the problem for which it was prescribed no longer exists. When such individuals develop a requirement for the medication and continue to use it, usually in increasing doses, they become addicts. Irrespective of the specific sedative–hypnotic drug, symptoms of chronic intake of large doses are similar. A tolerance develops; *i.e.*, increasingly large doses, two or three times the normal amount, become necessary to obtain a desired effect. If use of the drug then is stopped abruptly, a withdrawal syndrome, consisting of increased sensitivi-

ty of the central nervous system, develops. Changes occur in brain-wave patterns, which become similar to those of epileptics, and, in many instances, seizures occur. A characteristic delirium tremens may develop during chronic barbiturate intoxication, which is characterized by drowsiness accompanied, paradoxically, by sleeplessness. In some cases the drowsiness may change to a general restlessness.

In chronic intoxication from a sedative–hypnotic drug, psychotic states accompanied by displays of aggression, delusions, and hallucinations may occur. Damage to the peripheral organs, such as the liver and the kidneys, is not a sign, but loss of appetite and resultant loss of body weight are common. The treatment for chronic drug intoxication consists of a stepwise discontinuation of the drug. Suitable psychotherapy may be necessary to avoid relapses into drug use after detoxification.

Addiction to sedative–hypnotic drugs may occur among individuals who seek a euphoric effect from the drugs similar to that resulting from excessive use of alcohol; alcoholics sometimes use sedative–hypnotic drugs alone or in combination with alcohol. Addiction to drugs such as barbiturates rarely occurs from use of the sedative–hypnotic drugs alone; more often, combinations of barbiturates with amphetamine or a similar stimulant drug are the cause. The euphoric effects of stimulant and barbiturate combine, while the drowsiness caused by the barbiturate is antagonized by the stimulant. Such drug combinations are dangerous and may be fatal (see STIMULANT).

Suicide. Widespread use, comparatively easy access, and painless effects of sedative–hypnotic drugs have made them common methods for suicide in many countries. In Great Britain, for example, several thousand attempted suicides with these drugs are reported each year; and, in a Danish treatment centre serving about 1,500,000 inhabitants, as many as 2,000 cases of sedative–hypnotic poisoning are treated each year. The patients, generally in an unconscious state, are treated to remove the drug from the body, to counteract the depressive effects of the drug, and to prevent a long-lasting coma. Although the unabsorbed drugs once were removed directly from the stomachs of victims, newer and more effective ways have been developed, including the use of artificial kidneys and drugs that increase the rate of urine production. It is possible to increase the elimination rate of a drug fourfold with such procedures (see also DRUG AND DRUG ACTION).

Types of sedative–hypnotic drugs. *Barbiturates.* Barbiturates, used extensively for their hypnotic action, are derivatives of barbituric acid, which is formed from malonic acid and urea. Barbituric acid belongs to a class of organic compounds called diureides and has neither sedative nor hypnotic properties. Barbiturates with sedative–hypnotic action are formed by the substitution of various chemical groups on the barbituric acid molecule. These drugs may be arranged according to their duration of effect. Secobarbital acts rapidly to induce sleep, but its action is not prolonged; it is often administered before surgery when relatively brief sedation is desirable. Pentobarbital acts within about 30 minutes of administration to induce sleep and maintains a state of sleep overnight. Phenobarbital, the slowest acting widely used barbiturate, has the most prolonged effect and is especially valuable as a long-lasting sedative to calm persons in a nervous, jittery state.

Not only do the barbiturates exert sedative and hypnotic effects, but in excessively high dosage all of them are anesthetic and anticonvulsive. In order to produce sedation with barbiturates, a hypnotic dose normally is divided into three or four portions and administered at intervals throughout the day—usually in tablet or capsule form. Barbiturates that exert a sedative–hypnotic effect are sometimes called the true barbiturates to distinguish them from thiobarbiturates (*e.g.*, thiopental), which are used almost exclusively as anesthetics.

Minor tranquillizers. Meprobamate, tybamate, and the benzodiazepines (*e.g.*, chlordiazepoxide, diazepam, and nitrazepam) all are included among minor tranquil-

Treatment for chronic drug intoxication

lizers. Their effects are similar, but they vary widely both in chemical structure and in dosage. For instance, the amount of a benzodiazepine required to provide an active dose is 50 to 100 times less than that of either meprobamate or tybamate.

Although the effects of the minor tranquillizers resemble those of other sedative–hypnotic drugs, their mechanism of action may differ. When given to normal persons, minor tranquillizers induce a feeling of indifference to such outer disturbing influences as noise, but any actual superiority of minor tranquillizers in relieving anxiety is difficult to demonstrate. Minor tranquillizers are of some help in inducing normal sleep if sleeplessness is caused by anxiety. The anxiety-relieving effects of the minor tranquillizers generally are more pronounced than are the hypnotic ones; nitrazepam, however, does produce a definite hypnotic effect. Although the minor tranquillizers sometimes induce euphoria, they probably are less likely to do so than are some of the other sedative–hypnotic drugs.

Tranquillizers in anxiety relief

The minor tranquillizers affect muscles and certain reflexes; some are effective in stopping convulsions and may be the preferred drugs in treating convulsions in epileptics. In large doses, minor tranquillizers impair muscle coordination, produce drowsiness, and lower comprehension. In toxic doses, they have an anesthetic effect, which may result in death from acute respiratory failure or from cardiovascular collapse. The minor tranquillizers probably are less dangerous, however, than most sedative–hypnotic drugs, because much higher doses are required to cause death. Further discussion of these substances may be found under TRANQUILLIZER.

Other drugs with sedative–hypnotic effects. Chloral hydrate, derived from ethyl alcohol, once was widely used. But because it is a gastrointestinal irritant, has a disagreeable taste, and is administered in liquid form (inconvenient to take throughout the day), chloral hydrate is no longer extensively used as a sedative. It is an effective hypnotic drug, however, and induces long-lasting and satisfactory sleep rapidly, without causing the hangover effects commonly associated with barbiturates. Other alcohol derivatives with sedative–hypnotic action include amylene hydrate and ethchlorvynol; ethyl alcohol (ethanol) has limited hypnotic action.

Paraldehyde, a liquid polymer of acetaldehyde, is very powerful and quick-acting (ten to 15 minutes). Generally considered an innocuous drug, paraldehyde is used in a wide range of doses. It is sometimes used to treat non-epileptic convulsant states, and it often induces sleep in persons suffering pain.

For many years, bromides (*e.g.*, potassium, sodium, and ammonium bromide) were used as sedative–hypnotic drugs. When bromides are ingested, some substitution of chloride with bromide occurs in body fluids. The effects of a bromide depend not on the absolute dose of bromide but on the ratio between chloride and bromide. A calming action occurs with a ratio of one part bromide to four parts chloride. As the bromide content increases, drowsiness occurs; if the bromide concentration exceeds that of chloride, death occurs. Bromides have been replaced by newer and more effective sedative–hypnotic drugs with fewer side effects. Addiction to bromides, called bromism, once was relatively common.

A few drugs with sedative–hypnotic effects, called diphenylmethane derivatives, are related to antihistamines —substances used to treat allergic reactions and cold symptoms. The best known are hydroxyzine, azacyclonol, and an antihistamine called diphenhydramine. The anxiety-relieving effects of these drugs are less pronounced than are those of other sedative–hypnotic drugs. Diphenylmethane derivatives, therefore, often are used for reasons other than inducing sleep; in such cases, the induction of sleep may be an undesirable side effect. These drugs differ from others in the sedative–hypnotic group in that they affect the autonomic nervous system, which controls involuntary body functions. When administered in controlled doses, they prevent responses of certain body structures to nerve stimulation. In addition, large doses of the diphenylmethane derivatives do not in-

duce anesthesia and coma, but instead cause convulsions (see HISTAMINE AND ANTIHISTAMINES).

BIBLIOGRAPHY. This subject is covered mainly in specialized journals. The best general orientation may be obtained by studying the appropriate chapters in major textbooks. Suggested references are: T.A. BAN, *Psychopharmacology* (1969), with extensive bibliography; F.M. BERGER and J. POTTERFIELD, "The Effect of Anti-anxiety Tranquilizers on the Behavior of Normal Persons," in W.O. EVANS and N.S. KLINE (eds.) *The Psychopharmacology of the Normal Human*, pp. 38–113 (1969); C. CLEMMESEN, "Treatment of Acute Barbituric Acid Poisoning," *Int. Anesth. Clin.*, 4:295–307 (1966); H.F. FRASER, "Tolerance to and Physical Dependence on Opiates, Barbiturates, and Alcohol," *Ann. Rev. Med.*, 8:427–446 (1957); L. LASAGNA, "The Newer Hypnotics," *Med. Clin. N. Amer.*, 41: 359–368 (1957); I. OSWALD, "Drugs and Sleep," *Pharmacol. Rev.*, 20:273–303 (1968); S.K. SHARPLESS, "Hypnotics and Sedatives," in L.S. GOODMAN and A. GILMAN (eds.), *The Pharmacological Basis of Therapeutics*, 4th ed. (1970); M. SHEPHERD, M. LADER, and R. RODNIGHT, *Clinical Psychopharmacology* (1968).

(E.S.A.J.)

Sedimentary Facies

The term facies, as applied to sedimentary rocks (*q.v.*), derives from the work of a French-speaking Swiss geologist, Amanz Gressly, in the 1830s. Gressly studied the Mesozoic strata in the Jura Mountains and was impressed by the changes in the character of the strata and their contained fossils, as individual groups of beds were traced along stream valleys and mountain ridges. Previous workers had emphasized the differences among the kinds of sediments and fossils that appear in vertical succession at right angles to stratification planes. Vertical changes are responses to shifts in the environments at a particular site through spans of time or to variations in the character of material brought to the site and deposited. An abundant vocabulary for designation and description of vertical successions of strata already existed; these are the groups, formations, and members of present usage, which are the units shown on most geologic maps and cross sections. Gressly, however, had no terminology he could apply to the lateral changes observed within sequences of beds of the same age. For this purpose he used the word facies, meaning the "face" or aspect of the beds, which places stress on the differences in aspect encountered in beds of the same age.

Historical background

Gressly's term was readily applied by European geologists of the 19th century, although both usage and concept evolved in directions away from the original connotation of different but concurrent sedimentary environments. A distinction was drawn, for example, between similar (isopic) facies that recur with the passage of time in an area and differing (heteropic) facies that replace one another laterally in deposits of the same age. There arose a facies law, which essentially states that the facies that are heteropic in an area are inevitably isopic or vertically successive in the same area. This condition is true because sedimentation responds to shifting patterns of coexisting specific environments and sediment sources.

A further outgrowth of the facies concept was the designation of sequences of strata that could be identified as responses to particular environments. These include shallow-water facies, reef facies, and lagoonal facies, among others. Such usage prevails today, and application of the term has been extended to the inferred tectonic (deformational) conditions at the time of accumulation (orogenic [mountain formation] facies, geosynclinal [downward flexure of the earth's crust] facies, etc.), geographic position (boreal facies, tropical facies, etc.), or relation to mineral products (ore facies, oil-reservoir facies, etc.), among many others. All such terms are valid if they convey a sense of change or of contrast among differing conditions of sedimentary deposition.

Whereas application of the facies concept by European workers has stressed interpretation, especially environmental interpretation, of changes in the character of sedimentary rocks from place to place or at successive points in geologic time, the evolution of facies studies has followed a somewhat different course in North America. Two major factors contribute to the difference in ap-

Classical versus operational concepts

proach: vast areas of the interior of North America, in contrast to the areas of classical study in western Europe, are characterized by successions of layered sedimentary rocks that have suffered but little disturbance or disruption since their deposition; and these strata have been investigated by hundreds of thousands of boreholes drilled in search for minerals, mineral fuels, and water. Subsurface exploration only recently has risen to a comparable scale on other continents; in North America, it has produced an enormous array of data documenting rock type, rock geometry, and fossil content.

In response to these data, North Americans have emphasized facies studies that are primarily descriptive integrations in the form of maps and cross sections. These may assemble observations made at thousands of data points. Environmental interpretations are then derived by comparison and analogy of the synthetic integrative product with modern counterparts documented by ecologic, oceanographic, and related studies of present-day sedimentary environments. Such investigations have made it possible to decipher the evolving paleogeography and thus the geologic history of major parts of North America in great detail. The petroleum industry has made elaborate studies of the sedimentary facies associated with known oil and gas accumulations; the products of these studies are then applied to the exploration for and recognition of analogous facies patterns that are the clues to previously undiscovered oil and gas reserves. Similar methods have long been used as guides to exploration for coal, gypsum, salt, potash, phosphate, and other minerals with a well-defined relationship to sedimentary facies. More recently the approach has been extended to the search for lead, zinc, copper, uranium, and even gold.

In summary, there are at least two current concepts of sedimentary facies: classical and operational. In the classical concept, a sedimentary facies is a summation of the aspects of a sedimentary deposit, observed at a given place, that permits identification of the environment of deposition. Application of the classical concept is a highly developed art that invokes a simultaneous and commonly subjective environmental interpretation of mineralogical, textural, structural, and paleontologic criteria. The methodology of the operational concept, so called because it relies on a number of operations or procedures (some of them commonly employing electronic data processing), passes through stages of data acquisition, storage, retrieval, computation of quantitative expressions of aspect, and display of the variations of several aspects at a large number of observation points in the form of facies maps before environmental and other interpretations are made. The essentials of this operational methodology are described in later paragraphs; the following discussion of some of the principles of facies analysis derives very largely from the findings of the operational concept, combined with the findings of students of present-day depositional environments. See also SEDIMENTARY ROCKS; MOUNTAIN BUILDING PROCESSES; STRATIGRAPHIC BOUNDARIES; PETROLEUM; and EARTH, GEOLOGICAL HISTORY OF for some examples of the application of the facies concept.

CONTROLLING FACTORS AND KINDS OF FACIES

Sedimentary environments

The controls that govern the aspects of sedimentary accumulations, their geometric form and dimensions, composition, the properties that make texture or fabric, as well as the properties that make them sources or reservoirs for fossil fuels or other economic products, comprise a complex of factors. The most significant of these are the environment of deposition and the tectonic behaviour of the depositional site, the source of the sediment and the transport medium that carries it, and, finally, the postdepositional changes that affect the accumulation. The conditions under which sediment is deposited are controlled by the complex interaction of material, energy, and boundary-condition factors that combine to exert the most important influence on sedimentary facies. The materials include the sediment made available at the depositional site by transport of pre-existing rock particles or by precipitation from solution, plus the depositional medium in

which the accumulation of sediment takes place. The latter include air, waters of a great range of chemical (and nutritional) compositions, or, much more rarely, ice. Sedimentary aspect responds strongly to the kinetic energy released in the environment by currents and water waves and to the radiant energy of the sun, which, in the form of light and heat, controls the distribution of sediment-contributing organisms. Among boundary conditions, the most significant are those that define the geometrical features of the environment, such as depth of water, shape and extent of a delta, for example, or configuration of the depositional surface.

Although continental environments (lakes, streams, deserts, etc.) are identified with many sedimentary facies, by far the greater volume of ancient sediments observed in the geologic record was deposited in marine environments or in transitional environments at and near the border of a sea. Among the latter are included beaches and barrier bars, lagoons, coastal marshes and swamps, intertidal mud flats, and the complex of subenvironments that constitute delta systems. Shallow subtidal marine facies commonly exhibiting evidences of current and wave action, an oxygenated water mass, and sunlight penetration to the bottom dominate, in combination with transitional facies, the ancient sedimentary rocks that cover great areas of continental interiors and continental shelves. A spectrum of deepwater facies, extending from below the depth of penetration of sunlight and wave energy to abyssal depths of thousands of metres, is encountered on present-day continental slopes and rises and on the ocean floors. The same facies are evident in ancient oceanic and ocean-border sediments uplifted in mountain ranges at continental margins; similar facies are much less common in the records of continental interiors where only the central areas of deeply subsiding, "sediment-starved" basins show evidence of deepwater environments.

Tectonics

Erosion acts to reduce the elevation of high-standing land; sedimentation acts to fill depressions; the common equilibrium surface that both of these processes tend to approach is baselevel, which for present purposes is sea level. Were it not for continued uplift (positive tectonism), high areas would be reduced to baselevel; similarly, in the absence of subsidence (negative tectonism), shallow sedimentary basins on continents and continental margins would fill with thin accumulations of sediment. It is commonplace, however, to observe thick successions of sediment (hundreds of metres to a thousand metres and more thick) all representing transitional or shallow-water facies. Such could not be the case unless tectonic subsidence at the depositional site proceeded at approximately the same rate as sediment accumulation. Indeed, tectonics controls not only the thicknesses of stratigraphic successions but also grossly affects the distribution of environmental facies and their petrology.

Consider a marine basin such as the Gulf of Mexico. If there were no further subsidence of the Gulf, or if subsidence were markedly slower in rate than sedimentation, the deltas and intervening coastal deposits of the Mississippi, Colorado, Rio Grande, and other rivers that bring sediment from the continental interior would extend farther and farther into the Gulf, causing transitional environments to replace shallow-marine environments and continental environments to occupy the former positions of deltas, lagoons, coastal swamps, and beaches. These are the conditions of marine regression; the reverse, caused by an excess of the rate of subsidence over sedimentation, is marine transgression. In each case the subparallel belts of distinct transitional and shallow-marine environments may be gradually shifted distances of kilometres or even tens or hundreds of kilometres seaward or landward. Thus, the sedimentary facies resulting from deposition in these environments, although occupying a narrow zone (a beach, for instance) during an instant of time, may be spread as relatively thin blankets over very large areas. It is clear, then, that the interplay of rates of sediment accumulation and tectonic subsidence determines the length of time that a given environment prevails at a site of deposition, and, as a corollary, the same interrelationship deter-

Transgression and regression of the sea

mines the thickness and other geometric properties of the deposit representing a particular facies. Where equilibrium exists between sediment supply and subsidence, stillstand of environments occurs, and the accumulation of thicknesses of sediments of the same facies that are much greater than normal results.

Many sedimentary particles are chemically or physically unstable in the environments in which they are deposited, and tectonism at the depositional site becomes a factor in the mineralogic or textural character of the eventual deposit. Fine particles of clay or silt, for example, cannot remain long in the presence of the violent turbulent energy of a beach, nor can a feldspar grain long withstand the chemical activity induced in the same environment by alternate exposure to atmosphere and seawater. If the rate of subsidence is sufficiently high, the fine clays and chemically unstable feldspars can be buried rapidly, protected from the physical and chemical kinetics of the beach, and preserved in the rock record as grains in an impure, poorly sorted sandstone. Conversely, if subsidence is slow the beach will be reworked many times over, the clays and feldspar grains removed, and the result will be well-sorted sandstone made up almost entirely of quartz grains.

Terrigenous facies. It is convenient to separate the discussion of terrigenous facies, those sedimentary facies that result from the accumulation of particles eroded from older rocks and transported to the depositional site, from biogenic facies that represent accumulations of whole or fragmented shells and other hard parts of organisms and from chemical facies that represent inorganic precipitation of material from solution. Terrigenous sediments, often called clastic because they are formed from broken fragments of pre-existing rock, appear in many facies controlled by a number of factors other than depositional environment and tectonics.

Source and transport. The sedimentary grains carried to a depositional site reflect the mineralogy of the source area; its topographic relief and climate; and the character of the transporting rivers (or other media), their gradients and lengths, and the chemistry of their waters. A source area may expose a great variety of mineral grains for transport, but, if chemical weathering strongly predominates, only clays, fine quartz grains, and salts in solution will reach a depositional basin.

Postdepositional factors. Terrigenous facies commonly owe their aspect in large part to events and conditions that become effective after the sediment comes to rest on the depositional surface. Here, for example, detritus-feeding organisms, at the sediment–water interface or burrowing within, ingest the sediment, alter it chemically, and destroy the primary lamination, leaving trails, tubes, and castings.

Fine sediments, especially clays, are deposited with volumes of interstitial water as large as 80 percent. The increasing weight of accumulating sediment compresses the mass, squeezes out the water, and causes the clay and other mineral grains to become oriented with their long dimensions parallel to the depositional surface. This process, compaction, significantly reduces the volume of the accumulated sediment and causes large volumes of water to pass upward through the overlying deposits.

A number of other processes, lumped under the heading of diagenesis, affect sediments after deposition and reflect chemical and physical activity created as the sediments adjust to the burial environment and react with the water made available by compaction of underlying layers. Cementation, enlargement of grains, and replacement of metastable minerals by new (authigenic) species in equilibrium with the burial environment are common responses to diagenetic processes.

Biogenic facies. In common with chemical facies but in contrast to the land-derived sediments discussed above, biogenic facies almost exclusively reflect precipitation of mineral matter from the aqueous solutions that constitute the depositional medium. Coal and oil shale represent special and volumetrically trivial cases of biogenic sediments; the overwhelming mass of biogenic sediments in the geologic record consists of carbonates; silica is one to two orders of magnitude less abundant; by far the great majority of biogenic facies are marine in origin. Within the marine environment, biogenic facies respond to many of the controls exerted on the character and distribution of terrigenous facies, plus a number of other factors.

Geologic age. Biogenic facies are strongly influenced by the stage of evolution of marine organisms at the time of sediment accumulation. Biogenic facies of the Precambrian are completely dominated by algal contributions; increasing numbers of invertebrates acquired hard parts from Cambrian into Ordovician time, and thereafter carbonates reflect the rise (and eventual decline) of successive groups of organisms that attained dominance in marine communities (see FOSSIL RECORD).

Ecology. During any part of the Paleozoic Era and since that time, the organisms capable of contributing hard parts to biogenic sediments have been distributed according to their adaptation to specific environments; the character and distribution of biogenic facies similarly reflects the environment of deposition and the complex interrelationships of organisms in the environment.

Deep-marine bottoms, below the depth of penetration of light (benthos), cannot sustain a rich, bottom-dwelling biota. There, the major contributors to biogenic sediments are floating animals and plants (plankton) living at and near the surface and, on dying, adding their shells and tests to a planktonic facies accumulating on the bottom. Chalk is a common exemplar of this facies. Below depths of approximately 3,500 to 4,000 metres (11,550 to 13,200 feet), calcium carbonate dissolves in modern oceans, and bottoms significantly deeper lack the remains of carbonate hard parts. Instead the shells of silica-precipitating planktonic forms, chiefly radiolaria and diatoms, dominate the sediment that eventually lithifies to form the rock called chert.

The greatest number of carbonates on continents, in exposure or penetrated by the drill, were deposited in shallow-water marine environments. The resulting facies intimately reflect the nature and composition of the organic communities that inhabited the depositional site; this is the benthonic facies. Crinoidal, foraminiferal, and algal facies are examples dominated by a single group of organisms, sometimes by a single species; other facies are obviously the products of highly diverse biotas with many species, especially shelled invertebrates that contribute their hard parts to the accumulation of sediment. Each facies, simple or complex, is a response to a web of environmental factors; because of the detail available for observation, benthonic facies have a very high resolving power in identifying ancient environmental settings among successions of sedimentary rocks.

Benthonic facies may be classified according to the degree of kinetic energy interpreted to have been released at the depositional surface by waves or tidal currents. Low-energy facies are characterized by shells preserved in their growth positions or but little disturbed or fragmented and by a high range of particle sizes, including much fine material within and between biogenic shells. A number of environmental settings can be identified, such as the lagoonal facies that reflect the stresses placed on organic communities by seasonal or cyclical changes in salinity.

Most high-energy facies are marked by disarticulated, fragmented, and abraded hard parts, which commonly are graded according to size in response to wave and current action. Such facies may be spread as blankets by transgressing or regressing environments, or, under conditions of stillstand, relatively thick belts of accumulation may occur, representing the positions of carbonate banks. A special case is created by bottom communities that include sediment-binding or sediment-trapping organisms (calcareous algae and certain sponges, corals, and bryozoa among others). These create the wave-resistant framework of organic reefs that characterize present-day tropical marine environments. Where ancient reefs have been spread as blanket deposits by transgression or regression, the resulting facies is referred to as biostromal; designation as reef (or biohermal) facies is reserved for cases of long-continued stillstand during which thick accumulations form by superimposition of atolls, fringing and barrier reefs, or randomly distributed mounds.

Planktonic and benthonic facies

Chemical facies. Facies that represent physicochemical precipitation of sediment from solution without the intervention of biological agencies are termed chemical facies. Most such facies in the geologic record are marine, although the preserved deposits of saline lakes are well known and include a number of economically valuable accumulations.

The seas are saturated with calcium carbonate. Whenever the solubility of this carbonate is exceeded by removal of dissolved carbon dioxide, precipitation may result, typically as very fine needle-shaped crystals of the mineral aragonite that accumulate on the bottom as a carbonate mud. Where carbonate supersaturation occurs over shallow, wave-agitated bottoms, the product is an oolite facies composed of sand-sized spherical grains, each of which is formed by precipitation of concentric carbonate layers.

Seawater in lagoons or other areas of impeded circulation with the open sea may undergo evaporation at a rate faster than inflow, thus raising the concentration of dissolved salts to the point of precipitation and giving rise to evaporites (*q.v.*) or deposits of the evaporite facies. Precipitation of calcium sulfate ($CaSO_4$, gypsum or anhydrite) begins when the concentration is increased fivefold, and the common occurrence of this facies among ancient sediments is testimony to the frequency with which $CaSO_4$ solubility has been exceeded in the geologic past. A tenfold increase in concentration of seawater leads to precipitation of sodium chloride (NaCl, salt, the mineral halite). NaCl is the most abundant of marine salts, and it is not surprising that it constitutes the greatest volume of evaporite facies. Higher concentrations result in the deposition of potassium and magnesium chlorides and sulfates in various mineralogic combinations. These, the bittern salts, are much less common but are numbered among the most sought-after mineral deposits.

Other chemical facies include the greatest resources of phosphates and iron ore. Some phosphate deposits are clearly the results of postdepositional replacement of carbonates, whereas others are primary marine sediments that are thought to represent precipitation from upwelling deep, phosphate-laden waters at the margins of continental shelves. Sedimentary iron ores similarly reflect unusual depositional environments, combining partially isolated basins with, perhaps, a high degree of bacterial activity.

Postdepositional changes. Many of the primary sedimentary materials that constitute biogenic and chemical facies are relatively unstable in postdepositional environments and are grossly affected by diagenetic processes. The mineral aragonite, an important constituent of organic shells and the most common chemically precipitated form of calcium carbonate, is inevitably transformed to calcite. Both calcite and aragonite are unstable in the presence of water containing high concentrations of magnesium, by which they are converted to the double calcium–magnesium carbonate, dolomite (see LIMESTONES AND DOLOMITES). Dolomitization is the result of the reaction of high-magnesium waters on previously deposited limestones. Dolomite facies are widespread, commonly observed, and appear to be the product of percolation of such waters by capillary action or reflux seepage from saline lagoons and by the movement of waters along the groundwater table.

APPLICATIONS OF SEDIMENTARY FACIES

There are as many kinds of sedimentary facies as there are aspects to consider or goals to attain in the analysis of sedimentary rocks. For purposes of simplicity the following discussion is confined to facies defined by the composition of the rocks that they comprise; these are lithologic facies or lithofacies. Figure 1 illustrates the three-dimensional geometry of successive intertonguing rock types (limestone, shale, and sandstone) that results as depositional environments shift about and replace one another through spans of geologic time. The top of the block and the plane passing through the middle of the block (and connecting points *e* and *f*) are time surfaces; that is, each was a surface of deposition at an instant of time, and the intervening sediments were deposited during the same

(margin notes, left column:)
Calcium carbonate and evaporite facies

Phosphate and iron facies

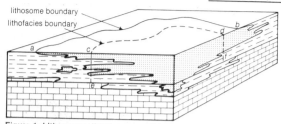

Figure 1: *Lithosomes, lithotypes, and lithofacies.*
Lithotypes are identified by the boundary *a–b*.
The clastic unit is divided into two lithofacies—one more than half sand and one more than half shale—by the boundaries *c–e* and *d–f* (see text).
From H. Wheeler and V. Mallory, *American Association of Petroleum Geologists Bulletin*, vol. 40, no. 11, pp. 2711–23 (November 1956)

span of time. Some workers refer to the three intertongued masses of rock as facies or lithofacies and would recognize limestone, shale, and sandstone facies within the block. In a more precise terminology each of these is designated a lithosome (literally, a rock body), and the term facies is reserved for a special usage in application of the operational facies concept.

Operational facies mapping. The four columns of Figure 2 show the lithologic aspect of a given unit of strata (such as that between the time surfaces of Figure 1) at points of observation that may be outcrops or boreholes. At each point the lithologic aspect may be expressed, as shown, by the percentages of the component rock types or by ratios among the components. The most commonly employed of the latter are the clastic ratio (the thickness of sandstone and shale divided by the thickness of limestone, dolomite, and other biogenic or chemical sediments) and the sand–shale ratio (the thickness of sandstone divided by the thickness of shale). At points *c* and *d* of Figure 1 the sand–shale ratio is 1 (half sandstone, half shale), and the lithofacies boundary shown connects other points of equal sand–shale ratio, dividing the unit between the two surfaces into two lithofacies, one dominated by sandstone and one by shale.

From W.C. Krumbein and L.L. Sloss, *Stratigraphy and Sedimentation*, 1st ed. (1951); W.H. Freeman and Co.

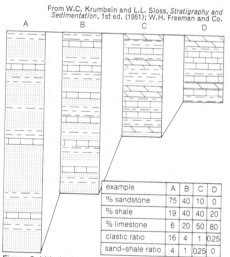

example	A	B	C	D
% sandstone	75	40	10	0
% shale	19	40	40	20
% limestone	6	20	50	80
clastic ratio	16	4	1	025
sand–shale ratio	4	1	025	0

Figure 2: Lithologic aspect of stratigraphic unit at four separate points of observation (boreholes or surface outcrops). The lithologic aspect at each point is expressed in terms of percentages of rock types and ratios among rock types.

Figure 3 is a facies map of an Early Cretaceous unit in the east Texas area. The points of observation are indicated, and lines connecting points of equal thickness (isopachs) of the unit are shown. Facies boundaries, defined by the ratios shown on the triangular diagram, divide the map area among eight lithofacies. Thus at any position in the large area covered, the thickness and rock character of the rock strata termed the Trinity Group in the south central U.S. can be determined from the map.

Once the raw data on the thicknesses of lithologic components are acquired, computers are capable of reducing these data to the desired percentages or ratios, plotting the figures in map form at each point of observation and

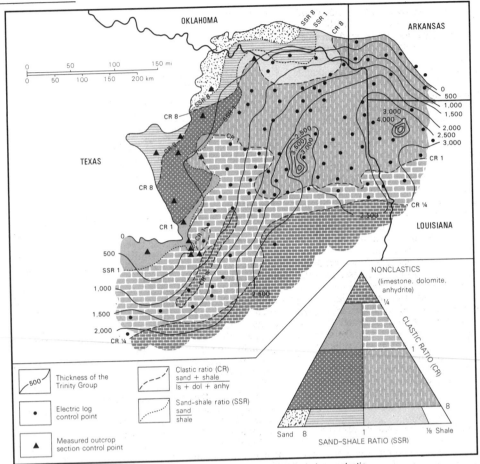

Figure 3: The Cretaceous Trinity Group showing the distribution of sand–shale nonclastic components and thickness.

Adapted from J.M. Forgotson, Jr., "Review and Classification of Quantitative Mapping Techniques," *The American Association of Petroleum Geologists Bulletin*, vol. 44, no. 1, pp. 83–100 (January 1960); The American Association of Petroleum Geologists, Tulsa

drawing the isopach lines and lithofacies boundaries to produce a finished map. Instrumental records of boreholes (electrical, geochemical, acoustic, and other digitized mechanical logs) produced in recent years can be scanned automatically to yield lithologic data suitable as input to the map-making computer program without human intervention beyond identification of the limits of the unit of strata to be mapped. The oil industry, which must cope with tens of thousands of borehole records in the search for new petroleum reserves, has been the leader in research and development of automated approaches to the production of facies maps.

Facies and paleogeography. The reconstruction of ancient lands and seas, more specifically the identification of the character and distribution of ancient environments, is enormously enhanced by interpretation of facies maps. Figure 4 is a paleogeographic interpretation of the east Texas area during the Early Cretaceous time of deposition of the Trinity Group. The sand concentrations evident along the northwest margin of the map area of Figure 3 obviously record the shifting positions of beaches. Although erosion has stripped Early Cretaceous sediments from much of Oklahoma and north central Texas, it can be presumed, by analogy with the present Gulf Coast, that the beaches formed barrier islands bounding lagoons and coastal swamps. The shales dominating the Trinity Group in the area around the common corner of Texas, Arkansas, and Louisiana are of the type formed by lithification of prodelta clays. It is probable, therefore, that the progenitor of the Mississippi River produced a large delta some 130,-000,000 years ago somewhere to the northeast of the facies map area, quite possibly in central Arkansas. Seaward of the delta clays and sand beaches the sediments become increasingly limy, suggesting approach to the clear, unmuddied waters of the open Early Cretaceous Gulf. The narrow trend of nearly pure limestone sur-

rounded by a mixture of lime and shale is indicative of the position of carbonate shell banks or, possibly, reefs. Trinity Group strata dip south beneath coastal Texas and the Gulf and are too deep to be reached by the drill. The presence of abundant limestone as far Gulf-ward as the limit of observation (the scalloped margin of the patterned area of the facies map), however, shows that a relatively shallow continental shelf, well above the carbonate compensation level, existed at least as far as the present shoreline.

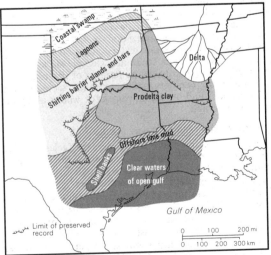

Figure 4: Early Cretaceous paleogeography in the area of deposition of the Trinity Group.

More detailed facies mapping, involving quantified expressions of aspects that relate directly to specific environmental settings, provides the basis for much more sophisticated paleographic reconstruction than is possible with the relatively simple example illustrated here. The fossil assemblages associated with the sediments, analyzed in terms of their water depth, temperature, salinity, and other requirements, lead to detailed biofacies maps of readily interpreted environmental significance. Primary structures of sedimentary rocks (cross-bedding ripple mark, sole marking, etc.) commonly reveal the transport directions of sediments brought to the site of deposition; vector-property maps displaying directional data are used in reconstructing ancient river systems, longshore current orientations, the slope direction of sea floors, and other paleogeographic elements. All of these approaches, and more, find employment in paleogeographic studies initiated for the practical purposes of mineral exploration as well as for consideration of broader problems, such as the ancient motions of sea floors and continents.

FURTHER QUANTITATIVE TREATMENT
OF SEDIMENTARY FACIES

The vast array of numerical data that is produced during routine operational facies mapping has allowed quantitative treatment of facies variability. The two examples below are among many that could be cited.

Trend-surface analysis. Trend analysis is a least-squares surface-fitting method by which systematic regional facies patterns are represented by low-order terms in the surface-fitting function, and local facies effects are represented by higher-order terms. The common problem is one of distinguishing local phenomena—a sandbar, for example—from regional effects created, say, by approach to a terrigenous sediment source such as an emergent landmass. If the goal of the study is location of the landmass, then it is necessary to remove the obscuring effects of local sandbars; conversely, if the problem is one of identifying sandbars, then it is the regional increase in sand toward the sediment source that clouds the picture. Least-squares mathematical surfaces are fitted to the facies data and "stripped" off to reveal underlying features that would be hidden on maps that combine both local and regional effects. Computer technology is available to perform the mathematical manipulations and produce the resulting maps.

Analysis of cyclical successions. It is a well-established characteristic of successions of sedimentary rocks that certain types of strata follow one another in a systematic, repetitive order, as in coal cyclothems (*q.v.*; cyclic, or repetitive, sequences of strata). The vertical cyclicity results from the natural systematic lateral arrangement of sedimentary environments and from the shift of these environments as the succession of strata is accumulated. It is predictable in a transgressive succession that barrier beach sands will overlie lagoonal muds and that the sands, in turn, may be followed by offshore sediments. The degree of predictability, however, is governed by both systematic and random factors. If, in a sequence of transgressive cycles, there is a progressive decrease in the supply of quartz grains, then there will be a systematic change in the kind of sediment above the lagoonal muds until the position of the beach sands is occupied, perhaps, by oolite grains or shell fragments.

Nonsystematic variations, such as responses to minor regressions or to the temporary influx of a new type of sediment, commonly referred to as "noise," are more difficult to assess. One approach is to express the likelihood that one type of rock follows another in terms of mathematical probabilities. Long study of cyclothems, for example, shows that there is a greater probability that a coal bed will be succeeded by a limestone than by a sandstone. Tabulation of the relative probabilities of each rock type in a cyclical succession forms the so-called Markov chain that postulates, within the limits of the determined probabilities, that the occurrence of each sediment type is controlled by the underlying sediment. In other words, a cyclothem limestone may be thought of as having a short-term, one-step "memory" of the underlying coal; the probability of limestone deposition is thus conditioned by the coal formed in the immediately pre-

Markov processes and vertical cyclical successions of strata

ceding span of time. Through the use of the computer and Markovian theory, it is possible to produce detailed simulations of successions of strata; such simulated successions find application to prediction in advance of exploratory drilling and to interpretation of data derived from geophysical surveys.

BIBLIOGRAPHY. W.C. KRUMBEIN and L.L. SLOSS, *Stratigraphy and Sedimentation*, 2nd ed. (1963), an intermediate-level text whose last four chapters concern many of the topics covered in this article; J.W. HARBAUGH and D.F. MERRIAM, *Computer Applications in Stratigraphic Analysis* (1968), an advanced treatment of trend-surface analysis and a number of other mathematical approaches to facies studies; P.E. POTTER and F.J. PETTIJOHN, *Paleocurrents and Basin Analysis* (1963), a comprehensive treatment of the vector properties of sediments and their application to facies analysis. The following four references are atlases of facies maps employing variations of the operational concept and including paleogeographic and tectonic interpretations: E.D. MCKEE *et al.*, "Paleotectonic Maps, Jurassic System," *U.S. Geol. Surv., Misc. Geol. Invest.* Map 1–175 (1956), "Paleotectonic Maps, Triassic System," ibid., Map 1–300 (1959); R.G. MCCROSSON *et al.* (eds.), *Geological History of Western Canada*, 2nd ed. (1965); and L.L. SLOSS *et al.* (eds.), *Lithofacies Maps: An Atlas of the U.S. and Southern Canada* (1960).

(L.L.Sl.)

Sedimentary Rocks

Sediments are deposits of solid material that accumulate upon the Earth's surface under the influence of various mediums (air, water, ice, gravity) and under the normal conditions of temperature and pressure that exist at the surface. Sedimentary rocks are the lithified equivalents of sediments, whether derived from previously formed rocks and minerals or from chemical and biochemical deposition. The processes of physical and chemical weathering prepare loose detrital sediment such as clay, silt, sand, and gravel for the processes of transportation, by gravity, mudflows, running water, glaciers, and wind action. These particles are transported to depositional sites—deserts, alluvial fans, submarine shelves and slopes, and deltas in lakes and oceans, among others. Upon reaching a site of deposition, the sediment is converted to sedimentary rocks by cementation, compaction, and induration. Hence, there is both a detrital fraction (the transported sediment) and a chemical fraction (various chemical precipitates) that make up the final sedimentary rock.

Definition, formation, and significance

Agents of transportation may sort out discrete particles, such as gravel to form conglomerate, sand to form sandstone, or silt and clay to form siltstone and claystone, which are called shale. Chemicals in solution in water bodies are precipitated or flocculated out to form certain types of limestone, dolostone, gypstone, rock salt, and other chemical sediments. Detrital particles of limestone may accumulate mechanically like any other sand, eventually forming limesand. Sedimentary rocks form only about 5 percent by volume of all rocks of the Earth's crust. The area of outcrop and exposure of sedimentary rocks, however, is about 75 percent of the total land area. The percentage probably is greater for ocean basins, though volcanic material is also being added to the daily increment of accumulation upon ocean floors. Sediments and sedimentary rocks therefore form only a thin, surficial veneer upon the Earth. Geologists have measured the thicknesses of outcropping sedimentary rocks and have calculated that the average thickness is about 2.4 kilometres (1.5 miles); thicknesses range from eight to 16 kilometres (five to ten miles) when a composite rock section is considered.

Sedimentary rocks contain the story of past periods of geologic time, because they have accumulated in some locality during each day of the Earth's past history. Billions of years ago the Earth was formed from the dust of a cosmic cloud. It then melted completely as a result of radioactive heating up and subsequently cooled some 4,500,000,000 to 5,000,000,000 years ago, the beginning of geologic time. Shortly thereafter the atmosphere and hydrosphere were formed from cooling and condensing gases and liquids derived from within the Earth. Weathering and running water were, therefore, among the first geological agents at work; sediment was transported from higher areas to the ocean basins, which then were gradually filling with water. Some gravelly sediment, now indurated into a conglomerate more than 3,500,000,000 years old, is known from Rhodesia, for example. During all of geologic time, sediment has formed at various places on Earth and in the oceans, ultimately to become compacted and cemented into sedimentary rocks. The process continues today, and during an average 24-hour period, for example, approximately 2,000,000 tons of sediment are transported by the Mississippi River past New Orleans, to accumulate in the Mississippi River Delta or in the Gulf of Mexico. The entire area is very slowly subsiding—*i.e.*, the crust of the Earth beneath the northern Gulf of Mexico is sagging—and the rate of sediment income just about balances the rate of subsidence. This is, therefore, a modern depositional site, and the sediment that accumulates today will eventually be transformed into sedimentary rocks in the future.

When properly understood and interpreted, sedimentary rocks reveal the story of past life groups (fossils) and of the evolutionary advancement from simple to complex organisms in the plant and animal kingdoms. They also provide information on ancient geography, termed paleogeography (*q.v.*), because a map of the distribution of sediments that formed in shallow oceans will indicate relationships of seas to landmasses in the past. It is also possible to study rock deformation—the various folds or bends in the strata and the faults that displace stratified rocks—and to determine the history of the formation of ancient mountain chains.

It is almost impossible to assess the importance of sedimentary rocks in terms of economics, because these rocks contain essentially the world's entire store of oil and gas, coal, phosphates, salt deposits, groundwater, and other natural resources. Sedimentary rocks are valuable as building stones, trim stone, patio slabs, and the like, and marbles and limestones also are sedimentary in origin. Limestones are used in cement making, in toothpastes and tooth powders, and in paints and chemicals. They serve as flux in steel plants, as crushed rock for highway construction, and for making burnt lime for mortar. Shales of certain types are used in the brick industry and to make clay pipes and similar items, whereas pure quartz sands provide industry with the raw materials for glassmaking, including optical glass. Other rock types, such as rock salt, phosphate rock, and gypsum (gypstone), are of tremendous value in man's economy, and many industrial minerals and metal ores are also derived from sedimentary rocks.

This article treats the classification and basic properties of sedimentary rocks, sedimentary structures and environments, and the geological distribution of sedimentary rocks. For detailed information on the more important sedimentary rock types, see the separate articles CONGLOMERATES AND BRECCIAS; SANDSTONES; GRAYWACKES; SHALES; LIMESTONES AND DOLOMITES; EVAPORITES; PHOSPHORITES; DURICRUSTS; and COALS. Stratigraphic aspects of sedimentary rocks are covered in detail in STRATIGRAPHIC BOUNDARIES and SEDIMENTARY FACIES, and additional information on the erosion, transportation, and deposition of sediment in several natural environments is presented in FLUVIAL PROCESSES; GLACIATION, LANDFORMS PRODUCED BY; WEATHERING; EARTH MOVEMENTS ON SLOPES; BEACHES; ALLUVIAL FANS; and JUNGLES AND RAIN FORESTS. See also CLAY MINERALS for coverage of this important sediment type.

CLASSIFICATION SYSTEMS

Early proposals

In general, geologists have attempted to classify sedimentary rocks on a natural basis, but some schemes have genetic implications (*i.e.*, knowledge of origin of a particular rock type is assumed), and many classifications reflect the philosophy, training, and experience of those who propound them. No single scheme to date has found universal acceptance, and discussion here will centre on some proposals.

The early editions of *A Handbook of Rocks*, beginning in 1896, showed that sedimentary rocks could be classified into clastic, chemical, and organic groups. A major contribution was made by the American geologist A.W. Grabau in 1904 in his *On The Classification of Sedimentary Rocks* and his revisions in 1913 of the monumental work *Principles of Stratigraphy*. Grabau combined textural and compositional terms in classifying and describing sedimentary rocks, and he distinguished between exogenetic and endogenetic types; the former are chiefly mechanical or clastic, having been derived from fragments of older rocks, whereas the latter are the nonclastic rocks and are chemical, organic, or biochemical in origin. His scheme of classifying sedimentary rocks involved the use of such prefixes as hydro- (for water-laid rocks), anemo- (for wind-deposited rocks), auto- (crushed or shattered rocks), and atmo- (rocks formed *in situ*). They were compounded with other terms designating composition and size, including rudaceous (gravelly texture), arenaceous (sandy texture), and lutaceous (silty and clayey texture). Many of Grabau's rock names have gained wide acceptance today, although the spelling has been changed slightly. The names calcirudite, calcarenite, and calcilutite—referring to calcareous conglomerate, sandstone, and shale—are popular, for example, among sedimentary petrologists. The name hydrocalcarenite in Grabau's system refers to a sandstone with discrete calcareous grains that was deposited in water. As another example, an anemosilicarenite is a wind-deposited, siliceous sandstone. The system has been criticized because some names are unwieldy and difficult to pronounce; moreover, rock origin must be known to choose the proper prefix.

The book *Rocks and Rock Minerals* was first published in 1908, and it has enjoyed various revisions. Sedimentary rocks are classified there according to their physical characteristics and composition into detrital and nondetrital rocks (see Table 1).

Table 1: Terms Designating Composition and Physical Characteristics	
detrital rocks	nondetrital rocks

Rudites (coarse)
Conglomerates (rounded clasts)
Breccias (angular clasts)
    Basal, or transgression
    Fanglomerates (in alluvial fans)
    Tillites (glacially transported)
Arenites (medium-grained)
Sandstone
Arkose (feldspar-rich)
Graywacke (sandstone with
    mud matrix)
Quartzite (orthoquartzite)
Lutites (fine-grained)
Siltstone
Shale
Mudstone or claystone
Argillite
Loess (transported and
    deposited by wind)
	Precipitates
	Chemical precipitates
	    (rocks formed by precipitation
	    from seawater or freshwater)
	Evaporites (products of
	    evaporation from saline brines)
	Duricrust rocks (hardened surface
	    or mean-surface layer of
	    any composition)
	Organic
	Zoogenic (made up of hard parts
	    of animals; *e.g.*, crinoidal
	    limestone)
	Phytogenic (made up of plant
	    remains; *e.g.*, algal limestone)

Other attempts were made to classify sedimentary rocks, and in 1948 a significant advance occurred. In that year three definitive articles were published in the *Journal of Geology* by the American geologists F.J. Pettijohn, R.R. Shrock, and P.D. Krynine. These classifications may be said to have provided the basis for all modern discussion of the subject. The nomenclature associated with several schemes of classifying clastic and nonclastic rocks will be discussed in the sections immediately following, but a rough division of sedimentary rocks based on chemical composition is shown in Figure 1.

Texture as a basis

Clastic rocks. An obvious physical feature of many rocks is texture; that is, the size, shape, and arrangement of the constituent grains. Texture may be coarse, medium, fine, or amorphous. When it is fragmental, and discrete grains can be recognized, the rock is a clastic sedimentary rock. Clastic material, for the most part, has been transported to the site of deposition and includes the gravelly sediment that forms conglomerate (if the particles are abraded and somewhat rounded) and breccia (if

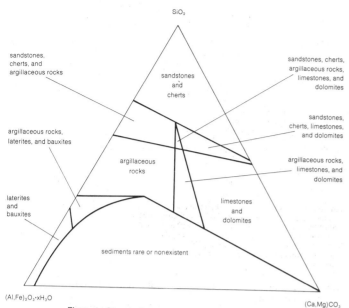

Figure 1: Chemical composition of sedimentary rocks.
From B. Mason, *Principles of Geochemistry* (1966); John Wiley and Sons

composed of angular particles). The following size grades can be recognized among coarse clastic sediments: granules; pebbles; cobbles; and boulders, or blocks (see Table 2). Medium clastics include the various sandstone (arenite) types; and fine clastics are the siltstones, mudstones, and shales. Some petrographers further subdivide sandstones as coarse, medium, and fine and may similarly classify fine clastic rocks.

There are many ways of classifying coarse, clastic sedimentary rocks. One such scheme is that of Grabau, previously mentioned, but the simplest method consists of giving a name together with a brief meaningful description of the characteristics of a particular conglomerate. Such a statement is, of course, applicable to all types of sedimentary rocks and need not be confined to the conglomerates. Thus, a pebble conglomerate means what the name implies—a coarse, clastic sedimentary rock whose discrete particles range from four to 64 millimetres in diameter. A description is necessary, however, to indicate the rock types that compose this variety of conglomerate. If the clasts, for example, consist of nearly equal amounts of granite and gneiss (crystalline and metamorphic rock types, respectively), such a rock could be called a granite–gneiss pebble conglomerate.

According to Pettijohn, gravels collected by ordinary water currents have an intact framework (*i.e.*, the clasts are in close proximity) and may be termed orthoconglomerates. Those deposited by mudflows, subaqueous turbidity flows and slides, and glacial ice tend to have a disrupted framework and may be termed paraconglomerates. As a further distinction, those conglomerates composed of a single rock type are termed oligomictic, whereas those containing many rock types are termed polymictic. This is but a sampling of the possible nomenclature for coarse clastic rocks.

Sandstones have long intrigued geologists, largely because of their relative abundance in the geologic column; they are present in rocks of every age and are also forming today. Certain groups of geologists have devoted great effort to the classification of these medium-textured, clastic sedimentary rocks, but no attempt will be made here to review all of the many schemes. There has been an effort on the part of one group of researchers to maintain the name sandstone, whereas others prefer to perpetuate the name arenite. Moreover, some authorities favour a classification based on the quartz–feldspar–clay content of a rock, whereas others consider the presence of rock fragments to be of principal significance. Classification schemes have been presented in the form of triangles, in which the three components used for classification occupy the corners, and in the form of tetrahedrons, which are more complicated but permit the use of four end members, or rock components.

Another approach of considerable merit is to classify sandstones in simplified tabular form, arranged according to mineral composition and textural maturity. Such a scheme emphasizes the importance of the degree of textural maturity (maturity of a sandstone refers to the relative absence or abundance of easily erodible or soluble constituents) of the medium-textured clastic sedimentary rocks. Immature graywackes, for example, tend to pass up the scale of maturity as they lose their less durable minerals and rock particles and eventually pass through rocks called subgraywackes into orthoquartzites

Three-component and other schemes

Table 2: Size Limits of Common Grades and Rock Terms

size	sedimentary particles					volcanic particles	
	rounded, subrounded, subangular			angular		fragment	aggregate
	fragment	aggregate		fragment	aggregate		
	boulder	boulder gravel		block		block*	volcanic breccia
256 mm		boulder conglomerate					
	cobble	cobble gravel cobble conglomerate	"roundstone"	...	breccia	bomb†	agglomerate
64 mm							
	pebble	pebble gravel pebble conglomerate		...		— 32 mm — lapilli — 4 mm —	lapilli tuff
4 mm							
2 mm	granule	granule gravel		...			
	sand	sand sandstone		— 1 mm — grit — ½ mm —		coarse ash	coarse tuff
1/16 mm						— ¼ mm —	
	silt	silt siltstone		...			
1/256 mm						fine ash	fine tuff
	clay	clay shale		...			

*Broken from previously consolidated igneous rock.   †Solidified from plastic material while in flight.
Source: from F.J. Pettijohn, *Sedimentary Rocks*.

(rocks with more than 90 percent quartz, approximately). Similarly, arkoses tend to lose their feldspar during weathering and erosion and then pass up the scale of maturity to grade into rocks that are called subarkoses and, again, ultimately into orthoquartzites (see further SANDSTONES).

One sandstone variety that has received much attention but whose precise definition is in question is the orthoquartzite mentioned above. To some this is no more than a handful of loose, essentially pure quartz sand, but most workers would argue that a loosely to moderately cemented quartz sandstone should be called quartzose sandstone. An orthoquartzite is properly defined as a clastic sedimentary rock composed of silica-cemented quartz sand. The cement is commonly deposited in continuity (when viewed through a microscope) with the quartz grains. Relatively pure orthoquartzites (ranging from as little as 80 percent to more than 95 percent quartz by composition) display intragranular fracture, equally across grains and cement. This is a requisite property of orthoquartzite, and quartzose sandstones, by contrast, lack this property.

Important related rock types include feldspathic orthoquartzite (or feldspathic sandstone if not truly an orthoquartzite), which contains a substantial percentage of feldspar of any kind, and protoquartzites, which are similar to orthoquartzites in all attributes but contain as much as 40 percent chlorite, micas, sericite, various other clays, and rock fragments. Such a rock is about midway between subgraywacke and graywacke in textural maturity.

Shale is a fine-textured clastic sedimentary rock with a preponderance of detrital components, having been indurated from silt and clay. Some shale a siltstone if it has an average grain size between 1/16 and 1/256 millimetre (0.0025 and 0.0002 inch) and claystone if discrete particles are mostly smaller than 1/256 millimetre, which is clay-size detrital material.

Shales are classified as essentially noncarbonate sedimentary rocks; fine and very fine grained carbonate rocks are called calcisiltites, calcilutites, or sometimes finegrained limestones or dolostones (dolomites). Shales are composed of the clay minerals, mostly silica and silicates, with accessory minerals of other composition. Shales can contain carbonates but not in excess of 50 percent of the bulk of the rock; otherwise, they fall into the limestone or dolostone scheme of classification (see further SHALES).

Nonclastic rocks. Nonclastic sedimentary rocks differ in many respects from their clastic counterparts, and there is no single classification that has been universally accepted. This is a reflection of the great variation in mineral composition, textures, and other properties of these rock types.

Limestones and dolostones make up the bulk among the nonclastic sedimentary rocks. Such rocks as ironstones (limonite, goethite, hematite, siderite, and chamosite), phosphorites (phosphate rock), coal- and oil-bearing rocks, carbonaceous and bituminous shales and limestones, evaporites (rock salt, gypsum, and other salts), chert, opal, and chalcedony occur in much lesser abundance, although locally these noncarbonate (or low-carbonate), nonclastic sedimentary rocks may form thick and widespread deposits. Classification schemes that would incorporate all types of noncarbonate, nonclastic sedimentary rocks have not been set forth, because no triangular or tetrahedral scheme could accommodate them all. Several of the major types of nonclastic rocks are shown in the tetrahedron in Figure 2. The organic corner of the tetrahedron identifies such nonclastic rocks as coal, lignite, and some richly bituminous rocks. Some carbonates and clastic material may be present, but these commonly compose much less than 50 percent of the bulk of such rocks. Coal consists principally of plant material that has been converted to a type of hydrocarbon, but it can pass into a carbonaceous shale, which is a clastic sedimentary rock. Similarly, an oil-rich nonclastic rock can grade into bituminous (petroliferous) shale, sandstone, or limestone. The same kinds of gradational possibilities occur in phosphatic, siliceous, and ferruginous rocks, and the tetrahedron in Figure 2 is designed to

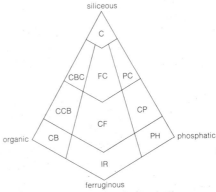

Figure 2: Common noncarbonate, nonclastic sedimentary rocks. C—cherts; CBC—carbonaceous chert; FC—ferruginous chert; PC—phosphatic chert; CCB—cherty carbonaceous rock; CF— cherty ironstone; CP—cherty phosphorite; CB— carbonaceous rock; PH—phosphorite and IR— ironstone.

aid in locating and identifying the more common nonclastic sedimentary rocks.

Limestones are, for the most part, originally deposited carbonate rocks and consist of 50 percent or more of calcite or aragonite (both $CaCO_3$). Dolostones (dolomites) are mostly secondary deposits or replacements of limestones; that is, the mineral dolomite [$CaMg(CO_3)_2$] replaces the calcite of limestones during diagenesis (postdepositional processes). Some very fine textured dolostones do form directly by precipitation from marine and lake brines in restricted environments, however, and these are primary deposits.

Most limestones have a granular texture, and the constituent grains vary from millimicrons (one micron equals .001 millimetre) to visible particles—or even to limestone conglomerates (the calcirudites). The grains may be classified as detrital (fragments of previously formed limestone), skeletal (fragments of fossil carbonate material), pelletal, lumpal, or coated grains. All such grains have been removed and deposited by waves and currents to a final site of deposition. By contrast, carbonate reefs, banks, and similar structures are accumulations of carbonate rock constructed by plants and animals *in situ*. In addition to limestones, there are such chemical and biochemical calcitic rock as tufa, travertine, caliche, calcrete, some tuffaceous limestones, cave deposits (dripstone), and others of lesser importance.

Certain limestones have been designated micritic by some authorities. Micrite is unconsolidated ooze or lime mud of chemical or mechanical origin, or consolidated equivalent. It is very fine textured and normally occurs as grains that are 0.05 millimetre (0.002 inch) in diameter or smaller. Pellets are grains of micritic material that lack significant internal structure and generally are approximately ovoid in shape. Most pellets in limestone range from silt-size to coarse sand-size (some are slightly larger); these spherical or subspherical to oval bodies are largely fecal in origin, having been excreted by shrimp, worms, snails, and the like. Coated grains include oolites, pisolites, and oncolites; these superficially resemble onions in that they have two or more accretionary rings around a central small nucleus. Oolites are spherical or subspherical accretionary grains generally less than two millimetres (0.08 inch) in diameter; pisolites are similar to oolites and range from two to about ten millimetres (0.4 inch) in diameter; and oncolites are still larger, ranging in diameter to 30 millimetres (1.2 inches), and may be spherical, subspherical, subovate, or biscuit shaped. Like oolites and pisolites, oncolites display an internal structure of concretionary rings and may (like their smaller counterparts) also have a fibro-radial structure. Lumps are composite grains possessing superficial re-entrants and are believed to have formed by a process of aggregation; lumps also may result from disruption of partially indurated lime mud at the site of deposition and incorporation in micritic or other limestone. Such limestones are called lumpal limestones.

Limestones and dolostones

Crusts, soils, and weathering products

Not really amenable to classification but of sufficient significance to warrant mention are some sedimentary crusts, soils, and weathering products. Duricrusts (*q.v.*) are peculiar deposits formed on gently sloping erosion surfaces in many parts of the world, consisting of armour-like precipitates that result from upward capillary migration of groundwaters during periods of aridity. Various carbonates are precipitated from these rising groundwaters, and aluminous, ferruginous, and siliceous materials also may form.

Residual soils are the products of weathering formed *in situ*. The character of these deposits results from the interaction of climate, drainage, and type of the parent rock. Regolith is a mantle of loose, incoherent rock material, of any origin or nature, which blankets the parent rock; saprolith is essentially the same; and saprolite is thoroughly decomposed, earthy, but not transported rock. It is a residual clay, silt, or other substance. In the piedmont area of North and South Carolina it commonly is reddish in colour and results from rather thorough decomposition *in situ* of old Paleozoic (225,000,000 to 570,000,000 years old) crystalline rocks. In humid regions the residual materials are enriched in hydroxides of aluminum and ferric iron during processes of weathering, and the end product is called laterite. It also is reddish in colour, and its formation requires high rainfall and high temperatures. Bauxite is a residual clay-size weathering product that is formed *in situ*, consisting largely of hydrated alumina (essentially $Al_2O_3 \cdot 2H_2O$). The principal ores of aluminum are obtained from bauxite; it is commonly gray to light gray in colour. Scree and talus are angular fragments of rock that occur at the bases of cliffs from which they were derived by weathering and erosion. Paleosols are buried soils, especially those developed during an interglacial episode and buried by later advances of ice. They are "fossil" soils and can occur interlayered in other types of sedimentary rocks. A final sedimentary material in this general category is sapropel, an aquatic ooze and sludge rich in organic matter.

PROPERTIES OF SEDIMENTARY ROCKS

Texture. Texture concerns the physical makeup of rock, namely, the size, shape, and arrangement (packing and fabric) of the discrete grains or elements of a sedimentary rock. Whereas mineral or chemical composition of sedimentary rock must be determined in order to classify these rocks and interpret their depositional history correctly, texture relates to the physical parameters of size grades: sorting, skewness of the size distribution, and the degree of particle abrasion, among others. Two main natural textural groupings exist for sedimentary rocks, namely, clastic (or fragmental) and nonclastic (commonly crystalline). A few rare types of sedimentary rocks are said to have an amorphous texture, but with the advent of the electron microscope many of these so-called featureless rocks were found to have a detrital or crystalline texture or both.

Grain size. Particle size is an important textural parameter of clastic rocks, because it provides information on the conditions of transportation, sorting, and deposition of the sediment and provides some clues to the history of events at the depositional site prior to final induration. To determine the sizes of the discrete particles that compose a sedimentary rock can pose a problem, particularly if the rock is firmly indurated (cemented, compacted, lithified). Various methods of setting up grade scales have been devised; a grade scale is a systematic division of a continuous range of sizes into classes or grades. Thus, particulate materials that make up sediments and sedimentary rocks can be weighed and their diameters measured by sieving through screens to determine their grade scales. The grade scale given in Table 3 is still one of the best methods of standardizing terminology, because each size grade or class differs from its predecessor by the constant ratio of 1:2, and each has a specific name to identify the particles included within it. The scale is a geometric grade scale, with a constant ratio between classes, and is well adapted to the description of sediments, because it gives equal significance to size ratios,

Size grades and grade scales

whether the ratios relate to gravel, sand, silt, or clay. The gravels and sands can be separated into discrete grade scales or size grades by using screens or sieves whose openings correspond to metric sizes. Silts and clays are relegated to their respective size grades by utilizing their settling velocities in water or in air to separate one size from another.

Table 3: Particle-Size Classification

grade limits (diameters in mm)	name	grade limits (diameters in mm)	name
Above 256	boulder	1/2–1/4	medium sand
256–128	large cobble	1/4–1/8	fine sand
128–64	small cobble	1/8–1/16	very fine sand
64–32	very large pebble	1/16–1/32	coarse silt
32–16	large pebble	1/32–1/64	medium silt
16–8	medium pebble	1/64–1/128	fine silt
8–4	small pebble	1/128–1/256	very fine silt
4–2	granule	1/256–1/512	coarse clay
2–1	very coarse sand	1/512–1/1,024	medium clay
1–1/2	coarse sand	1/1,024–1/2,048	fine clay

Source: C.K. Wentworth (1922).

Sorting of grains. The sorting of clastic sedimentary rocks measures the thoroughness with which a sediment has been winnowed by wind, washed by water, or worked by other transporting agents. The degree of sorting is a valuable indicator of the rate of sedimentation and the probable environment of deposition.

Determination of the degree of sorting in the laboratory with unconsolidated (or disaggregated) gravels and sands is readily accomplished, using a nest of sieves (screens) whose openings correspond to the grade sizes of the Wentworth or other scale. Sizes of silts and clays are determined in the laboratory using air elutriation or in settling tubes filled with water. Discrete size grades are separated according to their settling rates, and the percentage of material occurring in each size grade is obtained directly.

In order to determine the degree of sorting of indurated sedimentary rocks, a slabbed surface is prepared by cutting the rock, and the surface is then etched with acid or otherwise treated to cause the grains to stand out in relief. The grains can then be studied and counted.

All methods of ascertaining the grade sizes of clastic sediments and of sedimentary rocks result in compilation of data relating to the size frequency distribution. These data can be plotted in tabular form, as histograms (bar graphs), as size frequency curves, or as cumulative curves. Numerous techniques have been devised to illustrate these data; Figure 3 shows a few possibilities.

Some of the characteristics of size frequency distributions include skewness (a measurement of the symmetry of a histogram or of a size frequency curve), kurtosis (degree of peakedness of the histogram or curve), and the mean, or average (a measurement of the central tendency), as well as the quartiles. Some of these characteristics are also shown in Figure 3. The advantages of using these parameters is that they systematize determination of the degree of sorting of clastics and of the precise percentages of discrete grade sizes and designation of the clastic mixture as unimodal, bimodal, or even polymodal. These facts permit interpretation of the environment of sedimentation for the particular suite of sediments or sedimentary rocks involved.

Size frequency distribution

Grain roundness. Clastic rocks become abraded during their transit, and some degree of rounding usually occurs. Conglomerates, for example, are roundstones in that they have been abraded, and most (if not all) sharp corners have been worn off. Breccias, by contrast, are sharpstones and display varying degrees of angularity. The same is true of the arenites, or sandstones; thus, it is important to obtain some measurement of the degree of abrasion or perfection of roundness. Some geologists prefer to arrange sand grains in order of increasing abrasion, from those that are almost entirely unabraded and are thus angular to those that are well rounded. Figure 4 illustrates this arrangement, which is commonly used.

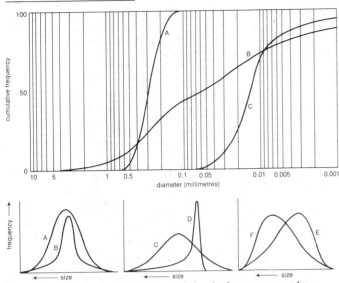

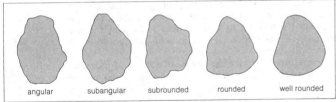

Figure 3: (Top) Typical cumulative size frequency curves for (A) beach sand; (B) glacial till; (C) loess. (Bottom) size frequency distribution curves for sediments that are (A) normal; (B) normal and peaked; (C) normal and scattered; (D) skewed to right and peaked; (E) asymmetrical, skewed to right; (F) asymmetrical, skewed to left.

From Krumbein and Pettijohn, *Manual of Sedimentary Petrography* (1938); Appleton-Century-Croft

Grains that are angular have maximum sharpness around their edges and show minimum abrasion on corners. Subangular grains indicate that the edges and corners have been abraded but retain their original form,

From F. Pettijohn, *Sedimentary Rocks*, 2nd Edition (1957); Harper and Row

| angular | subangular | subrounded | rounded | well rounded |

Figure 4: Roundness classes of sedimentary particles.

and their original surfaces are relatively little worn. Subrounded grains denote considerable attrition and abrasion, so that the entire surface has been worn from faces, angular grains, and crystal boundaries to a relatively smooth texture. Rounded grains approximate roundness and sphericity; edges, corners, and original surfaces have been so abraded that the entire remaining surface of the grain forms a smooth, broad curve. If some grains display perfect roundness and sphericity they may be termed well rounded.

Carbonate texture. Carbonate clastic rocks are similar in texture and may be lithoclastic or bioclastic. Lithoclastic means that the allogenic (detrital) materials are mainly inorganic and consist of grains of different kinds of minerals and rocks or rock fragments that are transported and redeposited as detrital grains and matrix. Thus, an arenite that consists of 50 percent or more (by bulk or by exposed area) of clasts of limestone derived from an earlier formed rock or partly indurated lime mud should be termed lithocalcarenite. Bioclastic indicates that the texture and composition is derived from allogenic materials that are high in organic material, commonly containing a variety of abraded skeletal fragments that have been transported and deposited as detrital material. The source of the clastic material is skeletal fragments, ranging in size from lutites (clays) and comminuted fossil detritus to calcarenite and even to rudaceous (gravelly) textured sediment, the calcirudites. Thus, a biocalcarenite is a clastic carbonate sedimentary rock consisting primarily of sand-size abraded skeletal grains; 50 percent or more of such a rock consists of sand-size fossil fragments.

Many carbonate sedimentary rocks are crystalline, however, rather than granular. In terms of crystal size, they can range from the macrocrystalline or megacrystalline—visible to the unaided eye—through those that are microcrystalline and cryptocrystalline (not visible). The term aphanic is useful to describe the texture of most micrites (and micritic limestones) and dolomicrites; individual crystals and grains (if present) are less than 0.01 millimetre (0.0004 inch) in size. A second designation, phaneric, refers to discrete particles, crystals, and grains that are larger than 0.01 millimetre in size, commonly visible to the unaided eye.

In addition, some degree of perfection of crystallinity can be noted in crystalline sedimentary rocks. Euhedral is a term applied to those crystals that are bounded by their own crystal faces, resulting in a relatively high degree of crystalline geometry. Those crystals whose faces are of a lower degree of perfection than euhedral forms are termed subhedral. Those crystals that are not bounded by their own crystal faces and have their outlines impressed on them by adjacent crystals are termed anhedral. They have a degree of geometry lower than subhedral forms. For further discussion of carbonate textures see LIMESTONES AND DOLOMITES.

Mass properties. Discussion of sedimentary rocks thus far has related to the problems of their classification and to some of the textural characteristics of sediments and sedimentary rocks. The association of the discrete particles in their aggregate, or bulk, state and the whole rock and its mass properties also warrant consideration. Some of the more significant of these properties are discussed here, in alphabetical order.

Cementation. The precipitation of mineral matter in the interstices of a clastic sediment provides cementation, particularly during and shortly following sedimentation. The final product is an indurated rock.

Cohesiveness. Cohering, or sticking together by surface forces, normally is displayed by unconsolidated (to weakly indurated), fine-textured clastic and carbonate sediments of particle size less than 0.01 millimetre.

Colour. The overall hue of sediment results from a combination of various grain colours, mineral inclusions, surface coating, weathered surfaces, matrix colour, and nature and hue of the cementing materials.

Compactibility. Rock becomes compacted when porosity is reduced in response to a decrease in volume under load. Finely textured sediments, such as silt and clay, normally are compacted more than sands and gravels.

Density. The mass per unit bulk volume of the sediment or rock, or its density, is a measure of the degree of packing of the components.

Elasticity. The ability of a strained body to recover its size and shape after deformation is its elasticity. If a rock such as shale, for example, is slowly bent, the degree to which it is able to regain its original size and shape without fracturing is a measure of its elasticity.

Electrical resistivity. Resistance to the passage of an electric current depends, of course, upon the nature of the sediment and the fluid content in its open spaces. Knowledge of the electrical resistivity of the various types of sedimentary rocks helps geologists to locate oil, gas, and water deposits below ground.

Magnetic susceptibility. Magnetization is acquired by rocks when in a magnetic field. In sediments, the susceptibility is largely related to the amount of magnetic minerals (magnetite, for example) that is present.

Packing. The mutual spatial relationships among the grains of a rock, or packing, reflect the degree to which grains are in contact with or interlocked among their neighbours.

Permeability. The ease of fluid flow through rocks, or permeability, is strongly influenced by particle size; coarse gravel, for example, has large openings among the cobbles and boulders, affording easy passage for fluids. Sands also have high permeability values, whereas clays (which have high cohesiveness) have low ones.

Porosity. Porosity, or the actual pore space in a rock, is expressed in percentages. Porosity is a function of the uniformity of particle size and shape and of the state of packing of the particles.

Consideration of the whole rock

Radioactivity. In sediments radioactivity is expressed in units equivalent to 10^{-12} gram of radium per gram of rock. Measured values average about 4.1 for pure quartz sandstones, 4.0 for limestone, 11.3 for gray shale, and 22.4 for dark-gray to black shale.

For further information on mass properties, see ROCKS, PHYSICAL PROPERTIES OF.

Geochemical properties. Minerals that make up sedimentary rocks are of two principal types, namely, allogenic (detrital) and authigenic. The former are obtained during the processes of weathering and are transported to or within the depositional site, whereas authigenic minerals form *in situ* within the depositional site in response to geochemical processes. The geochemical properties of sedimentary rocks, whether clastic or nonclastic, therefore result from certain chemical properties they inherited from earlier formed rocks and from the properties induced upon them during postdepositional epochs. Many igneous rocks contain minerals that are radioactive (some feldspars and zircon, for example). When such minerals occur as detrital grains in clastic sedimentary rocks, their absolute age and the source can generally be determined. Because only a few such minerals are commonly incorporated, however, the use of isotope techniques to determine the time of deposition of sedimentary rocks is limited.

Various clay minerals are present in sedimentary rocks and are of particular importance in most shales and in some limestones. Some of these clays are no more than fine to very fine textured detrital particles, whereas some may form authigenically in the site of deposition. Some of the important clays include kaolinite, halloysite, montmorillonite, illite, vermiculite, and chlorite (see further CLAY MINERALS).

Some zeolites (*q.v.*) are authigenic in origin, and their presence may shed light on the environmental conditions under which they formed. The zeolite analcite ($NaAlSi_2O_6 \cdot H_2O$), for example, commonly indicates formation in lakes (such as the Green River Formation of Utah, Colorado, and Wyoming). Heulandite, (Ca, Na_2) ($Al_2Si_7O_{18} \cdot 6H_2O$), results from the interaction of volcanic glass and saline waters that are commonly marine. In addition to zeolites, trace elements present in sedimentary rocks provide indications of either freshwater or marine environments. Marine clays may contain about 100 to 200 parts per million of boron, whereas freshwater clays have only about ten to 50 parts per million.

Diagenesis of sediments

The term diagenesis is a designation for all processes that act on sediments after their deposition. Such postdepositional processes may take place hundreds or even millions of years after sediment finally comes to rest; they include (1) formation of new minerals, (2) redistribution and recrystallization of substances in sediments, and (3) lithification. Diagenesis, therefore, includes all physicochemical, biochemical, and physical processes modifying sediments in the time between their deposition and their lithification at the low temperatures and pressures characteristic of surface and near-surface environments. Dolomitization is one process of diagenesis, whereby limestone is changed to dolostone.

Fabric. Fabric is the orientation or the lack of it of the elements of a rock. The texture of a rock therefore defines the fabric, because it is the arrangement or orientation of clasts and crystals in these rocks that controls its fabric—it is the way the rock is put together. Packing is a factor in the fabric because it concerns the spacing of the elemental constituents of sediments and sedimentary rocks, and this in turn determines the density. Genetically, there are two principal varieties of fabric, namely, primary (depositional or appositional) and secondary (or deformational). Primary fabric is syngenetic (it is determined while sediment is accumulating), whereas a deformation fabric is produced as a postdepositional process by external stress on the rock. It results from a rotation or from movements of the constituent elements under stress or from the growth of new elements. Fabric in clastics such as conglomerates and sandstones can be determined by plotting dimensional directions, such as

the long axes of pebbles or quartz-sand grains. Fabric in shales can be ascertained by plotting the platelike arrangement of mica and other clays and in carbonate rocks by plotting directional properties of clasts (pellets, skeletons, oolites) or of crystals and crystal patterns.

SEDIMENTARY STRUCTURES

Lamination and stratification

External stratification. Stratification (or bedding) is expressed by rock layers (units) of a general tabular or lenticular form that differ in rock type or other characteristics from the material with which they are interstratified (sometimes stated as interbedded, or interlayered). These beds, or strata, are of varying thickness and areal extent. The term stratum identifies a single bed, or unit, normally greater than one centimetre in thickness and visibly separable from superjacent (overlying) and subjacent (underlying) beds, or units. "Strata" refers to two or more beds, and the term lamina is sometimes applied to a unit less than one centimetre in thickness. Thus, lamination consists of thin units in bedded, or stratified, or layered, sequence in a natural rock succession, whereas stratification consists of bedded layers, or strata, in a geologic sequence of interleaved sedimentary rocks.

The individual beds, or layers, in an interbedded succession of rock strata will rarely be of approximately equal thickness. Examples do exist, however, notably in varved deposits (*q.v.*), which are laminated to thinly stratified layers of sediment that reflect seasonal or annual rhythms. For the preponderance of stratified sedimentary rocks the arrangement is one of unequal thickness, ranging from very thin laminae to discrete beds that measure a few to many feet in thickness. This is the normal sedimentary pattern for strata.

The terms thick and thin as applied to bedding, or stratification, are relative, reflecting the training of a particular geologist as well as his experience with a specific stratigraphic section or sections. Some quantitative values have been set forth, however, and these values and associated nomenclature are shown in Table 4.

Table 4: Quantitative Terms to Describe Layered Sedimentary Rocks			
descriptive terms for stratification	descriptive terms for cross-stratification	thickness	descriptive terms for splitting
Very thick-bedded	very thickly cross-bedded	greater than 6 ft	massive
Thick-bedded	thickly cross-bedded	3 ft to 6 ft	blocky
Medium-bedded	medium cross-bedded	1 ft to 3 ft	slabby
Thin-bedded	thinly cross-bedded	1 in. to 1 ft	flaggy
Laminated	cross-laminated	2 mm to 1 in.	platy (or shaly)
Thinly laminated	thinly cross-laminated	less than 2 mm	papery

Bedding types. It is common to discover a rhythmic pattern in a pile of stratified sedimentary rocks represented by a repetitive sequence of rock types (see further CYCLOTHEMS). In most instances of such cyclic sedimentation, the bedding, or stratification, is horizontal or essentially so; that is, the transporting, sorting, and depositing agents of wind, running water, and lake and ocean currents and waves accumulated the laminae and strata in flat-lying or horizontal arrangement. They are termed well-bedded, a type of primary stratification.

Primary stratification in sediments and sedimentary rocks can be cross-bedded (cross-stratified), graded, and imbricate and can also display climbing laminae, ripples, and beds. A simplified classification of cross-stratification into three principal types (simple, planar, and trough) is shown in Figure 5.

Graded and imbricate bedding

Graded bedding simply identifies beds, or strata, that grade upward from coarse-textured clastic sediment at their base to finer textured materials at the top (Figure 6). The stratification may be sharply marked so that one layer is set off visibly from those above and beneath it. More commonly, however, the layers are blended. This variety of bedding results from a check in the velocity of the transporting agent, and thus coarse-textured sediment (gravel, for example) is deposited first, followed upward by pebbles, granules, sand, silt, and clay. It is commonly associated with submarine density currents (*q.v.*).

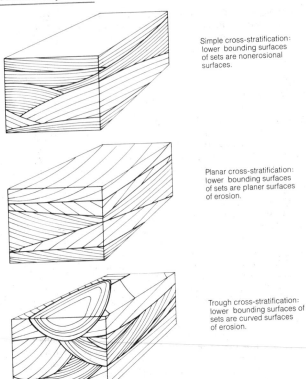

Figure 5: Basic elements of cross-stratification classification.

By courtesy of E.D. McKee and G.W. Weir, *Geological Society of America Bulletin*, vol. 64 (1953); Geological Society of America

Imbricate bedding is of a shingle structure in a deposit of flattened or disk-shaped pebbles or cobbles (Figure 6). That is, elongated and commonly flattened pebbles and cobbles in gravelly sediment are deposited so that they overlap one another like roofing shingles. Imbricate bedding forms where high-velocity currents move over a stream bed or where strong currents and waves break over a gradually sloping beach, thereby forming beach shingle.

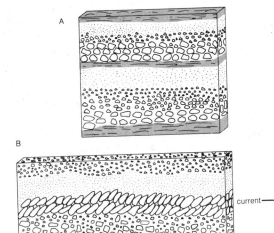

Figure 6: (A) Graded bedding. (B) Imbricate bedding.

Growth structures in sedimentary rocks are *in situ* features that accumulate largely as the result of organic buildups within otherwise horizontal or nearly flat-lying strata. Reefs and stromatolites are two common varieties of such growth structures. Reefs can consist of corals or any other organisms capable of constructing a rigid topographic deposit of carbonate in strongly agitated but shallow lake or ocean realms. Stromatolites are largely wavy–crinkly laminae or thin layers of carbonate that form when algae precipitate the lime from solution into a

buildup superficially resembling heads of cabbage or lettuce. A rather exotic growth structure is travertine; this calcium carbonate deposit is more common to caves in the form of stalactites, stalagmites, columns, and other dripstone, but it can also form in other openings in limestones, such as faults and joints.

Bedding-plane features.   Upper surfaces of beds commonly display primary sedimentary features that are classified as bedding-plane structures. A three-dimensional view may be obtained if some of these can be seen from the side as well as from the top of a pile of strata. They include such features as ripples (ripple marks), climbing ripples, rills, pits, mud cracks, trails and tracks, salt and ice casts and molds, and others. Bedding-plane markings and irregularities can be allocated to one of three classes: (1) those on the base of a bed (load and current structures and organic markings); (2) those within a bed (parting lineation); and (3) those on top of a bed (ripple marks, pits, impressions, mud cracks, tracks and trails of organisms, and others).

Deformation structures.   In addition to sedimentary structures that are normally associated with bedding planes, there are other sedimentary structures that result from deformation during or shortly after sedimentation but before induration of the sediment into rock. These are nontectonic features; that is, they are not bends and folds brought about by metamorphism or other causes. Deformation structures can be grouped into several classes, as follows: (1) founder and load structures, (2) convoluted structures, (3) slump structures, (4) injection structures, such as sandstone dikes or sills, and (5) organic structures. Pillow and convoluted structures are shown in Figures 7 and 8, and a plunge-trough structure in Figure 9.

From F.J. Pettijohn and P.E. Potter, *Atlas and Glossary of Primary Sedimentary Structures*; Springer-Verlag New York Inc.

Figure 7: Cross section of a large pillow structure in Thorold Sandstone (Silurian). New Jolly road cut, Hamilton, Ontario, Canada.

Structures found on the bottom of a bed are called sole markings, because they formed on the "sole" of the bed. Sole marks are commonly formed on sandstone and limestone beds that rest upon shale beds. They are termed casts, because they are fillings of depressions that formed on the surface of the underlying mud. They originate (1) by unequal loading upon the soft and plastic wet mud, (2) by the action of currents across the upper mud surface, or (3) by the activities of organisms on this surface. Load casts form as the result of downsinking of sandstone or limestone into the mud beneath. Current marks can form by the action of water currents on upper surfaces of the beds or by "tools" (such as wood and fossils) that are transported by currents over soft sediment.

A special variety of deformation structure that is common (but not necessarily limited) to limestones is the stylolite, a unique zigzag line that crosses rock surfaces. Stylolites may result from pressure-solution phenomena, which form a sutured pattern during compaction of wet sediment. Being common to limestones, they ordinarily form parallel to the horizontal bedding, or they parallel foreset bedding and cross-bedding. They may form at other angles in newly deposited sediment. The amplitude of the zigzag or up-and-down suture pattern is a measure of the amount of material that was dissolved and removed during compaction of the sediment.

From F.J. Pettijohn and P.E. Potter, *Atlas and Glossary of Primary Sedimentary Structures;* Springer-Verlag New York Inc.

Figure 8: Convolute lamination, Krosno Beds (Oligocene), from Mymon, central Carpathians, Poland.

SEDIMENTARY ENVIRONMENTS

"Sedimentary environment" refers to the complex of physical, chemical, and biological conditions under which a sediment accumulates. These conditions largely determine the properties of sediments deposited within the environment. A sedimentary rock, however, is a product not only of the environment but also of the transporting agent(s) involved. Moreover, its composition, texture, and other characters are determined to a large degree by the makeup of the source area (the provenance).

Any attempt to classify environments of sedimentation must take into account that there are not only marine and nonmarine realms of sedimentation but also mixed or transitional environments in nature.

Marine environments include the nearshore, rather shallow littoral zone, the offshore, moderately shallow zone, and deepwater realms. For mixed marine and nonmarine environments, such names as supralittoral, supratidal, and foreshore may be applied to that realm between the beach (or berm) and the water's edge at normal high tide. Other environments include the beach, estuary, and delta. Each environment, regardless of the name assigned, is associated with a set of criteria that constitutes the hallmark of the environment. The most commonly cited criteria for the recognition of sedimentary environments and source areas are given below.

Harold J. Bissell

Figure 9: Plunge-trough filling in Queantoweap Sandstone (Permian) southwest of Las Vegas, Nevada.

Marine environment. The marine environment consists of the shallow and deep littoral zones and the deepwater realm, as previously stated. The shallow littoral zone (high-energy or agitated realm) has the following characteristics: (1) gravelly, coarse bioclastic, and other materials are common; (2) moderately high textural range (boulders to mud) is present; (3) marine fossils are common and may be mixed with some nonmarine forms; (4) there is interbedding into beds of gravel, sand, silt, and clay, some of which are lenslike; (5) sedimentary structures such as ball-and-pillow, roll-and-plunge, and high-angle cross-bedding (Figure 10) may be present; (6) the map pattern of outcropping sediments or sedimentary rocks consists of elongate and linear belts parallel to the shoreline; (7) different textural variations grade laterally as well as vertically; (8) sedimentary features such as ripple marks, rill marks, rain and bubble pits, and mud cracks should be present in some beds; (9) within short distances (particularly at right angles to the depositional strike) there should be an apparent range in thickness of the various strata; (10) individual beds, lenses, and smaller units may display fair to excellent sorting, both texturally and mineralogically; (11) fossil bivalves and related invertebrates commonly are broken and disarticulated and, when cemented and indurated, form a conglomeration of shell debris termed coquina; (12) reefs, bioherms, and other organic buildups are common in limestone successions; and (13) disconformities are present or rather common.

From F.J. Pettijohn and P.E. Potter, *Atlas and Glossary of Primary Sedimentary Structures;* Springer-Verlag New York Inc.

Figure 10: Cross-bedding in calcareous sandstone of Loyalhanna Limestone (Mississippian), current from right to left. From abandoned quarry, Westmoreland County, Pennsylvania.

The deeper littoral zone (low-energy, minor agitated realm) has the following characteristics: (1) the average sediment is fine-sandy, silty, clayey, and limestone–dolostone; (2) moderately low textural range (local lenses only of gravelly material) is present; (3) lamination and stratification are fair to excellent; sorting is excellent; (4) marine fossils range from bedded shells with articulated valves to sparse isolated remains; (5) individual units as well as bedded geologic successions will be areally extensive, recognizable over a range from scores to hundreds of kilometres; (6) discrete strata, members, and formations do not vary greatly in thickness within short to moderate distances; (7) ripple marks may be present but commonly lack shells in the troughs, and mud cracks and raindrop prints are absent; (8) clastic and chemical sediments may interleave, or be interbedded; sandstones, siltstones, and shales may have limestone or dolostone interbeds; (9) lateral lithologic changes are subtle and extend over large areas; vertical lithologic changes are abrupt and sharp; (10) bedding or stratification planes are essentially horizontal; and (11) disconformities are not pronounced.

The bathyal, abyssal, and hadal zone (deepwater realm) has the following characteristics: (1) there are very fine textured silty and clayey sediments; (2) the textural range is extremely low, particularly among sediments that are silty and clayey only; (3) radiolarian and ribbon cherts and siliceous shales are present; (4) turbidites (graded sediments), graded bedding, chaotic, and other "out-of-place" coarse-textured materials may be sharply interbedded with finer sediments; (5) fossils of deepwater realms are present but scanty; turbidites may contain fossils obtained from the littoral zone or even from land areas; (6) burrowing structures may be present; (7) red and blue muds, possibly of volcanic-ash source, may be present; and (8) beds commonly range from thin to laminated and finely laminated and are not areally extensive.

Mixed marine and nonmarine environment. The mixed environment consists of the supralittoral zone, the beach, and the deltaic zones. The supralittoral zone has the following characteristics: (1) restricted environments have aphanic dolostone with algal crusts; (2) deposits are thin and not areally extensive, in bands parallel to coastline; (3) high-energy, high-storm deposits may have littoral fossils crudely mixed with supralittoral dolostones; (4) mud cracks and raindrop prints may be present; and (5) tree stumps may be in place or logs may be present in chaotic jumble.

Beach,
deltaic,
and
lacustrine
environ-
ments The beach zone has the following characteristics: (1) sandstones are cross-bedded with moderate- to high-inclination on foreset beds; (2) low textural range is present within cross-bedded sands; (3) stranded shells interlayered in beach sands display wave abrasion; some may represent life-forms common to the littoral zone, now stranded on the beach; (4) where beach shingle of flattened, disk-shaped pebbles is present, an imbricate structure is evident; (5) beach gravel (conglomerate) contains shells derived from the littoral zone crudely intermixed with gravel; (6) deposits are arranged in linear bands parallel to the coastline; (7) beach conglomerates are well cemented, in modern and ancient deposits; (8) land-derived logs and stumps and land-derived sediments are present; and (9) wind ripple marks and excellent sorting is present locally.

The deltaic zone has the following characteristics: (1) sandstones are arranged in linear bodies and are well sorted, with low textural range; (2) foreset dips (even in excess of 35°) are prevalent in the direction of streamflow; (3) lenses, pockets, and thin layers of carbonaceous shales are present; (4) much vegetation is derived from land; (5) there are rapid lateral and vertical lithologic changes; (6) tree stumps may occur in growth position; (7) mixtures of marine and nonmarine fossils are present; (8) there is a high textural range, except for localized thin units; (9) there are various sedimentary structures: scour, ball-and-pillow, burrowed units, roll-and-plunge, and slump overturning; (10) channel cut-and-fill features are present; (11) coarse-textured sediments grade into finer textured sediments; and (12) localized lacustrine deposits are present.

Nonmarine environment. The nonmarine environment consists of the lacustrine, eolian, fluvial, and glacial realms. The lacustrine realm (nearshore) has the following characteristics: (1) sediments are medium to coarse textured (sandstones to conglomerates); (2) there is a high textural range (boulders to clay—conglomerates to shales); (3) there is a strong contrast in bed thickness and areal extent; (4) some well-sorted pockets, lenses, and thin beds are present; (5) cross-bedding is characteristic; (6) fossils from surf or high-energy realm and some from land are present; (7) shingle gravels may be present; (8) there are contrasting vertical and lateral lithologic changes; (9) stratification planes may dip in all directions; (10) marsh mucks, delta lobes, channel cut-and-fill structures are present; (11) units are not uniformly thick or of areal extent; and (12) washed-in land plants (stumps, logs, and leaves) are present.

In areas of still water the lacustrine realm will exhibit different characteristics, which may be summarized as follows: (1) material is fine textured, and siltstones, shales, and mudstones are common; (2) there is a low textural range (silt to clay), except where turbidity currents have introduced coarse materials from land or nearshore; (3) definite, well-sorted layers and varves are common; (4)

laminae and beds are rather uniform in thickness; (5) fossil fish, bivalves, and other organisms of lake origin are present; (6) sediment is distributed continuously over large or small areas, according to the size of the lake; (7) evaporites and saline sediments may be present; (8) aphanic dolostones may be common; (9) oolites, pisolites, oncolites, and other accretionary limestone accumulations may be present; (10) tufa, travertine, and similar limestone buildups may be present; (11) bioherms are common and extensive; (12) montmorillonite clays are common; and (13) if present, illite clays contain little (ten to 50 parts per million) boron.

The
eolian,
fluvial,
and
glacial
environ-
ments The eolian realm has the following characteristics: (1) the textural range is low (fine-textured sandstones, extremely well sorted; if silty, well-sorted "adobes" or loess); (2) sediments are prominently cross-bedded into large-scale, sweeping, and festoon types; (3) they are sorted into irregular beds and lenses; (4) sediment is porous if original depositional fabric is preserved; (5) stratification planes are rarely horizontal and commonly dip up to 33°; (6) stratification planes may be crisscrossed and dip in all directions; (7) sand grains may display tiny pits resulting from sand blasting; (8) sand grains commonly are rounded to well rounded and spherical; (9) there is a strong contrast in thickness laterally and vertically; (10) fossils, if any, are of terrestrial forms; footprints may be present; and (11) ripple marks and raindrop imprints may show on cross-beds.

The fluvial realm has the following characteristics: (1) the textural range is high (blocks and boulders to mud or shale); (2) the sediment is nonsorted to poorly sorted; (3) it is lenticular in form—units thicken and thin rapidly and change in lithology; (4) channel sands and cut-and-fill structures are common; (5) log jams and logs in ancient stream channels may be common; (6) lenses and pockets of gravel may occur in fine sediment; (7) the sediment is distributed in belts (river flats and piedmont alluvial plains); some beds are linear "shoestring" sands with definite trends as distributaries or master-channel deposit; (8) when discrete sands of shoestring nature are mappable, a prevailing one-direction dip is characteristic; only locally are small opposing dips present; (9) the deposit diminishes in thickness uniformly in the direction of the divergence of dips; (10) lithologically, the sediment is likely to be heterogeneous; and (11) fossils, if present, are disarticulated, broken, and highly mixed.

The glacial realm has the following characteristics: (1) sediment is heterogeneous and largely nonsorted and may rest on glacially striated bedrock; (2) there is a high textural range, ranging from rock flour to unusually large blocks and boulders; (3) there is no stratification, except by glaciofluvial streams or as varves in glacial lakes; (4) most sediment is angular to subangular, unless derived from an already rounded conglomerate or gravel; (5) variation in thickness within short distances is unusually high; (6) sediment commonly is foreign to the area of outcrop (e.g., granitic and metamorphic rocks may occur far from their source area); (7) large angular and subangular blocks enclosed in tillites may display striations; (8) bases of glacial deposits contrast sharply with the substrate on which they rest; (9) deposits may contain paleosols (i.e., buried soil horizons); and (10) fossils, if any, are of terrestrial origin, save for fossils ripped from sediments over which the glacial material was transported.

DISTRIBUTION OF SEDIMENTARY ROCKS THROUGH TIME

Precam-
brian
through
Cenozoic
sediments **Rock-type variation.** Some of the oldest sedimentary rocks are of clastic origin; conglomerates dated in excess of 3,500,000,000 years old are known in Rhodesia. Other coarse-textured sedimentary rocks (or their metamorphic equivalents, the metaconglomerates) occur in many parts of the Earth. Sandstones (and their metamorphic equivalent, metaquartzites) and some carbonate rocks also are common in the Precambrian record (older than 570,000,000 years).

Sedimentary rocks of the Paleozoic Era (from 225,000,000 to 570,000,000 years ago) compose a vast spectrum of sandstones (commonly in the Lower Cambrian), shales, limestones, and dolostones. Lower Cambrian rocks commonly are sandstones, succeeded upward by shales, limestones, and dolostones. This oversimplified pattern is repeated at many places on Earth. Ordovician rocks (430,000,000 to 500,000,000 years old) are quite shaley, and the graptolite-bearing dark shales are common to many continents. Limestones and dolostones are abundant, and sandstones are less so in these marine sequences. Throughout the Silurian (395,000,000 to 430,000,000 years ago) and Devonian (345,000,000 to 395,000,000 years ago) periods much carbonate sediment was deposited—limestones and dolostones, with lesser amounts of sandstone and shale. During Late Paleozoic time (225,000,000 to 345,000,000 years ago) there accumulated much shale, limestone, sandstone, and ortho-quartzite (the latter is a fine-grained, tightly silica-cemented quartz sandstone), with minor dolostone. Of great significance is the presence of thick and areally extensive beds of workable coal at many places on various continents; the Upper Carboniferous (about 290,-000,000 years ago) is rich in economically valuable coal seams in North America, the British Isles, Europe, Asia, Australia, and Antarctica. Limestones, which underlie coal-bearing shales and sandstones in North America, are locally valuable as building stones. Many of the Paleozoic limestones, dolostones, and sandstones are rich in oil and gas.

Rocks of the Mesozoic Era (from 225,000,000 to 65,-000,000 years ago) include thick and extensive sandstones and shales, with thick conglomerates in some places. In other localities limestones are important. Numerous Triassic sedimentary rocks (190,000,000 to 225,000,000 years old) are reddish in colour and are termed red beds; the colour results mainly from the presence of admixed iron oxide compounds. Jurassic strata (136,000,000 to 190,000,000 years old) range from clay shales through siltstones, sandstones, and conglomerates. Limestones, interestingly enough, are very fine textured (micrite) on some continents, and those that contain clay are useful in production of cement. Evaporites (halite, potash, gypsum, and other salt deposits) are also present in Jurassic rocks. Cretaceous sedimentary rocks (65,-000,000 to 136,000,000 years old) contain thick sandstone, shale, conglomerate, and coal beds. Chalky sediments are present in the Cretaceous of Britain and in some other parts of the world.

During the Cenozoic Era (the last 65,000,000 years) great thicknesses of coarse- and medium-textured clastic rocks formed in many localities in subsiding depositional sites throughout the world. Shale, limestone, dolostone, and evaporites also formed. Nonmarine sediments of eolian, pluvial, fluvial, paludal, and lacustrine origin accumulated in continental-interior areas.

Few general summary statements can be made about glacial deposits. Continental ice sheets affected portions of the Northern Hemisphere during the Late Precambrian and the Pleistocene Epoch (from 10,000 to 2,500,000 years ago) and left evidence of their presence in the form of till and tillite deposits and glacial scratches during the Permian in parts of India, Australia, Antarctica, South Africa, South America, and a few other places. Wind action seems to have been at work throughout the geologic past, and some of the better known eolian deposits of the geologic column (the record of the rocks) include some Permian and Jurassic rocks. Marine deposits are characteristic of the Paleozoic and Mesozoic and on peripheral parts of most continents for the Cenozoic.

Geosyncline in the Gulf of Mexico

Rates of accumulation. The total thickness of some of the Cenozoic sedimentary rocks of the northern Gulf of Mexico that have been penetrated by drilling operations is more than 6,000 metres (20,000 feet). The total thickness of Cenozoic sedimentary rocks in this region, which have much clastic material, may be as great as 12,000 metres (40,000 feet). The duration of the Cenozoic Era was about 65,000,000 years, and a rate of sediment accumulation can therefore be obtained by simple division. Sedimentation in the Gulf of Mexico has probably not been uniform from day to day during the past 65,000,000 years; times of accelerated dumping of sediment into this

sinking geosyncline probably have alternated with times of reduced increment of materials. Furthermore, if compaction is not yet complete, the thickness value of 12,000 metres should be reduced somewhat. Nevertheless, on the average there has been a bit more than 0.0002 metre (0.0006 foot) of deposition per year (two metres in 10,-000 years) in this area.

For some Paleozoic sections, sampled from various places on different continents, the rate of sedimentation is estimated to have ranged from about 70 metres (230 feet) to as much as 800 metres (2,500 feet) per million years of geologic time. An average rate of about 200 metres (600 feet) per million years is realistic, and this is comparable to the Gulf of Mexico calculation.

Rate of sediment accumulation are not the same for every depositional site, nor do they maintain unusually rapid or unusually slow rates throughout all of geologic time. An illustration of this fact is found in the total Permian System exposed near the Hermit Trail in the Grand Canyon. The thickness is slightly less than 550 metres (1,800 feet), which gives an accumulation rate of roughly 11 metres (35 feet) per million years. The complete Permian section crops out just east of Las Vegas, Nevada, however, where the total thickness is about 2,100 metres (7,000 feet)—an accumulation rate of 40 metres (140 feet) per million years for the same system. The reason for this seeming disparity is that during the Permo-Triassic time what is now the Grand Canyon was a shelf, and the area to the west, near Las Vegas, was a different kind of depositional site—a geosyncline that subsided faster than the Grand Canyon shelf, thus permitting the accumulation of more sediment.

Sedimentary models. In any sedimentary environment, the sediment is derived from some source area, it is transported to the site of deposition by some agent, it is deposited, and under suitable conditions it may then be affected by organisms in the environment. This sequence has been formally designated a sedimentary model, one that can be further organized into a process–response environmental model; that is, certain processes and conditions lead to certain consequences, or responses. In this case, the process elements are the geometry, materials, energy, and biological elements of the environment, and the response elements are the geometry of the deposits, the properties of the sediments formed, and the areal variations in the sedimentary properties.

Process–response models

Perhaps hundreds of examples could be cited, but an outstanding one is the Queantoweap Sandstone (Permian), which is superbly exposed in the walls of the Grand Canyon of the Colorado River and from there westerly in outcrops and quarries west and southwest of Las Vegas. The boundary that encloses the outcropping Queantoweap Sandstone involves the Esplanade along the Grand Canyon region and proceeds westerly into southern Nevada in a relatively narrow band in a north–south direction but of considerable east–west extent. The geometry of the environment, therefore, is that of a delta plain across which mid-Permian streams meandered, developing delta lobes as the streams transported sand westerly toward the geosyncline that lay to the west in Nevada. The materials of the environment included mostly fine- to medium-grained quartz sand, which was washed clean by the energy of waves and currents in this environment. Biological entities included burrowing organisms, which churned up some of the sediment, particularly west and southwest of Las Vegas; there, the westerly flowing streams and currents during Permian time veered toward the south and progressively extended the delta lobes into a trough-like basin in the ancient geosyncline. Various organisms were effective in modifying the sediments there.

In response to the foregoing process elements, the westerly delta lobes formed superb cross-bedded clean quartz sandstones. By plotting the direction of inclination of the cross-strata (in this case, mostly westerly almost to Las Vegas), a determination of the direction of ancient current flow is made possible. Also, by mapping and plotting the areal extent of the outcropping Queantoweap and by measuring the thickness of the entire formation, a three-dimensional model results. West of Las Vegas, the azimuth of dip direction of cross-beds gradually but perceptibly changes, and foresets dip in a general southerly direction. Furthermore, numerous sedimentary structures such as ball-and-pillow, plunge-and-flow, flame structures, slump-and-overturn, and many others are developed. In general, foreset bedding defines the direction of the stream and other current flow from east to west out of what is now the Grand Canyon region nearly as far as Las Vegas; then these currents plunged into a linear downwarp or trough of the geosyncline and filled this trough from north to south. Sands were cleaned by the current winnowing of clay and silt, and in some places pure quartz sandstones are preserved in the outcrops as thin- to thick-bedded units.

Areal variations in the sedimentary properties of the Queantoweap Sandstone from the Grand Canyon region to the present Spring Mountains southwest of Las Vegas are not unusually striking. The easternmost outcrops are not as clean (i.e., finer material is admixed with the sands) as those farther west, and most sedimentary structures are those of small-scale cross-bedding. Progressively westward and thence southerly, the sandstones are better sorted, are cleaner, and have a low textural range. By contrast to those farther east, they display numerous sole markings and other sedimentary structures. Also, the formation progressively becomes thicker in overall vertical dimension from east to west.

BIBLIOGRAPHY. F.J. PETTIJOHN, *Sedimentary Rocks*, 2nd ed. (1957), a comprehensive, modern text that discusses and classifies all types of sedimentary rocks and treats various of their properties, with a bibliography at the end of each chapter; W.C. KRUMBEIN and L.L. SLOSS, *Stratigraphy and Sedimentation*, 2nd ed. (1963), a modern text that discusses and classifies sedimentary rocks relating them to the twin subject of stratigraphy, with emphasis on properties of sedimentary rocks and sedimentary processes, environments, and sedimentary tectonics, with a bibliography at the end of each chapter; HOWELL WILLIAMS, FRANCIS J. TURNER, and CHARLES M. GILBERT, *Petrography* (1954), discusses and classifies igneous, metamorphic, and sedimentary rocks; ALBERT V. CAROZZI, *Microscopic Sedimentary Petrography* (1960), a fairly recent text that discusses sedimentary rocks both petrologically (field) and petrographically (laboratory), including a list of references at the end of each chapter; ROBERT E. CARVER, (ed.), *Procedures in Sedimentary Petrology* (1971), a modern up-to-date text that treats in an excellent manner the procedures that should be followed in any investigation of sedimentary rocks, with 29 outstanding scholars each contributing a section of his specialty, including lists of references at the end of each section.

(H.J.Bi.)

Sediment Yield of Drainage Systems

Definitions and governing factors

When precipitation falls on the Earth's surface, that part of the total that does not evaporate or infiltrate into the soil is runoff. As it moves over the land surface, the runoff carries sediment eroded from the hillslopes. This water and the entrained sediment move for relatively short distances before they become concentrated and collected in stream channels. The network of streams that collect the runoff and its sediment load and that provide an efficient means of draining away the runoff is a drainage system. A drainage system is composed of a stream and its tributaries, to which water and sediment are contributed from the drainage area or drainage basin of the stream system (Figure 1). The rim of the basin or the boundary between adjacent drainage basins is the drainage divide. Each drainage basin has its own divide that delineates the drainage area of that stream system, the area from which both runoff and sediment are derived.

Drainage basins can be of any size, and they range from a few acres in areas with poorly defined divides to truly continental features (Table 1). The Continental Divide of the United States, for example, located largely on the crest of the Rocky Mountains, forms the boundary between the drainage basins of the Mississippi–Missouri river system and the Columbia, Colorado, and Rio Grande river systems. The drainage systems of major rivers are composed of smaller units, such as the third-order drainage system shown in Figure 1.

The individual channels of a system are frequently classified by number. Channels that receive no tributary contribution are first-order streams. The junction of two first-order streams forms a second-order stream, and so on. Of course, each small first-order stream has its own drainage area and drainage divide (Figure 1). Within this

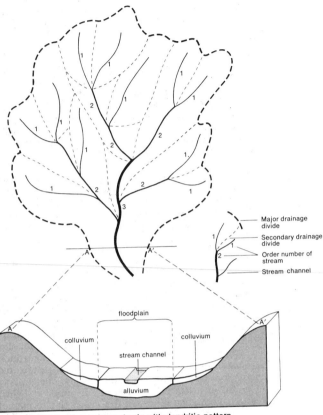

Figure 1: Third-order drainage basin with dendritic pattern (see text).

drainage area are the components of the drainage basin, hillslopes or valley-side slopes and stream channels.

Climate, morphology of the basin, rock type, and soil characteristics influence both runoff and the total quantity of surface water and sediment moving out of a drainage basin. The quantity of sediment moving through a specific cross section on a stream is the sediment yield of the drainage basin above that point. Sediment yield is, therefore, the total quantity of sediment exported from a drainage basin. Depending on the size of the basin, sediment yield may be almost negligible or it may amount to hundreds of tons of sediment per year (Table 1).

The sediment yield of drainage basins—both large and small—is of considerable economic as well as aesthetic

Importance to man

Table 1: Rivers of the World Ranked by Sediment Yield

	location	total drainage area (10³ sq mi)	average annual suspended load (000 tons)
Huang Ho	China	288	2,080,000
Ganges	India	369	1,600,000
Brahmaputra	Bangladesh	257	800,000
Yangtze	China	756	550,000
Indus	Pakistan	450	480,000
Ching (Huang Ho tributary)	China	22	450,000
Amazon	Brazil	2,722	400,000
Mississippi	U.S.	1,244	344,000
Irrawaddy	Burma	159	330,000
Missouri (Mississippi tributary)	U.S.	529	240,000
Lo (Huang Ho tributary)	China	10	210,000
Kosi (Ganges tributary)	India	24	190,000
Mekong	Vietnam	307	187,000
Colorado	U.S.	246	149,000
Red	Vietnam	46	143,000
Nile	Egypt	1,293	122,000

concern to man, especially in those areas where sediment yields are high. Large quantities of sediment moving out of drainage basins during floods may shorten the life of reservoirs, permanently damage agricultural lands, partially or completely fill stream or irrigation channels, destroy the spawning grounds of fish, and—perhaps of most immediate concern—partly fill one's residence with mud, silt, and sand.

Large sums of money are spent annually in an effort to decrease sediment yields or to restore property damaged by sediment deposition to its former value and use. The sediment yield of a drainage basin is one of a host of modern environmental factors of concern to the land manager, geologist, forester, civil engineer, and citizen.

This article treats the measurement of sediment yield, the sources of sediment and nature of deposition, and the variability of sediment yield in terms of the causative factors—*i.e.*, climate, soils and vegetation, and drainage basin morphology. The sediment-yield data employed in this article are largely derived from studies made in the United States. This is because records of long term are required for statistically valid conclusions, and such records are largely unobtainable elsewhere in the world.

For further information on the transportation of sediment by flowing water, see RIVERS AND RIVER SYSTEMS; FLUVIAL PROCESSES. See also HILL SLOPES; SOILS; WEATHERING; and EARTH MOVEMENTS ON SLOPES for insight into the origins of sediment; and LANDFORM EVOLUTION for a discussion of the consequences of the erosion processes involved. The article PHYSIOGRAPHIC EFFECTS OF MAN is of particular relevance with respect to the results of urbanization on sediment yield that are cited herein.

MEASUREMENT OF SEDIMENT YIELD AND SEDIMENT LOAD

The sediment yield of a drainage basin is expressed generally in two ways: either as a volume or as a weight—that is, as acre-feet (one-foot depth of material over one acre) or as tons. In order to adjust for the very different sizes of drainage basins, the yield frequently is expressed as a volume or weight per unit area of drainage basin—that is, as acre-feet per square mile or as tons per acre or as tons per square mile. The conversion between the two forms of expression is made by obtaining an average weight for the sediment (usually between 80 and 100 pounds per cubic foot) and calculating the total weight from the measured volume of sediment. Further, sediment yield is usually measured during a period of years, and the results are therefore expressed as an annual average—that is, as acre-feet or tons per square mile per year.

The sediment delivered to and transported by a stream is its sediment load. This can be classified into three types, depending on sediment size and the competence of the river. The coarsest sediment, consisting of boulders and cobbles as well as sand, moves on or near the bed of the stream and is the bed load of the river. The finer particles, silts and clays, are carried in suspension by the turbulent action of flowing water; and these fine particles, which are moved long distances at the velocity of the flowing water, comprise the suspended load of the river. The remaining component of the total sediment load is the dissolved load, which is composed of chemical compounds taken into solution by the water moving on or in the soils of the drainage basin. These three types of sediment comprise the total sediment load of the stream and, of course, the sediment yield of the drainage basin.

Measurement of the load The sediment load can be measured in different ways. Collection of water samples from a river and measurement of the sediment contained in each unit of water will, when sufficient samples have been taken and the water discharge from the system is known, permit calculation of annual sediment yield. Because sediment in a stream channel is transported in suspension, in solution, and as material rolling or moving very near the bed, the water samples will contain suspended and dissolved load and perhaps some bed load; but much of the bed load cannot be sampled by currently used techniques, as it moves too near the bed of a stream. It is fortunate, therefore, that the greatest part of the total sediment load is in the form of suspended load.

When a dam is constructed, the sediment transported by a stream is deposited in the still waters of the reservoir. In this case, both bed load and suspended load are deposited, but the dissolved load eventually moves out with the water released from the reservoir. Frequent, precise surveys of the configuration of the reservoir provide data on the volume of sediment that accumulates in the reservoir (Figure 2). Water samples can be taken to provide data

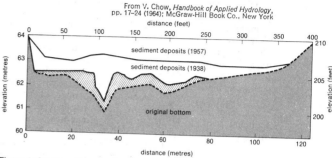

From V. Chow, *Handbook of Applied Hydrology*, pp. 17–24 (1964); McGraw-Hill Book Co., New York

Figure 2: Cross section of sediment deposits, Lake Barcroft, Virginia.

on the dissolved load transported into the reservoir; and when this quantity is added to the measurements of suspended and bed load, a reasonably accurate measure of sediment yield from the drainage basin above the reservoir can be obtained.

In areas where information on sediment yield is required but the necessary samples have not been taken (perhaps because of the infrequent occurrence of flow in ephemeral streams), estimates of sediment yields may be obtained from measurements of hillslope and channel erosion within the basin or by the evaluation of erosion conditions. As will be discussed later, certain characteristics of the drainage basin—such as the average slope of the basin or the number and spacing of drainage channels —may be used to provide an estimate of sediment yield.

All of the techniques utilized to measure sediment yield are subject to considerable error, but data sufficiently accurate for the design of water-regulatory structures can be obtained by sampling or by reconnaissance surveys of the drainage systems.

SOURCES OF SEDIMENT AND NATURE OF DEPOSITION

Erosion in drainage basins. The ultimate source of the sediment that is measured as sediment yield is the rock underlying the drainage basins. Until the rock is broken or weathered into fragments of a size that can be transported from the basin, the sediment yield will be low. The diverse mechanisms, both chemical and physical, that produce sediment and soil from rock are termed weathering processes. Depending on type of rock and type of weathering process, the result may be readily transported silts, clays, and sands or less easily transported cobbles and boulders.

Effects of weathering and breakdown of rocks

Most rocks have been fractured during the vicissitudes of geologic history, thereby permitting penetration of water and roots. Wedging by ice and growing roots produces blocks of rock that are then subject to further disintegration and decomposition by chemical and physical agencies. These rocks, if exposed on a hillslope, move slowly down the slope to the stream channel—the rate of movement depending on slope inclination; density of vegetation; frequency of freeze and thaw events; and the size, shape, and density of the materials involved. In addition, water moving through rocks and soil can dissolve soluble portions of rock or weathering products. This is especially important in limestone regions and in regions of warm, humid climate, where chemical decomposition of rocks is rapid and where the dissolved load of streams is at a maximum.

When sediment eroded from the hillslopes is not delivered directly to a channel, it may accumulate at the base of the slope to form a colluvial deposit (Figure 1). The sediment derived directly from the hillslope may be stored temporarily at the slope base; therefore, sediment

Sediment in storage

once set in motion does not necessarily move directly through the stream system. It is more likely, in fact, that a given particle of sediment will be stored as colluvium before moving into the stream. Even then, it may be stored as alluvium in the floodplain, bed, or bank of the stream for some time before eventually moving out of the drainage system. Thus there is a steady export of sediment from a drainage basin, but an individual grain of sediment may be deposited and eroded many times before it leaves the system.

The preceding suggests that, over a period of time, the total erosion within a drainage basin is greater than the sediment yield of the system. Proof of this statement is the fact that the quantity of sediment per unit area (area-feet or tons per mile) that leaves a drainage system decreases as the size of the drainage basin increases. This is partly explained by the decrease in stream gradient and basin relief in a downstream direction. That is, much sediment is produced in the steeper areas near drainage divides, and sediment production decreases downstream. Moreover, the increasing width of valleys and floodplains downstream and the decreasing gradient of the streams provide an increasing number of opportunities for sediment to be deposited and temporarily stored within the system.

Factors related to quantity of sediment Each of the components of the drainage system—hillslopes and channels—produces sediment; but the quantity provided by each will vary during the erosional development of the basin and during changes of the vegetational, climatic, and hydrologic character of the drainage system. Most rivers are flowing on the upper surface of an alluvial deposit, and considerable sediment therefore is stored in most river valleys. During great floods or during periods when floodplain vegetation is not an effective stabilizer of this sediment, large quantities may be flushed from the system as the channel widens and deepens. At these times, the sediment produced by stream-channel erosion is far greater than that produced by the hillslopes, and sediment yields will be far in excess of rates of hillslope erosion. Such cycles of rapid channel erosion or gullying and subsequent healing and deposition are common in arid and semi-arid regions.

Environments of deposition. It is clear that a great range of sediment sizes may be transported by a river. Sediment of small size (*e.g.*, suspended load), when set in motion by erosive agents, may be transported through a river system to the sea, where it may be deposited as a deep-sea clay. Most sedimentary particles, however, have a more eventful journey to their final resting place. (In a geologic context, this may be a temporary resting place; sediment, for example, when it reaches the coast, may be incorporated in a delta at the river mouth or be acted upon by tides, currents, and waves to become a beach deposit.)

Effects of climate and man on deposition If sediment is moved downstream into a progressively more arid environment, the probability of deposition is high. Thousands of feet of alluvial-fan deposits flank the mountains of the western United States, the basin-and-range terrain of Iran and Pakistan, and similar desert regions. In the arid climates of these areas, the sediment cannot be moved far, because the transporting medium—water—diminishes in a downstream direction as it infiltrates into the dry alluvium. In extremely arid regions, wind action may be important: the transport of sand-size and smaller sediment by wind may be the only significant mechanism for the transport within and out of some drainage systems in deserts.

Man's influence on river flow has become a major factor determining the place of deposition of sediment. The many dams that have been constructed for flood control, recreation, and power generation hold much of the sediment load of rivers in reservoirs. Furthermore, the contribution of sediment from the small upstream drainage systems has been decreased by the construction of stockwater reservoirs and various erosion-control techniques aimed at retaining both water and sediment in the headwater areas. Diversion of water for irrigation also decreases the supply of water available to transport sediment; and in many cases, the diversion actually moves

sediment out of the streams into irrigation canals and back onto the land.

Vast tonnages of sand and gravel, which have been deposited as floodplain and valley sediments, are being excavated and used in highway construction and all manner of concrete structures. This sediment is being permanently removed from the cycle of sediment movement and deposition.

FACTORS THAT INFLUENCE SEDIMENT YIELD

Of most concern to man are the factors that cause rapid rates of erosion and high sediment yields. The quantity and type of sediment moving through a stream channel are intimately related to the geology, topographic character, climate, vegetational type and density, and land use within the drainage basin. The geologic and topographic variables are fixed; but short-term changes in climatic conditions, vegetation, and land use produce abrupt alterations in the intensity of erosion processes and in sediment yields.

The sediment yield from any drainage system is calculated by averaging the data collected over a period of years (Table 1). It is, therefore, an average of the results of many different hydrologic events. The sediment yield for each storm or flood will vary, depending on the meteorological character of the storm event and the resulting hydrologic character of the floods. High-intensity storms may produce sediment yields well above the norm, whereas an equal amount of precipitation occurring over a longer period of time may yield relatively little sediment. During short spans of time (days or years), sediment yields may fluctuate greatly because of natural or man-induced accidents (floods and fires, for example); but over longer periods of time, the average sediment yield will be typical of the geologic and climatic character of a region.

Short-term variations. An example of a short-term change in sediment yield is provided by data on the sediment transported by the Colorado River in Arizona for the years 1926–54 (Figure 3). It is evident that sediment yield varied widely from year to year. It is greatest for years of highest runoff, but for a given amount of runoff, Drought-induced variations

By courtesy of the U.S. Geological Survey

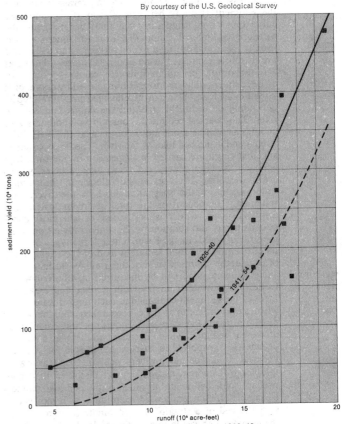

Figure 3: Relation of sediment yield and runoff for the 1926–40 and 1941–54 periods on the Colorado River at the Grand Canyon.

the maximum sediment yield may be twice the minimum sediment yield. These variations reflect the frequency of storms and their duration and intensity during the years of record.

Another interesting aspect of the relation is that in each of the years after 1940 the annual sediment load at the Grand Canyon was 50,000,000 to 100,000,000 tons less than would be expected on the basis of the curve fitted to the data for the period 1926–40 (Figure 3). This major decrease in sediment yield reflects some significant change in the hydrology of the Colorado River drainage basin. A study of the precipitation patterns for the years 1926–54 suggests that the change in the sediment yield–runoff relation beginning in 1941 is the result of a drought in the southwestern United States. The high-sediment-producing, weak-rock areas of the Colorado plateaus were affected by the drought; but the low-sediment-producing, hard-rock areas of the Rocky Mountains were not affected. Thus, during the years 1941–50 the amount of water delivered from the principal runoff-producing areas in Colorado, Wyoming, and northern Utah was normal; but runoff was considerably reduced from the high-sediment-producing areas in southern Utah and Arizona. The result was essentially normal runoff but greatly reduced sediment yield. Beginning in 1950 the drought encompassed the entire Colorado River Basin, and low runoff was recorded for the years 1950, 1951, 1953, and 1954; but the proportion of runoff produced by the high-sediment-producing areas remained low, as did the sediment yield.

It can be expected that sediment-yield rates will fluctuate with climatic variations. An average value of sediment yield obtained for a short period of record, therefore, may not provide a valid measure of the characteristic sediment yield to be expected over a longer period of years.

Variations induced by man and urbanization

A further example of short-term variation of sediment yield, in this case the result of man's activity on the landscape, is provided by data illustrating the change from natural conditions to conditions produced by upland farming and from farming conditions to urban conditions in the Piedmont region of the eastern United States. Sediment yields for forested regions normally are about 100 tons per square mile, and this was the case during the early part of the 19th century in this region (Figure 4). A

From M.G. Wolman, *Geografiska Annaler*, vol. 49 A, fig. 1, p. 386

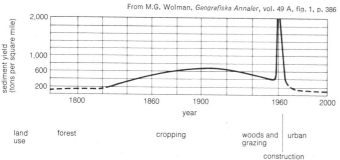

Figure 4: Schematic sequence of land use, sediment yield, and channel response from a fixed area.

significant increase in sediment yield occurred after 1820 as the land was occupied and farmed. During the period of intense farming, 1850–1930, the sediment yield reached 800 tons per square mile; but a decrease occurred between 1930 and 1960, as much land was permitted to revert to forest or grazing land. With the onset of construction and real estate development, however, vegetation was destroyed, and large quantities of sediment were eroded. The sediment yields for some small areas reached 2,000 tons per square mile during urbanization; but with the paving of streets, completion of sewage systems, and the planting of lawns, the sediment yields decreased markedly. In the future, they may eventually decrease to, or below the level of, the sediment-yield rates of natural conditions (pre-1810; Figure 4). This example demonstrates very clearly both long-term and short-term effects of man on sediment yield rates.

Another example of these short-term, man-induced fluctuations of sediment yield is provided by measurement of sediment accumulating in a reservoir in Fairfax County, Virginia (Figure 2). Before 1944 the sediment yield into the reservoir was about four acre-feet per square mile. At this time, the area was 76 percent pasture and woodland, with only 18 percent of the land under cultivation and 6 percent residential. After World War II, the population increased rapidly; and by 1953 much of the land formerly in pasture and woodland was converted to homesites, shopping centres, and streets; *e.g.*, 39 percent was pasture and woodland, less than 1 percent was cultivated, and 61 percent had become residential. Most of this change occurred between 1947 and 1957. The result of this conversion was a sixfold increase in sediment yield rates to 25 acre-feet per year. The increase was rapid as the percentage of watershed area under construction increased; however, sediment-yield rates decreased quickly following the peak of construction, as streets were paved and lawns became established.

In any drainage basin, even one not affected unduly by man, short periods of high sediment yield will alternate with periods of little export of sediment. Prime examples are small drainage basins in arid or semi-arid regions, where sediment yield occurs only during and following precipitation. Runoff and sediment yield can be zero between storms but high during and immediately following precipitation.

Seasonal and accidental variations

Even temperature variations have been demonstrated to influence sediment transport and sediment yields. Cooler water is more viscous, and this decreases the fall velocity of sediment particles and enables the stream to transport a larger amount of sediment. The sediment load of the Colorado River, for example, is greater during winter months because of this effect.

The disastrous effect of fire on sediment yields may be seen in the example of the conditions that followed a major storm and flood in the steep drainage basins of the San Gabriel and San Bernardino mountains of California in 1938. Maximum vegetational cover on these drainage basins is only 65 percent at best, and they are notoriously high sediment producers under the most favourable conditions. Sediment-yield rates were established for several drainage basins that had been subjected to fires as recently as one year before the storm and as long as 15 years before the storm. The results shown (Figure 5) further demonstrate the great effect of vegetational disturbance on sediment yields; for example, a drainage area with only 40 percent of the area burned had a 340 percent increase in sediment yield if the fire occurred one year before the storm. According to the information provided, the burned area one year after the fire had a 10 percent vegetational cover. Obviously, a storm immediately following the fire would have had even more disastrous consequences. Three years after the burn, a 35 percent vegetation cover had been established on the burned area, and sediment yields decreased markedly to only twice the yield preceding the fire. After seven years a 45 percent cover had been established on the burned area, and sediment yields were only 50 percent greater than preburn values. After 15 years, a 55 percent vegetal cover had been established, and sediment yields were almost normal. The decrease in sediment yield with increased plant cover is apparent. It is also obvious that an average value of sediment yield from a burned drainage basin for a 15-year period would be meaningless; with progressive re-establishment of vegetation, sediment-yield rates progressively decrease with time.

Long-term or average sediment yield. It has been estimated that modern sediment loads of the rivers draining to the Atlantic Ocean may be four to five times greater than the prehistoric rates because of man's influence. Even where man's influence is large, however, it is possible to recognize several other independent variables that exert a major influence on long-term sediment yield. These variables can be grouped into three main classes: geologic, geomorphic, and climatic–vegetational.

The major geologic influence on sediment yield is through lithology or the composition and physical prop-

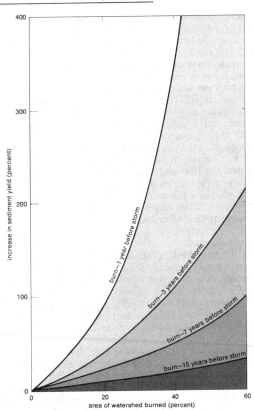

Figure 5: Increase in the sediment yields of southern California drainage basins following the 1938 storm. The several curves show the percentage increase in sediment yield in relation to the area burned and the date of burning (see text).

From Anderson and Trobitz, *Journal of Forestry*, vol. 47, p. 347 (1949)

rates apparently is caused primarily by the increasing percentage of precipitation that flows on the surface and causes erosion. Soils derived from the Wasatch Formation are extremely permeable, whereas the weathered and unweathered earth materials associated with the White River Group of sediments are highly impermeable.

Table 2: Sediment Yield from Rock Units of Cheyenne River Basin

rock unit	average annual sediment yield (ac-ft per sq mi)
Wasatch Formation (sandstone)	0.13
Lance Formation (sandy shale)	0.50
Fort Union Formation (sandstone and shale)	1.30
Pierre Shale Formation	1.40
White River Group (claystone)	1.80

Most drainage areas are composed of more than one rock type. In some areas, the sedimentary rocks have been folded, and rocks of different resistance are exposed, with hard rocks forming ridges and mountains and weak rocks forming valleys. The erosional development of such a terrain is complex, and the sediment produced by such a drainage basin will reflect the complex geologic situation, the greater part of the sediment yield being derived from the areas underlain by the rocks that are most susceptible to erosion.

Geomorphic variables

The character of the topography of a drainage basin significantly influences the quantity and type of runoff and sediment yield. The steeper a slope, the greater is the gravitational force acting to remove earth materials from the slope. In fact, the rate of movement of rocks and soil particles is directly related to the sine of the angle of slope inclination.

Steep slopes are readily eroded, and it follows that drainage basins with a great range of relief or steep average slope will produce not only higher sediment yields but coarser sediment. The average slope of a drainage basin can be expressed simply as a ratio of basin relief to basin length. Sediment yields increase exponentially with an increase in this relief–length ratio.

Another important characteristic of a drainage system is the spacing and distribution of drainage channels within the drainage basin (Figure 1). This is referred to as the texture of the topography, and it can be described by a ratio of total channel length to drainage area. This ratio is the drainage density of the system. A drainage density of five indicates that five miles of channel occur for every square mile of drainage basin. This number is an index of the efficiency of the drainage system; that is, high drainage density indicates numerous, closely spaced channels that provide an escape route for both runoff and its entrained sediment load.

When relief–length ratio (r), expressing the role of gravity, is combined with drainage density (d), expressing the efficiency of the drainage system, this yields a texture-slope product (rd), a parameter that describes the gross morphology of a drainage system. Hence it is not surprising that it is closely related to sediment yield of small drainage basins of similar geology and land use.

The relation between the texture-slope product and sediment yield is such that a high sediment yield can be expected from basins with a large drainage density and steep slope. For basins with similar relief–length ratios, those with the highest drainage density produce the greater quantity of sediment. In general, however, the basins with the highest drainage density are also those with the steepest slope.

Many geomorphic characteristics can be related to sediment yield, but it can be stated with assurance that the steeper and the better drained the system, the greater will be the quantity of sediment produced per unit area.

The relationship may be used to estimate yield from other drainage basins in the region from which these data were obtained. Similar relations may be developed for other regions when sufficient geomorphic data become available.

Influence of rock type and soils

erties of rocks and their resistance to weathering and erosion. An easily weathered and eroded shale, siltstone, or poorly cemented sandstone will provide relatively large quantities of sediment, whereas a lava flow, a well-cemented sandstone, or metamorphic and igneous rocks produce negligible quantities of transportable sediment. The highest known sediment yields that have been recorded are produced by the erosion of unconsolidated silts (loess). Loess is readily eroded, especially when the protecting vegetational cover is disturbed, as has happened in the high-sediment-producing areas of western Iowa and the Huang Ho Basin of China.

In general, sediment yield from drainage systems underlain by granitic rocks is from one-fourth to one-half that of drainage basins underlain by sedimentary rocks. There are exceptions. Limestone, which may be a massive rock, is highly resistant to erosion in arid regions, where mechanical or physical weathering is dominant; but it is highly susceptible to chemical weathering, especially solution, in humid regions. Most of the earth material removed from a limestone terrain will be transported as dissolved load, with some suspended load derived from erosion of the residual soil.

Another factor of importance in determining erosion rates is the permeability of earth materials. When soils are permeable, much of the water delivered to the surface infiltrates and does not produce surface runoff, thereby inhibiting surface erosion. This condition is characteristic of very sandy soils. When, on the other hand, soil materials are of low permeability (*e.g.*, clayey soils), a greater part of the precipitation runs off on the surface, thereby causing greater erosion and higher sediment yields. An example of this effect is provided by the five lithologic units underlying the Cheyenne River basin in eastern Wyoming. Each geologic formation is listed (Table 2) in order of decreasing permeability and infiltration capacity of the soils that were developed on these geologic units. All five of the units are relatively weak sedimentary rocks; therefore, the difference in sediment yield

In all studies, the sediment yield per unit area has been found to decrease as the size of the drainage basin increases. This reflects the previously discussed downstream decrease in gradient and slope, and the increase in area available for temporary storage of sediment. Thus total sediment yield per unit area invariably is related inversely to drainage area (Table 3). This relation can

Table 3: Effect of Size of Drainage Basins on Unit Sediment Yield	
basin size (sq mi)	average annual sediment yield (ac-ft per sq mi)
Under 10	3.8
10–100	1.6
100–1000	1.0
Over 1,000	0.5

also be detected among the data in Table 1. Other factors are involved, of course, but the largest drainage basins listed do not produce the largest quantity of sediment per unit area of drainage basin.

The morphology of a drainage basin is significantly related to sediment yield, but sufficient research has not yet been done to enable prediction of sediment yields from drainage basins in the diverse regions of the world.

Relationship between climatic and vegetational influences

It is difficult to separate the influences of climate and vegetation on erosion and sediment yield, because the primary effect of climate on sediment yield is determined by the interaction between vegetation and runoff. This effect is displayed by the contrast between the dissolved load and the suspended load and bed load transported by streams. Dissolved load increases from a negligible amount in arid regions to 150 tons per square mile in humid regions, where chemical weathering and groundwater contribution to river flow is greatest. The dense vegetational cover of humid regions retards runoff and aids infiltration, thereby enhancing the effects of chemical decomposition of the rocks and soils to produce soluble material. The available data also show a sharp increase in sediment yield (suspended and bed load) as precipitation increases from low to moderate amounts (Figure 6). In

From S. Schumm, *The Quaternary of the United States* (1965); Princeton University Press

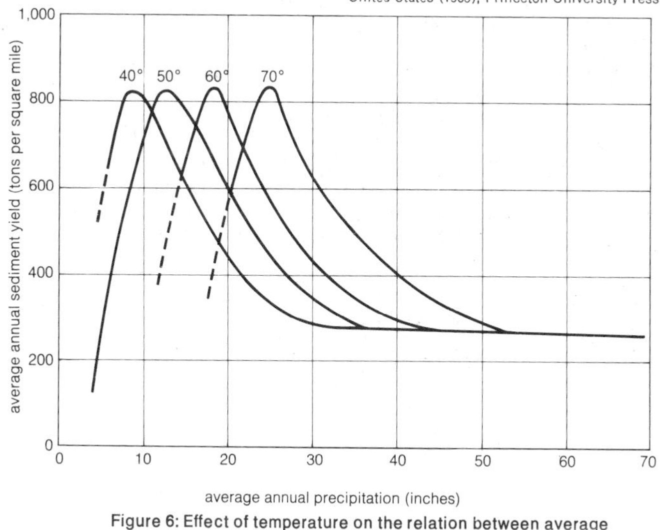

Figure 6: Effect of temperature on the relation between average annual sediment yield and mean annual precipitation.

semi-arid regions, however, the increase of vegetation density with increased precipitation exerts a significant influence on erosion; and sediment transport and sediment yield decrease as the climate becomes increasingly humid (Figure 6). This relationship can, of course, be significantly modified by man's activities. As the previously mentioned effect of urbanization demonstrates, removal of vegetation from the land in humid regions greatly accelerates erosion, and it may increase sediment yield to the maximum expected in semi-arid regions.

The graphs (Figure 6) also show the effects of average temperature on sediment yields. The hotter the climate, the more water is lost to evapotranspiration, and the critical zone where vegetation becomes dominant consequently shifts to areas of higher precipitation.

The effect of vegetational cover on sediment yield has been discussed previously for areas where fires have destroyed much of the cover and catastrophically increased erosion and export of sediment from the system (Figure 5). Additional data on the effect of vegetation on erosion rates reveal that with a 65 percent plant cover little erosion will occur, but as plant cover decreases erosion increases significantly. This relation may appear to be in conflict with that of Figure 6, which shows low sediment yields occurring in very arid regions, where vegetation cover should be least. It is true that the sediment concentration in the runoff from these arid regions is great, but runoff occurs so infrequently that the total quantity of sediment moved out of the system each year is scant.

Although erosion increases greatly with a decrease in plant cover between 20 percent and 15 percent, it cannot continue to increase at this high rate. At some point, the maximum rate of erosion of the soil will be achieved, and the curve will bend sharply to the left to intercept the vertical axis of the graph. At some value of low-plant-cover density, the influence of vegetation must be negligible; erosion then will be determined only by soil erodibility.

Although average precipitation significantly influences vegetation type and density and the sediment yield, it has been demonstrated that, for a given quantity of annual precipitation, sediment yields will be greatest where highly seasonal (e.g., monsoonal) climates prevail. Precipitation, when concentrated during a few months of the year, produces large quantities of sediment because of the higher intensity of the precipitation events and the long dry season when vegetational cover is weakened by drought.

Climate also plays a role in determining the type of sediment produced by a drainage basin. A study of the type of sediment deposited on the inner continental shelf reveals that the type of sediment (mud, sand, or gravel) is indeed influenced by climate. Mud, for example, is most abundant off shores of high temperature and rainfall, where chemical weathering is important. Gravel is common off areas of both low temperature and rainfall, where mechanical weathering is dominant. Sand is found everywhere, but it is most abundant in areas of moderate climate and in arid areas. Average temperature also may be important where the annual temperature is below the freezing point.

The preceding discussion of sediment yields has dealt solely with drainage basins subject to the common fluvial processes; however, in high mountains and at high latitudes, glaciers may occupy a drainage basin. The sediment yields from basins containing glaciers are significantly higher than from similar basins without glaciers. An unglaciated drainage basin in the Austrian Alps, for example, has an annual sediment yield of 91 tons per square mile, whereas an adjacent basin, 46 percent of which is occupied by a glacier, produces 3,900 tons per square mile of sediment annually.

BIBLIOGRAPHY. VEN TE CHOU (ed.), *Handbook of Applied Hydrology* (1964), contains 29 sections on all aspects of the hydrologic cycle. Chapters relevant to the topic of sediment yield are the following: H.A. EINSTEIN, "River Sedimentation," sect. 17, pt. 2, pp. 35–67; L.C. GOTTSCHALK, "Reservoir Sedimentation," sect. 17, pt. 1, pp. 1–34; and A.N. STRAHLER, "Quantitative Geomorphology of Drainage Basins and Channel Networks," sect. 4, pt. 2, pp. 39–76. R.J. CHORLEY (ed.), *Water, Earth, and Man: A Synthesis of Hydrology, Geomorphology, and Socio-Economic Geography* (1969), contains 37 chapters by 25 authors. Of special interest are the following: D.R. STODDART, "World Erosion and Sedimentation," pp. 43–66; R.J. CHORLEY, "The Drainage Basin as the Fundamental Geomorphic Unit," pp. 77–100; M.J. KIRKBY, "Erosion by Water on Hillslopes," pp. 229–238; and M.A. MORGAN, "Overland Flow and Man," pp. 239–258. UNITED STATES DEPARTMENT OF AGRICULTURE, *Proceedings of the Federal Interagency Sedimentation Conference, 1963* (1965), includes information on land erosion and control, sediment in streams, sedimentation in estuaries, harbours, and coastal areas, and sedimentation in reservoirs. J.J. HOLEMAN, "The Sediment Yield of Major Rivers of the World," *Wat. Resour. Res.*, 4:737–747 (1968), is a compilation of data on the sediment yield from all parts of the world.

(S.A.S.)

Seed and Fruit

A seed is the characteristic reproductive body of both angiosperms (flowering plants) and gymnosperms (conifers, cycads, and ginkgos). Essentially, it consists of a miniature, undeveloped plant (the embryo), which, alone or in the company of stored food for its early development after germination, is surrounded by a protective coat (the testa). Frequently small in size and making negligible demands upon their environment, seeds are eminently suited to perform a wide variety of functions the relationships of which are not always obvious: multiplication, perennation (surviving seasons of stress such as winter), dormancy (a state of arrested development), and dispersal. Pollination and the "seed habit" are considered the most important factors responsible for the overwhelming evolutionary success of the flowering plants, which number more than 300,000 species.

The superiority of dispersal by means of seeds over the more primitive method involving single-celled spores, lies mainly in two factors: the stored reserve of nutrient material that gives the new generation an excellent growing start and the seed's multicellular structure, which provides ample opportunity for the development of adaptations for dispersal, such as plumes for wind dispersal, barbs, and others.

Economically, seeds (and the fruits that contain them) are important primarily because they provide man with his most important foods; for example, the cereal grains, such as wheat, rice, and maize; the seeds of beans, peas, peanuts, soybeans, almonds, sunflowers, hazelnuts, walnuts, pecans, and Brazil nuts; the fruits of date palm, olive, banana, avocado, apple, and orange. Many fruits, especially those in the citrus family—limes, lemons, oranges, grapefruits—are rich in vitamin C (ascorbic acid); unpolished cereal grains in vitamin B_1 (thiamine); and wheat germ in vitamin E. Other useful products provided by seeds and fruits are abundant. Oils for cooking, margarine production, painting, and lubrication are available from the seeds of flax, rape, cotton, soybean, poppy, castor bean, coconut, sesame, safflower, the cereal grains of maize, and the fruits of olive and oil palm. Essential oils are obtained from such sources as juniper "berries," used in gin manufacture. Waxes such as those from bayberries (wax myrtles) and vegetable ivory from the hard fruits of a South American palm species are important products. Stimulants are obtained from such sources as the seeds of coffee, kola, guarana, and cocoa; and drugs, such as morphine, come from opium-poppy fruits. Spices—from mustard and nutmeg seeds; from the aril ("mace") covering the nutmeg seed; from fruits of anise, cumins, caraway, dill, vanilla, black pepper, red or chili pepper, allspice, and others—form a large group of economic products. Dyes (Persian berries, butternut brown, sap green) and ornaments (Job's tears from the grass *Coix*, used for curtains; *Abrus*, *Adenanthera*, and *Rhynchosia* seeds for necklaces; others for rosaries) are also provided by seeds and fruits.

GENERAL FEATURES

Seeds. *Angiosperm seeds.* In the typical flowering plant, or angiosperm, seeds are formed from bodies called ovules contained in the ovary, or basal part of the female plant structure, the pistil. The mature ovule contains in its central part a region called the nucellus that in turn contains an embryo sac with eight nuclei, each with one set of chromosomes (*i.e.*, they are haploid nuclei). The two nuclei near the centre are referred to as polar nuclei; the egg cell, or oosphere, is situated near the micropylar ("open") end of the ovule. With very few exceptions (*e.g.*, the dandelion), development of the ovule into a seed is dependent upon fertilization, which in turn follows pollination. Pollen grains that land on the receptive upper surface

(stigma) of the pistil will germinate, if they are of the same species, and produce pollen tubes, each of which grows down within the style (the upper part of the pistil) toward an ovule. The pollen tube has three haploid nuclei, one of them, the so-called vegetative, or tube, nucleus seems to direct the operations of the growing structure. The other two, the generative nuclei, can be thought of as nonmotile sperm cells. After reaching an ovule and breaking out of the pollen tube tip, one generative nucleus unites with the egg cell to form a diploid zygote (*i.e.*, a fertilized egg with two complete sets of chromosomes, one from each parent), which, through a limited number of divisions gives rise to an embryo. The other generative nucleus fuses with the two polar nuclei to produce a triploid (three sets of chromosomes) nucleus, which divides repeatedly before cell-wall formation occurs, producing the triploid endosperm, a nutrient tissue that contains a variety of storage materials—such as starch, sugars, fats, proteins, hemicelluloses, and phytic acid (a phosphate reserve). The events just described constitute what is called the double-fertilization process, one of the characteristic features of all flowering plants. In the orchids and in some other plants with minute seeds that contain no reserve materials, endosperm formation is completely suppressed. In other cases it is greatly reduced, but the reserve materials are present elsewhere—*e.g.*, in the cotyledons, or seed leaves, of the embryo, as in beans, lettuce, and peanuts, or in a tissue derived from the nucellus, the perisperm, as in coffee. Other seeds, such as those of beets, contain both perisperm and endosperm. The seed coat, or testa, is derived from the one or two protective integuments of the ovule. The ovary, in the simplest case, develops into a fruit. In many plants, such as the grasses and lettuce, the outer integument and ovary wall are completely fused, so that seed and fruit form one entity; thus seeds and fruits can logically be described together as "dispersal units," or diaspores. More often, however, the seeds are discrete units attached to the placenta on the inside of the fruit wall through a stalk, or funiculus. The hilum of a liberated seed is a small scar marking its former place of attachment. The short ridge (raphe) that sometimes leads away from the hilum is formed by the fusion of seed stalk and testa. In many seeds, the micropyle of the ovule also persists as a small opening in the seed coat. The embryo, variously located in the seed, may be very small (as in buttercups) or may fill the seed almost completely (as in roses and plants of the mustard family). It consists of a root part, or radicle, a prospective shoot (plumule or epicotyl), one or more cotyledons (one or two in flowering plants, several in *Pinus*), and a hypocotyl, which is a region that connects radicle and plumule (see Figure 1). A classification of seeds can be based on size and position of the embryo and on the proportion of embryo to storage tissue; the possession of either one or two cotyledons is considered crucial in rec-

Double fertilization in angiosperms

From (left) A.M. Mayer and A. Poljakoff-Mayber, *The Germination of Seeds* (1963); Pergamon Press Ltd.; (right) H.J. Fuller and O. Tippo, *College Botany*, revised edition, copyright 1954 by Holt, Rinehart & Winston, Inc.; reprinted by permission

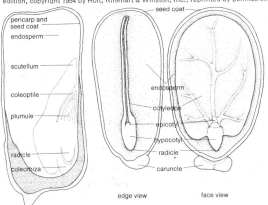

Figure 1: *Longitudinal sections of mature seeds.*
(Left) *Zea mays*, maize or Indian corn, a monocotyledonous caryopsis, or grain, which is actually both seed and fruit through the fusion of the seed coat with the ovary wall. (Centre and right) *Ricinus communis*, castor bean, a dicotyledonous seed, edge and face views.

ognizing two main groups of flowering plants, the Mono-cotyledones and Dicotyledones.

Seedlings, arising from embryos in the process of germination, are classified as epigeal (cotyledons above ground, usually green and capable of photosynthesis) and hypogeal (cotyledons below ground; see Figure 2). Particularly in the monocots, special absorbing organs may develop that mobilize the reserve materials and withdraw them from the endosperm; *e.g.*, in the grasses, the cotyledon has been modified into an enzyme-secreting scutellum ("shield") between embryo and endosperm.

From A.M. Mayer and A. Poljakoff-Mayber, *The Germination of Seeds* (1963); Pergamon Press Ltd.

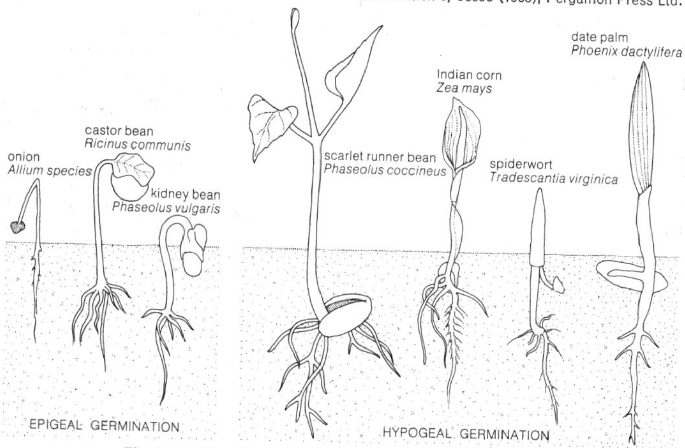

Figure 2: *Seedling morphology and germination modes.*
(Left) Epigeal germination. (Right) Hypogeal germination.

Gymnosperm seeds. In gymnosperms (plants with "naked seeds"—conifers, cycads, ginkgos) the ovules are not enclosed in an ovary but lie exposed on leaflike structures, the megasporophylls. A long time span separates pollination and fertilization, and the ovules begin to develop into seeds long before fertilization has been accomplished; in some cases, in fact, fertilization does not occur until the ovules ("seeds") have been shed from the tree. In the European pine *Pinus sylvestris*, for example, the female cones (essentially collections of megasporophylls) begin to develop in winter and are ready to receive pollen from the male cones in spring. During the first growing season, the pollen tube grows slowly through the nucellus, while within the ovule the megaspore nucleus, through a series of divisions, gives rise to a collection of some 2,000 nuclei, which are then individually enclosed by walls to form a structure called the female gametophyte or prothallus. At the micropylar end of the ovule, several archegonia (bottle-shaped female organs) develop, each containing an oosphere ("egg"). The pollen tube ultimately penetrates the neck of one of the archegonia. Not until the second growing season, however, does the nucleus of one of the male cells in the tube unite with the oosphere nucleus. Although more than one archegonium may be fertilized, only one gives rise to a viable embryo. During the latter's development, part of the prothallus is broken down and used. The remainder, referred to as "endosperm," surrounds the embryo; it is mobilized later, during germination of the seed, a process that occurs without delay when the seeds are liberated from the female cone during the third year after their initiation.

Fruits. The concept "fruit" is based on such an odd mixture of practical and theoretical considerations that it accommodates cases in which one flower gives rise to several fruits (larkspur) as well as cases in which several flowers cooperate in producing one fruit (mulberry). Pea and bean plants, exemplifying the simplest situation, show in each flower a single pistil, traditionally thought of as a megasporophyll or carpel. The carpel is believed to be the evolutionary product of an originally leaflike organ bearing ovules along its margin, but somehow folded along the median line, with a meeting and coalescing of the margins of each half, the result being a miniature, closed but hollow pod with one row of ovules along the

suture. In many members of the rose and buttercup families each flower contains a number of similar single-carpelled pistils, separate and distinct, which together represent what is known as an apocarpous gynoecium. In still other cases, two to several carpels (still thought of as megasporophylls, although perhaps not always justifiably) are assumed to have fused to produce a single compound gynoecium (pistil), whose basal part or ovary may be uniloculate (one cavity) or pluriloculate (with several compartments), depending on the method of carpel fusion. Most fruits develop from a single pistil. A fruit resulting from the apocarpous gynoecium (several pistils) of a single flower may be referred to as an aggregate fruit; a multiple fruit represents the gynoecia of several flowers. When additional flower parts, such as the stem axis or floral tube, are retained or participate in fruit formation, as in the apple, an accessory fruit results.

Certain plants, mostly cultivated varieties, spontaneously produce fruits in the absence of pollination and fertilization; such natural parthenocarpy leads to seedless fruits such as bananas, oranges, grapes, grapefruits, and cucumbers. Since 1934 seedless fruits of tomato, cucumber, peppers, holly, and others have also been obtained for commercial use by administering growth hormones, such as indoleacetic acid, indolebutyric acid, naphthalene acetic acid, and beta-naphthoxyacetic acid to ovaries in flowers (induced parthenocarpy).

Classification systems for mature fruits take into account the number of carpels constituting the original ovary; dehiscence (opening) versus nondehiscence; and dryness versus fleshiness. The properties of the ripened ovary wall, or pericarp, which may develop entirely or in part into fleshy, fibrous, or stony tissue, are important. Often, three distinct pericarp layers can be distinguished: the outer (exocarp), the middle (mesocarp), and the inner layer (endocarp). All purely morphological systems (*i.e.*, classification schemes based on structural features), including the one given in the Table and in Figure 3, are artificial. They ignore the fact that fruits can only be understood functionally and dynamically.

As strikingly exemplified by the word nut, popular terms often do not properly describe the botanical nature of certain fruits. A Brazil "nut," for example, is a thick-walled seed enclosed in a likewise thick-walled capsule along with several sister seeds. A coconut is a drupe (a stony-seeded fruit; see the Table) with a fibrous outer part. A walnut is a drupe in which the pericarp has differentiated into a fleshy outer husk and an inner hard "shell"; the "meat" represents the seed—two large, convoluted cotyledons, a minute epicotyl and hypocotyl, and a thin, papery seed coat. A peanut is an indehiscent legume fruit. An almond "nut" is the "stone"—*i.e.*, the hardened endocarp of a drupe usually containing a single seed. Botanically speaking, blackberries and raspberries are not "berries" but aggregates of tiny drupes. A juniper "berry" is comparable to a complete pine cone. A mulberry is a multiple fruit (see the Table) composed of small nutlets surrounded by fleshy sepals; a strawberry represents a much swollen receptacle (the tip of the flower stalk bearing the flower parts) bearing on its convex surface an aggregation of tiny achenes (small, single-seeded fruits; see the Table).

FORM AND FUNCTION

Seed size. In the Late Carboniferous Period (about 280,000,000 to 325,000,000 years ago) some seed ferns produced large seeds (12 × 6 centimetres [5 × 2 inches] in *Pachytesta incrassata*). This primitive, ancestral condition of large seeds is reflected in certain gymnosperms (*Cycas circinalis*, 5.5 × 4 centimetres; *Araucaria bidwillii*, 4.5 × 3.5 centimetres) and also in some tropical rain-forest trees with nondormant, water-rich seeds (*Mora excelsa*, 12 × 7 centimetres). The "double coconut" palm *Lodoicea maldivica* represents the extreme, with seeds weighing up to 27 kilograms (about 60 pounds). Herbaceous, nontropical flowering plants usually have seeds weighing in the range of about 0.0001 to 0.01 grams. Within a given family (*e.g.*, the pea family, Fabaceae or Leguminosae) seed size may vary greatly; in others it

Margin notes:

Delayed fertilization in gymnosperms

Criteria for classifying fruits

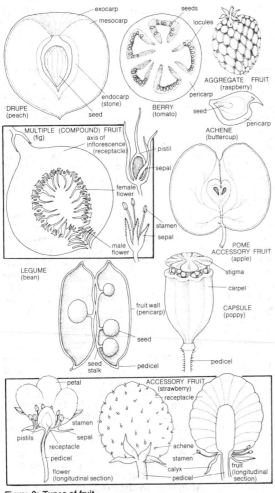

Figure 3: Types of fruit.
From H.J. Fuller and O. Tippo, *College Botany*, revised edition, copyright 1954 by Holt, Rinehart & Winston, Inc.; reprinted by permission

The smallest seeds

is consistently large or small, justifying the recognition of "megaspermous" families (*e.g.*, the beech, nutmeg, palm, and soursop families) and "microspermous" ones (*e.g.*, the milkweed, daisy, heather, nettle, and willow families). The smallest known seeds, devoid of food reserves, are found in orchids, saprophytes (non-green plants that absorb nutrients from dead organic matter—*e.g.*, Indian pipe, *Monotropa*; coral root, *Corallorhiza*), carnivorous plants (sundews, pitcher plants), and total parasites (members of the families Rafflesiaceae and Orobanchaceae, or broomrapes, which latter have seeds weighing about 0.001 milligrams—about 3.5 hundred-millionths of an ounce). Clearly, seed size is related to life-style—total parasites obtain food from their host, even in their early growth stages, and young orchids are saprophytes that receive assistance in absorbing nutrients from fungi that associate closely with their roots. In both cases only very small seeds that lack endosperm are produced. Dodders (*Cuscuta*) and mistletoes (*Viscum, Phoradendron*) live independently when very young and accordingly have relatively large seeds. Many plant species possess seeds of remarkably uniform size, useful as beads (*e.g.*, *Abrus precatorius*) or units of weight—one carat of weight once corresponded with one seed of the carob tree, *Ceratonia siliqua*. In wheat and many other plants, average seed size does not depend on planting density, showing that seed size is under rather strict genetic control. This does not necessarily preclude significant variations among individual seeds; in peas, for example, the seeds occupying the central region of the pod are the largest, probably as the result of competition for nutrients between developing ovules on the placenta. Striking evolutionary changes in seed size, inadvertently created by man, have occurred in the weed *Camelina sativa* subspecies *linicola*, which grows in flax fields. The

Classification of Fruits

major types	structure	
	one carpel	two or more carpels
Dry dehiscent	**Follicle**—at maturity, the carpel splits down one side, usually the ventral suture; milkweed, columbine, peony, larkspur, marsh marigold	**Capsule**—from compound ovary, seeds shed in various ways—*e.g.*, through holes (*Papaver*—poppies) or longitudinal slits (California poppy) or by means of a lid (pimpernel); flower axis participates in *Iris;* snapdragons, violets, lilies, and many plant families
	Legume—dehisces along both dorsal and ventral sutures, forming two valves; most members of the pea family	**Silique**—from bicarpellate, compound, superior ovary; pericarp separates as two halves, leaving persistent central septum with seed or seeds attached; dollar plant, mustard, cabbage, rock cress, wall flower
		Silicle—a short silique; shepherd's purse, pepper grass
Dry indehiscent	**Peanut fruit**—(nontypical legume)	**Nut**—like the achene (see below); derived from 2 or more carpels, pericarp hard or stony; hazelnut, acorn, chestnut, basswood
	Lomentum—a legume fragmentizing transversely into single-seeded "mericarps"; sensitive plant (*Mimosa*)	**Schizocarp**—collectively, the product of a compound ovary fragmentizing at maturity into a number of one-seeded "mericarps"; maple, mallows, members of the mint family (Lamiaceae or Labiatae), geraniums, carrots, dills, fennels
	Achene—small, single-seeded fruit, pericarp relatively thin; seed free in cavity except for its funicular attachment; buttercup, anemones, buckwheat, crowfoot, water plantain	
	Cypsela—achene-like, but from inferior, compound ovary; members of the aster family (Asteraceae or Compositae), sunflowers	
	Samara—a winged achene; elm, ash, tree-of-heaven, wafer ash	
	Caryopsis—achene-like; from compound ovary; seed coat fused with pericarp; grass family (Poaceae or Graminae)	
Fleshy (pericarp partly or wholly fleshy or fibrous)	**Drupe**—mesocarp fleshy, endocarp hard and stony; usually single-seeded; plum, peach, almond, cherry, olive, coconut	
	Berry—both mesocarp and endocarp fleshy; one-seeded: nutmeg, date; one carpel, several seeds: baneberry, may apple, barberry, Oregon grape; more carpels, several seeds: grape, tomato, potato, asparagus	
	Pepo—berry with hard rind; squash, cucumber, pumpkin, watermelon	
	Hesperidium—berry with leathery rind; orange, grapefruit, lemon	
	two or more carpels of the same flower plus stem axis or floral tube	carpels from several flowers plus stem axis or floral tube plus accessory parts
Fleshy (pericarp partly or wholly fleshy or fibrous)	**Pome**—accessory fruit from compound, inferior ovary; only central part of fruit represents pericarp, with fleshy exocarp and mesocarp and cartilaginous or stony endocarp ("core"); apple, pear, quince, hawthorn, mountain ash	**Multiple fruits**—fig (a "syconium"), mulberry, osage orange, pineapple, flowering dogwood
	Inferior berry—blueberry	
	Aggregate fleshy fruits—strawberry (achenes borne on fleshy receptacle); blackberry, raspberry (collection of drupelets); magnolia	

customary winnowing of flax seeds selects forms of *Camelina* whose seeds are blown over the same distance as flax seeds in the operation, thus staying with their "models." Consequently, *Camelina* seeds in the south of Russia now mimic the relatively thick, heavy seeds of the

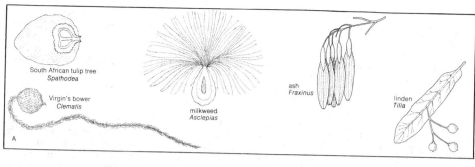

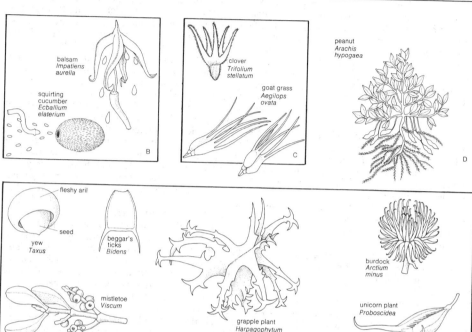

Figure 4: *Seed and fruit dispersal.*
(A) Wind-dispersed fruits and seeds. (B) Mechanically dispersed seeds. (C) Creeping and hopping fruits. (D) Limitation of seed dispersal, geocarpy, underground development of fruits resulting in confinement to areas near parent plant. (E) Animal-dispersed fruits and seeds.

Drawing by M. Moran based on (A,B,D; beggar's ticks, grapple plant, thistle, unicorn plant) *An Evolutionary Survey of the Plant Kingdom*, by R.F. Scagel, G.E. Rouse, J.R. Stein, R.J. Bandoni, W.B. Schofield, T.M.C. Taylor, © 1965 by Wadsworth Publishing Company, Inc., Belmont, California 94002, Reprinted by permission of the publisher; (C) S.K. von Marilaun, *The Natural History of Plants*, Holt, Rinehart and Winston, Inc.

oil flax that is grown there, whereas in the northwest they resemble the flat, thin seeds of the predominant fibre flax.

Seed size and predation. Seeds form the main source of food for many birds, rodents, ants, and beetles. Harvester ants of the genus *Veromessor*, for example, exact a toll of about 15,000,000 seeds per acre per year from the Sonoran Desert of the southwestern United States. In view of the enormous size range of the predators, which include minute weevil and bruchid-beetle larvae that attack the seeds internally, evolutionary "manipulation" of seed size by a plant species cannot in itself be effective in completely avoiding seed attack. With predation inescapable, however, it must be advantageous for a plant species to invest the total reproductive effort in a large number of very small units (seeds) rather than in a few big ones. The mean seed weight of those 13 species of Central American woody legumes vulnerable to bruchid attack is 0.26 gram; for the 23 species invulnerable by virtue of toxic seed constituents it is three grams.

Seed size and germination. Ecologically, seed size is also important in the breaking of dormancy. Being small, a seed can only "sample" that part of the environment immediately adjacent to it, which is not necessarily representative of the generally prevailing conditions. For successful seedling establishment, there is clearly a risk in "venturing out" too soon. The development in seeds of mechanisms acting as "integrating rain gauges" (see below) should be considered in that light.

The shape of dispersal units. Apart from the importance of shape as a factor in determining the mode of dispersal (*e.g.*, wind dispersal of winged seeds, animal dispersal of spiny fruits), shape also counts when the seed or diaspore is seen as a landing device. The flatness of the enormous tropical *Mora* seeds prevents rolling and effectively restricts germination to the spot where they land. In contrast, *Eusideroxylon zwageri* does not grow on steep slopes because its heavy fruits roll downhill. The grains of the grass *Panicum turgidum*, which have a flat and a round side, germinate much better when the flat rather than the convex side lies in contact with wet soil. In very small seeds, the importance of shape can be judged only by taking into account soil clod size and microtopography of the soils onto which they are dropped. The rounded seeds of cabbage species, for example, tend to roll into crevices, whereas the reticulate ones of lamb's quarters often stay in the positions in which they first fall. Several seeds have appendages (awns, bristles) that promote germination by aiding in orientation and self-burial. In one study, for example, during a six-month period, awned grains of *Danthonia penicillata* gave rise to 12 times as many established seedlings as de-awned ones.

Polymorphism of seeds and fruits. Some plant species produce two or more sharply defined types of seeds that differ in appearance (colour), shape, size, internal structure, or dormancy. In common spurry (*Spergula arvensis*), for example, the seed coat (part of the mother plant) may be either smooth or papillate (covered with tiny nipple-like projections). Here, the phenomenon is genetically controlled by a single factor, so that all the seeds of a given plant are either papillate or smooth. More common is somatic polymorphism, the produc-

Functional
aspects of
seed shape

tion by individual plants of different seed types, or "morphs." Somatic polymorphism occurs regularly in *Atriplex* and *Chenopodium*, in which a single plant may produce both large brown seeds capable of immediate germination and small black ones with some innate dormancy. Somatic polymorphism may be controlled by the position of the two (or more) seed types within one inflorescence (flower cluster) or fruit, as in cocklebur, or it may result from environmental effects, as in *Halogeton*, in which imposition of long or short days leads to production of brown and black seeds, respectively. Since the different morphs in seed (and fruit) polymorphism usually have different dispersal mechanisms and dormancies, so that germination is spread out both in space and in time, the phenomenon can be seen as an insurance against catastrophe. The most spectacular example of heterocarpy (*i.e.*, production of differing fruit) is found in the Mediterranean *Fedia cornucopiae* (family Valerianaceae), which has three astonishingly different kinds of fruits that show adaptations to dispersal by wind and water, ants, and larger animals, respectively.

DISPERSAL

The dispersing agents for seeds and fruits are indicated in such terms as anemochory, hydrochory, and zoochory, which mean dispersal by wind, water, and animals, re-

Categories of seed dispersal spectively. Within the zoochorous group further differentiation according to the carriers can be made: saurochory, dispersal by reptiles; ornithochory, by birds; myrmecochory, by ants. Or the manner in which the diaspores are carried can be emphasized, distinguishing endozoochory, diaspores carried within the animal; epizoochory, diaspores accidentally carried on the outside; and synzoochory, diaspores intentionally carried, mostly in the mouth as in birds and ants. See Figure 4 for examples of fruits and seeds that are adapted for dispersal by various means.

Dispersal by animals. Snails disperse the small seeds of a very few plant species (*e.g.*, *Adoxa*). Earthworms are more important as seed dispersers. Many intact fruits and seeds can serve as fish bait, those of *Sonneratia*, for example, for the catfish *Arius maculatus*. Certain Amazon River fishes react positively to the audible "explosions" of the ripe fruits of *Eperua rubiginosa*. Fossil evidence indicates that saurochory is very ancient. The giant Galapagos tortoise is important for the dispersal of local cacti and tomatoes. The name alligator apple for *Annona palustris* refers to its method of dispersal, an example of saurochory. Many mammals, ranging in size from mice and kangaroo rats to elephants, eat and disperse seeds and fruits. In the tropics, chiropterochory (dispersal by large bats such as flying foxes, *Pteropus*) is particularly important. Fruits adapted to these animals are relatively large and drab in colour, with large seeds and a striking (often rank) odour; they are accessible to bats because of the pagoda-like structure of the tree canopy, fruit placement on the main trunk, or suspension from long stalks that hang free of the foliage. Examples include mangoes, guavas, breadfruit, carob, and several fig species. In South Africa, a desert melon (*Cucumis humifructus*) participates in a symbiotic relationship with aardvarks—the animals eat the fruit for its water content and bury their own dung, which contains the seeds, near their burrows. Furry terrestrial mammals are the agents most frequently involved in epizoochory, the inadvertent carrying by animals of dispersal units. Burrlike seeds and fruits, or those diaspores provided with spines, hooks, claws, bristles, barbs, grapples, and prickles, are genuine hitchhikers, clinging tenaciously to their carriers. Their functional shape is achieved in various ways—in cleavers, or goose grass (*Galium aparine*), and enchanter's nightshade (*Circaea lutetiana*) the hooks are part of the fruit itself; in common agrimony (*Agrimonia eupatoria*) the fruit is covered by a persistent calyx (the sepals, parts of the flower, which remain attached beyond the usual period) equipped with hooks; in wood avens (*Geum urbanum*) the persistent styles have hooked tips. Other examples are

Examples of seed hitchhikers bur marigolds, or beggar's-ticks (*Bidens* species); buffalo burr (*Solanum rostratum*); burdock (*Arctium*); *Acaena*;

and many *Medicago* species. The last named, with dispersal units highly resistant to damage from hot water and certain chemicals (dyes), have achieved wide global distribution through the wool trade. A somewhat different principle is employed by the so-called trample burrs, said to lodge themselves between the hooves of large grazing mammals. Examples are mule grab (*Proboscidea*) and the African grapple plant (*Harpagophytum*). In water burrs, such as those of the water nut *Trapa*, the spines should probably be considered as anchoring devices.

Dispersal by birds. Birds, being preening animals, rarely carry burrlike diaspores on their bodies. They do, however, transport the very sticky (viscid) fruits of *Pisonia*, a tropical tree of the four-o'clock family, to distant Pacific islands in this way. Small diaspores, such as those of sedges and certain grasses, may also be carried in the mud sticking to waterfowl and terrestrial birds.

Synzoochory, deliberate carrying of diaspores by animals, is practiced when birds carry diaspores in their beaks. The European mistle thrush, *Turdus viscivorus*, deposits the viscid seeds of mistletoe (*Viscum album*) on potential host plants when, after a meal of the berries, it whets its bill on branches or simply regurgitates the seeds. The North American mistletoes (*Phoradendron*) are dispersed by various birds, and the comparable tropical species of the plant family Loranthaceae by flowerpeckers (of the bird family Dicaeidae), which have a highly specialized gizzard that allows seeds to pass through but retains insects. Plants may also profit from the forgetfulness and sloppy habits of certain nut-eating birds that cache part of their food but neglect to recover everything, or drop units on their way to the hiding place. Best known in this respect are the nutcrackers (*Nucifraga*), which feed largely on the "nuts" of beech, oak, walnut, chestnut, and hazel; the jays (*Garrulus*), which hide hazelnuts and acorns; the nuthatches; and the California woodpecker (*Balanosphyra*), which may embed literally thousands of acorns, almonds, and pecan nuts in bark fissures or holes of trees. Secondarily, rodents may aid in dispersal by stealing the embedded diaspores and burying them. In Germany an average jay may transport about 4,600 acorns per season, over distances of up to four kilometres (2.5 miles). Woodpeckers, nutcrackers, and squirrels are responsible for a similar dispersal of *Pinus cembra* in the Alps near the tree line.

Most ornithochores (plants with bird-dispersed seeds) have conspicuous diaspores attractive to such fruit-eating birds as thrushes, pigeons, barbets (members of the bird family Capitonidae), tucans, and hornbills (family Bucerotidae), all of which excrete the hard part undamaged.

Adaptations of seeds and fruits to bird dispersal Such diaspores have a fleshy, sweet, or oil-containing edible part; a striking colour (often red or orange); no pronounced smell; a protection against being eaten prematurely in the form of acids and tannic compounds that are present only in the green fruit; a protection of the seed against digestion—bitterness, hardness, or the presence of poisonous compounds; permanent attachment; and, finally, absence of a hard outer cover. In contrast to bat-dispersed diaspores, they occupy no special position on the plant. Examples are rose hips, plums, dogwood fruits, barberry, red currant, mulberry, nutmeg fruits, figs, blackberries, and others. The natural and abundant occurrence of *Evonymus* (cardinal's hat), essentially a tropical genus, in temperate Europe and Asia, can be understood only in connection with the activities of birds. Birds also contributed substantially to the repopulation with plants of the island Krakatau after the catastrophic eruption of 1883. Birds have made *Lantana* (originally American) a pest in Indonesia; the same is true of wild plums (*Prunus serotina*) in parts of Europe and *Rubus* species in Brazil and New Zealand.

Mimicry—the protection-affording imitation of a dangerous or toxic species by an edible, harmless one—is shown in reverse by certain bird-dispersed "coral seeds" such as those of many species in the genera *Abrus*, *Ormosia*, *Rhynchosia*, *Adenanthera*, and *Erythrina*. Hard and often shiny red or black and red, many such seeds deceptively suggest the presence of a fleshy red aril and thus invite the attention of hungry birds.

Water dispersal: red mangrove seedling *(Rhizophora mangle)* ready to drop into the water after germinating on tree.

Wind dispersal: woolly seeds produced by the seed pods of the kapok tree *(Ceiba pentandra)*.

Wind dispersal: winged fruits of the silver maple *(Acer saccharinum)*.

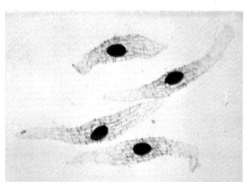

Wind dispersal: magnified view of seeds of lady's slipper *(Cypripedium)*, an example of the tiny seeds produced by orchids.

Water dispersal: a coconut *(Cocos nucifera)*, transported by the sea from a distant tropical island, germinating on a mainland beach.

Self-dispersal: plumes on the fruits of mountain mahogany *(Cercocarpus)*, which coil and uncoil to drive seeds into the soil.

Wind, water, and self-dispersal

Plate 1: (Top left) William E. Ferguson, (top centre) Norman Myers—Bruce Coleman Inc., (top right) Thase Daniel, (centre left) Rudolf Schmid, (bottom left) G.R. Roberts, (bottom right) Dennis Brokaw

Plate 2   Seed and Fruit

Naras melons *(Acanthosicyos horrida)* growing in the Namib Desert, South West Africa. Seeds are dispersed by the gemsbok oryx *(Oryx gazella)*, which feeds on the melons.

Seeds of rosary pea *(Abrus precatorius)*, which mimic fleshy red arils (accessory seed coverings) attractive to seed-eaters.

Acorns stored in the trunk of a digger pine *(Pinus sabiniana)* by the acorn woodpecker *(Melanerpes formicivorus)*.

Fleshy red appendages of fruits of the yew *(Taxus)*, which attract birds.

Animal dispersal

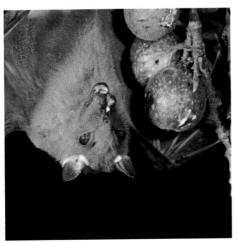

Epauletted fruit bat *(Epomophorus wahlbergi)* feeding on wild figs *(Ficus)*.

Curve-bill thrasher *(Toxostoma curvirostre)* with a berry in its beak.

Plate 2: (Top) Anthony Bannister from The Natural History Photographic Agency—EB Inc., (centre left) Walter Dawn, (centre) William E. Grenfell, Jr., (centre right) Rudolf Schmid, (bottom left) Jane Burton—Bruce Coleman Inc., (bottom right) Lois Cox

Dispersal by ants. Mediterranean and North American harvester ants (*Messor, Atta, Tetramorium,* and *Pheidole*) are essentially destructive, storing and fermenting many seeds and eating them completely. Other ants (*Lasius, Myrmica,* and *Formica* species) eat the fleshy, edible appendage (the fat body or elaiosome) of certain specialized seeds, which they disperse (see Figure 5). Most myrmecochorous plants (species of violet, primrose, hepatica, cyclamen, anemone, corydalis, *Trillium,* and bloodroot) belong to the herbaceous spring flora of northern forests. Tree poppy (*Dendromecon*), however, is found in the dry California chaparral; *Melica* and *Centaurea* species in arid Mediterranean regions. The so-called ant epiphytes of the tropics (*i.e.,* species of *Hoya, Dischidia, Aeschynanthus,* and *Myrmecodia*—plants that live in "ant gardens" on trees or offer the ants shelter in their own body cavities) constitute a special group of myrmecochores, providing oil in seed hairs, which in ancestral forms must have served in wind dispersal. The primary ant attractant of myrmecochorous seeds is not necessarily oil; instead, an unsaturated, somewhat volatile fatty acid is suspected in some cases. The myrmecochorous plant as a whole may also have specific adaptations; for example, Cyclamen brings fruits and seeds within reach of ants by conspicuous coiling (shortening) of the flower stalk as soon as flowering is over.

Plant and ant interrelationships

Fritz Schremmer

Figure 5: *Seed dispersal by ants.*
(Top left) Fruit of greater celandine (*Chelidonium majus*) opened to show dark seeds with light elaiosomes (fat bodies).
(Top right) Ant (*Myrmica laevinodes*) dispersing celandine seeds. (Bottom) Harvester ant (*Messor barbarus*) transporting cereal grains.

Dispersal by wind. In the modern world, wind dispersal (although numerically important) reflects the climatic and biotic poverty of certain regions; it is essentially a feature of pioneer vegetations. The flora of the Alps is 60 percent anemochorous, that of the Mediterranean garrigue 50 percent. By making certain assumptions (*e.g.,* for average wind velocity and turbulence) the "average limits of dispersal"—that is, the distance that 1 percent of the diaspores can reach—can be calculated for dispersal units of various construction and weight. This calculation yields values of ten kilometres (six miles) for dandelion (*Taraxacum officinale*) and 0.5 kilometre (0.3 mile) for European pine (*Pinus sylvestris*). Storms result in higher values—30 kilometres (20 miles) for poplar and 200 kilometres (125 miles) for *Senecio congestus.*
Too much success in dispersal may be ecologically futile, as exemplified by certain Florida orchids that arise from windblown West Indian seeds but do not multiply because of the lack of specific pollinators; usually certain bees or wasps. Anemochorous diaspores can be subdivided into flyers, dust diaspores, balloons, and plumed or winged diaspores; rollers, chamaechores or tumbleweeds; and throwers, ballistic anemochores. Dispersal by means of minute dust diaspores produced in huge quantities is comparable to spore dispersal in lower plants—a "saturation bombing" is required to find the very limited number of targets, or favourable growth habitats, that exist. Not surprisingly, it is practiced mostly by total parasites, such as broomrapes (in which the finding of the specific host is a problem), and saprophytes. The inflated, indehiscent pods of *Colutea arborea,* a steppe plant, represent balloons capable of limited air travel before they hit the ground and become windblown tumbleweeds. Winged fruits are most common in trees and shrubs, such as maple, ash, elm, birch, alder, and dipterocarps (a family of about 600 species of Old World tropical trees). The one-winged propeller type, as found in maple, is called a samara. When fruits have several wings on their sides, rotation may result, as in rhubarb and dock species. Sometimes accessory parts form the wings—for example, the bracts (small green leaflike structures that grow just below flowers) in *Tilia* (linden). Seeds with a thin wing formed by the testa are likewise most common in trees and shrubs, particularly in climbers—jacaranda, trumpet vine, catalpa, yams, butter-and-eggs. Most famous of these is the seed with a giant, membranaceous wing (15 centimetres) of *Macrozanonia macrocarpa,* a tropical climber of the cucumber family.

Winged fruits

Many fruits form plumes, some derived from persisting and ultimately hairy styles, as in clematis, avens, and anemones; some from the perianth, as in the sedge family (Cyperaceae); and some from the pappus, a calyx structure, as in dandelion and Jack-go-to-bed-at-noon (*Tragopogon*). Plumed seeds usually have tufts of light, silky hairs at one end (rarely both ends) of the seeds—*e.g.,* fireweed, milkweeds, dogbane. In woolly fruits and seeds, the pericarp or the seed coat is covered with cotton-like hairs—*e.g.,* willow, poplar or cottonwood, kapok, cotton, balsa, silk-cotton tree, and some anemones. In some cases, the hairs may serve double duty, in that they function in water dispersal as well as wind dispersal. In tumbleweeds, the whole plant or its fruiting portion breaks off and is blown across open country, scattering seeds as it goes; examples include Russian thistle, pigweed, tumbling mustard, perhaps rose of Jericho, and "windballs" of the grass *Spinifex* of Indonesian shores and Australian steppes. Poppies have a mechanism in which the wind has to swing the slender fruitstalk back and forth before the seeds are thrown out through pores near the top of the capsule.

Dispersal by water. Many beach, pond, and swamp plants have waterborne seeds, which are buoyant by being enclosed in corky fruits or air-containing fruits or both; examples of these plants include water plantain, yellow flag, sea kale, sea rocket, sea beet, and all species of Rhizophoraceae, a family of mangrove plants. Sea dispersal of the coconut palm has been well proved; the fibrous mesocarp of the fruit, a giant drupe, provides buoyancy. Once the nuts are ashore, the mesocarp also aids in the aboveground germination process by collecting rainwater; in addition, the endosperm has in its "milk" a provision for seedling establishment on beaches without much freshwater. A sea rocket species with seeds highly resistant to seawater is gaining a foothold on volcanic Surtsey Island south of Iceland. Purple loosestrife, monkey flower, *Aster tripolium,* and *Juncus* species (rushes) are often transported by water in the seedling stage. Rainwash down mountain slopes may be important in tropical forests. A "splashcup mechanism," common in fungi for spore dispersal, is suggested by the open fruit capsule with exposed small seeds in the pearlwort (*Sagina*) and mitrewort (*Mitella*). Hygrochasy, the opening of fruits in moist weather, is displayed by species of *Mesembryanthemum, Sedum,* and other plants of dry environments.

Self-dispersal. Best known in this category are the active ballists, which forcibly eject their seeds by means of

Explosive
fruits

various mechanisms. In the fruit of the dwarf mistletoe (*Arceuthobium*) of the western United States, a very high osmotic pressure (pressure accumulated by movement of water across cell membranes principally in only one direction) builds up that ultimately leads to a lateral blasting out of the seeds over distances of up to 48 feet with an initial velocity of about 60 miles per hour. Squirting cucumber (*Ecballium elaterium*) also employs an osmotic mechanism. In Scotch broom and gorse, however, drying out of the already dead tissues in the two valves of the seed pod causes a tendency to warp, which, on hot summer days, culminates in an explosive and audible separation of these valves, with violent seed release. Such methods may be coupled with secondary dispersal mechanisms, effected by ants in the case of Scotch broom and gorse or by birds and mammals, to which sticky seeds may adhere, in the case of *Arceuthobium* and squirting cucumber. Other active ballists are species of geranium, violet, wood sorrel, witch-hazel, touch-me-not (*Impatiens*), and acanthus; probable champions are *Bauhinia purpurea*, with a distance of 15 metres and the sandbox tree (*Hura crepitans*) with 14 metres. Barochory, the dispersal of seeds and fruits by gravity alone, is demonstrated by the heavy fruits of horse chestnut.

Creeping diaspores are found in grasses such as *Avena sterilis* and *Aegilops ovata*, the grains of which are provided with bristles capable of hygroscopic movements (coiling and flexing, in response to changes in moisture). The mericarps (a fruit fragment—see the Table: *Schizocarp*) or stork's bill (an *Erodium* species), when moistened, bury themselves with a corkscrew motion by unwinding a multiple-barbed, beak-shaped appendage, which, in the dry state, was coiled.

Atelechory, the dispersal over a very limited distance only, represents a waste-avoiding, defensive "strategy" that functions in further exploitation of an already occupied, favourable site. This aim is often achieved by synaptospermy, the sticking together of several diaspores, which makes them less mobile, as in beet and spinach; also, by geocarpy, which is either the production of fruits underground, as in the arum lilies *Stylochiton* and *Biarum*, in which the flowers are already subterranean, or the active burying of fruits by the mother plant, as in the peanut, *Arachis hypogaea*. In the American hog peanut (*Amphicarpa bracteata*), pods of a special type are buried by the plant and are cached by squirrels later on. Kenilworth ivy (*Cymbalaria*), which normally grows on stone or brick walls, stashes its fruits away in crevices after strikingly extending the flower stalks. Not surprisingly, geocarpy, like synaptospermy, is most often encountered in desert plants; however, it also occurs in violet species, in subterranean clover (*Trifolium subterraneum*)—even when it grows in France and England—and in *Begonia hypogaea* of the African rain forest.

GERMINATION

Dormancy and life-span of seeds.   Diaspore dormancy has at least three functions: (1) immediate germination must be prevented even when circumstances are optimal so as to avoid exposure of the seedling to an unfavourable period (*e.g.*, winter), which is sure to follow; (2) the unfavourable period has to be survived; and (3) the various dispersing agents must be given time to act. Accordingly, the wide variation in diaspore longevity can be appreciated only by linking it with the various dispersal mechanisms employed, as well as with the climate and its seasonal changes. Thus, the downy seeds of willows, blown up and down rivers in early summer with a chance of quick establishment on newly exposed sandbars, have a life-span of only one week. Tropical rain forest trees frequently have seeds of low life expectancy also. Intermediate are seeds of sugarcane, tea, and coco palm, among others, with life-spans of up to a year. *Mimosa glomerata* seeds in the herbarium of the Muséum National d'Histoire Naturelle in Paris were found viable after 221 years. In general, viability is better retained in air of low moisture content. Some seeds, however, remain viable under water—those of certain rush (*Juncus*) species and *Sium cicutaefolium* for at least seven years. Salt water

Seeds with
short life
expectan-
cies

can be tolerated for years by the pebble-like but floating seeds of *Caesalpinia* (*Guilandina*) *bonduc* and *C. bonducella*, species that, in consequence, possess an almost pantropical distribution. Seeds of the sacred lotus (*Nelumbo nucifera*) found in a peat deposit in Manchuria and estimated by radioactive-carbon dating to be 1,400 (±400) years old, rapidly germinated (and subsequently produced flowering plants) when the seeds were filed to permit water entry. In 1967 seeds of the arctic tundra lupine (*Lupinus arcticus*), found in a frozen lemming burrow with animal remains established to be at least 10,000 years old, germinated within 48 hours when returned to favourable conditions. The problem of differential seed viability has been approached experimentally by various workers, one of whom buried 20 species of common Michigan weed seeds, mixed with sand, in inverted open-mouthed bottles for periodic inspection. After 80 years, three species still had viable seeds.

Lack of dormancy.   In some plants, the seeds are able to germinate as soon as they have matured on the plant, as demonstrated by wheat, sweet corn, peas, and beans in a very rainy season. Certain mangrove species normally form foot-long embryos on the trees; these later drop down into the mud or seawater. Such cases, however, are exceptional. The lack of dormancy in cultivated species, contrasting with the situation in most wild plants, is undoubtedly the result of conscious selection by man.

Immature embryos.   In plants whose seeds ripen and are shed from the mother plant before the embryo has undergone much development beyond the fertilized egg stage (orchids, broomrapes, ginkgo, dogtooth violet, ash, winter aconite, and buttercups), there is an understandable delay of several weeks or months, even under optimal conditions, before the seedling emerges.

Role of the seed coat.   There are at least three ways in which a hard testa may be responsible for seed dormancy: it may (1) prevent expansion of the embryo mechanically (pigweed); or (2) block the entrance of water; or (3) impede gas exchange so that the embryos lack oxygen. Resistance of the testa to water uptake is most widespread in the bean family, the seed coats of which, usually hard, smooth, or even glassy, may, in addition, possess a waxy covering. In some cases water entry is controlled by a small opening, the strophiolar cleft, which is provided with a corklike plug; only removal or loosening of the plug will permit water entry. Similar seeds not possessing a strophiolar cleft must depend on abrasion, which in nature may be brought about by microbial attack, passage through an animal, freezing and thawing, or mechanical means. In horticulture and agriculture, the resistant coats of such seeds are deliberately damaged or weakened by man (scarification). In chemical scarification, seeds are dipped into strong sulfuric acid, organic solvents such as acetone or alcohol, or even boiling water. In mechanical scarification, they may be shaken with some abrasive material such as sand or be scratched with a knife.

Methods
of
over-
coming
resistant
seed coats

Frequently seed coats are permeable to water yet block entrance of oxygen; this applies, for example, to the upper of the two seeds normally found in each burr of the cocklebur plant. The lower seeds germinate readily under a favourable moisture and temperature regime, but the upper ones fail to do so unless the seed coat is punctured or removed or the intact seed is placed under very high oxygen concentrations.

Afterripening, stratification, and temperature effects. The most difficult cases of dormancy to overcome are those in which the embryos, although not underdeveloped, remain dormant even when the seed coats are removed and conditions are favourable for growth. Germination in these takes place only after a series of little-understood changes, usually called afterripening, have taken place in the embryo. In this group are many forest trees and shrubs such as pines, hemlocks, and other conifers; some flowering woody plants such as dogwood, hawthorn, ash, linden, tulip poplar, holly, and viburnum; fruit trees such as apples, pears, peaches, plums, and cherries; and flowering herbaceous plants such as iris, Solomon's seal, and lily-of-the-valley. In some species, one winter suffices for afterripening. In others, the pro-

Signif-
icance of
after-
ripening
require-
ment

cess is drawn out over several years, with some germination occurring each year. This can be viewed as an insurance of the species against flash catastrophes that might completely wipe out certain year classes.

Many species require moisture and low temperatures; for example, in apples, when the cold requirement is insufficiently met, abnormal seedlings result. Others (cereals, dogwood) afterripen during dry storage. The seeds of certain legumes—for example, the seeds of the tree lupin, the coats of which are extremely hard and impermeable—possess a hilum with an ingenious valve mechanism that allows water loss in dry air but prevents re-uptake of moisture in humid air. Of great practical importance is stratification, a procedure aimed at promoting a more uniform and faster germination of cold-requiring, afterripening seeds. In this procedure, seeds are placed for one to six months, depending on the species, between layers of sand, sawdust, sphagnum, or peat and kept moist as well as reasonably cold (usually 0° to 10° C [32° to 50° F]). A remarkable "double dormancy" has thus been uncovered in lily-of-the-valley and false Solomon's seal. Here, two successive cold treatments separated by a warm period are needed for complete seedling development. The first cold treatment eliminates the dormancy of the root; the warm period permits its outgrowth; and the second cold period eliminates epicotyl or leaf dormancy. Thus, almost two years may be required to obtain the complete plant. The optimal temperature for germination, ranging from 1° C (34° F) for bitterroot to 42° C (108° F) for pigweed, may also shift slightly as a result of stratification.

Many dry seeds are remarkably resistant to extreme temperatures, some even to that of liquid air (−140° C or −220° F). Seeds of Scotch broom and some *Medicago* species can be boiled briefly without losing viability. Ecologically, such heat resistance is important in vegetation types periodically ravaged by fire, such as in the California chaparral, where the germination of *Ceanothus* seeds may even be stimulated. Also important ecologically is a germination requirement calling for a modest daily alternation between a higher and a lower temperature. Especially in the desert, extreme temperature fluctuations are an unavoidable feature of the surface, whereas with increasing depth these fluctuations are gradually damped out. A requirement for a modest fluctuation—*e.g.*, from 20° C (68° F) at night to 30° C (86° F) in the daytime (as displayed by the grass *Oryzopsis miliacea*)—practically ensures germination at fair depths; and this is advantageous because a seed germinating in soil has to strike a balance between two conflicting demands, both depending on depth—on the one hand, germination in deeper layers is advantageous because a dependable moisture supply simply is not available near the surface; but, on the other hand, closeness to the surface is desirable because it allows the seedling to reach air and light rapidly and become self-supporting.

Light and seed germination. Many seeds are insensitive to light, but in a number of species germination is stimulated or inhibited by exposure to continuous or short periods of illumination. So stimulated are many grasses, lettuce, fireweed, peppergrass (*Lepidium*), mullein, evening primrose, yellow dock, loosestrife, and Chinese lantern plant. Corn (maize), the smaller cereals, and many legumes, such as beans and clover, germinate as well in light as in darkness. Inhibition by light is found in chive, garlic, and several other species of the lily family, jimson weed, fennel flower (*Nigella*), *Phacelia*, *Nemophila*, and pigweed (*Amaranthus*). Sometimes, imbibed (wet) seeds that do not germinate at all in darkness may be fully promoted by only a few seconds or minutes of white light. The best studied case of this type, and one that is a milestone in plant physiology, concerns seeds of the Grand Rapids variety of lettuce, which is stimulated to germination by red light (wavelength about 660 nanometres) but inhibited by "far red" light (wavelength about 730 nanometres). Alternations of the two treatments to almost any extent indicate that the last treatment received is the decisive one in determining whether the seeds will germinate.

Plants stimulated by light to germinate

Ecological role of light. Laboratory experiments and field observations indicate that light is a main controller of seed dormancy in a wide array of species. The absence of light, for example, was found in one study to be responsible for the nongermination of seeds of 20 out of 23 weed species commonly found in arable soil. In regions of shifting sands, seeds of Russian thistle germinate only when the fruits are uncovered, often after a burial period of several years. Conversely, the seeds of *Calligonum comosum* and the melon *Citrullus colocynthis*, inhabiting coarse sandy soils in the Negev Desert, are strongly inhibited by light. The survival value of this response, which restricts germination to buried seeds, lies in the fact that at the surface fluctuating environmental conditions may rapidly create a very hostile micro-environment. The seeds of *Artemisia monosperma* have an absolute light requirement but respond to extremely low intensities, such as is transmitted by a two millimetre thick sand filter. In seeds buried too deeply, germination is prevented. The responsiveness to light, however, increases with the duration of water imbibition. Even when full responsiveness to light has been reached, maximal germination occurs only after several light-exposures are given at intervals. In the field, this combined response mechanism acts as an integrating (cumulative) rain gauge because the seeds (as indicated) become increasingly responsive to light, and thus increasingly germinable, the longer the sand remains moistened. Certain *Juncus* seeds have an absolute light requirement over a wide range of temperatures; consequently, they do not germinate under dense vegetation or in overly deep water. In combination with temperature, light (in the sense of day length) may also restrict germination to the most suitable time of year. In birch, for example, seeds that have not gone through a cold period after imbibing water remain dormant after release from the mother plant in the fall and will germinate only when the days begin to lengthen the next spring.

Significance of seed light requirements

Stimulators and inhibitors of germination. A number of chemicals (potassium nitrate, thiourea, and ethylene chlorhydrin) and plant hormones (gibberellins and kinetin) have been used experimentally to break seed dormancy. Their mode of action is obscure, but it is known that in some instances thiourea, gibberellin, and kinetin can substitute for light.

Natural inhibitors, which completely suppress germination (coumarin, parasorbic acid, ferulic acid, phenols, protoanemonin, transcinnamic acid, alkaloids, essential oils, and the hormone dormin) may be present in the pulp or juice of fruits or in various parts of the seed. The effect of seed coat phenols, for example, may be indirect—being highly oxidizable, they may screen out much-needed oxygen. Ecologically, such inhibitors are important in at least three ways. Their slow disappearance with time may spread germination out over several years (a protection against catastrophes). Furthermore, when leached out by rainwater, they often serve as agents inhibiting the germination of other competitive plants nearby. Finally, the gradual leaching out of water-soluble inhibitors serves as an excellent integrating rain gauge. Indeed, it has been shown that the germination of certain desert plants is not related to moisture as such but to soil water movement—*i.e.*, to the amount and duration of rain received.

BIBLIOGRAPHY. L.V. BARTON, *Seed Preservation and Longevity* (1961), an excellent monograph reflecting many years of practical experience; M. BLACK, "Light-Controlled Germination of Seeds," *Symp. Soc. Exp. Biol. No. 23: Dormancy and Survival*, pp. 193–217 (1969), an up-to-date appraisal of the role of light reactions in germination; J.L. HARPER, P.H. LOVELL, and K.G. MOORE, "The Shapes and Sizes of Seeds," *Ann. Rev. Ecology and Systematics*, 1:327–356 (1970), a team of experts highlights the significance of seed shape and size for agriculture, dispersal, germination, physiology, evolution, etc.; D. KOLLER, "The Survival Value of Germination-Regulating Mechanisms in the Field," *Herb. Abstr.*, 34:1–7 (1964), careful observation, a thorough knowledge of germination physiology, and intelligent speculation combine to result in a fine review; P. MAHESHWARI (ed.), *Recent Advances in the Embryology of Angiosperms* (1963), an account of the progress in this area (embryology), by an old master; A.M. MAYER and A. POLJAKOFF-MAYBER, *The Germination of Seeds* (1963), a very readable, responsible account, presented in a well-organized, fairly concise manner; W.L. MCATEE, "Distribution of Seeds by Birds," *Am. Midl. Nat.*, 38:214–223 (1947), focusses on a group of dispersers well-known and attractive to many humans; S. ODUM, "Germination of Ancient Seeds," *Dansk Bot. Ark.*, vol. 24, no. 2 (1965), fascinating reading for historians and archaeologists; A.E. PORSILD, C.R. HARINGTON, and G.A. MULLIGAN "*Lupinus arcticus* Wats. Grown from Seeds of Pleistocene Age," *Science*, 158:113–114 (1967), an account of the almost incredible case in which 10,000-year-old seeds germinated to produce perfect plants; L. VAN DER PIJL, "The Dispersal of Plants by Bats," *Acta Bot. Neerl.*, 6:291–315 (1957), a monograph dealing with the intriguing animals that preceded us in the appreciation of tropical fruit; "Ecological Aspects of Fruit Evolution," *Proc. K. Ned. Akad. Wet.*, Series C, 69:597–640 (1966), a scholarly article covering various theoretical angles; *Principles of Dispersal in Higher Plants* (1969), a highly original and most stimulating little book, displaying a thorough knowledge of both tropical and temperate-region biology; H.N. RIDLEY, *The Dispersal of Plants Throughout the World* (1930), an almost inexhaustible source of information for the student of this field; E.J. SALISBURY, *The Reproductive Capacity of Plants* (1942), a truly thoughtful work that gives much more than the modest title suggests; J.C.T. UPHOF, "Ecological Relations of Plants with Ants and Termites," *Bot. Rev.*, 8:563–598 (1942), one of the very few articles in the English language that gives some information on the role of ants in seed dispersal; UNITED STATES DEPARTMENT OF AGRICULTURE, *Manual for Testing Agricultural and Vegetable Seeds*, Agriculture Handbook no. 30 (1952), of obvious practical importance; *Seeds: Yearbook of Agriculture, 1961* (1961), a treasure-trove of information, many-faceted; P.F. WAREING and I.D.J. PHILLIPS, *The Control of Growth and Differentiation in Plants* (1970), written with a physiologist's appreciation for the experimental approach, covers admirably various aspects of dormancy; F.W. WENT, "A Long-Term Test of Seed Longevity II," *Aliso*, 7:1–12 (1969), the latest results of Went's long-range experiments on differential longevity among seeds.

(B.J.D.M.)

Seine River

The Seine River, 485 miles (780 kilometres) long, with its tributaries drains an area of 30,000 square miles (78,000 square kilometres) in northern France; it is one of Europe's great rivers, and its drainage network carries most of the French inland waterway traffic. Since the early Middle Ages it has been above all the river of Paris, and the mutual interdependence of the river and the city that was established at its major crossing points has been indissolubly forged. The fertile centre of its basin in the Île-de-France was the cradle of the French monarchy and the nucleus of the expanding nation-state and is still its heartland and metropolitan region.

The Seine rises at 1,545 feet (471 metres) above sea level on the Mont Tasselot in the Côte d'Or region of Bourgogne (Burgundy) but is still only a small stream when it traverses porous limestone country beyond Châtillon. Flowing northwest from Bourgogne, it enters Champagne above Troyes and traverses the dry chalk plateau of Champagne in a well-defined trench. Joined by the Aube near Romilly, it bears west to skirt the Île-de-France in a wide valley to Montereau, where it receives the Yonne on its left bank. This tributary is exceptional in rising beyond the sedimentary rocks of the Paris Basin on the impermeable crystalline highland of the Morvan, a northward extension of the Massif Central. Turning northwest again, the Seine passes Melun and Corbeil as its trenched valley crosses the Île-de-France toward Paris. As it enters Paris, it is joined by its great tributary the Marne on the right, and after traversing the metropolis, it receives the Oise, also on the right. In its passage through Paris, the river has been trained and narrowed between the riverside quays that constitute France's major inland port. Flowing sluggishly in sweeping loops, the Seine passes below Mantes-la-Jolie across Normandie (Normandy) toward its estuary in the English Channel. Rouen, although 78 miles from the sea, is a major seaport but has been outstripped by the deepwater port of Le Havre on the broad estuary, which opens rapidly and extends for 16 miles below Tancarville. It experiences the phenomenon of the tidal bore, which is known as the *mascaret*.

From its source to Paris, the Seine traverses concentric belts of successively younger sedimentary rocks, infilling a structural basin, the centre of which is occupied by the limestone platforms of the Île-de-France immediately surrounding Paris. The rocks of this basin are inclined gently toward Paris at the centre and present a series of outward-facing limestone (including chalk) escarpments (*côtes*) alternating with narrower clay vales. The *côtes* are breached by the Seine and its tributaries, which have made prominent gaps. As they converge upon Paris, the trenchlike river valleys separate a number of island-like limestone platforms covered with very fertile, easily worked windblown soil (*limon*). These have provided rich cereal-growing land from time immemorial and constitute the Île-de-France. The lower course of the Seine, below Paris, is directed in a general northwesterly direction towards the sea, in conformity with the trend of the lines of structural weakness affecting the northern part of the basin. The English Channel breaches the symmetry of the basin on its north side, interrupting the completeness of the concentric zones. Still in the chalk belt, the river enters the sea. The geological background

The basin of the Seine presents no very striking relief contrasts. Within 30 miles of its source the river is already below 800 feet, and at Paris, 227 miles from its mouth, it is only 80 feet above sea level. It is thus slow flowing and eminently navigable, the more so because its regime is generally so regular. Most of the river basin is formed of permeable rocks, the absorptive capacity of which mitigates the risk of river floods. Precipitation throughout the basin is modest (generally 25 to 30 inches) and evenly distributed over the year as rain, with snow infrequent except on the higher southern and eastern margins. The Yonne, unique among the tributaries in being derived from impermeable, crystalline highlands, where there is also considerable winter snow, contributes most irregularity; but the Seine is the most regular of the great rivers of France and the most naturally navigable. Occasionally the summer level is considerably reduced, but sandbanks such as are so typical of the Loire do not appear; and low water is further masked by the regularization of the river that has been carried out to improve its navigability. Winter floods are rarely dangerous; but in January 1910 exceptionally heavy rainfall caused the river to rise above 28 feet at Paris, flooding the extensive low-lying quarters along its ancient meander loop (the Marais). To match this high level it is necessary to go back to February 1658; but in January 1955 again the river rose to more than 23 feet in Paris. The average flow at Paris is 10,000 cubic feet per second, as compared with the 1910 flood rate of 83,000. To regulate the flow, maintain the summer level, and protect the city from winter floods, large reservoirs have been built above Paris on the Yonne and Marne; and in 1960 work was begun on additional reservoirs on the Seine near Troyes and on the Marne at Champaubert-aux-Bois.

The Seine, especially below Paris, is a great traffic highway. It links Paris with the sea and the great maritime ports of Le Havre and Rouen. Vessels drawing up to 10 feet (3.20 metres) can reach the quays of Paris. Most of the traffic, which chiefly consists of heavy petroleum products and building materials, passes upstream to Paris. It more than doubled over the 1960s and was expected to reach 40,000,000 tons by 1975. The Lower Seine system is connected with that of the Rhine by way of the Marne, and the Oise links it with the waterways of Belgium. There are plans for further developing the inland waterways of this northwestern maritime gateway of Europe. The links with the Loire waterway and with the Saône–Rhône, dating from the 17th and 18th centuries, when connecting canals were built, are now of minor importance. Economic aspects of the river

BIBLIOGRAPHY. JACQUES GRAS, *Le Bassin de Paris méridional: étude morphologique* (1963), a comprehensive work on the relief of the Paris and Loire basins, as well as the Loing Valley and part of the Yonne Basin; ANDRE VIGARIE, *Les Grands Ports de commerce de la Seine au Rhin* (1964), a study of the seaports of Rouen, Le Havre, Dunkirk, Antwerp, Rotterdam, and Amsterdam and their historical development.

(A.E.Sm).

Seismograph

A seismograph is an instrument that makes a record of the ground oscillations caused by an earthquake, explosion, or other earth-shaking phenomenon. Although originally designed to record natural earthquakes, it now has many other uses.

An earlier seismic instrument called the seismoscope made no record of the ground oscillations but simply indicated that shaking had occurred. The term seismometer originally referred to an instrument that measures the amount of ground motion. Some seismographs are equipped with an electromagnetic device called a sensor that translates ground motions into electrical changes. A seismogram is a record made by a seismograph.

HISTORICAL DEVELOPMENT

A Chinese scholar, Chang Heng, invented a seismoscope that registered the occurrence of an earthquake as early as AD 132. Judging from the available descriptions of this device, it was cylindrical in shape with eight dragon heads arranged around its upper circumference, each with a ball in its mouth. Around the lower circumference were eight frogs, each directly under a dragon head. When an earthquake occurred, one of the balls dropped from the dragon's mouth and was caught by the frog's mouth, generating a sound. The ball probably was pushed out of the dragon's mouth by a loose vertical rod inside the device, which was shaken by the tremor. A device involving water spillage was made in 17th-century Italy. Later, a water-filled bowl and still later a cup filled with mercury were used for detecting earthquakes and tremors.

Mercury tube seismograph

In 1855 Luigi Palmieri of Italy designed a seismometer that consisted of several U-shaped tubes filled with mercury and oriented toward the different points of the compass. When the ground shook, the motion of the mercury made an electrical contact that stopped a clock and simultaneously started a recording drum on which the motion of a float on the surface of mercury was registered. This device thus indicated time of occurrence and the relative intensity and duration of the ground motion.

Pendulums. The basic problem in measuring ground motions is to attain a steady point that remains steady when the ground moves. Various types of pendulums have been used for this purpose. The simplest type is a common pendulum in which a heavy mass is suspended by a wire or rod from a fixed point (as in a clock). Other forms are the inverted pendulum, in which a heavy mass is fixed to the upper end of a vertical rod pointed at its lower end, and the horizontal pendulum, in which a rod with a mass on its end is suspended at two points so as to swing in a nearly horizontal plane instead of a vertical plane. In 1840 a seismometer based on the common pendulum was installed near Comrie in Perthshire, Scotland. In 1841 a seismometer based on the inverted pendulum was installed at six places near Comrie to register local shocks. This instrument recorded deflections of the pendulum on a fixed paper.

Milne's seismograph. Seismograph developments occurred rapidly in 1880 when Sir James Alfred Ewing, Thomas Gray, and John Milne, British scientists working in Japan, began to study earthquakes. Following a severe earthquake that occurred at Yokohama near Tokyo in that year, they organized the Seismological Society of Japan. This society continued active for about ten years; under its auspices, various devices, forerunners of today's seismograph, were invented. Among the instruments constructed in this period was Milne's now famous horizontal pendulum seismograph (Figure 1). A boom (B), to which the mass (M) is attached, is suspended horizontally by the pivot (P) and a silk thread (T) fixed to a point above the pivot. A thin plate (C), in which a narrow slit is cut parallel to the boom, is attached to the end of the boom (B). A similar plate with a slit at right angles to the upper plate is fixed on the top of the box containing a

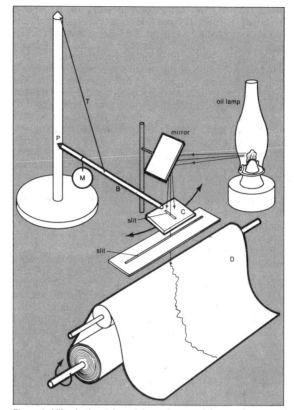

Figure 1: Milne horizontal pendulum seismograph (see text).
From *Bulletin of the Seismological Society of America* (1969), vol. 59, No. 1, p. 212

recording drum (D). A ray of light from an oil lamp passes through both slits and forms a small spot of light on a sheet of light-sensitive graph paper (bromide paper) wrapped on the recording drum. Milne successfully used this seismograph to record several earthquakes in Japan; then in England he established a small seismographic network using such instruments. Today's worldwide seismographic network was founded soon after.

Omori Fusakichi, the founder of Japanese seismology and inventor of the Omori horizontal pendulum seismograph, was a student of Milne and graduated from the science department of the University of Tokyo in 1890. He was among the Japanese scientists who began study of earthquakes in 1891 after the Mino-Owari earthquake struck central Japan. Japanese seismologists made significant contributions, particularly after they revived the Seismological Society of Japan following the great earthquake of 1923.

THE MODERN SEISMOGRAPH

General principles. If a common pendulum is free to swing in one direction and if the ground moves rapidly in the direction of freedom of the pendulum while the pendulum is motionless, the pendulum will remain in place through inertia. The same phenomenon will occur if the ground moves back and forth (oscillates). If the period of oscillation of the ground (the time necessary for one complete oscillation) is sufficiently shorter than the period of free oscillation of the pendulum, the pendulum will again remain motionless, and the movement of the ground relative to the pendulum can be recorded. The magnitude of this movement is commonly amplified in some way. This is the basic principle of the seismograph.

In actual practice, it often works out that the period of the pendulum is comparable to that of the ground oscillation; under these circumstances, the seismograph will not correctly record the earth's movement. The error, however, can readily be computed mathematically. A graphic curve showing the variation of magnification according to the oscillation period of the ground is called a magnification curve or response curve.

In general, then, the seismograph is an instrument in

which the relative motion of pendulum and ground is recorded. It is equally possible to take the ratio between the deflection of the pendulum and the velocity (or acceleration) of the ground. This ratio is called the velocity (or acceleration) sensitivity of the seismograph.

If free oscillation of the pendulum is not minimized, it will mask the proper recording of earth movements. The simplest way to reduce (damp out) the free oscillation of a pendulum is to suspend it in a viscous (thick) liquid of which the resisting force is proportional to the velocity of the pendulum. In practice, the required resisting force is exerted by a special device called a damper. An air damper produces its resisting force by the use of a piston moving in a cylinder. In an electromagnetic damper, the resisting force is created by electrical currents induced in a copper plate moving in a strong magnetic field.

Recording pendulum movement. The ground can move in any of three directions, two horizontal and one vertical. Since each kind of movement must be separately recorded, three pendulums, one for each direction, are needed for a complete seismograph.

In the mechanical method of recording movement, a sheet of smoked paper is wrapped around a rotating drum, so mounted as to move with the earth. A moving pen connected to the pendulum presses lightly on the paper. The rotating drum shifts slightly with each revolution so that recorded lines are not superimposed on each other. The drum rotates without interruption; one sheet of paper usually lasts 24 hours. Deflection of the pendulum is commonly magnified mechanically by single or double multiplying levers. Though this lever method is simple and economical the seismograph must have a heavy mass to overcome the friction between pen and paper. In consequence, some mechanical seismographs weigh one ton or more. In the optical lever method, pendulum motion causes a mirror to move; light is reflected by this mirror onto photosensitive paper wrapped on a drum. Thus there is no friction to affect the pendulum.

In the electromagnetic method, widely used today, a coil fixed to the mass of the pendulum moves in a magnetic field; the electric current generated in the coil operates a galvanometer exactly as a dynamo operates a motor. A mechanical damper is not needed, for damping force can be conveniently produced by electromagnetic action between the current in the coil of the pendulum and the magnetic field. If the current produced in the coil of the pendulum is amplified electronically, high magnification is obtainable. Certain short-period seismographs of this type used for the observation of micro-earthquakes attain a magnification as high as 1,000,000 or more. In ordinary seismographic observation, the time of initiation of ground oscillations is recorded. Marks are placed on the seismogram paper once a minute; an extra one identifies the hour.

Types of seismographs. Seismographs differ in the type of pendulum and magnifying and recording elements they employ. The horizontal pendulum seismograph was first used by John Milne of England, in 1883, though the horizontal pendulum had been used earlier by other scientists to observe the effect of the moon on the earth's gravity. Ernst von Rebeur-Paschwitz of Germany devised a horizontal pendulum for the same purpose in which two pivots were employed to suspend the pendulum. One day in 1889 he noticed that an unusual train of oscillations had been recorded by his instrument. He later learned that these coincided with a severe earthquake in Kyushu, Japan. This discovery demonstrated the feasibility of observing distant earth tremors by the use of a long-period pendulum and consequently gave European scientists an opportunity to make seismographic observations in their own countries, where no earthquakes occurred. The Milne seismograph was improved in 1927 by an optical lever that increased magnification. B.B. Galitzin of Russia also used a horizontal pendulum; he suspended a beam (with a weight attached) by two lines to make an electromagnetic seismograph.

The horizontal pendulum seismograph was improved greatly after World War II. The Press-Ewing seismograph, developed in the United States for recording long-period waves, is widely used throughout the world. This

Long-
distance
observa-
tion of
earth-
quakes

device employs a Milne-type pendulum, but the pivot supporting the pendulum is replaced by an elastic wire to avoid friction.

The inverted pendulum seismograph was first used by Emil Wiechert in Germany in 1904 (Figure 2). A large

From *Bulletin of the Seismological Society of America* (1969)

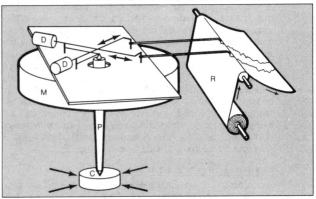

Figure 2: Wiechert inverted pendulum seismograph.

mass (M) is attached at the upper end of a strong pillar (P), and a double set of flat springs supports the pillar at its lower end (C). The mass has two-dimensional freedom; its movement is divided into two horizontal components by levers. A rigid framework supports a mechanical recording device (R) and piston-type air dampers (D).

A torsion pendulum seismograph was devised by J.A. Anderson and Harry O. Wood in the U.S. in 1924 (Figure 3). A small copper cylinder (C) is attached to a

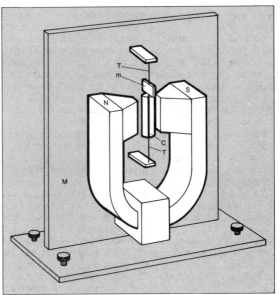

Figure 3: Anderson-Wood torsion pendulum seismograph.

tungsten wire (T) stretched nearly vertically. The mass can swing in a nearly horizontal plane around the wire; damping force is given to the mass by a strong magnetic field produced by U-shaped permanent magnet (M). Magnification as large as 2,800 is attainable by an optical lever using the mirror (m). This is the seismograph that was used by Charles F. Richter in the U.S. to define the magnitude scale of an earthquake (see EARTHQUAKES).

The vertical component seismograph employs a pendulum that oscillates vertically. The simplest pendulum of this type is a mass suspended by a helical spring. If a long oscillation period is desired, a long weak spring must be used; this is quite convenient. In 1881 Thomas Gray devised a vertical component seismograph employing a pendulum so suspended that the oscillation period can be increased without using a longer spring. Then J.A. Ewing showed that the period could be lengthened still more by lowering the point of attachment of the spring. This

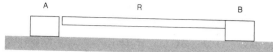

Figure 5: Strain seismograph.
From *Bulletin of the Seismological Society of America* (1935)

method of suspension was later applied to vertical component seismographs by Galitzin and Wiechert. Galitzin's instrument employs an electromagnetic recording device, while Wiechert's instrument uses a mechanical recording device with a heavy mass. Both were used widely in the first half of this century. In 1935 Lucien LaCoste in the U.S. devised a long-period vertical component pendulum using a new and different means of suspension. The LaCoste pendulum is so suspended that the upper end of the spring is fixed nearly above the rotation axis of the pendulum, which is composed of a horizontal rod and the mass. This method of suspension is very simple; the spring employed is of such a character that its initial length before the load is added is zero. The Press–Ewing vertical component seismograph uses a pendulum of the LaCoste type, with the period adjustable up to 30 seconds.

The electromagnetic seismograph was devised by Galitzin in 1907. A coil attached to a pendulum is arranged to move in the field produced by a magnet; the output of the coil indicates the magnitude of the earth's seismic movement, since the more rapidly the coil swings the larger is its output. A magnetic damper checks the oscillations, which would otherwise continue and prevent detection of the next tremor. More recently designed electromagnetic seismographs generally take advantage of coil movements parallel to the coil's axis, somewhat like the moving coil of a dynamic loudspeaker. Damping is accomplished by the current induced in the coil.

In 1932 Hugo Benioff, in the United States, applied an electromagnetic transducer to a short-period seismograph in a new way. Figure 4 is a schematic drawing of the Beni-

Adapted from H. Benioff, *Advances in Geophysics*

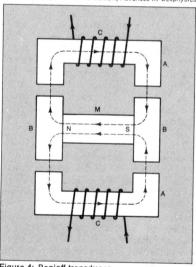

Figure 4: Benioff transducer.

off transducer as later improved. (M) is a permanent magnet that supplies magnetic field to the pole pieces (B,B). From the pole pieces, the field crosses the air gaps, dividing equally between two moving components (A,A). The structure consisting of magnet and pole pieces is fixed to the ground, and the armature assembly is fastened rigidly to the pendulum. Motion of the pendulum relative to the ground varies the lengths of the air gaps, one pair increasing while the other is decreasing. The resulting change in the magnetic field through the armatures induces an electromotive force (voltage) in the coils (C,C) surrounding the armatures that is proportional to the rate of change of the relative displacement. This voltage is measured by a galvanometer, a device for detecting small electrical currents. If an electronic amplifier is placed between transducer and galvanometer, a high-grain (magnification) seismograph is attainable. In instruments equipped with an electronic amplifier, magnetic tape recording is also possible.

All the seismographs hitherto described measure oscillatory motions of the ground at a given point. The strain seismograph, in contrast, employs no pendulum, and its operation depends on oscillation in the distance between two points on the ground. In Figure 5, (A) and (B) are

Strain seismograph

two piers separated by a distance, which may be 20 metres or more. One end of the rod (R) is fixed to the pier (B), and the other placed near the pier (A). Earth strains resulting from seismic waves produce variations in the separation of the two piers; these variations are observable as changes in the distance between the free end of the rod and pier (A). This seismograph was first devised in 1935.

APPLICATIONS OF THE SEISMOGRAPH

Detection and location of earthquakes. A seismograph records oscillation of the ground caused by seismic waves that travel from their point of origin through the earth or along its surface. The seismogram of a nearby earthquake is of simple pattern, showing the arrival of P waves, waves that vibrate in the direction of propagation; S waves, waves that vibrate at right angles to the direction of propagation; and surface waves. In case of distant earthquakes, the seismogram pattern is more complicated because it shows various sorts of seismic waves that originate from one point but then may be reflected or refracted within the earth's crust before reaching the seismograph. The relation between the arrival time of these seismic waves and the epicentral distance—*i.e.*, the distance from the point of origin—is expressed by a time–distance curve, in which the arrival time is read on the vertical axis and the epicentral distance on the horizontal axis. If the arrival times of various seismic waves are read on the seismogram at a station and compared with the standard time–distance curves, the epicentral distance from that station (the distance of the centre of the earthquake from the recording station) can be determined. Knowing the epicentral distance from at least three stations, the origin of the earthquake can be calculated by simple trigonometric methods.

Detection of microseisms. Seismographs sometimes detect small and long-continuing oscillations of the ground, called microseisms, that do not originate in earthquakes. The occurrence of some microseisms is related to storms at sea. The detectability of earthquakes is reduced by the masking effects of microseisms.

Detection and prediction of volcano activity. Eruption of a volcano is commonly accompanied by many small earthquakes, especially when a volcano resumes activity after a long dormant period. Observation with sensitive seismographs therefore plays an important role in the prediction of volcanic activity. Often a strong earthquake is preceded by small earthquakes. Observation of very small tremors with sensitive seismographs is helpful in predicting disastrous earthquakes.

Detection and policing of nuclear tests. The seismograph can be used for detecting remote nuclear underground tests. In this activity, the relatively faint seismic waves generated by an underground explosion must be distinguished from natural tremors. In one American installation, the Large Aperture Seismic Array (LASA), established in Montana in 1965, 525 seismometers were spread over an area of 30,000 square kilometres. Their signals are combined to attain a high degree of sensitivity to seismic events.

Seismic prospecting. If the seismic waves generated by an explosive charge are recorded by sensitive seismographs installed at various points in the neighborhood of the explosion, the underground structure can be determined by analyzing the time–distance curves of P waves, both direct waves and those reflected or refracted at the boundaries of underground layers. Depths of underground layers, their angle of inclination, and the speed of seismic waves in each layer can be determined. Velocity measurement of seismic waves caused by explosions was tried in England in 1851. Since discovery of a large oil field in the U.S. by this method in 1923, seismic prospecting has made rapid progress and is now used for oil and gas exploration. The improvement in the instruments and techniques achieved after World War II made it possible to determine the structure of the earth's crust to as deep as 40 or 50 kilometres by detonation of a small amount of explosive.

Other uses. Ground shocks caused by dynamite blasts in mines, quarries, public works, etc. can be measured by the seismograph. Preliminary examinations based on seismographic measurements make it possible to estimate the intensity of shocks, and thus evaluate the possibilities of damage, caused by a given amount of dynamite. Rock bursts, in which rocks are ejected suddenly in deep pits or tunnels, are caused by increase of stress in the surrounding rocks. Experience in mines shows that an increase of small shocks detectable by highly sensitive Geophones—portable seismometers for field use—generally indicates a rock burst hazard.

A strong motion seismograph is designed particularly to register strong motions of the ground for engineering purposes—*i.e.*, antiseismic construction in earthquake-prone areas such as Japan.

Detection of vibrations on the moon's surface by use of seismographs is of fundamental importance in determining the internal structure, physical state, tectonic (crust) activity, and composition of the moon. The first moon seismograph was installed and operated at Tranquility Base by Apollo 11 astronauts in 1969. It contains three long-period seismometers and a single-component, short-period, vertical seismometer. The remote recording device is operated from the earth.

SEISMOGRAPHIC STATIONS

Construction, operation, and essential equipment. A seismographic station is commonly built up on a hard rock foundation. It is desirable to install the seismographs in a vault to reduce temperature variation and artificial noise. A modern seismographic station is equipped with at least two sorts of seismographs; one is a short-period instrument like the Benioff short-period seismograph, and the other one a long-period instrument like the Press–Ewing seismograph. A correct time-marking system is essential. If seismic signals are noticed on the seismograms, the arrival time, amplitude, period of oscillation, etc. of each seismic phase (a train of oscillations caused by the arrival of a different sort of seismic wave) are read off. A station commonly publishes these data periodically in its seismological bulletins.

Number and location. The number of seismographic stations has been increasing since the end of World War II. The global seismographic network was improved greatly during the course of The International Geophysical Year (IGY) beginning in 1957. About 800 seismographic stations were in operation around the world in 1970. Many belong to national networks, such as those of the U.S.S.R. (about 100 stations), Japan (about 100 stations), and Canada (about 21 stations). Some belong to universities and other organizations. As part of a U.S. program, a worldwide network of standardized seismograph stations (116 stations) was built up in 61 countries after 1960 under the auspices of The U.S. Coast and Geodetic Survey (USCGS).

The International Association of Seismology, founded in 1905 and renamed the International Association of Seismology and Physics of the Earth's Interior (IASPEI) in 1951, began in 1918 to publish the International Seismological Summary (ISS), which contains lists of seismological data computed from information taken from the global stations. The ISS will soon move to the International Seismological Center newly established at Edinburgh. The Bureau Central Séismologique at Strasbourg publishes a list of the same kind, in the form of a fast bulletin. The USCGS works for rapid determinations of locations and magnitudes of earthquakes anywhere in the world. Certain stations, including many of those of World-Wide Standardized Seismograph Network, send their data promptly to the USCGS.

BIBLIOGRAPHY. J.A. EWING, *Earthquake Measurement* (1883), a classic paper describing various scientific attempts

for measuring earthquakes in the early days of seismology; E. WIECHERT, *Theorie der automatischen Seismographen* (1903), an historically important scientific paper describing the principle of the Wiechert seismograph; C.G. KNOTT, *The Physics of Earthquake Phenomena*, pp. 48–89 (1908), and G.W. WALKER, *Modern Seismology*, pp. 1–36 (1913), discussions of early 20th-century seismographs; B. GALITZIN, *Vorlesungen über Seismometrie*, pp. 48–89 (1914), a historically important description introducing the mathematical theory of the electromagnetic seismograph; A. IMAMURA, *Theoretical and Applied Seismology*, pp. 237–312 (1937), L.D. LEET, *Practical Seismology and Seismic Prospecting,* pp. 189–228 (1938), C.F. RICHTER, *Elementary Seismology*, pp. 210–231 (1958), and B.F. HOWELL, JR., *Introduction to Geophysics*, pp. 70–79 (1959), textbooks of seismology briefly explaining modern seismographs; P.L. WILLMORE, "The Detection of Earth Movements," in S.K. RUNCORN (ed.), *Method and Technique in Geophysics*, 1:231–276 (1960), a technical introduction to modern seismographs; J. DEWEY and P. BYERLY, "The Early History of Seismometry (to 1900)," *Bull. Seism. Soc. Am.*, 59:183–227 (1969), extensive bibliographical references.

(H.To.)

Selachii

The sharks, together with their close relatives, the rays, belong to one of the two great groups of living fishes, the class Chondrichthyes, or Selachii. The latter name is also used for an order that includes only the sharks. Many structural, physiological, biochemical, and behavioral peculiarities make these fishes of particular interest to scientists. The dissection of a small shark is the biology student's introduction to vertebrate anatomy. These fishes are, in a sense, living fossils, for many of the living sharks and rays are assigned to the same genera as species that swam the Cretaceous seas over 100,000,000 years ago. Although by any reckoning a successful group, the modern chondrichthyeds number far fewer species than the more advanced bony fishes, or telecosts; 200 to 250 species of sharks and 300 to 340 species of rays are known.

The danger some sharks and stingrays present to humans makes these animals fascinating and, at the same time, abhorrent. Perhaps for this reason, they figure prominently in the folklore and art of many tropical peoples whose living depends on the sea.

GENERAL FEATURES

Problems of taxonomy. The name Selachii refers to a category of fishlike vertebrates, which are given a variety of treatments by ichthyologists. Some consider the Selachii to be a class or subclass comprising all the modern sharks and rays; others restrict the name to an order limited to the modern sharks and certain extinct ancestral forms. Under the latter system, the rays (including the sawfishes, guitarfishes, electric rays, skates, and stingrays) are ranked as a separate order, and the two orders are placed in a class or subclass.

The chimaeras (Holocephali) bear many similarities to sharks and rays; *e.g.*, in skeletal structure, internal organs, and physiology. Ichthyologists commonly, although not unanimously, emphasize these similarities by grouping the modern and ancient sharks, rays, and chimaeras in the class Chondrichthyes, the cartilaginous fishes. Under this system, which is used in the present article, the sharks, skates, and rays are further grouped into one subclass, Elasmobranchii, and the chimaeras into another, Holocephali. A classification in which the elasmobranchs constitute one class (Selachii) and the chimaeras another (Helocephali) is found in FISH. Assigning the two groups class rank implies a degree of distinctness equal to that of the amphibians (Amphibia), reptiles (Reptilia), birds (Aves), and mammals (Mammalia).

Distribution and abundance. The majority of sharks and rays are marine fishes, but many enter estuaries; some travel far up rivers, and a few are reported to be permanent residents of freshwater. Most species live in the relatively shallow waters of continental margins or around offshore islands; a few roam far out in the vast spaces of the oceans. Some live at great depths, in midwaters or on the bottom; others are surface swimmers or inhabit the bottom in shallow waters.

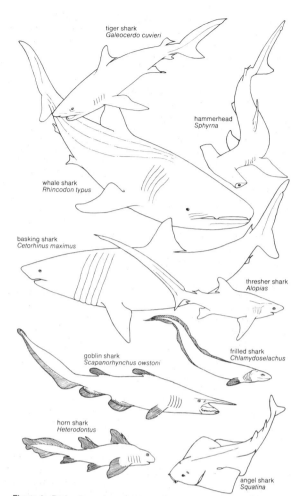

tiger shark
Galeocerdo cuvieri

hammerhead
Sphyrna

whale shark
Rhincodon typus

basking shark
Cetorhinus maximus

thresher shark
Alopias

goblin shark
Scapanorhynchus owstoni

frilled shark
Chlamydoselachus

horn shark
Heterodontus

angel shark
Squatina

Figure 1: Body plans of representative sharks.

Sharks and rays are poorly represented in fish markets of most countries. With limited demand for them, the damage they do to ordinary fishing gear, and the special care required to keep them marketable, fishermen avoid them if possible, or even discard those they happen to catch rather than bring them to port. Consequently, as a source of animal protein sharks and rays are generally underexploited, while the more highly valued bony fishes are generally overexploited. A possible consequence of this may be an increasing prominence of sharks and rays in the marine biota.

IMPORTANCE TO MAN

World catch of sharks and rays

Economic uses of elasmobranchs. *Sharks as food.* The Food and Agriculture Organization of the United Nations reports the world's total annual commercial catch of cartilaginous fishes in 1968 at 507,000 tons. Of these, 51 percent were sharks, 25 percent rays and their relatives, less than 1 percent chimaeras, and 24 percent various cartilaginous fishes. Countries of Asia accounted for 50 percent of the total; western Europe, 25 percent; U.S.S.R., 7 percent; Africa, 2 percent; South America, 10 percent; North America, 4 percent; and Oceania, 2 percent. The combined catch of these fishes by all the fisheries of the world has never exceeded 1.5 percent of all fish taken from the sea. Apart from their being generally less highly valued as food than bony fishes and therefore underexploited, they are much less numerous (*e.g.*, about 4 percent as many were taken during one systematic survey in the western Atlantic), and there are about 3 percent as many species.

The meat of sharks is marketed for food in all maritime countries. It may be prepared in various ways—fresh, salted, smoked, or pickled—offered in such forms as steaks, fillets, or flakes and under such names as shark, whitefish, grayfish, swordfish, sea bass, and halibut. The flesh is often rather strong tasting; this quality, however,

is one that can be removed by cleaning and washing and soaking the flesh in brine.

Since ancient times, Chinese people have used the dorsal fins of certain sharks and rays as the basis of an epicurean soup. To meet the demand for this product, they have imported fins from far-distant countries. The fins are prepared for market by removing the skin and flesh, leaving only the gelatin-rich cartilaginous rays, which are dried before shipment. Shark liver oil is used in various regions for tanning leather; for preserving wood; as a lubricant; as a folk medicine against rheumatism, burns, and coughs; as a general tonic; as a laxative; and as an ingredient of cosmetics. The liver of a basking shark yields 80 to 600 gallons of oil, which was used in lamps until petroleum products replaced animal oils for illumination. The discovery around 1940 that the liver of the soupfin shark of California is peculiarly rich in vitamin A led to an explosive development of a special fishery in California for this species and a search in other parts of the world for sharks having livers of comparable potency. Within a few years, however, the economic bubble burst, with the invention of a method for manufacturing synthetic vitamin A. The Australian school shark, that was used originally for vitamin A, is now caught for fish fillets.

Other shark products. The hard scales provide an abrasive surface to the skin of sharks and some rays, giving it a special value, as a leather called shagreen, for polishing hard wood. When heated and polished, shagreen is used for decorating ornaments and, in Japan, for covering sword hilts.

Shark leather is made in several countries, including the United States, from the skin of certain shark species after removal of the scales by a chemical process. A luxury product, much more durable than cowhide, shark leather is used for footwear, belts, wallets, and other accessories. The most suitable skins for leather are from tiger, dusky, brown, sand, blacktip, and nurse sharks.

In Greenland some Eskimos make rope from strips of the skin of the sleeper shark. Polynesians once added to the effectiveness of their war clubs with sharks' teeth. Sharks' teeth have some commerical value as curios. The Maori of New Zealand formerly paid high prices for mako sharks' teeth, which they wore as earrings.

Economic value of rays. About 126,000 tons of rays are marketed for food in various countries about the world, principally in Europe and Asia. By-products in local demand are skins of scaleless species for drumheads; those of scaly species are used for shagreen. Livers are used for oil, fins for gelatin. People of many tropical countries—Polynesia, Oceania, Malaysia, Central America, and Africa—have used the spines of stingrays for such various items as needles and awls, spear tips and daggers, and for the poison they contain. The entire tails of stingrays, complete with spines, have been used as whips in various tropical areas.

The electric rays, or numbfish, have little commerical value today. The ancient Greeks and Romans used the electric shock of *Torpedo* to relieve diseases of the spleen, chronic headaches, and gout. From the Greek word for electric ray, *narke*, comes the word narcotic. Today these fishes are of general interest chiefly as a source of acute irritation (if not danger) to bathers who happen to step on them and to fishermen who may be shocked when hauling in their wet nets.

Danger to man. Among the known shark species, 27 have been authoritatively implicated in attacks on persons or boats. Hospital and other records attest to many attacks on bathers, divers, and people awash in the sea following sea or air disasters. There are also many documented cases of sharks attacking small boats. A number of surviving victims have been able to identify the attacking animal as a shark; a few even reported the type of shark, such as a hammerhead. In many instances, witnesses have seen the assailant clearly enough to determine the species. Fragments of teeth left in wounds of victims or in the planking of boats have often been large enough to provide ichthyologists with the means for precise identification.

Attacks by sharks

In 1958 the American Institute of Biological Sciences established a Shark Research Panel at the Smithsonian Institution and Cornell University in order to gather historical and current records of shark attacks throughout the world. For the 35 years from 1928 to 1962, inclusive, the panel listed 670 attacks on persons and 102 on boats. Attacks occur most frequently throughout the year in the tropical zone between 21° north and south of the Equator; from midspring to midfall they extend as far north and south as the 42° parallels.

In Australia, New Zealand, South Africa, and along other coasts heavily infested with sharks, public beaches have been provided with lookout towers, bells, and sirens or nets, to protect bathers. Since 1937 Australia has used meshing offshore to catch the sharks. Gill nets suspended between buoys and anchors running parallel to the beach and beyond the breaker line have proved very effective in decreasing the danger of attack. The nets enmesh sharks from any direction, and even while touching neither the surface nor the bottom, and spaced well apart, they provide simple, effective control. South Africa has been using a similar protection system, although experiments with electrical barriers there were also in progress in the 1960s and 1970s.

The great majority of shark attacks seem to be in water warmer than 21° C (70° F), which presumably is also the habitat of the most dangerous species. Unfortunately, this rule does not apply to the most dangerous shark, the white shark, or man-eater (*Carcharodon carcharias*), which ranges into the cooler waters of both hemispheres.

By courtesy of New York Zoological Society

Sand shark (*Odontaspis taurus*).

The 27 species implicated by the Shark Research Panel in attacks on persons or boats are mostly large sharks with large, cutting teeth. Size, however, is not a dependable criterion, for man-eaters become dangerous when they are about one metre (three or four feet) long; and the largest ones, the basking shark and the whale shark, which grow to 12 and 18 metres (40 and 60 feet), respectively, subsist on minute planktonic organisms and on small schooling fishes. Although either might attack a boat if provoked, only two records of such occurrences have been reported, both in Scotland and both identified with the basking shark. More than 85 percent of all the

shark species are too small, too unsuitably toothed, or too sluggish or live at depths too great to be potentially dangerous. The most dangerous sharks include in addition to the white shark, the hammerheads (*Sphyrna*), tiger (*Galeocerdo*), blue (*Prionace*), and sand sharks (*Odontaspis*).

Most stingrays live in shallow coastal waters. Some move with the tides to and from beaches, mud flats, or sand flats. Anyone wading in shallow water where these fishes occur runs some risk of stepping on one and provoking an instant response—the ray lashes back its tail, inflicting an agonizingly painful wound that occasionally leads to fatal complications. Rays can be serious pests to shellfisheries, for they are extremely destructive to oyster and clam beds.

NATURAL HISTORY

Food habits. All sharks are carnivorous and, with a few exceptions, have broad feeding preferences, governed largely by the size and availability of the prey. The recorded food of the tiger shark (*Galeocerdo cuvieri*), for example, includes a wide variety of fishes (including other sharks, skates, and stingrays), sea turtles, birds, sea lions, crustaceans, squid, and even carrion such as dead dogs and garbage thrown from ships. Sleeper sharks (*Somniosus*), which occur mainly in polar and subpolar regions, are known to feed on fishes, small whales, squid, crabs, seals, and carrion from whaling stations. Many bottom-dwelling sharks, such as the smooth dogfishes (*Triakis* and *Mustelus*), take crabs, lobsters, and other crustaceans, as well as small fishes.

The two giant sharks, the whale shark (*Rhincodon typus*) and basking shark (*Cetorhinus maximus*), resemble the baleen whales in feeding mode as well as in size. They feed exclusively or chiefly on minute passively drifting organisms (plankton). To remove these from the water and concentrate them, each of these species is equipped with a special straining apparatus analogous to baleen in whales. The basking shark has modified gill rakers, the whale shark elaborate spongy tissue supported by the gill arches. The whale shark also eats small, schooling fishes.

The saw sharks (Pristiophoridae) and sawfishes (Pristidae) share a specialized mode of feeding that depends on the use of the long, bladelike snout, or "saw." Equipped with sharp teeth on its sides, the saw is slashed from side to side, impaling, stunning, or cutting the prey fish. Saw sharks live in midwaters; sawfishes, like most other rays, are bottom inhabitants.

Thresher sharks (*Alopias*) feed on open-water schooling fishes, such as mackerel, herring, and bonito, and on squid. The long upper lobe of the tail, which may be half the total length of the shark, is used to frighten the fish (sometimes by flailing the water surface) into a concentrated mass convenient for slaughter.

Most sharks and probably most rays segregate according to size, a habit that protects smaller individuals from predation by larger ones. Even among sharks of a size category, dominance between species is apparent in feeding competition, suggesting a definite nipping order. Other sharks keep clear of hammerheads (*Sphyrna*), whose manoeuvrability, enhanced by the rudder effect of the head, gives them an advantage. When potential prey is discovered, sharks circle it, appearing seemingly out of nowhere and frequently approaching from below. Feeding behaviour is stimulated by numbers and rapid swimming, when three or more sharks appear in the presence of food. Activity soon progresses from tight circling to rapid crisscross passes. Biting habits vary with feeding methods and dentition. Sharks with teeth adapted for shearing and sawing are aided in biting by body motions that include rotation of the whole body, twisting movements of the head, and rapid vibrations of the head. As the shark comes into position, the jaws are protruded, erecting and locking the teeth into position. The bite is extremely powerful; a mako shark (*Isurus*), when attacking a swordfish too large to be swallowed whole, may remove the prey's tail with one bite. Under strong feeding stimuli, the sharks' excitement may intensify into what is termed a feeding frenzy, in which not only the prey but

Feeding methods of larger sharks

also injured members of the feeding pack are devoured, regardless of size.

In most cases the initial attraction to the food is by smell. Laboratory studies have shown that sharks do not experience hunger in the normal sense of the word, and they are much more prone to be stimulated to feeding by the olfactory or visual cues announcing the appearance of prey.

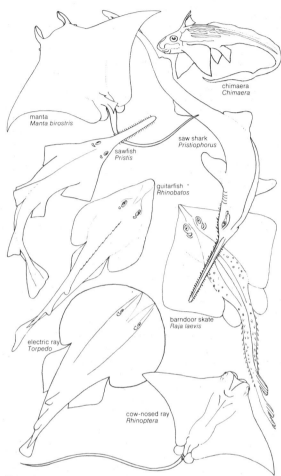

Figure 2: Body plans of representative selachii.

The majority of batoid fishes (members of the order Batoidei; i.e., rays and allies) are bottom dwellers, preying on other animals on or near the sea floor. Guitarfishes (Rhynchobatidae and Rhinobatidae), butterfly rays (Gymnuridae), eagle rays (Mylobatidae), and cownosed rays (Rhinopteridae) feed on invertebrates, principally mollusks and crustaceans. Whip-tailed rays (Dasyatidae) use their broad pectoral fins to dig shellfish from sand or mud. Skates (Rajidae) lie on the bottom, often partially buried, and rise in pursuit of such active prey as herring, trapping the victims by swimming over then settling upon them, a practice facilitated by the skates' habit of hunting at night.

Electric rays (Torpedinidae) are characteristically bottom fishes of sluggish habits. They feed on invertebrates and fish, which may be stunned by shocks produced from the formidable electric organs. With their electricity and widely extensible jaws, these rays are capable of taking very active fishes, such as flounder, eel, salmon, and dogfish. Shallow-water electric rays have been observed to trap fishes by suddenly raising the front of the body disk, while keeping the margins down, thereby forming a cavity into which the prey is drawn by the powerful inrush of water.

Most of the myliobatoid rays (seven recognized families of the suborder Myliobatoidea, which includes all of the typical rays) swim gracefully, with undulations of the broad, winglike pectoral fins. Some species, especially the eagle rays, frequently swim near the surface and even jump clear of the water, skimming a short distance through the air.

Manta, or devil, rays (Mobulidae) swim mostly at or near the surface, progressing by flapping motions of the pectoral fins. Even the largest often leap clear of the water. In feeding, a manta moves through masses of macroplankton or schools of small fish, turning slowly from side to side and using the prominent cephalic fins, which project forward on each side of the mouth, to fan the prey into the broad mouth.

Chimaeras and ghost sharks (Chimaeridae) dwell near the bottom in coastal and deep waters, to depths of at least 2,500 metres (about 8,000 feet). They are active at night, feeding almost exclusively on small invertebrates and fishes.

Reproductive behaviour. Mature individuals of some species of sharks segregate by sex, coming together only during the mating season, when the males, at least those of the larger, more aggressive species, stop feeding. Segregation is a behavioral adaptation to protect the females, one principal courting activity used by the male to induce cooperation of the female in mating being that of slashing her with teeth especially developed for that purpose. After mating, the sexes again separate. The pregnant females also tend to keep apart from the other females of like size. As the time of parturition approaches, the pregnant females move to particular areas, which presumably have properties of environment especially suitable as nursery grounds. When giving birth to their young, they stop feeding, and, soon after parturition is completed, they depart.

Nursery areas vary with species. Some sharks—e.g., the bull and sandbar sharks—use shallow waters of bays and estuaries; the silky shark uses the bottom far out on oceanic banks such as the Serrana Bank in the western Caribbean. The Atlantic spiny dogfish (Squalus acanthias) bears its young mostly during the winter far out on the continental shelf of northeastern America almost two years after mating.

Care of the young

A few skates that have been observed mating may be characteristic of other rays. The male seizes the female by biting the pectoral fin and presses his ventral surface against hers while inserting one, or in some species, both claspers into her cloaca. Male skates have one to five rows of clawlike spines on the dorsal side of each pectoral fin. These are retractile in grooves of the skin and are used to hold the female during mating.

The eggs of skates in aquaria have been observed to be extruded in series, usually of two but sometimes one, with rests of one to five days between extrusions. A female of a European skate, Raja brachyura, laid 25 eggs over a 49-day period in the aquarium located at Plymouth, England.

Although the mating of chimaeroids has not been observed, it is generally presumed that the mode of copulation is similar to that of sharks and that the male's frontal spine and anterior appendage of the pelvic fins are probably used in securing the female. Two eggs are laid simultaneously, one from each oviduct. They are often carried for a relatively long period before being laid, several hours or even days, each protruding for the greater part of its length.

FORM AND FUNCTION

Distinguishing features. The elasmobranchs are fishlike vertebrates differing from bony fishes in many respects. The skeleton is composed of cartilage and, although partly calcified (especially in the vertebrae), lacks true bone. There are five to seven fully developed gill clefts, opening separately to the exterior. Most sharks and all rays have an opening behind each eye, called a spiracle, which is a modified first gill cleft. The dorsal fin or fins and fin spines are rigid, not erectile. Scales, if present, are structurally minute teeth, called dermal denticles, each consisting of a hollow cone of dentine surrounding a pulp cavity and covered externally by a layer of hard enamel-like substances called vitrodentine. The scales covering the skin do not grow throughout life as they do in bony fishes, but have a limited size; new scales form

Shark scales

between existing ones as the body grows. Certain other structures, such as the teeth edging the rostrum (beak) of sawfishes and saw sharks, the stinging spines of sting rays, and the teeth in the mouth, are structurally modified scales. The teeth, arranged in rows in the mouth, are not firmly attached to the jaws but are imbedded in a fibrous membrane lying over the jaws. When a tooth becomes broken, worn, or lost, it is replaced by one moving forward from the next row behind; at the base of the innermost row are rudimentary teeth and tooth buds that develop and move forward as needed. A spiral membranous fold (spiral valve) extends through the intestine of all sharks, rays, and chimaeras.

The rays differ externally from sharks in having the gill openings confined to the lower surface; the eyes of the rays are on the dorsal surface, and the edges of the pectoral fins are attached to the sides of the head in front of the gill openings. Some rays lack scales, and others are variously armed with thorns, tubercles, or prickles, all of which are modified scales; the tails of some have long, saw-toothed spines equipped with poison glands. In the sawfishes the snout is prolonged into a long, flat blade armed on either side with teeth. Some skates and a few rays have electric organs by which they can administer electric shocks to enemies or prey.

The chimaeras have only one external gill opening. In the adult the skin on each side of the head is smooth and lacks scales; the teeth consist of six pairs of grinding plates. The dorsal fin and spine are erectile. Like male sharks and rays, male chimaeras have claspers that serve to transfer sperm to the female, but, in addition, they have an erectile clasping device, the tantaculum, in front of each pelvic fin; most species have another such organ on top of the head.

Senses. Although sharks are often said to have a low order of intelligence, they, as well as rays and chimaeras, have survived successfully over a long period of geologic time. They are well equipped to locate prey and their own kind; to direct the course of their seasonal migrations; to discriminate specific localities; to respond to variations of temperature; to react to attractive or repelling substances in the water; and perhaps even to feel objects some distance away from them. They can see, hear, smell, taste, feel, and maintain their equilibrium. The roles of the sense organs have been studied in only a few species, principally sharks, and consequently remain imperfectly understood.

The sense of smell is highly developed and probably the principal means of locating prey and guiding the predator toward it. Given a favourable direction of current, sharks can detect incredibly minute concentrations—fractions of a part per million (*i.e.*, less than 1×10^{-6} parts)—of certain substances in the water, such as blood.

Although their eyes are structurally and functionally adapted for seeing, it is believed that their visual acuity in discerning the form and colour of an object is limited. The importance of sight relative to smell increases as a shark approaches its target.

The hearing apparatus, located in the auditory capsule of the cranium, includes a system of semicircular canals, which are responsible for maintaining equilibrium. Sharks seem to be remarkably sensitive to sounds of low frequency and to possess extraordinary faculty for directional hearing. Whether or not hearing is more sensitive than smell has not yet been established.

Sensory organs identified as taste buds are located on the floor, sides, and roof of the mouth and on the throat, as well as on the tongue. Experiments on several species of large sharks indicate that they do discriminate food types, preferring tunas, for example, to other fish species. Under some conditions, however, they become less fastidious, going into a feeding frenzy in which they attack anything, including others of their own kind.

Sensory organs located in the skin of all sharks, rays, and chimaeras receive a variety of information—vibrations of low frequencies, temperature, salinity, pressure, and minute electrical stimuli, such as are produced by another fish in the vicinity. These organs are located in the lateral line system (a series of sensory pores along the side), in groups of pores on the head (ampullar organs), and in pit organs distributed on the back, flanks, and about the jaws.

Salt and water balance. Most marine vertebrates maintain lower concentrations of salts and other chemicals in their blood than are found in seawater, and so face a continuous problem of water loss to the environment, because of the tendency of water to move through membranes from regions of low salt concentration to regions of higher concentration. The marine cartilaginous fishes differ from almost all of the bony fishes (except the coelacanths and aestivating lungfishes) in being able to reabsorb in the renal (kidney) tubules most of their nitrogenous waste products (urea and trimethylamine oxide) and to accumulate these products in their tissues and blood, an ability termed the urea retention habitus. The concentration within the body thus exceeds that of the surrounding seawater, and water moves into the body with no expenditure of energy. When any of these fishes moves into freshwater, as many do, the urine flow to the outside increases; hence, the concentration of urea in the blood decreases. In the sawfish, for example, the increase of urine output is more than twentyfold; the blood urea concentration decreases to less than one-third the amount observed in marine forms. Purely freshwater elasmobranchs, such as the stingrays of the Orinoco and Amazon drainage systems, seem to lack the urea retention habitus.

The urea retention habitus

Respiration. Sharks with spiracles take in some water through them, but they breathe chiefly by opening the mouth while expanding the mouth-throat (bucco-pharyngeal) cavity and contracting the gill pouches to close the gill slits. With the mouth closed, they contract the bucco-pharyngeal cavity while dilating the gill pouches, thus drawing the water over the gills where the exchange of oxygen and carbon dioxide takes place. Then, with the mouth still closed, they contract the bucco-pharyngeal cavity and gill pouches and open the gill slits to expel the water. Most of the rays, on the other hand, take in water chiefly through the spiracles; these then close by contraction at their anterior margins, which bear rudimentary gill filaments and a spiracular valve. Folds of membrane on the roof and floor of the mouth prevent the water from passing down the throat and direct it to the gill openings. Skates, which usually hold the lower surface of the head slightly above the bottom, inhale some water through the mouth; mantas, which have small spiracles and live near the surface, respire chiefly through the mouth. Skates, stingrays, guitarfishes, and angel sharks frequently reverse the direction of flow through the spiracles, apparently to clear them of foreign matter. Chimaeras take in water chiefly through the nostrils, keeping the mouth closed for the most part. The water reaches the mouth primarily through grooves leading there from the nostrils.

Reproduction and development. All species of sharks, rays, and chimaeras produce large, yolk-rich eggs. These are fertilized internally, for which the males are equipped with two copulatory organs called claspers along the inner edges of the pelvic fins. Each clasper has a groove for guidance of sperm. The few published descriptions of mating sharks and rays are probably characteristic of the entire group. The male grasps one of the female's pectoral fins with his teeth to hold her in position as he inserts a clasper through a cavity (cloaca) and into a tube (oviduct). Males of most species probably use only one clasper at a time. The sperm travel to the anterior end of the oviduct, where they fertilize the eggs. The eggs then move down the oviduct past the shell gland, where they are covered by a shell or capsule.

In oviparous (egg-laying) species, which include some of the sharks, probably all the skates, possibly some of the guitarfishes, and all of the chimaeras, the eggs are enveloped in a horny shell, usually equipped with tendrils for coiling around solid objects or with spikelike projections for anchoring in mud or sand. The egg cases of most species are more or less pillow shaped; those of the horned sharks (Heterodontidae) are screw shaped with a spiral flange. The eggs of chimaeras are elliptic, spindle

Egg characteristics

shaped, or tadpole shaped and open to the exterior through pores and slits that permit entrance of water during incubation. An egg of the whale shark found in the Gulf of Mexico measured 30 centimetres (12 inches) long by about 14 centimetres (5½ inches) wide and was eight centimetres (three inches) thick. Protected by the shell and nourished by the abundant yolk, the embryo of an oviparous species develops for 4½ to 14¾ months before hatching.

The majority of sharks and most, possibly all, rays other than the skates are ovoviviparous (*i.e.*, the egg hatches within the mother). In this case, the egg is first coated in the shell gland with a temporary membranous capsule that lasts only during early development. After emerging from its capsule, the embryo remains in the oviduct of the mother, nourished by the yolk sac to which it remains attached. Embryos of some ovoviviparous sharks, notably the porbeagle (*Lamna nasus*), mako (*Isurus oxyrinchus*), and sand shark (*Odontaspis taurus*), ingest yolks of other eggs and even other embryos within the oviduct of the mother after the contents of their own yolk sacs are exhausted. In the majority of ovoviviparous sharks and rays, organically rich uterine secretions provide supplemental nourishment, which is absorbed by the yolk sac and in many cases by appendages borne on its stalk. In some genera of rays, vascular filaments producing these secretions extend through the spiracles and into the digestive tract of the embryos.

Several shark species are viviparous—*i.e.*, the yolk sac develops folds and projections that interdigitate with corresponding folds of the uterine wall, thus forming a yolk placenta through which nutrient material is passed from the mother.

Growth. Growth of a few shark species has been measured or estimated by the differences in length at the times of tagging and recapturing specimens, by statistical analysis of length in systematically collected samples, by the space between concentric circles on the centra of the vertebrae, and by periodic measurements of specimens kept in aquariums. All studies indicate a slow growth rate. During the ten years between birth and maturity, male Atlantic spiny dogfish grow an average of 47 centimetres (19 inches) and females 67 centimetres (26 inches). The Greenland shark (*Somniosus microcephalus*), which attains 6.5 metres (21 feet) or more (although rarely taken larger than about four metres [13 feet]), grows only about 7.5 millimetres (about 0.3 inch) per year. The annual growth increments of tagged juvenile whitetip reef and Galápagos sharks, both species that become at least 2.5 metres (eight feet) long, were found to be 31 to 54 millimetres (1.2 to 2.1 inches) and 41 millimetres (1.6 inches), respectively. The Australian school shark (*Galeorhincus australis*) grows about 80 millimetres (three inches) in its first year and 30 millimetres (one inch) in its 12th year. By its 22nd year, it is estimated to be approaching a maximum length of 160 centimetres (just over five feet).

The disk of the eastern Pacific round stingray (*Urolophus halleri*) increases in width on the average from 75 millimetres (three inches) at birth to 150 millimetres (six inches) when mature, when 2.6 years old. In the next five years it grows about 60 millimetres (2.4 inches) more toward its maximum recorded width of 25 centimetres (ten inches) in males or 31 centimetres (12.4 inches) in females. The males of European thronback rays (*Raja clavata*) are about 50 centimetres (20 inches) wide when they reach first maturity, about seven years after birth; females are 60 to 70 centimetres (24 to 28 inches) at first maturity, nine years after birth.

EVOLUTION AND CLASSIFICATION

Evolution. The earliest fossil remains of fishlike vertebrates are too fragmentary to permit tracing the modern fishes precisely to their origins. It is believed that the ancestral forms evolved during the Silurian Period (from about 430,000,000 to 395,000,000 years ago) in the upper reaches of streams. During the end of the Silurian and the beginning of the Devonian that followed, there appeared an exceedingly diverse group of armour-plated

Relationship to bony fishes

Figure 3: *Primitive sharklike fishes.*
(Above) *Hybodus* from the Mesozoic Era. (Below) *Cladoselache* from the Late Devonian Period.

fishes with jawlike structures, paired fins, and bony skeletal tissue. Paleontologists refer these to a distinct class, Placodermi (*q.v.*). Between the beginning and end of the Devonian (the latter about 350,000,000 years ago), the placoderms reached their peak in diversity and numbers and almost completely died out; only a few lingered another 10,000,000 years into the Early Mississippian (roughly, the Lower Carboniferous). During their flowering, the placoderms evidently gave rise to the Osteichthyes (the bony fishes) and the Chondrichthyes (the cartilaginous fishes). Although the lines of evolution remain to be discovered, it seems quite clear that the two groups evolved independently, the Chondrichthyes appearing much later than the Osteichthyes. Although a few sharklike forms remained in freshwater, the vast majority soon invaded the sea, perhaps in response to the arid Devonian climate. There they adapted to life in salt water by evolving the urea retention habitus (see above *Salt and water balance*). Their cartilaginous skeleton, far from representing an evolutionary stage antecedent to the Osteichthyes, as was once believed, is probably degenerate rather than primitive. Possibly their precursors were the petalichthyids, a group of Devonian sharklike placoderm fishes with ossified skeletons and well-developed fins.

The phyletic relationship of the chimaeras and the sharks and rays is a moot subject. Although both groups have many characteristics in common, such as the possession of a cartilaginous skeleton, placoid scales, teeth simply imbedded in gums, a spiral valve in the intestine, urea retention habitus, internal fertilization (for which the males have claspers) and absence of a swim bladder, the two groups may have evolved independently along parallel lines, the chimaeras from the pyctodonts, an order of Devonian placoderms with body form and tooth structure very suggestive of modern chimaeras.

The first fishes clearly identified with the Chondrichthyes were sharklike in form. One order, the Pleuracanthodii, consisting of one family of freshwater, sharklike fishes, appeared in Late Devonian, was abundant in the Carboniferous and Early Permian (until about 250,000,000 years ago), and disappeared during the Triassic Period, which followed. These fishes were characterized by the following features: the skeletal structure of both pectoral and pelvic fins had an axis with side branches (called the archipterygial type); the tail was almost symmetrical, being only slightly tilted upward; a long movable spine projected backward from the back of the head; the teeth had two divergent prongs and a central cusp set on a button-like base; the anal fin was two-lobed; and the males had claspers.

The other order, Cladoselachii, consisted of marine fishes known only from fossils of the late Middle Devonian, Carboniferous, and Early Permian periods. Their distinguishing characteristics were that each tooth had a long base composed of a bonelike tissue, from which rose three conical cusps, a tall central one and two smaller ones on either side; the body scales had several lobes or cusps; the jaws had double articulation, extending for-

Fossil sharklike fishes

ward to the snout; claspers were lacking; the outline of the caudal (tail) fin was almost symmetrical but with differing internal structure of the upper and the lower lobes.

The cladoselachians were probably ancestral to a group closer to modern sharks, the order Hybodontii. They probably represent an intermediate state in selachian evolution and are classified by some authorities in the order Selachii. Although the jaws had the primitive double articulation, the skeletal support of the pectoral and pelvic fins was close to that of modern selachians, with basal elements projecting outward into the fins. The teeth near the front of the mouth were generally sharp cusped; the cusps of those further back were sometimes reduced to a rounded crown. The front teeth were suitable for seizing prey; those in the back were suitable for crushing mollusks. The hybodonts appeared toward the end of the Devonian, flourished in the Late Paleozoic, and died out during the latter half of the Mesozoic, a few lasting into the Late Cretaceous (about 80,000,000 years ago).

The great period of radiation (diversification) in marine vertebrates characterizing the Mesozic ended in the Permian, and the chondrichthyed fishes, which had reached their greatest flowering during the Carboniferous, became greatly reduced, remaining so until the Jurassic (about 190,000,000 years ago), when the areas of the seas expanded and those of the land diminished. Then the six-gilled shark (*Hexanchus*), horned shark (*Heterodontus*), and guitarfishes appeared. By the end of the Cretaceous, most of the families and many genera of modern sharks, as well as those of skates and rays, were represented. The evolution of elasmobranch fishes, much as they are known today, had been accomplished.

Annotated classification. The most recent approaches to a comprehensive review of the chondrichthyeds are that of U.S. ichthyologists H.B. Bigelow and W.C. Schroeder and that by U.S. paleontologist Alfred S. Romer. The following synopsis, based on their work, provides principal identifying characteristics of all major Recent groups.

CLASS CHONDRICHTHYES (OR SELACHII)

Subclass Elasmobranchii (sharks and rays)

Chondrichthyeds with 5–7 pairs of gill clefts not covered by a fold of skin, opening separately to the exterior.

Order Selachii (sharks)

Elasmobranchs with gill clefts opening at least partly on the side of the body.

Suborder Notidanoidei. Sharks having 6 or 7 gill openings. Anal fin present.

Family Hexanchidae (cow shark and 7-gilled sharks). Lower Jurassic to present; marine. The cow shark (*Hexanchus griseus*), in deep water, down to 1,875 metres (about 6,000 feet). Distinguished by presence of 6 gill slits; teeth of lower jaw strikingly unlike those of upper, the 5 or 6 on either side of the central tooth being about twice as broad as high, their inner edges saw-toothed with 5–8 pointed cusps. Size up to at least 5 metres, estimated length at maturity about 2 metres. Ovoviviparous; 4.5-metre specimen contained 108 embryos. The 7-gilled sharks (*Heptranchias* and *Notorhynchus*) are widely distributed in warm and temperate continental waters.

Suborder Chlamydoselachoidei.

Family Chlamydoselachidae (frilled shark). Miocene to present. One modern species known, rather rare. Distinguished by 6 gill slits, the margins of the first being continuous across the throat. Size to about 2 m. Moderately deep water of the eastern North Atlantic from Portugal to Norway and in the North Pacific off California and Japan.

Suborder Heterodontoidei. Upper Devonian to present. Five gill openings on each side of body; anal fin present; 2 dorsal fins, each preceded by a spine. Marine.

Family Heterodontidae (Horned sharks, bullhead, Port Jackson shark). With 1 Recent genus and about 10 species. Oviparous; egg case screw shaped, a double spiral flange extending from apex to large end. Teeth in upper and lower jaws alike, those in front incisor-like, those on sides much larger and molar-like. Bottom dwellers out to about 180 m depth. Australia, New Zealand, East Africa, East Indies, China, Japan, eastern Pacific, north as well as south. Not known in Atlantic or Mediterranean. Size up to about 1.4 m.

Suborder Galeoidei (typical sharks). Five gill openings on each side of body; anal fin present; dorsal fin or fins not preceded by spines.

Family Odontaspididae (formerly *Carchariidae*) (sand sharks). Upper Jurassic to present. Marine. Caudal peduncle (narrow "stalk" of the tail) without lateral keels; with a distinct pit on its upper surface, but none on its lower. Teeth large, slender, smooth edged, lower eyelid without a nictitating membrane (a transparent extra eyelid). Development is ovoviviparous; maximum size varies with species, from around 2.8 to 6 m. One recent genus (*Odontaspis*) recognized, with some 6 species, found in warm temperate and tropical coastal waters of all oceans. Frequent shallow water near shore; sluggish except when feeding.

Family Scapanorhynchidae (goblin sharks). Lower Cretaceous to present. Marine. One genus, known from Japan, Portugal, and India, perhaps from Australia. Prominent elongation of the snout; protruding jaws. Maximum size to about 3.4 m. Probably ovoviviparous. A deepwater shark, fished commercially in Japan for its liver and flesh.

Family Isuridae. Upper Cretaceous to present. Three genera, marine, although at least 1 species (the white shark) occasionally strays into estuaries. Distinguished by 2 dorsal fins, of which the first is much larger than the second and the rear end of its base situated well in advance of the pelvic fins; caudal fin lunate (crescent shaped), its axis steeply raised. Teeth large. Ovoviviparous or viviparous. Circumglobal, occurring in boreal to warm temperate belts of all oceans in both hemispheres. Size in the great white shark (*Carcharodon carcharias*), to about 11 m.

Three genera, *Lamna, Isurus,* and *Carcharodon,* the last 2 dangerous to man, the great white shark unquestionably the most dangerous of all fishes.

Family Cetorhinidae (basking shark). Oligocene to present. Marine. Two dorsal fins, the first well in advance of pelvics; lunate caudal fin; gill openings extending around sides almost meeting at throat. Hundreds of minute teeth. Ovoviviparous. Embryonic development undescribed. Size at birth probably 1.5–1.8 m; maximum size to 13–14. Single genus (*Cetorhinus*) inhabiting temperate and boreal zones around the world. Whether basking sharks of the Northern and Southern hemispheres belong to a single species (*C. maximus*) is undetermined. Sluggish, inoffensive sharks, living at or near the surface, feeding wholly on plankton, which they sieve out of the water with their gill rakers.

Family Alopiidae (thresher sharks). Eocene to present. One genus, 5 species. Distinguished by the elongated upper lobe of the tail fin, which is almost as long as the rest of the body. Teeth small, bladelike. Ovoviviparous. Total length to about 6 m. Cosmopolitan at low and middle latitudes of all oceans. Harmless to man. Occasionally sold for food.

Family Orectolobidae (carpet and nurse sharks, wobbegongs). Upper Jurassic to present. Marine. Distinguished by the presence of 2 dorsal fins, the origin of the first over or behind the pelvic fins; nostril connected with mouth by a deep groove, its anterior margin with a well-developed fleshy barbel (tentacle). Teeth small, with several cusps; development ovoviviparous in some, oviparous in others. Some species (carpet sharks) live on the bottom and are ornamented with fleshy flaps along the sides of the head. Large family of many genera and species occurring mostly in western Pacific, Australasia, Indian Ocean, Red Sea. Only 1 species, the nurse shark, in Atlantic.

Family Rhincodontidae (whale shark). Distinguished from all other sharks by large, lunate tail, mouth at end of snout, 3 prominent ridges extending the length of body along the sides, back marked with round white or yellow spots and a number of white or yellow transverse stripes. Oviparous. Size said to reach over 18 m, the largest of modern fishlike lower vertebrates. One species only (*Rhincodon typus*); open waters of all oceans, mostly in tropics, but north to 42° north latitude (near New York) and to 33°55′ south (Table Bay, South Africa). Sluggish and inoffensive.

Family Scyliorhinidae (cat sharks, European dog shark, swell sharks). Upper Jurassic to present. Most with 2 dorsal fins (1 genus with 1); first dorsal fin situated far back on body, at least half of it behind the origin of the pelvic fins. Furrows are more or less developed at the angle of the jaws; teeth small, numerous, with several cusps. A large group of small sharks comprising many genera and species, occurring in temperate to tropical latitudes around the world. The swell sharks (*Cephaloscyllium*) can inflate the belly with air or water, presumably a defense mechanism. Of little, if any, commercial value; harmless to man.

Family Pseudotriakidae (false cat sharks). Distinguished by the base of the first dorsal fin being at least as long as the caudal fin. Teeth minute, numerous. One genus, *Pseudotriakis*; 2 species, 1 on both sides of the North Atlantic, the other in the western Pacific. Size to nearly 3 m. Deepwater sharks (taken down to 1,477 metres) rarely straying near shore and known only from a few specimens.

Family Triakidae (smooth dogfishes). Upper Cretaceous to present. The principal distinguishing feature is small, closely crowded teeth in series, rounded or somewhat compressed and with 3 or 4 cusps. True nictitating membrane lacking in eye. Development ovoviviparous or viviparous. Small sharks of coastal waters in tropical to temperate zones of all oceans. The family comprises at least 7 genera and numerous species. Smallest species, *Triakis barbour*, reaches only about 40 cm (16 in.); maximum size for others of family 150–175 cm. Although sharks of this family are generally considered harmless, there is one authenticated case of a California leopard shark (*Triakis semifasciata*) attacking a man in northern California.

Family Carcharhinidae. The largest family of sharks, with 13 genera and numerous species, including the tiger shark, the great blue, whalers, and many with various local common names. Upper Cretaceous to present. Two dorsal fins, the first in front of the pelvics. All species except 1 with well-developed nictitating membrane. Teeth bladelike, with only 1 cusp, only 1 or 2 rows functional along sides of jaws. Development either ovoviviparous or viviparous. The species range in maximum size from about 1.4–5.5 m. Members of this family occur from tropical to temperate zones in all oceans. Although most species are marine, several frequent brackish water or freshwater, and some occur in lakes that connect with the sea. The *Carcharinus leucas–gangeticus* group, a collection of several closely related species or subspecies, has a bad reputation; several cases of unprovoked attacks on persons are on record in both salt water and freshwater.

Family Sphyrinidae (hammerhead sharks). Upper Cretaceous to present. The most obvious distinguishing feature is the lateral expansion of the head in a hammer or bonnet form, with the eyes at the outer edges. Teeth large, triangular, smooth edged in some species, serrate in others. Viviparous or ovoviviparous; size varies with species, the largest (*Sphyrna mokarran*) is said to reach 6 m. Predacious. Marine, but occasionally straying into estuaries. Occur in tropical and temperate zones of all seas. Hammerheads have a sinister reputation of initiating unprovoked attacks, documented by authoritative cases on record.

Suborder Squaloidei (spiny dogfishes, bramble sharks, sleeper sharks, pygmy sharks). Upper Cretaceous to present. Widely distributed in all oceans from tropical to Arctic and sub-Antarctic latitudes; from shallow to deep depths. Anal fin lacking; snout not elongated into a beak; body subcylindrical (nearly round in section); not flattened dorsoventrally; margins of pectoral fin not expanded forward past first pair of gill openings.

Family Squalidae (spiny dogfishes, sleeper sharks and several others lacking common names). Upper Cretaceous to present. Distinguished by having about as many upper teeth in anterior row as in succeeding rows. Diverse habits, habitats, and sizes. Spiny dogfishes (*Squalus*) grow to about 120 cm; the Greenland sleeper shark to over 6 m; a pygmy shark (*Euprotomicrus*) to about 26 cm. Sleeper sharks (*Somniosus*) taken for food in waters around Iceland and west Greenland, but the fish must be dried before eating; otherwise it produces a mild poison.

Family Oxynotidae (prickly dogfish). Miocene to present. Distinguished by number of functional upper teeth increasing in each row from front to rear; dermal denticles large and prominent. Taken from depths of 60–530 m; 2 species known in eastern North Atlantic, Tasmania, and New Zealand.

Suborder Pristiophoroidei
Family Pristiophoridae (saw sharks). Cretaceous to present. Anal fin lacking, snout greatly elongated, each edge studded with sharp toothlike structures; upper eyelid is free; gill slits at the side of the head, not underneath as in the sawfish. Ovoviviparous. Marine. Indo-Pacific, South Africa, Tasmania, Australia, Philippines, Korea, Japan. The order comprises 1 family, 2 genera, *Pristiophorous*, with 5 gill openings, and *Pliotrema*, with 6. Good food fish, harmless to man.

Suborder Squatinoidei
Family Squatinidae (angel sharks). Upper Jurassic to present. Marine, widely distributed in continental temperate and warm waters of Atlantic and Pacific oceans, on or close to the sea bottom. Characterized by flattened body, eyes on upper surface; anterior margin of pectoral fins far overlapping gill openings, which are partly on side of body; no anal fin. Largest up to about 2.4 m. Ovoviviparous. One genus; possibly as many as 11 species.

Order Batoidei (rays, sawfishes, guitarfishes, skates, and stingrays)

Jurassic to present. Five gill openings, wholly on ventral

surface; pectoral fins united with sides of head forward past the gill opening. Differ from all sharks in lacking upper free eyelid.

Suborder Pristoidei
Family Pristidae (sawfishes). Jurassic to present. Distinguished by extension of snout into long, narrow, flattened blade armed on either side with teeth but without barbels; gills on lower side of body, as in other batoids. Ovoviviparous. Size varies with species; common Atlantic sawfish to at least 5.5 metres; species in Indian and Australian waters to over 7 metres. Widely distributed in tropical and subtropical zones of all oceans; occur in estuaries and run far up large rivers into freshwater; but whether they remain resident and reproduce in freshwater lakes is not clearly established. Six species are known.

Suborder Rhinobatoidei (guitarfishes). Lower Jurassic to present. Electric organs lacking; well-developed dorsal and caudal fins present; base of tail stout, not sharply marked off from rest of body. Most species ovoviviparous, some perhaps oviparous.

Family Rhynchobatidae. Cretaceous to Recent. Distinguished by caudal fin being conspicuously bilobed and somewhat lunate; posterior edge of pectorals does not reach foremargin of pelvics. Two genera, widely distributed in tropical and subtropical shallow waters of Indo-Pacific. Maximum size over 2 m.

Family Rhinobatidae. Caudal fin not bilobed; posterior edges of pectoral fins extending rearward at least as far as the origin of the pelvics. Small, rounded, closely set teeth. About 7 genera and 26 species; tropical and warm temperate shallow coastal waters of all oceans, in some localities entering freshwater and perhaps even permanently residing and breeding there. Size to about 1.8 m. Harmless to bathers.

Suborder Torpedinoidei (electric rays, numbfishes, torpedoes). Eocene to present. Distinguished principally by highly developed electric organs on either side of the head and gill chambers; the outlines of these organs visible externally in most species. Pectoral fins with the head form a circular or ovate disk. Skin of most species soft and entirely scaleless. Eyes small, fuctional in most species but rudimentary or obsolete in deepwater forms. Mostly sluggish bottom dwellers in all the oceans from tropical to temperate latitudes and from the intertidal zone to depths of at least 1,100 m. Three families, Torpedinidae, Narkidae, and Temeridae, distinguished by whether 1, 2, or no dorsal fins are present. Numerous genera and species. The largest electric rays of the genus *Torpedo* reach a length of about 180 cm; the smallest, of the genus *Narke*, less than 30 cm.

Suborder Rajoidei (skates). Lower Cretaceous to present. Moderately slender tail, on which the caudal fin is reduced to membranous fold or entirely lacking; outer margins of the pelvic fin are more or less concave or notched. Probably all species are oviparous. Three families are distinguished by whether 1, 2, or no dorsal fins are present.

Family Rajidae (the great majority of skates). Two dorsal fins. Upper surface of the body disk more or less rough with spines, thornlike denticles, or both. Some species with electric organs along the sides of the tail, which, as far as known, produce very weak shocks. Six genera, widely distributed from tropical to sub-Arctic belts of both hemispheres but with curious gaps in distribution; scarce, if present, in the Micronesian, Polynesian, and Hawaiian islands in the Pacific, in the western Atlantic between Yucatán and mid-Brazil, and in West Africa between Cape Verde and Walfish Bay. They occur from estuaries seaward, several species down to depths of over 500 m. Several species inhabit deep water, at last one being found at over 2,700 m. They live mostly on the bottom, often partially buried.

Family Arhynchobatidae. Distinguished from other skates by having a single dorsal fin. Single genus and species, *Arynchobatis asperrimus*, known only from New Zealand.

Family Anacanthobatidae. No dorsal fin; completely smooth skin; the pelvic fins so deeply notched as to form leglike structures anteriorly. Two genera, *Anacanthobatis* from Natal coast, South Africa, and *Springeria* from Gulf of Mexico.

Suborder Myliobatoidei. Upper Cretaceous to present. Distinguished by a slender tail, usually whiplike toward the tip; outer margin of the pelvic fins being straight or convex. Most with 1 or more saw-toothed, poisonous spines on upper surface of tail. Seven families are recognized. Tropical to warm temperate waters of all oceans, most abundant in shallow depths, entering brackish water and freshwater freely. One family is confined to freshwater.

Family Dasyatidae (whip-tailed rays). Lower Cretaceous to present. Caudal fin lacking; no distinct dorsal fin; tail, measured from the anus to the tip, longer than the breadth of the disk. Ovoviviparous. Tropical to warm temperate latitudes in all oceans. Generally in depths less than about 100 m, most abundant close to shore, including tidal embayments. The largest reaches at least 2 m in breadth. Five genera, 2 in tropical and subtropical rivers of South America. A peculiarity in the structure of the pelvis has been used to differentiate a separate family, Potamotrygonidae.

Family Gymnuridae (butterfly rays). Miocene to present. Distinguished by the body being more than 1.5 times as broad as long and the tail considerably shorter than the body. Saw-toothed spine on the back of the tail in some species but not all. Maximum breadth about 2 m. Shallow coastal waters of tidal embayments and river mouths in tropical to warm-temperature latitudes of all oceans.

Family Urolophidae (stingrays). Eocene to present. Distinguished by having well-developed tail fin supported by cartilaginous rays; tail with at least one large saw-toothed spine. Ovoviviparous. The numerous species look very much alike; the largest does not exceed about 70 cm in breadth. Tropical to warm temperate coastal waters less than about 70 m deep in western Atlantic and both sides of the Pacific from Japan to Tasmania, including the East Indies; they are unreported from eastern Atlantic or the Indian or African coasts of the Indian Ocean.

Family Myliobatidae (eagle rays). Upper Cretaceous to present. Distinguished from other myliobatoids by the forepart of the head projecting conspicuously beyond the rest of the body; eyes and spiracles on the sides of the head; tail as long as the disk or much longer and in most species bears a serrate venomous spine. Ovoviviparous. Some attain a width of about 2.5 m. Cosmopolitan, occurring in continental waters and around islands and island groups from tropical to temperate latitudes; 4 genera.

Family Rhinopteridae (cow-nosed rays). Upper Cretaceous to present. Similar to eagle rays except that the projecting head is deeply incised at the midline, forming two distinct lobes. Ovoviviparous. Maximum breadth about 2 m. Coastal waters of tropical and warm temperate latitudes of all oceans.

Family Mobulidae (devil rays, or mantas). Pliocene to present. Continental waters and around offshore island groups of tropical to warm temperate belts of all oceans. Distinguished by a pair of armlike structures (cephalic fins) projecting forward, on on each side of the head. Tail whiplike; with or without a serrate edged spine. Teeth minute, arranged in many rows. Maximum size (breadth) of smallest species about 60 cm; largest species at least 7 m.

Subclass Holocephali (chimaeras, ghost sharks). Upper Devonian to present. Cartilaginous skeleton, 4 pairs of gills, covered on each side of the body by an opercular fold of skin leading to a single external gill opening. First dorsal fin and spine erectile. Skin with small denticles along midline of back in some species and on tentacula and claspers of males. Teeth united to form grinding plates. Claspers of males are supplemented by an erectile organ, called tentaculum, in front of the pelvic fins, and all except one genus (*Harriotta*) have another club-shaped tentaculum on the forehead. Oviparous, laying elliptical, spindle-shaped, or tadpole-shaped eggs enclosed in brown horny capsules, remarkably large in proportion to the size of the parent. In breathing, chimaeroids take in water chiefly through the nostrils and thence through grooves leading to the mouth, which is generally kept closed. Variously distributed in temperate and boreal zones of all oceans, in coastal waters, and river estuaries and seaward down to over 2,500 m.

Order Chimaerae

Family Chimaeridae (ghost sharks, ratfishes, chimaeras). Lower Jurassic to present. Rounded short or conical snout. Claspers of males bifid or trifid. Size to about 1.5 m. Warm temperate and boreal latitudes of all oceans. Two genera, each with several species.

Family Callorhinchidae (elephant fish). Hoe-shaped proboscis. One genus (*Callorhinchus*) with a few species, which may eventually prove to be identical. Size to about 1.3 m. Restricted to cool temperate and boreal latitudes of Southern Hemisphere, generally taken in rather shallow water, sometimes entering estuaries and rivers.

Family Rhinochimaeridae (long-nosed chimaeras). Snout projecting into a long, straight point. Lateral line an open groove. Size to about 1.3 m. Probably cosmopolitan in middle latitudes of both hemispheres, taken in depths of 685–2,000 m.

Critical appraisal. Many of the elasmobranchs are particularly difficult subjects for taxonomic study. Differences between species are often subtle and hard to mea-sure. Lacking skeletal support such as that possessed by the bony fishes, captured sharks collapse along the soft undersides of the body when taken out of the water, thus reducing the accuracy of measurements. A satisfactory taxonomic study of any species requires adequate samples over a full range of sizes, representing the full geographical distribution of the species. The sampling must take into account rather large variations in body proportions between individuals of like size and different size groups and between populations inhabiting different regions of the total distribution. Hence, the identity of many species remains unsettled. The number of living species of sharks, now estimated at 200 to 250, tends to diminish as ichthyologists working in different parts of the world accumulate and exchange careful anatomical measurements of fresh specimens, discovering that fishes from widely separated areas, formerly thought to be distinct, are actually of the same species.

The rays, except the larger ones, are somewhat easier to work with. About 300 to 340 species have been described. Here again, however, the number tends to diminish as comparative studies in different parts of the world show many of them to be cosmopolitan.

The classification of chondrichthyed fishes is a somewhat controversial subject. An authoritative opinion as to how sharks, rays, and chimaeras should be grouped can be reached only from a comprehensive critical review of all available pertinent living and fossil material. Students continuously add to the accumulation of field measurements and museum specimens, and so such a classification needs to be revised from time to time. Because this revision involves a vast amount of work, it is not undertaken often.

BIBLIOGRAPHY. J.S. BABEL, "Reproduction, Life History, and Ecology of the Round Stingray, *Urolophus halleri* Cooper," *Fish Bull. Calif.* 127 (1967), an excellent natural history study of a ray; H.B. BIGELOW and W.C. SCHROEDER, "Sharks," *Fishes of the Western North Atlantic, Mem. Sears Fdn. Mar. Res.,* no. 1, pt. 1, pp. 59–546 (1948); "Sawfishes, Guitarfishes, Skates and Rays," and "Chimaeroids," *ibid.,* no. 1, pt. 2 (1953), the two most recent cosmopolitan syntheses in spite of emphasis on the western North Atlantic; "A Study of the Sharks of the Suborder Squaloidea," *Bull. Mus. Comp. Zool. Harv.,* vol. 117, no. 1 (1957), a revision of the group; P. BUDKER, *La Vie des requins* (1947; rev. Eng. trans., *The Life of Sharks,* 1971), a nontechnical, authoritative work; J.F. DANIEL, *The Elasmobranch Fishes,* 3rd rev. ed. (1934), a classic treatise on the anatomy of sharks and rays; D.H. DAVIES, *About Sharks and Shark Attack* (1964), an authoritative, nontechnical work about sharks, principally South African species; P.W. GILBERT (ed.), *Sharks and Survival* (1963), a collection of 22 papers about sharks, with emphasis on dangerous species, including a list of documented attacks throughout the world; P.W. GILBERT, R.F. MATHEWSON, and D.P. RALL (eds.), *Sharks, Skates and Rays* (1967), a collection of technical papers covering a wide range of subjects; E.W. GUDGER (ed.), *Archaic Fishes,* Bashford Dean Memorial Volume (1937), contains articles on the anatomy, reproduction, and development, of the frilled shark (*Chlamydoselachus anguineus*), and on natural history and development of Heterodontid sharks; H.W. MCCORMICK and T. ALLEN, with W.E. YOUNG, *Shadows in the Sea: The Sharks, Skates, and Rays* (1963), an authoritative, well-illustrated, nontechnical work; L.H. MATTHEWS and H.W. PARKER, "Notes on the Anatomy and Biology of the Basking Shark (*Cetorhinus maximus*)," *Proc. Zool. Soc. Lond.,* 120:535–576 (1950); P.M. ROEDEL and W.E. RIPLEY, "California Sharks and Rays," *Fish Bull. Calif.* 75 (1950), a handbook for identification of California species (of general use on the Pacific coast), illustrated with excellent photographs; A.S. ROMER, *Vertebrate Paleontology,* 3rd ed. (1966), a comprehensive review, with a classification of archaic and recent fishes; H.W. SMITH, *From Fish to Philosopher* (1961), a chapter on the elasmobranchs discusses their evolution and physiological adaptations to marine environment; D.W. STRASBURG, "Distribution, Abundance, and Habits of Pelagic Sharks in the Central Pacific Ocean," *Fish Bull. U.S. Dep. Interior,* 58:335–416 (1958), contains field observations and quantitative data on 12 species; G.P. WHITLEY, *The Fishes of Australia, Part I, The Sharks, Rays, Devil-Fish, and Other Primitive Fishes of Australia and New Zealand* (1940), a nontechnical book about Australian species.

(L.A.Wa.)

Seleucid Kingdom

The Seleucid Kingdom, or Empire (312–64 BC), one of the great powers of the Hellenistic Age, was created, along with Ptolemaic Egypt and other states, out of the Macedonian Empire of Alexander the Great. Originally it included a vast area extending from European Thrace east to the borders of India; when it was finally conquered by the Romans in the 1st century BC, the authority of the Seleucid kings was confined to Syria and Cilicia.

By courtesy of John Bartholomew & Son Ltd.

The Seleucid Kingdom c. 185 BC.

The dynasty. The kingdom's name is derived from that of its founder, Seleucus I Nicator, a Macedonian general who became prominent after Alexander's death. Seleucus was satrap (governor) of Babylonia under the Macedonian king Antigonus I from 321 to 316. In 312, allied with Ptolemy I of Egypt, he seized Babylonia for himself. From there he extended his domain eastward across Iran to the Indus River, establishing friendly relations with the Indian king Candragupta Maurya in 305. Around 304 he was proclaimed king of all the lands he had conquered (he had held that title in Babylonia since 309/308). He then pushed westward into Syria and Anatolia, defeating his rival Antigonus at Ipsus in 301 and completing his conquests by the annexation of the Thracian Cherronesus in 281. In the same year he was assassinated. Seleucus was succeeded by his eldest son, Antiochus I Soter (reigned 281–261). After Antiochus II (261–246), Seleucus II (246–225), and Seleucus III (225–223) came Antiochus III the Great (223–187), under whom the kingdom entered a new stage of its historical development. Antiochus III thoroughly reformed its administration; his innovations became a prototype for the states that succeeded the Seleucid Kingdom. The defeat of the Seleucids by Rome at Magnesia at the end of 190 or beginning of 189 marked the beginning of their decline.

The later Seleucids

Even among the later Seleucids there were significant personalities. This was less apparent in Seleucus IV (187–175) than in Antiochus IV Epiphanes (175–164/163), famous for his clashes with the Jewish Maccabeans. Antiochus V (164/163–162) was a minor and unable to rule. From the time of Demetrius I, the son of Seleucus IV (162–150), and Alexander Balas (150–145), who claimed to be the son of the fourth Antiochus, two mutually hostile branches of the dynasty existed. Demetrius II (145–139 and 129–125) was particularly opposed to Antiochus VII (139/138–129), the representative of the other line. When the latter fell in battle against the Parthians in 129, the ascendency of this line in the Seleucid Empire was permanently ended. The last rulers, Antiochus XIII and Philip II, reigned from 69 to 64 BC and from 65 to 64 BC, respectively. A final attempt by Philip II to seize the crown was thwarted by the Romans in the year 56 BC.

Significant regions of the kingdom. The Seleucid Kingdom reached its greatest extent at the death of Seleucus I, in the year 281.

The possession of the entire central and southern parts of Anatolia and, above all, the ancient Greek cities on Anatolia's west coast gave the Seleucids great economic power and cultural influence. (The Greek cities on the northern coast—Cyzicus, Heraclea, Trapezus, and others—retained their independence.) By controlling the Taurus passes between Anatolia and Syria and the Hellespont between Thrace and Anatolia, the Seleucids were able to dominate the important trade and communications routes between Europe and Asia. The invasion of Anatolia by the Celts in 278 did change the situation, but only temporarily. Possession of the ancient cultural areas of Syria and Phoenicia was equally important. The trade routes from the Middle and Far East passed through these lands and terminated at the Phoenician port cities. The trade of the Phoenician cities of Tyre, Sidon, and Berytos dominated almost the entire Mediterranean area. The settlements of the first Seleucids in northern Syria, such as Antioch, Seleucia, Laodicea, and Apamea, were not only manufacturing centres but also important garrisons for the army.

Sources of Seleucid strength

Seleucid culture and Hellenization. Syria became the centre of the Seleucid state and was the area most heavily influenced by the Greek culture of the Macedonians. In Babylonia, on the other hand, the traditions of the past lived on; the Mesopotamian cuneiform script, for example, continued to be used by the influential priestly caste, just as in pre-Seleucid times.

The ruling class in the Seleucid state was a Greek-speaking Macedonian aristocracy descended from the original conquerors. Below them was a class of Greek settlers, mostly soldiers, officers, and functionaries, located in the eastern provinces as well as in the Greek cities of Anatolia. Greek was spoken everywhere and Greek schools were to be found throughout the realm. Inscriptions in Greek have been found even in the areas farthest removed from traditional Greek centres. In many places, Greek theatre, performed by travelling actors, became popular. Inscriptions of Euripidean verse have been found in Armenia, and Greek was used for legal purposes at Susa in Iran.

On the whole, the Hellenistic culture was limited to the cities; in the countryside the indigenous national characteristics as well as the native languages of the Near East survived.

Thus resistance to Macedonian rule was centred mostly in rural areas (*e.g.,* the movement that established the Parthian state in the 3rd century BC, and the rising of the Maccabeans in the 2nd century). Antiochus IV (175–164/163), in his zeal to propagate Greek culture, raised a statue of the god Zeus in the temple at Jerusalem. He was supported by Hellenized Jewish aristocracy, but beginning in 165, upholders of traditional Judaism rose against him under Judas Maccabeus. After 25 years of struggle the Maccabeans won Judaea from the rule of the Seleucids.

Resistance to the Seleucids

For the Macedonians and Greeks who left their homelands in great numbers during the 3rd century BC, a broad new field of activity opened up under the Seleucids. In their domains, Greek-speaking people banded themselves into organizations; in these clubs as well as in private life, the traditions of Greek culture and the Greek language were zealously cultivated. Greek law was also important, as it formed the basis of personal and economic relations; and, indeed, the Greeks of the privileged class dominated the political and economic life of the kingdom.

Greek religion accompanied the Greeks to the Near East. Throughout the Seleucid domains, the cult of the Olympian gods coexisted with that of local deities. Greek temples were to be found everywhere—in Phoenicia, Syria, and even in distant Iran. Social contact with the indigenous peoples gave the Macedonians and Greeks access to the most diverse religions of the Near East—the cult of Mithra in Iran, Marduk and Ishtar in Babylonia, Astarte and Hadad in Syria and Phoenicia, the Magna Mater (Cybele) in Anatolia, and many others. They assimilated many of these, identifying the foreign gods with their own; but the capacity for assimilation was limited, and the wider Hellenistic civilization spread, the thinner the cover of genuine Greek religiosity became.

The "royal cult"

The kings themselves were accorded diverse honours, again in emulation of Alexander the Great, who had adopted this custom in his Asian territories. The "royal cult" was organized during the second generation of Seleucids by Antiochus I (281–261). The rulers adopted cult names, such as Soter ("the saviour"), Theos ("god"), and Epiphanes ("appearance of god"). This cult was intended to be a unifying influence on the various peoples and nations of the kingdom, but it was mainly official in character and does not seem to have had much popularity.

Because of the prestige of Greek culture, indigenous people often tried to become assimilated into the Greek class, assuming Greek names and participating in the life of the grammar schools. After the 2nd century BC, just when the initial impact of Hellenic culture was declining in the Near East, it was re-enforced by the arrival of the Hellenized Romans in the area; thus, Greek culture continued to be a strong influence there after the demise of the Seleucids.

Government and society. The fact that the Seleucid state had been formed through military conquest was apparent in all aspects of the administration. Seleucus I, like Alexander, adopted many features of the old Persian imperial administration, notably its division into satrapies. This form of administration had proved itself under the Achaemenian Persians and was, therefore, maintained, at least in the east. The provinces of Anatolia and the central areas of the kingdom were administered by *stratēgoi*, who combined military and civil authority. In the Iranian provinces satraps still controlled civil matters; military units, however, were commanded by their own officers, and controlling the entire Iranian East, probably from the Euphrates on, there was a "Supervisor of the Higher Satrapies." In the reforms of Antiochus III (223–187), this dualism was abolished; the heads of the provincial administration throughout the realm from that time on were *stratēgoi*, with special officials for financial affairs (*hoi epi tōn prosodōn*) to assist them. The entire empire was divided into satrapies, hyparchies, and toparchies, an organizational system that served as a model for the Parthians. Administrative centres were located at Sardis in the west and at Seleucia near the Tigris River in the east. Few details are known about the central government, but if the king was incompetent or a minor, a chancellor (*ho epi tōn pragmatōn*) was appointed (for example, Heliodorus during the reign of Seleucus IV).

The backbone of Seleucid power was the army, which included both the Macedonians, settled in military colonies throughout the kingdom, and mercenaries. The prestige of the Macedonians derived from the martial tradition of Alexander; from the end of the 3rd century their numbers began to decline, and gradually increasing numbers of the indigenous population were pressed into military service. Their contingents were of varying ability; the best being the Iranians and some of the peoples of Anatolia. The great Seleucid frontier fortresses were garrisoned mostly by mercenaries.

Taxation

The Seleucids in large measure continued the revenue policies of the Achaemenians and of Alexander. The most important direct tax was the *dekatē*, a tithe; indirect taxes included a duty on salt. There were also occasional special levies known as *stephanoi*. Though certainly less exacting than the Ptolemaic kings of Egypt in the demands they made on their subjects, the Seleucids must have drawn large revenues. The expenses involved in maintaining the court and army were heavy, but the surplus of revenue and the general prosperity of the kingdom were sufficient to make the kings and the leading men in the state very rich. All the categories within the empire—subject kings, dynasts, peoples, and cities—were liable to taxation in money or kind, but only in the case of the royal domains, where the land was cultivated by royal serfs ("the king's people"), were taxes collected directly by royal officials; in all other cases, collection was indirect and by stages. In accordance with their preference for a decentralized mode of government, and in order to encourage the growth of city life, the Seleucids commonly allotted large tracts of royal land to Greek cities and compelled feudal landowners and temple states to do the same. This process led to the gradual emancipation of the serfs on the land affected.

The social organization of the Seleucid Kingdom was that of most traditional Near Eastern states. Below the king were the *stratēgoi* and satraps in the imperial administration. The property-owning class and landed gentry were next. After this were the soldiers—Macedonians and mercenaries. At the bottom of the hierarchy was the great mass of serfs and peasants who formed the bulk of the population. In general, the bourgeois class was numerically weak and economically unproductive.

Territorial losses and decline. The kingdom lost much of its territory in Anatolia in the 3rd century. The Greek cities of the Aegean coast threw off their allegiance, and such states as Cappadocia and Attalid Pergamum achieved independence. Other territories were ceded to the Celts and to the kings of Pontus and Bithynia. The hill country of the Taurus Range in southern Anatolia was never properly subjugated, and the Seleucid possessions to the north and west of Cilicia were reduced, before the end of the century, to parts of Caria, Lydia, Aeolis, and the Troad (all on the Aegean seaboard), connected by a narrow corridor running through Phrygia and Lycaonia to Cilicia and Syria.

In the northeastern area of the empire, Parthia, Bactria, and Sogdiana became independent after the middle of the 3rd century. The submission of these districts to Antiochus III later (209–206) was of only passing effect. Coele Syria (Lebanon) and Palestine had been fought over by the Seleucids and the Ptolemaic kings of Egypt ever since the accession of Antiochus I (281); not until the reign of Antiochus III did they pass finally into Seleucid possession (c. 200). This acquisition and the short-lived subjugation of Armenia and the former eastern provinces of the empire counterbalanced the loss of all Anatolia north of Mt. Taurus by the Treaty of Apamea (188), which resulted from the defeat of Antiochus III at the hands of Rome and Pergamum.

After the death of Antiochus IV (164/163), the small state of Commagene in northern Syria emerged as an independent kingdom, as did Judaea in Palestine. In the east, all the provinces to the east of Media, Susiana, and Persis had been lost by the same date, either to the Parthians or to the kings of Bactria. In 145 Ptolemy VI of Egypt reoccupied Coele Syria and Palestine. In 141 the Parthians annexed Babylonia and Mesopotamia. By then everything to the east of the Euphrates, apart from a small foothold in northern Mesopotamia, had been lost; and the utter failure of the expeditions led by Demetrius II in 140–139 and Antiochus VII in 130–129 to recover the lost provinces meant that the kingdom was reduced to Syria and eastern Cilicia. Even this limited area was held only precariously in the final period of the dynasty.

BIBLIOGRAPHY. E.R. BEVAN, *The House of Seleucus*, 2 vol. (1902, reprinted 1966), a comprehensive presentation; A. BOUCHE-LECLERQ, *Histoire des Séleucides*, 2 vol. (1913–14); E. BIKERMAN, *Institutions des Séleucides* (1938), a valuable treatment of the court, and of the military organization and administration; H. BENGTSON, *Die Strategie in der hellenistischen Zeit II* (1944, reprinted 1964), contributions in the areas of administration and military organization of the Seleucids, *Griechische Geschichte*, 4th ed. (1969), see pp. 426 ff. for sources and new literature.

(He.B.)

Seleucus I Nicator

Seleucus I Nicator was the founder of the Seleucid dynasty and of the Seleucid Empire in Asia. A Macedonian noble and companion of Alexander the Great, he was one of the *diadochoi* ("successors") engaged in the struggle for the control of the empire after Alexander's death.

Born between 358 BC and 354 BC in Europus, Macedonia, the son of Antiochus (a general of Philip II of Macedonia, the father of Alexander the Great), he participated in the conquest of the Persian Empire as one of Alexander's officers, and in 326 he commanded the Macedonian infantry against King Porus of India in battle on the Hydaspes River. In 324 Alexander ordered a mass wedding ceremony at Susa (in Persia) to put into practice his ideal of uniting the peoples of Macedonia and Persia. On this occasion Seleucus married Apame, the daughter of Spitamenes, the ruler of Bactria. Of all the Macedonian nobles, he was the only one who did not repudiate his wife after Alexander's death.

Seleucus I, coin, late 4th–early 3rd century BC. In the British Museum.

By courtesy of the trustees of the British Museum; photograph, J.R. Freeman & Co. Ltd.

Ascension to power

After Alexander died (323), Seleucus was given the command of the *hetairoi* (companions) cavalry and took part in the regent Perdiccas' campaign to oust Ptolemy, the governor (satrap) of Egypt. In Egypt, however, he joined with others in the assassination of Perdiccas. When the empire was divided in 321, he was given the governorship (satrapy) of Babylon. At the same time Antigonus Monophthalmus (the One-Eyed) had been placed in command of a campaign against Eumenes of Cardia, a supporter of Perdiccas. In 317 Seleucus aided Antigonus but, after Eumenes' execution in 316, Antigonus demanded that Seleucus give an accounting of the income from his satrapy. Seleucus refused to give the accounting and escaped capture by fleeing to Ptolemy in Egypt.

From 316 to 312 Seleucus remained in Ptolemy's service. He took the initiative in forging a coalition among Ptolemy, Lysimachus (the ruler of Thrace), and Cassander (who laid claim to Macedonia) against Antigonus, whose desire to become the ruler of the whole of Alexander's empire was a threat to them all. In the resulting coalition war (315–311), Seleucus was made one of Ptolemy's generals and jointly with him commanded the Ptolemaic troops that defeated the force of Demetrius, the son of Antigonus, at the Battle of Gaza in southern Syria (312).

Seleucus once again turned his attention to returning to Babylonia, and in August 312 he was able to reconquer Babylon with only a small army. This conquest marked the beginning of the Seleucid era, which is dated Dios 1 (October 7), 312, in the Macedonian calendar and Nisan 1 (April 3), 311, in the Babylonian calendar. Antigonus ordered Nicanor, one of his generals, to invade Babylonia from the east and his son Demetrius to attack it from the west, but they failed to oust Seleucus. When Antigonus made peace with his enemies in 311, Seleucus was not included.

Consolidation of gains

Little is known about the next few years of Seleucus' reign; he presumably used them to consolidate his gains. In the year 305 he followed the example of the other successors and assumed the title of king (*basileus*). He embarked on an expansion of his kingdom throughout the Iranian east (the upper satrapies) as far as India, but his advance was eventually halted by Candragupta, the founder of the Maurya dynasty of India. In a pact concluded by the two potentates, Seleucus agreed to territorial concessions in exchange for 500 elephants.

Developments in the west also caused Seleucus to end his campaign in India (303). He had joined a coalition that Ptolemy, Cassander, and Lysimachus had once again formed against Antigonus and Demetrius. In the winter of 302 Seleucus was back in Asia Minor and, together with Cassander and Lysimachus, defeated Antigonus in the Battle of Ipsus (301). The victors divided the lands of

their enemy among them, with Seleucus being given Syria. The southern part of Syria, Coele Syria, had in the meantime been occupied by Ptolemy, who had not taken part in the war. This gave rise to the long series of Syrian wars between the Seleucids and Ptolemies. For the time being, however, Seleucus declined to enforce his claim; he merely transferred his capital from Seleucia on the Tigris to the newly founded city of Antioch on the Orontes (301–300).

Ptolemy, anxious to improve relations with Lysimachus, had given him his daughter Arsinoe in marriage. To provide a counterbalance, Seleucus asked for the hand of Stratonice, the daughter of Demetrius, and in 298 the wedding was held with much pomp at Rhosus in Syria. Soon, however, Seleucus' territorial demands (*e.g.*, the surrender of Cilicia and the cities of Tyre and Sidon) ruptured the previously harmonious relationship with Demetrius.

In 294 a sensational scandal occurred at the court of Seleucus. Antiochus, his son by Apama, fell in love with his beautiful stepmother, Stratonice, and his unrequited passion affected his health. Seleucus gave him Stratonice, assigned him as commander in chief to the upper satrapies, and appointed him coregent.

In 285 Seleucus took Demetrius prisoner, thus foiling his attempt to conquer Asia, and interned him in Apamea, where he died in 283. Subsequently, Seleucus intervened in dissensions in the house of Lysimachus, who had had his son Agathocles assassinated. In February 281 Lysimachus fell in a battle against Seleucus at Corupedium, and Seleucus gained control of Lysimachus' kingdom. He was now near his goal of re-establishing Alexander's empire. He crossed over to Europe to enter Macedonia, but at the end of August or beginning of September 281, he was murdered by Ptolemy Ceraunus, who had been passed over by his father, Ptolemy, as successor to the Egyptian throne. Seleucus' son and successor, Antiochus I, entombed his father's ashes in Seleucia, initiated (probably) the posthumous cult of his father, and ordered his veneration as Zeus Nicator.

Seleucus was an energetic ruler, creating the Seleucid Empire, which gained its greatest expansion under his rule. He took great interest in the administration of his territories and founded many new cities. He also encouraged scientific research: Patrocles explored the Caspian Sea and Megasthenes the Ganges River. A bronze bust—a very impressive likeness of him, conveying his imposing personality—was found in Herculaneum (in Italy) and is now in Naples. (J.Se.)

Seljuqs

The Seljuqs (Seljuks) were the ruling family of the Oğuz (Ghuzz) Turkmen tribes who invaded western Asia in the 11th century and founded a powerful empire, later to be divided into the principalities of Iran, Syria, and Asia Minor. The history of these invaders forms the first part of the history of the Turks in the Near and Middle East.

During the 10th century, in the course of the migrations and struggles of the Turkish peoples of Central Asia and southeast Russia, a group of nomadic Turks under a chief named Seljuq settled in the lower reaches of the Syr-Darya (Jaxartes) and later embraced Islām (see also ISLAM, HISTORY OF; INNER ASIA, HISTORY OF). They were incorporated in the frontier defense forces of the Sāmānids and moved to the vicinity of Bukhara c. AD 985. After the fall of the Sāmānids, they were established by Maḥmūd of Ghazna in the border regions of Khorāsān, but it was difficult to induce warlike nomads to live peacefully within a settled empire. While Maḥmūd's son Mas'ūd was busy waging war in northern India, the two grandsons of Seljuq, Chaghri (Chagri) Beg and Toghrïl (Tughril) Beg, saw the chance to win a realm of their own with the support of Persian nobles and religious leaders who were anxious to meet the threatening progress of heretic Shī'ite sects reinforced by the Būyid princes of western Iran and Iraq and the Fāṭimid Ismā'īlī caliphate of Egypt (see IRAN, HISTORY OF; EGYPT, HISTORY OF). When Mas'ūd saw the danger, it was too late: he was ut-

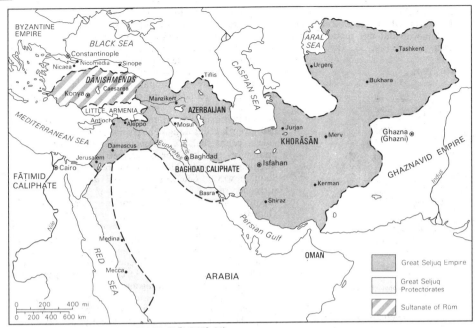

Seljuq Empire during the reign of Malik-Shāh (1073–92).
Adapted from *Westermann Historical Atlas*, Georg Westermann Verlag, Braunschweig (1965)

terly defeated at Dendenkan (Dandānqān) near Merv in 1040. Thereafter Chaghri Beg remained in control of the greater part of Khorāsān while Toghrïl, with a mixed army of Turkmen and regular Mamlūk (slave) troops, set out to conquer new territories in the west.

The great Seljuqs. Toghrïl Beg, a strong leader of men and a clear-headed statesman, achieved the creation of an empire that at his death (1063) included central and western Iran and Mesopotamia with Baghdad itself. There in 1055 Toghrïl undertook to deliver the caliph al-Qā'im from Būyid domination and to ally the house of Seljuq with the caliphate through marriage. Thereby the Seljuq conquests were identified with a restoration of the unity of the Muslim world under the Sunni caliphate. Alp-Arslan (1063 to 1072 or 1073), who succeeded both Chaghri and Toghrïl, and Malik-Shāh completed his conquering work. When Malik-Shāh I died in 1092, the Seljuq Empire included the whole of Iran, with the exception of the Ghaznavid realm of the Indian borderland, the whole of Mesopotamia, and Syria, including Palestine, to the frontier of Egypt. Furthermore, other Turkmen invaders closely akin to the Seljuqs had occupied the Asiatic provinces of the Byzantine Empire up to the Aegean Sea. The organization of the empire was the task of the vizier Niẓām al-Mulk (*q.v.*), who remained in power during the reigns of both Alp-Arslan and Malik-Shāh.

The main problem facing the Seljuqs was to persuade the Turkmen invaders, to whom they owed their victory, to live within the framework of the bureaucratic Iranian-Iraqi state. This problem was never completely solved. The Turkmen tribesmen had no interest in victory over heretics if their lands were unsuitable for stockbreeding or if pillage was not allowed; but on the northwestern frontier of Iran lay the Byzantine Empire, including half of Armenia, which was lacking religio-national homogeneity and the kind of military force able to fight against nomadic invaders. Love of plunder and zeal for a holy war drew the Turkmens into Byzantine territory, and, to prevent them from becoming quite estranged from him, the sultan had sometimes to lead them himself. Thus Alp-Arslan won immortal fame in the Muslim world when he defeated a huge Byzantine army at Manzikert in 1071, capturing the Byzantine emperor Romanus IV Diogenes. Thenceforth the Turkmens were able to settle in Asia Minor undisturbed.

The main feature of the Seljuq Empire was its religio-political character. The regime had to fight not only external wars but also wars against heretics within its frontiers, and to the Seljuqs Islām owes much of its later achievements.

The significance of the Great Seljuq state

Although *Madrasahs* (colleges) had been founded before the Seljuq period, Niẓām al-Mulk was the first official to establish a network of such institutions with the intention, presumably, of giving uniform training to administrators and religious scholars associated with the state. The head of orthodox Islām was the 'Abbāsid caliph, but, though he was permitted a degree of veneration and independence in Baghdad, he had little real political power in the empire. The sultans as well as the caliph considered it their duty to promote religious works; for this reason as well as to show their power they built many mosques, including the great mosque of Iṣfahān (the Masjed-e-Jāmī).

Strange as it may seem, the rule of the Turkish Seljuqs fostered rather than hampered the progress of Persian cultural autonomy. Before the Seljuq era a new form of Persian literature had developed in the Sāmānid territories of northeastern Iran and Transoxania. This was no longer written in the pure old language or in the alphabet of pre-Islāmic Iran but in the Arabic script with a number of borrowed Arabic words. At the same time the Būyids had favoured a form of Persian tradition that expressed itself in Arabic. Seljuq rule, on the other hand, led to the spread of literary Persian to the whole of Iran. The Turks had no cultural Islāmic tradition and almost no written literature. As the Iranians had been their instructors in Islām, they knew no cultural language other than Persian and showed no interest in the achievements of scholars or poets writing in Arabic. From the time of the Seljuqs onward, the Arabic language disappeared from the Iranian lands except in works of religious scholarship.

It is wrong to believe, as many have, that the pursuance of an Islāmic policy and of conquest in Anatolia led the Seljuqs to persecute the Christians. The plundering of the Turkmen armies in the Byzantine Empire no doubt caused much suffering and loss to Eastern Christianity, but inside the Seljuq Empire, as soon as order was restored, the lot of Christians was much the same as it had been before: the crusaders, who thought it must be otherwise, were judging conditions in Jerusalem by those prevailing in Anatolia (see also CRUSADES).

The later Seljuqs. Despite its successes there were weaknesses in the Seljuq Empire. It could not prevent the growth of the new terrorist sect, the Assassins, which was to inspire such dread in the medieval East and which began its activities with the murder of Niẓām al-Mulk (1092). Furthermore the Seljuqs, like the Būyids before them, could not rid themselves of the idea that sovereignty belonged to a family rather than to a single man; thus even the most powerful sultans thought it necessary to give provinces as appanages to their relatives. In the early years of the Seljuq conquests a practically independent principality had been founded in Kerman by a son of Chaghri Beg, Qāwurd (Kavurt), who extended his conquests to Oman on the Persian Gulf. Another independent but short-lived principality was created in Syria, partly for military reasons, by Malik-Shāh in favour of his brother Tutush.

When Malik-Shāh died, leaving several sons by different wives, all of them very young, the quarrels between them and their supporters resulted in a partition of the Seljuq heritage among Berk-yaruq, the eldest son; his brother Muḥammad, who received northwestern Iran; and a third brother, Sanjar, who was given charge of Khorāsān. When Berk-yaruq died in 1104, Muḥammad was able to establish only a measure of control in central and western Iran, and this broke down at his death (1118). Sanjar's realm in Khorāsān, however, attained a new power and glory, which were magnified in the eyes of posterity by the length of his reign and the disasters that befell him in his last years. It is necessary here only to recall his victories over the rival Turkish kingdom of the Qarakhanids in Transoxania and over the Ghaznavids of the Indian borderland. This was followed by his defeat in 1138 by new invaders from central Asia, the Karakitai, and by the revolt of his vassal in Khwārazm (Khorezmia). Finally came the general uprising of the Ghuzz (1153), which resulted in Sanjar's captivity, from which he escaped only to die in 1157. Years of disorder and misery ensued for Khorāsān until its final incorporation in a new Khorezmian empire in the reign of Tekish (Takash; 1172–1200).

The disintegration of the empire

Thereafter no territory was left in the former Seljuq Empire where a sultan could enjoy real power. When pretenders quarrelled they sought the help of high military officers, to whom they were obliged to abandon the government of whole provinces. This was especially so in the case of the *atabeg*s, officers who were entrusted with a kind of tutorship over minor princes. Tribal chiefs also profited by the disorders to make themselves independent, and the caliph himself thought the time ripe, if not to recover the ancient power of the ʿAbbāsids over the whole of the Muslim world, at least to secure a principality of his own in Iraq.

The first of the Seljuq lines to disappear was that in Syria. There Tutush's sons, Riḍwān (Ruḍwān) of Aleppo and Duqāq of Damascus, had quarrelled and were weakened by the attacks of the crusaders. Tughtigin, son of Būrī, the *atabeg* of Duqāq, founded a dynasty of his own (the Būrids) when his master died in 1104. In Aleppo the general feeling was against "Easterners," and the dynasty scarcely survived Riḍwān's death (1113). *Atabeg*s also were governing upper Mesopotamia around Mosul, and one of them, Zangī, united this province and Aleppo under his sway in 1128, thus creating a new dynasty there. Another *atabeg* dynasty, which was to last until the beginning of the 13th century, came to power somewhat later in Azerbaijan. These *atabeg*s "protected" the last Seljuqs of the Iranian line, who resided in Hamadan but had no powers except those granted them by their all-powerful tutors.

In the mid-12th century, the caliph again became independent, and when the last of the Iranian Seljuqs, Toghrïl III, tried to recover some of his lost influence, the caliph appealed to the *shāh* of Khorezmia the (Khwārazm-Shāh) for help. As a result Toghrïl died on the battlefield in 1194. Meanwhile other parts of the Seljuq heritage had met their fate at the hands of tribal chiefs. Even Arab tribes, such as the Mazyadids on the Iraqi borders, had taken advantage of the situation to win at least temporary autonomy. The principality of Kerman did not long survive the death (1170) of its sultan Toghrïl-Shāh. His sons quarrelled and called in foreign aid, with the result that the country was utterly devastated and fell an easy prey to a band of Ghuzz from Khorāsān under their chief, Malik Dīnār (1185). Ten years later it was incorporated in the Khorezmian Empire. Only in Anatolia did Seljuq power survive, and there it did not reach its peak until the 13th century.

The sultanate of Rūm. The invasion of Anatolia began as an uncoordinated movement of Turkmen tribesmen from Azerbaijan, and the expeditions of Toghrïl Beg and Alp-Arslan were aimed as much at controlling the tribesmen as at conquest. Alp-Arslan's victory at Manzikert (1071) destroyed the Byzantine frontier organization and enabled the Ghuzz to establish themselves in Byzantine territory, where they engaged as mercenaries in the struggles between the local commanders. Among a host of tribal chiefs the leading place was taken about 1075 by the sons of Toghrïl Beg's cousin Qutalmïsh (Kutlumush), who were violently hostile to Malik-Shāh. During the struggles of rival generals for the throne of Constantinople (1078–81) one after another of the contestants called for aid from the sons of Qutalmïsh and opened to them the gates of their cities, including Nicaea and Nicomedia (İzmit). By 1080 Sulaymān ibn Qutalmïsh held the greater part of Anatolia as the ally of the Byzantine emperor and rival sultan to Malik-Shāh. In 1084 Antioch (Antakya) was surrendered to him, but in 1086 he was killed near Aleppo in battle with Tutush and a coalition of Syrian princes. Malik-Shāh attempted to take advantage of Sulaymān's death, both by proposals for an alliance with the Byzantine emperor Alexius I Comnenus and by military expeditions into western Anatolia, but with little success; and on his death (1092), Sulaymān's son, Qïlïch (Kilij) Arslan (who had been captured by Malik-Shāh at Antioch), escaping from his captivity, reconstituted the sultanate. In the interval, however, northeastern Anatolia had been occupied by a rival Turkmen chief, Dānishmend of Sivas, whose successors engaged in a prolonged conflict with the Seljuq sultans.

Qïlïch Arslan I

The new sultan was immediately confronted with the First Crusade. The first crusader bands, under Walter the Penniless, were defeated at Nicaea (1096), but the Turks were severely defeated before Nicaea and at Dorylaeum (Eskişehir) in 1097 and driven into the interior, while the emperor Alexius reoccupied western Anatolia. After his victory over the next wave of crusaders (1101), Qïlïch Arslan, tempted by the disorders that had weakened the Seljuqs in Iraq, made a bid for the greater sultanate. He succeeded in capturing Mosul but was defeated by the forces of his kinsman of Aleppo and drowned in the Khābūr (Habor) river (1107).

This event proved decisive in determining the future development of the Sultanate of Rūm (the name used by the Turks for the Byzantine Empire). The Seljuqs, hemmed in between Byzantines and the crusading states in Syria and increasingly isolated from the east, gradually established an organized and settled Anatolian kingdom. Qïlïch Arslan was succeeded by his son Malik-Shāh (1107–16), and he by his brother Mas'ūd I (1116–55), who established his capital at Konya (Iconium). Mas'ūd's long reign was occupied by resistance to the encroachments of the Byzantines and by engagements and negotiations with the Dānishmendids, the crusaders, and his Muslim neighbours. During the reign of his son and successor, Qïlïch Arslan II (1155–92), the Armenians established a principality in Cilicia, but the Dānishmendids were finally subdued and their territories annexed to the sultanate.

Qïlïch Arslan's numerous sons, each of whom held the command of a city of the empire, embittered his old age by their mutual rivalry; and the eldest Quṭb ad-Dīn, tyrannized over him in his own capital, exactly at the time that Frederick I Barbarossa entered the sultan's dominions on his way to the Holy Sepulchre (1190). Konya itself was taken, and the sultan was forced to provide guides and provisions for the crusaders. Qïlïch Arslan lived two years longer, finally under the protection of his youngest son, Kay-Khusraw (Kaikhosrau), who held the capital after him until 1196, when his elder brother, Rukn ad-Dīn Sulaymān II, having vanquished his other brothers, ascended the throne and obliged Kay-Khusraw to seek refuge at the Byzantine emperor's court. Rukn ad-Dīn, who died in 1204, saved the sultanate from destruction and conquered Erzurum, which had been ruled for a considerable time by a separate dynasty; but Rukn ad-Dīn's son, Qïlïch Arslan III, was soon deposed, with Greek assistance, by Kay-Khusraw.

After the establishment of the Latin empire of Constantinople (1204), the Turks were the natural allies of the Greeks and the enemies of the crusaders and their allies, the Armenians. Kay-Khusraw, therefore, in 1207 took the important harbour of Attalia (Antalya) from the Italian Aldobrandini; but in 1211 he perished in battle with Theodore I Lascaris, emperor of Nicaea. His son and successor, Kay-Kā'ūs, made peace with Lascaris and extended his frontiers to the Black Sea by the conquest of Sinope (Sinop; 1214). On this occasion he took prisoner the Comnenian prince Alexius, who ruled the independent empire of Trebizond (Trabzon), and compelled him to acknowledge the supremacy of the Seljuqs, to pay tribute, and to serve in the armies of the sultan. Elated by this great success and by his victories over the Armenians in Cilicia, Kay-Kā'ūs attempted the capture of Aleppo, at this time governed by the descendants of Saladin, but the project was defeated by Ayyūbid resistance.

Kay-Kā'ūs' brother, 'Alā' ad-Dīn Kay-Qubādh (Kaikobad) I (1219–37), was the most powerful and illustrious prince of this branch of the Seljuqs. He extended his rule as far as Seleucia and desisted from further conquest only on condition that the Armenian princes would enter into the same kind of relation to the Seljuqs as had been imposed on the Comnenians of Trebizond. But his greatest military fame was won by a war that, however glorious, was to prove fatal to the Seljuq Empire in the future; in conjunction with his ally, the Ayyūbid prince Ashraf, he defeated the Khwārazm-Shāh, Jalāl ad-Dīn, near Erzincan (1230). During this war Kay-Qubādh put an end to a collateral dynasty of the Seljuqs of Erzurum and annexed its possessions. He also gained the city of Khilāt with dependencies that had recently been taken from the Ayyūbids by Jalāl ad-Dīn. This acquisition, however, led to a new war, as Kay-Qubādh's ally, the Ayyūbid prince, contested it. Sixteen Muslim princes, mostly Ayyūbids, of Syria and Mesopotamia, under the leadership of al-Malik al-Kamil, prince of Egypt, marched with considerable forces into Asia Minor against him. Happily for Kay-Qubādh, the other princes mistrusted the power of the Egyptian, and it proved a difficult task to penetrate through the mountainous, well-fortified accesses to the interior of Anatolia. The advantage thus rested with Kay-Qubādh, who extended his power in upper Mesopotamia. This expansion was pursued by his son Kay-Khusraw II.

The Seljuq
sultanate
assessed

The Seljuq sultanate of Anatolia can now be seen to have been one of the most important Muslim states of its age. Its population was a mixed one, including Christians, Armenians, Greeks, Syrians, and Iranian Muslims; but, when compared with the other Seljuq realms, of which the Turks had been only a small, if leading, element, it was really "Turkey" and was so called by its contemporaries. The Seljuqs of this line succeeded in establishing an administration largely based on the institutions of their Iranian-Seljuq neighbours, but it was modified by the Byzantine heritage and by its own evolution. With order and tolerance of all races and religions established, agriculture and mining activity revived, so that to foreigners Turkey seemed one of the richest of countries; meanwhile commerce was developed with the assistance of Italian merchants. In the cities beautiful buildings, several of which still survive, show the purity of an art related to, though not exactly identical with, the Iranian-Seljuq art of the same period. Literature, mostly in Persian, flourished, and, with it, mystical movements, such as that inspired by Jalāl ad-Dīn ar-Rūmī.

Yet this political organization and civilization were not really soundly based. The Seljuqs failed to tame, particularly in the frontier districts, the Turkmens, who, though partially settled, were impatient of centralized administration; they remained fond of petty wars against their Christian neighbours and still adhered to their traditional social and religious beliefs and practices. Newcomers from the countries invaded by the Khorezmians and Mongols added to their feeling of unrest. This helps to explain why, when the Mongol flood reached the frontiers of Turkey, which were no longer protected by the Khorezmian state, the Seljuq realm was no more able to resist than had been

the Muslim principalities of Iran. At the Battle of Köse Dagh (1243), between Erzincan and Sivas, the independence of the Seljuqs was lost forever.

The Mongol protectorate. The Mongols did not destroy the Seljuq state, but, in accordance with their plan, reduced it to vassalage. After the death of Kay-Khusraw II (1245) the quarrels between his sons led to a division of Asia Minor, 'Izz ad-Dīn Kay-Kā'ūs II taking the part west of the Halys and Rukn ad-Dīn Qïlïch Arslan IV the part to the east. When the former intrigued with the Mamlūks of Egypt and the Byzantine emperor, however, he was driven out and fled to Constantinople. The unity of the realm was thus restored, but the financial requirements of the Mongols and the intrigues of the great chiefs with them against one another quickly brought about a breakdown of the Seljuq administrative system. In the central provinces and cities, the all-powerful minister, the *perwane* Mu'īn ad-Dīn Sulaymān, who had Rukn ad-Dīn executed *c.* 1265, succeeded in maintaining the Iranian-Islāmic civilization of the recent golden age; to this end he cooperated with the Muslim viziers of the Mongol Īl-Khān of Iran, the suzerain of Anatolia. In the distant and mountainous districts, however, the Turkmen amirs, free from any form of government, established small principalities of their own: in the Taurus, on the Byzantine frontier; on the south Aegean coast, later even near the straits and the Black Sea. With their help and that of Baybars, the powerful Mamlūk sultan of Egypt, the most dreaded enemy of the Mongols, a group of Muslim nobles in Anatolia revolted during 1276–77 against the Mongol protectorate. The *perwane* himself had negotiated with them, and although he finally refused to join them, thus assuring the victory of the Mongols, he was executed. For a time the Seljuq sultanate was then no more than a Mongol province. Seljuq sultans, Kay-Khusraw II (died 1283), Mas'ūd III, and Farāmurz, still reigned nominally, but in the first years of the following century the dynasty ended in obscurity.

Thereafter the power of the Turkish amirates increased and the control of the Mongol Īl-Khāns of Iran became less effective until it also finally disappeared, in the 1330s.   (Ed.)

BIBLIOGRAPHY. Three works have been published in recent years that to a great extent supersede previous studies of the Seljuqs. The *Cambridge History of Iran,* vol. 5, *The Seljuq and Mongol Periods,* ed. by J.A. BOYLE (1968), contains chapters on all aspects of Seljuq history—government, religion, institutions, literature, and art. CLAUDE CAHEN, *Pre-Ottoman Turkey: A General Survey of the Material and Spiritual Culture and History, c. 1071–1330* (1968), covers the same topics for the sultanate of Rūm. Finally, GEORGE MAKDISI, *Ibn 'Aqīl et la résurgence de l'islam traditionaliste au XIe siècle* (1963), is of great importance for its analysis of politics and religion under the early Seljuqs.

Semantics

Semantics is the philosophical and scientific study of meaning. The term is one of a group of English words formed from the various derivatives of the Greek verb *sēmainō* ("to mean" or "to signify"). The noun semantics and the adjective semantic are derived from *sēmantikos* ("significant"); semiotic (adjective and noun) comes from *sēmeiōtikos* ("pertaining to signs"); semology from *sēma* ("sign") + *logos* ("account"); and semasiology from *sēmasia* ("signification") + *logos* ("account"). It is difficult to formulate a distinct definition for each of these terms because their use largely overlaps in the literature despite individual preferences. Semantics is a relatively new field of study, and its originators, often working independently of one another, felt the need to coin a new name for the new discipline; hence the variety of terms denoting the same subject. The word semantics has ultimately prevailed as a name for the doctrine of meaning, in particular, of linguistic meaning. Semiotic is still used, however, to denote a broader field: the study of sign-using behaviour in general.

Historical survey of the study of semantics. The concern with meaning, always present for philosophers and linguists, greatly increased in the decades following

World War II. The sudden rise of interest in meaning can be attributed to an interaction of several lines of development in various disciplines. From the middle of the 19th century onward, logic, the formal study of reasoning, underwent a period of growth unparalleled since the time of Aristotle. Although the main motivation for a renewed interest in logic was a search for the foundations of mathematics, the chief protagonists of this effort—notably the German mathematician Gottlob Frege and the English philosopher Bertrand Russell—extended their inquiry into the domain of the natural languages, which are the original media of human reasoning. The influence of mathematical thinking, and of mathematical logic in particular, however, left a permanent mark on the subsequent study of semantics.

Semantic theories of the Logical Positivists

This mark is nowhere more obvious than in the semantic theories offered by the Neopositivists of the Vienna Circle, which flourished in the 1920s and 1930s, and which was composed of philosophers, mathematicians, and scientists who discussed the methodology and epistemology of science. To such "logical" Positivists as the German-born philosopher Rudolf Carnap, for instance, the symbolism of modern logic represented the grammar (syntax) of an "ideal" language. Because the Logical Positivists were, at the same time, radical Empiricists (observationalists) in their philosophy, the semantics of their ideal language has been given in terms of a tie connecting the symbols of this language with observable entities in the world, or the data of one's sense experience, or both. Against such a rigid ideal as logic, natural language appeared to these philosophers as something primitive, vague, inaccurate, and confused. Moreover, since a large part of ordinary and philosophical discourse, particularly that concerning metaphysical and moral issues, could not be captured by the ideal language, the Positivistic approach provided a way to brand all such talk as nonsensical, or at least as "cognitively" meaningless. Accordingly, the Positivists engaged in a prolonged, and largely unsuccessful, effort to formulate a criterion of meaningfulness in terms of empirical verifiability with respect to the sentences formed in natural lanaguage.

Another source of dissatisfaction with the vernacular was made apparent shortly before World War II by the work of the American anthropological linguist Benjamin Lee Whorf. Whorf's famous thesis of linguistic relativity implied that the particular language a person learns and uses determines the framework of his perception and thought. If that language is vague and inaccurate, as the Positivists suggested, or is burdened with the prejudices and superstitions of an ignorant past, as some cultural anthropologists averred, then it is bound to render the user's thinking—and his mental life itself—confused, prejudiced, and superstitious. The Polish-American semanticist Alfred Korzybski, the founder of the movement called General Semantics, believed that the cure for such vague and superstition-laden language lay in a radical revision of linguistic habits in the light of modern science.

Natural language did not remain without champions in the face of this combined onslaught from the logicians and the Whorfians. A reaction started in England, first in Cambridge, then in Oxford. Influenced by the English philosopher George Edward Moore but more so by the "converted" Vienna-born Positivist Ludwig Wittgenstein, the philosophy of "ordinary language" (also known as the Oxford school) came into its own in the 1940s. According to the philosophers of this group, natural language, far from being the crude instrument the Positivists alleged it to be, provides the basic and unavoidable matrix of all thought, including philosophical reflections. Any "ideal" language, therefore, can make sense only as a parasitical extension of, and never as a substitute for, the natural language. Philosophical problems arise as a result of a failure to see the workings of man's language; they are bound to "dissolve" with improved understanding. These assumptions provided a mighty impetus to reflect upon the vernacular language, including its minute points of grammar and fine nuances of meaning. Indeed, some of the later representatives of this approach, particularly the English philosopher John L. Austin, became re-

nowned as much among linguists as among philosophers.

In the 1950s the science of linguistics itself rose to the challenges that had been coming chiefly from philosophical quarters. The development of transformational, or generative, grammar, initiated by the work of the U.S. linguists Zellig S. Harris and Noam Chomsky, opened a deeper insight into the syntax of the natural languages. Instead of merely providing a structural description (parsing) of sentences, this approach demonstrates how sentences are built up, step by step, from some basic ingredients. In the hands of the philosopher, this powerful new grammar not only served to counter the positivistic charge of imprecision laid against natural language but aided him in his own work of conceptual clarification. Moreover, the generative approach promised further results: since the late 1960s some steps have been taken to develop a generative semantics for natural languages, in addition to a generative syntax.

Influence of transformational grammar

PHILOSOPHICAL VIEWS ON MEANING

Meaning and reference. On a rather unsophisticated level the problem of meaning can be approached through the following steps. The perception of certain physical entities (objects, marks, sounds, and so on) might lead an intelligent being to the thought of another thing with some regularity. For example, the sight of smoke evokes the idea of fire, footprints on the sand makes one think of the man who must have passed by. The smoke and the footprints are thus signs of something else. They are natural signs, inasmuch as the connection between the sign and the thing signified is a causal link, established by nature and learned from experience. These can be compared with road signs, for example, or such symbols as the outline of a heart pierced by an arrow. The connection between the symbol and the thing signified in these cases is not a natural one; it is established by human tradition or convention and is learned from these sources. These nonnatural signs, or symbols, are widely used in human communication.

In this framework the elements of language appear to be nonnatural signs. The interest in words and phrases reaches beyond their physical appearance: their perception is likely to direct attention or thought to something else. Words, in fact, are the chief media of human communication, and, as the diversity of languages clearly shows, the link involved between words and what they signify cannot be a natural one. Words and sentences are like symbols: they point beyond themselves; they mean something. Smoke means fire, the pierced heart means love. Words mean the thing they make us think of; the meaning of the word is the tie that connects it with that thing.

Words as symbols

There are some words for which this approach seems to work very straightforwardly. The name Paris means (signifies, stands for, refers to, denotes) the city of Paris, the name Aristotle means that philosopher, and so forth. The initial plausibility of such examples created an obsession in the minds of many thinkers, beginning with Plato. Regarding proper names as words *par excellence*, they tried to extend the referential model of meaning to all of the other classes of words and phrases. Plato's theory of "forms" may be viewed as an attempt to find a referent for such common nouns as "dog" or for abstract nouns like "whiteness" or "justice." As the word Socrates in the sentence "Socrates is wise" refers to Socrates, for example, so the word wise refers to the form of wisdom. Unfortunately, whereas Socrates was a real person in this world, the form of wisdom is not something to be encountered anywhere, at any time, in the world. The difficulty represented by "Platonic" entities of this kind increases as one tries to find appropriate referents for verbs, prepositions, connectives, and so forth. Discussion of abstract entities such as classes (*e.g.*, the class of all running things) and relations (*e.g.*, the relation of being greater than . . .) abound in philosophical literature; Gottlob Frege even postulated "the True" and "the False" as referents for complete propositions.

There are many more serious problems besetting the referential theory of meaning. The first one, eloquently pointed out by Frege, is that two expressions may have the same referent without having the same meaning. For example, "the Morning Star" and "the Evening Star" denote the same planet, yet, clearly, the two phrases do not have the same meaning. If they had, then the identity of the Morning Star and the Evening Star would be as obvious to anybody who understands these phrases as the identity of a vixen with a female fox or a bachelor with an unmarried man is obvious to speakers of English. As it is, the identity of the Morning Star with the Evening Star is a scientific and not a linguistic matter. Thus, even in the case of names, or expressions equivalent to names, one has to distinguish between the denotation (reference, extension) of the name—*i.e.*, the object (or group of objects) it refers to—and its connotation (sense, intension)—*i.e.*, its meaning.

Denotation and connotation

The second problem with the theory of referential meaning arises from phrases that, though meaningful, pretend to refer but, in fact, do not. For example, in the case of such a definite description as "the present king of France," the phrase is meaningful although there is no such person. If the phrase were not meaningful, one would not even know that the phrase has no actual referent. Russell's analysis of these phrases, and the U.S. philosopher Willard V. Quine's similar treatment of such names as Cerberus, effectively detached meaning from reference by claiming that these expressions, when used in sentences, are equivalent to a set of existential propositions; *i.e.*, propositions without definite reference. For example, "The present king of France is bald" comes out as "There is at least, and at most, one person that rules over France, and whoever rules over France is bald." These propositions are meaningful, true or false, without definite reference.

Names, in fact, are very untypical words. The name of the Secretary General of the United Nations, U Thant, has no meaning in English. Whether it means anything in Burmese does not matter either; the reference is not affected by the meaning or the lack of meaning of the name. Names, as such, do not belong to the vocabulary of a language; most dictionaries do not list them. Thus, in spite of the initial plausibility, the idea of reference does not help in understanding the nature of linguistic meaning.

Meaning and truth. Despite the failure of referential meaning, many philosophers were quite unwilling to give up the idea that the meaning of linguistic expressions has something to do with objects, events, and states of affairs in the world. They reasoned that if language is used to talk about the physical environment, then there must be some connection between man's words and the things around him. If reference fails to provide the link, something else must.

In the face of referential failure Russell fell back on truth. The Positivists suggested verifiability as the criterion of empirical meaning. Indeed, at least in many cases, it stands to reason that to understand a sentence is to know what state of affairs would make it true or false. Such considerations motivate the aletheic (Greek *alētheia*, "truth") semantic theories, which claim that the notion of meaning is best explained in terms of truth rather than reference.

Tarski's semantic definition of truth

The most influential discussion of the notion of truth was offered by the Polish-born mathematician and logician Alfred Tarski in the 1930s. His semantic definition of truth is contained in the following formula (which he called [T]):

(T)   *X* is true if, and only if, *p*

in which "*p*" is a variable representing any sentence and "*X*" is a variable representing the name, or unique description, of that sentence. The easiest way to obtain such a unique description is to put the sentence in quotation marks. Thus, we get such instances of (T) as

"Snow is white" is true if, and only if, snow is white.

The above formula implies a distinction between the object language and the metalanguage. "*X*" represents the name of a sentence in the object language—*i.e.*, roughly, the language used to talk about things in the world. The instances of (T) themselves, however, are in the metalanguage, the language in which one can talk about both things in the world and sentences of the object language. Tarski claimed that no language can contain its own truth predicate, for if it did then it would permit the formation of such sentences as:

(S)   This very sentence is false.

Is the sentence (S) true or false? Clearly, it is true if, and only if, it is false, which is an intolerable paradox. Consequently, for any language the predicate ". . . is true" and other semantical predicates must belong to a language of a higher order (a metalanguage).

For this reason Tarski restricted his theory to clearly formalized, artificial languages, a decision that was very much in line with the positivistic tendencies of the 1930s. Nevertheless, the Tarski formula remained attractive even to some semanticists concerned with meaning in natural languages. For one thing, it seemed to succeed in pairing linguistic entities (named by the values of "*X*"; *e.g.*, the sentence "Snow is white") and nonlinguistic entities (named by the values of "*p*"; *e.g.*, the fact, or possible state of affairs, that snow is white). This correlation, however, is not very helpful because each one of the nearly infinite number of sentences one may form would have its "fact" as a counterpart, identifiable only by means of that very same sentence. Consequently, if linguistic meaning consisted in these correlations, no one could learn the meaning of any sentence at all and certainly not the meaning of all the sentences the speakers of a language are able to understand.

What was needed was a theory explaining the contribution of individual words—a clearly finite set—to the truth of sentences. Tarski himself, as well as other writers, suggested a repeatable procedure based on the notion of satisfaction. Snow, for example, satisfies the sentential function "*x* is white" because "Snow is white" is true. In much the same way, 3 satisfies the function "$2 \cdot x = 6$" because "$2 \cdot 3 = 6$" is true. Simply stated, the meaning of the predicate ". . . is white" is determined—and is learned—in terms of the set of objects of which it is true.

Limitations to the "meaning as truth" theory

As this approach is extended to cover the wide variety of words that exist in a natural language, however, its initial simplicity—and thereby its attractiveness—becomes progressively lost. This can be illustrated by "egocentric" words like "I," "you," "here," and "now"; by connectives like "since," "however," and "nevertheless"; and, if these appear trivial, by such crucial words as "believe," "know," and "intend," on the one hand, and "good" and "beautiful" on the other. Whereas it is plausible to say that, for instance, Joe and Mary satisfy the function "*X* loves *Y*," provided Joe loves Mary, it is more complicated to determine what would satisfy such functions as "*X* believes *Y*," "*X* knows *Y*," or "*X* intends *Y*." "*X*" is satisfiable by people, but the satisfaction of "*Y*" poses a problem. If one suggests such things as propositions, facts, and possibilities, one is confronted with abstract entities of a kind similar to those encountered in the Platonic theory of referential meaning. Again, can it be said that John and a unicorn will satisfy the function "*X* looks for *Y*"—if it is true that John looks for a unicorn?

Another difficulty arises concerning "good," "beautiful," and other words of moral or aesthetic judgment. If, for example, beauty is indeed "in the eye of the beholder," then what one person calls beautiful might not appeal to another, yet two people might keep arguing as to whether the thing is beautiful or not. Thus, people may seem to agree on the meaning of the word, yet remain at odds about its application. The meaning of such "emotive" words cannot be decided in terms of truth alone.

A more serious objection to the aletheic (truth) theory arises from the fact that many significant utterances of natural language are not true or false at all. Whereas statements, testimonies, and reports are true or false, orders, promises, laws, regulations, proposals, prayers, curses, and so forth are not assessed in terms of truth or falsity. It is not obvious that the employment of words in these speech acts is less relevant to their meaning than their use in speech acts of the truth-bearing kind.

Meaning and use. The difficulties just mentioned lead to another view concerning the notion of meaning, a theory that may be called the use theory. This view admits that not all words refer to something, and not all utterances are true or false. What is common to all words and all sentences, without exception, is that people use them in speech. Consequently, their meaning may be nothing more than the restrictions, rules, and regularities that govern their employment.

The use theory has several sources. First, in trying to understand the nature of moral and aesthetic discourse certain authors suggested that such words as "good" and "beautiful" have an emotive meaning instead of (or in addition to) the descriptive meaning other words have; in using them one expresses approval or commendation. If one says, for instance, that helping the poor is good, one does not describe that action, but says, in effect, something like "I approve of helping the poor, do so as well." Such is the role of these words, according to these thinkers, and to understand this role is to know their meaning.

Wittgen-
stein's
language
games

The second, and more important, stimulus for the use theory was provided by the work of Ludwig Wittgenstein. This philosopher not only pointed out the wide variety of linguistic moves mentioned above but in order to show that none of these moves enjoys a privileged status proposed the idea of certain language games in which one or another of these moves plays a dominant or even an exclusive role. One can imagine, for instance, a tribe whose language consists of requests only. Members of the tribe make requests and the other members comply or refuse. There is no truth in this language, yet the words used to make requests would have meaning. Human language as it exists in reality is more complex; it is a combination of a great many language games. Yet the principle of meaning, according to this theory, is the same: the meaning of a word is the function of its employment in these games. To Wittgenstein the question "What is a word really?" is analogous to "What is a piece in chess?"

Finally, John L. Austin offered a systematic classification of the variety of speech acts. According to him, to say something is to do something, and what one does in saying something is typically indicated by a particular performative verb prefixing the "normal form" of the utterance. These verbs, such as "state," "declare," "judge," "order," "request," "promise," "warn," "apologize," "call," and so on, mark the illocutionary force of the utterance in question. If one says, for instance, "I shall be there," then, depending on the circumstances, this utterance may amount to a prediction, a promise, or a warning. Similarly, the words of the commanding officer, "You will retreat" may have the force of a simple forecast, or of an order. If the circumstances are not clear, the speaker always can be more explicit and use the normal form; *e.g.*, "I promise that I shall be there" or "I order you to retreat."

To rephrase the conclusion already stated: the dimension of truth and falsity is not invoked by all the utterances of the language; therefore, it cannot provide an exclusive source of meaning. There are other dimensions, such as feasibility (in case of orders and promises), utility (in case of regulations and prescriptions), and moral worth (in case of advices and laws). These dimensions may be as much involved in the understanding of what one said and, consequently, in the meaning of the words the speaker used, as the dimension of truth.

As previously mentioned, philosophers professing the aletheic theory claimed that the meaning of a word should be explained in terms of its contribution to the truth or falsity of the sentences in which it can occur. The latest form of the use theory is an appropriate extension of the same idea. According to some exponents, the meaning of a word is nothing but its illocutionary act potential—*i.e.*, its contribution to the nature of the speech

Difficulties
with the
use
theory

acts that can be performed by using that word. One difficulty with this view is that the definition is too broad, to the extent of being unilluminating or useless. Given this definition, nobody would know what any word means without knowing the entire language completely because the possibilities of employing a given word are not only without limit but extend to every conceivable context and circumstance. As Wittgenstein stated so forcefully,

> The sign (the sentence) gets its significance from the system of signs, from the language to which it belongs. Roughly: understanding a sentence means understanding a language.

If this be the case, how can one account for the obviously gradual and prolonged process of learning a language? Indeed, the definition of the meaning of a word as illocutionary act potential seems to overstate the case. The obvious truth that the meaning of performative verbs, and other words closely tied to one illocutionary aspect or other, cannot be divorced from the nature of that type of speech act, does not entail that the meaning of an ordinary word, like "cat" or "running" is affected by any illocutionary force. Such words can occur in utterances bearing all kinds of illocutionary forces, so the contribution of these forces, as it were, cancel out. Nevertheless, what remains is the fact that all words are used to say something, in one way or another. The use theory would put a strong emphasis on the word "used" in the previous sentence. The next, and final, approach to meaning would stress the word "say."

Meaning and thought. In Wittgenstein's chess example, moves are made by moving the pieces. In a language, moves (saying something) are made by using words. And, according to the use theory, as a piece is defined by its move potential, so (the meaning of) a word is defined by its "saying" potential.

This analogy works only up to a certain limit. Whereas chess is only a game, the use of language is much more. One plays chess—or any other game—for its own sake; one speaks, however, with other ends in mind. Games, as it were, do not point beyond themselves; speech does. In order to see this, compare an ordinary conversation with such word games as children play—*e.g.*, exchanging words that rhyme, or words that begin with the same letter. These word games are language games and nothing more because the children use words according to certain rules. In doing so, however, they do not say anything except in the trivial sense of uttering words; nor are they called to understand what the other children say beyond the minimal feat of recognizing the words.

In real speech the situation is radically different. The point of using words in a real speech act is to be understood. If someone says, "It will rain tomorrow," his aim is to make the hearer believe that it will rain tomorrow. It is possible, of course, that the hearer or listener will not believe the speaker. Nevertheless, if the hearer understands what the speaker says, he will at least know that this is what the other person wants him to believe by saying what he says. Similarly, if one says, "Go home," and the listener understands what is said, then, whether or not the listener will actually go, he will at least know that this is what the speaker wants to bring about by using these words. Thus, the notion of saying something is inseparably tied to such concepts as belief, intention, knowledge, and understanding.

Speech
as an
expression
of thought

The view just outlined is a reformulation of a very traditional idea, namely, that speech is essentially the expression of thought. Words are used not to play a game with fixed rules but to express beliefs and judgments, intentions and desires; that is, to make others know, by the use of words according to fixed rules, that one has certain beliefs, desires, and so forth, and that one invites others to share them.

"Expression of thought" sounds rather vague. For one thing, what is a thought? Suppose John believes that Joe has stolen his watch. John can express this belief by saying, "Joe has stolen my watch" or "My watch has been stolen by Joe" or "It is Joe who has stolen my watch" and so on. Moreover, if John is a multilingual person, he can express the same belief in German, French, and so forth. These variants, called paraphrases and translations respectively, will express the same belief, the same thought. But whereas it makes sense to ask for the exact words of John's statement or to ask about the language in which it was made, it would be foolish to ask for the exact words of John's belief or to ask about the language in which it is framed. The alternative in "Do you believe that Joe has stolen the watch, or that the watch was stolen by Joe?" does not make sense. Consequently, the same thought—the same proposition, as some philosophers prefer to call it—can be expressed by using various linguistic media. In other words, the same thought can be encoded in various codes (languages) and in various ways in the same code (paraphrases) in much the same way as the same idea can be expressed in speech or in writing and the same numbers can be written by using Roman or Arabic numerals.

From this point of view, it appears that saying something involves encoding a thought and that understanding what one said involves decoding and recovering the same thought. The meaning of a sentence will consist in its relation to the thought it is used to encode. This may be viewed as the fundamental thesis of the psychological theory of meaning.

As previously explained, no theory of meaning can be adequate as long as it treats sentences as indivisible units. For, in the first place, the potentially infinite number of sentences would defy any attempt to learn their meaning one by one, and, second, such a theory could not account for the obvious ability of fluent speakers to understand entirely novel sentences. There must be, therefore, a correlation between certain recurring elements of sentences (roughly, words) and certain recurring elements of thoughts (roughly, concepts or ideas). Accordingly, the learning of the semantic component of a language will consist in the learning of these connections.

Synonyms and analytic propositions

In this learning process two notions play a prominent role: synonymy and analyticity. As the sentences that express the same thought stand in the relation of paraphrase (or translation), so words or phrases that code the same idea are related as synonyms—e.g., "vixen" and "female fox." Again, because one concept may include another, the sentence expressing this relation will record a conceptual truth or analytic proposition; e.g., "A dog is an animal." A definition, finally, will exhibit all parts of a concept by a combination of such propositions.

What concepts are and how they are related to words are topics that have been discussed throughout the history of philosophy. The following problems related to concepts pertain to the core of philosophical psychology: whether all concepts are derived from experience, as Aristotle and the Empiricists believed, or whether some of them at least are innate, as Plato and the Rationalists maintained; whether concepts exist prior to and independent from their verbal encodings, as the Realists and Conceptualists claimed, or whether they are nothing but a certain "field of force" accompanying the words, as the Nominalists thought.

It should be noted that these disputes, in a modern garb, still continue with undiminished force. Contemporary Empiricists still try to reduce most concepts to a configuration of sense data, or a pattern of nerve stimulation, while the Behaviourists attempt to explain understanding in terms of overt behaviour. Modern-day Rationalists reply by insisting on the unique spontaneity of human speech and by reviving the theory of innate ideas.

MEANING IN LINGUISTICS

Semantics in the theory of language. The science of linguistics is concerned with the theory of language expressed in terms of linguistic universals—i.e., features that are common to all natural languages. According to the widely adopted schema of the U.S. scholar Charles W. Morris, this theory must embrace three domains: pragmatics, the study of the language user as such; semantics, the study of the elements of a language from the point of view of meaning; and syntax, the study of the formal interrelations that exist between the elements of a language (i.e., sounds, words) themselves. Subsequently, certain authors spoke of three levels: the phonetic, the syntactic (the phonetic and syntactic together are often called grammatical), and the semantic level. On each of these levels a language may be studied in isolation or in comparison with other languages. In another dimension, the investigation might be restricted to the state of a language (or languages) at a given time (synchronic

Pragmatics, semantics, and syntax

study), or it might be concerned with the development of a language (or languages) through a period of time (diachronic study).

Semantics, then, is one of the main fields of linguistic science. Yet, except for borderline investigations, the linguist's interest in semantic matters is quite distinct from the philosopher's concern. Whereas the philosopher asks the question "What is meaning?", the typical questions the linguist is likely to ask include: "How is the meaning of words encoded in a language?" "How is this meaning to be determined?" "What are the laws governing change of meaning?" and "How can the meaning of a word be given, expressed, or defined?"

A few examples will suffice to illustrate some of these problems, and to show how the linguist's approach differs from that of the philosopher. In the matter of encoding, words are arbitrary signs; to some authors, particularly to the Swiss linguist Ferdinand de Saussure, this feature of arbitrariness represents an essential characteristic of all real languages. Nevertheless, in all languages there are clear cases of onomatopoeia—i.e., the occurrence of imitative words, such as "whisper," "snore," "slap," and, more remotely, "cuckoo."

There are several other issues that pertain to the question of encoding. Certain languages show a marked preference for very specific words, at least in certain domains, while lacking the corresponding general terms, which are the only ones occurring in other languages. The Eskimos, for instance, have a number of words denoting various kinds of snow, but no single word for snow. Similarly, in English, although there are distinct names for hundreds of animal species, there is no name for the very familiar animal species of which the female member is called cow and the male member bull.

There are also certain languages, such as English or Chinese, that for the most part prefer single words rather than the compounded phrases that other languages (e.g., German) seem to favour. Accordingly, whereas the English vocabulary is larger, the German words are more pliable, capable of entering into compounds often of great length and complexity. Such differences support De Saussure's distinction between lexicological and grammatical languages.

Context-bound and context-free words

Another distinction can be drawn concerning the relative frequency and importance of context-bound and context-free words. The meaning of such English words as "take," "put," and "get" depends almost entirely on the context—e.g., putting up with somebody has very little to do with putting off something or other. These can be compared with verbs like "canter" or "promulgate," which, by their very specific meaning, almost determine the context, rather than having their meaning determined by the context. Clearly, the context-bound type of word, such as "take" or "put," lends itself to idiomatic use, rather than the context-free word.

There are some obvious regularities in the change of meaning that are of interest to the linguist. One such regularity is the extension or transference of meaning based upon some similarities—i.e., the phenomenon of metaphor. For example, one can speak of the leg of the table, the mouth of the river, the eye of the needle, and the crown of the tree. These are anthropomorphic metaphors: the transfer goes from something belonging to an individual or close to him (his body, garments) to something more remote. The same principle operates in the extension of meaning from a domain close in interest rather than in physical proximity. Baseball-minded people are apt to speak of "not getting to first base," "striking out," or "scoring a hit" in contexts often remote from baseball. For a similar reason, many abstract concepts are denoted by words transplanted from the concrete domain. Such phrases as "grasping ideas," "seeing the point of a joke," "body of knowledge," "in the back of my mind," and many others, are the result of this very important move from the abstract to the concrete.

Meaning changes of another type are the result of emotive factors. The word democracy, for instance, has all but lost its original meaning and has become a word applicable to any system the speaker wants to praise. The contrary development is exhibited in the recent history of such words as "Fascist" and "aggression." In order to avoid derogatory connotations one is often forced, by social pressure, to use euphemisms, often to the detriment of clarity. Examples of this include the switch from "underdeveloped nations" to "developing nations," from "retarded children" to "exceptional children," and from "old people" to "senior citizens."

The preceding are but a few examples concerning coding and meaning change. The questions about the ways of finding out what a word means and about the manner of giving an adequate definition of a word deserve a more detailed account.

Meaning, structure, and context. Foreigners in a strange country and linguists are often confronted with the task of learning a new language. It is important to realize that in doing so they do not set out with a completely blank mind: they expect to learn a language (*i.e.*, a system of communication describable in terms of a large set of linguistic universals). They expect—consciously in the case of the linguist and unconsciously in the case of the layman—to find words and sentences, grammatical structures, and illocutionary forces in that language. And, on the semantic level, they expect words that will fit into the familiar semantic classes. They are confident, in other words, that the language they intend to master will be intertranslatable with their own.

Structure and language learning

Therefore, although at the very beginning their learning remains on the ostensive level (trying to find out the name of this or that kind of object), very soon they proceed to the level of first guessing, then establishing, the meaning of words from the contexts in which they occur. This has to be the case, for words that in any way can be viewed as "names" of objects (*i.e.*, that could be learned ostensively) form but a fraction of the vocabulary of any language. Anyone who doubts this should but try to list the words from this paragraph that could be learned ostensively. Moreover, linguists find no great difficulties in learning dead languages—*e.g.*, that of the ancient Egyptians—without any contact with any speaker, provided that a sufficiently large corpus of texts is available and that some clues are provided to the meaning of at least some words.

If any more evidence concerning this point is needed, one should remember that "pictorial" dictionaries are bound to remain on the kindergarten level, and that the mark of a good dictionary is the abundance of appropriate contexts. Thus, the contexts show the concept.

These intuitions are behind the U.S. philosopher Paul Ziff's semantic theory. According to Ziff, the meaning of a word is a function, first, of its complementary set, which consists of all the acceptable sentences in which the word can occur, and, second, of its contrastive set, which consists of all of the words that can replace that word in all of these sentences without rendering the sentences deviant. Clearly, the elaboration of the contrastive set will produce words more and more similar in meaning to the word in question, the limiting case being synonyms that can occur wherever the word in question can occur.

This theory is in need of further refinement. In the sentence "The cat sleeps," the fact that "cat" can co-occur with "sleep" undoubtedly casts some light on the meaning of these words (a cat is a kind of thing that can sleep). But there are a great number of sequences that could complete the frames "The cat sleeps and . . . ," ". . . said that the cat sleeps," and so forth. Clearly, the near infinity of the resulting sentences will not contribute anything to the meaning of "cat" beyond what the segment "the cat sleeps" already contributes.

Surface forms and underlying structures

Transformational grammar can be of assistance at this point. According to this approach, the sentences just considered are simply surface forms, each corresponding to an underlying structure, in which "cat" and "sleep" appear as forming an elementary, or kernel sentence (roughly: "a cat sleeps"). The essence of Ziff's insight can be reinterpreted in terms of the notions developed by Zellig S. Harris: co-occurrence (instead of complementary set) and co-occurrence difference (instead of contrastive set), both restricted to kernels. Because the voca-

bulary of a language is limited and the number of kernel structures is very small, the meaning of a word can be determined on the basis of a finite set of elementary sentences.

The contribution of grammar to semantic theory is by no means exhausted by this step. For the grammatical restrictions on a word represent, as it were, the "skeleton" of its meaning before the "flesh" is put on by the co-occurrences. The very first step in giving the meaning of a word is to specify its grammatical category—noun, verb, adjective, adverb, connective, and so forth—and not to speak of grammatical constants (such as the first, but not the second, "to" in "I want to go to Paris"), the meaning of which, if any, is entirely determined by their grammatical role. A refined grammar yields much more: the fact that the adjective "good," for example, unlike adjectives like "yellow" or "fat," can occur in the frames "(He is) good at (playing chess)"; "(The root is) good to (eat)"; "It is good that (it is raining)"; "It was good of (him) to (come)" says a great deal about the meaning of that word. The co-occurrences then complete the picture.

Lexical entries. Good dictionaries offer a variety of contexts for the items listed but, obviously, this is not enough. For one thing, no dictionary can list all the co-occurrences. There must be devices to sum up, as it were, the information revealed by the contexts. This is the role of dictionary definitions. The branch of scientific semantics that is concerned with the form and adequacy conditions of dictionary entries is called lexicography.

A systematic study of dictionary entries was presented in the 1960s by the U.S. philosophers Jerrold J. Katz and Jerry A. Fodor. According to them, the standard form of a dictionary entry comprises three kinds of ingredients: grammatical markers, semantic markers, and distinguishers. The grammatical markers describe the syntactic behaviour of the item in question in terms of a refined system of grammatical categories. The traditional division of words into nouns, adjectives, verbs, adverbs, and so on is but the first step in this direction. The class of nouns, for example, has to be subdivided into count nouns (like "cat"), mass nouns (like "water"), abstract nouns (like "love"), and so forth. The class of adjectives must be classified into subclasses that are fine enough to capture the grammatical peculiarities of such adjectives as "unlikely" or "good." The traditional subdivision of verbs into transitives and intransitives has to be completed to account for such verbs as "compare" or "order," which obviously involve three noun phrases ("someone compares something to something"), often of a particular kind ("human" nouns or noun clauses).

The idea of a semantic marker is merely a further elaboration of the traditional notions of genus and species. The result is a system of semantic markers that comprise such items as "physical object," "animate," "human," "male," "young" (in the case of the entry for "boy"), and others. Katz claims that the problems of synonymy, analyticity, and contradiction can be handled, at least in part, in terms of lexical items sharing some or all of their semantic markers.

Finally, the distinguisher completes the dictionary entry by giving, as it were, the leftover, if any, of the semantic information. There is no general form for the distinguisher; it may give the atomic weight (for elements), purpose (for tools), concise description (for animals), and so forth.

Generative semantics. According to the original formulation of generative or transformational grammar, the semantic and the syntactic components were regarded as distinct elements in the deep structure of a sentence. The syntactic component consisted of a relation of phrase markers giving the transformational structure of the sentence, usually represented by a "tree" diagram with the phrase markers as nodes (*e.g.*, "S" for sentence, "NP" for noun phrase). The semantic content entered through the process of lexical insertion—*i.e.*, the replacement of the phrase markers by words, the carriers of meaning. Lexical insertion was supposed to take place at the very beginning of the series of transformations leading up to the surface form of the sentence. The original input of mean-

Lexical insertion in a generative grammar

ing, as it were, was carried through the transformations yielding the semantical reading, or sense, of the whole sentence.

Several modern studies have attempted to demonstrate that this separation between syntax and semantics cannot be maintained. It appears that certain words in themselves indicate a structure analogous to syntactic structures. For example, consider "harden" and "break." To harden something is to cause that thing to become hard (or harder); to break something is to cause something to become broken. Because "harden" consists of two elements, "hard-" and "-en," thus it could be argued that the word itself is structured; "break" does not indicate any structure, yet its meaning clearly involves one. "Broken," therefore, carries a more basic semantic unit than "break." Again, in the case of such verbs as "remind," "allege," "blame," or "forgive," one feels that their meaning is highly structured, and, with some thinking, one can articulate the presuppositions of these words, which involve a great number of semantic units in a very complex relationship.

These and similar reasons support the theory of generative semantics, which denies a clear distinction between the semantic and the syntactic components. The transformations, in this theory, connect the surface structure of the sentence with its semantic representation (or according to some linguists, its logical form). Words, then, can encode either a semantic primitive (such as "blue") or a whole structure (such as "forgive") within the semantic representation. Thus, there is no definite point in the transformational history of the sentence at which lexical insertion must occur. The ultimate conclusion of this view is that, instead of the threefold division of semantics, syntax, and phonetics, all that is needed is the simple distinction between semantics and phonetics, corresponding to the distinction between meaning (as structured) and its verbal encoding. How much, finally, of the semantic structure can be attributed to a particular language, and how much can be ascribed to common (and possibly innate) elements of the human mind, remains a fascinating problem for continued study.

BIBLIOGRAPHY

Collections of essays: The best and most comprehensive selection of relevant papers is J.F. ROSENBERG and C. TRAVIS, *Readings in the Philosophy of Language* (1971). A good collection of earlier contributions, mainly from the Positivistic school, is found in L. LINSKY (ed.), *Semantics and the Philosophy of Language* (1952). J.A. FODOR and J.J. KATZ (eds.), *The Structure of Language* (1964), contains some fundamental papers on transformational grammar. J.H. GREENBERG (ed.), *Universals of Language* (1963), includes some key articles on scientific semantics. V.C. CHAPPELL (ed.), *Ordinary Language* (1964), offers some typical articles on ordinary language philosophy. R.M. RORTY, (ed.), *The Linguistic Turn* (1967), shows the development of linguistic philosophy in a broad selection of papers.

Books: W.P. ALSTON, *Philosophy of Language* (1964), is the best current introduction to philosophical semantics. M. BLACK, *Language and Philosophy* (1949), discusses some earlier views. L. BLOOMFIELD, *Language* (1933), contains a classic discussion of scientific semantics. B.L. WHORF, *Language, Thought and Reality,* ed. by J.B. CARROLL (1956), raises the issue of linguistic relativism. J.J. KATZ, *The Philosophy of Language* (1966), offers a semantic theory tied to generative grammar, the best expression of which is found in N. CHOMSKY, *Aspects of the Theory of Syntax* (1965). W.V. QUINE, *Word and Object* (1960); and P. ZIFF, *Semantic Analysis* (1960), represent two different but influential semantic theories. Some of the leading ideas for modern philosophical semantics come from C.L. STEVENSON, *Ethics and Language* (1944); J.L. AUSTIN, *How to Do Things with Words* (1962); L. WITTGENSTEIN, *Philosophical Investigations,* 3rd ed. (1968); and *The Blue and Brown Books: Preliminary Studies for the Philosophical Investigations,* 2nd ed. (1969).

(Z.V.)

Semiconductor Devices

Semiconductor devices are electronic circuit components, such as transistors, fabricated from a material that is neither a good conductor of electricity nor a good insulator; hence the name semiconductor. This article covers the preparation of semiconductor materials and the design, manufacture, and application of the more popular semiconductor devices. Specific devices are covered in greater detail in the articles THERMOELECTRIC DEVICES; LASER AND MASER. A more theoretical treatment of semiconductor action is given in SEMICONDUCTORS AND INSULATORS, THEORY OF. All the devices described in this article are discrete devices, as opposed to the more recent integrated devices described in the article INTEGRATED CIRCUITRY.

Semiconductor and junction principles. A wide range of semiconductor devices is available, made from a number of materials and by a variety of processes. The applications for these semiconductor devices cover the whole electromagnetic spectrum from ultraviolet frequencies to the control of direct current. There is now a semiconductor device suitable for practically any electronic application, even at extremely high frequencies and powers.

The materials known as semiconductors have electrical resistivities (the resistance of a cube of the material one centimetre on a side) in the range intermediate between insulators and metals. The resistivity of elemental semiconductors always decreases with increasing temperature, and these materials often show some decrease in resistivity when illuminated with light (photoconductivity). The most commonly used semiconductors are presently the elements germanium and silicon, but certain compounds, such as gallium arsenide, indium antimonide, and copper oxide, have useful semiconductor properties.

Electrons in an isolated atomic structure can exist only in certain definite energy levels. If an electron moves from one level to another, energy is either absorbed or emitted. The electrons in an atom that possesses relatively little energy move in orbits close to the atomic nucleus. If the electron absorbs energy from an outside source (for example, ultraviolet light), it may jump to a higher energy electron orbit, but these jumps always occur in discrete steps.

When a number of atoms are assembled in a group, as in a regular crystalline structure, the electrons are influenced by the electrical fields of neighbouring atoms as well as by the parent nucleus, causing the discrete energy levels to spread out into energy bands. These bands do not normally overlap; for any given atomic spacing there are permissible energy bands interspersed with gaps called forbidden energy gaps.

The outermost electrons of an atom are normally in what is called the valence band. If one of these electrons absorbs energy it is said to be excited; it may absorb enough energy to cause it to leave the valence band and jump temporarily to a conduction band, where it is free of the attractive force of the nucleus. In semiconductor materials, these conduction bands are often empty or only partially filled.

Electrons in the conduction band may be made to move easily by an electric field, and this drift is commonly known as a conduction current. The energy gap between the top level of the valence band and the lower level in the conduction band is the minimum energy (usually expressed in electron volts) required to produce a free electron in a crystal. Generally, a wider energy gap is related to a higher melting point.

The electrical conductivity of any material depends on the number of charge carriers available in the conduction bands, per unit volume, and on the rate at which these carriers move under the influence of an electric field. If a negatively charged electron is moved into a vacant level in the conduction band, this leaves a corresponding positive imbalance, or "hole," in the valence band.

Because of this concept it is convenient to think of electrical conduction as consisting of negative charges carried by electrons and positive charges carried by holes. In a pure semiconductor, conduction takes place by electron–hole pairs, but the electron and the hole have different mobilities; that is, they move with different velocities in an electric field. The differing electron and hole mobilities are caused by the fact that they start at different energy levels and travel under differing forces in opposite directions.

Electrical conduction in highly pure semiconductors

Electrical
conductivity
volts

(called intrinsic semiconductor material, with a ratio of impurities of about one part in 10^{12}) is poor and largely temperature dependent. The intentional addition of impurities, typically to a concentration of one part in 10^6, is known as doping and modifies the electrical characteristics to produce a much greater conduction. Such materials are called extrinsic, since the condition results from the external addition of impurities. Semiconductor materials have four electrons in the outer or valency shell, whereas the impurities have either five or three valency electrons. The elements antimony, arsenic, and phosphorus add electrons, or n (negative) carriers; and the elements aluminum, boron, and indium effectively provide more holes, known as p (positive) carriers. The small concentration of added impurities does not change the metallurgical characteristics of the basic semiconductor but modifies its electrical properties.

If a change in doping takes place over a short distance within a single crystal structure (described later), this produces a p–n junction, as illustrated in Figure 1A.

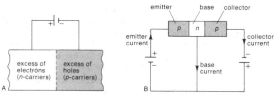

Figure 1: (A), A p–n junction. (B) The p–n–p transistor.

There will be an excess of holes in the p region, and so these holes are called majority carriers. A few thermally generated electrons will also exist in this region, and they are called minority carriers. Conversely, in the n region, the electrons are the majority carriers and the holes minority carriers. In the area of the p–n junction there are no free-charge carriers. This region is called the depletion layer and it acts as a dielectric (electrical insulator).

When a voltage is applied across this elementary junction with the polarities as shown, the charge carriers introduced by the impurities move in opposite directions away from the junction, and only a very small intrinsic current flows across the junction. If the polarity of the voltage is reversed, then the majority charge carriers flow across the junction. This means that the p–n junction acts as a rectifier, that is, it will conduct with one input-voltage polarity but will not conduct if this polarity is reversed.

Rectifier action — margin note

Rectifiers made from semiconductor materials were introduced commercially in the 1930s, long before the mechanism of the p–n junction was understood. The copper oxide diode, in which the boundary between copper and cuprous oxide forms the rectifying junction, is rarely used now. On the other hand, the selenium rectifier has a junction consisting of selenium and a tin–cadmium alloy. Due to the low cost of manufacture, selenium rectifiers, which give reasonable efficiency for power outputs up to ten kilowatts, are widely used and have been used in installations up to one megawatt, although it appears likely that junction devices will eventually replace such rectifiers.

The transistor. The transistor was invented by the U.S. scientists John Bardeen, Walter Brattain, and William Shockley in 1948. The name of this amplifying device was derived from the phrase "transfer resistor," since that is how the device appeared to operate in an electronic circuit. Early transistors were known as point-contact devices, in which the rectifying junctions were formed by two closely spaced fine wire springs in contact with a semiconductor surface. The point-contact transistors had a family resemblance to the simple "cat's whisker" diodes (rectifiers) that were used in early radio receivers. All modern transistors are of the junction type, usually produced by one of the processes to be described later. The transistor in its various forms is the most significant of the many semiconductor devices that have appeared so far.

The junction transistor exists in two complementary forms, the p–n–p and n–p–n transistors. The p–n–p transistor may be regarded as two p–n diodes joined back to back, with the first, forward biassed, providing the minority carriers for the second, reverse biassed, diode. This is illustrated in Figure 1B, in which the three terminals of the transistor are labelled with their usual names of emitter, base, and collector.

The construction of the p–n–p transistor is such that the impurity content of the narrow n-type base region is very much less than that in the p regions. This means that in the forward-biassed input circuit (from emitter to base) the flow of current carriers across the junction is mainly in the form of holes from the p to n regions. Some of these holes, which are minority carriers as far as the n-type region is concerned, recombine with electrons there. The majority, however, diffuse across the narrow base and flow to the collector, which is a high-resistance output circuit due to the applied reverse bias.

The circuit arrangement shown in Figure 2A is known as the common, or grounded, base configuration. The current gain is defined for the common-base connection as the change in collector current divided by the change in emitter current when the base-to-collector voltage is constant.

The other possible transistor circuit configurations are shown in Figures 2B and 2C, and are known as common emitter and common collector. The most useful amplifier circuit is common emitter, in which a small change in signal current to the base requires little power but can result in much greater power in the output circuit. This characteristic makes transistors useful as amplifiers, oscillators, and other circuit elements, as described later. A problem common to all transistors is the small "leakage current" that flows in the output circuit when the input current is zero. Since leakage current increases as the temperature increases, it increases the inherent power dissipation within a transistor as the environmental temperature is increased. However small the leakage current may be at room temperature, for any transistor there is a junction temperature at which thermal instability occurs, thus placing an upper limit on the temperature at which a transistor will operate satisfactorily.

Leakage current efficiency — margin note

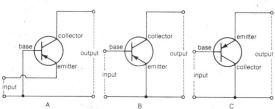

Figure 2: (A) Common base, (B) common emitter, and (C) common collector circuit configurations.

In the n–p–n transistor there are two n regions that sandwich in a narrow p region. Current flow from input to output is by means of free electrons. Because of the higher mobility of electrons compared with holes, n–p–n transistors can operate usefully at higher frequencies than can p–n–p transistors of the same dimensions. Since for the first decade of transistor history it was much more difficult to manufacture n–p–n than p–n–p transistors, most of the early semiconductor technology revolved around the p–n–p germanium transistor. This condition is no longer true, and the circuit designer can now choose from a variety of semiconducting devices that is almost bewildering in its range.

Preparation of semiconductor materials

TYPES OF SEMICONDUCTOR MATERIALS

Elemental materials. Semiconductor materials are divided into two categories: elemental and compound. Elemental semiconductors are usually composed of one element only in the undoped, or intrinsic state and are divided into valency groups according to the number of valence electrons they have, as shown in Table 1.

Germanium and silicon are by far the most commonly used elements in modern semiconductor devices.

Most semiconductor devices are constructed from a thin wafer, or slice, of properly doped material. Preparation involves the processing of germanium or silicon to pro-

Table 1: Significant Semiconductor Elements
(giving common chemical nomenclature)

group II 2 valence electrons	group III 3 valence electrons	group IV 4 valence electrons	group V 5 valence electrons	group VI 6 valence electrons
beryllium Be	boron B	carbon C	phosphorus P	sulfur S
magnesium Mg	aluminum Al	silicon Si	arsenic As	selenium Se
zinc Zn	gallium Ga	germanium Ge	antimony Sb	tellurium Te
cadmium Cd	indium In	lead Pb	bismuth Bi	
	thallium Tl			

duce thin, smooth, and polished wafers (typically two inches, or five centimetres, in diameter, 0.01 inch, or 0.025 centimetre, thick) that are properly doped with n or p-type impurities. The basic steps in wafer preparation are: material purification, single crystal growing, wafer processing, and epitaxy.

Material purification. Germanium occurs in nature as a low-level impurity in zinc and copper ores. It is extracted by chemical processes in the form of germanium dioxide and reduced to the elemental state by heating in hydrogen.

Semiconductor manufacturers purchase raw germanium that is fairly pure by commercial standards in the form of rods two inches (five centimetres) in diameter and five to six inches (13 to 15 centimetres) long. For semiconductor use, this raw germanium must be refined to a very pure condition. Refining is based on the principle that impurities are generally more soluble in molten than in solid germanium. The industrial process is called zone refining (see ZONE MELTING). The final product contains less than one impurity atom in 10^{12} of the pure germanium or silicon atoms.

Silicon is one of the most common of all the elements, occurring in the earth's crust as sand, mainly silicon dioxide, and in various silicate compounds. Also, large quantities of silicon tetrachloride, $SiCl_4$, and silicon trichlorosilane, $SiHCl_3$, are produced in the manufacture of silicones, and this source of supply is utilized for the preparation of very pure silicon for the semiconductor industry. The use of trichlorosilane is favoured because it is easier to remove such impurities as phosphorus and boron compounds from it. The trichlorosilane is purified by direct distillation (boiling point 32° C, or 91° F) using quartz containers to avoid contamination during the process. After purification, the trichlorosilane is reduced to pure silicon by heating in the presence of hydrogen. The hydrogen is bubbled through the trichlorosilane, which vaporizes and is taken with the hydrogen into a reaction chamber containing a thin, high-purity silicon rod heated to about 950° C (1,742° F). When the trichlorosilane decomposes, pure silicon is deposited onto the surface of the rod, building it up to a diameter between one and four inches (2.5 and ten centimetres), depending on the requirement. The hydrochloric acid vapour produced in the reaction is vented away.

Zone refining, as used with germanium, is not effective in purifying silicon. The high temperature needed to melt silicon, 1,420° C (2,588° F), causes problems. When in the molten state, silicon is easily contaminated by impurities in the container. Moreover, a common impurity in the low-grade silicon is boron, a Group III acceptor element (see Table 1). Boron has roughly equal solubilities in molten and solid silicon and so is difficult to remove by zone refining. Because of these factors, all purification of silicon is usually carried out by the chemical process described earlier, and purity levels of one part in 10^{10} are achieved. The silicon produced by the subsequent decomposition process is sufficiently pure for semiconductor use.

Crystal growing. The successful fabrication of a semiconductor device depends not only on the purity of the elemental semiconductor used but also on the regularity of the crystal structure. Polycrystalline or irregular crystal structure results in reduced carrier mobility and re-

duced carrier lifetime and so is not suitable for device fabrication. Most materials referred to as crystals are not single crystals but a collection of many single crystals of various shapes, sizes, and orientations. Such crystals are said to be polycrystalline.

A germanium bar that has been purified by zone refining is a polycrystalline material. For it to be useful as a semiconductor material, it must be grown into a single crystal. The process used to obtain single crystals of germanium large enough for device fabrication is called the Czochralski crystal-pulling technique. Solid polycrystalline germanium is placed in a graphite crucible inside a transparent quartz chamber through which a flow of argon is passed. Heat is applied to the germanium, generally from a radio-frequency power source. When the material is molten, the temperature is lowered to a value just above the melting point of germanium.

Next, a seed crystal (*i.e.*, a small single crystal of germanium) is lowered into the chamber until it just enters the top of the melted germanium. The seed is held in a clamp at the end of a long shaft. After the seed crystal has been dipped into the melt, it is rotated and raised by means of the shaft. Because the seed crystal is at a lower temperature than the melt, heat flows from the melt near the seed. The melt in contact with the seed solidifies onto it, the atoms arranging themselves into cubes to have the same orientation as the elementary cubes in the seed crystal. The heat that flows to the seed is radiated by the portion of the crystal above the melt.

The finished crystal is usually round, with a diameter depending on the melt temperature, the speed of rotation, and rate of withdrawal. The speed of rotation may be as high as 100 revolutions per minute and pull rates of one-half or two inches (1.3 or five centimetres) per hour are typical.

The growth of the crystal continues as it is rotated and raised. Typical germanium pulled crystals are two inches (five centimetres) in diameter by ten inches (25 centimetres) in length. When a crystal is grown from a high-purity germanium melt, a single crystal of intrinsic germanium results. It is the doped, or extrinsic, germanium, however, that is often desired for device fabrication. To grow a single crystal of n-type or p-type germanium, it is only necessary to add the donor- or acceptor-impurity atom to the melt before the growing process begins. Typical impurity concentrations are of the order of one atom to every 1,000,000 to 100,000,000 atoms of germanium or silicon.

The Czochralski method of growing single crystals is not often used with silicon because its higher melting point results in contamination from impurities in the quartz tube, especially when extremely pure crystals are required. Another problem is that when a doping material is added to the melt, the dopant impurity tends to vaporize from the molten silicon because of the high temperature. The method used in growing single-crystal silicon is known as the floating-zone method.

A cylindrical rod of polycrystalline silicon is supported vertically with a single crystal seed of the same diameter positioned under it. A molten zone is formed in the seed by radio-frequency heating and is slowly passed up the seed into the polycrystalline rod and up the rod to its top. As the silicon resolidifies onto the single-crystal seed, it does so in single-crystal form with the same orientation as the seed.

In addition to its use for single-crystal formation, this technique is sometimes used for final purification by making several zone passes up the single-crystal rod from bottom to top to reduce the concentration of many impurities. The impurity concentration and profile of the doped, single-crystal bar are checked by locally measuring the resistivity of the material as a function of the distance along the bar. This is carried out by a technique known as the four-point-probe method. The apparatus consists of a probe with four metal points arranged in a straight line. A conductor connects each metal point to an external circuit. To measure the resistivity of a sample at a particular spot, the probe is set down on the sample at that spot with all four points making contact with the

Czochralski crystal-pulling technique

Floating-zone method

Zone refining

surface of the semiconductor sample. Current is supplied to the crystal through the two outer probes and the voltage developed between the two inner probes, is measured with a voltmeter. The resistance of the material in the vicinity of the probe is equal to the measured voltage divided by the measured current. Resistivity depends on the voltage-to-current ratio and also on the probe dimensions. The device can thus be calibrated to read resistivity directly.

The tested semiconductor bar is then cut into wafers (typically 0.01 inch, or 0.025 centimetre, thick) with diamond-tipped saws. Subsequently, at least one side of each wafer is lapped (*i.e.*, the wafer is rubbed against a metal surface with a fine abrasive in between) and polished until it is smooth and flat. The wafers are then chemically treated to smooth the surface further and to remove any portion of the wafer surface in which the crystal structure has been damaged by the lapping and polishing operations.

Epitaxy. Epitaxy is a process in which a thin film of single-crystal silicon or germanium is deposited from a gaseous compound upon an existing wafer of the same material. The epitaxial film may be either *p*-type or *n*-type of specified impurity concentration. A reactor for the production of an epitaxial layer is composed of a long cylindrical quartz tube encircled by a radio-frequency induction coil. The wafers are placed on a rectangular graphite boat that is inserted in the inductively heated reactor. At the input of the reactor the different gases required for the reaction are introduced and controlled at a control terminal. For a silicon epitaxial film, the gases include silicon tetrachloride, hydrogen, nitrogen, and phosphine for *n*-type doping or biborane for *p*-type doping. The reaction produces either pure or doped silicon, as desired, which then deposits on the wafers. The gases from the reaction together with any inert gases used are carried at the end of the chamber to an exhaust vent. At the end of the epitaxial process the wafer is ready for device fabrication.

Intermetallic compound materials. Early developments in solid-state electronics were made with compound materials. The galena (lead sulfide) crystal detector and the selenium rectifier are examples of these early developments. A semiconductor compound is a substance containing two or more elemental semiconductors in a fixed ratio. Binary compounds contain two elemental semiconductors in a one-to-one ratio. The most useful types of binary compounds are those averaging four valence electrons per atom. They can usually be obtained from a one-to-one combination of Group III and Group V elements or Group II and Group VI elements (see Table 1). Intermetallic binary compounds (compounds formed of two metals) have crystal structures somewhat similar to elemental germanium and silicon and most have similar electrical characteristics. These compounds can be made extrinsic either by doping them (using Group VI atoms as donors and Group II atoms as acceptors) or by changing the compound ratio. Some of the intermetallic compounds have also shown electrical properties very different from those of elemental germanium and silicon, particularly in carrier mobilities and energy gaps. These properties are the bases of many useful new devices. Examples of compound semiconductor materials are gallium arsenide, indium antimonide, and zinc and cadmium sulfides.

Gallium arsenide. This material has a high energy gap and good carrier mobility and so is useful for microwave tunnel diodes, mixers, and the Gunn-effect diodes (see below). It is also used in light-emitting diodes and to make transistors for operation at very high temperatures.

Indium antimonide. This material has a low energy gap and very high mobility that makes it useful in infrared detectors, magnetoresistive (changes in electrical conductivity when a magnetic field is applied) and piezoresistive (changes in resistance when pressure is applied) devices.

Zinc and cadmium sulfides. These two materials, besides having high energy gaps and low mobilities, have electroluminescent properties (crystalline phosphors that

glow when struck by a beam of electrons), which make them useful for photoelectric devices.

Organic materials. There is a group of organic materials that exhibit semiconductor-like properties. Polyvinylidene chloride (saran) films, for example, can exhibit *p*–*n*-junction properties that are sensitive to ultraviolet radiation. Minute crystals of polyethylene, on the other hand, exhibit negative-resistance effects. In the early 1970s most work in organic semiconductors was at the research stage. The results indicated that the best hope for the utilization of these semiconductors lies in the field of biochemistry and biological systems.

Amorphous materials. These are amorphous (noncrystalline, lacking a lattice structure) materials such as certain glasses (*i.e.*, chalcogenide) and amorphous oxides that are neither crystalline nor pure. In other words, they are the antithesis of the crystalline materials that have traditionally been used in semiconductor devices. They do show, however, many striking electrical and optical similarities to crystalline semiconductors. The electrons in such amorphous materials, for instance, have bandlike energy structures, somewhat like those prevailing in crystals. They also exhibit reasonably distinct wavelength limits in their ability to absorb light, and their electrical conductivity varies exponentially with temperature over a wide temperature range.

Chalcogenide glasses lend themselves to a variety of processing techniques; they can be cast, extruded, rolled, hot-pressed, blown, painted, and deposited by evaporation. A thin-film Ovonic (after the United States scientist S.R. Ovshinsky) device exhibits switching characteristics. The attractiveness of amorphous materials lies in the fact that the essential characteristics of devices made from them do not depend critically on the fabrication method, and they are remarkably insensitive to accidental trace impurities. These materials, however, are still at the research stage, and many problems associated with their basic physics have to be solved before they gain wide acceptance.

BASIC FABRICATION TECHNIQUES

Doping. The techniques used to make all the semiconductor devices have many features in common, whether these be diodes, transistors, four-layer controlled rectifiers, or other devices. For this reason, the processes employed to fabricate transistors are of general application.

To achieve as large a current gain as possible within a transistor, the lifetime of the majority-charge carrier, in the base region, must be relatively long before recombination of a hole–electron pair takes place. This requires that the transistor be made from a single crystal of high quality. At the same time, to obtain other desirable transistor properties, the impurity content of the crystal must be accurately controlled. This is best achieved by refining the semiconductor material to maximum possible purity, as described previously, and then adding impurities under carefully specified conditions through one of the available doping techniques. In general terms, the high-frequency performance of a transistor depends on the base width, the impurity profile, and the transit time of the minority-charge carriers. In some devices it is possible to include different impurity concentration levels and profiles by sequential processes.

Alloying. During the decade from 1950 most transistors were made by the alloyed-junction process. Common examples are of indium alloyed into germanium wafers or aluminum into silicon wafers, to form *p*–*n*–*p* transistors. In the manufacture of a germanium-alloyed transistor, an *n*-type crystal is usually cut into small wafers 0.08 inch (two millimetres) square and 0.004 inch (0.1 millimetre) thick. When the indium melts, it dissolves a small amount of the germanium base and then, as the structure cools, the germanium recrystallizes, but it now contains some indium in the crystal structure, giving a *p*-type region. The alloying process is repeated on the other side of the base crystal to obtain the required two-junction structure. Contacts are soldered to the *n*-type base region and to the collector and emitter pellets. To minimize the base resistance the base contact is often in the form of a

Extrinsic compounds

Ovonic devices

ring around the emitter. Since most of the power is developed at the collector, this part of the transistor is made physically larger than the emitter.

It is difficult to alloy into a wafer of a thickness of less than 0.002 inch (about 0.05 millimetre) and extremely difficult to make alloyed-junction transistors with a base width narrower than 0.001 inch (0.025 millimetre) consistently. Also, the alloying process produces only a poorly defined boundary for the p–n junction. This results in a usable upper frequency limit of about ten megahertz for germanium-alloyed transistors. This technique has been superseded for the most part by other doping methods.

Diffusion. A region of semiconductor material may be converted from one type to another by solid and gaseous diffusion (the movement of impurity atoms into the crystalline structure of the material) without actually melting it. This process permits excellent control of impurity pen-

Controlling impurity penetration

etration, to within a few millionths of an inch, and is, therefore, attractive as a way of producing the thin base region necessary for a successful very high frequency device.

If a p-type germanium wafer is heated to near melting temperature in a donor-impurity atmosphere, such as antimony, then some of the impurity condenses on the wafer surface and tends to diffuse into the crystal. When the wafer is cool, the thin surface layer of the germanium will have changed from p to n type. The position of the junction below the germanium surface will be determined by the concentration of original impurity in the semiconductor wafer, the nature and temperature of the impurity vapour, and the time allowed for solid diffusion. Since the depth of impurity diffusion can be made extremely small with only moderate control of time and temperature, this method is attractive for industrial purposes.

One fact not properly understood is that n-type impurities diffuse fairly rapidly into germanium, but the diffusion rate of p-type impurities into germanium is so slow as to make it an unusable process. Diffusion of either n or p impurities into silicon is a viable process and can be employed to give a double-diffusion n–p–n transistor. With the use of this technique it is possible to make a transistor having a base width of 0.0005 millimetre (0.5 micrometre).

Ion implantation. This technique involves the doping of a semiconductor by implanting a dose of ions of the dopant into the semiconductor crystal. This is achieved by bombarding the semiconductor surface with an electrically controlled ion beam of high energy, approximately 10,000 electron volts. The motion and penetration of an ion beam into a crystal results from the kinetic energy of the beam and does not depend much on the crystal temperature. This means that the semiconductor processing steps can be varied substantially from those used in diffusion doping, giving the manufacturer more versatility in achieving his design objectives. The independence of crystal temperature allows the doping of a cold crystal, which, despite the fact that a final annealing (heating and slow cooling) step is usually required, allows the utilization of low-melting-temperature materials, and also high-diffusion-temperature materials, as dopants. The electrically controlled nature of the ion beam allows an extremely precise control of the number of ions implanted per unit surface area, which means electrical rather than thermal control of the p–n-junction depth and impurity profile. The flexibility of ion-implantation doping allows the creation of deep and shallow regions, high and low concentration of n and p dopants of very precise dimensions and penetration depths. The narrow emitter width required for high-frequency operation can be easily achieved by a 10,000-electron-volt boron beam directed through an emitter window of an aluminum mask 0.75 micrometre thick.

Masking and etching. The area of a wafer into which an impurity is diffused from a vapour may be approximately determined by masking the areas where diffusion is not desired. The final shape of the resulting p or n region may then be further defined by the use of an etching technique. The combination of these techniques together with that of epitaxy enables the production of

semiconductor devices within closely specified physical limits. Aluminum, for example, may be evaporated from a vapour into the surface of an n-type layer through a mask placed above the wafer surface. It is more common to have the mask as the surface material of the semiconductor wafer itself; *i.e.*, as an integral part of the semiconductor. The technique of making double-diffused silicon transistors depends on the selective-masking property of silicon dioxide. At high temperatures (above 1,300° C, or 2,370° F) a layer of this dioxide about five micrometres thick has very little inhibiting effect upon the diffusion of gallium into silicon from a gallium-rich atmosphere. But below 1,300° C, this same dioxide layer effectively masks the diffusion of boron, phosphorus, arsenic, or antimony. Using this property of silicon dioxide, together with photolithographic techniques of etching precisely defined holes in the dioxide layer (*i.e.*, by exposing a light-sensitive surface to light through a photographic mask), it is possible to produce high-performance double-diffused transistors. The cross section of a typical epitaxial-planar silicon transistor is shown in Figure 3. The impurity

Double diffusing

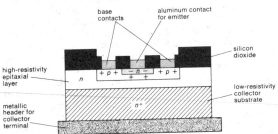

Figure 3: Cross section of an epitaxial-planar silicon transistor. The n^+ indicates heavy doping to give low resistivity.

diffuses laterally, under the surface of the dioxide, about the same distance that it diffuses normally to the surface. In this way the collector–base and base–emitter junctions are produced under the inert oxide layer and are thus sealed from contaminating chemicals during manufacture and encapsulation.

Design and manufacture of semiconductor devices

DEVICE ASSEMBLY AND PROCESSING

Several hundred semiconductor devices such as transistors, diodes, and thyristors can be formed on a single wafer of semiconductor material by the techniques described. These devices must be separated into individual chips, which are then individually packaged.

Chip separation. Several techniques are used in industry, of which the most important are the following:

Scribing and cleaving. The finished wafer is placed on a vacuum chuck capable of being moved and rotated horizontally. A diamond tool is then used to cut lines into the surface of the wafer in a grid pattern. The wafer is fractured along these lines, producing individual chips. These chips are then chemically cleaned from scribing dust and other foreign materials.

Etch cutting. The individual chips are masked with photo resist, a thin photosensitive film that is not affected by the etching solution, and the regions between them are removed (cut) by etching.

Ultrasonic cutting. A plane metal tool with numerous holes having the shape of the desired chip is placed in firm contact with a silicon wafer that is bathed in an abrasive slurry, a water mixture of fine abrasive powder. An ultrasonic transducer (a device that produces ultrasonic vibrations) drives the tool and causes it to grind completely through the silicon wafer, producing individual chips.

Laser scribing. A powerful laser beam mounted to permit motion of the beam along two axes (grid pattern) in a plane parallel to the wafer is used to scribe individual chips from the wafer.

Packaging. Semiconductor packages are prepared separately and serve the combined function of a heat sink (a device for dissipating heat from a heat-vulnerable component), a means of interconnecting one device with another, and a means of protecting the device against chemical contamination and mechanical damage. The two basic types of packages used in modern devices are the metal-can package and the plastic-epoxy package. Examples of different packages are shown in Figure 4.

By courtesy of Motorola Inc., Semiconductor Products Division

Basic packages

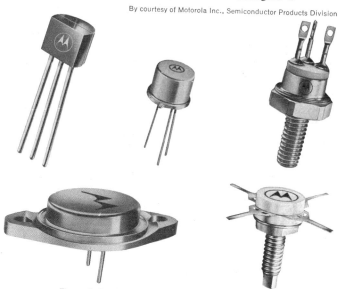

Figure 4: *Semiconductor packages.*
(Top, left to right) Small signal plastic, small signal metal, and medium power stud mounted. (Bottom, left to right) Power metal and rf (radio frequency) power.

Chip attachment. The attachment of a chip to its package is usually done by brazing (high-temperature soldering) using a brazing alloy such as gold–germanium. Two different methods are used.

The belt-furnace, or continuous, method employs a furnace with a long hollow tube surrounded by a suitably controlled heating element and containing a moving conveyor belt. Riding on the belt are metal or graphite jigs that can be loaded with headers, brazing preforms, and chips. These jigs progress through the furnace, where the thermal profile (temperature gradient) has been designed to bring them up to the bonding temperature (melting temperature of the brazing alloy) and, then, to cool them so that they can be safely handled.

The single-station method uses individually heated stations in which a single header or package is placed. The chips are picked up individually by an operator using a micromanipulator (a device for handling small articles) and placed on the package for bonding. The operator can observe the operation directly over the heated part.

Lead attachment. After the semiconductor chip has been attached to the package, it is necessary to make electrical connections between the chip and the package leads. A number of processes have been developed for making these connections.

The thermocompression bonding process involves the simultaneous application of heat and pressure to a very fine gold wire that makes the electrical connection between the proper contact point on the chip and the package leads.

In the wedge bonding technique, the header containing the chip is mounted on a heated column and positioned so that the point to which a lead attachment is desired is brought directly under a cross hair in the microscope. This cross hair has been previously aligned with the terminal positions of a swinging wedge that is to do the bonding. A second micromanipulator is used to bring the gold wire from a wire feeder into the position over the contact point. By pushing a button, the operator automatically brings the bonding wedge down on the wire to achieve the bonding. The header is then manipulated so that the cross hair is over the lead on the package, and the second bond is made at this point.

In the ball bonding method the bonding tool consists of a capillary tube whose bore is slightly larger than the bonding wire to be used. The bonding wire is initially fed through this capillary. A flame is used to melt the end of the wire to form a ball whose diameter is approximately twice that of the wire. This ball is then automatically drawn back snug against the end of the capillary, and the capillary is manipulated to the point at which bonding is desired. Then, in one continuous motion, the capillary is lowered and zeroed in on the target, and the ball is firmly compressed against the contact area of the chip, deforming the ball into a nailhead thermocompression bond. The capillary is then withdrawn an appropriate distance, and the flame is used to sever the wire and, also, to form a new ball.

These two techniques can be described as gold-wire-to-aluminum-contact-area bonding techniques. In recent years, the use of aluminum-alloy-to-aluminum bonding has been widely used because similar metals perform better in such circumstances than do dissimilar metals.

The soldering technique used for semiconductor device lead attachment is a modified version of the soldering process used in printed-circuit applications. The alloys of lead, together with silver, are usually the materials used. If compatibility with high-temperature processes such as hermetic sealing is required, however, such low-melting solders can be replaced with higher melting ones.

The beam-lead technique was developed primarily to batch-fabricate semiconductor devices. The technique consists of depositing an array of thick contacts on the surface of the semiconductor chip and then removing the excess semiconductor from under the contacts, thereby separating the individual devices and leaving them with semirigid beam leads cantilevered (supported at only one end) beyond the semiconductor. The contacts serve not only as electrical leads but also as the structural support for the devices; hence, the name beam leads. Chips of beam-lead circuits are mounted directly by the leads without aluminum or gold wire.

Beam-lead technique

Encapsulation. The semiconductor chip is welded into a metal package, and the metallized areas are connected to the package leads, usually by thermocompression bonding. Total protection of the device is then provided by means of a hermetically sealed (airtight) welded can that completely surrounds the device. The cans are generally baked out at a high temperature before welding in order to drive off any solvents or other contaminants on the surface. They are then brought into a controlled-atmosphere dry box, and the cans are welded to the header (the part that provides support and insulation), sealing in a portion of this controlled atmosphere.

The principal disadvantage associated with the metal package is the high cost associated with the individual sealing and leak-testing steps. Requirements of extreme reliability, as in military or aerospace applications, can justify the higher costs. The bulk of the other applications of semiconductor devices are satisfied by the use of plastic packages. Following the bonding of the chip and its wire leads to a metal lead frame, the whole assembly is coated with a plastic. When the plastic is set, the perimeter of the lead frame is cut away and the leads bent and trimmed to length. The process lends itself to more automation, and hence economy, than the hermetically sealed metal package. No plastics used at present, however, are completely impervious to water vapour, which can cause serious degradation of the semiconductor device's properties.

MOS technique. The metal-oxide-semiconductor (MOS) technique is employed in the construction of planar semiconductors; *e.g.*, the planar-epitaxial transistor of Figure 3. In this transistor structure all the junctions of the device (emitter to base and collector to base) are brought to the same plane, or surface (hence the name planar), which is eventually covered with silicon dioxide (SiO_2) except for a window opening to connect the terminals to the different regions. The major advantage of the silicon dioxide is the reduction of surface contaminants and impurities that cause surface leakage currents, degrading the transistor operation. When the coating of silicon dioxide is applied, the surface is said to be passivated, and the method is now widely used in the manufac-

Table 2: Semiconductor Devices

name of device	symbol	material	physical phenomena	application
Rectifier power diodes Small diodes		germanium; silicon selenium	unilateral conduction	power conversion and control, wave shaping and instrumentation; receiver detectors and mixers; switching and logic circuits
Breakdown (Zener) diodes		silicon	avalanche breakdown	voltage reference element in regulator and limiter circuits
Varactor diodes		silicon; gallium arsenide	voltage-controlled-depletion layer thickness	voltage-controlled capacitors in rf resoresonant circuits; rf frequency multipliers
Tunnel (Esaki) diodes		germanium; gallium arsenide	guided minority-carrier flow (tunnelling) producing negative-resistance effects	ultrahigh-frequency (UHF) oscillators and amplifiers
Schottky "hot carrier" diodes	*		majority-carrier conduction through metal-to-semiconductor junctions	UHF switching and detection
Step-recovery diodes	*	gallium arsenide	charge-controlled carrier lifetime	frequency multipliers; UHF switching
P–i–n diodes	*	gallium arsenide	variable conductance in the forward-biassed region	microwave dc-controlled switches and modulators
Gunn and Impatt diodes		gallium arsenide		microwave solid-state generator
Photo diodes		germanium and selenium compound semiconductors	conductive or generative modulation by radiation	light and infrared detector and sensors
Light-emitting diodes		gallium arsenide	radiation emission due to electron-energy-level transition	display system and instrumentation

*No standard symbol.

ture of field-effect transistors (transistors in which control is effected by application of an electric field) and integrated circuits (*q.v.*).

SEMICONDUCTOR DEVICES AND THEIR APPLICATIONS

Two-terminal p–n-junction devices. The unilateral conduction properties of the *p–n* junction are the basis of the operation of the solid-state junction diode that is mainly used for signal and power rectification. The *p–n* junction, however, exhibits a number of other useful phenomena that can be used in many practical applications; for example, the *p–n* junction exhibits variations in the depletion layer depth with voltage. It also exhibits avalanche breakdown characteristics; *i.e.*, nondestructive breakdown caused by the cumulative multiplication of carriers through field-induced impact ionization in the reverse direction. Such other phenomena as the controlled guidance of energy levels, the nonrectification at microwave frequencies (one gigahertz [10^9 hertz] and above), the peculiarities of charge storage (the ability to retain an electrical charge), and the light-emitting capabilities are only a few of the properties that the *p–n* junction possesses and are the basis of many useful *p–n* junction devices. Table 2 gives a summary of these semiconductor devices, symbols, materials, the fundamental physical properties in their operation, and the basic areas of application.

Junction diode. The semiconductor diode is a *p–n*-junction device with unilateral conduction properties. In power rectification, one or several devices are used in different configurations to convert alternating currents into direct currents. The same is done at lower power levels in instrumentation applications. The basic diode parameters (threshold voltage, leakage current, and breakdown voltage) are temperature sensitive. This characteristic is exploited to advantage to stabilize and compensate for temperature instabilities in the operation of solid-state amplifiers and oscillators. Especially constructed diodes, with small depletion capacitance (the capacitance of its depletion layer), are also used as detectors to separate audio frequency from intermediate frequency in radio-receiver circuits. Very low power diodes with idealized unilateral characteristics are used in switching, logic circuits of computer hardware, and digital communications systems.

Zener diode. This diode is a *p–n*-junction device using closely controlled impurity concentration to provide very sharp and well-defined breakdown voltage over a wide range (a few hundred millivolts to several hundred volts). Operation of the device in the reverse direction results in a constant voltage source that is used in many applications; *e.g.*, as a reference voltage in the regulator

section of a regulated power supply. Because of its voltage sensitivity and fast switching action, the Zener diode is also used for protecting electronic and meter circuits against voltage and current transients and for arc suppression in small circuit breakers. The Zener diode is often used together with a forward-biassed diode in series to produce a reference voltage unaffected by temperature changes for temperature-compensated amplifiers. The very low resistance of the Zener diode also makes it useful as a coupling element in direct-coupled amplifiers. Zener-diode control circuits are used for light dimming, relay control, ballast control, voltage multiplication, and many other industrial applications.

Varactor diode. The varactor (variable reactor) is a voltage-variable, reverse-biassed *p–n*-junction device whose effective capacitance can be varied by varying the applied voltage. It has a specially graded junction with an impurity profile that is determined by the desired application. Varactor diodes make possible the solid-state tuning of circuits by voltage variation. They are also useful in switching and frequency-multiplier circuits, for limiting and pulse shaping, and also in a special type of amplifier called a parametric amplifier.

Tunnel diode. The tunnel diode, sometimes called the Esaki diode, is a heavily doped semiconductor device with a vary narrow depletion region. Under very low forward-bias conditions (300 to 400 millivolts) and low dissipation, the electrons can tunnel or pass directly through the junction from the conduction energy band to an equal level in the valence band, producing a negative-resistance effect. If the forward bias is increased beyond 400 millivolts, the device conducts as a conventional diode. Tunnel diodes, because of inherent low noise, frequency stability, and high efficiency, find many applications in ultrahigh-frequency amplifiers, oscillators, and switching circuits.

Schottky diode. This is a diode with a metal–semiconductor junction instead of the usual *p–n* function. The current flow is the result of majority-carrier electrons at a relatively high energy level ("hot carriers") injected at forward bias. Because the mechanism of conduction across the junction involves majority carriers with a very short lifetime and very little recombination noise (noise resulting from the random process of electron–hole generation and recombination in the semiconductor material), the device is especially suitable for ultrahigh-frequency low-noise mixer and switching circuits.

Step-recovery diode. The step-recovery diode is a *p–n*-junction device with a graded junction whose impurity profile is designed to minimize stored-minority-carrier transit time. The nonlinear-junction capacitance variation is also minimized. The step-recovery diode is use-

Basic diode parameters

Uses of tunnel diodes

ful in microwave-frequency multipliers and microwave switching.

The p–i–n diode. This diode consists of a thin layer of high-resistivity intrinsic semiconductor between a heavily doped *p* (input) layer and another heavily doped *n* (output) layer. At microwave frequencies the device is equivalent to a capacitive high-resistance network, and in the forward direction under avalanche condition the *i* layer becomes flooded with holes, and the diode changes into a conductor. The device is used as a direct-current-controlled microwave switch. It can also be used as a modulator with the modulating signal producing the required variation in the input resistance.

Gunn and Impatt diodes. These devices, useful as microwave oscillators, are the result of recent research in the field of microwave diodes. The Gunn (after J.B. Gunn) diode operates basically like a tunnel diode in a pellet form mounted in a tunable microwave cavity. The Impatt (Impact Ionization Avalanche Transit Time) diode, on the other hand, generates microwave frequencies in the avalanche mode.

Photo diodes. These are *p–n*-junction devices designed in special packages equipped with light-focussing lenses. In the forward direction the device is photovoltaic (generates electricity when illuminated), while in the reverse direction it is photoconductive (conducts electricity when illuminated). These diodes are used as light sensors in many alarm systems, in control, and in industrial applications.

Light-emissive diodes. These are specially designed *p–n*-junction devices using gallium arsenide. The device emits infrared radiation under forward-biassed conditions. These devices, together with infrared photo diodes, are finding wide applications in the field of opto-electronic control systems and instrumentation and also in electronic surveying systems.

Injection lasers. The semiconductor diode laser is a higher power version of the light-emissive diode described earlier. By careful selection of the bias voltage, the junction cooling, and optical lens system, the coherent light radiation required for the laser can be achieved.

Transistors. *Amplifiers.* The most significant role of semiconductor devices is in electronic amplifiers. The majority of solid-state amplifiers have two *p–n* junctions, implying three layers of semiconductor material. The exceptions include the unijunction transistor, the field-effect transistor, and the tunnel diode. In general terms, the amplifying action of a transistor depends on a low-power input circuit controlling a higher power output circuit. In the frequently used common-emitter configuration, where the input impedance is of the order of a few thousand ohms, a small base current gives rise to a much larger collector current flowing out of the high-impedance collector circuit.

Types of electronic amplifiers Electronic amplifiers are usually classified into five groups: small-signal amplifiers, large-signal (*i.e.*, power) amplifiers, direct-current amplifiers, wide-band and tuned amplifiers, and feedback amplifiers.

The simple audio-frequency amplifier has limited use and can not deliver a worthwhile power output in other frequency ranges. The low-frequency response of transistor amplifiers is limited because of the extremely large values of coupling capacitors (*i.e.*, the capacitors that couple the output of one stage to the input of another stage) that are required. At very low frequencies and for direct-current applications, directly coupled amplifier stages are sometimes used. The inherent disadvantage in this arrangement is that of voltage drift, largely the result of temperature changes. Various compensating circuits have been designed to overcome this problem. A common alternative is to convert the direct-current signals to alternating current by means of a "chopper" circuit at the input to the amplifier. Numerous good-quality operational amplifiers for very low frequency applications, incorporating silicon transistors, are now available.

At the frequencies from about 100 kilohertz and upward, it is common to have the output circuit of the amplifier tuned to the required frequency band. The main considerations in the design of such amplifiers are the availability of transistors capable of giving useful gain at high frequency, the incorporation of any stray and inherent transistor capacitances into the tuned circuits, and effective compensation for unwanted feedback paths. At high frequencies, internal feedback in the transistor can be particularly troublesome. This factor varies considerably between transistors of different types. Transistors that have an exponential variation in impurity density across the base region, sometimes known as drift transistors, have a much lower feedback capacitance, with a generally better performance at very high frequencies, than transistors with constant base-impurity content.

The power dissipation within the transistor itself is a major consideration in nearly all amplifier applications. The semiconductor chip in a very high frequency transistor may have a volume of about 0.000001 cubic inch, and consequently heat must be conducted away quickly. In transistor amplifiers designed to produce more than 100 milliwatts of output power, the overall efficiency and the power dissipation become vital design considerations. A major aim is to reduce the standing, or quiescent, current to a minimum. Such a reduction is often accomplished in the push–pull type of circuit by using a pair of matched transistors. A major improvement was the advent of complementary *p–n–p* and *n–p–n* transistors, making it possible to produce transformerless amplifiers, a technique that greatly reduces the bulk and expense of audio equipment.

Oscillators. If a proportion of the output voltage from a transistor amplifier is fed back to the input and in step with the input, then the feedback reinforces the input and an oscillator circuit can be produced. In particular, a network of passive components can be connected to the transistor to give an output signal at one particular frequency. The losses in this network are made up by the gain of the transistor. The frequency of the electrical oscillation depends to some extent on the characteristics of the transistor, but suitable circuit design can make the output frequency and amplitude almost independent of any changes due to temperature variations from one transistor to another or to aging of the transistor.

In vacuum tubes, the majority of oscillators involve a tuned circuit with an inductance and capacitance. A significant proportion of transistor oscillators designed primarily for use at frequencies less than 100 kilohertz include a resistance–capacitance network to give a proper feedback signal. In this way it is possible to produce low-cost, small-size oscillator circuits that take full advantage of the transistor characteristics.

Digital circuits. Transistors are often used in pulse or switching circuits in such a manner that the transistor is driven from OFF to fully ON without remaining for any appreciable time in the normal, linear region of its operating characteristics. This is, in fact, the most efficient mode of using a transistor. In practice, a small collector current (a few microamperes in a small germanium transistor and a few nanoamperes [10^{-9} ampere] in a silicon device) does flow. In this case, both the junctions are reverse biassed. In practice, the transistor is "bottomed"; that is, it is conducting heavily and the current is limited by the external circuit. Under these circumstances base, collector, and emitter are at virtually the same potential. "Bottoming" the transistor

In these digital circuits the silicon device has the particular advantage of extremely low cut-off current, and the germanium transistor has a low internal voltage drop when fully switched on. These characteristics give rise to high efficiency and well-defined ON and OFF states.

The digital applications of transistors as gates, counters, and pulse amplifiers are really the heart of any digital computer. A vital feature of digital-circuit design is the speed with which a transistor can be switched through the active region of its characteristics. During the switching process a phenomenon known as "charge carrier storage" (which is electron storage in the case of an *n–p–n* transistor) occurs. In order to obtain transistor action it is necessary to establish and maintain a certain charge of current carriers in the base region. By considering current to be the result of the flow of charge into and out of a base store, a helpful approach to small and large signal calculations is obtained, which is often used in the design of digital circuits.

Four-layer (p–n–p–n) devices: thyristors. These devices are p–n–p–n four-layer devices, with two, three, or four external terminals. They have either unidirectional or bidirectional characteristics. The silicon-controlled rectifier and the triac are by far the most commonly used of all thyristor devices. The silicon-controlled rectifier is a reverse-blocking (unilateral) triode (three-terminal) thyristor. The triac, on the other hand, is a bidirectional triode thyristor. Physically, thyristors are three-junction p–n–p–n devices fabricated from successive layers, slices, or pellets of especially doped silicon. Examples of different thyristor constructions are shown in Figure 5.

By courtesy of General Electric Semiconductor Products Department, Syracuse, N.Y.

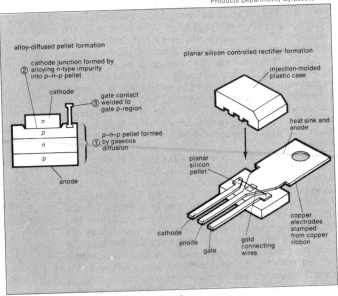

Figure 5: Thyristor constructions.

name	symbol
diac (bidirectional diode thyristor)	
SUS (silicon unilateral switch)	A K G
SBS (silicon bilateral switch)	A₂ A₁ G
LAS (light-activated switch) light-activated reverse-blocking diode thyristor	A K
LASCR (light-activated silicon-controlled rectifier) light-activated reverse-blocking triode thyristor	A K G
triac (bidirectional triode thyristor)	G
SCR (silicon-controlled rectifier) reverse-blocking triode thyristor	A K G
SCS (silicon-controlled switch) reverse-blocking tetrode thyristor	Gₐ A K G_K
LASCS (light-activated silicon-controlled switch) light-activated reverse-blocking tetrode thyristor	Gₐ A K G_K
A anode G gate K cathode	

Figure 6: Names and circuit symbols for a number of different thyristors, including three light-activated devices.
By courtesy of General Electric Semiconductor Products Department, Syracuse, N.Y.

Silicon-controlled rectifier. In the forward direction with no gate current, the device acts like an open switch until an appropriate gate signal is applied to the gate terminal, at which time it rapidly switches to the conducting state.

Once the silicon-controlled rectifier is turned on, it cannot be turned off by removing the gate current. It is turned off only if its current is reduced externally below the hold current. The silicon-controlled rectifier is thus a switching device that can be turned on by the proper application of sharp gate-current pulses and turned off usually every time its current is reduced below a minimum holding level. Silicon-controlled rectifier switches have the following advantages over power transistors: higher current capabilities, and better forward-blocking characteristics. Silicon-controlled rectifiers are low-frequency devices that are mainly used for power-frequency switching.

Triac. The triac is a p–n–p–n device especially constructed to provide bilateral operation instead of the unilateral action of the silicon-controlled rectifier. It is equivalent to two silicon-controlled rectifiers in inverse parallel connection.

Other thyristors. Other thyristors include the diac (bidirectional diode thyristor), the SUS (silicon unilateral switch) and the SBS (silicon bilateral switch). There is also a host of light-activated thyristors that add to the versatility and scope of the application of thyristors. Among these are the LAS (light-activated switch), the LASCR (light-activated SCR), and the LASCS (light-activated silicon-controlled switch). Figure 6 shows the circuit symbols for these and several other thyristors. Thyristors have replaced vacuum tubes and electromechanical devices as solid-state power conversion and control devices in industrial, control, and consumer circuit applications. This trend was prompted by the many attractive features and characteristics that these devices possess; among them are the following: (1) Reliability: using the now

Advantages of thyristors

proven planar and other processes, the packages are rugged and compact, with no vibrating mechanical parts. (2) Versatility: as indicated in Figure 6, the many types, and their triggering mechanisms, provide a variety of new devices. (3) Low power dissipation: a feature common to all solid-state devices. (4) Triggering sensitivity: most of these devices operate from low-level signal sources.

Microcircuits. Since about 1960, developments—in the field of microelectronic circuits, in general, and in monolithic integrated circuits, in particular—have dominated the field of electronics. The basic microcircuit tech-

Table 3: Thyristor Applications

Motor control	electric model trains; slot racing cars and other toys; sewing machines; movie projectors; food mixers; electric fans; servomotors
Temperature control	range surface unit (hybrid); chemical processing (photographic, etc.); food warmer tray; bearing temperature sensor; electric-blanket control
Light control	flame detectors; moving light signs ("chasers"); computer readout; harbour buoy markers; personal distress flashing equipment (marine, etc.); automotive warning systems; nixie and neon drivers; electroluminescent panel drivers; automatic focussing for colour slide projectors, movie projectors, etc.; sequential turn signal for automobiles
Pressure and liquid level controls	auto oil-pressure gauge; hot-water-boiler safety monitor; semiconductor strain-gauge monitor; hydraulic servos; machine-tool control systems; basement sump pump; automatic coffee maker; vending machine
Timing circuits	photo darkroom timer; oven timer; vending machine logic; industrial process control; automatic blender–mixer shutoff; sweep circuits; oscilloscopes
Remote control	armchair TV control; master switching stations for the home; garage door openers; power switch
Alarm and protection systems	burglar and other alarm systems; touch switch; electric door openers
Power electronic circuits	low-speed ring counters and shift registers; computer peripheral equipment; power flip-flops; constant current generators; oscillator–tone generators; pulse amplifiers; static switching; relay replacement; solenoid drivers; latching relay replacement; low-power inverters; thyratron tube replacement
Power supplies, etc.	voltage (battery charger sensor); current (electronic crowbar); safety circuits (for machine tools, etc.)

nologies used today are thick-film, thin-film, and monolithic integrated circuits (IC).

Film technology usually involves the deposition of a film of passive component patterns on the top of ceramic or other dielectric substrate or base material. Monolithic integrated circuits, on the other hand, are those circuits, like operational amplifiers or digital counters, in which all the components of the circuit, passive and active alike, are built into the same silicon chip. The individual components of the circuit cannot be separated without permanently destroying its intended electronic function. A hybrid microcircuit is a circuit assembly in which the passive components and their interconnection are formed by one of the film techniques. The monolithic active devices in the form of chips are bonded to the passive film base to complete the assembly.

The basic processes used in the fabrication of monolithic integrated circuits are similar to those used in the fabrication of the planar-epitaxial transistor described earlier, except that instead of building one transistor (by the successive application of photolithographic masking and selective diffusion), all the active and passive devices required for the circuit are built simultaneously. Integrated circuits can be classified into linear or digital types. The operational amplifier is the most common type of linear integrated circuit. It is now replacing the discrete small-signal transistor as the main building block in electronic instrumentation, industrial control systems, and consumer products. A typical monolithic operational amplifier will have about 15 transistors and diodes and about 20 resistors built on a 60-mil-square silicon chip, the whole encapsulated in a metal can with ten leads.

Digital integrated circuits form the main bulk of the market today. They are used as switching, logic, and memory elements in the computer field. They are also used in the field of data and digital communications. In a typical integrated-circuit memory, for example, several thousand transistors are packaged together in a three-dimensional array in silicon to form what is known as a large-scale integrated (LSI) memory (see also INTEGRATED CIRCUITRY).

Photo devices. Semiconductor photo-activated or photo-generative devices are an important class of semiconductor devices that play a role in industrial control, information transmission, digital data processing, power generation, and other industrial processes.

A correctly doped $p–n$ junction, when reverse biassed between 30 and 50 volts and equipped with a light-focussing lens, will exhibit variation in its background resistance under sufficient illumination. The junction will generate currents in the milliampere range for germanium and in the ampere range for silicon. A phototransistor amplifies the photoconductive current generated across the reverse-biassed base–emitter–base junction. The light applied to the base through a hole–lens assembly in the case is the input signal. The high impedance of a field-effect phototransistor allows the generation of relatively high gate voltages from small photocurrents. This fact, together with the field-effect transistor's inherent amplification, makes it one of the most sensitive photo devices.

The photo-transistor

SPECIALIZED FABRICATION TECHNIQUES

Construction. The epitaxial-planar transistor construction discussed earlier is the basis of most modern high-performance, silicon bipolar semiconductor devices. It is used for both small-signal and large-signal power devices. It has good stability, low noise, and high-frequency capability, usually up to 200 megahertz. Other specialized construction techniques are used to improve the capabilities of the devices and to enhance some of their parameters for specific applications.

Annular construction. This construction is usually employed to increase the power and breakdown-voltage capabilities of bipolar-junction transistors. For power transistors (Figure 7C), two annular rings are formed; both of the rings are concentric to the centre emitter element. This provides a large base area for better heat dissipation and also a maximum emitter perimeter. To increase the breakdown capabilities of a bipolar transistor, the star

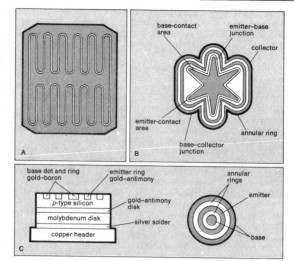

Figure 7: *Specialized transistor structures.*
(A) Parallel-connected emitters for increasing power and frequency capabilities; (B) annular structure for increasing voltage capabilities; (C) annular structure for increasing power-handling capabilities of an alloyed power transistor.

configuration (Figure 7B) is sometimes used. In this case, the base (n-type in a $p–n–p$ transistor) is surrounded by an annular protective band of p-type material. This low-resistance barrier effectively shorts the base currents, restricting their passage in the form of leakage. The annular band is also removed from the main emitter–base junction to avoid voltage breakdown.

Overlay. This construction is used to increase the power and frequency capabilities of radio-frequency transistors; *e.g.,* 50 watts at 50 megahertz. An example of this construction is shown in Figure 7A where a large number of emitters are connected in parallel to increase the emitter periphery.

Electron-beam technique. The ion-implantation technique described earlier is an example of a new approach to the manufacturing of semiconductor devices known as electron–ion-beam technology. Fine-focussed electron beams, which initially were employed in diagnostic tests on semiconductor devices, now are being utilized in the laboratory for creating devices and circuits with resolutions considerably higher than the values that can be achieved by photolithography. An electron beam, for example, has a spot size from five to 200 angstroms (an angstrom is 10^{-8} centimetre), as compared with 5,000 angstroms (the wavelength of visible light) used in conventional photolithography. These beams of charged particles are electrically controllable and thus can be programmed in intensity and positioned over wide ranges by electric signals. The high resolution of the beam-written pattern permits device operation at higher frequencies and at high packaging densities.

BIBLIOGRAPHY. The general area of semiconductor materials and physics is thoroughly covered in J.L. MOLL, *Physics of Semiconductors* (1964); M.J. BUERGER, *Crystal-Structure Analysis* (1960); C.A. HOGARTH (ed.), *Materials Used in Semiconductor Devices* (1965); A. MANY, Y. GOLDSTEIN, and N.B. GROVER, *Semiconductor Surfaces* (1965); A. GROVE, *Physics and Technology of Semiconductor Devices* (1967); C.L. HEMENWAY, R.W. HENRY, and M. CAULTON, *Physical Electronics*, 2nd ed. (1967); and A. VAN DER ZIEL, *Solid State Physical Electronics*, 2nd ed. (1968).

The general field of semiconductor technology with emphasis on integrated circuits is treated in R.M. BURGER and R.P. DONOVAN, *Fundamentals of Silicon Integrated Device Technology*, vol. 1, *Oxidation, Diffusion and Epitaxy*, vol. 2, *Bipolar and Unipolar Transistors* (1967–68); S. SCHWARTZ, *Integrated Circuit Technology* (1967); and G. SIDERIS (ed.), *Microelectronic Packaging: Interconnection and Assembly of Integrated Circuits* (1968).

Semiconductor device physics, characteristics, and applications are treated in E.J. ANGELO, *Electronics: BJT's, FET's and Microcircuits* (1969); J.F. GIBBON, *Semiconductor Electronics* (1966); J. MILLMAN and C.C. HALKIAS, *Electronics Devices and Circuits* (1967); J.W. BREMER, *Superconductive De-*

vices (1962); W. GOSLING, *Introduction to Microelectronic Systems* (1968); J.G. LINVILL and J.F. GIBBONS, *Transistors and Active Circuits* (1961); and C.S. MEYER, D.K. LYNN, and D.J. HAMILTON (eds.), *Analysis and Design of Integrated Circuits* (1968).

More specialized studies of individual devices and their applications appear in L.J. SEVIN, *Field-Effect Transistors* (1965); W.F. CHOW, *Principles of Tunnel Diode Circuits* (1964); L.A. BLACKWELL and K.L. KOTZEBUE, *Semiconductor-Diode Parametric Amplifiers* (1961); F.E. GENTRY *et al.*, *Semiconductor Controlled Rectifiers: Principles and Applications of p-n-p-n Devices* (1964); and S. WEBER (comp.), *Optoelectronic Devices and Circuits* (1964).

Classical semiconductor circuit analysis using discrete semiconductor devices is treated in J.R. ABRAHAMS and G.J. PRIDHAM, *Semiconductor Circuits: Theory, Design and Experiment* (1966), and *Semiconductor Circuits: Worked Examples* (1966); P. CUTLER, *Semiconductor Circuit Analysis* (1964); A.P. MALVINO, *Transistor Circuit Approximations* (1968); and R.B. ADLER, A.C. SMITH, and R.L. LONGINI, *Introduction to Semiconductor Physics* (1964).

Semiconductor circuit analysis using integrated circuit components is covered in D.L. SCHILLING and C. BELOVE, *Electronic Circuits: Discrete and Integrated* (1968); P.M. CHIRLIAN, *Integrated and Active Network Analysis and Synthesis* (1967); and R.W. NEWCOMB, *Active Integrated Circuit Synthesis* (1968).

(J.R.A./S.W.M.)

Semiconductors and Insulators, Theory of

One of the distinguishing characteristics used to differentiate many solid, liquid, and gaseous materials is their ability to transmit an electric current. In contrast to good electric conductors (*e.g.*, metals), through which electric current can flow easily, poor conductors (*i.e.*, semiconductors and insulators) offer more resistance to electric charges moving through them. Moreover, whereas heating reduces the electrical conductivity of good conductors and cooling enhances it, semiconductors and insulators are transformed into better conductors when heated and poorer ones when cooled. To explain these and related properties, which form the basis for the development of solid-state devices, it is first necessary to classify with greater refinement those substances that are electrical conductors.

GENERAL CONSIDERATIONS

Classification of solids by electrical resistivity. Electrical resistance (resistivity) is the opposition to electric current moving under the influence of a given voltage; it is expressed in units of ohms. The basic unit of resistivity is the resistance of a sample one centimetre long and one square centimetre in cross section; it is usually expressed in the units ohm-centimetres (ohm-cm). Because the resistance of a given solid depends on its length and cross-sectional area, electrical resistivity, symbolized by the Greek letter rho (ρ), is a convenient way to classify and compare materials. Electrical conductivity, symbolized by the Greek letter sigma (σ), is the reciprocal of electrical resistivity, $\sigma = 1/\rho$. The electrical resistivity of solids varies over many orders of magnitude, expressed as factors of ten or integral powers of ten (Figure 1).

At one end of the resistivity range are the superconductors (*e.g.*, lead below 7° K), which are extremely high in conductivity because they have no measurable resistance (this class of materials lies beyond the range of Figure 1). Lowest in resistivity on the scale illustrated are the metals (*e.g.*, silver and copper), with resistivities on the order of 10^{-6} ohm-centimetre. The next lowest group is the semimetals (*e.g.*, bismuth and arsenic), with only slightly higher resistivities. This group of good conductors is followed by two classes of materials, each covering a wide range of resistivities—the semiconductors, of which germanium and silicon are representative examples, and the insulators, such as fused quartz, with resistivities as large as 10^{18} ohm-centimetres and greater. Metal conductors find application in devices that transmit large currents for purposes of heating and lighting, for turning electric motors, to activate chemical reactions, and to achieve other goals that require an efficient flow of electrons. Such currents are controlled by insulators, resistors, capacitors, and, in

Good and poor conductors

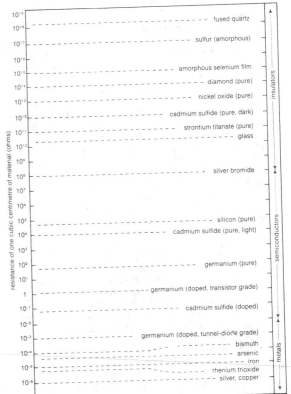

Figure 1: Electrical resistivity of materials at room temperature.

general, devices that are rugged enough to block or shunt the massive flow. In contrast, semiconductors transmit relatively weak currents, and the minute flow of electrons can be controlled with great precision by appropriate devices. One important application is the transistor, a semiconductor device that is used almost universally as a substitute for a radio or electronic tube because of its minute size, low power requirement, and cold operation. Another application is the crystal diode, a device that passes current more readily in one direction than another so that it can rectify (that is, change) alternating current into direct current.

General properties of semiconductors and insulators. Characteristic of the electrical resistivity of poor conductors is its great sensitivity to temperature, pressure, and frequency of electromagnetic radiation. It is also sensitive to its own purity and crystal perfection. For example, the resistivity of the insulator cadmium sulfide (CdS) decreases by 13 orders of magnitude (to one part in 10^{13} of the original value, because one order of magnitude is a factor of 10) upon the addition of less than 0.01 percent of a particular element, referred to as a type of impurity atom; the corresponding change in such typical semiconductors as silicon and germanium is six to seven orders of magnitude (Figure 1). On the other hand, the addition of impurities to typical metals produces a very much smaller change in resistivity, less than one order of magnitude, and the change is of the opposite sign; that is, the addition of impurities increases the resistivity.

Of particular interest is the dependence of resistivity on temperature. In fact, this property is used as a criterion for distinguishing semiconductors and insulators from metals. The resistivity of semiconductors and insulators characteristically increases by many orders of magnitude as the temperature is lowered from room temperature to 1° K (approximately —272° C or —458° F). On the other hand, the corresponding change in the resistivity of metals is a decrease of several orders of magnitude. That is, the resistivity of metals decreases with decreasing temperature, while that of semiconductors and insulators increases with decreasing temperature.

The classification of materials according to the magnitude and temperature dependence of their electrical resistivity can be quite different from a classification based on

Visual properties

visual inspection. Such semiconductors as silicon and germanium, for example, exhibit a metallic lustre, while a metal such as rhenium trioxide (ReO₉) is a reddish, almost transparent solid. Metallic lustre is associated with a high reflectivity at visible light frequencies and is usually, though not necessarily, found in materials with high direct-current conductivities. The electrical conductivity of all solids is dependent on the frequency of the electromagnetic radiation: for metals, conductivity tends to decrease with increasing frequency; for semiconductors and insulators, on the other hand, conductivity tends to increase with increasing frequency. Thus, at ultraviolet frequencies (higher than those of visible light, the optical region) the conductivity of all solid materials is about the same order of magnitude.

Although the conductivity at optical and ultraviolet frequencies is similar for the various classes of materials, the effect of light exposure on low-frequency conductivity (*i.e.*, alternating currents in the material of frequencies lower than those of the radiation) is different. For example, the direct-current conductivity of cadmium sulfide can change by eight orders of magnitude (100,000,000 times) upon exposure to visible light. The increase in electrical conductivity exhibited by certain solids when exposed to light is called photoconductivity. This effect is common in insulators and semiconductors, but it is not observed in metals and semimetals; in semiconductors, such as silicon and germanium, photoconduction is produced by infrared as well as by visible light excitation.

Photo-conductivity

HISTORY

The reason solids are classified according to their direct-current resistivities is partly because of a high correlation between this property and other physical properties. There is also a practical reason for doing so: most of the industrial applications of semiconductors and insulators make use of the low-frequency electrical properties. These applications characteristically exploit the great sensitivity of the resistivity of low-conductivity materials to small variations of external parameters. For example, the large photoconductivity of cadmium sulfide makes this an ideal material for an electrical switch triggered by light. Indeed, rectification (one-directional conduction) and other properties of semiconductors are exploited in the modern electronics industry and computer technology. In its infancy the electronics industry employed semiconductors as rectifiers in crystal sets for radio reception. These crystals were soon replaced by the then more reliable and effective vacuum tube, which controlled current by a relatively weak flow of free electrons through a vacuum, and which dominated the electronics industry for four decades until the invention of the transistor in 1948. (A transistor is a device that utilizes a semiconductor to control or to amplify, or both, small electrical currents. In 1956 three Bell Telephone Laboratories scientists, William Shockley, John Bardeen, and Walter Brattain, were awarded the Nobel Prize for Physics for their investigations of semiconductors and for their discovery of the transistor effect.) Because of this invention and the technological development that it inspired, semiconductor components have now mostly replaced vacuum tubes. Their compactness, simplicity, durability, and reliability are all responsible for the general industrial acceptance of solid-state devices for a variety of applications: from the transistor radio in the home to the hardware of giant computers; from solar cells for converting light into electricity to the electronic circuitry of rockets and satellites in the space program.

The discovery of the transistor is considered a milestone not only in the evolution of semiconductor physics but also in the development of solid-state physics in general. The solid-state research that was initiated to produce high-purity crystals and to study the properties of such materials has led to a better understanding of the basic physical properties of all solids, whether metals, semiconductors, or insulators. Such research has also led to the development of a variety of other technologically important devices, such as lasers, tunnel diodes, and Gunn oscillators. Insofar as semiconductors can, under appropriate conditions, exhibit superconducting and magnetic

properties, the field of semiconductor physics does, in fact, make contact with other broad areas of solid-state physics.

MECHANISMS OF CONDUCTION

In order to understand the nature of electronic conduction in semiconductors and insulators, it is necessary to study in some detail the conduction mechanisms appropriate to these materials. Electrical conduction is associated with the flow of charge between two electrodes attached to two points on these materials, from a positively charged anode to a negatively charged cathode or the reverse, and depends upon the concentration (*N*) of charged particles, or carriers, in the material. Whereas electrons are the dominant current carriers in metals, semimetals, and semiconductors, for some insulators both electrons and the heavier ions (charged atoms) contribute to the conduction of current.

Mobility of charged particles. To transport effectively electric charges from one electrode to another, the particles must resist collision and scattering along the path of the charge. Thus, charged particles in a solid are not accelerated indefinitely by the application of an external electric field (an electric field either pushes or pulls charged particles), because collisions force these particles to achieve some average velocity, called the drift velocity (v_D); each scattering event tends to randomize the velocity achieved in the acceleration process, so that after each such event the charged particle is effectively returned to zero average velocity, and the acceleration process caused by the electric field must begin again. The mobility, symbolized by the Greek letter mu (μ), which measures the effectiveness of the charge transport by a given charged particle in a conductor, semiconductor, or insulator, is thus defined as the drift velocity achieved through application of unit electric field (E), being equal to the drift velocity divided by the electric field; *i.e.*, $\mu = v_D/E$. That is, as the external field is increased, the drift velocity increases proportionately. Because the drift velocity depends on the magnitude of the applied electric field, the mobility of a particle of mass *m* and electric charge *e* can be more directly related to the mean time between scattering events, symbolized by the Greek letter tau, τ, through an equation in which mobility equals the product of the charge and the mean time between scattering events divided by the mass, or $\mu = e\tau/m$. In this way mobility is related directly to the interval of time between collisions; that is, to the effectiveness of a charged particle in avoiding collisions.

Drift velocity

Electrical conductivity (σ) equals the product of the mobility of each carrier (μ) and the concentration (number per unit volume) of carriers (N) with charge *e*; it may be defined as $\sigma = Ne\mu$. This definition of electrical conductivity is particularly useful for semiconductors and insulators because of the independence of the two factors, the carrier density factor (N), which is highly sensitive to such external parameters as temperature, optical excitation, and others, and the mobility factor (μ), which is sensitive to scattering mechanisms within the material.

Conductivity formula

Mobility in solids. Whereas conduction by ions is generally ineffective because of low mobility, conduction by electrons in metals, semimetals, semiconductors, and insulators is efficient. In fact, because of quantum mechanical principles, an electron travelling through a perfect crystal lattice is not scattered. The present understanding of electronic conduction in solids goes back to the classical Drude theory (1900), so called for Paul Drude, the German physicist who presented it, and according to which it was supposed that a dense gas of free electrons, interacting strongly with each other, existed in a metal. This theory has since been modified to explain why only a fraction of the available electrons participate in conduction and why the electron scattering times are longer than predicted by classical theory.

Electron diffraction. The wavelike nature of electrons gives rise to diffraction (resulting when obstacles interrupt a sequence of waves) rather than to scattering (resulting when a stream of moving particles meets an obstacle), as the wave traverses a crystal lattice (an orderly arrangement of atoms which act as obstacles). Thus, in certain directions the waves interfere constructively to yield diffraction peaks of intensity, whereas in other directions destructive interference results. From this point of view, although no scattering occurs, electronic conduction in a periodic (repeating) array of atoms is modified by the presence of the lattice. For most crystalline semiconductors and insulators, the effect of the periodic lattice on the conduction process can be described by an equation in which the electron mobility (μ) is equal to the product of the charge and the mean time between scattering events divided by a factor called the effective mass(m^*): $\mu = e\tau/m^*$ (see below *Theoretical approximations*). In semiconductors the effective mass tends to be considerably lower than the free electron mass (m)— *i.e.*, the mass of an electron at rest—whereas in insulators the effective mass tends to be higher than the free mass.

Electron scattering. The most important room temperature scattering mechanism in solids is usually the scattering of electrons by the thermal (heat) vibrations of the atoms of the lattice. Because of this mechanism, electrical resistivity varies with temperature, a relationship that is generally valid for materials in which the carrier density is independent of temperature. As the temperature is lowered, the thermal lattice vibrations become less important, and scattering is dominated by crystalline imperfections, such as lattice vacancies or interstitial atoms, lattice dislocations, impurity atoms, and crystal boundaries. Thus, electron scattering is increased by the addition of impurity atoms or by destroying the crystalline order of the solid; in fact, for amorphous (noncrystalline) materials, scattering by these imperfection mechanisms is important even at room temperature.

Because of the increasing importance of lattice vibrations with increasing temperature, the mobility of electrons in solids tends to decrease with increasing temperature. Moreover, because the carrier concentration (density) in metals and semimetals is essentially temperature independent, the increased scattering with increasing temperature leads to a characteristic decrease in conductivity with increasing temperature. For semiconductors and insulators the number of carriers is extremely temperature dependent; in fact, the carrier density increases exponentially with increasing temperature. Such a rapid increase in the carrier density completely overshadows the very much slower decrease in the mobility; thus the conductivity of semiconductors and insulators characteristically increases with increasing temperature.

Activation energy. The strong temperature dependence of the carrier density in semiconductors and insulators is intimately connected with an activation energy, or barrier, which restricts carriers to bound, nonconducting states. This barrier can be overcome by thermal excitation of the particles, which has an exponential temperature dependence through the Boltzmann factor that relates the temperature to the energy of the particle. Thus, the carrier density (N) is equal to the product of the density of the available bound carriers (N_0) and the exponential of minus the ratio of the activation energy (E_g) to twice the Boltzmann constant (k) times the absolute (Kelvin) temperature (T), or $N = N_0 \exp(-E_g/2kT)$. The temperature dependence is extremely high, especially in the temperature range below the characteristic temperature T, approximately equal to E_g/k. In insulators this region is generally equal to or greater than $10^5°$ K, and the room temperature conductivity is very small. For pure semiconductors, the characteristic temperature is equal to or greater than $T_c \geq 10^4°$ K, and even here the room temperature conductivity is low (Figure 1). Because of the strong temperature dependence of the conductivity in semiconductors, a constant temperature must be maintained for stable operation of semiconductor devices. In such devices it is important to minimize any power flow and power loss that could cause heating effects, because these would greatly increase the number of carriers, ultimately resulting in avalanche breakdown, a phenomenon that is similar to breakdown processes occurring in the air during a thunderstorm to produce lightning.

Conductivity in very pure semiconductors is characterized by extremely strong temperature dependence. As impurities are added, however, the temperature dependence of the carrier density becomes weaker; upon heavy doping with impurity atoms, the carrier density becomes essentially temperature independent, thus exhibiting semimetallic behaviour.

To gain a better understanding of the effect of impurity atoms on electrical conductivity, it is instructive to take a more microscopic view of a solid and to inquire into the nature of chemical bonding. In this way the interactions of single ions with their neighbours can be examined, and the microscopic interactions can be related to the macroscopic properties of the material. Contrasting with this chemical view of matter is the physical approach, whereby the solid is considered as an immobile structure composed of units arranged in a precise geometric pattern that can be repeated in any direction to extend the structure infinitely. Such a structure is periodic, and this periodicity is exploited to describe the electronic behaviour.

Chemical approach. Perhaps the most powerful application of the chemical approach has been directed toward the question of which atoms and crystal structures favour the formation of insulators, semiconductors, and metals. The approach is well illustrated by the important semiconductors silicon and germanium, which are chemically related to the element carbon and the atoms of which have the same chemical bonding as do the carbon atoms in diamond crystal structure.

Each carbon, silicon, or germanium atom has four valence electrons. (By gaining, losing, or sharing valence electrons, atoms can bind with one another.) Because there are about eight valence states of about the same energy the valence shells of carbon, silicon, and germanium are only half filled. To occupy the four remaining empty states and fill up the shell, each atom shares one electron with each of four neighbouring atoms. Thus, silicon and germanium (like carbon) crystallize in the diamond structure, in which each atom is bound to its four nearest neighbours in a tetrahedral arrangement.

Bonding characterized by the sharing of an electron between neighbouring atoms is called covalent bonding. The covalent bonds in diamond are so strong that it is extremely difficult to remove an electron from any bond. It is the strength of covalent bonding between carbon atoms that accounts for the extreme hardness of diamonds. In germanium and silicon, however, the covalent bonds are weaker because the valence electrons are in shells that are farther from the nucleus than the valence shell of the carbon atom. In such cases it is relatively easy to promote an electron from a covalent bond into a conducting state, and much of semiconductor technology is concerned with controlling the number of broken bonds that can contribute electrons to the conduction process. Increasing the temperature provides thermal energy for breaking bonds, thereby freeing electrons for conduction purposes.

Addition of impurities. The periodic table of the elements is an invaluable aid in comparing their properties. In the table, the elements are arranged in a sequence according to increasing numbers of protons in their nuclei and a corresponding increase of electrons around the nuclei. Elements that this system places in the same vertical column, or group, are similar because they have similar electron structures. The elements carbon, silicon, germanium, and tin are in Group IV of the periodic table. Impurities from neighbouring Groups V or III can be introduced substitutionally into the diamond structure of these elements. While the presence of the impurities has little effect on the crystal structure, they profoundly affect electrical conductivity. For example, antimony (Sb), an element in Group V, has five electrons in the valence shell, one electron more than that needed to satisfy the covalent bonding requirement. When antimony is used as an impurity atom in silicon, only a small amount of energy is needed to liberate the extra electron, which is weakly bound to the positively charged antimony ion (Sb^+). Impurities that donate electrons to the conduction pro-

(margin notes) Temperature effect

(margin notes) Chemical bonding

cess are called donors; here, electrical conduction is by negatively charged carriers and the materials are called *n*-type.

On the other hand, indium (In), an element in Group III, has only three electrons in its valence shell, which means a one-electron deficiency relative to the covalent bonding requirement. Because the covalent bond is so strong when indium is used as an impurity atom in silicon, the electron deficiency in the indium atom can be satisfied by taking an electron from a covalent bond elsewhere in the material. The covalent bond that now lacks an electron is called a hole and acts like a positive charge; it is free to hop from covalent bond to covalent bond in the material. Impurities that receive electrons are called acceptors; thus, an effective positive charge, a *p*-type, has been introduced into the conduction process.

Because the impurity atoms in semiconductors and insulators tend to be relatively well isolated from each other, the chemical approach is particularly fruitful. For example, the chemical mass-action law (the rate of a chemical reaction depends on the concentrations of the reacting substances) can be applied to determine the degree of ionization of the impurity atoms and hence the carrier density in the semiconductor.

Compound semiconductors. Silicon, germanium, diamond, and gray tin form the Group IV semiconductors, so called because their atomic structure puts them into the fourth group, or column, of the periodic table. (Other forms of carbon and tin, such as graphite and white tin, do not act as semiconductors.) A class of closely related materials is the III-V compound semiconductors, in which one atom of an element from the third group of the periodic table is surrounded by four neighbouring atoms of an element from the fifth group of the periodic table and conversely, so that the number of atoms from each group is equal. By transferring an electron from a fifth-group atom to a third-group atom, each lattice site becomes occupied by an ion surrounded by four oppositely charged ions in a tetrahedral arrangement, with the electronic bonding similar to that of the diamond structure. Actually, however, the crystal structure for the III-V compound semiconductors is the zinc-blende structure, which is like the diamond structure except that nearest-neighbour atoms are of a different species. An example of a III-V semiconductor is gallium arsenide, in which the bonding is mainly covalent, though some ionic bonding, and therefore Coulomb attraction (the electrostatic attraction between oppositely charged particles), exists between the oppositely charged ions. Because covalent bonding dominates these compounds, they have semiconducting properties similar to the Group IV materials.

Hopping process. The chemical structure approach is useful not only for understanding compound semiconductors but also for explaining molecular solids, which include all solids of organic molecules as well as such materials as solid hydrogen, which has a hexagonal arrangement of hydrogen (H_2) molecules. In molecular solids the dominant conduction mechanism is the hopping of a single electron from one molecular complex to another. Because this process typically involves an activation energy, however, it is not an efficient conduction mechanism. Consequently, molecular solids tend to be poor conductors of electricity.

Ionic crystal conduction

The hopping process is also an important conduction mechanism in ionic crystals. Here, however, the process involves either a lattice vacancy or an interstitial ion, rather than simply an electron. Just as in the case of electron hopping in molecular crystals, the hopping ions in ionic crystals must overcome a potential activation energy barrier by virtue of their thermal motion. The hopping barriers are lower for small ions than they are for larger ions; hence, a solid with small ions (*e.g.*, H^+ ions in ice) will tend to have relatively higher ionic conductivity. The relative sizes of the ions are important in determining the barrier height. In photosensitive materials, such as silver bromide (AgBr), the barrier of the smaller positive silver ions (Ag^+) is much less than that of the larger negative ions (Br^-), a difference that is an essential ingredient in the photographic process.

Amorphous solid semiconductors. The chemical approach has also proven to be very effective in dealing with amorphous solids that do not exhibit any long-range periodic structure. Such solids are noted for their durability, their insensitivity to variations of temperature and pressure, and their insensitivity to the introduction of impurities, vacancies, and interstitial atoms. The most common example of an amorphous material is glass, which consists mostly of a random array of silicon dioxide (SiO_2) molecules as well as impurities. The crystalline form of pure silicon dioxide is quartz, a well-ordered structure. When the ordering is destroyed, a glass results, and some of the properties of the material are changed. For example, fused quartz, the amorphous version of quartz, has a much lower conductivity than crystalline quartz; the ultraviolet properties of fused quartz and crystalline quartz, however, are almost identical.

Physical approach. While the chemical approach is advantageous in studying the more complicated materials, such as molecular and amorphous solids, the physical approach is probably more advantageous in dealing with simple, highly ordered crystalline solids, thus leading to an understanding of semiconductors and insulators. A crystalline solid is conceived of as an infinite, perfectly periodic array of atoms. Initially, this point of view may seem more complicated than that of the chemical approach, in which only a few interacting atoms are considered; a great deal of progress can be made, however, by exploiting the symmetry of the periodic structure, especially the translational symmetry (the movement of a configuration to new coordinates without changing its symmetry) of the perfectly periodic array.

Energy bands and gaps. As a direct consequence of translational symmetry, the discrete energy levels of the free atom spread out to form two kinds of energy bands in the solid, valence bands and conduction bands. The valence bands are those occupied by electrons and the conduction bands are normally unoccupied. If the conduction bands of a semiconductor become partly filled by thermal excitation, the solid becomes conducting. For materials in which the electrons are tightly bound to the atoms, the width of the energy bands is sufficiently small for each band of energy levels to be separated from neighbouring bands by an energy gap. Whereas there are no available valence states in the energy gaps, the number of available states in each energy band would be completely filled if each atom would contribute exactly two electrons.

The result for the number of available states is of great consequence because of the Pauli exclusion principle (*i.e.*, only one electron may occupy a particular energy state), and the result does, in fact, imply that every solid with an even number of electrons is an insulator, and every solid with an odd number is a metal.

Band degeneracies

The situation in actual solids is not quite so simple for several reasons. Band degeneracies (*i.e.*, several levels with the same energy) occur because of rotational point symmetries (the configuration remains unchanged upon performing a rotation) in the crystal structures. Such band degeneracies characteristically are present in the bands associated with the valence electrons of semiconductors that have the diamond and zinc-blende crystal structure. A second complication, prevalent in semimetals and metals, is the overlapping of neighbouring energy bands. Overlapping arises when the energy that binds electrons to their ion cores becomes weaker, causing electrons to move farther away, thus increasing the band widths and, consequently, decreasing the band gaps from a finite value to zero and, finally, to the overlapping condition. A third complication is associated with the complex arrangement of atoms within the solid. For example, the concept of band occupation given above indicates that solid hydrogen should be a metal (a hydrogen atom has only one electron, an odd number), whereas the solid is actually an insulator consisting of a hexagonal lattice of hydrogen (H_2) molecules. There is, however, a high-pressure phase of solid hydrogen that is metallic, because when the distance between interacting molecules is reduced, the crystal structure changes, with a resulting change in the electrical conductivity.

It is also possible to form, from the same atom, solids with different electrical properties depending on their crystal structure, a striking example being tin. White tin crystallizes in a tetragonal arrangement and is a high-conductivity metal, while gray tin is a covalently bonded semiconductor crystallizing in the diamond structure. In the case of tin, certain partly filled energy levels (p levels) of the free atom become conduction bands for metallic white tin, whereas the greater symmetry of the diamond structure of gray tin results in a splitting of the p bands into filled bonding and empty antibonding states, thus giving rise to semiconducting behaviour.

Theoretical approximations. The physical approach to the electronic properties of solids uses the translation symmetry of the periodic structure to establish the existence of valence and conduction energy bands. The detailed treatment of energy bands, however, is an exceedingly difficult matter and can be carried out only in an approximate way. Much of the theoretical work results in equations that employ only a small number of factors determined by experiment. Among these factors are the energy gap, which separates the occupied valence states from the empty conduction states, and the effective mass, which describes the dynamic motion of electrons in a solid. By introducing the effective mass concept, it is possible to treat the electrons in a solid as free electrons that possess a mass different from the free-electron mass.
Effective mass of electrons The effective mass approximation, whereby the effect of the periodic lattice is taken into account by introducing an effective mass, is extremely useful in dealing with many of the physical phenomena in semiconductors and insulators.

The lattice. The lattice, however, cannot be completely ignored. The atoms of the lattice are in a state of constant vibration, and the characteristic, or normal, mode frequencies of these lattice vibrations have been studied extensively for semiconductors and insulators. The number of normal modes of vibration is completely determined by the crystal structure and the number of atoms per unit cell. For example, in the diamond structure there are three acoustic (sound) modes and three optical (light) modes. The characteristic frequencies of lattice vibrations are determined by a variety of experimental techniques.

Lattice vibrations have an important influence on electrical conductivity because they provide the dominant scattering mechanism for solids at room temperature. In the scattering process, the energy of the electrons is either increased or decreased by the characteristic energies of the lattice. The conduction electrons contribute to both the electrical conductivity and the thermal conductivity of solids. Metals are characteristically good conductors of both heat and electricity, whereas electrical insulators are also typically good thermal insulators.

Statistical properties. The physical approach to solids uses the translational symmetry associated with the periodic lattice to establish the characteristic vibrational frequencies for the lattice. The physical view also exploits the statistical properties of a large ensemble of particles to determine such fundamental properties as the carrier densities of solids. Like electrons, ensembles of particles obey the Pauli exclusion principle, and the statistical behaviour of such ensembles is described by the Fermi-Dirac distribution function, $f(E)$, which expresses the probability that a given state of energy E will be occupied at temperature T. This relationship can be expressed by the following equation, in which the Fermi energy, or chemical potential, is symbolized by the Greek letter zeta, ζ, and k is Boltzmann's constant:

$$f(E) = [1 + \exp\{(E - \zeta)/kT\}]^{-1}.$$

The significance of the Fermi energy (ζ) is that, at $T = 0°$ K, all the states up to energy ζ are completely occupied, while those above energy ζ are completely empty. At higher temperatures a fraction of the states above the Fermi energy will be occupied and, consequently, some states below ζ will be empty in accordance with the distribution function $f(E)$. The distribution function can be applied directly to metals to find, at a given tempera-

ture, the number of excited electrons above the Fermi energy; such excited electrons are directly responsible for the electronic contribution to the specific heat of metals and for the electronic Pauli paramagnetism (permanent magnetism) of metals.

In applying the Fermi-Dirac distribution to semiconductors, it is necessary to take into account the presence of an energy gap above the valence bands that is forbidden to electron states. For pure semiconductors, at temperature equal to $0°$ K ($-273°$ C or $-460°$ F), the states below the energy gap are completely occupied, those above are completely empty, and the Fermi energy lies within the band gap. If the energy gap is small compared with the product of Boltzmann's constant and temperature, kT, then the Fermi-Dirac distribution function implies that the thermal energy will be strongly effective in exciting electrons into conduction states located in the conduction band. For every electron that is excited into a conduction state, an unfilled valence state is created in the valence bands; unfilled states are called holes and, for
Holes conduction purposes, behave very much like positive charges with masses comparable to electron masses.

For typical semiconductors, such as germanium and silicon at room temperature, the energy gap is very much greater than thermal energies, so that only a few thermally excited carriers are present. In this limit, the temperature dependence of the carrier concentration for both electrons and holes is exponential and of the form $N = N_0 \exp(-E_g/2kT)$, as explained above under *Activation energy*. Both the excited electrons and the holes that are left behind contribute to the conduction process, and for a semiconductor of high purity they are the predominant current carriers at room temperature.

Nonconducting states. The physical approach to solids is also useful in treating certain nonconducting excited states in semiconductors that are associated with the attraction of an electron to the hole that it has left behind. Such states, which are commonly called excitons, either
Excitons lie below the internal ionization energy of the solid or lie within the energy gap, just below the conducting states. An exciton can be transferred from one lattice site to another by a hopping mechanism. Excitons are generally more important in semiconductors and insulators with large band gaps, such as ionic crystals, than in those with small band gaps, although weak exciton effects have been observed in the latter. Because the exciton does not obey Fermi-Dirac statistics whereas the electron does, it is not possible to obtain a filled band of excitons. The Coulomb attraction of the exciton is in many ways suggestive of the attraction of the electron to the hydrogen ion in the hydrogen atom or of the electron to the positron (a negatively charged electron) in positronium (a short-lived system containing an electron and positron that revolve around a common centre). Theoretical treatments of excitons based on models similar to the hydrogen atom or to positronium have been very successful in explaining many of the characteristic properties of excitons.

Nonconducting states within the energy gap are also created by the presence of impurities. Because the free charges associated with impurities tend to screen the attraction between the electron and the hole associated with it, however, the exciton levels are generally observed in materials of higher purity than are desirable for the study of impurity levels.

Extrinsic and intrinsic semiconductors. From the physical point of view, shallow impurity levels in a solid (impurities that have a potential not too different from the host atoms) are generally treated by using models based on a hydrogen-like atom with an electron of effective mass. Impurity levels, unlike states within the conduction and valence bands, tend to be sharp, or discrete; in the simplest cases, the discrete donor (excess electron) levels lie just below the conduction band minimum, while the acceptor (deficiency of electrons) levels lie just above the valence band. Because these levels are easily ionized to create electrons or holes in conducting states, impurities provide a ready source of charged carriers for electrical conduction.

When conduction is dominated by impurity mechanisms, the semiconductor is called extrinsic, in contrast with intrinsic semiconductors, in which conductivity is mainly associated with the thermal excitation of carriers. An extrinsic semiconductor is generally classified as *n*- or *p*-type, depending on whether the impurity has an excess of negative charge (*n*-type) or a deficiency of negative charge (*p*-type). Under some circumstances, an intrinsic semiconductor can also be classified as *n*-type or *p*-type, because the mobility of the electrons and holes may be quite different although their carrier densities are closely equal. In such cases the conduction process itself is dominated by the carriers with the highest mobility.

Measurement of conductivity. A direct measurement of the carrier concentration in a semiconductor is obtained from a phenomenon, called the Hall effect after its discoverer, which makes use of the deflection of the electric current by a transverse direct-current magnetic field. The Hall measurement provides both the sign and concentration of the carriers. A separate measurement of the conductivity allows one to calculate the mobility of the carriers. Because these factors are so important for the characterization of semiconductors, conductivity and Hall-effect measurements are routinely carried out at room temperature and at liquid nitrogen temperature (77° K or −196° C, −321° F) when semiconducting crystals are produced. The temperature dependence of carrier density helps to determine whether the semiconductor is intrinsic or extrinsic.

Hall effect

The conductivity or resistivity of a solid is itself dependent on the magnitude and direction of the magnetic field relative to the current flow. This magnetoresistance effect is associated with the curling up of the electron trajectories in the magnetic field, thereby decreasing the mean free path (the average distance that a particle travels between successive collisions) of the carriers. Such experiments yield valuable information on the directional dependence (anisotropy) of the effective masses of the carriers.

The most direct information, however, on the effective mass for electrons and holes in semiconductors is provided by a cyclotron resonance experiment in which the charged particles can be considered to execute closed orbits in a plane perpendicular to the magnetic field. The experiments establish that the electrons in germanium have an effective mass that is approximately ten times smaller than the free-electron mass; even smaller effective masses have been found in other small-gap semiconductors.

Measurement of energy gaps. The other dominant parameter (a constant, in equations, to which any desired value can be given) that characterizes semiconductors and insulators is the band gap separating the valence states from the conduction states. The most direct measurement of this energy gap involves the excitation of an electron in a valence state to a state in the conduction band through the absorption of a photon (a discrete unit of light energy). The process, called the internal photoelectric effect (the action by which a substance emits free electrons as a result of absorbing light energy), is closely related to the photoelectric effect at a metallic surface. The energy gap is determined as the threshold for the onset of the photoelectric process and typically occurs at infrared or optical frequencies. Optical spectral techniques also provide a powerful tool for the study of discrete exciton and impurity states. The optical excitation of carriers is also exploited in a variety of photoconductive detectors, which are characterized by fast response, high sensitivity, and availability over a wide range of infrared and optical frequencies.

PRINCIPLES OF SEMICONDUCTOR APPLICATIONS

Photographic process. Perhaps the most common application of the photoelectric effect is in the photographic process. Although this process has been studied extensively for many years, the detailed mechanism is not yet completely understood. Photographic film contains small crystallites of silver salts, such as silver bromide or silver iodide, which are darkened when exposed to light and subsequently developed. The initial exposure to light sets the image in the photographic process; it is associated with the following mechanism.

The incident light frees an electron, which becomes trapped at some impurity site (*e.g.*, thallium). The silver ions, which have a relatively high mobility, diffuse through the lattice and migrate to those sites where the electrons have been trapped. At one of these sites the silver ion becomes neutralized, forming a neutral silver atom and thereby restoring the impurity site to its original state. In this way each impurity site can collect several neutral silver atoms, forming a collection of silver particles called the latent image. When the film is developed, the small silver particles in the latent image grow, and finally the silver salts that are in the ionic form are washed out, retaining the colloidal silver particles. In colour photography a separate image is formed for each of the three primary colours, red, green, and blue.

Luminescence. Also occurring in semiconductors and insulators is a process inverse to the photoelectric effect, one in which the recombination of an electron with a hole or with an impurity centre results in the emission of a photon. The effect, which is called luminescence, is essential in many devices using semiconductors and insulators; for example, a laser is a device that emits light by virtue of releasing radiation stored by creating electron and hole pairs.

Luminescence is also basic to the operation of scintillation counters, which are so important in detecting and measuring high-energy particles. In these devices a high-energy gamma ray (photons with frequencies much higher than visible light) is made to produce a larger number of photons in the visible range (photons with much lower frequencies). The mechanism for such photon production is as follows: the high-energy gamma ray generates very energetic electrons and holes that rapidly become degraded by collisions with other electrons; thus, when a highly energetic gamma ray is absorbed by an insulating material, such as sodium iodide (NaI), it effectively produces a large number of excited electrons, which, in turn, can recombine with an impurity centre or a hole by a luminescent process to produce many photons of visible light, which are then detected optically.

Hot-electron effects. Another property of semiconductors and insulators that has great practical significance is the nonlinear response (*i.e.*, nonproportionality) of the current flow to the applied electric field. For small electric fields the current flow is directly proportional to the applied electric field, and the electrical conductivity (the proportionality constant) is independent of the magnitude of the applied field. For sufficiently large electric fields, however, the conductivity itself can become dependent on the field, either increasing with increasing electric field (giving rise to avalanche effects), or decreasing, or even becoming negative. Nonlinear effects in semiconductors and insulators are sometimes called hot-electron effects because they involve a nonlinear dependence of the Fermi–Dirac distribution function on the applied electric field.

Avalanche breakdown, or sparking, is a common hot-electron effect in insulators. In the presence of a sufficiently large electric field, a conduction electron can pick up enough energy in a mean free path to induce ionization in the solid. With this mechanism for the creation of additional carriers, the current flow can increase catastrophically and the concomitant local heating can result in actual physical damage to the material. Similar avalanche processes occur in gases and are responsible for the operation of such devices as Geiger counters.

Avalanche breakdown

Practical devices are also based on hot-electron effects that result in a decrease in current flow with increasing applied electric field. Such a nonlinear effect (the Gunn effect) was discovered in gallium arsenide (GaAs) by a British-United States physicist, John B. Gunn, in 1963 and is the basis for the Gunn oscillator, which supplies large quantities of power at microwave frequencies. In such nonlinear semiconductors, small electric fields excite carriers into high-mobility conduction states; but above a certain threshold field, excitation into low-mobility states becomes energetically possible. With increasing electric fields, the low-mobility states are occupied with increasing probability, and a decrease in conductivity results. This negative conductivity is basic to the operation of the Gunn oscillator.

Junction effects.   Solid-state devices can make use of either bulk effects or junction effects. (Some typical examples of bulk-effect devices are Gunn oscillators, photoconductors, and ruby lasers.) Junctions exist between different semiconductors, or between semiconductors and metals, and are particularly important in devices based on a single junction.

When two dissimilar materials (in semiconductor electronics the most common are silicon, germanium, and gallium arsenide) are placed in contact, there will be a net flow of electrons from one material to the other until the Fermi levels or chemical potentials of the two materials are equal. Thus, in equilibrium, it is possible to take an electron across the junction between the two materials without the expenditure of any energy. In equilibrium there is no net current across the junction, and the hole current is equal and opposite to the electron current.

Perhaps the most common junction is the *p–n* junction, which is formed by contact between *n*-type and *p*-type samples of the same material. In the immediate neighbourhood of the junction there is a depletion layer, a region in which the carrier concentration is low, reflecting the fact that there are no allowed conduction states at the Fermi energy in this region of the crystal (see Figure 2B). In the depletion layer the electrons must tunnel (pass through at very high speeds) to overcome the potential barrier associated with the contact potential. For practical applications of *p–n* junctions it is important that the junctions be kept narrow and that their physical characteristics be carefully controlled.

The p-n junction

From S.M. Sze, *Physics of Semiconductor Devices* (1969); John Wiley & Sons, Inc.

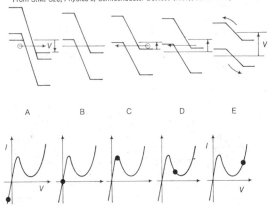

Figure 2: Simplified energy-band diagrams of tunnel diode at: (A) Reverse bias. (B) Thermal equilibrium. (C) Forward bias such that peak current is obtained. (D) Forward bias such that the valley current is approached. (E) Forward bias with thermal current flowing (see text).

The properties of the junction can be altered by superimposing a voltage across it or by modifying the junction characteristics (for example, the width). The effect of an external bias on a *p–n* junction is illustrated in Figure 2. Application of a reverse bias (Figure 2A) produces a large reverse current, which is illustrated by the dot directly below the *I-V* (ampere-voltage) curve. The reverse bias increases the potential of the *p*-type region relative to the *n*-type region, and conversely the forward bias increases the potential of the *n*-type region relative to the *p*-type region. Application of a forward bias (Figures 2C, 2D, 2E) eventually leads to a dramatic decrease in current or a negative conductivity as the number of available states vanish (Figure 2D). Other mechanisms, for example photon- or phonon-assisted tunnelling, provide some current for biassing voltages. Furthermore, by application of an extremely large forward bias, large currents once again become possible (Figure 2E).

A semiconductor in contact with a metal also forms a barrier with carriers removed, on the semiconductor side of the barrier. These junctions are important as rectifying

contacts and operate in the following manner: because the semiconductor effectively lowers the work function (energy needed to eject an electron) of the metal, electrons can be pulled out of the metal and into conducting states of the semiconductor with the application of reasonably small electrical fields. The reverse bias, however, does not produce currents, because the filled levels of the semiconductor are below the Fermi level of the metal.

Semiconductor and metal junctions

In addition to rectifying contacts, it is also possible to produce internal photoemission with a semiconductor–metal junction. The light can be incident on the junction, either through the semiconductor (it must be of low frequency so that bulk absorption does not occur) or directly onto the very thin metal coating that covers the semiconductor. In either arrangement, internal photoemission occurs at a lower threshold than for a metal-vacuum interface. The threshold can also be changed by the application of an external potential across the junction.

The internal photoemission process is basic to the operation of a solar cell, which consists of a *p–n* junction covering the entire external surface of a semiconductor. Light is absorbed in the *p–n* junction, creating a potential difference that in turn gives rise to a tunnelling current. Thus, the light is converted directly into electrical energy. The experimental conversion efficiency for the process is about 10 percent. Because solid-state electronics is widely used in space satellites, solar cells provide adequate power for the necessary circuitry.

A *p–n* junction not only can convert light into electrical energy but can also accomplish the inverse process; that is, convert electrical energy directly into light. The emitted radiation, which is produced by the recombination of holes and electrons that have been injected into the junction region by application of a forward bias, has a frequency characteristic of the energy gap. By polishing crystal faces on either side of a *p–n* junction, a resonant optical cavity, or Fabry–Perot interferometer, is formed from which the recombination radiation can be emitted coherently—that is, the emitted waves are in phase (in step) with each other—thereby producing laser action. Semiconducting diode lasers are of very small size and typically operate at an infrared frequency between 0.04 and two electron-volts, depending on the material. The tuning of a particular laser frequency is accomplished either by temperature variation or by application of an external magnetic field or mechanical stress.

Pressure effects.   Application of pressure results in a lattice deformation, which changes the lattice constant and hence the energy gap of the semiconductor; this mechanism is essentially that behind the pressure tuning of lasers. The same kind of mechanical deformation can also greatly influence the electric conductivity of a solid, and the resulting current flow gives rise to piezoelectric effects, the production of electric charges when certain crystals are deformed by mechanical stress, or, conversely, the deformation of a crystal caused by the application of a voltage. This conversion of mechanical motion into an electric current is exploited in such practical devices as phonograph pickups and sonar detectors. Piezoelectric materials that are used for such applications typically have a strong coupling between the electronic band structure and the characteristic modes for the lattice vibrations. An important class of piezoelectric materials are the ferroelectrics (ionic crystals in which the molecules are aligned with one another), such as barium titanate.

Magnetic effects.   Magnetism can occur in both insulators and semiconductors. Salts of nickel, cobalt, and iron, and of other atoms with partly filled *d*-shells (shells in which ten electrons are allowed) in the free atom, form insulating crystals with a variety of magnetic properties. Furthermore, oxides and sulfides of various rare-earth atoms form magnetic semiconductors. Among the many practical applications of magnetic insulators are magnetic memory cores in computers and magnetic gyrators for microwave devices.

Thermoelectric effects.   Semiconductors also have proved to be among the most useful materials for the production of devices based on thermoelectric power conversion. The Seebeck effect, discovered in 1821, represents a means of converting heat energy directly into electrical energy, whereas the Peltier effect (1834) represents a means of using electrical energy for refrigeration. Practical devices based on these two effects make use of a junction between two dissimilar conductors. For thermoelectric generation (Seebeck effect), a potential difference is set up across a junction when it is heated. In thermoelectric refrigeration (Peltier effect), cooling of a junction results when a current is passed through it. A current passing down a wire or through a junction represents the transport of both charge (electric current) and kinetic energy (heat current). Lattice-thermal conduction provides a mechanism for curtailing the temperature difference established by the flow of kinetic energy. The presence of p- and n-type materials on either side of a $p–n$ junction provides high-mobility carriers of opposite sign, which act to enhance thermoelectric generation. The $p–n$ junctions in the semiconductors lead telluride (PbTe) and bismuth telluride ($Bi_2 Te_3$) have been found to be among the best materials for thermoelectric refrigeration. Although these devices have not replaced mechanical refrigerators for economic reasons, they can be effectively applied in situations that exploit their small size and weight, such as outer-space travel.

BIBLIOGRAPHY. C. KITTEL, *Theory of Semiconductors and Insulators: Introduction to Solid State Physics*, 3rd ed. (1966), a comprehensive, modern text dealing with all basic physical concepts in semiconductors and insulators; S.M. SZE, *Physics of Semiconductor Devices* (1969), a basic engineering text giving a detailed description of modern semiconductor devices; W. SHOCKLEY, *Electrons and Holes in Semiconductors* (1950), a classic text giving physical insight into the properties of semiconductors and the operation of early transistors; *Scientific American*, vol. 217, no. 3 (1967), a special issue devoted to materials, including the following nontechnical articles that relate to semiconductors and insulators: H. EHRENREICH, "The Electrical Properties of Materials"; H. REISS, "The Chemical Properties of Materials"; A. JAVAN, "The Optical Properties of Materials"; and SIR NEVILLE MOTT, "The Solid State." C.E.K. MEES and T.H. JAMES (eds.), *Theory of the Photographic Process*, 3rd ed. (1966), a comprehensive book covering all aspects of the photographic process; the solid state models are covered particularly well in the articles by F. MOSER and R.S. VAN HEYNINGEN.

Semmelweis, Ignaz Philipp

Semmelweis, who has been called "the saviour of mothers" for his discovery of the cause of puerperal fever, also introduced antiseptic prophylaxis and thus opened a new era in medical science.

By courtesy of the Semmelweis Medical Historical Museum and Library, Budapest

Semmelweis, detail of an oil painting by A. Canzi, 1857. In the Semmelweis Medical Historical Museum and Library, Budapest.

He was born in Buda, Hungary, on July 1, 1818. Educated at the Universities of Pest and Vienna, he received his doctor's degree from Vienna in 1844 and was appointed assistant at the obstetric clinic in Vienna. He soon became involved in the problem of childbed fever, or puerperal infection, the scourge of maternity hospitals throughout Europe. Although most women delivered at home, those who had to seek hospitalization because of poverty, illegitimacy, or obstetrical complications faced mortality rates ranging as high as 25–30 percent. Some thought that the infection was induced by overcrowding, poor ventilation, the onset of lactation, or "miasma." Semmelweis proceeded to investigate its cause over the strong objections of his chief, who, like other continental physicians, had reconciled himself to the idea that the disease was unpreventable. *(margin: Early interest in childbed fever)*

Semmelweis observed that among women in the first division of the clinic, the death rate from childbed fever was two or three times as high as among those in the second division, although the two divisions were identical with the exception that students were taught in the first and midwives in the second. He put forward the thesis that perhaps the students carried something to the patients they examined during labour. The death of a friend from a wound infection incurred during the examination of a woman who died of puerperal infection and the similarity of the findings in the two cases gave support to his reasoning. He concluded that students who came directly from the dissecting room to the maternity ward carried the infection from mothers who had died of the disease to healthy mothers. He ordered the students to wash their hands in a solution of chlorinated lime before each examination.

Under these procedures, the mortality rates in the first division dropped from 18.27 percent to 1.27 percent, and in March and August of 1848 no woman died in childbirth in his division. The younger medical men in Vienna recognized the significance of Semmelweis' discovery and gave him all possible assistance. His superior, on the other hand, was critical—not because he wanted to oppose him but because he failed to understand him.

In the year 1848 a liberal political revolution swept Europe, and Semmelweis took part in the events in Vienna. After the revolution had been put down, Semmelweis found that his political activities had increased the obstacles to his professional work. In 1849 he was dropped from his post at the clinic. He then applied for a teaching post at the university in midwifery but was turned down. Soon after that, he gave a successful lecture at the Medical Society of Vienna entitled "The Origin of Puerperal Fever." At the same time, he applied once more for the teaching post, but although he received it, there were restrictions attached to it that he considered humiliating. He left Vienna and returned to Pest in 1850.

He worked for the next six years at the St. Rochus Hospital in Pest. An epidemic of puerperal fever had broken out in the obstetrics department, and at his request, Semmelweis was put in charge of the department. His measures promptly reduced the mortality rate, and in his years there it averaged only 0.85 percent. In Prague and Vienna, meantime, the rate was still from 10 to 15 percent.

In 1855 he was appointed professor of obstetrics at the University of Pest. He married, had five children, and developed his private practice. His ideas were accepted in Hungary, and the government addressed a circular to all district authorities ordering the introduction of the prophylactic methods of Semmelweis. In 1857 he declined the chair of obstetrics at the University of Zürich. Vienna still remained hostile toward him, and the editor of the *Wiener Medizinische Wochenschrift* wrote that it was time to stop the nonsense about the chlorine hand wash.

In 1861 Semmelweis published his principal work, *Die Ätiologie, der Begriff und die Prophylaxis des Kindbettfiebers*. He sent it to all the prominent obstetricians and medical societies abroad, but the general reaction was adverse. The weight of authority stood against his teachings. He addressed several open letters to professors of medicine in other countries, but to little effect. At a conference of German physicians and natural scientists, most of the speakers—including the pathologist Rudolf Virchow—rejected his doctrine. The years of controversy gradually undermined his spirit. In 1865 he suffered a *(margin: Publication of his major work)* breakdown and was taken to a mental hospital, where he died on August 13, 1865. Ironically, his illness and death were caused by the infection of a wound on his right hand, apparently the result of an operation he had performed before being taken ill. He died of the same disease against which he had struggled all his professional life.

Semmelweis' doctrine was subsequently accepted by medical science. His influence on the development of knowledge and control of infection was hailed by Joseph Lister, the father of modern antisepsis: "I think with the greatest admiration of him and his achievement and it fills me with joy that at last he is given the respect due to him."

BIBLIOGRAPHY. The first comprehensive biography of Semmelweis was SCHUERER VON WALDHEIM, *Ignaz Philipp Semmelweis* (1905). A recent work by G. GORTVAY and I. ZOL-TÁN, *Semmelweis élete és munkássága* (1966; Eng. trans., *Semmelweis: His Life and Work*, 1968), is critical of some of the romantic legends that have grown up around him.

(I.Z.)

Seneca

Lucius Annaeus Seneca, orator, tragedian, stylist, philosopher, statesman, and multimillionaire, was the leading intellectual figure in Rome in the middle of the 1st century AD. In the first phase of Nero's reign (AD 54–62) he and his friends virtually ruled the Roman world, giving a period of (relatively) good government. In his 40 surviving books the thoughts of a versatile but unoriginal mind are expressed and amplified by the resources of an individual style, brief, pointed, rhetorical, and epigrammatic. Their influence on later European culture has been pervasive but subject to fluctuation. So has Seneca's reputation; scholars have been and are divided on his merits as a writer and as a man.

By courtesy of the Staatliche Museen zu Berlin

Seneca, marble bust, 3rd century, after an original bust of the 1st century. In the Staatliche Museen, Berlin.

The problem of reconciling the gap between moral principles and political conduct is unrealistic. Seneca's thought evolved; Nero's autocracy degenerated. Seneca could justly say, at the end of his life, "I point out to others the right way, which I have learned late, and tired out with wandering." As tutor and adviser of princes, his record appears to be better, on a larger scale, than that of Plato or Aristotle. On the other hand, his wealth is not easily condoned by his plea that neither poverty nor opulence affect the philosopher, for it derived from estates (property in Rome, vineyards in Campania, an estate in Egypt, doubtless others), whose profits went into usury. A story that his action in recalling his loans precipitated the rebellion of Boudicca in Britain is first found in the *Roman History* of Dio Cassius, written in the 3rd century.

Early life and family

Seneca, second son of a wealthy family, was born about 4 BC at Corduba in the romanized province of Baetica. The father Lucius Annaeus Seneca (Seneca the Elder) had been famous in Rome as a teacher of rhetoric: the

mother Helvia was of excellent character and education: the older brother was Gallio, met by St. Paul in Achaea in AD 52: the younger brother was the father of the poet Lucan. An aunt took Lucius as a boy to Rome; there he was trained as an orator and educated in philosophy in the school of the Sextii, which blended Stoicism with an ascetic neo-Pythagoreanism. Seneca's health suffered, and he went to recuperate in Egypt, where his aunt was now the wife of the prefect, Gaius Galerius. Returning to Rome about the year 31, he began a career in politics and law. Soon he fell foul of the emperor Caligula, who was deterred from killing him only by the argument that his life was sure to be short.

In 41 the emperor Claudius banished him to Corsica on a charge of adultery with the princess Julia Livilla, the emperor's niece. In that uncongenial milieu he studied natural science and philosophy and wrote the three treatises entitled *Consolationes*. The influence of Agrippina, the emperor's wife, had him recalled to Rome in 49. He became praetor in AD 50, married Pompeia Paulina, a wealthy woman, built up a powerful group of friends, including the new prefect of the guard Sextus Afranius Burrus, and became tutor to the future emperor Nero.

The murder of Claudius in 54 pushed Seneca and Burrus to the top. Their friends held the great army commands on the German and Parthian frontiers. Nero's first public speech, drafted by Seneca, promised liberty for the Senate and an end to the influence of freedmen and women. Agrippina, Nero's mother, was resolved that her influence should continue; and there were other powerful enemies. But Seneca and Burrus, provincials from Spain and Gaul, understood the problems of the Roman world. They introduced fiscal and judicial reforms and fostered a more humane attitude toward slaves. Their nominee Corbulo defeated the Parthians; in Britain a more enlightened administration followed the quashing of Boudicca's rebellion. But as Tacitus, the historian (c. 56–117), says, "Nothing in human affairs is more unstable and precarious than power unsupported by its own strength." Seneca and Burrus were a tyrant's favourites. In 59 they had to condone—or to contrive—the murder of Agrippina. When Burrus died in 62 Seneca knew that he could not go on. He received permission to retire, and in his remaining years he wrote some of his best philosophical works. In 65, Seneca's enemies denounced him as having been a party to the conspiracy of Piso. Ordered to commit suicide, he met death with fortitude and composure.

Philosophical works and tragedies

The *Apocolocyntosis divi Claudii* (*The Pumpkinification of the Divine Claudius*) stands apart from the rest of Seneca's surviving works. A political skit, witty and unscrupulous, its theme is the deification—or "pumpkinification"—of Claudius. The rest divide into philosophical works and the tragedies. The former expound an eclectic version of "Middle" Stoicism, adapted for the Roman market by Panaetius of Rhodes (2nd century BC), and developed by his compatriot Poseidonius in the 1st century BC. Poseidonius lies behind the books on natural science, *Naturales quaestiones*, where lofty generalities on the investigation of nature are offset by a jejune exposition of the facts. Of the *Consolationes*, *Ad Marciam* consoles a lady on the loss of a son; *Ad Helviam matrem*, Seneca's mother on his exile; *Ad Polybium*, the powerful freedman Polybius on the loss of a son but with a sycophantic plea for recall from Corsica. The *De ira* deals at length with the passion of anger, its consequences, and control. The *De clementia*, an exhortatory address to Nero, commends mercy as the sovereign quality for a Roman emperor. *De tranquillitate animi*, *De constantia sapientis*, *De vita beata*, *De otio*, consider various aspects of the life and qualities of the Stoic wise man. *De beneficiis* is a diffuse treatment of benefits as seen by giver and recipient. *De brevitate vitae* demonstrates that our human span is long enough if time is properly employed—which it seldom is. Best written and most compelling are the *Epistulae morales*, addressed to Lucilius. Those 124 brilliant essays treat a range of moral problems not easily reduced to a single formula.

Of the 10 "Senecan" tragedies, *Octavia* is certainly, and *Hercules Oetaeus* is probably, spurious. The others handle familiar Greek tragic themes, with some originality of detail. Attempts to arrange them as a schematic treatment of Stoic "vices" seem too subtle. Intended for playreadings rather than public presentation, the pitch is a high monotone, emphasizing the lurid and the supernatural. There are impressive set speeches and choral passages; but the characters are static, and they rant. The sole representatives of classical tragedy known to the Renaissance world, these plays had a great influence, notably in England. Shakespeare's *Titus Andronicus*, John Webster's *The Duchess of Malfi*, and Cyril Tourneur's *Revengers Tragaedie*, with their ghosts, witches, cruel tyrants, and dominant theme of vengeance, are the progeny of Seneca's tragedies.

Stature and influence

Hostile propaganda pursued Seneca's memory. Quintilian, 1st-century rhetorician, criticized his educational influence; Tacitus was ambivalent on Seneca's place in history. But his views on monarchy and its duties contributed to the humane and liberal temper of the age of the Antonines (Antoninus Pius, Marcus Aurelius, and Commodus; AD 138–192). Meanwhile, the spread of Stoicism kept his philosophy alive: new horizons opened when it was found to have Christian affinities. There was a belief that he knew St. Paul, and a spurious collection of letters to substantiate it. Studied by Augustine and Jerome, he consoled Boethius in prison. His thought was a component of the Latin culture of the Middle Ages, often filtered through anthologies. Known to Dante, Chaucer, and Petrarch, his moral treatises were edited by Erasmus; the first complete English translation appeared in 1614. In the 16th to 18th centuries Senecan prose, in content and style, served the vernacular literatures as a model for essays, sermons, and moralizing. Calvin, Montaigne, and Rousseau are instances. As the first of "Spanish" thinkers, his influence in Spain was always powerful. Nineteenth-century specialization brought him under fire from philosophers, scientists, historians, and students of literature. But recent scholarly work and the interest aroused by the bimillenary commemorations of his death in Spain in 1965 suggest that a Senecan revival may be under way.

MAJOR WORKS

PHILOSOPHICAL TREATISES: *Dialogi* (Eng. trans., "Loeb Series," 2 vol., 1917) comprising: *Ad Marciam de consolatione* (AD 40; *Consolation to Marcia*); *Ad Helviam matrem de consolatione* (c. AD 42; *Consolation to Helvia*); *Ad Polybium de consolatione* (c. AD 42; *Consolation to Polybius*); *De providentia* (?AD 41–42; *On Providence*); *De constantia sapientis* (after AD 47; *On the Constancy of the Wise Man*); *De ira* (after AD 42; *On Anger*); *De otio* (?AD 63–65; *On Leisure*); *De tranquillitate animi* (?AD 63–65; *On Tranquillity of Mind*); *De brevitate vitae* (?AD 55; *On the Shortness of Life*); *De clementia* (AD 55–56; *On Mercy*); *De vita beata* (? c. AD 58–59; *On the Happy Life*); *De beneficiis* (after AD 56; *On Benefits*). *Epistulae morales ad Lucilium* (AD 63–65; Eng. trans. by R.M. Gummere, "Loeb Series," 3 vol., 1917–25); *Naturales quaestiones* (AD 63–65; Eng. trans. by A. Geikie and J. Clarke, 1910).

SATIRE: *Apocolocyntosis divi Claudii* (c. AD 54; *The Pumpkinification of Claudius*, 1951).

TRAGEDIES: all dates unknown—*Phaedra; Troades; Thyestes; Phoenissae; Medea; Oedipus; Agamemnon; Hercules furens; Hercules Oetaeus* (? not Senecan); *Octavia* (not Senecan)—Eng. trans. by F.J. Miller, *Seneca's Tragedies*, "Loeb Series," 2 vol., 1917.

BIBLIOGRAPHY

Texts and commentaries: (*Dialogi*): A. BOURGERY and R. WALTZ, 4 vol. (1922–42). (*Epistulae morales*): L.D. REYNOLDS, 2 vol. (1965), an excellent edition. (*Naturales quaestiones*): P. OLTRAMARE, 2 vol. (1929).

General works: No full-length definitive study of Seneca exists in English. C.W. MENDELL, *Our Seneca* (1941), is good on Seneca the writer. R. WALTZ, *Vie de Sénèque* (1909); and P. GRIMAL, *Sénèque* (1948), are also useful. A.L. MOTTO, *Seneca Sourcebook* (1970), is a guide to Seneca's thought as reflected in his extant prose works; F.L. LUCAS, *Seneca and Elizabethan Tragedy* (1922), is a good introduction to the subject, although written before recent advances in Senecan studies. Comprehensive surveys of recent scholarship include A.L. MOTTO in *Classical World*, 53:13–18, 37–48, 70–71 (1960), addenda, 54:111–112 (1961), and 74:147–158, 177–191 (1971), on the prose works; and M. COFFEY in *Lustrum*, 2:113–186 (1957), on the tragedies.

(D.R.D.)

Senegal

Situated at the western extremity of Africa's tropical zone, the Republic of Senegal (République du Sénégal) has an area of 78,684 square miles (203,793 square kilometres), and a population of about 3,755,000 people. It is bounded to the north and to the northeast by the Sénégal River, which separates it from Mauritania; to the east by the Falémé, a tributary of the Sénégal River, which separates it from the Mali; to the south by Guinea and Portuguese Guinea (Guinea Bissau); and to the west by the Atlantic Ocean. The Gambia constitutes a finger of territory 20 miles wide and 200 miles long that thrusts from the coast eastward deep into Senegal.

Senegal—which gained its independence in 1960, first as part of the short-lived Mali Federation and then as a sovereign state in its own right—is among the principal peanut- (groundnut-) producing countries of the world; its light soils and its climate are particularly well suited to this crop. While food crops such as millet are important, the entire economy of Senegal in fact depends literally on its peanut exports. The economy itself is operated in the spirit of "African socialism" of which the Senegalese government is one of the foremost champions; while it is a planned economy, the moderate controls to which it is subjected are applied in an indicative rather than an authoritarian manner. Private investors, whether foreign or Senegalese nationals, are encouraged to establish new enterprises; an investment code grants tax exemptions and permits the withdrawal of profits. Nationalization has been avoided except for the marketing of agricultural products, for which the state has created the Office de Commercialisation Agricole (Agricultural Marketing Board), which conducts marketing operations for the international business companies active in the country. The economic life of Senegal is characterized by its adherence to the franc currency zone, as a result of which the country benefits from French financial support. French is the official language.

Politically, Senegal is a parliamentary democracy, operating under a decentralized presidential regime which in theory permits a multiparty system, but, in fact, encourages the development of a one-party system within which group interests as well as individual interests may find expression. The principal role in political life is played by the president of the republic, in cooperation with a prime minister nominated by him, and a national assembly elected by universal suffrage.

Senghor's leadership

The liberal regime established in Senegal is based on a spirit of participation and of dialogue, associated with a conception of the black African heritage known as *négritude*—a conception which has been expounded by Léopold Sédar Senghor (*q.v.*), a Senegalese poet who is president of the republic. Senegal itself has been defined as a land of *négritude*—that is to say, the home of a historic ideology of cultural liberation and of political independence. (For coverage of associated physical features see GAMBIA RIVER; and SENEGAL RIVER; for coverage of the capital city, see DAKAR; for historical aspects, see WEST AFRICA, HISTORY OF.)

THE LANDSCAPE

Relief. Senegal is a flat country, lying in the depression known as the Senegal-Mauritanian Basin. Altitudes of more than about 330 feet are found only at Cap Vert and in the southeast of the country. The country as a whole falls into three structural divisions. These are: first, Cap Vert, which forms the western extremity and consists of a grouping of small plateaus made of hard rock of volcanic origin; second, the southeastern and the eastern parts of the country that consist of the fringes of ancient massifs (mountain masses) contiguous with those buttressing the massif of Fouta Djallon on the Guinea frontier, with the highest point reaching an altitude of 1,640 feet; third, an immense but shallow basin lying between Cap Vert to the west and the edges of the massif to the east.

Washed by the Canary Current, the Atlantic coast of Senegal is sandy and surf beaten. Like the rest of the country, it is low except for the Presqu'île du Cap Vert, which represents the westernmost point of the African continent and which shelters Dakar (*q.v.*), the finest port in Africa. To the south of Cap Vert the surf on the coast is less heavy. To the south of the Saloum River mouth, the coast consists of rias (drowned valleys) and is increasingly fringed with mangroves.

Drainage and soils. The country is drained by the Sénégal, Saloum, Gambie (Gambia), and Casamance rivers, all of which are subjected to a climatic regime characterized by a dry season and a rainy season. Of these rivers, the Sénégal (*q.v.*), which rises in the Fouta Djallon highlands and was for long the main route providing access to the interior, is the most important. After traversing the old massifs over the Guina and Félou waterfalls, the river rapidly drops downward. At Dagana it forms the so-called False Delta, which supplies Lac de Guiers on

The False Delta

the left bank. At the head of the delta is Richard-Toll (the Garden of Richard), named for a 19th-century French nursery gardener. The slope of the land is so gentle on this stretch of the river that at low water, salty seawater flows about 125 miles upstream. The island on which the town of Saint-Louis stands, at the mouth of the river, is situated about 300 yards from the sea in the False Delta whose true mouth lies 10 miles to the south.

Despite its apparent uniformity, Senegal contains a great diversity of soils. These fall generally into two types —the valley soils and those found elsewhere.

The valley soils. The soils of the Sénégal and Saloum river valleys, in their middle courses, are alluvial and consist of sandy limes or clays. Near the river mouths the soils are salty and favourable for grazing. Similar condi-

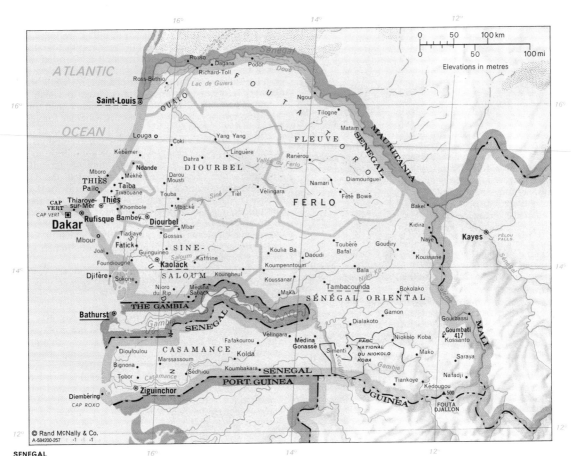

SENEGAL

tions are associated with the Gambie and Casamance rivers, except that near their mouths the banks are muddy, while their upper courses have sandy clay soils.

Other soils. Many different types of soils are found in the various regions. In the northwest the soils are ochre-coloured and light, consisting of sands combined with iron oxide. These soils, called "Dior soils," constitute the wealth of Senegal; the dunes they form are highly favourable to peanut cultivation, while the soils between the dunes are suitable for other food crops, such as sorghum. In the southwest the plateau soils are sandy clays, frequently laterized (leached into red residual iron-bearing soils). In the centre and the south the country is covered by a layer of laterite hidden under a thin covering of sand. These soils afford only sparse grazing during the rainy season. In Casamance heavily leached clay soils with a high iron content predominate. Whether they are deep, as in western Casamance, or shallow, as in the southeast of the region, they are suitable for cultivation.

Climate. The Senegalese climate is conditioned by two general factors: first, the tropical latitude and second, the movement of air masses that in turn are governed by anticyclones over the Azores and St. Helena—regions of high pressure over northern Africa and regions of low pressure near the Equator. The prevailing winds fall into two categories—those which are dry and those which bring rains.

The dry winds consist of the trade winds—both from the continent and from the sea—and the harmattan; they bring no rains at all, apart from a very light precipitation which, to the Wolof people of Senegal, is known as the "Heug." The rain-bearing winds blow from the west-northwest, resulting from the high-pressure system centred on St. Helena in the southern Atlantic. In summer these monsoon winds bring rains which become progressively lighter towards the north of the country.

From the combination of these various factors, three principal climates may be distinguished, each of them associated with a characteristic type of vegetation.

The coastal (Canarian) climate. This climate occurs along a coastal strip about ten miles wide running from Saint-Louis to Dakar. Its winters are cool, with minimum temperatures reaching about 63° F (17° C) in January, and maximum temperatures in May not exceeding 81° F (27°C). The rains begin in June, reach their height in August, and cease in October. The average rainfall is about 20 inches.

The Sahelian climate. This occurs in a zone bounded to the north by the Sénégal River and to the south by a line running from Thiès (a town on Cap Vert) to Kayes in the neighbouring country of Mali. The month of January is very cool, especially in the mornings before sunrise, when the temperature drops to about 57° F (14° C); maximum temperatures rise higher than 95° F (35° C). In May, minimum temperatures do not fall below about 72° F (22° C), while maximums often rise above 104° F (40° C). The dry season is quite distinct, and lasts from November to May. Certain places, such as Podor and Matam, are particularly noted for their dryness and for the heat of the sun. Between July and October the rainfall averages about 14 inches, moderating the temperature somewhat. Maximum temperatures at this season amount to about 95° F (35° C).

The Sudanic climate. This occurs in the remainder of Senegal. Regional nuances are in evidence. Thus, from north to south three subdivisions may be recognized, each characterized by the amount of average annual rainfall. First, in the Kaolack-Tambacounda subdivision, rainfall averages between 29 and 39 inches, occurring on about 60 days between June and October. Cultivation without irrigation is possible. Second, in the Gambian region, the rainfall frequently amounts to 50 inches, resulting in the growth of a continuous belt of light forest and patches of herbaceous undergrowth. Third, in the Casamance region, rainfall everywhere exceeds 50 inches, falling on 90 days of the year. The forest is dense and green, and is continuous, without undergrowth. Oil palms, mangroves, and rice fields are characteristic of this climate zone. The Sudanic climate in general is very hot, humid, and un-

comfortable. The town of Kaolack, for example, has a heavy climate that is rendered more oppressive by salt wind.

Animal life. While it is true that large mammals have disappeared from the western part of the country, due to human settlement, such animals as elephants, antelopes, lions, panthers, cheetahs, and jackals may still be encountered in the interior. Herds of warthogs abound in the marshes, especially those of the False Delta. Hares are ubiquitous, and monkeys of all types congregate in noisy bands, above all in the upper Gambia and upper Casamance river valleys. Among the great numbers of birds the quelea, or "millet eater," which is destructive of crops, may particularly be noted, as well as the partridge and the guinea fowl. Reptiles are numerous, and include boa constrictors, pythons, cobras, and venomous snakes. Crocodiles, hippopotamuses, and turtles are to be found in the rivers. The rivers and the coastal waters are rich in fish and crustaceans.

Traditional regions. While such physical factors as geology, soil, climate, and vegetation have resulted in regional differentiation, man has also been a determining factor in the delimitation of different regions, each marked by a traditional type of human settlement. Thus from north to south five principal traditional regions may be distinguished.

The Ferlo region. This is the central region of Senegal; very extensive, it is distinguished by its semidesert aspect and by the poverty of its soils. Vegetation appears only in the south, the north consisting of the Sahelian type of savanna parkland (an intermediate zone between the Sahara and the savanna proper); it affords light grazing for the flocks of nomadic Fulan (Peul) pastoralists.

Fouta–Toro. This region is based upon the Sénégal River, extending approximately from Bakel in the east to Dagana in the north and consisting of a strip of territory that is relatively densely inhabited. Cultivated lands, which are watered by the river and its tributaries in the dry season, are of importance thanks to highly developed agricultural and pastoral use of the soils and vegetation. Most of the region is inhabited by Tukulor people. Fouta–Toro is bounded to the west by the False Delta, also known as the Oualo, which is peopled by the Wolof, who cultivate millet and carry on stock raising, employing Fulani shepherds.

The Dianbour, Cayor, Djolof, and Baol region. This is a diverse area situated between the Ferlo region and the Atlantic, and extending from the Oualo in the north to Cap Vert in the south. The soils are sandy, the winters cool, and peanuts are the primary crop. The population is as diverse as the region itself and includes Wolofs in the north, Serer in the Thiès region, and Lebu on Cap Vert.

The Sudan region. This vast region is bounded by Cap Vert to the northeast, the Ferlo to the north, and the lower Casamance Valley to the southwest. It is composed of the following subregions—The "Little Coast", the Sine-Saloum *région*, Rip, Yacine, Niani, Boundou, Fouladou and the valleys of the Gambia and upper Casamance rivers. In general, the region benefits from ample rainfall which becomes abundant towards the south. The clayey soil is suitable for agriculture, despite the lateritic crust which appears intermittently. The region, as a result, is relatively densely peopled. The estuaries are muddy and salty, with marshy saline depressions known as *tannes* occurring occasionally. The region as a whole is inhabited by a very diverse population composed of all the ethnic groups living in Senegal; the majority are, however, Malinke (Mandingo).

The lower Casamance region. This is a small but strongly characterized region. It is covered by dense vegetation of the Guinean type. Mangroves, oil palms, and raffia palms predominate. The rainy climate favours the cultivation of rice, which has long been a specialty in this part of the country.

Rural settlement. The great majority of the Senegalese population lives in the countryside. There are about 13,000 villages, each with an average population of more than 200 persons. Usually each village has a shaded public gathering place, a mosque, and a water source, whether

Rainfall in the Sudanic area

a well, a spring, or a small stream. The village is administered by a chief who is either traditionally nominated or appointed by the government. Religious life is directed either by a person literate in Arabic, called a marabout, or by a leading sorcerer. Various types of village may be distinguished, according to ethnic characteristics.

The Wolof village. Whether it is situated in the western Ferlo or the Cayor regions, the Wolof village is small, being inhabited by about a hundred farmers. The houses are built of locally obtained materials. Each village may easily be moved from place to place, as the topography provides no natural obstacles to this. Harvests are kept in straw granaries, located far from the compounds for fear of fires. In the eastern Saloum region, the Wolof village is surrounded by three concentric zones of vegetation. The first of these—the inner zone—consists of fields and vegetable gardens and is known as the Tol-keur (literally "kitchen garden"). The second circle consists of land that has been exhausted, except for peanut cultivation, and it is known as the Diatte. The third, the farthest from the village, is the Gor, in which cereal crops are cultivated.

The Malinke village. The typical village of the Sudanic region of Casamance consists of a Malinke agglomeration; it is a heritage from the epoch when the Sudanic peoples conquered the region. Each village has between 200 and 300 inhabitants living in enclosed compounds and crowded together in geometrically aligned rectangular huts. Agriculture and stock raising are the principal activities. The chief of each village is generally a marabout, conservative in his ways.

The Serer village. This differs from the Wolof and Malinke village because of its family compounds, called M'Binds, being loosely dispersed; each M'Bind is autonomous. On the islands at the mouth of the Saloum River, the houses of the Serer Niominke people are solidly built and trim. The granary is located in the compound.

The Dyola village. These are substantial rural agglomerations with populations of up to 5,000 people or more. One of the characteristics of this type of village is that it is usually built on the edge of a plateau, or on ground which overlooks the rice fields with which Dyola life is associated. As in the Serer villages, the compounds are not grouped in any distinguishable organization hierarchy. The houses are the best built and the most permanent among the different types of village dwellings to be found. On occasion they constitute veritable fortifications, for example, in the Thionck-Essyl and Oussouye regions; the villages of the Essyl region are often equipped with a rainwater tank. The Dyola and Serer villages have no chiefs with authority or prestige comparable to those of the Wolof or Malinke villages.

Urban settlement. The town of Saint-Louis was founded in 1633, and Dakar in 1857; other towns were, however, more recently founded. All the towns are of colonial origin. Dakar, as was formerly Saint-Louis, is the political and administrative capital. The other towns usually owe their foundation to the peanut trade, for which they were collection points which later developed into urban centres. These towns were often stops along the railroad lines, as at Thiès, Tivaouane, Mékhé, and Louga (between Dakar and Saint-Louis), or Khombole, Bambey, Diourbel, Gossas, Kaffrine, and Koungheul (between Thiès and Kayes, Mali). Certain ports also became towns: among these are Kaolack, Foundiougne, and Fatick (on the Sine-Saloum rivers), and Ziguinchor, Sédhiou, and Kolda (on the Casamance River). With the exception of Dakar, Saint-Louis, Rufisque, Thiès, and Kaolack, these towns have not as yet emerged, as it were, from their rural cocoons. Furthermore, all of the towns—including Saint-Louis, Rufisque, and Gorée, all of which had great importance in the past—are today dependent upon Dakar, which has become the focus of attraction for the whole of Senegal.

Apart from the division of the countryside into traditional regions, one may observe that the best lands in Senegal are concentrated in the west and in the river valleys. The remainder of the land becomes increasingly poor and less and less settled as one continues toward the north or toward the east.

PEOPLE AND POPULATION

Linguistic, ethnic, and religious groups. The scientific study of languages in Senegal has not progressed far enough for even a rough type of classification to be attempted. Specialists nevertheless recognize certain imprecise groupings. These are: (a) the Atlantic (West Atlantic) group, including Wolof, Lebu, Serer, Tenda, and Diola; (b) Fulfulde, the Fulani (Peul) language, which also shares some of the characteristics of the Atlantic group; Fulfulde possesses numerous linguistic particularities, and has a complex grammar; and (c) the Mande group, including Bambara, Diula, Malinke, and Soninke (Sarakole). There are seven major ethnic and religious groups, and a number of other less significant groups.

The major groups are located in the Sahel and savanna regions which formerly supported the ancient empires of the western Sudan, such as Ghana, Mali, and Songhai. Until recently the societies composing this grouping were strictly hierarchical in organization, consisting of the princely caste, the nobility, the free men, the lower castes, and finally the slaves. The grouping consists of the following peoples:

The Wolof. Numbering 1,200,000 people, the Wolof represent about one third of the total population. Their language is the most widely used in the republic. The Wolof predominate in the sandy western region. In the Cayor district they are initiates of the Tijānī Muslim brotherhood; the other brotherhoood, that of the Murīdīs, is very influential, and its expansion towards the southern part of the country is concurrent with that of peanut cultivation. Members of the Murīdīs brotherhood, strong adherents of Islām, are primarily agriculturalists.

The Serer. Numbering about 600,000, the Serer are densely settled in the western part of the southern Ferlo region. They are experienced farmers, practicing both cultivation and cattle raising. Originally animist by religion, they are now becoming increasingly either Muslim or Catholic.

The Fulani. Also known as the Peuls, Foulah, Fulbe, and Fellata, this group numbers about 500,000; distributed throughout Senegal, the Fulani are particularly found in the Ferlo, the Upper Casamance, and Oualo regions, where their settlements are substantial. Characteristically nomadic pastoralists, many of them have today become settled agriculturalists, above all in the Fouta-Toro region and on the Senegal–Guinea border. They are Muslim.

The Tukulor. Numbering 350,000, the Tukulor (or Toucouleur) are often hard to distinguish from either the Wolof or the Fulani, with both of whom they have often intermarried. The name Tukulor (or Toucouleur) is a distortion of the name of the ancient realm of Tekrour. The Tukulor live primarily in the middle course of the Sénégal River Valley, in the Senegalese part of the Fouta region, and between Bakel and Dagana. They are also found in dispersed groups living on the Gambie and Saloum rivers. They were the first Senegalese people to become Muslim, having accepted Islām probably in the 11th century; many of them are literate in Arabic. Primarily farmers, they are increasingly migrating to the towns, particularly to Dakar and Saint-Louis.

The Dyola. Numbering between 200,000 and 250,000, the Dyola occupy the Lower Casamance Valley and the southwest of the Gambie Valley. They are skilled farmers, specializing in rice growing, but turning more and more to the cultivation of peanuts and millet as the distance from the sea increases. In the Fogni district they are Muslim, but the majority remain animist. Some few have accepted Christianity.

The Malinke. The Malinke (or Mandingo) came originally from the Niger River Valley, and have spread out into various regions of Senegal, especially into the Gambie, Upper Casamance, and Saloum river valleys. Farmers and energetic traders, they number about 200,000; they are Muslim.

The Sarakole, or Soninke. This is a minority group, numbering less than 65,000, and is of Berber descent. They represent an extension into Senegal of the Malinke families of Mali. They are in the process of abandoning

(marginal notes)
Tribal villages

Major towns

an unfruitful agricultural terrain in order to migrate towards the towns where they often become small traders. They are Muslim.

The numerically less significant Senegalese comprise such peoples as the Maures, who live especially in the north of the country where they are stock raisers or traders; the Lebu of Cap Vert, who are fishermen and often wealthy landowners; and the Bassari, an ancient people who are found in the rocky highlands of Fouta Djallon.

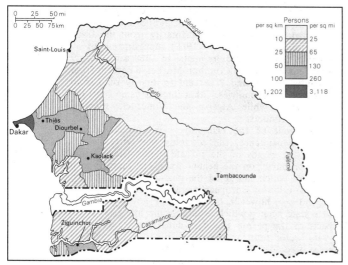

Population density of Senegal.

Demography. The population of Senegal consists of 3,755,000 people with an average population distribution of about 50 people per square mile. The birthrate is 4.6 percent, and the death rate 2.3 percent, giving a rate of increase of 2.4 percent a year.

Migration to the towns as well as to the peanut-growing lands of the west is taking place at a pace that is assuming disturbing proportions. The rural zones which are becoming depopulated by migration are the Fleuve (River) *région* in the north, the Sénégal Oriental (Eastern Senegal) *région* in the southeast, and the Casamance *région* in the southwest. The towns and peanut plantations are also attracting migrants from the neighbouring countries of Mali and Guinea, but in numbers that are now becoming insignificant. Other groups of foreigners include Mauritanians, Syrians (or Lebanese), and Europeans, who all live in the towns. The pattern of internal migration has resulted in the highest concentration of population occurring in the Cap Vert *région*, where it amounts to over 3,000 persons per square mile. In the Thiès *région* the concentration is 186 persons per square mile; the proportion drops to about 61 persons per square mile in the Sine-Saloum, Diourbel and Casamance *régions*, while in the rest of the country the population distribution is 13 persons per square mile. All of this means that about two-thirds of the country's population lives west of a line running north to south from Saint-Louis through Louga to Linguère and to Koumpenntoum near the Gambia frontier, an area comprising about one quarter of Senegal's territory.

The population as a whole is young, with 43 percent being less than 15 years old, 51 percent being between the ages of 15 and 59, and 6 percent being 60 years old or older. The major cause for concern lies in the drift towards the towns, which is creating an increasingly acute administrative problem. In Dakar, for example, the population is increasing at a rate of from 6 to 7 percent a year, which if maintained will result in the population of the city doubling every 12 years.

Coastal population (margin note)

THE NATIONAL ECONOMY

Resources. The economy is essentially agricultural and, as mentioned, is primarily based upon the peanut crop. The known mineral resources are only of relative importance, consisting of phosphates of lime, located at Taïba near Tivaouane, about 60 miles north of Dakar,

Senegal, Area and Population				
	area		population	
	sq mi	sq km	1960–61 census	1970 estimate
Régions				
Cap Vert	212	550	444,000	649,000
Casamance	10,946	28,350	530,000	601,000
Diourbel	12,952	33,547	503,000	607,000
Fleuve	16,988	44,000	345,000	372,000
Sénégal Oriental	25,792	66,800	151,000	227,000
Sine-Saloum	9,245	23,945	727,000	772,000
Thiès	2,549	6,601	410,000	527,000
Total Senegal	78,684	203,793	3,110,000	3,755,000
Source: Official government figures.				

with reserves estimated at 115,000,000 tons; aluminum phosphates at Palo Dial, near Thiès, with reserves estimated at 100,000,000 tons; titanium-bearing sand deposits at Djifère, on the shores of Sangomare Bay, which contain ilmenite (the principal ore of titanium, an element used in making steel), zircon (the chief ore of zirconium, also used in steel metallurgy), and rutile (titanium dioxide, used to coat welding rods); salt from the saltworks of Kaolack, which have a considerable potential production. Prospecting for petroleum deposits has so far been without result.

Biological resources include 8,696,064 acres of forest, much of which is located in the Casamance area; these do not, however, yield any commercial products. Production of gum arabic, which is obtained from acacia trees elsewhere in the country, has declined until it is only of secondary significance. The herbaceous vegetation nevertheless permits a relatively important amount of stock raising. By improving the grazing land available, Senegal has the potential to increase the numbers of its cattle herds to a considerable extent.

The waters off Senegal, particularly those at some distance from the shore, are rich in schools of fish, although the coastal waters are also known for their large variety of fish; in this respect Senegal is better endowed than most other tropical countries on the Atlantic seaboard.

The production of cheaper electricity depends on the construction of the Guina hydroelectric project on the Sénégal River. In the early 1970s electricity is being produced at thermal generating centres which are located at Dakar.

Sources of national income. *Agriculture.* Agriculture occupies at least 75 percent of the economically active population, and provides the basis for industry as well. Although a certain balance between the raising of livestock and peanut cultivation is maintained, it is the peanut production which earns the foreign exchange that the country needs.

Importance of the peanut crop (margin note)

The main problem affecting national agriculture is the dependence upon the peanut crop, and the saying "When peanuts do well we all do well" is still valid. In 1970, when for various reasons production dropped to 600,000 tons, Senegal found itself on the verge of economic catastrophe. About 2,942,000 acres are devoted to peanut cultivation, producing an annual yield of about 1,000,000 tons. Each year the sale of peanut crop results in much economic activity throughout Senegal; the resulting wealth has favoured the development of the smaller towns. The traffic in peanuts has also resulted in the establishment of the river ports of Kaolack, Foundiougne, Fatick, Sédhiou, and Kolda. Much of the activity at Dakar itself is due to the peanut trade.

Apart from peanuts, which are an export crop, a number of food crops are also grown. About 2,559,000 acres are devoted to sorghum and pennisetum (a genus of Old World grasses), resulting in an annual production of about 630,000 tons of grain. Rice is cultivated both in naturally wet areas and by irrigation. Its large-scale cultivation is restricted to Casamance, to the Sénégal River Valley, and to the Sine-Saloum area. About 207,000 acres are used for rice, of which 15,000 acres are used for experimental purposes at Richard-Toll. A further 74,000 acres are being brought into cultivation between Dagana and Saint-Louis. More than 150,000 tons are now produced annually. In addition, about 50,000 tons of maize, 175,000 tons of cassava (manioc), 15,000 tons of beans, and 25,000 tons of sweet potatoes are grown each year.

Livestock. The climate and the savanna type of vegetation encourage the raising of livestock, which is carried on in almost all regions, but is especially characteristic of the north. In 1970 the cattle population was estimated to amount to more than 2,600,000 head. There were also about 2,950,000 sheep and goats, 192,000 horses, 170,000 donkeys, 30,000 camels, and about 93,000 pigs. Stock raising is not a major source of income for the farmer; in addition to the difficulty of improving livestock strains, the fact that stock raising is often conducted for reasons of prestige alone provides an economic drawback.

Fishing. About 20,000 people, possessing about 5,000 canoes, engage in full-time fishing. While many fish are obtained from the rivers, the greater part of the catch is obtained from the sea. Due to the modernization of fishing techniques annual production, which amounted to only about 83,000 tons in 1957, had risen to 189,000 tons by 1970. A fleet of 26 trawlers and more than 60 tuna-fishing boats are now in service.

Mineral production. Of secondary significance in the national economy, mineral production, as already mentioned, consists of phosphate of lime, of which 998,000 tons were obtained in 1970, nine-tenths of which was for export; phosphate of aluminum from Pallo, of which 130,000 tons were produced in 1970; and lesser amounts of ilmenite, zircon, and rutile.

Industry. Industrial production in Senegal is more developed than in most West African countries and accounts for 15 percent of the total national revenue. Both processing and handicraft industries are established. About 90 percent of the processing industry is located in the Cap Vert *région* where six oil processing plants process 500,000 tons of peanuts a year. Two of these plants are established in Dakar, the remaining four being in the towns of Rufisque, Kaolack, Diourbel, and Ziguinchor. In addition, there are six fish canneries, one shoe factory with an output of 500,000 pairs of shoes a year, and one cement manufacturing plant with an output of 240,000 tons of cement a year. Both the shoe factory and the cement plant are located at Rufisque. Other industries, all of which are located in Dakar, include two flour mills, a textile plant, a sugar refinery, a tobacco factory, and a brewery, in addition to a naval shipyard, chemical plants, and an automobile assembly plant.

About 40,000 craftsmen are engaged in traditional handicrafts; the more skilled among them are established at Dakar and Saint-Louis.

There are altogether about 350 industrial enterprises employing 29,000 wage earners. It has been estimated that the value of industrial production rose by 75 percent between 1962 and 1967.

Energy. About 90 percent of energy is produced in Dakar, and is distributed through Saint-Louis via Thiès, Tivaouane, Mékhé, Louga, and other towns along the coastal strip. Kaolack and Mbour are also supplied from Dakar.

Role of Senegal as a West African financial centre

Financial services. In finance, Senegal has benefited from the fact that in colonial times it was the principal territory of the administrative grouping known as French West Africa. The Senegalese currency is the franc CFA, the franc issued by the Communauté Financière Africaine. (CFA Fr. 277.71 = $1.00 U.S.; CFA Fr. 666.50 = £1 sterling, on December 1, 1970.) It has a value of 50 francs CFA to the French franc. Goods entering the country from the franc zone are liable to a simple fiscal tax; those from the Common Market countries enjoy a preferential tariff. There are a considerable number of banks offering financial services. Currency is issued by the Banque Centrale des États de l'Afrique de l'Ouest, which is the agency of the West African Monetary Union to which Senegal belongs, and which includes all French-speaking West African territories with the exception of Guinea. Other financial institutions include the Société Immobilière du Cap Vert (a building society); the Banque Nationale de Dévelopement du Sénégal; the Union Sénégalaise de Banque; and three private banks.

Foreign trade. The value of imports is usually greater than the value of exports. In 1971, for example, imports were valued at $218,000,000, and exports at $125,000,000. The principal imports are rice, sugar, petroleum products, machinery, textiles, and chemicals. The principal exports are peanuts and peanut products (representing almost 50 percent of the total), phosphates, leather, and canned fish. About 75 percent of Senegal's exports go to the franc zone, in which France is the principal trading partner. A fraction of exports go to Guinea, Cameroon, the Common Market countries (4 percent of the total), the sterling bloc, the Scandinavian countries, and Japan. Imports are also primarily from the franc zone, with France alone (in 1969) supplying about 40 percent of Senegal's requirements. In 1969 a further 19 percent came from the Common Market, 6 percent from the United States, and 7 percent (primarily rice) from Southeast Asian countries. Other imports came from the sterling zone, while Algeria and Venezuela supplied petroleum products.

Management of the economy. *The private sector.* Before independence, the economy was virtually entirely in the hands of the private sector. Since it depended primarily on the peanut trade, the large French companies which marketed the peanuts also controlled the importation of European manufactured goods. After independence, however, the Senegalese government created a state agency which is responsible for virtually all aspects of the peanut trade; in consequence, while the private sector remains important in the economy as a whole, it receives its impulse from the state. An investment code is composed of various guarantees and long-term tax concessions, as a result of which investment has been attracted from many quarters.

In 1968 there were almost 3,000 private enterprises in Senegal, of which more than half were in Dakar. These enterprises employed 60,000 persons. Transportation, services, commerce, and industry are in general the responsibility of the private sector.

The public sector. The public sector is of primary importance in a country in which, for historic reasons, a middle class in the western sense has never existed. The intervention of the state, moreover, is not a recent phenomenon; already in existence during the colonial era, it has been given a new form since independence by the creation of the Office de Commercialisation Agricole (Agricultural Marketing Board). Apart from buying and selling peanuts, rice, and millet, the board also sells fertilizer, seed, tools, and equipment, and is thus the primary instrument used by the state in giving form to its policy of "African socialism." Between 30,000 and 40,000 persons are employed by the public sector.

The Agricultural Marketing Board

Taxation. As already mentioned, the government encourages investment by granting tax benefits. Most governmental revenue is obtained from indirect taxes, which take the form of local taxes on alcoholic beverages, gasoline, tobacco, firearms, automobiles, and commerce. Direct taxation consists of land taxes, professional licenses, and personal taxes, such as taxes on profits, and income taxes.

Trade unions. Since the end of World War II, Senegalese trade unionism has undergone many mutations. Until 1955 French-speaking African workers in general belonged to the French trade-union movement. In that year, however, they broke away to create the Union Générale des Travailleurs d'Afrique Noire, of which the Senegalese affiliate was the Union Nationale des Travailleurs Sénégalais. This remained the only Senegalese union until the occurrence of disturbances in May and June 1968 which began at the University of Dakar, and in which the Union Nationale des Travailleurs Sénégalais actively participated. As a result, the Senegalese government and the governmental party, the Union Progressiste Sénégalaise, decided to associate trade unionism into the governmental structure; a new union, the Confédération Nationale des Travailleurs Sénégalais, subsequently split away from the Union Nationale des Travailleurs Sénégalais in 1969. The result has been a situation rare in Africa—the coexistence of two trade unions, one governmental, the other affiliated with the opposition. It would appear that the governmental union draws its strength from the rural areas, while the stronghold of the other remains in Dakar.

Economic policies. Economic life is characterized by two factors. The first is the division of the country into two regions—the western region which is wealthy and dynamic, and the remainder, and larger part, of the country which remains poor and economically stagnant, depending upon a subsistence economy. The second factor is the existence of a single crop economy, which leads to partial unemployment, an insufficient income, and a dependence on an unpredictable climate and the international market. The single crop economy consequently produces a "budget of poverty," resulting in savings so slim as to be virtually nonexistent, and a problematical degree of development that remains primarily dependent upon foreign aid.

In seeking to break this circle, the government introduced its first economic plan in 1958; its primary result was to create a consciousness of the need for further planning. The second plan, which covered the period from 1964 to 1969, sought to diversify agricultural production by encouraging the cultivation of other crops in addition to peanuts. Other steps taken were the creation of the Office de Commercialisation Agricole and the Africanization of personnel in banking and commerce.

Future problems. Among the many problems to be faced, three types may be cited—those relating to neighbouring countries, internal problems, and those related to the future. They may be enumerated as follows: (1) Problems with neighbouring countries: Senegal has experienced some problems with Mali, as well as with Guinea which is attempting to make its way outside the French-speaking community; with Mauritania which is attempting to do without the services of the port of Dakar; and above all with The Gambia, with whom a serious dispute exists. Senegal has experienced disappointment in the failure of the Senegambian Federation that was to have joined the two countries together; furthermore, as a result of this failure, the Senegalese economy has been injured by a great amount of smuggling. (2) Internal problems: The internal situation is still more acute. An inflammatory situation resulted from the abrupt drop in peanut production in the 1970 season, for which the government had forecast a harvest of 1,100,000 tons, whereas barely 600,000 tons were produced. The discrepancy appears to have been caused by the poor performance of the Office de Commercialisation Agricole. Despite a rise in peanut prices on the world market, the price paid to the Senegalese farmer dropped. Thus the 1,700,000 Senegalese peanut cultivators each received an average payment of no more than 134 French francs a head, a circumstance which caused widespread discontent. The situation was not improved by the fact that Senegalese nationalists began to press for the nationalization of the country's entire economic life. (3) The future: Faced with this situation, the government took various measures to safeguard the future. An African banker was appointed to the presidency of the Dakar Chamber of Commerce; the trade union movement was to some extent incorporated in the government with the creation of the Confédération Nationale des Travailleurs Sénégalais; reforms were instituted within the Office de Commercialisation Agricole; and a third four-year plan, covering the period from 1969 to 1973, was published which envisaged an increased agricultural production.

Relations with The Gambia

Transportation. *Road transport.* The development of a transport network has taken place primarily in the western part of the country, within the area bounded by Saint-Louis, Kaolack, and Dakar. Despite the fact that the remainder of the country is insufficiently developed, Senegal's transport system nevertheless compares favourably to that of many other West African countries. Most of the 5,800 miles of roads, of which 1,300 miles are paved, are concentrated in western Senegal.

Rail transport. The rail system includes a line from Saint-Louis to Dakar, with a branch line running from Louga inland to Linguère, and the line from Dakar to the Niger River, at Koulikoro, with two branch lines running from Diourbel to Touba and from Guinguinéo to Kaolack. The two main lines meet at the junction of Thiès, which is also the site of railroad repair workshops. The railroad system is suffering from the competition offered by road transport.

Ports. Senegal's four ports are Kaolack, Ziguinchor, Saint-Louis, and Dakar. Only Dakar (*q.v.*) is an international port, the other ports handling only local traffic. In addition to its facilities as a commercial port, Dakar is also in the process of creating a fishing harbor. It is, however, suffering from the competition presented by Nouadibou (Port-Étienne) in Mauritania, and by the port of Las Palmas in the Canary Islands, which is 50 percent cheaper in its port fees. Partly because of these factors, as well as because of the fact that Dakar has been affected by the granting of independence to the former French West African territories of which it was once the administrative capital, its traffic in both passengers and goods has diminished in recent years.

Dakar's role in international shipping

Air transport. The international airport of Dakar-Yoff at Daka is served by a number of airlines. Traffic has diminished slightly in recent years. Domestic services are provided by Air Afrique. There are local airports at Thiès, Saint-Louis, Ziguinchor, Kaolack, Rosso, Podor, Matam, Tambacounda, Kédougou, Sementi, and Kolda.

River transport. Since the end of the 19th century the rivers, of which the Sénégal River has always been the most important, have lost much of their importance. The Sénégal (*q.v.*) is navigable all year round from Saint-Louis to Podor by boats drawing about three feet of water. Other reaches are only navigable in the rainy season; Kayes in Mali, for example, can be reached only at that time. Despite the competition of the railroad, fleets of canoes still provide river transport. Activity on the Saloum River is due to the presence of the peanut port of Kaolack, while traffic on the Casamance is due to the port of Ziguinchor.

ADMINISTRATION AND SOCIAL CONDITIONS

The constitutional framework. Senegal now has its third constitution since independence. It was adopted by referendum on February 22, 1970, by a majority of 99.9 percent of the voters. Like its predecessors, it proclaims its attachment to fundamental human rights, respect for political, trade union, and religious freedoms, and also for individual and collective property rights. The Senegalese state is a social, democratic, and lay (noneccle-siastical) state, with French as its official language.

Government. *The central government.* The most important innovation in the new constitution is the establishment of a decentralized presidential regime. The president of the republic no longer rules directly, as in the past, but through the intermediary of a prime minister whom he nominates and who is responsible to him alone. The president retains special powers concerning justice, foreign policy, and defense. In other spheres his decisions must be approved by the ministers, who thus share the responsibility for presidential decisions. The president is elected for five years, and cannot serve more than two terms in office. Ministers are appointed by the president, who has the right to dissolve the government in case of a vote of censure in the national assembly. Judicial, executive, and legislative powers are separated. Deputies exercise a check on the executive power by means of commissions of inquiry, oral and written questions, and motions of censure.

The office of the president

Regional government. Senegal is divided into seven *régions*, 28 *départements* (provinces), and 94 *arrondissements* (districts). The *régions* and their capitals are the following: Cap Vert (Dakar), Thiès (Thiès), Diourbel (Diourbel), Fleuve (Saint-Louis), Sine-Saloum (Kaolack), Casamance (Ziguinchor), and Sénégal Oriental (Tambacounda). Each *région* is administered by a governor whose role is coordinative; he is assisted by two deputy governors, one dealing with administration, and the other with development. A regional assembly composed of general councillors deals with local taxation. In each *département* the prefect represents the republic, as well as the ministers; he sees to the implementation of laws, and supervises the local administrative units. In the *arrondissement* he is assisted by a local official (*chef d'arrondissement*). Several towns operate autonomously with elected municipal councils.

The political process. National Assembly and municipal council elections are held every five years, as also are presidential elections.

Political parties. Due to the fact that Senegalese played a pioneering role in the development of a modern political system in the territories of French West Africa, the political-party system is solidly entrenched, and the concept of a single-party system is generally held to be repugnant. A plethora of parties is not, however, considered desirable. Party political life, therefore, tends to be dominated by the governmental party, the Union Progressiste Sénégalais, which in 1963 succeeded in winning the adherence of two parties of the intellectual elite—the Bloc des Masses Sénégalaises and the Parti du Régroupement Africain, the principal opposition party—which then merged with it. Another party, the Parti Africain d'Independance has been outlawed since 1960. The Union Progressiste Sénégalais is committed to the socialization of the economy within the framework of "African socialism," and to the quest for African unity.

The participation of the citizen. At the beginning, political life was of concern only to a very limited élite consisting of the intellectuals, the traditional chiefs, and above all the inhabitants of four communes—Saint-Louis, Dakar, Rufisque, and Gorée—who had been French citizens since 1916. After World War II universal suffrage was introduced by stages, with the electorate increasing from 192,000 voters in 1946 to 890,000 in 1958. The number of voters has since grown larger; by the early 1970s it numbered about 1,500,000. Senegalese citizens today participate in the elections of the president, of the deputies to the national assembly, of regional councillors, and of municipal councillors.

The electorate

De facto political developments. In addition to participation in political party and trade union activities, other institutions also permit participation in the political process. These include societies for mutual assistance, which are organized both on a regional and on a village basis; youth associations; and religious groupings, which are most influential. The present disinclination of farmers to cooperate economically constitutes, in effect, a method of exerting political pressure on the government.

Justice. Justice is administered in the *départements* by justices of the peace and in the regions by courts of first instance. Criminal cases are judged by assize courts held at Saint-Louis, Kaolack, Ziguinchor, and Dakar. Dakar is the seat of the Court of Appeal.

The Army. The Senegalese army has 7,900 men; 2,000 of these are French (500 sailors, 300 airmen, and 1,200 soldiers) who are maintained in Senegal under a military agreement. The army as a whole includes infantry companies, parachutists, engineers, and communications units, as well as a Garde Républicaine, a constabulary, and naval and air force units. There are 200 officers. Supreme command of the army is vested in the president. Direct command is exercised by a single commander in charge of land, sea, and air forces acting under the orders of the prime minister. The Senegalese army has inherited from the French army a significant armament and a strong organization; it constitutes a fundamental element in Senegalese political life.

Administration. *Education.* In addition to continuing the educational expansion begun during the colonial period, Senegal has made particular efforts to increase school enrollment in rural areas. In primary education, school enrollment rose from 23 percent of the primary school age population in 1959 to 40 percent in 1969, and it is expected that the proportion will shortly reach 50 percent. There are 138 secondary schools, among which the Lycée Faidherbe at Saint-Louis and the Lycée Van Vollenhoven at Dakar are the most renowned and the oldest. Technical education is expanding; technical training is provided by a number of institutions, including l'École Nationale des Travaux Publics and the Lycée Technique Maurice Delafosse in Dakar, the Lycée Technique Andre Peytavin in Saint-Louis, and the Centre d'Enseignement de Pêche at Thiaroye-sur-Mer.

University education was begun in Dakar in 1957. The University of Dakar, now completed, had an enrollment of 3,380 students in 1970. Following disturbances in 1968, Senegal concluded an agreement with France on higher education by the terms of which the University of Dakar will become oriented to its African context. The Africanization of courses has meant that university degrees, with the exception of those gained in medicine, are no longer equivalent to those obtained in France.

The Africanization of university courses

Health services. Although still insufficient, Senegal nevertheless has a considerable range of medical facilities. They include 10 hospitals, 285 clinics, 44 maternity homes, and various services specializing in various diseases, such as tuberculosis, poliomyelitis, syphilis, and leprosy. The Senegalese Red Cross is also active, while environmental studies are conducted by the French Office de la Recherche Scientifique et Technique Outre-Mer in cooperation with the World Health Organization.

Housing. In rural areas dwellings, which are usually well constructed, are roofed with straw, while walls are either made of earth or straw. In more prosperous villages, roofs are sometimes of corrugated iron, and walls are sometimes of cement brick. Houses in the towns are of cement with roofs either of tile or of corrugated iron; many families are usually crowded together. The drift from the countryside and the expansion of town populations has frequently resulted in the proliferation of shanty towns.

Police services. The Ministry of the Interior is responsible for police services, which are under the control of the Director General for Security, who heads the Garde Républicaine, the central city police station, the national constabulary, and some mobile brigades. These forces are officered by a team of magistrates and administrators.

Social welfare. *Wages and cost of living.* Both wages and the cost of living are highly variable. In rural areas annual income averages between 15,000 and 20,000 francs CFA (between 300 and 400 French francs). In periods of crisis, as for example in 1970, the average rural annual income fell to 13,000 francs CFA (260 French francs). Migrant rural workers who seek temporary employment in towns often raise their wages to an average of 50,000 francs CFA (1,000 French francs) a year. Employees in minor posts in towns—orderlies, cooks, and chauffeurs employed by the administration—enjoy a relatively privileged standard of living, earning wages of between 50,000 and 100,000 francs CFA (1,000 to 2,000 French francs) a year. Those in clerical positions in commerce and industry earn salaries which may amount to 150,000 francs CFA (3,000 French francs). The highest salaries are earned by professors, members of the liberal professions, French expatriates, and international civil servants.

The standard of living in the countryside is low. Manufactured products are more expensive than in the city, which despite often startling social inequalities, may appear to be a kind of paradise in comparison with living conditions in the countryside. About 63 percent of all the wages in the country, for example, are earned in Dakar alone, although only one-eighth of the population lives there. As a result the cost of living in Dakar in 1969, according to United Nations statistics, was the highest of any city in the world.

Health conditions. Thanks to the efforts of doctors during the colonial era, Senegal is rid of the plagues which raged in the early 20th century. If yellow fever, tuberculosis, smallpox, and similar diseases are still to be encountered they at least no longer assume epidemic proportions. In rural areas, however, sanitary conditions leave much to be desired, due to the lack of training and facilities. It must be admitted, however, that this situation is due, above all, to the fact that sanitary facilities are primarily concentrated in Dakar, which recently accounted for three-fifths of the total budgetary expenditure for health. There is one doctor for every 1,000 inhabitants in Dakar, whereas the ratio is one to every 15,000 inhabitants elsewhere in Senegal. Out of 140 midwives, 90 are

Health facilities in Dakar

located in Dakar. The death rate for children between the ages of one and four is five times higher in rural Senegal than it is in Dakar. Life expectancy in the capital is 60 years, whereas in the countryside it is only 38.

Social and economic divisions. As is emphasized by the foregoing, the most marked socioeconomic cleavage in Senegal today is between those living in towns and those living in the country. This division results from the modernizing process which has taken hold in the western fringes of the country.

Country life, in its traditional communal village form, is still followed by 80 percent of Senegalese. The family is extended and lives, under the authority of its most elderly member, in a compound consisting of a group of thatched dwellings, engaging in agriculture for a livelihood. The influence of the marabouts—interpreters of the Qur'ān—remains uncontested. Liquid funds are virtually nonexistent, a subsistence economy being followed.

The way of life of the city dwellers stands in contrast to this, since it typifies the modernizing process at work in Senegal. To speak of city life, moreover, is virtually tantamount to speaking of Dakar, since 75 percent of town dwellers live in this one city. The primary factor distinguishing the rural farmer from the town dweller is monetary income, since the inhabitants of the towns earn from 10 to 12 times more than those living elsewhere. Better lodging, better food, better education, and better health conditions are available in the towns. Socially the city dweller, particularly in Dakar, follows a way of life which represents a break with the traditional values of communal village life in its pure form. As worker, clerk, or trader, the town dweller follows a timetable that is governed by the clock instead of by the seasonal rhythms of the countryside. In the towns Tukulor, Wolof, Fulani, Serer, and Dyola tend to define themselves as Senegalese rather than in terms of their community of origin and feel themselves to be a part of the nascent Senegalese nation.

Senegal today, in sum, presents two distinct aspects to the contemporary observer. On the one hand stands Dakar, the capital, with its inhabitants in communication with international society and a universal civilization; on the other stands the remainder of the country, following a provincial pattern of life which has lost is primary impulse and which is growing increasingly stagnant.

CULTURAL LIFE AND INSTITUTIONS

The cultural milieu. Both the rhythm of life in Senegal and the Senegalese mentality have evolved over a long period of time in a setting which was unacquainted with technology in the Western sense of the word. The attitudes of Senegalese in their relations with nature are consequently different from those of Europeans in general. Fear, magic, and collectivism are dominant in traditional Senegalese life. Writing is absent, or constitutes at best no more than the prerogative of the few. The cultural heritage is preserved in oral tradition of which the guardians have been the most experienced, that is to say the oldest, men. Society thus forms a hierarchy, at the summit of which stand the oldest people.

The social hierarchy

The state of the arts and popular culture. The traditional Senegalese cultural heritage remains much alive. Rites and initiations are actively practiced in rural areas —for example, by the Bassari of Kédougou. Among Muslims, youths must be circumcised before being accorded the responsibilities of adulthood.

Art, sculpture, music, and dance remain typically Senegalese in expression. Sculpture is characterized by abstraction and by the ideogram; a sculptured gazelle, for example, may be represented solely by its horns and its neck, while an elephant may be represented only by the immense fan formed by its ears and its trunk. The Senegalese artist thus neglects the material aspect in order to give free rein to ideas and to feelings. Similarly, in the absence of written music, the imagination of the musician is released. Without falling into the realm of fantasy, the *griot* (a West African kind of troubadour) recites poems, or tells of warrior deeds, drawing upon his own sources of inspiration. Both dance and music owe much to im-

provisation, which, combined with rhythm, produces an intense effect upon the entire community.

Senegalese literature is incarnated by President Léopold Sédar Senghor. The quality and the importance of his work resulted in his election, in France in 1970, to the Académie des Sciences Morales et Politiques. He is the poet associated with *négritude*, a concept that he has defined as consisting on the one hand of an attitude of defense of the traditional values of black Africa, and on the other of tension towards the modernization of these same values. From this concept Senghor has drawn his political philosophy not only concerning Senegal but the whole of black Africa. Besides Senghor one may also cite the names of Birago Diop, who has revived local legends, as well as of such writers as Ousmane Socé, David Diop, Alioune Diop, Cheikh Anta Diop, Cheikh Amidou Kâne, Abdoulaye Sadji, Abdoulaye Ly, Sembène Ousmane, and Bakary Traoré, all of whom are known for works which combine intelligence with the savour of Senegalese life.

Cultural institutions. Since the World Festival of Negro Arts was organized at Dakar in 1966, a number of existing institutions have been reoriented towards African traditions, while new institutions have also been created. Among the new institutions are the Musée Dynamique, the Théâtre Daniel Sorano, and the Tapestry Factory of Thiès. The existing institutions which have undergone some transformations are the Institut Fondamental d'Afrique Noire, the Maisons de la Jeunesse et de la Culture, and the craft village of Soumbedioune in Dakar, which has become a centre for Senegalese sculpture and goldsmithing.

Press and radio. Senegal was the first of the former French West African territories to have a press. The *Moniteur du Senegal* was founded in 1854, to be succeeded by the *Journal Officiel du Sénégal*. A nonofficial press has also long thrived in Senegal. For a long time the principal independent publication was the daily *Paris-Dakar* which, when Senegal became independent, was renamed *Dakar Matin*. In 1970 both *Dakar Matin* and the publication of the government party, *L'Unité Africaine*, gave way to a new publication *Soleil du Sénégal*. Other important Dakar newspapers are *Afrique Nouvelle* and *Le Moniteur Africain*, while magazines include *Africa* and *Bingo*. Radio Sénégal broadcasts both in French and in English, as well as in several African languages. In 1971 there was no television service.

FUTURE PROSPECTS

In the economic and social sphere, Senegal, of all the West African states of French expression, is the one which has benefitted the most from a modern economic infrastructure. Development was, however, intended to serve colonial ends and envisaged Senegal as playing the leading administrative role among the former French West African territories. It is the reorientation of Senegal towards more restricted national policy goals that is at present causing many problems for the government. Of all the constraints to which Senegal is now subjected, the most serious arise from overdependency upon a single crop economy. Since 1965 the government has been attempting to alter the situation by encouraging crop diversification. This policy has, however, placed the government on the horns of a cruel dilemma: on the one hand the preferential prices accorded by France were ended in 1967, so that it became necessary to increase production in order to compensate for the loss of revenue; on the other hand the necessity of diversifying crops requires a diminution in the proportion of peanuts produced. This situation has become further aggravated by the increasingly serious deficit in the balance of trade. In 1970, finally, serious and dramatic perspectives on the future were opened by the disinclination of the rural population to maintain peanut production as a result of the defective operation of the Agricultural Marketing Board.

It is clear to many that the dominance of peanut production in the national economy must be replaced by diversification, and that this measure should be accompanied by another step—the organization of a West African

The
Organiza-
tion of
Senegalese
Riverain
States

economic grouping. Senegal is already attempting to attain this end by forming—in cooperation with the neighbouring states of Mali, and Mauritania—the Organisation pour la Mise en Valeur du Fleuve Sénégal (Organization for the Development of the Sénégal River) for the purpose of achieving the harmonious development of the potentialities of the Senegalese river valley. Senegal argues that it deserves more understanding than it is given by virtue of the originality of the political and economic course that it has been following; that it has chosen to safeguard human values, rather than to sacrifice them for the sake of spectacular economic development—a policy which has placed it in the western camp in the contemporary world. The struggle that it is pursuing to rehabilitate the values of *négritude* when confronted with technical civilization is also proving a rewarding task.

BIBLIOGRAPHY. The most important geographical, economic, and sociological studies are: M. CROWDER, *Senegal: A Study in French Assimilation Policy* (1962); J.S. TRIMINGHAM, *A History of Islam in West Africa* (1962); H. DESCHAMPS, *Le Sénégal et la Gambie*, 2nd ed. (1968); P. PELISSIER, *Les paysans du Sénégal* (1967); A. SECK and A. MONDJANNAGNI, *L'Afrique Occidentale* (1967); R.J. HARRISON CHURCH, *West Africa*, 6th ed. (1968); A. SECK, *Dakar: Métropole Ouest-Africaine* (1970); C. CAMARA, *Saint-Louis-du-Sénégal* (1968); and P. FOUGEYROLLAS, *Modernisation des hommes, l'exemple du Sénégal* (1967).

(Ca.C.)

Sénégal River

The Sénégal River, 1,015 miles (1,633 kilometres) long, is one of West Africa's longest rivers. Two of its three headstreams rise in the Fouta Djallon plateau, after which it flows northwestward and then westward to drain into the Atlantic Ocean. For 533 miles of its course, it forms the boundary between the Islamic Republic of Mauritania to the north, and the Republic of Senegal to the south. In medieval times, reports of its existence as the "River of Gold" reached European navigators. From the 16th to the 20th centuries, the river formed a route of advance for French colonial influence.

Course of the river. Of the various headstreams of the river, the Falémé and Bafing rise in the Primary sandstones of the Fouta Djallon plateau in Guinea, while the Bakoye rises in western Mali. The Bafing and Bakoye meet at Bafoulabé in the Republic of Mali to form the Sénégal, 650 miles from its mouth; the stream is then joined by the Falémé near Bakel, below Kayes. From here onward the Senegal–Mauritania boundary lies on the right bank, so that the river belongs to Senegal; nevertheless, a modus vivendi (temporary arrangement pending a settlement) permits the use of the river by Mauritania.

From Bakel to Dagana, a distance of 385 miles, the river flows through an alluvial valley as much as 12 miles wide. Floods come in early September at Bakel, reaching Dagana by mid-October. Water level rises 12 feet, the flow is 300 times greater than in the dry season, and the river occupies the entire valley. As the floods retreat, maize (corn), sorghum, sweet potatoes, tomatoes, pulses (plants of the pea family), and cucurbits (plants of the gourd family, such as pumpkins and watermelons) are planted, in that order. The river has many branches, called *marigots*, with meanders, cutoffs (new and shorter channels formed by the water cutting across bends in the river's course), and hollows (depressions in the river's valley), the latter permitting cultivation with sorghum and rice. This is the most populated part of the valley.

The
Sénégal
Delta

Below Dagana, 165 miles from Saint-Louis, the Sénégal enters its delta. The river floods more widely, and water and soils are saline. The delta is visited by nomads but is sparsely settled. The mouth has been deflected southward by the offshore Canary Current and by trade winds blowing from the north; the result has been the formation of a long sandspit, the Langue de Barbarie. Saint-Louis lies in the river's estuary, which has such a dangerous bar that its port was supplanted by Dakar, 163 miles to the south, after a Dakar to Saint-Louis railway link opened in 1885.

Climate, vegetation, and animal life. The Bafing and Falémé sources receive 80 inches of annual rainfall, mostly from late March to early November; the Bakoye

Basin receives less. The Sénégal Valley proper receives 10 to 30 inches of rain annually, from late May to mid-October, with mean maximum temperatures of about 105° F (41° C) in April, and mean minimum ones of about 62° F (17° C) in January. Rainfall diminishes downstream, and the climate of Saint-Louis is similar to that of Dakar.

Typical trees of the valley are acacias, notably *Acacia nilotica*, which grows profusely on banks, and *A. senegal*, which provides the gum arabic of commerce, and grows on drier slopes. The grass *Vetiverea nigritiana* grows in tufts in wet depressions. In dry areas near the valley sides *Acacia albida*, *Balanites aegyptiaca* (a shrub with leathery leaves), and grasses are common.

The river is overfished. Nile perch are common. Spoonbills, herons, egrets, and weaver birds are widespread. Among the animals on the river banks hedgehogs, monitor lizards, and warthogs are fairly common.

The riverine peoples. Below Dagana the peoples of the valley are Wolofs; from Dagana they are Tukulors (Toucouleurs) to upstream of Matam, where Soninke (Sarakole) dominate. Throughout the Sénégal River region small groups of usually nomadic Fulani and Mauri (more commonly Maure or Moors) are found. Villages average about 300 people, who grow millet on the rainfed lands and use the floodlands for other crops. Both areas provide pasture for the livestock of nomads.

Exploration. French ships entered the estuary at least as early as 1558. From a French fort established in 1638, reconnaissance parties went 160 miles upriver to Podor. In 1659 a larger fort was erected on N'Dar Island in the estuary and named Saint-Louis-du-Sénégal after the French king Louis IX (St. Louis). This became a base for French exploration of the river and for trade in slaves, gum, gold, skins, ivory, beeswax, and ostrich feathers. André Brüe built a post, Saint-Joseph-de-Galam, 400 miles upstream in 1698, and parties sent by him reached the Félou Falls above Kayes soon after. Some went up the Falémé, where another fort was built. Pierre David penetrated far up that river in 1744.

Rice
cultivation

Resource exploitation. Rice cultivation on lands from which floods have retreated has been locally improved by embankments, with sluices constructed mainly on the Senegalese river bank; diesel pumps are also being tried on the Mauritanian bank. At Richard-Toll, near Dagana, about 14,000 acres are irrigated by means of a dam across the Taoué, a tributary stream up which Sénégal floods penetrate to Lake Guiers. The dam admits this fresh water and retains it by closing the sluices at the end of the flood, thereby preventing the admission of tidal saltwater during the dry season. Rice and, more recently, sugarcane are grown by the use of mechanized equipment and paid labour. Rice yields have been disappointing because of saline soils and the depredations of the quelea bird. In the delta a 50-mile-long embankment controls the entry of floodwater to 78,000 acres, part of which has been prepared for cultivation. This scheme has yet to prove itself. Chinese technicians from Taiwan help with most schemes.

River traffic. Extension of a railway from Kayes to Dakar, completed in 1924, diverted traffic that previously went by river, after which the valley became an economic backwater. Local traffic is carried by boats drawing nine feet or less as far as Podor all year round, and as far as Kayes (566 miles from the river's mouth) from early August to mid-October. Most traffic plies between the river ports of Rosso, Bogué and Kaédi, in Mauritania. Minor ferries exist at Rosso and Kayes; there is a dry season causeway across the river at Kayes.

Prospects for the future. The Organisation des États Riverains du Sénégal (the Organization of Senegalese Riverain States) comprising Guinea, Mali, Mauritania, and Senegal, promotes cooperation on the river and beyond, but political differences have limited its effectiveness. The construction of one or more dams has been proposed to improve flood control and produce power, but their justification is unclear.

BIBLIOGRAPHY. ANDRE VILLARD, *Histoire du Sénégal* (1943), is a comprehensive yet concise source, which may be supplemented by J. BLACHE, "Le Trafic au Sénégal à la fin du XVIIIe siècle," *Revue de Géographie Alpine,* 55:469–490 (1967). The most detailed study of the modern valley is J.L. BOUTILLIER *et al., La Moyenne Vallée du Sénégal* (1963), which may be supplemented for the river itself by A. MINOT, "Contribution à l'étude du fleuve Sénégal," *Bulletin du Comité d'Etudes Historiques et Scientifiques de l'Afrique Occidentale Française,* 17:385–416 (1934). L. PAPY, "La Vallée du Sénégal," *Les Cahiers d'Outre-Mer,* 4:277–324 (1951), provides further detail on agriculture; see also R.J. HARRISON CHURCH, *West Africa,* 6th ed. ch. 12 (1968), on Senegal as a whole.

(R.J.H.–C.)

Senghor, Léopold

Equally distinguished as poet, statesman, and advocate of *négritude*—the literary and artistic expression of the black African experience—Léopold Sédar Senghor was born on October 9, 1906, in the picturesque Senegalese town of Joal, the son of a prosperous trader of the Serer tribe. He spent his first seven years in a small village. His first ambition was to become "a teaching priest to work toward the intellectual emancipation of my race." He therefore attended school at a nearby Catholic mission and a seminary. When he was 20, he realized that the priesthood was not his calling and transferred to the lycée (secondary school) in Dakar. Born into a large family, he learned early to get along with people: white and black, Muslim and Christian, and members of both the Serer and the Wolof tribes. Yet, even as a youngster, he was described by an older brother as stubborn. He held tenaciously to certain convictions, one of which was his faith in the importance of African cultural values. As Jean Rous, one of his biographers, relates, when the director of the seminary "denounced [black African] backwardness in civilization," young Senghor retorted "that we, too, had a civilization."

Early life

By courtesy of the United Nations

Senghor, addressing the United Nations General Assembly, 1961.

In 1928 Senghor went to Paris on a partial scholarship and continued his formal studies at the famous Lycée Louis-le-Grand and at the Sorbonne, where he formed a lifelong friendship with his classmate Georges Pompidou, who later was to become premier and, eventually, president of France. During these years Senghor discovered the unmistakable imprint of African art on modern painting, sculpture, music, and literature, which confirmed his belief in Africa's potential contribution to what he would later call "the civilization of the universal." He learned that distinguished anthropologists, such as Leo Frobenius, had written enthusiastically of the African heritage and character. With the other two originators of the concept of *négritude,* Aimé Césaire of Martinique and Léon G. Damas of French Guiana, he read and discussed works by the black writers of America's so-called Harlem Renaissance of the '20s and translated some of their

poetry into French. Despite his respect for European poetry and Western political thought, he upheld the importance of his African heritage and exhorted his compatriots "to assimilate, not be assimilated."

In 1935 he became the first African agrégé, the highest rank of qualified teacher in the French school system, and began "teaching French to French youngsters" in Tours. Two years later he was transferred to a lycée near Paris. Drafted in 1939, at the beginning of World War II, he was captured in 1940 and spent two years in Nazi concentration camps, where he wrote some of his finest poems. On his release, he joined the French Resistance.

After the war he became a member of the French Constituent Assembly. There he was chairman of the subcommittee that passed on the grammatical correctness of the new constitution. In 1946 he was sent as one of Senegal's two deputies to the National Assembly in Paris. Elected on the Socialist (SFIO) ticket, Senghor soon realized that only an African party would accord top priority to African needs. Rejecting the RDA (Rassemblement Démocratique Africain), which in those early years was affiliated with the Communists, he founded the BDS (Senegalese Democratic Bloc) in 1948 and defeated Lamine Gueye, the SFIO candidate, by a wide margin in the 1951 elections for the French National Assembly. Five years later he became mayor of Thiès, Senegal's railroad centre, and was re-elected deputy.

Political career

When the French Parliament passed (1956) the *loi cadre,* which gave a large measure of self-government to the African territories, Senghor was one of the first to oppose the act. The *loi cadre* emphasized territorial rather than federal government, and Senghor realized this would result in the proliferation of small, unviable states. To counter this disintegration of West Africa and French Equatorial Africa, he helped to found and supported a series of parties that were dedicated to establishing a federal African unity. But none of these was as successful as the RDA. On the home front he rejoined forces with Lamine Gueye to create the UPS (Senegalese Progressive Union), which is still the governing party of Senegal. On the broader African scene, he was cofounder of the Convention Africaine in 1957 and the PRA (Party of African Regrouping) in 1958. The alliance of the UPS, the Senegal section of the PRA, and the Union Soudanaise became the PFA (African Federation Party) in 1959; Senghor was cofounder and president. This party led to the creation of the so-called Mali Federation in 1959. Senegal, former French Sudan (now the Republic of Mali), Dahomey, and Upper Volta, all of which had voted against an immediate rupture with France in the September 1958 referendum, were expected to become charter members of the new federation. Dahomey and Upper Volta defected, however, and only Senegal and the French Sudan remained. In December 1959 Senghor made his eloquent, successful appeal to French President Charles de Gaulle for independence. The Mali Federation lasted only until the following August, when the two component states separated. Senegal became a republic, and Senghor was unanimously elected president.

A second major crisis for Senghor occurred in late 1962, when Prime Minister Mamadou Dia, longtime protégé of Senghor, attempted a coup d'etat. Again the Senegalese rallied behind Senghor, and Mamadou Dia was sentenced to life imprisonment. A new constitution was ratified, and Senghor was re-elected President. In 1968 he received a mandate for a third term.

As the chief executive of a new country with few known resources except peanuts, fish, and phosphates, Senghor tried to modernize Senegal's agriculture, to instill a sense of enlightened citizenship, to combat corruption and inefficiency, to forge closer ties with his African neighbours, to continue cooperation with the French, and to establish peaceful relations with the rest of the world. He advocated an African socialism based on African realities, free of both atheism and excessive materialism. He described the kind of socialism he is seeking as open, democratic, humanistic socialism that shuns such slogans as "dictatorship of the proletariat." A vigorous spokesman for Third World, he protests unfair terms of

Assessment

trade that work to the disadvantage of the agricultural nations.

His concern with political and economic issues strengthened his espousal of *négritude*, which he defined as "the sum total of cultural values of the Negro-African world." The first World Festival of Negro Arts was held in Dakar in April 1966 under the sponsorship of his government, the African Society of Culture, and UNESCO (United Nations Educational, Scientific, and Cultural Organization). For both his literary and his political works, he has been awarded honorary doctorates by universities on four continents. In December 1969 he became the first African member of the French Academy of Moral and Political Sciences, filling the vacancy caused by the death of the former German chancellor Konrad Adenauer.

Senghor's career is replete with paradoxes. Although a Catholic and a Serer, he heads a predominantly Muslim, Wolof nation. An outstanding intellectual, he draws his main support from the peasants. A distinguished poet, he is also a professional politician of great skill. The theoretician of *négritude*, Senghor believes, with the French scientist and philosopher Teilhard de Chardin, in the eventual emergence of a planetary civilization, and he includes this idea in the Senegalese national anthem: "The Bantu is a brother, and the Arab, and the white man."

BIBLIOGRAPHY. The major works of Senghor are: *Poèmes* (1964), containing poems previously published in his *Chants d'ombre* (1945), *Hosties noires* (1948), *Chants pour Naëtt* (1949), *Ethiopiques* (1956), and *Nocturnes* (1961); *Selected Poems*, trans. by JOHN REED and CLIVE WAKE (1964); *Anthologie de la nouvelle poésie nègre et malgache de langue française*, ed. by SENGHOR with a famous preface by JEAN-PAUL SARTRE (1948); *Liberté*, 2 vol. (1964–71), essays, prefaces, and speeches by Senghor; *Pierre Teilhard de Chardin et la politique africaine* (1962); and *On African Socialism*, trans. by MERCER COOK (1964), three essays.

Works about Senghor include: JEAN ROUS, *Léopold Sédar Senghor: La vie d'un président de l'Afrique nouvelle* (1967), a short biography by a personal friend and political adviser; ARMAND GUIBERT, *Léopold Sédar Senghor* (1961), biography, poetry, an interview, and press comments (in French); and I.L. MARKOVITZ, *Léopold Sédar Senghor and the Politics of Negritude* (1969), a scholarly study of the man and of his theory on the evolution of *négritude*.

(W.M.C.)

Sennacherib

Sennacherib (Akkadian, Sin-akhkhe-eriba [the God Sin Has Replaced the Brothers]) was king of Assyria from 704 to 681 BC. He was the son and successor of Sargon II, from whom he inherited an empire that extended from Babylonia to southern Palestine and into Asia Minor. As king he waged campaigns in Babylonia and rebuilt the city of Nineveh.

By courtesy of the trustees of the British Museum

Sennacherib leading a military campaign, relief from Nineveh, *c.* 690 BC. In the British Museum.

Before his accession he served, with ability demonstrated by his extant reports, as a senior administrator and diplomat in the north and northwest of the empire. The main problem of his reign was in Babylonia, where the growth of the power of the Chaldean and Aramaean tribes seriously disturbed the old urban centres, whose interests in commerce and need for safe trade routes made them usually pro-Assyrian. Political instability was worsened by the interference of Elam (southwestern Iran), so that between 703 and 689 Sennacherib had to undertake six campaigns in that area; his attitude toward the capital city, Babylon, changed from acceptance of native rule to hostility.

Campaigns in Babylonia

The peace was broken in 703 by a tribal insurrection under the Chaldean Merodach-Baladan (Marduk-apal-iddina), with Elamite military assistance. By skillful generalship Sennacherib recovered northern Babylonia and appointed a native Babylonian, Bel-ibni, as subking. His army there devastated the tribal areas in southern Babylonia, though he spared major Babylonian cities, except for a few that had gone over to the tribesmen. Elamite interference in Babylonia probably dictated a campaign in 702 against the petty kingdoms of the Zagros Mountains, vassals of Elam, to forestall a possible Elamite thrust by that route toward eastern Assyria.

In 701 a rebellion, backed by Egypt, though probably instigated by Merodach-Baladan (II Kings 20:12–18; Isa. 39:1–7), broke out in Palestine. Sennacherib reacted firmly, supporting loyal vassals and taking the rebel cities, except for Jerusalem, which, though besieged, was spared on payment of a heavy indemnity (II Kings 18:13–19:36; Isa. 36:1–37:37). The biblical narrative has been interpreted as implying two campaigns against Jerusalem, but this receives no support from Assyrian sources.

Further intrigues by Merodach-Baladan necessitated another Assyrian campaign into the Chaldean area in 700. Merodach-Baladan thereupon took refuge in Elam, where he soon died. Sennacherib's hardening attitude toward Babylon was marked by the introduction of direct Assyrian rule through the replacement of Bel-ibni by Sennacherib's son Ashur-nadin-shum. This gave Babylonia a brief period of stability, during which Sennacherib undertook campaigns in Cilicia and the north. But continuing Elamite support for disaffected Chaldean tribesmen led in 694 to a further attack on southern Babylonia, coupled with a seaborne invasion of Elam across the Persian Gulf. Elam reacted by raiding northern Babylonia, capturing Ashur-nadin-shum, and installing a nominee who reigned for 18 months until removed during a fresh Assyrian attack.

Another Chaldean leader, Mushezib-Marduk, now seized Babylon and, by opening the temple treasuries, bought massive military support from Elam. In 691 the Assyrian and Elamite armies met at Halule on the Diyālā, where Sennacherib, though claiming a victory, suffered losses that left him temporarily impotent. In 689 he returned to besiege Babylon, capturing it after nine months. Abandoning attempts to conciliate this great cult centre, Sennacherib systematically sacked Babylon; a text exists that probably represents a theological justification for this impiety.

Sennacherib's most enduring work was the rebuilding of Nineveh, his official residence as crown prince. On his accession he made it his capital, building a splendid new palace Shanina-la-ishu (Nonesuch). Using prisoners of war for labour, he extended and beautified the city, laying out streets, enlarging squares, restoring and extending public buildings, and erecting a great inner wall, nearly eight miles (13 kilometres) long, which completely encircled the city, and an outer wall; both walls still stand. Around his capital he established plantations of fruit trees and parks of exotic trees and plants; among his introductions was the cotton plant, described as "the wool-bearing tree." To irrigate the plantations, for which at times the Tigris and Khosr rivers fell too low, Sennacherib sought springs and streams in the hills north of Nineveh and led them by six miles (ten kilometres) of canal and a massive stone aqueduct to feed the Khosr. He also undertook building activities in other cities, particularly Ashur.

Building and technological achievements

Sennacherib claimed to be "of clever understanding," a boast supported by his initiatives in technology. He had surveys undertaken for new sources of alabaster and building stone, and he discovered new stands of giant timber in mountain forests. He devised a new and less laborious method of bronze casting and introduced more convenient equipment for raising water from wells. He showed considerable logistic ability in his seaborne attack on Elam, in which ships built in Nineveh were taken by Phoenician sailors down the Tigris, overland to a canal of the Euphrates, and thence to the Persian Gulf.

Sennacherib died in January 681 by parricide, probably at Nineveh. He was survived by his principal wife Naqia, mother of his heir Esarhaddon, whose non-Assyrian name suggests that she was of either Jewish or Aramaean origin.

Because of his attack on Jerusalem, Sennacherib receives prominence in the Bible. Isaiah regarded Sennacherib as God's instrument (II Kings 19:23–28; Isa. 37:24–29); the prophet did not condemn the King's military activities as such, though punishment was decreed for his arrogance in not acknowledging the divine source of his power.

In *The Story of Ahikar* (a pre-Christian Oriental work), Sennacherib is seen as a king of apparently good repute, under whom the sage Ahikar served; where this same story is alluded to in the book of *Tobit*, however, the King is cast in an evil role. A similar ambivalence is shown in Jewish Talmudic tradition, where Sennacherib, though called an evil man, is also regarded as the ancestor of the teachers of the celebrated Rabbi Hillel.

Classical tradition retained a memory of Sennacherib's activities not only in Babylonia but also in Cilicia, where the building of Tarsus, on the plan of Babylon, was attributed to him. He was also credited with building a temple at Athens. Herodotus' story of an attempted invasion of Egypt frustrated by mice eating the Assyrian bowstrings and quivers may reflect a plague epidemic during Sennacherib's Palestinian campaign; this possibly underlay the story (in II Kings 19:35; Isa. 37:36) of the decimation of the Assyrian army by God's destroying angel, which inspired Lord Byron's poem "The Destruction of Sennacherib."

BIBLIOGRAPHY. D.D. LUCKENBILL (trans.), *The Annals of Sennacherib* (1924), edits all relevant texts then known. This is supplemented by a bibliography and an interesting new text by A.K. GRAYSON, "The Walters Art Gallery Sennacherib Inscription," *Archiv für Orientforschung*, 20:83–96 (1963). T. JACOBSEN and SETON LLOYD, *Sennacherib's Aqueduct at Jerwan* (1935), offers the definitive account of that structure. H.W.F. SAGGS, *The Greatness That Was Babylon*, pp. 118–222 (1962), gives a general account of Sennacherib.

(H.W.F.S.)

Sensorimotor Skills

Even in the age of automation motor skills must be acquired and utilized. Proficiency in a wide range of activities is dependent upon one's ability to move accurately and within specified time limits. The growing child must master a long list of complex skills as he matures—feeding and dressing himself, riding a bicycle, throwing and catching balls—if he is to be considered successful by his parents and his friends. Social competence hinges to a great extent upon the ability to exhibit proficiency in the contemporary dances; many vocations and professions require abilities to move the fingers, limbs, and body in precise ways. The manual dexterity of the dentist, the ferocious movements of the professional athlete, and the creative efforts of the artisan have in common the necessity to acquire various motor skills and subskills for the assurance of success.

While many modern conveniences have purportedly made life's activities simpler and have apparently reduced the demands upon human beings to learn skills, many other actions demanded of men today require more proficiency. Cars move at higher speeds, requiring quicker and more precise reactions on the part of their operators; the simple radio has been replaced by the colour television set with its multitude of dials; the foxtrot and waltz have been replaced with the more complex dances that require different rhythm patterns to be maintained simultaneously in several parts of the body. Hobbies and recreational pursuits of wide variety are sought by man in an apparent effort to exercise and to extend his capacities to perform motor skills. Painting and needlework require precision by smaller muscle groups, while tennis, swimming, and the like require the coordination of both large and small muscle groups working in unison.

The term "skill" denotes a movement that is reasonably complex and the execution of which requires at least a minimal amount of practice. Thus skill excludes reflex acts. One does not become skilled at sneezing or at blinking the eyes when an object approaches. At the same time, it has become increasingly apparent to scientists investigating the performance and acquisition of motor acts that the performance of complex skills is closely linked to sensations arising from the things the performer looks at, sensations from the muscles that are involved in the movement itself, as well as stimuli received by other sensory end organs. Thus the term "sensorimotor skill," denoting the close relationship between movement and sensation in the acquisition of complex acts, is found within the research literature with increasing frequency.

Definitions

Simple components of bodily skills.   Most of life's skills are continuous and complex and contain a multitude of integrated components; however, these complex skills may be analyzed by examination of their component parts.

The performance of a skill may be broken down into several time intervals. Initially the performer must be attentive and alert enough to be receptive to some kind of sensory information, which may in turn lead toward some kind of motor act. For this to occur the performer usually becomes aware of some kind of stimulus that is intense or distinctive enough to be perceived as different from other sensory information.

Reception of stimulus and selection and initiation of response

As this cue occurs the performer then must make a decision to act or not to act; and this is generally dependent upon his past experience within similar situations and with similar stimuli, as well as upon his feelings about his personal capabilities. If he decides to act, the next thing that occurs is the selection of an appropriate motor response from the entire "collection" of motor responses that he has acquired.

In the laboratory, a subject's reaction time is the time between the presentation of some kind of stimulus and the performer's initiation of response. The individual's speed of reaction in such situations is dependent upon a number of variables, including the intensity of the stimuli; for example, a person will initiate a movement more quickly to increasingly louder sounds until a limit is reached. If too loud a sound is presented it will delay the onset of the movement and result in a longer reaction time. Similarly, a longer reaction time will be recorded in such experiments if the subject is aware that he will have to initiate a complex movement or if the subject must choose from among a number of stimuli before initiating a movement (*e.g.*, if he must move only if one of a number of various coloured lights is turned on).

The quality of the movement then initiated is dependent upon a number of other factors, the precision of the act required, the past experience of the performer in similar skills, the speed of the movement, the force of the motor act, as well as body part or parts to be moved.

Factors that affect quality of motor response

The efficient performance of many types of extremely simple motor skills may be limited by inherent response capacities built into the human nervous system. Finger tapping at more than ten times per second for example is not usually possible. A person's ability to keep a body part relatively steady may be disturbed by natural, regular, and rather predictable oscillation rates of the limbs, fingers, and of the total body (evidenced in measures of body sway).

Individuals vary greatly in their ability to exercise force with various body parts. At the same time, there are limits beyond which it is not realistic to expect humans to go when evidencing strength in various tasks.

Careful experimentation reveals that because of the complexity of the human motor system it is unlikely that an individual ever repeats an apparently similar movement in precisely the same way. Thus the acquisition of skill in a given task involves the performance of a reasonably consistent response pattern, which varies, within limits, from trial to trial.

It is a common observation that there seem to be a number of basic motor abilities that may underlie the performance of a number of life's activities. This subject was investigated rather extensively during the 1950s and 1960s. The intercorrelation of performance scores elicited from thousands of young adult subjects who participated in these investigations revealed that there are in fact a number of basic abilities that contribute to the efficient performance of both fine and gross motor skills. Although a detailed examination of these abilities is not possible here, in general it was revealed that there are five components of what might be broadly referred to as "manual dexterity," including fine finger dexterity, arm-wrist speed and aiming ability. Similar research has explored the manner in which performance scores group themselves in skills in which larger muscles are involved. It was found, for example, that there are several kinds of strengths, including static strength (pressure measured in pounds exerted against an immovable object); this is independent of what was termed "dynamic strength" (moving the limbs with force). Muscular flexibility and balancing ability were similarly dissected into several components. Thus discussion of a single quality in human movement is inaccurate. Rather, one should refer to several specific types of ability.

Motor skills may also be classified by reference to the more general characteristics of the tasks themselves rather than by measuring and intercorrelating the scores elicited by human subjects. It is common, for example, to find the dichotomy "fine" and "gross" motor skill, in which the latter label is applied to acts in which the larger muscles are commonly involved, while the former classification denotes actions of the hands and fingers. One researcher has proposed a three-way classification system, separating human movements into "body transport movements," in which the total body moves in space; limb movements; and manual (hand) actions. In general, however, most skills incorporate precise movements of both larger and smaller muscle groups working in harmony. The basketball player must use his larger skeletal muscles to run and jump but at the same time must employ a fine "touch," evidencing accurate finger control, when dribbling the ball. On the other hand, when a person sits at a desk and writes, the large postural muscles that contribute to the writer's stability are invariably active.

Complex, integrated skills. Most of life's skills are not simple ones. They are rhythmic at times and almost always are composed of several integrated parts. Such skills often are often controlled by the organization of visual information available to the performer, particularly during the early stages of learning. At the same time, the individual's ability to analyze the mechanics of a motor task, his verbal ability, and other intellectual and perceptual attributes may influence his acquisition of a skill.

Motor-skill learning has been divided by some authors into three phases. In the first, or cognitive phase, the learner attempts to achieve some understanding of the requirements of the task. Studies of effectiveness of verbal and cognitive pretraining attest to the importance of this initial phase for skilled learning. In the second, or intermediate phase, the learner acquires new response patterns, recognizes the similarity and differences between old and new actions, and gradually eliminates inappropriate motions while instilling the proper ones into the complex skill. In the final phase of skill learning, the skilled act becomes increasingly automatic and less dependent upon external cues. Improvement in performance continues during this final stage but usually at a decreasing rate.

Some researchers employ the cybernetic term "feedback" to explain the manner in which a highly complex motor skill is performed. This basic concept generally hypothesizes that the human being is a type of self-correcting servomechanism. And within such a model several types of feedback systems may be used to explain the mechanisms of human skill. During the initial stages of skill acquisition, for example, discrete "bits" of visual

information relative to limb location and object location (if an object is to be dealt with) are employed during the performance of the task to correct the movements of the limb, as when a person reaches toward a glass of water. Thus the direction and speed of the arm are controlled by constant and regular visual monitoring, just as are the initial attempts of a young child to write the letter *a*.

The external stimuli that afforded information concerning the location of the hand and pencil during the writing of the letter *a* and the position of the arm, hand, and water glass in the first example cited form only part of the regulatory feedback system. There are also internal sources of feedback. The mature performer is aware of the positions of his arm when he cannot see it. Most adults can write their names without watching their hands, or can reach for a glass of water with only a minimum of attention directed toward the location of the vessel they are seeking.

The close and important relationships between sensation and movement are revealed in experiments in which subjects are given lenses to wear that invert and/or reverse their visual field and are required to learn a new set of movement responses to events in their visual world.

In another experiment the subjects were required to transfer pins from one hole to another with a small pair of pliers. The subjects viewed their performance in a television monitor, which permitted the experimenter to eliminate the subject's view of the pins; the pliers; his own hand; or any combination of pins, pliers, or hand. Improvement in the task was possible under all conditions, and even when all visual information was eliminated the subject learned by apparent reference to the kinesthetic cues arising from the movements of his hands.

In addition to information from the performer's own visual and muscular systems, cues from other sources contribute to the execution of sensorimotor skills. This information may consist of some kind of formal instructions prior to attempting the task or may consist of knowledge given at the completion of the task concerning the relative accuracy evidenced.

In general it has been found that formal instructions about the mechanics and execution of the task are more effective during the earlier than during the latter stages of skill acquisition. Information relative to task success at the completion of performances is usually more effective if delayed several seconds to give the performer time to integrate the sensory information obtained from his own visual and muscular systems.

In addition to instructions in the performance of a task offered by another person, it is apparent to many teachers of motor skills and to most experimenters that, as people perform, they silently verbalize instructions to themselves. In one recent experiment it was found that one group of mature college-age youth, left alone in a gymnasium to work out their own unique skill deficiencies, were able to perform badminton skills better than was a second group that was exposed to formal instruction. In general, however, the research indicates that appropriate instructions properly placed within a learning schedule raise final performance levels.

Emphasis should be placed, however, upon matching proper instructions to the attributes important during various levels of skill acquisition. In a limited number of tasks it has been demonstrated that perceptual components, knowledge of mechanical principles, and awareness of spatial relations were most important during initial stages of learning; while various motor attributes, reaction time, movement speed, and the like, assumed greater importance during the final stages of skill learning. Final performance was accelerated, in experiments in which these principles were accounted for, by the appropriate placement of instructions just before the emergence of important perceptual, intellectual, and motor factors within a learning schedule.

Much attention has been paid to the influence of the duration and placement of practice sessions upon performance and learning. A vast array of practice schedules has been studied, including schedules in which practice sessions were closely spaced in time, those in which a

---

Basic abilities that contribute to motor skills

Other classifications of motor skills

Three phases of learning motor skills

External and internal feedback

The timing of formal instructions

prolonged rest was permitted between trials, and various other combinations of spaced and massed practice.

It is usually found that relatively brief practice sessions followed by prolonged rest periods, at least equal in time to the practice sessions, promote the best terminal performance. It is probable that practice sessions should be shorter when less interesting skills or those that are physically taxing are to be acquired, whereas when the task is interesting and not physically fatiguing, performance may be facilitated if the practice sessions are closely spaced in time.

Reasons for plateaus in motor learning curves

When successive performance measures are plotted, a learning curve is obtained that often reveals periods during which no improvement is apparent. These learning "plateaus" often are accounted for by the suggestion that the performer is taking time to build up larger response units from smaller ones. For example, the early studies of this phenomenon utilized the sending rates of telegraphers. It was hypothesized that initially the sender responded to discrete letters, while later he responded to whole words, and finally tapped out phrases. The time taken to integrate letter, word, and phrase responses, during which no apparent improvement occurred, corresponded to plateaus in the learning curve. More recent thinking on this subject, however, suggests other reasons for plateaus in motor learning curves. The hypothesis has been advanced that while response accuracy does not always evidence continual improvement, the intellectual components of the task may be mentally rehearsed by the performer in the absence of measurable progress.

Retention. Good retention is the goal of most people practicing motor skills. The literature indicates that motor skills are more easily retained than are most types of verbal material; however, the differences in retention obtained are often traceable to the relative difficulty and rhythmicity of the task rather than to the fact that one type of act is primarily verbal and the other motor. Easiest to retain is poetry, just as are rhythmic motor skills; more difficult to retain are skills in which there is some kind of irrational pairing of stimuli to response (*e.g.*, moving a lever to a given position when one of ten light cues appears), just as are words having no meaning to the learner.

Factors affecting retention of motor skills

Retention of motor skills depends more upon how well a skill was learned than upon the specific conditions under which performance levels were obtained during initial practice. Overlearning that exceeds a given criterion of success by 50 or 100 percent usually elicits greater retention than if high performance levels have not been achieved initially.

Another factor that governs retention is whether the learner knows in advance that he is to be retested in a given skill. In several recent studies it has been found that groups of subjects who were given instructions that they would be retested for retention, retained more than did other groups who were afforded no similar instructions. If people know they will be held responsible for the re-performance of a skill, they apparently learn the skill with closer attention to the task than those who do not believe that they will later have to perform the skill.

Summary and overview. Skill acquisition involves two major processes. First on the one hand, the performer gains increasing facility in dealing with the sensory information available; he begins to attend to relevant cues, while ignoring information that is extraneous to the performance of the task. Second, the individual smooths his response pattern by dropping out inappropriate components and adopting and integrating relevant movement. Recent research indicates that this process continues for prolonged periods, the final stages of learning being marked by extremely subtle adjustments, involving the finite pairing of eye movements to other movements and the regulation of breathing.

Progress in the understanding of sensorimotor skill will be achieved when an increasing number of tasks within industry, education, and sports are analyzed to determine the general ability traits that contribute to each. Further effectiveness in the instruction of motor skills will occur when more skills are analyzed during the various stages of their acquisition to determine the ability traits important to each phase. With this information it will be possible to design instructional programs that better match the ability trait structure underlying specific skills, and at the same time to determine at what point during a learning schedule (initial, intermediate, or later stages) various types of instruction should be inserted.

Evaluation of sensorimotor skill. Motor-skill tests may sample relatively simple response capacities, such as simple reaction time to an auditory cue, or more complex and prolonged responses, as when an operator attempts to keep two cursors perpendicular to each other and crossing on a moving dot on a television-type screen.

Measurement of motor skills

Some motor-skill tests are found exclusively in a laboratory setting. One of the more common of these is the pursuit rotor task, in which the subject must attempt to hold a flexible stylus and keep its end on a dime-sized circle rotating along the edge of a phonograph-like disk.

Other frequently researched tasks require the subject to coordinate his arms and legs in a device resembling the controls of an airplane, while reacting to some kind of visual display of lights indicative of the position of the "airplane." Motor-skill tests in the laboratory similar to motor skills seen in everyday life may be classified according to the response complexity and/or duration of response elicited from the subject, as well as by the complexity or the sensory information to which the subject is required to respond.

BIBLIOGRAPHY. Standard texts in motor learning include J.B. OXENDINE, *Psychology of Motor Learning* (1968); and B.J. CRATTY, *Movement Behavior and Motor Learning*, 2nd ed. (1967). Books by P.M. FITTS and M.I. POSNER, *Human Performance* (1967); and E.A. BILODEAU (ed.), *Acquisition of Skill* (1966), analyze in detail the sensory components of sensorimotor learning and also the influence of the knowledge of results upon learning. B. KNAPP, *Skill in Sport* (1963), is directed toward understanding the essentials of athletic skills. E. FLEISHMAN, "Human Abilities and Verbal Learning" in R.M. GAGNE (ed.), *Learning and Individual Differences* (1967); and A.W. MELTON (ed.), *Categories of Human Learning* (1964), contain excellent material on motor skill learning, emphasizing individual differences in skilled performance and learning.

(B.J.C.)

Sensory Reception

Sensory reception is the means by which an organism is able to react to changes in its external or internal environment, in particular through the activation of specific parts, which transform the energy change involved into vital processes. In many instances, environmental changes are transmitted from the receptor organ to other parts of the body by specialized cells, but in unicellular organisms such transformations are made by specialized organelles, such as light-sensitive "eye spots" or cilia sensitive to mechanical disturbances. In all higher animals, sensory reception is the special function of sensory neural elements, which "translate" changes into nerve impulses. The biological significance of such a feature is that it allows an organism to make appropriate reactions to changed circumstances; without such provisions it would be in constant danger of injury or death at the slightest environmental alteration. In general, the more highly evolved the organism, the greater the number of environmental changes sensed and the more precisely each is analyzed. Some organisms, however, possess special senses developed for perceiving environmental changes not registered by, nor relevant to, other species.

There are some environmental conditions that are sensed readily by certain animals but only poorly or not at all by man. Man, of course, has taken advantage of the sharpened senses of other animals, as when he uses the acute smell of pigs for gathering truffles and of dogs in hunting and more recently for discovering contraband (*e.g.*, marihuana); the keen vision of falcons and hawks in falconry; and the heightened hearing sense of guard dogs.

Specialized senses

Classification of sensory systems. *According to location of receptors.* In general, sense cells, or receptors, located superficially in an organism receive signals from outside the organism and are parts of the exteroceptive system. Receptors located inside the body receive signals from changes taking place inside the body and belong to the enteroceptive system. On activation, sense cells cause reactions appropriate to their location; they are said to respond with their local sign. For example, a decapitated frog reacts to stimulation of the skin by precisely directed limb movements aimed at wiping away the stimulus. Local sign in man is expressed by a conscious awareness of the spot being stimulated, as when a person locates a thorn in the skin. This is not true for vision, hearing, and smell, however, the sources of which are localized away from the body surface. Although some authorities believe that projection in space is learned, especially in man, for most animals such ability seems to be innate. In many cases, enteroreceptors stimulate channels that are never brought into consciousness; the presence of a local sign is thus shown only by the appropriateness of the resulting reactions. Internal pain is remarkable in that it is usually "misdirected" (referred) to the body surface in well-established patterns, according to its origin, a considerable help in medical diagnosis.

According to type of stimulus. More than one type of energy applied to a sense cell can, if strong enough, generate a nerve impulse, which will be interpreted by the central nervous system (CNS) as a change in the specific energy to which the cell is sensitive and will cause the same results as if the appropriate stimulus were present. Thus, a specific reflex action can be brought about by natural stimulations, such as touch of the skin, as well as by electrical stimulation of the nerve fibres activated by such touch. Each type of sense cell thus causes a specific output reaction and a specific sensation, which is the modality perceived. In other words, if the optic nerve could be functionally connected to the ear and the acoustic nerve to the eye, lightning would be heard and thunder seen (see SENSORY RECEPTION, HUMAN).

Selectivity with regard to specific energy changes comes about in diverse ways, the simplest of which is the localization of the sense cell in such a way that it is protected from unwanted stimuli and by the use of accessory structures that make it extremely sensitive to the wanted one. The sense cells in the eye, for instance, are protected from any but the most severe changes in mechanical pressure; at the same time, the eye's optical properties focus the incoming light on the layer of sense cells constituting the retina. The hair cells of the ear, which are very sensitive to rapid changes in air pressure because of the ear's structure, are also well protected from other mechanical disturbances by shock-absorbing fluid.

Another main factor that differentiates types of sense cells is the presence of specific receptor sites for reacting with the energy to which they are specifically sensitive. Certain cells, for example, can be specifically stimulated by a given substance and no other, at least in the small concentrations required for reaction. Cells with such narrow reaction ranges are rare, however; more often, each cell has a wider spectrum, as is the case of the photoreceptors of the eye with regard to colour. Photoreceptors comprise three types of cell, each with a definite optimum but reactive to well-overlapping band widths, thereby providing for a range of colour vision. In other cases, it is the threshold (the lowest energy level) to any given stimulus that varies in different cells; this variation provides for measurement of the intensity of the stimulus. In many cases, however, intensity is coded by the frequency of the nerve impulses each receptor sends to the central nervous system.

The actual amounts of energy that can be transformed into a nerve impulse are sometimes amazingly small. One or a few photons of light absorbed may suffice not only for reception and transformation into a nerve impulse in several optic fibres but also for visual perception.

Photo-receptors

Photoreceptors are sensitive to light changes. They contain photopigments for absorption of light. The variety of photopigments in different cells determines the number of colours that can be distinguished. It is interesting to note that in insects, among other animals, colour sensitivity is extended into the ultraviolet range, though it is short in the red range. Cells especially sensitive to infrared radiation are found in the remarkable pit organs of vipers, which enable the snake to locate warm-blooded prey from a distance even when it freezes into immobility.

In the skin of warm-blooded animals, nerve endings, with or without accessory structures, are present that react especially to warming or to cooling (see THERMORECEPTION).

Taste and smell

Well-known organs of chemical reception are those of smell and of taste. Except in cases in which there is great specificity to one substance, as, for example, the sex attractant in insects, the spectrum of chemoreceptive cells is broad. The sense of taste was long thought to be mediated by narrow, separate fibres for acid, bitter, sweet, and sour sensations; this viewpoint is now being replaced by one in which the spectra are considerably wider. Frogs have been shown to have taste cells that react specifically to distilled water. Chemoreceptors are also present as enteroreceptors, a well-known example being the carotid body in certain vertebrates; this organ monitors oxygen pressure in the carotid artery, which supplies the brain with blood.

Mechanoreceptors are the most widespread type of sense receptor and the most varied with regard to localization, sensitivity, and type of nerve-impulse firing. There are numerous subdivisions of the mechanoreceptive sense, such as touch, pain, sound, gravity, and muscle tone. Examples in humans include the naked nerve endings in the cornea of the eye; the Pacinian corpuscles in the skin, with their multilayered sheathlike covers; and the hair cells in the inner ear. Impulse formation may continue for as long as stimulus lasts, thus giving a continuous (tonic) type of discharge, or be limited and proportional to the rate of change of the stimulus, thus producing an abrupt (phasic) discharge. A remarkable type of mechanoreceptor occurs in the elastic organs of crustacean legs; movement-sensitive cells fire for the time a joint moves in one direction, and others fire for the opposite movement (see MECHANORECEPTION and SOUND RECEPTION).

Electro-reception

Electroreception is known only in certain fishes. Electrosensitive cells are accompanied by an organ that sends out small or large voltage changes. The sense cells occur along the long axis of the fish, enabling it both to discover food objects in the surrounding water and to locate other fish. This system is a great aid for navigation in murky water (see BIOELECTRICITY).

Certain animals appear to be able to orient to environmental changes for which no specific sense cells are known. Among these, magnetism is the most outstanding example. In fish, magnetic fields may well be received by electroreceptors. In insects and birds, which seem to perceive magnetic fields, no special sense cells have been implicated. The wide variety of phenomena considered as extrasensory perception in man may be based on direct influence on central-nervous elements, thus bypassing sensory input channels.

Evolution of sensory systems. Specific sensory abilities do not show a clear evolutionary progression, most likely because the development of any type of sense depends on many other factors in the total ecology of a given organism. Vision, for instance, is sometimes poor or absent in a species of a class in which other members have a highly developed visual system: examples include cave-dwelling species, relatives of sighted emergent species.

Mechanical stimuli are effective in all forms of life. Specialized organs, however, appear very early in animal evolution; such organs include gravity and light receptors in jellyfish. In more advanced members of the phyla Mollusca and Arthropoda, greatly developed sense organs occur, some of which show an amazingly close resemblance to vertebrate organs; *e.g.*, *Octopus* eyes and semicircular canals (for equilibrium). There is always a close relationship between the presence of highly developed sense organs and a region of the central nervous system; the latter is needed to "process" the incoming information in order to abstract the cues of importance to a given animal. The fact that such elaborate systems exist does not exclude the possibility of much shorter and simpler pathways, which provide for more localized and quicker reactions; for instance, the blink reflex, caused by the sudden approach of an object to the eye, bypasses the visual cortex of the brain.

Sensory information. Although sensory information must be coded into a flow of nerve impulses for transmittal over distances, interactions between adjacent sense cells and sensory neurons also occur. Nerve cells can influence each other by mutual connections that result in membrane potential changes (electrical differences) in one when the other is stimulated. Similar effects are often caused by nerve impulses. When a number of nerve cells (neurons) with adjacent receptive fields are activated, it is common to find that the ones receiving the strongest stimulation suppress the response of those that are stimulated less. This action leads to a sharper difference at boundaries of stimulated and nonstimulated areas; thus, contrasts can be enhanced by this process, known as lateral inhibition. Certain sense cells have the property of being active, usually at a low rate, when not stimulated. This activity can then be either increased or decreased by appropriate stimuli. It is by such means that neurons indicating visual movements in one direction or sounds changing from one frequency to another obtain their selectivity. Such elaborations can be performed at different levels of the central nervous system. In the higher mammals, for instance, the fibres forming the optic nerve are mainly of two types, with small visual fields, one in which light in the centre of the field excites while light in the surrounding field inhibits, and vice versa. In animals even as highly developed as the rabbit, more complex integration has taken place in the visual periphery, and optic fibres can indicate such features as the movement of oriented lines in specific directions, which in cats and monkeys does not seem to occur before units in the brain have sampled the incoming information.

Lateral inhibition

From this and other information it is clear that the use the animal makes of its senses is highly correlated with the type of sensory integration taking place in the nervous system. The ways by which a given stimulus is analyzed are varied and as yet only partially understood. It is, however, possible to build models that can be of mutual benefit for engineering and sensory information processing. By feeding back part of the incoming signal to earlier steps in the information processing, stability is greatly enhanced both in organisms and in machines.

BIBLIOGRAPHY. E.D. ADRIAN, *The Basis of Sensation: The Action of the Sense Organs* (1928), a basic work in the field of sensory physiology; *Cold Spring Harbor Symposia on Quantitative Biology*, vol. 30, *Sensory Receptors* (1965), a report of current concepts and research in the field; JOHN FIELD (ed.), *Handbook of Physiology*, sect. 1, *Neurophysiology*, vol. 1 (1959), a comprehensive treatise on historical as well as current concepts of sensory reception.

(C.A.G.W.)

Sensory Reception, Human

Ancient philosophers called the human senses "the windows of the soul," and Aristotle enumerated at least five senses—sight, hearing, smell, taste, and touch—and his influence has been so enduring that many people still speak of the five senses as if there were no others. Yet, the human skin alone is now regarded as participating in (mediating) a number of different modalities or senses (*e.g.*, hot, cold, pressure, and pain). The modern sensory catalogue also includes a kinesthetic sense (sense organs in muscles, tendons, and joints) and a sense of balance or equilibrium (so-called vestibular organs of the inner ear stimulated by gravity and acceleration). In addition, there are receptors within the circulatory system that are sensitive to carbon dioxide gas in the blood or to changes in blood pressure; and there are receptors in the digestive tract that appear to mediate such experiences as hunger and thirst.

Not all receptors give rise to direct sensory awareness; circulatory (cardiovascular) receptors function largely in reflexes that adjust blood pressure or heart rate without the person being conscious of them. Though perceptible as hunger pangs, feelings of hunger are not exclusively mediated by the gastric (stomach) receptors. Some brain cells may also participate as "hunger" receptors. This is especially true of cells in the lower parts of the brain (such as the hypothalamus) where some cells have been found to be sensitive to changes in blood chemistry (water and other products of digestion) and even to changes in temperature within the brain itself.

CLASSIFICATION OF THE SENSES AND GENERAL CONSIDERATIONS OF SENSATION

Basic features. One way to classify sensory structures is by the stimuli to which they normally respond; thus, there are photoreceptors (for light), mechanoreceptors (for distortion or bending), thermoreceptors (for heat), chemoreceptors (*e.g.*, for chemical odours), and nociceptors (for painful stimuli). This classification is useful because it makes clear that various sense organs can share common features in the way they convert (transduce) stimulus energy into nerve impulses. Thus, auditory cells and vestibular (balance) receptors in the ear and some receptors in the skin all respond similarly to mechanical displacement (distortion). Because many of the same principles apply to other animals, their receptors can be studied as models of the human senses. In addition, many animals are endowed with specialized receptors that permit them to detect stimuli that man cannot sense. A snake (the pit viper) boasts a receptor of exquisite sensitivity to "invisible" infrared light; some insects have receptors for ultraviolet light and for pheromones (chemical sex attractants and aphrodisiacs unique to their own species) thereby also exceeding human sensory capabilities.

Classification by stimuli

Regardless of their specific anatomical form, all sense organs share basic features. (1) They contain receptor cells which are specifically sensitive to one class of stimulus energies, usually within a restricted range of intensity. Such selectivity means that each receptor can be said to have its own "adequate" or proper or normal stimulus, as, for example, light is the adequate stimulus for visual experience. Nevertheless, other energies ("inadequate" stimuli) can also activate the receptor if they are sufficiently intense. Thus, one may "see" pressure when, for example, the thumb is placed on a closed eye and one experiences a bright spot (phosphene) seen in the visual field at a position opposite the touched place. (2) The sensitive mechanism for each modality is often localized in the body at a receiving membrane or surface (such as the retina of the eye) where transducer neurons (sense cells) are to be found. Often the sensory organ incorporates accessory structures to guide the stimulating energy to the receptor cells; thus, the normally transparent cornea and lens within the eye focus light on the retinal sensory neurons. In some cases, blindness can be cured by surgically removing a lens that has grown opaque from cataract in order to permit light once again to reach the retina. Additional postoperative optical correction in the form of a contact lens or eyeglasses is necessary to compensate for the missing lens. Retinal nerve cells themselves are more or less shielded from nonvisual sources of energy by the surrounding structure of the eye; but mild electrical currents delivered to most sense organs, including the eye, can produce sensory experiences appropriate to the specific organ. The generalized electrical nature of neural function largely accounts for the effectiveness of such currents in evoking a full range of different sensations. (3) The primary transducers or sensory cells in any receptor structure normally connect (synapse) with secondary, ingoing (afferent) nerve cells that carry the nerve impulse along. In some receptors, such as the skin, the individual primary cells possess threadlike structures (axons) that may be yards long, winding from just beneath the skin surface through subcutaneous tissues until they reach the spinal cord. Here each axon from the skin terminates and synapses with the next (second-order) neuron in the chain. By contrast, each primary receptor cell in the eye has a very short axon that is contained entirely in the retina, making synaptic contact with a network of several types of second-order (internuncial) cells, which, in turn, make synaptic contact with third-order neurons called bipolar cells, all still in the retina. The bipolar-cell axons extend afferently beyond the retina, leaving the eyeball to form the optic nerve, which enters the brain to make further synaptic connections. If this visual system is considered as a whole, the retina may be said to be an extended part of the brain on which light can directly fall. (4) From such afferent nerves, still higher order neurons make increasingly complex connections with anatomically separate pathways of the brainstem and deeper parts of the brain (*e.g.,* the thalamus) that eventually end in specific receiving areas in the cerebral cortex (the convoluted outer shell of the brain). Different sensory receiving areas are localized in particular regions of the cortex; *e.g.,* occipital lobes in back for vision, temporal lobes on the sides for hearing, and parietal lobes toward the top of the brain for tactual function.

Sensory
parts of
the brain

Approaches to the study of sensing. The science of the human senses is truly interdisciplinary. Philosophers, physicians, anatomists, physical scientists, physiologists, psychologists, and others have all joined in studying sensory activities. Some of their earliest work was anatomical, an approach that continues to be fruitful. Physical scientists, particularly physicists and chemists, made especially important contributions to an understanding of the nature of stimulus energies (*e.g.,* acoustic, photic, thermal, mechanical, chemical); in the process, they also carried out many fundamental measurements of human sensory function. Hermann L.F. von Helmholtz, a 19th century German scientist who was a physicist, physiologist, and psychologist, studied the way in which sound waves and light are received (sensed or detected) and also how they are interpreted (perceived) by people.

Modern studies of sensation have been enhanced by contemporary devices permitting the precise production and control of sensory stimuli. With other kinds of instruments, physiologists have been able to probe the electrical signals generated by sensory cells and afferent nerve fibres to provide a biophysical analysis of sensory mechanisms. Psychophysics embraces the study of the inner (private, subjective) aspects of sensation in terms of outer (public, objective) stimulus energies. One of the oldest and most classical approaches to the study of sensation, psychophysics includes the study of people's reports of their sensations when they are stimulated: of their ability, for example, to match tones of equal loudness, to detect stimulus differences, and to estimate sensory magnitude or intensity under conditions of controlled stimulation. Psychophysical research continues as an active enterprise particularly among modern psychologists.

An old philosophical notion that "mind" is but a clean slate or tablet (*tabula rasa*) until written on by impressions from the senses no longer seems fully tenable; human infants, for example, show inborn (innate) ways of sensing or perceiving at birth. In its modern form, the problem of learned versus innate factors in sensory experience is studied in terms of the extent to which the genetically determined structure and function of sense organs and brain depend upon stimulation and experience for their proper maturation. Poverty of stimulation (sensory deprivation) in an infant's early life increasingly is being documented as detrimental to the full flowering of mature perceptual and intellectual functions. Since this sort of evidence may indeed lend some support to the notion of the *tabula rasa*, modern investigators give credence both to nativistic (based on heredity) and empiricistic (based on learning) interpretations of human sensory function (see also LEARNING, PERCEPTUAL).

A distinction between the discriminatory (epicritic) and emotional (protopathic) features of sensations was made by Sir Henry Head (1861–1940), a British neurologist, who noted, for example, that after a sensory nerve from the skin had been cut, the first sensations to recover as the nerve healed appeared to be diffuse, poorly localized, and extremely unpleasant. He theorized that this initial lack of sharp discrimination associated with unpleasant experience reflected the properties of a primitive protopathic (emotional) neural system which regenerated first. He held that this system subserves pain and the extremes of temperature and pressure sensation usually associated with an affective (emotional) tone. Because recovery of

Emotional
aspects of
sensation

fine tactual discrimination, sensitivity to lightly graded stimuli, and the ability to localize points touched on the skin returned later, Head posited the existence of another discriminatory system. While later research has not confirmed his theory, the sequence of changes in the recovery following nerve injury is most typical.

Chemical-visceral sensations particularly have hedonic (pleasure–pain) properties. Most people tend to refer to odours and tastes as pleasant or unpleasant; thus, the chemical senses are closely tied to motivation, to preferences, or to aversions. Although reflex licking or sucking is stimulated by tactual stimulation of lips and mouth, newborn infants tend to suck longer and harder when the stimulus has clear hedonic value; *e.g.,* avidly turning their lips toward a nipple to get a sweet taste. (See also EMOTION; MOTIVATION.) Apparently, one's sweet tooth is largely nativistic, in that it requires little prior learning. The craving for salt (especially heightened under conditions of salt deprivation) likewise appears to be widespread throughout the animal kingdom without prior learning. The role of taste and smell as innate factors in behaviour may not be quite so influential in man as in other animals. Man's food habits and preferences are strongly overladen with custom and tradition; that is, they are learned in large measure.

In the modern era, the language of communication engineering has been found to be useful in describing human senses. Thus, each sensory modality may be described as a channel that receives stimulus information (input), that processes and stores the information, and that retrieves it as needed for the effective behaviour (output) of the individual. In addition, modern engineering has provided devices (*e.g.,* radio, television, radar, the electron microscope) that serve to extend the range and power of man's senses; in the last analysis, however, all such devices convert (transduce) their information back to a form of stimulus energy that is directly perceptible to the unaided senses. Thus a television set is a transducer that converts imperceptible electromagnetic waves into visual and auditory signals. For some special purposes, people may employ alternative sensory channels, as when blind people use Braille or other tactual input as substitutes for the missing visual channels. While the chemical senses have little function in symbolic communication among people, the use of perfumes in romantic signalling is a notable exception. In general, however, the human chemical senses are more directly involved in physiological survival; *e.g.,* warning that a putrid fish is dangerous to eat. One's physical well-being also rests heavily on his proprioceptors (for sensing his own bodily position) and on his sense of balance. These structures, monitoring (feeding back information on) his bodily orientation in space, provide crucial sensory feedback for guiding one's movements (see also PERCEPTION OF MOVEMENT).

CUTANEOUS (SKIN) SENSES

It was observed above that studies of cutaneous (skin) sensitivity yield evidence that man's senses number more than five. There is evidence for two pressure senses (for light and for deep stimulation), for two kinds of temperature sensitivity (warm and cold), and for a pain sense. In the 1880s, experimental findings that the human skin is punctate (selectively sensitive at different points) gave clear indication of a dissociation among functions once lumped together as the sense of touch. Mapping the skin with a fine bristle or with a narrow-tipped (warm or cold) cylinder showed that there were different spots of maximum sensitivity to pressure, warm, and cold. When stimulated between the spots on the skin, people reported no such sensations. Pain spots also can be located with a finely pointed needle, but the punctate character is less striking since pain seems to be widespread when stimulus intensity is increased. The number of spots is greatest for pain, next for touch, then for cold, and least for warm. Efforts to identify specific receptor cells for each of these sensitive points have been the subject of much debate and still pose a problem that is not completely settled.

Mapping
sensitive
spots of
skin

Nerve function. Microscopic examination of the skin reveals a variety of nerve terminals; there are free nerve endings (which are most common), so-called Ruffini endings, and encapsulated endings, such as the pacinian corpuscle, Meissner's corpuscle, or Krause end bulb, all named for investigators who discovered them (Figure 1).

From E. Gardner, *Fundamentals of Neurology*, 5th ed. (1968); W.B. Saunders Company, Philadelphia

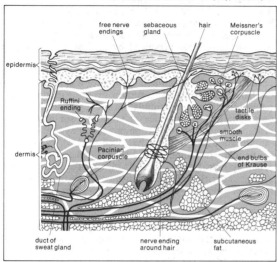

Figure 1: Microscopic view of human skin.

At one time it was thought that each of these specialized structures mediated one of the cutaneous modalities, but efforts to extirpate (surgically remove) the nerve endings under the spots have yielded only questionable data. Further, the cornea of the eye shows only free nerve endings; yet pain, pressure, and some temperature sensations can be elicited by stimulating the corneal surface.

Electrical recordings from the cutaneous nerves of laboratory animals suggest a much wider variety of receptors than are encompassed by the reports people give of their sensations. Some nerve endings seem to respond only to one type of stimulus (*e.g.*, to pressure stimuli of very light weight or to slight temperature changes); others exhibit a broad range of sensitivity. There are some receptors that show combined sensitivity to both temperature and pressure. In some cases only special types of mechanical stimulation (such as rubbing) may be effective. Furthermore, there is an extensive overlap in the areas of skin (receptor fields) for the individual nerve fibres examined, suggesting that there is a neural integration of overlapping afferent inputs of skin nerves. A model of the sensory system that envisages only a single nerve fibre serving one tactual spot is clearly contradicted.

On the other hand, some tactual receptors (*e.g.*, Pacinian corpuscles) respond only to mechanical deformation. This corpuscle is an onion-shaped structure of non-neural (connective) tissue built up around the nerve ending; indeed, the distinctive corpuscle, if anything, reduces the mechanical sensitivity of the nerve terminal itself. If the onion-like capsule is entirely removed, mechanical sensitivity not only remains but is somewhat greater than when the capsule is present.

Variations in sensory nerve fibres

In addition to the differences in the sensory end structures of the skin, the afferent nerve fibres (axons) from them also show diversity. The nerve fibres range in size from large myelinated (sheathed) axons of 10 to 15 microns diameter down to extremely small unmyelinated fibres measuring only tenths of microns across. Fatter axons tend to conduct nerve impulses more rapidly than do small fibres; when axons of different diameters form a single bundle (a nerve), they constitute a so-called mixed nerve. Thus, electrical records from a mixed nerve show what are labelled A (fast), B (medium), and C (slow) components that reflect the typical speeds at which axons of different diameters conduct. Although such specialized capsules as Pacinian corpuscles tend to be associated with larger diameter axons, and temperature-sensitive endings tend to be associated with medium-size fibres, a unique

relation of each of the skin modalities with one of the A, B, or C fibre groups cannot be supported. All of the cutaneous senses seem to be associated with some fibres of all diameters; furthermore, the C fibres (once thought to be restricted to the pain function) display quite specific sensitivities to nonpainful stimuli applied to the skin.

A major neural pathway for tactual impulses runs along the back (in the dorsal columns) of the spinal cord. Afferent fibres enter the cord from the cutaneous nerves and ascend without synaptic break in one (the ipsilateral) dorsal column. This is a very rapidly conducting pathway shared by fibres that mediate sensations of deep pressure and also kinesthesis. Other tactual, temperature, and pain information crosses the spinal cord close to the level of entry of the sensory fibres and ascends to the brain in contralateral pathways of the cord (the lateral and ventral spinothalamic tracts).

Each of the nerves distributed along the spinal cord contains a sensory bundle that serves a well-defined strip of skin (a dermatome) about an inch or more wide on the body surface. Successive spinal nerves overlap, so that each place on the skin represents two and sometimes three dermatomes; this yields a segmented pattern of strips over the body from head to toe. All dermatomes feed into a single relay centre (the sensory thalamus) deep within the brain, where a precise three-dimensional layout of tactual sensitivity at the body surface can be found. The neurons in this part of the thalamus (the ventral posterolateral nucleus) are specific to particular skin senses (such as pressure) and form small and precise receptor fields. There is a second more diffuse thalamic system (in the posterior thalamic nuclei) where the receptor fields are large, perhaps bilateral, on the left and right sides, perhaps including one whole side of the body. The receptor fields here or the types of stimuli to which they respond are not clearly delineated.

The dissociation of cutaneous senses is dramatically demonstrated in the course of some diseases; for example, in a disorder called syringomyelia, degeneration of the central canal of the spinal cord leads to loss of pain and temperature sensitivity. Nevertheless, the sufferer still can experience pressure. In some instances there may be a complete absence of pain sensitivity with disastrous consequences for the welfare of the afflicted person. Such individuals are bruised and cut and even lose parts of the body because they are unable to sense the dangerous (painful) characteristics of stimuli. Among people born with total absence of the pain sense, there may not be demonstrable anatomic abnormality. Still other instances of dissociation of pain versus pressure occur in surgical procedures (such as tractotomy) in which spinal tracts or parts of the nerves leading into the brainstem are selectively cut. Such operations are designed specifically to relieve pain without unduly diminishing pressure sensitivity.

Pathways from the specific (ventral posterolateral) thalamus end (or project) in a narrow band of brain cortex (the posterior rolandic cortical sensory area in man) where there is a point-for-point representation of the body surface on the cortical surface. The cortical projection of the more diffuse (posterior) thalamic system is less well charted. There thus appears to be a dissociation between those tactual structures that are highly specific and those that are more generalized.

Tactual psychophysics. The mixture of sensitivities within a given patch of skin provides a ready basis for the concept of adequate stimulation. Sometimes, for example, a cold spot responds to a very warm stimulus, and the person experiences what is called paradoxical cold. The **Paradoxical cold** sensation of heat from a hot stimulus presumably arises from the adequate stimulation of warmth receptors combined with the inadequate or inappropriate (albeit effective) stimulation of cold and pain receptors.

Human ability to barely detect pressure (*i.e.*, the human pressure threshold) generally appears when a tension of about 0.85 grams per square millimetre of skin surface is applied on the back of the hand. Thus a force of 85 milligrams applied to a stimulus hair (or bristle) of 0.1 square millimetre is just about enough to elicit the experience of pressure. The energy of impact at pressure threshold is very much greater than that required for hearing or seeing, the skin requiring on the order of 100,000,000 times more energy than the ear and 10,000,000,000 times more energy than the eye. Differential pressure discrimination (the ability to detect just noticeable differences in intensity) requires changes of roughly 14 percent at maximum sensitivity.

Adaptation to pressure is well known; one's awareness of a steadily applied bristle fades and ultimately disappears. As a result people are rarely aware of the steady pressure of their clothing unless movement brings about a change in stimulation. Most dramatic and perhaps best known among tactual experiences is adaptation to thermal stimulation. Continued presentation of a warm or cold stimulus leads to reduction or disappearance of the initial sensation and an increase in threshold values. Total obliteration of thermal sensation through adaptation occurs in the range from about 16° to 42° C (61° to 108° F). If one hand is placed in a bowl of hot (40° C [104° F]) water and adapted to that, and at the same time the other hand is adapted to cold (20° C [68° F]) water, then when both hands are simultaneously placed in lukewarm (30° C [86° F]) water, the previously cooled hand feels warm and the other hand feels cold. This effect was once interpreted as evidence for a single temperature sense, but careful study shows that there are indeed two kinds of temperature receptors, both of which show adaptation. Cold receptors are characterized by an electrical discharge on sudden cooling, normally showing no response to sudden warming; similarly appropriate electrical responses are made by warmth receptors. Both receptors show steady discharges selectively depending on temperature; maximum discharge typically occurs between 38° to 43° C (100° to 109° F) for individual warmth cells and between 15° and 34° C (59° and 93° F) for cold receptors. These temperature receptors show no electrical response to weak mechanical stimulation in either laboratory animals or human subjects.

Pain · Pain is least understood among all the human senses. The pattern of stimulation is more crucial in pain than in any other sense. A single brief electric shock to the skin or to an exposed nerve may not elicit the experience of pain; yet it tends to become painful upon repetitive stimulation. Cutaneous pain is often sensed more sharply than is pain associated with deep tissues of the body (e.g., viscera). Certain areas of the body are relatively analgesic (free of pain); for example, the mucous lining of the cheek into which one can bite shallowly without discomfort. The organs of the abdominal cavity are usually insensitive to cutting or burning, but traction or stretching of hollow viscera is painful (as when the stomach is distended by gas). Pain displays sensory adaptation, although the process appears to be more complex than it is for other sensory modalities. Thus, the intensities of headaches, toothaches, and pains from injury often show cyclic fluctuations, possibly from such factors as changes in blood circulation or in degree of inflammation. The visceral pains, those of dental origin, or of diseased tissues can be reduced by analgesic drugs, which tend to be less effective on cutaneous pain. Pain has a strong emotional context (see PAIN, THEORIES OF). In certain cases, after frontal lobotomies (a type of brain surgery) have been performed, a person may report that he still feels the pain of a pin prick or other irritation but that he does not find it as disturbing or emotionally disruptive as he did before the lobotomy. Many phenomena indicate the powerful role of the brain and spinal cord in sensing potentially painful sensory input. Indeed, according to one theory, a so-called gate control system in the spinal cord modulates (increases or decreases) sensory input from the skin to determine whether the input is perceived as painful. This theoretical formulation also may account for moment-to-moment fluctuations in the intensity of perceived pain despite the absence of any stimulus change. Such brain-mediated factors as emotional tension or past psychological experience are held to influence pain perception by acting upon this spinal gate control system.

Itching seems to bear the same relation to pain as tickle does to pressure. The experience usually lasts long Itching · enough to demand attention and (like tickle) normally leads to a response such as rubbing or scratching the affected area. A number of skin disorders are accompanied by itching, presumably from a fairly low level of irritation in the affected area (which also may be produced in undiseased skin). While a single shock by a low-intensity electrical spark normally produces no sensation, a repetitive pattern of such shocks may induce an itch not unlike that produced by an insect bite. Itching also may occur as an aftereffect of the sharp pricking sensation produced by single strong shocks, presumably because the nerves continue to produce a patterned afterdischarge following the cessation of the stimulus. Nonpainful tactile pattern stimulation is exemplified by vibration. Different frequencies of vibration are readily discriminated and a tactual communication system employing vibrations on the skin has been devised, particularly for people who cannot see or hear. Further research will probably reveal other ways of utilizing the fine discriminatory capacities of the cutaneous senses as substitutes for other sensory avenues of communication.

KINESTHETIC (MOTION) SENSE

It is a common experience that, with the eyes closed, one is aware of the positions of his legs and arms and can perceive the active or passive movement of a limb and its direction. The term kinesthesis (literally "feeling of motion") has been coined for this sensibility.

Nerve function. Four types of sensory structures are widely distributed in muscles, tendons, and joints (Figure 2): (1) the neuromuscular spindle consists of small, fine

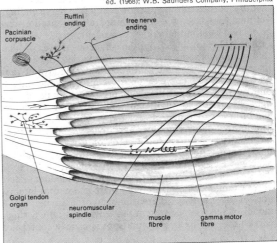

From E. Gardner, *Fundamentals of Neurology*, 5th ed. (1968); W.B. Saunders Company, Philadelphia

Figure 2: Sensory structures of muscle, tendon, and joint. Arrows indicate direction of conduction. (Motor nerves and motor nerve endings on contractile muscle fibres not shown.)

muscle fibres around which sensory fibre endings are wrapped; (2) the Golgi tendon organ consists of sensory nerve fibres that terminate in a rich branching encapsulated within the tendon; (3) joint receptors (as in the knee) consist of "spray-type" endings (Ruffini) and Golgi-type and Pacinian corpuscles within the joints; and (4) free nerve endings. All these receptors combine to provide information on active contraction, passive stretch of muscle fibres, and tension whether produced actively or passively. In passive stretch both the muscle-spindle receptors and the tendon receptors send trains of impulses over their sensory (afferent) nerves; in active contraction the spindles show a silent period of neural activity when tension on the parallel fibres is unloaded, while the tendon receptors discharge just as when stretch is passive.

The muscle spindle is contractile in response to its own small-diameter, so-called gamma motor (efferent) fibre. The receptors and the gamma fibres of the muscle spindle form a neuromuscular loop that serves to insure that tension on the spindle is maintained within its efficient operating limits. The excitability of the muscle spindle also can be influenced through other neural pathways that control the general level of excitability of the central nervous system (brain and spinal cord). Activity of the descending reticular formation (a network of cells in the brainstem) may enhance the contraction of the spindle and hence influence its neural discharges.

The knee jerk

Muscle and tendon receptors combine to play an intimate and crucial role in the regulation of reflex and voluntary movement. Much of this control is automatic (involuntary) and not directly perceptible except in the aftereffects of movement or change of position. The knee jerk that follows a tap just below the kneecap of a freely hanging leg is one such involuntary reflex. Sensory (afferent) impulses from stretching the receptors (*e.g.*, in the muscles) relay to the spinal cord and activate a path to the motor (efferent) nerves leading back to the same muscle. The knee jerk is a purely spinal reflex response (the brain is not required) which is tested usually to determine nerve damage or other interference with the spinal-cord motor mechanisms. Besides producing loss of knee jerk, a disease such as syphilis may lead to locomotor ataxia (a clumsy and stumbling gait) when the germ (called a spirochete) attacks the sensory nerves of the cord's dorsal column. The result is that the sufferer has difficulty sensing the position of his limbs. Another general function of the muscle receptors is the maintenance of muscle tone (or tonus: partial contraction) to permit rapid response (fast reaction time) to stimulation. In normal conditions the muscle has tone and is ready to go; but, when it is without motor stimulation (deafferented), the muscle is flaccid, showing little tone. One's upright posture depends on the tonus of opposing (extensor and flexor) muscles in response to the effects of gravity.

The exact contribution of the muscle receptors to sensation is not entirely understood. It seems clear, however, that they are not essential to the sensation of bodily position. It has been suggested that the appreciation of passive movement of the limbs probably comes largely from the joints, since, after anesthetizing the overlying skin and muscles (*e.g.*, with cocaine), sensibility to the limb movement seems little affected. Evidence also shows that very few of the impulses arising from the muscle receptors themselves reach the cerebral cortex; instead, they ascend in the spinal pathways to another part of the brain (the cerebellum) where they interact in the automatic control of bodily movement. Impulses arising from the joint receptors, on the other hand, have been recorded in both the thalamus and brain cortex, the degree of angular displacement of a joint being reflected systematically in these structures by the frequency of nerve impulses. Symptoms of some diseases also emphasize the importance of joint sensitivity. When bone disease, for example, destroys only the joint receptors the person's ability to appreciate posture and movement is lost.

Cerebellar disorders

The feedback system. The feedback system leading to muscle tonus is a most delicately balanced mechanism. The gamma loop feeds back information that serves to maintain the muscle tonus and postural adjustments appropriate to the efficient performance of different voluntary actions. The afferent input from the muscle spindles via the spinal cord to the brain's cerebellum traverses an extensive circuit involving interactions of excitatory and inhibitory processes, the end result of which helps insure smooth and finely coordinated movements. Disease or other neurological damage in the cerebellum is characterized by distortions of movement and posture. Some sufferers of cerebellar disorders display crude, overactive motor activity (ballistic movement) that overshoots the mark in attempted voluntary coordination. Other victims of cerebellar disease display what resemble a drunken gait, jerkily stumbling and swaying along. By relying on other sensory cues (*e.g.*, visual and tactual), some people are able to compensate for awkward and uncoordinated movements associated with cerebellar damage.

VESTIBULAR SENSE (EQUILIBRIUM)

Function of the inner ear. The human inner ear contains parts (the nonauditory labyrinth or vestibular organ) that are sensitive to acceleration in space, rotation, and orientation in the gravitational field. Rotation is signalled by way of the semicircular canals, three bony tubes in each ear that lie embedded in the skull roughly at right angles to each other. These canals are filled with fluid (endolymph); in the ampulla of each canal are receptor cells with fine hairs that project up into the fluid to be displaced as the endolymph lags behind when rotation begins. When rotation is maintained at a steady velocity, the fluid catches up, and stimulation of the hair cells no longer occurs until rotation suddenly stops, again circulating the endolymph. Whenever the hair cells are thus stimulated, one normally experiences a sensation of rotation in space. During rotation one exhibits reflex nystagmus (back-and-forth movement) of the eyes. Slow displacement of the eye occurs against the direction of rotation and serves to maintain the gaze at a fixed point in space; this is followed by a quick return to the initial eye position in the direction of the rotation. Stimulation of the hair cells in the absence of actual rotation tends to produce an apparent swimming of the visual field, often associated with dizziness and nausea; compensatory postural adjustments commonly follow.

Two sacs or enlargements of the vestibule (the saccule and utricle) react to steady (static) pressures; *e.g.*, those of gravitational forces. Hair cells within these structures are covered by a gelatinous cap in which are embedded small granular particles of calcium carbonate (otoliths) that weigh against the hairs. When iron particles are implanted in the same structures of a fish, they may be displaced by externally applied magnets. In this way the fish can be made to assume inverted or other unusual positions in the water. In man, unusual stimulation of the vestibular receptors and semicircular canals also can give rise to sensory distortions in visual and motor activity. The resulting discord between one's visual and motor responses and the external space (as aboard ship in a heaving sea) often leads to nausea and disorientation (*e.g.*, seasickness). In space flight these sensory systems usually are not stimulated except as the weightless astronaut affects them by his own movements. Such abnormal gravitational and acceleratory forces apparently contribute to the nausea or disequilibrium sometimes reported by people in outer space. Training before space flight reduces the likelihood and severity of these symptoms.

Seasickness

Factors affecting equilibrium. In some diseases (*e.g.*, ear infections), irritation of vestibular nerve endings occurs, and the sufferer may be subject to falling as well as to spells of disorientation and vertigo (dizzy confusion). Similar symptoms may be induced by flushing hot and cold water into the outer opening of the ear, since the temperature changes produce currents in the endolymph of the semicircular canals. This caloric (temperature) effect is used in clinical tests for vestibular functions and in physiological experiments. Externally applied electrical currents may also stimulate the nerve endings of the vestibule. When current is applied to the right mastoid bone (just behind the ear), nystagmus to the right tends to occur, associated with a reflex right movement of the head; movement tends to the left for the opposite mastoid. In man, destruction of the labyrinth in only one ear causes vertigo and other vestibular symptoms, such as nystagmus, inaccurate pointing, and tendency to fall. Very often symptoms of sweating and flushing appear, indicating involvement of other (autonomic) parts of the nervous system. Discomfort, disorientation, nausea, and vertigo may gradually subside, and a complete recovery from the one-sided vestibular disability may occur after one or two months. Following complete loss of vestibular function on both sides, the symptoms are much less likely to occur. Some disturbance of equilibrium is present, however; when blindfolded, the person has difficulty in maintaining normal posture or locomotion. This is especially pronounced when he is submerged in water; he tends to become disoriented and is as likely to swim downward as upward in trying to reach the surface (see also EAR AND HEARING, HUMAN).

TASTE (GUSTATORY) SENSE

The sensory structures for taste in man are the taste buds, clusters of cells contained in goblet-shaped structures (papillae) that open by a small pore to the mouth cavity. A single bud contains about 50 to 75 slender cells, all arranged in a banana like cluster pointed toward the gustatory pore (see also CHEMOREPTION). These are the taste receptor cells, which differentiate from the surrounding epithelium, grow to mature form, and then die out to be replaced by new cells in a turnover period as short as seven to ten days. The various types of cells in the taste bud appear to be different stages in this turnover process. Slender nerve fibres entwine among and make contact usually with many cells. In man and other mammals, taste buds are located primarily in fungiform (mushroom-shaped), foliate, and circumvallate (walled-around) papillae of the tongue or in adjacent structures of the palate and throat. Many gustatory receptors in small papillae on the soft palate and back roof of the mouth in human adults are particularly sensitive to sour and bitter, whereas the tongue receptors are relatively more sensitive to sweet and salt. Some loss of taste sensitivity suffered among wearers of false teeth may be traceable to mechanical interference of the denture with taste receptors on the roof of the mouth.

Locations of taste buds

Nerve supply. There is no single sensory nerve for taste in vertebrates. In man, the anterior (front) two-thirds of the tongue is supplied by one nerve (the lingual nerve), the back of the tongue by another (the glossopharyngeal nerve), and the throat and larynx by certain branches of a third (the vagus nerve), all of which subserve touch, temperature, and pain sensitivity in the tongue as well as taste. The gustatory fibres of the anterior tongue leave the lingual nerve to form a slender nerve (the chorda tympani) that traverses the eardrum on the way to the brain stem. When the chorda tympani at one ear is cut or damaged (by injury to the eardrum), taste buds begin to disappear and gustatory sensitivity is lost on the anterior two-thirds of the tongue on the same side. Impulses have been recorded from the human chorda tympani, and good correlations have been found between the reports people give of their sensations of taste and of the occurrence of the afferent nerve discharge. The taste fibres from all the sensory nerves from the mouth come together in the brainstem (medulla oblongata). Here and at all levels of the brain, gustatory fibres run in distinct and separate pathways, lying close to the pathways for other modalities from the tongue and mouth cavity. From the brain's medulla, the gustatory fibres ascend by a pathway to a small cluster of cells in the thalamus and thence to a taste-receiving area in the anterior cerebral cortex.

Physiological basis of taste. No simple relation has been found between chemical composition of stimuli and the quality of gustatory experience except in the case of acids. The taste qualities of inorganic salts (such as potassium bromide, a sedative) are complex; epsom salt (magnesium sulfate) commonly is sensed as bitter, while table salt (sodium chloride) is typical of sodium salts, which usually yield the familiar saline taste. Experiences of sweet and bitter are elicited by many different classes of chemical compound.

Types of taste receptors

Theorists of taste sensitivity classically posited only four basic or primary types of human taste receptors, one for each gustatory quality: salty, sour, bitter, and sweet. Yet, recordings of sensory impulses in the taste nerves of laboratory animals show that many individual nerve fibres from the tongue are of mixed sensitivity, responding to more than one of the basic taste stimuli, such as acid plus salt or acid plus salt plus sugar. Other individual nerve fibres respond to stimuli of only one basic gustatory quality. Most numerous, however, are taste fibres subserving two basic taste sensitivities; those subserving one or three qualities are about equal in number and next most frequent; fibres that respond to all four primary stimuli are least common. Mixed sensitivity may be only partly attributed to multiple branches of taste nerve endings. In man, experiences of sugars, synthetic sweeteners, weak salt solutions, and the taste of some unpleasant medicines are blocked by a drug (gymnemic acid) obtained from *Gymnema* bushes native to India. Among some laboratory animals, gymnemic acid blocks only the nerve re-

sponse to sugar, even if the fibre mediates other taste qualities. Such a multiresponsive fibre still can transmit taste impulses (*e.g.*, for salt or sour), so that blockage by the drug can be attributed to chemically specific sites or cells in the taste bud.

In some species of animals (*e.g.*, the cat), specific taste receptors appear to be activated by water; these so-called water receptors are inhibited by weak saline solutions. Water taste might be considered a fifth gustatory quality in addition to the basic four.

The qualities of taste. *Sour.* The hydrogen ions of acids (*e.g.*, hydrochloric acid, HCl) are largely responsible for the sour taste; but, although a stimulus grows more sour as its hydrogen ion (H^+) concentration increases, this factor alone does not determine sourness. Weak organic acids (*e.g.*, the acetic acid in vinegar) taste more sour than would be predicted from their hydrogen ion concentration alone; apparently the rest of the acid molecule affects the efficiency with which hydrogen ions stimulate.

Salt. Although the salty taste is often associated with water-soluble salts, most such compounds (except sodium chloride) have complex tastes such as bitter-salt or sour-salt. Salts of low molecular weight are predominantly salty, while those of higher molecular weight tend to be bitter. The salts of heavy metals such as mercury have a metallic taste, although some of the salts of lead (especially lead acetate) and beryllium are sweet. Both parts of the molecule (*e.g.*, lead and acetate) contribute to taste quality and to stimulating efficiency. In man the following series for degree of saltiness, in decreasing order, is found: ammonium (most salty), potassium, calcium, sodium, lithium, and magnesium salts (least salty). The order appears to vary for other animals.

Sweet. Except for some salts of lead or beryllium, the sweet taste is associated largely with organic compounds (such as alcohols, glycols, sugars, and sugar derivatives). Human sensitivity to synthetic sweeteners (*e.g.*, saccharin) is especially remarkable; the taste of saccharin can be detected in a dilution 700 times weaker than that required for cane sugar. The stereochemical (spatial) arrangement of atoms within a molecule may affect its taste; thus, slight changes within a sweet molecule will make it bitter or tasteless (Figure 3). Several theorists

From R.W. Moncrieff, *Chemical Senses* (1944); Leonard Hill Books

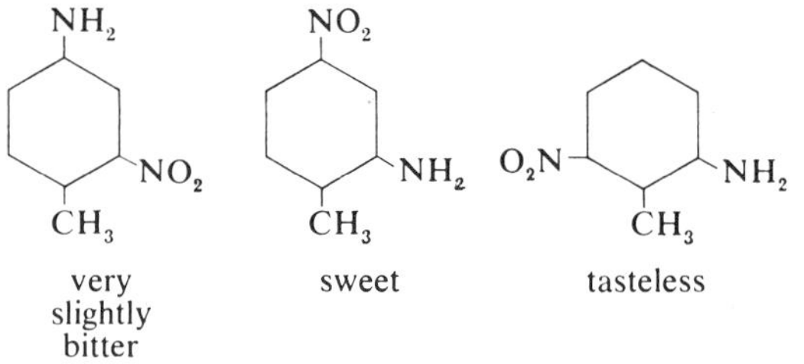

very slightly bitter   sweet   tasteless

Figure 3: Effects of molecular rearrangement on taste sensation (see text).

have proposed that the common feature for all of the sweet stimuli is the presence in the molecule of a so-called proton acceptor, such as the OH (hydroxyl) components of carbohydrates (*e.g.*, sugars) and many other sweet-tasting compounds. It has also been theorized that such molecules will not taste sweet unless they are of appropriate size.

Bitter. The experience of a bitter taste is elicited by many classes of chemical compounds and often is found in association with sweet and other gustatory qualities. Among the best known bitter substances are such alkaloids (often toxic) as quinine, caffeine, and strychnine. Most of these substances have extremely low taste thresholds and are detectable in very weak concentrations. The size of such molecules is theoretically held to account for whether or not they will taste bitter. An increase in molecular weight of inorganic salts or an increase in length of chains of carbon atoms in organic molecules tends to be associated with increased bitterness.

A substantial minority of people exhibit specific taste blindness, an inability to detect as bitter such chemicals as

Taste blindness

PTC (phenylthiocarbamide). Taste blindness for PTC and other carbamides appears to be hereditary (as a recessive trait), occurring least frequently among American Indians and Africans, in about a third of Europeans, and in roughly 40 percent of the people in Western India. Evidence for such taste blindness among other animals has been observed only in anthropoid apes; apparently it appeared at a relatively late stage of evolution. Taste blindness for carbamides is not correlated with insensitivity to other bitter stimuli, the reasons for this being poorly understood.

Factors affecting taste sensitivity. Fluids of extreme temperature, especially those that are cold, may produce temporary taste insensitivity. People generally seem to taste most acutely when the stimulus is at or slightly below body temperature. When the tongue and mouth are first adapted to the temperature of a taste solution, sugar sensitivity increases with temperature rise, salt and quinine sensitivity decrease, and acid sensitivity is relatively unchanged. Gustatory adaptation (partial or complete disappearance of taste sensitivity) may occur if a solution is held in the mouth for a period of time. The effect of one adapting stimulus on the person's sensitivity for another one (cross adaptation) is especially common with substances that are chemically similar and that elicit the same taste quality. Adaptation to sodium chloride will reduce one's ability to sense the saltiness of a variety of the inorganic salts but will leave undiminished or even enhance such qualities as bitterness, sweetness, or sourness that were part of the taste of the salt before adaptation. Likewise, adaptation by one acid may reduce sensitivity to the sourness of other acids.

Contrast effects

Adaptation studies often are complicated by so-called contrast effects; for example, people say that distilled water tastes sweet following their exposure to a weak acid. Water may take on other taste qualities as well; following one's adaptation to a sour-bitter chemical (urea), water may taste salty. Adaptation tends to diminish or enhance the effect of a subsequent stimulus depending on whether the two stimuli normally elicit the same or a contrasting taste. Thus the adapted sweetness of water and all normally sweet-tasting substances are enhanced after one has tasted acid (sour). The bitterness of tea and coffee or the sourness of lemon are masked or suppressed by sugar or saccharin.

The human gustatory difference threshold (for a just noticeable difference in intensity) is approximately a 20 percent change in concentration. For very weak taste stimuli, however, the threshold sensitivity is poorer.

Food choice. One's ability to taste is intimately concerned in his eating habits or in his rejection of noxious substances. One of the earliest reflex responses of the infant, that of sucking, can be controlled by gustatory stimuli. Sweet solutions are sucked more readily than is plain water; bitter, salty, or sour stimuli tend to stop the sucking reflex.

Among insects, a very specific feeding reaction (proboscis extension) is so automatic that it is widely used as an index of taste stimulation. If a common housefly is held relatively immobile in wax, different parts of the mouth, legs, and body readily may be stimulated by a drop of solution. Sugar solution will make the fly extend its proboscis when a drop is applied to the legs or mouth parts. A fly that has been starved will show a positive response to a weak sugar solution that ordinarily would not affect one that is satiated. Addition of salt or acid to the sugar solution inhibits this response.

Many animals provide clear examples of beneficially selective feeding behaviour. Laboratory rats, when given unhampered choice of carbohydrates, proteins, vitamins, and minerals (each in a separate container), show consistent patterns of self-selection that may be modified by physiological stresses and strains. A rat made salt-deficient by removal of its adrenal glands, for example, will increase its intake of sodium chloride sufficiently to maintain health and growth; normally, such gland removal is fatal in the absence of salt-replacement therapy. Histories of similar effects have been reported in human beings, one dramatic case being that of a child with adrenal disorder who kept himself alive by satisfying an intense salt craving.

Among human adults, past experience shows a strong influence on eating habits, sometimes to the point that physiological well-being suffers. Food habits and other factors play a significant role in eating behaviour.

Poisonous substances often are unpalatable, but not invariably. Lead acetate, sometimes called sugar of lead, once was used as a sweetening agent with disastrous results before its potentially fatal effects were appreciated. Many palatable substances, including some synthetic sweeteners, are toxic; taste alone is not a reliable guide to safety. A rat poison, alpha-naphthylthiourea (ANTU), was developed in a relatively insoluble and therefore tasteless form; soluble forms of ANTU had all been rejected by the animals. Taste aversions also may be readily established by conditioning, even for substances that have been normally preferred. In one study, a rat tasted saccharin solution three hours before being exposed to enough radiation to become sick. When the animal recovered, it was found to have a strong aversion to the taste of saccharin. Other aversions selectively can be produced by injecting the individual with a nauseating drug following specific taste experience. An unusual finding is that long delays of up to several hours in the time between the presentation of the taste stimulus and the induction of illness do not prevent the conditioning. In most other studies, only brief intervals (perhaps up to minutes in duration) have been found to result in successful conditioning. Bait shyness developed by wild rats that survive poisoning strongly suggests conditioned taste aversion. Positive preferences also are subject to conditioning, as when the tastes of drugs or vitamins become associated with the feelings of well-being they generate.

SMELL (OLFACTORY) SENSE

In mammals the olfactory receptors are located high in the nasal cavity. The yellow-pigmented olfactory membrane in humans covers about 2.5 square centimetres on each side of the inner nose. The olfactory sense receptor is a long thin cell ending in several delicate hairs (cilia) that project into and through the mucus that normally covers the nasal epithelium or lining (Figure 4). Electron microscope photographs show from six to 12 olfactory cilia per cell. The end of each receptor narrows to a fine nerve fibre, which, along with many others, enters the

Olfactory receptors

From *Physiological Psychology* by Peter M. Milner. Copyright © 1970 by Holt, Rinehart and Winston, Inc. Reprinted by permission of Holt, Rinehart and Winston, Inc. (After DeLorenzo, 1963)

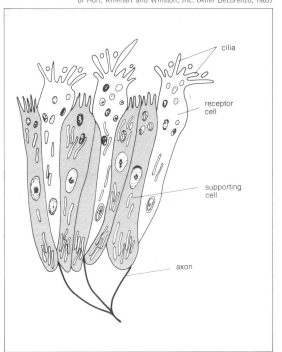

Figure 4: Olfactory lining of the nose.

olfactory bulb of the brain through a fine channel in the bony roof of the nasal cavity. The olfactory membrane of a young rabbit contains about 100,000,000 ciliated receptor cells that provide as much area as total skin surface of the animal.

Pain endings of the trigeminal nerve fibres are widely distributed throughout the human nasal cavity, including the olfactory region. Relatively mild odorants, such as orange oil, as well as the more obvious irritants, such as ammonia, stimulate such free nerve endings as well as the olfactory receptors.

Odorous molecules may be carried to the olfactory region by slight eddies in the air during quiet breathing, but vigorous sniffing brings a surge into the olfactory region. Odour sensitivity may be impaired by blocking the nasal passages mechanically, as when membranes are congested by infection.

It is generally agreed that the antennae of insects are their principal olfactory sites, but specific mouth parts may also bear endings for smell. The nonliving outer covering (cuticle) of such structures has been shown to be pierced by many ultramicroscopic holes through which odorous molecules enter, presumably to dissolve the fluid underneath. In vertebrates (such as man), olfactory stimulation occurs only after the odour molecule is dissolved in the mucus that covers the olfactory membrane. In spite of the wide biological gap between them, odour sensitivity of man and that of insect display certain similarities of mechanism.

Olfactory bulbs

In vertebrates the olfactory nerve fibres enter either of two specialized structures (olfactory bulbs), stemlike projections under the front part of the brain, to end in a microscopic series of intricate basket-like clusters called glomeruli. Each glomerulus receives impulses from about 26,000 receptors and sends them on through other cells, eventually to reach higher olfactory centres at the base of the brain. There are also fibres that cross over from one olfactory bulb to the other. When the olfactory bulbs are removed by surgery, the individual's ability to discriminate odours is lost; details of higher brain centres for smell are still unclear.

Olfactory qualities. The vocabulary of odour is rich with the names of substances that elicit a great variety of olfactory qualities. One of the best known published psychological attempts at classification was in 1916 on the basis of tests of more than 400 different scents on human observers. On the basis of the apparent similarities of perceived odour quality or confusions in naming, it was concluded that there were six main odour qualities: fruity, flowery, resinous, spicy, foul, and burned.

Electrical activity can be detected readily with fine insulated wires inserted into the olfactory bulb. Those portions of the bulb toward the anterior or oral (mouth) region in the rabbit are found to be more sensitive to water-soluble substances, whereas the more posterior or aboral (away from the mouth) parts of the olfactory bulb are more sensitive to fat-soluble substances. In addition, when very fine electrodes are used, individual cells (so-called mitral cells) are found to be sensitive to different groups of chemicals. Evidence for the existence of only a few primary receptors, however, does not emerge from such studies; a variety of different combinations of sensitivity has been found. Similarly, recordings from the primary receptor nerve fibres reveal different patterns of sensitivity. Electrical recording of this type also shows that olfactory sensitivity can be enhanced by a painful stimulus, such as a pinch on the foot of an experimental animal. This appears to be a reflex that serves to enhance the detection of dangerous stimuli in the environment. Different parts of the olfactory neural pathways seem to be selectively tuned to discriminate different classes of olfactory information. Thus, the third- and fourth-order olfactory neurons found beyond the olfactory bulb of the rat seem particularly concerned with distinguishing the odour of sexually receptive females. These neurons appear to be especially important in the preference the male rat shows for the smell of urine from a female in heat.

Odorous substances. To be odorous, a substance must be sufficiently volatile for its molecules to be given off and carried into the nostrils by air currents. The solubility of the substance also seems to play a role; chemicals that are soluble in water or fat tend to be strong odorants, although many of them are inodorous. No unique chemical or physical property that can be said to elicit the experience of odour has yet been defined.

Characteristics that impart odour

Only seven of the chemical elements are odorous: fluorine, chlorine, bromine, iodine, oxygen (as ozone), phosphorus, and arsenic. Most odorous substances are organic (carbon-containing) compounds in which both the arrangement of atoms within the molecule as well as the particular chemical groups that comprise the molecule influence odour. Stereoisomers (*i.e.*, different spatial arrangements of the same molecular components) may have different odours. On the other hand, a series of different molecules that derive from benzene all have a similar odour. It is of historic interest that the first benzene derivatives studied by chemists were found in pleasant-smelling substances from plants (such as oil of wintergreen or oil of anise), and so the entire class of these compounds was labelled aromatic. Subsequently, other so-called aromatic compounds were identified that have less attractive odours.

The scent of flowers and roots (such as ginger) depends upon the presence of minute quantities of highly odorous essential oils. Although the major odour constitutents can be identified by chemical analysis, some botanical essences are so complex that their odours can be duplicated only by adding them in small amounts to synthetic formulations.

Odour sensitivity. In spite of the relative inaccessibility of the human olfactory receptor cells, odour stimuli can be detected at extremely low concentrations. Olfaction is said to be 10,000 times more sensitive than taste. A human threshold value for such a well-known odorant as ethyl mercaptan (found in rotten meat) has been cited in the range of 1/400,000,000th of a milligram per litre of air. A just-noticeable difference in odour intensity may be apparent when there is a 20 percent increase in odorant strength, but at low concentrations as much as 100 percent increase in concentration may be required. Temperature influences the strength of an odour by affecting the volatility and hence the emission of odorous particles from the source; humidity also affects odour for the same reasons. Hunting dogs can follow a spoor (odour trail) most easily when high humidity retards evaporation and dissipation of the odour. Perfumes contain chemicals called fixatives, added to retard evaporation of the more volatile constituents. The temporary anosmia (absence of sense of smell) following colds in the nose may be complete or partial; in the latter case, only the odours of certain substances are affected. Paranosmia (change in perceived odour quality) also may occur during respiratory infections. Changes in sensitivity are reported to occur in women during the menstrual cycle, particularly in regard to certain odorants (steroids) related to sex hormones. Olfactory sensitivity also is said to become more acute during hunger.

Factors affecting odour sensitivity

Human adaptation to odours is so striking that the stench of a slaughterhouse or chemical laboratory ceases to be a nuisance after a few minutes have passed. Olfactory adaptation, as measured by a rise in threshold, is especially pronounced for stronger odours. Cross adaptation (between different odours) may take place; thus, eucalyptus oil may be difficult to detect after one becomes adapted to camphor. Adaptation long was regarded solely as the result of changes in the olfactory receptor; however, electrical recordings show that the receptor cells in the nose seem to adapt only partially. Rhythmic discharges continue in the olfactory bulb long after the experimenter ceases to detect the odour that is stimulating the experimental animal. Apparently, some olfactory adaptation may occur in the brain as well as in the sense organ.

Odour blending and flavour. The ancient art of perfumery and the modern science of odour control depend on mixing and blending. Two different odours presented together may be readily identifiable. The more they resemble each other, the greater will be the tendency to blend;

yet trained workers usually can discriminate the components of a successfully blended perfume. The substantially greater intensity of one odour may mask another. Masking, however, is less effective than chemical conversion or physical collection (removal) as a basis for odour control. Some odorants also may be removed by passing air through activated charcoal.

Flavours and the sense of smell

The distinctive flavours of food are known largely through the sense of smell. Flavour is the composite of experiences from many senses, but the aroma of roast beef and the delicate bouquet of wine are mainly olfactory in origin. Flavour technology has assumed a well-entrenched place in the food industry; it is common practice for manufacturers to use flavour panels of several trained members to judge the flavour of new food products. Using psychophysical methods with adequate statistical control, such panels are very reliable and can detect qualities so subtle that they defy the methods of physics and chemistry. In using large, untrained consumer panels, the emphasis is on acceptability, often an emotional reaction to the product. Such untrained judgments are unstable and may vary among individuals because of idiosyncrasy or differences in experience. The strong cheese odour so palatable to the gourmet can produce revulsion in the uninitiated.

Effects on behaviour. Recognition of friend or foe by social insects may depend upon olfactory cues: certain ants attack their own kind furiously if deprived of the sense of smell by amputation of their antennae; bees entering a strange hive are put to death because the scent of a foreign hive clings to them. Bees also have a specialized organ on the end of the abdomen that deposits a scent on a newly discovered food source to guide other foraging workers. The scents of flowers attest to the evolutionary importance of odour; those flowers that attract insects most efficiently are the likeliest to be pollinated and to reproduce their kind.

The effect of odours on the sexual behaviour of invertebrates is most striking; a female moth, for example, was observed to attract more than 100 males during relatively brief observation periods of about six hours. The physiological basis for the attraction can be traced to specific odour attractants (pheromones), molecules produced by the scent glands of the female. Pheromones also function in defense and as alarms of impending danger. The specific sex attractant of the female silk moth (*Bombyx*) has been identified and synthesized. It has been found that the antennae of the male silk moth contain olfactory receptors specifically sensitive to the female pheromone but that the females have no receptors to detect their own attractiveness.

Mammals in the wild state appear to utilize their odour glands for sexual attraction. Laboratory rats show a preference for the branch of a maze that has been scented with the odour of a sexually receptive female. It is likely that some rudiments of these effects operate in man. The most sexually provocative perfumes have a high proportion of musk or musklike odour. Genuine musk is derived from the sexual glands of the musk deer and is chemically related to human sex hormones; odour sensitivity in humans varies with the menstrual cycle.

Among laboratory animals the secretion of reproductive hormones can be markedly influenced by odour stimulation. This seems to be an innate physiological process rather than the result of learning. A most dramatic effect (pregnancy block) is observed when the odour of a strange male is presented to a recently mated female. The normal hormonal changes following copulation are blocked under these conditions, and the fertilized egg fails to survive. A related study of the periodicity and length of menstrual cycle in women exposed to the normal odours of men suggests there may be similar effects among people. The behaviour of civilized man, molded and shaped by custom and culture though it is, has many of its roots in his basic sensual appetites.

BIBLIOGRAPHY. E.G. BORING, *Sensation and Perception in the History of Experimental Psychology* (1942), a classic historical account of the early work in sensation and perception; J. FIELD (ed.), *Handbook of Physiology, Section 1, Neu-rophysiology*, vol. 1 (1959), a technical and detailed review of modern sensory physiology; F.A. GELDARD, *The Human Senses* (1953), a scholarly overview of the senses, suitable as an introduction to the subject; D.R. KENSHALO (ed.), *The Skin Senses* (1968), a rather specialized report of a symposium held in 1968 that gives the reader with a special interest in this field a good idea of current research; P.M. MILNER, *Physiological Psychology* (1970), an advanced textbook in general physiological psychology with a good section on the senses; C. PFAFFMANN (ed.), *Olfaction and Taste, III* (1969), a somewhat specialized but good overview of current research in both olfaction and taste; J.S. WILENTZ, *The Senses of Man* (1968), an excellent popular account for the general reader that serves as a good introduction to the field.

(C.Pf.)

Seoul

Now the capital of the Republic of Korea (South Korea), Seoul (Sŏul-t'ŭkpyŏlsi meaning special city of Seoul) has been the capital of Korea since 1394. The name itself means capital in the Korean language. The city was popularly called Seoul in Korean during the Yi dynasty (1392–1910) and during the period of Japanese rule (1910–45), although the official names in those periods were Han-sŏng and Kyŏngsŏng respectively. Seoul became the official name of the city after 1945 with the founding of the Republic of Korea. In 1970 it was a fast-growing metropolis of some 5,500,000 people. It is also a rapidly changing city in a transitional stage between traditional and modern urban society.

History. The earliest historical mention of Seoul and the surrounding area dates from the 1st century BC. During the Three Kingdoms period (57 BC–AD 668) of Silla, Koguryŏ, and Paekche, the Seoul area formed a borderland between the three countries and during the early part of the period was most closely associated with the Kingdom of Paekche. According to legend, Paekche's capital, Wirye-sŏng, located at Chiksan, was raided so often that King Onjo, the founding king of Paekche, moved back to Pukhan, a place north of the Han-gang (Han River), in about 6 BC. It is believed that Pukhan was at the foot of Tobong-san (Tobong Mountain), in the northeastern section of present-day Seoul.

It was not, however, until King Munjong of Koryŏ built a summer palace in 1068 that a fairly large settlement existed on the present site of the city.

After the annexation of Korea to Japan, the name of the Seoul area was changed to Kyŏng-sŏng in 1911, and minor changes were made in the boundary. Seoul served as the centre of Japanese rule, and modern technology was imported. Roads were paved, old gates and walls partly removed, new Western-style buildings built, and streetcars introduced.

Seoul under Japanese rule

After the end of Japanese control, Seoul came directly under the control of central government instead of under the administration of Kyŏnggi-do (Kyŏnggi Province) in which it lies. In 1962 it was placed directly under the prime minister instead of, as previously, the ministry of home affairs.

The contemporary city. *City plan.* Seoul was a suitable site for a capital city because of its location at the centre of undivided Korea and on the navigable Han-gang, one of the major rivers flowing into the Yellow Sea. Before the Korean War, small vessels used to navigate the 37 miles up to Seoul. Presently, however, the demilitarized zone that divides Korea into North and South and that runs partly through the mouth of the river has deprived Seoul of its role as a river port.

Central Seoul is located in the lowland of a topographic basin surrounded by low hills of around 1,000 feet. The basin, circled by a wall along the ridges of the hills, is drained by a small tributary of the Han-gang, which is mostly covered by streets or expressways. Main streets and major shopping areas occupy the lower part of the basin. The growth of the city, however, has resulted in buildings spilling out in all directions, firstly out of the four major gates of the old castle toward Yongsan and Yŏngdŭng-p'o to the south, Mia-dong Suyu-dong to the north, Map'o and Hongje-dong to the west, and Ch'ŏng-nyangni to the east. The present boundary of Seoul was

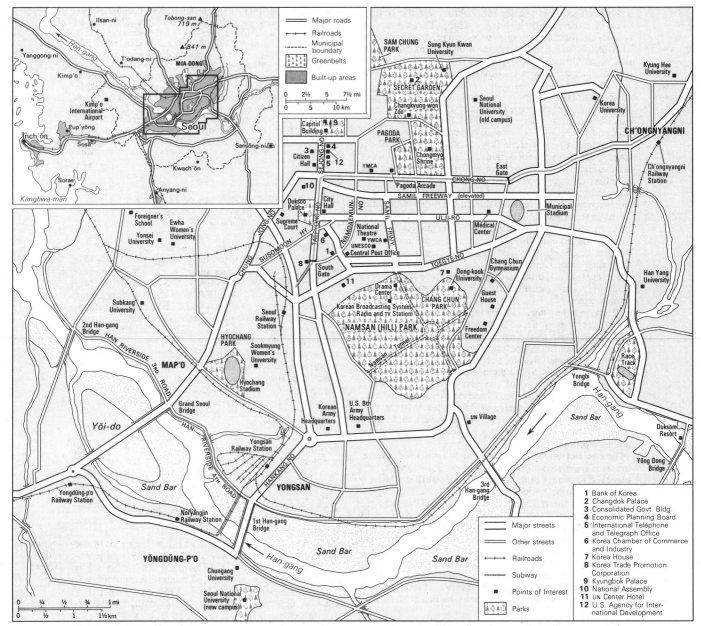

Central Seoul and (inset) its metropolitan area.

set up in 1963 encompassing 237 square miles (613 square kilometres), more than twice the 1948 city area of 103 square miles. The entire area of the present city, however, is not all built up. The boundary foresees a much larger future city, and many square miles of suburbs and farmlands are included.

Street patterns in the city centre are basically rectangular. Main streets, such as Chong-no and Ulji-ro, are oriented east to west, but, toward the foot of the surrounding hills, topographic irregularities have some influence on the pattern. Outside the basin area of the central city, however, there are some ten radiating streets, and three circular ones, interconnecting the radiating streets, are under construction. The capitol and other government offices are concentrated along Sejong-no; banks, department stores, and other business offices, along Namdaemun-no and Taepyong-no. The area of Chong-no, Myongdong, and Ulji-ro constitutes the central business district.

Climate. Seoul's climate is characterized by a large annual range of temperature: the coldest month, January, has a mean temperature of 23° F (−5° C); and the warmest month, August, 78° F (25° C). Yearly precipitation in the city is about 49.6 inches, with a heavy concentration in the summer months. During the 1960s air pollution in the basin and in Yŏngdŭng-p'o, an industrial

area, became a serious problem, caused largely by the increasing number of automobiles and factories. The river also became so polluted that, except in a limited area, swimming was no longer possible.

Transportation. Although Seoul is a very old city, it has a mostly paved, sturdy, and relatively wide road system as a result of the construction of new modern roads and the improvement of old ones. Transportation facilities, however, are not quite adequate for the large and expanding population, resulting in crowded streets. Streetcars, consequently, had to be eliminated in 1969 and were to be replaced by subways, which were under construction early in the 1970s. Buses and a circular railroad were the main forms of public transport but could not accommodate all commuters in rush hours. Since the mid-1960s automobiles have increased rapidly in number: in 1970 there were 60,442—about three times the number in 1966. About one-third of passenger vehicles are taxicabs and buses. Seoul depends mostly on railways for transportation of goods and materials from and to distant provincial cities. The capital is the hub of six railway lines connecting it with most provincial cities and ports, including Inch'ŏn and Pusan. Railways are still important for passenger transport also. Kimp'o, located in the western part of Seoul, is the only international

Kwanghwa Gate with the Unified Government Building to the right in downtown Seoul.
Kim Chon-Kil

airport in Korea and serves also as the centre of the national airline network.

Current development plans

There are several long-term plans to permit Seoul to expand rapidly but in orderly fashion. Establishment of satellite cities, functional centres, dispersal of industry, and urban renewal of the old section are some of the projects under serious consideration. In order to slow the city's growth, a circular zone about three to six miles wide at a distance of about 9.3 miles from the city centre has been established as a green belt. The building of houses and other industrial plants is not allowed in this area, only agriculture and forestry being permitted.

Demography. The population of Seoul has grown very rapidly since 1950, from 1,690,000 to over 5,500,000 in 1970. During the decade 1960–69, the population more than doubled, until its density reached 23,400 persons per square mile, one of the highest in the world. The most densely populated areas were distributed within and outside the old city, while newly developed residential areas in the suburbs had a relatively low density. Koreans constituted nearly all of the population; foreign residents, numbering about 10,000, were mostly Chinese. The sex ratio showed an almost equal proportion, females very slightly outnumbering males.

Housing. Housing shortages have been a chronic problem. Numerous blocks of municipal apartment buildings have been constructed for low-income residents in the old city, and several new residential sections are being prepared. Houses in the lowland and adjacent areas outside the old-city wall are mostly traditional, tile-roofed wooden structures, but new houses in the suburbs are one story and are something akin to Western style. All houses have *ondol* ("heated") floors designed for the cold winter. Coal is used as fuel to warm the *ondol,* but gases extracted from coal are increasingly in demand.

Principal employers

Economic life. Manufacturing (27.9 percent), commerce (34.8 percent), and service industry (20.4 percent) together comprised about 83 percent of all economic activity in 1970. Textiles, machinery, and chemical industries were the most important sectors in manufacturing. Food processing, printing, and publishing were also important. Most of the manufacturing plants are small-scale, and three-quarters of the some 700 textile plants accommodate less than 100 workers.

The two most important shopping centres, located near South and East gates, serve the whole country as well as Seoul. Banks are not much utilized since checking accounts are unpopular. To encourage savings, high interest rates of more than 17 percent a year are offered by banks, but loans are not easily available because of the shortage of capital in the banks. Accordingly, small companies are highly dependent on private loans.

Social conditions. Because of the rapid expansion of the city, water, sewage disposal, and electricity facilities are inadequate, despite strenuous efforts to keep up with demand. The city has relatively good medical facilities, with 70 hospitals containing over 7,000 beds. There are many smaller medical facilities, including small clinics. There are also many herb doctors. Fires occur frequently during winter and spring because of the cold, dry season and the many wooden structures, placing a heavy demand on the city's fire services.

Education. Compulsory education applies only to the six-year elementary school, but 94 percent of elementary school graduates (1970) go on to the three-year middle school, 89 percent of middle-school graduates (1969) to the three-year high school, and 33 percent of high-school graduates to colleges and universities. There is a serious shortage of elementary-school facilities because of the rapid increase of population, resulting in very crowded classrooms. There are some 38 colleges and universities in Seoul, a total of more than 87,000 students being enrolled in 1970. Major universities are Seoul National, Yonsei, Korea, Ewha Woman's, Sung Kyun Kwan, and Dong-kook universities. The Korea Advanced Institute of Science was established in 1971 to produce natural scientists and was expected to·begin receiving students in 1974.

Cultural life and recreation. Important musical organizations in Seoul are the National Classical Music Institute, engaged in preservation of the traditional court music of Korea—and in education of its musicians—and two symphony orchestras, the Korean National Symphony Orchestra and Seoul Symphony Orchestra. There are also a national theatre, over 100 cinemas, Duksookung Art Gallery, national and private museums, and four public libraries.

Newspapers and broadcasting

Main offices of major nationwide daily newspapers, the government newspaper, and two English language newspapers are all located in Seoul. Early in the present decade there were six radio broadcasting stations and three television stations, one of which is owned by the government; most families had at least one radio and there was approximately one television set for every four families.

Surrounded by hills, Seoul has numerous large and small parks within easy reach. Changkyong-won, which is an old palace containing in its grounds a modern zoo and a botanical garden, attracts a large number of citizens and tourists throughout the season from spring to autumn. Seoul Athletic Field has a main stadium that can accommodate 57,500 people and smaller attached areas for baseball, tennis, volleyball, and swimming. One large open athletic ground has a capacity of 25,000. Many national games are also held in Hyochang Athletic Ground and Chang Chun Gymnasium, both of which have a large capacity.

BIBLIOGRAPHY. ALLEN D. and DONALD N. CLARK, *Seoul: Past and Present* (1969), is a well written and comprehensive guidebook. EDWARD B. ADAMS, *Through Gates of Seoul*, 2 vol. (1970–71), is a more extensive work, well prepared and containing numerous pictures and maps, some in colour. The *Statistical Yearbook of Seoul* (annual), provides official statistics, with a brief history of Seoul in Korean and English.

(C.Le.)

Sergipe

Sergipe is a state (*estado*) of Brazil located on the southern coast of that country's northeastern bulge into the Atlantic. It is bounded on the east by the Atlantic, on the south and west by the State of Bahia, and on the north by the State of Alagoas, from which it is separated by the São Francisco River. The state has limited agricultural and other natural resources, and the per capita income in the state is 50 percent below the national average. The second smallest Brazilian state, it has an area of 8,492 square miles (21,994 square kilometres). Its population in the early 1970s was over 900,000. The state capital is Aracaju. Sergipe is named after Serigy, a gallant native chief.

History
Located between the captaincies of Pernambuco and Bahia (the latter being at the time the seat of d'el the general government) in the 16th century, Sergipe Rei, as it was then called, was conquered and settled by cattlemen and sugar planters from Bahia. The aborigines were easily subdued by the superior firearms of Cristóvão de Barros, who founded the city of São Cristóvão, the first capital, in 1590. In 1820 Sergipe became an independent captaincy. It became a province of the empire in 1824 and a state of the republic in 1889.

The natural environment. The state is divided into two major geographic regions, a narrow, low, heavily forested coastal region, and a higher zone of rough open country, including tablelands rising to mountainous areas in the west. The northern part of the state drains into the São Francisco River, the southern part into the Atlantic. Small rivers, that are frequently dry in their upper reaches, include the Japaratuba, the Sergipe, the Cotinguiba, the Vasa Barris, the Piauí, and the Real.

Sergipe's climate is typical of the northeastern region of Brazil. The coastal area is hot, with adequate rainfall extending into the São Francisco Valley; the interior is hot and dry and subject to both flood and drought. There are two well-defined seasons, winter (May to September) and summer (October to April). The annual mean temperature is 78° F (26° C). The warmest month, January, has an average of 80° F (27° C) and the coldest month, August, has an average of 75° F (24° C) at Aracaju. The average annual rainfall is 49 inches (1,250 millimetres) at Aracaju.

Vegetation is distributed as follows: 34 percent tropical forests, 50 percent thorny deciduous scrub woodland, known as *caatinga*, and 16 percent coastal vegetation. The forests of the coastal zone have been practically devastated. Only palms and cashew trees still abound. Bird life includes varieties of tinamou and there are some mammals such as deer and cavies and armadilloes.

Population. Sergipe has a population of over 900,000. Population density is 107 persons per square mile (41 per square kilometre), with the heaviest concentrations in the coastal and central regions. Forty-six percent of the population is urban. The most populous cities are Aracaju, the capital (almost 180,000), Estância (over 20,000),

Propriá (over 18,000), and Itabaiana, Lagarto, and São Cristóvão (each over 10,000). About three-fourths of the people are of mixed racial origin. The state is experiencing the processes of gradual ethnic amalgamation that are characteristic of all Brazilian states. The language is Portuguese. The predominant religion is Roman Catholicism.

Administration and social conditions. The governor of the state and the members of the state legislature are elected in accordance with the state constitution and laws. The auxiliary organs of the state government at Aracaju include the State Economic Development Council; the Industrial Company of Sergipe, which is charged with the development of research, plans, and projects; the Sergipe State Bank; the Welfare Institute; and the Superintendency of Public Works.

There are 25 hospitals in the state with five located in the capital and 41 in the interior. There are 4.9 hospital beds per 1,000 inhabitants in the capital and 2 per 1,000 in the interior.

Primary education is compulsory. About 100,000 pupils attend primary schools, with about 20,000 in the capital and 80,000 in the interior. At the intermediate level there are about 23,000 pupils, with 16,000 of these in Aracaju and 7,000 in the interior. There has been an increase in public intermediate education facilities, which have a capacity for 7,000 students, as well as in those for primary education. Higher education is furnished by the Universidade Federal de Sergipe, founded in 1967, in Aracaju. The university has a capacity for 1,000 students.

Education

Eighteen cities, or about one-fourth of those in the state, have operating water systems, and systems for 12 more cities have been planned. Seventy-one of the 74 county seats and 30 villages have electricity. A program of rural electrification is underway; 12 projects are in the starting phase and others being developed.

Economy. The economy is predominately agricultural. Ninety percent of the industrial sector is made up of traditional industries: sugarcane, textiles, and small food-processing enterprises (manioc meal, rice, coconut meal, and milk). The Aracaju Industrial District, an area of 314 acres, was developed in 1960 to attract new industries.

Eight products—cotton, rice, sugarcane, coconut, beans, tobacco, manioc (cassava), and maize (corn)—represented 52 percent of the agricultural production in 1967. Agriculture is concentrated on the lower, fertile lands, the higher interior being devoted primarily to raising livestock. Livestock includes about 825,000 cattle, as well as hogs, sheep, and goats. Horses, mules, and asses also are raised. Sergipe's petroleum reserves are being increasingly exploited, with production surpassing 30,000 barrels of oil a day in 1970 as compared with 9,000 in 1966. The reserves are located principally in the northeast and on the Aracaju maritime platform. There are also reserves of 140,000,000 tons of rock salt, 14,600,000 tons of potassium, and reserves of potter's clay, kaolin, gypsum, limestone, and manganese.

Agricultural products

Transportation and communications. Sergipe has 3,165 miles of roads, 757 miles of which are state, 2,159 miles municipal, and 199 miles federal; about 140 miles are asphalted. The Viação Férrea Federal Leste Brasileira (Brazilian East Federal Railway Transit System) covers 183 miles in the state. Construction of a railway bridge over the São Francisco River to link Sergipe (Propriá) to Alagoas (Pôrto Real do Colégio), began in 1971. Although maritime transport has been insignificant, projects have been initiated to improve the harbour of the Rio Sergipe. River transportation on the São Francisco and other rivers is also being developed. The Aeroporto de Santa Maria has a paved runway 6,600 feet long. The Brazilian Mail and Telegraph Enterprise is responsible for communication in Sergipe as a whole. The capital is linked to the system of the Brazilian Telecommunications Enterprise.

Cultural life and institutions. Sergipe's past is rich in outstanding national literary figures, such as Tobias Barreto, Sílvio Romero, Fausto Cardoso, João Ribeiro, and Hermes Fontes. Sergipe has half a dozen newspapers and some magazines. Its principal cultural institutions are the Academia Sergipana de Letras, the Instituto Histórico e Geográfico de Sergipe, the Galeria de Artes Álvaro Santos, the Biblioteca Pública do Estado de Sergipe, and the Museu São Cristóvão, which is quite rich in colonial art.

Two popular forms of merrymaking are notable, the Chegança, of Iberian origin, and the *bumba-meu-boi*, created by the *caboclos* (or backwoodsmen, Indians or Portuguese–Indian half-breeds), both of which are danced and sung. Traditional festivals are the June carnivals; the Festa da Laranja (Feast of the Orange), in Buquim; the Festa de Nossa Senhora de Conceição (Feast of Our Lady of the Immaculate Conception), the patron of Aracaju; the Feirinha de Natal, a Christmas festivity in Aracaju; and the Festa de Bom Jesus dos Navegantes (Feast of Good Jesus of the Navigators), a river procession held on January 1 since 1857.

BIBLIOGRAPHY. IVO DO PRADO, *A Capitania de Sergipe* (1919), is a documented account of the founding of Sergipe that also deals with the question of the border with Bahia. FELISBELLO FREIRE, *História de Sergipe* (1855), covers the period 1525–1855. See also J. PIRES WYNNE, *História de Sergipe, 1575–1930*, vol. 1 (1970).

(J.da.S.R.F.)

Serpentes

The reptile suborder Serpentes, one of three suborders of the order Squamata, includes only the snakes, a widely known and much misunderstood group of animals. The closest relatives of the snakes are the lizards (suborder Sauria) and the wormlike amphisbaenians (suborder Amphisbaenia).

Arms and legs gone, no ears, only one functional lung, voiceless, eyelids missing—a human being in such condition would be institutionalized and under constant care. Snakes have not only survived these losses but have become highly successful in a great variety of ecological roles. Fearless, independent, and usually solitary, the snake has capitalized upon these apparent deficiencies to become an efficient second- and third-level predator, focussing perhaps 70 percent of its existence on tracking down, catching, and digesting its living prey. The elongate, limbless body of the snake permits it to be soundless in motion, invisible at rest, and almost unlimited in its access to hiding places, such as nests, tree holes, crevices, brier patches, gopher tunnels, and other shelters where small vertebrated animals seem to feel themselves safe from their enemies. Most of the remainder of the snake's existence is dedicated to continued survival in an antagonistic world that is usually either too hot or too cold and is full of other organisms challenging the snake's right to live. With its body temperature almost totally dependent upon the surroundings, the snake must seek out both nightly and seasonal resting places where rising temperatures eventually can be relied upon to rekindle its abilities to move, to sense, and to reproduce. Reproduction demands only a few percent of the male snake's existence, for it consists of little more than a sudden burst of highly seasonal activity followed by an immediate return to the more pressing activities of food search. The female devotes slightly more time to reproductive activities, because she must eventually seek out a suitable place to deposit the eggs or to give birth to a usually good-sized brood. This, too, however, is an act of short duration, followed immediately by return to the continuing problems of daily existence.

Snakes are found around the world in practically every kind of habitat and in all regions except near the poles. They are not successful competitors with man, and only a few diminutive species with very secretive habits find it possible to share living space with humans. When man moves in, practically all reptiles share the fate of large mammals and predatory birds—they must move out or die, because man is not and never has been a particularly good coexisting species except with those organisms that he bends to his will, such as corn or horses, or with those capable of capitalizing upon his presence, such as pigeons and rats. Of the reptiles, the snake is the most distasteful to man, and snake species are quickly wiped out. In rural

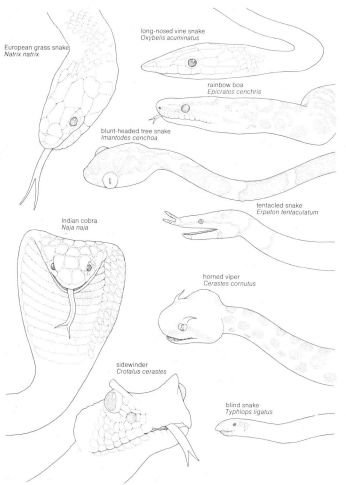

Figure 1: Variation of snake head shapes.
Drawing by M. Moran

areas, man pays the penalty for this eradication in an inevitable increase in the natural prey of the snakes, including rats, mice, and other rodents.

Importance to man

After the unfortunate episode in the Garden of Eden, perhaps the first relationship between man and snakes that one thinks of is envenomation from poisonous snakebite. The likelihood of any individual human encountering a venomous snake during his lifetime has been reduced to almost zero as a result of the tremendously increased world population, the concentration of humans in cities, where poisonous snakes cannot survive, and the reduction in overall numbers of snakes as a consequence of the invasion and destruction of their habitats by man. At the same time, the likelihood of any one poisonous snake, sometime during its life, finding itself in a position in which it must bite a human in self-defense increases geometrically, as a consequence of the enormously inflated human population, man's ever-increasing mobility, and the increased utilization of remote areas for recreation purposes of all sorts. One of these likelihoods is offset by the other, and the overall number of bites per year by venomous snakes around the world remains rather constant, at about 1,000,000 per year. Of this 1,-000,000, perhaps 30,000 to 40,000 result in death, with most of the deaths occurring in areas such as tropical Africa and Asia because of the inadequate medical facilities for proper treatment. It has been estimated that in the United States about 1,000 bites occur each year, with approximately 15 resulting in death. Records for bites by the viper in England indicate that only seven deaths occurred between 1899 and 1945 and only one death between 1945 and 1960, with the latter a consequence of treatment rather than of the bite. A large percentage of the bites in the United States occur when the snakes are

Snakebite

handled for various reasons. These reasons include care in zoos, the extraction of venoms, exhibition by showmen in carnivals and sideshows, the maintenance of snakes as pets or curiosities, and their inclusion in religious ceremonies by various sects. Practically all of the time-honoured remedies or first-aid measures for snakebite treatment are more dangerous in the hands of the inexperienced than is the bite itself. If any kind of medical care is available within an hour or less, nothing more than a light tourniquet is needed as emergency treatment.

No snake has ever regularly hunted man, but man continues to engage in seeking out the snake. The uses that man finds for snakes are not extensive, but each of them results in the decimation of wild populations. Snakes are collected as a source of rare and exceedingly expensive leather for belts, pocketbooks, shoes, and gloves. There is a phenomenal traffic in live snakes for purposes of display or as pets, including the flow to zoos, circuses, carnivals, or roadside "snake farms," as well as to the amateur snake fancier with a large collection in his basement. There are perhaps 40–50 research laboratories and antivenin institutes around the world, in which either snakes or snake venoms are used, and live snakes are needed in fairly large numbers for the work. An indication of the numbers of animals involved in this kind of traffic is given by data from the United States Department of the Interior on importations, taken from customs reports. During 1968 and 1969, more than 3,344,000 specimens of living reptiles (including snakes) were brought into the United States. It is difficult to determine how many of these reptiles were snakes, but perhaps a quarter to a third of the total would be a reasonable estimate, which would mean that almost 1,000,000 snakes were shipped into the United States in those two years. The mortality rate among such snakes is high, but those that survive bring prices from about $5 to as much as $1,500, and, therefore, this is a multimillion-dollar business. The snake roundup, or snake rodeo, has become recognized as a tourist attraction in the United States, and such events take place in about a dozen different cities each year. The emphasis is on capturing and killing rattlesnakes or copperheads, but usually any snake will do, and the slaughter is always extensive. This phenomenon will die out as the number of available snakes decreases. Distaste for snakes has often led legislatures or monarchs to promise bounties for those killed in areas under their jurisdiction, and such bounties invariably result in the importation of animals from many miles away. In a single year, 1889, 578,415 snakes were turned in for bounties in India. Although Western cultures have never developed the taste, in some parts of Asia the snake is considered a choice delicacy and, by some, even as somewhat of an aphrodisiac.

Snakes as symbols

The serpent is a recurrent figure in religious beliefs, ceremonies, activities, and legends. The decidedly unhuman appearance of the snake, its unwinking eye, its reputed ability to deliver unexpected and sudden death, the fear, hatred, and loathing with which it is regarded by many, the folktales and legends that have surrounded it in practically every culture, all have combined to produce religious overtones in many different parts of the world. While in many religions the snake is primarily a symbol, direct worship of the snake as a godlike creature (not as an indirect representation) is not uncommon. Python worshippers are found in Africa, and the cobra cults of India are well known. Quetzalcoatl was the feathered serpent of the Aztecs. The serpent is a symbol for the snake-handling Protestant sects of the United States, the snake dancers of the Hopi Indians, and perhaps the Burmese snake charmers, who end their ceremonies with a kiss on the top of a cobra's head. Handling of snakes is done both as a gesture of belief and faith in the power of the gods and as an act of defiance of the same power. Bites and fatalities are about equally distributed in both cases.

Natural history

INTERACTION WITH THE ENVIRONMENT

While not exactly at the mercy of the environment, the snake is largely dependent upon it and must devote much of its day-to-day existence to coping with the vagaries and changes taking place in its surroundings. The problem varies with latitude and altitude, for the actions and reactions of a snake in temperate North America are distinct from those of one living in the American tropical lowlands but are similar to those of another living at higher altitudes in the Andes of Ecuador. No matter where they live, snakes are subjected to pressures from the biotic, or living, parts of the environment as well as from the abiotic, the physical, or nonliving, parts. But the amount or degree of challenge to the snake from different segments of the environment changes drastically depending upon the region it inhabits. The individual living in the hot, humid tropics of Africa, with comparatively constant temperatures close to optimum throughout the year and ample moisture from both rainfall and the surroundings, finds that its environmental problems involve competition with other members of its own species for food supply, the challenge of other species of snakes and perhaps other vertebrates for possession of the ecological niche, and the constant pressure of the predator that finds it a tasty morsel. The viper (*Vipera berus*) living within the Arctic Circle of Europe, on the other hand, is the only snake species present in the area and lives practically unchallenged in its niche but is faced permanently with situations in its physical environment that are substandard for survival, so that death from overheating, freezing, or dehydration is a repetitive threat. These differences among animals from different parts of the world are reflected in their life histories, and it is neither possible nor legitimate to speak of the "life history of the snake" unless one speaks only of a single region or, perhaps, of a single species.

In the tropical regions, life continues at approximately the same activity level year after year. The only break in the rhythm comes in the dry season and this only when the dry season is not just a period of slightly less rainfall. Snakes may enter a short period of dormancy at such times, which is, at least in part, a consequence of the effect the dry season has upon their prey. This dormant period is similar to the hibernation in winter by temperate-area snakes, although little is known about the physiological changes that may or may not take place in tropical dormancy. At higher latitudes and altitudes, during periods of maximum stress, which for most snakes are the cold months, the animals must seek out a place where they can be completely inactive and nonreactive, where their inability to respond to the stimulus of danger is compensated for by the absence of danger, and where the surrounding extremes of low temperature and low humidity are mitigated to the point that they remain within the limits of the tolerance capacity of snakes. Such places are few and far between, and good hibernacula (dens used for hibernation) are recognized and utilized year after year, with snakes of several different species often sharing a den. It seems likely that the snakes do not remember the location of a hibernaculum but utilize the simple expedient of following a scent trail left by other snakes randomly seeking a den, with the scent growing more and more strong as successive snakes arrive from greater and greater distances. Many of the changes that occur in the individual snake after arriving at the hibernaculum are direct results of its dependence upon the environment, and, as its body cools, the heartbeat and respiration slow almost to a stop and there is no muscular activity, little digestion, and no defecation. Physiological changes that are not correlated with or responsive to the surroundings also take place, but not to a degree comparable to those occurring in a hibernating mammal, and there is no "alarm system" to stir the snake into activity if a tolerance limit is passed. In such a case, the snake simply dies. At the end of the cold season, the snake is totally dependent upon the changes in its surroundings to bring it back to activity; it cannot rouse itself. The stimuli are felt by all almost simultaneously, and snakes emerge by the dozens or even by the hundreds from some denning places. In some species, copulation takes place immediately after enough of the sun's rays have been absorbed to permit the development of an interest in the surroundings; in others, copulation is the final act before entering

Hibernation

hibernation, and the sperm lie dormant in the dormant female. Fertilization of the egg can take place immediately after copulation, but in some species at least, the female can store the sperm for several years, using them to fertilize successive batches of eggs.

BEHAVIOUR

Interactions between individuals. Snakes in both tropical and temperate regions tend to be solitary in their habits. The denning and mating aggregations are, for the most part, the only social events of the season. Sea snakes differ in this respect, sometimes being seen travelling in large troops, which seems to indicate an urge to aggregate. Female sea snakes (Hydrophiidae) also congregate in large numbers in seawall caves at parturition time, but this may have no social significance, since it seems to be a consequence of availability of a safe place for the young to be born rather than aggregational behaviour per se. There is some tendency for females of certain species in temperate areas to use a single site for egg deposition. Hunting of food is strictly an individual act for snakes; there are no known instances of cooperative hunting, as seen in some mammal and bird species. Hiding places and basking sites are occasionally shared; this again is a consequence of availability, and in the tropics, where hiding places abound, it is rare to find more than one snake at a time under a log or a rock. Except for these few weak instances, there is no development in snake populations of social behaviour. There is no establishment of social hierarchies, no territoriality, and perhaps no dominance. The combat dance engaged in by two males of the same species, where the bodies are entwined anteriorly and raised higher and higher off the ground until finally one snake overthrows the other, certainly establishes a dominant individual, but there is no indication that awareness of this dominance is retained by either snake. A dominance that must be reestablished at every encounter does not contribute to a social structure. It has been suggested that the combat dance is essentially a homosexual encounter, with each male attempting to copulate with the other.

Combat dances

Reproduction. The occurrence of mating immediately after emergence from hibernation allows snakes to take advantage of the fact that the females are accessible, concentrated, and receptive. The males are equally concentrated, so pair formation and copulation is a simple matter. Males of some species have nuptial tubercles on various parts of the body, used to stroke or massage the female and, presumably, to arouse her sexually. Even when obvious tubercles are absent, the male uses a rubbing technique to stimulate the female, and in some species a muscle ripple moving along the male's body will provide a lateral caress. There are many descriptions in the literature of courtship dances done by snakes, in which the bodies are entwined and as much as one-third lifted off the ground, the coils ebbing and flowing with silent grace. Unfortunately, in many of these reports, the snakes were not captured and sexed, and the observer simply assumed that a male and female were involved. Recent work, where the snakes have been sexed, tends to indicate that the dance often, if not always, involves two males and is of little or no significance in reproduction. In any event, copulation is achieved after a comparatively brief courtship through the insertion of a hemipenis in the female's cloaca (a common urogenital chamber, lying just anterior to the anus). The hemipenis is one of a pair of mirror-image intromittent organs lying in the base of the male's tail, posterior to the anus, and strictly reserved for mating, for the urinary passages empty directly into the cloaca of the male. Either hemipenis can be used in copulation and must be everted, through a process of turning itself inside out. This is achieved primarily by engorgement of the organ with blood. The everted organ is heavily armed with spines, spinules (minute spines), flounces, calyces, and other ornaments, all of which appear to play a role in ensuring that the male is securely attached to the female for the entire period until the sperm have been deposited. The sperm pass along a deep groove in the hemipenis, which, although open along one margin when examined in a dead snake, clearly forms a tubular passage as a result of the pressures of the engorged margins of the groove. After release, the sperm may immediately move up the oviducts and fertilize eggs just released from the ovary, or they may be stored by the female and released later to achieve fertilization. Once fertilization has occurred, the egg begins to accumulate additional layers from the shell glands in the oviduct. In some species, this continues until a firm yet pliable, leathery shell has been formed, permeable to both gases and liquids but capable of retaining much of its liquid content unless in a very dry place. The female then deposits the entire clutch of eggs in a protected, damp, warm, and usually dark place, often along with clutches from other females of the same species, for the same stimuli that lead snakes to congregate for hibernation also bring them to the same places for egg laying. Many species immediately abandon the eggs, some remain with the clutch and certainly appear to be protecting them from external danger, and a very few actually assume the role of a brood hen, maintaining a body temperature measurably higher than the surroundings, presumably assisting in incubation. In certain species, additional layers of membranous material are deposited around the embryo, but the calcareous (calcium-containing) shell does not form. Instead, the embryo is retained in the oviduct and continues its development there. This is termed ovoviviparous development, since it is simply an egg retained in the oviduct, in contrast to viviparous, the condition seen in mammals, where the fetus develops in the uterus and establishes a placental connection with the uterine wall to permit exchange of materials with the maternal circulation. But, while an umbilical connection does not develop, there is now considerable evidence of exchange of materials between mother and fetus across their contiguous, highly vascularized membranous surfaces, and the distinction between the two types of development is so blurred in some species as to become specious.

Egg laying

Regardless of the devices used to provide it with protection, the snake fetus is always brought to term before the onslaught of environmental conditions that could result in its death. The embryonic turtle can sleep away its first winter in the egg and hatch the following spring none the worse for the experience, but there is as yet no evidence that snakes can do the same. The contrast may result from the fact that the female turtle can scoop out a hole deeply enough that freezing temperatures may not affect her brood, but the female snake is restricted, both by her limblessness and by the nature of the egg itself, to egg laying on or near the surface, where below-freezing temperatures are unavoidable. In the tropics, evidence is scanty, but it would appear that there is an endogenous (*i.e.*, controlled from within) rhythm there as well, since young are not produced throughout the year.

EARLY DEVELOPMENT AND GROWTH

The young snake, whether from an egg or born alive, comes equipped with a sharp cutting device on its upper lip, the egg tooth. It slashes its way out of the rubbery eggshell with this tooth or, in the case of the live-born, cuts its way out of the soft membranes and is instantly competent to cope with its surroundings. Almost invariably, the first act of a newborn snake is to extend its tongue and taste the surroundings, conveying to the Jacobson's organ (a sensitive region in the roof of the mouth) chemical information perhaps more significant than the visual cues picked up by the pair of very inexperienced eyes. Young snakes begin to feed immediately after hatching, displaying considerable ability in the capture and consumption of prey. Venomous snakes are born with functional venom glands and fangs and are capable of immediate utilization of their most formidable weapons. Some of the viperid snakes are born with a bright-green tail tip (contrasting strongly with the rest of the body colour), which they are capable of waving and shaking in a way that attracts the attention of possible prey. Within a very short time after birth, the first sloughing of the skin takes place, and the egg tooth is shed at about the same time.

The rate of growth is correlated with availability of

food and temperatures high enough to permit full metabolic activity. When all factors are optimum, snakes grow surprisingly fast. A brood of California rosy boas born on October 26, 1965, more than doubled their lengths by July 26, 1966. In this nine-month period they had reached lengths only a few inches shorter than their mother, an adult close to maximum length for the species. It has been suggested that all snakes grow rapidly until they reach sexual maturity, after which time growth slows but very seldom stops completely. Snakes have indeterminate growth, which means there is no terminal point in time or size for growth in their lifetime, but they can continue to increase in length until they die. Sexual maturity is reached in about two years by many snakes. In the larger species, sexual maturity comes later, after four or five years or more.

MOLT

A regularly recurrent event during the activity period of all snakes is the shedding, or molting, of the skin. Dormant individuals do not shed, but quite often this is one of the first events to take place after the end of dormancy. The integument of all animals represents the primary buffer between internal structures and the environment, and it is constantly subject to wear, tear, and other damage. The first line of defense against damage, especially when the skin is completely broken, is the formation of a blood clot, a scab, cellular reorganization, and scar formation. The second line of defense is the constant production of new cells in the deeper layers of the skin to provide replacement cells on the surface for those lost or worn away. In snakes, the replacement procedure has been modified to a considerable degree. The replacement cells are not constantly produced independently of each other but are all on the same cycle and are cohesive into a complete unit. When this unit is functional, the old skin lying external to it becomes a threat to continued good health. At this point, the snake's eyes become a milky blue, an indication of a physiological loosening of the skin that forms the eye cap. This loosening is duplicated all over the body, although not so obviously. Shortly, the eyes clear, and the snake rubs loose the skin around the mouth and nose and crawls out of it completely, leaving a new, functional skin resplendent in fresh, bright colours. The rattlesake sheds its skin in the same fashion as all other snakes, but the process is highly modified at the tail tip, where successive layers of keratinized, hardened epidermis are interlocked, or nested, to form the rattle, a device used to ward off death or injury to the snake caused by large mammals, including man. The use of the rattle is reasonably successful with buffalo, cattle, or horses but spectacularly unsuccessful with man, because, through this advertising, the rattling snake precipitates either its death or capture but seldom its escape.

LOCOMOTION

The snake has overcome the handicap of absence of limbs by developing several different methods of locomotion, some of which are seen in other limbless animals, others being unique. The first method, called serpentine locomotion, is shared with almost all legless animals, such as some lizards, the caecilians, earthworms, and others. This is the way most snakes move and has been seen by any zoo visitor. The body assumes a position of a series of S-shaped horizontal loops, and each loop pushes against any resistance it can find in the environment, rocks, branches, twigs, dust, sand, pebbles, etc. The environment almost always provides sufficient resistance to make movement possible, and many snake species never use any other method of locomotion than this. Such species, when placed on a surface providing no resistance, such as smooth glass, are unable to move, whipping and thrashing around without progress. Other methods of terrestrial movement also involve at least some resistance by the environment but usually less than the first. One of these is known as "concertina" locomotion, because the snake in action resembles the opening and closing of an accordion or concertina. First the tail and the posteriormost part of the body are securely anchored, then the head and the

rest of the body are extended as far forward as possible from that secure base. At the maximum extension, the head and the fore part of the body are anchored and the posterior part drawn up as close as possible in the accordion-like folds. A second cycle follows the first, and the snake progresses. Tree snakes, such as *Imantodes* and *Oxybelis*, modify this technique to move from branch to branch and have a strongly compressed body that permits surprising amounts of the body to be stiffened and extended, using a modified I-beam effect for rigidity. The

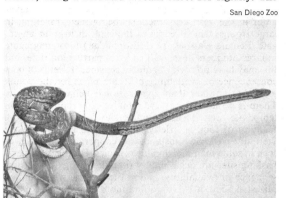

San Diego Zoo

Figure 2: In typical method of locomotion, Bahaman boa *(Epicrates striatus)* extending itself to reach branch at right (not shown).

third method is called "caterpillar" or "rectilinear" locomotion, because the body moves in a straight line, using a flow of muscle contractions along the sides that looks like a caterpillar in motion. The body musculature is used for sequential lifting, anchoring, and pushing against individual ventral scales, which results in an inching along. It is used by large, heavy-bodied snakes, such as the boas and some of the vipers. The fourth method is the least dependent on friction with the substrate and, in fact, was developed because of the failure of the substrate to provide sufficient resistance for any of the previously described methods. This method, called sidewinding, characterizes snakes living in the desert, where the sand simply gives way under any kind of push. The sidewinder does not progress forward when in motion but actually goes sideways. The snake, lying extended on the sand, lifts the anterior part of the body, moves it five to six inches to the side, and rests that part on the sand, maintaining a lifted loop to the rest of the body. This lifted loop is then progressively shifted along the body to the end of the tail, at which time the entire snake has moved five to six inches to the side from its previous position. By the time the first loop reaches the end of the tail, a new loop has already lifted the head and started down the body, and the snake looks like a coiled spring rolling across the sand. There is no rolling involved, however, since the ventral surface is always in contact with a substrate and usually leaves its impression behind in the sand, like a footprint. A nonterrestrial method of locomotion is swimming. Most snakes use a somewhat frantic serpentine locomotion in water, and the water provides enough resistance to allow progress, but one would be hard put to say whether snakes are natural swimmers or cannot swim at all but simply take advantage of their natural buoyancy to crawl through the water. The true sea snakes, however, have a morphological adaptation that gives rise to a clearly distinct method of locomotion. The tail is compressed from side to side to form an oar, or paddle, and swimming efficiency is not only improved but raised almost to the level of an art by these snakes.

Form and function

GENERAL FEATURES

The most characteristic aspect of the snake form is the elongate body and tail and the absence of limbs. Fragments of limbs and girdles still survive in a few species of snakes, and in some snakes of the family Boidae the remnant forms a tiny, external spur on either side of the

Body
propor-
tions

body at the anus, which is used by the male during courtship to stimulate the female. There is no snake in which the limb remnants still retain a function in locomotion. The body is usually slender, although there are some very heavily bodied species. The body shape is correlated with activity level, with the slender species moving about all the time and the heavy forms leading a sedentary life. The pit vipers, for example, while not always long snakes, are often big snakes. It seems likely that these snakes evolved in the direction of heaviness only after the development of a heat-sensitive depression, the loreal pit, located between the eye and the nostril, and the venom apparatus, which enabled them to stay in one place and wait for their prey to approach, rather than engaging in a continuous, active search for food. Similarly, some of the largest boid snakes (boas, anacondas, and pythons) have labial pits that function in the same way as the loreal pit of the vipers, so they, too, can be sedentary and grow fat. Arboreal snakes are the most elongated and slender of all, with the tail (the region posterior to the anus) often longer than the body and the body often strongly compressed laterally, which permits greater rigidity of the body frame while crawling from branch to branch. Burrowing snakes are seldom large, and the true burrowers, the Typhlopidae and Leptotyphlopidae, living all their lives like earthworms, are the tiniest snakes of all. The burrowers have almost no tail, although some of them retain a spiny tail tip, which probably serves the animal as an anchoring point when crawling through the soil. The tail in the sea snakes is flattened to form an oar, used to scull through the water. Sea snakes are almost totally helpless on land, locomoting only with the utmost of difficulty.

The skin. The entire body and tail in snakes are covered with scales, which are cornified folds in the epidermal layers of the skin. These scales are usually arranged in longitudinal rows, the numbers and arrangement of which are characteristic of the species. The scales may be large and shield shaped, in which case the number of rows is low, from 8 to 29 or 30, or they may be very small, rounded, and occasionally with the centre raised, in which case the number of rows can be as high as 90 or 100. A single scale may be very smooth and shiny (as in the rainbow snakes), it may have a raised ridge (keel) along its centre, it can be heavily striated, or it may even have a raised spine in the centre, as in the Javanese wart snake. The scales in some species have sensory structures on the posterior margins called apical pits, and all scales have various micro-ornamentations, consisting of hairlike projections, holes, spinules (small spines), and other specializations visible only through an electron microscope. The scales on the ventral surface of the body are modified into broad plates in the majority of species and are used in locomotion. The sea snakes and the blind snakes lack such ventrals, the scales being small, as on the dorsal surface, and there are several other species, such as the anaconda, in which the ventrals are very reduced in size. This appears to be a secondary loss of the enlarged ventrals, correlated with life in an environment where locomotion is achieved in other ways, such as swimming or movement in burrows.

Coloration. The colours and colour patterns seen in snakes are often bright, occasionally spectacular, and in some species even beautiful. Snake colours are produced in two ways, either by pigment deposited in the skin or by differential diffraction of light as a consequence of the physical properties of the skin itself. When seen on a unicolour or uniform background, most snakes are obvious, and their colour patterns seem bold and prominent. When the animals are placed in their natural habitat, however, the significance of the colour patterns becomes obvious. The many lines running at sharp angles to the elongated lines of the body, the triangles or rectangles of colour, the blotches, spots, bands, or lozenges, all become highly disruptive to the eye, and the snake disappears into its surroundings. Blotched or spotted snakes tend to be sedentary and heavy bodied, while striped and the occasional unicolour snakes are usually active species. In both cases, the coloration is protective, since a coiled,

sedentary snake has its body outline completely obscured by the overlapping patterns, while the stripes on a crawling snake eliminate the sensation of motion until they suddenly narrow at the tip of the tail and the snake disappears.

Although in most snakes the colours are such that they help the animal to hide, there are some species that seem to be advertising their presence rather than trying to hide it. Their patterns are aposematic, or warning, in nature, and let a possible enemy or predator know that he runs some risk in an encounter with the snake. The warning is effective, of course, only if the intruder is knowledgeable concerning its significance and can take heed. This implies a teaching and learning sequence, with the dangerous snake as "teacher" and the predator as "student." For this reason, it has been suggested that the bright colours of the highly (and often fatally) venomous coral snakes did not evolve as warnings of the snakes' own poison but as mimics of some other venomous species, less dangerous, but still able to teach the predator the significance of the warning coloration. There is no evidence that avoidance of aposematic species is instinctive; on the contrary, naïve predators readily attempt to take aposematic forms. A predator that dies in its first encounter with a dangerous species cannot act as a selective force favouring the coloration of that species. There are quite a few mildly poisonous rear-fanged snakes, brightly banded in red, black, and yellow (colours found in the coral snakes), that can make a predator suffer a sufficiently painful lesson that it will avoid contact with all similarly coloured snakes, including the fatally venomous coral snakes and the completely harmless milk snakes (*Lampropeltis*). (For a complete discussion of the evolution of mimicry, see MIMICRY.)

Warning
coloration

Skull and sense organs. Snakes rely on several senses to inform them of their surrounding. The pits, found in the region between the nostril and the eye in the pit vipers (the viperid subfamily Crotalinae) and in the scales of the lip line in some boids, are sensitive to very slight changes in temperature in their surroundings. These snakes feed almost exclusively on animals, such as birds and mammals, that maintain a constant body temperature and can therefore be located by the snake through the reception of the heat of the warm body. The heat lost by even a small rodent is sufficient to alert a waiting viper and enable it to direct a fast strike at the animal as it passes by. Death follows rapidly, and the snake follows the dying animal at a leisurely pace, perhaps in full awareness that it will not go far. The boids use the same technique for detecting warm prey, but after striking they retain the grip, killing by constriction.

Tempera-
ture
detection

The eye of the snake is lidless and covered by a transparent cap of epidermis, which is shed with the rest of the skin at each molt. Animals active during the day usually have round pupils, while the nocturnal species have a vertical or slit pupil that opens up in the dark, as does that of a cat, but closes more effectively in bright light, protecting the sensitive, dark-adapted retina. The eye has been almost completely lost in the burrowing families, in which it is visible only as a black spot buried under the flesh and bone of the head. Arboreal snakes often have a bulging, laterally placed eye, permitting them to see activities directly below as well as above and around them. The structure of the eye in snakes indicates that their lizard ancestor was probably a burrower and that all aboveground activity by snakes is a secondary invasion from an ancestral life underground.

The reception of sound is entirely by bone conduction within the skull. The snake has no external ear, but it still retains a few of the vestiges of the internal ear, which are connected to other skull bones in such a way as to permit transmission of some earth-borne sound waves.

The skull of snakes is characterized by mobility. It is light, with a reduced number of bones, and there are hinge joints at several levels that permit slight rotation or movement of one segment upon another. The only compact unit is the central braincase, with all other skull bones little more than attachments to it. The flexibility of the skull and the jawbones attached to it is a major com-

Teeth and fangs

pensatory factor to balance the loss of limbs. The snake replaces manipulation of digits with manoeuvrability of skull bones.

The jaws of snakes are highly mobile and are usually heavily armed with teeth. The upper jaw can move to and fro on hinged joints and can also rotate slightly. In most snakes, the upper jaw is connected to the lower jaw by a joint that acts as a pivot point, and, in eating, all toothed bones on one side of the mouth move forward as a unit. In some tree snakes (the colubrid subfamilies Dipsadinae and Pareinae), the connection between the upper jaw and the quadrate is lost, and there are four independent units rather than two. These snakes feed excusively on small, slippery prey, such as slugs and snails, and this jaw modification permits them to hold their food with three jaws while the fourth is advanced. The maxillary bone (the main bone of the upper jaw) of most snakes is elongated, with many teeth, but in the Viperidae (Old World vipers, New World rattlesnakes, and other pit vipers) only one functional fang remains, on a short, blunt, rotatable maxillary. The position usually occupied by the maxillary has been taken by the pterygoid bone. In the Elapidae (cobras and relatives) the maxillary bears a single fang in a fixed position, sometimes followed by a few smaller, solid teeth. In several different evolutionary lines of snakes, the posterior one or two teeth on the maxillary have enlarged and changed, usually in the direction of developing a groove or canal on the anterior edge to conduct a flow of venom. These are the rear-fanged snakes, usually (although not always) nonlethal to man. Snake teeth are usually long, slightly recurved, and needle-sharp. This facilitates swallowing and prevents loss of food, because the only direction in which a food item, which may be alive when swallowed, can go to escape the teeth is down the throat. Modifications in food habits have often been accompanied by changes in tooth structure or the loss of

Drawing by M. Moran

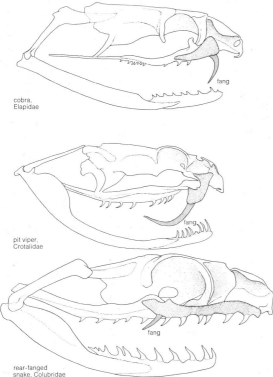

cobra,
Elapidae

fang

pit viper,
Crotalidae

fang

rear-fanged
snake, Colubridae

fang

Figure 3: Skulls of representative poisonous snakes.

teeth. The egg-eating snakes, for example, have only a few peglike teeth left. The burrowing blind snakes have very reduced dentition and have often lost the teeth of one jaw entirely.

The vertebral column of snakes is highly elongated and includes many more vertebrae than almost any other kind of vertebrated animal. Since there are no limb girdles

associated with the skeleton, there are no good delimiters of regions, and snakes are generally regarded as having only two kinds of vertebrae, precaudal and caudal. A pair of ribs is associated with each precaudal vertebra except for a few immediately behind the head, but, by definition, there are no ribs on caudal vertebrae. Each vertebra articulates with its neighbours at five different points: first, at the contact point between the centra (the main, central bodies of the bones), which is a ball-and-socket joint; then two points at the zygapophyses (projections from the centra), with articulating surfaces that lie dorsally and ventrally; and finally the zygosphenes and zygantra, found almost exclusively in snakes, the zygosphene being a projecting shelf on the neural arch (the upper part of the vertebra) and the zygantrum, a pocket into which the zygosphene fits and within which it can swivel. These five points permit lateral and vertical rotation while preventing almost entirely any twisting of the vertebral column, thus achieving both flexibility and rigidity. The vertebra may bear on its ventral surface a long, posteriorly directed projection called a hypapophysis. The presence or absence of this structure on the vertebrae of the posterior third of the body has been of considerable importance in snake classification, because large groups of species show this as a common characteristic. In the egg-eating snakes (members of the colubrid subfamily Dasypeltinae), the hypapophyses of a series of vertebrae a short distance behind the head have developed anteriorly directed tips that have a distinct coating of enamel-like substance. These serve as eggshell breakers, projecting through a gap in the dorsal intestinal wall, where they can rip into an egg when the snake constricts the muscles of the body as it passes the hypapophyseal points. The crushed shell is regurgitated, and the contents of the egg pass on to the stomach. The vertebrae of the tail tip in the rattlesnake are highly modified to form a "shaker" for the rattle.

The hypapophysis

Urogenital system. The urogenital system in snakes is not very distinctive from that of other vertebrates. The testes and ovaries tend to be staggered as a consequence of the elongation of the body, with the right usually lying anterior to the left. Snakes do not have a urinary bladder, and kidney wastes are excreted in a solid state as uric acid. As mentioned above, the male snake has two separate intromittent organs, the hemipenes. This structure is not homologous with the penis of mammals but seems to represent a completely different solution to the problem of internal fertilization. It is a saclike structure that must be turned inside out to be inserted in the cloaca of the female and can be removed only by turning it back to inside in, because to draw it out directly would damage the female considerably. The hemipenis is extremely variable in its overall appearance and structure; the cloaca of the female is often similarly constructed, thus preventing cross-fertilization by males of related species.

SPECIALIZATIONS FOR SECURING FOOD

The most essential and time-consuming activity for a snake during nondormant periods, regardless of its habitat, is the pursuit, capture, and digestion of food. There are many morphological and behavioural modifications to be observed in snakes that facilitate food gathering. Some of these changes are widespread and found in practically every kind of snake. Jacobson's organ, for example, is located in the roof of the mouth and is capable of detecting minute quantities of various chemical substances when they are picked up externally on the delicate, double-tipped tongue and thrust into the organ for analysis. It is so significant and useful that it has never been lost by any snake species. While important primarily in trailing and recognition of prey, the Jacobson's organ is also used in detection of enemies, in trailing other snakes of the same species, and in courtship.

Some snakes have specialized salivary glands that elaborate a potent poison, along with either grooved or tubular teeth to permit internal injection of the venom. This device for rapid immobilization of prey has proven successful whenever it has occurred, and several different lines of evolution can be detected both in the type of injector

Figure 4: (Top left, top right, bottom left) Egg-eating snake *(Dasypeltis)* approaching and swallowing egg of a hen. (Bottom right) Eggshell that has been regurgitated after snake has consumed its contents.
Carl Gans

Types of venom

tooth and in the chemical composition or mode of action of the venoms. The types of injector tooth include the long, tubular fang of the viperids; the short, hollow fang on a fixed maxillary seen in the elapids; and the several kinds of grooved tooth on the posterior end of the maxillary. In the latter case, there is little doubt but that the development of grooving has taken place several different times in different places. As for the venoms, it is true that the terms neurotoxic, hemotoxic, and cardiotoxic, once used to describe the different effects, are clearly misleading and are too simple for accurate statements concerning venom composition, but it is still accurate to say that some of the components of venoms cause changes in the red blood cells, coagulation defects, and blood-vessel injury, while others produce deleterious changes in sensory and motor functions and in respiration, and still others have a direct effect on the heart. Some venoms kill very rapidly, such as that of *Bothrops insularis* of Queimada Island, off the Brazilian coast, which would lose as prey most of the birds it bites if they could fly very far away. Other venoms kill more slowly, and the snake bites, retires, and waits, finally trailing the bitten prey, using the tongue and the Jacobson's organ until it finds the already stiffening body. Some snakes, in particular the rear-fanged species, bite, chew, and hold on, eventually bringing the hindmost maxillary teeth into play, which permits the injection of toxins.

Constriction

Other feeding specializations are not so widespread among species, and some are restricted to a single group. Many of the boids and some of the colubrids utilize a constriction method for killing their food. The prey is struck and held by the teeth, and a series of body coils are rapidly thrown around it. These coils tighten until respiration is impossible and suffocation results, but very seldom are bones crushed or broken. The snail-eating snakes have a series of modifications of the teeth, the toothed bones, and the lower jaw that permit the insertion of the lower jaw into a shell to pull out the snail's body. One genus of sea snakes, *Microcephalophis*, has a tiny head and a long neck with the same diameter as the head, which can be inserted deeply into very narrow holes inhabited by its prey. An Asiatic water snake, *Erpeton*, has a pair of elongate tentacles on its snout that appear to function as sighting devices to guide the strange, stiff-bodied strike at a passing fish. There is a great correlation between the difficulty in catching a particular kind of prey and the development of morphological and behavioural devices to help solve the problem. The blind snake living in a termite nest needs no more than its tongue and

Jacobson's organ to permit it to recognize the soft-bodied, defenseless termites, and its eyes and most of its teeth have been lost. But the rattlesnake, seeking the most elusive prey of all in the agile, aware, sensorily acute small mammal, has a full armament of equipment, including the facial pit, the venom gland, the rotatable maxillary bone, the tubular fang, and two functional eyes.

Evolution and classification

EVOLUTIONARY ORIGINS

The oldest fossil definitely identifiable as a snake is *Dinilysia*, from the Upper Cretaceous (about 80,000,000 years ago) of Argentina, considered to be most closely related to the aniliids and others in the superfamily Booidea. Some fossils from earlier deposits have been called snakes, but American paleontologist Alfred S. Romer has tentatively regarded them as lizards. Snake bones are delicate and do not tend to fossilize well. Most snakes are small, and fossil hunters in the past tended to concentrate on larger, more spectacular specimens. Modern techniques have begun to turn up a wealth of material, much of very small size, including snake skull bones and vertebrae. Much of this material is from Pliocene, Pleistocene, and older Recent deposits, and it often either is identifiable with modern genera or else shows close resemblance to them.

Relation to lizards

Snakes are, thus, a comparatively young group of animals. They arose from a lizard ancestor probably very similar to the modern varanids (monitor lizards). *Dinilysia* shows certain characters very similar to those found in the Bornean lizard *Lanthanotus*, a platynotan lizard related to the Varanidae. Several theories have been proposed as to the habitat preference of the snake ancestor, including aquatic, terrestrial in savanna-like situations, or burrowing. Strong support for the burrowing hypothesis has come from study of the eye. Losses (such as the movable eyelid) caused by ancestral adaptation to burrowing were not regained by the descendant nonburrowing snakes, and other devices to cope with vision problems were developed and refined.

The phenomenal adaptive radiation that produced the many different species of colubrid snakes (a category that includes the vast majority of familiar snakes), now found in practically every kind of habitat and efficiently capitalizing upon almost every kind of terrestrial animal as food, was a very recent event. It probably took place entirely within the Tertiary (from about 65,000,000 to 2,500,000 years ago), and represents a triumph over the handicap of limb loss, which is often a blind alley in evolution. The development of over 2,000 species of snakes occupying practically all available niches is an achievement equivalent to the concomitant emergence and differentiation of the birds or perhaps even that of the mammals.

DISTINGUISHING TAXONOMIC FEATURES

Herpetologists have used a variety of characteristics in the recognition of higher taxonomic units within the snakes, but one tendency has characterized most of the classifications set up by different authors over the years. This has been to base the classification on contrasting conditions of a very few characteristics, occasionally only one. Characteristics used either by themselves or in combinations with one or two others have included the following: the manifold variations in the structure of the hemipenis; the presence or absence of various projections, knobs, folds, shelves, and other modifications of the individual vertebrae; the different types of maxillary teeth and their arrangement on the bone; arrangement and relationships of bones in the skull; presence or absence, location, origin, and insertion of muscles, primarily cranial, but occasionally those of the body; and the type of retina in the eye. If any one of these is emphasized over most others in a classification, that classification will be very different from other systems, because these characteristics are not closely associated genetically and do not tend to group themselves together but vary quite independently. Taxa at the lower levels of classification (genera and species) are usually recognized on the basis of external characteristics that permit easy identification, even though these cannot be used to indicate phylogenetic relationships. These characteristics include the shape, presence or absence, fusion, division, and relationships of the plates of the head; the numbers of rows of dorsal scales and their ornamentation with keels, striae, pits, etc.; the size, number, and condition of ventral, anal, and subcaudal scales; shape of body or head or both; and, in some cases, coloration.

ANNOTATED CLASSIFICATION

The classification presented here represents a conservative summary of the views expressed by G. Underwood, H.W. Parker, H.G. Dowling, A.S. Romer, A. Bellairs, and other prominent herpetologists in the recent literature. Careful analysis of the classifications offered by these authors shows that the major differences are in the level of taxonomic recognition given to a particular group rather than in the allocation of a group with regard to phylogenetic position.

SUBORDER SERPENTES

Reptiles without limbs and with the body greatly elongated; with a very high number of vertebrae in both body and tail, each individual vertebra with zygosphene and zygantrum and almost all those of the body with a pair of attached ribs. Pectoral girdle completely absent; pelvic girdle usually absent, but present as a vestige in primitive species. Outer ear and tympanum lacking, sound reception entirely by bone conduction. Bones of both jaws usually flexible, loosely attached to the skull and to each other, plentifully supplied with teeth in most species, forming poison fangs in some. The braincase is platytrabic.

Superfamily Typhlopoidea (or Scolecophidia)

Diminutive, wormlike snakes that usually retain vestiges of the pelvic girdle and 2 common carotid arteries. Skull compact, with the bones solidly united, which facilitates burrowing; dentition very reduced, with no teeth on the pterygoid, premaxillary, or palatine bones. Intercostal arteries to almost all body segments.

Family Typhlopidae (blind snakes or worm snakes)

Maxillary bone bears teeth arranged transversely and can be rotated slightly on its attachment to the skull; dentary bone usually lacks teeth (present in anomalepine species). Either there is a single pelvic bone or the girdle is absent entirely. Circumtropical in distribution; practically no fossils are known, except for a few specimens from the Tertiary of Europe.

Family Leptotyphlopidae (slender blind snakes)

Maxillary bone bears no teeth and is quite firmly united with the skull; teeth are always present on the dentary. The pelvic girdle made of of 3 bones. Tropics of Latin America to southwestern United States, Africa, and southwestern Asia. No fossils are known.

Superfamily Booidea (or Henophidia)

Moderate-sized to very large snakes. Often with vestiges of the pelvis and associated bones, sometimes visible externally as a rudimentary hind limb. There are two common carotid arteries. The coronoid bone of skull usually present; parasphenoid bone does not form part of the optic foramen; supraorbital bone absent in all except some members of the Boidae. Dentition well developed on all jawbones, usually including the premaxillary. Intercostal arteries running to almost all body segments are present.

Family Aniliidae

The femur present as an anal spur in males, and pelvis made up of a single bone. No hypapophyses on the body vertebrae. Ventral scales only slightly larger than dorsal scales, not extending across the full width of the belly. Premaxillary bone with teeth; forms a suture (tight seam) with the maxillary; dentary immovable. One genus, *Anilius;* known only from the Recent of South America; a brightly coloured snake, with red, black, and yellow rings around the body.

Family Xenopeltidae (sunbeam snakes)

Femur absent; no trace of the pelvic girdle. Hypapophyses on the anterior vertebrae. The ventral scales enlarged. Premaxillary bone toothed; forms a suture with the maxillary. Dentary hinged on the surangular bone and movable. One genus, *Xenopeltis,* burrowing snakes from India and elsewhere in Asia. No fossils known.

Family Uropeltidae (shieldtail snakes)

Femur absent; there may or may not be pelvic rudiments. No hypapophyses on the vertebrae. Ventral scales usually not more than twice as broad as the neighbouring dorsal scales. No teeth on the premaxillary, which forms a suture with the maxillary. Dentary fixed on the surangular and, thus, immovable. A family of burrowing snakes, found only in southern Asia. No fossils known.

Family Boidae (pythons, boas, and wood snakes)

Femur often present; pelvic vestiges occuring in all but a few genera. Hypapophyses present on vertebrae. Ventral scales broad, extending across the entire belly, except in a very few groups. Premaxillary may or may not bear teeth; does not form a suture with the maxillary. Circumtropical; it includes all of the giant snakes as well as several genera of small, secretive snakes. Bones from apparent boids have been found in Tertiary deposits around the world. The family is divided into subfamilies in different ways by different authors. The subfamilies Boinae, for the large New World constrictors, and the Pythoninae, for the Old World pythons, are almost universally recognized.

Family Acrochordidae (wart snakes)

Femur and all pelvic vestiges absent; hypapophyses present throughout the vertebral column. Ventral scales cannot be differentiated from dorsals. Premaxillary bone toothless and free of maxillary bone; dentary not hinged or any part of it free. One genus, *Acrochordus;* aquatic snakes found in Australia, the East Indies, and southeastern Asia. No fossils known.

Superfamily Colubroidea (or Caenophidia)

This superfamily includes the major number of snakes, which have in common the complete absence of any vestiges of the limb girdles and have only the left common carotid artery. Skull quite flexible, with several joints and sutures that permit movement of one part on another. Coronoid bone absent. No teeth on the premaxillary; characteristically, maxillary, palatine, pterygoid, and dentary bones all are toothed; some groups have a fang, or grooved tooth, at the posterior end of the maxillary. Intercostal arteries occur at intervals of several body segments.

Family Colubridae

Maxillary bone comparatively fixed in position, cannot be rotated; usually elongate and armed with teeth throughout its length. Posteriormost maxillary teeth grooved or hollow in some groups, but these fangs are preceded by a series of normal teeth in practically every instance. Hypapophyses may be present on vertebrae throughout the body or may be absent posteriorly, and this character has been used to divide the family into smaller groups. Tail usually long and ending in a point. Found all over the world where snakes occur; species make up the majority of snakes everywhere except Australia. Most of the following subfamilies are recognized by herpetologists, and some authors raise several of them to familiar status.

Subfamily Dasypeltinae (egg-eating snakes). Perforated esophagus and a series of elongated, enamel-tipped vertebral hypapophyses, which pass through the perforations and can crush eggshells. Teeth extremely reduced and peglike. Two genera, found in Africa and Asia.

Subfamilies Pareinae and Dipsadinae. Two small subfamilies of arboreal snakes, specialized for snail eating. These adaptations, including specially modified lower jaw, have evolved separately in the Asian Pareinae and the South American Dipsadinae.

Subfamily Xenodontinae. Large, bladelike posterior maxillary teeth, a large adrenal gland, and several other characters. Two of the genera, *Lystrophis* and *Heterodon,* have pointed, recurved, digging snouts not seen in *Xenodon.*

Subfamily Homalopsinae. Aquatic, fish-eating snakes, lacking grooved teeth. Stout body with a short tail. Southeast Asia, the East Indies, and Australia.

Subfamily Colubrinae. Widespread and often abundant group; contains most of the familiar harmless snakes of Europe and North America. Highly variable in coloration, size, and structure. Many nonpoisonous; some rear-fanged (but rarely dangerous to man); many kill by constriction. About 1,500 species.

Family Viperidae (vipers, rattlesnakes, moccasins, and relatives)

The maxillary bone rides on a hinged joint and is armed with a long, sharp tooth with a canal through it for injection of poison; no other teeth on the maxillary except for replacement fangs. Hypapophyses present on the vertebrae throughout the body.

Subfamily Viperinae (Old World vipers). No heat-sensitive pit or excavation in the maxillary bone. Found throughout Europe, Asia, and Africa but not in Australia. Fossils from Miocene of Europe.

Subfamily Crotalinae (pit vipers). Heat- or infrared-sensitive pit present on the side of the head between the nostril and the eye; maxillary bone with deep excavation in its outer surface to accommodate the pit organ. Widely distributed in the New World; one of the larger groups includes rattlesnakes. A few species also known from Asia. Fossils from Pliocene and Pleistocene of North America.

Family Elapidae (cobras, mambas, coral snakes and relatives)

Maxillary bone is shortened, fixed in position; cannot be rotated. Anteriormost tooth on the maxillary a short, fixed, hollow poison fang, usually but not always followed by a few other teeth. Hypapophyses are present on all body vertebrae. Tail rounded and normal, ending in a narrow tip. Elapids are also found abundantly in Asia, Africa, Central America, and South America; especially numerous in Australia, comprising, with sea snakes, more than two-thirds of snake species; rarely enter the United States; do not occur in Europe except as possible fossils.

Family Hydrophiidae (sea snakes)

The maxillary bone much like that of the elapids. Hypapophyses are present on the vertebrae throughout the body. The tail and part of the body compressed vertically into a large, oarlike swimming device. Found in the tropical western Pacific and Indian oceans; only one genus proven to have reached the Pacific coast of the New World.

CRITICAL APPRAISAL

The classification of snakes cannot yet be considered to have achieved the relative stability that characterizes bird and mammal classification. Authorities continue to disagree both on the taxonomic rank to be accorded certain groups and on the relationships of many groups. Romer, for example, recognizes the Xenopeltinae and Loxoceminae as subfamilies of the Aniliidae. Underwood, on the other hand, treats the first as a family, Xenopeltidae, and considers the Loxoceminae to be a subfamily of the Boidae. The Anomalepinae are regarded by some authors as sufficiently distinct from the Typhlopinae to warrant family status.

Emphasis on one characteristic, such as the presence or absence of a pelvis, profoundly affects the classification. Some authorities remove from the Uropeltidae all genera with pelvic remnants, placing them in the Aniliidae. Others have excluded from the Boidae all genera that lack pelvic remnants.

The family Colubridae has troubled taxonomists for nearly two centuries, many attempts having been made to break it into workable groups other than those currently recognized. The conservative view still recognizes only a few small, distinct subfamilies and several large grab-bag subfamilies. Many groups have been separated from the Colubrinae as subfamilies within the Colubridae or even as distinct families.

In older classifications, the pit vipers have sometimes been separated from the Old World vipers as the family Crotalidae.

BIBLIOGRAPHY. CARL GANS *et al.* (eds.), *Biology of the Reptilia* (1969–), a multivolume work, made up of contributions by specialists, that will eventually summarize current knowledge about the class Reptilia, with emphasis on morphology, embryology and physiology, and ecology and behaviour; GEORGE A. BOULENGER, *Catalogue of the Snakes in the British Museum, Natural History*, 3 vol. (1893–96), a classic work, the only attempt ever made in the English language to list, describe, and furnish an aid in the identification of all the snakes of the world; GARTH UNDERWOOD, *A Contribution to the Classification of Snakes* (1967), a highly technical discussion of relationships among the various kinds of snakes; JAMES A. PETERS, *Dictionary of Herpetology* (1964), contains extensive information about snakes and other reptiles, in a readily accessible form; ROGER CONANT, *A Field Guide to Reptiles and Amphibians of the United States and Canada East of the 100th Meridian* (1958), and ROBERT C. STEBBINS, *A Field Guide to Western Reptiles and Amphibians* (1966), extensively illustrated manuals for field identification of snakes, as well as other reptiles; CLIFFORD H. POPE, *The Giant Snakes* (1961), an entertaining discussion of the very large snakes, such as the anaconda and boa constrictor, and *Snakes Alive and How They Live* (1937, reprinted 1958), although somewhat outdated, still a readable account of snake natural history; ALBERT H. and ANNA A. WRIGHT, *Handbook of Snakes of the United States and Canada*, 2 vol. (1957), de-tailed descriptions of all the kinds of snakes known on the North American continent, with many photographs; COLEMAN J. and OLIVE B. GOIN, *Introduction to Herpetology* (1962), a textbook designed for undergraduate classes at the college level; KARL P. SCHMIDT and ROBERT F. INGER, *Living Reptiles of the World*, pp. 175–279 (1957), a popular account, aimed at the general public, profusely illustrated with colour photographs; RAMONA and DESMOND MORRIS, *Men and Snakes* (1965), a thorough review of man's relationships with snakes, including culture, mythology, medicine, and exploitation; H.W. PARKER, *Natural History of Snakes* (1965), one of the handbook guides to the British Museum, and *Snakes* (1963), a factual account of the general biology of snakes; LAURENCE M. KLAUBER, *Rattlesnakes: Their Habits, Life Histories, and Influence on Mankind*, 2 vol. (1956), a thorough summary, not only of rattlesnakes but of all snakes, their biology and relationships with man; HOBART M. SMITH, *Snakes As Pets* (1965), a guide to the care and feeding of snakes in captivity; JAMES A. OLIVER, *Snakes in Fact and Fiction* (1958), a popular account of the snake, with both true and imaginative stories about size, food, numbers, and other bits of natural history; WOLFGANG BUCHERL, E.E. BUCKLEY, and V. DEULOFEU (eds.), *Venomous Animals and Their Venoms*, 2 vol. (1968–71), a discussion of the classification, distribution, and biology of venomous snakes, with detailed discussions of their venoms as well as treatment of snakebite; SHERMAN A. and MADGE R. MINTON, *Venomous Reptiles* (1969), an entertaining and often anecdotal account of venoms, venomous reptiles, their bites and the treatment of bites, and the intricate relationships of snakes with man and his cultures.

(J.A.P.)

Sesshū

Of all the many distinguished painters Japan has produced, Sesshū is usually considered to have been the most outstanding. This estimate is based not only on the excellence of his work but on his eminence as a Zen monk and man of learning. The tradition of the Zen-Buddhist-inspired style of ink painting (*sumi-e*) finds its ultimate expression in his art. Although basing his work on Chinese models, he adapted them to Japanese artistic ideals and aesthetic sensibilities, transforming an artistic style imported from China in the 14th century into something characteristically Japanese.

Sesshū was already hailed during his lifetime as the greatest Japanese painter of his time, a verdict ratified by later generations of artists, many of whom imitated his style or were influenced by his work even as late as the

By courtesy of the National Museum, Tokyo

"Winter Landscape" by Sesshū, ink on paper. In the Tokyo National Museum. 46 cm x 29 cm.

19th century. Several painters even used his name; these included the great 16th century master Hasegawa Tōhaku, who proudly signed himself Sesshū of the fifth generation. An entire school of Japanese painting, the Unkoku school, devoted itself to continuing his artistic heritage.

In contrast to many of the masters of Japanese art about whose lives little is known, the biography and artistic career of Sesshū are recorded in detail. He was born in 1420 in the village of Akahama in Okayama Prefecture (formerly called Bitchu Province). His family name was Oda; his original personal name is no longer known. In 1431, at the age of ten, he was enrolled at the local Zen temple, known as Hofuku-ji, where he received the name Tōyō, meaning "willowlike" (perhaps because he was slender and graceful). Zen Buddhist temples were the artistic and cultural centres of the period as well as the centres of spiritual life. As a young novice, therefore, Sesshū undoubtedly received not only religious guidance but also instruction in calligraphy and painting.

Early career at Shōkoku-ji

Around 1440, he left his native province for Kyōto, then the capital city and the intellectual and artistic focus of Japan. The young monk lived at Shōkoku-ji, a famous Zen temple adjacent to the Imperial Palace of the Ashikaga shoguns, who were great art patrons. Shūbun, the most famous Japanese painter of the day, was the overseer of the buildings and grounds at Shōkoku-ji. In addition to studying painting under Shūbun, Sesshū studied Buddhism under the famous Zen master Shurin Suto. Although there are no paintings that can be assigned with certainty to this early period of Sesshū's career, it is believed that he must have worked in the style of Shūbun, who was profoundly influenced both in choice of subject matter and style by the Chinese painters of the Sung period (960–1279). Sung masters enjoyed great favour with the Japanese Zen painters, and their work was eagerly collected by Japanese connoisseurs and artists alike. The young Sesshū, therefore, must have had many opportunities to study masterpieces of Chinese painting.

After spending 20 years in Kyōto, Sesshū left the capital for Yamaguchi in the western part of the island of Honshu, a city that had become an important cultural centre under the Ōuchi clan. In Yamaguchi, the artist became the chief priest of the Unkoku-ji, and it was at this time, probably in 1466, that he began to call himself Sesshū ("Snow Boat"). It seems certain that one of the reasons Sesshū chose to move to Yamaguchi was his desire to go to China. Strategically located, this section of Japan was the staging point for many expeditions to the Asian mainland. The Ōuchi lords, in fact, had a trade permit that enabled them to conduct very profitable commercial transactions with China.

Journey to China

Sesshū succeeded in joining one of these Japanese trading missions as an art expert and landed in 1468 at Ning-po in southern China. He was to act as a "purchaser priest," who would buy Chinese paintings for his patrons and would also study at the Chinese Zen monasteries. Sesshū was disappointed with contemporary Chinese painting, which, under the Ming dynasty (1368–1644), had turned away from the spiritual and aesthetic ideas prevalent during the Sung period. Nevertheless, the magnificent scenery of China, as well as the contact with the Ch'an (Chinese word for Zen) monasteries, was a source of great inspiration to Sesshū, who often referred to these experiences in his later life. As a distinguished visitor from Japan, Sesshū was treated with great respect. He was honoured with the "First Seat" (that is, the seat next to the abbot in the famous Ch'an monastery of Mt. T'ien-t'ung) which led him to sign several of his paintings "Occupant of the First Seat at T'ien-t'ung." He also travelled to the Chinese capital of Peking. A friend who accompanied him on this trip reported that Sesshū was invited to paint the walls of one of the halls of the Ministry of Rites at the Imperial Palace. It is not known whether this story is true or whether it is an exaggeration of some other invitation, but it does indicate in what high esteem this Japanese master was held by his Chinese contemporaries. What Sesshū's painting of this period may have looked like is perhaps best exemplified by a set of four landscape scrolls (Tokyo

National Museum) that are signed "Tōyō, Japanese Zen Priest," a designation hardly necessary if they were painted in Japan.

Having been honoured at the Imperial Court in Peking and at the most celebrated Zen monastery in China, Sesshū was at the height of his career. In 1469 he returned to Japan where his fame had greatly increased. It is believed that he first went back to Yamaguchi but eventually (probably in 1476) built a charming rustic retreat across the strait near Oita in Bungo Province. He called his new house and studio Tenkai Zuga-rō ("heaven created painting pavillion") as a tribute to the peace and beauty of the setting. Sesshū painted some of his most outstanding works here and received many visitors who wished to hear about his trip to China or to study painting under him.

Retreat near Oita

After many trips through northern Kyushu and other sections of Japan, Sesshū again returned to Yamaguchi in 1486 and rebuilt his studio. It is not certain if he also lived in Iwami, as some sources suggest, nor is it known in what place he died, although the year of his death was 1506. Several temples claim the honour of being his burial site.

A large body of work has been assigned to Sesshū, but the question of authenticity is particularly vexing. Some of the paintings usually attributed to him are accepted without question on the basis of their outstanding quality, provenance, or inscriptions. Many others bearing his seal and signature are merely assigned to him because of their style and may be school pieces produced by his numerous followers. The largest group of authentic Sesshū scrolls are those in the Tokyo National Museum, which, in addition to four early landscapes believed to have been painted in China, has three of the major works of his maturity. Two of them are hanging scrolls (kakemono) representing autumn and winter. The third is a landscape painted in the haboku, or splashed-ink technique, and therefore usually referred to as the "Haboku-sansui" scroll. Painted in 1495, this work was given by Sesshū to his pupil Sōen when he returned to Kamakura after studying under the master.

The so-called long landscape scroll, or "Sansui Chōkan" (probably painted in 1486) is generally considered his masterpiece and is often regarded as the greatest Japanese ink painting. Depicting the four seasons, beginning with spring and ending with winter, it extends over 50 feet (15 metres). Though based in both theme and style on Chinese models, it nevertheless is Japanese in character; for heavier lines, sharper contrasts of dark and light tones, and a flatter effect of space are employed than was customary in Sung painting. Almost equally outstanding is another horizontal landscape scroll in the Asano Collection. Believed to be somewhat earlier in date, the inscription says that it was painted in 1474 at the request of his pupil Tōetsu. Its style is far freer and more subtle. A very different kind of landscape painting is the "Amano-Hashidate" scroll (c. 1502–05) in the Kyōto National Museum. Much more detailed and realistic, it is almost like a topographic view of a particular place.

Sesshū's masterpiece

In addition to these landscapes, Sesshū painted a large number of Buddhist pictures that were often directly inspired by Zen teachings. The most famous of these is the scroll dated 1496 showing Bodhidharma and Hui K'o (1496; Sainen-ji, Aichi Prefecture). Painted in heavy, vigorous lines, it reveals how Hui K'o cut off his arm in order to demonstrate his seriousness to Bodhidharma, the founder of Zen Buddhism who is called Daruma in Japan.

Sesshū also painted decorative screens. Perhaps the best of the ones attributed to him is the pair of six-fold screens showing birds and flowers in the Kosaka Collection in Tokyo. Painted in a realistic yet decorative manner, with slight additions of colour, they reveal yet another aspect of the artist's genius. In contrast to the landscapes and Zen pictures that are inspired by the paintings of Sung China, these pictorial compositions are closer to the type of decorative painting that flourished in China during the Ming period.

While his most celebrated works are all in Japan, other pictures attributed to Sesshū are located in the West, especially in United States collections. The Boston Museum of Fine Arts, for example, has seven paintings attributed to him, but the only one that is at all likely to be by Sesshū himself is a pair of screens depicting falcons and monkeys, which has Sesshū's seal and signature, as well as an inscription saying it was painted during the artist's 72nd year. Other works that may be authentic are found in the Cleveland Museum of Art and the Seattle Art Museum. The great bulk, however, of the many scrolls traditionally attributed to Sesshū both in Japan and in the West are generally considered to be school pieces or copies inspired by the work of the master.

MAJOR WORKS

There are only a few authenticated works by Sesshū, the most important of which are listed below.

"Four Seasons Landscape," four landscape scrolls (*c.* 1470–90; Tokyo National Museum); "Autumn Landscape," hanging scroll (*c.* 1470–90; Tokyo National Museum); "Winter Landscape," hanging scroll (*c.* 1470–90; Tokyo National Museum); "Short Scroll Landscape" (*c.* 1474–90; Asano Collection, Odawara); "Portrait of Masuda Kanetaka" (1479; Masuda Collection, Tokyo); "Long Scroll Landscape," or "Sansui Chōkan" (*c.* 1486; Mōri Collection, Yamaguchi); "Haboku-Sansui," scroll (1495; Tokyo National Museum); "Daruma and Hui K'o," scroll (1496; Sainen-ji, Aichi); "Ama-no-Hashidate," scroll (*c.* 1502–05; Kyoto National Museum); "Flowers and Birds," pair of 6-fold screens (undated; Kosaka Collection, Tokyo).

BIBLIOGRAPHY. J.C. COVELL, *Under the Seal of Sesshū* (1941), the only detailed and scholarly study of Sesshū in English; E. GRILLI, *Sesshū* (1957), a brief English survey of the life and art of Sesshū (well illustrated).

(H.Mu.)

Set Theory

Between the years 1874 and 1897, the German mathematician and logician Georg Cantor (*q.v.*) created a theory of abstract sets of entities making it into a mathematical discipline. This theory grew out of his investigations of certain concrete problems regarding certain types of infinite sets of real numbers (see ANALYSIS, REAL). A set, wrote Cantor, is a collection of definite, distinguishable objects of perception or thought conceived as a whole. The objects are called elements or members of the set.

The theory had the revolutionary aspect of treating infinite sets as mathematical objects that are on an equal footing with those that can be constructed in a finite number of steps. Since antiquity, a majority of mathematicians had carefully avoided the introduction into their arguments of the actual infinite (*i.e.*, of sets containing an infinity of objects conceived as existing simultaneously, at least in thought). Since this attitude persisted until almost the end of the 19th century, Cantor's work was the subject of much criticism to the effect that it dealt with fictions; indeed, that it encroached on the domain of philosophers and violated the principles of religion. Once applications to analysis began to be found, however, attitudes began to change, and in the 1890s Cantor's ideas and results were gaining acceptance. By 1900, set theory was recognized as a distinct branch of mathematics.

At just that time, however, it received a severe setback through the derivation of several contradictions in its superstructure (see below *Cardinality and transfinite numbers*). The main thrust of this article is to present an account of one response to such contradictions as these. The purpose of the development here related has been to provide an axiomatic basis for the theory of sets analogous to that developed for elementary geometry. The degree of success that has been achieved in this development, as well as the present stature of set theory, has been well expressed in the Bourbaki *Éléments de mathématique:* "Nowadays it is known to be possible, logically speaking, to derive practically the whole of known mathematics from a single source, The Theory of Sets." (R.R.S.)

Introduction to set theory

FUNDAMENTAL SET CONCEPTS

If the elements and sets to be considered are restricted to some fixed class of objects, such as the letters of the alphabet, the universal set (or the universe), denoted by *U,* can then be defined as that which includes all of the elements—the set of all of the 26 letters. Thus, if *A* is a set, it will be understood that *A* is a subset of *U.* Another set may now be defined that includes all of the elements of *U* that are not elements of *A.* This set, called the complement of *A,* is denoted by *A'.* (Some writers, employing the convention of "difference sets," speak of "the complement of *A* with respect to *U,*" which they denote by "$X - A$.")

The empty (or void, or null) set, symbolized by "∅," contains no elements. One description of the empty set is that of all whole numbers that are neither even nor odd.

Operations on sets. The symbol ∪ is employed to denote the union of two sets. Thus, the set *A* ∪ *B*—read "*A* union *B*" or "the union (or join) of *A* and *B*"—is the set that consists of all elements belonging either to set *A* or set *B.* If sets *A* and *B,* however, have one or more members in common, their union will not duplicate those members. A committee, for example, consisting of Jones, Blanshard, Smith, and Hixon (Committee *A*) may for some common purpose sit in joint session with Committee *B,* consisting of Blanshard, Morton, Hixon, and Peters. Clearly, the union of Committees *A* and *B* must then consist of six members rather than eight, viz., Jones, Blanshard, Smith, Morton, Hixon, and Peters.

The intersection operation is denoted by the symbol ∩. *A* ∩ *B*—read "*A* intersect *B*" or "the intersection of *A* and *B*"—is defined as that set comprised of all elements that belong to both *A* and *B.* Thus the intersection of the two committees in the foregoing example is the set consisting of Blanshard and Hixon.

If the set *E* denotes all positive even numbers and the set *Q* denotes all positive odd numbers, then the union of the two yields the entire sequence of positive natural numbers, and their intersection is the empty set. Any two sets the intersection of which is the empty set are said to be disjoint.

A product of two sets *A* and *B,* called a Cartesian product, is denoted by *A* × *B.* This product is defined in terms of ordered pairs, analogous to the coordinates (or *x* and *y* values) of points on a Cartesian grid in analytic geometry. It is conventional to denote such pairs by enclosure in parentheses. If (*a, b*) and (*c, d*) are ordered pairs, then (*a, b*) = (*c, d*) if and only if $a = c$ and $b = d$. The Cartesian product *A* × *B* may now be defined as the set consisting of all ordered pairs (*x, y*) for which *x* is an element of *A* and *y* is an element of *B.* An example is easily constructed: $A = \{x, y\}$, $B = \{3, 6, 9\}$, $A \times B = \{(x, 3), (x, 6), (x, 9), (y, 3), (y, 6), (y, 9)\}$.

Relations involved in set theory. The relations between sets can be of many sorts; *e.g.*, "is a subset of" (⊆), "is equivalent to" (~), "is a complement of" ('), "is in one-to-one correspondence with," and "has the same cardinal number as" (see below). In addition, pairing relations, defined in terms of some specific criterion, can exist between the individual elements of a set. Examples of pairing relations are: "is parallel to" (∥), "is equal to" (=), "is less than" (<), and "is the same colour as." More broadly conceived, pairing can include the relations depicted on charts and graphs, on which, for example, calendar years may be paired with automobile production figures, weeks with Dow-Jones averages, and degrees of angular rotation with the lift accomplished by a cam.

The relation of one-to-one correspondence between two sets can be conceived as one in which each element of a set *A* is matched with an element of another set *B.* If $A = \{x, z, w\}$, for example, and $B = \{4, 3, 9\}$, then *A* is in one-to-one correspondence with *B* if and only if a matching such as 4 with *x,* 3 with *z,* and 9 with *w* obtains without any element in either set left unmatched as a remainder.

Many relations display identifiable similarities. The relations "is parallel to," "is the same colour as," and "is in one-to-one correspondence with," for example, all bear the stated relation to themselves as well as to other ele-

---

Marginal notes:

Empty set

Union, intersection, and Cartesian product

Pairing relations between elements

Controversy over the actual infinite

ments; thus, these relations are said to be reflexive. These same relations share, in addition, the property that, if an element bears the stated relation to a second element, then the second also bears that relation to the first—a property known as symmetry. Relations also have the property that, if two elements bear the stated relation to a third element, then they bear it to one another as well—a property known as transitivity.

Those relations that have all three properties—reflexivity, symmetry, and transitivity—are called equivalence relations. In an equivalence relation, all elements related to a particular element are related to each other, thus forming what is called an equivalence class. For the relation "is parallel to," for example, the equivalence class of a particular line ℓ is the set of all lines parallel to ℓ.

Equivalence classes and numbers

For each of the equivalence classes of sets, it is possible to construct an ordered set—for which not only the membership but also the sequence of its elements is significant—that can be used to name the class.

With appropriate qualifications, the cardinal of the empty set $\emptyset$ can be defined as 0; *i.e.*, $n(\emptyset) = 0$. The number 1, then, is assigned to be the cardinal of the set $\{0\}$ that contains only a single element; it is thus called the successor of 0. Similarly, the number 2, the cardinal of $\{0, 1\}$, is called the successor of 1; and 3, the cardinal of $\{0, 1, 2\}$, is the successor of 2. Continuing in this manner, the set $\mathfrak{N}$ of the natural numbers in the proper sequence $\{0, 1, 2, 3, 4, \cdots\}$ is obtained, for which the ordering is given by the successor relation.

It is this ordering that is used when one learns to count. The words one, two, three, four, $\cdots$ in proper sequence are associated with the elements in the set that are being counted. If this process stops, the set is said to be finite. Otherwise, it is said to be infinite.

There is a technical difference between cardinal and ordinal numbers. The distinction can be seen in the way these numbers are used.

A number used to designate the size of a set—*i.e.*, to answer the question, "How many?"—is used cardinally. Any use that depends on the position of the number in the prescribed sequence is the ordinal use of the number. The number at the top or bottom of the page is an example of the ordinal use of the number. (Jo.Ha.)

ESSENTIAL FEATURES OF CANTORIAN SET THEORY

At best, the foregoing description presents only an intuitive concept of a set. Essential features of the concept as Cantor understood it include: (a) that a set is a grouping into a single entity of objects of any kind; and (b) that, given an object x and a set A, exactly one of the statements "x is an element of A" (symbolized $x \in A$) and "x is not an element of A" (symbolized $(x \notin A)$) is true and the other is false. The definite relation that may or may not exist between an object and a set is called the membership relation.

A further intent of this description is conveyed by what is called the principle of extension, viz., that a set is determined by its members: that sets A and B are equal (symbolized $A = B$) if and only if every element in A is also in B and every element in B is in A; or, in other terms, $x \in A$ implies $x \in B$ and vice versa. There exists, for example, exactly one set the members of which are 2, 5, and 7; and this set will be written by listing its elements in some order (which order is immaterial) between small braces, possibly $\{5, 2, 7\}$.

Extension and abstraction

A set A is finite if for some natural number n there is a pairing of the elements of A with those of the initial segment $0, 1, \cdots, n - 1$ of the natural numbers $0, 1, 2, \cdots$ in their usual order. This definition amounts to classifying a set as finite if it has a natural number n as its cardinal number (see below *Cardinality and transfinite numbers*). In principle, the brace notation is adequate for defining all finite sets.

To define infinite (*i.e.*, nonfinite) sets, Cantor used (sentential) formulas. The phrase "x is a professor" is an example of a formula; if the symbol "x" in this phrase is replaced by the name of a person, there results a declarative sentence that is true or false. The notation "$S(x)$" will be used to represent such a formula. The phrase "x is a professor at university y and x is a male" is a formula with two variables. If the occurrences of x and y are replaced by names of appropriate, specific objects, the result is a declarative sentence that is true or false. Given any formula $S(x)$ that contains the letter "x" (and possibly others) but not the letter "A," Cantor's principle of abstraction asserts the existence of a set A such that for each object x, $x \in A$ if and only if $S(x)$ holds. The unique (because of the principle of extension) set A corresponding to $S(x)$ is symbolized by $\{x \mid S(x)\}$ and read "The set of all objects x such that $S(x)$." For instance, $\{x \mid x$ is blue$\}$ is the set of all blue objects. This illustrates the fact that the principle implies the existence of sets the elements of which are all objects having a certain property. It is actually more comprehensive. For example, it asserts the existence of a set B corresponding to "Either x is an astronaut or x is a natural number." Astronauts have no property in common with numbers (other than both being members of B). The formula "$x \neq x$" defines the only set without elements. It is called the empty set and symbolized by $\emptyset$. The empty set is finite, for its members can be paired with those of the initial segment defined by $n = 0$.

Equivalent sets. Cantorian set theory is thus founded on the principles of extension and abstraction. To describe some results based upon these principles the notion of equivalence of sets will be defined. The set A is defined as equivalent to the set B (symbolized $A \sim B$) if and only if there exists a third set the members of which are ordered pairs such that: (a) the first member of each pair is an element of A and the second is an element of B, and (b) each member of A occurs as a first member and each member of B occurs as a second member of exactly one pair. Thus, if A and B are finite and $A \sim B$, then the third set that establishes this fact provides a pairing or matching of the elements of A with those of B. Conversely, if it is possible to match the elements of A with those of B, then $A \sim B$, because a set of pairs meeting requirements (a) and (b) can be formed (if $a \in A$ is matched with $b \in B$, then the ordered pair (a, b) is one member of the set). By thus defining equivalence of sets in terms of the notion of matching, it is formulated independently of finiteness. As an illustration involving infinite sets, $\mathfrak{N}$ may be taken to denote the set of natural numbers $0, 1, 2, \cdots$ (some authors exclude 0 from the natural numbers). Then $\{(n, n^2) \mid n \in \mathfrak{N}\}$ establishes the equivalence of $\mathfrak{N}$ and the set of the squares of the natural numbers.

Equivalence and subsets

A set B is included in, or is a subset of, a set A (symbolized $B \subseteq A$) if every element of B is an element of A. (So defined, a subset may possibly include all of the elements of A, so that A can be a subset of itself.) If, in addition, the converse is false (hence $B \neq A$), then B is said to be properly included in, or is a proper subset of, A (symbolized $B \subset A$). Thus, if A is $\{3, 1, 0, 4, 2\}$, both $\{0, 1, 2\}$ and $\{0, 1, 2, 3, 4\}$ are subsets of A; but the latter is not a proper subset. A finite set is nonequivalent to each of its proper subsets. This is not so, however, for infinite sets, as is illustrated with the set $\mathfrak{N}$ in the earlier example. (The equivalence of $\mathfrak{N}$ and its proper subset of the even natural numbers was essentially the paradox noted by Galileo in 1638.)

Cardinality and transfinite numbers. The application of the notion of equivalence to infinite sets was first systematically explored by Cantor. His initial significant finding was that the set of all rational numbers (see ANALYSIS, REAL; ARITHMETIC) is equivalent to $\mathfrak{N}$ but that the set of all real numbers is not equivalent to $\mathfrak{N}$. The existence of nonequivalent infinite sets justified Cantor's introduction of transfinite cardinal numbers as measures of size for such sets. Cantor defined the cardinal of an arbitrary set A as the concept that can be abstracted from A taken together with the totality of other equivalent sets. Gottlob Frege, in 1884, and Bertrand Russell, in 1902, both mathematical logicians, defined the cardinal number $\overline{\overline{A}}$ of a set A somewhat more explicitly, as the set of all sets that are equivalent to A; this definition thus provides a place for cardinal numbers as objects of a universe whose only members are sets.

Infinite sets and power sets

These definitions are consistent with the usage of natural numbers as cardinal numbers. A natural number, 2 for example, is first assigned to the set $\{0, 1\}$ as a measure of its size; then 2 is assigned to every set equivalent to $\{0, 1\}$. Turning matters around, 2 is the concept that can be abstracted from the collection of sets equivalent to $\{0, 1\}$, or 2 may be defined as this collection of sets. Intuitively, a cardinal number, whether finite (*i.e.*, a natural number) or transfinite (*i.e.*, nonfinite), is a measure of the size of a set. Exactly how a cardinal number is defined is unimportant; what is important is that $\overline{\overline{A}} = \overline{\overline{B}}$ if and only if $A \sim B$.

To compare cardinal numbers, an ordering relation—denoted by $<$—may be introduced by means of the definition: $\overline{\overline{A}} < \overline{\overline{B}}$ if A is equivalent to a subset of B and B is equivalent to no subset of A. Clearly this relation is irreflexive $\overline{\overline{A}} \not< \overline{\overline{A}}$ and transitive $\overline{\overline{A}} < \overline{\overline{B}}$ and $\overline{\overline{B}} < \overline{\overline{C}}$ imply $\overline{\overline{A}} < \overline{\overline{C}}$.

When applied to natural numbers used as cardinals, $<$ coincides with the familiar ordering relation for $\mathfrak{N}$, so that $<$ is an extension of that relation.

The symbol $\aleph_0$ (aleph null) is standard for the cardinal number of $\mathfrak{N}$ (sets of this cardinality are called denumerable) and $\aleph$ (aleph) is usually used for that of the set of real numbers. Then $n < \aleph_0$ for each $n \in \mathfrak{N}$ and $\aleph_0 < \aleph$.

This, however, is not the end of the matter. If the power set of a set A—symbolized $P(A)$—is defined as the set of all subsets of A, then, as Cantor proved, $\overline{\overline{A}} < \overline{\overline{P(A)}}$ for every set A—a relation that is known as Cantor's theorem. It implies an unending hierarchy of transfinite cardinals: $\overline{\overline{N}} = \aleph_0, \overline{\overline{P(N)}}, \overline{\overline{P(P(N))}}, \cdots$ Cantor proved that $\aleph = \overline{\overline{P(N)}}$ and was led to the question whether there is a cardinal number between $\aleph_0$ and $\aleph$, which is known as the continuum problem. A solution was completed in 1963 (see below).

There is an arithmetic for cardinal numbers based on natural definitions of addition, multiplication, and exponentiation (squaring, cubing, and so on), which deviates, however, from that of the natural numbers when transfinite cardinals are involved. For example, $\aleph_0 + \aleph_0 = \aleph_0$ (because the set of integers is equivalent to $\mathfrak{N}$), $\aleph_0 \cdot \aleph = {}^0\aleph_0$ (because the set of ordered pairs of natural numbers is equivalent to $\mathfrak{N}$), and $c + \aleph_0 = c$ for every transfinite cardinal c (because every infinite set includes a subset equivalent to $\mathfrak{N}$).

The extension of the natural numbers as cardinal numbers to transfinite numbers described earlier is a typical facet of Cantorian set theory.

The so-called Cantor paradox, discovered by Cantor himself in 1899, is the following: By the principle of abstraction, the formula "x is a set" defines a set U. It is the set of all sets. Now $P(U)$ is a set of sets and so $P(U)$ is a subset of U. By the definition of $<$ for cardinals, however, if $A \subseteq B$, then it is not the case that $\overline{\overline{B}} < \overline{\overline{A}}$. Hence, by substitution, $\overline{\overline{U}} \not< \overline{\overline{P(U)}}$. But by Cantor's theorem, $\overline{\overline{U}} < \overline{\overline{P(U)}}$. This is a contradiction. In 1902, Bertrand Russell devised another paradox of a less technical nature. The formula "x is a set and $(x \notin x)$" defines a set R of all sets not members of themselves. Using proof by contradiction, however, it is easily shown that (A) $R \in R$. But then by the definition of R it follows that (B) $(R \notin R)$. Together, (A) and (B) form a contradiction.

Axiomatic set theory

The attitude adopted in an axiomatic development of set theory is that it is not necessary to know what the "things" are that are called "sets" nor what the relation of membership means. Of sole concern are the properties assumed about sets and the membership relation. Thus, in an axiomatic theory of sets, the terms set and membership relation $\in$ are undefined. The assumptions adopted about these notions are called the axioms of the theory. Its theorems are the axioms together with the statements that can be deduced from the axioms using the rules of inference provided by a system of logic.

Criteria for the choice of axioms include: (A) their consistency (*i.e.*, that it should be impossible to derive as theorems both a statement and its negation), (B) their plausibility (*i.e.*, that they should be in accord with intuitive beliefs about sets), and (C) their richness (*i.e.*, that desirable results of Cantorian set theory can be derived as theorems).

These points are elaborated upon below.

POSTULATES OF AXIOMATIC SET THEORY

The Zermelo–Fraenkel axioms: discussion. The first axiomatization of set theory was given in 1908 by Ernst Zermelo, a German mathematician. From his analysis of the paradoxes, he concluded that they are associated with sets that are "too big," such as the set of all sets in Cantor's paradox. Thus, the axioms that Zermelo formulated are restrictive insofar as the asserting or implying of the existence of sets is concerned. As a consequence, there is no apparent way, in his system, to derive the known contradictions from them. On the other hand, the results of classical set theory short of the paradoxes can be derived. Zermelo's axiomatic theory is here discussed in a form that incorporates modifications and improvements suggested by later mathematicians, principally Thoralf Albert Skolem, a pioneer in metalogic, and Abraham Adolf Fraenkel, an Israeli mathematician. In the literature on set theory, it is called Zermelo–Fraenkel set theory (symbolized ZF), though it would seem historically more correct to call it Zermelo–Fraenkel–Skolem set theory. The ten axioms are first discussed and then formally listed (see below *The Zermelo-Fraenkel axioms: formal presentation*).

Schemas for generating well-formed formulas. In the axioms that follow, "set" and "$\in$" are undefined terms. Lowercase Latin letters are used for variables; and variables denote sets. Equality (symbolized $=$) is taken as part of the underlying logic.

The first axiom (see axiom 1, below) conveys the idea that, as in classical set theory, a set is determined by its members. It should be noted that this is not merely a logically necessary property of equality but an assumption about the membership relation as well.

The set defined by the second axiom (see 2) is the empty (or null) set $\emptyset$.

For an understanding of the third axiom (see 3) considerable explanation is required. Zermelo's original system included the assumption (*Aussonderung* axiom) that, if a formula $S(x)$ is "definite" for all elements of a set s, then there exists a set the elements of which are precisely those elements x of s for which $S(x)$ holds. This is a version of the principle of abstraction, for it provides for the existence of sets corresponding to formulas. It restricts that principle, however, in two ways. Instead of asserting the existence of sets unconditionally, it can be applied only in conjunction with pre-existing sets. Further, only "definite" formulas (for which Zermelo offered only a vague description) may be used. Clarification was given, however, by Skolem (1922) by way of a precise definition of what will be called simply a formula of ZF. Using tools of modern logic, the definition may be made as follows:

a. For any variables x and y, $x \in y$ and $x = y$ are formulas (such formulas are called atomic).

b. If A and B denote formulas and x is any variable, then each of the following is a formula: If A, then B; A if and only if B; A and B; A or B; not A; for all x, A; for some x, B.

Formulas are constructed recursively (in a finite number of systematic steps) beginning with the (atomic) formulas of (a) and proceeding via the constructions permitted in (b). "Not $(x \in y)$," for example, is a formula (which is abbreviated to $x \notin y$), and "There exists an x such that for every y, $y \notin x$" is a formula. A variable is free in a formula if it occurs at least once in the formula without being introduced by one of the phrases "for some x" or "for all x." Henceforth, a formula P in which x occurs as a free variable will be called a "condition on x" and symbolized $P(x)$. The formula "For every y, $x \in y$," for example, is a condition on x. It is to be understood that a formula is a formal expression—*i.e.*, a term

Zermelo's pioneering work

Intuitive
inter-
pretation

without meaning. Indeed, a computer could be programmed to generate atomic formulas and build up from them other formulas of ever-increasing complexity using logical connectives ("not," "and," etc.) and operators ("for all" and "for some"). A formula acquires meaning only when an interpretation of the theory is spelled out; *i.e.*, when (A) a nonempty collection (called the domain of the interpretation) is specified as the range of values of the variables (thus the term set is assigned a meaning, viz., an object in the domain), (B) the membership relation is defined for these sets, (C) the logical connectives and operators are interpreted as in everyday language, and (D) the logical relation of equality is taken to be identity among the objects in the domain.

The terminology "a condition on x" for a formula in which x is free is merely suggestive; relative to an interpretation, such a formula does impose a condition on x. Thus, the intuitive interpretation of the third axiom schema is: given a set a and a condition on x, $P(x)$, those elements of a for which the condition holds form a set. It provides for the existence of sets by separating off certain elements of existing sets. Calling the third axiom schema an axiom schema is appropriate, for it is a schema for generating axioms—one for each choice of $P(x)$.

Axioms for compounding sets. Although the third axiom schema has a constructive quality, further means of constructing sets from existing sets must be introduced if some of the desirable features of Cantorian set theory are to be established. Each of the next three axioms is of this sort.

Using five of the axioms (see 2–6), a variety of basic concepts of classical set theory (*e.g.*, the operations of union, intersection, and Cartesian product; the notions of relation, equivalence relation, ordering relation, and function) can be defined with ZF. Further, the standard results about these concepts that were attainable in classical set theory can be proved as theorems of ZF.

Axioms for infinite and ordered sets. If I is an interpretation of an axiomatic theory of sets, the sentence that results from an axiom when a meaning has been assigned to "set" and "∈," as specified by I, is either true or false. If each axiom is true for I, then I is called a model of the theory (see METALOGIC: *Model theory*). If the domain of a model is infinite, this fact does not imply that any object of the domain is an "infinite set." An infinite set in the latter sense is an object d of the domain D of I for which there is an infinity of distinct objects d' in D such that $d'Ed$ holds (E standing for the interpretation of ∈). Though the domain of any model of the theory of which the axioms thus far discussed are axioms is clearly infinite, models in which every set is finite have been devised. For the full development of classical set theory, including the theories of real numbers and of infinite cardinal numbers, the existence of infinite sets is needed; thus the seventh axiom (see 7) is included.

The existence of a (unique) minimal set, ω, having properties expressed in the seventh axiom can be proved; its distinct members are $\emptyset$, $\{\emptyset\}$, $\{\emptyset, \{\emptyset\}\}$, $\{\emptyset, \{\emptyset\}\}$, $\{\emptyset, \{\emptyset\}\}$, $\cdots$. These elements are denoted by 0, 1, 2, 3, $\cdots$ and are called natural numbers. Justification for this terminology rests with the fact that the Peano axioms, which can serve as a base for arithmetic, can be proved as theorems. Thereby the way is paved for the construction within ZF of entities that have all the expected properties of the real numbers.

The origin of the next axiom was Cantor's recognition of the importance of being able to well-order arbitrary sets; *i.e.*, to define an ordering relation for a given set such that each nonempty subset has a least element. The virtue of a well-ordering for a set is that it offers a means of proving that a property holds for each of its elements by a process (transfinite induction) similar to mathematical induction. Zermelo (1904) gave the first proof that any set can be well-ordered. His proof employed a set-theoretic principle that he called the axiom of choice, which, shortly thereafter, was shown to be equivalent to the so-called well-ordering theorem. One form of this principle is expressed as an eighth axiom (see 8).

Intuitively, the axiom asserts the possibility of making a simultaneous choice of an element in every nonempty member of any set; this guarantee accounts for its name. The assumption is significant only when the set has infinitely many members. Zermelo was the first to explicitly state the axiom, although it had been used but essentially unnoticed earlier. It soon became the subject of vigorous controversy because of its unconstructive nature. Some mathematicians rejected it totally on this ground. Others accepted it but avoided its use whenever possible. Some changed their minds about it when its equivalence with the well-ordering theorem was proved as well as the assertion that any two cardinal numbers c and d are comparable (*i.e.*, that exactly one of $c < d$, $d < c$, $c = d$ holds). There are many other equivalent statements, though even today there are a few mathematicians who feel that the use of the axiom of choice is improper. To the vast majority, however, it, or an equivalent assertion, has become an indispensable and commonplace tool.

Schema for transfinite induction and ordinal arithmetic. One more axiom has been added to the list of axioms (with modifications) postulated by Zermelo. When Zermelo's eight were found to be inadequate for a fullblown development of transfinite induction and ordinal arithmetic, Fraenkel and Skolem independently proposed an additional axiom schema to eliminate the difficulty. As modified by John von Neumann, a Hungarian-born U.S. mathematician, it says, intuitively, that if with each element of a set there is associated exactly one set, then the collection of the associated sets is itself a set; *i.e.*, it offers a way to "collect" existing sets to form sets. As an illustration, each of ω, $P(\omega)$, $P(P(\omega))$, $\cdots$ is a set in the theory based on the first eight axioms. But there appears to be no way to establish the existence of the set having these sets as its members. An instance of the next schema, however, provides for its existence.

Intuitively, the ninth axiom or schema (see 9) is the assertion that if the domain of a function is a set then so is its range. That this is a powerful schema (in respect to the further inferences that it yields) is suggested by the fact that the third axiom can be derived from it and that, when applied in conjunction with the sixth axiom, the axiom of pairing can be deduced. The ninth axiom has played a significant role in developing a theory of ordinal numbers. In contrast to cardinal numbers, which serve to designate the size of a set, ordinal numbers are used to determine positions within a prescribed sequence. Following an approach conceived independently by Zermelo and von Neumann, if x is a set, the successor x' of x is the set obtained by adjoining x to the elements of x ($x' = x \cup \{x\}$). In terms of this notion the natural numbers, as defined above, are simply the succession 0, 0', 0'', 0''', $\cdots$; *i.e.*, the natural numbers are the sets obtained starting with $\emptyset$ and iterating the prime operation a finite number of times. The natural numbers are well-ordered by the ∈ relation, and with this ordering they constitute the finite ordinal numbers. The axiom of infinity secures the existence of the set of natural numbers; and this set, $\aleph\omega$, is the first infinite ordinal. Greater ordinal numbers are obtained by iterating the prime operation beginning with ω. An instance of the ninth axiom or schema asserts that ω, ω', ω'', $\cdots$ form a set. The union of this set and ω is the still greater ordinal that is denoted by $\omega2$ (employing notation from ordinal arithmetic). A repetition of this process beginning with $\omega2$ yields the ordinals $(\omega2)'$, $(\omega2)''$, $\cdots$; next after all of those of this form is $\omega3$. In this way the sequence of ordinals ω, $\omega2$, $\omega3$, $\cdots$ is generated. An application of the ninth axiom schema then yields the ordinal that follows all of these in the same sense in which ω follows the finite ordinals; using notation from ordinal arithmetic, it is ω^2. At this point the iteration process can be repeated. In summary, the axiom of replacement makes possible the extension of the counting process as far beyond the natural numbers as one chooses.

In the ZF system, cardinal numbers are defined as certain ordinals. From the well-ordering theorem (a consequence of the axiom of choice), it follows that

Cardinal
and ordinal
numbers

every set a is equivalent to some ordinal number. Also, the totality of ordinals equivalent to a can be shown to form a set. Then a natural choice for the cardinal number of a is the least ordinal to which a is equivalent. This is the motivation for defining a cardinal number as an ordinal that is not equivalent to any smaller ordinal. The arithmetics of both cardinal and ordinal numbers have been fully developed. That of finite cardinals and ordinals coincides with the arithmetic of the natural numbers. For infinite cardinals, the arithmetic is uninteresting since, as a consequence of the eighth axiom, the sum and product of two such cardinals are each equal to the maximum of the two. In contrast the arithmetic of infinite ordinals is interesting and presents a wide assortment of oddities.

In addition to the guidelines already mentioned for the choice of axioms of ZF, another guideline is taken into account by some set theorists. For the purposes of foundational studies of mathematics, it is assumed that mathematics is consistent; for otherwise any foundation would fail. It may thus be reasoned that, if a precise account of the intuitive usages of sets by mathematicians is given, an adequate and correct foundation will result. Traditionally, mathematicians deal with the integers, with real numbers, and with functions. Thus an intuitive hierarchy of sets in which these entities appear should be a model of ZF. It is possible to construct such a hierarchy explicitly from the empty set by iterating the operations of forming power sets and unions in the following way.

The first level of the hierarchy is composed of the sequence of sets $s_0 = \emptyset, s_1, \cdots, s_n, \cdots$, in which s_{n+1} is the power set of s_n. The second level consists of the sets at the first level together with those sets obtained by iterating the power set operation any finite number of times. The third level has as its members the union of all sets constructed thus far together with those obtainable by iterating the power set operation as before. The hierarchy of sets envisaged, therefore, consists of all sets that can be obtained by proceeding to an arbitrarily large transfinite level. The domain of the intuitive model of ZF is conceived as the union of all sets in the hierarchy. In other words, a set x is in the model if it is an element of some set of the hierarchy.

Axiom for eliminating infinite descending species. From the assumptions that this system is sufficiently comprehensive for mathematics and that it is the model to be "captured" by the axioms of ZF, it may be argued that models of the first nine axioms that differ sharply from this system should be ruled out. The discovery of such a model led to the formulation by von Neumann of the tenth axiom (see 10).

This axiom eliminates from the models of the first nine axioms those in which there exist infinite descending $\in$-chains (*i.e.*, sequences $x_1, x_2, x_3, \cdots$ such that $x_2 \in x_1, x_3 \in x_2, \cdots$), a phenomenon that does not appear in the heuristic model described above. (The existence of models having such chains was discovered by D. Mirimanoff in 1917.) It also has other attractive consequences; *e.g.*, a simpler definition of the notion of ordinal number is possible. Yet there is no unanimity among mathematicians whether there are sufficient grounds for adopting it as an additional axiom, since it does not have the immediate plausibility that even the axiom of choice has nor has it ever been shown to have any mathematical applications.

The Zermelo–Fraenkel axioms: formal presentation.

(1) *Axiom of extension.* If a and b are sets and if, for all x, $x \in a$ if and only if $x \in b$, then $a = b$.

(2) *Axiom of the empty set.* There exists a set a such that for all x, it is false that $x \in a$.

(3) *Axiom schema of separation.* If a is a set, there exists a set b such that for all x, $x \in b$ if and only if $x \in a$ and $P(x)$. Here, $P(x)$ is any condition on x in which b is not free (it must be bound by a quantifier such as "all" or "some").

(4) *Axiom of pairing.* If a and b are sets, there exists a set (symbolized $\{a, b\}$ and called the unordered pair of a and b) having a and b as its sole members.

(5) *Axiom of union.* If c is a set, there exists a set a such that $x \in a$ if and only if $x \in b$ for some member b of c.

The intuitive hierarchy of sets

(6) *Axiom of power set.* If a is a set, there exists a set b such that $x \in b$ if and only if $x \subseteq a$.

(7) *Axiom of infinity.* There exists a set a such that $\emptyset \in a$ and, if $x \in a$, then $(x \cup \{x\}) \in a$, in which $x \cup \{x\}$ is the set x with x adjoined as a further member.

(8) *Axiom of choice.* If a is a set the elements of which are nonempty sets, then there exists a function f with domain a such that for member b of a, $f(b) \in b$.

(9) *Axiom schema of replacement.* If a is a set and $B(x, y)$ a formula (in which x and y are free) such that for $x \in a$ there is exactly one y such that $B(x, y)$, then there exists a set b the members of which are the y's determined by $B(x, y)$ as x ranges over a.

(10) *Axiom of restriction.* Every nonempty set a contains an element b such that $a \cap b = \emptyset$; *i.e.*, a and b have no elements in common.

The von Neumann–Bernays–Gödel axioms: discussion. The second axiomatization of set theory originated with von Neumann in the 1920s. His formulation differed considerably from ZF because the notion of function, rather than that of set, was taken as primitive. In a series of papers beginning in 1937, however, the Swiss logician Paul Bernays, a collaborator with the formalist David Hilbert, modified the von Neumann approach in a way that put it in much closer contact with ZF. In 1940, the Czech-born logician Kurt Gödel, known for his undecidability proof, further simplified the theory. This version will be called NBG.

For expository purposes it is convenient to adopt two undefined notions for NBG: class and the binary relation, $\in$, of membership (though, as is also true in ZF, $\in$ suffices). In the axioms, capital Latin letters are used as variables. For the intended interpretation, variables take classes—the totalities corresponding to certain properties—as values. A class is defined to be a set if it is a member of some class; those classes that are not sets are called proper classes. Lowercase Latin letters are used as special restricted variables for sets. For example, "for all x, $A(x)$" stands for "for all X, if X is a set, then $A(X)$"; *i.e.*, the condition holds for all sets. Intuitively, sets are intended to be those classes that are adequate for mathematics, and proper classes are thought of as those collections that are "so big" that, if permitted to be sets, contradictions would follow. In NBG, the classical paradoxes are avoided by proving in each case that the collection on which the paradox is based is a proper class—*i.e.*, is not a set.

Comments about the axioms that follow are limited to features that distinguish them from their counterpart in ZF. The axioms are listed later (see 11–20, below *The von Neumann–Bernays–Gödel axioms: statement*).

The third axiom or schema (see 13) is presented in a form to facilitate a comparison with the third axiom schema of ZF. In a detailed development of NBG, however, there appears, instead, a list of seven axioms (not schemas) that state that for each of certain conditions there exists a corresponding class of all those sets satisfying the condition. From this finite set of axioms, each an instance of the above schema, the schema (in a generalized form) can be obtained as a theorem. When obtained in this way, the third axiom schema of NBG is called the class existence theorem.

In brief, the fourth to eighth axioms of NBG (see 14–18) are axioms of set existence. The same is true of the next axiom, which for technical reasons is usually phrased in a more general form.

Finally there may appear in a formulation of NBG an analogue (see 20) of the last axiom of ZF.

A comparison of the two theories that have been formulated is in order. In contrast to the ninth schema of ZF (see 9), that of NBG (see 19) is not an axiom schema but an axiom. Thus, with the comments above about the third axiom in mind, it follows that NBG has only a finite number of axioms. On the other hand, since the ninth axiom or schema of ZF provides an axiom for each formula, ZF has infinitely many axioms—which is unavoidable because it is known that no finite subset yields the full system of axioms. The finiteness of the axioms for NBG makes the logical study of the system simpler. The relationship between the theories may be

Comparison of ZF and NBG axiomatizations

summarized by the statement that ZF is essentially the part of NBG that refers only to sets. Indeed, it has been proved that every theorem of ZF is a theorem of NBG and that any theorem of NBG that speaks only about sets is a theorem of ZF. Finally, it has been shown that ZF is consistent if and only if NBG is consistent.

The von Neumann–Bernays–Gödel axioms: statement.

(11) *Axiom of extension.* If A and B are classes and if, for all (sets) x, $x \in A$ if and only if $x \in B$, then $A = B$.

(12) Same as axiom (2).

(13) *Axiom schema for class formation.* If $P(x)$ is a condition on x in which (a) only set variables are introduced by the phrase "for all" or "for some" and (b) B is not free, then there exists a class B such that $x \in B$ if and only if $P(x)$.

(14) *Axiom of pairing.* Same as axiom (4).

(15) *Axiom of union.* Same as axiom (5).

(16) *Axiom of power set.* Same as axiom (6).

(17) *Axiom of infinity.* Same as axiom (7).

(18) *Axiom of choice.* Same as (8).

(19) *Axiom of replacement.* If (the class) X is a function and a is a set, then there exists a set b such that $y \in b$ if and only if for some x, $(x, y) \in X$ and $x \in a$; *i.e.*, the range of the restriction of a function X to a domain that is a set is also a set.

(20) *Axiom of restriction.* Every nonempty class A contains an element b such that $A \cap b = \emptyset$.

LIMITATIONS OF AXIOMATIC SET THEORY

The fact that NBG avoids the classical paradoxes and that there is no apparent way to derive any one of them in ZF does not settle the question of the consistency of either theory. One method for establishing the consistency of an axiomatic theory is to give a model; *i.e.*, an interpretation of the undefined terms in another theory such that the axioms become theorems of the other theory. If this other theory is consistent, then that under investigation must be consistent. Such consistency proofs are thus relative: the theory for which a model is given is consistent if that from which the model is taken is consistent. The method of models, however, offers no hope for proving the consistency of an axiomatic theory of sets. In the case of set theory and, indeed, of axiomatic theories generally, the alternative is a direct approach to the problem.

If T is the theory of which the (absolute) consistency is under investigation, this alternative means that the proposition "There is no sentence of T such that both it and its negation are theorems of T" must be proved. The mathematical theory (developed by the formalists) to cope with proofs about an axiomatic theory T is called proof theory, or metamathematics. It is premised upon the formulation of T as a formal axiomatic theory; *i.e.*, the theory of inference (as well as T) must be axiomatized. It is then possible to present T in a purely symbolic form; *i.e.*, as a formal language based on an alphabet the symbols of which are those for the undefined terms of T and those for the logical operators and connectives. A sentence in this language is a formula composed from the alphabet according to prescribed rules. The hope for metamathematics was that by using only intuitively convincing, weak number-theoretic arguments (called finitary methods), unimpeachable proofs of the consistency of such theories as axiomatic set theory could be given.

Gödel's theorem and the consistency of S That hope suffered a severe blow in 1931 from a theorem proved by Gödel about any formal theory S that includes the usual vocabulary of elementary arithmetic. By coding the formulas of such a theory with natural numbers (now called Gödel numbers) and by talking about these numbers, Gödel was able to make the metamathematics of S to become part of the arithmetic of S and hence to be expressible in S. The theorem in question asserts that the formula of S that expresses (via a coding) "S is consistent" in S is unprovable in S if S is consistent. Thus, if S is consistent, then the consistency of S cannot be proved within S; rather, methods beyond those that can be expressed or reflected in S must be employed. Because, in both ZF and NBG, elementary arithmetic can be developed, Gödel's theorem applies to these two theories. Although there remains the possibility of a finitary proof of consistency that cannot be reflected in the foregoing systems of set theory, no hopeful, positive results have been obtained.

Other theorems of Gödel when applied to ZF (and there are corresponding results for NBG) assert that if the system is consistent, then (A) it contains a sentence such that neither it nor its negation is provable (such a sentence is called undecidable), (B) there is no algorithm (or iterative process) for deciding whether a sentence of ZF is a theorem, and (C) these same statements hold for any consistent theory resulting from ZF by the adjunction of further axioms. Apparently ZF can serve as a foundation for all of present-day mathematics because every mathematical theorem can be translated into and proved within ZF, or within extensions obtained by adding suitable axioms. Thus, the existence of undecidable sentences in each such theory (which entails the existence of true sentences of ZF not provable in ZF) points out the hopelessness of any attempt to base all of conceivable mathematics on a single axiomatic theory and hence implies the inadequacy of the axiomatic approach to mathematics, in particular, via axiomatic set theory.

PRESENT STATUS OF AXIOMATIC SET THEORY

The foundations of axiomatic set theory are in a state of significant change as a result of recent discoveries. The situation is analogous to the 19th-century revolution in geometry, set off by the discovery of non-Euclidean geometries. It is difficult to predict the ultimate consequences of these late 20th-century findings for set theory, but already they have had profound effects on attitudes about certain axioms and have forced the realization of a continuous search for additional axioms. These discoveries have focussed attention on the concept of the independence of an axiom. If T is an axiomatic theory and S is a sentence (*i.e.*, a formula) of T that is not an axiom, and if $T + S$ denotes the theory that results from T upon the adjunction of S to T as a further axiom, S is said to be consistent relative to T if $T + S$ is consistent and independent of T whenever both S and $\sim S$ (the negation of S) are consistent relative to T. Thus, assuming that T is consistent, if S is independent of T, then the addition of S or $\sim S$ to T yields a consistent theory. The role of the axiom of restriction (AR) can be clarified in terms of the notion of independence. If ZF′ denotes the theory obtained from ZF by deleting AR and either retaining or deleting the axiom of choice (AC), then it can be proved that if ZF′ is consistent, AR is independent of ZF′.

Relations of axiom of choice to continuum hypotheses Of far greater significance for the foundations of set theory is the status of AC relative to the other axioms of ZF. The status in ZF of the continuum hypothesis (CH) and its extension, the generalized continuum hypothesis (GCH) are also of profound importance. (If $q(a)$ denotes "There does not exist a set b such that $\overline{\overline{a}} < \overline{\overline{b}} < \overline{\overline{P(a)}}$," then CH is $q(a)$ for $\overline{\overline{a}} = \aleph_0$ and GCH is $q(a)$ for all infinite sets a.) In the following discussion of these questions, ZF denotes Zermelo–Fraenkel set theory without AC. The first finding was obtained by Gödel in 1938. He proved that AC and GCH are consistent relative to ZF (*i.e.*, if ZF is consistent, then so is ZF + AC + GCH), by showing that a contradiction within ZF + AC + GCH can be transformed into a contradiction in ZF. In 1963, Paul J. Cohen, a Stanford mathematician, proved that (1) if ZF is consistent, then so is ZF + AC + $\sim$CH, and (2) if ZF is consistent, then so is ZF + $\sim$AC. Since in ZF + AC it can be demonstrated that GCH implies CH, Gödel's theorem together with Cohen's establishes the independence of AC and CH. For his proofs Cohen introduced a new method (called forcing) of constructing interpretations of ZF + AC. The method of forcing is applicable to many problems in set theory, and since 1963 it has been used to give independence proofs for a wide variety of highly technical propositions. Some of these results have opened new avenues for attacks on important foundational questions.

Status of the continuum hypothesis The current unsettled state of axiomatic set theory can be sensed by the responses that have been made to the question of how to regard CH in the light of its independence from ZF + AC. Someone who believes that set theory deals only with nonexistent fictions will have no concern about the question. But for most mathematicians sets actually exist; in particular, ω and $P(\omega)$ exist. Further, it should be the case that every nondenumerable subset of $P(\omega)$ either is or is not equivalent to $P(\omega)$; *i.e.*, either CH is true or is false. Followers of this faith regard the axioms of set theory as describing some well-defined reality—one in which CH must be either true or false. Thus there is the inescapable conclusion that the present axioms do not provide a complete description of that reality. A search for such axioms is in progress. One who hopes to prove CH as a theorem must look for axioms that restrict the number of sets. There seems to be little hope for this restriction, however, without changing the intuitive notion of the set. Thus the expectations favour the view that CH will be disproved. This disproof requires an axiom that guarantees the existence of more sets; *e.g.*, of sets having cardinalities greater than those that can be proved to exist in ZF $+$ AC. So far, none of the axioms that have been proposed that are aimed in this direction (called "generalized axioms of infinity") serves to prove $\sim$CH. Although there is little supporting evidence, the optimists hope that the status of the continuum hypothesis CH will be settled in the near future.   (R.R.S.)

BIBLIOGRAPHY. N. BOURBAKI, *Éléments de mathématique, théorie des ensembles* (1966; Eng. trans., *Theory of Sets*, 1968); G. CANTOR, *Beiträge zur Begründung der transfiniten Mengenlehre* (1895–97; Eng. trans., *Contributions to the Founding of the Theory of Transfinite Numbers*, 1915), of historical interest; P.J. COHEN, *Set Theory and the Continuum Hypothesis* (1966), contains proofs of the independence of AC and CH; K. GOEDEL, *The Consistency of the Axiom of Choice and of the Generalized Continuum-Hypothesis with the Axioms of Set Theory*, rev. ed. (1953); W.S. HATCHER, *Foundations of Mathematics* (1968), presents an overall view of axiomatic set theory and its relationship to the foundations of mathematics; E. MENDELSON, *Introduction to Mathematical Logic* (1964), contains a formal development of NBG; J.R. SHOENFIELD, *Mathematical Logic* (1967), contains a development of ZF and the independence proofs; R.R. STOLL, *Set Theory and Logic* (1963), contains an informal development of ZF; P. SUPPES, *Axiomatic Set Theory* (1960).

(Jo.Ha./R.R.S.)

Seurat, Georges

In his short life of only 31 years, Georges Seurat earned an illustrious place in the history of 19th-century French painting as the leading exponent of the Neo-Impressionist school. Beginning with the analyses of colour and light of the Impressionists, who immediately preceded him, and elaborating on them through the observations of scientists, he perfected the technique of pointillism, creating huge compositions with tiny, detached strokes of pure colour too small to be distinguished when looking at the entire work but making his works shimmer with brilliance. Working with infinite deliberation, he completed only seven such works, which nonetheless represented a significant new direction in the course of modern art.

Georges-Pierre Seurat was born on December 2, 1859, in Paris, the son of Antoine-Chrisostôme Seurat, a 44-year-old property owner, originally from Champagne, and Ernestine Faivre, a Parisienne. His father, a singular personality who had been a bailiff, spent most of his time in Le Raincy, where he owned a cottage with a garden (in which Seurat often painted). The young Seurat lived primarily in Paris with his mother, his brother Émile, and his sister Marie-Berthe. At the time of the Paris Commune, in 1871, when Paris rebelled against the French state and set up its own government, the prudent family temporarily withdrew to Fontainebleau.

While attending school, Georges began to draw, and, beginning in 1875, he took a course from a sculptor, Justin Lequien. He officially entered the École des Beaux-Arts in 1878, in the class of Henri Lehmann, a disciple of Ingres, who painted portraits and conventional nudes. In the school library Seurat discovered a book that was to inspire him for the rest of his life: the *Essai sur les signes inconditionnels de l'art* (1827; "Essay on the Unmistakable Signs of Art"), by Humbert de Superville, a painter-engraver from Geneva; it dealt with the future course of aesthetics and with the relationship between lines and images. Seurat was also impressed with the

work of another Genevan aesthetician, David Sutter, who combined mathematics and musicology. Throughout his brief career, Seurat manifested an unusually strong interest in the intellectual and scientific bases of art.

In November 1879, at the age of 20, Seurat went to Brest to do his military service. There he drew the sea, beaches, and boats. When he returned to Paris the following autumn, he shared a studio with another painter, Édmond-François Aman-Jean, who then joined him in Lehmann's class. But Seurat and Aman-Jean departed from the policies of the École des Beaux-Arts in admiring the warm landscapes of Jean-Baptiste Millet at the Louvre. The two friends often frequented dance halls and cabarets in the evening, and in spring they took the passenger steamer to the island of La Grande Jatte, the setting of Seurat's future paintings. Seurat exhibited at the official Salon—the state-sponsored annual exhibition —for the first time in 1883. He displayed portraits of his mother and of his friend Aman-Jean. The same year he began his studies, sketches, and panels for "Une Baignade, Asnières." When the picture was refused by the jury of the Salon in 1884, Seurat decided to participate in the foundation of the Groupe des Artistes Indépendants, an association "with neither jury nor prizes," where he showed his "Baignade" in June. *(margin: Early exhibition at the Salon)*

During this period, he had seen and been strongly influenced by the monumental symbolic paintings of Puvis de Chavannes. He also met the 100-year-old chemist Michel-Eugène Chevreul and experimented with Chevreul's theories of the chromatic circle of light and studied the effects that could be achieved with the three primary colours, yellow, red, and blue, and their complements. Seurat fell in with Paul Signac, who was to become his chief disciple, and painted many rough sketches on small boards in preparation for his masterpiece, "Sunday Afternoon on the Island of La Grande Jatte." In December 1884 he exhibited the "Baignade" again, with the Société des Artistes Indépendants, which had grown out of the earlier association and was to be of immense influence in the development of modern art.

Seurat spent the winter of 1885 working on the island of La Grande Jatte and the summer at Grandcamp, in Normandy. The Impressionist master Camille Pissarro, who was temporarily converted to the technique of pointillism, was introduced to Seurat by Signac during this period. Seurat finished the painting "La Grande Jatte" and exhibited it from May 15 to June 15, 1886, at an Impressionist group show. This picture demonstration of his technique aroused great interest. Seurat's chief artistic associates at this time, painters also concerned with the effects of light on colour, were Signac and Pissarro. The unexpectedness of his art and the novelty of his conception excited the Belgian poet Émile Verhaeren. The critic Félix Fénéon praised Seurat's method in an avant-garde review. And Seurat's work was exhibited by the eminent dealer Durand-Ruel in Paris and in New York. *(margin: Influence of "La Grande Jatte")*

In 1887, while he was temporarily living in a garret studio, Seurat began work on "Les Poseuses." This painting was to be the last of his compositions on the grand scale of the "Baignade" and "La Grande Jatte"; he thought about adding a "Place Clichy" to this number but abandoned the idea. In the following year he completed "Les Poseuses" and also "La Parade." In February 1888 he went to Brussels with Signac for a private viewing of the exposition of the Twenty (XX), a small group of independent artists, in which he showed seven canvases, including "La Grande Jatte."

Seurat participated in the 1889 Salon des Indépendants, exhibiting landscapes. He painted Signac's portrait at this time. His residence at this point was in the Pigalle district, where he lived with his mistress, Madeleine Knobloch, a girl of 21. On February 16, 1890, Madeleine presented him with a son, whom he officially acknowledged and entered in the register of births under the name of Pierre-Georges Seurat. During that year Seurat completed the painting "Le Chahut," which he sent to the exhibition of the Twenty (XX) in Brussels. During that period he also painted the "Jeune Femme se poudrant," a portrait of his mistress, though he continued to conceal *(margin: Liaison with Madeleine Knobloch)* his liaison with her even from his most intimate friends. He spent that summer at Gravelines, near Dunkirk, where he painted several landscapes and planned what was to be his last painting, "Le Cirque."

As if from some sort of premonition of his impending death, Seurat showed the uncompleted "Cirque" at the eighth Salon des Indépendants. As an organizer of the exhibition, he exhausted himself in the presentation and hanging of the works. He caught a chill, developed infectious angina, and, before the exhibition was ended, he died on Easter Sunday, March 29, 1891. On the following day Madeleine Knobloch presented herself at the town hall of her district to identify herself as the mother of Pierre-Georges Seurat. The child, who had contracted his father's contagious illness, died April 13, 1891. Seurat was buried in the family vault at Père Lachaise cemetery. In addition to his seven monumental paintings, he left some 40 smaller paintings and sketches, about 500 drawings, and several sketchbooks. Though a modest output in terms of quantity, they show him to have been among the foremost painters of one of the greatest periods in the history of art.

MAJOR WORKS

PAINTINGS: "Casseurs de pierre, Le Raincy" (c. 1880–81; private collection, Paris); "Maison dans les arbres" (1881; Museum and Art Gallery, Glasgow); "Les Pêcheurs à la ligne" (1883; Pierre Lévy Collection, Troyes, France); "Une Baignade, Asnières" (1883–84; National Gallery, London); "Sunday Afternoon on the Island of La Grande Jatte" (1884–86; Art Institute of Chicago); "Le Bec du Hoc, Grandcamp" (1885; Tate Gallery, London); "The Bridge at Courbevoie" (1886; Courtauld Institute Galleries, London); "The Asylum and the Lighthouse, Honfleur" (1886; Chester Beatty Collection, London); "Les Poseuses" ("The Models"; 1887–88; Barnes Foundation, Merion, Pennsylvania); "La Parade" ("Invitation to the Side-Show"; 1887–88; Metropolitan Museum of Art, New York); "Sunday at Port-en-Bessin" (1888; Rijksmuseum Kröller-Müller Otterlo); "Le Chahut" (1889–90; Rijksmuseum Kröller-Müller Otterlo); "A Young Woman Holding a Powder-puff" (1889–90; Courtauld Institute Galleries, London); "The Channel at Gravelines, Evening" (1890; Museum of Modern Art, New York); "Le Cirque" ("The Circus"; 1890–91; Louvre, Paris).

DRAWINGS: "Le Marchand d'oranges" (1881; Louvre, Paris); "Le Labourage" (1881; Louvre); "Paysans" (1882–83; Louvre); "La Mère de l'artiste" (1882–83; Metropolitan Museum of Art, New York); "Au concert européen" (1886–87; Museum of Modern Art, New York).

BIBLIOGRAPHY. CESAR DE HAUKE (comp.), *Seurat et son oeuvre*, 2 vol. (1961), is a basic work that serves as a general catalog to the works of Seurat and complements HENRI DORRA and JOHN REWALD, *Seurat* (1959). LUCIE COUSTURIER, *Seurat* (1921; 2nd ed., 1926), gives a lively literary portrait (in French) of the man and the painter. This biographical information was enhanced by GUSTAVE COQUIOT, *Seurat* (1924), also in French. Other general studies include DANIEL C. RICH, *Seurat and the Evolution of "La Grande Jatte"* (1935, reprinted 1969); JACQUES DE LAPRADE, *Georges Seurat* (1945, reissued as *Seurat*, 1951); MEYER SCHAPIRO, "New Light on Seurat," *Art News*, 57:22–24, 44–45, 52 (1958); ANTHONY BLUNT, *Seurat*, with an essay by ROGER FRY (1965); JOHN RUSSELL, *Seurat* (1965); and PIERRE COURTHION, *Georges Seurat* (1969). On Seurat's technique and aesthetic theories, JULES CHRISTOPHE, "Georges Seurat," in *Les Hommes d'aujourd'hui*, vol. 8 (1890), is basic. The major works on Seurat's drawings are GUSTAVE KAHN, *Les Dessins de Georges Seurat, 1859–1891*, 2 vol. (1928); GERMAIN SELIGMAN, *The Drawings of Georges Seurat* (1946); and ROBERT L. HERBERT, *Seurat's Drawings* (1962).

(P.Co.)

Seven Years' War

The Seven Years' War is the name history has given to the last great conflict involving all the major powers of Europe, except Turkey, before the French Revolutionary Wars. One aspect of the conflict—the specifically Franco-British aspect—can be understood as an extension of the so-called French and Indian War, a colonial struggle that broke out in North America and in India before 1756 but ended simultaneously with the Seven Years' War. Further, it is possible to regard the French campaigns in the western areas of the Holy Roman Empire, against electoral Hanover (dynastically united with Great Britain)

and its allies, Brunswick and Hesse-Kassel, as well as the Spanish entry and the consequent Portuguese involvement in the last phase of the war, as by-products of the colonial struggle. From such a point of view, then, the Seven Years' War properly is the Austro-Prussian War of 1756–63, in which Russia was also deeply committed against Prussia until the beginning of 1762 and in which Sweden likewise played a part against Prussia. On the other hand, a British alliance with Prussia and a French one with Austria, together with the geographical contiguity of Hanover and Prussia, interwove the fortunes and problems of the two sets of belligerents so closely that, for a practical appreciation, the European campaigns at least should be surveyed as factors of a single war, complex although not incoherent. British and European historians, in fact, are often inclined, regardless of chronology, to use the expression Seven Years' War to include also the French and Indian War. The present article is concerned mainly with the campaigns involving Prussia in central and eastern Europe; but the European campaigns of the war between Great Britain-Hanover and France, with the naval war on the French coast, are also noted. (For the colonial theatres of the war see UNITED STATES, HISTORY OF THE; CANADA, HISTORY OF; INDIAN SUBCONTINENT, HISTORY OF THE; and BRITAIN AND IRELAND, HISTORY OF.)

The origins of the war. The outbreak of the war in Europe was caused largely by the attempt of the Austrian Habsburgs to win back the rich province of Silesia, which had been wrested from them by Frederick II the Great of Prussia during the War of the Austrian Succession (1740–48). The great Austrian diplomat Graf Wenzel von Kaunitz engineered an alliance that ranged Austria, Saxony, Sweden, Russia, and France against Prussia. Prussia concluded an alliance with Great Britain, which since 1754 had been at war with France in the New World. The alignment of Austria with France, and of Great Britain with Hanover and Prussia, marked a reversal of long-standing enmity between these countries and constitutes what is known as the "Diplomatic Revolution" (see also EUROPEAN DIPLOMACY AND WARS [c. 1500–1914]). By 1756 the major powers of Continental Europe were poised for an attack on Prussia. Frederick the Great, a believer in attacking first, invaded Saxony on August 29 to detach that country from its alliance.

The Prussian advance into Saxony, 1756. Crossing the Saxon frontier with 70,000 Prussians, Frederick entered Dresden, the Saxon capital, on September 10, while the Saxon Army of not more than 20,000 men fell back on Pirna to the southeast. The Elector, Frederick Augustus II (also king of Poland as Augustus III), and his minister, Heinrich von Brühl, were offered assurances of Prussia's good intentions, which they naturally mistrusted. An Austrian force of 32,000, under Maximilian Ulysses von Browne, was moving from Bohemia to unite with the Saxons. To prevent this junction, Frederick advanced southward into Bohemia; and Browne was severely defeated at Lobositz (Lovosice; midway between Dresden and Prague) on October 1. Returning to Saxony, Frederick received the capitulation of the Saxons at Pirna (October 16), whereupon he took nearly all of them into his own service. The Elector and Brühl retired to Poland.

Russia might have sent forces to Austria's help at once but for the problem of the route they would have to take —namely, the route across Poland. Poland was a sphere of French influence that had maintained itself by opposition to Russian designs. For the perfect achievement of an anti-Prussian coalition, it was most desirable, as Kaunitz saw, for Russia and France to come to terms. The Russians, however, saw the new contingency as an occasion for extracting concessions from France with regard not only to Poland but to Sweden and to Turkey as well. The views of the French foreign ministry, ready to admit a swift passage of Russian troops across Polish territory in order to smash Prussia and so to relieve France of the obligation to help Austria, came into conflict with the *secret du roi* (the secret diplomacy of the king), the primary purpose of which had been to exclude the Russians from Poland at any cost.

In Great Britain, the accession of the Elder William Pitt

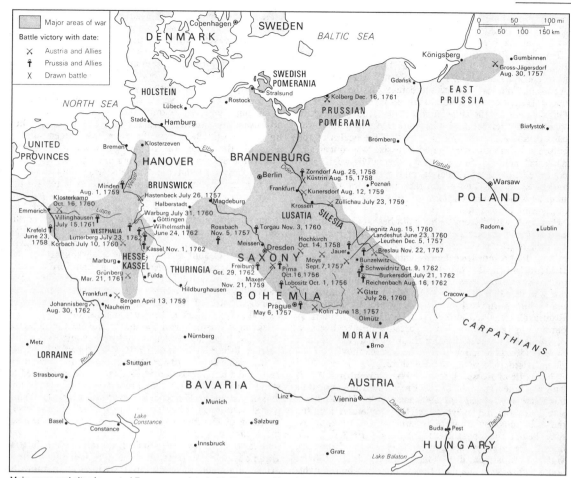

Main areas and sites in central Europe associated with the Seven Years' War.
Adapted from H.C. Darby and Harold Fullard (eds.), *The New Cambridge Modern History*, vol. XIV, Atlas (© 1970), Cambridge University Press; maps © George Philip & Son, Ltd. 1970

to office in November 1756 was to have a decisive effect on the development of the war. Pitt (later earl of Chatham) realized the importance of the colonial theatres of the war and devoted his enormous energy to the success of British arms in India and North America.

Alliances against Prussia, 1757. After weeks of negotiation at cross purposes, the French representative in St. Petersburg obtained Russia's accession to the First Treaty of Versailles by signing a secret promise of French help to Russia, in the event of an attack by Turkey, on January 11, 1757 (December 31, 1756, old style). This contradiction of the long-standing Franco-Turkish entente was immediately disavowed by the French government; and a personal letter from Louis XV to Russia's Empress Elizabeth, the first of an important series, finally secured Russian accession to the treaty without the objectionable secret promise (April 19). An Austro-Russian offensive alliance against Prussia was concluded on February 2, 1757, the parties each undertaking to put 80,000 men into the field and forswearing any separate peace, while secret articles provided for a partition of Prussia.

The Second Treaty of Versailles

On May 1, 1757, Austria and France signed the Second Treaty of Versailles, an offensive alliance against Prussia, with further provision for territorial adjustments elsewhere. Austria was to recover Silesia but would cede the Austrian Netherlands for partition between Louis XV and his Spanish Bourbon cousin, Philip, duke of Parma, Piacenza, and Guastalla, whose Italian possessions should then revert to Austria. Militarily, France was to maintain 105,000 men in Germany, in addition to the contingent to be supplied to Austria (which was raised from 24,000 to 30,000), and was to grant an annual subsidy of 12,000,000 livres to Austria.

By a large majority of votes in the Council of Princes of the *Reich,* Austria had secured the declaration of a "war of the Empire" against Prussia. Though Hesse-Kassel, Brunswick, and, naturally, Hanover opposed it, some Protestant states supported Austria, despite Frederick's attempt to pose as the champion of Protestantism against an Austro-French Catholic coalition.

In central Europe the Prussians in April 1757 advanced into Bohemia again. In the Battle of Prague, on May 6, the 66,000 Austrians under Browne and Prince Charles of Lorraine were routed by Frederick's force of 64,000 before they could be reinforced by another Austrian force under Leopold Joseph, Graf von Daun. The Austrians lost more than 14,000 men; 16,000 escaped to join Daun; the rest took refuge in Prague itself, which the Prussians, whose losses were about the same, proceeded to besiege. A month later Daun, with more than 50,000 men, moved forward to relieve Prague; and Frederick went to meet him with 34,000. The Battle of Kolín, on June 18, was a great victory for Daun. Raising the siege of Prague, the Prussians evacuated Bohemia. The retreat fell just short of being a rout.

Prussia meanwhile was exposed to attack from several directions. The French had begun their campaign in the spring by sending 100,000 men against the Hanoverians and their allies, who formed the so-called Army of Observation under William Augustus, duke of Cumberland, a younger son of King George II. Defeated at Hastenbeck, on the Weser southwest of Hanover, on July 26, 1757, Cumberland withdrew to Stade, near the Elbe estuary, abandoning the defense of the electorate and of Brunswick. A few weeks later, on September 8, the duc de Richelieu, to whom the French command had been transferred, forced Cumberland to sign the Convention of Klosterzeven, which stipulated the disbanding of the Army of Observation. Richelieu then advanced on Prussia's western frontier; and at the same time another French army of 24,000, under the Prince de Soubise (Charles de Rohan), was crossing Franconia, to join the Army of the *Reich*, namely Austria's German allies, under Joseph Friedrich of Saxe-Hildburghausen. Furthermore, Sweden,

Richelieu takes command

having signed an alliance with France and Austria on March 21, invaded Prussian Pomerania in September so as to annex it, whether Russia approved or not.

The main Russian army of 90,000 men crossed into Polish territory in July and entered East Prussia in August; and on August 30, its general, Stepan Fyodorovich Apraksin, inflicted a crushing defeat on the Prussians under Hans von Lehwaldt at Gross-Jägersdorf west of Gumbinnen. To the stupefaction of the world, Apraksin then began a retreat. It now appears that his conduct was caused, at least partly, by the fact that the health of the empress Elizabeth, who hated Prussia, was uncertain, while her heir, the future emperor Peter III, was a self-confessed adorer of Frederick and an opponent of the anti-Prussian war. This meant that any general or statesman who did too much harm to Prussia was risking the displeasure of his future master.

Frederick, with Saxony as his main base, decided first to confront the danger from the west, leaving Frederick Francis of Brunswick-Bevern to face the Austrians in Silesia. To prevent Richelieu's joining Soubise and Saxe-Hildburghausen, he marched first toward Halberstadt; but Austrian successes in Silesia, where Brunswick-Bevern was defeated at Moys (Zgorzelec) on September 7, made him turn eastward again, while Ferdinand of Brunswick remained to observe Saxe-Hildburghausen. A daring Austrian raid on Berlin forced a further diversion of Frederick's forces. Finally, hearing that Soubise and Saxe-Hildburghausen were together on the move in Thuringia, Frederick went to meet them.

The Battle of Rossbach followed on November 5, 1757. The combined strength of the French and the Army of the *Reich* was at least 41,000, against the 21,000 Prussians; but the aggressive Saxe-Hildburghausen and the more cautious Soubise were at variance; and when at last they began the engagement for which Frederick had hoped, the greatly superior mobility of the Prussians, with the brilliant cavalry leadership of Friedrich Wilhelm von Seydlitz, won the day. In less than two hours' fighting, the Allies lost 7,000 men, the Prussians only 550.

Encouraged by the news of Rossbach, the British government, on the insistance of Pitt, repudiated Cumberland's Convention of Klosterzeven. It decided to reinforce the Hanoverians and to transfer the command in western Germany to Ferdinand of Brunswick. In September, a British naval expedition against the French base of Rochefort had been a failure.

In Silesia, the Austrians took Schweidnitz (Świdnica) on November 11 and Breslau (Wrocław) on November 22. Frederick arrived from Thuringia to support Brunswick-Bevern. In the Battle of Leuthen (Lutynia), on December 5, 1757, he won the greatest of his victories. With 43,000 men, he attacked the 72,000 under Charles of Lorraine and routed them with an unexpected cavalry charge followed by a heavy artillery bombardment. As against Frederick's losses of rather more than 6,000, Charles lost 22,000 men, including 12,000 taken prisoner. Breslau fell to the Prussians again.

In the course of the winter, Lehwaldt drove the Swedes back into their own part of Pomerania, where they were able to hold the Prussians outside Stralsund. Frederick's spectacular victories, combined with Apraksin's retreat, completely altered the fortune of the war.

The Prussian offensive of 1758. William Fermor, a Scottish émigré in the Russian service, had taken Apraksin's place in the autumn of 1757. On January 22, 1758, the East Prussian capital, Königsberg (Kaliningrad), surrendered to him. With the onset of spring, however, the thawing of the snows made the northern roads impassable, and Fermor was temporarily immobilized. In Russia itself, the still anti-French Aleksey Bestuzhev-Ryumin was arrested, and power came into the hands of his rival, Mikhail Illarionovich Vorontsov.

Ferdinand of Brunswick, with his Anglo-Hanoverians, launched a successful offensive against the French in Westphalia; and on March 27 he crossed the Rhine at Emmerich, near the Dutch frontier. On June 23, with 40,000 men, he defeated the Comte de Clermont (Louis de Bourbon-Condé), with 70,000, at Krefeld; and the

effect of this victory, which enabled him to hold all northwestern Germany, was scarcely offset by subsequent French successes farther to the south, in Hesse and in Thuringia. The British on April 11 signed a new treaty with Prussia, promising an annual subsidy of 4,000,000 talers (£670,000), while both parties undertook not to make a separate peace with any of the belligerents.

Frederick began the year's campaign with an offensive in Silesia, where Schweidnitz fell on April 16. He then advanced into Moravia, to lay siege to Olmütz (Olomouc). In July, however, the Austrians forced him to abandon the siege. In the north, meanwhile, a new Swedish attack on Prussian Pomerania was being fended off by Lehwaldt; but the Russians were on the march again, going southwestward from East Prussia toward the Oder River and Brandenburg.

To evade interception by the Austrians, Frederick had to march first northwestward into Bohemia, then northward across Silesia. Fermor's 52,000 Russians, having reached the Oder, began a siege of Küstrin (Kostrzyn) on August 15, but Frederick was at Frankfurt an der Oder by August 20. He then moved around Fermor's east flank and, with a total of 36,000 men, attacked the Russians at Zorndorf (Sarbinowo) on August 25. In the bloodiest battle of the war, the Russians' casualties were 42,000 (21,000 killed), the Prussians, 13,500.

Leaving Christoph von Dohna to pursue the defeated Russians, Frederick hastened back to Saxony, to save his brother Prince Henry from attack by superior Austrian forces under Daun, outside Dresden. Daun fell back until he found a strong position at Kittlitz, where he decided to stand with his 90,000 men. Frederick, with 37,000, advanced as far as Hochkirch, never thinking that Daun would venture an offensive. Daun's attack, in the early morning of October 14, took the Prussians by surprise; but Daun, who lost 7,500 men (the Prussians 9,500) was unable to interfere with Frederick's retreat into Silesia. Daun advanced on Dresden again, but the news of Frederick's approach through Lusatia caused him to withdraw to Pirna in November.

Hochkirch in any case put new spirit into the French, who after Krefeld and Zorndorf had been inclined to despair of their European war. The duc de Choiseul became foreign minister in December, in the place of the exhausted François-Joachim de Bernis, whose overtures for peace had been scorned by the British government.

French and Russian campaigns in 1759. The Third Treaty of Versailles, already drafted by the end of December 1758, was signed in March 1759 and ratified in May. By this, the French obligations of direct help to Austria in men and money were considerably reduced, and the plan of 1757 concerning the Austrian Netherlands and Parma was discarded. The French, however, were still to maintain 100,000 men in Germany.

On April 13 Ferdinand of Brunswick, who had advanced against the French in southwestern Germany, was defeated by the duc de Broglie (Victor-François) at Bergen, near Frankfurt am Main; and on July 9 Broglie took Minden on the Weser. When Marshal Louis-Georges-Erasme de Contades joined Broglie, the French had 60,000 men against Ferdinand's 43,000 Anglo-Hanoverians; but on August 1, in the Battle of Minden, Ferdinand contrived to lure Contades into an engagement that resulted in the complete rout of the French.

Choiseul had relieved France of its heavier commitments to Austria in order to prosecute the war against Great Britain with greater vigour. He planned an invasion, with landings around London and in Scotland. To transport and escort the expeditions, the Mediterranean fleet from Toulon was summoned to join the Atlantic fleet at Brest; but on its way northward the former fleet was attacked and scattered by Admiral Edward Boscawen in the Battle of Lagos (August 19), off the Portuguese coast. Meanwhile, Edward Hawke was blockading Brest. Later, when Hawke withdrew to English waters (November 9), the Brest fleet took to sea. Then Hawke reappeared, and in the Battle of Quiberon Bay (November 20–21) the French suffered a decisive defeat, with damaging losses. Not only had the invasion project to be

Frederick's victory at Leuthen

Battle of Zorndorf

British naval supremacy

dropped but also British naval superiority was established for the rest of the war.

Minden, Lagos, and Quiberon Bay, together with outstanding successes in North America—the capture of Ft. Niagara on July 24–25 and, of far more significance, that of Quebec on September 18—made 1759 the *annus mirabilis,* or "wonderful year," for the British. From its strong position, the government began negotiations for peace with France. But, while on the one hand its terms were too stiff, on the other, its proposals were made in association with its Prussian ally, who at the end of the year was in no situation to expect favourable treatment from its enemies. Furthermore, Austria and Russia strongly objected to France's treating separately with the British.

In May 1759 the Russian command had been transferred from Fermor to Pyotr Semyonovich Saltykov. Advancing across Poland through Poznań into Brandenburg with 70,000 men, Saltykov defeated 26,000 Prussians, under C.H. von Wedel, at Züllichau (Sulechów), east of Krossen (Krosno), on July 23. He then moved down the Oder toward Frankfurt, while Daun, from Saxony, sent 35,000 Austrians, under Gideon Ernst von Laudon, northward to join forces with him. Frederick, who had been facing Daun, promptly marched northward also, hoping to prevent the Austro-Russian junction; but he failed to do so. Having joined forces with Wedel and Friedrich von Finck, so that he finally disposed of about 50,000 men, Frederick boldly assailed the enemy in their strong position at Kunersdorf (Kunovice), east of Frankfurt, on August 12. The result was a disaster for Frederick, who in six hours lost more than 18,000 men. He wrote despairingly to one of his ministers, ". . . I tell you the truth, I believe everything is lost." Saltykov, however, made no immediate use of his victory; but Daun, advancing against the diminished Prussian forces in Saxony, took Dresden on September 14.

Attempts at junction between Daun and Saltykov were frustrated by Frederick's skillful movements after Kunersdorf; and when Saltykov was forced by lack of supplies to retire from the scene, Frederick turned on Daun again. Finck, who had been sent with more than 12,000 men to attack Daun's rear, was surprised by 42,000 of Daun's men at Maxen, south of Dresden, and forced to surrender (November 21). The year had been a bad one for Frederick, but by extraordinary exertion he was again able to take the field.

The Silesian campaign of 1760.   For the campaign of 1760, Russia and Austria chose Silesia as the main field of operations: Saltykov, from Poznań, was supposed to march southward (instead of westward into Brandenburg) and to join forces with Laudon. The latter, on June 23, destroyed a Prussian force at Landeshut (Kamienna Góra) and, on July 26, captured the stronghold of Glatz (Kłodzko). Frederick, meanwhile, had first moved eastward against Laudon, then had turned back to besiege Dresden (July 12) on hearing that Daun was moving to Laudon's support. When Daun also turned back, Frederick raised his siege and marched through Meissen and Lusatia into Silesia. While 20,000 Russians, under Zakhar Grigorevich Chernyshev, occupied Prince Henry of Prussia in the vicinity of Breslau, the Austrians were converging on Frederick; but on August 15, at Plaffendorf, near Liegnitz (Legnica), Laudon launched a sudden attack on Frederick's columns in the hope of preventing their escape from encirclement but was beaten off with heavy Austrian losses. A ruse of Frederick's tricked Chernyshev into retreating, and the Austro-Russian plan for a decisive victory in Silesia came to nothing.

Most of Saxony remained defenseless against Daun, and Brandenburg was open to the Russians. A detachment under G.G. Totleben took Berlin in the night of October 8–9 and was able to retire unmolested on October 13, when Frederick was approaching from Silesia. Daun was able to concentrate 64,000 men around Torgau, against which Frederick marched with about 45,000. The Battle of Torgau, Frederick's last major victory, began on November 3. The Austrian artillery devastated his attacking troops, but Frederick sent wave after wave forward until at last the Austrian line was broken; and, on the arrival

of Frederick's general, Hans Joachim von Zieten (who should have appeared earlier), the Austrians gave up the struggle and retreated. Frederick had lost 13,000 men, Daun 11,000 (including 7,000 captured).

In western Germany, Broglie won a victory at Korbach on July 10, 1760, but this was offset by Ferdinand's victory at Warburg on July 31. Hanover was again saved from French invasion, but a subsequent advance of Ferdinand's troops across the Rhine was reversed by Charles-Eugène-Gabriel de Castries at Klosterkamp on October 16.

George II of Great Britain died on October 25. His grandson and successor, George III, was far more attached than he to British, as distinct from Hanoverian, interests and had a strong dislike for William Pitt, earl of Chatham, who was the foremost exponent of the Anglo-Prussian alliance. Without the British subsidies, Prussia could not have fought on.

Disputes within the anti-Prussian coalition, 1761.   By March 1761, when George III's favourite, John Stuart, the 3rd earl of Bute, became British secretary of state for the northern department, the members of the anti-Prussian coalition were at variance in their attitudes toward the war: France wanted a negotiated peace with the British; Austria desired a general congress of the powers, at which the retrocession of Silesia might have been obtained from Prussia; and the Russian Empress was still bent on war until Prussia could be carved up. Formal discussions between the French and the British broke down in July because Pitt finally insisted that, whereas the British would go on supporting Prussia, the French should reduce their support of Austria to a minimum and virtually abandon Germany and that the British should keep all their colonial conquests. Choiseul would not submit to this dictation. To counter it, he fell back on a plan that he had long had in mind—the introduction of Spain into France's war against Great Britain. In August a "Family Compact" was concluded between Louis XV of France and Charles III of Spain. Spain would declare war on Great Britain if France had not obtained peace by May 1, 1762, and France would see that Spanish claims against Great Britain were met at the final peacemaking. When the British government refused to declare immediate war on Spain, Pitt resigned office (October 5, 1761).

[marginal note: Entry of Spain into the war]

Meanwhile, the fighting in western Germany went on as usual. Ferdinand advanced southward from Westphalia but was repulsed by Broglie at Grünberg, between Fulda and Marburg (Maribor), on March 21, 1761; and a French counterthrust into Westphalia was checked by Ferdinand at Vellinghausen, in the middle valley of the Lippe River, on July 15. By October the French had made considerable progress eastward. The capture of Belle-Île-en-Mer, off the Breton coast of France, was achieved by a British expedition in April–June.

For Prussia, Frederick's first concern was to prevent the junction, in Silesia, of Laudon's 72,000 Austrians, based on Glatz, with a Russian army of 50,000 under Aleksandr Borisovich Buturlin. He concentrated his available forces around Schweidnitz, but after two months of skirmishing and marching the Allies effected their junction between Liegnitz and Jauer (Jawor) on August 23. Cut off from the north and outnumbered by three to one, Frederick entrenched himself at Bunzelwitz, where his enemy did not dare to attack him. When Buturlin withdrew to the north in September, leaving only 20,000 Russians under Chernyshev in Silesia, Frederick could move toward Brandenburg; but Laudon took Schweidnitz on October 1, so that the Austrians could count on wintering in Silesia. In Saxony, meanwhile, Daun made gradual progress against Prince Henry; and on the Pomeranian coast the fortress and harbour of Kolberg (Kołobrzeg) fell to the Russians under Pyotr Aleksandrovich Rumyantsev on December 16. No longer sure that he could rely on a British subsidy (since Pitt had gone), Frederick saw that only luck could save him from destruction the next year.

The Prusso-Russian alliance of 1762.   Frederick's salvation came with the death of the empress Elizabeth on January 5, 1762, bringing the Prussophile Peter III to the Russian throne. On May 5, Peter made peace with Frederick; and on May 22 the Treaty of Hamburg was con-

The
Russians
change
sides

cluded between Prussia and Sweden, through Peter's mediation. Next, in June, Peter not only allied himself with Frederick for action against Denmark over his ancestral Holstein but even instructed Chernyshev to help Frederick to expel the Austrians from Silesia. In July, when Peter was deposed and murdered, Catherine II the Great, his widow and successor, countermanded his positive measures against Denmark and Austria; but she did not renew the war against Frederick.

Daun had been given the Austrian command in Silesia in Laudon's place. Before Catherine's recall of Chernyshev had become effective, when Frederick was trying to recapture Schweidnitz, Daun marched to relieve it but was defeated at Burkersdorf (Burkatów) on July 21. His second attempt at relief was similarly defeated, at Reichenbach (Dzierżoniów), on August 16; and on October 9 Schweidnitz again fell to the Prussians.

In Saxony, on October 29, Prince Henry and Seydlitz together won a considerable victory over the Austrians and their German allies at Freiburg. Austria and Prussia signed an armistice on November 24.

In the west, the British government declared war on Spain on January 2, 1762, three months after its rejection of Pitt's advocacy of the same measure and four months ahead of the Family Compact's deadline for Spain's intervention. The Spaniards then attacked Portugal, which the British promptly reinforced. The Portuguese fortress of Almeida fell to the Spaniards on August 25; and overseas they took Colonia del Sacramento, on the estuary of the Río de la Plata, opposite Buenos Aires. These Spanish successes were counterbalanced by the British capture of Havana, in Cuba (August 13), and of Manila, in the Philippines (October 5). In the same year three important West Indian islands had fallen to the British: Martinique and St. Lucia in February, Grenada in March.

In western Germany, Ferdinand of Brunswick won victories over Soubise at Wilhelmsthal (June 24) and over Prince Xavier of Saxony at Lutterberg (July 23) and took Göttingen (August 16). The French had a success at Johannisberg, near Nauheim, August 30, but lost Kassel on November 1.

The end of the war. Russia's defection from the anti-Prussian alliance convinced Austria that nothing was to be gained from prolonging the war. After the removal of Austria's objections, France could soon come to terms with Great Britain, which in turn had no interest in continuing to back Prussia in a quarrel about Silesia with Austria alone. France in October induced the disappointed Spaniards to join in the negotiations with the British; and on November 3, 1762, anticipating the Austro-Prussian armistice by three weeks, Great Britain and France signed preliminaries of peace, at Fontainebleau. By the Treaty of Paris (February 10, 1763), which settled the colonial aspects of the war, Britain won North America and India and became the undisputed leader in overseas colonization. By the Treaty of Hubertusburg (February 15, 1763) Frederick maintained Silesia and thereby elevated Prussia to a major European power.

Several factors account for Prussia's survival and ultimate victory: the inherent weakness of the anti-Prussian coalition, the "dictatorship" of William Pitt, and the last minute defection of Russia. But what served Prussia best was Frederick himself—his courage, his endurance, and his unbreakable will.

BIBLIOGRAPHY. For general accounts of diplomacy and the fighting, largely from the Prussian side, see RICHARD P. WADDINGTON, *La Guerre de sept ans*, 5 vol. (1899–1914), incomplete but still the best account; CURT JANY, *Geschichte der königlich-preussischen Armee bis zum Jahre 1807*, vol. 2 (1928), by a military historian; MAX IMMICH, *Geschichte des europäischen Staatensystems von 1660 bis 1789* (1905), an old but still valuable study of diplomatic developments; WALTER L. DORN, *Competition for Empire, 1740–1763*, ch. 7 (1940), the story mainly from the British and French points of view; JULIAN S. CORBETT, *England in the Seven Years' War*, 2 vol. (1907), particularly good on tactics and strategy; RICHARD LODGE, *Great Britain and Prussia in the Eighteenth Century* (1923); BASIL WILLIAMS, *The Life of William Pitt, Earl of Chatham*, 2 vol. (1913, reprinted 1966), laudatory but very useful; and A. BOURCET, *Études sur la politique du duc de Choiseul* (1907). For a critical study of French policy in Russia, see L.J. OLIVA, *Misalliance* (1964). Z.E. RASHED, *The Peace of Paris, 1763* (1951), stresses politics in England as a factor in peacemaking. See also books cited in the articles on the sovereigns, statesmen, and generals mentioned in the text above.

Seville

Seville (Sevilla) is the capital of the Provincia de Sevilla, in the Andalusia region of southern Spain. An inland port, it is the chief city of Andalusia and the fourth largest in Spain. It was important in history as a cultural centre, and it served as a capital for Muslim Spain and later as a centre for Spanish exploration of the New World. In the 1970s it had a population of about 548,000.

Ancient Seville. Its position on the Guadalquivir Estuary and its rich soil enabled Seville, already populated in the Paleolithic Period, to develop greatly in the Neolithic, when floods facilitated a precocious grain agriculture, documented by the presence of many silos. Dolmens left from this period were rich in artifacts, including gold and copper from the Sierra Morena and bell-shaped vessels, indicating European expansion.

Earlier
cities
at or near
the site of
Seville

At the end of the Bronze Age, a city appeared that may have been Seville and the name of which, Tartessus, was given to a river and a kingdom. Rich from agriculture, stock raising, and mining (copper, gold, and silver from Ríotinto), the Tartessians trafficked in tin from the Cassiterides (the Scilly Isles or Cornwall, in England). Biblical quotations and Greek historians confirm the existence of treasures, such as that of El Carambolo, near Seville, where Tartessus' material wealth was uncovered. Such riches attracted Greeks, Phoenicians, and Celts.

The fall of Tartessus was brought about by the spread of iron rather than by Carthaginians, as is generally believed. The Carthaginians were resisted by Turdetan princes of the lower Guadalquivir Valley (c. 500 BC). The Second Punic War in 206 BC included a Roman victory at Ilipa Magna, about eight miles north of what is now Seville, and the founding of Italica (about five miles to the northwest), the birthplace of the Roman emperors Trajan and Hadrian. Later excavation there revealed a high level of urbanization, noteworthy inscriptions, sculptures and mosaics, and a huge amphitheatre. But Italica, built on shifting soil, fell in favour of Hispalis (Seville), the walls of which had been built before Caesar and which inherited Italica's population. Seville's prosperity erased the traces of Hispalis; the columns of Calle Mármoles ("Street of Sculptures") and a few inscriptions remain.

Archivo Mas, Barcelona

The cathedral and the Giralda (right), Seville.

Razed by the Vandals and fertilized by the presence of the Byzantines, Seville reached an apogee in the late Visigothic period, personified in the towering figure of St. Isidore (died AD 636), a politician, bibliophile, and historian, whose *Etymologiae*, a synthesis of ancient culture, was the instructional encyclopaedia of Europe's high Middle Ages.

Muslim Seville. Delivered to the Muslims in 711 by its Jewish inhabitants (whom the Visigoths had persecuted), Seville welcomed the first emir, ʿAbd al-Azīz. Córdoba's status as a capital, however, kept Seville rebellious, fired by the discontent of its many rich Christians (Mozarabs, or *mozárabes*) and Jews and its Arab nobles. Under ʿAbd ar-Raḥmān II, the *qāḍī* ʿUmar ibn Adabbas built, with Roman and Visigothic materials, the mosque whose remains are still to be found in El Salvador. In 844, Normans razed Seville but were defeated and lost 30 ships, many of which remained in the swampland around the Guadalquivir. A second wall was built, enclosing a wider area than the Roman one. ʿAbd ar-Raḥmān III took Seville *c.* 918 through trickery and constructed an *alcazaba*, or fort, the door of which was recently found.

With the caliphate destroyed in 1031, Seville was the principal factional kingdom under the ʿAbbādids: Abū al-Qasim Muḥammad; al-Muʿtaḍid (ruled 1042–69), who expanded his kingdom by resisting Ferdinand I of Castile; and al-Muʿtamid (ruled 1069–91), a great poet who fought Alfonso VI and the Berber Almoravids. Seville flourished culturally in a climate of political tension, economic weakness, and religious laxity. The fall of Toledo in 1085 and the pressure of religious enthusiasts forced al-Muʿtamid to call on the Almoravids, who defeated the Christians at az-Zallāqah and dethroned the "party kings" (*mulūk aṭ-ṭawāʾif*). Al-Muʿtamid died an exile in Morocco.

In the 12th century, under both the Almoravids and their successors the Almohads, Seville was the European capital of an African empire to which it lent its cultural achievement and prestige. Ibn-ʿAbdūn's *ḥisbah* treatise describes a Seville that had Muslim, Mozarab, and Hebrew communities, a garrison of watchful Bedouins, noisy markets, beautiful mosques, and cemeteries. The high point of Almohad rule saw population growth, a flourishing economy, the rebirth of poetry, and the construction of more representative monuments: new and more extensive walls of undulating design, the new mosque, one of the largest in Islām, with surrounding commercial districts, a new fort, the first boat bridge over the Guadalquivir, the gardens of Bohaira, the fortresses of Iznalfarach and Alcalá de Guadaira, and the Tower of Gold (Torre del Oro, 1220).

Medieval Christian Seville. With the Almohads defeated in the Battle of Las Navas de Tolosa in 1212, Ferdinand III reconquered the valley of the Guadalquivir. Seville fell to the Christians in 1248 and experienced a complete demographic change with the Repartimiento —the exit of Muslims from the city and its repopulation by Christians. Princes, prelates, great lords, and the military orders received extensive gifts of land, so that small Muslim holdings gave way to large landed estates, with the ensuing pre-eminence of the nobility and economic disequilibrium.

Alfonso X chose to live in Seville, thus colouring the city with courtly refinements and intellectual activity. He founded a school for Latin and Arabic and worked on his prodigious encyclopaedia and the *Cántigas de Santa María* (a series of poems). The cathedral was placed in the old mosque, but Alfonso introduced Gothic architecture in a palace next to the fort, the church of Santa Ana, and the Tower of Silver (Torre de la Plata), while continuing to respect the Almohad tradition in the arsenals (*atarazanas*).

Between the 13th and the 14th centuries the land became impoverished because of strife among the nobles, the consolidation of the kingdom of Granada, and the pressure of the Marīnids from Morocco in the Strait of Gibraltar. Alfonso XI defeated the Marīnids in 1340; he improved Seville's administration and gave a lift to the economy through olive agriculture, a soap industry, and commerce in oil as far as the Near East. Guilds were organized, and parish churches were rebuilt uniformly in the Mudejar style, a mixture of Muslim and Western elements. Pedro I, beloved by the residents of Seville, built a palace there that is the principal part of the Alcázar and an echo of the Alhambra.

In the 15th century Seville became illustrious. The cathedral (built in 1403–1506) was one of the largest in the world. The Canary Islands and much of the kingdom of Granada were conquered and colonized from Seville. With the peace and good government of the Catholic monarchs Ferdinand and Isabella, the city grew and prospered despite the expulsion of the Jews (1492) and the establishment of the Inquisition (1478). Seville's great opportunity had arrived: to be the centre of the exploration and exploitation of America through the Casa de Contratación (House of Trade), established in 1503 to regulate commerce between Spain and the New World.

Apogee and decadence. Seville was the richest and most populated city of Spain in the 16th century (some 60,000 inhabitants around 1500, more than 100,000 in 1565, and some 150,000 in 1588). Charles V married Isabella of Portugal in the Alcázar; the Magellan–Elcano expedition embarked from Saulúcar de Berrameda, Seville's outpost, on its first trip around the world; and treasures arrived from Mexico and Peru. European bankers and merchants frequented the market of the *gradas* (the steps), and a fever for luxury invaded the city. The University prospered; the town hall was built in the fine, richly ornamented plateresque style; the cathedral received its gigantic main altarpiece, shrine, and sacristy; and Nebrija wrote the first Castilian grammar (*Gramática castellana*).

This brilliance, however, was fleeting and partially ephemeral. No industries were created to supply America. Most banking and commerce was handled by foreigners, who were enriched by the gold and silver coined in the world's most active mint. The Emperor's war debts ruined the treasury and the city. In the 17th century political and economic decadence contrasted with a great flowering of culture: the painters Velásquez, Zurbarán, Murillo, the sculptor Juan Martínez Montañés, and Fernando de Herrera are the glories of Seville and of Spain. The picaresque novel documented the disillusionment, the poverty, and the genius, as did *The Exemplary Novels* (*Novelas ejemplares*) on Sevillian themes by Cervantes, who conceived of *Don Quixote* while confined in Seville's jail.

In the 18th century the Bourbons stimulated an economic revival. The countryside around Seville was filled with enormous villas. The Fábrica de Tabacos (Tobacco Factory) was built, as were the present university and the Maestranza bull ring. Excavations in Italica were initiated, and new settlements were made in the Sierra Morena. In the 19th century the French invasion, revolutions, and civil war halted these developments. In 1847 the April Fair, an annual gala following Easter, was born. The Iberoamerican Exposition of 1929 initiated a new renaissance in Seville; and the swampland was placed under cultivation, an effort that involved important irrigation works and a degree of industrial development. In the mid-20th century the city's area and population more than tripled.

BIBLIOGRAPHY

Topography: Though nearly 70 years old, W.M. GALLICHAN, *The Story of Seville* (1903), is a good general account on which the later A.F. CALVERT, *Seville*, illustrated (1907), occasionally draws. E.A. PEERS, *Royal Seville* (1926), voices personal impressions. A picture book is YVES BRAYER, *Seville* (1959), with notes. A personal account by NINA C. EPTON, *Andalusia* (1968), devotes a chapter to Seville, while RAFAEL LAFFON, *Seville*, 3rd ed. (1958), is a useful short guide.

History and art: A good, brief, general survey is J. HAZANAS, *Historia de Sevilla* (1932), while the early era receives attention in Muslim Seville in IBN SAHIB AL-SALA, *Sevilla bajo los almohades* (1969). J. DE M. CARRIAZO, *Anecdotario Sevillano del siglo XV* (1947); and S. MONTOTO DE SEDAS, *Sevilla en el Imperio* (1938), cover more modern times. On artistic and archaeological aspects, J. GESTOSO Y PEREZ, *Sevilla monumental y artística*, 3 vol. (1889–92), is a general work; see also A. SANCHO CORBACHO, *Arquitectura barroca Sevillana del siglo XVIII* (1952). On economic history, a fundamental work is R. CARANDE THOBAR, *Carlos V y sus banqueros*, 3 vol. (1943–67); works on special aspects of economic history are H. and P. CHAUNU, *Séville et l'Atlantique, 1504–1650*, 12 vol. (1955–60); and R. PIKE, *Enterprise and Adventure: The Genoese in Seville and the Opening of the New World* (1966).

(J. de M.C.)

Centre of New World exploration and exploitation

European capital of an African empire

Sewage Systems

Sewage systems are physical systems for the collection of waste water and its treatment before discharge back into the environment. Domestic waste water includes the used water of businesses and office buildings as well as dwellings; industrial waste water is that discharged during industrial operations. In addition to waste water, sewage systems also handle the flow of storm water, either separately or, more commonly, as part of a single system.

The volume of waste water discharged by a community is closely related to the volume of water supply required by it, and keeping the two separate has been one of the most critical problems of modern city engineers.

Because of the time required to plan, finance and build sewage disposal facilities, the engineer who designs such facilities is obliged to make an estimate of future population and industrial growth. The type of industry present or foreseen is important owing to the wide range of water-volume use by various industries—up to 50,000 gallons of water may be used to produce a ton of steel, and up to 100,000 to produce a ton of paper.

The complex and still evolving modern metropolitan sewage system has grown out of a long past, including many disastrous experiences with water-borne diseases and, more recently, other environmental problems such as ecological damage.

HISTORY

Ancient systems.   Drainage systems may be traced to the early Christian Era and earlier; surviving examples include the city of Pompeii (1st century AD) and the even earlier Minoan sites on the island of Crete. Such ancient communities provided for conveying away roof water and rainwater from the pavements. Clay pipes for drain lines were the counterpart of lead pipe conveying water to certain buildings, though these refinements were chiefly limited to the official or wealthy class. In Rome drain water was conveyed to the Tiber principally by surface drains, but as early as the 6th century BC part of the cloaca maxima, the main sewer, was vaulted; in the 3rd century AD the entire sewer was vaulted. In addition to carrying storm runoff, the Roman system served a major source of waste water, the public baths.

Roman engineers introduced their techniques throughout their vast empire; even today, at such ancient bathhouses as that at Bath, England, may be seen the lead pipes bringing water in and the drains for discharge of used water.

The Middle Ages.   The early Middle Ages witnessed few developments in the field of drainage; in the rude garrison towns and frontier outposts of northwest Europe the disposal of human waste was largely in keeping with the injunction contained in the 23rd chapter of Deuteronomy that prescribed withdrawal outside the camp. But in the rapidly growing cities of the high Middle Ages, the first attempts at organized waste removal were made. Privy vaults, usually built to serve several families, were periodically cleaned. The system was none too satisfactory; wealthy families preferred to live adjacent to or over a watercourse, with the "garderobe" (privy) corbelled out over the water; London Bridge was a favourite residence because of its convenience in this respect. A more significant advance introduced in some places was the cesspool. But throughout the Renaissance wastes were universally dumped in city gutters to be flushed through the drains by floods.

Public health aspects.   Not surprisingly, the crude sanitary arrangements of Europe contributed to the spread of epidemics. John Snow, a 19th-century English physician, compiled a list of outbreaks of cholera that he believed had moved westward from India over a period of centuries, reaching London and Paris in 1849. Snow traced a London recurrence of 1854 to a public well, known as the Broad Street Pump, in Golden Square, which he determined was being contaminated by nearby privy vaults. This was a noteworthy epidemiological achievement, especially since it predated by several years the discovery of the role of bacteria in disease transmission.

When the public health dangers became apparent, Londoners first, and soon after other European city dwellers, were ordered to discharge wastes into the drainage system originally provided to carry storm-water runoff only. It might be said that here stream pollution had its birth, as the concentration of such an organic load on a river like the Thames at London was more than the stream could assimilate without nuisance. The resulting stench was such that burlap saturated in chloride of lime was hung in the windows of Parliament House in an attempt to kill the odours. That experience developed into pressure for the treatment of sanitary wastes. Similar treatment demands arose in the large cities of Germany, which had also experienced major waterborne epidemics. Such catastrophes have today been virtually eliminated by vastly improved sanitation of water and modern water-pollution control. In the infectious hepatitis epidemic of 1955–56 in Delhi, India, a laxity in water-treatment techniques was shown to be the cause of the outbreak.

A major contributor to water pollution problems as they reached major intensity first in England during the early 19th century and in the United States and western Europe a little later was the Industrial Revolution, with its combination of concentration of population and industry. Few major industrial users of water, in their early years of development, paid serious attention to waste products that left the plant. Even today, approximately 50 percent of the total wood used in a modern paper mill goes into the industrial waste-water stream and must be removed by treatment of the waste water. Textile mills discharge some waste fibres and also frequently discharge multicoloured dyes.

Industry and water pollution

DEVELOPMENT OF TREATMENT METHODS

Early treatment techniques simulated natural methods of purification. It was observed that moderate amounts of organic wastes discharged into a watercourse eventually went through a natural purification process. In time the receiving water, as well as the waste water itself, regained a status of natural purity. If too much organic matter was imposed upon a watercourse, however, the water was badly degraded and would become a nuisance to sight and smell as well as become uninhabitable for fish and other aquatic life. Because of the absorptive capacity of the soil and the value of organic material as fertilizer an early attempt at disposal was that of sewage farming, the spreading of raw sewage on the land. This met with particular favour in the large cities of Europe and was employed in Berlin and Paris until relatively recent years. This practice was followed in the early years of experimentation in Britain, but soon gave way to methods of treatment in which the final solids removed from the waste water could be used for organic fertilizers or soil conditioners. Such methods included plain sedimentation and, later, chemical precipitation or sedimentation aided by flocculation chemicals.

Development of the trickling filter.   Even these methods were insufficient in many cases and further treatment of the waste water was necessary. Again, observing nature, workers sought to expose the waste-water flow to oxygen from the air by various means. An early attempt consisted of filling a large tank with stones from three to eight inches in average diameter and flooding the interstices with the settled waste water. After contact of several hours, the tank was drained and much organic matter remained on the surface of the stones enmeshed in the zoogleal (massive bacterial) growths that occurred there. Such a treatment scheme required several such tanks so they could be rotated on a fill-and-draw basis. Because of the labour involved with this manipulation and a desire for something better, the next big step was toward a so-called trickling or sprinkling filter. This was not a filter in the usual sense, but a large shallow concrete tank filled with medium-size stones, over whose surface the settled waste water was allowed to trickle, draining from the bottom of the unit. Such filters were operated intermittently so that air had free access to the zoogleal growths that formed on the filter stones and accomplished the oxidization of material from the waste-water flow.

Activated-sludge process. During the years 1912–15, the British developed another process that proved to be still more effective in the removal of organic material from the waste water. Recognizing the trickling filter as merely a means of bringing together the organic matter in the waste water and air as a source of oxygen, British engineers reasoned that by releasing compressed air in a tank of waste water they could achieve a greater measure of control, and hence degree of treatment. They also observed that the circulation of some of the sludge gave a vast area for the same biological action that was going on in the trickling filter, by combining the organisms carried by the sludge, oxygen supplied by the incoming air, and new food supplied by the settled waste water entering the aeration tanks. By varying the amount of air and the amount of sludge returned to the process, higher levels of treatment could be obtained. Because the sludge was teeming with bacterial and associated biological life, the sludge was called "activated" and the process called the "activated-sludge process." It proved highly efficient and was rapidly adopted by cities around the world with severe treatment problems.

MODERN TRENDS

A water-pollution control plant has been described as "a river wound up at one point," because a treatment plant accomplishes, within a few hours, what a river requires days or even weeks to do. In the 1970s nearly all communities needed increasing waste-water treatment; in addition to the greater load from growing populations and industrial activity, there has been a significant increase in most parts of the world in both the stringency and level of enforcement of water-pollution control laws. One result of this pressure has been a search for methods to increase the levels of treatment or, specifically, the removal of organic material from the waste water. Practices of the past have employed biological and physical processes because of their economy.

Chemical treatment. With the increased demands for treatment effectiveness, serious consideration is now being given to the return to chemical precipitation methods. These methods were tried briefly in the 19th century; they were given up, however, because of high costs. The increased value placed by the 20th century on stream cleanliness tends to justify such higher costs, and the treatment plant of the immediate future will probably include chemical precipitation in addition to physical and biological processes.

Separate storm and waste-water sewers. Although most sewer systems still combine storm water and domestic waste water, it is generally recognized that separate systems are highly desirable. Where a combined system is used, heavy rainfall overloads treatment plants, with the result that untreated overflow becomes a source of pollution. Furthermore, where the two streams are kept separate, it is possible to handle each in accordance with the level of treatment required. One proposed method of handling storm runoff is that it be piped to holding reservoirs underground and gradually run through treatment plants.

Recycling. Even further, because of the exhaustion or near exhaustion of water supplies in some areas, there has been a major trend, particularly in the arid parts of the world, to treat waste waters to a level that will allow reuse of the water for various purposes. For many years such treated waters have been used for irrigation, industrial cooling, and certain other industrial processes. Studies are proceeding to reclaim water for many other purposes, with a growing likelihood of eventual reclamation and treatment to the level of drinking water. In the United States, the city of Dallas, Texas, is studying the possibilities of reuse because the city has developed virtually all of the freshwater sources within its reach. Many cities with similar problems, in the U.S. and elsewhere, will soon be studying reuse. The United States government has been carrying on an intensive research program in this area for several years. It is clear that the relation between water supply and water-pollution control is growing steadily closer.

Better law enforcement

Modern urban sewage treatments can best be described by reference to a specific city. The Washington, D.C., system has many aspects typical of any large modern city, though its early history is not representative of many others. The town's first bathtubs were installed in the White House and the Capitol, for the members of Congress in the 1840s; in 1850 the U.S. Congress authorized the Corps of Engineers of the U.S. Army to develop a city-wide water supply from the Potomac River. At this point Washington caught up with New York, London, and Paris, which were also encountering the problem of disposing of used water along with wastes. Washington's solution was the same as that of other cities; the existing system of culverts and drains, built for street drainage only, was extended and developed into a sewer system for the disposal of domestic waste water from residences, government offices, and businesses. The system followed the drainage pattern of the city street network and in general made a system of pipes with a sewer available to each private property. At the same time, again in common with other cities, street drains were built to empty into the nearest surface watercourse without any thought of degradation of the water quality. This was in spite of the fact that an engineering study and report (1890) recommended that all extensions of the sewer system separate storm runoff from domestic waste water.

With continued growth of the city, the District of Columbia constructed in the first decade of the 20th century a series of intercepting sewers and a pumping station to lift the domestic waste water into an outfall line for discharge into the Potomac River south of the city. At the same time pumping facilities were installed for the lifting of storm water drainage directly into the nearby Anacostia River. It was impossible to keep domestic and storm flow completely separate, but practical separation was attempted.

With the accelerated growth of the 1920s, concern over pollution of the Potomac increased. The Potomac estuary had a remarkable ability to assimilate pollution because of the large "flats" on both sides of the river that were kept in a state of constant circulation by tidal variations, but a study made by the Public Health Service in 1932 revealed that the river was in such a condition that low flow would bring about serious pollution effects. As a result, Congress decided to proceed with the construction of facilities for the treatment of waste water. This again was in line with decisions being made in many U.S. and European cities at the same period.

Treatment plant at Blue Plains, D.C. During 1934–38 a plant was constructed on the left bank of the Potomac at Blue Plains, D.C., to accommodate a flow of 130,000,000 gallons per day and serve a population of 650,000. Initially, with the help of the Federal Emergency Administration of Public Works, money was allowed for construction of a plant that would remove 90 percent of the organic matter from the waste-water flow. That level of treatment was in accordance with the Public Health Service recommendation contained in the 1932 report. Instead of constructing the plant in accordance with that recommendation, the District of Columbia decided to eliminate the second step in the treatment and construct a sedimentation plant, generally known as primary treatment. The plant was able to remove about 36 percent of the organic matter when it went into operation in August 1938, but as the population load increased, accelerated by World War II, the plant was unable to maintain this level and year by year efficiency dropped until it was regularly under 30 percent.

During World War II, initial plans were made for the relief of the treatment burden, and by 1950 the District of Columbia had begun major construction to increase the capacity of the plant and make further plans for inclusion of secondary treatment.

Activated-sludge plant. The activated-sludge process pioneered in Britain had by now been widely tested. Washington constructed a high-rate activated-sludge treatment plant in anticipation of 70 percent removal of organic matter. While the new plant brought a major improvement in the river, there was no real possibility of keeping up with the pollution burden, even though the plant grew to a capacity of 290,000,000 gallons daily. In the early 1970s the District planned to extend treatment to a much higher level—once more, a decision being forced on many cities of the United States, Europe, and Asia.

Coordination with surrounding areas.   One of the awkward problems confronting city engineers of the 20th century in nearly all countries has been the impossibility of isolating a metropolitan area from neighbouring regions. Rivers carry pollution from city to city, even country to country. In Washington the problem was encountered in a relatively mild form; much of the Maryland suburban area drains into Rock Creek and the Anacostia River, which flow through the District of Columbia; to try to keep the two streams as clean as possible the District of Columbia and the Washington Suburban Sanitary Commission (of Maryland) entered into an agreement to handle each other's flow at a reasonable cost. All the domestic waste water of the suburban areas is now connected into District sewers, with payments made to handle the waste waters. As part of the agreement, the Maryland Commission helps to finance both the construction and the operation of the District of Columbia Water Pollution Control Plant.

Other developments.   With continued growth and rising pollution control standards of the 1960s and 1970s, Washington like most other major cities has been turning toward additional treatment, including chemical treatment. One proposal calls for achieving so high a level of treatment that the Potomac estuary into which the effluent flows could be used as an emergency water source.

Another direction in which Washington had headed in company with many other modern cities is toward separation of systems. This is a tedious and expensive process, requiring piping changes on private property. Its long-range wisdom, however, is irrefutable. The redevelopment of certain major areas, such as southwest Washington, has given favourable opportunities for large-scale separation.

An important advance in financing improvements has been adopted by Washington: the sewer-service charge on all those served by the drainage system. This system has been followed more and more by drainage systems serving both municipalities and industry.

Since about 1959 the D.C. sewer system has been interconnected with the areas in Maryland that naturally drain through the District via the Potomac River and major areas in Virginia related to the intercepting sewer serving Dulles International Airport near Herndon, Virginia. As a result of this connection the area served increased by 436 square miles in Maryland and 228 square miles in Virginia. The Metropolitan area in Arlington County and much of the Virginia suburban area adjacent to Arlington County are served by other treatment plants.

Present treatment facilities.   At the District of Columbia Water Pollution Control Plant (see illustration) the raw waste water enters the plant pumping station and is treated in the following successive steps: grit removal, preliminary sedimentation, aeration, and final sedimentation. In addition, chlorine treatment may be given the flow prior to preliminary sedimentation or it may be given to the final effluent. With the first application, the effect of chlorine is to minimize odours from the sedimentation tanks. When fed to the final effluent, chlorine has a disinfectant effect.

The purpose of the sedimentation tanks, both preliminary and final, is to separate solids from the waste-water flow; the solids removed must be given further treatment. At the D.C. plant these solids are exposed to anaerobic digestion and dewatering on vacuum filters. The final product is a moist cake with approximately 70 percent water, suitable for land application as a soil conditioner. During the digestion of sludge, a gas consisting of approximately two-thirds methane is produced that is burned for heat for the plant buildings and to provide some power generation. The sludge gas has a heat value of about 600

Gas production

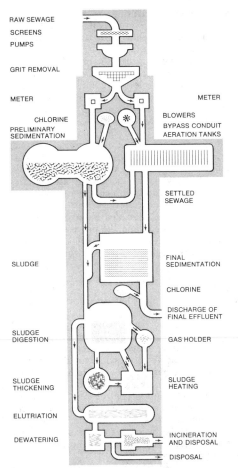

Basic steps in the sewage disposal process of the District of Columbia Water Pollution Control Plant.

RAW SEWAGE
SCREENS
PUMPS
GRIT REMOVAL
METER
METER
CHLORINE
BLOWERS
PRELIMINARY
BYPASS CONDUIT
SEDIMENTATION
AERATION TANKS
SETTLED SEWAGE
SLUDGE
FINAL SEDIMENTATION
CHLORINE
DISCHARGE OF FINAL EFFLUENT
SLUDGE DIGESTION
GAS HOLDER
SLUDGE THICKENING
SLUDGE HEATING
ELUTRIATION
INCINERATION AND DISPOSAL
DEWATERING
DISPOSAL

BTU (British thermal units) per cubic foot and the quantity produced is about one cubic foot per person, per day. A sludge gas engine of 1,200 horsepower drives an 800-kilowatt generator for production of electric power. Initially, the power produced supplied about 95 percent of the needs of the plant, but with the growth of the plant, power requirements have increased rapidly and now the gas engine supplies only a minor proportion of the electric power. It supplies, however, through its jacket water-cooling system, a large amount of the heat necessary to maintain active biological digestion in the sludge digestion tanks.

The total cost of the plant exceeds $25,000,000 and the annual operating costs in the late 1960s approximated $2,500,000. Over 250 persons are employed in operation and maintenance.

The full extent of the undertaking may be appreciated when the vast waste-water collection system serving property throughout the area is visualized. In the District of Columbia alone, over 1,700 miles of sewers serve this purpose, while 2,700 miles in the Maryland area give similar service to the properties of that jurisdiction. The maintenance of the system is a major activity, as 200 men are engaged in regular maintenance and minor construction related to the sewer system in the District of Columbia alone. Proper maintenance involves regular inspection of the lines and periodic cleaning to avoid difficulties that could cause great inconvenience and possibly property damage to those served by the drainage system.

WORLDWIDE SEWAGE DISPOSAL PROBLEM

Sewage disposal in non-Western areas is progressing at a rapid pace. The growth of cities and industries has made it necessary for such areas to have public water supplies. The full advantages of a public water supply cannot be realized without a proper drainage system that will remove promptly the used waste water along with the wastes contributed by its use. The advanced state of public health protection from persons living in an environment served by proper water and sewer service is properly credited to the advantage of these services.

Since World War II Japan has been converting from its outdated agricultural utilization of raw sewage to the modern water-carried drainage system. To build such a system in a metropolis like Tokyo with its population exceeding 11,000,000 is truly a herculean task. The traditional communal bathhouses of Tokyo neighbourhoods eventually will be replaced by household plumbing systems. Thailand, India, Pakistan, and many countries on the African continent are following this pattern. Eastern as well as western Europe has its pollution problems; such densely populated countries as Romania, Czechoslovakia, Hungary, and Poland have intensive programs of water-pollution control under way. In areas where water is extremely short, such as Israel and South Africa, reclamation after full waste-water treatment is practiced. In Windhoek, South West Africa, approximately one-third of the waste water is circulated back to the domestic water supply; plans are being made to increase the return to 50 percent. This is accomplished by following the conventional methods of waste-water treatment with more refined techniques to restore the water to a completely satisfactory public-health quality. At the same time the chemical characteristics of the water are improved, and hardness is reduced. The city of Bangkok, Thailand, is pursuing a gigantic program involving complete reconstruction of its water system and its sewer system along the most modern lines, including a high degree of recycling.

Recirculation

Future problems in the field include proper means of financing the construction and operation of sewer systems including such appurtenances as pumping stations and plants for the control of water pollution, but most significantly higher and higher degrees of waste-water treatment. Research in progress in many countries of the world promises to achieve a high degree of reclamation, and even recycling at reasonable cost.

The control of water pollution is not dependent wholly on the civil and environmental engineers who customarily design the facilities for the collection and treatment of waste waters. For the intelligent operation of such structures, the cooperation of chemists, biologists, bacteriologists, and limnologists (freshwater scientists) has been considered essential for many years. Now, with the added emphasis on ecology and environment, the application of the principles of these broad fields of biology must also be included to meet the problems of the growing world population and its demands for a greatly improved environment.

BIBLIOGRAPHY. M.M. COHN, *Sewers for Growing America* (1966), a modern description of waste-water collection systems, their history, and the water-pollution problem created; G.M. FAIR, J.C. GEYER, and D.A. OKUN, *Water and Wastewater Engineering*, 2 vol. (1966–68), and H.E. BABBITT and E.R. BAUMANN, *Sewerage and Sewage Treatment*, 8th ed. (1958), popular texts in sanitary engineering; *Waste Treatment Proceedings* (1960), a symposium report. Physical descriptions of various city systems are provided by published reports of most municipal sanitary agencies.

(R.E.F.)

Sex and Sexuality

Sex, sexuality, and reproduction are all closely interwoven into the fabric of living things, both animal and plant. All relate to the propagation of the race and the survival of the species. Yet there can be sex without sexuality, and reproduction need not be sexual, although for most forms of life sexual reproduction is essential both for propagation and long-term survival. (For the process of sex in human beings, see SEXUAL BEHAVIOUR, HUMAN.)

SEXUAL AND NONSEXUAL REPRODUCTION

Since the life-span of all individual forms of life, from microbes to man, is limited, the first concern of any particular population is to produce successors. This is reproduction, pure and simple. Among lower animals and plants it may be accomplished without involving eggs and sperm. Ferns, for example, shed millions of micro-

scopic, nonsexual spores, which are capable of growing into new plants if they settle in a suitable environment. Many higher plants also reproduce by nonsexual means. Bulbs bud off new bulbs from the side. Certain jellyfish, sea anemones, marine worms, and other lowly creatures bud off parts of the body during one season or another, each thereby giving rise to populations of new, though identical, individuals. At the microscopic level, single-celled organisms reproduce continually by growing and dividing successively to give rise to enormous populations of mostly identical descendants. All such reproduction depends on the capacity of cells to grow and divide, which is a basic property of life. In the case of most animals, however, particularly the higher forms, reproduction by nonsexual means is apparently incompatible with the structural complexity and activity of the individual.

Nonsexual reproduction

Although nonsexual reproduction is exploited by some creatures to produce very large populations under certain circumstances, it is of limited value in the long run. Such so-called vegetative forms of reproduction, whether of animals or plants, result in individuals that are genetically identical with the parent. All have exactly the same genetic, or inherited, traits, for better or worse. If some adverse environmental change should occur, all would be equally affected and none might survive. At the best, therefore, nonsexual reproduction can be a valuable and perhaps an essential means of propagation, but it does not exclude the need for sexual reproduction.

Sexual reproduction not only takes care of the need for replacement of individuals within a population but gives rise to populations better suited to survive under changing circumstances. In effect it is a kind of double assurance that the race or species will persist for an indefinite time. The great difference between the two types of reproduction is that individual organisms resulting from nonsexual reproduction have but a single parent and are essentially alike, whereas those resulting from sexual reproduction have two parents and are never exact replicas of either. Sexual reproduction thus introduces a variability, in addition to its propagative function. Both types of reproduction represent the capacity of individual cells to develop into whole organisms, given suitable circumstances. Sex is therefore something that has been combined with this primary function and is responsible for the capacity of a race to adapt to new environmental conditions.

Sex cells. The term sex is variously employed. In the broad sense it includes everything from the sex cells to sexual behaviour. Primary sex, which is generally all that distinguishes one kind of individual from another in the case of many lower animals, denotes the capacity of the reproductive gland, or gonad, to produce either sperm cells or eggs or both. If only sperm cells are produced, the reproductive gland is a testis, and the primary sex of the tissue and the individual possessing it is male. If only eggs are produced, the reproductive gland is an ovary, and the primary sex is female. If the gland produces both sperm and eggs, either simultaneously or successively, the condition is known as hermaphroditic. An individual, therefore, is male or female or hermaphrodite primarily according to the nature of the gonad.

As a rule, male and female complement each other at all levels of organization: as sex cells; as individuals with either testes or ovaries; and as individuals with anatomical, physiological, and behavioral differences associated with the complemental roles they play during the whole reproductive process. The role of the male individual is to deliver sperm cells in enormous numbers in the right place and at the right time to fertilize eggs of female individuals of the same species. The role of the female individual is to deliver or otherwise offer eggs capable of being fertilized under precise circumstances. In the case of hermaphrodite organisms, animal or plant, various devices are employed to ensure cross-fertilization, or cross-pollination, so that full advantage of double parentage is obtained. The basic requirement of sexual reproduction is that reproductive cells of different parentage come together and fuse in pairs. Such cells will be genetically different to a significant degree, and it is this feature that is essential to the long-term well-being of the race. The other sexual distinctions, between the two types of sex cell and between two individuals of different sex, are secondary differences connected with ways and means of attaining the end.

Sexuality: complementary mating types. The complementarity of both male and female sex cells and male and female individuals is a form of division of labour. Male sex cells are usually motile cells capable of swimming through liquid, either freshwater, seawater, or body fluids, and they contribute the male cell nucleus but little else to the fertilization process. The female cell also contributes its nucleus, together with a large mass of cell substance necessary for later growth and development following fertilization. The female cell, however, is without any capacity for independent movement.

In other words, small male cells (sperm cells, spermatozoa, or male gametes) are burdened with the task of reaching a female cell (egg, ovum, or female gamete), which is relatively large and awaits fertilization. A full complement of genes is contributed by both nuclei, representing contributions by both parents, but, apart from the nucleus, only the egg is equipped or prepared to undergo development to form a new organism. A comparable division of labour is seen in the distinction between male and female individuals. The male possesses testes and whatever accessory structures may be necessary for spawning or delivery of the sperm, and the female possesses ovaries and what may be needed to facilitate shedding the eggs or to nurture developing young. Accordingly there is the basic sex, which depends on the kind of sex gland present, and sexuality, which depends on the different structures, functions, and activities associated with the sex glands.

The role of each sex

THE ADAPTIVE SIGNIFICANCE OF SEX

When two reproductive cells from somewhat unlike parents come together and fuse, the resulting product of development is never exactly the same as either parent. On the other hand, when new individuals, plant or animal, develop from cuttings, buds, or body fragments, they are exactly like their respective parents, as much alike as identical twins. Any major change in environmental circumstances might exterminate a race since all could be equally affected. When eggs and sperm unite, they initiate development and also establish genetic diversity among the population. This diversity is truly the spice of life and one of the secrets of its success; sex is necessary to its accomplishment.

In each union of egg and sperm, a complete set of chromosomes, representing a complete set of genes, is contributed by each cell to the nucleus of the fertilized egg. Consequently, every cell in the body inherits the double set of chromosomes and genes derived from the two parental cells. Every time a cell divides, during the long period of development and growth, each daughter cell receives exact copies of the original two sets of chromosomes. The process is known as mitosis. Accordingly, any fragment of tissue has the same genetic constitution as the body as a whole and therefore inevitably gives rise to an identical individual if it becomes separated and is able to grow and develop. Only in the case of the tissue that produces the sex cells do cells divide differently, and genetic differences occur as a result.

During the ripening of the sex cells, both male and female, cell divisions occur (known as meiosis) that result in each sperm and egg cell having only a single set of chromosomes. In each case the set of chromosomes is complete—*i.e.*, one chromosome of each kind—but each such set is, in effect, drawn haphazardly from the two sets present in the original cells. In other words, the single set of chromosomes present in the nucleus of any particular sperm or egg, while complete in number and kinds, is a mixture, some chromosomes having come from the set originally contributed by the male parent and some from the female. Each reproductive cell, of either sex, therefore contains a set of chromosomes different in genetic detail from that of every other reproductive cell. When these in turn combine to form fertilized eggs or fertile

seeds, the double set of chromosomes characteristic of tissue cells is re-established, but the genetic constitution of all such cells in the new individual will be the same as that of the fertilized egg—two complete sets of genes, randomly derived from sets contributed by the two different parents. Variation is thus established in two steps. The first is during the ripening of the sex cells, when each sperm or egg receives a single set of chromosomes of mixed ancestry. None of these cells will have exactly the same combination of genes characteristic of the respective parent. The second step occurs at fertilization, when the pair of already genetically unique sex cells fuse together and their nuclei combine, thus compounding the primary variation.

Reproduction and evolution. Sexual reproduction appears to be a process serving two opposing needs. The individuals produced must be almost exactly like their parents if they are to succeed; *i.e.*, to grow and reproduce in turn, under the prevailing circumstances. At the same time they should exhibit a wide range of differences so that some at least can survive under different environmental circumstances. The first business of reproduction is to produce perfect working copies of the parental organism, without any mistakes. The second is to introduce novelties; *i.e.*, new models that make possible other life styles. Extreme conservatism, in either sexual or nonsexual reproduction, may be disastrous to the species in the long run. Extreme variability may also be detrimental, resulting in the production of too high a percentage of misfits. A delicate balance has to be struck. Variability is necessary but must be kept within bounds. Sex is responsible for controlled diversity, without which adaptation and evolution could not take place.

Signifi-
cance
of
reproduc-
tion

Natural selection operates in two ways on this basic diversity inherent in any particular population or community. In a stable environment, where there is little change during a long period of time, except for the regular changes associated with the seasons and the daily cycle, those individuals most likely to survive and produce offspring are precisely those that are most like their parents at all stages of their existence. The more radical departures from the established types fail either to grow or to compete successfully and consequently do not reproduce. The less radical departures struggle along but leave progeny in proportionately smaller numbers. If, however, a significant long-term change occurs in the environment, the previously established types are likely to suffer, while other types that previously had been weeded out generation by generation now may be favoured. They may become the more successful at surviving and growing and consequently replace themselves more readily than do others. They, in turn, become the establishment, and the older type is jeopardized. A constant interplay persists between a changeable environment and a variable population. This is adaptation. If environmental change continues in the same general direction, adaptation also continues in the initial direction, and eventually significant evolution becomes apparent.

The variability or diversity resulting from sexual reproduction is vital in two ways. It permits the process of natural selection to work and allows a population of organisms to adapt to new conditions. It also serves as a corrective mechanism. During nonsexual reproduction, particularly of single-cell organisms, large populations of virtually identical individuals are readily built up and maintained for a great many generations. Sooner or later, however, more and more abnormalities appear and, usually, a general waning of vigour ensues. When such organisms subsequently fuse together in pairs, equivalent to sexual reproduction, a rejuvenation and re-establishment of healthy strains generally follows.

Life cycles adjusted to environmental change. Both sexual and nonsexual reproduction may be exploited or adjusted to meet widely fluctuating environmental conditions, especially those of a regular seasonal character. This phenomenon is particularly striking in the case of the smaller or simpler forms of animal and plant life that have a life-span of a year or less. The seeds of annual plants germinate in the spring, grow and set seed in turn during the summer, and die in the fall. Only the sexually produced seeds persist and represent the species during the long winter season. Certain small, though common, freshwater creatures have a similar cycle. The microscopic eggs of *Hydra* and of *Daphnia*, for example, lie at the bottom of ponds throughout the winter, each within a tough protective case. In late winter or early spring, a new generation of hydras develops, each individual becoming attached to a stone or vegetation and feeding on small crustaceans by means of its long slender tentacles. The daphnias, or so-called water fleas, emerge at about the same time and grow rapidly to maturity. In both cases the growing season, usually from spring until fall, is a time for intensive reproduction by whatever means is most effective. Hydras bud off new hydras continually, each new hydra repeating the process, with the size of populations limited only by available food. Only late in the season, when the food supply drops off and the temperature drops, does the riotous splurge of nonsexual reproduction come to an end. Then each individual ceases to bud and produces either minute ovaries or testes, and in some species, both. Eggs become fertilized, encased, drop into the mud, and await the coming of the following spring, while the parental creatures die as living conditions worsen with approaching winter. Such is a general pattern of life, widely seen among creatures whose individual existence is measured in weeks or months but whose race must persist in some form at all times if extinction is to be avoided.

So it is with *Daphnia* and many others. The *Daphnia* also changes according to the times, but it alternates between one form of sexual reproduction and another. Sexually, it is exquisitely adapted to the little world in which it lives. Under ideal conditions every member of a *Daphnia* community is female. All those first hatching out from winter eggs in the spring are females. Each produces a succession of broods during the month or two of its individual existence, all offspring being females. Each such female, generation after generation, during the spring and summer season, produces eggs that develop at once without need or opportunity of being fertilized. No males in fact are present. Every individual is a self-sufficient breeding female. Population explosions occur wherever environmental circumstances are good. Eventually, however, conditions inevitably change for the worse, either because of effects inherent in any population explosion or because every season comes to an end. Food becomes scarce because of too many consumers; space becomes crowded and in some degree polluted; chilly days succeed the warmth of summer. Whatever it is, and well before disaster can strike, the creatures respond in remarkable ways. On the first signal that conditions may be getting less than good, a certain number of the eggs produced by a population of *Daphnia* develop into males, each with testes in place of ovary, together with certain secondary sexual characteristics. A scattering of males through the virgin paradise, however, is only a first step, a preparedness in case conditions go from bad to worse. If there has been a false alarm, the females continue to produce female-producing eggs that develop parthenogenetically—*i.e.*, without benefit of fertilization—and the males die off without performing any sexual function. But if the environmental signal means the beginning of the end of congenial conditions, a cell in the ovary of each female grows to form a larger egg than usual, and it is of a type that must be fertilized. Then mating between the sexes takes place, and these special, fertilized eggs become thickly encased and alone survive the winter season after becoming separated from the parent.

Wherever small aquatic creatures live in bodies of water that may freeze in winter or dry up in summer, similar adaptations are seen in many forms of life besides hydras and water fleas. Certain small fish, known as the annual fishes, have individual life-spans of about six months. The life-span itself is in fact adapted to the period during which active existence is possible in their particular habitat. When the water holes, swamps, and puddles in which they live begin to dry up, mating takes place, and the fertilized eggs drop into the mud. The parents die, and the

eggs remain in a state of suspended development until the next rainy season occurs. The race must go on whatever the circumstances, and all sex is directed toward this end.

THE ORIGIN OF SEX AND SEXUALITY

All sexual reproduction, no matter how large or small the organisms may be, is a performance of single cells. Only at the level of single cells can the essential genetic recombinations be accomplished. So in every generation new life begins with the egg, which is a single cell, however large it may be. Egg and sperm unite at fertilization, but the fertilized egg is as much a single cell as before. When did it all begin? The generally accepted answer is that the fundamental, or molecular, basis of sexuality is an ancient evolutionary development that goes back almost to the beginning of life on earth, several billion years ago, for it is evident among the vast world of single-celled organisms, including bacteria.

In these lowest forms of life, sex and reproduction are distinct happenings. Reproduction is accomplished in most cases entirely by fission, which is simply cell division repeated regularly, as long as the environmental conditions permit. As long as crowding and other adverse changes are avoided, cells divide, and the daughter cells grow and divide again, for weeks or months on end. This process occurs in both plantlike and animal-like single-celled organisms and in bacteria as well. Under certain other conditions, such cell organisms come together and fuse in pairs, a form of sexual behaviour at its primary level and comparable to the fusion of an egg and sperm. In all such cases, a combined cell is produced in which nuclear exchange or recombination has occurred. Pairing off of this sort takes place sooner or later in all forms of unicellular life, even where no outwardly distinguishable differences can be detected between the pairing individuals. The lack of discernible differences between the members of mating pairs, however, does not mean that pairing occurs between identical individuals. In the much investigated *Paramecium* and other protozoan organisms, two separate populations of cells may continue to increase almost indefinitely by ordinary cell division of single individuals, but when two such populations are mixed together, mating generally occurs immediately between individuals from the two different sources. The fusion, or pairing, has essentially the same function as the fusion of the male and female nucleus during the process of fertilization of eggs of higher forms. It is the basis of sex, the essential event in all cases being the genetic or chromosomal recombination.

Individual mating cells (*i.e.*, eggs, sperm, or even whole single-celled organisms) may be called gametes whether or not they are distinguishable from one another. Yet even among the various single-celled organisms, mating commonly occurs between individuals of two different kinds. This kind of mating is seen most often among the single-celled organisms known as flagellates. In some species the gametes may be alike and all are motile, progressing through the water by means of one or more whiplike flagella similar to the tail of a sperm. In other species, all individuals may still be motile, but pairing occurs between individuals of different sizes. In still others, one of the two mating types may be very small and motile, and the other, large, with stored nutritional material, and nonmotile. All degrees of differentiation between male and female gametes can be found, and it is probable that the basic and characteristic distinction between the sex cells of both animal and plant life in general was established very early in the course of evolution, during the immense period of time when virtually all living organisms consisted of single cells.

This division of labour between mating types, male and female, respectively, is nature's way of attaining two ends. These are the bringing together of the gametes so that fusion may take place and the accumulation of reserves so that development of a new organism can be accomplished. The first calls for as many motile cells as possible; the second calls for cells as large as possible. These different requirements are practically impossible to satisfy by a single type of cell. Accordingly, and especial-

Partheno-
genesis

Kinds of
gametes

ly in multicelled animals of all sorts, male gametes, or spermatozoa, are extremely small, extremely motile, and are produced in enormous numbers. The larger the number, the greater the likelihood that some will encounter and fertilize eggs. On the other hand, the female gametes, or ova, individually need to be as large as possible since the larger the size and the more condensed the internal nutritional reserves, the farther along the path of embryonic development the egg can travel before hatching must occur and the new organism must fend for itself. Nevertheless, eggs in general are caught between the desirability of being individually as large as they can be and the persisting need to be produced in reasonably large numbers, so that an assortment of differing individuals is produced from a single pair of parents. A large number of offspring ensures that a proportion, at least, will survive the environmental hazards faced by all developing organisms in some degree.

Differentiation of the sexes. Animals and plants, apart from microscopic kinds of life, consist of enormous numbers of cells coordinated in various ways to form a single organism, and each consists of many different kinds of cells specialized for performing different functions. Certain tissues are set aside for the production of sexual reproductive cells, male or female as the case may be. Whether they are testes or ovaries or, as in some animals and plants, both together in the same parental individual, they are typically contained within the body, and therefore the sex cells usually need to be passed to the outside in order to function. Only in certain lowly creatures such as hydras is there a simpler state, for in hydras the testes and ovaries form in the outermost layer of cells of the slender, tubular body, and the sex cells when ripe burst directly from the simple, bulging gonads into the surrounding water. With few other exceptions, in all other creatures the gonads are part of the internal tissues and some means of exit is necessary. In some, such as most worms, all that is needed are small openings, or precisely placed pores, in the body wall through which sperm or eggs can escape. In most others, more is needed and a tubular sperm duct or an oviduct leads from each testis or ovary, through which the sex cells pass to the exterior. This is minimal equipment, except where none is needed. The gonad and its duct is accordingly comparable to other glands in the body; that is, the gland is generally a more or less compact mass of cells of a particular, specialized kind, together with a duct for passage of the product of the tissue to the site of action. Gonads secrete —i.e., produce and transmit—sex cells that usually act outside the body.

Differentiation between the sexes exists, therefore, as the primary difference represented by the distinction between eggs and sperm, by differences represented by nature of the reproductive glands and their associated structures, and lastly by differences, if any, between individuals possessing the male and female reproductive tissues, respectively.

Sex cells, sexual organs, other sexual structures, and sexual distinction between individuals constitute a series of evolutionary advances connected with various changes and persisting needs in the general evolution of animals and, to some degree, of plants as well. In other words, no matter how large or complex a creature may become, it still needs to deliver functional sex cells to the exterior. This condition is almost always the case for sperm cells. Among aquatic animals, particularly marine animals whose external medium, the ocean, is remarkably similar chemically to the internal body fluid medium of all animals, eggs are also in most cases shed to the exterior, where development of the fertilized eggs can proceed readily. Even so, time and place are important. Starfish, sea urchins, and many others, for instance, accumulate mature eggs and sperm in the oviducts and sperm ducts until an appropriate time when all can be shed at once. When one member of a group of such creatures begins to spawn, chemicals included in the discharge stimulate other members to do the same, so that a mass spawning takes place. One might say that the more they are together the more variable their offspring may be. This situation

actually is the crux of the matter for nearly all forms of life, because while it may be possible for a single individual to possess both male and female gonads, producing both sperm and eggs, it remains generally desirable, if not essential, that eggs be fertilized by sperm produced by another individual. Cross-fertilization results in a much greater degree of variability than does self-fertilization. The existence of two types of individuals, male and female, is the common means of ensuring that cross-fertilization will be accomplished, since then nothing else is possible. Where the sexes are separate, therefore, all that is necessary is that members of the opposite sex get together at a time and place appropriate for the initial development of fertilized eggs. Typically, spawning of this sort is a communal affair, with many individuals of each sex discharging sex cells into the surrounding water. This process is only suitable, however, when eggs are without tough protective cases or membranes; that is, only when eggs are readily fertilizable for some time after being shed and while drifting in the sea. In this circumstance there is no need for individuals of the opposite sex to mate in pairs, nor is such mating practiced.

The value of cross-fertilization

Mating. Mating between two individuals of the opposite sex becomes necessary when eggs must be fertilized at or before the time the eggs are shed. Whenever eggs have a protective envelope of any kind through which sperm cannot penetrate, fertilization must take place before the envelope is formed. The envelope may at first be a gluey liquid, which covers the egg and solidifies as a tough egg case, as in all crustaceans, insects, and related creatures. It may be a thick membrane of protein deposited around the egg, as in fishes generally; or it may be a material that swells up as a mass of jelly surrounding the eggs after the eggs have been shed, as in frogs and salamanders. And finally, it may be a calcified shell, as in birds and reptiles. In all of these organisms the sperm must reach the egg before the protective substance is added, except in those forms in which a small opening or pore persists in the egg membrane through which sperm can enter.

When and how such eggs need to be fertilized depends on the nature of the protective membranes and the time and place of their formation. The jelly surrounding frog and toad eggs, for instance, swells up immediately after the eggs are shed. Mating and fertilization must take place at the time of spawning. Male frogs mount the back of female frogs and each clasps his mate firmly around the body, which not only helps press the egg mass downward but brings the cloacal opening of male and female close together. Eggs and sperm are shed simultaneously, and the eggs are fertilized as they leave the female body. Fish eggs are also fertilized as or shortly after they are shed, although fish have no arms and mating generally is usually no more than a coming together of the two sexes side by side, so that simultaneous shedding of sperm and eggs can be accomplished. In other creatures the mating procedure may be much more complicated, depending on various circumstances. Crustaceans such as crabs and lobsters, for example, mate in somewhat the same manner as frogs, with the male holding on to the female by means of clawlike appendages and depositing sperm at the openings of the oviducts, which are typically situated near the middle of the undersurface of the body.

Mating modifications imposed by the land environment. Greater problems arise on land than in water. Eggs produced by truly terrestrial creatures are either retained in the parental body during their development or must be fully protected from drying up. Protective membranes must be tough indeed. More importantly, however, sperm cells must still be deposited where they can swim toward the eggs, for they cannot survive or function except in a watery solution of dilute salts. In all terrestrial creatures, except those that return to water to breed, sperm can survive only in the body of the male or female organism. All insects, therefore, must mate in order for eggs to be fertilized, and all have appendages at the rear of the body that serve as a copulatory device capable of being used even when in flight. Sperm is injected into the female's duct or storage sac, either for immediate fertilization or for later use. The queens of bees, ants, and termites, in fact, mate once and for all during a nuptial flight and thereafter use the stored sperm to fertilize all the eggs they subsequently produce.

The land vertebrates have to cope with much the same breeding circumstances as the insects. Man is more aware of these procedures because they happen mostly in much larger creatures and also because he has some fellow feeling for them. Reptiles, birds, and even the most primitive surviving mammals—namely, the platypus and spiny anteater of Australasia—produce yolky eggs encased in a more or less rigid calcareous shell. Moreover, within the shell, a thick layer of albumen surrounds the egg proper. Both the albumen and the shell are added after the ovum leaves the ovary and during its passage down the oviduct. Fertilization must take place, if at all, as the eggs enter the oviduct, for neither the albumen nor the shell can be penetrated by spermatozoa. Sperm must therefore be introduced into the female and must be able to make their way up to the end of the oviduct, which is a very long journey for so small a cell. An enormous number must begin the journey to make sure that some will reach the goal.

Sexual anatomy. In reptiles and birds of both sexes, as in amphibians and fish, a single opening to the exterior serves jointly for both the intestine and reproductive duct. This is the cloaca, or vestibule. Nevertheless, copulation of a sort occurs in all three groups of terrestrial vertebrates: the reptiles, birds, and mammals. With the exception of man, the male always mounts the female from the rear or back, and in both reptiles and birds the cloacal openings are pressed closely together to form a continuous passage from one individual to the other. With one exception, the archaic tuatara (*Sphenodon*) of New Zealand, all present-day reptiles have an erectile penis, derived from the cloacal wall, that delivers the sperm into the proper duct. One mating may serve for a long time, and there are cases known in which female snakes have laid fertile eggs after months and sometimes years of isolation in captivity. On the other hand, a penis of any sort is lacking in most kinds of birds, and the pressing together of the cloacal apertures seems to serve well enough. The most advanced copulatory procedure is that of mammals. In mammals the cloaca has become replaced by separate openings for the reproductive duct and intestine, respectively. Eggs have become microscopic, devoid of shell, yolk, and virtually all albumen, although they still need to be fertilized as they enter the upper end of the oviduct. A well-developed, erectile penis is always present in the male for the ejaculation of stored sperm well up the reproductive passage of the female. Accordingly, the two sexes have become strikingly differentiated anatomically, with regard to delivery of sperm, compared with the seemingly primitive anatomical equipment of birds.

Courtship. The coming together of two members of the opposite sex is a necessary preliminary to mating. It may be accomplished by two individuals independently of any larger congregation, or it may result from two individuals pairing off within a breeding population that may have assembled even from the ends of the earth. In the one the problem is to find one another; in the other the problem is to find the appropriate place, called the staging area. In both cases timing and some sort of navigation are important. Mass assembly appears to be the more effective, although a local crowd of any kind of animal may be an open invitation to predators, human or otherwise, and may on occasion become disastrous.

The searching out of a solitary individual by another of the opposite sex can be a difficult matter. In the dark depths of the ocean, for instance, where fish and other marine life forms are extremely scarce and scattered, the chance of encounter is rare indeed. The small angler fish (*Photocorynus spiniceps*) that cruise around at great depths are most unlikely to meet a member of the opposite sex at a time or place when the female happens to be ready to shed her eggs. As a form of insurance to this end, however, any small, young male that happens to meet a large female, apparently at any time, immediately fastens on to her head or sides by his jaws and thereafter

Necessity of internal fertilization in land animals

lives a totally parasitic existence sustained by the juices of the female body. Sperm thus becomes available at any time the female may produce eggs to be fertilized.

On land this individual procedure of searching out is common among insects and the more predatory mammals. Male crickets and cicadas sound their familiar signals, by night or by day, which attract any females within hearing distance. More remarkable are those insects and other creatures that produce living light, in some cases for no apparent purpose but in others, such as the firefly, for signalling between the sexes in the dark of summer nights. The male individuals, always more dispensable than females, fly freely at considerable risk, flashing their light at regular intervals. The light of the female, perched more safely on some tall grass, winks back as though it were a landing light, and so they come together. Each of the several species of firefly has its own flash code, or rhythm, and any wasteful attempt at interspecies mixing is avoided. On the same principle, female moths send their personal perfume into the night air, and those males that detect the scent fly toward the source, the winner taking all. Mammals also depend mainly on their sense of smell, being generally colour blind, not too attentive to sound, and, apart from the grazing and browsing creatures, mainly active at night. The scented sex appeal of a cat in heat, whether domestic or wild, excites all the males in the neighbourhood and, with or without the sound of voice, male and female come quickly together in the dark. In all of these, courting is mostly uncalled for since only ready-to-mate individuals are involved in this sexual searching in the dark.

Sexual attractants

Courting is necessary whenever the male is a supplicant. A female may not be ready to mate, and stimulation in the form of dance or song may be required to create the mood; or, as is commonly the case, there is a surplus of available and eager males, and one must be chosen among many. However it may be, courting is most practiced not only when the female is in command of the final outcome but also when the mating procedure presents certain difficulties. A small male spider dances before a larger and ever ravenous female in an effort to induce her sexual interest rather than her hunger. Birds especially, however, depend on courtship as a preliminary to mating. The mating of birds represents copulation in its simplest form, without benefit of significant anatomical devices. Bird wings are a poor substitute for arms in a sexual embrace. Consequently the fullest cooperation between male and female is essential to success. In most birds a long-lasting, often lifetime, bonding becomes established between a male and female, a bonding that is usually reinforced by ritual behaviour at certain intervals, particularly during the onset of each breeding season and on various occasions when the individuals meet after short periods of separation. In some species a new mate may be taken each season or, as in sparrows, a general promiscuity may prevail.

One important aspect of courtship concerns the question of recognition. In gull colonies, for instance, members of the opposite sex look very much alike, and, at least to humans, the various individuals of one sex or the other may appear exactly the same. The advantages, with regard to successful production, incubation, and rearing of eggs and young, of permanent or semipermanent mate selection, however, are as great in gull colonies as elsewhere. The preliminaries to such a mutual selection not only establish a bond, by various posturings, but also establish the many small idiosyncrasies of action that add up to individuality and make one bird distinguishable among many within a colony, at least to its mate.

Many different forms of sex-oriented behaviour have consequently evolved among birds, depending on the character and particular needs of the various species. Penguins apparently not only look alike to human observers but also to themselves. Penguins seemingly have trouble even distinguishing between the sexes. Being unable to dance or sing, though they can make a lot of noise, male penguins can do little more than offer a pebble to a prospective female. If she accepts it as a token contribution to nest making, the match is on. If it is rejected, the suitor may have picked an unready female or even another male. In the case of most birds, however, the male can either sing, particularly the smaller kinds, or can strut and dance, with wings and feathers displayed, and some species, such as the lyre bird, continue to enchant the female by sight and sound together. In general, the need for physical mating has led to courtship and an emotional bonding between mating pairs throughout much of the animal kingdom at the higher level, particularly among birds and mammals. These are primarily utilitarian functions relating to the survival of the species, but in their fullest expression they represent what seem to man to be among the finest attributes of life.

SEX PATTERNS

Since the great value of sex as distinct from reproduction is the reassortment and recombination of genes every generation, sex cells from two separate parents ordinarily give rise to the greatest variation, unless the parental individuals are themselves too closely related to each other. The presence of male and female individuals, respectively, generally produced in approximately equal numbers, is characteristic of so much of the animal kingdom that it appears to be the natural state. All that is certain, however, is that this condition has evolved as the most effective means to the particular end, and it may have done so independently among the various more or less unrelated groups of animals. The condition of separate sexes is not a universal fact, and two sexes within the same individual is typical of the more sluggish or actually attached kinds of animal life. Earthworms, slugs, land snails, flatworms, tapeworms, barnacles, sea squirts, and some others are all double-sexed individuals, or hermaphrodites. All have ovaries and testes producing mature eggs and sperm at the same time. Nevertheless, cross-fertilization is accomplished, and self-fertilization, even though possible, is generally avoided. Of those kinds of animal life mentioned above, all except the sea squirts have well-encased eggs that need to be fertilized before being laid. Mutual copulation, whereby each member of a mating pair of individuals introduces sperm into the body of the other member, is characteristic of these creatures, with the exception of the sea squirts.

*Hermaph-
rodites*

When animals shed sperm and comparatively naked eggs into the surrounding water, as is the case in sea squirts, self-fertilization is difficult to avoid. Most creatures have evolved an effective separation of the sexes between different individuals. Even so, there are more ways than one of accomplishing this. The common means is to produce male and female individuals that are constitutionally different, yet an equally effective procedure is for all individuals to be constitutionally the same but to become mature as male or female at different stages of the growth cycle. The oyster on its rock changes sex from male to female and back again once or twice a year. Certain shrimps also are hermaphrodites. Each young shrimp of this kind grows up to be a male and is fully and functionally a male when about half the size of the females. As the next season approaches, his testes shrink, no more spermatozoa are produced, and ovaries begin to enlarge. As full growth is reached, the shrimp that had been a male becomes a typical female, ready to mate again, but this time with a young male of a newer generation. The system works as well as any other and clearly has its points. In fact the hagfish, not a true fish but a more primitive jawless vertebrate, also changes sex regularly, from year to year.

Sex differences in animals. In many animals, sexual differences are apparent in addition to the primary sex differentiation into males with testes and females with ovaries and apart from the accessory structures and tissues associated with the presence of one kind of sex gland or the other. Secondary sex differentiation in sexually distinct individuals is to be seen in many forms. In humans, for example, the beard and deep voice of the male and the enlarged breasts of the female are features of this sort. The great claw of the fiddler crab, the antlers of a moose, the great bulk and strength of a harem master in a fur seal colony, the beautiful fan tail of the peacock, and the bright feathers of other birds, are all dintinctively male characteristics, and all are associated with the sexual drive of males. Females, by and large, are of comparatively quiet disposition and relatively drab appearance. Their function is to produce and nurture eggs, as safely and usually as inconspicuously as possible. The male function is to find and fertilize the female, for which both drive and display are generally required.

It is the business of sperm to be active and so find an egg. Similarly it is the business of males to find a female and mate with her if possible. The male drive, or male eagerness, is a consequence of this special function of males. In nature, males possessing a strong eagerness to mate will find more females and leave more progeny than males lacking in sex drive. The progeny moreover will tend to inherit the drive of the parent. Males therefore are generally competitive with other males, with a premium placed on physical strength and sex drive and also on various devices for the attraction and stimulation of the female. The various exclusively male features already listed are all examples of characteristics of this sort, and they are related to the securing of female mates rather than the actual fertilization of eggs or to the problems of survival and adaptation.

Seasonal or periodic sexual cycles. In most animals sexual reproduction is seasonal or rhythmical, and so is sexual behaviour, whether in the form of courtship, drive, or other activities that lead to mating. In the marine fireworm of the West Indies, for instance, individuals of both sexes live in crevices on the sea floor but come out to breed where their fertilized eggs can drift and develop in the water above. But they can only find one another by means of the luminescence they themselves produce, which is an eerie light visible only in complete darkness. Each spring or summer month they emerge and swim to the surface about one-half hour after sunset when all daylight is gone but only before the moon can rise, a situation that confines them to a monthly breeding period of three or four days after the full of the moon. They follow a lunar rhythm. So do the grunion, a common fish along the southern California coast. Here again mating takes place when all is dark and the tide is high. Pairing occurs in the wash of the waves on the sand; fertilized eggs become immediately buried and there develop until the next high spring tides reach and wash the upper level sand nearly two weeks later. The mysterious biological clocks that apparently all living things possess adjust the rhythms of life to the needs of the particular organism. Some of these timing processes call internal signals on a regular day and night basis; others, on a somewhat longer cycle that keeps pace with the moon rather than the sun; and many, especially in the larger animals, run on a seasonal, or annual, cycle. Many activities are brought into line with the regular changes occurring in the environment. Sex and reproduction, however, are adjusted mainly with regard to two functions; namely, safety while mating, which is therefore commonly in the dark, and the launching of the new generation at a time or season when circumstances are most favourable.

*Biological
control of
sexual
cycles*

Birds lay eggs, and most mammals deliver their young in early spring, when the months ahead are warm and food is plentiful. Sex for the most part is adjusted to this end. Among the mammals, for example, the period of development within the womb varies greatly, from less than three weeks in the smallest to almost a year in the largest and certain others. Yet with few exceptions, the time for birth is in the spring. The time for mating in most cases is accordingly adjusted to this event: the larger the offspring at birth, the earlier the mating must take place. The horse and the great whales mate in spring and deliver in spring; roe deer mate in summer and deliver in spring; goat and sheep mate in the fall and deliver in spring. Even the elephant, which has a 22-month pregnancy, delivers in spring but must mate in early summer two years before. In small creatures, however, such as mice, rats, hamsters, and shrews, where the gestation, or pregnancy, period is about three weeks, reproduction is still seasonal, but there is time during the warmer months for several broods to be conceived and raised. In others, expediency may prevail, and mating may occur at a time to suit the convenience of the pairing animals. The little brown bat, for instance, mates in the fall, and yet ovulation does not take place until winter has passed; the spermatozoa survive the winter in the uterus and fertilize the eggs when they in turn arrive there five or six months later. In some other creatures mating occurs at a convenient time, eggs are fertilized, but development itself is suspended at an early stage for a time so that hatching or birthing, depending on the kind of animal, takes place when circumstances are suitable.

In all of this, the time of the mating season is clearly regulated, both with regard to the physiological condition of the animal and to the environmental conditions. The urge and capacity to mate depends on the ripeness of the gonads, male or female. In most animals the reproductive glands wax and wane according to the seasons; that is, with an annual rhythm or else with a shorter cycle. Hormones are mainly in control of this rhythm. Sex hormones, male or female, respectively, are produced by the gonads themselves and cause or maintain their growth and at the same time cause the various secondary sexual characteristics of the male or female individual to become enhanced. Male hormone increases masculinity, even when injected into a female. Female canaries injected with male hormone no longer behave as females and shortly begin to sing loud and long and commence the courtship activities of a male. A hen thus injected grows a larger comb, starts to crow, and begins to strut.

The production of these hormones is in turn controlled by hormones of the pituitary gland. Pituitary hormones stimulate ovarian or testicular tissue, which secretes the sex hormones. The sex hormones not only maintain the growth of the sexual tissues generally but inhibit the secretion of pituitary hormones, so that the process does not get out of hand. The pituitary activity, however, is also influenced by external conditions, particularly by stimuli received indirectly from light. The annual growth of ovaries or testes that occurs in late winter and early spring in frogs, reptiles, birds, and mammals is initiated by the steadily increasing period of daylight. In response to this changing day length, female frogs are packed with eggs and male frogs are ready to croak by the time the mating period arrives. The large eggs of reptiles and birds are ready to be fertilized, and the males are showing whatever they may have to display at the proper time. In mammals, the female comes into heat, the uterus undergoes the preparatory changes for taking care of fertilized eggs, and the male usually has but one thought in his mind. But as daylight ceases to lengthen, the sexual drive slowly diminishes.

SEX DETERMINATION

The determination of the sex of an individual, with regard to both the primary sex—*i.e.*, whether the ovaries or the testes develop—and the various secondary sexual characteristics may be rigorously controlled from the start of development or may be subject to later influences of a hormonal or environmental nature. However this may be, in order to appreciate the action of the control systems, the point of departure is that animals were primitively hermaphrodite, that during early stages of evolution every individual probably possessed both male and female gonads. Differentiation into separate sexes, each possessing male or female gonads but not both at the same time, is a device to ensure cross-fertilization of eggs, whether this is accomplished by having the two types of sexual gland mature at different stages of the growth of the individual, as in some shrimp and others, or whether by the production of two distinct types of individuals, as in most species of animals. This point of view is important because the question ceases to be how testes are caused to develop in the male organism and ovaries in the female but how, in a potentially double-sexed organism, the development of one or the other sex is suppressed. That such is the case is seen as clearly as anywhere in the human condition itself. Neither sex is completely male or female. Females have functional, well-developed mammary glands. Males also have mammary glands, undeveloped and nonfunctional although equipped with nipples. Males have a penis for delivering sperm, but females have a small, nonfunctional equivalent—the clitoris. These are secondary sexual features, to be sure, but the difference between the sexes is in the degree of their development, not a matter of absolute presence or absence.

The basis for this is seen in the very beginnings of the development of the reproductive system, in frog, mouse, and man alike. In the young embryo a pair of gonads develop that are indifferent or neutral, showing no indication whether they are destined to develop into testes or ovaries. There are also two different duct systems, one of which can develop into the female system of oviducts and related apparatus and the other into the male sperm duct system. As development of the embryo proceeds, either the male or the female reproductive tissue differentiates in the originally neutral gonad of the mammal.

In the frog and other lower vertebrate animals, the picture is even clearer. The original gonad consists of an outer layer of cells and an inner core of cells. If the individual is to be a male, the central tissue grows at the expense of the outer layer. If it is to be a female, the outer tissue grows at the expense of the central core tissue. If both should grow, which is a possibility although a rare occurrence, the individual will be a hermaphrodite. Anything that influences the direction taken therefore may be said to determine sex.

Sex chromosomes. In most species of animals the sex of individuals is determined decisively at the time of fertilization of the egg, by means of chromosomal distribution. This process is the most clear-cut form of sex determination. When any cell in the body divides, except during the formation of the sex cells, each daughter cell receives the full complement of chromosomes; *i.e.*, copies of the two sets of chromosomes derived from the sperm cell and egg, respectively. The two sets are similar except for one pair of chromosomes. These are the so-called sex chromosomes, and the pair may be exactly alike or they may be obviously different, depending on the sex of the individual. The sex chromosomes are of two types, which are designated X and Y, and the pair of sex chromosomes may consist of two X chromosomes or of an X and Y paired together. In mammals (including man) and flies, the cells of males contain an XY pair and the cells of females contain an XX pair. On the other hand, in butterflies, fishes, and birds, the cells of females contain an XY pair and those of males contain an XX pair. In either case the Y chromosome is generally smaller than the X chromosome and may even be absent. What is most important concerning chromosomal sex determination is whether the cells of the individual contain one X chromosome or two X chromosomes. Human beings, for example, have cells with 22 pairs of nonsexual chromosomes, or autosomes, together with an XX pair or an XY pair. The female has a total of 46 functional chromosomes; the male has 45 plus a Y, which is mainly inert. Sex determination thus becomes a matter of balance. With one X chromosome plus the 44 autosomes in every cell, the whole course of development of primary and secondary sexual characteristics is toward the male; with two X chromosomes plus the autosomes in every cell, the whole system is swung over to the female.

The manipulation of this control system is readily accomplished during the special process of cell division that takes place in the gonads to produce sperm and eggs and their subsequent union at fertilization. In mammals, for example, since all cells in the female contain two X chromosomes, all the eggs will receive a single X chromosome when they are formed. All eggs are accordingly the same in this respect. In contrast, all cells in the male have the XY constitution, and therefore, when the double set of chromosomes is reduced to a single set during the formation of the spermatozoa, half of the spermatozoa will receive an X and half will receive a Y. Consequently, when an egg is fertilized by a sperm, the chances are about equal that the sperm will carry an X or will carry a Y, since the two types are inevitably produced in equal numbers. If it carries an X, the XX female constitution results; if a Y, then the XY male constitution results.

Early develop-ment of reproduc-tive systems in young animals

Abnormal chromosome effects. Occasionally, however, the processes of chromosomal reassortment and recombination occurring during sex cell formation and fertilization depart somewhat from the normal course. Sperm and eggs may be produced that are oversupplied or undersupplied with sex chromosomes. Fertilized eggs in humans may, for instance, have abnormal sex chromosome constitutions such as XXX, XXY, or XO. Those with the triple-X chromosome constitution have all the appearance of normal females and are called, in fact, superfemales, although only some will be fertile. Those with the XO (one X, but lacking Y altogether) constitution, a much more common condition, are also feminine in body form and type of reproduction system but remain immature. Individuals with the XXY constitution are outwardly males but have small testes and produce no spermatozoa. Those with the more abnormal and relatively rarer constitutions XXXXY and XXYY are typically mentally defective and in the latter case are hard to manage. Thus abnormal combinations generally result in an infertility on the one hand and an abnormal sexuality in the whole system, for either too little or too much of what is ordinarily good can be disastrous.

Very different kinds of abnormal development resulting from faulty chromosomal distribution are particularly observable in insects. The most common form in flies is an individual that is male on one side, female on the other, with a sharp line of demarcation. In other cases one-quarter of the body may be male and three-quarters female, or the head may be female and the rest of the body, male. These types are known as gynandromorphs, or sexual mosaics, and result from aberration in the distribution of the X chromosomes among the first cells to be formed during the early development of the embryo. This condition is unknown among higher animals.

Parthenogenesis. The unfertilized, ripe egg possesses all the potentiality for full development. The process of fertilization by a spermatozoon introduces the nucleus of the male sex cell into the female egg, a process that increases the differences between parent and offspring and may determine the sex of the new individual and also stimulates the egg to begin development. These two functions are separate. Parthenogenetic development, without benefit of sperm, occurs naturally in various kinds of animals besides the waterflea (*Daphnia*), already described. Artificial, or experimental, parthenogenesis is readily brought about in many other species and by a variety of means. Mature, unfertilized eggs of starfish, sea urchins, various worms, and other marine invertebrate animals can be caused to develop by treatment with a weak organic acid. Unfertilized frog eggs can be readily caused to develop by gentle pricking of the egg surface with the tip of a fine glass needle that has been dipped in lymph. In nature the eggs of various creatures can develop with or without the aid of spermatozoa. The sex of parthenogenetically developed individuals, insofar as it depends on the chromosomal constitution of the developing egg, is consequently affected. Frog eggs developing parthenogenetically become males, since only one X chromosome is present in each cell. In nature, where varying conditions call for various responses, the system is usually more complicated, although based on the general relationship that individuals with the XX constitution will be female and those with a single X will be males. A queen honeybee, for instance, begins her reproductive life with a store of sperm received from a male during her nuptial flight. Throughout spring and summer almost all eggs become fertilized and develop into females (either as nonfertile female workers or as new fertile queens, depending on the nature of food received during growth). Toward the end of summer, when the sperm supply runs low, eggs cease to be fertilized and, when laid, develop into drones, ready to mate with a new queen should occasion arise. In other cases, even parthenogenetically developing eggs may become female individuals through a process of chromosome doubling, which takes place in the mature but unfertilized eggs. Thus certain wasps, waterfleas, and others are able to produce many exclusively female generations in succession.

Effects of environment on sex determination. Sex chromosomes, however, do not determine sex directly but do so through their control of such cell activities as metabolism and hormone production. Their determinative influence, indirect though it is, may be complete. On the other hand, environmental conditions may play the dominating role. In the case of *Bonellia*, a unique kind of marine worm, all eggs develop into small larvae of a sexually indifferent kind. Those that settle freely on the sea floor grow into comparatively large females, each of which has a long, broad extension, the proboscis, at its front end. Those larvae that happen to settle on the proboscis of a female, however, fail to grow beyond a certain minute size and become dwarf males, permanently attached to the female body. The sex-determining factor appears to be the environmental carbon dioxide tension, which is relatively high at the surface of living tissue.

Hormones. Because in most developing animals the reproductive gland is essentially neutral to begin with, there is generally some possibility that agents external to the gland, particularly chemical agents—*i.e.*, hormones—circulating in the blood system, may override the sex-determining influence of the sex chromosomes. In the chick, for example, the sex can be controlled experimentally by such means until about four hours after hatching. If a female chick is injected on hatching with the male sex hormone, testosterone, it will develop into a fully functional cock. Even when injected at later stages of growth, the male hormone causes extra early growth of the comb, crowing, and aggressive behaviour after being injected in either male or female chicks. Female sex hormones, such as estrogen, on the other hand, stimulate early growth of the oviduct in the female and feminize the plumage and suppress comb growth when injected in the male.

This susceptibility of the reproductive glands, and sexuality in general, to the influence of sex hormones is particularly acute in mammals, where the egg and embryo, unprotected by any shell, develop in the uterus exposed to various chemicals filtering through from the maternal blood stream. A developing embryo eventually produces its own sex hormones, but they are not manufactured in any quantity until the anatomical sex of the embryo is already well established. One of the curious things about sex hormones, however, is that the reproductive glands are not the only tissues that produce them. The placenta, through which all exchange between fetus and mother takes place, itself produces tremendous amounts of female sex hormone, together with some male hormone, which are excreted by the mother during pregnancy. This condition is true of humans, as well as of mice and rats. As a rule these hormones are produced too late to do any harm, but not always. The female embryo is fairly immune inasmuch as additional female hormone merely causes a child to be more feminine than usual at an early age. Male embryos, however, may be seriously affected if the female hormone catches them at an early stage. Boy babies may be born that are truly males but under the impact of the feminizing hormone appear superficially to be females and are often raised as such. As a rule, even when older, they have more or less sterile, undescended testes; an imperfect penis; well-developed breasts; an unbroken voice; and no beard. One in a thousand may be like this and on occasion may have won in women's Olympic competitions. In other cases, those somewhat less severely affected, during adolescence when the hidden testes begin to secrete their own male hormones in abundance, the falsely female characteristics become suppressed, and the voice, beard, breasts, and sexual interest take on the pattern of the male. What were thought to be girls in their youth change into the men they were meant to be upon reaching maturity.

BIBLIOGRAPHY. C.N. ARMSTRONG and A.J. MARSHAL (eds.), *Intersexuality in Vertebrates Including Man* (1964), a collection of articles by various authors dealing with all aspects of intersexuality in many kinds of animals, including humans, from physiological and genetic viewpoints; C.R. AUSTIN, *Fertilization* (1965), a concise general account of the nature of reproductive cells, the basic process of fertilization of the egg, and the various adaptive devices employed by animals and plants to ensure successful and normal fertilization, writ-

Sexual mosaics

Production and effects of sex hormones in mammals

ten for biology students; M. BASTOCK, "The Physiology of Courtship and Mating Behavior," *Advances in Reproductive Physiology*, 2:9-51 (1967), a review intended for biologists, but of general interest; N.J. BERRILL, *Sex and the Nature of Things* (1953), an award-winning inclusive account of sex, its diversity, and its significance in relation to evolution and animal behaviour, for the lay reader; *The Person in the Womb* (1968), a treatment of human development from conception to infancy, including the determination of sex at conception and the influence of hormones on sexuality during pregnancy; W.S. BULLOUGH, *The Vertebrate Reproductive Cycles*, 2nd ed. (1961), a short, concise account of reproduction, particularly in birds and mammals, with emphasis on hormonal and seasonal controls of sexual maturity and reproduction; L.J. and M.J.G. MILNE, *The Mating Instinct* (1954, paperback ed. 1968), very inclusive and detailed descriptions of the courting and mating behaviour of animals, extensively illustrated photographically; G. PINCUS, *The Control of Fertility* (1965), a highly scientific discussion, by a pioneering authority, of the reproductive process in man and other mammals, with emphasis on the action of hormones on sex cell production, on the first stages of development, and on the problems of fertility; H. WENDT, *The Sex Life of Animals* (1965), a very descriptive account of courting and mating, and sexuality generally, throughout the animal kingdom, translated from an earlier German edition; G.C. WILLIAMS, *Adaptation and Natural Selection* (1966), an illuminating and thoughtful discussion of sexual reproduction in relation to the processes of biological evolution and adaptation.

(N.J.B.)

Sexual Behaviour, Human

Sexual behaviour may be defined as any activity—solitary, between two persons, or in a group—that induces sexual arousal. There are two major determinants of sexual behaviour: the inherited sexual response patterns that have evolved as a means of ensuring reproduction and that are a part of each individual's genetic inheritance, and the degree of restraint or other types of influence exerted on the individual by society in the expression of his sexuality. The objective of this article is to describe and explain both sets of factors and their interaction. It begins with an analysis of the range of human sexual behaviour in terms of the number and gender of the participants and goes on to describe the physiological processes involved in such activity and in the life cycle of the individual. Having thus established the physiological determinants involved, the article moves on to an account of the influence of learning and conditioning in the early years of life and the range, development, and therapy of sexual problems that are often directly related to this early conditioning and to other socially induced inhibitions. In the final section human sexuality is discussed in a much broader cultural and historical perspective, describing varying attitudes and degrees of permissiveness in different cultures and historical periods, common means of social control of sexual activity, and the influence of such factors as religion and socio-economic developments, and concluding with legal regulations of sexual activity. (For a discussion of homosexuality and other deviations, see SEXUAL DEVIATIONS.)

It should be noted that taboos in Western culture and the immaturity of the social sciences for a long time impeded research concerning human sexual behaviour, so that by the early 20th century scientific knowledge was largely restricted to individual case histories that had been studied by such European writers as Sigmund Freud, Havelock Ellis, and Richard, Freiherr von Krafft-Ebing. By the 1920s, however, the foundations had been laid for the more extensive statistical studies that were conducted before World War II in the United States. Of the two major organizations for sex study, one, the Institut für Sexualwissenschaft in Berlin (established in 1897), was destroyed by the Nazis in 1933. The other, the Institute for Sex Research, begun in 1938 by the American sexologist Alfred Charles Kinsey at Indiana University, Bloomington, undertook the study of many aspects of human sexual behaviour. Much of the following discussion rests on the findings of the Institute for Sex Research, which comprise the most comprehensive data available. The only other country for which comprehensive data exist is Sweden.

Physiological and psychological aspects

TYPES OF BEHAVIOUR

Human sexual behaviour may conveniently be classified according to the number and gender of the participants. There is solitary behaviour involving only one individual, and there is socio-sexual behaviour involving more than one person. Socio-sexual behaviour is generally divided into heterosexual behaviour (male with female) and homosexual behaviour (male with male or female with female). If three or more individuals are involved it is, of course, possible to have heterosexual and homosexual activity simultaneously.

In both solitary and socio-sexual behaviour there may be activities that are sufficiently unusual to warrant the label deviant behaviour. The term deviant should not be used as a moral judgment but simply as indicating that such activity is not common in a particular society. Since human societies differ in their sexual practices, what is deviant in one society may be normal in another.

Solitary behaviour. Self-masturbation is self-stimulation with the intention of causing sexual arousal and, generally, orgasm (sexual climax). Most masturbation is done in private as an end in itself but is sometimes practiced to facilitate a socio-sexual relationship.

Masturbation, generally beginning at or before puberty, is extremely common in males, particularly among young males, but becomes less frequent or is even abandoned when socio-sexual activity is available. Consequently, masturbation is most frequent among the unmarried. Fewer females masturbate; in the United States, roughly one-half to two-thirds have done so, as compared to nine out of ten males. Females also tend to reduce or discontinue masturbation when they develop socio-sexual relationships. There is great individual variation in frequency, so that it is impractical to try to define what range could be considered "normal."

The myth persists, despite scientific proof to the contrary, that masturbation is physically harmful. Neither is there evidence that masturbation is immature behaviour; it is common among adults deprived of socio-sexual opportunities. While solitary masturbation does provide pleasure and relief from the tension of sexual excitement, it does not have the same psychological gratification that interaction with another person provides; thus, extremely few people prefer masturbation to socio-sexual activity. The psychological significance of masturbation lies in how the individual regards it. For some, it is laden with guilt; for others, it is a release from tension with no emotional content; and for others it is simply another source of pleasure to be enjoyed for its own sake.

The majority of males and females have fantasies of some socio-sexual activity while they masturbate. The fantasy not infrequently involves idealized sexual partners and activities that the individual has not experienced and even might avoid in real life.

Since the masturbating person is in sole control of the areas that are stimulated, the degree of pressure, and the rapidity of movement, masturbation is often more effective in producing sexual arousal and orgasm than is socio-sexual activity, during which the stimulation is determined to some degree by one's partner.

Orgasm in sleep evidently occurs only in humans. Its causes are not wholly known. The idea that it results from the pressure of accumulated semen is invalid because not only do nocturnal emissions sometimes occur in males on successive nights, but females experience orgasm in sleep as well. In some cases orgasm in sleep seems a compensatory phenomenon, occurring during times when the individual has been deprived of or abstains from other sexual activity. In other cases it may result from external stimuli, such as sleeping prone or having night clothing caught between one's legs. Most orgasms during sleep are accompanied by erotic dreams.

A great majority of males experience orgasm in sleep. This almost always begins and is most frequent in adolescence, tending to disappear later in life. Fewer females have orgasm in sleep, and, unlike males, they usually begin having such experience when fully adult.

Attitudes toward masturbation

Orgasm in sleep is generally infrequent, seldom exceeding a dozen times per year for males and three or four times a year for the average female.

Most sexual arousal does not lead to sexual activity with another individual. Humans are constantly exposed to sexual stimuli when seeing attractive persons and are subjected to sexual themes in advertising and the mass media. Response to such visual and other stimuli is strongest in adolescence and early adult life and usually gradually declines with advancing age. One of the necessary tasks of growing up is learning to cope with one's sexual arousal and to achieve some balance between suppression, which can be injurious, and free expression, which can lead to social difficulties. There is great variation among individuals in the strength of sex drive and responsiveness, so this necessary exercise of restraint is correspondingly difficult or easy.

Socio-sexual behaviour. By far the greatest amount of socio-sexual behaviour is heterosexual behaviour between only one male and one female. Heterosexual behaviour frequently begins in childhood, and, while much of it may be motivated by curiosity, such as showing or examining genitalia, many children engage in sex play because it is pleasurable. The sexual impulse and responsiveness are present in varying degrees in most children and latent in the remainder. With adolescence, sex play is superseded by dating, which is socially encouraged, and dating almost inevitably involves some physical contact resulting in sexual arousal. This contact, labelled necking or petting, is a part of the learning process and ultimately of courtship and the selection of a marriage partner.

Petting
and
foreplay Petting varies from hugging, kissing, and generalized caresses of the clothed body to techniques involving genital stimulation. Petting may be done for its own sake as an expression of affection and a source of pleasure, and it may occur as a preliminary to coitus. This last form of petting is known as foreplay. In a minority of cases, but a substantial minority, petting leads to orgasm and may be a substitute for coitus. Excluding foreplay, petting is usually very stereotyped, beginning with hugging and kissing and gradually escalating to stimulation of the breasts and genitalia. In most societies petting and its escalation are initiated by the male more often than by the female, who generally rejects or accepts the male's overtures but refrains from playing a more aggressive role. Petting in some form is a near-universal human experience and is valuable not only in mate selection but as a means of learning how to interact with another person sexually.

Coitus, the insertion of the penis into the vagina, is viewed by society quite differently depending upon the marital status of the individuals. The majority of human societies permit premarital coitus, at least under certain circumstances. In more repressive societies, such as modern Western society, it is more likely to be tolerated (but not encouraged) if the individuals intend marriage. Marital coitus is usually regarded as an obligation in most societies. Extramarital coitus, particularly by wives, is generally condemned and, if permitted, is allowed only under exceptional conditions or with specified persons. Societies tend to be more lenient toward males than females regarding extramarital coitus. This double standard of morality is also seen in premarital life. Postmarital coitus (*i.e.*, coitus by separated, divorced or widowed persons) is almost always ignored. Even societies that try to confine coitus to marriage recognize the difficulty of trying to force abstinence upon sexually experienced and usually older persons.

In the United States and much of Europe, there has been, within the last century, a progressive trend toward an increase in premarital coitus. Currently in the United States, at least three-quarters of the males and over half of the females have experienced premarital coitus. The proportions for this experience vary in different groups and socio-economic classes. In Scandinavia, the incidence of premarital coitus is far greater, exceeding the 90 percent mark in Sweden, where it is now expected behaviour.

Extramarital coitus continues to be openly condemned but is becoming more tolerated secretly, particularly if mitigating circumstances are involved. In some areas, such as southern Europe and Latin America, extramarital coitus is expected of most husbands and is accepted by society if the behaviour is not too flagrant. The wives do not generally approve but are resigned to what they believe to be a masculine propensity. In the United States, where at least half the husbands and one-quarter of the wives have extramarital coitus at some point in their lives, there have recently developed small organizations or clubs that exist to provide extramarital coitus for married couples. Despite the publicity they have engendered, however, extremely few individuals have belonged to such organizations. Most extramarital coitus is done secretly without the knowledge of the spouse. Most husbands and wives feel very possessive of their spouses and interpret extramarital activity as an aspersion on their own sexual adequacy, as indicating a loss of affection and as being a source of social disgrace.

Human beings are not inherently monogamous but have a natural desire for diversity in their sexuality as in other aspects of life. Some societies have provided a release for these desires by suspending the restraints on extramarital coitus on special occasions or with certain individuals, and in modern Western society a certain amount of extramarital flirtation or mild petting at parties is not considered unusual behaviour.

Sexuality
in
ceremony
and
religion Discussion of socio-sexual behaviour would be incomplete without some note of the role it has played in ceremony and religion. While the major religions of today are to varying degrees anti-sexual, many religions have incorporated sexual behaviour into their rites and ceremonies. The ancient and continuing interest of man in the fertility of food plants, animals, and himself makes such a connection between sex and religion inevitable, particularly among peoples with uncertain food supplies. In most religions the deities were considered to have active sexual lives and sometimes took a sexual interest in humans. In this regard it is noteworthy that in Christianity sexual behaviour is absent in heaven and sexual proclivities are ascribed only to evil supernatural beings: Satan, devils, incubi, and succubi (spirits or demons who seek out sleeping humans for sexual intercourse).

Whether or not a behaviour is interpreted by society or the individual as erotic (*i.e.*, capable of engendering sexual response) depends chiefly on the context in which the behaviour occurs. A kiss, for example, may express asexual affection (a mother kissing a child or a kiss between relatives), respect (as a French officer kissing a soldier after bestowing a medal on him), reverence (kissing the hand or foot of a pope), or it may be a casual salutation and social amenity. Even something as specific as touching genitalia is not construed as sexual if done for medical reasons. In other words, the apparent motivation of the behaviour determines its interpretation.

Individuals are extremely sensitive in judging motivations: a greeting kiss, if protracted more than a second or two, takes on a sexual connotation, and recent studies show that if an adult male at a party stands closer than the length of his hand and forearm to a female, she generally imputes a sexual motive to his proximity. Nudity is construed as erotic or even as a sexual invitation—unless it occurs in a medical context, in a group consisting of but one gender, or in a nudist camp.

PHYSIOLOGICAL ASPECTS

Sexual response. Sexual response follows a pattern of sequential stages or phases when sexual activity is continued. First, there is the excitement phase marked by increase in pulse and blood pressure, an increase in blood supply to the surface of the body resulting in increased skin temperature, flushing, and swelling of all distensible body parts (particularly noticeable in the penis and female breasts), more rapid breathing, the secretion of genital fluids, vaginal expansion, and a general increase in muscle tension. These symptoms of arousal eventually increase to a near maximal physiological level, the plateau phase, which is generally of brief duration. If stimulation is continued, orgasm usually occurs. Orgasm is marked by a feeling of sudden intense pleasure, an abrupt increase in pulse rate and blood pressure, and spasms of the pelvic muscles causing vaginal contractions in the female and ejaculation by the male. Involuntary vocalization may also occur. Orgasm lasts for a few seconds (normally not over ten), after which the individual enters the resolution phase, the return to a normal or subnormal physiological state. Up to the resolution phase, males and females are the same in their response sequence, but, whereas males return to normal even if stimulation continues, continued stimulation can produce additional orgasms in females. In brief, after one orgasm a male becomes unresponsive to sexual stimulation and cannot begin to build up another excitement phase until some period of time has elapsed, but females are physically capable of repeated orgasms without the intervening "rest period" required by males.

Genetic and hormonal factors. While all normal individuals are born with the neurophysiology necessary for the sexual-response cycle described above, inheritance determines the intensity of their responses and their basic "sex drive." There is great variation in this regard: some persons have the need for frequent sexual expressions; others require very little; and some persons respond quickly and violently, while others are slower and milder in their reactions. While the genetic basis of these differences is unknown and while such variations are obscured by conditioning, there is no doubt that sexual capacities, like all other physiological capacities, are genetically determined. It is unlikely, however, that genes control the sexual orientation of normal humans in the sense of individuals being predestined to become homosexual or heterosexual. Some severe genetic abnormality can, of course, profoundly affect intelligence, sexual capacity, and physical appearance and hence the entire sexual life.

Genetic combinations in the sexes

While the normal female has 44 autosomes plus two X-chromosomes (female) and the normal male 44 autosomes plus one X-chromosome and one Y-chromosome (male), many genetic abnormalities are possible. These are females, for example, with too many X-chromosomes (44 + XXX) or too few (44 + X) and males with an extra female chromosome (44 + XXY) or an extra male chromosome (44 + XYY). No 44 + YY males exist—an X-chromosome is necessary for survival, even in the womb.

One's genetic makeup determines one's hormonal status and the sensitivity of one's body to these hormones. While a disorder of any part of the endocrine system can adversely affect sexual life, the hormones most directly influencing sexuality are the androgens (male sex hormones), produced chiefly in the testicles, and the estrogens (female sex hormones), produced chiefly in the ovaries. In early embryonic life there are neither testicles nor ovaries but simply two undifferentiated organs (gonads) that can develop either into testicles or ovaries. If the embryo has a Y-chromosome, the gonads become testicles; otherwise, they become ovaries. The testicles of the fetus produce androgens, and these cause the fetus to develop male anatomy. The absence of testicles results in the development of female anatomy. Animal experiments show that, if the testicles of a male fetus are removed, the individual will develop into what seems a female (although lacking ovaries). Consequently, it has been said that humans are basically female.

After birth and until puberty, the ovaries and testicles produce comparatively few hormones, and little girls and boys are much alike in size and appearance. At puberty, however, these organs begin producing in greater abundance, with dramatic results. The androgens produced by boys cause changes in body build, greater muscular development, body and facial hair, and voice change. In girls the estrogens cause breast development, menstruation, and feminine body build. A boy castrated before puberty does not develop masculine physical characteristics and manifests in adult life more of a feminine body build, lack of masculine body and facial hair, less muscular strength, a high voice, and small genitalia. A girl who has her ovaries removed before puberty is less markedly altered but retains a childlike body build, does not develop breasts, and never menstruates. Castrated individuals or persons producing insufficient hormones can be restored to a normal condition by administration of appropriate hormones.

Beyond their role in developing the secondary sexual characteristics of the body, the hormones continue to play a role in adult life. An androgen deficiency causes a decrease in a man's sexual responsiveness, and an estrogen deficiency adversely affects a woman's fertility and causes atrophy of the genitalia. A loss of energy may also result in both men and women.

Androgen seems linked in both males and females with aggressiveness and strength of sexual drive. When androgen is given to a female in animal experiments, she becomes more aggressive and displays behaviour more typical of males—by mounting other animals, for example. Estrogen increases her sexual responsiveness and intensifies her female behaviour. Androgen given to a male often increases his sexual behaviour, but estrogen diminishes his sex drive.

Role of androgen and estrogen

In humans the picture is more complex, since human sexual behaviour and response is less dependent on hormones once adulthood has been reached. Removing androgen from an adult male reduces his sexual capacity; but this occurs gradually, and sometimes the reduction is small. Giving androgen to a normal human male generally has little or no effect since he is already producing all he can use. Giving him estrogen reduces his sex drive. Administration of androgen to an adult human female often increases her sex drive, enlarges her clitoris, and promotes the growth of facial hair. Giving estrogen to a normal woman before menopausal age generally has no effect whatsoever—probably because human females, unlike other female mammals, do not have hormonally controlled periods of "heat" (estrus).

Hormones have no connection with the sexual orientation of humans. Male homosexuals do not have more estrogens than normal males (who have a little) nor can their preferences be altered by giving them androgen.

Nervous system factors. The nervous system consists of the central nervous system and the peripheral nervous system. The brain and spinal cord constitute the central system, while the peripheral system is composed of (1) the cerebrospinal nerves that go to the spinal cord (afferent nerves), transmitting sensory stimuli and those that come from the cord (efferent nerves) transmitting impulses to activate muscles, and (2) the autonomic system, the primary function of which is the regulation and maintenance of the body processes necessary to life, such as heart rate, breathing, digestion, and temperature control. Sexual response involves the entire nervous system. The autonomic system controls the involuntary responses; the afferent cerebrospinal nerves carry the sensory messages to the brain; the efferent cerebrospinal nerves carry commands from the brain to the muscles; and the spinal cord serves as a great transmission cable. The brain itself is the coordinating and controlling centre, interpreting what sensations are to be perceived as sexual and issuing appropriate "orders" to the rest of the nervous system.

The parts of the brain thought to be most concerned with sexual response are the hypothalamus and the limbic system, but no specialized "sex centre" has been located in the human brain. Animal experiments indicate that each individual has coded in its brain two sexual response patterns, one for mounting (masculine) behaviour and one for mounted (feminine) behaviour. The mounting pattern can be elicited or intensified by male sex hormone and the mounted pattern by female sex hormone. Normally, one response pattern is dominant and the other latent but capable of being called into action when suitable circumstances occur. The degree to which such inherent patterning exists in humans is unknown.

While the brain is normally in charge, there is some reflex (*i.e.*, not brain-controlled) sexual response. Stimulation of the genital and perineal area can cause the "genital reflex": erection and ejaculation in the male, vaginal changes and lubrication in the female. This reflex is mediated by the lower spinal cord, and the brain need not be involved. Of course, the brain can override and suppress such reflex activity—as it does when an individual decides that a sexual response is socially inappropriate.

Development and changes of the reproductive system.
One's anatomy and sexuality change with age. The
changes are rapid in intra-uterine life and around puberty but are much slower and gradual in other phases of
the life cycle.

Intra-
uterine
sexual
develop-
ment

The reproductive organs first develop in the same form
for both males and females: internally there are two
undifferentiated gonads and two pairs of parallel ducts
(Wolffian and Müllerian ducts); externally there is a genital protrusion with a groove (urethral groove) below it,
the groove being flanked by two folds (urethral folds).
On either side of the genital protrusion and groove are
two ridgelike swellings (labioscrotal swellings). Around
the fourth week of life the gonads differentiate into either
testes or ovaries. If testes develop, the hormone they
secrete causes the Müllerian duct to degenerate and almost vanish and causes the Wolffian duct to elaborate
into the sperm-carrying tubes and related organs (the vas
deferens, epididymis, and seminal vesicles, for example).
If ovaries develop, the Wolffian duct deteriorates, and the
Müllerian duct elaborates to form the fallopian tubes,
uterus, and part of the vagina. The external genitalia
simultaneously change. The genital protrusion becomes
either a penis or clitoris. In the female the groove below
the clitoris stays open to form the vulva, and the folds on
either side of the groove become the inner lips of the
vulva (the labia minora). In the male these folds grow
together, converting the groove into the urethral tube of
the penis. The ridgelike swellings on either side remain
apart in the female and constitute the large labia (labia
majora), but in the male they grow together to form the
scrotal sac into which the testes subsequently descend.

At the time of birth both male and female have all the
neurophysiological equipment necessary for sexual response, although the reproductive system is not at this
stage functional. Sexual interests, sexual behaviour, and
sexual response are seen with increasing frequency in
most children from infancy on. Even newborn males
have penile erections, and babies of both sexes seem to
find some pleasure in genital stimulation. What appears
to be orgasm has been observed in infant boys and girls,
and, later in childhood, orgasm definitely can occur in
self-masturbation or sex play.

Puberty may be defined as that short period of time
(generally two years) during which the reproductive
system matures and the secondary sexual characteristics
appear. The ovaries and testes begin producing much
larger amounts of hormones, pubic hair appears, female
breasts develop, the menstrual cycle begins in females,
spermatozoa and viable eggs are produced, and males
experience voice change and a sudden acceleration in
growth. Puberty generally occurs in females around age
12–13 and in males at about 13–14, but there is much
individual variation. With puberty there is generally an
intensification or the first appearance of sexual interest.
Puberty marks the beginning of adolescence.

Adolescence, from a physical viewpoint, is that period
between puberty and the attainment of one's maximum
height. By the latter point, which occurs around age 16 in
females and 18 in males, the individual has adult anatomy and physiology. In late adolescence the majority of
individuals are probably at their peak in terms of sexual
capacity: the ability to respond quickly and repeatedly.
During this period the sex drive is at its maximum in
males, although it is difficult to say whether this is also
true of females, since female sexuality, in many societies,
is frequently suppressed during adolescence.

Following adolescence there are about three decades of
adult life during which physiological changes are slow
and gradual. While muscular strength increases for a
time, the changes may best be described as slow deterioration. This physical decline is not immediately evident in
sexual behaviour, which often increases in quantity and
quality as the individual develops more social skills and
higher socio-economic status and loses some of the inhibitions and uncertainties that often impede adolescent sexuality. Indeed, in the case of the United States female, the
deterioration is more than offset by her gradual loss of
sexual inhibition, and the effect of age is not clear until

menopausal symptoms begin. In the male, however, there
is no such masking of deterioration, and the frequency of
sexual activity and the intensity of interest and response
slowly, but inexorably, decline.

If one must arbitrarily select an age to mark the beginning of old age, 50 is appropriate. By then, most females
have experienced menopausal symptoms, and most males
have been forced to recognize their increasing physical
limitations. With menopause, the female genitalia gradually begin to atrophy and the amount of vaginal secretion
diminishes—this is the direct consequence of the cessation of ovarian function and can be prevented, or the
symptoms reversed, by administering estrogen. If a female has had a good sexual adjustment prior to menopause and if she does not believe in the fallacy that it
spells the end of sexual life, menopause will have no
adverse effect on her sexual and orgasmic ability. There is
reason to believe that if a woman remains in good health
and genital atrophy is prevented, she could enjoy sexual
activity regardless of age. Males in good health are also
capable of continuing sexual activity, although with an
ever-decreasing frequency, throughout old age. The male
has more difficulty in achieving erection, cannot maintain
erection as long, and must have longer and longer "rest
periods" between sexual acts. The amount of ejaculate
becomes less, but most old males are still fertile. The
Cowper's gland secretion (called "precoital mucus") diminishes or disappears entirely. According to Kinsey's
data, about one-quarter of males are impotent by age 65,
one-half by age 75, and three-quarters by age 80. One
must remember, however, that some unknown but certainly substantial proportion of this impotence may be
attributed to poor health.

Sexual
changes
in later
life

In general, the female withstands the onslaughts of age
better than the male. The reduction in the frequency of
marital intercourse or even its abandonment is more often than not the result of male deterioration.

PSYCHOLOGICAL ASPECTS

Effects of early conditioning.   Physiology sets only very
broad limits on human sexuality; most of the enormous
variation found among humans must be attributed to
the psychological factors of learning and conditioning.

The human infant is born simply with the ability to
respond sexually to tactile stimulation. It is only later and
gradually that the individual learns or is conditioned to
respond to other stimuli, to develop a sexual attraction to
males or females or both, to interpret some stimuli as
sexual and others as nonsexual, and to control in some
measure his or her sexual response. In other words, the
general and diffuse sexuality of the infant becomes increasingly elaborated, differentiated, and specific.

The early years of life are, therefore, of paramount
importance in the development of what ultimately becomes adult sexual orientation. There appears to be a
reasonably fixed sequence of development. Before age
five, the child develops a sense of gender identity, thinks
of himself or herself as a boy or girl, and begins to relate
to others differently according to their gender. Through
experience the child learns what behaviour is rewarded
and what is punished and what sorts of behaviour are
expected of him or her. Parents, peers, and society in
general teach and condition the child about sex not so
much by direct informational statements and admonitions as by indirect and often unconscious communication. The child soon learns, for example, that he can
touch any part of his body or someone else's body except
the anal–genital region. The child rubbing its genitals
finds that this quickly attracts adult attention and admon-
ishment or that adults will divert him or her from this
activity. It becomes clear that there is something peculiar
and taboo about this area of the body. This "genital
taboo" is reinforced by the great concern over the child's
excretory behaviour: bladder and bowel control is
praised; loss of control is met with disappointment, chiding,
and expressions of disgust. Obviously, the anal–genital
area is not only a taboo area but a very important one as
well. It is almost inevitable that the genitalia become
associated with anxiety and shame. It is noteworthy that

Develop-
ment
of genital
taboo

this attitude finds expression in the language of Western civilizations, as in "privates" (something to be kept hidden) and the German word for the genitals, *Scham* ("shame").

While all children in Western civilizations experience this anti-sexual teaching and conditioning, a few have, in addition, atypical sexual experiences, such as witnessing or hearing sexual intercourse or having sexual contact with an older person. The effects of such atypical experiences depend upon how the child interprets them and upon the reaction of adults if the experience comes to their attention. Seeing parental coitus is harmless if the child interprets it as playful wrestling but harmful if he considers it as hostile, assaultive behaviour. Similarly, an experience with an adult may seem merely a curious and pointless game, or it may be a hideous trauma leaving lifelong psychic scars. In many cases the reaction of parents and society determines the child's interpretation of the event. What would have been a trivial and soon-forgotten act becomes traumatic if the mother cries, the father rages, and the police interrogate the child.

Some atypical developments occur through association during the formative years. A child may associate clothing, especially underclothing, stockings, and shoes with gender and sex and thereby establish the basis for later fetishism or transvestism. Others, having been spanked or otherwise punished for self-masturbation or childhood sex play, form an association between punishment, pain, and sex that could escalate later into sadism or masochism. It is not known why some children form such associations whereas others with apparently similar experience do not.

Around the age of puberty, parents and society, who more often than not refuse to recognize that children have sexual responses and capabilities, finally face the inescapable reality and consequently begin inculcating children with their attitudes and standards regarding sex. This campaign by adults is almost wholly negative—the child is told what not to do. While dating may be encouraged, no form of sexual activity is advocated or held up as model behaviour. The message usually is "be popular" (*i.e*, sexually attractive), but abstain from sexual activity. This anti-sexualism is particularly intense regarding young females and is reinforced by reference to pregnancy, venereal disease, and, most importantly, social disgrace. To this list religious families add the concept of the sinfulness of premarital sexual expression. With young males the double standard of morality still prevails. The youth receives a double message, "don't do it, but we expect that you will." No such loophole in the prohibitions is offered young girls. Meanwhile, the young male's peer group is exerting a prosexual influence, and his social status is enhanced by his sexual exploits or by exaggerated reports thereof.

Effects of the double standard on the sexual relations of the young

As a result of this double standard of sexual morality, the relationship between young males and females often becomes a ritualized contest, the male attempting to escalate the sexual activity and the female resisting his efforts. Instead of mutuality and respect, one often has a struggle in which the female is viewed as a reluctant sexual object to be exploited, and the male is viewed as a seducer and aggressor who must succeed in order to maintain his self-image and his status with his peers. This sort of pathological relationship causes a lasting attitude on the part of females: men are not to be trusted; they are interested only in sex; a girl dare not smile or be friendly lest males interpret it as a sign of sexual availability, and so forth. Such an aura of suspicion, hostility, and anxiety is scarcely conducive to the development of warm, trusting relationships between males and females. Fortunately, love or infatuation usually overcomes this negativism with regard to particular males, but the average female still maintains a defensive and skeptical attitude toward men.

Western society is replete with attitudes that impede the development of a healthy attitude toward sex. The free abandon so necessary to a full sexual relationship is, in the eyes of many, an unseemly loss of self-control, and self-control is something one is urged to maintain from infancy onward. Panting, sweating, and involuntary vo-

calization are incompatible with the image of dignity. Worse yet is any substance once it has left the body: it immediately becomes unclean. The male and female genital fluids are generally regarded with disgust—they are not only excretions but sexual excretions. Here again, societal concern over excretion is involved, for sexual organs are also urinary passages and are in close proximity to the "dirtiest" of all places—the anus. Lastly, many individuals in society regard menstrual fluid with disgust and abstain from sexual intercourse during the four to six days of flow. This attitude is formalized in Judaism, in which menstruating females are specifically labelled as ritually unclean.

In view of all of these factors working against a healthy, rational attitude toward sex and in view of the inevitable disappointments, exploitations, and rejections that are involved in human relationships, one might wonder how anyone could reach adulthood without being seriously maladjusted. The sexual impulse, however, is sufficiently strong and persistent and repeated sexual activity gradually erodes the inhibitions and any sense of guilt or shame. Further, all humans have a deep need to be esteemed, wanted, and loved. Sexual activity with another is seen as proof that one is attractive, desired, valued, and possibly loved—a proof very necessary to self-esteem and happiness. Hence, even among the very inhibited or those with weak sex drive, there is this powerful motivation to engage in socio-sexual activity.

Most persons ultimately achieve at least a tolerable sexual adjustment. Some unfortunates, nevertheless, remain permanently handicapped, and very few completely escape the effects of society's anti-sexual conditioning. While certain inhibitions and restraints are socially and psychologically useful—such as deferring gratification until circumstances are appropriate and modifying behaviour out of regard for the feelings of others—most people labour under an additional burden of useless and deleterious attitudes and restrictions.

Sexual problems. Sexual problems may be classified as physiological, psychological, and social in origin. Any given problem may involve all three categories; a physiological problem, for example, will produce psychological effects, and these may result in some social maladjustment.

Physiological problems of a specifically sexual nature are rather few. Only a small minority of people suffer from diseases of or deficient development of the genitalia or that part of the neurophysiology governing sexual response. A large number of persons, however, experience, at some point in life, sexual problems that are by-products of other pathologies or injuries. Vaginal infections, for example, retroverted uteri, prostatitis, adrenal tumours, diabetes, senile changes of the vagina, and cardiovascular conditions may cause disturbance of the sexual life. In brief, anything that seriously interferes with normal bodily functioning generally causes some degree of sexual trouble. Fortunately, the great majority of physiological sexual problems are solved through medication or surgery. Generally, only those problems involving damage to the nervous system defy therapy.

Psychological problems constitute by far the largest category. They are not only the product of socially induced inhibitions, maladaptive attitudes, and ignorance but also of sexual myths held by society. An example of the latter is the idea that good, mature sex must involve rapid erection, protracted coitus, and simultaneous orgasm. Magazines, marriage books, and general sexual folklore reinforce these demanding ideals, which cannot always be met and hence give rise to anxiety, guilt, and feelings of inadequacy.

Premature ejaculation is a common problem, especially for young males. Sometimes this is not the consequence of any psychological problem but the natural result of excessive tension in a male who has been sexually deprived. In such cases, more frequent coitus solves the problem. Premature ejaculation is difficult to define. The best definition is that offered by the American sexologists, William Howell Masters and Virginia Eshelman Johnson, who say that a male suffers from premature ejaculation if

Premature ejaculation and its therapy

he cannot delay ejaculation long enough to induce orgasm in a sexually normal female at least half the time. This generally means that vaginal penetration with some movement (although not continuous) must be maintained for more than one minute. The average United States male ejaculates in two or three minutes after vaginal penetration, a coital duration sufficient to cause orgasm in most females the majority of the time. Various methods of preventing premature ejaculation have been tried. One is for the male to excite the female more during the foreplay so that she reaches orgasm more rapidly after penetration, but this technique often excites the male as well and defeats its purpose. Another common method is for the male to think of nonsexual matters, which may prove effective but reduces his pleasure. The most effective therapy is that advocated by Masters and Johnson in which the female brings the male nearly to orgasm and then prevents the male's orgasm by briefly compressing the penis between her fingers just below the head of the penis. The couple come to realize that premature ejaculation can thus be easily prevented, their anxiety disappears, and ultimately they can achieve normal coitus without resorting to this squeeze technique.

Erectile impotence is almost always of psychological origin in males under 40; in older males physical causes are more often involved. Fear of being impotent frequently causes impotence, and, in many cases, the afflicted male is simply caught up in a self-perpetuating problem that can only be solved by achieving a successful act of coitus. In other cases, the impotence may be the result of disinterest in the sexual partner, fatigue, distraction because of nonsexual worries, intoxication, or other causes—such occasional impotency is common and requires no therapy. Some males, however, are chronically impotent and require psychotherapy or behaviour therapy. Such impotency is thought to be the result of deep-seated causal factors such as unconscious feelings of hostility, fear, inadequacy, or guilt. Primary impotence, the inability to ever have achieved erection sufficient for coitus, is more difficult to treat than the far more common secondary impotence, which is impotence in a male who was formerly potent.

Ejaculatory impotence, the inability to ejaculate in coitus, is quite rare and is almost always of psychogenic origin. It seems associated with ideas of contamination or with memories of traumatic experiences. Occasional ejaculatory inability may be expected in older men or in any male who has exceeded his sexual capacity and should cause no concern.

Vaginismus and dyspareunia

Vaginismus is a powerful spasm of the pelvic musculature constricting the vagina so that penetration is painful or impossible. It seems wholly due to anti-sexual conditioning or psychological trauma and serves as an unconscious defense against coitus. It is treated by psychotherapy and by gradually dilating the vagina with increasingly large cylinders.

Dyspareunia, painful coitus, is generally physical rather than psychological. It is mentioned here only because some inexperienced females fear they cannot accommodate a penis without being painfully stretched. This is a needless fear since the vagina is not only highly elastic but enlarges with sexual arousal, so that even a small female can, if aroused, easily receive an exceptionally large penis.

Disparity in sexual desire constitutes the most common sexual problem. It is to some extent inescapable, since differences in the strength of the sexual impulse and the ability to respond are based on neurophysiological differences. Much disparity, however, is the result of inhibition or of one person having been subjected to more sexual stimuli during the day than the other. The husband who has been seeing attractive females periodically during his work day and who may have had an opportunity to relax on his way back from the office or store is naturally more interested in coitus than his harried wife who has remained at home caring for children and doing housework. Another cause of disparity is a difference in viewpoint. Often a male will anticipate coitus as a palliative to compensate for the trials and tribulations of life, whereas many females are interested in sex only if the preceding hours have been reasonably problem-free and happy. Even in cases of neurophysiological differences in sex drive, the less-motivated partner can be trained to a higher level of interest, since most humans operate well below their sexual capacities.

Psychological fatigue, a growing disinterest in sexual behaviour with a particular partner, sometimes constitutes a problem. Humans are subject to monotony, and coitus may become routine or even a chore. Lessening frequencies of marital coitus are more often the result of this than of age. The solution lies in varying the time, the setting, and in breaking away from habitual techniques and positions.

Preferences for or antipathies toward particular positions, techniques, or times not infrequently cause trouble. One partner may desire mouth–genital contact or anal stimulation that the other partner finds disagreeable or perverse. Some wish to have coitus in the light, others insist upon darkness; some prefer morning, others evening. The possibilities of disagreement are legion. Even if disagreements stemming from needless inhibition are overcome, there still remain disparities in preference, and these should be met by the philosophy that, by giving pleasure to another, one obtains pleasure. Needless to say, no partner should insist upon that which is abhorrent to the other after the latter has made honest attempts to cooperate.

Anorgasmy and frigidity

Lack of female orgasm, anorgasmy, is a very frequent problem. One should differentiate between females who become sexually aroused but do not reach orgasm and those who do not become aroused. Only the latter merit the label frigid. It is common for females not to achieve orgasm during the first weeks or months of coital activity. It is almost as though many females must learn how to have orgasm, for after having had one, they respond with increasing frequency. In some cases, the female initially has no idea how to copulate effectively and simply lies passive, expecting the male to bring her to orgasm. Other females resist orgasm because the feeling of being swept away and losing control is frightening. In most cases, however, anorgasmy is simply the result of years of inhibition—having been trained since childhood to avoid yielding to the sexual impulse, it is difficult to metamorphose into a responsive and orgasmic being. In the final analysis, anorgasmy is psychological in origin; few, if any, females lack the neurophysiology necessary for orgasm, and anthropology shows that in sexually permissive societies virtually all females have little difficulty in attaining orgasm in coitus.

Anorgasmy is treated by removing inhibitions, teaching coital techniques, and by inducing orgasm through noncoital methods. The effective therapist should also impress upon the female that not reaching orgasm is no sign of failure or inadequacy on her part or her partner's and that sexual activity is very pleasurable to both, even if orgasm does not ensue. Indeed, some females derive great pleasure and satisfaction without orgasm, a fact that should be made known to anxious husbands. Too great a concern over orgasm defeats itself. As Kinsey once pointed out, thinking is the enemy of sexual pleasure, and a female can scarcely have orgasm if she is worrying about whether she will attain it or not and if she senses that her partner is mentally turning the pages of a marriage manual.

Lastly, sexual problems are often perpetuated by the inability of the partners to communicate freely their feelings to one another. There is a curious and unfortunate reticence about informing one's partner as to what does or does not contribute to one's pleasure. The partner must function on a trial and error basis, ever on the alert for signs indicating the efficacy of his or her efforts. This muteness is even more pronounced when it comes to an individual making suggestions to the partner. Many persons feel that a suggestion or request would be interpreted by the partner that he or she had been inept or at least remiss. As with any other problems, sexual problems can be overcome or ameliorated only if the individuals concerned communicate effectively.

Social and cultural aspects

The effects of societal value systems on human sexuality are, as has already been mentioned, profound. The U.S. anthropologist G.P. Murdock has summarized the situation, saying:

All societies have faced the problem of reconciling the need of controlling sex with that of giving it adequate expression, and all have solved it by some combination of cultural taboos, permissions, and injunctions. Prohibitory regulations curb the socially more disruptive forms of sexual competition. Permissive regulations allow at least the minimum impulse gratification required for individual well-being. Very commonly, moreover, sex behavior is specifically enjoined by obligatory regulations where it appears directly to subserve the interests of society.

The historical heritage is, of course, the foundation upon which the current situation rests. Western civilizations are basically Greco-Roman in social organization, philosophy, and law, with a powerful admixture of Judaism derived from Christianity. This historical mixture contained incompatible elements: individual freedom was cherished, yet there was a great emphasis on law and proper procedure; the pantheism of the Greeks and Romans clashed with Judeo-Christian monotheism; and the sexual permissiveness of the Greeks met the fanatical anti-sexuality of early Christianity.

Effects of Christianity on sexual attitudes

In terms of sex, the most important factor was Christianity. While other vital aspects of human life, such as government, property rights, kinship, and economics, were influenced to varying degrees, sexuality was singled out as falling almost entirely within the domain of religion. This development arose from an ascetic concept shared by a number of religions, the concept of the good spiritual world as opposed to the carnal materialistic world, the struggle between the spirit and the flesh. Since sex epitomizes the flesh, it was obviously the enemy of the spirit. While Judaism subscribed to this dichotomous philosophy, it did have the saving grace of largely exempting marriage from its anti-sexuality. This was not the case with early Christianity, in which sex in any form outside of marriage was unmitigated evil and, within marriage, an unfortunate necessity for procreation rather than pleasure. The powerful anti-sexuality of the early Christians (note that neither God nor Christ has a wife and that marriage does not exist in heaven) was in part due to their apocalyptic vision of life: they anticipated that the end of the world and the Last Judgment would soon be upon them. There was no time for a gradual weaning away from the flesh; an immediate and drastic approach was necessary. Indeed, such excessive anti-sexuality developed that the church itself was finally moved to curb some of its more extreme forms.

As it became evident that human existence was going to continue for some unforeseeable length of time and as occasional intelligent theologians made themselves felt, anti-sexuality was ameliorated to some extent but still remained a foundation stone of Christianity for centuries. This attitude was particularly unfortunate for women, to whom most of the sexual guilt was assigned. Women, like the original temptress Eve, continued to attract men to commit sin. They were spiritually weak creatures prone to yield to carnal impulses. This is, of course, a classic example of projecting one's own guilty desires upon someone else.

Ultimately, legal control over sexual behaviour passed from the church to the state, but, in most instances, the latter simply perpetuated the attitudes of the former. Priests and clergymen frequently continued to exert powerful extralegal control: denunciations from the pulpit can be as effective as statute law in some cases. Although religion has weakened as a social control mechanism, even today, liberalization of sex laws and relaxation of censorship have often been successfully opposed by religious leaders. On the whole, however, Christianity has become progressively more permissive, and sexuality has come to be viewed not as sin but as a God-given capacity to be used constructively.

Apart from religion, the state sometimes imposes purely secular restrictions. The more totalitarian a government, the more likely it is to restrict or direct sexual behaviour. In some instances, this is simply the consequence of a powerful individual (or individuals) being in a position to impose his (or their) ideas upon the public. In other instances, one cannot escape the impression that sex, being a highly personal and individualistic matter, is recognized as antithetical to the whole idea of strict governmental control and supervision of the individual. This may help explain the rigid sexual censorship exerted by most totalitarian regimes. It is as though such a government, being obsessed with power, cannot tolerate the power the sexual impulse exerts on the population.

PERMISSIVENESS AND SOCIAL CONTROL

Societies differ remarkably in what they consider socially desirable and undesirable in terms of sexual behaviour and consequently differ in what they attempt to prevent or promote. There appear, however, to be four basic sexual controls in the majority of human societies. First, to control endless competition, some form of marriage is necessary. This not only removes both partners from the competitive arena of courtship and assures each of a sexual partner, but it allows them to devote more time and energy to other necessary and useful tasks of life. Despite the beliefs of earlier writers, marriage is not necessary for the care of the young; this can be accomplished in other ways. Second, control of forced sexual relationships is necessary to prevent anger, feuding, and other disruptive retribution. Third, all societies exert control over whom one is eligible to marry or have as a sexual partner. Endogamy, holding the choice within one's group, increases group solidarity but tends to isolate the group and limit its political strength. Exogamy, forcing the individual to marry outside the group, dilutes group loyalty but increases group size and power through new external liaisons. Some combination of endogamy and exogamy is found in most societies. All have incest prohibitions. These are not based on genetic knowledge. Indeed, many incest taboos involve persons not genetically related (father–stepdaughter, for example). The prime reason for incest prohibition seems to be the necessity for preventing society from becoming snarled in its own web: every person has a complex set of duties, rights, obligations, and statuses with regard to other people, and these would become intolerably complicated or even contradictory if incest were freely permitted.

Four major areas of sexual control

Fourth, there is control through the establishment of some safety-valve system: the formulation of exceptions to the prevailing sexual restrictions. There is the recognition that humans cannot perpetually conform to the social code and that well-defined exceptions must be made. There are three sorts of exceptions to sexual restrictions: (1) Divorce: while all societies encourage marriage, all realize that it is in the interest of society and the individual to terminate marriage under certain conditions. (2) Exceptions based on kinship: many societies permit or encourage sexual activity with certain kin, even after marriage. Most often these kin are a brother's wife or a wife's sister. In addition, sexual "joking relationships" are often expected between brothers-in-law, sisters-in-law, and cousins. While coitus is not involved, there is much explicit sexual banter, teasing, and humorous insult. (3) There are, in addition, exceptions based on special occasions, ranging from sexual activity as a part of religious rites to purely secular ceremonies and celebrations wherein the customary sexual restrictions are temporarily lifted.

Turning to particular forms of sexual behaviour, one learns from anthropology and history that extreme diversity in social attitude is common. Most societies are unconcerned over self-masturbation since it does not entail procreation or the establishment of social bonds, but a few regard it with disapprobation. Sexual dreams cause concern only if they are thought to be the result of the nocturnal visitation of some spirit. Such dreams were once attributed to spirits or demons known as incubi and succubi, who sought out sleeping humans for sexual intercourse.

Petting among most preliterate socities is done only as

a prelude to coitus—as foreplay—rather than as an end in itself. In some parts of sub-Saharan Africa, however, petting is used as a premarital substitute for coitus in order to preserve virginity and avoid pregnancy. There is great variation in petting and foreplay techniques. Kissing is by no means universal, as some groups view the mouth as a biting and chewing orifice ill-suited for expressing affection. While some societies emphasize the erotic role of the female breast, others—such as the Chinese—pay little attention to it. Still others regard oral stimulation of the breast unseemly, being too akin to infantile suckling. Although manual stimulation of the genitalia is nearly universal, a few peoples abstain because of revulsion toward genital secretions. Not much information exists on mouth–genital contact, and one can say only that it is common among some peoples and rare among others.

A considerable number of societies manifest scratching and biting in conjunction with sexual activity, and most of this is done by the female. Sadomasochism in any other form, however, is conspicuous by its absence in preliterate societies.

An enumeration of the societies that permit or forbid premarital coitus is complicated not only by the double standard but also by the fact that such prohibition or permission is often qualified. As a rough estimate, however, 40 to 50 percent of preliterate or ancient societies allowed premarital coitus under certain conditions to both males and females. If one were to count as permissive those groups that theoretically disapprove but actually condone such coitus, the percentage would rise to perhaps 70.

Frequency of marital coitus

In marital coitus, when sexual access is not only permitted but encouraged, one would expect considerable uniformity in frequency of coitus. This expectation is not fulfilled: social conditioning profoundly affects even marital coitus. On one Irish island reported upon by a researcher, for example, marital coitus is best measured in terms of per year, and among the Cayapas of Ecuador, a frequency of twice a week is something to boast of. The coital frequencies of other groups, on the other hand, are nearer to human potential. In one Polynesian group, the usual frequency of marital coitus among individuals in their late 20s was ten to 12 per week, and in their late 40s the frequency had fallen to three to four. The African Bala, according to one researcher, had coitus on the average of once or twice per day from young adulthood into the sixth decade of life.

Marital coitus is not unrestricted. Coitus during menstruation or after a certain stage of pregnancy is generally taboo. After childbirth a lengthy period of time must often elapse before coitus can resume, and some peoples abstain for magical reasons before or during warfare, hunting expeditions, and certain other important occasions or ceremonies. In modern Western society one finds menstrual, pregnancy, and postpartum taboos perpetuated under an aesthetic or medical guise, and coaches still attempt to force celibacy upon athletes prior to competition.

Extramarital coitus provides a striking example of the double standard: it is expected, or tolerated, in males and generally prohibited for females. Very few societies allow wives sexual freedom. Extramarital coitus with the husband's consent, however, is another matter. Somewhere between two-fifths and three-fifths of preliterate societies permit wife lending or allow the wife to have coitus with certain relatives (generally brothers-in-law) or permit her freedom on special ceremonial occasions. The main concern of preliterate societies is not one of morality, but of more practical considerations: does the act weaken kinship ties and loyalty? Will it damage the husband's social prestige? Will it cause pregnancy and complicate inheritance or cause the wife to neglect her duties and obligations? Most foreign of all to Western thinking is that of those peoples whose marriage ceremony involves the bride having coitus with someone other than the groom, yet it is to be recalled that this practice existed to a limited extent in medieval Europe as jus primae noctis, the right of the lord to the bride of one of his subjects.

Sexual deviations and sex offenses are, of course, social definitions rather than natural phenomena. What is normative behaviour in one society may be a deviation or crime in another. One can go through the literature and discover that virtually any sexual act, even child–adult relations or necrophilia, has somewhere at some time been acceptable behaviour. Homosexuality is permitted in perhaps two-thirds of human societies. In some groups it is normative behaviour, whereas in others it is not only absent but beyond imagination. Generally, it is not an activity involving most of the population but exists as an alternative way of life for certain individuals. These special individuals are sometimes transvestites—that is, they dress and behave like the opposite sex. Sometimes they are regarded as curiosities or ridiculed, but more often they are accorded respect and magical powers are attributed to them. It is noteworthy, however, that aside from these transvestites, exclusive homosexuality is quite rare in preliterate societies.

In conclusion, the cardinal lesson of anthropology is that no type of sexual behaviour or attitude has a universal, inherent social or psychological value for good or evil—the whole meaning and value of any expression of sexuality is determined by the social context within which it occurs.

SOCIO-ECONOMIC FACTORS

Differences in sexual behaviour between classes within technologically developed societies are very marked. Civilizations are made up of class hierarchies, and the different subgroups normally develop their own value systems. Most of the knowledge of the sexual behaviour and attitudes of ancient cultures is that of the upper or ruling class; the behaviour and feelings of the slaves and peasants were seldom recorded. There is the impression—probably a correct one—that throughout history the lower socio-economic class was the most permissive. Sex has always been one of the few pleasures of the poor and oppressed. On the other hand, one must not overlook the fact that a fanatical Puritanism can also flourish at the bottom of the social scale, and, hence, one can never assume that low status and sexual permissiveness are inevitably linked.

The Kinsey studies showed considerable social class differences in sexuality in the United States, chiefly in that the lower class was more tolerant of nonmarital coitus. More recent studies indicate that these class differences have rapidly broken down. Increased literacy and the influence of mass media have made the population more homogeneous in sexual attitudes. One can find, moreover, reversals of the previous pattern: a lower class person on the way up the social ladder may be quite conservative in his sexual views, feeling that this facilitates upward mobility, whereas the person secure in his or her high social status often feels that he or she can afford to flout convention. Actually, the most sexually liberal are those at the very bottom, who have nothing to lose, and those at the very top, who are beyond social retribution.

Breakdown of class differences in sexual behaviour

The great middle class remains the bastion of traditionalism, and it is here that the double standard of morality is most prominent. The intellectualized liberalism of the upper level seeps down only slowly, and the pragmatic egalitarianism of the lower level does not penetrate far upward.

Systems of production and distribution have had a growing influence on sexual behaviour since the Industrial Revolution. The old family pattern was inexorably disrupted by the rise of the industrial state. Children were no longer kept at home to share in the work and be economic assets but left for school or for nonfamily employment, and the degree of parental control diminished. The "working wife" employed outside the home, once found only among the impoverished, has gradually become the typical wife. With her enhanced economic power and her greater association with people outside the home, she became less a chattel. As the population left the family farm and tight-knit small communities for anonymous big-city existence, not only parental but societal controls over behaviour were weakened. Society became increasingly nomadic with improved transportation and job opportunities. Cultural and ethnic subgroups that formerly would have had little contact were thrown together in the same schools, factories, offices, and neighbourhoods.

All of this vast uprooting and rearranging naturally altered sexual attitudes and behaviour. The individual no longer had the option of choosing to conform or depart from a rather clear-cut sexual moral code but instead was faced with a multiplicity of choices of varying degrees of social acceptability. The major sexual change—one still in progress—was the emancipation of women, which brought with it an increasing acceptance of premarital sexual activity, the concept of woman as a human being with her own sexual needs and rights, and the possibility of terminating an unhappy marriage without incurring serious social censure. A second major change was the erosion of simplistic value systems: with increased mobility and social mixing, the individual learned that the values and attitudes he or she had unquestioningly accepted were not necessarily shared by neighbours and co-workers. As a result, life became not only more complex but more permissive. This growing tolerance has in recent decades extended, to a limited extent, to homosexuality. There is no evidence that homosexuality or other deviant behaviour has measurably increased as a result of society's urbanization and technological progress, but one gains the impression of an increase simply because these topics, previously unmentionable, are now openly discussed in the mass media.

While the old monolithic value systems broke down and individuals were accorded a wider variety of choices in terms of sexual life, there developed a paradoxical trend toward homogeneity as a result of mobility, the mass media, and increasing economic parity. Geographical and social-class differences in sexual attitudes and behaviour have steadily lessened. The plumber's family and the banker's family are now indistinguishable in terms of dress; both have automobiles; their offspring attend the same schools; and they share the same newspapers, magazines, and television programs. One might summarize by saying that society is homogeneous in that everyone now has available a wide diversity of sexual attitudes and activities.

LEGAL REGULATION

Sex laws, the origins of which, as mentioned above, are found within the church, are unique in one important respect. Whereas all other laws are basically concerned with the protection of person or property, the majority of sex laws are concerned solely with maintaining morality. The issue of morality is minimal in other laws: one can legitimately evict an impoverished old couple from their mortgaged home or sentence a hungry man for stealing food. Only in the realm of sex is there a consistent body of law upholding morality.

Early examples of sex laws

The earliest sex laws of which there is knowledge are from the Near East and date back to the 2nd millennium BC. They are remarkable in three respects: there are great omissions—certain acts are not mentioned whereas others receive detailed attention; some laws seem almost contradictory; and penalties are often extraordinarily severe. One obtains the distinct impression that these laws were case law—that is, laws formulated upon specific cases as they arose rather than being the result of lengthy judicial deliberation done in advance. These laws influenced Judaic and, hence, Christian thinking, and some were immortalized in the Bible, chiefly in Leviticus.

As mentioned earlier, when secular law replaced religious law, there was rather little change in content. In Europe the Napoleonic Code represented a break with tradition and introduced some measure of sexual tolerance, but in England and the United States there was no such rift with the past. In the latter country, as each new state joined the union, its sex laws simply duplicated, to a great extent, those of pre-existing states; legislators were disinclined to debate sexual issues or to risk losing votes by discarding or weakening sex laws.

Sex laws may be grouped in three categories: (1) Those

concerned with protection of person. These are based on the element of consent. These otherwise logical laws become problematic when society deems that minors, mental retardates, and the insane are incapable of giving consent—hence, coitus with them is rape. (2) Those concerned with preventing offense to public sensibilities. Statutes preclude public sexual activity, exhibitionism, and offensive solicitation. (3) Those concerned with maintaining sexual morality. These constitute the majority of sex laws, covering such items as premarital coitus, extramarital coitus, incest, homosexuality, prostitution, peeping, nudity, animal contact, transvestism, censorship, and even specific sexual techniques—chiefly oral or anal. Laws relating to sexual conduct and morality are generally far more extensive in the United States than in western Europe and most other areas of the world.

In recent years, in Europe and the United States, a number of highly respected legal, medical, and religious organizations have deliberated on the whole issue of the legal control of human sexuality. They have been unanimous in the conclusion that, while the laws protecting person and public sensibilities should be retained, the purely moral laws should be dropped. Specifying what consenting adults do sexually in private, it is argued, should not be subject to legal control.

In the final analysis, sexuality, like any other vital aspect of human life, must be dealt with on an individual or societal level with a combination of rationality, sensitivity, and tolerance if society is to avoid personal and social problems arising from ignorance and misconception.

BIBLIOGRAPHY. An anthropological overview of sex is given in DONALD S. MARSHALL and ROBERT C. SUGGS (eds.), *Human Sexual Behavior: Variations in the Ethnographic Spectrum* (1971); GEORGE P. MURDOCK, *Social Structure* (1949); and CLELLAN S. FORD and FRANK A. BEACH, *Patterns of Sexual Behavior* (1951); the latter also covers mammalian behaviour. Data on sexual behaviour and attitudes in the United States are in ALFRED C. KINSEY et al., *Sexual Behavior in the Human Male* (1948) and *Sexual Behavior in the Human Female* (1953); while IRA L. REISS, *The Social Context of Premarital Sexual Permissiveness* (1967), provides more recent information on attitudes. General information may be found in JAMES L. MCCARY, *Human Sexuality* (1967), a book that also serves as an excellent sex manual. The best single volume on homosexuality is that of DONALD J. WEST, *Homosexuality* (1968). Genetic, hormonal, and gender matters are summarized in two technical volumes: RICHARD GREEN and JOHN MONEY (eds.), *Transsexualism and Sex Reassignment* (1969); and ROBERT J. STOLLER, *Sex and Gender: On the Development of Masculinity and Femininity* (1968). Sexual physiology is comprehensively treated in WILLIAM H. MASTERS and VIRGINIA E. JOHNSON, *Human Sexual Response* (1966), while their second volume, *Human Sexual Inadequacy* (1970), deals with behaviour therapy. The history of Judeo-Christian attitudes toward sex is presented in detail in L.M. EPSTEIN, *Sex Laws and Customs in Judaism* (1968); and DERRICK S. BAILEY, *Sexual Relation in Christian Thought* (1959). Sex laws are covered by three volumes: RALPH SLOVENKO (ed.), *Sexual Behavior and the Law* (1965); EDWARD SAGARIN and DONAL E.J. MACNAMARA, *Problems of Sex Behavior* (1968); and the AMERICAN LAW INSTITUTE, *Model Penal Code*, 2 vol. (1955–57).

(P.H.Ge.)

Sexual Deviations

Sexual deviation is defined here as any pattern of behaviour including a habitual, preferred, compelling need for sexual gratification by any technique other than willing coitus between man and woman and involving actions that directly result in genital excitement. "Preferred" is a key word in the definition because sexual behaviour that is chosen as desirable is thus distinguished from sexual acts that are prescribed by others or that are momentary, casual, or experimental; such acts would be deviant acts, but they may or may not signal deviation. If a pagan ritual required a celebrant to have intercourse with an animal, for instance, the act would not be considered in the pattern of deviation, because the person is simply obeying a societal code and would presumably not prefer animals under ordinary circumstances. Overall, the criterion of definition here is man's evolutionary and biological need to reproduce the species; and there is intended no social or cultural implication that deviant behaviour is, or is not, unhealthy, immoral, sinful, useless to society, or contrary to natural law. The only exception in this article is the inclusion of incest, which, though culturally and not physiologically defined, is universally tabooed in one form or another.

Statistical frequencies. The first generalization to apply to all sexual deviations concerns the problem of determining prevalence. Despite a century of scientific study, it is not possible to state precisely for any population how many people are involved in any particular deviation. Published statistics have dubious accuracy because of such errors as poor definition; improper sampling techniques; and denial due to guilt, embarrassment, and secrecy that attends sexual deviation in all societies. Even the Institute for Sex Research (Indiana University), founded by Alfred C. Kinsey (1894–1956), which has demonstrated the possibility of determining the rate of deviation in a given population, still admits the imprecision of its findings and the need for further refinement of statistical techniques. Thus, for the time being, one must be satisfied with approximations and such imprecise measures of frequency as "occasionally," "rarely," "extremely," and "very."

Therapies. Second, there are no adequate statistics on results of theory. Although psychoanalysts may point to psychoanalysis as the preferred treatment for sexual deviations, there is not a single published work demonstrating, in significant numbers of cases and with adequate controls, how effective treatment actually is. The same can be said for all other methods of treatment, although the next decade may determine the reliability of behavioral techniques. Such techniques involve "conditioning" a patient to canalize his desires into new directions by associating his acts with rewarding or punishing stimuli. The individual, for instance, may be rewarded for acts progressively like the act to be preferred until that act finally occurs and is rewarded (positive conditioning). Or an act to be abandoned may be accompanied by electric shocks or other punishments until that act is habitually avoided (aversion therapy).

Whatever the future holds, however, one can say now that all sexual deviations are difficult to treat and the outcomes are uncertain. This is true because the pleasure inherent in the behaviour is intense, and the alternatives so much less so. If cure means to give up what is most pleasurable, even the best intentions may not adequately motivate a patient.

Causes. Third, in spite of the immense literature dealing with the causes of deviation—biological, psychological, or a combination of both—there is little sure knowledge. The hypotheses, however, generally fall into one of the following categories:

1. Willful sinning.

2. Atavism, degeneracy, or hereditary taint. These causes imply, along with a connotation of disgust, an inherited biological inferiority.

3. Animal instinct. If some behaviour, such as licking another animal's genitals, occurs in a number of mammalian species, then human beings, being mammals, may be instinctively inclined to practice such behaviour.

4. Neurophysiological causes. If, by subjecting an animal's brain to neurophysiological, biochemical, or microscopic stimuli under laboratory conditions, one can induce an animal to engage in a certain behaviour, then a similar behaviour found in human beings may be due to the functioning or malfunctioning of corresponding brain centres in man.

5. Genetic causes. Studies of chromosomes and genes are insufficiently advanced to determine whether or not they comprise an ultimate biological basis for sexual deviations. Studies of single families, however, have been offered as evidence of hereditary factors when the same deviation is found in two generations or among many members of the same family and when social or psychological influences can be proved to be minimal. (Identical twins raised apart have often been the subject of such research.)

6. Endocrine causes. Variations in the makeup and

amounts of crucial hormones do affect sexual behaviour. Although it may be excessive to say that a person's behaviour is thus genetically "controlled," his behaviour can certainly be said to be "pushed" in certain directions or "influenced." One hypothesis suggests that there is a narrow time period before or after birth when an unusual dose of a sex hormone can permanently alter gender development so that, for instance, a male rat at maturity will act as if it were a female. If this occurs at the critical period in human beings, changes of masculinity and femininity may result, perhaps associated with changes in sexual practices.

7. Environmental imprinting. From birth on, intense and complex interactions between members of a family and other associates will shape (by reward and punishment, conditioning, and identification) the behaviour and sexual choices of the developing individual. In extreme cases, as has been demonstrated in some birds and animals, there is a critical period during which an infant, exposed to the proper environmental (nonbiological) stimuli, can have his behaviour permanently redirected. (A bird, for instance, may forever after seek a human being rather than another bird as an affectionate and erotic object.) Such behaviour may be insusceptible to forgetting or extinction.

8. Intrapsychic causes. In an attempt to deal with the genetically controlled development of his sex drive, a growing child, threatened by the power of his parents to castrate, abandon, or kill, may work out compromises (deviations) in order to preserve himself and his (now disguised) libido.

9. Societal causes. In different societies and eras certain types of sexual behaviour will be encouraged or punished and will be defined as normal or aberrant. These codes govern or influence sexual practices. In addition, certain codes or taboos, such as the forbidding of nudity, may set up tensions, the resolution of which may be sexual deviations.

No proof exists that any of the causative theories listed above is wrong, and thus each has its worthy proponents. There is a growing agreement, however, that, excepting certain rare and specific cases in which biological abnormalities can be demonstrated, almost all sexual deviations are the result of postnatal, psychological (societal and intrapsychic) influences and that future studies of infant and child development, including studies of family dynamics, will reveal the specific causes of deviation.

Popular misconceptions. The fourth generalization to be made about sexual deviations is that popular conceptions should not interfere with a realistic attempt to understand various forms of deviation. There is no relation between practicing a sexual deviation and being "oversexed"; for what is meant by being "oversexed"? The capacity to perform sexually more than the user of the term? The single-mindedness with which satisfaction is pursued? The bizarreness of the sexual act? Such vagueness has no practical value in analyzing deviation. Similarly, despite contrary public opinion, there is generally no progression from a "minor" deviation to "major" one (even if one could define which are minor and which are major). Each deviation is necessary to its possessor, and he would no more get pleasure from a different deviation than would a more normal person. Progressive deviation, however, should not be confused with multiple deviation, which is common. Fetishism, sadomasochism, and homosexuality with a preference for anal intercourse may all be present in the same person.

The dynamics of deviation. A final generalization: the overall force that causes one's sexual drive to bend, detour, or deviate is seemingly psychic aggression, arising from fear or anxiety, especially in childhood when sexual conditions begin to form. The fear may be inspired by the presumed danger of other people and by the attack of one's own conscience because of the incestuous desires of childhood. Later, when the final form of the deviation is evolving, fear may be surmounted by attacking others. Thus, in the deviant act one can always find—disguised or overt, in fantasies that accompany the act or in the act itself—a hostility toward a sexual object. It seems that

Problems in determining the prevalence of deviations

one function of sexual deviations is to degrade the opposite sex. Conversely, one element of the deviant act may serve as a defense: protecting oneself against attack. In fetishism, for instance, an inanimate object may replace a human being for sexual pleasure because it never complains, is always willing, and never accuses or fights back.

The Freudian interpretations

Understanding of sexual deviations was greatly increased with the work of Sigmund Freud, especially with the publication in 1905 of the *Three Essays on the Theory of Sexuality*. This work single-handedly lifted the subject out of the realm of simple description or vague theorizing and into a much more fruitful search for causes and psychological mechanisms. In particular, it removed sexual deviations from a state of therapeutic hopelessness inspired by the earlier belief that they were the result of untreatable, subtle, biological degeneracy. Although recognizing that sexual desire had biological sources, Freud emphasized the part that psychological events play in developing both normal and abnormal sexual behaviour. From data collected in the psychoanalyses of his patients, he concluded that most sexual deviations are the result of the thwarting of the normal processes of development to heterosexuality, primarily through demands made on the growing child to curb his many libidinal desires. Through an intense and complicated process of threat and approval, a child learns, particularly from his mother (who funnels into him her idiosyncratic version of her society's mores) that his cannibalistic voraciousness, his unlimited joy in dirtying himself with excrements, or his completely selfish genital needs are simply not acceptable. Since these needs are ultimately biological, they cannot be made to disappear but can only be molded, delayed, and disguised —in time, as much disguised from the individual as from the outside world. These disguises take two main forms: sexual deviations and neuroses.

For Freud, crucial for the development of deviations was the castration complex and the Oedipal situation causing it. In a boy the original unlimited love for his mother must be severely modified if he is to develop into an independent individual; additionally, he cannot hope to have his mother exclusively when his father has prior possession. That circumstance—and the threat of his father's strength—makes the little boy fear that his father could punish him for his sexual desires by removing that most intensely pleasurable organ, his penis. On the other hand, said Freud, little girls, discovering early that they do not have a penis, feel that the humiliating and depriving act of castration has already been performed in the forgotten past, making them inferior and envious of males. How to survive these painful relations with parents and to salvage sexual pleasure are for Freud the main tasks of childhood libidinal development; and, depending on what the parents do and how the child reacts to what is done, one gets various degrees of distortion of normal sexual development.

Sexual deviation may result from either or both of two processes. First, there is fixation, whereby a stage in development, because experienced too intensely, is clung to, thus delaying progress to the next stage or distorting it. Excessive concentration on learning bowel control, for instance, can focus the child excessively on anal sensations; and when he enters the stage of genital ascendancy (penile or clitoral), he (or she) may associate seminal or vaginal fluid with excremental filth or poison. The second process is regression, whereby one more or less reaches psychosexual maturity but, under pressure of severe distress, retreats to a more primitive libidinal state. Pedophilia (see below), for instance, sometimes appears for the first time in a man becoming senile.

Although many aspects of Freud's theory have been questioned or modified, no attack has yet demonstrated the falsity of his claims that infants and children have sexual lives, that eroticism is attached not only to the genitals but also to many other parts of the body, that the sexual pleasures of childhood can be maintained relatively intact into adult life, that sexual desire is tamed only with great difficulty in most societies, that the taming does not destroy sexual instincts but merely makes them take

on different appearances, that infants and children have highly charged libidinal relations with their parents that must be resolved for successful living as an adult, that infantile sexuality lives on in both normal sex practices and sexual deviations, and that there are discoverable in early life psychological forces that produce sexual deviations in an adult.

HOMOSEXUALITY

Homosexuality, very generally defined, is a preference for sexual relations with a person of the same sex. Though the most prevalent deviation, its frequency is unknown, largely because its being considered both sinful and illegal in most societies makes people with this preference unlikely to reveal themselves to authorities. It may be the most prevalent deviation because it is closest to heterosexuality in offering the pleasure of being sexually with a willing object recognized as quite human.

Problems in defining homosexuality

The definition of homosexuality would seem easy enough, and yet authorities disagree, primarily because of the difficulty in determining to what degree a person performing a homosexual act prefers it to some other act. Some experts, for instance, believe that much of adolescent homosexuality is due to the social restrictions on overt heterosexuality, making homosexuality a matter of *faute de mieux:* something adopted for the lack of something better. Likewise, men isolated from women during wartime or imprisonment may turn to transient homosexuality. This is called facultative homosexuality.

The issue of who is a homosexual is further complicated by the fact that many people have conscious or unconscious homosexual desires. They may express them in fantasies or in reading or watching films on the subject, or they may even sense excitement in aborted homosexual acts revealed in affectionate gestures. The homosexual interests of many people appear in dreams, in hatred of homosexuals, or in a man's fear of not seeming manly or a woman's fear of not seeming feminine. According to some analysts, even some cases of paranoid psychosis, drug addiction, alcoholism, and myriad other psychiatric conditions are due to fear of homosexual impulses. In the end, if one accepts Freud's statement that all human beings possess undercurrents of homosexuality because they are biologically and thus psychologically bisexual, the task of precise definition would seem impossible.

Nevertheless, there is a growing consensus that a homosexual can be defined at least relatively: although homosexual tendencies can be found under many circumstances, a homosexual is a person who in fantasy or reality habitually prefers sexual relations with a person of the same sex. That being so, one finds that most people are heterosexual, a smaller number can enjoy both sexes (bisexualism), and a still smaller number exclusively prefer people of the same sex.

The character of homosexuality. *The male homosexual.* Male homosexuals have often been classified in a polarizing fashion: active and passive, insertor and insertee, masculine and effeminate, obligatory and facultative. Such dichotomies all presume that there are masculine homosexuals and feminine ones—the latter identifying themselves with women, being quieter, gentler, more effeminate, and more prone to live and work in ways reminiscent of females and especially preferring to assume a woman's receptive role in sexual acts as much as anatomically possible. Too many homosexuals, however, enjoy alternating in masculine and feminine roles to permit such simple classification. The Kinsey seven-point scale avoids the issue by merely rating people from exclusively heterosexual to exclusively homosexual in their choice of sexual partners throughout life.

Male homosexuals can be habitually effeminate, intermittently so, or habitually masculine. The most effeminate restrict their behaviour to their version of a woman's role, not only mimicking nonsexual femininity but also enjoying being seduced and overpowered by their partner, receiving penises into their anus, mouth, or hand and disliking the insertor role.

They dress flamboyantly and effeminately, with a few resorting even to women's clothes, as at "drag balls" and beauty contests. This cross-dressing is not sexually exciting, as it is for the transvestite, nor does it indicate a desire to be a female, as it does for the transsexual (see below *Transsexualism and Transvestism*). The effeminate homosexual loves his penis and abhors penisless creatures. He is still so identified with the female role, however, that he can appear as a woman for a short time and enjoy being complimented on his feminine appearance. It is understood by the observers and himself that he has a penis under his costume.

Most male homosexuals are less effeminate, revealing their effeminacy only when safely with other homosexuals. They alternate sexually between active and passive roles, and some also can perform heterosexually and not infrequently marry and have children. Finally, there are habitually masculine men, who, with no apparent wish to simulate femaleness, still choose other males exclusively for sexual pleasure, with a few even exaggerating their masculinity in dress and manner.

There is as yet no way to judge accurately the prevalence of homosexuality and all its characteristics. But the growing number of studies and surveys in such countries as the U.S., Great Britain, and Sweden tends to loosen society's attitudes toward sexuality; and changes in attitudes in turn make such studies easier, with homosexuals more willing to reveal themselves.

The female homosexual. Like their male counterparts, female homosexuals can be very masculine ("butch"), alternatively masculine and feminine, or always feminine ("femme"). The "butch" may dress and act like a man, but this is simply mimicry in the reverse manner of the effeminate male homosexual. These women proclaim their dislike of maleness, especially penises, and, in the extreme, state that men have value only as repositories of sperm. In sexual relations they take a masculine role, playing the seducing and active role, sometimes with artificial penile devices. They prefer "femmes" and rarely have sexual relations with other masculine women. Many believe, because men are unnecessary, that women make the best lovers for women and that a "butch" can seduce any woman, including a normal heterosexual. There is thus an apparent paradox that such women may get along well with effeminate men, closely imitate masculinity in sexual and other ways, and yet hate maleness.

Those who consider themselves bisexual can be masculine (though not so much as "butches") or feminine, switching roles at will. The "femmes" are feminine in dress and behaviour and incapable of simulating masculinity. Though appearing normally heterosexual, they need masculine women (*i.e.*, penisless "men"), finding sexual relations with males unappealing. At times in a "butch-femme" relation the "butch" is the man, but she may also perform as a powerful, punishing, and threatening mother: her partner may behave as a daughter. Thus affectionate mother-daughter roles can combine with threatening sadomasochistic ones.

Female homosexual relations are usually more stable than are male relations because more emphasis is placed on non-erotic companionship. Thus long-lasting liaisons are more likely and may even include the raising of children. Either the child is "adopted" nonlegally or one of the women becomes pregnant so that the two can raise their own child (the necessary male of course being discarded soon after conception).

The homosexual subculture. In modern societies in which homosexuality is condemned but still prevalent, homosexuals usually congregate in large cities, where urban anonymity permits them to develop underground communities. After working in the "straight" (heterosexual) world all day, they can lift their disguises in exclusively "gay" (homosexual) bars where they can meet, talk, dance, drink, and otherwise feel free from observation, censure, or arrest. Helping to increase their sense of solidarity as protection against an intolerant majority has been the gradual invention of their own private language, a jargon of such expressions as "gay," "straight," "butch," and "femme." Additionally they may create homosexual organizations for social, scientific, and political action favouring homosexuality.

A "sexual" subculture has also developed. In most cities, in addition to bars, there are parks, beaches, public toilets, and bathhouses known to male homosexuals for finding sex partners. These bars and other meeting places are familiar to the police, but, recognizing their social value, the authorities usually leave them alone so long as the rest of society is not victimized. Only when occasional public pressure is exerted for a "cleanup" do the police act, invariably, however, permitting an expeditious return to normalcy. In business and the professions male homosexuals dominate certain areas of the creative and performing arts, hairdressing, interior decorating, and fashion designing. In such nonsexual settings effeminate men, protected from female anatomy, often find women congenial. Female homosexuals of masculine persuasion often prefer working in masculine professions, in which their strong motivation can be highly effective.

Comparative views of homosexuality. Male homosexuality was highly valued in ancient Greece, but experts disagree over whether the literary praise of homosexuality meant that it was acceptable for society in general or only for the elite. Others disagree whether the idealized Greek homosexual relation between an older, wiser man and his young patron minimized sexuality or was decidedly sexual as well as philosophic. At any rate, many Greek writers represented homosexuality as ennobling and normal. Ancient Greece also exemplifies the more casual or indifferent attitude toward female homosexuality throughout history, women being considered inferior creatures and their homosexuality not worthy of much comment.

The Greek's congeniality for homosexuality is said to have influenced such neighbours as the Persians and to have been transmitted along with other Greek traditions into the Roman Empire. The Greek view, however, contrasts with the Judaic attitude of respecting heterosexuality for its familial function and strongly disapproving of homosexuality, though not until later times, evidenced in the later books of the Old Testament, was it seen as an abomination punishable by death. This scorn was transmitted to early Christianity, fortified with the belief that far better than any sexual relations at all was abstinence. (To the church's discomfort, those most able to abstain from heterosexuality may lean toward homosexuality.)

Data regarding the Orient are so scattered as to warrant only surmises, though homosexuality was known throughout the Orient in ancient and modern times. As with other civilizations over wide stretches of time, it was alternately accepted and condemned in China, Japan, and India and expressed at times in male prostitution. Clellan S. Ford and Frank A. Beach, reporting on 76 preliterate societies, found 28 in which adult homosexual activities were "totally absent, rare, or carried on only in secrecy" and 48 in which homosexuality was "normal and socially acceptable for certain members of the community." What especially catches the eye in such societies is cross-dressing, a mode of behaviour often cited by anthropologists but usually without proof that it goes beyond masquerading or ritual to involve genital acts. Where true homosexuality does exist, natives, when questioned, have simply been amused that it could conceivably be banned. Nevertheless, M.K. Opler has noted:

Actually, no society, save perhaps ancient Greece, pre-Meiji Japan, certain top echelons in Nazi Germany, and the scattered examples of such special status groups as the berdaches, Nata slaves, and one category of Chukchee shamans, has lent sanctions in any real sense to homosexuality.

Among modern countries, homosexuality seems to find least disfavour in such countries as the Scandinavian nations, The Netherlands, and Japan and to be most condemned in authoritarian countries such as the Soviet Union and in some Latin American countries where *machismo* or manliness is strongly dictated by tradition. In the U.S., which seems moving toward more sexual tolerance, Alfred Kinsey and his group estimated in 1948 that 4 percent of American males were exclusively homosexual throughout their lives, and 10 percent during at least three years of their adult lives; 30 percent had at least some incidental homosexual experience. The estimates for females, reported in 1953, were less specific on "exclusive"

Historical and cross-cultural data

homosexuality but noted that 13 percent had at least a "homosexual experience" reaching orgasm prior to age 45, or 28 percent a "homosexual response." The validity of such estimates, however, has been subject to debate.

Comparative legal aspects. Generally in all countries there are no laws against homosexuality per se but rather against acts evidencing homosexual gratification, such as sodomy, fellatio, or mutual masturbation. Usually there are also general provisions against "conduct outrageous to public decency," used to ensure the imposition of some penalty when overt homosexuality or some serious crime cannot be proved. Almost all countries—even those having repealed laws against homosexual activities between "consenting adults in private"—reserve severe punishment for an adult having homosexual relations with a minor. In Scandinavia, for instance, homosexual relations are punishable only when one of the persons is under 18 years of age or when the person is between 18 and 21 and demonstrably a victim of superior age and experience. In Great Britain the lower age is 18 (since 1970, the age used in definitions of adulthood in all legal matters); and in those states of the U.S. (Illinois and Connecticut) adopting the principle of "consenting adults," the lower age is 21. (Almost all states of the U.S. still outlaw all "unnatural" or homosexual acts, regardless of the age of the participants.) Japan, France, and some other European countries not only prohibit adults taking advantage of minors but also prohibit any person of authority, such as an employer or guardian, taking advantage of an inferior, such as an employee or ward. Although free to engage in acts involving consent and privacy, anyone using intimidation or violence is subject to severe penalty.

The Soviet criminal code takes a traditional conservative approach to homosexual relations. All sexual relations between men are punishable by a prison term of up to five years, and the penalty is severer when force or superior age or position is used. Communist China, on the other hand, though punishing force, fraud, or the misuse of authority, apparently has no legal proscription against homosexuality between consenting adults in private.

Laws regarding homosexuality may not always reflect public conscience on the matter or the degree of enforcement by authorities.

Cross-species data. All vertebrates, including man, have sufficient equipment to indulge in homosexual behaviour. A male stickleback fish, for instance, may push a nesting female aside, perform on the nest as if female, and then be approached by a dominant male as a female; smaller male iguana lizards are regularly sexually engaged by stronger males; male roosters, bending over, may be mounted by other roosters; cows in heat mount other cows; and dogs, cats, horses, rabbits, lions, and many other species mount others of the same sex. In young primates there is much play activity with members of the same sex that is typical of adult sexual behaviour. Two cases have been reported of male monkey pairs who had well-motivated and coordinated anal intercourse.

This great mass of data, however, cannot answer the question whether any of these animals is a homosexual. No adult animals other than human beings are known to prefer orgasmic intercourse regularly with their own sex.

Theories of causation of homosexuality. *Genetic theories.* Theories that homosexuality can be hereditary have been popular for more than 100 years, but no real evidence exists that aberrations running through generations or among blood relations are not the result of living in similar or identical environments. One study by F.J. Kallmann in 1952 indicated that among identical twins both were homosexual if one was homosexual; among fraternal twins this condition did not necessarily hold true. Kallmann's study, though impressive, has not been confirmed by subsequent research. Other studies have shown that male homosexuals tend to be born of older mothers; but, although genetic abnormality could be involved (as it is in mongolism), the reason may be simpler: older mothers may find their last son more precious and so rear him differently from their other children.

Constitutional and hormonal theories. Recognizing that all human beings are constitutionally bisexual (the hu-

man fetus of either sex having rudimentary reproductive organs of the opposite sex), researchers have conducted various experiments to redirect male or female behaviour. Sex hormones, for instance, once were considered prime movers of masculinity and femininity. Treating effeminate male homosexuals with male hormones, however, has not resulted in more manliness but rather in an intensification of their sexual excitement with the same effeminate behaviour as before. All theories in this class are thus still inconclusive.

Psychoanalytic theories. According to Freudian theory, usually either boys are too fearful of wanting their mothers sexually and thus turn from her and all like her to the safety of those with penises, or they experience intense relations with their mother and so identify with her femaleness that they take the same love objects (males). In some instances, according to Freud, hatred of a brother, in murderous intensity, is covered over with love; such a hate-ridden love seems to underlie the hostility often found in male homosexual pairs. In other instances, a homosexual looks for a youth reminding him of himself at a younger, idealized age, feeling safer with someone more like himself than with a female. Others are said to be homosexual in order to assume the strength or masculinity they lack, much in the manner of cannibals who eat part of another to incorporate prized qualities. In general, psychoanalysts consider homosexuality a result of severe anxiety in childhood, not a variant of normality.

In Freudian theory, the Oedipus complex is crucial to understanding female homosexuality as well. Failing to establish a loving relation with her father, a little girl may turn from hopes of heterosexuality and return to an earlier stage of love with her mother, who is same-sexed. Excessive penis envy may predispose her to this retreat. Wanting to be male makes her reject her vagina and femininity and overemphasize her clitoris as a phallus. Trying to be like a male and, out of envy, revenging herself on males, she turns from heterosexuality, becomes like her father, and takes women for her lovers.

Learning theories. Learning theories differ from Freudian theories in placing greater emphasis on the power of reward and punishment and general environmental conditioning to shape sexual preferences. A high proportion of homosexuals, for instance, come from disturbed home backgrounds, where they experienced difficulty in identifying with the parent of their own sex. In the case of male homosexuals, there may be an overwhelming mother who binds her son too closely to her through a mixture of overprotection and threats and a father who is unreachable because he is passive, often absent, or so punitive that his son can never have a warm relation with him. Such theories of reward and punishment are similar to certain sociological theories that emphasize the cultural forces forming family beliefs. Whether one's society and thus one's family glorifies homosexuality as in Greece, or puts a taboo on it in such a way as surreptitiously to point up its pleasures, the child is conditioned somehow to the attractions of homosexuality. In societies, on the other hand, that tend toward heterosexual permissiveness for children, without severe rewards and punishments—such as the Israeli *kibbutzim*—homosexuality seems to be rare or nonexistent.

Treatment of homosexuality. The treatment of choice is psychoanalysis and related psychotherapies. Reports of such treatment are consistently optimistic (that is, provided that the treatment is not forced upon the homosexual but is requested because the condition is distressing) and show rates of remission from one-third to one-half of the patients. Success is less likely if the patients at an early age exhibited strong cross-gender behaviour; marked effeminacy as a young boy or tomboyishness as a young girl. No other treatment seems so successful; the only other therapy that is apparently causing remissions is behaviour conditioning (aversion therapy). Nevertheless, although several patients have given up homosexual practices with such treatment, most have not become heterosexual. Treatments involving hormones and other drugs such as tranquilizers, hypnosis, exhortations, imprisonment, and suggestion have all failed.

Marginal notes:

Legal principle of homosexual acts between "consenting adults in private"

Oedipal conflict and homosexuality

The "disturbed home" and homosexuality

DEVIATIONS FOCUSSING ON GENDER IDENTITY

Transsexualism. Transsexualism is a condition in which a biologically normal person believes himself (or herself) to be truly a member of the opposite sex, despite anatomical evidence to the contrary. A transsexual does not simply imitate members of the opposite sex in clothing or manner but becomes adept at seeming to be one. In the fantasy life of childhood, expressed in play, the boy, for instance, invariably takes the female role, and his interest in stories is always focussed on women's activities; unlike a transvestite (see below), he dresses in girls' clothes without sexual excitement. This feminine interest never wavers, though it may be somewhat driven underground at school, only to re-emerge in adolescence, when he habitually behaves with extreme femininity and may even pass successfully in the world as a woman. A female transsexual, of course, experiences a similar reversal.

A transsexual may attempt to be surgically and hormonally transformed. In the male, this consists of removal of facial and body hair, the use of estrogens to develop female secondary sex characteristics, especially breasts; the surgical thinning of the larynx; and a genital "sex change" through removal of testes, amputation of the penis, and creation of an artificial vagina from retained penile skin, other skin, or intestinal grafts, and scrotal tissue. In the female, the operation consists of the use of testosterone to create facial and body hair, a lowering of the voice, and clitoral enlargement; the removal of the breasts, ovaries, tubes, and uterus; the closure of the vagina; and, rarely, a skin grafting to produce a nonfunctioning phallus. There are no known cases of adult transsexuals who have lost their desire to change sex through psychotherapy or psychoanalysis. In a few little boys given treatment along with their parents, however, the process of feminization seems to have been reversed.

Causes of trans-sexualism

Biological theories of the causes of transsexualism rest on animal experiments that have revealed a critical prenatal or infantile period during which, for instance, a single dose of opposite-sex hormone, without demonstrable brain damage, will produce permanent change in the development of masculine or feminine behaviour. More reliable, however, are psychological and environmental theories that have shown that transsexuals derive from disturbed families. The mothers of male transsexuals, for example, usually themselves experience powerful transsexual tendencies in childhood but later put on feminine facades—without heterosexual interests, however—and married men who were distant, passive, perhaps not effeminate but unable to assert themselves in a masculine and fatherly manner. Only one son becomes transsexual, usually the youngest and the one to whom the mother is particularly attracted because of a special quality of infantile beauty and grace and whom the mother keeps in excessively close, blissful relations with her for years—often keeping him physically next to her for many hours, day and night, even when as old as four years, and generally making him feel so much a part of her that there is no normal process of separation that children must go through as they develop. With his mother encouraging him and his father either absent or uninterested, the boy develops unimpeded in a feminine manner, his mother becoming concerned only later when talk arises about her very girlish boy. No similar history or etiology of female transsexuals is known, although there is belief that, unlike the males, the females may be more nearly homosexuals of the very masculine variety. Some female transsexuals tell of a close, tender relation in childhood with an inadequate father who either died or left the family; their mothers were generally aggrieved women who encouraged them to assume many characteristics of the role of father.

Transvestism. Transvestism here refers not to cross-dressing that is momentary, casual, or ritualistic or adopted for theatrical entertainment but rather to the condition in which one habitually develops sexual excitement fetishistically by wearing clothes of the opposite sex. True transvestism apparently exists only in males and begins when an adolescent or man first finds himself in a woman's garment and is struck by the most intense sexual tension, leading to masturbation and powerful orgasm.

One type, whose cross-dressing remains simply fetishistic, concentrates on a single favourite garment, such as shoes or underwear. In a second type, the condition progresses; the man gradually becomes interested in dressing completely as a woman, feeling transiently like a woman, and learning to appear and carry himself so like a woman that he can go out into the world without detection. Although the sexual excitement combines with the sense of being a woman, such men are no more apt to be homosexual than other men and, in spite of their occasional cross-dressing, spend most of their time appearing masculine and choosing masculine professions. They usually marry. They do not wish to become females; they preserve their genitals, finding in them the source of their greatest sexual pleasure.

No evidence exists that transvestism has genetic, anatomic, or hormonal roots; and reports of a higher than predicted incidence of electroencephalographic abnormalities among transvestites still need confirmation. The psychoanalytic theory of causation presumes that the small boy, fearful that sexual desires for his mother will lead to castration by his father, seeks out a "homosexual" solution by fantasying that donning female clothes permits him to be a phallic, uncastrated woman. A modification of this theory derives from the finding that boys who become transvestites are often first put in female clothes by a woman or girl who despises maleness and relishes humiliating males. Either she openly despises maleness or she assumes a loving, succouring, "motherly" behaviour, unaware of her wish for a weakened (effeminate) male.

Despite a large literature on psychotherapy as treatment for transvestism, no successes are reported, nor are drugs effective. If success in treatment is defined as the removal of the desire for fetishistic cross-dressing, then the only successes reported are those with aversion therapy: patients have had rapid remission, lasting up to several years, when treated over a period to low-voltage but painful electric shocks or to inductions of violent vomiting in the presence of exciting garments.

Intersexuality. Intersexuality is the condition of having both male and female biological characteristics. An intersexual individual may have the external or internal features of both sexes, the external genitals of one sex and the gonads of the other sex, or any other obvious or covert blend of male and female characteristics. Related terms are gynandromorphism and hermaphroditism.

Such biological abnormalities can lead to deviation behaviour. An infant appearing externally like a normal female but otherwise being entirely male, for instance, will be raised by the unsuspecting parents as a girl, who grows to accept the femaleness without question. In adolescence, however, when the male hormones start their effects, "she" will react in the same way as a biologically normal girl to the hated masculinizing of her body. When the anatomic abnormality is obvious and the parents do not know whether the child is clearly male or female, however, the child can develop a "hermaphroditic identity," believing itself to be different from all other people and feeling emotionally both male and female or neither. Another noteworthy variety of intersexuality is Klinefelter's syndrome, usually marked by the presence of a third sex chromosome (XXY) in males rather than the normal two (XY) and involving markedly defective testes. Appearing to be anatomically normal males at birth, such children are reared unequivocally as boys but nonetheless on occasion become so feminine in childhood that, like transsexuals, they wish to grow up to be women and take on feminine behaviour.

DEVIATIONS FOCUSSING ON SPECIAL SEX OBJECTS

Pedophilia. In pedophilia the object of sexual pleasure is a prepubescent child. Pedophiles are probably always men, whose objects are more often little girls than little boys and whose behaviour rarely involves sadistic attacks (which seem frequent only because of the great publicity attending such acts) and usually involves fondling the child or persuading the child to manipulate his genitals or engage in some degree of oral or anal sodomy.

According to most published case histories, the male pedophile's childhood is disturbed by a broken home (the scene of divorce, separation, or death) and marked by a higher than average incidence of social and sexual activities with girls his own age. Reaching adolescence, however, he becomes shy and fearful of the sexual and bodily maturity of the girls, becomes inhibited, and rather than turning to homosexuality, returns to the variety of safer females—little girls—with whom he was more comfortable and successful as a boy. Pedophiles actually are often married and have children, even though they find little sexual gratification or affection with their wives, and they chronically struggle with overt neurosis or even mild psychosis. One rare type is the senile man, who, because of his waning sexual capacity for adult women and his weakening sense of morality, recalls the sexual pleasures of childhood and takes to fondling little girls.

As for the molested child, whether or not the act is psychologically traumatic depends upon how old and how willing the child is, whether the man is a stranger, whether there is pleasure or pain, and what private fantasies the child assigns to the act. In some instances there are little girls who participate so actively as to be seducers—not because they are "oversexed" or monstrous but because, growing up fearful and unloved in a shattered family, they learn how sex can bring attentiveness appearing like affection or can serve as a medium of taunting revenge.

As with many other deviations, the most hopeful therapy involves increasing the man's insight into the sources of his need by means of psychoanalysis, group therapy, or other psychotherapy. The success of such treatments, however, is still undetermined.

Fetishism. In psychiatric usage, fetishism denotes deriving sexual excitement directly from an inanimate object or a body part (such as hair or hair ribbon, feet or shoes, underclothing) and, though the mode of using these objects varies (kissing, fondling, smelling, and other physical actions), there is usually masturbation. The fetish serves as a substitute for a wanted but too dangerous whole, live person and seems to possess human qualities, despite perhaps its apparent oddness. Some fetishists, for instance, focus on garments that have been worn and contain the odour of the absent owner. Even if new, the clothes usually suggest intimacy, as in the case of garments worn close to the skin. A rather common practice is stealing and then masturbating into the hair cut from a woman.

Fetishism is found mostly in males, rarely in females. According to psychoanalytic theory (involving the Oedipal complex and castration fears), a small boy observes the anatomical differences between the sexes, comes to realize that his prized penis can be lost because there are penisless creatures, and then begins in fantasy to create a "penis" for women by considering some item of clothing or other fetish as the phallus. As the boy grows older, though, his "ego is split": unconsciously the eroticized fetish stands for the female's penis, even though consciously he recognizes the reality of female genitals. The shortcoming of such a theory, however, is its failure so far to show why one boy will be fetishistic and another not or why fetishism should exist in females. Nonpsychoanalytic theorists explain the condition more simply. Some consider the cause to be conditioning: on some occasion a special sexual arousal was associated with a neutral object, and thereafter, through reinforcement, the object developed in importance. Others suggest the process of imprinting: just as an infant chick can erotically fix on a piece of wood if the piece of wood is presented as the first strong external stimulus in its life, so may a neutral object be imprinted in the first few years of a child's life.

When there are multiple fetishes and other sexual deviations involved, the prognosis for treatment is poor, but when there is the problem of a single fetish, the chances of success increase. Such fetishism has been removed by hypnosis, insight psychotherapy (including psychoanalysis), and aversion therapy.

Incest. Incest refers to culturally prohibited sexual relations between certain family members—the exact members being defined differently from society to society, although every society known to history has had some incest taboos. Although prohibitions against incest have been rationalized on the grounds of the alleged dangers of inbreeding (see CONSANGUINITY), such defenses are largely modern afterthoughts. Incest taboos have more practical social origins: marrying outside the family assures a wider circle of allies and various economic advantages, and it also preserves the family (with its procreative and childrearing functions) by precluding the disruptive jealousies that incest might arouse among family members. Whatever the origins, however, incest comes to be socially viewed with intense disgust, even when personal fantasies rather than actual incest are involved.

Freud's psychology of human behaviour centred on the incest taboo and the resultant struggle against it, which he called the Oedipal conflict. The struggle results because, in Freud's view, sexual desire, most prominently toward the parent of the opposite sex, is found universally in small children. In other words, although biologically the desire may be unusual, it must be curbed because it is socially "unnatural."

The severest taboo has always been against mother-son sexual relations, which have been so dramatized in mythologies and generally so execrated by mankind that the act almost never occurs outside of fantasies. In those rare cases reported in modern times, the mother's sexual object was not an adult son but rather a child or defenseless adolescent, and the mother was usually nearly or actually psychotic. On the other hand aborted incestuous activity between mother and son, such as genital manipulation or sensual kisses and embraces, is so common as to be considered at the root of many cases of psychiatric disorder. _{Types of incest}

Intercourse between father and daughter is more common, with countless cases reported every year. Not infrequently the father, usually an ineffectual man with a history of heavy drinking, has sexual relations with more than one daughter, though one is usually favoured. The man's wife hates her sexual "obligations," helping to cause him to turn to their daughter and often even surreptitiously pushing her daughter onto her husband. All the while she blinds herself to the evidence of incest, even accusing the daughter of having a "dirty mind" should the daughter speak up. In any event, the father-daughter incest may proceed for years, eventually to be dissolved by the daughter, at the latest in her 20s. Although such a continuing experience may not arouse much guilt in father or daughter, both sensing the mother's collusion, they may suffer severe conscious anxiety and guilt should the mother indeed interfere at the outset.

Society uses primarily primitive measures for treating the participants in incest, namely, imprisonment and in an earlier day death. Modern psychotherapy, however, may assist a person, particularly a parent, in reducing the intensity of his incestuous wishes and assist the victim in handling his feelings of guilt or rage.

Bestiality. Bestiality is a sexual deviation in which animals are the preferred objects for achieving sexual gratification. Its frequency is overestimated in the public imagination because of the stories of boys or men isolated on farms and ranches and experimentally sex-playing with animals; such males, however, presumably would prefer females if they were available. Bestiality as a pattern of deviation is rare.

The deviation may arise as the result of fear and inadequacy in approaching members of the opposite sex and often also as the result of a strong previous development of bestial patterns (conditioning). Humiliation is avoided with a compliant animal, and revenge is possible: often bestiality in men is accompanied by overt sadism; the man gets excitement simply from inflicting pain upon, or even killing, the animal and, more rarely, from having intercourse with the animal as well. Bestiality in women (less common than in men) is usually a form of masturbation, the animal being used to rub against or lick the woman's genitals. There seems no real sexual desire for animals, but only the fear of rejection and humiliation by men.

Because only a handful of cases have ever been reported to have been treated, no preferred therapy is known.

Necrophilia. Necrophilia involves sexual gratification with a corpse, which may be mutilated after the sexual act. It is to be distinguished from extreme forms of sadism, in which a person is murdered and while dying is subjected to intercourse or masturbation. The necrophiliac is not a murderer. The condition apparently occurs only in men, is extremely rare, and is ordinarily associated with overt psychosis.

The essential rationales for the necrophiliac's excitement are, first that the woman, being dead, is absolutely undangerous and, second, that he is revenged upon womankind, represented by the dead woman. Such people have not been studied adequately, however, to determine what has happened in their lives that specifically directs their needs. There are no reliable reports on treatment.

DEVIATIONS FOCUSSING ON SPECIAL PATTERNS OF ACTS

Exhibitionism. Exhibitionism is the deviation in which sexual excitement or gratification is achieved by exposing one's genitals publicly or semipublicly, almost always to members of the opposite sex, adults or children. It is reported only in males and obviously only in societies in which such exposure is looked upon as sinful and indecent.

The typical exhibitionist is a shy, passive male with strong feelings of inadequacy and impotency and with little capacity for developing affectionate or sexual relations with a woman, even though he may be married. The impulse to expose himself usually occurs when he is feeling especially inadequate; he furtively exposes his penis (usually erect), masturbates, and looks for signs that his victim is impressed or shocked—but he does not wish her to respond sexually. That would terrify him. The danger and apprehension surrounding the act contribute to the excitement; both psychiatrists and courts recognize that exhibitionists seem to feel the need to be caught. (Next to homosexuality, exhibitionism is the deviation most frequently dealt with by the courts.)

The act of exposure for an exhibitionist is thus not an act of seduction or anticipation of a sexual relationship as it is among homosexuals or among some women expressing their femininity seductively in loose or revealing dress. Nor is it like the showing-off of prepubescent boys, since the exhibition for them is not itself sexually exciting or like the foreplay of heterosexuals who are trying to create excitement in their partners. Instead the exhibitionist is one who considers himself unmanly, yet prefers women and attempts in the act of exposure to prove to allegedly skeptical women that he indeed does have a penis and is potent. The exposure can also be meant to express the dirtying of women by the penis and its ejaculate.

There is no reason to believe that exhibitionism has biological causes, since it occurs only in societies in which covering the genitals is crucial and especially in societies of a puritanical nature. Usually the exhibitionist has had early childhood relations with a domineering woman, especially his mother, who had puritanical attitudes toward sex. He grows up shy and immature, with no adequate outlet for his sexual tensions. Strongly identifying with females, such as his mother, but also being masculine enough to desire manliness, he must demonstrate that he too is not penisless and that indeed he has a penis capable of impressing or shocking women.

Although there is cautious optimism about treatment, the degree of success is still indeterminate. Individual psychotherapy and aversion therapy have produced few cures, though they occasionally succeed in conditioning a man to frustrate his urge and reduce his need to be caught. Group therapy has been used extensively because of the considerable populations of imprisoned exhibitionists, but such treatment seems similarly effective in producing discretion, not cure.

Voyeurism. Voyeurism is the deviation in which one achieves sexual excitement and gratification through clandestine peeping. Voyeurs, seemingly all males, usually avoid any sexual approach to females and instead concentrate on watching females in the nude or in the act of undressing or on couples in sex play and find release in masturbating in the course of such peeping.

In societies placing restrictions on nudity, young men are given to curiosity about sexual activities and females and to viewing pornographic drawings, photographs, and motion pictures as partial compensation for their sexual needs. Whereas females in such societies are taught from childhood to conceal themselves and prevent their being looked at, males are indoctrinated to the challenge of this modesty and the forbidden excitement of catching a glimpse. Furthermore, visual pleasures are ubiquitous in restrictive societies, as attested by the popularity of nude and seminude pictures and entertainment.

Given these general circumstances, why do some males develop a habitual, preferred need for peeping and voyeuristic activities? The answers are unclear. A voyeur is often the youngest child and a child whose sexual curiosity or tension has been heightened by the provocative feminine behaviour of a mother or sisters. Like the exhibitionist, he typically feels shy, inadequate, and fearful of the opposite sex, but he achieves his compensatory feelings of potency and superiority in the act of violating unseen the privacy and modesty of the woman being watched. Intensifying the excitement may be the risks and dangers often associated with peeping. Also, fantasies of identifying with a male partner can contribute to a sense of achievement.

Voyeurism seems difficult to treat and, although various forms of psychotherapy have tended to help patients to curb their impulses to peep, few cures are known.

Sadism. Sadism is the condition in which one achieves sexual excitement or gratification through inflicting physical pain. The sex object can be human or animal, adult or child, a person of the opposite or the same sex. The sadistic activity can be whipping, biting, binding, chaining, knifing, slashing, or other more exotic inflictions—or in extreme cases mutilation or murder or both. It can involve stereotyped ritual or vary from victim to victim in kind and intensity. The sadistic activity may itself be sufficiently exciting to induce the sadist's orgasm or may lead up to sexual intercourse or sodomy. The condition is most often found in males. Women who perform sadistic acts during sexual relations are often not sexually excited but have been put to use by masochistic men.

Various possible causes of sadism have been offered. One suggests that sadism grows out of a child's frustration, neglect or rejection by others and the consequent desire to prove one's importance and superiority by delivering retribution upon others. Another theory relates sadism and masochism (see below *Masochism*), suggesting that they represent an exaggeration of the active or passive, aggressive or submissive roles that human beings tend to assume. Other approaches tie sadism more closely to the sexual act: a sadist may be one who feels impotent and fears that he might fail sexually in approaching the opposite sex; to preserve his self-esteem and demonstrate his power, he takes the "easier," though more destructive, avenue of sadistic attack. Or the sadist may be one whose puritanical upbringing has led him to consider sexual relations sinful and depraved; the sadistic acts are punishment of others for allegedly having lustful tendencies or engaging in sexual relations. (Extreme sadists of the murderous type, for example, are known to mutilate the genitals or breasts of their victims.)

At different times Freud tended toward various hypotheses: in an early essay he noted that "the history of human civilization shows beyond any doubt that there is an intimate connection between cruelty and the sexual instinct" and that sadism is thus an intensified primary urge (masochism being "a transformation of sadism"); later he pointed to man's "death wish" or ultimate drive to be inanimate (a masochistic tendency) and stated that sadism is a secondary transformation of this self-destructive urge, an attempt to turn the destruction away from oneself and onto the outside world, where it can be better borne. In any event, Freud emphasized that masochism is often hidden behind sadism; the victim is present within the attacker, either overtly, when the sadist for brief moments becomes himself a masochistic object of attack, or covertly, when throughout the activities he identifies with his victim vicariously.

It is uncertain whether or not there is a successful treatment for sexual sadism. There are a few reports of men treated by psychoanalysis or psychotherapy who, after

Freudian conceptions of sadomasochism

treatment, were driven less (or perhaps not at all) to inflict pain upon others; but programs of group therapy, particularly among convicted sadist offenders, have yet to demonstrate their curative or ameliorative effects. Thus far there are not adequate reports of the success of aversion treatment.

Masochism. Masochism is the condition in which sexual pleasure is derived from the sensation of physical pain. The pain may be either self-inflicted or inflicted by others and can involve such activities as flagellation, pin sticking, binding, spanking, or semi-strangulation. Masochistic sexual fantasies are ubiquitous in women, but overt masochistic behaviour to the point of sexual excitement seems more prevalent in men.

The interpretations of masochism often parallel the interpretations of sadism (see above *Sadism*); many authorities consider masochism a mirror image of sadism, with both tendencies found in varying degrees in the same person. Freud related masochism both to the "death instinct" (the wish for one's own dissolution) and to sadism turned round on oneself. Others have suggested that masochism is a means of holding sadistic impulses in check, and there are indeed examples of persons having long experienced masochistic roles, only to explode, turn sadistic, and kill their attackers when their defenses suddenly fail.

Other attempts to explain the causes of masochism are more closely related to childhood experiences. It is suggested, for instance, that masochistic behaviour may arise when one believes that sexual relations are sinful or disgusting. When fantasying or engaging in sexual pleasures, therefore, the individual must atone or pay for his sin by means of self-torture. Other evidence suggests a relation between masochistic development and a lack of love and affection in childhood. A child who is neglected by his or her parents and who receives attention only when punished may turn repeatedly to punishment to get attention. Later, punishment translates into an assurance of being wanted and loved. Masochism may also be associated with martyrdom, a way of transferring guilt to others.

Persons with a masochistic life style are difficult to treat, particularly when their behaviour is coupled to the sadistic behaviour of a spouse or lover. As in the case of sadism, psychoanalysis and psychotherapy can be used to develop a patient's insight into his non-rational convictions; but the success of such therapies is still indeterminate for this deviation.

Rape. In psychiatric usage, rape is the act of taking sexual relations by force or threat and without the victim's consent. There is no term for the deviation itself (such as "rapism"), the habitual preference for forcible sexual relations. In legal usage the term rape extends to relatively nondeviational acts such as those involved in a man's obtaining consent through fraud or false pretenses, in a woman's submitting willingly and then retaliating with accusations, and in an adult's having nonforcible sexual relations with a minor (statutory rape) or a mentally incompetent. For obvious anatomical reasons, the deviation is found exclusively in males, about half of whom (according to court records) are married and living with their spouses when committing rape upon other women.

Deviational rape is a form of sadism in which the man achieves excitement only in the awareness that he is harming the woman, as evidenced by her struggles or anguish; behind this awareness lies a fantasy of revenge or a feeling that women are inferior and not worthy of decent treatment. Such attitudes often derive from childhood experiences in which the boy was rejected or humiliated by women and subjected to physical punishment excessive for the boy's misbehaviour. Rapists usually come from families in which violence is frequent between parents or between parents and children. In psychoanalytic theory involving the Oedipal complex, deviational rape represents a displaced attempt to force a rejecting mother into sexual relations.

Although psychoanalysis or related psychotherapies should help the motivated patient to discover the sources of his hatred of women and to find more acceptable means of gratifying his needs, there are as yet no reliable reports of successful treatment.

Satyriasis and nymphomania. Satyriasis and nymphomania refer to excessive or exaggerated sexual desire and activity on the part of males and females, respectively. The difficulty in drawing a meaningful line between "normal" and "excessive" sexual desire or activity is obvious. Satyriasis and nymphomania, which are psychologically induced, should be distinguished, however, from hypersexuality, a biological condition caused by brain lesions or hormonal imbalances and marked by extremely intense sexual desires and frequent spontaneous erection of the penis or clitoris.

A person who centres his or her life on sexual pleasures may do so for various reasons: to escape from one's problems, to compensate for the frustrations of life when few other pleasures are available, or to lend support to one's feelings of adequacy as man or woman. Such pleasures may be sought within marriage, in a variety of deviant sexual acts, or in a pattern of promiscuity. The promiscuous satyr and nymphomaniac—specifically, the person with an overpowering, tormenting need for sexual relations with a never-ending number of partners—will be dealt with here, since their attributes are more markedly deviational and definable.

In one variety of males and females, the purpose of such promiscuity is not sexual gratification per se but rather conquest and the proof of superiority over the opposite sex. The satyr or Don Juan, for instance, who operates on the fantasied belief that women are domineering and cruel must attempt to humiliate all women endlessly in an insatiable search for his self-esteem. Seduction is his aim, not sexual intercourse, unless such is necessary to hide his real purposes or to fix the woman dependently on him. The nymphomaniac of parallel design is trying to outdo men, who have been hated and envied since early childhood for their social and anatomical power. The nymphomaniacal woman needs to demonstrate repeatedly that she is better than any man and can outperform him in that most prideful competition, sexual intercourse. Such a woman has another device, in addition to changing partners, for humiliating a man: she insists that he have intercourse "one more time." Then, no matter how many times he manages, she needs "one more time" and in this way wins.

In another variety of satyriasis and nymphomania, the never-ending (and thus painful) search for mates is a search for a fantasied ideal man or woman. Genital sensation is secondary or unimportant; the test is not to outdo or outlast one's partner in sexual intercourse but to find some idealized virtue or quality. A woman may be wanting a sense of peace and safety, for which she searches in man after man. A man may be testing for purity but, in successfully seducing a woman, he proves she is not his pure woman ("the perfect mother").

Without treatment, the satyric or nymphomaniacal sufferer tries to cure the incurable with endless liaisons and thus runs the risk of developing a gradual sense of hopelessness as the years pass, sometimes eventuating in acute depression or even suicide. Such hopelessness derives not only from his or her enslavement to seduction (with all the energy that such requires) but also from the process of aging and reduced attractiveness and potency (physiological or psychological), forcing him or her to rely more on wiliness than on youthful prowess.

Because of the often underlying fears of not being manly or feminine enough (*i.e.*, of being homosexual), the patient must get insight into the roots of the condition if he or she is to be freed from its thralldom. This requires extensive psychotherapy or psychoanalysis.

OTHER DEVIATIONS

Abstinence. Abstinence is the conscious avoidance of sexual relations. As a mode of self-restraint, it can be distinguished from biological states (such as aging, castrations, genetic disorders, or malnutrition) that prevent sexual activity or desire. There are several modes or degrees of abstinence, among them those involving (1) full masturbation; (2) masturbation short of orgasm; (3) excitement engendered by fantasy, without masturbation and with or without orgasm; (4) disguised sexual excitement;

as in religious frenzies containing unacknowledged sexual imagery or in various kinds of veiled sadistic or masochistic abuse; and (5) total self-denial, without any detectable sexual excitement or substitution.

There are also various motivations for abstinence, such as extreme commitment to a moral or intellectual purpose (private or institutional) requiring abstinence, or extreme fear of punishment from one's conscience. There are also rare persons who, though biologically normal, are effortlessly abstinent.

Compared to most other deviations, abstinence is a common pattern in those societies in which religious and ethical systems place a premium upon physical denial. As a test of motivation and as a respectable offering to higher powers, abstinence has been pursued for thousands of years in almost every culture. Its value in focussing sexual frustration into other productive channels of behaviour is as strong today as in earlier eras.

Deviational masturbation. Masturbation is self-stimulation of the genitals, commonly to orgasm, using the hand, some other bodily part, or an inanimate instrument. It is the most common cause of orgasm in both males and females prior to marriage. The frequency of the practice depends on the intensity of one's sex drive, emotional conflicts, and the availability of other outlets.

Although most psychiatrists and psychologists consider masturbation an expected practice on the path to heterosexual relations, it serves equally to gratify in fantasy many of the sexual deviations discussed above. Additionally, it can be deviational if it persists out of fear of heterosexual relations or if it is so associated with shame or guilt as to cause serious personality disorders of a broader nonsexual nature. Folkways deploring masturbation as a "vile habit" are common in many societies historically, causing chronic guilt and sense of inferiority in some young people.

Although masturbation itself may not be sexually deviant in a statistical sense, the fantasies accompanying it usually are. In mild form, these may be simply voyeuristic, but in more involved storytelling, deviation appears. For instance, a person may, while masturbating, fantasy being beaten, raped, or humiliated or taking revenge upon members of the opposite sex. Because such fantasies may appear even in nondeviational heterosexuals, however, they point up the fact that sexual deviation is a relative, not an absolute, state.

Polymorphous-perverse personality. The term polymorphous-perverse personality refers to an individual who is indiscriminate in his object or mode of sexual behaviour. Although the capacity to imagine oneself in almost any deviant act is general, few people can or need to perform such acts. Some individuals, however, can enjoy almost any potential inducer of orgasm, whether the sex object be man, woman, child, beast or inanimate object and whether the method involves the object's genitals or some other body part. This lack of discrimination, because it resembles the sensual activities of small children, is thought to result from a person's inability to develop sexually beyond early stages of life.

Although the condition is occasionally found in the mentally retarded (who fail to develop well beyond childhood) and in persons disturbed by brain lesions as in senility, most people with a polymorphous-perverse personality are either nearly or wholly psychotic persons or nonpsychotic persons who, in sexual and nonsexual areas of living, are unable to develop lasting, affectionate relations with others.

Minor deviations. The variety of deviant sexual acts seems limited only by a human being's anatomy and physiology and his capacity for invention and fantasy. Thus there are innumerable other sexual acts and patterns—such as cunnilingus (oral stimulation of the vulva or clitoris) and fellatio (oral stimulation of the penis); buggery, or anal intercourse; acts involving urination or defecation; frottage, or rubbing against other persons for sexual excitement (as in crowded buses or subways); and coprolalia, or using obscene language. Most such behaviour would not be defined as deviant if the acts are momentary, experimental, for variety, or part of fore-play. These acts would be considered in the realm of sexual deviation if they involved a habitual and preferred practice (such as the need not only to use obscene language for piquancy during intercourse but as a hostile act with strangers, as in obscene telephone calls). Some, of course, are elements of other deviations, such as homosexuality or sadomasochism.

It should also be noted that such conditions as pyromania and kleptomania may be sexual deviations when they are demonstrably associated with sexual excitement or gratification.

BIBLIOGRAPHY. C.E. ALLEN, *Textbook of Psychosexual Disorders* (1962), a general text describing in detail and with case material all the sexual deviations, their causes and treatment, from a psychodynamic viewpoint; I. BIEBER *et al.*, *Homosexuality: A Psychoanalytic Study* (1962), the most extensive study published of the psychodynamics of homosexuality and of the usefulness of psychoanalysis in treatment; HAVELOCK ELLIS, *Studies in the Psychology of Sex*, 4 vol. (1936), a classic work, emphasizing case descriptions of the sexual deviations; C.S. FORD and F.A. BEACH, *Patterns of Sexual Behaviour* (1951), an overview especially stressing the relationship of animal research and anthropological data to understanding normal and abnormal sexual behaviour in Western society; SIGMUND FREUD, *Three Essays on the Theory of Sexuality* (1905), the original fundamental study of normal and abnormal sexuality, from the psychoanalytic viewpoint; ALFRED C. KINSEY *et al.*, *Sexual Behavior in the Human Male* (1948), *Sexual Behavior in the Human Female* (1953), the most extensive attempts to describe statistically sexual practices in American males and females; RICHARD KRAFFT-EBING, *Psychopathia Sexualis* (1886; Eng. trans. by H.E. WEDECK, 1965), another classic, primarily descriptive, collection of case studies; J. MARMOR (ed.), *Sexual Inversion: The Multiple Roots of Homosexuality* (1965), a series of essays by authorities on aspects of homosexuality ranging from biological through psychoanalytic to social; R.J. STOLLER, *Sex and Gender* (1968), a study on earliest roots of masculinity and femininity, using highly deviant subjects as "natural experiments" for revealing more normal processes of gender development.

(R.J.S.)

Seychelles

The Seychelles Archipelago, a colony of the United Kingdom, is situated in the Indian Ocean 4° south of the Equator and approximately 900 miles from the coast of East Africa. It consists of 85 islands made up of two main groups: the Mahé group of 40 islands and islets of granitic formation; and islands of coralline formation which are scattered, some of them as far as 600 miles from Mahé. These latter are, for the most part, but little over sea level, whereas the granitic islands are mountainous, the highest reaching 2,971 feet (906 metres).

The islands have a total area of 107 square miles (278 square kilometres), of which the Mahé group take up some 90 square miles. Mahé itself is some 55 square miles. The next largest is Praslin, where a unique double coconut (coco-demer) and the black parrot are to be found.

The average temperatures of the Seychelles are 84° F (29° C) maximum and 77° F (25° C) minimum. The calm seasons, when the humidity is high and therefore the temperature seems hotter, are October and November and March to May. From December to February the northwest monsoon may bring a little rain, but the wind provides excellent surfing on the western side of Mahé. Hurricanes, cyclones, or typhoons are unknown. Annual rainfall, which is variable, averages 92 inches.

(C.G.de C.)

History. It is possible that the Arabs, adventuring in their dhows in the 9th century, were the first to see the Seychelles. It is certain that the Portuguese visited them in the 16th century and made charts; they called them the "Seven Sisters," by which name they were known until the French located them again in 1768.

There were no indigenous inhabitants, nor did the Portuguese attempt to settle the islands, which, during the early 18th century, proved to be ideal hideouts for pirates, who are said to have landed their booty and to have hidden it in various caches. British and French warships hunted the pirates vigorously until the last of them, Olivier le Vasseur, was captured.

Arrival of the Europeans

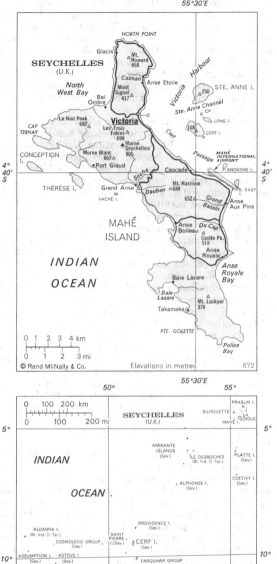

The people. The original French colonists were in the 19th century joined by deportees from France, by a few British, and by African slaves freed from Arab dhows by the British Navy. Asians from China, India, and Malaysia arrived later in smaller numbers. They were mostly traders and shopkeepers. Intermarriages left only few families of pure European descent. The census of 1960 put the total population at 41,041. The 1971 census recorded that the population had risen to about 52,400. About one-third of the islands are inhabited, but four-fifths of the population lived on Mahé; and Victoria, the only sizable town, had more than 13,000 inhabitants.

Composition of the population

Seychelles, Area and Population				
	area		population	
	sq mi	sq km	1960 census	1971 census*
Island groups				
Coralline Islands				
Alphonse	0.7	1.8	90	40
Assumption	4.3	11.1	30	60
Astove	1.9	4.9	50	9
Bird	0.3	0.8	50	20
Coetivy	3.6	9.3	200	120
Cosmoledo	1.7	4.4	60	20
D'Arros	0.6	1.6	100	40
Denis	0.5	1.3	70	30
Marie Louise	0.2	0.5	20	10
Platte	0.5	1.3	20	30
Poivre	1.0	2.6	20	40
Providence	0.6	1.6	80	40
Remire Reef	0.1	0.3	10	3
St. Pierre	0.6	1.6	50	50
Granitic Islands				
Frigate	0.8	2.1	90	30
La Digue and satellites	5.6	14.5	2,000	2,000
Mahé and satellites	58.7	152.0	33,000	45,200
North	0.8	2.1	50	30
Praslin and satellites	17.3	44.8	4,000	4,200
Recif	0.1	0.3	10	10
Silhouette	6.3	16.3	800	400
Total Seychelles	107.4†	278.2†‡	41,000§‖	52,400§

*Preliminary census figures. †Includes 1.2 sq mi (3.1 sq km) of uninhabited land. ‡Converted area figures do not add to total because of rounding. §Figures do not add to total given because of rounding. ‖Excludes the population of Aldabra, Farquhar, and Desroches, which became part of British Indian Ocean Territory in 1965.
Source: Official government figures.

English is the official language and the medium of instruction in schools, although French is allowed in the courts and governing council. The commonly spoken language is a creole patois, a mixture of clipped French, much of it archaic, with words from African dialects and a few mutilated English words. Most of the population is Roman Catholic. Less than one-tenth is Anglican, and there are a few Seventh-day Adventists, Hindus, Muslims, Buddhists, Parsis, and pagans. Witchcraft and voodoo also have their devotees. Street processions on saints' days with pilgrimages to a mountain church and picnics are very popular. There is little native culture, but tortoiseshell ornaments, lacework, raffia, and coco-demer mats and fans are sold to tourists. (Ed.)

Economic life. Copra continues to be the mainstay of the islands' economy, its quality and reputation on the world's markets being well maintained by the rigorous inspection services of the agricultural department and the cooperation of the growers. Production for export has decreased considerably, however, because many hotels are being built and large swathes of coconut palms are being felled to make room for them. Exports have also been reduced because of an increase in population and local consumption.

Cinnamon bark and cinnamon, which at one time formed part of the colony's main exports, are also on the decrease. Cinnamon leaf oil production has been reduced to a very small tonnage because of the high salary of local labourers and the low prices offered on the American market. Guano exports go mainly to the island of Mauritius, where it is used on the sugarcane plantations.

Since the completion in 1971 of an international airport, the primary means of access to the islands has become air

In 1742 the French governor of Mauritius, which was then known as Île de France, dispatched a Captain Lazare Picault to explore the islands to the north. Picault eventually anchored in a bay on the southwest coast of Mahé, but he stayed only for a few days in November of that year. He was sent back two years later and landed where Victoria now stands on May 30, 1744. He then renamed the island Mahé. The French made no real attempt to annex Mahé and its surrounding islands until 1756, when the frigate "Le Cerf" was sent to forestall the British, who were thought to be looking for islands to use as a naval base. A stone claiming possession was set up, and the flag of France was hoisted. The master of "Le Cerf" gave the name of Séchelles to the group in honour of the controller general of finance to Louis XV. The British later altered the spelling to Seychelles. No actual colonization took place until about 1768, when the first colonists began to arrive from Mauritius. The small colony appears to have made rapid progress, for in addition to coconuts, the people grew maize, cotton, and coffee. By the early 19th century the population, composed of Frenchmen, their African slaves, and a few east Indians, had grown to more than 2,000. War between France and Britain broke out in 1778, but the islands were not affected until 1794 when Captain Newcome in HMS "Orpheus" arrived with four other ships to take on supplies and demanded capitulation. The Seychelles were finally ceded to Britain in 1815 by the Treaty of Paris.

services originating from London or from African or Asian cities. A mail and passenger ship from Bombay calls every two months en route to East and South Africa, and a government launch operates between the main islands.

Administration. The administrative capital is Victoria on Mahé. The islands are governed by a governor and commander in chief, assisted by a council of ministers consisting of a chief minister, four ministers, an ex officio attorney general, a financial secretary, and a deputy governor. There is also a legislative assembly consisting of 15 members elected under universal adult suffrage, three official members, and a speaker. The governor does not preside over the assembly.

Political parties

The colony has two main political parties: the Seychelles Democratic Party (SDP), which won ten seats in the 1970 general elections, and the Seychelles People's United Party (SPUP), which won only the five remaining seats, though it won 44 percent of the total votes cast. A third party known as Le Parti Seychellois (LPS) failed to win any seat at the elections. Under the 1970 constitution, the governor has powers over the civil service, law and order, government press and radio, defense, and foreign affairs.   (C.G.de C.)

BIBLIOGRAPHY. A more detailed description of these islands may be found in WILLIAM TRAVIS, *Beyond the Reefs* (1959); and ATHOL THOMAS, *Forgotten Eden: A View of the Seychelles Islands in the Indian Ocean* (1968). On the history, see J.T. BRADLEY, *The History of the Seychelles*, 2 vol. (1940); and on the economy, J.W.F. ROWE, *Report on the Economy of the Seychelles and Its Future Development* (1959); and the biennial *Colonial Report on the Seychelles* (HMSO).

Sforza, Ludovico

One of the most magnificent of the Renaissance princes, a patron of Leonardo da Vinci and other great artists, Ludovico Sforza was at the same time typical of his time and rank in his ruthless pursuit of personal power. He won a leading position in Italy by his subtle and unprincipled diplomacy and his boundless trust in himself and his destiny.

Alinari

Sforza, detail from the Sforzesca altarpiece by the Master of the Pala Sforzesca (1480–1520). In the Brera, Milan.

Rise to power

Ludovico Sforza was born at Vigevano, Pavia, on July 27, 1452, the second son of Francesco Sforza, who had made himself duke of Milan. While still a child, he received the epithet il Moro (the Moor) because of his dark complexion and black hair. Brought up at his father's refined court, he remained, after his father's death in 1466, in the service of the new ruler, his elder brother Galeazzo Maria. When Galeazzo was murdered, however, in 1476, leaving the dukedom to his seven-year-

old son Gian Galeazzo II, Ludovico first revealed his appetite for power, plotting to win the regency from the child's mother, Bona of Savoy. The plot failed, and Ludovico was exiled but eventually, through threats and flattery, won a reconciliation with Bona and brought about the execution of her most influential adviser and chief minister, Cicco Simonetta, in 1480. Shortly afterward, he compelled Bona to leave Milan, and Ludovico assumed the regency for his nephew, becoming the virtual head of state.

From that moment he entered the arena of "equilibrium politics," by which a precarious balance was maintained among the major Italian states—Milan, Venice, Florence, the Papal States, and Naples. Taking advantage of the rivalry between these states, he established Milan's supremacy. Distrusting Venice, he remained on good terms with Florence and its Medici ruler, Lorenzo the Magnificent. He secured useful alliances with Ferdinand I, king of Naples, whose granddaughter Isabella was married in 1489 to Gian Galeazzo, and with the Borgia pope Alexander VI, through the influence of Ludovico's brother Ascanio, who was a cardinal. In 1491 Ludovico married Beatrice d'Este, the beautiful and cultured daughter of the Duke of Ferrara. The marriage proved to be unusually harmonious, in spite of Ludovico's mistresses; and Beatrice bore him two sons, Massimiliano and Francesco, both of whom later became dukes of Milan.

With lavish but enlightened patronage of artists and scholars, Ludovico made the court of Milan the most splendid not only in Italy but in Europe. Leonardo da Vinci and the architect Donato Bramante were among the many artists, poets, and musicians who gathered in Milan. Ludovico sponsored extensive work in civil and military engineering, such as canals and fortifications. The court and the common people alike rejoiced in Ludovico's magnificent celebrations; the Milanese, however, though enjoying considerable well-being, were increasingly burdened by taxes.

Resentful of the overshadowing splendour of the court of Ludovico and Beatrice, Gian Galeazzo, the rightful ruler of Milan, and his wife Isabella left Milan to establish another court at Pavia. Isabella was more outraged by Ludovico's flagrant usurpation of the ducal powers than even her husband, who had only a passing interest in politics. She appealed to her grandfather, Ferdinand I, who intervened in 1492, ordering Ludovico to surrender control of the duchy to Isabella and Gian Galeazzo.

Ludovico refused and, fearing a war with Naples, formed an alliance with two foreign sovereigns, the emperor Maximilian I and King Charles VIII of France. For an enormous sum of money Maximilian not only bestowed upon Ludovico the title of duke of Milan in 1494, legitimizing his usurpation, but also married Bianca Maria, Gian Galeazzo's sister. Charles VIII, who was contemplating the seizure of the kingdom of Naples from Ferdinand, received Ludovico's promise of help.

Alliance with Maximilian I and Charles VIII

The campaign of Charles VIII to conquer Naples in 1494–95 threw the whole of Italy into confusion and eventually alarmed even Ludovico himself. He joined the league led by Venice, which, in spite of Charles's initial successes, soon expelled him from Italy. Ludovico was the ultimate victor in this affair, achieving for a time maximum safety and almost unlimited power; both Gian Galeazzo and Ferdinand died in 1494, and Charles VIII himself soon became reconciled with him. Ludovico is reported to have said at the time that Pope Alexander was his chaplain, the emperor Maximilian his general, the governing Signoria of Venice his chamberlain, and Charles VIII his courier. The illusion, however, did not last long.

Charles VIII died in 1498 and was succeeded by Louis XII, a descendant of the first duke of Milan. Louis claimed the duchy and with the support of Venice and a Milanese population oppressed by Ludovico's taxation quickly conquered it. When the Milanese had in turn tired of Louis's rule, Ludovico, who sought refuge with Maximilian, tried to retake Milan with German and Swiss mercenaries. His Swiss troops, however, refused to fight for him in a crucial battle, and in April 1500 Ludo-

Ludovico's fall

vico was captured by the French while attempting to escape, disguised as a Swiss. His fall was celebrated all over Italy. He was imprisoned in the castle of Loches in Touraine, from which he tried in vain to escape. He died there, still unresigned, on May 27, 1508.

The memory of Ludovico was clouded for centuries by Machiavelli's accusation that he "invited" Charles VIII to invade Italy, paving the way for subsequent foreign domination. The charge was perpetuated by later historians who espoused the ideal of national independence. More recent historians, however, placing the figure of Ludovico in its Renaissance setting, have re-evaluated his merits as a ruler and given a more equitable assessment of his achievement.

BIBLIOGRAPHY. The personality of Ludovico Sforza is described with full particulars in F. MALAGUZZI-VALERI, *La Corte di Lodovico il Moro*, 4 vol. (1913–23; 2nd ed. of vol. 1 only, 1929); and compendiously in E. VERGA, *Storia della vita milanese* (1909; 2nd ed., 1931). Concise biographies are: S.A. NULLI, *Lodovico il Moro* (1929); and P. PIERI, "Ludovico il Moro," in *Enciclopedia Italiana*, vol. 21 (1934). Biographical information may also be found in the best works on the Sforza Family: C. SANTORO, *Gli Sforza* (1968), an excellent book with an exhaustive bibliography; L. COLLISON MORLEY, *The Story of the Sforzas* (1933); and G. FRANCIOSI, *Gli Sforza* (1932). The politics of Ludovico Sforza and the Renaissance in Milan are dealt with in detail by various authors in TRECCANI'S *Storia di Milano*, vol. 7 (1956) and vol. 8 (1957).

(Al.B.)

Shaftesbury, Anthony Ashley Cooper, 1st Earl of

Anthony Ashley Cooper, the 1st earl of Shaftesbury, whose political career extended over more than 40 years, is best known as the most prominent and skillful opponent of Charles II's pro-Catholic policies. He was born at Wimborne St. Giles, Dorset, on July 22, 1621. From his maternal grandfather, Sir Anthony Ashley, and his father, Sir John Cooper, he inherited estates in Dorset and Wiltshire, and although some were lost through litigations during his minority, his inheritance was large enough to enable him to contemplate a career in politics at an early age. On February 25, 1639, he married Margaret, the daughter of Lord Coventry, Charles I's Lord Keeper; this marriage ended with her death ten years later. When still only 18, he had been elected to the Short Parliament (April–May) of 1640, but his election to the Long Parliament of the same year was disputed and he was not allowed to take his seat.

Role in the Civil War Though the Civil War broke out in 1642, Cooper did not take up arms for the King until the summer of 1643, and in February 1644 he went over to the side of Parliament, dissatisfied with the political and religious influences uppermost at the Royalist Court in Oxford (the

By courtesy of the National Portrait Gallery, London

The 1st Earl of Shaftesbury, painting from the studio of J. Greenhill, c. 1672–73. In the National Portrait Gallery, London.

king's headquarters) at that time. He took an active part in the operations in Dorset in 1644. There is little evidence of his activities between 1645 and 1652, other than his marriage to Lady Frances Cecil, the Earl of Exeter's sister, in 1650, and that he became a member of a commission to aid a parliamentary committee that was to examine projects for law reform. It may have been this commission membership that secured his nomination to the Barebones Parliament (July–December) of 1653. In December 1653 he helped to persuade the more conservative majority of that Parliament to resign its powers to Oliver Cromwell, the victorious Puritan leader. As a result, he was appointed to the Council of State established by the Instrument of Government that set up the Protectorate—with Cromwell as Lord Protector—and elected to the first Parliament that met under its terms, in 1654. His association with Cromwell ceased at the end of that year, however, probably because he disliked a regime that seemed increasingly more military than parliamentary. In 1655 (his second wife had died in 1654) he married as his third wife, Margaret Spencer, the niece of the earl of Southampton, the leading Cavalier peer remaining in England after Charles's execution, but there is no evidence that he positively favoured a Royalist Restoration until 1660, when every other possible political alternative had proved unsuccessful. On May 8 he was appointed one of the 12 commissioners sent by the House of Commons to Holland to invite Charles II to return, and after Charles had done so, Cooper was admitted to Charles's Privy Council.

Office under Charles II From 1660–73 he held office under Charles II, becoming Lord Ashley in 1661 and earl of Shaftesbury in 1672. During this period his intelligence, his capacity for business, and his ability as a speaker in the House of Lords were generally recognized, but because of his equivocal political past he was at first given only the then minor office of chancellor of the exchequer. By the end of the 1660s, however, he had been admitted to the King's "Cabinet Council" and in 1672 he became lord chancellor—the last to preside in Chancery with no formal legal training other than a short spell in Lincoln's Inn (one of the four legal schools and societies). His name has been associated with three particular acts of policy between 1670 and 1673: the Stop of the Exchequer of 1672, which by suspending the repayment of debt for twelve months gave Charles the use of his revenue for naval preparations; the Declaration of Indulgence of the same year; and the third Dutch war of 1672–74. The first of these is now known to have been the responsibility of Sir Thomas Clifford; the second reflected his consistent desire to secure toleration for Dissenters (religious groups that did not belong to the Church of England), though the King and Clifford intended the bill primarily as relief for Catholics; the third was, in Shaftesbury's mind, a natural continuation of the commercial rivalry with the Dutch. Earlier, in 1670, he signed a sham Anglo-French treaty supposedly to reduce the commercial supremacy of the Dutch, but he was unaware that the previous secret Treaty of Dover had provided for Charles to declare himself a Catholic, a prospect he could never have condoned. In 1673 he supported the first Test Act, designed to exclude Catholics from office, and opposed the marriage of the King's brother and heir, James, duke of York, a Catholic, to another Catholic. Later in that same year, Charles, feeling that he could no longer trust his chancellor, dismissed him.

In the years that followed, Shaftesbury gradually became the most formidable politician in the Whig opposition or "Country Party," against the King and his Lord Treasurer, Danby, until, in 1678, a certain Titus Oates gave information about an alleged extensive Catholic plot to kill Charles and put James on the throne. This gave Shaftesbury his first real chance to acquire a wide base of support. Though he had not contrived the tale—nor did he prompt Oates to come forward at first—he realized he could exploit the situation to his own advantage. In the ensuing national panic, Shaftesbury took control of the political chaos, organized an elaborate party network, exercised great control over elections, and acquired a

The
Exclusion
Bill

large following in Parliament. His strategy was primarily aimed at securing the passage of the Exclusion Bill, which would keep Catholic James from the throne, using Charles's illegitimate son, the duke of Monmouth, a puppet of Shaftesbury, as a possible claimant to the throne. Although the bill passed in the Commons, it was rejected by the Lords because of the King's strong opposition. Shaftesbury rode to the next Parliament, at Oxford on March 21, 1681, with an armed following, but Charles dissolved it within a week, leaving him helpless, without a following, and, as the general panic dissolved, without a cause. He was seized on July 2, 1681, and committed to the Tower of London, but he was acquitted of the trumped-up charge of treason by a London grand jury in November. Shortly before the trial the most famous attack on him, John Dryden's satire *Absalom and Achitophel*, appeared. In the absence of another Parliament, Shaftesbury could do little more. After privately discussing the possibility of rising against the government, he fled the country in November 1682, and died in Holland in January 1683.

Shaftesbury was a man of intelligence, charm, and wide and usually enlightened interests, including those related to colonization. In 1663, he was given a grant, along with seven others, of the province of Carolina in North America, and was appointed president of the Council of Trade and Foreign Plantations from 1672 to 1674. The philosopher John Locke, who helped him to draft the *Fundamental Constitutions* of Carolina and superintended the surgical operation that saved his life in 1668, was a member of his household from 1667 to 1675. Recent scholarly work on Locke has stressed the importance of his connection with Shaftesbury and has modified the impression of the earl left by Dryden's partisan satires and other unfavourable, sometimes unjust, evaluations through history.

BIBLIOGRAPHY. The most recent biography is K.H.D. HALEY, *The First Earl of Shaftesbury* (1968), an attempt to demonstrate a consistency of political outlook throughout Shaftesbury's various changes in his career. Earlier biographies are W.D. CHRISTIE, *A Life of Anthony Ashley Cooper, First Earl of Shaftesbury* (1871); and L.F. BROWN, *The First Earl of Shaftesbury* (1933). The best general account of the reign of Charles II is in D. OGG, *England in the Reign of Charles II*, 2 vol., 2nd ed. (1955). ANDREW BROWNING, *Thomas Osborne, Earl of Danby and Duke of Leeds, 1632–1712*, 3 vol. (1944–51), is a biography of Shaftesbury's most important rival. See also M. LEE, *The Cabal* (1965); and J.R. JONES, *The First Whigs* (1961).

(K.H.D.H.)

Shaka

In the first quarter of the 19th century the tribal structure of southern Africa was convulsed by wars generated by Shaka, the ruthless founder of the Zulu Empire. In less than a decade as the paramount chieftain of the Zulu clan, he revolutionized the techniques of tribal warfare and fashioned an efficient and terrifying fighting force that created havoc throughout the area of present-day Natal and beyond.

Shaka was born about 1787, the son of Senzangakona, chieftain of the Zulu, and Nandi, an orphaned princess of the neighbouring Langeni clan. Because his parents belonged to the same clan, their marriage violated Zulu custom, and the stigma of this extended to the child. The couple separated when Shaka was six, and Nandi took her son back to the Langeni, where he passed a fatherless boyhood among a people who despised his mother and made him the butt of endless cruel pranks. In 1802 the Langeni drove Nandi out, and she finally found shelter with the Dletsheni, a subclan of the powerful Mtetwa. When Shaka was 23, the Mtetwa paramount chieftain, called up Shaka's Dletsheni age group for military service. For the next six years, he served with brilliance as a warrior of the Mtetwa Empire.

Senzangakona died in 1816, and Dingiswayo released Shaka from service and sent him to take over the Zulu. The eldest son of Senzangakona's Great Wife had already mounted the throne; messengers slew him even before Shaka arrived.

Shaka, lithograph by W. Bagg, 1836.
By courtesy of the trustees of the British Museum; photograph, J.R. Freeman & Co. Ltd.

The Zulu, at this time, probably numbered fewer than 1,500, occupying an area on the White Umfolozi River, perhaps ten miles on a side. They were among the smallest of the more than 800 Eastern Nguni–Bantu clans, but from the day of Shaka's arrival they left forever the ranks of the sleepy upcountry clans and commenced their march to greatness. Shaka ruled with an iron hand from the outset, meting out instant death for the slightest opposition.

His first act was to reorganize the army. Like all the clans, the Zulu were armed with oxhide shields and spindly throwing spears. Battles were little more than brief and relatively bloodless clashes in which the outnumbered side prudently gave way before extensive casualties occurred. Shaka first rearmed his men with a long-bladed, short-hafted stabbing assegai, which forced them to fight at close quarters. He then instituted the regimental system based on age groups, quartered at separate kraals (villages) and distinguished by uniform markings on shields and by various combinations of headdress and ornaments. He also developed standard tactics, which the Zulu used in every battle. The available regiments (known collectively as the *impi*) were divided into four groups. The strongest, termed the "chest," closed with the enemy to pin him down, while two "horns" raced out to encircle and attack the foe from behind. A reserve, known as the "loins," was seated nearby, with its back to the battle so as not to become unduly excited, and could be sent to reinforce any part of the ring if the enemy threatened to break out. The battle was supervised by *indunas*, or officers, who used hand signals to direct the regiments. An *impi* consistently covered 50 miles a day, living off grain and cattle requisitioned from the kraals it passed, and accompanied by boys who carried the warriors' sleeping mats and cooking pots.

Shaka fought for extermination, incorporating the remnants of the clans he smashed into the Zulu. He first sopped up the small clans in his vicinity, starting with the Langeni; he sought out the men who had made his boyhood a misery and impaled them on the sharpened stakes of their own kraal fences. In less than a year, the Zulu—and their army—had quadrupled in number. In 1817 Dingiswayo—still Shaka's overlord—was murdered, and the last restraint on Zulu expansion removed. Within two years, Shaka bested the only clans large enough to threaten him, the Ndwandwe and the Qwabe, and in a series

Reorganization of the army

The
Mfecane
of the
1820s

of annual campaigns he then struck at and smashed the complex network of clans living to the south of the Zulu territories. By 1823 present-day Natal was a depopulated ruin of smoking kraals, and the terrified survivors had broken up tribal patterns as far away as the Cape Colony.

Although Shaka's depredations were limited to the coastal area, they led indirectly to the *Mfecane* ("the Crushing") that devastated the inland plateau in the early 1820s. Marauding clans, fleeing the Zulu wrath and searching for land, started a deadly game of musical chairs that broke the clan structure of the interior and left 2,000,000 dead in its wake. The Boer Great Trek of the 1830s passed through this area, succeeding only because virtually no one was left to oppose them.

The first Europeans came to Port Natal (present-day Durban) in 1824. A dozen settlers of the Farewell Trading Company established a post on the landlocked bay and soon made contact with Shaka, whose kraal Bulawayo lay 100 miles to the north. Fascinated by their ways and their artifacts, but convinced that his own civilization was much superior, he permitted them to stay. Two of the early settlers, Henry Francis Fynn and Nathanial Isaacs, became fluent Zulu linguists, and most of what is known of early Nguni history stems from their writings.

In 1827 Nandi died, and with his mother's death Shaka became openly psychotic. About 7,000 Zulus were killed in the initial paroxysm of his grief, and for a year no crops were planted, nor could milk—the basis of the Zulu diet staple—be used. All women found pregnant were slain with their husbands, as were thousands of milch cows, so that even the calves might know what it was to lose a mother.

Early in 1828 Shaka sent the *impi* south in a raid that carried the warriors clear to the borders of the Cape Colony. They had no sooner returned, expecting the usual season's rest, than he sent them off to raid far in the north. It was too much for his associates, and two of his half-brothers, Dingane and Mhlangana, together with an *induna* named Mbopa, murdered him on September 22, 1828.

Shaka—who seems to have had at least a tendency to homosexuality—left no offspring, despite a harem of 1,200 women. (He consistently killed any woman there found pregnant.) He ruled by the sheer force of his personality, building, by scores of daily executions, a fear so profound that he could afford to ignore it. His subjects no more thought of resisting him than a mouse would gainsay an elephant.

Shaka dominates the history of the Eastern Nguni–Bantu, and as the founder of a Zulu Empire he has already passed into legend. He was highly intelligent and, at least on the tactical level, something of a military genius. He, nevertheless, lacked the political sagacity of a Dingiswayo or a Mshweshwe, who founded the Sotho nation from the debris of the *Mfecane*. Shaka's only objective was to destroy all that he encountered, subordinating as much land and as many people as possible to his personal hegemony. In that process, he created an armed nation so monolithic that it survived the mismanagement of two incompetent successors and lasted for 50 years, until the British destroyed it in the Zulu War of 1879.

BIBLIOGRAPHY. D.R. MORRIS, *The Washing of the Spears: A History of the Rise of the Zulu Nation under Shaka and its Fall in the Zulu War of 1879* (1965), a detailed account; JAMES STUART and D.M. MALCOLM (eds.), *The Diary of Henry Francis Fynn* (1950), and NATHANIEL ISSACS, *Travels and Adventures in Eastern Africa*, ed. by LOUIS HERRMAN, 2 vol. (1936–37), primary sources by two of the first Europeans to have prolonged contact with Shaka; A.T. BRYANT, *Olden Times in Zululand and Natal* (1929), an extensive history of the Eastern Nguni–Bantu clans during the Shakan era.

(D.R.M.)

Shakespeare, William

Widely regarded as the greatest writer of all time, William Shakespeare occupies a position unique in world literature. Other poets, such as Homer and Dante, and novelists, such as Leo Tolstoy and Charles Dickens, have

transcended national barriers; but no writer's living reputation can seriously compare with that of Shakespeare, whose plays, written in the late 16th and early 17th centuries for a small repertory theatre, are now performed and read more often and in more countries than ever before. The prophecy of his great contemporary, the poet and dramatist Ben Jonson, that Shakespeare "was not of an age, but for all time," has been marvellously fulfilled. It may be audacious even to attempt a definition of his greatness, but it is not so difficult to describe the variety of gifts that enabled him to create imaginative visions of pathos and mirth that, whether read in the book or witnessed in the theatre, fill the mind and linger there. He is a writer of great intellectual rapidity, perceptiveness, and poetic power. Other writers have had these qualities. But with Shakespeare the keenness of mind was applied not to abstruse or remote subjects but to human beings and their complete range of emotions and conflicts. Other writers have applied their keenness of mind in this way. But Shakespeare is astonishingly clever with words and images, so that his mental energy, when applied to intelligible human situations, finds full and memorable expression, convincing and imaginatively stimulating. As if this were not enough, the art form into which his creative energies went was not remote and bookish but involved the vivid stage impersonation of human beings, commanding sympathy and inviting vicarious participation. Thus many of Shakespeare's great merits can survive translation into other languages and into cultures remote from that of Elizabethan England.

By courtesy of the Folger Shakespeare Library, Washington, D.C.

Shakespeare, first proof of an engraved portrait by Martin Droeshout, from the frontispiece of the First Folio edition of Shakespeare's plays, 1623. In the Folger Shakespeare Library, Washington, D.C.

This article is divided into the following sections:

I. Shakespeare the man

HIS LIFE

Although the amount of factual knowledge available about Shakespeare is surprisingly large for one of his station in life, many find it a little disappointing, for it is mostly gleaned from documents of an official character. Dates of baptisms, marriages, deaths, and burials; wills, conveyances, legal processes, and payments by the court —these are the dusty details. There is, however, a fair number of contemporary allusions to him as a writer, and these add a reasonable amount of flesh and blood to the biographical skeleton.

Early life in Stratford. The parish register of Holy Trinity Church, Stratford-on-Avon, Warwickshire, shows that he was baptized there on April 26, 1564; his birthday is traditionally celebrated on April 23. His father, John Shakespeare, was a burgess of the borough, who in 1565 was chosen an alderman and in 1568 bailiff (the position corresponding to mayor, before the grant of a further charter to Stratford in 1664). He was engaged in various kinds of trade and appears to have suffered some fluctuations in prosperity. His wife, Mary Arden, of Wilmcote, Warwickshire, came from an ancient family and was the heiress to some land. (Given the somewhat rigid social distinctions of the 16th century, this marriage must have been a step up the social scale for John Shakespeare.)

Education at Stratford's grammar school

Stratford enjoyed a grammar school of good quality, and the education there was free, the schoolmaster's salary being paid by the borough. No lists of the pupils who were at the school in the 16th century have survived, but it would be absurd to suppose the bailiff of the town did not send his son there. The boy's education would consist mostly of Latin studies—learning to read, write, and speak the language fairly well and studying some of the classical historians, moralists, and poets. Shakespeare did not go on to the university, and indeed it is unlikely that the tedious round of logic, rhetoric, and other studies then followed there would have interested him.

Instead, at the age of 18 he married. Where and exactly when are not known, but the episcopal registry at Worcester preserves a bond dated November 28, 1582, and executed by two yeomen of Stratford, named Sandells and Richardson, as a security to the bishop for the issue of a license for the marriage of William Shakespeare and "Anne Hathaway of Stratford," upon the consent of her friends and upon once asking of the banns. (Anne died in 1623, seven years after Shakespeare. There is good evidence to associate her with a family of Hathaways who inhabited a beautiful farmhouse, now much visited, two miles from Stratford.) The next date of interest is found in the records of the Stratford church, where a daughter, named Susanna, born to William Shakespeare, was baptized on May 26, 1583. On February 2, 1585, twins were baptized, Hamnet and Judith. (The boy Hamnet, Shakespeare's only son, died 11 years later.)

How Shakespeare spent the next eight years or so, until his name begins to appear in London theatre records, is not known. There are stories—given currency long after his death—of stealing deer and getting into trouble with a local magnate, Sir Thomas Lucy of Charlecote, near Stratford; of earning his living as a schoolmaster in the country; of going to London and gaining entry to the world of theatre by minding the horses of theatregoers; it has also been conjectured that Shakespeare spent some time as a member of a great household and that he was a soldier, perhaps in the Low Countries. In lieu of external evidence, such extrapolations about Shakespeare's life have often been made from the internal "evidence" of his writings. But this method is unsatisfactory: one cannot conclude, for example, from his allusions to the law that Shakespeare was a lawyer; for he was clearly a writer, who without difficulty could get whatever knowledge he needed for the composition of his plays.

Career in the theatre. The first reference to Shakespeare in the literary world of London comes in 1592, when a fellow dramatist, Robert Greene, declared in a pamphlet written on his deathbed:

Greene's attack on the "upstart" dramatist

> There is an upstart crow, beautified with our feathers, that with his *Tygers heart wrapt in a Players hide* supposes he is as well able to bombast out a blank verse as the best of you; and, being an absolute *Johannes Factotum*, is in his own conceit the only Shake-scene in a country.

It is difficult to be certain what these words mean; but it is clear that they are insulting and that Shakespeare is the object of the sarcasms. When the book in which they appear (*Greenes, groats-worth of witte, bought with a million of Repentance*, 1592) was published after Greene's death, a mutual acquaintance wrote a preface offering an apology to Shakespeare and testifying to his worth. This preface also indicates that Shakespeare was by then making important friends. For, although the puritanical city of London was generally hostile to the theatre, many of the nobility were good patrons of the drama and friends of actors. Shakespeare seems to have attracted the attention of the young Henry Wriothesley, the 3rd earl of Southampton; and to this nobleman were dedicated his first published poems, *Venus and Adonis* and *The Rape of Lucrece*.

One striking piece of evidence that Shakespeare began to prosper early and tried to retrieve the family fortunes and establish its gentility is the fact that a coat of arms was granted to John Shakespeare in 1596. Rough drafts of this grant have been preserved in the College of Arms, London, though the final document, which must have been handed to the Shakespeares, has not survived. It can scarcely be doubted that it was William who took the initiative and paid the fees. The coat of arms appears on Shakespeare's monument (constructed before 1623) in the Stratford church. Equally interesting as evidence of Shakespeare's worldly success was his purchase in 1597 of New Place, a large house in Stratford, which as a boy he must have passed every day in walking to school.

It is not clear how his career in the theatre began; but from about 1594 onward he was an important member of the Lord Chamberlain's Company of players (called the King's Men after the accession of James I in 1603). They had the best actor, Richard Burbage; they had the best theatre, the Globe; they had the best dramatist, Shakespeare. It is no wonder that the company prospered. Shakespeare became a full-time professional man of his own theatre, sharing in a cooperative enterprise and intimately concerned with the financial success of the plays he wrote.

Unfortunately, written records give little indication of the way in which Shakespeare's professional life molded his marvellous artistry. All that can be deduced is that for 20 years Shakespeare devoted himself assiduously to his art, writing more than a million words of poetic drama of the highest quality.

Private life. Shakespeare had little contact with officialdom, apart from walking—dressed in the royal livery as a member of the King's Men—at the coronation of King James I in 1604. He continued to look after his financial interests. He bought properties in London and in Stratford. In 1605 he purchased a share (about one-fifth) of the Stratford tithes—a fact that explains why he was eventually buried in the chancel of its parish church. For some time he lodged with a French Huguenot family called Mountjoy, who lived near St. Olave's Church, Cripplegate, London. The records of a lawsuit in May 1612, due to a Mountjoy family quarrel, show Shakespeare as giving evidence in a genial way (though unable to remember certain important facts that would have decided the case) and as interesting himself generally in the family's affairs.

Shakespeare's financial interests

No letters written by Shakespeare have survived, but a private letter to him happened to get caught up with some official transactions of the town of Stratford and so has been preserved in the borough archives. It was written by one Richard Quiney and addressed by him from the Bell Inn in Carter Lane, London, whither he had gone from Stratford upon business. On one side of the paper is inscribed: "To my loving good friend and countryman, Mr. Wm. Shakespeare, deliver these." Apparently Quiney thought his fellow Stratfordian a person to whom he could apply for the loan of £30—a large sum in Elizabethan money. Nothing further is known about the transaction, but, because so few opportunities of seeing into Shakespeare's private life present themselves, this begging letter becomes a touching document. It is of some interest, moreover, that 18 years later Quiney's son

Thomas became the husband of Judith, Shakespeare's second daughter.

Shakespeare's will (made on March 25, 1616) is a long and detailed document. It entailed his quite ample property on the male heirs of his elder daughter, Susanna. (Both his daughters were then married, one to the aforementioned Thomas Quiney and the other to John Hall, a respected physician of Stratford.) As an afterthought, he bequeathed his "second-best bed" to his wife; but no one can be certain what this notorious legacy means. The testator's signatures to the will are apparently in a shaky hand. Perhaps Shakespeare was already ill. He died on April 23, 1616. No name was inscribed on his gravestone in the chancel of the parish church of Stratford-on-Avon. Instead these lines, possibly his own, appeared:

Good friend, for Jesus' sake forbear
To dig the dust enclosed here.
Blest be the man that spares these stones,
And curst be he that moves my bones.

EARLY POSTHUMOUS DOCUMENTATION

Shakespeare's family or friends, however, were not content with a simple gravestone, and, within a few years, a monument was erected on the chancel wall. It seems to have existed by 1623. Its Latin epitaph, immediately below the bust, attributes to Shakespeare the worldly wisdom of Nestor, the genius of Socrates, and the poetic art of Virgil. This apparently was how his contemporaries in Stratford-on-Avon wished their fellow citizen to be remembered.

The tributes of his colleagues. The memory of Shakespeare survived long in theatrical circles, for his plays remained a major part of the repertory of the King's Men until the closing of the theatres in 1642. The greatest of Shakespeare's great contemporaries in the theatre, Ben Jonson, had a good deal to say about him. To William Drummond of Hawthornden in 1619 he said that Shakespeare "wanted art." But, when he came to write his splendid poem prefixed to the Folio edition of Shakespeare's plays in 1623, he rose to the occasion with stirring words of praise:

Triumph, my Britain, thou hast one to show
To whom all scenes of Europe homage owe.
He was not of an age, but for all time!

Besides almost retracting his earlier gibe about Shakespeare's lack of art, he gives testimony that Shakespeare's personality was to be felt, by those who knew him, in his poetry—that the style was the man. Jonson also reminded his readers of the strong impression the plays had made upon Queen Elizabeth I and King James I at court performances:

Sweet Swan of Avon, what a sight it were
To see thee in our waters yet appear,
And make those flights upon the banks of Thames
That so did take Eliza and our James!

Shakespeare seems to have been on affectionate terms with his theatre colleagues. His fellow actors John Heminge and Henry Condell (who, with Burbage, were remembered in his will) dedicated the First Folio of 1623 to the Earl of Pembroke and the Earl of Montgomery, explaining that they had collected the plays ". . . without ambition either of self-profit or fame; only to keep the memory of so worthy a friend and fellow alive as was our Shakespeare, . . ."

Anecdotes and documents. Seventeenth-century antiquaries began to collect anecdotes about Shakespeare, but no serious life was written until 1709, when Nicholas Rowe tried to assemble information from all available sources with the aim of producing a connected narrative. There were local traditions at Stratford: witticisms and lampoons of local characters; scandalous stories of drunkenness and sexual escapades. About 1661 the Vicar of Stratford wrote in his diary: "Shakespeare, Drayton, and Ben Jonson had a merry meeting, and it seems drank too hard; for Shakespeare died of a fever there contracted." On the other hand, the antiquary John Aubrey wrote in some notes about Shakespeare: "He was not a company keeper; lived in Shoreditch; wouldn't be debauched, and, if invited to, writ he was in pain." Rich-

ard Davies, archdeacon of Lichfield, reported, "He died a papist." How much trust can be put in such a story is uncertain. In the early 18th century, a story appeared that Queen Elizabeth had obliged Shakespeare "to write a play of Sir John Falstaff in love" and that he had performed the task (*The Merry Wives of Windsor*) in a fortnight. There are other stories, all of uncertain authenticity and some mere fabrications.

When serious scholarship began in the 18th century, it was too late to gain anything from traditions. But documents began to be discovered. Shakespeare's will was found in 1747 and his marriage license, in 1836. The documents relating to the Mountjoy lawsuit already mentioned were found and printed in 1910. It is possible that further documents of a legal nature may yet be discovered, but as time passes the hope becomes more remote. Modern scholarship is more concerned to study Shakespeare in relation to his social environment, both in Stratford and in London. This is not too easy, because the author and actor lived a somewhat detached life: a respected tithe-owning country gentleman in Stratford, perhaps, but a rather rootless artist in London.

Portraits. Curiosity about what Shakespeare looked like has not been adequately satisfied. Two representations have indisputable claims to authenticity: a half-length bust in the Stratford-on-Avon parish church, which was in position within a few years of his death; and an engraving used as a frontispiece to the Folio edition of his plays in 1623. The family must have approved the memorial statue, and presumably his friends must have thought the engraving a reasonable likeness. The bust shows Shakespeare with a pen in his hand; the face is rather round, but the high forehead is striking. The engraving is by Martin Droeshout, a member of a family of Flemish artists resident in London, and it has provided the image by which Shakespeare is now best known. The "Chandos" portrait (so called because the Duke of Chandos once owned it) in the National Portrait Gallery, London, seems to have been owned by Sir William Davenant. It resembles the bust and the engraving to a certain extent and could have been a portrait painted in Shakespeare's lifetime. Many other portraits alleged to be of Shakespeare began to appear in the later 17th century and in the 18th century. These are artists' "creations," fabrications, or downright forgeries.

The Droeshout engraving

II. The poet and dramatist

THE INTELLECTUAL BACKGROUND

Shakespeare lived at a time when ideas and social structures established in the Middle Ages still informed men's thought and behaviour. Queen Elizabeth I was God's deputy on earth, and lords and commons had their due places in society under her, with responsibilities up through her to God and down to those of more humble rank. The order of things, however, did not go unquestioned. Atheism was still considered a challenge to the beliefs and way of life of a majority of Elizabethans, but the Christian faith was no longer single—Rome's authority had been challenged by Martin Luther, John Calvin, and a multitude of small religious sects. Royal prerogative was challenged in Parliament; the economic and social orders were disturbed by the rise of capitalism, by the redistribution of monastic lands under Henry VIII, by the expansion of education, and by the influx of new wealth from discovery of new lands.

An interplay of new and old ideas was typical of the time, when official homilies exhorted the people to obedience, while the Italian political theorist Niccolò Machiavelli expounded a new practical code of politics that caused Englishmen to fear the Italian "Machiavillain" and, yet prompted them to ask what men do, rather than what they should do. In *Hamlet*, disquisitions—on man, belief, a "rotten" state, and times "out of joint"—clearly reflect a growing disquiet and skepticism. The translation of Montaigne's Essays in 1603 gave further currency, range, and finesse to such thought, and Shakespeare was one of many who read them, making direct and significant quotations in *The Tempest*. In philosophical inquiry the question "how?" became the impulse for ad-

Popularity of the plays

vance, rather than the traditional "why?" of Aristotle. Shakespeare's plays written between 1603 and 1606 unmistakably reflect a new, Jacobean distrust. James I, who, like Elizabeth, claimed divine authority, was far less able than she to maintain the authority of the throne. The so-called Gunpowder Plot (1605) showed a determined challenge by a small minority in the state; James's struggles with the House of Commons in successive Parliaments, in addition to indicating the strength of the "new men," also revealed the inadequacies of the administration.

POETIC CONVENTIONS AND DRAMATIC TRADITIONS
The Latin comedies of Plautus and Terence were familiar in Elizabethan schools and universities, and English translations or adaptations of them were occasionally performed by students. Seneca's rhetorical and sensational tragedies, too, had been translated and often imitated, both in structure and rhetoric. But there was also a strong native dramatic tradition deriving from the medieval miracle plays, which had continued to be performed in various towns until forbidden during Elizabeth's reign. This native drama had been able to assimilate French popular farce, clerically inspired morality plays on abstract themes, and interludes or short entertainments that made use of the "turns" of individual clowns and actors. Although Shakespeare's immediate predecessors were known as "university wits," their plays were seldom structured in the manner of those they had studied at Oxford or Cambridge; instead, they used and developed the more popular narrative forms. Their subplots, for example, amplified the main action and theme with a freedom and awareness of hierarchical correspondences that are medieval rather than classical.

Changes in language. The English language at this time was changing and extending its range. The poet Edmund Spenser led with the restoration of old words, and schoolmasters, poets, sophisticated courtiers, and travellers all brought further contributions from France, Italy, and the Roman classics, as well as from farther afield. Helped by the growing availability of cheaper, printed books, the language began to become standardized in grammar and vocabulary and, more slowly, in spelling. Ambitious for a European and permanent reputation, the essayist and philosopher Francis Bacon wrote in Latin as well as in English; but, if he had lived only a few decades later, even he might have had total confidence in his own tongue.

Shakespeare's literary debts. In Shakespeare's earlier works his debts stand out clearly: to Plautus for the structure of *The Comedy of Errors;* to the poet Ovid and to Seneca for rhetoric and incident in *Titus Andronicus;* to morality drama for a scene in which a father mourns his dead son, and a son his father, in *Henry VI;* to Marlowe for sentiments and characterization in *Richard III* and *The Merchant of Venice;* to the Italian popular tradition of commedia dell'arte for characterization and dramatic style in *The Taming of the Shrew;* and so on. But he did not then reject these influences; rather, he made them his own, so that soon there was no line between their effects and his. In *The Tempest* (which is perhaps the most original of all his plays in form, theme, language, and setting) folk influences may also be traced, together with a newer and more obvious debt to a courtly diversion known as the masque, as developed by Ben Jonson and others at the court of King James.

THEATRICAL CONDITIONS
The Globe and its predecessor, the Theatre, were public playhouses run by the Chamberlain's Men (later the King's Men), a leading theatre company of which Shakespeare was a member. To these playhouses almost all classes of citizens, except the Puritans, came for afternoon entertainment. The players were also summoned to court, to perform before the monarch and assembled nobility. In the summer they toured the provinces, and on occasion they performed at London's Inns of Court (associations of law students), at universities, and in great houses. Popularity led to an insatiable demand for plays:

repertories were always changing, so that early in 1613 the King's Men could present "fourteen several plays." The theatre soon became fashionable too, and in 1608–09 the King's Men started to perform on a regular basis at the Blackfriars, a "private" indoor theatre where high admission charges assured the company a more select and sophisticated audience.

Shakespeare's first associations with the Chamberlain's Men seem to have been as an actor. He is not known to have acted after 1603, and tradition gives him only secondary roles, such as the ghost in *Hamlet* and Adam in *As You Like It*, but his continuous association must have given him direct working knowledge of all aspects of theatre: like Aeschylus, Molière, Bertolt Brecht, or Harold Pinter, Shakespeare was able to work with his plays in rehearsal and performance and to know his actors and his audiences and all the different potentialities of theatres and their equipment. Numerous passages in Shakespeare's plays show conscious concern for theatre arts and audience reactions. Prospero in *The Tempest* speaks of the whole of life as a kind of "revels," or theatrical show, that, like a dream, will soon be over. The Duke of York in *Richard II* is conscious of how

> . . . in a theatre, the eyes of men,
> After a well-graced actor leaves the stage
> Are idly bent on him that enters next,
> Thinking his prattle to be tedious.

And Hamlet gives expert advice to visiting actors in the art of playing.

In Shakespeare's day, there was little time for group rehearsals, and actors were given the words of only their own parts. The crucial scenes in Shakespeare's plays, therefore, are between two or three characters only, or else are played with one character dominating a crowded stage. Female parts were written for young male actors or boys, so Shakespeare did not often write big roles for them or keep them actively engaged on stage for lengthy periods. Writing for the clowns of the company—who were important popular attractions in any play—presented the problem of allowing them to use their comic personalities and tricks and yet have them serve the immediate interests of theme and action.

Theatre is a collaborative art, only occasionally yielding the right conditions for individual genius to flourish and develop, and Shakespeare's achievement must at least in part be due to his continuous association with the Chamberlain's and King's Men, who were as practiced in acting together as he was to become in writing for them.

CHRONOLOGY
Despite much scholarly argument, it is often impossible to date a given play precisely. But there is a general consensus, especially for plays written 1585–1601, 1605–07, and 1609 onward. The following list of first performances is based on external and internal evidence, on general stylistic and thematic considerations, and on the observation that an output of no more than two plays a year seems to have been established in those periods when dating is rather clearer than others.

1589–92	*1 Henry VI, 2 Henry VI, 3 Henry VI*
1592–93	*Richard III, The Comedy of Errors*
1593–94	*Titus Andronicus, The Taming of the Shrew*
1594–95	*The Two Gentlemen of Verona, Love's Labour's Lost, Romeo and Juliet*
1595–96	*Richard II, A Midsummer Night's Dream*
1596–97	*King John, The Merchant of Venice*
1597–98	*1 Henry IV, 2 Henry IV*
1598–99	*Much Ado About Nothing, Henry V*
1599–1600	*Julius Caesar, As You Like It*
1600–01	*Hamlet, The Merry Wives of Windsor*
1601–02	*Twelfth Night, Troilus and Cressida*
1602–03	*All's Well That Ends Well*
1604–05	*Measure For Measure, Othello*
1605–06	*King Lear, Macbeth*
1606–07	*Antony and Cleopatra*
1607–08	*Coriolanus, Timon of Athens*
1608–09	*Pericles*
1609–10	*Cymbeline*
1610–11	*Winter's Tale*
1611–12	*The Tempest*
1612–13	*Henry VIII, The Two Noble Kinsmen*

Shakespeare's two narrative poems, *Venus and Adonis* and *The Rape of Lucrece*, can be dated with certainty to the years when the Plague stopped dramatic performances in London, in 1592 and 1593–94, respectively, just before their publication. But the sonnets offer many and various problems; they cannot have been written all at one time, and most scholars set them within the period 1593–1600. "The Phoenix and the Turtle" can be dated 1600–01.

PUBLICATION

During Shakespeare's early career, dramatists invariably sold their plays to an actor's company, who then took charge of them, prepared working promptbooks, and did their best to prevent another company or a publisher from getting copies; in this way they could exploit the plays themselves for as long as they drew an audience. But some plays did get published, usually in small books called quartos. Occasionally plays were "pirated," the text being dictated by one or two disaffected actors from the company that had performed it or else made up from shorthand notes taken surreptitiously during performance and subsequently corrected during other performances; parts 2 and 3 of the *Henry VI* (1594 and 1595) and *Hamlet* (1603) quartos are examples of pirated, or "bad," texts. Sometimes an author's "foul papers" (his first complete draft) or his "fair" copy—or a transcript of either of these—got into a publisher's hands, and "good quartos" were printed from them, such as those of *Titus Andronicus* (1594), *Love's Labour's Lost* (1598), and *Richard II* (1597). After the publication of "bad" quartos of *Hamlet* and *Romeo and Juliet* (1597), the Chamberlain's Men probably arranged for the release of the "foul papers" so that second—"good"—quartos could supersede the garbled versions already on the market. This company had powerful friends at court, and in 1600 a special order was entered in the Stationers' Register to "stay" the publication of *As You Like It, Much Ado About Nothing*, and *Henry V*, possibly in order to assure that good texts were available. Subsequently *Henry V* (1600) was pirated, and *Much Ado About Nothing* was printed from "foul papers"; *As You Like It* did not appear in print until it was included in *Mr. William Shakespeares Comedies, Histories & Tragedies*, published in folio (the reference is to the size of page) by a syndicate in 1623 (later editions appearing in 1632 and 1663).

The only precedent for such a collected edition of public theatre plays in a handsome folio volume was Ben Jonson's collected plays of 1616. Shakespeare's folio included 36 plays, 22 of them appearing for the first time in a good text. (For the Third Folio reissue of 1664, *Pericles* was added from a quarto text of 1609, together with six apocryphal plays.) The First Folio texts were prepared by John Heminge and Henry Condell (two of Shakespeare's fellow sharers in the Chamberlain's, now the King's Men), who made every effort to present the volume worthily. Only about 230 copies of the First Folio are known to have survived.

The texts of *Venus and Adonis* (1593) and *The Rape of Lucrece* (1594) are remarkably free from errors. Shakespeare presumably furnished a fair copy of each for the printer. He also seems to have read the proofs. The sonnets were published in 1609, but there is no evidence that Shakespeare oversaw their publication (see below *III. Understanding Shakespeare: The contribution of textual criticism*).

POETIC AND DRAMATIC POWERS

The early poems. Shakespeare dedicated the poem *Venus and Adonis* to his patron, Henry Wriothesley, 3rd earl of Southampton, whom he further promised to honour with "some graver labour"—perhaps *The Rape of Lucrece*, which appeared a year later and was also dedicated to Southampton. As these two poems were something on which Shakespeare was intending to base his reputation with the public and to establish himself with his patron, they were displays of his virtuosity—diploma pieces. They were certainly the most popular of his writings with the reading public and impressed them with his

(margin, left) Shakespeare's bid for fame

poetic genius. Seven editions of *Venus and Adonis* had appeared by 1602 and 16 by 1640; *Lucrece*, a more serious poem, went through eight editions by 1640; and there are numerous allusions to them in the literature of the time. But after that, until the 19th century, they were little regarded. Even then the critics did not know what to make of them: on the one hand, *Venus and Adonis* is licentiously erotic (though its sensuality is often rather comic); while *Lucrece* may seem to be tragic enough, the treatment of the poem is yet somewhat cold and distant. In both cases the poet seems to be displaying dexterity rather than being "sincere." But Shakespeare's detachment from his subjects has come to be admired in more recent assessments.

Above all, the poems give evidence for the growth of Shakespeare's imagination. *Venus and Adonis* is full of vivid imagery of the countryside; birds, beasts, the hunt, the sky, and the weather, the overflowing Avon—these give freshness to the poem and contrast strangely with the sensuous love scenes. *Lucrece* is more rhetorical and elaborate than *Venus and Adonis* and also aims higher. Its disquisitions (upon night, time, opportunity, and lust, for example) anticipate brilliant speeches on general themes in the plays—on mercy in *The Merchant of Venice*, suicide in *Hamlet*, and "degree" in *Troilus and Cressida*.

There are a few other poems attributed to Shakespeare. When the *Sonnets* were printed in 1609, a 329-line poem, "A Lovers complaint," was added at the end of the volume, plainly ascribed by the publisher to Shakespeare. There has been a good deal of discussion about the authorship of this poem. Only the evidence of style, however, could call into question the publisher's ascription, and this is conflicting. Parts of the poem and some lines are brilliant, but other parts seem poor in a way that is not like Shakespeare's careless writing. Its narrative structure is remarkable, however, and the poem deserves more attention than it usually receives. It is now generally thought to be from Shakespeare's pen, possibly an early poem revised by him at a more mature stage of his poetical style. Whether the poem in its extant form is later or earlier than *Venus and Adonis* and *Lucrece* cannot be decided. No one could doubt the authenticity of "The Phoenix and the Turtle," a 67-line poem that appeared with other "poetical essays" (by John Marston, George Chapman, and Ben Jonson) appended to Robert Chester's poem *Loves Martyr* in 1601. The poem is attractive and memorable, but very obscure, partly because of its style and partly because it contains allusions to real persons and situations whose identity can now only be guessed at.

The sonnets. In 1609 appeared *SHAKE-SPEARES SONNETS. Never before Imprinted*. At this date Shakespeare was already a successful author, a country gentleman, and an affluent member of the most important theatrical enterprise in London. How long before 1609 the sonnets were written is unknown. The phrase "never before imprinted" may imply that they had existed for some time but were now at last printed. Two of them (nos. 138 and 144) had in fact already appeared (in a slightly different form) in an anthology, *The Passionate Pilgrim* (1599). Shakespeare had certainly written some sonnets by 1598, for in that year Francis Meres, in a "survey" of literature, made reference to "his sugared sonnets among his private friends," but whether these "sugared sonnets" were those eventually published in 1609 cannot be ascertained—Shakespeare may have written other sets of sonnets, now lost. Nevertheless, the sonnets included in *The Passionate Pilgrime* are among his most striking and mature, so it is likely that most of the 154 sonnets that appeared in the 1609 printing belong to Shakespeare's early 30s rather than to his 40s—to the time when he was writing *Richard II* and *Romeo and Juliet* rather than when he was writing *King Lear* and *Antony and Cleopatra*. But, of course, some of them may belong to any year of Shakespeare's life as a poet before 1609.

(margin, right) Contemporary reference to Shakespeare's "sugared sonnets"

The order of the poems. Elizabethan sonnet sequences (following the example of their Italian and French models) were generally in some kind of narrative order.

Sir Philip Sidney's *Astrophel and Stella*, moreover, and Edmund Spenser's *Amoretti* each tells a reasonably well authenticated story.

Shakespeare's sonnets, however, do not give the impression of an ordered sequence as it exists in Sidney, Spenser, and others. It is only at times that a narrative can be sensed, frequently breaking off, then resuming later or reverting to an earlier stage of the "story." It is therefore often argued that there was an original order, which has been lost, and many efforts have been made to recover, by ingenious analysis, Shakespeare's "intended" order. Although some interesting observations about associations between widely separated sonnets have been the result, none of the schemes carries any conviction. Most critics feel that it is hopeless to try to replace the order of the 1609 edition with anything convincingly better, arguing that the sonnets have no pretensions to be complete or adequate as a narrative. They are mixed in mood, in quality, and in distinction. Some seem open, addressed to all the world. Some seem too cryptic and personal ever to be intelligible.

It is equally uncertain whether the 1609 arrangement bears any relation to the order in which the sonnets were actually written. It may reasonably be supposed that the printer followed, more or less, the order in which the sonnets appeared in manuscript (or manuscripts). It is quite likely, however, that single leaves of the manuscript got out of order (for the numbers attached to each poem could well be a printer's addition), which, if so, might explain why some groups or pairs of sonnets seem to be oddly separated.

Sonnets 1 to 17 are variations on one theme. A handsome young man is being persuaded to marry and beget offspring who will preserve his beauty in a new generation, though he himself will lose it as he grows old. Gradually this theme gives place to the idea that the beloved will survive through the poet's verse. (There is no discussion of the relative merits of the two kinds of immortality.)

Sonnets 18 to 126 are on a variety of themes associated with a handsome young man (who is presumably, but not necessarily, the youth of 1 to 17). The poet enjoys his friendship and is full of admiration, promising to bestow immortality on the young man by the poems he writes in his honour. But sometimes the young man seems cold. Sometimes he provokes jealousy by his admiration of another poet. The climax of the series comes when the young man seduces the poet's woman. But eventually the poet reconciles himself to the situation and realizes that his love for his friend is greater than his desire to keep the woman.

The "dark lady" of the late sonnets

Sonnet 126 seems a kind of concluding poem (and is not in sonnet form). Then begins a new series, principally about a dark lady by whom the poet is enthralled, though well aware of her faults. At one point, she is stolen from him by his best friend. This faithlessness of both friend and woman wounds his disappointment deeply. He nevertheless tries to rise above his disappointment. (The two concluding sonnets are impersonal translations of a familiar Renaissance theme about Cupid.)

Artistic invention or real experience. Various persons are addressed or referred to in the poems, though whether they are real people or fictions of Shakespeare's dramatic imagination is not entirely clear. But if the "story" of the sonnets is an invention, then it is badly invented, showing nothing of the skill in storytelling that Shakespeare elsewhere reveals. The relationships between "characters," moreover, are so obscure, so irritatingly cryptic, that it is difficult to believe Shakespeare was divising the story for artistic purposes. The very clumsiness and obscurity of the narrative, if it is considered a fiction, are a strong argument that the sonnets are close to real experience; yet a degree of fictionalization in the sonnets would be in accord with Shakespeare's lifelong devotion to writing plays and with the pervasive "impersonality" of his art as a dramatist.

Some critics have been tempted to declare that it does not matter who the young man and the dark lady were— that the poetry is the important thing. Though as a ges-

ture of impatience this mood is understandable, the world will continue to be curious about the circumstances of these poems, and, if historical documents should be discovered bringing hard facts to bear on the matter, the sonnets would surely be reinterpreted in the light of those facts. But for now, the sonnets on the whole retain an obstinate privacy that is a bar to enjoyment and therefore must be judged a fault, one that would hinder altogether the appreciation of any poems less brilliant. The sonnets do not quite "create a world" within which they can be apprehended. There is the sense of a missing (or unascertainable) body of experience and reference that falls short of poetical mystery.

Human experience in the poems. From the beginning of the 19th century, explorations of Shakespeare's personality have constantly been made by studying the sonnets. William Wordsworth proclaimed that "with this key Shakespeare unlocked his heart." But many readers feel that Shakespeare the man is elusive in the sonnets, just as he is in the plays. It has been natural to look in the poems for "personal details" about the author. One can observe allusions to his insomnia, to his disapproval of false hair and painted cheeks, to his love of music, and, according to some, to his bisexuality. It does not amount to very much.

Attempts to discover details of his life in the poems

The experiences of love and friendship, as related in the sonnets, must be described as disheartening and disenchanted. On the plane of human experience, they are full of disappointment, separation, anxiety, estrangement, self-accusation, and failure. The triumph, or near triumph, of death and of time is deeply felt. Only on the transcendental plane and in the faith in the permanence of poetry does a positive or affirmative attitude assert itself and compensate for the outcast state of the poet and the dateless night of death. On the whole they are quieter and closer to normal human experience than are the plays. The storms of passion are absent. Instead, there is a refined analysis of feeling, somehow more characteristic of the method of Jane Austen and Henry James than of Shakespeare the playwright. There are, of course, many moments of comparable moral scrupulousness in the plays, but they come incidentally and sometimes a little irrelevantly, perhaps, or awkwardly. In the sonnets Shakespeare brilliantly controls the shifting texture of the words in accordance with the variations in mood and tone. Generally, a careful analysis of the words reveals the tone in which a sonnet should be read, though, it must be admitted, this can be ambiguous.

The attractions of the sonnets are indeed very great. They win the admiration of readers by a variety of virtues. They express strong feeling, but they preserve artistic control. They have a density of thought and imagery that makes them seem the quintessence of the poetical experience. They delight by a felicity of phrase and verse movement, no less memorable than that familiar in the plays. They have, in recent years, received more exegesis than any of Shakespeare's plays, except perhaps *Hamlet* and *King Lear*. This is not necessarily a testimony to their value, for they have a tantalizing quality that encourages continued commentary. But it would be ungenerous not to relate this keen interest in the sonnets to an appreciation of their poetic power, of their unembarrassed exploration of intimate human relationships, and of their sensitivity to the tragedy of human aspirations and the triumph of time.

The early plays. Although the record of Shakespeare's early theatrical success is obscure, clearly the newcomer soon made himself felt. His brilliant two-part play on the Wars of the Roses, *The Whole Contention between the two Famous Houses, Lancaster and Yorke*, was among his earliest achievements. He showed, in *The Comedy of Errors*, how hilariously comic situations could be shot through with wonder and sentiment. In *Titus Andronicus* he scored a popular success with tragedy in the high Roman fashion. *The Two Gentlemen of Verona* was a new kind of romantic comedy. The world has never ceased to enjoy *The Taming of the Shrew*. *Love's Labour's Lost* is an experiment in witty and satirical observation of society. *Romeo and Juliet* combines and interconnects a tragic situation with comedy and gaiety. All this represents the probable achievement of Shakespeare's first half-dozen years as a writer for the London stage, perhaps by the time he had reached 30. It shows astonishing versatility and originality.

Henry VI, 1, 2, and 3. In *The Contention*, a two-part chronicle play (called in the First Folio *2 Henry VI; 3 Henry VI*), Shakespeare seems to have discovered the theatrical excitement that can be generated by representing recent history on the stage—events just beyond living memory but of great moment in the lives of present generations. The civil wars (popularly known as the Wars of the Roses) resulted from the struggle of two families, York and Lancaster, for the English throne. They had ended in 1485 with Richard III's defeat at the Battle of Bosworth, when Henry Tudor, as Henry VII, established a secure dynasty. Queen Elizabeth I was the granddaughter of Henry VII, so the story of York and Lancaster was of great interest to Shakespeare's contemporaries. In *2 Henry VI* the power struggle turns around the ineffective King Henry VI, until gradually the Duke of York emerges as contender for the throne. The climaxes of *3 Henry VI* include the murder of the Duke of York by the Lancastrians and, in the final scene, the murder of King Henry by Richard (York's son and the future Richard III). Shakespeare already showed himself a master of tragic poetry, notably in the speech of the captured York (wounded, mocked by a paper crown on his head, and awaiting death under the cruel taunts of Queen Margaret) and in the meditation of the King on the miseries of civil war. The vigorous and comic scenes with Jack Cade, a rebel leader, and his followers anticipate the kind of political comment that Shakespeare handled with greater subtlety in introducing the mobs of plebeians in *Julius Caesar* and *Coriolanus*.

His early mastery of tragic poetry

A third play, *1 Henry VI*, about the early part of the reign of King Henry VI, concerns events preceding the opening of the first part of *The Contention*. This is less successful, and it is uncertain whether it was a first effort at a historical play, written before *The Contention*, or a preparatory supplement to it, written subsequently and less inspired. It was printed in the 1623 Folio as the first part of *King Henry VI; The Contention* appeared as the second and third parts of *King Henry VI*, on what authority is not known.

The Comedy of Errors. The title of this, Shakespeare's shortest play, speaks for itself (though the opening scene is, unexpectedly, full of pathos). The play is based on Plautus' *Menaechmi*, a play of the comic confusions deriving from the presence of twin brothers, unknown to each other, in the same town; but Shakespeare has added twin servants, and he fills the play with suspense, surprise, expectation, and exhilaration as the two pairs weave their way through quadruple misunderstandings. The play already reveals Shakespeare's mastery of construction.

Titus Andronicus. This play was highly popular and held the stage for many years. Its crude story, its many savage incidents, and its poetic style have led some critics to think it not by Shakespeare. But the tendency of recent criticism is to regard the play as wholly or essentially his, and, indeed, when considered on its own terms as a "Roman tragedy," it displays a uniformity of tone and reveals a consistency of dramatic structure as a picture of the decline of the ancient world (though, by the standards of Shakespeare's later Roman plays, this picture is much confused).

The Two Gentlemen of Verona. Shakespeare took this play's story from a long Spanish prose romance called *Diana*, by Jorge de Montemayor. He added new characters—including Valentine, one of the "Two Gentlemen," whose "ideal" friendship with Proteus is so developed that the plot is more than a love story; indeed, the play glorifies friendship to an extent that, by modern conventions, is absurd. The abrupt last scene suggests that something has gone wrong with the text, and certainly Shakespeare was never again so ready to abandon common sense in motivating the behaviour of his lovers. But it is also clear that Shakespeare is here feeling

his way toward a new kind of high comedy, later to find expression in *The Merchant of Venice* and *Twelfth Night*.

The Taming of the Shrew. Often played as a boisterous farce, this play is actually a comedy of character, with implications beyond the story of the wooing, wedding, and taming of Katharina, the "shrew," by Petruchio, a man with a stronger will than her own. Shakespeare arouses more interest in these two than farce permits. They gain, for example, by contrast with the tepid, silly, or infatuated lovers (Bianca, Lucentio, Hortensio, and Gremio), and their relationship is given an admirable vitality and energy; while in the play's last scene Katharina's discourse on wifely submission—if spoken with sincerity and genuine tenderness and without irony—has a moving quality in performance. The Italianate play about the shrew taming is set inside another play (concerning a trick played upon Christopher Sly, a drunken tinker), which gave Shakespeare an opportunity for some brilliant English country scenes. Originally, Sly was made the "audience" of the shrew play, a device that is abandoned after a little while (that is, in the text of the 1623 Folio). Probably the players' company came to abandon the Christopher Sly framing because the Katharina and Petruchio story was too strong not to be acted directly at the real audience in a theatre.

Love's Labour's Lost. Once regarded as obsolete, depending too much upon temporary and irrecoverable allusions, this play has come to life in the theatre only during the past 50 years. Its rejection by the theatre was a background for 18th- and 19th-century critics such as John Dryden, Dr. Johnson, and William Hazlitt, all of whom had severe things to say about it. But, once the play had been recovered for the theatre, it was discovered that it is full of humanity, exploring the consequences of man being made of flesh and blood. The central comic device is that of four young men, dedicated to study and to the renunciation of women, meeting four young women; inevitably they abandon their absurd principles. For variety, and as an escape from the pretty, gay, young royalty and courtiers, there is an entertaining band of eccentrics who are allowed their "vaudeville" turns: Sir Nathaniel the curate, Holofernes the schoolmaster, Dull the constable, Costard the clown, and Jaquenetta the country girl; linking both groups is Don Adriano de Armado the ineffable (who begins by being a bore but becomes interesting as he becomes pathetic). Toward the end, the play takes on a new dramatic vitality through a brilliant *coup de théâtre:* the sudden arrival of Mercade as the messenger of death and the herald of responsibility. The deliberate abstention from the customary conclusion of comedy is remarkable: "Jack hath not Jill," but he will have her after a twelvemonth, when he has done something to deserve her. Thus the play ends with hope—perhaps the best kind of happy ending.

Romeo and Juliet. The most complex work of art among these early plays of Shakespeare, *Romeo and Juliet* is far more than "a play of young love" or "the world's typical love-tragedy." Weaving together a large number of related impressions and judgments, it is as much about hate as love. It tells of a family and its home as well as a feud and a tragic marriage. The public life of Verona and the private lives of the Veronese make up the setting for the love of Juliet and Romeo and provide the background against which their love can be assessed. It is not the deaths of the lovers that conclude the play but the public revelation of what has happened, with the admonitions of the Prince and the reconciliation of the two families.

Shakespeare enriched an already old story by surrounding the guileless mutual passion of Romeo and Juliet with the mature bawdry of the other characters—the Capulet servants Sampson and Gregory open the play with their fantasies of exploits with the Montague women; the tongues of the Nurse and Mercutio are seldom free from sexual matters—but the innocence of the lovers is unimpaired.

Romeo and Juliet made a strong impression on contemporary audiences. It was also one of Shakespeare's first plays to be pirated; a very bad text appeared in 1597. Detestable though it is, this version does derive from a performance of the play, and a good deal of what was seen on stage was recorded. Two years later another version of the play appeared, issued by a different, more respectable publisher, and this is essentially the play known today, for the printer was working from a manuscript fairly close to Shakespeare's own. Yet in neither edition did Shakespeare's name appear on the title page, and it was only with the publication of *Love's Labour's Lost* that publishers had come to feel that the name of Shakespeare as a dramatist, as well as the public esteem of the company of actors to which he belonged, could make an impression on potential purchasers of playbooks.

The histories. For his plays on subjects from English history, Shakespeare primarily drew upon Raphael Holinshed's *Chronicles*, which appeared in 1587, and on Edward Hall's earlier account of *The union of the two noble and illustre famelies of Lancastre and York* (1548). From these and numerous secondary sources he inherited traditional themes: the divine right of royal succession, the need for unity and order in the realm, the evil of dissension and treason, the cruelty and hardship of war, the power of money to corrupt, the strength of family ties, the need for human understanding and careful calculation, and the power of God's providence, which protected his followers, punished evil, and led England toward the stability of Tudor rule.

The Tragedy of King Richard III. In this play, the first history to have a self-contained narrative unity, Shakespeare accentuated the moment of death as a crisis of conscience in which man judges himself and is capable of true prophecy. He centred the drama on a single figure who commits himself to murder, treason, and dissimulation with an inventive imagination that an audience can relish even as it must condemn it; and in defeat Richard discovers a valiant fury that carries him beyond nightmare fear and guilt to unrepentant, crazed defiance.

The Tragedy of King Richard II. In the group of histories written in the late 1590s, Shakespeare developed themes similar to those of *Richard III* but introduced counter-statements, challenging contrasts, and more deeply realized characters. The first of this group, *Richard II*, concentrates on the life and death of the King, but Bolingbroke, his adversary, is made far more prominent than Richmond had been as Richard III's adversary. The rightful king is isolated and defeated by Act III, and in prison he hammers out the meaning of his life in sustained soliloquy and comes to recognize his guilt and responsibility. From this moment of truth, he rediscovers pride, trust, and courage, so that he dies with an access of strength and an aspiring spirit. After the death of Richard, a scene shows Bolingbroke, now Henry IV, with the corpse of his rival in a coffin; and then Bolingbroke, too, recognizes his own guilt, as he sits in power among his silent nobles.

1 Henry IV; 2 Henry IV. In the two plays that bear his name, Henry IV is often in the background. The stage is chiefly dominated by his son, Prince Hal (later Henry V), by Hotspur the young rebel, and by Sir John Falstaff. The secondary characters are numerous, varying from prostitutes and country bumpkins to a Lord Chief Justice and country gentlemen. There is a tension underlying the two-part play that sounds in the King's opening lines:

> So shaken as we are, so wan with care,
> Find we a time for frighted peace to pant,
> And breathe short-winded accents of new broils
> To be commenced in stronds afar remote.

When the Earl of Warwick counsels hope, the King sees how "chances mock, and changes fill the cup of alteration":

> O, if this were seen,
> The happiest youth, viewing his progress through,
> What perils passed, what crosses to ensue,
> Would shut the book, and sit him down and die.
> (Act III, scene 1, 51–56)

Yet the two plays of *Henry IV* are full of energy. In Falstaff—that "reverend vice . . . that father ruffian,

that vanity in years"—Shakespeare has created a character who becomes a substitute father of license and good fellowship for Prince Hal and who comments on the political situation with inglorious, reckless, egotistical good sense. Falstaff is Shakespeare's major introduction into English history. His characterization is wholly original, for, although Shakespeare uses something of the earlier "vice" figure from early tragedies and comedies, something of the glutton and coward from allegorical, or morality, plays, something of the braggart soldier and the impotent old lecher from neoclassical comedy, he also studied life for this character of an out-of-work soldier, a knight without lands or alliances, a childless man whose imagination far outruns his achievement.

King John. Already in *King John*, Shakespeare had developed a subsidiary character to offset kings and princes. Here the Bastard, the son of Sir Robert Faulconbridge, is a supporter of the King and yet has soliloquies, asides, and speeches that mock political and moral pretensions. King John provides the central focus of the play, which ends with his death, but Shakespeare presents him on a rapidly changing course, surrounded by many contrasting characters—each able to influence him, each bringing irresolvable and individual problems into dramatic focus—so that the King's unsteady mind seems no more than one small element in an almost comic jumble of events.

Henry V. *Henry V* is the last of this group of history plays and the last until *Henry VIII* at the end of Shakespeare's career. Structurally the King is again central and dominant, but the subsidiary characters far outnumber those of the earlier plays. In the first two acts Henry is shown in peace and war, politic, angry, confident, sarcastic, and then vowing to weep for another man's revolt. There is an account of Falstaff's death, and, after scenes of military achievement, there is a nervous watch before the Battle of Agincourt when the King walks disguised among his fearful soldiers and prays for victory while acknowledging his own worthless repentance for his father's treason. The presentation of the battle avoids almost all fighting on stage, but recruits, professional soldiers, and dukes and princes are all shown making preparation for meeting defeat or victory. The King's speech to his troops before battle on St. Crispin's Day is famous for its evocation of a brotherhood in arms, but Shakespeare has placed it in a context full of ironies and challenging contrasts. The picture of two nations at war is full of deeply felt individual response: a boy comes to realize that his masters are cowards; a herald is almost at a loss for words; a common soldier has to justify his heart before his king. Just before the conclusion, the King woos the French princess; she knows almost no English, and so he is forced to plead on the merits only of his simplest words, a kiss, and the plain fact of himself and his "heart." There is no doubt that Kate marries Henry because he has won a battle and peace is necessary, but Shakespeare has developed the comedy and earnestness of their wooing so that the need for human trust and acceptance is also evident. This play is presented by a chorus, which speaks in terms of heroism, pride, excitement, fear, and national glory. But at the end, when the King prays that the oaths of marriage and peace may "well kept and prosperous be," the chorus speaks for the last time, reminding the audience that England was to be plunged into civil war during the reign of Henry V's son. The last of a great series of history plays thus concludes with a reminder that no man's story can bring lasting success.

The Roman plays. *Julius Caesar.* After the last group of English history plays, Shakespeare chose to write about Julius Caesar, who held particular fascination for the Elizabethans. He was soldier, scholar, and politician (Francis Bacon held him in special regard for the universality of his genius); he had been killed by his greatest friend (Shakespeare alluded to the "bastard hand" of Brutus in *2 Henry VI*); and he was seen as the first Roman to perceive and, in part, to achieve the benefits of a monarchial state. His biography had appeared in Sir Thomas North's translation, via a French version, of

(margin note left) Shakespeare's sources for the history plays

(margin note right) Falstaff's characterization

(margin note right) The Elizabethans' fascination with the figure of Julius Caesar

Plutarch's *Parallel Lives,* published as *The Lives of the noble Grecians and Romanes* in 1579, which Shakespeare certainly read. To all of this, Shakespeare's response was surprising: Caesar appears in three scenes and then is murdered, before the play is half finished. But a variety of characters respond to and reflect upon the central fact of the great man. This is the dramatic strategy of an ironist, or of a writer who wishes to question human behaviour and to observe interactions and consequences. In fact, Caesar influences the whole play, for he appears after his death as a bloodstained corpse and as a ghost before battle. Both Brutus and Cassius die conscious of Caesar and even speak to him as if he were present. And then his heir takes command, to "part the glories" of what is for him a "happy day."

In other ways *Julius Caesar* is shaped differently from the histories and tragedies that precede it, as if in manner as in subject matter Shakespeare was making decisive changes. The scene moves only from Rome to the battlefield, and with this new setting language becomes more restrained, firmer and sharper. Extensive descriptive images are few, and single words such as "Roman," "honour," "love," "friend," and proper names are repeated as if to enforce contrasts and ironies. In performance this sharp verbal edge, linked with commanding performances and the various excitements of debate, conspiracy, private crises, political eloquence, mob violence, supernatural portents, personal antagonisms, battle, and deaths, holds attention. The play has popular appeal and intellectual fascination.

For six or seven years Shakespeare did not return to a Roman theme, but, after completing *Macbeth* and *King Lear,* he again used Plutarch as a source for two more Roman plays, both tragedies that seem as much concerned to depict the broad context of history as to present tragic heroes.

Antony and Cleopatra. The language of *Antony and Cleopatra* is sensuous, imaginative, and vigorous. "*Feliciter audax* ["happily bold"] is the motto for its style comparatively with his other works," said the poet Samuel Taylor Coleridge. Almost every character seems to talk of kingdoms and to envision heroic deeds: Dolabella, the Roman soldier, says that his "love makes religion to obey" Cleopatra in her last imprisonment; Antony's servant is called Eros, who kills himself before his "great chief"; his soldiers have seen his eyes "glow like plated Mars"; his enemies say that, even in defeat, he "continues still a Jove." Octavius knows, as he closes for the kill, that great issues are at stake. Yet, while the issues are thus enlarged (or inflated), the protagonists do not reveal themselves to an audience as they do in *Hamlet, Othello, Lear,* or *Macbeth.* Antony has soliloquies only in defeat, and then he addresses the sun or fortune, rather hearts or his queen, rather than seeking to hammer out his thoughts or to explore his own response. In the last scene, however, the focus concentrates intensely on a single character, when Cleopatra, prepared for death in robe and crown, believing in immortality, and hearing the dead Antony mock "the luck of Caesar," seems indeed to be transfigured:

... Husband, I come:
Now to that name my courage prove my title!
I am fire, and air; my other elements
I give to baser life. ....

(Act IV, scene 2, 278 ff.)

Coriolanus. The hero of *Coriolanus* has still fewer soliloquies: one in rhyme as he arrives, a renegade in Antium, and another of a few sentences when he stands alone in the marketplace waiting for the citizens to express their choice of him for consul. Through many guises, the audience sees the same man: as a young nobleman in peacetime, as a soldier going to battle, as bloodstained fighter and then victor, as candidate for consul in the "napless garment of humility," as a muffled, banished renegade, and then as leader of the Volscians, enemies of Rome.

In this play Shakespeare's customary contrasts and ironies, which lead an audience to discover meanings for themselves, are replaced by repetitions within the single

The tragic intensity of Cleopatra's death scene

narrative line: there are three Forum scenes, four family scenes, a succession of fights, four scenes of mob violence, and continual attempts to argue with Coriolanus and deflect him from his chosen course. The language is sometimes elaborate, but does not have the poetic richness of *Antony and Cleopatra*; images are compact, sharply effective. Those moments when the audience is drawn most intently into the drama are strangely silent or understated. The citizens "steal away" instead of volunteering to fight for their country; their tribunes stay behind to organize their own responses. When the banished Coriolanus returns at the head of an opposing army, he says little to Menenius, the trusted family friend and politician, or to Volumnia, his mother, who have come to plead for Rome. His mother's argument is long and sustained, and for more than 50 lines he listens silent, until his resolution is broken from within: then, as a stage direction in the original edition testifies, he "holds her by the hand, silent." In his own words, he has "obeyed instinct" and betrayed his dependence; he cannot

stand
As if a man were author of himself
And knew no other kin.

(Act V, scene 3, 35 ff.)

His desire for revenge is defeated, and the army retreats. Volumnia is hailed as "patronness and life of Rome," but she is silent while the drums, trumpets, and voices greet her. Coriolanus is seen only once more, in the enemy city where he is accused of treachery and is assassinated in the kind of mob violence he has previously withstood. So *Coriolanus* finishes with the audience observing a hero helpless to prevent his own death and with patterns of political, social, and personal behaviour repeated without hope of change. Nowhere has Shakespeare shown an aspect so severe as in the silent moments of this Roman tragedy, during which the actor is at a loss for words.

The "great," or "middle," comedies. The comedies written between 1596 and 1602 have much in common and are as well considered together as individually. With the exception of *The Merry Wives of Windsor,* all are set in some "imaginary" country. Whether called Illyria, Messina, Venice and Belmont, Athens, or the Forest of Arden, the sun shines as the dramatist wills. A lioness, snakes, magic caskets, fairy spells, identical twins, disguise of sex, the sudden conversion of a tyrannous duke or the defeat offstage of a treacherous brother can all change the course of the plot and bring the characters to a conclusion in which almost all are happy and just deserts are found. Lovers are young and witty and almost always rich. The action concerns wooing; and its conclusion is marriage, beyond which the audience is scarcely concerned. Whether Shakespeare's source was an Italian novel (*The Merchant of Venice* and *Much Ado About Nothing*), an English pastoral tale (*As You Like It*), an Italian comedy (the Malvolio story in *Twelfth Night*), or something of his own invention (probably *A Midsummer Night's Dream,* and parts of each), always in his hands story and sentiments are instinct with idealism and capable of magic transformations. *The Merry Wives of Windsor* differs from the other comedies in that it is set not in an imaginary country but in Windsor and the rural life of Shakespeare's own day. Fantasy occurs at the end, however, when the characters enter a land of make-believe around the folk fertility symbol of Herne, the Hunter's oak in the forest; and, as they leave to "laugh this sport o'er by a country fire," quarrels are forgotten. The more overtly fantastic plays, in their turn, contain observations of ordinary and (usually) country life.

Much Ado About Nothing is distinctive in many ways, for there is no obvious magic or disguise of sex. But many misunderstandings arise in a masked dance, and the play concludes with a pretended death and a simulated resurrection from behind yet another mask; moreover, the two main characters, Beatrice and Benedick, are transformed from within by what is called "Cupid, the only matchmaker."

In some ways these are intellectual plays. Each comedy has a multiple plot and moves from one set of characters

The blend of fantasy and everyday experience in the comedies

to another, between whom Shakespeare invites his audience to seek connections and explanations. Despite very different classes of people (or immortals) in different strands of the narrative, the plays are unified by Shakespeare's idealistic vision and by an implicit judgment of human relationships, and all their characters are brought together—with certain significant exceptions—at, or near, the end.

The "outsider." The plays affirm truth, good order, and generosity, without any direct statement; they are shapely and complicated like a dance or like a game of chess. Yet at the general resolution all is not harmony: some characters are held back from full participation. At the end of *A Midsummer Night's Dream*, for example, the lovers' more callow comments on the rustics' play of *Pyramus and Thisbe* mark them as irresponsive to the imaginative world of Bottom and his fellows, who project themselves into their play's heroics almost without fear of failure; they are also distinct from the duke, Theseus, who says of the amateur performers:

> The best in this kind are but shadows: and the worst are no worse, if imagination amend them.

In *The Merchant of Venice*, most of the unresolved elements in the comedy are concentrated in the person of Shylock, a Jew who attempts to use justice to enforce a terrible, murderous revenge on Antonio, the Christian merchant, but is foiled by Portia, in disguise as a lawyer, who turns the tables on the Jew by a legal quibble and has him at the mercy of the court. This strange tale is realized with exceptionally credible detail: Shylock is a moneylender, like many in Shakespeare's London, and a Jew of pride and deep religious instincts; the Christians treat him with contempt and distrust, and, when one of them causes his daughter to elope and steal his money and jewels, he suffers with an intensity equalled only by that of his murderous hatred of all Christians. In a scene written in prose that gives at one time both histrionic power and sensitive, personal feeling, Shylock identifies his cause with basic human rights:

> I am a Jew ... Hath not a Jew eyes? hath not a Jew hands, organs, dimensions, senses, affections, passions? fed with the same food, hurt with the same weapons, subject to the same diseases, healed by the same means, warmed and cooled by the same winter and summer, as a Christian is? If you prick us, do we not bleed? if you tickle us, do we not laugh? if you poison us, do we not die? and if you wrong us, shall we not revenge?
>
> (Act III, scene 1, 50 ff.)

The happiness that follows the thwarting of his revenge, however, cannot be celebrated with full unison while there are reminders that he never reached "the beautiful mountain," Belmont.

In *As You Like It*, the melancholy character Jaques leaves the play before the concluding dances. He has seen, and voiced, the limitations of each of the pairs of lovers and is determined to hear more and learn more from the tyrant duke, so mysteriously converted to a "religious life." In *Twelfth Night*, Malvolio the steward is gulled by practical jokes that take advantage of his self-esteem; he is the last character to come onstage in the final scene, and he refuses reconciliation; he leaves after a noticeable silence with only these words: "I'll be revenged on the whole pack of you." This comedy has yet other "outsiders"; alone at the end, Feste the fool sings a strange song in which the whole of life is reduced to a melancholy tale sung by a knowing idiot. *Twelfth Night* is probably the last of the "great" comedies, and it is the saddest.

Wit and ambiguity. Incidental images, too, strike deep into the audience's remembrance of pain, fear, and suffering. In *Twelfth Night*, barren mountains, salt sea, and the smoke of war, storms, imprisonment, death, and madness are all invoked. When the king and queen of fairies quarrel in *A Midsummer Night's Dream*, Titania's speech evokes a world of chaos:

> The ox hath therefore stretched his yoke in vain,
> The plowman lost his sweat, and the green corn
> Hath rotted ere his youth attained a beard:
> The fold stands empty in the drowned field,
> And crows are fatted with the murrion flock ...
>
> (Act II, scene 1, 81 ff.)

Yet the poetry also celebrates happiness and joy with a clearer note and quicker interplay of thought than had been achieved in English before. So, in *Twelfth Night*, from Orsino:

> Then let thy love be younger than thyself,
> Or thy affection cannot hold the bent:
> For women are as roses, whose fair flower,
> Being once displayed doth fall that very hour.

From Olivia:

> Cesario, by the roses of spring,
> By maidhood, honour, truth, and everything,
> I love thee so that, maugre all thy pride,
> Nor wit nor reason can my passion hide.

And from Viola:

> And all those sayings will I over-swear,
> And all those swearings keep as true in soul,
> As doth that orbed continent the fire
> That severs day from night.

The wit and ambiguity through which the apparent meanings are laced with further indications of love, yearning, sexuality, unrest, and happiness glance continuously through the dialogue, especially perhaps in *Much Ado About Nothing*. Often the disguise of identity or sex or else misunderstandings or intentional counterfeiting serve to accentuate the varying levels of consciousness expressed; moments of near unmasking, or of recognition, hold the attention firmly. Witty debates between lovers were not unfamiliar; they had held the stage more than 10 years earlier in John Lyly's fantastic comedies that had been played at court by very young child actors. But never before had sharpness of wit been so matched by gentleness or fineness of sentiment.

Perhaps the most extraordinary achievement of these comedies—which change in mood so rapidly, which are so funny and yet sometimes dangerous and sad, which deal both with fantasy and eloquence—is that the recurrent moments of lifelike feeling are so expressed in words or action that an audience shares in the very moment of discovery. Sometimes this is a second thought, as in Viola's

> I am all the daughters of my father's house,
> And all the brothers too ... and yet I know not ...

Sometimes it is a single phrase—Sir Andrew Aguecheek's "I was adored once too"—and on several climactic occasions it is held in a song, whether of happiness, sorrow or peace, or of the "good life":

> O mistress mine, where are you roaming?
> O, stay and hear, your true-love's coming,
>   That can sing both high and low.

The structure of these comedies can be explained, their stage devices and language analyzed; but essentially they remain on the wing, alive with the "fancy" of art and sentiment. Puck's epilogue to the *Dream* is often quoted as their characteristic note:

> If we shadows have offended,
> Think but this, and all is mended,
> That you have but slumbered here
> While these visions did appear ...

But Rosalind's epilogue to *As You Like It* is also apposite:

> ... I am not furnished like a beggar; therefore to
> beg will not become me: my way is to conjure you ...

The great tragedies. It is a usual and reasonable opinion that Shakespeare's greatness is nowhere more visible than in the series of tragedies—*Hamlet, Othello, King Lear*, and *Macbeth*. *Julius Caesar*, which was written before these, and *Antony and Cleopatra* and *Coriolanus*, which were written after, have many links with the four. But, because of their rather strict relationship with the historical materials, they are best dealt with in a group by themselves. *Timon of Athens*, probably written after the above-named seven plays, shows signs of having been unfinished or abandoned by Shakespeare. It has its own splendours but has rarely been considered equal in achievement to the other tragedies of Shakespeare's maturity.

Hamlet. Judged by its reception by the civilized world,

[margin note left: Shylock]

[margin note right: The "fancy" of art and sentiment in the great comedies]

Hamlet must be regarded as Shakespeare's most successful play. It has unceasing theatrical vitality, and the character of Hamlet himself has become a figure of literary mythology. Yet *King Lear* became for a time the fashionable play in 20th-century criticism, with many critics arguing that in *Hamlet* Shakespeare did not make a psychologically consistent play out of a plot that retained much of the crudity of an earlier kind of "revenge" drama—that he was trying to transform a barbaric "revenge" hero into a subtle, Renaissance prince but did not succeed in this impossible task.

Even if this opinion has become unacceptable, it nevertheless taught critics to look for elements other than psychological consistency. In particular, it is worth concentrating not on Elizabethan attitudes toward revenge but on Shakespeare's artistic balance in presenting the play's moral problems. It is likely that an artist will make his work more interesting if he leaves a dilemma morally ambiguous rather than explicit. The revenge situation in *Hamlet*, moreover, is one charged with emotional excitement as well as moral interest. Simply put, the good man (Hamlet) is weak, and the bad man (Claudius) is strong. The good man has suffered a deep injury from the bad man, and he cannot obtain justice because justice is in the hand of the strong bad man. Therefore the weak good man must go around and around in order to achieve a kind of natural justice; and the audience watches in suspense while the weak good man by subtlety attacks and gets his own back upon the strong bad man and the strong bad man spends his time evading the weak good man. Hamlet is given a formidable opponent: Claudius is a hypocrite, but he is a successful one. He achieves his desired effect on everybody. His hypocrisy is that of a skilled politician. He is not dramatically shown as being in any way unworthy of his station—he upholds his part with dignity. He is a "smiling villain" and is not exposed until the final catastrophe. The jealous Hamlet heaps abuse upon him, but Shakespeare makes Claudius the murderer self-controlled. Thus, theatrically, the situation is much more exciting.

Against this powerful opponent is pitted Hamlet, the witty intellectual. He shares his wit with the audience (and a few favoured characters such as Horatio), who thus share his superiority over most other personages in the play. His first words are a punning aside to the audience, and his first reply to the King is a cryptic retort. His sardonic witticisms are unforgettable ("The funeral baked meats/Did coldly furnish forth the marriage tables"; and "More honoured in the breach than the observance"). Hamlet is an actor in many parts of the play. The range of language in the roles he affects shows that his mimetic powers are considerable. He is skillful in putting on "an antic disposition" and gives a very funny performance in talking to Polonius. He condescends to talk the silly bawdry of Rosencrantz and Guildenstern. He can mimic Osric's style to perfection. He quarrels with Laertes beside Ophelia's grave in a display of verbosity that exceeds the modesty of nature in much the same way as does that of Laertes.

Besides Claudius, set off against Hamlet is Polonius. He is wrong in his judgments, one after another, and this leads to the audience's rejection of his political and human values. In all circumstances he seems slightly ridiculous—a foil for Claudius as he is for Hamlet. His astuteness suffers by comparison with that of the King. His philosophical view of life is hollow compared with Hamlet's. Hamlet has as many general maxims as Polonius; but his seem to be the product of a far more refined sensibility and of an ability to respond truthfully to experience. It is these qualities in the somewhat enigmatic characterization of Hamlet that have won him the fascinated admiration of the world.

Othello. Trusting to false appearances and allowing one's reason to be guided by one's passions had been a theme of many of Shakespeare's comedies. In *Othello* he showed that the consequences of so doing can be tragic rather than comic. Shakespeare adapted the story from an Italian model. His principal innovation consisted in developing the character of Iago, the villain, whose mo-

(margin: Hamlet himself as an actor)

tives are represented as complex and ambiguous. Clearly Shakespeare was keenly interested in a villain who could successfully preserve an appearance of honesty; the bad as well as the good can be "the lords and owners of their faces" (Sonnet 94). Iago is made a plausible villain by being so interesting. He is an actor who enjoys playing his role of "honesty." Shakespeare makes him take the audience into his confidence at every stage of his plotting, and, as a consequence, they have a kind of non-moral participation in his villainy.

The pure and deep love between Desdemona and Othello is stressed from the beginning. Again and again the moral and intellectual stature of Othello is elevated by Shakespeare. He quells tumults in the streets with a few words; he bears himself with dignity before the Venetian council, defending himself compellingly from bitter accusations by Brabantio and accepting his military burden with quiet confidence. Even Iago, in the opening scene of the play, grudgingly admits the dependence of the Venetians on his valour. After his terrible murder of Desdemona, Othello's contrition is agonizing enough to swing the sympathies of the audience back to him.

King Lear. For Shakespeare's contemporaries, Lear, king of Britain, was thought to have been a historical monarch. For Shakespeare, however, although he gave the play something of a chronicle structure, the interest lay not in political events but in the personal character of the King. The main theme of the play is put into the mouth of the evil Regan, speaking to the pitiful Gloucester:

> O sir, to wilful men
> The injuries that they themselves procure
> Must be their schoolmasters.
>
> (Act II, scene 4, 301)

The various stages of Lear's spiritual progress (a kind of "conversion") are carefully marked. He learns the value of patience and the worth of "unaccommodated man." He begins to realize his own faults as a king and almost understands his failure as a father. He begins to feel for the "poor naked wretches" and confesses, "O I have ta'en too little care of this." His initial instability of mind, almost a predisposition to madness, is shown from the beginning. His terrible rages and curses, first upon Cordelia and later upon Goneril and Regan, and his ranting and tyrannical language all foreshadow his breakdown. His faithful counsellor is plain with him: "Be Kent unmannerly/When Lear is mad"; and his daughters shrewdly judge him: "he hath ever but slenderly known himself." He is painfully conscious of approaching madness, but gradually the bombast of his sanity gives place to a remarkable kind of eloquence, flowing easily and never incoherent. His "ravings" are intelligible to the audience, however perturbing they may seem to the other characters on the stage. They express a point of view that, had he understood it earlier, would have saved him from many errors of judgment. The mode of speech of the mad King contrasts strongly with the congenital inconsequentiality of his fool and the assumed madness of Edgar as "Poor Tom."

(margin: Lear's predisposition to madness)

King Lear has a distinct underplot, a separable story of the fortunes of Gloucester—another father suffering from "filial ingratitude" and from his false judgment of the characters of his children. This underplot is introduced in the opening scene, in some detail, as if it were of as much importance as the main plot. The stages by which Gloucester similarly learns by suffering are clearly indicated. He begins by being the cheerful sinner, but gradually his sense of pity and duty become stronger, and he reveals himself to Edmund: "If I die for it (as no less is threatened me), the King my master must be relieved." This revelation of his good intentions to the treacherous Edmund leads directly to his downfall and to his being blinded.

Two of the "good" characters, Edgar and Albany, also grow in moral stature and strength in the course of the play. At first, Edgar seems rather ineffectual, quite unable to cope with the villainy of his half brother Edmund; but eventually he emerges as a strong character, confirmed by suffering and by compassion; able to fight and overcome Edmund in the ordeal at arms; and eventually, as one of the survivors, he is entrusted, along with Albany, with the future of the kingdom. Albany, too, is gradually built up, from being the weak husband of Goneril to being the spokesman of virtue and justice, with an authority able to cope with the force of Edmund's malignant energy.

Yet the representatives of goodness and of hope in *King Lear* do not emerge dynamically, and it has been difficult for champions of Shakespeare's moral and religious orthodoxy to combat the pessimism and nihilism that most readers experience when reading the play—precisely the qualities that have made it a favourite in the 20th century.

The historical basis of *Macbeth*

Macbeth. *Macbeth* is the only play of Shakespeare that seems, to a large extent, to be related to the contemporary historical situation. It was intended to interest the new monarch, James VI of Scotland, who became James I of England. This was a matter of professional importance; for Shakespeare's company of actors had been taken over by the King on his accession, entitled to wear the royal livery as his retainers (as they did when they walked in the procession at his coronation). But more important than the flattering of the King was the way *Macbeth* satisfied public interest. For its subject was regicide, commonly regarded as the supreme crime. And the public had been profoundly moved by an attempted regicide in November 1605—the famous "Gunpowder Plot" —which the English people, even after three and a half centuries, have still not forgotten. The reign of Macbeth, king of Scotland, belonged, for Shakespeare and his audiences, to Scottish history of many centuries past. But the play of *Macbeth*, both in its treatment of the events of the story and in its details, was devised by Shakespeare with a very clear consciousness of the mood of his own times.

It is the first task of criticism to interpret the success of *Macbeth*, to explain how Shakespeare transformed a crude and horrible story of murderous ambition into a satisfying imaginative vision of good and evil. There are two principal artistic methods by which he effected this transformation. First, he made his play highly poetical; it is audacious in style, relying upon concentrated, brilliant brevity of phrase. So great is the imaginative verbal vigour that some critics, sensitive to poetry but unsympathetic to the theatre, have almost forgotten that *Macbeth* is a play and have encouraged readers to treat it rather as a poem. Second, Shakespeare has consistently humanized the two murderers, so that they almost become sympathetic—and, by making them husband and wife, their human relationship is as interesting as their motives for evil actions. This humanizing process is the key to Shakespeare's success in the play. His control of the reactions of an audience is an achievement of theatrical art, not of intellectual or moral subtlety.

Timon of Athens. *Timon of Athens* is yet another of Shakespeare's experiments—the exploration of a new kind of tragic form. Certain usual elements of Shakespearean tragedy are reduced in importance or eliminated from the structure of the play: the story, or "plot," is simple and lacks development. There is no maturing of characters—the only change is the single one of Timon, who moves from a fixed character of universal generosity to one of universal hatred. In the first half of the play, there is a consistent effort to build up a world around Timon in terms of which his behaviour can be judged. As he perceives characters and situations unrealistically and responds to them disproportionately, it becomes clear that his is a dream world. Into that world—as the audience watches, with some pain—reality intrudes. The second half of the play, however, is simply a series of interviews between Timon and his visitors, seemingly arranged solely to bring them under his curses; Timon's frenzied vituperation of his fellowmen becomes almost unbroken monotone. Eventually Timon rages himself to death, leaving Alcibiades to lament his death and punish his enemies.

Of the various explanations put forward for the uneven quality of the writing in *Timon of Athens* (collaboration; incomplete revision; completion by an inferior dramatist), much the most probable is that this is Shakespeare's rough draft of a play. It certainly has close analogies with the great plays of the few years to which its composition belongs (iterative words and iterative imagery, ironic preparation and anticipation, "chorus" statements by disinterested observers, plot and subplot parallel, both complementary and contrasted). If it is a rough draft, then it presents a unique opportunity of getting close to Shakespeare's method of writing. It would prove that he put structure before composition; that he went straight ahead drafting the structure of a play, unifying it by means of theme, imagery, and ironic preparation, and paying less attention to prose–verse form and to the characterization of minor personages. It would indicate that his pen wrote speeches quickly, not wasting much time at first about verse form, putting down the gist of what the character had to say, sometimes with imagery that came to him on the spur of the moment, incorporating lines or half lines of blank verse and even occasionally rhymed couplets—all to be "worked up" later. Nor, by judging the play "unfinished," are its worth and importance diminished: certain parts may be roughly written, but the imaginative conception has a wholeness that imperfect composition does not obscure.

Timon of Athens a unique opportunity of seeing Shakespeare's working method

The "dark" comedies. Before the death of Queen Elizabeth I in 1603 the country was ill at ease: the House of Commons became more outspoken about monopolies and royal prerogative; uncertainty about the succession to the throne made the future unsettled. In 1603 the Plague again struck London, closing the theatres. In 1604 Shakespeare's patron, the Earl of Southampton, was arrested on charges of treason; he was subsequently released, but such scares did not betoken confidence in the new reign. About Shakespeare's private reaction to these events there can be only speculation, but three of the five plays usually assigned to these years have become known as "dark" comedies for their distempered vision of the world.

Troilus and Cressida. *Troilus and Cressida* may never have been performed in Shakespeare's lifetime, and it fits no single category. Based on Homer (as translated by George Chapman) and on 15th-century accounts of the Trojan War by John Lydgate and William Caxton, it explores the causes of strife between and within the Greek and Trojan armies and might well have been a history play of a newly questioning and ironic kind. But Shakespeare was also influenced by Geoffrey Chaucer's love poem, *Troilus and Criseyde*, and for the first time portrayed sexual encounters outside the expectation of marriage. Cressida desires Troilus (and later Diomedes) with physical as well as idealistic longing; she considers love frankly as a chase and acts on the principle

> That she was never yet that ever knew
> Love got so sweet as when desire did sue.

As in Shakespeare's earlier comedies, these lovers are contrasted with others—but with a difference, for they are set beside the shallow and jaded routine of Helen's life with Paris and the assembled Trojans, and beside the jealous humours of Achilles, lounging in his tent with Patroclus. Into Cressida's last scene, when she begs Diomedes to come to her tent, Shakespeare has further introduced three lookers-on who comment directly: the enslaved Troilus watching with the politically wily Ulysses and, at another corner of the stage, Thersites. The audience cannot identify simply with any one of the five characters but, instead, must take note of each varying discord.

In his ubiquitous commentary, Thersites, perhaps the most notable single invention in the play, expresses revulsion against the pursuit of both honour and love. When the lovers have left the stage he has the last word:

> Would I could meet that rogue Diomed! I would croak like a raven; I would bode, I would bode. . . . Lechery, lechery! Still wars and lechery! Nothing else holds fashion. A burning devil take them!

He proclaims Agamemnon "both ass and ox"; Ajax he would scratch from head to foot, to make the "loathsomest scab in Greece"; and as Menelaus and Paris fight

Thersites' revulsion from the pursuit of honour and love

in the last battle, he sees them as "bull" and "dog," cuckold and cuckold maker—and then he saves his own life by cowardice. Yet he is not the only commentator in the play. Priam sits on his throne, between his disputing sons; Ulysses arouses Achilles by praising Ajax; and Cassandra cries out from a supernatural certainty of doom. Pandarus describes the handsome warriors as food for love and hurries forward to take purient pleasure in Cressida's excitement.

Pandarus also speaks the epilogue, and something of the play's irony may be gauged by contrasting his weak and broken appearance as he speaks the last words with that of Prologue, who, dressed in armour, had announced the scene of Troy, the "princes orgulous," and all the brave and massy consequences of war. No history play by Shakespeare had run such a gamut from the heroic to the petty and familiar. Although the earlier comedies sometimes start with tyrannies and loss, they all conclude with a dance or, at their least hopeful, with a procession offstage until a "golden time convents." Nor could this play be called a tragedy, for, despite the death of Hector and the loss of all Troilus' hopes beyond those of hatred and revenge, there is no scope in the last disordered and inglorious battle for the intensity of tragedy. The stature of every character has been progressively diminished.

All's Well That Ends Well; Measure for Measure. The other two comedies of 1601–04, are less completely original. Both *All's Well That Ends Well* and *Measure for Measure* centre on stories of love that lead to marriage, and both end with complicated denouements superintended by a benevolent king or duke. The fantasy of the earlier comedies, however, is largely missing, and, although there are clowns, they haunt brothels or a prison, or they "love as an old man loves money, with no stomach." Subplots are about cowardice in battle or fornication. Only *Measure for Measure* has a song, and that "pleases" the woe of Mariana deserted by her unworthy Angelo.

The intensity of the "dark" comedies

Perhaps the most important element in both comedies is a new intensity. In *All's Well*, Helena's soliloquies of frustrated love and, sometimes, the brevity of her speech reveal her inner struggles; and a few words from her graceless husband indicate his new loss of assurance. In *Measure for Measure*, Isabella pleading for her brother's life and defending her chastity or the Duke disguised as a friar persuading Claudio to disdain life both carry their arguments fiercely and finely; and Angelo is shown twice in soliloquy, tempted to what he knows is evil by Isabella, whom he knows is good:

> When I would pray and think, I think and pray
> To several subjects....
>
> (Act II, scene 4, 1 ff.)

In this comedy the intensity of much of the dialogue, the overt religious and legal concerns, and the variety of plot and subplot in Shakespeare's earlier manner all combine to make a searching, unsettling, and, in the opinion of most judges, precarious play, a comedy that reaches its general conclusion only with difficulty, with adroitness, compromise, or dramatic necessity.

Although such issues are present in *All's Well*, they are more in the background, and Shakespeare ostensibly considers other themes—inherited virtue opposed to virtue achieved by oneself, the wisdom of age over against the impressionability of youth, and the need for each man to make his own choice, even if wrongly.

Only during the 20th century have the three "dark" comedies been frequently performed in anything like Shakespeare's texts, an indication that their questioning, satiric, intense, and shifting comedy could not please earlier audiences.

The latest plays. *Pericles, Cymbeline, The Winter's Tale, The Tempest,* and *Henry VIII,* written between 1608 and 1612, are commonly known as Shakespeare's "late plays," or his "last plays," and sometimes, with reference to their tragicomic form, they are called his "romances." Works written by an author in his 40s hardly deserve to be classified as "late" in any critical sense, yet these plays are often discussed as if they had been written by a venerable old author, tottering on the edge of a well-earned grave. On the contrary, Shakespeare must have believed that plenty of writing years lay before him, and indeed the theatrical effectiveness and experimental nature of *Cymbeline, The Winter's Tale,* and *The Tempest* in particular make them very unlike the fatigued work of a writer about to break his staff and drown his book.

One of the common characteristics of these plays is that, although they portray a wide range of tragic or pathetic emotions, events move toward a resolution of difficulties in which reconciliations and reunions are prominent. They differ from earlier comedies in their structural emphasis on a renewal of hope that comes from penitence and forgiveness, together with a faith in the younger generation, who by love will heal or obliterate the wounds inflicted in the past.

There is also an extravagance of story and an unreality of motivation, both prompting the use of the label "romances." From *Coriolanus,* the most austere of his tragedies, Shakespeare turned immediately to *Pericles,* a fantastically episodic play set in a vaguely pre-Christian world. He no longer saw antiquity through the eyes of a historian like Plutarch but through the bright fictions of the imitators of late Greek romances, Heliodorus and Achilles Tatius. In *The Winter's Tale,* for instance, where events are determined by the god Apollo from his oracle on the island of Delphos, the kingdoms of Bohemia and Sicilia nevertheless contain Warwickshire country festivals and conycatchers; and Queen Hermione boldy asserts: "The Emperor of Russia was my father."

Some critics have attributed this change in theatrical manner to Shakespeare's boredom with everything except poetry; others have pointed to a revival of interest in romantic tragicomedy (in *Phylaster,* by Beaumont and Fletcher, many characteristics of Shakespeare's latest plays are discernible, but the precise date of this play is questioned, and thus it is difficult to decide whether the fashion was set by Beaumont and Fletcher with their play or by Shakespeare with *Pericles*). It is at least likely, however, that Shakespeare himself was the pioneer and originator of a new style. The King's Men took over the Blackfriars Theatre in 1608. It was a more expensive theatre, and it has reasonably been conjectured that its facilities influenced Shakespeare to produce a new kind of play for a sophisticated audience more responsive to imaginative experiment in drama.

Pericles. The first scenes of *Pericles* are often feeble in expression, frequently unsyntactical, and sometimes scarcely intelligible. The second half is splendidly written, in Shakespeare's mature style. It is now generally supposed that the inadequate parts of the play are due to its being a reconstruction of the text from the actors' imperfect memories. For the second half of the play, either the printer had a manuscript of good quality or the actors' memories were more accurate. Ben Jonson called it "a mouldy tale." Certainly it was a very old one. There was a Greek prose fiction on the story, which survives in a Latin translation. Versions of it are found in many European languages. John Gower, Chaucer's friend and contemporary, had included the story in his poem *Confessio amantis,* and there were two separate prose renderings in Shakespeare's time.

The stylistic maturity of the second half of *Pericles*

Cymbeline. The main theme of *Cymbeline*—Posthumus' wager on the chastity of his wife, Imogen—Shakespeare derived from a story in Boccaccio's *Decameron.* But he put this Italianate intrigue into a setting that, for his audience, was authentic. Cymbeline, king of Britain, and his two sons, Guiderius and Arviagus, who succeeded him, were, for Shakespeare's audience, historical monarchs. The play is carefully set in the pre-Christian Roman world. The Romans who invade Britain are recognizably derived from the same kind of exploration of the antique world that had produced *Julius Caesar, Antony and Cleopatra,* and *Coriolanus.*

Shakespeare shows great dramatic skill in weaving together many different elements of plot, period, and place. The open-air scenes in Wales, Iachimo's concealment in a trunk in Imogen's bedchamber, the supposed deaths of

Posthumus and of Imogen disguised as Fidele, the battle between the Britons and Romans, the vision of the eagle-borne Jupiter—all these in preparation for the amazing complications of the final scene of the play, where (it has been calculated) there are 24 distinct "revelations" in 455 lines.

The Winter's Tale. In *The Winter's Tale* Shakespeare's audacity had increased. He introduced a similar combination of heterogeneous civilizations. But he also abandoned a unity of development in the story: he made a break of 16 years in the middle of the play, introducing the figure of Time to persuade the audience to accept the rapid shift of dramatic time. Shakespeare similarly challenged their confidence by the pathos of the deaths of the little boy Mamillius and, seemingly, of his mother Hermione, followed by the repentance of her jealous husband Leontes. He also allows Antigonus a most attractive character, to be eaten by a bear. Shakespeare clearly intended the audience to become involved only at certain moments of the play, by intensifying particular episodes without allowing emotional commitment to the whole plot. Three times his characters use the phrase "like an old tale," as if they were themselves commenting on its incredibility. What might have been the most moving scene or series of scenes in this group of plays—the revelation of Perdita's true birth—is related only at second hand by a number of anonymous gentlemen. Presumably, Shakespeare did not wish to anticipate or reduce the theatrical effect of the final scene, in which the "statue" of Hermione comes to life. Or perhaps, having already shown a similar scene of recognition of father and long-lost daughter in *Pericles*, he did not wish to repeat himself.

Ingredients in the plot of *The Tempest*

The Tempest. *The Tempest* shows even greater excellence in the variety of its ingredients. There is story enough, including two assassination plots. There is a group of quickly differentiated and interesting characters; there is elaborate dancing and singing; there is an inset entertainment, a marriage masque performed by the goddesses Iris, Ceres, and Juno; there is a theatrical "quaint device," the introduction and vanishing of a banquet; there is a tender love affair; there are marvellous comic turns. Yet a mood of seriousness is felt throughout the play; questions about freedom, about the instinct for revenge, and the conflicting claims of generosity are being asked; there is a sense of subtle seriousness when Prospero speaks his cryptic epilogue as an actor appealing for the good opinion of his audience.

Most of the action of the plot has taken place in the past; only the climax of reconciliation and the events immediately leading up to it are represented. But, although the "unity of time" is almost preserved, the amount of mental progress, the number of mental events, is large. The newcomers to Prospero's island grope their way toward repentance; the Prince finds his way to true love, after his previous tentative explorations; and Miranda awakens to womanhood. Caliban, the subhuman creature, rebels and then comes to learn the error of his ways; Ariel, the supernatural sprite, finds the means of regaining his freedom. Prospero resumes his political authority as duke and pardons all.

The play has a most interesting double focus, geographically speaking. Openly it is a story of Naples and Milan, a world of usurpations, tributes, homages, and political marriages that is familiar in Jacobean tragedy. At the same time the contemporary excitement of the New World permeates the play—a world of Indians and the plantations of the colonies, of the wonders and terrors and credulities of a newly discovered land. A lesser dramatist would surely have set his play far away in the west of the Atlantic to take advantage of this contemporary excitement. Perhaps with a surer theatrical instinct, Shakespeare offered his audience a familiar Italianate fictional world, which then became shot through with glimpses of the New World, too exciting to be fictional.

Henry VIII. *Henry VIII* is a play that has offered many difficulties to criticism. It has had a long and interesting stage history, but, from the mid-19th century, judgment has been confused by doubts about Shakespeare's sole authorship of the play, for many scenes and splendid speeches are written in a style very close to that of John Fletcher (see below *Collaborative and attributed plays*). The best of recent criticism, however, is inclined to restrict itself to consideration of the play as it stands. Although a story of English history, it differs from the "histories" that Shakespeare had written earlier, during the reign of Queen Elizabeth I. It is more episodic—more of a pageant and a series of loosely connected crises—than a skillfully plotted drama. It has a different sort of unity: three tragic episodes involving the deaths of Buckingham, Wolsey, and Queen Katharine) led to the prophecy of a new age. For Anne Boleyn's infant, whose christening closes the play, inspires Thomas Cranmer, archbishop of Canterbury, to a marvelous speech about the glories of her future reign as the first Elizabeth. Thus *Henry VIII*, in spite of many differences, resembles Shakespeare's other late plays in its emphasis on the way in which past tragic events lead to reconciliation and to hope for the new generation.

Collaborative and attributed plays. The busy competition of Elizabethan theatre encouraged collaboration between authors and was almost the rule in some companies. Naturally, therefore, scholars have sought "other hands" in Shakespeare's plays, but, following the magisterial arguments of the distinguished scholar Sir Edmund Chambers, critical opinion has held that each play in the Folio edition of 1623 is substantially Shakespeare's. The possibility remains that parts of the earliest plays, especially *1 Henry VI* and *The Taming of the Shrew*, may derive from earlier plays by other hands. Stronger than this, however, are arguments that parts of *Henry VIII* were written by John Fletcher, who from 1608 onward wrote frequently for the King's Men. Fletcher's name has been linked with Shakespeare's elsewhere, most notably in the play *The Two Noble Kinsmen*, published as their joint work in 1634. Internal evidence of style and structure suggests that Shakespeare planned the whole work and wrote Act I; that then a need for haste arose and Fletcher took over responsiblity for Acts II, III and IV, leaving Shakespeare to complete Act V. Some such story could account for a curious lack of cohesion in the writing and also for the closeness of the theme to interests apparent in Shakespeare's latest plays.

The search for "other hands" in Shakespeare

In his own lifetime and in later ages, several plays were attributed to Shakespeare (often with no justification at all). In his own handwriting, however, are 147 lines of a scene in *The Booke of Sir Thomas More*, a play written in about 1595 by a group of five authors (probably including Thomas Dekker, Anthony Munday, and Henry Chettle) and then suppressed by the censor. The attempts of Sir Thomas to quell the anti-alien riots are linked in sentiment to Shylock episodes from *The Merchant of Venice* and echo the plays of the 1590s in imagery and versification. Among the printed texts that have been ascribed to Shakespeare is the anonymous *Edward III* (1596); the stylistic evidence adduced for his authorship of an episode in which the King woos the Countess of Salisbury might, however, be the work of an imitator. Several plays were added to his works in the third edition of the Folio (1664): *Locrine* (1595), *Sir John Oldcastle* (1600), *Thomas Lord Cromwell* (1602), *The London Prodigal* (1605), *The Puritan* (1607), and *A Yorkshire Tragedy* (1608). None is now considered to be of his authorship. Other plays, too, were printed as Shakespeare's, indicating the extent of his prestige—a brand name that could sell even rotten fish. No other dramatist of his time was so misused.

SHAKESPEARE'S READING

With a few exceptions, Shakespeare did not invent the plots of his plays. Sometimes he used old stories (*Hamlet, Pericles*). Sometimes he worked from the stories of comparatively recent Italian writers, such as Boccaccio—using both well-known stories (*Romeo and Juliet, Much Ado About Nothing*) and little-known ones (*Othello*). He used the popular prose fictions of his contemporaries in *As You Like It* and *The Winter's Tale*. In writing his historical plays, he drew largely from Plutarch's *Lives of*

Shakespeare's plots

the *Noble Grecians and Romans* for the Roman plays and the chronicles of Edward Hall and Ralph Holinshed for the plays based upon English history. Some plays deal with rather remote and legendary history (*King Lear, Cymbeline, Macbeth*)—though it seemed more genuinely historical to Shakespeare's contemporaries than it does today. Earlier dramatists had occasionally used the same material (there were, for example, earlier plays called *The Famous Victories of Henry the fifth* and *King Leir*). But, because many plays of Shakespeare's time have been lost, it is impossible to be sure of the relation between an earlier, lost play and Shakespeare's surviving one: in the case of *Hamlet* it has been plausibly argued that an "old play," known to have existed, was merely an early version of Shakespeare's own.

Availability of literary contacts and accessibility of books

Shakespeare was probably too busy for prolonged study. He had to read what books he could, when he needed them. His enormous vocabulary could only be derived from a mind of great celerity, responding to the literary as well as the spoken language. It is not known what libraries were available to him. The Huguenot family of Mountjoys, with whom he lodged in London, presumably possessed French books. There was, moreover, a very interesting connection between Shakespeare and the book trade. For there survives the record of apprenticeship of one Richard Field, who published Shakespeare's two poems *Venus and Adonis* and *Lucrece*, describing him as the "son of Henry Field of Stratford-upon-Avon in the County of Warwick, tanner." When Henry Field the tanner died in 1592, John Shakespeare the glover was one of the three appointed to value his goods and chattels. Field's son, bound apprentice in 1579, was probably almost exactly the same age as Shakespeare. From 1587 he steadily established himself as a printer of serious literature—notably of Sir Thomas North's translation of Plutarch (1595, reprinted in 1603 and 1610). There is no direct evidence of any close friendship between Field and Shakespeare. But it cannot escape notice that one of the important printer-publishers in London at the time was an exact contemporary of Shakespeare at Stratford, that he can hardly have been other than a schoolfellow, that he was the son of a close associate of John Shakespeare, and that he published Shakespeare's first poems. Clearly, a considerable number of literary contacts were available to Shakespeare, and many books were accessible.

That Shakespeare's plays had "sources" was already apparent in his own time. An interesting contemporary description of a performance is to be found in the diary of a young lawyer of the Middle Temple, John Manningham, who kept a record of his experiences in 1602 and 1603. On February 2, 1602, he wrote:

At our feast we had a play called *Twelfth Night, or What You Will*, much like *The Comedy of Errors*, or *Menaechmi* in Plautus, but most like and near to that in Italian called *Inganni*. . . .

The first collection of information about sources of Elizabethan plays was published in the 17th century—Gerard Langbaine's *Account of the English Dramatick Poets* (1691) briefly indicated where Shakespeare found materials for some plays. But, during the course of the 17th century, it came to be felt that Shakespeare was an outstandingly "natural" writer, whose intellectual background was of comparatively little significance: "he was naturally learn'd; he needed not the spectacles of books to read nature," said John Dryden in 1668. It was nevertheless obvious that the intellectual quality of Shakespeare's writings was high and revealed a remarkably perceptive mind. The Roman plays, in particular, gave evidence of careful reconstruction of the ancient world.

The first collection of source materials, arranged so that they could be read and closely compared with Shakespeare's plays, was made by Mrs. Charlotte Lennox in the 18th century. More complete collections appeared later, notably those of John Payne Collier (*Shakespeare's Library*, 1843; revised by W. Carew Hazlitt, 1875). These earlier collections have been superseded by one edited by Geoffrey Bullough as *Narrative and Dramatic Sources of Shakespeare* (7 vol., 1957–72).

It has become steadily more possible to see what was original in Shakespeare's dramatic art. He achieved compression and economy by the exclusion of undramatic material. He developed characters from brief suggestions in his source (Mercutio, Touchstone, Falstaff, Pandarus), and he developed entirely new characters (the Dromio brothers, Beatrice and Benedick, Sir Toby Belch, Malvolio, Paulina, Roderigo, Lear's fool). He rearranged the plot with a view to more effective contrasts of character, climaxes, and conclusions (*Macbeth, Othello, The Winter's Tale, As You Like It*). A wider philosophical outlook was introduced (*Hamlet, Coriolanus, All's Well That Ends Well, Troilus and Cressida*). And everywhere an intensification of the dialogue and an altogether higher level of imaginative writing together transformed the older work.

Acquaintance with the literary achievements of other writers

But, quite apart from evidence of the sources of his plays, it is not difficult to get a fair impression of Shakespeare as a reader, feeding his own imagination by a moderate acquaintance with the literary achievements of other men and of other ages. He quotes his contemporary Christopher Marlowe in *As You Like It*. He casually refers to the *Aethiopica* ("Ethiopian History") of Heliodorus (which had been translated by Thomas Underdown in 1569) in *Twelfth Night*. He read the translation of Ovid's *Metamorphoses* by Arthur Golding, which went through seven editions between 1567 and 1612. Chapman's vigorous translation of Homer's *Iliad* impressed him, though he used some of the material rather sardonically in *Troilus and Cressida*. He derived the ironical account of an ideal republic in *The Tempest* from one of Montaigne's essays. He read (in part, at least) Samuel Harsnett's *Declaration of egregious popish impostors* and remembered lively passages from it when he was writing *King Lear*. The beginning lines of one sonnet (106) indicate that he had read Edmund Spenser's poem *The Faerie Queene* or comparable romantic literature.

He was acutely aware of the varieties of poetic style that characterized the work of other authors. A brilliant little poem he composed for Prince Hamlet (Act II, scene 2, line 115) shows how ironically he perceived the qualities of poetry in the last years of the 16th century, when poets such as John Donne were writing love poems uniting astronomical and cosmogenic imagery with skepticism and moral paradoxes. The eight-syllable lines in an archaic mode written for the 14th-century poet John Gower in *Pericles* show his reading of that poet's *Confessio amantis*. The influence of the great figure of Sir Philip Sidney, whose *Arcadia* was first printed in 1590 and was widely read for generations, is frequently felt in Shakespeare's writings. Finally, the importance of the Bible for Shakespeare's style and range of allusion is not to be underestimated. His works show a pervasive familiarity with the passages appointed to be read in church on each Sunday throughout the year, and a large number of allusions to passages in Ecclesiasticus (Wisdom of Jesus the Son of Sirach) indicates a personal interest in one of the uncanonical books.

III. Understanding Shakespeare
SYMPATHETIC EXPLORATION OF THE TEXTS

On opening the works of Shakespeare, a reader can be held by a few lines of verse or a sentence or one complex, glittering, or telling word. Indeed, Shakespeare's supreme mastery of words and images, of sound, rhythm, metre, and texture, as well as the point, neatness, and lyricism of his lines, has enslaved countless people.

The next step in understanding, for most readers, is an appreciation of individual characters. Many of the early books on Shakespeare were about his "characters," and controversy about them still continues. Appreciation of the argument of the plays usually comes on insensibly, for Shakespeare is not a didactic playwright. But most persistent readers gain an increasing sense of a unity of inspiration, of an alert moral judgment and idealistic vision, both in the individual plays and in the works as a whole.

When the plays are seen in performance, they are further revealed in a new, three-dimensional, flesh and blood reality, which can grow in the minds of individual play-goers and readers as they become more experienced in response to the plays' many suggestions.

But, while various skills and learned guidance are needed for a developed understanding of Shakespeare, the directness of his appeal remains—the editors of the First Folio commended the plays to everyone "how odd soever your brains be, or your wisdoms." Perhaps most essentially, the plays will continually yield their secrets only to imaginative exploration.

(margin note: Shakespeare's direct appeal to readers*)*

CAUSES OF DIFFICULTY

Questions of authorship. The idea that Shakespeare's plays and poems were not actually written by William Shakespeare of Stratford has been the subject of many books and is widely regarded as at least an interesting possibility. The source of all doubts about the authorship of the plays lies in the disparity between the greatness of Shakespeare's literary achievement and his comparatively humble origin, the supposed inadequacy of his education, and the obscurity of his life. In Shakespeare's writings, people have claimed to discover a familiarity with languages and literature, with such subjects as law, history, politics, and geography, and with the manners and speech of courts, which they regard as inconceivable in a common player, the son of a provincial tradesman. This range of knowledge, it is said, is to be expected at that period only in a man of extensive education, one who was familiar with such royal and noble personages as figure largely in Shakespeare's plays. And the dearth of contemporary records has been regarded as incompatible with Shakespeare's eminence and as therefore suggestive of mystery. That none of his manuscripts has survived has been taken as evidence that they were destroyed to conceal the identity of their author.

The claims put forward for Bacon. The first suggestion that the author of Shakespeare's plays might be Francis Bacon, Viscount St. Albans, seems to have been made in the middle of the 19th century, inquiry at first centring on textual comparison between Bacon's known writings and the plays. A discovery was made that references to the Bible, the law, and the classics were given similar treatment in both canons. In the later 19th century a search was made for ciphered messages embedded in the dramatic texts. In *Love's Labour's Lost*, for example, it was found that the Latin word "honorificabilitudinitatibus" is an anagram of *Hi ludi F. Baconis nati tuiti orbi* ("These plays, the offspring of F. Bacon, are preserved for the world.") Professional cryptographers of the 20th century, however, examining all the Baconian ciphers, have rejected them as invalid, and interest in the Shakespeare–Bacon controversy has diminished.

Other candidates. A theory that the author of the plays was Edward de Vere, 17th earl of Oxford, receives some circumstantial support from the coincidence that Oxford's known poems apparently ceased just before Shakespeare's work began to appear. It is argued that Oxford assumed a pseudonym in order to protect his family from the social stigma then attached to the stage and also because extravagance had brought him into disrepute at court. Another candidate is William Stanley, 6th earl of Derby, who was keenly interested in the theatre and was patron of his own company of actors. Several poems, written in the 1580s and exhibiting signs of an immature Shakespearean style, cannot well have been written by Shakespeare himself. One of these is in Derby's handwriting, and three of them are signed "W.S." These initials are thought by some to have been a concealment for Derby's identity (for some such motives as were attributed to Oxford) and to have been later expanded into "William Shakespeare."

(margin note: Edward de Vere, earl of Oxford*)*

Shakespeare has also been identified with Christopher Marlowe, one theory even going so far as to assert that Marlowe was not killed in a tavern brawl in 1593 (the corpse of another being represented as his own) but was smuggled to France and thence to Italy where he continued to write in exile—his plays being fathered on Shakespeare, who was paid to keep silent.

(margin note: Christopher Marlowe*)*

The case for Shakespeare. In spite of recorded allusions to Shakespeare as the author of many plays in the canon, made by about 50 men during his lifetime, it is arguable that his greatness was not as clearly recognized in his own day as one might expect. But on the other hand, the difficulties are not so great as many disbelievers have held, and their proposals have all too often raised larger problems than they have resolved. Shakespeare's contemporaries, after all, wrote of him unequivocally as the author of the plays. Ben Jonson, who knew him well, contributed verses to the First Folio of 1623, where (as elsewhere) he criticizes and praises Shakespeare as the author. John Heminge and Henry Condell, fellow actors and theatre owners with Shakespeare, signed the dedication and a foreword to the First Folio and described their methods as editors. In his own day, therefore, he was accepted as the author of the plays. Throughout his lifetime, and for long after, no person is known to have questioned his authorship. In an age that loved gossip and mystery as much as any, it seems hardly conceivable that Jonson and Shakespeare's theatrical associates shared the secret of a gigantic literary hoax without a single leak or that they could have been imposed upon without suspicion. Unsupported assertions that the author of the plays was a man of great learning and that Shakespeare of Stratford was an illiterate rustic no longer carry weight, and only when a believer in Bacon or Oxford or Marlowe produces sound evidence will scholars pay close attention to it and to him.

Linguistic and historical problems. Since the days of Shakespeare, the English language has changed, and so have audiences, theatres, actors, and customary patterns of thought and feeling. Time has placed an ever-increasing cloud before the mirror he held up to life, and it is here that scholarship can help.

Problems are most obvious in single words. In the 20th century, "presently," for instance, does not mean "immediately," as it usually did for Shakespeare, or "will" mean "lust" or "rage" mean "folly" or "silly" denote "innocence" and "purity." In Shakespeare's day, words sounded different, too, so that "ably" could rhyme with "eye" or "tomb" with "dumb." Syntax was often different, and, far more difficult to define, so was response to metre and phrase. What sounds formal and stiff to a modern hearer might have sounded fresh and gay to an Elizabethan.

Ideas have changed, too, most obviously political ones. Shakespeare's contemporaries almost unanimously believed in authoritarian monarchy; they accepted a police state and recognized divine intervention in history. Most of them would have agreed that a man should be burned for ultimate religious heresies. It is the office of linguistic and historical scholarship to aid the understanding of the multitude of factors that have significantly affected the impressions made by Shakespeare's plays.

Textual and editorial problems. None of Shakespeare's plays has survived in his handwritten manuscript, and, in the printed texts of some plays, notably *King Lear* and *Richard III*, there are passages manifestly corrupt, with no clue to the words Shakespeare once wrote. Even if the printer received a good manuscript, small errors could still be introduced. Compositors were less than perfect; they often "regularized" the readings of their copy, altered punctuation because they lacked the necessary pieces of type, or made mistakes because they had to work too hurriedly. Even the correction of proof sheets in the printing house could further corrupt the text, since such correction was usually effected without reference to the author or to the manuscript copy; when both corrected and uncorrected states are still available, it is often the uncorrected version that is preferable. Correctors are undoubtedly responsible for many errors now impossible to right.

OVERCOMING SOME DIFFICULTIES

The contribution of textual criticism. The early editors of Shakespeare saw their task chiefly as one of correction and regularization of the faulty printing and imperfect texts of the original editions or their reprints. Many changes in the text of the quartos and folios that are now accepted derive from Nicholas Rowe (1709) and Alexander Pope (1723–25), but these editors also introduced many thousands of small changes that have since been rejected. Later in the 18th century, editors compiled collations of alternative and rejected readings. Samuel Johnson (1765), Edward Capell (1767–68), and Edmond Malone (1790) were notable pioneers. Their work reached its most comprehensive form in the Cambridge edition in nine volumes by W.G. Clark, J. Glover, and W.A. Wright, published in 1863–66. A famous one-volume Globe edition of 1864 was based on this Cambridge text.

Each major editor had added to the great number of annotations on textual problems and on linguistic and historical difficulties, and in 1871 was published the first of a series of large volumes, one or two for each play, called "A New Variorum Edition," which aimed at bringing all previous textual scholarship together. The series remains incomplete, but A.W. Pollard published his *Shakespeare Folios and Quartos* in 1909 and, together with R.B. McKerrow, Sir Walter Greg, and Charles Sisson, began a concerted study of the manuscript plays surviving from Elizabethan theatres and the practice of Elizabethan printers. Their work was summed up in Greg's study *The Shakespeare First Folio* (1955) and Fredson Bowers' *On Editing Shakespeare and the Elizabethan Dramatists* (1955). By this time a new phase of bibliographic and textual inquiry had begun, and Bowers, with Alice Walker, Charlton Hinman, and others, began studying the smallest minutiae of each substantive early edition. Computers will analyze the huge mass of their detailed information and make available the full results of their investigations. Also, individual compositors who set in type the early editions are being identified, and already something of their work habits and habitual errors is known. Processes of correction in the Elizabethan printing houses are also being studied more intensively. Before the end of the 20th century, a new edition of Shakespeare may appear in which a multitude of small errors have been removed. But even then, nothing will compensate for the loss of Shakespeare's manuscripts, and numerous important readings and details of presentation will still have to be supplied by educated guesses.

The "New Variorum Edition"

Historical, linguistic, and dramatic studies. Since the end of the 19th century, many other problems that hinder the understanding of Shakespeare's texts have been at least partly overcome thanks to extensive investigation into, for example, his syntax, vocabulary, and word usage —especially with regard to other Elizabethan and Jacobean literature. Such technical works, as well as studies of current theories of composition (the use of rhetoric, metaphor, and simile), have provided material for critical analysis, as have works that examine the ideas and life-style of Shakespeare's contemporaries. An increasingly large proportion of research is devoted to an investigation of contemporary literary and dramatic conventions.

LITERARY CRITICISM

Literary critics and the theatre. Shakespeare criticism must take into account the certainty that Shakespeare intended his plays to be acted, that he was the professional playwright of a repertory company, that the success of a play in performance by his company was what determined his income, and that during his lifetime he apparently made no effort (or perhaps was too busy) to gain a "literary" reputation from his plays. Yet, his contemporaries had no doubt about his literary eminence. Heminge and Condell, his fellow players, and Ben Jonson, his fellow playwright, commended the great Folio of 1623 to "the great variety of readers."

The tension between the critics and the theatre

The situation has been complicated by the fact that the history of Shakespeare criticism and the stage history of his plays have run parallel but separate courses. It is fair to say that, from about the mid-18th century onward, there has been a constant tension between the critics and the theatres regarding treatment of Shakespeare. Although Dr. Johnson was the contemporary of David Garrick, Coleridge and Hazlitt the contemporaries of Ed-

mund Kean, Dowden of Sir Henry Irving, and Bradley of Beerbohm Tree, the links between these critics and actors were not notably strong. Theatregoers were usually impressed by character impersonations rendered by virtuoso actors, while readers became more and more impressed by an awareness and admiration of the special artistic form of the plays. Rather than by stage performances, Shakespeare criticism was influenced by the dominant literary forms of each age: by the self-revelatory poem of the Romantic period, the psychological and ethical novel of the Victorians, the fragmentary revelations of the human condition in 20th-century poetry. It is a platitude that each age finds what it wants to find in Shakespeare. It will only see what it can. It can only see what it must. But Shakespeare critics, if criticism is to be in a healthy condition, must pay more than lip service to that fact. However deeply embedded in its contemporary situation, good criticism, like all intellectual feats, is a leaping out of the situation. The history of Shakespeare criticism is a subject of more than scholarly interest. It is a cautionary tale. Sometimes it is an awful warning.

The progress of Shakespeare criticism. As a basis for the criticism of an author's work, it is reasonable to begin by inquiring how his contemporaries assessed his achievement. But contemporary literary criticism was surprisingly silent about the plays actually being written (though critics were reasonably articulate about the plays they thought ought to be written). Collections of references made to Shakespeare later, during the 17th century, show that many important writers paid little attention to him. Ben Jonson's reputation was, for a variety of reasons, probably superior for the first half of the century. He was, moreover, the most vocal literary critic of the early 17th century, and he thought of Shakespeare as a naturally gifted writer, who failed to discipline himself. From his criticism derived the distinction between "nature" and "art" that for long proved to be a pertinacious and unproductive theme of Shakespeare criticism. It was further encouraged by John Milton, when he contrasted Jonson's "learned sock" with Shakespeare's "native wood-notes wild" (which refers to the comedies but came to be treated as a general statement, especially the epithet "wild"). A good deal of the spirit of Ben Jonson's cavillings, rather than his magnificent praise in the poem prefixed to the Folio of 1623, was continued by later 17th-century and 18th-century critics, censuring Shakespeare's carelessness, his artistic "faults."

John Dryden (died 1700) was the first great critic of Shakespeare. Much concerned with his own art as a dramatist, he judged Shakespeare in a practical spirit. For 100 years after him, the best literary criticism of Shakespeare was an elaboration and clarification of his opinions. Dryden on some occasions praised Shakespeare in the highest terms and boldly defended the English tradition of the theatre, maintaining that, if it was contrary to the revered classical precepts of Aristotle, it was only because Aristotle had not seen English plays; had he seen them, his precepts would have been different. Dryden nevertheless at times attributes artistic "faults" to Shakespeare, judging him according to Neoclassical principles of taste that derived from France and soon prevailed throughout Europe. Shakespeare's dramatic art was so different from that of the admired tragedy of the times (that of Corneille and Racine) that it was difficult for a critic to defend or interpret it in reasonable terms. The gravest charge was the absence of "poetical justice" in Shakespeare's plays. Although some of the better 18th-century critics, such as Joseph Addison and Dr. Johnson, saw the limitations of "poetical justice" as an artistic theory, they nevertheless generally felt that the ending of *King Lear*, especially, was intolerable, offending all sense of natural justice by the death of Cordelia. The play was thus given a "happy ending"—one congruent with "poetical justice"—by the poet and playwright Nahum Tate: Lear was restored to his authority, and Cordelia and Edgar were to be married and could look forward to a prosperous reign over a united Britain. This change was approved by Dr. Johnson, and the revised play held the stage for generations and was the only form of *King Lear* performed on the stage until the mid-19th century.

In the early 18th century the cumbrous folio editions were replaced by more convenient editions, prepared for the reader. Nicholas Rowe, in a six-volume edition of 1709, tidied up the text of the plays, adding scene divisions, lists of dramatis personae, indications of locality, and so on. Rowe thus made a start in turning Shakespeare's plays into literature to be read, yet without neglecting the theatrical environment from which they emerged. Rowe was himself a practicing and successful dramatist, and on the whole he gave a good lead to the dramatic criticism of the plays. The preface to Alexander Pope's edition of 1725, however, had an unhappy influence on criticism. Shakespeare's natural genius, he felt, was hampered by his association with a working theatre. Pope fully accepted the artistic form of Shakespeare's writings as due to their being stage plays. But he regarded this as a grave disadvantage and the source of their artistic defectiveness. Lewis Theobald took the opposing view to Pope's, claiming that it was an advantage of Shakespeare that he belonged to the theatrical profession. Dr. Johnson similarly realized that methods of producing the plays on the stage influenced the kind of illusion created. In the splendid preface to his edition (1765), Johnson dismissed, once and for all in English criticism, the Neoclassical theories of "decorum," the "unities," and the mutual exclusiveness of tragedy and comedy—theories now seen as irrelevant to Shakespeare's art and as having confused the discussion of it. In many ways Johnson was the source of the notion of Shakespeare as a realistic dramatist, whose mingling of tragic and comic scenes was justified as "exhibiting the real state of sublunary nature," in which laughter and tears, rejoicing and misery, are found side by side.

Johnson censured Shakespeare as a dramatic artist for his lack of morality. Shakespeare, he wrote, "sacrifices virtue to convenience, and is so much more careful to please than to instruct, that he seems to write without any moral purpose." Later critics have felt compelled to controvert or to circumvent such a judgment. But Johnson's preface, if it did not give the discussion of Shakespeare's artistry a fresh start, cleared away some of the dead or irrelevant doctrines.

During the rest of the 18th century, after Johnson, it was scholarship rather than criticism that advanced in England. The best of literary criticism of the time was in the discovery of new subtleties in Shakespeare, especially in characterization; indeed, the acceptance of Shakespeare as a dramatic artist largely came about through his evident powers of characterization (to which probably the growth of the realistic novel in the 18th century had made readers more sensitive), and inadequate attention was paid to other aspects of his dramatic craftsmanship. There was nothing in England comparable to the brilliant Shakespeare criticism of Lessing, Goethe, and August von Schlegel in Germany. The latter's essay on *Romeo and Juliet* of 1797 demonstrated that, apart from a few witticisms, nothing could be taken away from the play, nothing added, nothing rearranged without mutilating the work of art and confusing the author's intentions. Here modern Shakespeare criticism begins. Indeed, from the time of Lessing, in the 18th century, to the mid-19th century, German critics and scholars made substantial and original contributions to the interpretation of Shakespeare, indicating Shakespeare's superlative artistry, at a time when in England he was admired more as a great poet and a brilliant observer of mankind than as a disciplined artist.

Samuel Taylor Coleridge, the greatest English critic of Shakespeare, vigorously denied that he had been affected by Schlegel (though he acknowledged the influence of Lessing), but there are many similarities between the two. His criticism—which has to be put together from reports of his lectures, from his notebooks, and from memories of his conversation, for he never succeeded in writing an organized book on Shakespeare—at first censured Shakespeare's lack of artistry, but in his lectures, given from 1810 onward, and in his *Biographia Literaria*

(1817), he demonstrated that Shakespeare's "irregularities" were in fact the manifestations of a subtle intelligence. It was the purpose of criticism to reveal the reasons why the plays are as they are. Shakespeare was a penetrating psychologist and a profound philosopher; but Coleridge claimed that he was an even greater artist, and his artistry was seen to be "unconscious" or "organic," not contrived. Thus the dominant literary forms of Coleridge's age, which were those of self-revelatory poetry, influenced the criticism of the age: Hamlet was felt to speak with the voice and feeling of Shakespeare, and, as for the sonnets, William Wordsworth, whose greatest achievement was writing a long poem on the growth of his own mind, explained that Shakespeare "unlocked his heart" in his sonnets.

These critical opinions were inclined to degenerate in inferior hands in the course of the 19th century: the belief in Shakespeare's all-pervading artistry led to over-subtle interpretations; the enthusiasm for character analysis led to excessive biography writing outside the strictly dramatic framework; and the acknowledged assessment of Shakespeare's keen intelligence led to his being associated with almost every school of thought in religion, politics, morals, psychology, and metaphysics. Nevertheless, it was the great achievement of the Romantics to have freed criticism from preoccupation with the "beauties" and "faults" in Shakespeare and to have devoted themselves instead to interpreting the delight that people had always felt in the plays, whether as readers or theatregoers. Shakespeare's "faults" now became "problems," and it was regarded an achievement in literary criticism to have found an explanation for some hitherto difficult or irreconcilable detail in a play. Many of the most brilliant writers of Europe were critics of Shakespeare; and their utterances (whether or not they may be regarded as having correctly interpreted Shakespeare) are notable as recording the impressions he made upon great minds.

SHAKESPEARE'S INFLUENCE

Today Shakespeare's plays are performed throughout the world, and all kinds of new, experimental work finds inspiration in them: " . . . in the second half of the twentieth century in England," wrote the innovative theatre director Peter Brook, "we are faced with the infuriating fact that Shakespeare is still our model."

Shakespeare's influence on English theatre was evident from the start. John Webster, Philip Massinger, and John Ford are among the better known dramatists who borrowed openly from his plays. His influence is evident on Restoration dramatists, especially Thomas Otway, John Dryden, and William Congreve. John Osborne, Harold Pinter, Samuel Beckett, and George Bernard Shaw are among 20th-century writers in whose works Shakespearean echoes are to be found. Many writers have taken over Shakespeare's plots and characters: Shaw rewrote the last act of *Cymbeline*, Tom Stoppard invented new characters to set against parts of *Hamlet* in *Rosencrantz and Guildenstern Are Dead* (1968), and Edward Bond used *King Lear* as the starting point for his own *Lear* (1971).

Shakespeare has also influenced dramatists and theatre directors outside his own country. In Germany, English acting troupes were welcomed early in the 17th century, and the German version of *Hamlet, Der bestrafte Brudermord* ("Fratricide Punished"), testifies to the immediate influence of that play. His influence on later European dramatists ranges from a running allusion to Hamlet in Anton Chekhov's play *The Seagull* to imitation and parody of *Richard III* in Bertolt Brecht's *Arturo Ui*, adaptation of *King John* by Max Frisch, and André Gide's translation and simplification of *Hamlet*.

Shakespeare's influence on actors since his own day has been almost as widespread. Many European and American actors have had their greatest successes in Shakespearean roles. In England very few actors or actresses reach pre-eminence without acting in his plays. Each player has the opportunity to make a part his own. This is not because Shakespeare has created only outlines for others to fill but because he left so many and varied

Pope's theory that Shakespeare's natural genius was hampered by writing for the theatre

Coleridge's critical opinions

invitations for the actor to call upon his deepest, most personal resources.

Theatre directors and designers after Shakespeare's time, with every technical stage resource at their command, have returned repeatedly to his plays, which give opportunity for spectacle and finesse, ritual and realism, music and controlled quietness. Their intrinsic theatricality, too, has led to adaptations into very different media: into opera (as Verdi's *Otello*) and ballet (as versions of *Romeo and Juliet* from several nations); into sound recordings, television programs, and films. Musicals have been made of the comedies (as *Kiss Me Kate* from *The Taming of the Shrew*); even a tragedy, *Othello*, was the inspiration of a "rock" musical in 1971 called *Catch My Soul*, while *Macbeth* has yielded a political-satire show called *Macbird!* (1967).

Shakespeare has Hamlet say that the aim of theatre performance is to "hold the mirror up to nature," and this is what the history of his plays, from their first production to the latest, shows that he has, pre-eminently, achieved.

MAJOR WORKS

PLAYS: (probable dates of performance given): *2 Henry VI*, *3 Henry VI* (1589–91); *1 Henry VI* (1591–92); *Richard III*, *The Comedy of Errors* (1592–93); *Titus Andronicus*, *The Taming of the Shrew* (1593–94); *The Two Gentlemen of Verona*, *Love's Labour's Lost*, *Romeo and Juliet* (1594–95); *Richard II*, *A Midsummer Night's Dream* (1595–96); *King John*, *The Merchant of Venice* (1596–97); *1 Henry IV*, *2 Henry IV* (1597–98); *Much Ado About Nothing*, *Henry V* (1598–99); *Julius Caesar*, *As You Like It* (1599–1600); *Hamlet*, *The Merry Wives of Windsor* (1600–01); *Twelfth Night*, *Troilus and Cressida* (1601–02); *All's Well That Ends Well* (1602–03); *Measure for Measure*, *Othello* (1604–05); *King Lear*, *Macbeth* (1605–06); *Antony and Cleopatra* (1606–07); *Coriolanus*, *Timon of Athens* (1607–08); *Pericles* (1608–09); *Cymbeline* (1609–10); *The Winter's Tale* (1610–11); *The Tempest* (1611–12); *Henry VIII* (1612–13).

POEMS: (dates of publication given): *Venus and Adonis* (1593); *The Rape of Lucrece* (1594); "The Phoenix and the Turtle" (1601); *Sonnets* with "A Lovers complaint" (1609).

BIBLIOGRAPHY

Modern editions: One-volume editions of Shakespeare's *Works* are by GEORGE L. KITTREDGE (1936), PETER ALEXANDER (1954), HARDIN CRAIG (1951), and CHARLES J. SISSON (1954). Editions giving one volume for each play are ALFRED HARBAGE (gen. ed.), *The Pelican Shakespeare*, rev. ed. (1969); SYLVAN BARNET (gen. ed.), *The Signet Classic Shakespeare*, 27 vol. (1963–66); and the still incomplete revision of *The Arden Shakespeare*, ed. by UNA ELLIS-FERMOR, H.F. BROOKS, and H. JENKINS (1951–   ); and T.J.B. SPENCER (gen. ed.), *The New Penguin Shakespeare*; the *New Cambridge Edition* is also one volume for each play, but the early publications of the comedies and some histories are now considered eccentric (gen. eds., SIR A.T. QUILLER-COUCH, J.D. WILSON et al.). The *New Variorum Edition*, started by HORACE HOWARD FURNESS in 1871, is still in progress, and the completeness of its textual apparatus and notes ensures continual usefulness.

Textual studies: WALTHER EBISCH and LEVIN L. SCHUCKING published a comprehensive *Shakespeare Bibliography* in 1931 (supplemented in 1937 for the years 1930–35). The account is updated by GORDON R. SMITH, *A Classified Shakespeare Bibliography, 1936–1958* (1963). The *Shakespeare Quarterly* (New York) publishes an annual classified bibliography, while the *Shakespeare Survey* (London) publishes annual accounts of "Contributions to Shakespearian Study," together retrospective articles on work done on particular aspects during the present century. JOHN BARTLETT, *A New and Complete Concordance . . . to Shakespeare* (1894); and CHARLES T. ONIONS, *A Shakespeare Glossary*, 2nd ed. rev. (1919), are both still most useful reference works and are kept in print. On textual criticism as applied to Shakespeare, the following works represent latest thinking and practice: FREDSON BOWERS, *Bibliography and Textual Criticism* (1964) and *On Editing Shakespeare* (1966); WALTER W. GREG, *The Editorial Problem in Shakespeare*, 3rd ed. (1954), and *The Shakespeare First Folio* (1955); CHARLTON HINMAN, *The Printing and Proof-Reading of the First Folio of Shakespeare*, 2 vol. (1963); E.A.J. HONIGMANN, *The Stability of Shakespeare's Text* (1965); RONALD B. MCKERROW, *An Introduction to Bibliography for Literary Students* (1927); ALFRED W. POLLARD, *Shakespeare Folios and Quartos: A Study in the Bibliography of Shakespeare's Plays, 1594–1685* (1909); ALICE WALKER, *Textual*

Problems of the First Folio (1953); and FRANK P. WILSON, *Shakespeare and the New Bibliography*, rev. ed. by HELEN GARDNER (1970). Facsimile editions of quartos and folio, which are necessary for any close work on textual problems, have been edited by WALTER W. GREG et al., *Shakespeare Quarto Facsimiles* (1939 and in progress); and by CHARLTON HINMAN, *The Norton Facsimile of the First Folio* (1968).

Biographies: A lively account of the various efforts that have been made to write a biography of Shakespeare from the available materials, with the help of imaginative interpretation, is SAMUEL SCHOENBAUM, *Shakespeare's Lives* (1970). The first detailed life of Shakespeare was written by NICHOLAS ROWE, *Some Account of the Life of Mr. William Shakespeare* (1709; photographic facsimile, 1948). EDMOND MALONE, from 1780 onwards added much new material; his final account is in the 1821 Variorum Edition. The best of the 19th-century biographies were J.O. HALLIWELL-PHILLIPPS, *Outlines of the Life of Shakespeare* (1881; last revision, 1887); and SIDNEY LEE, *A Life of William Shakespeare* (1898; 14th ed., 1931). The standard work is E.K. CHAMBERS, *William Shakespeare: A Study of Facts and Problems*, 2 vol. (1930), of which there is a useful abridgment by CHARLES WILLIAMS, *A Short Life of Shakespeare with Sources* (1933). More recent works are E.I. FRIPP, *Shakespeare, Man and Artist*, 2 vol. (1938); PETER ALEXANDER, *Shakespeare's Life and Art* (1939, reprinted 1961); HAZELTON SPENCER, *The Art and Life of William Shakespeare* (1940, reprinted 1970); M.M. REESE, *Shakespeare: His World and His Work* (1953); G.E. BENTLEY, *Shakespeare: A Biographical Handbook* (1961), supplemented by his *Profession of Dramatists in Shakespeare's Time, 1590–1642* (1971); PETER QUENNELL, *Shakespeare* (1963); and A.L. ROWSE, *William Shakespeare* (1963). Studies of special aspects of the life and environment include JOHN LESLIE HOTSON, *Shakespeare Versus Shallow* (1931, reprinted 1970); THOMAS W. BALDWIN, *William Shakspere's Petty School* (1943) and *William Shakspere's Small Latine and Lesse Greeke*, 2 vol. (1944, reprinted 1966); and MARK ECCLES, *Shakespeare in Warwickshire* (1961). A valuable collection of background material is contained in *Shakespeare's England: An Account of the Life and Manners of His Age*, ed. by SIDNEY LEE and CHARLES T. ONIONS, 2 vol. (1916). Also helpful are E.M.W. TILLYARD, *The Elizabethan World Picture* (1943, reprinted 1966); and *Shakespeare in His Own Age*, ed. by ALLARDYCE NICOLL (1964). The standard works on the theatre of Shakespeare's professional life are E.K. CHAMBERS, *The Elizabethan Stage*, 4 vol. (1923); and GLYNNE WICKHAM, *Early English Stages 1300–1660* (vol. 2 on 1576–1600, published in two pt., 1963–72). Other helpful studies are ALFRED HARBAGE, *Shakespeare's Audience* (1941); A.M. NAGLER, *Shakespeare's Stage* (1958); and BERNARD BECKERMAN, *Shakespeare at the Globe, 1599–1609* (1962). Special aspects of the environment that throw light on the mentality of the dramatist are RICHMOND NOBLE, *Shakespeare's Biblical Knowledge and Use of the Book of Common Prayer* (1935, reprinted 1970); R. MUSHAT FRYE, *Shakespeare and Christian Doctrine* (1963); PAUL A. JORGENSEN, *Shakespeare's Military World* (1956); GEORGE W. KEETON, *Shakespeare's Legal and Political Background* (1967); and K.M. BRIGGS, *The Anatomy of Puck* (1959) and *Pale Hecate's Team* (1962), on belief in fairies and witchcraft. A survey of the theories that someone other than William Shakespeare of Stratford-upon-Avon was the author of the plays published under his name has been written by H.N. GIBSON, *The Shakespeare Claimants: A Critical Survey of the Four Principal Theories Concerning the Authorship of the Shakespearean Plays* (1962). See also R.C. CHURCHILL, *Shakespeare and His Betters* (1958); and FRANK W. WADSWORTH, *The Poacher from Stratford* (1958). The possibility of cryptic messages in the plays was conclusively investigated in W.F. and E.S. FRIEDMAN, *The Shakespearean Ciphers Examined* (1957). The following are some of the principal exponents of the theories: (*Bacon*): EDWIN DURNING-LAWRENCE, *Bacon Is Shake-speare* (1910, reprinted 1971); A.B. CORNWALL, *Francis the First, Unacknowledged King of Great Britain and Ireland . . .* (1936); see also J.M. ROBERTSON, *The Baconian Heresy* (1913, reprinted 1970). (*Edward de Vere, 17th Earl of Oxford, 1550–1604*): J.T. LOONEY, "*Shakespeare*" *Identified* (1920); PERCY ALLEN, *The Story of Edward de Vere as William Shakespeare* (1932); HILDA AMPHLETT, *Who Was Shakespeare?* (1955, reprinted 1970); GILBERT SLATER, *Seven Shakespeares* (1931), proposes Oxford and a group of his collaborators. (*6th Earl of Derby*): ABEL LEFRANC, *Sous le masque de "William Shakespeare,"* 2 vol. (1918–19) and *À la découverte de Shakespeare*, 2 vol. (1945–50). (*Marlowe*): CALVIN HOFFMAN, *The Man Who Was Shakespeare* (1955).

Critical studies: Early opinion about Shakespeare up to 1700 is collected in *The Shakespeare Allusion-Book*, ed. by

JOHN MUNRO, 2 vol. (1909), rev. by E.K. CHAMBERS (1932, reprinted 1970); and in G.E. BENTLEY, *Shakespeare and Jonson: Their Reputations in the Seventeenth Century Compared* (1945). Eighteenth-century criticism is surveyed in DAVID NICHOL SMITH, *Shakespeare in the Eighteenth Century* (1928) and in his collection of *Eighteenth Century Essays on Shakespeare* (1903; 2nd ed., 1963); his anthology *Shakespeare Criticism: A Selection* (1916), includes work up to about 1825. Dr. Johnson's criticism has been conveniently excerpted in *Johnson on Shakespeare*, ed. by WALTER RALEIGH (1908) and *Samuel Johnson on Shakespeare*, ed. by W.K. WIMSATT (1960). T.M. RAYSOR prepared the standard edition of *Coleridge's Shakespearean Criticism* (1930; 2nd ed., 2 vol., 1960), but a useful compilation is *Coleridge on Shakespeare*, ed. by TERENCE HAWKES (1969). These can be supplemented by *Coleridge on Shakespeare: The Text of the Lectures of 1811–12*, ed. by R.A. FOAKES (1971). General surveys of the development of criticism are given by LOUIS MARDER, *His Exits and His Entrances* (1963); ALFRED HARBAGE, *Conceptions of Shakespeare* (1966); and A.M. EASTMAN, *A Short History of Shakespearean Criticism* (1968). The best brief accounts are by T.S. ELIOT and J. ISAACS, "Shakespearian Criticism," in *A Companion to Shakespeare Studies*, ed. by HARLEY GRANVILLE-BARKER and G.B. HARRISON (1934, reprinted 1960); and by M.A. SHAABER, "Shakespeare Criticism: Dryden to Bradley," and STANLEY WELLS, "Shakespeare Criticism Since Bradley," in *A New Companion to Shakespeare Studies*, ed. by KENNETH MUIR and SAMUEL SCHOENBAUM (1971). The situation outside Britain may be studied in *Shakespeare in Europe*, a collection edited by OSWALD LE WINTER (rev. ed., 1970). PATRICK MURRAY, *The Shakespearian Scene: Some Twentieth-Century Perspectives* (1969), gives a shrewd survey of recent criticism. The following 20th-century works may be regarded as having had a substantial effect on the criticism of Shakespeare. HARLEY GRANVILLE-BARKER, *Prefaces to Shakespeare* (5 series, 1929–47; 4 vol., 1963), set the plays firmly in their theatrical environment. Enquiries into the artistic conventions of Shakespeare's time were the basis of the criticism of LEVIN L. SCHUCKING, *Die Charakterprobleme bei Shakespeare* (1919; Eng. trans., *Character Problems in Shakespeare's Plays*, 1922); E.E. STOLL, *Art and Artifice in Shakespeare* (1933); O.J. CAMPBELL, *Shakespeare's Satire* (1943, reprinted 1971); and W.W. LAWRENCE, *Shakespeare's Problem Comedies*, 2nd ed. (1969). G. WILSON KNIGHT, *The Wheel of Fire* (1930), *The Imperial Theme* (1931), *The Shakespearian Tempest* (1932), and later books; and L.C. KNIGHTS, *How Many Children Had Lady Macbeth?* (1933), showed how Shakespeare achieved poetical and symbolic effects. The study of Shakespeare's imagery is best represented by the pioneer work of CAROLINE F.E. SPURGEON, *Shakespeare's Imagery and What It Tells Us* (1935); and WOLFGANG CLEMEN, *The Development of Shakespeare's Imagery* (1951), followed by ROBERT B. HEILMAN, *This Great Stage: Image and Structure in King Lear* (1948) and *Magic in the Web: Action and Language in Othello* (1956). An understanding of the intellectual and social background of the plays was notably advanced by WILLARD FARNHAM, *The Medieval Origin of Elizabethan Tragedy* (1936) and *Shakespeare's Tragic Frontier* (1950); HARDIN CRAIG, *The Enchanted Glass: The Elizabethan Mind in Literature* (1936); C.L. BARBER, *Shakespeare's Festive Comedy* (1959); THEODORE SPENCER, *Shakespeare and the Nature of Man*, 2nd ed. (1949); and L.B. CAMPBELL, *Shakespeare's "Histories": Mirrors of Elizabethan Policy* (1947). Some of the notable explorations of the artistry of the plays are MADELEINE DORAN, *Endeavors of Art* (1954); BERTRAND EVANS, *Shakespeare's Comedies* (1960); and ANNE RIGHTER, *Shakespeare and the Idea of the Play* (1962). JAN KOTT, *Szkice o Szekspirze* (1962; Eng. trans., *Shakespeare, Our Contemporary*, 1964), has been very widely read and influential on theatrical productions.

(J.R.Br./T.Sp.)

Shales

The sedimentary rocks that occur in nature generally are classified as clastic, chemical, or organic, depending upon their principal mode of origin. The clastic or particulate rocks are further divided on the basis of grain size, the coarsest being conglomerates or rudites, and the finest-grained, consisting of particles finer than sand size (1/16 to 2 millimetres) derived principally from the weathering of continental (*i.e.*, nonmarine) rocks, are called shales or lutites. Those lutites that are laminated (bedding thicknesses are less than one centimetre) and fissile (tend to split into thin layers, generally parallel to bedding) or both are called shales. A bipartite name is often used, with a prefix such as clay, silt, or mud indi-

cating the dominant grain size and the suffix shale or stone indicating the presence or absence of lamination and fissility. Commonly the term shale is used interchangeably with lutite, perhaps because such shales make up 50 percent of all sedimentary rocks, and a lutite fraction is a significant component in many more.

In addition to weathered continental debris, many shales contain appreciable chemical precipitates and volcanically derived components. Fragments or hard parts of calcareous and siliceous micro-organisms and fine particles of calcium carbonate that are precipitated by chemical or biochemical means are often present. Organic matter also is commonly an important component. Some fine-grained material is formed by chemical alteration *in situ*, partly as the reaction product of original fine clastic detritus (transported particles) but mostly from the formation of clay minerals and zeolites (a group of silicate minerals that readily exchange some of their ions—charged atoms—with those of the immediate environment) by reaction of volcanic flows and ejecta with sea (or lake) water, forming extensive marine volcanic muds or continental bentonite (a type of clay) beds.

The properties of shales are largely determined by the fine grain size of the constituent minerals. The accumulation of fine clastic detritus generally requires a sedimentary environment of low mechanical energy (one in which wave and current actions are minimal), although some fine material may be trapped by plants or deposited as weakly coherent pellets in more agitated environments. The properties of the clay mineral constituents of lutites are particularly important, even when they do not make up the bulk of a rock. The clay minerals have a platy (rarely fibrous) form and are electrically charged with charge balance achieved by associated ions. The plates may bond together face-to-face, and the interlayer and edge ions may be exchangeable with ions from surrounding waters. The clays also may absorb water; hydration of interlayer cations (positively charged atoms) leads to clay swelling that ranges from a few angstrom units (one angstrom unit equals 10^{-8} centimetre) to a widely dispersed state. The charge interactions between clay particles allows their association in a very open fabric of high porosity but low permeability. The potential for variation of fabric leads to plasticity at moderate water content: at higher water content the sediment may undergo sudden liquefaction (thixotropic behaviour).

The average abundance of organic matter in shales is about 1 percent, compared with 0.3 percent in limestones and 0.05 percent in sandstones; lesser amounts exist in the open ocean muds, and more than 30 percent is contained in muds entrapped in marsh environments. More than 75 percent of all buried organic matter is found in shales. With abundant deposition of suitable types of organic matter and its preservation in the sediment, the complex sequence of events leading to petroleum accumulation may begin. Low-temperature thermal degradation produces disseminated hydrocarbons, and, if the hydrodynamic situation is suitable, these may migrate to porous reservoir rocks. Further maturation and gravitational segregation may then lead to economic accumulations of natural gas and crude oil.

Some organic-rich shales called oil shales contain kerogen (a chemically complex mixture of solid hydrocarbons from macerated plant matter) in sufficient amounts to make feasible petroleum production by distillation.

Both shales and clays are among the most important nonmetallic raw materials and find many applications, largely in the ceramics industry. Over a suitable range of moisture content, clays are plastic and will retain a molded shape when dried, allowing a variety of products (*e.g.*, pottery, porcelain, bricks, sewer pipes, electrical insulators) to be formed. Partial melting on firing leads to glassy interparticle bonds and a permanently hard product. The proportions of clay minerals, quartz, and feldspar that are used influence the manufacturing process and the final product. The plasticity depends largely on the clay-mineral content, whereas quartz reduces dry shrinkage, increases mechanical strength, and increases porosity and permeability. Feldspar acts like quartz and

Constituents and general properties

Economic importance

also lowers fusion temperature. Shales with high alumina content and low flux content have fusion temperatures above 1,500° C (2,700° F) and are used as refractories. The fired colour of a ceramic body is determined by trace pigments.

Shales and clays are used as sources of alumina and silica in portland cement, and kaolinitic clays are used as fillers and surface coatings in paper and plastics. Some types are also used extensively in the oil industry as constituents of drilling muds.

Shales are unsatisfactory structural materials. They have relatively low compressive strength, particularly if the water content is high, and clay minerals will expand if permitted to absorb water. The low coefficient of friction of shales, particularly when moist, makes them unsuitable as structural and dam foundations. Their high initial water content may allow serious compaction problems when they are subjected to a load. A notable example is the sinking of Mexico City, built on old lake sediments containing a high percentage of clay minerals.

This article treats the physical properties of shales, including their structure and fabric, the origin of shales, and their abundance and distribution in the geological record. For further information on the properties of clays, see CLAY MINERALS, and for coverage of the general transportation and deposition of sedimentary particles that precede final compaction and lithification of sedimentary rocks, see SEDIMENTARY ROCKS. See also MARINE SEDIMENTS; OIL SHALES; and PETROLEUM for related information. Structural problems pertaining to the presence of shales and clays are covered in EARTH MOVEMENTS ON SLOPES.

PHYSICAL PROPERTIES

Grain size, mineralogy, and chemistry. Lutites consist of an admixture of silt- and clay-sized particles. Silt is abundant in sediments, but, except for rare, thin blanket deposits of loess (predominantly windblown deposits), it generally occurs admixed with other grain sizes. The clay minerals make up more than 50 percent of all sediments, and more than 95 percent of all sediments contain appreciable clay minerals. The bulk of the clay minerals occur in shales, however, and sediments dominated by clay-sized particles are much more abundant than those dominated by silt. Quartz and feldspar generally dominate the silt fraction.

> The clay content

Reported shale grain-sized distributions depart markedly from those characteristic of most coarser sediments. Sorting is generally poor, and skewing toward the finer fraction is common. Fine quartz and feldspar are transported as single-grain entities, but the clay minerals may be transported and deposited as individual plates or as aggregates; the state of aggregation of clay minerals strongly influences their hydraulic behaviour. Old estimates suggesting rarity of clay shales and an average silt-to-clay ratio of about 2:1 were probably in error because of overestimation of silt in microscope observations and the difficulties of making settling-rate analyses. Recent electron-microscope and X-ray-diffraction analyses suggest that clay minerals constitute about 60 percent of the average shale.

The mineralogy of shales is highly variable. In addition to clay minerals (60 percent), the average shale contains quartz and other forms of SiO_2, notably amorphous silica and cristobalite (30 percent), feldspars (5 percent), and the carbonate minerals calcite and dolomite (5 percent). Iron oxides and organic matter (around 0.5 and 1 percent, respectively) are also important. Older estimates greatly underestimated clay minerals because of incorrect assignment of potassium to feldspar minerals. The most abundant clay mineral is illite; montmorillonite and mixed-layer illite-montmorillonite are next in abundance, followed by kaolinite, chlorite, chlorite-montmorillonite, and vermiculite. The quartz-to-feldspar ratio generally mirrors that of associated sands. In pelagic (deep-sea) sediments, however, feldspar may be derived from local volcanic sources, whereas quartz may be introduced from the continents by wind, upsetting simple patterns. A large number of accessory minerals occur in shales. Some of

these are detrital (*i.e.*, are transported grain fragments), but diagenetic or *in situ* varieties (*e.g.*, pyrite, siderite, and various phosphates) and volcanically derived varieties (*e.g.*, zeolites, zircon, biotite) have been noted.

The bulk of the weathering products of igneous rocks (those derived by crystallization from silicate melts) are incorporated in shales, and it is not surprising that the average shale is chemically little different from the average igneous rock. The differences reflect mainly the differentiation or selective distribution of sodium and magnesium to seawater, calcium and magnesium to limestones, and silicon to sandstones. One estimate of average shale composition in percent by weight is SiO_2, 58.1; Al_2O_3, 15.4; Fe_2O_3, 4.02; FeO, 2.45; MgO, 2.44; CaO, 3.11; Na_2O, 1.3; K_2O, 3.24; CO_2, 2.63; H_2O (110° C), 5; and other components, 2.31. Many trace metals are enriched in shales, particularly in organic-rich varieties. Variations in shale composition, generally quite minor, may reflect the silt-to-clay ratio, differential leaching of the source rock, the relative importance of biogenic components, and depositional variations in mineralogy throughout a basin. Pelagic muds of the South Pacific volcanic province differ from average shale, particularly in their greater abundance of soda (Na_2O), and geochemical calculations suggest that some shales (and some limestones also) may have an important volcanic component. The influence on shale composition will depend on the extent to which the calcium, magnesium, and iron leached from the (basaltic) volcanic material either form carbonates and iron oxides admixed with the plagioclase feldspar, clay minerals, and zeolites of the residual mud or are removed and deposited elsewhere.

> Relation to igneous rocks

Older shales tend to differ chemically from modern ones. It is sometimes difficult to determine whether this reflects variations in weathering and depositional conditions through time or whether the older shales sampled simply reflect selective preservation of certain environments and increased frequency of samples subjected to higher grades of diagenesis (*i.e.*, of alteration during the processes of rock formation)—metamorphism and metasomatism. Lower values of carbon dioxide and water in older shales represent loss during incipient metamorphism. Studies of younger shales show increased reduction of iron (accompanying oxidation of organic matter) with increasing depth of burial. The higher $Fe^{2+}:Fe^{3+}$ ratio found in older shales probably reflects this, although iron compounds may have been exposed to less efficient oxidation processes on weathering or to more reducing depositional environments on a younger Earth. Other major elements decrease, relative to chemically inert alumina, potassium, and, possibly, total iron increase in older shales.

Colour. The colours of the common abundant minerals in shales are nearly white. The wide variety of rock colour observed is caused by small amounts of finely disseminated pigmenting material. The common pigments are organic matter and various iron-bearing minerals. A high organic content, often supplemented by very fine pyrite, gives a black colour. In general, the higher the organic content, the darker the shale, but in oil shales this may lead to a brown colour. The colour of iron-bearing minerals is controlled by oxidation state rather than by abundance of iron, and local variations in oxidation potential (*e.g.*, local concentrations of decomposing organic tissue, worm burrowing, or periodic exposure and aeration of tidal flats) may lead to colour mottling or banding. Hematite and limonite (ferric iron) impart reddish and purple colours. Blue, green, gray, and black colours generally indicate reducing conditions and ferrous iron, although the green clay mineral glauconite is rich in ferric iron. Many calcareous and siliceous shales are devoid of pigment and exhibit light gray or buff colour. In general, marine muds of the continental slope and continental rise are blue or green, whereas deep-sea muds are red.

Structure. Some shales, particularly those formed in lagoons, small lakes, or on floodplains, occur in relatively elongate or lenticular formations. The geographic requirements for a low-energy depositional environment of muds, however, coupled with their generally low deposi-

> Bedding thickness and extent

tional rates, lead to the common occurrence of shales in extensive thin sheets. The wide extent of the environment may allow persistence over long time periods, and shale sequences many thousands of feet thick are found in geosynclinal regions where great depositional troughs existed in the Earth's crust. By contrast, the high-energy environment of sand deposition is usually restricted to relatively narrow zones such as river channels and along shorelines, and sheet formation requires lateral migration of such environments through time. The wide extent of some shale formations, a few feet thick and of different age in different localities, also requires environment migration. The source of the sediments may affect formation geometry. The silty muds of river deltas occur as lobate masses. In these, as in other subaerial environments, formations are often quite irregular.

Shales are generally characterized by very thin bedding or lamination because of grain-size variations or changes in mineralogy (*e.g.*, different proportions of calcite or organic matter). Some, but by no means all, of these may reflect seasonal variations in mineral detritus or biologic productivity. Silt rarely forms thick deposits, except in windblown loess deposits. When not intimately associated with clays or sands, it occurs as thin lenses within the shales. Thick, homogeneous clay sequences are more common. The silts show the current scour and cross-bedding (micro-cross-bedding) features associated with sands. Water-saturated silts are particularly susceptible to differential compaction and soft sediment flowage. Dewatering of muds may lead to mud cracks. These are susceptible to re-erosion and transport as soft shale pellets, some being hydraulically equivalent to sand grains. On close examination, massive clay shales are often found to consist of aggregates of pellets. These may be transported clay floccules, re-eroded shale pellets, or fecal pellets. Burrowing by mud-dwelling organisms may homogenize sediments by wholly or partially destroying depositional laminae. Many shales are characterized by nodules and concretions because of element migration and accumulation under chemical gradients set up largely by localized accumulation of decaying biologic tissue.

Fabric. The water content of detrital sediments is, in general, inversely related to particle size, and some freshly deposited muds may contain up to 90 percent water by volume. The fabric of muds and shales is strongly influenced by the properties of the clay minerals, in particular their small size, high specific surface, platy morphology, and properties of water absorption and cation exchange. Depending on the type of clay minerals and the nature of the geochemical environment, the particles may be deposited individually from a dispersed state or as floccules (face-to-face, edge-to-edge, or face-to-edge associations of clay plates). The freshly deposited mud undergoes particle rearrangement and dewatering, either by subaerial dehydration (leading to mud cracks), by spontaneous expulsion of water from an unstable gel (syneresis), or as a result of the pressure of newly deposited sediments. At moderate water contents the sediments exhibit plastic behaviour, and structures caused by foundering and flow are common. Large-scale flowage may lead to diapiric (piercement type) mud intrusion. Muds with higher water content are metastable, and, when subjected to stress by earthquakes, sediment load, etc., the interparticle bonds may be broken, the particles will pack more closely, and oversaturation with water may lead to sudden initiation of flow as a viscous liquid.

The best fissility (tendency to split into layers) in shales is associated with a high degree of orientation of clay plates parallel to bedding. This may be the result of compactional rearrangement of flocculated particles or, perhaps, of diagenetic growth of clay minerals with orientation influenced by overburden pressure, but in most cases it is developed early, at deposition or during the first few metres of burial. This preferred orientation may result from the settling of clay plates particle by particle from a dispersed state or by particle rearrangement, a process for which a high initial water content appears necessary. Biogenic siliceous and calcareous matter decrease fissility. A high organic content and perhaps also deposition

Role of water content

from low-salinity waters are associated with high fissility, apparently through their effect on promoting clay dispersion or weak flocculation.

ORIGIN OF SHALES

Transportation and deposition of sediments. The formation of fine-grained sediments generally requires weak transporting currents and a quiet depositional basin. Water is the common transporting medium, but ice-rafted glacial flour (silt produced by glacial grinding) is a major component in high-latitude oceanic muds, and windblown dust is prominent, particularly in the open ocean at low and intermediate latitudes. Shale environments thus include the deep ocean; the continental slope and rise; the deeper and more protected parts of shelves, shallow seas, and bays; coastal lagoons; interdistributory regions of deltas, swamps, and lakes (including arid basin playas); and river floodplains. The deep-sea muds are very fine, but an orderly sequence from coarse sediments in high-energy nearshore environments to fine sediments at greater depths is rarely found. Sediments at the outer edges of present-day continental shelves are commonly sands, relict deposits of shallower Pleistocene (from about 10,000 to 2,500,000 years ago) glacial conditions, whereas muds are currently being deposited in many parts of the inner shelf. The nearshore deposition of clay minerals is enhanced by the tendency of riverborne dispersed platelets to flocculate in saline waters (salinity greater than about four parts per 1,000) and to be deposited just beyond the agitated estuarine environment as aggregates hydraulically equivalent to coarser particles. Differential flocculation leads to clay-mineral segregation, with illite and kaolinite near shore and montmorillonite farther out to sea. Advance of silty and sandy delta-slope deposits over clays also leads to complex grain-size patterns.

Shales may be deposited in environments of periodic agitation. Sediments deposited on submarine slopes are frequently mechanically unstable and may be redistributed by slumping and turbidity currents (density currents that result from an increase in sediment concentration) to form thick accumulations (possible present-day eugeosynclinal equivalents) on the lower continental slope and rise. Part of the shale in many graywacke-shale alternations (a graywacke is a sandstone with a muddy matrix and a high proportion of rock fragments) may be of turbidite origin. The fine matrix of the graywackes is partly original fine sediment, but much is probably the later diagenetic and metamorphic alteration product of chemically unstable rock fragments. Fine sediment can be deposited in marshes and on tidal flats. Trapping by marsh plants and binding of muds in fecal pellets are important. Because of electrochemical interactions among fine particles, muds plastered on a tidal flat by an advancing tide are difficult to re-erode on the ebb. This may lead, as in the present-day Waddenzee, in The Netherlands, to a size increase from nearshore tidal flat muds to lag sands seaward. Fine floodplain sediments may dry out to coherent shale pellets, and these, on re-erosion, can be redistributed as sands and gravels.

Diagenetic changes. The minerals deposited in a sedimentary basin may not be in physicochemical equilibrium among themselves and with the water. At any point on the sea floor, for example, there are too many aluminosilicate minerals to constitute an equilibrium assemblage, and common biogenic constituents (amorphous silica, magnesium-calcite, and aragonite) are metastable. Diagenetic reconstitution (alterations following deposition but prior to final lithification) is expected because of observed changes in water composition in laboratory experiments; there is some evidence for such reaction in nature. Clays entering the sea undergo a rapid re-equilibration of their exchange cations, and potassium and chloritic (iron- and magnesium-rich) interlayers may become strongly incorporated in some clays. Diagenetic palygorskites are associated with midoceanic ridge hydrothermal activity. Most unequivocal examples of marine diagenesis involve iron-rich clays. For example, glauconite and chamosite are shown to be diagenetic by

Reaction with seawater

their virtual restriction to marine sediments and to specific depth zones in present seas, by their occurrence in special micro-environments (concentrations of organic tissue), and by the smaller number of clay mineral types in glauconite pellets than in the surrounding muds. The montmorillonites formed with zeolites from volcanic material in the oceans are also iron rich.

The distribution of clay minerals in the present deep ocean can be related to source-area mineralogy and wind- and water-current patterns. Chlorite is concentrated at high latitudes where mechanical (glacial) weathering is dominant, whereas low-latitude concentration of kaolinite reflects intense chemical weathering on the adjacent continents. Illite (and quartz) concentrations in the central North Pacific are related to the path of midlatitude jet streams. Only the montmorillonite (and zeolite) concentration of the South Pacific, Indian Ocean, and Red Sea indicates extensive diagenesis, utilizing chemically reactive volcanic material. Nearshore gradients of proportion of different clay minerals are better explained by transport phenomena such as differential flocculation than by extensive diagenesis. Reaction is limited by the relatively short exposure time of clay minerals before burial (about one year) and the armouring of grains by reaction products.

The euxinic environment

Little further reaction occurs among the silicates on shallow burial, but dissolved silica levels are raised by the solution of siliceous diatoms, one-celled marine organisms, and bacterial attack of organic matter releases nutrient elements and alters the physicochemical properties of the sediment. In some cases, this leads to the formation of diagenetic sulfides and phosphates. This is particularly important in euxinic environments, in which stagnant conditions prevent introduction of oxygen to bottom waters from the atmosphere. Considerable amounts of organic matter (black shales) with their nutrient elements and adsorbed trace metals are thus incorporated into the sediment rather than being oxidized in the sea floor. With increased temperature of deeper burial (several thousand metres), extensive reconstitution of the silicates and carbonates occurs. The most obvious change is the evolution of montmorillonite, through mixed-layer minerals, toward illite and chlorite. Kaolinite and some feldspars and micas become unstable, and their breakdown provides elements for new mineral growth. There may be some additions from greater depth and some element exchange with associated sands, however.

SHALES IN THE GEOLOGICAL RECORD

Abundance and distribution. Estimates of the abundance of shales by direct measurement of stratigraphic sections have ranged from 42 to 57 percent of all sedimentary rocks. Independent estimates of lutites have been made by geochemical calculations, allocating the elements weathered from primary igneous rocks to the oceans and to major sediment types. Such estimates suggest that lutites should make up 70 to 80 percent of all sedimentary rocks. The discrepancy is partially resolved by recognition of a lutite fraction admixed in sandstones and limestones and of a high lutite content (more than 90 percent) in deep-ocean sediments, which are rarely incorporated into the sedimentary rock record of the continents. One difficulty, however, is uncertainty about the total amount of sediment in the oceans.

Apart from dominance of volcanically derived sediments during Precambrian time (all Earth history prior to 570,000,000 years ago) and an increase in carbonates at the expense of shales around the beginning of post-Precambrian time, the proportions of shales in the preserved sedimentary record are relatively constant through time. At any given time and place, however, the amount of shale deposited depends in part on the environment of the source area and depositional basin. For example, shale accumulations on stable continental shelves generally make up less than 20 percent of relatively thin deposits, whereas mobile belts—depositional troughs that are loci for later mountain building—are often characterized by thick accumulations of which shale is the dominant rock. About 80 percent of all the fine continental debris currently delivered to the ocean passes through Southeast Asia from adjacent high-altitude sources. The chances of a shale being preserved in the record depend on its resistance to weathering (relatively low) and to the tectonic environment of its deposition. This latter factor influences its chances of alteration by metamorphism after burial or its chances of exposure by erosion.

Contained fossils. The low mechanical energy of deposition, the infrequency of reworking of the sediment by currents (particularly in the abundant offshore marine varieties), and the fine grain size all aid in the greater preservation of fossils in shales. The fine grain size allows delicate molding and casting of biological remains. Because of the great degree of compaction of shales, many fossils are compressed and preserved as thin films, but the formation of concretions about remains may retain accurate shapes and details of structure. Putrefaction gases may prevent collapse of even such large delicate forms as cephalopods until they are incorporated into hard concretions. Shales of volcanic-ashfall origin may also provide excellent preservation. Many shales are deposited in environments connected to the open sea, and bottom conditions are suitable for the preservation of free-floating and swimming organisms. Shales have proved to be excellent hosts for the preservation of such delicate fossils as the graptolites, whose rapid evolution and ready dispersal allow detailed intercontinental correlation of time and rocks (see further STRATIGRAPHIC BOUNDARIES).

Preservation of fossils in shales

Microfossils also may be preserved in shales, often in large enough numbers to permit statistical analyses of their populations. Plant spores reflect changing vegetation patterns, and their remains in lake deposits allow reconstruction of regional climatic changes.

Present deep-sea and continental-slope muds and their ancient equivalents are characterized by virtual absence of benthos- or bottom-dwelling organisms; only a few burrowing organisms are present, and biologic degradation is carried out by anaerobic bacteria. Sulfur-reducing varieties may lead to pyritic fossilization in which pyrite (iron sulfide) replaces organic tissues. Phosphatic brachiopods, plant spores, and other such resistant forms, as well as radiolarians, foraminiferans, and rare invertebrates, are found. This characteristic of absence of benthos organisms applies particularly to black shales, regardless of the water depth. In other marine shales benthonic fossils are more abundant, however.

Shales formed in lakes may contain the remains of freshwater fish, mollusks, ostracods, insects, calcareous algae, pollen, etc. Occasionally terrestrial plants and vertebrates may be washed into the basin and preserved.

Famous shales. Shales are ubiquitous throughout the geological record and are of great importance in sedimentological and stratigraphic studies. A limited number of types are encountered again and again, however, and a particular shale generally attains more than local significance only as the host of important fossils or by virtue of its economic value.

The oldest known shales are carbonaceous varieties of the 3,200,000,000-year-old Figtree Series of South Africa. Associated cherts contain bacterial remains, and the shales contain organic compounds of probable biologic origin. An abundant fauna of soft-bodied creatures not normally fossilized has been preserved as detailed carbonaceous imprints in the Middle Cambrian Burgess Shale of British Columbia (the Cambrian Period began 570,000,000 years ago and ended 500,000,000 years ago). These remains provide perspective on the nature of early life, whose preserved remains, generally restricted to the hard parts of organisms, are not generally representative of life assemblages. Similar details of animal tissue (*e.g.*, marine ichthyosaurs) are preserved in the Lower Jurassic shales of Holzmaden, West Germany. Shale partings in the uppermost Precambrian Ediacara sandstone of South Australia also preserve traces of soft-bodied creatures (coelenterates, worms, arthropod-like forms, echinoderms, probable mollusks), showing an unexpectedly advanced metazoan evolution. Early and continued study of the Ordovician and Silurian shales of Wales have been important in the development of the

Figtree Series and the Burgess Shale

geologic time scale, concepts of sedimentation and mountain building, and of fossil (graptolite) zonation.

Black shales are often of economic importance as sources of petroleum products and metals, and this importance will probably increase in the future. The lacustrine Eocene Green River Shales of Colorado–Wyoming–Utah are potentially rich petroleum sources and are undergoing exploratory extraction. Bituminous layers of the Early Permian Irati Shales of Brazil are similarly important. These shales contain the remains of the marine reptile *Mesosaurus*, also found in South Africa, and have played a prominent part in the development of the concepts of continental drift. The very widespread thin Chattanooga Shale (Devonian-Mississippian) of the eastern United States has been exploited for its high (up to 250 parts per 1,000,000) uranium content. The Permian Kupferschiefer is a bituminous shale rich in metallic sulfides of primary sedimentary or early diagenetic origin; it covers a large area of central Europe as a band generally less than one metre thick, and in East Germany and in Poland there is sufficient enrichment in copper, lead, and zinc for its exploitation as an ore.

BIBLIOGRAPHY. F.J. PETTIJOHN, *Sedimentary Rocks*, 2nd ed. (1957), a classic text that includes a discussion of the petrography, origin, and geological associations of shales; W.C. KRUMBEIN and L.L. SLOSS, *Stratigraphy and Sedimentation*, 2nd ed. (1963); and C.O. DUNBAR and JOHN RODGERS, *Principles of Stratigraphy* (1957), describe the lithology and stratigraphic relations of shales; R.M. GARRELS and F.T. MACKENZIE, *Evolution of Sedimentary Rocks* (1971), evaluates the role of shales in the Earth's surface and near-surface geochemical budget; GEORGES MILLOT, *Géologie des argiles* (1964; Eng. trans., *Geology of Clays*, 1970), reviews mineralogical and geochemical transformations of clays and contains numerous examples of shale deposits with interpretation of their origins.

(K.C.B.)

Shamanism

Shamanism is a religious phenomenon centred on the shaman, an ecstatic figure believed to have power to heal the sick and to communicate with the world beyond. The term applies primarily to the religious systems and phenomena of the north Asian, Ural-Altaic (*e.g.*, Vogul, Ostyak, Samoyed, Tungus), and Paleo-Asian (*e.g.*, Yukaghir, Chukchi, Koryak) peoples.

NATURE AND SIGNIFICANCE

The term shamanism comes from the Tunguso-Manchurian word *šaman*. The noun is formed from the verb *ša-* ("to know"); thus, "shaman" literally means "he who knows." Various other terms are used by other peoples among whom shamanism exists.

There is no single definition of shamanism that applies to the elements of shamanistic activity found in North and South America, in southeast India, in Australia, and in small areas all over the world as well as to the phenomena among the north Asian, Ural-Altaic, and Paleo-Asian peoples. It is generally agreed that shamanism evolved before the development of class society in the Neolithic Period and the Bronze Age; that it was practiced among peoples living in the hunting-and-gathering stage; and that it continued to exist, somewhat altered, among peoples who had reached the animal-raising and horticultural stage. According to some scholars, it originated and evolved among the more developed societies that bred cattle for production. Opinions differ as to whether the term shamanism may be applied to all religious systems in which the central personage is believed to have direct intercourse through an ecstatic state with the transcendent world that permits him to act as healer, diviner, and psychopomp (escort of souls of the dead to the other world). Since ecstasy is a psychosomatic phenomenon that may be brought about at any time by persons with the ability to do so, the essence of shamanism lies not in the general phenomenon but in specific notions, actions, and objects connected with the ecstatic state.

Among the peoples of northern Asia, shamanism developed into a more definitely articulated and specialized form than among other peoples. Shamanism as practiced there is distinguished by its special clothing, accessories, and rites as well as by the specific world view connected with them. North Asiatic shamanism in the 19th century, which may be taken as the classical form, was characterized by the following traits:

(1) A specialist (man or woman) is accepted by the society as being able to communicate directly with the transcendent world and thereby also possessed of the ability to heal and to divine; this person is held to be of great use to society in dealing with the spirit world. (2) This figure has special physical and mental characteristics; he is neurasthenic or epileptic, with perhaps some minor defect (*e.g.*, six fingers or more teeth than normal), and with an intuitive, sensitive, mercurial personality. (3) He is believed to have an active spirit or group of spirits to assist him and may also have a passive guardian spirit present in the form of an animal or a person of the other sex—possibly as a sexual partner. (4) The exceptional abilities and the consequent social role of the shaman are believed to result from his being the "choice" of the spirits, though the one who is chosen—often an adolescent—may resist his selection, sometimes for years. Torture by the spirits, appearing in the form of illness, breaks the resistance of the shaman candidate and he (or she) has to accept the vocation. (5) The initiation of the shaman, depending on the belief system, may happen on a transcendent level or on a realistic level, or sometimes on both, one after the other. While the candidate lies as if dead, in a trance state, the body is cut into pieces by the spirits of the Yonder World or is submitted to a similar trial. The reason for cutting up his body is to see whether he has more bones than the average person. After awakening, the rite of symbolical initiation, climbing the World Tree, is occasionally performed. (6) By falling into ecstasy at will, the shaman is believed to be able to communicate directly with the spirits either by his soul leaving the body to enter their realm or by acting as their mouthpiece, like a medium. (7) One of the distinguishing traits of shamanism is the combat of two shamans in the form of animals, usually reindeer or horned cattle. The combat rarely has a definite purpose but rather seems to be a deed the shaman is compelled to do. The outcome of the combat means well-being for the victor and destruction for the loser. (8) In going into ecstasy, as well as in his mystical combat, certain objects are used: drum, drumstick, headgear, gown, metal rattlers, and staff. (The specific materials and shapes of these instruments are useful for identifying the types and species of shamanism and following their development.) (9) Characteristic folklore texts and shaman songs have come into being as improvisations on traditional formulas in luring calls and imitations of animal sounds.

As an ethnological term, shamanism is applied primarily to the religious systems of those regions in which all these traits are present together. In addition, there are primitive religions in which some of the above criteria are missing but which are still partially shamanistic; *e.g.*, among the Chukchi of northeast Siberia, the specialist chosen by the spirits does not fall into ecstasy. Such religious systems may be regarded as marginally shamanistic.

Phenomena similar to some of the traits of shamanism may be found among primitive peoples everywhere in the world. Such detached traits, however, are not necessarily shamanistic. The central personalities in such systems—sorcerers, medicine men, and the like—may communicate with the other world through ecstasy, but, unlike the shaman, they have attained their position through deliberate study and the application of rational knowledge. Although they perform ceremonies as priests, hold positions of authority, and possess magical abilities, the structure and quality of their transcendental activities are entirely different from that of the shaman.

WORLD VIEW

The universe. The classic world view of shamanism is found among the peoples of northern Asia. In their view, the universe is full of heavenly bodies peopled by spiritual beings. Their own world is disk-shaped—saucer-like—with an opening in the middle leading into the Netherworld; the Upper World stands over the Central World, or Earth, this world having a manyfold vault. The Earth, or Central World, stands in water held on the back of a colossal monster that may be a turtle, a huge fish, a bull, or a mammoth. The movement of this animal causes earthquakes. The Earth is surrounded by an immense belt. It is connected with the Upper World by the Pillar of the World. The Upper World consists of several strata—three, seven, nine, or 17. On the navel of the Earth stands the Cosmic Tree, which reaches up to the dwelling of the upper gods.

Gods, spirits, and souls. All three worlds are inhabited by spirits. Among the Mongolian and Turkish peoples, Ülgen, a benevolent deity and the god of the Upper World, has seven sons and nine daughters. Among the Buryats of southern Siberia, Tengri (often identified with Ülgen) also has children, the Khatʿs—the western ones being good and the eastern ones wicked. The gods of the Buryats number 99 and fall into two categories: the 55 good gods of the west whose attribute is "white," and the 44 wicked gods of the east whose attribute is "black." The leader of the latter is Erlen khan, a figure equivalent to Erlik khan of the Altai Kizhi people, who is the ruler of the Underworld. Besides gods and the progeny of gods—both sons and daughters—other spirits also inhabit all the three worlds. Fire is also personified, as is the Earth itself. Such personifications are represented in idols as well. Man, besides his body, consists of a soul, even of several souls. Man also has a mirror soul, which can be seen when looking into water, and a shadow soul, which is visible when the sun is shining.

SOCIAL ROLE, PERSONALITY STRUCTURE, AND FUNCTIONS OF THE SHAMAN

Social role. The extraordinary profession of the shaman naturally distinguishes him socially. The belief that he communicates with the spirits gives him authority. Furthermore, the belief that his actions may not only bring benefit but also harm makes him feared. Even a good (white) shaman may do harm, and a wicked (black) shaman, who is in contact with the spirits of the Lower World, is very alarming. In consequence of his profession, the shaman cannot go hunting and fishing and cannot participate in productive work; therefore, he must be supported by the community, which considers his professional activity necessary. Some shamans make use of their special position for economic gain. Among the reindeer-raising Evenki of northern Siberia, poor families have to pay yearly one animal, and rich ones pay two, three, or even four, to the shaman for his activities. A saying of the Altai Kizhi illustrates this situation: "If the beast becomes ill, the dogs fatten; if man becomes ill, the shaman fattens."

Special economic position of the shaman

Among the Evenki, it was the duty of every member of the clan to aid the shaman economically. When distributing the fishing spots in the spring and in the summer, the part of the river most abundant in fish was given to the shaman and even the fishing devices were set up for him. He was aided in grazing and herding the reindeer in autumn, and in winter the members of the clan went hunting in his stead. Even furs were presented to the shaman occasionally. The social authority of the shaman was shown through the honours bestowed on him and the practice of always giving him the best food. Generally, the shaman was never contradicted, nor was any unfavourable opinion expressed about him behind his back.

Such an economic and social position resulted in the shaman attaining political power. As early as 1752, for instance, it was noted that the Tungus shaman was also the leader of his clan. Along the Yenisey River, shamans led armed groups of the Evenki on the left and the right banks who fought against each other. In the northern forest regions of Mongolia, the shamans stood at the head of the tribes and clans. In the fight of the Buryats against the Russians in the 17th and 18th centuries, the shaman always led the fight. The ruler of one domain among the Vadeyev Samoyed in northern Siberia was a shaman as well as a reigning prince. Among the Eskimo of North America and Asia, the positions of leader and of shaman are often occupied by the same person: indeed, the two Eskimo terms *angakok* ("shaman") and *angajkok* ("leader") have the same root.

Personal makeup and selection. Scholars generally agree that the shaman acquires his profession through inheritance, learning, or an inner call, or "vocation," but each of these terms requires some qualification. "Inheritance" means that the soul of a dead shaman or the so-called shaman illness is inherited. "Learning" here does not usually mean the study of exact knowledge and explicit dogma, for the shaman, it is believed, is taught by the spirits. The inner "call" is in reality not the call of the person but of the spirit who has chosen him and who forces him to accept his vocation. This compulsion is unavoidable. "Had I not become shaman, I would have died," said a Gilyak (southeast Siberia). The future shaman of the Altai Kizhi was subjected to terrible torture until, finally, he grasped the drum and began to act as a shaman.

The compulsory nature of shamanism as a vocation

According to the abundant literature on the subject and the experience of investigators in the field, no one voluntarily ventures into the shaman role, nor does a candidate have time to study the role. Such study, however, is not necessary, because peoples born into a culture with shamanistic beliefs know them thoroughly, and when the "call" arrives, the future shaman can learn specific practices by close observation of active shamans, even the technique of "ecstasy." The shamanistic view of the world and spirits is already familiar to him. The various qualitative categories by which shamans are distinguished—small, intermediate, and great—are explained by the category of the spirit who chose the shaman. It is evident, however, that this depends on the personal abilities of the shaman himself, his mental capacities, his dramatic talent, and his power to make his will effective. All of these elements add to the quality of his shaman performance, the art expressed in it.

The shaman is born to his role, as is evident in certain marks distinguishing him from ordinary men. He may be born with more bones in his body—*e.g.*, teeth or fingers—than other people. Therefore, he does not become a shaman simply by willing it, for it is not the shaman who summons up the spirits, but they, the supernatural beings, who choose him. They call him before his birth. At the age of adolescence, usually at the period of sexual ripening, the chosen one suddenly falls into hysterics with faintings, visions, and similar symptoms, being tortured sometimes for weeks. Then, in a vision or a dream, the spirit who has chosen him appears and announces his being chosen. This "call" is necessary for the shaman to acquire his powers. The spirit who has chosen him first lavishes the unwilling shaman-to-be with all sorts of promises and, if he does not win his consent, goes on to torment him. This so-called shaman illness will anguish him for months, perhaps for years, as long as he does not accept the shaman profession. When the candidate finally gives way to the compulsion and becomes a shaman, he falls asleep and sleeps for a long time—three days, seven days, or thrice three days. During the "long sleep," the candidate, according to belief, is cut into pieces by the spirits, who count his bones, determining whether he truly has an "extra bone." If so, he has become a shaman. Some people, such as the Mongolians and the Tunguso-Manchurians, still initiate the shaman. They introduce him to the supernatural beings, and he symbolically ascends the "tree-up-to-the-heavens," that is, the pole representing it.

The central activity of the shaman is ecstasy at the wish of his clients, and some have inferred from this that he is a psychopath. A person becomes a shaman at puberty, according to this view, when, especially in sub-Arctic and Arctic climatic conditions, changes in his constitution and nervous system may result in the loss of mental balance and in various mental disorders. Social and ethnic factors also may be seen to support the psychopathological factor. A person born with certain marks knows he is destined to the vocation and becomes apprehensive

The shaman as psychopath

of the call of the spirits. His fears of the event, according to this theory, create the hallucinations, and the hallucinations reinforce the belief.

Types and functions. *Differences in quality and degree.* Shamans differ greatly in quality and in degree. Difference of quality is manifest in the kind of spirits the shaman communicates with. "White" shamans, for example, apply to a benevolent deity and the good spirits, while "black" shamans call on a wicked deity and the wicked spirits.

The difference in degree is exemplified in the Yakut belief (in northeastern Siberia) that the souls of the future shamans are reared upon an immensely high tree in the Upper World, in nests at various heights. The greatest shamans are brought up close to the top of the tree, the intermediate ones toward the middle, the smaller ones on the lower branches. Hence, shamans may be classified into three groups: great, intermediate, and last, according to their powers.

Basic tasks. It is the obligation of the shaman to know all matters that human beings need to know in everyday life but are unable to learn through their own capacities. He foresees events distant in time and space, discovers the place of a lost animal, forecasts prospects for fishing and hunting, and assists in increasing the gain. Besides these everyday functions, he is a healer and a psychopomp. He fulfills all these obligations by communicating with the spirits directly whenever he pleases.

The shaman's assistance is necessary at the three great events of life: birth, marriage, and death. If a woman bears no child, for instance, then, according to the belief of the Goldi, in the Amur region of northeast Asia, the shaman ascends to heaven and sends an embryo soul (*omija*) from the tree of embryos (*omija muoni*). Among the Buryats, the shaman performs libations after birth to keep the infant from crying and to help him develop more quickly. Among the Goldi, when death occurs the shaman is necessary to catch the soul of the deceased floating in the universe and to escort it to the Yonder World. Illness is believed to be caused by the spirits, who must be appeased for a cure to be effected. Among the Ostyak of northern Siberia, the shaman decides how many reindeer should be sacrificed to appease the spirit who causes an illness. Among the Altai Kizhi, he states which *körmös* (soul of the dead) caused the disaster and what to do to conciliate it. Illness might be caused by the soul having left the patient's body and fallen into the hands of spirits who are angry with it and therefore torment it; the shaman liberates the strayed soul. Illness may also be caused by spirits entering into a man; the shaman cures it by driving the spirits out.

Forms of ecstasy. The shaman may fulfill his obligations either by communicating with the spirits at will or through ecstasy. The latter has two forms: possession ecstasy, in which the body of the shaman is possessed by the spirit, and wandering ecstasy, in which his soul departs into the realm of spirits. In passive ecstasy, the possessed gets into an intense mental state and shows superhuman strength and knowledge; he quivers, rages, struggles, and finally falls into an unconscious trancelike condition. After accepting the spirit, the shaman becomes its mouthpiece—"he becomes him who entered him." In active ecstasy, the shaman's life functions decrease to an abnormal minimum, and he falls into a trancelike condition. The soul of the shaman, it is believed, then leaves his body and seeks one of the three worlds, or strata, of heaven. After awakening, he relates his experiences, where he wandered, and with whom he spoke. There are cases of possession ecstasy and wandering ecstasy combined, when the spirit first enters the shaman and then leads his soul to the world of supernatural beings. Scholars differ as to which is the original and which the derivative form; *e.g.*, the historian of religions Mircea Eliade does not consider possession ecstasy to be essential to shamanism.

SYMBOLISM IN OBJECTS AND ACTIONS

The shaman attains the ecstasy necessary for communicating with the spirits through the performance of the shaman rite, which requires certain appurtenances.

Dress. He wears a ritual gown, which usually imitates an animal—a deer, a bird, a bear. Similarly, the headdress is a crown made of antlers or a band to which feathers of birds have been pierced. The footwear is also symbolic—iron deer hooves, birds' claws, or bears' paws. The clothing of the shamans among the Tofalar (Karagasy), Soyet, and Darhat are decorated with representations of human bones—ribs, arm and finger bones. The shamans of the Goldi–Ude tribe perform the ceremony in a singular shirt and in a front and back apron on which there are representations of snakes, lizards, frogs, and other animals.

Drums, sticks, and other objects. An important device of the shaman is the drum, which always has only one membrane. It is usually oval but sometimes round. The outer side of the membrane, and the inside as well among some peoples, is decorated with drawings; *e.g.*, the Turks, or Tatars, of Abakan mark the Upper and Lower World. The handle is usually in the shape of a cross, but sometimes there is only one handle in a vertical direction or in the shape of the letter Y or X. The drumstick is made of wood or horn and the beating surface is covered with fur. In some cases, the drumstick is decorated with human and animal figures, and rattling rings often hang down from it. During the ecstasy brought on by the sound of the drum, the spirits move to the shaman—into him or into the drum—or the soul of the shaman travels to the realm of the spirits. In the latter case, the shaman makes the journey on the drum as if riding on an animal, the drumstick being his lash. Sometimes the shaman makes the journey on a river and the drum is his boat, the drumstick his oar. All this is revealed in the shaman song. Besides the drum, the Buryat shaman sometimes makes the journey with sticks ending in the figure of a horse's head. The shaman of the Tungus people, who raise reindeer, makes the journey on a stick ending in the figure of a reindeer's head. Among some people, the shaman wears a metal disk, a "shaman-mirror."

Drama and dance. Shamanic symbolism is impressively presented in dramatic enactment and dance, as observed among the peoples where the shamanistic rites survived longest (such as the Samoyed, Tofalar, Buryat, and Tungus). The shaman, garbed in his ritual robes, lifts his voice in song to the spirits. This song is always improvised, with certain obligatory images and similes, dialogue, and refrains. The performance always takes place in the evening. The theatre is the conical tent, or yurt; the stage is the space around the fire where the spirits are invoked. The audience consists of the invited members of the clan, awaiting the spirits in awe. The stage lighter and decorator, the shaman's assistant, tends the fire so as to throw fantastic shadows onto the wall. All these effects help those present to visualize everything that the recited action of the shaman narrates. The shaman is an actor, dancer and singer, and a whole orchestra. This restless figure is a fascinating sight, with his cloak floating in the light of a fire in which anything might be imagined. The ribbons of his gown flit around him, his round mirror reflects the flames, and his trinkets jingle. The sound of his drum excites not only the shaman but also his audience. An integral characteristic of this drama is that those who are present are not mere objective spectators but rather faithful believers, and their belief enables the shaman to achieve results, as in healing mental illnesses. Among some people—the Altai Kizhi, for instance—a tall tree is set into the smoke opening at the top of the tent, symbolizing the Tree of the World. The shaman ascends the tree to the height of the Upper World, which is announced to his audience by the text of his song.

CONTEMPORARY RESIDUES
AND RECONSTRUCTIONS OF SHAMANISM

The residues of shamanism may be found among peoples who have been converted to religions of a later stage of culture; *e.g.*, Finno-Ugrian peoples who became Christians, Turkic peoples in Central Asia and Asia Minor who became Muslim, and Mongolians who became Buddhists. Among the Finns, the *tietäjä*, a figure equiva-

The shaman as healer

The drum as symbolic bearer of the shaman

The shaman Tulayev of the Karagas, Siberia, photographed in 1927. He wears a deerskin coat, embroidered with a rib cage and holds a drumstick of fur-covered reindeer horn and a deerskin-covered drum. The shaman's soul is said to "ride" the soul of the animal whose skin is stretched over his drum and to use the drumstick as a knout.
By courtesy of the Staatliches Museum fur Volkerkunde, Munich

lent to the shaman, is also born with one more tooth than normal. Among the Osmanlı Turks of Asia Minor, the horned headwear of the shaman is remembered in popular belief. Among people who formerly believed in shamanism but later were converted to various world religions (e.g., Christianity or Islām), former shamanism may be revealed through an analysis of their folklore and folk beliefs. An example of such a case is the discovery of former Hungarian shamanism. In north Asia, shamanism appears in various forms that may be attributed to differences in cultural phases. In the most northern parts, among the Chukchi, Koryak, and Kamchadal, the shaman does not exist as a member of a special profession: a suitable member of the family—often an old woman—performs the activity of the shaman. Often the shamans are of "changed sex"—effeminate men who have adopted feminine clothing and behaviour at the command of their "spirit." Among the Yukaghir of Arctic Siberia, shamanism is part of the cult of the clan; so also among pockets in the Obi-Ugrian peoples, and among all three Altaic peoples: Turkic, Mongol, and Manchu-Tungusic. These are instances of definitely professional shamanism, which, however have been excluded by so-called higher religions. Shamanism was excluded among the Khalkha-Mongolian and eastern Buryats, who became Buddhists, and among the Kazakh and Kirgiz who adopted Islām, and it was greatly changed and developed into an atypical form by the Manchurians.

Certain scholars have investigated ecstatic actions that may be adjudged outside the area of shamanism in the strictest sense. Mircea Eliade has studied North and South America, Southeastern Asia and Oceania, Tibet, and China, and S.P. Tokarev has also studied Africa. Some scholars suppose that the phenomena of shamanism spread to the two American continents when the first settlers migrated from Asia. The shamanistic phenomena in the Shintō religion of Japan are attributed to the migration of nomadic peoples from the territory bordering Northern Korea. No such theory of migration has yet

been developed to explain the "shamanism" of Southeast Asia and Oceania. Those who oppose this broad usage of the term shamanism argue that an apparent structural similarity among phenomena in widely separated areas does not justify an assertion of a common source or that typological similarity must be distinguished from a genetic connection. For them, shamanism may be attributed only to a precise pattern of cultural phenomena in a specific, well-defined territory, one that forms a concrete, systematic whole, such as the religious systems of the peoples mentioned at the beginning of this article.

BIBLIOGRAPHY. A thorough description of the shamanism of the peoples of Siberia is given in M.A.C. CZAPLICKA, *Aboriginal Siberia* (1914); and in MIRCEA ELIADE, *Le Chamanisme et les techniques archaïques de l'extase* (1951; Eng. trans., *Shamanism: Archaic Techniques of Ecstasy*, 1964). The latter not only deals with phenomena in Central and Northern Asia but also from North and South America, Southeast Asia, and Oceania. See especially the chapters on "Shamanic Ideologies and Techniques Among the Indo-Europeans" and "Shamanic Symbolisms and Techniques in Tibet, China, and the Far East." The English translation includes an extensive bibliography. Shamanism among the Finno-Ugrian Siberian peoples is described by UNO HOLMBERG in *The Mythology of All Races*, vol. 4 (1927). A very thorough summary of the world view and specific traits of shamanism in North Asia, based on a good knowledge of literature on the subject in Russian, may be found in GEORG NIORADZE, *Der Schamanismus bei den sibirischen Völkern* (1925). The shamanism of the same territory, but only the traits considered most significant, has been discussed by AKE, OHLMARKS, *Studien zum Problem des Schamanismus* (1939). The volume *Glaubenswelt und Folklore der siberischen Volker* (1963; Eng. trans., *Popular Beliefs and Folklore Tradition in Siberia*, ed. by V. DIOSZEGI, 1968) contains studies on the shamanistic conceptions of the Lapp, Hungarian, and Siberian peoples.

(V.D.)

Shanghai

Shanghai (in Pin-yin romanization, Shang-hai), whose name literally means "on the sea," is one of the world's largest seaports and a major industrial and commercial centre of the People's Republic of China. It is located on the coast of the East China Sea between the mouth of the Yangtze River to the north and the bays of Hangchow and Yü-p'an to the south. The municipality covers a total area of 2,200 square miles (5,800 square kilometres), which includes the city itself, surrounding suburbs, and an agricultural hinterland. China's most populous urban area, metropolitan Shanghai contains between 5,500,000 and 6,000,000 inhabitants and the municipality, a total of about 10,800,000.

Shanghai was the first Chinese port to be opened to Western trade, and it long dominated the nation's commerce. Since the Communist rise to power in 1949, however, it has become an industrial giant whose products supply China's growing domestic demands. The city has also undergone extensive physical changes with the establishment of suburbs and housing complexes, the improvement of public works, and the provision of parks and other recreational facilities. Shanghai has attempted to eradicate the economic and psychological legacies of its exploited past and to create a burgeoning, and purely Chinese, urban area. (For a related physical feature see YANGTZE RIVER.)

HISTORY

As late as the 5th to 7th centuries AD, the Shanghai area, then known as Shen or Hu Tu, was sparsely populated and undeveloped. Despite the steady southward progression of Chinese settlement, the exposed deltaic position of the area retarded its economic growth.

During the Sung dynasty (960–1126) Shanghai emerged from its somnolent state as a small, isolated fishing village. The area to the west around T'ai Hu (T'ai Lake) had developed a self-sustaining agricultural economy on protected reclaimed land and was stimulated by an increase in population resulting from the southward migration of Chinese fleeing the invading Mongols in the north. The natural advantages of Shanghai as a

The city's origins

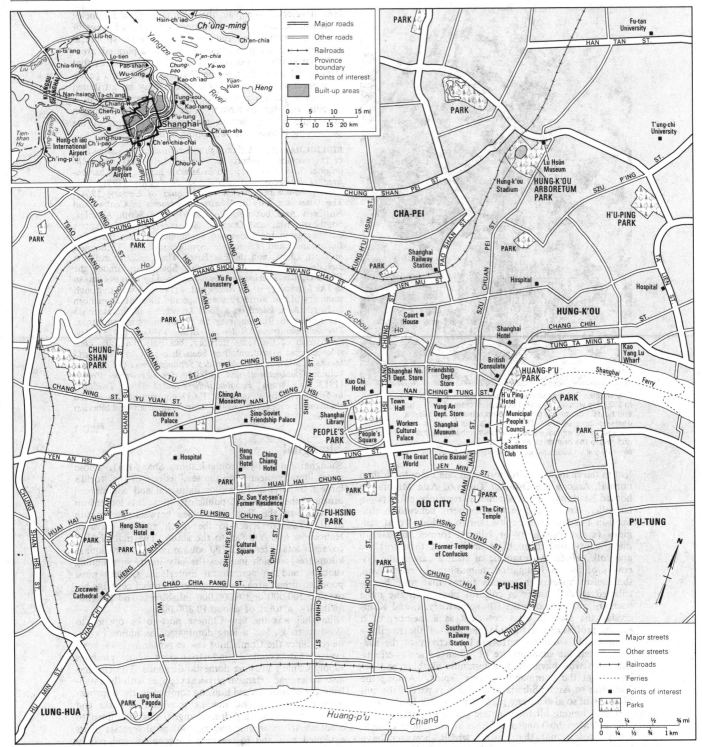

Central Shanghai and (inset) its metropolitan area.

deepwater port and shipping centre were recognized as coastal and inland shipping expanded rapidly. By the beginning of the 11th century, a customs office was established; and by the end of the 13th century, Shanghai was designated as a county seat and placed under the jurisdiction of Kiangsu Province.

During the Ming dynasty (1368–1644), roughly 70 percent of the cultivated acreage around Shanghai was given to the production of cotton to feed the city's cotton-and silk-spinning industry. By the middle of the 18th century there were more than 20,000 persons employed as cotton spinners.

After the 1850s, the predominantly agricultural focus of the economy was quickly transformed, when the city became the major Chinese base for Western commercial imperialism. Following their humiliating defeat by Great Britain in 1842, the Chinese surrendered Shanghai and signed the Treaty of Nanking, which opened the city to unrestricted foreign trade. The British, French, and Americans took possession of designated areas in the city within which they had special rights and privileges, and the Japanese received a concession in 1895 under the terms of the Treaty of Shimonoseki.

The opening of Shanghai to foreign business immediately led to the establishment of major European banks and multipurpose commercial houses. The city's prospects as a leading centre of foreign trade were further enhanced when Canton, a rival port in the southeastern coastal province of Kwangtung, was cut off from its hinterland by the Taiping Rebellion (1850–64). Impelled by

The
impact of
Western
imperial-
ism

this potential threat to the uninterrupted expansion of their commercial operations in China, the British obtained rights of navigation on the Yangtze in 1857. As the natural outlet for the vast hinterland of the Lower Yangtze, Shanghai rapidly grew to become China's leading port and by 1860 accounted for about 25 percent of the total shipping tonnage entering and departing the country.

Shanghai did not, however, show promise of becoming a major industrial centre until the 1890s. Except for the Chiang-nan Arsenal organized by the Ch'ing dynasty (1644–1911) in the early 1860s, most industrial enterprises were small-scale offshoots of the larger foreign trading houses. As the flow of foreign capital steadily increased after the Sino-Japanese War of 1894–95, light industries were established within the foreign concessions, which took advantage of Shanghai's ample and cheap labour supply, local raw materials, and inexpensive power.

By contrast, local Chinese investment in Shanghai's industry was minimal until World War I diverted foreign capital from China. From 1914 through the early 1920s, Chinese investors were able to gain a tenuous foothold in the scramble to develop the industrial economy. This initial involvement was short-lived, however, as the post-World War I resurgence of Western and Japanese economic imperialism—followed closely by the Depression of the 1930s—overwhelmed many of the newly established Chinese industries. Competition became difficult, as cheaper foreign goods were dumped on the Shanghai market, and labour was attracted to relatively higher paying jobs in foreign-owned factories. Prior to the Sino-Japanese War of 1937–45 the Japanese had gained control over about half of the city's yarn-spinning and textile-weaving capacity.

The 1920s was also a period of growing political awareness in Shanghai. Members of the working class, students, and intellectuals became increasingly politicized as foreign domination of the city's economic and political life became ever more oppressive. When the agreements signed by the United Kingdom, the United States, and Japan at the Washington Conference of 1922 failed to satisfy Chinese demands, boycotts of foreign goods were instituted. The Chinese Communist Party was founded in Shanghai in 1921, and four years later the Communist Party led the "May 30" uprising of students and workers. This massive political demonstration was directed against feudalism, capitalism, and official connivance in foreign imperialistic ventures. The student-worker coalition actively supported the Nationalist armies under Chiang Kai-shek, but the coalition and the Communist Party were violently suppressed by the Nationalists in 1927.

Founding of the Chinese Communist Party

Shanghai was occupied by the Japanese during the Sino-Japanese War of 1937–45, and the city's industrial plants suffered extensive war damage. In the brief interim before the fall of Shanghai to the People's Liberation Army (PLA) in 1949, the city's economy suffered even greater dislocation through the haphazard proliferation of small, inefficient shop industries, rampant inflation, and the absence of any overall plan for industrial reconstruction.

After 1949, Shanghai's development was temporarily slowed because of the emphasis on internal regional development, especially during the period up to 1960 when close cooperation was maintained with the Soviet Union. With the cooling of relations after 1960, Shanghai has resumed its key position as China's leading scientific and technological research centre, with the nation's most highly skilled labour force.

THE CONTEMPORARY CITY

The city site. The province-level municipality (*shih*) of Shanghai has a total area of 2,200 square miles and is bordered by Kiangsu Province on the north and west and Chekiang Province on the south. It includes the city of Shanghai; the nine mainland counties (*hsien*) of Pao-shan, Chia-ting, Ch'ing-p'u, Sung-chiang, Chin-shan (Chu-ching), Shang-hai (Hsin-chuang), Feng-

hsien (Nan-ch'iao), Nan-hui, and Ch'uan-sha; and approximately 30 islands in the mouth of the Yangtze and offshore to the southeast in the East China Sea. The largest island, Ch'ung-ming, has an area of 270 square miles (1,220 square kilometres), extends more than 40 miles (65 kilometres) upstream from the mouth of the Yangtze, and is the tenth county in the greater Shanghai Municipality.

The city's composition

The mainland portion of the city lies on an almost level deltaic plain with an average elevation of 10 to 16 feet above sea level. It is crisscrossed by an intricate network of canals and waterways that connect the municipality with the T'ai Hu region to the west.

The environment. The city's maritime location fosters a mild climate characterized by minimal seasonal contrast. The average annual temperature is about 61° F (16° C); the July maximum averages about 80° F (27° C), and the average January minimum is about 37° F (3° C). About 45 inches of precipitation fall annually, with the heaviest rainfall in June and the lightest in December.

As China's greatest industrial agglomeration, Shanghai has been increasingly plagued by pollution. Industrial relocation and new construction away from the city centre have helped alleviate air pollution, while water pollution has been tackled in a comprehensive manner since 1968. The Su-chou and Huang-p'u rivers, which flow through the city, are being purified; and attempts to recycle industrial waste materials are encouraged as a contribution to the more comprehensive and efficient use of natural resources.

The city plan. The central urban core, composed of the city proper and ten contiguous counties, has an area of roughly 20 square miles. It radiates toward the north, west, and south from the confluence of the Su-chou Ho and the Huang-p'u Chiang, a tributary of the Yangtze. Surrounding the central core is a transitional zone on both banks of the Huang-p'u, which encompasses a partially rural area of about 160 square miles. It includes several self-contained villages and the industrial satellite towns of T'ao-p'u, P'eng-p'u, Ts'ao-ho-ching, Min-hang, Wu-sung, Ho-chia-wan, and Wu-ching. The banks of the Su-chou, an important inland waterway connection to the interior hinterland, are occupied by a westward arterial extension of the transitional zone. To the south, however, the transitional zone terminates abruptly a few miles south of the central Shanghai urban core, at the Huang-p'u. Eastern Shanghai (P'u-tung), directly across the Huang-p'u from the central business district, was founded in 1870 as one of the earliest industrial areas; it was also notorious as the city's most extensive and appalling slum. Several of the post-1949 industrial workers' residential complexes are now located there.

The physical perspective of downtown Shanghai is much the same as in the pre-Communist period. Because of the policy of developing integrated residential and industrial complexes in suburban areas, central city development and renewal has been given low priority. Many of the pre-World War II buildings, which housed foreign commercial concerns and diplomatic missions, still dominate the area.

Extending southward and westward from the confluence of the Su-chou and Huang-p'u rivers, central Shanghai has a gridded street pattern and includes the area originally contained within the British concession. The area is bounded on the east along the Huang-p'u by Chung Shan Tung Lu (Chung Shan Tung Street); on the west by Hsi Tsang Chung Lu; and on the south by Yen An Tung Lu, which was built on the former Yang-ching-p'ang Canal that separated the British from the French concessions. Chung Shan Tung Lu has several hotels, the central administrative offices of Shanghai, and a residence for foreign seamen. The main commercial artery, Nan Ching Tung Lu, runs westward from the eastern road. On this street are Shanghai's largest retail establishment—the Shanghai No. 1 Department Store (which handles 150,-000 customers daily), restaurants, hotels, and the central communications and telegraph building.

A portion of the commercial centre of Shanghai along the Su-chou Ho.
Paolo Koch—Photo Researchers

The Hung-k'ou district lies to the north and east of the Su-chou Ho. It was originally developed by American and Japanese concessionaires and in 1863 was combined with the British concession to the south to create the International Settlement. It is an important industrial area, with shipyards and factories spread out along the bank of the Huang-p'u in the eastern section of the district. Its best known building, the Shanghai Hotel (Shang-hai Ta-hsia), overlooks the Huang-p'u; and the district is also the site of Shanghai's main railroad station.

The old Chinese city, which is now part of central Shanghai, is characterized by a random and labyrinthine street pattern. Until the early 20th century the area was surrounded by a three-mile wall. It is now circumscribed by the two streets of Jen Min Lu and Chung Hua Lu, which follow the course of the original wall; and it is bisected by the main north–south artery, Ho Nan Nan Lu (South Ho Nan Street).

Western Shanghai is primarily residential in character and is the site of the Sino-Soviet Friendship Palace, a permanent industrial exhibition hall. To the southwest, the district of Ziccawei (in Mandarin, Hsu-chia-hui) became a centre of Christian missionary activity in China in the 17th century. During the late 1800s, Jesuit priests established a major library, a printing establishment, an orphanage, and a meteorological observatory in the area.

Land-use patterns in metropolitan Shanghai mirror pre-1949 real-estate market conditions. Much of the high-value land given over to industrial plants, warehouses, and transport facilities lies close to the Huang-p'u and Su-chou rivers. South of the Su-chou, which is traversed by about 20 bridges within the city, residential areas extend south from the industrial strip to the Huang-p'u. North of the Su-chou, residential areas are less clearly demarcated, and there is a more gradual merging of city and country in the transitional zone. Continuous urban settlement is bounded on the north by the two major east–west arteries of Chung Shan Pei Lu and Szu P'ing Lu.

Retail trade is concentrated in the old central business district, although the volume of trade conducted here has diminished with the establishment of the new industrial satellite towns and new villages on the periphery of Shanghai.

Transportation. Shanghai is China's major transport centre. The central city is both a sea and river port, with the Huang-p'u Chiang serving as an excellent harbour; at high tide, oceangoing vessels can sail up the river to the city.

The port of Shanghai

In the early 1950s, the harbour was divided into a number of specialized districts. P'u-tung, on the east bank of the Huang-p'u, is used for the storage of bulk commodities and for transportation maintenance and repair facilities, while P'u-hsi, on the west bank, and Fu-hsing Tao (Fu-hsing Island) are the sites of general cargo wharves. Kao Yang Lu Wharf and I-hui contain general and bulk cargo wharves, and the Su-chou Ho is lined with riverine and small-craft terminals and cargo-handling facilities. The ocean terminals constructed since 1952 are at Jih-hui Chiang, south of the city, and at Chang-hua-peng, to the north at Wu-sung.

Heavily used inland-waterway connections, via the Su-chou Ho, and an extensive canal network are maintained with Soochow, Wu-hsi, and Yang-chou in Kiangsu Province, and with Hangchow, in Chekiang Province.

The railway network reflects the efforts that have been made since 1949 to reorient the city's industrial economy to give maximum support to domestic development needs. Before World War II, Shanghai was the terminus of two major rail lines south of the Yangtze—the Hu-ning line, from Nanking to Shanghai, and the Hu-han-jung line, from Shanghai to the port of Ning-po in Chekiang Province. A short spur line also ran from Shanghai to Wu-sung.

Railway facilities

Additional spur lines, built since 1949, connect the new industrial districts to the main trunk routes. Among these newly constructed spurs are the Wen-tsao-pin and Min-hang lines and several short spurs emanating from Nan-hsiang (just west of the central city) to Ho-chia-wan, Peng-p'u, and T'ao-p'u.

Shanghai is served by two airports, the older Lung-hua Airport, a few miles south of the city used mainly for domestic flights, and the Hung-ch'iao International Airport, southwest of Shanghai, one of China's busiest.

Intraurban transport by electric trolleybus, trolley, and motorbus has been substantially improved since 1949; and there are more than 900 miles of transit routes throughout the city.

Demography. Shanghai's population has been estimated at between 6,000,000 and 11,500,000 persons. The wide range of estimated figures is due to a lack of differentiation in statistics between the city itself and Shanghai Municipality. The greater municipality can be divided into three distinct population zones—the densely populated central city, the transitional zones, and the rural hinterland, which is one of the world's most densely settled agricultural areas.

Population densities vary from a maximum of about 125,000 persons per square mile in the urban core to between 1,500 and 2,500 persons per square mile in the hinterland. The transitional zone, which is considered part of metropolitan Shanghai, has a density of roughly 15,000 to 18,000 persons per square mile. It would appear, then, that the population of metropolitan Shanghai is roughly 5,500,000 to 6,000,000 and that of the hinterland over 4,000,000.

Within metropolitan Shanghai, there are few, if any, concentrations of ethnic minority groups. The majority of the population is of Han Chinese origin. There is undoubtedly a significant Chinese Christian community, as well as a foreign community, although it is impossible to estimate their size.

Housing. Shanghai has made considerable progress since 1949 in providing new housing for its growing population. Construction of integrated, self-sufficient residential complexes in conjunction with industrial, agricultural, and commercial development throughout metropolitan and suburban Shanghai has helped disperse population from the overcrowded central city and has led to dramatic changes in the urban and suburban landscape.

The concept of state-supported housing was introduced in 1951 with the development of Ts'ao-yang Hsin Ts'un (Ts'ao-yang New Village) in an existing industrial zone on Shanghai's western periphery. Two- and three-story standardized structures were supplied with running water, adequate drainage, and modern sewage facilities. Attention was also given to landscape beautification, and to the building of nurseries, schools, recreational facilities, shops, and post offices.

Following the construction of the Ts'ao-yang Hsin Ts'un, at least ten other residential complexes have been built, housing more than 1,000,000 persons. Some of them were constructed with the partial support of government bureaus or industrial enterprises to satisfy the needs of their employees. Two of the earliest complexes in this category were the Railroad Village and the Post and Telegraph Village.

Five major housing developments were built in the former slum area of Yang-shu-p'u. These include the villages of An-shan, K'ung-chiang, Ch'ang-pai, Feng-ch'eng, and the Feng-nan Erh Ts'un. Other complexes are those at P'eng-p'u, Chen-ju, I-ch'uan, Jih-hui, and Ch'iang-wan. Some of these are in relatively remote suburban locations in the transitional and hinterland zones near older rural marketing centres. The P'eng-p'u workers' housing project is typical. Some 15,000 to 20,000 persons who work in nearby factories live in a garden–apartment complex that includes apartment buildings, administrative offices, workshops, clinics, and a nursery. The adjacent fields supply wheat, clover, beans, cabbage, melons, and rapeseed (for cooking oil) for consumption by the inhabitants of the complex.

The economy. Shanghai has become the nation's leading industrial and manufacturing centre because of a distinctive combination of factors. These include the availability of a large, highly skilled, and technologically innovative work force; a well-grounded and broadly based scientific-research establishment supportive of industry; a tradition of cooperation among producers; and excellent internal and external communication and supply facilities.

The industrial establishment supplies a wide variety of semimanufactured and finished products to factories throughout China. In 1970, for example, an exhibition of Shanghai-made machines and machine tools designed for provincial industries included such specialized products as high-capacity wire-drawing dies, multiple-use lathes,

China's leading industrial centre

and equipment for assembling radios and other electronic equipment. Many of these precision-ground products were made in the Shanghai Machine Tool Plant (China's largest), which employs 6,000 workers. The machine industry also produces mining machinery, printing presses, equipment for sugar refineries and cement factories, cars and trucks, and industrial ball bearings. It supports a growing shipbuilding industry and is presently developing a giant turbo-generator capable of generating 125,000 kilowatts of electricity.

The iron and steel industry, though not of the first order in terms of actual production or productive capacity, was one of the earliest to be established in China. In the 1950s, the blast-furnace capacity of the industry was enlarged, and attempts were made to integrate the operations of the iron and steel industry more closely with the machine-manufacturing industry.

The chemical and petrochemical industries are almost fully integrated, and there is increasing cooperation among individual plants in the production and supply of chemical raw materials for plastics, synthetic fibres, dyes, paint, pharmaceuticals, agricultural pesticides, chemical fertilizers, synthetic detergents, and refined petroleum products. Shanghai has also taken the lead in supplying plants and equipment for the nationwide network of small chemical-fertilizer plants.

The textile industry has been reorganized to assure efficient utilization of the mills' productive capacity at all stages of the manufacturing process. More than 160 textile mills cooperate in their use of raw materials and have established cooperative relationships with plants that manufacture rubber shoes, tires, zippers, industrial abrasives, and conveyor belts.

Shanghai is also a primary source of a wide variety of consumer goods such as watches, cameras, radios, fountain pens, glassware, stationery products, leather goods, and hardware. Since 1962, factories producing such goods have made a special effort to meet consumer demands and to produce durable and attractive products. Special teams of industrial designers and factory workers interview customers in large stores to determine their preferences.

The retail trade in manufactured consumer goods is managed by the First Bureau of Commerce, which is directly responsible to the Shanghai Municipal Revolutionary Committee, the chief municipal administrative body. A number of commercial corporations under the Bureau are responsible, in turn, for the wholesaling, distribution, and warehousing of specific commodity groups. A separate corporation manages the larger retail stores, while the smaller retail establishments and some specialized wholesaling organizations are controlled by local commerce bureaus in the various districts of the city.

Shanghai's two major banks—the People's Construction Bank and the Bank of Communications—function as administrative organs of the Ministry of Finance. They are responsible for the disbursement and management of capital investment funds for state enterprises. The two British banks, the Hong Kong and Shanghai Banking Corporation and the Chartered Bank, maintain Shanghai branch offices that underwrite foreign trade transactions and exchange foreign currency in connection with trading operations. Remittances from Chinese living abroad (mainly in Hong Kong and in a number of Southeast Asian countries) are managed and collected by the three overseas Chinese banks, the Bank of East Asia, the Chi-Yu Bank, and the Overseas Chinese Banking Corporation.

Industrial products are exported from Shanghai to all parts of China. Imports are mainly unprocessed food grains, petroleum and coal, construction materials, and such industrial raw materials as pig iron, salt, raw cotton, tobacco, and oils. In domestic trade, Shanghai still imports more than it exports. In foreign trade, however, the value of exported commodities exceeds that of imported goods, and the proportion of manufactured exports is steadily increasing.

Political and governmental institutions. As a first-order, province-level administrative unit, Shanghai Munici-

Banking operations

pality is, in theory, directly controlled by the central government in Peking. It is difficult, however, to gauge the precise nature of this relationship. Since the Cultural Revolution of the late 1960s, China's administrative apparatus at all levels of the hierarchy has been in a process of readjustment so as to bring governmental organization in line with political reality. Prior to 1966, central administrative authority was shared by representatives of the central government and the Communist Party. From 1966 through 1968, however, this joint leadership was shattered, and both party and governmental institutions were subject to drastic reorganization and realignment.

The Shanghai Municipal Revolutionary Committee, the top governing body in the municipality, was established in 1967 after a chaotic period in which a number of popular-based revolutionary organizations seized control of the city for brief periods. The committee is composed of representatives of the army; the mass revolutionary organizations, such as workers, peasants, and students; and some former Communist Party officials. It would appear at this time that the semblance of a unified party–governmental administrative structure is being re-established.

Public utilities. Public works improvements since 1949 include the installation and improvement of drainage and sewage treatment facilities, public water supply systems, street lights, and public refuse bins. Roads have been widened and repaired, flood walls constructed in low-lying areas subject to tidal inundation, and housing built. The Chao-chia-pin drainage project drains approximately five square miles in southwestern Shanghai. The course of the Jih-hui Chiang, a stream that frequently flooded before draining into the Huang-p'u Chiang, has been filled in and a large sewer installed that now channels the stream flow directly into the main river. The sea walls surrounding Shanghai have also been strengthened and enlarged; two long sea walls extend east of the Huang-p'u for a total of more than 13 miles.

Shanghai is also one of China's major electric power generating centres. About 500,000 kilowatts of electric power can be generated by coal-fired thermal plants; and the Shanghai area is linked via a major transmission network with Nanking to the northwest and with Hangchow and Hsin-an-chiang (the site of a new hydroelectric generating facility) in Chekiang Province to the southwest. China's largest gas works, the Wu-ching works at Lunghua, is capable of producing about 35,000,000 cubic feet of coking coal gas daily.

Health and safety. Shanghai's health-care facilities range from thousands of small clinics associated with factories, schools, retail establishments, and government offices to several major research and teaching hospitals. The Shanghai No. 6 Hospital, a typical medium-sized institution, has 580 beds and a staff of 700. Most hospitals have facilities for practicing and teaching both traditional Chinese and Western medicine. Medical schools have concentrated on the training of "barefoot" doctors, practitioners with sufficient medical skills to supply basic care to people in rural areas.

Public security is maintained by both military and police units. During the Cultural Revolution, the army assumed a greater degree of control over civilian militia and police. Before 1966, the Shanghai Public Security Bureau was responsible for all security matters. It consisted of a number of sections, including a political-assistance group; a secretariat; agencies for political, internal security, and criminal investigation; a public-order section; and detention and technical experiments offices.

Education. Shanghai is China's leading centre of higher education and scientific research. There are about 25 universities—including Fu-tan, Chiao-t'ung, T'ung-chi, and the Hua-tung Shih-Fan ta-hsueh—with a total enrollment of more than 50,000 students. In addition, about ten technical and higher education institutes train another 10,000 students. Many factories have affiliated work–study colleges to equip workers for more highly skilled jobs. In 1960 the Shanghai Municipal Part-Work Part-Study Industrial University was established through the cooperation of more than 1,000 industrial establish-

Work and college programs

ments. In the early 1960s, about one-fourth of the city's total work force of approximately 1,000,000 workers was enrolled in one of these schools.

The Shanghai Branch of the Chinese Academy of Sciences, China's leading scientific research and development body, is located in Shanghai. Since the Cultural Revolution, research work under the academy's auspices has been directed toward the solution of practical production problems. In Shanghai, therefore, much research is being carried out under the joint auspices of the academy and individual industrial establishments.

Cultural life. Shanghai's cultural attractions include museums, historical sites, and scenic gardens. The Shanghai Museum has an extensive collection of sculpture and pictorial art, and the Shanghai Revolutionary History Memorial Hall displays photographs and objects that trace the city's evolution. The Ta Shih-chieh ("Great World"), founded in the 1920s, is Shanghai's leading theatrical centre and offers revolutionary folk operas, dance performances, plays, story readings, and specialized entertainment forms typical of China's national minority groups. The city also has many workers' and children's recreational clubs and several large motion picture theatres, including the Kuang-ming Theatre.

The old Chinese city houses the 16th-century Yu-Yüan Garden, an outstanding example of late Ming garden architecture, and the Former Temple of Confucius. Other points of attraction are the Ch'ing dynasty Lung Hua Pagoda, the Sino-Soviet Friendship Palace, and the tomb and former residence of Lu Hsün, a 20th-century revolutionary writer.

The major publishing houses of Shanghai are a branch of the People's Literature Publishing House (at Peking) and the People's Educational Publishing House. In addition to the large branch of the Central Library of the Chinese Academy of Sciences, Shanghai has five other libraries with collections totalling more than 5,000,000 volumes. Shanghai's art and music schools include a branch of the Central Conservatory (Tientsin), the Shanghai Conservatory, and the Shanghai Institute of Drama.

Shanghai has two leading newspapers—the *Chieh-fang jih-pao* ("Liberation Daily") and the *Wen Hui Pao*. The television station was established in 1958. Stations serve as advertising media as well as vehicles for the dissemination of news and political propaganda. Other extensively used advertising media in Shanghai include magazines, billboards, telephone directories, and motion pictures.

The mass media

Parks, open spaces, and playing fields were notably expanded after 1949. Two of the earliest to be opened for public use were the People's Park in central Shanghai and the Huang-p'u Park on the shore of the Huang-p'u Chiang. Every section of the city has large parks and playing fields. Among the largest are the Hung-k'ou Arboretum, Park, and Stadium in the north; the Peace Park and Hup'ing Park and playing field in the northeast; the P'u-tung Park in eastern Shanghai, the Hu-nan and Fu-hsing parks in the south, and the Chung-shan Park on the western periphery of the central city.

BIBLIOGRAPHY. RHOADS MURPHEY, *Shanghai: Key to Modern China* (1953), is an authoritative study of Shanghai's pre-World War II political and economic organization. Special attention is given to the city's role as a trading and manufacturing centre, as well as to its relationship with the hinterland. For the post-1949 period, NEALE HUNTER, *Shanghai Journal* (1969), recounts the author's experiences as an English teacher in the Shanghai Foreign Language Institute during the Cultural Revolution; and *Nagel's Encyclopedia-Guide to China* (1968), describes historically and artistically important places. More scholarly accounts of the organization and management of Shanghai's industry, trade, and financial institutions may be found in AUDREY G. DONNITHORNE, *China's Economic System* (1967); and BARRY M. RICHMAN, *Industrial Society in Communist China* (1969). Economic and political developments are treated in CHRISTOPHER HOWE, "The Level and Structure of Employment and the Sources of Labor Supply in Shanghai, 1949–1957," and LYNN T. WHITE III, "Shanghai's Polity in Cultural Revolution," in J.W. LEWIS (ed.), *The City in Communist China* (1971). An earlier study by CHRISTOPHER HOWE, "The Supply and Administration of Urban Housing in Mainland China: The Case of Shanghai," *China Quarterly*, 33:73–97 (1968), also concentrates on conditions in Shanghai.

(B.Bo.)

Shansi

Shansi (Shan-hsi in Pin-yin romanization) is a province (*sheng*) of northern China. With an area of about 60,700 square miles (157,200 square kilometres) and a population of about 20,000,000 people, Shansi is roughly rectangular in shape; it is bounded by the provinces of Hopeh to the east, Honan to the south and southeast, Shensi to the west, and by the Inner Mongolian Autonomous Region to the north. The name Shansi, which means Western Mountains, testifies to the rugged terrain of the territory. The largest city and provincial capital T'ai yüan, is located in the centre of the province.

Shansi has always held a strategic position as a gateway to the fertile plains of Hopeh and Honan. Since ancient times, it has also served as a buffer zone between China proper and the Mongolian and Central Asian steppes. A key route for military and trading expeditions, it was also one of the major avenues for the entrance of Buddhism into China from India. Today it is important for its vast reserves of coal and iron, which form the basis of heavy industrial development, and for its production of cotton for export. (For a related physical feature, see HUANG HO [RIVER].)

History. Pollen analyses from western and southern Shansi reveal that several cereal plants were grown there as early as the 5th to the 3rd millennium BC. During the Western Chou period, from about 1122 to 771 BC, the fief of Chin (now a colloquial and literary name for Shansi) was established in the area of modern Ch'ü-wo (Hou-ma) along the Fen Ho in the southwest.

Under the Han dynasty (206 BC to AD 220) Shansi assumed what was to become its traditional role as a buffer state between the pastoral nomads to the north and west and the sedentary Chinese farmers to the south and east. Through successive dynasties, the political status of the region varied with the relative strength or weakness of the Chinese central government. A predilection for political autonomy was paralleled by a sense of commercial initiative and aggressiveness that led to the rise in the 18th and 19th centuries AD of a class of Shansi bankers and merchants famous throughout China.

From the end of the Han dynasty until the reunification of the empire under the Sui dynasty in 581, Shansi came under the dominance of several short-lived dynasties, most prominent of which was the Northern Wei dynasty (AD 386 to 534). Buddhism prospered for the first time during the Northern Wei period; it was from Shansi that the Chinese Buddhist monk Fa-hsien (*q.v.*) began his legendary journey to India. The Buddhist cave sculptures dating from this period and preserved at Yün-kang today constitute some of China's most precious art treasures.

From the 7th century until the end of the 14th century, control over the area shifted back and forth among local military leaders, invading Turkic and Mongol forces, and representatives of the Chinese dynasty in power. Some stability was restored during the Ming dynasty (1368–1644), when many of the present-day towns and cities were built.

Antiforeign feeling ran high during the latter years of the Ch'ing (Manchu) dynasty (1644–1911), despite the fact that there was relatively little foreign influence in the province. A few manufacturing establishments were set up in T'ai-yüan in 1898, and a French- and Chinese-financed railway between T'ai-yüan and Cheng-ting in western Hopeh was built from 1904 to 1907. In 1900, antiforeign feeling took a violent form when an English mission church in T'ai-yüan was burned by the I-ho t'uan (a secret society that came to be popularly known as the "Boxers"), and foreigners and Chinese Christian converts were killed. This led to the outbreak of the so-called Boxer Rebellion, which eventually spread to Peking.

After the overthrow of the Ch'ing dynasty in 1911, the Shansi warlord Yen Hsi-shan (1883–1960) ruled as an absolute dictator until the end of World War II. Yen was instrumental in the establishment of the nucleus of a heavy industrial base and the opening of the T'ung-p'u railway—a north–south extension of the existing T'ai-yüan–Cheng-ting line—in 1934.

During the Sino-Japanese War of 1937 to 1945, the Japanese developed coal resources in the T'ai-yüan Basin and expanded heavy industry. They were, however, continually harassed by Communist guerrillas who operated from mountain bases. The agricultural and handicrafts cooperatives established at these bases were instrumental in facilitating economic and social recovery after Communist forces assumed control of Shansi in 1949.

The natural landscape. Two-thirds of the province is composed of a vast plateau that lies at average elevations of between 1,000 and 3,000 feet above sea level. The plateau is bounded by the Wu-t'ai Shan (Wu-t'ai Mountains) and Heng Shan on the north, the T'ai-hang Shan on the east, and the Lü-liang Shan on the west. The eastern mountains average between 5,000 and 6,000 feet in height and reach their maximum elevation at Shih-kao Shan (8,300 feet or 2,530 metres). The highest peak in the west, Kuan-ti Shan, reaches an elevation of 9,135 feet (2,785 metres), while the northern ranges are crowned by Wu-t'ai Shan at 9,495 feet (2,894 metres).

The Huang Ho (Yellow River) flows through a mountain gorge from north to south and forms the western border with Shensi Province. At Feng-ling-tu, the river turns sharply eastward and forms part of the southern border with Honan Province. The southwest corner of the province is part of the highland region that extends from Kansu to Honan provinces and is covered with a layer of loess (a loamy deposit formed by wind).

The Fen Ho Valley is comprised of a chain of linked, loess-filled basins that crosses the plateau from northeast to southwest. The largest of the valley's basins is the 100-mile-long T'ai-yüan Basin. North of T'ai-yüan are three detached basins—Ning-wu, Hsin-hsien, and P'ing-ting—which are isolated areas of cultivation. Further north, the Ta-t'ung Basin forms a separate feature.

Several rivers drain eastward and southeastward, cutting valleys and ravines through the T'ai-hang Shan and the Wu-t'ai Shan. Among these are the Hu-t'o Ho and its tributaries the Cho-chang-pei Yüan, the Ch'ing-chang, the Cho-chang, and the Ching. In the west, several rivers cut across the Lü-liang Shan and drain into the Huang Ho. In addition to the Fen Ho, which flows southward through two-thirds of the province, these include the Lan-i Ho, the Ch'iu-shui Ho, the San-ch'uan Ho, the Ch'u-chan Shui, the Hsin-shui Ho, and the Sou Shui. The northern mountains are drained chiefly by the Sang-kan Ho, which flows eastward toward Peking.

In the mountains, several types of light-brown and brown forest soils are common, with meadow-steppe varieties found at higher elevations. Alluvial soils in the central and southern portions of the province are formed mainly of calcareous (lime-bearing) brown soils deposited by the Fen Ho. There are also loess and lime deposits. Natural organic materials are not abundant, and salinity—caused by a high degree of surface evaporation—is excessive.

Shansi has a semi-arid climate. The mean annual rainfall ranges from less than 10 inches a year in the northwest to a maximum of 20 inches in the southeast. Between 70 and 80 percent of the annual rainfall occurs between June and September. Temperatures range from a January mean of 17° F (−8° C) and a July mean of 77° F (25° C) at T'ai-yüan, to a January mean of 3° F (−16° C) and a July mean of 72° F (22° C) at Ta-t'ung.

Winter droughts are common because the plateau is subject to the full force of the dry winter northwestern wind that blows from the Mongolian plateau. In summer, the southeastern monsoon (a rain-bearing wind) is blocked by the T'ai-hang Shan. Hailstones are a common natural hazard, as are frequent floods, particularly along the course of the Fen Ho.

Vegetation distribution primarily depends on the direction in which the mountain slopes face. The southern slopes are characteristically covered by species such as oak, pine, buckthorn, and honey locust, which are more tolerant to drier conditions than those such as linden,

Early settlements

The Boxer Rebellion

Mountains and plateaus

The climate

hazel, maple, and ash that prevail on the more humid northern slopes. The province has long been cultivated, and such natural vegetation as remains consists mainly of shrubs and grasses; isolated forests occur on the north-facing slopes.

Destruction of the original forest cover in ancient times eliminated most animal species, although several species of steppe rodents—including the hamster and the vole (a small rodent-like animal)—are still prevalent.

People and population. Most of the province's 20,000,000 people are of Han (Chinese) origin and speak the Northern Mandarin dialect of Chinese. The small minority populations include the Hui, or Chinese Muslims, in the T'ai-yüan–Yü-tz'u area, and some Mongols and Manchus around Ta-t'ung.

Roughly 85 percent of the populace live in agricultural villages. The highest rural densities occur in the T'ai-yüan Basin, in the southeast around Ch'ang-chih, and in the Fen Ho Valley. In these areas, densities range from 500 to 800 persons per square mile. The average population density is about 330 persons per square mile. In some of the more remote mountain areas there are fewer than 130 persons per square mile.

The main cities

The two principal urban areas are T'ai-yüan, the provincial capital and leading industrial and mining complex (1970 estimated population 2,725,000), and Ta-t'ung (1964 estimated population 500,000), a mining and rail transport centre near the borders of Hopeh Province and the Inner Mongolian Autonomous Region. Other manufacturing and transport centres include Yü-tz'u and Yang-ch'üan, both east of T'ai-yüan, and Ch'ang-chih in the southeast. Smaller cities are Ch'ü-wo (Hou-ma) and Lin-fen, both situated in the fertile Fen Ho Valley; Fen-yang, immediately southwest of T'ai-yüan; and Yün-ch'eng, on the Chieh Ch'ih salt lake in the southwest.

Administration and social conditions. The chief provincial administrative unit is the Shansi Provincial Revolutionary Committee. Formed in 1967 during the Cultural Revolution, it is composed of representatives of revolutionary mass organizations, members of the People's Liberation Army, and revolutionary cadres. The province is divided into two types of regional administrative units—the municipality (*shih*) and the special district (*chuan-ch'ü*). There are three municipalities—Ta-t'ung in the north, T'ai-yüan in the T'ai-yüan Basin, and Yang-ch'üan in the east. The five special districts are Yen-pei in the extreme northeast, Hsin-hsien in the north, Chin-chung in the centre of the province, Chin-tung-nan in the southeast, and Chin-nan in the southwest. On the local level, there are 96 counties (*hsien*) and one municipality—Ch'ang-chih in the Chin-tung-nan Special District.

The educational and medical institutions that were established in Shansi, mainly through foreign initiative, between 1898 and 1910 played a minor role in ameliorating widespread poverty, illiteracy, and substandard health conditions that then prevailed. Shansi University, founded in T'ai-yüan by an English missionary in 1902, was one of the first in China to offer Western curricula in liberal arts, law, and medicine but had an enrollment of no more than 400 students from its inception until 1949.

Since 1949, about a dozen technical schools for agriculture, mining, forestry, and machine technology have been established, as have about ten senior middle schools and more than 90 primary schools. Less than five percent of the population is now illiterate, and work-study facilities in factories are common. Educational planning centres on the practical requirements of industrial and technological development.

The four medical colleges and affiliated hospitals in T'ai-yüan offer treatment and full courses of study in both Western and traditional Chinese medicine. There are also smaller clinics in the industrial and mining areas. Public works projects include a centralized water supply system based at Lan-ts'un that regulates the flow of the underground water supply of the T'ai-yüan Basin; modernized sewerage and waste disposal facilities in the major cities; housing projects; and extensive "green belt"

areas that are planted with thousands of trees. Sports stadiums, physical education facilities, and three large parks have been built within the T'ai-yüan metropolitan area.

The economy. *Sectors of the economy.* Shansi is a major coal-producing region, and, together with Hopeh Province, it accounts for nearly 20 percent of China's total coal production. Estimated reserves of 400,000,000,-000 tons include both anthracite and high-grade coking coal; these have supported the development of heavy industry as well as the thermal generation of electricity. The major mining operations, in order of annual production capacity, are located at Ta-t'ung, Hsi-shan, Yang-ch'üan, Fen-hsi, and Hsien-kang. Another 150 smaller coal mines are widely distributed throughout the province.

Mineral resources

Iron ore is mined from vast deposits in the Ma-an Shan district of central Shansi, which have an estimated reserve of 100,000,000 tons. The largest titanium and vanadium (metallic elements used in alloys such as steel) deposits in China are located near Fen-hsi. Some silver and zinc is mined near Ta-t'ung; copper is mined in the southwestern mountains; and edible salt is produced from Chieh Ch'ih (Chieh Lake), near Yün-ch'eng in the southwest.

Most of the province's industries are concentrated in the T'ai-yüan–Yü-tz'u region. The iron and steel industry produces ingot steel, pig iron, and finished steel products. Heavy machinery and industrial chemicals and chemical fertilizers are produced, as are cement, paper, textiles, milled flour, and wine.

Other iron and steel centres include Yang-ch'üan, Ch'ang-chih, Ta-t'ung (which also produces cement and mining machinery), and Lin-fen. Manufacturing is important in P'ing-wang, Yü-hsien, Shou-yang, Ning-wu, Fen-hsi, and Ling-shih-hsien.

T'ai-yüan is an important electricity-generating centre. The thermal generating capacity exceeds 150,000 kilowatts; in addition, the basin is linked to the hydroelectric plant at San-men Gorge on the Huang Ho in Honan Province.

Because of widespread erosion, only about one-third of the province is under cultivation. Extensive soil and water conservation efforts since 1949 have taken the form of terracing, afforestation, the digging of irrigation canals, diking of cultivated plots, soil desalinization, and land reclamation along rivers.

In the extreme north, the short growing season and long, cold winter limit cultivation to one annual crop of spiked millet, spring wheat, naked oats (oats with no covering on the kernels), potatoes, and sesame. In the rest of the province—except for the mountainous areas—the longer growing season permits three crops in two years or two crops in one year. Winter wheat, millet, soybeans, kaoliang (a variety of grain sorghum), corn, and cotton are raised in adequately irrigated areas. Some tobacco and peanuts are produced in the central basins and on the Huang Ho flood plain as well as such fruits as grapes, apricots, persimmons, apples, peaches, and plums.

Agricultural production

Only 10 percent of Shansi's cultivated acreage is devoted to cash crops. Shansi is the largest provincial producer of cotton, and sesame is grown both for its oil seeds and for its fibre. Other cash crops include castor beans, rape seeds, and Indian hemp.

The relatively low ratio of population to land over much of Shansi's hilly terrain has traditionally fostered animal husbandry. Before 1949, unsettled political and economic conditions interfered with the development of high-quality animal strains. Sheep are raised for their high wool yields. Domestic animals include pigs, horses, yellow oxen (for transport), donkeys, and chickens.

Transportation. Shansi relies heavily on three major rail lines, both for intraprovince transport and for shipping raw materials, industrial commodities, and foodstuffs outside the province. The longest of these, the T'ung-p'u trunk line, runs for 518 miles from Ta-t'ung to Feng-ling-tu in the southwest corner of the province. An additional 75 miles of branch lines connect the main line with newly opened industrial and mining sites. The

Ching-pao line from Peking to Pao-t'ou, Inner Mongolia, passes through Ta-t'ung; it carries the northern region's coal eastward to Hopeh Province and the Yangtze Delta region and westward to Lan-chou, Kansu Province, via the Pao-t'ou–Lan-chou railway. Central and eastern Shansi coal is carried eastward on the double-tracked Shih-t'ai (or Cheng-t'ai) line, which runs between T'ai-yüan and Shih-chia-chuang, Hopeh. A spur connects Yüan-p'ing, on the main T'ung-p'u route, with O-k'ou in the northeast, whereas the rich southeastern agricultural area is served by a line from Ch'ang-chih to Chiao-tso, Honan.

Long-distance, all-weather roads are not extensive; most roads serve as feeder routes to the rail lines. A road links T'ai-yüan to northern Shensi Province via Chun-tu on the eastern shore of the Huang Ho. It carries industrial products to Shensi and hides and other mountain products to Shansi. Other important long-haul highways run between T'ai-ku (just south of Yü-tz'u) and Honan Province, between Ch'ang-chih and Han-tan, Hopeh.

The Fen Ho is navigable for small flat-bottomed boats below Hsin-chiang. Freight traffic on the Fen, as well as on the north–south section of the Huang Ho, is insignificant, however.

Cultural life. Shansi's long-standing position as an avenue of communication between the North China Plain, the Mongolian steppes, and Central Asia gave rise to a

Ancient
handicrafts

rich and varied cultural and folkloric tradition. Several distinctive forms of Shansi opera became popular under the Ming and Ch'ing dynasties. Metalworking has been a specialty of Shansi craftsmen since the 2nd millennium BC. The province was also famous for the uniquely sculpted decorative tiles and glazed pottery figures used for temple decoration. The Chin-ssu, near T'ai-yüan, is Shansi's best known temple complex; it was originally built in the 5th century AD. During subsequent periods, it served as a monastery and as the centre for several religious cults.

BIBLIOGRAPHY. YI-FU TUAN, *China* (1969), is a comprehensive and eminently readable account of the evolution and modification of the Chinese cultural landscape since prehistoric times. The final section of the book is concerned with landscape changes after 1850, with special attention given to developments since 1949. Although not focussed specifically on Shansi and Shantung, it stands as the outstanding concise statement of China's historical and contemporary geographical configurations. YU-TI JEN, *A Concise Geography of China* (1964), provides a brief introduction to the subject, organized along traditional lines, with sections on Shansi and Shantung. *The Physical Geography of China*, 2 vol. (1969), prepared originally by a group of Soviet earth scientists, is authoritative, but somewhat difficult to read because of awkward translation. Most topics bearing upon the physical geography of Shansi and Shantung are adequately treated. Four atlases are useful reference works: ALBERT HERRMANN, *An Historical Atlas of China*, new ed. (1966); *Communist China Administrative Atlas* (1969); *Communist China Map Folio* (1967); and *People's Republic of China Atlas* (1971). *Nagel's Encyclopedia-Guide to China* (1968) describes historically and artistically important places. An excellent documentary account of the period from 1948 to 1949 is found in WILLIAM HINTON, *Fanshen* (1966). Articles on current economic and political developments in Shansi and Shantung sometimes appear in the serials: *China Quarterly*, *Far Eastern Economic Review*, *China News Analysis*, *China Reconstructs*, and *China Pictorial*.

(B.Bo.)

Shantung

Shantung (Shan-dong in Pin-yin romanization) is a north coastal province of the People's Republic of China across the Yellow Sea from Korea. It has an area of 59,300 square miles (153,600 square kilometres). Shantung is China's second most populous province, its estimated population of 57,000,000 in 1970 being exceeded only by that of Szechwan; its average population density of 961 persons per square mile is exceeded only by that of Kiangsu Province.

The province consists of two distinct segments: an inland zone bounded by the provinces of Hopeh to the north and west, Honan to the southwest, and Anhwei and Kiangsu to the south; and a peninsula (the Shantung Peninsula) extending some 200 miles seaward from the Wei and Chiao-lai river plains, with the Gulf of Chihli (Po Hai) to the north and the Yellow Sea to the south, giving it a longer coastline than any other Chinese province (750 miles). The peninsula, which encloses the Gulf of Chihli on the south, is separated from the Liaotung Peninsula to the north by a 100-mile-wide strait extending from P'eng-lai on the north coast of the Shantung Peninsula, to Port Arthur (Lü-shun), a rail terminus at the tip of the Liaotung Peninsula in Liaoning Province.

The inland zone, covering roughly two-thirds of the province's total area, includes a hilly central region centred on the famous T'ai Shan (Mt. T'ai) complex, and a fertile and intensively farmed agricultural area surrounding the central mountainous mass on the north, west, and south, which forms part of the Huang Ho (Yellow River) Basin and the North China Plain. The provincial capital, Tsinan, is situated just west of T'ai Shan and three miles south of the Huang Ho, which flows from southwest to northeast through the province before emptying into the Gulf of Chihli.

The
Shantung
Peninsula

The Shantung Peninsula, in contrast, is entirely an upland area, and, with its seaward orientation and indented coastline, has traditionally depended on fishing, mining, and port-related activities. Long a focal area in the evolution of Chinese civilization and institutions, the province's natural inland-peninsular division is paralleled by a dual orientation in its past and present political and economic configurations. The eastern peninsula, with its seaward focus, historically has coveted autonomy, whereas the larger and more densely settled inland portion has been closely tied to the inward-facing empire.

The name Shantung means "Eastern Mountains" and was first officially used during the Chin dynasty in the 12th century. For an associated physical feature, see HUANG HO (RIVER).

HISTORY

A Neolithic culture—known as the Lung-shan because of archaeological remains discovered near the township of that name—existed on the Shantung Peninsula in the 3rd millennium BC; it played a key role in the establishment of a common rice-based cultural grouping that apparently spread along the Pacific seaboard from the Shantung Peninsula to Taiwan and eastern Kwangtung.

Western Shantung formed part of the Shang Kingdom (1766–c. 1122 BC). By the Spring and Autumn (Ch'un ch'iu) Period (722–481 BC) it had become the centre of political and military activity that resulted from the eastward expansion of the Chou, following their conquest of the Shang. One of the small southern Shantung states was Lu, the birthplace of Confucius and Mencius. Also in the "Eastern Territory"—an early name for Shantung—was Ch'i, extending over the major part of Shantung Peninsula; it became an important economic centre, exporting hemp clothing, silk, fish, salt, and a unique variety of purple cloth to all parts of China. Beginning in the Six Dynasties period (AD 222–589), Shantung became North China's leading maritime centre, receiving commodities from the South China coastal area (now Fukien and Kwangtung) for transshipment to destinations north and south of the Huang Ho. Thus, Shantung has been a part of China from its very beginning as an organized state.

In 1293 the Grand Canal (Yün Ho), running generally north to south, was completed, making western Shantung a major inland trading route. (The 1,200-mile-long canal is one of the longest in the world; it connects Peking with the Yangtze River; and sections of it may have been begun as early as the 5th century BC). Yet even after the completion of the canal, maritime trade still remained important to Shantung, and the peninsula retained its dominant economic position. In the great agricultural areas of the province, however, early deforestation and the long-established practice of clearing land for cultivation without providing for flood prevention and control measures, led to serious and ultimately disastrous erosion and wastage of valuable agricultural land. In the 19th

The
Grand
Canal

century this problem was intensified by shifts in the course of the Huang Ho. From 1194 until the early 1850s the Huang Ho followed the original bed of the Huai River along the Shantung–Kiangsu border before emptying into the Yellow Sea. After 1855, when a series of devastating floods was followed by extensive dike construction, the river changed to its present course some 250 miles to the north. Hardships and food shortages from floods and other natural calamities increased in intensity throughout the 19th and 20th centuries. This resulted in a substantial emigration of Shantung peasants to the Northeast (Manchuria) and to the Inner Mongolian Autonomous Region, with more than 4,000,000 emigrating between 1923 and 1930.

In the closing decade of the 19th century, Shantung came under the influence of German, British, and Japanese interests. It was occupied briefly by Japanese troops after the Sino-Japanese War of 1894 to 1895. In 1897 Germany landed troops, and in 1898 a treaty was signed by which China ceded to Germany, for 99 years, two entries to Chiao-chou Wan (Bay) and the islands in the bay and granted the right to construct a naval base and port, Tsingtao. Germany used Tsingtao as a base to extend its commercial influence throughout the peninsula; it developed coal mines and constructed a railway (1905) from Tsingtao to Tsinan. Similarly, in 1898 Great Britain obtained a lease for Wei-hai-wei (modern Wei-hai), another strategic port near the northern tip of the peninsula. This was in response to the Russian occupation of Port Arthur. With the advent of World War I, Japan took over German interests in the peninsula and in 1915 compelled the Chinese to give official recognition to their renewed occupation, which they maintained until 1922.

In the Sino-Japanese War of 1937 to 1945, even though the Japanese had gained control of most of Shantung by the end of 1937, they miscalculated Chinese strength and suffered a serious defeat—their first—at T'ai-erh-chuang, in southern Shantung, in 1938. In the postwar struggle between the Chinese Communists and Nationalists, Shantung came under Communist control by the end of 1948, with Tsinan falling in the autumn of that year.

THE LANDSCAPE

The hill regions

Shantung is dominated by two hill masses to the east-northeast of the Grand Canal and to the south-southwest of the present course of the Huang Ho. These hills are geologically similar to the mountains of the eastern Manchurian region, the Liaotung Peninsula, and Korea to the northeast. They are formed mainly of ancient crystalline shales and sedimentary rocks on their flanks and of hard, very ancient rocks with granitic intrusions in their core. Both masses are detached remnants of China's most ancient geologic core. The easternmost (peninsular) mass is connected to the Liaotung Peninsula by a submerged ridge, emerging periodically in the Gulf of Chihli as the Ch'ang-shan Ch'ün-tao (archipelago). In fairly recent geological times, the Shantung hill masses stood as islands in an inland sea that separated them from the T'ai-hang Shan (mountains) of Shansi to the west.

Relief and drainage. *The plains areas.* A broad, marshy depression, the Chiao-lai Plain (sometimes known as Wei-hsien Valley), extends for about 100 miles from Lai-chou Wan (bay) in the Gulf of Chihli, south to Chiao-chou Wan in the Yellow Sea, near Tsingtao, and westward into the North China Plain. This plain ranges in width from 18 to 30 miles and has an average elevation of less than 150 feet. Its generally flat surface is interrupted occasionally by bedrock-derived monadnocks, or residual rocks or hills, that have resisted erosion. Another depression, part of the inland zone of western Shantung, forms the central segment of the North China Plain. It slopes eastward into a northwest–southeast trough skirting the western perimeter of the central Shantung hill mass and is filled with a mixture of loess (a loamy soil, deposited by wind) and alluvial materials (sand, clay, and gravel), along with more recently deposited alluvium, resulting from the building up of the Huang Ho flood plain. Five narrow lakes forming part of the Grand Canal system—Tung-p'ing Hu, Nan-yang Hu, Tu-

shan Hu, Chao-yang Hu, and Wei-shan Hu—stretch out along this depression and are also linked to a series of saline marshes (indicative of earlier swamp conditions) that separate the fertile margin at the western edge of the central hills from the main sections of the North China Plain to the south and west.

The two hill masses. Of the two main hill masses, the westernmost (inland) complex is the most extensive. It consists of a northern series of three parallel faulted ranges—the Hsing Shan, Lu Shan, and T'ai Shan, that stretch northeastward for more than 200 miles—and a more diversified, lower, and more exposed southern portion. The granitic T'ai Shan, dominated by Mt. T'ai, the most famous of China's five sacred mountains, attains a maximum elevation of over 5,000 feet just above the city of T'ai-an. While the elevation of the three northern ranges averages from 1,000 to 3,000 feet, several other peaks exceed this level. Drainage is predominantly radial and subject to the prevailing configuration of the mountains. The only navigable river (other than portions of the Huang Ho) is the Hsiao-ch'ing Ho which emerges from a small spring-fed lake in a limestone outcrop zone near Tsinan and flows parallel to the Huang Ho, before emptying into Lai-chou Wan. The southern hills, in contrast, are drained by several rivers in arable valleys, typified by those of the Tung-wen Ho system, which eventually terminate in the marshy plain east of the Grand Canal in Kiangsu Province. The most prominent of these are the Tung-wen, the I, the Shu, and the Hsin-shu.

The mountains of the peninsular mass to the east seldom rise above 700 feet. Here, surface erosion has etched irregular and deeply cut valleys, and rounded hills contrast sharply with small intermontane basins. Both the north and south coasts of the peninsula are rocky, with hills dropping precipitously to the sea and separating a series of intensively cultivated crescent-shaped plains. The granitic bedrock of the peninsular core is sometimes broken by igneous intrusions, most notably on Lao Shan, northeast of Tsingtao with an elevation of 3,700 feet.

Soils. The soils of Shantung fall into two broad categories associated with upland or lowland distributions. The so-called Shantung brown soils are found over most of the two major hill masses and include a variety of brown forest and cinnamon-coloured soils formed through clay accumulations and sod processes. Although the depth of the soil cover varies with altitude because of severe erosion (especially on the northwest-facing surfaces), these soils are quite consistent in their composition. Typically, they are either leached brown forest soils or slightly leached calcareous (chalky) brown soils.

Shantung brown soils

A distinctive variant of the typical Shantung brown soil is the recalcified soil (soil that has again been made hard or stony by the deposit of calcium salts); it is found on the northern perimeter of the central hill mass. This area, subject to the full blast of the northwest winter monsoon (rain-bearing winds) has been inundated for centuries with limestone dust of loessal origin. The accumulation of this surface cover has outpaced the soil's ability to leach out the limestone, with the result that many soils in the area have a characteristic upper layer as well as a lower layer of calcium carbonate.

Calcareous alluvial soils predominate in both lowlands and plains. They are usually quite fertile, depending on both the length of time they have been cultivated and their proximity to urban centres (where heavier fertilization with human and animal wastes results in rich, dark-coloured soils). Silty alluvium covers most portions of the North China Plain area of the province. Variants include a clayey calcareous alluvium that appears in western and southern Shantung in low-lying areas away from rivers and a sandy calcareous alluvium found along the present and past courses of the Huang Ho. Before 1949, when the Huang Ho frequently flooded, sandy materials were deposited close to the riverbanks. The winds blew the lighter sandy loams into 45-to-60-foot dunes that moved unchecked over fertile farmlands. More limited distributions of noncalcareous alluvium are formed of loam and sand deposits eroded from the hilly brown forest soils. Those in Shantung usually occur at the base of

The stone ginger soil

granitic and sandstone hills and are composed of sandy or fine gravelly loams. Another distinctive soil type found in central and western Shantung on the North China Plain is the subsurface *sha-chiang t'u,* or "stone ginger soil." This appears at the lowest elevations of alluvial plains where surface water remains unevaporated for several months until the dry season and also in sections of the plains subject to annual alluvial inundation. Such soils are located anywhere from one to six feet below the surface and are always covered with alluvium or redeposited loess. Their name derives from the appearance of lime concretions that resemble the shape of ginger roots. Other *sha-chiang t'u* soils develop impervious layers of limestone hardpan up to 20 inches thick.

Climate. Shantung falls within the North China climatic region, which extends from the Huai Ho in the south to the Hopeh-Liaoning border in the north; it is characterized by a continental climate with cold winters and hot, dry summers. Climatic variation prevails, however, between the peninsular and inland zones of the province. The inland zone, especially in its northern sections, is subject to the full effect of the winter monsoon, when cold, northwesterly winds continue through December. By March, when the Siberian high-pressure concentration weakens, wind direction gradually reverses, and warmer, southeasterly winds prevail throughout the summer.

The inland zone. In the inland zone, annual precipitation ranges from 10 inches in northwest Shantung to 20 to 24 inches as one approaches the mouth of the Huang Ho. Of the total annual precipitation, only 2 to 6 percent falls during the winter, with 70 to 80 percent occurring in summer. The interior areas of Shantung are also subject to severe winter and spring dust storms, sometimes followed by droughts and frequent summer floods.

Rainfall and temperature

Temperatures in the inland zone range from a mean January reading of 25° F (−4° C) in the northern interior to a mean of 82° F (28° C) in July. In common with the rest of the North China Plain, this area is subject to freezing temperatures from one to three months, with frosts common from late October to April. It is also not unusual for rivers to freeze over for extended periods during the winter months. In the interior zone, the growing season extends 200 to 250 days.

The maritime zone. The maritime orientation of the Shantung Peninsula tends to modify the climatic extremes of the inland zone. The northern half of the peninsula is subject to winter snow and rainstorms and to extensive coastal ice from the mouth of the Huang Ho to Wei-hai and Chefoo (Yen-t'ai); the southern half is somewhat warmer. Mean January temperatures range from 25° F (−4° C) on the northern coast of the peninsula to 32° F (0° C) in the south. Northwest winds pick up moisture as they pass over the Gulf of Chihli and deposit snow on north-facing slopes. There is less temperature differential during the hot summer months when the mean July temperature is 79° F (26° C), but the ports of Chefoo and Tsingtao are cooler than interior stations. Maximum summer temperature in these ports rarely exceeds 77° F (25° C).

Sea fog is common along the north and south coasts of the peninsula, with an average of eight fogbound days in February at Wei-hai increasing to 15 to 20 days during June and July. Because of the high relative humidity, annual mean precipitation over the peninsula reaches 31 inches, with less seasonal contrast than in the interior of the province. Heaviest precipitation occurs on the south-facing slopes of the central and peninsular hill masses. Spring droughts on the peninsula are also less common because of the high relative humidity.

Vegetation and animal life. *Plant life.* The limited natural vegetation that remains in the intensively cultivated inland zone of Shantung is found in minor depressions in the flat, alluvial landscape. Species there included reeds, grassy legumes, and several varieties of shrubs, notably tamarisk. Halophytic (salt-tolerant) vegetation is common in alkaline and saline soil areas along the coasts of the Gulf of Chihli and southern Shantung near the Kiangsu border. Many of the halophytic shrubs are har-

Halophytic (salt-tolerant) plants

vested for fuel and are used for salt manufacture. Lien-liu, a shrub with long willowy branches, is used for basket weaving, while other plants are woven into thatch mattings and sunshades. Poplar, pine, and arbor vitae (an aromatic evergreen tree of the cypress family) are planted around settlements, along roads, and on the coasts to deter the movement of sand dunes.

The mountainous zones of Shantung are almost completely deforested, with only 2 percent of the area covered by scattered deciduous and coniferous forests interspersed among barren, eroded hills. Residual coniferous forests are found on higher foothills and mountain slopes, while deciduous trees appear on the lowest hills and on fan-shaped heaps of alluvial detritus at the base of mountains. Several types of pine grow at higher elevations on rocky, shallow soils in association with Alpine meadow species. On the lower slopes and in the valleys, mixed oak, elm, cedar, linden, ash, maple, and chestnut forests appear along with such economically important fruit trees as apple, pear, apricot, and peach. Other deciduous species found at the lower elevations include the pagoda, or "Chinese scholar's tree," the white mulberry, Persian walnut, the silk tree, and the acacia.

For centuries Shantung forests were overharvested for fuel and timber, and natural regeneration became extremely difficult. With a long dry season young trees had difficulty becoming established, and heavy summer rains eroded the thin soil cover. Since 1949, reforestation and closer regulation of timber harvesting has resulted in more extensive growth.

Despite the obliteration of much of Shantung's natural vegetation cover, the peninsular zone still exhibits an interesting mixture of northern and southern vegetation. Along with common northern plants, uniquely southern varieties, such as wingnut, magnolia, and styrax, are common.

Animal life. Through long periods of human settlement, intensive cultivation, and destruction of forests, animal life has suffered drastic declines. Animals include roe deer and field and harvest mice; birds include mandarin ducks, dollar birds (belonging to the roller group), and large owls. Even with recent attempts at reforestation, formerly extensive populations of native birds and mammals have almost vanished. Species of insects, beetles, and moths, however, are still unusually diverse and varied.

POPULATION

Shantung's population is predominantly Northern Mandarin-speaking and of Han Chinese origin, but there are small concentrations of Hui (Chinese Muslims) in Tsinan, the capital, in Chou-ts'un (just west of Tzu-po), and in Chi-ning and Lin-ch'ing (trading centres on the Grand Canal in western Shantung near the Hopeh border). The population, over 90 percent rural, is fairly evenly distributed over the level, cultivated areas of the province.

Urban settlement. The two largest cities are Tsingtao and Tsinan, with estimated populations of 2,000,000 and 1,000,000, respectively, followed by the Tzu-po conurbation, a leading mining and industrial zone at the northern edge of the central hill mass, about 20 miles east of Tsinan, with a combined population of over 800,000. Tzu-po includes the important mining, glass and pottery centre of Po-shan and the smaller towns of Chang-chou, Tzu-ch'eng, Hung-shan, Lu-chia-chuang, Po-t'ou, and Nan-ting. Other cities with populations of between 100,-000 and 500,000 include: Chefoo and Wei-hai, ports and fishing centres on the northeast coast of the Shantung Peninsula; Wei-fang, an industrial and commercial town on the central Chiao-lai Plain; and Hsin-t'ai, another mining town south of Po-shan. Smaller cities with populations of from 50,000 to 100,000 include I-tu, a transport junction between Tzu-po and Wei-fang; Yen-chou, a rail centre in the southwest; and Chi-ning. Te-chou, a minor industrial town on the Grand Canal, north of Lin-ch'ing; T'ai-an, in central Shantung at the base of Mt. T'ai; and Ho-tse, a rail junction and special district (*chuan-ch'ü*) seat in the southwest, all have populations of 30,000 to 50,000 persons.

Principal cities and towns

Rural settlement. The greatest rural population densities are found in three areas: The first is one of the earliest settled places in the province where irrigation works were constructed as long ago as the Han dynasty (206 BC–220 AD); it lies along the foothills of the central hill mass, bounded by Tsinan on the northwest, T'ai-an on the southwest, and I-tu to the northeast. The second, the southwestern Ho-tse–Ting-t'ao–Chi-ning area, is bounded on the northwest by the Huang Ho and on the southwest by the former course of the Huang Ho. This area was frequently subject to flood, but because of its fertility and level terrain gradually became densely settled. The third area constitutes a fertile, irrigated strip along the north coast of the Shantung Peninsula between I-hsien and Lung-k'ou; this was a major zone of emigration during the 1920s and 1930s when Shantung farmers left to settle in Manchuria.

Before 1949, Shantung was seriously affected by an imbalance in the ratio of population to land. With 95 percent of the population engaged in agriculture, the per capita holdings were extremely small. Since 1949, the government of the People's Republic has encouraged the emigration of Shantung farmers to the Manchurian and to other underpopulated regions, such as the Sinkiang Uighur Autonomous Region in the northwest.

ADMINISTRATION AND SOCIAL WELFARE

Government. Shantung is divided into nine special districts (*chuan-ch'ü*) and four municipalities (*shih*) directly under provincial administration. At the lowest administrative level there are 107 counties (*hsien*) and five smaller cities (also designated *shih*) administered by the county. Although the total number of counties has not changed since the 1930s, local adjustments in the area and number of the counties were made in connection with the establishment of the special districts by the People's government after 1949. The special districts, while never officially acknowledged in the 1954 Constitution of the People's Republic of China, have facilitated major improvements in administrative efficiency and control and play an important role in the process of administrative streamlining leading to implementation of central government directives at the provincial and subprovincial levels. The Shantung Provincial Revolutionary Committee, the chief provincial administrative body, was established in 1967.

The special districts and people's communes

Rural people's communes, made up of production teams and production brigades, serve as the lowest level administrative units. In many special districts, county seats operate as coordinating centres for the production and distribution of agricultural and industrial commodities produced in the communes under their administrative jurisdiction. In most of the agricultural areas of Shantung, the communes are spatially coterminous with the pre-1949 townships (*hsiang*) and function economically as natural marketing areas.

Social conditions. Before 1949, Shantung was a particularly hard-pressed area because of the pressure of population on the land; because of the common occurrence, especially since the later half of the 19th century, of such natural hazards as floods, droughts, dust storms, excessive soil salinization and alkalinization, and insect infestations; and because of frequent military and civil disturbances. Few serious attempts had ever been made by officials of either the Ch'ing (Manchu) dynasty (1644–1911) or, later, by the Republic of China to ameliorate the difficult social conditions of the peasant population. With the exception of missionary financed and controlled undertakings in areas under foreign influence or administration, such as Tsingtao, Chefoo, and Tsinan, modern intensive health-care facilities were virtually nonexistent, and there was only token support for public higher education. Water supplies, environmental sanitation facilities, and public housing were similarly inadequate to the needs of the populace, and public health services were neglected and understaffed.

Public health and recreation. Since 1949, the public health services in both rural and urban areas have been improved, and formerly common ailments such as kala azar, (a severe infectious disease transmitted by the sand fly), leprosy, and a variety of nutritional deficiency diseases have been eliminated. Most large and medium cities now have adequate water-supply systems, often built in conjunction with multi-purpose water conservancy schemes to improve and stabilize the watersheds of nearby rivers. Near Tsingtao the watershed storage facilities of the Chang-ts'un and Yuan-t'ou rivers have been enlarged, and the Lao-shan reservoir northeast of the city furnishes an ample supply of potable water. Similarly, in T'ai-an, central Shantung, a modern high-pressure water system has been installed and is coordinated with the Huang-ch'ien reservoir outside the city. Along with water supply, the construction of sewage treatment facilities in many cities has also helped raise public-health standards.

Multi-purpose systems of water supply

Not only has extensive tree planting enhanced the beauty of most Shantung cities, but "turning green" has been officially designated as a primary task of urban reconstruction in order to ameliorate the effects of harsh climates and to improve health conditions. In Tsingtao alone, some 4,000,000 trees were planted from 1949 to 1959; while in Tsinan, a green belt has been built on the site of some dilapidated sections of the ancient city wall. Along with urban reforestation, recreational facilities have been expanded, improved, and made readily available for public use. Many famous temples, hot springs, shrines, parks, lakes, and museums are frequented by the populace. In Tsinan, a city famous for its 72 hot springs where, for centuries, poets, scholars, and officials enjoyed diverse pleasures, several new parks have been built and old buildings restored. Tsingtao, known as the most pleasant beach resort in North China, is also famous for its parks. Ten public parks are complemented by six large beaches. The city is also famous for its workers' convalescent facilities and recreation clubs near picturesque Lao Shan.

Education. Most of Shantung's institutions of higher education are located in the provincial capital, Tsinan, with smaller or special-purpose schools scattered widely throughout the province. Among those in Tsinan are the Shantung Medical College, and the Shantung Institute of Technology. Shantung University is in Tsingtao. The Shantung Provincial Museum and Shantung Library are located in Tsinan. A small teachers' training college and a water-conservancy institute are located in Ch'ü-fu, a county seat in the Chi-ning special district, which is most famous as the ancestral home of Confucius and his lineal descendants, the Kungs. Facilities for primary and secondary education throughout the province have also been expanded and improved.

Higher education complex in Tsinan

THE ECONOMY

Shantung has a diversified agricultural and industrial economy. With the highest ratio (more than 60 percent) of cultivated to available arable land of any Chinese province, a broad range of food and cash crops are grown for internal consumption and export to other provinces and overseas. The province's industrial base has been expanded since the establishment of the People's Republic of China in 1949. Before World War II, light industrial enterprises in Tsinan and Tsingtao produced limited quantities of machine tools, electrical components, textile products, processed foods, and alcoholic beverages—primarily for export overseas, mainly in response to foreign commercial initiative. Despite the fact that the province often suffered a food deficit, agricultural products, such as vegetable oil, cotton, peanuts, and tobacco, were continuously exported along with salt, coal, iron ore, and bauxite.

Since 1949, relatively greater emphasis has been given to the development of industry and mining at the expense of agriculture, although the absolute overall level of agricultural output continues to rise, attributed, in part, to increased mechanization. By 1960, Shantung also had 18 state farms—ten arable (crop raising) and eight livestock.

Agriculture. The leading food crops—wheat, soybeans, kaoliang (grain sorghum), spiked millet, corn (maize), and sweet potatoes—account for 90 percent of the total cultivated acreage of the province. The remaining arable land is given over to cash crops, chiefly cotton, peanuts, tobacco, and fruit. More than 30 to 40 percent of the food crop acreage is planted to wheat, followed by soybeans (15 to 20 percent), kaoliang and spiked millet (sharing about 10 percent), and corn and sweet potatoes (10 to 15 percent).

Principal cash crops

The cash crops are grown on only 10 percent of the province's cultivable land, yet contribute substantially to agricultural earnings. Cotton, a leading cash crop, is grown throughout the province but is concentrated in the western and northern sections on the intensively irrigated lands near the mouth of the Huang Ho.

Shantung's other major cash crop, peanuts, is grown over approximately the same number of acres as cotton, but its cultivation is centred in the peninsular uplands and in the south central sector. The large variety of peanuts grown in Shantung is especially well suited for oil pressing, and Shantung is a leading manufacturer of peanut oil for cooking. Shantung's average annual peanut crop amounts to between one-third and one-half of the total national output, and some of the crop is exported.

Other cash crops include tobacco, grown chiefly on irrigated land in the vicinity of I-tu and Wei-fang; hemp, produced on low ground in the southwest; and fruit, grown on the lower slopes of the central and peninsular hill masses. Common fruits include peaches, pears, apricots, apples, grapes, persimmons, and dates.

Animal husbandry plays an important role. The most common animals are yellow oxen and donkeys. Both are used as draft animals, with oxen more prevalent in the level areas in the north and west and donkeys in the uplands. Some sheep are also raised in the uplands.

Sericulture (silkworm raising), another important subsidiary activity, has been carried out in Shantung for hundreds of years. The popular fabric known as shantung was originally a rough-textured tussah, or wild silk, cloth made in the province. Silkworm raising is most common in the central hills near I-tu, Lin-ch'ü, Tzu-ch'uan, and Lai-wu, and most of the raw silk is sent to other provinces for processing and spinning.

Irrigation and flood control

Irrigation and flood control are crucial to the success of Shantung's agricultural economy and the province was one of the first to put irrigation districts (after 1958) under commune control. Before World War II, only 3 percent of the province's cultivable land was irrigated, with major irrigation works being situated throughout the level zones north and west of the central hill mass, and on the peninsular north coastal plain. The irrigated areas have been continuously expanded since 1949, and by the early 1970s more than 90 percent of the cultivable and sown acreage of the province was irrigated. Irrigation water is derived chiefly from wells, although much effort also has been given to the construction of multipurpose flood control and irrigation systems associated with the natural watersheds of rivers. The most extensive projects have been carried out on the Hsiao-ch'ing Ho system south of the Huang Ho near Tsinan and Tzu-po Shih. Canals, dikes, and retention dams have been built and riverbeds widened and straightened.

Fishing. Shantung's seaward orientation and its excellent harbours, as well as the convergence of cold and warm currents in offshore waters, have fostered a thriving ocean fishing industry, complemented by the intensive development of pisciculture in the province's western lake region. Trawlers and smaller fishing craft operate from more than 70 ports around the peninsula and off the Huang Ho delta. The leading ports, by tonnage of fish landed, are Tsingtao, Chefoo, Wei-hai, Shih-tao, and Lung-k'ou. Annual fish production comes to more than 600,000 tons—second only to Kwangtung Province. The ocean catch, amounting to nearly 90 percent of the annual total, consists mainly of eels, herring, gizzard-shad, fish roe, and several varieties of shrimp and crab. Freshwater varieties raised artificially are chiefly carp and crucian carp.

Minerals and mining. Shantung's industrial base is supported by extensive mining activities. Coal mines were originally developed by German concessionnaires between 1898 and 1915. The annual production capacity of one of the earliest and largest coal-mining complexes, Po-shan (part of Tzu-po Shih), approaches 6,000,000 tons, or nearly 70 percent of the province's total. Other pre-1949 mining sites, since enlarged, include Chai-wang, south of Tsao-chuang, near the Kiangsu border; and T'ao-chuang, in the south central hills north of Chi-ning. Newly developed mines, largely mechanized, are at Chiu-jung-ch'eng, at the tip of the peninsula; Hsin-wen (Sun-ts'un), in the central hills south of Tzu-po; and Fei-ch'eng, west of T'ai-an also in the central hills.

Major iron-ore deposits are located north of Tzu-po at Chin-ling-chen, with reserves estimated at 100,000,000 tons; minor deposits are found near Tsao-chuang and Tsingtao. Some bauxite is mined near Tzu-po Shih (Nanting), and gold is scattered throughout the peninsular hills. One major oil field is in operation at Sheng-li, in the Huang Ho delta region north of Tzu-po.

Edible salt is produced on both the north and south coasts of the Shantung Peninsula. Production from the largest field, along the shores of Chiao-chou Wan near Tsingtao, accounts for over three-fifths of the province's total. Salt, formerly exported in large quantities to Japan, is largely consumed domestically.

Industry. The province is still especially well-known for its light industrial products, despite post-1949 gains in heavy industry. The leading manufacturing centres, accounting for nearly 80 percent of the province's total industrial output, are Tsingtao, Tsinan, Tzu-po, and Wei-fang, all situated along the Tsinan–Tsingtao railway and all but Wei-fang with major thermal electric installations.

Light industry and handicrafts

Tsingtao, the major manufacturing centre, has a large textile industry—five-sixths of the province's total plants—a locomotive works, industrial chemical, tire, and machine-tool factories. Pre-World War II oil pressing (peanut oil), cigarette making, flour milling, brewing, and beverage distilling installations are still important. Tsinan—long famous for its silks, precious stones, handicrafts, munitions, flour, and electrical components—now also manufactures trucks, agricultural machinery, machine tools, precision instruments, industrial chemicals, chemical fertilizers, paper, and textiles. Tzu-po produces glass, porcelain and ceramics, silk and textiles; while Wei-fang is an important food-processing centre, and has metal-processing and textile factories. Other, secondary industrial centres include Nan-ting, Hsin-t'ai-hsien, Han-chuang, Tsao-chuang, I-hsien, Tung-liang-chuang, and Chefoo.

Some of Shantung's better known handicraft goods are embroidered tablecloths from Chefoo and Lin-tzu (east of Tzu-po), straw braids for hat weaving from P'ing-tu (east of Wei-fang), poplins, pottery, and ceramics.

Transportation and communications. Shantung's first railways were built in the first decade of the 20th century during the time of the German concession. One of the lines traverses the province from north to south and another east and west, connecting Tsingtao and Tsinan. Since 1949 new lines have been built, and some sections of the existing routes converted to double track. A major new trunk line was completed in 1956, from Tsingtao north to Chefoo. The province has a total of 518 miles of rail trunk lines and 90 miles of branch lines.

Shantung's highways connect every district in the province, but most of them have earthen surfaces and are used either for short-haul transport or as feeder routes for the three major railways. Of the roughly 6,000 miles of roads in the province, only about a quarter are suitable for all-weather use. Nevertheless, truck traffic accounts for more than 60 percent of the total annual vehicular movement over Shantung's highways, as compared with only 20 percent (estimated) in other North China provinces.

Limited use of inland waterways

Except for portions of the Huang Ho and of the Hsiao-ch'ing Ho in northern Shantung, part of the Grand Canal in the west, and the I Ho in the southeast, inland-waterway transport is limited. The chief route—for shallow-draft craft only—extends upstream from Li-chin, about 50 miles inland from the mouth of the Huang Ho, for about 125 miles to Ch'i-ho, the main Huang Ho river port in Shantung and just northwest of Tsinan. The Grand Canal is navigable only to a limited extent south of the Huang Ho.

Shantung has a number of excellent seaports. Tsingtao, the largest in tonnage handled, can berth vessels of more than 10,000 deadweight tons at its piers. On the north coast of the peninsula, Chefoo, Wei-hai, and Lung-k'ou can handle vessels up to 6,000 tons. Coastal shipping also plays an important role in Shantung's economy. Tsingtao alone handles over a third of the province's intraprovince trade. Goods transshipped at Tsingtao for coastal distribution within Shantung include cotton cloth, coal, general cargo, and fertilizer. Salt, tobacco, chemicals, coal, processed foods, and sea products are shipped southward along the China coast as far as Foochow and Swatow, as well as to points along the Gulf of Liaotung and the Liaotung Peninsula to the north. Trade between Tsingtao and Shanghai and Tsingtao and Dairen (Lü-ta) is particularly heavy.

CULTURAL LIFE AND INSTITUTIONS

Temples and shrines

Shantung's rich cultural and folklore tradition is most clearly evidenced in the temples, shrines, legends, and cults associated with T'ai Shan (Mt. T'ai) and with the temple and tomb of Confucius at Ch'ü-fu, north of Chining. Since 1949, despite official disavowal of their religious, parareligious, animistic, and superstitious connotations, the temples, shrines, and their surrounding areas have been restored, renovated, and converted to public parks so as to assure their preservation as important symbols of the national cultural heritage. T'ai Shan—known also as *tung-yüeh*, or "Eastern Peak," to distinguish it from the "Southern Peak" (in Hunan); the "Central Peak" (Honan); the "Western Peak" (Shensi); and the "Northern Peak" (Shansi)—is the most prominent of these five sacred mountains where the emperors once offered sacrifices to Heaven and Earth. It was also the place where for centuries Buddhists, Taoists, and Confucianists built more than 250 temples and monuments to honour deified historical personages and to immortalize the sacred presence and supernatural powers of the supreme mountain deity, the T'ai Shan. The mountain rises precipitously to a height of 5,069 feet (1,545 metres); as the highest peak in the central Shantung hill mass, it affords spectacular views of the surrounding areas from its summit. The mountain was deified at least as early as Han times (2nd century BC–2nd century AD), and in the Sung dynasty it was elevated by the emperor, Chen-tsung, to the position of "Equal with Heaven." Incantations and prayers offered to the T'ai Shan deity by countless emperors are inscribed in steles along the ascent to the summit, and the temples are distributed in T'ai-an and on the mountain itself. T'ai Shan was also thought to be the gathering place for souls of deceased persons.

The Temple of Confucius, Confucius' tomb, and the residence of the Kungs (Confucius' lineal descendants) at Ch'ü-fu are also maintained as national historic monuments. Both the temple and the Kung residence are laid out with elaborate temples, monuments, pavilions, and gates, and have collections of steles dating, in some cases, from the Han dynasty.

There are no television stations in the province but there are several theatres and cinemas in Tsiman. Tsingtao has a municipal museum, as well as a Marine Products Museum.

BIBLIOGRAPHY. Sources of information on Shantung are given in the bibliography of the article SHANSI.

(B.Bo.)

Shāpūr II of Persia

Shāpūr (reigned AD 309–379) was tenth in the long line of the "kings of kings" who ruled the Sāsānian Empire of Persia (Iran). A general who personally led vast armies in battle, he was a remarkable tactician and a consummate politician who succeeded in spreading dissension among his enemies. Though usually merciful and just, he was savage in his persecution of Christians and unfeeling

in the enslavement and forced resettlement of prisoners of war in Persia. But in those few words of his own that have survived, he speaks of his virtuous conduct and of his clear conscience. Shāpūr's unflagging devotion to the empire brought it to the zenith of its power and glory.

Shāpūr II, gold coin, 4th century. In the British Museum.
By courtesy of the trustees of the British Museum; photograph, J.R. Freeman & Co. Ltd.

The name Shāpūr, "son of a king," was common in the Sāsānian period and was often given to sons other than princes. Numerical designations were not used to distinguish kings of the same name; instead, the family genealogy was cited. Thus, in one inscription, Shāpūr styles himself,

the Mazdāh-worshipping god Shāpūr, king of kings of Iran and non-Iran, who is a scion of the Gods, the son of Hormizd (Ormizd II), the grandson of Narses.

According to tradition, he was a posthumous child proclaimed king by the Persian nobility at his birth in 309, in preference to his brothers. After a regency, he apparently took the realm into his own hands in 325 at the age of 16.

A contemporary account describes his appearance and courage in battle:

And he himself, mounted on his charger, and being taller than the rest, led his whole army, wearing instead of a crown a golden figure of a ram's head inlaid with jewels; being also splendid from the retinue of men of high rank and of different nations which followed him . . . He rode up to the gates [of Amida]; escorted by the cohort of his royal guard; and while pushing on more boldly, so that his very features might be plainly recognized, his ornaments made him such a mark for arrows and other missiles, that he would have been slain, if the dust had not hindered the sight of those who were shooting at him; so that after a part of his robe had been cut off by a blow of a javelin, he escaped to cause vast slaughter at a future time.

In 337 Shāpūr sent his forces across the Tigris River, the uneasy frontier, to recover Armenia and Mesopotamia, which his predecessors had lost to the Romans. Until 350 conflict raged in northern Mesopotamia, with neither side a clear-cut victor. Shortly after 337, Shāpūr took an important policy decision. Although the state religion of the Sāsānian Empire was Mazdaism (Zoroastrianism), Christianity flourished within its boundaries. The Roman emperor Constantine the Great had granted toleration to Christians in 313. With the subsequent Christianization of the empire, Shāpūr, mistrustful of a potential force of a fifth column at home while he was engaged abroad, ordered the persecution and forcible conversion of the Christians; this policy was in force throughout his reign.

Persecution of Christians

In 358 he was ready for a second encounter with Rome and sent an ambassador to the emperor Constantius II, bearing presents and a letter wrapped in white silk. This letter read, in part,

I Sapor, king of kings, partner of the stars, brother of the sun and the moon, to Constantius Caesar my brother send much greeting. . . . Because . . . the language of truth ought to be unrestrained and free, and because men in the highest rank ought only to say what they mean, I will reduce my propositions into a few words . . . Even your own ancient records bear witness that my ancestors possessed all the country up to the Strymon and the frontier of Macedonia. And these lands it is fitting that I who (not to speak arrogantly) am superior to those ancient kings in magnificence, and in all eminent virtues, should now reclaim. But I am at all times thoughtful to remember that, from my earliest youth, I have never done anything to repent of.

When Constantius politely refused to hand over these lands, Shāpūr marched into northern Mesopotamia, this time with marked success. In 363, however, the emperor Julian led a huge army into Persia, creating havoc and advancing to the very gates of Ctesiphon on the Tigris, a major Sāsānian city. Julian was mortally wounded in a skirmish, and his successor, Jovian, was compelled to accept an ignominious 30 years' truce and surrender of five Roman provinces.

Conquest of Armenia   Shāpūr then turned his attention to the subjugation of Armenia. He defeated its pro-Roman ruler and attempted to force Zoroastrianism on the country. The Romans, however, regained their influence in Armenia, and a precarious balance between Romans and Persians existed about 374. For five years, Armenia was weakened by internecine strife, and one of Shāpūr's last acts was to win it over by discreet gifts. Shāpūr's death in 379 left Persia with its territory considerably augmented: he had pacified the eastern frontier and gained control over Armenia; the Persian Empire had never been stronger. But war with Rome had become habitual and eventually undermined the strength of the Sāsānians.

As did the other great rulers of his line, Shāpūr considered himself an heir of the great Achaemenid Empire and strove to renew its glory. Indeed, his letter to Constantius contains a distant echo of the wording of the inscriptions of Darius I the Great, the Achaemenid ruler, when he writes of his devotion to truth and righteousness. Shāpūr was called a god, and he lived up to this exalted status, becoming irascible, even violent, when individuals summoned to his presence appeared to pay insufficient respect to his awesome majesty.

The figure of Shāpūr survives. A large silver plate has a scene in relief that shows him hunting lions with bow and arrow, and countless silver coins portray his face in profile. At Bishapur in southwestern Iran, a tremendous rock-cut relief depicts him seated on a throne and witnessing a triumph of his army: in the top row he is flanked by nobles of the court, and the lower row contains soldiers who present captives and trophies of victory.

BIBLIOGRAPHY. *The Roman History of Ammianus Marcellinus During the Reigns of the Emperors Constantius, Julian, Jovianus, Valentinian, and Valens*, trans. by C.D. YONGE (1902), is a detailed, often fascinating, account of Rome's wars against major enemies. The information on those with the Sāsānian Empire is not duplicated by any other source. SIR PERCY SYKES, *A History of Persia*, vol. 1 (1915, 3rd ed. reprinted 1958), is a major work, although the facts are not always documented and parts are now outdated (contains an extensive bibliography).

(D.N.W.)

Shaw, George Bernard

The most significant British playwright since the 17th century, George Bernard Shaw was more than merely the best comic dramatist of his time, for some of his greatest works for the stage—*Caesar and Cleopatra*, the "Don Juan in Hell" episode of *Man and Superman, Major Barbara, Heartbreak House*, and *Saint Joan*—have a high seriousness and prose beauty unmatched by his stage contemporaries. A visionary and mystic whose philosophy of moral passion permeates his plays, Shaw was also the most trenchant pamphleteer since Swift; the most readable music critic in English; the best theatre critic of his generation; a prodigious lecturer and essayist on politics, economics, and sociological subjects; and the most prolific letter writer in literature. Impudent and irreverent, always a showman, he used his buoyant "Shavian" wit to keep himself in the public eye to the end of his 94 years; his wiry figure, bristling beard, and dandyish cane were as well-known throughout the world as his plays.

Early life and career.   George Bernard Shaw was born on July 26, 1856, in Dublin, the third and youngest child (and only son) of George Carr Shaw and Lucinda Elizabeth Gurly Shaw. Technically, he belonged to the Protestant "ascendancy"—the landed Irish gentry; but his fa-

George Bernard Shaw.
© Karsh

ther (first a sinecured civil servant and then an unsuccessful grain merchant) was too impractical and intemperate to sustain anything more than a "downstart" atmosphere of genteel impecuniosity, which to his son was more humiliating than being born poor. At first tutored by a clerical uncle, Shaw then attended—briefly—both Protestant and Catholic day schools. Before he was 16, he was working in a land agent's office.

Music pervaded the Shaw household. When Shaw was a child his mother turned for consolation not only to music but also to her music teacher, George John Vandeleur Lee, a mesmeric figure in Irish music circles, who, by 1886, shared households in Dublin with the Shaws. When his mother and sisters left his father in Dublin and followed Lee to London in 1875, young Shaw followed the next year.

Shaw in his 20s suffered continuous frustration and poverty. For a brief period, he produced ghost-written musical criticism for Lee, and from late 1879 to mid-1880, he worked for the Edison Telephone Company of London. It was his last non-literary employment. Living with his mother and elder sister Lucy (Agnes, his other sister, had died in 1876), he depended upon their pound a week from a family bequest and his mother's earnings as a music teacher. He spent his afternoons in the British Museum reading room, writing novels and reading what he had missed at school, and his evenings in search of additional self-education in the lectures and debates that characterized contemporary middle class London intellectual ferment.

His fiction failed utterly. The semi-autobiographical and aptly titled *Immaturity* (1879; published 1930) repelled every publisher in London. His next four novels, similarly refused, soon padded propagandist magazines edited by Shaw's Socialist friends. Shaw later pronounced *The Irrational Knot* a forerunner of the dramatist Henrik Ibsen, of whom he had not yet heard, for the hero marries at the beginning and abandons his wife at the end. With his halfhearted attempts at job hunting still fruitless, he began *Love Among the Artists*, in which the neglect of "a British Beethoven" among dilettantes and mediocrities reflected Shaw's passionate belief in his own talents and his bitterness at being thwarted; midway through the manuscript he was stricken during the 1881 smallpox outbreak in London, but he stubbornly completed the unsalable novel. The next year he began another, *Cashel Byron's Profession*. Its exuberance belied Shaw's lack of success, and its core ("immoral" and "retrograde" professions—in this case, prizefighting—as an indictment of society) anticipated such early plays as *Mrs. Warren's*

Failure at fiction

Profession. (In 1901 he satirized this novel in a burlesque Elizabethan blank-verse adaptation. *The Admirable Bashville* [performed 1902].) The Socialism in *Cashel Byron* had been an afterthought, most of it inserted for its magazine appearance after a lecture in 1882 by the U.S. economist Henry George spurred Shaw to a reading of Marx. The new gospel was also the stimulus for his last novel, *An Unsocial Socialist,* which broke down under the weight of its incongruities, among them a runaway husband, a finishing school for girls, and ponderous paraphrases from Marx's *Capital.* A fragment posthumously published as *An Unfinished Novel* in 1958 (but written 1887-88) was his final false start in fiction (but for a 1932 *Candide*-like novella, *The Adventures of the Black Girl in Her Search for God*).

Despite his failure as a novelist in the 1880s, Shaw found himself during this decade. He became a vegetarian, a Socialist, a spellbinding orator, a polemicist, even tentatively a playwright. He became the force behind the newly founded (1884) Fabian Society, a middle class Socialist group that aimed at the transformation of English society not through revolution but through "permeation" (in Sidney Webb's term)) of the nation's intellectual and political life. Shaw involved himself in every aspect of its activities, most visibly as editor of one of the classics of British Socialism, *Fabian Essays in Socialism* (1889), to which he also contributed two sections.

Pamphleteer and platform speaker A pamphleteer and platform speaker of rare dialectical skill, he spoke to crowds of any size, often as frequently as three times a week, and always without compensation. The experience forged the forceful prose of his missionary books *The Quintessence of Ibsenism* (1891, 1913) and *The Perfect Wagnerite*—on behalf of Ibsen and the composer Richard Wagner, respectively—and *The Common Sense of Municipal Trading*—the result of his years, from 1897 to 1903, as vestryman and borough councillor of St. Pancras Parish, London. His early journalism ranged from bread-and-butter book reviews in the *Pall Mall Gazette* (1885-88) and art criticism in the *World* (1886-89) to brilliant (and often brilliantly digressive) musical columns in the *Star* (as "Corno di Bassetto"—basset horn) from 1888 to 1890 and in the *World* (as "G.B.S.") from 1890 to 1894. With passionate objectivity (but for his Wagnerism), he scorned mediocrity and applauded excellence in a manner consistent with his contention that the true critic "is the man who becomes your personal enemy on the sole provocation of a bad performance, and will only be appeased by good performances." Recruited by Frank Harris to the *Saturday Review* as theatre critic (1895-98), he campaigned there to displace the artificialities and hypocrisies of the Victorian stage (Shaw called them "Sardoodledom"—an allusion to the prolific French dramatist Victorien Sardou) with a theatre of vital ideas.

First plays. With the "New Drama" in England little more than "a figment of the revolutionary imagination," Shaw determined that since "I had rashly taken up the case . . . rather than let it collapse I manufactured the evidence." That effort became his primary activity during the 1890s. Shaw began his first major experiment as playwright in 1884, when the critic William Archer suggested a collaboration (Archer to supply the plot, Shaw, the dialogue). Eight years later, in 1892, Shaw completed the abortive drama on his own; *Widowers' Houses* had two performances and created a newspaper sensation. Combining Ibsen, Socialism, and slum landlordism, it flouted the threadbare romantic conventions that were still being exploited, even by the most daring new playwrights.

Next, unafraid to satirize himself, Shaw in *The Philanderer* invented an "Ibsen Club" and even ridiculed the socially emancipated "New Woman," thereby mocking two new movements he championed. No one would produce the play, but Shaw, undeterred, began the sardonic *Mrs. Warren's Profession.* The lord chamberlain, as the censor of plays, refused it a license although its ostensible subject—prostitution—was treated remorselessly and without the titillation of fashionable comedies about "fallen women."

Shaw's first volume of collected plays, *Plays, Pleasant and Unpleasant,* was published in 1898. Labelling the first three "unpleasant," Shaw explained that "their dramatic power is used to force the spectator to face unpleasant facts." The "pleasant" plays were Shaw's attempt to find the producers and audiences that his mordant comedies put off. "To me," he explained, "[both] the tragedy and comedy of life lies in the consequences, sometimes terrible, sometimes ludicrous, of our persistent attempts to found our institutions on the ideals suggested to our imaginations by our half-satisfied passions, instead of on a genuinely scientific natural history." *Arms and the Man,* in a spoof-Balkan setting, satirized romantic falsifications of love, war, and upward mobility and was itself romanticized (unauthorized by Shaw) in the Oscar Straus operetta *Der tapfere Soldat* (1908), translated as *The Chocolate Soldier* (1909). In *Candida,* the wife—who represents herself in a tour de force "auction scene" as being compelled to choose between her clergyman husband (a well-meaning Christian Socialist) and an immature young poet—chooses her stuffy husband, while the interloper renounces what Shaw later called "the small beer of domestic happiness" for the larger creative purpose he senses within himself. The two other "pleasant" plays were of lighter weight. The one-act *Man of Destiny,* about Napoleon I, was described by Shaw as merely "a bravura piece to display the virtuosity of two performers"; his antidote to the "older, coarser Napoleon" of previous plays, it was his first study in greatness. First volume of collected plays

The strain of writing these plays, while his critical and political work went on unabated, so sapped his strength that a minor illness became a major one. In 1898, during the process of recuperation, he married his unofficial nurse, Charlotte Payne-Townshend, an Irish heiress and friend of Beatrice and Sidney Webb. The apparently celibate marriage lasted all their lives, Shaw having satisfied his sexual needs in premarital affairs with an aggressive widow and several actresses, and his later emotional requisites in paper-passion correspondences with Ellen Terry, Mrs. Patrick Campbell, and others.

Shaw's next collection, *Three Plays for Puritans* (1901), continued what became the traditional Shavian preface —an introductory essay in an electric prose style dealing as much with the themes suggested by the plays as the plays themselves. The texts, made available to the wider reading public for many of whom the plays were inaccessible even when produced, included—a Shaw innovation —stage directions and descriptions in narrative form rather than in the brevity of directorial jargon. In *The Devil's Disciple*—a play set in New Hampshire during the American Revolution and written as an inversion of traditional melodrama—Dick Dudgeon, the black sheep of his family (because he rejects Puritan masochism and hypocrisy), heroically substitutes for a rebel minister condemned to the gallows, acting spontaneously out of some instinctive imperative. As with Caesar and similar Shavian protagonists, virtue is a quality, not an achievement. The Shavian preface

In his preface to *Caesar and Cleopatra,* Shaw lays down the challenge "Better than Shakespear?" but evades it by dramatizing a 16-year-old Cleopatra rather than the 38-year-old temptress of Shakespeare's *Antony and Cleopatra.* In addition, Shaw's Caesar in Egypt has not yet been enticed into the domestic demagoguery against which Brutus reacts in Shakespeare's *Julius Caesar.* Shaw's feline Cleopatra, however, is a logical precursor to Shakespeare's; and his Caesar, as much philosopher as soldier in this mentor-disciple play, is meant to be a study in credible magnanimity and "original morality" rather than a superhuman hero on a stage pedestal—in Shaw's words, a hero "in whom we can recognize our own humanity." In this seriocomic chronicle play, Shaw rises to prose-poetic eloquence and wisdom.

International importance. In *Man and Superman* Shaw took the legend of Don Juan as found in Mozart's opera *Don Giovanni* and made it a dramatic parable prefiguring the philosophy expounded in Henri Bergson's *Creative Evolution* (1907). Shaw described a purposeful and eternal movement toward ever-higher organisms; he saw this to be a more satisfactory explanation of the nature of things than "blind" Darwinian evolution and one that restored a sense of divinity to the universe as well. Subtitled "A Comedy and a Philosophy," the play on the surface is a comedy of manners about the relations between the sexes in which a resourceful young woman schemes to capture her man, who is a social philosopher and Socialist propagandist. The action provides the basis for Shaw to explore the intellectual climate of the new century in a series of interlocking debates and discussions. Its nonrealistic third act, the "Don Juan in Hell" dream scene (performed 1907), is often played independently: mythic counterparts to the major characters in *Man and Superman*, including Don Juan and the devil, play out a dramatic quartet that is spoken theatre at its most operatic.

The eminent poet William Butler Yeats asked Shaw to write a play for the Irish Literary Theatre, Dublin, but when Shaw presented him with *John Bull's Other Island*, Yeats timidly rejected it. Although its politics have dated, the play when performed as a period piece reveals Shaw's perceptiveness about the Irish character, and it remains one of his most amusing comedies. The minor but exquisitely drawn character of the unfrocked priest Father Keegan is one of his earliest explorations of the religious rebel as saint.

Shaw had already become established as a major playwright on the Continent by the performance of his plays there, but, curiously, his reputation lagged in England. It was only with the production of *John Bull* in London, with a special performance for Edward VII, that Shaw's stage reputation was belatedly made in England. He backed the actor-manager Harley Granville-Barker's management of the Royal Court Theatre, not only with his own capital but also with his plays; and in the years of their association (1904–07), Shavian drama reached a seldom-equalled level of performance.

Exploration of religious consciousness

Shaw continued, through high comedy, to explore religious consciousness and to point out society's complicity in its own evils. In *Major Barbara*, Shaw has his heroine, a major in the Salvation Army, discover that her estranged father, a munitions manufacturer, may be a dealer in death but that his principles and practice, however unorthodox, are religious in the highest sense, while those of the Salvation Army require the hypocrisies of often-false public confession and the donations of the distillers and the armourers, against which it inveighs. In *The Doctor's Dilemma*, Shaw produced a comedy with a seriocomic death scene, a satire upon the medical profession (representing the self-protection of professions in general) and upon both the artistic temperament and the public's inability to separate it from the artist's achievement. In *Androcles and the Lion*, Shaw dealt with true and false religious exaltation, combining the traditions of miracle play and Christmas pantomime into a philosophical farce about early Christianity; its central theme, recurrent in Shaw, is that one must have something worth dying for—an end outside oneself—in order to make life worth living. His other plays of the prewar period include self-described pot-boilers, discussion-drama, and serious farce.

Possibly Shaw's comedic masterpiece, and certainly his funniest and most popular play, *Pygmalion*, was claimed by Shaw to be a didactic drama about phonetics, and its anti-heroic hero, Henry Higgins, is a phonetician; however, the play is a humane comedy about love and class, about a Cockney flower girl trained to pass as a lady and the repercussions of the experiment's success. It has been both filmed (1938), winning an Academy Award for Shaw for his screenplay, and adapted into an immensely popular musical, *My Fair Lady* (1956).

Works after World War I. World War I was a watershed for Shaw. At first he ceased writing plays, publishing instead a controversial pamphlet. "Common Sense About the War" (*New Statesman*, supplement, November 14, 1914), which called Britain and its Allies equally culpable with the Germans and argued for negotiation and peace. It made him notorious. Some of his anti-war speeches were erased from history by newspaper censorship, and he was ejected from the Dramatists'

Club, although he was its most distinguished member. Only when the nation was ground down by astronomical casualties and home-front austerities did a more rational attitude toward him prevail. In *Heartbreak House*, Shaw exposed, in a country-house setting on the eve of war, the spiritual bankruptcy of the generation responsible for the bloodshed. Combining discursive high comedy with a new symbolism, he produced a sombre vision owing much in mood to Chekhov's *Cherry Orchard* and, in its patriarchal protagonist, to Shakespeare's *Lear*.

Shaw's parable of creative evolution

Attempting to keep from falling into "the bottomless pit of an utterly discouraging pessimism," Shaw wrote five linked plays under the collective title *Back to Methuselah;* together they comprise a parable of creative evolution that progresses from the Garden of Eden to AD 31,920. The first of the five plays, *In the Beginning*, through Adam and Eve (and the Serpent) and Cain and Abel, dramatizes the need to have aspirations beyond mere subsistence. (Serpent: "You see things; and say 'Why?' But I dream things that never were; and I say 'Why not?' "). The *Gospel of the Brothers Barnabas*, set just after World War I, indicts the politicians who made the war and suggests that sufficient longevity to learn from experience—perhaps 300 years—might be willed. Two undistinguished characters from the cycle's second play prove to be still alive in *The Thing Happens*, in AD 2170, and longevity has given them wisdom. In *The Tragedy of an Elderly Gentleman*, a survivor from the dwindling race of short-livers confronts the passionless and ascetic long-livers, who possess extraordinary powers over nature, but—to the Gentleman—no soul. And in the last play, *As Far as Thought Can Reach*, humans are born, fully developed, from eggs and after a brief adolescent phase of physical pleasure live lives of contemplative ecstasy achieved through creative use of intellect; and Shaw speculates, in satire ranging from bright to bleak, about the values of escaping from "this machinery of flesh and blood."

The canonization of Joan of Arc in 1920 reawakened within Shaw ideas for a chronicle play about her. The Maid became not only a Catholic saint and martyr but a Shavian one as well, a combination of practical mystic, heretical saint, and inspired genius. Joan, as the superior being (in the Inquisitor's words), "crushed between those mighty forces, the Church and the Law," is the personification of the tragic heroine, but to Shaw classical tragedy was not enough: thus, in the dream-epilogue, he moves from satire to litany and transforms the play from a tragedy of inevitability to an embodiment of the paradox that humankind fears—and often kills—its saints and heroes and will go on doing so until the very qualities it fears become the general condition of man. Acclaim for *Saint Joan* resulted in a Shavian apotheosis, including the 1925 Nobel Prize for Literature.

Success of Saint Joan

In his last plays Shaw intensified his explorations into tragicomic and nonrealistic symbolism, using an extravagance reminiscent of the comedy of the ancient Greek master Aristophanes; it was designed to explode the verisimilitude Shaw had taken from Ibsen and to remind audiences that these were performances in a theatre. For the next five years, he wrote nothing for the theatre but worked on his collected edition of 1930–38 and the encyclopaedic political tract "The Intelligent Woman's Guide to Socialism and Capitalism" (1928). Then he produced the Platonic "political extravaganza" *The Apple Cart*, a futuristic high comedy that emphasized Shavian inner conflicts between his lifetime of radical politics and his essentially conservative mistrust of the common man's ability to govern himself. His later plays included apocalyptic imagery, warning that 1914–18 was about to be repeated. The deliberately absurd *Too True to Be Good* (performed 1932; published 1934) is a dream-fantasy including a Bunyanesque prophet, a Lawrence of Arabia caricature, and a burglar-turned-preacher who, as the curtain closes upon him, suggests Shaw confronting his own obsolescence. (From their first meeting in 1922 until Lawrence's death in 1935 the Shaws treated the colonel–turned–private—"Private Meek" in the play—as a surrogate son, Lawrence even implicitly acknowledging the relationship in his legal change of name to T.E. Shaw in 1927.) In *On The Rocks* (performed 1933; published 1934), he predicts the collapse of parliamentary government in a protofascist, depression-ridden England, and in *The Simpleton of the Unexpected Isles* (performed 1935; published 1936), set in a futuristic South Seas, he satirizes a eugenic solution to human problems and ends with a Day of Judgment. In *Geneva* (performed 1938; published 1939; revised 1947), Shaw lampoons the futile League of Nations, and the dictators Hitler, Mussolini, and Franco appear on the stage, thinly disguised; that the despots are treated so lightly suggests that Shaw's flirtation with dictatorships, which arose out of the 1914–18 disillusionment with democracies, was slow in dying, the one with Stalin stubbornly enduring to the end. *In Good King Charles's Golden Days* (performed and published 1939), his last play before World War II, is a throwback to the mood of *The Apple Cart*, a warm yet discursive high comedy in which Charles II, Sir Isaac Newton, Charles James Fox, Nell Gwyn, and luminaries of 17th-century England debate leadership, science, art, and religion; in it Shaw again dwells upon the major preoccupation of his later years: "The riddle of how to choose a ruler is still unanswered," says Charles, "and it is the riddle of civilization."

Late works after World War II. After a wartime hiatus, Shaw, now in his 90s, produced several more plays. In *Farfetched Fables* (performed 1950; published 1951), a farce in six short scenes, Shaw again attempted to see ironically into a timeless future; *Shakes Versus Shav* (performed 1949; published 1951) is a brief puppet play in which the "rival" playwrights confront each other. A last playlet, *Why She Would Not* (published 1956), is a fantasy with only flashes of the earlier Shaw.

When Shaw's wife, Charlotte, died of a lingering illness in 1943, in the midst of World War II, Shaw, frail and feeling the effects of wartime privations, made permanent his retreat from his London apartment to his country home at Ayot St. Lawrence, a Hertfordshire village in which he had lived since 1906. He died there at 94 on November 2, 1950, having continued to write and to maintain the indomitable "G.B.S." persona to the end.

Although Shaw left his estate for research into a 40-letter phonetic alphabet, his residual legatees, the British Museum, the Royal Academy of Dramatic Art, and the National Gallery of Ireland, overturned the will in their favour, settling a token sum for an alphabet competition and publication of *Androcles and the Lion* in the winning system (1962). He also directed the public trustee to publish his work under the name of Bernard Shaw, hoping thus to forever eliminate from his authorized writings the "George" he disliked.

Influence on drama Shaw left no school of playwrights as such. Yet his development of a drama of moral passion and of intellectual conflict and debate, his revivifying the comedy of manners, his ventures into symbolic farce and into a theatre of disbelief helped shape the theatre of his time and after. By bringing a bold critical intelligence to his many other areas of interest, he helped mold the political, economic, and sociological thought of three generations.

MAJOR WORKS

PLAYS AND DRAMATIC PIECES: *Widowers' Houses* (performed 1892, published 1893); *Mrs. Warren's Profession* (performed 1902, published 1898); *Arms and the Man* (performed 1894, published 1898); *Candida* (performed 1897, published 1898); *You Never Can Tell* (performed 1899, published 1898); *The Man of Destiny* (performed 1897, published 1898); *The Philanderer* (performed 1898, published 1898); *The Devil's Disciple* (performed 1897, published 1901); *Caesar and Cleopatra* (performed 1901, published 1901); *Captain Brassbound's Conversion* (performed 1900, published 1901); *Man and Superman* (performed 1905, published 1903); *John Bull's Other Island* (performed 1904, published 1907); *Major Barbara* (performed 1905, published 1907); *The Doctor's Dilemma* (performed 1906, published 1911); *The Shewing-Up of Blanco Posnet* (performed 1909, published 1911); *Getting Married* (performed 1908, published 1911); *Misalliance* (performed 1910, published 1911); *Fanny's First Play* (performed 1911, published 1914); *Overruled* (performed 1912, published 1916); *Androcles and the Lion* (performed 1912, published 1916); *Pygmalion* (per-

formed 1913, published 1916); *Heartbreak House* (performed 1920, published 1919); *Back to Methuselah* (performed 1922, published 1921); *Saint Joan* (performed 1923, published 1924); *The Apple Cart* (performed 1929, published 1930).

OTHER WRITINGS: (POLITICAL): *Fabian Essays in Socialism* (1889); *The Common Sense of Municipal Trading* (1904, 1908); "Common Sense about the War" (1914); "The Intelligent Woman's Guide to Socialism and Capitalism" (1928); "What I Really Wrote About the War" (1931); "Everybody's Political What's What?" (1944). (NOVELS): *An Unsocial Socialist* (serialized in *To-Day* 1884, published as book 1887); *Cashel Byron's Profession* (serialized in *To-Day* 1885-86, published as book 1886); *The Irrational Knot* (serialized in *Our Corner* 1885–87, published as book 1905); *Love Among the Artists* (serialized in *Our Corner* 1887–88, published as book 1900). (MISCELLANEOUS): *The Quintessence of Ibsenism* (1891, 1913); *The Perfect Wagnerite* (1898); *Dramatic Opinions and Essays* (1907); *The Adventures of the Black Girl in Her Search for God* (1932).

BIBLIOGRAPHY. DAN H. LAURENCE, *Bernard Shaw: A Bibliography*, 2 vol. (1973).

Major collections: Berg Collection of the New York Public Library, British Museum, Cornell University, Harvard University, National Library of Ireland (Dublin), University of North Carolina, University of Texas.

Editions: Collected Edition, 33 vol. (1930–38); Constable Standard Edition, 18 vol. (1931–50); *The Bodley Head Bernard Shaw: Collected Plays with Their Prefaces*, 7 vol. (1970–). *Complete Plays*, 1 vol. (1931 and subsequent enlargements). *Complete Prefaces*, 1 vol. (1934 and subsequent enlargements). Individual plays are also available in the Penguin and Bobbs-Merrill paperback series. (*Reviews in collected editions*): *London Music in 1888–89* (1937); *Music in London 1890–94*, 3 vol. (1932); *Our Theatres in the Nineties*, 3 vol. (1932). (*Posthumous collections*): *Shaw on Theatre*, ed. by E.J. WEST (1958; rev. by DAN H. LAURENCE, 1961); *Shaw on Shakespeare*, ed. by EDWIN WILSON (1961); *How to Become a Musical Critic*, ed. by DAN H. LAURENCE (1961); *Religious Speeches of Bernard Shaw*, ed. by W.S. SMITH (1963); *Shaw on Language*, ed. by ABRAHAM TAUBER (1963); *Platform and Pulpit*, ed. by DAN H. LAURENCE (1961); *The Matter with Ireland*, ed. by DAN H. LAURENCE and DAVID H. GREENE (1962); *Shaw: The Chucker-Out*, ed. by ALLAN CHAPPELOW (1969), a miscellany of uncollected notes, journalism, speeches; *Bernard Shaw's Nondramatic Literary Criticism*, ed. by STANLEY WEINTRAUB (1972); *The Road to Equality*, ed. by LOUIS CROMPTON (1971), Socialist lectures; *Devilling in London*, ed. by DAN H. LAURENCE (1973), early journalism.

Correspondence: Collected Letters, ed. by DAN H. LAURENCE, 5 vol. (1964–); *Ellen Terry and Bernard Shaw*, ed. by CHRISTOPHER ST. JOHN (1931); *Bernard Shaw and Mrs. Patrick Campbell*, ed. by ALAN DENT (1952); *Advice to a Young Critic and Other Letters* (to R. Golding Bright), ed. by E.J. WEST (1955); *Shaw's Letters to Granville Barker*, ed. by C.B. PURDOM (1956); "The Nun and the Dramatist" (correspondence with Dame Laurentia McLachlan), *Cornhill*, no. 1008, pp. 415–458 (1956), and *In a Great Tradition*, ed. by the BENEDICTINES OF STANBROOK (1956); *To a Young Actress* (Molly Tompkins), ed. by PETER TOMPKINS (1960).

Autobiography: *Sixteen Self Sketches* (1949), collects and revises some earlier pieces and adds several new ones; *Shaw: An Autobiography*, 2 vol., ed. by STANLEY WEINTRAUB (1969–70), creates a patchwork autobiography from Shaw's myriad memoir writings and asides, and includes as appendix his last will and testament.

Translations: Freely adapted S. TREBITSCH's *Frau Gittas Sühne* as *Jitta's Atonement* (1920–21; pub. in *Translations and Tomfooleries*, 1926). Shaw's own works have been translated into all major languages, in some cases in his own lifetime the translations even appearing before publication in English.

Concordance: E. DEAN BEVAN, *A Concordance to the Plays and Prefaces of Bernard Shaw*, 10 vol. (1972).

Biography: ARCHIBALD HENDERSON, *George Bernard Shaw* (1911; rev. and augmented, 1932 and 1956); FRANK HARRIS, *Bernard Shaw* (1931); HESKETH PEARSON, *Bernard Shaw* (1943, augmented 1961); ST. JOHN ERVINE, *Bernard Shaw* (1956); ALLAN CHAPPELOW (ed.), *Shaw: The Villager and Human Being* (1961); B.C. ROSSET, *Shaw of Dublin: The Formative Years* (1964); STANLEY WEINTRAUB, *Private Shaw and Public Shaw* (1963), *Journey to Heartbreak: The Crucible Years of Bernard Shaw, 1914–18* (1971); JANET DUNBAR, *Mrs. G.B.S.* (1963); J.P. SMITH, *The Unrepentant Pilgrim* (1965).

Criticism: Early works include: H.L. MENCKEN, *George Bernard Shaw: His Plays* (1905); G.K. CHESTERTON, *George Bernard Shaw* (1909, augmented 1935); JULIUS BAB, *Bernard Shaw* (1910, rev. 1926; in German); and P.P. HOWE, *Bernard Shaw: A Critical Study* (1915). Later criticism includes: E. STRAUSS, *Bernard Shaw: Art and Socialism* (1942); STEPHEN WINSTEN (ed.), *G.B.S. 90* (1946); ERIC BENTLEY, *Bernard Shaw* (1947); WILLIAM IRVINE, *The Universe of G.B.S.* (1949); C.E.M. JOAD, *Shaw* (1949); ALICK WEST, *George Bernard Shaw: A Good Man Fallen Among Fabians* (1950); DESMOND MacCARTHY, *Shaw* (1951); A.H. NETHERCOT, *Men and Supermen*, 2nd ed. rev. (1966); RAYMOND MANDER and JOE MITCHENSON, *A Theatrical Companion to Shaw* (1954); J.B. KAYE, *Bernard Shaw and the Nineteenth-Century Tradition* (1958); R.M. OHMANN, *Shaw: The Style and the Man* (1962); MARTIN MEISEL, *Shaw and the Nineteenth-Century Theatre* (1963); J.I.M. STEWART, in *Eight Modern Writers* (1963); D.P. COSTELLO, *The Serpent's Eye: Shaw and the Cinema* (1965); LOUIS CROMPTON, *Shaw the Dramatist* (1969); B.F. DUKORE, *Bernard Shaw, Director* (1971); MARGERY MORGAN, *The Shavian Playground* (1972). Also *The Shavian* and *The Shaw Review* (both issued 3 times per year).

(S.We.)

Shelley, Percy Bysshe

Shelley was a poet, philosopher, reformer, novelist, and essayist. In a period of great poetry he wrote the greatest lyrical drama, the greatest tragedy, the greatest poem on love, the greatest pastoral elegy, and a body of short and long poems that many believe are unequalled in range of form and style, imagery and symbolism.

He was, however, not merely a man who wrote rapturous poetry. He was an idealist who loved mankind and a philosopher who sought reality and truth through reason and knowledge. He was also a rebel against all forms of wrong, to which he was as sensitive "as a nerve o'er which do creep/The else unfelt oppressions of this earth," a reformer of these evils in politics, religion, and conventional opinions and customs.

By courtesy of the National Portrait Gallery, London

Shelley, oil painting by Amelia Curran, 1819.
In the National Portrait Gallery, London.

EARLY YEARS

Childhood and education. Percy Bysshe Shelley was born on August 4, 1792, at Field Place, the family estate, near the market town of Horsham, in Sussex. He was the eldest son of Timothy Shelley (baronet, 1815), one of the wealthiest of the landed gentry, a Whig member of Parliament, and a follower of the Duke of Norfolk.

Shelley's difference from the common or normal man must not be overlooked. Most people, talented and untalented, have personal oddities and eccentricities. Shelley's difference is far deeper and very important. During a conversation Shelley's mother asked advice as to a proper school for her son Percy Bysshe. Her friend said offhand: "Oh, send him somewhere where they will teach him to think for himself." Mrs. Shelley replied: "Teach him to think for himself? Oh, my God, teach him rather to think like other people!" Shelley also felt keenly his difference from the common man. More than once he refers to

himself as an imprisoned spirit, and in his "With a Guitar, to Jane" he identifies himself with Shakespeare's delightful spirit Ariel.

Shelley attended Syon House Academy, Brentford, Middlesex, while his cousin Thomas Medwin was there. Then came four years at Eton College, where he was dubbed "Mad Shelley." In October 1810 he took up residence at Oxford as a member of University College. His father accompanied him and introduced him to his former booksellers, Slatter and Munday, with the request that they indulge his son in his "printing freaks." These freaks began at Eton with the publishing of the short Gothic novel *Zastrozzi* (1810) and a volume of poems entitled *Original Poetry by Victor and Cazire* (Shelley and his sister Elizabeth), 1810. A second Gothic novel, *St. Irvyne*, was published at Oxford early in 1811.

Early works at Oxford

On the very first evening in the college dining hall occurred an event that was of great importance in Shelley's life: he met another beginning student, by name Thomas Jefferson Hogg, the son of John Hogg, a nonpracticing barrister of a well-established family at Norton, Yorkshire. Shelley and Hogg took an instant mutual liking and spent their days and evenings together, to almost the entire exclusion of others. They talked, walked, read, and studied philosophy and inevitably were regarded as oddities. In his life of Shelley, Hogg portrays himself as a man with his feet on the ground, loving Shelley but partly because he was amused by his eccentricities. This is a false view; Hogg shared all of his friend's enthusiasms and extravagances. Through Shelley's praise of her, Hogg fell in love with Shelley's sister Elizabeth; he made love to both of Shelley's wives and married one of Shelley's favourite friends, Jane Williams.

Shelley was happy with his freedom and thought four years far too short a time for reading and study. He was therefore greatly shocked when he was expelled by his college, on March 25, 1811, for "contumaciously refusing" to answer any questions about a brief pamphlet called "The Necessity of Atheism." This pamphlet, a digest of the arguments of Locke and Hume, he and Hogg had sent to the bishops and archbishops and the heads of the colleges. The authorship became known at once, except for Hogg's complicity. When Hogg also refused to answer questions, he too was expelled. The friends left the university together, on March 26, for London.

The preceding Christmas holidays had been very unhappy. In addition to persecution at home for his religious opinions, Shelley suffered the loss of his first serious love. His lovely cousin Harriet Grove, a year older than Shelley, alarmed by the opinions expressed by Shelley in his letters, consulted her parents, and their engagement, existing by common consent of their families, was broken off.

Shelley and Hogg, at their fathers' insistence, soon separated, though Shelley put up a stiff resistance and capitulated only after significant concessions had been made. Father and son now disliked each other heartily, and their relations were soon broken for life by Shelley's elopement with and marriage to Harriet Westbrook; all further communications were to be carried on through Timothy Shelley's London solicitor. The father outlived the son by 22 years but never forgave him and took no pride in his growing fame.

Marriage to Harriet Westbrook

Harriet Westbrook (1795–1816) was the beautiful 16-year-old daughter of John Westbrook of London, a wealthy retired tavern keeper. Shelley became acquainted with Harriet through his sisters Mary and Hellen, who attended the same school at Clapham. Harriet agreed with Shelley's radical views and gave him the companionship and encouragement the lonely radical needed. Shelley's love for her appears to have been ardent and sincere when they were married at Edinburgh, on August 29, 1811, by Scotch law. During his vacation Hogg joined them in Edinburgh. They returned with him to York, where he was studying law. Shelley left Harriet there for a trip south to recruit funds, his allowance having been stopped. During his absence Hogg attempted to seduce Harriet, who told Shelley. The poet instantly fled the city with his wife and her sister Eliza, whom Harriet had summoned and who remained a member of the family from then on.

Years in the Lake District. The Shelleys settled at Keswick, in the Lake District, hoping to meet the older poets Wordsworth, Coleridge, and Robert Southey, but they had to content themselves with Southey, whose liberalism and poetry Shelley had ardently admired. He was disappointed, however, when he found Southey to be a conservative who uttered platitudes about morals, religion, politics, and the errors of youth and immaturity.

Shelley now discovered that the philosopher William Godwin was still alive. On January 3, 1812, he wrote to Godwin, introducing himself, and on the 16th he sent a colourful sketch of his life. He wrote that while at Eton he had read Godwin's masterpiece, *An Enquiry Concerning Political Justice* (1793). This work had been relatively popular for a few years and had influenced Wordsworth and Coleridge. For Shelley it became a master guide. To the end of his life he read it with the highest regard for its ideas and veneration for the intellectual powers of its author. No book has ever so completely furnished another great writer with his principal ideas.

Influence of William Godwin on Shelley

William Godwin was a professional writer, primarily a philosopher, who wrote essays, biographies, histories, novels, and books for children. He married Mary Wollstonecraft, author of *A Vindication of the Rights of Woman* (1792), and was the father of Mary Wollstonecraft Godwin, Shelley's second wife. In those years he was a powerful writer and a man of strict integrity. After the death of Mary Wollstonecraft, he married Mrs. Mary Jane Clairmont, a woman of uncertain origin with two children of her own, Claire and Charles. Mary Wollstonecraft left a daughter, Fanny, by Major Gilbert Imlay, and Godwin and Mrs. Clairmont had a son William. Quite a mixed household it was. Mrs. Godwin was heartily disliked by the writer Charles Lamb and by most of Godwin's friends.

When Shelley wrote to him, Godwin had already degenerated into a cunning and impecunious man who spent a good part of his time borrowing and then borrowing again to repay the first loan. The young man now addressing him might therefore be useful; he was the son of a member of Parliament soon to be a baronet and the heir to a great fortune. Godwin's speculations proved to be correct for a time, for as soon as he was of age, Shelley borrowed large sums on bonds, the greater part of the proceeds going to Godwin to set him firmly on his financial feet. But it was all in vain, and in 1818 Shelley stopped ruining his own future estate in efforts to save Godwin. He said to him in a letter of August 7, 1820:

> I have given you within a few years the amount of a considerable fortune, & have destituted myself, for this purpose of realising it of nearly four times the amount. . . . this money, for any *advantage* that it ever conferred on you, might as well have been thrown into the sea. Had I kept in my own hands this £4 or £5,000 & administered it in trust for your permanent advantage I should have been indeed your benefactor.

Godwin never forgave Shelley.

The years 1812 and 1813 did much to mature the young Shelley. His two trips to Ireland and wanderings in Wales and northwest Devonshire enlarged his knowledge of the physical world: the sea, mountains, a foreign country. His efforts to free the Irish people from the Act of Union, which brought about the union of Great Britain with Ireland and to bring about Catholic emancipation widened his understanding of politics and social reform; in fact, he learned by experience and Godwin's admonitions the slowness with which practical reform can be accomplished and the still more important lesson that the reform of men's minds must precede practical reforms. Virtually all of Shelley's activities as a practical reformer are confined to his prose works of this time.

Trips to Wales and Ireland

His intellectual life grew in his association with Godwin, whom he finally got to know personally on October 4, 1812, and those to whom Godwin introduced him in Ireland and England. He also came to know Thomas Hookam, Jr., a publisher and bookseller; and the youthful Thomas Love Peacock, a thorough classicist and poet who became famous for his short satirical novels. Peacock became one of Shelley's closest friends, and it was he more than anyone else who, in 1817, turned Shelley to a serious study of the Classical writers.

Shelley had not neglected poetry. He had written enough to make a short volume and a long poem entitled *Queen Mab,* which was finished in February 1813.

On July 17 or 18, 1812, while the Shelleys were at Lynmouth, North Devonshire, Miss Elizabeth Hitchener had joined them, presumably as a permanent inmate. She and Shelley were to supply the world with the ideas and arguments they deemed necessary for the liberation of mankind.

Miss Hitchener was a school teacher of 29, tall, thin, dark, with long, black hair. She was introduced to Shelley in 1811 by his favourite uncle, Captain John Pilfold, of the Royal Navy, whose daughter was one of Elizabeth's pupils; her father kept a public house. Shelley was powerfully attracted to Elizabeth, for this woman thought independently and liberally. He began a correspondence that is very curious and instructive: it shows with starkness his tendency to idealize intellectual women.

Finally, his incessantly repeated invitation that she should live with them, in which Harriet joined, led her to attach herself to his family. The result was disastrous. It soon became clear that she was more interested in Shelley than in human freedom. After changing her name from Elizabeth to Portia to Bessy, then to the Brown Demon, the Shelleys expelled her on November 8, 1812. On December 3 he described her to Hogg as "an artful, superficial, ugly, hermaphroditical beast of a woman." Quite unfair, but expressive of his feelings.

Queen Mab sums up poetically this practical reforming phase of Shelley's life. Biographically the poem is of great importance, and no other poem is so complete an expression of all of Shelley's principal ideas. To class it as a bad piece of juvenilia, as some have done, is sheer folly. Its 2,014 lines of blank verse and unrhymed lyrical verse were written with great intensity, and the wonder is that Shelley already knew distinctly the functions of poetry and of didactic verse; for him "didactic poetry is my abhorrence." To the soul of Ianthe, Queen Mab shows the earth of the past, present, and future: excoriated tyranny, organized religion, war, commercialism, and marriage. Long philosophical notes or essays (the first, "The Necessity of Atheism") explain the main ideas in clear-cut language and forceful logic. To accept Shelley's half-derogatory, half-amused remarks about the poem in 1821 as his full view of it, is a mistake.

Biographical importance of *Queen Mab*

Queen Mab was begun in February 1812 and completed in February 1813. Shelley wished to have it published, but no publisher would risk the danger of prosecution. He therefore printed it privately and distributed copies among his friends.

The events of 1814–16 not only broadened Shelley but led him to mature as man and poet. His residence in Bracknell brought him more satisfying intellectual companionship with the widow of Jean-Baptiste Chastel de Boinville and her clever and talented daughter Mrs. Cornelia Turner, as well as intimacy with the vegetarian family of John Frank Newton, whose *The Return to Nature, or a Defense of the Vegetable Regimen* (1811) Shelley adopted as authoritative.

Harriet was not happy with these people and was often away from home. In fact, a dangerous estrangement between Shelley and Harriet, which began in 1813, was growing, so that by April 1814, the possibility of a separation existed. The birth of their daughter Ianthe rather aggravated than improved the situation. Hogg is of the opinion that Harriet became a conventional wife who desired new hats, greater stability, and the pleasure of her husband's rank. However that may be, it is beyond any doubt that Shelley and Mary Godwin fell instantly in love when they met at Godwin's house on May 5 or 6, 1814, after her return on March 30 from a protracted stay in Scotland. Mary (1797–1851) was 16, pretty, highly intellectual, and accustomed to unconventional thought, being the child of the famous Mary Wollstonecraft and the philosopher Godwin. She was the kind of person whom Shelley said his wife must be: "one who can feel poetry and understand philosophy."

Elopement with Mary Godwin. The two eloped on July 28, 1814, and accompanied by Claire Clairmont, who knew French, they toured France and Switzerland for six weeks but had to return home (down the Rhine and through Holland) because of lack of funds. From Troyes, France, Shelley wrote the famous letter to Harriet inviting her to join them.

In London, Shelley had to go into hiding for a while to avoid arrest, to haunt the offices of lawyers and money-lenders, chiefly to raise large sums for Godwin, who now refused all personal contact; moreover, Harriet gave birth to his son Charles Bysshe on November 30. Through these harrowing months, which included the frequent shifting of lodgings, Shelley and Mary were nevertheless happy. They read incessantly, enjoyed again the company of Thomas Hogg, now pursuing his law studies in London, and were buoyed up by their love for each other.

Comparative peace came to them upon the death of Shelley's grandfather, Sir Bysshe, on January 6, 1815. Most of Shelley's ruinous debts were paid, and the sum of £1,000 a year settled upon him.

On August 3, Shelley and Mary took a pleasant cottage at Bishopsgate, near the entrance to Windsor Park, where they often had the company of Peacock, who lived at Marlow. Late in the summer of 1815, Shelley made a boat trip up the Thames, stopping at Oxford and getting as far up the now shallow stream as Lechlade; his companions were Mary, Peacock, and Charles Clairmont.

Shelley had been suffering from bad health. He had consulted the eminent London physician Sir James Henry Lawrence, who said he had tuberculosis. When he returned to Bishopsgate after the boat trip, Shelley produced his first truly great poem, *Alastor, or the Spirit of Solitude,* published with a few short poems early in 1816. Though some of his later poems are greater, none is more beautiful. The blank verse is influenced by John Milton and Wordsworth but is distinctly Shelleyan, as are the melody of sound and richness of imagery and metaphor and symbolism, which differ so much from *Queen Mab* and are to be henceforth his mode of expression. And in *Alastor,* Shelley introduces the most important theme in his poetry: that of vision and pursuit. It is repeated in varying combinations in the "Hymn to Intellectual Beauty," the "Dedication" of *The Revolt of Islam, Epipsychidion,* "Adonais," "The Zucca," and *The Triumph of Life.*

On January 24, 1816, Mary gave birth to their son William at Bishopsgate; August 16 found them in a cottage on the shores of Lake Geneva, Switzerland. Just above them, Lord Byron occupied the Villa Diodati, famous because Milton had stayed there in 1639. Mutual visits, animated conversations, reading, and excursions on the water led to daily intimacy. Especially notable is the ten-day trip around the lake taken by the poets. Unfortunately, what might have been a most gratifying friendship was complicated by the birth of a daughter, fathered by Byron, to Claire Clairmont on January 12, 1817; she was named Allegra by Byron.

On returning to England in September, Shelley took lodgings at Bath. Here, on December 15, he learned that Harriet Shelley had taken her own life by drowning, in London. Her death was a terrible shock to Shelley, and he was denied possession of his two children by the Lord Chancellor, which intensified his suffering. On December 30, 1816, at St. Mildred's Church and in the presence of Godwin, with whom he had become reconciled, he married Mary Wollstonecraft Godwin.

It was at this time that James Henry Leigh Hunt became a beloved and lifelong friend of Shelley, to whom he now gave the assistance he so desperately needed: deep personal sympathy, a temporary refuge in his home at Hampstead, intellectual stimulation, new friends, zeal for the liberal causes to which Shelley was devoted, and encouragement as a poet.

Hunt had won popular admiration when, in 1812, he had published a severe article on the Prince Regent in

The Examiner and had then spent two years (1813–14) in prison for libel, as did his brother John, printer and publisher of the article. Equally important to Shelley was Hunt's publication on December 1, 1816, of a short article on "Young Poets", John Keats, Shelley, and John Hamilton Reynolds. Throughout his long life, Hunt was Shelley's chief defender against personal attack and criticism of his poetry; hence, Shelley had good reason to address Hunt, as he often did, as his dearest friend.

Shelley had long wished to own a house and to settle down. Only once was he to make the experiment. In February 1817 he settled in Albion House, Marlow, Buckinghamshire, a small town 30 miles (50 kilometres) up the Thames River, where Peacock lived. He bought the lease and furnished the house. The experiment lasted a year and was not a complete success. Here he and Mary read aloud to each other in the evenings, and here Shelley felt the full influence of Peacock's classicism, which led him to a devotion to the classics that is impossible to exaggerate. They were abetted in this by Hogg, who visited both Peacock and Shelley. Other visitors were Godwin, and Leigh Hunt and his large family, including Mrs. Hunt's sister Bessy Kent. Here Mary put together her useful *History of a Six Weeks' Tour* (1817), wrote her famous *Frankenstein* (published 1818), and gave birth to their daughter, Clara, on September 2. And, in the first six months at Albion House, Shelley wrote his longest poem, *Laon and Cythna* (renamed *The Revolt of Islam,* 1818). During this period Shelley assisted the poor of the neighbourhood by visiting them and supplying them with blankets.

But the couple were not ideally happy, for they, especially Mary, lived in a state of uneasiness and embarrassment in the presence of Claire Clairmont, who was also there with Byron's child Allegra. Her equivocal state of being a "Mrs." who was bringing up someone else's child became impossible; Shelley's reputation was in danger. In March 1818 they therefore left England to turn over to Byron at Venice the child he freely offered to accept and rear as his own, provided he had nothing to do with her mother.

Shelley was persuaded by his friends and publisher to make a few alterations in *Laon and Cythna.* These consisted mainly in changing the relationship of Laon and Cythna from brother and sister to Laon and an orphan, who are in love and share the same ideals about freedom, and toning down a few denunciatory expressions about God. The title was altered to *The Revolt of Islam* as more suitable.

The poem, in Spenserian stanzas, united the themes of *Queen Mab* and *Alastor*: the lover of mankind and the poet dying young. In a letter to Godwin, Shelley says he wrote the poem with the ardor of a dying man. His overall purpose was to show his contemporaries that they should not lose hope because the French Revolution had failed. It was but one of many revolutions that must occur before universal good is victorious over universal evil. The poem has a superfluous profusion of cloud and other natural imagery and shows that Shelley is not at his best as a narrative poet. Much of the poetry, however, has a greater variety and power than any previous composition.

YEARS IN ITALY

To the reasons already given for the Shelleys' migration to Italy must be added two more: Shelley's health and the fear that his children by Mary might be taken from him by law, as Harriet's had been. But not even to Godwin or his friends did he ever make all his motives clear.

Personal life. They stopped briefly at Milan, Como, Pisa, and spent a month at Leghorn (May 9–June 11). On April 28, from Milan, they had sent Allegra to Byron in Venice in the care of one of their maids. Though Claire was of very great importance in Shelley's life, her relationship with Byron became so complicated that it is necessary to omit her hereafter, except for the necessary details. It should be noted, however, first, that Shelley was always very fond of Claire, who lived in his house most of the time during his union with Mary. Second, she was

Marginal notes (left column): Meeting with Lord Byron

Marginal notes (right column): Influence of Thomas Love Peacock on Shelley highly imaginative, nervous, and demonstrative, the antithesis of Mary; in consequence Mary and Claire could never live happily together, even through the many years after Shelley's death. At certain times Mary required Shelley to make arrangements for Claire to live elsewhere. Third, Shelley was obliged to be the arbiter between Byron and Claire, a painful task that he managed with great understanding and delicacy.

At Leghorn, the Shelleys made fast friends of John Gisborne, his wife Maria, and her young engineer son by a previous marriage, Henry Reveley. John Gisborne, Shelley said, was "an excessive bore. His nose is something quite Slawkenburgian." Maria had led an adventurous life and soon after Mary's birth in 1797 had been proposed to by Godwin, who needed a wife to care for his baby daughter. Maria at once won the love and admiration of the Shelleys. She fitted the type of woman Shelley always admired, regardless of age: she was intellectual, learned, liberal, strong in character.

In August, Claire's anxiety about Allegra induced Shelley to make with her the long and exhausting journey from the Baths of Lucca to Venice. She stopped at Padua, her presence to be kept a secret, while Shelley went on to Venice to meet Byron, who was delighted to see him and offered the use of his villa at Este, the Capuccini, a lovely mainland estate that Byron himself had never used. Shelley wrote hastily and eagerly to Mary, asking her to bring their family there at once. She did so, but as a result their baby girl Clara died (September 24). Mary secretly blamed Shelley and Claire for this calamity, and the strained relations, her "coldness," led Shelley to write (or alter) *Julian and Maddalo* and a group of poems, including "Lines Written Among the Euganean Hills," which are, in his own words, "my saddest verses raked up into one heap." Mary would never again be the radiant mate whom he had addressed in the "Dedication" of *The Revolt of Islam*. Not until after his death did Mary realize how she had become "cold moonshine" to Shelley. Her repentance was very bitter, as her poem "The Choice" reveals.

Death of Shelley's daughter

Better things also occurred at Este. Shelley wrote the first act of *Prometheus Unbound* and entered upon the period of his greatest achievement as a poet.

The Shelleys left Este early in November to spend the winter at Naples, which they reached on December 1. They made several excursions about the beautiful bay—to Pompeii, Paestum, Sorrento, Mt. Vesuvius—and visited the museums. Shelley wrote wonderful travel letters to Peacock for his English friends; but otherwise the creative spirit lay dormant in him. It came to life again in Rome, where from March to June 10, 1819, they revelled in this "Paradise of exiles," this "Niobe of nations." Amid the vast ruins of the Baths of Caracalla he wrote Acts II and III of *Prometheus Unbound*. He began *The Cenci*. Misfortune, however, continued to dog the Shelleys. Their three-year-old son William died on June 7 and left them childless. He was buried in what is now the old section of the English Protestant Cemetery in Rome, the loveliness of which, Shelley said, "might make one in love with death."

Leaving Rome on June 10, the Shelleys spent the summer at Montenero, near Leghorn. Here Shelley finished *The Cenci* with unusual rapidity. From October 2 to January 25, 1820, they lived in Florence rather uncomfortably, Shelley because of bad health and the cold weather. Mary's deep melancholy was much relieved by the birth of a son, named Percy Florence after Shelley and the city of his birth, on November 12. He was to be Mary and Shelley's only surviving child.

The removal to Pisa late in January 1820 was to be their last, except for summers at the baths of Pisa, about four miles from the city, occasional trips to Leghorn and Lucca, and the final summer at Casa Magni, near Lerici; for in Pisa they had for the first time put down roots.

Shelley went to Pisa chiefly to consult the famous Italian physician Andrea Vaccà Berlinghieri. Here he became the nucleus of a considerable group of people, English, Irish, Italian and Greek. On November 1, 1821, Byron and the Gambas joined them. The "Pisan Circle" is quite a study in itself. It consisted of former members of Shelley's circle—the Gisbornes, Shelley's cousin Thomas Medwin, and an adventurous Cornishman named Edward John Trelawny—and new acquaintances, among whom Edward Ellerker Williams, and his wife Jane and the "Masons" were of special importance. The Williamses had come to Pisa to meet Shelley. They arrived there on January 15 or 16, 1821, and became the Shelleys' closest associates. With meticulous regularity Edward Williams kept a daily journal of this period. Of quite a different sort were the "Masons," much older and highly cultivated people. Though known in the town as "Masons," they were in reality Lady Mountcashell and George William Tighe. The former had separated from Lord Mountcashell in 1805 after bearing him several children. She and Tighe had settled in Pisa in 1814 and had two daughters. Mrs. Mason, also an intellectual, became closely attached to the Shelleys and was especially helpful to Claire Clairmont.

The "Pisan Circle"

Mature works. During his four years in Italy, Shelley had composed not only the universally known "Ode to the West Wind," "To a Skylark," and "The Cloud," but also a series of major poems wherein his true greatness lies. They are *Rosalind and Helen* (1817–18; 1819), *Julian and Maddalo* (1818; 1824), *Prometheus Unbound* (1818–19; 1820), *The Cenci* (1819), *The Masque of Anarchy* (1819; 1832), *Peter Bell the Third* (1819; 1839), *The Witch of Atlas* (1820; 1824), *Oedipus Tyrannus, or Swellfoot the Tyrant* (1820), *Epipsychidion* (1821), "Adonais" (1821), *Hellas* (1821; 1822), and *The Triumph of Life* (fragment: 1822; 1824). Double dates indicate composition and date of publication.

Prometheus Unbound, a lyrical drama, is his greatest poem, which many believe is the greatest long poem in English since Milton's *Paradise Lost*. It is a modern myth still valid for the astronomical universe, just as the ancient myth as treated by the Greek dramatist Aeschylus was valid for the age in which it was composed. Though the narrative can be read as an interesting story, it is as a whole and in its parts an elaborate symbol of the triumph of the universal principle of good (Prometheus) over the universal principle of evil (Jupiter). Many readers miss the universality of the theme because they are preoccupied with identifying Prometheus with the mind of man and as the champion of mankind. He is those, indeed, but more. He is the champion of the gods, too, and of all that is good. The poem is intended to inculcate "beautiful idealisms of moral excellence," through the imagination and the heart, not through reason. The beauty and diversity of verse forms is not matched elsewhere. The last act (written as a kind of afterthought in December 1819) has been called "the greatest lyrical outburst in poetry."

Composition of Prometheus Unbound

The Cenci is astonishingly different from *Prometheus Unbound*. It is the greatest tragedy of the period, and it is the only one of Shelley's works to go into a second edition in his lifetime. Moreover, it is the only work in which he dealt with real human beings. Shelley wrote the play for the stage, and it would have been accepted gladly had not the theme of incest made public performance in his day impossible. Shelley had learned much about human beings as they are and about the necessities of dramatic style and construction. The straightforward, forceful, unadorned style, the noble character of Beatrice, and the monstrosity of Cenci are sharp contrast to the rich ornamentation of the ethereal beings of *Prometheus Unbound* and other of his poems. Mary encouraged Shelley to seek public recognition with more poems like *The Cenci*; Shelley laughed at her gently in *The Witch of Atlas*.

Epipsychidion is often regarded as the greatest poem on love in the language. Shelley was apparently planning a poem on his spiritual life, when a beautiful Italian girl, Teresa Emilia Viviani, was introduced to him and his family. She was ardent, poetical, philosophical, 19 years old, and a victim of parental tyranny. Her father, a nobleman and governor of Pisa, kept her in the Convent of Santa Anna until he could find a husband for her. Shelleys' poem was precipitated and changed in direction when he thought that at last he had found the perfect woman, an incarnation of the veiled maid of *Alastor*, of intellectual beauty. The poem he wrote in an almost hypnotic state is in three parts. The first is addressed to Emilia and concludes with plain and eloquent lines on his concept of marriage and true love. The second traces his spiritual life and is Shelley's most pronounced presentation of the vision and pursuit theme. It differs from *Alastor*, in that now the poet pursues not the vision of intellectual beauty but one among human beings who incarnates the essential qualities of this divine vision. There are experiences recounted with one whose "touch was as electric poison," and others, until he was rescued by Mary, who sustained him during the horrors of Harriet's suicide. Then Emilia, the perfect one, came. In a beautiful passage borrowed from Milton, Shelley likens himself to the Earth ruled by the "Twin Spheres of light," the Sun and Moon (Emilia and Mary). The third part is an invitation to Emilia to join him in living in an earthly paradise on an isolated Greek isle. In a few concluding lines, Shelley sends his poem as an invitation to his friends to join him in a perfect social order governed by reason and the highest ideals of love. Shelley invented the word "Epipsychidion" and in the poem translates it as "this soul out of my soul." Along with the poem should be read his prose fragment "On Love," which gives his broader views on love. It should be noted that the poem is in iambic pentameter couplets, which move with rare rapidity and fluency.

Shelley's most perfect poem

Shelley considered "Adonais" his most perfect poem. When in March he heard of the death of Keats, at Rome on February 23, 1821, he was deeply moved, not so much by the physical removal of a friend as by the early loss of a poet who had suffered neglect and abuse as Shelley himself had done. In slowly meditating the proper form to signify the loss, Shelley chose the Classical pastoral elegy. Though following the traditional structure and clearly using details suggested by the Classical poets, but especially Milton's "Lycidas," Shelley composed his poem of 55 Spenserian stanzas with feverish enthusiasm in the first days of June. On it he lavished all his art. It was printed at Pisa under his personal supervision, for he intended to present to the public a poem that was free from reform and political, religious, and social opinions distasteful to them. When the reviews proved as obtuse as ever, Shelley was so bitterly disappointed that he found it impossible for a considerable time to write again.

The following stanzas mark the opening of the four divisions of the poem, the fourth being an addition to the traditional structure: (I: stanza 1) "I weep for Adonais—he is dead!/O, weep for Adonais"; (II: stanza 18) reflections on life and death; the death of winter, the renewed life, joy, and beauty of spring; (III: stanzas 38–39) "Dust to the dust! but the pure spirit shall flow/Back to the burning fountain whence it came,/ . . . Peace, peace! he is not dead, he doth not sleep—/He hath awakened from the dream of life—" (IV: stanza 47) "Who mourns for Adonais? Oh, come forth,/Fond wretch! and know thyself and him aright"; truth is beyond the grave.

Hellas was occasioned by the beginning of the Greek Revolution, in 1821. Though Shelley called it only an "improvise," it is more than that, and three of its choruses are famous.

The Triumph of Life (a fragment) was Shelley's last major poem. Strongly influenced by the *Triumphs* of Petrarch, especially "The Triumph of Love," it reflects the philosophy first found in "Adonais," that the world of so-called reality is a world of illusion and asserts that all are the victims of life except Socrates and Christ. Though the poem stops with that passionate cry of his whole life—"Then, what is life?"—it does not leave the reader without hope. Again the vision and pursuit theme makes one feel the presence of the ideal and impels one to pursue it, even though it is beyond the grave.

It must not be forgotten that Shelley wrote a considerable quantity of prose. In it he expresses more clearly his ideas than he does in his poetry. "A Philosophical View of Reform" (1819–20; 1920) shows a sensible approach to practical reform. Most of his prose is fragmentary. Even the famous "A Defence of Poetry" (written 1821)

is but the first of three projected parts. For power of analysis and beauty of expression, the "Defence" is unsurpassed. Unfortunately, it was not published until 1840.

Though Shelley thirsted for fame, his poetry could never be popular, for it is addressed to the "highly refined imagination of the more select classes of poetical readers."

The death of Byron's daughter Allegra on April 20, 1822, caused the Shelleys and Williamses to begin their projected summer on the coast precipitately and early; they wished to remove Claire from the vicinity of Byron before she knew of her terrible loss. They rented Casa Magni at San Terenzo, facing Lerici, on the Gulf of Spezia, and occupied it on April 8.

Death. On July 1, Shelley sailed his trim yacht, the "Don Juan," with Williams to Leghorn to welcome Leigh Hunt and his wife and six children to Italy, to help them settle in Byron's *palazzo* in Pisa, and to make some definite arrangements with Byron concerning *The Liberal*, a periodical Byron wished to establish and had, through Shelley, brought Leigh Hunt to Italy to edit. On the return trip on July 8, a sudden squall struck and sank the boat, and Shelley and Williams were drowned.

Trelawny took charge of recovering the body, cremating it on the shore at Viareggio, and sent the ashes to Rome for burial in the new section of the Protestant Cemetery. Some weeks after the burial, Trelawny visited the grave, with which he was much dissatisfied. With his limited means he bought a plot up against the old Roman wall, built two tombs, to one of which he transferred the ashes of Shelley; he also enclosed the plot and decorated it with cypresses and laurels. To Shelley's wife Mary he wrote an account of these transactions. The second grave, he said, was not for Mary but for himself. Fifty-nine years later his ashes were buried in the long-empty tomb next to Shelley. Trelawny had known Shelley personally only during the last six months of his life.

Immediately after her husband's death Mary resolved to devote her life to the ordering, preservation, and publication of Shelley's manuscripts and to write a biography. In 1824 she published *Posthumous Poems*; Shelley's father, Sir Timothy, however, frustrated further publication until 1839, and in the *Poetical Works* Mary's invaluable notes are primarily biographical.

All of Shelley's intimate friends later made contributions of importance to Shelley's biography: Thomas Medwin and Thomas Jefferson Hogg wrote biographies, and Leigh Hunt and Thomas Love Peacock published works of a more miscellaneous kind. Each of these friends felt that Shelley was the most important influence in his life.

MAJOR WORKS

VERSE: *Queen Mab, a Philosophical Poem* (1813); *The Cenci, a Tragedy in Five Acts* (1819); *Prometheus Unbound* (1820); *Epipsychidion* (1821); "Adonais" (1821); *Hellas, a Lyrical Drama* (1822); *Posthumous Poems*, ed. by Mary Shelley (1824).

PROSE: "A Philosophical View of Reform" (written 1819, first published 1920) and "A Defence of Poetry" (written 1821, published 1840) are included in *Political Tracts of Wordsworth, Coleridge, and Shelley*, ed. by R.J. White (1953).

BIBLIOGRAPHY. The following are valuable for the scholar; there is no general bibliography for the general reader unless that in the *New Cambridge Bibliography of English Literature*, vol. 3 (1969), can be so classed: H. BUXTON FORMAN, *The Shelley Library* (1886); RUTH S. GRANNIS, *A Descriptive Catalogue of the First Editions in Book Form of the Writings of Percy Bysshe Shelley* (1923); T.J. WISE, *A Shelley Library* (1924); SEYMOUR DE RICCI, *A Bibliography of Shelley's Letters, Published and Unpublished* (1927).

Collections: There are three great collections of Shelley's manuscripts and materials. First is the unrivalled collection in the Bodleian Library, which consists mainly of two-thirds of the Shelley family papers. Second is the collection of Lord Abinger, who owns the third part of the Shelley family papers. The third-ranking collection is that of the Carl H. Pforzheimer Library. Unfortunately, public use of these materials is not possible until the Library has published them in the projected eight volumes of its *Shelley and His Circle, 1773–1822*, ed. KENNETH N. CAMERON, vol. 1–2 (1961) and 3–4 (1970), have been published. Smaller but valuable collections are at the British Museum, the University of Texas, and the Henry E. Huntington Library.

Works: The editions cited below are both useful and valuable: *Posthumous Poems* (1824); *Poetical Works* (1839), and *Essays, Letters from Abroad, Translations, and Fragments* (1840), ed. by MARY SHELLEY; *Poetical Works* (1876) and *Prose Works* (1880), ed. H. BUXTON FORMAN; *Complete Poetical Works,* ed. by THOMAS HUTCHINSON (1904); *Shelley's Literary and Philosophical Criticism,* ed. by JOHN SHAWCROSS (1909); *Poems,* ed. by C.D. LOCOCK (1911); *Complete Works,* ed. by ROGER INGPEN and WALTER E. PECK, 10 vol. (1926–30), and known as the Julian Edition, is the best complete edition of the works today; *Shelley's Prose,* ed. by DAVID LEE CLARK (1954), is inferior but makes the prose works of Shelley more easily accessible; *Letters of Shelley,* ed. by F.L. JONES (1964).

Biography: Basic biographical materials by Shelley's friends are MARY SHELLEY's Notes for the *Poetical Works* (1839), her *Journal* (1947) and *Letters* (1944); and *Maria Gisborne and Edward E. Williams, Shelley's Friends: Their Journals and Letters* (1951), ed. by F.L. JONES; *The Journals of Claire Clairmont,* ed. by MARION K. STOCKING (1968); JAMES HENRY LEIGH HUNT, *Lord Byron and Some of His Contemporaries* (1828) and *Autobiography* (1850); THOMAS MEDWIN, *Life of Shelley* (1847; ed. by H. BUXTON FORMAN, 1913); T.J. HOGG, *Life of Percy Bysshe Shelley* (1858; goes only to 1814), is an authorized life denounced after publication by Shelley's son and his wife; LADY JANE SHELLEY, *Shelley Memorials* (1859), contains important documents refuting Hogg; E.J. TRELAWNY, *Recollections of the Last Days of Shelley and Byron* (1858; 2nd ed., *Records,* 1878, is less reliable); THOMAS LOVE PEACOCK, *Memoirs of Shelley,* ed. by H.F.B. BRETT-SMITH (1933). Hogg, Trelawny, and Peacock, with an Introduction by Humbert Wolfe, were published together in 1933; this is now the standard reference for the books above. In 1882 PERCY FLORENCE and LADY JANE SHELLEY arranged, transcribed, and printed in chronological order a great quantity of their family collection, including Mary Shelley's *Journal*; the privately printed volumes (3, sometimes 4) are rare and very valuable. Scholarly biographies are NEWMAN I. WHITE, *Shelley* (1940; corrected ed., 1947; 1-volume condensation, *Portrait of Shelley,* 1945), which is masterly and definitive; D.F. MACCARTHY, *Shelley's Early Life from Original Sources* (1872); EDWARD DOWDEN, *Life of Percy Bysshe Shelley* (1886), the standard life until White's 1940 biography, and still of great importance; A.H. KOSZUL, *La Jeunesse de Shelley* (1910); HELEN ROSSETTI ANGELI, *Shelley and His Friends in Italy* (1911); ROGER INGPEN, *Shelley in England* (1917), which utilizes for the first time the Shelley-Whitton papers; WALTER E. PECK, *Shelley: His Life and Work* (1927); EDMUND BLUNDEN, *Shelley: A Life Story* (1946); D.G. KING-HELE, *Shelley: His Thought and Work* (1960), which deservedly has been very popular.

Criticism: In criticism the following are all solid contributions: MATTHEW ARNOLD, "Shelley," in *Essays in Criticism,* 2nd Series (1888), in which a great critic made the worst mistake of his career; FRANCIS THOMPSON, *Shelley* (1889), in beautiful poetic prose; E.S. BATES, *A Study of Shelley's Drama The Cenci* (1908); A.C. BRADLEY, "Shelley's View of Poetry," in his *Oxford Lectures on Poetry* (1909); A. CLUTTON-BROCK, *Shelley: The Man and the Poet* (1910, revised 1923); CARL GRABO, *A Newton Among Poets: Shelley's Use of Science in Prometheus Unbound* (1930) and *The Magic Plant: The Growth of Shelley's Thought* (1936), the first comprehensive work of its kind; A.M.D. HUGHES, *The Nascent Mind of Shelley* (1947); CARLOS BAKER, *Shelley's Major Poetry* (1948), excellent; KENNETH N. CAMERON, *Young Shelley: The Genesis of a Radical* (1950), the best book on his early prose.

(F.L.J.)

Shensi

Shensi Province (Shen-xi in Pin-yin romanization) is a province of China, bordered by the Huango Ho and Shansi Province in the east, by the Ningsia Hui Autonomous Region and Kansu Province on the west, the Inner Mongolian Autonomous Region to the north, by Szechwan Province in the south, and Hupeh and Honan provinces in the southeast. Its total area is 75,600 square miles (195,800 square kilometres). In 1970 its estimated total population was 21,000,000. The capital is Sian. (For an associated physical feature, see HUANG HO [RIVER].)

HISTORY

Northern Shensi. *The early period.* The northern parts of Shensi, particularly the Wei Ho Valley (which runs from west to east across the centre of the province), were some of the earliest settled parts of China. In the valley some remains of the Mesolithic Period have been found, while there are New Stone Age (Neolithic) Yang-shao culture sites spreading along the whole of the west–east corridor through Kansu, the Wei Ho Valley, and the Huang Ho Valley into Honan, showing that this was already an important route for the movement of peoples. Chinese Neolithic culture was probably first developed in the Wei Ho Valley. It remained an important centre of the later Neolithic Lung-shan culture and then became the first home of the Chou people, who, in 1122 BC, invaded the territories of their overlords, the Shang, to the east, and set up a dynasty that exercised some degree of political authority over much of North China. Until 771 BC, the political centre of the Chou was at Hao, near modern Sian.

For the early agriculturalists, working the ground with primitive stone-tipped tools, the slopes of loess (unstratified windborne deposits of loam) and river terraces provided ideal farmland—light, stone free, and fertile. The natural cover, too, was mostly grass and scrub and could be easily cleared for temporary cultivation.

After the 8th century BC the Chou lost much of their authority and moved their capital eastward to Lo-yang in Honan Province, after which Shensi became something of a backwater. Gradually, however, the pre-dynastic Ch'in state, which controlled the area, began to develop into a strong centralized polity of a totally new kind, able to mobilize mass labour for vast construction projects, such as the part of the Great Wall of China built between Shensi and the Ordos Desert. One of the greatest of these tasks was the completion in the Wei Ho Valley of a very large and efficient irrigation system based on the Cheng-kuo and Pai-kung canals and centred around the junction of the Ching Ho with the Wai Ho. This system, completed in the 3rd century BC, watered some 450,000 acres (180,000 hectares) and provided the powerful economic base for the Ch'in's eventual conquest of the whole of China.

The middle period. In 221 BC Hsien-yang, in Shensi, became the capital of the Ch'in dynasty, which unified China for the first time; it was a city of vast wealth, the focus of a nationwide road system. The area remained extremely populous and was a major centre of political authority for the next millennium. The Han (206 BC to AD 221), successors of the short-lived Ch'in dynasty, made their capital Ch'ang-an, near Hsien-yang. Later, in the 6th century, when after some centuries of disunion the Sui (581 to 618) again unified the empire, their capital —Ta-hsing—was on the same site as Ch'ang-an, which also was the capital of the T'ang (618–907). Ch'ang-an, as the capital was now once more known, was by far the largest and most magnificent city in the world in its day and was immensely wealthy. But by this time the irrigation system upon which Shensi primarily depended had begun to deteriorate, soil erosion and deforestation had begun to be problems, and the productivity of the area declined. The maintenance of a huge metropolis of more than 1,000,000 people in the area consequently necessitated the difficult and costly transportation of vast quantities of grain and provisions from the eastern plains and the Yangtze Valley. The capital remained in Shensi largely because the area (known as Kuan-chung—literally Within the Passes) was easily defended and was of crucial importance as a frontier with China's neighbours. After the sack of Ch'ang-an in 882, however, no dynasty ever again had its capital in the Northwest, and the area rapidly declined in importance as the economic centre of the empire gradually gravitated toward the Yangtze Valley and the South. During the next millennium Shensi became one of the poorest and most backward of China's provinces.

The early modern period. Under the Mongols, from 1279 onward, Shensi as a provincial unit assumed approximately its present form, incorporating the area formerly known as Shan-nan (literally South of the Mountains), or Li-chou. During this era, however, Shensi underwent many changes. In the course of the Yüan dynasty (1279 to 1368), the province was devastated and largely

Ancient construction projects

depopulated as a result of the Mongol conquest. Subsequently there emerged a large Muslim element in the population. The area suffered badly from rebellion and disorders following the collapse of Mongol rule after about 1340, when two independent regimes—those of Chang Ssu-tao in the Northwest and of Li Ssu-chi around Ch'ang-an—controlled most of Shensi. Later it was one of the areas in which disaffection with Ming rule (which began in 1368) first appeared in the late 1620s, and it was somewhat badly damaged in the fighting leading up to the Ch'ing conquest in 1644. Under Ming rule Shensi Province also incorporated Kansu, but under the Ch'ing dynasty (1644–1911) the two were separated once more.

The 19th and 20th centuries. By the 19th century Shensi was seriously impoverished. Although only marginally affected by the Taiping Rebellion (1850 to 1864) in its last stages, eastern and southern Shensi were slightly disturbed by the Nien Rebellion between 1853 and 1868. It then suffered the terrible Muslim Rebellion of 1862 to 1878, which affected much of the western and northern parts of the province. Although the effects of the rebellion and its savage suppression were not as terrible as in Muslim Kansu, about 600,000 were killed in Shensi, and the resulting destruction left the province in a serious plight.

Periodic famines

As this rebellion was coming to an end, Shensi was also affected by one of the worst drought famines of modern times. It had virtually no rain from 1876 to 1878, and, when the government tried to remedy the situation in 1877, poor transport facilities prevented effective relief. Perhaps 4,000,000 or even 5,000,000 people died in Shensi alone, with some single counties in the fertile Wei Ho Valley losing more than 100,000 dead. As a result of the terrible death toll in the last decades of the 19th century, Shensi became a haven for a wave of land-hungry immigrants from Szechwan and Hupeh provinces.

The end of the empire in 1911 brought yet further deterioration in living conditions. In 1912 the governors of Shensi and Kansu became engaged in a destructive civil war of an unusually brutal and violent character; the war, often affecting the whole province, continued until 1921, after which the province became involved in a still larger war between Yü-hsiang Feng and the Chihli warlords. In 1926 the capital, Sian, was besieged and badly damaged; the death toll numbered nearly 100,000 from starvation alone.

In the earlier years of the 20th century, Shensi also suffered badly from periodic famines, which occurred in 1915, in 1921, and finally in 1928. This last famine was as severe as that of 1877–78; it is estimated that at least 3,000,000 people died of starvation, after which a wave of epidemics increased the death toll still further. Whole counties were virtually depopulated. This time, however, some measures of relief were forthcoming. The International Famine Relief Organization began to rehabilitate the derelict irrigation system of the Wei Ho Valley, while the extension of the Lunghai Railway into the province meant that, if in the future famine should threaten, relief supplies could quickly be moved into the province.

A further political upheaval followed in 1936, when Communist armies, driven out of their bases in Kiangsi, passed through the western parts of Shensi. They then established themselves in Yen-an in northern Shensi, which was to be the base from which they conducted their war of resistance against the Japanese and from which, after the end of World War II, they successfully undertook the conquest of all China. In Shensi itself they controlled the territory of the present Yen-an and Yü-lin, special districts from 1937 onward.

Southern Shensi. The history of the southern part of the province has been more placid. Until the late 17th century the area was very sparsely peopled, and much of it, apart from the Han-chung basin, is still virgin forest. In the period after about 1680, the introduction of maize (corn) and sweet potatoes, followed in the 18th century by the Irish potato, made upland farming possible. A pattern emerged of growing rice in the valley bottoms, maize on the lower mountain slopes, and Irish potatoes on the higher land. Southern Shensi, with its great

amounts of vacant land, attracted immigrants on a large scale after severe famines and crop failures had occurred in Hupeh and Szechwan provinces in the 1770s. In the early 19th century, immigrants from central and southern China constituted as much as 90 percent of the population in some parts.

Rapid and often reckless development of the uplands, however, often led to soil erosion, rapid loss of fertility, and declining crop output. Local disaffection broke out in the so-called White Lotus Rebellion of 1796–1804, which was centred in the Szechwan–Shensi–Hupeh–Honan border regions. After its suppression, however, the area remained generally peaceful: in the 20th century it escaped the worst excesses of the northwestern warlords' civil wars, as well as of the repeated famines that occurred in northern Shensi.

LANDSCAPE AND ENVIRONMENT

Relief. Shensi Province comprises three distinct natural regions—the mountainous southern region, the Wei Ho Valley, and the northern upland plateau.

The three natural regions

The mountainous southern region forms the drainage area of the upper Han Shui, which is a northern tributary of the Yangtze. The Han Shui flows between two great mountain complexes that structurally form part of a great, single fold zone. These complexes are the Ta-pa Shan, forming the boundary with Szechwan Province to the south, and the Tsinling Shan—the major environmental divide between northern and central China—to the north. The Ta-pa Shan is an impressive range, 5,000 to 6,000 feet (1,500 to 1,800 metres) in height, with individual peaks reaching altitudes of up to 8,000 feet (2,400 metres). Its northern flank in Shensi is very heavily dissected by the complex pattern of the Han Shui's southern tributaries. There is only one major break in this mountain chain; it occurs in the far southwest of the province where the Chia-ling Chiang, which rises to the north in the Tsinling Shan, cuts through the Ta-pa Shan chain to flow into Szechwan on its way to join the Yangtze at Chungking. This valley forms the major communication route from the Wei Ho Valley in central Shensi to Szechwan and the southwest.

The Han Shui Valley itself broadens out near the city of Han-chung into a fertile and densely cultivated basin about 60 miles (100 kilometres) long and 10 miles (16 kilometres) broad. Further downstream the valley again narrows, after which the river flows between mountains and through deep gorges, only emerging into the plain once more in Hupeh Province.

The Tsinling Shan to the north of the Han Shui Valley forms an even more impressive barrier than the Ta-pa Shan. Structurally a continuation of the great Kunlun Mountains to the west, it runs continuously across Shensi from west to east at an average height of some 8,000 feet, with individual peaks, such as T'ai-pai Shan, reaching 13,500 feet. East of Sian the Hua Shan branches off the main range to the northeast, running eastward to the south of the Wei Ho and Huang Ho valleys into Honan. The main range, however, merges into the Fu-niu Shan (which has a northwest to southeast axis) and the Hsiung-erh Shan (which has a southwest to northeast axis) in Honan.

The Tsinling Shan forms a very broad mountain belt, divided into three parallel west to east zones. The northern and highest zone consists of ancient metamorphic rocks with massive intrusions of granite. It is divided from the Wei Ho Valley to the north by a line of faults that make its northern face rise abruptly in clifflike ranges from the plain. The middle zone is composed of intensely folded younger rocks. The southern zone, again, consists of metamorphic rocks that are younger than those of the northern range and mostly consist of metamorphic limestones and granite intrusions. The main watershed is in the highest northern zone. The southern slope of the range, draining into the Han Shui, is deeply sculptured by an extremely complex drainage pattern.

Only three passes of any importance cross the Tsinling Shan. These are the San-kuan Shan-k'ou (San-kuan Pass) south of Pao-chi, which leads to the Chia-ling Chiang

Valley and thus into Szechwan; the Kao-kuan Shan-k'ou south of Sian, which leads to the Han-chung Basin; and the Lan-t'ien Shan-k'ou southeast of Sian, which affords a route to the town of Shang-hsien and thence to Nan-yang in Honan on the way to northern Anhwei Province. The second major region is the Wei Ho Valley, a tributary of the Huang Ho, which flows west–east across the province from its headwaters in Kansu to join the Huang Ho at T'ung-kuan. This valley is a major geological trough, bounded on the south by a vast complex of faults and fractures along the base of the Tsinling Shan. This is a zone of considerable seismic instability, especially vulnerable to earthquakes. The northern border of the Wei Ho trench is less abrupt, and the large northern tributaries of the Wei Ho, the Ching Ho and Lo Ho, have themselves formed quite extensive alluvial plains in their lower courses that are continuations of the Wei Ho plain. The plain consists largely of loess (which also mantles parts of the northern face of the Tsinling Shan), as well as of redeposited loess washed off the plateau to the north. The rivers are heavily silted.

The third region, to the north, is the great upland plateau of northern Shensi. Structurally this is a basin of largely undisturbed sedimentary rocks of immense thickness. Its raised western rim forms the Liu-p'an Shan, which extends from the far west of Shensi northward into Kansu and the Ningsia Hui Autonomous Region. A minor northwest to southeast axis forms the Ta-liang Shan and Huang-lung Shan, which constitute the watershed between the Lo Ho system and the northern part of the province, which drains directly into the Huang Ho. On the eastern border of the basin the Huang Ho flows north–south through a narrow, gorgelike trough. In this section it falls some 2,000 feet in less than 500 miles, and it is mostly unnavigable, with frequent rapids, culminating in a very deep, narrow gorge and falls at Lung-men.

The whole of this basin plateau, which is mostly above 3,000 feet, is a peneplain (a region reduced almost to a plain by erosion) covered with a deep mantle of loess, blown from the Gobi and the Ordos Desert by the prevailing northwesterly winds of the winter season. Much of the area is covered to a depth of 150 or even 250 feet, and the loess completely masks the original relief and structure of the region. The loess, in turn, has been heavily eroded, leaving a characteristic landscape of almost vertical walls, cliff faces, and deep ravines. This erosion has been intensified by the effects of human occupation, which have destroyed the natural vegetation cover.

Climate.   The Tsinling Shan is not only a physical divide, but it also divides Shensi into two sharply differentiated climatic regions. The southern mountain area has a subtropical climate, similar to that of the Middle Yangtze Basin or of Szechwan. Mean temperatures in January are from 37° to 39° F (3° to 4° C), and the frost-free growing season is from 260 to 280 days, although the summer and autumn are not so hot as in the Middle Yangtze region. Total precipitation is between 30 and 40 inches (750 to 1,000 millimetres), falling mostly between May and October. The driest part of the year is spring and early summer, when irrigation is necessary. But in general the climate is hot and moist. Needless to say, in an area of such rugged and varied topography, there are great local variations.

The Wei Ho Valley has a much drier and somewhat colder climate. Average winter temperatures are about 32° F (0° C), and the frost-free period lasts for about 240 days. Total precipitation is between 20 to 25 inches, mostly falling between May and October, with a sharp peak in September and October. Rainfall is generally deficient in spring and early summer, but the climate is not seriously dry. It is, however, an area subject to severe and prolonged droughts. On the Loess Plateau further north and west the climate grows progressively drier and colder. The extreme north and west have only about 10 inches of annual precipitation, most of which occurs in late summer and autumn, when evaporation loss is at its maximum. The growing season and frost-free period become progressively shorter until in the north the former is only about 190 days. In this area agriculture depends

on techniques for minimizing evaporation losses and in conserving moisture in the soils. The northern frontier with the Inner Mongolian Autonomous Region, roughly coinciding with the line of the Great Wall, remains an important cultural divide. Beyond it conditions for agriculture become precarious in the extreme.

Vegetation and animal life.   The vegetation in the northern and southern zones is also sharply differentiated. The southern mountain area forms a part of the mixed deciduous and evergreen broad-leaved forest zone that formerly covered the Lower Yangtze and Han Shui basins; this region is characterized by a very rich variety of vegetation that includes more than 50 broad-leaved genera and a dozen or more coniferous genera. Owing to the difficulty of access, large areas of natural timber still remain standing.

The northern slopes of the Tsinling Shan and the lower Wei Ho Valley were originally covered with deciduous broad-leaved forest. The bulk of northern Shensi, except for the pure steppe (treeless plain) of the northern and western borders, was originally part of the so-called northwestern forest steppe area, where deciduous broad-leaved woodland grows only on the highest ground and around watercourses, most of the area being covered by grass or low, drought-resistant scrub. This northern area has been intensively cultivated since the first millennium BC, and its natural vegetation has been virtually destroyed.

POPULATION AND ADMINISTRATION

The people and their settlement patterns.   The people are virtually entirely Chinese and speak the Peking dialect of Mandarin. There are no ethnic minorities or minority languages. Some Chinese Muslim (Hui) communities remain in the south and northwest of the province. Most of the population is settled in the Wei Ho and Fen Ho valleys; the uplands are more sparsely settled. The chief cities are Sian, with a population estimated at 2,500,000 in the early 1970s; Pao-chi, with 180,000 in 1958; and Hsien-yang and Han-chung, each with 70,000 in 1953. An-k'ang, San-yüan, Fu-feng, Wei-nan, T'ung-ch'uan, and Yü-lin in 1953 all had populations between 20,000 and 50,000. Most of the province's county seats are very small indeed. Sian is the provincial metropolis besides being the main communication centre and chief industrial city; it is also an important administrative, educational, and cultural centre. It has an important university, a medical college, and an institute of art and music, as well as libraries and museum collections. Pao-chi is an important road and rail transportation centre. San-yüan and Hsien-yang are both satellite cities of Sian, as well as rail and road transport centres. Han-chung is the main communication and administrative centre for the southern region.

Administration.   Sian, the provincial capital, is an independent municipality directly subordinated to the province. The rest of the province is organized into eight special districts (*chuan-ch'ü*); the northern plateau area is divided between the Yü-lin Special District in the far north and the Yen-an Special District further south; the Wei Ho Valley area (from west to east) is divided into the special districts of Pao-chi, Hsien-yang, and Wei-nan; and the mountainous southern area is divided into the Han-chung, An-k'ang, and Shang-lo special districts. At the second administrative level, the province is divided into 93 counties (*hsien*) and three county-level municipalities (*shih*)—Hsien-yang, Pao-chi, and T'ung-ch'uan. For purposes of economic planning, the province, together with Kansu and Sinkiang Uighur Autonomous Region, forms part of the northwestern economic region.

ECONOMY AND TRANSPORTATION

Resource exploration.   *Agriculture.* The southern part of the province forms a portion of the southwestern highland and basin area, which is characterized by double cropping, wet-field agriculture, and forestry production. Most of the cultivated land is below 3,000 feet. The Han-chung Basin grows rice intensively, followed by winter wheat, but in the mountain zones of the Ta-pa Shan and Tsinling Shan the main cereal crops are maize and winter wheat. Such subtropical crops as tea, tung oil, and citrus fruits are grown. Apples, pears, apricots, and grapes are also widely produced, but only in the Han-chung Basin is more than 20 percent of the land under cultivation.

The Wei Ho Valley area is very intensively cultivated. As described above, it was the first area of China to be irrigated on a large scale. Well over half of the total area is under cultivation, and it supports a dense agricultural population. The valley area produces some rice, good winter wheat, tobacco, and cotton, but millet, barley, and corn are also increasingly important crops, as is kaoliang (a variety of grain sorghum). On the higher ground, millet, oats, and buckwheat are common. Hemp and sesame are important subsidiary crops, particularly in the upper Wei Ho and the Ching Ho valleys; in the latter area oats are an important fodder crop. Normally three crops are raised every two years.

The northern plateau is too cold in the winter for winter wheat to survive. It forms a part of the Inner Mongolian dry agricultural and pastoral zone. Spring-sown wheat and millet are the main grain crops, and these depend largely on the availability of irrigation water. Grazing becomes particularly important toward the northern and western borders, and the growing season is so short that only one crop yearly is possible. Over most of the northern region less than 25 percent of the land is cultivated, and in the north and west it is less than 10 percent.

Conservation and reclamation. The whole of Shensi, north of the Tsinling Shan, had in the past suffered badly from soil erosion as a result of the destruction by man of natural vegetation. As a part of the very large-scale Huang Ho multipurpose conservancy scheme, first decided upon in 1955, it was judged essential to reduce the enormous silt load discharged into the Huang Ho by the Wei Ho and its other west-bank tributaries. As a result, a great effort has since been made to spread terraced cultivation in Shensi. The plan also calls for the construction of great numbers of dams in the loess uplands to retain silt before it reaches the Huang Ho. These small dams quickly silt up, forming new farmland. At the same time, ambitious projects have been begun to sow grass on denuded land, to plant trees to protect the new terraced fields and slopes, and to prevent gullying. An even more ambitious plan is the planting of a belt of trees a mile or more wide, mostly consisting of drought-resistant poplar, elm, or willow, in an attempt to contain the spread of sand dunes from the Ordos Desert. This belt extends southwestward for about 375 miles from Yü-lin Special District in northern Shensi across the Ningsia Hui Autonomous Region and into Kansu, skirting the edge of the desert.

The irrigation system has also been greatly extended.
The irrigation system The ancient irrigation systems of the Wei Ho and Ching Ho valleys, restored (after centuries of neglect) following the famine of 1932, have been extended, while great numbers of small dams and wells have also been constructed to increase the irrigated area.

Mineral resources. The basin in the north of the province has enormous coal reserves, second in size only to those of Shansi. In the early 1970s, however, the only important modern mines were those at T'ung-ch'uan, on the border of the Wei Ho Valley. The whole basin is also an area with good prospects as an oil-producing district, but again production in the early 1970s was limited to Yen-ch'uan and Yen-ch'ang, near Yen-an, and the exploitation of these was hampered by lack of adequate transportation. There are minor coal and oil-shale deposits in the Han Shui Basin in the south, where there are also iron-ore deposits. The Tsinling Shan contains some minor gold-producing areas (mostly in the west), as well as some minor deposits of manganese and other minerals. But, in general, coal and oil form the only major resources of the province.

Power resources. The coal produced at T'ung-ch'uan feeds two large thermal generating plants at Sian (both generating more than 100,000 kilowatts), as well as a smaller plant at Pao-chi. Pao-chi, Sian, and T'ung-ch'uan are linked by a power grid that extends to the unfinished hydroelectric station at San-men on the Huang Ho, from

where it is also linked to Lo-yang and Cheng-chou in Honan and the industrial centres of T'ai-yüan and Yang-ch'üan in Shansi. This will form the most extensive power grid in China outside the Northeast region.

Industry. The only major industrial area in Shensi is that centred around Sian. Both Sian and the nearby cities of Hu-hsien and Hsien-yang are centres for the cotton-textile industry, with large modern plants. Sian is also an important centre for the production of electrical equipment and for engineering and chemical manufacturing. The first heavy industry in the province was the large iron and steel plant set up at Sian in 1958; in 1960 it was reported to have an annual capacity of 500,000 tons of pig iron. This was temporarily shut down in 1962, following the failure of the Great Leap Forward. It was brought into production again in 1971.

There are minor centres of industry at Pao-chi and at Shih-ch'üan in the Han Shui Valley, near An-k'ang, and Yao-hsien, near T'ung-ch'uan, has a large and important cement plant. Also, a small petrol refinery is located at Yen-ch'ang. But, apart from Sian, which ranks 15th among Chinese cities in industrial capacity and which since 1949 has become a regional industrial metropolis, the province remains virtually unindustrialized.

Transportation. The Wei Ho Valley since prehistoric times has formed part of the main east–west route running from the North China Plain in the east to the Kansu Corridor and the steppelands in the west. Sian is a natural route centre, where the great east to west route meets the routes that cross the Tsinling Shan to the south and southeast, an alternative route to the northwest via the Ching Ho Valley, and routes to the Ordos region in the north and to the Fen Ho Valley and Shansi to the northeast. All these routes are now followed by modern highways. In the south a highway crosses the province from east to west, joining Han-chung, in southwest Shensi, with Wu-han, in Hupeh Province to the east, and Lan-chou, in Kansu Province to the west. In the far southwestern corner of Shensi, a main highway follows the route of the ancient Man Post Road from Pao-chi southwestward to Ch'eng-tu in Szechwan. Apart from these trunk routes, only the Wei Ho Valley has an adequate road network. *Road and rail routes*

The first railway to reach Shensi was the Lunghai line, the great east–west trunk line from the sea at Lien-yün-kang in Kiangsu, via the industrial centres of K'ai-feng, Cheng-chou, and Lo-yang in Honan. This line was extended to T'ung-kuan in 1932, to Sian in 1934, and to Pao-chi in 1937. Much of the railway was destroyed during the war with Japan but was reconstructed in the late 1940s and extended westward to T'ien-shui, in Kansu. Also at this time a branch was constructed from Hsien-yang, near Sian, to T'ung-ch'uan, the site of the only large coalfield in the area. Construction of another line from Sian to cross the Huang Ho near Lung-men and join the main trunk line through Shansi at Ch'ü-wu was still incomplete in the early 1970s. A second major new rail link was the line from Pao-chi southwest to Ch'eng-tu in Szechwan, where it links with various lines to the southwest. The northern part of the province is still without adequate communications. Sian is an important centre of air traffic, with regularly scheduled flights to Peking, T'ai-yüan, Lan-chou, Pao-t'ou, and Central Asia, and to Ch'eng-tu, Chungking, and Wu-han.

BIBLIOGRAPHY. The best available description of the physical features and natural environment of the province in a Western language remains that in *China Proper*, ed. by PERCY M. ROXBY, 3 vol. (1944–45). For the climatic regime of the area, see the excellent study by CHU PING-HAI, *The Climate of China* (1968; orig. pub. in Chinese, 1962). An incomplete description of soils and other physical factors is included in VIKTOR A. KOVDA, *Soils and Natural Environment of China*, 2 vol. (1960; orig. pub. in Russian, 1959); while a general and not entirely reliable picture is given in V.G. KALMYKOVA and I.K. OVDIYENKO, *Geographical Survey of North-West China*, 3 vol. (1958; orig. pub. in Russian, 1957). Some economic and social information is included in THEODORE SHABAD, *China's Changing Map*, rev. ed. (1972); in T.R. TREGEAR, *A Geography of China* (1965), and in his more specialized *Economic Geography of China* (1970). On the historical geography of the area, there is a wealth of information on the earliest periods in K.C. CHANG, *The Archaeology of Ancient China*, rev. ed. (1968). There also are some good materials in the imaginative historical geography by Y.F. TUAN, *China* (1969); and a great deal of information in the classical work on Chinese economic and social history by P.T. HO, *Studies on the Population of China, 1368–1953* (1959). There is an excellent political-administrative map in the C.I.A. publication, *Communist China Administrative Atlas* (1969).

(D.C.T.)

Sheridan, Richard Brinsley

Richard Brinsley Butler Sheridan, though best remembered as the author of brilliant comedies of manners, was also important as an English politician and orator. His genius both as dramatist and politician lay in humorous criticism and the ability to size up situations and relate them effectively. These gifts were often exercised in the House of Commons on other men's speeches and at Drury Lane Theatre in the revision of other men's plays. They are seen at their best in *The School for Scandal*, in which he shaped a plot and dialogue of unusual brilliance from two mediocre draft plays of his own. In person he was often drunken, moody, and indiscreet, but he possessed great charm and powers of persuasion. As a wit he delivered his sallies against the follies of society with a polish that makes him the natural link in the history of the British comedy of manners between William Congreve and Oscar Wilde.

By courtesy of the Lord Plunket

Sheridan, oil painting by Sir Joshua Reynolds, 1788–89. In the Lord Plunket Collection.

Formative years. Sheridan's birth date is not known, but he was baptized (mistakenly as "thos. Brinsley") at St. Mary's Church, Dublin, on November 4, 1751, the third son of Thomas and Frances Sheridan. His grandfather Thomas Sheridan had been a companion and confidant of Jonathan Swift; his father was the author of a pronouncing dictionary and the advocate of a scheme of public education that gave a prominent place to elocution; and his mother gained some fame as a playwright.

The family later moved to London, and Sheridan never returned to Ireland. He was educated (1762–68) at Harrow, and in 1770 moved with his family to Bath. While there he corresponded with a school friend then at Oxford, and together they wrote *Jupiter*, a farce, which, after revision, Sheridan renamed *Ixion*. They also collaborated (1771) in a metrical version of the epistles of the fifth-century writer Aristaenetus who compiled two books of love stories taken from Plato, Lucian, and Plutarch. Sheridan's poems *The Ridotto of Bath* and "Clio's Protest" also date from this period.

In Bath Sheridan fell in love with Elizabeth Ann Linley (1754–92), whose fine soprano voice had, from an early age, delighted audiences at the concerts and festivals conducted by her father, Thomas. In order to avoid the unpleasant attentions of a Welsh squire, Thomas Mathews

Education and marriage

of Llandaff, she decided to take refuge in a French nunnery. Sheridan accompanied her to Lille in March 1772, but returned to fight two duels that same year with Mathews, in London in May, where he disarmed Mathews, and at Bath in July, where he was bodily wounded. Meanwhile, Elizabeth had returned home with her father, and Sheridan was ordered by his father to Waltham Abbey, Essex, to pursue his studies. He was entered at the Middle Temple in April 1773, but after a week broke with his father, gave up a legal career, and married Elizabeth at Marylebone Church, London.

Dramatic career. After his marriage Sheridan turned to the theatre for a livelihood. His comedy *The Rivals* opened at Covent Garden Theatre, London, in January 1775. It ran an hour longer than was usual, and, because of the offensive nature and poor acting of the character of Sir Lucius O'Trigger, it was hardly a success. Drastically revised and with a new actor as Sir Lucius, its second performance nine days later won immediate applause. The situations and characters were not entirely new, but Sheridan gave them freshness by his rich wit, and the whole play reveals Sheridan's remarkable sense of theatrical effect. Characteristic is the genial mockery of affectation displayed by some of the characters. Even the "malapropisms" that slow down the play give a proper sense of caricature to the character of Mrs. Malaprop.

The Rivals

Some of the play's success was due to the acting of Lawrence Clinch as Sir Lucius. Sheridan showed his gratitude by writing the amusing little farce *St. Patrick's Day; Or, The Scheming Lieutenant* for the benefit performance given for Clinch in May 1775. Another example of his ability to weave an interesting plot from well-worn materials is seen in *The Duenna*, produced the following November. The characters are generally undeveloped, but the intrigue of the plot and charming lyrics and the music by his father-in-law Thomas Linley and his son gave this ballad opera great popularity. Its 75 performances exceeded the 62, a record for that time, credited to John Gay's *The Beggar's Opera* (1728), and it is still revived.

Thus, in less than a year Sheridan had brought himself to the forefront of contemporary dramatists. David Garrick, looking for someone to succeed him as manager and proprietor of Drury Lane Theatre, saw in Sheridan a young man with energy, shrewdness, and a real sense of theatre. A successful physician, Dr. James Ford, agreed with Garrick's estimate and increased his investment in the playhouse. In 1776, Sheridan and Linley became partners with Ford in a half-share of Drury Lane Theatre. Two years later they bought the other half from Willoughby Lacy, Garrick's partner. Sheridan had put only £1,300 into the enterprise; the transaction had been possible only because Garrick and Ford had backed him with mortgages in the belief that Drury Lane would flourish under his direction.

Drury Lane Theatre

In fact, Sheridan's interest in his theatre soon began to seem rather fitful. Nevertheless, he was responsible for the renewed appreciation of Restoration comedy that followed the revival of the plays of William Congreve at Drury Lane. In February 1777 he brought out his version of Vanbrugh's *The Relapse* (1696) as *A Trip to Scarborough*, again showing his talent for revision. He gave the rambling plot a neater shape and removed much indelicacy from the dialogue, but the result was disappointing, probably because of the loss of much of the play's former gusto.

What Sheridan learned from the Restoration dramatists can be seen in *The School for Scandal* produced at Drury Lane in May 1777. That play earned him the title of "the modern Congreve." Although resembling Congreve in that its satirical wit is so brilliant and so general that it does not always distinguish one character from another, *The School for Scandal* does contain two subtle portraits in Joseph Surface and Lady Teazle. There were several Restoration models (*e.g.*, Mrs. Pinchwife in Wycherley's *The Country-Wife* and Miss Hoyden in Vanbrugh's *The Relapse*) for the portrayal of a country girl amazed and delighted by the sexual freedom of high society. Sheridan softened his Lady Teazle, however, to suit the more refined taste of his day. The part combined innocence and

The School for Scandal

sophistication and was incomparably acted. The other parts were written with equal care to suit the members of the company, and the whole work was a triumph of intelligence and imaginative calculation. With its spirited ridicule of affectation and pretentiousness, it is often considered the greatest comedy of manners in English.

Sheridan's flair for stage effect, exquisitely demonstrated in scenes in *The School for Scandal*, was again demonstrated in his delightful satire on stage conventions, *The Critic*, which since its first performance in October 1779 has been thought much funnier than its model, *The Rehearsal* (1671), by George Villiers, the 2nd duke of Buckingham. Sheridan himself considered the first act to be his finest piece of writing. Although Puff is little more than a type, Sir Fretful Plagiary is not only a caricature of the dramatist Richard Cumberland but an epitome of the vanity of authors in every age.

Political career. Sheridan continued to adapt plays and to improvise spectacular shows at Drury Lane, but as a succession of acting managers took over the burden of direction his time was increasingly given to politics. His only full-length later play was the artistically worthless but popular patriotic melodrama *Pizarro* (1799), based on a German play on the conquest of Peru. Sheridan had become member of Parliament for Stafford in September 1780 and was undersecretary for foreign affairs (1782) and secretary to the treasury (1783). Later he was treasurer of the Navy (1806–07) and a privy councillor. The rest of his 32 years in Parliament were spent as a member of the minority Whig party in opposition to the governing Tories. His critical acumen and command over language had full scope in his oratory and were seen at their best in his speeches as manager of the unsuccessful impeachment of Warren Hastings, governor general of India.

Party posts

He was recognized as one of the most persuasive orators of his time but never achieved greater political influence in Parliament because he was thought to be an unreliable intriguer. Some support for this view is to be found in his behaviour during the Regency Crisis (1788–89) following the temporary insanity of George III when Sheridan acted as adviser to the unpopular self-indulgent Prince of Wales, later George IV. He encouraged the Prince to think that there would be a great majority for his being regent with all the royal powers simply because he was heir-apparent. In the country at large this was seen as a move by Charles James Fox and his friends to take over the government and drive out Prime Minister William Pitt. Sheridan was also distrusted because of his part in the Whigs' internecine squabbles (1791–93) with Edmund Burke over the latter's implacable hostility to the French Revolution. He was one of the few members courageous enough openly to defend those who suffered for their support of the French Revolution. Indeed, Sheridan liked taking an individual stand, and although he supported Fox in urging that the French had a right to choose their own way of government, he broke with Fox once the French became warlike and threatened the security of England. He also came out on the side of the Tory administration when he condemned mutineers who had rebelled against living conditions in the British Navy (1797). Much to Fox's disgust, Sheridan, although a Whig, gave some support to the Tory administration of Prime Minister Henry Addington, later 1st Viscount Sidmouth (1801–1804).

In November 1806, Sheridan succeeded Fox as member for Westminster—although not, as he had hoped, as leader of the Whigs—but he lost the seat in May 1807. The prince of Wales then returned him as member for the "pocket borough" of Ilchester, but his dependence on the prince's favour rankled with Sheridan, for they differed in their attitude on Catholic emancipation. Sheridan, who was determined to support emancipation, stood for election as member from Stafford again in 1812, but could not pay those who had previously supported him as much as they expected and as a result was defeated.

Last years. Sheridan's financial difficulties were largely brought about by his own extravagance and procrastination, as well as by the destruction of Drury Lane Theatre by fire in February 1809. With the loss of his parliamenta-

ry seat and his income from the theatre, he became a prey to his many creditors. His last years were beset by these and other worries—his circulatory complaints and the cancer that afflicted his second wife, Esther Jane Ogle. She was the daughter of the dean of Winchester, whom he had married in April 1795, three years after Elizabeth's death. Pestered by bailiffs to the end, Sheridan died in London on July 7, 1816. Even in decline, he had made a strong impression on Byron, who wrote a *Monody on the Death of the Right Honourable R.B. Sheridan* (1816), to be spoken at the rebuilt Drury Lane Theatre.

MAJOR WORKS

PLAYS: *The Rivals*, 1775; *St. Patrick's Day; Or, The Scheming Lieutenant*, 1775; *The Duenna*, 1775 (comic opera); *A Trip to Scarborough*, 1777 (Sheridan's version of Sir John Vanbrugh's *The Relapse; or, Virtue in Danger*); *The School for Scandal*, 1777; *The Critic; or a Tragedy Rehearsed*, 1779, *Pizarro* (1799) (adapted from August von Kotzebue's *Die Spanier in Peru*).

POEMS: *The Ridotto of Bath*, 1771; *The Rival Beauties. A poetical Contest*, 1772 (including "Clio's Protest"); *Verses to the Memory of Garrick Spoken as a Monody*, 1779.

BIBLIOGRAPHY

Editions and bibliography: *The Plays and Poems*, ed. by R. CROMPTON RHODES, 3 vol. (1928, reprinted 1962), is the standard text. It should be supplemented by RICHARD L. PURDY's excellent edition of *The Rivals: A Comedy As It Was First Acted at the Theatre-Royal in Covent-Garden* (1935); and by GEORGE H. NETTLETON's texts of *The Rivals*, *The School for Scandal*, and *The Critic*, in *British Dramatists from Dryden to Sheridan*, ed. by Nettleton and A.E. CASE (1939). Annotated editions of *The Rivals* (1968) and *The School for Scandal* (1971), have been prepared by C.J.L. PRICE, who is also responsible for a critical edition of all the plays (1973). No full bibliography of Sheridan's work has been published; valuable bibliographical material may be found in J.P. ANDERSON's lists in L.C. SANDERS, *Life of Sheridan* (1890); in *Sheridan's Major Dramas*, ed. by GEORGE H. NETTLETON (1906); in the works by SICHEL (see below) and RHODES (see above); in IOLA A. WILLIAMS, *Seven XVIIIth-Century Bibliographies* (1924, reprinted 1968); and in the critical edition of the plays, ed. by Price.

Bibliography and criticism: THOMAS MOORE, *Memoirs of the Life of the Right Honourable Richard Brinsley Sheridan*, 5th ed., 2 vol. (1827, reprinted 1971), is indispensable. WILLIAM SMYTH, *A Memoir of Mr. Sheridan* (1840), is a brief but vivid account from personal acquaintance. W. FRASER RAE, *Sheridan*, 2 vol. (1896); and W. SICHEL, *Sheridan*, 2 vol. (1909), are full accounts, printing much new material, but are not altogether reliable. R.C. RHODES, *Harlequin Sheridan* (1933, reprinted 1969), provides a scholarly review of evidence about disputed passages in Sheridan's life; LEWIS GIBBS, *Sheridan* (1947, reprinted 1970), gives a useful summary of accepted material. JEAN DULCK, *Les Comédies de R.B. Sheridan* (1962), is a close examination of Sheridan's achievement from the French point of view. *The Letters of Richard Brinsley Sheridan*, ed. by C.J.L. PRICE, 3 vol. (1966), prints 972 letters in detail; they are mainly concerned with his life in politics and the theatre, but they also include some delightful ones to his second wife.

(C.J.L.P.)

Sherman, William Tecumseh

An American Civil War general, William Tecumseh Sherman became one of the chief architects of modern warfare when he combined with Gen. Ulysses S. Grant in unified campaigns to crush the Confederate armies and destroy the South's resources for waging war.

Born February 8, 1820, at Lancaster, Ohio, and named Tecumseh in honour of the famous Shawnee chieftain, he was one of eight children of Judge Charles R. Sherman, who died when the boy "Cump" was only nine. Thomas Ewing, a warm family friend and a Whig political force in Ohio, adopted Cump as "the brightest of the lot." His foster mother, a devout Catholic who feared that no priest would baptize a child with a heathen name, added William to the boy's name. When Sherman was 16, Ewing obtained an appointment to West Point for his adopted son, whom Eastern relatives saw as "an untamed animal just caught in the Far West." Cadet Sherman excelled in engineering, geology, rhetoric, and philosophy. He also did well in collecting demerits.

Early years

After graduation Sherman was sent to fight Seminole

Sherman.
By courtesy of the Library of Congress,
Washington, D.C.

Indians in Florida; he encountered no Indians but was delighted with the young ladies of St. Augustine. Transferred to Ft. Moultrie, South Carolina, within easy reach of Charleston, he enjoyed four years of "horse-racing, picnicking, boating, fishing, swimming, and God knows what not." He also thought of becoming an artist.

The Mexican War, in which so many generals of the Civil War received their experience, passed Sherman by. He was stranded in California as an administrative officer. In 1850 Sherman married Ellen Ewing, daughter of his adoptive father, who was then serving as secretary of the interior in Washington. They settled in St. Louis.

He was bored by his commissary duties of purchasing cattle in Kansas and Missouri. The lure of gold in California led him to resign from the army on September 6, 1853, and join the St. Louis banking firm of Lucas, Turner and Co. as its representative in San Francisco. In the collapse of the gold rush, he had accumulated a debt of $13,000; he thereupon declared himself "the Jonah of banking." Other disappointments followed. As a self-taught lawyer his legal career came to an end in Leavenworth, Kansas, with his first case—proving anew, as he declared, that he had become "a dead cock in a pit." The army would not reinstate him.

Old friends, Southerners Braxton Bragg and P.G.T. Beauregard, found Sherman employment as superintendent of a Southern military college (now the University of Louisiana). He loved being a schoolmaster, but with Louisiana's secession from the Union he returned north and became president of the Fifth Street Railroad in St. Louis. The war, he told one of his daughters, demonstrated that "men are blind and crazy." He distrusted Pres. Abraham Lincoln yet used the influence of his younger brother, Senator John Sherman, to obtain appointment in the U. S. Army as a colonel in May 1861.

Civil
War
years

Raised to a generalship after the first Battle of Bull Run (July 21, 1861), Sherman begged Lincoln not to trust him in an independent command. Nevertheless, he was placed in charge of troops in Kentucky until his hallucinations concerning the Confederate force opposing him caused him to ask for so many reinforcements that he was publicly called insane. He then served as a commander under Generals Henry Halleck and Grant.

Grant had a calming influence upon Sherman. Together they fought brilliantly to capture Vicksburg (1862–63), shattering the Confederate defenses and opening the Mississippi River to Northern commerce once more. When, in 1864, Grant went east to fight Confederate general Robert E. Lee, Sherman led three armies in the invasion of Georgia that brought the fall of Atlanta. Both Grant and Lincoln doubted the wisdom of Sherman's celebrated "March to the Sea" from Atlanta to Savannah with 60,-000 men. But a cocky Sherman reached the Atlantic coast in time to offer President Lincoln the city of Savannah

for a Christmas present. Grant plunged into the Wilderness to trap Lee in Virginia; Sherman marched north through the Carolinas; and the war entered its climactic phases.

Sherman declined all opportunities to run for political office, saying he would not run if nominated and would not serve if elected. When Grant became president in 1869, he made Sherman commanding general of the army, a post he held until 1884. Sherman remained a soldier until the end, though he expressed his view of warfare in the often-quoted phrase, "War is hell." His friends accused him of keeping a carpetbag packed so that he could leave at an instant's notice upon invitation to address an audience. He died in New York City on February 14, 1891.

BIBLIOGRAPHY. The definitive biography of Sherman is LLOYD LEWIS, *Sherman: Fighting Prophet* (1932). SHERMAN'S own *Memoirs*, 2 vol. (1875), are charming, straightforward, and highly critical of numerous Confederate heroes. EARL SCHENCK MIERS, *The General Who Marched to Hell* (1951), depicts Sherman's temperament and fighting style. Collections of Sherman's letters have been ed. by RACHEL SHERMAN THORNDIKE, *The Sherman Letters: Correspondence Between General and Senator Sherman from 1837 to 1891* (1894); and M.A. DE WOLFE HOWE, *Home Letters of General Sherman* (1909). Some glimpses of the Sherman whom soldiers and southerners knew are given in the diaries of HENRY HITCHCOCK, *Marching With Sherman*, ed. by HOWE (1927); and EMMA LECONTE, *When the World Ended*, ed. by MIERS (1957).

(E.S.Mi.)

Shinran

Shinran was an important Japanese philosopher and religious reformer who insisted on the salvation of all human beings, poor and rich, low and high, and who, to achieve these aims, established the Jōdo Shinshū ("True Pure Land School") sect of Buddhism in 1224. Historically speaking, this school of Buddhism retained Indian devotionalism and provided it with a Buddhistic foundation of compassion (maitrī-karuṇā) in contrast to the self-disciplined Buddhism (Tendai, Zen) that concentrated on wisdom (prajñā), and had few effective means of saving less well-endowed human beings. Shinran took seriously the salvation of the masses. His belief was that perfect intercommunion of Amida Buddha (the Buddha who ruled over the Western Paradise) and all sufferers and, thus, the salvation of all could be achieved through the mere calling of the name of Amida Buddha (Namu-Amida-Butsu).

By courtesy of the International Society
for Educational Information, Tokyo

Shinran, ink on paper by Sen-ami, middle of the 13th
century. In the Nishi-Hongan-ji, Kyōto, Japan.

Shinran was born to Hino Arinori near Kyōto in AD 1173. Orphaned at an early age, he entered the Tendai priesthood when he was nine and was given the name Hannen Shōnagon-no-Kimi in 1182 by the priest Jichin (Jien), the head of Shōren-in. For 20 years Shinran studied Buddhism on Mt. Hiei, where an eminent Bud-

Early life
and career

dhist monk, Dengyō Daishi, had established the centre of the Tendai school, which taught that the Buddha uses skillful means to enlighten men.

Despite the most rigorous asceticism, Shinran failed to find the assurance of salvation. A long spiritual struggle in quest of salvation had occupied his early years as a monk of the Tendai school, which had been weakened by its political affiliation with the aristocracy. Moreover, at the beginning of the Kamakura period (1192–1333), the decline of the aristocratic class and its fierce struggles with the military class for political supremacy brought so much confusion and distress that the people began to accept a pessimistic view of history, according to which, with the passage of time after the Buddha's death, the world would gradually become degenerate and the Buddha's teaching would become decadent.

Shinran then came down from Mt. Hiei for 100 days to continue his quest for salvation in the Rokkakudō, in Kyōto (the "Hexagonal Temple"). It was at this time that he met the Buddhist saint Hōnen, founder of the Jōdo ("Pure Land") sect, who had been preaching to the masses the message: "Anyone who only calls Amida's Name shall be saved without fail, for the Name-Call is not a human contrivance, but the select way given in Amida's Original Vow." This practice of calling Amida's name is known as *nembutsu*. In his 29th year, "Shinran abandoned ascetic practices and took refuge in the Original Vow." In his 33rd year, Shinran was allowed to copy Hōnen's main work, *Senchaku-shū* ("Book on the choice of *nembutsu*"), and drew a portrait of Hōnen. The *Senchaku-shū* was a great source of inspiration to Shinran, for copies of the document were entrusted only to a few close disciples. Shinran's study under Hōnen came to an end in 1207, when the government issued an edict against Hōnen's *nembutsu* movement (focussed on the invocation of the Buddha's name). The oppression had its centre in Kōfuku-ji at Nara and at Enryaku-ji on Mt. Hiei. As a result, Hōnen was exiled to Tosa Province, Shinran to Echigo, and two other *nembutsu* teachers were decapitated. Soon after his arrival in Echigo, Shinran married Eshinni, in violation of the Buddhist precept of celibacy for the priesthood.

Shinran's biography *Denne*, written by Kakunyo in 1295, ascribes a strong evangelistic impulse to his move to Kanto in eastern Japan, where, between 1212 and 1235 or 1236, he lived an academic and missionary life. In this period he compiled a monumental anthology, *Kyōgyōshinshō* ("Teaching-Action-Faith-Attainment," in six volumes), around 1224. In this work Shinran made an original contribution to Buddhist philosophy with the interpolation of faith between action and attainment. His ministry also had great success. Leaving behind a body of devoted believers, he had sown seeds that were later to bear fruit when ecclesiastical institutions were set up.

Works · After 20 years he left Kanto for Kyōto, where his fellow believers were in a miserable plight from constant oppression after Hōnen's death. Moreover, in 1256 Shinran had to disown Zenran, his oldest son, who tried to control the community with a heretical interpretation of the faith. This was the most tragic experience in Shinran's long life. Despite spiritual depressions and economic difficulties, he completed his *Kyōgyōshinshō* and compiled a number of derivative works to make his teachings accessible to the masses. Among these writings, *Wasan* ("Poems"), *Gutokushō* ("An Exposition of Buddhism and Amida's Vow"), and *Yuishinshōmoni* ("A Commentary on Seikaku's Book of Faith") are regarded as important books.

Shinran died quietly on November 28, 1262, in Kyōto, where he had been born 90 years before. Shinran's teaching of justification by faith alone, and especially his teaching concerning the spiritual priesthood of all devotees, contained democratic implications that the mass of the people were later to apply in the service of a social and religious reformation. Shinran's religion, Jōdo Shinshū, has become the largest school of Buddhism in Japan today.

BIBLIOGRAPHY. For further information on Shinran, see ALFRED BLOOM, *The Life of Shinran Shonin: The Journey to Self-Acceptance* (1968); KAKUNYO, *The Life of Shonin Shinran* (Eng. trans. 1911); CHOJUN OTANI, *Pages trad. du japonais* (1969); SHUNJO, *Honen, the Buddhist Saint: His Life and Teaching*, trans. with historical introduction and explanatory and critical notes by HARPER H. COATES and RYUGAKU ISHIZUKA (1925); SHINRAN SHONIN, *Buddhist Psalms*, trans. by SHUGAKU YAMABE and L.A. BECK (1921); GESSHO SASAKI, *A Study of Shin Buddhism* (1925).

(G.H.S.)

Shintō

Shintō is the name given to indigenous religious beliefs and practices of Japan. The word Shintō literally means "the way of *kami*" (*kami* means "mystical," "superior," or "divine," generally sacred or divine power, specifically the various gods or deities) and came into use in order to distinguish indigenous Japanese beliefs from Buddhism, which had been introduced into Japan in the 6th century AD.

By courtesy of the Japan National Tourist Organization

Procession at Toshogu Shrine Festival at Nikko, Japan, May 17–18.

NATURE AND VARIETIES

Shintō consists of the traditional Japanese religious practices as well as the beliefs and life attitudes which are in accord with these practices. Shintō is more readily observed in the social life of the Japanese people and in their personal motivations than in a pattern of formal belief or philosophy. Shintō remains closely connected with the Japanese value system and the Japanese people's ways of thinking and acting.

Three major types of Shintō · Shintō can be roughly classified into the following three major types: Shrine Shintō, Sect Shintō, and Folk Shintō. Shrine Shintō (*Jinja Shintō*), which has been in existence from the beginning of Japanese history to the present day, constitutes a main current of Shintō tradition. Shrine Shintō includes within its structure the now defunct State Shintō (*Kokka Shintō*)—based on the total identity of religion and state—and has close relations with the Japanese Imperial Family. Sect Shintō (*Kyōha Shintō*) is a relatively new movement consisting of 13 major sects which originated in Japan around the 19th century. Each sect was organized into a religious body by either a founder or a systematizer. Folk Shintō (*Minzoku Shintō*) is an aspect of Japanese folk belief that is closely connected with the other types of Shintō. It has no formal organizational structure nor doctrinal formulation but is centred in the veneration of small roadside images and the agricultural rites of rural families. These three types of Shintō are interrelated: Folk Shintō exists as the substructure of Shintō faith, and a Sect Shintō follower is usually a parishioner (*ujiko*) of a certain Shrine Shintō shrine at the same time.

HISTORY TO 1900

Much remains unknown about religion in Japan during the Paleolithic and Neolithic ages. It is unlikely, however, that the religion of these ages has any direct connection with Shintō. Yayoi culture, an early West Japan culture which originated in north Kyūshū around the 3rd or 2nd century BC, is directly related to later Japanese culture and hence to Shintō. Among the primary Yayoi religious phenomena were agricultural rites and shamanism.

Early clan religion and ceremonies. In ancient times small states were gradually formed at various places. By the middle of the 4th century AD a nation with an ancestor of the present Imperial Household as its head had probably been established. The constituent unit of society in those early days was the *uji* (clan or family), and the head of each *uji* was in charge of worshipping the clan's *uji-gami*—its particular tutelary or guardian deity. The prayer for good harvest in spring and the harvest ceremony in autumn were two major festivals honouring the *uji-gami*. Divination, water purification, and lustration (ceremonial purification), which are mentioned in the Japanese classics, became popular and people started to build shrines for their *kami*.

Kami

Ancient Shintō was polytheistic. People found *kami* in nature, which ruled seas or mountains, as well as in outstanding men. They also believed in *kami* of ideas such as growth, creation, and judgment. Though each clan made the tutelary *kami* the core of its unification, such *kami* were not necessarily the ancestral deities of the clan. Sometimes *kami* of nature and *kami* of ideas were regarded as their tutelary *kami*.

Two different views of the world were present in ancient Shintō. One was the three-dimensional view in which the Plain of High Heaven (Takama-no-hara, the *kami*'s world), Middle Land (Nakatsu-kuni, the present world), and the Hades (Yomi, the world after death) were arranged in vertical order. The other was a two-dimensional view in which this world and Perpetual Country (Tokoyo), a utopian place of boundless wealth, pleasure, and peace) existed in horizontal order. Though the three-dimensional view of the world (also characteristic of North Siberian and Mongolian shamanistic culture) became the representative view observed in Japanese myths, the two-dimensional view of the world (also present in Southeast Asian culture) was dominant among the populace.

Early Chinese influences on Shintō. Confucianism is believed to have reached Japan in the 5th century AD, and by the 7th century it had spread among the people, together with Chinese Taoism and Yin-Yang (harmony of two basic forces of nature) philosophy, and stimulated the development of Shintō ethical teachings. With the development of centralization of political power, Shintō began to develop as a national cult as well. Myths of various clans were combined and reorganized into a pan-Japanese mythology with the Imperial Household as its centre. The *kami* of the Imperial Household and tutelary *kami* of powerful clans became the *kami* of the whole nation and people, and offerings were made by the state every year. Such practices were systematized supposedly around the Taika Reformation (645). By the beginning of the 10th century about 3,000 shrines were receiving state offerings. As the power of the central government declined, the system ceased to be effective, and after the 13th century only a limited number of important shrines continued to receive the Imperial offerings. Later, after the Meiji Restoration (return to traditional Imperial system) in 1868, the old system was revived.

The encounter with Buddhism. Buddhism was first introduced into Japan in AD 538 and developed gradually. In the 8th century there emerged tendencies to interpret Shintō from a Buddhist viewpoint. Shintō *kami* were viewed as protectors of Buddhism; hence shrines for tutelary *kami* were built within the precincts of Buddhist temples. *Kami* were made equivalent to *deva* (the Buddhist Sanskrit term for "gods") who rank highest in the Realm of Ignorance, according to Buddhist notions. Thus *kami*, like other creatures, were said to be suffering because they were unable to escape the endless cycle of transmigration; help was therefore offered to *kami* in the form of Buddhist discipline. Thus from the mid-8th

century Buddhist temples were even built within Shintō shrine precincts, and Buddhist *sūtras* (scriptures) were read in front of *kami*. By the late 8th century *kami* were thought to be avatars, or incarnations, of Buddhas and *bodhisattvas*. *Bodhisattva* names were given to *kami*, and Buddhist statues were placed even in the inner sanctuaries of Shintō shrines. In some cases also Buddhist priests were in charge of the management of Shintō shrines.

Shintō-Buddhist syncretism

After 1192, during the Kamakura shogunate, theories of Shintō-Buddhist amalgamation were established. Two representative examples of such amalgamation were Shingon Shintō and Tendai Shintō. According to Shingon Shintō—also known as Ryōbu ("Two Aspects") Shintō—the principal source of the whole universe was considered to be the cosmic Buddha, Mahā-Vairocana (the Great Illuminator). According to Tendai Shintō—also called Ichijitsu ("One Reality") Shintō—only the Buddha-nature was the source of all things. These two sects also brought various Buddhist rituals of an esoteric nature into Shintō. Buddhistic Shintō was popular for several centuries and influenced the majority of Shintō shrines until its extinction at the Meiji Restoration.

Shintō reaction against Buddhism. Watarai, or Ise, Shintō was the first theoretical school of anti-Buddhistic Shintō in that it attempted to exclude Buddhist accretions and tried to formulate a pure Japanese version. Watarai Shintō appeared in Ise during the 13th century as a reaction against the Shintō-Buddhist amalgamation. Konton (chaos), or Kizen (non-being), was the basic *kami* of the universe for Watarai Shintō and was regarded as the basis of all beings, including the Buddhas and *bodhisattvas*. Purification, which had been practiced since the time of ancient Shintō, was given much deeper spiritual meanings. *Shōjiki* (uprightness or righteousness) and prayers were emphasized as the means by which to be united with *kami*.

Yoshida Shintō, which was started by Yoshida Kanetomo (1435–1511) in Kyōto, inherited various aspects of Watarai Shintō and also showed some Taoist influence. Its fundamental *kami* (the source of all things and beings in the universe) was Taigen Sonjin (the Great Exalted One). According to its teaching, if one is truly purified, his heart can be the *kami*'s abode. The ideal of inner purification was a mysterious state of mind in which one worshipped the *kami* that lived in one's own heart. Although the Watarai and Yoshida schools were thus free of Buddhistic theories, the influence of Chinese thought was still present.

Neo-Confucian Shintō. In 1603 the Tokugawa Shogunate was founded in Edo (Tokyo), and contact between Shintō and Confucianism was resumed. Scholars tried to interpret Shintō from the standpoint of Neo-Confucianism, which became an official subject of study for warriors, and from that of the Chinese Wang Yang-ming school of philosophy. Scholars emphasized the unity of Shintō and Confucian teachings. Yoshikawa Koretaru (1616–94) and Yamazaki Ansai (1618–82) were two representative scholars of Confucian Shintō. They added Neo-Confucian interpretations to the traditional theories handed down from Watarai Shintō, and each established a new school. The T'ai Chi ("Supreme Ultimate") of Neo-Confucianism was regarded as identical with the first *kami* of the *Nihon-shoki*, or *Nihongi* ("Chronicles of Japan"). One of the characteristics of Yoshikawa's theories was his emphasis on political philosophy. Imperial virtues (wisdom, benevolence, and courage), symbolized by the *sanshu-no-shinki* ("Three Sacred Treasures"), and national ethics, such as loyalty and filial piety, constituted the way to rule the state. Yamazaki Ansai further developed this tendency and advocated both mystic pietism and ardent emperor worship.

Yoshikawa Koretaru and Yamazaki Ansai

Revival of Shintō. Revival Shintō is one of the Kokugaku ("Japanese studies") movements which started toward the end of the 17th century. Advocates of this school maintained that the norms of Shintō should not be sought in Buddhist or Confucian interpretations but in the beliefs and life-attitudes of their ancestors as clarified by philological study of the Japanese classics. Moto-ori

Norinaga (1730–1801) represented this school. His emphasis was on the belief in *musubi* (the mystical power of becoming or creation), which had been popular in ancient Shintō, and on a this-worldly view of life, which expected the eternal progress of the world in ever-changing mutations. These beliefs, together with the inculcation of respect for the Imperial line and the teaching of absolute faith—according to which all problems beyond human capability were turned over to *kami*—exercised great influence on modern Shintō doctrines.

The most important successor of Moto-ori in the field of Shintō was Hirata Atsutane (1776–1843), who showed the influence of Roman Catholic teachings in some respects —derived from the writings of Jesuits in China—and introduced the idea of a creator god and retribution for ethical and religious failings in another world. These doctrines, however, were not accepted into the main current of Shintō. Hirata developed the philological studies started by Moto-ori and trained many capable disciples. He also wrote prayers, worked out formulas for family cults of tutelary *kami* and ancestors, and promoted Shintō practices. His criticism of the Tokugawa shogunate, based on the spirit of ancient Shintō, and his call to unite all the people under the emperor enlisted many supporters and served as one of the factors in bringing about the Meiji Restoration in 1868.

Formation of Sect Shintō. From the end of the Tokugawa period to the beginning of Meiji (1867–68), new religious movements emerged out of the social confusion and unrest of the people. What these new movements taught differed widely: some were based on mountain-worship groups, which were half Buddhist and half Shintō; some placed emphasis on purification and ascetic practices; and some combined Confucian and Shintō teachings. New religious movements such as Kurozumi-kyō (*kyō* means "religion," or "religious body"), founded by Kurozumi Munetada (1780–1850), Konkō-kyō (Konkō is the religious name of the founder of this group which means, literally, "golden light") by Kawate Bunjirō (1814–83), and Tenri-kyō (*tenri* means "divine reason or wisdom") by Nakayama Miki (1798–1887) were based mostly on individual religious experiences and aimed at healing diseases or spiritual salvation. These sectarian Shintō groups, amounting to 13 during the Meiji period (1868–1912), were stimulated and influenced by Revival Shintō. They can be classified as follows:

1. Revival Shintō sects: Izumo-ō-yashiro-kyō (or Taisha-kyō), Shintō-tai-kyō, Shinri-kyō
2. Confucian sects: Shintō-shūsei-ha, Shintō-taisei-kyō
3. Purification sects: Shinshū-kyō, Misogi-kyō
4. Mountain worship sects: Jikkō-kyō, Fusō-kyō, Ontake-kyō (or Mitake-kyō)
5. "Faith-healing" sects: Kurozumi-kyō, Konkō-kyō, Tenri-kyō

SHINTO LITERATURE AND MYTHOLOGY

Shintō has no founder. When the Japanese people and Japanese culture became aware of themselves, Shintō was already there. Nor has it any official scripture that can be compared to the Bible in Christianity or to the Qur'ān in Islām. The *Kojiki* ("Records of Ancient Matters") and the *Nihongi* or *Nihon shoki* ("Chronicles of Japan") are regarded in a sense as sacred books of Shintō. They were written in AD 712 and 720 respectively and are compilations of the oral traditions of ancient Shintō. But, they are also books about the history, topography, and literature of ancient Japan. It is possible to construct Shintō doctrines from them by interpreting the myths and religious practices they describe.

Stories partially similar to those found in Japanese mythology can be found in the myths of Southeast Asia; and in the style of description in Japanese myths, some Chinese influence is detectable. The core of the mythology, however, consists of tales about Amaterasu Ō-mikami ("Sun Goddess"), the ancestress of the Imperial Household, and tales of how her direct descendants unified the Japanese people under their authority. In the beginning, according to Japanese mythology, a certain number of *kami* simply emerged, and a pair of *kami*,

Kojiki and *Nihongi* ("Nihon shoki")

Izanagi and Izanami, gave birth to the Japanese islands, as well as to the *kami* who became ancestors of the various clans. The "Sun Goddess," the ruler of Takama-no-hara, the Moon Ruler (Tsukiyomi-no-mikoto), and the ruler of the nether regions (Susanowo-no-mikoto) were the most important among them. A descendant of the "Sun Goddess," Jimmu Tennō, is said to have become the first emperor of Japan. Japanese mythology says that the Three Sacred Treasures (*sanshu-no-shinki;* the mirror, the sword, and the jewels), which are still the most revered symbols of the Imperial Throne, were first given by the "Sun Goddess" to her grandson. The Grand Shrine of Ise is dedicated to this ancestral goddess and is the most highly respected shrine in Shintō.

The Japanese classics also contain myths and legends concerning the innumerable *kami* (*yaho-yorozu-no-kami;* literally, yaho=800, yorozu=10,000, no=of). Some of them are the tutelary deities of clans and later became the tutelary *kami* of their respective local communities. Many others, however, were not enshrined in sanctuaries and have no direct connections with the actual Shintō faith. Little attention had been paid to Shintō mythology until the development of Revival Shintō, and even today it is not really well known except by Shintō priests and scholars.

DOCTRINES

Concept of the sacred. At the core of Shintō are beliefs in the mysterious power (*musubi*, creating and harmonizing power) of *kami* and in the way or will (*makoto*, truth or truthfulness) of *kami*. The nature of *kami* cannot be fully explained in words because *kami* transcends the cognitive faculty of man. Devoted followers, however, are able to understand *kami* through faith and usually recognize various *kami* in polytheistic form.

Kami and *makoto*

Parishioners of a Shintō shrine believe in their tutelary *kami* as the source of human life and existence. Each *kami* has a divine personality and responds to truthful prayers. *Kami* also reveals *makoto* to men and guides them to live in accordance with it. According to the traditional Japanese way of thinking, truth manifests itself in empirical existence and undergoes transformation in infinite varieties in the empirical conditions of time and space. *Makoto* is not an abstract ideology. It can be recognized every moment in every individual thing in the encounter between man and *kami*.

In Shintō all the deities are said to cooperate with one another, and life lived in accordance with *kami*'s will is believed to produce a mystical power that gains the protection, cooperation, and approval of all the particular *kami*.

Precepts of truthfulness and purification. As the basic attitude toward life, Shintō emphasizes *makoto-no-kokoro* (heart of truth) or *magokoro* (true heart), which is usually translated as "sincerity, pure heart, or uprightness." This attitude follows from the revelation of *kami*'s truthfulness in man. It is, generally, the sincere attitude of a man in doing his best in the work he has chosen or in his relationship with others, and the ultimate source of such a life-attitude lies in man's awareness of the divine.

Although Shintō ethics do not ignore individual moral virtues such as loyalty, filial piety, love, and faithfulness, it is generally considered more important to seek for *magokoro*, which constitutes the dynamic life-attitude that brings forth these virtues. *Magokoro* was interpreted as "bright and pure mind" or "bright, pure, upright, and sincere mind" in ancient scriptures. In other words, it is the pure state of mind. Purification, physical and spiritual, is stressed in Shintō even today to produce such a state of mind. It is a necessary means to make communion between *kami* and man possible and to enable man to accept *kami*'s blessings.

Nature of man and other beliefs. In Shintō it is commonly said that "Man is *kami*'s child." First, this means that man was given his life by *kami* and that his nature is therefore sacred. Second, it means that daily life is made possible by *kami*, and, accordingly, the personality and life of man are worthy of respect. Man must revere the basic human rights of everyone (regardless of race, nationality, and other distinctions) as well as his own. The concept of original sin is not found in Shintō. On the contrary, man is considered to have a primarily divine nature. In actuality, however, this sacred nature is seldom revealed in man. Purification is considered symbolically to remove the dust and impurities that cover man's inner mind.

Role of the individual in the history of his family

Shintō is described as a "religion of *tsunagari*" (continuity or communion). The Japanese, while recognizing each man as an individual personality, do not take him as a solitary being separated from others. On the contrary, he is regarded as the bearer of a long, continuous history that comes down from his ancestors and continues in his descendents. He is also considered as a responsible constituent of various social groups.

Moto-ori Norinaga stated that the human world keeps growing and developing while continuously changing. Similarly Japanese mythology speaks of an eternity of history in the divine edict of the "Sun Goddess." In its view of history, Shintō adheres to the cyclical view, according to which there is a constant recurrence of historical patterns. Shintō does not have the concept of the "last day": there is no end of the world or of history. One of the divine edicts of the "Sun Goddess" says:

> This Reed-plain-1,500-autumns-fair-rice-ear Land is the region which my descendants shall be lords of. Do thou, my August Grandchild, proceed thither and govern it. Go! and may prosperity attend thy dynasty, and may it, like Heaven and Earth, endure forever.

Modern Shintōists interpret this edict as revealing the eternal development of history as well as the eternity of the dynasty. From the viewpoint of finite individuals, Shintōists also stress *naka-ima* (middle present), which repeatedly appears in the Imperial edicts of the 8th century. According to this point of view, the present moment is the most valuable of all conceivable times. In order to participate directly in the eternal development of the world, it is required of Shintōists to live fully each moment of life, making it as worthy as possible.

Historically, the *uji-gami* of each local community played an important role in combining and harmonizing different elements and powers. The Imperial system, which has been supported by the Shintō political philosophy, is an example of unity and harmony assuming the highest cultural and social position in the nation. After the Meiji Restoration (1868), Shintō was used as a means of spiritually unifying the people during repeated wars. Since the end of World War II the age-old desire for peace has been restressed. *The General Principles of Shintō Life* proclaimed by the Association of Shintō Shrines in 1956 has the following article: "In accordance with the Emperor's will, let us be harmonious and peaceful, and pray for the nation's development as well as the world's co-prosperity."

RITUAL PRACTICES AND INSTITUTIONS

Shintō does not have a weekly religious service. People visit shrines at their convenience. Some may go to the shrines on the 1st and 15th of each month and on the occasions of *matsuri* (rites or festivals), which take place several times a year. Devotees, however, may pay respect to the shrine every morning.

Matsuri

Rites of passage. Various Shintō rites of passage are observed in Japan. The first visit of a newborn baby to the tutelary *kami*, which will be between 30 and 100 days after his birth, is to initiate the baby as a new adherent. The Shichi-go-san festival on November 15 is the occasion for children of three, five, and seven years old respectively to visit the shrine to give thanks for *kami*'s protection and to pray for their healthy growth. January 15 is Adults' Day. Youth in the village used to join the local young men's association on this day. At present it is the commemoration day for those Japanese who have attained their 20th year. The Japanese usually have their wedding ceremonies in Shintō style and pronounce their wedding vows to *kami*. Shintō funeral ceremonies, however, are not popular. The majority of the Japanese are Buddhist and Shintōist at the same time and have their funerals in Buddhist style. A traditional Japanese house has two family altars: one, Shintō, for their tutelary *kami* and the goddess Amaterasu Ō-mikami, and another, Buddhist, for the family ancestors. Pure Shintō families, however, will have all ceremonies and services in Shintō style. There are other Shintō *matsuri* (rites) concerning occupations or daily life, such as a ceremony of purifying a building site or for setting up the framework for a new building, a firing or purifying ceremony for the boilers in a new factory, a completion ceremony for a construction works, or a launching ceremony for a new ship.

Varieties of festival, worship, and prayer. Each Shintō shrine has such grand festivals every year as the Spring Festival (*Haru-matsuri*, or *Toshi-goi-no-matsuri;* prayer for good harvest), Autumn Festival (*Aki-matsuri*, or *Niiname-no-matsuri;* Shintō thanksgiving), Annual Festival (*reisai*) and Divine Procession (*shinkō-shiki*). Divine Procession usually takes place on the day of Annual Festival, and sacred palanquins (*mikoshi*, miniature shrines carried on the shoulders) are transported through the district. The order of rituals at a grand festival is usually as follows: (1) Purification rites (*harai*)—commonly held at a corner of the shrine precincts before participants come into the shrine, but sometimes held within the shrine before beginning a ceremony. (2) Adoration—the chief priest and all the congregation bow to the altar. (3) Opening of the door of the inner sanctuary (by the chief priest). (4) Presentation of food offerings—rice, *sake* wine, rice cake, fish, bird, seaweed, vegetables, salt, water, etc., are offered, but not animal meat, because of the taboo on shedding blood in the sacred area. Generally, cooked food used to be offered to *kami*, but nowadays uncooked food is more often used. In accordance with this change, the idea of entertaining *kami* changed to that of thanksgiving. (5) Prayer—the chief priest recites *norito* (prayers). The models for *norito* are ancient Shintō prayers that were compiled in the early 10th century, based on the old belief that spoken words would have spiritual potency. (6) Sacred music and dance. (7) General offering—participants in the festival make symbolic offerings using little branches of the evergreen sacred tree with strips of white paper tied on them. (8) Taking offerings away—food and symbolic offerings are taken away. (9) Shutting the door of the inner sanctuary. (10) Final adoration. (11) Feast (*naorai*).

Ritual at festivals

Bob and Ira Spring

Shintō priest performing a purification rite before a portable shrine at the Komitake Festival, celebrating the opening of the Funatsu Trail to the summit of Mt. Fuji after the melting of the winter snow.

In the olden days *naorai*, a symbolic action for participants to hold communion with *kami* by having the same food offered to the deity, came in the middle of the festival ceremony. The custom is still observed sometimes at the Imperial Household and some old shrines. Most of the shrines, however, today have communion with *kami* by drinking the wine that was offered to *kami* after the festival instead. Since World War II it has become popular to have a brief sermon or speech before the feast.

Most Shintō festivals are observed generally in accordance with the above-mentioned order. On such occasions as the Annual Festival, various special rites may be held; *e.g.*, special purification (*misogi*) and abstinence (*o-komori*), a divine procession of a sacred palanquin (*o-miyuki*) or of boats (*funa-matsuri*), a ceremonial feast (*tōya-matsuri*), *sumo* wrestling, horseback riding (*kwabe-uma*), archery (*matoi*), a lion dance (*shishi-mai*), and a rice planting festival (*o-taue-matsuri*).

Types of shrines. A simple *torii* gate stands at the entrance of the shrine precincts (see illustration). After proceeding on the main approach, a visitor will come to an ablution basin where he is to clean his hands and rinse his mouth. Usually he will make a small offering at the oratory (*haiden*) and pray. Sometimes a visitor may ask the priest to conduct rites of passage or to offer special prayers. The most important shrine building is the inner sanctuary (*honden*), in which a sacred symbol called *shintai* (*kami* body) or *mitama-shiro* (divine spirit's symbol) is enshrined. Usually it is a mirror, but sometimes it is a wooden image, a sword, or some other object. In any case, it is carefully wrapped and placed in a container, and it is forbidden to see it. Only the chief priest is allowed inside the inner sanctuary.

Shintai and mitama-shiro

In the beginning Shintō had no shrine buildings. At each festival people placed a tree symbol at a sacred site or built a temporary shrine to invite *kami*. Later they began to construct permanent shrines where *kami* were said to stay permanently. The *honden* of the Grand Shrine of Ise and Izumo Shrine (in Shimane Prefecture) illustrate two representative archetypes of shrine construction. The style of the former probably developed from a storehouse for crops, especially for rice, and that of the latter from ancient house construction. In the course of time, variations of shrine architecture were adopted and additional buildings were attached in front of the *honden*. The *honden* and *haiden* are in many cases connected by a hall of offering (*heiden*) where prayers are usually recited. Large shrines also have a hall for liturgical dancing (*kagura-den*).

Other practices and institutions. *Uji-gami* belief is the most popular form of Shintō in Japan. The term *uji-gami* originally referred to the *kami* of an ancient clan. After the 13th century the term was used in the sense of the tutelary *kami* of a local community, and all the members in the community were considered to be that *kami*'s adherents (*ujiko*). Even today a *ujiko* group will consist of the majority of the residents in a given community. A Shintōist, however, can believe at the same time in shrines other than his own local shrine. It was only after World War II that some large shrines also started to organize believers' groups (*sūkeisha*). The Believers' Association of the Meiji Shrine, for instance, has approximately 200,000 members living around Tokyo.

Kokugakuin University and Kōgakkan University are the primary training centres for Shintō priests. Though anyone who goes through certain training processes may be a priest (or a priestess), many priests are, in fact, from the families of hereditary Shintō priests.

SHINTO RELIGIOUS ARTS

The Japanese from ancient times have valued emotional and aesthetic intuitions in expressing and appreciating their religious experiences. They found symbols of *kami* in natural beauty and the forces of nature, and they developed explicitly religious poetry, architecture, and visual arts. Shrine precincts are covered with green trees and are places of a serene and solemn atmosphere, which is effective in calming worshippers' minds. In the larger shrines, surrounded by expansive woods with mountains as their background, a harmony of nature and architecture may be achieved. The Grand Shrine of Ise and Izumo Shrine still retain the ancient architectural styles. After the 9th century an intricate form of shrine construction was developed adopting both Buddhist and Chinese architectural styles and techniques. The curving roof style is one example. Unpainted timbers are most

frequently used, but wherever Buddhistic Shintō was popular, Chinese vermilion-lacquered shrines were also built. A *torii* gate always stands in front of a shrine. Various kinds of *torii* can be seen in Japan, but their function is always the same: to divide the sacred precincts from the secular area. A pair of sacred stone animals called *koma-inu* (dogs of Kokuryō, an ancient Korean kingdom) or *karajishi* (lions of Tang) are placed in front of a shrine. Originally they served to protect the sacred buildings from evil and defilements. After the 9th century they were used for ornamental purposes on ceremonial occasions at the Imperial Court and later came to be used at various shrines generally. Some of the stone lanterns (*ishi-dōrō*) used at the shrines are works of art. The dedicator's name and the year are inscribed on the lanterns to inform viewers of the long tradition of faith and to urge them to maintain it.

Torii: the sacred gates

Compared with the Buddhist statues, images of *kami* are not outstanding either in their quality or quantity. Images of *kami* were, in fact, not used in ancient Shintō until after the introduction of Buddhism into Japan. These are placed in the innermost part of the *honden* and are not the objects of direct worship by the people. *Kami* icons are not worshipped at shrines.

The history of the shrine, its construction arrangements, and ritual processions are recorded in picture scrolls (*emakimono*), and at the older shrines there are many votive pictures (*ema*)—small wooden picture plaques—that have been dedicated by the people from former times. Other articles, such as specimens of calligraphy, sculpture, swords, and arms, dedicated by the Imperial families, nobles, or feudal lords, are also kept at shrines. Several hundred such items and shrine constructions have been designated by the Japanese government as national treasures and important cultural properties.

The traditional religious music and dance of shrines were performed for the purpose of entertaining and appeasing *kami*, rather than to praise them. *Gagaku* (literally "elegant music") involves both vocal and instrumental music, specifically for wind, percussion, and stringed instruments. *Gagaku* with dance is sometimes called *bugaku*. *Gagaku* was patronized by the Imperial Household as court music and was much appreciated by the upper classes from the 9th to the 11th century. Later some of the more solemn and graceful pieces were used as ritualistic music by shrines and temples. Today *gagaku* is widely performed at larger shrines. The authentic tradition of *gagaku* has been transmitted by the Institute of Music of the Imperial Household (established in 701).

Religious music and dance

Apart from *gagaku* there are also *kagura* (a form of indigenous, religious music and dance based on blessing and purification), *ta-asobi* (a New Year's dance-pantomime of the cycle of rice cultivation), and *shishi-mai* (lion dance), which developed originally from magico-religious dances, and are now danced for purification and as prayers. *Matsuri-bayashi* is a gay lively music with flutes and drums to accompany divine processions. Some organizations of both Shrine and Sect Shintō have recently begun to compose solemn religious songs to praise *kami*, making use of Western music. It is expected that such songs will be used in the future along with the traditional music. (See also VISUAL ARTS, EAST ASIAN; MUSIC, EAST ASIAN; DANCE AND THEATRE, EAST ASIAN.)

POLITICAL AND SOCIAL ROLES

Until the end of World War II, Shintō was closely related to the state. Offerings to *kami* were made every year by the government and the Imperial Household, and prayers were offered for the safety of the state and people. The *matsuri-goto* (the affairs of worship) offered by the emperor from olden days included not only ceremonies for *kami* but also for ordinary matters of state. "Shintō ceremonies and political affairs are one and the same" was the motto of officials. Administrators were required to have a religious conscience and develop political activities with *magokoro*.

This tradition was maintained as an undercurrent throughout Japanese history. Villagers prayed to the tutelary *kami* of the community for their peace and welfare, and promoted unity among themselves with village festivals. After the Meiji Restoration, the government treated Shintō like a state religion and revived the system of national shrines, which dated from the 10th century. In order to propagate Revival Shintō as the foundation of the national structure, they initiated the "great promulgation movement" in which the emperor was respected like *kami*. Although the Japanese constitution enacted in 1889 guaranteed freedom of faith under certain conditions, priority was, in fact, given to Shintō. In elementary schools Shintō was taught to children, and most of the national holidays were related to Shintō festivals. Shintō of this nature was called State Shintō and came under the control of the Bureau of Shrines in the Ministry of Home Affairs.

Relation of State and Sect Shintō

State Shintō was regarded as a state cult and a national ethic and not as "a religion." The free interpretation of its teachings by individual Shintō priests was discouraged. Priests of the national shrines were prohibited from preaching and presiding over Shintō funerals. By 1945 there were 218 national and approximately 110,000 local shrines. The number of Sect Shintō groups was limited to 13 after the organization of Tenri-kyō. Legally these 13 sects were treated as general religious bodies, similar to Buddhism and Christianity, and came under the supervision of the Ministry of Education.

After the end of World War II, the Supreme Commander for the Allied Powers ordered the Japanese government to disestablish State Shintō. All financial support from public funds and all official affiliation with Shintō and Shintō shrines were also discontinued. State rites performed by the emperor were henceforth to be regarded as the private religious practices of the Imperial family. These rulings were carried into the new Japanese constitution in 1947. Presently, Shrine Shintō is faced with two serious problems. The first is determining how the traditional unifying function of Shintō can be promoted in local communities or in the nation without interfering with freedom of faith. The second is the necessity of harmonizing Shintō with rapid modernization, especially in organizing believers and dealing with human problems or the meaning of life.

The number of Shintō shrines has been decreasing since the beginning of the Meiji era, in part because a municipal unification plan in 1889 called for the shrines of tutelary *kami* to be combined with the municipality. As of 1968, there were about 80,000 shrines, most belonging to the Association of Shintō Shrines, established in 1946. Another 1,000 shrines are independent or belong to small groups. Shintō believers number about 60,000,000.

About 15 percent of 16,251 Sect Shintō churches were damaged during World War II. Although they were not affected by the occupation policies after the war, many sects, in fact, went through difficult years because of unrest among the people and disunion within their own organizations. At present, Tenri-kyō in particular is most active among the Sect Shintō groups and is extending its missionary activities overseas to East Asia, North and South America, etc. As of 1968 the number of some of the major sects is approximately as follows: Izumo-ō-yashiro-kyō—1,530,000; Shinri-kyō—688,000; Shinshū-kyō—523,000; Ontake-kyō—655,000; Kurozumi-kyō—605,000; Konkō-kyō—521,000; Tenri-kyō—1,846,000.

PLACE OF SHINTO IN JAPANESE AND WORLD RELIGION

Shintō together with Buddhism is closely related both culturally and socially to the life of the Japanese people. Its relationships to other religions in Japan are generally cooperative and harmonious. Most Shintōists believe that cooperation between different religions could contribute to world peace, but this is not to imply a facile religious syncretism. Shintōists insist on maintaining their own characteristics and inner depth while working toward the peaceful coexistence of human beings.

BIBLIOGRAPHY. MASAHARU ANESAKI, *History of Japanese Religion* (1930, reissued 1955), a classical and standard book on Japanese religion; W.G. ASTON (trans.), *Nihongi: Chronicles of Japan from the Earliest Time to AD 697*, 2 vol. (1896, reissued 1956), a standard translation into English; D.L. PHILIPPI (trans.), *Koji-ki* (1968), a new translation with introduction of the work by Ō-no-Yasumaro Ō (d. 723), using recent achievements of Japanese philological studies; D.C. HOLTOM, *The National Faith of Japan* (1938, reissued 1965), the best book on Shintō written by a foreigner, strong in history and political philosophy; TSUNETSUGU MURAOKA, *Studies in Shinto Thought*, trans. by D.M. BROWN and J.T. ARAKI (1964), a dependable description of Shintō thought by an eminent philologist; NOAFUSA HIRAI, *Japanese Shinto* (1966), a brief general sketch of Shintō.

(N.H.)

Ship

A ship is a relatively large floating vessel capable of operating in the deep ocean. In modern times the term usually applies to vessels of over 500 tons that can negotiate the open seas, as opposed to "boat," a term reserved for smaller craft. Submersible ships are an exception to this convention in that regardless of their large size and unlimited operational ability they are generally called boats. The same is true of ore-carrying vessels on the U.S. Great Lakes, which are always called ore boats. In reference to sailing vessels, the word ship signifies three or more masts with square rigging.

A fuller history of sailing ships will be found in SAILS AND SAILING SHIPS. The present article briefly treats the historical development of all types of ships, oared, sailed, and combinations of the two, before the advent of steam propulsion; traces the development of the metal-hulled steamship; and describes the various types of modern ships and propulsion systems. Air-cushion vehicles are described in the article AIR-CUSHION MACHINES.

This article is divided into the following sections:

I. Ships of oar and sail

Historians are not unanimous in their determination of the birth of ships, but from the evidence it is safe to conclude that man ventured on water before 6000 BC, probably at first on a log, later on logs tied together. It has been argued that a raft is not technically a ship, because it depends for support on the buoyancy of its material rather than on the displacement of water. Prehistoric man, however, used primitive tools or fire to hollow out logs to form the earliest displacement vessel, the dugout canoe, still in use in some corners of the Earth. Other forms of early floating devices were fashioned from hides of animals inflated with air and sealed or stretched over branches to make lighter and faster canoes. The North American Indian's birchbark canoe is a similar device, using bark insted of hides.

Propulsion for the earliest craft was by hand or leg paddling, later by a flattened piece of wood, which evolved into the canoe paddle. The sequence of improved technology, improved tools, and availability of better materials and fastening methods, resulting in lighter and stronger hulls and more efficient propulsion, was repeated many times in the history of the ship.

ANCIENT SHIPS

Many of the most primitive types of ships still exist for special purposes. Log rafts are used in some regions in which seas are so rough that stiffer structures would be beaten to pieces. The efficiency of the outrigger canoe in giving the least possible frictional surface to the water for the most support against tipping under sail is still widely used by natives in the South Pacific and in Hawaii. Other surviving ancient types include the Arab dhows and the Chinese junk.

Egyptian and Minoan ships. From rock drawings dating from 6000 BC in Egypt and from descriptions in legends and stories, it is known that relatively large ships were developed in the eastern Mediterranean; and on the Nile River in Egypt, ships were built of bundles of reeds, the ends of which were bound together and bent upward to form the bow and stern of the ship so that in profile the ship was crescent shaped. This kind of construction was dictated not by choice but by the lack of large trees suitable for making dugouts or straight, heavy-strength members. Further to the east, across the Red Sea, where there were trees, early shipbuilders used a different method. They started with a canoe dug out from a stout log and graduated to building slanted sides fastened to a bow and stern boards to keep out the water and increase the carrying capacity. The result was a flat-keeled boat with square corners at the ends. These ships were also immortalized in rock drawings. By 3000 BC the reed boats of Egypt were venturing into the Mediterranean as far as Crete and Lebanon to bring back logs and other materials. Because these ships had no keel, they were held in shape by a taut cable, running on deck from the bow to the stern, which could be tightened as required. They were rowed and were steered by long oars over the stern. Later, sails were devised to move the ships when the wind was from the stern, which in the Nile was an advantage, because the wind normally blew upriver, so that the ships could sail up against the current and either pole or row down with the current. As successful and numerous as the Egyptian ships were, had not others invented a ship built around a sturdy log, ship development would have ceased, because without the strength and stiffness of a central structural member such as a keel or keels, larger and faster ships would have been impossible.

By about 2000 BC in Crete, the Minoans had developed ships using a log keel with ribs and planking on the sides joined at the stem and stern. To protect the bow against damage from waves, the heavy keel was bent upward and forward of the joint between the two sides of the ship, thus giving the ship a double, or bifid, bow.

During this period, nearly all ships were narrow beamed for their length to facilitate rowing. In the absence of navigational devices, the ships were restricted to moving on rivers, along coasts, or in narrow seas. Merchant ships and warships were very similar, although a warship development of the bifid bow became the sharpened ram projecting forward near the waterline. When the ram was used, it produced a great stress on the bow of the galley. In order to overcome this, heavy timbers were fastened lengthwise along the sides of the galley to help support the bow from damage. These timbers were known as whales (wales). Later, in addition to their original purpose of attacking other war vessels, it was found that they stiffened the ship so it did not have the unpleasant habit of bending in the middle when a wave passed under. In more modern times the strength members have been put inside the hull and are called longitudinals. To conserve the energy of the crew, these galleys included one or more large, square sails. Such galleys could not sail into the wind, and in battle the sail was never used; to set sail was a sign of defeat.

Phoenician merchant ships. The great merchants of the Mediterranean world, the Phoenicians of Tyre and Sidon, found that galleys were inefficient for trading voyages, because the large crews needed were expensive to feed, and the long narrow hull provided little space for cargo. The first merchant ships were descendants of the old Egyptian reed boats in that their hull form was broad and short, earning them the nickname of the round ship. They were built up from a heavy keel with ribs and a stem and stern post. A single large square sail furnished propulsion (see Figure 1). Such ships may have sailed around Africa. It is known that they sailed in the Atlantic as far north as Britain to trade for tin.

Margin note: The Phoenician round ship

By courtesy of the Museum of The Philadelphia Civic Center

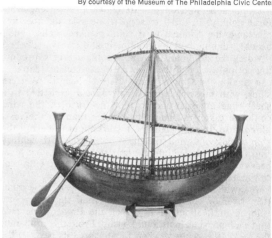

Figure 1: Model of a Phoenician ship, 13th century BC. In the Museum of the Philadelphia Civic Center.

Greek and Roman ships. In the Greek era the galley developed from an open, undecked craft up to 100 feet (30 metres) long and driven by a single row of oars 25 on a side to the ships used in the Battle of Salamis in 480 BC, about 150 feet (45 metres) in length with an outrigger (*parado*) on which the oarlocks were fixed. Width including outrigger was 20 feet (six metres). The oars were arranged in two banks (biremes) or three banks (triremes). In the next few hundred years larger galleys were tried but were found to be too cumbersome to manoeuvre, and so the final development of the war galley produced a ship of about 150 feet with a full deck or decks and a strong ram. They were called quinquiremes, a term the meaning of which is still in dispute. Some authorities believe it refers to a ship having five banks of oars, and others interpret it to mean five men to each oar. While the galley was the predominant military ship, the vast Mediterranean commerce in the Greek era was carried on with the round ships of Phoenician design.

The Romans brought little change in ships except the addition of the corvus, a bridge at the bows of a war galley to accommodate boarding parties. Roman grain ships grew to new sizes, measuring some 90 feet (27 metres) in length and 28 feet (nine metres) in beam, capable of carrying about 250 tons of cargo and over 300 passengers. Such heavy oared ships required more sail to drive them as well as to help in manoeuvring. Though they could still not sail into the wind, they were able to hold a course with their sails hauled around to take the wind on the quarter (about 45° from dead astern), an important step forward. These ships proved their seaworthiness in regular commerce with the British Isles.

Oriental ships. While the peoples of the Mediterranean were developing ships from those of the Egyptians, at about the same time China, with its vast land areas and poor road communications, was turning to water for transportation. The development in China followed a slightly different pattern from that of the Mediterranean. Starting with a dugout canoe, the Chinese joined two canoes with planking, forming a square punt, or raft. Next, the side, the bow, and the stern were built up with planking to form a large, flat-bottomed wooden box. The

Margin note: The Chinese junk

Margin note (left column): Flat-keeled boats

bow was sharpened with a wedge-shaped addition below the waterline. At the stern, instead of merely hanging a steering oar over one side as did the Western ships, Chinese shipbuilders contrived a watertight box, extending through the deck and bottom, that allowed the steering oar or rudder to be placed on the center line, thus giving better control. The stern was built to a high, small platform at the stern deck, later called a castle in the West, so that, in a following sea, the ship would remain dry, and when hove to or anchored she would turn with her bow to the wind. Thus, in spite of what to Western eyes seemed an ungainly figure, the Chinese junk was an excellent hull for seaworthiness as well as for beaching in shoal (shallow) water. Her principal advantage, however, not apparent from an external view, was great structural rigidity. In order to support the side and the bow planking, the Chinese used solid planked walls (bulkheads), running both longitudinally and transversely and dividing the ship into 12 or more compartments, producing not only strength but also protection against damage.

In rigging the Chinese junk was far ahead of Western ships, with sails made of narrow panels, each tied to a sheet (line) at each end so that the force of the wind could be taken in many lines rather than on the mast alone; also, the sail could be hauled about to permit the ship to sail somewhat into the wind. By the 15th century junks had developed into the largest, strongest, and most seaworthy ships in the world. Not till about the 19th century did Western ships catch up in performance.

Meanwhile, in the island kingdom of Japan, little other than river or coastal dugouts and small ships were developed until about 81 BC, when the Emperor decreed that each province must build a ship. From this time until the early 17th century, when Japan closed its ports to the world, Japan developed its ships rapidly. From drawings in the 15th century, Japan had ships comparable to the best Western vessels. But soon after, the closure of Japanese ports halted progress until the mid-19th century, when Japan recommenced building ships.

Northern ships.   In the European north, where the seas were cold and unfriendly, the peoples of the Scandinavian countries developed still another form of ship. Because they also started from the log, some authorities hypothesize that in early times Minoans fleeing invaders had taught the northern people how to build ships. In any case, the first northern ships were very similar to the Minoan ships with the bifid bow. Because these ships had to weather higher seas, the bifid was not developed into a ram, for in pitching in a heavy sea the ram put great stress on the ship and tended to break her back. Instead,

Viking ships

the Vikings developed double-ended ships, having both a sharp bow and a sharp stern, built high against following seas. To survive in the strong gales of the northern waters, the single large square sail on the Viking ship was made of leather or cloth with reinforcing leather strips. Over the stern a long oar was suspended from one side, extending below the bottom of the keel, to improve stability. The hull form in the centre (amidships) was much broader than that of the galleys of the south, and overall there was a smooth, flowing curve from the high bow through the well-rounded midships to the high stern, a good design still used in lifeboats and whaleboats today. Another feature was the covering of the oar ports with sliding plugs to keep out the water when the oars were not in use. Many pictorial representations of Viking galleys show shields slung over the oar ports, which may be the locations they were placed when the ship was in port, but at sea this placement would have interfered with the operation of the oars. The planks were fastened to the ribs by lashings rather than by bolts or pegs, giving the ship a flexibility that reduced the stress in heavy seas. Even more important was a northern merchantman, the knorr, broader and deeper-hulled than the long ships and the first northern ships to sail into the wind. In about the 14th century the knorr developed into a standard merchant ship, the design of which governed north European shipbuilding for over 400 years. This later version, called the cog, was given a true stern rudder for better handling and a long spar extending forward

called a bowsprit. Modified by a built-up castle in the stem or stern to provide a platform for soldiers, the cog became the standard man-of-war.

RIGGING

Medieval developments.   Meanwhile, in the Mediterranean a change in rigging had permitted ships to sail closer to the wind. Traders may have observed Chinese junks with their lug rig or the Arab dhows of the Indian Ocean. In the Indian Ocean the monsoon winds blow toward India in the summer and Africa in the winter. For this situation the Arabs developed the dhow, with a long stem and a sharp bow to run well before the wind and a square sail with only a top spar. It could be placed so that the spar was nearly vertical, allowing the rest of the sail to lie nearly in the fore and aft plane of the ship for sailing with the wind and could be placed horizontal to support the square sail for sailing before the wind.

To summarize the problem of a rig to permit sailing before or into the wind, it may be noted that, when the simple square sail is placed 90 degrees to the centreline of a ship with the wind coming from directly astern, the force of the wind literally blows the ship along at a speed somewhat less than that of the wind. If the wind is from the side of the ship, however, the sail must be placed at an angle to the wind. In this case, the phenomenon known as aerodynamic lift, which supports aircraft in flight, comes into play and produces a force nearly perpendicular to the surface of the sail, driving the ship forward and simultaneously causing her to drift to leeward (downwind), depending on how deep the ship is. As the ship begins to move forward in the water, the sail reacts not directly to the direction and velocity of the wind but to the force that is the sum of the wind and the motion of the ship (the vector), producing a greater force at the sail. For this reason, a ship can sail faster than the prevailing wind, a common characteristic of well-designed racing ships. In iceboats where resistance to motion is small this effect can build up to high speeds (90 to 100 miles [145 to 160 kilometres] per hour). To work this way a sail must have a tight, straight luff (edge facing the wind) and a gentle curve from the luff to leach (edge further from the wind) resembling the upper surface of an airplane wing (see SAILS AND SAILING SHIPS).

Problems of sailing into the wind

The first attempts at sailing into the wind of the Chinese and the Norsemen were made simply by attaching ropes (sheets) to the ends of the top and bottom spars and leading these sheets one forward and the other aft, to hold the spars at a desired angle to the wind, permitting sailing within 80 degrees of the wind. The Arabs found that, by leaving off the bottom spar, tilting the top spar nearly vertical, and varying the tension on the sheets, the best curve of the sail could be obtained. This rig became known as the lateen after an innovation that eliminated the luff and produced a triangular sail.

About the 9th century the Byzantines built carvel-planked (smooth-sided) ships with the new lateen rig that could sail to within about 60° of the wind, giving them a great manoeuvring and navigational advantage over earlier ships. Their round form helped their sailing qualities, and the smooth carvel sides offered less skin friction to the water, giving at once a commodious ship with good sailing qualities and the ability to sail generally in the desired direction without too much concern for the wind direction. This development was the final stage of the southern ship, which had inherited 6,000 years of Mediterranean experience. These ships grew over the next two to three hundred years to large and cumbersome ships called nefs, which had two and three masts, all lateen rigged, and displaced over a thousand tons.

The full-rigged ship.   In about the 13th century the sturdy square-sailed cogs of the north appeared in the Mediterranean and met the lateen-rigged nefs of the south. Over the next few years the features of the two types merged in the carrack, which became the prototype for the western European ocean ship. The carrack was a three-masted ship with carvel hull planking and external whales for strengthening. It had the centreline rudder and the graceful rounded lines of the northern parent. Its rig was a mixture of north, south, and ancient Roman. By happy coincidence, at nearly the same time, the magnetic compass made its appearance, equipping the carrack with a fundamental navigational aid.

The swift evolution of the carrack into the classic ship that served as both warship and merchantman for the Western world consisted mostly of details. The drudgery of handling the large square sails brought forth sets of smaller sails on the forward masts, with the lower being the driving sail, called the course sails, then upper and lower topsails, resulting in the full-rigged ship.

Copper cladding. From the beginning there had been a problem of bottom fouling and attacks by a boring worm called *Teredo navalis.* These had been dealt with by coating with tar or other substances or sheathing with lead, with indifferent success. Ships had been small enough so that their crew either could careen them (tip them over with weights in the water until most of one side of the bottom showed) or could haul them out on a gently sloping beach and clean and treat their bottoms. As sails became more efficient and ships became larger, these practices were not nearly as practical. During the late 18th century the British tried coating the bottoms with sheets of copper, which at first caused severe corrosion of the iron fastenings but later proved to be very effective with bronze fastenings, and by the end of the 18th century most ships of any significance had copper-clad bottoms to protect them.

Ships grew with the efficiency of their sailing rigs from the 80- or 90-foot (24- or 27-metre) lengths of the 15th century to the 2,000- and 3,000-tonners of the early 19th century.

The clippers. The last period of the wooden sailing ships produced some of the fastest and most beautiful ships of the entire era. The Industrial Revolution brought pressure for speed in shipping, while trade among Europe, North America, and the Orient was blossoming, particularly in tea, which had become the staple beverage in England. Grown almost solely in China, tea was a seasonal crop, its leaves being picked each summer. Rivalry developed between ships to bring the first shipments each year to England and North America. As a result, the sailing ship achieved its finest development, in the form of the China clipper, just as the steamship matured to displace it.

The term clipper, first applied to a class of small, swift Chesapeake Bay schooners and brigs (Baltimore clippers), was given in 1833 to a larger ship, built in Baltimore, named the "Ann McKim," which became the prototype of a new type of ship for the North Atlantic packet service. Built for speed and stability to handle the greatest possible area of sails and to offer the least resistance to the water, the clippers had a radically new set of hull lines, a sharp cutwater at the bow widening very gradually toward the midship section, giving actually a concave shape to the waterlines. This conformation still is a very popular form for the underwater portion of a fast ship— V sections forward and U sections aft. The hull was designed to give minimum weight with adequate strength, another modern principle for a fast ship. The first ship built to the new design, the "Rainbow," made a round trip from New York to Canton, China, in six months, 14 days, a new record, on her maiden voyage. In the 1840s and 1850s the demand for clipper ships was so great that the shipyards on the East Coast of the United States were mass producing them. British shipbuilders and owners quickly joined the competition. The Civil War in America ended American supremacy and left the field to the British; competition between the Clyde builders and the Aberdeen builders produced the finest clippers of all. The British clippers were built of hardwoods that lasted much longer and remained dryer than the American clippers. In the 1860s the British used composite structure to insure that their ships would be as dry as possible. Their ribs were formed of iron, on which the hull planks were fastened. These ships were very strong, and at least one, "Cutty Sark," launched in 1869 and sailed in commerce for over 30 years, is still preserved in a dry dock in Greenwich. Some of the clippers reached speeds of 21 knots (21 nautical miles per hour) and even averaged 16 to 18 for a full day's sailing.

By the 1870s the Suez Canal had been opened, the transcontinental railroad was opened across North America, and steamships were gaining dependability and acceptance. The day of the clipper ship thus ended barely 30 years after it started, and with it ended the age of sail.

II. The age of steam and iron

FROM SAIL TO STEAM

The first steamboats. Though Robert Fulton is generally credited with the invention of the steamboat, it is well known that he had been preceded by several others. Salomon de Caus of France experimented with steam power for a boat as early as 1615, as did Denis Papin, a French Huguenot physicist, a century later. The first steam-powered boats to actually run followed James Watt's improvement of the steam engine in 1775. Among others, John Fitch demonstrated one in the United States in 1787 and by 1790 had built several. Fitch was unlucky in attracting backers and lacked the funds to continue development. His original model was powered by a set of six paddles suspended from either side of the boat and moved forward and aft by the action of the steam piston. He later built a craft with three paddles in the stern that attained a speed of eight miles (13 kilometres) per hour. All of these earliest steamboats used chains attached to ratchet wheels or other crude methods to convert the reciprocating motion of the piston rod of the single steam piston. In Scotland, however, William Symington aroused interest with his use of a crank, the capacity of which to convert linear to rotary motion is still the basic principle of reciprocating steam machinery. With the crank device, Symington built the 56-foot (17-metre) "Charlotte Dundas," named after the daughter of his financial backer, in 1801. Its piston developed ten horsepower and enabled it to act as a tug in the canals of Scotland, probably the first commercially successful steam-driven vessel.

Robert Fulton developed a steamboat that he demonstrated on the Seine in 1803 with indifferent success, but, undaunted, he had the "Clermont" built and shipped to the United States, where it was demonstrated on the Hudson River in 1807. The "Clermont," nearly three times the length of the "Charlotte Dundas," steamed up the Hudson under its own power at an average speed of five miles (eight kilometres) per hour. After a few improvements it was renamed the "North River" and went into regular service between New York and Albany. Highly successful financially, it enabled Fulton to continue his work and produce many more ships.

A contemporary of Fulton's, John Stevens, in 1804 applied the principle of the Archimedes screw, a rotating helix, to drive a ship. His boat ran, but insufficient skill of the workmen who fabricated the propeller prevented him from perfecting his device. Stevens, however, formulated lasting principles in steam engineering. He said that a ship, to be successful, should have a multitube boiler, high-pressure steam, direct connection of the steam engine to the propeller, and a short, four-bladed, helical propeller. Although the number of blades has varied, Stevens' predictions have been remarkably accurate. While development continued in the United States, a number of shipbuilders on the Clyde River in Scotland, close to large foundries and machine works, led steamboat building in Europe.

For its first 50 years, steam power was looked on with mistrust, not totally unfounded in view of the wooden construction of the ships, yet the steam engines themselves were remarkably dependable, perhaps because of their simplicity. Nearly all ships of this period were equipped with sails as well as steam and relied mainly on sail to conserve their wood fuel supply. Such was the case with the "Savannah," built by Moses Rogers, a sea captain and engineer, who interested backers in Savannah, Georgia, in developing a steam-equipped ship to cross the Atlantic. Purchasing an unfinished sailing packet in New York, Rogers added a two-boiler reciprocating steam engine. The ship was about the size of a modern seagoing tug. The engine produced at most 75 horsepower, equalled by some modern outboard motors. Among noteworthy characteristics of the engine and propulsion system were the use of seawater for boiler feed; coal-fired instead of wood-fired boilers, collapsible paddle wheels to be stowed on deck in severe storms, and a full set of sails.

Although the "Savannah" was especially outfitted for passenger comfort, people were apprehensive of taking passage in it, and in 1819 it sailed with no passengers and no cargo. Rogers took it all the way to Russia with no mechanical troubles reported, but the vessel remained a financial failure and in the end was stripped of its power plant and sold as a sailing packet. Despite its own fate, the "Savannah" was followed by many successors; by 1839 there were 776 steam-propelled ships registered in the British Isles alone. A series of Atlantic crossings under sail and steam culminated in 1827 in the all-steam crossing by the British-built Dutch ship "Curaçao," a ship of 438 tons with steam-driven paddle wheels capable of 50 horsepower each. A short time later the "Royal William," a Canadian ship of 830 tons and 200-horsepower engines, made regular scheduled crossings.

An important contribution to the success of the new ships came from Robert Napier, a British ship designer who observed that the bluff bows of old-fashioned sailing ships caused considerable turbulence. Experimenting in a model tank, Napier developed a sharp cutwater bow that allowed easier passage of the steamship, thus improving its speed. One of Napier's associates was a merchant named Samuel Cunard, who with several others formed a company that obtained a subsidy from the British government to carry mail. With this help they built the four ships that began the famous Cunard Line, the "Britannia," the "Acadia," the "Caledonia," and the "Columbia." They were not large, being about 200 feet (60 metres) long with 34-foot (ten-metre) beam and displacing 1,150 tons. Their power of 750 horsepower enabled them to cross the Atlantic on a regular basis, the "Britannia" doing it in 14⅓ days.

In the United States in 1850, a new line called the Collins Line was formed with the purpose of surpassing the Cunard ships. This line built five large paddle-wheel steamers of 1,000 horsepower using a cylinder of eight-foot (2.4-metre) diameter with a nine-foot (2.7-metre) stroke. The Collins ships displaced 2,860 tons and carried extensive sail. Their speed of 13 knots won them temporary dominance in the Atlantic trade.

Development of steam power.   In all these early steamships the steam pressures were very low, at first as little as three to five pounds per square inch above atmospheric pressure. To grasp the problem confronting the marine engineers of the 19th century, a brief description of the low-pressure steam engine is necessary. In it, wood or coal was burned in proximity to water in a square boiler, causing the water to boil and form steam at a pressure above atmospheric. This steam was led into the cylinder, in which its expansive force pushed the piston to the end of the cylinder; valves then opened to allow the steam to escape to the condenser and be returned to the liquid state. The water, pressurized by pumps to a pressure slightly higher than that existing in the boiler, was reintroduced into the boiler to continue the cycle. Where water was plentiful, the cycle could be even further simplified by exhausting the steam from the engine directly to the atmosphere and pumping in new water to the boiler.

The expansive force, or pressure, of steam depends upon its temperature. In the low-pressure cylinder, during the stroke, the steam expanded to at or below atmospheric temperature and pressure. Because this represented only a relatively modest drop, the power generated was weak. After 50 years of steamboats, maximum steam pressure possible was about 20–30 pounds per square inch at the boiler. To increase power output, the size of the pistons was increased, or more were added. The largest pistons could deliver up to 1,000 horsepower. By the 1860s the boxlike low-pressure boiler had reached the limit of its potential. In the 1870s a new approach was tried. A British warship, HMS "Iris" was given a boiler built in the form of a cylinder. The experiment was a success; a much

higher steam pressure was achieved without structural failure of the boiler. Within a decade, steam pressures multiplied six times.

With this increased pressure available, a further refinement could be introduced. The hot, high-pressure steam could be used more than once. It could be expanded through the original high-pressure cylinder and discharged to power a second, lower pressure but larger cylinder (double expansion) and even a third (triple expansion). Improved condensers brought the exhaust of the last cylinder to well below atmospheric pressure. With these improvements, the reciprocating steam engine approached the peak of its development by the turn of the 20th century, producing better than 20,000 horsepower per engine from an initial steam pressure of slightly over 200 pounds per square inch. Engines such as these drove the North Atlantic liners of the day, but the size of the reciprocating engine was placing a limit on its further development, because at these powers the lowest pressure cylinders were nearing ten feet (three metres) in diameter, and, with their large structural foundations and braces to take the load of the tons of metal reversing every stroke, they were becoming extremely heavy.

The turbine.   A continuing demand for greater speed and power brought the adoption of a newer form of engine, the turbine. Reciprocating machinery remained in vogue for moderate powered ships, however, and many still remain in service because of their simplicity of operation and maintenance, their long life, and dependability, ideal qualities for merchant ships relying on low-cost operation. One of the added advantages of the reciprocating engine was that it could be timed to turn at the relatively slow speed that is required of an efficient ship propeller, thus removing an added complication arising with the turbine.

The principle of the turbine, which is the reaction or impulse or both of a current of pressurized water, steam, or gas against a series of curved blades on a central rotating spindle, had been known for some time when, in 1884, an English engineer, Charles A. Parsons, patented a turbine in which the rotor wheel was driven by the reaction of a steam jet from its periphery (reaction turbine), and shortly afterward a Swedish inventor, Carl de Laval, patented a turbine in which the jet of steam impinged on the turbine blade (see also TURBINE). Because these turbines were inherently efficient devices that were not limited in size, they developed rapidly, and by the start of the 20th century they were in service. Initially, the real advantages of the turbines, high efficiency and light weight, were not exploited; directly connected to the relatively slow-turning propellers, they had to be made large and inefficient. The first solution for faster ships was to use several propellers (multiple screws) and turn them at higher than optimum speeds and to divide the turbines into several units, the lowest pressure units becoming very large in diameter. The Parsons and De Laval turbines

Reduction gearing.   About 1910 the real solution to the problem appeared in the form of new transmissions. These took three forms. The solution in Germany was to provide a hydraulic speed-reducing coupling in the propeller shaft so that the turbine could run at its more efficient high speed while the propeller could run at its slower optimum speed. In Britain a similar result was achieved by fitting mechanical reduction gearing between the turbine and the propeller shaft; and in the United States the turbines were used to drive electric generators, which in turn drove electric motors attached to the propeller shaft, and, by motor control, the best speed for each could be obtained. The net result of any of these systems was to open the way for rapid development of high-powered fast ships with improved range of operation, because these devices allowed the turbine and propeller designers to achieve about 25 percent improvement in overall efficiency. Ultimately, most ships adopted mechanical gearing. Electric drive, because of its lower efficiency and higher cost, is usually reserved for ships requiring very fine control of engines from the bridge or ships such as dredges in which there are high requirements for electric power. Because of poor efficiency, hydraulic couplings have almost disappeared except for certain specialized uses.

In the early cylindrical boilers the fire was still brought through the water in tubes, as in the old box types. The system was perpetuated in the so-called Scotch boiler widely used with reciprocating machinery in merchant ships requiring only moderate pressures; above a certain point such a boiler becomes too massive to be practical. Shortly after the introduction of the Scotch boiler, its successor, the water-tube boiler, was invented. Its perfection took several years because of difficulties in circulation and watertightness, but in the end it supplanted the fire-tube boiler in all high-powered ships. As the name implies, the water-tube boiler uses a furnace in which the fire is contained and through which water is passed in tubes between upper and lower cylindrical drums. Water-tube boilers originally employed natural circulation, using the lower density of hot water to keep the water flowing through the tubes. Later, in order to increase efficiency further and reduce size and weight, pumping was introduced to force circulation, thus achieving faster heating rates.

DEVELOPMENTS IN HULL DESIGN AND PROPULSION SYSTEMS

Hull materials and fabrication. From earliest times the custom was to build the hull from the most readily available natural material. In Egypt this meant reeds; in Crete it meant wood; and so it went for most of the shipping nations until the early and middle part of the 19th century. When iron first became available, the concept of putting to sea in a vessel built of a material heavier than water was not accepted by shipbuilders any more than by the general public. The fact that the ship is supported by the water it displaces rather than by the buoyancy of its material could not overcome the fear of sinking should the hull be ruptured. The beginning of iron shipbuilding was the construction by an iron founder in Scotland of an iron barge in 1787, a venture that met with ridicule. But in 1818 Thomas Wilson, also of Scotland, built an iron sailing ship, the "Vulcan," to haul coal in coastal and river traffic; the vessel proved so durable that it was still in service 60 years after its launching. In 1821 the "Aaron Manby," with a hull of iron, made the passage from Birmingham, where it was built, to France, where it entered service on the river Seine. There followed several smaller iron ships built in England and Scotland. Most were sailing craft and designed for service on inland waterways, a use that did not arouse popular apprehension over sinking so much as for oceangoing service. A significant event in 1834 helped to change the image of iron ships, when a number of wooden ships and one iron steamer, the "Garryowen," were driven ashore in a storm. After the storm the "Garryowen" was able to refloat itself and proceed, while the wooden vessels were either badly damaged or lost. This graphic demonstration of the superior hull strength of iron over wood quickly led to the widespread adoption of iron as a hull material. From 1850 through about 1880, iron was the principal material for ships' hulls.

Wood was finally abandoned for other reasons. In 1853 Russia first used explosive shells in warfare at sea, and the wooden ships that had resisted solid shot well splintered and came apart with exploding shells. Another reason was economic. The wooden ship cost more to build and maintain than her iron successor. Finally, because of difficulty in fastening and inherent strength, the size of ships built from wood was limited to about 300 feet (100 metres). Iron plates formed to the shape of the ship, joined by rivets to each other and to the frames of the ship, produced a more homogeneous structure than wooden hulls, which had a weakness wherever the ends of planks were connected. After 1880, steel offered superior ductility and strength to produce lighter and stronger hulls and soon replaced iron.

In the 20th century, engineers were long aware of the possible superior strength of welding over riveting, but the problems of incomplete welds or of cracking kept widespread use of welding for hulls from developing until nearly World War II, when welding's advantages in mass production became an overriding consideration. Great numbers of ships were then built with all of the connections in their hulls welded. During the latter part of the war and shortly thereafter, several mysterious ship losses occurred. In a few cases, tankers with all-welded hulls cracked in two while riding at anchor. The problem of welding ships was studied by metallurgists and shipbuilders, and it was found that some steels at low temperatures, such as are found in the wintertime in the North Atlantic, became very brittle and so sensitive to small cracks and notches that under the right conditions they cracked with almost explosive speed and violence. Remedies for these weaknesses were found by inserting riveted joints in these ships at critical points, a practice that stopped the running of cracks. For later ships a change in the composition and treatment of the steel was made to avoid the notch sensitivity. The episode was a good illustration of the unsuspected problems that have made shipbuilders and designers traditionally conservative.

With the solution of the cracking problems, all-welded ships became the rule. As the search for higher speeds continued, newer hull materials were introduced. In the case of very high speed cutters and hydrofoils or air-cushion ships, almost exclusive use has been made of high-strength alloys of aluminum. Investigations continue in even higher strength materials, such as titanium, for highly stressed elements.

The screw propeller. From the introduction of steamships, both the paddle wheel and the screw propeller were available for propulsion, and at first the paddle wheel predominated. Of itself, the paddle wheel is a very efficient device and is competitive with even modern propellers. The drawbacks that led to its being replaced include its vulnerability to damage; its unhappy trait of coming out of the water when the ship rolls violently in a heavy sea, complicating steering; and the fact that, because it operates close to the surface of the water, it is susceptible to excessive slipping under heavy load at slow speed and high thrust (driving power). The propeller, on the other hand, is well submerged and if well designed can have good low-speed thrust as well as high-speed efficiency. Its disadvantages are underwater resistance of shafts and struts, the need to make the penetration of the hull by the shaft watertight, and vulnerability to underwater obstacles. In 1845 the British Admiralty staged a tug-of-war between HMS "Rattler," a screw-propelled ship designed and built by Isambard Kingdom Brunel, and a merchant ship equipped with paddle wheels, the "Alecto." Both ships were about 800 tons and about equal power. The event was held on a calm sea, and the "Rattler" towed the "Alecto" away at about two to two and a half knots. This test was hailed as a proof that the screw propeller was superior to the paddle wheel, because it was under those conditions of very slow speed and high thrust. Whether the paddle wheel would fare so badly at speed in an efficiency run was not determined, but from that day forward the screw propeller was favoured, and nearly all ships are fitted with propellers today, except for river steamers that are faced with shoal-water operation and some ships operating on sheltered lakes.

Other forms of propulsion have developed to fill various specialized needs, such as the air propeller to supply thrust for high-speed boats designed to traverse swamps and for some air-cushion vessels. The simple air screw seems to have many advantages for propulsion, but its prohibitive size for larger powers at the relatively slow speed of ships has restricted its use.

III. The modern ship

The changes in the early steamships during the age of iron ships followed the developments in power, propulsion, and hull materials already discussed. A typical ship of the 1840s was the "Sarah Sands," 186 feet (57 metres) long, 33-foot (ten-metre) beam, 1,400 gross tons, equipped with 300 horsepower in two cylinders. The Inman Line built a succession of ships of iron with screw propellers that set a new standard. For example, the "City of Washington" was 2,870 tons and 358 feet (109

Scotch boiler and water-tube boiler

Adoption of welding in ship construction

Drawbacks of the paddle wheel

metres) long with a 40-foot (12-metre) beam. In 1852 the last Cunard wooden ship was built, the "Arabia," with a sea speed of 13 knots on 3,250 horsepower.

DEVELOPMENTS IN SHIPBUILDING

Specifications of the "Great Eastern"

The "Great Eastern." In nearly every development of ships, the fundamental motive that brought on the building of a better ship was economic need. So, too, was the case of the largest ship of its time and perhaps the most revolutionary single step in shipbuilding—the "Great Eastern." It was conceived in the mind of one of the great builders of his time, the "Little Giant," Isambard Kingdom Brunel, also an outstanding bridge and railroad builder. From his knowledge of naval architecture Brunel realized that, the larger a ship is, the less power it takes to drive it; or, stated another way, the longer the ship, the faster it will travel with about the same power. At the time, the mid-19th century, steamships were just beginning to come of age and compete with sailing ships. Their weakest feature was their lack of sufficient fuel for long voyages, and in the 1850s the most lucrative employment was the China tea trade, in which round-trip speed was important. Putting these factors together, Brunel sold the idea to a syndicate of building, with existing technology, a steamship five times as large as the largest ship then afloat. The result was a remarkable ship, over 690 feet (210 metres) long, of nearly 19,000 gross tons. To give adequate strength, it was fashioned out of ⅞-inch (22-millimetre) iron plates and was the first ship to have a double bottom. In addition, it was divided into 22 massive compartments by fore and aft- and transverse-subdivision bulkheads, making it comparable to modern ships in strength and capacity to survive damage. It was powered by three separate means of propulsion, a pair of 58-foot (18-metre) paddle wheels, a 28-foot (nine-metre) screw propeller driven by a separate steam engine, and, as an additional safety measure and to conserve fuel, the enormous spread of 6,500 yards of sail. Its fuel capacity gave it sufficient endurance to make the round trip of 22,000 miles (35,000 kilometres) from England to Ceylon and return without refueling.

Launching a ship of such unprecedented size created unprecedented problems, and the launch effort ended in failure. The ship was stuck on the ways for almost four months, bursting some of the most powerful hydraulic jacks in the country before it was finally set afloat in 1858. By this time the original £780,000 cost had been exceeded, and, because there was no government subsidy, the backers went bankrupt. After several changes of ownership and more difficulty, it finally went on an unprofitable voyage to the United States and was put on exhibition in several places to attempt to gain funds for its owners. It never was sent on the route for which it was designed, or it might have set records; but instead it gained a measure of fame for laying the transatlantic cable and the cable to India. It was a technical marvel, but, because financing and other problems did not permit it to perform its design mission, it was an economic failure. Not approached in size or efficiency for over 50 years, the "Great Eastern" led the way to the ship revolution of the second half of the 19th century.

The transatlantic liners. The rivalry for the record for the fastest passage of the Atlantic by steam spurred most of the developments in shipbuilding during this period, each company adopting new technology as fast as it was proved practical. By 1874 the ocean liners had reached the speed of 16 knots and had cut the Alantic crossing time to seven days. Their displacement had risen to over 5,000 tons. By 1881, ships of 7,000 to 8,000 tons and steam pressures of over 100 pounds brought speeds of 20 knots. Steel had arrived as a hull material, and double, triple, and quadruple expansion engines rapidly reduced fuel requirements by nearly 50 percent. Finally, in 1899 the "Oceanic" was built, measuring 704 feet (215 metres) in length, after a half century, the first ship to exceed the size of the "Great Eastern." German shipbuilders of this time took command of the Atlantic speed records with the "Deutschland," which raced across the ocean at from 22 to 23 knots.

Another event in this great change in the face and power of ships was the demonstration of Parsons' "Turbinia." Parsons experimented with a turbine-driven boat in secret, and, when he had achieved a reasonable balance between turbine speed and propeller speed, he took his boat to Queen Victoria's Diamond Jubilee Review of the Fleet. Before the large crowd of onlookers, he proceeded to weave his way in and out between the ships of the fleet at a previously unheard of speed of 34½ knots. After this unorthodox demonstration, the turbine was accepted as a means of propulsion for the future high-speed ships. About the same time, Rudolf Diesel in Germany was discovering the principles of the diesel cycle, which was to result in one of the most economical means of marine propulsion.

Between 1900 and 1914, all of the innovations in technology seemed to come into focus with the age-old principle that a larger, longer ship was easier to drive and more comfortable to ride. Ships grew to gigantic proportions. Geared turbines had made high powers easier to produce, and steam pressures were in the area of 300 pounds per square inch. The largest of the prewar monsters was the German "Vaterland," of 904-foot (276-metres) length and 54,000 tons.

The "Vaterland"

During World War I the "Vaterland" was seized by the U.S., used as a troop transport, and later refurbished under the direction of William Francis Gibbs, a New York naval architect, who was to become for the United States what I.K. Brunel was to the 19th century in England. It was converted to oil, and many structural changes were made to improve its resistance to damage. Renamed the "Leviathan," for years it dominated the Atlantic. Shortly after its refit, it set a new speed record of 27.48 knots average speed for over 25 hours.

In 1929–30 the Germans launched the "Bremen" and the "Europa," which, while moderate in size, had better engineering and hull design and thus gave them the transatlantic speed record. These ships exploited a new hull-design idea, the bulbous bow, in which the bow of the ship was made sharp at the waterline to cut the waves but flattened out further down, giving greater buoyancy, and easier changes of direction to the water. In addition, this greater buoyancy below the water reduced pitching of the ship and made it ride easier.

The next record holder was the giant 79,280-ton "Normandie," which in 1935 reduced the transatlantic record to four days, three hours, and two minutes at an average speed of over 30 knots. It used a turbo-electric drive.

In the 1920s and 1930s the world's commerce was being hauled in many less glamorous ships, some with Scotch boilers and reciprocating engines, about 400 feet (120 metres) long and steaming at an economical 13 to 14 knots. The diesel engine had started to displace steam, because the fuel consumption and the crew requirements of the diesel made it more economical to operate, even though its maintenance costs were higher.

World War II ships. World War II, with its tremendous production of new tonnage of all types, brought several new standards. In steamships, superheated steam (600 pounds per square inch and 850° F [450° C]) became nearly a standard for high-powered ships, some going as high as 1,000 pounds per square inch. In the light of boiler-maintenance problems, some engineers considered that a more modest pressure might have been more prudent, but "higher, lighter, and faster" was the watchword of the times. A military type of ship developed from a British prototype was introduced in several sizes during the course of the war. Its most widely used version was labelled the LST (landing ship tank), which could load or unload wheeled vehicles through a bow door, could transfer them to another deck through a ramp device, and could turn them around on a turntable. The great utility of this slow-moving, pedestrian-looking ship caused it to inspire many changes in ships of the postwar period.

In World War II, as in its predecessor, the momentum of war and the necessity of speed produced building programs that are unequalled in peacetime. Shortly after the start of the war, a British purchasing mission came to the

World
War II
Liberty
ships

United States to contract for 60 ships, 441 feet (134 metres) long, of 10,490 tons displacement, with reciprocating steam engines and coal-fired Scotch boilers, as simple and rugged a merchant ship as could be devised. Shortly afterward, the same designers redesigned this ship for the U.S. war effort, giving it oil-fired watertube boilers, but otherwise left them identical to the British ships. The U.S. program to produce emergency ships got under way in April 1941, when the first keel was laid; the "Patrick Henry" was launched on September 27, 1941. In all, 2,610 Liberty (or Ec-2) ships were built. Many records were set in this effort, including the launching of a ship within ten days of the laying of the keel, with completion and delivery four days later. Altogether, the U.S. shipbuilding effort in World War II produced 5,874 merchant-type ships of 57,205,407 deadweight tons, over one-third of the world tonnage at the beginning of the war. As in World War I, the tonnage was of mixed types and quality. Barracks, barges, and drydocks were built of iron-enriched concrete. Few if any wooden ships were built, but some older wooden hulls were converted to war service. Mass production of ships, the coming of age of welded steel as a hull material, standardization of machinery components and plants, and the many special-purpose ships and craft that were developed during the war left an important heritage in design and construction.

Postwar developments. After World War II, the arrival of fast, dependable air travel across the oceans signalled the beginning of the end of the era of the super passenger liners. The speed differential between a jet aircraft and even the swiftest liners made performance differences between ships somewhat irrelevant, but even toward the end of the superliner era new records were set. In the 1970s France has in service the longest passenger ship in the world, the "France." It is 1,035 feet (315 metres) long, aluminum in its superstructure lightens its displacement, and it is equipped with fin stabilizers protruding from its sides below the water to reduce roll. Its modern plant is powered by 1,000-pounds-per-square-inch steam at 1,052° F, and 175,000 horsepower drives it at a speed of slightly over 35 knots. This combination of improvements, however, did not gain for the "France" the speed record, which belongs to a ship ten years its elder, the 1952-launched "United States," the holder of the Atlantic records for both east and west crossings. The "United States," the personal project of noted designer William Francis Gibbs, on its maiden voyage set a record of three days, ten hours, and 40 minutes. The record is likely to stand, because the competition of air travel makes it improbable that the expense and effort required to build a superliner to surpass it will be economically feasible (see Figure 2).

Two noteworthy technical developments of the postwar period were nuclear propulsion and hydrofoils (both

discussed below). Far more significant in its impact on merchant shipping was the advent of containerization, a revolution that began in the late 1960s.

SPECIAL TYPES OF SHIPS

Container ships. The military success of prepackaged shipments to overseas points during World War II and the rising costs of stevedore services and labour in general stimulated consideration of the use of standardized containers for shipping materials. At first, the relatively poor volumetric efficiency in the stowage of the ship delayed acceptance of the concept. Studies of the savings available in turnaround time, lower insurance rates because of reduced pilferage and damage, better customer satisfaction, and the greater facility of transshipping from sea terminal to land transportation slowly made their weight felt.

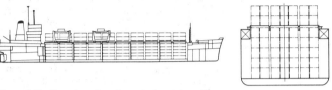

Figure 3: Profile and section of a typical container ship.

Standard containers that fitted into cells created in container ships, on trailer trucks, and on rail cars were adopted (20 by eight by eight feet (about six by 2.5 by 2.5 metres). The containers were fabricated of light, strong aluminum alloys, usually of corrugated construction to provide requisite stiffness. They were provided with lifting pads to allow easy hoisting and with fittings to permit them to be fastened to truck beds. They became the unit of transit in a complete transportation system from point of origin to destination. Packed and sealed at the warehouse, the container is transmitted by road or rail to a port, at which specially designed high-speed lifting cranes take it from the carrier either to temporary pierside stowage or directly to the container ship. The ship is equipped with a cellular grid of belowdecks compartments opening to the weather deck, designed to receive the containers and hold them in place until unloading at the port of destination. The ship is filled to the deck level with containers, the hatches are closed, and one or two layers of containers, depending upon the size and stability of the ship, are loaded on the hatch covers on deck. Upon arrival at the port of destination, specially designed lifting gear removes the containers in a matter of hours and loads them to trucks or trains or to temporary terminal stowage. In another few hours, the ship can be filled with containers for another port and can be under way. An additional economy is the low cost of the crew of the ship while in port awaiting loading or unloading. Further, because each ship can make more trips than before, container fleets require fewer vessels. There is also less pilferage and, hence, lower insurance rates and, finally, the assurance to the shipper that his shipment will not require any further handling until it arrives at its designation (see Figure 3).

Advantages
of
container
ships

Among the disadvantages is the fact that each ship does not carry quite as much total volume of cargo with containers as with regular bulk stowage, because the containers themselves take space and, since they are square in shape, do not fill in all the nooks and crannies created by a ship-shaped hull form. Further, a rather substantial capital investment is needed in port facilities, such as special berths, weight-handling equipment, storage areas, and links to land transportation, all of which must be made by the ports that receive or ship via container ship if its full potential savings are to be realized.

Since 1965 there has been a worldwide upsurge in port development, spurred by the adoption of container shipping. As early as 1967, 20 percent of all tonnage from New York was in containers. In the early 1970s several weekly scheduled container-ship lines were operative between European and American ports, as well as on the longer routes to the Mediterranean and Far Eastern ports.

From Laurence Dunn, Passenger Liners

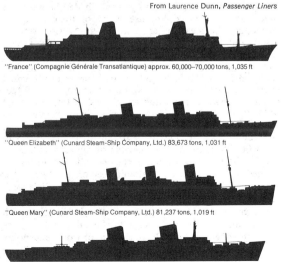

"France" (Compagnie Générale Transatlantique) approx. 60,000–70,000 tons, 1,035 ft

"Queen Elizabeth" (Cunard Steam-Ship Company, Ltd.) 83,673 tons, 1,031 ft

"Queen Mary" (Cunard Steam-Ship Company, Ltd.) 81,237 tons, 1,019 ft

"United States" (United States Lines, Inc.) 53,329 tons, 990 ft
Figure 2: Silhouettes of several post–World War II passenger liners.

Developments in containers include an increase in maximum size to 40 feet (12 metres) in length, with several ships able to carry large or small containers interchangeably. There are also refrigerated containers for perishables, open-top containers, and many other improvements.

The newer ships being built or converted to this service are moderate-sized merchant ships but of a higher average speed than in the past; in fact, few modern ships are built for speeds of less than about 20 knots. Greater use is being made of small, compact power plants to provide more space for containers. One new ship of the more common variety is the "Elbe Express." Built in 1969, it is equipped with fin stabilizers to help prevent damage to containerized cargo, and its nine-cylinder Diesel engine, giving 15,750 horsepower, drives it at 20 knots with good efficiency. It can carry either 786 standard 20-foot containers or 300 40-foot containers and 136 20-foot containers. Twenty-one 40-foot refrigerated containers can be accommodated. Special equipment includes six mooring winches to insure accurate positioning of the ship under cranes in port and special tanks to list (tip) and trim (level) the ship to permit a symmetrical loading or unloading without excessive list or trim. Its crew numbers only 33, including two stewardesses. Its route is from the continent of Europe via Britain to the United States East Coast ports.

Roll-on–roll-off. Another offspring of the specialized ships of World War II is the so-called roll-on–roll-off ship, which uses the general principles of the landing-ship tank but on a much larger scale. The ship is equipped with bow or stern openings (ports) and in most cases with side ports from which ramps can be extended to shore. Through these ports, vehicle traffic is efficiently ramped to the many decks within the ship. In essence, the inside of the ship is arranged to resemble a seagoing parking garage. Large sliding or folding watertight doors preserve the integrity of watertight bulkheads within the ship by giving sufficient compartmentation to withstand some flooding. Sealing the large doors that cover the openings in the hull offers a certain problem but one that modern mechanisms have satisfactorily solved. The general outline of the ship, in view of its relatively low density of cargo, is rather beamy, with a high deckhouse covering much of the ship's superstructure, to afford more parking decks. To insure stability, fixed ballast is usually included in these ships, along with water ballast to adjust load and stability. The engineering plants of these ships are commonly twin engines of compact variety, such as geared diesel, so arranged that the engine spaces are at either side of the ship, allowing valuable free space between them for vehicle passage.

An example of such a ship is the Japanese "Aoi Maru," designed for the Japanese coastal trade. It has four car decks above the weather deck and three within the hull itself, giving it a capacity of 737 cars (Japanese compact-size), but its areas can also accommodate moderate-sized buses and trucks. To avoid the problem of bow sealing, no port is included in the bow. Its speed is 19.5 knots.

Ferryboats. A close kin to the roll-on–roll-off ship is the ferryboat, built for protected waters over a predetermined, usually short route. Ferries have been in existence for hundreds of years. Some of the earliest were unpowered rafts towed back and forth across a stream by ropes pulled by men or horses. In other cases, the barges or rafts were towed by small boats or tugs. The modern powered ferryboat is usually relatively small—100 to 200 feet (30 to 60 metres) in length—and broad in the beam to accommodate two to four lanes of vehicles on either side of a narrow centre section containing access and exhaust systems. The ships are usually double-ended, with propellers and rudders at both ends and separate sets of controls in pilothouses at the top of both ends of the ship. At each terminal a specially devised slip is built so that the ship can, in any condition of tide or current, dock end first, with almost no manoeuvring. A shore-based bridge is lowered to the deck to allow the vehicles to discharge and another load to come aboard.

Much larger ships have been used to carry trains across

bodies of water such as the English Channel, although, because of their seaworthiness requirements, these might better be classed as seagoing ships than ferries. Ferries on longer inland routes, such as Puget Sound, in the northwestern United States, are of much more conventional hull form. In fact, the "Chinook," a Puget Sound ferry, somewhat resembles a destroyer; its propulsion plant is a wartime diesel destroyer escort plant, its bow is conventional, and with its 4,800-horsepower twin screws it makes over 17 knots.

Since World War II, construction of bridges over waterways that interrupt heavily travelled routes has considerably reduced the need for ferries.

Icebreakers. Many ports and harbours of the world are above the latitudes that provide ice-free navigation year around; consequently, ships that can break ice to provide lanes for other ships have been a necessity. These ships do not rush into ice and break it up by the impact of their hull against the edge of the ice, although this is possible with very thin ice of only a few inches thickness. Rather, the ship is designed to ride up over the ice as it proceeds along its path, and then, when the ice by a wedging action has picked up more of the weight of the ship than it can support by its shear strength, the hull falls through the ice, leaving a hole slightly larger than the ship's width. Thus, the hull lines of the icebreakers are broad, with very shallow draft at the bow and stern and gentle increases in draft to the midship section. The waterline of the ship must be reinforced with layers of plating and supported by a close-knit grill of stiffeners to protect against the constant collisions with solid ice. Because propeller damage is an obvious hazard, an icebreaker is usually provided with three screw arrangements, with the centre screw protected by a tunnel or flute in the bottom of the ship. It is also common practice to provide propellers at both ends of the ship, so that, if one end is imprisoned by ice, the other may be able to move the ship enough to get free. The propellers are built with large hubs to which each blade is individually bolted, so that single blades that are broken or bent can be replaced.

While sailing ships operated in ice at times, and some were strengthened to withstand the squeeze of the ice, the first genuine icebreaker that deserves the name was the "Ermak," built in Britain for the Russian government in 1899. It had 1½-inch (38-millimetre) steel plating on its waterline, displaced 10,000 tons, and had over 10,000 horsepower in steam engines. As today, it had three screws aft and an additional one in the bow. It was so successful at its task that it has served as a prototype of nearly all following icebreakers. One of the outstanding differences that has developed is in the propulsion. Modern ships have used electric drive extensively to obtain the fine control of the propellers needed, and, because the centre screw is the most protected, the propulsion system is so balanced that the centre screw carries 50 percent of the power, with the other 50 percent divided between the two outer propellers. Because many of their ports are icebound, the Russians are perhaps the world's leading users and builders of icebreakers. The world's largest icebreaker is also the world's first nuclear surface ship— the "Lenin," built in Leningrad in 1957. Displacing 16,-000 tons, it is 440 feet (134 metres) long and 90½ feet (27½ metres) in beam, with a maximum draft of 30 feet (nine metres). It has three screws with a total of about 44,000 horsepower from an atomic–steam–turbine–electric power plant. Its free route speed is 18 knots. It is protected at the sides by a stiffened ice belt of 1.5 to 2 inches (four to five centimetres) of high-strength steel. While the best weight-to-horsepower ratio would be obtained by using one large atomic reactor, the "Lenin" is fitted with three, two of which can carry the ship's load, leaving the third as a reserve reactor. The principal advantage of the nuclear reactor is that it imparts an almost unlimited cruising range to the ship. In heavy ice an icebreaker must do a huge amount of work, expending large amounts of fuel, to make a few miles a day. In conventional ships, the fuel supply is limited, and operations must at some times be curtailed to insure that fuel will not be exhausted, while on the "Lenin," with for

The "Elbe Express"

The "Aoi Maru"

How an icebreaker operates

The "Lenin"

Figure 4: *Below-deck arrangement of a typical tanker.*
(A) Profile; (B) Plan view.
By courtesy of Newport News Shipbuilding and Dry Dock Co.

practical purposes an unlimited fuel endurance, power can be used in whatever amounts the situation demands. Next to the submarine, in which nuclear power makes possible almost an entirely new type of ship, the icebreaker represents the most advantageous marine use of nuclear power. The overall cost of nuclear-power installation, however, has discouraged construction of more such icebreakers.

Tankers. Perhaps the simplest ship to build and operate is the tanker. In essence, the tanker is a floating group of tanks contained in a ship-shaped hull, propelled by an isolated machinery plant at the stern. Each tank is substantially identical to the next throughout the length of the parallel-sided middle body of the ship. The tanks are fitted with heating coils to facilitate pumping in cold weather. Within the tanks are the main, or high-suction, pipes, running several feet from the bottom to avoid sludge. Below them, low-suction piping, or stripping lines, removes the lowest level of liquid in the tank. Tanks are filled either through open trunks leading from the weather deck or from the suction lines with the pumps reversed. Because tankers, except for military-supply types, usually move a cargo from the source to a refinery or other terminal with few manoeuvres en route, the machinery plant is called on only to produce at a steady rate the cruise power for the ship; consequently, considerable use of automatic controls is possible, thus reducing the size of the crew to a minimum. In view of the simplicity of inner arrangement, the tanker lends itself to mass production perhaps more than any other ship type. Because of the limited crew requirements and the low cost per ton for initial building and outfitting, the tanker has led the way in rapid expansion in the size of ships (see Figure 4).

For reasons already stated, larger ships are superior to smaller ones. The interaction of the wave train set up by the passage of the bow and that from the passage of the stern establishes a relationship between the speed of the ship and its length, such that, at a critical speed-to-length ratio, the addition of great amounts of power result in little if any increase in speed, while, below this ratio, the power requirements of a ship drop off radically, till, at low speed-to-length ratios, very small powers are required. Simply put, the longer the ship, the less power is required to drive it at a given speed. Hence, when ships of very high speed are desired, such as ocean passenger liners, lengths of up to 1,000 feet (300 metres) were used. In the case of the tanker, where economy is paramount, and speeds in the order of 15 to 18 knots are sufficient, the greater length of the ship reduces power requirements to very low amounts.

Early in the history of merchant ships, the carrying of oil was viewed with caution. Before the 1880s, oil transported across the seas was carried by loading it in barrels

and stowing it in ordinary merchant ships. In 1886, however, a 300-foot (90-metre) German ship, the "Gluckauf," was launched, designed to carry oil in tanks against the ship's hull plating. By 1900 the idea of the tanker was so well established that 99 percent of the oil carried at sea was carried in tankers. Originally about the same size as other merchant ships, tankers were designed differently. For safety, the machinery was placed aft, with only enough superstructure forward to provide protection for the decks from water washing across and an elevated platform for ship control. The caution about the carrying of oil at sea has persisted to this day in that passengers are never carried in the same ship as cargo oil. Gradually, the size of oil tankers increased as the demand for the service grew, and the need for economical operation to compete for cargo continued, until those of the 1970s nearly stagger the imagination. The Universe-class tankers, built in Japan, the largest in service in the early 1970s, are of 326,000 tons deadweight. Dimensions are 1,132 feet (345 metres) in length and 175 feet (53 metres) in beam, with a loaded draft of 81 feet (25 metres), dwarfing the largest of the old-fashioned ocean liners. Such a ship is able to average over 15 knots on only 37,400 shaft horsepower. Complications arose with the introduction of such large ships; most of the harbours of the world are dredged to no more than 50 feet (15 metres) in the main channels, and special port facilities had to be arranged. One solution that is used in Kuwait, where much oil is shipped, is to build an artificial island in deep water, connected to shore by a pipeline, to load and unload tankers.

The first tanker

Presumably, the length of tankers will ultimately be limited only by the strength of available materials, for in the 1970s the monstrous Universe ships were surpassed by a new class of tankers ordered from Japan by a British corporation and designed for 477,000 deadweight tons. A Dutch company has developed an offshore buoy mooring and servicing system that will handle all ships now building or contemplated, up to and including ships of 1,000,000 deadweight tons or three times as large as the largest now afloat.

Along with the great increase in numbers and size of tankers have come specialized uses of tankers for products other than oil. A major user is the natural-gas industry, which ships natural gas by tanker to areas such as the British Isles. For shipment, gas is cooled and converted to liquid at −260° F (−162° C), pumped aboard the tanker for transit in aluminum tanks surrounded by heavy insulation to prevent absorption of heat and keep the liquid from evaporating during the voyage. So popular was this type of tanker that in 1970 orders were placed for 46 such ships, more than doubling the capacity of the existing fleet. The cost of these ships is rather high, because steel cannot be used for the containers. The cold liquid gas, in contact with steel, would make the steel as brittle as glass. Aluminum is therefore used, sometimes backed by balsa wood, backed in turn by steel. A special nickel–steel alloy known as Invar has been used in this application.

Other materials, such as iron ore, can be carried in a tanker in the form of slurry. The bulk dry cargo is mixed with high-velocity water jets, forming a pumpable mixture to load the tanker; at the other end of the voyage, jets in the bottom of the tankers again mix the cargo with water to permit pumping ashore. The ships using this system have been reported to be much more economical to operate than ordinary dry bulk cargo ships.

Other cargo that has been shipped by tankers includes wine, molten sulfur, and methane gas. A novel type of tanker is the Mobil Pegasus, by today's standards moderate-sized, only 1,017 feet (310 metres) long and 63 feet (19 metres) in draft for a total deadweight of 212,000 tons. The innovative feature of this ship is the fact that it is the first tanker to be built with a second bottom inside the hull. In this space is run all the piping to the tanks and to controls. The bottoms of the tanks above this are smooth so that no pockets of oil are formed when pumping out, and, since the tanks drain through a hole in the bottom, no stripping pipes are needed. In addition, the double bottom space allows what ballasting is necessary to be done outside the cargo oil tanks, reducing the possibility of polluting cargo.

A noteworthy tanker exploit was the voyage of "Manhattan," a 150,000-ton ship refitted with a heavily reinforced bow, that with the aid of two icebreakers was able to force her way through the Northwest Passage from Alaska to the Atlantic coast in 1969, breaking ice floes as thick as 15 feet and ridges as high as 40 in the process. This voyage, a first for a merchant ship, may foretell a new profitable route to extract oil from the newly discovered rich Alaskan fields later in the 1970s.

Nuclear ships. From the end of World War II, when the power generation capability of nuclear power was being developed, it was realized that, if a practical nuclear-power plant could be fitted into a submarine, a new type of ship could at last be realized—a true submarine instead of merely a short-term submersible. A large number of such submarines were ultimately built, with virtually unlimited underwater cruising range (see SUBMARINE). A few nuclear-powered surface naval ships have also been built. Civil applications of marine nuclear power have so far been limited. As mentioned above, the Soviet Union built a successful icebreaker, the "Lenin," in 1957, and in 1962 the potential of nuclear power for an ordinary merchant ship was explored when the "Savannah," sponsored by the United States Atomic Energy Commission and Maritime Commission, was delivered. A modern shelter-deck ship of 12,220 gross tons with accommodations for 60 passengers, "Savannah" made about 20 knots on her 22,000-horsepower nuclear-power geared steam-turbine plant. Named for the ocean-steam pioneer of 1818, it was designed to demonstrate the feasibility of nuclear-power plants, as the first "Savannah" had done for steam power. "Savannah" represented a reversal of the usual progression to higher temperatures and pressures, because it produced steam at 480 pounds per square inch for its turbines. "Savannah" performed its function reasonably well in that it was a ship around which many of the regulatory and procedural problems could be solved and in which the technical feasibility of this type of ship could be demonstrated. But it could not compete with other dry-cargo ships and was never used commercially.

Another nuclear ship being evaluated for commercial service in 1970s was the "Otto Hahn," operated in Germany by the Society for the Evaluation of Nuclear Energy in Shipbuilding and Navigation. It is reported to have a smaller and more compact power plant than the "Lenin" or "Savannah," giving it a better safety factor against collision. To date, no nuclear ship has been produced and operated by a commercial enterprise, because of the high initial costs and the difficulties in crew training. As nuclear cores become longer lasting and conse-

quently reduce fuel costs and downtime (for overhaul and repair), and as other factors become more favourable, it is not considered impossible that this source of power could be important in ships.

Hydrofoils. The search for speed on water has been frustrated by the combination of the resistance created by the ship in making waves and by the friction of water flowing past the hull. The combination of these factors makes the power demands of a ship at very high speed prohibitive. One method of overcoming this situation is offered by the hydrofoil. This craft is so designed that the hull of the ship is lifted entirely out of the water as it gains speed and is supported on hydrofoils, wings shaped like those of an aircraft but made much stronger and smaller; because the density of water is about 600 times that of air, a relatively small lifting surface in water will lift as much as a large wing in air.

The mode of operation of these craft is for the hull to support its weight, when at rest or steaming slowly, by its own buoyance. As speed is increased, the foils pick up more and more of the weight until at "takeoff" all of the weight is transferred to the foils and the ship is "flying."

The likeness to an aircraft is more than one of nomenclature. The problems of weight control are critical; because the same laws apply in foils as in aircraft, every pound of weight creates drag that must be supported by power. Thus, the hulls are built of light alloys and the foils of such materials as high-strength steel or titanium. Power is supplied by the lightest possible source, such as aircraft-type gas turbines. Propulsion is a special problem, because the power in a ship is normally generated in the hull and must be transmitted a considerable distance to the water. For this reason, several early hydrofoils used air-screw propulsion. Later, a water jet in which water is pumped out of the stern at high velocity was developed to provide low-weight propulsion.

Control and stability of foils is similar to that of aircraft, except that the control of altitude must be much more precise, for the range of motion can be only the distance from the surface of the water to the foil submergence, usually not over ten feet (three metres). All of the early foils relied on their geometry for control. The most prevalent foil system is the surface system, in which the foil surface intersects the surface of the water at an angle, so that, when more lift is needed, the foil simply submerges farther and with more surface in the water produces enough lift to regain equilibrium. These types have been arranged in single Vs or in a ladder pattern, with several foils one above the other to increase the lift faster as more submergence is attained. All the early systems relied on the surface of the water for control and consequently produced a rather rough ride. Later developments produced electronic means of sensing the clearance of the hull from the water and signalling control-surface changes to fully submerged foils that operate nearly independent of the surface and hence provide both a smoother ride and greater seakeeping ability.

The first hydrofoil may have been a French patent application in 1897 by the Comte de Lambert, who drove a catamaran hull fitted with four transverse "hydroplanes." There is some doubt that this boat actually used the hydrofoil principle at all; it may have been only a specialized planing boat. The first true hydrofoil was operated by an Italian inventor, Enrico Forlanini, between 1898 and 1905 and was supported by a set of hydrofoils. While little is known of the performance of this craft, another Italian inventor operated a craft of this type at 50 miles (80 kilometres) per hour.

Hydrofoils reached a pinnacle of performance and publicity when a boat built by Alexander Graham Bell and Casey Baldwin set the world's water speed record in 1918 with a speed of 60 knots. The craft, the HD 4, was powered by two Liberty aircraft engines of 350 horsepower each and was equipped with a set of ladder-type foils. While the boat was far ahead of its time, its efficiency by later standards was rather low. In the early 1930s several effective surface-piercing foil boats were developed, and World War II gave a major stimulus. In Germany, craft of up to 80 tons and speeds of nearly 60

Carrying dry cargo by tanker

The nuclear ship "Savannah"

Alexander Graham Bell's hydrofoil

knots were built, but Allied bombs prevented this effort from reaching operational status. After the war the United States, Canada, the Soviet Union, Britain, and Germany all launched development efforts. A boat developed by a U.S. windmill builder was supported by four V foils, one at each corner of the boat, that gave excellent stability. Because there was no supporting structure in the water, only lifting surface, it was most efficient, having the highest lift-to-drag ratio attained up to that time.

A breakthrough came in the early 1950s, when the laboratories of Massachusetts Institute of Technology in conjunction with the ship-designers firm of Gibbs and Cox developed a sonic device to measure the distance from the bow of the ship to the water and to use this measurement to control fully submerged foils. The new device was tried on a standard power yacht converted to a set of tandem, fully submerged foils with great success. The speed of the boat was more than tripled and its seakeeping ability in heavy seas greatly enhanced.

By the early 1970s the technology was available to construct and operate hydrofoils of up to 500 tons with speeds from 40 to 50 knots. Several passenger ferries employed the hydrofoil principle; one in the Soviet Union, the "Meteor," had a capacity of 150. The U.S. Navy's "Plainview," of about 300 tons, had speed in excess of 40 knots, and test craft have reached speeds in excess of 80 knots on foils under controlled conditions.

The LASH ship. A recent development in shipping is the LASH (lighter-aboard-ship) vessel, designed to carry nearly any cargo in steel lighters or barges, each about 60 feet (18 metres) long and 30 feet (nine metres) wide and capable of handling 500 tons of cargo (see Figure 5).

From *Business Abroad* (January 1971)

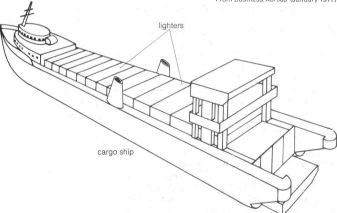

lighters

cargo ship

Figure 5: A group of lighters (small cargo vessels) loaded aboard a specially designed cargo ship. The combination is referred to as LASH (lighter aboard ship).

The hull of the ship is generally conventional except that its superstructure is dominated by a large travelling crane supported by legs from each side of the ship. At the stern the tracks for the crane extend well aft of the deck, so that barges that are picked up from the deck may be lowered directly into the water, or, in reverse, barges can be picked up directly from the water and placed in their stowage position aboard. The ship can also carry containers (for a complete description of LASH ships and some other recent developments in this area, see MATERIALS HANDLING and TRANSPORTATION, WATER).

Ferrocement boats. Ferrocement construction, under development since 1965, involves the use of common waterproof cement or concrete applied over a metal rod or lath (wire-mesh) core to form the hull and subdivisions of a boat hull. The low cost of the materials (portland cement, metal lath, reinforcing rods, and wooden forms) is somewhat offset by the relatively high amount of labour involved in plastering the successive layers required for the completed hull. In underdeveloped countries, however, where labour is plentiful and inexpensive, this material is widely used. Its resistance to rot and corrosion and ease of repair offer some of the advantages of plastic construction, while the weight of the hull is considerably greater than that of aluminum or plastics. Its cost to the private boat builder who is furnishing his own labour is undoubtedly the lowest of any material now used. For further information on shipbuilding, see SHIP DESIGN AND CONSTRUCTION.

IV. Ship maintenance

When ships were small, the ship's crew was able to perform not only routine maintenance but also major repairs. As ships grew larger and more complicated, they came to require specialized facilities. Such facilities are collectively called a shipyard. A shipyard consists of one or more dry docks or marine railways to expose the bottoms of the ships for cleaning and painting (normally every 18 or 36 months) and a series of long, high-reach cranes to take loads in and out of ships for repair. Waterfront facilities are supplemented by shops for shipfitting, machining, electric and electronic work, carpentry, pipe welding, painting, and rigging.

Conventional ships are sent into shipyards on a regular schedule for bottom cleaning and overhaul. Though schedules vary among ship types and services, vessels are generally sent to shipyards once in every one to three years. A considerable amount of preplanning is required before the ship's entry to the shipyard. The operators of the ship and representatives of the shipyard meet, usually three to six months in advance of the overhaul, to determine needed repairs and other work. The owners and the repair yard then arrange the ordering of the necessary materials to perform the repairs.

Since modern ships have become more and more complicated advance planning in maintenance is vital. Electronic parts and control devices may need to be ordered several months in advance; the owner cannot afford to leave his vessel idle. In the case of submarines or nuclear-powered vessels, planning for repair may start from 18 months to two years in advance.

In addition to formal overhaul in the yard, ships require day-to-day cleaning, lubrication, adjustment, and minor repairs to continue to operate during their time at sea. This work is normally done by the crew, using onboard supplies. Since a ship at sea is dependent on itself for all such services as fresh water, heat, light, and refrigeration, the responsibility of the crew members is a great and personal one.

A new approach to maintenance, intended to increase the time that the ships are in service and to reduce the direct labour required of the crew, has recently appeared. Machinery components small enough and so packaged that they can be removed from the ship easily and replaced by new or overhauled components are provided. Even those parts that may be replaced at sea are installed in modules that can be stored and installed easily when needed. Although the initial cost of the ship may be increased, this is offset by savings in maintenance.

An extreme example of this modular concept of ship maintenance is the adoption of gas-turbine power for some of the newer high-speed container ships. The principle advantage of this type of power has been its very low weight per horsepower, which made its use attractive in hydrofoils and high-speed boats. Gas turbines are now used in many aircraft installations and thus are mass produced. Even more important from the economic viewpoint, they are mass serviced. In addition, the gas-turbine installation is more compact than any other type of power, permitting more room for cargo, and is light enough to be removable from the ship for servicing. Replacement of units, which can be accomplished in less than 12 hours in some installations, permits ships to remain in service without extended stays in port. In a container ship, for example, engines can be replaced while the ship is being loaded for her turn around, without any loss in time at sea. These advantages have overcome the disadvantages of higher fuel costs of gas turbines. The "Adm. William Callaghan," the largest roll-on–roll-off ship afloat in the early 1970s, was powered by a combination of gas turbines totalling 50,000 horsepower.

While the use of gas turbines increases the amount, weight, and cost of fuel needed, the reduction in crew

Shipyard facilities

Gasturbine power

and ease of maintenance (a gas turbine is so light and compact that it can be hoisted out of the ship and replaced in a few hours) tip the economic balance. The same procedure is used in modular electronic units, complicated control units, and even in the electrical-generating units themselves. Of course, the new method of overhaul and repair by module requires a much more sophisticated planning and control system ashore to ensure that a new or repaired unit is available when and where it is needed without an excessive inventory of parts being accumulated. Computers are used to assist in such control.

BIBLIOGRAPHY. EDWARD LEWIS, ROBERT O'BRIEN, and the EDITORS OF LIFE, *Ships* (1965), a popular well-illustrated volume on ships and their design and use; A.C. HARDY, *The Book of the Ship* (1949), a brief but thorough description of various types of ships; CHRISTOPHER LLOYD, *Ships and Seamen from the Vikings to the Present Day* (1961), an excellent pictorial history of ships and the men who sailed them; E.E. SIGWART (comp.), *Merchant Ships: World Built* (annual), a pictorial and descriptive catalog of each year's new ships; HERBERT LEE SEWARD (ed.), *Marine Engineering*, 2 vol. (1942–44), a fundamental source of information on the design and use of marine power plants; HENRY B. CULVER, *Forty Famous Ships* (1936), on ships from the time of Christ to the Queen Mary; PHYLLIS FLANDERS DORSET, *Historic Ships Afloat* (1967), a tabulation of preserved ship relics; RUPERT SARGENT HOLLAND, *Historic Ships* (1926), a summary of facts and stories of famous ships; CHARLES GIBSON, *Wandering Beauties* (1960), an excellent compilation of tales, facts, and descriptions of sailing ships; J.S. MORRISON and R.T. WILLIAMS, *Greek Oared Ships, 900–322 B.C.* (1968), a special treatment of the ancient ships of Greece; FRANK O. BRAYNARD, *By Their Works Ye Shall Know Them* (1968), a complete description of the life and ships of William Francis Gibbs; WARREN TUTE, *Atlantic Conquest* (1962), another good source on the Atlantic and its conquerors; ROBERT DOLLAR, *One Hundred-Thirty Years of Steam Navigation* (1931), a firsthand account of ships and shippers; WARREN ARMSTRONG, *Atlantic Highway* (1962), an interesting account of transoceanic ships and their adventures; HOWARD IRVING CHAPELLE, *The Baltimore Clipper: Its Origin and Development* (1965), an excellent account of a link in the chain leading to the Clippers; ALBERT COOK CHURCH, *Whale Ships and Whaling* (1960), a history with good illustrations; JAMES DUGAN, *The Great Iron Ship* (1953), the story of the *Great Eastern*; FREDERIC C. LANE, *Ships for Victory* (1951), a history of the shipbuilding programs of World War II; CHARLES BOSWELL, *The America* (1964), the story of the yacht *America*; FRANK O. BRAYNARD, *S.S. Savannah* (1963), the story of the first steamer across the Atlantic; CARLO M. CIPOLLA, *Guns, Sails and Empires: Technological Innovations and the Early Phases of European Expansion, 1400–1700* (1965), an exhaustive analysis of Oriental ships; G.R.G. WORCESTER, *Sail and Sweep in China: The History and Development of the Chinese Junk . . .* (1966), another source on Oriental ships; JOHN D. HARBRON, *Communist Ships and Shipping* (1962), an overview of shipping developments behind the iron curtain; PATRICK FINLAY (ed.), *Jane's Freight Containers* (annual), a fascinating addition to the "Jane's Series" for those interested in modern shipping developments (see also *Jane's Merchant Ships*); T.M. BUERMAN, P. LEEHEY, and JAMES J. STILLWELL, "An Appraisal of Hydrofoil Supported Craft," *Trans. Inst. Mar. Engrs.*, vol. 65, no. 8 (1954), a basic source document on the design and performance of hydrofoils; S.W. LANK and O.H. OAKLEY, *Application of Nuclear Power to Icebreakers* (1959), a tentative design analysis including a Russian description of the *Lenin*. Current information may be found in the Society of Naval Architects and Marine Engineers *Transactions* (monthly); and the *Marine Engineering Log* (monthly)—see especially vol. 75, no. 13 (1970), an excellent source for modern merchant ship developments.

(Ja.J.S.)

Ship Design and Construction

Ship design and construction today is a complicated compound of art and science. In the great days of sail, vessels were designed and built on the basis of practical experience; ship construction was predominantly a skill. With the rapid growth and development of the physical sciences, beginning in the early 19th century, it was inevitable that hydrokinetics (the study of fluids in motion), hydrostatics (the study of fluids at rest), and the science of materials and structures should augment the shipbuild-er's skill. The consequence of this was a rapid increase in the size, speed, commercial value, and safety of ships.

HISTORY

From antiquity until the 19th century. Man has been a boatbuilder since remotest antiquity. It is probable that primitive man first took to the water on a log or a raft. Later, the invention and application of paddles enabled man to progress from rafts to dugout canoes. The paddle led eventually to the lever and so to the use of oars. Much later came the harnessing of wind and the application of sails. Excavations in Crete have shown that seagoing craft were constructed in the eastern Mediterranean as early as 5000 BC. In ancient Egypt, ships built of planks were used on the Nile. By about 2800 BC the basic principles of boatbuilding had evolved, with transverse and longitudinal strengths provided by different parts of the structure. The largest Roman ships, which exceeded 100 feet (30 metres) in length, were carvel-built; that is, the oak planks were laid flush at the seams over closely spaced ribs. These craft were propelled by oars and by a primitive form of rectangular sail. Later, the triangular lateen sail on its long slantwise yard appeared on Roman ships; this had first been used by Arab dhows sailing the Red Sea and Indian Ocean. A striking development in Scandinavian waters was the Viking ship, of fine form, but clinker-built—that is, with the planks on its sides overlapping, and propelled mainly by oars and carrying a simple sail. The ship was of wood—plank construction with cross beams—of the open-boat, undecked type. A seagoing ship peculiar to Chinese and Japanese waters was the junk, a flat-bottomed boat with square sails of matting (see also SAILS AND SAILING VESSELS).

Progress continued from the Middle Ages onward, with considerable advances in sail design. Sails entirely supplanted oars in all large European vessels, except in the Mediterranean. As ships grew larger, they were decked over, and more decks were fitted with "castles" at bow and stern. In Portugal, Henry the Navigator (1394–1460) encouraged the building of new types of ships. Portugal's achievements in navigation were due in part to Henry's enlightened policy of experiment and trial on actual vessels. Sporadic attempts to test ship forms were made in Italy, France, Sweden, and England but to little practical effect. Ships remained essentially unchanged from the 15th to the 19th century, when a fast new vessel of revolutionary design was constructed in North America in 1812. The clipper ship followed, a triumph of empiricism and craftsmanship; it was capable of very high speeds, the result of hulls designed for minimum water resistance, and greater sail area.

Developments since the 19th century. A more profound revolution in shipbuilding followed the substitution of steam engines for sails and the substitution of iron for wood in hull construction. Iron, in turn, was replaced by steel, with a substantial saving in weight. In the decades-long period of transition from sail to steam, side-paddle wheels were first used but were gradually ousted by the screw propeller. The first propeller-driven ship was put into service in 1839, but it was not until about 1850 that steam navigation entered upon its era of unprecedented development, during which the steam engine evolved into a propulsive force of great power and economy. At the turn of the 20th century, the steam turbine appeared and soon became a rival to the reciprocating steam engine, eventually supplanting it. More powerful than even the largest reciprocators, the steam turbine, because of its comparatively small size, greatly changed the size and proportions of ships, and cut costs of operation.

The first decade of the 20th century also saw the heavy-oil engine come into use. Though the first of these was not notably successful, by 1912 the marine diesel engine was established. From that time onward, the steam turbine and the heavy-oil engine enjoyed a keen rivalry. They were joined later by the gas turbine and the nuclear power plant.

Impact of science and technology. From early days shipbuilding was practiced in most of the maritime Eu-

[margin notes: Wooden seagoing vessels; Steam navigation]

ropean nations, notably in Britain, The Netherlands, Germany, Italy, and in the countries of the Baltic Sea. Before 1850, U.S. shipbuilders were supreme in the building of sailing vessels. The U.K. industry was at that time handicapped by the shortage of suitable timber supplies; moreover, it could not compete in price with either U.S. or Baltic shipbuilders. The introduction and development of iron and steel ships, however, gave the U.K. an enormous, if temporary, advantage because of Britain's wealth of coal and iron, together with its early and successful application of steam propulsion.

Modern shipbuilding

For a time old and new practices were mingled; sails were used to drive iron ships, wooden hulls were propelled by steam engines, and composite ships—framed with iron sections and planked with wood—were driven by both systems. The size of wooden ships had been limited by timber's inherent shortcomings as a structural material; ships made of iron and steel could be larger.

Despite the rapid progress in the design and construction of ships, the greatest technical innovations were in their engines. After a century of development, the steam engine was eclipsed by the direct-driven steam turbine, at first, only for the largest and fastest vessels; later, by the aid of gearing, for vessels of moderate size and speed. It was natural that in Britain, the home of steam, the steam turbine should be the favoured engine. In Europe, notably in Germany, Switzerland, and Denmark, the heavy-oil engine was preferred.

In the period from 1850 to 1890, the shipbuilding industry in Britain grew so rapidly that for a time it produced more than 80 percent of the world output of ships, and even from 1910–14, 60 percent. Over the next half century other countries increasingly moved into the world's shipbuilding industry, notably Japan and the U.S.S.R.

Since World War II, scientific research has resulted in a general improvement, both in the propulsive performance of ships and in their structural qualities. The widespread adoption of welding, the introduction of prefabrication, as well as technical planning and improvements in managerial efficiency, have combined to revolutionize the industry.

Trend to larger ships. Since the early 1960s, the dimensions and complexity of ships have increased remarkably. By the end of the 1960s, oil tankers of about 325,000 tons deadweight had been built and much larger hulls were under construction. Ore carriers and other types have also grown in size, while specialized ships have replaced the general bulk-cargo vessels. Probably the most significant innovation has been the container ship, which carries prepacked cargo in standard containers eight feet square (2.4 metres) in cross section and 20 feet (6.1 metres) or 40 feet (12.2 metres) in length. The governing principle has been that the cost of transportation decreases as ship size increases. The unit cost of carrying oil in a 200,000-ton tanker is 25 percent lower than in a 16,000-ton vessel. Moreover, a larger ship requires a proportionally smaller crew than does a smaller ship and, in the early 1970s, the wages bill for a ship greatly exceeded the cost of fuel, a predominant item for all ships until the late 1950s. In addition to larger size, modern ships are capable of attaining higher average service speeds, which permit these ships to spend more days out at sea and fewer days in port.

Container ships

Ship design

PRINCIPLES OF NAVAL ARCHITECTURE

Naval architecture is the branch of engineering concerned with the design and construction of ships. Merchant vessels range in size from mammoth tankers to tugs and trawlers; naval ships range from aircraft carriers to patrol craft. The basic principles of naval architecture apply to all vessels, irrespective of size and type: a ship design must guarantee safety, stability, strength, and speed completely adequate for the requirements and conditions of the vessel's operations.

The measurements of ships are given in terms of length, breadth, and depth. The length, L, between perpendiculars, is the distance on the summer (maximum) load waterline, from the forward side of the stem at the ex-

treme-forward part of the vessel to the after side of the rudder post at the extreme rear, or to the centre of the rudder stock, if there is no rudder post. The beam, B, is the greatest breadth of the ship. The depth, D, is measured at the middle of the length, from the top of the keel to the top of the deck beam at the side of the uppermost continuous deck. Draft is the summer draft, measured from the keel. These terms, together with several others of importance in ship design, are illustrated in Figure 1.

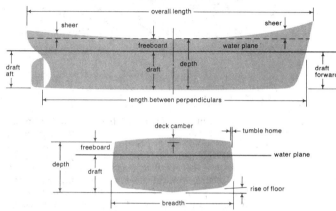

Figure 1: Terms used in ship construction.

Certain form coefficients are useful as indications of a vessel's shape characteristics. The commonest is the block coefficient, which is the ratio of the actual displacement of the vessel to the displacement of a rectangular block with the same length, breadth, and draft as the vessel. The block coefficient thus indicates the relative fineness or slenderness of the vessel and varies from about 0.5 in a fine, fast ship to 0.85 in a full, slow-speed oil tanker. The midship area coefficient is the ratio of the immersed area of a vessel's midship section (the transverse section at the middle of the length) at any draft to the area of a rectangle of which the breadth is equal to the breadth of the vessel and the depth is equal to the given draft.

Form coefficients

The prismatic coefficient is the ratio of the actual displacement of a vessel to the displacement of a prism of length equal to the vessel's length and of the same cross section as the vessel's immersed midship area. The water plane of a ship is the horizontal section of the ship at the waterline. The water plane area coefficient is the ratio of the actual area of a vessel's water plane to the area of a rectangle having the length of the ship and a breadth equal to the widest part of the water plane.

HYDRODYNAMICS AND HYDROSTATICS

When a body is immersed in a liquid, the upthrust of the water that holds up the body equals the weight of the fluid displaced by the body; this is Archimedes' principle. This upthrust is called buoyancy. Hence, when a body is floating freely in a fluid, the weight of the body equals the buoyancy, which equals the weight of the fluid displaced. The watertight volume of a ship above the waterline is called the reserve buoyancy. This is important in the assignment of the minimum service freeboard, freeboard being the distance between the waterline and the deck below which all bulkheads are made watertight. Minimum service freeboard determines the maximum permissible draft, the vessel's ability to survive flooding after damage, and its weather qualities in a seaway. The centre of gravity of the volume of water displaced by a ship floating at rest is called the centre of buoyancy. Its position is largely determined by the underwater shape of the vessel and is specified by its distance above the keel and from amidships. For equilibrium, the centre of gravity of the ship and its contents must lie in the same vertical plane as the centre of buoyancy. If a weight already on board is moved aft, for example, the ship's centre of gravity will move aft, but for equilibrium the vessel will adjust its position until the new centre of buoyancy is in the same vertical plane as the new centre of gravity.

Centre of buoyancy

Stability and trim. Figure 2 shows a transverse section of a ship floating at a waterline W_1L_1, displaced from its

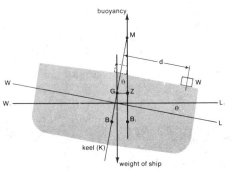

buoyancy

weight of ship

keel (K)

Figure 2: Stability shown in a transverse section of a floating ship (see text).

original waterline WL. One condition of equilibrium has been defined above. A second condition is that the centre of gravity of the ship must be in such a position that, if the vessel is inclined, the forces of weight and buoyancy tend to restore the vessel to its former position of rest. At small angles, vertical lines through B_1, the centre of buoyancy when the vessel is inclined at an angle θ, intersect the centre line at M, the metacentre, which means "change point." If M is above G (the centre of gravity of the ship and its contents), the vessel is in stable equilibrium. When M coincides with G, there is neutral equilibrium. When M is below G, the forces of weight and buoyancy tend to increase the angle of inclination, and the equilibrium is unstable.

The distance GM is termed the metacentric height and the distance GZ, measured from G perpendicular to the vertical through B_1, is termed the righting level or GZ value. Weight and buoyancy are equal and act through G and B_1, respectively, to produce a moment (tendency to produce a heeling motion) ΔGZ, where Δ is the displacement or weight in tons.

Stability at small angles, known as initial stability, depends upon the metacentric height GM. At large angles, the value of GZ affords a direct measure of stability, and it is common practice to prepare cross-curves of stability from which a curve of GZ can be obtained for any particular draft and displacement.

Transverse stability should be adequate to cover possible losses in stability that may arise from flooding, partially filled tanks, and the upward thrust of the ground or from the keelblocks when the vessel touches the bottom on being dry-docked.

The case of longitudinal stability, or trim, is illustrated in Figure 3. There is a direct analogy with the case of

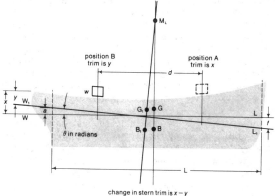

position B
trim is y

position A
trim is x

θ in radians

change in stern trim is $x - y$

Figure 3. Longitudinal section of floating ship showing change in stern trim as deck load W is shifted from position A to position B (see text).

transverse stability. When a weight originally on board at position A is moved a distance d, to position B, the new waterline W_1L_1 intersects the original waterline WL at the centre of flotation (the centre of gravity of the water

plane area WL), the new centre of buoyancy is B_1 and the new centre of gravity is G_1.

For a small angle of trim, signified by the Greek letter theta (θ),

$$\theta = (a + f)/L$$
$$wd = \Delta GM_L (a + f)/L$$

Thus if $(a + f) = 1$ inch $= 1/12$ foot, $wd = \Delta GM_L/12L$ and this represents the moment to change trim one inch.

The inclining experiment. A simple test called the inclining experiment provides a direct method of determining GM, the metacentric height, in any particular condition of loading, from which the designer can deduce the position of G, the ship's centre of gravity. If a weight w (tons) is transferred a distance d (feet) from one side of the ship to the other and thereby causes an angle of heel θ (theta) degrees, measured by means of a pendulum or otherwise, then $GM = wd/\Delta \tan \theta$ (see Figure 2).

For any particular condition, KB and BM can be calculated, GM is found by the inclining experiment, whence $KG = KM - GM$. It is simple to calculate the position of G for any other condition of loading.

Ship motions. Ship motions are defined by the movements from the equilibrium position of the ship's centre of gravity along the three axes shown in Figure 4 and by

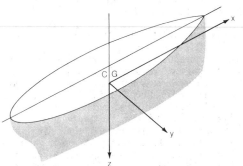

Figure 4: Coordinate axes of ship motions (see text).

rotations about axes approximately parallel to these. The linear displacements along the horizontal (x), lateral (y), and vertical (z) axes are termed surge, sway, and heave, respectively. The rotations about the corresponding body axes are respectively termed roll, pitch, and yaw (veering off course). Roll, pitch, and heave are oscillatory because hydrodynamic forces and moments oppose them.

Ship motions are important for many reasons. A ship should be able to survive any sea that may be encountered and, in addition, to behave well and to respond to control. In brief, a ship should respond to the action of the sea in such a manner that the amplitudes of its motions and its position never become dangerous, and so that the accelerations it undergoes are kept within reasonable limits. Propulsive performance always deteriorates when a vessel is rolling, pitching, or heaving. Hence these motions are made as small as possible.

Ship motions are excited by waves, whose growth is governed by the wind velocity at the sea surface, the area of water, or distance, over which the wind blows (the "fetch"), and the length of time during which the wind has been blowing (the "duration"). Any seaway is always a complex mixture of waves of different lengths, as wind itself is a complex mixture of gusts. All wave components do not travel in the same direction, but the directions of most of them in a single storm lie within 30° of each other. Regular trains of waves of uniform height and length are rarely, if ever, encountered. Most seas are confused and can be considered as made up of many separate component waves that differ in height and length. Pitching, rolling, and heaving are all excited by the changing pattern of surface waves in relation to the speed and course of the ship. In practice, it is possible to damp one motion only—that of rolling. The fitting of bilge keels (finlike longitudinal projections along the part of the underwater body of a ship between the flat of the

Rolling, pitching, heaving

bottom and the vertical topsides) has this effect, and still more effective means are the activated fin stabilizer (a device along the side of a ship activated by a gyroscope and used to keep the ship steady) and the passive or flume stabilizing tank, filled with water inside the ship.

Location of vibration symptoms

Ship vibration. Vibration is undesirable in any ship, and especially in passenger vessels. The main causes of vibration are: (1) unbalanced forces and couples (or moments) in main machinery, auxiliary machinery, and propellers; (2) propeller-excited forces and moments arising in the wake of the ship; (3) impacts from sea waves. Vibration may be local, occurring in structural parts or members only; or it may be general, arising when the hull vibrates like a girder. Though the local type is almost impossible to predict when the ship is being designed, it can usually be cured at little expense, often by the addition of local stiffening or pillar support. Though general vibration can be avoided in many instances by careful design, alleviation presents formidable difficulties in a completed vessel.

The hull of a ship is a girder that varies in cross section, sometimes with large openings in the decks, and is subjected to nonuniform loads arising from the distributions of weight and buoyancy. Additionally, the hull is subjected to acceleration forces arising from the ship's motions in a seaway and from wave impacts. Forces and moments from the main and auxiliary machinery that cause vibration can be made as small as possible, but forces and moments from the propellers and from waves are inevitable. Furthermore, this circumstance holds for each condition of loading—intermediate between-load draft, when the ship is fully loaded with cargo, and ballast draft, when the ship is empty of cargo, but the ballast tanks (which are filled with water to give the ship stability when it is empty of cargo) are full. Though it is almost impossible to calculate all of the possible modes and frequencies of vibrations to which a ship will be subjected, it is possible to compute with some reasonable degree of accuracy the fundamental modes of vertical and horizontal vibrations. Though the accuracy of calculated results for higher modes decreases as the order of vibration increases, reasonable approximations can be obtained. The results of such calculations are sometimes presented to indicate the ranges of engine revolutions per minute at which vibration difficulty may occur.

Resistance and propulsion. The motion of a surface vessel, whether towed or propelled, is characterized by three effects. They are: resistance to motion, formation of a wave pattern, and change of both draft and trim, as compared with draft and trim at rest.

When a vessel is in motion, friction exists between the hull surface and the water touching it; the vessel's motion also causes pressure between the hull surface and the adjacent fluid. These two forces cause waves. The relation of these forces to various ship designs is often studied on small models in experimental tanks.

Any propelling device operates by accelerating, and so increasing the momentum of, the fluid that passes through it. For the great majority of surface vessels, the screw propeller provides an efficient and convenient method of propulsion. The propeller may be described as a device for obtaining a propulsive thrust from a rotary motion.

Ships are usually propelled by one or more propellers situated at the stern. Thus the propeller works in a region where water flow is disturbed by the hull—*i.e.*, in the "wake," where the water has already been set in motion by the passage of the ship.

The action of the propeller increases flow velocities over the hull near the stern and thus reduces fluid pressure in this region. Consequently, there is in effect an addition to the resistance of the hull, commonly termed resistance augment or thrust deduction.

Efficiency of propulsion is generally defined at any speed as the ratio between the power required to tow the vessel and the power absorbed by the propeller(s). The propulsive qualities of a vessel are ascertained by means of: (1) resistance tests with the naked hull; (2) resistance tests with the hull, plus any appendages that affect propulsion (*e.g.*, the struts that support the propeller); (3)

self-propulsion tests. The optimum hull has the minimum increase of resistance in waves; hence further tests may be made in waves.

Propellers for high-speed vessels present special difficulties, notably cavitation, which may be described as the formation and collapse of cavities in a stream of flowing liquid as a result of pressure changes within the stream caused by changes in the velocity of flow. Cavitation tunnels are employed for the appropriate propeller investigations. Cavitation is overcome by increasing the propeller blade area and by modification of the blade section shape.

Manoeuvrability. Increases in the size and speed of ships bring problems of safe operation in congested waters and control at high speed in waves. Therefore, designs necessarily represent a compromise between manoeuvrability and course-keeping ability. Ship operators desire maximum manoeuvrability in port to minimize the need for assistance from tugs and to reduce delays in docking. They also desire a ship that can hold a steady course at sea with the minimum use of helm. These aims, however, are mutually conflicting.

Rudders and steering

A ship is steered by means of one or more rudders arranged at the stern or, in rare cases, at the bow. There are many types and shapes of rudders, depending upon the type of ship, design of stern, and number of propellers. When a yaw—that is, a change of angle about a vertical axis through the centre of gravity—is started, a turning moment is set up and the ship swings off course unless the swing is corrected by rudder action. This turning effect arises because the hull's centre of lateral resistance is much nearer the bow than the ship's centre of gravity.

Good course keeping demands directional stability. This is aided by design features that bring the centre of lateral resistance nearer to the ship's centre of gravity. These measures, however, increase the diameter of the ship's turning circle, requiring a design compromise. In warships, in vessels operating in confined waters, and in tugs, a small turning circle is essential. In merchant ships, rapid manoeuvring is required only in port; accordingly, the everyday function of the rudder is to ensure the maintenance of a steady course with the minimum use of helm. In this sense, turning circle properties are of less practical significance than the effect of small rudder angles.

STRUCTURAL STRENGTH

In still water, the loads acting on a hull include weight, fluid pressure, and buoyancy. In a seaway, additional forces arise from the wave-induced alteration of buoyancy distribution, from the ship's motions, from vibration, and from static and dynamic fluid pressures, including wave impact and slamming. The resultant loading on the main hull girder can be resolved into distributions along the length of shearing force, the bending moment in both vertical and horizontal planes, and the twisting moment.

Stresses acting upon the ship

The maximum stresses usually arise from the longitudinal vertical bending moment when the vessel is moving at right angles to a train of waves. As indicated above, this bending moment is considered as the sum of two components: first, the still water bending moment, due to the unequal distribution of weight and buoyancy along the ship length; and, second, the wave bending moment, which arises from differences in buoyancy distribution between the still-water and wave surfaces. The first of these components is governed by the disposition of weights within the ship and can often be minimized by skill and ingenuity at the design stage. The second is governed by the shape of the hull and the length and height of waves encountered. The length of a wave is the horizontal distance from the lowest point of one wave (the trough) to the lowest point of the next, or from the highest point of one wave (crest) to the highest point of the next. The height of a wave is measured vertically from the trough to the crest of any single wave. It is customary to assume that the worst conditions are when the length of the wave equals the ship length or when the midpoint of the ship is either at the crest or in the trough. Height of wave was formerly taken to be $1/_{20}$ of its length, but a common present-day practice is to assume that height h is the square root of the length l times the factor 1.1 $(h = 1.1 \sqrt{l})$.

With the wave crests at the ends of the ship, the supporting buoyancy is mainly at the ends of the ship, while with the wave crest at amidships the support is mainly at amidships. In the former case the greatest bending moment acting on the structure will occur when there is a concentration of weight amidships. Similarly, with a wave crest at amidships, the greatest bending moment will occur when there is concentration of weight toward the ends. The former case is known as sagging and the latter case as hogging.

In addition to stresses arising from the vertical forces which tend to bend the hull and which have their origin in heavy seaways and in engine pulsations, shear stresses are often investigated, notably in the longitudinal bulkheads of oil tankers. In container ships, where there is little actual deck area because of the large hatchways, special structural reinforcement is required to obtain the necessary strength. High superstructures, extending over a large fraction of the length, are a characteristic feature of passenger liners; and the design of such superstructures presents special problems. Transverse strength also poses difficult problems, notably in oil tankers, container ships, and bulk carriers.

The design of all structures is based upon experience, and experience is nowhere more requisite than in the design of ships. The great majority of ships are built according to the requirements of the classification societies of their countries, which publish rules and regulations for the construction of ships. To build a vessel of the classification specified by the owner, the shipbuilder must conform to these rules and regulations; he is thereby spared much difficult and tedious calculation work.

Steel is the main structural material in shipbuilding. The permitted types, composition, and qualities of mild and high-tensile steel, together with the approved manufacturing and the requisite tests, are specified in the classification society rules. The rules also cover the composition, manufacture, and tests appropriate to castings, forgings, and other manufactured components. Aluminum alloys, with good resistance to corrosion and the necessary strength properties, are used for the construction of erections on deck, notably in the superstructures of passenger ships, where their relative lightness makes ship stability properties more easily attainable. In the early 1970s it was thought that no new material was likely to replace steel as the main structural material within that decade, although composite materials might do so eventually. High-tensile steels were increasingly being used in the construction of very large tankers, bulk carriers, and container ships. Wood and wood substitutes are often employed for the sheathing of weather decks. Various synthetic materials with good fire-resisting properties can be used in accommodation spaces.

Spacing of watertight bulkheads. Typical ship hazards are stranding—when the bottom may be holed—and collision, when spaces within the hull may become flooded. Dry-cargo ships are protected against stranding by their double bottom construction. All ships must have a collision bulkhead, bulkheads to enclose the machinery space, and others—the number of which depends, in cargo and passenger ships, on their length. Oil tankers are well subdivided by both transverse and longitudinal bulkheads because a large number of separate tanks is required. In all vessels, but especially in passenger ships, the number and spacing of transverse watertight bulkheads must be adequate for safety under specified conditions of flooding. The extent to which a compartment open to the sea will flood depends on the permeability of its contents, this being defined as the ratio of the volume that can be occupied by water to the total volume. Formulas for the permeability of different compartments are laid down by governments, according to international agreement. Calculations to determine the floodable length—that is, the length at any point in the ship that may become flooded, without resulting in the immersion of any part of the margin line, which is three inches (76 millimetres) below

the deck to which the bulkheads extend—are made on the basis of an assumed permeability. The rule book also specifies formulas which ensure that one, two, or three adjacent compartments may be flooded before the margin line is immersed. Ships are thus described as having one-, two-, or three-compartment standards. The product of the floodable length and the factor of subdivision gives the permissible length of compartment. In the case of passenger ships, calculations must be made to discover whether their stability remains adequate under flooding.

Safety. In most maritime countries, a government department assumes responsibility for specifying and enforcing standards of safety in merchant vessels relating to maximum allowable draft, lifesaving appliances, stability, bulkhead subdivision, carriage of dangerous cargoes, lights and signals, and so on. These departments employ surveyors who supervise the testing, fitting, and inspection of all lifesaving appliances and other equipment essential for the safety of passengers and crew. Official inquiries are made into accidents, strandings, collisions, or wrecks, when loss of life is incurred.

The classification societies, such as Lloyd's Register of Shipping in England, the American Bureau of Shipping, Det Norske Veritas, Bureau Veritas, Registro Italiano Navale, Germanischer Lloyd, and Nippon Kaiji Kyokai, undertake the task of determining appropriate technical standards in ship construction and classification. Standards are laid down in the rules and regulations published by these societies, together with detailed specifications for the composition, quality, and testing of all materials of construction. The societies' surveyors are responsible for the testing of materials and for supervising the construction and repair of ships and their machinery. An owner specifies that a ship built to his order obtain a certain classification-society class because, for insurance purposes, this ensures a definite standard of strength and workmanship and a minimum freeboard. In the U.K., Lloyd's Register of Shipping is empowered by the Board of Trade to assign freeboards. Lloyd's also publishes annually its register book, which gives technical information for all merchant ships in service throughout the world and is kept up-to-date by the regular issue of supplements.

THE NAVAL ARCHITECT

A naval architect asked to design a ship may receive his instructions in a form ranging from such simple requirements as "an oil tanker to carry 100,000 tons deadweight at 15 knots" to a fully detailed specification of precisely planned requirements. He is usually required to prepare a design for a vessel that must carry a certain weight of cargo (or number of passengers) at a specified speed with particular reference to trade requirements; high-density cargoes, such as machinery, require little hold capacity, while the reverse is true for low-density cargoes, such as grain.

Deadweight is defined as weight of cargo plus fuel and consumable stores, and lightweight as the weight of the hull, including machinery and equipment. The designer must choose dimensions such that the displacement of the vessel is equal to the sum of the deadweight and the lightweight tonnages. The fineness of the hull must be appropriate to the speed. The draft—which is governed by freeboard rules—enables the depth to be determined to a first approximation.

After selecting tentative values of length, breadth, depth, draft, and displacement, the designer must achieve a weight balance. He must also select a moment balance because centres of gravity in both longitudinal and vertical directions must provide satisfactory trim and stability. Additionally, he must estimate the shaft horsepower required for the specified speed; this determines the weight of machinery. The strength of the hull must be adequate for the service intended; detailed scantlings (frame dimensions and plate thicknesses) can be obtained from the rules of the classification society. These scantlings determine the requisite weight of hull steel.

The vessel should possess satisfactory steering characteristics, freedom from troublesome vibration, and should

Marginal notes:

Materials in shipbuilding

Classification societies

Major design factors

comply with the many varied requirements of international regulations. Possessing an attractive appearance, the ship should have the minimum net register tonnage, the factor on which harbour and other dues are based. (The gross tonnage represents the volume of all closed-in spaces above the inner bottom. The net tonnage is the gross tonnage minus certain deductible spaces that do not produce revenue. Net tonnage can therefore be regarded as a measure of the earning capacity of the ship, hence its use as a basis for harbour and docking charges.) Passenger vessels must satisfy a standard of bulkhead subdivision that will ensure adequate stability under specified conditions if the hull is pierced accidentally or through collision.

Compromise plays a considerable part in producing a satisfactory design. A naval architect must be a master of approximations. If the required design closely resembles that of a ship already built for which full information is available, the designer can calculate the effects of differences between this ship and the projected ship. If, however, this information is not available, he must first produce coefficients based upon experience and, after refining them, check the results by calculation.

Training. There are four major requirements for a good naval architect. The first is a clear understanding of the fundamental principles of applied science, particularly those aspects of science that have direct application to ships—mathematics, physics, mechanics, fluid mechanics, materials, structural strength, stability, resistance, and propulsion. The second is a detailed knowledge of past and present practice in shipbuilding. The third is personal experience of accepted methods in the design, construction, and operation of ships; and the fourth, and perhaps most important, is an aptitude for tackling new technical problems and of devising practical solutions.

The professional training of naval architects differs widely in the various maritime countries. University degrees in naval architecture are offered by many universities and polytechnic schools; such academic training must be supplemented by practical experience in a shipyard.

Trends in design. The introduction of calculating machines and computers has facilitated the complex calculations required in naval architecture and has also introduced new concepts in design. There are many combinations of length, breadth, and draft that will give a required displacement. Electronic computers make it possible to prepare a series of designs for a vessel to operate in a particular service and to assess the economic returns to the shipowner for each separate design. Such a procedure is best carried out as a joint exercise by owner and builder. As ships increase in size and cost, such combined technical and economic studies can be expected to become more common.

Shipbuilding

THE SHIPYARD

The wooden ship was constructed on a building berth, around which timbers and planking were cut and shaped, and then fitted together on the berth to form the hull. A similar practice was followed with iron vessels and, later, with the earlier steel ships, as these tended to be replicas of wooden hulls. Gradually iron came to be used more effectively in its own right, rather than as a substitute for timber. The berth or slipway from which the vessel is launched is an assembly area, rather than a ship construction site. In many shipyards the number of launching berths has been reduced to increase the ground area available for prefabrication sheds. Greater ease of fabrication means that, despite the reduction in the number of berths, more ships can be built and construction costs lowered.

Organization. A shipbuilder undertakes to deliver to the client by a certain date and for a stated sum a vessel with specific dimensions, capabilities, and qualities, a vessel that has been tested on trial and is ready for service. The function of a shipyard is the production of completed ships in accordance with the shipbuilder's undertakings. The raw materials for construction and finished items to be installed on board are delivered there. The labour force in the yard consists of various workmen—

(margin left) The building berth

steelworkers, welders, shipwrights, blacksmiths, joiners, plumbers, turners, engine fitters, electricians, riggers, and painters.

Management is headed by a chairman and a board of directors, consisting usually of about 6 to 12 members from the technical, commercial, and secretarial departments, with one or more representing outside interests. The chief departments are the design, drawing, and estimating offices, planning and production control, the shipyard department—responsible for construction up to launching—and the outside finishing department, which is responsible for all work on board after launching. Other departments are responsible for buying and storekeeping and the yard maintenance.

The construction of the hull is only one of a shipbuilder's responsibilities. As soon as a contract is placed, he must negotiate with subcontractors for the supply of items that shipyards do not produce—the electric power plant, propulsion machinery, shafting and propellers, engine-room auxiliaries, deck machinery, anchors, cables, and furniture and furnishings. Production planning and control is therefore a complex undertaking, covering subcontracts, assembly, and installation, in which costs must be kept as low as possible.

Layout. In the early 1970s, shipyard practice was to have few building berths and extensive areas around them for the construction of large components of the steel hull. Building berths slope downward toward the waterway, to facilitate launching. Building basins, or dry docks, are sometimes used for the construction of very large vessels, because it is convenient to lower, rather than to lift, large assemblies, and this method also eliminates problems associated with launching. Extensive water frontage for the building berths is unnecessary. The main requirement is a site of considerable depth, rather than width, with a large area extending inland from the berths. Steel plates and sections are delivered to the shipyard at the end of the area farthest from the berths. There they are stored in a stockyard and removed, as needed, for cleaning, straightening, shaping, and cutting. Separate streams of plates and rolled sections converge toward the prefabrication shop, where they are used to build structural components or subassemblies. The subassemblies are transported to an area nearer the berths, where they are welded together to form large prefabricated units, which are then carried by cranes to the berth, to be welded into position on the ship.

(margin right) Prefabrication

In practice, there are many variations in this general procedure. At the Götaverken shipyard at Arendal, Norway, for example, partly fitted-out sections of the ship are fabricated in sheds and welded to sections already completed. As the vessel becomes built up with component sections, it is moved out of the covered area into a building dock and further sections are attached until the ship is complete. Water is then admitted to the dock and the ship is floated out for completion in the fitting-out basin. An example of an outstanding shipbuilding facility is the Harland and Wolff building dock in Belfast, Northern Ireland, completed in 1970, then the largest of its kind in the world: 1,825 feet (556 metres) long, 305 feet (93 metres) wide, and 38 feet (12 metres) deep. It is large enough for the construction of a 1,000,000-ton deadweight tanker. The dock is spanned by a travelling crane capable of lifting prefabricated structures of 840 tons maximum weight.

PLANNING

Delivery of a completed ship by a specified date requires careful planning. Following the introduction of the critical path method of planning and control by the U.S. E. I. du Pont de Nemours & Company about 1959, new techniques were adopted in many shipyards.

The critical path method is the basis of network analysis, which is used in planning complex production projects. The network, and information derived from it, is used for overall planning of a project and also for detailed planning with production progress control. The network gives a logical, graphical representation of the project, showing the individual elements of work and

(margin right) Critical path method

their interrelation in the planned order of execution. Each element of work is represented by an arrow, the tail of which is the starting point of activity and its head the completion. The arrows are drawn to any suitable scale and may be straight or curved. An event, which represents the completion of one activity and the beginning of another, is usually indicated by a circle and described further by a number within the circle. But each activity need not be completed before the next activity is begun. The logical order of steelwork in a hull, for example, is: (1) detailed drawings of steelwork; (2) ordering of steel; (3) manufacture and delivery of steel; (4) storing of steel material in stockyard; (5) shotblasting, cleaning, and forming operations; (6) subassembly work; and (7) erection of structure on berth. These operations can be represented on a ladder type of diagram. Many such diagrams—ladder and other types—go toward making up the complete aggregate operation of building a ship. When the proper sequence of operations is decided upon, times must be allocated to each operation to ensure that the men in charge understand their obligations. Planning, based on realistic estimates of times and costs, must begin at the precontract stage, so that, throughout the building program, a clear plan, with scheduled dates for each major section, is available. Detailed networks must be prepared for each of the major sections, showing dates for completion. The earliest and latest permissible starting and finishing times are indicated for each activity.

The critical path of a project is a series of activities whose duration cannot be increased without delaying the completion of the project as a whole. In large networks there may be more than one critical path. Up to about 100 activities can be dealt with manually but, for more complex cases, the numerical work is done by computer. The spare time available for a series of activities; *i.e.*, the maximum time these activities can be delayed without retarding the total project, is aggregated into a "total float." This is regarded as a factor of safety to cover breakdowns, mishaps, and labour troubles. Intelligent and experienced use of critical path methods can provide information of great value. Savings in production costs depend upon the use that management makes of this information.

From contract to working plans. Before an order is placed, the main technical qualities of the ship are decided upon and a general-arrangement drawing of the vessel, showing the disposition of cargo, fuel, and ballast, and crew and passenger accommodation is prepared. This plan provides a complete picture of the finished vessel. It is accompanied by detailed specifications of hull and machinery. This general-arrangement plan and the specifications form the basis of the contract between shipowner and shipbuilder.

As soon as an order is confirmed, drawing offices and planning departments produce working plans and instructions. Since ships are usually constructed according to the rules of a classification society, the stipulated structural plans are normally submitted to the society for approval. The spacing of bulkheads in passenger ships, for example, must be approved by the appropriate authority. For all ships, passenger and cargo, the approval of the maximum permissible draft must be sought from the classification society. Necessary working drawings include the lines plan and detailed plans of the steel structure—shell plating, decks, erections, bulkheads, and framing—as well as accommodation spaces, plumbing, piping, and electrical installations, and main and auxiliary machinery layout. The planning and production department prepares a detailed progress schedule, fixing dates for the completion of various stages in the construction. A berth in the yard is allocated to the ship, arrangements for the requisite materials, labour, personnel, and machines are made, and precautions are taken to ensure that the many interrelated operations will progress according to the timetable.

The lines plan; fairing. A lines plan, usually a 1/48 life-size scale drawing of a ship, is used by designers to calculate required hydrostatic, stability, and capacity conditions. Full-scale drawings formerly were obtained from the lines plan by redrawing it full size and preparing a platform of boards called a "scrive board" showing the length and shape of all frames and beams. Wood templates were then prepared from the scrive board and steel plates marked off and cut to size.

An alternative to the full-scale scrive board is a photographic method of marking off, introduced about 1950 and widely adopted. The lines plan is drawn and faired (mathematically delineated to produce a smooth hull free from bumps or discontinuities) to a scale of one-tenth full-size by draftsmen using special equipment and magnifying spectacles. The formerly used wood templates are thus replaced by specially prepared drawings, generally on one-tenth scale. Photographic transparencies of these drawings are then projected full size from a point overhead onto the actual steel plate. The plate is then marked off to show the details of construction, such as position of stiffening members, brackets, and so on. This optical marking-off system is much more economical in terms of space and skilled labour than the older method.

By the 1960s, digital computers were being used to fair the preliminary lines plan by a numerical method. Faired surfaces can be produced to a specified degree of accuracy and the lines can be drawn by a numerically controlled drawing machine, bringing the process under continuous scrutiny. Tapes can be produced for use in numerically controlled plate-burning machines, which cut plates to shape, and for the automatic cold bending of frames and curved girders. Fairing calculations produce data that can be fed back into a computer, and programmed to generate hydrostatic and stability data and other information.

FABRICATION AND ASSEMBLY

Since 1930, rivetting has been progressively supplanted by welding. This has proved more than a mere alteration in the method of connecting structural components because welding facilitates prefabrication of large component parts of the main hull structure.

Before welding came into wide-scale use every ship was constructed on the building berth. The keel was laid, floors laid in place, frames or ribs erected, beams hung from the frames, and this skeleton, framed structure was held together by long pieces of wood called ribbands. Plating was then added and all the parts of the structure were rivetted together. In other words, the ship was built from the keel upward.

The modern method is to construct large parts of the hull, for example, the complete bow and stern. Each of these parts is built up from subassemblies or component parts, which are then welded together to form the complete bow or stern. These sections of the ship are manufactured under cover in large sheds, generally at some distance from the building berth, before being transported to the berth and there fitted into place and welded to the adjacent section. The advantages of this procedure are that work can proceed under cover, unhampered by bad weather, and the units or component parts can be built up in sequences to suit the welding operations—not always possible at the building berth itself.

A number of techniques can be used to weld together two pieces of the same metallic material. The ideal weld is a continuity of homogeneous material, with the same composition and the same physical properties as the parts being joined. In steel shipbuilding, metal arc welding is produced by an electric arc formed between the parts to be joined; the fusion material is supplied by a coated electrode. The welding electrode consists of a core rod that is deposited as weld metal; it is flux coated to protect the molten metal from the atmosphere during deposition and to supply certain metallurgical properties to the weld. A great deal of research has gone into the production of the best possible coated electrodes for specific duties. The main advantages of welding over rivetting are: (1) a lighter structure (because overlaps are eliminated), (2) improved watertightness and oiltightness, (3) smoother surfaces, and (4) reduced hull upkeep. Certain precautions, however, are necessary. The design of the structure must be adapted for welding because structural details

Marginal notes:

General-arrangement drawing

Numerical method of fairing

The welding electrode

which can be rivetted are seldom suitable for welding. The joints must be carefully prepared beforehand for welding. Incomplete penetration, lack of fusion, porosity, and cracking are typical weld defects that must be avoided. Hard spots must be avoided and gradual tapering off of stiffness is necessary if defects in service are to be minimized (see also WELDING, BRAZING, AND SOLDERING).

LAUNCHING, OUTFITTING, AND TRIALS

Launching. Apart from certain small craft built on inland waterways, which are launched sideways, the great majority of ships are launched stern first from the building berth. Standing structures called ways, constructed of concrete and wooden blocks, spaced about one-third of the vessel's beam apart, support the ship under construction. The slope of the standing ways—which are often cambered (slightly curved upward toward the middle or slightly curved downward toward the ends) in the fore and aft direction—ranges from one-half to three-quarters of an inch per foot of length (from 42 to 62 millimetres per metre of length); ways extend from a position near the bow to past the stern and for a certain distance into the water. Over these standing ways is built the launching cradle, which consists of sliding ways on which are built poppets, or supporting structures, of timber to provide support for the hull. Between standing ways and launching ways is a layer of lubricant.

During construction the ship is supported by at least one line of blocks under the keel, with side supports and shores as necessary. As the vessel nears completion, the standing ways are built under it, the sliding ways are superimposed, and the cradle is built up. The weight of the vessel is transferred gradually to the standing ways. The full weight must not be supported by the ways for too long because the thickness of lubricant would be reduced by squeezing and its properties would be adversely affected. It is common to fit launching triggers which, when released at the moment of launching, permit the sliding ways to move over the standing ways.

As a vessel moves down the ways, the forces operating are: its weight acting down through the centre of gravity, the upward support from the standing ways, and the buoyancy of the water. As it travels further, the buoyancy increases and the upthrust of the ways decreases, with the weight remaining constant. As the centre of gravity passes the after end of the standing ways, the moment of the weight about the end of the ways tends to tip the ship stern first. At this position and for some time later, it is essential that the moment of buoyancy be greater than the moment of weight about the after end of the ways, thus giving a moment to keep the forward end of the sliding ways on the standing ways; otherwise there would be concentration of weight at the end of the ways, causing excessive local pressure. Calculations are made to determine the most important factors in launching, namely, the moment at which the stern lifts, the difference between weight and buoyancy when the stern lifts, the existence of a moment against tipping, and the equality of weight and buoyancy before the vessel reaches the after end of the ways to ensure that the cradle will not drop off the end of the standing ways.

Launching into a restricted waterway

The launching of a vessel into a restricted waterway requires the application of a retarding force. Usually piles of chains are laid alongside the sides of the ship to act as drags, and these are secured to chain plates by wire cables, fixed temporarily to the hull. As the vessel slides down the launching ways, the drags come serially into operation after, or sometimes before, the bow has cleared the after end of the ways. Launching can be a hazardous operation. If the lubricant is ineffective, the vessel will not move. If the stern does not lift as the vessel slides down the ways, the ship may tip about the way ends. The bow may sustain damage when it drops into the water at the end of the ways and may damage the slipway when the stern lifts. Excessive loads on the poppets may cause their collapse.

Outfitting. After launching, the ship is berthed in a fitting-out basin for completion. The main machinery, together with auxiliaries, piping systems, deck gear, life-boats, accommodation equipment, plumbing systems, and rigging are installed on board, along with whatever insulation and deck coverings are necessary. Fitting out may be a relatively minor undertaking, as with a tanker or a bulk carrier, but in the case of a passenger vessel, the work will be extensive. Although fitting-out operations are diverse and complex, as with hull construction there are four main divisions: (1) collection and grouping of the specified components, (2) installation of components according to schedule, (3) connection of components to appropriate piping and/or wiring systems, and (4) testing of completed systems.

In the early 1970s, the tendency in planning was to divide the ship into sections, listing the quantities of components required and times of delivery. Drawings necessary for each section are prepared and these specify the quantities of components required. A master schedule is compiled, specifying the sequences and target dates for completion and testing of each component system. This schedule is used to marshal and synchronize fitting work in the different sections and compartments.

Trials. As the vessel nears completion a number of tests are made. The naval architect makes a careful assessment of the weight of the finished ship and checks its stability and loading particulars by reference to data for the ship's lightweight and centre of gravity, obtained from a simple inclining experiment. The inclining test also provides a check on calculations.

Before the official sea trials, dockside trials are held for the preliminary testing of main and auxiliary machinery. Formal speed trials, necessary to fulfill contract terms, are often preceded by a builder's trial. Contract terms usually require the speed to be achieved under specified conditions of draft and deadweight, a requirement met by runs made over a measured course.

Speed trials

It is usual to conduct a series of progressive speed trials, when the vessel's performance over a range of speeds is measured. The essential requirements for a satisfactory measured course are: adequate depth of water; freedom from sea traffic; sheltered, rather than exposed waters; and clear marking posts to show the distance. Whenever possible, good weather conditions are sought. With a hull recently docked, cleaned, and painted, sea-trial performance can provide a valuable yardstick for assessing performance in service. Ideally, the ship should be run on trial in the fully loaded condition; but this is difficult to achieve with most dry-cargo ships. It is, however, comparatively simple to arrange in oil tankers, by filling the cargo tanks with seawater. Large vessels with a low displacement–power ratio must cover a considerable distance before steady speed is attained; hence they need to make a long run before entering upon the measured distance.

MODERN TRENDS

The rapid expansion of world trade, combined with the closure of the Suez Canal in 1967, has created a great demand for shipping of all types, but particularly for large vessels to carry bulk raw materials, such as oil, ore, and grain. The number of ships above 50,000 tons gross more than trebled in the succeeding years, and a tanker of 476,000 tons deadweight was on order at the end of 1970. Almost 90 percent of the ships on order were either tankers or bulk cargo carriers. Simultaneously, there has been a rapid expansion of the container ship fleet which, because of these ships' greater productivity, is likely to supersede much of the existing dry-cargo ship fleet, leading to a net reduction in the number of ships in service. Ship passenger transport continues to decline as air transport becomes relatively cheap, but passenger vessels continue to find employment in the tourist and cruise fields.

The effect of these changes on the shipbuilding industry has been profound. Shipyards have had to be reorganized and, in many cases, rebuilt to cope with the demand for very large ships. This has necessitated vast capital expenditure, and in a period of fierce world competition there have been amalgamations of small firms into large shipbuilding groups. In Britain, for example, in the 1960–70 decade the number of shipbuilding companies producing ships over 400 feet (120 metres) in length declined from 36 to about 12, while the output remained substantially the same.

By concentrating on the construction of large tankers and bulk carriers, Japan has become the leading ship-building nation, with an annual output of about 9,000,000 tons—nearly half the world total. At the beginning of the 1970s, only three shipyards in Britain were capable of producing very large tankers. West Germany specialized in container-ship production and now has a large share of that trade. Thus, increasingly, the trend was for particular shipyards to specialize in certain types of vessels, and the day of the shipyard with facilities to build practically any type of vessel was over.

Propulsion

Marine engineering is a branch of mechanical engineering. Its distinctiveness lies in the special features of engine design and operation that are necessary for ship propulsion. Otherwise, production processes, organization, and other matters have a similar basis.

A shipowner considers the following factors before ordering a ship: (1) capacity and deadweight on suitable draft, (2) speed, (3) first cost, (4) running and maintenance charges, and (5) general suitability. Items (1) and (2) indicate the purchaser's requirements. Items (3), (4), and (5) are computed by the engine builder.

Factors affecting choice of engine

The choice of propelling machinery is influenced by the engine power necessary for the required ship speed; the effects of the weight and space of engines plus fuel bunkers on the dimensions of the ship; fuel costs; upkeep costs —including overhaul, replacements, and consumable stores; and special considerations, such as personnel required. The choice of alternatives in marine propulsion may be grouped into two basic classes: diesel engines and geared steam turbines. The diesel engine is available in double-acting two-stroke; single-acting two-stroke or single-acting four-stroke direct drive; and in indirect drive systems, such as geared diesel engines and diesel-electric systems. It is usually possible to determine, without elaborate analysis, which type of machinery is most suitable for a particular vessel engaged in a particular trade. Occasionally, however, detailed investigation is necessary.

STEAM INSTALLATIONS

Steam generators. Immediately after World War II general mercantile practice favoured boiler pressures of 450–600 pounds per square inch (psi) with steam temperatures of 750–825° F (400–440° C). Occasionally, installations were built with levels as high as 850 psi and 900° F (480° C). In the early 1970s, pressures of 600–800 psi and temperatures of 800–900° F (425–480° C) became general; but higher ranges (*e.g.* 900–1200 psi and 1,000° F [540° C]) were accepted.

The following design data apply to a typical steam generator: normal evaporation, 180,000 pounds (82,000 kilograms) of water per hour; steam pressure/temperature, 880 psi, 990° F (530° C); feed temperature, economizer inlet, 280° F (140° C); temperature air heater outlet, 250° F (120° C); carbon dioxide in funnel gases, 15 percent; boiler efficiency, 86.8 percent. Such a generator normally would be provided with four fuel injectors, directed downward, arranged in the combustion chamber roof. Combustion air from the atmosphere is delivered by motor-driven fans. The furnace is surrounded by a wall of water-filled tubes, to which the heat of combustion is transmitted. The steam thus generated rises to a horizontal steam drum and from there it flows through pipes to the superheater, to be further heated by combustion gases. Finally, it is conveyed to the turbine. Hot gases rising from the superheater flow to the economizer, through which feedwater is circulated on its way from the feed heating system to the boiler. The products of combustion finally rise to the funnel and thence into the atmosphere (see STEAM POWER).

Steam turbines. A succession of evolutionary changes has brought steam-turbine practice to its present level. Two-turbine units are now standard for all except low-power installations, and these are single-turbine sets (see TURBINE).

Gearing. Reduction gearing between the steam turbines and the propeller enables the prime mover to rotate at speeds sufficiently high to ensure maximum thermal efficiency, while propeller revolutions are low enough to realize the maximum propulsive efficiency. In this respect the geared turbine has an advantage, compared with the direct-driven diesel engine.

Double- and single-reduction gearing

Double-reduction gearing is the most widely applied arrangement, the ratio of reduction ranging between 30 to 1 and 60 to 1; the lower values are for low-pressure turbines, and the higher values for high-pressure turbines. Single-reduction gearing, in which the ratio may be from 12 to 1 up to 20 to 1, has only limited applications.

For twin-screw ships, the propeller revolutions are usually of the order of 110 to 120 per minute (rpm). For single-screw vessels, the propeller may revolve at 90 to 100 rpm. Where the ship form permits, propellers of large diameter may be installed, as in single-screw ships with a large cross section (*e.g.* tankers); in such ships the revolutions may be as low as 80 per minute, to the great advantage of propulsive efficiency.

INTERNAL COMBUSTION ENGINES

Diesel engines. Heavy-oil engines, commonly termed diesel engines, operate on a cycle comprising four phases: suction, compression, expansion, and exhaust. Fuel is injected at the end of the compression stroke. In the so-called four-stroke cycle, each of the phases occupies one stroke; that is, the complete cycle extends over two revolutions. The earliest marine engines were of this form and were heavy and costly. The next step was to complete the four-phase cycle in one revolution, hence the term two-stroke cycle. In this cycle, the revolution is divided into three approximately equal periods, for compression, combustion and expansion, exhaust and scavenge. In all the early engines, combustion air was drawn from the atmosphere and the engines were termed atmospheric induction engines. Air density determines the maximum fuel weight that can be burned; it therefore determines the power that can be developed. If the charge-air density is increased by the interposition of a compressor between the atmosphere and the cylinder, then the weight of air is increased and a greater weight of fuel can be burned, with a proportionate increase in power output. The compressor, or blower, is driven by a gas turbine utilizing the heat energy of the exhaust gases. This is the principle of exhaust turbocharging. Single-acting, two-stroke, exhaust turbo-pressure-charged engines are almost standard in marine practice (see DIESEL ENGINE).

Geared engines. When engine powers were moderate, there was little or no need for geared engines. With the trend to larger direct-coupled engines, the scope for geared units, as an alternative method of propulsion, has widened. Moreover, there is greater opportunity for variation with geared engines than with direct-coupled engines. In general terms, the advantages of geared drive are: (1) greater reliability, by having more than one engine per screw; (2) when the ship is running light or partly loaded, one or more of the engines can be shut down and the others operated at their most efficient ratings; (3) maintenance is easier because the engines are of more manageable size; (4) engines can be overhauled one after the other at sea; (5) by modifying the number of engines per ship and cylinders per engine, the propelling machinery of a fleet of vessels of different sizes and powers can be standardized upon a single cylinder size, with advantage to initial cost, delivery time, and replacements.

Flexible couplings

Geared engines occasionally have been made with a heavy flywheel as the only damping agent between engine and gearing. More commonly, however, a flexible coupling of some kind is interposed between engine and gearing: to serve as a cushion, preventing the transmission of detrimental torque pulsations from engine to gearing; to function as a quick-disconnecting clutch for use when manoeuvring; and to limit the transmissible torque to, say, 1.5 to 2.5 times its normal value and thus obtain a measure of protection should one of the engines stop suddenly.

A flexible coupling can be mechanical, electrical, hydraulic, or pneumatic. A mechanical coupling cannot easily be made to serve as a clutch. Cost, weight, space, and reliability are the factors to be considered when comparing forms of coupling. The gearing is always single-reduction. The efficiency of the energy transmission, from engine to propeller, is approximately 92 percent for a geared installation and about 97 percent for a direct-coupled engine.

Diesel-electric drive. An alternative to geared engines is the diesel-electric drive, in which a diesel engine powers an electric generator and the propellers are powered by electric motors. Its advantages are similar to those of the geared arrangement. With the exception of small powers, however, direct-current machinery is too heavy and too costly to compete with geared systems; and alternating current and high voltages are accompanied by certain problems, especially those associated with manoeuvring and reversing.

GAS TURBINES

The gas turbine has not fulfilled the expectation at the beginning of the 1940s that it would become popular as a marine prime mover. By the 1970s, it was being applied to certain types of naval vessels, but it has seldom been used for mercantile ship propulsion. One of its basic problems is the low efficiency of the compressor; moreover, the metallurgical problems associated with the very high temperatures required for efficient operation are difficult to surmount (see also TURBINE).

NUCLEAR PROPULSION

In principle, the difference between a conventional steam installation and a nuclear power plant is that the combustion chamber in the former is replaced by a reactor using enriched uranium, the process of nuclear fission being utilized as the source of heat (see NUCLEAR REACTOR). The steam produced is fed into a normal set of steam turbines. The essential part of the reactor system is enclosed within a sealed, shielded structure capable of containing the products of any possible rupture in the reactor when in service. The weight of the shielding structure is more than three times that of the reactor system proper. The thickness of the surrounding concrete wall may vary from 30 to 48 inches (760–1200 millimetres).

Many forms of reactor are in use or under investigation in land plants. There are about 25 possible types of ship reactor. Nuclear plants for merchant ship propulsion ultimately may take the form of a direct-cycle reaction gas turbine, thus eliminating steam and other forms of intermediate heat exchange. Such a cycle may be a pressurized gas reactor coupled directly to a gas turbine. In the early 1970s, pressurized water was preferred as the primary coolant-moderator medium in marine installations; it was a logical development from high-pressure marine boilers.

The first nuclear propelled merchant vessel, the 21-knot NS "Savannah," launched in 1959, made clear the great potentialities of the system. This vessel is propelled by a single-screw, two-cylinder geared turbine arrangement delivering 21,000 shaft horsepower (shp). Steam pressure is only 460 psi, 475° F (245° C)—below the usual 650 psi, 875° F (470° C) level of conventional marine boilers.

A conventional steamer of the same size and power as the "Savannah" is limited in its steaming range to 13,000 nautical miles before refuelling. The nuclear-powered ship can travel 350,000 nautical miles before fuel renewal is necessary. Whereas fuel for a fuel-oil fired ship is paid for when purchased at routine intervals, in a nuclear ship the first fuel charge must be built-in. Thus the initial capital cost is high.

THE ENGINE ROOM

Engine-room auxiliary machines. In addition to the main propulsion machinery, an engine room contains a number of auxiliary machines. These auxiliaries fall into two groups: (1) those needed for ship services, and (2) those attendant upon the propulsion machinery. In the first group are the bilge, ballast, sanitary, freshwater, and general service pumps. The bilge pump deals with leakage water, and the ballast pump is used to empty the double-bottom ballast tanks before cargo is shipped.

In steam installations, pumps are required for main condenser circulation and water extraction, boiler feed, and fuel-burning equipment. There are also evaporators, feed heaters, forced- and induced-draft fans, soot collectors, an auxiliary condenser with circulating pump, forced lubricating pumps, and oil purifiers. Pumps needed for diesel propelling engines include water-circulating pumps for cylinder jackets, lubricating oil pumps, filters and purifiers, oil transfer and surcharging pumps, and an auxiliary boiler for fuel heating and other services. Water pumps are almost invariably of the vertical, motor-driven, centrifugal type. Cogwheel or screw pumps, as well as reciprocators, are commonly used for pumping fuel (see also PUMP). {Pumps}

Electric power for all purposes is provided by turbo-generators or by diesel-driven generators. Some of the auxiliaries run continuously at full load; others run intermittently, often at reduced load. To determine the total power requirements of the electric generators, the rated horsepowers of the various units are added and multiplied by a diversity factor that may vary between say, 0.60 and 0.75. On deck, there are cargo winches, capstan machinery, anchor winches, steering gear, and, perhaps, stabilizers. Although operated by the deck department, the upkeep of this equipment is undertaken by the engineering staff.

The piping systems for bilge, ballast, fuel oil, and other services, although out of sight under the floorplates, are elaborate and costly. In cargo liners and tankers, the total weight of piping is 20 to 27 percent that of the main engines; the cost of pipework can be 35 to 45 percent that of the main engines.

Engine-room automation. Automation, to a greater or lesser degree, is standard. The makers of proprietary engines have their own characteristic systems. There are differences of opinion regarding the extent to which propelling engines and auxiliary equipment should be automatically and remotely controlled, and the number of engineers that should be available at a central console. The American Bureau of Shipping, Lloyd's Register of Shipping, Bureau Veritas, and Det Norske Veritas have each published memoranda and guidance notes; but none has issued mandatory regulations.

BIBLIOGRAPHY. D.G.M. WATSON, "Estimating Preliminary Dimensions in Ship Design," *Trans. Instn. Engrs. Shipbldrs. Scotl.,* 105:110–174 (1961–62), a comprehensive treatment of merchant ship design, rich in factual information and providing a series of useful graphs—an ingenious method of designing by volume is explained; T. LAMB, "A Ship Design Procedure," *Mar. Technology,* 6:362–405 (1969), a most useful treatment of the subject, covering all types of merchant ships, with an extensive bibliography; R.V. TURNER, M. HARPER, and D.I. MOOR, "Some Aspects of Passenger Liner Design," *Trans. R. Instn. Nav. Archit.,* 105:379–414 (1963), a thoroughly practical paper dealing with the resistance, machinery, performance, stability, strength, and general arrangement of large passenger vessels; F.G. FASSETT, JR. (ed.), *The Ship-building Business in the United States of America,* 2 vol. (1948), deals exhaustively with all aspects of shipbuilding to date of publication.

Marine engineering: H.L. SEWARD (ed.), *Marine Engineering,* 2 vol. (1942–44), on all forms of prime movers, thermodynamics, and metals; J.H. MILTON, *Marine Steam Boilers,* 2nd ed. (1961, reprinted 1969), on natural and forced circulated boilers, superheaters, and classification society rules; A. STODOLA and L.C. LOEWENSTEIN, *Steam and Gas Turbines,* 6th ed., 2 vol. (1927); H. ROXBEE COX (ed.), *Gas Turbine Principles and Practice* (1955), on thermodynamics, compressor and turbine design, materials, and fuels; C.C. POUNDER et al., *Marine Diesel Engines,* 4th ed. (1971), a study of all well-known types, design, construction, and maintenance; L.R. FORD, *Practical Marine Diesel Engineering,* 4th ed. (1943), on operation and maintenance, with questions and answers; S. GLASSTONE and A. SESONSKE, *Nuclear Reactor Engineering* (1963), prepared and compiled under auspices of U.S. Atomic Energy Commission.

(C.C.P./J.F.C.C.)

Shock, Electrical

An electrical shock is the perceptible and physical effect of an electrical current that enters the body. The shock may range from an unpleasant but harmless jolt of static electricity, received after one has walked over a thick carpet on a dry day, to a lethal discharge from a power-line. The present article is focussed primarily upon the dangerous and often lethal shocks from house currents.

In the middle of the 18th century, after the invention of the electrical condenser, also called a capacitor (a device for the accumulation and storage of electrical charges), numerous experiments were carried out to discover the physical effects of electricity and its effects on animals. In one such experiment by Benjamin Franklin, the American editor, scientist, and statesman, a pullet was "struck dead" by an electric shock through the head and was revived by someone's repeatedly blowing into its lungs. It is important to note that in that experiment the current was passed directly through the pullet's head. Two years later, during a similar experiment with lightning in St. Petersburg (Leningrad), the investigator accidentally received a heavy discharge along the same current pathway and was killed. This difference in effect is just one example of the variability of the effects of electricity. Some of these variations are discussed in the paragraphs that follow (see also LIGHTNING).

The advent of town electrical-distribution systems, toward the end of the 19th century, may be said to have made electric shock a hazard of everyday life. From the beginning of the 20th century to the present, deaths from electric shock have increased manyfold in industrially developed countries. The consumption of electricity has meanwhile increased even more rapidly, so that the average number of deaths per gigawatt-hour (million kilowatt-hours) is actually falling (see Table).

	Deaths Due to Electric Shock			
year	country	number of deaths per annum	average consumption (gigawatt-hour)	deaths per gigawatt-hour
1910	England and Wales	26	...	...
	Sweden	5	...	...
1950	England and Wales	89	42	2.1
	Sweden	41	18	2.3
	France	181	29	6.2
	U.S.	955	329	2.9
1960	England and Wales	117	93	1.3
	Sweden	30	35	0.9
	France	184	65	2.8
	U.S.	989	753	1.3
1965	England and Wales	126	149	0.8
	Sweden	28	49	0.6
	France	203	94	2.2
	U.S.	1,071	1,055	1.0

Type of current responsible for most deaths

The great majority of deaths occur from alternating current at house-current frequencies of 60 hertz (cycles per second) in North America and 50 hertz in Europe, and it is shocks from this type of current that will be considered in the present article. Most of the deaths occur from contact with conductors at less than 500 volts. That is not to say that high voltages are less dangerous, but they are generally present only on apparatus and supply lines operated by utility companies, which try hard to ensure that only trained and authorized persons have access to them.

The effects of electric shock on the human body depend on the current that flows—the amperage—rather than on the force of the current, or voltage. The electrical resistance of the human body is variable and may in fact alter considerably during the passage of an electric shock. Therefore, except in broad terms, applied voltage is not a consideration. This leads to difficulties in the investigation of accidents, for the electrical engineer is often able to state only the voltage applied, but the physician thinks in terms of the current that flowed.

Another important consideration is the path that the current takes through the body. Looked at as an electrical conductor, the body behaves as a solution of electrolytes in a leathery container. The greatest current density therefore occurs along the axis joining the two points of contact. As the distance perpendicular to the line of current flow increases, the density of current rapidly falls off. Thus, those organs most likely to be affected are those that lie close to the direct path of the current. As the great majority of electrical fatalities are due to currents passing between an arm (usually the right) and the legs, the current passes through the chest and affects the organs within it. Except in those extremely unusual accidents in which the head makes one of the points of contact, the brain does not lie on or near the pathway of the current.

Causes of death. An electric shock may directly cause death in three ways: asphyxia, persistent respiratory arrest, and ventricular fibrillation.

Asphyxia. A person may be unable to let go of a conductor of electrical current because of the uncontrollable contraction of the forearm muscles. In the same way a current traversing the body through the chest holds the chest muscles in an uncontrollable contraction and the victim is unable to breathe. Unless he is freed or manages to release himself, he will die within a few minutes.

Persistent respiratory arrest. The early experimenters directed electric currents through the heads of the experimental animals and produced persistent arrest of respiration. From this, and similar evidence, arose the widely accepted belief that restoration of breathing by artificial respiration was the correct and sufficient first-aid treatment for all victims of electric shock. As has been said above, accidents in which currents pass through the head are quite uncommon, but in such instances artificial respiration by itself would be an appropriate treatment. During electroconvulsive therapy (electric shock treatment), used for treatment of some psychiatric illnesses, an electric current is passed across the head, and respiratory arrest is an extremely rare complication.

Ventricular fibrillation. At the end of the 19th century it was shown that an electric shock can cause the heart to function in such an uncoordinated fashion that the circulation stops. This condition, called ventricular fibrillation, is not peculiar to electric shock and may occur in a number of other conditions. Untreated, ventricular fibrillation results in death within three to five minutes; only rarely in human beings does the heart revert spontaneously to a normal rhythm.

An electric shock will cause ventricular fibrillation only if the current passes through the heart at the moment when the ventricles (the main pumping chambers of the heart) are starting to relax. It has been shown that, during this vulnerable period, the greater the current the shorter the time it takes to cause ventricular fibrillation. It is generally believed that ventricular fibrillation is the most common cause of death in electric shock.

First-aid treatment. It has been seen that, although electric shock may bring about death in a number of ways, all of these result in either the arrest of respiration or the arrest of the circulation (due to disordered heart action) or both. First aid is therefore directed at treatment of these conditions. Arrest of respiration is now almost universally treated by mouth-to-mouth artificial respiration, and circulatory arrest by external massage of the heart (cardiac massage). Both of these are effective if started promptly within three minutes of the accident—and if applied correctly. There is no time to learn these techniques from books or posters after the accident, and persons who are likely to be first on the spot in an emergency should have a thorough practical training beforehand. This is particularly the case with external cardiac massage, which may itself cause death or serious injury if carried out incorrectly. Because of these dangers, external cardiac massage should be used only when it is really necessary as a life-saving procedure. Not only should the potential rescuer know how to carry out external cardiac massage, but he must be able to recognize quite clearly the indications for starting.

Artificial respiration and cardiac massage

Aftereffects. Although the great majority of victims of electric shock, excluding those who have been burned, either die or recover completely, a very small number suffer from aftereffects, which may be temporary but are sometimes permanent. These may include cataract of the eye, a form of angina (attacks of pain beneath the breastbone), or various disorders of the nervous system. All sorts of conditions that might have started in any event are commonly attributed by uncritical observers to an electric shock that occurred perhaps weeks or months earlier. Such tendencies lead one to skepticism, but careful study of accident records including the current pathway and the clinical details have convinced a number of observers that some manifestations actually are sequelae. Nevertheless, it must be emphasized that such aftereffects of accidental electric shock are extremely rare.

BIBLIOGRAPHY. C.F. DALZIEL and W.R. LEE, "Lethal Electric Currents," *IEEE Spectrum*, 6:44-50 (1969), a general review by an electrical engineer and a physician on lethal electric currents, with references to many original papers; W.R. LEE, "Electric Shock," *The Practitioner*, 199:306–313 (1969), a short review by a physician on the history, effects, and treatment of electric shock, with references to many original papers.

(W.R.L.)

Shock, Physiological

Physiological shock may be defined as acute progressive circulatory failure in which defective tissue perfusion occurs. This definition is derived from the one constant feature of physiological shock, the failure of adequate blood flow through the capillaries, the smallest of the blood vessels. As a result of this failure, an inadequate supply of oxygen and nutrients is delivered to the tissues, and the removal of metabolic waste products from the tissues is incomplete.

All, or some, of the following features may be present: a raised pulse rate, each pulse being diminished in strength, or "thready"; diminished arterial blood pressure; a cold, sweaty skin; rapid, deep respirations (breathing called air hunger in this context); mental confusion; dilated pupils; a dry mouth; and diminished flow of urine.

Many classifications of various types of shock have been developed, the most popular being one that relates the state to its cause; *e.g.*, hemorrhage (bleeding) or sepsis (invasion by pus-forming organisms). This classification has the advantage of possessing diagnostic and therapeutic implications, but unfortunately the cause of shock is often uncertain. Alternatively, the state may be called hypovolemic if it is associated with a reduction in blood volume or normovolemic if no blood-volume diminution has occurred. Shock can also be subdivided into "warm hypotension," if the sufferer has lowered blood pressure and warm dry skin, and "cold hypotension," if the skin is cold.

Components of normal circulation

In order to comprehend the various mechanisms associated with the onset of shock, it is necessary to understand the functioning of the normal circulation, as it is described in detail in the article CIRCULATION AND CIRCULATORY SYSTEMS. Essentially there are five circulatory components: (1) the heart, whose muscle, called the myocardium, pumps blood around the circulatory system; (2) the arteries; elastic-walled vessels whose final subdivisions are the arterioles, which act as sluice gates to regulate both the flow of blood into the capillary bed and the pressure in the arterial tree; (3) the capillaries; tiny, thin-walled vessels at which vital metabolic exchanges between blood and tissues occur; (4) the veins; large, relatively thin-walled vessels conducting blood back to the heart; and (5) the blood, comprised chiefly of plasma fluid and red blood cells. Malfunction of any one of these can lead to inadequate blood flow and permeation of the tissues, and thus cause shock.

THE TYPES OF SHOCK AND THEIR RECOGNITION

Shock due to inadequate blood volume. Hemorrhage is the commonest cause of shock. In the "average man" (weighing 70 kilograms, or about 154 pounds) the blood volume is about five litres (about 5.3 quarts), and the loss of any part of this will initiate certain cardiovascular reflexes. Hemorrhage results in a diminished return of

venous blood to the heart, the output of which therefore falls, causing diminution of the arterial blood pressure. When this occurs pressure receptors (baroreceptors) in the aorta and carotid arteries will initiate remedial reflexes either through the autonomic (nonvoluntary) nervous system by direct neural transmission or by epinephrine (adrenaline) secretion into the blood from the adrenal gland. The reflexes comprise increase in the rate and power of heart beat, increasing its output; constriction of arterioles leading to nonessential capillary beds (notably the skin and some viscera); and constriction of the veins, diminishing the large proportion of the blood volume normally contained therein. By these means arterial blood pressure will tend to be maintained, thus preserving blood flow to the vital areas such as the brain and the myocardium. After continued acute blood loss of 20–30 percent of the blood volume, the compensatory mechanism will begin to fail, the blood pressure will begin to fall, and shock will ensue.

Increased sympathetic (autonomic) nervous activity thus accounts for the fast pulse rate, pallor, and coldness of the skin in shock and, in addition, is the cause of increased sweating and dilation of the pupils of the eyes. Air hunger and mental confusion are caused by the inadequate carriage of oxygen, and decreased urine flow stems from a diminution in the renal (kidney) blood flow. This diminution, if severe, can lead to kidney failure. If acute blood loss continues beyond about 50 percent, the inadequacy of flow through vital circulations will lead to death.

Loss of whole blood is not necessary for the blood volume to be low, for plasma loss through burnt areas of the skin, or dehydration following inadequate intake of fluid, or exceptional fluid loss can lead to contraction of the blood volume to levels capable of causing shock (see DEHYDRATION).

Shock due to inadequate cardiac output. *Cardiogenic shock.* Sudden interference with the blood supply to the heart muscle, as by a thrombosis (clotting) in a coronary artery, causes damage to the muscle with resultant diminution in its contractile force. The output of the heart falls; if the decline is severe, a fall in blood pressure stimulates the baroreceptors and, in the way just described, shock results. This occurs in a substantial number of myocardial infarcts (death of sections of heart muscle). But low heart output alone may not account for the shock, for in chronic heart failure the cardiac output may be low without such a response in the peripheral circulation.

Shock from functioning of heart

Pulmonary embolus. A thrombus is a blood clot that remains fixed to the blood vessel wall at its point of origin. The clot is called an embolus if it breaks loose from its point of origin. A pulmonary embolus results when a venous thrombus breaks loose from its original site (usually in a pelvic or leg vein), passes along the veins to the heart, and on to a pulmonary artery or subdivision. By the bulk of the clot or because of reflex constriction of the remainder of the pulmonary arterial tree, blood flow through the lung is obstructed. This reduces cardiac output, and shock may follow; in addition breathing is noticeably faster and deeper.

Dissection of the aorta. Degenerative changes in the lining layer (intima) of an artery can lead to the stripping of this layer from the vessel wall (dissection) by the flow of the blood, which works into the interstices of the arterial wall. Thus the passageway of the vessel (lumen) is effectively blocked, and, should this occur in the thoracic aorta—usually at the site of a localized dilation (aneurysm)—diminished cardiac output leads to shock.

Cardiac tamponade. The heart is enclosed in a membranous sac (the pericardium) whose lubricated smooth inner layer facilitates unimpeded movement during the heart's contraction and refilling. The thin layer of pericardial fluid may suddenly increase or a hemorrhage into the sac may occur, which can compress the heart, preventing adequate filling between contractions. This compression of the heart by surrounding fluid, a condition called cardiac tamponade, causes diminution in cardiac output that can lead to shock.

Shock due to increased circulatory capacity. If widespread dilation of the veins or of the capillary beds occurs, the blood volume is no longer sufficient to fill the larger space and shock ensues.

Bacteremic shock. Infection anywhere in the body may spread to the circulation, and the presence of organisms in the blood stream—bacteremia—may lead to shock. Bacteria are conveniently divided into "gram-positive" and "gram-negative" grouped according to their reaction to a special gram stain.

Gram-negative bacteremia, the more common and more lethal type, is frequently caused by *Escherichia coli, Proteus, Pseudomonas,* or *Klebsiella* organisms; the first of these normally inhabits the intestine. The clinical picture of gram-negative bacteremia is much like that of hemorrhage, although no blood has been lost, with a rapid, thready pulse; a cold, sweaty skin; and low blood pressure. A fever may occur, in addition to the local signs of the associated infection. The cause of the type of reaction is uncertain.

The response to bacteremia from gram-positive organisms such as *Staphylococcus* and *Streptococcus* is different. Widespread dilation of the blood vessels results in a warm, dry skin and a full volume pulse in spite of lowered blood pressure.

In both types of bacteremia the condition may be exacerbated by contraction in blood volume. This follows fluid loss, *e.g.,* that lost in the peritoneal cavity in peritonitis—inflammation of the peritoneum, the membrane that lines the abdominal cavity; in the tissues in streptococcal infection; or through the intestine in enteritis (inflammation of the intestine).

Reaction to foreign material in bloodstream; fainting

Anaphylactic shock. Anaphylactic shock is discussed in detail in the article ALLERGY AND ANAPHYLACTIC SHOCK. An anaphylactic reaction follows the entrance of a specific foreign material into the bloodstream of a person whose body has become sensitized against it by previous contact. When this happens, intense constriction of the lung bronchi occurs, interfering seriously with respiration; blood pressure may fall precipitously because of the release of substances (serotonin, histamine, and bradykinin) that cause dilation of the arterioles and venules with increase in the capillary-wall permeability. Thus the circulatory capacity is increased, and fluid is lost into the tissues.

Psychogenic shock. Psychogenic shock causes fainting, probably by initiating dilation of the vessels of the muscles. Blood pressure falls, the skin becomes cold and sweaty, and the pulse rate increases. Decrease in blood flow to the brain leads to light-headedness and loss of consciousness. As soon as the affected person is prone cerebral blood flow improves and the circulation recovers.

Drugs and shock. Most anesthetic drugs—nitrous oxide is a notable exception—have a profound effect on the circulation, decreasing contractility of the heart muscle and increasing circulatory capacity by dilating the blood vessels. In addition, the normal postural circulatory reflexes are lost, so that pooling of blood in the legs is liable to occur if the affected person is tilted to a head-up position. This is of particular importance after an operation, when sitting up too soon can lead to low blood pressure and insufficient blood flow to the brain.

Overdosage of certain drugs, notably barbiturates, narcotics, and tranquillizers, blocks normal circulatory reflexes and causes dilation of the blood vessels, leading to a fall in blood pressure that often is accompanied by a slow, full-volume pulse.

Neurogenic shock. The maintenance of the tone of the blood vessels by the autonomic nervous systems may be affected by severance of one of these nerves or by its interruption of the flow of nervous impulses. Thus, spinal anesthesia—injection of an anesthetic into the space surrounding the spinal cord—or severance of the spinal cord results in a fall in blood pressure because of dilation of the blood vessels in the lower portion of the body and a resultant diminution of venous return to the heart.

Endocrine causes of shock. The endocrines play a vital role in the regulation of normal metabolic processes, and it is not surprising that part of the picture in malfunction relates to the circulation. Detailed description is found in ENDOCRINE SYSTEM DISEASES AND DISORDERS.

Inadequate secretion by the adrenal cortex, the outer substance of the adrenal gland, leads to shock both by diminution of myocardial efficiency and by decrease in the blood volume. Functional disorders of the pituitary, the adrenal medulla (the inner substance of the adrenal gland), the thyroid, and the parathyroids can all lead to circulatory upset and shock.

Refractory and irreversible shock. The terms refractory shock and irreversible shock are widely used in professional literature. Refractory shock exists when in spite of apparently adequate therapy the shock state continues. Commonly the treatment proves later to have been inadequate, in which case the shock was not true refractory shock. This often occurs after a major injury in which there is internal bleeding, leading to underestimation of true blood loss and therefore to inadequate transfusion.

Definitions of refractory and irreversible shock

In certain cases, though the therapy actually is appropriate, shock persists; if patients in such cases respond to further special treatment, then this is true physiologic refractory shock. If the patient fails to respond, and death follows, then the diagnosis of irreversible shock is made retrospectively.

The concept of refractory and irreversible shock can be clarified by reference to animal experiment. If a tube is inserted into the femoral artery of a dog and about 20 percent of the dog's blood volume is removed, the animal goes into shock. If the blood is immediately replaced, the animal recovers. If replacement of the blood is delayed, then reinfusion later on may not result in reversal of the shock state, which is thus refractory; infusion of additional intravenous fluid will cause pulse and blood pressure to return to normal. If the dog is allowed to remain in the shock state for too long before reinfusion, no therapeutic measure will result in more than transient recovery and death will be inevitable. This is therefore irreversible shock. Clearly fundamental change must occur in the circulatory components to cause the refractory, or irreversible state, but, in spite of extensive research, it is not yet clear where the defect lies. The possibilities are:

The heart. It is possible that in severe or prolonged shock states the myocardial blood supply is diminished sufficiently to damage the heart's pumping action temporarily or permanently. Alternatively it may be that noxious products of inadequately perfused tissues may circulate and affect the heart muscle.

The peripheral circulation. While the flow of blood through major vessels is under the control of the nerves, circulation through the capillary beds is of a more primitive type and is under the influence of local metabolic products. In this way local tissue requirements control the microcirculation by effecting the capillary sphincters and by shunts between the small artery, or arteriole, and the small vein, or venule. Normally only one third of the capillaries, containing about 5 percent of the blood volume, are open at any given moment. In shock, arteriolar constriction causes inadequate flow through the tissues and local waste products increase. These cause dilation of the capillary sphincters and opening of the whole capillary bed, which thus contains an increased proportion of the blood volume. Further, the post-capillary sphincter (being less sensitive to lack of oxygen) is less widely dilated than the precapillary one so that the capillaries become further engorged with slowly flowing blood, and fluid leaks through the vessel walls into the tissues. Thus the body is further deprived of circulating blood volume.

Disseminated intravascular coagulation. It has been suggested that widespread clotting of the blood occurs during capillary stagnation. This leads to severe damage to the cells unsupplied by flowing blood. Later, when the clot is dissolved under the influence of enzymes that dissolve the fibrin of the clots, the flow through these areas carries toxic metabolic products to vital organs such as the heart, kidney, or liver, and the ensuing damage leads to irreversibility of shock.

Possibility of clotting in capillaries

Endotoxin. In experiments on dogs, hemorrhage leads to diminution of blood flow to the bowel to such a degree that damage to its lining results. Intestinal bacteria, or their products, may then breach this unhealthy mucous membrane and enter the circulation, perpetuating the shock state. Though other experimental evidence lends support to this theory, there is little evidence that this sequence of events occurs in man, in whom the changes in blood flow to the bowel are much less severe.

Reticuloendothelial system. Spread throughout the body is a system of cells, called reticuloendothelial cells, whose function is to absorb toxins from the bloodstream. It seems possible that these may be incapacitated by the shock state and may thus permit the accumulation of substances that contribute to prolongation of the state. This may be particularly true of the reticuloendothelial cells of the liver, since a period of low blood pressure may deprive them of the ability to absorb noxious substances arriving in the blood from the intestine. These substances are normally filtered out in the liver.

Identification of the causes of shock. It must be emphasized that although the types of shock have been categorized for clarity of description, several causes may actually be present in any given instance. For example, in peritonitis—inflammation of the lining membrane of the abdominal cavity—bacteria enter the bloodstream as a result of the infection, and fluid loss into the peritoneal cavity leads to a low blood volume. In pancreatitis, inflammation of the pancreas, the cause of shock may be threefold: bleeding and escape of fluid into the tissues may lead to diminished blood volume; there may be increased release of the vasodilator bradykinin, leading to increased circulatory capacity; and bacteremia, the presence of bacteria in the bloodstream, may exist. In severe infection with *Streptococcus* organisms, there may be bacteremia, a low blood volume from loss of fluids into the tissues, and toxic damage to the heart muscle.

Hemorrhage may present no recognition difficulties, since losses of blood from the intestine or from wounds and fractures are usually apparent, but the bleeding may not be evident if it occurs in the chest or abdomen after trauma or if the blood fails to drain from deep-seated operative wounds.

When bacteremia occurs there is often an obvious source of infection such as peritonitis, pneumonia, or urinary tract infection, but such loci of infection may be small or deep-seated, so that final proof of cause has to be determined from culture of the blood.

Cardiogenic shock usually occurs only along with typical features of coronary thrombosis—severe central chest pain perhaps radiating to the arm or neck and showing typical changes on an electrocardiogram (ECG). Myocardial infarction, the death of a section of heart muscle, can occur without causing any signs; it may happen while a person is under anesthesia, for example, and it does not always produce typical changes in the ECG at first. Furthermore, low blood pressure from any cause can result in ECG changes, further obscuring the cause of shock.

Lodging of a clot in a pulmonary blood vessel—pulmonary embolus—often occurs without clinical evidence of formation of the clot in a vein of the leg or pelvis but is usually distinguishable by a severe shortness of breath in the absence of pulmonary physical signs. It may be difficult, however, to differentiate pulmonary embolus from pneumonia with bacteremia.

MANAGEMENT AND PROGNOSIS

Treatment is directed at the specific cause, when the cause is known.

Shock due to inadequate blood volume and cardiac output. *Hemorrhage.* When it is possible to anticipate blood loss, and to measure it accurately—*e.g.*, during an operation—losses may be immediately replaced before significant volume depletion can occur.

More often, however, hemorrhage is unexpected; it may not be possible to measure the amount of blood lost. If shock occurs in an otherwise healthy person weighing 70 kilograms, or about 154 pounds, then at least one litre of blood (or slightly over one quart) has been lost and generally is replaced by transfusion into a vein. But since a preliminary matching between recipient serum and donor cells must be carried out, and cannot be done in less than twenty minutes, other fluid is usually given intravenously during the delay. The fluid chosen, such as plasma or a solution of the carbohydrate dextran, must contain molecules large enough to keep the solutions within the blood vessels.

The doctor judges the adequacy of the volume given from the rising blood pressure and falling pulse rate with increasing pulse volume. Monitoring central venous pressure (CVP) helps in accurate volume replacement.

Burns. Since the main loss from burns is plasma and electrolytes, these require replacement in proportion to the area of the burn and the size of the patient and are calculated from a suitable formula.

Dehydration. Pure water loss rarely occurs. Thus, low blood volume is treated by intravenous infusion of a balanced salt or electrolyte solution, though an initial circulatory boost with a large-molecule solution may be required.

Dissection of the aorta. Major arterial dissections are treated where possible by removal of the section of diseased artery. When this is not possible an opening is made in the loosened intima at the far end of the dissection, to allow blood to return to the main channel.

Cardiac tamponade. Usual emergency treatment is by removal of the fluid that is compressing the heart. If there is a wound in the heart muscle, allowing leakage of blood from the heart into the pericardium, the opening must be closed.

Shock due to increased circulatory capacity. *Bacteremic shock.* Bacteremic shock, exceeded in frequency only by cardiogenic and hemorrhagic shock, is most often caused by gram-negative organisms. There are three aspects of treatment: collections of pus are drained as soon as possible; the circulatory volume is increased to compensate for enlargement of the vascular bed; and appropriate antibiotics are administered.

Anaphylactic shock. The essence of treatment of anaphylactic shock is the injection of epinephrine (adrenaline), whose effects include an increase in the heart rate and constriction of the blood vessels, followed by an antihistamine, to counteract the reaction to the foreign substance, and a bronchodilator, to ease breathing.

Psychogenic shock. Persons suffering from psychogenic shock are placed flat or with head slightly lower than the rest of the body, to restore a good flow of blood to the brain and bring about recovery from the fainting.

Shock from drug use. Dangerously low blood pressure may be raised by decreasing the dose of the drug (such as an anesthetic agent), by speeding its elimination from the body, or by the administration of a substance that constricts the blood vessels.

Neurogenic shock. Neurogenic shock does not usually require specific therapy; indeed, spinal anesthetics may be given with a view to producing a low blood pressure so as to diminish bleeding during an operation. If blood pressure becomes critically low, the legs are sometimes elevated and a vasoconstrictor administered.

Undiagnosable and refractory shock. A major problem in the treatment of shock occurs when the doctor cannot be sure of its cause, either because of a lack of diagnostic criteria or because failure to respond to specific therapy has placed the diagnosis in doubt. In particular, the doctor must differentiate between shock that results from inadequate cardiac output and shock due to absolute or relative blood volume deficiency. The latter type improves when measures are taken to increase blood volume, while in the former type such treatment overloads the failing heart, giving rise to edema of the lungs, which can cause death.

In cases in which there is doubt about the volume of intravenous replacement or the rate at which it should be given, a long, fine tube may be threaded through a peripheral vein until its tip lies in the superior vena cava, the last venous channel before the heart. Although the pressure in this vein—central venous pressure (CVP)—does not give an accurate measure of the blood volume, it does give an indication of the ability of the heart to deal with returning venous blood. Thus, broadly speaking, if intra-

Measures taken when cause is undetermined

venous fluids are given, with clinical improvement and no gross change in the CVP, a volume deficiency is deemed to be present and treatment is by further volume replacement. If rapid rise in CVP follows intravenous fluid administration, then a cardiac deficiency is present and no further intravenous volume therapy is given.

Other measures that may be taken in addition to a trial of volume therapy include administration of wide-spectrum antibiotics (antibiotics effective against a wide range of bacteria), oxygen, and, if there is evidence of failing heart, digitalis. Any tendency toward a decline in blood alkalinity is corrected.

Monitoring effectiveness of treatment   If the shock remains undiagnosed and refractory, the effectiveness of further treatment can sometimes be checked by such direct measurements as of the blood volume, the cardiac output, and the blood pressure in the pulmonary artery. If such measurements are not possible, the doctor may have some indication of progress by observation of the physical signs and response to therapy listed in the accompanying Table.

Clinical Indicators of Circulatory Dynamics	
indicator	significance
Pulse volume	Cardiac output
Skin temperature	Arteriolar constriction
Urine output	Visceral perfusion
CVP upper normal range	Adequate circulatory volume

In the past, drugs such as norepinephrine have been used to constrict the arterioles in an attempt to elevate blood pressure. Because arteriolar spasm resulting from such measures prevents adequate flow to the capillaries and results in tissue damage, modern therapy utilizes agents that diminish constriction of the arterioles and thus improve blood flow and tissue perfusion. This type of therapy increases the overall circulatory capacity and consequently may need to be accompanied by further volume replacement therapy, the actual amount being controlled by reference to the CVP.

Prognosis. During the course of treatment, some indication of outlook may be had from measurement of the lactic acid in the blood. The higher its level, the greater is the chance of irreversibility.

The outlook may also depend on the cause of shock and the speed and vigour with which it is treated. At one end of the scale the mortality of immediately treated shock following hemorrhage is small, while at the other, severe cardiogenic shock carries a mortality rate of about 80 percent. In septic shock the mortality is about 50 percent.

SALIENT FEATURES OF PHYSIOLOGIC SHOCK

Shock is a failure of blood flow through the tissues and is most commonly seen after hemorrhage, myocardial infarction, sepsis, or pulmonary embolus. Clinically it is characterized by fast, thready pulse, low blood pressure, and cold sweaty skin, though many variants are found. Treatment usually involves elimination of blood volume deficiency and sepsis and improvement of myocardial action. When therapy initially fails, additional treatment with arteriolar dilators sometimes improves perfusion of the tissue with blood. Blood flow is seen to be more important than blood pressure.

BIBLIOGRAPHY.   M.H. WEIL and H. SHUBIN (eds.), *Diagnosis and Treatment of Shock* (1967), a full account of the various aspects of the subject, with a large section on clinical management; R.M. HARDAWAY *et al.*, "Intensive Study and Treatment of Shock in Man," *J.A.M.A.*, 199:779–790 (1967), a detailed report of studies of shocked patients treated in the specialized unit at the Walter Reed Army Institute, Washington; S.G. HERSHEY (ed.), *Shock* (1964), a collection of monographs by distinguished authors that emphasizes the range of opinions on this subject; R.T. GRANT and E.E. REEVE, *Observations on the General Effects of Injury in Man with Special Reference to Wound Shock* (1951), a report of the authors' considerable experience in the investigation of shock following trauma, the definitive work of that time; R.M. HARDAWAY, *Syndromes of Disseminated Intravascular Coagulation: With Special Reference to Shock and Hemorrhage* (1966), including numerous references; J.H. BLOCH *et al.*, "Theories of the Production of Shock," *Brit. J. Anaesth.*, 38:234–250 (1966), a learned and unbiassed account of the many facets of the etiology and pathogenesis of shock; L.D. MacLEAN *et al.*, "Treatment of Shock in Man Based on Hemodynamic Diagnosis," *Surg. Gynec. Obstet.*, 120:1–16 (1965), a paper emphasizing the variety of physiological upsets found in shock, with an outline of a therapeutic regimen.

(W.G.Pr.)

Shooting

Shooting, as the subject of this article, is the sport—or art —of firing at targets of various kinds with rifles, shotguns, or handguns (pistols and revolvers) as an exercise in which accurate marksmanship is the goal.

Rifles may be divided into four subclasses: modern cartridge rifles (big bores and small bores), muzzle-loading rifles, benchrest rifles, and air rifles. (Benchrest rifles are heavy target guns that in competition are cradled, usually on a sandbag rest on a solid platform called a benchrest.)

Shotguns for competition shooting consist of two basic classes: guns for trap shooting, frequently with one barrel only; and shotguns of several gauges for skeet shooting, a fairly modern clay bird sport developed about 1924. (For the use of modern shotguns and rifles in taking big and small game, flying wildfowl, and upland birds, see HUNTING, SPORT.)

Handguns used in competitive target shooting include local police and armed forces service weapons and, more frequently, small-calibre pistols of various types; rifled air pistols now are also used. Air rifles and rifled air pistols are new in formal competition, having been introduced in 1966 at the world championship matches held in Wiesbaden, West Germany.

This article covers the history of target shooting, its development as an organized sport, and the principal competitive events that have evolved for the various firearms. For the history and development of firearms and for technical information, see GUNS, SPORTING AND TARGET. See also SMALL ARMS, MILITARY.

HISTORY

Shooting at a mark as a test of skill had its beginnings long before the advent of firearms (*c.* AD 1300). It seems reasonable to assume that the first archers, some 50,000 years ago, may have loosed their arrows at a practice target, perhaps a large stone, to prove the accuracy of their equipment and their ability. Certainly target archery with the longbow and the crossbow was a widespread sport in much of Europe, Asia, and the Far East as early as the 15th century. Because the origin of firearms is still uncertain, it is not known whether sport shooting existed coevally with the use of guns in warfare, but game shooting with firearms is recorded as early as the 16th century, by which time matchlock guns had been in use almost 100 years. The matchlock, fired by a match, or wick, controlled by a trigger, at last allowed the shooter to take and sustain aim at birds on the wing. Soon thereafter, toward the end of the 16th century, the rifled wheel lock, fired by a spark, appeared, and formal target shooting, particularly in the German areas of central Europe, became popular. Rifling—the spiral or helical grooves cut into a smoothbored barrel to impart spin to the bullet and thus improve its accuracy—existed at least by 1480 if not earlier, though instances of it were vastly outnumbered by barrels of smooth, uncut interiors, suitable for firing both solid ball and small shot.

Origins in archery

Target shooting with rifles. The history of target shooting with guns is largely the history of shooting at targets with rifles. Elaborately decorated Germanic wheel locks, profusely engraved and inlaid with gold and silver, appeared in the late 16th century. These had rifled bores and, sometimes, quite sophisticated peep or aperture rear sights that were fully adjustable. Since such guns were probably too valuable to have been hunting arms, it has been assumed they were intended for target shooting.

Early evidences. It is generally held that rifled shoulder arms of finest quality were made throughout Europe, especially in Germany, by 1525. The Turin armoury is known to have owned at least one rifled iron gun in 1476. A shooting match was held in Eichstädt in 1477 in which participants, probably matchlock shooters, competed at a range of 200 metres (220 yards). This is the earliest known recorded instance of shooting at a mark.

Shooting in Switzerland. Target rifle shooting certainly took place early in Switzerland. A painting from 1506 depicts target shooting with the crossbow; another shows a rifle shooting setup that is quite modern. Three enclosed and covered shooting booths are pictured, the contestants firing at targets in the background. Each target frame is flanked by a small hut, inside which a target marker is concealed during the actual shooting; after the shot the marker indicates to the marksman and the judges the value of the hit via a staff or pole. The judges and score-keepers are seen in the right foreground, seated at a table under a roof. Several wind flags are shown flying, and spectators are seen watching the shooting. This shooting took place at Zürich in 1504.

If shooting facilities and range appointments of such advanced degree were extant in 1504, then it can easily be argued that target shooting with firearms had existed in Switzerland in the 15th century, most likely as early as 1450–75. Shooting at a mark with the crossbow had been a popular sport in that country for at least 100 years earlier, so the sporting use of the rifle followed naturally.

Popularity in Europe and Great Britain. By the 16th century target shooting with rifled arms was a popular pastime in much of Europe, especially in the Germanic countries. In 1517 the cardinal Luigi d'Aragona wrote:
. . . every place and every village (in Germany) has its shooting park, where anyone interested in crossbow or rifle shooting—or in any other weapon—may go to practise.

Early targets

Many museums in Germany possess wooden targets dating from as far back as 1540. These were special targets, made to honour such occasions as marriages, and were painted in a large range of subject matter—portraits, scenics, and so on. Such targets were shot at by the assembled guests sometime during the ceremonies and then given to the host as a memento.

From that time on, target rifle shooting grew rapidly until, by the end of the 18th century, the sport was enjoyed over most, if not all, of Europe. In Spain the use of the rifle—and its problems—was thoroughly understood as early as 1644, when Alonso Martínez de Espinar wrote at length in his *Arte de Ballesteria y Monteria* (Madrid; 1644) on the details and peculiar aspects of rifling, including the rates of twist and number of spiral grooves. In Great Britain target rifle shooting was a popular and refined sport before 1800. In 1776 an English patent was granted to Patrick Ferguson (1744–80) on a breech-loading, flintlock, single-shot rifle, an arm that was to see some service in the American Revolution. Ferguson was a dedicated rifleman; in the 1750s, having been posted to the Caribbean as a young subaltern, his personal luggage on arrival included some dozen rifles.

The first book in English on target rifle shooting was published in London in 1808: *Scloppetaria: Or considerations on the Nature and Use of Rifled Barrell Guns . . . by a Corporal of Riflemen* (pseudonym of Capt. Henry Beaufoy). The contents are advanced and knowledgeable, while the illustrations show intricate and useful gun sights and other accoutrements of the serious rifleman. Some of the aperture sight designs are quite modern.

Sport rifle shooting in Russia. While hunting for sport had existed in Russia from the 16th century, shooting at a mark did not, apparently, make a start until the early 18th century.

A.A. Yuriev, in *Sporting Rifle Shooting* (Moscow; 1957), says that the first recorded instance of target shooting was in 1737, when the empress Anna ordered the establishment of a target-shooting range at the imperial court. The marks shot at were, in fact, live birds, not paper targets, but the object of these competitions was not the obtainment of game for the table. The marksmen were given valuable awards—gold- and diamond-studded cups—and the royal shooting contests soon became a tradition.

In 1806 the Society of Shooting Amateurs was formed in St. Petersburg (modern Leningrad), largely by army and guard officers. Their chief interest was in handgun shooting, which, at that time, would have been with flintlock pistols.

In that same city the first public shooting range, or club, was founded in 1834. Shooting could be done with rifles, smoothbores, or handguns on payment of a nominal fee. Many more such public shooting grounds had appeared in various Russian cities by the 1850s.

In the 1890s several other shooting societies were established: among these were the Russian Athletic Society, with a shooting range on club property; the St. Petersburg Club of Sports Amateurs; the St. Petersburg Society of Salon Shooting; and the Riga Shooting Society.

In 1897 the Imperial Society of Reglemented Hunting published rules for rifle-shooting competitions, particularly for military-style rifles. The next year in the society's first formal tournament, in Khabarovsk, some 130 competitors, using the Berdan Mark II rifles of 1870, shot at 466 feet (142 metres). The bull's-eye of the target was 28 inches (70 centimetres). A second contest the same year brought out over 200 participants.

In 1899 the Southern Russian Shooting Society, just formed, offered for the first time gold and silver award badges, in two categories, to successful sharpshooters.

The first All-Russian Championship-drawing shooting competition, from all over Russia, was held at Kiev in 1913. A like event took place at Riga in 1914.

After World War I—and in part, perhaps, because of its stimulus, as was the case in the U.S. and elsewhere in the West—organized target shooting grew rapidly, especially small-bore-rifle shooting. Following World War II the interest in sport shooting expanded greatly, more so than anywhere else, probably, except for the U.S.

The continuing successes of Soviet marksmen in the Olympic Games and World Championship events need little elaboration.

The American frontier. Rifle shooting in the North American colonies was a way of life on the frontier and in the farming settlements west of the Atlantic seaboard. The flintlock Kentucky rifle, so-called, appeared about 1750. Most were made then, and for many years thereafter, in the Lancaster area of Pennsylvania. Most of the gunmakers were of German extraction, and the rifle they had evolved differed greatly from its central European ancestor. Since shots at relatively long range were common, the new rifle was long in the barrel, up to 48 inches (122 centimetres) and longer, its diameter, or calibre, averaging about one-half inch (1.3 centimetres), compared to its forebear, the jäger (hunter) rifle, of Europe. These were often heavy and bulky looking, of calibres as large as .80 inch (20 millimetres), their barrels some 30 inches (76 centimetres) long.

The Kentucky rifle

Because the Kentucky rifle barrels were long, a larger charge of powder could be used, thereby imparting to the smaller round lead ball a much increased velocity, which in turn meant a flatter shooting trajectory and greater accuracy, resulting in effective use to 200 yards (180 metres) and more—then considered quite a long range.

Target shooting became common on the frontier and grew in popularity throughout the entire 19th century. Virtually every village and settlement was the scene for a shooting match on weekends and holidays. Some of the larger events attracted an entry list of a hundred or more marksmen. White paper was scarce along the frontier, and a common target was a piece of board blackened in the smoke of a fire or charred. On this a cross was slashed with a knife, and the ball that hit closest to the intersection—or upon it—was the winner. Shooting at a wooden figure of a bird atop a tall pole, after the fashion of crossbowmen in the Middle Ages, was also popular. Live turkey shooting—the bird tethered behind a box or rock, and only his head and neck visible—was a standard event.

By 1830 shooting clubs began to form, particularly in the more heavily populated East but also in many towns and cities in the Midwest. Target shooting from a bench or rest was an old activity before 1840. Between 1840 and 1848 the accuracy level of rifles improved as the result of two developments: the introduction of a magnifying telescopic sight, probably in the middle 1830s, and the invention in 1840 of a device called the false muzzle or patent muzzle, which was removable from the barrel after loading and permitted an elongated bullet to be seated into the barrel without deformation or distortion. The new bullet was ballistically superior to the round lead ball hitherto in general use, especially for the 40- and 80-rod (220- and 440-yard; 200- and 400-metre) shooting early bench marksmen preferred. The telescope sight, attached to the rifle and carrying crosshairs at its optical centre, was a far better means of sighting and holding the centre of the bull's-eye.

Sometime in the 1850s a benchrest shooting club was formed in Vermont. Called the National Rifle Club—though its annual matches were more regional than nationwide in scope—its members established a high reputation for their skill and their scores in shooting relatively heavy-barrelled muzzle-loading rifles from what were, essentially, shooting platforms or machine rests. In 1871 the National Rifle Association was founded (an organization with well over a million members in the early 1970s.) A weekly paper called *The Rifle* was inaugurated a few years later. Other journals devoted to both target events and hunting came into being.

Long-range shooting. Research on various rifles and projectiles, conducted by the English military from about 1800, focussed interest on long-range shooting at targets of over 600 yards (550 metres). Early in the 1850s volunteer rifle brigades devoted to this kind of shooting were formed. Many of their members were among the finest shots in the United Kingdom, and so popular was the activity and so intense had been the earlier studies of rifles and bullets that, in July 1860, on the occasion of the first prize meeting of the new British National Rifle Association, Queen Victoria had been persuaded to fire the opening shot. Shooting continued with increasing interest at Wimbledon Common (outside London) and at numerous other ranges. A 2,100-yard (1,900-metre) range existed in Scotland.

During the period 1853–77, improvements in firearms included the reduction of bore diameter (from the previously common calibre .58 to .45; *i.e.*, from $\frac{58}{100}$ inch to $\frac{45}{100}$) and a sharp alteration in the rate of twist of the rifling, from a standard twist (in the issue Enfields) of one turn in four feet (1.2 metres) to one turn in 20 inches (51 centimetres). At the same time an elongated bullet was introduced, at first of hexagonal cross section for use in a hexagonal barrel. The longer bullet proved ballistically superior to the bullet of the same weight but reduced length then in common use, requiring much less elevation of the sights at the longer ranges, and at the same time giving far greater accuracy on the 600- to 1,000-yard (550- to 900-metre) targets commonly used by the long-range shooters. W.E. Metford, a civil engineer with a lifelong interest in all that pertained to rifles, demonstrated, in long-range matches, that his design of bullet, a quite smooth cylinder, and his matching rifled bore were superior to the hexagonal bullet. In 1865 he produced his first "small bore" rifle, one of .45 calibre and with a depth of groove only .004 inch (.1 millimetre) deep. That rifling pattern is virtually identical to the rifling used today throughout the world.

During the 1870s and 1880s there was a gradual change-over from the caplock muzzle-loading rifle to the breechloader. Breechloaders had existed, in fact, from the earliest days of firearms, but none had been fully successful until the advent of the metallic cartridge case, which formed a perfect barrier to leaking burning gases, which had been an early problem with breech-loading rifles.

Nevertheless, the early breechloaders were not yet as accurate as the highly developed muzzle-loaders. In 1873 an Irish rifle team, competing at Wimbledon against the best teams from England and Scotland, won the matches by a substantial margin and then challenged U.S. marksmen to an 800-, 900- and 1,000-yard (700-, 800-, and 900-metre) match to be held at Long Island in September 1874. The U.S. team, however, though it had not shot at distances over 600 yards (550 metres), won the match

by three points, shooting breech-loading rifles against the Irish muzzle-loading caplocks.

Interest in long-range shooting grew greatly in the last third of the 19th century and continued until quite recently. All of the English-speaking countries participated in this essentially military-inspired form of target shooting. International competitions were held frequently, with teams from as far away as Australia and New Zealand making the journeys to England as late as the 1930s.

Schuetzen shooting. Of Germanic-Swiss ancestry, Schuetzen shooting was practiced throughout much of central Europe for centuries and in a practically unchanged manner. Although this form of target shooting had many adherents as early as the 1850s, it was not until the 1880s that Schuetzen shooting became a national sport. Schuetzen shooting was performed in the standing, or offhand, position. Targets were 100 or 200 yards (90 or 180 metres) from the firing points when the matches were held outdoors. In the winter months indoor galleries were used and the ranges were usually 25 yards (23 metres). While the use of any rifle type was generally permitted, the rifle of choice among serious marksmen was a single shot of fairly heavy weight (as much as 17 to 18 pounds [7,700 to 8,200 grams] or more). These carried highly refined sights, capable of minute adjustments, or a telescope. The butt plate was made with long prongs or extensions that went under and over the upper arm and palm rests, a device attached to the underside of the rifle, usually to the fore-end, and held in the shooter's left hand as a means of supporting and directing the muzzle-heavy barrel. Triggers were carefully tuned and adjusted. Superb shooting was done with the Schuetzen rifle in this period. The sport began to decline in Europe and the United States in the 1920s.

The .22 rifle and growth of the sport. Following the end of World War I, interest in target rifle shooting grew rapidly throughout the world. Shooting clubs and associations soon numbered in the thousands. There had been, of course, many such establishments prior to World War I, some of them dating to the mid-19th century, but by the 1930s numerous small villages and hamlets offered public or private facilities where rifles and other firearms could be shot.

Many of these new facilities came into being because of the rapid growth of small-bore—.22-calibre rimfire—shooting. The .22-calibre rimfire cartridge (a cartridge with a firing charge in the rim set off by a blow from the hammer) appeared in the 1870s, but serious match shooting with small-bore rifles had its major beginnings in England only after the Boer War. In that conflict, British military authorities learned that British military marksmanship was poor, especially in comparison with that of the Boers, many of whom were bush dwellers and countrymen long familiar with the hunting rifle. In the resulting push to upgrade military trainees' shooting abilities, it was soon found that the .22 rifle offered many advantages over the much larger and heavier service rifle: rifles, ammunition, ranges (200 yards instead of 1,000 yards), backstops, and other equipment were all less expensive. The shooter's initial equipment costs were thus much lower, and the major component—his rifle—lasted satisfactorily for many thousands of rounds of ammunition, unlike the big-bore rifle, which frequently lost its required accuracy after a thousand or so bullets had gone through its barrel. Interest in target shooting with the small-bore .22-calibre rifle quickly spread to civilian shooters and attracted and held many new marksmen.

Target shooting with handguns. The history of handguns roughly parallels that of long guns, but, perhaps because they are so much more difficult to aim and shoot accurately, they have never been as widely used in warfare or for sport in hunting or target shooting. In the days when men might be challenged to a duel with pistols, they perforce, if prudent, had to practice shooting for accuracy; and a large and romantic role has been ascribed to the six-shooter revolver in the taming of the American frontier in the West. But, aside from widespread use by the police forces in many nations, handguns usually have

Improvements in bores and bullets

Breechloaders

The six-shooter

been used as secondary hunting weapons—many sportsmen carry a .22 pistol for use in case of an emergency, and big-game hunters often carry a heavy gun, such as a .44 magnum, as a backup weapon—and for self-defense.

Pistol shooters, nevertheless, are among the most avid devotees of the sport of marksmanship. Evidence of the considerable interest in target shooting with handguns is the fact that pistol shooting was added to the official program of the National Rifle Association national championships in 1900, and three events in target pistol shooting were included in the first of the modern series of Olympic Games held in 1896.

Target shooting with shotguns. The original purpose of shooting at targets with shotguns was to improve the skills required for shooting game, usually upland game birds or ducks or other waterfowl, by simulating the various conditions that occur in actual field shooting. This required moving targets, and for many years live birds, usually pigeons, were used for this purpose. The pigeons were released from simple box traps and, the direction of the birds' flight being unpredictable, served as a challenge to the shooters' skill. In England about the end of the 18th century, pigeon shooting developed into a sport with rules and regulations governing the number of traps, their placement and distances from the shooter, the weight of shot allowed, and so on. In the 19th century pigeon shooting became popular in England and in Europe, and international competitions and sweepstakes were held annually at Monaco and elsewhere.

As pigeon shooting increased in popularity the supply of live birds was soon critical, and a substitute was found in glass balls that were flung out in various directions by spring-loaded devices. Late in the 19th century various types of saucer-shaped clay targets were tried, from which evolved the modern disk-type clay targets called "birds" or "clay pigeons," which are thrown or scaled through the air from mechanical devices called traps (after the box traps from which live pigeons are released).

Trapshooting. The sport was introduced into the United States about 1830 by Cincinnati, Ohio, sportsmen. The evolution of targets followed the same sequence of live birds, glass balls, and clay disks that had occurred in England. The first successful clay target and modern trap in the United States was developed in Cincinnati in 1880. Trapshooting for some years was also known, especially in England, as inanimate bird shooting, the Inanimate Bird Shooting Association being founded there in 1893.

Trapshooting is a long-range, clay-target sport. A single sunken trap house, from which the targets are propelled into the air at varying angles, is 16 yards (15 metres) in front of the shooter's station. The target is usually rising at the time of shooting and, on the average, when hit is about 35 yards (32 metres) from the marksman.

Skeet shooting. In skeet shooting the same targets and traps used in trapshooting are employed, but the pattern of shooting is different. Skeet shooting is a short-range, clay-target sport requiring two trap houses and eight shooting stations. It originated in the United States as a method of informal shooting practice for upland hunters who wanted a greater variety of shooting angles than was possible in trapshooting.

Between 1915 and 1920 definite rules governing the sport were instituted. At that time the shooting area was a complete circle of 25-yard (23-metre) radius, with the stations marked off like the face of a clock. A ground-level trap, located at the 12 o'clock position, threw the targets toward the 6 o'clock point. In 1923 the radius of the circle was reduced to 20 yards (18 metres), and, at about the same time, a second trap was placed at 6 o'clock that threw targets over 12 o'clock, and the 12 o'clock trap was elevated about ten feet (3 metres) above the ground. By shooting from stations in only half the circle and using both traps to throw targets, all of the shooting angles remained, and the range could be set up in a smaller area with no danger to spectators, who formerly had been required to move with the marksmen.

The term skeet, derived from an old Norse word for "shoot," was adopted in the U.S. after a 1925 nationwide contest to name the new sport.

Other events. Other less formal target shotgun events have been devised, usually to simulate the shooting of a particular kind of game. One of these is the so-called grouse walk or quail walk, in which the shooter walks along a woodland path and shoots at clay-bird targets that are released, either singly or in pairs, from traps hidden in the bushes alongside the path. Other events simulate the shooting of "springing teal," "running rabbits," or other small game. Shotguns are also used with paper targets in simulation of old-time live turkey shoots; in one form a small central mark on the target must be struck by a pellet, or, in case it is not hit, the pellet hole nearest the mark is the winner.

Regulation. The governing body for trapshooting in the United States is the Amateur Trapshooting Association, which came into being at the end of the 19th century as the Interstate Association of Trapshooters and conducted tournaments for both live-bird and clay-target shooting. In 1900 the name of the organization was changed to the American Trapshooting Association. It existed as an organization controlled by firearms manufacturers until 1923, when it was decided to make the sport completely independent and the name was changed to its present form, in part because of the increasing numbers of Canadian members.

The National Skeet Shooting Association was organized in 1925, and the first national championships, which were held at a different place each year, were in 1927.

In Great Britain the governing body is the Clay Pigeon Shooting Association of London. With the introduction of the standard clay targets at the close of the 19th century, the name of the Inanimate Bird Shooting Association was changed to the Clay Bird Shooting Association in 1903, and the association became known by its present name in 1928. The association annually awards the Coronation Cup to the best all-round performer in skeet.

Clay-pigeon shooting, the common term for all inanimate-target shotgun shooting in Europe, is popular in most continental nations, particularly the U.S.S.R., Romania, Italy, Belgium, France, Greece, Finland, and Sweden. Live-pigeon shooting is still popular in Italy, France, and Spain.

International organization and competition. Hundreds of local clubs and dozens of state and regional associations and national federations are devoted to one or more aspects of sport shooting. More than 100 federations from 90 countries belong to the International Shooting Union (ISU), with headquarters at Wiesbaden, West Germany. The ISU was founded in 1907 and reorganized after World War I, in 1919. It conducts the world championships and regulates shooting competition in the Olympic Games.

World championship competitions are with the small-bore rifle, free rifle, centre-fire pistol, free pistol, rapid-fire pistol (.22-calibre), air rifle, air pistol, and shotgun. Army rifle matches are fired with a military weapon designated by the International Shooting Union. The running-deer and running-boar matches are fired with relatively light rifles, calibre .22 rimfire or .222 centre-fire, and telescope sights are permitted.

The small-bore rifle competition consists of firing from three positions (standing, prone, kneeling) at a range of 50 metres. Three-position matches are held at 300 metres in the free-rifle (unrestricted as to rifle design and accessories) and army-rifle competitions.

Free-pistol matches are conducted at 50 metres, while centre-fire and rapid-fire competition is at 25 metres.

Running-deer and running-boar competition is conducted at 100 metres, with the shooters firing at rapidly moving silhouette targets. Clay-pigeon (trapshooting) and skeet matches are also conducted.

Except as noted, only metallic sights are permitted in ISU competitions.

Shooting has been a recognized Olympic sport since the first modern Olympic Games in 1896. In addition to the more regular events of shooting competition, however, Olympic shooters have also taken part in such events as live-pigeon shooting and competition with duelling pistols. One of the five events in the modern, or military,

Rules for skeet shooting

pentathlon, included in the Olympic Games since 1912, is shooting a pistol or revolver at a 25-metre standing silhouette target. In the winter Olympic Games the biathlon is a combination of cross-country skiing and rifle shooting.

Growth of interest and participation. Interest in competition shooting under International Shooting Union rules and auspices—and participation therein—has grown tremendously over the past 20 years or so. The first post-World War II World Shooting Championship matches were held at Stockholm in 1947. Sixteen different events were staged, with marksmen from 11 countries entered in the various contests. At that time this was considered an excellent turnout and the shoot a highly successful affair.

In the intervening years these world matches (now held every four years) became successively more popular, both in number of events scheduled and in entries, until in 1966 the World Shooting Championships took place at Wiesbaden, in West Germany. This 39th running of the matches saw 52 nations participating in 37 shooting contests for rifle, shotgun, handgun, and air-arm awards. Competitors numbered 1,390, a new record.

In October of 1970 the 40th World Shooting Championship matches were held at Phoenix, Arizona, the various events spanning 13 days. This was the first time these matches had been held in the United States since 1923. The latter contest was something of a fiasco—only two countries took part, the U.S. and Canada, shooting for seven events.

The number of competitors at Phoenix fell to 704, about half the number appearing at Wiesbaden, but an even 50 nations were represented. The United States is a long way from Europe, where the majority of those who enter the ISU matches live and where most of the World Shooting Championships have been held.

Twenty of the 50 countries won at least one gold (first place), silver (second), or bronze (third) medal at Phoenix; but, as has been the case in recent years, the U.S.S.R. and the United States garnered most of the awards. Several world records were toppled at Phoenix, both in individual and team events, and with rifled firearms and smoothbore guns—in the running-boar matches by a Swedish shooter; in the air rifle by a German; in the rapid-fire pistol, individual, by an Italian; in rapid-fire pistol, team, by the Czech team; and in the ladies' air pistol, team (see below).

Women competitors and events. Women may compete as members of men's teams (team scores are derived from the individual's shooting performance), but there were at Phoenix six separate events scheduled for women, including rifle, handgun, and shotgun matches. The most outstanding shooting at Phoenix, and the most surprising, was the winning of a gold medal by Capt. Margaret Murdock (U.S. Army) in the free-rifle matches, a three-position event (40 shots each, while standing, kneeling, and prone) at 300 metres (330 yards). The rifles used in this event are without restrictions except as to weight (not to exceed eight kilograms [18 pounds]) and calibre (not over eight millimetres), and only metallic sights may be used, without optics of any kind. The free rifle, therefore, may be quite a heavy arm, and it usually weighs 13–15 pounds (six–eight kilograms).

Captain Murdock, the only woman among 46 contestants in the match, won her gold medal in the standing position, the first and only woman ever to do so. The standing position is the most difficult of the three, yet Mrs. Murdock's score was only one point under the previous world record. Captain Murdock also won the Ladies Standard Rifle Match, making her the only double gold medallist among the American contingent.

The Soviet women's team took their first gold medal at Phoenix in winning the ladies' air pistol matches (four stages) and established a new world record at the same time.

International-U.S. differences. Participation by American shooters in the World Shooting Championship matches and in the similar Olympic matches has increased more than has ISU-controlled shooting worldwide.

This has come about in spite of two serious problems. One problem has been that, while the considerable costs of hosting a World Shooting Championship program have been underwritten in whole or great part by the host nation virtually without exception in all other countries, in the United States the costs have been met by private and local groups and voluntary contributions, without the aid of government funds.

The second reason why more American shooters, until recent years, have not participated in ISU and Olympic matches lies in the distinctly different modes of shooting in the United States, compared with competition marksmanship under ISU regulations. American shooters, of all classes and types, have long used targets and ranges based on the English systems of measurement—ranges set out in feet and yards, targets designed with, for example, a two-inch ten-ring at 100 yards, and so on. Much of the world's shooting, however, is done under the metric system, and certainly all ISU competitions are so conducted. American shooters generally, and for a variety of reasons, have been reluctant to adopt the metric system for U.S.-held events; this has also meant a lack of facilities available for metric-system practice. In addition to the cost involved in converting scores of targets and thousands of shooting ranges to the metric system, there are the ISU matches themselves, many of them markedly different from U.S.-style events, many others having no full counterpart in American match programs. Another hurdle facing American marksmen—and perhaps the hardest one—has been and is the increasingly more difficult task of scoring well on ISU targets. For example, in the ISU free-pistol match, fired at 50 metres (55 yards) offhand with a .22 rimfire (5.6-millimetre) single-shot handgun (the free pistol is one almost without restrictions as to weight, barrel length, stocks, and trigger pull; the only requirements are that it shall not have optical sights and that the grip or stock may not offer support to the shooter's arm), the target has a ten-ring measuring 1.97 inches (five centimetres); the 50-yard (45-metre) U.S. targets' ten-rings are 3.39 inches (8.61 centimetres) across, and they are five yards closer to the shooter. American marksmen have been shooting "possibles" for many years, which is to say the full score, or 100 out of a possible 100. They are loath to give their own targets up, for in ISU matches the possibles are noted for their rarity.

The American clay-bird shooter, long used to breaking 100 and 200 birds without a miss—with much longer "straights" not unusual—in the stiffest competition, finds such ISU events much more difficult. (For further details on this kind of shooting, see below *Shotgun-shooting events.*)

The foregoing account of the differences between ISU and American shooting is, necessarily, simplified. For a detailed analysis and a full explanation of the various ISU matches, plus a comparison of shooting under U.S. rules, see the latest issue of the *NRA Illustrated International Shooting Handbook,* published by the National Rifle Association.

THE SPORT OF SHOOTING

Rifle-shooting events. Marksmanship with rifled arms is commonly practiced with paper targets (fixed or movable) at various distances, from ten metres (11 yards) for air pistols and rifles to 1,000 yards (900 metres) and more with centre-fire rifles. Handgun ranges may be anything from a few yards (combat shooting, quick-draw techniques) to 50 metres (international competition).

Formal match shooting with rifles may call for one or more of several positions to be assumed by the shooter. In the least steady, the standing or offhand stance, the rifleman cradles the butt of the stock into his shoulder, grasping the grip or small of the stock (wrist) with his right hand (if he is right-handed), his forefinger tip pad (usually) touching the trigger. His left hand grasps the fore-end of the rifle, directing his aim at the target. In the case of heavily-recoiling centre-fire rifles, the right hand is also used to press the butt firmly against the hollow of the shoulder in order to better absorb the rifle's thrust on

Reluctance to adopt metric system

Standing, kneeling, sitting, and prone positions

firing. The left elbow is classically held directly under the rifle, for optimum support and steadiness. The offhand rifleman usually stands at or near 90° to the target, the rifle positioned across his chest, but this classic stance is not mandatory. The shooter's aiming eye is held close to the peep sight (or aperture, a movable disk in the rear sight having a hole in its centre), sighting through this—not at it—to a front sight usually surrounded by a hood to exclude light; this may be a square post or another but larger aperture that encircles the target bull's-eye.

The kneeling position, somewhat steadier than standing, finds the rifleman with his right knee on the ground (or shooting mat). He may sit on his right foot, side or heel, if he wishes to and the rules permit. His left foot is flat on the ground, his left knee supporting his left forearm or, less steadily, his left elbow. His knee and left arm are directly under the rifle for support. The other aspects of hold and aiming are the same as for standing and sitting.

In the sitting position the shooter faces some 45° to the right of the target, his knees raised and spread, his heels dug into the ground (if permitted by the rules and if feasible). The outside of his upper arms lies against the inside of his knees, his hands supporting and aiming the rifle as described earlier.

The orthodox prone position has the rifleman face down, his body angled about 45° to the target. His elbows, forming two legs of a tripod, in effect, support the rifle. His left elbow is placed under the rifle for support. His legs are spread apart, flat to the ground. The rifle is aimed and held as before, except that the buttplate impinges to a degree on the shooter's collarbone.

Much freedom of choice is exercised by the shooter in assuming the prone (and other) positions. Often he lies at other than the conventional 45°, and his legs may be in almost any position—crossed, one knee partially raised, and so on. Individual comfort and a position he has found best for his shooting are the criteria.

In all rifle-shooting positions a sling (usually a strap of leather) is frequently used to further steady the position. The forward sling end is attached to the rifle somewhere toward the front, the rear portion going around the shooter's upper arm or attaching to a leather cuff encircling the left arm above the biceps muscles.

Trigger control

Maintaining sight alignment and trigger control are vitally important in rifle (and handgun) target shooting. While the amount of applied weight against the trigger (pull) to effect its release varies with the style and class of the arm being used, successful shooters train themselves to complete the trigger letoff with minimum disturbance of the sight picture. The fleshy pad of the forefinger first joint is usually placed on the trigger, the pressure gradually increased as sight alignment is observed, the shooter holding a part breath during the process.

Under current ISU rules, air rifle shooting is done only in the regular standing position, with the target ten metres away. The only calibre allowed is 4.5 millimetres (.177 inch); the pellet is of soft lead. Spring-air guns or carbon-dioxide-powered guns may be used. Very light triggers are in common use, so maximum trigger control is a prime requirement. Shooting techniques and the like are the same as with the cartridge rifle.

Handgun-shooting events. Target shooting with handguns has been marked by a gradual decline in popularity of revolvers in favour of autoloading pistols, both rimfire and centre-fire. Most modern revolvers are of double-action design; the trigger may be pulled to effect discharge of the gun, but this entails bringing the hammer from rest to full cock and then forward to fire. This technique, which may call for as much as ten pounds (4.5 kilograms) of effort or more, tends to affect steady aim. As a result, target shooting with revolvers is almost invariably done in single-action form; the hammer is brought to full cock manually, by the thumb in one-hand (extended arm) shooting, the thumb repositioned on the gun, and the much lighter and crisper trigger pulled off. Additional time is needed to thumb-cock the hammer, time the shooter needs in the timed-fire and rapid-fire stages common to formal handgun matches.

With the autoloading pistol the shooter can concentrate on sight alignment and trigger control, or watching the clock or his practiced rhythm in the fast fire courses. The autoloader does as its name implies—chambers a fresh cartridge after a shot is fired, rapidly and without attention.

Holding and aiming the hand gun

In conventional paper-target shooting, the handgunner may adopt any standing position that is comfortable. Generally, the right-handed shooter stands at 20° to 90° away from the target, facing left, his right arm extended and about level (when ready to fire). His elbow is "locked," particularly when firing centre-fire guns. This carries the recoil straight back and upward, allowing fast and precise return to the shooting position for the next shot. The manner of grasping the handgun may vary with the individual, but maintaining the chosen grip undisturbed is important. Even minor alterations in holding usually impair results at the target. Holding the sights of a handgun in correct alignment is far more important than it is with rifles because of the quite short sight radius; *i.e.*, distance between rear and front sights. Even a slight error in this alignment is magnified many times at the target some ten to 50 yards (nine to 45 metres) away. In slow-fire handgun shooting the marksman generally holds a half breath, too, but that is not so readily done in timed and rapid fire.

For reasons of safety and better control of shooters and their arms, formal handgun competition (and rifle matches as well) is controlled by one or more assigned officials. Shooting commences on signal, the shooters in position, their guns held to point downwards and toward the targets. Another command or signal ends the firing.

Open sights are standard in handgun competition. The usual rear sight carries a square or rectangular notch in a vertical-standing metal leaf, a common width being .125 inch (.3 centimetre). A similar flat-topped post is used for the front sight, so dimensioned that a small amount of light may be seen at either side when the post is held central and level with the rear sight opening.

Such "iron," or metallic, open sights on target handguns are invariably capable of being adjusted in precise increments of movement both laterally (commonly called "windage") and vertically. Such movement is frequently by clicks, audible and visual, so that the shooter may make such adjustments in the often-dark confines of a shooting booth. These precise sight movements are a necessity if a given brand or type of ammunition is to print or cut the target at its centre. The individual shooter's particular method of aiming and sighting his handgun adds to the need for controlled sight adjustment. Low-cost handguns usually have fixed (nonadjustable) sights, generally integral with the gun frame or barrel.

Shotgun-shooting events. Formal clay-bird shooting takes place under well-established rules. These regulations differ in Europe and elsewhere from those in force in the U.S. In both straight trapshooting and skeet, international rules require a clay bird to be a bit harder than U.S. targets (thus more difficult to break), to fly at greater velocity from the throwing machines (traps), and thus fly farther. In international shooting the contestant's gun must be held at his side, the butt visible below his bent arm. Under U.S. rules the gun may be fully mounted at the shoulder, ready to fire when the target appears on call from the shooter. International rules also permit an unknown (up to three seconds) delay before the called bird is thrown from the trap house. In the U.S. the clay bird is propelled immediately following the shooter's call or other vocal signal to the referee or trap house attendant.

International and U.S. rules

Formal trapshooting and skeet shooting in the U.S. are team events, teams ordinarily consisting of five shooters (women as well as men, though the latter predominate greatly). Scoring, however, is on an individual basis. In trapshooting each contestant takes his turn at shooting from one of five stations (arranged in a shallow semicircle), these shooting positions being 16 yards (15 metres) from the trap house on single clay birds (see Figure 1) unless the match is a "handicap" type. Shooters are handicapped on the basis of their ability, and high-

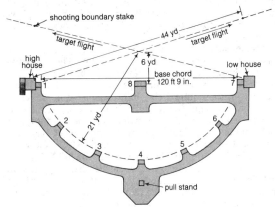

trap house

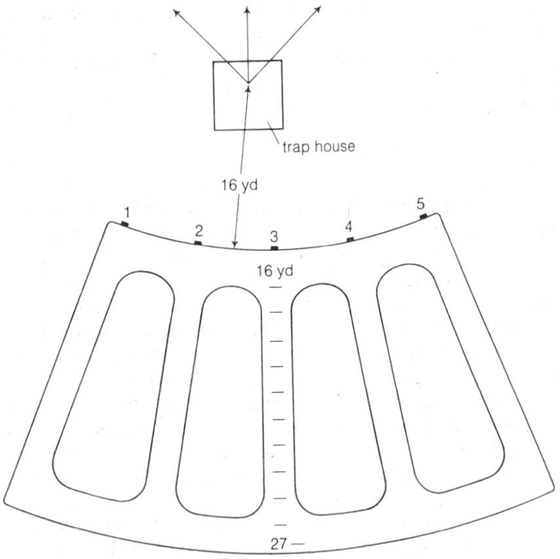

16 yd

1   2   3   4   5

16 yd

27 —

Figure 1: Layout of a trapshooting field.

scoring shooters may have to fire from 18 to 27 yards (16 to 25 metres) away from the trap house. The trap house opening lies at about ground level; the birds are thrown at various lateral angles (up to 22° from either side of the house) away from the shooter—angles unknown beforehand to the contestant.

The usual singles event at trap consists of 100 shots per man, but in "doubles," where two clays are thrown at the same time, 50 to 100 shots are usually fired in one event.

Skeet shooting is similar to trapshooting in that shotguns and the same type of clay target are used and that a round consists of 25 shotshells (the standard box or carton) to be fired by each shooter. The skeet layout (see Figure 2) has eight stations, seven of them arranged in a half-circle; station 8 lies in the centre, between the two trap houses. Station 1 is sited at the "high house," station 7 at the "low house," stations 2 through 6 located a uniform distance apart on the rest of the quadrant. Both houses in skeet throw targets along fixed lines of flight, thereby differing from trapshooting. These flight paths cross at a point equidistant from each house but six feet (two meters) from the central station.

shooting boundary stake

44 yd

target flight   target flight

high house   6 yd   low house

base chord
120 ft 9 in.

1   8   7

21 yd

2   6

3   5

4

□— pull stand

Figure 2: Layout of a skeet shooting field.

A round of skeet consists of 16 single shots; *i.e.*, eight targets from each house, plus four pair of doubles from stations 1, 2, 6, and 7. If all 24 clay birds are broken (or "dead"), the 25th shot is an "optional" and may be fired at any station. If a bird is missed at any previous station, however, that shot is repeated at that time.

Guns used in skeet are generally open bored; *i.e.*, they throw shot patterns in a larger circle at given ranges than the trap gun does. The skeet target, correctly broken, is hit at closer ranges than is the case with straight trap. Double-barrelled guns are generally thought to be ade-

quate when half of the shot charge hits inside a 30-inch (76-centimetre) circle at 40 yards (37 metres) from one barrel and 55 to 60 percent from the other. Because of the fast gun swinging required in skeet, barrels tend to be short—26 to 28 inches (66 to 71 centimetres)—but any length may be used.

Four gun classes are recognized for skeet shooting. All-bore allows any gauge up to and including 12. Twenty-gauge requires a gun of that gauge or smaller. (The bore or gauge number was originally the number of lead balls, each the diameter of the bore, that would weigh one pound.) Small bore calls for a 28-gauge or .410 (the .410 is calibre .41), while subsmall bore may be shot only with the .410. Shot loads and sizes in these four gauges are restricted, respectively, to: 1⅛-oz., ⅞-oz., ¾-oz., and½-oz. (32, 25, 21, and 14 g), all shot pellets to be size 9 or larger. All shotgun types are used at skeet except single shots. Autoloading and pump guns (also called slide—or trombone action) are quite popular in the U.S. (and abroad to a somewhat lesser extent), but double-barrelled guns, both side-by-side and over-under forms, are regaining some of their lost popularity. Double guns had all but disappeared from the U.S. market because of high manufacturing cost, until the 1960s saw an influx of European-made models at moderate prices that sold well. Many of these are offered as "skeet specials," which is to say with single trigger, selective automatic ejectors (these propel the fired empty cases forcibly from the chambers and to some distance), with fore-ends "beavertail" style—that is, broad fore-end stocks that let the hand grasp them for better directional control. Both skeet and trap butt-stocks are generally of straighter profile and a bit longer than the stocks found on field (hunting) guns. This results in the shot charge being thrown higher at normal target distances. Shotguns ordinarily have only a front sight (on clay target guns there may be a middle sight, placed about halfway along the barrel) acting as a rear sight.

Shot patterns and gun classes

BIBLIOGRAPHY

General: Of the many books extant on firearms, relatively few are on shooting as such. JACK O'CONNOR *et al.*, *The Complete Book of Shooting* (1966); LARRY KOLLER, *How to Shoot* (1964), and C.E. CHAPEL, *The Art of Shooting* (1960), cover field and target use of shotguns, rifles, and handguns comprehensively and well.

Rifle shooting: JAROSLAV LUGS, *A History of Shooting* (1968), is what the title implies, with emphasis on marksmanship and exhibition shooting with rifle and handgun. N.H. ROBERTS and K.L. WATERS, *The Breech-Loading Single-Shot Match Rifle* (1967), is an outstanding work on Schuetzen (offhand) and rest shooting in the United States from about 1840 to the 1920s. The NATIONAL RIFLE ASSOCIATION of America publishes books and brochures on target shooting of all types, as does its counterpart, the British NRA. Two titles available from the NRA of America that will be most helpful are the *NRA Shooting Handbook* (1961) and the *NRA International Shooting Handbook* (1960). Some excellent books on rifle shooting, out of print but not yet replaced by studies of equal worth, are T.F. FREMANTLE, *The Book of the Rifle* (1900); and H. OMMUNDSEN and E.H. ROBINSON, *Rifles and Ammunition* (1914). The former is a superb history of British rifles and rifle shooting from the 18th century; the latter a well-illustrated, comprehensive volume on British and continental military rifle shooting. E.C. CROSSMAN, *Small Bore Rifle Shooting* (1927), and *Military and Sporting Rifle Shooting* (1932), both first-rate texts despite their age, are not in print.

Handgun shooting: Target handgunning in its many phases is well treated in P.C. FREEMAN, *Modern Pistol Shooting* (1968); PAUL B. WESTON, *The Handbook of Handgunning* (1968); and C. GAYLORD, *Handgunner's Guide* (1960).

Shotgun shooting: JACK O'CONNOR, *The Shotgun Book* (1965), is an excellent work, with material as well on gun selection, choice of gauges and chokes, and cartridges. A first-class text on target (clay-bird) shooting, from the British viewpoint is PERCY STANBURY and G.L. CARLISLE, *Clay Pigeon Marksmanship* (1964). GOUGH THOMAS, *Gough Thomas's Gun Book* (1969); and MICHAEL BRANDER, *The Game Shot's Vade Mecum* (1965), furnish a wealth of information for the British shotgunner, with good coverage on marksmanship and its attainment. B. HARTMAN, *Hartman on Skeet* (1967); and D. LEE BRAUN, *Trapshooting with D. Lee Braun* (1969), are excellent choices for the clay-bird-shooting aspirant. F.E. SELL,

Sure-Hit Shotgun Ways (1967), devotes over a third of its pages to a fast method of learning to shoot the smoothbore gun.

(J.T.A.)

Shorthand

Shorthand is a method of writing rapidly by substituting characters, abbreviations, or symbols for letters, words, or phrases. Other names for shorthand are stenography (close, little, or narrow writing), tachygraphy (swift writing), and brachygraphy (short writing). Because shorthand can be written rapidly, the shorthand writer is able to record the proceedings of legislative bodies, the testimony of law courts, or dictation in business correspondence. In addition, shorthand has been used through the centuries as a cultural tool; for example, George Bernard Shaw wrote his plays in shorthand, and Samuel Pepys recorded his diary in shorthand. Furthermore, Cicero's orations, Martin Luther's sermons, and Shakespeare's plays were all preserved by means of shorthand. Today, in every industrial nation of the world, shorthand is used to conduct operations in business, industry, and the professions.

Background and development. Through the centuries shorthand has been written in systems based on orthography (normal spelling), on phonetics (the sounds of words), and on arbitrary symbols, such as a small circle within a larger circle to represent the phrase, "around the world." Most historians date the beginnings of shorthand with the Greek historian Xenophon, who used an ancient Greek system to write the memoirs of Socrates. It was in the Roman Empire, however, that shorthand first became generally used. Marcus Tullius Tiro, a learned freedman who was a member of Cicero's household, invented the *notae Tironianae* ("Tironian notes"), the first Latin shorthand system. Devised in 63 BC, it lasted over a thousand years. Tiro also compiled a shorthand dictionary. Among the early accomplished shorthand writers were the Emperor Titus, Julius Caesar, and a number of bishops. With the beginning of the Medieval Age in Europe, however, shorthand became associated with witchcraft and magic, and disappeared.

The "Tironian notes"

While he was archbishop of Canterbury, Thomas Becket (1118?–70) encouraged research into Tiro's shorthand. By the 15th century, with the discovery in a Benedictine monastery of a lexicon of Ciceronian notes and a Psalter written in Tironian shorthand, a renewed interest in the practice was aroused. Somewhat influenced by Tiro's system, Timothy Bright designed an English system in 1588 that consisted of straight lines, circles, and half circles. (Tiro's method was cursive, based on longhand script.) Bright's system was called *Characterie: an Arte of Shorte, Swifte, and Secrete Writing by Character.*

The 17th century produced four important inventors of shorthand systems: John Willis, who is considered to be the father of modern shorthand; Thomas Shelton, whose system was used by Samuel Pepys to write his famous diary; Jeremiah Rich, who popularized the art by publishing not only his system but also the Psalms and the New Testament in his method of shorthand; and William Mason, whose method was used to record sermons and to translate the Bible in the years following the Reformation. Mason's system was later adapted and became the official system of the British Parliament.

Several other systems were invented in the next decades, but most of them were short-lived. One of the most successful was that of the British stenographer Samuel Taylor, who invented a system in 1786 that was based on that of one of his predecessors. Taylor's method was adapted into French, Spanish, Portuguese, Italian, Swedish, German, Dutch, Hungarian, and other languages.

The Industrial Revolution brought a demand for stenographers in business. Because the geometric systems then in use required a high standard of education and long training in the system, a need existed for a method that would be easier to learn. The German Franz Xaver Gabelsberger (1789–1849) turned away from geometric methods and developed a simple cursive system. Gabelsberger has been considered by many to have been one of

Figure 1: Alphabet of Gabelsberger shorthand, 1834.
From Hans Glatte, *Shorthand Systems of the World*

the world's leaders in the field of shorthand. His system, which he called "Speech-sign art," was based on Latin longhand characters and had a neatness and beauty of outline that is unsurpassed. It enjoyed a spontaneous success and spread to Switzerland, Austria, Scandinavia, Finland, and Russia. Its simplicity made it an easy matter to translate it into other languages, and in 1928 it became the Italian national system.

Modern symbol systems. Sir Isaac Pitman (1813–97), an educator who advocated spelling reform, was knighted by Queen Victoria for his contributions to shorthand. Pitman had learned Taylor's method of shorthand but saw its weakness and designed his own system to incorporate writing by sound, the same principle he advocated in phonetic longhand spelling. He published his system in 1837, calling it *Stenographic Sound-Hand*. It consisted of 25 single consonants, 24 double consonants, and 16 vowel sounds. Similar, related sounds were represented by similar signs, shading was used to eliminate strokes, the shortest signs were used to represent the shortest sounds, and single strokes were used to represent single consonants. At first, the principle of positioning to express omitted vowels—*i.e.*, writing the word above, on, or below the line of writing—was reserved until later lessons, after the theory had been presented. Later, positioning was introduced with the first lesson.

Pitman's system

In 1852, Isaac Pitman's brother, Benn Pitman, brought the system to America, where, with several slight modifications, it became the method most extensively used in the United States and Canada. An investigation in 1889 stated that 97 percent of the shorthand writers in America used the Isaac Pitman system or one of its modifications. The percentage is much lower today, but Pitman shorthand is still the major system in New York City, Philadelphia, Chicago, and all of Canada. In addition, Pitman shorthand has been adapted to Afrikaans, Arabic, Armenian, Dutch, French, Gaelic, German, Hebrew, Hindi, Italian, Japanese, Persian, Spanish, and other languages.

The Irish-born John Robert Gregg (1867–1948) taught himself an adaptation of Taylor's shorthand at the age of ten. Fascinated by shorthand, he then studied Pitman by himself but disliked its angles, shading, and positioning. Later, while in his early teens, he read a history of shorthand by Thomas Anderson, a member of the Shorthand Society of London. In his book, Anderson listed the essentials of a good shorthand system, stating that no method then in use possessed them. These essentials, which made a lasting impression on Gregg, included the following: independent characters for the vowels and consonants, all characters written with the same thickness, all characters written on a single line of writing, and few and consistent abbreviation principles.

Gregg was 18 when he invented his own system and 21 when he published it in pamphlet form, *Light-Line Phonography* (1888). The Gregg system was predominantly a curve-motion shorthand with circles, hooks, and loops. Based on the ellipse or oval and on the slope of longhand,

Gregg's light-line phonography

its motion was curvilinear. Obtuse angles were eliminated by natural blending of lines, vowels were joined, shading was eliminated, and writing was lineal, or in one position.

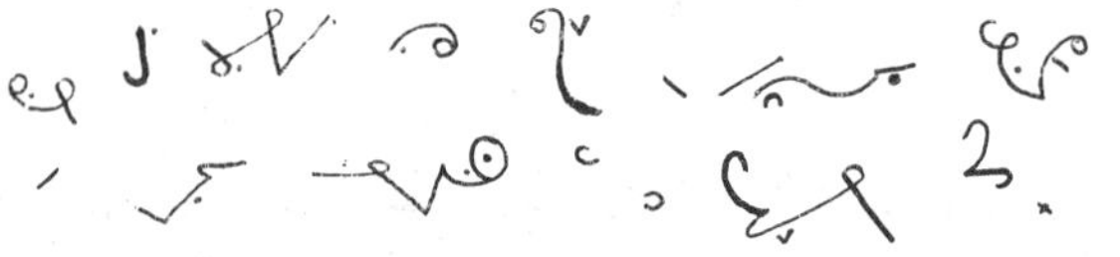

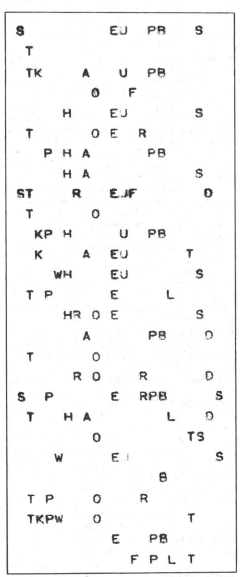

PITMAN

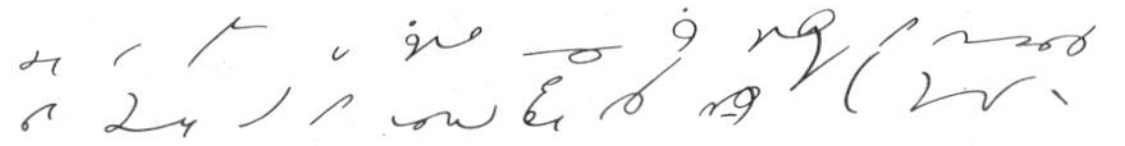

GREGG

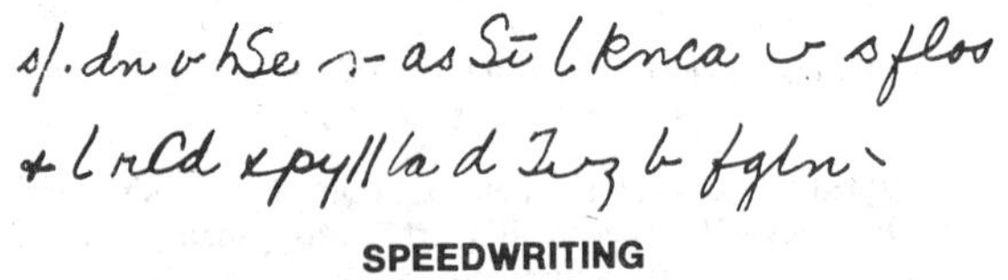

SPEEDWRITING

Figure 2: Modern systems of shorthand recording the same sentence: "Since the dawn of history man has strived to communicate with his fellows and to record experiences that would otherwise be forgotten."

In 1893 Gregg brought his system to America, and Light-Line Phonography became Gregg Shorthand. The inventor found that, except for the eastern coastal cities, shorthand was virtually unknown. Also, at that time American secondary education had embarked upon a new idea, that of teaching shorthand in the high schools. Gregg travelled through the Midwest, the West, and the South, selling his system and demonstrating his teaching methods with great success. The Gregg system is now taught in over 90 percent of the schools teaching shorthand in the United States. It has also spread to Canada and to the British Isles. Gregg shorthand is published in English, French, Spanish, and Portuguese by the parent company. In addition, other companies publish Gregg shorthand in Hebrew, Russian, Italian, Tagalog, Japanese, Thai, Chinese, Erse (Scottish Gaelic), Esperanto, Sinhalese, and Polish.

A German system of importance is the Stolze-Schrey method. Wilhelm Stolze invented his system at about the same time as Gabelsberger and along similar lines. In 1885, Ferdinand Schrey, a Berlin merchant, attempted to simplify the Gabelsberger system. Sometime later the Stolze and Schrey methods were merged and became the leading system in Germany and Switzerland. Stolze-Schrey shorthand was also adapted to other languages, including Danish, Dutch, English, French, Italian, Norwegian, Polish, Russian, and Spanish.

Modern abbreviated longhand systems. The system of Speedwriting shorthand was created around 1924 by Emma Dearborn, an instructor at Columbia University. Her method was designed to be taken down on the typewriter; but in 1942 it was changed to be written by hand with pen or pencil. Speedwriting shorthand uses the letters of the alphabet and the known punctuation marks to represent sounds. For example, the sound of "ch" is written with a capital C; the word "each" is thus written "eC." Over 20,000 words in the Speedwriting dictation can be written with a total of 60 rules and a list of approximately 100 brief forms and standard abbreviations. Speedwriting shorthand is taught in seven languages—English, Spanish, Italian, Portuguese, German, Flemish, and Afrikaans—in 28 countries. There are an estimated 600 licensed schools throughout the world that are teaching this system.

Forkner Alphabet shorthand was first published in 1952 in the U.S. The author, Hamden Forkner, spent ten years in research before publishing the first edition of the new system, which uses a combination of conventional letters and a few symbols for the hard-to-write letters and sounds. For example, H is expressed by a short dash above the line. This same short dash through the letter C gives the "ch" sound, through the longhand S it gives

"sh," and across the T it designates "th." Abbreviations are used for a number of common words. Forkner Alphabet shorthand is now taught in high schools and business colleges in the U.S.

Another U.S. method, Hy-Speed Longhand, was first published under that title in 1932. Based on Andrew J. Graham's *Brief Longhand,* published in 1857, its principles include the omission of silent letters and most vowels, the substitution of letters, numbers, or signs, and the combination of certain letters.

Stenoscript ABC Shorthand is a phonetic system using only longhand and common punctuation marks. It originated in London in 1607 and was revised by Manuel Claude Avancena, who published a modern edition in 1950. Stenoscript has 24 brief forms that must be memorized; e.g., *ak* stands for acknowledge, *ac* for accompany, *bz* for business, and *gvt* for government.

Stenospeed originated in 1950 in the U.S.; the first publication was called Stenospeed High Speed Longhand, but in 1951 the system was revised under the name of Stenospeed ABC Shorthand. It is used by many schools in 20 states of the U.S. as a standard text. Stenospeed has also been programmed for use with teaching machines.

Other alphabetic or partially alphabetic systems have also been devised since the early 1950s.

Machine shorthand. A method of recording speech by using machines became commercially feasible around 1906, when the Stenotype machine was invented by Ward Stone Ireland, a U.S. stenographer and court reporter.

Figure 3: Stenotype shorthand recording the same sentence as in Figure 2.

Stenograph
and
Stenotype
machines

At present, the Stenograph and Stenotype machines are used in offices to some extent, but they are principally employed for conference and court reporting. Both machines have keyboards of 22 keys; they are small, light, and silent. Because the operator uses all fingers and both thumbs, any number of keys can be struck simultaneously. The machines print roman letters on a strip of paper that folds automatically into the back of the machine. The operator controls the keys by touch and is thus able to watch the speaker.

To operate the machine, the fingers of the left hand control the keys that print consonants occurring before vowels. These keys print on the left side of the tape. The thumbs control the vowels, which are printed in the centre of the tape, and the fingers of the right hand control the consonants that follow the vowels, which are printed on the right side of the tape. There are not separate keys for each letter of the English alphabet, thus, those letters for which there are no keys are represented by combinations of other letters. Abbreviations are used for some of the most frequent words, giving the operator the ability to write two or three words in one stroke.

The advantages given for machine shorthand include greater speed, interchangeability of notes, and greater volume, in that other typists familiar with the system can transcribe the notes. Disadvantages include the cost of the machine, the inconvenience of moving the machine from place to place, and the difficulty of revising notes once they have been taken, in addition to reading back dictation when desired. Machine shorthand has proved itself in the reporting field, however. Reporting speeds are attained in less time than is needed with pen shorthand; and machine shorthand reporters now do most of the convention reporting and a large part of the court reporting, legislative reporting, and reporting of hearings in the United States.

Voice
transcrib-
ing
machines

Alternatives to shorthand. Machines for voice transcribing are used in modern offices as an alternative to pen or machine shorthand; in fact, they are found in most offices of any size. The advantages of such dictating equipment include the following: the equipment is always available, even though the secretary may not be; the dictator can dictate his thoughts immediately—in his office, in his home, in his car, or on a plane; he can dictate as rapidly as he wishes, unhampered by his secretary's recording skill; and dictation belts can be mailed back to the typist for transcription. Disadvantages of voice transcribing machines are the impossibility of teamwork during the dictation process and the necessity of a high degree of dictating skill when using dictating equipment. In addition, urgent matters usually cannot be dictated and transcribed without some delay.

BIBLIOGRAPHY. E.H. BUTLER, *The Story of British Shorthand* (1951), a complete history of early shorthand systems with emphasis on modern British systems; H. GLATTE, *Shorthand Systems of the World* (1959), a short history that emphasizes the extent to which important systems spread to countries other than those in which they originated; L.A. LESLIE (ed.), *The Story of Gregg Shorthand: Based on the Writings of John Robert Gregg* (1964), a complete history that emphasizes the early life of John Robert Gregg, his invention of Gregg shorthand, his promotion of the system in the U.S., and his method of teaching; ISAAC PITMAN, *A History of Shorthand* (1852, rev. ed. 1934), a chronological history of shorthand systems with emphasis on British systems to the end of the 19th century; A.R. RUSSON, *Methods of Teaching Shorthand* (1968), the history of shorthand instruction.

(A.R.R.)

Short Story

The short story is a kind of prose fiction, usually more compact and intense than the novel and the short novel (novelette). Prior to the 19th century it was not generally regarded as a distinct literary form. But although in this sense it may seem to be a uniquely modern genre, the fact is that short prose fiction is nearly as old as language itself. Throughout history man has enjoyed various types of brief narratives: jests, anecdotes, studied digressions, short allegorical romances, moralizing fairy tales, short myths, and abbreviated historical legends. None of these

constitutes a short story as the 19th and 20th centuries have defined the term, but they do make up a large part of the milieu from which the modern short story emerged.

Many of the elements of storytelling common to the short story and the novel are discussed at greater length in the article NOVEL. The short stories of particular literary cultures, along with other genres, are discussed in articles such as LITERATURE, WESTERN; and LITERATURE, EAST ASIAN; and in articles on the arts of various peoples —*e.g.,* SOUTH ASIAN PEOPLES, ARTS OF.

Analysis of the genre

As a genre, the short story has received relatively little critical attention, and the most valuable studies of the form that exist are often limited by region or era (*e.g.,* Ray B. West's *The Short Story in America,* 1900–1950). One recent attempt to account for the genre has been offered by the Irish short story writer Frank O'Connor, who suggests that stories are a means for "submerged population groups" to address a dominating community. Most other theoretical discussions, however, are predicated in one way or another on Edgar Allan Poe's thesis that stories must have a compact, unified effect.

By far the majority of criticism on the short story focusses on techniques of writing. Many, and often the best of the technical works, advise the young reader—alerting him to the variety of devices and tactics employed by the skilled writer. On the other hand, many of these works are no more than treatises on "how to write stories" for the young writer, and not serious critical material.

The sketch
and the tale

The prevalence in the 19th century of two words, "sketch" and "tale," affords one way of looking at the genre. In the United States alone there were virtually hundreds of books claiming to be collections of sketches (Washington Irving's *Sketch Book,* William Dean Howells' *Suburban Sketches*) or collections of tales (Poe's *Tales of the Grotesque and Arabesque,* Herman Melville's *Piazza Tales*). These two terms establish the polarities of the milieu out of which the modern short story grew.

The tale is much older than the sketch. Basically, the tale is a manifestation of a culture's unaging desire to name and conceptualize its place in the cosmos. It provides a culture's narrative framework for such things as its vision of itself and its homeland or for expressing its conception of its ancestors and its gods. Usually filled with cryptic and uniquely deployed motifs, personages, and symbols, tales are frequently fully understood only by members of the particular culture to which they belong. Simply, tales are intracultural. Seldom created to address an outside culture, a tale is a medium through which a culture speaks to itself and thus perpetuates its own values and stabilizes its own identity. The old speak to the young through tales.

The sketch, by contrast, is intercultural, depicting some phenomenon of one culture for the benefit or pleasure of a second culture. Factual and journalistic, in essence the sketch is generally more analytic or descriptive and less narrative or dramatic than the tale. Moreover, the sketch by nature is *suggestive,* incomplete; the tale is often *hyperbolic,* overstated.

The primary mode of the sketch is written; that of the tale, spoken. This difference alone accounts for their strikingly different effects. The sketch writer can have, or pretend to have, his eye on his subject. The tale, recounted at court or campfire—or at some place similarly removed in time from the event—is nearly always a recreation of the past. The tale-teller is an agent of *time,* bringing together a culture's past and its present. The sketch writer is more an agent of *space,* bringing an aspect of one culture to the attention of a second.

It is only a slight oversimplification to suggest that the tale was the only kind of short fiction until the 16th century, when a rising middle class interest in social realism on the one hand and in exotic lands on the other put a premium on sketches of subcultures and foreign regions. In the 19th century certain writers—those one might call the "fathers" of the modern story: Nikolay Gogol, Hawthorne, E.T.A. Hoffmann, Heinrich von Kleist, Prosper Mérimée, Poe—combined elements of the tale with ele-

Modern
fusions

ments of the sketch. Each writer worked in his own way, but the general effect was to mitigate some of the fantasy and stultifying conventionality of the tale and, at the same time, to liberate the sketch from its bondage to strict factuality. The modern short story, then, ranges between the highly imaginative tale and the photographic sketch and in some ways draws on both.

The short stories of Ernest Hemingway, for example, may often gain their force from an exploitation of traditional mythic symbols (water, fish, groin wounds), but they are more closely related to the sketch than to the tale. Indeed, Hemingway was able at times to submit his apparently factual stories as newspaper copy. In contrast, the stories of Hemingway's contemporary William Faulkner more closely resemble the tale. Faulkner seldom seems to understate, and his stories carry a heavy flavour of the past. Both his language and his subject matter are rich in traditional material. A Southerner might well suspect that only a reader steeped in sympathetic knowledge of the traditional South could fully understand Faulkner. Faulkner may seem, at times, to be a Southerner speaking to and for Southerners. But, as, by virtue of their imaginative and symbolic qualities, Hemingway's narratives are more than journalistic sketches, so, by virtue of their explorative and analytic qualities, Faulkner's narratives are more than Southern tales.

Whether or not one sees the modern short story as a fusion of sketch and tale, it is hardly disputable that today the short story is a distinct and autonomous, though still developing, genre.

History of the short story

ORIGINS

The evolution of the short story first began before man could write. To aid himself in constructing and memorizing tales, the early storyteller often relied on stock phrases, fixed rhythms, and rhyme. Consequently, many of the oldest narratives in the world, such as the famous Babylonian tale the *Epic of Gilgamesh* (c. 2000 BC), are in verse. Indeed, most major stories from the ancient Middle East were in verse: "The War of the Gods," "The Story of Adapa" (both Babylonian), "The Heavenly Bow," and "The King Who Forgot" (both Canaanite). These tales were inscribed in cuneiform on clay during the 2nd millennium BC.

The earliest tales extant from Egypt were composed on papyrus at a comparable date. The ancient Egyptians seem to have written their narratives largely in prose, apparently reserving verse for their religious hymns and working songs. One of the earliest surviving Egyptian tales, "The Shipwrecked Sailor" (c. 2000 BC), is clearly intended to be a consoling and inspiring story to reassure its aristocratic audience that apparent misfortune can in the end become good fortune. Also recorded during the 12th dynasty were the success story of the exile Sinuhe and the moralizing tale called "King Cheops [Khufu] and the Magicians." The provocative and profusely detailed story "The Tale of Two Brothers" (or "Anpu and Bata") was written down during the New Kingdom, probably around 1250 BC. Of all the early Egyptian tales, most of which are baldly didactic, this story is perhaps the richest in folk motifs and the most intricate in plot.

The earliest tales from India are not as old as those from Egypt and the Middle East. The *Brāhmaṇas* (c. 700 BC) function mostly as theological appendixes to the Four Vedas, but a few are composed as short, instructional parables. Perhaps more interesting as stories are the later tales in the Pāli language, *The Jātaka*. Although these tales have a religious frame that attempts to recast them as Buddhist ethical teachings, their actual concern is generally with secular behaviour and practical wisdom. Another, nearly contemporaneous collection of Indian tales, *The Pañca-tantra* (c. AD 500), has been one of the world's most popular books. This anthology of amusing and moralistic animal tales, akin to those of "Aesop" in Greece, was translated into Middle Persian in the 6th century; into Arabic in the 8th century; and into Hebrew, Greek, and Latin soon thereafter. Sir Thomas North's English translation appeared in 1570. Another noteworthy collection is

The Ocean of Rivers of Stories, a series of tales assembled and recounted in narrative verse in the 11th or 12 century. Most of these tales come from much older material, and they vary from the fantastic story of a transformed swan to a more probable tale of a loyal but misunderstood servant.

During the 2nd, 3rd, and 4th centuries BC, the Hebrews first wrote down some of their rather sophisticated narratives, which are now a part of the Old Testament and the Apocrypha. The book of Tobit displays an unprecedented sense of ironic humour; Judith creates an unrelenting and suspenseful tension as it builds to its bloody climax; the story of Susanna, the most compact and least fantastic in the Apocrypha, develops a three-sided conflict involving the innocent beauty of Susanna, the lechery of the elders, and the triumphant wisdom of Daniel. The Old Testament books of Ruth, Esther, and Jonah hardly need mentioning: they may well be the most famous stories in the world.

Nearly all of the ancient tales, whether from Israel, India, Egypt, or the Middle East, were fundamentally didactic. Some of these ancient stories preached by presenting an ideal for readers to imitate. Others tagged with a "moral" were more direct. Most stories, however, preached by illustrating the success and joy that was available to the "good" man and by conveying a sense of the terror and misery that was in store for the wayward.

The early Greeks contributed greatly to the scope and art of short fiction. As in India, the moralizing animal fable was a common form; many of these tales were collected as "Aesop's fables" in the 6th century BC. Brief mythological stories of the gods' adventures in love and war were also popular in the pre-Attic age. Apollodorus of Athens compiled a handbook of epitomes, or abstracts, of these tales around the 2nd century BC, but the tales themselves are no longer extant in their original form. They appear, though somewhat transformed, in the longer poetical works of Hesiod, Homer, and the tragedians. Short tales found their way into long prose forms as well, as in Hellanicus' *Persika* (5th century BC, extant only in fragments).

Herodotus, the "father of history," saw himself as a maker and reciter of *logoi* (things for telling, tales). His long *History* is interspersed with such fictionalized digressions as the stories of Polycrates and his emerald ring, of Candaules' attractive wife, and of Rhampsinitus' stolen treasure. Xenophon's philosophical history, the *Cyropaedia* (4th century BC), contains the famous story of the soldier Abradates and his lovely and loyal wife Panthea, perhaps the first Western love story. The *Cyropaedia* also contains other narrative interpolations: the story of Pheraules, who freely gave away his wealth; the tale of Gobryas' murdered son; and various anecdotes describing the life of the Persian soldier.

Moreover, the Greeks are usually credited with originating the romance, a long form of prose fiction with stylized plots of love, catastrophe, and reunion. The early Greek romances frequently took shape as a series of short tales. The *Love Romances* of Parthenius of Nicaea, who wrote during the reign of Augustus Caesar, is a collection of 36 prose stories of unhappy lovers. *The Milesian Tales* (no longer extant) was an extremely popular collection of erotic and ribald stories composed by Aristides of Miletus in the 2nd century BC and translated almost immediately into Latin. As the variety of these short narratives suggests, the Greeks were less insistent than earlier cultures that short fiction be predominantly didactic.

By comparison the contribution of the Romans to short narrative was small. Ovid's long poem, *Metamorphoses*, is basically a reshaping of over 100 short, popular tales into a thematic pattern. The other major fictional narratives to come out of Rome are novel-length works by Petronius (*Satyricon*, 1st century AD) and Apuleius (*The Golden Ass*, 2nd century AD). Like Ovid these men used potential short story material as episodes within a larger whole. The Roman love of rhetoric, it seems, encouraged the development of longer and more comprehensive forms of expression. Regardless, the trend away from didacticism inaugurated by the Greeks was not reversed.

(Marginal notes)

The earliest tales extant

The didacticism of early tales

Beginnings of the romance

Proliferation of forms. The Middle Ages was a time of the proliferation, though not necessarily the refinement, of short narratives. The short tale became an important means of diversion and amusement. From the Dark Ages to the Renaissance, various cultures adopted short fiction for their own purposes. Even the aggressive, grim spirit of the invading Germanic barbarians was amenable to expression in short prose. The myths and sagas extant in Scandinavia and Iceland indicate the kinds of bleak and violent tales the invaders took with them into southern Europe.

In contrast, the romantic imagination and high spirits of the Celts remained manifest in their tales. Wherever the Celts appeared—in Ireland, Wales, or Brittany—stories steeped in magic and splendour also appeared. This spirit, easily recognized in such Irish mythological tales as *Longes mac n-Uislenn* (probably composed in the 9th century), infused the chivalric romances that developed somewhat later on the Continent. The romances usually addressed one of three "Matters": the "Matter of Britain" (stories of King Arthur and his knights), the "Matter of France" (the Charlemagne cycle), or the "Matter of Rome" (stories out of antiquity, such as "Pyramus and Thisbe," "Paris and Helen"). Many, but not all, of the romances are too long to be considered short stories. Two of the most influential contributors of short material to the "Matter of Britain" in the 12th century were Chrétien de Troyes and Marie de France. The latter was most gifted as a creator of the short narrative poems known as the Breton lays. Only occasionally did a popular short romance like "Aucassin and Nicolette" (13th century) fail to address any of the three Matters.

Also widely respected was the exemplum, a short didactic tale usually intended to dramatize or otherwise inspire model behaviour. Of all the exempla, the best known in the 11th and 12th centuries were the lives of the saints, some 200 of which are extant. The *Gesta Romanorum* ("Deeds of the Romans") offered skeletal plots of exempla that preachers could expand into moralistic stories for use in their sermons.

Among the common people of the late Middle Ages there appeared a literary movement counter to that of the romance and exemplum. Displaying a preference for common sense, secular humour, and sensuality, this movement accounted in a large way for the practical-minded animals in beast fables, the coarse and "merry" jestbooks, and the ribald fabliaux. All were important as short narratives, but perhaps the most intriguing of the three are the fabliaux. First appearing around the middle of the 12th century, fabliaux remained popular for 200 years, attracting the attention of Boccaccio and Chaucer. Some 160 fabliaux are extant, all in verse.

Often, the medieval storyteller—regardless of the kind of tale he preferred—relied on a framing circumstance that made possible the juxtaposition of several stories, each of them relatively autonomous. Since there was little emphasis on organic unity, most storytellers preferred a flexible format, one that allowed tales to be added or removed at random with little change in effect. Such a format is found in *The Seven Sages of Rome*, a collection of stories so popular that nearly every European country had its own translation. The framing circumstance in *The Seven Sages* involves a prince condemned to death; his advocates (the seven sages) relate a new story each day, thereby delaying the execution until his innocence is made known. This technique is clearly similar to that of *The Arabian Nights*, another collection to come out of the Middle Ages. The majority of the stories in *The Arabian Nights* are framed by the story of Scheherazade in "A Thousand and One Nights." Records indicate that the basis of this framing story was a medieval Persian collection, *Hezar Efsan* ("Thousand Romances," no longer extant). In both the Persian and Arabian versions of the frame, the clever Scheherazade avoids death by telling her king-husband a thousand stories. Though the framing device is identical in both versions, the original Persian stories within the frame were replaced or drastically altered as the collection was adapted by the Arabs during the Muslim Mamlūk period (AD 1250–1517).

(margin) Exempla and fabliaux

(margin) The framing circumstance

Refinement. Short narrative received its most refined treatment in the Middle Ages from Chaucer and Boccaccio. Chaucer's versatility reflects the versatility of the age. In "The Miller's Tale" he artistically combines two fabliaux; in "The Nun's Priest's Tale" he draws upon material common to beast fables; in "The Pardoner's Tale" he creates a brilliantly revealing sermon, complete with a narrative exemplum. This short list hardly exhausts the catalogue of forms Chaucer experimented with. By relating tale to teller and by exploiting relationships among the various tellers, Chaucer endowed *The Canterbury Tales* with a unique, dramatic vitality.

Boccaccio's genius, geared more toward *narrative* than toward *drama*, is of a different sort. Where Chaucer usually reveals a character through his actions and assertions, Boccaccio seems more interested in his stories as pieces of action. With Boccaccio, the characters telling the stories, and to a large part the characters within the stories, are of subordinate interest. Like Chaucer, Boccaccio frames his well-wrought tales in a metaphoric context. The trip to the religious shrine at Canterbury provides a meaningful backdrop against which Chaucer juxtaposes his earthy and pious characters. The frame of the *Decameron* (from the Greek *deka*, ten, and *hēmera*, day) has relevance as well: during the height of the Black Plague in Florence, Italy, ten people meet accidentally in a church and agree to amuse and divert each other by telling ten stories each. Behind every story, in effect, is the inescapable presence of the Black Death. The *Decameron* is fashioned out of a variety of sources, including fabliaux, exempla, and short romances.

Spreading popularity. Immediately popular, the *Decameron* produced imitations nearly everywhere. In Italy alone, there appeared at least 50 writers of *novelle* (as short narratives were called) after Boccaccio.

Learning from the success and artistry of Boccaccio and, to a lesser degree, his contemporary Franco Sacchetti, Italian writers for three centuries kept the Western world supplied with short narratives. Sacchetti was no mere imitator of Boccaccio. More of a frank and unadorned realist, he wrote—or planned to write—300 stories (200 of the *Novelle* ["Short Stories"] are extant) dealing in a rather anecdotal way with ordinary Florentine life. Two other well-known narrative writers of the 14th century, Giovanni Fiorentino and Giovanni Sercambi, freely acknowledged their imitation of Boccaccio. In the 15th century Masuccio Salernitano's collection of 50 stories, *Il novellino* (1475), attracted much attention. Though verbosity often substitutes for eloquence in Masuccio's stories, they are witty and lively tales of lovers and clerics.

With Masuccio the popularity of short stories was just beginning to spread. Almost every Italian in the 16th century, it has been suggested, tried his hand at *novelle*. Matteo Bandello, the most influential and prolific writer, attempted nearly everything from brief histories and anecdotes to short romances, but he was most interested in tales of deception. Various other kinds of stories appeared. Agnolo Firenzuolo's popular *Ragionamenti di amore* ("The Reasoning of Love") is characterized by a graceful style unique in tales of ribaldry; Anton Francesco Doni included several tales of surprise and irony in his miscellany, *I marmi* ("The Marbles"); and Gianfrancesco Straparola experimented with common folktales and with dialects in his collection, *Le piacevoli notti* ("The Pleasant Nights"). In the early 17th century, Giambattista Basile attempted to infuse stock situations (often of the fairy-tale type, such as "Puss and Boots") with realistic details. The result was often remarkable—a tale of hags or princes with very real motives and feelings. Perhaps it is the amusing and diverting nature of Basile's collection of 50 stories that has reminded readers of Boccaccio. Or, it may be his use of a frame similar to that in the *Decameron*. Whatever the reason, Basile's *Cunto de li cunti* (1634; *The Story of Stories*) is traditionally linked with Boccaccio and referred to as *The Pentamerone* ("The Five Days"). Basile's similarities to Boccaccio suggest that in the 300 years between them the short story may have gained repute and circulation, but its basic shape and effect hardly changed.

(margin) Boccaccio and Chaucer

(margin) Italian short narratives

This pattern was repeated in France, although the impetus originally provided by Boccaccio was not felt until the 15th century. A collection of 100 racy anecdotes, *Les Cent Nouvelles Nouvelles*, "The Hundred New Short Stories" (c. 1460), outwardly resembles the *Decameron*. Marguerite de Navarre's *Heptameron* (1559; "The Seven Days"), an unfinished collection of some 70 amorous tales, admits a similar indebtedness.

In the early 17th century Béroalde de Verville placed his own Rabelaisian tales within a banquet frame in a collection called *Le Moyen de parvenir*, "The Way of Succeeding" (c. 1610). Showing great narrative skill, Béroalde's stories are still very much in the tradition of Boccaccio; as a collection of framed stories, their main intent is to amuse and divert the reader.

As the most influential nation in Europe in the 15th and 16th centuries, Spain contributed to the proliferation of short prose fiction. Especially noteworthy are: Don Juan Manuel's collection of lively exempla *El Conde Lucanor* (1328–35; "Count Lucanor"), which antedates the *Decameron*; the anonymous story "The Abencerraje," which was interpolated into a pastoral novel of 1559; and, most importantly, Miguel de Cervantes' experimental *Novelas ejemplares* (1613; "Exemplary Novels"). Cervantes' short fictions vary in style and seriousness, but their single concern is clear: to explore the nature of man's secular existence. This focus was somewhat new for short fiction, heretofore either didactic or escapist.

A new concern

Despite the presence of these and other popular collections, short narrative in Spain was eventually overshadowed by a new form that began to emerge in the 16th century—the novel. Like the earlier Romans, the Spanish writers of the early Renaissance often incorporated short story material as episodes in a larger whole.

Decline of short fiction. The 17th and 18th centuries mark the temporary decline of short fiction. The causes of this phenomenon are many: the emergence of the novel; the failure of the Boccaccio tradition to produce in three centuries much more than variations or imitations of older, well-worn material; and a renaissant fascination with drama and poetry, the superior forms of classical antiquity. Another cause for the disappearance of major works of short fiction is suggested by the growing preference for journalistic sketches. The increasing awareness of other lands and the growing interest in social conditions (accommodated by a publication boom) produced a plethora of descriptive and biographical sketches. Although these journalistic elements later were incorporated in the fictional short story, for the time being fact held sway over the imagination. Travel books, criminal biographies, social description, sermons, and essays occupied the market. Only occasionally did a serious story find its way into print, and then it was usually a production of an established writer like Voltaire or Addison.

Perhaps the decline is clearest in England, where the short story had its least secure foothold. It took little to obscure the faint tradition established in the 16th and 17th centuries by the popular jestbooks, by the *Palace of Pleasure* (an anthology of stories, mostly European), and by the few rough stories written by Englishmen (*e.g.*, Barnabe Rich's *Farewell to Military Profession*, 1581).

During the Middle Ages short fiction had become primarily an amusing and diverting medium. The Renaissance and Enlightenment, however, made different demands of the form. The awakening concern with secular issues called for a new attention to actual conditions. Simply, the diverting stories were no longer relevant or viable. At first only the journalists and pamphleteers responded to the new demand. Short fiction disappeared, in effect, because it did not respond. When it did shake off its escapist trappings in the 19th century, it reappeared as the "modern short story." This was a new stage in the evolution of short fiction, one in which the short form undertook a new seriousness and gained a new vitality and respect.

EMERGENCE OF THE MODERN STORY

The 19th century. The modern short story emerged almost simultaneously in Germany, the United States,

France, and Russia. In Germany there had been relatively little difference between the stories of the late 18th century and those in the older tradition of Boccaccio. In 1795 Goethe contributed a set of stories to Schiller's Journal, *Die Horen*, that were obviously created with the *Decameron* in mind. Significantly, Goethe did not call them "short stories" (*Novellen*) although the term was available to him. Rather, he thought of them as "entertainments" for German travellers (*Unterhaltungen deutscher Ausgewanderten*). Friedrich Schlegel's early discussion of the short narrative form, appearing soon after Goethe's "entertainments," also focussed on Boccaccio (*Nachrichten von den poetischen Werken des G. Boccaccio*, 1801).

A new type of short fiction

But a new type of short fiction was near at hand—a type that accepted some of the realistic properties of popular journalism. In 1827, 32 years after publishing his own "entertainments," Goethe commented on the difference between the newly emergent story and the older kind. "What is a short story," he asked, "but an event which, though unheard of, has occurred? Many a work which passes in Germany under the title 'short story' is not a short story at all, but merely a tale or what else you would like to call it." Two influential critics, Christoph Wieland and Friedrich Schleiermacher, also argued that a short story properly concerned itself with events that actually happened or could happen. A short story, for them, had to be realistic.

Perhaps sensitive to this qualification, Heinrich von Kleist and E.T.A. Hoffmann called their short works on fabulous themes "tales" (*Erzählungen*). Somewhat like Poe, Kleist created an expression of human problems, partly metaphysical and partly psychological, by dramatizing man's confrontations with a fantastic, chaotic world. Hoffmann's intriguing tales of exotic places and of supernatural phenomena were very likely his most influential. Another important writer, Ludwig Tieck, explicitly rejected realism as the definitive element in a short story. As he noted in his preface to the 1829 collection of his works and as he demonstrated in his stories, Tieck envisioned the short story as primarily a matter of intensity and ironic inversion. A story did not have to be realistic in any outward sense, he claimed, so long as the chain of consequences was "entirely in keeping with character and circumstances." By allowing the writer to pursue an inner, and perhaps bizarre, reality and order, Tieck and the others kept the modern story open to nonjournalistic techniques.

In the United States, the short story, as in Germany, evolved in two strains. On the one hand there appeared the realistic story that sought objectively to deal with seemingly real places, events, or persons. The regionalist stories of the second half of the 19th century (including those by G.W. Cable, Bret Harte, Sarah Orne Jewett) are of this kind. On the other hand, there developed the impressionist story, a tale shaped and given meaning by the consciousness and psychological attitudes of the narrator. Predicated upon this element of subjectivity, these stories seem less objective and are less realistic in the outward sense. Of this sort are Poe's tales in which the hallucinations of a central character or narrator provide the details and facts of the story. Like the narrators in "The Tell-Tale Heart" (1843) and "The Imp of the Perverse" (1845), the narrator of "The Fall of the House of Usher" (1839) so distorts and transforms what he sees that the reader cannot hope to look objectively at the scene. Looking through an intermediary's eyes, the reader can see only the narrator's impressions of the scene.

Evolving in two strains

Some writers contributed to the development of both types of story. Washington Irving wrote several realistic sketches (*The Sketch-Book*, 1819–20; *The Alhambra*, 1832) in which he carefully recorded appearances and actions. Irving also wrote stories in which the details were taken not from ostensible reality but from within a character's mind. Much of the substance of "The Stout Gentleman" (1821), for example, is reshaped and recharged by the narrator's fertile imagination; "Rip Van Winkle" (1819) draws upon the symbolic surreality of Rip's dreams.

The short prose of Nathaniel Hawthorne illustrates that

neither type of modern story, however, has exclusive rights to the use of symbol. On a few occasions, as in "My Kinsman, Major Molineux" (1832), Hawthorne's stories are about symbolic events as they are viewed subjectively by the central character. Hawthorne's greater gift, however, was for creating scenes, persons, and events that strike the reader as being actual historical facts and also as being rich in symbolic import. "Endicott and the Red Cross" (1837) may seem little more than a photographic sketch of a tableau out of history (the 17th-century Puritan leader cuts the red cross of St. George out of the colonial flag, the first act of rebellion against England), but the details are symbols of an underground of conflicting values and ideologies.

The "impressionist" story

Several American writers, from Poe to James, were interested in the "impressionist" story that focusses on the impressions registered by events on the characters' minds, rather than the objective reality of the events themselves. In Herman Melville's "Bartleby the Scrivener" (1856) the narrator is a man who unintentionally reveals his own moral weaknesses through his telling of the story of Bartleby. Mark Twain's tales of animals ("The Celebrated Jumping Frog," 1865; "The Story of Old Ram," 1872; "Baker's Blue Jay Yarn," 1879), all impressionist stories, distort ostensible reality in a way that reflects on the men who are speaking. Ambrose Bierce's famous "An Occurrence at Owl Creek Bridge" (1891) is another example of this type of story in which the reader sees a mind at work —distorting, fabricating, and fantasizing—rather than an objective picture of actuality. In contrast, William Dean Howells usually sought an objectifying aesthetic distance. Though Howells was as interested in human psychology and behaviour as any of the impressionist writers, he did not want his details filtered through a biassed, and thus distorting, narrator. Impressionism, he felt, gave license for falsifications; in the hands of many writers of his day, it did in fact result in sentimental romanticizing.

But in other hands the impressionist technique could subtly delineate human responses. Henry James was such a writer. Throughout his prefaces to the New York edition of his works, the use of an interpreting "central intelligence" is constantly emphasized. "Again and again, on review," James observes, "the shorter things in especial that I have gathered into [the Edition] have ranged themselves not as my own impersonal account of the affair in hand, but as my account of somebody's impression of it." This use of a central intelligence, who is the "impersonal author's concrete deputy or delegate" in the story, allows James all the advantages of impressionism and, simultaneously, the freedom and mobility common to stories narrated by a disembodied voice.

In at least one way, 19th-century America resembled 16th-century Italy: there was an abundance of second- and third-rate short stories. And, yet, respect for the form grew substantially, and most of the great artists of the century were actively participating in its development. The seriousness with which many writers and readers regarded the short story is perhaps most clearly evident in the amount and kind of critical attention it received. James, Howells, Harte, Twain, Melville, and Hawthorne all discussed it as an art form, usually offering valuable insights, though sometimes shedding more light on their own work than on the art as a whole.

Poe's notion of the unity of effect

But the foremost American critic of the short story was Edgar Allan Poe. Himself a creator of influential impressionist techniques, Poe believed that the definitive characteristic of the short story was its unity of effect. "A skillful literary artist has constructed a tale," Poe wrote in his review of Hawthorne's *Twice-Told Tales* in 1842.

If wise, he has not fashioned his thoughts to accommodate his incidents; but having conceived, with deliberate care, a certain unique or single *effect* to be wrought out, he then invents such incidents—he then combines such events as may best aid him in establishing this preconceived effect. If his very initial sentence tend not to the out-bringing of this effect, then he has failed in his first step. In the whole composition there should be no word written of which the tendency, direct or indirect, is not to the one pre-established design.

Poe's polemic primarily concerns craftsmanship and artistic integrity; it hardly prescribes limits on subject matter or dictates technique. As such, Poe's thesis leaves the story form open to experimentation and to growth while it demands that the form show evidence of artistic diligence and seriousness.

French short stories

The new respect for the short story was also evident in France, as Henry James observed, when in 1844 Prosper "Mérimée with his handful of little stories was appointed to the French Academy." As illustrated by "Columba" (1841) or "Carmen" (1845), which gained additional fame as an opera, Mérimée's stories are masterpieces of detached and dry observation, though the subject matter itself is often emotionally charged. Nineteenth-century France produced short stories as various as 19th-century America—although the impressionist tale was generally less common in France. (It is as if, not having an outstanding impressionist storyteller themselves, the French adopted Poe, who was being ignored by the critics in his own country.) The two major French impressionist writers were Charles Nodier, who experimented with symbolic fantasies, and Gérard de Nerval, whose collection *Les Filles du feu* (1854; "Daughters of Fire") grew out of recollections of his childhood. Artists primarily known for their work in other forms also attempted the short story—novelists like Honoré de Balzac and Gustave Flaubert and poets like Alfred de Vigny and Théophile Gautier.

One of the most interesting writers of 19th-century France is Alphonse Daudet, whose stories reflect the spectrum of interest and techniques of the entire century. His earliest and most popular stories (*Lettres de mon moulin*, 1866; "Letters from My Mill") create a romantic, picturesque fantasy; his stories of the Franco-Prussian War (*Contes du Lundi*, 1873; "Monday's Tales") are more objectively realistic, and the sociological concern of his last works betrays his increasing interest in naturalistic determinism.

A master of the objective story

The greatest French storywriter, by far, is Guy de Maupassant, a master of the objective short story. Basically, Maupassant's stories are anecdotes that capture a revealing moment in the lives of middle class citizens. This crucial moment is typically recounted in a well-plotted design, though perhaps in some stories like "Boule de suif" (1880; "Ball of Tallow") and "The Necklace" (1881) the plot is too contrived, the reversing irony too neat, and the artifice too apparent. In other stories, like "The House of Madame Tellier" (1881), Maupassant's easy and fluid prose captures the innocence and the corruption of human behaviour.

Russian writers

During the first two decades of the 19th century in Russia, fable writing became a fad. By all accounts the most widely read fabulist was Ivan Krylov whose stories borrowed heavily from Aesop, La Fontaine, and various Germanic sources. If Krylov's tales made short prose popular in Russia, the stories of the revered poet Aleksandr Pushkin gained serious attention for the form. Somewhat like Mérimée in France (who was one of the first to translate Pushkin, Gogol, and Turgenev into French), Pushkin cultivated a detached, rather classical style for his stories of emotional conflicts (*The Queen of Spades*, 1834). Also very popular and respected was Mikhail Lermontov's "novel," *A Hero of Our Time* (1840), which actually consists of five stories that are more or less related.

But it is Nikolay Gogol who stands at the headwaters of the Russian short story; Dostoyevsky noted that all Russian short story writers "emerged from Gogol's overcoat," a punning allusion to the master's best known story. In a manner all his own, Gogol was developing impressionist techniques in Russia simultaneously with Poe in America. Gogol published his *Arabesques* (1835) five years before Poe collected some of his tales under a similar title. Like those of Poe, Gogol's tales of hallucination, confusing reality and dream, are among his best stories ("Nevsky Prospect" and "Diary of a Madman," both 1835). The single most influential story in the first half of the 19th century in Russia was undoubtedly Gogol's "Overcoat" (1842). Blending elements of realism (natural details from the characters' daily lives) with elements of fantasy (the central character returns as a ghost), Gogol's story seems to anticipate both the impressionism of Dostoyevsky's "Underground Man" and the realism of Tolstoy's "Ivan Ilych."

Ivan Turgenev appears, at first glance, antithetical to Gogol. In *A Sportsman's Notebook* (1852) Turgenev's simple use of language, his calm pace, and his restraint clearly differentiate him from Gogol. But like Gogol, Turgenev was more interested in capturing qualities of people and places than in building elaborate plots. A remaining difference between the two Russians, however, tends to make Turgenev more acceptable to 20th-century readers: Turgenev studiously avoided anything artificial. Though he may have brought into his realistic scenes a tale of a ghost ("Bezhin Meadow," 1852), he did not attempt to bring in a ghost (as Gogol had done in "The Overcoat"). In effect, Turgenev's allegiance was wholly to detached observation.

Developing some of the interests of Gogol, Fyodor Dostoyevsky experimented with the impressionist story. The early story "White Nights" (1848), for example, is a "Tale of Love from the Reminiscence of a Dreamer" as the subtitle states; the title of one of his last stories, "The Dream of the Ridiculous Man" (1877), also echoes Poe and Gogol. Though sharing Dostoyevsky's interest in human motives, Leo Tolstoy used vastly different techniques. He usually sought psychological veracity through a more detached and, presumably, objective narrator ("The Death of Ivan Ilich," 1886; "The Kreutzer Sonata," 1891). Perhaps somewhat perplexed by Tolstoy's nonimpressionist means of capturing and delineating psychological impressions, Henry James pronounced Tolstoy the masterhand of the disconnection of method from matter.

The Russian master of the objective story was Anton Chekhov. No other storywriter so consistently as Chekhov turned out first-rate works. Though often compared to Maupassant, Chekhov is much less interested in constructing a well-plotted story; nothing much actually happens in Chekhov's stories, though much is revealed about his characters and the quality of their lives. While Maupassant focusses on event, Chekhov keeps his eye on character. Stories like "The Grasshopper" (1892), "The Darling" (1898), and "In the Ravine" (1900)—to name only three—all reveal Chekhov's perception, his compassion, and his subtle humour and irony. One critic says of Chekhov that he is no moralist—he simply says "you live badly, ladies and gentlemen," but his smile has the indulgence of a very wise man.

The 20th century. In the first half of the 20th century the appeal of the short story continued to grow. Literally hundreds of writers—including, as it seems, nearly every major dramatist, poet, and novelist—published thousands of excellent stories. William Faulkner suggested that writers often try their hand at poetry, find it too difficult, go on to the next most demanding form, the short story, fail at that, and only then settle for the novel. In the 20th century Germany, France, Russia, and the U.S. lost what had once appeared to be their exclusive domination of the form. Innovative and commanding writers emerged in countries that had previously exerted little influence on the genre: Sicily, for example, produced Luigi Pirandello; Czechoslovakia, Franz Kafka; Japan, Akutagawa Ryūnosuke; Argentina, Jorge Luis Borges. Literary journals with international circulation, such as Ford Madox Ford's *Transatlantic Review, Scribner's Magazine,* and Harriet Weaver's *Egoist,* provided a steady and prime exposure for young writers.

As the familiarity with it increased, the short story form itself became more varied and complex. The fundamental means of structuring a story underwent a significant change. The overwhelming or unique event that usually informed the 19th-century story fell out of favour with the storywriter of the early 20th century. He grew more interested in subtle actions and unspectacular events. Sherwood Anderson, one of the most influential U.S. writers of the early 20th century, observed that the common belief in his day was that stories had to be built around a plot, a notion that, in Anderson's opinion, appeared to

Increasing complexity of the short story

poison all storytelling. His own aim was to achieve form, not plot, although form was more elusive and difficult. The record of the short story in the 20th century is dominated by this increased sensitivity to—and experimentation with—form. Although the popular writers of the century (like O. Henry in the U.S. and Paul Morand in France) may have continued to structure stories according to plot, the greater artists turned elsewhere for structure, frequently eliciting the response from cursory readers that "nothing *happens* in these stories." Narratives like Ernest Hemingway's "A Clean Well-Lighted Place" may seem to have no structure at all, so little physical action develops; but stories of this kind are actually structured around a psychological, rather than physical, conflict. In several of Hemingway's stories (as in many by D.H. Lawrence, Katherine Mansfield, and others), physical action and event are unimportant except insofar as the actions reveal the psychological underpinnings of the story. Stories came to be structured, also, in accordance with an underlying archetypal model: the specific plot and characters are important insofar as they allude to a traditional plot or figure, or to patterns that have recurred with wide implications in the history of mankind. Katherine Anne Porter's "Flowering Judas," for example, echoes and ironically inverts the traditional Christian legend. Still other stories are formed by means of motif, usually a thematic repetition of an image or detail that represents the dominant idea of the story. "The Dead," the final story in James Joyce's *Dubliners,* builds from a casual mention of death and snow early in the story to a culminating paragraph that links them in a profound vision. Seldom, of course, is the specific structure of one story appropriate for a different story. Faulkner, for example, used the traditional pattern of the knightly quest (in an ironic way) for his story "Was," but for "Barn Burning" he relied on a psychologically organic form to reveal the story of young Sarty Snopes.

The decline of the plot

No single form provided the 20th-century writer with the answer to structural problems. As the primary structuring agent, spectacular and suspenseful action was rather universally rejected around midcentury since motion pictures and television could present it much more vividly. As the periodicals that had supplied escapist stories to mass audiences declined, the short story became the favoured form of a smaller but intellectually more demanding readership. The Argentine Borges, for example, attracted an international following with his *Ficciones,* stories that involved the reader in dazzling displays of erudition and imagination, unlike anything previously encountered in the genre. Similarly, the American Donald Barthelme's composition consisted of bits and pieces of, *e.g.,* television commercials, political speeches, literary allusions, eavesdropped conversations, graphic symbols, dialogue from Hollywood movies— all interspersed with his own original prose in a manner that defied easy comprehension and yet compelled the full attention of the reader. The short story also lent itself to the rhetoric of student protest in the 1960s and was found in a bewildering variety of mixed-media forms in the "underground" press that publicized this life style throughout the world. In his deep concern with such a fundamental matter as form, the 20th-century writer unwittingly affirmed the maturation and popularity of the genre; only a secure and valued (not to mention flexible) genre could withstand and, moreover, encourage such experimentation.

BIBLIOGRAPHY. Perhaps the most informative recent study of narrative, though not necessarily short narrative, that incorporates both theoretical and historical material is R.E. SCHOLES and R.L. KELLOGG, *The Nature of Narrative* (1966). K.P. KEMPTON examines the genre, emphasizing theme and meaning, in *The Short Story* (1947). An excellent analysis of story techniques is offered in SEAN O'FAOLAIN, *The Short Story* (1948). BRANDER MATTHEWS' well-known theoretical discussion, *The Philosophy of the Short Story* (1901, reprinted 1931), is predicated on Poe's theories. A provocative thesis regarding the nature of stories is presented in FRANK O'CONNOR, *The Lonely Voice: A Study of the Short Story* (1963). H.S. SUMMERS has collected some of the more important discussions of the form in *Discussions of the Short Story* (1963). *Storytellers and*

Their Art, ed. by G. SAMPSON and C. BURKHART (1963), contains comments of various authors on the form. More specialized discussions of the form are contained in F.L. PATTEE, *The Development of the American Short Story* (1923); R.B. WEST, *Short Story in America, 1900–1950* (1952); E.K. BENNETT, *A History of the German Novelle*, 2nd ed. rev. by H.M. WAIDSON (1961); and S. TRENKNER, *Greek Novella in the Classical Period* (1958). An important discussion of short narratives from the standpoint of the folklorist is S. THOMPSON, *The Folktale* (1946).

(A.J.H.)

Shostakovich, Dmitry

Dmitry Shostakovich has been the most important composer to have emerged in Russia within the Soviet period. Though he has produced operas, some choral works, a large number of able film scores, and some significant piano music and songs, Shostakovich is primarily a symphonic and chamber music composer, whose 15 symphonies, 13 string quartets, six concertos, piano trio, and piano quintet establish him as the most important Russian composer of instrumental music since Tchaikovsky.

EB Inc.

Shostakovich.

Birth and early life

Shostakovich was born in St. Petersburg on September 25 (September 12, old style), 1906, the son of an engineer. He entered the Petrograd (formerly St. Petersburg, now Leningrad) Conservatory in 1919, where he studied the piano with the pianist Leonid Nikolayev until 1923 and composition until 1925 with the Russian composers Aleksandr Glazunov and Maximilian Steinberg, the latter the son-in-law of Nikolay Rimsky-Korsakov. He participated in the Chopin International Competition for Pianists in Warsaw in 1927 and received an honorable mention but made no subsequent attempt to pursue the career of a virtuoso, confining his public appearances as a pianist to performances of his own works.

Even before his keyboard success in Warsaw, he had made a far greater impact as a composer with the precocious *First Symphony* (1924–25), which quickly achieved worldwide currency. The symphony's stylistic roots were numerous; the influence of men as diverse as Tchaikovsky and Paul Hindemith (and, avowedly, Shostakovich's contemporary Sergey Prokofiev) is clearly discernible. In the music Shostakovich was to write in the next few years he submitted to an even wider range of influences. The cultural climate in the Soviet Union was remarkably free at that time: even the music of Igor Stravinsky and Alban Berg, then in the avant-garde, was played. The Hungarian composer Béla Bartók and the German Paul Hindemith visited Russia to perform their own works, and Shostakovich himself openly experimented with avant-garde trends. His satiric opera *The Nose* (composed 1927–28; first performed 1930), based upon Nikolay Gogol's story, displayed a comprehensive awareness of what was new in Western music, although already it seems as if the satire is extended to the styles themselves, for the avant-garde sounds are contorted with wry humour. Not surprisingly, Shostakovich's incomparably finer second opera, *Lady Macbeth of the Mtsensk Dis-*

trict (composed 1930–32; first performed 1934; later renamed and successfully revived as *Katerina Izmaylova*), marked a stylistic retreat. Yet even this more accessible musical language was now too radical for the authorities.

From 1928, when Joseph Stalin had inaugurated his First Five-Year Plan, an iron hand fastened on Soviet culture, and in music a direct and popular style was demanded. Avant-garde music and jazz were banished, and for a while even the unproblematic Tchaikovsky was out of favour. Shostakovich did not experience immediate official displeasure, but when it came, it was devastating. It is said that it was Stalin's personal anger at what he heard when he attended a performance of *Lady Macbeth of the Mtsensk District* in 1936 that precipitated the official condemnation of the opera and of its creator. Shostakovich was bitterly attacked in the official press, and both the opera and the until then unperformed *Fourth Symphony* (1935–36) were withdrawn. The composer's next major work was his *Fifth Symphony* (1937), which he described as "A Soviet artist's reply to just criticism." A trivial, dutifully "optimistic" work might have been expected; what emerged was compounded largely of serious, even sombre and elegiac music, presented with a compelling directness that scored an immediate success with the public and even the authorities.

The shock of official disfavour

With the *Fifth Symphony*, Shostakovich escaped from the stylistic instability of his earlier works, finally forging the personal style that he used in his subsequent compositions. The Austrian composer Gustav Mahler was a clear progenitor of both the *Fourth* and *Fifth* symphonies, but the latter represented a drastic shift in technique. Whereas the earlier symphony had been a sprawling work, founded upon a free proliferation of melodic ideas, the first movement of the *Fifth* was marked by melodic concentration—certain particles providing the main bases of music that grows organically to a relentless climax. This singlemindedness is reflected elsewhere in Shostakovich's work in his liking for the monolithic Baroque structures of the fugue and chaconne, each of which grows from, or is founded upon, the constant repetition of a single melodic idea. This almost obsessive concern with the working out of a single expressive character can also be seen in the recurrence from work to work in his mature music of certain thematic ideas, notably various permutations founded upon the juxtaposition of the major and minor third (already clear in the *Fifth Symphony*), and the four-note cell D-E♭-C-B derived from the composer's initials in their German equivalent (D. Sch.), interpreted according to the labels of German musical notation (in which "S," spoken as "Es," equals E♭ and "h" equals B).

In 1937 Shostakovich was appointed a teacher of composition in the Leningrad Conservatory, and the German attack on the Soviet Union in 1941 found him still in that city. He composed his *Seventh Symphony* (1941) in beleaguered Leningrad during the latter part of that year, and the work achieved a quick fame, though this sprang more from the quasi-romantic circumstances of its composition than from its musical quality, which is often banal. Indeed, Shostakovich has always been an unequal composer. When some extramusical force has conditioned the music, empty rhetoric and impoverished invention have all too often resulted. After evacuation to Kuybyshev in 1942, Shostakovich settled in Moscow in 1943 as a teacher of composition at the conservatory, and from 1945 he taught also at the Leningrad Conservatory.

Shostakovich's works written during the mid-1940s contain some of his best music, especially the *Eighth Symphony* (1943), the *Piano Trio* (1944), and the *Violin Concerto No. 1* (1947–48). Their prevailing seriousness, even grimness, was to contribute to Shostakovich's second fall from official grace. Under the gathering clouds of the Cold War, the Soviet authorities sought to impose a firmer ideological control, demanding a more accessible musical language than some composers were currently using. In Moscow in 1948, at a now notorious conference presided over by Andrey Zhdanov, a prominent Soviet theoretician, the leading figures of Soviet music, including Shostakovich, were attacked and disgraced.

As a result, the quality of Soviet composition slumped in the next few years, and Shostakovich produced a number of poor pieces. His personal influence was reduced by the termination of his teaching activities at both the Moscow and Leningrad conservatories. Yet Shostakovich was not completely intimidated, and in his *String Quartet No. 4* (1949), and especially in his *Quartet No. 5* (1951), he offered a splendid rejoinder to those who would have had him renounce completely his style and musical integrity. His *Tenth Symphony*, composed in 1953, the year of Stalin's death, flew in the face of Zhdanovshchina (Zhdanovism) yet, like his *Fifth Symphony* of 16 years earlier, compelled acceptance by sheer quality and directness.

Success of the Tenth Symphony

Since then Shostakovich's biography has been essentially a catalog of his works. He has been left to pursue his creative career largely unhampered by official interference. He did, however, experience some difficulty over the texts by the Russian poet Yevgeny Yevtushenko on which he based his *Thirteenth Symphony* (1962), and the work was suppressed after its first performance. Yet he has clearly been undeterred by this, and his deeply impressive *Fourteenth Symphony* (1969), cast as a cycle of 11 songs on the subject of death, is not the sort of work to appeal to official circles. The composer had visited the United States in 1949, and in 1958 he made an extended tour of western Europe, including Italy, where he had already been elected an honorary member of the Accademia Nazionale di Sta. Cecilia, Rome; and Britain, where he received an honorary doctorate of music at Oxford University. In 1966 he was awarded the Royal Philharmonic Society's Gold Medal.

Despite the brooding typical of so much of his music, which might suggest an introverted personality, Shostakovich is noted for his apparent gregariousness. Since Sergey Prokofiev's death in 1953, he has been the undisputed head of Russian music. There is no reason to doubt that he is a sincere Communist, and he has even participated in political conferences. Yet as a composer he has always refused to be a mere cipher of official politics. Indeed, he appears to have flourished in the tension between his own creative drives and the demands of authority, writing much of his best music when his fiercely independent creative thought has, under the abiding pressure from his masters for comprehensible expression, been channelled into a musical language of the utmost directness.

MAJOR WORKS

OPERAS: *The Nose* (first performed 1930); *Lady Macbeth of the Mtsensk District* (1934; later known as *Katerina Izmaylova*, and performed in the revised version, 1962).

BALLETS: *The Golden Age* (1930); *Bolt* (1931); *Bright Rivulet* (1935).

ORCHESTRAL WORKS: 15 symphonies, including *No. 1* (composed 1924–25), *No. 5* (1937), *No. 7* (*Leningrad*, 1941), *No. 10* (1953), *No. 14* (a cycle of 11 songs, 1969).

CONCERTOS: (VIOLIN): *No. 1* (1948) and *No. 2* (1967). (CELLO): *No. 1* (1959) and *No. 2* (1965). (PIANO): *No. 1* (1933) and *No. 2* (1957).

CHAMBER MUSIC: 13 string quartets; *Piano Quintet* (1940); two piano trios, the first of which (op. 8) has been repudiated by the composer.

PIANO: Two sonatas; *24 Preludes and Fugues* (1951).

CHORAL: *The Execution of Stepan Razin* (1964).

BIBLIOGRAPHY. DAVID A. RABINOVICH, *Dmitry Shostakovich* (1959; orig. pub. in Russian), is a fairly recent general book in English on the composer; however, it is marred by its political bias. The most useful study of the music is contained in NORMAN KAY, *Shostakovich* (1971). Though not recent, GERALD ABRAHAM, *Eight Soviet Composers* (1943), contains valuable critical comment. ALEXANDER WERTH, *Musical Uproar in Moscow* (1949), is an account of the upheaval surrounding the Zhdanov conference of 1948 and yields valuable insight into the pressures under which Shostakovich has had to work.

(D.C.Br.)

Siam and Thailand, History of

The present state of Thailand was officially known as Siam before 1939 and from 1945 to 1949.

The Thai peoples emerged out of historical obscurity about one thousand years ago when they began moving southward and westward from the China landmass to the northern parts of the Indochinese Peninsula. They moved into lands from Assam in the west to northern Vietnam in the east, where most of the indigenous peoples were already under the influence of Indian culture.

The Thai culture before this time cannot be precisely delineated, since there are no documents describing it. It was once assumed that the Thai peoples were the founders and rulers of the kingdom of Nanchao, an independent state that flourished from the 8th to the 13th century in China's Yunnan province, but recent studies have indicated that the rulers of this state were not Thai. The culture of the Thai, then, can only be estimated on the basis of elements that continue to exist among most peoples speaking Thai languages today. The Thai language itself, in various dialect forms, is spoken by a wide variety of people living today in Burma, Thailand, Laos, Vietnam, and southern China. The Thai are people of the lowlands; their homes are in river valleys, and their economy is dependent on river waters. The Thai are subsistence farmers whose principal crop is rice. In the rice fields, their technology includes the use of the plow and the harrow for breaking the land and the hand sickle for harvest. Individual land holdings are typical, but cooperative efforts to build dikes or to harvest fields are common. Animals are domesticated, including the water buffalo and ox for labour and the pig and fowl for food.

Early Thai culture

Family relationships are important among the Thai, but they have no concept of the extended family or clan, and no caste system. Women occupy a high position: they may inherit property, and widows are free to remarry.

The earliest Thai religious beliefs were animistic. Spirits were thought to inhabit various natural sites—large trees, high rocks or mounds, the living quarters of families, and the rice kernel, the habitat of the rice goddess. Other spirits were the ghosts of the dead. Spirits could be benevolent or malevolent; offerings were made to them and ceremonies performed to ensure their favour.

When the Thai settlers in Southeast Asia began to emerge into history, they possessed sufficient social cohesion and political order to establish a number of petty principalities. Thai chronicles, although written long after the events they describe, point to the emergence by the 13th century of several small Thai states in what is now North Burma, the Yunnan province of China, and Assam in India, as well as in Thailand. In the 13th century several of these states rose to prominence, thanks partly to the rise of the Mongols, who sent armies to defeat Burma, Vietnam, and Champa but accepted Thai vassal status, and partly to the weakened condition of the Indianized states that had long been powerful in the area.

In the centre of the Indochinese Peninsula two peoples, the Mon and the Khmer, bore the impress of the culture of India in religion, government, the arts, and literature. The Mon, in lower Burma and central Thailand, and the Khmer, in the Mekong Valley, had created distinctive and vigorous cultures and powerful political states. By the 13th century, the Mon had suffered from the depredations of the stronger Khmer, retaining political independence only in a relatively small state, Haripunjaya, in what is now northern Thailand. Mon culture, however, continued to be strong throughout central and northern Thailand. Particularly noteworthy was the devotion of the Mon peoples to Theravāda Buddhism. The Khmer, after an extraordinary burst of military and cultural expansionism under King Jayavarman VII (reigned 1181–*c.* 1219), began to decline in political power. The times were propitious for the emergence of the Thai.

Sukhothai and Chiangmai. Two principal Thai states emerged in what is now Thailand during the 13th century: Sukhothai in the Central Plain and Chiangmai in the north. Sukhothai was founded around 1220 after a Thai revolt against Khmer rule at an outpost of the Khmer empire. Chiangmai was founded in 1296, shortly after the Thai defeat of the Mon state of Haripunjaya.

From the outset, both Thai states showed that the Thai had already absorbed many elements of the cultures of the peoples around them. There are, in fact, reasons to assume that the political emergence of the Thai did not represent any drastic change in the ethnic character of Thailand. It seems likely that the Thai, who for centuries had been filtering into the area, at the time of their rise were a minority of the population but were able to rise to dominance because of superior organizational ability and military prowess. The subsequent expansion of the Thai may reflect their ability to retain social supremacy and to absorb large numbers of non-Thai peoples.

Among the cultural borrowings of the Thai, one of the most profound and important was their acceptance, from the Mon, of Theravāda Buddhism. Thai animistic beliefs did not disappear—they persist even today—but to them were added the humanistic and philosophic concepts of a popular and egalitarian world religion.

Sukhothai under King Ramkhamhaeng

Sukhothai, regarded by the Thai today as their first historical kingdom, achieved a considerable expansion by the end of the 13th century. Little is known of Sukhothai during its first two reigns, but its third king, Ramkhamhaeng (reigned 1279?–?1317), has left a remarkable stone inscription that is the earliest example of writing in the Thai language. The Ramkhamhaeng inscription, dated 1292, pictures the Thai state as rich and prosperous, active in trade, and benevolently governed by a paternal monarch. According to the inscription, the state taxed its citizens modestly; treated all citizens, including non-Thai, alike; and provided justice for all. And "all its citizenry, all chiefs and nobles, everyone everywhere, all men and women, all groups, believe in Buddhism." The kingdom is described as extensive, covering much of central Thailand down to Nakhon Si Thammarat on the peninsula, but excluding the plain of the Chao Phraya River below Nakhon Sawan, a region once dominated by the Khmer but apparently during Ramkhamhaeng's reign governed as an independent state called Lavo.

Allowing for some royal exaggeration of the virtues of the state, much of Ramkhamhaeng's description rings true. It seems clear that the Thai rulers of Sukhothai were proud of the differences between their social order and that of their Khmer predecessors and adversaries. The

emphasis on their human and humane king, on their low tax burden, on their popular Buddhist faith was undoubtedly meant to point out the contrast with the very different "god-king" status of the Khmer monarch, the heavy exactions in taxes and labour of the Khmer state, and the high cost and remoteness of the aristocratically oriented Khmer Hindu cults.

Although much of Sukhothai "high" culture was a result of culture borrowing—Buddhism from the Mon, the system of writing from the Cambodians, art techniques and styles from various sources—many of these cultural borrowings were transmuted into Thai forms. Particularly outstanding were Thai bronze sculptures of the Buddha cast with great skill in distinctive and original forms. Thai ceramics, inspired apparently by Chinese Sung ware, were produced in great quantity at kilns in Sawankhalok; their high quality made them prized in trade.

King Ramkhamhaeng combined the abilities of effective ruler, warrior, and patron of Buddhism and the arts. His successors did not have his range. His son, Loe Thai (reigned 1317?–?47), the fourth king of the dynasty, poured his energies into religion, and a weakening of the state was the eventual outcome. Sukhothai apparently regained some power under King Lu Thai (reigned 1347?–74), but it fell under the domination of a new Thai state to the south in 1378.

The Ayutthaya Period (1350–1767). The successor state to Sukhothai was the Thai kingdom of Ayutthaya that had emerged around 1350. According to tradition, Ayutthaya's first king, Ramathibodi I, inherited the states of Lavo and U Thong (their capitals correspond to the towns of Lop Buri and Suphan Buri in Thailand today) and combined them into a single strong kingdom. Ayutthaya was located in the centre of the rich rice plains of the Chao Phraya Basin, a region strongly subject to the influences of the Khmer, the Mon, and the Burmese. From the outset it appears to have competed successfully for power with Sukhothai and with the Khmer. By the early 15th century it had absorbed Sukhothai and devastated the eroding Cambodian kingdom.

During the first century after the foundation of Ayutthaya, many changes reflecting the influence of Cambodia occurred in Thai society, particularly on the upper levels. Under King Trailok (reigned 1448–88) further changes were made and former changes were codified; the character of the Thai state was permanently transformed.

The most significant of the changes concerned the nature and organization of government. The self-image of Sukhothai kings had been that of a father bringing riches, justice, and the benefits of Buddhism to his people. In Ayutthaya these ideals were expanded and overlaid with the Khmer view of the ruler as god-king. Court ceremonials and court Brahmans were introduced to bring to kingship the magical attributes of divine intermediary. The court calendar swelled with ceremonies for the manipulation of cosmic forces to promote the success and prosperity of the state. (These ceremonies are described in a voluminous [718-page] 19th-century work in Thai by King Chulalongkorn, "The Royal Ceremonies of the Twelve Months.") In a practical way, new techniques for centralizing power, including a bureaucratic system of government, were introduced. Members of royalty who had been serving as provincial officials were replaced by appointed nobles. A hierarchy of princes and nobles was established whereby the relative status of each was formalized. A system of patrons and clients extended throughout the population so that, theoretically, every man fulfilled obligations—in loyalty and goods and services—to someone above him and received, in return, protection from a patron. Commoners paid their military service, compulsory labour services, and taxes to local masters who, in turn, were subject to higher masters above them. The apex of the pyramid of patronage was the king himself.

The formal hierarchical system awarded each man *sakdi na*, or "dignity marks," in which the position of each man was equated with an acreage of land. Ordinary freemen were actually allowed to take possession of twenty-five *rai* of land, equal to about ten acres, to represent their *sakdi na*. The rank of officials of the government and members

Ayutthayan government

From *Atlas of South-East Asia*

Ayutthaya kingdom c. 1400.

of the royal family was also expressed in the acreage terms of *sakdi na;* the acreage indicated could number in the hundreds or thousands. But for nobles and princes the term stood for power and position, for "dignity," and not for actual landed estates. High royal and noble officials were, in fact, required to live and work in the capital.

Many of the principles of government were enacted into codes of law, and a large body of law is reputed to date back to the reign of King Ramathibodi I. The basis of law was Hindu, and the codes were probably transmitted to the Thai from Mon sources. These codes were expanded a century later. They included laws on evidence, on slavery, on robbery, on divorce. A Palace Law spelled out the duties of members of the royal family, rules of succession, and court procedures. The institution of the rank of *uparat* also dates back to the mid-15th century. Often inappropriately termed "Second King" by Western visitors to Thailand, this rank was Indian in origin and was, in fact, the highest princely rank awarded to a member of the royal family. The *uparat* functioned as general of the armies and had some claim to being the heir apparent.

By and large, in the context of the times and in comparison with neighbouring states, Thailand in Ayutthaya was a strong and well-governed state. There were, however, periodic internal disorders, products, it would seem, of contests for power between and within the royal and noble elites. In order to retain power a king had to preserve a balance of strength between princes and nobles. The prime ingredient for power was population, for land was plentiful and people were scarce. If a king allowed too many clients to fall under the control of his relatives, the princes, or even of his own bureaucratic officials, the nobles, political conflict would likely ensue. Many such conflicts are recorded—one of the bloodiest resulting from the usurpation of the throne by a high noble early in the 17th century. This noble, whose position was essentially that of minister of the Southern Provinces, paved his way to the throne by putting two kings to death, and after his accession as King Prasatthong, some 3,000 persons, members of the former ruling dynasty and other potential rivals, were executed. One prince who had followed the established practice of seeking sanctuary by becoming a Buddhist monk was first lured out of his monastery and then put to death.

Ayutthayan society and culture

The mass of the people in Ayutthayan times, the peasant farmers, were divided into two main classes: freemen and slaves. Freemen had the right to till an area of land equivalent to ten acres. The obligations of the freemen to government in taxes and labour were paid to local patron-officials. This link was all-important. The way to improve one's status was to gain special favour through a patron or, if he were unable to help, to find a new patron who might give special favour. Exactions on freemen, it would seem, were seldom excessive. The fact of underpopulation meant that freemen could escape onerous obligations or an overly demanding patron by moving and clearing new land; the existence of numerous decrees against this practice testifies to its existence and prevalence. Another "escape" for freemen was slavery. There were many so-called slaves in Ayutthayan times; the term slave, however, is misleading—the great majority of slaves could better be called bondsmen, for the "slave" was usually also a peasant-farmer who could own land and could redeem his status by repayment of his debt.

Theravāda Buddhism in Ayutthayan times continued to supply an element of social cohesion in the Thai state. From king to peasant, all Thai regarded themselves as Buddhists despite the introduction of court Brahmanism on the top levels of society and the continued persistence of animism on all levels. Buddhism, indeed, was thoroughly acculturated in Ayutthayan times. On the popular level, Buddhist amulets and reliance on monks with magic power interpenetrated the more sublime ideas of the doctrine. At court, one king, Trailok, in 1458 cast 500 images of the Buddha in order to prevent repetition of the great famine that had occurred in 1457. The Buddhist monastic establishment itself played an important social role, providing moral and practical education for boys and giving young men who spent some time as monks the opportuni-

ty to "gain merit" for themselves and their parents. For men who chose to remain monks, the monastic order constituted a society parallel to secular society that allowed for considerable social advancement.

In its relationships with outside states, Ayutthayan Thailand was comparatively strong. Warfare was endemic, and the sway, or empire, of Ayutthaya fluctuated considerably during its 400-year history. But Thai dominance of the central Chao Phraya Plain remained unchallenged. Most of the wars were petty campaigns during the dry season, when the terrain permitted the movement of men and the agricultural cycle made their absence from the fields possible. Most of the wars were contests for sovereignty over border principalities. Some were essentially raids to acquire population—*i.e.*, agricultural manpower and skilled artisans—and transportable wealth.

Ayutthaya's emergence in the 14th century in an area once ruled by Cambodia brought on a series of wars with Cambodia. By the early 15th century Ayutthaya had reduced Cambodia to vassal status, and, although Cambodia was frequently able to throw off its dependency, the balance of power between the two states thereafter continued to favour the Thai. Ayutthayan dominance over Sukhothai, achieved early in the 15th century, brought the kingdom into confrontation with the northern Thai states of Chiangmai and Laos. During the reign of King Trailok these wars reached a peak of intensity, and Ayutthaya went to war with Chiangmai seven times. In order to improve his military position with respect to Chiangmai, King Trailok in 1463 moved his capital to the northern town of Phitsanulok, where it remained throughout the rest of the reign. Ayutthaya was unable to retain power over Chiangmai, and Chiangmai had periods of independence and periods of dependency on Burma throughout the Ayutthayan period; it was not until the late 18th century that Thailand finally succeeded in gaining permanent control over Chiangmai.

Ayutthayan–Burmese rivalry

The most powerful rival of the Thai in the Indochinese Peninsula was Burma. On two occasions when the ethnically diverse area of Burma was welded together into a political whole, Burmese imperial expansion extended into Thailand. One series of campaigns started around 1549. In the first engagement of this series, according to the Thai chronicles, the Thai king Maha Chakkraphat (reigned 1548–69) found himself in difficulties and was rescued by his wife, Queen Suriyothai, who lost her life in the incident. The campaigns ended in 1569 in a Thai defeat, and the country was overrun by Burmese forces. Burmese troops were garrisoned in Thailand, and the Burmese placed on the throne a Thai king who accepted Burmese suzerainty. Thailand remained a Burmese vassal-state for 15 years. In 1584–87, a Thai prince, Naresuan, since regarded by the Thai as a national hero, led a successful revolt against the Burmese and re-established Thailand's independence. In another period of Burmese unity and expansionism in the 18th century, the Burmese succeeded again in 1767 in capturing the Thai capital at Ayutthaya. The Burmese armies did not remain for long; they withdrew after sacking the Thai capital and thus ending the Ayutthaya period of Thai history.

Ayutthaya's relations with most other Asian states were limited to trade and the exchange of occasional embassies. The pursuit of friendly relations with China, started in Sukhothai times, was carried on throughout the Ayutthayan period. These relations were typical of those existing between China and outlying states: the Thai acknowledged the "elder brother" position of China and sent tributary missions triennially to the Chinese court. This formal suzerain–vassal relationship had little political significance but was willingly maintained by the Thai for the very real benefits it brought in the way of trade. Thailand, as a registered vassal, was permitted to send ships to China to purchase silks, pottery, and other luxury goods that were much in demand among the Thai upper classes. Thai trading vessels, and Chinese ships emanating from Thai ports, also conducted a lively trade in such commercial centres as Malacca, Vietnam, Java, and India.

Relations of a different sort were maintained with Ceylon; they were religious contacts. Some of the principal religious leaders in Sukhothai had come from Ceylon. Ceylon was looked to in Sukhothai and Ayutthayan times as the font of Theravāda Buddhist knowledge, and several religious missions were sent to Ceylon to obtain religious instruction, religious texts, and religious relics. During the 18th century, Buddhism in Ceylon underwent a serious decline, and a reversal in the religious relationship occurred. Ceylon then turned to Thailand for aid in purifying its ordination and other religious practices. One Thai mission that went to Ceylon in 1753 stayed for three years and performed some 700 ordinations for monks and 3,000 for novices. The Thai missions of this period established a Thai school of Buddhism in Ceylon, called Syāmvaṃsa, that still existed in the 1970s.

European contacts

In long-range terms the most significant foreign contacts of Thailand—and the rest of Asia—were those with Europeans, who began arriving in the 16th century. By any standard, however, the European impact on Thai society in Ayutthayan times was slight. Portuguese diplomats, traders, and missionaries began arriving at the court of Ayutthaya shortly after the Portuguese capture of Malacca in the Malay Peninsula in 1511. Portuguese trade and missionary activities never became very important; the largest group of Portuguese in Thailand were adventurers who assumed roles as mercenaries in the Thai armies and who introduced some Western military techniques to Thai warfare. In the 17th century the Dutch and English began to arrive and to establish trading centres near the capital and in peninsular Thailand. The growth of Dutch trading interests throughout Eastern Asia was reflected in the emergence of the Dutch as the leading Western traders in Thailand. By 1664 the Dutch, by threatening the use of force, had obtained a treaty giving them monopolies over certain portions of Thailand's external trade. The Thai, seeking to offset Dutch power, welcomed the arrival of French missionaries in the 1660s, and in 1684 initiated a series of diplomatic exchanges between the courts of Ayutthaya and Versailles. The principal French spokesmen for promoting expansion of French interests in Thailand were clerics who, misunderstanding the characteristic Thai attitude of religious toleration, became convinced that the Thai king Narai (reigned 1657–88) could be converted to Catholicism. The arrival in 1687 of a large French mission that included some 600 soldiers aroused Thai fears, and in 1688 a coup by anti-Western Thai leaders led to the expulsion of the French and the beheading of their chief advocate at the Thai court, a colourful Greek adventurer, Constantine Phaulkon, who had become a Thai noble and a leading counsellor of the king. The Thai coup of 1688 inaugurated a new Thai policy of minimizing contacts with Westerners—a policy that was to continue for 150 years.

The Thon Buri and early Bangkok Periods (1767–1868). The Ayutthayan Period in Thai history came to an end as a result of the successful Burmese invasion of 1767. A new period began with the rise of a provincial noble, Phraya Taksin, who succeeded in ousting the Burmese and eliminating Thai rivals to political power. Taksin established a new capital for the kingdom at Thon Buri, on the Chao Phraya River some 40 miles south of the ruined city of Ayutthaya. The new capital was somewhat less accessible to Burmese armies and more accessible to foreign merchants—principally Chinese—who brought desired products and whose trade could be taxed to provide significant revenues for the government. King Taksin followed a policy of political reunification, including the reclaiming of vassal states that had broken off from Thai suzerainty at the time of the Burmese invasion. A campaign in Cambodia led by Thailand's leading general, Chao Phraya Chakkri, was under way in 1781 when a palace coup took place in Thon Buri. Taksin, who had apparently become mad and imagined himself an incarnate Buddha, was deposed. Chakkri hastily returned to the capital, where a group of officials invited him to assume the throne. He did so in 1782, thus establishing a new dynasty, the Chakkri dynasty, that continues to head the Thai state. One of the first acts of the new king was to move the capital across the Chao Phraya River to Bangkok.

There is much continuity in the history of Thailand from

Ayutthaya to Thon Buri-Bangkok. The ethos of the state, the customs and livelihood of the people, underwent no marked change. Taksin and the first Chakkri kings were primarily engaged in a policy of restoration both internally and externally. Law codes, religious works, and literary texts were rewritten. New temples and palaces were built using the patterns, and even the very bricks, of old Ayutthaya. The first three Chakkri kings were all restorers. Rama I (reigned 1782–1809) continued the policy of military reunification and brought Cambodia and other lost territories back into vassal status. He also gathered whatever evidence survived from Ayutthaya to re-establish court rituals and to set down comprehensive law codes and authoritative texts for the Buddhist canon. Rama II (reigned 1809–24) paid much attention to arts and letters. The King himself was an outstanding poet and, together with a team of court poets, wrote definitive Thai versions of the Hindu *Rāmāyaṇa* and other classical works. Rama III (1824–51), during whose reign the British defeat of the Burmese kingdom (1826) ended the Thai–Burmese rivalry, was able to expand the Thai empire in the south and in the north. In the south he strengthened Thai control over vassal states in the Malay Peninsula; in the north he was able to absorb most of the territory of the Lao kingdom of Wiangchan (Vientiane) after he put down a revolt by the leader of that vassal state, Chao Anu. Rama III's armies also fought several campaigns in Cambodia against the Vietnamese, who were extending their power into Cambodian lands during the early 19th century. These campaigns ended in 1845, and negotiations that followed led to an agreement that Cambodia should be a tributary state to both Thailand and Vietnam.

The early Chakkri kings

Although restoration of Ayutthayan society was a prime goal during the early Bangkok Period, there were differences between Ayutthaya and Bangkok. For one thing, restoration is conscious traditionalism, which is not quite the same as tradition itself. For another, the restoration policy necessarily led to choices, choices that the Thai may have presumed were made on the basis of authority but in fact were often made on the basis of utility. The reform of the law code in 1805, for example, began after the King discovered in a contested divorce case that the law was not just. In the traditional Thai view, law is of divine origin; it is immutable, and the role of government is not to enact law but to administer it. An unjust law, then, could only be explained as a false law. The reform of 1805 was therefore seen as a work of removing falsifications, although in fact it was a work of reformation.

Some basic social changes in the early Bangkok Period seem also to have been introduced in order to prevent the recurrence of the internal weaknesses and political factionalism that had contributed to Ayutthaya's downfall. Labour-service requirements on freemen were reduced, and payment of obligations in money rather than services was encouraged. These moves can be seen as an attempt by the monarchy to focus greater strength in the royal house, to bring more of the population under the patronage of the king rather than that of the princes.

Other changes in the early Bangkok Period came from the outside and reflect general changes in the Asian scene: the growth of commerce, the great increase in Chinese migration, and the revival of European interest in eastern Asia. In the late 18th and early 19th centuries, trade, primarily with China, seems to have undergone rapid expansion, thanks in part to the growth in numbers of Chinese immigrants acting as merchants and entrepreneurs. The principal Thai export item in the early 19th century was sugar, a new industry that began because of Chinese enterprise.

Chinese immigration assumed the proportions of a flood. By the mid-19th century, approximately half of Bangkok's estimated population of 400,000 were Chinese; these newcomers greatly increased commercial activity in Thailand and came to control much of the country's internal trade.

Revival of Western interest in eastern Asia, which at the start was primarily British interest in China, brought Western traders and diplomats to "rediscover" Thailand in the early 19th century. The Westerners were politely received, and the Thai agreed to sign limited treaties (with

Britain in 1826 and the United States in 1833), but the Thai remained suspicious of Western nations and relations with the West were kept to a minimum.

The acceleration of Western demands for free trade and diplomatic representation in Thailand—underlined by the British conquests in Burma, expansion in Malaya, and forced opening of China—led to a change in Thailand's foreign policy under King Mongkut (Rama IV). During his reign, which lasted from 1851 to 1868, Thailand signed treaties granting trade privileges to Britain (1855), the United States (1856), France (1856), and other Western states. These treaties held Thai taxation on imports and exports to a low level and permitted the establishment of foreign consulates with extraterritorial powers. They led to greatly expanded trade with the West, to development of commercialized rice farming in Thailand's Central Plain, and to a considerable expansion of foreign influences in the country.

The reign of King Mongkut is noted particularly for his enlightened appreciation of the requirements in foreign policy. The monarch realized that the Western countries had the power to enforce their will on him and decided to treat peaceably with them on the best terms possible. Concessions in trade were subsequently followed by concessions in territory: Thailand relinquished its sovereign rights in Cambodia to the French in 1867. Western influences on internal affairs, however, were limited to the acceptance of some innovations introduced by Western missionaries, including printing and vaccination, and the hiring of some Western military instructors, technicians, and teachers, including Anna Leonowens, whose romanticized report of Mongkut's reign was a popular book and in the 20th century became the basis of a musical comedy, *The King and I*. Perhaps more indicative of the monarch's attitude toward Western culture was his sponsorship of a reformed sect of Thai Buddhism, the Thammayut, that aimed at purification of Buddhist practice. This reform seems clearly to have been motivated by the desire to make Buddhism less vulnerable to the criticisms of Western missionaries. In fact, Thai Buddhists were little attracted to Christianity; even to the present, very few Thai have become Christians.

King Chulalongkorn and internal reform. King Mongkut was succeeded in 1868 by his fifteen-year-old son, King Chulalongkorn (Rama V: reigned 1868–1910), who, after a five-year period of regency, assumed full powers in 1873. Chulalongkorn continued his father's concessionistic policy toward the West, and territory was surrendered to the French in Laos and Cambodia in 1893, 1904, and 1907 and to the British in Malaya in 1909. The large concession of all Lao vassal territories east of the Mekong River to France in 1893 was made with extreme reluctance; the Thai attempted to enlist British support against the French, but the reluctance of the British to give support and the arrival of French gunboats in the Chao Phraya River with guns trained on the palace gave the Thai little choice but to concede. In 1896 the rival French and British imperial powers agreed to recognize the central part of Thailand as a neutral buffer zone that should remain free.

To the policy of accommodation to the West, Chulalongkorn added the first effective program of internal reform. There were enormous political difficulties in bringing these internal changes about, for many undercut the bases of power of influential men at court. The young King proceeded gradually and was aided by a few gifted and far-sighted leaders of "Young Siam," most notably the King's half-brother, Prince Damrong. The internal reforms accomplished during Chulalongkorn's reign included the creation of a highly centralized bureaucracy, the strengthening of government revenues, the drawing of vassals and outlying dependencies into the regular provincial administration, the abolition of slavery and labour-service requirements, the end of the formalized system of patron–client relationships, the beginning of new state services such as public education, and the introduction of technical improvements such as railway and telegraph lines. The first tentative move toward internal reform was undertaken in 1873 and was aimed at reducing inef-

ficiencies in revenue collection so that a larger share of government revenues would come directly to the King. Other measures, such as the creation of a Council of State and Privy Council in 1874, were designed to improve the political position of the king as compared with that of older conservative officials. In the mid-1880s a few Western-style ministries of government were created. These reforms were consolidated in 1892 when the government was completely reorganized into ministries with functional responsibilities for the interior, foreign affairs, justice, finance, war, public works, education, agriculture, the capital, the royal household, and royal services. The model for all these reforms was the West; their purpose was to provide Thailand with the internal strength to meet the challenge of the West. The policy of internal reform was successful: Thailand retained its independence; the country grew stronger; the monarchy, by promoting reform, retained its leadership.

Chulalongkorn's policies were continued by his sons who succeeded him: Vajiravudh (Rama VI: reigned 1910–25) and Prajadhipok (Rama VII: reigned 1925–35). King Vajiravudh opened Thailand's first university, which was named after his father; in 1921 he made primary education compulsory. Vajiravudh strengthened the Thai army and navy. He stressed military preparedness and created a paramilitary organization, the "Wild Tiger Corps," for civil servants. In 1917 he took Thailand into World War I on the side of the Allies, and at the war's end the Thai were able to begin the process of the complete removal of the "unequal provisions" pertaining to Western extraterritorial and fiscal rights that had first been imposed by the 1855 treaty. King Vajiravudh's major work was the promotion of Thai nationalism. He is best known in Thailand today for a great volume of literary works—poems, plays, and essays. And a large body of this work stressed the need for the Thai people to be united, to be committed to their nation, religion, and king.

King Prajadhipok reigned as absolute monarch for seven years; the most notable event during his reign was a coup d'etat in 1932 that brought an end to absolute monarchy in Thailand. Prajadhipok did not have the inclination to rule that his elder brother and father had had, and he turned many affairs of state over to his royal relatives. These relatives, believing government expenses were excessive, embarked on a policy of economizing. This policy, enlarged during the worldwide depression of the 1930s, adversely affected numbers of governmental officials, civil and military, and so contributed to the disaffection of younger members of the ruling elite.

Thailand since 1932. The coup d'etat of 1932 represented the joining together of several discontented elements of the educated ruling class. It was carried out by a group of young men, moved variously by unhappiness with Prajadhipok's retrenchment policies, with the domination of government by members of the royal family, with disappointment of personal hopes for position and power, with a monarchic institution that they considered anachronistic, and with the lack, as they saw it, of social and economic progress in Thailand. The intellectuals of the coup, led by a young lawyer who had been schooled in France, Pridi Phanomyong, made plans for a constitutional regime that would build a democracy in Thailand and inaugurate far-reaching social and economic reforms.

The bloodless coup, carried out on June 24, 1932, succeeded in seizing control of the army, imprisoning the royal officials, and winning the King's acceptance of a new constitutional regime.

The disparate elements comprising the coup party soon broke up into factions in the new government. The principal factions were the conservative military leaders, on the one hand, and the more radical civilians, on the other, the latter led by Pridi Phanomyong. When it appeared that the assembly, composed of coup members, would accept a socialistic economic plan presented by Pridi Phanomyong, the King dissolved the assembly. Fear that the King would retain control of the government led the coup military leaders to force the reconstitution of the assembly, now sympathetic to the military. This was followed by an attempted royalist counter coup. By the end of 1933, when the dust had settled, the new Thai constitutional regime was under the control of the conservative military faction, and for the most part it has remained so ever since.

During the period from 1939 to 1941 the government, headed by Field Marshal P. Pibul Songgram, embarked on a strongly nationalistic policy that was chauvinist at home, irredentist and pro-Japanese abroad. Thailand's leaders, whose policy was always to promote Thai independence, appreciated the fact that the country was small and defenseless against a big power. In the 19th and early 20th centuries, when the major power was Britain, the Thai government had been pro-British; in 1941, with Japanese armies at the Cambodian border, the Thai government saw no alternative but to become an ally of Japan.

At the end of World War II, governments headed or supported by the civilian leader, Pridi Phanomyong, came to power. These governments, in effect supported by the Allied Powers, lasted for two years. The civilian governments were faced by problems created by the war, corruption, and the death by gunshot in 1946 of the young king Ananda Mahidol (Rama VIII), who had succeeded Prajadhipok after his abdication in 1935. Late in 1947 the army, sensing that Allied interest in Thai internal affairs had declined, ousted the civilian government, accusing its leaders of regicide.

During the 1950s and '60s, there were disputes within the military, some attempted coups, some changes in leadership, but the essential fact of military dominance at the top remained unchanged. For nine years, from 1948 to 1957, the Thai premier was Pibul Songgram, who played the role of arbiter of competing military factions. By 1957 the army faction led by Field Marshal Sarit Thanarat had gained predominance of power, and it seized control of the government. Sarit assumed the position of head of state in 1958, and, to underline his intention of ruling without interference, he abolished the constitution and dispensed with the formality of elections. After Sarit's death in 1963, his successor as commander in chief, Field Marshal Thanom Kittikachorn, assumed the premiership. In 1968 a new constitution was inaugurated, and in 1969 a partly elected assembly was reconstituted.

Governments in Thailand in recent years have followed a pro-American and anti-Communist foreign policy, sending troops to fight on the U.S. side in both Korea and Vietnam, and allowing the U.S. to maintain military bases in Thailand.

BIBLIOGRAPHY. General histories include: W.A.R. WOOD, *A History of Siam*, 2nd ed. (1933), essentially a chronicle of reigns; and PRINCE CHULA CHAKRABONGSE, *Lords of Life* (1960), a sympathetic account stressing the Bangkok period. A general account of the Chinese minority is G.W. SKINNER, *Chinese Society in Thailand: An Analytical History* (1957). A brief survey of Buddhist developments is PRINCE DHANI NIVAT, *A History of Buddhism in Siam* (1965). On the Ayutthaya period, see E.W. HUTCHINSON, *Adventurers in Siam in the Seventeenth Century* (1940); and H.G. QUARITCH WALES, *Ancient Siamese Government and Administration* (1965). The early Bangkok period is discussed in KLAUS WENK, *The Restoration of Thailand under Rama I, 1782–1809* (1968); WALTER F. VELLA, *Siam under Rama III, 1824–1851* (1957); and AKIN RABIBHADANA, *The Organization of Thai Society in the Early Bangkok Period, 1782–1873* (1969). For developments that followed the opening of the country to the West, see ABBOT LOW MOFFAT, *Mongkut: The King of Siam* (1961); WALTER F. VELLA, *The Impact of the West on Government in Thailand* (1955); JAMES C. INGRAM, *Economic Change in Thailand Since 1850* (1955); and DAVID K. WYATT, *The Politics of Reform in Thailand: Education in the Reign of King Chulalongkorn* (1969).

(W.F.V.)

Sibelius, Jean

Occupying a special position not only in the music of Finland and Scandinavia but in the development of the symphony, Jean Sibelius possessed the most powerful musical personality to have emerged in any of the Scandinavian countries, and his seven symphonies show an exceptional mastery of form. Two themes run through his art: an overpowering love of nature and of the northern

Sibelius, photograph by Karsh, 1949.
© Karsh

landscape, and a preoccupation with myth, in particular the mythology enshrined in the Finnish national epic, the *Kalevala*.

Born in Hämeenlinna, Finland, on December 8, 1865, Sibelius early showed a talent both for the violin and for composition. After studying in Helsinki, he went abroad to Berlin in 1889 and to Vienna the following year. The first performance of his *Kullervo Symphony*, Opus 7 (completed, 1892), established him as the leading Finnish composer of his generation, a position consolidated by the *Four Legends*, Opus 22 (one of which is the famous "Swan of Tuonela"), and by patriotic works such as *Karelia*, Opus 11, and *Finlandia*, Opus 26, all written during the 1890s. A measure of his success is the fact that the Finnish Senate voted him a small life pension in 1897, before he had composed his *Symphony No. 1 in E Minor*, Opus 39 (1899). The 1890s show him developing as a nationalist composer, working within the Romantic musical tradition and responding positively to the influence of Tchaikovsky. After the *Symphony No. 2 in D Major*, Opus 43 (1901), and the *Violin Concerto in D Minor*, Opus 47 (1903, revised in 1905), there is an undoubted change in his style prompted by discontent with the musical language of post-Romanticism and the development of a stronger sense of classical discipline. The year 1900 marked the beginning of his international career. Championed by conductors, such as his countryman Robert Kajanus, and by several noted European musicians of the day, as well as by such important critics as Rosa Newmarch and Ernest Newman, Sibelius' music gradually won acceptance abroad.

Early Romantic works

He made numerous visits to the rest of Europe before World War I and also went in 1914 to the United States, for which country he had written *The Oceanides* (*Aallottaret*), Opus 73 (1914), one of his masterly tone poems. Earlier, in 1909, he was operated on for throat cancer; this experience may account for the greater austerity and depth of the *Symphony No. 4 in A Minor*, Opus 63 (1911), as well as for the seriousness and concentration of his other music of this period, *The Bard*, Opus 64 (1913), and *Luonnotar*, Opus 70 (1913). During World War I he wrote many lighter instrumental pieces in the hope of repeating the enormous success of *Valse triste*, Opus 44 (1903), the rights to which he had sold outright and which had made his publishers a fortune.

His career during the years up to 1926 is a record of ceaseless creative activity, but after the *Symphony No. 7 in C Major*, Opus 105 (1924), *Tapiola*, Opus 112 (1925), and *The Tempest*, Opus 109 (1926), he virtually ceased composing, though promises of an eighth symphony were made to Serge Koussevitzky, Sir Thomas Beecham, and other major conductors. In the 1930s Sibelius' popularity soared to unprecedented heights in England, and the great claims made on his behalf by British musicologist Cecil Gray and other critics doubtless had an

Personality

inhibiting effect on a composer who was highly self-critical and given to self-doubt. He lived in quiet retirement until his death from a cerebral hemorrhage at the age of 91, on September 20, 1957, at his home in Järvenpää.

As a man Sibelius was far more complex than has been generally supposed, and, although his life was outwardly uneventful, he lived it to the full. He was sensitive to criticism, and his keen self-criticism was responsible for the suppression of the early quartet and the *Kullervo Symphony* as well as the destruction of the *Symphony No. 8*, which he had certainly completed by 1929. He was generous by nature and scarcely recorded an unkind word about his contemporaries. His practical circumstances were not comfortable until the 1920s, although he loved travel almost as much as he did his native Finland and had a love of good wine and cigars.

Each of his symphonies is totally fresh in its approach to structure: one cannot distill from the earlier symphonies any set of rules that can be applied to his later works. It was equally difficult to foresee, from the vantage point of one symphony, the character of the next. The heroism of the *Symphony No. 5 in E Flat Major*, Opus 82 (1915, revised 1916, 1919), is far removed from the quietism of the *Symphony No. 6 in D Minor*, Opus 104 (1923), while the *Seventh Symphony*, a one-movement structure of remarkable unity, seems to explore the epic world of man pitting himself against nature. All show a seemingly infinite capacity for evolving new material from simple germinal ideas.

Sibelius' contributions to the development of the symphonic poem are no less significant. They reveal a power to encompass the imaginative world of Finnish mythology within the strongest formal framework. *Pohjola's Daughter*, Opus 49 (1906), is as perfect an example of the narrative tone poem as any of those written by his German contemporary Richard Strauss, yet it is totally satisfying as pure music to the listener ignorant of its program. *Tapiola* is, however, his most original and awe-inspiring tone poem, for it is here that his vision is most intense. Sibelius, like Hector Berlioz in 19th-century France or Gustav Mahler somewhat later in Austria, was one of the great masters of the orchestra: each line seems conceived directly in terms of the instrumental timbre (tone colour) in which it is cast. So personal is his idiom in *Tapiola* that it is not susceptible of imitation. Sibelius composed prolifically in the smaller orchestral forms, though with varying degrees of success. His incidental music to his contemporary Maurice Maeterlinck's Symbolist drama *Pelléas et Mélisande* or to Shakespeare's *The Tempest* shows with what skill he could communicate atmosphere with so few strokes and the minimum of orchestral means. He composed about 100 songs, mostly to Swedish texts, some of great lyrical power. Though he wrote a great deal of chamber music in his youth, he composed only one quartet in maturity, *Voces intimae*, Opus 56 (1909), a work that reaffirms the depth of his classical sympathies as much as it demonstrates his mastery of the medium.

MAJOR WORKS
Orchestral music

SYMPHONIES: Eight symphonies: *Kullervo Symphony*, Op. 7 (1892); *No. 1 in E Minor*, op. 39 (completed, 1899); *No. 2 in D Major*, op. 43 (1901); *No. 3 in C Major*, op. 52 (1907); *No. 4 in A Minor*, op. 63 (1911); *No. 5 in E Flat Major*, op. 82 (1915, rev. 1916, 1919); *No. 6 in D Minor*, op. 104 (1923); *No. 7 in C Major*, op. 105 (1924); *No. 8* (destroyed).
SYMPHONIC TONE POEMS: *En Saga*, op. 9 (1892); "The Swan of Tuonela," No. 3 of *Four Legends*, op. 22 (1893); *Finlandia*, op. 26 (1899, rev. 1900); *Pohjola's Daughter*, op. 49 (1906); *The Bard*, op. 64 (1913); *Tapiola*, op. 112 (1925).
INCIDENTAL MUSIC: *Pelléas et Mélisande*, op. 46 (1905); *The Tempest*, op. 109 (1926).
CONCERTOS: *Violin Concerto in D Minor*, op. 47 (1903, rev. 1905).

Chamber music

String quartet in D Minor (*Voces intimae*), op. 56 (1909); various works for violin and piano.

Piano music

Various sets of *Pieces*; *Sonata in F Major*, op. 12 (1893).

Vocal music

Luonnotar, tone poem for soprano and orchestra, op. 70 (1913); about 100 songs, including *Höstkväll* (*Autumn Evening*, op. 38, no. 1, 1903); *Svarta Rosor* (*Black Roses*, op. 36, no. 1, 1899); *Våren flyktar hastigt* (*Spring Flies Speedily*, op. 13, no. 4, 1891); *Var det en dröm?* (*Was It a Dream?*, op. 37, no. 4, 1902); *Flickan kom ifrån sin älsklings möte* (*The Maid Came from Her Lover's Tryst*, op. 37, no. 5, 1901).

BIBLIOGRAPHY. L. SOLANTERA (comp.), *The Works of Jean Sibelius* (1955); and F. BLUM, *Jean Sibelius: An International Bibliography on the Occasion of the Centennial Celebrations* (1965), are two bibliographies on the composer. Considerable information may also be found in the Sibelius-museum, Turku, and in the Sibelius family archives. ERIK TAWASTSTJERNA, *Sibelius* (1968), is the first of three volumes (in Finnish, soon to be translated into English) based on hitherto unpublished material, correspondence, and diaries; it is likely to remain the definitive study of the composer. See also KARL EKMAN, *Jean Sibelius, en konstnärs liv och personlighet* (1935; Eng. trans., *Jean Sibelius: The Life and Personality of an Artist*, 1935; and *Jean Sibelius: His Life and Personality*, 1936), the first comprehensive study of the composer by a Finn; CECIL GRAY, *Sibelius: The Symphonies* (1931), the most influential study of Sibelius in the 1930s and 1940s; ROBERT LAYTON, *Sibelius* (1965), a succinct biographical and critical study; SIMON PARMET, *Sibelius symfonier* (1955; Eng. trans., *The Symphonies of Sibelius*, 1959), a study written from a conductor's standpoint; and GERALD ABRAHAM (ed.), *Sibelius: A Symposium* (1947), predominantly critical and unfailingly illuminating.

(R.Lay.)

Siberian Cultures

Siberia is an immense land area running from the Urals on the west to the Sea of Japan and the Pacific on the east, and from the steppes of Kazakhstan and Outer Mongolia on the south to the Arctic Ocean on the north. It presents a variety of climates and natural habitats but falls into three major zones: a fringe of arid or semi-arid steppe on the south; a wide forested belt in the middle; and, along the northern edge, a band of tundra subject to permafrost and with numerous tidal rivers and lakes.

PEOPLES AND LANGUAGES

Before the large-scale influx of Europeans in the mid-17th century, Siberia was inhabited by a large number of ethnic groups, most of them very small. The culture of these peoples was adapted to the natural and climatic conditions of the three zones mentioned above. In the south were pastoral nomads with herds of sheep and horses. In the forest areas lived hunters and gatherers of wild foods. Most of the latter groups kept some reindeer of a large and sturdy breed for purposes of transport and occasionally milked them but consumed them as food only in case of absolute necessity. The nomads of the northern tundra kept fairly large herds of domestic reindeer, which provided them with their principal means of sustenance and which they drove along fixed routes according to the season. Other parts of the tundra were inhabited by still more primitive nomadic groups who hunted wild reindeer and fished. Finally, the shores of the Arctic Ocean and of the Sea of Okhotsk were settled by groups of maritime hunters living off whales, walruses, and seals.

Agriculture was unknown in Siberia until the beginning of massive Russian colonization in the mid-17th century, and it is even now possible only on the West Siberian plain (Omskaya, Tomskaya, Kemerovskaya, and Novosibirskaya *oblasti* [regions]) as well as in a relatively few favoured locations in other places—the Khabarovsky and Primorsky (Maritime) *kraya* (territories), for example. Animal husbandry—dairy farming, beef cattle, and the raising of the Siberian stag, or maral, for meat—is more widely distributed. The Yakut, who are the largest indigenous ethnic group, are raisers of cattle and horses; they represent an incursion of Central Asian pastoral nomads into the northern Siberian environment.

The indigenous population of Siberia before the coming of Europeans was divided into a large number of usually small ethnic groups, the boundaries between which shifted over time and were often arbitrary. The important social unit under Siberian conditions was probably not the tribe but the clan. Instances are known in which members of the same clan belonged to two or even three different tribes but considered themselves bound to each other by clan obligations in respect of marriage and mutual aid. The Siberian ethnic groups belong to a number of different linguistic stocks, the most important of which are: Turkic (Yakut, Siberian Tatars, and a number of small groups along the southern fringe); Tunguso-Manchurian (the numerous and widely scattered groups of Tungus [Evenki] and Evens [Lamuts]); Finno-Ugric (Khanty [Ostyaks], Mansi [Voguls]); Mongolic (Buryats); and the so-called Paleosiberian family (Koryaki, Yukaghiry, Gilyaki [Nivkhi], and some others) consisting of a number of languages that do not fit elsewhere but whose interrelationship has yet to be demonstrated. The shifting and fluid nature of ethnic boundaries resulted in parts of one tribe often engaging in types of economic activity and assuming other cultural patterns characteristic of another tribe. Hence the older ethnographic sources frequently speak of "Yukaghirized Tungus" or the like. Such assimilated groups often acquired a different name from either the main body of their former tribe or from the one to which they were assimilated.

CULTURAL PATTERNS

Social organization. Except for the Yakut, who are considered by Soviet scholars to have been in a stage of incipient feudalism at the time of the first intensive European contact, the Siberian peoples were without exception small, extremely primitive, and loosely organized. The major organizational unit over large parts of the year was the camp group, similar in constitution to the horde among the Australian Aborigines in that it consisted of a core of members of one descent group, with the addition of women from other groups and some male hangers-on. The overall kinship pattern was patrilineal, but Russian and Soviet scholars have identified numerous phenomena that, in their opinion, show the previous existence of a matrilineal pattern. These phenomena include not only the kinship terminology itself but also important elements in the religion, such as the fact that the shaman wore modified female dress and had in certain respects a hermaphrodite personality. The camp group cooperated in economic activity on a regular basis and controlled the important economic resources. The concept of private property in the Western sense was lacking, except among the Yakut and in regard to domestic reindeer.

Social stratification was rudimentary, with one significant exception. For administrative convenience, the Russian authorities appointed certain members of the local ethnic groups to represent these groups in dealings with the Russians. These individuals, referred to in the Russian sources as "princelings," gained opportunities for enrichment and came to form a kind of incipient nobility. In addition, Soviet scholars point to the existence, just prior to the Revolution, of individuals who controlled large herds of reindeer and who could call upon the services of their poorer fellow clansmen—that is, people who were on their way to becoming feudal lords. It is difficult to determine from the sources whether this development was the result of a natural evolution or was due entirely to Russian contact.

As among primitive peoples, the nuclear family (parents and children) among the Siberian tribes was not clearly separated out in its economic and child-rearing functions from the larger kin group. Children were introduced early to economic activities and were taught the basic skills by older relatives. The same skills were also inculcated by special games and contests, some of which are still being used for the same purposes. Such games were a common feature of the rites of passage for both boys and girls. The professions of shaman and blacksmith, which were the only separate professions among most Siberian groups, were acquired by apprenticeship to older practitioners, but these professions called in addition for evidence of special aptitude and election on the part of the apprentice.

Kinship patterns (margin)

Technology and economy. The technology and applied art of the Siberian peoples relied heavily on such materials as horn, mammoth ivory, wood, and the skins of birds, mammals, and fish. The latter were processed in various ways and either tailored into garments or used whole as containers. Iron was obtained by trade with groups close to the sources of supply in the south, or with the Russians. The smelting of iron from ore was unknown, but some groups used a small portable forge to produce such items as smoking pipes (from old gun barrels), stands for storing women's jewelry, and various pieces of harness. The standard weapons before the introduction of firearms were the bow and arrow and barbed spear with a head of mammoth or walrus ivory. The bow in common use was compound, since the wood available was not in sufficiently large pieces to permit the making of a simple bow. Fire was made by the bow-drill method, in which a shaft was spun in a socket by means of tightly wound cords, friction igniting the tinder. In addition to the skin containers mentioned above, many Siberian groups made vessels of wood or birch bark decorated with natural colouring in intricate patterns. Pots for cooking were made of metal and were bought from the Russians. The same was true of small griddles, which were used for preparing unflavoured pancakes of wheat flour; these were considered a delicacy. Clothing was made of cured skins with or without the fur and was elaborately decorated. In certain areas capes and boots were made from fishskin, processed so as to be waterproof. Skins were also used to cover boats and to make bags for clothing and small pieces of equipment.

Aboriginal hunting methods included the use of nets made out of rawhide strips in which reindeer became tangled, to be dispatched with spears. Another favourite device of the reindeer hunter was a movable blind behind which a hunter on skis concealed himself, shooting through a small hole. Nets of rawhide, gut, or string were used for fishing, along with hooks and lines similar to those used by the European peoples.

Means of transport were adapted to the tundra or forest environments: sleds drawn by dog teams, with runners of walrus ivory or metal, sleighs drawn by reindeer, skis, snowshoes, and riding reindeer. In the summer, boats, either of birch bark or covered with skins, were important.

Dwellings were generally portable and made of poles and skins, or (among the more southerly groups) of poles covered with brush and a layer of sod. These latter dwellings were of semi-dugout form. A distinctive type of house was the *balagan,* constructed on runners and moved by means of reindeer. Finally, the maritime sea mammal hunters had more or less permanent dwellings the structures of which were supported on the rib bones of whales. Such houses are very ancient, going back to Paleolithic times.

Types of dwellings (margin)

With the gradual exploration and conquest of Siberian territory by the Russians, various changes took place in the economy of the native peoples. The introduction of firearms, steel spring traps, metal utensils, and the like, led to more efficient hunting and fishing technology. The native peoples were drawn into the ambit of the fur trade and were subject to a special tax, first in furs and later in money. The effect of European contact at this stage, however, was limited and did not affect the basis of the subsistence economy. Other than hunting equipment and supplies needed for the fur trade, only luxury goods—vodka, tobacco, cloth, salt, sugar, tea, and flour in very small quantities—reached the native inhabitants through the trade network.

Religious belief and practice. The religious system of the Siberian peoples was firmly anchored to their subsistence activities. The central figure of their religious life, at least as far as the society as a whole was concerned, was the shaman, who acted as intermediary between the natural and supernatural worlds. The shaman was at once a physician, a counsellor of the community in regard to subsistence activities, and a defender of it by magical means against the attacks of other groups. The shamanistic ritual was embellished with the full skills of the shaman in poetry, song, ventriloquism, and magic. The ritual took the form of a dramatic representation of the shaman's journey to the world of the spirits and his return.

The mythical world of the Siberian peoples was conceived of as being on three levels, which were connected either by a "world tree" or by a river, or both (the parallel with ancient Norse mythology is striking). The position of shaman was acquired through a "call," usually during adolescence, that was manifested through a peculiar illness from which the victim could only recover by agreeing to assume the role of shaman. Certain characteristics of a shaman—his hermaphrodite personality, for example, and the fact that he was thought to have organs other than the natural ones implanted in his body —have close parallels among other primitive peoples in widely scattered parts of the world and even in the residual religious phenomena found in more complex societies.

Besides the rites and ceremonies performed by the shaman on behalf of the group at large or of individuals, there were also private ceremonies conducted by individuals in connection with hunting and fishing activities or with important milestones in personal life. On such occasions, the shaman was often not present—perhaps because his participation would have involved an additional expense.

Artistic expression.   The folklore of the Siberian peoples includes an origin myth, shamanistic songs, proverbs, and some rudimentary epics. Many groups have a rich tradition of graphic art, in terms both of sculpture in the round and incised drawing on mammoth or walrus ivory. The assortment of musical instruments is meagre: besides the drum (or more accurately tambourine) used by the shaman and as an accompaniment for dancing, there are only a small jew's harp of wood and metal and a few bone and reed pipes. Some of the Far Eastern peoples have primitive stringed instruments, the idea of which was apparently borrowed from the Chinese people.

Early Russian influence

Russian cultural influence (apart from the mere availability of Western trade goods) was present in various places but was neither universal nor profound. On the southern fringes of the Siberian area—on the Altai upland and in the vicinity of Lake Baikal—there were considerable settlements of Russian peasants, and the native population had begun to acquire agricultural skills. Certain groups—some of them, like the Yakut, fairly large —had been nominally Christianized, and a few individuals attended schools sponsored by the Russian Orthodox Church. Western medicine was available in a few places, but the mortality rate remained extremely high, especially among children. A factor the importance of which was certainly considerable was the tsarist government's policy of exiling political dissidents to remote areas. This affected the type of Russians with whom the native population in many places came into contact. In addition, there were long-established Russian peasant societies in certain parts of Siberia, in many cases the descendants of exiled religious dissidents. Such people, known as Sibiryaks or "local Russians," have a culture and an outlook differing markedly from those of the people of European Russia. Physical and cultural hybridization with the native population has given rise to a wide range of intermediate groups, some of which still retain their own ethnic identity.

THE SIBERIAN PEOPLES TODAY

After the Revolution of 1917, the Soviet government adopted in principle the goal of comprehensive economic and social development of the Siberian area. Approximately the first 15 years subsequent to the Revolution were devoted chiefly to exploration and planning, and the area was exempted from the requirements of the first five-year plan for the development of the Soviet national economy. Considerable progress was made in education and public health, but these measures were of limited effectiveness among the peoples whose way of life had been and remained nomadic. Institutions such as the Northern Division of the Leningrad Institute of Living Eastern Languages (established in 1926 and later transformed into the Institute of the Peoples of the North), however, performed an important function, despite the very small numbers of persons involved, in training the first professional cadres of physicians, paramedical workers, and teachers for the northern peoples.

During the 1920s and early 1930s, the languages of a number of small Siberian peoples were reduced to writing for the first time, and elementary school books were published in these languages. In connection with this and other practical tasks, a considerable amount of ethnographic research was undertaken. The publication of books in the languages of some very small groups, and instruction in these languages in the elementary schools, were later abandoned as being uneconomical, or as working counter to the general policy goal of integration of the population of the Soviet Union into a single and unified whole.

Until the end of World War II, however, the basic economic patterns of Siberian native life remained largely unchanged. Collectivization of the hunting, fishing, and reindeer economies (agriculture had been collectivized in the rest of the country during the early 1930s) was hardly even attempted until the end of World War II in most areas, or until the early 1950s in the more remote places. Small cooperative production units of a traditional type, using the native technology and often based on kinship groups, had existed up to that time but represented no sharp break with the pre-Revolutionary situation.

The Soviet policy and practice with regard to the peoples of the Siberian North represent a unique experiment in the integration of small, primitive, formerly tribal groups into a complex modern industrial state. The severity of the climate and the former backwardness of the people, both in a social and a technological sense, are such stubborn factors in the story of cultural change that no serious student of the Soviet Union can fail to admire what has been achieved, notwithstanding serious shortcomings in the planning and implementation of government policy.

Indigenous population and ethnic affiliation

In surveying the present situation, a few statistics are in order. According to 1970 census data, there are 151,000 indigenous peoples of the North, Siberia, and the Far East (as against 130,000 in 1959). Native language may be used as an index of ethnic affiliation: in 1970, 67.4 percent of these peoples considered the language of their nationality to be their native language (75.9 percent in 1959). In addition, 52.5 percent were fluent in Russian, and 7.1 percent were fluent in the language of another nationality. There are 26 ethnic groups, all increasing in size, a change from the pre-Revolutionary situation in which most were dying out. There has been a consistent attempt throughout the Soviet period to foster ethnic awareness among the Siberian peoples, even, in some cases, when the awareness had to be created. "National in form, socialist in content" was the slogan created by Soviet premier Joseph Stalin to describe the kind of culture the regime thought appropriate for the Soviet system, and even though Stalin has been discredited, the idea still remains.

Particularly since World War II, the Siberian peoples have been developing under conditions of unprecedented industrialization, almost all of it with labour and tools imported from European Russia. The total population of the Soviet North has risen to 3,000,000. Well into the 1960s, however, the small peoples of the North were predominantly rural, and even urban residency was likely to mean that the family had moved into a large fishing cooperative, or that many young people were away attending school, where for the most part they became doctors, teachers, and cultural or government workers. In some instances the large-scale influx of Europeans has irreparably damaged the traditional way of life of the Siberian peoples, not least because educated young people are unwilling and often physically unable by training or capacities to carry on the occupations of their forefathers. Technological means exist by which reindeer can be herded and waters fished more easily, but the skill to operate and maintain the equipment must be acquired, not, as previously, within the family group but in schools of a radically different type. Change of this type has been slow in coming to the North but will increase in proportion to capital investment in the area.

Soviet policy for the peoples of the Siberian North, particularly with respect to education, faces a dilemma that in the long run is inescapable. This dilemma can be baldly stated as follows: to dismantle the traditional economy, turn the small peoples into an industrial labour force, and supply the North completely from the outside; or to develop the traditional economy and pursue the industrialization of the North exclusively with an imported labour force. No clear choice has yet been made between these two alternatives, and the result is that the educational system is ill-adapted to either one. It goes without saying that if the first alternative is chosen, there will soon be little left of the traditional culture of the small Siberian peoples, and the slogans that have been prevalent up to now will lose their meaning.

Which elements of native Siberian culture can be expected to survive industrialization, urbanization, and the changes in status which accompany them? Certain aspects of material culture will certainly persist for many years to come—native clothing, for example, which is warmer than present synthetics and more readily available. Kinship ties will continue to be important, although the increasing number of mixed marriages may alter the traditional patterns. Other elements of the native culture will have to be nurtured, perhaps artificially. In 1970, for example, there was the premiere of the first Kamchadal (Itelmen) ballet, *Emem Kutkh*, based on a Kamchadal legend of a battle between good and evil and staged in Petropavlovsk-Kamchatsky; the ballet was subsequently sent on tour to the Mongolian People's Republic. The Kamchatka Kamchadals numbered 1,300 by the 1970 census. It should be noted that aside from the ballet's value as an example of Soviet cultural policy, the theme itself is universal enough to appeal to a wide variety of people. Ideally, the unique culture of the Siberian peoples will not be lost but will blend with and enrich Soviet culture as a whole.

BIBLIOGRAPHY. Detailed discussions of Soviet development policy in the Far North, its ethnographic background, and sociological effects may be found in STEPHEN P. and ETHEL DUNN, "The Transformation of Economy and Culture in the Soviet North," *Arctic Anthropology*, 1:1–28 (1963); ETHEL DUNN, "Educating the Small Peoples of the Soviet North: Further Thoughts on the Limits of Culture Change," and "Education and the Native Intelligentsia in the Soviet North: The Limits of Culture Change," *ibid.*, 5:1–31 (1968), *ibid.*, 6:112–122 (1970). V.I. BOIKO, "Direction and Motivations of Potential Migration of Peoples of the Lower Amur," *Soviet Sociology*, 9:567–578 (1971), provides data on urbanization among small peoples of the Far East. TERENCE ARMSTRONG, *Russian Settlement in the North* (1965) and "The Administration of Northern Peoples: The USSR," in RONALD ST. J. MACDONALD (ed.), *The Arctic Frontier*, pp. 57–88 (1966), are historical and political studies by a Canadian scholar, one of the few Westerners dealing with technological development in the Soviet North; V. IANOVSKII, "Man in the North," *Soviet Sociology*, 7:16–26 (1969), gives interesting impressions of "the northern experience" by a prominent Soviet journalist. I.S. GURVICH, "Directions to be Taken in the Further Reorganization of the Economy and Culture of the Peoples of the North," *Soviet Anthropology and Archeology*, 1:22–30 (1962), provides an interesting and important discussion of technical problems and limitations of culture change for northern peoples. V. DIOSZEGI (ed.), *Glaubenswelt und Folklore der sibirischen Völker* (1963; Eng. trans., *Popular Beliefs and Folklore Tradition in Siberia*, 1968), gives interesting data on traditional Siberian ethnography, especially religion and magic, in relation to similar phenomena among other peoples. M.G LEVIN and L.P. POTAPOV (eds.), *The Peoples of Siberia* (1964; orig. pub. in Russian, 1956), is a semi-popular Soviet book providing detailed information on traditional Siberian culture and economy, with brief sections on modern conditions. W. BOGORAZ, *The Eskimo of Siberia* (1913) and *The Chukchee*, 3 pt. (1904–09), are classic ethnographies of small Siberian groups, reflecting mainly the situation before intensive Russian contact. H.N. MICHAEL (ed.), *Studies in Siberian Shamanism* (1963), contains translations from Soviet literature and gives data on traditional Siberian ethnography, particularly religion and magic, in relation to similar phenomena occurring among various other peoples.

(S.P.D./E.D.D.)

Sicily

The largest and one of the most densely populated islands in the Mediterranean Sea, Sicily (with several small adjacent islands) is an autonomous region of Italy. Its northern shore, site of the capital, Palermo, is lapped by the Tyrrhenian Sea; to the east it looks across the narrow Strait of Messina to the toe of the Italian peninsula; and it lies about 100 miles (160 kilometres) northeast of Tunisia, in North Africa. The 9,830 square miles (25,460 square kilometres), 9,927 square miles (25,710 square kilometres) with adjacent islands, of Sicily (Italian Sicilia) held a population of 4,582,000 in 1971. *(margin: Location and general character of the island)*

Sicily's strategic location at the centre of the Mediterranean has made the island a turbulent crossroads of history, a pawn of conquest and empire, and a melting pot for a dozen or more ethnic groups whose warriors or merchants sought its shores virtually since the dawn of recorded history. The island and its people have lived much by the sea, flourishing when the Mediterranean traffic was intense and stagnating when it waned. Only a few days' sailing time from the ancient civilizations of Greece and the Aegean, Sicily was at times the major western outpost of the high culture of those regions. Its land also lies open to climatic influences from all directions. In spite of these many forces that so often have reshaped its political and social life and of the economic depression that continues to plague it, Sicily has been able to establish one of the most distinct identities among the Italian regions, a distinctiveness that is guarded jealously by its inhabitants. (For information on related topics, see the articles ITALY; ITALY AND SICILY, HISTORY OF; and MEDITERRANEAN SEA.)

The natural and human landscape. *Surface features.* The landscape of Sicily is mainly one of mountains, sometimes reaching almost to the coasts, and of irregular coastal plains on which all the main cities are located. The present topography is the result of the fact that the rocks erode easily in a climate marked by intense exposure to the sun, persistent drought during the long summers, and the sea winds.

The mountains are continuations of the Apennines of the Italian peninsula and the Atlas Mountains of northwestern Africa, which are parts of the discontinuous Alpine–Himalayan mountain belt circling much of the Earth from Asia to southern Europe and northern Africa. In northeastern Sicily the Peloritani chain rises suddenly from the Strait of Messina and continues the landscape of the Calabrian Apennines of the mainland, though without the typical high plateaus. The higher reaches have little or no vegetation and are deeply scarred by currents that, at lower altitudes, produce frequent flash floods and sweep away both rubble and fertile sediments. Forests of chestnut, beech, or Mediterranean scrub climb above the cultivated lower slopes. Maximum altitudes are about 4,300 feet (1,300 metres). *(margin: The mountain chains)*

The Nebrodi and Le Madonie chains to the west are higher, reaching 5,900 and 6,600 feet, respectively. The forms are similar, though in Le Madonie they tend to be stark, standing out like great limestone massifs or peninsulas. Le Madonie is known for its underground drainage, which provides water to Palermo. Inland, the mountains gradually diminish in height toward the south, with great expanses of virtual tableland known for its sulfurous, desolate conditions; grasses and twisted olive trees dominate the landscape. The Iblei chain in the southeast is of volcanic origin and presents a refreshing scene of brightly coloured vegetation.

To the northeast of this chain, the great mass of Mt. Etna rises to 10,703 feet (3,263 metres), the highest point in Sicily which is a region of strong seismic activity. One of the world's most active volcanoes and the biggest in Europe, Mt. Etna covers half the province of Catania and rises above the provincial capital of that name. It is thought that this massive mountain was gradually built by extruded volcanic debris from beneath the sea to its present height. Luxuriant wild and cultivated trees and *(margin: Mt. Etna)*

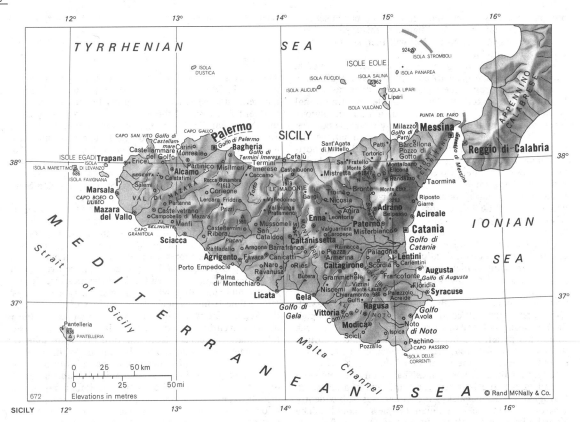

shrubs cover its sides wherever a cover of decomposed debris occurs. Underground water and springs are plentiful for the many vineyards and citrus orchards of the region.

Climate. Sicily's most notable climatic factors are its southern latitude, its insularity, its elevations decreasing from north to south, and the moderate atmospheric pressure characteristic of the Mediterranean. Latitude and the pattern of winds make it a sun-drenched island, and desert winds from Africa often scourge the southern and central regions during the May to October summers.

Summer temperatures often climb over 85° F (29° C), but the climate is even more influenced by the rainfall, which is irregular in quantity from year to year but regular in its uneven annual distribution, virtually all of it falling in late autumn and winter. Northwestern and central regions receive only about 25 inches (635 millimetres) a year; the south receives about 15 inches; Messina, in the northeast, receives about 39 inches. Much of the fall is lost through deforestation (less than 4 percent of the island is woodland) and the soil's resultant inability to hold the torrents from the mountains; and, though the amounts are similar to those on the Italian mainland at equivalent latitudes, the irregularity of the fall and its concentration in short downpours contributes significantly to the island's agricultural depression and rural poverty. Neither irrigation facilities nor discoveries of underground water have begun to counteract this natural blight.

Vegetation and animal life. Only on the higher slopes does the chestnut replace the laurel, perhaps the most characteristic Sicilian tree. Pines grow on Mt. Etna, on whose upper reaches grow the low, isolated shrubs and grasses of the Alpine zone. Of the cultivated plants, only the flowering ash is native; the olive, grape, almond, pomegranate, hazel, and other fruit and nut trees, however, date from antiquity. Arabs introduced the date palm and citrus trees, though the common orange is of 16th-century Chinese origin, and other species came a century later from the Americas. Of the few animal species, the invertebrates, birds, and fish outnumber mammals, though remains of vanished large mammals occasionally are encountered in caves. Overall, the animal population represents a transitional zone between Italy and Africa.

The people of Sicily. *Ethnic composition.* Sicily was already inhabited toward the end of the Pleistocene Epoch (more than 10,000 years ago), and throughout its history has received peoples of every coast on the Mediterranean. According to archaeologists, anthropologists, philologists, and historians, the peoples living there in the remotest times, the Sicani, were of Mediterranean origin. Some of the physical features of the present-day population may be traced to them: elongated heads, small stature, and dark pigmentation of the eyes and hair. Interbred with them were the Elimi, who left their mark mainly on the towns of Segesta, Erice, and Entella; they may have come in small numbers from neighbouring Africa.

Then the Siculi, a short-headed Eurasian people who spoke an Italic language akin to Latin, came down the peninsula from the central and eastern Alps; they seem to have infiltrated slowly and in small waves among these ancient Mediterranean peoples. The Siculi and Sicani seem to have formed the most homogeneous group of the island's population. But as early as the transition from the Bronze to the Iron Age, they appear to have been molested by Greek pirates, coinciding and in a sense competing with Etruscan pirates in the lower Tyrrhenian. Some pirate groups appear to have established themselves on the island, forcing the inhabitants to withdraw inland and fortify their new settlements. Later, between the 8th and 6th centuries BC, migrations from Greece seem to have been more frequent and of larger size. The new peoples —among them Ionians from Euboea and Samos, Aeolians and Achaeans from Boeotia, and Dorians from Corinth and other locations—had apparently left their homelands to settle on the island.

At more or less the same time, the Carthaginians, Semites from the North African coast, set up some of their trading posts along the western coast of Sicily. Some of the tyrants then welcomed exiles from the neighbouring continent and recruited labourers to cultivate the land and mercenaries to fight their battles from the Italian peninsula, Greece, Asia, and Africa. These new immigrants remained and merged with their predecessors, an example that was later followed by Romans, Vandals, Goths, and Byzantines, who came for reasons of war or conquest.

From Arabia, Egypt, Syria, and Mesopotamia came the

Diversity of ethnic stocks and physical types

Muslims, who took only 80 years to conquer Sicily, settling mainly in the northern regions, while the Berbers were more predominant in the south. Many Sicilian Christians converted to Islām. Around the year 1000 the Normans arrived and held the island for more than a century; then came the Swabians, who held it for three-quarters of a century. The tall stature, blond hair, blue eyes, and pink colouring of some present-day Sicilians may be traceable to them. The Aragonese also governed Sicily for more than a century.

By courtesy of the Italian Government Travel Office

The town of Taormina on the island of Sicily. Mt. Etna is in the background.

Demography.   The Sicilian population is the most urbanized of the provinces in southern Italy; yet it displays many characteristics of a rural population, a fact attributable primarily to a generally low standard of living. The greatest proportion live in the provinces of Palermo and Catania, and only a small fraction live outside the narrow coastal strip around the island. Migrants long have been driven from the interior not only by the barrenness but also by malaria and by the land-tenure system, *latifundium*, characterized by large estates ruling over great wheat-growing acreages. Contemporary statistics show marriages, live births, and infant mortality to be proportionately greater than throughout Italy as a whole, though overall death rates are lower. Births exceed deaths by about 13 percent.

The region's economy.   *Incomes.*   The per capita income of Sicilians is less than three-quarters of that for Italy as a whole. If only employed persons were accounted for, however, the disparity would be less, since, as in all poor regions, the number of dependents per employed worker is higher than in more affluent areas. Only the province of Syracuse approximates the national average, while Agrigento has less than one-half the average.

The tertiary sector of the economy—retailing and services—plus the civil service account for about one-half the island's income. Industry has gradually outstripped agriculture to contribute the greater proportion of the other one-half, especially in Palermo; only in Trapani and Agrigento is agricultural income greater. Much of this industry, moreover, is based on the processing of the products of farm, forest, fishery, and mine.

Components.   Agriculture employs about one-quarter of the labour force, and some 95 percent of Sicily's land area is given over to it and to forestry. One-quarter of this is sown in wheat, which does not require great fertility. In ancient Rome, Sicily was known as one of the breadbaskets of the republic and empire. Citrus fruits (including nine-tenths of Italy's entire lemon production) and vegetables, however, provide the largest part of agricultural exports to the peninsula and abroad. Dams, flood- and erosion-control measures, and irrigation canals are among the major projects begun to assist the farmer, but much remains to be done.

Among the more promising aspects of industry, which

Agri-
culture,
industry,
and energy
resources

employs about one-third of all workers, have been the discoveries of petroleum and the building of refineries to complement the plants producing chemicals, pharmaceuticals, and synthetics. These are in addition to the small-scale food- and sulfur-processing plants and apparel manufacturing. Mineral production also includes limestone, asphalt, and salt.

Virtually all of Sicily's energy is generated in thermal plants; hydro potentiality is nil. The three main ports—Palermo, Catania, and Messina—have extensive shipping facilities and are interconnected by single-track railways. Main highways between cities are adequate, but secondary roads are poor. Many interior communities are reachable only by track.

Governmental involvement.   Since World War II, the national government has given Sicily and other areas of southern Italy special funds to improve transportation facilities and other public works and to prepare them for industrial development. In its turn, the regional government took numerous steps to ease the location and capitalization of industry. Years of political instability and shortage of resources, however, have tended to impede even the legislated goals, and observers find it impossible to estimate when the generally backward economy of the region can be given a major stimulus.

Administration and social conditions.   *Structure of government.*   An Italian constitutional statute of 1948 made Sicily an autonomous region, divided into nine provinces with 379 communes. Government is parliamentary, with the president elected from among the members of the regional assembly. With the assembly's executive committee, he promulgates laws and may attend meetings of the Italian council of ministers and speak on Sicilian matters. He represents the federal government and is charged with maintaining order with the national police force. A Sicilian separatist movement won minority support after World War II, but faded in the 1950s.

The social milieu.   Life in much of the interior remains at a primitive level, with inadequate water supplies and sanitation, and rampant disease. Unemployment is chronic everywhere, except around the developing petroleum-producing and petroleum-processing centres.

The regional government exercises complete control of primary education, but the illiteracy rate remains twice that of Italy as a whole. The universities in Palermo, Messina, and Catania are required to maintain national standards. The well-stocked civil service provides a well-organized system of social services that are generally of low calibre. Good housing and medical services, even in the cities, tend to be in short supply as well.

A peculiar feature of the separateness of Sicilian life from that of mainland Italy is the persistence of the Mafia, an organization dating from the Middle Ages that gradually evolved into a paralegal criminal brotherhood. It gives certain parts of the island virtually a dual government, standard of conduct, and system of enforcement—one is the legitimate regime and the other a shadow but a pervasive social, economic, and political network maintaining its powers through violence. In recent years it has tended to move away from the rural areas, in which it was spawned, to urban Sicily, in which through its traditional code of silence and frequently violent settlement of disputes it directs its activities at legitimate businesses through extortion and terror.

Cultural life.   Sicily has made its contribution to Italian literature and art. The poets of the Sicilian school at the court of the emperor Frederick II were important in the development of Italian lyrical poetry in the vernacular early in the 13th century. The Byzantine and Norman architecture of the island with its splendid mosaic murals is celebrated. In the 15th century the great painter Antonella da Messina introduced the Flemish technique of oil painting to Italy.

In more recent times, in the realm of the "fine" arts, Palermo has its opera house and Catania its Bellini Theatre, named in honour of the island's major musical celebrity, the opera composer Vincenzo Bellini. In literature the influences of two Sicilians, the novelist Giovanni Verga and the playwright Luigi Pirandello, have pro-

foundly affected the shape of modern Italian literature
and have had great influence far beyond the shores of the
Mediterranean. In 1959 the Sicilian poet Salvatore Quasimodo was awarded the Nobel Prize for Literature.

Sicily has been called the cradle of the Italian popular
song. Various kinds of song exist locally: love songs are
the most numerous, followed by the work songs of such
occupations as fishing (the *mattanza*, or tuna fishing
song) and by the sung accompaniments to the many
children's games. The songs of the beggars and the musical cries of the street vendors are still heard, though they,
like much traditional culture, are disappearing under the
homogenizing influence of radio and television and of
modern life in general.

Silicy has strong traditions of folk art. The elaborately
painted carts of the peasants, which are features of the
provinces of Catania and Palermo, depict on their sideboards scenes of combat between the Christian knights
and the Saracens. Though no extant carts predate the
19th century, their art may commemorate the era of
Sicilian prosperity under the Norman kings and the
themes of chivalric quest popular in the epic poetry of
that time. Similar themes run through many of the puppet dramas, which remain popular on the island. Silversmiths' and goldsmiths' work, to be seen especially in Palermo, and peasant filigree settings for gems are of the
most intricate refinement, and Sicilian embroidery has an
uninterrupted tradition many centuries old.

Popular religious festivals make up colourful occasions
for the sun-bleached land. The processions of triumphal
cars of the feasts celebrating St. Rosalia in Palermo, the
Annunciation in Trapani, and St. Lucia in Syracuse, as
well as the historical pageants featuring symbolic figures
of Christians and Saracens and of Normans and Turks in
combat to the accompaniment of fireworks and dancing,
represent the gayer sides of Sicilian life.

BIBLIOGRAPHY. ALDO PECORA, *Sicilia* (1968), is an informative, general work. Geography and physical description may be found in OLINTO MARINELLI, *Sicilia* (1968); GUSTAVO CUMIN, *La Sicilia* (1944); and FRANCIS M. GUERCIO, *Sicily: The Garden of the Mediterranean, the Country and Its People*, 2nd ed. (1954). Land use and economics are covered in FERDINANDO MILONE, *Sicilia* (1960), on the interaction of nature and man; JOHN P. COLE, *Italy* (1964); VERA C. LUTZ, *Italy: A Study in Economic Development* (1962), with an acute understanding of the south; MARGARET CARLYLE, *The Awakening of Southern Italy* (1962); and NUNZIO PRESTIANNI, *L'economia agraria della Sicilia* (1946), which is technical but interesting. On archaeology, see MARGARET GUIDO, *Sicily: An Archaeological Guide* (1967); L. BERNABO BREA, *La Sicilia prima dei Greci*, 4th ed. (1966; Eng. trans., *Sicily Before the Greeks*, rev. ed., 1966); and the various writings of PAOLO ORSI. See also periodicals and other publications of the Instituto Centrale di Statistica, the Banco di Sicilia, and organs of the Sicilian regional government and of the University of Sicily.

Sidney, Sir Philip

Sir Philip Sidney was admired as the ideal gentleman of
his age in England, the complete Renaissance man: he
was a master of social graces, an idealistic politician, a
brave military leader, learned in the arts and sciences of
his time, the best writer of English prose, and, after
Edmund Spenser, the best English poet of his generation.

He was born at Penshurst, in Kent, on November 30,
1554, the eldest son of Sir Henry Sidney and his wife,
Lady Mary Dudley, daughter of the Duke of Northumberland, and godson of King Philip II of Spain. After
Elizabeth I succeeded to the throne, his father was appointed lord president of Wales (and later served three
times as lord deputy of Ireland), while his uncle, Robert
Dudley, was created earl of Leicester and became the
Queen's most trusted adviser. In keeping with such a
family background, the young Sidney was intended for a
career as a statesman and soldier. At the age of ten he
entered Shrewsbury School, where his classmate was
Fulke Greville (later a court official under Elizabeth),
who became his lifelong friend and was his early biographer. In February 1568 he began a three-year period of
studies at Christ Church, Oxford, afterward travelling in

Europe, between May 1572 and June 1575, perfecting his
knowledge of Latin, French, and Italian. He also gained
firsthand knowledge of European politics and became
acquainted with many of Europe's leading statesmen.

By courtesy of the trustees of the Warwick Castle
Resettlement; photograph, Courtauld Institute of Art, London

Sidney, detail of an oil painting by an unknown
artist, 1576. In the Warwick Castle Collection.

His first court appointment came in the spring of 1576,
when he succeeded his father as cupbearer to the Queen,
a ceremonial position. Then in February 1577, when he
was only 22, he was sent as ambassador to the German
emperor Rudolf II and the elector Palatine Louis VI,
carrying Queen Elizabeth's condolences on the deaths of
their fathers. But along with this formal task, he also had
secret instructions to sound out the German princes on
their attitude toward the formation of a Protestant league
—the chief political aim being to protect England by
associating it with other Protestant states in Europe that
would counterbalance the threatening power of Catholic
Spain. Sidney apparently brought back enthusiastic reports on the possibilities of forming such a league; but the
cautious Queen sent other emissaries to check on his
reports, and they returned with less optimistic accounts of
the German princes' reliability as allies. He did not receive another major official appointment until eight years
later.

He, nevertheless, continued to busy himself in the politics and diplomacy of his country. In 1579 he wrote
privately to the Queen advising her against a proposal
that she enter into a marriage with the Duke of Anjou,
the Roman Catholic heir to the French throne. Sidney,
moreover, was a member of Parliament for Kent in
1581 and 1584–85. He corresponded with foreign statesmen and entertained important visitors—including the
French Protestant envoy Philippe de Mornay in 1577, the
German Calvinist Prince Casimir in 1578, the Portuguese
pretender Dom Antônio in 1581, and later a number of
Scottish lords. Sidney was among the few Englishmen of
his time with any interest in the newly discovered Americas, and he supported maritime explorations by the navigator Sir Martin Frobisher. In 1582 Richard Hakluyt,
who published accounts of English explorers' enterprises,
dedicated his *Divers voyages, touching the discoverie of
America* to him. Sidney later became interested in the
project to colonize the American colony of Virginia, sent
out by Sir Walter Raleigh, and he intended to set out
himself in an expedition with Sir Francis Drake against
the Spaniards. He had wide-ranging intellectual and artistic interests, discussed art with the painter Nicholas Hilliard and chemistry with the scientist John Dee, and was a
great patron of scholars and men of letters. More than 40
works by English and European authors were dedicated
to him—works of divinity, ancient and modern history,
geography, military affairs, law, logic, medicine, poetry

Early
career
and
writings

Artistic
and
intellectual
interests

—indicating the breadth of his interests. Among the many poets and prose writers who sought his patronage were Edmund Spenser, Thomas Watson, Abraham Fraunce, and Thomas Lodge.

Sidney was an excellent horseman and became renowned for his participation in tournaments—elaborate entertainments, half athletic contest and half symbolic spectacle, that were a chief amusement of the court. He hankered after a life of heroic action, but his official activities were largely ceremonial—attending on the Queen at court and accompanying her on her progresses about the country. In January 1583 he was knighted, not because of any outstanding accomplishment but in order to give him the qualifications needed to stand in for his friend Prince Casimir, who was to receive the honour of admittance to the Order of the Garter but was unable to attend the ceremony. In September he married Frances, daughter of Queen Elizabeth's secretary of state, Sir Francis Walsingham. They had one daughter, Elizabeth.

Because the Queen would not give him an important post, he had turned to literature as an outlet for his energies. In 1578 he composed a pastoral playlet, *The Lady of May,* for the Queen. By 1580 he had completed a version of his heroic prose romance, the *Arcadia.* It is typical of his gentlemanly air of assumed nonchalance that he should call it "a trifle, and that triflingly handled," whereas it is in fact an intricately plotted narrative of 180,000 words.

Early in 1581 his aunt, the countess of Huntington, had brought to court her ward, Penelope Devereux, who later that year married the young Lord Rich. Some time afterward Sidney fell in love with her, and during the summer of 1582 he composed a sonnet sequence, *Astrophil and Stella,* recounting the first stirrings of his passion, his struggles against it, and his final abandonment of his suit to give himself instead to the "great cause" of public service. These sonnets, witty and impassioned, brought Elizabethan poetry at once of age. About the same time he wrote his *Defense of Poesy,* an urbane and eloquent plea for the social value of imaginative fiction, which remains the finest work of Elizabethan literary criticism. In 1584 he began a radical revision of his *Arcadia,* transforming its linear dramatic plot into a many-stranded, interlaced narrative. He left it half finished, but it remains the most important work of prose fiction in English of the 16th century. He also composed other poems and later began a paraphrase of the Psalms. He wrote for his own amusement and for that of his close friends; true to the gentlemanly code of avoiding commercialism, he did not allow his writings to be published in his lifetime.

The incomplete revised version of his *Arcadia* was not printed until 1590; in 1593 another edition completed the story by adding the last three books of his original version (the complete text of the original version remained in manuscript until 1926). His *Astrophil and Stella* was printed in 1591 in a corrupt text, his *Defense of Poesy* in 1595, and a collected edition of his works in 1598, reprinted in 1599 and nine times during the 17th century.

Although in July 1585 he finally received his eagerly awaited public appointment, his writings were to be his most lasting accomplishment. He was appointed, with his uncle, the Earl of Warwick, as joint master of the ordnance, an office that administered the military supplies of the kingdom. In November the Queen was finally persuaded to assist the struggle of the Dutch against their Spanish masters, sending them a force led by the Earl of Leicester. Sidney was made governor of the town of Flushing and was given command of a company of cavalry. But the following 11 months were spent in ineffective campaigns against the Spaniards, while Sidney was hard put to maintain the morale of his poorly paid troops. He wrote to his father-in-law that if the Queen did not pay her soldiers she would lose her garrisons but that for himself the love of the cause would never make him weary of his resolution, because he thought "a wise and constant man ought never to grieve while he doth play his own part truly, though others be out."

On September 22, 1586, he volunteered to serve in an action to prevent the Spaniards from sending supplies

Revision of the Arcadia

into the town of Zutphen. The supply train was heavily guarded, and the English were outnumbered; but Sidney charged three times through the enemy lines, and, even though his thigh was shattered by a bullet, he rode his horse from the field. He was carried to Arnhem, where his wound became infected, and he prepared himself religiously for death. In his last hours he confessed:

> There came to my remembrance a vanity wherein I had taken delight, whereof I had not rid myself. It was the Lady Rich. But I rid myself of it, and presently my joy and comfort returned.

He died on October 17, 1586, not yet 32 years of age.

He was buried at St. Paul's Cathedral in London on February 16, 1587, with an elaborate funeral of a type usually reserved for great noblemen. The universities of Oxford and Cambridge and scholars throughout Europe issued memorial volumes in his honour, while almost every English poet composed verses in his praise. He won this adulation even though he had accomplished no action of consequence—it would be possible to write a history of Elizabethan political and military affairs without so much as mentioning his name. It is not what he did but what he was that made him so widely admired: the embodiment of the Elizabethan ideal of gentlemanly virtue.

MAJOR WORKS

The Countesse of Pembrokes Arcadia (1590, consisting of the revised books i, ii, and part of iii; 2nd ed., "augmented and ended," 1593, adds original books iii–v; 3rd ed., 1598, also includes *Certaine Sonets* and *The Lady of May*); *Syr P.S. His Astrophel and Stella* (1591), an unauthorized corrupt text; a slightly corrected edition of the same year; a better text also contained in the 1598 edition of the *Arcadia; The Defense of Poesy* (1595; another edition, of the same year, entitled *An Apologie for Poetrie*); *The Psalmes of David* (first printed 1823—only the first 43 by Sidney, the rest by his sister).

BIBLIOGRAPHY. M.W. WALLACE, *The Life of Sir Philip Sidney* (1915); J.M. OSBORN, *Young Philip Sidney, 1572–1577* (1972); JOHN BUXTON, *Sir Philip Sidney and the English Renaissance* (1954), on his patronage; N.L. RUDENSTINE, *Sidney's Poetic Development* (1967); *The Complete Works of Sir Philip Sidney,* ed. by A. FEUILLERAT, 4 vol. (1912–26), diplomatic texts of the earliest editions; *Poems,* ed. by W.A. RINGLER, JR. (1962), and *The Countess of Pembrokes Arcadia (The Old Arcadia),* ed. by JEAN ROBERTSON (1973), critically reconstructed texts.

(W.A.Ri.)

Siemens Family

Four brothers in the Siemens family made substantial contributions to technology during the last half of the 19th century. Ernst Werner and Karl Wilhelm (later Sir William), in collaboration with Karl and Friedrich, were pioneers in the development and expansion of the electrical and steel industries. The technical advances they achieved, such as the dynamo and the open-hearth process, were all made possible by discoveries in pure science and illustrate the trend—the application of science to technology—that has since characterized the growth of industry.

By courtesy of (left) the trustees of the British Museum; photographs (left), J.R. Freeman & Co. Ltd., (right) Interfoto-Friedrich Rauch, Munchen

(Left) Sir William Siemens, engraving after a portrait by Rudolf Lehmann (1819–1905). (Right) Werner von Siemens, drawing by Ismael Gentz, 1887.

Werner and Karl

Werner von Siemens, the eldest son, was born on December 13, 1816, in Lenthe, Germany. After attending grammar school at Lübeck, he joined the Prussian artillery at age 17 for the training in engineering his father could not afford. His next three years at the Berlin Artillery and Engineering School were the happiest of his life. While in prison briefly at Magdeburg for acting as second in a duel between brother officers, he carried out chemistry experiments in his cell. These led, in 1842, to his first invention: an electroplating process. The death of his father in 1840 left him responsible for the bringing up of nine younger children; thus he had to supplement his army pay. His appointment in about 1841 to the artillery workshops in Berlin gave him an opportunity to do research, which in turn set the direction of his life's work. When he saw an early model of an electric telegraph, invented by Sir Charles Wheatstone in 1837, he realized at once its possibilities for international communication and invented improvements for it. A specialist on the electric telegraph, he laid an underground line for the army in 1847 and, at the same time, persuaded a young mechanic named Johann Georg Halske to start a telegraph factory with him in Berlin. In 1848, during hostilities with Denmark at Kiel, he laid a government telegraph line from Berlin to the National Assembly of Frankfurt, as an army officer on loan to the Ministry of Commerce, and supervised the laying of lines to other parts of Germany. In 1849 he resigned his commission to become a telegraph manufacturer; this attracted him more than a career in the army or managing the new Prussian state telegraphs.

The firm of Siemens and Halske prospered rapidly, and in 1852 Werner married Matilda Drumann, a professor's daughter, by whom he had four children. When she died, he married another professor's daughter by whom he had two more children. Werner and his brother Karl, who was born on March 3, 1829, established subsidiary factories in London, St. Petersburg, Vienna, and Paris. Under Werner's direction, the firm of Siemens and Halske, with which William was also associated, laid cables across the Mediterranean and from Europe to India. Werner's continued research efforts and his inventions in electrical engineering appeared as new products, including in 1866 the self-excited generator, a dynamo that could be set in motion by the residual magnetism of its powerful electromagnet, which replaced the inefficient steel magnet. In that year he also was a member of the Prussian Chamber of Deputies and, always a Liberal, voted against the increased military budget. Later, he was raised to the rank of nobility and received many honours. Werner died at Charlottenburg, Berlin, on December 6, 1892.

William

William Siemens (christened Karl Wilhelm), who was born at Lenthe, Hanover, April 4, 1823, was first intended by his parents for a business career. After private tutoring he was sent to a commercial school at Lübeck in order to enter his uncle's bank. But Werner, deciding that engineering was more suitable, sent him to a technical school at Magdeburg for three years. Financed by his uncle, he then studied chemistry, physics, and mathematics for a year at the University of Göttingen, where his brother-in-law was a professor of chemistry. Through his brother's influence he became an apprentice-student, without fee, in an engineering factory making steam engines in Magdeburg. While there, he determined to sell Werner's electroplating process; after modest success in Hamburg, William travelled to London, arriving in March 1843 with only a few pounds in cash. He sold the process of Elkingtons of Birmingham for £1,600. He returned to Germany to complete his studies and then went again to England in February 1844 with the intention of selling two further inventions: a chronometric, or differential, governor to control speed in steam engines, invented by Werner and developed by himself; and a copying process improved by the two brothers. But he could not repeat his first success.

Finding that the patent laws in England were encouraging, William boldly decided to settle there as an inventor, but he found it difficult to make a living until his water

meter, invented in 1851, began to earn large royalties. He could now afford an office in London and a house in Kensington, where he lived with Karl and Friedrich until his marriage in 1859 to Anne Gordon, the sister of an engineering professor at the University of Glasgow. The same year he also received British citizenship. Before then, he had developed his life's work, which involved heat and electricity. Beginning in 1847, William and his brother Friedrich, who was born December 8, 1826, attempted to apply to industrial processes the regenerative principle, by which heat escaping with waste gases was captured to heat the air supplied to a furnace, thus increasing efficiency. The technical difficulties of applying it to the steam engine could not be overcome, but Friedrich obtained an English patent in 1856 for a method of heat regeneration in metallurgy. In 1861 William used this principle in his patent for the open-hearth furnace that was heated by gas produced by low-grade coal outside the furnace. This invention, first used in glassmaking, was soon widely applied in steelmaking and eventually supplanted the earlier Bessemer process of 1856. William's achievements were recognized by his membership in the Institution of Civil Engineers in 1860 and by his election as a fellow of the Royal Society in 1862. Tempted by the prospect of profits as well as royalties, he started his own steelworks at Landore, South Wales, in 1869, but, although it flourished for some years, he was losing money by the 1880s.

William's work in telegraphy

Meanwhile, he had made yet another reputation and fortune in electric telegraphy. Beginning in 1850, he had acted as English agent for Siemens and Halske of Berlin, a connection he maintained until 1858, when he became managing partner of the separate London firm founded under the same name; the firm was engaged in electrical testing for cable firms and in manufacturing of apparatus. As an expert in electrical cable, he was interested in cable laying. In 1863 he established a factory at Charlton, Kent; in 1865 the name of the London and St. Petersburg branches of the firm was changed from Siemens and Halske to Siemens Brothers (William, Werner, and Karl), while the Berlin branch retained the name of Siemens and Halske. The firm specialized in contracting and manufacturing electrical equipment. After acting jointly with Siemens and Halske, the English firm alone laid, in 1874, the electrical cable from Rio de Janeiro to Montevideo, an operation in which two ships were lost. In 1875, when the firm laid the first direct link from Britain to the United States, William assisted in the design of a new type of ship, the "Faraday."

Thereafter, looking into the future, he worked on electric lighting and electric traction. He invented improvements in arc lights and had them installed in the British Museum and elsewhere. A few months before he died he was responsible for the Portrush electric railway in Northern Ireland. He played a full part in professional life; he acted as president of professional organizations including the British Association for the Advancement of Science, received degrees from various universities and many foreign orders, and was knighted in the year of his death, on November 19, 1883, in London. He left a large fortune but no children. His contributions were commemorated by a window in Westminster Abbey.

BIBLIOGRAPHY. WILLIAM POLE, *The Life of Sir William Siemens* (1888), is the only book-length biography, written by an eminent engineer. WERNER VON SIEMENS, *Lebenserinnerungen* (1892; Eng. trans., *Personal Recollections*, 1893; *Inventor and Entrepreneur: Recollections*, 2nd ed., 1966), gives interesting details of family relationships and industrial enterprises. The *Dictionary of National Biography*, vol. 18 (1897–98, reprinted 1921–22), contains a scholarly entry that refers mainly to Sir William Siemens.

(P.W.K.)

Siena

Siena was an important medieval commercial centre. Siena today is an agricultural and administrative centre and the capital of the province (*provincia*) of Siena in the region (*regione*) of Tuscany (*Toscana*) in central Italy. Its population was about 69,000 in the early 1970s.

History. The site of Siena was an Etruscan settlement that later became the Roman city of Sena Julia. This colony disappeared, but a new Siena developed on or near the old site, which provided a relatively secure inland refuge from the barbarians who invaded the disintegrating Roman Empire in the 4th and 5th centuries AD.

Thanks to its position on the Via Francigena, the medieval route southward to Rome, Siena flourished under the Lombard kings, who ruled it through royal representatives, or *gastaldi*. The Lombard ruling class gradually fused with the older aristocracy and seized power in the surrounding countryside, or *contado*. These local lords made themselves independent of the Holy Roman emperor, but in the city itself they had, during the 11th century, to share their predominance with the local bishop.

Extensive land reclamation in the fertile *contado*, which produced oil, grain, and wine, increased the total wealth of the area and permitted a growth of urban life. In the 12th century the prospering townsfolk began to replace the rule of local lords and bishops with their own self-governing commune and councils, expanding their hegemony into the countryside and defending it against the emperors, from whom they finally won recognition of their independence. In 1240 the older nobility (the *magnati* or *grandi*) had to accept a governing council with a large measure of popular representation; and in 1277 the *magnati* were completely excluded from government office. Economic rivalry and territorial conflict with neighbouring Florence, which was anti-imperial, or Guelf, made Siena the centre of pro-imperial Ghibellinism in Tuscany. The Sienese reached the peak of political success on Sept. 4, 1260, when their army crushed the Florentines at Montaperti.

This triumph was founded on spectacular economic developments. In the 13th century Sienese merchants were transferring funds for the popes and were trading at the Champagne fairs and in Bruges and London. Siena became a great banking centre, where high interest rates brought great profits. The city, however, lacked both a good local water supply and a maritime port; it developed no real industry and was unable to compete demographically or commercially with its rival Florence. The imperial cause declined, and the popes moved their custom to Florentine banks. Siena suffered from wars and famines and from the general economic decline that afflicted most of Europe. These disasters culminated in the catastrophic visitations of the Black Death, which first reached the city in 1348; the population, perhaps 50,000 within the walls and double that in the *contado*, was probably halved by the plague.

The Ghibelline triumph at Montaperti was short-lived. The popes hit at Sienese business and credit, while the imperialists were decisively crushed at Tagliacozzo in 1268; soon after, Siena itself became Guelf and the Ghibelline nobility lost its share of power. For some two centuries a privileged class of lesser nobles and merchants ruled Siena under various forms of republican government that afforded power to a restricted group of oligarchs, who provided experience, continuity, and stability in public affairs, even if they provoked party strife and endless conspiracy among the many who were excluded. There were repeated and turbulent struggles between representatives of the older aristocracy, the newer rich, many of whom came from the *contado*, and the lesser populace, though class distinctions were seldom clear-cut because the landed nobility often engaged in business while many successful merchants married into the aristocracy and purchased country estates. After 1385 entrance into the governing class was increasingly limited, and the urban ruling elite transformed itself into a new aristocracy based on political privilege and investments in land.

Despite these political and economic problems, the Sienese maintained an overall prosperity that was slow to evaporate and that enabled them to embellish their city. Duccio's great "Maestà," painted (1308–11) to celebrate the victory at Montaperti, adorned the grandiose Gothic cathedral, schemes for the completion of which were largely abandoned after the Black Death. Beautiful churches, palaces, towers, and fountains reflected the inhabitants' civic pride, while the town centre, the concave Piazza del Campo, was dominated by the Palazzo Pubblico (1297–1310), seat of the government, and by its slender bell tower, the Torre del Mangia (1338–48). The council chambers of the Palazzo Pubblico displayed edifying frescoes of the Virgin, painted by Simone Martini, and of an allegory of good government, painted by Ambrogio Lorenzetti. In the decades of economic and moral depression following the Black Death, Siena entered an era of heightened religiosity, during which the city produced its two great mystic saints, Catherine and Bernardino; this spiritual movement was reflected in the lyrical madonnas painted by Sassetta and a succession of Sienese artists.

Foto Grassi

The Piazza del Campo, Siena; right is the Palazzo Pubblico (1297–1310), from which rises the Torre del Mangia (1338–48).

Siena retained its independence during the 15th century, but economic stagnation continued as capital was invested in land rather than in commerce, social mobility was reduced to a minimum, and Florence blocked expansion northward toward the main markets of Tuscany and the European lands beyond. In 1487 an exiled aristocrat, Pandolfo Petrucci, seized power and ruled with brutal tyranny through a period of French and Spanish invasions until his death in 1512. His regime was continued by his family until 1524. In 1526 Siena was compelled to seek assistance against the Florentine pope Clement VII from the emperor Charles V, whose protection was subsequently transformed into a Spanish domination that lasted until 1552. Two years later the Spaniards besieged the city; a prolonged and heroic defense drastically reduced the population and ended with the surrender of Siena in April 1555. In 1557 Philip II of Spain ceded the city to Cosimo I de' Medici of Florence. Siena's independence was at an end.

Thenceforth Siena's fortunes followed those of Tuscany and its grand dukes, under whose rule the economy became even more predominantly agrarian. In 1861 Siena, together with the rest of Tuscany, was absorbed into the new Kingdom of Italy.

The modern city. Siena survives as a charming provincial town. It is an archbishopric and a university city. It has some light industry, but it is not on a major national motorway or rail route, although there is a fast road to Florence. Siena thrives on the visitors attracted by its artistic treasures and medieval monuments, by the ancient Palio with horse races in the Piazza del Campo, and above all by its Old-World beauty.

BIBLIOGRAPHY. The best introduction is F. SCHEVILL, *Siena: The History of a Mediaeval Commune* (1909), reprinted with an important introduction discussing the modern scientific literature by W. BOWSKY (1964). On the early his-

(margin notes:) Growth of urban life · Oligarchic rule · Economic stagnation and loss of independence

tory, see E. SESTAN, "Siena avanti Montaperti," *Bullettino senese di storia patria*, vol. 68 (1961). Useful works in English include: L. DOUGLAS, *A History of Siena* (1902); and E. HUTTON, *Siena and Southern Tuscany* (1955). T. BURCKHARDT, *Siena: The City of the Virgin* (Eng. trans. 1960), is beautifully illustrated and contains interesting excerpts from chronicles and documents. I.M. ORIGO, *The World of San Bernardino* (1962), pictures local society; while key problems, artistic and otherwise, receive brilliant treatment in M. MEISS, *Painting in Florence and Siena after the Black Death: The Arts, Religion and Society in the Fourteenth Century* (1951, reprinted 1964).

(A.T.L.)

Sierra Leone

Sierra Leone is a sovereign republic in West Africa, bordered on the north and east by the Republic of Guinea, on the south by Liberia, and on the west by the Atlantic Ocean. One of the smaller African countries, it has an area of 27,925 square miles (72,325 square kilometres), and it is larger than Togo and The Gambia but smaller than Dahomey. Its population of about 2,600,000 is large in relation to the nation's size by African standards. The national capital of Freetown commands the third-largest harbour in the world after Rio de Janeiro and Sydney.

The country owes its name to the Portuguese explorer Pedro de Cintra, the first European to sight and map Freetown Harbour, in the 15th century. The original Portuguese name of Serra Lyoa (Lion Mountains) referred to the range of hills that surrounds the harbour.

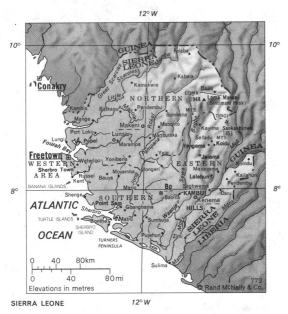

SIERRA LEONE

Although most of the nation's population is engaged in subsistence agriculture, Sierra Leone is also a mining centre. Its land yields important quantities of diamonds, iron ore, bauxite, and other minerals. Increasing urbanization has resulted in the gradual depopulation of the rural areas and the growth of a jobless population in the cities. The political troubles of the country after independence in 1961 were perhaps ameliorated by the creation of a republican constitution in 1971. (For history see WEST AFRICA, HISTORY OF.)

THE NATURAL LANDSCAPE

Relief features. The country can be divided into four distinct physical regions. The coastal swamp region extends along the Atlantic for about 200 miles. It is a flat, low-lying, and frequently flooded plain that is between 20 and 40 miles wide and is composed mainly of sands and clays. Its numerous creeks and estuaries contain mangrove swamps. Parallel ridges, often separated by silting lagoons, are common and sometimes form the actual coast. The Sierra Leone Peninsula, which is the site of Freetown, is a region of thickly wooded mountains that

run parallel to the sea for about 25 miles. The Peninsula Mountains rise from the coastal swamps and reach 2,913 feet (888 metres) at Picket Hill.

Inland from the coastal plain is the interior plains region. In the north it is comprised of featureless grasslands (savanna) that are known as "Bolilands" (*Boli* being a Temne word for those lands which are flooded in the rainy season and dry and hard in the dry season, and on which only grass can grow). In the south the plains comprise rolling wooded country where isolated hills rise abruptly to more than 700 feet. The interior contains a variety of landforms ranging from savanna-covered plateau surfaces to rocky scarp and hill country. The region is composed mainly of granite with a thick lateritic (iron-bearing) crust; to the west it is bounded by a narrow outcrop of mineral-bearing metamorphic rocks known as the Kambui Schists. Rising above the plateau are a number of mountain masses; in the northeast the Loma Mountains are crowned by Bintimani Peak at 6,390 feet (1,948 metres), and the Tingi Hills rise to 6,079 feet in Sankanbiriwa.

Drainage and soils. The country's drainage pattern is dense. Numerous rivers rise in the well-watered Fouta Djallon highlands of Guinea and flow in a general northeast to southwest direction across Sierra Leone to empty into the Atlantic Ocean. Their middle courses are interrupted by rapids that restrict navigability to their lower reaches. River levels show considerable seasonal fluctuations. During the dry season, levels generally decrease, and the rivers of the plateau region become mere shallow channels. In the rainy season, however, levels increase and the rivers' lower reaches are usually flooded.

The drainage system has nine major rivers and a series of minor coastal creeks and tidal streams. From north to south, the principal rivers are the Great Scarcies, Little Scarcies, Rokel (known in its lower course as the Sierra Leone River), Gbangbaia, Jong, Sewa, Wanje, Moa, and Mano. The Mano forms the country's frontier with Liberia. The river basins are small compared to the major basins of Africa; the largest is the Sewa River Basin, of over 5,000 square miles.

The major rivers

In most areas, the dominant soils are of the weathered and leached ferrallitic (iron-bearing) type. Red to yellowish-brown in colour, they contain much oxide of iron and aluminum, and are acid. Kaolin (China) clays are important, but under cultivation a light, readily workable, free-draining soil is available, whose productivity depends largely on the nutrients provided from the vegetation previously cleared and burned. In the coastal plains ferrallitic soils, developed on sandy deposits, are poor, but slightly better results are obtained where the soils derive from basic igneous rocks. At the foot of the main escarpment, on the Sula mountain plateau, and elsewhere an iron-rich crust forms a surface that is intractable for agricultural production. In the northeast, ferrallitic soils have been modified to produce a "grit" soil with a relatively high clay and silt content. Swamp soils occur over large areas. In coastal and estuarine areas where mangrove is the natural vegetation, productive soils can be acquired by clearance, but careful water control is sometimes needed to prevent toxicity.

Climate. The climate is tropical and is characterized by the alternation of the wet and dry seasons. Conditions are generally hot. Mean monthly temperatures range from 77° F (25° C) to 83° F (28° C) in low-lying coastal areas; inland the range may be from 73° F (23° C) to 82° F (28° C). In the northeast, where extremes of temperature are greater, mean daily minimums fall to 56° F (13° C) in January, and mean daily maximums rise to 90° F (35° C) in March. During the rainy season, from May to October, the dominant humid air masses blow from the Atlantic. The sky is cloudy, the winds are southwesterly, sunshine is minimal, and rainfall is almost a daily occurrence, especially during July and August. The rainy season usually begins with a series of violent line squalls marked by thunder and lightning. Precipitation is greater on the coast than inland; over 150 inches of rain falls annually on the Peninsula Mountains, while the northeast receives about 80 inches a year.

The dry season, from November to April, is characterized by the dry harmattan wind that blows from the Sahara. Conditions are hazy and dusty, with prevailing northeast winds of low relative humidity. The sky is often clear and blue, and rainless weather is common.

The rainy season tends to be cooler than the dry season by about 10° F (6° C). The relative humidity during the rains may be as high as 90 percent for considerable periods, particularly during the wettest months, from July to September.

Vegetation and animal life. The distribution of plants and animals has been influenced by such factors as relief and soil types and, perhaps more importantly, by farming methods. Remnants of the extensive original forest cover remain in the Gola Forest reserve in the southeastern hill country near the Liberian border. Secondary forest is now dominant, and valuable timber species, such as *Khaya* (African mahogany) and African teak, that were common in the original forests are now rare. The secondary forest is characterized by other tree species, such as the prevalent fire-resistant palm tree, which is a valuable source of palm oil and kernels.

The prevalence of savanna vegetation increases to the north as rainfall decreases. The savannas owe their present extent and character largely to the erosion produced by farming, grazing, and the use of fire. There are some small areas of climax savanna (a closed woodland of broad-leaved, low-growing trees) and tall tussocky grasses, but these are only remnants of a much wider spread. Other savannas are derived from forest, and are characterised by fire-resistant savanna trees with tall grasses. Tracts of tall-grass savanna also occur. Along the coast, mangrove swamps constitute the main vegetation community, especially in the saline tidal areas of river estuaries. These swamps are being extensively cleared for rice cultivation. Piassava, a kind of raphia palm, is common in the swamps of the south.

Coastal mangrove swamps

Large game animals, such as elephants, leopards, lions, wolves, and buffalo, are rarely seen. Various species of monkeys and chimpanzees are common in the forest zones, while tiger cats, porcupines, antelope, and bush-pigs are more generally distributed. There is a wide variety of insects, including the malaria-carrying mosquito and the tsetse fly, a carrier of trypanosomiasis (sleeping sickness). Hippopotamuses, crocodiles, and alligators occupy the rivers. The coastal waters, estuaries, and rivers such as the Sierra Leone and Sherbro, also contain a wide variety of fish, such as tuna, barracuda, and mackerel, and lobsters and sharks. Bird life includes parrots, owls, kingfishes, green pigeons, African magpies, vultures, and many other species.

The human imprint. Villages of about 35 buildings and 300 inhabitants dominate the rural landscape. Modernization is slowly altering the traditional pattern of rural settlement; the old circular village form with a tight cluster of houses is rapidly yielding to the linear village along a road or the regular gridiron pattern with adequate spacing between houses. Economic activity still centres largely around rice farming. The extended family provides farm labour both for rice farming and cash crop production. Fishing is becoming increasingly important. The rearing and herding of cattle is largely confined to the north and to groups of pastoral Fulani. The small shopkeeper is typical of the villages, as are the tailor and carpenter. Traditional crafts, such as metalworking, cloth dyeing and weaving, and woodworking, are rapidly disappearing with the increased importation of cheap manufactured goods.

Urban development

Except for Freetown, the development of large towns occurred only after World War II. Because of the incipient nature of urbanism, functional specialization is rudimentary and occurs mainly in the development of the small, central business district, the most prominent feature being the daily market of petty traders, the majority of whom are women.

Freetown is a long, narrow city of about 200,000 inhabitants. Central Freetown—the administrative and commercial hub of the city—houses government buildings and embassies, the law courts, hotels, and the Roman Catholic and Anglican cathedrals. Eastern Freetown is mainly residential, with retail trading concentrated along major roads; there are also a few impressive mosques in the area. Further east is the port area. Western Freetown is functionally similar to the east; it also contains the nation's main stadium, the central prison, and the administrative offices of New England Ville. On Mount Aureol, overlooking the city, is Fourah Bay College, black Africa's first institution of higher learning.

Bo, located in the southeast on the railway, is the second largest town, with a population of 30,000. An early administrative and educational centre, it has shown rapid expansion and has engulfed several surrounding villages. Commerce and retail trade are located in the centre of town near the important daily market. Its role as an educational centre has increased steadily, and Bo now contains many schools, including the famous Bo Government Secondary School, founded in the early 20th century.

Other important towns include Kenema, east of Bo, which has grown as a result of diamond mining, and Makeni, in the north, which is a provincial capital and major commercial centre. Mining has also been important to Koidu, Sefadu, Yengema, and Jaiama in the east and Lunsar in the north. Port Loko, Kabala, Bonthe, Moyamba, Kailahun, Kambia, Pujehun, and Magburaka are administrative centres that have also developed such functions as retail trading and produce marketing.

PEOPLE AND POPULATION

Population groups. There are about 18 ethnic groups that exhibit similar cultural features, such as secret societies, chieftaincy, patrilineal descent, and farming methods. The Mende, found in the east and south, form the largest group; they numbered almost 673,000 in 1963. They are closely followed by the Temne (649,000) in

Sierra Leone, Area and Population				
	area		population*	
	sq mi	sq km	1963 census	1970 estimate
Area				
Western Area	256	663	195,000	250,000
Provinces				
Eastern	5,876	15,219	546,000	632,000
Northern	13,925	36,066	898,000	1,040,000
Southern	7,868	20,378	542,000	628,000
Total Sierra Leone	27,925	72,325†	2,180,000†	2,550,000

*Census results exclude, and estimates include, adjustment for underenumeration estimated at 5 percent. †Figures do not add to total given because of rounding. Source: Official government figures.

the north. Other major groups include the Limba (183,000), Kuranko (81,000), Susu (67,000), Yalunka (15,000), and Loko (64,000), in the north; the Kono (105,000) and Kissi (49,000) in the east; and the Sherbro (75,000), in the southwest. Minor groups include the coastal Bullom, Vai, and Krim and the Fulani and Malinke (Mandingo), who are immigrants from Guinea concentrated in the north and east. The 42,000 Creole —descendants of freed slaves who colonized the coast in the 19th century—are found mainly in the Western Area and Freetown. Ethnic complexity is further enhanced by the presence of Lebanese and Indian traders in urban centres.

Krio, a language derived from English and a variety of African languages, is the mother tongue of the Creole and the country's lingua franca. Among the indigenous languages, the Mande group is the most widespread; it includes the Mende, Kuranko, Kono, Yalunka, Susu, Vai, and Malinke languages. The Mel group, which is similar to the Bantu languages of Central and eastern Africa, includes the Temne, Krim, Kissi, Bullom, Sherbro, and Limba languages. English is the official language and is used extensively in administration, education, and commerce. Arabic is used among Lebanese traders and adherents of Islām.

Linguistic patterns

(Left) Workers washing gravel for diamonds near Kenema. (Right) Rice harvesters of the Susu tribe on their way to work on the Great Scarcies River.
(Left) A.F. Kersting, (right) Camera Press—Publix

In the late 1960s about two-thirds of the population practiced a variety of animist religions. About 28 percent of the people were Muslims and 6 percent Christians. Islām is most influential in the north, and Christianity is more prevalent in the southern and western cities.

Demography. Fertility and mortality rates are high; the crude birth and death rates approximate 45 and 23 per 1,000 population, giving a natural rate of increase of 22 per 1,000. The population is young, with more than 50 percent under 25 years and only 8 percent over 60 years. Emigration from rural areas to the urban centres is common; immigrants are particularly attracted to Freetown and the diamond-mining areas. There is also a floating immigrant population of Ghanaian fishermen along the coast. Areas of predominant emigration tend to show an excess of females, since migrants are usually men. Areas of predominant immigration, such as Freetown, show an excess of males.

The average population density of more than 92 persons per square mile (1970 estimate), far higher than the average for Africa as a whole, is exceeded only by a few countries, such as Nigeria. Areas of sparse population are found in the mountainous and infertile north and the swampy coastal areas of the south and southwest. Population is dense in the west, particularly in the Kambia and Port Loko districts, where intensive swamp-rice cultivation has produced a rural population distribution sometimes as high as 250 per square mile. In the east profitable cash crop production and diamond mining have created dense population patterns. The Western Area has the highest density, almost 1,000 per square mile, largely as a result of immigration to Freetown and its suburbs. Separating the eastern and western high-density zones is a middle belt of moderate population density. There is a similar moderate zone in the southwest.

Future population trends indicate increasing emigration to the urban centres from rural areas as well as an appreciable increase of the rural population in the southwest following advances in the mechanical cultivation of swamp-rice.

THE NATIONAL ECONOMY

The economy is dominated by mining industries, which account for 85 percent by value of the nation's total exports, while agriculture accounts for about 15 percent. Minerals are fairly widespread and include iron ore, diamonds, chromite, and reserves of rutile (titanium dioxide) that are among the world's largest. Other minerals include bauxite, columbite (a black mineral of iron and columbium), pyrochlore, gold, platinum, monazite, corundum, cassiterite, talc, and vermiculite. Major concentrations of those minerals have been found in the Kono and Kenema districts, along the Sewa River Val-

Mineral resources

ley, on the western coastal plain, along a central axis stretching south of Kabala to Mongeri, and in the Peninsula Mountains.

Forest covers almost 1,160 square miles, the most important area of which is the Gola Forest. Biological resources include about 240,000 head of tsetse-resistant Ndama cattle, mainly in the savanna belt. The coastal waters provide rich fishing grounds for bonga, herring, snappers, tuna, shrimps, and lobsters. The hydroelectric power potential is appreciable, although none of the country's rivers had been harnessed for electricity by the early 1970s.

Sources of national income. Agriculture is carried out largely by traditional methods. About 75 percent of the population are engaged in production for the domestic and export markets. Rice, the main food crop, is widely cultivated on swampland and upland farms. Swamp-rice cultivation is concentrated in the lower reaches of river basins, of which the Scarcies is the most important. Efforts are being made to reduce upland-rice farming with its attendant soil erosion in favour of swampland farming with its superior yields. Other food crops include millet, peanuts, cassava, sweet potatoes, and oil palms. Vegetable gardening is important around the major urban centres, where markets are available to farmers.

The major cash crops are palm kernels, cocoa, coffee, piassava, and ginger. Production is carried out entirely by small-scale farmers. Timber (which includes *Guarea cendrata*, a cedar-scented, pink, mahogany-type wood, and the *Lopjara plata* variety *procera*, or red ironwood) is produced for the domestic market; there are major sawmills located in the Gola Forest; the main furniture factory is in Kenema.

Mining is the most important industry in terms of employment in the modern sector and in exports, and is second only to agriculture in its contribution to the national economy. Diamonds are mined by the National Diamond Mining Company (Diminco), which is jointly owned by the government (51 percent) and the Sierra Leone Selection Trust (SLST), a subsidiary of a London mining firm, the Consolidated African Selection Trust (49 percent), and also by a few private companies, and vast numbers of private prospectors. Mining methods range from mechanical grab lines with washing and separator plants to crude hand digging and panning. About half of the diamonds are gem stones found in river gravels, especially along the Sewa–Bafi river systems. In 1935 the SLST obtained an initial 99-year concession covering virtually the whole country; in 1956 the lease area was renegotiated and reduced to the Yengema and Tongo fields. The surrendered SLST areas were opened to licensed diggers, and the government opened diamond-buying offices in

The mining industry

Koidu, Kenema, and Bo, partly as a measure against smuggling.

The Sierra Leone Development Company (SLDC) has been mining iron ore at Marampa since 1935. Mining is open-cast (open-cut) and completely mechanized. The ore is processed and taken about 50 miles by the company's railway to the port of Pepel for shipment abroad. During 1963 the Sierra Leone Ore and Metal Company (Sieromco) opened open-cast bauxite mines at Mokanji Hills. The ore is shipped to Europe for reduction and refining into aluminum. Rutile is found in the southwest; in 1965 rutile production was begun, and production and prospecting activities were in progress in the early 1970s.

Industrialization is restricted largely to import substitution. Manufacturing is concentrated in Freetown, and production is mainly of consumer goods, such as cigarettes, sugar, alcoholic beverages, soap, tires, textiles, mineral fuels, and lubricants. Although factories are small and employ less than 1,000 workers each, their role in economic diversification is important. In the provinces industries are concerned exclusively with the processing of agricultural and forest produce, such as rice, timber, and palm oil. Traditional industries, such as fish curing and leatherwork, continue.

Electricity is provided by thermal power stations with a combined installed capacity of 76,000 kilowatts. Power-development plans centre upon Bumbuna Falls on the Rokel or Seli River.

Financial services The Bank of Sierra Leone is the nation's central bank; it issues currency, maintains external reserves, and acts as banker and financial adviser to the government. The National Development Bank is charged with providing finances to investors within the country. In 1971 a National Co-operative Bank was established, and a National Commercial Bank and an Agricultural Co-operative Development Bank are to be established in the future. Their function will be to provide credit and technical assistance to farmers. Commercial banking is handled by Barclays Bank of the United Kingdom and the Standard Bank of Sierra Leone. Post Office Savings banks are found in all main towns, and there are also various kinds of thrift and credit societies.

Foreign trade is expanding substantially, although its character still reflects the colonial nature of the economy. An excessive reliance is placed upon a few primary products, most of which go to the United Kingdom and western Europe. Minerals and agricultural products account for the bulk of exports. Imports, however, are becoming more diversified; they include machinery, textiles, vehicles, fuel, and food products. Japan, Hong Kong, and Burma are new significant trading partners, while trade with other African countries is small.

Transportation. A 311-mile government railway was completed in 1916 as a means of opening the country to commerce and of ensuring effective British occupancy. The railway runs east from Freetown to Pendembu; the branch line from Bauya to Makeni in the north is now closed. The entire line is being phased out because of its limited carrying capacity and inability to meet the needs of an expanding economy.

Roads, originally developed as a feeder system to the railway, have become the principal transport carrier. The road network is dominated by a series of highways radiating from Freetown to inland urban centres. About 5,000 miles of roads exist, and are maintained by the government, local authorities, and private companies; about 500 miles of road within Sierra Leone are paved. The road system is being nationalized and modernized to meet the needs of rapidly expanding traffic. In addition, road links with Conakry, Guinea, and Monrovia, Liberia, are being modernized at the present time.

Inland waterways carry a considerable volume of mineral ores, piassava, and food products. Launches and sailing boats are important, especially on the southern route to Bonthe and the northern route to the Great and Little Scarcies. Freetown, with the finest natural harbour in West Africa, is the country's principal port. Its eight berthing facilities handle all imports and agricultural exports. The general ports of Bonthe and Sulima are silting

Port facilities

up and commercially moribund. Specialized ports include Point Sam, which handles all bauxite and rutile exports, and Pepel on the Sierra Leone River, which handles iron-ore exports.

The international airport of Lungi is situated on the north bank of the Sierra Leone River opposite Freetown. It can accommodate commercial jets and a large annual volume of traffic. Domestic air transport is limited, but there are regular flights from Hastings near Freetown to Bo, Kenema, and Yengema. Domestic services are provided by Sierra Leone Airways, which—together with various African and European airlines—also offers international flights.

Management of the economy. Private capital dominates mining concerns, commerce, and banking. European, Lebanese, and Indian interests are predominant, and participation by Sierra Leoneans is small. The public sector features the Sierra Leone Produce Marketing Board (SLPMB), which has a monopoly on cash crops, and other public corporations, such as that of road transport, which is entirely owned by the government. Government revenue is derived from direct and indirect taxes. In addition to import and export taxes, the government can also rely on company, excise, income, and mining taxes for revenue.

Sierra Leone has a national labour congress, with about 20,000 members, comprising 20 percent of all wage and salary earners, who are grouped into 12 unions. There are also employers' associations, and there is a chamber of commerce. Arrangements exist for establishing minimum wages, but unions can negotiate with management concerning fringe benefits.

Contemporary economic policies focus essentially on internal development, economic diversification, industrialization based mainly on import substitution, the increase of exports, and the insurance of financial stability. In the early 1970s the government of Sierra Leone actively participated in partnership with private enterprises in the mining industry, in oil refining, and in Sierra Leone Airways.

The main problems facing the country are unemployment, rural emigration, and excessive reliance on a few primary products for foreign-exchange earnings. On the other hand, the diversity of natural resources, along with expanding educational facilities and trends toward political stability all seem to point toward a bright economic future.

ADMINISTRATION AND SOCIAL CONDITIONS

Government structure. The constitution of 1971 created Sierra Leone a republic within the Commonwealth of Nations. The former office of governor general was replaced by that of an executive president as head of state. The combined offices of vice president and prime minister are held in rotation, by decision of the cabinet for a period of five years. The House of Representatives is composed of a speaker and 78 members, 66 of whom are elected from constituencies that are established by an electoral commission. The other 12 representatives are paramount chiefs representing the 12 administrative districts of the three provinces. The chiefs are hereditary rulers whose local powers have been largely superseded by those of officials of the central and local government. Their influence remains important, however, particularly in matters of traditional culture and justice.

Local government The country is divided into two units—the Western Area, which was the former Crown Colony of Sierra Leone, and three provinces, the former Protectorate of Sierra Leone.

The Western Area, with a population of about 250,000, contains the capital of Freetown, which has a city council consisting of a mayor, aldermen, and councillors representing the six wards of the city. It has the usual local government committees.

The provinces have a population of about 2,300,000. Northern Province is divided into five districts, Southern Province into four districts, and Eastern Province into three districts. Each of these provinces is under the central political control of a resident minister, and each district is headed by a district officer who is, in turn, responsible to a provincial secretary, the chief adviser to the resident minister.

The districts are subdivided into about 146 chiefdoms, which are controlled by paramount chiefs and chiefdom councillors. The chiefdoms are further divided into sections and villages.

In addition, there are District Councils, which in some cases override the chiefdom administrations. The councils deal largely with local matters and are under the indirect control of the central government. Town Councils also have been established in the larger provincial towns of Bo, Kenema, Makeni, Koidu, and Bonthe.

Elections have been held regularly every five years since independence with one year's interruption of military rule. Most people belong to political parties although tribal influence is strong. There are two political parties—the Sierra Leone People's Party (SLPP) and the All People's Congress (APC). The parties operate in a manner similar to that of political parties in the United Kingdom; the party that receives a majority of seats forms a government, and the other party operates as the opposition.

Justice and the armed forces.   The laws of Sierra Leone follow the pattern of British law. Until 1971 the framework of the courts was equally similar, and the final court of appeal was the Privy Council in London. Since the adoption of a republican constitution, however, the highest court is the Supreme Court, headed by the chief justice.

There are local courts that take account of indigenous laws and customs, Magistrate Courts administering the English-based code, a High Court, and a Court of Appeal. Nearly all of the judges, magistrates, and lawyers are Sierra Leone Africans trained in British universities and the Inns of Court in London. There are presiding officers in the local, magistrate, and juvenile courts who are not qualified lawyers but who are citizens of wide experience.

The attorney general is a cabinet minister and the political head of the State Law Office, which is administered by a solicitor general.

The president is commander in chief of the armed forces. There is an army of 1,500–2,000 men, a para-military force of 300, and a civil police force of about 3,000 including female police. The army served in Africa and Burma during the world wars and has been used internally to suppress rebellions and strikes. There were unsuccessful military coups d'etat in 1967 and 1971. A defense pact with neighbouring Guinea allows for the exchange of army personnel. A similar agreement is also projected with Liberia.

Administrative services.   Since the early 1960s, there has been a great increase in the number of children attending schools. More schools have been built and more teachers trained to meet the growing need. Significant contributions have been made by overseas bodies, such as church societies, and by volunteer corps from the United States, the United Kingdom, and Canada. There is no free or compulsory education at any level, but the government awards many scholarships.

There are about 1,000 primary schools, 80 secondary schools, 2 technical institutes, and several vocational schools, trade centres, and teacher-training colleges in the country. The University of Sierra Leone consists of Fourah Bay College, founded in 1827; Njala College, founded in 1964; and an Institute of Education, founded in 1968. Fourah Bay College was for a long time the only university-level institution in black Africa, and its alumni are scattered far and wide in positions of responsibility.

Most health and welfare services are provided free by the central government. There are also a few hospitals belonging to religious societies and mining companies and private doctors. The fee-paying government nursing home in a suburb of Freetown is used by wealthy Africans and some overseas visitors. Every district in the interior has at least one hospital. The major hospitals with specialist facilities are in Freetown and Bo; they are staffed by highly qualified doctors who have been trained in Europe and the United States.

The Public Health Section controls port and airport sanitation, schemes for the control and eradication of malaria and other infectious or endemic diseases, and the sanitation of Freetown. In other areas sanitation is under the control of district health authorities and town councils supervised by doctors who are appointed by the central government.

The Endemic Diseases Control Unit concentrates on the mass treatment of such diseases as sleeping sickness, yaws, and leprosy. Smallpox, yaws, and measles have been almost completely eradicated.

There are slum areas at the edges of most of the main cities. Several low-cost housing schemes are in various stages of development. There are adequate middle-income houses in the urban areas and luxury villas on hilly sites.

There is a fascinating variety of housing in the interior districts, depending on the availability of materials. Roofs are made of grass in the savanna region and of bamboo in the forest areas. Walls may be circular or rectangular and constructed of dried mud bricks, palm fronds, or, more generally, lattice pole work filled with mud and coated with clay or chalk. There is usually a veranda or shaded porch. In most villages and towns along the roads, houses are roofed with corrugated zinc and the walls constructed of cement. In Freetown and Bonthe, some houses remain that were built of wood or laterite stone in a Brazilian or Victorian Colonial style and roofed with slate.

The Sierra Leone Police Force was constituted in 1894; the Frontier Police Force and the Court Messenger Force have been disbanded. The police force carries out traffic duties, riot control, and first aid and combats illicit diamond mining. Most of the senior officers were trained in the United Kingdom; they are not armed, except when on special duty.

Social conditions.   The main employer of labour is the government, followed by the mining and commercial establishments. But most persons, especially in the rural areas, are engaged in agriculture. There is a seasonal exodus to the diamond areas, where both legal and illicit mining are carried out.

There are no hereditary ruling classes, except for the families of paramount chiefs in the provinces. As the chiefdoms are usually small and their political influence restricted, the privileged position of the chief's family is confined to a small local area.

In the cities successful politicians, high government officials, professional men and women, and university teachers constitute an elite, the members of which earn incomes far above those of average workers. This is a potential source of danger, since most of the elite are of Creole origin. It is hoped that the spread of education and the growth of regional cities will correct this imbalance by the 1990s.

The concentration of economic power in the hands of Lebanese and Afro-Lebanese diamond merchants is also inflammatory, as there are few wealthy African contractors and exporters.

Unemployment is high among the illiterate and partially educated Africans who have moved into the towns from the rural areas. Extreme poverty is not widespread because family and friends usually give support to those unemployed. Hunger, unemployment, and poor housing are increasing, however, and the 1970s will be difficult years unless there is a massive infusion of external capital to establish new industries.

Housing

Economic
divisions
of the
population

CULTURAL LIFE AND INSTITUTIONS

The most outstanding feature of the country's cultural life is its dancing. The Sierra Leone Dance Troupe is internationally known and has performed in many foreign cities. The different communities of the nation have their own styles of costume and dance. In addition, certain closed societies, such as the Wunde, the Sande (Bundu), and the Gola, have characteristic ceremonial dances. A wide range of agility, gracefulness, and rhythm is displayed; in addition, there are elements of symbolism in most of the dances. Drums, wooden xylophones (called balaphones), and various stringed instruments provide the musical background.

The Poro society for men and the Sande society for girls play an educational role in village culture.

The Vai script has the distinction of being one of the few indigenous scripts in Africa. Some of the local languages are written in European script, but a few, especially the ones in the Muslim areas in the north, have been transcribed into Arabic.

Handicrafts. The carving of various wooden masks in human and animal figures for the dances is especially advanced in the southern region. The Sande mask worn on the head of the chief dancer during the ceremony attending the reappearance of the female initiates from their period of seclusion is perhaps the most well-known carved figure in Sierra Leonean art. It is a symmetrically stylized black head of an African woman with an elaborate plaited pyramidal coiffure adorned with various figures and with a facial expression of grave dignity and beauty.

Ivory figures are characteristic of the Sherbro, Bullom, and Temne peoples of the coastal and northern regions. Fine examples of these figures, which were bought or commissioned by Portuguese traders during the 16th century, are still extant. There are also steatite human figures, sometimes distorted, called *nomoli*, which certainly date earlier than the 16th century and were probably used for ancestor worship or fertility rites. At present, they are used for ceremonies to ensure abundance of crops.

Containers or rattles are carved from gourds, and are decorated with intricate geometrical patterns that are burnt into them.

The weaving and dyeing of cloth

The weaving of blue or brown cloth of thick texture with linear designs is carried out in the southern and eastern regions by the Mende and the Kono. The cloth is made into coats for men or wrapped around as a lower garment by women and is also used as a bedspread. In the north, among the Temnes, imported cotton or satin is dyed with indigo, the red juice of the kola nut, or imported dyes into beautiful patterns by tie dyeing. In the west, baskets are made with dyed raffia, and patterned slippers are fashioned from dyed wool.

Painting and literature. There is an active school of modern artists who are trained in Europe and the United States and whose paintings have been exhibited locally and abroad. Olayinka Burney Nicol, Hassan Bangura, John Vandi, Koso Thomas, and Gladys Metzger are among the most well-known artists.

The Vernacular Literature Bureau produces school texts, information bulletins, and collections of folktales in indigenous languages, such as Mende and Temne. There has been a literary tradition in Freetown since the 19th century. One of the most prolific writers was James Africanus Beale Horton, who wrote books and pamphlets on politics, science, and medicine while he was a medical officer in the British army between 1857 and 1871.

There were also 19th-century works on exploration by such Sierra Leone Africans as Samuel Crowther, a bishop of the Anglican Protestant faith, and another clergyman John Cristopher Taylor. Sierra Leone is represented in most anthologies of African- and English-language poetry and short stories. In addition, the modern novels and short stories of Sarif Easmon, William Conton, and Eldred Jones give a vivid picture of modern life in the country.

The Sierra Leone National Museum in Freetown contains historical, ethnographic, and archaeological collections. Fourah Bay College and Njala University College both have libraries; the former houses the public archives. The Sierra Leone Library Board has a central library in Freetown and branch libraries and book-van libraries in the provinces.

Press and broadcasting. The two daily newspapers—the *Daily Mail* and *The Nation*—are controlled by the government; they have the widest circulation. There are

also weekly papers published in Mende (*Seme Loko*), Temne (*Akera Kakethemne*), and English (*We Yone* and the *People*). Learned journals are published by the University of Sierra Leone, of which *Sierra Leone Studies* and the *Sierra Leone Language Review* are the best known.

The government-controlled Radio Sierra Leone broadcasts in English and local languages. Its programs, particularly of news and discussion groups, reach about 40 percent of the population. The government-controlled television service can only be received in the Freetown area.

PROSPECTS FOR THE FUTURE

The country has potential wealth in its agricultural and mining resources, and industrialization, although recent, is making rapid progress. Improvements in road communications and transport will certainly result in a greater exploitation and utilization of these assets. The spread of education, intermarriage, and the establishment of workers' unions that cut across tribal lines are all factors that will lessen intercommunal rivalry and will result in a more united and progressive country.

BIBLIOGRAPHY. Publications by the MINISTRY OF INFORMATION AND BROADCASTING, Freetown, Sierra Leone, include well-illustrated pamphlets that appear at regular intervals and contain up-to-date information. The *Report* by the MINISTRY OF EDUCATION (annual) gives educational developments and statistics. A valuable source of information is the *Sierra Leone Yearbook*, published in Freetown. The CENTRAL BANK OF SIERRA LEONE also produces regular bulletins. An *Atlas of Sierra Leone* (1966), produced by the DIRECTORATE OF SURVEYS AND LANDS, gives useful information and detailed maps of the country and of street plans of some of its important urban areas.

J.I. CLARKE (ed.), *Sierra Leone in Maps* (1969), is an admirably illustrated symposium by members of the staff of the Department of Geography, University of Sierra Leone. For history, see CHRISTOPHER FYFE, *A History of Sierra Leone* (1962) the major work; and ALEXANDER P. KUP, *The Story of Sierra Leone* (1964). GEOFFREY J. WILLIAMS, *A Bibliography of Sierra Leone 1925–67* (1971), emphasizes articles on the communities of the provinces and includes a list of previous bibliographies. MARTIN L. KILSON, *Political Change in a West African State: A Study of the Modernisation Process in Sierra Leone* (1966); and JOHN CARTWRIGHT, *Politics in Sierra Leone 1947–67* (1970), give an account of modern political developments. For economic studies, see RALPH GERALD SAYLOR, *The Economic System of Sierra Leone* (1968); H.L. VAN DER LAAN, *The Sierra Leone Diamonds: An Economic Study Covering the Years 1952–1961* (1965); and SIAKA STEVENS in the *Report of the Duke of Edinburgh's Study Conference* (1956). F.W.H. MIGEOD, *A View of Sierra Leone* (1925), contains a valuable account of the culture of peoples of the provinces. K.L. LITTLE, *The Mende of Sierra Leone*, rev. ed. (1967), gives an account of the most numerous community in Sierra Leone; as does W.T. HARRIS and HARRY SAWYER, *The Springs of Mende Belief and Conduct* (1968). An account of the Limba peoples is given by RUTH H. FINNEGAN, *Survey of the Limba People of Northern Sierra Leone* (HMSO 1963). These three are the major communities in Sierra Leone. ARTHUR T. PORTER, *Creoledom* (1963); and JOHN PETERSON, *Province of Freedom* (1969), are good socio-historical accounts of the Sierra Leone Creoles.

The lives of distinguished Sierra Leoneans are well set out in M.C.F. EASMON, *Eminent Sierra Leoneans* (1961); CHRISTOPHER FYFE, *Africanus Horton, 1835–1883: West African Scientist and Patriot* (1972); DAVIDSON NICOL (ed.), *Black Nationalism in Africa, 1867* (British title, *Africanus Horton: The Dawn of Nationalism in Modern Africa*; 1969); and J.D. HARGREAVES, *A Life of Sir Samuel Lewis* (1958). *Modern African Stories*, a collection by ELLIS AYITEY KOMEY and EZEKIEL MPHALELE (1964), contains selections by Sierra Leone writers. The autobiographical *Kossoh Town Boy*, by R.B.W.A. COLE (1960), gives a vivid picture of Sierra Leone Creole childhood.

(D.S.H.W.N./S.M.S.)

Sierra Nevada Range

The Sierra Nevada is a major mountain range of western North America, running along the eastern edge of the state of California. Its great mass is the uplifted complement of the Great Valley (Central Valley) depression to the west. Extending over 250 miles (400 kilometres) northward from the Mohave Desert to the Cascade Range of northern California and Oregon, the Sierra Nevada is about 50 miles wide. Its magnificent skyline and spectacular landscapes make it one of the most beautiful of the great physical features of the United States. As a recreation centre, its year-round facilities prove a magnet to the inhabitants of the huge urban areas of California, and it has considerable importance as a source of power and water. It was the focus of the celebrated California Gold Rush of 1849.

The Sierra Nevada is an asymmetrical range with its crest and high peaks decidedly toward the east. The peaks range from 11,000 to 14,000 feet above sea level, with Mt. Whitney, at 14,494 feet (4,418 metres), the highest peak in the conterminous United States.

Much of the rock is granite or a near relative of granite. There are dividing bands of metamorphosed (heat- and pressure-altered) sedimentary rock, all that is left of a once extensive sedimentary basin.

History of scientific study. For many readers, the naturalist John Muir's *My First Summer in the Sierra*, a diary of camping and exploration in 1869, is one of the classics of American geographical writing. Muir, the founder of the Sierra Club (1892), a conservationist group concerned with the preservation of the scenic resources of the Sierras and like areas of the United States, dedicated his book to members of the club in 1911.

Geologists have studied the Sierra Nevada from the late 19th century onward. Especially significant studies concern the Mother Lode system, Jurassic stratigraphy and its relation to intrusive granites, glacial erosion, placer gold, multiple intrusions, isotope ages, and chronology and nature of emplacement.

Geological background. It has long been recognized that the Sierra Nevada is a tilted block of the Earth's crust. A fault bounds the block on the east, and it was along this that the great mass that became the Sierra Nevada was uplifted and tilted westward. This explains the asymmetry of the range. As the block was uplifted the abrupt, east-facing escarpment was cut into by the erosive action of wind, rain, frost, and ice, and a series of steep-gradient canyons developed. Though the massive uplift started possibly 15,000,000 years ago, much of it occurred in the last 2,000,000 years. Altogether, the vertical movement along the fault amounted to at least 15,000 feet, and possibly more.

The gentle west-facing slope has been dissected by a series of streams, relatively long in comparison to those of the eastern slope. Such rivers as the Yuba, American, Mokelumne, Merced, and Kern have carved deep, V-shaped valleys into the predominant granite. These rivers drain into the Sacramento River in the Great Valley on the north, and into the San Joaquin on the south. By means of these two large rivers the range's drainage ultimately reaches the Pacific Ocean through San Francisco Bay.

During the Ice Age, which started about 2,000,000 years ago and ended in North America just 11,000 years ago, the river-eroded valleys were covered several times by great glaciers. Glacial climates came and dissipated at least five times, and each time excessive snows built snow and ice fields and long glaciers. The ice carved the V-shaped valleys into U-shaped ones, and in few ranges of the world are the forms more crisp and inspiring than in the Sierra Nevada. In the high snow fields, steep-walled basins, called cirques, were carved from the mountain sides by ice action. The resulting rock debris was transported by the glaciers down into terminal moraines, the tonguelike deposits of waste at the glaciers' end. These moraines, like the U-shaped valleys, are classical in their development. The glacial features are chiefly responsible for the scenic beauty and are the focus of the Yosemite, Kings Canyon, and Sequoia national parks. The several episodes of glacial chronology must be related to the progressive uplift of the Sierra Nevada block, and this is a remarkable story, explored in detail by geologists.

Geological and geophysical analyses have led to the conclusion that the region occupied by eastern California

The basic tilted block

and western Nevada was once a broad and long northward-trending basin, called a geosyncline, in which layers of sedimentary rock were laid down mostly in marine waters. Continued subsidence of this vast downwarp in the Earth's surface brought the lower sediments into successively higher temperature zones, where heat conducted from the Earth's interior resulted in the melting of the rock layers. In consequence, the granite rocks of the range were created, for, after the sediments were melted, they became mobile and proceeded, in part, to intrude upward into overlying layers of rock.

Careful mapping by geologists shows that the granite of the Sierra Nevada has been intruded as a number of separate masses, each with recognizable boundaries and its own mineralogical compositions. Further, radioactive dating techniques show that the intrusive masses are of three separate age groups. The first originated in Triassic time (about 190,000,000 to 225,000,000 years ago) and was an easterly group of intrusive bodies, mostly exposed in ranges east of the Sierra Nevada. The second occurred in Jurassic time (about 136,000,000 to 190,000,000 years ago) and was made up of a westerly lying group of intrusions now exposed along the west slopes of the Sierra Nevada. The third occurred in Late Cretaceous time (about 80,000,000 to 90,000,000 years ago) and makes up a central area of granite, now composing the high Sierras.

In Yosemite National Park a remarkable series of no fewer than nine separate intrusive masses has been mapped and ordered chronologically. Again, field surveys of the interrelationships of these masses have been confirmed by isotopic dating techniques, and this group of granite bodies is now seen as belonging to the third general age group mentioned above.

Environmental aspects. Gold nuggets were found in 1848 at Sutters Fort on the Coloma River, and the tremendous gold rush that followed was to be of fundamental significance in the historical evolution of the western United States. By the 1970s about $1,800,000,000 worth of gold had been produced. The nuggets, found in the stream gravels of the lower western slopes of the Sierra Nevada, probably come from the quartz vein of the Mother Lode (see below). Not only did the present river bottom gravels contain the nuggets, but the older gravel layers forming terraces on either side of the streams were also gold bearing. In places where these old river gravels had been buried by solidified lava flows, mining operations proceeded under the lava beds. Large dredges were built to handle huge volumes of gold-bearing gravels and concentrate the gold. As a result, where lush meadows once existed, there are now only rows of barren gravel ridges to mark the progress of the dredges. The rivers were muddied for miles below. Fortunately, this ruinous disturbance of a scenic and ecologically important environment was long ago condemned, and this type of industry has now almost ceased to exist. Fabulously rich gold mines were also developed in the Mother Lode vein system, which was traced for about 150 miles (250 kilometres) in a northerly direction along the west side of the Sierra Nevada. Some of the mines are still operating.

The moist Pacific winds drop many feet of snow each year on the Sierra Nevada, and thus the mountains become a life-sustaining watershed for many of the nearly 20,000,000 people who now reside in California. The large streams of the wide western slope drain into the Great Valley, where the most prolific truck farms, orchards, vineyards, and grain, alfalfa, and cotton fields existing in the United States are now found. Some of the drainage seeps underground and is pumped for irrigation, and the Great Valley itself provides an extensive and fine underground reservoir for water storage. Many power plants along the streams provide electric power for the Great Valley cities and smaller communities. Water that drains from the east slopes is gathered and conducted in large aqueducts to the metropolitan centres of southern California, notably to Los Angeles. Considerable lumber is harvested from the rich upper slopes of the Sierras, although the finest timber stands of the region are to be

The sequence of granites

Gold mining

found in the Coast Ranges of northern California, Oregon, and Washington.

The vast growth of population in the densely settled regions of the west coast of the United States, and the attendant thirst for outdoor recreation, have placed heavy demands on the scenic Sierra Nevada area. On a national holiday, more than 40,000 people may invade the Yosemite National Park, or more than a thousand make the hike to the summit of Mt. Whitney. The whole area is ideal for summer camping, hiking, nature studies, and fishing, and great for winter skiing. Already the national forest and national park staffs are taxed to the limit in keeping the streams pure, the campgrounds clean, and nature relatively undefiled, and the situation appears to be deteriorating rather than improving. The Sierras are a great natural blessing but will require great vigilance in future environmental control if this status is to be maintained.

Recreation

BIBLIOGRAPHY. P.C. BATEMAN and J.E. EATON, "Sierra Nevada Batholith," *Science*, 158:1407–1417 (1967), current theory on the origin of the granites of the Sierra Nevada, with a graphic presentation of the sequence of development; JOHN MUIR, *My First Summer in the Sierra* (1911), the full text of Muir's explorations; D. BROWER (ed.), *Gentle Wilderness: The Sierra Nevada* (1968), extracts from the text of Muir's work, richly illustrated by Sierra landscape photographs; W. HAMILTON, "Mesozoic California and the Underflow of Pacific Mantle," *Bull. Geol. Soc. Am.*, 80:2409–2430 (1969), current theory on the mobility of the earth's crust of the western U.S., showing the relation of the Sierra Nevada to similar components of the crust; A. KNOPF, "The Mother Lode System of California," *Prof. Pap. U.S. Geol. Surv. 157* (1929), a thorough description of the Mother Lode and its mines; W. LINDGREN, "The Tertiary Gravels of the Sierra Nevada of California," *ibid. 73* (1911), a good description of the placer gravels of the Sierra Nevada, with considerable history of placer mining; F.E. MATTHES, "Geological History of the Yosemite Valley," *ibid. 160* (1930), a beautifully illustrated and scientifically accurate account of the glacial features and chronology of the Yosemite Canyon.

(A.J.E.)

Sigillography

Sigillography is the study of seals. A sealing is the impression made by the impact of a hard engraved surface on a softer material, such as clay or wax, once used to authenticate documents in the manner of a signature today; the word seal (Latin *sigillum*; old French *scel*) refers either to the matrix (or die) or to the impression. Seals are usually round or a pointed oval in shape or occasionally triangular, square, diamond, or shield-shaped.

Medieval matrices were usually made of latten—a kind of bronze—or of silver. Ivory and lead were occasionally used, gold very rarely. Steel was used from the 17th century. Matrices could include intaglio gems. The usual material for the impression was sealing wax, made of beeswax and resin, often coloured red or green. In southern Europe, notably in the papal Curia, lead and occasionally gold were used. Shellac, the wax used today, was introduced in the 16th century.

Purposes of seals

Seals were used to establish the authenticity of such documents as charters and legal agreements and for the verification of administrative warrants. In southern Europe, early medieval documents were drawn up by notaries and authenticated with their written *signa,* but this never replaced seals in northern Europe. Forgeries were manufactured as early as the 12th century, indicating how important seals had become. From that time, also, seals were used to close folded documents and thus to guarantee their secrecy. Seals were also used to affirm assent; for example, by a jury. Under the Statute of Cambridge (1388), sealed letters were used in England for the identification of people and their places of origin.

Sigillography is used to assist other historical studies. Many impressions have survived from the medieval period. Those attached to documents are most valuable, because the documents may date their use precisely and the seal may confirm the documents' authenticity. Unattached seals may still provide useful evidence from their inscription or design. Fragmentary seal impressions are often difficult to interpret. Fewer matrices have survived and often without related impressions. Seals often reflect the taste of the owner. They provide evidence for changes in fashion in both secular and ecclesiastical costume and for the development of armour. Seals indicate heraldry before the earliest rolls of arms and are an original source for armorial bearings, which thereby enables the historian to trace the distinctions or alliances between various families and so contributes to genealogy. Craftsmen's seals often display tools connected with trade. Depictions of towns, churches, castles, and monasteries, although conventional, can often aid the architectural historian. Seals can also be used profitably for studying ancient ships, particularly their shape and details of masts and rigging. The main difficulty in studying seal designs is that they were often conservative, especially since seals were often replaced with an exactly similar design. (J.Ch.)

Seals in antiquity. Seals with designs carved in intaglio were used throughout antiquity. They were of two main types—the cylinder and the stamp. The cylinder first appeared in Mesopotamia in the late 4th millennium BC and continued to be used there until the 4th century BC. It was also widespread in Elam, Syria, and Egypt (3rd millennium BC) and in Cyprus and the Aegean (2nd millennium BC). Stamp seals preceded cylinders, first appearing in Mesopotamia in the 5th millennium BC and developing over a period of about 1,500 years until largely replaced by the cylinder in the 3rd millennium. Early stamp seals were also used in Iran, northern Syria, and southeastern Anatolia during the 4th and 3rd millennia; in Anatolia their use was continued in the 2nd millennium by the Hittites. In Mesopotamia the stamp seal gradually came into use again in the 8th–6th centuries, effectively replacing the cylinder by the 3rd century BC. In Egypt the scarab largely replaced the cylinder seal early in the 2nd millennium BC and continued as the main type until replaced by the signet ring in Roman times. In the Aegean, various types of stamp seals were used throughout the 2nd and much of the 1st millennium BC, until in Hellenistic and Roman times the signet ring became dominant.

The uses of ancient seals are known from textual references and ancient sealings, both on lumps of clay and on documents found in excavations. In historical times most prominent citizens, including women, carried their own seals. That the rank or office of the owner was often included in the inscription indicates that many of these may have been official seals. Kings had their own seals, and high officials could hold the king's seal as a mark of delegated authority.

Uses of ancient seals

Seals came into use before the invention of writing for the securing of jars, bales, bags, baskets, boxes, doors, etc., and this use continued throughout ancient times. The method was either to shape clay over the stopper or lid or to make a fastening with cord and place clay around the knot and then impress it with the seal.

The sealing of written documents, of which the two major ancient classes were clay tablets and papyrus scrolls, became regularly established in the latter part of the 3rd millennium BC. The clay tablet was the main vehicle of writing in Mesopotamia, where cuneiform was used into the Christian Era, and this method spread to Elam, Anatolia, Syria, and Egypt; clay tablets were also used in the Aegean Bronze Age. The tablet was inscribed while the clay was soft, and seal impressions were applied at the same time.

The main kinds of sealed cuneiform documents were contracts, accounts, and letters. Contracts were sealed by the contracting parties and by witnesses and commonly encased in clay "envelopes," on which the text was either repeated or summarized and the seals again impressed. Two special kinds of contract were the royal grant to a subject, impressed with the royal seal of the grantor, and the treaty between nations, a number of examples of which have been recovered, some of them bearing impressions of the seals of the royal contracting parties. Account tablets were sealed to authenticate the transfer of goods. A letter was often encased in an "envelope" and the sender's seal impressed on the outside to identify him to the recipient and, in the case of official letters, to authenticate any commands contained in the letter.

In Egypt, papyrus documents may be assumed from soon after 3000 BC, but surviving evidence dates mostly from the latter part of the 3rd millennium onward. The method of sealing a papyrus document was to roll it into a tube, tie a strand or cord around the centre, and seal a clay lump over the knot. This method continued into the Christian Era, from which time a great number of Greek papyri have survived in Egypt. It was not until the 1st millennium BC that this kind of document, including by then leather and parchment, came into wide use outside Egypt. The spread of this kind of document, on which the space for a seal was small, probably played some part in the gradual replacement of the cylinder by the stamp seal.

No documents or sealings have been discovered from ancient India, but the still undeciphered inscriptions on the seals may include personal names, perhaps of merchants, who could have used the seals in much the same ways as their Near Eastern contemporaries, with whom they are known to have had commercial contacts.

Since seals were used throughout ancient times and are sufficiently durable to have survived in very large numbers, they form one of the few classes of ancient objects in which a continuous development can be traced. The great majority bear artistic representations, so their chief value is for art history, but, since these include details of environment (plants, animals), equipment (plows, chariots, musical instruments), or dress, they also contribute to cultural history.

Further information is provided by the inscriptions on seals. The existence of rulers known only from king lists may sometimes be confirmed by the discovery of their seals, and in some cases rulers are known only from their seals, which, because they often mention the names of their fathers, the cities that they ruled, and the chief gods that they served, form a valuable historical source. The assembling of tablets and sealings bearing the impressions of private seals can contribute to the reconstruction of business archives and the destinations of traded goods, thus providing valuable material for economic analysis, and far-flung trade contacts can be deduced from foreign seals in excavations (e.g., Indus Valley seals in Babylonia). Personal names are an important source for ethnic analysis, and inscribed seals, because they often name the owner's father and even grandfather, provide material for this as well as for genealogical reconstruction.

(T.C.M.)

Medieval European seals. The connection between Roman and medieval seals lies in the use of seals in the chanceries of the Merovingian and Carolingian kings. Many Ottonian seals had busts of the emperors. Royal seals of medieval type, with the ruler enthroned and bearing his insignia, appear from the 11th century. The use of seals by bishops and nobles became usual at this time and was widespread by the 12th century. By the 13th century, seals were used by all classes, including small landowners; and, by the 14th century, simple seal matrices could be bought ready-made.

Spread of sealing in medieval times

The quality of engraving varied greatly. Some delicately designed seals date from the 12th century, such as the silver seal of Isabella of Hainaut, queen of France in 1180–90. The silver equestrian seal of Robert Fitzwalter is a notable example of the 13th century, the period of the finest seal engraving.

The names of several engravers of medieval seals are known: for example, Luke, who engraved the seal of Exeter, and Walter de Ripa, who engraved the first great seal of Henry III of England.

Forms of medieval seals. Seal matrices may be single or double, thus producing an impression on either one or both sides of the wax. Single matrices, the older type, often have a ridge along the back and end in a loop. Double matrices, known from the 11th century onward, are flat, with two to four projecting lugs pierced with holes in which vertical pins keep the halves aligned.

Sealing both sides of the wax makes detaching the seal more difficult, and so in medieval times the reverse was often sealed by a counterseal for greater security. The official seal of an institution was often countersealed by the seal of an official, such as a town by its mayor. Single seals were often fitted with a handle; the most common type was a six-sided cone ending in a trefoil. In some matrices the centre screwed outward, enabling the device to be used without a legend. On many seals the back was marked with a cross to indicate the top.

Seals could be either applied to the surface of a document or appended from it by a strip of material. Application was the earlier system, although papal bulls were always appended. Appended seals appeared in England in the 11th century and in France in the 12th; seals were appended either on a tongue of parchment cut across from the bottom of the document or on a tag of parchment, leather, or silk inserted through a cut in the document. Some documents had many seals. Seals were often protected by woven bags or by boxes of wood, metal, or ivory known as skippets.

The legend, often abbreviated, usually declared the name of the owner or institution; it often began with a cross and the word *sigillum*, followed by the name in the genitive case. Latin remained in fashion for inscriptions, though English and French are occasionally found from the 13th century, more frequently on personal seals. On English seals roman capitals were used in the 11th and 12th centuries and Lombardic ones in the 13th and early 14th centuries. Black letter (Gothic script) was first used in England in the 14th century and was quite popular in the 15th century, although Lombardic often continued for capitals. Roman capitals reappeared in the 16th century.

The legend

Royal and official seals. The great seal, or seal of majesty (a round seal showing the seated ruler with the royal insignia), first appeared in Europe on the seal of the emperor Henry II of Germany (ruled 1002–24), in France on the seal of Henry I (ruled 1031–60), and in England on the double seal of Edward the Confessor (ruled 1042–66). The seal of William I of England (ruled 1066–87) had the King on one side and an equestrian figure on the other. The kings of France adopted double seals under Louis VII (ruled 1137–80).

The development of lesser royal seals can be illustrated by the growth of English government. Deputed great seals were used for the major legal courts and for France, Ireland, and Wales. The expansion of the kings' affairs caused the addition of smaller, more personal seals, such as the signet. The Chancery did not control these seals, and this freedom led to the evolution of autonomous offices. The privy seal appeared early in the 13th century in the custody of the clerks of the king's chamber. It was soon transferred to the wardrobe clerks, and gradually its importance increased until by the early 14th century the keeper of the privy seal was the third minister of state. The keepership gained further prestige in midcentury, when the great seal was entrusted to the keepers who went abroad with Edward III. As the privy seal grew in importance, the king preferred another small seal for authenticating correspondence and warrants. Under Edward II (ruled 1307–27) there was a secret seal distinct from the privy seal. By 1400 the signet, as the secret seal was then called, was in the charge of the king's secretary. The signet rather than the privy seal became the originating force in administration, and from 1540 there were two secretaries, each with two signets. The privy seal and signet seal were both single armorial seals.

Royal officials had their own seals. Circular admirals' seals, dating from the late 14th century to the 17th century, include a fine group of 15th-century bronze matrices. The seals show ships in great detail, with the sails displaying the arms of the admiral.

Religious seals. The principal episcopal seal was the seal of dignity, always a pointed oval. From the 11th to the 14th century it usually depicted the standing figure of the bishop, from the 13th century with a canopy above him. In the mid-14th century the standing figure was often replaced by a saint or a religious scene, with the bishop praying beneath—a form that had been used earlier on episcopal counterseals. The seal of Thomas Arundel, archbishop of Canterbury (1396), depicts the mar-

Bishops' and monastic seals

tyrdom of Becket in the centre of an elaborate series of niches, with the archbishop below.

Monastic seals, usually double-sided and of high quality, normally show the buildings of the monastery, religious scenes, or the patron saint. They were distinct from abbots' and priors' seals, which were similar to those of bishops. Notable was the elaborate four-part matrix of Boxgrove Priory (mid-13th century). The seal of Merton Priory (1241), considered the finest English medieval seal, had the Virgin and child on one side with St. Augustine of Hippo on the other.

Papal bulls were doubled-sided lead seals appended to the document on strings. The earliest known is that of Deusdedit (reigned 615–618). The usual design, with the head of the Apostles Peter and Paul on one side and the pope's name on the other, first appeared under Paschal II (reigned 1099–1118). Although this style of portrayal of the heads was changed in the Renaissance, the design has not been altered.

Town seals. The possession of a common seal was an important part of a town's independence. Town seals were almost always round and often double. Many towns still possess their original matrices. The earliest in England date from around 1200, when many towns received their charters. The seal of Exeter has been dated to *c.* 1180. Maritime towns often depicted a ship with a furled sail; inland towns often showed the guildhall or the town itself. The seal of Rochester depicted the Norman castle within a wall. Counterseals often bore the figures of saints. Later medieval town seals were less common and beginning with the 14th century were often single seals.

Commercial seals. Commercial seals in England were considerably increased during the reign of Edward I, when double-sided bronze dies occurred for various customs, subsidies, and the delivery of wool and hides. Their obverse displayed the arms of England, and the reverse had the same device without the shield. The seals of merchants and craftsmen often displayed either merchants' marks or tools connected with their trade.

Personal seals. The earliest class of personal seals was that of greater barons of the 12th century, who used the device of a fully armed equestrian knight. Their shields often provide the earliest evidence for the use of heraldic charges. Some greater barons used a double seal with an equestrian obverse and an armorial reverse. The most usual type of personal seal was a single seal with the arms of the owner. Women's seals were usually pointed ovals and showed the lady standing, sometimes between shields. Nonheraldic personal seals displayed a variety of devices, such as stars, fleurs-de-lis, armorials, and religious subjects. The inscription sometimes indicated the owner, although it may simply have related to the device, as on those that bore the device of a squirrel and the inscription "I krack nuts."   (J.Ch.)

Modern use of seals. The use of seals declined as the use of signatures grew. Personal fob seals were in fashion from the 17th to the early 19th century; often they were gems in gold settings that were carried in the fob or breeches pocket and were used to seal folded private correspondence before the envelope was introduced. States and institutions continued to use seals for the formal ratification of their acts, but few of these seals maintained the medieval vigour of design.

Chinese and Japanese seals. The private seals used in China (*t'u-chang*) and Japan (*ingyō*), commonly square and reading merely "seal of so and so" (XX *chih yin*), served as a confirmation of signature or a sign to be verified but have not the legal status of a signature. They are made of ivory, wood, or jade. Used by artists and collectors to mark their paintings and books, there is hardly a limit to their fanciful designs and phraseology. A man might own scores of seals, using his many sobriquets, especially those suggesting unworldly and rustic tastes. A seal is impressed in red ink—made of cinnabar in water and honey or suspended in sesame oil, hempseed oil, etc.—held ready on a pad of cotton or moss. The characters most often appear in line, but they are sometimes reserved against the inked ground.

The first record of a seal in China is from 544 BC. Actual

bronze seals survive from the 5th century BC, and the practice of sealing must be some centuries older. The emblematic characters cast on Shang dynasty bronze vessels (13th–11th century BC) imply the use of something like a seal for impressing on the mold. The royal seal and other seals of high office were termed *hsi;* other seals of rank and appointment were *chang.* The imperial *hsi* (called *pao* beginning in the T'ang period, AD 618–907) was traditionally lárge and square, made of jade or ivory. The most famous one belonged to Shih Huang Ti (ruled 221–210 BC); it had as its knob a one-horned dragon and is fabled to have been handed down to the present day.

The official and, no doubt, the personal use of seals began in Japan with the copying of Chinese institutions in the 7th century AD. Both in China and in Japan modern seals generally employ the "small seal" character (*chuan shu*), the "great seal" character being reserved in the past for the ruler and high officers. To the historian the importance of the Far Eastern seals is greater in the earlier periods, and in China they yield more information than in Japan. Thus, seals recovered archaeologically throw light on government appointments made in the Han period, particularly in the reign of Han Wu Ti (140–87 BC), when they were tokens of rank given to internal officials and some external client rulers. Gold seals of the "King of the Han Wei-nu county," found near Fukuoka in 1784, and that of the "King of Tien" excavated near K'un-ming in 1956 have implications of this kind. But in post-Han times the seals have served little if at all as primary historical documents, and in writings on East Asia it is chiefly the art historian who appeals to their testimony in authenticating paintings and calligraphies.   (W.W.)

"Small" and "great" seals

BIBLIOGRAPHY. The best general account is SIR HILARY JENKINSON, *Guide to Seals in the Public Record Office* (1954). JOSEPH H. ROMAN, *Manuel de sigillographie française* (1912), is a longer study mainly on French seals. The basic catalog for European seals and impressions is WALTER DE GRAY BIRCH, *Catalogue of Seals in the Department of Manuscripts in the British Museum*, 6 vol. (1887–1900). Seal matrices are discussed by ALEC B. TONNOCHY in the *Catalogue of British Seal-Dies in the British Museum* (1952). ALFRED B. WYON, *The Great Seals of England from the Earliest Period to the Present Time* (1887), provides a systematic and well-illustrated account of English Great Seals. A full discussion of Classical seal use, with bibliography and occasional reference to Near Eastern sources, is given in the article "Signum," by WENGER in *Pauly-Wissowa Real-Encyclopädie*, vol. 2, col. 2361–2448 (1923); and details of use in the Aegean and Greece are conveniently given in JOHN BOARDMAN, *Greek Gems and Finger Rings* (1970). No adequate study exists of the uses of seals in ancient western Asia. See at present, however, ELENA CASSIN, "Le Sceau: un fait de civilisation dans la Mésopotamie ancienne," *Annales*, pp. 742–751 (1960); and M.I. ROSTOVTSEFF, "Seleucid Babylonia: Bullae and Seals of Clay with Greek Inscriptions," *Yale Classical Studies* 3:1–114 (1932). A very full bibliography of ancient Eastern seal publications from which information on use may be gleaned is given by HANS H. VON DER OSTEN in *Ancient Oriental Seals in the Collection of Mr. Edward T. Newell*, pp. 168–190 (1934); and in *Altorientalische Siegelsteine der Sammlung Hans Silvius von Aulock*, pp. 156–219 (1957), but no more recent convenient bibliography exists; systematic study of use must depend mainly on the examination of sealed texts. For Egypt, P.E. NEWBERRY, *Scarab-Shaped Seals* (1907), provides a brief account, now much in need of revision. Books on Chinese and Japanese seals deal mainly with those of painters, calligraphers, and collectors. ROBERT H. VAN GULIK, *Chinese Pictorial Art As Viewed by the Connoisseur* (1958), has the most illuminating discussion of the artist's use of seals. See also VICTORIA CONTAG and WANG CHI-CH'IEN, *Seals of Chinese Painters and Collectors of the Ming and Ch'ing Periods*, rev. ed. (1966); and CH'EN CHIH-MAI, *Chinese Calligraphers and Their Art* (1966).

(J.Ch./T.C.M./W.W.)

Sikhism

Sikhism is the religion of an Indian group founded in the Punjab (more correctly Pañjāb) in the late 15th century AD by Gurū Nānak. Its members are known as Sikhs.

There are now about 9,000,000 Sikhs, of whom over 85 percent live in the state of Punjab. The majority of the remainder are in Haryāna state and Delhi, or are scattered in other parts of India. Some Sikhs have also settled in Malaysia, Singapore, East Africa, England, the United States, and Canada. The word Sikh is derived from the Pāli *sikkha* or Sanskrit *śiṣya*, meaning "disciple." Sikhs are disciples of their ten Gurūs (religious teachers), beginning with Nānak (b. 1469) and ending with Gobind Singh (d. 1708).

HISTORY AND BACKGROUND

Religious and cultural origins. Sikhism was a historical development of the Hindu Vaiṣṇava Bhakti movement—a devotional movement among followers of the god Viṣṇu (Vishnu)—that began in Tamil country and was introduced to the north by Rāmānuja (*c.* AD 1050–1137). In the 14th and 15th centuries, and after prolonged confrontation with Islām, the movement spread across the Indo-Gangetic Plain. The Bhaktas (devotees) maintained that God, though known by many names and beyond comprehension, is the one and the only reality; that all else is illusion (*māyā*); and that the best way to approach God is through repetition of his Name (Sanskrit *nāma*), singing hymns of praise (Punjabi *kīrtan*), and meditation under the guidance of a Gurū. Traditional Hindu religion and society were hierarchically structured; the Brahmin priests claimed a monopoly over religious matters and the people were divided into castes. The Bhakti movement opposed the Brahmin monopoly and the caste system.

Hindu Vaiṣṇava and Islāmic Ṣūfī origins

Kabīr (AD 1440–1518), a medieval mystic poet and religious synthesist, was the link between Hindu Bhakti and Islāmic Ṣūfism (mysticism), which had also gained a considerable following among Indian Muslims. Ṣūfīs (mystics) also believed in singing hymns and in meditation under guidance of a leader. They welcomed non-Muslims in their hospices. Sikhism drew its inspiration from both Bhaktas and Ṣūfīs.

By courtesy of the Victoria and Albert Museum, London

The first Sikh Gurū Nānak (d. 1539) conversing with the tenth and last Gurū Gobind Singh (1675–1708). The imaginary meeting is expressive of the religion's development from a pacifist to a militant brotherhood. Painting of the Guler school, *c.* 1820. In the collection of Mohan Singh, Punjab, India.

The Ten Gurūs: Nānak and his tradition. Nānak was born in 1469 in the village of Rāi Bhoi dī Talvaṇḍī, 40 miles from Lahore (in present-day Pakistan). His father was a revenue collector belonging to the Bedī (conversant with the Vedas—the revealed scriptures of Hinduism) subcaste of Kṣatriyas ("Warriors"). Nānak received an education in traditional Hindu lore and the rudiments of

Islām. Early in life he began associating with holy men. For a time he worked as the accountant of the Afghān chieftain at Sultānpur. There a Muslim family servant, Mardānā, who was also a rebec player, joined him. Nānak began to compose hymns. Mardānā put them to music and the two organized community hymn singing. From the offerings made, they organized a canteen where Muslims, as well as Hindus of different castes, could eat together. At Sultānpur Nānak had his first vision of God, in which he was ordered to preach to mankind. He disappeared while bathing in a stream. When he reappeared on the third day, he proclaimed: "There is no Hindu, there is no Mussulman."

Sikh tradition relates that Nānak also undertook four long voyages: east as far as Assam; south through the Tamil country to Ceylon; north to Ladakh and Tibet; and west as far as Mecca, Medina, and Baghdad. He spent the last years of his life in Kartārpur (in present-day Pakistan), where he raised the first Sikh temple. Before he died in 1539 he nominated one of his disciples, Aṅgad, as his successor.

Aṅgad (Gurū 1539–1552) was followed by another disciple, Amar Dās (Gurū 1552–1574), who later nominated his son-in-law, Rām Dās Soḍhī (Gurū 1574–1581) as his successor. Thereafter, the office of Gurū remained in the Soḍhī family. Rām Dās was succeeded by his youngest son, Arjun Mal (Gurū 1581–1606), who, before his execution in Lahore on May 30, 1606, nominated his son Hargobind (Gurū 1606–1644). The seventh Gurū, Har Rāi (Gurū 1644–1661), was Hargobind's grandson, who, after his tenure, nominated his young son Hari Krishen (Gurū 1661–1664), who died of smallpox at the age of 13. Tegh Bahādur (Gurū 1664–1675), who succeeded him, was the son of the sixth Gurū, Hargobind. Before his execution in Delhi on November 11, 1675, Tegh Bahādur passed succession to his son, Gobind Rāi (Gurū 1675–1708).

The founding of the Khālsā. The execution of two Gurūs and persecution by the Mughals compelled the Sikhs to take to arms. This was given religious sanction when, on the Hindu New Year Day (April 13, 1699), Gobind Rāi baptized five Sikhs into a new fraternity he called the Khālsā, "the pure" (from the Persian *khāleṣ,* also meaning "pure"), and gave them a common surname, Singh ("lion"). Kaur "lioness" is the corresponding name given all Sikh women. Gobind Rāi's military career was not very successful. He lost most of his followers including his four sons. He was hounded out of the Punjab and assassinated at Nanded (Mahārāshtra) on October 7, 1708. Before his death he declared the succession of Gurūs at an end. The military leadership of the Sikhs devolved upon Bandā Singh Bahādur (1670–1716). For eight years Bandā defied the Mughals and devastated large tracts of eastern-central Punjab, until he was captured and, along with 700 of his followers, executed in Delhi in the summer of 1716.

The surname Singh

For a few years the Khālsā disappeared into the hills. But when Mughal power was weakened by the incursion in 1738–39 of the Persian Nāder Shāh, they re-emerged into the plains. They organized themselves under *misls* (from Persian *mēsāl*, meaning both "example" and "equal"), and began to extract protection money from towns and villages. The series of invasions by Ahmad Shāh Durrānī, 1747–1769, completely disrupted Mughal administration. In the battle of Panipat in 1761, the Afghāns destroyed rising Marāthā power in the north. In the power vacuum thus created, the Sikhs moved in as rulers of the Punjab.

The Sikh Empire of Ranjit Singh. In the years of turmoil between the Persian and Afghān invasions, Sikh *misls* had operated in loosely defined areas. Two main divisions emerged: Cis-Sutlej, the area between the Sutlej and the Jamuna rivers, and the Trans-Sutlej, between the Sutlej and the Indus rivers. In 1761 Sikhs wrested the capital city of Lahore from the Mughal governor.

Ranjit Singh's (1780–1839) *misl*, the Śukerchakīās, was based at Gujrānwāla, north of Lahore. Ranjit took possession of the capital in 1799 and two years later had himself crowned maharaja of the Punjab. The English, who had advanced beyond Delhi, took the Cis-Sutlej

Ranjit Singh

states under their protection and compelled Ranjit Singh to accept the Sutlej River as the south-eastern limit of his kingdom. There, after Ranjit Singh systematically brought the Trans-Sutlej region under his suzerainty, he took Multan in 1818 and Kashmir in 1819. In the following winter he extended his domain beyond the Indus River into the land of the Pathans.

Ranjit Singh modernized his army by employing European officers. This army defeated the Pathans and Afghāns and extended Sikh power to the Khyber Pass. Ranjit Singh died in June 1839.

Relations between the Sikhs and the British. After taking the Cis-Sutlej states under protection, the English began to think in terms of extending their empire up to the Indus River. Even during Ranjit Singh's lifetime they had begun to interfere in the affairs of Afghanistan, and had persuaded him to join in an Anglo-Sikh expedition to Kabul. After the death of Ranjit Singh the Sikh kingdom disintegrated rapidly. Ranjit's eldest son, Kharak Singh, who succeeded him, was deposed by his own son, Naonihal Singh, and died of excessive use of opium. On the same day, Naonihal Singh was mortally injured when a gateway collapsed on his head. Kharak Singh's widow, Chand Kaur, occupied the throne for a few months until she was deposed and later murdered by Ranjit Singh's second son, Sher Singh. On September 15, 1843, Sher Singh, his son Pratap Singh, and Chief Minister Dhian Singh Dogra were murdered by Chand Kaur's kinsmen, who in their turn were slain by Dhian Singh's son, Hira Singh Dogra. Ranjit Singh's youngest son, Dalip Singh, was proclaimed maharaja with his mother, Jindan Kaur, as regent and Hira Singh Dogra as prime minister. Power passed, however, into the hands of the pañcāyat (elected council) of the Khālsā Army, which compelled the Dogra to flee Lahore and then slew him in flight.

The English began to move their troops to the Sikh frontier and commandeered boats to cross the Sutlej. On December 11, 1845, the Khālsā Army crossed the river to intercept a British force led by their commander-in-chief and the governor general. In a series of bitterly contested battles at Mudki (December 18, 1845), Ferozeshah (December 21, 1845), Aliwal (January 28, 1846), and Sabraon (February 10, 1846) the Khālsā were defeated. The British annexed the territory between the Sutlej River and the Beas, forced the Sikhs to reduce their Army, and on their failure to pay war indemnity of 1½ crores of rupees, to cede Jammu and Kashmir, which were then sold to Gulab Singh Dogra. A British resident was posted at Lahore to administer the rest of the Sikh kingdom during the minority of Dalip Singh.

Administrative measures taken by the resident aroused resentment among the people. The banishment of Jindan Kaur, the queen mother, on charges of conspiracy brought matters to a head in the winter of 1848 and touched off a general Sikh uprising. A bloody but inconclusive battle was fought at Chiliānwāla (January 13, 1849); however, at Gujrāt (February 21, 1849) the Khālsā were totally defeated and laid down their arms. The Sikh kingdom was annexed and Maharaja Dalip Singh was exiled from the Punjab.

Sikh role in the Indian Mutiny

After many years of chaos, the Punjab was administered efficiently and fairly. Consequently when the Indian Mutiny broke out in 1857, the province stayed loyal to the British and the Sikhs took a prominent role in suppressing the Mutiny. For this loyalty and help they were rewarded by grants of land. The proportion of Sikhs in the British Army was increased. A regulation was passed requiring Sikh soldiers to observe Khālsā traditions. With the reclamation of desert lands through an extensive system of canals, unprecedented prosperity came to the Punjab. Sikhs were the most favoured settlers. By the turn of the century, though they numbered under 12 percent of the population of the province, they were paying 25 percent of the land revenue and 40 percent of the land revenue and water rates combined. Sikh loyalty was evidenced in World War I, in which Sikhs formed over 20 percent of the British Indian Army.

The depression that followed the war led to widespread disturbances, climaxed in the shooting, on April 13, 1919,

at Amritsar of over 400 men. Sikhs also clashed with the authorities over the possession of their *gurdwārās* ("temples"), which were under the control of hereditary priests. The Sikh masses turned from their British connection to join Gandhi's freedom movement. The progressive introduction of democratic reforms further reduced their earlier privileged status under British rule. Their participation on the British side in World War II was considerably less enthusiastic than it had been in 1914–18.

The division of the subcontinent into India and Pakistan in 1947 found the Sikh population divided equally on both sides of the boundary line. Since the partition had been preceded by savage Sikh–Muslim riots, 2,500,000 Sikhs were compelled to leave Pakistan.

Sikhism since 1947. The government of free India abolished privileges previously extended by the British to religious minorities, including the Sikhs. Thus, the proportion of Sikhs in defense and civil services declined. The partition also adversely affected the Sikh agricultural classes, who had abandoned rich farmlands in Pakistan and changed places with Muslims of east Punjab whose holdings were much smaller. The decline in their fortunes nurtured a sense of grievance and gave birth to agitation for a Punjabi-speaking province in the Republic of India in which the Sikhs would form a majority of the population. This demand was conceded after the Indo-Pakistan War in 1965. In the present-day Indian Punjab, Sikhs form 51 percent of the population.

SIKH LITERATURE, MYTH, AND LORE

Canonical and noncanonical. The earliest source materials on Nānak are the *janam-sākhīs* ("life stories"), written 50 to 80 years after the death of the Guru. Most Sikh scholars reject them and rely instead on the Guru's compositions incorporated in the *Ādi Granth* and the *Vārs* (heroic ballads) composed by Bhāī Gurdās (d. AD 1629). Neither Nānak's hymns nor Gurdās' *Vārs*, however, are specific regarding the events of Nānak's life. Other historical writing was done during the 18th and the 19th centuries, notably by Manī Singh (died 1734), Kirpāl Singh Bhallā (died 1741), Sarūp Dās Bhallā (1776), and Santokh Singh (1823). For the rest, Sikh historians rely heavily on records of Mughal court historians.

The canonical work

There is only one canonical work: the *Ādi Granth* (first volume) compiled by the fifth Guru, Arjun, in AD 1604. There are at least three recensions (versions) of the *Ādi Granth* that differ from each other in minor detail. The version accepted by Sikhs as authentic is said to have been revised by Gobind Singh in AD 1704. The *Ādi Granth* contains nearly 6,000 hymns composed by the first five Gurūs: Nānak (974), Angad (62), Amar Dās (907), Rām Dās (679), and Arjun (2,218). Gobind incorporated 115 hymns of his father Tegh Bahādur in it. Besides the compositions of the Guru, the *Ādi Granth* contains hymns of the Bhakta saints and Muslim Ṣūfīs, notably Farīd, and of a few of the bards attached to the courts of the Gurūs. The hymns are divided into 31 *rāgas* (musical modes), meant to be sung except for Nānak's *Japī* (a morning prayer) that is spoken.

The *Dasam Granth* (tenth volume) is a compilation of writings ascribed to Guru Gobind. Scholars are not agreed on the authenticity of the contents of this *Granth*, and it is not accorded the same sanctity as the *Ādi Granth*.

Traditions of the Khālsā are contained in the *Rahatnāmās* (codes of conduct) by several contemporaries of Gurū Gobind Singh.

Myths and lore. Although the Gurūs themselves disclaimed miraculous powers, a vast body of *sākhīs* ("stories") recounting such miracles grew up, and with them *gurdwārās* ("temples") commemorating the sites where they were performed. It also became an article of belief that the spirit of one Guru passed to his successor "as one lamp lights another." This notion gained confirmation through the fact that the Gurūs used the same poetic pseudonym, "Nānak", in their compositions.

A composition about which little is known, but which has played an important role in Sikh affairs, is a collection of prophecies, *Sau Sākhī* (hundred tales), ascribed to Gurū Gobind Singh. Various versions are known to have been published prophesying changes of regimes and the advent of a redeemer who will spread Sikhism over the globe.

DOCTRINES OF SIKHISM

Use of Hindu cosmogony

Views on the nature of man and the universe. Speculation on the origin of the cosmos is largely derived from Hindu texts. Sikhs accept the cyclic Hindu theory of *saṃsāra*—birth, death, and rebirth—and *karman*, whereby the nature of a man's life is determined by his actions in a previous life. Man is, therefore, equal to all other creatures, except insofar as he is sentient. Human birth is his one opportunity to escape *saṃsāra* and attain salvation.

Concept of the Khālsā. Khālsā is a concept of a "chosen" race of soldier-saints committed to five principles: a Spartan code of conduct (consisting of abstinence from liquor, tobacco, and narcotics; and devotion to a life of prayer) and a crusade for *dharmayudha*—the battle for righteousness. The number five has always had mystic significance in the Punjab—"land of the five rivers." "Where there are five, there am I," wrote Gobind Singh. The first Khālsā were *pañj piyāres*—the five beloved ones.

The aim of all young Sikhs should be to take *pahul* ("baptism") and thus become Khālsā. The *sahajdhārī* ("slow-adopter") is assumed to be preparing himself gradually for the initiation.

The notion of the five K's. The five emblems of the Khālsā, all beginning with the letter *k*, have no scriptural basis, but are mentioned in the *Rahatnāmās*, written by Gobind Singh's contemporaries. The most important of the K's is *keṣa* ("hair"), which the Khālsā must retain unshorn. A Khālsā who cuts off his hair is a *patit* ("renegade"). The sanctity of unshorn hair is older than Guru Gobind Singh—the founder of the Khālsā—for many of the earlier Gurūs also followed the tradition (common among certain sects of Hindu ascetics as well) of letting their hair and beards grow.

The other four K's are *kaṅghā* ("comb"); *kacch* ("drawers"), worn by soldiers; *kirpān* ("sabre"); and *karā* ("bracelet") of steel, commonly worn on the right arm. The usually accepted explanation of the *karā* is that it is the Gurū's charm against evil—a variation of the Hindu *rakhri* tied by sisters on the wrist of their brothers to keep them from harm.

Monotheism. Unity of the godhead is emphasized in Sikhism. Nānak used the Hindu Vedāntic concept of *Om*, the mystic syllable, as a symbol of God. To this he added the qualifications of singleness and creativity and thus constructed the symbol *ik* ("one") *Om Kār* ("creator"), which was later given figurative representation as ੴ. The opening lines of his celebrated morning prayer, *Japjī*, which are known as the *Mul Mantra* ("root belief") of Sikhism define God as the One, the Truth, Creator, immortal, and omnipresent. God is also *nirankār*—formless—and beyond human comprehension. Sikh scriptures use many names, both Hindu and Muslim, for God. Nānak's favourite names were *Sat-Kartār* (True Creator) and *Sat-Nām* (the True Name). Later the word *Wāh-Gurū* (Hail Gurū) was added and is now the Sikh synonym for God.

Concepts of spiritual authority. The sole repository of spiritual authority is the *Ādi Granth*. In the event of disputes, spiritual or temporal, a conclave is summoned to meet at the Akāl Takht ("Throne of the Timeless"), a building erected by the sixth Gurū, Hargobind, facing the Harimandir temple in Amritsar. Resolutions passed at the Akāl Takht have spiritual sanction.

Aniconic orientation and anti-ritualism

Views on idolatry and rituals. Sikhism forbids representation of God in pictures and the worship of idols. Nevertheless the *Ādi Granth* itself has become an object of worship and as such is known as *Granth Sahib* (the *Granth* personified). It is "roused" in the morning and placed under an awning draped in fineries. Devotees do obeisance and place offerings before it. In the evening it is put to rest for the night. On festival days it is taken in procession through the streets. Most rituals centre on the *Ādi Granth*. The nonstop recitation from cover to cover by a relay of readers (*akhand-path*), which takes two days and nights, has become very popular.

Social consequences of beliefs. The main consequence of Sikh belief has been a gradual breaking away from the Hindu social system and the development of Sikh separatism. The singular worship of the *Ādi Granth* excludes worship of all other objects common among Hindus (*i.e.*, the sun, rivers, trees, etc.) and also puts a stop to the practice of ritual purifications and pilgrimages to the Ganges. Since every Sikh is entitled to read the scripture, Sikhs do not have a priestly caste similar to the Brahmins in Hinduism. Sikh insistence on commensality (eating together) at the *Gurū ka laṅgar* ("kitchen of the Gurū") destroyed the traditional Hindu pattern of caste among them and substituted a far less rigid social structure. Sikhs are grouped into three broad categories based largely on ethnic differences: Jāṭs (agricultural tribes), non-Jāṭs (erstwhile Brahmins, Kṣatriyas and Vaiśyas—the three highest groups of the traditional Hindu social system), and Mazahabis (untouchables). The Jāṭs, though Śūdras (lowest group inside caste system), are pre-eminent; the Mazahabis, though converts from Hindu outcastes (untouchables outside the caste system), and still discriminated against, have a much higher status than untouchables in Hindu society (see also CASTE SYSTEMS).

PRACTICES AND INSTITUTIONS

The Gurū and the disciple. The guidance of the Gurū toward the attainment of *mokṣa*—release—is absolutely essential. The Gurū or the Satgurū—true Gurū—is accorded a status only a shade below that of God. His function is to point the way to the realization of the truth, to explain the nature of reality, and to give the disciple the gift of the divine word (*nām-dān*). Although the line of Gurūs ended with Gobind Singh and Sikhs regard the *Ādi Granth* as their "living" Gurū, the practice of attaching oneself to a *sant* ("saint") and elevating him to a status of a Gurū has persisted and is widely practiced.

Recitation of Nāma. Sikhism is often described as *Nāmmārga* ("the way of *Nāma*") because it emphasizes the constant repetition (*Jap*) of the name of God and the *gurbāni* (the divine hymns of the Gurūs). *Nāma* cleanses the soul of sin and conquers the source of evil, *haumain* ("I am")—the ego. Thus tamed, the ego becomes a weapon to overcome lust, anger, greed, attachment, and pride. *Nāma* stills the wandering mind and induces a super-conscious stillness (*divya drṣti*), opens the *dasam duār* (tenth gate—the body has only nine natural orifices) through which enters divine light; and thus a person attains the state of absolute bliss.

Rites of passage and other ceremonies. No specific rites are prescribed for birth, but the practice of chanting the first five verses of Nānak's *Japjī* is practiced among some Sikhs. A few days later the child is brought to the *gurdwārā*. The *Ādi Granth* is opened and the child given a name beginning with the letter of the first word on the left page. When a child has learned some Gurmukhi script he is initiated into reading the *Ādi Granth*. The most important ceremony is that of *pahul* ("baptism"), usually administered on attaining puberty. The initiate takes *amrit* ("nectar") and is admitted to the Khālsā fraternity. A Sikh marriage (*karaj*) requires the groom and bride to go round the *Ādi Granth* four times to the chanting of wedding hymns. On death, there is continual chanting of hymns till the body is prepared for cremation. A final *ardāsā* ("supplicatory") prayer is said before the funeral pyre is lit. Ashes of the dead are usually immersed in the Beas at Kīratpur—or in one of the Hindu sacred rivers, preferably the Ganges.

Sacred times and places. Early hours of the dawn are ambrosial hours (*amritvelā*) most appropriate for prayer and meditation. Though not specifically prescribed as such, *gurdwārā*s with historical associations are, in fact, places of pilgrimage. Pre-eminent amongst them is the Harimandir at Amritsar. Nankāna, the birthplace of Nānak (now in Pakistan) comes second. There are also four thrones (Akāl Takhts) that are accorded special sanctity; these are at Amritsar, Anandpur, Patna and Nanded. The last two are the places where Guru Gobind Singh was born and died. From all of them, proclamations can be made to all the Khālsā.

Pilgrimage places

The ceremony of pahul, which initiates Sikhs into the Khālsā brotherhood. Five members prepare the initiating drink (*amrit*, "nectar") by mixing sweets in water with a dagger, while the initiates wait in the background. The ceremony usually takes place when a boy reaches puberty, but may be undergone at a later age. On entering the brotherhood, initiates adopt the five K's; *kesa* (uncut "hair" and beard), *kangha* ("comb"), *kacch* ("soldier's shorts"), *kara* ("steel bracelet"), and *kirpan* ("double-edged dagger").

Marc Riboud—Magnum

The first Sikh place of worship, built by Nānak at Kartārpur, was like Hindu temples, known as *dharamsālā* ("place of faith"). At a later stage, Sikhs coined their own name for their temples—*gurdwārā*—gateway to the Gurū. There are over 200 historical *gurdwārā*s associated with the Gurūs, which are controlled by the Shiromanī Gurdwārā Prabandhak Committee (S.G.P.C.) set up by the Sikh Gurdwāras Act of 1925. Offerings made at *gurdwārā*s are used for their upkeep as well as for the operation of Khālsā schools and colleges.

Besides historical *gurdwārā*s, every place with a sizable Sikh population is likely to have a *gurdwārā* of its own. In well-to-do homes, a room is often set apart for this purpose.

The only object of worship is the *Ādi Granth*. Worshippers make their offerings of money and flowers and receive *karāh-prasād*, a batter made of flour, *ghī* (clarified butter), and sugar.

Sikhs observe all festivals celebrated by the Hindus of northern India. In addition, they celebrate the birthdays of the first and the last Gurū and the martyrdom of the fifth (Arjun) and the ninth (Tegh Bahādur). The biggest fair is on the first of Baisākh (March/April), which is also the birthday of the Khālsā itself.

The Khālsā Sangat. The Sangat—congregation—is usually known as the *Sādh-sangat* (congregation of holy men)—and thus is invested with sanctity. The Sangat in each *gurdwārā* elects its own governing body and decisions are taken by vote. As a rule women do not participate in the deliberations. The S.G.P.C. at Amritsar is the general governing body of Sikhism.

Sectarian differences. The first dissenters from the mainstream of Sikhism were followers of Nānak's elder son, Śri Chand, known as the Udāsīs. The order inclined towards asceticism and later furnished priests (*mahants*) for *gurdwārā*s. They were ousted from control by the S.G.P.C. in 1925. Followers of Rām Rāi, who was passed

(margin) Minor subgroups and orders

over by Har Rāi (seventh Gurū) in favour of the younger son Hari Krishen (eighth Gurū), broke away to become Rām Rāiyās. They have their headquarters in Dehra Dūn, Uttar Pradesh.

Khālsā who do not believe that the line of Gurūs ended with Gobind Singh have continued the tradition of having a living Gurū. Among these, the Bandaī Khālsā (followers of Bandā Bahādur) are now extinct; but two other groups, the Nāmdhārīs and Nirankārīs, worship living Gurūs.

Sikh welfare and educational institutions. The S.G.P.C. is the chief welfare organization of the Sikhs. The Sikh Educational Conferences, meeting annually since 1908, are the chief educational organizations credited with the setting up of innumerable schools. In 1965 two religio-social organizations, the Gurū Gobind Singh Foundation and the Gurū Nānak Foundation, set up to commemorate the 300th and 500th birth anniversaries of the last and the first Gurūs, respectively, have endowed many university chairs for the study of Sikhism and the publication of material on Sikh history and religion.

POLITICAL AND SOCIAL ROLE IN INDIA SINCE INDEPENDENCE

Caste attitudes. The three-tiered-caste structure among the Sikhs, viz., Jāts, non-Jāts, and Mazahabis, is in a state of flux. Among the educated urban classes it is fast breaking up, but in the villages a form of apartheid persists, excluding Mazahabis from community wells. State laws provide untouchables with free schooling, preference in services, and reservation of seats in village councils. State legislatures and the Indian Parliament have encouraged the underprivileged to maintain their separate identity.

Church–state relations. The Sikh religion and politics have always been intimately connected, and belief in a Sikh state is an article of faith. *Rāj karey Gā Khālsā*—"the Khālsā shall rule"—is chanted at the conclusion of every service and was one of the motivations of the demand for a Sikh-dominated state, now in existence, with Chandīgarh as its capital (transferred to the Punjab in February 1970).

The place of Sikhism in Indian religions. Close religious and social affiliation with Hinduism has always presented a danger to Sikhism as a separate socio-religious system. The tendency of the younger generation of Sikhs to abandon Khālsā emblems of unshorn hair and beard have increased the rate of lapse back into Hinduism. Efforts are made to combat this tendency by emphasizing features that are unique to Sikhism and elements that the faith has imbibed from non-Hindu sources, chiefly Ṣūfīstic Islām.

BIBLIOGRAPHY. J.D. CUNNINGHAM, *History of the Sikhs*, 2nd ed. (1853), was the first scholarly work on the Sikhs up to the first Anglo-Sikh war of 1845–46. His interpretation of Sikhism as an eclectic Hindu–Muslim faith remained unquestioned till McLeod's work in 1968. Cunningham was censured for suggesting that British designs on the Sikh kingdom provoked Sikh aggression. M.A. MACAULIFFE, *The Sikh Religion*, 6 vol. (1909), is a compilation of all the legends about the Sikh Gurūs based on *Janam-sākhīs* and on saints whose writings are in the Sikh scriptures; full of literal translations of Sikh hymns. SHER SINGH, *Philosophy of Sikhism* (1944), is a scholarly work interpreting Sikhism as an offshoot of Vaiṣṇavite Hinduism. A selection of hymns from the *Ādi Granth* and Gobind Singh's *Dasam Granth* carried out by a panel of Sikh scholars may be found in *Selections from the Sacred Writings of the Sikhs*, trans. by T. SINGH *et al.* (1960). KHUSHWANT SINGH, *A History of the Sikhs*, 2 vol. (1963–66), interprets Sikhism as an aspect of Panjabi nationalism and ends with a note of warning about the future of Sikhs. See also KHUSHWANT SINGH, *Ranjit Singh, Maharajah of the Punjab* (1963), a biography based on Persian, Panjabi, and English sources, and (trans.), *Hymns of Guru Nanak* (1969), a selection of Nānak's hymns with a short introduction. W.H. MCLEOD, *Gurū Nānak and the Sikh Religion* (1968), casts serious doubts on source material on the life of Nānak, reflects the theory of Sikhism as an eclectic faith and asserts that it is a branch of Hindu Vaiṣṇavism tinged with yogism.

(K.S.)

Sikkim

Sikkim, a country in the eastern Himalayan mountains, has an area of 2,818 square miles (7,299 square kilometres) and a population of about 200,000. It is the smallest of three contiguous Himalayan kingdoms, the other two being Nepal, which lies to the west, and Bhutan, which lies to the east. To the north Sikkim is bounded by China (Tibet), and to the south by India. Although Sikkim is a sovereign state, since 1950 its relations with India have been governed by a treaty, by the terms of which India has undertaken to defend Sikkim's territorial integrity and to accept responsibility for its foreign relations and strategic communications.

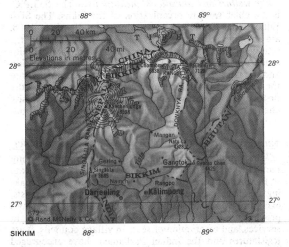

SIKKIM

As the smallest country in Central Asia, Sikkim throughout its history has had to battle constantly to retain its identity. It is primarily an agricultural country. The head of state, who has his seat in Gangtok, the capital, is the *chogyal* (temporal and spiritual king). Buddhism is the state religion.

Sikkim has great extremes of altitude and climate within its borders; its lowest point is about 700 feet above sea level, and its highest is the peak of Kānchenjunga (Khangchendzonga; 28,208 feet), the third-highest mountain in the world. (For coverage of an associated physical feature, see HIMALAYAN MOUNTAIN RANGES. For historical aspects, see INDIAN SUBCONTINENT, HISTORY OF THE).

Relief, drainage, and soils. The topography of the country is so mountainous that level ground is rare. Sikkim is bounded on the west, north, and east by a horseshoe-shaped ring of high mountain ranges. To the west, the Singalila Range separates Sikkim from Nepal, culminating its northern extremity in the Kānchenjunga Massif (mountainous mass); besides Kānchenjunga itself, the massif includes many other peaks, all of which are over 20,000 feet high. The northern section of the horseshoe is formed by the main axis of the Himalayan mountains, running from west to east. The eastern boundary of the state is formed by the Donkhya Range, which stretches south from the Himalayas near Tista Kangse, a glacier.

Much of Sikkim forms the drainage basin of the Tista River, which originates in the extreme northeast, near the Chinese frontier. From its source the river descends steeply, dropping about 16,000 feet within 65 miles to Rongphu (Rangpo). The mountains of the north, east, and west are composed of hard gneissic (coarse-grained) rocks, which are to a considerable extent resistant to weathering. The central and southern parts of the country, which are the least elevated and most populated, are formed of comparatively soft materials, being partly composed of schistose (medium- or coarse-grained) or foliated rocks, which are easily eroded.

Climate, vegetation, and animal life. The great range of altitude leads to immense variations in climate and vegetation. The rainfall, except near the northern boundary, is very heavy, averaging 140 inches annually at Gangtok. From October to February the weather is generally clear. In March thunderstorms begin, later giving way to the southeast monsoon winds, which bring rain from mid-June to late September.

The type of vegetation varies with altitude, and three categories may be distinguished. These are the tropical type, which occurs at altitudes up to 5,000 feet; the temperate type, which occurs between 5,000 and 13,000 feet; and the Alpine type, which occurs between 13,000 feet and the perpetual snowline, which begins at 16,000 feet. In the lowest regions tropical forests of tall shady trees occur, accompanied by a luxuriant undergrowth of shrubs. Canes, palms, bamboos, ferns, and orchids are abundant. In the temperate region, forests of oak, laurel, maple, magnolia, alder, and birch, as well as coniferous forests of fir, hemlock, and spruce, and rhododendron scrub form the predominant vegetation. The Alpine zone is characterized by such flowers as primulas, gentians, blue poppies, aconites, and Himalayan rhubarb. Altogether more than 4,000 species of plants occur in Sikkim. There are 40 species of rhododendron, which vary from two feet to 60 feet in height. There are also more than 450 different species of orchid.

There is a rich bird life, and between 500 and 600 different species have been enumerated. Nearly 600 species of butterflies have been recorded, many of them brightly coloured. The wildlife includes mountain sheep, Tibetan antelope, wild ass, musk deer, panda, Himalayan wild goat, spotted deer, and wild boar.

Landscape and population. Most of the population lives in the central, western, or southern parts of the country. In the far north the land is snowbound and uninhabitable. As there are few flat areas, villages are few; the people live in small homesteads scattered on the slopes of the hills. The population density is 70 per square mile. About 90 percent of the people are farmers; due to the isolation of their farms they tend to be self-sufficient. About 60 percent of the people in Sikkim own their own land, and the remainder are tenant farmers. Maize and rice are the two chief crops, with maize and potatoes becoming the staple above 5,000 feet. In the northern valleys, a partially pastoral economy still endures, based on yak and sheep herding. The annual growth rate of the present population, which numbers about 200,000, is estimated at 1.9 percent.

Gangtok, the capital and seat of government, which is at an altitude of 5,600 feet, has a population of 13,000. A conscious effort is being made by the government to discourage too great a population flow to the capital to avoid depopulating other parts of the country. As a part

Crops and livestock

Sikkim, Area and Population				
	area		population	
	sq mi	sq km	1961 census	1971 estimate
Districts				
Eastern	367	951	...	84,440
Northern	1,736	4,496	...	13,565
Southern	269	697	...	52,692
Western	446	1,155	...	57,912
Total Sikkim	2,818	7,299	162,189	208,609
Source: Official government figures.				

of this effort, the district administration centres in the north, south, and west of the country have been provided with the same facilities as those available in Gangtok, which is the headquarters for the eastern region. Mangen (Mangang) is headquarters for the northern region, Gezing (Gyalzing) for the western, and Namchi for the southern. In Gangtok itself there are six schools with a total school population of about 4,000 children. Gangtok hospital has nine doctors and 200 beds. Among the places of interest in Gangtok are the Namgyal Institute of Tibetology, the Royal Chapel, the Cottage Industries Institute (a training school, manufacturing centre, and a shop), and the open market. There are two film theatres.

The people and their history. The Lepchās have no legends of migration, and it is possible that they are indigenous to the country. They speak a Tibeto-Burman language, using a script that was devised for the language by King Chagdor Namgyal at the beginning of the 18th century. Most Lepchās have accepted Buddhism, although the pre-Buddhist Lepchā religion, Bon, has influenced Sikkimese Buddhism. The Lepchās

Climatic variation

are expert weavers and are knowledgeable about jungle plants.

Other tribes that are either indigenous to Sikkim or that may have entered the country from the trans-Himalayas in the prehistoric period are Mongolian Magars and Tsongs. The Magars are mentioned as one of the groups to have celebrated the coronation in 1642 of the first *chogyal* of Sikkim, Phuntsog (Penchoo) Namgyal. The Magars are renowned warriors and form an important part of the Sikkim Guards. The name Sikkim seems to have derived from the Tsong term *sukkim*, meaning "new house" or "happy house." The second *chogyal*, Tensung Namgyal, married a Tsong.

Migrations into Sikkim

The Bhutias, a Tibetan-speaking group who entered Sikkim in the 13th century, previously lived a pastoral life on the plateaus of Tibet; they belonged to the Rnying-ma-pa sect of Mahāyāna Buddhism (representing a liberal tendency in that religion). Their migration, which was from Kham in Tibet, was led by a prince of the Namgyal dynasty, from which the present *chogyal* is descended. In adapting to the lusher geography of Sikkim, most of them settled down as farmers, although some still prefer to live in the high valleys of northern Sikkim, herding yak and sheep.

Over the years the Bhutia group came into increased contact with the Lepchas and intermarried with them.

The largest migration to Sikkim took place in the mid-19th century, when various tribes entered from northern and eastern Nepal. The first large migratory group were the Newars, a Tibeto-Burman group skilled in metalwork; the ruling *chogyal* granted them the right to mine copper and to mint a Sikkimese coinage. The Newars were followed by the Gurungs, Tamangs, Rais, and Sherpas; these were Mongoloid peoples who were adept at farming at high altitudes. To accommodate the influx of settlers, new lands were opened to cultivation. As pressure on the land grew intensive, new methods of farming were introduced, including the terracing of steep slopes. Other groups migrating from Nepal included clans of the Chettri, the Bahuns, and the Bishu Karmas, all of whom were probably Aryans in origin. The various Nepalese tribes spoke their own languages; today, most of them speak Gurkhali Nepali. By religion the newcomers were mainly Hindus of a peculiarly Himalayan type. They brought with them a pantheon of both Hindu and Buddhist deities. Today many clans worship deities of both religions; in both Nepal and Sikkim, Buddhist and Hindu beliefs have traditionally interacted or amalgamated over the centuries. Today, in addition to Hinduism and Buddhism, both Christianity and Islām are also established.

Sikkim, as a small country, has been obliged to struggle to maintain its territorial integrity. In the mid-18th century Sikkim fought a series of wars with Bhutan over territory. In the latter part of the 18th century the expansionism of the Nepalese ruler Prithvi Narayan Shah obliged Sikkim to defend its western borders, which had extended as far as Ilām, Nepal. Prithvi Narayan Shah,

The wars with Nepal

after consolidating control over the various regions of Nepal, began a series of wars with Sikkim that were to last for nearly a century. For a short time the Nepalese rulers occupied part of western Sikkim but were obliged to relinquish part of it in 1793 and the Terai, or submontane part, in 1816. In 1839 the British East India Company obtained Darjeeling from Sikkim as a health resort. After the British were established in Darjeeling, British advocates of an expansionist policy attempted to bring independent Sikkim within their sphere of influence and succeeded in annexing the submontane regions. The annexation led to troubles, but after the defeat of Sikkimese troops by the British an Anglo-Sikkimese treaty was signed in 1861. By the terms of this treaty, the British obtained such concessions as the right to build a road through Sikkim to Tibet, while Sikkim's sovereignty was recognized, thus establishing it as a buffer state between British India and Tibet. In 1890, after a series of Tibetan incursions across the frontier of Sikkim, an Anglo-Chinese convention was concluded whereby China acknowledged the special relationship of the Anglo-Indian government with the kingdom of Sikkim, while at the same time the boundary between Sikkim and China was defined. A British political officer was subsequently appointed to assist the *chogyal*.

After India attained independence in 1947, a treaty was subsequently signed between Sikkim and the Republic of India in 1950. By the terms of this treaty Sikkim was deemed to be an Indian protectorate, and an Indian representative, who was simultaneously accredited to Tibet and Bhutan, was sent to Sikkim. This period was a difficult one in Sikkim's history. Political parties had been formed for the first time and social distinctions were sharply felt. At the same time some factions exerted considerable pressure to persuade Sikkim to accede to India. Today Sikkim's political system has matured. Four elections have been held. There are three principal parties—the Sikkim State Congress, the Sikkim National Party, and the Sikkim National Congress. Since 1953 there has been a coalition of the three parties within the government. The present *chogyal* is Palden Thondup Namgyal, who was crowned in 1965. The Gyalmo (Queen) is interested in education and handicrafts.

The present government

The national economy. The economy of Sikkim is primarily agricultural. The principal cash crops are cardamom (a spice plant), potatoes, mandarin oranges, maize, rice, soybeans, and ginger. Sikkim is the world's principal source of cardamom, producing about 2,000 tons a year. The forests occupy about 35 percent of the land area and are rich in valuable timber; they include large tracts of coniferous forest suitable for making wood pulp. Timber and various medicinal herbs are exported. A tea industry has recently been established. The principal minerals exported are copper concentrate and graphite. Because of the heavy rainfall and steep terrain the potential for hydroelectrical production is considerable. A variety of fruits are canned for export. Local crafts include carpet weaving, silversmithing, and the making of paper by hand. There is great potential for tourism, the woodpulp industry, floriculture, and the production of hydroelectric power for export. At present most of Sikkim's trade is with India, and foreign aid is obtained only from India, which provides the equivalent of $4,000,000 a year in rupees.

Transport and communications. Road transport is the main means of communication, and it is nationalized. More than 930 miles of paved roads connect all the major towns and many minor townships. Despite the immense difficulties posed by the rough terrain and climatic conditions, Sikkim possesses the best road system in the region. There is a network of government radio stations in the interior, and there is telephonic communication between the principal towns. Gangtok is 75 miles from the nearest airport, which is at Bāghdogra, and 70 miles from the nearest railway station, which is at Siliguri; both of these are in the Indian plains.

Administration and social conditions. The *chogyal* is assisted in governing by the Sikkim Council, which is composed of 24 representatives, of which 18 are elected and six nominated. Council members hold portfolios of education, health, forestry, excise, the bazaar, agriculture, public works, transport, and press and publicity. The secretaries to the government are directly responsible for home affairs, land revenue, and finance. In 1972 the *chogyal* assumed all executive powers previously held by the *sidlon*, or prime minister; these included positions as president of the council and head of the civil service. The official language is English.

The *chogyal* and the Sikkim Council

The district headquarters of north, south, and west Sikkim are the centres for development in these areas; Gangtok, as mentioned earlier, constitutes the headquarters for the eastern region. Each district headquarters has a hospital, a secondary school, law courts, and a forestry office, while the various departments, such as police, development, and agriculture, have representatives in each region. The Sikkimese civil service has personnel of a high standard, but further training is often required at junior levels. Apart from the governmental administration, a local system of village government permits each community to formulate and carry out decisions on matters of immediate concern to it; this village system is particularly strong in the north.

There are more than 200 schools and 28 dispensaries in the country; no person lives more than two miles from a school. Three development plans have so far been completed; the fourth development plan covers the period from 1971 to 1976. The average per capita income is about 650 rupees (U.S. $87); extremes of wealth and poverty are not to be found in Sikkim.

Cultural life. Sikkim's cultural life is related to Tibetan religious and aesthetic traditions, but it retains a unique character from the various indigenous tribes of Sikkim and their pre-Buddhist customs. The cultural climax of the year is represented by the national day, Phanglhapsol, when masked dances are performed in honour of the presiding national deity and of the mountain Kānchenjunga. There are also many secular folk dances. Music is an important part of the school curriculum. The Namgyal Institute of Tibetology has the third-largest collection of Tibetan books in the world, exceeded only by the libraries of Leningrad and Peking. An institute in Gangtok specializes in weaving, painting, and carpentry and has helped to revive cottage industries throughout the country. Many monasteries are repositories of artistic treasures, including wall paintings, thang-kas (religious paintings mounted on brocade), and bronze images.

Cottage industries

Sikkim generally depends on Indian newspapers, although a government newspaper is printed every weekday; there is also an independent English-language publication published every other week and a monthly paper in Nepali. There are no radio or television services.

Prospects for the future. Sikkim has attained a standard of living higher than that in many neighbouring regions of Asia. Under a pragmatic administration, development is being fostered while at the same time an attempt is being made to retain the best traditional, spiritual, and social values inherited from the past. Its political system seems to have successfully united democracy with traditional modes of ruling, thereby avoiding the sharp conflicts between the old and the new that sometimes occur in developing nations. Much remains to be done to tap the country's resources; more industrial development, in particular, is needed as, with the growth of population, agriculture will increasingly need to be supplemented with other modes of employment. Further training is required in several fields; there is a particular need for teacher training.

Sikkim is fortunate in the degree of national cohesion that it has attained; it is the only one of the Himalayan kingdoms to have an elected council. It is also fortunate in possessing clearly demarcated boundaries, and in enjoying correct relations with its neighbours. A sense of national purpose and identity has done much to consolidate all groups in Sikkim and to dispel the anxieties that caused disturbances a generation ago. Current concern focusses upon the emergence of Sikkim's national personality within the larger comity of nations.

BIBLIOGRAPHY. C.U. AITCHISON, *A Collection of Treaties, Engagements and Sunnuds Relating to India and Neighbouring Countries*, 5th ed. (1929), includes the texts of three 19th-century treaties with Great Britain and a brief historical sketch of Sikkim; CHARLES A. BELL, *Tibet Past and Present* (1924), contains a discussion of Sikkim's history and politics, based on the author's experience as Political Officer in Sikkim for over 10 years; J.C. GAWLER, *Sikkim, with Hints on Mountain and Jungle Warfare* (1873), contains official reports of British retaliations against Sikkim for purported kidnappings of British subjects inside British territory; GEOFFREY GORER, *Himalayan Village: An Account of the Lepchas of Sikkim* (1938), an ethnological study of this society in the village of Lingthem; JOSEPH DALTON HOOKER, *Himalayan Journals*, rev. ed., 2 vol. (1855), a classic work that discusses comprehensively the history, religion, customs, and botany of Sikkim in the 19th century; MARCO PALLIS, *Peaks and Lamas* (1939), a popular, anecdotal account of mountaineering and a form of Mahāyāna Buddhism in Sikkim; THE ROYAL WEDDING COMMITTEE, *Sikkim: Facts and Figures* (1963), a digest of essential data and statistics on Sikkim.

(K.C.Pr.)

Sikorsky, Igor

An outstanding pioneer of aircraft design, Igor Sikorsky is also known for his successful development of the helicopter in the 1930s. This contribution, and others in fixed-wing design, changed the course of flight history.

Sikorsky was born in Kiev, Russia, on May 25, 1889. His father was a graduate physician and professor of psychology in the local university. His mother also was a physician but never practiced professionally. Her great interest in art and in the life and work of Leonardo da Vinci undoubtedly stimulated her son's early interest in experimenting with model flying machines; when he was 12 years old he made a small rubber-powered helicopter that could rise in the air.

By courtesy of Sikorsky Aircraft

Sikorsky.

In 1903 he entered the Naval Academy in St. Petersburg (Leningrad), with the intention of becoming a career officer, but his interest in engineering led to his resignation from the service in 1906. After a brief period of engineering study in Paris, he returned to Kiev and entered the Kiev Polytechnic Institute. Following a reasonably successful academic year, however, he concluded that the abstract sciences and the higher mathematics as then taught had little relationship to the solution of practical problems, and he left the school, preferring to spend his time in his own shop and laboratory.

A trip through Europe in the summer of 1908 brought him into contact with the accomplishments of the Wright brothers and the group of European inventors who were trying to match their progress in flight. Returning to Kiev, Sikorsky came to the conclusion that the way to fly was "straight up," as Leonardo da Vinci had proposed, a concept that called for a horizontal rotor. Assisted financially by his sister Olga, he returned to Paris in January 1909 for further study and to purchase a light-weight engine.

Back in Kiev in May of 1909 he began construction of a helicopter. Its failure revealed some of the practical obstacles. A second machine with a larger engine tested in 1910 also failed to fly. He then made a major decision: "I had learned enough to recognize that with the existing state of the art, engines, materials, and—most of all— the shortage of money and lack of experience . . . I would not be able to produce a successful helicopter at that time." In fact, he had to wait 30 years before all conditions could be met.

First flying machine

For the time being he decided to enter the fixed-wing field and began construction of his first airplane. Sikorsky's S-1 biplane was tested early in 1910, and, although its 15-horsepower engine proved inadequate, a redesigned airframe with a larger engine (S-2) carried him on his first short flight. The S-3, S-4, and S-5 followed in quick succession, each a refinement over its predecessor, and each adding to his piloting experience. Finally, by the summer of 1911, in an S-5 with a 50-horsepower engine, he was able to remain in the air for more than an hour, attain altitudes of 1,500 feet (450 metres), and make short cross-country flights. This success earned him International Pilot's License Number 64.

The subsequent S-6 series established Sikorsky as a serious competitor for supplying aircraft to the Russian Army. Characteristically, he soon took a giant step: the first four-engined airplane, called "Le Grand," the precursor of many modern bombers and commercial transports, which he built and flew successfully by 1913. Among its innovative features, not adopted elsewhere until the middle 1920s, was a completely enclosed cabin for pilots and passengers.

In the period of disruption following the Russian Revolution and the collapse of Germany, Sikorsky saw little opportunity for further aircraft development in Europe. He decided to start over again in the United States and in March 1919 landed in New York as an immigrant.

After several lean years as a lecturer and school teacher, while trying to find a place for himself in the contracting postwar aircraft industry, he and a few associates, some of them former Russian officers, formed their own company, the Sikorsky Aero Engineering Corporation. They set up shop in an old barn on a farm near Roosevelt Field on Long Island. Sikorsky became a U.S. citizen in 1928. By 1929 the company, having become a division of United Aircraft Corporation, occupied a large modern plant at Bridgeport, Connecticut, and was producing S-38 twin-engined amphibians in considerable numbers. In 1931 the first S-40, the "American Clipper," pioneered Pan American World Airways mail and passenger routes around the Caribbean and to South America. By the summer of 1937 Pan American began transpacific and transatlantic service with the first four-engined S-42 "Clipper III," the last of the Sikorsky series, the ancestor of which had been "Le Grand" of 1913.

The "American Clipper"

By the late 1930s changing requirements for military and commercial air transport forecast the termination of the large flying boat, and Sikorsky returned to his first love, the helicopter. Once again he was involved in "advanced pioneering work . . . where extremely little reliable information and no piloting experience whatever were available." The essential aerodynamic theory and construction techniques that had been lacking in 1910, however, were now available. Early in 1939, with a well-trained engineering group at his disposal, he started the construction of the VS-300 helicopter. As he said later, "There was a great satisfaction in knowing that, within a short period of time, good engineering along a novel line produced encouraging results." On September 14, 1939, the plane lifted off the ground on its first flight. Its designer was at the controls; during his entire career Sikorsky always insisted on making the first trial flight of any new design himself. On May 6, 1941, in an improved machine, he established an international endurance record of 1 hour, 32.4 seconds.

First flight of the VS-300

It is doubtful that Sikorsky at that time fully envisioned the remarkable development of the vertical lift machine in the next 30 years. Certainly he did not anticipate widespread use of the helicopter as an offensive military weapon as in Vietnam. He regarded it as a useful tool for industry and air commerce but primarily as an effective device for rescue and relief of human beings caught in natural disasters, such as fire, flood, or famine. He estimated that over 50,000 lives had been saved by helicopters.

Igor Sikorsky's active professional life covered virtually the entire span of practical flight by man, from the Wright brothers to space exploration. Few in aviation can claim such a span of personal participation, or personal contribution with such a wide range of innovative ideas. He only complained that of all his past predictions, those that he lived to regret were on the "too conservative" side.

Sikorsky retired as engineering manager for his company in 1957 but remained active as a consultant until his death on October 26, 1972, at Easton, Connecticut. In addition to his wife (married in 1924), he left one daughter and four sons, all of whom have professional careers. Sikorsky received many honorary doctorates in science and engineering, honorary fellowships in leading scientific and technical societies in the United States and Europe, and the highest medals and awards in aviation, including the Cross of St. Vladimir from Russia; the Sylvanus Albert Reed Award for 1942 from the Institute of Aeronautical Sciences in New York; the United States Presidential Certificate of Merit in 1948; the Daniel Guggenheim Medal and Certificate for 1951; the Elmer A. Sperry Award for 1964; and the National Defense Award in 1971.

BIBLIOGRAPHY. CHARLES DOLLFUSS and HENRI BOUCHE, *Histoire de l'aéronautique* (1932), contains photos of "Ilya Mounametz," the first 4-engined Sikorsky bomber and of Sikorsky bombers on the Russian front; IGOR I. SIKORSKY, *Recollections and Thoughts of a Pioneer* (1964), transcript of a recording of Sikorsky's lectures to the Wings Club, reviewing his own career and accomplishments and including his views on the future trends of aviation development; *The Story of the Winged-S: Late Developments and Recent Photographs of the Helicopter*, rev. ed. (1967), an autobiography, including a detailed account of the author's life and work through 1938, with supplementary chapters on his first helicopter experiments of 1939–40 and later work; see also a definitive study by F.J. DELEAR, *Igor Sikorsky: His Three Careers in Aviation* (1969).

(S.P.J.)

Silica Minerals

Silica minerals make up approximately 12 percent of the Earth's crust and are second only to the feldspars in mineral abundance. Free silica occurs in many crystalline forms with a composition very close to that of silicon dioxide (SiO_2), 46.75 percent by weight of silicon and 53.25 percent oxygen. Quartz is by far the most commonly occurring form. Tridymite, cristobalite, and the hydrous silica mineral opal are uncommon, and vitreous (glassy) silica, melanophlogite, coesite, and stishovite have been reported from only a few localities. Several other forms have been produced in the laboratory but have not been found in nature.

Quartz is the only natural silica mineral used in significant quantities; millions of tons are consumed annually by many industries. The sand that is an essential ingredient of concrete and mortar is largely quartz, as are the sandstone and quartzite used as building stones. Crushed sandstone and quartzite are used for road and railway construction, roofing granules, and for riprap—erosion-control linings of river channels. Quartz is hard (7 on Mohs scale of mineral hardness, on which diamond is 10) and resists fracture because it lacks easy cleavage (*i.e.*, the tendency to split along crystallographic planes). These properties, combined with its ready availability, lead to its use as a sandpaper abrasive and in sandblasting; for polishing and cutting glass, stone, and metal; and for providing traction on stairs, streets, and rails. Large amounts of relatively pure quartz are used in refractory products, such as insulating and firebricks, foundry molds, and electrical insulators, because of the combination of its high melting temperatures, low coefficients of expansion, inertness of the high-temperature forms of silica, and low costs.

Uses of quartz

Relatively pure quartz is required in large tonnages as an ingredient for glass and porcelain manufacture. High purity quartz is fused to make premium grades of chemical and optical glass for which one or more of its desirable properties of low thermal expansion, high shape stability, elasticity, low solubility, and transparency to various kinds of light can justify the greatly increased costs involved. Fibres of vitreous silica are essential for precision instruments, such as balances, galvanometers, and gravimeters. Large tonnages of quartz of various qualities are used as raw materials for processes in which silica is not the final product. These include the production of water glass, or sodium silicate, various sols—very fine dispersions of solids in liquids—that are used as hydrophobic coatings, organic silicates and silicones, silicon carbide, silicon metal, smelting flux, and alloying in metallurgy.

Quartz and its innumerable varieties have been used since antiquity as semiprecious gems, ornamental stones, and collector's items and are very popular today. Precious opal, a hydrous form of silica, has been one of the most attractive gemstones since Roman times.

This article treats the properties of the silica minerals, including their physical and chemical characteristics and crystallography, and their formation and occurrence in nature. For further information on crystal structure and mineralogical properties in general, see CRYSTALLOGRAPHY and MINERALS. See also SILICATE MINERALS; GEMSTONES; SILICEOUS ROCKS; and SANDSTONES for coverage of related minerals, gem varieties, and principal occurrences in sedimentary rocks. The occurrence of shock-related varieties, such as coesite and stishovite, is covered in the article METEORITE CRATERS.

Physical and chemical properties. The crystallographic structures of the silica minerals, with the exception of stishovite, are three-dimensional arrays of linked tetrahedra, each of which consists of a silicon atom coordinated (surrounded and bonded) by four oxygen atoms. (For a comprehensive description of the nature of several kinds of bonds, see CHEMICAL BONDING.) The tetrahedra are usually quite regular, and the silicon–oxygen bond distances are 1.61 ± 0.02 Å (one angstrom unit [Å] equals 10^{-8} centimetres). The principal differences among the silica minerals are related to the geometry of the tetrahedral linkages, which may cause small distortions within the silica tetrahedra. High pressure forces silicon atoms to coordinate with six oxygen atoms, thus producing nearly regular octahedra in the stishovite structure.

The silica minerals when pure are colourless and transparent and have a vitreous lustre. They are nonconductors of electricity and are diamagnetic (inert in a magnetic field). All are hard, strong, and fail by brittle fracture under an imposed stress.

Some of the more important physical properties of the silica minerals are compared in the Table. All except low tridymite and coesite (among the crystalline varieties) have relatively high symmetry. There is a linear relationship between the specific gravity values listed in the Table and the arithmetic mean of the indices of refraction (measures of the velocity of light that is transmitted in different crystallographic directions) for silica minerals composed of linked tetrahedra. This relationship (Figure 1) does not extend to stishovite because it is not made up of silica tetrahedra. Melanophlogite is notable because it plots below vitreous silica on the graph; one other poorly defined silica polymorph, called silica W, may also plot below vitreous silica. The specific gravities of silica minerals are less than those of most of the dark-coloured silicate minerals associated with them in nature; in general, the lighter coloured rocks have lower specific gravity for this reason.

Marginal note: Crystallographic properties

Some Physical Properties of Silica Minerals

phase	symmetry	cell* parameters	specific gravity	hardness
Quartz (α-quartz)	hexagonal; trigonal trapezohedral	$a = 4.913$Å $c = 5.405$Å	2.651	7
High quartz (β-quartz)	hexagonal; hexagonal trapezohedral at 575° C	$a = 4.999$Å $c = 5.457$Å at 575° C	2.53 at 600° C	7
Low tridymite	monoclinic (?)	$a = 18.54$Å $b = 4.99$Å $c = 23.83$Å $\beta = 105.6°$	2.26	7
High tridymite	orthorhombic	$a = 8.74$Å $b = 5.05$Å $c = 8.24$Å at 200° C	2.20 at 200° C	7(?)
Low cristobalite	tetragonal	$a = 4.97$Å $c = 6.93$Å	2.32	6–7
High cristobalite	isometric	$a = 7.15$Å at 1,300° C	2.20 at 500° C	6–7
Keatite	tetragonal	$a = 7.456$Å $c = 8.604$Å	2.50	?
Melanophlogite	isometric	$a = 13.402$Å	1.99	6–7
Coesite	monoclinic	$a = 7.16$Å $b = 12.39$Å $c = 7.16$Å $\beta = 120°$	2.93	7.5
Stishovite	tetragonal	$a = 4.179$Å $c = 2.665$Å	4.28	?
Vitreous silica	amorphous	—	2.203	6
Opal	poorly crystalline or amorphous	—	1.99–2.05	5.5–6.5

*The unit cell of a mineral is the smallest volume that contains a complete sample of the atomic composition and symmetry. It is described in terms of crystallographic axes and the angles at which they intersect. These axes are designated a, b, and c when of unequal length (monoclinic and orthorhombic symmetry); if a equals b, then only a and c cell lengths are given, and if a, b, and c are all equal (isometric symmetry) then only a is given. Hexagonal symmetry is related to three a axes of equal length that are 120° apart; the c axis is perpendicular to the plane containing these a axes. In monoclinic symmetry, two axes intersect obliquely, and the angle formed is designated β.

From B.J. Skinner and D.E. Appleman, *American Mineralogist*, (1963); Mineralogical Society of America

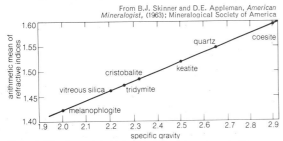

Figure 1: The linear plot obtained for silica minerals made up of linked tetrahedra (see text).

Silica minerals are insoluble to sparingly soluble in strong acids except hydrofluoric acid. There is a fair correlation between specific gravity and the solubility in hydrofluoric acid. The less dense phases dissolve rapidly in cold acid; quartz dissolves slowly in cold acid and rapidly in hot; coesite is nearly insoluble in cold and slowly soluble in hot acid; and stishovite is nearly insoluble even in hot hydrofluoric acid. All silica minerals are dissolved by strong alkali, particularly in hot and concentrated solutions, and by some fused salts, such as ammonium bifluoride.

Descriptions and characteristics. *Quartz.* Quartz occurs in many varieties in almost all types of igneous,

sedimentary, and metamorphic rocks. It has also been found in meteorites and in some lunar rocks.

Quartz crystals lack a centre of symmetry or planes of symmetry and have one crystallographic axis (c) perpendicular to three polar axes (a) that are 120° apart. One end of a polar axis is different from its other end; when mechanical stress is applied on such an axis, opposite electrical charges develop on each end. This leads to important applications in electronics as a frequency control and in pressure gauges and other devices. The lack of symmetry planes parallel to the vertical axis allows quartz crystals to occur as two types: left-handed or right-handed (enantiomorphism). Left-handed quartz is less than 1 percent more abundant than right-handed quartz. The structural tetrahedra spiral upward through the crystal in the sense of the handedness parallel to the c axis. Similarly, if polarized light—which is light vibrating in a single plane—is transmitted by a quartz crystal along the c axis direction, the plane is rotated in the direction of the handedness by tens of degrees per millimetre, the amount depending on the wavelength of the light. This property is used in the manufacture of optical instruments such as monochromaters.

Marginal note: Left-handed and right-handed quartz crystals

Twinning—the symmetrical juxtaposition of two or more crystals of the same mineral species—is ubiquitous in quartz, even if not conspicuous to the eye. One general class of twins occurs with the two sets of a axes parallel to each other, and the twinned portions may be complexly intergrown so that they penetrate each other. When the two crystals are of the same handedness and the a axes are of opposite electrical polarity, such twinning constitutes the Dauphiné law, which is also known as electrical twinning. When one of the crystals is left-handed and the other right-handed, this also causes the parallel a axes to be of opposite electrical polarity; this type is called Brazil, or optical, twinning. In another general class of quartz twins, the sets of a axes of the twinned crystals are inclined to each other, and the crystals ordinarily do not penetrate one another. This twinning is the Japan law.

The requirements for high purity crystals free from

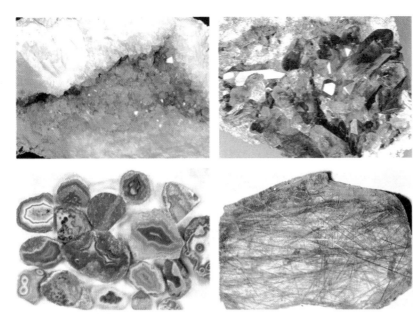

Figure 2: *Quartz varieties.*
(Top left) Amethyst geode from Nova Scotia. (Top right) Smoky quartz from St. Gotthard, Switzerland. (Bottom left) Quartz agate from Mexico. (Bottom right) Rutilated quartz from Madagascar.

By courtesy of (top right, bottom right) the Field Museum of Natural History, Chicago, (bottom left) Joseph and Helen Guetterman collection; photographs, (top right, bottom left, bottom right) John H. Gerard—EB Inc., (top left) Emil Javorsky—EB Inc.

twinning for electronic frequency applications have led to the development of industrial synthesis methods based on the differences in silica solubility with temperature. Nutrient crystals are placed in the hot portion of a solution-filled autoclave, and an oriented seed crystal free from twinning is placed in the cooler portion. Crystals weighing thousands of grams can be grown in a few weeks.

Quartz shows less range in chemical composition than do most other minerals, but it commonly contains tens to hundreds of parts per million of aluminum atoms substituting for silicon atoms, with charge balance maintained by the incorporation of small atoms, such as hydrogen, lithium, or sodium. Titanium, magnesium, or iron atoms substituting for silicon atoms also have been reported, but anionic substitution (*i.e.*, substitution for the negative ion, oxygen) is limited because the linkage of the tetrahedra is disrupted.

Colours of quartz varieties   Coloured varieties of quartz are numerous and have many causes. Most colours result from mechanically incorporated admixtures within fine-crystallized or granular quartz, but some coarse-crystallized varieties, such as amethyst (violet), citrine (yellow), milky quartz, smoky quartz or morion (black), or rose quartz, may be coloured by ions other than silicon and oxygen that occur within the crystal structure (see Figure 2). Small fractions of 1 percent by weight of iron, aluminum, manganese, titanium, hydrogen, and small alkali atoms, such as lithium and sodium, have been shown to be the cause of different colours. Heat treatment or various irradiation treatments under oxidizing or reducing atmospheres are used to change one coloured variety to another. Citrine is commonly produced by heat treating amethyst at 250°–400° C (500°–750° F), for example.

Quartz may contain inclusions of other minerals, such as rutile (rutilated quartz), asbestiform amphiboles (tigereye is the yellow-brown variety from South Africa; hawk's-eye, the blue variety), or platy minerals, such as mica, iron oxides, or chlorite (aventurine).

Chalcedony.   Chalcedony is white, buff, or light tan, finely crystallized or fibrous quartz that forms rounded crusts, rinds, or stalactites (mineral deposits suspended from the roofs of caverns) in volcanic and sedimentary rocks as a precipitate from moving solutions. If chalcedony is conspicuously colour banded, it may be called agate; onyx is agate with alternate bands of white and black or dark brown. Some concentrically banded "eye" agate nodules contain cores of coarsely crystalline quartz, and other agates are mottled or variegated in colour.

Arborescent or dendritic (branching) dark-coloured patterns set in a lighter field are called moss agate or Mocha stone. Translucent red chalcedony is called carnelian, and translucent brown shades are called sard; both are pigmented by admixed iron oxides.

Chrysoprase, plasma, and prase are names for green varieties of chalcedony coloured by admixed green minerals, such as chlorite, fibrous amphiboles, or hydrous nickel silicates. Bloodstone and heliotrope are green chalcedony with red spots. Much chalcedony is coloured by artificial methods.

Jasper, chert, and flint.   Jasper is opaque red, brown, or yellow quartz that contains much admixed material. Touchstone, or basanite, is black or dark gray jasper that has been used to estimate the composition of precious alloys by the colour of their streak (powder). Chert and flint are finely crystallized varieties of gray to black quartz that occur as nodules or bands in sedimentary rocks.

High quartz (β-quartz).   High quartz, or β-quartz, is the more symmetrical form quartz takes at sufficiently high temperatures (about 573° C [1,063° F] at one atmosphere of pressure), but the relationship is pressure-sensitive (see Figure 3). High quartz may be either left- or right-handed, and its *c* axis is one of sixfold symmetry rather than threefold symmetry; thus, many of the twin laws of ordinary quartz cannot occur. High quartz twins typically involve inclined sets of axes, for example. High quartz can form directly from silicate magma or from high-temperature gases or solutions. It invariably undergoes the transition to ordinary quartz (low quartz) on cooling, and all ordinary quartz, when heated above the transition temperature, is transformed into high quartz. The transformation involves only displacement of the linkage between the tetrahedra, and no bonds are broken. Much quartz that formed originally as high quartz in volcanic rocks has lost all morphological or twinning evidence of its origin and is virtually indistinguishable from ordinary quartz on any other basis. **Transition from high quartz to low quartz**

Tridymite.   Tridymite, an uncommon silica mineral, may occur as a primary magmatic phase (*i.e.*, as a direct result of crystallization from a silicate melt) in siliceous rocks but is most abundant in voids in volcanic rocks where it probably was deposited metastably (*i.e.*, formed instead of the form more stable at existing conditions of temperature and pressure) from hydrous gases. Tridymite also forms in contact-metamorphosed rocks; *e.g.*, those that were close to very hot basic intrusions. It has been found in meteorites and is common in lunar basalts. It occurs in quantity in firebricks and other siliceous refractories. Natural tridymite has no specific commercial use.

Tridymite characteristically forms thin plates made up of three crystals in twin relationships; hence the name, which means triplet. The tridymite structure can be considered as cross-linked hexagonal sheets of tetrahedra perpendicular to the c-axis that approximate hexagonal closest packing of the oxygen atoms. (This is one of the two ways in which spheres can be packed together in space with the greatest possible density and still have a periodic arrangement, the other way being cubic closest packing.) These sheets may be stacked in regular, random, or irregular sequences, and the stacking can be different in parts of the same crystal. So much crystallographic complexity results that confusion exists as to the precise stacking arrangements. The stacking sequence and tetrahedral linkage within a sheet can change easily with temperature change, the transition temperatures being sensitive to the original stacking sequence and the composition. The high tridymite that is stable at one atmosphere pressure, from about 867° C (1,593° F) to 1,470° C (2,678° F), contains two sheets and has orthorhombic symmetry (related to three mutually perpendicular crystallographic axes of unequal length), though it is dimensionally hexagonal. Tridymite retains an orthorhombic cell as a subcell at lower temperatures but may contain as many as 20 sheets. Such tridymite also has pseudohexagonal symmetry (i.e., appears to have sixfold symmetry but does not), but most carefully studied samples are actually monoclinic at room temperature. Terrestrial low tridymite does not show the characteristic monoclinic supercell of extraterrestial samples. This probably is related to the influence of conditions of formation on stacking sequences. Tridymite transforms sluggishly to quartz because the transformation requires tetrahedra to be disrupted and relinked.

Tridymite can be synthesized with high purity, but natural material commonly contains as much as 2 percent by weight of sodium and aluminum oxides substituting for silica, as well as fractions of 1 percent of titania, ferric iron, magnesia, calcium oxide, or potassium oxide.

Cristobalite. Cristobalite is probably more abundant in nature than tridymite, although it seldom forms as distinctive crystals. The devitrification (transformation from the glassy to the crystalline state) of siliceous volcanic glasses yields abundant tiny crystallites of cristobalite, and the mineral is also deposited metastably from hot hydrous gases in cavities and cracks of many volcanic rocks. It has been found in lunar basalts and in meteorites and is common in silica refractories exposed to very high temperatures.

Cristobalite is made up of sheets of silica tetrahedra that can be considered to be stacked in sequences of three sheets normal to a threefold axis; this approximates cubic closest packing of the oxygen atoms. Isometric high cristobalite is the stable phase at one atmosphere of pressure from about 1,470° C (2,678° F) to melting, and this form can be supercooled over the range 270°–175° C (520°–350° F) before it transforms reversibly to a metastable tetragonal form. The latter is called low cristobalite and shows complex polysynthetic twinning (twins of three or more individual crystals conforming to the same twin law). As might be expected from its open structure and high temperature of origin, substitution of small alkali and aluminum atoms for silicon atoms may amount to several percent in cristobalite, and minor amounts of other coupled substitutions are known.

Opal. Opal is poorly crystalline or amorphous hydrous silica that is compact and vitreous and most commonly is translucent white to colourless. Precious opal reflects light with a strong play of brilliant colours across the visible spectrum, red being the most valued colour. Opal forms by precipitation from silica-bearing solutions near the Earth's surface. Electron microscopy has shown that many opals are composed of spheres of tens to a few thousand angstrom units in size (one angstrom unit equals 10^-8 centimetres) that are arranged in either hex-

agonal or cubic close packing. The spheres are composed of hydrous silica that may be either almost cristobalite-like, tridymite-like, mixtures of both, or random and nondiffracting. The specific gravity and refractive index are lower than those of pure silica minerals and tend to fall along lines extending from cristobalite, tridymite, and vitreous silica (see Figure 1) toward the point for water (the index of refraction of water is 1.33, and the specific gravity is 1). The play of colours in precious opal arises from domains of regularly oriented spheres that satisfy Bragg's law (relating the angle of reflection of X-rays from a crystal to the spacing of crystallographic planes and the wavelength of the incident radiation) for the wavelength of visible light observed. When heated, opal may lose as much as 20 percent of its weight of water, fracture, and then crystallize to any one of the silica minerals described above.

Opal usually contains 4 to 9 percent water, but lower and much higher values have been observed. The contents of alumina, ferric oxide, and alkalis are variable but may amount to several percent in light coloured opals and more if pigmenting minerals are also present. Precious opal has been synthesized. Opaline silica is a friable hydrous silica found near hot springs and geysers.

Vitreous silica. Vitreous silica is supercooled liquid silica. It has been observed in nature as the result of fusion of quartz by lightning strikes or by shock associated with large meteorite impacts and may approach artificial, very pure silica glass in composition and physical properties.

Melanophlogite. Melanophlogite is a cubic silica mineral with a gas-hydrate structure containing many large voids. In nature these are filled with 6 to 12 percent by weight of compounds of hydrogen, carbon, and sulfur, which may be necessary for mineral growth. If these compounds are destroyed by heating, they do not cause the crystal to collapse, but the free carbon formed does darken it. Melanophlogite occurs with bitumen and forms at temperatures below 112° C (234° F) on native sulfur crystals in Sicily.

Keatite. Keatite is a tetragonal form of silica known only from the laboratory, where it can be synthesized metastably over the range of temperatures from about 300° to 600° C (600°–1,200° F) and 400 to 4,000 bars (standard atmospheric pressure at sea level is 1,013.3 millibars, or slightly more than one bar, which equals 760 millimetres of mercury) in the presence of steam. It has negative thermal expansion along the a axes and positive thermal expansion along the c axis, so that the overall expansion is very low or negative.

Coesite and stishovite. Coesite and stishovite are rare dense forms of silica observed in nature only where quartz-bearing rocks have been severely shocked by a large meteorite impact, such as Meteor Crater, Arizona. Coesite is made up of tetrahedra arranged like those in feldspars (q.v.). Stishovite is the most dense form of silica and consists of silicon that is octahedrally coordinated with oxygen. Both coesite and stishovite have been synthesized and found to be stable only at high pressures (Figure 3).

Occurrence in magmas and solutions. Silicon and oxygen are the two most abundant elements in the Earth's crust, in which they largely occur in combination with other elements as silicate minerals. Free silica, SiO_2, appears as a mineral in crystallizing magma only when the relative abundance of SiO_2 exceeds that of all other cations available to form silicates. Silica minerals thus occur only in magmas containing more than about 47 percent by weight of SiO_2 and are incompatible with minerals with low cation/silica ratios—such as olivine, nepheline, or leucite. Basaltic and alkalic igneous magmas therefore can crystallize only minor amounts of silica minerals, and sometimes none are produced. The gas released from such rocks can dissolve the silica component, however, and later precipitate it as silica minerals upon cooling. The amount of silica minerals crystallized from magma increases with increasing silica content of magma, reaching 40 percent in some granites and rhyolites. In granitic pegmatite, where a hydrous gas was

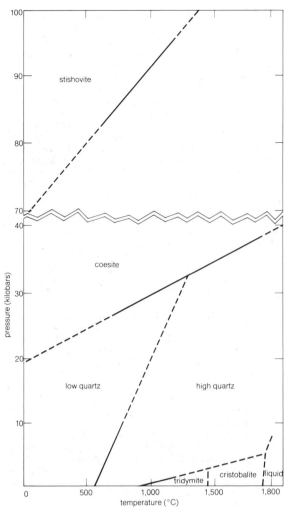

Figure 3: Silica phase diagram.
From F.R. Boyd and J.L. England, *Journal of Geophysical Research* vol. 65, p. 752 (1960)

stone, which, when all pore space is eliminated by selective solution and nearby deposition during metamorphism, form tough, pore-free quartzite.

The silica content of seawater is highly variable because it is removed by plankton (floating organisms). An estimate for average upper ocean waters is 4.3 parts per million, but values of 0.1 part per million can occur at the surface. Deep sea sediments are highly siliceous from the accumulation of the siliceous skeletons of single-celled plants and animals (diatoms and radiolaria), sponges, and other organisms.

Gases or solutions escaping from cooling rocks, especially volcanic or intrusive igneous rocks, commonly are saturated with silica and other compounds that, as they cool, precipitate quartz along their channelways to form veins. The quartz may be fine-grained (as chalcedony), massive granular, or in coarse crystals as large as tens of tons. Most of the natural colourless quartz crystals—the "rock crystal" found in collections or used in jewelry and electronic and optical apparatus—were formed in this way. Famous localities for rock crystal are the Swiss Alps; Herkimer County, New York; Minas Gerais, Brazil; Hot Springs, Arkansas; and the Malagasy Republic.

Rock crystal, spring deposits, and glass sands

The emergence of heated silica-bearing solutions onto the surface results in rapid cooling and the loss of complexing anions. Rapid precipitation of fine-grained silica results in formation of siliceous sinter or geyserite, as at Mammoth Hot Springs in Yellowstone National Park.

Quartz is mechanically resistant and relatively inert chemically during rock weathering in temperate and cold climates. Thus, it becomes enriched in river, lake, and beach sediments, which commonly contain more than one-half quartz by weight. Some strata consist almost entirely of quartz over large lateral distances and tens or hundreds of feet in thickness. Known as glass sands, these strata are important economic sources of silica for glass and chemical industries. Quartz-bearing strata are abundant in metamorphic terrains. The reincorporation of

present in addition to magma, igneous-appearing rocks composed largely or almost completely of quartz can occur because of transport of silica through the hydrous gas.

Solubility of silica minerals

The solubility of silica minerals in natural solutions and gases is of great importance. The solubility of all silica minerals increases regularly with increasing temperature and pressure (Figure 4) except in the region of 340°–550° C (640°–1,020° F) and 0–600 bars, where retrograde solubility occurs because of changes in the physical state of water. The solubility of quartz in steam reaches at least 22 percent by weight at 10,000 bars and 1,055° C (1,931° F). The solubility of silica increases in the presence of anions such as OH^- and CO_3^-, which form chemical complexes with it.

Quartz is the least soluble of the forms of silica at room temperature. In pure water its solubility at 25° C (77° F) is about 6 parts per million, that of vitreous silica being at least 10 times greater. The amount of dissolved silica in hot springs has been utilized to measure the temperature at the depth from which the water emanates, because the major control of silica solubility appears to be with quartz. Typical temperate climate river water contains 14 parts per million of silica, and enormous tonnages of silica are carried away in solution annually from weathering rocks and soils. The amount so removed may be equivalent to that transported mechanically in many climates. In tropical climates, waters enriched in organic acids may leach silica completely to form lateritic residual soils enriched in hydrous iron and aluminum oxides. Silica dissolved in moving groundwater may form hollow spheroids lined with crystals called geodes, or it may cement loose sand grains together to form concretions and nodules or even entire sedimentary beds into sand-

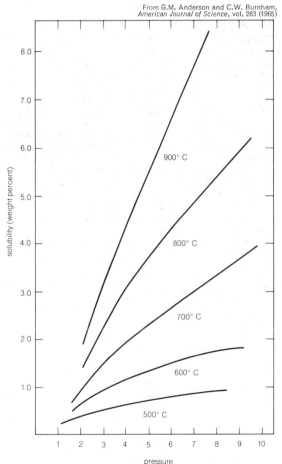

From G.M. Anderson and C.W. Burnham, *American Journal of Science*, vol. 263 (1965)

Figure 4: Solubility of quartz in pure water.

free silica into complex silicates and the solution and redeposition of silica into veins is characteristic of such terrains.

The silica phase diagram.   The pressure-temperature fields of stability of silica minerals as presently understood are shown in Figure 3. The experimentally determined boundaries are drawn with heavy lines. No data have been obtained for certain boundaries because of slow reaction rates or difficulties in obtaining the required conditions. Traces of water, for example, are necessary for reactions to take place over much of the diagram. Stability fields are not shown for keatite, melanophlogite, opal, or the low forms of tridymite and cristobalite because they have not been demonstrated. Quartz is the stable phase of silica under the physical conditions that prevail over most of the Earth's crust. Coesite is possible at depths of about 100 kilometres (60 miles) in the Earth's mantle, but free silica is not thought to be abundant there. Stishovite would require even greater depths of burial, and no rocks that occur on the Earth's surface have been buried so deeply.

BIBLIOGRAPHY. H.C. DAKE, F.L. FLEENER, and B.H. WILSON, *Quartz Family Minerals* (1938), a popular illustrated account of quartz varieties and localities for the mineral collector; W.A. DEER, R.A. HOWIE, and J. ZUSSMAN, "Silica Minerals," in *Framework Silicates*, vol. 4 of *Rock-Forming Minerals* (1963), an abbreviated technical summary of crystallography, physical properties, chemistry, and occurrence of silica minerals, with copious references to the literature through 1962; CLIFFORD FRONDEL, *Dana's System of Mineralogy*, 7th ed., vol. 3, *Silica Minerals* (1962), a definitive and encyclopaedic treatise of all aspects of the mineralogy of silica minerals through early 1962, with historical perspective and attention to localities; R.B. SOSMAN, *The Phases of Silica* (1965), a treatment from the physical chemist's point of view with the strengths and weaknesses of each observation or experiment critically examined—helpful discussions of solutions, gels, and phase equilibria with water; R.W.G. WYCKOFF, *Crystal Structures*, 2nd ed., vol. 1 (1963), a detailed and critical evaluation of the crystal structures of silica minerals.

(D.B.S.)

Silicate Minerals

Silicate minerals are compounds of silicon (Si) and oxygen (O) that occur as the major constituents of the rocks that form the Earth's crust. Although more than 1,000 minerals have been recognized, the igneous rocks, born from molten silicate material deep below the Earth's crust, of which they comprise about 95 percent, are made up of only a few—all silicates. Sedimentary rocks, which are made of pre-existing rocks for the most part, contain large amounts of silicate minerals, and metamorphic rocks, formed by the alteration of igneous or sedimentary rocks, also consist largely of silicates. Furthermore, silicate minerals are important constituents of meteorites and lunar samples. Spectral analysis of the outer regions of the Sun shows silicon to be the sixth most abundant element, following hydrogen, helium, oxygen, carbon, and nitrogen. Chemical analyses of meteorites reveal silicon to be third in abundance, after oxygen and iron, and estimates of its cosmic abundance rank it seventh, following hydrogen, helium, oxygen, neon, nitrogen, and carbon. Thus it is clear that silicon is an important element in the Earth–Moon system, the solar system, and the cosmos; and it follows, then, the minerals that contain silicon—the silicate minerals—are of like importance.

Economic importance of silicate minerals

Silicate minerals have great economic importance as well. Some fibrous amphiboles (asbestos) are used in the textile industry, for manufacturing rope, brake linings, nonflammable cements, and shingles. Tremolite and anthophyllite have been used for filtering fruit juices and chemicals. Montmorillonite (sometimes called bentonite) is used in drilling muds. Igneous and metamorphic silicate rocks are used for building and monumental materials. The very abundant feldspar minerals are used as additives in paint and as a mild abrasive as well as in the manufacture of glass and in ceramics. Some silicates are prized as gems; among these are emerald, aquamarine, and morganite, all varieties of beryl; peridot; moonstone, amazonstone, peristerite, and labradorite, all

feldspars; garnet; jadeite and nephrite, the two forms of jade; opal, onyx, chalcedony; agate, bloodstone, and quartz, all forms of silica; staurolite; tourmaline; and zircon. Spodumene and lepidolite are ore minerals of lithium. Muscovite and phlogopite are used in radio tubes, in capacitors, and in insulating of heating elements. Pyrophyllite is used in ceramics, paints, soap, textiles, cosmetics, and rubber. Quartz is sometimes used as an abrasive, and high-quality quartz crystals are used for precision electronic control components and for optical lenses. Andalusite, kyanite, and sillimanite are used in the preparation of mullite, a high-temperature refractory. Vermiculite is used for home insulation, concrete aggregate, agricultural chemicals, and fertilizers. Wollastonite is used in ceramics, especially for single-fired wall tile. Zircon is an ore mineral of zirconium and also of hafnium.

This article treats the chemical composition and crystal structure of the silicate minerals, their classification, and their occurrence and distribution in the Earth's crust and mantle and in meteorites and the moon. For further detail on any of the specific groups of silicate minerals that are here covered in overview fashion, see FELDSPARS; FELDSPATHOIDS; OLIVINES; PYROXENES; AMPHIBOLES; CLAY MINERALS; MICAS; SILICA MINERALS; and ZEOLITES. Additional information on crystal structure and chemical bonding in general is given in the articles CRYSTALLOGRAPHY; CHEMICAL BONDING. See also EARTH, STRUCTURE AND COMPOSITION OF; MOON; METEORITE; and METEORITE CRATERS for details on the several principal environments of silicate minerals.

CRYSTAL STRUCTURE AND CHEMICAL COMPOSITION

The SiO_4 tetrahedra and SiO_6 octahedra.   The fundamental unit of all silicates formed at low to moderate pressures is the silicate tetrahedron, an SiO_4 group in which one silicon atom (Si) is surrounded by and bonded to (coordinated with) four oxygen atoms (O_4), each at the corner of a regular tetrahedron (a solid that has four triangular faces). Although this tetrahedron does show various distortions from regular shape in different minerals, it is not broken down until extremely high pressures, where silicon assumes a new coordination, forming SiO_6 groups, in which one silicon atom is surrounded by six oxygen atoms, each at the corner of an octahedron (a solid with eight triangular faces that looks like two pyramids joined at the bases). This increased coordination (four to six) results in the higher density minerals that would be expected at high pressure.

Silicate minerals can be thought of as three-dimensional arrays of oxygen atoms that contain void spaces (crystallographic sites) where various cations (positively charged atoms) can enter. Other than the tetrahedral and octahedral sites, the positions of the silicon atoms in 4-fold and 6-fold coordination, respectively, 8-fold and 12-fold sites, are also quite common. A correlation exists between the size of a cation and the type of a site it can occupy: the larger the cation, the greater the coordination, because large cations have more surface area for oxygen atoms to make contact with than small cations. The most common cations that occur in silicate minerals include, from smallest to largest, silicon (Si^{4+}), aluminum (Al^{3+}), ferric iron (Fe^{3+}), titanium (Ti^{4+}), magnesium (Mg^{++}), ferrous iron (Fe^{++}), lithium (Li^+), manganese (Mn^{++}), sodium (Na^+), calcium (Ca^{++}), and potassium (K^+). Tetrahedral (4-fold coordination) sites commonly are occupied by silicon and aluminum; octahedral (6-fold) sites by aluminum, iron, titanium, magnesium, lithium, manganese, and sodium; 8-fold sites by sodium, calcium, and potassium; and 12-fold sites by potassium.

Chemical substitution.   Elements with similar ionic radii often can substitute for one another in a mineral. In such cases, a complete substitutional series may be found, as between magnesium silicate, Mg_2SiO_4, and iron silicate, $Fe_2^{2+}SiO_4$ (olivine minerals), for example. Between these pure magnesium and pure iron compounds, called end-members, substitution of one for the other can occur in any amount, and thus any magnesium-to-iron ratio may be observed in natural minerals. If the discrepancy in the size or charge, or both, of cations is large, only limited substitution, also called solid solution because one end-member can be thought of as being "dissolved" in the other, will be observed, and a miscibility gap may occur between compositional end-members.

Silicates as geothermometers and geobarometers

Silicate minerals act as tiny probes that record the detailed evolutionary history of the rocks that contain them. For example, the composition or crystal structure of a mineral (its detailed arrangement of atoms) may give clues to its temperature history (geothermometry) or pressure history (geobarometry). The amount of substitution (solid solution) between compositional end-members commonly increases with temperature, and thus the miscibility gaps usually decrease in size with increasing temperature. In addition, the way that cations are distributed between the different crystallographic sites in the oxygen three-dimensional network is commonly a function of temperature. For example, if a mineral contains two different cations and two different crystallographic sites, the distribution of the cations among the sites usually becomes more random with increasing temperature. Thus, when calibrated, the degree of substitution (solid solution) between compositional end-members and the degree of randomness (disordering) of cation distributions in a mineral structure is useful in deducing the thermal history of rocks.

The element aluminum plays an interesting role in silicate structures because it can enter both octahedral and tetrahedral sites. As pressure is increased, however, aluminum prefers octahedral coordination (6-fold) rather than tetrahedral (4-fold). This increased coordination of aluminum in silicates results in minerals with higher density, as would be expected from a high pressure of formation. Thus, in some silicates, it is possible to correlate the amount of aluminum in octahedral coordination with the pressure history of a rock (geobarometry).

CLASSIFICATION OF SILICATES

Because the basic building block of a silicate structure is the SiO_4 tetrahedron, most of the important rock-forming silicate minerals can be divided into groups based on the degree to which the SiO_4 tetrahedra are linked together (degree of polymerization).

A common structure is one that contains isolated SiO_4 groups (Figure 1A). If the charge on the silicon atom is considered as $+4$ and that on the oxygen as -2, a SiO_4 group has a total charge of $[1(+4) + 4(-2)]$, or -4. To achieve electrical neutrality in a silicate structure, therefore, cations must be present in addition to silicon; their charges must total $+4$ for each SiO_4 group.

Another common silicate structure type has double tetrahedron groups (Figure 1B) in which one oxygen atom is shared by two tetrahedra. The formula for this structural group is Si_2O_7, and the charge on the group is $[2(+4) + 7(-2)]$, or -6. Thus, cations must be added with charges totalling $+6$ for each Si_2O_7 group for an electrically neutral structure.

Further polymerization may result in a third structure type—infinite single chains (Figure 1C) in which each tetrahedron shares two oxygen atoms. The formula for these chains is (SiO_3), with a charge of -2 on each SiO_3 group. Another type of chain, a double chain (Figure 1D), occurs when two single chains are linked by the sharing of one oxygen atom between every second tetrahedron on each chain. The formula can be derived by counting the silicon and oxygen atoms in a portion of the double chain and can be expressed as (Si_4O_{11}), in which each Si_4O_{11} group has a -6 charge. In both the single and double chain structures, the negative charges on the groups require additional cations in the structure.

A fourth basic structure type contains infinite sheets of tetrahedra, in which each tetrahedron shares one oxygen atom with each of three other tetrahedra (Figure 1E); the basic unit in these sheets has the formula $(Si_4O_{10})^{4-}$. The tetrahedra are linked to form interconnected six-member rings.

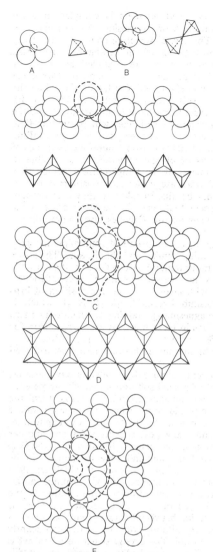

Figure 1: *Important silicate structure types.* (A) Isolated tetrahedra, with the formula $[SiO_4]^{-4}$. (B) Double tetrahedra, with the formula $[Si_2O_7]^{-6}$. (C) Single tetrahedral chain, in which the basic structural unit (in dashed ring) has the formula $[SiO_3]^{-2}$. (D) Double tetrahedral chain, in which the basic unit has the formula $[Si_4O_{11}]^{-6}$. (E) sheet, in which the basic unit has the formula $[Si_4O_{10}]^{-4}$.

From *Crystallography and Crystal Chemistry: An Introduction* by F. Donald Bloss. Copyright © 1971 by Holt, Rinehart and Winston, Inc. Reprinted by permission of Holt, Rinehart and Winston, Inc.

The last structure type to be considered is an infinite three-dimensional network of tetrahedra, in which each tetrahedron shares all of its oxygen atoms. This structure has no residual negative charge; because it is electrically neutral, it does not contain appreciable amounts of any other cations.

Substitution of aluminum (charge $+3$) for silicon (charge $+4$) will change the negative residual charge on a silicate group; for example, if an aluminum atom is substituted for one silicon atom in the basic formula for a sheet structure, the formula $(Si_4O_{10})^{4-}$ becomes $(Si_3AlO_{10})^{5-}$. Thus, in the three-dimensional network structures (framework structures), substitution of aluminum for silicon leaves a residual charge on the framework, as in the feldspars; the feldspar mineral albite has the formula $NaAlSi_3O_8$, in which the substitution of the aluminum atom is balanced by the addition of a sodium atom with a charge of $+1$.

Isolated or double tetrahedral group silicates. The olivine mineral group has two important end-members, forsterite, or magnesium silicate (Mg_2SiO_4), and fayalite, or iron silicate (Fe_2SiO_4). The solid-solution series

Olivines

between these two end-members is complete and involves the substitution of magnesium for ferrous iron, $Mg^{2+} \rightleftarrows Fe^{2+}$. The crystal structure consists of an array of SiO_4 groups between which octahedral sites exist. These octahedral positions are occupied by Mg^{2+}, or Fe^{2+}, or both. The magnesium end-member (forsterite) melts at approximately 1,900° C (3,450° F), while the iron end-member (fayalite) melts at 1,200° C (2,190° F), and thus in a crystallizing basaltic silicate melt (molten rock) the magnesium-rich olivines will precipitate first, and the olivine crystals that precipitate later with falling temperature will be richer in iron. Therefore, by means of chemical analysis of olivine minerals, it is possible to make some estimates of the temperature at which they crystallized. Olivines are important constituents of terrestrial and lunar basalts. In addition they are components of other rocks that occur in the lower crust of the Earth or the upper mantle. Olivines also commonly occur in meteorites.

Humites
The humite group is comprised of four minerals: norbergite, chondrodite, humite, and clinohumite. The structures of the humite minerals are related to those of the olivine minerals and consist essentially of layers of forsterite intergrown with layers with the composition of brucite, or magnesium hydroxide $[Mg(OH)_2]$, which is composed of magnesium-containing octahedra. The two main substitutions in these minerals are ferrous iron for magnesium, $Fe^{2+} \rightleftarrows Mg$, and fluorine for hydroxide, $F \rightleftarrows (OH)$. The humite minerals occur in metamorphosed carbonate rocks.

Garnets
The garnet minerals are usually divided into two groups, each composed of a solid-solution series with three end-members. Pyrope, almandine, and spessartine form the pyralspite group of aluminum silicates in which divalent cations (atoms with a charge of +2) of magnesium, ferrous iron, and manganese substitute for one another in the R position in the general formula $R_3Al_2Si_3O_{12}$. Uvarovite, grossularite, and andradite are included in the ugrandite group of calcium silicates in which trivalent cations (atoms with a charge of +3) of chromium, aluminum, and ferric iron substitute for one another in the R position in the general formula $Ca_3R_2Si_3O_{12}$. There is far less solid solution between the two groups because this would involve substitution of atoms of significantly different atomic radii. The crystal structure of garnet is comprised of silicate tetrahedra arranged to provide octahedral and 8-fold sites; the octahedral sites are occupied by the trivalent cations Cr^{3+}, Al^{3+}, or Fe^{3+}, and the 8-fold sites can be occupied by Ca^{2+}, Mn^{2+}, Fe^{2+}, and Mg^{2+}. The pyrope end-member is stabilized at high pressures, and thus the amount of this end-member in a garnet specimen gives an indication of the pressure at which it formed.

Alumino-silicates
The aluminosilicate mineral group contains three important members: andalusite, kyanite, and sillimanite—all with the chemical formula Al_2SiO_5. The difference between the members of this group does not involve chemical composition but involves instead the way the atoms are arranged in their crystal structures; these minerals are therefore polymorphs.

The structure of sillimanite is comprised of AlO_6 octahedra, SiO_4 tetrahedra, and AlO_4 tetrahedra; it has half of its aluminum in octahedral coordination and half in tetrahedral coordination. To express this concisely, the formula can be written as $Al^{VI}Al^{IV}Si^{IV}O_5$. The crystal structure of andalusite is comprised of AlO_6 octahedra, SiO_4 tetrahedra, and irregular AlO_5 groups in which the aluminum atom is surrounded (coordinated) by five oxygen atoms. Its formula can be written as $Al^{VI}Al^VSi^{IV}O_5$. The last member of the aluminosilicate group, kyanite, has a structure comprised of only AlO_6 octahedra and SiO_4 tetrahedra. Thus, both Al atoms are in octahedral coordination, and the formula for kyanite can be written $Al^{VI}Al^{VI}Si^{IV}O_5$.

The aluminosilicate minerals offer an unusually good opportunity to relate mineral crystal structures, temperature–pressure conditions, and natural occurrence. Figure 2, which illustrates some of these relations in a diagrammatic form, indicates which polymorph will occur at

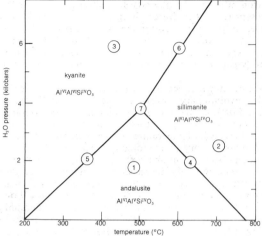

Figure 2: Temperature-pressure stability of the various forms of aluminosilicate.
From M.J. Holdaway, *American Journal of Science*, vol. 271 (1971); Yale University

specific temperature and pressure combinations. At low temperatures and pressures, andalusite (region 1 on Figure 2) forms; with increasing temperature, sillimanite (2) becomes the stable mineral, whereas increasing pressure results in kyanite (3). At high pressures all of the aluminum is in octahedral coordination, and the densest polymorph, kyanite, forms, whereas at high temperatures the least dense mineral, sillimanite, forms, with half the aluminum in tetrahedral coordination. Along any of the lines on the diagram (4,5,6) two polymorphs can coexist; along line 4 andalusite and sillimanite coexist, along line 5 andalusite and kyanite coexist, and along line 6 kyanite and sillimanite coexist. When two forms are coexistent, the temperature and pressure conditions of their formation falls along these lines; either temperature or pressure, but not both, can be varied independently to achieve a new set of conditions where this is possible. At point 7 on the diagram, andalusite, kyanite, and sillimanite coexist; this point is fixed, and neither temperature nor pressure can be varied to achieve another set of conditions.

These relationships can be used in geobarometry and geothermometry of natural rock systems because, depending on the number of polymorphs existing in a rock, it is possible to make estimates of temperature and pressure conditions with various degrees of certainty. If a rock contains only one aluminosilicate, then only broad temperature–pressure estimates can be made corresponding to regions 1, 2, or 3 on the diagram. If two polymorphs coexist in a rock, then the possible combinations are limited to the univariant lines 4, 5, and 6, and, if all three polymorphs are present, then the conditions are uniquely defined, within the certainty of the experimental determination.

Mullite, a related compound, can be formed from the aluminosilicate polymorphs by heating them to extremely high temperatures. The following reaction may occur:

$$3Al_2O_3 \cdot 3SiO_2 \rightarrow Al_2O_3 \cdot 2SiO_2 + SiO_2$$
$$\text{aluminosilicate} \qquad \text{mullite} \qquad \text{silica}$$

($3Al_2O_3 \cdot 3SiO_2$ is just a convenient way of writing the formula of the aluminosilicates instead of $3Al_2SiO_5$.) Thus, the reaction involves liberation of some silica, and mullite contains proportionally more aluminum than the aluminosilicate polymorphs. Mullite is of commercial value as a high-temperature refractory material.

Epidotes
In minerals of the epidote group, silicon occurs both in isolated tetrahedra and double tetrahedral groups. Important members of this group are epidote, a calcium and ferric iron silicate $[Ca_2Fe_3^{3+}Si_3O_{12}(OH)]$, and the polymorphs zoisite and clinozoisite, calcium and aluminum silicates $[Ca_2Al_3Si_3O_{12}(OH)]$. Extensive substitution occurs in the group, which may be given the general formula $X_2Y_3Z_3(O,OH)_{13}$. The X position can be occupied by calcium (Ca^{2+}), cerium (Ce^{3+}), lanthanum

(La^{3+}), yttrium (Y^{3+}), thorium (Th^{4+}), ferrous iron (Fe^{2+}), and both divalent and trivalent manganese (Mn^{2+} and Mn^{3+}); the Y position can be occupied by aluminum (Al^{3+}), ferrous and ferric iron (Fe^{2+} and Fe^{3+}), divalent and trivalent manganese (Mn^{2+} and Mn^{3+}), and titanium (Ti^{4+}); and the Z position can be filled by either silicon (Si^{4+}) or beryllium (Be^{2+}) ions. Zoisite has the restricted composition expressed above, but clinozoisite (which has a different crystal structure) shows extensive substitution of ferric iron for aluminum to give a composition nearer that of epidote. In zoisite, clinozoisite, and epidote, the calcium ions occupy irregular 7-fold or 8-fold sites, whereas the aluminum or the ferric iron ions occupy octahedral (6-fold) sites. The epidotes are common in metamorphic rocks, those derived from pre-existing igneous or sedimentary rocks by changes in pressure and temperature.

Melilites
The melilite group consists essentially of a solid-solution series between åkermanite, or calcium magnesium silicate (Ca$_2$MgSi$_2$O$_7$), and gehlenite, or calcium aluminum silicate (Ca$_2$Al$_2$SiO$_7$). The crystal structure contains double groups of SiO$_4$ tetrahedra. In addition to a large 8-fold site occupied by the calcium ions, an additional tetrahedral (4-fold) site exists that is occupied by aluminum in gehlenite and magnesium in åkermanite; this tetrahedral coordination of magnesium is rare in silicates. The melilite minerals are characteristic of high-temperature metamorphic rocks formed from impure carbonates.

Pyroxenes
Chain silicates. Pyroxenes comprise undoubtedly the most important group of ferromagnesian minerals—those containing ferrous iron (Fe^{2+}) and magnesium (Mg^{2+})—in the Earth–Moon system and, in addition, are important in meteorites; they almost certainly will prove to be an important silicate type on other planets as well. Pyroxenes are important not only because of their abundance but also because they are capable of revealing their detailed evolutionary history. The most important pyroxene minerals are part of a threefold solid-solution series, in which substitution takes place between wollastonite, a calcium silicate (Ca$_2$Si$_2$O$_6$) abbreviated as Wo; enstatite, a magnesium silicate (Mg$_2$Si$_2$O$_6$) abbreviated as en; and ferrosilite, a ferrous iron silicate (Fe$_2$Si$_2$O$_6$) abbreviated fs. A convenient way to represent the pyroxene solid-solution series is as a triangular diagram that represents the composition of the pyroxenes as percentages of the three end-members. Triangular compositional diagrams such as these are rather easy to read: if a mineral composition plots on a corner of the triangle, only one end-member is present (in this case, either wo, en, or fs); if the composition plots on one of the bounding lines, the mineral is a solid solution between two of the end-members (en–fs, fs–wo or wo–en); if the composition plots within the triangle, all three end-members are present in solid solution. The actual position of a mineral's chemical analysis on the diagram gives the proportions of the three end-members: the closer the analysis plots to an end-member, the more of it in solid solution.

Figure 3A represents such a diagram and gives a generally accepted nomenclature for intermediate members. The apex of the triangle represents pure wollastonite (Ca$_2$Si$_2$O$_6$); a point on the base directly below the apex represents a composition of MgFeSi$_2$O$_6$, or species that contain equal numbers of enstatite (Mg$_2$Si$_2$O$_6$) and ferrosilite (Fe$_2$Si$_2$O$_6$) formula units. In like manner a point on the side of the triangle directly opposite the right-hand corner represents a composition of CaMgSi$_2$O$_6$, or that of pure diopside, abbreviated di. A point opposite the left-hand corner represents a composition of CaFeSi$_2$O$_6$, or that of pure hedenbergite, abbreviated hed. The compositional region bounded by the diopside, hedenbergite, enstatite, and ferrosilite is known as the pyroxene quadrilateral; minerals with compositions that fall above the di–hed line no longer possess a pyroxene crystal structure.

The crystal structure of the pyroxenes contains infinite chains of linked silicate tetrahedra (see Figure 1C). Each tetrahedron contains a tetrahedral (4-fold coordi-

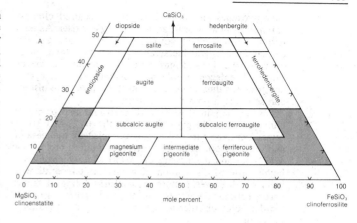

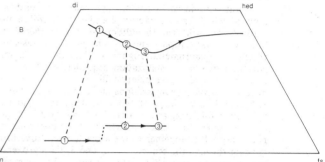

Figure 3: (A) Nomenclature of clinopyroxenes in the system CaMgSi$_2$O$_6$–CaFeSi$_2$O$_6$–Mg$_2$Si$_2$O$_6$–Fe$_2$Si$_2$O$_6$; (B) one important type of pyroxene crystallization trend (see text).
Modified from A. Poldervaart and H.H. Hess, "Pyroxenes in the Crystallization of Basaltic Magma," *Journal of Geology*, vol. 59 (1951); University of Chicago Press

nation) site. In addition, there are octahedral (regular 6-fold) sites, called $M(1)$ sites, and irregular 6-fold to 8-fold sites, called $M(2)$ sites. The tetrahedral sites may be filled with silicon as well as aluminum ions; the $M(1)$, or octahedral, sites can be occupied by aluminum (Al^{3+}), magnesium (Mg^{2+}), ferrous or ferric iron (Fe^{2+} or Fe^{3+}), trivalent chromium (Cr^{3+}), divalent manganese (Mn^{2+}), or titanium (Ti^{4+}) ions. The $M(2)$ sites can be occupied by calcium (Ca^{2+}), sodium (Na$^+$), manganese (Mn^{2+}), ferrous iron (Fe^{2+}), lithium (Li$^+$), or magnesium (Mg^{+2}) ions; when such a site is occupied by a large cation (*i.e.*, calcium or sodium), it essentially has an 8-fold coordination, but when it is occupied by one of the smaller ions it has a 6-fold coordination. Within the pyroxene crystal structure, the tetrahedral chains are arranged in layers that alternate with layers containing the $M(2)$ and $M(1)$ sites. Various stacking possibilities for these tetrahedral and octahedral layers result in three different crystal structure types: orthopyroxenes, which crystallize in the orthorhombic system, and have a unit cell (the basic crystal building block) with three mutually perpendicular cell edges of unequal lengths; primitive clinopyroxenes, which crystallize in the monoclinic system and have a unit cell with three unequal cell edges, two of which are perpendicular and the third of which is inclined to the plane of the other two; and the C-centred clinopyroxenes, which also crystallize in the monoclinic system and have a unit cell like that of the primitive clinopyroxenes, except that the arrangement of atoms in the unit cell is slightly more symmetrical.

The orthopyroxenes and primitive clinopyroxenes have chemical compositions that plot close to the line in the pyroxene quadrilateral connecting enstatite and ferrosilite, called the enstatite–ferrosilite join. Therefore, these pyroxenes have the rather small magnesium and iron atoms in the $M(2)$ site, which thus has a 6-fold coordination. C-centred clinopyroxenes have compositions that plot near the diopside–hedenbergite join. It follows that they are enriched in calcium, and thus the $M(2)$ site has an 8-fold coordination.

At low temperatures, there is incomplete solid solution between the calcium-poor orthopyroxenes and primitive clinopyroxenes and the calcium-rich *C*-centred clinopyroxenes; in other words, a miscibility gap exists. As temperature is increased, however, the miscibility gap decreases in size, and increased solid solution takes place between the low-calcium and high-calcium pyroxene groups. The degree of solid solution between these pyroxene groups is thus an indication of the temperature history and serves as a powerful geothermometer.

Close to the join at which orthopyroxenes and primitive clinopyroxenes, the pigeonites, exist, the $M(2)$ and $M(1)$ crystallographic sites are largely occupied by magnesium and ferrous iron. At low temperatures the iron prefers the $M(2)$ site and magnesium the $M(1)$ site, which gives a highly ordered distribution of atoms. As temperature is increased, however, a more random distribution of atoms occurs between these sites, which gives increased disorder; the degree of disorder is, therefore, another temperature indicator.

Natural basaltic rocks contain pyroxenes the compositions of which can be expressed rather well within the pyroxene quadrilateral. In addition, these pyroxenes show orderly crystallization trends which can be represented within the quadrilateral. Figure 3B illustrates one important pyroxene crystallization sequence. With falling temperature and degree of crystallization of the basaltic melt, the pyroxene compositions move in the progression 1, 2, and 3. The two point 1s on the diagram are joined by a line; this line, called a tie line, indicates that the two pyroxenes (one calcium rich and the other calcium poor) crystallize together at the same temperature. Progressing through the sequence 1, 2, and 3, the pyroxenes are becoming richer in iron, because they contain more of the fs (ferrosilite) end-member. Thus, the iron-to-magnesium ratio in naturally occurring pyroxenes provides information about the rock's place in the crystallization sequence: those rocks rich in magnesium crystallized early, and those rich in iron crystallized late.

In addition to having use as geothermometers and as indicators of their place in a crystallization sequence, pyroxenes have potential as geobarometers. One example of the usefulness of pyroxenes as geobarometers, but certainly not the only one, concerns the pyroxene jadeite, sodium aluminum silicate ($NaAlSi_2O_6$). In terrestrial crustal rocks the feldspar mineral albite, a different sodium aluminum silicate ($NaAlSi_3O_8$) that will be discussed in detail below, is an important constituent. In this mineral all of the aluminum is in tetrahedral (4-fold) coordination. When pressure is increased, however, as in the lower crust, upper mantle, or in a meteorite-impact-induced shock event, albite becomes unstable and breaks down to jadeite ($NaAlSi_2O_6$) and quartz (SiO_2). In jadeite all of the aluminum is in octahedral (6-fold) coordination, and the mineral assemblage jadeite + quartz is denser than albite. The reaction can be written:

$$NaAl^{IV}Si_3O_8 \rightarrow NaAl^{VI}Si_2O_6 + SiO_2,$$
$$\text{albite} \qquad \text{jadeite} \qquad \text{quartz}$$

in which the superscripts indicate the coordination of al. Thus, the amount of jadeite in a pyroxene gives some indication of the pressure history.

Pyroxenoids The pyroxenoids, an interesting group of minerals somewhat similar to but not as abundant or important as the pyroxenes, have structures that contain chains of SiO_4 tetrahedra. The pyroxene chain (Figure 1C) has a repeating two-tetrahedra unit along it. This means that, on a line drawn from any point on a tetrahedron parallel to the chain direction, that point will be repeated at a distance of two tetrahedra along the chain. In pyroxenoids, however, the repeat distance varies from one mineral to another. In wollastonite, calcium silicate ($CaSiO_3$), the repeat distance is three tetrahedra; in rhodonite, manganese and calcium silicate [$(Mn, Ca)SiO_3$], it is five; in pyroxmangite, a manganese, calcium, iron, and magnesium silicate [$(Mn, Ca, Fe^{2+}, Mg)SiO_3$], it is seven; and in ferrosilite III, an iron silicate, it is nine. In general, the repeat distance increases as the mean radius of the cation decreases. A new lunar mineral, pyroxferroite, has essentially the same structure as pyroxmangite. Wollastonite is

a common mineral in metamorphosed limestone that has been subjected to high temperatures.

Amphiboles Among the important rock-forming minerals the amphiboles are perhaps the most complicated. Their crystal structures are capable of accommodating cations of diverse size and charge. A general chemical formula for amphiboles can be written as $AX_2Y_5Z_8O_{22}(OH, F)_2$, in which the A position can be potassium or sodium; the X position can be calcium, sodium, manganese, ferrous iron, lithium, or magnesium; the Y position can be filled with manganese, ferrous or ferric iron, magnesium, chromium, titanium, or aluminum; and the Z position can be filled with silicon or aluminum. Important species include anthophyllite, grunerite, tremolite, ferrotremolite, edenite, tschermakite, ferrotschermakite, pargasite, ferrohastingsite, glaucophane, magnesioriebeckite, riebeckite, and richterite, all of which are end-members in the various solid-solution series exhibited by the amphiboles. In addition to these end-members, important intermediate members include hornblende (calcium and aluminum rich), cummingtonite (a solid solution between anthophyllite and grunerite), and gedrite (aluminum- and sodium-rich anthophyllite).

An amphibole quadrilateral can be constructed that is directly analogous to the pyroxene quadrilateral. The four end-members are tremolite, calcium magnesium silicate [$Ca_2Mg_5Si_8O_{22}(OH)_2$]; ferrotremolite, calcium iron silicate [$Ca_2Fe_5^{2+}Si_8O_{22}(OH)_2$]; anthophyllite, magnesium silicate [$Mg_7Si_8O_{22}(OH)_2$]; and grunerite, ferrous iron silicate [$Fe_7^{2+}Si_8O_{22}(OH)_2$]. The calcium-rich join includes tremolite and ferrotremolite, whereas the calcium-poor join includes anthophyllite and grunerite.

Amphibole structures contain double chains of silicate tetrahedra (Figure 1D). In addition, there are sites with three types of coordination: the A site, a large site with up to a 12-fold coordination; the $M(4)$ site, an irregular site with 6-fold to 8-fold coordination; and the $M(1, 2, 3)$ sites, regular octahedral (6-fold) sites. The A site is occupied by those cations that can be in the A position in the general chemical formula, but sometimes it is vacant; similarly, the $M(4)$ site is occupied by the cations in the X position and the $M(1, 2, 3)$ sites by those in the Y position. Amphibole structures, like pyroxene structures, can be considered in terms of alternating tetrahedral and octahedral layers. Different structural arrangements of these layers and certain distortions result in three important structure types that correspond to the three different pyroxene structures: orthoamphiboles, primitive clinoamphiboles, and C-centred clinoamphiboles.

Orthoamphiboles and primitive clinoamphiboles have compositions near the anthophyllite–grunerite join and thus are calcium poor. In these structures, the $M(4)$ site is occupied by ferrous iron and magnesium and has a 6-fold coordination. C-centred clinoamphiboles have compositions near the tremolite–ferrotremolite join and are therefore calcium rich. In these amphiboles, the $M(4)$ site is largely occupied by calcium and has an 8-fold coordination. At low temperatures there is limited miscibility (solid solution) between the calcium-poor group (orthoamphiboles and primitive clinoamphiboles) and the calcium-rich group (C-centred clinoamphiboles). The amount of mixing between these groups increases with temperature; although this relation has potential in geothermometry, as with the pyroxenes, the amphibole geothermometer has not been properly calibrated.

In orthoamphiboles and primitive clinoamphiboles the $M(4)$ and $M(1, 2, 3)$ sites are largely occupied by ferrous iron and magnesium. At low temperatures the ferrous iron is concentrated largely in the $M(4)$ site, whereas the magnesium is concentrated in $M(1, 2, 3)$; at higher temperatures a more disordered distribution obtains. Again as in the pyroxenes, a second type of geothermometer is available, which involves the degree of disorder of the ferrous iron and magnesium ions between two kinds of sites.

A third striking analogy between the pyroxenes and the amphiboles concerns the aluminum-rich end-members. In the pyroxenes, the aluminous pyroxene jadeite forms at the expense of the sodium feldspar albite under high-pressure conditions. Similarly, in amphiboles the aluminous end-member glaucophane, a sodium magnesium aluminosilicate $[Na_2Mg_3Al_2Si_8O_{22}(OH)_2]$, forms at the expense of albite at high pressures. Glaucophane forms preferentially over jadeite in rocks formed under high pressures when hydrous conditions prevail.

Thus, as in pyroxenes, amphiboles offer potential as geothermometers and geobarometers. Pyroxenes and amphiboles are not redundant in this application, however, because the two groups of minerals commonly form in different pressure and temperature regimes, with the amphiboles commonly forming at lower temperatures and under more hydrous conditions.

Sheet silicates. Sheet silicate structures are characterized by silicate tetrahedral layers (Figure 1E), octahedral layers, and, in some instances, interlayer cations. The tetrahedral (4-fold) sites can be occupied by silicon or aluminum; the octahedral (6-fold) sites commonly are occupied by magnesium, ferrous and ferric iron, aluminum, and titanium; and the interlayer sites (up to 12-fold coordination) are occupied by sodium or potassium ions or by water molecules or hydronium ions (water with an added proton, H_3O^+). Two groups of structures are defined: in the dioctahedral structures, two-thirds of the octahedral sites are occupied by cations and one-third are vacant; in the trioctahedral structures, all the octahedral sites are filled.

Trioctahedral micas Trioctahedral mica minerals have an octahedral layer, designated TRI, that is usually occupied by magnesium (Mg^{+2}) and ferrous iron (Fe^{+2}) ions with a $+2$ charge. It is possible to develop the various trioctahedral minerals by combining silicate tetrahedral layers (T) with trioctahedral layers (TRI) in various combinations. A simple member of this series is obtained by forming composite layers containing one tetrahedral layer (T) and one trioctahedral layer (TRI); these composite layers are designated concisely as T–TRI. A structure can be built by stacking T–TRI layers—i.e., T–TRI, T–TRI, T–TRI, etc. The bonding between T and TRI is rather strong, but that between one T–TRI layer and the next is very weak. Thus, these structures have excellent cleavage; that is, they can be broken readily between the composite layers. Antigorite, a mineral with this structure, has the chemical formula $Mg_3(Si_2O_5)(OH)_4$.

Another trioctahedral structure can be derived by constructing a tightly bonded composite layer of two T layers and one TRI layer—i.e., T–TRI–T. When stacked, the structure would thus consist of the sequence T–TRI–T, T–TRI–T, T–TRI–T, etc. Again, good cleavage exists between the composite layers. Talc is such a mineral, with the formula $Mg_3(Si_4O_{10})(OH)_2$.

A third member of the trioctahedral group can be derived if one-fourth of the silicon atoms in the tetrahedral (4-fold) sites are replaced by aluminum atoms. Because of the charge difference (silicon has a $+4$ charge, aluminum only a $+3$), this leaves a residual charge on the T–TRI–T layers; interlayer cations enter the structure to achieve electrical neutrality. An example of such a structure has potassium (K) as the interlayer cation; its structure can be represented as (T–TRI–T)K(T–TRI–T)K(T–TRI–T)K(T–TRI–T), etc. In these structures the bonding between adjacent T–TRI–T layers is stronger than before because of the presence of an interlayer cation; however, the cleavage is still good. Biotite micas are examples of this type; the group is a solid-solution series with two important compositional end-members: annite $[KFe_3^{2+}(Si_3Al)O_{10}(OH)_2]$ and phlogopite $[KMg_3(Si_3Al)O_{10}(OH)_2]$.

Still another trioctahedral structure can be derived by filling half of the tetrahedral sites by aluminum and half by silicon. The negative residual charge is thus increased, and calcium, which has a $+2$ charge, can enter the structure. The structure can be represented as (T–TRI–T)Ca(T–TRI–T)Ca(T–TRI–T), etc. A mineral representative is the brittle mica xanthophyllite, with the formula $CaMg_3(Al_2Si_2)O_{10}(OH)_2$. The bonding between T–TRI–T layers is stronger because of calcium's greater charge, and thus the cleavage is not as pronounced.

An additional member of the trioctahedral group can be formed by adding interlayer water molecules to the structure of talc. Such a structure can be represented as (T–TRI–T)H_2O(T–TRI–T)H_2O(T–TRI–T), etc. The addition of water between the layers causes the structure to expand, which gives such minerals the name swelling micas. A mineral example is vermiculite, with the formula $Mg_3(Si_4O_{10})(OH)_2 \cdot H_2O$.

Dioctahedral micas A parallel development can be made for dioctahedral micas. Addition of one T layer to one dioctahedral layer (DI) yields a structure T–DI, T–DI, T–DI, etc. As expected, there is weak bonding between individual T–DI layers. A mineral representative is kaolinite, with the formula $Al_2(Si_2O_5)(OH)_4$.

Another member can be derived from T–DI–T layers; it has the structure T–DI–T, T–DI–T, T–DI–T, etc. Again, the bonding is weak between composite layers, and the cleavage is good. Pyrophyllite, $Al_2(Si_4O_{10})(OH)_2$, represents this group.

Addition of aluminum to one-fourth of the sites previously occupied by silicon allows the addition of a monovalent interlayer cation (charge of $+1$), either sodium or potassium; the structure can be represented as (T–DI–T)(Na, K)(T–DI–T)(Na, K)(T–DI–T). The cleavage is not as good as in the dioctahedral micas without interlayer cations. Muscovite is the potassium end-member of this group $[KAl_2(Si_3Al)O_{10}(OH)_2]$, and paragonite is the sodium end-member $[NaAl_2(Si_3Al)O_{10}(OH)_2]$.

When half of the tetrahedral sites are occupied by silicon and half by aluminum, the structure of the mineral margarite $[CaAl_2(Si_2Al_2)O_{10}(OH)_2]$ can be derived and represented as (T–DI–T)Ca(T–DI–T)Ca(T–DI–T). This brittle mica does not have as good cleavage as do the other dioctahedral micas.

Addition of water to pyrophyllite results in montmorillonite, a dioctahedral swelling mica with the formula $Al_2(Si_4O_{10})(OH)_2 \cdot H_2O$.

The micas can be used as geobarometers as well as geothermometers. Solid solution between the potassium-rich dioctahedral mica, muscovite, and the sodium-rich dioctahedral mica, paragonite, is not complete at low temperatures but increases with increasing temperature; this relationship has been calibrated rather well by experimental studies. Thus, the chemical compositions of coexisting muscovite and paragonite solid solutions in natural rocks can yield information about the thermal history of the rock. Furthermore, as with the pyroxenes and the amphiboles, the amount of aluminum in octahedral coordination in a mica may be indicative of its pressure history. For example, under high pressures phlogopite, which has its aluminum in tetrahedral (4-fold) coordination, is converted at the expense of potassium–feldspar into the mica phengite, which has its aluminum in octahedral (6-fold) coordination and is thus denser. The reaction proceeds as follows:

$$KMg_3(Al^{IV}Si_3)O_{10}(OH)_2 + 2KAl^{IV}Si_3O_8 + 3SiO_2$$
$$\text{phlogopite} \qquad \text{K-feldspar} \quad \text{quartz}$$
$$+2H_2O \rightarrow 3KMgAl^{VI}Si_4O_{10}(OH)_2.$$
$$\text{water} \qquad \text{phengite}$$

Silica minerals **Framework silicates.** There are six important polymorphs of silica, silicon dioxide (SiO_2); these include low quartz, high quartz, tridymite, cristobalite, coesite, and stishovite, all of which have the silica composition but have different crystal structures. The structures of all except stishovite are made up of SiO_4 tetrahedra with all four corners linked to other tetrahedra, but even though they are made up of three-dimensional frameworks, their densities vary significantly because the arrangements of the tetrahedra differ.

At low temperatures and pressures, low quartz is the stable form. If the pressure is held at one atmosphere and the temperature is raised, high quartz becomes the stable form in the temperature range 573°–870° C (1,063°–1,600° F), tridymite in the range 870°–1,470° C (1,600°–2,680° F), and cristobalite above 1,470° C until it melts at 1,720° C (3,130° F). The high-temperature polymorphs have lower densities than the low-temperature polymorphs. If pressure is increased, all will transform to coesite; this transition takes place at approximately 20 kilobars (one bar = 29.5 inches of mercury) at room temperature and approximately 40 kilobars at 1,900° C (3,450° F). Although coesite is denser than most of the silica polymorphs, it still has silicon in tetrahedral coordination. The high density results from tight packing of the SiO_4 tetrahedral groups. At extremely high pressures (near 160 kilobars), silica has the very dense stishovite structure. In this structure silicon is in octahedral coordination; octahedral coordination of silicon may well be the important silicon coordination in the lower mantle of the Earth.

Feldspars

The feldspar minerals are the most abundant mineral group in the Earth's crust, where they make up 60 percent of the rocks and, thus, are an extremely important group of silicates. They, like the forms of silica discussed above, have framework structures, but, unlike the silica polymorphs, they have some of the tetrahedral (4-fold coordination) silicon atoms replaced by aluminum. The substitution results in a residual negative charge on the framework structure caused by the charge difference between aluminum and silicon, and other cations can be accommodated—e.g., sodium, calcium, or potassium. Feldspars are less important in the mantle of the Earth. Their relatively low-density crystal structures give way to denser structures under high-pressure conditions.

The three most important end-members are potassic feldspar ($KAlSi_3O_8$), the sodic feldspar albite ($NaAlSi_3O_8$), and the calcic feldspar anorthite ($CaAl_2Si_2O_8$). There is limited solid solution between potassic feldspar and albite (mutual substitution between potassium and sodium ions) at low temperatures because of the great disparity in ionic radii between the potassium ion, with a radius of about 1.5 angstrom units (symbolized Å; 1 Å = 10^{-8} centimetre), and the sodium ion, with a radius of about one angstrom. At high temperatures the amount of solid solution increases, which makes this relationship useful in tracing the temperature history of feldspar-bearing rocks.

There is little solid solution between anorthite and potassic feldspar at any temperature. This is perhaps due not only to the size discrepancy of cations (about the same as between sodium and potassium because the ionic radius of calcium is very similar to that of sodium) but also to the difference in charge, because calcium ions have a +2 charge, whereas potassium ions only have a +1 charge.

Because the ionic radii of calcium and sodium are similar, there is complete solid solution between albite and anorthite at high temperatures, but the substitution involves four cations (coupled substitution) instead of the usual two, $Na^{1+}Si^{4+} \rightleftharpoons Ca^{2+}Al^{3+}$ (sodium and silicon reversibly replacing calcium and aluminum), and this results in some small miscibility gaps in this series at low temperature.

The crystal structure of anorthite ($CaAl_2Si_2O_8$) is a framework of linked SiO_4 and AlO_4 tetrahedra with large void spaces that are occupied by calcium. There is the same number of aluminum and silicon atoms in the crystal structure, and the tetrahedra are arranged so that every SiO_4 tetrahedron is linked to four AlO_4 tetrahedra, and every AlO_4 tetrahedron is linked to four SiO_4 tetrahedra. This relationship is a general rule in silicate mineralogy—i.e., that AlO_4 tetrahedra tend not to share corners with other AlO_4 tetrahedra. This perfectly ordered distribution remains essentially intact even at high temperatures and so offers little in the way of geothermometry for anorthite-bearing rocks.

In albite ($NaAlSi_3O_8$) the aluminum-to-silicon ratio is 1 to 3 rather than 1 to 1 as in anorthite; this offers more freedom in the arrangement of the silicon and aluminum atoms in the albite structure. Although all of the silicon and aluminum occupy tetrahedral (4-fold) sites in the albite structure, these tetrahedra sites differ in detail; the four types have slightly different distortions and are referred to as T1(0), T1(m), T2(0) and T2(m). At low temperatures most of the aluminum occupies the T1(0) site, and the silicon atoms occupy T1(m), T2(0), and T2(m), which gives a highly ordered distribution. At high temperatures (about 1,000° C, or 1,800° F) the aluminum and silicon atoms have a much more random distribution. Thus, order–disorder relationships between silicon and aluminum are very useful in determining the temperature history of albite-bearing rocks.

In potassic feldspar, as in albite, the aluminum-to-silicon ratio is 1 to 3, and again the possibility of order and disorder of aluminum exists. In the low-temperature form, called microcline, the potassic feldspar has four distinct tetrahedral sites, referred to as T1(0), T1(m), T2(0), and T(m), just as in albite. At low temperatures the aluminum–silicon distribution is highly ordered, with aluminum in T1(0) and silicon in T1(m), T2(0), and T2(m). As temperature is increased, microcline changes to orthoclase, which has only two distinct tetrahedral sites—T1 and T2 sites. In the orthoclase structure, aluminum preferentially occupies the T1 sites, but the overall aluminum–silicon distribution is more disordered than in microcline. As the temperature is increased further, orthoclase becomes sanidine, with a very disordered distribution of the aluminum and silicon atoms. Thus, as in albite, the aluminum–silicon distribution in potassic feldspar provides a powerful geothermometer.

The feldspathoid minerals take the place of feldspars when igneous rocks are deficient in silica; important species include leucite, kalsilite, nepheline, sodalite, noselite, and cancrinite.

Feldspathoids

Leucite, potassium aluminum silicate ($KAlSi_2O_6$), is the commonest potassium-containing feldspathoid; it occurs frequently in potassic rocks that are poor in silica.

Nepheline, sodium aluminum silicate ($NaAlSiO_4$), and kalsilite, a potassium aluminum silicate ($KAlSiO_4$), form a solid solution series; both end-members (i.e., nepheline and kalsilite) have a framework structure with half the silicon atoms replaced by aluminum. Electrical neutrality is achieved by the addition of sodium or potassium ions (Na^+ or K^+) into structural cavities in the framework. Extensive substitution exists between sodium and potassium at elevated temperatures, but at low temperatures a large miscibility gap exists because of the significant difference between the ionic radii of sodium and potassium. Again, as with the feldspar minerals, the amount of solid solution between these two end-members serves as a geothermometer. Nepheline and kalsilite are found in igneous and metamorphic rocks in which the silica content is low; in these rocks nepheline commonly is present instead of the feldspar albite, which is richer in silica.

In sodalite, noselite, and cancrinite, the tetrahedral framework units have a negative residual charge of −6. In this case, however, electrical neutrality is not achieved by the addition of positively charged metal ions alone; anions or anionic groups—ions or ion groups with a negative charge such as chloride (Cl^-), sulfate (SO_4^{2-}), or bicarbonate (HCO_3^-)—are added to these structures as well. Charge balance is achieved as follows: in sodalite, $(8\ Na^+)^{8+} + (framework)^{6-} + (2Cl^-)^{2-} = 0$ residual charge; in noselite, $(8\ Na^+)^{8+} + (framework)^{6-} + (SO_4^{2-})^{2-} = 0$; and in cancrinite, $(8\ Na^+)^{8+} + (framework)^{6-} + (2HCO_3^-)^{2-} = 0$.

Although not considered feldspathoid minerals, the scapolites bear resemblances to both the feldspathoids and the feldspars. The scapolites are a solid-solution series between two important end-members: marialite, a chloride-containing sodium aluminum silicate [$Na_4Al_3(Si_9O_{24})Cl$] that can be said to be made up of three albite ($NaAlSi_3O_8$) formula units and one sodium chloride (NaCl) formula unit; and meionite, a carbonate containing calcium aluminum silicate ($Ca_4Al_6Si_6O_{24}CO_3$) that can be said to be made up of three anorthite ($CaAl_2Si_2O_8$) formula units and one calcium carbonate ($CaCO_3$) formula unit. These minerals have framework structures with aluminum-to-silicon ratios ranging from 1 to 3 in marialite to 1 to 1 in meionite. Large central cavities in the structures accommodate the anionic chloride (Cl^-) and sulfate (So_4^{2-}) group, whereas smaller cavities accommodate the sodium and calcium ions. Other anionic groups can substitute into the scapolite structure, including fluoride, bisulfate, and hydroxide ions. Scapolites can form over a wide range of temperatures and pressures and are found both in metamorphic and igneous rocks.

Scapolites

Another mineral that bears a strong resemblance to the feldspathoids and also to the zeolites is the mineral analcime [$Na(AlSi_2O_6)\cdot H_2O$]. Analcime has a framework structure that contains large cavities capable of accommodating both sodium ions and water molecules. It is a primary constituent of some igneous rocks that are rich in sodium and poor in silica.

Zeolites The zeolite minerals are hydrated aluminosilicates that have very open three-dimensional framework structures and form at low temperatures. As in the case of the feldspars, aluminum atoms in the tetrahedral framework result in a negative residual charge, which is compensated by the entrance of additional cations (*e.g.*, lithium, sodium, potassium, magnesium, calcium, strontium, and barium) into the large holes. Because these holes can also be occupied by water molecules, zeolites have the property of reversible hydration and dehydration. Compared to the feldspars, zeolites have the cations loosely bonded in their structures, and these cations essentially rattle around in the large structural cavities. The randomness of cations and water molecules make it difficult to determine the crystal structures of many members of this very complex silicate group. The large cavities in zeolite structures allow a second type of coupled substitution—*i.e.*, two cations for one cation, as two sodium ions for one calcium ion: $2Na^{1+} \rightleftharpoons Ca^{2+}$.

Zeolites are commonly divided into three main groups, but recent work has shown that this is not rigorously correct; the three groups are the natrolite group, the heulandite group, and the chabazite group. In considering these groups, account is taken of the bonding strength in various directions in the structures. Therefore, although all zeolites are three-dimensional frameworks, the strong bonding linkages may be considered as being linear in one group of zeolites, two-dimensional (planar) in a second, and three-dimensional in another. The natrolite group of zeolites has strong linear bonding linkages, which gives members of this group a fibrous appearance; members of the group include natrolite, mesolite, scolecite, thomsonite, gonnardite, and edingtonite. The heulandite group has strong two-dimensional linkages, and thus members of the group commonly have a platy appearance; members of this group include heulandite, stilbite, and epistilbite. The chabazite group of zeolites has bond linkages of approximately the same strength in all three dimensions; members of this group include harmotome, phillipsite, chabazite, gmelinite, levyne, and faujasite.

A general correlation exists between the number of tetrahedra in various rings or loops in the tetrahedral framework and the minimum diameter of the widest channel (MDWC). Harmotome and phillipsite have four- and eight-membered rings and an MDWC of 3.2 Å; levyne has four-, six-, and eight-membered rings and an MDWC of 2.7 Å; erionite has four-, six-, and eight-membered rings and an MDWC of 3.6 Å; chabazite has four-, six-, and eight-membered rings and an MDWC of 3.9 Å; gmelinite has four-, six-, eight-, and 12-membered rings and an MDWC of 6.4 Å; fanjasite has four-, six-, and 12-membered rings and an MDWC of 9 Å. It is apparent that the degree of openness of zeolite structures varies considerably from one to the next.

Zeolites are useful as crystalline ion exchangers, drying agents, and molecular sieves. The cation exchange property means that if a zeolite with a certain cation content is put into an aqueous solution with a different cation content, an exchange of cations will take place, resulting in a more similar cation content of both solid and solution. Zeolites are useful as drying agents, but they must first be dehydrated. Because zeolites have the property of reversible hydration, they will take up water molecules again, and thus containers of dehydrated zeolites may be placed in areas to remove moisture from the air, as for example in areas for precise weighing of materials. A third use of zeolites is as molecular sieves. This property results because of the range of structural channel sizes discussed above. Molecules with diameters larger than the channelways are excluded, whereas molecules with smaller diameters can enter. Because of this, zeolites provide an effective way of separating (sieving) materials on a molecular scale.

Zeolites typically occur in low-temperature environments in the Earth's crust. They fill small openings (vesicles or fissures) in late-stage igneous rocks, can form in sedimentary rocks, and occur in very low-grade metamorphic rocks (those formed at low temperatures).

OCCURRENCE OF SILICATES

In the Earth's crust. Igneous rocks are composed largely of a few silicate minerals, namely feldspars, (about 60 percent), amphiboles and pyroxenes (about 17 percent), quartz (12 percent), micas (about 4 percent), and olivine. The igneous rocks are classified according to their mineral content: for example, syenites are rocks containing potassic feldspar, micas, and amphiboles; granites contain potassic feldspar, sodium–calcium feldspars, micas, and amphiboles; gabbros contain sodium–calcium feldspars and pyroxene; peridotites contain pyroxene and olivine; dunites are pure olivine rocks.

Sedimentary rocks result largely from the breakdown of pre-existing rocks, mainly igneous rocks, by the action of air and water. The minerals formed in igneous rocks are stable at high temperatures, but, after the rocks have cooled and hydrous conditions prevail, many are broken down to other low-temperature, usually hydrous minerals, which may be carried and redeposited by water.

The silicate minerals that form sedimentary rocks fall into two genetic groups: first, those resistant minerals that have not been altered from their composition in the parent igneous rock and, second, those that have been newly formed. The first silicate minerals that are broken down from igneous rock parents are usually those that formed at the highest temperatures; thus, olivine and anorthite-rich feldspars are broken down readily. The later stage (lower temperature) silicate minerals, such as albite-rich feldspar, potassic feldspar, muscovite mica, and quartz, are more resistant and may occur as unchanged constituents in sedimentary rocks. Silicates that form from the breakdown of pre-existing high-temperature silicate minerals usually have layer structures, such as the kaolinites, montmorillonites, and some zeolites.

Metamorphic rocks can be formed from pre-existing igneous, sedimentary, or other metamorphic rocks. They are formed within a temperature range between the low-temperature conditions under which sedimentary rocks are formed to the high temperatures (about 700° C, or 1,300° F) at which igneous rocks may be generated. Metamorphic silicates include the aluminosilicate minerals, andalusite, kyanite, sillimanite; cordierite, a framework silicate containing magnesium and ferrous iron; garnets; chlorite, a sheet silicate rich in magnesium and ferrous iron; talc; staurolite and chloritoide, hydrous iron- and aluminum-rich silicates; amphiboles; pyroxenes; feldspars; and micas. Metamorphic rocks are commonly classified according to the pressure and temperature conditions under which they formed (metamorphic facies concept). The minerals present at the various pressure–temperature combinations are largely a function of rock composition. At low to moderate pressures the progression from low-temperature to high-temperature facies is as follows: the greenschist facies, which include quartz, muscovite, microcline, albite, zoisite–epidote, tremolite, chlorite, and chloritoid; the epidote–amphibolite facies, which include quartz, kyanite, muscovite, microcline, albite, zoisite–epidote, cummingtonite, talc, anthophyllite, tremolite, hornblende, chlorite, chloritoid, almandite, and biotite; and amphibolite facies, which include quartz, kyanite–sillimanite, muscovite, microcline, plagioclase, zoisite–epidote, wollastonite, cummingtonite, anthophyllite, forsterite, tremolite, diopside, hornblende, cordierite, almandite, staurolite, and biotite; the granulite facies, which include quartz, kyanite, sillimanite, orthoclase, plagioclase, wollastonite, orthopyroxene, forsterite, diopside, augite, pyrope–almandite, and biotite. At low temperatures and high pressures (200°–300° C [400°–600° F], five to eight kilobars) the glaucophane schist facies is represented. It includes, in addition to many of the above, the high-pressure minerals glaucophane, jadeite, and phen-

The two genetic groups of sedimentary silicates

gite. The high pressure, high-temperature eclogite facies contain jadeite-rich pyroxene and pyrope-rich garnets.

In the Earth's mantle. The Earth's mantle extends from depths of approximately 36 kilometres (22 miles) to 2,900 kilometres (1,800 miles), which represents a pressure range of 10–1,400 kilobars and a temperature range of roughly 600–6,000° C (1,100°–11,000° F). The mantle is sometimes divided into three parts: the upper mantle (36–400 kilometres, 10–160 kilobars), the transition zone (400–1,000 kilometres, 160–450 kilobars) and the lower mantle (1,000–2,900 kilometres, 450–1,400 kilobars).

Unlike the parts of the crust of the Earth that can be observed and sampled, the mineralogic nature of the mantle has to be deduced largely on theoretical grounds. The constraints on the theoretical mineralogic combination of the mantle include the temperature gradients, pressure gradients, mean density of the Earth, moment of inertia of the Earth (related to the distribution of mass in the Earth), and the velocity of seismic waves in the mantle. In addition, there are some samples of the upper mantle that have been delivered to Earth's surface: inclusions of rock carried up in deeply derived basalts; and inclusions in diamond pipes, which are thought to be derived with explosive violence from the Earth's mantle. Any model of the mantle, then, must be compatible with both the constraints and the actual samples. In addition, it must be able to account for the composition of igneous rocks derived from the mantle.

The problem of mantle mineralogy has been reviewed by S.P. Clark and Alfred E. Ringwood, and the ideas expressed here are largely theirs. The upper mantle may be represented by four important mineral assemblages (minerals occurring together) and include:

I. olivine + amphibole
II. olivine + aluminum-poor pyroxene + calcium–sodium feldspar (plagioclase)
III. olivine + aluminum-rich pyroxene + spinel
IV. olivine + aluminum-poor pyroxene + garnet.

The Clark–Ringwood model for the transition zone assumes a chemical composition comprised largely of magnesium oxide (MgO) and silica (SiO_2), corresponding to a mixture of the olivine mineral forsterite (Mg_2SiO_4) and the pyroxene mineral enstatite ($MgSiO_3$). These minerals would be stable to a depth of about 400 kilometres (approximately 160 kilobars). With increasing depth into the transition zone, Clark and Ringwood propose the following reactions (the Roman superscripts indicate coordination):

I. $2MgSi^{IV}O_3 \rightarrow Mg_2SiO_4 + Si^{IV}O_2$
   pyroxene   olivine   stishovite

II. $Mg_2Si^{IV}O_4 \rightarrow MgSi^{IV}O_4$
   olivine   spinel structure
                  (closer packing
                   of SiO_4
                   groups)

III. $Mg_2Si^{IV}O_4 + Si^{VI}O_2 \rightarrow 2MgSi^{VI}O_3$
    spinel   stishovite   ilmenite
                                  structure

IV. $Mg_2Si^{IV}O_4 \rightarrow MgSi^{VI}O_3 + MgO$
   spinel   ilmenite   periclase
                 structure

This series of transformations should be complete at about 1,000 kilometres (approximately 450 kilobars) and result in a density increase from 3.2 to 3.9 grams per cubic centimetre. It is apparent that the general sequence from crust to upper mantle through the transition zone involves an increase in coordination of aluminum atoms from 4-fold to 6-fold, an increase in packing density of SiO_4 groups, and an increased coordination of silicon from 4-fold to 6-fold.

The lower mantle appears to be more homogeneous and may be made up largely of magnesium silicate ($MgSiO_3$) with the ilmenite structure and magnesium oxide (MgO) with the periclase structure.

In meteorites and in the Moon. Silicate minerals are important in meteorites and lunar samples, which pro-

vide solid extraterrestrial material for mineralogic study. The silicate minerals occurring in meteorites include the silica polymorphs quartz, tridymite, and cristobalite, as well as olivine, pyroxenes, and plagioclase. Thus, for those meteorites studied, the range of silicates observed is far more limited than on Earth. This may reflect a much more extensive study of terrestrial silicates, a smaller compositional range for silicate meteorites, and a more limited temperature and pressure range for many meteorites.

The Apollo 11, 12, 14, 15, 16, and Luna-16 missions have provided a wealth of lunar samples. Apollo missions 11, 12, 15, and Luna-16 sampled mare regions (low, dark, relatively smooth areas), and the samples returned were largely basalts. The silicates found in these rocks included the pyroxenes augite and pigeonite, anorthite-rich feldspar, olivine, and the silica polymorphs (cristobalite and tridymite); pyroxenes are the most abundant and important constituents of these basaltic rocks. In addition to these common silicate minerals, a new silicate mineral was discovered, pyroxferroite $Ca_{1/7}(Fe,Mg)_{6/7}SiO_3$. This mineral has a structure that contains chains of SiO_4 tetrahedra and octahedral (6-fold) and 8-fold sites, which accommodate the calcium, ferrous iron, and magnesium. It is one of the last minerals to crystallize from the basaltic melt. Detailed study of these rocks demonstrated that they crystallized rapidly at or near the lunar surface under extremely anhydrous and reducing conditions.

The Apollo 14, 15, and 16 missions sampled the lunar highlands (lighter in colour, older, and displaying rough surface areas heavily pockmarked by meteorite impact craters) and provided samples different from the mare areas. These samples contained far more feldspar (anorthite-rich) and also contained orthopyroxene. Most of these rocks are breccias (rocks formed by breaking up of previously existing rock largely by meteorite impact) the most abundant constituent mineral of which is feldspar.

Although the samples provided information about the distribution of silicate minerals in lunar mare and highlands regions, far less is known about the interior of the moon. Because samples of the lunar interior are lacking, information on it is based largely on theoretical ground. Based on such reasoning, it appears that a pyroxene–olivine lunar interior is likely.

BIBLIOGRAPHY. F. DONALD BLOSS, *Crystallography and Crystal Chemistry* (1971), a general textbook on crystallography and crystal chemistry; NORMAN L. BOWEN, *The Evolution of the Igneous Rocks* (reprinted 1956), a classic work on experimental silicate systems and their application to petrologic problems; S.P. CLARK and A.E. RINGWOOD, "Density Distribution and Constitution of the Mantle," *Rev. Geophys.*, 2:35–88 (1964), a thorough review of this problem, utilizing geochemical, petrological, geothermal, and seismic data; *Dana's System of Mineralogy*, vol. 3, 7th ed. rev. by CLIFFORD FRONDEL (1962), a detailed account of the silica minerals; *Dana's Manual of Mineralogy*, 17th ed. rev. by CORNELIUS S. HURLBUT, JR. (1959), an introductory text of mineralogy; W.A. DEER, R.A. HOWIE, and J. ZUSSMAN, *Rock-Forming Minerals*, vol. 1–4 (1962–63), four volumes concerning the mineralogy of the rock-forming silicates; K.F. FISCHER and W.M. MEIER, "Crystal Chemistry of the Zeolites: A Summary of Recent Results," *Fortschr. Miner.*, 42:50–86 (1964), a review article on the crystal chemistry of zeolites; BRIAN MASON, *Meteorites* (1962), a detailed account of the geochemistry, mineralogy, and petrology of meteorites; and *Principles of Geochemistry*, 3rd ed. (1966), a general textbook concerning the geochemistry of the Earth, meteorites, and solar system; WALTER LOEWENSTEIN, "The Distribution of Aluminum in the Tetrahedra of Silicates and Aluminates," *Am. Miner.*, 39:92–96 (1954); SEELEY W. MUDD, *Industrial Minerals and Rocks*, 3rd ed. (1960), a detailed account of the uses of minerals but not including the common sulfide and oxide ore minerals; J.J. PAPIKE *et al.*, *Pyroxenes and Amphiboles: Crystal Chemistry and Phase Petrology* (1969), recent crystal chemical, mineralogical, and petrologic studies on amphiboles and pyroxenes; S.M. STISHOV and S.V. POPOVA, "New Dense Polymorphic Modification of Silica," *Geokhimiya*, 10:837–839 (1961), one of the first reports on the important new mineral, stishovite.

(J.J.Pa.)

Siliceous Rocks

The siliceous rocks are those sedimentary rocks that consist largely or almost entirely of free silica (SiO_2), in the form either of quartz or varieties of amorphous silica and cristobalite. By custom the term includes rocks that have formed as chemical precipitates of one type or another but exclude rocks high in free silica content that are of detrital or fragmental origin, such as the quartz arenites, those sandstones composed almost entirely of quartz grains. Though many of the siliceous sediments are relatively pure silica, the same rock types may be mixed with clays, carbonates, or detrital grains of sand and silt so that they are impure. By far the most abundant type of siliceous rock is chert, a common constituent of strata of every age and character.

This article deals with the general characteristics and occurrence of siliceous rocks and their origins within the framework of the biogeochemistry of silica. For further information on diagenesis, the alteration of sediments to solid rocks, see SEDIMENTARY ROCKS; see also SHALES; SANDSTONES; and LIMESTONES AND DOLOMITES for specific rock types involved. For an expanded treatment of the role of organisms, see ELEMENTS, PHYSIOLOGICAL CONCENTRATION OF; and MARINE SEDIMENTS. The formation of siliceous crusts is treated in the article DURICRUSTS.

OCCURRENCE AND CHARACTERISTICS

Types of siliceous rocks

Chert is a dense, more or less microcrystalline rock, composed of chalcedony and quartz, that occurs in beds and nodules. Flint, a term that is used synonymously with chert, tends to be used more for references to artifacts such as arrowheads. Various other names have been used for chert, including silexite, hornstone, and phthanite. Porcellanite is a variety of chert, equally dense and hard, that breaks in the manner of unglazed porcelain. Jasper is a coloured chert; the most abundant variety is mixed with iron oxide that makes it red and brown in colour. Such rocks contain much nonsiliceous material, chiefly clay and calcium or magnesium carbonate (calcite or dolomite). Novaculite is a bedded chert (deposits exhibit stratification); the name has been applied mainly to formations of Paleozoic age in the Ouachita Mountains of Arkansas and Oklahoma and, to some extent, to rocks of the same age in the Marathon Mountains of Texas.

Marine and hot spring deposits. Many siliceous rocks called chert are composed almost entirely of siliceous fossils. Thus, diatoms (one-celled marine plants) sink to form diatomaceous oozes on the sea floor, which ultimately may become diatomaceous earths or, if well indurated, diatomite, a hard rock. In the same way, radiolaria (one-celled marine animals) form oozes, earths, and radiolarites. The radiolarians or radiolarian cherts of the Alpine chain are the most famous representatives in the geologic column (the strata that represent all of geological time). Other names used for siliceous fossil earths are infusorial earth, or kieselguhr, and tripoli.

Yet another mode of occurrence of siliceous deposits is as sinters and encrustations formed by evaporation in and around hot springs. There are many names applied to these kinds of deposits; most frequent are siliceous sinter, geyserite (if associated with geysers), and fiorite. The areal extent and total volume of the deposits associated with hot springs and geysers are relatively small, but it is not known how much silica is deposited under the sea or in the interstices of rocks by rising hydrothermal solutions. In contrast, the areal extent and volume of cherts, both bedded and nodular, is large. Some formations containing abundant chert are known to have covered many tens of thousands of square miles in their former extent. Cherts also may be a prominent constituent of many stratigraphic sections (the sequence of strata in a given locale); and though quantitatively small compared to the total amount of clastic rocks (those consisting of aggregates of individual grains) and limestone, they are probably the most abundant chemically precipitated rock type after limestone. Much of their total volume is distributed in small beds and nodules, mainly in carbonate rock sections, and tends to be underestimated.

Various forms of siliceous rocks have found a wide variety of uses from prehistoric times on. The earliest important use was that of chert or flint for the making of weapons in early prehistoric cultures. Another former use for flint was its use in firearms. In modern times chert pebbles have been found useful as grinding agents in ball mills. Diatomaceous earths are used for fine abrasives (as are crushed cherts of various kinds), for molded refractories, and for some fluid filtering purposes. As a major source of silica, the siliceous rocks can be used as the raw material for the making of portland cement, as crushed rock for secondary roads, and as raw material for the making of chemical compounds of silicon. In some localities they are used for building stone.

Physical properties. The diverse origins of siliceous rocks are reflected in the variety of their physical characteristics. Cherts range from almost pure white through tones of cream and buff to dark grays and blues and black. The colours come from impurities, the most common of which are iron impurities, usually finely disseminated ferric oxide (hematite), that colour the rock yellow, brown, and red. The jaspers may represent various mixtures of hematite and silica. Included clay gives a gray or gray-blue colour, whereas finely dispersed organic matter produces a dark blue or black colour. Diatomaceous and radiolarian oozes and earths are white to cream coloured unless they are mixed with large amounts of clay. The sinters and geyserites are white to varying shades of gray.

Porosity, hardness, texture, and composition

The porosity of cherts is very low, usually less than a few percent; and electron micrographs have shown that this porosity is distributed as very tiny cavities and holes. Thus, the permeability is immeasurably small. In contrast, the diatomaceous earths may be very porous and permeable; the pore space between the fossil skeletons may be as high as 50 percent if the rock is not cemented at all. The bulk specific gravity (density of a bulk specimen) of the rock, therefore, may range from a value near that of quartz (2.65) to very low values, depending on its porosity. The cherts tend to have relatively high specific gravities and will be particularly high if much iron is included. Almost all cherts are hard, and some particularly dense varieties may approach seven (the value of quartz) on the Mohs scale of hardness. The siliceous earths are softer because of the friability of the skeletal remains of diatoms and radiolaria, although the silica substance itself is hard. Chert is brittle and breaks with a conchoidal fracture, two properties that made it so suitable for prehistoric arrows, spears, and axes.

The composition of cherts, in terms of free silica present, ranges from opaline silica, a type of amorphous silica, through a form of disordered cristobalite similar in some respects to amorphous silica, to a chalcedonic silica that consists largely of microcrystalline quartz, perhaps with an admixture of cristobalite or amorphous silica. Composition varies with age; the oldest cherts are entirely microcrystalline quartz, whereas younger rocks have more amorphous silica or cristobalite. The siliceous oozes and earths are composed entirely of the untransmuted skeletons of diatoms and radiolaria, which are amorphous silica. The common nonsilica components of siliceous rocks —carbonate (calcite and dolomite), clay minerals, and iron oxides—contribute calcium, magnesium, sodium, potassium, aluminum, and iron, the presence of which is shown by chemical analyses. There is usually a fine-grained fraction of detrital quartz in cherts. The texture of cherts under the microscope is that of a fine-grained microgranular rock composed of interlocking and intergrown tiny crystals of quartz. Chalcedonic quartz, commonly present in many cherts, is composed of radiating sheaves and fibres of material whose index of refraction (ratio of velocity of light in air to the velocity in the substance) is slightly lower than that of quartz (1.54; 1.55), a property that may be the result of occluded water in tiny holes in the structure. Opaline silica is isotropic (its properties of light transmission are the same in all directions) with an index of refraction from 1.41 to 1.46. Electron microscopy of cherts has revealed a great range of textures, ranging from equigranular to those exhibiting complex intergrowths of different size crystals with vary-

Chert
nodules
and
horizons

ing morphology. The oldest fossils known, those of cells of primitive algae, have been noted by microscopic and electron microscopic studies of Precambrian cherts.

Bedding and sedimentary structures. The bed-thickness characteristics of siliceous rocks are linked to their composition and origin. The bedded cherts are those that show continuous beds of wide areal extent, with more or less uniform thickness. Such beds usually range in thickness from less than an inch to a foot and are most commonly several inches thick. A succession of these layers makes up a thicker unit of chert, varying from one foot to hundreds of feet in thickness. The beds may alternate with beds of siliceous clay or shale or with limestones and dolomites. In contrast, the nodular cherts have a much more uneven bedding development. The chert beds may be stratigraphic horizons (zones that represent a given time interval) along which many chert nodules occur, or they may be continuous beds that pinch and swell, composed of coalesced nodules. Some formations have been traced laterally from a zone in which a few nodules are present, through one in which nodules are abundant, to one in which the nodules are completely coalesced to make a continuous bed. The siliceous earths tend to be more or less evenly bedded.

The common sedimentary structures of cherts are the nodules. A nodular character, however, is entirely missing from the bedded cherts. In some bedded cherts one can sometimes see faint traces of current bedding and ripples. Bands of reddish or brownish colour are common in many cherts; they may cut across the bedding and thus indicate their postdepositional origin. Cherts are in some places deformed by contemporaneous or postdepositional movements that give rise to contorted bedding, intrusions of a chert layer into overlying or underlying beds, and brecciation, the breakage and reconsolidation of angular chert fragments. One variety of siliceous rock is actually a silicified limestone; some of these limestones were originally oolitic, that is, they were composed of rounded carbonate grains that had formed by precipitation about various nuclei. Thus, in a few instances, a siliceous oolite rock results. None of the primary siliceous rocks, the bedded cherts, contains such oolites, and the nodular cherts are oolitic only when the nodules have replaced sections of oolitic limestone.

ORIGIN OF THE SILICEOUS ROCKS

The origin of chert and the siliceous rocks has been the subject of controversy for as long as the rocks have been studied (Figure 1). There is little doubt as to the origin

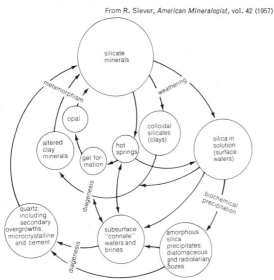

From R. Siever, *American Mineralogist*, vol. 42 (1957)

Figure 1: Silica cycle.

of the diatomaceous and radiolarian oozes and earths. Sediments in all stages of development have been found. It is clear that they form by the sedimentation of the shells and other hard parts of siliceous organisms that live in surface waters, such as diatoms, radiolaria, and

siliconflagellates, together with the spicules of siliceous sponges. It is probable that portions of such shells, or the entire shells of the most fragile species, dissolve as they fall through the lower part of a seawater column that is undersaturated with respect to silica. Freshwater diatomaceous earths form in lakes as they do in the oceans. The transformation of such unindurated (relatively soft) siliceous sediments into hard cherts has been partly traced by studies of Tertiary cherts that show all intermediate stages. The hardness and denseness of the cherts comes from the precipitation of silica in the void spaces between skeletal fragments, the source of the silica being the more soluble parts of the skeletons themselves. The net result of the dissolution and reprecipitation process is the making of a hard rock out of soft sediment, with an accompanying loss of many identifiable fossils and an increase in bulk density of the rock. Although the fossils in older cherts, those of the Paleozoic, are harder to see, they contain siliceous sponge spicules and radiolarians. The Precambrian cherts, however, contain no recognizable fossil remains other than the organic remains of algae; and it is doubtful that such algae secreted silica at that early evolutionary stage.

Role of
organisms
and their
remains

The interrelation of siliceous organisms, sedimentary deposits, and the geochemistry of oceans or lakes is fairly well understood. Most of the silica-secreting organisms require silica as an essential nutrient, usually coupled with phosphate. As a result, abundant populations of these organisms are found in those surface waters of the oceans overlying upwellings that supply sufficient quantities of nutrients from deep water, or in nearshore areas where nutrients are supplied from the land. Important locales for the supply of dissolved silica are regions surrounding active volcanoes or submarine extrusive volcanics, where the seawater becomes enriched in silica by the continuous alteration and hydrolysis of volcanic glass. In such regions the silica-secreting population more or less maintains a balance with the supply of dissolved silica; the solid biogenic amorphous silica sediments sink to the bottom of the sea. These organisms, then, are the vital link between volcanism and siliceous sediment formation. Such an association has been known for many years from work on bedded cherts in volcanic geosynclinal terrains, which are sites of ancient and modern mountain building.

Volcanism
and the
supply of
silica in
oceans and
lakes

The formation of siliceous sediments in some freshwater lakes is the result of much the same process, the abundance of dissolved silica promoting extensive growth of diatoms. In some alkaline lakes, however, the dissolved solids in the water inhibit or prevent much biological growth, and inorganic precipitates of silica may form. This process apparently occurs through an intermediate mechanism precipitating first a variety of sodium silicate (named magadiite for Lake Magadi in Africa) that later converts to free silica by the leaching of sodium. Such alkaline lakes are almost all restricted to volcanic-rich terrains, where the source of dissolved silica and alkalies comes from alteration of volcanic material, demonstrating again a clear relationship between volcanism and chert formation.

Origin of nodular chert. The origin of the nodular cherts is tied to a much different kind of environment. Where the bedded cherts show little or no evidence of postdepositional origin other than cementation and have every appearance of a primary sedimentary deposit, the nodular cherts in limestones appear to be almost entirely the product of diagenesis, whereby the rock is extensively altered after deposition. The evidence for this is the commonly seen replacement texture, in which primary sedimentary features, such as fossils, bedding, and oolites, are partially or completely replaced by secondarily precipitated silica. A key observation in such rocks is the presence of the remains of siliceous organisms in the chert nodule—usually sponge spicules and radiolaria in Paleozoic formations—and the absence of such fossils in the limestone bed between nodules. Because it is most unlikely that the original fossil distribution bore any relation to the nodules, which follow somewhat braided paths and cut across bedding, it must be concluded that the fossils were originally distributed more or less evenly through the largely limy sediment and that subsequently silica through much of the rock dissolved and reprecipitated as inorganic silica in the form of nodules. Such redistribution of silica in an early stage of diagenesis may have been caused by localized clumpings of decaying organic matter in the sediment. These could give rise to a lateral variation in pH (acidity-alkalinity index) and dissolved organic matter, both of which are known to affect the solubility of silica.

The nodules are typically distributed along some bedding planes but are absent in others, even though there seem to have been no obvious differences in permeability between the beds. This suggests that the beds that contain nodules were laid down during times in which the silica-secreting organisms were particularly abundant. The lateral variation between the occurrence of occasional nodules and their coalescence to form lumpy beds of continuous nodular chert suggests that the population of organisms increased toward the source of dissolved silica. Because there seems to be no association with volcanic activity for most of these formations, the source was probably solid and dissolved land-derived material from a nearby shoreline.

Mixed siliceous sediments. The mixed siliceous sediments, those intermediate between chert and shale or chert and limestone, are the products of varying amounts of dilution of the chemically precipitated silica by solid terrigenous detritus or by biogenically formed carbonate. Some highly siliceous shales have been shown to have formed by diagenetic redistribution of siliceous organisms; others show no identifiable fossil remains and may be the result of redistribution and cementation by nonbiogenic silica. The source of the nonbiogenic silica may have been groundwaters that were enriched with silica by passing through volcanic rocks in some stage of weathering and alteration. By convention, siliceous shales do not include very silty shales, which contain large amounts of fine-grained detrital quartz and thus show high proportions of SiO_2 in a chemical analysis.

Many types of both clastic and chemical sediments may become impregnated with secondarily precipitated silica; sandstones that have become completely cemented by silica are the most common. If the original sandstone were composed chiefly of quartz grains, the cemented rock, which may have the appearance of a true quartzite in which the rock splits across the grains of sand, is practically a monomineralic rock. It is less common to find sandstones with smaller quantities of quartz completely cemented by silica. The silica may be the result of pressure solution, a process by which quartz grains dissolve at points of grain-to-grain contact and the whole rock loses pore space and becomes more compact. Other sources of silica are clay minerals, which under appropriate chemical conditions may transform to a less siliceous clay, releasing silica into solution in the process.

Modern siliceous analogues. Though contemporaneous siliceous oozes and freshwater silica deposits are clearly the modern analogues of the process that formed many of the ancient siliceous rocks, until recently there have been few observations in modern sediments of opaline silica forming as an early diagenetic product. Small amounts of opaline silica have been found in the Coorong Swamp, an intermittently hypersaline and desiccated inlet of the sea in South Australia. A program of deep drilling in the bottom sediments of the oceans of the world, initiated in 1968 by the U.S. National Science Foundation, has resulted in knowledge of the commonplace and relatively abundant occurrence of chert and other siliceous sediments in the stratigraphic columns beneath the deep sea. Such cherts appear to be similar to their ancient continental analogues and to have formed in the same way, that is, by diagenetic reorganization of a biogenic silica deposit. The evidence of these deep-sea cherts is proof that siliceous deposits need not be uplifted or subject to any special conditions to become cemented; the norm is an isochemical redistribution of silica, in which there is no addition or subtraction of material from outside the bed.

Siliceous shales and sandstones and nonbiogenic silica

CHERTS IN THE GEOLOGICAL RECORD

Although cherts are widespread in the geologic columns of the continents, they are most prominent in two associations. These are nodular cherts occurring with shallow-water platform limestones (miogeosynclinal) and bedded cherts occurring with graywacke and volcanic rocks (eugeosynclinal). Both associations are known from all parts of the geological record. Most of the famous cherts come from the eugeosynclinal suite. The Arkansas novaculite comes from the eugeosynclinal sections of the Ouachita Geosyncline, the Alpine radiolarian cherts from the Tethyan eugeosynclinal facies, and the Franciscan and Monterey cherts (Figure 2) from the far western parts of the Cordilleran Eugeosyncline. Nodular cherts, less well known by formation name, are similarly distributed in the stable continental interior and shallow-water deposits of the major geosynclines of the world.

By courtesy of the U.S. Geological Survey; photograph, M.N. Bramlette

Figure 2: Lenticular chert beds along the Californian coast two miles northwest of Pismo Beach. The scale is five inches long.

Precambrian cherts are noted for a third association, that with bedded iron formations. The taconites of the Lake Superior region of North America are bedded cherts associated with some of the most famous iron ores of the world, an association which stimulated much speculation on its origin. No remains of possible silica-secreting organisms have ever been found in such Precambrian cherts; and there seems little basis for speculation that siliceous sponges and radiolaria had evolved that early but that all traces of them have been lost in subsequent diagenesis. It seems probable, rather, that these cherts are the product of chemical sedimentation in large lakes or arms of the sea, where the seasonal overturn of the water column (known in many modern lakes) would have given rise to seasonal alternations of silica and iron bands. There would have been no biogenic silica deposits and, in their absence, the solubility of amorphous silica could have been exceeded in such water bodies. Thus, the silica would have precipitated as a finely particulate gel that would quickly have dewatered and compacted.

Bedded iron formation in Precambrian rocks

BIBLIOGRAPHY. F.J. PETTIJOHN, *Sedimentary Rocks*, 2nd ed., ch. 11, pp. 428–448 (1957), the best textbook summary of the subject; H.A. IRELAND (ed.), *Silica in Sediments* (1959), many papers covering all aspects of the subject; M.N. BRAMLETTE, "The Monterey Formation of California and the Origin of its Siliceous Rocks," *Prof. Pap. U.S. Geol. Surv. 212* (1946), a classic study of a famous formation.

(R.Si.)

Silurian Period

The time interval of 430,000,000 to 395,000,000 years ago is termed the Silurian Period. As indicated on the geological time scale (*q.v.*), the Silurian is a division of the Paleozoic Era. The rocks deposited during Silurian time comprise the Silurian System, which was named in 1835

Establishment of the Silurian System

Table 1: General Subdivisions and Local Rock Sequences of the Silurian Period

Lower Silurian (Llandoverian) — Lower (A_1-A_4)	Middle (B_1-B_3)	Upper (C_1-C_6)	Wenlockian — Wenlock Shales	Wenlock Limestone	Ludlovian — Eltonian	Bringewoodian	Leintwardinian	Whitcliffian	Pridolian — Ludlow Bone Bed	lower half of Downtonian	series / stage — region
shale, sandstone, and mudstone			Wenlock Shales	Wenlock Limestone	Eltonian	Bringewoodian	Leintwardinian	Whitcliffian	Ludlow Bone Bed	lower half of Downtonian	Welsh borderland (Britain)
Kilfillian Formation		Garheugh Formation; Carghidown Beds; Kirkmaiden Beds; Hawick Rocks	Riccarton Beds								Southern Uplands (Britain)
	unnamed Silurian strata (subsurface)		Visby Marls; Högklint Group; Slite Group	Mulde Marl	Hemse Group			Eke Group	Hamra Group	Sundra Group	Gotland (Sweden)
Rastrites	Shale		Cyrtograptus Shale; Retiolites Beds	Hemingü Beds	Colonus Shale				Oved-Ramsåsa Group		Skåne (Sweden)
Liten	Shales			Liten Limestone	Kopanina Limestone				Pridoli Limestone		Prague region
Lower	Graptolite	Slates					Ocherous Limestone				Thuringia
		Argile Schisteuses									Morocco (Africa)
	Tanezzuft	Shale					Aracus Sandstone				central Sahara (Africa)
		Table Mountain Sandstone									South Africa
Juuru Stage	Raikkula Stage	Adavere Stage	Jaani Stage	Jaagarahu Stage	Kaarma Stage	Paadla Stage	Kuressaare Stage	Kaugatuma Stage	Ohesaare Stage		Estonia
Kitaigorod Horizon		Muksha Horizon		Malinovetski Horizon				Skala Horizon			Podolia (U.S.S.R.)
Kosyu Horizon		Adak Horizon	Filipelsk Horizon	Sedelsk Horizon	Gerdyusk Horizon				Greben Horizon		western Urals (Chernishev Range)
unnamed Llandovery Volcanics			unnamed Wenlock Volcanics		Elkino Series		Zhuravlik Series		Turin Series		eastern Urals (Is River)
limestone and shale											Siberian Platform
Lungmachi Shale	Lojoping Series						Shamao Series				China (Yangtze region)
Melbourne Group							Yering Group				Melbourne area (Australia)
Mundoonan Sandstone	Hawkins Series	Bango Group	Douto Group	Yass Group	Laidlaw Group; Barrandella Shale	Hume Limestone	Black Bog Shale	Dalmanites Beds	green and black shale		Yass area (Australia)
Cancañiri Graywacke	Llallagua Formation	Pampa Shale			Catavi Sandstone			Ventilla Shale			Bolivia
Caparo		Formation									Venezuela
Allen Bay Formation	Cape Phillips Formation						Read Bay Formation				Arctic Canada
		western assemblage; Roberts Mountains Formation									central Nevada
black slate and graywacke			unnamed limestone					upper graywacke and sandstone			southeastern Alaska
Laketown Dolomite											eastern Nevada and Utah
Manitoulin Dolomite; Cabot Head Shale	Moss Lake Formation; Burnt Bluff Group (Lime Island Dolomite, Byron Dolomite)	Hendricks Dolomite	Manistique Group (Schoolcraft Dolomite, Cordell Dolomite)		Engadine Dolomite			Point Aux Chenes Shale	St. Ignace Dolomite		northern Michigan (North America)
Grimsby Sandstone	Kodak Sandstone; Reynales Formation; Maplewood Formation; Wallington Formation	Upper Sodus; Williamson Shale; Irondequoit Island; Rockway Member; upper member; Rochester Shale			Lockport Group			Vernon Shale; Salina Group (Syracuse Salt, Camillus Shale)	Bertie Group	Akron Dolomite	New York State
Ellis Bay Formation	Becsie Formation; Gun River Formation	Jupiter Formation	Chicotte Formation								Anticosti Island, Canada
	Quoddy Formation		Dennys Formation		Edmunds Formation				Pembroke Formation		southeastern Maine
Carys Mills Formation	Spragueville	Formation					Perham Formation; upper member				Presque Isle, Maine
Glencoe Brook Formation	Kerrowgare	Formation									northern Nova Scotia
Beechhill Cove Formation	lower member Ross Brook Formation	middle member Ross Brook Formation	upper member Ross Brook Formation	French River Formation	Doctor's Brook Formation	McAdam Brook Formation		Moydart Formation	Stonehouse Formation		northern Nova Scotia

by Sir Roderick Impey Murchison after the warlike Silures. The latter were inhabitants at the time of the Roman occupation of the Welsh borderland where Murchison and his successors studied the complicated rock system of the type Silurian, subdividing it and establishing its graptolitic and shelly faunas as independent worldwide standards for correlation. In most of the rest of the world, however, the Silurian has, until recently, been one of the most neglected and thus most poorly known sequences—an ironic contrast to the wide attention given to the lower part of Murchison's original Silurian, the Ordovician, which was not split off as an independent system until 1879.

Rocks are identified as Silurian (or a specific part of it) from comparison of their contained fossils with those of the type marine sequence in Wales and Shropshire or in relationship to or correlation with other rocks so dated. By definition, therefore, the Silurian includes all deposits formed during the same time as those in the type sequence, regardless of origin, location, or local relationships. The principal Silurian subdivisions for selected regions are outlined in the accompanying correlation table, emphasizing marine sequences as the basic local standards (see Table 1).

Silurian deposits contain some of the earliest good fossils of various fishes, although fish originated tens of millions of years earlier. An aberrant possible vertebrate relative, *Monograptus*, the last surviving bladelike graptolite, burst into a flowering of short-lived species whose flexible external skeletons are used to divide the Silurian marine deposits of the world into time-equivalent zones. Also important in subdividing the Silurian marine deposits of the world into time-equivalent zones are the brachiopods and conodonts. The evidence of widespread Silurian marine shallow-water invertebrates and the sediments is interpreted to signify mild climates, not markedly zoned latitudinally.

The responses of Silurian rocks to local conditions of erosion and weathering account for some of the world's distinctive landscapes. Undercutting of weak sedimentary layers beneath massive Late Silurian dolomites at the outlet of Lake Erie created and maintains Niagara Falls. The picturesque glade country of Tennessee consists of isolated grassy areas on infertile shales surrounded by wooded areas on more calcareous shales or limestones of Late Silurian age. Beautiful Wenlock Edge in Shropshire is an east dipping Silurian limestone ridge, and much of Wales, the Lake District of England, and the Southern Uplands of Scotland are underlain by Silurian rocks. The Swedish island of Gotland is the type site of the Gotlandian; picturesque Visby, its capital and ancient Hanseatic harbour, is built around a Silurian reef limestone. In the U.S., Early Silurian sandstones crest many of the ridges in the central Appalachians.

Mountain-building deformation older than the oldest local Silurian deposits is indicated by Silurian overlap across folded Ordovician rocks in portions of the Acadian region of east central North America (Taconic folding or orogeny), the Angara Shield region of Central Asia (from the southeastern Altai, Sayan, and Tuva to the Amur River's middle reaches), a few restricted areas in northwestern Europe, and eastern Australia (Benambran orogeny). Similar relationships indicate later deformation between Silurian and overlying Devonian in eastern Victoria and New South Wales, Australia (Bowning orogeny), and in a few minor regions of northwestern Europe (Caledonian orogeny). Strong evidences of volcanism throughout the Silurian of portions of eastern Australia, a few localities within the Pacific border of North America, the Acadian region, the eastern Urals, and Kazakhstan and the thick sequences of coarse detrital sediments in eastern Australia, south Scotland, Ireland (except for the northern portions), western Scandinavia, and the eastern Appalachian trough, however, seem to imply continued crustal instability in the borderlands and the Ural–Kazakhstan region during the Silurian. Broadly speaking, however, the bulk of the Silurian sediments (platform carbonates, platform mudstones, and nonmarine platform sediments together with platform regions subject to subaerial erosion) indicate widespread shallow seas over the present

land masses of the Northern Hemisphere, both widespread shallow seas and low-lying land areas in Australia and South America, and land only in most of Africa below the Equator, as well as in Antarctica.

Silurian rocks have yielded about 10 percent of U.S. iron, 20 percent of its salt, and a little oil and gas. They also serve, especially where mainly limestone and dolomite, as host for many metallic mineral deposits, including important gold and tin ores in eastern Australia. And they are exploited industrially for cement, agricultural lime, and building stone. Petroleum from Algeria and Libya as well as the central Sahara is mostly from the Silurian.

This article treats the rocks, life, and environments of Silurian time. For additional relevant information, see also the articles EARTH, GEOLOGICAL HISTORY OF; ORDOVICIAN PERIOD; DEVONIAN PERIOD; SEDIMENTARY FACIES; STRATIGRAPHIC BOUNDARIES; PALEOZOIC ERA, LOWER; and FOSSIL RECORD.

SILURIAN ROCKS

Sedimentary rocks. Silurian rocks formed under differing local physical or chemical conditions, with different sources of sediment supply, and various biologic migration routes. For this reason, they have a characteristic stamp, or facies, that may tell a great deal about their origin and ecology. Facies variations of rocks and accompanying fossil assemblages may be lateral (in space), vertical (in time), or both. Similar sedimentary facies that do not differ drastically in age, and some that do, are likely to contain similar fossils, and different facies of the same age ordinarily contain different assemblages of fossils (see also FOSSIL RECORD).

The stratigraphic correlation of unusual facies to deposits of known age is determined from field relations or is based on ubiquitous fossils of restricted time span. Species of graptolites, brachiopods, and conodonts, so characteristic of Silurian as well as of Ordovician beds, have proved especially useful in indicating the probable contemporaneity of contrasting sedimentary facies. Graptolites are generally excellent guide fossils that are interpreted as animals that floated at the surface of the water all or much of their lives instead of living somewhere below the surface like most planktonic species or floating only temporarily like the larval stages of so many aquatic organisms. This would explain their being buried, not only with the open-sea sediments of their normal living environment but also in many different shallow-water deposits, together with bottom-living shelly fossils.

Silurian stratified rocks may best be divided into the following broad categories: (1) platform carbonates (including both limestone and dolomite suite rocks), (2) platform mudstone, (3) terrigenous and volcanic (geosynclinal rocks), and (4) nonmarine. The usage of the term platform is here defined for the Silurian, as well as for the rest of the Early Paleozoic, as a large (minimum dimension in thousands of kilometres), relatively planar, vertically stable portion of a continent. The platform carbonate rocks are characterized by a relatively small thickness (seldom exceeding 300 metres but in a few minor instances reaching 1,200 or 1,500 metres) of either limestone and calcareous shale (limestone suite) or dolomite (dolomite suite) predominating over each other by a large factor except at major facies boundaries and including relatively minor amounts of clean-washed, well-sorted quartz sand, light-coloured nodular chert, glauconite, and nonmarine strata. The platform mudstones are characterized by a relatively small thickness (seldom exceeding 300 metres, except in central China where 1,200 to 1,500 metres is not unusual) of mudstone, shale, and siltstone, often highly carbonaceous and containing limestone nodules or concretions with less abundant interbeds of very argillaceous limestone. The terrigenous and volcanic rocks are restricted to the so-called geosynclinal regions, which, where present, border the Silurian platforms. The terrigenous and volcanic rocks are characterized by overall thicknesses of 3,100 to 4,600 or even 6,100 metres. Limestone is uncommon, never making up more than 5 percent of the total volume; dolomite is almost unknown. The predominant rock types in this category are sandstone containing much

Sedimentary facies and their distribution

silt and mud, graywacke, together with bedded chert and minor amounts of conglomerate made up chiefly of pre-Silurian rocks, plus large amounts of both light- and dark-coloured volcanic rocks in certain regions of certain geosynclines. Nonmarine rocks may occur on platforms, as broad, thin sheets of mudstone, siltstone, and sandstone or as restricted occurrences in the geosynclines.

North and South American platforms

The platforms of the Silurian include the following: (1) North American, (2) South American, (3) Old World, and (4) Australian. The North American Platform is characterized by a broad platform carbonate sheet extending from the Arctic islands to Mexico and from Anticosti Island to Nevada. Limestone suite rocks are peripheral to dolomite suite rocks. Terrigenous and volcanic geosynclinal rocks occur in the northern Appalachians from Newfoundland to Long Island Sound. These geosynclinal strata are bounded to the west by a linear island, Appalachia, which extended from the northern Gaspé region southwest along the Sutton Mountain, Green Mountains, Jersey Highland, and eastern valley and ridge regions to at least central Tennessee. Terrigenous rocks occur farther to the south in northern Alabama and Georgia as well as in the subsurface of northern Florida. On the southern border of the North American Platform occur the terrigenous rocks of the Ouachita Geosyncline in Oklahoma and Arkansas, as well as in the subsurface of adjoining states. On the west, the North American Platform is bordered by the poorly known terrigenous rocks (volcanic rocks are present in only a very minor amount) of central Nevada and Idaho, northern California, northeast Washington, southeast Alaska, western British Columbia, and the western Yukon Territory. The Silurian of the bulk of Alaska to the west of the Yukon Territory is too poorly known to be added to this picture. To the north of the North American Platform occur the widespread terrigenous sediments present in the northern Arctic islands of Canada and portions of northwestern Greenland.

The South American Platform is very poorly known but appears to consist of a northern and western half covered by platform mudstone and a southeastern portion possibly covered in part by nonmarine strata. Silurian geosynclinal rocks have not been recognized in South America.

The Old World Platform consists of a number of subdivisions. On the northwest it is bounded by the Caledonian Geosyncline, which is present in the western and northwestern portions of the British Isles and is concluded to extend into and through western Scandinavia (Norway west of the Oslo region and the mountainous border region of central Norway and Sweden), from where its northern limits are very uncertain. In the north central region the Old World Platform is partially divided by a geosyncline extending from the northern three-fourths of the north island of Novaya Zemlya down through the northeastern portion of the south island, northeastern Vaigach Island, eastern Pai-Hoi, the eastern Urals, and the entire southern Urals, plus Kazakhstan. This Ural-Kazakhstan Geosyncline, chiefly volcanic in character, appears to terminate in the middle of the Old World Platform against the west side of the Angara Shield. A third geosyncline, characterized by volcanics, may be present along the southeastern side of the Japanese islands. The western portions of the Old World Platform may be divided into an eastern half characterized by platform carbonates (this includes the Russian Platform plus its extension into portions of the Near East and Central Asia) and a western to southwestern half characterized by platform mudstones up to the Caledonian Geosyncline and bounding islands on the west and a shoreline region on the south extending from Sierra Leone to eastern Libya, southeastern Turkey, and then southeast into the Persian Gulf region. This shoreline region gradually prograded during the Silurian until by the end of the period it was situated as far north as central Algeria. South of this shoreline region in both Africa and Arabia was an area above sea level—with the possible exception of southernmost Africa, which may have been briefly subject to shallow-water sedimentation. It is possible that peninsular India was a part of this same great land area during the Silurian. In northeastern Asia the Siberian Platform seg-

Old World and Australian platforms

ment of this Old World Platform extended from the Altai–Sayan–Tuva–Lake Baikal–Amur region on the south to the lower Yenisei through Kolyma region on the east, bearing a cover of platform carbonate rocks, which grades to the south into the nonmarine beds on the northern border of the Angara Shield. The precise eastern and southeastern as well as northern boundaries of the Siberian Platform carbonate rocks are unknown but may have extended well beyond the limits discussed here. The bulk of China, including the vast Yangtze River region, is characterized by thick platform mudstone in the lower half of the Silurian, succeeded by shelly sandstone on the north and shelly limestone on the south, which suggests that the Angara Shield to the north was rising during the latter half of the Silurian and shedding debris to both north and south. Southeastern Asia is characterized by the presence of both platform mudstone and platform carbonate rocks, with a common boundary extending southerly from the Shan states of Burma through the Isthmus of Kra into the vicinity of Kuala Lumpur.

Silurian rocks of the Australian Platform are virtually unknown except for a borehole penetrating carbonate rocks on Dirk Hartogs Island, the westernmost part of the continent; but it is concluded that most of this platform was subject to subaerial conditions—except for the easternmost fringe, which graded laterally into the Tasman Geosyncline, and possibly to the north in the Papua region.

Volcanic deposits. Volcanism is relatively subordinate during the Silurian as contrasted with some other periods. The most important site of Silurian volcanism is to be found within the Ural–Kazakhstan Geosyncline, where important centres of volcanism, chiefly andesitic and basaltic, extend along the east slope of the Urals from the polar through the central Urals, both east and west slopes of the southern Urals, and in Kazakhstan. Very minor dark-coloured volcanics of Late Silurian age exist in the Prague region, where they raised the sea bottom high enough locally to support a rich shelly fauna whose skeletal debris forms the fringing limestones of this area, which grade laterally into the typical deeper water platform mudstones so characteristic of North Africa and central and western Europe, as well as the Balkans and Turkey. Volcanics are also known from the southeastern Silurian deposits of Japan. Within the Caledonian Geosyncline, volcanics are very rare, known from only a few minor, scattered occurrences. Within the Appalachian Geosyncline, volcanics are abundant in a narrow belt extending from eastern Massachusetts through coastal Maine, adjacent New Brunswick, western Nova Scotia, westernmost portions of the Cobequid Mountains), Gaspé (central and southern), northern New Brunswick, northern Maine, and northern New Hampshire. In the Cordilleran Geosyncline, minor volcanics are known in the Klamath Mountains and southeastern Alaska. Within the Tasman Geosyncline of eastern Australia, minor occurrences of volcanics are known in eastern Victoria, eastern New South Wales, and possibly in Queensland.

Uralian Geosyncline deposits

SILURIAN LIFE

Characteristics and evolution. The record of Silurian invertebrate life shows an elaboration of Ordovician lineages. It has, however, novel and distinctive features of its own, such as expansion of the corals and echinoderms and a general evolutionary development of the dominant groups of brachiopods, graptolites, and conodonts. And it differs from the Devonian record in the types of corals and brachiopods present and in many less striking features. The faunal changes at both the Ordovician and Devonian boundaries may best be regarded as transitional, reflecting the slow progress of evolution.

Silurian fishes are the oldest preserved, except for isolated occurrences of fragments in the Middle and Upper Ordovician of the North American Rocky Mountains. Silurian plants also are the oldest preserved, except for questionable Cambrian plants reported from eastern Siberia, Estonia, and northern India and less doubtful Middle Ordovician plants recently described from near Prague. This distribution pattern is attributable to the rarity of preserved pre-Silurian terrestrial deposits.

Table 2: Ranges of Representative Genera in the Silurian Period

series	stage	graptolite zones	coral zone	conodont zones	brachiopod zones
Upper Silurian	Pridolian	Monograptus angustidens		zone VII — eosteinhornensis	
		Monograptus transgrediens			
		Monograptus perneri			
		Monograptus bouceki			
		Monograptus lochkovensis			
		Monograptus ultimus			
	Ludlovian	35 Monograptus leintwardinensis		zone VI latialatus and crispus	
		34 Monograptus scanicus		zone V siluricus	
		33 Monograptus nilssoni		crassa and ploeckensis	
Upper Silurian	Wenlockian	32 Monograptus ludensis		sigtta	
		31 Cyrtograptus lundgreni			
		30 Cyrtograptus ellesi (= C. rigidus E & W)			
		29 Cyrtograptus linnarssoni		zone IV patula	
		28 Cyrtograptus rigidus (= C. symmetricus E & W)			
		27 Monograptus riccartonensis	Paleocyclus		
		26 Cyrtograptus murchisoni			
Lower Silurian	Llandoverian Upper (C₁–C₆)	25 Monograptus crenulatus		zone III amorphognathoides	
		24 Monograptus griestoniensis			
		23 Monograptus crispus		zone II celloni	
		22 Monograptus turriculatus			
		21 Monograptus sedgwicki			
	Llandoverian Middle (B₁–B₃)	20 Monograptus convolutus			
		19 Monograptus gregarius		icriodina bearing	
	Llandoverian Lower (A₁–A₄)	18 Monograptus cyphus		zone I	
		17 Orthograptus vesiculosus		pre-icriodina	
		16 Akidograptus acuminatus			

Brachiopod zone genera (with ranges shown): Janius, Hedeina, Harpidium, Pentamerifera, Brooksina, Lissocoelina, Kirkidium, Callipentamerus, Pentameroides, Capellinella, Rhipidium, Pentamerus, Plectatrypa, Atrypa, Spirigerina, Meristina, Resserella "elegantula", Skenidioides, Howellella, Dalejina, Eocoelia sulcata, Eocoelia curtisi, Eocoelia intermedia, Eocoelia hemisphaerica, Costistricklandia gaspiensis, Stricklandia lens ultima, Stricklandia lens progressa, Stricklandia lens intermedia, Stricklandia lens typica, Stricklandia lens prima, Microcardinalia mullochensis, Ehlersella, "P" borealis, Virgiana, Platymerella, Kulumbella, Protatrypa, Eospirigerina, Cryptothyrella, Dalmanella, Eostrophodonta, Mendacella.

The characteristics and evolution of Silurian or any other fossil life are of interest not only from an aesthetic and scholarly point of view but also because they provide us with a practicable means of consistently telling fossil time. Radiogenic methods of absolute age determination do not yet suffice for general dating or correlation of the Paleozoic rocks, even though a very few apparently reliable dates are used to set, approximately, the hands of the paleontological clock in terms of years. From the fossils also can be deduced much of the history, ecology, and geography of ancient times, always in connection with the characteristics and positions of the rocks. Ecologic deductions are greatly aided by the tracks, trails, and burrows of different organisms; these are almost the only traces of life in some deposits, such as the Silurian of the eastern Appalachian trough.

Invertebrates and associated fossils. In the Silurian, as with other fossiliferous rocks, the invertebrate and noncellular (or unicellular) organisms are the true indices of time, on the basis of which nearly all meaningful stratigraphic correlation with the standard marine sequence is founded. The form sequence of the monograptid graptolites illustrates well how such correlation may be accomplished either by relating stage of evolution to time or by the empirical knowledge of the ranges of specific mor-

[margin: Graptolites and stratigraphic correlation]

phologic types. Correlation, or paleoecological analysis, in practice, however, is also made by analysis of the total biotal characteristics of the problem sample, considered in relation to lithology and sequence of the enclosing sediments. Ranges of representative genera (shown in Table 2) illustrate how Silurian fossiliferous sediments can be dated, using apparent terminal ranges of a variety of fossils. (In Table 2 the symbols e, d, c, and f stand for *Microcardinalia triplesiana*, *M. raberensis*, *Plicostricklandia castellana*, and *P. multilirata*, respectively.)

The graptolites, despite their suggested close alliance to the vertebrates, are at best invertebrate chordates and, in this sense, are among the most conspicuous and distinctive Silurian invertebrates. The monograptids are the evolutionary culmination of the simply saw-blade-like forms of graptolites and appear to be exclusively Silurian and Early Devonian.

Moreover, only a few species of two genera (*Diplograptus* and *Climacograptus*) of their Ordovician ancestors carried over into the Silurian, and these only into the lower part. The Silurian graptolite assemblage thus consists almost entirely of *Monograptus*, of short-lived derivative genera from it or older forms, and of occasional reticulate colonies such as persisted into the Devonian. The time subdivision of Silurian rocks is based largely on short-ranged species of *Monograptus*, and many of the same species are present around the world.

Corals and stromatoporoids are subordinate to the graptolites as Silurian time indicators but far ahead of them in range of evolutionary diversification. Compound corals particularly flourished, including the tabulates, which reached their greatest expansion, and fasciculate tetracorals, which did not attain their acme until the Devonian. Horn corals of simple types were more abundant and more complicated than Ordovician, less so than Devonian relatives. Stromatoporoids had also to await the Devonian for their climax, and no Silurian or other common Paleozoic coelenterate is anything like its modern relatives. Presumably, however, they did have the same alternation of sessile and free-floating generations as typifies the living representatives of the phylum, which would account for wide distribution of identical species in favourable environments. Unlike the graptolites, which apparently could drift even after death, they are not found far from their place of life except as a result of unusual events.

Bryozoa are about as common as they were in the Ordovician, with a slight dwindling of stony types and an increase of the more delicately ornamented twiglike cryptostomes. Locally they made small mounds at the bottom of the Silurian seas, as represented by the ball reefs of the Rochester Shale in western New York State.

Among Silurian brachiopods, the globular, short-hinged, and commonly large pentamerids were the most distinctive forms. Short-hinged, spire-bearing brachiopods were essentially new, although there are common Ordovician forms. The wide-hinged spiriferoids began the expansion that was to flower in Devonian and Lower Carboniferous time. A number of new genera and families make their first appearance near the base of the late Llandovery, the most marked faunal break occurring within the Silurian or even at its boundaries.

The pelecypods continued to expand slowly from Ordovician beginnings, and the prosobranch gastropods became important fossils in continuance of a long progressive expansion to modern times. Among the cephalopods, ammonitoid progenitors appeared and nautiloids dwindled. Some distinctive Ordovician groups of nautiloids were missing completely (*e.g.*, Endoceratidae), and others died out during the Silurian (*e.g.*, Ascoceratida). As if to emphasize their decline, no important new nautiloid groups appeared.

Among the arthropods, trilobites continued their slow decline from a Cambrian maximum, and ostracods and merostomes both expanded slightly. Among the latter, eurypterids became much more common, while the aglaspids were missing, but xiphosurans ancestral to living *Limulus* are recorded. Ostracods are locally abundant and are useful Silurian index arthropods, particularly within the Appalachian region for the late Llandovery through Pridoli and in the Baltic region, coastal Maine, adjacent New Brunswick, and Nova Scotia for the Ludlow and Pridoli. Trilobites, despite their general decline showed an expansion of bizarre spiny types, perhaps as an adaptation to floating or camouflage, forced by increasing competition for the nutrient-rich bottom niches or predation. Allied developments may have caused the eurypterids to enter freshwater in later Silurian time, from which, according to one theory, they eventually chased the fishes.

Crinoids were the most successful Silurian echinoderms, enjoying their greatest recorded expansion of numbers and kinds. Unlike their commoner living relatives, these lilies of the sea were stalked forms; if they were equally colourful, their colonies must have been the showy marine gardens of Silurian time. Cystoids also were common and, although much more primitive, were similar in living habits and appearance to the crinoids.

Noncellular invertebrates, or the Protista (Protophyta and Protozoa), are abundant in some Silurian deposits. Chitinous and agglutinated Foraminifera have been described from North America, the Baltic, and England, and Radiolaria are occasionally reported, but little is known in detail of these Silurian records.

An important, but problematical, Silurian group is the Chitinozoa, consisting of minute, black, chitinous, vase-shaped to club- or ball-shaped organisms. Equally important are the enigmatic, minute acritarchs. Revelation of such tiny organisms by chemical treatment of apparently unfossiliferous rocks sometimes permits the correlation of deposits whose position cannot be closely established by other methods.

Of growing importance are the conodonts, a group of toothlike objects of unknown affinity, and only recently intensively studied.

Fishes, land plants, and associated fossils. Silurian occurrences of fish and plant fossils are more numerous and complete than in older rocks. They are, however, mostly, though not entirely, restricted to the upper part of the system, and the fossils are not demonstrably more advanced than their predecessors. Conversely, they are greatly surpassed in number and variety by Devonian records. In the Late Silurian, in fact, the arthropods appeared to be making more headway than the vertebrates in colonizing the lands. The arachnids were represented by the scorpionid *Paleophonus*, from the Upper Silurian of both sides of the Atlantic. Millipedes are reported to occur in association with eurypterids (water-dwelling, scorpion-like creatures) in Wales. Neither scorpion nor millipede was surely air breathing, but both were at least evolving in that direction. In the estuarine to questionably marine or freshwater deposits, where the early fishes are most commonly found, is also an abundance of eurypterid remains. Indeed, the Silurian and Devonian saw the climax of this group, which comprised the greatest arthropod predators of all time, perhaps including principal foes of the early fishes and possible ancestors of the arachnids.

The simple, externally armoured, mainly backboneless, earliest fishes and the primitive early plant assemblages are discussed in a separate article on the DEVONIAN PERIOD.

SILURIAN PALEOGEOGRAPHY

Continental stability. The vast continental platforms of the Silurian (Old World, Australian, North American, and South American) appear to have been very stable in a vertical sense, as shown by their relatively uniform veneer of platform carbonate, platform mudstone, and nonmarine sediments, considered together with the position of the strandlines and community boundaries. The strandlines and community boundaries provide third-order level lines of a sort. Evidences of intra-Silurian tectonism are almost wholly lacking except for the very minor Salinic Disturbance of the northern Appalachians. Minor disconformities upon the continental platforms record, at best, relatively trivial vertical movements.

Northwestward strandline migration from the central Sahara to Morocco and Algeria during the Silurian indicates a steady rising of that continent, but the total change in elevation is no more than a few hundred metres as indicated by the sediment thicknesses. Gradual sinking of a series of islands off the eastern coast of the U.S. and extending from north central Spain through northwestern France, south central England, and west central Scandinavia, occurred during the Silurian. Gradual shoreline migration to the south occurred during the Llandovery and early Wenlock Stages on the northern margins of the Angara Shield, followed by similar migration to both the south and north as the shield slowly rose again during the latter half of the Silurian. Shorelines gradually encroached upon the Russian platform during the Llandovery until by late Llandovery time it must have been completely covered. Geosynclinal records of marine sedimentation are in some regions quite complete, in others fragmentary. Where adequate information is available it is obvious that a complex geography—an alternation of islands (both volcanic and basement complex in type), shallow waters, and deeper waters—was present within the geosynclines.

Subsequent to the Silurian, large areas of the former platforms have been incorporated with younger geosynclines and orogenic belts, viz., Rocky Mountains, Atlas, Timan, Hercynian chains of the Old World, Great Basin, Carpathians, Alpine chains of Europe and the Near East, Pyrenees, Cantabrians, Himalayan chains, Tien Shan, Sette-Daban, Altai-Sayan, Andean chains, and Southeast

Marginal notes:

Corals, bryozoa, brachiopods, and pelecypods

Trilobites and ostracods

Colonizers of land areas

Vertical movements and strandlines

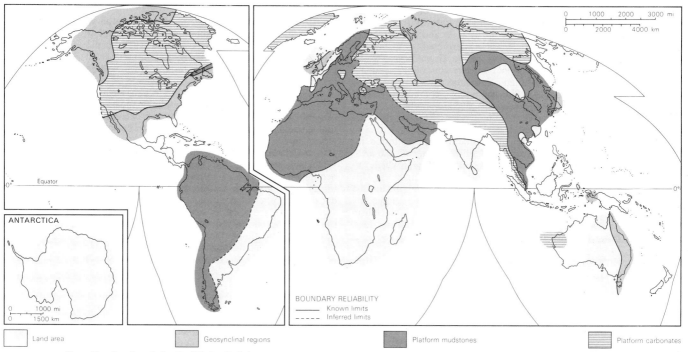

Depositional regions during the Silurian Period.

BOUNDARY RELIABILITY
— Known limits
- - - Inferred limits

Land area   Geosynclinal regions   Platform mudstones   Platform carbonates

Silurian evidence of continental drift

Asian chains. It is obvious that the Silurian, as well as the preceding Cambro-Ordovician, was an interval of relative orogenic and geosynclinal quiescence, with the presence of vast, stable platforms, contrasting markedly with the smaller platforms and greater degree of orogenic and geosynclinal activity characterizing many subsequent time intervals (see also PALEOGEOGRAPHY).

Relative continental positions and sediment sources. The relatively uniform sheet of platform mudstone covering North Africa, Turkey, and the bulk of Europe west of the U.S.S.R., considered together with the shoreline extending across Africa from Sierra Leone to the Kufra Basin, coupled with similar relations in southeast Turkey and other portions of the Near East, indicates that this region formed one continental block during the Early Paleozoic (Cambro-Ordovician relationships are not far different). Relations between Asia and Eurafrica plus the Near East are less certain, because of the paucity of data for the West Siberian Lowlands, Tibet, Afghanistan, Iran, and the Himalayan region, but there are no compelling reasons why Asia should have been dissociated from Eurafrica during the Silurian. From a Silurian point of view, the modern Mediterranean Sea and its Tethyan predecessor are merely a more complicated Red Sea; *i.e.*, a portion of a shield (Arabian and Nubian in the case of the Red Sea) sundered subsequent to the Silurian.

The relative position of Australia is enigmatic, particularly in view of the total absence of information between Malaya and New Guinea. Possibly Australia has always been isolated.

The position of South America relative to Africa is equivocal: Silurian data are consistent with either continental drift (*q.v.*) away from Africa or for its present position having obtained during the Silurian. The position of North America vis-à-vis Europe is similarly equivocal from a Silurian point of view. Data for the Silurian on opposite sides of Bering Strait are too scanty to provide an adequate basis for speculation.

The source of terrigenous sediment poses serious questions about continental relationships. The platform mudstones of Africa, Europe, and the Near East may be easily accounted for by postulating Africa south of the central Sahara, plus portions of Arabia, and possibly peninsular India plus the western Indian Ocean as sources. The platform mudstones of South America are too poorly known, relative to possible sources upon that continent, to prove a problem at present. The platform mudstones of China and Southeast Asia may call upon the Angara Shield and

potential sources in the Yellow and South China seas. The Tasman Geosyncline may call upon the Australian Platform as a source. The Caledonian and Appalachian Geosynclines require exterior sources, but the available continental shelves may be adequate. The Franklinian Geosyncline as well as the terrigenous Silurian abutting the Kara Sea (chiefly in Novaya Zemlya and the Taimyr Peninsula) may require a source within the confines of the present Arctic Ocean. Too little is known of either the Cordilleran or Ouachita Geosynclines to make them worthy of consideration.

The presence of Silurian platforms adjacent to or near modern ocean shorelines raises questions about the permanence and relative position in time of the continents. Such problem areas include the abrupt termination of the North American Platform against the San Andreas–Gulf of California lineament, the termination of the Russian Platform carbonates against the White and Barents seas, of the Siberian Platform carbonates against the Laptev and East Siberian seas, of the Eurafrican Platform mudstones against the Atlantic, of the South American Platform mudstones against the Atlantic and Pacific, of Africa south of the central Sahara against the Atlantic and Indian oceans, of southern Australia against the Southern (Antarctic) Ocean, and of the platform carbonates of Southeast Asia against the Bay of Bengal. There are at present no satisfactory solutions, although continental drift and oceanization have been offered. Continental drift would, in some cases, bring together regions of widely contrasting geology, viz., Australia and Africa or southern Asia, or require the removal of large segments of present continents (the bulk of Central America) or open up vast chasms for which no geological evidence exists (a wide separation between southern Turkey and Syria). Oceanization, on the other hand, requires such vast transfers of material within the mantle and deeper crust of the earth as to beggar the imagination of the geochemist and geophysicist (see SEA-FLOOR SPREADING; ISLAND ARCS; and EARTH, STRUCTURE AND COMPOSITION OF).

Climate and general ecology. Widespread reef formation by Silurian corals and stromatoporoids (hydrozoan relatives) couples with the evidence for high calcium metabolism furnished by laterally equivalent limestones and dolomites to imply extensive warm, shallow seas in present continental areas and little latitudinal or seasonal temperature variation. Interference of mountainous tracts with prevailing winds or other special meteorologic circumstances created local conditions in the middle latitudes such as those under which the Late Silurian salt and gypsum deposits of New York State and the Michigan Basin originated. If deposits, interpreted as glacial, in Bolivia, northern Argentina, and Africa prove to be basal Silurian, they would suggest conditions adequate to support basal Silurian continental glaciation (see also CLIMATIC CHANGE). Silurian animal community distributions are consistent with this glacial hypothesis, but the absence of proved tillite in intervening Brazil is still puzzling.

The relatively cosmopolitan shallow-water Silurian invertebrates of the Northern Hemisphere suggest the presence of widespread, uniform conditions under which migration from one region to another was unhindered. This situation contrasts strongly with that existing during the preceding Late Ordovician interval and the succeeding Early Devonian interval, both times of high provincialism relative to the Silurian. (Low-level provincialism does, however, exist during the Silurian.) Combined ecologic, lithologic, and biogeographic data suggest that South America south of Venezuela, Europe (south from Brittany and the Caucasus), the Near East, and Africa may have possessed a climate cooler than that existing in such places as North America, northern Europe (including the Urals), Central Asia, Siberia, eastern Asia and Australia.

Ecological variation and environmental factors Principal ecologic variations appear to have been connected with physical, chemical, and biologic factors. Faunas best interpreted as marine and indicative of hypersaline conditions are known in the Late Silurian of the Michigan Basin and adjacent areas and are characterized by an abundance of ostracods (chiefly smooth), eurypterids, and a few other invertebrates, including mollusks and brachiopods. Faunas best interpreted as brackish occur in a few regions, including parts of the central Appalachians, the Welsh Borderland, Midland Valley of Scotland, Tuva, and the Siberian platform, for which a mixture of lingulid and rhynchonellid brachiopods, homolanotid trilobites, fish, eurypterids, and the bellerophontid gastropod *Plectonotus* are characteristic. Nonmarine deposits are characterized chiefly by an association of fish together with certain types of eurypterids. The reef environments, which have been little investigated ecologically, appear to have provided a multitude of niches controlled in all probability by both biologic and physicochemical factors. The ecologic influence of depth and temperature, or more probably temperature varying directly with depth, has been considered for the Silurian shallow-water marine animal communities. In those portions of the Northern Hemisphere inferred to have been relatively warm, there is a definite sequence, proceeding away from the shoreline toward deep water, of shallow-water animal communities. At the shoreline is found a *Lingula* community, followed away from the shoreline successively by an *Eocoelia* community, a *Pentamerus* community, a *Stricklandia* community, a *Clorinda* community, and finally a pelagic community characterized by graptolites to the exclusion of most shelly organisms. The depth control of these communities is confirmed by a few occurrences of interbedded lava flows, which when thin do not alter the sequence of communities but when thick result in nearer shore; i.e., shallower water communities occurring on top of the flows and farther from shore; i.e., deeper water communities below. The occurrence of the pelagic community next to the Lingula community in those portions of the Northern Hemisphere concluded to have been relatively cool suggests that water temperature is ecologically the most important variable controlling the distribution of Northern Hemisphere and Australian shallow-water marine invertebrates. Otherwise the absence in this vast region of the *Eocoelia* through *Clorinda* communities is difficult to explain. The sole exception to these generalizations is in the Istanbul region, where late Llandovery *Stricklandia* and Llandovery through Pridoli age shells occur. Recent studies are developing a depth zonation for Paleozoic graptolites, including Silurian plankton, by comparing Paleozoic plankton faunas with benthic faunas whose depth values are known.

WORLD DISTRIBUTION OF SILURIAN DEPOSITS

The paleogeographic map (see the Figure) shows where Silurian marine deposits and nonmarine regions of different ages might have been in existence on the present continental areas. Naturally a map for any instant of the 30,-000,000 years or so of Silurian time would look different in detail from this highly generalized scheme, particularly if the Paleozoic condition of the ocean basins were known. This map and the correlation table together give a general view of Silurian stratigraphy and paleogeography that supplements the condensed discussion of outcrop regions below.

Great Britain. Silurian sediments of the type region in Wales and western England and extending into southern Scotland were deposited in a northeast–southwest-trending subsiding area (the Caledonian Geosyncline) and bordering shelf seas to the east. The basin or geosynclinal facies is characterized by graptolite-bearing slates and shales, flaggy and shaly siltstones, sandstones, and mixed, coarse detritus about 5,000 to 10,000 feet thick. This facies is typically developed in Wales, the Lake District of northwestern England, the Southern Uplands of Scotland, and much of Ireland. The shelf facies consists of shales (including mudstones), limestones, and siltstones with a shelly fauna and a maximum thickness of perhaps 1,000 metres in typical development. It thins eastward to disappear toward the inferred Silurian seashore in the subsurface of central England. Complete gradation in sedimentary facies, thickness, and fauna occur from shelf to basin along the margins of the subsiding trough, with some persistent zones of graptolitic shale that correlate between facies and record the history of downwarping. The type area of south Wales and the Welsh borderland is intermediate between extreme developments of either shelf or basin facies. Northward in the Midland Valley of Scotland, the sediments suggest approach toward the northwest side of the geosyncline as is also true in portions of northwestern Ireland. **Caledonian Geosyncline deposits**

At many places in the Welsh borderland the oldest Silurian deposits in Britain are separated from underlying rocks by unconformity. Preceding crustal movements, of which the profuse Ordovician volcanicity is one indication, may have brought the southeastern part of the British subsiding area generally above water in the waning stages of the Ordovician. Subsidence, with sharply waning volcanism, was almost immediately renewed, however, and continued intermittently to near the end of the Silurian. Onset of the Caledonian orogeny, chiefly at the end of the Early Devonian, forever reversed the process and made mountains where the sea had been from Wales to Scandinavia.

Subdivisions of the British sequence are shown on the correlation table. The oldest interval, the Llandoverian (or Valentian), saw the beginning of a sharp distinction between basin graptolitic shale facies and calcareous and, in part, sandy shelf facies. This distinction was well marked in the Wenlockian or middle division, when the importance of the calcareous facies was increased by growth of coral-stromatoporoid reefs and colonies on the shelf. In Ludlovian time the same distinction continued. It finally disappeared in Pridoli time with the cessation of marine conditions coincident with the lower half of the Downtonian.

European continent. The same Caledonian Geosyncline, in and along which were deposited the Silurian sediments of Britain (except for eastern England), continued northeastward to western Scandinavia, with a bordering shelf sea that extended eastward. Best known Scandinavian sequences are in southern Norway, southern Sweden, and Gotland. That of south Sweden (Skåne) is a somewhat deformed but essentially complete platform succession of graptolitic shales with limestone interbeds increasing toward the top. This grades northwestward to the fine-textured and richly fossiliferous, but also structurally disturbed, intermediate to platform facies of limestones and shales north of Oslo. Southeastward it goes into the thin, calcareous, relatively flat-lying platform facies of Gotland and Estonia. Later Caledonian deformation from a northwest direction folded the Norwegian sequence and **Scandinavian sequences and facies**

that of south Sweden but did not noticeably affect Gotland or the eastern Baltic. The Silurian section of Gotland, important because it comprises the type Gotlandian (synonym of Silurian as here used), is a thin but richly fossiliferous succession of limestones and calcareous shales. Many of the hills (*klintar*) of Gotland are coral-stromatoporoid reefs, marvellously exposed for study.

Between the Baltic and Brittany, the Silurian is represented by shales and mudstones rich in graptolites and a few pelecypods, with small amounts of limestone, commonly strongly metamorphosed and discontinuous. Eastward in the Harz and Thuringian uplifts the section is similar. The Armorican Massif itself (Brittany) displays the same Silurian facies—500 metres or so of graptolitic, black shales with sandstone at the base.

In the Bohemian (or Czechoslovakian) Massif around Prague is the famous Silurian sequence of Joachim Barrande and J. Perner, which is somewhat deformed by post-Middle Devonian movements. This is prevailingly of graptolitic shales with at first inconspicuous limestone bands. The calcareous fraction increases toward the top until the whole sequence goes over to gray and black limestones, with both bedded and reef facies and some volcanics. Total thickness is somewhat under 200 metres. This sequence represents a large span of Silurian time during which sediments presumably accumulated in a relatively shallow sea connected with Brittany and surrounding regions as far distant as North Africa. Similar well-known exposures are present in the Montagne Noire of south central France, Sardinia, Spain, the eastern Bavarian Alps, Austria, Romania, Poland, Denmark, Yugoslavia, Greece, Bulgaria, Portugal, and Andorra.

U.S.S.R. Platform carbonates rim the Russian Platform, including occurrences in the Baltic states, Volhynia, Podolia, Odessa, the west slope of the Urals from the central Urals north, Timan, Kanin Peninsula, western Pai-Hoi, southwestern Vaigach Island and south island of Novaya Zemlya, and the southern quarter of the north island of Novaya Zemlya. Similar carbonates occur in Russian Turkistan and may well have been continuous with those of the Russian platform as well as the Chinese Tien Shan. Geosynclinal accumulations of mudstone, siltstone, and related clastic rocks occur in northern and northeastern portions of Novaya Zemlya, Vaigach, and Pai-Hoi. The eastern slopes of the Urals, both slopes of the southern Urals, and Kazakhstan are occupied by geosynclinal deposits of volcanic type. The Altai–Sayan is occupied by interbedded carbonate and terrigenous sediments intermediate in character between those of the geosyncline and the adjacent Siberian Platform. The Siberian Platform (including the Kolyma Massif and the Sette–Daban Silurian) is covered by a thin veneer of carbonate rocks and subordinate shale. The Silurian carbonates of both Severnaya Zemlya and the New Siberian Islands are probably isolated portions of the Siberian Platform. On the northwest of the Siberian Platform, carbonates grade into the graptolitic clastic rocks of the northern Taimyr Peninsula. To the south the Siberian platform Silurian abuts the near-shore sediments of the southeastern Altai–Sayan, Tuva, and the Amur region, which flanked the emergent Angara Shield.

Near East. The Silurian of the Near East is merely an extension of that present in North Africa. Platform mudstone rich in graptolites occurs widespread in Turkey, grading to the southeast into near-shore sandstones. Similar sandstones with rare marine intercalations occur in Syria, Jordan, and Saudi Arabia. Graptolitic mudstones occur in southwestern Iran, and carbonates in central and northeastern Iran.

Asia. Silurian platform carbonates that were originally continuous with that of the Russian Platform occur in Afghanistan, Kashmir, Spiti, Nepal, the Shan states of Burma, and the western portions of Malaya bordering the Straits of Malacca. Platform mudstone is widespread in eastern, southeastern, and central China, extending south into northern Thailand, Indochina, and the eastern part of Malaya. Minor land areas are believed to have been present in southeastern China. During the upper half of the Silurian, the graptolitic platform mudstones of China

Deposits
of the
Russian
and
Siberian
platforms

gave way to shelly limestone to the south and shelly, clastic rocks to the north. The Silurian of Japan contains carbonate rocks in the north and volcanic, clastic, and carbonate rocks elsewhere.

Australia. The known Silurian of Australia is limited to the eastern coast (Victoria, New South Wales, and Queensland) and Tasmania. Known Silurian sections consist dominantly of fine clastics. Interbedded with these locally are graptolitic shales and limestones or calcareous shales with a shelly fauna and volcanics. Northeast of Melbourne are clastic beds that represent the whole of the Silurian. In the Yass district of New South Wales the section is only about 1,000 metres thick but is famed for the rich and beautifully preserved fossils of its Yass Beds and Lower Hume Limestones and Shales. In eastern Victoria and New South Wales the Ordovician and Silurian are separated by an orogenic interval, the Benambran orogeny. Silurian crustal unrest culminated with compressive movements and deep-seated igneous intrusions locally (eastern Victoria and adjacent New South Wales) termed the Bowning orogeny and considered a phase of the more inclusive Caledonian orogeny. When the Devonian seas reinvaded eastern Australia their deposits came to rest on the folded and erosionally truncated edges of such eastern Silurian rocks.

On the west, Silurian carbonates, dated by conodonts, are known from a borehole on Dirk Hartogs Island, the westernmost point of the continent. To the north, graptolitic Llandovery shale and limestone containing corals are known from two areas in Papua. (Geologically New Guinea and the Sahul shelf form part of Australia.)

South America. The poorly known Silurian of South America may be divided into the marine-platform mudstones known in the north (Venezuela and the Amazon region of Brazil) and west (Bolivia, Argentina, and Paraguay) and the possibly Silurian nonmarine rocks known in portions of the continent from southeastern Brazil to the Falkland Islands and southern Argentina.

Africa. Platform mudstones rich in graptolites and certain pelecypods are widespread in North Africa from Sierra Leone on the southwest to the Kufra Basin on the Egyptian–Libyan frontier. To the southeast of this line they grade into nonmarine beds. This shoreline gradually migrates during the Silurian, until near the end of the period it comes to rest in Morocco and Algeria far to the northwest. This regional shift results from the Silurian marine beds to the southeast, representing only a fraction of early Llandovery time, whereas those to the northwest represent the entire period; *i.e.*, North Africa was gradually rising during the Silurian. Glacial tillites are known from the very base of the Silurian in parts of Africa. A single occurrence of shallow-water invertebrates in the Table Mountain Sandstone of South Africa of probable late Llandovery-Wenlock age represents the only marine Silurian south of the Sahara. The intervening region was above sea level during the Silurian.

North America. The widespread Silurian deposits of North America may for convenience be considered under the following categories: (1) platform carbonates of the continental interior and (2) terrigenous geosynclinal deposits: (*a*) Appalachian Geosyncline, (*b*) Ouachita Geosyncline, (*c*) Cordilleran Geosyncline, and (*d*) Franklinian Geosyncline. The platform carbonates are well known in both the surface and subsurface, as indicated in the following list of occurrences: Anticosti Island, northwestern Gaspé, western portions of the central and southern Appalachians, surface and subsurface of the midcontinent (including western Pennsylvania, New York, Ontario, Ohio, Michigan, Wisconsin, Illinois, Kentucky, Indiana, Iowa, Kansas, Nebraska, northwest Alabama, Missouri, Arkansas, and Oklahoma), Llano region of Texas, Permian Basin of Texas and New Mexico plus outcrops in southeastern New Mexico and western Texas, Hudson Bay region of Ontario and Quebec, Lake Timiskaming, Laramie Range of Wyoming, Great Basin (including western Utah, southeastern Idaho, eastern Nevada, southeastern California), Chihuahua, possibly southern Sonora, Williston Basin (including the Dakotas, Wyoming, Saskatchewan, and Manitoba), southern British Colum-

Crustal
movements
in eastern
Australia

bia, northeastern British Columbia, central and eastern Yukon and Northwest territories, southern portion of the Canadian Arctic Archipelago, southern Baffin Island, Foxe Basin region, and portions of northwestern and northeastern Greenland.

Appalachian deposits of Silurian age

The Appalachian geosynclinal deposits are widespread from northern Newfoundland southwest through Nova Scotia, New Brunswick, Quebec south of the St. Lawrence River, Maine, and New England from the Connecticut River region east and south to Long Island Sound. The Appalachian geosynclinal Silurian is separated from the platform carbonates by a linear island Appalachia, which shed clastic debris to both east and west to form dual aprons of both nonmarine and marine clastic rocks paralleling the shorelines. This island gradually submerged during the Silurian until, by Pridoli time, it formed only a small fraction of its early Llandovery extent. Sedimentary iron ores, Clinton Ores, are near-shore phenomena known on the west side of Appalachia intermittently and are of varying ages from New York to Alabama. Similar iron deposits related to land areas are also known in the Silurian of northern Maine and Nova Scotia.

Ouachita geosynclinal deposits are known from exposures in Arkansas, Oklahoma, and Tamaulipas, plus subsurface occurrences in Texas and Mississippi.

Cordilleran geosynclinal deposits are known in a north–south strip extending from near Bishop, Calif., through central Nevada to southeastern Idaho, in northern California (Klamath Mountains and Taylorsville district), northeast Washington (Metaline quadrangle), northern British Columbia, adjacent Yukon and Alaska (Road River Formation), and in southeastern Alaska.

Franklinian goesynclinal deposits are known from the northern parts of the Canadian Arctic Archipelago (Cape Phillipa Formation, Cape Rawson Formation, and their clastic equivalents) and portions of northwesternmost Greenland.

Isolated occurrences in central and western Alaska as well as in the subsurface of northern Florida are difficult to relate to the aforementioned units and may represent remnants of additional major platforms of platform carbonate (Alaska) and platform mudstone (Florida) character.

BIBLIOGRAPHY. RODERICK IMPEY MURCHISON, "On the Silurian System of Rocks," *Lond. Edinb. Dubl. Phil. Mag.,* 7:46 (1835); *The Silurian System,* 2 pt. (1839); and A. GEIKIE, *The Founders of Geology,* 2nd ed. (1905), are of historical interest. The basic sources today are the Silurian Correlation charts now being published by the Geological Society of America, edited and written by W.B.N. BERRY and A.J. BOUCOT, with many co-authors. These charts present the physical and biological bases for correlation in some detail and outline the rock types, paleogeography, fossil zonation, and paleoecology for the Silurian Period and System. W.B.N. BERRY and A.J. BOUCOT, "Pelecypod-Graptolite Association in the Old World Silurian," *Bull. Geol. Soc. Am.,* 78:1515–1522 (1967), gives the evidence for concluding that Silurian deposits of the Mediterranean region were deposited under a colder regime than that occurring to the North; "Continental Stability—A Silurian Point of View," *J. Geophys. Res.,* 72:2254–2256 (1967), presents additional evidence.

(A.J.Bo.)

Silver Products and Production

For thousands of years silver has been used for its aesthetic and monetary value. Today it is fundamentally an industrial commodity and will become even more so in the future. In the early 1970s the United States became the last large nation to eliminate silver from all coins, though some smaller nations retained it.

Comparison with other noble metals

Silver is in the precious-metal group because of its scarcity and price. Although it is widely distributed in nature, the total amount in the Earth's crust is quite small compared with other metals. As a consequence it costs about 500 times more than iron and about 50 times more than copper. Among the noble metals, however, it is relatively abundant and costs about $\frac{1}{20}$ as much as gold and $\frac{1}{50}$ as much as platinum. Noble metals are not easily changed to an oxide form by air or oxygen and consequently can

be found in the elemental form or as an alloy in nature. They can be used for electrical contacts at which arcing (sparking) occurs, and they are excellent conductors of electricity. Silver is the best conductor of electricity and heat among all metals and is used as the electrical and heat-conductance standard against which other metals are measured in percentage terms. Copper, for example, has a relative electrical conductance of 95 percent and a thermal conductance of 73.7 percent.

Because of its resistance to atmospheric oxidation, as well as its beauty and value, silver has been used since antiquity for ornaments, jewelry, and coins. It is the whitest of all metals and has excellent ductility and malleability; pure silver, however, can be easily scratched and tarnishes quickly in the presence of certain sulfur compounds. Silver objects have been found in ancient tombs unaffected by air pollution but have tarnished rapidly in areas in which coal containing sulfur is burned. The reflectivity of silver, particularly to that part of the spectrum visible to the human eye, is one of the highest among metals. When properly polished and under favourable conditions, about 95 percent of the light striking the surface is reflected. Further information on physical and chemical properties of silver and its occurrence is contained in the articles TRANSITION ELEMENTS AND THEIR COMPOUNDS and NATIVE ELEMENTS.

History. The Latin name for silver is *argentum,* meaning white and shining, and from it the chemical symbol Ag was obtained. Silver ornaments, vessels for ceremonial services, and decorations have been found in royal tombs dating back to 4000 BC. The Egyptian Code of Menes, about 3000 BC, decreed that "one part of gold was equal to two and one-half parts of silver in value," perhaps the first gold standard. Records show that gold and copper were the first metals to be worked by man, with silver third. The Romans, who probably advanced the science of metallurgy further than any other people up to their time, had large plants to produce silver for ornaments and decoration. The Roman process, in which the silver was separated from the ore by heating in a furnace, was used throughout the Middle Ages, when silver–copper mines were worked in central Europe. In the 16th century the Spaniards discovered enormous silver deposits in South and Central America, and during the 19th century, a so-called patio process, involving grinding silver ore in the presence of salts, water, and mercury to make an amalgam (alloy), was developed in Mexico. The amalgam (mercury and silver and gold if present) was heated in a retort to drive off the mercury, leaving the silver and gold; the mercury was recovered by condensation. Spanish America supplied the world with silver until the Comstock Lode strike of 1859 in the Sierra Nevada area in the United States.

The cyanide process (see below), developed in the latter part of the 19th century, is still used today for ores containing only gold and silver values. About 1910 a froth flotation process was introduced. In this process, particles of sulfides of copper, lead, and zinc containing small amounts of silver and gold are made to adhere to rising air bubbles, which are skimmed off. The froth flotation process today accounts for about 75 percent of the world production of silver.

Occurrence. In the early 1970s, most of the silver produced from ores was associated with the sulfides of lead, copper, and zinc. These so-called argentiferous ores may contain from a trace to several thousand troy ounces of silver per ton of ore. Precious metals are generally sold by troy ounces, one troy ounce equalling 31.1 grams, or 1.097 avoirdupois ounces.

Silver ore associations

Unlike gold, silver is found in many naturally occurring minerals. The most important is galena (lead sulfide), followed by argentite (silver sulfide), cerargyrite (or chlorargyrite; silver chloride), polybasite (silver antimony sulfide), proustite (silver arsenic sulfide), pyrargyrite (or stephanite; silver antimony sulfides), and others. Deposits of native silver (generally an alloy) are commercially important and widespread. Sylvanite (gold and silver telluride) ores are of commercial value in some areas. Arizona, Utah, and Colorado in the United States are large producers of silver as a by-product from copper, lead, and zinc ores. Low grade porphyry copper ores mined in Arizona assay about 0.6 percent copper and about 0.1 ounce of silver per ton of ore. In Canada, silver is found in the Canadian Shield around Sudbury, Ontario, as part of the nickel–copper–cobalt ores, in British Columbia, and in the Yukon Territory. Large silver deposits at Cerro de Pasco, Peru, have been worked since the 17th century. Mt. Isa and North Broken Hill in Australia are becoming large producers.

Extraction and refining. Many methods are employed for the extraction of silver or silver and gold from ores, scrap, alloys, and used photographic materials. Most of the silver produced today is a by-product from the treatment of copper, lead, and zinc ores, and consequently any large increase in silver implies an increase in copper, lead, and zinc or vice versa. Silver occurring with copper ores is first extracted with the copper and recovered as a silver–gold anode mud after electrolysis. Silver occurring with lead ores is recovered from the lead bullion as a silver–gold dross (see LEAD PRODUCTS AND PRODUCTION). Silver occurring with zinc ores, which also contain lead, is recovered with the lead bullion as a by-product (see ZINC PRODUCTS AND PRODUCTION).

The cyanide process is generally used on ores that contain only silver or silver and gold as the valuable constituent. The ore is pulverized and leached with a dilute sodium cyanide water solution. The silver and gold form water-soluble sodium–silver–gold complexes. The resulting mixture is filtered and the solids discarded. The filtrate is generally treated with finely divided zinc dust that causes the silver and gold to precipitate from the solution. This precipitate is filtered off, melted, and cast into bullion bars.

Silver is recovered from used photographic film by burning the film and dissolving the silver in the ashes with nitric acid. The silver is precipitated with sodium chloride and the resulting precipitate filtered off and cast into bars. Silver is also recovered from photographic processing solutions by replacing the silver with another metal, such as zinc, by electrolysis or by chemical precipitation with chemicals such as sodium hydroxide or sodium sulfide.

The method used in refining the crude silver or silver–gold bullion obtained from these metallurgical processes depends upon its purity and the amount of bullion to be refined. For bullion containing a large amount of impurities, smelting in a small furnace with lead oxide, fluxes, and a reducing agent produces slag that is further processed in a lead smelter. The resulting lead bullion, containing the silver and gold, is melted in the presence of air. The oxidized lead (a liquid oxide) is evaporated or absorbed by a cupel (holding vessel), a process called cupellation. The end product is an alloy of silver and gold called doré, a high purity alloy. The cupel material (the liquid lead oxide absorber) can be cement or bone ash.

The two most important methods for separating silver and gold in silver–gold bullion are electrolysis and parting. In electrolysis, a silver nitrate water solution is employed, with silver, gold bullion, or doré serving as the anode (positive electrode). Pure silver is deposited at the cathode (negative pole), which can be a pure thin sheet of silver or stainless steel. The resulting cathode silver or silver stripped from the stainless steel cathode is melted and cast into bars assaying about 999.0+ fine of silver. Gold is recovered from the anode mud.

Silver and gold alloys are stated in terms of fineness, given by the parts of silver or gold per 1,000 of alloy. Sterling silver contains 92.5 percent silver and 7.5 percent of another metal, usually copper as a hardening agent; such silver is therefore 925 fine.

In the parting, or wet, method the doré or silver–gold bullion is placed in a bath of hot concentrated sulfuric acid or strong nitric acid, and the silver is allowed to dissolve. Gold is recovered from the residue. The clear solution contains a soluble silver sulfate or nitrate; it is treated with ferrous sulfate to precipitate the silver, which is filtered off and melted into bars assaying 995+ fine of silver. This method is applicable to doré or very high purity silver–gold bullion containing two or more

Electrolysis and parting

parts of silver to one part of gold. Additional silver may be added to achieve this ratio, as ratios of less than two to one will not dissolve in the acid.

Uses. *Pure metal applications.* In the 1970s coinage accounted for only about 8 percent of the world's silver production. The rest went to industrial production, with photography accounting for about 30 percent of this total, a proportion expected to increase in the future. Photographic silver is used in the form of halides, such as silver bromide. Television cassettes contain film using silver halides. Electrical and electronic equipment also accounts for a large percentage of silver consumption. Silver solders are used extensively in refrigeration units, air conditioners, automobiles, and electrical appliances. Brazing, soldering, and welding use substantial amounts of silver. Silver–copper alloys are used in welding and, in some cases, as contacts in relays for computers, tabulators, and other applications requiring high strength at elevated temperatures. Inexpensive though intricate electrical circuits for radios, television, computers, and other electronic devices may be made by stamping or printing a given circuit on insulating panels with silver ink. Silver is used in certain cold epoxy solders to bond microminiature electronic devices without heat and in some electronic adhesive applications. Silver–magnesium–nickel alloys are used for high thermal-conductivity applications and relay switches operating at high temperatures. Silver coatings on ceramics, glass, mica, and other insulators are widely used in electronic devices.

Silverware, plated and sterling, takes another large share of the production. An average sterling teaspoon contains about one ounce of silver. Electroplated ware also takes a considerable amount of silver. Thin plates of silver for bone replacement in the human body, silver wire to prevent movement of broken bones, and drainage tubes of silver are useful in medicine because the silver exhibits germicidal properties. These properties may result from the ability of silver to absorb oxygen. Liquid silver, for example, can absorb about 20 times its volume of oxygen. Silver water purifiers developed to make water bacteria free for space explorers are now also used by campers and sportsmen. High-silver batteries, requiring less space, maintaining higher voltages, and lasting longer than conventional batteries, are used for such applications as hearing aids. Because of the higher power per unit of weight, silver batteries are used in space travel, submarines, and portable television cameras.

Manufacturers of airplanes and diesel locomotives have been using a silver-base-alloy bearing containing 3 to 5 percent lead, which is much less subject to seizure (freezing) than Babbitt metal and has excellent oiliness under severe conditions. Because of its excellent reflectability, silver is used extensively as a coating on glass and other materials for making mirrors. Coatings may be applied in many ways, but generally the process uses an ammonium hydroxide–silver nitrate solution, which is applied to the surface, and a reducing agent, such as sugar, Rochelle salt, or formaldehyde, which is added to precipitate a layer of metallic silver. The process is hazardous because of the formation of ammonium nitrate; explosions may occur on the slightest disturbance.

Silver coatings

Silver in colloidal form (very fine particles) is used as a catalyst in certain vapour-phase organic chemical reactions, such as the manufacture of various types of alcohols. Cesium–silver alloys are used in some types of photoelectric cells. Dental amalgams are alloys of silver–tin–mercury that can be molded at temperatures of the mouth and harden quickly to give a polished surface.

Silver is also used in the manufacture of jewelry and art objects. Jewelry silvers are alloys containing around 80 percent silver and 20 percent copper.

Applications of compounds. Silver is easily tarnished by sulfur, sulfur oxides, and hydrogen sulfide. The black tarnish can be removed by household silver polish, which generally contains fine abrasive material, or by an electrolysis kit that removes the tarnish with no loss of silver. An antitarnish dip of 1.5 percent tin chloride water solution, used for five to 30 seconds and followed by a water rinse, may prevent tarnishing. Silver dissolves rapidly in strong or dilute nitric acid to form water-soluble silver nitrate. Silver nitrate solutions are used as fungicides in treating certain plants for disease control and as a starting point to make other materials, such as silver for photographic film and plates and for mirrors. The halogen compounds of silver are by far the most important; silver bromide makes possible the modern photographic industry. In photography the glass plate or film merely serves to hold the light-sensitive emulsion, generally silver bromide crystals, in suspension in some type of a gelatin. Silver chloride, a white crystal material practically insoluble in water, is made by adding hydrochloric acid to a silver nitrate solution. Silver iodide, a yellow crystal material, is made in a similar manner. In recent years large amounts of finely divided silver iodide, which has a crystal structure similar to ice, have been used for cloud seeding to produce rainfall and to reduce the violence of hurricanes. Its effectiveness for this purpose is open to some question, but one ounce of silver as silver iodide under the right conditions might produce as much as 3,000,000 gallons of water as rain.

Table 1: Silver Production*
(in millions of troy ounces)

	1950	1965	1970
Mexico	49.1	40.3	40.2
United States	42.3	39.8	44.5
Canada	23.2	32.3	43.9
Peru	13.4	36.5	37.0
Bolivia	6.6	4.1	5.0
Total	198.6	257.4	246.6
Total consumption	201.5	406.9	397.2

*Non-Communist world.

Argentic fluoride (AgF_2), a dark brown solid formed when fluorine reacts with argentous fluoride (AgF), is a powerful oxidizing agent and a good fluorinating agent. Silver sulfadiazene is used in preventing infection resulting from burns because it combats bacteria by attacking the wall and not the nucleus of the cell.

Economic importance. The production of silver by the Soviet Union is believed to be about equal to that of the United States, approximately 43,000,000 ounces per year.

Total world production of silver up to 1970 was just under 30,000,000,000 accumulated ounces, of which about 80 percent was derived from ores of the Western Hemisphere and about 20 percent was produced by the United States. India probably has the world's largest supply of refined silver, with perhaps 4,000,000,000 ounces in the form of artifacts.

Table 2: Silver Consumption*
(in millions of troy ounces)

	1950 industrial	1950 coinage	1965 industrial	1965 coinage	1970 industrial	1970 coinage†
United States	120.0	24.6‡	137.0	320.3‡	135.0	0.8‡
Great Britain	12.4	—	25.0	—	25.0	—
West Germany	7.6	—	54.6	—	48.2	—
Canada	5.2	3.4	5.3	20.4	5.9	—
Japan	—	—	25.0	5.8	45.5	—
Total	157.4	44.1	346.6	380.6	357.6	40.3

*Non-Communist world. †By 1970 less than 10 percent of the silver production was used for coinage. ‡Obtained from United States Treasury stocks.

BIBLIOGRAPHY. A. BUTTS, *Silver: Economics, Metallurgy, and Use* (1967), contains recent information on silver in general. J. NEWTON, *An Introduction to Metallurgy* (1938), is an excellent book for general fundamentals concerning extractive metallurgy. L ADDICKS, *Silver in Industry* (1940), contains a complete history of the properties, types of alloys, and uses of silver. The AMERICAN SOCIETY FOR METALS, *Metals Handbook*, 8th ed. (1961), is a standard reference handbook for properties and selection of metals. UNITED STATES BUREAU OF MINES, *Minerals Yearbook* (annual), gives statistics on production, value, and location for all metals and nonmetals.

(S.L.Sm.)

Simpson, George Gaylord

Through his studies of the early history of mammals, George Gaylord Simpson established himself as one of the leading paleontologists of the 20th century. Among his important contributions were his studies of South American mammals, which shed much light on the subject of the intercontinental migration of animal species.

Simpson was born in Chicago on June 16, 1902, and received his doctorate from Yale University in 1926. He chose for his thesis the mammals of the Mesozoic Era, which are important for the understanding of mammalian evolution, but evidence of their existence consists mainly of tantalizing fragments of jaws and teeth. The materials were located chiefly in the Peabody Museum at Yale and the British Museum in London. Simpson produced substantial quarto monographs on the two collections, making his reputation as an able worker in mammalian paleontology.

In 1927 he joined the staff of the American Museum of Natural History, New York City, where he was to continue research in paleontology for three decades. The first 15 years were highly productive; he published about 150 scientific papers, many of considerable importance. A few dealt with lower vertebrates, but nearly all were on mammalian paleontology. In his first years in New York City he was interested in the fauna of the later Tertiary and Pleistocene of Florida, and he published a number of works on this topic. For the most part, however, his interests were in the early history of mammals, and most of his publications in the 1930s were concerned with this field. He studied the Cretaceous mammals of Mongolia and North America, especially the Paleocene fauna of the latter continent. This resulted in a major work on the Paleocene fauna of the Fort Union beds of Montana, in which about 50 mammals of a variety of primitive types were found. The breadth of his studies of mammalian evolution led to the writing of a detailed classification of mammals that is standard in the field.

In the Tertiary a series of mammalian fauna lived in South America that were quite unlike those of any other continent. These of the late Tertiary and Pleistocene forms were fairly well known, but little was known of the earlier history of the peculiar South American groups. Hence, in the early 1930s, he made three expeditions to Patagonia to collect new material and re-study specimens already described; as a result of these efforts, the early history of the Tertiary mammals of South America became vastly better known. He published several dozen papers on these forms in the later 1930s and afterward two volumes summarizing their early history.

During World War II Simpson served the U.S. Army in staff work, principally in North Africa. On his return to the American Museum, he became curator in charge of the active department of paleontology, as well as a professor at Columbia University. This restricted the time available for research, but his scientific productivity remained undiminished. While his descriptive work in paleontology continued, his interests spread to other fields. The possibility of applying mathematical methods to paleontology had already led to his coauthorship of a work on quantitative zoology. A consideration of the successive faunas of the various continental areas led to studies of the problems of the intercontinental migrations of animal species. Problems of taxonomy and classification are intimately connected with evolutionary studies, and, in addition to giving a thorough consideration of principles of classification in his work on mammalian classification, he published in 1961 a volume on *The Principles of Animal Taxonomy*. In a series of lectures on *The Meaning of Evolution*, which appeared in book form in 1949, he discussed the philosophical implications of the acceptance of evolutionary theory, which attracted worldwide attention. In the postwar period there was a renewed study of evolutionary theory by geneticists, systematists, and paleontologists. Simpson took a major part in such studies; his principal publications in the area were his volumes *Tempo and Mode in Evolution* (1944) and *Major Features of Evolution* (1953).

In 1958 Simpson left New York City to spend a decade

Work in mammalian paleontology

Evolutionary theory

as an Alexander Agassiz Professor of Paleontology at the Harvard Museum of Comparative Zoology. After that he moved to Tucson, Arizona, where he was affiliated with the University of Arizona.   (A.S.R.)

Sinai Desert

The Sinai Desert forms a triangular peninsula linking Africa with Asia. It lies between the Gulf of Suez and the Suez Canal on the west and the Gulf of Aqaba and the Negev desert on the east, and it is bounded by the Mediterranean Sea on the north and the Red Sea to the south. It has an area of 23,500 square miles (61,000 square kilometres). Its greatest extent is about 130 miles from east to west and about 240 miles from north to south. Usually regarded as being geographically part of Asia, the Sinai Peninsula is the northeastern extremity and a desert governorate of Egypt, adjoining Israel on the east; but since the Arab–Israeli War of 1967 it has been occupied by Israeli forces.

The earliest information about Sinai in written form dates back to 3000 BC, when the ancient Egyptians recorded their exploration there in search of copper ores. But the name Sinai seems to have been known much earlier than this and may have been derived from the original name of one of the most ancient religious cults of the Near East, that of the moon god Sin. Mt. Sinai is famous as the scene of the giving of the Law to Moses, but there is doubt as to which of the mountains of Sinai is the actual site.

The landscape. *Relief.* Geologically speaking, Sinai occupies an ancient block, a portion of the African Precambrian Shield (from 4,600,000,000 to 570,000,000 years old), which rose between two rifted areas and became tilted down in a northward direction and, during the time interval from the Precambrian to the Quaternary Period (which began 2,500,000 years ago), was subject to both long and short transgressions of the Mediterranean Sea. The Sinai Desert is separated by the Gulf of Suez and the Suez Canal from the Eastern Desert of Africa, by continuing eastward into the Negev desert without marked change of relief. The Eastern Desert is also known as the Arabian Desert, but is not to be confused with the Arabian Desert on the Arabian Peninsula (*q.v.*). Two principal regions may be recognized in Sinai. The first region is the southern complex of high mountains, including such peaks as Mt. Catherine (Jabal Katrīnah) which is 8,651 feet high, Umm Shawmar (8,482 feet), ath-Thabt (7,997 feet), and Jabal Mūsā, or Mt. Sinai (7,482 feet); it is essentially built of igneous rocks (those formed by solidification from a molten state) and is sharply incised by deep, canyon-like wadis (seasonal watercourses) that drain toward the Gulf of Suez or the Gulf of Aqaba. This gaunt mountain mass is separated from the Gulf of Suez by a narrow coastal plain, but on its eastern side it rises precipitately from the Gulf of Aqaba. The second region, flanking this mass on the north and forming two-thirds of Sinai, is a great plateau sloping from heights of more than 3,000 feet downward to the Mediterranean. It is characterized by the extensive plain of Wādī al-'Arīsh, by a number of island-like massifs (mountain masses), and by broad western and northern coastal plains with extensive sand dunes.

Drainage. A conspicuous ridge runs from the south round Sinai in a great horseshoe curve, from which three main drainage basins have developed: the northern (or Mediterranean) drainage basin, in which Wādī al-'Arīsh acts as a master stream, empties into the Mediterranean near the town of al-'Arīsh; the eastern (Gulf of Aqaba and Dead Sea) basin and the western (Gulf of Suez) basin are both drained by a number of small arteries.

Soils. In Sinai, metamorphic rocks (those formed under heat and pressure) and igneous rocks predominate in the south; sedimentary rocks (mainly limestone) in the centre and north. Such rocks are either barren or covered with a mantle of young, unconsolidated deposits. They are provisionally termed soils, although they lack organic matter and appear to be undeveloped. These soil deposits can be classified as rock debris (20 percent), desert detri-

tus (50 percent), subdesert soils (25 percent), and hydromorphic soils—those formed by water—5 percent. The rock debris is dominant in the south. The desert detritus occurs in the centre and north and includes the stretches of alluvial soils of Wādī al-'Arīsh and the dune complex of northwest Sinai. The subdesert soils include loesslike deposits (predominantly silt, with subordinate amounts of fine sand and clay) and are found in the northeast and parts of the western coastal plain. The hydromorphic soils, which are localized in the northwest corner, are related to the soils of the Nile but have been subjected to strong salinization processes.

Climate. Sinai falls within the great arid belt crossing northern Africa and southern Asia. Aridity is manifested in Sinai by degraded soil surface, sand-dune expanses, salinization, and dry watercourses (wadis). That less arid climatic conditions formerly prevailed is demonstrated by occasional terraces of thick alluvial and lacustrine (lake-originated) deposits. In the northern, or Mediterranean, region of low relief, the climate in winter is unstable, with relatively high rainfall (five inches); in summer it is dry and intensely hot with a clear sky, and in spring and autumn it is unstable again, with khamsin winds (hot, southerly winds, associated with Egypt) and occasional torrential rain. In the central and southern, or Red Sea, region, comprising most of Sinai, the climate differs because of the mountainous nature of the terrain. In winter, ice caps cover the prominent peaks, but rainfall is very sparse. Nights are cold, even though the summer heat is intense. In northern Sinai the average maximum winter temperature is 68° F (20° C), while the minimum is 45° F (7° C); the summer maximum averages 99° F (37° C) and the minimum 64° F (18° C). In southern Sinai the maximum winter average is 81° F (27° C), while the minimum is 55° F (13° C); the summer average maximum is 95° F (35° C), while the minimum is 77° F (25° C).

Vegetation and animal life. Vegetation in the Sinai Desert is mostly ephemeral, but perennial scrub survives on the steep southern slopes and on the plateau to the north. Succulents and salt-tolerant plants, such as tamarisks, are found on the subdesertic coastal plains.

Animals are rare, but the species represented include ibex, gazelles, sand foxes, leopards, wildcats, jackals, hares, hedgehogs, and moles. Falcons and eagles are indigenous, and there are also seasonal migrants, such as quail, partridge, and grouse.

The inhabitants. The scanty population of Sinai (130,000 in 1966) is mostly concentrated in the northern fringe, where water supplies are adequate, as well as in the western fringe, where petroleum and manganese industries have also developed. About 80,000 are settled, and 50,000 are Bedouins. The settled population is engaged in agriculture and land reclamation (at al-'Arīsh, Sheikh Zweid) and in the petroleum (Sudr, Abū Rudays), mining (Abū Zanīmah), and fishery industries (Bi'r al-'Abd, at̤-Ṭur). The wandering Bedouin tribes migrate, seeking water and pasturage—few are attracted to industry or even agriculture. They comprise southern and northern groups. The southern group, known as Twara (a name referring to their chief village, at̤-Ṭur) inhabit all Sinai south of Darb al-Ḥāji (the old pilgrim route from Suez to al-'Aqabah via an-Nakhl); the principal tribes of this group are the Eleigat of northwest Sinai, the Sawallha of southwest Sinai, and the Umm Zeina of east Sinai, particularly along the Gulf of Aqaba. The northern group has no distinctive title and consists of a collection of tribes who have mostly migrated from Arabia. It includes principally the Tarabin (the largest tribe in Sinai), the Tiaha of east central Sinai, the Hueitat of west central Sinai, and the Aiada and the Eheiwat of northwest Sinai.

In the mountainous south a community of Orthodox Christian monks living in the Monastery of St. Catherine, which was founded by the emperor Justinian, in AD 530, is still in existence.

Transport and communication. Sinai is connected to the west bank of the Suez Canal by ferryboats at Suez, Ismailia, al-Qantarah, and Port Said and by a railway bridge at al-Firdān.

Marginal notes:

The southern mountains

The Bedouin

Types of aridity

Before 1936 the principal roads were desert tracks running from west to east. The northernmost of these was a track linking al-Qanṭarah on the Suez Canal with Rafaḥ on the Mediterranean coast. There are two central tracks —the Syrian track, which runs between Ismailia on the canal and Abū 'Uwagilāh, and a track running from Suez to al-Quṣaymah via al-Ḥasana (a route known since the 16th century BC). The southernmost track is the most important in Sinai and is variously known as Darb al-Ḥājj, al-Darb al-Sultany, or Darb al-Khutalia; dating from the 13th century BC, it was the pilgrims' road running from Suez to Aqaba via an-Nakhl.

After 1936, paved roads and railway lines were constructed in Sinai for military purposes. Still more roads were constructed after World War II to serve the petroleum industry, particularly in the west. Paved roads in Sinai have a total length of about 900 miles. There are 250 miles of railway lines, a telephone network, three airports—at al-'Arīsh (the principal airfield), Abū Rudays, and aṭ-Ṭur—and three small-sized harbours located at Abū Zanimah and aṭ-Ṭur on the Gulf of Suez and at Sharm ash-Shaykh at the southern tip of the peninsula. At Abū Rudays and at Sudr on the Gulf of Suez, crude oil is pumped into tankers through hoses.

Natural resources. *Water resources.* The economic development of Sinai depends upon the finding of water. Surface water is supplied by the many usually dry watercourses, which sculpture the surface of the desert and become filled with water during rainy years. Such years, while irregular, usually occur once every decade. The most important of these water supplies is that contributed by the Wādī al-'Arīsh Basin, which drains an area of about 7,700 square miles. Attempts to conserve the surface water in this wadi, as well as in many others, date back to prehistoric times; ancient masonry and earth dikes across such wadis are still preserved. A modern masonry dam was constructed across Wādī al-'Arīsh at ar-Ruāfa, some 30 miles south of al-'Arīsh, in 1946. The initial capacity of that dam was estimated at 100,000,000 cubic feet. Groundwater is provided by natural springs, shallow, hand-dug wells, and deep-drilled wells.

Geological strata containing water consist of the Nubian Complex, fissured limestone, marly sandstone, and calcareous sandstone. The Nubian Complex consists of a series of strata, predominately of sandstone, which are exposed in southern Sinai and occasionally in the north. In these strata water is stored under pressure: in some localities of lower altitude, it gushes strongly to the surface. It consists of a type of fossil water between 25,000 and 40,000 years old.

The fissured limestone, dating from the Cretaceous Period (from 65,000,000 to 136,000,000 years old) and from the Eocene Epoch (from 38,000,000 to 54,000,000 years old), occupies about 50 percent of Sinai's area; its potential as a groundwater carrier is little understood. Some natural springs in northeast Sinai receive their water supply from it.

Marly sandstone strata, formed in the Neogene Period (within the past 26,000,000 years), occur in west Sinai and form an aquifer, or water carrier, of secondary importance, containing brackish water.

Calcareous (chalky) sandstone strata, locally known as al-Kurkar and belonging to the Early Quaternary Period (*i.e.*, from about 2,500,000 to 7,000,000 years old), are found only in the coastal zone between al-'Arīsh and Rafaḥ, in the Sinai area, but also extend farther eastward into the Gaza Plain. Al-Kurkar forms a basin within which water exists under pressure; it accumulates from both local and regional precipitation, as well as through upward leakage from underlying water-bearing layers.

In addition to all these strata, accumulations from recent wadis and from sand-dune areas act as the main sources of water for shallow, hand-dug wells.

Mineral resources. Since the time of the ancient Egyptians, Sinai has attracted miners. The mineral ores exploited at present are manganese and ferromanganese (with reserves estimated at between 9,000,000 and 14,000,000 tons), gypsum and anhydrite (calcium sulfate), clays, salts, and glass sands. Other deposits discov-

ered but not exploited include copper ore, phosphates, iron ore, coal, lead and zinc, sulfur, feldspar, quartz, and black shale. Further prospecting and surveying is needed for their development. Such minerals as building stones, dolomite, sands, and gravels await use in future urban and industrial development.

Petroleum, first discovered in 1910 in Jabal Tanakah, in west Sinai, is the most important mineral exploited in Sinai. Petroleum production was begun by large petroleum companies in 1935, especially in north central and west Sinai. In 1944, deep drilling operations were begun in these areas, as a result of which a number of oil fields —Sudr, 'Asal, Matārimah, Fayrān, al-Balā'im, Rudays— were discovered in western Sinai. Between 1921 and 1965, petroleum production in Sinai increased from about 200 to about 3,000,000 tons.

Agricultural resources. The few inhabitants occupied with agriculture are predominantly engaged in grazing livestock and in cultivating barley after the rainy season. The animal wealth of Sinai in 1960 was estimated at about 5,000 camels, 3,000 donkeys, 7,500 sheep, 9,000 goats, and 1,000 cows. The main areas of cultivation are the delta of Wādī al-'Arīsh, the coastal strip between al-'Arīsh and Rafaḥ, and scattered patches in west Sinai (Qatia, 'Uyūn Mūsā, Abū Zanimah, Wādī Fayrān, aṭ-Ṭur). Reclamation efforts are directed toward improving the soil and water conservation and to the siphoning of the Nile water to northwest Sinai.

BIBLIOGRAPHY. H. AWAD, *La Cartographie et la morphologie de la Péninsule du Sinaï* (1950), deals with general topography and geomorphology. F.W. MOON and H. SADEK, *Topography and Geology of Northern Sinai* (1921), describes the drainage systems and the geology of the northern part. M. EL GABALY, *The Soil Water Supply and Agriculture in Northeast Sinai* (1954); and T. KADDAH MALEK, *Soil Survey of the Northwest Sinai Project* (1956), deal with the soils in the northern region. Records of the Meteorology Department of Egypt, although not complete, give detailed information on the climate. See also ABDEL HAKIM M. SOBHI, *The Inhabitants of Sinai* (1960), on the demography; and A. ALY SHATA, *The Structural Development of the Sinai Peninsula* (1954); and R. SAID, *The Geology of Egypt* (1962), for geological information.

(Ab.A.S.)

Sind

Sind, or Sindh, is the southeastern province of Pakistan. Bounded by the neighbouring Pakistani provinces of Punjab and Baluchistan on the north and west and India on the east and southeast, it extends along 150 miles of the Arabian Sea coast on the southwest and covers an area of 54,407 square miles (140,913 square kilometres).

Sind is essentially part of the Indus River Delta and has derived its name from that river, which has been known to the people as the Sindhu. The province of Sind, which has a population of about 14,000,000, was established in 1970, with the integration of Hyderābād and Khairpur Divisions and the District of Karāchi. The city of Karāchi, with a population in 1972 of 3,469,000 (metropolitan area), is the provincial capital. (For related physical features, see INDUS RIVER; THAR DESERT.)

History. The Indus civilization, represented by the archaeological findings at Mohenjo-daro, Amri, and Kot Diji, existed from 2300 to 1750 BC, after which there is a gap of more than a millennium before its earliest recorded history began, with Sind's annexation to the Persian Empire under Darius I (reigned 522–486 BC). Nearly two centuries later, Alexander the Great stormed through the region in 326 and 325 BC. After Alexander's death, Sind came under the domination of the empires of Seleucus Nicator, Candragupta Maurya (305 BC), the Indo-Greeks and Parthians (3rd–2nd century BC), and the Scythians and the Kuṣāṇas (100 BC–AD 200). Under the Kuṣāṇa emperor Kaniṣka (c. AD 78–103), Sind embraced Buddhism. From the 3rd to the 7th century, the area remained under the Sāsānids, and Sind came to be ruled by the Samma chiefs of the local Rai Dynasty as feudatories of Persia. A Brahmin priest subverted Samma rule in 622 and brought Sind under Brahmin rule, which ended with the Arab invasion in 711.

The Arab conquest

The Arab conquest of Sind heralded the entry of Islām into the subcontinent. As-Sind included the present Sind, Baluchistan, and southern Punjab; it became an administrative province of the Umayyad and 'Abbāsid empires from 711 to c. 900, with its capital at al-Manṣūrah, 45 miles northeast of Hyderābād. With the weakening of central authority in Baghdad, the Arab governors in as-Sind established their own dynastic rule during the 10th century. The first Sindian dynasty of the Sūmras was established between 1058 and 1348 and was followed by the Samma Chiefs of Sind from 1349 to 1520.

Over the next two centuries Sind came under the outside domination of the Arghūns (1520–56), the Tarhāns (1556–96) and the Mughals (1591–1700), followed by the independent Sindhian dynasties of the Kalhōrās (1700–82) and the Tālpur Baluch (1782–1843), who lost Sind to the British in 1843. Except for the princely state of Khairpur, all of Sind was annexed to the Bombay Presidency. In 1937 it was established as a separate province; but after Pakistan independence, it was integrated into the province of West Pakistan from 1955 to 1970, together with Khairpur state. Upon dismemberment of the province of West Pakistan in 1970, Sind was re-established as a separate province.

The landscape. *Relief.* From north to south, Sind assumes a pattern of three parallel belts—a central stretch of rich alluvial plain bisected by the long, winding, silvery line of the Indus, flanked on the west by the rocky range of the Khīrthar Range and bounded on the east by a sandy desert belt.

The Khīrthar Range consists of three parallel tiers of ridges. The easternmost section is steep on the west but has a long gradient to the east. The central ridge has flat tops and rounded sides broken by deep ravines and fissures, whereas the westernmost tier consists of a vast plateau or tableland with some peaks rising above 7,000 feet. This mountainous belt has little soil and is mostly dry and barren. The easterly desert region first appears in the north as low dunes and vast flats. Continuing southward, the Achhrro Thar (White Sand Desert) occurs in the middle of the belt and is followed by the Thar Desert (*q.v.*) in the southeast.

The central riverine belt—360 miles long and about 20,000 square miles in area—constitutes the Valley of the Indus. The fertile plain, gradually sloping down from north to south, in its long gradient forms the three flat regions known as *siro* (the upper), *vichole* (the middle), and *larr* (the lower). The variety of soils includes *pakki*, or *patt*, the flat level land of old alluvium forming the northern strips of the Sukkur, Jacobābād, and Lārkāna districts; *reti-wari*, the soft reddish rocky soil of the belt skirting the northwesterly rocky range; *kacho*, the fertile silt alluvium in the narrow inundated belt of the Indus; *wariasi*, an admixture of soft clay and sand; *chiki*, the composite fine clay and soft sand on both sides of the inundated belt; and *kalar*, or alkaline soil, found mostly in the *larr* region.

Climate. A subtropical region, Sind is hot in summer and cold in winter. Temperatures frequently rise above 115° F (46° C) between May and August, and the minimum average temperature of 36° F (2° C) occurs during December and January. The annual rainfall averages about seven inches, falling mainly during July and August. The southwesterly monsoon wind begins to blow in mid-February and continues until the end of September, whereas the cool northerly wind blows during the winter months from October to January.

Vegetation and animal life. Except for the irrigated Indus Valley, the province is arid and has scant vegetation. The dwarf palm, *kher* (*Acacia rupestris*), and *lohirro* (*Tecoma undulata*) trees are typical of the western hill region. In the central valley, the babul tree is the most dominant and occurs in thick forests along the Indus banks. The *nīm* (*Azadirachta indica*), *bēr* (*Zizyphus vulgaris*) or *jujuba*, *lai* (*Tamarix orientalis*), and *kirirr* (*Capparis aphylla*) are among the more common trees. Mango, date palms, and the more recently introduced banana, guava, orange, and chiku are the typical fruit-bearing trees. The coastal strip and the creeks abound in semi-aquatic and aquatic plants, and the inshore Indus deltaic islands have forests of *timmer* (*Avicennia tomentosa*) and *chaunir* (*Ceriops candolleana*) trees. Water lilies grow in abundance in the numerous lakes and ponds, particularly in the lower Sind region.

Among the wild animals, the *sareh* (Sind ibex), *urial* or *gadh* (wild sheep), and black bear are found in the western rocky range, where the leopard is now rare. The *pirrang* (large tiger cat or fishing cat) of the eastern desert region is also disappearing. Deer occur in the lower rocky plains and in the eastern region, as do the *charakh* (striped hyena), jackal, fox, porcupine, common gray mongoose, and hedgehog. The *Sindhi phekari*, red lynx or caracal cat, is encountered in some areas. *Pharrho* (hog deer) and wild bear occur particularly in the central inundation belt. There is a variety of bats, lizards, and reptiles, including the cobra, *lundi* (viper), and the mysterious Sind krait of the Thar region, which is supposed to suck the victim's breath in his sleep. Crocodiles are rare and inhabit only the backwaters of the Indus and its eastern Nāra channel. Besides a large variety of marine fish, the plumbeous dolphin, the beaked dolphin, rorqual, or blue whale, and a variety of skates frequent the seas along the Sind coast. The Pallo (sable fish), though a marine fish, ascends the Indus annually from February to April to spawn.

The people. *Population groups.* Although the population is of mixed ethnic origins, the background of many groups remains visible. The Indus Valley of Sind has been the terminal for sizable migrations, particularly from the west. Of the more ancient groups of Panyas, Takkas, and Mēds, only the progeny of the Mēds has survived as the Mehs, or Muhannas—the professional fishermen living along the Indus and its channels, around the lakes, and in the southern deltaic region. Among the other ethnic groups who form the bulk of the indigenous population are Sammas and the related Lakhas, Lohānās, Nigamaras, Kahahs, and Channas; the Sahtas, Bhattīs, and Thakurs (the present Sodhas of Thar Pārkar) of Rājput origin; and the Jāts and Lorras, both admixtures of the ancient Scythian and the later Baluch peoples. The Jokhia, Burfat, and other sizable ethnic groups inhabiting the western rocky region also appear to be the remnants of early indigenous groups. With the advent of Islām (711), a number of groups of Arab, Persian, and Turkish origin settled in Sind, the most numerous of whom were the Baluch who, beginning from the 13th century, migrated to Sind and made it their second homeland after Baluchistan.

A great change occurred in the composition of the population with the influx of Muslim refugees from India after the partition of the subcontinent in 1947. As early as 1951, more than four persons in every 10 in Karāchi and more than one in every 10 in the rest of Sind were refugees from India. Earlier, since the opening of irrigation barrages on the Indus in the 1930s, there had also been a regular flow of settlers from the other present-day Pakistani provinces. Thus, the ethnographic pattern of Sind continues to undergo a change that is marked and visible.

Linguistic patterns

Sindhi, Seraiki, and Baluchi are the main indigenous languages spoken in Sind. Besides the standard Sindhi speech of the middle Sind region, Sindhi is spoken in five main dialects. Brahui is spoken in the northwestern districts by the migrating communities from Baluchistan; and Dhatki—a dialect of Rajasthani—is spoken in southeastern Thar Pārkar District. With the entry of numerous linguistic groups from India, varieties of languages have come to be spoken in the urban areas. Of these, the most numerous is Urdu, followed by Punjabi, Gujarati, Rajasthani, and Pashto. In schools, English is taught as a compulsory foreign language in upper grades and is spoken by all educated adults.

Most of the population is Muslim. The Hindus of Thar Pārkar District and the Christians and Parsis (Zoroastrians) of the city of Karāchi constitute the province's minority religious groups.

Patterns of settlement. The ever-increasing population, large-scale immigration, and the process of agricultural development and industrialization have changed the settlement pattern in both rural and urban areas. The population has doubled since 1947 and is concentrated in the cities and the irrigated central valley. With the extension of the irrigation system of the Indus, areas formerly barren have come under cultivation, and the semi-nomadic way of life has changed to that of permanent settlement. In 1947, some 15 percent of the population was urban; by the early 1970s the percentage had increased to 45. This trend towards urbanization is part of the historic process, but agricultural development since the 1930s and rapid industrial expansion since the 1950s have lent momentum to it.

Urban and industrial growth

The process of industrial growth has entailed alterations in the population's occupational structure, whereas large-scale movements have tended to accentuate local inequalities in the scope of social and economic development.

A number of urban areas have grown significantly, while a few rural areas have been consistently shrinking. By 1961 the total national urban population had increased 57 percent from 1951; two-thirds of that increase was accounted for by cities with a population of more than 100,000. Of the largest cities in Pakistan, Karāchi and Hyderābād are in Sind, and Sukkur grew to more than 100,000 in 1961.

Administration and social conditions. *The government.* The head of the province is the governor, who is appointed by the president of Pakistan. The province has an elected legislature called the Sind Assembly. The majority party, with the chief minister as the leader, forms the government. Until the early 1970s, Sind province consisted administratively of the three divisions of Karāchi, Hyderābād, and Khaipur, but was then divided into 11 districts, each of which is headed by a commissioner who is also a district magistrate. The districts are Karāchi (including the city of Karāchi), Hyderābād, Dādu, Sānghar, Thar Pārkar, Tatta (Thatta), Khairpur, Nawābshāh, Sukkur, Jacobābād, and Lārkāna. A district is divided into *taluka*s, each headed by a *mukhtiārkār*; a *taluka* is further divided into *tappa*s and a *tappa* into *deh*s, which are the smallest revenue units in the province. Law and order are maintained by an inspector general of police. For dispensation of justice and recruitment to government service, Sind and Baluchistan have a joint High Court and a joint Public Service Commission.

Health. The provincial government has a permanent department of health, which is responsible for the organization and expansion of health services administered through the Directorate of Health. Along with the modern allopathic system, which alone is public supported, the age-old indigenous *ṭibbī* (traditional) system is also widely practiced by private *ḥakīm*s (professional doctors of this system). Since 1947, medical facilities have been extended to all parts of the province. Besides a number of private hospitals and clinics, there are about 40 civil hospitals, more than 300 dispensaries, 75 rural health centres, two tuberculosis sanitariums, one epilepsy hospital, one mental hospital, and a dozen or so tuberculosis and dental clinics. In addition, there are child-health centres, midwifery and maternity services, mobile health units, and facilities for the training of nurses.

Health problems

Despite considerable progress, medical facilities remain inadequate, particularly in the rural areas. The problem of educating the general public to adopt preventive measures and seek timely medical advice needs to be tackled more effectively. The developmental health program of the early 1970s centred upon the provision of curative facilities, the prevention and control of epidemics, the checking of adulteration of food and drugs, the eradication of malaria, the control of smallpox, the strengthening of tuberculosis control projects, the extension of school health services, and the improvement of facilities for treatment in the medical colleges and their attached hospitals.

Education. The provincial department of education is responsible for policy and planning; except for the universities which are virtually autonomous, all educational institutions are under departmental control.

Primary school education is of five years duration, middle school of three years, and high school of two years. Primary schools have been extended to village areas, middle schools to bigger villages and small townships, high schools to the *taluka* towns, and colleges to the district headquarters. There are also teacher-training schools and technical, vocational, and commercial institutes. The institutions of higher education include colleges for secondary teacher training, for medicine, agriculture, and engineering, as well as the University of Karāchi in Karāchi, the University of Sind in Hyderābād, and an institute of education.

Welfare. Since the 1950s, welfare work has been organized and extended to a number of selected rural and urban areas through a system of community development projects. The program is administered by the provincial directorate of social welfare. Vocational training is one of the projects' significant activities, which are also designed to serve religious and recreational needs. Some special institutions, such as a socio-economic centre, a home for the destitute, and orphanages, have been established on a permanent basis.

The provincial Sind Family-Planning Board administers the family-planning program, which was started in six districts in 1965 and later expanded into all 11 districts. Some 600 clinics and 6,800 sales agents bring supplies and services within the reach of all, while family-planning workers, the lady health visitors, and other paramedical staff provide the necessary motivation and advice.

The Sind family-planning program

The Directorate of Labour Welfare maintains industrial relations conducive to higher productivity and promotes the welfare of all the workers employed in industrial establishments, factories, mines, docks, and other utilities by insuring their health and safety and improving their employment conditions. Employment exchange agencies and vocational guidance units render job-finding and job-placement services to the unemployed.

The Sind Employees' Social Security Institution, established in 1965, is an autonomous organization the governing body of which includes representatives of both employees and the government. It administers relief in the form of maternity, sickness, and injury benefits; total or partial disablement gratuities and pensions; and death grants and survivor's pensions. Nonmonetary benefits include medical care through social security dispensaries and polyclinics.

The economy. *Agriculture, fishing, and forestry.* The mainstay of Sind's economy is agriculture, and 38 percent of the provincial area is under cultivation. Production increased substantially after 1961 because of the advance in agricultural research and extension services, use of inorganic fertilizers, development of agricultural engineering, and construction of more than 1,000 miles of surface drains to counter the effects of waterlogging and salinity. Major crops include cotton, wheat, rice, sugarcane, corn (maize), millet, and oilseeds. Fruit orchards have been extended, and a substantial increase has been achieved in the production of mangoes and bananas. Fruit-bearing date palms are also important.

Livestock includes cattle, buffalo, sheep, goats, camels and poultry. The Red Sindhi and Tharee cows are the best dairy animals, and the Sakrai and Dia-ee are the best camel breeds for transport. The potential for animal husbandry for commercial production has not been fully exploited. The government maintains two livestock farms that are engaged primarily in experimentation and research. The Fourth Five-Year Plan for 1970–75 gives priority to the improvement of livestock, increased livestock products, and increased veterinary services.

With its 150 miles of coastline and hundreds of square miles of inshore backwaters, Sind has a high potential for marine fishing. The varieties found in abundance include prawns and shrimp, pomfrets, *palla* (shad), and *khagga* (catfish). The Indus and its deltaic branches, abandoned beds (*dhora*s) and irrigation canals, and the numerous freshwater lakes (*dhandh*s) constitute a rich reservoir for the breeding and production of freshwater fish, such as *kurirro* (*Cyprinus denticulatus*) and *thelhi* (*Catla buchanani*). About 1,700 acres have been developed on the Gudu Barrage for fish production.

Sind has more than 2,655,000 acres of forests managed by the Forest Department and the Agricultural Development Bank of Pakistan. The productive areas are exploited for both timber and firewood.

Mining and quarrying. The few known metallic minerals include celestite, laterite, and bauxite. Clays, gypsum, anhydrite (a mineral of calcium sulfate), limestone, chalk, dolomite (a mineral of calcium magnesium carbonate), silica sand, bentonite (a clay mineral), sulfur, flint, and lake salt all are available in large quantities. Coal, gas, and petroleum also occur. The resources exploited include coal, china clay, clay, chalk, fuller's earth, gravel, lake salt, limestone, and silica sand.

In 1970 about 89,000,000 tons of various petroleum products were produced in Sind, in excess of the provincial demand by about 2,000,000 tons. About 90 percent of the province's total energy was provided by oil and gas. In the early 1970s all of the transmission and distribution mains for the supply of gas were based on the Sūi gas field of Baluchistan.

Water and power development. The West Pakistan Water and Power Development Authority (WAPDA) was established to unify and coordinate the development of resources in Pakistan. The WAPDA's main water-development schemes in Sind are the Gudu Barrage, which irrigates 2,900,000 acres and a forest area of 223,000 acres; the Karachi Irrigation Project to irrigate 84,000 acres and supply water for industrial and domestic use; the North Rohri Fresh Groundwater Project, involving the construction and electrification of almost 1,270 tubewells; and the salinity control and reclamation projects in Khairpur, Lārkāna, and Shikārpur. The Gudu Barrage has been completed and handed over to the Irrigation Department and the Agricultural Development Bank.

The WAPDA power system, with a total installed capacity of 1,300,000 kilowatts, has four grids, two of which are in Sind. These are the Sukkur Thermal Grid Area, with a capacity of 25,000 kilowatts, which is to electrify Upper Sind, and the Hyderābād Thermal Grid Area in Lower Sind, with a capacity of 43,700 kilowatts.

The Kotri Gas Power Station, with an installed capacity of 42,250,000 kilowatts, has been linked with the Lower Sind Grid. The Gudu Steam Power Station was under construction in the early 1970s near Kashmor in Upper Sind; its plans called for two units of 110,000 kilowatts each for the first stage and one unit of 200,000 kilowatts for the second stage. The Water and Soil Investigation Division (WASID) of WAPDA also has four subprojects in Sind.

Industry. Sind is a highly industrialized area. It accounts for one-third of the entire cotton production of the country and contains almost half of the country's cotton textile mills. Four large cement factories turn out more than 60 percent of the country's cement production. The expanding sugar industry is expected to have a dozen large mills in operation by the mid-1970s.

Sind Industrial Trading Estates Ltd. has developed industrial Parks, or estates, at Karāchi, Kotri, Hyderābād, and Tando Ādam. Another project is planned at Sukkur. By 1970 the West Pakistan Industrial Development Corporation (WPIDC) had completed 15 industrial projects in Sind and was constructing four more. The corporation's Fourth Plan Program, for 1971 to 1975, called for investment in a machine tool factory, a chemicals and fertilizer complex, and a heavy electric complex.

The West Pakistan Small Industries Corporation (WPSIC) promotes cottage and other small industries. In Sind, WPSIC, established by the early 1970s, had 21 projects in the public sector, including two small-industry developments, or estates, four service centres, an artisans' workshop, a handicraft development centre, five handicraft sales centres, and an artisans' gallery.

Transport and communications. Communications are by road, rail, water, and, to a small extent, air. The network of roads of all types extends to more than 13,000 miles. Two highways traverse the province from south to north—the National Highway runs on the eastern bank of the Indus and leads to Multān and Lahore in the Punjab; and the Indus Highway, along the western bank

of the Indus, leads to Sibi and Quetta in Baluchistan. The 97-mile Karāchi–Hyderābād limited access highway was opened in 1970. Numerous feeder roads connect townships in the interior with the main roads.

The Pakistan Western Railway system starts at Karāchi and bifurcates at Kotri on the Indus into two main lines. The Hyderābād–Nawābshāh–Rohri line leads to Lahore, and the Kotri–Sehwān–Lārkāna–Jacobābād line leads to Quetta. A main-line connection from Hyderābād runs eastward through Mīrpur Khās to the Indian border at Khokhropār. There are also eight different link and loop sections extending to some 600 miles. In the city of Karāchi, the 19-mile Karāchi Circular Railway was completed and opened to passenger traffic in 1970.

The railway system

The Indus and some of its channels, particularly in the lower delta, have served as the main waterways since time immemorial. Country boats continue to ply the Indus, transporting grain, hay, timber, and firewood. Along the 150 miles of seacoast and the numerous creeks and abandoned mouths of the Indus, country boats and launches transport fish, grain, firewood, and other supplies.

Karāchi Airport maintains both domestic and international services. Within Sind, air services are in a preliminary stage of development. Hyderābād, 120 miles from Karāchi, is connected by flights from Karāchi en route to Quetta and Lahore. Special weekly services operate from Karāchi to Mohenjo-daro. The airstrip at Nawābshāh is subsidiary to Karāchi Airport; eventually, it and airstrips at Jacobābād and Sukkur will prove important centres for travel and commercial transport from north to south.

Cultural life. Separated from the rest of the subcontinent by a vast desert belt on the east, by ocean on the south, mountain ranges on the west, and a bottleneck of the Indus on the north, Sind long remained an isolated and self-contained region. With comparatively less borrowing from the outside, Sind has therefore stamped its arts and crafts, games and sports, music, and folklore with a typical originality. The continuity of the ancient artistic tradition is manifest today in superb pottery; in work with glazed tile, lacquer, leather, and straw; and in carpetmaking, needlework, embroidery, quilt making, the making of hand prints, and the designing of textiles.

Melas (fairs) and *malakhara*s (wrestling festivals) are the most popular recreation. *Malh* is the distinctive style of Sindhi wrestling, and the training of horses and camels to run in different styles is typical of Sindian riding and sport. Falconry is a time-honoured pastime. The method of catching the *palla* fish in the Indus by floating on an earthen pot is the distinctive technique of Sindhi fishermen. Bullock-cart racing and cockfighting are popular in some areas.

The music tradition in Sind goes back to early times. Its early professional minstrels, the Loras, carried Sindian music to ancient Iran, where it flourished as Luryan music; and the large variety of musical instruments confirms the existence of a long-standing musical tradition. The renowned poet Shāh ʿAbd-ul-Laṭīf of Bhit (died 1752) founded a new music tradition of *Shāh jō rāga* in which thematic music primarily based on popular themes was interpreted by folk melodies.

The literary tradition has been influenced by the region's history of disastrous floods and storms. The story of *Dodo-Chanēsar* is the theme of a great epic of the Sūmra period. *Mōmul-Rāno, Nūrī-Jām tamachi, Suhnī-Mehar, Līlan-Chanēsar,* and *Sassī Punnūn* are among the famous age-old romances of Sind. The story of *Umar-Mārūī* represents the lofty character of a village girl who prefers the company of her own simple people to the comforts of a king's palace and resists the temptation to leave her poor family to become a queen. The story of *Sōrath-Rai Daiāch* demonstrates the generosity of a munificent king and his love and appreciation of music, for which he lays down his life.

Traditional culture is greatly strained under the impact of modern development. It is mainly in the vast rural countryside and its more isolated areas where traditions have been perpetuated, although in a much diluted form. Unless sociocultural institutions attempt to preserve the traditional culture, it is likely to succumb to the growing

Water-development projects

Cultural
institu-
tions

impact of such developments as modern education and Westernization, agricultural development, industrialization, the extension of transport and communications, the use of mass communication, continued immigration, and urbanization.

The Sindhi Adabi (literary) board, functioning at Hyderābād, has published more than 200 works in Sindhi, Persian, Arabic, Urdu, and English, covering Sindhi language, literature, folklore, history, and lexicography. The Shāh 'Abd-ul-Laṭīf Cultural Centre at Bhit Shāh, 35 miles north of Hyderābād, has conducted research and published works on the life, music, and poetry of Shāh 'Abd-ul-Laṭīf. The preliminary development of the Sind-Provincial Museum and Library, both located at Hyderābād, was completed by the early 1970s. The Mehran Arts Council at Hyderābād is concerned with the development of the fine arts, crafts, and general culture and has published useful monographs on the traditional arts and crafts, early musical tradition, and musical instruments of Sind.

Karāchi is the stronghold of the national press, publishing half a dozen widely circulated dailies in either English or Urdu. The interior of the province is served mainly by a local press, which includes four widely circulated dailies. Radio stations at Karāchi and Hyderābād broadcast national and provincial programs in Sindhi, Urdu, and English.

BIBLIOGRAPHY. SIR MORTIMER WHEELER, *The Indus Civilization*, 3rd ed. (1968); and F.A. KHAN, *The Indus Valley and Early Iran* (1964), are among the more recent works that deal with the beginning, development, and external relationships of the Indus Valley civilization. H.T. LAMBRICK, *Sind: A General Introduction* (1964), details the ancient history, though the more significant contribution lies in his delineation of the characteristic features of physical geography; MANECK PITHAWALLA, *A Physical and Economic Geography of Sind, the Lower Indus Basin* (1959), gives greater details of physiography, geology, hydrography of the Indus, climatic conditions, vegetation and animal life. H.M. ELLIOT and J. DOWSON, *The History of India As Told by Its Own Historians*, vol. 1 (1867), provides in English translation the more significant but copious extracts from the native histories in Persian and other sources. M.R. HAIG, *The Indus Delta Country* (1894), is a scholarly monograph that remains unsurpassed in its discussion of the changing courses of the Indus, particularly in the lower deltaic region. R.F. BURTON, *Sindh, and the Races That Inhabit the Valley of the Indus* (1851), contains general information on the ethnology and sociocultural conditions in Sind in the mid-19th century; while S.S. ANSARI, *Musalman Races Found in Sind* (1901), gives in alphabetical order a brief account (sometimes based on hearsay) of the different Muslim groups, communities, tribes, and racial stocks of Sind. H.T. SORELY, *Shah Abdul Latif of Bhit* (1940, reprinted 1966), in dealing with the poetry and biography of the renowned poet, Shāh 'Abd-ul-Laṭīf, presents a study of the literary, social and economic conditions in 18th-century Sind. The *Sindhi Folklore Project* of the Sindhi Abadi Board, Hyderābād, Sind, directed by N.A. BALOCH (1958–), is an extensive study and documentation of Sindhi folklore. N.A. BALOCH, *Traditional Arts and Crafts of Hyderabad Region* (1966); and *Musical Instruments of the Lower Indus Valley of Sind* (1966), are elementary brochures in English on these subjects. The *Census of Pakistan, 1961* (General Report, and the Sind District Volumes); H.T. SORELY, *The Gazetteer of West Pakistan: The Former Provinces of Sind, Including Khaifur State* (1968); and the *Sind Annual*, provide the latest information and statistical data on administrative and developmental aspects.

(N.A.B.)

Singapore

The Republic of Singapore is a city-state situated at the southern tip of the Malay Peninsula, about 85 miles (137 kilometres) north of the Equator. It consists of Singapore Island, which is diamond-shaped and 210 square miles (544 square kilometres) in extent, and 50 other islets, only half of which are inhabited, which make up another 16 square miles (42 square kilometres). To the north the main island is separated from West Malaysia by Johor Strait, a narrow channel crossed by a road and rail causeway more than half a mile long. The southern limits of the state run through Singapore Strait where outliers of the Riau-Lingga Archipelago, which forms a part of

Indonesia, extend to within ten miles (16 kilometres) of the main island. Singapore has a population of about 2,100,000, of which three-quarters are Chinese.

The largest port in Southeast Asia, and the fourth largest port in the world, Singapore owes its growth and prosperity to its focal position at the southern extremity of the Malay Peninsula, dominating the Strait of Malacca that leads from the Indian Ocean to the South China Sea. Once a British colony, and now a member of the Commonwealth of Nations, Singapore joined the federation of Malaysia on its formation in 1963. When friction subsequently developed between the Malay-dominated central government and the Chinese-dominated Singapore administration, Singapore accepted Malaysia's invitation to leave the federation and become an independent state, which it did on August 9, 1965.

Size and
regional
importance

Since 1965, despite a large and rapidly growing population concentrated on a minute geographical base, Singapore has reduced its birth rate, rehoused many of its people, initiated a program of industrial expansion, and raised national income to the highest per capita level of any Southeast Asian nation. Singapore was formerly the principal British naval and air base in Asia, but its strategic role lately has been eroded by developments in nuclear warfare, as well as by the withdrawal of British power from Asia (for coverage of an associated physical feature, see MALACCA, STRAIT OF; for coverage of historical aspects, see MALAYA, HISTORY OF).

The natural environment. Nearly two-thirds of the main island is less than 50 feet (15 metres) in altitude. Bukit Timah, the highest summit, is only 581 feet high (177 metres); with other peaks, such as Bukit Panjang and Bukit Mandai, it forms a block of rugged terrain in the centre of the island. To the west and south are lower scarps with marked northwest-southwest trends, such as Bukit Faber Ridge. The eastern part of the island is a low plateau cut by erosion into an intricate pattern of hills and valleys. These physical units reflect their geological foundations: the central hills are formed from granitic rocks, the scarplands from highly folded and faulted sedimentary rocks, and the eastern plateau from uncompacted sands and gravels. A dense network of short streams drains the island, but floods are locally severe, owing to low gradients and to excessive runoff of water from cleared land. Many streams, especially those draining northwards, have broad, mangrove-fringed estuaries that extend far inland.

None of the soils is even reasonably fertile, but those derived from the granites tend to be better than most. Soils developed from the sedimentary rocks are variable, but many contain hard pans (compacted layers) that restrict plant roots and impede soil drainage. The soils of eastern Singapore are extremely infertile. All have suffered extensive degradation (loss of material through erosion) as a result of generations of careless exploitation.

Singapore, being in an equatorial region, experiences uniformly high temperatures throughout the year, with the mean monthly average varying from about 81° F (27° C) in June to 77° F (25° C) in January. The daily range is much greater, averaging 12° F (7° C), but the maritime location and constant humidity keep maximum temperatures relatively modest: the highest temperature ever recorded was only 95° F (35° C). As temperatures are so uniform, the incidence of rainfall defines the seasons; rainfall in turn depends on air-mass movements, which are affected by the presence of the Asian and Australian land masses. Between December and March, for example, the northeast trade winds that blow at that season are reinforced by outflows of surface air from Asia, bringing the strongest winds and heaviest precipitation of the year; rainfall averages over ten inches a month in both December and January. From May to September surface winds from the southern hemisphere are strengthened by the Australian high pressure belt and reach the Singapore-Malaya region. Winds are generally light during this season, however, and rainfall drops to around six inches in June and July. From April to May and from October to November sluggish air movements are common, and intense afternoon showers bring monthly rainfall averages

Climate

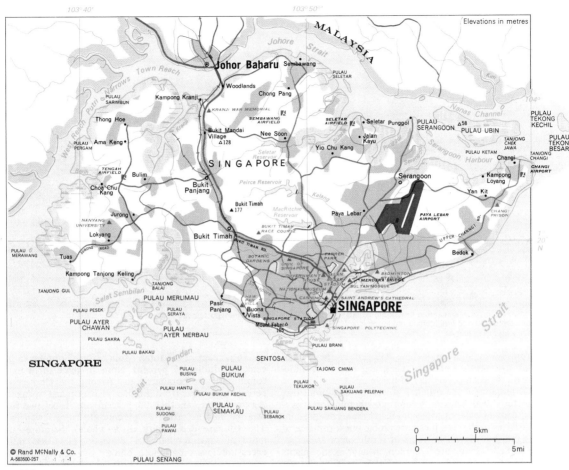

Elevations in metres

© Rand McNally & Co.
A-563500-257

Downtown Singapore seen across one of the canals. Barges in the foreground transport goods between the docks and freighters in the harbour.
Sven Gillsater—Tiofoto Bildbyra

of from seven and ten inches. Altogether, the annual rainfall averages about 100 inches, and rain falls somewhere on the island every day of the year.

Little remains of the original vegetation or animal life, except for 4,000 acres of second growth rain forest preserved around catchment areas. Some mangrove vegetation survives in the Kranji estuary on the northwest side of the island, but elsewhere tracts of scrub, or of *Imperata* grass called lalang, are common. Many exotic plants have been introduced for ornamental use. The largest native animals are the long-tailed macaque (an Asian species of monkey), the slow loris (a large-eyed tailless nocturnal lemur), and the scaly anteater. Birds are numerous, especially those, such as the Indian mynah bird, the brahminy kite (a kite with reddish-brown plumage and a white head and breast), and the house swallow, which have adapted to a symbiotic relationship with man. Reptiles, such as cobras and lizards, are also common. Fringing coral reefs with their associated fish and wildlife occur around many parts of the coast.

Human settlement. The city of Singapore stands on the southern part of the main island. Urbanization has reduced differences between city and country. Today built-up areas cover ·50 square miles (128 square kilometres), or 24 percent of the main island. In the older parts of the city (along Singapore River, in the Rochore-Kallang floodplain, and in the low hills behind the harbour), rows of narrow-fronted Chinese shops, with their upper floors subdivided into living cubicles, line the streets. Similar shops stand along the main roads that radiate from the city. Behind their facades lie extensive suburbs composed partly of bungalows, semi-detached residences, and apartments, and partly of rural types of dwellings, such as wooden huts roofed with *atap* (thatch made from the *Nypa* species of palm tree) or corrugated iron. Such huts are common in all the rural districts, and in squatter settlements in the city. The traditional Malay *kampong*s (villages built on stilts) are seldom seen, except in fishing villages on some of the smaller islands.

The port of Singapore occupies the southern coast of the main island south of the Singapore River. It consists of two partly sheltered areas of water—the Eastern Roads, which are subdivided by an offshore breakwater, and the Western Roads. The two roadsteads are connected by the deepwater channel of Keppel Harbour, with its miles of berths, docks, warehouses, and other facilities, which runs between the main island and islands to the south. A few miles further west is the new port, Jurong.

People and population. As a result of past immigration, the population is diverse. Chinese predominate, form-ing 76 percent of the total. Malays form another 15 percent, and Indians 7 percent. None of these three major communities is homogeneous. Among the Chinese, 40 percent originate from Fukien province and speak the Amoy dialect; another 23 percent are Teochews from Swatow, and a further 19 percent are from Kwangtung. The Chinese community as a whole, therefore, uses mutually incomprehensible dialects. Linguistic differences are less pronounced among the Malays, but the group includes Indonesians speaking Javanese, Boyanese, and other dialects. The Indian group is most diverse, consisting of Tamils (60 percent), Malayalis, and Sikhs; it is also considered to include the Pakistani and Sinhalese communities.

Because of this diversity, no fewer than four official languages are recognized—English, Mandarin, Malay, and Tamil. English remains the main medium for administration, commerce, and industry; nearly 60 percent of all schoolchildren attend English-language schools. Mandarin, the national language of China, transcends dialect barriers; one-third of the school population is taught in that language. Malay, like English, is widely used for interracial communication and plays an especially useful role in view of the close ties between Singapore and Malaysia.

Official languages

Religious affiliations reflect ethnic patterns. Over 70 percent of all Chinese profess some degree of attachment to Confucianism, Buddhism, or Taoism, or to some combination thereof. Virtually all Malays, and some Indians, adhere to Islām, which is the formal religion of about 16 percent of the population. The remaining population is either Christian or Hindu.

In 1970 there were 2,075,000 people in Singapore, and from immigration and natural increase combined, the population had been growing for many decades at the rapid rate of 3 percent a year. As a result, the proportion of young people to those of employable age is higher than it is among the advanced industrial nations. Since 1958 annual growth rates have, however, fallen dramatically. In 1970 the birthrate was 22 per 1,000, and the death rate was 5 per 1,000, resulting in a rate of natural increase of 17 per 1,000. With the ending of large-scale immigration after World War II, the sex ratio among the population has become more balanced, with 1,049 males per 1,000 females.

In the state as a whole, the density of population averages about 9,400 per square mile, but a more revealing statistic shows that 1,700,000 people, or 85 percent of the total population, live on 28 square miles. Of these, 750,-000 occupy multistoried apartments that cover a mere 2.2 square miles. By contrast, rural areas of Singapore have densities of between only 1,900 and 2,700 per square mile. The most crowded areas are still the older parts of the city, where densities of more than 110,000 per square mile were recorded in 1966. In new housing developments, such as those at Queenstown and Toa Payoh, densities of 65,000 per square mile are normal.

Singapore, Area and Population				
	area		population	
	sq mi	sq km	1957 census†	1970 census†
Administrative areas*				
Bukit Panjang	35.6	92.2	62,000	107,000
City	37.6	97.4	912,000	1,247,000
Jurong	60.1	155.7	51,000	104,000
Katong	42.3	109.6	199,000	305,000
Serangoon	47.3	122.5	208,000	298,000
Southern Islands	3.5	9.1	14,000	13,000
Total Singapore	226.4	586.4	1,446,000‡	2,075,000‡

*These areas have no administrative function (the government of Singapore is unitary); they provide a useful geographical breakdown of the population. †Excluding residents abroad, numbering 27,299 in 1957 and 47,959 in 1970; also excluding transients afloat, numbering 3,466 in 1957 and 4,565 in 1970. ‡Figures do not add to total given because of rounding.
Source: Official government figures.

The economy. With an urban population engaged largely in trade, finance, and industry, Singapore's economy differs markedly from that of most Southeast Asian countries, which are primarily based on the production of raw materials. In 1970 the per capita gross national product was about Sing$2,682—more than twice that of Malaysia or the Philippines, but only about 60 percent of that of Japan. The monetary unit is the Singapore dollar (Sing$3.06 equalled $1.00U.S.; Sing$7.35 equalled £1 sterling on December 1, 1970).

Resources. The state has few natural resources, apart from small amounts of brick clays, rock aggregates, and building sand. The natural vegetation provides only firewood and a few poles. Local catchment areas are small, obliging Singapore to use water from Johor state in West Malaysia. The low-lying relief does not permit hydroelectric development, so that energy has to be generated from imported fuels.

Sources of national income. In 1970, about 55 square miles (140 square kilometres), or nearly a quarter of the total area, was devoted to agriculture. Although more than half the agricultural acreage is used for the cultivation of rubber and coconuts, most of the 20,000 registered farms produce vegetables, fruit, and livestock for local markets. Over 40,000 tons of fresh vegetables, representing half the total demand, were produced in 1970. Singapore is self-sufficient in pig, poultry, and egg production. Some 14,300 tons of marine fish were caught in local waters, and supplies are augmented by fish raised in freshwater ponds on farms. Total fish production nevertheless accounts for only one-quarter of total consumption. The joint contribution of agriculture and fishing to the gross domestic product fell from about 6 percent in 1961 to under 3 percent in 1970.

The manufacturing sector, on the other hand, has expanded rapidly and now forms nearly one-fifth of the total gross domestic product—a proportion nearly equal to that of the entrepôt trade. In 1971 there were nearly 1,880 industrial establishments with a combined work force of 148,587. Manufacturing plants produce transport equipment and petroleum products, and process food. The ship-repairing and ship-building industry is growing rapidly. In 1970 four power stations with a total generating capacity of 644 megawatts, producing a total of 2,220,000,000 kilowatt-hours, met industrial and domestic needs. The other major energy source was coal gas, of which about 1,600,000,000 cubic feet was used in 1969.

Financial services are available both from modern banks and insurance companies, and from traditional thrift societies and money lenders. In 1970 there were 37 commercial banks with combined assets of more than Sing$5,000,000,000. Almost two-thirds of all bank credit

was advanced for general commerce and trade, but the proportion devoted to industry is growing, with encouragement from such official bodies as the Development Bank of Singapore. Other sources of finance include finance companies, building societies, insurance firms, and co-operatives. A stock exchange handled Sing$1,100,000,000 worth of securities in 1969. Commodity markets, especially for rubber, pepper, and tin, form an important element in the economy.

The total value of foreign trade in 1971 was Sing$14,000,000,000, representing one-third of the total gross domestic product. Singapore continues to perform its traditional entrepôt function of shipping raw materials from the region in exchange for finished products from the industrial nations. Malaysia, the U.S., the United Kingdom, China, and South Vietnam are—after Japan—Singapore's principal trading partners. Rubber and petroleum together account for 28 percent of the value of all trade. Crude rubber, imported from West Malaysia and Indonesia, is shipped to Japan, the U.S., China, the Soviet Union, and Britain. Petroleum from the Middle East is refined in Singapore, and the resulting fuel oils, diesel oils, gasoline, and other products are exported to South Vietnam, Thailand, Japan, and Hong Kong. Other significant items in foreign trade include timber, spices, and rice. The export of machinery, vehicles, and textiles is also increasing.

Management of the economy. The economy of Singapore is basically of the free-enterprise type. The private sector therefore has an essential role, and is expected to generate the increased productivity necessary for progress. At the same time the government is strongly committed to developmental goals, and its influence is pervasive.

In 1970 investment by the private sector amounted to Sing$978,000,000, or about 70 percent of gross capital formation, while government development expenditure totalled Sing$425,000,000, or about 30 percent.

The main sources of government revenue are excise duties (mainly on liquor, tobacco, motor vehicles, and petroleum products) and income tax (mostly from companies). Tax relief may be granted to new manufacturing and export enterprises; to encourage the entrepôt trade, free trade zones have been established. Revenue from all sources amounted to about Sing$1,307,200,000 in 1971, while total expenditure amounted to about Sing$1,942,800,000 resulting in a deficit. Overseas assets, however, totalled almost Sing$4,400,000,000, of which government surpluses amounted to nearly Sing$990,000,000.

About 25 percent of all workers are trade unionists. Most of those employed in the public sector and most employees of the larger, foreign-directed firms are unionized. There are 156 separate unions, led by the National Trades Union Congress, whose main objectives are to secure welfare benefits for workers by established procedures. The government regulates collective bargaining and compulsory arbitration, and it also provides a wide range of services, including training courses and a workers' superannuation scheme. Organized management is represented by two bodies, and there are, in addition to these, chambers of commerce representing different ethnic groups.

The country's limited area, a rapid population growth, and a weakening entrepôt role have virtually obliged Singapore to develop its manufacturing industries. Between 1961 and 1971, the number of manufacturing establishments rose by 235 percent from 560 to 1,880, the number of workers rose by 438 percent from 27,600 to 148,600, and the value of total manufacturing output rose in value by 832 percent from Sing$518,000,000 to Sing$4,310,000,000. Despite these advances, the economy still depends on external factors over which the state has no control, such as fluctuations in the price of rubber on the world market. The internal problem of providing full employment for an expanding population has yet to be solved; the work force of 444,000 in 1970 represented only 39 percent of the population of working age; *i.e.,* those between the ages of 15 and 59. In the industrial sector productivity per worker has grown more slowly than total output, and the cost of capital investment in manu-

Margin notes:
Agricultural production

Sources of revenue

Employment

facturing has risen from about Sing$4,800 per worker in 1961 to Sing$12,700 per worker in 1969.

Transportation. As the fourth largest port in the world, Singapore is a major transportation nucleus. In 1971, it handled nearly 38,000 vessels and 48,000,000 tons of cargo. Roughly one-half of all ships were engaged in the coastal and interisland trade conducted between Singapore and Indonesia, but the extent of this barter trade is poorly documented. Seaborne passenger movements declined in 1968 owing to competition from air transport and the continued closure of the Suez Canal. Railroads with a one-metre gauge connect Singapore with West Malaysia. There are over 1,200 miles of motorable roads used by more than 313,000 motor vehicles. More than 20 international and pan-Malaysian airlines use Paya Lebar Airport, which handled over 1,600,000 passengers and 25,700 metric tons of freight in 1971.

Administration and social conditions. Singapore is a parliamentary democracy based on the Westminster model. The government consists of a head of state, a president with nominal powers, and a fully elected, unicameral Parliament of 58 members. The electorate includes every adult citizen who is a registered voter, and voting is compulsory. The parliamentary majority selects the prime minister and cabinet from its own ranks. Since 1959 the government has been virtually synonymous with the Peoples' Action Party, led by Prime Minister Lee Kuan Yew. After three successive elections, the party now holds all the parliamentary seats. In each constituency there is a Citizens' Consultative Committee, designed to act as a link between government and people. Each committee explains official policies and transmits demands or grievances to the government. Similar exchanges are conducted with organized labour, which has six seats in Parliament.

Close liaison is maintained between the political and administrative arms of government. The administrative structure comprises various ministries and statutory boards. These are staffed by some 65,000 civil servants whose technical competence and integrity are monitored by a Public Service Commission, an independent body responsible for controlling standards, appointments, and discipline. A similar body maintains the status and assures the independence of the judiciary. Justice is administered by the Supreme Court and by courts of minor jurisdiction such as magistrates' and criminal district courts. Appeals can be made from the lower to the higher courts, with final appeal to the judicial committee of the Privy Council in London. Legal assistance in civil actions is available for the poor. The Shariah Court has jurisdiction in matters of Islāmic law.

Defense. The armed forces of Singapore consist of six infantry battalions with supporting artillery, armour, engineer, and signal units. The training of fighter pilots and of personnel for local missile defenses began recently. There is also a flotilla of fast naval patrol boats. Military conscription for 18-year-olds was introduced in 1967. Those not selected for the statutory two-year period of service with the regular forces are obliged to serve on a part-time basis with either the Peoples' Defence Force, the Special Constabulary, or the Vigilante Corps (a paramilitary force largely made up of youths).

Education

Social conditions. Primary education in any one of the four official languages is free for children of Singapore citizens, but the learning of a second language is compulsory. Secondary education is available in technical, commercial, and academic subjects; courses are combined to prevent premature specialization. In 1970 there were more than 500 schools at which more than 500,000 children were enrolled. Existing school facilities are sufficient to meet anticipated future demands. There are also three technical institutes with a combined enrollment of 4,000 students. The University of Singapore and Nanyang University provide academic and professional courses to postgraduate levels. There are separate institutes to train teachers, nurses, radiographers, and seamen; over 80 centres offer adult education. Total government expenditure on education in 1971 was more than Sing$196,000,-000, or roughly Sing$392 per student.

The range and quality of medical services is notably high, with one doctor for every 1,500 persons, and one dentist for every 5,300 persons. Government and private hospitals provide a ratio of about four hospital beds for every 1,000 people; nonhospital care is dispensed from numerous out-patient clinics and mobile centres. Official campaigns to keep Singapore clean are conducted periodically. Singapore's most significant achievement is in family planning, a distinction that it shares with few other nations; it resulted in a drop in the birthrate from 32 per 1,000 in 1964 to 22 in 1970.

Medical services

A housing and development board, established by the government, is responsible for building homes for families with low incomes. By the early 1970s it had completed nearly 144,000 home units, most of which are in high-rise apartment buildings, grouped into neighbourhood units, each with its own school, parking lot, community centre, and social facilities. All together, official programs housed over 650,000 people, or nearly one-third of the total population, in the 1960s alone. With more than 1,000 housing units being built each month, the severe housing shortages of the fifties have now been overcome. Nearly a quarter of all government apartments built have been sold to individual families. More than 16,000 residential units have been privately built since 1961, mostly in the suburbs.

The police force comprises 6,000 regulars and 9,000 members of the Special Constabulary. The force patrols the islands by land and water in order to maintain internal security. Traffic management, crime prevention, and political subversion are also matters under police jurisdiction. A police academy trains recruits and serving personnel.

The average weekly wage is about Sing$46.00; male earnings are twice those of females. The working week ranges from about 45 hours for workers in commercial and service occupations, to 48 hours for construction workers. Since 1960 the consumer price index has risen by slightly more than 11 percent; food, which represents half of all consumer expenditure, has risen by 12 percent, as has the cost of housing.

Health conditions in Singapore compare favourably with those of the advanced nations. Life expectancy for all races and sexes is over 68 years; infant mortality is only 21 per 1,000 live births, and infectious diseases are of negligible significance. With the reduction in communicable diseases, cardiovascular diseases and malignant neoplasms account for an increased proportion of deaths. The government and voluntary associations, headed by the Council of Social Service, provide welfare services for the aged, sick, and unemployed. Welfare grants totalling Sing$3,500,000 were paid in 1970.

Divided into ethnic groups, society is stratified by income and education. Income tax records show that there are only about 92,000 taxpayers, who form only 8 percent of the population of working age, or 23 percent of the work force. Of these, nearly half have assessable incomes below Sing$6,000 a year, 32 percent have incomes of from Sing$6,000 to Sing$10,000, and 12 percent have incomes of from Sing$10,000 to Sing$12,000. In education, about one-quarter of all persons aged ten and above have had no education at all, and just over 30 percent have had only a primary education. Current educational levels, however, compare favourably with those of most other nations, with attendance rates of from 80 to 85 percent for children aged six to 14, 40 to 45 percent for those aged 15 to 19, and about 5 percent for those aged 20 to 24.

Income levels

Cultural activities. As might be expected, cultural activities in Singapore are largely derivative, springing from one or another of the major civilizations of China, India, Indonesia, or the West. Traditional Chinese and Indian music, painting, and drama are actively practiced by numerous cultural societies and professional groups. Popular culture, based on modern mass media of communication, is far more widespread. Malay music, which has adopted the rhythms of Western orchestras, has a general appeal. Musical films that popularize Hindustani and Tamil songs have a considerable following. Films from Hong Kong, Taiwan, and the United States attract multiracial audiences, with attendances averaging 600,-000 per week. Several Chinese, English, Indian, and Malay newspapers with a total daily circulation of over 400,000 copies serve a largely literate population. Magazines published in the West, Hong Kong, and Japan have wide appeal. Broadcasting is a government monopoly; radio programs in English, Chinese, Malay, and Tamil are transmitted daily on three separate channels. There are also two television channels.

Prospects for the future. Among developing nations, Singapore has an outstanding record of progress. The success it has so far achieved is largely due to the realism shown by government and people alike. Recognizing problems, yet capitalizing on advantages, they have initiated a determined program to make the small state more viable. While it is perhaps too early to judge whether Singapore can ultimately survive as an independent entity, its achievements in its first years of independence augur well for the future.

BIBLIOGRAPHY

General works: E.H.G. DOBBY, "Singapore, Town and Country," *Geogrl. Rev.,* 30:84–109 (1940); OOI JIN-BEE and CHIANG HAI DING (eds.), *Modern Singapore* (1969). Current information may be found in the (Singapore) *Monthly Digest of Statistics,* the *Singapore Year Book,* and the *Yearbook of Statistics.*

Environment: R. HO, "The Physical and Human Background," in *Impact of Man on Humid Tropics Vegetation* (1960); S. NIEUWOLT, "Uniformity and Variation in an Equatorial Climate," *J. Trop. Geogr.,* 27:23–39 (1968); I.E.M. WATTS, "Rainfall of Singapore Island," *Malay. J. Trop. Geogr.,* 7:1–68 (1955).

People: W. NEVILLE, "The Areal Distribution of Population in Singapore," *J. Trop. Geogr.,* 20:16–25 (1965); YOU POH-SENG, "The Population of Singapore, 1966," *Malay. Econ. Rev.,* 12:59–96 (1967).

Economy: C.T. EDWARDS, *Public Finances in Malaya and Singapore* (1970); FIRST NATIONAL CITY BANK, *Singapore: Foreign Investment Guide* (1969); GOH KENG SWEE, *Decade of Achievement* (1970); H. HUGHES and YOU POH-SENG, *Foreign Investment and Industrialization in Singapore* (1969).

Government and politics: A. JOSEY, *Lee Kuan Yew and the Commonwealth* (1969); TAE YUL NAM, "Singapore's One-Party System," *Pacif. Affairs,* 42:465–480 (1969–70).

Social services and conditions: M. FREEDMAN and M. TOPLEY, "Religion and Social Realignment among the Chinese in Singapore," *J. Asian Stud.,* 21:3–23 (1961); C. GAMBA, "Some Social Problems in Singapore," *Aust. Q.,* 26:99–106 (1954); B.B. KAYE, *Upper Nankin Street, Singapore: A Sociological Study of Chinese Households Living in a Densely Populated Area* (1966); SINGAPORE HOUSING AND DEVELOPMENT BOARD, *Annual Report.*

(Rt.H.)

Singing

In recitation and declamation, as in singing, the voice is sustained beyond the requirements of speech. But in song, the voice is sustained at greater length than in the others, and its sound distributed over a wider range of pitch.

Every individual normally has in his throat at birth a reed instrument, the two vocal cords in his larynx, which, with his breath, and assisted by the areas of the sinuses, mouth, and other areas of the throat, neck, and head that serve as resonance chambers (*i.e.,* vibrating with the voice's sound, enhancing it, and increasing its volume), produce rudimentary music when he speaks. Physiologically, what distinguishes singing from speaking is the manner in which the breath is expended to vibrate the vocal cords. Singing requires more breath, and ever more breath the louder, higher, and longer one sings. It also requires that the emission of breath be more firmly controlled. A pertinent analogy is the function of the instrumentalist's breath in playing a reed instrument—*e.g.,* a clarinet, an oboe, or a saxophone.

A further distinction between singing and speaking is the control required, in singing, of the movement and reflexes of the larynx. As one sings higher, the larynx tends to rise sympathetically and at a certain point becomes an interference causing the voice to break, or crack. Not much movement of the larynx occurs within a singer's normal range, usually about an octave and a third. Beyond that,

Song and speech (margin note)

either above or below, an element of technical accomplishment sets the professional off from the unschooled amateur.

WESTERN ART SINGING

Western art singing is distinguished most strikingly by its volume. Singers of other cultures may have a wider range, particularly a greater upward extension; but it is doubtful that they have sung, or have been inclined or encouraged to sing, louder. And in Western singing, singers once sang even higher than they do today. Such ranges were acquired only at the expense of the large, ample, resonant tone which the requirements and conventions of opera have rendered fashionable, even indispensable, in Western music.

Related to concern for volume and range is a concern with pure sound, with the tone quality, or timbre, and with colour, with what is felt to be the sheer beauty or majesty of the voice itself. Both singers and their listeners, in Western music more than any other, have tended to lose sight of song's roots in language and to think of singing as a purely instrumental production. This has occurred at various critical junctures in the history of Western singing and has invariably precipitated a reaction in favour of a more linguistic approach to song and singing.

The bel canto era. *Aesthetic reorientation.* It is with one of these crises that the history of Western singing, in terms familiar to a contemporary audience, began in Italy, in the first decade of the 17th century, when the elaborate contrapuntal (based on interwoven melodies) vocal forms of the late Renaissance were felt to have reached such a peak of complexity that the words no longer mattered. A reaction was led by the Camerata, a circle of Florentine intellectuals who sought to recover the monodic technique (melody supported by expressive harmonies) they believed to have been employed in classical Greek drama, and the result was opera. Western singing ever since then, whether operatic or not, has reflected in its objectives, techniques, and criteria the trends and exigencies of operatic fashion and vocal production.

Little is known about Western singing prior to that time. Musicologists know what the troubadours and the German minnesingers (noble medieval poet-composers) sang, but they do not know exactly what kind of sound they made while singing. The same is true of singing in the medieval church. It may be said, however, that from multiple-voiced singing, cultivated in Europe as in no other civilization, both in church and out, evolved the devices of melodic ornamentation found in later monodic styles and the traditional voice categories of soprano, alto, tenor, and bass.

Early singing styles (margin note)

The most decisively influential figure in the crisis referred to above was the composer Giulio Caccini. Rebelling against the artificiality of the multiple-voiced music of his time and particularly against the want of any expressive relationship between text and melodic contour, he devised a style of solo singing, essentially recitative in character, over an instrumental accompaniment, in which the florid conventions of multiple-voiced song were harnessed to prosody and to the expression of the appropriate emotions. The style he inaugurated was brought to an early maturity in the operas of Claudio Monteverdi.

Caccini's objectives, laid down in a discourse, *Le nuove musiche,* in 1602, and refined and elaborated a century later by Pier Francesco Tosi in his *Observations on the Florid Song* (1723), may be summarized as a mellifluous kind of singing aimed at an agreeable, well-rounded tone, an even scale from bottom to top, a nicety of intonation, an eloquence of phrase and cadence, a purity of vowels, a mastery of the devices of ornamentation and embellishment, invention and taste in improvisation, and a disciplined avoidance of shouting, nasality, harsh or open sounds, disjointed registers, undue vehemence, and other evidence of vulgarity or negligent schooling. These became the precepts of a school of singing now referred to as bel canto, or "beautiful song."

The work of Giulio Caccini (margin note)

Role of the castrati. The foremost early exponents of this kind of singing, and those whose example established the criteria of Western singing that have prevailed with some modifications to the present, were castrated males known as castrati, or *evirati* ("emasculated"). By fateful coincidence, castrati were introduced into the churches of Italy, and subsequently elsewhere, at about the same time that the reforms signallized by Caccini were beginning to take hold in the Italian musical theatre. The castrati, too, were a reflection of the excessive complexity of late Renaissance multiple-voiced song. Women's voices were barred from the Roman Catholic Church in obedience to St. Paul's injunction "Let your women keep silence in the churches." By the end of the 16th century, church music had become so exacting that a boy was approaching vocal mutation by the time he had developed the requisite skills. Male falsetto voices proved unsatisfactory, and castration, never condoned by church or civil authority, but accepted once performed, provided the solution.

Women were also excluded from the theatre in many centres of Catholic Europe; and, by the middle of the 17th century, castrati, playing both male and female roles, were making notable careers in opera. The greatest of them dominated Italian opera throughout most of the 18th century, and a few survived in the theatre into the first three decades of the 19th. They survived in the church even longer, and the last of them, Alessandro Moreschi, who died in 1922, was director of music at the Sistine Chapel until his retirement in 1913 and made phonograph records shortly after the turn of the century.

Prominence of castrati in opera

The significant fact of a castrato's life was that it could have no satisfactory fulfillment other than singing. He would have begun his studies at the age of six or seven and would have proved to be an exceptional choirboy; otherwise, he would not have been castrated. His studies would be continued in the most rigorous manner for another four or five years. He would have developed an extraordinary chest expansion, an exemplary use of the diaphragm to support and control the emission of breath, an agile and supple throat, great virtuosity and imagination in vocal display and ornamentation, and, in a majority of cases, a notable degree of personal vanity.

And it was vanity, among prima donnas as well as castrati, that brought on the next crisis in Western singing. The virtues of textual expression so prized by Caccini and Tosi, gave way, toward the middle of the 18th century, to extravagant and competitive vocal athleticism. Words, and music, too, were lost in an orgy of exhibitionistic vocal self-indulgence. Gluck's opera *Orfeo ed Euridice* (1762) was an early symptom of reaction in favour of a simpler kind of singing and fidelity to music, drama, and text. In a manifesto accompanying his *Alceste*, in 1767, Gluck emphasized music's—and the singer's—subservience to the concerns of drama; and in the operas he composed for Paris between 1774 and 1779, he perfected the practice of his preaching.

Modification of the bel canto tradition. Vocal vainglory was not extinguished. But it began to be tempered both by the requirements and the character of opera as it evolved after Gluck in the late-18th- and early-19th-century masterpieces of Mozart, Beethoven, Rossini, Donizetti, and Vincenzo Bellini. The new operas tended to favour the exigencies of drama over the specialties and convenience of the singers; and the singers had to substitute real acting for the conventional posturing of earlier opera. The unmutilated male, who had heretofore taken second place to castrati and prima donnas, now came into his own; and tenors and basses began to rival female sopranos and contraltos for top billing and top fees.

Prominence of the orchestra in the 19th century

Theatres were becoming larger, and so was the opera orchestra, reflecting the evolution of symphonic forms in Austria and Germany, and assuming a dramatic function rather than serving merely as an accompanist. The size and assertiveness of the orchestra became critical—and decisive—toward the mid-19th century in the operas of Giacomo Meyerbeer, Verdi, and Wagner. Especially in the later music dramas of Wagner, sheer weight of orchestral sound forced the singer to unprecedented vocal exertions. With Verdi it was the vehemence of dramatic utterance rather than the presumptions of the orchestra that called for louder and more emphatic singing than

would have been thought seemly in the age of bel canto. But the orchestra, too, was a factor, mitigating against a perpetuation of the florid traditions of European singing. Singers found it difficult, if not impossible, to be at once forceful and elegant. Nor were they encouraged to try. A strong reaction had set in, especially in Germany, against vocal improvisation and embellishment of any kind. What had seemed the ultimate in vocal virtue and accomplishment from the 17th to well into the 19th century was now anathematized as presumptuous and impudent frippery.

Florid song did not die. It lived on in the surviving operas of the older repertoire. But it tended to become stereotyped and, even as a stereotype, the property of specialists. Whereas until about 1830 all singers were expected to be masters of the devices of bel canto, they were now categorized as dramatic, lyric, coloratura (specialist in florid song), and so on. The traditional range classifications of soprano, alto, tenor, and bass were also widened to admit the mezzo-soprano, the baritone, and the bass-baritone. A further departure from the canons of bel canto was implicit in the newer requirement of bringing more voice to the upper extremes of the vocal range. Western music had been growing louder since Haydn's time. Singers had to raise their voices in order to be heard. Their success was felt to be exciting, but a fundamental change of taste was involved. Even a Caruso's high C would have seemed vulgar to the vocal connoisseurs of the age of bel canto.

The art of the singer, as it had flourished in the 17th and 18th centuries, was inhibited throughout the 19th not only by the growth and burgeoning prestige of the orchestra but also by the new dominance of the composer. Whereas the composer formerly had worked for the singer, much as composers and arrangers work for the popular singer today, tailoring the music to his art and convenience, the singer was now seen as the servant of the composer. Improvisation and artful deviation, which in former times had been a singer's prerogative, even a requirement—as they are for the popular singer now—were outlawed in favour of fidelity to what a composer had written.

The second half of the 20th century produced a predictable reaction in favour of the singer, with a revival of public enthusiasm for nearly forgotten operas by Rossini, Donizetti, and Bellini, and even of the true bel canto operas of Handel, and the emergence of singers capable of acquiring the requisite technique and of accepting the creative responsibility imposed by music which left much to the singer's invention and discretion. The popular singer, too, relieved by the microphone of the necessity of raising his voice, and exploiting the improvisatory conventions of jazz, employs intuitively many ornaments and expressive devices nearly identical to those of bel canto. Concurrently, the vocal requirements of avant-garde music extend beyond those of traditional operatic singing to include wider flexibility of timbre, techniques such as *Sprechstimme* (musically pitched speech), and improvisational fantasy drawing on sounds formerly excluded from the trained singer's vocal resources.   (H.Pl.)

Popular and avant-garde singing

FOLK AND NON-WESTERN SINGING

Singers conform their style to the vocal and musical conventions of their culture as closely as their training and talent permit. When they overstep the bounds of proper vocalizing in a given cultural context, they rouse feelings of shame, amusement, or anger among their hearers. This is because singing, like speech, is a language. Therefore its use of tone, metre, and much more must be bound by formal conventions if it is to communicate effectively. An operatic performance of a folk song sounds just as inappropriate as would a folk rendition of Wagner at the Metropolitan Opera. Every vocalist is likely to feel that his tradition of singing is the most natural and beautiful one—and so it is—in its own cultural setting. In fact, history has witnessed a myriad of singing styles, as varied as culture itself, each one capable of bringing joy or ecstasy to one branch of the human family.

In this century, song hunters, armed with portable re-

Cross-cultural analysis of singing styles

corders, have explored the limits of this global ocean of song. In fact, no other aspect of human behaviour has been so universally recorded. A number of general conclusions about the relation of singing style and culture emerge from a survey of these recordings. In order to avoid culture bias on the part of the investigators, all aspects of song performance must be described, including, for example, voice qualities, dynamics, embellishment style, and the organization of the performing group, as well as melody, metre, and harmony. If so described, performance pattern seems to vary in clear-cut ways from culture to culture, defining culture areas and tracing the main human migrations, as do language and design. The discovery that singing style varies with culture pattern makes it possible to study song as a cultural phenomenon, to observe its symbolic and social functions, and to note how musical traits co-vary with known facts of human behaviour and geography.

The method employed in the above-mentioned survey was an empirical rating system of 37 measures in the form of numerical scales on which a trained observer could record his judgment of the relative presence or absence of such easily observable features of performance as level of volume, degree of ornamentation, or length of phrase. The specific scales chosen were those that produced the clearest and most consistent typology among more than 400 songs drawn from every world region. These judgmental rating scales, carefully defined and numerically weighted, were then applied to 4,000 song performances from cultures from every culture area. Coded numerical data on economy, politics, stratification, family, division of labour, religion, sexual mores, and other features of social organization were available for 233 of these cultures. The correlation between features of singing style and aspects of social and cultural organization was studied in relation to this small but representative sample of societies. With the help of the computer, a number of relationships of a high order of statistical significance were then established between singing style on the one hand and social structure and human geography on the other. These hypotheses seem very helpful in explaining the way song style varies from region to region.

Hypotheses relating singing style to social structure. Measured against a scale of economic productivity, the songs of simple producers such as hunters tend usually to be repetitious in text, slurred in enunciation, full of wide melodic intervals, non-embellished, and accompanied by no more than one or two instruments playing in simple rhythmic unison, often to a one-beat rhythm. It is much easier to join in music so relatively empty of information than in the singing of complex societies, in which songs usually have a heavy text load, precise enunciation, narrower intervals, and, if the society is highly stratified, employ many forms of embellishment along with complex orchestras playing polyrhythms, counterpoint, or heterophony. This finding suggests the existence of a general principle: dominant song style constantly restates the level of economic development a culture has reached and the order of complexity normal to its communications.

The organization and integration of the singing group, however, reflects another aspect of social structure—the texture of relations within groups. Solo performance is most frequent when the individual normally works on his own, as do hunters, fishers, and pastoralists, as well as modern farmers and free enterprisers. Group singing is the rule in collective agricultural societies, like those of black Africa, Oceania, and eastern Europe, where cooperative groups till the fields. Whether the chorus performs in unison or sings in parts, however, seems to be related to the sexual division of labour. Where males dominate production, as they generally do in hunting, pastoral, and Western farm economies, one melodic part or unison prevails. Part singing that allows for at least an upper (female) and a lower (male) voice part occurs among gatherers and collective agriculturalists. In these economies, women share or dominate the main productive activity, and usually take a prominent part—with males—in other public activities. Thus, polyphony, where indigenous, seems to stand for sexual complementarity.

Choral singing and vocal blend

The cohesiveness or level of voice blending in unrehearsed choral performance apparently depicts the relative solidarity or diffuseness of community life. Among small solitary groups, like permanent work teams or clan villages, such as those of the Pueblos of the southwest United States, unity flows out of lifelong sharing and cooperation. In cultures whose continuance depends upon impermanent teams, like hunting parties, or in complex cultures, in which highly individuated and changeful social relations are the rule, there is a preference for diffuse, highly individualized group singing in which every voice stands out. In diffusely organized performances one often observes a heavy load of text, consonants, and embellishments, as well as noisy features like harshness, nasality, and vocal narrowness or squeeze. These noisy qualities, which interfere with vocal blend and thus with part singing, are most common in non-complementary, usually male-dominated cultures. Vocal harshness or rasp appears among choruses of hunters, fishers, and other groups in which young males are trained for aggressiveness. Again, vocal narrowness and nasality are heard in societies in which fathers and brothers invoke severe sanctions against female premarital coitus. It is postulated that this male control of female sexuality produces tensions that are voiced in the familiar high-pitched wailing style heard in the Orient and the Mediterranean, where women, until recently, lived in purdah. In the survey of major singing styles that follows, principal musical and performance traits are discussed and at times related to the hypotheses set forth above.

Singing traits of major cultural regions. *African gatherers.* The Bushman and Pygmy people living close to the source of man's known beginnings have a music that might have come from the Garden of Eden. In their complementary, chiefless, egalitarian, and pacifist societies, men and women, old and young, are linked in close interdependence by preference and not by force. Here, where bands of gathering women bring home most of the food, group singing is not only contrapuntal but polyrhythmic, a playful weaving of four and more strands of short, flowing, canon-like melodies (each voice imitating the melody of the others), sounding wordless streams of vowels in clear, bell-like yodelling voices. Free counterpoint of this type may have been man's first song style, for variants of this style appear throughout the world in refuge areas and among gatherers—not only in Africa but also, for example, among the Sajek of Taiwan, the Dani of New Guinea, the Paleosiberian Yukaghir and Ainu, the Pomo of California, and the Jívaro, Motilones, and Guarauno (Warao) of South America.

Sibero-American hunters. Solos are uncommon among collectivist gatherers, but frequent among hunters. A guttural, raspy, punchy, slurred, nonsense-syllable kind of soloizing seems to be one main style of the Arctic, from the Lapps of northern Europe across Siberia to the Chukchee and in the whole of aboriginal North America. Its special prominence in South America, especially among the primitive hunter-fishers of Patagonia, may be another piece of evidence that the first Americans arrived across the land bridge from Siberia. Many North American Indian songs are performed by men in a related style, notable for its vigour. It employs wide intervals, much nonsense material, and weaves generous, descending cadences into rather freely structured, big strophic forms (consisting of five or more phrases repeated in a set pattern). Vocal rhythms are often complexly irregular and accompanied by one-beat patterns. The main choral style of these freedom-loving, virile pathfinders and incipient producers is grandly noisy, pulsing, and freely diffuse. Among the surprisingly puritanical Plains Indians, a thrilling, narrow-voiced, high-pitched yelling style developed; in contrast, in the settled clan villages of the southeastern and southwestern United States and in eastern Brazil another variant of the basic style is performed in striking tonal and rhythmic blend with wider, deeper voices.

American Indian singing styles

Nuclear American incipient. There is another great American singing style found from the Valley of Mexico south through the isthmus of Panama, in the whole ancient terrain of the Incas, and along the eastern jungle rim of the Andes, thence blending with forms of the two previously mentioned styles in the riverine plains to the east. The geographical spread of this style, together with the rather complex, heterophonically related orchestras common to it, suggests that it once linked the ancient high cultures of Mexico and Peru and spread thence to simpler nearby peoples. Today it is practiced largely by seminomadic gardening peoples of the South American forests. Their unstable social relations are apparently reflected in diffuse, highly individualized choralizing, and their dependence on feminine agricultural labour correlates with their use of polyphony that often veers toward vocal heterophony. Frequency of irregular and one-beat metres, wide melodic intervals, and guttural vocalizing link the nuclear American style with that of the Sibero-American hunters, but the frequency of a pattern of soft, nonraspy, high-pitched delivery points in another direction. This gentle, somehow childlike vocal stance occurs, in combination with the heterophonic choral style just described, in only one other region on the globe—in tribal societies in Melanesia and Melaysia—one more indication of an ancient cultural connection between the two zones. In the Malaysian form, however, appear the sure signs of Old High Culture influence (see below)—vocal tensions, embellishment, and explicit text.

Pacific gardeners. Out of the complex weave of migrating cultures through the Pacific islands, three main Oceanic song style patterns emerge. The first is the noisy, unison, rhythmically complex, horn-accompanied style found throughout aboriginal Australia, reminiscent of American hunter singing. The second is the tense-voiced, wordy, highly ornamented, heavily orchestrated solo and heterophonic choral style occurring through the Malay Archipelago, where the influence of Far Eastern music is clear. The third is the varied polyphonic traditions of the gardening peoples of New Guinea, Melanesia, Micronesia, and Polynesia.

Only the third stylistic complex may be briefly considered here. One of its elements is a low-energy, diffuse, harmonizing style that seems old because it is found in enclaves of refugees in the interiors of islands from Taiwan to the Solomon Islands. A second, far more widespread strain might be called Papuan, since its centre seems to be the Eastern Highlands of New Guinea. Its prototypical performance setting is a ceremonial food exchange between two clans or two neighbouring gardener tribes, when tightly packed formations of males, body-painted, oiled, and wearing elaborate headdresses of feathers, flowers, and leaves parade for each other's admiration and display the yams and pigs that their women have, in the main, produced. As they dance, feast, and exchange gifts, they sing in thunderous unison choruses, each man rattling an irregular tattoo on the hourglass-shaped drum he carries. One-phrase melodies, slurred consonants, much repetition, and one-beat, unison-organized orchestras are musical traits correlating with the simplicity of these economies. The relatively wide, noise-free, often polyphonic choruses usually achieve remarkable unity, in spite of the irregular or free rhythms employed.

This endlessly fertile and powerful Papuan type has been often reinvented or widely diffused, because similar patterns are found in tribal India, the Balkans, and especially in East Africa, all through the zone of early tropical agriculture. In cantometric analysis this Papuan pattern links New Guinea with Micronesia and Melanesia as well, and, in other manifestations, it is found throughout Polynesia. The Polynesians also behave in social unison with an unsurpassed cohesiveness, in spite of the fact that their rather complex culture and their concern with geneologies motivate them to sing long, complexly textured poems in precise enunciation. Many of these chants are restrained within a narrow compass of notes, are dominated by free or irregular metres, and have a drone harmonic structure (*i.e.*, a melody sung against a long, sustained note). Just as characteristic is the dance drama, enacted by well-rehearsed male and female squads singing in polyvoiced antiphony (alternating groups of singers), the musical dynamics moving from a sinuous and gentle attack to aggressive fortissimo in which no syllable should be missed and no ancestor's name mispronounced.

Black African. Black Africa's predominant style belongs to the set of wide-voiced, superbly cohesive, polyphonic choralizing found among tropical village gardeners from Nigeria to the South Pacific island of Pukapuka. To this stylistic complex black Africa adds very much from its endlessly rich rhythmic, harmonic, and orchestral traditions. African vocal style is so varied that it can be called playful; where most other singers take a vocal stance and maintain it, Africans play with register, rasp, volume, emphasis, nasality, narrowing, glottalizing, yodelling, and a dozen other vocal effects, using them as intermittent decorative ploys. Black African style is especially characterized by changefulness—by song leaders and instrumentalists constantly shifting roles, varying the melody, complicating the rhythmic pattern, finding new chords, increasing tension and volume, and then relaxing —with accompanying voices and instruments moving hard behind.

Indeed, in black African antiphony, choruses and ensembles do not allow a moment of silence before they respond; they leap in before the other part is finished and overlap theirs with it, a feat that is easier to describe than to perform. This sociable overlapping of parts, found wherever Africans make music—in the Sahara, in Madagascar, in America, as well as across the whole dark continent—makes the African such a master of synchrony that he can match and answer change as it occurs, so giving rise to the polyrhythmic interaction between voices and instruments and between choruses and orchestras for which Africa is famed.

As a symbol of social solidarity, the complexly integrated character of black African song style reinforces the complementary and unified structure of African society, in which ritual, work, socializing, and even politics are enlivened with multi-part group dancing and singing. Its open-throated, bawdy, body-rocking style reflects the high value that Africans place on the erotic. In all this it appears likely that tall black Africans, moving south from the northern savanna, learned much from the small aboriginal jungle dwellers, the Pygmies and the Bushmen, who still today excel at rhythm, playful vocalizing, and polyphony. The black Nilotes and Cushites of East Africa do not share all these gifts, though they are clearly Africans. The core style, however, gives most of black Africa, in spite of its musical diversity, a stylistic unity that no other such large area can boast of. The pattern survived virtually intact through the Atlantic passage and centuries of deculturation in slavery. In Brazil, among sizable minorities who still speak African languages, many songs are simply West African. West Indian song style is often indistinguishable from West African except that melodic fragments of western European or Creole origin appear. In the United States the slaves learned to create western European strophes, or stanzas, thus producing ballads such as "Frankie and Albert" and spirituals such as "Go Down Moses." Adapting western European harmonic materials, they created a new world of chords found in their spirituals and popular music. They learned to make European instruments sing in a playful African vein, and so produced fiddle breakdowns (improvisations), the minstrel tunes, piano ragtime, and instrumental jazz. Even so, their manner of playing and singing remained basically African.

European peasant. Perhaps the oldest of the three main European folk song traditions is the one found in central and eastern Europe, site of Neolithic agricultural villages. Here a highly cohesive, often polyphonic style, basically similar to those of Africa and Oceania, has endured for many centuries, apparently reflecting the communal, complementary culture pattern of the region. This area early received hard-grain plow agriculture and dairying from the Middle East as it also gradually acquired the musical instruments developed by the great ancient civilizations. Yet middle Europe remained sufficiently isolated so that a world of regional musical styles could flower alongside new and productive types of agriculture. Dozens of folk polyphonies, both instrumental and vocal, can be found from the Caucasus Mountains north across the Russian plains, east along the Baltic, in the mountainous sectors of central Europe, and in the Balkans. This region, where the agricultural cycle, the country dance, and music making are all highly cohesive and integrated, is the most likely zone of origin for European fine art music. Its distinctive traits—clear, wide voices; complex texts, precisely enunciated, yet sung in perfect concert; strings of strophic melodies; orchestras of strings and horns joined in accompanying rather than polyrhythmic relationships; and part singing based on separate melodic movement—are uniquely common in both its folk and fine art traditions.

This central Old European zone includes southern Germany, northern Italy, and Spain, with northeastern France and Wales as its westernmost extensions. It gave rise to art music institutions such as the orchestra and church choir and to the system of harmony and ensemble that influenced all western European popular music, vocal and instrumental. Since its inception, the popular music industry has been controlled by persons taking for granted Old European stylistic standards of vocal and instrumental style and circumstances of performance. Accordingly, the music of Tin Pan Alley is shaped to fit those standards, both in elements surrounding the vocal performance—such as the orchestras and the harmonies, tempi, and musical forms—and also in the concert of the choruses; and, above all, in vocal delivery and enunciation. Jazz was made to conform by dressing the players in uniforms and placing them in orchestral sections under a director's baton. Both the register-breaking black vocal style, with its gamut of vocal effects, and the thin, nasal voices of white Midwesterners were modified through voice lessons, disguised with close miking and echo chambers, and hidden behind large orchestras. Rock, the latest of the musical developments stemming from the crowded urban black ghettos, was given an overlay of Old European vocal and instrumental style by the Beatles and a regimented polish by professional techniques such as multi-track recording.

Northwestern European. Among the almost unbroken victories of this central European tradition, a few defeats have been caused by the stubborn preference of other cultures for their own singing traditions. Strongest of these in America was the ballad style of northwestern Europe. This zone of shepherds, fisherman, woodsmen, and isolated farmers has long favoured the turn-by-turn singing of unaccompanied solo narrative songs the purpose of which was to tell a tale rather than to create a musical mood. This tradition gave rise to most English-language folk songs of the United States and Canada—the workaday ballads of the lumberjacks, cowboys, and miners. What counted in a singer was a good memory and the ability to "sing it out plain and clear." The singer was a neutral-voiced storyteller, permitted a bit of embellishment in the Irish tradition but committed to maintaining a poker face and letting the story tell itself. The burdens, or refrains, of the sea chanteys were handled in roaring individualized unison.

In the southern backwoods of the United States the narrow-voiced, ornamented style of the Scots-Irish took hold and flowered, perhaps reflecting in its tense-voiced delivery the emotional tensions of frontier Protestantism with its painful sanctions against fleshly pleasure. At one time it was the pride of mountain singers to keep their tone a straight continuation of the wailing notes of a fiddle accompaniment. When the backwoods opened up to black five-string banjo and guitar music and little singing ensembles were formed, these individualized, high, lonesome mountain voices produced a thrilling steam-whistle unison; then, with town ways and mill employment freeing their women, it gave rise to the wailing harmonized style called "hillbilly."

Southern poor whites found a style to their liking in hillbilly as black urbanized workers had earlier found their favourite style in the blues. The blues, although it reflects its African roots in playful vocalizing, descending cadences, and polyrhythmic overlapping with its accompaniment, still joins the mainstream of northwestern

European music. The centre of this tradition is in its adherence to the brief three or four phrase strophe (stanza), set to simple metres. For centuries the great majority of the songs in this region have been such simple strophes, and the whole of American folk and pop songs are variations on this formal theme. Europe's herdsmen and husbandmen, and America's fiddlers, bluesmen, and popular song composers have been mainly preoccupied with the creation of these compact melodic packages.

Old High Culture. This zone of the ancient high civilizations, including the European southern Mediterranean, North Africa, the Middle East, India, and the Far East, is united by a common cultural heritage and a common performance style. The Middle Eastern culture complex of grain agriculture, hoofed animal husbandry, cities, writing, and empire spread through this vast area thousands of years ago, presumably carrying a suitable song style in its van. Sea and caravan trade routes kept alive the exchange between the farthest ends of this region so that in spite of its variety of languages, arts, and local historical developments it has many things in common. A complex system of irrigation agriculture supported by specialized pastoralism, a highly centralized political system, and a multilayered social stratification seem to be mirrored in the flowery textual style and in long through-composed (nonstrophic) melodies that are elaborately enunciated and heavily ornamented with passing notes, quavers, glottal shakes, melismata (many notes to one syllable), glides, and rhythmic variation. The Oriental bard addressing an all-powerful emperor, the priest supplicating the deity, the lover crying out to his distant adored, all employ a variant of this flowery, elaborate, and placatory style. Everywhere, from raspy-voiced west Sudan to the pressed-back and squeezed-white tone of Indonesia and Japan, the vocal delivery tends to be tense, high-pitched, and nasal, a symbolic parallel to the severe system of constraints that separate the sexes and bear, with painful heaviness, upon the women of this zone. Similarly, the radical centralization of authority in the state, the community, and the family and the radical system of punishment and law that reinforced this system may be related to the predominance of solo bardic performances, which comprise almost two-thirds of all singing in this region. Sometimes singing without accompaniment, more often accompanied by one heterophonically related instrument or by a large and elaborate orchestra, and in a wealthy setting, the bards of old High Culture for six or seven millennia have had free play with their passive and often reverent audiences. Because through the content of their recitations they supported and reinforced the centralized imperial systems, these bards had the leisure to specialize, to devote themselves exclusively to the arts of song style, gesture, music, and poetry and to develop systems of orchestration and music theory. European music owes much to these masters. Young Western composers and instrumentalists are turning to them today, finding excitement in the endless games of schooled elaboration, improvisation, and virtuosity, yet savouring also the endless and tender melancholy of their melodies. This is an unexpected development at the dawn of the atomic age, perhaps a sign of an Oriental level of stratification emerging in Western democratic society.

(A.Lo.)

BIBLIOGRAPHY

Western art singing: GIULIO CACCINI, *Le nuove musiche* (1602), most readily available in English in W. OLIVER STRUNK, *Source Readings in Music History*, pp. 377–392 (1950), a seminal document establishing what were to become the fundamental principles, both technical and aesthetic, of *bel canto*; PIER FRANCESCO TOSI, *Opinioni de' cantori antichi e moderni, o sieno osservazioni sopra il canto figurato* (1723; Eng. trans., *Observations on the Florid Song; or, Sentiments on the Ancient and Modern Singers*, 1742, reprinted 1905), a more specific discourse drawing upon the author's experience of singers and singing in Italy and elsewhere a century after Caccini's precepts had become generally accepted; FRANZ HABOCK, *Die Kastraten und ihre Gesangskunst* (1927), the definitive work on the life, times, and art of the castrati; ANGUS HERIOT, *The Castrati in Opera* (1956), less comprehensive than Haböck, but the principle source available in English; MANUEL GARCIA, *Traité complet de l'art du chant*

Hillbilly and blues

(1847; Eng. trans., *Hints on Singing*, 1894), a further refinement and elaboration of the principles previously established, and taking into account the newer trends in operatic fashion, especially as reflected in the operas of Rossini, Donizetti, and Bellini; HENRY PLEASANTS, *The Great Singers: From the Dawn of Opera to Our Own Time* (1966), a survey of the history of Western singing as reflected in the lives and careers of a selective list of singers from the end of the 17th century to the present, with glossary and bibliography; and "A Shorter Vocabulary of Vocalism," *Stereo Review*, pp. 69–72 (May 1971), a layman's guide to the terminology and techniques of Western singing.

Folk and non-Western singing: JOHN BLACKING, *Venda Children's Songs* (1967), a fine analysis of the relation of song style and melody in one African tribe; VICTOR A. GRAUER, "Some Song-Style Clusters: A Preliminary Study," *Ethnomusicology*, 9:265–271 (1965), gives an analysis of the Gatherer style; FRANCES HANNETT, "The Haunting Lyric: The Personal and Social Significance of American Popular Songs," *Psychoanal. Q.*, 33:226–269 (1964), analyzes the emotional content of the American popular song tradition; BESSIE JONES and BESS LOMAX HAWES, *Step It Down: Games, Plays, Songs, and Stories from the Afro-American Heritage* (1972), a presentation of the performance style of a great black American folksinger; ALAN LOMAX, *The Folk Songs of North America* (1960), a mapping and discussion of the song styles of North America together with 400 illustrative songs; "The Homogeneity of African–Afro-American Musical Style," in NORMAN E. WHITTEN, JR. and JOHN F. SZWED (eds.), *Afro-American Anthropology* (1970), on the style regions of Africa and their relation to Afro-American song; *Folk Song Style and Culture* (1968), a book-length presentation of the ideas in this article along with a number of methods for measuring and comparing aesthetic performance; and, with NORMAN BERKOWITZ, "The Evolutionary Taxonomy of Culture," *Science*, 177:228–239 (1972), shows how song style analysis can lead to a classification of human cultures; NORMAN N. MARKEL (ed), *Psycholinguistics: An Introduction to the Study of Speech and Personality* (1969), the best summary of the features of language that are the background to singing style; DAVID P. MCALLESTER, *Enemy Way Music* (1954), a full description of Navaho singing style; ALAN P. MERRIAM, *The Anthropology of Music* (1964), a general description of the methods of conventional ethnomusicology with comments on the acquisition of style; *African Music on LP: An Annotated Discography* (1970), a full bibliography of African music on records with many annotations on musical style; PAUL J. MOSES, *The Voice of Neurosis* (1954), the best essay in English on the relationship of vocal qualities to individual psychology; CURT SACHS, *The Wellsprings of Music*, ed. by JAAP KUNST (1962), posthumously published essays of one of the great musicologists with illuminating comments on style; and *The Rise of Music in the Ancient World, East and West* (1943), a summary of Near Eastern and Mediterranean music with many comments on style; BRUNO NETTL, *North American Indian Musical Styles* (1954), a mapping of American Indian musical regions; and *Music in Primitive Culture* (1956), a general introduction to world musicology with some reference to style features; EGON WELLESZ (ed.), *The New Oxford History of Music*, vol. 1, *Ancient and Oriental Music* (1957), a discussion of a number of culture regions from the stylistic point of view.

(H.Pl./A.Lo.)

Sinkiang Uighur

Sinkiang Uighur Autonomous Region (in Pin-yin romanization Xin-jiang-wei-wu-er Zu-zi-chü) occupies the northwestern corner of the People's Republic of China. It is bordered by Mongolia to the northeast, the Soviet Union to the northwest, Afghanistan and the disputed territory of Jammu and Kashmir to the southwest, the Tibetan Autonomous Region to the southeast, and the Chinese provinces of Tsinghai and Kansu to the east. China's largest political unit, it covers 635,800 square miles (1,646,700 square kilometres), or one-sixth the national area. The population of about 8,000,000 is composed of numerous ethnic groups, the largest of which is the Uighurs. The Uighurs follow the Islāmic religion and work at agriculture and animal husbandry. The capital city of Urumchi is a busy commercial and industrial centre.

The Chinese name Sinkiang, or New Dominion, was applied to the area when it came under Chinese rule in the 3rd century BC. The region was long known to Westerners as Chinese Turkistan to distinguish it from Russian Turkistan.

Sinkiang is an area of lonely, rugged mountains and vast desert basins. Its indigenous population of agriculturalists and pastoralists inhabit oases strung out along the mountain foothills or wander the arid plains in search of pasturage. Since the establishment of firm Chinese control in 1949, serious efforts have been made to integrate the regional economy into that of the nation. Agriculture has been improved, mining increased, power stations built, and industry introduced. Previously isolated from the rest of China, Sinkiang is now connected to neighbouring provinces by road and rail, and transportation to the Soviet Union has been improved. Despite the great increase in the Chinese population, the ethnic groups are officially encouraged to develop their own cultures. *Economic development*

For related physical features, see ALTAI MOUNTAINS; KUNLUN MOUNTAINS; PAMIR MOUNTAIN AREA; TARIM RIVER; TAKLA MAKAN DESERT; and TIEN SHAN (MOUNTAINS). For a more detailed discussion of history, see TURKISTAN, HISTORY OF.

History. Southern Sinkiang was controlled by China during the Han dynasty (206 BC–AD 220). It then passed under the rule of local Uighur rulers until it was conquered by the Mongol leader Genghis Khan in the 13th century and in the 18th century by the Mongolian-speaking Kalmucks. Sinkiang again came under Chinese control during the Ch'ing (Manchu) dynasty (1644–1911) and was made a province of China in 1884. Because of the region's remote location, the rule of the central government was nominal; the province was governed by semi-independent warlords, occasionally under pressure from the Soviet Union. Sinkiang came under the rule of the Chinese Communists in 1949 and, in accordance with the government's ethnic policy, became the Sinkiang Uighur Autonomous Region in 1955.

The landscape. *Relief.* Sinkiang can be divided into five physiographic regions: the Northern Highlands, the Dzungarian Basin, the Tien Shan (Celestial Mountains), the Tarim Basin, and the Kunlun Mountains. These regions run roughly from east to west, the high mountains alternating with large, lower basins.

In the north, the Northern Highlands extend in a semicircle along the Mongolian border. The major range in this area is the Altai Mountains, with average heights of approximately 4,500 feet above sea level. The slopes of the Altai Mountains on the Chinese (western) side are relatively gentle, with numerous rolling and dome-shaped hills.

The triangular-shaped Dzungarian Basin, or Dzungaria, with an area of 270,000 square miles (700,000 square kilometres), is bordered by the Altai Mountains on the northeast, the Tien Shan on the south, and the Chun-ka-erh-a-la-t'ao Shan on the northwest. The basin is open on both the east and west. It contains a ring of oases at the foot of the enclosing mountains and a steppe and desert belt in the centre of the depression.

The Tien Shan occupies nearly one-fourth of the area of Sinkiang. The mountains stretch into the region from the Soviet Union and run eastward from the border for about 1,000 miles. They are highest in the west and taper off slightly to the east. The highest peaks are Khan-tengri, which rises to an elevation of 22,949 feet (6,995 metres) on the Sino-Soviet border, and Sheng-li, which attains 24,406 feet (7,439 metres), 13 miles to the south. The Tien Shan is perpetually covered by snow, and numerous long glaciers descend its slopes from extensive snow fields.

The Tarim Basin is surrounded by the Tien Shan to the north, the Pamir Mountains to the west, and the Kunlun Mountains to the south. It occupies about 55 percent of Sinkiang, extending 850 miles from west to east and about 350 miles from north to south. The basin consists of a central desert, alluvial fans at the foot of the mountains, and isolated oases. The desert—the Takla Makan—covers more than 270,000 square miles (700,000 square kilometres) and is absolutely barren. The core of the basin has an elevation ranging from about 4,000 feet (1,200 metres) above sea level in the west to about 2,500 feet (760 metres) in the east. The Turfan Depression at *The Tarim Basin* the eastern end of the Takla Makan, however, is 505 feet (154 metres) below sea level.

The Kunlun Mountains form the northern rampart of the Tibetan Plateau. With elevations up to 24,000 feet, the central part of the range forms an almost impenetrable barrier to movement from north to south. There are passes on the west and east such as the Karakoram in Kashmir and the K'u-erh-kan in Sinkiang. In the east the A-erh-chin Shan-mo turns northeast and eventually merges with the Nan Shan in southern Kansu Province, China.

Drainage and soils. The drainage pattern of Sinkiang is unique. The only stream whose waters reach the sea is the O-erh-ch'i-ssu, which rises in north central Sinkiang, crosses into the U.S.S.R., and joins the Ob, which empties into the Arctic Ocean. Other streams in Sinkiang issue from the mountains and disappear into inland deserts or salt lakes. The principal river is the Tarim, which is fed by largely intermittent streams that rise in both the Kunlun Mountains and the Tien Shan. It flows eastward across the Tarim Basin into the salt lake of Lop Nor and ends in marshes west of the lake.

Climate. Remote from the ocean and enclosed by high mountains, Sinkiang is cut off from marine climatic influences. It therefore has a continental dry climate. The Tien Shan separates the dry south from the slightly less arid north, and the northern slopes of the Tien Shan are more humid than those on the south.

Rainfall is not only small, but it fluctuates widely from year to year. Average January temperatures in the Tarim Basin are about 20° F (−7° C), compared with 5° F (−15° C), in many parts of Dzungaria. In the summer, average temperatures north of the Tien Shan are lower than they are south of the mountains. In Dzungaria, July averages vary from 70° F (21° C) in the north to 75° F (24° C) in the south. In the Tarim Basin, July temperatures average about 80° F (27° C). The hottest part of Sinkiang is the Turfan Depression, where a maximum of 118° F (48° C) and a July mean of 90° F (32° C) have been recorded.

Vegetation and animal life. Because of the great expanses of desert, the plant life of much of Sinkiang is monotonous. There are pine forests in the Tien Shan and tugrak woods in many places on the edge of the Takla Makan Desert. Apart from these trees, the most common are varieties of poplars and willows. In the Tien Shan and other mountains, there is a great assortment of wild plants and flowers, many of which have never been classified and of which little is known.

Animal life is of greater interest, and big-game hunting is an attraction of the Tien Shan. These and other mountains are inhabited by antelopes, ibex (wild goats), wapiti (elks), vaious wild sheep, leopards, wolves, bears, lynx, and marmots (burrowing rodents). There are wild horses in the north, wild camels near Lop Nor, and wild yaks (large, long-haired oxen) and wild asses on the Tibetan frontier. Deer, wild boar, wild cats, foxes, and hares are also found. Bird life is extensive, especially in the Lop Nor district. The few varieties of fish are mostly of the carp family. Snakes are not numerous and appear to be harmless; scorpions and centipedes, however, abound. During the summer, horse flies, mosquitoes, flies, and midges are thick in the woods. A great variety of butterflies are seen in the mountains.

The people. *Population groups.* Sinkiang is inhabited by 13 different ethnic groups, of which the largest are the Uighurs and the Chinese. Other groups include the Mongolians and Khalkans, Hui (Chinese Muslims), Kazakhs, Uzbeks, Tungusic-speaking Manchus and Sibos, Tadzhiks, Tatars, Russians, and Tahurs. In 1953 the Uighurs accounted for almost 75 percent of the total population of 4,900,000; there were only about 1,000,000 members of non-Chinese groups and about 300,000 Chinese. By the mid-1960s the Chinese population had increased to 2,600,000, or almost one-third of the total population of 8,000,000; there were 4,000,000 Uighurs.

The Chinese migration altered the pattern of population distribution. In 1953 only 1,300,000 people lived north of the Tien Shan in the Dzungarian Basin, and three-fourths

of the population lived south of the mountains in the Tarim Basin. The Chinese influx was directed mainly to Dzungaria because of its resource potential. By 1970 the population was believed to be evenly divided between the two basins, with a Uighur majority in the south and a majority of Chinese in the north. The Kazakhs, the third largest minority group, are nomadic herdsmen in the steppes of Dzungaria; they are especially concentrated in the Upper Ili Valley.

There are two major language groups in the region. The Mongolians speak languages of the Mongolian branch of the Altaic group, and the Uighurs, Kazakhs, and Uzbeks speak the Turkic branch of the Altaic group. The Tadzhiks, however, belong to the Iranian branch of the Indo-European language group. Mongolian, Uighur, and Kazakh are written languages in everyday use; Mongolian has its own script, while Uighur and Kazakh are written in the Arabic script.

The largest Muslim groups in China are the Uighurs and the Hui. The Kazakhs and Tadzhiks also follow Islām, and the Mongolians are adherents of Buddhism.

Settlement patterns. There are many differences in rural settlement patterns in the north and south. Oasis agriculture in the Tarim Basin occupies about 40 percent of the population, and only 2 percent are engaged in animal husbandry. North of the Tien Shan, the grasslands support 35 to 40 percent of the population, who are pastoralists.

In the early 1970s, there were four major cities in the province. Urumchi (Chinese Wu-lu-mu-ch'i), the regional capital, had grown from a population of 80,000 in 1949 to about 500,000 by 1970. Formerly an agricultural centre for the Dzungarian Basin, it has undergone considerable industrial development. Karamai, also in Dzungaria, had a population of more than 40,000 in 1958; in the early 1960s it was developed as a centre of the petroleum industry. Kuldja (Chinese I-ning) is located in the Upper Ili Valley near the Soviet border. With a population of 85,000 in 1958, it was an administrative town with a growing food-processing industry. Kashgar is the largest city of the Tarim Basin, with a population in 1960 of 140,000; it is an ancient centre for the manufacture of handicrafts such as textiles, rugs, and tanned leather.

Administration and social conditions. *Government.* The administrative structure of Sinkiang reflects the governmental policies of recognition of ethnic minorities and self-administration, in which local leaders are appointed to governmental positions. The Sinkiang Uighur Autonomous Region is divided on the subprovincial level into three types of administrative units. There are two municipalities (*shih*) of Karamai (K'o-la-ma-i) and Urumchi (Wu-lu-mu-ch'i); the area to the southeast of Urumchi —including the towns of Toksun (T'o-k'o-hsün), Turfan (T'u-lu-fan), and Shan-shan—is under direct regional administration. There are five autonomous districts (*tzu-chih-chou*): Bayan Gol Mongol (Pa-yin-kuo-leng-meng-ku), Boro Tala Mongol (Po-erh-t'a-la-meng-ku), Ch'ang-chi Hui (Chang-chi-hui-tsu), Ili Kazakh (I-li-ha-sa-k'o), and Kizil Su Kirghiz (K'o-tzu-lo-su-k'o-erh-k'o-tzu). The six areas (*ti-ch'ü*) include A-k'o-su, Ha-mi, Ho-t'ien, K'a-shih, A-le-t'ai, and T'a-ch'eng, the last two of which are under the administration of the Ili Kazakh Autonomous District.

Below the subprovince level, there are two municipalities of Kuldja and Kashgar, 73 counties (*hsien*), and six autonomous counties (*tzu-chih-hsien*).

Education. Before World War II the educational system was minimal; attendance appeared to be voluntary and the teaching halfhearted. Since 1949, educational facilities have been broadened. Institutions of higher learning, concentrated in Urumchi, include the Sinkiang University; the Sinkiang "August First" Institute of Agriculture, which offers a course on water conservation; the Sinkiang Institute of Minorities, which offers courses in art, Chinese language and literature, history, and science; the Sinkiang Medical College; and the Sinkiang Institute of Languages, which offers instruction in Russian, English, French, and German language and literature. The provincial library and museum are also in Urumchi.

[margin notes]
Changing demographic patterns

Urban settlement

Institutions of higher learning

The economy. *Sources of income.* Because of the dry climate, more than 90 percent of the cultivated land in Sinkiang depends entirely on irrigation. The various nationalities in the region have had rich experience in water-conservancy techniques, of which the Kareze system in the Turfan and Ha-mi depressions is a fine example. The present cultivated area can be more than doubled with the further utilization of Sinkiang's mountain glaciers, rivers, and underground water.

About half of the total crop area is sown into winter and spring wheat. Maize (corn), another important crop, is grown more extensively in the south than the north. Rice, kaoliang (Chinese sorghum), and millet are also produced in large quantities. Long-staple cotton is produced in the Turfan Depression and the greater Tarim Basin. Sinkiang is one of China's main fruit-producing regions; its sweet Ha-mi melons, seedless Turfan grapes, and Ili apples are well-known. Livestock includes about 25 percent of China's sheep, which yield about 60 percent of the nation's wool.

Mineral resources

Mineral resources include deposits of lead, zinc, copper, and molybdenum and tungsten (metallic elements used in strengthening steel), none of which are of industrial significance. Gold is produced from placer and lode deposits on the southern slopes of the Altai Mountains, where uranium is also believed to be mined. Significant quantities of petroleum are produced at Karamai, whose Uighur name means Black Soil.

Sinkiang's industry is powered by thermal and hydroelectric stations in the major cities. Heavy industry includes an iron and steel works and a cement factory at Urumchi and a farm-tool plant at Kashgar. Industries processing agricultural products have been established near the sources of raw materials. They include the cotton mill in Kashgar, the silk mill in Khotan in the south, the cotton mill in Shih-ho-tze, the woolen-textile mill in the Kazakh pastoral area of northern Sinkiang, the beet-sugar mill in the Ma-na-ssu reclamation area (northwest of Urumchi), and processing factories for the animal products of the pastoral areas.

Transportation. Roads encircle the Tarim Basin, along the foothills of the surrounding mountains, and run along the northern foothills of the Tien Shan in Dzungaria. The two basins are connected by a road that crosses the Tien Shan near Urumchi. There are roads leading to the Soviet Union in the north through passes in Dzungaria and in the south through the pass at Kashgar, the historic gateway of the silk trade between Asia and Europe. The region is also connected by road to the Chinese provinces of Kansu and Tsinghai in the southeast.

A railway crosses Sinkiang from Kansu Province through Ha-mi, Urumchi, and the Dzungarian Gate (a pass in the Pamir Mountains); it connects with the Soviet railway system at Aktogay, Kazakh S.S.R. Air services radiate from Urumchi east to Ha-mi, south to Khotan, west to Kuldja, and north to A-lo-t'ai.

Cultural life. The various indigenous peoples of Sinkiang exhibit their own cultures. The dominant Uighurs are sedentary farmers whose social organization is centred upon the village. There is little political unity, and the villages are virtually autonomous. The Uzbeks, related to the population of the Uzbek S.S.R., are also agriculturists who exhibit some remnants of their ancient nomadic way of life. Tadzhiks are related to those of the Tadzhik S.S.R. Agriculturalists, they are also skilled in handicrafts and trade.

The Kazakhs are pastoralists related to the people of the Kazakh S.S.R. They migrate seasonally in search of pasturage and live in dome-shaped, portable tents known as yurts. Livestock includes sheep, goats, and some cattle; horses are kept for prestige. The basic social unit is the extended family; political organization extends through a hierarchy of chiefs. Although there is a concept of national origin, the chiefs are seldom united.

Like the Kazakhs, the Mongolians are pastoralists who live in yurts, but their society is more firmly organized. The basic social unit is the nuclear family. There is an established political hierarchy of groups, the smallest of which is a group of several households known as a *bag*.

The average person, or free nomad (*arat*), owes allegiance to nobles (*taiji*) and princes (*noyan* or *wang*). National power, however, is fragmented.

BIBLIOGRAPHY. GEORGE B. CRESSEY, *China's Geographic Foundations* (1934), a classic and basic text, although rather old; and *Land of the 500 Million: A Geography of China* (1955), a standard text; BASIL DAVIDSON, *Turkestan Alive* (1957), primarily a travel book, sympathetic to the Communist regime; A.R. FIELD, "Strategic Development in Sinkiang," *Foreign Affairs*, 39:312–318 (1961); WERNER HANDKE, *Die Wirtschaft Chinas: Dogma und Wirklichkeit* (1959); D.J.M. HOOSON, "A New Soviet Heartland?" *Georgl. J.*, 128:19–29 (1962); HUMAN RELATIONS AREA FILES, *A Regional Handbook on Northwest China* (1956); W.A. DOUGLAS JACKSON, *The Russo-Chinese Borderland: Zone of Peaceful Contact or Potential Conflict?* (1962), a political geography approach; OWEN LATTIMORE, *Pivot of Asia: Sinkiang and the Inner Asian Frontiers of China and Russia* (1950), an early study on the importance of Sinkiang; V.P. PETROV, "New Railway Links Between China and the Soviet Union," *Geogrl. J.*, 122:471–477 (1956); THEODORE SHABAD, *China's Changing Map*, 2nd ed. (1972), a political and economic geography text based on provincial units; UNITED STATES CENTRAL INTELLIGENCE AGENCY, *Communist China Administrative Atlas* (1969); UNITED STATES DEPARTMENT OF THE INTERIOR, BUREAU OF MINES, *Foreign Minerals Survey*, vol. 2, *Mineral Resources of China* (1948), a basic reference document (also referred to as Dickerman).

(C.-M.H.)

Sino-Tibetan Languages

In the narrowest sense, the Sino-Tibetan languages include the Chinese and Tibeto-Burman languages. In terms of numbers of speakers, they comprise the world's second largest language family (after Indo-European), including over 300 languages and major dialects. In a wider sense, Sino-Tibetan has been defined as also including the Tai (or Daic), Karen, and Miao-Yao languages and even the Yenisey-Ostyak (or Ket) language in Northern Siberia (the latter affiliation seems rather untenable). Some linguists connect the Austro-Asiatic or Austronesian (Malayo-Polynesian) families, or both, with Sino-Tibetan; a suggested term for this most inclusive group, which seems to be based on premature speculations, is Sino-Austric. Other scholars see a relationship of Sino-Tibetan with the Athapascan and other languages of North America, but proof of this is beyond reach at the present state of knowledge.

Sino-Tibetan languages were known for a long time by the name of Indochinese, which is now restricted to the languages of Indochina. They were also called Tibeto-Chinese until the now universally accepted designation Sino-Tibetan was adopted. The term Sinitic also has been used in the same sense, as well as for the Chinese subfamily exclusively. (In the following discussion of language groups, the ending *-ic,* as in Sinitic, indicates a relatively large group of languages, and *-ish* denotes a smaller grouping.)

Areas in which the languages are spoken

Sinitic languages, commonly known as the Chinese dialects, are spoken in China and on Taiwan and by important minorities in all the countries of Southeast Asia (by a majority only in Singapore). In addition, Sinitic is spoken by Chinese immigrants in many parts of the world, notably in Oceania and in North and South America; altogether there are some 600,000,000 speakers of the Chinese dialects. Sinitic is divided into a number of languages, by far the most important of which is Mandarin (or Northern Chinese). Mandarin, which includes Modern Standard Chinese (which is based on the Peking dialect), is not only the most important language of the Sino-Tibetan family but also has the most ancient writing tradition still in use of any modern language. The remaining Sinitic language groups include Wu (including Shanghai dialect), Hsiang (Hunanese), Kan (or Kan-Hakka), Yüeh, or Cantonese (including Canton and Hong Kong dialects), and Min (including Fuchow, Amoy, and Taiwanese).

Tibeto-Burman languages are spoken in Tibet and Burma; in the Himalayas, including Nepal, Sikkim, and Bhutan; in Assam and in Bangladesh; as well as by hill tribes all over mainland Southeast Asia and West China (Kansu, Tsinghai, Szechwan, and Yunnan provinces). The total number of speakers is approximately 25,000,000. Tibetic (*i.e.*, Tibetan in the widest sense of the word) comprises a number of dialects and languages in Tibet and the Himalayas. Burmic (Burmese in its widest application) includes Lolo, Kachin, Kuki-Chin, the obsolete Hsi-hsia, or Tangut, and other languages. The Tibetan writing system (from the 7th century) and the Burmese (from the 11th century) are derived from the Indo-Aryan (Indic) tradition; the Hsi-hsia system (11th–13th century in Northwest China) was based on the Chinese model. Pictographic writing systems, which show some influence from Chinese, were developed within the last 500 years by Lolo and Moso tribes in West China. In modern times many Tibeto-Burman languages have acquired writing systems in Roman (Latin) script or in the script of the host country (Thai, Burmese, Indic, and others).

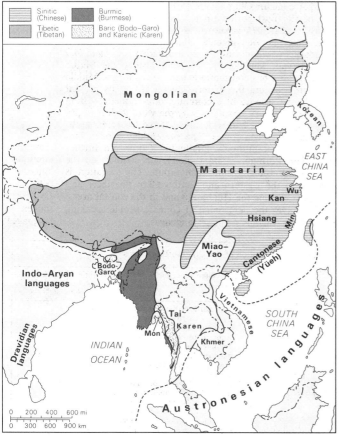

Distribution of the Sino-Tibetan languages.

CLASSIFICATION OF THE LANGUAGES

The old literary languages, Chinese, Tibetan, and Burmese, are generally considered as representatives of three major divisions within Sino-Tibetan (Sinitic, Tibetic, and Burmic). A fourth literary language, Thai, or Siamese (written from the 13th century), represents what was accepted for a long time as a Tai or Daic division of Sino-Tibetan or as a division of a Sino-Tai family (see also TAI LANGUAGES). This relationship is now more commonly considered nongenetic in that most of the shared vocabulary is more likely to be cultural loans than derivations from a common ancestral language.

Sinitic stands apart from Tibetic and Burmic on many grounds (vocabulary, morphology, syntax, and phonology). Most scholars agree on combining Tibetic and Burmic into a Tibeto-Burman subfamily, which also includes Bodo-Garo or Baric but not Karenic. If Karenic is Sino-Tibetan, it must be set up as an independent member of a Tibeto-Karen group that includes Tibeto-Burman. The special affinities between Sinitic and Karenic (especially in syntax) are secondary. The two closely related language groups, Miao and Yao (also known as Mnong and Man), may be very remotely related to Sino-Tibetan;

Problems in classifying Karenic

they are spoken in West China and northern mainland Southeast Asia and may well be of Austro-Tai stock.

In attempting to determine the exact interrelationship of the Tai (Daic) languages, Karenic, Sino-Tibetan, and several other marginal tongues, scholars must keep in mind that a discernable layer of Sino-Tibetan features in a given language may have been superimposed upon an older, non-Sino-Tibetan foundation (called the substratum language). Attributing a language to Sino-Tibetan or to another family may depend entirely on the ability of scholars to identify the substratum. Thus, if Tai is not considered as a division of Sino-Tibetan, it is because the substratum has been recognized as Austronesian; if Karen is still included among Sino-Tibetan languages on some level, it is perhaps because identification of a substratum is still lacking. Among the languages classified as Sino-Tibetan, a great many are known only from word lists or have not yet been described in a way that makes valid comparisons possible.

A number of Sino-Tibetan languages are enumerated below together with their most likely affiliation. Some scholars believe the Tibetic and Burmic divisions to be premature and that for the present their subdivisions (such as Bodish, Himalayish, Kirantish, Burmish, Kachinish, Kukish) should be considered as the classificatory peaks around which the Sino-Tibetan languages group themselves as members or more or less distant relatives. Certainly the stage has not yet been reached in which definite boundaries can be laid down and ancestral Proto-, or Common, Tibetic and Proto-, or Common, Burmic can be undisputedly reconstructed.

Tibetic languages. The Tibetic (or Bodic, from Bod, the Tibetan name for Tibet) division comprises the Bodish-Himalayish, Kirantish, and Mirish language groups.

Table 1: Tibetic (Bodic) Languages*		
	areas where spoken	number of speakers†
Bodish-Himalayish		
Bodish languages		
Tibetan (with branches and dialects)	Tibet, Sikkim, Nepal, sporadically in India, in Bhutan, Kashmir, the Chinese provinces of Kansu, Tsinghai, and Szechwan	3,000,000
Central group: Lhasa, Khams, Kagate, Jad, Nyamkat (Mnyamskad)		
Southern group: Spiti, Sharpa, Sikkim, Lhoke		
Northern group: Ambo (Ngambo), Chone		
Western group: Balti, Purik (Burig), Ladak (Ladwags)	Kashmir	
Derge	China	
Gurung	central Nepal	
Gyarung (Rgyarung)	Tibet, Szechwan	
Himalayish languages		100,000
Kanauri branch: Thebor, Bunan, Kanashi, Chitkhuli, Manchati, Rangloi, Chamba Lahuli		
Almora branch: Rangkas, and others		
Kirantish (Bahing-Vayu)		200,000
Eastern (Bahing) branch: Bahing, Sunwari, Dumi; Khambu, Rodong, Waling, Lambichong, Lohorung, Limbu, Yakha	eastern Nepal	
Western (Vayu) branch; Vayu, Chepang; Magari (perhaps)	central Nepal	
Mirish (Mishingish)	Assam, Tibet	
Miri (Mishing)		
Abor		
Dafla (Nyising)		
Other Tibetic languages		
Newari	central Nepal	several hundred thousand
Hruso (Hurso, Aka)	northern Assam	
Digaro (Taying)	Assam, Tibet	
Miju	Assam, Tibet	
Dhimal	Darjeeling area	
*Represents approximately 6,000,000 speakers. †Approximate.		

Burmic languages. The Burmic division comprises Burmish, Kachinish, and Kukish.

A number of Tibeto-Burman languages that are difficult to classify have marginal affiliations with Burmic. The

Table 2: Burmic Languages

	areas where spoken	number of speakers
Burmish (Burmese-Lolo)		
Burma branch	west China, Burma, Indochina	
Burmese and its dialects (Rangoon, Mergui, Intha, Danu, Yaw, Taungyo, Tavoyan, Arakanese)		15,000,000
Maru (Lawng)		
Lashi (Letsi)		
Atsi (Tsaiwa)		
Lolo branch		
Northern group: Lisu, Nyi (I), Ahi, Lolopho		
Southern group: Akha, Lahu		
Moso (Nakhi)*		
Ch'iang*		
Kachinish		
Kachin (Chingpaw)†	Kachin State in Burma, adjoining Assam, Shan State, Yunnan	180,000
Kukish (Kuki-Chin)		
Kuki branch	border region of Burma-South Assam-Bangladesh	
Central Kuki: Lushai, Lakher, Lai (Haka)		
Northern Kuki: Thado, Kamhau (Tiddim), Siyin (Sizang)		
Southern Kuki: Sho, Yawdwin, Chinbok, Khami (with Khimi)		
Old Kuki: Rangkhol, Bete (Biate); Anal, Lamgang; Aimol, Purum	spoken by dispersed tribes driven out from their original home on the Burma-India border	
Western Kuki: Empeo, Maram, Kwoireng, Kabui, Khoirao‡		
Lahupa languages§ (Tangkhul, Maring, Khoibu)		
Nāga branch	Nāgāland	
Northern: Ao		
Eastern group: Rengma, Sema (Simi), Angami		
Lepcha (Rong)‖	Sikkim, east Nepal, west Bhutan	

*These stand in a not clearly defined relationship to Lolo. †For cultural, non-linguistic reasons, Maru, Lashi, and Atsi are often grouped with Kachin. ‡In Manipur and Cachar. §These languages are similar to Kuki. ‖Usually compared to the northern Nāga branch of Kukish, but has Baric and Himalayish affinities.

Luish languages (Andro, Sengmai, Kadu, Sak, and perhaps also Chairel) in Manipur and adjacent Burma resemble Kachin; Nung (including Rawang and Trung) in the Kachin State of Burma and in Yunnan has similarities with Kachin; and Mru, with 20,000 speakers in Arakan and Chittagong Hills, Meithei (Mhithlei) in Manipur, and Mikir in Assam seem close to Kukish.

Baric languages. The Baric, or Bodo-Garo, division consists of a number of languages spoken in Assam and falls into a Bodo branch (not to be confused with Bodic Tibetic, and Bodish, a subdivision of Tibetic) and a Garo branch.

A group of Sino-Tibetan languages in Nāgāland (Nagish, not to be confused with the Nāga branch of Kukish; including Mo Shang, Namsang, and Banpara) has affinities to Baric.

Table 3: Baric (Bodo-Garo) Languages

	areas where spoken	number of speakers*
Bodo branch	the plains of Assam	
Bodo		200,000
Dimasa		15,000
Garo branch	the hills of Assam	300,000+
Achik, Abeng, Dacca Atong, Rabha, Ruga, Koch		

*Approximate.

Karenic languages. The Karenic languages of the Karen State of Burma and adjacent areas in Burma and Thailand include the two major languages of the Pho (Pwo) and Sgaw, which have about 2,000,000 speakers. Taungthu (Pa-o) is close to Pho, and Palaychi to Sgaw. There are several minor groups.

Chinese, or Sinitic, languages. Chinese as the name of a language is a misnomer. It has been applied to numerous dialects, styles, and languages from the middle of the 2nd millennium BC. Sinitic is a more satisfactory designation for covering all these entities and setting them off from the Tibeto-Karen group of Sino-Tibetan languages. *Han* is a Chinese term for Chinese as opposed to non-Chinese languages spoken in China. The Chinese terms for Modern Standard Chinese are *kuo-yü* "national language" and *p'u-t'ung-hua* "common language." Reconstructed prehistoric Chinese is known as Proto-Sinitic (or Proto-Chinese); the oldest historic language of China is called Archaic or Old Chinese (8th–3rd century BC), and that of the next period up to and including the T'ang dynasty (618–907) is known as Ancient or Middle Chinese. Later periods include Old, Middle, and Modern Mandarin ("Mandarin" is a translation of *kuan-hua* "civil servant language"). Through history the Sinitic language area has constantly expanded from the "Middle Kingdom" around the eastern Huang Ho to its present size. The persistence of a common, non-phonetic writing system for centuries explains why the word dialect rather than language has had widespread usage for referring to the modern speech forms. The present-day spoken languages are not mutually intelligible (some are further apart than Portuguese and Italian), and neither are the major subdivisions within each group. The variation is slightest in the western and southwestern provinces and the greatest along the Huang Ho and in the coastal areas. Table 4 gives the percentage of Chinese people speaking each of the various Chinese languages.

Absence of intelligibility between Chinese spoken languages

Table 4: Distribution of the Chinese Languages

	areas where spoken	ratio of speakers to total population (percentage)*
Mandarin	China, north of the Yangtze River; a narrow belt south of the Yangtze River in Kiangsi, Anhwei, and Kiangsu; Szechwan, Yunnan, and Kweichow; small parts of Hunan	70†
Wu	Kiangsu and Chekiang	8+
Hsiang	Hunan	5
Kan‡	Kiangsi and a corner of Hupei	2+
Hakka‡	east and north Kwangtung; parts of Fukien, Kiangsi, Kwangsi, Taiwan, Hunan, Szechwan; sporadically in other provinces	4
Yüeh (Cantonese)	Kwangtung, south Kwangsi, Hong Kong, Macao	5
Min§	Fukien, west Kwangtung, Hainan, Taiwan, south Chekiang	4+

*A Chinese estimate from the 1950s gives the following figures of number of speakers: Mandarin 387,000,000; Wu 46,000,000; Hsiang 26,000,000; Kan-Hakka 33,000,000; Yüeh 27,000,000; Min 22,000,000. †Figure applies to those people speaking Mandarin as the mother tongue as opposed to speaking it as a second language. ‡Kan and Hakka are often combined as Kan-Hakka, or simply Kan. §Min is subdivided into Northern Min, in North Fukien with little over 1 percent of the national population, and Southern Min, in the remainder of the Min-speaking area with 3 percent of the population.

A vernacular written tradition exists mainly in Peking Mandarin and in Cantonese. An unwritten storytelling tradition has survived in most languages. The school and radio language is Modern Standard Chinese in China as well as in Taiwan and Singapore. In Hong Kong, Cantonese prevails as the school language and in the communication media. Modern Standard Chinese is the accepted written language for all Chinese.

Non-Chinese Sino-Tibetan languages of China include some Lolo-type languages (Burmish)—I (Yi, or Nyi), with over 3,000,000 speakers in Yunnan, Szechwan, Kweichow, and Kwangsi; Hani (or Akha) with fewer than 100,000 speakers in Yunnan; Lisu, with approximately

250,000 speakers in Yunnan; Lahu, with 150,000 speakers in Yunnan; Moso or Nasi, with 150,000 speakers in Yunnan and Szechwan; and Achang by the Burmese border. Other Sino-Tibetan languages in Yunnan and Szechwan (with fewer than 100,000 speakers each) are Kachin and the closely related Tsaiwa; Ch'iang, Gyarung, Hsifan; and Pai (or Minchia, perhaps an Austro-Asiatic language).

COMMON SINO-TIBETAN FEATURES

At the end of the 18th and during the first half of the 19th century, a great number of languages were discovered by Western scholars in the Himalayas, in India, and in China, and word lists and grammatical sketches began to appear. By the late 19th century a foundation had been laid for Sino-Tibetan comparative studies.

The comparative method for determining relationships

The comparative method for determining genetic relationship among languages was worked out for Indo-European during the latter part of the 19th century. It rests on the assumption that sound correspondences in related words and morphological units, as well as structural similarities on all levels (phonology, morphology, syntax), can be explained in terms of a reconstructed common language, or protolanguage. The morphology and syntax of Sino-Tibetan languages are for the most part rather simple and nonspecific, and the length of time involved in the separation of subfamilies and divisions is such that comparative phonological statements are often hard to reduce to the form of concise correspondences and laws.

A number of features have been delineated as common for the Sino-Tibetan languages. Many of them can be shown to be of a typological nature, the result of diffusion and underlying unrelated language strata.

Typological similarities. *Monosyllabicity.* The vast majority of all words in all Sino-Tibetan languages are of one syllable, and the exceptions appear to be secondary (*i.e.,* words that were introduced at a later date than Common, or Proto-, Sino-Tibetan). Some suffixes in Tibeto-Burman are syllabic, thus adding a syllable to a word, but they have a highly reduced set of vowels and tones ("minor syllables"). These features are, however, shared by contiguous languages not clearly attributable to Sino-Tibetan on the basis of shared basic vocabulary items (namely, Austro-Asiatic and Miao-Yao).

Tonality. Most Sino-Tibetan languages possess phonemic tones, which indicate a difference in meaning in otherwise similar words. There are no tones in Purik, a Western Tibetan language; Ambo, a Northern Tibetan tongue; and Newari of Nepal. Balti, another Western Tibetan language, has pitch differences in polysyllabic nouns. The tones of the remaining Tibetan dialects can be accounted for by positing an original and older system of voiced and voiceless initial sounds that eventually resulted in tones. In several Himalayish languages, tones are linked with articulatory features connected with the end of the syllable or are linked with stress features, as also in Kukish Lepcha.

Most Baric languages lack tones altogether; and Burmic, Karenic, and Sinitic tonal systems can be reduced to two basic tones ultimately probably accounted for by different syllabic endings. What can be reconstructed for Proto-Sino-Tibetan, the language from which all the modern Sino-Tibetan languages developed, are a set of conditioning factors (as, for example, certain syllabic endings) that resulted in tones; the tones themselves cannot be reconstructed. Again the features that encouraged the development of tones are not uniquely Sino-Tibetan; similar conditions have produced similar effects in Tai and Miao-Yao and—within the Austro-Asiatic languages —in Vietnamese and in the embryonic form of two registers (pitches or musical range) also in Cambodian.

Affixation. Most Sino-Tibetan languages possess or can be shown to have at one time possessed derivational and morphological affixes—*i.e.,* word elements attached before or after or within the main stem of a word that change or modify the meaning in some way. Many prefixes can be reconstructed for Proto-Sino-Tibetan: *s-* (causative), *m-* (intransitive), *b-, d-, g-,* and *r-,* and many more for certain language divisions and units. Among the

Prefixes and suffixes

suffixes, *-s* (used with several types of verbs and nouns), *-t,* and *-n* are inherited from the protolanguage. The problem of whether Proto-Sino-Tibetan made use of *-r-* and *-l-* infixes (besides perhaps semivocalic infixes) has not been solved. Whether clusters containing these sounds were the result of prefixation to roots beginning in *r* and *l* (and *y*) or came about through infixation is not clear.

Initial consonant alternation. Voiced and voiceless initial stops alternate in the same root in many Sino-Tibetan languages, including Chinese, Burmese, and Tibetan (voiced in intransitive, voiceless in transitive verbs). The German Oriental scholar August Conrady linked this morphological system to the causative *s-* prefix, which was supposed to have caused devoicing of voiced stops. (Voicing is the vibration of the vocal cords, as occurs, for example, in the sounds *b, d, g, z,* and so on. Devoicing, or voicelessness, is the pronunciation of sounds without vibration of the vocal cords, as in *p, t, k, s*). Such alternating of the initial consonant cannot itself be reconstructed for the protolanguage.

Vowel alternation. The morphological use of vowel gradation ("ablaut") is well-known from Indo-European languages (*e.g.,* the vowel change in English "sing, sang, sung") and is found in several Sino-Tibetan languages, including Chinese and Tibetan. In Tibetan the various forms of verbs are differentiated in part by vowel alternation; in Sinitic some related words ("word families") are kept apart by vowel alternation. A conditioning factor outside the vowel (perhaps stress or sandhi, the modification of a sound according to the surrounding sounds) may have been responsible for the Sino-Tibetan ablaut systems.

Indistinct word classes. Especially in the older stages of Sino-Tibetan, the distinction of verbs and nouns appears blurred; both overlap extensively in the Old Chinese writing system. Philological tradition as well as Sinitic reconstruction show, however, that frequently when the verb and the noun were written alike, they were pronounced differently, the difference manifesting itself later in the tonal system. Verbs and nouns also used different sets of particles. In this respect, Chinese resembles Tai and Austro-Asiatic, whereas Tibetan is more similar to the Altaic languages (for example, Turkish, Mongol).

Use of noun classifiers. The Sino-Tibetan noun is typically a collective term, designating all members of its class—*e.g.,* "man" meaning "all human beings." In a number of modern Sino-Tibetan languages, such a noun can be counted or modified by a demonstrative pronoun only indirectly through a smaller number of non-collective nouns, called "classifiers," in constructions such as "one *person* man," "one *animal* dog," and so on, much like parallel cases in Indo-European (in English, "one head of cattle"; in German, *ein Kopf Salat* "one head of lettuce"). The phenomenon is absent in Tibetan and appears late in Burmese and Chinese. Furthermore, classifiers are not exclusively Sino-Tibetan; they exist also in Miao-Yao, Tai, Austric, and Japanese. In Classical Chinese, Tai, and Burmese, the classifier construction follows the noun; in modern Chinese, as in Miao-Yao, it precedes it. Classifiers are of later origin and do not belong to Proto-Sino-Tibetan.

Classifiers for nouns

Word order. Although the word order of subject–object–verb and modified–modifier prevails in Tibeto-Burman, the order subject–verb–object and modifier–modified occurs in Karenic. In this respect Chinese is like Karen, although Old Chinese shows remnants of the Tibeto-Burman word order. Tai employs still another order: subject–verb–object, and modified–modifier, like Austric but unlike Miao-Yao, which follows the Karen and Chinese model. Word order, even more than any of the other distinguishing features, points to diffusion from several centres, or to unrelated substrata.

Phonological correspondences. The hypothesis that the Sino-Tibetan languages are all related and derive from a common source depends on phonological correspondences in shared vocabulary more than on any other argument. It is ironic that the clearest and most convincing results should have been obtained from studies of the

Sinitic-Tai similarities, which probably do not indicate a true case of genetic relationship. In 1942 it was shown that most of the words in this grouping were cultural loans (then thought of as Chinese loanwords in Tai, now believed to a very large extent to be borrowings in the opposite direction).

A comparison of Old Chinese and Old Tibetan made by Walter Simon in 1929, although limited in some ways, pointed to enough sound resemblances in important items of basic vocabulary to eliminate the possibility of coincidental similarities between unrelated languages. A few examples of similar words in Old Tibetan and Old Chinese, respectively, follow: "bent," *khyog* and *khyuk;* "eye," *mig* and *myok;* "friend," *grogs* and *gyug;* "kill," *gsod* and *sat;* "die" *shi* and *syər;* "sun," *nyi* and *ńye;* "life," *srog* and *serŋ.* The U.S. linguist Paul Benedict brought in material from other Sino-Tibetan languages and laid down the rule that the comparative linguist should accept perfect phonetic correspondences with inexact though close semantic equivalences in preference to perfect semantic equivalences with questionable phonetic correspondences. New material and competent descriptions later made it possible to reconstruct important features of common ancestral languages within major divisions of Sino-Tibetan (notably Lolo, Baric, Tibetic, Kachin, Kukish, Karenic, Sinitic).

Interrelationship of the language groups. The position of Proto-Sino-Tibetan can be defined in terms of a chain of interrelated languages and language groups: Sinitic is connected with Tibetic through a body of shared vocabulary and typological features, similarly Tibetic with Baric, Baric with Burmic, and Burmic with Karenic. The chain continues at both ends, connecting Sinitic to Tai and Tai to Austronesian (Malayo-Polynesian) and also connecting Karenic with Austro-Asiatic. Considerations of basic vocabulary versus cultural loans and diffusion versus inheritance have led scholars to believe that only the members of the chain from Sinitic to Karenic share a common ancestral language; especially Sinitic and Karenic are under suspicion for containing only superstrata of Sino-Tibetan origin.

Proto-Tibeto-Burman was monosyllabic. Some grammatical units may have had the form of minor syllables before the major syllable (**ma-*, **ba-*) or after the major syllable (**-ma*, **-ba*). (An asterisk [*] indicates that the form it precedes is unattested and has been reconstructed as a possible ancestral form.) The consonants were three voiceless stops (*p, t, k*), which were aspirated in absolute initial position, three voiced stops (*b, d, g*), and three nasal sounds (*m, n, ŋ* [as the *-ng* in "sing"]). There were five continuant sounds (*s, z, r, l,* and *h*) and two semivowels (*w, y*). In final position there was only one set of stops, but there were a number of initial and final clusters mainly resulting from the addition of prefixes and suffixes. Three degrees of vowel opening existed with two members in each: *i* and *u, e* and *o, a* and *aa* (short and long *a*). Length may have been relevant also with the *i* and *u* and *e* and *o* vowels. The conditioning factors that led to the development of tones can be shown to have been voiced–voiceless contrast in initial and final consonants and consonant clusters. Because the conditioning factors were involved with morphological process (affixation and consonant alternation), tonal systems could also acquire certain grammatical or structural functions. An independent morphological system was vowel alternation.

The sound system of Proto-Karenic appears closely related to that of Proto-Tibeto-Burman. The tonal classes can be reduced to two, which connect Karen to Burmic, Sinitic, Tai, and Miao-Yao.

Greater dissimilarity is encountered with respect to Proto-Sinitic. The contrast of aspirated and unaspirated voiceless stops in initial position is most likely the result of lost initial cluster elements as in Proto-Tibeto-Burman. The voiced stops also possess the aspirated–unaspirated distinction. Unlike Tibeto-Burman, two series of stops in syllable final position are posited for Old Chinese, but whether the contrast involved aspiration or voicing is not clear. One series is in general without an exact corre-

spondence in Tibeto-Burman languages, but Burmish Maru and Kuki-oid Mru both have final stops in a number of these words. Similar isolated cases are found in Tibetan and in Tai.

Old Chinese has two more relevant points of articulation, or sound-producing positions of the mouth, than Proto-Tibeto-Burman: palatal (in which the tongue surface touches the palate) and retroflex (in which the tip of the tongue is curled upward toward the palate). But these two types of sounds may be explained as the result of influence from lost Proto-Sinitic medical sounds (a palatal *-y-* and a retroflex *-r-*). The relationship between these specific medial sounds and similar elements in Tibeto-Karen is, however, not certain. Dental affricate sounds in Old Chinese, which begin as stops with complete stoppage of the breath stream and conclude as fricatives with incomplete air stoppage and audible friction, can at least be explained partly as metathesized (transposed) forms of prefix *s-* plus a dental sound in Proto-Sinitic (*e.g., st* changes to *ts*). Old Chinese possessed initial consonant clusters containing *-l-* as a second element, so Proto-Sinitic can reasonably be supposed to have had the same three medial elements as Proto-Tibeto-Burman: *-y-*, *-l-*, and *-r-*. There are few, if any, traces in Old Chinese of the more complicated clusters and the minor syllables of Tibeto-Burman.

The vowel system of Old Chinese as reconstructed (1940) by the linguist Bernhard Karlgren to account especially for the language of the "Classic of Poetry" (a collection of poetry, entitled the *Shih Ching,* from around 800–600 BC) seems surprisingly complicated as compared to that of later Sinitic and to that of Proto-Tibeto-Burman. Probably some of the vowels were in reality diphthongs or combinations of vowels plus consonants.

As in Karen and Burmese-Loloish, the tones of Sinitic can be reduced to two (the modern Sinitic languages have from two to as many as eight or nine). Monosyllabicity of roots and morphological affixation were characteristic features of Proto-Sino-Tibetan as of Proto-Tibeto-Karen.

CHARACTERISTICS OF THE MODERN CHINESE LANGUAGES

All modern Sinitic languages—*i.e.,* the "Chinese dialects"—share a number of important typological features. They have a single syllabic structure of the type consonant–semivowel–vowel–semivowel–consonant. Some languages lack one set of semivowels, and, in some, gemination (doubling) or clustering of vowels occurs. The languages also employ a system of tones (pitch and contour) and sometimes glottal features and occasionally stress. For the most part, tones are lexical (*i.e.,* they distinguish otherwise similar words); in some languages tones also carry grammatical meaning. Non-tonal grammatical units (*i.e.,* affixes) may be smaller than syllables, but usually meaningful units consist of one or more syllables. Words can consist of one syllable, of two or more syllables each carrying an element of meaning, or of two or more syllables that individually carry no meaning. For example, Modern Standard Chinese *t'en* "sky, heaven, day" is a one-syllable word; *jih-t'ou* "sun" is composed of *jih* "sun, day," a word element that cannot occur alone as a word, and the noun suffix *t'ou;* and *hu-t'ier* "butterfly" consists of two syllables, each having no meaning in itself (this is a rare type of word formation). The Southern languages have more monosyllabic words and word elements than the Northern ones.

The Sinitic languages distinguish nouns and verbs with some overlapping, as do Sino-Tibetan languages in general. There are noun suffixes that form different kinds of nouns (concrete nouns, diminutives, abstract nouns, and so on), particles placed after nouns indicating relationships in time and space, and verb particles for modes and aspects. Adjectives act as one of several kinds of verbs. Verbs can occur in a series (concatenation) with irreversible order (*e.g.,* the verbs "take" and "come" placed next to one another denote the concept "bring"). Nouns are collective in nature, and only classifiers (see above) can be counted and referred to singly. Specific particles are used to indicate the relationship of nominals (*e.g.,* nouns

Chain of interrelated languages

Vowel system of Old Chinese

Sinitic grammatical characteristics

and noun phrases) to verbs, such as transitive verb–object, agent–passive verb; in some of the languages this system forms a sentence construction called ergative, in which all nominals are marked for their function and the verb stays unchanged. Final sentence particles convey a variety of meanings, such as "question, command, surprise, new situation." The general word order of subject–verb–object and complement and modifier–modified is the same in all the languages, but the use of the preposed particles and verbs in a series varies considerably. Grammatical elements of equal or closely related values in various languages are very often not related in sounds.

The Sinitic languages fall into a Northern and a Southern group. The Northern languages (or Mandarin dialects) are closer to each other than the Southern ones (Wu, Hsiang, Kan, Yüeh, Min).

Modern Standard Chinese (Mandarin). Modern Standard Chinese is based on the Peking dialect, which is of the Northern, or Mandarin, type. It employs about 1,300 different syllables. There are 22 initial consonants, including stops (made with momentary, complete closure in the vocal tract), affricates (beginning as stops but ending with incomplete closure), aspirated consonants, nasals, fricatives, liquid sounds (l, r), and a glottal stop. The medial semivowels are y (i), ʮ ($ü$) and w (u). In final position, the following occur: nasal consonants, ŗ (retroflex r), the semivowels y and w, and the combinations ŋr and wr. There are nine vowel sounds, including three varieties of i (retroflex, apical, and palatal). Several vowels combine into clusters.

The four tones of Mandarin

There are four tones: (1) high level; (2) high rising crescendo; (3) low falling diminuendo with glottal friction (with an extra rise from low to high when final); (4) falling diminuendo. Unstressed syllables have a neutral tone, which depends on its surroundings for pitch. Tones in sequences of syllables that belong together lexically and syntactically ("sandhi groups") may undergo changes known as tonal sandhi, the most important of which causes a third tone before another third tone to be pronounced as a second tone. The tones influence some vowels (notably e and o), which are pronounced more open in third and fourth tones than in first and second tones.

A surprisingly low number of the possible combinations of all the consonantal, vocalic, and tonal sounds are utilized. The vowels i and $ü$ and the semivowels y and ʮ never occur after velar sounds (e.g., k) and occur only after the palatalized affricate and sibilant sounds (e.g., $t\acute{s}$), which in turn occur with no other vowels and semivowels.

There are many alternative interpretations of the distinctive sounds of Chinese; the interaction of consonants, vowels, semivowels, and tones sets Modern Standard Chinese apart from many other Sinitic languages and dialects and gives it a unique character among the major languages of the world. The two most widely used transcription systems (romanizations) are Wade-Giles (first propounded by Sir Thomas Francis Wade in 1859 and later modified by Herbert A. Giles) and the official Chinese transcription system today, known as the *pinyin zimu* ("Pin-yin phonetic spelling") or simply Pin-yin (adopted in 1958). The accompanying romanization table presents both the Wade-Giles and the Pin-yin systems. In Wade-Giles, aspiration is marked by ' (p' t', and so on). The semivowels are y, $yü$, and w in initial position; i, $ü$, and u in medial; and i and u (but o after a) in final position. Final retroflex r is written rh. The tones are indicated by raised figures after the syllables (^{1}, ^{2}, ^{3}, ^{4}).

The Pin-yin system indicates unaspirated stops and affricates by means of traditionally voiced consonants (e.g., b, d) and aspirated consonants by voiceless sounds (e.g., p, t). The semivowels are y, yu, and w initially; i, iu, and u medially; and i and u (o after a) finally. Final retroflex r is written r. The tones are indicated by accent markers, $1 = ^-$, $2 = ^\prime$, $3 = ^\vee$, $4 = ^\grave{}$, (e.g., $m\bar{a}$, $m\acute{a}$, $m\check{a}$, $m\grave{a}$ = Wade-Giles ma^1, ma^2, ma^3, ma^4).

Wade-Giles is used in the following discussion of Modern Standard Chinese grammar.

The most common suffixes that indicate nouns are *-erh* (as in *ch'ang-erh* "song"; cf. *ch'ang* "sing"), *-tzu* (as in *fang-tzu* "house"), and *-t'ou* (as in *mu-t'ou* "wood"). A set of postposed noun particles express space and time relationships (*-li* "inside," *-hou* "after"). An example of a verbal affix is *-chien* in *k'an-chien* "see" and *t'ing-chien* "hear." Important verb particles are *-le* (completed action), *-kuo* (past action), *chih* or *-che* (action in progress). The directional verbal particles *-lai* "toward speaker" and *-ch'ü* "away from speaker" and some verbal suffixes can be combined with the potential particles *te* "can" and *pu* "cannot"—e.g., *na-ch'ü-lai* "take out," *na-pu-ch'ü-lai* "cannot take out"; *t'ing-chien* "hear," *t'ing-te-chien* "can hear." The particle *te* indicates subordination and also gives nominal value to forms for other parts of speech (e.g., *wo* "I," *wo-te* "mine," *wo-te shu* "my book," *lai* "to come," *lai-te* "coming," *lai-te jen* "a person who comes"). The most important sentence particle is *le*, indicating "new situation" (e.g., *hsia-yü-le* "now it is raining," *pu-lai-le* "now there is no longer any chance that he will be coming"). *Ko* is the most common noun classifier (*i* "one," *i-ko-jen* "one person"); others are *so* (*i-so-fang-tzu* "one house") and *pen* (*liang-pen-shu* "two books").

Grammatical features of modern standard Chinese

Adjectives can be defined as qualitative verbs (*hao* "to be good") or stative verbs (*ping* "to be sick"). There are equational sentences with the word order subject–predicate—e.g., *wo-ihih pei-ching-jen* "I am a Peking-person (i.e., a native of Peking)"—and narrative sentences with the word order subject (or topic)–verb–object (or complement)—e.g., *wo ch'ih-fan* "I eat rice," *wo chu tsai pei-ching* "I live in Peking." The proposed object takes the particle *ba* (*wo da ta* "I beat him," *wo ba ta da le yi dun* "I gave him a beating"), and the agent of a passive construction takes *bei* (*wo bei ta da le yi dun* "I was given a beating by him").

Standard Cantonese. The most important representative of the Yüeh languages is Standard Cantonese of Canton, Hong Kong, and Macao. It has fewer initial consonants than Modern Standard Chinese (p, t, ts, k and the corresponding aspirated sounds ph, th, tsh, kh; m, n, ŋ; f, s, h; l, y), only one medial semivowel (w), more vowels than Modern Standard Chinese, six final consonants (p, t, k, m, n, ŋ), and two final semivowels (y and w). The nasals m and ŋ occur as syllables without a vowel.

Cantonese tonal system

There are three tones (high, mid, low) in syllables ending in *-p*, *-t*, and *-k*; six tones occur in other types of syllables (mid level, low level, high falling, low falling, high rising, low rising). Two tones are used to modify the meaning of words (high level °, and low-to-high rising *), as in *yin°* "tobacco," but *yin* "smoke" and *nöy** "daughter," but *nöy* "woman." Some special grammatical words also have the tone °. There is no neutral tone and little tonal sandhi.

There are more than 2,200 different syllables in Standard Cantonese, or almost twice as many as in Modern Standard Chinese. The word classes are the same as in Modern Standard Chinese. The grammatical words, although phonetically unrelated, generally have the same semantic value (e.g., the subordinating and nominalizing particle $k\varepsilon$, Modern Standard Chinese *te*; m "not," Modern Standard Chinese *pu*; the verbal particle for "completed action" and the sentence particle for "new situation," both *le* in Modern Standard Chinese, are Standard Cantonese *tsɔ* and *lɔ*, respectively).

Min languages. The most important Min language is Amoy from the Southern branch of Min. The initial consonants are the same as in Standard Chinese. There are two semivowels (y, w), six vowels and several vowel clusters, plus the syllabic nasal sounds m and ŋ functioning as vowels, the same semivowels as in Standard Cantonese, and, in addition, a glottal stop (ʔ) and a meaning-bearing feature of nasalization, as well as a combination of the last two features. There are two tones in syllables ending in a stop, five in other syllables. Tonal sandhi operates in many combinations.

Fuchow is the most important language of the Northern branch of Min. The very extensive sandhi affects not only tones but also consonants and vowels, so that the phonetic manifestation of a syllable depends entirely on interac-

Table 5: Romanization of Chinese, and Chinese Numerals

printed	name	EB preferred (Wade-Giles)	alternative (Pin-yin)	approximate pronunciation	printed	name	EB preferred (Wade-Giles)	alternative (Pin-yin)	approximate pronunciation
ㄅ	po	p	b	*baby*	ㄤ	ang	ang	ang	Fr. r*ang*
ㄆ	p'o	p'	p	*pepper*	ㄟ	ei	ei	ei	f*ade*
ㄇ	mo	m	m	*maim*	ㄣ	en	en	en	*undo*
ㄈ	fo	f	f	*fifty*	ㄥ	eng	eng	eng	h*ung*
ㄉ	te	t	d	*did*	ㄡ	yu	ou⊕	ou	*know*
ㄊ	t'e	t'	t	*tie*	ㄨㄥ	ung	ung	ong	Austr. b*oong*
ㄋ	ne	n	n	*no*	ㄧㄚ	ia	ia	ia	*yard*
ㄌ	le	l	l	*lily*	ㄧㄝ	ieh	ieh	ie	*yip*, id*ea*
ㄍ	ko	k	g	*go*	ㄧㄠ	iao	iao	iao	*yowl*
ㄎ	k'o	k'	k	*kin*	ㄧㄡ	iu	iu	iu	*yoke*
ㄏ	ho	h	h	Ger. Bu*ch**	ㄧㄢ	ien	ien	ian	*yen*
ㄐ	chi	ch	j	*jeer*†	ㄧㄣ	in	in	in	*kinky*
ㄑ	ch'i	ch'	q	*cheap*†	ㄧㄤ	iang	iang	iang	*Yonkers*♀
ㄒ	hsi	hs	x	Ger. Bü*ch*er	ㄨㄚ	ua	ua	ua	*guava*
ㄗ	tzu	ts‡	z	bi*ds*	ㄨㄛ	o	o**	uo	*wooer*
ㄘ	tz'u	ts'§	c	bi*ts*	ㄨㄞ	uai	uai	uai	*wide*
ㄙ	ssu	s‖	s	*sand*	ㄨㄟ	ui	ui††	ui	*way*
ㄓ	chih	ch	zh	*jug*†	ㄨㄢ	uan	uan	uan	Fr. d*ouame*
ㄔ	ch'ih	ch'	ch	*chug*†	ㄨㄣ	un	un	un	Fr. j*eune*, Ger. t*un*
ㄕ	shih	sh	sh	*shy*	ㄨㄤ	uang	uang	uang	*Wong*♀ (Chinese surname)
ㄖ	jih	j	r	¶	ㄩㄝ	üeh	üeh	üe	new w*icket*
ㄧ	i	y	y	*yard*	ㄩㄢ	üan	üan	üan	new w*en*
ㄨ	wu	w	w	*we*	ㄩㄣ	ün	ün	ün	new w*indow*

vowels

printed	name	EB preferred (Wade-Giles)	alternative (Pin-yin)	approximate pronunciation
ㄚ	ia	a	a	cot♀
ㄜ	e	eᵟ	e	c*o*mmand
ㄧ	i	i	i	b*ea*t
ㄓㄔㄕㄖ	chih, chi'ih, shih, jih	ih□	i	maj*or*♀
ㄗㄘㄙ	tzu, tz'u, ssu (szu)	u◇	i	b*ir*d♀
ㄛ	o	o	o	w*oo*d
ㄨ	wu	u	u	f*oo*d
ㄩ	yü	ü	ü▲	Ger. f*üh*len
ㄦ	erh	erh	er	j*ourney*+
ㄞ	ai	ai	ai	s*i*te
ㄠ	ao	ao	ao	n*ow*
ㄢ	an	an	an	n*on*

numerals

Chinese/Japanese	Arabic	Chinese/Japanese	Arabic	Chinese/Japanese	Arabic
〇	0	十一	11	二十二	22
一	1	十二	12	二十三	23
二	2	十三	13	二十四	24
三	3	十四	14	二十五	25
四	4	十五	15	二十六	26
五	5	十六	16	二十七	27
六	6	十七	17	二十八	28
七	7	十八	18	二十九	29
八	8	十九	19	三十	30
九	9	二十	20	一百	100
十	10	二十一	21	一千	1,000

*Velar, heavily aspirated *h*.   †*j* and *ch* in *jeer* and *cheap* are followed by front vowels; *j* and *ch* in *jug* and *chug* are followed by back vowels.   ‡Written *tz* before *ŭ*.   §Written *tz'* before *ŭ*.   ‖Written *ss* or *sz* before *ŭ*.   ♀In U.S., not British, pronunciation.   ᵟWritten *o* after *k, kh, h*.   □Occurs only after *ch, ch', sh, j*.   ◇Occurs only after *tz, tz', ss (sz)*; standard Wade-Giles uses *ŭ*.   ▲Written without umlaut after *j, a, x*.   +Retroflex *r*, with tongue at hard palate, slightly curled back.   ⊕Written *u* after *y*.   **Written *uo* after *k, k', h, sh*.   ††Written *uei* after *k, k'*.

tion with the surroundings. There are three initial labial sounds (*p, ph, m*), five dental sounds (*t, th, s, l, n*), three palatal sounds (*tś, tśh, ń*), and five velars (*k, kh, h, ?*, and ŋ). Syllables can end in -*k*, -ŋ, -? (glottal stop), a semi-vowel, or a vowel. The tones fall into two classes: a comparatively high class comprising high, mid, high falling, and high rising (only in sandhi forms) and a rather low one, comprising low rising and low rising-falling (circumflex). Certain vowels and diphthongs occur only with the high class, others occur only with the low class, and the vowel *a* occurs with both classes. Sandhi rules can cause tone to change from low class to high class, in which case the special vowels also change.

Other Sinitic languages. *Hakka.* Of the Kan (Kan-Hakka) languages, Hakka of Mei-hsien in Kwangtung is best known. It has the same initial consonants, final consonants, and syllabic nasals as Standard Cantonese; the vowels are close to Modern Standard Chinese. Medial and final semivowels are *y* and *w*. There are two tones in syllables with final stops, four in the other syllabic types.

Suchow. Suchow is usually quoted as representative of the Wu languages. It is rich in initial consonants, with a contrast of voiced and voiceless stops as well as palatalized and non-palatalized dental affricates, making 26 consonants in all. (Palatalized sounds are nonpalatal sounds formed with simultaneous movement of the tongue toward the hard palate. Dental affricates are sounds produced with the tongue tip touching the teeth and then drawing slightly away to allow air to pass through, producing a hissing sound.) Medial semivowels are as in Modern Standard Chinese. In addition, there are also ten vowels and four syllabic consonants (*l, m, n,* ŋ); -*n* and -ŋ occur in final position, as do the glottal stop and nasalization.

Shanghai dialect. The Shanghai dialect belongs to Wu. The prevalent tendency is for there to be only two tones or registers (high and low), which are related in an automatic way to the initial consonant type (voiceless and voiced).

Hsiang languages. The Hsiang languages, spoken only in Hunan, are divided into New Hsiang, which is under heavy influence from Mandarin and includes the language of the capital Ch'ang-sha, and Old Hsiang, closer to the Wu languages, as spoken for instance in Shuang-feng. Old Hsiang has 28 initial consonants, the highest number for any major Sinitic language, and 11 vowels, plus the syllabic consonants *m* and *n*. It also uses five tones, final *n* and *ŋ*, and nasalization, but no final stops.

HISTORICAL SURVEY OF CHINESE

Vocabulary. Old Chinese vocabulary already contained many words not generally occurring in the other Sino-Tibetan languages. The words for "honey" and "lion," probably also "horse," "dog," and "goose," are connected with Indo-European and were acquired through trade and early contacts. (The nearest known Indo-European languages were Tocharian and Sogdian.) A number of words have Austro-Asiatic cognates and point to early contacts with the ancestral language of Muong-Vietnamese and Mon-Khmer; *e.g.*, the name of the Yangtze River, **klawŋ*, Cantonese *kɔŋ*, Modern Standard Chinese *chiang*, is still the word for "river," pronounced *kroŋ* and *kloŋ*, in some modern Mon-Khmer languages. Words for "tiger," "ivory," and "crossbow" are also Austro-Asiatic. The names of the key terms of the Chinese calendar ("the branches") have this same non-Chinese origin. It has been suggested that a great many cultural words that are shared by Chinese and Tai are Chinese loanwords from Tai. Clearly, the Chinese received many aspects of culture and many concepts from the Austro-Asiatic and Austro-Tai peoples whom they gradually conquered and absorbed or expelled.

From the first century AD China's contacts with India, especially through the adoption of Buddhism, led to Chinese borrowing from Indo-Aryan (Indic) languages, but, very early, native Chinese equivalents were invented. Sinitic languages have been remarkably resistant to direct borrowing of foreign words. In modern times this has led to an enormous increase in Chinese vocabulary without a corresponding increase in basic meaningful syllables. For instance, *t'ieh-lu* "railroad" is based on the same concept expressed in the French *chemin de fer*, using *t'ieh* "iron" and *lu* "road"; likewise, *tien-hua* "telephone" is a compound of *tien* "lightning, electricity" and *hua* "speech." A number of such words were coined first in Japanese by means of Chinese elements and then borrowed back into Chinese. The reason that China has avoided the incorporation of foreign words is first and foremost a phonetic one; such words fit very badly into the Chinese pattern of pronunciation. A contributing factor has been the Chinese script, which is ill-adapted to the process of phonetic loans. In creating new words for new ideas, the characters have sometimes been determined first and forms have arisen that cannot be spoken without ambiguity ("sulfur" and "lutecium" coalesced as *liu*, "nitrogen" and "tantalum" as *tan*). It is characteristic of Modern Standard Chinese that the language from which it most freely borrows is one from its own past: Classical Chinese. In recent years it has borrowed from Southern Sinitic languages under the influence of statesmen and revolutionaries (Chiang Kai-shek was originally a Wu speaker and Mao Tse-tung a Hsiang speaker). Influence from English and Russian (in word formation and syntax) has been increasingly felt.

Chinese practices in word borrowing and word creation

Historical periods: pre-Classical Chinese. The history of the Chinese language can be divided into three periods, pre-Classical (*c.* 1500 BC–*c.* AD 200), Classical (*c.* 200–*c.* 1920), and post-Classical Chinese (with important forerunners as far back as the T'ang dynasty).

The pre-Classical Chinese is further divided into Oracular Chinese (Yin dynasty [*c.* 1766–*c.* 1122 BC]), Archaic Chinese (Chou and Ch'in dynasties [1122–206 BC]), and Han Chinese (Han dynasty [206 BC–AD 220]).

Oracular Chinese is known only from rather brief oracle inscriptions on bones and tortoise shells. Archaic Chinese falls into Early, Middle (*c.* 800–*c.* 400 BC), and Late Archaic. Early Archaic is represented by bronze inscriptions, parts of the "Classic of History" (*Shu Ching*), and parts of the "Classic of Poetry" (*Shih Ching*). From this period on, many important features of the pronunciation of the Chinese characters have been reconstructed (see below). The grammar depended to a certain extent on unwritten affixes. The writing system kept apart forms with or without infixes. Early Archaic Chinese possessed a 3rd person personal pronoun in three cases (nominative *kyəg*, or *ghyəg*, accusative *cyəg*, genitive *kywat*). No other kind of written Chinese until the post-Classical period possessed a nominative of the 3rd person pronoun, but the old form survived in Cantonese (*khöy*) and is also found in Tai (Modern Thai *khăw*).

Archaic Chinese— Early, Middle, and Late

Middle Archaic Chinese comprises the earliest writings of the Confucian school. Important linguistic changes had taken place, which became still more pronounced in Late Archaic, the language of the two major Confucian and Taoist writers, Meng-tzu (Mencius) and Chuang-tzu, as well as of other important philosophers. The grammar by then had become more explicit in the writing system, with a number of well-defined grammatical particles, and it can also be assumed that the use of grammatical affixes had similarly declined. The process used in verb formation and verb inflection that later appeared as tonal differences may at this stage have been manifested in other suprasegmental features, such as different types of laryngeal phonation. The word classes included nouns, verbs, and pronouns, all with several subclasses and particles. The use of a consistent system of grammatical particles to form noun modifiers, verb modifiers, and several types of embedded sentences (*i.e.*, sentences that are made to become parts of another independent sentence) disappeared in Han Chinese and was gone from written Chinese until the emersion of post-Classical Chinese. In Modern Standard Chinese the subordinating particle *te* combines the functions of several Late Archaic Chinese particles, and the verb particle *le* and the sentence particle *le* have taken over for other Late Archaic forms.

Han and Classical Chinese. Han Chinese developed more polysyllabic words and more specific verbal and nominal (noun) categories of words. Most traces of verb formation and verb conjugation began to disappear. An independent Southern tradition (on the Yangtze River), simultaneous with Late Archaic Chinese, developed a special style, used in the poetry *Ch'u Tz'u* ("Elegies of Ch'u"), which was the main source for the refined *fu* (prose poetry). Late Han Chinese developed into Classical Chinese, which as a written idiom underwent few changes during the long span of time it was used. It was an artificial construct, which for different styles and occasions borrowed freely and heavily from any period of pre-Classical Chinese but in numerous cases without real understanding for the meaning and function of the words borrowed.

At the same time the spoken language changed continually, as did the conventions for pronouncing the written characters. Soon Classical Chinese made little sense when read aloud. It depended heavily on fixed word order and on rhythmical and parallel passages. It has sometimes been denied the status of a real language, but it was certainly one of the most successful means of communication in the history of mankind. It was the medium in which the poets T'ao Yüan-ming (365–427), Li Po (701–762), and Tu Fu (712–770) and the prose writer Han Yü (768–824) created some of the greatest masterpieces of all times and was the language of the Neo-Confucianist philosophy (especially of Chu Hsi [1130–1200]), which was to influence the West deeply. Classical Chinese was also the language in which the Italian missionary Matteo Ricci (1552–1610) wrote in his attempt to convert the Chinese Empire to Catholic Christianity.

Post-Classical Chinese. Post-Classical Chinese, based on dialects very close to the language now spoken in

Northern China, probably owes its origin to the Buddhist storytelling tradition; the tales appeared in translations from Sanskrit during the T'ang dynasty (618–907). During the Sung dynasty (960–1279) this vernacular type of language was used by Buddhists and Confucianists alike for polemic writings; it also appeared in indigenous Chinese novels based on popular storytelling. From the Yüan dynasty (1279–1368) the vernacular was used also in the theatre.

Modern Standard Chinese has a threefold origin: the written post-Classical language, the spoken standard of Imperial times (Mandarin), and the vernacular language of Peking. These idioms were clearly related originally, and combining them for the purpose of creating a practical national language was a task that largely solved itself once the signal had been given. The term National Language (*kuo-yü*) had been borrowed from Japanese at the beginning of the 20th century, and, from 1915, various committees considered the practical implications of promoting it. The deciding event was the action of the May Fourth Movement of 1919; at the instigation of the liberal savant Hu Shih, it rejected Classical Chinese (also known as *wen-yen*) as the standard written language. (Hu Shih also led the vernacular literature movement of 1917; his program for literary reform appeared on January 1, 1917.) The new written idiom has gained ground faster in literature than in science, but there can be no doubt that the days of Classical Chinese as a living medium are numbered. After the establishment of the People's Republic of China some government regulation was applied successfully, and the tremendous task of making Modern Standard Chinese understood all over China was effectively undertaken. In what must have been the largest scale linguistic plan in history, untold millions of Chinese, whose mother tongues were divergent Mandarin or non-Mandarin languages or non-Chinese languages, learned to speak and understand the National Language; with this effort literacy was imparted to great numbers of people in all age groups.

The writing system. The Chinese writing system is non-alphabetic. It applies a specific character to write each meaningful syllable or each nonmeaningful syllabic that is part of a polysyllabic word.

When the Chinese script first appeared, as used for writing Oracular Chinese (from *c.* 1500 BC), it must already have had a considerable development behind it. Although many of the characters can be recognized as originally depicting some object, many are no longer recognizable. The characters did not indicate the object in a primitive nonlinguistic way but only represented a specific word of the Chinese language (*e.g.*, a picture of the phallic altar to the earth is used only to write the word earth). It is therefore misleading to characterize the Chinese script as pictographic or ideographic; nor is it truly syllabic, for syllables that sound alike but have different meanings are written differently. Logographic (*i.e.*, a system using symbols representing entire words) is the term that best describes the nature of the Chinese writing system.

Verbs and nouns are written by what are or were formerly pictures, often consisting of several elements (*e.g.*, the character for "to love" depicts a woman and a child; the character for "beautiful" is a picture of a man with a huge head-dress with ram's horns on top). The exact meaning of the word is rarely deducible from even a clearly recognizable picture, because the connotations are either too broad or too narrow for the word's precise meaning. For example, the picture "relationship of mother to child" includes more facets than "love," a concept that, of course, is not restricted to the mother–child relation, and a man adorned with ram's horns undoubtedly had other functions than that of being handsome to look at, whereas the concept "beautiful" is applicable also to men in other situations, as well as to women. Abstract nouns are indicated by means of concrete associations. The character for "peace, tranquillity" consists of a somewhat stylized form of the elements "roof," "heart," and "(wine) cup." Abstract symbols have been used to indicate numbers and local relationships.

Related words with similar pronunciations were usually written by one and the same character (the character for "to love, to consider someone good" is a derivative of a similarly written word "to be good"). This gave rise to the most important invention in the development of the Chinese script—that of writing a word by means of another one with the same or similar pronunciation. A picture of a carpenter's square was primarily used for writing "work, craftsman; to work" and was pronounced *kuŋ*; secondarily it was used to write *kuŋ-* "to present," *ghuŋ* "red," *kuŋ* "rainbow," *klawŋ* "river," and others. During the Archaic period this practice was developed to such a degree that too many words came to be written as one character. In imitation of the characters that already consisted of several components an element was added for each meaning of a character to distinguish words from each other. Thus "red" was no longer written with a single component but acquired an additional component that added the element "silk" on the left; "river" acquired an additional component of "water," and so on. The original part of the character is now referred to as its phonetic and the added element as its radical.

During the Ch'in dynasty (221–206 BC) the first government standardization of the characters took place, carried out by the statesman Li Ssu. A new, somewhat formalized style known as seals was introduced—a form that generally has survived until now, with only such minor modifications as were necessitated by the introduction of the writing brush around the beginning of the Christian Era and printing around AD 600. As times progressed, other styles of writing appeared, such as the regular handwritten form *k'ai* (as opposed to the formal or scribe style *li*), the running hand *hsing*, and the cursive hand *ts'ao*, all of which in their various degrees of blurredness are explicable only in terms of the seal characters.

The Ch'in dynasty standardization comprised somewhat over 3,000 characters. In addition to archaeological finds, the most important source for the early history of Chinese characters is the huge dictionary *Shuo-wen*, compiled by Hsü Shu in *c.* AD 100. This work contains 9,353 characters, a number that certainly exceeds that which it was or ever became necessary to know offhand. Still, a great proliferation of characters took place at special times and for special purposes. The *Kuang-yün* dictionary of 1007 had 26,194 characters (representing 3,877 different syllables in pronunciation). The *K'ang-hsi tzu-tien*, a dictionary of 1716, contains 40,545 characters, of which, however, fewer than one-fourth were in actual use at the time. The number of absolutely necessary characters has probably never been much over 4,000–5,000 and is today estimated at fewer than that.

By the 20th century the feeling had become very strong that the script was too cumbersome and an impediment to progress. The desire to obtain a new writing system necessarily worked hand in hand with the growing wish to develop a written language that in grammar and vocabulary approached modern spoken Chinese. If a phonetic writing were to be introduced, the classical language could not be used at all because it deviates so markedly from the modern language. None of the earlier attempts gained any following, but in 1919 a system of phonetic letters (inspired by Japanese kana) was devised for writing Mandarin. (In 1937 it received formal backing from the government, but World War II stopped further progress.) In 1929 a National Romanization, worked out by the author and language scholar Lin Yü-t'ang, the linguist Yuen Ren Chao, and others, was adopted. This attempt also was halted by war and revolution. A rival Communist effort known as *Latinxua*, or Latinization of 1930, fared no better. An attempt to simplify the language by reducing the number of characters to little over 1,000 failed because it did not solve the problems of creating a corresponding "basic Chinese" that could profitably be written by the reduced number of symbols.

The government of the People's Republic of China has taken several important steps toward solving the problems of the Chinese writing system. The first and basic step of making one language, Modern Standard Chinese, known all over the country has been described above. In

Adoption of the National Language

Logographic form of writing

Ch'in dynasty standardization of characters

Attempts at phonetic writing system

1956 a simplification of the characters was introduced that made them easier to learn and faster to write. Most of the abridged characters were well-known unofficial variants, used in handwriting but previously not in printing; some were innovations. In 1958 a romanization known as the phonetic system, or *pinyin zimu* (see Table 5), was introduced. This system is widely taught in the schools and is used for many transcription purposes and for teaching Modern Standard Chinese to non-Chinese peoples in China and to foreigners. The Pin-yin is conceived as a script that will gradually replace characters.

Reconstruction of protolanguages. For reconstructing the pronunciation of older stages of Sinitic, the Chinese writing system offers much less help than the alphabetic systems of such languages as Latin, Greek, and Sanskrit within Indo-European or Tibetan and Burmese within Sino-Tibetan. Therefore, the starting point must be a comparison of the modern Sinitic languages, with the view of recovering for each major language group the original common form, such as Proto-Mandarin for the Northern languages, Proto-Wu and others for the languages south of Yangtze. Because data are still lacking from a great many places, the approach has until recently been to compare major representatives of each group for the purpose of reconstructing the language of the important dictionary *Ch'ieh-yün* of AD 601 (Sui dynasty), which mainly represents a Southern language type. One difficulty is that the language in a given area represents a mixture of at least two layers: an older one of the original local type, antedating the language of the *Ch'ieh-yün*, and a younger one that is descended from the *Ch'ieh-yün* language or a slightly younger but closely related tongue—the so-called T'ang-koine or the standard spoken language of the T'ang dynasty (618–907). The relationship of the protolanguages is further complicated by the fact that different substrata of non-Chinese stock underlie most if not all of the major languages.

Influence of the T'ang layer on Sinitic

The degree to which the Sinitic languages have been influenced by the T'ang (or Middle Chinese) layer varies. In the North the Old Chinese layer still dominates in phonology; in Min the two layers are kept clearly apart from each other and the Middle Chinese layer is most important in the reading pronunciation of the characters; in Yüeh both Chinese layers are of the Southern type and are typologically close to a Tai substratum.

The Old Chinese layer is characterized by early decay of final consonants, late development of tones from sounds or suprasegmental features located toward the end of the syllable, change of final articulation type because of similar initial type (as in syllables with voiced glottal activity both at the opening and at the end that lose the final voicedness; a phenomenon later manifested as a tonal change), and influence of sounds and tones in a syllable on those of surrounding ones (sandhi).

The New Southern stratum in Sinitic languages is characterized by early change of final articulation types into tones, extensive development of registers according to type of initial consonant, and late or no loss of final stops. The Old layer cannot be the direct ancestor of the New layer. The division into Northern and Southern dialects must be very old. It might be better to speak of a T'ang and a pre-T'ang layer or a T'ang or Han layer (the Han dynasty, 206 BC–AD 220, was one of extensive settling in most parts of what is now China proper).

For a long time it was assumed that the *Ch'ieh-yün* dictionary represented the language of the capital of the Sui dynasty, Ch'ang-an in the present province of Shensi, but recent research has demonstrated that its major component was the language of the present-day Nanking area with a certain attempt at compromise with Northern speech habits. As its first criterion for classifying syllables, the *Ch'ieh-yün* dictionary takes the tones, of which it has four: *p'ing*, *shang* (transcribed as :—e.g., *pa*:), *ch'ü* (transcribed as -—e.g., *pa*-), and *ju*, or even, rising, falling, and entering ("checked") tones. The entering tone comprised those syllables that ended in a stop (*-p*, *-t*, *-k*). The rising and falling tones may have retained traces of the phonetic conditioning factor of their origin, voiced and voiceless glottal or laryngeal features, respectively.

Tones of the *Ch'ieh-yün* dictionary

The even tone probably was negatively defined as possessing no final stop and no tonal contour.

Next, the dictionary is divided according to rhymes, of which there are 61, and, finally, according to initial consonants. Inside each rhyme an interlocking spelling system known as *fan-ch'ieh* was used to subdivide the rhymes. There were 32 initial consonants and 136 finals. The number of vowels is not certain, perhaps six plus *i* and *u*, which served also as medial semivowels. There were probably more vowels than in either Archaic Chinese or in Modern Standard Chinese, another indication that the development of the Northern Chinese phonology has not passed the stage represented by *Ch'ieh-yün*.

There are additional sources for reconstructing the *Ch'ieh-yün* language: Chinese loanwords in Korean and Japanese (Japan has two different traditions—Go-on, slightly older than *Ch'ieh-yün* but representing a Southern language type like *Ch'ieh-yün*, and Kan-on, contemporary with *Ch'ieh-yün* but closer to the Northern tradition) and Chinese renderings of Indo-Aryan (Indic) words. Voiced stops are recovered through Wu, Hsiang, and Go-on (e.g., Modern Standard Chinese *t'ien* "field," Wu and Hsiang *di*, Go-on *den*, *Ch'ieh-yün dhien*), final stops especially through Yüeh and Japanese (e.g., Modern Standard Chinese *mu* "wood," Yüeh *muk*, Go-on *mok*[*u*], *Ch'ieh-yün muk*), and retroflex initial sounds from Northern Chinese (e.g., Modern Standard Chinese *sheng* "to live," *Ch'ieh-yün* ʂɐŋ [the ʂ is a retroflex]).

Early Archaic Chinese is the old stage for which the most information is known about the pronunciation of characters. The very system of borrowing characters to write phonetically related words gives important clues, and the rhymes and alliteration of the "Classic of Poetry" (*Shih Ching*) furnish a wealth of details. Even though scholars cannot always be sure that prefixes and infixes are correctly recovered, and though the order in which recoverable features were pronounced in the syllable is not always certain (*rk-* or *kr-*, *-wk* or *-kw*, and so on), enough details can be obtained to determine the typology of Old Chinese and to undertake comparative work with the Tibeto-Burman and Karenic languages. The method employed in this part of the reconstruction of Chinese has been predominantly internal reconstruction, the use of variation of word forms within a language to construct an older form. As knowledge of the old layer of modern languages and dialects increases, however, the comparative method, which draws on similarities in several related tongues, gains importance. Through further internal reconstruction, features of the Proto-Sinitic stage, antedating Archaic Chinese, can then be restored.

TIBETO-BURMAN LANGUAGES—
HISTORY AND CHARACTERISTICS

The Tibeto-Burman languages have evolved from the ancestral language, Proto-Tibeto-Burman, in vastly different ways and at their own pace, in accordance with the geographical and social factors that have determined the fate of Central and South Asian peoples. Some tribes have been stationary; others have swept over huge areas. As a result, conservative or archaic features do not occur in only one contiguous part of the language area and innovations in another. The nearest genetic relations are often not identical with the closest typological ones.

Tibetan. Of the modern Tibetan languages and dialects, the Western ones have preserved initial consonant clusters and final stops most faithfully and have had the least compensational development of tones. Most Central languages and dialects, including Lhasa, have lost all consonant clusters and final stops and in the process have acquired a larger inventory of single consonants and a system of tones. These changes and reductions are linked to a similar reshaping of certain grammatical processes of word formation that now operate only through suprasegmental and syllabic elements. To a surprising degree, however, Modern Central Tibetan possesses grammatical categories identical with or very similar in content, though not in form, to those of Classical Tibetan (a similar relationship as that of Modern Standard Chinese to Old Chinese). The relationship of nouns to the main

Influence of geography and social factors on Tibeto-Burman languages verb is indicated through postposed particles, the agent of a transitive verb indicated as the one by whom the action is performed, and the subject of an intransitive verb expressed as the object or goal of the action. Nominal modifiers precede nouns, and verbal modifiers follow them. The main verb, always placed after all nouns, is followed by particles expressing aspect and tense.

Old Tibetan pronunciation can be reconstructed by comparison of modern dialects and through the very conservative alphabetic script of Indian origin that goes back to the 7th century AD and found its present form in the 9th century. The orthography is far removed from present-day Standard Tibetan pronunciation.

Old Tibetan is one of the most archaic of the Tibeto-Burman languages. It retained Tibeto-Burman final stops and final *-r, -l, -s* and also the initial voiced consonants. Many Old Tibetan consonant clusters may be referred to Proto-Tibeto-Burman. The case particles and complicated verbal conjugation perhaps represent an elaboration on somewhat simpler tendencies in the protolanguage.

Hima-layish languages Some Himalayish languages are in certain respects as archaic as Tibetan, although most initial clusters are gone. An old feature is the connection of voiced–voiceless initial consonants with intransitive–transitive verbs. Because they have developed the feature of incorporating agent and object pronouns in verbs (and of possessive pronouns in nouns), these have been known as "pronominalizing" languages. An influence from contiguous Indo-European languages seems possible, but not certain.

Some Kirantish languages retain consonant clusters and voiced initial consonants; others give up both. Bahing has maintained the connection between voicedness and transitivity. Within Mirish, which has kept voiced initial sounds, Abor retains final stops and Dafla has some initial consonant clusters. Kachinish is quite conservative; prefixes are well retained as are voiced initial consonants, although some reshuffling has taken place in this respect.

Burmese. Within Burmish, Modern Standard Burmese has undergone a set of radical changes. Initial *ts-* and *tsh-* have become *s-* and *sh-*; *s* has become θ (*th* as in "thin"); *y-* and *r-* have coalesced as *y-*, and *ky-* and *kr-* as a palatal *c* (*ty*). Furthermore, all final consonants except nasals have coalesced as glottal stops, and all nasals have resulted in nasalization of the preceding vowel. In addition, the quality of vowels has been greatly altered. As was the case in Tibetan, in spite of great phonetic changes, grammatical categories are close to those scholars envisage for Proto-Tibeto-Burman. Cases of nouns and aspects of verbs are expressed through postposed particles.

Among the Burmese dialects, Arakanese is especially conservative, and the closely related language Maru is one of the most archaic within Tibeto-Burman in respect to final consonants. The Lolo languages lost most consonant clusters, as did all Burmish languages, but tend otherwise to be conservative in their treatment of initial sounds and radical in the loss and change of final consonants. Nung has retained final stops lost in Burmish (*-r, -l, -s*) and possesses a set of prefixes like Kachin.

The Burmese writing system Study of the Burmese writing system, in combination with comparative linguistic work, makes possible the reconstruction of Old Burmese. The language of the Myazedi inscription of 1113 is close in its sound system to written Burmese in its present form, which dates back to at least the 15th century. The writing system was taken over from the Mon people, who had developed their writing from Pyu, a Sino-Tibetan language known in Burma from *c.* AD 500. It is alphabetic of an Indian type but represents a separate Southern line of development.

Old Burmese is phonetically further from Proto-Tibeto-Burman than is Tibetan. Initial clusters are mostly gone but are felt in the development of initial consonants. Some clusters with *-w-* and liquid sounds were retained. The tonal system of Burmese (unlike that of Tibetan) developed to compensate for the loss of final features.

The Baric languages maintain a few older prefixes and developed some of their own. They tend to retain or merge *r* and *l*. The relationship of voicedness and transitivity is retained, but a great reshuffling of initial consonants took place, as it did also in Meithei and Kukish. The Kukish languages are found in all stages of development, but many of them are among the most archaic and most important for the reconstruction of Tibeto-Burman. Prefixes are best preserved in Old Kuki and in the Naga branch, whereas vowels seem very archaic in Lushai of the Central branch (the Lushai vowels have a difference of length that must in some way be explained in terms of Proto-Tibeto-Burman). Some Kukish languages incorporate pronouns in verbs. Mru, distantly related to Kukish, is noted for a number of archaic features, including final consonants lost elsewhere in Tibeto-Burman.

BIBLIOGRAPHY

General works: PAUL BENEDICT, *Sino-Tibetan: A Conspectus* (1971), a comprehensive and original study; G.A. GRIERSON, *Tibeto-Burman Family,* in the *Linguistic Survey of India,* vol. 3 (1909), a wealth of material but of uneven quality; FRANK M. LEBAR, GERALD C. HICKEY, and JOHN K. MUSGRAVE, *Ethnic Groups of Mainland Southeast Asia* (1964), an excellent reference work; HENRI MASPERO, "Langues de l'Asie du Sud-Est," in ANTOINE MEILLET and MARCEL COHEN (eds.), *Les Langues du Monde,* new ed., pp. 524–644 (1952), the most authoritative concise treatment of Sino-Tibetan to date; C.F. and F.M. VOEGELIN, "Languages of the World: Sino-Tibetan," *Anthropological Linguistics,* vol. 6 and 7 (1964–65), much information of a semitechnical nature; ROBERT SHAFER, *Introduction to Sino-Tibetan,* 3 vol. (1966–), a comprehensive and extensive, but technical, series; and *Bibliography of Sino-Tibetan Languages,* 2 vol. (1957–63), indispensable for further research.

Chinese: NICHOLAS C. BODMAN, "China: Historical Linguistics," in THOMAS A. SEBEOK (ed.), *Current Trends in Linguistics,* vol. 2, pp. 3–58 (1967); KUN CHANG, "China: Descriptive Linguistics," *ibid.,* pp. 59–90; YUEN-REN CHAO, *Mandarin Primer* (1948), excellent chapters on script and grammar; and with LIEN-SHENG YANG, *Concise Dictionary of Spoken Chinese* (1947), the best dictionary of modern Chinese, with an excellent introduction; JOHN DeFRANCIS, *Nationalism and Language Reform in China* (1950), informative and readable; and "China: Language and Script Reform," in *Current Trends in Linguistics,* vol. 2, pp. 130–150 (1967); SOREN EGEROD, "China: Dialectology," *ibid.,* pp. 91–129, technical in nature; R.A.D. FORREST, *The Chinese Language,* 2nd ed. rev. (1965), a standard reference work that also treats related and contiguous languages; BERNHARD KARLGREN, *Études sur la phonologie chinoise,* 4 pt. (1915–26), an epoch-making work but very technical; *Compendium of Phonetics in Ancient and Archaic Chinese* (1954), also technical; *Grammata Serica: Script and Phonetics in Chinese and Sino-Japanese* (1957), the standard dictionary of Old Chinese characters; *Sound and Symbol in Chinese,* rev. ed. (1962), very readable, but somewhat out of date; *The Chinese Language* (1949), a popular account of phonetic reconstructions; and *Easy Lessons in Chinese Writing* (1958), an interesting account of the etymology of Chinese characters; PAUL KRATOCHVIL, *The Chinese Language Today* (1968), very readable and up to date.

Tibeto-Burman and Karen: KUN CHANG, "China: National Languages," in *Current Trends in Linguistics,* vol. 2, pp. 151–176 (1967), treats minority languages in China; ROBERT B. JONES, *The Burmese Writing System* (1953), offers the best description; *Karen Linguistic Studies* (1961), up to date but technical; ROY A. MILLER, *The Tibetan System of Writing* (1956), offers the best description of the subject; "The Tibeto-Burman Languages of South Asia," *Current Trends in Linguistics,* vol. 5, pp. 431–449 (1969), informative and up to date; STUART N. WOLFENDEN, *Outlines of Tibeto-Burman Linguistic Morphology* (1929), the classic statement.

(S.C.E.)

Sinus

The word sinus is primarily an anatomical term meaning a hollow, cavity, recess, or pocket; a large channel containing blood; a suppurating tract; or a cavity within a bone. Two types of sinus, the blood-filled and the air-filled sinus, deserve particular attention.

The cranial venous sinuses are spaces between the layers of dura mater, which covers the brain, and are lined with endothelium similar to that lining veins. These sinuses receive blood from the veins of the brain, and all eventually drain into the principal vein of the neck—the internal jugular. Communications between these intracranial venous sinuses and veins outside the skull such as those in the nose, are important because they offer a direct path by which infection in the nose may reach the brain.

Among these sinuses the cavernous sinus is of particular interest, since it lies on each side of the pituitary gland and contains not only venous blood but also the internal carotid artery and several cranial nerves.

Paranasal air sinuses. The air sinuses, four on each side, are cavities in the bones that adjoin the nose. They are outgrowths from the nasal cavity and retain their communications with it by means of drainage openings or ostia. Consequently, their lining is mucous membrane similar to that found in the nose. The mucus secretion formed is propelled by small, hairlike processes called cilia through the ostia of the sinuses to the nasal cavity. From there it is eventually swallowed or expelled. All sinuses are absent or small at birth; they gradually enlarge until puberty, when they usually grow rapidly.

Frontal sinuses

The two frontal sinuses are situated in the frontal bone immediately above and between the eye sockets or orbits. They are usually unequal in size and have the shape of an irregular pyramid with its apex directed upward. The thin bony wall separating the two cavities sometimes is absent.

It is rare to recognize the frontal sinuses until the age of seven years, and their maximum growth occurs after puberty. They vary considerably in size and are usually larger in the male than in the female, averaging, when fully developed, approximately 3 cm in height, 2.5 cm in width, and 2 cm in depth. The front or anterior wall is thick skull bone; behind the sinuses lies bone covering the brain, and the floor of the sinuses slopes toward their openings into the nose.

The maxillary sinuses are not only the largest of the air sinuses but also the first to appear, being present in the fourth month on intra-uterine life. Each is a pyramidal space, its roof formed by the floor of the orbit, or eye socket, and its floor by the palate and teeth-bearing bone. The roots of the upper jaw teeth may project through the floor into the sinus cavity or may be so closely related to the floor that extraction leads to the formation of an opening between mouth and sinus (oro-antral fistula). The maxillary sinuses reach their maximum size by about age 12, when all the permanent teeth except the third molars have erupted. The nerves supplying the upper teeth run through the front wall of the sinus and may be irritated during acute antral infections with resultant toothache.

Ethmoidal sinuses

The ethmoidal sinuses, from 3 to 18 thin-walled cavities between the nasal cavities and the eye sockets, make up the ethmoidal labyrinths. Their walls form most of the inner walls of the eye sockets and are joined together by a thin perforated plate of bone at the roof of the nose. This bone, the cribriform plate, transmits the olfactory nerves that carry the sense of smell.

The sinuses contained within each labyrinth are arranged in three noncommunicating groups, all of which open into the nasal cavity. All produce mucus whose function is to lubricate the cilia lining the nasal passages.

The sphenoidal sinuses are situated back of the nose in the sphenoidal bone, which forms a forward part of the base of the skull and contains the depression or fossa for the pituitary gland. The sinuses are separated from each other by a bony wall or septum that is rarely in the midline, and they discharge their mucus through an opening in the front wall of the sinus into the nose.

These sinuses appear before birth but remain small until the age of 10, when they grow rapidly; rapid growth also occurs at about puberty. Sphenoidal sinuses are important in the surgical approach to the pituitary gland for patients with breast cancer or pituitary tumours.

Functions of the paranasal sinuses. Comprehensive studies on the comparative anatomy and physiology of the nose and paranasal sinuses have been made in man and in lower animals. The presence of the sphenoidal and frontal sinuses in carnivores such as the dog, hyena, and tiger is related to an increased area of olfaction and consequent improvement in the sense of smell. Ethmoidal air cells are found only in higher apes and man and are probably the result of restriction of the olfactory area.

The maxillary sinuses are largest in man, in the higher apes, and in capuchin and howler monkeys; they are absent in baboons, lorises, and tapirs. It has been suggested that these sinuses play a part in phonation, that they aid in conservation of heat from the nasal fossae, and that they serve to lighten the skull, but evidence for these theories is lacking.

Infections

Diseases of the sinuses. Acute infections of all the paranasal sinuses usually result from infections of the upper respiratory tract such as the common cold. Acute sinusitis may occur at any time after the sixth month. By the age of four years the maxillary sinus is the one most commonly affected. General diseases, such as measles, frequently precipitate acute sinusitis, as may the penetration of infected water from swimming.

Treatment is directed primarily toward overcoming the infecting organism by the use of systemic antibiotics such as penicillin and toward encouraging drainage of the sinuses with vasoconstricting nose drops and inhalations. In most cases the condition will resolve within several days. If infection persists, the pus localized in any individual sinus may need to be removed by means of a minor surgical procedure known as lavage, in which the maxillary or sphenoidal sinuses are irrigated with water or normal saline solution. Any residual infection will be displaced into the nasal cavity through the normal openings. Persistence of purulent nasal discharge after adequate antibiotic therapy or repeated lavage may indicate the presence of a chronic infection that necessitates surgery. Pain is not a feature of chronic sinusitis.

Polyps, consisting of swollen nasal lining, may grow from both the maxillary and ethmoidal sinuses and cause nasal obstruction. They occur most commonly as a result of nasal allergy and require surgical removal.

Cancers affecting the paranasal sinuses are rare, especially in the sphenoidal and frontal area. They occur most commonly among the Bantu of South Africa, where they are related to the long-term use of homemade carcinogenic snuff. Recently, however, it has been shown that certain woodworkers in the furniture industry have a greatly increased incidence of nasal sinus cancer.

BIBLIOGRAPHY. Additional information on the various phases of this subject may be found in the following texts: V.E. NEGUS, *Comparative Anatomy and Physiology of the Nose and Paranasal Sinuses* (1958); W.G. SCOTT-BROWN (ed.), *Diseases of The Ear, Nose and Throat*, 2nd ed., 2 vol. (1965); and A.W. PROETZ, *Essays on the Applied Physiology of the Nose* (1941).

(D.F.N.H.)

Siphonaptera

Fleas, which comprise the order Siphonaptera, are parasites that live on the exterior of the host (*i.e.*, are ectoparasitic); they are bloodsucking insects, important carriers of disease, and sometimes serious pests. As the chief agent transmitting the Black Death (bubonic plague) in the Middle Ages, they were an essential link in the chain of events that killed a quarter of the population of Europe.

Size and distribution

Fleas are small, wingless insects with a tough cuticle bearing many bristles and frequently combs (ctenidia) of broad, flattened spines. The adult flea varies from about 0.1 to 1 centimetre in length and feeds exclusively on the blood of mammals (including man) and birds. With more than 1,600 species and subspecies known, the order is still a small one compared with many other groups of insects; however, it is widely distributed. The rat flea and the mouse flea have been carried all over the world by man; native species of fleas are found in the Arctic Circle and south polar regions, the Arabian deserts and tropical rain forests, as well as the more temperate zones.

Medical and economic importance. Infestation by fleas may cause severe inflammation of the skin and intense itching. Although many animals acquire partial immunity after constant or repeated attacks, occasionally individuals (especially man) become sensitized after exposure and develop allergies. Species that attack man and livestock include the cat flea (*Ctenocephalides felis*), the so-called human flea (*Pulex irritans*), the dog flea (*Ctenocephalides canis*), the sticktight flea (*Echidnophaga gallinacea*), and the jigger, or chigoe, flea (*Tunga penetrans*). Poultry may be parasitized by the European chicken flea (*Ceratophyllus gallinae*) and (in the U.S.) by the western chicken flea (*Ceratophyllus niger*).

Certain fleas that feed primarily on rodents or birds sometimes attack man, particularly in the absence of their usual prey. When rats are dying of bubonic plague, their hungry fleas, themselves infected with plague bacilli and seeking food elsewhere, can transmit the disease to man, especially in buildings heavily infested with rats. The Oriental rat flea (*Xenopsylla cheopis*) is the most efficient carrier of plague, but other species of fleas (*e.g., Nosopsyllus fasciatus, Xenopsylla brasiliensis, Pulex irritans*) can also transmit the disease to man. Although there are occasional cases of plague in tropical regions, the disease in man has been controlled by early diagnosis and antibiotics. Plague (sylvatic plague), a widespread disease in hundreds of species of wild rodents throughout the world, is maintained by fleas that parasitize these animals. More than 100 species of fleas are known to be infected by the plague bacillus, and an additional ten species are implicated as carriers of the classic type of urban plague. (See INFECTIOUS DISEASES.)

Fleas, particularly *Xenopsylla cheopis*, are believed to be the principal carriers of murine typhus, a rickettsial disease of man; rats and mice are sources of infection. Fleas are considered important in the maintenance and spread of many locally restricted infections among rodents and other mammals, including tularemia and Russian spring-summer encephalitis. Fleas transmit myxomatosis, a viral disease of rabbits used deliberately to control rabbits in areas where they are severe pests (*e.g.*, in Australia). Fleas are probable carriers of a filarial worm of dogs and serve as the intermediate host of a common tapeworm (*Dipylidium caninum*) of dogs and cats (and occasionally children). If heavily infested, animals can suffer severe damage or be killed by the effects of flea bites and considerable loss of blood. Fleas are subject to parasitism by external mites; internal nematode worms; and bacterial, fungal, and protozoan infections.

The female chigoe, or jigger, flea (not to be confused with "chigger," a larval mite), burrows into the skin of its host, generally on the feet, and lives within a cyst that forms around it. Intense itching accompanies the development and enlargement of the cyst as the abdomen of the pregnant flea swells to the size of a pea; secondary infections may constitute serious complications.

Natural history. *Life cycle.* Details of the life cycle are available for a few species only. The four stages are the egg, larva, pupa, and adult. Pearly white, oval eggs are deposited on the body of, or in the nest or habitat of, the

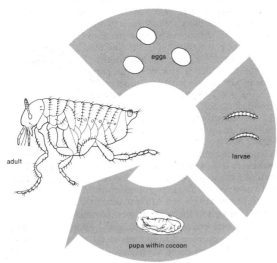

Stages in the life cycle of fleas.

host animal. The larva, a small legless caterpillar, feeds on organic debris, such as dried excrement, dried bits of skin, dead mites, or dried blood found in the host's nest. The parent fleas pass freshly imbibed blood rapidly through their gut to produce fecal matter for the nourishment of their offspring, which is essential to the successful metamorphosis of certain species of flea larvae. After three (exceptionally, two) molts, the larva spins

a silk cocoon that includes debris from the nest; this is the beginning of the pupal stage. The pupa emerges as an adult some days or months later. Depending upon the species or environmental conditions, the time required for a complete life cycle varies from two weeks to several months. The life-span of the adult flea varies from a few weeks (*e.g., Echidnophaga gallinacea*) to a year or more (*Pulex irritans*). The life cycle of the European rabbit flea (*Spilopsyllus cuniculi*) and its host are perfectly synchronized. The sexual development of male and female fleas is under the direct control of the rabbit's sex hormones. Thus, the eggs of the female flea mature successfully only if she is feeding on a pregnant doe rabbit. When the young rabbits are born, both flea sexes now mature and leave the parturient doe for the nestlings and the nest, where they copulate and lay their eggs, thus assuring the flea larvae a suitable habitat for development. If the sex hormones of the female rabbit are controlled artificially by the administration of synthetic progestins (contraceptives), the sexual development of the female flea is also arrested. Although no similar case is yet known among other species of fleas, it has been recorded that rat fleas are less fertile if fed on baby mice than on their parents and that the mouse flea (*Leptopsylla segnis*) is more prolific if reared on family units rather than on individual adult mice. It seems likely, therefore, that the influence of the hosts' hormones is more widespread than hitherto suspected.

Parasitism. Some fleas (*e.g.,* shrew fleas and rabbit fleas) are highly host specific; other species parasitize a variety of mammals. The cat flea infects not only the domestic cat but dogs, foxes, civets, mongooses, opossums, leopards, and other mammals including man if accustomed hosts are not available. Related mammals tend to be parasitized by fleas that are themselves related. Thus the rabbitlike pikas (*Ochotona*) living in the Rocky Mountains are infested with two peculiar genera of fleas that occur also on pikas in the mountains of Asia; this indicates a close phylogenetic relationship between these geographically separated hosts. Bird fleas have adapted themselves in relatively recent times to their avian hosts. These share several common adaptive features; one of the most obvious responses to the new environment is an increase in the number of comb spines on the upper surface of the thorax.

It is interesting that monkeys and apes do not harbour fleas, nor do horses or the majority of ungulates. The most heavily parasitized group of mammals are the rodents (*e.g.*, rats, mice, squirrels). Their habit of nest building in holes favours development of flea larval stages; animals with no permanent home tend to have fewer fleas.

Although both flea sexes feed avidly and repeatedly on blood (a single male exception never feeds), they survive for various periods away from the host. The rabbit flea, for example, can live for nine months at temperatures around the freezing point without feeding.

Form and function. Anatomically, adult fleas are a rather uniform but distinctive group, with many interesting modifications and few obvious links with other orders. The compressed body and backwardly projecting spines or combs enable them to move swiftly through hairs or feathers of the host. The mouthparts, modified for sucking blood, include barbed stylets that aid both in penetration of the flea into the host skin and in attachment of species that spend long periods fixed to the host (*e.g.*, the stick-tight fleas). Generally fleas that live on diurnal hosts have well-developed eyes; species that parasitize subterranean hosts (*e.g.*, moles or nocturnal animals like bats) have poorly developed eyes or none at all. The most impressive adaptations are highly developed jumping legs and the powerful muscles that control them. During their evolution, fleas, like the majority of parasitic insects, lost their wings. Certain parts of the flight mechanism have been retained, however, and incorporated in the jumping mechanism. Because fleas are able to leap horizontal or vertical distances 200 times their body length and to develop an acceleration of 200 gravities, they have been described as insects that fly with their legs. Certain species that live in nests high above the ground or in other unusual habi-

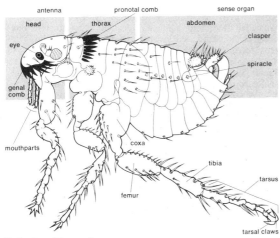

Body plan of the cat flea.
By courtesy of R. Traub

tats crawl rather than jump. An incidental use of the unusual strength of fleas is in "flea circuses" in which they pull miniature carts and perform other feats.

Control. In controlling fleas it is best to treat simultaneously both the breeding sites of fleas and the infested host, since, as mentioned earlier, the larval and pupal stages usually develop away from the host's body. For infested animals a commercial dust, spray, dip, or aerosol containing an insecticide such as pyrethrum, rotenone, malathion, or methoxychlor is used. Methoxychlor and malathion may continue to kill fleas for a few weeks after application. The long-acting chlorinated hydrocarbons, such as lindane and chlordane, can be applied to the fur of certain infested animals (but not to cats or dogs). In some regions, however, fleas have become resistant to these hydrocarbon insecticides, and new toxicants are required. Organic phosphorus compounds offer promise as systemic insecticides. When animals to be protected are fed these compounds, the fleas feeding on them die. For the control of larval and adult fleas away from the host, dieldrin, lindane, or malathion may be applied to the pens and haunts of the affected animals. Repellents containing benzyl benzoate, phthalate compounds, or diethyltoluamide are effective in preventing attack by fleas.

Evolution, paleontology, and classification. The Siphonaptera form a small group of insects probably descended from an ancestor of the Mecoptera (scorpionflies), with which they share certain characteristics. Both groups have a spined gizzard (proventriculus), sexual differences in the number of ganglia in the ventral nerve cord, six rectal glands, and a simple type of ovary. The males have a similar type of spermatozoon, unique in the phylum Arthropoda, in which a motile flagellum, or tail, lacking the outer ring of nine tubules, is deployed around the mitochondria (cell organelles). A fossil flea, discovered in Australia, is claimed to be 200,000,000 years old. Two other known fossil fleas come from the Baltic amber (Oligocene) and are similar to "modern" fleas in all but specific details.

Distinguishing taxonomic features. Although taxonomic separation of these groups rests upon a combination of superficially trivial morphological characteristics, they do reflect the fundamental differences between the groups. At the family or generic levels, classification is based principally upon shape of head and thorax, arrangement of combs, various modifications of the highly specialized male copulatory organ and female reproductive organs, general chaetotaxy (arrangement of bristles), and other characteristics.

Annotated classification. Fleas of today can be divided into three superfamilies: the Pulicoidea, Malacopsylloidea, and Ceratophylloidea. The Pulicoidea are generally adapted more to life on the host's body than are the latter two, which spend more time in the nest.

Order Siphonaptera (fleas)
Small, wingless, laterally compressed insects; adults ectoparasitic on warm-blooded vertebrates; eyes present or lacking; antennae short and stout, reposing in grooves; mouthparts adapted to piercing and sucking, maxillary and labial palps present; thoracic segments free; legs with large coxae, tarsi five-segmented; larvae elongated, legless, caterpillar-like; pupae with appendages free, enclosed in cocoons.

Superfamily Pulicoidea. Outer internal ridge of midcoxa of leg absent; mesonotum (dorsal sclerite of mesothorax) without pseudosetae under collar; metepimeron extending far upward, with first abdominal spiracle placed above the metepisternum; metanotum (dorsal sclerite of metathorax) and abdominal terga (dorsal surface) without apical spines or spinelets; spiracles circular; abdominal terga (segments II–VII) with, at most, one row of bristles; no bristles above spiracle of terga VIII; sensillium with either 8 or 14 pits each side; hind tibia of leg without an apical tooth outside; one family Pulicidae with genera *Pulex, Xenopsylla, Tunga,* and others.

Superfamily Malacopsylloidea. Rod of the lateral sclerites of the mesothorax (mesopleural rod) not forked; anterior tentorial arm present in head; no genal combs (spines on the anteroventral border of head) or pronotal combs (spines on the dorsal sclerite of the prothorax); ventral margin of pronotum never bilobed; fifth tarsal segment of leg always with four pairs of bristles (Neotropical region and extreme south Nearctic); two families, Malacopsyllidae and Rhopalopsyllidae.

Superfamily Ceratophylloidea. All fleas that do not possess combinations of characters listed above are included with the Ceratophylloidea, 12 families are included.

Critical appraisal. There is general agreement among flea specialists regarding the basic classification of the order, but it is probable that the family Hystrichopsyllidae will be accorded the rank of a superfamily.

BIBLIOGRAPHY. G.P. HOLLAND, "The Siphonaptera of Canada," *Tech. Bull. Dep. Agric. Can. 70* (1949), the best work on identification, affinities and host-relations of relevant North American fauna; "Evolution, Classification and Host-Relations of Siphonaptera," *A. Rev. Ent.,* 9:123–146 (1964), a critical review of the literature; G.H.E. HOPKINS and M. ROTHSCHILD, *An Illustrated Catalogue of the Rothschild Collection of Fleas (Siphonaptera) in the British Museum (Natural History),* 5 vol. (1953–71), indispensable for global identification and general morphology of families treated to date; W.L. JELLISON, "Fleas and Disease," *A. Rev. Ent.,* 4:389–414 (1959), a summary of the medical importance of fleas; P.T. JOHNSON, "A Classification of the Siphonaptera of South America with Descriptions of New Species," *Mem. Ent. Soc. Wash.,* 5:1–299 (1957), sole opus on South American fleas, well-prepared and well-illustrated; M. ROTHSCHILD, "Fleas," *Sci. Am.* 213:44–53 (Dec. 1965), an account of interesting aspects of the biology and behaviour of fleas; "The Rabbit Flea and Hormones," in *The Biology of Sex,* ed. by A. ALLISON, pp. 189–199 (1967), reviews findings on hormonal interrelationships of the rabbit flea and its host; and with T. CLAY, *Fleas, Flukes and Cuckoos,* 3rd ed. (1957), information on bionomics and habits of bird fleas and other bird parasites; R. TRAUB, *Siphonaptera from Central America and Mexico* (1950), includes generic revisions and the first study on comparative anatomy of the aedeagus of fleas; *United States Department of Agriculture,* "Fleas—How to Control Them," Leaflet no. 392 (n.d.), one of a series of pamphlets on methods of control.

(M.L.R./R.T.)

Sipuncula

Peanutworms (phylum Sipuncula) are elongated, often spindle-shaped, unsegmented marine worms. The head usually has one or more rings of tentacles. The worms vary in length from a few to 300 millimetres or more in length. Though rare, they may be locally common on seabeds throughout the oceans of the world. Peanutworms are bottom-dwelling (benthic) animals; most burrow in the mud or sand between tide levels or in oozes of the deepest ocean trenches. Some species have other habitats and live in discarded mollusk shells, in sponge siphons, in corals, among the twisted tubes of encrusting polychaetes (marine annelid worms), and even in tangled roots of marine plants.

Life cycle. Externally the sexes are alike and separate, with one exception. Gametes (mature germ cells) are shed into the body cavity and collect in nephridia (excretory organs) that become modified as egg- and sperm-storage organs; they are emitted into the sea from nephridiopores. Fertilization takes place outside the body. The trocho-

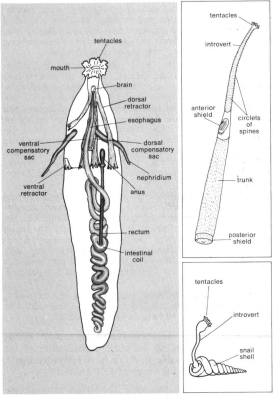

Sipunculids.
(Left) *Sipunculus nudus.* (Top) *Aspidosiphon.* (Bottom)
Phascolion.

From *Invertebrate Zoology* by Paul A. Meglitsch. Copyright © 1967 by Oxford University Press, Inc. Reprinted by permission

phore (free swimming) larva, which results from spiral cleavage of the zygote (cell formed by two gametes), undergoes metamorphosis to its characteric shape.

Form and function. Peanutworms consist of a muscular trunk, cylindrical to globular in shape, and a slender, anterior introvert (retractible proboscis) that is muscular, highly extensible, and capable of being withdrawn into the trunk by retractor muscles. Hooks or spines are often present toward the tip of the introvert, while glandular pores and papillae are scattered over both trunk and introvert. Within the body cavity (coelom) a long alimentary canal spirals backward from the mouth to the posterior region of the trunk, then forward to the dorsal anus near the anterior end of the trunk. A contractile vessel, or compensatory sac associated with the esophagus, extends forward to the tentacles. Fluid passes to extended tentacles, returning to the vessel as they contract; both this and coelomic fluid contain blood cells with hemerythrin. One or two nephridia discharge to the exterior. Gonads develop at the base of the ventral retractor muscles.

Classification and phylogeny. Peanutworms have few external characters and, apart from the arrangement of tentacles in relation to the mouth and the presence of a cap or shield at the anterior and posterior ends of the trunk, most distinguishing features can be detected only by dissection. Longitudinal trunk muscles may be in the form of bands or fused into a continuous sheet. The number of retractor muscles and the presence of protractor muscles in the musculature of the introvert are important. Other internal characters include presence of integumentary canals, the number of nephridia, and the presence of a postesophageal loop in the intestine.

Annotated classification. The following classification is based on the system proposed by A.C. Stephen and S.J. Edmonds (1972). Peanutworms once were included with priapulans and spoonworms (see ECHIURA) in the phylum Gephyrea; Adam Sedgwick (1898) gave them phylum rank. Presently four families are recognized.

PHYLUM SIPUNCULA

Unsegmented, coelomate, bilaterally symmetrical marine invertebrates; body divided into muscular trunk and protus-ible introvert; mouth, situated at extremity of introvert, usually partly or wholly surrounded by tentacles or by a tentacular fold; long alimentary canal; anus situated anteriorly in the mid-dorsal line near or on the base of the introvert; setae (bristles) and anal vesicles absent; about 320 species.

Family Sipunculidae

Numerous tentacles or a tentacular fold form a ring around mouth; anterior cap or shield absent; integumentary canals or sacs in body wall; longitudinal body wall musculature in separate bundles.

Family Golfingiidae

Tentacles variable, digitiform, leaflike, dendritic (branching) or lobular; anterior cap or shield and integumentary canals or sacs absent; longitudinal body wall musculature a continuous sheet.

Family Aspidosiphonidae

Tentacles wholly or partly surround mouth; anterior cap or shield present; integumentary canals or sacs absent; longitudinal body wall musculature in bundles or a continuous sheet.

Family Phascolosomatidae

Tentacles never surround mouth, form a horseshoe-shaped, broken ring; anterior cap or shield absent; integumentary canals or sacs usually absent; longitudinal body wall musculature in bundles or a continuous sheet.

Critical appraisal. The affinities of the peanutworms are obscure. Their development, like that of spoonworms, resembles that of annelids in that spiral cleavage and a trochophore larva occur. They differ from annelids, however, in their unsegmented bodies and absence of setae. They differ from spoonworms by the absence of setae, anterior anus, absence of anal vesicles, and presence of tentacles surrounding the mouth at the tip of the introvert. Fossils from the Middle Cambrian have been considered to be sipunculan (see FOSSIL RECORD).

BIBLIOGRAPHY. L.H. HYMAN, "Phylum Sipunculida," in *The Invertebrates*, vol. 5 (1959), the best general account in English; R.B. CLARK, "Systematics and Phylogeny: Annelida, Echiura and Sipuncula," in M. FLORKIN and B.T. SCHEER (eds.), *Chemical Zoology*, vol. 4, pp. 1–68 (1969), less morphological approach than Hyman; G.E. and N. MACGINITIE, *Natural History of Marine Animals*, 2nd ed. (1968), an ecological viewpoint; A.C. STEPHEN and S.J. EDMONDS, *The Phyla Sipuncula and Echiura* (1972), includes descriptions of all the known species and an exhaustive bibliography; A. TETRY, "Classe des sipunculiens," in P.P. GRASSE (ed.), *Traité de zoologie*, vol. 5 (1959), a well-illustrated summary of morphological variation, development, and physiology (in French).

(R.W.S.)

Sirenia

Sirenians, or sea cows, are a group of large aquatic mammals that have become rare or extinct as a result of exploitation by man for meat and oil. The largest, Steller's sea cow (*Hydrodamalis gigas*), which reached lengths of about 8 metres (about 24 feet), was eaten out of existence by hungry seal hunters within a few decades of its discovery in 1741 in the Bering Sea. The remaining forms, the dugong (*Dugong dugon*) and manatees (three species of *Trichechus*), if their stocks were allowed to rebuild themselves, could again become of economic importance. Being the only large aquatic herbivores, other than some turtles, they could provide meat from the vast expanses of marine and freshwater vegetation, at present quite unused by man, and so bring another marginal area into production.

Dugongs and manatees are both usually seen up to lengths of three to four metres (10 to 13 feet), but larger specimens, up to 6 metres (20 feet), have been mentioned in tales of early travellers.

The dugong seems to have had a wider distribution in the past, but in recent times it has been restricted to the warm coastal waters of the Indo-Pacific region. Throughout most of its range it is now much depleted in numbers but exists from the Solomon Islands in the east to the head of the Red Sea in the west and from the Philippine Islands and the Persian Gulf in the north to Brisbane, Perth, and Mozambique in the south. It is entirely marine and rarely even enters estuaries. Manatees, however, seem more adaptable and inhabit the coastal, estuarine, and riverine waters of the tropical and subtropical Atlantic region: *T. senegalensis* from West Africa; *T. manatus,* with two subspecies, from the Caribbean; and *T. inunguis,* landlocked in the Amazon Basin.

Drawing by J. Helmer based on photograph courtesy of (Manatees) Field Museum of Natural History; from (Dugong) G.M. Allen, *Extinct and Vanishing Mammals of the Western Hemisphere;* Cooper Square Publishers

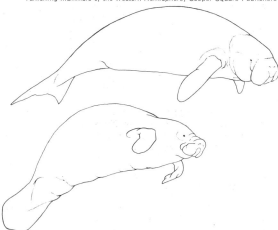

Body plans of two major sirenian groups.
(Top) dugong (*Dugong dugon*); (bottom) manatee (*Trichechus manatus*).

Natural history. Sea cows tend to live in groups, and dugongs particularly may be highly gregarious at times. An enormous herd, three and a half by one and a half miles in extent, was recorded off Brisbane, Australia, early in the last century. Both genera are totally aquatic, living almost continuously submerged, and this, coupled with their wary and surreptitious habits, makes them exceptionally difficult to study. They are unable to come out of the water, but manatees placed on land nearby may just manage to return to their natural environment by vigorous wriggling of the body. Breathing is by frequent brief visits to the surface, where the tip of the snout is protruded and the nostrils silently opened by muscular valves. A manatee has been known to last as much as 16½ minutes between taking breaths. Manatees may also be seen lying at the surface, usually with only their backs visible above the water. Even when basking thus, they are extremely sensitive to sound or disturbance and will silently submerge. On occasion both dugongs and manatees will thrust their heads entirely out of the water, and they sometimes may even disport themselves like cumbersome seals.

Extremely little is known of the breeding biology of sea cows and particularly of the time scale involved. Manatees are known to be long-lived, and dugongs are believed to have similar lifespans. But there is no information about age of maturity, rate of growth, or number of young produced in a lifetime. Mating in manatees has been observed with the animals in very shallow water lying on their sides. Gestation is known to occupy more than 152 days, and the normal birth is a single calf, which receives much maternal care. Very occasionally twin fetuses are found in dugongs. Suckling from the single pair of pectoral mammary glands normally occurs in a horizontal postion, but the occasional suckling of a young one held vertically by a flipper may have given rise to the mermaid myth. There is no marked difference in size between the sexes.

Sea cows are totally herbivorous. Whereas Steller's sea cow fed on marine algae, the dugong and manatees feed entirely on green higher plants, a circumstance that limits their distribution to relatively shallow waters. The habit of the dugong is to feed where there is good growth of "dugong grass" (*Zostera*, etc.), the leaves and underwater stems of which are pulled off by the animal's powerful lips. Manatees seem prepared to feed on marine or freshwater plants whether growing on the bottom, floating at the surface, or even growing on banks of rivers up to a foot above water level. It is this catholicity that has led to the experimental use of manatees in Guyana to keep clear

irrigation and transport channels in cane fields that otherwise must be cleared by hand. Virtually the sole enemy of both the dugong and manatees is man. There does not seem to be any commercial exploitation of these animals at present, but both are hunted sporadically and locally for food with the use of nets or harpoons. The dugong still has a considerable residual stock off northern Australia and with protective legislation enforced, could have a valuable future. Manatees, because they come into more confined waters, are still in danger of extermination.

Form and function. Sea cows have torpedo-shaped bodies and, like whales, have lost all external trace of hindlimbs. Their tails likewise are flattened horizontally and provide the main propulsive force in swimming. The forelimbs are small and may help in turning and manoeuvring. Though usually somewhat sluggish, sea cows are capable of considerable speeds for short distances.

The main distinguishing characteristics between the dugong and the manatees are that the former have a downturned snout and a forked tail, while the latter have a straight snout and rounded tail. Both have immensely thick, tough skin, which is nearly hairless. In the dugong there are individual hairs about six millimetres (¼ inch) long, spaced five to seven centimetres (two or three inches) apart. There is no substantial layer of blubber beneath the skin, but the body contains much fat. The eyes are small and circular, without lids, and the minute external ear openings are to be found only by careful examination. All of the bones are of exceptional density. Sea cows, particularly the dugong, have a much enlarged and intensely muscular upper lip, the corners of which serve to pluck the vegetation on which the animal feeds. In the dugong there are remains of two incisors, the second of which becomes large in the adult, remaining unerupted in the female and erupting to form a tusk in the male. There are basically six cusped molars in each jaw, which fall out progressively from the front so that only two remain in the adult. These teeth, together with horny pads at the front of each jaw, crush the food. In manatees each jaw has a series of 20 to 30 crushing molars, which move progressively forward during the life of the animal. Manatees are also exceptional in having only six vertebrae in the neck, instead of the seven standard in mammals. Almost nothing is known about the physiological processes of these animals.

Classification and paleontology. Sea cows comprise the order Sirenia of the superorder Subungulata, which also includes elephants and hyraxes. Two points of resemblance with elephants are the mode of tooth succession and the pectoral position of the mammary glands. The extensive fossil record indicates that the Sirenia date from the Eocene, about 50,000,000 years ago. More than 20 genera of fossil sirenians have been described. They seem to have been widespread near the coasts of the warmer seas of the world, and some think that the manatee is of more recent origin and has replaced the dugong in the Atlantic region.

BIBLIOGRAPHY. G.M. ALLEN, "Extinct and Vanishing Mammals of the Western Hemisphere, with the Marine Species of All the Oceans," *Spec. Publs. Am. Comm. Int. Wildl. Prot.,* no. 11 (1942), provides information on the causes of extinction and the basis for conservation of sirenians; C. BERTRAM, *In Search of Mermaids: The Manatees of Guiana* (1963), is a readable popular account of the biology of manatees; C.K. and G.C.I. BERTRAM, "The Sirenia as Aquatic Meat-Producing Herbivores," *Symp. Zool. Soc.* (*London*), no. 21, pp. 385–391 (1968), contains an extensive bibliography of the literature on the Sirenia.

(G.C.L.B./C.K.B.)

Śivajī

Śivajī (Shivaji), called the "Grand Rebel," a Marāthā hero of 17th-century India, was the founder of an independent Marāthā kingdom in the Deccan, in the south central part of the subcontinent. A great statesman and social reformer, he was also a master of guerrila warfare. He breathed new life into a moribund race that for centuries had resigned itself to abject serfdom and led them against Aurangzeb, a powerful Mughal ruler. Above all, in a place and age stained by religious savagery, he stands

Aquatic behaviour

Distinguishing features

almost alone as one who practiced true religious tolerance.

Śivajī was probably born on February 19, 1630 (some say April 1627), of a line of prominent nobles. India at that time was under Muslim rule: the Mughals in the north and the Muslim sultans of Bijāpur and Golkundā in the south. All three ruled by right of conquest, with no pretense that they had any obligations toward the ruled. Śivajī, whose ancestral estates were situated in the Deccan, in the realm of the Bijāpur sultans, found the Muslim oppression and religious persecution of the Hindus so intolerable that, by the time he was 16, he had already convinced himself that he was the divinely appointed instrument of the cause of Hindu freedom—a conviction that was to sustain him throughout his life. Collecting a band of followers, about 1655 he began to seize the weaker Bijāpur outposts. In the process, he destroyed a few of his influential coreligionists who had aligned themselves with the sultans. All the same, his daring and military skill, combined with his sternness toward the oppressors of the Hindus, won him the heart and mind of the common man. His depredations grew increasingly audacious, and several minor expeditions sent to chastise him proved ineffective.

When the Sultan of Bijāpur, in 1659, sent agianst him an army 20,000 strong under Afẓal Khān, Śivajī, pretending to be intimidated, enticed the force deep into difficult mountain terrain and then killed Afẓal Khān at a meeting to which he had lured him by submissive appeals. Meanwhile, picked troops that had been previously positioned swooped down on the unwary Bijāpur army and routed it. Overnight, Śivajī had become a formidable warlord, possessing the horses, the guns, and the ammunition of the Bijāpur army.

Alarmed by Śivajī's rising strength, the Mughal emperor Aurangzeb ordered his viceroy of the south to march against him. Śivajī countered by carrying out a daring midnight raid right within the Viceroy's encampment, in which the Viceroy lost the fingers of one hand and his son was killed. Discomfitted by this reverse, the Viceroy withdrew his force. Śivajī, as though to provoke the Mughals further, attacked the rich coastal town of Surat and took immense booty.

Aurangzeb could hardly ignore so flaunting a challenge and sent out his most prominent general, Mīrza Raja Jai Singh, at the head of an army said to number 100,000 men. The pressure exerted by this vast force, combined with the drive and tenacity of Jai Singh, soon compelled Śivajī to sue for peace and to undertake that he, accompanied by his son, would attend Aurangzeb's court at Āgra to be formally accepted as Mughal vassals. In Āgra, hundreds of miles from their homeland, Śivajī and his son were placed under house arrest, where they lived under the threat of execution. Undaunted, Śivajī feigned illness and, as a form of penance, began to send out enormous baskets filled with sweets to be distributed among the poor. On August 17, 1666, he and his son had themselves carried past their guards in these baskets. His escape, possibly the most thrilling episode in a life filled with high drama, was to change the course of Indian history. His followers welcomed him back as their leader, and within two years he not only had won back all the lost territory but had expanded his domain. He collected tribute from Mughal districts and plundered their rich mart; he reorganized the army and instituted reforms for the welfare of his subjects. Taking a lesson from the Portuguese and English traders who had already gained toeholds in India, he began the building of a naval force and was thus the first Indian ruler in modern times to appreciate that sea power was essential for trade as well as defense.

Almost as though prodded by Śivajī's meteoric rise, Aurangzeb intensified his persecution of Hindus; he imposed a poll tax on them, connived at forcible conversions, and demolished temples, erecting mosques in their places.

In the summer of 1674, Śivajī had himself enthroned with great fanfare as an independent sovereign. The suppressed Hindu majority rallied to him as their leader. He ruled his domain for six years, through a Cabinet of eight ministers. A devout Hindu who prided himself as the protector of his religion, he broke tradition by command-

Escape from Āgra

Independent sovereign

ing that two of his relatives, who had been forcibly converted to Islām, should be taken back into the Hindu fold (Hinduism admits no converts); yet even though both Christians and Muslims often imposed their creeds on the populace by force, he respected the beliefs and protected the places of worship of both communities. Many Muslims were in his service. After his coronation, his most noteworthy campaign was in the south, during which he forged an alliance with the sultans and thereby blocked the grand design of the Mughals to spread their rule over the entire subcontinent.

Śivajī had several wives and two sons. His last years were shadowed by the apostasy of his elder son, who, at one stage, defected to the Mughals and was brought back only with the utmost difficulty. The strain of guarding his kingdom from its enemies in the face of bitter domestic strife and discord among his ministers hastened his end. The man Macaulay called "the Great Śivajī" died after an illness on April 3, 1680, in the mountain stronghold of Rājgarh, which he had made his captial.

BIBLIOGRAPHY. DR. BALKRISHNA, *Shivaji the Great*, 2 vol. (1932), the most detailed factual account using newly discovered Dutch sources; J.N. SARKAR, *Shivaji and His Times*, 6th ed. rev. (1961), a study by one of the greatest authorities, based chiefly on Persian sources; H.G. RAWLINSON, *Shivájí the Maráthá: His Life and Times* (1915), a readable account by a British historian; N.S. TAKAKHAV, *The Life of Shivaji Maharj, Founder of the Maratha Empire* (1921), a detailed account for the general reader, based mainly on Marathi sources; V.B. KULKARNI, *Shjivaji: The Portrait of a Patriot* (1963), compact account for the general reader.

(R.R.D.)

Skeletal System, Human

Man, as a member of the great group of vertebrates, has an internal skeleton as framework for his body as a whole. This framework consists of many individual bones and cartilages. There are bands of fibrous connective tissue, the ligaments and tendons, in intimate relationship with the parts of the skeleton, but they are not, in a strict sense, considered a part of it.

The present article is concerned primarily with the gross structure and the function of the skeleton of the normal human adult. Details of tissue structure of cartilage and bone, of the complex developmental processes that bring the skeleton to its mature state, and of the diseases that affect the skeletal tissues and the joints are dealt with in the articles BONE; BONE DISEASES AND INJURIES; JOINT; JOINT DISEASES AND INJURIES.

The human skeleton, like that of other vertebrates, consists of three subdivisions, each with origins distinct from the others and each presenting certain individual features. These are (1) the axial, comprising the vertebral column—the spine—and much of the skull; (2) the visceral, comprising the lower jaw, some elements of the upper jaw, and the branchial arches, including the hyoid bone (the branchial arches are barlike ridges and the bones and cartilages that derive from them on either side of the throat and the head of the embryo, corresponding to the bars that support the gills of fish; for the hyoid, see below *The hyoid: example of the anchoring function*); and (3) the appendicular, to which the hip and shoulder girdles and the bones and cartilages of the limbs belong.

Three subdivisions of skeleton

When the relation of these three divisions of the skeleton to the soft parts, such as the nervous system, the alimentary respiratory, and circulatory systems, and the voluntary muscles, are considered, it is clear that the functions of the skeleton are of three different types—support, protection, and motion. Of these functions, support is the most primitive and the oldest, just as the axial part of the skeleton was the first to evolve. The vertebral column, corresponding to the notochord in lower organisms, is the main support of the trunk.

The central nervous system lies largely within the axial skeleton, the brain being well protected by the cranium (see below *The cranium: example of the protective function*) and the spinal cord by the vertebral column, by means of the bony neural arches (the arches of bone that encircle the spinal cord) and the intervening ligaments.

A distinctive characteristic of man as compared with

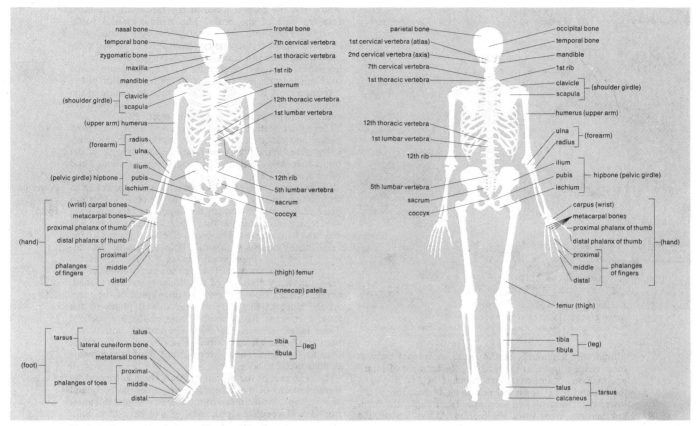

Figure 1: Front and back views of human skeleton.
From *Cunningham's Textbook of Anatomy*, edited by G.J. Romanes and published by Oxford University Press as an Oxford Medical Publication

Protective function of skeleton

other mammals is his erect posture. The human body is, to some extent, like a walking tower that moves on pillars, represented by the legs. Tremendous advantages have been gained from this erect posture, the chief among which has been the freeing of the arms for a great variety of uses. Nevertheless, erect posture has created a number of mechanical problems; in particular, weight bearing. These problems have had to be met by adaptations of the skeletal system.

Protection of the heart, lungs, and other organs and structures in the chest creates a problem somewhat different from that of the central nervous system. These organs, the function of which involves motion, expansion, and contraction, must have a flexible and elastic protective covering. Such a covering is provided by the bony thoracic basket, or rib cage, which forms the skeleton of the wall of the chest, or thorax. The connection of the ribs to the breastbone—the sternum—is in all cases a secondary one, brought about by the relatively pliable rib (costal) cartilages. The small joints between the ribs and the vertebrae permit a gliding motion of the ribs on the vertebrae during breathing and other activity. The motion is limited by the ligamentous attachments between ribs and vertebrae.

The third general function of the skeleton is that of motion. The great majority of the skeletal muscles are firmly anchored to the skeleton, usually to at least two bones and, in some cases, to many bones. Thus, the motions of the body and its parts, all the way from the lunge of the football fullback to the delicate manipulations of a handicraft artist or of the use of complicated instruments by a scientist, are made possible by separate and individual engineering arrangements between muscle and bone.

In this article, the cranium, the hyoid bone, the rib cage, and other parts of the skeleton are considered in terms of their sharing in these functions.

BONES OF THE AXIAL AND VISCERAL SKELETON

The cranium: example of the protective function. The cranium—that part of the skull that encloses the brain—is sometimes called the braincase, but its intimate relation

to the sense organs for sight, hearing, smelling, and taste and to other structures makes such a designation somewhat misleading.

The cranium is formed of bones of two different types of developmental origin—the cartilaginous, or substitution, bones, which replace cartilages preformed in the general shape of the bone; and membrane bones, which are laid down within layers of connective tissue. For the most part, the substitution bones form the floor of the cranium, while membrane bones form the sides and roof.

Development of cranial bones

The range in the capacity of the cranial cavity is wide but is not directly proportional to the size of the skull, because there are variations also in the thickness of the bones and in the size of the air pockets, or sinuses. The cranial cavity has a rough, uneven floor, but its landmarks and details of structure generally are consistent from one skull to another.

The cranium forms all the upper portion of the skull, with the bones of the face situated beneath its forward part. It consists of a relatively few large bones, the frontal bone, the sphenoid, two temporal bones, two parietal bones, and the occipital bone (see below). The frontal bone underlies the forehead region and extends back to the coronal suture, an arching line that separates the frontal bone from the two parietal bones, on the sides of the cranium. In front, the frontal bone forms a joint with the two small bones of the bridge of the nose and with the zygomatic bone (which forms part of the cheekbone; see below *The facial bones and their complex function*), the sphenoid, and the maxillary bones. Between the nasal and zygomatic bones, the horizontal portion of the frontal bone extends back to form a part of the roof of the eye socket, or orbit; it thus serves an important protective function for the eye and its accessory structures.

Each parietal bone has a generally four-sided outline. Together, they form a large portion of the side-walls of the cranium. Each adjoins the frontal, the sphenoid, the temporal, and the occipital bones and its fellow of the opposite side. They are almost exclusively cranial bones, having less relation to other structures than the other bones that help to form the cranium.

Parietal bones

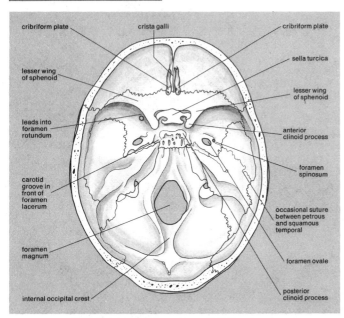

cribriform plate

crista galli

cribriform plate

lesser wing
of sphenoid

sella turcica

lesser wing
of sphenoid

leads into
foramen
rotundum

anterior
clinoid process

carotid
groove in
front of
foramen
lacerum

foramen
spinosum

occasional suture
between petrous
and squamous
temporal

foramen
magnum

foramen ovale

internal occipital crest

posterior
clinoid process

Figure 2: Internal surface of base of skull.
From *Cunningham's Textbook of Anatomy* edited by G.J. Romanes and published
by Oxford University Press as an Oxford Medical Publication

Important landmarks of the skull, useful not only in measurement but also in specifying the location of injury and of X-ray examination, are found at the four angles of the parietal bone: the upper rear angle is the lambda; the lower rear, the asterion; the upper front angle, the bregma; and the lower front, the pterion. At the lambda, the two parietal bones meet the occipital bone, which forms the back of the cranium. The asterion marks the location, within the cranium, of the lateral venous sinus, a large channel for venous blood that runs between layers of the outermost covering of the brain, the dura mater. The asterion is also the point at which parietal, occipital, and temporal bones meet. The bregma, the upper front corner, lies at the juncture of the parietal bones with the frontal bone. The pterion, the lower front joint, is the region of juncture of frontal, parietal, and sphenoid bones and, in some skulls, is the site of an irregular, isolated bone, called a wormian bone.

The interior of the cranium shows a multitude of details, reflecting the shapes of the softer structures that are in contact with the bones.

Internal surface of the vault

The internal surface of the vault is relatively uncomplicated. In the midline front to back, along the seam, called the sagittal suture, between the two parietal bones, is a shallow depression—the groove for the superior longitudinal venous sinus, a large channel for venous blood. A number of depressions on either side of it mark the sites of the pacchionian bodies, structures that permit the venous system to absorb cerebrospinal fluid. The large, thin-walled venous sinuses all lie within the cranial cavity. While they are thus protected by the cranium, in many places, they are so close beneath the bones that a fracture or penetrating wound may tear the sinus wall and lead to bleeding. The blood frequently is trapped beneath the outermost and toughest brain covering, the dura mater, in a mass called a subdural hematoma.

Conspicuous markings on the internal surface of the projection of the sphenoid, called the great wing, and on the internal surfaces of the parietal and the temporal bones are formed by the middle meningeal artery and its branches, which supply blood to the brain coverings. Injury to these vessels may lead to extradural hematoma, a mass of blood between the dura mater and the bone.

In contrast to the vault and sides of the cranium, the base presents an extremely complicated aspect. It is divided into three major depressions, or fossae, in a descending stair-step arrangement from front to back. The fossae are divided strictly according to the borders of the bones of the cranium but are related to major portions of the brain. The anterior cranial fossa serves as the bed in which rest the frontal lobes of the cerebrum, the large forward part of the brain. The middle cranial fossa, sharply divided into two lateral halves by a central eminence of bone, contains the temporal lobes of the cerebrum. The posterior cranial fossa serves as a bed for the hemispheres of the cerebellum (a mass of brain tissue back of the brainstem and beneath the rear portion of the cerebrum) and for the forward and middle portion of the brainstem. Major portions of the brain are thus partially enfolded by the bones of the cranial wall.

There are openings in the three fossae for the passage of nerves and blood vessels, and the markings on the internal surface of the bones are from the attachments of the brain coverings—the meninges—and venous sinuses and other blood vessels.

Anterior cranial fossa

The anterior cranial fossa shows a crestlike projection in the midline, the crista galli ("crest of the cock"). This is a place of firm attachment for the important falx cerebri, a subdivision of dura mater that separates the right and left cerebral hemispheres. On either side of the crest is the cribriform (pierced with small holes) plate of the ethmoid, a midline bone important as a part both of the cranium and of the nose. Through the perforations of the plate run many divisions of the olfactory, or first cranial, nerve, coming from the mucous membrane of the nose. At the sides of the plate are the orbital plates of the frontal bone, which form the roofs of the eye sockets. Their inner surfaces are relatively smooth but have a number of sharp irregularities more obvious to the touch than to the sight. These irregularities mark attachments of dura mater to bone.

The rear part of the anterior cranial fossa is formed by those portions of the sphenoid bone called its body and lesser wings. Projections from the lesser wings, the anterior clinoid (bedlike) processes, extend back to a point beside each optic foramen, an opening through which important optic nerves, or tracts, enter into the protection of the cranial cavity after a relatively short course within the eye socket.

Middle cranial fossa

The central eminence of the middle cranial fossa is specialized as a thronelike or saddlelike seat for the pituitary gland. The posterior portion of this seat, or sella turcica ("Turk's saddle"), is actually wall-like and is called the dorsum sellae. The pituitary gland is, thus, situated in almost the centre of the cranial cavity. It is covered over also by the brain coverings and has no connection with the exterior of the cranium except by blood vessels.

The deep, lateral portions of the middle cranial fossa contain the temporal lobes of the cerebrum. In the forward part of the fossa are two important openings: one, the superior orbital fissure, opening into the eye cavity, and the other, the foramen rotundum, for the passage of the maxillary nerve, which serves the upper jaw and adjacent structures. Farther back are the conspicuous foramen ovale, an opening for the mandibular nerve to the lower jaw, and the foramen spinosum, for the middle meningeal artery, which brings blood to the dura mater.

Also in the middle fossa, near the apex of that part of the temporal bone called the petrous (stonelike) temporal bone, is the jagged opening called the foramen lacerum. The lower part of the foramen lacerum is blocked by fibrocartilage, but through its upper part passes the internal carotid artery, surrounded by a network of autonomic nerves, as it makes its way to the interior of the cranial cavity.

The delicate structures of the internal ear are not entrusted to the cranial cavity as such but lie within the petrous portion of the temporal bone in a bony labyrinth into which the thin-walled membranous labyrinth, with its areas of sensory cells, is more or less accurately fitted but with an adequate space for protective fluid, the perilymph, between bone and membrane.

Posterior cranial fossa

The posterior cranial fossa is above the vertebral column and the muscles of the back of the neck. The foramen magnum, the opening through which the brain and spinal cord make connection, is in the lowest part of the fossa. Between its forward margin and the base of the dorsum sellae is a broad, smooth, bony surface called the clivus (Latin for "hill"). The bridgelike pons and the pyramid-like medulla oblongata of the brainstem lie upon the clivus, separated from the bone only by their coverings. Near the foramen magnum are ridges for attachment of folds of the dura mater.

In the sides of the posterior cranial fossa are two transverse grooves, each of which, in part of its course, is separated by extremely thin bone from the mastoid air cells back of the ear. Through other openings, the jugular foramina, pass the large blood channels called the sigmoid sinuses and also the 9th (glossopharyngeal), 10th (vagus), and 11th (spinal accessory) cranial nerves as they leave the cranial cavity.

The vessels, as well as the cranial nerves, are subject to injury at the openings into or from the cranial cavity and in special areas, such as close to the mastoid air cells. In the latter location, mastoiditis may lead to enough breakdown of bone to allow disease-bearing organisms to reach the other structures within the cranial cavity.

The hyoid: example of the anchoring function. The primary function of the hyoid bone is to serve as an anchoring structure for the tongue. The bone is situated at the root of the tongue in the front of the neck and between the lower jaw and the largest cartilage of the larynx, the voice box. It has no articulation with other bones and has, thus, a purely anchoring function.

The hyoid consists of a body, a pair of larger horns, the greater cornua, and a pair of smaller horns, the lesser cornua. The bone is more or less in the shape of a U, and the body forms the central part, or base, of the letter. In the act of swallowing, the hyoid bone, tongue, and larynx all move upward rapidly.

From *Cunningham's Textbook of Anatomy* edited by G.J. Romanes and published by Oxford University Press as an Oxford Medical Publication

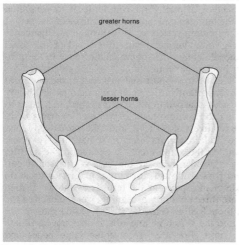

Figure 3: Hyoid bone.

The greater cornua are the limbs of the U. Their outer ends generally are overlapped by the large sternocleidomastoid muscles. The lesser cornua are small projections from the places somewhat arbitrarily called the junctions of the body and the greater cornua. The hyoid bone has certain of the muscles of the tongue attached to it.

The hyoglossus muscles originate on each side from the whole length of the greater cornua and also from the body of the hyoid. They are inserted into the posterior half or more of the sides of the tongue. The hyoid bone anchors them when they contract to depress the tongue and to widen the oral cavity. The two geniohyoid muscles originate close to the point at which the two halves of the lower jaw meet; the fibres of the muscles extend downward and backward, close to the central line, to be inserted into the body of the hyoid bone. Contraction of the muscles pulls the hyoid bone upward and forward.

Inserting into the middle part of the lower border of the hyoid bone are the sternohyoids, long muscles arising from the breastbone and collarbone and running upward and toward each other in the neck.

Other muscles attached to the hyoid bone are the two mylohyoid muscles, which form a sort of diaphragm for the floor of the mouth; the thyrohyoid, arising from the

Muscles anchored by the hyoid bone

thyroid (the largest) cartilage of the larynx; and the omohyoid, which originates from the upper margin of the shoulder blade and from a ligament, the suprascapular ligament.

The position of the hyoid bone with relation to the muscles attached to it has been likened to that of a ship steadied as it rides when anchored "fore and aft." Through the muscle attachments, the hyoid plays an important role in mastication, in swallowing, and in voice production.

At the beginning of a swallowing motion, the geniohyoid and mylohyoid muscles elevate the bone and the floor of the mouth simultaneously. These muscles are assisted by the stylohyoid and digastric muscles. The tongue is pressed upward against the palate and the food is forced backwards.

The facial bones and their complex functions. The larger part of the skeleton of the face is formed by the maxillae. Though they are called the upper jaws, the extent and functions of the maxillae include much more than serving as complements to the lower jaw, or mandible. They form the middle and lower portion of the eye socket. They have the opening for the nose between them, beneath the lower borders of the small nasal bones. A sharp projection, the anterior nasal spine, is formed by them at the centre of the lower margin of the opening for the nose, the nasal aperture.

The upper jaws

The infraorbital foramen, an opening into the floor of the eye socket, is the forward end of a canal through which passes the infraorbital branch of the maxillary nerve, the second division of the great fifth cranial nerve. It lies slightly below the lower margin of the socket.

The alveolar margin, containing the alveoli, or sockets, in which all the upper teeth are set, forms the lower part of each maxilla, while a lateral projection from each forms the zygomatic process, forming a joint with the zygomatic, or malar (cheek), bone.

The left and right halves of the lower jaw, or mandible, originally are two distinct bones, but in the second year the two bones fuse at the midline to form one. The horizontal, central part on each side is the body of the mandible. The upper portion of the body is the alveolar margin, corresponding to the alveolar margins of the maxillae. The projecting chin, at the lower part of the body in the midline, is said to be characteristic of the human skull. On either side of the chin is the mental foramen, an opening for the mental branch of the mandibular nerve, the third division of the fifth cranial nerve.

The lower jaw

The ascending parts of the mandible at the side are called rami (branches). The joints by means of which the lower jaw is able to make all its varied movements are between a rounded knob, or condyle, at the upper back corner of each ramus and a depression, called a glenoid fossa, in each temporal bone. Another, rather sharp projection at the top of each ramus and in front, called a coronoid process, does not form part of a joint. Attached to it is the temporalis muscle, which serves with other muscles in shutting the jaws.

On the inner side of the ramus of either side is a large, obliquely placed opening into a channel, the mandibular canal, for nerves, arteries, and veins.

The zygomatic arch, forming the cheekbone, consists of portions of three bones: the maxilla, in front; the zygomatic bone, centrally in the arch; and a projection from the temporal bone to form the rear part. The zygomatic arch actually serves as a firm bony origin for the powerful masseter muscle, which descends from it to insert on the outer side of the mandible and which shares with the temporalis and lateral and medial pterygoid muscles the function of elevating the mandible to bring the lower against the upper teeth, thus achieving bite.

The spine: its role in protection, anchoring, and weight bearing. In speaking earlier of the three major functions of the skeleton (support, protection, motion), it was indicated that the assumption of the erect posture during the development of the human species has led to a need for adaptation and changes from the arrangements seen in the quadrupeds. The very form of the human vertebral column is due to such adaptations and changes.

The
curvature
of the
spine

The vertebral column is not actually a column but, rather, a sort of spiral spring in the form of the letter S. The newborn child has a relatively straight backbone. The development of the curvatures occurs as the supporting functions of the vertebral column in man—holding up the trunk, keeping the head erect, serving as an anchor for the extremities—are developed.

The S-curvature makes it possible for the vertebral column to absorb the shocks of walking on hard ground or on pavement; a straight column would conduct the jarring shocks directly from the pelvic girdle to the head. The curvature meets the problem of the weight of the viscera. In an erect animal with a straight column, the column would be pulled forward by the viscera. Additional space for the viscera is provided by the concavities of the thoracic and pelvic regions.

From *Cunningham's Textbook of Anatomy* edited by G.J. Romanes and published by Oxford University Press as an Oxford Medical Publication

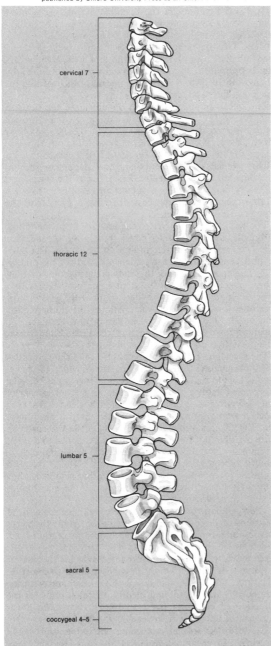

cervical 7

thoracic 12

lumbar 5

sacral 5

coccygeal 4–5

Figure 4: Backbone, from the left side.

Weight distribution of the entire body is also effected by the S-curvature. The upper sector, to a large extent, carries the head; the central sector, the thoracic viscera—the organs and structures in the chest—and the lower sector,

the abdominal viscera. If the column were straight, the weight load would increase from the head downward and be relatively great at the base. Lastly, the S-curvature protects the vertebral column from breakage. The doubly bent spring arrangement is far less vulnerable to fracture than would be a straight column.

The protective function of the skeleton is perhaps most conspicuous in relation to the central nervous system, although it is equally important for the heart and lungs and some other organs. A high degree of protection for the nervous system is made possible by the relatively small amount of motion and expansion needed by the component parts of this system and by certain physiological adaptations relating to circulation, to the cerebrospinal fluid, and to the meninges, the coverings of the brain and spinal cord. The brain itself is snugly enclosed within the boxlike cranium. Sharing in the protection afforded by the cranium is the pituitary gland, or hypophysis.

For the spinal cord, with its tracts of nerve fibres travelling to and from the brain, the placement in relation to the spinal column is somewhat like that of a candle in a lantern. Normally, there is considerable space between the nervous and the bony tissue, space occupied by the meninges, by the cerebrospinal fluid, and by a certain amount of fat and connective tissue. In front are the heavy centrums, or bodies, of the vertebrae and the intervertebral disks—the tough, resilient pads between the vertebral bodies—while in back and on the sides the cord is enclosed and protected by the portion of each vertebra called the neural arch. Between the neural arches are sheets of elastic connective tissue, the interlaminar ligaments, or ligamenta flava. Here some protective function has to be sacrificed for the sake of motion, because a forward bending of part of the column leads to separation between the laminae and between the spines of the neural arches of adjoining vertebrae. It is through the ligamenta flava of the lower lumbar region (the small of the back) that the needle enters the subarachnoid space in the procedure of lumbar puncture.

Besides its role in support and protection, the vertebral column is important in the anchoring of muscles. Many of the muscles attached to it are so arranged, in fact, as to move either the column itself or various segments of it. Some are relatively superficial, and others are deep lying. The large and important erector spinae, as the name implies, holds the spine erect. It begins on the sacrum (the large triangular bone at the base of the spinal column) and passes upward, forming a mass of muscle on either side of the spines of the lumbar vertebrae. It then divides into three columns, ascending over the back of the chest. Although slips (narrow strips) of the muscle are inserted into the vertebrae and ribs, it does not terminate thus, for fresh slips arise from these same bones and continue on up into the neck, until one of the divisions, known as the longissimus capitis, finally reaches the skull.

Anchoring
function
of the
spine

Small muscles run between the transverse processes (projections from the sides of the neural rings) of adjacent vertebrae, between the vertebral spines (projections from the centres of the rings), and also from transverse process to spine, giving great mobility to the segmented bony column.

The anchoring function of the spinal column is of great importance for the muscles that arise on the trunk, in whole or part from the column or from ligaments attached to it, and that are inserted on the bones of the arms and legs. Of these muscles, the most important for the arms are the latissimus dorsi (drawing the arm backward and downward and rotating it inward), the trapezius (rotating the shoulder blade), the rhomboideus, and the levator scapulae (raising and lowering the shoulder blade); for the legs, the psoas (loin) muscles.

The rib cage. The rib cage, or thoracic basket, consists of the 12 thoracic (chest) vertebrae, the 24 ribs, and the breastbone or sternum. The ribs are curved, compressed bars of bone, each succeeding rib, from the first, or uppermost, becoming more open in curvature. The place of greatest change in curvature of a rib, called its angle, is found several inches from the head of the rib, the end that forms a joint with the vertebrae.

Structure
and
functions
of ribs

The first seven ribs are attached to the breastbone by cartilages called costal cartilages; these ribs are called true ribs. Of the remaining five ribs, which are called false, the first three have their costal cartilages connected to the cartilage above them. The last two, the floating ribs, have their cartilages ending in the muscle in the abdominal wall.

Through the action of a number of muscles, the rib cage, which is semirigid but expansile, increases its size. The pressure of the air in the lungs thus is reduced below that of the outside air, which moves into the lungs quickly to restore equilibrium. These events constitute inspiration (breathing in). Expiration (breathing out) is a result of relaxation of the respiratory muscles and of the elastic recoil of the lungs and of the fibrous ligaments and tendons attached to the skeleton of the thorax. A major respiratory muscle is the diaphragm, which separates the chest and abdomen and has an extensive origin from the rib cage and the vertebral column. The configuration of the lower five ribs gives freedom for the expansion of the lower part of the rib cage and for the movements of the diaphragm.

BONES OF THE APPENDICULAR SKELETON

Shoulder girdle and pelvic girdle compared and contrasted. The upper and lower extremities of man offer many interesting points of comparison and of contrast. They and their individual components are homologous; *i.e.*, of a common origin and patterned on the same basic plan. A long evolutionary history and profound changes in function of these two pairs of extremities have led, however, to considerable differences between them.

The pelvic
girdle

The girdles are those portions of the extremities that are in closest relation to the axis of the body and that serve to connect the free extremity (the arm or the leg) with that axis, either directly, by way of the skeleton, or indirectly, by muscular attachments. The connection of the pelvic girdle to the body axis, or vertebral column, is by means of the sacroiliac joint. On the contiguous surfaces of the ilium—the rear and upper part of the hipbone—and of the sacrum—the part of the vertebral column directly connected with the hipbone—are thin plates of cartilage. The bones are closely fitted together in this way, and there are irregular masses of softer fibrocartilage in places joining the articular cartilages; at the upper and posterior parts of the joint there are fibrous attachments between the bones. In the joint cavity there is a small amount of synovial fluid. Strong ligaments, known as anterior and posterior sacroiliac and interosseous ligaments, bind the pelvic girdle to the vertebral column. These fibrous attachments are the chief factors limiting motion of the joint, but the condition, or tone, of the muscles in this region is important in preventing or correcting the sacroiliac problems that are of common occurrence.

The pelvic girdle consists originally of three bones, which become fused and each of which contributes a part of the acetabulum, the deep cavity into which the head of the thighbone, or femur, is fitted. The flaring upper part of the girdle is the ilium; the lower anterior part, meeting with its fellow at the midline, is the pubis; and the lower posterior part is the ischium. Each ischial bone has a prominence, or tuberosity, and it is upon these tuberosities that the body rests when seated.

The
pectoral
girdle

The components of the girdle of the upper extremity, the pectoral girdle, are the shoulder blade, or scapula, and the collarbone, or clavicle. The head of the humerus, the long bone of the upper arm, fits into the glenoid cavity, a depression in the scapula. The pectoral girdle is not connected with the vertebral column by ligamentous attachments, nor is there any joint between it and any part of the axis of the body. The connection is by means of muscles only, including the trapezius, rhomboids, and levator scapulae, while the serratus anterior connects the scapula to the rib cage. The range of motion of the pectoral girdle and, in particular, of the scapula is enormously greater than that of the pelvic girdle.

Another contrast, in terms of function, is seen in the shallowness of the glenoid fossa, as contrasted with the depth of the acetabulum. It is true that the receptacle for the head of the humerus is deepened somewhat by a lip of fibrocartilage, the glenoid labrum, which, like the corresponding structure for the acetabulum, aids in grasping the head of the long bone. The range of motion of the free upper extremity is, however, far greater than that of the lower. With this greater facility of motion goes a greater risk of dislocation, and, of all joints of the body, that of the shoulder is most often the site of dislocation.

Long bones of arms and legs: comparison and contrast. The humerus and the femur are corresponding bones of the arms and legs, respectively. While their parts are similar in general, their structure has been adapted to differing functions. The head of the humerus is almost hemispherical, while that of the femur forms about two-thirds of a sphere. There is a strong ligament passing from the head of the femur to further strengthen and ensure its position in the acetabulum.

The anatomical neck of the humerus is only a slight constriction, while the neck of the femur is a very distinct portion running from the head to meet the shaft at an angle of about 125°. Actually, the femoral neck is developmentally and functionally a part of the shaft. The entire weight of the body is directed through the femoral heads along their necks and to the shaft. The structure of the bone within the head and neck and the upper part of the shaft of the femur would do credit to an engineer who had worked out the weight-bearing problems involved.

From *Cunningham's Textbook of Anatomy* edited by G.J. Romanes and published by Oxford University Press as an Oxford Medical Publication

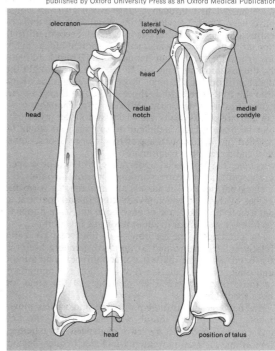

Figure 5: (Left) Forearm, radius and ulna bones. (Right) Lower leg, fibula and tibia bones.

The forearm and the lower leg have two long bones each. In the forearm are the radius—on the thumb side of the forearm—and the ulna; in the lower leg, the tibia (the shinbone) and the fibula. The radius corresponds to the tibia and the ulna to the fibula. The knee joint not only is the largest joint in the body but also is perhaps the most complicated one. The bones involved in it, however, are only the femur and the tibia, although the smaller bone of the leg, the fibula, is carried along in the movements of flexion, extension, and slight rotation that this joint permits. The very thin fibula is at one time in fetal development far thicker relative to the tibia than in the adult.

At the elbow, the ulna forms with the humerus a true hinge joint, in which the actions are flexion and extension. In this joint, a large projection of the ulna, the olecranon, fits into the well-defined olecranon fossa, a depression of the humerus.

Radius
and ulna

The radius is shorter than the ulna. Its most distinctive feature is the thick, disk-shaped head, which has a smoothly concave superior surface to articulate with the head, or capitulum, of the humerus. The head of the radius is held against the notch in the side of the ulna by means of a strong annular, or ring-shaped, ligament, which, at the same time, leaves the head free to rotate. As the head rotates, the shaft and outer end of the radius are swung in an arc. In the position of the arm called supination, the radius and ulna are parallel, the palm of the hand faces forward, and the thumb is away from the body. In the position called pronation, the radius and ulna are crossed, the palm faces to the rear, and the thumb is next to the body. There are no actions of the leg comparable to the supination and pronation of the arm.

Hands and feet: comparison and contrast. The skeleton of the wrist, or carpus, consists of eight small carpal bones, in two rows of four each. That of the ankle, or tarsus, has seven bones, and, because of the angle of the foot to the leg and the weight-bearing function, they are arranged in a more complicated way. The bone of the heel, directed downward and backward, is the calcaneus, while the "keystone" of the tarsus is the talus, the superior surface of which articulates with the tibia.

In the skeleton of the arms and legs, the outer portion is specialized and consists of elongated portions made up of chains, or linear series, of small bones. In an evolutionary sense, these outer portions appear to have had a complex history and, within man's own mammalian ancestry, to have passed first through a stage when all four would have been "feet," serving as the weight-bearing ends of extremities, as in quadrupeds in general. Second, all four appear to have become adapted for arboreal life, as in the lower primates, the "four-handed folk." Third, and finally, the assumption of an upright posture has brought the distal portions of the hind, now lower, extremities back into the role of feet, while those of the front, now upper, extremities have developed remarkable manipulative powers and are called hands. At what place in the primates a foot becomes a hand is difficult to say, and one might be justified, in fact, in speaking of hands in raccoons, squirrels, and some other nonprimates.

In man, the metatarsal bones, those of the foot proper, are larger than the corresponding bones of the hands, the metacarpal bones. The tarsals and metatarsals form the arches of the foot, which give it strength and enable it to act as a lever. The shape of each bone and its relations to its fellows are such as to adapt it for this function.

Fingers and toes The phalanges—the toe bones—of the foot have bases relatively large compared to the corresponding bones in the hand, while the shafts are much thinner. The middle and outer phalanges in the foot are short in comparison to those of the fingers. The phalanges of the great toe have special features.

The hand is an instrument for fine and varied movements. In these, the thumb with its skeleton, the first metacarpal bone and the two phalanges, is extremely important. Its free movements include, besides flexion, extension, abduction (ability to draw away from the first finger), and adduction (ability to move forward of the fingers), which are exercised in varying degrees by the great toe also, a unique action, that of opposition, by which it can be brought across, or opposed to, the palm and to the tips of the slightly flexed fingers. This motion forms the basis for the handling of tools, weapons, and instruments.

BIBLIOGRAPHY. G.J. ROMANES (ed.), *Cunningham's Textbook of Anatomy*, 10th ed. (1964), contains a detailed discussion of the subject with a comprehensive description of the features of each individual bone; J.E. FRAZER, *Anatomy of the Human Skeleton*, 6th ed. (1965), a classic in the field of osteology; C.M. GOSS (ed.), *Gray's Anatomy of the Human Body*, 28th ed. (1966), a full descriptive treatise, brought up-to-date and well-illustrated; G.H. BARNETT, "Joints and Movement" in F. GOLDBY and R.J. HARRISON (eds.), *Recent Advances in Anatomy*, 2nd ed., ch. 12, pp. 404–422 (1962), and M.C. HALL and D.S. KINOSHITA, *Architecture of Bone* (1966), two works useful for an understanding of the functional aspects and the structural adaptations of bone; F. KAHN, *Man in Struc-* *ture and Function* (1960; pub. orig. in German, 1939), a treatment of the subject for the interested lay reader.

(W.A.)

Skeletal Systems

The skeleton is the supportive framework of an animal body. In vertebrates it is mainly internal and consists mostly of bone and cartilage; in invertebrates it is sometimes external and may consist of a variety of nonbony, noncartilaginous materials. In addition to its supportive function, the animal skeleton may provide protection, facilitate movement, and aid in certain sensory functions.

Support of the body is achieved in many Protozoa by a simple stiff, translucent, nonliving envelope called a pellicle. In nonmoving (sessile) coelenterates, such as coral, whose colonies attain great size, it is achieved by dead structures, both internal and external, which form supporting axes. In the many groups of animals that can move it is achieved either by external structures known as exoskeletons or by internal structures known as endoskeletons. Many animals remain erect or in their normal resting positions by means of a hydrostatic skeleton; *i.e.*, fluid pressure in a confined space.

The protective function alone of a skeleton may be provided by structures situated on the body surface; *e.g.*, the lateral sclerites of centipedes and the shell (carapace) of crabs. These structures carry no muscle and form part of a protective surface armour. The scales of fish, the projecting spines of echinoderms (*e.g.*, sea urchins), the minute, needlelike structures (spicules) of sponges, and the tubes of hydroids, raised from the body surface, are similarly protective. The bones of the vertebrate skull protect the brain. In the more advanced vertebrates and invertebrates many skeletal structures provide a rigid base for the insertion of muscles as well as providing protection.

The skeleton facilitates movement in a variety of ways, depending on the nature of the animal. The bones of vertebrates and the exoskeletal and endoskeletal units of the cuticle of arthropods (*e.g.*, insects, spiders, crabs) support opposing sets of muscles (*i.e.*, extensors and flexors). In other animal groups the hydrostatic skeleton provides such support.

In a limited number of animals, the hard skeleton transmits vibrations that are sensed by the hearing mechanism. In some forms—*e.g.*, bony fishes and fast-swimming squids—it aids in the formation of buoyancy mechanisms that enable the animal to adjust its specific gravity for travelling at different depths in the sea.

SKELETAL ELEMENTS

General features. Certain types of skeleton usually characterize particular animal phyla, but there are a limited number of ways in which an animal can form its skeleton. Similar modes of skeleton formation have been evolved independently by different groups to fulfill similar needs. The cartilaginous braincase of the octopus and squid, which are invertebrates, has a microscopic structure similar to the cartilage of vertebrates. The calcareous (*i.e.*, calcium-containing) internal skeleton of the echinoderms is simply constructed but is essentially not far different from the much more elaborate bones of vertebrates. Skeletal fibres of similar chemical composition occur in unrelated animal groups; for example, coiled shells of roughly similar chemical composition are present in gastropods (*e.g.*, snails), brachiopods (*e.g.*, lamp shells), and cephalopods (*e.g.*, chambered nautilus). The mechanical properties of different skeletal types vary considerably according to the needs of animals of particular size ranges or habits; *e.g.*, aquatic, terrestrial.

Skeletal elements are of six principal types: so-called hard structures, semirigid structures, connective tissue, hydrostatic structures, elastic structures, and buoyancy devices.

Cuticular structures. Hard structures may be either internal or external. They may be composed of bone (calcareous or membranous structures that are rigid), crystals, cuticle, or ossicles (*i.e.*, minute plates, rods, or spicules).

Fish scales The scales of some fishes (*e.g.*, sturgeon) may be heavy, forming a complete external jointed armour; calcareous deposits make them stiff. They grow at their margins, and their outer surfaces become exposed by disintegration of the covering cell layer, epithelium. Other fish scales—*i.e.*, those of most modern bony fishes—are thin, membranous, and flexible. The external shells of gastropods and bivalve mollusks (*e.g.*, clams, scallops) are calcareous, stiff, and almost detached from the body. The laminated, or layered, shell grows by marginal and surface additions on the inner side. Muscles are inserted on part of the shell, and the body of the animal can be withdrawn into the protection of the shell. Chambered calcareous shells formed by cephalopods and by protozoans of the order Foraminifera become so large and so numerous that the broken remains of the shells may constitute a type of sand covering large areas of tropical beaches; the pieces may also consolidate into rock. Protozoa of the order Radiolaria form skeletons of silica in the form of very complicated bars. The body of the animal flows partly inside and partly outside among the bars.

Coral skeletons are also partly inside and partly outside the animal. Calcareous depositions below a young coral polyp (*i.e.*, an individual member of the animal colony) are secreted by the ectoderm (generally, the outermost of three basic tissue layers), fixed to the surface to which the animal is attached, and thrown up into ridges, which form a cup into which the polyp can contract. A spreading of the base and the formation of more polyps on the base are followed by a central humping up of the soft tissue and further secretion of skeleton. An upright branch is thus formed, and, in time, large branching corals many feet high may arise from the sea floor. Most of the soft tissue is then external to an axial calcareous skeleton, but in rapidly growing corals the skeleton is perforate, and soft tissue lies both inside and outside it. Protection of the animal is provided by the skeletal cups into which each polyp can contract, but usually neither the whole colony nor a single animal has mobility.

The starfishes, brittlestars, and crinoids (Echinodermata) have many types of calcareous ossicles in the mesoderm (generally, the tissue layer between the gut and the outermost layer). These form units that articulate with each other along the arms, spines that project from the body covering and articulate with ossicles, and calcareous jaws (in sea urchins), functioning in complex endoskeletal systems. Less well organized calcareous deposits stiffen the body wall between the arms of the starfish.

Crystals form the basis of many skeletons, such as the calcareous triradiate (three-armed) and quadradiate (four-armed) spicules of calcareous sponges. The cellular components of the body of the sponge usually are not rigid and have no fixed continuity; cells from the outer, inner, and middle layers of a sponge are freely mobile. Spicules, which may be of silica, often extend far from the body. They can be shed at times and replaced by new spicules. Skeletal fibres are present in many sponges.

Calcareous spicules, large and small, form an important part of the skeleton of many coelenterates. Huge, needle-like spicules, projecting beyond the soft tissue of sea pens (pennatulids), for example, both support the flanges that bear feeding polyps and hinder browsing by predators. Minute internal spicules may be jammed together to form a skeletal axis, as in the red coral. In some corals (Alcyonaria), spicules combine with fibres made of keratin (a protein also found in hair and feathers) or keratins with amorphous calcite (noncrystalline calcium carbonate) to form axial structures of great strength and size, enabling colonies to reach large, bushlike proportions.

Skeletons consisting of cuticle but remote from the body surface give support and protection to other coelenterates, the colonial sedentary hydroids, and form tubes in which pogonophores (small, threadlike aquatic animals) live. Exoskeletons that are superficially similar but quite different from hydroids and pogonophores in both manner of growth and internal support occur in the graptolites, an extinct group, and in the protochordates, *Rhabdopleura* and *Cephalodiscus*. Some graptolites, known only from fossil skeletal remains many millions of years old, had skeletons similar to those of *Rhabdopleura*.

In segmented and in many nonsegmented invertebrates,

cuticle is secreted by the ectoderm and remains in contact with it. It is thin in annelid worms (*e.g.*, the earthworm) and thicker in roundworms (nematodes) and arthropods. In many arthropods the cuticle is infolded to form endoskeletal structures of considerable complexity. Rigidity is imposed on parts of the cuticle of arthropods either by sclerotization or tanning, a process involving dehydration (as in crustaceans and insects), by calcification (as in millipedes), or by both, as in many crabs. In most arthropods the body and legs are clearly segmented. On the dorsal (upper) side of each segment is a so-called tergal sclerite of calcified or sclerotized cuticle, usually a ventral (lower) sternite and often lateral pleurites; *i.e.*, side plates. There may be much fusion of sclerites on the same segment. Sometimes fusion occurs between dorsal sclerites of successive segments, to form rigid plates. Leg sclerotizations are usually cylindrical.

Internally, apodemes are hollow rods or flanges derived from the cuticle; they extend inward from the exoskeleton. Apodemes have a function similar to the bones of vertebrates, for they provide sites for muscle insertion, thereby allowing the leverage that can cause movement of other parts of the skeleton independent of hydrostatic forces. The apodemal system is most fully developed in the larger and more swiftly moving arthropods. The cuticle is a dead secretion and can only increase in thickness. At intervals an arthropod molts the entire cuticle, pulling out the apodemes. The soft body rapidly swells before secreting a new, stiff cuticle. The molting process limits the upper size of cuticle-bearing animals. Arthropods can never achieve the body size of the larger vertebrates, in which the bones grow with the body, because the mechanical difficulties of molting would be too great. The mechanical properties of bone limit terrestrial mammals to about the size of a 12-ton elephant. In water, however, bone can support a heavier animal, such as a blue whale weighing 100 tons. Bone is mechanically unsuited to support an animal as bulky as, for example, a large ship.

Limitation of size by molting

Semirigid structures. Flexible cuticular structures on the surface of unsegmented roundworms and arthropods are just as important in providing support as are the more rigid sclerites. Mobility between the sclerites of body and legs is maintained by regions of flexible cuticle, the arthrodial membranes. Some sclerites are stiffened by closely packed cones of sclerotization at their margins, forming rigidity structures that combine rigidity and flexibility.

The so-called mesoglea layer, which lies between the ectoderm and endoderm (the innermost tissue layer) of coelenterates, is thin in small species and massive in large ones. It forms a flexible skeleton associated with supporting muscle fibres on both the ectodermal and endodermal sides. In many branched alcyonarian, or soft corals, the mesoglea is filled with calcareous spicules, which are not tightly packed and thus permit the axis of each coral branch to bend with the swell of the sea. As a result, soft corals, which are sessile and colonial, are very strong and can resist water movements without breaking. In this respect they are unlike the calcareous corals, which break in violent currents of water. The often beautifully coloured, gorgonian corals, or sea fans, are supported by an internal horny axis of keratin. They, too, bend with the water movements, except when very large. In some forms the horny axis may be impregnated with lime. The horny axes are often orientated in complex branches set in one plane, so that the coral forms a feeding net across a prevailing current. Certain chordates also possess a flexible endoskeleton; the rodlike notochord occurs in adult lampreys and in most young fishes. Running just within the dorsal midline, it provides a mechanical basis for their swimming movements. In the higher vertebrates the notochord is surrounded by cartilage and finally replaced by bone. In many protochordates, however, the notochord remains unchanged. Cartilage, too, forms flexible parts of the endoskeletal system of vertebrates, such as between articulating bones and forming sections of ribs.

Connective tissue. Connective tissue forms sheets of varying complexity below the ectoderm of many animals, existing as fine membranes or as complex superficial layers of fibres. Muscles inserted on the fibres form subepithelial complexes in many invertebrates; and vertebrate muscles are often inserted on firm sheets of connective tissue (fascia) deep in the body that are also formed by these fibres. Particular concentrations of collagen fibres, oriented in different directions, occur superficially in the soft-bodied *Peripatus* (a caterpillar-like terrestrial invertebrate). In coelenterates they also occur deep in the body. In many arthropods, collagen fibres form substantial endosternites (*i.e.,* ridges on the inner surface of the exoskeleton in the region of the thorax) that are isolated from other skeletal structures. These fibres are not shed during molting, and the endosternites grow with the body. The fibres do not stretch, but their arrangement provides firm support for muscles and sometimes permits great changes in body shape.

The hydrostatic skeleton. The hydrostatic skeleton is made possible by closed, fluid-filled internal spaces of the body. It is of great importance in a wide variety of animal groups because it permits the antagonistic action of muscles used in locomotion and other movements. The fluid spaces are part of the gastrovascular cavity in the Coelenterata, part of the coelomic cavity (between the gut and the body wall) in the worms, and hemocoelic (*i.e.,* in a type of body cavity consisting of a complex of spaces between tissues and organs) or vascular in mollusks and arthropods. As the exoskeleton becomes more rigid and the apodemal endoskeleton more fully developed in arthropods, the importance of the hemocoele in promoting antagonistic muscle action decreases. In larger and more heavily sclerotized species the hydrostatic skeleton is no longer of locomotory significance; the muscles work directly against the articulated skeleton, as in vertebrates.

Skeletal structure of jellyfishes

Elastic structures. In the larger medusae, or jellyfishes (Coelenterata), the musculature is mainly circular. By contracting its bell-shaped body, the jellyfish narrows, ejecting water from under the bell thus pushing the animal in the opposite direction from that of the water. There are no antagonistic muscles to counteract the contracted circular muscles. A passive, slow return of the bell to its expanded shape is effected largely by the elasticity of the mesoglea layer, which crumples during the propulsive contraction. After the circular muscles relax, the distorted mesoglea fibres pull them out to expand the bell. In many of the larger mammals, elastic fibres are used more extensively. The elephant and whale for example, possess an abundance of elastic tissue in their musculature.

Elasticity of surface cuticle assists recovery movements in roundworms and arthropods, but the stresses and strains that cuticle can withstand are limited. Special sensory devices (chordotonal organs) convey the extent of stress in the cuticle to the animal's nervous system, thus preventing the generation of stresses great enough to damage the structure. There are also elastic units in the base of the wings of some insects. These rather solid elastic structures alternately store and release energy. They have probably been important in the evolution of the extremely rapid wing beat of some insects.

Buoyancy devices. Buoyancy devices are complex structures that involve both hard and soft parts of the animal. In vertebrates they may be closely associated with or form part of the auditory apparatus. A chain of auditory ossicles in mammals transmits vibrations from the tympanic membrane to the internal ear; simpler devices occur in the cold-blooded land vertebrates. In the roach fish, which has sensitive hearing, a chain of four so-called Weberian ossicles connects the anterior, or forward, end of the swim bladder to the auditory organs of the head. Sound vibrations cause changes in volume in the anterior part of the bladder and are transmitted to the nervous system through the ossicles. The swim bladder of other fishes appears to be a buoyancy organ and not skeletal; however, cephalopods capable of swimming rapidly in both deep and shallow water possess air-filled buoyancy organs. The calcareous coiled shell of the bottom-living *Nautilus* is heavy and chambered; the animal lives in the large chamber. The shell behind is coiled and composed of air-filled chambers that maintain the animal in an erect position. When the

entire, coiled, lightly constructed shell of *Spirula* sinks into the body, the animal has internal air spaces that can control its buoyancy and also its direction of swimming. In cuttlefish and squids, a shell that was originally chambered has become transformed into a laminated cuttlebone. Secretion and absorption of gases to and from the cuttlebone by the bloodstream provide a hydrostatic buoyancy mechanism enabling the squids to swim with little effort at various depths. This device has probably made it possible for some species to grow to a length of 18 metres (59 feet). Some siphonophores (Coelenterata) have a chambered, gas-filled float, its walls stiffened with a chitin-like structure in *Velella*.

Cuttlebone

INVERTEBRATE SKELETON

Skeleto-musculature of a mobile coelenterate. A sea anemone provides an example of the way in which a hydrostatic skeleton can act as the means by which simple sheets of longitudinal and circular muscle fibres can antagonize each other to produce contrasting movements. The fluid-filled space is the large digestive, or internal, cavity of the body. If the mouth is slightly open when both longitudinal and circular muscles of the trunk contract, fluid flows out of the internal space, and the body shrinks. If the mouth is closed, the internal fluid-filled space cannot be compressed; thus, the body volume remains constant, and contraction of the longitudinal muscles of the trunk both shortens and widens the body. Contraction of the circular muscles pulls out relaxed longitudinal muscles, and the body lengthens. Appropriate coordination of muscular action working against the hydrostatic skeleton can produce locomotion movements—such as burrowing in sand or stepping along a hard surface—by billowing out one side of the base of the animal, the other side of the base contracting and forcing fluid into the relaxed, dilated portion. The forward dilated part sticks to the surface, and its muscles contract, pulling the animal forward.

From (A) E.J. Batham and C.F.A. Pantin, "Activity in the Sea Anemone Metridium Senile," *Journal of Experimental Biology* (1950), reprinted by permission of Cambridge University Press; (B) T.J. Parker and W.A. Haswell, *Textbook of Zoology*, 2nd ed. (1962), St. Martin's Press, Inc., Macmillan Co., Ltd.; (C) A. Schepotieff, "Die Anatomie von Rhabdopleura," *Zoologische Jahrbucher Abteilung fur Anatomie* (1907), Gustav Fischer Verlag; (D) A. Dendy, "On the Origin, Growth and Arrangement of Sponge Spicules," *Quarterly Journal of Microscopial Sciences*, vol. 1 (1966), Cambridge University Press

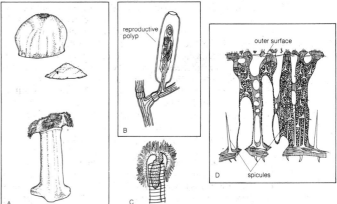

Figure 1: *Skeletal systems of lower invertebrates.*
(A) *Metridium* in three conditions; (B) *Obelia;* (C) *Rhabdopleura;* (D) *Grantia.*

The circular muscles lie outside a substantial layer of skeletal mesoglea fibrils; longitudinal muscles are internal to the layer. The muscle fibres are attached at either end to the mesoglea fibres, which, like vertebrate bones, cannot stretch. Unlike bones, however, the mesoglea sheet is able to change its shape, because its components (fibrils) are set in layers at an angle to each other and to the long axis of the body. Alteration in length and width of the body is accompanied by changes in the angle between two sheets of mesoglea fibrils; thus, support for the muscles can vary greatly in position. The range in change of shape of the sea anemone is implemented by simple muscles and connective tissue mesoglea fibrils. The movements are characteristically slow, often occurring so slowly as to be invisible to the naked eye. Faster movements would engender greater increases in internal pressures, thus placing a needless burden on the musculature. All coelenterates utilize this slow hydrostatic–muscular system, but, as described for the jellyfish, some faster movements are also possible.

Skeleto-musculature of an earthworm. The hydrostatic skeleton of many other animals is provided by the body cavity, or coelom, which is situated outside the alimentary canal and inside the body wall. In an earthworm the body cavity of each segment of the trunk is separated from that of the next by a partition, so that the segmented body possesses a series of more or less isolated coelomic, fluid-filled spaces of fixed volume. The body wall contains circular and longitudinal muscles and some minor muscles. As in the sea anemone, skeletal connective-tissue fibres form the muscle insertions. As a worm crawls or burrows, a group of segments shorten and widen, their total volume remaining the same; contact with the ground is maintained by projection of bristle-like structures from the cuticle (setae). Groups of short, wide segments are formed at intervals along the body; the segments between these groups are longer, narrower, and not in contact with the ground. As the worm crawls, the thickened zones appear to travel backward along the body, because the segments just behind each zone thicken, widen, and cling to the ground, while the segments at the front end of each wide zone free themselves from the ground and become longer and narrower. Thus, the head end of the body intermittently progresses forward over the ground or enters a crevice as the longitudinally extending segments are continuously being lengthened outward from the front end of each thickened zone. It is therefore only the long narrow segments that are moving forward. This mechanism of crawling by the alternate and antagonistic action of the longitudinal and circular muscles is made possible by the hydrostatic action of the incompressible coelomic spaces. The movements of most other annelid worms are also controlled by a hydrostatic skeleton.

Skeleto-musculature of arthropods. In arthropods the skeleton is formed in part by the cuticle covering the body surface; by internal connective-tissue fibres; and by a hydrostatic skeleton formed by the hemocoele, or enlarged, blood-filled spaces. The cuticle may be flexible or stiff, but it does not stretch. In the Onychophora (*e.g.*, *Peripatus*) the cuticle is thin and much folded, thus allowing great changes in the body shape. The muscular body wall, as in annelids, works against the hydrostatic skeleton in the hemocoele. Each leg moves in a manner similar to the body movement of a sea anemone or *Hydra*. But a unique lateral isolating mechanism allows suitable hydrostatic pressures to be available for each leg. Muscles of a particular leg thus can be used independently, no matter what the other legs may be doing or what influence the body movements may be having on the general hemocoele.

In most adult arthropods the cuticle is less flexible than is that in the Onychophora, localized stiff sclerites being separated by flexible joints between them; as a result, the hydrostatic action of the hemocoele is of less importance. Cuticle, secreted by the ectodermal cells, may be stiffened by deposition of lime or by tanning (sclerotization). Muscle fibres or their connective-tissue supports are connected to the cuticle by tonofibrils within the cytoplasm of ectodermal cells.

The joints between the stiffened sclerites consist of undifferentiated flexible cuticle. Between the distal (*i.e.*, away from the central body axis) leg segments of many arthropods the flexible cuticle at the joint is relatively large ventrally (*i.e.*, on the lower side) and very short dorsally (*i.e.*, on the upper side), thus forming a dorsal hinge. Flexor muscles (for drawing the limb toward the body) span the joint and cause flexure of the distal part of the leg. There are no extensor muscles, however, and straightening of the leg when it is off the ground is effected by hydrostatic pressure of the general hemocoele and by proximal depressor muscles that open the joint indirectly. Between the proximal leg segments (*i.e.*, those closer to the point of insertion of the limb into the body), pivot

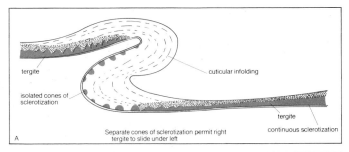

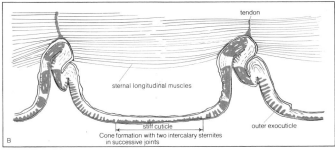

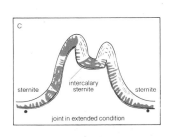

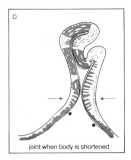

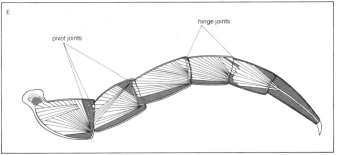

Figure 2: *Skeletal features of a centipede and a millipede.*
(A–D) Trunk intersegments of burrowing centipede, *Geophilus,* allow the body to change shape while still presenting a complete external armour of sclerites. (E) The proximal joints in a millipede leg function in a pivotal fashion; the distal joints act as hinges.
From (A–D) *Zoological Society of the Linnean Society* (1965) and (E) (1958)

joints are usually present. They are composed of a pair of imbricating, or overlapping, facets near the edges of the overlapping cylinders that cover the leg segments, one pair on the anterior face of the leg and another on the posterior face. A pair of antagonistic muscles span the leg joint and move the distal segment up or down, without reference to hydrostatic pressure.

The more advanced arthropods—those with the most elaborate sclerites and joints—are no longer dependent upon hydrostatic forces for skeleto-muscular action. Evolution away from the hydrostatic skeleton has made possible faster and stronger movements of one cuticular unit upon another. The type of skeleto-musculature appropriate for fast movements, such as rapid running, jumping, or flying, are quite different from those producing strong movements, such as those used by burrowing arthropods.

The flexible edges of the sclerites of burrowing centipedes (Geophilomorpha) enables them to change their shape in an earthworm-like manner, while preserving a complete armour of surface sclerites at all times. This is made possible by the fact that the marginal zones of the sclerites bear cones of sclerotization that are set in the flexible cuticle, thus permitting flexure in any direction without impairing strength. The surface of the arthropodan cuticle is rendered waterproof, or hydrofuge, by a variety of structures, such as waxy layers, scales, and hairs. These features enable the animals not only to resist desiccation on land but to exist in damp places without uptake of water—a process that could cause swelling of the body and lead to death. The cuticular endoskeleton is formed by an infolding of surface cuticle. Sometimes transverse plates are formed, as in the cephalothorax of lobsters, which covers both head and the thorax.

Connective-tissue fibres form substantial endoskeletal units in arthropods. The fibres are not united to the cuticle and are not shed during molting; rather, they grow with the body. A massive and compact endosternite (internal sternite), formed by connective-tissue fibres, frequently lies below the gut and above the nerve cord. In *Limulus*, the horseshoe crab, muscles from the anterior margin of the coxa (the leg segment nearest the body) are inserted on the endosternite, as are other muscles from the posterior margin.

The jointed cuticular skeleton of arthropods enables them to attain considerable size, up to a few metres in length, and to move rapidly. These animals have solved most of the problems presented by life on dry land in a manner unequalled by any other group of invertebrates. They have also evolved efficient flight by means of wings derived from the cuticle. The arthropods can never achieve the body size of the larger vertebrates, although mechanically they perform as well as smaller vertebrates. As mentioned above, the major limiting factor to size increase is the need to molt the exoskeleton.

Skeleton of echinoderms. Among the invertebrates, only the echinoderms possess an extensive mesodermal skeleton that is stiffened by calcification—as in vertebrates—and also grows with the body. The five-rayed symmetry of echinoderms may be likened to the vertebral axis of vertebrates. It is similarly supported; a series of ambulacral ossicles in each ray roughly corresponds with the vertebrae of vertebrates. The ossicles articulate with each other in mobile echinoderms such as starfishes and form the basis of the rapid movements of the arms of crinoids, brittlestars, and similar forms. The ambulacral ossicles and, in many cases, the surface spines provide protection for superficial nerve cords, which extend along the arms and around the mouth. The ossicles also protect the tubes of the water-vascular system, a hydraulic apparatus peculiar to echinoderms. In sea urchins a spherical, rigid body is formed by the five arms coming together dorsally around the anus; the ambulacral ossicles are immobile, and the body wall between the ambulacra is made rigid by a layer of calcareous plates below the ectoderm, which completes the continuous spherical skeleton. Locomotion is carried out by extensible tubefeet, soft structures that are pendant from the water-vascular system. Mobile spines also serve for locomotion in many classes, the base of the spine articulating with a part of some stable ossicle. The fine internal structure of echinoderm sclerites bears no resemblance to that of bone.   (S.M.M.)

VERTEBRATE SKELETON

General features.   In vertebrates the adult skeleton is usually formed of bone or cartilage, living substances that grow with the animal, in contrast to the many types of invertebrate skeleton that do not grow or are dead secretions, deposits, or crystals. The internal position of bones and their central position in limbs provide firm support for small and large animals. Muscles can be inserted on all surfaces of the skeleton, in contrast to the limitations of the cuticular skeleton of arthropods, in which muscles occur on only one side. Antagonistic muscles are easily placed upon vertebrate bones to allow contrasting movements at the joints between them.

The component parts of the skeletons of vertebrates, although remarkably uniform in basic plan, are subject to wide superficial differences, which are associated with each class and with adaptations for particular habits or environments. The axial skeleton consists of the skull and the vertebral column. The appendicular skeleton supports the fins in fish and the legs in tetrapods (four-legged animals) and is associated with limb girdles, which become progressively more closely linked with the vertebral column in the higher vertebrates. Superficially there may be an exoskeleton of scales; some scales on the head may be incorporated into the skull.

Swimming of a typical fish occurs by undulations passing along a greater or lesser part of the body. The mechanism for caudal (tail) propulsion involves the vertebral column, the axial musculature, and the lateral surfaces of the body and caudal fin. The vertebral column of the fish can be regarded as a series of rigid units hinged to each other by surfaces that allow the body to bend only sideways. On each side of the vertebral chain lie the great axial muscles of the body; the fibres of this complex group of muscles are more or less parallel to the long axes of the vertebrae. One pair of vertebrae and their associated musculature form the fundamental unit of propulsion. The muscles on the two sides of each vertebral articulation shorten alternately, the surface of the body becoming concave, or bent inward, on the side on which the muscles are shortened and convex, or bent outward, on the side on which they are stretched. The whole tail of the fish is essentially a chain of such units in which the phase of muscular contraction at any one link is slightly ahead of that of the next posterior unit and slightly behind that of the next anterior unit. Each wave of contraction passes tailward along the body, which is thus propelled forward. The greatest thrust against the water is exerted by the tail end. Ribs of various kinds lie between and support the segmental muscles. The fins and their skeletal supports are used as balancing and steering organs. The paired fins are set horizontally in cartilaginous fish, which do not have a swim bladder, and vertically in most bony fishes, in which rapid vibrations or small angular movements provide exact steering. In the air-breathing lungfish, fins are used for stepping on the bottom in a manner that superficially resembles stepping by the legs of a salamander. Indeed, the land vertebrates evolved from extinct fishes that used their fins for stepping; the pentadactyl (*i.e.*, with five digits) skeleton and the form of the forelegs and hindlegs of land vertebrates similarly evolved from the fins of such fishes.

An unjointed elastic notochord is present in the protochordate amphioxus, in the tail of larval ascidians (tunicates), and in the adult cyclostomes (lamprey and hagfish), but there are no vertebrae. Segmental series of muscles are present as in fish, and the resultant swimming movements of these muscles, working with the elastic notochord, are similar to those in fish.

The lateral body undulations caused by the trunk musculature, as seen in fish, are the main propulsive agents in amphibians such as the newt. The feet raise the body from the ground but otherwise serve only to anchor the body while the vertebral musculature allows forward progression by straightening the flank. The same propulsive mechanism serves for locomotion in water and on land. In the reptiles, birds, and mammals a transition of the locomotory force from the body to the limbs occurs. When the vertebral muscles contract isometrically (*i.e.*, against such great pressure that the muscle is unable to shorten), so as to prevent body undulations, the energy for propulsion comes from the limbs. Hands and feet are directed forward, as is the knee; and the elbow is directed backward. The limbs are no longer outstretched laterally but move ventrally below the body. The bones at the heel and elbow are extended to form levers that give origin to powerful extensor muscles of the foot and hand, thus contributing to a locomotory thrust against the ground. The elimination of lateral undulations of the vertebral column as the main propulsive agent is accompanied by the development of dorso-ventral flexibility of the chain of vertebrae; the distance between successive footfalls would be less if the vertebral column remained rigid. Swimming in whales is accomplished by dorso-ventral tail beats, in contrast to that in fish (which beat the tail laterally). The swimming musculature of whales evolved from the nonswimming musculature of terrestrial ances-

The fish skeleton in swimming

The whale skeleton in swimming

tors. Long antagonistic muscles extend from the whale's skull to the tail and implement the dorso-ventral motion, in contrast to propulsion by means of segmental muscles in fish.

The structure of the vertebrae provides a basis for many movements, including those mentioned above. Mobility sometimes is extreme, as in the necks of certain birds, in which the imbricating, or overlapping, centra (*i.e.*, the main, ventral portion of a vertebra that articulates with that of the adjacent vertebrae) can flex in any direction yet remain firmly interlocked, because the adjacent articular surface of the bony centra are saddled-shaped. The extensive mobility of snakes is mediated by its vertebral structure and its well-developed ribs; in this case, mobility is lost but greater stability achieved by fusion of two or more vertebrae.

The limbs of tetrapods and their limb girdles have become much modified in association with particular habits, such as rapid running, jumping, swimming, and burrowing. The limb bones remain relatively unspecialized in slow-moving animals and in those with climbing ability. Accomplished runners differ from man and the monkeys in that the proximal sector of the leg (humerus in the forelimb, femur in the hindlimb)—*i.e.*, the portion closer to the limb's insertion in the body proper—is short. This sector carries many locomotory muscles but does not project far—if at all—from the trunk. Beyond the short, strong femur and humerus, the limb bones of running animals are elongated, slender, and strong. The distal part of the leg (*i.e.*, that portion further from the trunk) must be narrow and light if it is to move rapidly through a wide angle. The wrist and knee are far from the ground, and in horses and other ungulates (*i.e.*, hoofed animals) the animal stands on its toenails and fingernails (hooves); the whole hand and foot are raised from the ground, thus contributing to leg length.

Embryology of vertebrate skeletons. When the early embryo consists of only two tissue layers, ectoderm and endoderm, a longitudinal thickening appears as the result of multiplication of the ectodermal cells. This thickening, the primitive streak, gives rise to the notochord and to the third basic layer, the mesoderm. The longitudinal axis of the embryo is first laid down by the formation of a cylindrical mass of cells, the notochord, proliferated from the primitive (Hensen's) node at the anterior end of the streak. The notochord lies ventral to the developing central nervous system and forms the first supporting structure for the developing embryo.

In fishes such as the shark, cartilaginous vertebrae form around the notochord and to some extent compress it. It persists, nevertheless, as a continuous structure through the length of the vertebral column. In the higher vertebrates, including man, the notochord is a temporary structure, persisting only as a minute canal in the bodies of the vertebrae and in the central part of the so-called nucleus pulposus of the intervertebral disks.

As the notochord is being laid down, cells proliferate from each side of the primitive streak, forming the mesoderm, which spreads out laterally and, as a result of migration and multiplication of cells, soon comes to occupy most of the space between the ectoderm and the endoderm on each side of the notochord. The mesodermal sheets soon become differentiated into (1) a mass lying on each side of the notochord (paraxial mass) that undergoes segmentation into hollow blocks, the mesodermal somites; (2) a lateral plate that becomes separated into an outer layer, the somatopleuric mesoderm, against the future body wall, and an inner layer, the splanchnopleuric mesoderm, against the endoderm of the future gut; and (3) an intermediate mass, the nephrogenic cord, which gives rise mainly to the genitourinary system.

The segmentation of the paraxial mesoderm is a fundamental feature of the development of the vertebrates. The axial skeleton and associated structures develop from part of the mesodermal somite; the appendicular skeleton arises from the somatopleuric mesoderm of the lateral plate. Each somite differentiates into (1) a lateral and superficial plaque, the dermatome, which gives rise to the integumentary tissue; (2) a deeper lateral mass, the myo-

tome, which gives rise to the muscles; and (3) a medial ventral mass, the sclerotome. The sclerotomic cells from each pair of somites migrate until they enclose the notochord, separating it from the neural tube dorsally and from the aorta (the principal blood vessel) ventrally. The sclerotomic tissue retains its original segmentation and condenses to form the forerunner, or blastema, of the centrum of the future vertebra. From each posterolateral half of the condensation, extensions pass backward and eventually meet posteriorly around the neural tube to form the blastema of the neural (dorsal) arch of the vertebra. In the interspaces between adjacent myotomes of each side, an extension from each sclerotomic mass passes laterally and forward to form the costal, or rib, element. It is only in the thoracic (midbody) region that the costal elements develop into ribs. In the other regions the costal elements remain rudimentary (undeveloped). The mesenchymal blastema of the future vertebra becomes chondrified; *i.e.*, the mesenchymal cells are converted into cartilage cells. In this cartilaginous vertebra, ossification (bone-forming) centres appear, and the cartilage is gradually replaced by bone. The mesenchyme of the embryonic ribs also undergoes chondrification and later ossification. In the thoracic region, in which costal elements are best developed, a cartilaginous sternal bar forms, connecting the anterior, or growing, ends.

The appendicular skeleton begins to develop in the primitive limb bud in the core of mesenchyme that is derived directly from the unsegmented somatopleuric mesoderm. This mesenchyme condenses to form the blastemal masses of the future limb bones. Soon the mesenchyme becomes transformed into the cartilaginous precursors of the individual bones (except in the clavicle). The cartilaginous models determine the general shape and relative size of the bones. There is convincing evidence that the shape of the bones of higher vertebrates is determined by factors inherent in the tissues, and that, once development has begun, extrinsic influences provide the proper conditions for maintaining the normal structure.

The first mesenchymal condensations of the appendicular skeleton are in the region of the future girdles; those for the shoulder girdle appear a little earlier than those for the pelvic girdle. The mesenchymal condensations for the other bones of the limbs appear in order of their proximity to the trunk.

Vertebral column and thoracic skeleton. The notochord constitutes the earliest structure that stiffens the embryo and appeared in animals before the true vertebral column evolved. A vertebra includes a centrum and a neural arch surrounding the spinal cord.

Lower chordates and fishes. Possession of the notochord distinguishes members of the most advanced phylum, Chordata. In the sea squirts (Urochordata) the notochord is present in the tail region of the larva but disappears after the animal transforms into the adult. In amphioxus (Cephalochordata), the notochord is permanent and extends the whole length of the body. In the cyclostome fishes (Agnatha), the most primitive group within the subphylum Vertebrata, the notochord and its sheath persist throughout life; rudimentary cartilaginous neural arches are found in the adult lamprey. Among the sharks (Selachii), modern representatives possess a vertebral column composed of cartilaginous, partly calcified centra that have their origin within the sheath of the notochord, thus causing its partial absorption. Among the bony fishes (Osteichthyes), the sturgeon has a persistent notochord with a fibrous sheath upon which appear paired cartilaginous arches: dorsally, the neural arches and, ventrally, the hemal arches. The vertebrae of the more advanced bony fishes, such as the salmon and cod, are completely ossified; each centrum develops in the sclerotomic mesoderm outside the notochordal sheath. This is known as perichordal development.

Amphibians and higher vertebrates. In amphibians a vertebra is formed from the sclerotomic tissues of two somites, the tissue from the posterior part of one somite joining that from the anterior part of the somite behind it. In living reptiles the vertebrae are completely ossified.

Margin notes:

Development of the notochord

Development of appendicular skeleton

Mam-
malian
vertebrae

The neural arch has a spinous process and pre- and post-zygapophyses (additional articulating surfaces); at the junction of the arch and centrum is a facet for articulation of the head of a rib. Groups of vertebrae can be distinguished; *e.g.*, the cervical vertebrae are recognizable because the neck is differentiated from the body.

The fibrocartilaginous intervertebral disks uniting the centra of crocodiles have been identified as representing so-called intercentra. Ribs are present in the cervical, thoracic, and lumbar regions of the column.

The sternum may be calcified but is seldom ossified in the reptiles. In the lizards it is a cartilaginous plate articulated with the coracoid processes of the pectoral girdle and with the anterior thoracic ribs. The sternum is absent in the turtles and in the snakes; in the crocodiles it is a wide plate joined by the coracoid processes and by two pairs of ribs.

The skeletons of modern birds show reptilian features with some specialized adaptations to their bipedal locomotion (*i.e.*, by means of one pair of legs) and their power of flight. The neck is very flexible. With its variation in length the number of cervical vertebrae ranges from 25 in the swan to nine in certain small birds. The tendency for the vertebrae to fuse in certain regions is characteristic of birds. The sternum, a very large bone, is positioned like a shield in front of the chest. In flying birds a median keel, the carina, projects ventrally, providing additional surface for the attachment of the pectoral muscles that move the wings. The flightless birds, such as the ostrich, have a keelless, raftlike sternum.

In mammals the vertebral centra articulate by means of intervertebral disks of fibrocartilage. Bony disks (epiphyses) formed on the generally flat ends of the centra are characteristic of mammals. Regional differentiation in the mammalian backbone is marked. The number of vertebrae in each group, excepting the caudal vertebrae, is moderately consistent, though there are some exceptions to the group averages. Whereas seven cervical vertebrae are the rule, there are nine or ten in the three-toed sloth and only six in the two-toed sloth and the manatee. The thoracic vertebrae commonly number 13 or 14, although they vary from nine in some whales to 24 in the two-toed sloth. The average number of lumbar vertebrae is about six; but there are two in the duck-billed platypus and 21 in the dolphin. Rib elements are fused to the transverse processes of the cervical vertebrae, and in the lumbar vertebrae they form the so-called transverse processes.

There is an increase in the number of vertebrae that compose the sacrum. In the early developmental stages of the human fetus, the beginnings of the hipbones lie opposite those segments of the spinal column that form the lower lumbar and upper sacral vertebrae. As development proceeds, the sacroiliac joints become established between the hipbones and the upper sacral vertebrae. The sacrum, derived from the 25th to the 29th vertebrae, inclusive, becomes a single bone by their fusion. The whales and sea cows lack a sacrum, although vestiges of a pelvis occur. In some anteaters the posterior sacral vertebrae are fused with the ischium (a bone on each side of the pelvic girdle) through ossification of a connecting ligament. The sacrum of some armadillos consists of 13 vertebrae, caudal vertebrae having become fused with it. The cervical vertebrae of some whales are fused together, because the whale is spindle-shaped for swimming and has no need for a mobile neck such as occurs in most mammals. The centrum of the atlas (first cervical vertebra) of most mammals fuses with that of the axis (second cervical vertebra) and projects from it, but in the duck-billed platypus, as in the reptiles, it is a separate bone.

The spinous processes of the thoracic vertebrae, excepting the last, point caudally (*i.e.*, toward the tail), and those of the lumbar vertebrae generally point cranially (*i.e.*, toward the head) at the transitional zone between these groups. Spines of one or two thoracic vertebrae are upright; these are known as anticlinal spines. Lying ventral to the intervertebral disks in some mammals (*e.g.*, whale, pangolin) are paired ossicles, the intercentra, which are homologous (of similar origin) with the ante-

rior arch of the atlas. The tail vertebrae vary in number from none in the bat to 49 in the pangolin.

The ribs in mammals correspond in number of pairs to the number of thoracic vertebrae. The ventral ends of the ribs join the costal cartilages, the relations of which follow, with minor variations, the pattern for the human skeleton. Sternal ribs, connecting the more anterior vertebral ribs with the sternum, may be cartilaginous, calcified, or ossified. The mammalian sternum is composed of several pieces: the presternum anteriorly, followed by the mesosternum, made up of a number of segments, and a terminal xiphisternum.

Appendicular skeleton. *General features.* Paired appendages are not found in ancestral vertebrates and are not present in the living cyclostomes (*e.g.*, lampreys, hagfishes). Appendages first appeared during the early evolution of the fishes. Usually two pairs of appendages are present, fins in fish and limbs in land vertebrates. Each appendage includes not only the skeletal elements within the free portion of the limb but also the basal supporting structure, the limb girdle. This portion of the appendage lies partly or wholly within the trunk and forms a stable base for the fin or limb. Each girdle consists of ventral and dorsal masses. In lower fishes these are composed of cartilage; in bony fishes and in land vertebrates they become partly or completely ossified.

The anterior appendages, the pectoral fins or forelimbs, articulate with the pectoral girdle, which is situated just behind the gill region in fish and in a comparable position at the junction of the neck and thorax in land vertebrates.

The posterior appendages, called pelvic fins, or hindlimbs, articulate with the pelvic girdle, which is situated in the trunk region usually just in front of the anus or cloaca (the ventral, posterior body opening in many lower vertebrates). It is by way of the girdles that the weight of the body of land vertebrates is transmitted to the limbs. Because the hindlimb is usually of greater importance in weight bearing, especially in bipedal vertebrates, it articulates with the vertebral column by means of the costal elements of the sacral vertebrae. The vertebrae to which the pelvic girdle are attached usually fuse to form the sacrum. In fishes, however, a sacrum as such does not develop, since the posterior appendages usually do not support the body weight but are used only in locomotion.

The origin of paired fins has been much debated, and many theories have been put forward in explanation. According to the widely accepted fin-fold theory, the paired limbs are derived from the local persistence of parts of a continuous fold that, in ancestral vertebrates, passed along each side of the trunk and fused behind the anus into a single fin. The primitive paired fins were attached to the body by a broad base and carried no weight. Their main function, it would appear, was to act as horizontal stabilizing keels, which tended to prevent rolling movements and possibly also front-to-back pitching movements.

Most authorities agree that the limbs of land vertebrates evolved from the paired fins of fishes. Limbs and fins are thought to have their ancestral counterparts in the fins of certain lobe-finned fishes (Crossopterygii, a nearly extinct group of which the coelacanth is a living example). The skeleton of the primitive fin consists of a series of endoskeletal rods, each of which undergoes subdivision into a series of three or four pieces. The basal pieces tend to fuse into larger pieces. The most anterior of the basal pieces fuses across the midline with its fellow of the opposite side to form a primitive girdle in the form of a cartilaginous bar. The more distal pieces persist to form the dermal (*i.e.*, on or near the body surface) fin rays.

Pectoral girdle. In a cartilaginous fish such as the dogfish the pectoral girdle consists of a U-shaped endoskeletal, cartilaginous, inverted arch with its ends extending dorsally.

In all other major groups of vertebrates the pectoral girdle is a composite structure. It consists of endoskeletal structures to which secondary dermal components are added as the result of ossification of dermal elements. The components become ossified to form dermal bones.

Origin
of paired
fins

In primitive bony fishes such as the lungfishes, sturgeon, and coelacanths, the main element added is a vertically placed structure, the cleithrum, which supports the scapu-

Adapted from (A) H.V. Neal and H.W. Rand, *Comparative Anatomy*, Copyright 1950; used with permission of McGraw-Hill Book Company; (B) from D.P. Quiring, *Functional Anatomy of the Vertebrates*, Copyright 1936; used by permission of McGraw-Hill Book Company

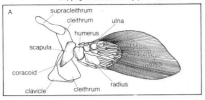

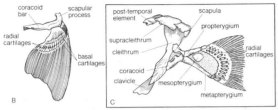

Figure 3: Fins of (A) crossopterygian, (B) cartilaginous, and (C) teleost fish.

la. The cleithrum may be joined by a supracleithrum, which in turn is surmounted by a posttemporal element (*i.e.*, at the rear of the skull). The most ventral of the added dermal bones are the clavicles, which unite below the gill chambers with each other or with the sternum. In the holostean fishes (*e.g.*, gar) the clavicle is lost, leaving only the cleithrum.

In tailed amphibians such as newts and salamanders the dermal elements of the pectoral girdle have been completely lost, and only the endoskeletal parts remain, mainly as cartilaginous bars. This retrogression is probably the result of their adaptation chiefly to an aquatic mode of life in which less support is required by the girdles. The ventral part of the girdle forms the coracoid process and the dorsal part the scapula; the latter is the only part that becomes ossified. Only a rudimentary sternum develops.

In most reptiles the primary girdle for the forelimb consists of a scapula and a single coracoid process. The pectoral girdle of the lizard consists of bones formed in cartilage: the scapula and the large coracoid process, forming the glenoid cavity (*i.e.*, the cup-shaped structure in which the humerus articulates), and the dermal bones —the clavicle and interclavicle. The latter is a single T-shaped bone, with the stem in the midline; it is in contact with the sternum. The curved clavicles articulate with each other at their medial ends (*i.e.*, toward the body midline). The cartilaginous suprascapula is present.

The pectoral girdle in birds In birds the pectoral girdle is essentially similar to that in reptiles. The precoracoid process forms a stout bar that reaches to the sternum. The wishbone, or furcula, which forms from the dermal part of the girdle, consists of two clavicles united in the midline by the interclavicle. Carinate birds (those with a keeled sternum) have a sabre-shaped scapula and a stout coracoid process joined by ligaments at the point at which is found the glenoid cavity for articulation with the humerus. The coracoid process is joined to the sternum; at its dorsal end is the acrocoracoid process. The furcula stands in front of the coracoid processes, its ends connected by ligaments with the acrocoracoid process and with the rudimentary acromion process of the scapula. The girdle of the flightless ratite birds (those with a flat sternum) is little developed, being represented by an ankylosed, or fused, scapula and coracoid process.

Among mammals, the monotremes have two coracoid processes, which articulate medially with the presternum and laterally with the scapula. The coracoids enter into the formation of the glenoid cavity. Also present are an interclavicle (episternum) and an investing clavicle, resembling the bones in reptiles. The clavicle articulates with the acromion process of the scapula. In the opossum the scapula has a spine ending in the acromion, with which

the clavicle articulates. A much-reduced coracoid fuses with the scapula and does not meet the sternum. The scapula of placental mammals has a spine ending, generally, in an acromion; the body of the bone is triangular. In mammals that use the forelimb for support in standing, the vertebral margin is the shortest, and the long axis of the scapula runs from it to the glenoid cavity; but in those whose forelimb is used for prehension, or grasping, such as in the primates, or for flight, such as in the bats, the vertebral margin is elongated, and the distance from it to the glenoid cavity is decreased. The long axis is thus parallel with that of the body instead of being transverse. In the placental mammals the coracoid, although developing independently, has dwindled to a beaklike process and fuses with and becomes part of the scapula. It does not articulate with the sternum.

The clavicle is present generally in those placental mammals that have prehensile (capable of grasping) forelimbs (primates, many rodents and marsupials, and others) or whose forelimbs are adapted for flying (bats). In many mammals it is suppressed or reduced, as in cats, or absent, as in whales, sea cows, and hoofed animals.

Pelvic girdle. The pelvic girdle of the elasmobranch fishes (*e.g.*, sharks, skates, and rays) consists of either a curved cartilaginous structure called the puboischial bar or a pair of bars lying transversely in the ventral part of the body anterior to the cloaca; projecting dorsally on each side is a so-called iliac process. Connected with the process is a basal cartilage carrying a series of radialia, the skeleton of the paired pelvic fins. The pelvic girdles of many bony fishes are situated far forward, near the gills.

There are marked variations in the form of the pelvic girdle in the amphibians. In the frog the three parts of the hipbone (ilium, ischium, and pubis) are present. The pubic elements, however, remain wholly cartilaginous. The hipbone is characterized by the great length and forward extension of the ilium. The girdle is connected with the costal element of one vertebra, thus establishing a sacral region of the vertebral column. The acetabulum (the cup-shaped structure in which the femur articulates) is situated at the junction of the three elements.

The pelvic girdle of some reptiles has a loose connection with the spine. In most reptiles the ilium is joined to two sacral vertebrae. Both the pubic and the ischial parts usually meet in the so-called ventral symphysis, from which a cartilage or bone, the hypoischium, projects backward to support the margin of the cloacal orifice, and another, the epipubis, projects forward. A few snakes (*e.g.*, boas) retain vestiges of a pelvic girdle and limb skeleton.

In most birds the ilium extends forward and backward and is fused with the many vertebrae, forming a synsacrum. The slender ischia and pubes do not form symphyses except in the ostrich.

In most mammals the ilium articulates with the sacrum, and the pubes meet in a symphysis anteriorly. A cotyloid bone, formed in the cartilage in the bottom of the acetabulum, is usually found. The symphysis pubis is not present in certain mammals (*e.g.*, moles). In monotremes and marsupials, the marsupial bones that support the pouch have been regarded as part of the epipubis.

Limbs. The pectoral fin of the elasmobranchs has basal cartilages articulating with the pectoral girdle. They carry a number of radial cartilages consisting of varying numbers of short segments; beyond these are delicate fin rays.

The proximal segment of the pelvic fin of sharks is supported by a single basal cartilage and by one or two radialia. In the pectoral fin of the primitive ray-finned fish *Polypterus*, three elements constitute the proximal segment of the fin: two bony rods, the propterygium and the metapterygium, on the margins and an intermediate, partly ossified cartilage, the mesopterygium.

The adoption of an upright position of the trunk, as seen in certain lemurs and in the great apes, has brought about further modification. In man the lower limbs are used for bipedal locomotion, thus freeing the upper limbs for prehensile use. Many of the great apes have developed the use of the upper limb for an arboreal life; hence, they are Modifications for an upright position sometimes distinguished as brachiators; *i.e.*, animals whose locomotion is by swinging with the arms from branches or other supports.

From (top) *Zoological Journal of the Linnean Society* (1956)

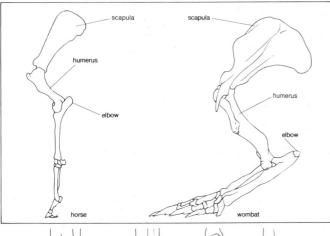

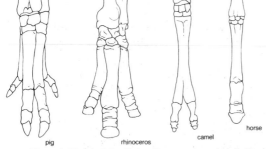

Figure 4: (Top) Left forelimbs of horse and wombat; (bottom) left forefeet of ungulates.

The skeleton of the free limb of the land vertebrate is divisible into three segments: proximal, medial, distal.

The proximal segment consists of a single bone (the humerus in the forelimb, the femur in the hindlimb). The humerus articulates by its rounded head with the glenoid cavity of the scapula and by condyles with the bones of the forearm. Its shaft is usually twisted and has ridges and tuberosities for the attachment of muscles.

The femur is essentially cylindrical; the ends are expanded. At the proximal end, for articulation with the acetabulum, is the rounded head; near it are usually two elevations (trochanters) for muscle attachment. Three trochanters are characteristic of certain mammals; *e.g.*, horse and rhinoceros. Distally, the femur expands into two condyles for articulation with the tibia. In many types there is an articular facet on the lateral surface for the head of the fibula.

The medial segment of the limb typically contains two bones, the radius and the ulna in the forelimb, the tibia and the fibula in the hindlimb. In the forelimb the radius is anterior, or preaxial (*i.e.*, its position is forward to that of the ulna), in the adjustment of the limb for support and locomotion on land. Mammals in which the radius is fixed in pronation—*i.e.*, in which the forelimb is rotated so that the shaft of the radius crosses in front of that of the ulna—are called pronograde. The radius transmits the weight of the forepart of the body to the forefeet; but it is the ulna that makes the elbow joint with the humerus; into its proximal end are inserted the flexor and extensor muscles of the forelimb.

The tibia and fibula are separate in salamanders and newts, united in frogs and toads. In land reptiles the tibia articulates with both condyles of the femur and with the so-called tritibiale of the ankle. The fibula articulates with the postaxial femoral condyle and with the tritibiale and fibulare. The tibia of birds is long, the fibula reduced. In mammals the fibula is generally reduced and may be fused with the tibia and excluded from the knee joint.

The distal segment of the limb comprises the carpus, metacarpus, and phalanges in the forelimb and the tarsus,

metatarsus, and phalanges in the hindlimb. A typical limb has five digits (fingers or toes), which contain the phalanges.

The carpus and tarsus of the higher vertebrates have probably been derived from a primitive structure by the fusion or suppression of certain of its elements. The bones of a generalized carpus (or tarsus) end in three transverse rows: a proximal row of three bones, the radiale (or tibiale), intermedium, and ulnare (or fibulare); a distal row of five carpalia (or tarsalia), numbered one to five from the radial (or tibial) margin; and an intermediate row of one or two centralia.

In many urodele amphibians (*e.g.*, salamanders) the carpus is generalized. In the frogs and toads, however, it is more specialized, only six carpals being present, the third, fourth, and fifth carpalia probably having fused with either or both centralia. In birds the radiale and ulnare are distinct, but the distal bones are fused with the metacarpus to form a carpometacarpus. In mammals various examples of fusion and suppression occur. In man the radiale forms the scaphoid bone; the intermedium forms the lunate bone; the ulnare forms the triquetral. The pisiform bone in man is probably the remains of an extra digit. It may, however, be a sesamoid bone; *i.e.*, an ossification within a tendon. The trapezium and trapezoid are carpalia 1 and 2; the capitate is derived from carpal 3; carpalia 4 and 5 have fused to form the hamate. An os centrale is present in the carpus of many monkeys. In mammals the number of digits varies, but the number of phalanges in each digit present usually corresponds with that of man. In some species, however, the phalanges are more numerous, as when the limb is modified to form a paddle (*e.g.*, in whales).

The tarsus of urodele amphibians has the typical arrangement of bones. In the frogs and toads the intermedium is absent; two long bones are the tibiale and fibulare. Among the reptiles there is much variation in the composition of the tarsus. Generally, the joint of the ankle is intratarsal, the row of tarsalia being distal to the hinge. In most living reptiles the tibiale and intermedium fuse to form the talus. In birds the ankle hinge is of the reptilian pattern in being intratarsal. The three tarsal cartilages of the embryo fuse to form the talus, which fuses with the tibia to form the tibiotarsus. The tarsalia fuse with the ends of the united metatarsals to make a tarsometatarsus. In the mammalian tarsus the talus is generally composed of the fused tibiale and intermedium, but in some a centrale is included to form a tritibiale. The ankle joint is not intratarsal but is located between the bones of the leg and the first row of tarsal bones, usually the tibia and the talus.

Suppression of digits in hoofed mammals frequently has occurred in the following sequence: the pollex (first digit) is the first to be suppressed, then the minimus (fifth digit), the index (second digit), and finally the annularis (fourth digit). Among the even-toed ungulates (*i.e.*, the artiodactyls; *e.g.*, pig and hippopotamus) the pollex has disappeared, and the other four digits are present, although the second and fifth digits are much reduced. In the camel only the third and fourth digits persist and are of equal importance. Among the odd-toed ungulates (*i.e.*, the perissodactyls; *e.g.*, horse) the right digit is dominant; the others are reduced to rudiments or splints.

Fusion and suppression of carpal bones

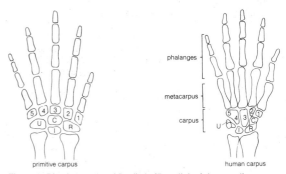

Figure 5: Distal segment of forelimb. (R, radiale; I, intermedium; U, ulnare; C, centrale; 1–5, carpalia)

Joints. The junctions between the bony or cartilaginous units of vertebrate skeletons and between the body-wall ossicles of sea urchins (Echinodermata) are often kept rigid by dovetailed margins. One skeletal unit, however, may move freely on another, as shown by the ambulacral ossicles along the arms of brittlestars, crinoids, and starfishes among the echinoderms and by the leg bones and vertebrae of vertebrates in which joints that permit various types of movement exist.

Joints between the bony or cartilaginous units of vertebrate skeletons are very simple in animals with a cartilaginous skeleton. When bone replaces cartilage, however, stronger and more elaborate joints form. Flat, articulating, cartilaginous surfaces between the vertebral centra of sharks do not permit extensive movement, but it is sufficient for these animals. In sharks, intervertebral cones of notochord persist, with conical ends projecting into the ends of adjacent vertebrae. Joints between bones and cuticular sclerites may permit movement in one plane only, as in most arthropodan joints and the interphalangeal joint in man. Between some bones (*e.g.*, the human femur and pelvis) there is a ball-and-socket device, by which a ball-like articular facet rotates in a concavity, the acetabulum. The femur can thus move in a variety of planes. The bony vertebrae of fishes, amphibians, reptiles, and birds possess centra articulating with one another in a ball-and-socket manner. The terrestrial animals strengthen the ball-and-socket articulation and sometimes restrict its movement by additional imbricating facets (zygapophyses). Snake vertebrae interlock firmly with one another; a hemispherical posterior projection from each articulates with an anterior concavity (*i.e.*, a cup-shaped depression) on the vertebra in front of it. The freely moving joints permit a twisting movement, with extra support being gained by two sets of sliding facets between each pair of consecutive vertebrae. Ball-and-socket joints, common in vertebrates, are easily contrived in animals with an endoskeleton. Among invertebrates are some remarkable parallels. In certain millipedes (Juliformia) heavy circular sclerites encompass each segment and slightly overlap. Rotation of one skeletal ring upon the next, as well as flexion, is possible. The animal can thus curve its hard body in any direction. It can curl up dorso-ventrally with the legs in the middle of a spiral, then walk with the legs on the ground and at right angles to the coiled position. Echinoderms also possess many ball-and-socket joints, such as at the base of spines in sea urchins.

Various types of strong hinge joints, easily contrived by an arthropod, also occur in vertebrates. The joint between the skull and the first vertebra in mammals is a strong hinge. A pair of occipital condyles on the skull that articulate against shallow concavities on the anterior face of the vertebra permit a nodding movement of the head. The strongest hinge joints in arthropods also bear a double articulation, as in the leg of the spider and in *Scutigera*, the fastest running centipede. Hinge joints in vertebrates are often composite, being formed or supported by the incorporation of several small bones, as in the human wrist. To facilitate cursorial, or running, habits, flexion is limited to one plane.

A series of small bones at the wrist or ankle can, in contrast, provide, in addition to strength, a marked flexibility in many directions. A leg that can flex in various directions is usually achieved in arthropods by a series of pivot joints. Each joint is set in a different plane along the leg, so that the combined action of the several joints enables the leg to move in any direction. Single endoskeletal joints of vertebrates supply a variety of movements with greater ease; no duplication is necessary.

In vertebrates, the joints between bones are constructed in a variety of ways. They fall, however, into two main categories, the synovial joint and the nonsynovial joint. In the former, known also as diarthrosis, a cleft occurs between the free surfaces of two skeletal parts; during movements these surfaces slide on each other. In the nonsynovial type, known also as synarthrosis, the skeletal parts are connected by nonosseous material that permits bending or twisting. The range of movement is greater in

the synovial than in the nonsynovial type. In the course of vertebrate evolution the nonsynovial type appears to have preceded the synovial. The latter is unusual in fishes, but the majority of the joints in man and other mammals are of this form. The amphiarthrosis is an intermediate type of joint in man. In this type the connecting material between the bones contains a cavity, but movement depends on bending of the connecting material.

Some of the strongest movements in arthropods (*e.g.*, in the legs of Polydesmida, an order of millipedes) are also implemented by a joint possessing cavities that contain synovial fluid in which imbricating cuticular facets slide against one another. Levers exist in vertebrates in the heel bone and in the human elbow projection (olecranon process).

Movements at joints are commonly produced by voluntary muscular action. Such movements are distinguished as "active," as against those produced by the application of external force, whether by manipulation or by the energy of moving parts or gravity, which are known as "passive" movements.

Muscles may be situated to act only on one joint (uniarticular muscles), but many muscles can act on two or more joints (bi- and multi-articular muscles). A multiarticular muscle will act on only one joint if the remaining joints under its control are fixed by other muscles. Muscles, however, rarely contract as isolated units. They usually act as a group; this is known as the "group action of muscles." The intricate adjustment and coordination of muscular tensions that are required for posture and movement are under the control of the central nervous system.

PROPERTIES OF BONE AND ITS DEVELOPMENT

Vital properties. The essential bone-forming cell is the osteoblast. It can give rise to bone even if transplanted to tissue in which bone formation does not usually occur. If a portion of the whole thickness of the periosteum (the fibrous tissue that surrounds bone) is transplanted, it forms bony tissue. It can thus be employed for reconstruction of bone following disease or injury.

Although the general form of the skeleton is hereditary, it is also influenced by mechanical factors, such as pressure on the cartilage at the end of a bone (epiphysis) or stresses applied to the external surface; *e.g.*, from adjacent muscles. The effect of pressure on bone depends on whether the bony surface is covered by periosteum or by cartilage. In the case of the periosteum, which has blood vessels, pressure causes impairment of blood supply and absorption of underlying bone. The direct pressure exerted by an abnormal expansion of the aorta on the sides of the vertebrae thus brings about absorption of bone but not of the cartilaginous intervertebral disks. The impressions corresponding to the gyri, or ridges of the brain's cerebral cortex that are found on the internal surface of the skull, are probably produced by the slight but constant pressure of the growing brain in the young person. On the other hand, pressure on cartilage, which has no blood supply, does not cause absorption.

Internal strains stimulate bone formation. If a tibia is removed, thus leaving the fibula to bear more weight, the fibula's thickness tends to approach that of the tibia. If strains are reduced—*e.g.*, by muscular paralysis—the trabeculae, or layers of bone, become thinner, though there may be no change in external form; meanwhile, the lacunae, or spaces within the bone, and the haversian canals (structures that contain nerves and blood vessels) of compact bone become larger. If a bone becomes bent through pathological softening (*e.g.*, from rickets), a thick strut of bone forms along the concavity of the bend.

When the direction of stress is altered, bony reconstruction takes place. The internal structure is thus changed in the bones of the feet when their customary relative positions are disturbed. If the tibia and femur are united by surgical removal of the knee-joint surfaces, with resultant bony union (*i.e.*, ankylosis) at the knee, the internal bone structure is altered in such a way as to correspond closely with what are believed to be the lines of stress under the new conditions. The fact that the bony fragments in a

Ball-and-socket joint

Synovial and non-synovial joints

Absorption of bone due to pressure

badly set fracture become smoothed with an internal reconstruction at the site of union is further evidence of the structural adaptation of bone to changed conditions.

When a bone is fractured, some bone tissue adjacent to the fracture is absorbed, and a mass of tissue termed callus, at first uncalcified, makes its appearance between and around the broken ends. Cartilage formation commonly takes place in the callus even when the fracture is in a membrane bone; e.g., the parietal bone of the skull. Callus also contains osteoblasts derived from both periosteum and endosteum, the connective tissue within a bone. The formation of callus is greater if there is pressure and movement between the broken ends of the bone and is most pronounced on the concave side when the bony fragments are at an angle. Bony union is effected by calcification and subsequent ossification of the callus. Regeneration of bone is more active in the shafts of long bones, lower jaw, and ribs than in the skull and the spongy ends of long bones.

Bone elasticity

Physical properties. Bones are not absolutely rigid but possess some degree of elasticity. By virtue of this quality, stresses can produce a transient deformation that is followed by recovery of the original form. The bones of a young person are more elastic than are those of an elderly person.

A fracture is produced when stresses exceed the normal limits of elasticity. Adult bone gives way suddenly when the breaking point is reached. The degree of force necessary to produce a fracture depends partly on the thickness of the bone and partly on the direction of the force in relation to structure. It has also been shown that the speed at which the force is applied affects the breaking point.

The primary stresses may be classified as compression, tension, and shear. Combinations of these may secondarily give rise to bending and twisting. A shear stress is encountered in a long bone when a force is exerted obliquely to the long axis. When directed at an angle of 45°, the shear stress equals the compression stress. Twisting stresses represent a special variety of shear, and their results are well exemplified in the spiral form of many so-called torsion fractures. Bending stresses produce compression on one side of the shaft and tension on the other side; in the bone's interior, however, there is a zone in which no stress occurs; this zone is occupied by marrow. The cortical (non-marrow) layer is especially thick in the middle of the shaft, the point at which the greatest bending stresses usually occur.

In compact bone the breaking stresses are comparable with those of materials widely employed in engineering. In the case of tension stresses, compact bone is comparable to cast iron; for compression stresses it is comparable to wrought iron, with minor variations depending on the direction of the stress relative to the "grain" of the haversian canals. Breaking stresses have a lower value in the bone of old persons and in paralyzed limbs, because of the relative diminution of calcium salts and the thinning of trabeculae (layers of bone).

The skull bones respond to stress in a manner quite unlike that of the long bones. The force of impact of a penetrating object on the outer layer of compact bone in the skull is transmitted through the diploe, the middle, spongy layer of bone, to a larger area of the inner wall, also of compact bone; damage to the inner wall is correspondingly more extensive.

Greenstick fracture

The bones of young persons, although richer in fibrous tissue than are those of adults, are poorer in calcium salts and therefore less resistant to tension than to compression. For this reason, bending of the long bones frequently produces a greenstick fracture, in which the bone breaks only partially, on the side opposite that toward which the bending occurs.

The smaller bones and the ends of long bones have a thinner cortical layer than the shafts of long bones, and their internal trabeculated structure enables them to withstand a great variety of stresses applied in many directions. In the neck of the femur, for example, a series of bony sheets running in one direction is intersected by another series situated approximately at right angles to it.

The arrangement of the trabeculae corresponds approximately to the lines of pressure and possibly also to the lines of tension. Stress apparently plays some direct part in determining both the direction of bone formation in the young and the reorganization of pre-existing bone in the adult.

Development of bone. *General features.* In most parts of the body, bone formation takes place in relation to an existing cartilaginous model, which it eventually replaces (endochondral ossification). In certain situations, on the other hand, bone formation takes place in dense connective tissue (intramembranous ossification). The former type is seen in the early stages of the development of most bones of the body; the latter occurs mainly in the calvaria (*i.e.,* the outer surface) of the skull and around the shafts of long bones. In both cases the process of ossification generally commences in a localized region called a centre of ossification and then spreads. Some of these centres appear long before birth; others (epiphyseal centres) appear only after birth (or sometimes immediately before).

Intramembranous ossification. Intramembranous ossification is the simpler of the two types of osteogenesis, or bone development, and probably the more primitive. As in the formation of cartilage, the first indication of membrane bone formation is a condensation produced by multiplication of mesenchymal cells to form a membranous mass. The cells, which lie parallel to each other, are compressed to form either smooth membranous sheets that may be very extensive, as in the blastemal vault of the cranium, or irregular membranous condensations, as in the regions in which irregular-shaped bones will be laid down. In further development, intercellular fibres of collagen, a rather inelastic protein, are deposited by the mesenchymal cells of the condensations.

In the region in which an ossification centre develops, the osteoblasts become arranged in closely packed layers along small bundles of the collagenous fibres. Their cytoplasm increases considerably, and their nuclei become eccentrically located. The fibrous material between the osteoblasts swells until it occupies all of the intercellular space. Prior to the deposition of calcium, this material, called osteoid, represents the organic matrix of the bone. **Osteoid** Soon after the appearance of the osteoblasts and presumably by virtue of the physiological action of these cells, calcium salts in the form of crystalline spicules are deposited in the intercellular spaces and within the immediately adjacent osteoid. These spicules constitute primary bone. A noticeable increase in the number of very small blood vessels (capillaries) occurs at these ossification centres. This increased vascularity is probably correlated with special metabolic activity. Later, the blood vessels become those of the blood-forming bone marrow, which is invariably associated with the later stages of bone formation.

As development proceeds, transformation of more mesenchyme cells into osteoblasts occurs; the latter form further spicules, extending in all directions through the membrane. In flat bones this extension is largely two-dimensional in direction; the spicules and trabeculae of the young bone thus form a radiate pattern from the centre. The structure of such an ossification area now consists of a mass of vascular primary bone with a condensed sheet of vascular mesenchyme (periosteum) on its surfaces. Most of the differentiated osteoblasts are located on the inner surface of the periosteum, where the skeletal element can be thought of as growing by accretion. This inner cellular layer of the periosteum is called the cambium layer, in contrast to the outer, much thicker section, known as the fibrous layer. A rich network of fine blood vessels and capillaries occupies the zone of transition between the cambium and fibrous layers.

For a while, such a membrane bone is more or less spongy throughout, but in the early fetal stages a process of absorption and redeposition of bony substance commences. This process continues until full growth has been attained. Soon after it begins, spongy, or cancellous, bone occupies the central portion of the mass, and a layer of compact bone forms on each surface by the continued addition of new sheets of bone from the cambium layer of the periosteum. Compact bone is therefore often called periosteal bone. Vascular tissue is very sparse in the compact bone but fills all the spaces in the cancellous bone. Here it soon becomes hematopoietic (*i.e.*, capable of producing blood cells) and is called red bone marrow.

As each successive layer of compact bone is laid down, some osteoblasts become trapped in the newly deposited matrix. Each cell so isolated becomes a bone cell, or osteocyte, and occupies a small space, a bone lacuna, in the interstitial bony substance. New osteoblasts develop from the outer periosteal layer which, in its turn, is reinforced by new cells from the undifferentiated surrounding mesenchyme. The osteoblasts that remain on the surface of the bone persist as the deepest cells of the periosteum and assume a fibroblast-like appearance unless stimulated to form new bone. If this occurs, they assume the characteristics of osteoblasts.

Cellular
changes
prior to
ossifica-
tion

Endochondral ossification. The first indication that ossification is about to occur is an enlargement of the chondrocytes (cartilage cells) in the centre of the bone shaft. Glycogen (animal starch) accumulates within them, and their cytoplasm becomes highly vacuolated; *i.e.*, filled

Adapted from L.B. Arey, *Developmental Anatomy* (1965); W.B. Saunders Company

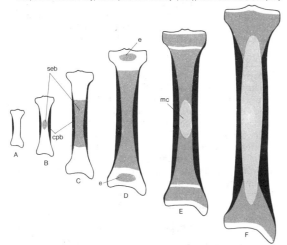

Figure 6: *Ossification and growth in long bone of a mammal.*
(A) Cartilaginous stage; (B) and (C) deposit of spongy endochondral bone (seb) and compact perichondral bone (cpb); (D) appearance of epiphysis (e) at either end; (E) appearance of marrow cavity (mc); (F) union of epiphysis with shaft and enlargement of marrow cavity.

with globule-like spaces. The matrix between these cells becomes impregnated with calcium salts, and the cartilage cells degenerate. As these changes in the cartilage occur, the perichondrium of the middle of the shaft acquires osteogenic (*i.e.*, bone-producing) properties and is then called the periosteum. The cells of its internal layer become transformed into osteoblasts, which rapidly lay down a delicate cylinder of compact periosteal bone around the centre of the shaft. This cylindrical ossification is intramembranous because it is formed by the periosteum and does not actually replace any preformed cartilage. Accompanying these changes, a vascular bud derived from the inner layer of the periosteum penetrates to the calcified cartilaginous matrix in the centre of the shaft (the future diaphysis, or bone shaft proper) at the so-called irruption canal. This vascular bud consists of a network of actively growing capillaries together with mesenchymal cells, some of which become osteoblasts, others chondroclasts, which break down and remove the calcified cartilage matrix, causing several cartilage lacunae to coalesce. The larger spaces, called primary areolae, are occupied immediately by osteogenic tissue. The osteoblasts range themselves along the remaining strands of calcified cartilage. As a result of their activity, layers of bone are deposited on the cartilaginous strands, just as they are upon the fibrous strands in the case of membrane bone formation. These bony layers unite with one another and with the superficial layer of compact bone, forming primitive cancellous bone, the

spaces of which are called secondary areolae. In addition to the chondroclasts and osteoblasts, multinucleate giant cells (osteoclasts) also appear in the vascular bud. The osteoclasts seem to be active in absorbing bone in situations in which redeposition and rearrangement of bone is to occur.

The changes considered thus far result in the establishment of the primary, or diaphyseal, centre of ossification. At each end of the centre the cartilage cells and lacunae are arranged in parallel rows, with the largest cells and lacunae in continuity with the region of ossification. The enlarged cartilage cells show degenerative changes, and the matrix around them becomes calcified. If cartilage from this zone of provisional calcification is examined, and inspection is made progressively toward a free end of the combined bony–cartilaginous model, the cells of the columns are found to decrease in size and the columnar arrangement to disappear. The cells, however, are still crowded. Such a growth region is found usually near each extremity of the cartilaginous portion of the developing bone. By the activity of the growth region the cartilage at each end of the model increases in length. The region of cartilage proliferation is carried progressively away from the original site of ossification, since most of the new cartilage cells proliferate toward the diaphyseal ossification centre. As they approach the region of ossification, the cartilage cells thus produced become arranged in columns. They also show progressive degenerative changes, and calcification of the matrix occurs preparatory to the extension of the ossification into it. This extension results from the activity of the osteoblasts and associated blood vessels, which together form an advancing zone of bone formation in the degenerating calcified cartilage. The latter is continuously replaced by the activity of the cartilage growth centre.

The process of cartilage growth and the extension of ossification into it proceeds until, at birth, the result is a bony shaft with cartilaginous extremities. The latter are, for the most part, ossified after birth by the appearance within them of secondary (epiphyseal) centres of ossification. These are established in a manner similar to that of the endochondral primary (diaphyseal) centre. When this occurs, a gradient is formed in two directions from the cartilaginous growth centre—short columns of cartilage cells extending toward the epiphyseal centre and longer ones toward the diaphysis. This arrangement ensures growth in length on the diaphyseal side of the growth centre and increase in size of the cartilaginous epiphysis. Some growth also takes place from the epiphyseal centre toward the articular surface, but this appears to be merely enough to ensure the proper modelling of the extremities of the bone. Increase in thickness of the cartilage model distal to the region of periosteal ossification takes place by continued transformation of the inner perichondrium into cartilage.

The diaphysis increases in girth by the deposition (by accretion) of periosteal bone. This is accompanied by resorption of the original endochondral bone of the shaft and the establishment of the marrow cavity. The epiphysis appears to grow in width chiefly by the lateral (peripheral) extension of the epiphyseal endochondral ossification centre. In later postnatal stages of bone growth the mass of cartilage between diaphysis and epiphysis decreases in thickness to form a comparatively thin structure, the epiphyseal cartilage, or epiphyseal plate, which is of great importance for the growth of the bone. At the termination of growth in any bone the epiphyseal plate disappears, and the epiphysis unites with the diaphysis. As a result, no further longitudinal growth of the bone is possible. The number and situation of epiphyseal centres vary in different bones. In a long bone such as described, there is at least one epiphyseal centre at each end; in some there may be two or more. In some smaller bones (phalanges, metacarpals, metatarsals), an epiphyseal centre is found only at one extremity, the other end being ossified by the extension of the diaphysis to the articular cartilage. In small bones, such as carpals and tarsals, ossification proceeds from a single endochondral centre until the definitive adult size is reached. In irregular bones, such as the scapula, pelvic girdle, and the vertebrae, one or more primary centres occur, and usually several secondary centres take part in the ossification of the borders and processes. (W.J.H.)

BIBLIOGRAPHY. T.H. BRYCE, *Osteology and Arthrology*, vol. 4 of *Quain's Elements of Anatomy*, 11th ed. (1915), a comprehensive account of bones and joints; R.B. CLARK, *Dynamics in Metazoan Evolution* (1964), deals with some aspects of the coelomate condition, hydrostatic skeletons, metamerism, and their evolution; D.J. CUNNINGHAM, *Textbook of Anatomy*, 9th ed. by J.C. BRASH (1951), a detailed description of the anatomy of the human skeleton; D.V. DAVIES (ed.), *Gray's Anatomy*, 34th ed. (1967), a detailed description of the anatomy of the human skeleton; J. GRAY, *Animal Locomotion* (1968), a comprehensive, comparative account of the coordination and mechanisms of vertebrate locomotion, with some chapters on invertebrates (the approach is for the non-specialist, but the treatment is mathematical and neurological); W.J. HAMILTON (ed.), *Textbook of Human Anatomy* (1956), a concise and readable account of the anatomy of the skeleton of man; S.J. HICKSON, *Introduction to the Study of Recent Corals* (1924), a well-illustrated book for the non-specialist; L.H. HYMAN, *Comparative Vertebrate Anatomy*, 2nd ed. (1942); S.M. MANTON, "The Evolution of Arthropodan Locomotory Mechanisms," pt. 1–11 *J. Linn Soc. (Zool.)* (1950–72), a series dealing with habits and locomotory mechanisms, showing how they are correlated with structure and with the evolution of the various arthropodan groups; D.P. QUIRING, *Functional Anatomy of the Vertebrates* (1950); A.S. ROMER, *The Vertebrate Body*, 4th ed. (1970), an excellent account of the evolution of the skeleton in vertebrates; J.Z. YOUNG, *The Life of Vertebrates*, 2nd ed. (1962), and *An Introduction to the Study of Man* (1971).

(W.J.H./S.M.M.)

Skepticism

As a philosophical attitude, skepticism is the doubting of knowledge claims set forth in various areas. Skeptics have challenged the adequacy or reliability of these claims by asking what they are based upon or what they actually establish. They have raised the question whether such claims about the world are either indubitable or necessarily true, and they have challenged the alleged grounds of accepted assumptions. Practically everyone is skeptical about some knowledge claims; but the Skeptics have raised doubts about any knowledge beyond the contents of directly felt experience. The original Greek meaning of *skeptikos* was "an inquirer," someone who was unsatisfied and still looking for truth.

Skepticism in history

From ancient times onward Skeptics have developed arguments to undermine the contentions of dogmatic philosophers, scientists, and theologians. The Skeptical arguments and their employment against various forms of dogmatism have played an important role in shaping both the problems and the solutions offered in the course of Western philosophy. As ancient philosophy and science developed, doubts arose about basic accepted views of the world. In ancient times Skeptics challenged the claims of Platonism, Aristotelianism, and Stoicism, and in the Renaissance those of Scholasticism and Calvinism. After Descartes, Skeptics attacked Cartesianism (*q.v.*) and other theories justifying the "new science." Later, a Skeptical offensive was levelled against Kantianism and then against Hegelianism. Each Skeptical challenge led to new attempts to resolve the difficulties. Skepticism, especially since the Enlightenment, has come to mean disbelief—primarily religious disbelief—and the Skeptic has often been likened to the village atheist.

VARIOUS SENSES AND APPLICATIONS

Skepticism developed with regard to various disciplines in which men claimed to have knowledge. It was questioned, for example, whether one could gain any certain knowledge in metaphysics (the study of the nature and significance of being as such) or in the sciences. In ancient times a chief form was medical Skepticism, which questioned whether one could know with certainty either the causes or cures of diseases. In the area of ethics doubts were raised about accepting various mores and customs and about claiming any objective basis for making value distinctions. Skepticisms about religion have questioned

the doctrines of different traditions. Certain philosophies, like those of Hume and Kant, have seemed to show that no knowledge can be gained beyond the world of experience and that one cannot discover the causes of phenomena. Any attempt to do so, as Kant argued, leads to antinomies, contradictory knowledge claims. A dominant form of Skepticism, the subject of this article, concerns knowledge in general, questioning whether anything actually can be known with complete or adequate certainty. This type is called epistemological Skepticism.

Kinds of epistemological Skepticism can be distinguished in terms of the areas in which doubts are raised; that is, whether they be directed toward reason, toward the senses, or toward knowledge of things-in-themselves. They can also be distinguished in terms of the motivation of the Skeptic—whether he is challenging views for ideological reasons or for pragmatic or practical ones to attain certain psychological goals. Among the chief ideological motives have been religious or antireligious concerns. Some Skeptics have challenged knowledge claims so that religious ones could be substituted—on faith. Others have challenged religious knowledge claims in order to overthrow some orthodoxy. Kinds of Skepticism also can be distinguished in terms of how restricted or how thoroughgoing they are—whether they apply only to certain areas and to certain kinds of knowledge claims or whether they are more general and universal.

Epistemological Skepticism

ANCIENT SKEPTICISM

Historically, skeptical philosophical attitudes began to appear in pre-Socratic thought. In the 5th century BC, the Eleatic philosophers, known for reducing reality to a static One (see ELEATICISM), questioned the reality of the sensory world, of change and plurality, and denied that reality could be described in the categories of ordinary experience. On the other hand, the Ephesian philosopher of change Heracleitus and his pupil Cratylus thought that the world was in such a state of flux that no permanent, unchangeable truth about it could be found; and Xenophanes, a wandering poet and philosopher, doubted whether man could distinguish true from false knowledge.

A more developed Skepticism appeared in some of Socrates' views and in a couple of the Sophists (*q.v.*). Socrates, in the early Platonic dialogues, was always questioning the knowledge claims of others; and in the *Apology*, he said that all that he really knew was that he knew nothing. Socrates' enemy, the Sophist Protagoras, contended that man is the measure of all things. This thesis was taken as a kind of skeptical relativism: no views are ultimately true, but each is merely one man's opinion. Another Sophist, Gorgias, advanced the skeptical-nihilist thesis that nothing exists; and if something did exist, it could not be known; and if it could be known, it could not be communicated.

The putative father of Greek Skepticism is Pyrrho of Elis (*c.* 360–*c.* 270 BC), who tried to be a living Skeptic. He avoided committing himself to any views about what was actually going on and acted only according to appearances. In this way he sought happiness or at least mental peace.

The first school of Skeptical philosophy developed in Plato's Academy (see PLATONISM AND NEOPLATONISM) in the 3rd century BC and was thus called "Academic" Skepticism. Starting from the skeptical side of Socrates, its leaders, Arcesilaus (*c.* 315–*c.* 240 BC) and Carneades (214/213–129/128 BC), set forth a series of epistemological arguments to show that nothing could be known, challenging primarily the two foremost schools, those of the Stoics and Epicureans. They denied that any criteria could be found for distinguishing the true from the false; instead, only reasonable or probable standards could be established for knowledge. This limited or probabilistic Skepticism was the view of the Academy until the 1st century BC, when Cicero was a student there. His *Academica* and *De natura deorum* are the main sources for knowledge of this movement. (St. Augustine's *Contra academicos* is an answer to Cicero's views.)

The other major form of ancient Skepticism was Pyr-

Academic and Pyrrhonian schools

rhonism, apparently developed by medical Skeptics in Alexandria. Beginning with Aenesidemus (1st century BC), this movement, named after Pyrrho, criticized the Academic Skeptics because they claimed to know too much, namely, that nothing could be known and that some things are more probable than others. The Pyrrhonians advanced a series of tropes, or ways of opposing various kinds of knowledge claims, in order to bring about *epochē* (suspense of judgment). The Pyrrhonian attitude is preserved in the writings of one of its last leaders, Sextus Empiricus (2nd or 3rd century AD). In his *Outlines of Pyrrhonism* and *Adversus mathematicos,* Sextus presented the tropes developed by previous Pyrrhonists. The ten attributed to Aenesidemus showed the difficulties to be encountered in ascertaining the truth or reliability of judgments based on sense information, owing to the variability and differences of human and animal perceptions. Other arguments raised difficulties in determining whether there are any reliable criteria or standards—logical, rational, or otherwise—for judging whether anything is true or false. To settle any disagreement, a criterion seems to be required. Any purported criterion, however, would appear to be based on another criterion, thus requiring an infinite regress of criteria, or else it would be based upon itself, which would be circular. Sextus offered arguments to challenge any claims of dogmatic philosophers to know more than what is evident; and in so doing he presented in one form or another practically all of the skeptical arguments that have ever appeared in subsequent philosophy.

Sextus said that his arguments were aimed at leading people to a state of *ataraxia* (unperturbability). People who thought that they could know reality were constantly disturbed and frustrated. If they could be led to suspend judgment, however, they would find peace of mind. In this state of suspension they would neither affirm nor deny the possibility of knowledge but would remain peaceful, still waiting to see what might develop. The Pyrrhonist did not become inactive in this state of suspense but lived undogmatically according to appearances, customs, and natural inclinations.

MEDIEVAL SKEPTICISM

Pyrrhonism ended as a philosophical movement in the late Roman Empire, as religious concerns became paramount. In the Christian Middle Ages the main surviving form of Skepticism was the Academic, described in St. Augustine's *Contra academicos.* Augustine, before his conversion, had found Cicero's views attractive and had overcome them only through revelation. With faith, he could seek understanding. Augustine's account of Skepticism and his answer to it provided the basis for medieval discussions.

In Islāmic Spain, where there was more contact with ancient learning, a form of antirational Skepticism developed among Muslim and Jewish theologians. Al-Ghazāli, an Arab theologian of the 11th and early 12th centuries, and his Jewish contemporary Judah ha-Levi (*c.* 1075/*c.* 1085–*c.* 1141), who was a poet and physician as well as a philosopher, offered skeptical challenges (much like those later employed by the occasionalist Nicolas Malebranche and by David Hume) against the contemporary Aristotelians in order to lead people to accept religious truths in mystical faith. This kind of fideism also appears in the late Middle Ages in the German cardinal and philosopher Nicolaus of Cusa's advocacy of learned ignorance as the way to religious knowledge.

MODERN SKEPTICISM

Modern Skepticism emerged in the 16th century, not from medieval views but from the intellectual crises of the Renaissance and Reformation and from the rediscovery of the Skeptical classics. The voyages of exploration; the humanistic rediscovery of the learning of ancient Greece, Rome, and Palestine; and the new science—all combined to undermine confidence in man's accepted picture of the world. The religious controversy between the Protestants and Catholics raised fundamental epistemological issues about the bases and criteria of religious

knowledge. At the same time the texts of Cicero and Sextus became available again. (Sextus' *Outlines of Pyrrhonism* [*Hypotyposeis*] was published in Latin in 1562, his *Adversus matematicos* in 1569, and the Greek texts of both in 1621.)

In the Reformation. The fundamental skeptical issues raised by the Reformation appeared in the debate between the outstanding humanist scholar Erasmus and Luther. Erasmus, using Academic skeptical materials, insisted that the issues in dispute could not be resolved, that one should therefore suspend judgment and remain with the church. Luther insisted, on the other hand, that true and certain religious knowledge could and must be gained through conscience. Erasmus' view developed into a Christian Skepticism, accepting traditional Christianity on faith after seeing that no adequate evidence existed. Luther's view, and later that of Calvin, proposed a new criterion—that of inner experience—while the Catholics of the Counter-Reformation employed Pyrrhonian and Academic arguments to undermine the criterion.

Following after Erasmus, another humanist, Giovanni Pico della Mirandola II (nephew of the famous count of the same name) and H.C. Agrippa von Nettesheim, a stormy occult philosopher and physician, employed the skeptical arguments against Scholasticism, Renaissance Naturalism, and many other views to win people to the "true religion." The Catholic scholar Gentian Hervet, in the preface to his 1569 edition of Sextus, saw the Skeptical arguments as the definitive answer to Calvinism and the way to true Christianity.

In the 17th century. The new concern with Skepticism was given a general philosophical formulation by Michel de Montaigne and his cousin Francisco Sanches. Montaigne in *Apology for Raimond Sebond* and Sanches in *Quod nihil scitur,* both written in 1576, explored the human epistemological situation and showed that man's knowledge claims in all areas were extremely dubious. Montaigne recommended living according to nature and custom and accepting whatever God reveals, and Sanches advocated recognizing that nothing can be known and then trying to gain what limited information one can through empirical scientific means.

Montaigne's Skepticism was extremely influential in the early 17th century. His followers, Pierre Charron, J.-P. Camus, La Mothe Le Vayer, and others, further popularized his views. Various French Counter-Reformers used the arguments of Montaigne and Sextus to undermine Calvinism. Montaigne's Skepticism opposed all sorts of disciplines, including the new science, and was coupled with a fideism that many suspected to be insincere.

In the 1620s efforts to refute or mitigate this new Skepticism appeared. A Christian Epicurean, Pierre Gassendi, himself originally a Skeptic, and Marin Mersenne, one of the most influential figures in the intellectual revolution of the times, while retaining epistemological doubts about knowledge of reality yet recognized that science provided useful and important information about the world. The constructive Skepticisms of Gassendi and Mersenne, and later of members of the Royal Society of England like Bishop John Wilkins and Joseph Glanvill, developed the attitude of Sanches into a hypothetical, empirical interpretation of the new science.

René Descartes offered a fundamental refutation of the new Skepticism, contending that, by applying the skeptical method of doubting all beliefs that could possibly be false (due to suffering illusions or being misled by some power), one would discover a truth that is genuinely indubitable, viz., "I think, therefore I am" (*cogito ergo sum*), and that from this truth one could discover the criterion of true knowledge, viz., that whatever is clearly and distinctly conceived is true. Using this criterion, one could then establish: God's existence, that he is not a deceiver, that he guarantees our clear and distinct ideas, and that an external world exists that can be known through mathematical physics. Descartes, starting from Skepticism, claimed to have found a new basis for certitude and for knowledge of reality. Throughout the 17th century Skeptical critics—Mersenne, Gassendi, the re-

Fideistic views

Christian Skepticism

Cartesian Skepticism

viver of Academic philosophy Simon Foucher, and Pierre-Daniel Huet, one of the most learned men of the age—sought to show that Descartes had not succeeded, and that, if he sincerely followed his skeptical method, his new system could only lead to complete Skepticism. They challenged whether the *cogito* proved anything, or whether it was indubitable; whether Descartes' method could be successfully applied, or whether it was certain; and whether any of the knowledge claims of Cartesianism were *really* true. Nicolas Malebranche, the developer of occasionalism, revised the Cartesian system to meet the Skeptical attacks only to find his efforts challenged by the new Skeptical criticisms of Foucher and by the contention of the Jansenist philosopher Antoine Arnauld that Malebranchism led to a most dangerous Pyrrhonism.

Various English philosophers culminating in Locke tried to blunt the force of Skepticism by appealing to common sense and to the "reasonable" man's inability to doubt everything. They admitted that there might not be sufficient evidence to support the knowledge claims extending beyond immediate experience. But this did not actually require that everything be doubted; by using standards of common sense, an adequate basis for many beliefs could be found. Blaise Pascal, who presented the case for Skepticism most forcefully in his *Pensées*, still denied that there can be a complete Skepticism; for nature prevents it. Lacking rational answers to complete Skepticism, man's only recourse lies in turning to God for help in overcoming doubts.

Pierre Bayle

The culmination of 17th-century Skepticism appears in the writings of Pierre Bayle, especially in his monumental *Dictionnaire historique et critique* (1697–1702). Bayle, a superb dialectician, challenged philosophical, scientific, and theological theories, both ancient and modern, showing that they all led to perplexities, paradoxes, and contradictions. He argued that the theories of Descartes, Spinoza, Leibniz, and Malebranche, when skeptically analyzed, cast in doubt all information about the world, even whether a world exists. Bayle skillfully employed Skeptical arguments about such things as sense information, human judgments, logical explanations, and the criteria of knowledge in order to undermine confidence in human intellectual activity in all areas. Bayle suggested that man should abandon rational activity and turn blindly to faith and revelation; he can therefore only follow his conscience without any criterion for determining true faith. Bayle showed that the interpretations of religious knowledge were so implausible that even the most heretical views, like Manichaeism, known for its cosmic dualism of good and evil, and Atheism, made more sense. As a result Bayle's work became "the arsenal of the Enlightenment," and he was regarded as a major enemy of religion.

In the 18th century. Most 18th-century thinkers gave up the quest for metaphysical knowledge after imbibing Bayle's arguments. George Berkeley, an Empiricist and Idealist, fought Skeptical doubts by identifying appearance and reality and offering a spiritualistic metaphysics. He was immediately seen as just another Skeptic since he was denying the world beyond experience.

David Hume

Bayle's chief 18th-century successor was David Hume. Combining empirical and skeptical arguments, Hume charged that neither inductive nor deductive evidence could establish the truth of any matter of fact. Knowledge could only consist of intuitively obvious matters or demonstrable relations of ideas but not of anything beyond experience; the mind can discover no necessary connections within experience nor any root causes of experience. Beliefs about the world are based not upon reason or evidence nor even upon appeal to the uniformity of nature but only on habit and custom. Beliefs cannot be justified. Belief that there is an external world, a self, a God is common; but there is no adequate evidence for it. Although it is natural to hold these convictions, they are inconsistent and epistemologically dubious. "Philosophy would render us entirely Pyrrhonian, were not Nature too strong for it." The beliefs that a man is forced to hold enable him to describe the world scientifically, but when he tries to justify them he is led to complete Skepticism.

Before he goes mad with doubts, however, Nature brings him back to common sense, to unjustifiable beliefs. Hume's fideism was a natural rather than a religious one; it is only animal faith that provides relief from complete doubt. The religious context of Skepticism from Montaigne to Bayle had been removed, and man was left with only his natural beliefs, which might be meaningless or valueless.

The central themes in Hume's Skeptical analysis—the basis of induction, of causality, knowledge of the external world and the self, proofs of the existence of God—became the key issues of later philosophy. Hume's contemporary Thomas Reid hoped to rebut Hume's Skepticism by exposing it as the logical conclusion of the basic assumptions of modern philosophy from Descartes onward. Such disastrous assumptions should be abandoned for commonsensical principles that have to be believed. As Hume and Kant saw, Reid had not answered Hume's Skepticism but had only sidestepped the issue by appealing to commonsensical living. This provided, however, neither a theoretical basis for beliefs nor a refutation of the arguments that questioned them.

Kant and his critics

Kant saw that Hume had posed a most fundamental challenge to all human knowledge claims. To answer him, it had to be shown not that knowledge is possible but *how* it is possible. Kant combined a Skepticism toward metaphysical knowledge with the contention that certain universal and necessary conditions are involved in having experience and describing it. In terms of these it is possible to have genuine knowledge about the forms of all possible experience, space and time, and about the categories in which all experience is described. Any effort to apply this beyond all possible experience, however, leads into contradictions and Skepticism. It is not possible to know about things-in-themselves nor about the causes of experience.

Though Kant thought that he had resolved the Skeptical problems, some of his contemporaries saw his philosophy as commencing a new Skeptical era. G.E. Schulze (or Schulze-Aenesidemus) a notable critic of Kantianism, insisted that, on Kant's theory, no one could know any objective truths about anything; he could only know the subjective necessity of his views. The Jewish critic Salomon Maimon contended that, though there are such things as a priori concepts, their application to experience is always problematical, and whether they apply can only be found through experience. Hence, the possibility of knowledge can never be established with certainty. Assured truth on the basis of concepts is possible only of human creations, like mathematical ideas, and it is questionable whether these have any objective truth. The thesis that human creativity is the basis of truth, however, was soon to be developed by Johann G. Fichte, a leading German Idealist, as a new way of transcending Skepticism.

Another Skeptical critic of Kant, J.G. Hamann, saw in Hume's and Kant's work a new basis for fideism. If knowledge of reality cannot be gained by rational means, then one must turn to faith. Based on Hume's efforts, Hamann advanced an antirational Skepticism in an effort to convince Kant to become a fideistic Christian. Hamann's kind of fideism was also developed in France by Catholic opponents of the French Revolution and liberalism—like Joseph de Maistre and Hugues-F.-R. de Lamennais.

Existentialism

In recent and contemporary philosophy. Irrational Skepticism was developed into Existentialism (*q.v.*) by Søren Kierkegaard in the 19th century. Using traditional Skeptical themes to attack Hegelianism and liberal Christianity, Kierkegaard stressed the need for faith. Only by an unjustified and unjustifiable "leap into faith" could certainty be found—which would then be entirely subjective rather than objective. Modern neo-orthodox and Existentialist theologians have argued that Skepticism highlights man's inability to find any ultimate truth except through faith and commitment. Nonreligious forms of this view have been developed by Existentialist writers like Albert Camus, combining the epistemological Skepticism of Kierkegaard with the religious and value Skepticism of Nietzsche. The rational and scientific examination of the world shows it to be unintelligible and absurd; and if God is dead, as Nietzsche proclaimed, then the world is ultimately meaningless. But it is necessary to struggle with it. It is thus through action and commitment that one finds whatever personal meaning he can, though it has no objective significance.

Other kinds of Skepticism appear in various forms of recent and contemporary philosophy. The English Idealist F.H. Bradley used classical Skeptical arguments in his *Appearance and Reality: A Metaphysical Essay* to contend that the world could not be understood empirically or materialistically; true knowledge could be reached only by transcending the world of appearance.

George Santayana, an American critical Realist, in *Scepticism and Animal Faith*, presented a naturalistic Skepticism. Any interpretation of immediate or intuited experience is open to question. To make life meaningful, however, men make interpretations by "animal faith," according to biological and social factors. The resulting beliefs, though unjustified and perhaps illusory, enable them to persevere and find the richness of life.

Types of Skepticism also appear in Logical Positivism (see POSITIVISM AND LOGICAL EMPIRICISM) and various forms of linguistic philosophy (see ANALYTIC AND LINGUISTIC PHILOSOPHY). The attack on speculative metaphysics developed by the physicist and early Positivist Ernst Mach, by Bertrand Russell, and by Rudolf Carnap, a leader in the Vienna Circle, where Logical Positivism was nourished, incorporated a Skepticism about the possibility of gaining knowledge beyond experience or logical tautologies. Russell and the important philosopher of science Karl Popper have further stressed the unjustifiability of the principle of induction, and Popper has criticized theories of knowledge based upon empirical verification. A founder of linguistic analysis, Fritz Mauthner, has set forth a Skepticism in which any language is merely relative to its users and thus subjective. Every attempt to tell what is true just leads one back to linguistic formulations, not to objective states of affairs. The result is a complete Skepticism about reality—a reality that cannot even be expressed except in terms of what he called godless mystical contemplation. Mauthner's linguistic Skepticism bears some affinities to the views expressed in Ludwig Wittgenstein's *Tractatus Logico-Philosophicus*.　(R.H.P.)

SKEPTICISM IN INDIA

Though the formulations sound very different, similar Skeptical strains also appeared in the history of non-Western thought, especially in India. The *Upaniṣads* themselves, philosophic Scriptures of the later Vedic period, reflected a Skeptical climate of thought; and the Buddha, typically, sidestepped speculative issues, the discussion of which could only delay the business of salvation. The more-or-less orthodox system of Sāṃkhya already had distrusted Scripture and based itself upon perception and its implications.

Others went further. The sect of Ājīvikas ("those observing restrictions concerning livelihood") similarly frustrated the probings of metaphysics. Based upon the deterministic doctrines of Gośāla Maskariputra, a contemporary of the Buddha, the Ājīvikas denied the efficacy of human action to speed or delay one's salvation; events merely happened as fated until the eon had run its course. Still more extreme were the Cārvākas (also known as Lokāyatas, "the This-Worldly"), who denied not only revelation but also all deductions from sense data. To the Cārvākas, only sense perception counts; hence there is no soul, and mind is merely a gas of the body. The views of these two schools were perennially quoted, but only to be condemned.

Buddhist Skepticisms

The Buddha's willful Agnosticism was continued by the Mādhyamika school of Mahāyāna (the "School of the Middle"), which, particularly in the person of Nāgārjuna (*c*. 2nd century AD), demolished arguments based on too literal an acceptance of the objective world as real. Nāgārjuna preferred the paradox that objective reality was void (*śūnya*) of significance, but that under Pharmakāya ultimate reality could only be grasped by a synthesis of objective antitheses. Likewise despairing of any positive statements about what is felt to be real, Dharmakīrti, a Buddhist monk of the 7th century AD, expressed his Skepticism in speaking of man's momentary and ineffable contact with the real, the nature of which is lost when he presses it (as he must) into cognitive relationships.

Akin to the acosmism of the Mādhyamika Buddhists was the nonduality doctrine of Śaṃkarācārya, the great Vedāntin. But, while his views were comparable, they were based upon the very Veda that the Buddha had rejected. His Skepticism was thus fideistic, combining an Agnosticism about the world of common experience with an utter faith in the ultimate reality and purposefulness of the soul, onto which the categories of discursive thought are erroneously, and distortingly, projected.

On a nonphilosophical level Skepticism regarding the apperception of the world and reality continued through the history of Indian religion. The authority of the learned and the wise was continually questioned and at times derided. The trend has run its course through various devotional and reform movements and is finally reflected in recent attitudes, both on the right and on the left, that are Skeptical of the faiths of imported modernities.　(Ed.)

CRITICISM AND EVALUATION

In Western thought Skepticism has raised basic epistemological issues. In view of the varieties of human experience, it has questioned whether it is possible to tell which are veridical. The variations that occur in different perceptions of what is presumed to be one object raise the question of which is the correct view. The occurrence of illusory experiences raises the question of whether it is really possible to distinguish illusions and dreams from reality. The criteria employed can be questioned and require justification. On what basis does one tell whether he has the right criteria? By other criteria? Then, are these correct? On what standards? The attempt to justify criteria seems either to lead to an infinite regress or to just stop arbitrarily. If an attempt is made to justify knowledge claims by starting with first principles, what are these based upon? Can it be established that these principles cannot possibly be false? If so, is the proof itself such that it cannot be questioned? If it is claimed that the principles are self-evident, can one be sure of this, sure that he is not deceived? And can he be sure that he can recognize and apply the principles correctly? Through such questioning, Skeptics have indicated the basic problems that an investigator would have to resolve before he could be certain of possessing knowledge; *i.e.*, information that could not possibly be false.

Criticisms

Critics have contended that Skepticism is both a logically and a humanly untenable view. Any attempt to formulate the position will be self-refuting since it will assert at least some knowledge claims about what is supposed to be dubious. Montaigne suggested that the Skeptics needed a nonassertive language, reflecting the claim of Sextus that the Skeptic does not make assertions but only chronicles his feelings. The strength of Skepticism lies not in whether it can be stated consistently but upon the effects of its arguments on dogmatic philosophers. As Hume said, Skepticism may be self-refuting, but in the process of refuting itself it undermines dogmatism. Skepticism, Sextus said, is like a purge that eliminates itself as well as everything else.

Critics have claimed that anyone who tried to be a complete Skeptic, denying or suspending all judgments about ordinary beliefs, would soon be driven insane. Even Hume thought that the complete Skeptic would have to starve to death and would walk into walls or out of windows. Hume, therefore, separated the doubting activity from natural practical activities in the world. Skeptical philosophizing went on in theory, while believing occurred in practice. Sextus and the contemporary Norwegian Skeptic Arne Naess have said, on the other hand, that Skepticism is a form of mental health. Instead of going mad, the Skeptic—without commitment to fixed positions—can function better than the dogmatist.

Some recent thinkers like A.J. Ayer and John Austin

have contended that Skepticism is unnecessary. If knowledge is defined in terms of satisfying meaningful criteria, then knowledge is open to all. The Skeptics have raised false problems, because it is, as a matter of fact, possible to tell that some experiences are illusory since we have criteria for distinguishing them from actual events. We do resolve doubts and reach a state of knowledge through various verification procedures, after which doubt is meaningless. Naess, in his book *Scepticism*, has sought to show, however, that, on the standards offered by Ayer and Austin, one can still ask if knowledge claims may not turn out to be false and hence that Skepticism has still to be overcome.

Evaluation   Skepticism throughout history has played a dynamic role in forcing dogmatic philosophers to find better or stronger bases for their views and to find answers to the Skeptical attacks. It has forced a continued re-examination of previous knowledge claims and has stimulated creative thinkers to work out new theories to meet the Skeptical problems. The history of philosophy can be seen, in part, as a struggle with Skepticism. The attacks of the Skeptics also have served as a check on rash speculation; the various forms of modern Skepticism have gradually eroded the metaphysical and theological bases of European thought. Most contemporary thinkers have been sufficiently affected by Skepticism to abandon the search for certain and indubitable foundations of human knowledge. Instead, they have sought ways of living with the unresolved Skeptical problems through various forms of naturalistic, scientific, or religious faiths.

BIBLIOGRAPHY

Primary sources: The basic statements and arguments of various forms of Skepticism are given in: (Academic Skepticism)—CICERO, *Academica* and *De natura deorum*, both with trans. by H. RACKHAM, Loeb Classical Library (1956). (Pyrrhonian Skepticism)—SEXTUS EMPIRICUS, *Adversus Mathematicos*, with trans. by R.G. BURY, Loeb Classical Library: vol. 1–2, *Against the Logicians* and *Outlines of Pyrrhonism* (1933–36); vol. 3, *Against the Physicists, Against the Ethicists* (1936); vol. 4, *Against the Professors* (1959–60); and *Scepticism, Man and God: Selections from the Major Writings of Sextus Empiricus*, ed. by P. HALLIE, trans. by S.G. ETHERIDGE (1964). (Renaissance Skepticism)—MICHEL DE MONTAIGNE, "L'Apologie de Raimond Sebond," in PIERRE VILLEY (ed.), *Les Essais de Michel de Montaigne*, new ed. (1922). (Skepticism and fideism)—BLAISE PASCAL, *Pensées*, ed. by L. BRUNSCHVICG (1951). (Skepticism in relation to modern philosophy)—PIERRE BAYLE, *Dictionnaire historique et critique*, esp. the articles "Pyrrho" and "Zeno of Elea," both of which appear in BAYLE's *Historical and Critical Dictionary: Selections*, trans. and ed. by RICHARD H. POPKIN (1965); DAVID HUME, *Dialogues Concerning Natural Religion*, ed. by N. KEMP SMITH (1947); *Enquiries Concerning the Human Understanding and Concerning the Principles of Morals*, 2nd ed. (1957), and *A Treatise of Human Nature*, both ed. by L.A. SELBY-BIGGE (1958).

Secondary sources: The standard studies of ancient Skepticism are: EDWYN R. BEVAN, *Stoics and Sceptics* (1959); VICTOR BROCHARD, *Les Sceptiques grecs* (1887); NORMAN MACCOLL, *The Greek Sceptics from Pyrrho to Sextus* (1869); MARY MILLS PATRICK, *The Greek Sceptics* (1929); LEON ROBIN, *Pyrrhon et le scepticisme grec* (1944); and EDUARD ZELLER, *The Stoics, Epicureans and Sceptics*, trans. by O.J. REICHEL (1880). A recent fine study of the epistemological problems involved in ancient Skepticism is CHARLOTTE L. STOUGH, *Greek Skepticism* (1969). See also RAOUL RICHTER, *Der Skeptizismus in der Philosophie* (1904–08); RICHARD H. POPKIN, "Skepticism," *Encyclopedia of Philosophy*, vol. 7, pp. 449–461 (1967), which contains a bibliography on the subject; these examine Skepticism from ancient times to the 19th century. JOHN OWEN, *The Skeptics of the French Renaissance* (1893), is an interesting discussion of Renaissance and 17th-century Skepticism, though not particularly scholarly. DON CAMERON ALLEN, *Doubt's Boundless Sea: Skepticism and Faith in the Renaissance* (1964); and RICHARD H. POPKIN, *The History of Scepticism from Erasmus to Descartes*, rev. ed. (1968), which contains a lengthy bibliography, are studies of Renaissance Skepticism and its impact on philosophy and religion. RICHARD H. POPKIN, "Berkeley and Pyrrhonism," *Review of Metaphysics*, 5:223–246 (1951–52); "David Hume and the Pyrrhonian Controversy," *ibid.*, 6:65–81 (1952–53); "David Hume: His Pyrrhonism and His Critique of Pyrrhonism," *Philosophical Quarterly*, 1:385–407 (1950–51); "The High Road to Pyrrhonism," *American Philosophical Quarterly*, 2:1–15 (1965); "The Skeptical Crisis and the Rise of Modern Philosophy," *Review of Metaphysics*, 7:132–151, 307–322, 499–510 (1953–54); "The Skeptical Precursors of David Hume," *Philosophy and Phenomenological Research*, 16:61–71 (1955–56); and "Scepticism in the Enlightenment," in T. BESTERMANN (ed.), *Studies on Voltaire and the Eighteenth Century*, 26:1321–1345 (1963), are specialized studies on aspects of Skepticism in relation to modern philosophy. ARNE NAESS, *Scepticism* (1968), is a most interesting attempt to clarify Skepticism in relation to contemporary thought and to defend it as a viable outlook today.

(R.H.P.)

Skiing

Skiing is a way of moving over snow by the use of a pair of long flat runners, called skis, attached to the shoes or boots. It is practiced for recreational, competitive, or utilitarian purposes. On the level or slight grades, the skier uses a gliding gait, assisted by a ski pole in each hand; downhill, he slides effortlessly over the snow, turning to avoid obstacles, to reduce speed, or to change direction. Ski jumping is usually performed on especially designed inclines of varied size.

Skiers, at first, had to climb to gain heights from which to ski down. In the early 1900s only the mountain railways or aerial cable cars of the Alps were available for uphill transportation of skiers. Since the early 1930s, many new devices have been built for this purpose, including chair lifts, gondola lifts, T-bar and J-stick tramways, platter pulls, and, in the U.S. and Canada, rope tows (especially on small slopes for beginners) and other devices. Such aids greatly promoted the popularity of skiing, for they made possible four or five times as much downhill skiing in a day as when the skier had to climb uphill. The development of snow-making machines permitted the enjoyment of the sport in areas with only marginally adequate snow and during seasons other than winter. In the Scandinavian and eastern European countries, touring and cross-country skiing remained the more popular sports.

Competitive skiing comprises the Nordic, or classic, events (cross-country racing and jumping) and the Alpine, or downhill, events (downhill or straight racing, and slalom and giant slalom racing between series of set gates). The biathlon is a military competition consisting of a cross-country course and rifle target shooting.   *The types and appeal of skiing*

The pleasure of downhill skiing lies in the comparatively effortless and speedy manner in which the skier descends a snow-covered slope, controlling the direction of his skis and his speed in accordance with his skill. Cross-country skiing, or ski touring, and ski mountaineering have an appeal similar to that of hiking and mountaineering. The popularity of skiing is attested to by its rapid growth in all parts of the world where there is snow and hilly or mountainous country. Some of the chief attractions of the sport are that there is virtually no limit to the degree of skill that can be acquired, that snow conditions to be coped with are of infinite variety and constantly changing, that no two trails or slopes are the same, and the appeal of the out-of-doors and the scenery.

This article relates the history of skiing, the development of the modern Alpine sport, international competitive skiing, and world organization of the sport, and describes the basic equipment and principles of the basic movements. Only the basic movements are defined in the paragraphs under that title, and no effort is made to describe how to ski. (Most ski books deal with technique: examples are listed in the bibliography.)

History.   The oldest skis that have been found, in bogs in Sweden and Finland, are believed to be between 4,000 and 5,000 years old, and a rock carving of two men on skis found near the Arctic Circle in Norway dates from 2000 BC. Unconfirmed 3rd-century-BC Chinese reports refer to skis being used in the north. It is recorded that the Vikings used skis in the 10th and 11th centuries, and somewhat later the historian Olaus Magnus reported the swiftness with which ski-clad Laplanders pursued game. Skis are also mentioned in Norse mythology, in which Ull (sometimes Skade) was the ski god and Undurridis the ski goddess.

The earliest known pictorial representation of skiing, a rock carving from Rodoy, Norway, dating from 2000 BC.
By courtesy of the Norwegian Ski Museum

Skis are referred to in continental European literature as early as the 17th century, for instance in a book by the Austrian J.W. von Valvasor, *Die Ehre des Herzogtums Krain* ("The Honour of the Duchy of Carniola"). These were isolated and ephemeral instances and had no historical significance.

Skis were first used for practical purposes rather than for sport—to get from one place to another. Such uses have continued until modern times, especially in Norway, Sweden, Finland, and the eastern European countries.

In 1200 King Sverrir of Norway sent out men on skis to reconnoitre before the battle of Oslo. Ski troops were also used in Sweden as early as 1452. In the 15th, 16th, and 17th centuries, skis were used in warfare in Finland, Norway, Poland, Russia, and Sweden. In 1716, the first ski-equipped troops were organized in Norway. The first skiing manual, written by Capt. Jens Emmahusen of Trondheim, was published in 1733. From 1767, ski competitions were arranged for the troops, with money awarded as prizes.

Ski touring, or cross-country skiing, in the hills and mountains as a sport was a natural development from utilitarian skiing. Ski mountaineering, distinguished by the need to use ropes and ice axes, followed later. The first important expedition in the Alps was the traverse of the main massif of the Bernese Oberland by a party of five Germans headed by Wilhelm Paulcke in 1897. Thereafter, German, French, Austrian, Italian, and British skiers made many first ascents on skis of Alpine peaks and high passes. Among the other ski mountaineers of this early period were Payot of France, F.F. Roget and Marcel Kurz of Switzerland; and, a little later, Count Aldo Bonacossa of Italy and Sir Arnold Lunn of Great Britain.

Development of skiing as a sport. Recreational skiing undoubtedly was engaged in throughout the times when skis were used chiefly for practical purposes. However, up to the mid-1800s, bindings were primitive, consisting only of toestraps, which allowed insufficient control of the skis for jumping or turning. One of the earliest civilian competitions was a cross-country race at Tromsö, Norway, in 1843. A milestone in the competitive sport came about 1860, when Sondre Nordheim, from Morgedal, Telemark, Norway, first used willow or cane bindings around the heel from each side of the toe strap to fasten the boots to the skis. Nordheim also designed skis with incurving sides, which became the pattern for all modern skis. With this equipment, he evolved the Christiania turn, a graceful, sweeping swing across the fall-line, and the Telemark turn, with the outside ski weighed and leading (for information on turns and other movements see below, *Basic movements*). Competitive skiing also started in California in the 1860s, on straight downhill courses, using skis 12 feet long and only leather toe straps.

The thrills of negotiating occasional small jumps that occurred on many natural downhill runs, where pioneer skiing took place, led the more adventurous to seek out larger and larger jumps and eventually to improve them artificially. The interest in ski jumping grew rapidly. The first big contest was held at Huseby Hill, Oslo, Norway, in 1879, with the king and 10,000 spectators in attendance.

This contest was moved to the Holmenkollen Hill in 1892.

It was the Norwegian jumpers and men who had visited Norway who brought skiing to the Alps of central Europe, where the steep hillsides, mountains, and glaciers required a different technique and more controllable skis than the more rolling terrain of Scandinavia. But a strong influence on the development of interest in Alpine skiing was Fridtjof Nansen's account of his 1888 expedition across Greenland on skis, *Paa Ski Over Grönland*, which was translated into English, French, and German in 1891. Among those inspired by the book was Mathias Zdarsky who became outstanding in the development of a new way of skiing, methods of instruction, and better equipment, and who taught his "Lilienfeld" technique to large classes in Austria.

Other pioneers of this period included Wilhelm Paulcke of Germany and F. Huitfeld of Norway and, a little later, W.R. Rickmers and Henry Hoek of Germany, Col. Georg Bilgeri of Austria, Col. Christoph Iselin of Switzerland, and Vivian Caulfeild of Great Britain.

In the 20th century skiing became increasingly popular, attracting more and more devotees in Europe and North America. It spread rapidly in Australia and New Zealand in the 1930s, in Chile and Argentina in the 1940s, and in Japan in the 1950s. With the considerable expansion of holiday skiing after World War II, skiers appeared on snow covered slopes around the world, in Yugoslavia and Greece, for example, in the Pyrenees in central Spain and Portugal, in Morocco and Algeria, in the U.S.S.R., in Lebanon, Turkey, and Iran, in the Andes in Argentina and Chile, and in India. The world alpine championships were held in the southern hemisphere for the first time at Portillo, Chile, in 1966. The skiing and other events of the 1972 Olympic Winter Games were held at Sapporo, Japan.

Modern skiing and ski schools. All forms of Alpine skiing progressed during the early 1900s. One outstanding innovator initiated the modern surge in the sport. He was Hannes Schneider of St. Anton, Austria, the outstanding competitor of his time, whose "Arlberg" technique, featuring the crouched position and the stem Christiania, as well as the position of "vorlage," or putting the weight forward, led to the present way of skiing. He started teaching at St. Anton in 1907, and his systematized ski school became the model for those of many other countries. Schneider taught in a methodical progression from snowplow to control speed or stop, through slow snowplow turn, more rapid stem turn, and stem Christiania, to free parallel swing initiated with only a slight quick stem (for descriptions of movements see below *Basic movements*). His school became very popular, and he soon found graded classes and additional instructors necessary. During World War I, he further developed his methods while training Austrian mountain troops.

As more efficient techniques were developed, largely by competition, these also were taught, and attendance at ski schools increased. The first examination for teachers of skiing was held in Austria in 1925. This examination became increasingly exacting over the years, and other countries, including Switzerland, France, Italy, Germany, Canada, and the U.S., adopted similar tests, with certification considered a mark of professional competence. In each of these countries a uniform national system is taught in all or most of the schools, but in some places an eclectic or original method may be used.

Switzerland instituted courses for teachers in the early 1930s, and under the leadership of Christian Rubi the Swiss ski schools promoted a uniform method of instruction. While Schneider's Arlberg ski school put great emphasis on the stem and stem turns as the basis of its technique, the Swiss avoided what they considered excessive attention to these positions, and later the French schools, too, took a more direct route to "parallel" skiing. Émile Allais and Paul Gignoux brought the French theories to the forefront when they challenged the value of teaching the basic stem and body rotation. Ahead of their time were Eugen Matthias, physiologist of the University of Munich, and Giovanni Testa, head of the ski school in St. Moritz, who in the mid-1930s first taught the reverse

Ski touring and mountaineering

Ski jumping

The "Arlberg" technique

The Swiss schools

(or inside) shoulder technique and the technique of turning with knees together. Their book, *Natürliches Skilaufen* (1936), attracted considerable attention, but was not at the time recognized as prophetic of what was to come.

Since World War II, the techniques taught and the sequence of instruction in the ski schools of the various countries have tended to become more similar. In particular, less emphasis is placed on a thorough and almost exclusive grounding in the stemmed turns. Instead, a parallel position of the skis is inculcated, and to make this habitual, early stress is placed on sideslipping, traversing, edge control, and straight running of slopes. The chief differences are between the Austrian system of rhythmic short-swinging (short swings and counterswings across the fall-line; *wedeln*) turns, distinguished by counterrotation and leading with the inside shoulder in turning, as first advocated by Matthias; and the French turning style of *projection circulaire*, in which the shoulders are kept almost square to the direction of movement during a turn.

Among the important factors leading to these developments were the introduction of the steel edge in the 1930s, and the great increase of ski lifts, beginning in the late 1940s. The former facilitated the learning of parallel, narrow-tracked, and precise running and turning. The latter greatly increased the numbers of skiers and multiplied the number of runs each one could make downhill, so that little skiing could be done on virgin snow, and nearly all runs were made on well-packed trails and slopes, thus promoting the development of the short-swinging, with alternate pole-planting, and the *wedeln* techniques.

Organization of the sport. The International Ski Federation (Fédération Internationale de Ski, or FIS) founded in 1924, is the world governing body of the sport. It is composed of the various national ski associations or federations, and these, in turn, are usually composed of individual ski clubs. Two of its chief functions are to set the rules of competition for each branch of the sport, and to sanction the quadrennial world championships and the international calendar comprising all other important events. It also sets the rules of eligibility.

The world's first ski club was the Trysil in Norway, formed in 1861. The first in the United States was organized at Berlin, New Hampshire, in 1872. The Ski Club of Great Britain, founded in 1903, was the sport's first national administrative body. It was superseded by the National Ski Federation of Great Britain (1964). The first intercollegiate ski meet, with Dartmouth, McGill, and Montreal, was held in Quebec, at Shawbridge, in 1914. The first meet between the British Universities Ski Club and the Swiss Academic Ski Club was held in 1927.

The International Association for Ski Instruction (Interski) holds a congress every three years at which teams from the chief skiing countries demonstrate the methods of instruction used by their schools.

Competitive skiing. Downhill races are run on defined courses of a length, steepness, and difficulty appropriate to the skill and endurance of the entrants. For men's Olympic and world championship events, a vertical descent of between 800 and 1,000 metres is prescribed. The limits for women are 300 metres lower. Courses may be between 2.4 and 5 kilometres long, although some races are considerably longer. Average speed of the winners is usually between 64 and 80 kilometres per hour (40 to 50 miles per hour). Speeds of more than 161 km/hr (100 mph) have been recorded on special short courses.

A slalom course is defined by gates formed by pairs of poles with flags, between which the runner must pass. The course is carefully set to test the skill and judgment of the competitor. For Olympic and world championship races, the men's course must have a vertical descent of between 180 and 220 metres. Fifty-five to 75 gates are required for men, 40 to 60 for women. For less important competitions, courses are shorter and less difficult. Sir Arnold Lunn is credited with initiating the modern slalom in the early 1920s, and with being chiefly responsible for its recognition (and that of the downhill) by the FIS in 1930.

The giant slalom has characteristics of both the downhill and the slalom. The gates are set wider and further apart, the length of the course approaches that of the downhill, and the average speeds achieved are between those of the other two Alpine events. The best Alpine competitors have come from Austria, France, Italy, Switzerland, and, more recently, Canada and the U.S.

The World Cup, inaugurated in 1967, is a competition in which skiers can accumulate points in the three Alpine disciplines in many designated meets during the winter.

Cross-country races are held over rolling terrain. The standard distances in international competition are 15, 30, and 50 km for men, and 10 and 5 km for women. In the relay race, four men each run a 10-km course, and three women a 5-km course. The Vasa race in Sweden is 56 mi (90 km) long.

Jumping competitions are held on carefully graded and prepared hills, classified according to size as 100-m, 80-m, 70-m, etc. The approach, or inrun, usually starts on a scaffold or tower; down this incline the jumper, in a crouched position, accumulates speed until he reaches the takeoff, where he leaps outward, upward, and forward. The best competitors lean far over toward the points of their skis in order to minimize wind resistance and to get an aerodynamic lifting effect to increase the length of their jump. The landing is made on the steep landing hill in a more upright position with the shock of contact taken up by the knees. After the slope levels off, the jumper stops by turning on the outrun. The performance is decided half by the distance covered and half on form, as marked by the judges, who attribute style marks.

The best jumpers and cross-country runners have come largely from the Scandinavian countries, Finland, and eastern Europe, especially from the U.S.S.R., but some also from the Alpine countries.

A combination of the results of the downhill and slalom,

Downhill, slalom, and giant slalom

Cross-country racing and jumping

(Left, centre) Pictorial Parade, (left) D.P.A., (centre) *Paris Match*, (right) *Sports Illustrated*—Tony Triolo © Time Inc.

(Left) Skier airborne in leap during men's downhill race (Egon Zimmermann [Austria]) at Innsbruck, Austria, 1964. (Centre) Skier running gate in the giant slalom (Karl Schranz [Austria]) at the Arlberg-Kandahar competition, Austria, 1969. (Right) Airborne skier (Bjørn Wirkola of Norway) stretches out over skis.

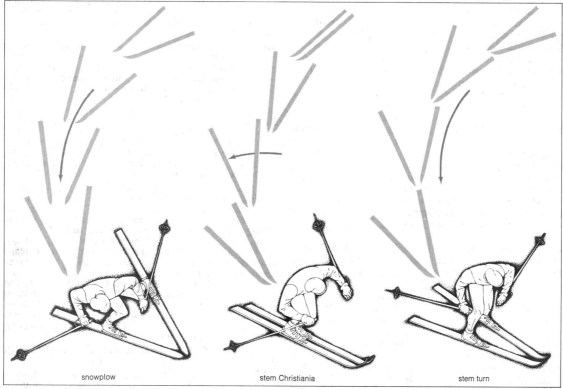

straight running   sideslipping   traversing

snowplow   stem Christiania   stem turn

Basic skiing movements.

and sometimes the giant slalom, events is called the Alpine combined, and the jump and 15 km cross-country together are called the Nordic combined.

The Winter Olympic Games were initiated in 1924 at Chamonix, France, but included only Nordic ski events. The same was true of the St. Moritz, Switzerland (1928), and Lake Placid, New York (1932), Olympics. Alpine events for men and women were introduced at Garmisch-Partenkirchen, Germany, in 1936. World Ski Championships, sanctioned by the FIS, are now held every fourth year, between the Olympics. The first was in 1925, at Johannesbad, Czechoslovakia. The Alpine events were first included in these championships at Mürren, Switzerland, in 1931. The oldest international event decided on the results of a downhill and a slalom, is the Arlberg-Kandahar race, first held in 1928, which now rotates between Mürren, St. Anton, Chamonix, Sestriere (Italy), and Garmisch, and in 1971 was held in the United States, at Sugarloaf Mountain, Maine. Lunn and Schneider were its founders. Other famous competitions are the Holmenkollen, the world's senior ski meeting, in Norway, the Parsenn Derby and the Lauberhorn in Switzerland, and the Hahnenkamm in Austria.

For a complete record of Winter Olympics winners see ATHLETIC GAMES AND CONTESTS: *Olympic record.* For Nordic and Alpine World Champions, World Cup winners, World Biathlon champions, and progressive world ski-jumping records see SPORTING RECORD in the *Ready Reference and Index.*

The sport of skiing. *Basic equipment.* The three chief types of skis, downhill (including slalom), jumping, and cross country (racing and touring), have certain characteristics in common. They are pointed, turned up, and usually slightly wider at the front (the tip or shovel) and are squared at the rear (or tail). They are thickest in the midsection under the foot, thinnest just before the ends, and are built with a slight arch, or camber, so as to distribute the skier's weight along the length of the ski. The stiffness of the camber may vary to accord with the use to which the skis are to be put. Over the years skis have been refined in their shape and camber and in precision of stiffness. The running surface, or sole, has been improved to reduce friction and increase durability.

Skis vary in length, the downhill ski for the average adult man being a little less than seven feet (210 centimetres) long, although much shorter skis, slower but more manoeuvrable, are enjoying some vogue, particularly in teaching beginners and novices. Skis were formerly fashioned from one piece of wood, usually hickory, but after the 1930s laminated constructions were also used. After 1950, plastic running surfaces were introduced to increase speed and durability, and skis of metal, usually with a wood or plastic core, became increasingly popular. The downhill ski, which is about three inches (7.6 cm) in width, typically has a shallow groove running longitudinally along the centre of the bottom; this imparts directional stability. In addition, skis have sharp edges of steel along the bottom in order to bite into hard snow or ice.

Skis: types and construction

Jumping skis are longer (about 8 ft [244 cm]), wider, thicker, and heavier, and ordinarily have three grooves in the bottom, and no steel edges. Cross-country skis are narrower and lighter than downhill skis. They have one groove and often are of laminated wood. Skis for touring have metal edges; cross-country racing skis do not.

For downhill skiing, the skier wears closefitting, heavy leather or plastic boots with flat and stiff soles in order to exercise precise control over the skis. The boots are firmly attached to the skis by bindings, often with release features, designed to free the skier's foot in case of falls. Many improvements in bindings have been developed. For jumping and cross country a lighter and more flexible boot is used, with a binding that allows the heel to be raised.

For downhill skiing a light pole, or stick, of metal or bamboo, about four feet long, is carried in each hand. For cross-country skiing the pole is typically longer and lighter. These aid the skier in pushing himself along on the level and in climbing. They are also used in maintaining balance when running downhill and to assist in turning. Each pole has a wrist strap at the top and a ring or wheel near the bottom, which prevents the point from sinking too deeply into the snow. Various waxes, depending on temperature and snow conditions, are used on the bottoms of skis to prevent snow from sticking to them and to reduce friction. To aid in climbing, special waxes are used, and sometimes strips of sealskin or plush are strapped or stuck to the bottoms of the skis to prevent backsliding.

Refinements in ski equipment after World War II were accompanied by a great increase in the proficiency of the average recreational or competitive skier. As the parallel (skidded) technique supplanted the earlier stemmed (steered) turns, speed and manoeuvrability were greatly increased.

Basic movements. Brief identifications of the basic skiing movements referred to above and commonly taught in most schools follow. The best way to learn these movements is with a certified instructor.

Formerly the fundamental of instruction, stemmed turns are based on placing one or both skis at an angle to the direction of movement. The chief turning force is the shifting of weight from one ski to the other. The snowplow turn is made from a snowplow, or double stem (skis in a V), position by shifting the weight to one ski and exerting outward-turning pressure with that heel to make a steered turn. The stem turn is made from traversing, with skis parallel, by stemming (angling out) the upper ski and turning as in the snowplow. The stem Christiania is similar except that during the turn the skis are brought parallel and the rest of the turn is skidded with them in this position, while the Christiania is a swing from a slight initial stem that continues across the fall line. A jump turn is executed while in motion by lifting both skis from the snow with the aid of one or both poles, and turning them in the air. The kick turn is a sharp turn made from a stationary position by lifting one ski into a vertical position, letting it drop into the desired direction, and placing the other ski next to it. The *ruade* is a turn made by lifting the heels of the skis clear of the snow.

Sideslipping is useful on hard-packed trails, and as it also inculcates the parallel ski position and teaches edge control, has become a basic of modern instruction. The skis are skidded sideways by flattening them to disengage the edges and pushing the heels downhill and the skis out from under the body.

Traversing is running downhill and diagonally across the fall line with skis parallel and close together for greater control.

For running downhill in the fall line, the skis are flat, parallel, close together, and equally weighted. The goal is a stable, relaxed position, slightly forward leaning (*vorlage*), with smooth movements to adjust the skier's centre of gravity to changing conditions of snow and slope. The reverse position (*rücklage*), with the body back and the weight on the heels, was formerly considered a fault, but this position may be preferable with some types of equipment.

BIBLIOGRAPHY

History: A.H.M. LUNN, *History of Ski-ing* (1927) and *The Story of Ski-ing* (1952); C.M. DUDLEY, *60 Centuries of Skiing* (1935); J.K. HUNTER and O. GULBRANDSEN, *Ski-ing in Great Britain* (1963); E. MEHL, *Grundriss der Weltgeschichte des Schifahrens* (1964), a history of world skiing.

Technique and teaching: Col. Bilgeri's *Handbook on Mountain Skiing*, trans. by H. HOLME (1929), one of the earliest books of instruction; E. ALLAIS and P. GIGNOUX, *Ski Français* (1937); W. AMSTUTZ, *Ski-ing from A–Z* (1938); B. RYBIZKA, *Hannes Schneider Ski Technique*, new ed. (1946); AUSTRIAN ASSN. OF PROFESSIONAL SKI TEACHERS (eds.), *The New Official Austrian Ski System*, trans. by R. PALMEDO (1958); C.M. HUTER, *Wedeln: The New Austrian Skiing Technique* (1960); F. HOPPICHLER, *Neige et Style* (1960); J. FRANCO and M. MAURO, *Ski de France* (1962); J. CALDWELL, *The Cross Country Ski Book* (1964); PROFESSIONAL SKI INSTRUCTORS OF AMERICA, *The Official American Ski Technique* (1964); G. TESTA, *Das Skibuch* (1967), a recent book by an early technique innovator; E. MCCULLOCH, *Ski The Champions' Way* (1967).

Ski resorts and mountaineering: F.F. ROGET, *Ski Runs in the High Alps* (1913), various tours, an early classic; D.R. BROWER (ed.), *Manual of Ski Mountaineering*, 2nd ed. (1946); H.R. FEDDEN, *Alpine Ski Tour* (1956), an account of the famous Haute Route, from Chamonix to Sass Fe; J. RIDDELL, *Ski Runs of Switzerland* (1957), and with J. ODDIE, *Ski Runs of Austria* (1958); SKI CLUB OF GREAT BRITAIN, *Handbook on Ski Touring and Glacier Touring* (1961); R. PALMEDO, *Ski New Horizons*, 3rd ed. (1968), a guide to the world's ski resorts; A. RAND, *Ski North America: The Top 28 Resorts* (1969), a guide to the major ski resorts of the U.S. and Canada; W. PAUSE, *Ski Heil* (1969), a description, with maps, of the best-known ski runs of the Alps.

Miscellaneous: M. ZDARSKY, *Fuer Skifahrer* (1916), a small collection of essays by "the father of Alpine skiing"; G. SELIGMAN, *Snow Structure and Ski Fields* (1936), the classic technical work on this subject; S. KRUCKENHAUSER, *Snow Canvas* (1937), a handsome book by this famous photographer and leading authority on ski teaching and technique; R. PALMEDO (ed.), *Skiing: The International Sport* (1937), an anthology of articles by the then leading authorities on the sport, many illustrations; V.A. FIRSOFF, *Ski Track on the Battlefield* (1943), military skiing from the sixth century to 1942; E. BOWEN, *The Book of American Skiing* (1963), an eloquent account, in words and pictures; EDS. OF SKI MAG., *America's Ski Book* (1966), an authoritative anthology; M.H.N. MILNE and M.F. HELLER, *The Book of European Skiing* (1966); C.W. CASEWIT, *Ski Racing*, 2nd ed. (1969).

Periodicals: *Der Winter* (Germany); *Ski* (Great Britain); *Ski, Skier, Skiing,* and *Ski Racing* (U.S.).

Annuals: *American Ski Annual* (American Ski Association); *British Ski Year Book* (Ski Club of Great Britain); and *Annuario* (Argentine Ski Club).

(Ro.Po.)

Skin, Human

The apparent lack of body hair distinguishes man at once from all other large land mammals. Regardless of individual or racial differences, man's body seems to be more or less hairless, and it has become fashionable to refer to man as a naked ape, although he is neither naked nor an ape. Certainly, the larger part of human skin is covered with hair so vestigial as to seem absent; yet in certain areas hair grows profusely. These may be referred to as "epigamic" areas, and they have no other useful purpose than that of sexual attraction. Lacking a full coverage of hair, skin has attained adaptive changes in structure that give it strength and resilience. Although skin is the organ with which one is most familiar, man is still hopelessly ignorant about many of its anatomical, physiological, and biochemical properties and with most of its numerous disorders.

"Epigamic" areas

THE SKIN AS A WHOLE

The characteristic features of skin change from the time of birth to old age. In infants and children it is velvety, dry, soft, and largely free of wrinkles and blemishes. Children younger than two years sweat poorly and irregularly; their sebaceous glands function minimally. At adolescence, hair grows larger and becomes more pigmented, particularly in the scalp, axillae, pubic eminence, and face of men. General skin pigmentation increases, localized pigmented foci appear mysteriously, and acne lesions often develop. Hair growth, sweating, and sebaceous secretion begin to blossom in adolescence and reach full bloom in adults. As one ages, anatomical and physiological alterations and exposures to sunlight and wind all leave indelible marks, particularly upon skin not protected by clothing. The dry, wrinkled, flaccid skin of old people has suffered many abuses and is a relic of a fine organ system.

Human skin, more than that of any other mammal, exhibits many gross and subtle topographic differences, for example, those between the palms and the backs of one's hands and fingers. The skin of the eyebrows is thick, coarse, and hairy; that on the eyelids is thin, smooth, and covered with almost invisible hairs. The face is seldom visibly haired on the forehead and cheek bones. It is completely hairless in the vermilion border of the lips, yet coarsely hairy over the chin and jaws of men. The surfaces of the forehead, cheeks, and nose are normally oily, in contrast with the relatively greaseless lower surface of the chin and jaws. The skin of the chest, pubic areas, scalp, axillae, abdomen, soles of the feet, and ends of the fingers differs as much structurally and functionally as it would if the skin in these different areas belonged to different animals.

Man's skin is thicker than that of many other mammals and is thicker on the dorsal than the ventral parts. It is elastic to accommodate size increases and decreases of the body it encases and to accommodate the many subtle movements that characterize the human body. The extent of elasticity is an individual property, largely dictated by regional, racial, and genetic factors; taut in some persons, the skin is easily stretched in others. Skin repairs expertly and with dispatch the perennial minor injuries it suffers and, given an opportunity, repairs major injuries almost equally well.

Since its surface is constantly shedding, it is renewing itself at all times. Its many nerves record all modalities of sensibility of touch, pain, and temperature, and it is therefore the largest sense organ of the body. Finally, the skin is the largest organ of personal identification and sexual attraction, being molded and marked differently in every individual and endowed with numerous subtle and gross epigamic adaptations.

Structure and nerve distribution

The skin is fashioned in such a way that it attains maximal strength and protection from the environment while remaining delicately in communication with it. Skin achieves maximal strength and pliability by being composed of numbers of layers oriented in such a way that each complements the others structurally and functionally. To allow a communication with the environment, countless nerves, some modified as specialized receptor end organs and others more or less structureless, come as close as possible to the surface layer, and nearly every skin organ is enwrapped by skeins of fine sensory nerves. The distribution of skin nerves supports what is already known from physiology: in most areas the skin is adapted for light-touch sensibility rather than deep pressure.

Human skin is enormously well supplied with blood vessels; it is pervaded with a tangled, though apparently orderly, mass of arteries, veins, and capillaries. Such a supply of blood, far in excess of the maximum biological needs of the skin itself, is evidence that the skin is at the service of the blood vascular system, functioning as a cooling device. To aid in this function, sweat glands pour water upon its surface, the evaporation of which absorbs heat from the skin. Sweat glands thus are ancillary devices of the blood vascular system. If the environment is cold and body heat must be conserved, cutaneous blood vessels contract in quick, successive rhythms, allowing only a small amount of blood to flow through them. When the environment is warm, they contract at long intervals, providing a free flow of blood. During muscular exertion, when great quantities of heat generated must be dissipated, blood flow through the skin is maximal. In addition to its control of body temperature, skin also plays a role in the regulation of blood pressure. Much of the flow of blood can be controlled by the opening and closing of certain sphincter-like vessels in the skin. These vessels allow the blood to circulate through the peripheral capillary beds or

to bypass them by being shunted directly from small arteries to veins.

In addition to an overly abundant, complex vascular bed, skin is also riddled by an intricate mesh of lymph vessels. In the more superficial parts of the dermis, minute lymph vessels that appear to terminate in blind sacs are affluents of a superficial lymphatic net that in turn opens into vessels that become progressively larger in the deeper portions of the dermis. The deeper, larger lymph vessels are embedded in the loose connective tissue bed surrounding veins. The walls of lymph vessels are so flabby and collapsed that they often escape notice in specimens prepared for microscopic studies. Their abundance, however, has been demonstrated by the injection of vital dyes inside the dermis and the observation of the clearance of the dye. Since lymph vessels have minimal or no musculature in their walls, the circulation of lymph is sluggish and largely controlled by such extrinsic forces as pressure, skeletal muscle action, massaging, and heat. Any external pressure exerted, even from a fixed dressing, interferes with its flow. Since skin plays a major role in immunological responses of the body, its lymphatic drainage is as significant as its blood vascular system.

Skin is an array of different layers, each layer of the stack having its own properties. Although the layers do not display a true orthogonal pattern, they nonetheless make skin comparable to plywood, which has much greater strength than a single board of the same thickness. There are two principal layers; on the surface is the entirely cellular epidermis, and beneath it the fibrous dermis. The epidermis is relatively thin and is itself veneered, being composed of four or five variably distinct layers. The dermis is much thicker and composed of two layers. It is the dermis that gives bulk to the skin; leather is tanned dermis.

Dermis and epidermis

PARTICULAR ASPECTS OF THE SKIN

The surface of the skin. The intact surface of the skin is pitted by the orifices of sweat glands and hair follicles and is furrowed by intersecting lines that delineate characteristic patterns. Every individual has roughly similar markings on any one part of the body, but the details are unique. The lines are oriented to indicate the general direction of elastic tension. Countless numbers of them, deep and shallow, together with the "pores," give each area of the body a characteristic topography; like the deeper furrows and ridges on the palms and soles, they are mostly established before birth. The fine details of each surface of the body are peculiar to each individual. Fingerprints are used as a means of personal identification because they have a high relief, more visible patternings, and can be obtained easily (see below *Dermatoglyphics*).

Not all lines on the surface of the skin are congenital; some are acquired after birth as a result of use or damage. Furrows on the forehead and face, those extending from the corners of the mouth to the wings of the nose, and others are acquired from years of wrinkling the brow or from certain fixed facial expressions such as frequent smiling; these and similar lines represent an accentuation of preexisting congenital lines that become strongly emphasized in old age. As the skin becomes less firm with aging, it also forms wrinkles. Certain occupations leave skin marks, which, depending upon duration and severity, may be transient or permanent.

The ventral surfaces of the hands and feet are etched by distinct alternating ridges and grooves that together comprise dermatoglyphics. The crest of each ridge is pockmarked at spaced intervals by the small, conical depressions of the orifices of sweat glands. The ridges follow variable courses, but their arrangements in specific areas have a consistent structural plan. Though apparently continuous, ridges have many interruptions and irregularities, branching and varying in length. Every small area of surface has ridge details not matched anywhere in the same individual or in any other individual, even in identical twins. This infallible signature makes dermatoglyphics the best-known physical characteristic for personal identification.

The epidermis. The epidermis is thicker on the palms

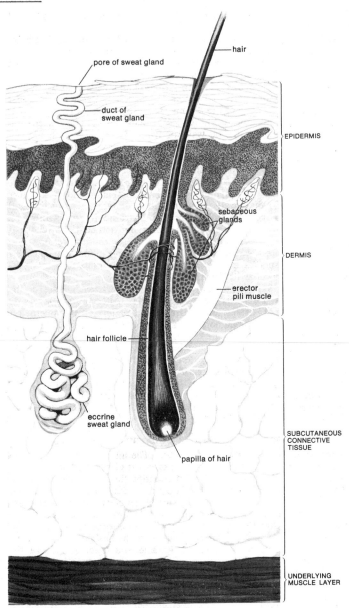

- hair
- pore of sweat gland
- duct of sweat gland
- EPIDERMIS
- sebaceous glands
- DERMIS
- erector pili muscle
- hair follicle
- eccrine sweat gland
- papilla of hair
- SUBCUTANEOUS CONNECTIVE TISSUE
- UNDERLYING MUSCLE LAYER

Section through human skin and underlying structures.
Adapted from *Cunningham's Textbook of Anatomy* edited by G.J. Romanes and published by Oxford University Press as an Oxford Medical Publication

General structure

and soles than it is anywhere else and is usually thicker on dorsal than on ventral surfaces. Omitting the fine details, it is divisible everywhere into a lower layer of living cells and a superficial layer of compact dead cells. All the cells, living or dead, are attached to one another by a series of specialized surfaces called attachment plaques or desmosomes. Thus, instead of being completely fused, the membranes of adjacent cells make zipper-like contacts, with fluid-filled spaces between the contact areas. This structural pattern insures a concatenation of cells to one another so that they cannot be sloughed off easily, and at the same time it also allows nutrient fluids to seep in from the vessels in the dermis. Epidermal cells, which multiply largely at the base in contact with the dermis, gradually ascend to the surface, manufacturing keratin as they go; they finally die in the upper part, forming a horny layer.

The epidermis is an epithelium of variable thickness. It is thickest on friction surfaces and thinnest over the eyelids, the lower parts of the abdomen, and around the external genitalia. Unlike that of most other mammals, it has an intricately sculptured underside and does not lie flat upon the dermis. Seen from the underside, there are straight and branching ridges and valleys, columns and pits, all finely punctuated. The complexity of the underside varies according to topography, and each pattern is characteristic of certain areas. Because of this unevenness, it is al-

most impossible to state the exact thickness of the epidermis. Furthermore, individual differences, sex, and aging have an enormous influence on the structure of the underside. Such labyrinthine patterns give human epidermis two unique advantages: it attains a more intimate connection with the subjacent dermis than if the surface were flat, and its source of dividing cells, the building blocks of the horny layer, is greatly increased.

The two major layers of the epidermis are a viable malpighian layer at the bottom, in contact with the dermis, and a dead corneal, or horny, layer on the surface. The cells of the malpighian layer that rest upon the dermis comprise the basal layer. Above the basal cells is a variously stratified prickle cell or "spinous" layer. Its upper cells blend gradually into a granular layer, so called because its cells contain particles of various sizes that stain with basic dyes and are called keratohyaline granules. The granular layer is often several cells deep in normally thick epidermis such as that in the palms and soles. A hyaline, transitional layer one to three cells deep is above the granular layer, interposed between it and the horny layer. In friction surfaces, the backs of the hands, and a few other surfaces, the hyaline layer attains considerable thickness.

Epidermal cells make contact with each other by way of many punctate areas of adhesion. When the epidermis is

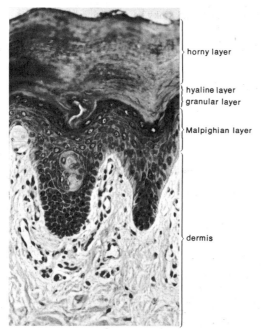

horny layer

hyaline layer
granular layer

Malpighian layer

dermis

Photomicrograph of a vertical section of epidermis from a finger.

William Montagna

Cell
division
in
epidermis

dehydrated, its cells remain in contact with one another, but the membrane at the points of adhesion between two adjacent cells is stretched out, giving rise to artifactual structures called "intercellular bridges." Midway between each intercellular bridge, at the actual place of contact, the adjacent cell membranes attain a spindle-shaped swelling, a "desmosome," that has received much attention from electron microscopists. The membranes of the basal cells above the dermis, not being in contact with the membranes of other cells, have half desmosomes, or hemidesmosomes. The cells of the basal layer of the epidermis are columnar or cuboidal, with the long axis usually oriented perpendicularly to the surface. As these cells divide and ascend to the surface, they become progressively larger and of different shapes, oriented horizontally to the surface and increasingly flattened until they reach the dead horny layer, where their appearance becomes scalelike in form.

Reproducibility and differentiation in the epidermis must occur linearly. Cells divide at a constant rate, lest they become depleted with the continual shedding at the surface of the horny layer. Division occurs chiefly in the basal layer, but where the epidermis is very thick, it also occurs a little higher. Cell division in the epidermis is rhythmic and cyclic. It has been estimated that normal human-skin epidermal cells take about 27 days, or roughly one month, to travel from the basal layer to the surface. Under certain pathological conditions (for example, psoriasis), the renewal process is greatly accelerated and may occur in one week or less.

Histologists who are accustomed to dehydrating and embedding skin in paraffin and sectioning it vertically have often dismissed the horny layer as a flimsy structure of no great structural interest. Under the light microscope such preparations show the horny layer as a fragmented, lacy, structureless residue above the granular layer. This debris has little resemblance to the horny layer in living skin; in fresh-frozen sections it is thicker and always compact. The electron microscopist has found that this layer has a precise architecture and that even under minor disturbance its integrity is altered. It can be stripped in individual layers with adhesive tape, or removed intact with vesicating agents. When intact, the horny layer is a substantial structure of closely bound cells, which, though dead, are well-organized entities. Interposed between external and internal environments, the epidermis is sensitive to changes in both. Having no intrinsic vascular supply, the epidermis is dependent upon the dermis, from which nutritive and other essential substances seep in

through the intercellular spaces to guide its growth and differentiation.

The cells of the epidermis readily adapt to internal and external changes, and they have superlative regenerative powers. Epidermal metabolic activity is geared primarily to the replacement of cells lost on the surface and to the production of highly specific chemical substances that prevent both penetration by noxious substances and the escape of vital substances from within.

The most important mission of the malpighian layer is to form the dead outer covering of the horny layer. This is the final product of epidermal differentiation. The substances manufactured by epidermal cells have been loosely called "keratin." There is confusion as to what is meant by keratin, because a number of substances with distinctly different chemical composition are known by this name. Keratin in the horny layer is a mixture of sulfur-poor fibrous protein surrounded by a sulfur-rich amorphous protein, the two components enclosed in a thickened, cornified plasma membrane. The process of keratinization begins as soon as cells move up from the basal into the spinous layer and when fibrous proteins, microfilaments, begin to form. In their ascension to the surface, cells increase in size and in their content of filaments. In the granular layer proteinous keratohyalin granules are also synthesized, and the cells become replete with both fibrous proteins and granules. In the next stop upward from the granular layer, the granules and most cell organelles become dissipated as a sulfur-rich amorphous substance that stabilizes the horizontal orientation of the filamentous proteins. In the meantime, cell membranes keratinize by becoming a sulfur-rich amorphous protein in their own right. This melange is epidermal keratin. The horny layer also synthesizes lipids, waxes, and sterols, which combine to give it sturdiness and plasticity.

The skin of human beings is variously coloured, with remarkable individual variations occurring even within members of the same race. In addition to the blood in the superficial vessels, the colour of human skin is determined by melanin, a pigment manufactured by special dendritic cells, melanocytes, that reside mostly below or between the basal cells of the epidermis. The number of melanocytes per surface area in any one part of the body is roughly the same within and between races, and the blondest Europeans may have as many melanocytes as the darkest Negro. This means that the quality rather than the quantity of these cells determines the intensity of pigmentation in the skin. When, on exposure to sunlight, the skin becomes tanned, the resident melanocytes have not increased in number; only their activity has increased. Melanocytes are an integral part of the epidermis, having migrated there from the neural crest during embryonic life. These cells can be compared to unicellular glands with long, thin, branching, streamer-like processes that worm their way between the epidermal cells in their immediate vicinity, making up a constellation of epidermal cells around each melanocyte. Melanin is produced inside the cytoplasm and travels to the dendrites. Epidermal cells in contact with the melanin-laden dendrites actually phagocytose the tips of the dendrites. Once inside the epidermal cells, melanin granules tend to move above the nucleus, forming a shroud over it. Such an orientation of melanin suggests that it is there to protect the cells from damaging ultraviolet rays, and experimental evidence in tissue culture has left no doubt that this is the case.

In addition to protecting the skin from ultraviolet light irradiation, epidermal pigmentation forms epigamic markings. The heavy pigmentation of the nipples and areolae of breasts, as well as that in the labia minora, or penis and scrotum, functions solely as a sexual attractant.

In addition to pigment-producing cells in the basal layer, the epidermis also contains branched cells farther up in the spinous layer. These cells of Langerhans have the same shape as melanocytes but form no melanin, and, in spite of much imaginative investigation, no one seems to know what they do.

Still another type of cells, "Merkel cells," is said to be normally resident at the base of the epidermis. Apparently associated with nerves that penetrate the epidermis, Mer-

Pigmenta-
tion of skin

kel cells have been demonstrated well only in the skin of some mammals. There is little doubt that they are also present in human skin, but they have not been shown satisfactorily.

Even in perfectly normal skin, one finds variable numbers of lymphocytes between epidermal cells. There has been much speculation about their significance, but it remains obscure. Actually, lymphocytes are encountered often in all epithelia, and their presence may reflect only their wandering proclivity; once inside the epidermis, they simply die.

The epidermis is a precisely tailored tissue, adapted in every detail to protect the body against its environment. Its architecture, the balance in the rates of the wear and replacement of its cells, the physical and chemical properties of the horny layer, the specific kinds of keratin and lipids that it produces, all cooperate in safeguarding the integrity of the organism against the environment.

The pilary system.   Man's body hair has little protective value even in hirsute persons. Eyelashes and eyebrows, the hairs inside the external ears and nostrils, and those around the anogenital orifices have obviously useful functions, and scalp hair is often thick enough to afford some protection. Beard and mustache, and axillary and pubic hair, are embellishments. Other than minimal protection and adornment, the only important biologic role of man's hair is its participation in the sensory mechanism.

All hair follicles are surrounded by sensory nerves, and pressure on the hair shaft is transmitted to these nerves. Other mammals, including subhuman primates, have highly specialized sensitive hair follicles around the eyes, lips, and muzzle. These "tactile" hairs, known as vibrissae or whiskers, are particularly large in nocturnal mammals. The follicles from which they emerge are rich in nerves and are surrounded by a sinus filled with blood. Man is the only animal with no sinus hair follicles; but his hair follicles, particularly those of the face, are well supplied with nerves, and his skin is probably more sensitive than that of any other mammal.

Except for those on the scalp, beard, and mustache, most body hairs grow to a predictable length peculiar to the body area and individual; they are shed periodically and are subsequently replaced by other hairs of the same length. Hairs do not grow continuously; the follicles that produce them have precisely controlled periods of growth and rest. If this were not the case, we would require periodic shearing, as do sheep.

Hair and its functions

Hairs are manufactured by follicles, tubelike organs attached to the epidermis at the surface and extending through most or all the depth of the skin. The bottom of a follicle is shaped like a scallion, the bulbous part representing the growing end. Follicles grow at an angle to the surface. Two-thirds of the way up on the obtuse angle is a bulge; attached to it are wisps of smooth muscle fibre that on contracting pull the follicle to a more or less perpendicular position. This action also puckers the skin into a mound on the surface, a "goose pimple."

In the centre of the follicle is the hair, with a root extending to the bulbous end. After a period of growth, when the hair has reached its characteristic length, the terminal part of the hair attains a clubbed, rather than a cylindrical, shape. Fibrous rootlets anchor the club to the surrounding tissue of the follicle. While forming the club, the follicle shrivels up, the lower part becoming largely dissipated. A resting follicle can be recognized at once by the clubbed hair, by its short size, and its uniquely different structure.

Follicles remain dormant for variable periods of time. When they become active again, they reconstruct a bulb that manufactures a new hair. As the new hair works its way to the surface, it loosens the club hair from its moorings and causes it to be shed.

Hairs vary in colour, diameter, and contour. The different colours result from variations in amounts, distribution, and types of melanin pigment in them, as well as from variations in surface structure, causing light to be reflected in different ways. Hairs may be coarse or so thin and colorless as to be nearly invisible. Straight hairs are round, while wavy hairs are alternately oval and round. Very curly and kinky hairs are shaped like twisted ribbons.

Human hair grows about one-third of a millimetre per day. This means that if the colour or shape of a hair is altered as it is formed, several days must elapse before the effect is visible on the surface. Tales of the hair's becoming entirely gray overnight stem from fantasies.

The hair follicles of the scalp differ from the others in their ability to grow sometimes for years without interruption, producing hair of considerable length. It is surprising, therefore, that the human scalp, in which the hair follicles are dense and grow vigorously, should become bald in such large number of individuals. Baldness is not a disease but a systematic involution of hair follicles culminating in organs similar to the primitive embryonic follicles, without necessarily a diminution in absolute numbers. There are about 150,000 hairs on the scalp.

All human beings are, to a degree, bald. Until late in fetal life, the forehead is indistinguishable from the scalp, with no line of demarcation between the two. After the fifth month of gestation, the follicles in the rest of the scalp grow larger, but those of the forehead do not. After birth the hairs on the forehead become even smaller and nearly invisible. The hair line of newborn infants is usually indistinct; the familial pattern of a hair line is established late in childhood, through a process that is identical with that of baldness. When male pattern baldness sets in, in the late 20s or earlier, the follicles affected do exactly the same things as those at the hair line. Involution of hair follicles also takes place elsewhere on the body of infants. Newborn infants are often more hirsute than they are months or even years later. In rare cases of hirsutism, the forehead may be as heavily clothed with hairs as the scalp.

Baldness is a natural tendency of the follicles of the scalp to become very small as individuals become mature and is a secondary sex characteristic.

The sebaceous glands.   The sebaceous glands usually grow attached to hair follicles and pour their secretion, sebum, inside the canal of the follicle. Hairs emerging on the surface of the skin are coated with sebum. In a few areas of the body, disproportionately large sebaceous glands are associated with very small hair follicles; in other areas, the glands are altogether free of follicles.

The outstanding structural feature of sebaceous glands is their mode of forming sebum. Undifferentiated glandular cells gradually synthesize and accumulate fat globules in their cytoplasm and become progressively larger and distorted. When they have finally utilized all their vital resources, they die and disintegrate. Sebum is the accumulation of dead, fragmented sebaceous cells and other cellular debris from the pilary canal. The pressure created by sebum in the body of the glands, capillary traction through the ducts, and movements and compression of the skin all aid the glands in pouring their sebum onto the surface.

Scientists who have searched for the specific functions of sebum have had scant success. This semiliquid mixture of bizarre fatty acids, triglycerides, waxes, cholesterol, and cellular detritus does not emulsify readily, is toxic to living tissues, and seems to serve little purpose except as an emollient. Some investigators have dismissed sebum as a useless substance and sebaceous glands as archaic organs that do greater harm than good. Yet man has more and larger glands than most mammals, and there is a specific plan in their distribution: they are largest and most numerous on the face and around the anogenital surfaces. The skin around the nose, mouth, and forehead and over the cheekbones has beds of gigantic glands, the secretion of which keeps these surfaces constantly oily. The sebaceous glands evenly spaced in rows at the border of the eyelids, meibomian glands, are so large that they are easily seen with the naked eye when one everts the eyelids before a mirror. The glands on the genitalia produce copious amounts of smegma.

Only man has rich populations of sebaceous glands on the hairless surfaces of the lips; these glands increase in number and size as individuals mature. The inside of the cheeks also has many large sebaceous glands, and occasionally there are glands even on the gums and tongue. No one knows their significance.

The size and function of sebaceous glands are controlled mostly by androgenic hormones. The glands, large in newborn infants, become smaller during childhood, begin to enlarge in early puberty, and attain full growth in adults. They are larger and more active in men than in women; the level of the total output of sebum, a valid index of their activity, closely parallels the levels of androgenic hormones in individuals. The development of these glands is minimal in eunuchs, but increases when they are treated with androgens.

In spite of our ignorance of its biological significance, sebum is abundantly secreted upon certain specific surfaces of the body; and it cannot be assumed that sebaceous glands, so prominent on the human body, are necessarily archaic.

The sweat glands. The two categories of sweat glands are those called apocrine, which are usually associated with hair follicles, and eccrine, which are not. The two types share practically no biologic properties; they have distinctly different origins, different structures, and different functions.

Most other mammals have numerous apocrine glands on the hairy skin; eccrine glands are usually absent from the hairy skin and limited to friction surfaces. In nonhuman primates there is a tendency for the number of eccrine sweat glands over the body to increase in progressively advanced animals at the same time that the number of apocrine glands becomes reduced. Prosimians have only apocrine glands in the hairy skin; eccrine glands begin to appear in some of the higher forms. The great apes either have equal numbers or have more eccrine than apocrine glands. Man has the most eccrine glands, with apocrine glands restricted to specific areas.

Strictly speaking, apocrine glands have nothing to do with sweating. They appear late in fetal development (5 to 5½ months), nearly everywhere on the body, and mostly associated with hair follicles. Most of these rudiments disappear within a few weeks except in the external ear canal, in the axilla, on the nipples of the breasts, around the navel, and on the anogenital surfaces; single glands may be found anywhere. From this, one might speculate that the ancestors of man had apocrine glands widely distributed over the body, and the embryonic rudiments may be reminders of the history of a once widespread organ system. In the areas mentioned above, the glands are large and numerous. In the axilla, they are so large that the coils press upon each other, forming adhesions and cross-shunts of such complexity that the glands are more spongy than tubular. The complex of these large apocrine glands interspersed with an equal number of eccrine sweat glands in the axilla comprises what is known as the axillary organ, one of the most characteristic features of man's skin. Other than man, only chimpanzees and gorillas have axillary organs.

In spite of their large size, apocrine glands secrete only small amounts of a milky, viscid, pale gray, whitish, yellow, or reddish fluid that contributes very little to axillary sweat. If eccrine glands were not there, the axilla would be relatively dry.

Fresh and sterile eccrine and apocrine secretions are fairly odourless. When in contact with bacteria on the surface of the axilla, apocrine sweat is decomposed and emits the characteristic axillary odour. The odour of individual human beings comes mostly from apocrine secretion, with some contribution from sebum. Since the body odours of all other animals have a social or sexual significance, it can be assumed that this is the archetypal purpose of apocrine secretion, even in man.

Apocrine glands are dispensable organs, unnecessary to the biological economy of modern man. They are primarily scent glands that secrete in response to a variety of stressful stimulations. The presence of eccrine sweat in the same areas provides a vehicle in which the viscid, concentrated apocrine secretion is diluted, brought into contact with micro-organisms that decompose it, and distributed over larger surfaces to allow a better aeration and thus a stronger odour.

In most mammals eccrine sweat glands are either absent or limited to the friction surfaces. Eccrine glands are found in the hairy skin of some primates; chimpanzees and gorillas have more eccrine than apocrine glands, and man has 2,000,000 to 5,000,000 of them, with an average distribution of 150 to 340 per square centimetre. They are most numerous on the palms and soles and then, in decreasing order, on the head, trunk, and extremities. Some individuals have more glands than others, but there is no difference between the number in men and in women.

Eccrine sweat glands

The specific function of sweat glands is to secrete water upon the surface so that it can cool the skin when it evaporates. The purpose of the glands on the palms and soles, however, is to keep these surfaces damp, to prevent flaking or hardening of the horny layer, and thus to maintain tactile sensibility. A dry hand does not grip well and is minimally sensitive. Sweat glands, then, can be divided into those that respond to thermal stimulation, the function of which is thermoregulation, and those that respond to psychic stimuli and keep friction surfaces moist. This makes a clear-cut division between the glands on the hairy surfaces and those on the palms and soles. The axilla, though a hairy surface, has adjacent fields that respond either to thermal or to psychic stimuli but not to both. In addition to thermal and psychic sweating, some individuals sweat on the face and forehead in response to certain chemical substances. The glands on the palms and soles develop at about 3½ months of gestation, whereas those on the hairy skin are the last appendages to form, appearing at 5 to 5½ months, when all the other structures are already formed. This dyschrony may represent a fundamental difference in the evolutionary history of the two types of glands. Those on palms and soles, which appear first and are present in all but the hooved mammals, may be more ancient; whereas those glands in the hairy skin, which respond to thermal stimuli, may be more recent organs.

The sweat glands on the hairy skin of subhuman primates probably function subliminally or not at all, although they are structurally similar to those of man. The skin of monkeys and apes remains dry even in a hot environment. Profuse thermal sweating in man, then, seems to be a new function. Eccrine sweat glands respond to a variety of drugs with different properties; they often respond differently in different individuals under nearly identical conditions and sometimes even respond differently in the same individual. Notwithstanding these apparent vagaries in function, eccrine sweat glands are indispensable to man and function perennially though insensibly. Their secretion is controlled by the autonomic nervous system. Sweating is essential for keeping the body from becoming overheated.

Nails. A major characteristic of primates is that their fingers and toes terminate in nails rather than in claws. One can speculate that the development of nails into flattened plates reflects the discontinuation of their use for digging or for defending and attacking. In a broad sense, nails are analogous to hair, having similar composition (keratin) and some basic structural entities. Even the genesis and mode of growth are comparable, but not identical, with those of hair. Although apparently simple structures, nails are formed by complex and still poorly understood structural entities, referred to as nail organs. Unlike hair, nails grow continuously, with no normal periods of rest; if their free edges were protected from wear, they would extend to prodigious lengths, growing in a twisted fashion like a ram's horns. Nails grow about 0.1 mm per day or roughly one-third more slowly than hair. Growth is somewhat slower in winter than in summer and slower in infants and old people than in vigorous young adults. It requires about three months for a whole nail to replace itself. A number of factors can alter normal nail growth, among them age, trauma, poisons, and organic disorders. Habitual nail biting speeds up growth, and certain occupational uses can cause increase in thickness. The nail-forming organ is particularly sensitive to physiologic changes; during stressful periods, prolonged fever, and in response to noxious drugs, nails become cracked, thinner, thicker, furrowed, or otherwise deformed, or they may be shed. Such sensitivity of response should make nails relatively good indices of the health of individuals; but because of their ready response to so many internal and external factors, and because changes in them often occur without a known reason, signs of abnormality can be misleading or difficult to interpret. Like hair, the visible part of the nail plate is a dead structure. Defects inflicted upon it by mechanical means that do not disturb the underlying living tissue are eventually cast off at the free border.

Nail root   Nails have a root, buried underneath the skin, a plate that is firmly attached to a nail bed underneath, and a free edge. Depending upon its thickness and the quality of its surface, the nail plate may be pink or whitish; the nail itself is translucent and colourless, allowing the colour of the blood in the superficial capillaries in the nail bed to show through. At its base the nail plate may have a whitish, arched marking called a lunula. Always present on thumb nails, lunulae may be present or absent in the other fingers and are nearly always absent in the little finger. There are variations in different individuals and even between the two hands of the same person; such variations are probably controlled by genetic factors.

The nail itself consists of firmly cemented keratinized cells, flattened horizontally to the surface. Whereas the surface of nail plates appears to be smooth, it is lined by parallel, longitudinal furrows, more strongly etched in some persons than in others and always more prominent in the aged. These markings have some correspondence to the more pronounced grooves and ridges on the undersurface of the plate.

Nails grow from the matrix at the base of the nail root. During the early part of the journey, matrix cells multiply and move forward, synthesizing keratin, underneath the fold of skin (eponychium) at the base of the nail. Once exposed to the surface, the nail is fully formed. The nail plate seems to glide over the nail bed but is firmly attached to it. The entire tissue, nail bed and plate, most likely moves forward as a unit. The nail bed has often been called sterile matrix, since it adds little or nothing to the nail plate. Yet under certain pathologic conditions, it assumes keratinizing activities that result in a variably thickened or deformed nail plate.

Less effective than claws in digging or gouging, the flattened nail is still an excellent adaptation that has added much to the development of manipulative skills. Nails not only protect the tips of fingers but also give them firmness and the ability to pick up or make contact with minute objects. Claws would be useless for such functions.

Summation. The outstanding features of the skin of man are its apparent nakedness and the ability to sweat profusely. Since the only hairs that grow luxuriantly upon his body have no practical value in protecting him from his environment, man's hair is largely ornamental. Baldness is universal and represents another sign of man's advancing nakedness. As man's skin lost its hair cover, it underwent many adaptive changes. The outer horny layer, while remaining thin to allow suppleness, attained remarkable biological ruggedness, protecting the skin from physical and chemical injury and from the invasion of micro-organisms. The skin is employed by the blood vascular system to serve as its major cooling device and as a safety factor to control blood pressure. To better perform its thermoregulatory services, skin has developed eccrine sweat glands, which pour water upon its surface so that it can absorb body heat as it evaporates. Since heat is generated constantly, the glands secrete perennially; when greater amounts of heat are produced by muscle action or a hot environment, sweating becomes profuse. The sweat on the palms and soles functions to keep these surfaces soft, enhancing grip and tactile sensibility. Though apparently identical in structure and function, the glands on the hairy skin and those on the palms and soles have different ontogenetic histories, different central controls, and different functional purposes.

Continuously exposed to trauma, skin has inherent mechanisms that enable it to adapt to new situations and to withstand the onslaught of injurious environmental conditions.

BIBLIOGRAPHY. W. MONTAGNA, *The Structure and Function of Skin*, 2nd ed. (1962), the only textbook in English that describes the details of structure and function of human skin; S. ROTHMAN, *Physiology and Biochemistry of the Skin* (1954), the only comprehensive accumulation of information, although somewhat outdated, on the physiology and composition of human skin; W. MONTAGNA and R.L. DOBSON (eds.), *Advances in the Biology of Skin*, vol. 9, *Hair Growth* (1969), a compendium of the most recent data on the problems of hair growth; A.J. ROOK, D.S. WILKINSON, and F.J.G. EBELING (eds.), *Textbook of Dermatology*, 2 vol. (1968), the most outstanding work on normal and pathologic human skin; W. MONTAGNA and W.C. LOBITZ, JR. (eds.), *The Epidermis* (1964), an accumulation of nearly all available knowledge on the epidermis from differentiation to composition; E.H. MERCER, *Keratin and Keratinization* (1961), an excellent book, comprehensive and well-written, on keratinization.

(W.M.)

Skin Diseases

Although the skin is normally and conveniently regarded as a single organ, it is by no means homogeneous over the body, nor even in any single area (see SKIN, HUMAN). The transplantation of a piece of skin from one body site to another, except to the exact position on the opposite side, will make clear that it is out of place. Each skin area has characteristics sufficiently different that they can be recognized visually, although it is not always possible to describe the differences in exact words by scientific measurements.

Each area of skin consists, from the inside out, of a fat layer, a dermis, and an outer covering or epidermis. The dermis contains the special appendages for producing hair and nails, glands, connective tissue, a special arrangement of blood vessels and mechanisms to control blood flow, a specialized lymphatic system, nerve endings to detect a variety of sensations, cells with special functions, and muscle for moving the hairs and skin.

The human epidermis contains two types of melanocyte cells, for producing pigment, and three "races" of epithelial cells. These latter cells operate to form the hair follicle, the sweat duct openings, and the rest of the epidermis.

All of these elements of the skin's structure are blended into a cohesive whole, but disease may affect them individually, severally, or all together.

The skin surface is divided by body part involved into the following main and special areas (it will be noted that there is overlap among them): (1) the trunk and limbs; (2) the chest, abdomen, upper and lower back; (3) the head and neck; (4) the scalp, face, eyelids, ears, front, back, and sides of neck; (5) the genitalia and perianal area; (6) the arm and forearm, the thigh and leg, and buttocks; (7) the front and back, or flexor and extensor, aspects of the limbs; (8) the hands and feet, dorsa, and palms or soles; (9) the main folds or flexures, such as the knee and elbow, sides of the neck, armpits and groins, under the breasts, the natal cleft, and around the umbilicus; (10) other special areas such as the ear canal and the lips.

The range of diseases of human skin is extremely wide. Because skin is visible, many temporary or permanent symptomless changes, which would pass unnoticed in an internal organ, can be observed. The great diversity of skin changes is partly attributable to the differences between human skin and that of animals as a result of evolutionary development, partly because of its complex multiple structure, and partly because the skin can be affected by almost every known pathogenetic process. Moreover, the physical signs of a skin disease may vary in so many different ways that they are often recorded by the observer as different diseases until more is known about their causation.

The diagnosis of skin diseases is determined from the patient's history of his complaint, a detailed examination of the skin lesions, and special investigative procedures. Examination of the skin consists of analyzing the signs of disease in three parameters: first, the distribution of any lesions, noting both the affected and unaffected areas; second, the various individual elements of which each lesion is composed; and third, the pattern or arrangement (or absence of it) of any lesions on the skin.

SKIN LESIONS

Arrangement of lesions

The elemental lesions, or individual elements or spots of skin abnormality, may be present in various degrees, in almost any combination, and arranged in numerous different ways. The result is that the number of pictures which skin rashes may present is virtually limitless, no two being identical. They may have a uniform pattern over the affected areas or be distributed at random. Certain configurations are sufficiently characteristic to have diagnostic significance, although not all the lesions will be arranged in the same pattern. Examples of recognizable patterns are: (1) annular (ring-shaped), arcuate (arched), or polycyclic (in many rings); (2) concentric rings; (3) disks and plaques, or flat areas that tend to coalesce; (4) large sheets with ill-defined borders; (5) linear or streaked; (6) retiform (in the shape of a net) and variegated; (7) grouped in clusters; (8) symmetrical or asymmetrical; (9) universal or generalized.

Examination of the lesion. The analysis of a skin rash in this manner produces morphological descriptions and diagnostic nomenclature under which skin diseases have been classified in the past. Knowledge of the anatomy, physiology, biochemistry, and biology of the skin has advanced so much in the past few decades that progress is now being made towards a classification on the basis of pathology and biological changes and the factors responsible for them. With suitable test procedures, it is possible to analyze the cellular and subcellular structure of individual parts of the skin; the functional activity of the separate elements such as production of keratin, the fibrous protein in the outer skin, and cell growth, sweat delivery and absorption, hair growth, pigment production, distribution, and removal, and cutaneous permeability; and also some of the biochemical pathways in the tissues.

The most important procedure, however, is a detailed histological examination of one or more biopsy specimens from the affected areas, in order to observe and attempt to interpret the changes in terms of pathological processes.

Pathological types. The skin is susceptible to all of the types of pathological change that affect other tissues. These include congenital abnormalities, effects of trauma, inflammation, metabolic disorders, neoplasia, and degenerative changes.

In addition, the skin, like other tissues, exhibits many diseases, such as psoriasis and rheumatoid arthritis, that do not readily fit in to any of the above pathological types, though future research may provide more information. Several different concepts of disease have been proposed at various times to explain them, for example, stress, psychosomatic factors, and auto-immunity. However, each of these concepts so far lacks convincing proof.

Congenital abnormalities

Each of the different components incorporated in the skin may be the site of a congenital and familial, or inherited, abnormality. The aberration may be generalized throughout the skin or localized to a small, large, or multiple area. A localized abnormality, called a nevus (a mole or birthmark, although it need not actually be present at birth), is a congenital abnormality, in structure or function, of cells, tissues, or organs. Such abnormalities are most frequently found in the skin and may serve as distinctive markings on passports or police records. A nevus may remain unchanged throughout life or resolve itself over several years, be slowly progressive, or sometimes give rise to malignant change after a long period of time.

Examples of generalized congenital abnormalities are epidermolysis bullosa and xeroderma pigmentosum. In epidermolysis bullosa, a genetic defect in the adhesion mechanism between the dermis and epidermis permits mild trauma to break the adhesion and allow tissue fluid to flow into the gap and form a blister. Xeroderma pigmentosum involves a genetic defect in the normal enzyme

mechanism for excising and replacing a radiation-damaged segment of the gene chain in the cell nuclei.

The skin is more exposed to trauma than any other tissue. An injury may be physical or chemical, or caused by actinic, or radiant, energy; the damage may be temporary or permanent. Continuous or intermittent trauma may result in skin thickening, such as callosities (abnormal hardnesses), and corns, while more acute trauma—whether physical or chemical—can cause erosions, ulcers, or burns, followed by permanent scarring if the dermis is injured. Less severe chemical injury can lead to inflammation and dermatitis.

Excessive actinic radiation, whether from the sun, X-rays, or other source, will, if acute, cause dilatation of capillaries, along with redness and swelling, followed by scaling, as in sunburn, with subsequent stimulation of the melanocytes to produce suntan. Prolonged exposure to actinic radiation may produce damage to the dermal connective tissue which may be irreversible and later induce skin cancer in the epithelium (see also RADIATION INJURY).

Inflammation

Many skin diseases are manifestations of acute or chronic inflammation. The main causes of such inflammation are (1) infective agents, (2) physical and chemical agents, and (3) immunologic changes. Almost every type of biological agent can infect the skin—viruses, Rickettsia, bacteria, fungi, worms, and arthropods. The discovery of modern antibiotics and chemotherapeutic drugs, and the improvement of public health measures, has greatly reduced the incidence of this type of infection among inhabitants of developed countries. In the developing nations of Africa and Asia, however, infection still accounts for at least 60 percent of all skin diseases.

In contrast, physicochemically induced inflammation is more common in developed and industrialized countries. The principal manifestation is dermatitis, or eczema. (There is no uniform agreement in the use of the words eczema and dermatitis, but there is an increasing tendency among dermatologists to regard them as synonyms.) Dermatitis is a pathological change in the upper dermis and epidermis that can have many different causes. Contact dermatitis is produced by contact of the skin with physical or chemical agents, including drugs, cosmetics, or even clothing, as well as a wide variety of industrial and domestic products.

With the development of modern immunology, many skin diseases of previously unknown cause have been found to be associated with (though not necessarily caused by) immunologic reactions. Some examples are lupus erythematosus, which may also be systemic; pemphigus, with its crops of blisters; dermatomyositis, an inflammation of the skin and the subcutaneous tissues and muscles; and vasculitis, an inflamation of the vessels in the subcutaneous tissues.

The two well-established types of allergic reaction in the skin are urticaria, or skin eruptions, caused by an immunoglobulin antibody circulating in the blood, and allergic contact dermatitis mediated by lymphocytes. Immunologic reactions are also the mechanisms mostly responsible for inflammatory diseases such as erythema multiforme, erythema nodosum, drug-caused eruptions, the rashes of such infectious fevers as measles and scarlet fever, and reactions to such infections as those of tuberculosis, syphilis, and ringworm.

Metabolic disorders

The normal metabolic activities of the human body may be upset when certain internal organs malfunction and thus bring about a variety of diseases. Manifestations of these diseases may show specific and diagnostic changes in the skin. Cells in the skin alone, moreover, may produce abnormal or excessive amounts of metabolic products such as lipid, mucin, and amyloid, causing pathological skin conditions. A dietary deficiency of protein produces the skin and hair changes of a disease known as kwashiorkor; lack of vitamin A causes a dry skin change called phrynoderma; vitamin B deficiency causes dry, fissured lips and sore tongue; while insufficient dietary vitamin C causes hemorrhages in the skin and horniness around the hair follicles (see also VITAMIN; NUTRITION

AND DIET, HUMAN; NUTRITIONAL DISEASES AND DISORDERS).

Each of the cell types contributing to the structure of the dermis and epidermis may undergo benign or malignant change. At times the distinctions between nevi and benign and malignant growths are ill-defined and difficult to determine.

Aging in the skin is principally a connective tissue change in the dermis that produces the typical signs. The structural arrangement of the fibres is modified, the tissue becomes less elastic, and its mass diminishes. The changes are greatly enhanced by continued exposure to ultraviolet light and hence are most prominent on the sun-exposed skin of such people as farmers, seamen, and those living in sunny, tropical climates. The changes are much less pronounced in Negro and Mongoloid than in Caucasian skin, and, among Caucasians, less in the skin of brunettes than that of blondes.

THE EPIDERMIS

The upper (outer) part of the dermis and the papillae are so intimately related to the epithelium of the epidermis that they can be regarded as a single dermo-epidermal unit in disease processes. The dermis controls and influences the growth of the epidermis, so that the source of pathological change in the epidermis is frequently sought in the dermis.

Congenital abnormalities. Since the principal function of the epidermis is to form the horny layer of keratin, lipid, and other components of the outer skin, disease affecting the epidermis is often characterized by a patchy or generalized disturbance of keratinization. Ichthyosis ("like fish skin"), a genetic disorder in which the horny layer develops visible flakes, is thought to be caused by an enzyme "error" in the synthesis of the keratin layer, probably in the formation of its biomolecular arrangement. The condition may, however, be acquired in association with Hodgkin's disease (a malignant lymphosarcoma), or from treatment with a drug, triparanol, which interferes with lipid metabolism. Hyperkeratosis is the formation of excessive keratin. Thick keratin, or callus, is normal on certain sites, such as the heels, but it may be induced (a callosity) by persistent friction or pressure, often as a result of certain occupations or habits. Examples are to be found on the hands of carpenters, shoemakers, upholsterers. A corn is an impacted mass of keratin caused by pressure over a bony point. An increase of keratin may be the result of a genetic abnormality (keratodermia) affecting the palms and soles (and, less commonly, other areas) in varied patterns. One type is associated with cancer of the esophagus. Sometimes the whole epidermis over small or large areas is malformed (an epidermal nevus), producing a rough, heaped-up or warty surface.

To cure the condititon surgically, the underlying dermis must be excised at the same time. Seborrheic warts (or basal cell papillomas) are the extremely common flesh coloured or brown-to-black pigmented warty lesions that are found especially on the trunk in middle-aged and older people. They are benign proliferations of the basal cell layer of the epidermis, which contains the melanocytes and forms a small, cauliflower-like proliferation containing keratin crypts and cysts. They may be regarded as late-developing nevi.

Dandruff. An extremely common disturbance of normal keratinization is dandruff, in which the rate of cell turnover of the epidermis is uneven and may be as high as two or three times normal, in certain places on the scalp. The horny layers in these areas are irregular and distorted, the keratinocytes being malformed or nucleated (separating in large groups). This irregular horny layer provides a milieu in which normal surface bacteria and yeasts multiply considerably. This condition of the scalp is not considered to be primarily infectious because reduction of the organisms by appropriate drugs does not cure it.

Infections. Skin surface normally is never sterile. At birth, or soon after, it becomes populated with bacteria, which all but the most stringent measures fail to remove.

The three main resident organisms on the surface are micrococci, diphtheroids, and the acne bacillus. Transient organisms, in a "carrier state" without inducing an infection, are commonly found in many diseases, such as psoriasis or eczema, in which the horny layer is abnormal.

Pathogenic infective agents may penetrate under the horny layer, often through a small break in the skin, and cause inflammation. Staphylococci and streptococci produce impetigo, in which the bacteria are present with pus cells in blisters filled with serous fluid, covered by the horny layer. Streptococci may spread more extensively and deeper through the skin, producing conditions of erysipelas and cellulitis. These are readily cured with appropriate antibiotics.

Many viruses are epidermotropic; they invade epidermal cells, gaining entrance either from outside, via a breach in the horny layer, or from inside, by way of the bloodstream or even the peripheral nerves. The most common ones are the viruses causing warts and molluscum contagiosum ("water warts"). Though most frequent on the hands and feet, including the soles (plantar warts), warts may occur anywhere. When the virus invades the nuclei of epidermal cells it stimulates growth so that a small tumour is produced. These may resolve spontaneously or following psychic influences (by hypnosis or "wart charming"), or may have to be removed or destroyed by physical or chemical means. In western Europe, as well as much of the rest of the civilized world, over the past two decades there has been an enormous increase of warts, and no effective drug has been found to cure them, nor has immunization been successful.

Herpes simplex ("fever blisters," "cold sores") and herpes zoster (shingles) are two virus infections that appear as small clusters of vesicles in which the epidermal cells they invade are killed. But the virus is itself then neutralized by an antibody. Examples of other virus infections are orf ("sheep pox"), milkers' nodes, and hand, foot, and mouth disease.

Herpes infections

Fungi and yeasts live preferentially in dead material at temperatures lower than blood heat. The keratinous horny layer is ideally suited and many different species of fungi may infect human skin, producing mild or acute inflammation by their secretions, which diffuse through the epidermis. The ecology of human fungal infections throughout the world is constantly changing. In two decades, for example, infection with *Trichophyton rubrum*, a species of ringworm, has spread westward over the Pacific Ocean and United States and eastward over Asia and Europe from China, where it has been endemic for years. But the discovery and use of the antibiotic griseofulvin, one of the few antifungal antibiotics, has greatly diminished the problem. This drug, when given by mouth, is incorporated into the horny layer during the synthesis of keratin.

For about ten years there has been almost a pandemic of yeast infections with *Candida albicans*. Often a commensal, or symbiotic, type of organism that inhabits the mouth, gut, and vagina, is helped to spread on the skin and mucous membranes by medication with broad-spectrum antibiotics, and corticosteroid and antimitotic drugs; anticandida antibiotics nystatin and amphotericin, B, however, are available for treatment.

Parasites. The skin surface is constantly exposed to parasites. Some live on or in the skin (scabies and lice), while most merely feed on it. In scabies ("the itch") the female mite (*Sarcoptes scabiei hominis*) burrows into the horny layer to lay eggs. Most of the itching and rash of scabies is due to an allergic reaction to the mite or its products. An attack does not confer immunity, and large epidemics appear in cycles of about 20 years. Pubic and head lice (*Phthirus pubis* and *Pediculus humanus capitis*) have crablike claws by which they cling to the large hairs and lay their eggs (nits) on them. Body lice (*Pediculus humanus corporis*) live and lay their eggs on woollen clothing. All of these parasites feed by puncturing the skin and sucking blood; the inflammatory papules and excoriations follow this traumatic puncture. Various parasitic worms, especially in tropical countries, may penetrate and live in the skin or pass on through to infest

Abnormalities of the keratin

other organs. There are numerous other parasites including bedbugs, fleas, mosquitoes, and ticks, which feed on human blood and cause itchy papules when inflammatory agents in their saliva are injected into the skin. They may also be vectors for organisms producing localized skin infections, such as leishmaniasis, or systemic diseases, such as malaria and typhus. There are many effective parasiticidal drugs available for prophylaxis and treatment.

Psoriasis, eczema, and lichen planus. Three important diseases of the dermo-epidermal layer are psoriasis, eczema, and lichen planus. Usually, but not always, clinically and histologically distinctive, they do not appear to have a single precise cause but seem to be of multifactorial origin, resulting from an interplay of genetic, environmental, and internal factors. They pursue a fluctuating course, are subject to relapses, are completely reversible and responsive to potent corticosteroid drugs.

Psoriasis, an ancient disease (probably the biblical leprosy), is a genetic disorder inherited as a dominant trait with incomplete penetrance (it does not always affect individuals who possess the gene). One to two percent of the population in Britain, for example, carry the gene. It may affect any or every part of the skin, the favourite sites being the extensor aspect of the knees and elbows, the scalp and the trunk. The eruption of lesions may be precipitated by physical trauma such as a scratch or wound, streptococcal throat infections, and, on occasion, psychic trauma. It is rare in early childhood and attains peaks of onset in the second and fifth decades of life.

The two distinctive features of its pathology are an increased epidermopoiesis, or epidermal cell turnover (three to four times the normal), and the immigration of polymorphonuclear leukocytes (white blood cells) into the upper layers of the epidermis, forming micro-abscesses and visible pustules if large enough. The capillaries in the dermal papillae are tortuous. The process can be reversed simply by the use of cytotoxic agents, but the mechanisms by which it is controlled or triggered in the first place remain obscure. The disease is usually benefitted by sunlight, being worse in winter than summer, and less common on the face and exposed parts, but how ultraviolet light exerts this action is not yet known.

As previously mentioned, the terms dermatitis and eczema are increasingly recognized as synonymous. They refer to a pathological change that can be induced in any person's skin and may be precipitated by a variety of causes including trauma, chemical agents, infections, and disorders of metabolism and circulation. Dermatitis is a major skin disease in highly developed countries but almost unknown among the Eskimo of Alaska. Distinctive features of the condition are capillary dilatation and release of fluid, which penetrates between the damaged prickle cells of the epidermis, and swelling and destruction of the epidermal cells to form small vesicles. Normal keratinization is disrupted, so that the horny layer is malformed and allows the leakage of the fluid onto the surface.

Cases of dermatitis are normally classified according to the pattern or arrangement of the disease over the skin surface, apart from contact dermatitis, which occurs at any site where the responsible agent comes into contact. About two-thirds of dermatitis cases can be categorized into contact, atopic, seborrheic, discoid, and varicose patterns. The atopic (from the Greek: "different, strange") pattern is a genetic disorder, inherited as an incomplete dominant (see also ALLERGY AND ANAPHYLACTIC SHOCK). It is frequently associated with asthma, hay fever, and food allergies, all of which, but not the dermatitis, are found in individuals whose serum contains the special immunoglobulin IgE. These people also show physiological abnormalities of their cutaneous vessels and sweat apparatus, and a small number of them develop a type of cataract of the lens in the eye.

Contact dermatitis is the only pattern that can readily be produced experimentally. One type (irritant) results from a direct toxic or damaging action on the epidermal cells by substances such as alkalis, detergents, oils, and solvents; the other type (allergic) occurs only if the individual has been sensitized by a previous exposure and has acquired a special cell-mediated immunologic sensitivity to the particular substance (allergen). To induce contact sensitivity such substances, and there are a wide range of them, must form an irreversible covalent bond with a homologous protein or polypeptide. Lymphocytes and macrophage cells in the skin, intact cutaneous lymphatic vessels, and lymph nodes are other essential components in the process. When the contact allergen encounters specifically sensitized lymphocytes in the skin, the changes of dermatitis result. The pharmacodynamic mediators of the reaction are possibly a protein and a prostaglandin hormone, but this is not yet proved. Contact dermatitis is of great importance as a cause of occupational illness and in many countries such industrial dermatitis accounts for more than half the claims for compensation. The common allergens responsible include many metals (nickel, chromium, cobalt, and beryllium), aniline, paraphenylenediamine, and related chemicals containing an amino group in the *para* position on a benzene ring, many drugs and therapeutic substances, additives used in the manufacture of rubber, and synthetic resins, as well as a wide range of natural products, including flowers, shrubs, ivies, balsams and other trees, and turpentine (see also POISONOUS ANIMALS AND PLANTS).

Lichen planus is a common skin disease in Europe, the United States, and West Africa. It is characterized by purplish, flat-topped, angulated papules, arranged singly, in sheets or in rings. It produces similar changes in most of the mucous membranes, in the mouth, and on the genitalia. It is characterized histologically by necrosis of the basal cell layer of the epidermis and a dense, inflammatory infiltrate around it. The only known causes, albeit of only a small percentage of the patients affected, are certain drugs and contact with some colour-film developer chemicals. The usual drugs responsible are organic gold and arsenic salts, atabrine, and amiphenazole. During World War II many servicemen developed an especially severe form of lichen planus as a result of taking a daily tablet of atabrine for malarial prophylaxis. The mechanism is almost certainly immunologic, since a further small dose induces a rapid relapse, but there is no evidence that such a mechanism is operative in all individuals affected with lichen planus.

Cancer. All grades of skin cancer are found among Caucasians living in sunny climates. The principal types are intraepidermal, or cancer *in situ*; basal-cell epithelioma (rodent ulcer); and squamous cell epithelioma. There may be racial differences (basal-cell cancer is rare in the Japanese), and there is sometimes a strong genetic predisposition to its development, as in the mendelian dominant basal-cell nevus syndrome, or the recessive xeroderma pigmentosum. Chronic exposure to inorganic arsenic, in the form of medicine, paints, sheep dip, and pesticides, or accidental exposure, causes cancer of both the skin and internal organs. Exposure of the skin to coal tar and its derivatives, or to many mineral oils widely used in the engineering industry, produces grades of skin cancer from "tar warts" to malignant and fatal epitheliomas. Apart from the head and hands and arms, the male genitalia can be affected (scrotal cancer) by oil soaking through the clothing. The minimal period of exposure required is about ten years.

Pigmentation and melanocytes. The pigment-cell system, consisting of basal- and high-level melanocytes of the epidermis, shows only three common types of disease—variations in the production of pigment, nevoid proliferation, and malignant growth.

Pigment production by melanocyte cells is a complex biological process. The copper-containing, metalloenzyme-tyrosinase system is influenced not only by metabolic and hormonal changes in the body but also by local disease in the skin, especially inflammation. The normal stimulus to the enzyme is ultraviolet light of wavelengths 290 to 315 nanometres (billionths of a metre), producing suntan. The response is greatly increased by the ingestion or local application of a group of chemicals called psoralens, which are found in many plant products and are now made synthetically.

Inflammatory diseases in the skin, such as eczema, psoriasis, lichen planus, and infections, as well as trauma to the epidermis, will often induce a temporary increase or decrease of pigmentation. The general control of melanocyte function is by the melanocyte-stimulating hormone secreted by the pituitary gland, and skin-lightening factor (melatonin) secreted by the pineal gland. Diseases of these and other endocrine glands (*e.g.*, Addison's disease and thyrotoxicosis) cause increased or decreased pigmentation by disturbing the normal balance of these hormones. Protein, and therefore tyrosine, deficiency (as in kwashiorkor) or appropriate enzyme deficiency (as in phenylketonuria) will cause decreased melanin formation.

Vitiligo. Loss of pigmentation occurs in vitiligo (leukoderma). This is a common familial disease and is a serious social and cosmetic disability, most particularly in the more pigmented peoples of Asia and Africa. Circumscribed depigmented patches appear and in some cases become confluent over large areas of the body or even universal. The melanocytes lose the capacity to make melanin, but the nature of the cell damage is not known. In some patients the melanocytes can be stimulated to produce pigment again by exposure to ultraviolet light after topical application or internal administration of 8-methoxy psoralen.

Depigmentation

Depigmentation similar to vitiligo can be produced by inhibiting the tyrosinase system with substances such as hydroquinones, 4-isopropylcatechol and *p*-tertiary butylphenol. Hence, Caucasians can be made as black as Negroes by injections of a melanocyte-stimulating hormone, and Negroes can be made as white as albinos with hydroquinone; but there are hazards associated with such procedures.

Proliferation of melanocytes to form a mole, a melanocyte nevus, is extremely common. They may be flat (macular) or raised (papular), large or small, and all shades of colour from that of normal skin to jet black. They are normally only of cosmetic interest, but their importance is that uncontrolled growth of melanocytes constitutes a malignant melanoma, one of the most dangerous tumours known.

Melanocytes are sometimes found producing melanin pigment in the deeper layers of the dermis. A patch of such cells is normal in Mongoloid babies at birth but much less frequently found in other races. It is called a Mongolian spot or blue nevus. The black melanin pigment appears blue through the skin, in the same way that a tattoo with carbon black looks blue. There is a particular optical relationship between collagen and the pigment that leads to a subtractive colour mixing in the light reflected from the dermis.

Melanin pigment shed by melanocytes or extravascular blood pigment (hemosiderin) or pigment injected by tattoo is engulfed by tissue macrophages or histiocytes, although some may persist free in the dermal tissue. Some of the pigments used by tattooists, in addition to carbon, are insoluble compounds of cobalt, cadmium, and chromium. Occasionally the tattooed person may develop an allergic reaction to one of these metals.

THE DERMIS

The collagen, or elastic fibres of the dermis, may be congenitally malformed and constitute a connective tissue nevus; such nevi are especially associated with a more serious genetic disease called tuberous sclerosis or epiloia, with epilepsy from brain lesions and small papular lesions on the face (adenoma sebaceum). Overelasticity of the skin, capillary fragility, "double joints," and other genetic abnormalities of the biomolecular organization of this tissue are seen in various conditions called cutis laxa, pseudoxanthoma elasticum, and the Ehlers-Danlos syndrome.

Chronic granulomatous inflammation

Although the dermis may be affected by many types of acute inflammation, the most important type is chronic granulomatous inflammation. A granuloma is formed in the dermis by masses of large epithelioid or histiocytic cells, and often giant multinucleate cells, with varying admixtures of lymphocytes and other inflammatory cells.

Granulomas with the histiocytes lined up around the edge are particularly seen in granuloma annulare, a condition that appears as small, beaded papulonodular rings, especially on backs of the hands and fingers. It is frequent in children and often resolves spontaneously. In adults it may be much more widespread and associated with diabetes mellitus. A similar granulomatous change in which the histiocytes contain large quantities of fat is found in necrobiosis lipoidica, which appears as papular, and later atrophic, plaques on the shins, usually in individuals with diabetes mellitus. A third variety of palisaded granuloma comprises the large dermal rheumatoid nodules, mostly over bony prominences, in patients with rheumatoid arthritis.

Granulomas without palisading of the histiocytes may be produced as a reaction to any foreign body or abnormal material in the dermis but are more often caused by allergy or hypersensitivity to infective or chemical agents. Some of the diseases in which these reactions appear are tuberculosis, syphilis, leprosy, deep mycoses, leishmaniasis, lymphogranuloma, and sarcoid. They are also seen as a result of sensitization to such chemical substances as beryllium and zirconium, or of sensitization by colloidal silica.

Injury and inflammation may result in scarring—fibrosis of the connective tissue fibres. It can involve excessive production of fibrous tissue that may be temporary (hypertrophic scar or "proud flesh") or long lasting, as a keloid.

After about age 20 the dermal connective tissue undergoes changes in its fibre configuration, making it less extensible. This change is progressive and accompanied by atrophy as senescence progresses. Similar alterations are produced by corticosteroid drugs and sometimes, to a lesser degree, by increased secretions of certain adrenal hormones during puberty and pregnancy, as a result of which any severe stretching of the skin causes small breaks in the fibres seen as purplish streaks ("striae atrophicae") on the hips, abdomen, back, and axillary folds. The changes are usually not reversible.

Connective tissue diseases

The connective tissue of the dermis is affected in important and related diseases—lupus erythematosus, scleroderma, and dermatomyositis. Each of these diseases has its principal manifestations in the skin, although each affects internal organs as well, and it is the progressive involvement of the internal organs that may prove fatal. Scleroderma ("hard skin") is more frequently seen as localized patches of indurated, waxy skin, harmless, and resolving spontaneously. Lupus erythematosus also occurs more often as fixed red, scaly patches with much dilatation of the blood vessels, especially over the face, and may resolve spontaneously, or with treatment, over several years. But the systemic forms of scleroderma, lupus erythematosus, and dermatomyositis are serious diseases with a mortality rate of about 50 percent. All three occur more frequently in women than in men. Scleroderma is associated with Raynaud's disease—arterial spasm in the fingers, which go white and anaesthetic ("dead fingers") in response to cold. Dermatomyositis mainly involves the skin and muscles, and in such patients over age 40, more than half are found to have some form of internal cancer.

Pathologically, the main changes in these diseases are in the dermis and the blood vessels. In scleroderma, the fibres are normal, but the ground substance is thickened so that the dermis appears to be expanded in depth and homogenized. In lupus erythematosus the upper dermis is edematous—*i.e.*, contains much extracellular fluid—and has a thickened basement membrane, while the basal cells of the epidermis may degenerate and die. In dermatomyositis the edema fluid contains mucin, the chief constituent of mucus. In all three there is varying infiltration of lymphocytic cells accompanied by damage to small blood vessels.

These three diseases, once grouped together as so-called collagen or connective tissue disease, are now regarded as autoimmune diseases. The affected individuals are found to have various types of auto-antibodies in their blood, the most important being the antinuclear factor.

Metabolic
disorders

Metabolic disorders may result in the deposition of excess materials in the dermis and cause visible disease. Uric acid salts are deposited in gout, calcium salts in calcinosis, lipids in xanthomatosis, an abnormal protein in amyloidosis, mucin in myxedema, and porphyrins in porphyria. The appearances of the skin are usually sufficiently characteristic to be diagnostic.

One manifestation of the presence of excess porphyrins (as a result of abnormal metabolism in the bone marrow or the liver) is abnormal sensitivity to ultraviolet light, which causes small blisters on the skin. The wavelength responsible is 400 nanometre, the peak absorption band for porphyrin. Photosensitivity of the skin has become more common in recent years. Apart from porphyria and certain idiopathic (*i.e.*, of unknown cause) light-provoked rashes, the most important causative agents are photosensitizing drugs, such as sulfonamides (antibacterial), phenothiazines (psychotropic), thiazides (diuretics), sulfonyl ureas (hypoglycemic), halogenated salicylanilides (germicidal), and nalidixic acid (urinary antiseptic). After exposure to ultraviolet light, patients taking these drugs may develop redness, swelling, or blisters on the exposed parts.

The blood vessels. Dermal blood vessels are involved in many skin diseases. They can be malformed in various ways, producing hemangiomas or vascular nevi. They control temperature by dilatation and contraction, but this control may be disturbed in patients with Raynaud's disease (episodic spasm of digital arteries) and chilblains.

The dermal vessels will dilate and may release plasma, white blood cells, or red cells in response to inflammation from any cause—physical, chemical, or immunological. The vessel walls themselves may be damaged in a disease process. Vasodilatation and edema with inflammatory cells is found in erythemas of many types such as rosacea on the face, erythema nodosum and erythema multiforme on the limbs, urticaria, purpura, and vasculitis. The individual areas are usually small, making up a rash of scattered macules, papules, or nodules. Many of the infectious fevers, such as scarlatina, measles, and secondary syphilis, are of this type. But many widespread red, scaly rashes have no precisely identifiable cause, although they produce recognizable patterns, such as pityriasis rosea (reddish branny scales) or annular erythemas (red or pink rings).

The hair and pilo-sebaceous follicles. The hair follicles with their sebaceous glands are special invaginations of the epidermis and dermis, so that the formation of hair is similar to that of the horny layer. Although the epidermis grows and produces a horny layer continuously, each hair follicle has a cyclical growth pattern. A scalp hair grows for about three years and then the follicle rests for about three months before producing a new hair. This hair cycle may be interfered with by many types of local disturbance such as trauma, inflammation, or vascular insufficiency; and by general factors such as nutritional deficiencies, excesses of certain types of radiation, some drugs, major internal diseases, prolonged high fever, and metabolic changes. Severe infective illnesses like typhoid frequently cause the hair to involute and rest for about three months, after which it rapidly falls out as the new hairs start to grow. The commonest drugs to cause a diffuse hair loss are anticoagulants and antimitotic agents used for the treatment of malignant disease and after transplantation surgery.

Temporary
hair loss

The process of production of hair by a follicle is complicated, and there are a wide variety of genetic disorders in any one of which one facet may be faulty, resulting in a sometimes, but not always, remediable hair abnormality. Examples are beaded hair (monilethrix), ringed hair (pili annulati), and twisted hair (pili torti).

There are different types of hair follicles over the body surface producing variations from the fine and almost invisible lanugo (downy) hair to the large coarse scalp, pubic, and male beard hair. The two main factors that influence the type of hair are genetic and hormonal. Androgen production at puberty produces both a change from straight to V-shaped in the forehead hairline in boys, as well as the development of coarse beard, axil-

lary, pubic, and body hair. The common type of male-pattern baldness (alopecia) on the scalp may start at any time after puberty as recession at the temples and thinning over the crown. It is produced by the male hormone, testosterone, acting on genetically predisposed follicles. The follicles are not destroyed but gradually regress to the stage of those producing small lanugo hairs.

Patches of hair loss are due to localized disease affecting the hair follicles. The commonest in alopecia areata, in which the hair roots are the site of inflammation, but ringworm infections, by proliferating in the hair shaft, cause the hair to break off and fall out. These changes are normally reversible, but the hair roots may be permanently damaged and scarred by some skin diseases such as lichen planus, lupus erythematosus, and scleroderma and by excessive X-irradiation. One of the most important diseases of the hair and sebaceous gland units (the pilosebaceous follicles) is acne vulgaris. The clinical signs are blackheads (comedones), papules, pustules, cysts, and scars, together with excessive oiliness of the skin (seborrhea). The effects are produced in both boys and girls by androgenic hormones (produced in the testes and adrenal glands at puberty) acting on susceptible follicles in the so-called acne areas—the face, chest, and back. How the effect is produced on the follicle is not precisely known. The sebaceous gland enlarges and the follicle wall becomes damaged and its opening blocked. Once occluded, the gland and follicle keratinize to form a horny cyst. If anaerobic organisms (principally the acne bacilli—*Corynebacterium* or *Proprionibacterium acnes*) are trapped in the cyst, they metabolize the sebum to produce irritant fatty acids. These acids cause inflammation and abscesses, which eventually resolve and may leave scars. The most valuable forms of treatment are ultraviolet light, desquamating local applications, and the systemic administration of tetracycline antibiotics.

Acne
vulgaris

It is possible for similar changes to be brought on in pilosebaceous follicles on any area of skin by contact with bromides and iodides, mineral oils, tar and pitch, chlorinated naphthalenes and chlorodiphenyls, as a result of either external or systemic exposure.

Sweat glands. The eccrine sweat glands (*i.e.*, exocrine sweat glands as opposed to the apocrine, in which the secretions are concentrated at the free end of the cell and thrown off with that part of the cell) are under the control of the autonomic nervous system and produce sweat as a result of three types of stimuli. First, there is a normal low-grade secretion by all the glands of "insensible" perspiration amounting to about half a litre (about a pint) per day. Second, there is thermal sweating, in which a rise of temperature will induce all the glands to increase secreting. Third, emotional stimuli produce increased secretion from the glands on the forehead, palms and soles, in the armpits and around the anogenital area. Inability to secrete adequate sweat (anhidrosis) is usually a congenital abnormality. Hyperhidrosis is the abnormal excessive secretion of sweat, usually on the palms and soles and in the axillae.

Prickly heat (miliaria) results from the occlusion of the sweat pore openings as a result of maceration and blockage in a hot, humid climate. The gland continues to secrete and the pressure may rupture the sweat duct at its junction with the epidermis, resulting in spillage of sweat into the epidermis with consequent inflammation.

Nails. A nail is formed by an invagination of the skin, similar to that forming a hair follicle. The specialized area of dermis and epidermis produces a type of hard keratin with a higher proportion of sulfur-containing amino acids.

Like the rest of the skin or the hair follicle, the nail matrix may be congenitally abnormal and produce many varieties of malformed nails, as for example pachyonychia congenita (thickened nails). The matrix may also be the site of trauma and produce a deformed nail; the damage may be temporary or permanent.

The most common causes of diseased nails are chronic paronychia—an inflammation resulting from loss of the thin cuticle from exposure to water and alkalis—fungus infections, trauma, psoriasis, impaired circulation, and

Chronic
paronychia

dermatitis. Chronic paronychia is an occupational hazard of dishwashers, barmaids, and vegetable preparers. When the cuticle is lost, water, bacteria, and yeasts seep under the nail fold and cause inflammation.

Fungi can infiltrate the nail plate itself and disrupt its structure, causing variable degrees of deformity, but generally resulting in thickening and crumbling of the plate. Psoriasis frequently affects the nails. The most common change is a thimble-like pitting on the surface, but separation of the plate from the nail bed (onycholysis) and thickening are also seen.

Any disease of the skin, such as dermatitis, lichen planus, or psoriasis and chilblains, and other forms of interference with the blood supply, may also affect the nail matrix and produce irregular growth of the nails.

Quite apart from specific diseases, variations from the normal pattern are frequently seen—white patches, splitting of the tips, brittleness, ridging, curvature, and other minor abnormalities too numerous to mention.

BIBLIOGRAPHY. A.J. ROOK, D.S. WILKINSON, and F.J.G. EBBLING, *Textbook of Dermatology* (1968), a standard textbook covering all aspects of dermatology; W. MONTAGNA, *The Structure and Function of Skin*, 2nd ed. (1962), a detailed textbook of anatomy and biology of normal skin; W.F. LEVER, *Histopathology of the Skin*, 4th ed. (1967), a standard textbook of the histology of skin diseases; P.D. SAMMAN, *The Nails in Disease* (1965), a small monograph on common nail disorders; L. SCHWARTZ, L. TULIPAN, and D.J. BIRMINGHAM, *Occupational Diseases of the Skin*, 3rd ed. (1957), a standard textbook of occupational dermatoses; T.B. FITZPATRICK, *Dermatologic Differential Diagnosis* (1962), an elementary textbook of morphological diagnosis of skin diseases; A.J. ROOK and G.S. WALTON (eds.), *Comparative Physiology and Pathology of the Skin* (1965), selected papers on skin diseases in animals.

(C.D.C.)

Slang

Difficult to define, slang consists basically of unconventional words or phrases that express either something new or something old in a new way. It is flippant, irreverent, indecorous; it may be indecent or obscene. Its colourful metaphors are generally directed at respectability, and it is this succinct, sometimes witty, frequently impertinent social criticism that gives slang its characteristic flavour. Slang, then, includes not just words but words used in a special way in a certain social context. The origin of the word slang itself is obscure; it first appeared in print around 1800, applied to the speech of disreputable and criminal classes in London. The term, however, was probably used much earlier. Other related types of nonstandard word usage include cant and jargon, synonyms for vague and high-sounding or technical and esoteric language not immediately intelligible to the uninitiate. In England, the term cant still indicates the specialized speech of criminals, which, in the United States, is more often called argot. The term dialect refers to language characteristic of a certain geographic area or social class.

The development of slang. Slang emanates from conflicts in values, sometimes superficial, often fundamental. When an individual applies language in a new way to express hostility, ridicule, or contempt, often with sharp wit, he may be creating slang, but the new expression will perish unless it is picked up by others. If the speaker is a member of a group that finds that his creation projects the emotional reaction of its members toward an idea, person, or social institution, the expression will gain currency according to the unanimity of attitude within the group. A new slang term is usually widely used in a subculture before it appears in the dominant culture. Thus slang—*e.g.*, "sucker," "honkey," "shave-tail," "jerk" —expresses the attitudes, not always derogatory, of one group or class toward the values of another. Slang sometimes stems from within the group, satirizing or burlesquing its own values, behaviour, and attitudes; *e.g.*, "shotgun wedding," "cake eater," "greasy spoon." Slang, then, is produced largely by social forces rather than by an individual speaker or writer who, single-handed (like Horace Walpole, who coined "serendipity" more than 200 years ago), creates and establishes a word in the language. This is one reason why it is difficult to determine the origin of slang terms.

Creators of slang. Civilized society tends to divide into a dominant culture and various subcultures that flourish within the dominant framework. The subcultures show specialized linguistic phenomena, varying widely in form and content, that depend on the nature of the groups and their relation to each other and to the dominant culture. The shock value of slang stems largely from the verbal transfer of the values of a subculture to diametrically opposed values in the dominant culture. Names such as fuzz, pig, fink, bull, and dick for policemen were not created by officers of the law. (The humorous "dickless tracy," however, meaning a policewoman, *was* coined by male policemen.)

Occupational groups are legion, and while in most respects they identify with the dominant culture, there is just enough social and linguistic hostility to maintain group solidarity. Terms such as scab, strike-breaker, company-man, and goon were highly charged words in the era in which labour began to organize in the United States; they are not used lightly even today, though they have been taken into the standard language.

In addition to occupational and professional groups, there are many other types of subcultures that supply slang. These include sexual deviants, narcotic addicts, ghetto groups, institutional populations, agricultural subsocieties, political organizations, the armed forces, Gypsies, and sports groups of many varieties. Some of the most fruitful sources of slang are the subcultures of professional criminals who have migrated to the New World since the 16th century. Old-time thieves still humorously refer to themselves as FFV—First Families of Virginia.

In criminal subcultures, pressure applied by the dominant culture intensifies the internal forces already at work, and the argot forming there emphasizes the values, attitudes, and techniques of the subculture. Criminal groups seem to evolve about this specialized argot, and both the subculture and its slang expressions proliferate in response to internal and external pressures.

Sources. Most subcultures tend to draw words and phrases from the contiguous language (rather than creating many new words) and to give these established terms new and special meanings; some borrowings from foreign languages, including the American Indian tongues, are traditional. The more learned occupations or professions like medicine, law, psychology, sociology, engineering, and electronics tend to create true neologisms, often based on Greek or Latin roots, but these are not major sources for slang, though nurses and medical students adapt some medical terminology to their slang, and air force personnel and some other branches of the armed services borrow freely from engineering and electronics.

Linguistic processes forming slang. The processes by which words become slang are the same as those by which other words in the language change their form or meaning or both. Some of these are the employment of metaphor, simile, folk etymology, distortion of sounds in words, generalization, specialization, clipping, the use of acronyms, elevation and degeneration, metonymy, synecdoche, hyperbole, borrowings from foreign languages, and the play of euphemism against taboo. The English word trip is an example of a term that has undergone both specialization and generalization. It first became specialized to mean a psychedelic experience resulting from the drug LSD. Subsequently, it generalized again to mean any experience on any drug, and beyond that to any type of "kicks" from anything. Clipping is exemplified by the use of "grass" from "laughing grass," a term for marijuana. "Funky," once a very low term for body odour, has undergone elevation among jazz buffs to signify "the best"; "fanny," on the other hand, once simply a girl's name, is currently a degenerated term that refers to the buttocks (in England, it has further degenerated into a taboo word for the female genitalia). There is also some actual coinage of slang terms.

Characteristics of slang. Psychologically, most good slang harks back to the stage in human culture when animism was a worldwide religion. At that time, it was

The specialized languages of subcultures

Primitive
origins
of slang

believed that all objects had two aspects, one external and objective that could be perceived by the senses, the other imperceptible (except to gifted individuals) but identical with what we today would call the "real" object. Human survival depended upon the manipulation of all "real" aspects of life—hunting, reproduction, warfare, weapons, design of habitations, nature of clothing or decoration, etc.—through control or influence upon the *animus*, or imperceptible phase of reality. This influence was exerted through many aspects of sympathetic magic, one of the most potent being the use of language. Words, therefore, had great power, because they evoked the things to which they referred.

Civilized cultures and their languages retain many remnants of animism, largely on the unconscious level. In Western languages, the metaphor owes its power to echoes of sympathetic magic, and slang utilizes certain attributes of the metaphor to evoke images too close for comfort to "reality." For example, to refer to a woman as a "broad" is automatically to increase her girth in an area in which she may fancy herself as being thin. Her reaction may, thus, be one of anger and resentment, if she happens to live in a society in which slim hips are considered essential to feminine beauty. Slang, then, owes much of its power to shock to the superimposition of images that are incongruous with images (or values) of others, usually members of the dominant culture. Slang is most popular when its imagery develops incongruity bordering on social satire. Every slang word, however, has its own history and reasons for popularity. When conditions change, the term may change in meaning, be adopted into the standard language, or continue to be used as slang within certain enclaves of the population. Nothing is flatter than dead slang. In 1910, for instance, "Oh you kid" and "23-skiddoo" were quite stylish phrases in the U.S. but they have gone with the hobbleskirt. Children, however, unaware of anachronisms, often revive old slang under a barrage of older movies rerun on television.

Some slang becomes respectable when it loses its edge; "spunk," "fizzle," "spent," "hit the spot," "jazz," "funky," and "p.o.'d," once thought to be too indecent for feminine ears, are now family words. Other slang survives for centuries, like "bones" for dice (Chaucer), "beat it" for run away (Shakespeare), "duds" for clothes, and "booze" for liquor (Dekker). These words must have been uttered as slang long before appearing in print, and they have remained slang ever since. Normally, slang has both a high birth and death rate in the dominant culture, and excessive use tends to dull the lustre of even the most colourful and descriptive words and phrases. The rate of turnover in slang words is undoubtedly encouraged by the mass media, and a term must be increasingly effective to survive.

Transience
and
persistence

While many slang words introduce new concepts, some of the most effective slang provides new expressions—fresh, satirical, shocking—for established concepts, often very respectable ones. Sound is sometimes used as a basis for this type of slang, as, for example, in various phonetic distortions (*e.g.*, pig Latin terms). It is also used in rhyming slang, which employs a fortunate combination of both sound and imagery. Thus, gloves are "turtledoves" (the gloved hands suggesting a pair of billing doves), a girl is a "twist and twirl" (the movement suggesting a girl walking), and an insulting imitation of flatus, produced by blowing air between the tip of the protruded tongue and the upper lip, is the "raspberry," cut back from "raspberry tart." Most slang, however, depends upon incongruity of imagery, conveyed by the lively connotations of a novel term applied to an established concept. Slang is not all of equal quality, a considerable body of it reflecting a simple need to find new terms for common ones, such as the hands, feet, head, and other parts of the body. Food, drink, and sex also involve extensive slang vocabulary. Strained or synthetically invented slang lacks verve, as can be seen in the desperate efforts of some sportswriters to avoid mentioning the word baseball—*e.g.*, a batter does not hit a baseball but rather "swats the horsehide," "plasters the pill," "hefts the old apple over the fence," and so on.

The most effective slang operates on a more sophisticated level and often tells something about the thing named, the person using the term, and the social matrix against which it is used. Pungency may increase when full understanding of the term depends on a little inside information or knowledge of a term already in use, often on the slang side itself. For example, the term Vatican roulette (for the rhythm system of birth control) would have little impact if the expression Russian roulette were not already in wide usage.

Diffusion of slang. Slang invades the dominant culture as it seeps out of various subcultures. Some words fall dead or lie dormant in the dominant culture for long periods. Others vividly express an idea already latent in the dominant culture and these are immediately picked up and used. Before the advent of mass media, such terms invaded the dominant culture slowly and were transmitted largely by word of mouth. Thus a term like snafu, its shocking power softened with the explanation "situation normal, all fouled up," worked its way gradually from the military in World War II by word of mouth (because the media largely shunned it) into respectable circles. Today, however, a sportscaster, news reporter, or comedian may introduce a lively new word already used by an ingroup into millions of homes simultaneously, giving it almost instant currency. For example, the term uptight was first used largely by criminal narcotic addicts to indicate the onset of withdrawal distress when drugs are denied. Later, because of intense journalistic interest in the drug scene, it became widely used in the dominant culture to mean anxiety or tension unrelated to drug use. It kept its form but changed its meaning slightly.

Slang and
the mass
media

Other terms may change their form or both form and meaning, like "one for the book" (anything unusual or unbelievable). Sportswriters in the U.S. borrowed this term around 1920 from the occupational language of then legal bookmakers, who lined up at racetracks in the morning ("the morning line" is still figuratively used on every sports page) to take bets on the afternoon races. Newly arrived bookmakers went to the end of the line, and any bettor requesting unusually long odds was motioned down the line with the phrase, "That's one for the end book." The general public dropped the "end" as meaningless, but old-time gamblers still retain it. Slang spreads through many other channels, such as popular songs, which, for the initiate, are often rich in double entendre.

When subcultures are structurally tight, little of their language leaks out. Thus the Mafia, in more than a half-century of powerful criminal activity in America, has contributed little slang. When subcultures weaken, contacts with the dominant culture multiply, diffusion occurs, and their language appears widely as slang. Criminal narcotic addicts, for example, had a tight subculture and a highly secret argot in the 1940s; now their terms are used freely by middle class teen-agers, even those with no real knowledge of drugs.

Uses of slang. Slang is used for many purposes, but generally it expresses a certain emotional attitude; the same term may express diametrically opposed attitudes when used by different people. Many slang terms are primarily derogatory, though they may also be ambivalent when used in intimacy or affection. Some crystallize or bolster the self-image or promote identification with a class or ingroup. Others flatter objects, institutions, or persons but may be used by different people for the opposite effect. "Jesus freak," originally used as ridicule, was adopted as a title by certain street evangelists. Slang sometimes insults or shocks when used directly; some terms euphemize a sensitive concept, though obvious or excessive euphemism may break the taboo more effectively than a less decorous term. Some slang words are essential because there are no words in the standard language expressing exactly the same meaning; *e.g.*, "freakout," "barn-storm" "rubberneck," and the noun "creep." At the other extreme, multitudes of words, vague in meaning, are used simply as fads.

Slang
expressing
emotional
attitudes

There are many other uses to which slang is put, according to the individual and his place in society. Since most slang is used on the spoken level, by persons who probably are unaware that it is slang, the choice of terms naturally follows a multiplicity of unconscious thought patterns. When used by writers, slang is much more consciously and carefully chosen to achieve a specific effect. Writers, however, seldom invent slang.

It has been claimed that slang is created by ingenious individuals to freshen the language, to vitalize it, to make the language more pungent and picturesque, to increase the store of terse and striking words, or to provide a vocabulary for new shades of meaning. Most of the originators and purveyors of slang, however, are probably not conscious of these noble purposes and do not seem overly concerned about what happens to their language.

Attitudes towards slang. With the rise of naturalistic writing demanding realism, slang began to creep into English literature even though the schools waged warfare against it, the pulpit thundered against it, and many women who aspired to gentility and refinement banished it from the home. It flourished underground, however, in such male sanctuaries as lodges, poolrooms, barbershops, and saloons.

Slang in literature By 1925 a whole new generation of U.S. and European naturalistic writers was in revolt against the Victorian restraints that had caused even Mark Twain to complain, and today any writer may use slang freely, especially in fiction and drama. It has become an indispensable tool in the hands of master satirists, humorists, and journalists. Slang is now socially acceptable, not just because it is slang but because, when used with skill and discrimination, it adds a new and exciting dimension to language. At the same time, it is being seriously studied by linguists and other social scientists as a revealing index to the culture that produces and uses it.

Slang in English-speaking areas. In looking at slang in the English-speaking world, authorities see not only a strong historical tradition for the production and use of slang but also conditions fertile for its continued growth. There are, for example, strong dominant cultures within which there have been powerful vertical movements of people into the middle class; large blocks of foreign immigrants, along with a multitude of the subcultures mentioned earlier; and, most important, channels of communication with foreign cultures and subcultures and an established language that has long proved its ability to absorb and utilize slang. There is, furthermore, a solid literary tradition hospitable to slang, some terms tending to become part of the literary language.

England. England may indeed be the mother of slang wherever English is spoken, not only because of centuries of production but also because of the wide distribution of Englishmen throughout the world. Today, however, British slang is distinctive and tends to be insular. It has absorbed much lively material from Irish, Scottish, and Welsh speech forms, as well as foreign terms from the more recent immigration of Asians, Africans, and West Indians. Some of these expressions were well established abroad during the colonial period. Within the present generation there has been a large-scale invasion of American slang (decried by some Britishers), largely derived from criminal sources. Perhaps the leading domestic source is the colourful speech of the Cockneys of London.

More recently developed British subcultures, not far removed from that of the Cockneys, and hostile to either the Establishment or to other nonconformist subcultures or both, are the Mods, Teddy-boys, Rockers, and Suedeheads, or Skinheads. In addition, drug addiction increased dramatically in the 1960s, with a concentration in younger age groups. Each of these subcultures has developed its own special characteristics, particularly its life-style, and language; some of their expressions may flavour British slang in the future.

Preservation of British terms in Australian slang *Australia.* In Australia, still a frontier country, slang is in lively production. Because it was heavily settled by transported convicts until 1868, it still preserves many terms from 18th- and 19th-century British criminal usage, especially rhyming slang, which may be somewhat archaic in Britain today. There are also many adaptations of words from native aboriginal languages, together with earthy metaphors originated by the sundowners, swagmen, and drovers in the bush, the Australian versions of hoboes, itinerant workers, and cattle and sheep drivers. The larrikins who constitute the city street gangs also contribute a steady stream of urban slang to a language that is, perhaps, about to reach its literary maturity.

Canada and the United States. Canada and the United States share a great body of common slang, though there are differences. Canada, for instance, still has close ties with England, and much more British slang finds its way, both via print and the spoken word, into Canada than into the United States. Further, Canada is a bilingual country and more French slang filters into Canadian English than into British English; this French is different in nature from continental French and its slang vocabulary is little known or used in France. There are also more terms of Indian and Eskimo origin than appear in slang in the United States. In addition, large blocks of only partially assimilated immigrants from Scandinavia and central Europe, as well as from Scotland, England, and Ireland, still exist. Sizable urban enclaves in the areas of Vancouver, the Toronto-Detroit-Buffalo triangle, and Montreal have both occupational and criminal subcultures feeding slang into the dominant culture. For many reasons, native slang does not have the currency in journalism and literature that it enjoys in the United States.

Slang in European languages. Several other European languages that, during the past, have contributed considerably to British and especially to American slang have well-developed slang systems of their own.

Spanish. Spain, with a long picaresque tradition in both life and literature, absorbed much argot from criminal subcultures into the printed language beginning in the 16th century. Cervantes, like Shakespeare, knew slang and used it well. This slang, along with the subcultures producing it, spread to the New World and proliferated through all Spanish settlements, with usage in each country developing along somewhat different lines. Modern continental Spanish slang is heavily indebted to the large indigenous Gypsy population. England was influenced most by continental Spanish, the United States by Caribbean, and especially Mexican, slang. Today, while Mexican slang contains some archaic Spanish terms, it is Mexican slang heavily dominated by *caló* (a semicriminal argot) and contains many aboriginal words, creations based on American English, and terms originated by the Pachucos, Mexican-American youths along the Mexican border. This is the Spanish slang, along with that of Cuban and Puerto Rican enclaves in many American cities, that most influences American usage today. Frequently it is clipped or anglicized so that it is not readily recognized as Spanish, as in the case of "pot" (marijuana, itself a *caló* word) from *potiguaya*, in turn cut back from *potación de guaya* (a strong intoxicant made of ripe cannabis seedpods soaked in wine or brandy).

French. French has a long tradition of slang production. There are, for example, criminal subcultures in Marseille that probably date back to the days of Roman colonialism. Slang today is as popular with literary men as it is with the man in the street. Recent immigration from Algeria has coloured French slang heavily. As in most other European cultures, the Gypsies continue to contribute to slang. Under the policing of the French Academy, backed during the 1960s by General DeGaulle, there was an official campaign, largely unsuccessful, to bar American slang from the French language. While French formerly contributed some words to American slang, and even more to British slang, it adds little today.

Italian. The Italians, especially urban Italians, are major makers of slang for home consumption. Sicily, however, has contributed the secret argot of the Mafia, which exists both in Italy and in the United States but remains largely secret in both countries, though Italian police have attempted to study it. Italians borrow freely from the slang terms of other European languages and, since World War II, from American slang, which is still popular in Italy though officially deplored.

Romanian. Romania, once a Roman prison colony,

has a rich slang heritage, particularly from the Gypsies, who are numerous. Also, Romania's policy of giving Gypsies work permits and gradually incorporating them into the dominant culture promises to encourage a wider infusion of Romany terms into the standard language. From the Balkans to Scandinavia, older Gypsy terms heavily infiltrate criminal argots and general slang.

Yiddish
slang *German.* In German, where *Hochdeutsch* (High German) dominates the standard language, slang has little recognition in literature, though many colourful idioms exist in the several regional dialects, and among males of the dominant culture there is a current *arschloch-humor* (anal humour), which is primarily scatalogical and remains on a spoken level. Yiddish, on the other hand, is rich in colourful metaphor and, in larger cities like Hamburg and Berlin, established a place for itself in theatrical and literary usage before World War I. Although German proper has contributed little to slang in other languages, Yiddish, with its roots in Middle High German, has put many terms into international circulation. German scholars have given close attention to the collection and analysis of older traditional nonstandard language usage under the categories of *Gaunersprache* and *Rotwelsch*, which are criminal argots; in fact, Martin Luther gave Europe one of its first German compilations of the language of Gypsies, fake friars, wandering Jews, and rogues in the preface of the *Liber Vagatorum* ("Book of Vagabonds"; 1528).   (D.W.M.)

BIBLIOGRAPHY. The transiency of most slang makes compiling a bibliography difficult. Otherwise undistinguished fiction may show certain varieties with high comprehension and sensitivity; almost any Sunday newspaper supplement may have a casual report on the usage of some currently newsworthy subculture; many studies, such as the PETER TAMONY series, *Americanisms: Content and Continuum*, may be known only to the professional scholar.

The most comprehensive critical bibliography is provided by DAVID W. MAURER in his updating of H.L. MENCKEN, *The American Language*, 4th ed. abridged ch. 11 of (1963); useful also are the quarterly bibliographies in *American Speech*, and the annual ones prepared by the PERMANENT INTERNATIONAL COMMITTEE ON LINGUISTICS.

For English, *Slang and Its Analogues* (1890–1904, reprinted 1970), by JOHN S. FARMER and WILLIAM ERNEST HENLEY, is still the most comprehensive work. More contemporary but less careful are various works by ERIC PARTRIDGE, notably *A Dictionary of Slang and Unconventional English*, 7th ed. rev. (1970, frequently updated), and *A Dictionary of the Underworld* (1950). FRANCIS GROSE, *A Classical Dictionary of the Vulgar Tongue* (1785; ed. with notes by PARTRIDGE, 1931, reprinted 1968), is an historical landmark; more specialized is JULIAN FRANKLYN, *Dictionary of Rhyming Slang* (1960). For American slang the only dictionary of consequence is that of HAROLD W. WENTWORTH and STUART B. FLEXNER (eds.), *Dictionary of American Slang* (1960, with supplement, 1967). More specialized are ROBERT S. GOLD, *A Jazz Lexicon* (1964); and HYMAN E. GOLDIN, FRANK O'LEARY, and MORRIS LIPSIUS (eds.), *Dictionary of American Underworld Lingo* (1950). DAVID W. MAURER has provided many studies of specialized argots, as in *The Big Con* (1940), *The Argot of the Racetrack* (1951), *Whiz Mob* (1955, 1964) and with VICTOR H. VOGEL, *Narcotics and Narcotic Addiction*, 3rd ed. (1967). For Canadian slang, see MARK E. ORKIN, *Speaking Canadian English* (1970); and WALTER S. AVIS, *A Bibliography of Writings on Canadian English 1857–1965* (1965); for that of Australia and New Zealand, SIDNEY J. BAKER, *The Australian Language* (1945), *The Drum: Australian Character and Slang* (1960), and *New Zealand Slang* (1941); and G.W. TURNER, *The English Language in Australia and New Zealand* (1966).

Comprehensive treatments of slang in other languages are even rarer than those in English. For French, see ALBERT DAUZAT, *Les Argots* (1929); and GEORGE SANDRY and MARCEL CARRERE, *Dictionnaire de l'argot moderne* (1953). Less comprehensive is CARLA PEKELIS, *A Dictionary of Colorful Italian Idioms* (1965). Depending on their orientation, most introductions to linguistics or to modern English have some discussion of the origin and significance of slang.

(S.B.F./R.McD.)

Slavery, Serfdom, and Forced Labour

The feature common to all forms of servitude surveyed in this article is the social sanction that permits one person

or group to compel the involuntary labour of another person or group. In all cases the bonded individual—whether slave, serf, indentured servant, or otherwise—is obliged to perform personal service for his lord or master under conditions that make him socially inferior and are restrictive of his freedom of action.

Certain forms of service, actually or allegedly involuntary, are not included within the range of this article. Military conscription, including impressment, is excluded because it rests on the age-old principle that every able-bodied citizen owes military service, however socially unequal the method of his selection. Metaphorical or extended uses of the term slave are also avoided. The expression wage slave, for instance, was used by Marxists in reference to labourers under capitalism and by U.S. slaveholders in the antebellum South to refer to Northern industrial labourers. Advocates of democracy have sometimes attributed slavery to citizens of totalitarian states.

The article is divided into the following sections:

I. Forms of involuntary servitude

SLAVERY

Degrees
of
slavery A slave is one who is owned by another and deprived of most or all rights and freedoms, hence the term chattel slave, denoting personal property at law. The slave is dependent on the whim of the owner, who may generally force him to any service and, at least in principle, may usually even dispose of his life. The term slavery, however, does embrace differing degrees of social status. Slaves in ancient Rome, for instance, could be educated and could, in many cases, acquire property and the means of buying their freedom. Black slaves in the antebellum Southern U.S., on the other hand, were expressly forbidden by law to receive an education or acquire property and thus could rarely attain on their own the means to buy their freedom. Very possibly the most extreme form of slavery was represented by the *Sklavenarbeiter*, or slave labourers, of Nazi Germany—Jews, Slavs, and other conquered peoples who, unlike most slaves, were often not even cared for as valued capital. As one survivor reported,

> We were not slaves; our status was much lower. True, we were deprived of freedom and became a piece of property which our masters put to work. But here the similarity with any known form of slavery ends, for we were a completely expendable piece of property. . . . The equipment in the shop was well maintained. It was operated with care, oiled, greased and allowed to rest; its longevity was protected. We, on the other hand, were like a piece of sandpaper which, rubbed once or twice, becomes useless and is thrown away to be burned with the waste.
>
> <div align="right">(W. Manchester, <i>The Arms of Krupp</i>,
Little, Brown, 1968, p. 522)</div>

Effects of
pastoral-
ism and
agriculture **Origins of slavery.** Explanations of the origins of slavery are necessarily speculative, constituting *post hoc* rationalizations. It would seem, however, that through the hunting and food-gathering stages of civilization, slavery probably was unknown; the hunter or food gatherer simply would have had no use for a slave, who would have been more of a burden than an asset for his master, as he would have been an additional mouth to feed. This reasoning seems to be supported by the fact that such hunters' societies as have survived into historical times, as for example those of most of the American Indians and of the Australian aborigines, do not seem ever to have practiced slavery.

In any event slavery as an institution definitely made its appearance when tribes reached the pastoral, as distinct from the hunter, stage. Even then it was modest as far as the number of slaves was concerned because the care of flocks required only a few hands. Furthermore, life was simple and there was little difference between the condition of a slave and that of the wives, sons, or daughters of his master, who were also subject to the latter's absolute authority.

The exploitation of slave labour increased at the agricultural stage. But as long as agriculture retained the character of a subsistence economy, slavery continued to bear on the whole the "patriarchal," or "domestic," character of the pastoral period.

Effects of market economy and urbanism **Expansion of slavery.** The real change in the character of slavery, as well as its expansion, came as a result of the change from a subsistence to a market economy. When large tracts of land fell into the hands of a relatively few wealthy landowners, and only one or a few staple products were cultivated, it was generally profitable to employ the labour of slaves working in large gangs. Under these conditions the slaves became an anonymous multitude, and their treatment was quite different and much harsher than when they still were considered members of their master's household. Examples of this type of "praedial," or "plantation," slavery existed in ancient Greece and Rome and in New World plantation economies.

In the cities slaves were used not only in the domestic service of the master and his family in all kinds of capacities and exploited for the satisfaction of the master's lust or of his artistic tastes but also for work in mining, industry, commerce, and the like. Slave girls staffed the brothels and filled the harems of the ancient world. At times there also were slave policemen and slave warriors. Among the latter, some achieved great power and sometimes took the place of their masters and even founded dynasties. Such cases, of course, were exceptional, and usually slaves were treated as an inferior class or caste.

Sources of slaves. It would seem that individuals were reduced into slavery mainly by capture or force; as punishment for some offense; by birth from slave parents; by sale for nonpayment of debt; or by sale by parents, guardians, or chieftains.

Undoubtedly, capture is the most ancient source of slaves. And once the need for slave labour increased, expeditions were undertaken with the specific view of capturing human beings to reduce them into slavery. Thus slave raiding and kidnapping became the major means of supply. They were practiced in antiquity as well as in modern times—until the end of the 19th century and perhaps even later.

Slavery as punishment Punishment for crime is also an ancient source of slaves. When society took the right to punish for crime into its own hands, criminals usually became publicly rather than privately owned slaves, as in the case of condemned criminals sentenced to the galleys. Although slavery of this kind seems to have disappeared, a certain analogy to it may be found in penal servitude and perhaps also in forced or compulsory labour employed by some colonial powers and imposed by certain governments upon political opponents.

A third source of slaves—birth—was the consequence of the acceptance of the idea that the slave was the property of his master. Consequently, the child born of slave parents belonged to their owner; however, birth has been a less important source of slaves than one would imagine: in particular, under the conditions of mass slavery such as those that prevailed on the Roman latifundia, and later on American plantations, there were usually a far greater number of men than women among the slaves. Furthermore, it was often more profitable to buy grown-up slaves

than to wait until children reached an age where they could be put to work.

Another major source of slaves was sale. This needs some explanation. Insofar as slaves were considered as objects of property, they were subject to sale—and the main purpose of slave raiding was to supply the slave market. In these cases, sale is not considered as the source of slavery, as the individuals concerned already were slaves (by capture or kidnapping, birth, sentence, or prior sale).

In many societies, however, it has been possible for a free individual to sell a person under his authority—a wife or concubine, a child or grandchild, or a ward—into slavery for money or other consideration; or a tribal chieftain might sell individuals, families, or groups under his jurisdiction or sanction their forced removal by traders. Although the sale of persons into chattel slavery has been virtually eliminated, it must be stressed that practices leading to similar results frequently have outlived legal prohibitions. One such practice has been the sham adoption of children, especially girls, of extremely poor households by wealthier people who pay a certain price to the natural parent and thereafter exploit the child. Such practices were widespread even in the 20th century in China and other countries of Southeast Asia, where they were known under the Chinese name of *mui tsai* ("little sister") and also in certain regions of South America, where the "adopted" child was frequently of Indian origin. Sham adoption

CONTRACT LABOUR

Closely related to slavery resulting from sale was the practice of contract labour, in which an individual surrendered his freedom to quit his work or his master, usually for a specified period. His entry into service may have been voluntary, as in the case of indentured servants who gained some financial advantage (such as transportation costs to a new land), or it may have been involuntary, as in the case of debtors enslaved for nonpayment of debts or criminals whose sentences have been commuted to indentured servitude. During the period of subjection, in any event, the individual's labour had at least one of the features of slavery in that he was not free to leave and was subject to coercive measures if he tried.

Debt bondage. In a considerable number of civilizations, an insolvent debtor either became his creditor's slave or could be sold by the latter to a third person. Usually the condition arose from a pledge by a debtor of his personal services, or those of a person under his control, as security for a loan. The main feature of such an arrangement is that the value of services furnished is not applied toward the liquidation of the debt. Consequently the individual pledged has practically no hope ever to escape his servile condition. And, as it is not unusual in such cases that the debt remains due after the death of the original debtor, thereby devolving on his next of kin, the servile station may become hereditary. Despite measures taken to put an end to servitude for debt, it has survived in many regions even in the second half of the 20th century. It occurs mainly in underdeveloped agricultural countries, but even economically more advanced countries have not been entirely exempt from it. In agricultural communities it often happens that the lender of money or credit is at the same time a wealthy local landlord, while the debtors are the impoverished farmers. In more industrialized communities, the moneylender either directly exploits the debtor's labour for his own profit or hires him out to some third party. "Temporary" debt slavery

Colonial indenture. In colonial times, indentured service was a form of contract labour; in the middle and later 19th century, Chinese and Indian labourers, commonly called coolies, moved great distances under contractual arrangements. Deception, kidnapping, and coercion were widely used as means of obtaining control of defenseless persons, usually unskilled and poorly educated adult males. North American indentured servants

North American indentured labour began with the founding of the colonies and existed concurrently with free labour and slavery until the American Revolution. Its subjects were males and females of western European and mainly British origin. The terms of indenture were harsh to favourable, depending upon the strength of the individual's position and the preferences of his master. The harshest terms and the longest indentures were imposed upon criminals whose death sentences (often for political offenses and numerous crimes now regarded as misdemeanours) were commutable upon entry into colonial indentures.

At the other extreme, those able to negotiate the terms of indenture were able to obtain contracts generally patterned after English apprenticeship customs and were usually free after five to seven years of service. Colonial laws gave some protection to the indentured servant but also sanctioned and enforced performance of the contract whether oral or written.

Chinese and Indian overseas labourers

The indenture of Chinese and Indians also was associated with colonial developments but occurred later, following the abolition of slavery in areas other than the American colonies. Indian emigrant labourers were brought into British, French, and Dutch African colonies and also into Ceylon, Malaya, and the Caribbean. Chinese labourers served in many of these areas and also in Peru, Western Samoa, New Zealand, and Hawaii. The Chinese, Japanese, and Hindustani workers who came to California in the latter 19th century were commonly regarded as coolies, but they were mainly free immigrants, some of whom had completed or escaped from indenture contracts. Their numbers included those who remigrated from the sugar plantations of Hawaii. Although Asian indenture was not free of kidnap, decoy, and fraud, it was basically a noncompulsory system to the extent that the governments of China and India were able to protect the interests of their nationals by legislation and negotiation. Poverty in the home country was the foundation of Asiatic indenture. In contrast, American colonial indenture, though founded partly on poverty, was also fed by a harsh penal code characterized by political and religious intolerance.

Debtor's labour and chain gangs

Peonage. A form of contract labour commonly associated with deception or circumvention is peonage. Early in the history of Mexico, the conquerors worked out a plan by which the poor, especially the Indians, could be forced to do the work of the planters and mine operators. The word peon became synonymous with the English word labourer, but it later was restricted in its meaning to those labourers who were compelled to serve their creditors to pay debts that by contract they had pledged themselves to pay in labour. For example, although the Thirteenth Amendment to the U.S. Constitution and congressional legislation prohibited any such involuntary servitude in the United States, the former slave-holding states devised certain legislation, following emancipation, to make labour compulsory. Under these state laws, employers deceived ignorant men by inducing them to sign contracts for labour in payment of debts and deceived those who might have to pay fines imposed by the courts to sign other similar contracts. In rural districts far removed from the populous centres, the chain-gang system of forced labour, under the pretense of farming out the services of penal offenders, resulted in great injustice. The practice of leasing short-term prisoners, both white and black, to managers of labour camps was continued in a few of the Southern states.

SERFDOM

Distinctions between serfs and slaves

According to customary legal distinctions, slaves were chattel to be treated at will, whereas serfs, though bound to a lord, were attached to a hereditary plot of land, liable only for certain dues and services and by right protected from being maimed or killed. In fact, however, serfs almost everywhere very often could be bought and sold without land and frequently were subject to almost unlimited discipline from their masters. In any case, the vast majority of serfs were peasants. This means that they obtained their subsistence from a plot of land. This, rather than their place in public law, was the essential feature differentiating serfs from slaves. The slave was an instrument of production owned by a master who provided him with food and clothing. The serf provided his own food and clothing from his own productive effort. Under for-

tunate circumstances he could produce more than his own subsistence requirements and accumulate reserves of his own. He was, however, a dependent peasant; this meant that a substantial proportion of the surplus product of his holding was taken by his overlord. Alternatively, or additionally, the lord used the serf's labour for the cultivation of the portion of his land that was not held by tenants. The payment of rent in money, in kind, or in labour was not, however, the only or even the essential sign of the serf's dependence, for rents are paid by freemen as well as by serfs. The essential additional mark of serfdom was lack of freedom of movement of the peasant family and restrictions on the free disposal of its property. When the peasant could leave his holding, and if necessary his village, without obtaining a lord's permission, he was no longer a serf.

CORVÉE, OR STATUTE, LABOUR

Although the term corvée applied originally to the regular work that both serfs and freedmen owed a lord, it later became synonymous with statute labour, a specified amount of labour on public projects required by law. The corvée was revived when money payment did not provide sufficient labour for public projects. This might occur when public revenues were low, when there was a shortage of labour, or when the available labour did not customarily seek outside employment. It was revived in France in 1726 for road work and was finally abolished during the French Revolution. In England and Scotland statute labour on roads was used from the 16th through the 19th centuries, by which time the turnpike system had begun to take over the main roads. Compulsory labour in Africa was instituted by Europeans to overcome the African's alleged resistance to leaving the village to work for wages. In French West Africa, for example, the corvée was applied until 1946; all able-bodied African males were obliged to work about 15 days a year on public works. In the Peoples Republic of China today, civilians may be drafted to spend a certain number of days (usually ten) a year on road work, repairing dikes, and so forth.

The basic distinction between the corvée and ordinary forced labour is that the corvée is a general and periodic short-term obligation; forced labour is usually prescribed for a long or indefinite period as a method of discipline or discrimination on a highly selective basis.

II. Slavery in antiquity

THE ANCIENT NEAR EAST

Royal slavery

Sources of slaves. Warfare was the earliest source of slaves in the ancient Near East and always remained a relatively important one. Originally captives seem to have been slaughtered; later, women and then men were spared to serve their captors: the Sumerian word for slave woman means literally "woman from a foreign land" and appears at an earlier date than that for a man slave. Some prisoners passed into private possession, but most of them became the property of the kings (in Egypt all captives belonged in the first instance to Pharaoh), who either kept them or dedicated them to service in temples. The numbers of royal (state) and temple slaves thus created often grew considerably. They were the only large aggregations of slaves in preclassical times; and, except perhaps in late Assyrian times, there seems to have been no equivalent of the great private slave households of Roman times.

The supply of slaves by war was supplemented by purchase, usually from among neighbouring peoples. "House born" slaves, however, enjoyed a slightly higher social status, and masters often supplied their slaves with "wives" or "husbands" in order to obtain them. An important source of slaves lay within the native population itself. At least from the 3rd dynasty of Ur in Babylonia (c. 2100 BC), and no doubt earlier, and from the Old Kingdom in Egypt (c. 2686–c. 2160 BC) self-sale or the sale of children in order to pay debts was widespread. Unlike the ordinary form of slavery, debt slavery was recognized as a social evil that should be held in check.

Many Babylonian kings, notably in the Old Babylonian period (c. 1800–1600 BC), issued decrees liberating debt slaves and abolishing public and private debt. The Hebrew sabbatical year (the seventh) in which Israelite debt slaves were to go free was paralleled in the Code of Hammurabi by which such persons were to be released upon completing three years' work for their creditor. It is not known how far and for how long these laws were observed, though Jeremiah castigates their evasion (Jer. 34:8–17). Poor Jews were forced to sell their children into slavery to pay their taxes after returning from the Babylonian Captivity (Neh. 5:1–5).

Slaves, freemen, and freedmen

Status of slaves. Slaves and freemen were not often or strictly divided racially or culturally as they have been in more recent slave societies. Moreover, between slave and freeman there existed a variety of semifree classes dependent on king or temple, and even free citizens were commonly liable to labour service (corvée). Nevertheless a slave was not a human being before the law but a "head" like an animal. He seems to have enjoyed no protection from his master, and if he was injured by someone else, the case was considered as one of damage to his master's property. Hebrew law provided that if a master beat his slave to death and the victim lingered on for a day or two, the master went unpunished "for the slave is his money" (Ex. 21:20–21). In the circumstances, runaways were numerous, and in Babylonia the laws of Hammurabi prescribed death for harbouring a fugitive; other societies, notably among the Hebrews, were more lenient. Probably most masters found that it paid to treat slaves reasonably well, and sometimes inducements were held out to them, such as the privilege of retaining small gratuities or the prospect of ultimate liberation. Manumission (freedom) was often granted on condition that the freedman (who was frequently adopted) should support his ex-master during his lifetime; any failure to do so led to re-enslavement. The freedman thus was in an intermediate position between slavery and complete freedom; he might be required to remain for life or a definite time with, or perform some special duty or service for, his former master or a person named by him, and his failure or refusal to do so would subject him to being again reduced to slavery.

The capacity of slaves to carry on business on their master's behalf was recognized, under rigid safeguards, in Babylonian times. By the Neo-Babylonian period (c. 620 BC), slaves carrying on business—as merchants, bankers, artisans, tenant farmers—and living on their own were commoner; some of them even owned slaves of their own. Any property acquired by a slave, however, remained legally the possession of his master, the slave making a payment for the privilege of engaging in business.

Slave occupations

Economic importance. Slaves were to be found in almost every field of work in preclassical antiquity, but in the absence of reliable statistics it is impossible to estimate the total economic importance of slave labour.

Most privately owned slaves in cities were domestics; in the country they worked alongside their masters in the fields. They seem never to have presented a threat to the existence of free tenant farmers, though true slave farmers existed on large estates in the Assyrian Empire, and could be bought and sold either with the land they worked or separately. This was probably exceptional, because of the conditions of the period. Slaves seem to have been rarer in skilled trades and professions, though slave apprentices are mentioned, especially in Neo-Babylonian times, in contracts concluded between their owners and master craftsmen. Skilled workmen were also to be found among the temple slaves but were probably exceptional there also. In general, craftsmen were freemen. It seems certain, therefore, that any threat to the economic conditions of free persons by slaves was confined to the unskilled, and it can only have been acute in times of an overabundant supply of labour, but to judge from the retention of unpopular forced-labour service, a shortage of labour was much commoner.

GREECE AND ROME

Slaves are mentioned in the Homeric poems, which probably reflect the conditions of the early 1st millennium BC, and they play a prominent role in the legal code of Justinian

(AD 527–565). During these 15 centuries, slavery was an accepted institution, never seriously challenged. In the 5th and 4th centuries BC, it is true, some philosophers questioned slavery like all other fundamental human institutions, such as the state and the family. As Plato was not much interested in the problem, we know little of the debate, but it appears from Aristotle that some philosophers declared that slavery was contrary to nature and therefore unjust. Aristotle himself took an opposite view. According to him, many—indeed the majority—of the human race lacked those higher qualities of the soul that were necessary for freedom. Slavery was not only good for the master, who was provided with living instruments, but for the slave, who received guidance that he was incapable of providing for himself. Aristotle admitted that in practice men free by nature were enslaved "by accident," and natural slaves were allowed to be free; but although the institution was not always properly used, it was fundamentally natural and good. Later philosophical schools, like the Cynics and Stoics, who preached the brotherhood of man, held that slavery was contrary to nature, but they did not suggest its abolition. Freedom and slavery, like all material concerns, were, they taught, matters of indifference. To Christians there were neither bondmen nor freemen in Christ, but in this world they counselled masters to be kind to their slaves and slaves to be obedient to their masters. The doctrine of the Roman law was summed up by Justinian in the sentence, quoted from the 2nd-century lawyer Florentinus: "Slavery is an institution of the jus gentium (law of nations), whereby a man is, contrary to nature, subjected to the ownership of another." No other legal institution is expressly admitted to be contrary to natural law, but after this formal acknowledgment of philosophical theory, the Roman lawyers formulated the practical rules governing slavery without demur.

Philosophical, religious, and legal views of slavery

Sources of Greek and Roman slaves. The sources of slaves were many and varied. In primitive Athens and Rome, insolvent debtors might be enslaved by their creditors. This was forbidden by Solon at Athens in the 6th century BC and in the late 4th century BC in Rome, but the rule probably prevailed longer in many communities. With the extension of Roman law to the whole empire, slavery for debt ceased to be legal. In Greece, children exposed and abandoned by their parents became the slaves of those who reared them. Roman law varied on this point until Justinian in the 6th century declared that all exposed infants were free. Poor parents also sometimes sold their children. This was prohibited by Roman law but was nevertheless not uncommon, especially under the later empire; the sale of newborn infants was legally recognized by Constantine the Great. A freeman might, under Roman law, allow himself to be sold into slavery and could not reclaim his freedom if he was over 20 and had received a part of the price paid for him. A few offenses were punished both in Greece and Rome by sale into slavery, and under the empire a common penalty for crimes among the lower orders was slavery in the state mines and quarries.

Debt slavery and the law

The principal sources of slaves, however, were war, piracy and kidnapping, breeding, and import from barbarian lands. Victors in war always possessed, and frequently exercised, the right of selling captives. With the establishment of the principate (27 BC) conditions changed, however. Under Augustus there were still wars of conquest and many thousands of barbarian prisoners were enslaved, but thereafter large-scale wars were rare. Peace reigned within the empire, piracy and brigandage were effectively suppressed and, without these two major sources, slaves could be imported only from beyond the Rhine, the Danube, and the Euphrates. In these circumstances, slaves became scarcer and their price rose. Breeding in these circumstances became necessary and profitable.

Economic importance. There were few activities that were not common to freemen and slaves. The latter were, of course, excluded from political life and only citizens could hold magistracies (public office). Slaves were, moreover, excluded from military and naval service; only in moments of extreme crisis were slaves enrolled in the armed forces, being freed for the purpose. Domestic service, however, was reserved for slaves; it is almost unknown in classical antiquity to find a freeman as a personal servant. It is often stated on the basis of statements in Plato, Aristotle, and Cicero that the Greeks and Romans regarded manual work, with the exception of agriculture, as degrading for freemen and only fit for slaves. The great majority of Athenian citizens, however, either were peasants, craftsmen, or labourers and felt no shame in the fact; they worked even in the mines. But while the hardest manual labour was tolerated, any employment that involved being subject to another man's orders was considered servile and degrading, even if the work was managerial and not manual. This attitude seems to have been widespread in the Greek and Roman world, and it had far-reaching effects on the economy.

It meant in the first place that slaves (or freedmen) were normally employed in secretarial and managerial posts. In 4th-century Athens, bank managers were often slaves or freedmen of the bank owners. Within the sphere of agriculture the bailiff, who was directly responsible to his owner, was normally a slave, even though the estate was worked by free tenants and free casual labour. In the early principate in Rome a curious anomaly arose. The emperor's principal secretaries and accountants, who were slaves or freedmen, inevitably became politically influential and important and came to do the work of secretaries of state and ministers of finance. This situation caused great bitterness among the senatorial aristocracy, but it was only after a century that the problem was solved, when the offices of the imperial household came to be regarded as public rather than as domestic posts and became acceptable to members of the equestrian order, though not to senators.

Secondly, it was virtually impossible for any industrial enterprise to expand beyond the scope of a household business without the use of slave labour. A freeman would accept casual jobs, usually on a contract basis, but he was generally unwilling to submit himself to regular work under a master's orders. A craftsman might employ members of his family and perhaps apprentices, but if he wished to expand his business he had to buy slaves. Except when slaves were very cheap, this meant a heavy and risky capital outlay, and as a result industry tended to be on a small scale, unless conditions were exceptionally favourable, as in mining.

Slavery reached its high-water mark in Rome in the 2nd and 1st centuries BC. Not only were slaves very abundant and cheap, owing to the prevalence of wars and piracy, but the Roman upper classes were immensely wealthy and were building up huge estates (*latifundia*). The result was the introduction of agricultural slavery on a vast scale. The peasantry were progressively expropriated, and their lands either cultivated by slave gangs or converted into ranches manned by slave herdsmen. This is the only period of antiquity in which large-scale revolts occurred, in Sicily in 135–132 and 104–100 BC and the rising of Spartacus in Italy in 73–71 BC, and the difficulty with which these revolts were suppressed proves the large numbers involved. Slaves were also employed on a vast scale in the mines; there are said to have been as many as 40,000 in the silver mines of New Carthage in Spain.

In the later empire, despite the fall in the price of slaves, there developed hereditary groups of agricultural slaves who could not legally be sold apart from the land; their status in law and practice more and more resembled that of free tenants, who on their side were being converted into serfs and were bound to a given piece of land. Convicts were used in certain state quarries, but miners were, in general, freemen. The chief innovation of the age was the establishment by Diocletian, in the 3rd century, of state weaving and dyeing factories manned by slaves; but by the 4th century these slaves had become hereditary groups whose status differed little from that of freemen.

Social conditions. It is obviously impossible to generalize on the condition of slaves in classical antiquity. All slaves were liable to the arbitrary cruelty of their masters; their only legal remedy was to escape to a sanctuary and

demand to be sold to another master. Antoninus Pius (AD 138–161) ruled that the killing of a slave by his master was homicide, but Constantine (306–337) absolved the master if the slave died as a result of flogging. In practice there were great differences between various categories of slaves. In the mines slaves often were ruthlessly worked to death, and the chained gangs on the land were brutally treated. On the other hand, a private secretary or a nurse might be treated as one of the family, and a craftsman in charge of a workshop or a sea captain in command of a ship enjoyed de facto most of the rights of a freeman. Miners and agricultural slaves had little hope of freedom, while domestic servants could reasonably hope to be manumitted, and craftsmen and shopkeepers had a fair chance of buying their freedom.

The fact that slavery was universally accepted as a normal social institution made relations between slaves and masters easier. Slavery was regarded as a misfortune but not as a wrong, and slaves felt no resentment against their masters unless they were ill-treated. There was, moreover, no distinction of race or colour between slaves and freemen. In classical Greece most slaves were barbarians, but there were many Greek slaves (although no Greek was a slave in his own city) and free barbarians, and there was no marked racial or cultural cleavage between the Greeks and the neighbouring barbarian peoples. In the Roman Empire slaves were, for the most part, from the same stock as the provincials. Nor was there any marked distinction in the kind of work done by freemen and slaves. There were slaves in the professions and skilled trades and free manual workers. Slaves were not distinguishable by dress or any outward mark from free persons in the same walk of life, and the intermarriage between slave and free, though legally null, was not uncommon in the lower ranks of society. A manumitted slave did not in Greek cities become a citizen, citizenship being a strictly hereditary privilege, but he ranked like any other resident alien. In Roman law he became a citizen if manumitted in proper legal form, though he did not enjoy full civic rights, being ineligible to serve in the army or to hold public office or become a city councillor. (Ed.)

III. Servitude in ancient India and China

SLAVERY AND THE CASTE SYSTEM IN INDIA

India's oldest legal treatise, called the Laws of Manu (variously dated between the 2nd century BC and 2nd century AD), contains articles apparently dating back to the 12th century BC and identifying six types of servants: the captive taken under a flag or in a battle; the domestic who enters someone's service for maintenance; the serf born of a woman slave in the master's home; the man who has been bought or won; one inherited in an estate; the one who is a slave as punishment for not being able to pay a fine. Any one of these enslaved persons could attain freedom, however, under the following conditions: (1) the enslaved war prisoner could attain freedom if he left in his place a slave who could perform the duties his master had charged him with; (2) the person condemned to slavery for debts could be freed if he paid his master what was owed him; (3) a slave saving his master's life was considered free before the law and deserving of a reward. But in all these cases of liberation, the tacit consent of the master was necessary for the slave to exercise his right to be free.

More abundant than slavery was serfdom. Within the rigid classification of social classes in ancient India, the Śūdra caste was obliged to serve the Kṣatriya, or warrior, caste, the Brahmins, or priests, and the Vaiśyas, or farmers, cattle raisers, and merchants. There is an unbreakable barrier, however, separating these castes from the inferior Śūdra caste, the descendants of the primitive indigenous people who lived in serfdom. Below this there was yet a final class, the lowest and unworthy and without a social category, made up of the pariahs, who lived by begging. The separation that the pariahs were obliged to maintain was rigorous, not only in terms of caste but also in terms of their daily lives, because pariahs were positively forbidden to approach a person in a higher caste; even when begging alms, they had to maintain a certain distance.

Even the servile Śūdra despised the pariah, although the former lived forever afraid of and subject to the other classes.

Not even from an economic standpoint did the Śūdra find the opportunity for a door to open the way toward his betterment. In those times it was not a person's economic wealth that gave him his social rank but rather his social and racial level; and thus one of Manu's laws says: "Although able, a Śūdra must not acquire excess riches, since when a Śūdra acquires a fortune, he vexes the Brāhmaṇs with his insolence." The barrier separating the servile castes took on extreme cruelty in some laws:

A man of low caste who dares to contest a man of a higher caste must be branded below the hip and exiled. If he raises a hand or a stick to a superior, the hand shall be cut off; and if in a moment of rage he kicks him, that foot shall then be cut off. Should he inflict injuries upon a man of a higher caste, a hot dagger shall be put into his mouth.

The legal condition of the Śūdra left him only death as a means of improving his condition.

SLAVERY AND PEASANT SERFDOM IN CHINA

The sale and purchase of slaves did not exist in China as a formal business, although there were in fact enslaved serfs and also men or women who became slaves for the following reasons: (1) impoverished persons could surrender themselves to slavery in order to avoid dying of starvation; (2) criminals committing high treason could be made into slaves in public service or at the royal palace; (3) the children of these condemned ones could be castrated and used as overseers and eunuch slaves in the harems; (4) adulterous women, expelled from the home, often had no other recourse but to offer themselves as slaves; (5) debtors sliding into insolvency could be taken into slavery by creditors. This practice was in existence from the most primitive times and continued in China until the 16th century.

Serfdom in China In China, extreme serfdom generally made slavery unnecessary. The landowner did not need the purchase of men for labour, because the serfs, theoretically free but in practice subject to the most cruel serfdom, worked as slaves. The Chinese landholders obtained all of the serfs they needed and in fact more than necessary, since the great fecundity of the peasant couples kept them in good supply. The rural serfs paid their tribute in labour; they worked the lord's lands, while some women helped to pay tribute by weaving silk.

In the social history of the Chinese Empire, the various dynasties that succeeded each other for millennia are usually distinguished by some predominant cultural characteristic, but there is an inalterable parallelism in all of the epochs with respect to serfdom. From the Shang dynasty, when history and legend unite (2nd millennium BC), there is evidence of an industrious agricultural people working servilely on the lands of the lords. In the Chou dynasty (1122–221 BC), when feudalism was organized by means of a tributary system, the rural population was oppressed by great vigilance in the collection of tribute; and the farmer lived practically dedicating his life to the lord, who required his oppressive share whether the harvest was good or bad, and drove the serf into extreme poverty. During times of famine (caused by poor harvests or wars between the lords), the parents either abandoned their children with the hope that fortune would save them from starvation or they would offer them as slaves to a lord who would feed them. The Chou dynasty was the epoch of the great philosophers, Confucius, Mencius, and Lao-tzu. According to Lao-tzu, it was necessary to return to the natural life, to the simplicity of primitive work, in which each family depended upon its efforts with the land and fed only themselves and did not enrich the lords. Confucius, on the contrary, less a philosopher than a moralist, partisan of order at any cost, espoused education as the means of attaining progress for the lower social classes. These were times of rivalries between the lords, until one of them, Ch'in Shih Huang-ti, brought to an end the feudal anarchy of the Chou dynasty and founded the absolute monarchy of the Ch'in dynasty (221–206 BC), which scorned the philosophers and the words of the

texts, imposed a harsh militarism, and completed the most gigantic effort of an enslaved populace: the Great Wall of China. But the workers who performed this forced labour were farmers who knew that the Great Wall would defend the country from the frequent incursions of the Tartars, who put them in danger of being enslaved or being robbed. The following dynasty, the Han (206 BC–AD 220), was a return to intellectualism, which implemented the standards of Confucius and his followers; then Buddhism infiltrated into China from India and, in spreading humanitarian ideas, influenced behaviour toward the worker and tended to soften the oppression of the serfs. Nevertheless, with all of the luxury, culture, and refinement of the imperial court, which reached its maximum splendour with the T'ang dynasty (AD 618–907), the misery of the people and their enslavement grew.

Tenant farmers and agricultural labourers who worked on the large private estates continued to be free in theory but were in practice at the mercy of the landowners. They could be bought and sold; they could be arbitrarily punished; they had virtually no rights before the law. This form of landlordism and tenant farming continued from these early times up until the modern period.

THE PEASANTRY IN JAPAN

By the 8th century AD Japan had been greatly influenced by Buddhist ideas and views of life emphasizing mercy and tolerance, but the Buddhist foundations of Japanese life were apparently insufficient to free the slaves and serfs characteristic of the landed economy. The manor, or *shōen* in Japan, remained one of the major features of social organization. It contained the lord and his retinue and at least three types of labourers: the "free workers," who were only nominally free, for without land of their own they were really immobile; the serfs who went with the land (and whose condition was remarkably similar to the serfs of medieval Europe); and the land and household slaves.

In the centuries that followed, however, so much new land was put under cultivation that the great landowners found it difficult to find additional slave labourers or serfs and thus had to rely more and more on the services of freemen or runaway serfs, who themselves were showing a new kind of enterprise and occupying new plots of land. The general effect of the labour shortage was to improve the treatment of slaves and serfs and thus gradually to reduce the old distinctions between free and unfree. The general effect of the occupation of new plots of land was to encourage the development of individual enterprise and a sense of devotion to one's own land in Japan. All this was to shape strongly the character and status of the Japanese peasant into modern times.   (L.Bo.)

IV. Servitude in Muslim lands and Europe

THE PERSISTENCE OF SLAVERY

The Muslim world. Slavery continued under the Eastern Roman and Byzantine Empire, and the appearance of Islām gave a new character or direction to the institution. Muḥammad found slavery well established in Arabia when he began to preach the new religion in the first years of the 7th century. His attitude toward it as revealed in the Qur'ān (Koran) was similar to that of the Christian churches: he did not condemn slavery but taught that slaves should be treated with humanity and that the liberation of a slave was a pious and meritorious act. *The Qur'ānic view*

But the appearance of Islām was followed by wars of conquest that covered vast areas in Asia, northern Africa, and eastern and southern Europe. After the Arabs came other Muslim invaders, including the Ottoman Turks. All these wars led to the capture of numerous prisoners, often reduced to slavery, although usually the civilian population was left free on condition of paying taxes to the conquerors. During the Crusades, Christians also enslaved many of their Muslim prisoners. This brought about a considerable increase in the slave traffic, not only in Muslim lands but in Christian Europe as well. Even the church's strenuous efforts to prevent the sale of Christians by Christians were not always successful: Hanseatic, Venetian, and Genoese slave traders bought Syrians, *Muslim–Christian reprisals*

Serbians, Bulgarians, Armenians, and others from the Turks and resold them elsewhere. The fall of Constantinople in 1453 was followed by a marked increase of sales. Another source of slavery in Muslim lands was the capture of seamen and passengers in the Mediterranean by buccaneers operating from North Africa. "Slave charities" were established in England and other European countries to redeem these Christian prisoners, and diplomatic efforts were made to curb the Muslim slave trade. Muslim slavers also raided territories in various parts of black Africa or purchased slaves from African chieftains.

It must be noted, however, that slavery in Muslim countries, which continued for centuries and survived legally, or at least in custom, in a few of them, has always been very different from that which existed in Rome and in the Americas after their colonization by Europeans. Gang slavery for work in the fields or in industry and mining was almost unknown in the Islāmic world. Most of the slaves were employed in wealthy households for domestic service and were well treated, in accordance with the prescriptions of the Qur'ān. The one really cruel Muslim institution was that of the eunuchs, which involved emasculation. Women slaves in harems became their masters' concubines or even legitimate wives. Furthermore, Muslim society was not usually race or colour conscious. Liberated slaves of whatever origin were readily absorbed as equal members of the community, and examples of slaves or former slaves reaching the highest positions were numerous. Perhaps the most famous example of all is the case of the Mamlūk slave dynasty, which ruled Egypt for more than two and a half centuries (1250–1517), during which period one slave ruler succeeded another in the same way as normally a son succeeds his father.

Spain and Portugal. In Spain and Portugal, slavery continued to exist, not only through the period of Arabic, or Moorish, dominance but also after their reconquest by the Christians in the 15th century. Naturally, the defeated Muslims were the first to be reduced into slavery. But soon the Portuguese set out to import slaves from Africa as well. The first black slaves were imported in 1444 by Portuguese captains of Prince Henry the Navigator, who had obtained them as ransom in exchange for Moorish prisoners. Later, the Portuguese engaged directly in the slave trade and established factories (trading posts) for that purpose on the coast of Guinea.

Black slaves were imported in ever-increasing numbers into southern Portugal and neighbouring regions of Spain, where Seville became an important slave market. These regions had greatly suffered from wars between Christians and Muslims, and their populations had been largely depleted. Imported Africans were employed not only for service in wealthy households but also for work in the fields and for a variety of tasks in the cities, especially as stevedores in the harbours. Because the Portuguese, and to a lesser degree also Spaniards, as a result of the many conquests, had little race or colour consciousness, the various elements of the population mixed relatively freely and ultimately merged.

EUROPEAN SERFDOM

Origins of serfdom. One of the sources of the servile population of medieval Europe was the body of slaves of the late Roman Empire and of the barbarian states that succeeded the empire. As early as the 2nd century AD, the slackening of production for the market caused changes in estate management. Large estates that had been worked by slave gangs housed and fed by the estate owner were divided into peasant holdings, some of which were granted to the slaves, who, however, were not necessarily freed. In some cases enfranchisements did put the former slave on a level with free members of society, but for the most part even the freedman continued to be under the protection of his former master and owed him loyalty and services.

The bulk of the peasants of the late empire and early Middle Ages were neither slaves nor freedmen but *coloni*. These *coloni* might have taken up holdings granted by a proprietor or they might have surrendered their own

lands to him in return for protection, receiving back their land as a dependent tenement. This surrender and reissue of land frequently accompanied the act by which a person commended himself to a great man and swore fealty to him, though the act of commendation did not necessarily involve any land transaction. It was made in order to obtain protection (especially in the empire) from the state tax gatherer and (especially in the disorders of the early Middle Ages) from invaders and oppressive neighbours. Whatever the origin of the *coloni*, a problem concerning them, which was as old as the Roman Empire, was to prevent them from leaving their land. The solution was to bind them to their holdings. This was done, probably originally for fiscal reasons, by the emperor Constantine in AD 332. But it was so useful to the landlords that by the 6th century it was still firmly established, and *coloni*, though legally free, were treated as an inferior element in society.

A significant element of the new servile condition was the labour services owed on the landlord's own (demesne) land. In theory, these labour services were no more symptoms of servile tenure than other forms of rent or service. But in practice the exaction of labour services required the exercise by the landlord's agents of labour discipline. This was recognized as one of the clearest signs of a man's personal subjection.

In the 9th and 10th centuries, the serfs, in the strict sense of the word, those who in fact were called *servi*, were mainly those descended from the former slave population, though many on the big estates who were not called *servi* (*e.g.*, the *coloni*) had conditions of life that were virtually servile. In the next three centuries, economic and political conditions in Europe changed considerably. Population increased; commerce and industry developed; towns grew up; and, both within the old territories of the Carolingian Empire and in sparsely occupied Slavonic lands east of the Elbe, forests and marshes were opened up for cultivation. Politically there was, first of all, a disintegration of the old forms of authority, both central and local and, from the 12th century, a reconstitution of feudal monarchies, duchies, and counties. Statistical evidence about serfdom during this period is scanty, but by the 13th century it is clear that there was an immense increase in the number of dependent peasants, whether in the territories of present-day France, England, or western Germany. It has been shown that this increase in the numbers of peasants whose social and economic condition was virtually equivalent to servility did not occur, as was once believed, as a result of the spread of the legal status of the Carolingian *servi* to the *coloni*, freedmen, and other categories of dependent peasants on the big estates.

Social conditions and statuses. The *servi* were considered to be personally subjected to one master "to the very bones." Their condition was hereditary, usually through the mother. They had no legal rights in the public courts. They could not normally enter the clerical order. The only way in which their servile status could be ended was by an act of enfranchisement or manumission by their master. Since these serfs constituted a hereditary caste, the only way in which their numbers grew over the centuries was by natural increase. This was offset by manumissions and by escape. By the middle of the 13th century, the serfs in the stricter juridical sense of the word were relatively no more numerous than four centuries earlier. The increase was in the numbers of dependent peasants whose status was socially, if not juridically, servile. They were servile because lords at all levels in the feudal hierarchy were strengthening their rights (or seizing rights) of private jurisdiction through the right of command, *bannum,* exercised not merely over their tenants but over all inhabitants within their area of jurisdiction. Even the juridically free tenants had no redress against the lord who had appropriated for himself a jurisdiction that had once been public.

In the case of both types of lordship, whether personal or real or in many instances a mixture of both, there were three principal obligations shared by serfs and by other dependent peasants. The first obligation was the payment to the lord of a head payment, or *capitagium* (French *chevage*). This was common to serfs, to enfranchised

Black slavery in Portugal

Coloni

Labour services owed by the serf

Obligations of the serf to the lord

men, to those who had commended themselves to a religious overlord, and to other dependent peasants. It was not a heavy payment, but it was the sign that the payer accepted his dependence on the lord. Next was the obligation (*forismaritagium*) to obtain the lord's permission for marriage outside the social group or outside the lord's domain. This was particularly important in the case of juridical serfs, for if a male serf married a free woman, the offspring followed the mother's condition. But in the case of both juridical serfs and dependents, marriage outside the domain was (apart from flight) the most serious threat to the lord's future supply of tenants and labourers. The third principal obligation was that of surrendering part of the peasant inheritance to the lord at the death of the servile or subject tenant. This *mainmorte* of the serf was the whole or a substantial part of the inheritance, where there were no direct heirs to succeed. If there were direct heirs, the lord would allow the inheritance to go to them, so that they could continue production and pay rent. Subject peasants who were not juridical serfs had a modified obligation, that of paying the best beast or chattel, but this was paid whether the direct heirs succeeded or not. These were the three most common symbols of dependence; other symbols included the payment of an arbitrary tallage, a seigneurial tax, which was a burden shared by juridical serfs and subject peasants alike.

This necessarily simplified description of serfdom, and peasant dependence between the 9th and 13th centuries must be tempered with the recognition that from region to region there were varying degrees of dependence and of servile obligations.

Decline of serfdom in the west. As early as the end of the 13th century, the French monarchy, largely for fiscal reasons, began a policy of individual manumission of serfs on crown lands. Perhaps the most significant early initiatives, however, came from the heads of the Italian communes, which were among the most powerful rulers of the peninsula. Their motives were mixed and included the wish to weaken the power of the landowning nobility, to increase the number of free taxpayers to the commune, and to increase the urban labour force. These real motives were covered by moralizing. The enfranchisement of serfs by Bologna in 1256–57 was attributed to the realization that slavery was the consequence of the fall of man, that man's natural condition is freedom, and that Bologna was the home of freedom.

By the 14th century, economic conditions in western Europe were favourable to the replacement of the servile by the free peasant tenant. The growth of the power of central and regional governments permitted the enforcement of peasant-landlord contracts (as in métayage, or stock and land-lease contracts) without the need for peasant servility. The final abandonment of labour services on demesnes removed the need for the direct exercise of labour discipline. The drastic population decline after 1350, as a result of the Black Death, altered the land-to-labour ratio in favour of tenants. And, not least, peasant risings, which were endemic in England, France, Italy, and Spain in the 14th and 15th centuries, culminating in the German Peasant War of the early 16th century, also forced more favourable terms of peasant tenure. Although the new peasants were not necessarily better off economically than their servile forebears, their status in society conformed to their economic position rather than to the legal classification of their holdings or their persons.

Prolonged serfdom in eastern Europe. This favourable evolution was not shared by the peasants of eastern Europe. In the later Middle Ages, peasant status from eastern Germany to Muscovy deteriorated sharply; a second serfdom began that was prolonged well into modern times, in Russia until 1861. Peasant conditions in eastern European countries before the 14th century do not seem to have been worse than those of the west. In some ways they were better, for in eastern Germany, Poland, Bohemia, Moravia, and Hungary the colonization of forest land had led to the establishment of many free-peasant communities. But a combination of political and economic circumstances reversed these developments.

Emancipation in the Italian communes

Eastern Europe from the Baltic to the Balkans in the 14th and 15th centuries suffered wars even more devastating than those of western Europe. These not only diminished the peasant population and increased the area of uncultivated land, as in the west, but also increased the power of the nobility at the expense of central governments. In eastern Germany, Prussia, Poland, and Russia this development coincided with an increased demand for grain from western Europe. To profit from this demand, landlords took back peasant holdings, expanded their own cultivation, and made heavy demands for peasant labour services. Not until the end of the 18th century were the peasants of the Austro-Hungarian Empire freed from a serfdom that was defined by the Emperor Joseph II himself as the absence of freedom of movement, of freedom of marriage, and of the right to learn a profession according to one's choice. Not until Alexander II's Emancipation ukase of 1861 were the serfs of Russia similarly given personal freedom, together with allotments of land.

V. Early modern plantation slavery
INTRODUCTION AND DEVELOPMENT OF SLAVERY IN THE NEW WORLD

Exploitation of Indian labour. The Spanish conquistadors in the New World first endeavoured to use the native Indian population as labour. In this connection it may be observed that although slavery was not a general institution in the Americas before the arrival of Europeans, it certainly existed in some regions, and particularly in parts of Central America. For example, Cortés left a description of the great marketplace, at Tlaltelolco near Tenochtitlán (present Mexico City), and of the large number of male and female slaves brought there "for sale as the Portuguese bring Negroes from Guinea." The Spaniards themselves shipped a number of captured Indians to the home country, either as presents for the sovereigns or for sale. In America, however, Indians were generally subjected by the Spaniards to institutions more reminiscent of serfdom, such as *repartimiento* or *encomienda*, and were more often exploited in hard agricultural work than in outright slavery. Only in the mines was the situation different; there labour was more akin to outright slavery.

Whatever the case, difficulties arose. First, Indians proved to be less docile than had been thought and sometimes rebelled or more often disappeared in the surrounding forests. Second, they often lacked physical vigour and succumbed in large numbers to diseases brought over from Europe. In addition, their employers found themselves at odds with the Roman Catholic missionaries. The missionaries' main preoccupation was the evangelization of the pagan population, and consequently they wanted it to be treated gently. The Spanish king Ferdinand II, the Catholic, adopted a solution midway between the desires of the settlers for abundant and cheap labour and the much more lenient attitude of missionaries; Indians could be forced to work but only under certain prescribed conditions, including humane treatment and the payment of a remuneration. But the last prescriptions of the edict often were disregarded.

Even the subsequent introduction of black slaves from Africa did not put an end to the exploitation of Indians, and both forms of servitude existed side by side. In the Spanish possessions on the mainland, the servitude of Indians was prevalent; from it evolved peonage. Certain remnants of this condition survived as late as the second half of the 20th century, thus outliving the abolition of chattel slavery. On the other hand, in the Caribbean island colonies—not only of the Spaniards but also of the British, French, Dutch, and Danes—the aboriginal Indian population suffered total extinction in the course of time.

The importation of African slaves. The harsh treatment of Indian slaves eventually prompted Bartolomé de Las Casas, Roman Catholic bishop of Chiapas, to approach the new Spanish king, Charles I, with the proposal that each Spanish settler should be permitted to bring over a certain number of black African slaves. In 1517 this idea was accepted, although in somewhat modified form, and a Spanish nobleman was granted, by letters patent, a license to import each year a specified number of Africans into Hispaniola on

Deterrences to Indian slavery

the condition of paying duties to the royal treasury. Soon thousands of blacks were brought, not only into Hispaniola but also into the other islands of the Caribbean and later to the mainland. There black slavery prevailed and, with the development of sugar plantations, assumed colossal proportions beginning at the end of the 17th century. Thus a measure of mercy conceived for the protection of Indian natives became the origin of one of the cruelest institutions of all time—black plantation slavery.

Similar events occurred in Brazil, after the coast of that country fell under Portuguese domination. Indian aborigines were directly enslaved in large numbers with perhaps even more inhumanity than in Spanish possessions. When sugar, and later coffee, plantations developed on the vast latifundia, however, the Portuguese adopted the same solution as the Spaniards and imported blacks as slaves in ever-increasing numbers.

Slavery on tobacco and cotton plantationsIn the North American English possessions, perhaps the striking fact is that black slavery as a systematic institution appeared relatively late: the first shipload of slaves arrived, almost by chance, in Virginia in 1619 and in a Dutch, and not a British, ship. At first slavery developed extremely slowly, and in Virginia in 1681 there were still only 2,000 black slaves as against 6,000 indentured labourers of European origin. It was only after intensive cultivation of tobacco developed, and a little later also of rice, that slavery took root in the colony, so that the number of slaves reached 59,000 in 1714. From then on, it increased steadily, mainly through new arrivals, reaching 263,000 in 1754. But a few years later the increase slowed down, and at the time of the American Revolution it even seemed that slavery might gradually disappear. The reason was that tobacco rapidly exhausted the land on which it was grown, so that it had to be used for other crops, by far less profitable. It was only with the introduction of cotton, and particularly after the invention of the cotton gin in 1793, that the trend was once again reversed and the number of slaves increased steadily until it reached the census figure of 4,441,830 on the eve of the Civil War in 1860.

Thus, the development of the institution of slavery in Central and South America and, later, in parts of North America was intimately connected with the growth of the plantation economy. Black slaves also worked in the mines, as stevedores in the ports, and in other heavy work; served as domestic servants of all kinds; and were trained in various trades. But it was after the development of sugar, tobacco, and cotton plantations that the slave trade between the west coast of Africa and the Americas reached enormous proportions, becoming the most lucrative trade of the time and constituting a considerable proportion of traffic as a whole.

Growth of the triangular slave trade. The English became the most important importers of slaves, although the French, the Dutch, and others also took part in the commerce, to supply their own colonies or the larger and richer Spanish possessions. On the other hand, the Portuguese reserved the monopoly of traffic to Brazil to their nationals.

The slave shipsThis trade was usually triangular. Ships set out first from a home port, such as Liverpool or Bristol in the case of the British, for the Atlantic coast of Africa. They carried liquor, firearms, cotton goods, and various trinkets that were exchanged for slaves brought from the African hinterland to one of the numerous factories established along what became known as the Slave Coast (Gulf of Guinea). Then came the so-called middle voyage from Africa toward the West Indies or one of the colonies or countries on the American continents: this leg of the trip was the slave trade proper. Although usually shortened by favourable winds, it represented a true torture for the involuntary passengers. They were closely packed in the hull to save space and often chained in order to avoid rebellion or to prevent them from jumping into the sea. Even by standards of the time, food was inadequate and water scarce. There was no proper ventilation, nor were sanitary installations provided. It has been calculated that at least 20 percent of all the blacks transported did not survive the voyage. Once they arrived at their destination, survivors were either directly delivered to their prospective employers or more often kept in stockades to await a purchaser. The ship then undertook the third and last leg of the voyage—homeward—loaded with the various staples produced on the American plantations. One of the chief items of the trade was molasses, from which rum was distilled and used for the purchase of more slaves on the next trip.

Treatment of slaves. Policies regarding the treatment of slaves varied widely among the colonies. By way of generalization, it may perhaps be said that slaves fared better in colonies of Catholic and Latin nations than in those of Protestant countries. One reason for this is that the link between the mother country and its dependencies was much closer for the first group than for the second. Consequently, the metropolitan authorities, through their agents, tried to exercise at least a minimum of control over planters. These countries, namely, Spain, Portugal, and France, promulgated detailed laws concerning the treatment of slaves, of which the most famous is the French *Code Noir* (Black Code) put into force by King Louis XIV in 1685. This compilation contained a number of relatively mild prescriptions, which were, however, often disregarded. Even more liberal was the Spanish Slave Code promulgated in 1789. In the British possessions, on the other hand, white settlers often were granted self-government. Consequently they were free to promulgate regulations as they saw fit. These often were extremely stringent, as in the case of the Barbados Code, imitated in Virginia and elsewhere. Beginning with the last years of the 17th century, however, under the impact of the antislavery movement both at home and in certain American colonies, improvements were sometimes introduced in the British dependencies.The black codes

Another factor affecting the situation of black slaves in the colonies of Roman Catholic nations was the interest taken in their lot by the clergy. One partial expression of this influence was the enactment of already mentioned codes by metropolitan authorities. But the Roman Catholic clergy also tried to exert authority upon slaveowners on the spot. For example, the clergy encouraged church marriages for slaves and opposed the separation of families. On the other hand, the Anglican clergy did not seem to show similar interests in the slaves, and in many British possessions and U.S. states the law expressly prohibited legally binding slave marriages. But here too the situation in some cases changed under the influence of the Quakers and of certain Protestant dissidents.

A third difference came as a result of the attitude of the peoples themselves. As already noted, the Portuguese and Spaniards had relatively far less race or colour prejudice. Mating between white men and black women was a common phenomenon in all colonies. The rule everywhere was that the child inherited its mother's condition and consequently was born a slave. It was customary, however, in Roman Catholic lands for the master to grant manumission to his child and sometimes also to the mother. Manumission was also frequently granted for long and devoted services of a domestic slave, in particular to nurses who had looked after the master's children. As a result, for example, in Haiti under French domination, a class of free and relatively well-to-do mulattoes gradually emerged. In Brazil, where toleration toward the half-castes and even full blacks was much more in evidence, a number of free persons of African descent had reached positions of eminence even before the liberation that came in 1888; this, in turn, fostered still more the spirit of nondiscrimination and had its effect on the condition of slaves, particularly those in direct contact with their masters. It would be excessive to say that in Anglo-Saxon territories, including the Southern United States, similar situations never occurred. But there the colour line was drawn once and for all, and a person having a small strain of African blood was a "Negro," whether slave or free. In addition, some of the colonial statutes prohibited manumission or made it extremely difficult.Status of freedmen and mixed bloods

What is certain is that the condition of slaves in all countries depended greatly upon their position and the tasks they had to perform. Those in domestic service were usually a kind of privileged elite, although here againStatus and occupation of slaves there were many gradations depending upon the nature of the job, the character of the master, and personal qualities of the slave himself. The next category was that of slaves exercising various trades. The third—and most numerous —included the slaves working on plantations. Here were the worst excesses, particularly if the estate was large and the absentee landowner had to rely on an agent who hired supervisors. Nonetheless, in order to maintain a balanced picture, one must always remember that published accounts usually dealt with either the best or the worst examples. Probably on the whole the situation of slaves was not much worse than that of indentured labourers brought over from Europe. At times it might have been even better because the master had reason to take care of his slave, who represented capital, whereas he had no similar incentive in regard to the labourer. But, of course, the condition of the slave was permanent and even hereditary, whereas an indentured man retained important rights under colonial laws and became free at the expiration of his contract. Furthermore, the condition of slavery itself was degrading. This was keenly felt by many blacks, particularly those who had been brought over from Africa and sold into slavery; a person born into slavery was more likely to accept his condition with resignation. But rebellion was an ever-present threat, and uprisings occurred from time to time in various parts of the slave world—in Brazil and Haiti (which thus gained its independence from France), for example, and also in the British possessions. Nor was the danger absent in some of the Southern U.S. states, although the Civil War proved that it had been greatly exaggerated: during the entire period Southern slaves showed a surprising passivity and toward the end some of them were even called upon to serve in the forces of the Confederacy.

ANTISLAVERY MOVEMENTS IN THE WESTERN HEMISPHERE

Altogether probably more than 15,000,000 blacks were transported to the Western Hemisphere, and before 1800 far more African slaves than English or European colonists crossed the Atlantic—mostly to the West Indies and South America. But despite its inhumanity and size, the slave system aroused little protest until the 18th century. Rational thinkers of the Enlightenment then began to criticize it for its violation of the rights of man, and pietistic or evangelical religious groups condemned it for its unchristian and brutal qualities. In Britain and America, the Quakers, who began their criticism in 1671, were the first significant opponents of slavery, and the dynamics of the antislavery movement were largely religious throughout. Consequently, the leaders were always more concerned with ending the sin of slavery than with finding a constructive social policy for the slaves. In France, where the Société des Amis des Noirs ("Society of the Friends of the Blacks") was founded in 1788, the rational factor was stronger than the evangelical.

By the late 18th century, moral disapproval of slavery was widespread, and antislavery reformers gained a number of deceptively easy victories. In Britain, Granville Sharp, working almost alone, secured a decision in the Somersett case (1772) that West Indian planters could not hold slaves in England, since slavery was contrary to English law. In America, leading figures of the revolutionary period, such as Thomas Jefferson and Benjamin Franklin, condemned slavery. Between 1777 and 1804 all of the states north of Maryland abolished it—some by gradual, others by immediate action. Meanwhile, in the South, numerous and vigorous antislavery societies enjoyed considerable success in persuading owners to manumit their slaves voluntarily.

These victories, however, had little effect upon the centres of slavery, the great plantations of the Deep South, the West Indies, and South America. The antislavery movement, therefore, slowly turned to the problem of slavery in these areas, and as it did so, it passed through three major phases.

Efforts to outlaw the slave trade. The first phase involved British and American efforts to prohibit the importation of African slaves into the British colonies and the United States. English Quakers began actively to cam-

Quaker opposition

paign for such a prohibition in 1783. In 1787 the Abolition Society, consisting mostly of Quakers, was formed. Under William Wilberforce, who led the movement in Parliament, and Thomas Clarkson, who devoted many years to the tireless collection of evidence concerning the evils of the trade, the antislavery forces waged an unremitting contest against powerful opposition. The trade to the British colonies was finally abolished in 1807.

The Abolition Society

Meanwhile, in the United States, the Constitutional Convention in 1787 had considered placing in the constitution a prohibition of the trade, but, in order to conciliate Southern interests that opposed immediate action, the convention agreed to a provision that congress might prohibit the trade after 20 years. Accordingly, in 1807 the United States also prohibited it.

Efforts toward abolition (emancipation). Antislavery men had hoped that when the supply of new slaves was stopped, slavery itself would gradually wither away. But this did not follow, and in its second phase abolitionism concentrated upon the emancipation of populations already in slavery. Most of the Spanish possessions in America abolished slavery when they won independence in the first quarter of the 19th century. (Slavery, though, continued in countries such as Cuba and Puerto Rico, which remained under Spanish rule.) In Britain antislavery leaders organized the Anti-Slavery Society in 1823, made Thomas Fowell Buxton their parliamentary leader in place of the aging Wilberforce and, after another prolonged and dramatic contest, finally succeeded in 1833 in passing a law to free all slaves in the British colonies after a 5- to 7-year period of apprenticeship, with compensation to their owners. In 1848 France also abolished slavery in its West Indian colonies. This was France's second attempt, for the French revolutionists in 1794 had proclaimed emancipation, but the internal struggle over this question in Haiti had led to bloody and violent uprisings. During a vain attempt to restore French control of the island, Napoleon re-established slavery (1802), and it continued in other French colonies until 1848.

France's abolition of slavery in the West Indies

The British abolition movement had a deep influence in the United States. As the cotton economy developed, slavery gained new vigour and the South began to defend slavery in positive terms. Discouraged by these developments and disappointed by the limited results of their appeals to gradualism and persuasion and their attempts to colonize free Negroes in Liberia, U.S. antislavery men turned, about 1830, to a more militant policy. Denouncing all slaveholders, they demanded immediate abolition by law. In this aggressive program the most conspicuous and most extreme leader was William Lloyd Garrison, editor of the *Liberator* (1831) and founder of the American Anti-Slavery Society (1833). But Garrison's actual following was small, and it is quite possible that a greater influence was exercised by the burning evangelist Theodore Dwight Weld, who, with his "Seventy Apostles," carried the gospel of antislavery to pulpits throughout the North. Also, the activity of free Negroes, of whom Frederick Douglass was the most important, is not to be underestimated.

U.S. abolitionism laboured under the handicap that it threatened the harmony of North and South in the Union and it ran counter to the constitution, which left the question of slavery to the individual states. Therefore the Northern public remained unwilling to adopt abolitionist policy and distrustful of abolitionist extremism, as illustrated by John Brown's raid at Harpers Ferry (1859). Even when convinced of the evil of slavery as they were by Harriet Beecher Stowe's *Uncle Tom's Cabin* (1852), most Northerners rejected abolitionism. But they were prepared to resist the spread of slavery into new territories. The election of Abraham Lincoln as president on this issue in 1860 led to the secession of the Southern states and to the Civil War (1861–65). The war, in turn, led Lincoln, who had never been an abolitionist, to emancipate the slaves in areas in rebellion (1863) and led further to the freeing of all other slaves by the Thirteenth Amendment to the Constitution in 1865.

U.S. Civil War

Efforts to stop slave smuggling. Meanwhile, the third phase of the abolition movement had already begun, as

Britain took the lead in efforts to break up the remaining slave trade. All leading countries, by this time, had enacted laws against the trade, but smuggling was extensive and open. In fact, the closing of U.S. and British markets had merely deflected the trade to Cuba, Brazil, and elsewhere, and as late as 1850 more than 50,000 slaves a year were being transported. A new organization, the British and Foreign Anti-Slavery Society, was therefore formed in 1839 under the leadership of Joseph Sturge. While this society kept up a public agitation, the British government sought to obtain international agreements to stop the trade by means of an effective naval patrol, but the profitability of the trade and jealousy of British naval power both stood in the way. In 1862, however, the United States signed a treaty conceding the right of search, which was necessary for effective enforcement. After this treaty, the slave trade was quickly reduced to a trickle. Later, the worldwide reaction against slavery led to abolition in Cuba, between 1880 and 1886, and in Brazil, between 1883 and 1888.

The system of African slavery as a Western phenomenon, after shaping the destiny of three continents and dominating the history of three centuries, had largely ceased to exist.

VI. Forced labour in the late 19th and the 20th centuries

EARLY INTERNATIONAL EFFORTS TO SUPPRESS SLAVERY AND FORCED LABOUR

Pre-World War I agreements. In the second half of the 19th century, the exploration of Africa revealed all the horrors of slave raiding and of the traffic in human beings that was going on completely unchecked in a vast territory covering the basins of the Nile and the Congo and the region of the great African lakes. Slave caravans fanned out from the interior to the shores of the Mediterranean, the Red Sea, the Persian Gulf, and the Indian Ocean. Some of the slaves brought there were sold for local employment, but most were sent farther, usually in small native craft, to Turkey, Arabia, Iran, and other eastern countries.

The occupation, at least nominally, of the newly explored African lands by European powers offered an opportunity to strike at the root of the evil. The new authorities, particularly the British, worked to halt the overland traffic and slave raiding. An international diplomatic conference at Berlin in 1885, called for the purpose of delimiting the spheres of influence in the Congo Basin, presented the first opportunity for the coordination of the action already undertaken by individual European administrations. The General Act of Berlin, which applied only to the so-called Conventional Basin of the Congo, required all of the powers concerned "to strive for the suppression of slavery and especially of the Negro slave trade."

The Second Brussels Conference of 1890, however, was a far more important event. Its outcome was the General Act of Brussels, which for a quarter of a century constituted the fundamental charter of international efforts to suppress slavery. One of the important facts about the General Act of Brussels was the number of its signatories: in addition to all the major European powers and the United States, Turkey, Persia (Iran), and Zanzibar were parties thereto. The participation of the last three countries was particularly significant because at the time they still recognized the institution of slavery. But perhaps the major feature of the General Act was the broadness of the subjects covered by its provisions. These included recommendations for taking various measures of vigilance in countries of origin and transit, such as the establishment of permanent military posts and the use of patrols for stopping slave raiding and the conveyance of slaves by land. These acts, and some others connected with them, were to be treated as criminal offenses. Other provisions dealt with measures to be taken for the welfare of liberated or fugitive slaves and their repatriation.

The League of Nations and the International Labour Organisation. The outbreak of World War I in 1914 brought to a standstill the international efforts inaugurat-

ed by the General Act of Brussels. At the close of the war, the principal Allied Powers (Belgium, the British Empire, France, Italy, Japan, Portugal, and the United States) thus signed a new convention at Saint-Germain-en-Laye on September 10, 1919, designed to revive the "endeavour to secure the complete suppression of slavery in all its forms and of the slave trade by land and sea."

The Saint-Germain Convention coincided with the creation of the League of Nations, which took up the general problem of slavery in 1920. In 1924 the League set up a Temporary Slavery Commission of experts to collect information on slavery proper (including so-called domestic slavery), slave raiding and the slave trade, and also on such other institutions and practices as serfdom; purchase of girls as brides; sham adoption of children to exploit their work; various forms of indenture, or reducing to servitude, of persons for debt or for other reasons; and systems of compulsory labour, both public and private. The commission recommended the conclusion of an international convention covering all these matters.

When the League of Nations Assembly adopted the International Slavery Convention in 1926, however, it created ambiguity as to its scope. It decided not to include the subject of forced or compulsory labour, which it referred for further study and action to the International Labour Organisation. As a consequence, the ILO produced the Convention of 1930 "outlawing" the use of forced labour, defined as "all work or service which is exacted from any person under the menace of any penalty and for which the said person has not offered himself voluntarily." It excluded from the category of forced labour compulsory military service and, later, national service required of conscientious objectors, normal civic obligations and "minor communal services," prison labour performed "under the supervision and control of a public authority," and work in the case of *force majeure*. This term relates to work exacted "in the event of war or of a calamity or threatened calamity, such as fire, flood, famine, earthquake, violent epidemic or epizootic diseases, invasion by animal, insect, or vegetable pests, and in general any circumstance that would endanger the existence or well being of the whole or part of the population."

In specific terms, perhaps the League's most successful efforts were to suppress slavery, through the mandate system, in the former Ottoman territories and German colonies. The League also succeeded in bringing around the two nations then most notoriously associated with slavery: Ethiopia was denied entry into the League until it had undertaken a definite program of eliminating slavery (despite the later Italian seizure of Ethiopia, the country lived up to this undertaking and abolished slavery in 1942 upon recovering its independence), and Liberia availed itself of the League's financial and technical assistance to do away with intertribal slavery and some other forms of servitude, including forced labour.

FORCED LABOUR IN MODERN STATES

A number of 20th-century states have resorted to forced labour for economic and political reasons. Persons either suspected of opposition to the regime or considered racially or nationally unfit have been summarily arrested and placed under long or indefinite terms of confinement in concentration camps, remote labour colonies, or industrial camps. There the inmates have been forced to labour, usually under dire conditions. Those unable to work have often died from starvation (or been exterminated outright), and those who have not starved have frequently died from overwork. Although such forced-labour punishment has been established in various forms under many regimes, both totalitarian and colonial, it has been used most extensively in Nazi Germany and the Soviet Union. Millions of persons have been confined, punished, and exploited in concentration camps and labour colonies.

Nazi slave labour. In Nazi Germany, concentration camps (*Konzentrationslager*) were first established for the confinement of opponents of the Nazi Party, mostly leaders of the Communist and Social Democratic parties. But political opposition soon was enlarged to include others,

African slave caravans to the East

General Act of Brussels

ILO Convention of 1930

particularly such persecuted minorities as the Jews. In the anti-Jewish pogrom of 1939, 20,000 Jews were taken into "protective custody" and sent to the concentration camps. By 1939 six major camps had been established: Dachau, Sachsenhausen, Buchenwald, Mauthausen, Flossenbürg, and Ravensbrück.

The outbreak of World War II created a tremendous demand for labour in Germany, and Nazi authorities turned to the concentration camp population to augment the labour supply. From 1940 to 1942 nine new camps were established: Auschwitz, Neuengamme, Gusen, Natzweiler, Gross Rosen, Lublin, Niederhagen, Stutthof, and Arbeitsdorf. Thousands of forced labourers from countries occupied by Germany were placed in concentration camps and auxiliary labour camps.

By the end of September 1944 there had been put to work in the Third Reich some 2,000,000 prisoners of war (the majority Russians and Ukrainians) and some 7,500,000 foreign civilian men, women, and children—Poles, Russians, Ukrainians, French, Belgians, Dutch, Danes, Norwegians, Luxembourgers, Czechs, Slovaks, Hungarians, Yugoslavians, Greeks, Italians, and Algerians. Although some of the non-Jewish civilians from western Europe arrived initially as "volunteers" (*Freiwillige*), subsequently to be turned into slave labourers (*Sklavenarbeiter*), almost all of the millions were rounded up by force, transported to Germany in boxcars, and put

Conditions in concentration camps to work in factories, mines, and fields under conditions that were degrading and brutal. Housing was so deplorable, rations were so meagre, and work was so excessive that few persons could survive long internment. Crematoriums were established in some camps to dispose of the bodies of the dead. Toward the end of the war, when food and fuel supplies became exhausted, thousands died of starvation and disease. The Allied forces found the quick and the dead lying side by side in the barracks. Camp after camp presented a scene of horror.

From 1942 to 1943, the highly efficient organizer of Nazi war production and economy, including the provision of labour, was Albert Speer, who was subsequently sentenced at Nuremberg in 1946 to 20 years' imprisonment. The slave labour program itself was under the subordinate charge of Fritz Sauckel, as deputy general for labour allocation (*Generalbevollmächtigter für den Arbeitseinsatz*). Sauckel was hanged at Nuremberg in 1946.

Corrective labour camps of the Soviet Union. During the first years of the Soviet regime, the Cheka (All-Russian Extraordinary Commission for Repression of Counterrevolution and Sabotage) was the primary repressive instrumentality of the state. The Cheka was given the power to exile persons to concentration camps without judicial trial. It was replaced in 1922 by the OGPU (United Government Political Administration). At that time there were 23 concentration camps in various locations in the U.S.S.R.

Although its powers were not absolute, the OGPU could arrest and send to concentration camps, without trial, persons accused of political offenses, such as espionage and counter-revolution, as well as those accused of certain criminal offenses, such as looting and illegal border crossing. In 1923 the OGPU established a concentration camp on Solovetski Island in the White Sea in which prisoners were first used extensively for forced labour. Thereafter, the Soviet concentration camp system became a gigantic organization for the exploitation of inmates through work.

The OGPU established many corrective labour camps in northern U.S.S.R. and Siberia, especially during the first five-year plan, 1928–32, when thousands of rich peasants (kulaks) were driven from their farms under the collectivization program. The inmates of the camps in northern U.S.S.R. were used principally in the lumbering and fishing industries and on large public-works projects, such as the construction of the White Sea–Baltic Sea canal. The inmates of the Siberian camps were used principally in lumbering and mining. In 1932 the OGPU set up corrective labour camps for gold mining in the Arctic taiga along the Kolyma River in far eastern Siberia.

The OGPU was replaced by the NKVD (People's Com-

missariat of Internal Affairs) in 1934. Thereafter the corrective labour-camp system was administered by the NKVD, which had its own paramilitary force. The Stalinist purges of 1937–38 brought additional thousands of political "unreliables" into the camps. By 1939, a vast The Stalinist purges system of concentration camps, utilized primarily for forced labour, existed across the northern reaches of European Russia and Siberia. These camps were said to be essentially institutions of slavery. Inmates were housed in rough barracks and were inadequately clothed for the severe Arctic climate. The standard rations of bread and soup were scarcely adequate to maintain life. Camp commandants were credited with the amount of work produced against the amount of food consumed. As a consequence, the prisoners were driven to, and often beyond, the limits of human endurance.

The occupation of eastern Poland in 1939 and the incorporation of the Baltic states into the Soviet Union in 1940 led to incarceration in concentration camps of large numbers of non-Soviet citizens from those areas. Following the outbreak of war with Germany in 1941, the camps received prisoners of war and Soviet nationals accused of collaboration with the enemy. After the war, Soviet soldiers who had allowed themselves to be captured were sent to the camps. The powers of the NKVD were transferred to the MVD (Ministry of Internal Affairs) in 1946 and then, in turn, to the KGB (Soviet State Security Service) in 1954. Under the MVD and KGB corrective labour camps continued to serve as primary instruments not only of political control but also of the economic structure until the mid-1950s. After a worldwide survey of forced labour conducted in 1953 by the UN ad hoc Committee of Three had exposed certain conditions in the Soviet Union, the severer features of the Soviet labour system apparently were mitigated (even though the Soviet bloc had boycotted the committee's work). Soviet sources indicate that about one-third of the corrective labour camps were converted, in 1956, to the relatively milder corrective labour colonies, following a series of rebellions and strikes between 1953 and 1955.

THE UNITED NATIONS AND THE ILO

The United Nations and human rights. After the conclusion of World War II, when the United Nations organization replaced the League, the question of combatting slavery in its different forms came once again to the fore. The General Assembly, at its third session (1948), adopt- Universal Declaration of Human Rights ed the Universal Declaration of Human Rights, which in article 4 states that "1. No one shall be held in slavery or servitude; slavery and the slave trade shall be prohibited in all their forms."

Following the fourth session of the General Assembly, in 1949, an ad hoc committee of four members was set up "to survey the field of slavery and other institutions or customs resembling slavery." This body, in 1951, presented a report to the Economic and Social Council outlining a program for action. The basic ideas were that the League of Nations' 1926 Slavery Convention, binding 45 states, should be maintained in operation and brought into the framework of the UN, which, however, should also prepare a new international instrument to make sure that not only chattel slavery but also other institutions and practices already studied by the League of Nations, and servitude of women resulting from marriage practices, should be brought to an end. In addition, mindful of another experience of the former League, the Ad Hoc Committee recommended the creation of a Standing Committee of Experts to supervise the application of both the old and the new conventions.

Continued existence of slavery and other forms of servitude. The UN implemented the first recommendation in 1953 by executing a protocol transferring to its secretary general the powers and duties of the League's Secretariat in regard to the 1926 Slavery Convention. The conclusion of a supplementary convention was implemented in 1956, after a number of further studies, summarized in a report presented in 1955 by Hans Engen of Norway. In his introduction he pointed out that he endeavoured "to extract . . . only those statements which, in his view, would assist the [Economic and Social] Council in surveying the extent to which slavery, and practices resembling slavery, exist in the world today." He stated, however, that the documentation was in some respects incomplete and unverified. It must also be added that a number of governments concerned either denied the information in the report, stated that it was inaccurate or out-of-date, or indicated measures had been taken to combat the objectionable practices reported. The material in the report on the continued existence of slavery (including "domestic slavery") and the slave trade concerned a number of countries in the Arabian Peninsula. Mention also was made of a few countries in Southeast Asia, Africa, and South America. The material on serfdom concerned mainly countries in Asia, although certain regions in Africa and Central America also were mentioned. The material related to "traditional forms of unpaid or underpaid personal services exacted by landowners and other employers of labour, or their agents" concerned a number of South and Central American countries, certain regions in Africa, in East and Southeast Asia, and in the north of the Arabian Peninsula. The material related to debt bondage, including pledging and pawning of third persons as security for debt, concerned a number of countries in East and Southeast Asia, in the north of the Arabian Peninsula, in various parts of Africa, and in Latin America. The material related to the exploitation of children, notably under the guise of adoption, concerned various countries of East and Southeast Asia, South America, and Africa. The material related to the "purchase" of wives and the "inheritance" of widows concerned mainly territories in Africa, northern Australasia, South America, and Asia.

The Supplementary Convention on the Abolition of Slavery, the Slave Trade, and Institutions and Practices Similar to Slavery (1956) retained the 1926 definition of slavery but supplemented it with a description of the various institutions and practices similar to slavery, referred to above, in respect to which all of the signatory states agreed to "take all practicable and necessary legislative and other measures to bring about progressively and as soon as possible [their] complete abolition or abandonment."

ILO Convention of 1957

Further efforts of the International Labour Organisation. Another significant postwar attack on forced labour was the ILO's convention number 105, adopted in 1957 and, by the early 1960s, ratified by 91 member states and made applicable to 52 nonmetropolitan territories. The convention condemned the use of forced labour (1) as a means of political coercion or education or as a punishment for holding or expressing political views, or views ideologically opposed to the established social, political or economic system; (2) as a method of mobilizing or using labour for purposes of economic development; (3) as a means of labour discipline; (4) as punishment for having participated in strikes; (5) as a means of racial, social, national, or religious discrimination. Of the Communist bloc countries, only Poland had ratified the 1957 convention by the early 1960s.

The 1962 review by the ILO upon the operation of the convention observed that, despite various improvements, forms of forced labour "are still rife in many countries." Countries were cited in which "the expression of political opinions which do not conform to those held by the organization in power (or at least in one case on certain fundamental questions) is prohibited by various legal provisions which entail forced labour, contrary to the convention." These countries were South Africa, Spain, the U.S.S.R., and the United Arab Republic. In another group of countries—Burma, China, Republic of the Congo, Fiji, Kenya, Liberia, Northern and Southern Rhodesia (later Zambia and Rhodesia), Portugal (overseas provinces), Ruanda-Urundi (later Rwanda and Burundi), the Solomon Islands, Sudan, and Swaziland—the law "expressly provided for the possibility" of compulsory labour in normal times on public works. The ILO declared that such requirements should be terminated.

Another section of the report pointed out that a group of countries—principally nonmetropolitan areas but including Denmark and India—provided in legislation for forced labour in public works in ways that unduly widened the concept of work for "minor communal services." In such cases work was permitted that was only indirectly of benefit to "the members of the community" from which the labour is exacted or that "is for the benefit of more than the village community." Clearly there remained adequate scope for detailed debate in each case on the problem of borderline instances of alleged forced labour.

In general, the ILO has strongly emphasized the need to develop competent forms of labour inspection in order to reduce the possibility of undetected forced labour.

BIBLIOGRAPHY

General: C.W.W. GREENIDGE, *Slavery* (1958); C.J.M. LE-TOURNEAU, *L'évolution de l'esclavage dans les diverses races humaines* (1897); SIR G.F. MACMUNN, *Slavery Through the Ages* (1938); J.J. NIEBOER, *Slavery As an Industrial System*, 2nd rev. ed. (1910); A. TOURMAGNE, *Histoire de l'esclavage ancien et moderne* (1880).

Slavery in antiquity: H.A. WALLON, *Histoire de l'esclavage dans l'antiquité*, 2nd ed., 3 vol. (1879); I. MENDELSOHN, *Slavery in the Ancient Near East* (1949), *Legal Aspects of Slavery in Babylonia, Assyria and Palestine* (1932); R.P. DOUGHERTY, *The Shirkûtu of Babylonian Deities* (1923); A.M. BAKIR, *Slavery in Pharaonic Egypt* (1952). For slavery among the ancient Hebrews, see A. BARNES, *An Inquiry into the Scriptural Views of Slavery* (1857); and M.J. RAPHALL, *Bible View of Slavery* (1861).

Slavery in Greece and Rome: M.I. FINLEY (ed.), *Slavery in Classical Antiquity* (1961); W.L. WESTERMANN, *The Slave Systems of Greek and Roman Antiquity* (1955); R.H. BARROW, *Slavery in the Roman Empire* (1928, reprinted 1968); W.W. BUCKLAND, *The Roman Law of Slavery* (1908).

Medieval serfdom: The Cambridge Economic History of Europe, 2nd ed., vol. 1, *The Agrarian Life of the Middle Ages* (1966); G. DUBY, *L'économie rurale et la vie des campagnes dans l'occident médiéval*, 2 vol. (1962); J.W. THOMPSON, *An Economic and Social History of the Middle Ages, 300–1300*, new ed., 2 vol. (1959); G. VERLINDEN, *L'esclavage dans l'Europe médiévale* (1955). For medieval England, see G.C. HOMANS, *English Villagers of the Thirteenth Century* (1941); F. POLLOCK and F.W. MAITLAND, *History of English Law Before the Time of Edward I*, 2nd ed., 2 vol. (1898); P. VINOGRADOFF, *Villainage in England* (1892, reprinted 1968). For France, see M.L.B. BLOCH, *Mélanges historiques*, vol. 1 (1963); for Austria, see E.M. LINK, *The Emancipation of the Austrian Peasant, 1740–1798* (1949). For serfdom in Russia, see J. BLUM, *Lord and Peasant in Russia: From the Ninth to the Nineteenth Century* (1961); B.D. GREKOV, *Kiev Rus* (1953; Eng. trans., 1959); R.E.F. SMITH, *The Enserfment of the Russian Peasantry* (1968).

Slavery in Asia and North Africa: For the Far East, see R. LINGAT, *L'esclavage privé dans le vieux droit siamois* (1931); Y. TAKEKOSHI, *The Economic Aspects of the History of the Civilization of Japan*, vol. 1 (1930, reprinted 1967). For India, see D.R. BANAJI, *Slavery in British India* (1933); G.S. GHURYE, *Caste and Class in India*, 2nd ed. (1957); and R.S. SHARMA, *Sūdras in Ancient India* (1958). For slavery in Africa, see R. COUPLAND, *The Exploitation of East Africa, 1856–1890*, 2nd ed. (1968); and G. MARTIN, *Histoire de l'esclavage dans les colonies françaises* (1948).

Slavery in the New World: For South America and the Caribbean, see R.R. MILLER, *Slavery and Catholicism* (1957); H.H.S. AIMES, *A History of Slavery in Cuba, 1511 to 1868* (1907, reprinted 1967); and G. FREYRE, *The Masters and the Slaves*, trans. from the Portuguese by S. PUTMAN, 2nd Eng. ed. rev. (1956). For British colonies in the New World, see SIR T.F. BUXTON, *The African Slave Trade*, 2nd ed. (1968); B. EDWARDS, *The History, Civil and Commercial, of the British West Indies*, 5th ed., 5 vol. (1818–19); R.B. MORRIS, *Government and Labor in Early America* (1946); H. RUSSELL, *Human Cargoes: A Short History of the African Slave Trade* (1948). For slavery in North America after the Declaration of Independence, see H. APTHEKER (ed.), *A Documentary History of the Negro People in the United States* (1951); F. BANCROFT, *Slave Trading in the Old South* (1959); J.E. CAIRNES, *The Slave Power*, 2nd ed. (1862, reprinted 1969); E. DONNAN (ed.), *Documents Illustrative of the History of the Slave Trade to America*, 4 vol. (1930–35, reprinted 1965); N.W. EPPES, *The Negro of the Old South* (1925); B. MANDEL, *Labor: Free and Slave* (1955); D.P. MANNIX, *Black Cargoes* (1962); F.L. OLMSTED, *The Slave States Before the Civil War* (1959); U.B. PHILLIPS, *American Negro Slavery* (1918); J.R. SPEARS, *The American Slave Trade*, abr. ed. (1960); K.M. STAMPP, *The Peculiar Institution: Slavery in the Ante-Bellum*

South (1956); H. WISH (ed.), *Slavery in the South* (1964), a collection of contemporary accounts.

International efforts toward abolition: The following books refer to the abolition movement in the 18th and 19th centuries. For Latin America, see R. CEPERO BONILLA, *Azúcar y abolición*, 2nd ed. (1960). For abolition in the French West Indies, see M.D. KENNEDY, *Lafayette and Slavery: From His Letters to Thomas Clarkson and Granville Sharp* (1950); and for the abolition movement in the British colonies, W.L. BURN, *Emancipation and Apprenticeship in the British West Indies* (1937); T.F. BUXTON, *The African Slave Trade and Its Remedy*, 2nd ed. (1840); T. CLARKSON, *The History of the Rise, Progress, and Accomplishment of the Abolition of the African Slave-Trade by the British Parliament*, new ed., 2 vol. (1839, reprinted 1968); R. COUPLAND, *Wilberforce* (1923); *The British Anti-Slavery Movement* (1933); F.J. KLINGBERG, *The Anti-Slavery Movement in England* (1926, reprinted 1968); W.L. MATHIESON, *British Slavery and Its Abolition, 1823–1838* (1926, reprinted 1967), *Great Britain and the Slave Trade, 1839–1865* (1929, reprinted 1967); O.A. SHERRARD, *Freedom from Fear: The Slave and His Emancipation* (1959); and H.A. WYNDHAM, *The Atlantic and Emancipation* (1937).

For the abolition movement in the United States, see G.H. BARNES, *The Antislavery Impulse, 1830–1844* (1933); T.E. DRAKE, *Quakers and Slavery in America* '(1950); W.E.B. DU BOIS, *The Suppression of the African Slave-Trade to the United States of America, 1638–1870* (1896, reprinted 1969); D.L. DUMOND, *Antislavery: The Crusade for Freedom in America* (1961); *A Bibliography of Antislavery in America* (1961); S.M. ELKINS, *Slavery: A Problem in American Institutional and Intellectual Life*, 2nd ed. (1968); J.H. FRANKLIN, *From Slavery to Freedom*, 3rd ed. (1967); H. HENKLE, *Let My People Go: The Story of the Underground Railroad and the Growth of the Abolition Movement* (1941); A.Y. LLOYD, *The Slavery Controversy, 1831–1860* (1939).

The text of the League of Nations Slavery Convention of 1926 and a list of League of Nations documents relating to slavery are given in the United Nations document *The Suppression of Slavery: Memorandum Submitted by the Secretary General* (1951). Other UN documents on slavery may be found through the *Index to United Nations Documents*. See also the *United Nations Yearbook* (annual); and *Year Book on Human Rights* (annual).

Types of servitude existing in the 20th century: For forced labour, see S. SWIANIEWICZ, *Forced Labour and Economic Development* (1965); and reports of the INTERNATIONAL LABOUR OFFICE. For slavery and forced labour in the Far East, see B. LASKER, *Human Bondage in Southeast Asia* (1950); A. WINNINGTON, *The Slaves of the Cool Mountains* (1959); and YUAN-LI WU, *An Economic Survey of Communist China* (1956). For the Middle East, see M. GAUDEFROY-DEMOMBYNES, *Les institutions musulmanes* (1921); W.H. INGRAMS, *Arabia and the Isles* (1952); A.K.S. LAMBTON, *Landlord and Peasant in Persia* (1953); and R. O'SHEA, *The Sand Kings of Oman* (1947). For former colonial territories in Africa, see E. BERG, "French West Africa," in W. GALENSON (ed.), *Labor and Economic Development* (1959); E. DE JONGHE, *Les Formes d'asservissement dans les sociétés indigènes du Congo belge* (1949); LORD LUGARD, *Africa Emergent*, rev. ed. (1949); and C. TISSERANT, *Ce que j'ai connu de l'esclavage en Oubangui-Chari* (1955). For Portuguese Africa, see J. DUFFY, *Portuguese Africa* (1959) and *Portugal in Africa* (1962).

(Ed.)

Slavic Languages

The Slavic, or Slavonic, languages, constituting a separate branch of the Indo-European language family, are closer to the Baltic languages than to any other Indo-European subgroup, but they share certain linguistic innovations with the other eastern Indo-European languages (such as Indo-Iranian and Armenian) as well. From their original area situated between the Oder and the Dnepr rivers, the Slavic languages have spread to the territory of the Balkans (Bulgarian, Serbo-Croatian), central Europe (Czech and Slovak), eastern Europe (Polish, Ukrainian, Russian), and the northern parts of Asia (Russian). The number of native speakers for the entire branch is about 260,000,000. In addition, Russian is used as a second language by most inhabitants of the Soviet Union. Some of the Slavic languages have been used by writers of worldwide significance (*e.g.*, Russian, Polish, Czech) and the Church Slavonic language is an important means of communication within the Eastern Orthodox Church.

LANGUAGES OF THE FAMILY

The Slavic language group is divided schematically into three branches: South Slavic, with two subgroups—Serbo-Croatian-Slovene and Bulgarian-Macedonian; West Slavic, with three subgroups—Czech-Slovak, Sorbian, and Lekhitic (Polish and related tongues); and East Slavic comprising Russian, Ukrainian, and Belorussian.

Three branches of Slavic

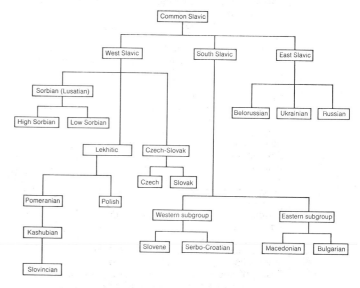

In the spoken Slavic dialects (as opposed to the sharply differentiated literary languages) the linguistic frontiers are not always apparent. There are several transitional dialects and mixed forms of speech that connect the different languages, with the exception of the area where the South Slavs are separated from the other Slavs by the non-Slavic Romanians, Hungarians, and German-speaking Austrians. But even in this latter domain, some vestiges of the old dialectal continuity (between Slovene and Serbo-Croatian, on the one hand, and Czech and Slovak, on the other) that was later interrupted can be traced; the same traces of the old links are seen in comparing Bulgarian and Russian dialects. Thus the traditional schematic division of the Slavic group into three separate branches is not to be taken as the real model of historical development. It would be more realistic to represent the historical development as a process in which tendencies to differentiate and to reintegrate the cognate dialects have been continuously at work, bringing about the remarkable degree of uniformity in the different dialects. Still it would be an exaggeration to suppose that communication between any two Slavs is possible without any linguistic complications. The myriad differences between the dialects and languages in phonological and phonetic realization as well as in the spheres of semantics and morphology may cause misunderstandings even in the simplest of conversations; and the difficulties are greater in the language of belles lettres, even in the case of closely connected languages. For a Slav to master effectively a second Slavic language demands time and work.

South Slavic. Bulgarian is spoken by almost 8,000,000 people in Bulgaria and adjacent areas of other Balkan countries and the Soviet Union. There are two major groups of Bulgarian dialects: an Eastern one that became the basis of the literary language in the middle of the 19th century and a Western one that influenced the literary language. Bulgarian texts prepared before the 16th century were written mostly in an archaic language that preserved some features of Old Bulgarian (10th to 11th centuries) and Middle Bulgarian (beginning in the 12th century).

Although the vocabulary and grammar of the early texts written in the Old Church Slavonic language include some Old Bulgarian features, the language was nevertheless based originally on a Macedonian dialect. Old Church Slavonic was the first Slavic language to be put down in written form, by SS. Cyril and Methodius. The modern Macedonian language, spoken by more than 1,000,000 people in Yugoslavia and Greece, was the last Slavic language to attain a standard literary form; during World War II, its central dialects of Prilep and Veles were elevated to this status. The Central Macedonian dialect is closer to Bulgarian, while the Northern dialect shares some features with the Serbo-Croatian language. Modern Macedonian dialects may be considered as links between the Eastern (Bulgarian) subgroup of South Slavic and the Western (Serbo-Croatian) subgroup.

The Western subgroup of South Slavic includes the dialects of Serbo-Croatian, among them those of the Prizren-Timok group, which are close to some North Macedonian and West Bulgarian dialects. The literary Serbo-Croatian language was formed in the first half of the 19th century on the basis of the Shtokavian dialects that extend over the greater part of the Serbo-Croatian territory in Yugoslavia. These dialects are called Shtokavian because they use the form *što* (*shto*) for the interrogative pronoun "what?". They are distinguished from the Chakavian dialects of western Croatia, Istria, the coast of Dalmatia (where a literature in that dialect developed in the 15th century), and of some islands in the Adriatic; in those areas *ča* (*cha*) is the form for "what?". A third main group of Serbo-Croatian dialects, spoken in northwestern Croatia, uses *kaj* rather than *što* or *ča* and is therefore called Kajkavian. In all, more than 15,000,000 people speak Serbo-Croatian.

Dialects of Serbo-Croatian

The Slovene language is spoken by almost 2,000,000 persons in the Socialist Republic of Slovenia in federal Yugoslavia and in the adjacent areas of Italy and Austria. It has some features in common with the Kajkavian dialects of Croatia and includes many dialects with great variations between them. In Slovene (particularly its Western and Northwestern dialects) some traces can be found of old links with the West Slavic languages (Czech and Slovak).

West Slavic. To the West Slavic branch belong Polish and some remnants of other Lekhitic languages (Kashubian and its archaic variant Slovincian), Low and High Sorbian (also called Lusatian or Wendish), Czech, and Slovak. Approximately 40,000,000 people speak Polish in Poland, in some regions of Czechoslovakia and the Soviet Union, and in the United States and Canada. The main Polish dialects are Great Polish (in the northwest), Little Polish (in the southeast), Silesian, and Mazovian. The last dialect shares some features with Kashubian. There are about 200,000 native speakers of Kashubian remaining in Poland on the left bank of the Lower Vistula River. Slovincian belongs to the Northern group of Kashubian dialects, which is distinguished from a Southern group. Kashubian dialects (including Slovincian) are considered to be the remnants of a Pomeranian subgroup that belonged to the Lekhitic group. Lekhitic also included Polabian, which was spoken up to the 17th and 18th centuries by the Slavic population of the Elbe (Labe) River region. (At that time a dictionary and some phrases in the language were written down.)

The Polabian language bordered the Sorbian dialects, which are still spoken by about 120,000 inhabitants of Lower Lusatia and Upper Lusatia in East Germany. There are three main groups of Sorbian dialects: High Sorbian (Upper Sorbian), one of whose dialects in the area of Bautzen (Budyšin) is the basis of the literary language; Low Sorbian (or Lower Sorbian); and East Sorbian, the remnants of which are spoken in the area of Muskau (Mužakow).

Czech is spoken by over 9,000,000 people in the western part of Czechoslovakia (Bohemia, Moravia, and Silesia); its dialects are divided into Bohemian, Moravian, and Silesian groups. The literary language is based on the Central Bohemian dialect of Prague. The Slovak literary language was formed on the basis of a Central Slovak dialect in the middle of the 19th century. Western Slovak dialects are close to Moravian and differ from the Central and the Eastern dialects, which have features in common with Polish and Ukrainian. More than 4,000,000 people speak Slovak; they are located mostly in Slovakia.

East Slavic. Russian, Ukrainian, and Belorussian (White-Russian) comprise the East Slavic language group. Russian is the native language of about 130,000,000 people and is widely used by many others in the Soviet Union and in some other eastern European countries. Its main dialects are divided into a Northern Great Russian group, a Southern Great Russian group, and a transitional Central group.

Russian, Ukrainian, Belorussian

Ukrainian dialects are classified into Northern, Southeastern, Southwestern, and Carpathian divisions (the last group having features in common with Slovak); the literary language is based on the Kiev-Poltava dialect. More than 41,000,000 people speak Ukrainian in the Soviet Ukraine, and there are more than 500,000 Ukrainian speakers in Canada and the United States.

More than 9,000,000 people speak Belorussian in the Belorussian Soviet Socialist Republic. Its main dialectal groups are Northwestern Belorussian, some features of which may be explained by contact with Polish, and Northeastern Belorussian. The dialect of Minsk, which served as a basis for the literary language, lay on the border between these two groups.

HISTORICAL SURVEY

The Slavic protolanguage. Each branch of Slavic originally developed from a dialect of Proto-Slavic, the ancestral parent language of the group, which in turn developed from an earlier language that was also the antecedent of the Proto-Baltic language. Both Slavic and Baltic share with the eastern Indo-European languages (called satem languages) the same change of Indo-European palatalized $\acute{k}$ and g sounds (consonants modified by bringing the front of the tongue up to or toward the hard palate) into spirants of the s and z type (*e.g.*, in Proto-Slavic *sъto* "hundred" contrasts with Latin *centum*, etc.). The Slavic and Baltic branches are distinguished by such innovations as: (1) the change of the old Indo-European syllabic r, n, and m (which functioned as vowels) to *ir, ur,* and related variants; (2) the same patterns of stress in nouns and verbs; and (3) the same reshuffling of the verbal system to produce two forms of the past tense in $-\bar{a}$ and $-\bar{e}$.

Some scholars believe that, after the common Indo-European area had been divided into different dialect zones (approximately after the 3rd millennium BC), a protodialect developed in the Baltic and Slavic areas that had many features peculiar to only these two branches of Indo-European. At the same time this protodialect was connected with certain western Indo-European protodialects called Old European that are identified as the source of a number of river names. The ancient Baltic and Slavic names of rivers (hydronyms), such as the Russian Oka, are of the same type as those found in the central European area. The dialects of the Slavic protolanguage spoken near the Carpathian Mountains in the upper Vistula area may have been part of the intermediate zone situated between the western Indo-European dialects (Germanic, Celtic, Italic, and so on) and the eastern Indo-European ones; in addition to Baltic and Slavic in the north, this intermediate zone included the Indo-European languages of the Balkans (Illyrian, Thracian, Phrygian). The domain of the Proto-Balto-Slavic dialect may have been situated to the east of the Germanic and other Old European dialects, to the north of Ancient Balkanic (including Illyrian), and to the west of Tocharian. The exact geographical borders of the Balto-Slavic domain appear impossible to determine, but they may well have been located in eastern Europe around present-day Lithuania and to the east and south of it. The later diffusion of Slavic languages southward into the Carpathian region may represent the spread of one of the dialects of this Old Baltic domain. The oldest Slavic protolanguage may be described as the result of the historical transformation of the Baltic protolanguage (but not vice-versa).

Domain of Proto-Balto-Slavic

Until the middle of the 1st millennium AD, the Slavs were known to other people as the inhabitants of the vast territories between the Dnepr and the Vistula. In the 6th century AD the Slavs expanded to the Elbe (Labe)

Distribution of the Slavic languages in Europe.

River and the Adriatic Sea and across the Danube River to the Peloponnese. In that period, according to the oldest references of Greek and Latin sources about the Slavs, they were already divided into several groups. The Slavic language, however, was uniform in its phonological and grammatical structure, with important dialectal variations occurring only in the vocabulary. The main phonological difference between the oldest pattern common to Baltic and Slavic and the later one that characterized Slavic alone was that in Slavic all syllables became open (*i.e.*, a syllable could end only in a vowel). Thus, all consonants at the end of a syllable were lost. This led to a reshuffling of most of the inflectional endings.

The next period in Slavic linguistic history began with the loss of the reduced vowels, called *yers* (*jeri*), that resulted from Indo-European short *ĭ* and *ŭ*; this loss caused a wide-ranging change in many words and forms. Although this process was common to all the Slavic dialects, which were still connected with each other at that period, it took place slowly and at different rates in different dialects, beginning in the 10th to the 12th century and expanding from the southwest to the northeast. After the loss of the *yers*, which gave different results in different dialectal groups (see Table 3), the uniformity of the Slavic language area began to disappear, and separate branches and languages emerged. An important clue to the date of the dissolution of Slavic unity is the separate development in different Slavic dialects of the name of the emperor Charlemagne (742–814). This name must have entered into Slavic in the postulated form **korljь* ("Karl") before the dissolution took place. Subsequently the proper name became the generic term for "king." The segment *-or-* in the postulated form appears differently in the modern Slavic languages—compare Bulgarian *kral*, Serbo-Croatian *kralj*, Slovene *králj* (*i.e.*, South Slavic *-ra-*), Russian *korol* (*i.e.*, East Slavic *-oro-*), Czech *král*, Polish *król*.

Emergence and early development of the Slavic languages. The separate development of South Slavic was caused by a break in the links between the Balkan and the West Slavic groups that resulted from the settling of the Magyars in Hungary during the 10th century and from the Germanization of the Slavic regions of Bavaria and Austria. Some features common to Slovak and Slovene may possibly have developed before the West–South break. The eastward expansion of dialects of Balkan Romanian (a Romance language) led to a break in the connection between the South and the East Slavic groups around the 11th–12th centuries. The history of the Balkan Slavs was closely connected with Byzantium, in contrast to that of the Lekhitic and Sorbian subgroups of the Western Slavs, which was connected with west European culture.

Disruption between South Slavic and West Slavic groups

An effort on the part of the Slavs to counteract the influence of the Western Christian Church (which was associated with the German Empire) was the motive behind the introduction of the Old Church Slavonic language into the liturgy in Great Moravia, the first Slavic national state. Founded in the 9th century, Great Moravia united different groups speaking West Slavic dialects. In 863 its prince, Rostislav, invited St. Cyril (Constantine) and his brother St. Methodius to create a national church with a language and writing of its own. Prior to that time some Christian texts in Moravia had been translated into Slavic from Latin (and partly perhaps from Old High German); these have been preserved only in later copies.

The second period in the history of the Old Church Slavonic language (893–1081) occurred in the Bulgarian kingdoms of Symeon (893–927) and Peter (927–969) and in the kingdom of Samuel (997–1014), and was connected with the literary activity of many Bulgarian scholars who translated numerous Greek texts into Slavic and also produced a small number of original works. In the writings of the period of Symeon and Peter, Western (Macedonian) features were substituted for Eastern Bulgarian ones.

Development of the individual Slavic languages. Both the Western (Macedonian) and Eastern (Bulgarian) variants (recensions) of the Old Church Slavonic language are preserved in manuscripts of the 11th century, while the East Slavic (Russian) variant is reflected in the oldest dated Old Church Slavonic manuscript, Ostromir's Evangelium (1056), and in many later texts. The Moravian variant must be reconstructed on the basis of some later texts (such as the Kiev fragments of the beginning of the 11th century) dating from after the break with the Great Moravian tradition. In some documents of the 10th and 11th centuries, the Bohemian variant (sharing some West Slavic peculiarities with Moravian) has been preserved. Several features are common to the Moravian and Bohemian varieties of the Old Church Slavonic language, to the Slovene (Pannonian) variant reflected in the Freising fragments (late 10th century), and to the Croatian Old Church Slavonic tradition that is attested from the 12th century, as well as to the Serbian tradition. All these variants of the Old Church Slavonic language have some peculiarities that are to be explained as the result of the interaction of the original system with that of a local dialect. At about 1000 all Slavic languages were so close to one another that such interaction was possible.

Reflection of Old Church Slavonic variants in various manuscripts

From these local variants of the Old Church Slavonic language that are preserved in the manuscripts of the 10th to the 12th centuries, one should distinguish the later local Church Slavonic languages (Russian, with its different variants; Middle Bulgarian; Serbian, which was replaced by the Russian variant in Serbia in the 18th century; Croatian; and the Romanian variant of Church Slavonic, which was used as a literary and church language of Romania from the 14th to the 18th centuries). From the linguistic point of view, these later Church Slavonic literary languages differ from the earlier varieties in their systems of vowels; the early nasalized vowels were replaced by different later reflexes, and the reduced vowels (*yers*), with the exception of those followed by a syllable containing another *yer*, were generally lost. These changes in the sound pattern were accompanied by changes in vocabulary that were the result of cultural factors.

After the schism between the Eastern (Orthodox) and Western (Roman) Christian churches in the 11th century and the beginning of the Crusades, the Church Slavonic language fell out of use in all West Slavic countries and in the western part of the Balkan Slavic region. The only exception was the renaissance of Croatian Church Slavonic in the 13th century. At the end of the same century, the first Czech verses in the local dialect were written; they were the precursors of the rich poetic literature in the Old Czech language that appeared in the 14th century. The early Czech literary language was marked by the influence of Latin, which had replaced the Bohemian variety of Old Church Slavonic as a literary language.

In the earliest period of its development, the Polish literary language was modelled on the Czech pattern. After the Christianization of Poland, Latin (and later German) loanwords entered the Polish language in their Czech form. The Czech influence is seen in the Polish literary language until the 16th century (the "Golden Age"), when Renaissance tendencies resulted in the creation of texts that had aesthetic merit and were at the same time stylistically close to everyday speech. Later on the Polish literary language was enriched by cross-fertilization with Ukrainian and Belorussian.

In the 16th century in Dalmatia, a rich poetic literature in Croatian was created by poets who were influenced by the Italian Renaissance and who also wrote in Italian and Latin. A Slovene translation of the Bible was published in 1575–84 and Kashubian and Sorbian religious texts were also produced during this period. The comparatively early rise of the West Slavic (and western South Slavic) languages as separate literary vehicles was related to religious and political factors that resulted in the decline of the western variants of the Church Slavonic language.

In contrast, the continuing use of Bulgarian Church Slavonic and different variants of Russian Church Slavonic made it difficult to construct literary languages for Bulgarian and Russian based on everyday speech. Bulgarian texts were written in Bulgarian Church Slavonic until the 16th century. After that the language of the so-called Damaskinar (Damascene) literature was developed, closer to the popular speech; its development, however, was hampered under Turkish rule. Most of the Old East Slavic (Old Russian) literary texts were written in a mixture of Russian Church Slavonic and the Old Russian vernacular language; only a few documents, particularly some parts of the chronicles (annals), are written entirely in Old Russian. The proportion of South Slavic (Church Slavonic) and East Slavic (Old Russian) elements in each text is different depending on its stylistic peculiarities.

In the middle of the 17th century, the old Great Russian variant of the Church Slavonic language in the official Russian Orthodox Church was replaced by a new variant taken from the southwestern East Slavic tradition, a form that incorporated some Ukrainian and Belorussian elements. This development was connected with a split in the Orthodox Russian Church; the Old Believers, who split off from the main body of the church, continued to use the archaic Great Russian variant, while Patriarch Nikon's new variant, based on the southwestern tradition, was adopted by the official church and is used in it to this day. Because the Ukrainian tradition includes many West Slavic elements, this reform, which occurred after the incorporation of the Ukraine into the Russian Empire, was a step in the direction of the Westernization of the Russian language that took place soon after Peter the Great began his attempts to reconstruct and Westernize the whole Russian way of life.

Linguistic results of religious schism

In the 18th and 19th centuries, many waves of loanwords from different Western languages entered the Russian language. While some of the syntactic structures earlier had been formed on Germanic and Latin patterns, many western European semantic characteristics penetrated into the Russian language as a result of the intensive French–Russian bilingualism of the Russian upper classes at the end of the 18th and the beginning of the 19th century. The great Russian literature of the 19th and the early 20th century (up until Tolstoy's death in 1910) created a literary language close to everyday speech, especially to that of the villages. In the official style of Russian, however, Church Slavonic elements still dominate, as can be seen even in general newspaper articles.

The concept of a language that would unite all the Slavs has remained in the back of the Slavic consciousness, not as a real aim but rather as an important symbol. The most interesting attempt to unite different chronological and local Slavic strata was carried out by the Serbian Romantic writer Vuk Stefanović Karadžic. In modern literature one might cite the experiments at unification of Velemir Khlebnikov, a Russian futurist writer, and of the Polish poet Julian Tuwim, who created a Polish–Russian symphony of sounds in some of his poems.

Standardization of the modern Slavic languages. Among the Slavic languages that attained their standard literary form at a later stage in Slavic history than those mentioned above is Ukrainian. It was used in some literary texts in the late 18th century and in turn influenced the language of Gogol, one of the greatest Russian writers of the 19th century, to the extent that the language of some parts of Gogol's early texts may be described as a mixed Russian–Ukrainian dialect. In the 19th century and especially in the first decades of the 20th century, a number of great poets wrote in Ukrainian. The movement toward national liberation led to the introduction of many neologisms into the language, which persisted even after some attempts were made toward the artificial unification of the East Slavic area. After World War I, the Belorussian language became a standard language in the Belorussian Soviet Socialist Republic.

Status of modern Slavic languages

Since World Wars I and II, all of the Slavic languages have acquired the status of either the main language of an independent state (*e.g.,* Bulgarian and Polish) or the language of an autonomous part of a state (*e.g.,* Russian, Ukrainian, and Belorussian in the Soviet Union; Serbo-Croatian, Slovene, and Macedonian in Yugoslavia; Czech and Slovak in Czechoslovakia). Only the minor languages are exceptions: Kashubian is used officially only in some cultural performances, and Low and High Sorbian are now taught in schools in East Germany. The extent of dialectal variation in the different languages ranges from a very great degree in Slovene to a much smaller degree in some areas of such languages as Polish and Russian. Radio and other mass media have been among the main influences leading to linguistic consolidation. Languages like Polish, Czech, and Russian, which have served as a basis for great literatures, have become models for others that are only now being put to literary use (although for such languages as Kashubian and, to some degree, for High and Low Sorbian, the folk literature remains much more important as a model than individual literary works and translations of past centuries).

LINGUISTIC CHARACTERISTICS

A number of distinguishing characteristics set off the Slavic languages from other Indo-European subgroups. On the whole, Slavic auxiliary words tend to be unstressed and to be incorporated into a single phonetic group or phrase with autonomous stressed words. Inflection (*i.e.,* the use of endings, prefixes, and vowel alternations) has persisted as the main method of differentiating grammatical meanings, although to a lesser degree in the nouns than in the verbs because many functions of the noun case endings may also be expressed by prepositions. Verbal categories have retained their complex archaic character. The movable stress pattern common to most South and East Slavic languages has had a profound influence on versification in these languages.

Many linguistic devices found both in the oral tradition and in individual literary works of the different Slavic languages may be traced to common ancestral forms. An exuberant use of diminutives and metaphoric figures marks the Slavic oral tradition. It seems possible to reconstruct a common Proto-Slavic model of the universe as seen through linguistic expression. The main feature of such a model is the recurrence of binary (two-way) contrasts, as is evidenced by such cue words as *bogъ* "god" from "a portion allotted by the gods" and *ne-bogъ* "not having his portion, having bad fortune." Such pairing of

opposites bears a striking resemblance to the ancient Iranian dualistic view of the world, a view that evidently influenced the Slavs to a degree not yet fully appreciated.

As compared with the common Indo-European scheme, the pre-Slavic cultural linguistic heritage seems in some degree simpler, evidently as a result of the loss of direct contact with the Southern civilizations that served as a pattern for pre-Indo-European culture. Later developments were caused largely by western European and Greek (particularly Byzantine Christian) influences and by contacts with eastern cultures, which led to innovations in the vocabularies of the East Slavic and South Slavic languages. In some instances, whole series of designations for objects were borrowed into Russian and other East Slavic languages from eastern sources.

Influence of other cultures on Slavic vocabularies

All Slavic languages are synthetic, expressing grammatical meaning through the use of affixes (suffixes and, in verbal forms, also prefixes), vowel alternations partly inherited from Indo-European, and consonant alternations resulting from linguistic processes peculiar to Slavic alone. Although analytical methods of expressing grammatical meanings (through prepositions and other "empty" grammatical words) are present in older strata of the language, they are used to the exclusion of all other means only in the case system of Modern Bulgarian and Macedonian. The tendency toward analytic expression is noticeable in contemporary everyday Russian speech, but the drift of the Slavic languages in this direction (as in the development of the western European languages) has been held back by the stabilization of the language resulting from mass communication and education.

Phonological characteristics. The Slavic systems of distinctive sounds are rich in consonants, particularly in spirants and affricates. This is especially true in comparison with the protolanguage and with other Indo-European languages. The affricates (which are consonant sounds begun as stops, with complete stoppage of the breathstream, and released as fricatives, with incomplete stoppage) have resulted historically from a succession of different processes of palatalization that have occurred in Slavic and are one of the most characteristic features of Slavic phonology. Palatalization is the process whereby the pronunciation of an originally nonpalatal sound is changed to a palatal sound by touching the hard palate with the tongue; it is also the process whereby a nonpalatal sound is modified by simultaneously moving the tongue up to or toward the hard palate. Originally, palatalization was connected with the adaptation of a consonant to the following vowel within a syllable, specifically, with the adaptation of a consonant to a following front vowel. This adaptation gave rise to "soft" (palatalized) syllables, composed of palatalized consonants followed by front vowels. The *j* sound, as *y* in English "year" (from older nonsyllabic Indo-European *i*), tended to palatalize the preceding consonant either by merging with it or by giving rise to consonant groups such as *bl'* from *bj* (*by*). As palatalized stop consonants (for instance *k', g', t', d'*) became increasingly differentiated from the corresponding nonpalatalized series (*k, g, t, d*), the palatalized stops tended to develop further into affricates (with the subsequent development of voiced affricates into spirants). Thus palatalized *k'* before the ancient front vowels developed into the affricate *č* (as *ch* in English "church"), and palatalized *g'* in the same environment changed to ʒ (as *j* in "judge"), which became the spirant sound *ž* (as *z* in "azure") in all Slavic languages. Before front vowels resulting from ancient diphthongs, palatalized *k'* changed to a *ts* sound, written as *c* (*e.g.,* Old Church Slavonic *cěna* "price," Serbo-Croatian *cijéna*, Russian *cena*, cognate to Lithuanian *káina*), and *g'* changed to a *dz* sound, which later changed to *z* (Old Church Slavonic [*d*]*zelo* "very," Old Czech *zielo*, Belorussian *do zěla*, cognate to Lithuanian *gailas*). The sounds *t'* (from *tj*) and *d'* (from *dj*) changed, respectively, into different stops, affricates, and spirants according to special rules in the separate Slavic dialects (see Table 1).

Development of palatals, affricates, and spirants

These processes of assibilation of the palatalized velar (*k', g'*) and dental (*t', d'*) sounds happened repeatedly in the history of the individual Slavic languages. Palataliza-

Table 1: Development of Proto-Slavic *tj, *dj

Proto-Slavic	Old Church Slavonic	South Slavic				East Slavic	West Slavic		
		Bulgarian	Macedonian	Serbo-Croatian	Slovene	Russian	Polish	Czech	High Sorbian
*tj > *t'	št	št	ḱ	ć	č	č	c	c	
*dj > *d'	žd	žd	ǵ	đ	j	ž	ʒ	z	
*svetja "candle"	sve šta	svešt	sveḱa	svijeća	sveča	sveča	świeca	svíce	sweca
*medja "bound(ary)"	mežda	mežda	meǵa	međa	meja	meža	mieʒa (miedza)	meze	meza

*Indicates an unattested, reconstructed form.

tion (softness) as a distinctive feature of most consonant sounds has been preserved in East Slavic; for example, in Modern Russian palatalized (or soft) *t', d', s,' z'* contrast with nonpalatalized (or hard) *t, d, s, z.* (The contrast between the palatalized *k'* and the hard *k* is just now in the process of development.) Some West Slavic languages also have this palatalized–nonpalatalized contrast, while others do not. Czech, Slovak, and Serbo-Croatian, which have the usual three sets of labial, dental, and velar consonants inherited from the proto-language, have developed a special, additional series of palatal stops. In all of the Slavic languages, voiced stop consonants (pronounced with vibrating vocal cords) contrast with voiceless stop consonants (pronounced without vibrating vocal cords).

The tendency to increase the number of different spirants (nonstops) is connected with the processes of palatalization. In the Ukrainian and the Southern Russian dialects and in Belorussian, Czech, Slovak, High Sorbian, and some Slovene dialects there also developed a voiced velar spirant sound, corresponding to the voiceless velar spirant of the Proto-Slavic language. The nasal vowels ę and ǫ that had developed in Proto-Slavic from older combinations of vowels with nasal consonants (still retained in Baltic) have been preserved only in some Lekhitic languages and in some South Slavic dialects, especially those of Slovene (see Table 2). The vowel systems are especially rich in those Slavic languages that have preserved prosodic differences in pitch (tone) and quantity (length)—Serbo-Croatian, Slovene, and Northern Kashubian. The reshaping of the Slavic vowel systems is in large measure a result of the loss of the *yers,* which had different effects in different dialects (see Table 3).

Slavic vowel systems

Table 2: Development of Proto-Slavic Nasal Vowels Compared with Baltic

English translation	Lithuanian	Serbo-Croatian	Polish	Russian
"I spin"	sprendžiu	predem	przędę	pryadu
"snipe, woodcock"	slanka	šljuka	słonka	sluka (obs.)
"soft"	minkštas	mek	miękki	myagky
"wise"	mañdras	mudar	mądry	mudry

Prosodic differences in vowel quantity have been preserved in Czech and Slovak, in which new vowels developed as a result of contraction. A fixed stress accent is found in the West Slavic languages as well as the Western and Central Macedonian dialects, in contrast to Proto-Slavic, Serbo-Croatian, Slovene, Bulgarian, and the East Slavic languages. In Czech and Slovak, as well as in Sorbian and Southern Kashubian, stress is fixed on the first syllable of the word, but in Polish, Eastern Slovak, and Southern Macedonian, it falls on the next to the last syllable of the word, while in Western Macedonian it falls on the third syllable from the end. The Slavic languages with a nonfixed placement of stress reflect the Proto-Slavic (and Indo-European) distinction between two types of noun and verb paradigms: (1) the paradigm with movable stress in which the stress (indicated here by ') falls on the root in some forms and on the inflectional ending in others (*e.g.,* "head" in Russian is *golová* in the nominative case and *gólovu* in the accusative, these forms derive from Proto-Slavic *golvá, *gólvǫ [an asterisk indicates an unattested, reconstructed form]) and (2) the paradigm in which the stress is fixed on the stem (*e.g.,* "willow" in Russian is *íva* in the nominative case, *ívu* in the accusative, from *íva, *ívǫ).

Grammatical characteristics. Most Slavic languages reflect the old Proto-Slavic pattern of seven case forms (nominative, genitive, dative, accusative, locative, instrumental, vocative), which occurred in both the singular and the plural. In the dual number the cases that were semantically closest to each other were represented by a single form (nominative–accusative, instrumental–dative, genitive–locative). The dual number is preserved today only in the westernmost area (*i.e.,* in Slovene and Sorbian) and in the archaic Slovincian language. The trend toward the modern, more analytical type of construction using prepositions and away from the synthetic type using case endings exclusively (as in Proto-Slavic and the archaic Slavic languages), is evident in the gradual elimination of the use of the dative and locative forms without prepositions. The end result of this development is seen in Bulgarian and Macedonian, in which noun declension has almost completely disappeared and has been replaced by syntactic combinations using prepositions. In the other South Slavic languages and in the western part of the West Slavic area (Sorbian and Czech), the same tendency to lose some of the distinctions between cases may be seen, but to a lesser degree. In the other West Slavic languages and in East Slavic, on the other hand, the old system of cases has been preserved in spite of the large number of loanwords and other neologisms that have no case distinctions at all (*e.g.,* borrowed Russian nouns like *kino* "cinema," or acronyms ending in a vowel like *Rayono* "district people education department").

The declension of pronouns has been preserved in all Slavic languages. The old combinations of adjectives with pronouns gave rise to the definite forms of adjectives. These forms still contrast with the indefinite forms in South Slavic, but in the other languages the indefinite forms have either been gradually lost or else have been preserved only to serve a special function, that of predicate noun. In Bulgarian and Macedonian, as well as in some northern East Slavic dialects, an article is used, placed after the noun (*e.g.,* in Macedonian, *kniga-ta* "book-the"). The noun may be combined with either an article, as in the above example, or with a deictic (pointing) pronominal element—*e.g.,* in Macedonian, *kniga-va* "this book here," or *kniga-na* "that book there," In addition to three noun genders (masculine, feminine,

The seven case forms

Table 3: Results of Loss of Yers

English translation	Proto-Slavic	Russian	Bulgarian	Macedonian	Serbo-Croatian	Czech	Polish	High Sorbian	Low Sorbian
"day"	dьnь < *dĭnĭ	den' (d'en')	den	den	dan	den	dzień	dzeń	źeń
"dream"	sъnъ < *sŭnŭ	son	sъn	son	san	sen	sen	son	son

*Indicates an unattested, reconstructed form.

Verb tenses

neuter), many Slavic languages distinguish animate and inanimate noun forms of some cases; and in some West Slavic languages, Ukrainian, and Bulgarian, personal and nonpersonal noun forms are differentiated.

In the modern Slavic languages the verb is inflected to show present and past tenses. In the early history of the individual Slavic languages, however, a distinction was made between the aorist (originally differentiated as to voice, as in Baltic and Greek) and the imperfect; this distinction is still preserved in modern South Slavic (with the exception of Slovene) and Sorbian. (The aorist is a verb form indicating the occurrence of an action without reference to its completion, repetition, or duration; the imperfect is a verb tense designating a continuing state or an uncompleted action, especially in the past.) Slavic has almost no traces of the Indo-European old perfect tense, but, from combinations with the verbal noun in *-l*, new perfect forms were created that were differentiated from the pluperfects. Later these perfect forms came to be used as past tense forms in different Slavic languages. The most striking feature of the Slavic verb is the existence of paired stems to express the perfective (completed) and imperfective (uncompleted) aspects of the same verb—*e.g.*, Russian *dat'* "to give" (*i.e.*, "to complete the process of giving"), *davat'* "to be in the process of giving."

The present tense form of a perfective verb may be used to express future meaning, which can also be indicated by other means. In most South Slavic languages it is expressed by combinations (originally syntactic) with the verb "to want." The eastern South Slavic languages, Bulgarian and Macedonian, have lost the infinitive forms of the verb as a result of the influence of non-Slavic Balkan languages. These same Slavic languages have developed verb forms to differentiate between an action witnessed by the speaker and one not witnessed (hence only reported) by him.

A striking feature of Slavic syntax is the widespread use of possessive adjectives (*e.g.*, Russian *bozheskaya milost* "the mercy belonging to God") instead of the genitive case of the noun (*milost boga* "the mercy of God"). Word order in the Slavic languages is characterized by a gradual shift of the verb toward the medial position; originally the initial position was more characteristic. Other important features of Slavic syntax are related to this medial positioning of the verb and the consequent occurrence of the verb before the object. For example, grammatical elements are often placed before nouns; today they follow nouns only in some set phrases like Old Church Slavonic *boga radi* "for God's sake," with *radi* following the noun *boga* "God's."

Originally the verb occupied the initial position, which throws light on the origin of the reflexive verbal forms; these may be traced to the Proto-Slavic combination of the verb with a reflexive pronoun that occurred immediately after the verb and was pronounced as part of one accentual unit with the verb. Words other than pronouns that occurred immediately after verbs were also pronounced as a unit with them (these called enclitics).

The rules for the shift of the stress in syntactic combinations with enclitics were identical for verbs and nouns. Depending on the intonation of the word preceding the enclitic, the stress could be shifted either to the enclitic (as in Bulgarian *zim'ŭs* "this winter") or to the proclitic or preceding unstressed particle or word (as *na* in Serbo-Croatian *ná brijeg* and Russian *ná bereg* "on the shore").

Vocabulary. The original vocabulary of general terms common to Baltic and Slavic is still retained in most of the Slavic languages. In prehistoric times Proto-Slavic borrowed a number of important social and religious terms from Iranian (*e.g.*, *bogŭ* "God," *mirŭ* "peace"). Later, special terms were borrowed by East Slavic and South Slavic from different eastern languages (especially Turkish) as a result of the political domination of the Tatars in Russia and of the Turks in the Balkan area. After the Renaissance, loanwords were taken from classical and western European languages (especially German and French) into all of the Slavic languages. Church Slavonic

Borrowings from Iranian, eastern languages, and western European languages

in its different variants remained the main source of innovations in vocabulary in East Slavic and in some South Slavic languages. The Slavic languages make extensive use of prefixes and suffixes to derive new words and thereby enrich the vocabulary; *e.g.*, Russian *čern-y* "black," *čern-i-t'* "to blacken," *o-čern-i-t'* "to slander." Several prefixes may be combined to modify the meaning of a verb (*e.g.*, Ukrainian *po-na-vi-pisuvati*, in which three prefixes are added to the verb "to write" to convey the meaning "to write out copiously"; Bulgarian *is-po-razboleyase*, in which the added prefixes intensify the meaning "to develop an illness"). Many derivational suffixes are common to most Slavic languages—*e.g.*, the very productive suffix *-stvo* (as in Russian *khristian-stvo* "Christianity," Ukrainian *pobratim-stvo* "fraternity," Polish *głup-stvo* "foolishness, trifle," Macedonian *golem-stvo* "high status, arrogance"). The archaic type of derivation by compounding, inherited from Indo-European, was particularly productive in Church Slavonic under the stimulus of Greek. Compounding remains one of the methods of creating new terms, especially technical terms (*e.g.*, Russian *vodokhranilishche* "reservoir" from *voda* "water" and *khranilishche* "depository"), but is far less important than affixation. Some Slavic languages typical-

Table 4: The Russian Alphabet

Cyrillic letters				equivalent		approximate pronunciation
printed		written		EB preferred	Akademiya Nauk	
capital	lower-case	capital	lower-case			
А	а	𝒜	𝑎	a		*fa*ther
Б	б	ℬ	𝑏	b		*ba*by
В	в	ℬ	𝑣	v		*vi*vid
Г	г	𝒢	𝑧	g		*go**
Д	д	𝒟	∂𝑔	d		*di*d
Е	е	ℰ	𝑒	e or ye†	e or je	b*e*t or *ye*t
Ё	ё	ℰ	𝑒̈	o or yo‡	'o, o, or jo	*yo*re
Ж	ж	𝒥ℋ	𝑥	zh	ž	a*z*ure
З	з	𝒵	𝑧	z		*z*one
И	и	𝒰	𝑢	i‖	i *or* ji	ma*chi*ne
Й	й	𝒰	𝑢̆	y‖	j	*boy*
К	к	𝒦	𝑘	k		*ki*n
Л	л	𝒜	𝑙	l		*li*ly
М	м	ℳ	𝑚	m		*ma*i*m*
Н	н	ℋ	𝑛	n		*no*
О	о	𝒪	𝑜	o		*o*rder
П	п	𝒫	𝑛	p		*pe*pper
Р	р	𝒫	𝑝	r		e*rr*or (trilled)
С	с	𝒞	𝑐	s		*s*and
Т	т	𝒯	𝑚	t		*ti*e
У	у	𝒴	𝑦	u		r*u*le
Ф	ф	𝒫	𝜑	f		*fi*fty
Х	х	𝒳	𝑥	kh	ch	Ger. Bu*ch*
Ц	ц	𝒰	𝑢	ts	c	ca*ts*
Ч	ч	𝒰	𝑧	ch	č	*ch*in
Ш	ш	𝒰	𝑤	sh	š	*sh*y
Щ	щ	𝒰	𝑤	shch	šč	ra*sh ch*oice
Ъ	ъ		𝑧	omit	,,	§
Ы	ы		𝑤	y‖		rh*y*thm
Ь	ь		𝑏	omit	'	¶
Э	э	𝒵	𝑧	e		*e*cho
Ю	ю	𝒥𝒪	𝑤	yu	'u or ju	*yo*uth
Я	я	𝒥𝒜	𝑥	ya	'a or ja	*ya*rd

*Pronounced as *v* in genitive endings *-ego* and *-ogo*. †*e* after consonant; *ye* initially or after vowel, ъ, or ь. ‡*o* after ж, ч, ш, щ; *yo* elsewhere. §Hard sign; hardens preceding consonant or separates syllables. ‖In transliterating the adjectival endings -**ий** and -**ый**, the first vowel should be omitted. ¶Soft sign; softens or palatalizes preceding consonant or separates syllables.

Table 5: The Serbo-Croatian Alphabet

letters				letters			
Croatian		Serbian		Croatian		Serbian	
capital	lower-case	capital	lower-case	capital	lower-case	capital	lower-case
A	a	А	а	L	l	Л	л
B	b	Б	б	Lj	lj	Љ	љ
C	c	Ц	ц	M	m	М	м
Č	č	Ч	ч	N	n	Н	н
Ć	ć	Ћ	ћ	Nj	nj	Њ	њ
D	d	Д	д	O	o	О	о
Dž*	dž*	Џ	џ	P	p	П	п
Đ†	đ†	Ђ	ђ	R	r	Р	р
E	e	Е	е	S	s	С	с
F	f	Ф	ф	Š	š	Ш	ш
G	g	Г	г	T	t	Т	т
H	h	Х	х	U	u	У	у
I	i	И	и	V	v	В	в
J	j	J	j	Z	z	З	з
K	k	К	к	Ž	ž	Ж	ж

*Alphabetized in *Britannica* as *dz*.   †Alternatively, *dj*.

Table 6: The Bulgarian Alphabet

Cyrillic letters				equivalents	approximate pronunciation
printed		written			
capital	lower-case	capital	lower-case		
А	а	𝒜	a	a	*father*
Б	б	Ƃ	б	b	*baby*
В	в	ℬ	в	v	*vivid*
Г	г	𝒯	г	g	*go*
Д	д	𝒟	дg	d	*did*
Е	е	ℰ	е	e	*bet*
Ж	ж	𝒲	ж	zh	a*z*ure
З	з	𝒵	з	z	*zone*
И	и	𝒰	и	i	mach*i*ne
Й	й	𝒰̆	й	y	*boy*
К	к	𝒦	к	k	*kin*
Л	л	ℒ	л	l	*lily*
М	м	ℳ	м	m	*maim*
Н	н	ℋ	н	n	*no*
О	о	𝒪	о	o	*order*
П	п	𝒯	п	p	*pepper*
Р	р	𝒫	р	r	*error* (trilled)
С	с	ℭ	с	s	*sand*
Т	т	𝒯	т	t	*tie*
У	у	𝒴	у	u	*rule*
Ф	ф	𝒫	ф	f	*fifty*
Х	х	𝒳	х	kh	Ger. Bu*ch*
Ц	ц	𝒰	ц	ts	ca*ts*
Ч	ч	𝒱	ч	ch	*chin*
Ш	ш	𝒲	ш	sh	*shy*
Щ	щ	𝒰	щ	sht	Ger. *st*ill
Ъ	ъ		ъ*	ŭ	*above*
	ь		ь		†‡
Ю	ю	𝒥𝒪	ю	yu	*youth*‡
Я	я	𝒜	я	ya	*yard*‡

*ŭ can occur initially in only a few words.   †When transliterated, this is represented by an apostrophe. In modern orthography ' is used medially and finally for the y consonant before o and is pronounced *yonder*.   ‡When ya, yu, and 'o are preceded by consonants they are themselves pronounced like a, u, and o, respectively, but cause the preceding consonant to be palatalized. The softening is less great in Bulgarian than it is in Russian.

ly derive new words by means of a condensed suffixing (*e.g.*, Czech *železnice* "railroad," from *železo* "iron" combined with a noun-forming suffix; *hledisko* "point of view," from *hled* "look" combined with a noun-forming suffix), while others tend to use phraseological combinations of words (*e.g.*, Russian *vodokhranilishche*, or the adjective *železnodorožny* "railroad," from *zeleznaya doroga* "iron road" combined with an adjective-forming suffix).

Writing systems. The first writing system used for Slavic was the Glagolitic system invented by St. Cyril. Quite original in pattern, it reflected accurately the sound system of the Macedonian dialect. The forms of its letters can be traced to several different alphabets, mainly Greek and Semitic ones. Glagolitic was widely used in the first three centuries of Slavic literature but was gradually replaced by the Cyrillic alphabet, created in the 10th century and still used to write all the East Slavic languages, Bulgarian, Macedonian, and Serbian.

Other Slavic languages use the Latin (roman) alphabet. To render the specific distinctive sounds of a Slavic language, either Latin letters are combined or diacritic signs are used (*e.g.*, Polish *sz* for the *sh* sound in "ship," Czech *č* for the *ch* sound in "church"). An orthographic system devised by the Czech religious reformer Jan Hus was adopted into different West Slavic systems of writing, including Czech, Slovak, and Sorbian. Polish spelling was patterned after the Czech spelling of the 14th century. Most of the Slavic writing systems are closely related to the sound patterns of the individual languages and are constructed either to symbolize the distinctive sounds of the language or to render the same morphemes by the same groups of letters despite differences in pronunciation in various forms. Modern Russian spelling reflects a morpheme-based principle.

BIBLIOGRAPHY. ROMAN JAKOBSON, *Slavic Languages*, 2nd ed. (1955), is the best short structural sketch. A useful general survey is REINHOLD TRAUTMANN, *Die slavische Völker und Sprachen* (1947). The comparative grammar is described in the following works: ANTOINE MEILLET, *Le Slave commun*, 2nd ed. rev. (1934), the best introduction to Proto-Slavic from the point of view of Indo-European; VACLAV VONDRAK, *Vergleichende slavische Grammatik*, 2 vol. (1924–28), rich in material; JOOSEPPI J. MIKKOLA, *Urslavische Grammatik*, 3 vol. (1913–50), condensed, but not quite up-to-date now. The general drift of the languages is seen in RAJKO NAHTIGAL, *Slovanski jeziki*, 2nd ed. (1952). A traditional approach to the history of the phonemic systems is exemplified in САМУИЛ БОРИСОВИЧ БЕРНШТЕЙН, *Очерк сравнительной грамматики славянских языков*, vol. 1 (1961); ANDRE VAILLANT, *Grammaire comparée des langues slaves*,

vol. 1 (1950); and PEETER ARUMAA, *Urslavische grammatik*, vol. 1 (1964); recent developments in the diachronic phonology are summarized in ROMAN JAKOBSON, *Selected Writings*, 2nd ed., 6 vol. (1971–); FRANTISEK MARES, *The Origin of the Slavic Phonological System and Its Development Up to the End of Slavic Language Unity* (1965); GEORGE SHEVELOV, *A Prehistory of Slavic* (1964); CHRISTIAN S. STANG, *Slavonic Accentuation* (1957); and NICHOLAS VAN WIJK, *Les Langues slaves, de l'unité à la pluralité*, 2nd ed. rev. (1956). The dialectal differentiation of Proto-Slavic from the point of view of comparative phonology is analyzed in ANTONI FURDAL, *Rozpad języka presłowiańskiego w świetle rozwoju głosowego* (1961); and HENRIK BIRNBAUM, "The Dialects of Common Slavic," in HENRIK BIRNBAUM and JAAN PUHVEL (eds.), *Ancient Indo-European Dialects* (1966). The problem of the original territory and migrations of the speakers of Proto-Slavic is discussed in the light of linguistic and archaeological evidence in the following works: TADEUSZ LEHR-SPLAWINSKI, *O pochodzeniu i praojczyźnie Słowian* (1964), a brilliant survey using archaeological data; KAZIMIERZ MOSZYNSKI, *Pierwotny zasiąg języka prasłowiańskiego* (1957), employs a strictly linguistic approach, and is hardly convincing; K.H. MENGES, *An Outline of the Early History and Migrations of the Slavs* (1953), cites important Oriental sources; MARIJA GIMBUTAS, *The Slavs* (1971), provides an archaeological and linguistic survey of Slavic migrations to Central Europe and the Balkan Peninsula; and S.H. CROSS, *Slavic Civilization Through the Ages* (1948, reprinted 1963), provides some general information. The only reliable Common Slavic etymological dictionary remains the unfinished work of ERICH BERNEKER, *Slavisches etymologisches Wörterbuch*,

2nd ed., vol. 1 (1924). Of essential value for proof of the close links between Slavic and Baltic is REINHOLD TRAUTMANN, *Baltisch-Slavisches Wörterbuch* (1923); the study of verbal forms is presented in CHRISTIAN S. STANG, *Das slavische und baltische Verbum* (1942); and H. KOLLN, *Oppositions of Voice in Greek, Slavic and Baltic* (1969). For the accentual pattern of Slavic as compared to Baltic, see especially ВЛАДИСЛАВ МАРКОВИЧ ИЛЛИЧ-СВИТЫЧ, *Именная акцентуация в балтийской и славянском* (1963). The only English textbook introduction to concrete data on each language remains R.G.A. DE BRAY, *Guide to the Slavonic Languages,* rev. ed. (1969).

(V.V.I.)

Slavic Religion

Slavic religion as a term is taken here to include only the relevant beliefs and practices of the ancient Slavic peoples of eastern Europe. Slavs are usually subdivided into East Slavs (Russians, Ukrainians, and Belorussians), West Slavs (Poles, Czechs, Slovaks, and Lusatians), and South Slavs (Serbs, Croats, Slovenes, Macedonians, and Bulgars).

In antiquity the Slavs were perhaps the most numerous branch of the Indo-European family of peoples. The very late date at which they came into the light of recorded history (even their name does not appear before the 6th century AD) and the scarcity of relics of their culture make serious study of them a difficult task. Sources of information about their religious beliefs are all late and by Christian hands.

SLAVIC WORLD VIEW

Since *patria potestas*—*i.e.*, paternal power in the form of absolute authority—was absent from their family structure and monarchical government from their civil society, the Slavs' pantheon of deities was without a centre or a hierarchy of divinities. As in Baltic religions each supernatural being was active in its own particular sphere without contact with other deities. Although contacts with the Indo-European world are evident (as found, for example, in the concepts of a celestial god and a god of lightning), the Slavic religious atmosphere was substantially different from that of other Indo-European peoples.

Socially the Slavs were organized as exogamous clans (based on marriages outside blood relationship) or, more properly, as sibs (related by blood) since marriage did not cancel membership in the clan of one's birth—a type of organization unique among Indo-European peoples. The elected chief did not have executive powers. The world had been created, in the Slavic view, once and for all, and no new law ought to modify the way of life transmitted by their ancestors. Since the social group was not homogeneous, validity and executive power were attributed only to decisions taken unanimously in an assembly, and the deliberations in each instance concerned only the question of conformity to tradition. Ancient Slavic civilization was one of the most conservative known on earth.

According to a primitive Slavic belief, a forest spirit, *leshy,* regulates and assigns prey to hunters. Its food-distributing function may be related to an archaic divinity. Though in early times the *leshy* was the protector of wild animals, in later ages it became the protector of flocks and herds. In early 20th-century Russia, if a cow or a herdsman did not come back from pasture, the spirit was offered bran and eggs to obtain their return.

Varieties of spirits

Equally ancient is the belief in a tree spirit that enters buildings through the trunks of trees used in their construction. Every structure is thus inhabited by its particular spirit: the *domovoy* in the house, the *ovinnik* in the drying-house, the *gumenik* in the storehouse, and so on. The belief that either harmful or beneficial spirits dwell in the posts and beams of houses is still alive in Bosnia, Slovenia, and the Poznań area. Old trees with fences around them are objects of veneration in Serbia and Russia and among the Slavs on the Elbe River. In 19th-century Russia a chicken was slaughtered in the drying house as a sacrifice to the *ovinnik.* This vegetal spirit is also present in the sheaf of grain kept in the "sacred corner" of the dwelling under the icon and venerated along with

it, and also in noncultivated plant species that are kept in the house for propitiation or protection, such as branches of the birch tree and bunches of thistle. Such practices evidence the preagrarian origin of these beliefs. Similar to the *leshy* are the field spirit (*polevoy*), and, perhaps, the water spirit (*vodyanoy*). Akin to the *domovoy* are the spirits of the auxiliary buildings of the homestead.

MYTHOLOGY

Cosmogony. A myth known to all Slavs tells how God ordered a handful of sand to be brought up from the bottom of the sea and created the land from it. Usually, it is the Devil who brings up the sand; in only one case, in Slovenia, is it God himself. This myth is diffused throughout practically all of Eurasia and is found in ancient India as well.

A 12th-century German missionary, Helmold, left a record of his surprise in encountering among the Slavs on the Baltic a belief in a single heavenly God, who ignored the affairs of this world, having delegated the governance of it to certain spirits begotten by him. This is the only instance in which the sources allude to a hierarchy of divinities, but its centre is empty. The divinity mentioned by Helmold is a *deus otiosus; i.e.,* an inactive god, unique in the mythology of the Indo-European peoples. Such a deity is, however, also found among the Volga Finns, the Ugrians, and the Uralians.

Helmold's *deus otiosus*

Principal divine beings. Common to this Eurasian area is another divinity, called by Helmold and in the *Knytlinga saga* (a Danish legend that recounts the conquest of Arkona through the efforts of King Valdemar I of Denmark against the pagan and pirate Slavs) Zcerneboch (or Chernobog), the Black God, and Tiarnoglofi, the Black Head (Mind or Brain). The Black God survives in numerous Slavic curses and in a White God, whose aid is sought to obtain protection or mercy in Bulgaria, Serbia, and Pomerania. This religious dualism of white and black gods is common to practically all the peoples of Eurasia.

The Kiev Chronicle (also called the *Chronicle of Nestor*)—a 12th- to 13th-century account of events and life in the Kievan state—enumerates seven Russian pagan divinities: Perun, Volos, Khors, Dazhbog, Stribog, Simargl, and Mokosh. A Russian glossary to the Greek writer John Malalas' (6th century) *Byzantine Chronicle* mentions a Svarog, apparently the son of Dazhbog. Of all these figures only two, Perun and Svarog, are at all likely to have been common to all the Slavs. In Polish, *piorun,* the lightning, is derived from the name of Perun, and not vice versa. In the province of Wielkopolska the expression *do pierona*—meaning "go to the devil"—has been recorded. In the expression, *pieron/piorun* is no longer the lightning but the being who launches it. The curse is considered to be so strong that little boys in school will refuse to read it. Uncertain or indirect traces of Perun are also encountered among the Carpathians and in Slovenia and Serbia. The lightning-wielding Perun cannot be considered the supreme god of the Slavs but is rather a spirit to whom was given the governance of the lightning.

In Estonia the prophet Elijah is considered to be the successor to Ukko, the ancient spirit of lightning. Similarly, the prophet Elijah replaces Elwa in Georgia and Zeus in Greece. It is therefore probable that, among the Slavs also, Elijah is to be considered a successor of Perun. According to a popular Serbian tradition, God gave the lightning to Elijah when he decided to retire from governing the world. The Serbian story agrees with Helmold's description of the distribution of offices by an inactive God. Elijah is a severe and peevish saint. It is rare that his feast day passes without some ill fortune. Fires—even spontaneous combustion—are blamed on him.

A similar complex may be seen if the Slavic Perun is equated with Perkūnas, the lightning deity of the Lithuanians. In Latvia, creatures with black fur or plumage were sacrificed to Perkun, as they were to the fire god Agni in ancient India. Such deities are therefore generic deities of fire, not specifically celestial and even less to be regarded as supreme. Scholarly efforts to place Perun at the centre of Slavic religion and to create around him a pantheon of deities of the Greco-Roman type cannot yield appreciable results. Russian sources treat Svarog, present as Zuarasici among the Liutici of Rethra (an ancient locality in eastern Germany), as a god of the drying-house fire. But the Belorussians of Chernigov, when lighting the drying-house fire, invoke Perun and not Svarog, as if Svarog (apparently from *svar*, "litigation" or "dispute," perhaps referring to the friction between the pieces of wood used to produce ignition) were an appellation of Perun.

Folk conceptions. In a series of Belorussian songs a divine figure enters the homes of the peasants in four forms in order to bring them abundance. These forms are: *bog* (God); *sporysh*, anciently an edible herb, today a stalk of grain with two ears, a symbol of abundance; *ray* (paradise); and *dobro* (the good). The word *bog* is an Indo-Iranian word signifying riches, abundance, and good fortune. *Sporysh* symbolizes the same concept. In Iranian *ray* has a similar meaning, which it probably also had in Slavic languages before it acquired the Christian meaning of paradise. *Bog*, meaning "riches," connotes grain. The same concept is also present in Mordvinian *pa* and *riz*—where their provenance is certainly Iranian. Among the Mordvins, Paz, like the Slavic Bog, enters into the homes bringing abundance. The adoption of the foreign word *bog* probably displaced from the Slavic languages the Indo-European name of the celestial God, Deivos (Ancient Indian Deva, Latin Deus, Old High German Ziu, etc.), which Lithuanian, on the other hand, has conserved as Diēvas.

Among the heavenly bodies the only object of Slavic veneration was the moon. The name of the moon is of masculine gender in Slavic languages (Russian *mesyats*; compare Latin *mensis*). The word for sun (Russian *solntse*), on the other hand, is a neuter diminutive that may derive from an ancient feminine form. In many Russian folk songs a verb having the sun as its subject is put in the feminine form, and the sun is almost always thought of as a bride or a maiden.

It is to the moon that recourse is had to obtain abundance and health. The moon is saluted with round dances and is prayed to for the health of children. During lunar eclipses, weapons are discharged at the monsters who are said to be devouring the moon, and weeping and wailing express the sharing of the moon's sufferings. In Serbia the people have always envisioned the moon as a human being. Such appelations as father and grandfather are customarily applied to the moon in Russian, Serbo-Croatian, and Bulgarian folk songs. At Risano (modern day Risan, Yugoslavia) in the days of Vuk Karadžić (1787–1864)—the father of modern Serbian literature—it was said of a baby four months old that he had four grandfathers. In Bulgaria the old people teach small children to call the moon Dedo Bozhe, Dedo Gospod (uncle God, uncle Lord). Ukrainian peasants in the Carpathians openly affirm that the moon is their god and that no other being could fulfill such functions if they were to be deprived of the moon. In two Great Russian supplications the sickle moon is invoked as "Adam"—the final phase of a fully developed moon worship in which the moon becomes the progenitor of the human family.

PRACTICES, CULTS, AND INSTITUTIONS

Places of worship. Though the idols of which the Russian chronicles speak appear to have been erected out-of-doors, the German chronicles provide detailed descriptions of enclosed sacred places and temples among the Baltic Slavs. Such enclosures were walled and did not differ from profane fortifications—areas usually of triangular shape at the confluence of two rivers, fortified with earthwork and palisades, especially on the access side. The fortifications intended for religious purposes contained wooden structures including a cell for the statue of a god, also made of wood and sometimes covered in metal. These representations, all anthropomorphic, very often had supernumerary bodily parts: seven arms, three or five heads (Trigelavus, Suantevitus, and Porenutius). The temples were in the custody of priests, who enjoyed

prestige and authority even in the eyes of the chiefs and received tribute and shares of military booty. Human sacrifices, including eviscerations, decapitations, and trepanning, had a propitiatory role in securing abundance and victory. One enclosure might contain up to four temples; those at Stettin (Polish Szczecin), in northwest Poland, were erected in close proximity to each other. They were visited annually by the whole population of the surrounding district, who brought with them oxen and sheep destined to be butchered. The boiled meat of the animals was distributed to all the participants without regard to sex or age. Dances and plays, sometimes humorous, enlivened the festival.

Communal banquets and related practices. The custom of communal banquets has been preserved into modern times in Russia in the *bratchina* (from *brat*, "brother"), in the *mol'ba* ("entreaty" or "supplication"), and in the *kanun* (short religious service); in the Serbian *slava* ("glorification"); and in the *sobor* ("assembly") and *kurban* ("victim, prey") of Bulgaria. Formerly, communal banquets were also held by the Poles and the Polabs (Elbe Slavs) of Hannover. In Russia the love feasts are dedicated to the memory of a deceased person or to the patron saint of the village, in Serbia to the protecting saint from whom the *rod* or *pleme* ("clan") took its name. Scholars no longer have any doubts of the pagan nature of these banquets. The Serbian *slava* is clearly dedicated to a saint held to be the founder of the clan. These saints are patrons or founders, and are all men who have died. When the Serbs celebrate the *slava* of the prophet Elijah or of the archangel Michael they do not set out the "dead man's plate" (the *koljivo*, boiled wheat), because Elijah and Michael are not dead. In certain localities in Serbia even the women given in marriage to another clan, the so-called *odive*, have to be present at the *slava*. They return with their children (according to the ancient matrilineal conception of the offspring), but not with their husbands who belong to another clan and celebrate another *slava*. More akin to the ancient pagan feasts of the Baltic is the Serbian *seoska slava* or *slava* of the village in which the whole population of the place takes part and they consume in common the flesh of the victims prepared in the open air. Such feasts are votive. In Russia sometimes the animals (or their flesh) are first brought into the church and incensed. Even at the beginning of the 20th century there were small villages in Russia where cattle were butchered only on the occasion of these festivities, three or four times a year. *The Homily of Opatoviz* (attributed to Herman, bishop of Prague) of the 10th–11th centuries emphatically condemns the love feasts as well as the veneration of statues and Slavic worship of the dead and veneration of saints as if they were gods. As in the Christian Era the saints entered the line of ancestors, so perhaps in pagan antiquity, ancient divinities (Perun, Svarog) were taken over as tribal progenitors. The Slavs did not record genealogies (exogamous societies have no need of them), and the founders of their clans were mainly legendary. The social unit sought to assure for itself the favour of powerful figures of the past, even of more than one, representing them in several forms on the same pillar or giving to their statues supernumerary bodily parts that would express their superhuman powers. A hollow bronze idol, probably ancient Russian, was found at Ryazan (U.S.S.R.). The idol has four faces with a fifth face on its breast.

The eastern Finns and the Ugrians venerated their dead in the same way, similarly representing them as polycephalic (multiple-headed), and also held communal banquets in their honour. Wooden buildings (the so-called *continae*) in which the faithful Baltic Slavs used to assemble for amusement, to deliberate, or to cook food have been observed in the 20th century among the Votyak, the Cheremis, and the Mordvins, but especially among the Votyak. Such wooden buildings also existed sparsely in Slavic territory in the 19th century, in Russia, particularly in the Ukraine, as well as here and there among the South Slavs.

If it is supposed that, as among the Finns and the Ugrians, each clan venerated its own divine ancestor in a

Worship of celestial bodies (left margin)

Temple ceremonies (right margin)

separate building, this would explain why many sacred enclosures would contain more than one *contina*—three at Carentia (the island of Garz at the mouth of the Oder River) and four at Stettin.

The custom of second interment

The system of idolatry of the Baltic area was essentially manistic (pertaining to worship of ancestors). It is not irrelevant that until the 19th century there survived here and there throughout the Danubian–Balkan region the custom of reopening graves three, five, or seven years after interment, taking out the bones of the corpses, washing them, wrapping them in new linen, and reinterring them. Detailed descriptions of this procedure have come particularly from Macedonia and Slovenia. Among East and West Slavs only faint echoes of the custom of a second interment survive in folk songs. In the former guberniya (administrative subdivision) of Vladimir, east of Moscow, as late as 1914, when a grave was to be dug, a piece of cloth was taken along with which to wrap the bones of any earlier corpse that might be unearthed in the process of digging. Such corpses would then be reinterred with the newly deceased. In protohistoric times the tumuli (mounds) of the mortuaries of the Krivichi, a populous tribe of the East Slavs of the northwest, the so-called long *kurgans* (burial mounds), contained cinerary urns buried in the tumulus together and all at one time. Such a practice could occur only as the consequence of collective and simultaneous cremation. There must, therefore, have existed a periodic cremation season or date, as for the opening of the tombs in Macedonia and as has been verified elsewhere in comparing the South Asian areas of second interment, in preparation for which the corpses are temporarily exhumed. The cremations by the Krivichi are of exhumed bones. In the Volga region today the Mordvins still burn the disinterred bones of the dead in the flames of a "living fire" ignited by friction.

Considering the religious past of the Slavs, it is not surprising that manism was strong enough to epitomize and overwhelm all or practically all of their religious views. The seasonal festivals of the Slavs turn out to be almost entirely dedicated to the dead, very often without the participants realizing it, as in the case of the Koljada (Latin Kalendae)—the annual visit made by the spirits of the dead, under the disguise of beggars, to all the houses in the village. It is possible that the bones of the disinterred were kept for a long period inside the dwellings, as is still sometimes done in the Tyrol of Austria, and that the sacred corner—now occupied by the icon—was the place where they were kept.

The spirits of the departed are not only venerated but also feared, especially the spirits of those who were prematurely deprived of life and its joys. It is believed that such spirits are greedy for the good things thus lost and that they make attempts to return to life—to the peril of the living. They are the prematurely dead, the so-called unclean dead. Particularly feared are maidens who died before marriage and are believed to be addicted to the kidnapping of bridegrooms and babies. One annual festival in particular, the Semik (seventh Thursday after Easter) was dedicated to the expulsion of these spirits. They are called *rusalki* in Russia, *vile* or *samovile* in Serbo-Croatia and Bulgaria.

The belief in vampires

The dead person who does not decompose in the grave becomes a vampire, a word and concept of Slavic origin. To save the living from a vampire's evil deeds, it is necessary to plant a stake in the grave so that it passes through the heart of the corpse or else to exhume the corpse and burn it. Since the classes of unclean dead are believed to have been constantly increasing (in Macedonia, for example, it is believed that all those born in the three months between Christmas and Lady Day are unclean), it will be seen that all of the dead—once objects of veneration and piety—will at some point be in danger of rancor, fear, and eventual disregard. A Christian clergy that has lent its presence at the exhumation and destruction of vampires has thereby contributed unwittingly to the preservation of this last phase of Slavic paganism into modern times.

There are other rites associated with second interment of which the Slavs have forgotten the purpose, such as the cemetery pyres—fires lit on top of the tombs—or the assiduous watering of graves. In Polynesia and South America where second interment is practiced, these same acts have the purpose of fostering decomposition of the corpses in order to hasten exhumation.

Numerous other ritual acts are performed by the Slavs, for the most part related to this complex of beliefs. In 19th-century Russia, if a man encountered the procession of naked women who were plowing a furrow around the village at night in order to protect it from an epidemic, he was inevitably killed. It was a chthonic (underworld) being to which, in those same times, human sacrifices were offered in Russia (more rarely in Poland and Bulgaria), since the victims were often buried alive. In most cases they were either voluntary victims or chosen by lot from among the devotees. Since such acts were punished by the law of the state, the sacrifices were performed in secrecy and are difficult to document.

BIBLIOGRAPHY. The sources for Slavic paganism were collected by C.H. MEYER, *Fontes historiae religionis slavicae* (1931); and reproduced in the appendix of the Italian translation of A. BRUCKNER, *Mitologia slava* (1923; pub. orig. in Polish, 1918). Brückner's work and the more recent work by V. PISANI, "Il paganesimo balto-slavo," in *Storia delle religioni*, ed by P. TACCHI VENTURI, pp. 587–632 (1934), represent the two most valiant attempts to furnish an Indo-European interpretation of Slavic paganism. For the critical side of the problem these two works remain indispensable. For the archaeological aspects, see C. SCHUCHHARDT, *Arkona, Rethra, Vineta* (1926). HELMOLDUS, "Chronica Slavorum" may be found in *Monumenta Germaniae historica*, vol. 21 of the series "Scriptorum" (1869). In the same series are the texts of the other German chroniclers and biographers. Descriptive exposition of the whole is in L. NIEDERLE, *Slovanské starožitnosti* (1911); and in B.O. UNBEGAUN, "La Religion des anciens Slaves," in A. GRENIER, *Les Religions étrusque et romaine . . .*, pp. 389–445 (1948). An attempt to find in the folklore traces of a more ancient mythology was made by W.R.S. RALSTON, in *The Songs of the Russian People, As Illustrative of Slavonic Mythology and Russian Social Life* (1872). A collection of materials and interesting suggestions in the same field is found in V.J. MANSIKKA, *Die religion der Ostslaven* (1922). For ethnography, see D. ZELENIN, *Russische (ostslavische) Volkskunde* (1927); K. MOSZYNSKI, *Kultura ludowa Słowian*, 3 vol. (1930–39); E. SCHNEEWEIS, *Grundriss des Volksglaubens und Volksbrauchs der Serbokroaten* (1935); P. CARAMAN, *Obrzęd kolędowania u Słowian i u Rumunów* (1933); and P. BOGATYREV, *Actes magiques, rites et croyances en Russie Subcarpathique* (1929). See also J. MACHAL, "Slavic Mythology," in *The Mythology of All Races* (1918).

(E.G.)

Sleep

Sleep is a normal, easily reversible, recurrent, and spontaneous state of decreased and less efficient responsiveness to external stimulation. The state contrasts with that of wakefulness, in which there is an enhanced potential for sensitivity and an efficient responsiveness to external stimuli. The sleep–wakefulness alternation is the most striking manifestation in higher vertebrates of the more general phenomenon of periodicity in the activity or responsivity of living tissue (see PERIODICITY, BIOLOGICAL). There is no single, perfectly reliable criterion of sleep. Sleep is defined by the convergence of observations satisfying several different motor, sensory, and physiological criteria. Occasionally, one or more of these criteria may be absent during sleep or present during wakefulness, but even in such cases there usually is little difficulty in achieving agreement among observers in the identification of the two behavioral states.

THE NATURE OF SLEEP

Sleep usually requires the presence of flaccid or relaxed skeletal muscles and the absence of the overt, goal-directed behaviour of which the waking organism is capable. Part of the recurring fascination with sleep talking and sleepwalking stems from their apparent violation of this latter criterion. Were these phenomena continuous, rather than intermittent, during a behavioral state, it is indeed questionable whether the designation "sleep" would continue to be appropriate. The characteristic posture associated with sleep in man and in many but not all

Motor and sensory criteria used in defining sleep

animals is that of horizontal repose. The relaxation of the skeletal muscles in this posture and its implication of a more passive role toward the environment are symptomatic of the reduced behavioral repertoire of sleep.

Indicative of the decreased sensitivity of the human sleeper to his external environment are the typical closed eyelids (or the functional blindness associated with sleep while the eyes are open) and the presleep rituals that include seeking surroundings characterized by reduced or monotonous levels of sensory stimulation. Three additional criteria, reversibility, recurrence, and spontaneity, distinguish the insensitivity of sleep from that of other states. Compared to that of hibernation or coma, the insensitivity of sleep is more easily reversible; *i.e.*, sleep may be defined in terms of the possibility of "waking up." Although the occurrence of sleep is not perfectly regular under all conditions, it is at least partially predictable from a knowledge of the duration of prior sleep periods and of the intervals between periods of sleep; and, although the onset of sleep may be facilitated by a variety of environmental or chemical means, sleep states are not thought of as being absolutely dependent upon such manipulations.

In experimental studies, both with subhuman vertebrates and with man, sleep also has been defined in terms of physiological variables generally associated with recurring periods of inactivity identified behaviourally as sleep. For example, the typical presence of certain electroencephalogram (EEG) patterns (brain patterns of electrical activity as recorded in tracings) with behavioral sleep has led to the designation of such patterns as "signs" of sleep. Conversely, in the absence of such signs (as, for example, in a hypnotic trance) it is felt that true sleep is absent. Such signs as are now employed, however, are not invariably discriminating of the behavioural states of sleep and wakefulness. Advances in the technology of animal experimentation have made it possible to extend the physiological approach from externally measurable manifestations of sleep such as the EEG to the underlying neural (nerve) mechanisms presumably responsible for such manifestations. As a result, it may finally become possible to identify structures or functions that are invariably related to behavioral sleep and to trace the evolution of sleep through comparative anatomical and physiological studies of structures found to be critical in the maintenance of sleep behaviour in the higher vertebrates.

In addition to the behavioral and physiological criteria already mentioned, subjective experience (in the case of the self) and verbal reports of such experience (in the case of others) are used at the human level to define sleep. Upon being alerted, one may feel or say, "I was asleep just then," and such judgments ordinarily are accepted as evidence for identifying a prearousal state as sleep, but such subjective evidence can be at variance with behavioristic classifications of sleep.

Problems in defining sleepMore generally, problems in defining sleep arise when evidence for one or more of the several criteria of sleep is lacking or when the evidence generated by available criteria is inconsistent. Do subhuman species sleep? Other mammalian species whose EEG and other physiological correlates are akin to those observed in human sleep demonstrate recurring, spontaneous, and reversible periods of inactivity and decreased critical reactivity. There is general acceptance of the designation of such states as sleep. As one descends the evolutionary scale below the birds and reptiles, however, and such criteria are successively less well satisfied, the unequivocal identification of sleep becomes more difficult. Bullfrogs (*Rana catesbeiana*), for example, seem not to fulfill sensory threshold criteria of sleep during resting states. Tree frogs (genus *Hyla*), on the other hand, show diminished sensitivity as they move from a state of behavioral activity to one of rest. Yet the EEGs of the alert rest of the bullfrog and the sleeplike rest of the tree frog are the same. There are parallel problems in defining sleep at different stages in the development of a single individual. At full-term birth in the human being, for instance, a convergence of nonsubjective criteria clearly seems to justify the identifica-

tion of periods of sleep, but it is more difficult to justify the attribution of sleep to the human fetus.

Problems in defining sleep may arise from the effects of artificial manipulation. For example, the EEG patterns commonly used as signs of sleep can be induced in an otherwise waking organism by the administration of certain drugs. Sometimes, also, there is conflicting evidence: a person who is "awakened" from a spontaneously assumed state of immobility with all the EEG criteria of sleep may claim that he had been awake prior to this event. In such troublesome cases, and more generally, it is becoming common to qualify attributions of sleep with the criteria upon which such attributions rest—*e.g.*, "behavioral sleep," "physiological sleep," or "self-described sleep." Such terminology accurately reflects both the multiplicity of criteria available for the identification of sleep and the possibility that these criteria may not always agree with one another.

DEVELOPMENTAL PATTERNS OF SLEEP AND WAKEFULNESS

Length of time spent in sleepHow much sleep does a person need? While the physiological bases of the need for sleep remain conjectural, rendering definitive answers to this question impossible, much evidence has been gathered on how much sleep people do in fact obtain. Perhaps the most important conclusion to be drawn from this evidence is that there is great variability among individuals in total sleep time. For adults, anything between six and nine hours of sleep as a nightly average is not unusual, and 7½ hours probably best expresses the norm. Such norms, of course, inevitably vary with the criteria of sleep employed. The most precise and reliable figures on sleep time, including those cited here, come from studies in sleep laboratories, where EEG criteria are employed.

Age consistently has been associated with the varying amount, quality, and patterning of electrophysiologically defined sleep. The newborn infant may spend an average of about 16 hours of each 24-hour period in sleep, although there is wide variability among individual babies. During the first year of life, total sleep time drops sharply; by two years of age, it may range from 9 to 12 hours. Decreases to approximately six hours have been observed among the elderly.

As will be elaborated below, EEG sleep studies have indicated that sleep can be considered to consist of several different stages. Developmental changes in the relative proportion of sleep time spent in these sleep stages are as striking as age-related changes in total sleep time. For example, the newborn infant may spend 50 percent of total sleep time in a stage of EEG sleep that is accompanied by intermittent bursts of rapid eye movements (REMs, indicative of a type of sleep that in some respects bears more resemblance to wakefulness than to other forms of sleep; it is discussed later in this article), while the comparable figure for adults is approximately 25 percent, and for the aged is less than 20 percent. There is also a decline with age of EEG stage 4 (deep slumber).

Aspects of sleep patterningSleep patterning consists of (1) the temporal spacing of sleep and wakefulness within a 24-hour period and (2) the ordering of different sleep stages within a given sleep period. In both senses, there are major developmental changes in the patterning of sleep. In alternations between sleep and wakefulness, there is a developmental shift from polyphasic sleep to monophasic sleep (*i.e.*, from intermittent to uninterrupted sleep). At birth, there may be five or six periods of sleep per day alternating with a like number of waking periods. With the dropping of nocturnal feedings in infancy, and of morning and afternoon naps in childhood, there is an increasing tendency to the concentration of sleep in one long nocturnal period (see Figure 1). The trend to monophasic sleep probably reflects some blend of the effects of maturing and of pressures from a culture geared to daytime activity and nocturnal rest. Among the elderly there may be a partial return to the polyphasic sleep pattern of infancy and early childhood, namely, more frequent daytime napping and less extensive periods of nocturnal sleep. Significant developmental effects also have been observed in spacing of stages within sleep. In the adult, REM sleep rarely occurs at sleep onset, while, in newborn infants, sleep-onset REM sleep is typical.

It would be difficult to overestimate the significance of the various age-related changes in sleep behaviour for a general theory of sleep. In the search for the functional significance of sleep or of particular stages of sleep, the shifts in sleep variables can be linked with variations in waking developmental needs, in the total capacities of the individual, and in environmental demands. It has been suggested, for instance, that the high frequency and pre-emptory character of REM sleep in the newborn infant may reflect a need for stimulation from within to permit orderly maturation of the central nervous system (CNS).

From E.J. Murray, *Sleep, Dreams and Arousal*, p. 297 (1965); Appleton-Century-Crofts

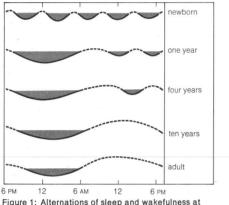

Figure 1: Alternations of sleep and wakefulness at specified ages. The shading indicates periods of sleep.

Another interpretation of age-related changes in REM sleep stresses its possible role in processing new information, the rate of acquisition for which is assumed to be relatively high in childhood but reduced in old age. As these views illustrate, developmental changes in the electrophysiology of sleep are germane not only to sleep but also to the role of CNS development in behavioral adaptation.

PSYCHOPHYSIOLOGICAL VARIATIONS IN SLEEP

That there are different kinds of sleep has long been recognized. In everyday discourse there is talk of "good" sleep or "poor" sleep, of "light" sleep and "deep" sleep; yet, only in the second half of the 20th century have scientists paid much attention to qualitative variations within sleep. Sleep was formerly conceptualized by scientists as a unitary state of passive recuperation. Revolutionary changes have occurred in scientific thinking about sleep, the most important of which has been increased sensitivity to its heterogeneity.

This revolution may be traced back to the discovery of sleep characterized by rapid eye movements (REM sleep), first reported by the physiologists Eugene Aserinsky and Nathaniel Kleitman in 1953. REM sleep proved to have characteristics quite at variance with the prevailing model of sleep as recuperative deactivation of the central nervous system. Various central and autonomic nervous system measurements seemed to show that the REM stage of sleep is more nearly like activated wakefulness than it is like other sleep. It now has become conventional to consider REM ("paradoxical") and non-REM (NREM or "orthodox") sleep as qualitatively different. Thus the earlier assumption that sleep is a unitary and passive state has yielded to the viewpoint that there are two different kinds of sleep, a relatively deactivated NREM phase and an activated REM phase.

Non-rapid eye movement sleep. NREM sleep itself is conventionally subdivided into several different stages on the basis of EEG criteria. Stage 1 is observed at sleep onset or after momentary arousals during the night and is defined as a low-voltage mixed-frequency EEG tracing with a considerable representation of theta-wave (four to seven hertz, or cycles per second) activity. Stage 2 is a relatively low-voltage EEG tracing characterized by intermittent, short sequences of waves of 12–14 hertz ("sleep

Stages of NREM sleep

spindles") and by formations called K-complexes, biphasic wave forms that can be induced by external stimulation, as by a sound, but that also occur spontaneously during sleep. Stages 3 and 4 consist of relatively high-voltage (over 50-microvolt) EEG tracings with a predominance of delta-wave (one to two hertz) activity; the distinction between the two stages is based on an arbitrary criterion of amount of delta-wave activity, with greater amounts classified as stage 4. Unlike the basic distinction between NREM and REM, differences among NREM sleep stages generally are regarded as quantitative rather than qualitative.

The EEG patterns of NREM sleep, particularly of stages 3 and 4 (tracings of slower frequency and higher amplitude), are those associated in other circumstances with decreased vigilance. Furthermore, after the transition from wakefulness to NREM sleep, most functions of the autonomic nervous system decrease their rate of activity and their moment-to-moment variability. Thus, NREM sleep is the kind of seemingly restful state that appears capable of supporting the recuperative functions assigned to sleep. There are, in fact, several lines of evidence suggesting such functions for NREM stage 4: (1) increases in such sleep, in both man and laboratory animals, have been observed after physical exercise; (2) the concentration of such sleep in the early portion of the sleep period (*i.e.*, immediately after wakeful states of activity) in human beings; and (3) the relatively high priority that such sleep has, among human beings, in "recovery" sleep following abnormally extended periods of wakefulness.

Rapid eye movement sleep. REM sleep is a state of diffuse bodily activation. Its EEG patterns (tracings of faster frequency and lower amplitude than in NREM stages 2–4) are at least superficially similar to those of wakefulness. Most autonomic variables exhibit relatively high rates of activity and variability during REM sleep; for example, there are higher heart and respiration rates and more short-term variability in these rates than in NREM sleep, increased blood pressure, and, in males, full or partial penile erection. In addition, REM sleep is accompanied by a relatively high rate of gross body motility, periodic twitching of the muscles of the face and extremities, relatively high levels of oxygen consumption by the brain, increased cerebral blood flow, and higher brain temperature. An even more impressive demonstration of the activation of REM sleep is to be found in the firing rates of individual cerebral neurons, or nerve cells, in experimental animals: during REM sleep such rates exceed those of NREM sleep and often equal or surpass those of wakefulness. Another distinguishing feature of REM sleep, of course, is the intermittent appearance of bursts of the rapid eye movements, whence the term is derived.

For both man and animals, REM sleep now is defined by the concurrence of three events: low-voltage, mixed-frequency EEG; intermittent REMs; and suppressed tonus of the muscles of the facial region (*i.e.*, suppression of the continuous slight tension otherwise normally present). This decrease in muscle tonus and a similarly observed suppression of spinal reflexes are indicative of heightened motor inhibition during REM sleep. Animal studies have identified the locus ceruleus, in the pons, as the probable source of this inhibition. (The pons is in the brain stem directly above the medulla oblongata; the locus ceruleus borders on the brain cavity known as the fourth ventricle.) When this structure is surgically destroyed in experimental animals, they periodically engage in active, apparently goal-directed behaviour during REM sleep, although they still show the unresponsivity to external stimulation characteristic of the stage. It has been suggested that such behaviour may be the acting out of the hallucinations of a dream.

An important theoretical distinction is that between REM sleep phenomena that are continuous and those that are intermittent. Tonic (continuous) characteristics of REM sleep include the low-voltage EEG and the suppressed muscle tonus; intermittent events in REM sleep include the REMs themselves and, as observed in the cat, spikelike electrical activity in those parts of the brain concerned with vision and in other parts of the cerebral cortex. The

The three events defining REM sleep

various intermittent events of REM sleep tend to occur together, and it seems to be these moments of intermittent activation that are responsible for much of the difference between REM sleep and NREM sleep. The spiking mentioned is observed occasionally in NREM sleep, an occurrence that has been interpreted by some theorists as suggesting that REM sleep is not qualitatively unique in its capacity to support intermittent activation and that between NREM and REM sleep the differences may be less striking than the differences in eye movement and in EEG have indicated.

Sequences of NREM and REM sleep. The usual temporal progression of the two kinds of sleep in the adult human is for a period of approximately 70–90 minutes of NREM sleep (the stages being ordered 1–2–3–4–3–2) to precede the first period of REM sleep, which may last from approximately 5 to 15 minutes. NREM–REM cycles of roughly equivalent total duration then recur through the night, with the REM portion lengthening somewhat, and the NREM portion shrinking correspondingly, as sleep continues. Approximately 25 percent of total accumulated sleep will be spent in REM sleep and 75 percent in NREM sleep. Most of the latter will be EEG stage 2. The high proportion of stage 2 NREM sleep is attributable to the loss of stages 3 and 4 in the NREM portion of the NREM–REM cycles after the first two or three (see Figure 2).

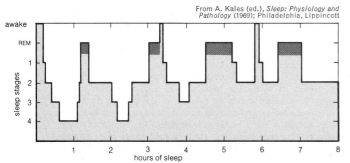

From A. Kales (ed.), *Sleep: Physiology and Pathology* (1969); Philadelphia, Lippincott

Figure 2: Nocturnal sleep pattern in young adults. Note the absence of stage 4 and the decreased length of NREM periods during the latter part of the night and the short first REM period.

Light and deep sleep. Which of the various NREM stages is light sleep and which deep sleep? The criteria used to establish sleep depth are the same as those used to distinguish sleep from wakefulness. In terms of motor behaviour, motility decreases (depth increases) from stages 1 through 4. By criteria of sensory responsivity, thresholds generally increase (sleep deepens) from stages 1 through 4. By most physiological criteria, NREM stages 3 and 4 are particularly deactivated (deep). Thus, gradations within NREM sleep do seem fairly consistent, with a continuum extending from the "lightest" stage 1 to the "deepest" stage 4.

Problems of defining depth in REM sleep

Relative to NREM sleep, is REM sleep light or deep? The answer here seems to be that by some criteria REM sleep is light and by others it is deep. For example, in terms of muscle tone, which is at its lowest point during sleep in REM sleep, it is deep. In terms of its relatively high rates of intermittent fine and gross body motility, REM sleep would have to be considered light. Arousal thresholds during REM sleep are variable, apparently as a function of the meaningfulness of the stimulus (and of the possibility of its incorporation into an ongoing dream sequence). With a meaningful stimulus (*e.g.*, one which cannot be ignored with impunity), the capacity for responsivity can be demonstrated to be roughly equivalent to that of "light" NREM sleep (stages 1 and 2). With a stimulus having no particular significance to the sleeper, thresholds can be rather high. The discrepancy between these two conditions suggests an active shutting out of irrelevant stimuli during REM sleep. By most physiological criteria related to the autonomic and central nervous systems, REM sleep clearly is more like wakefulness than like NREM sleep, but drugs that cause arousal in wakefulness, such as amphetamine, suppress REM sleep. In terms of subjective response, recently awakened sleepers often de-

scribe REM sleep as having been "deep" and NREM sleep as having been "light." The subjectively felt depth of REM sleep may reflect the immersion of the sleeper in the vivid dream experiences of this stage.

Thus, as was true in defining sleep itself, there are difficulties in achieving unequivocal definitions of sleep depth. Several different criteria may be employed, and they are not always in agreement. REM sleep is particularly difficult to classify along any continuum of sleep depth. The current tendency is to consider it a unique state, sharing properties of both light and deep sleep. The fact that selective deprivation of REM sleep (elaborated below) results in a selective increase in such sleep on recovery nights is consistent with this view of REM sleep as unique.

Autonomic variables. Some autonomic physiological variables have a characteristic pattern relating their activity to cumulative sleep time, without respect to whether it is REM or NREM sleep. These variables are viewed by some authorities as incidental rather than essential features of the state of sleep, which is conceived in terms of the central nervous system. Such variables presumably reflect constant or slowly changing features of both kinds of sleep, such as the cumulative effects of immobility and of relaxation of skeletal muscles on metabolic processes. Body temperature, for example, drops during the early hours of sleep, reaching a low point after five or six hours, then rises toward the morning awakening.

Behavioral variables. Behaviorally, it has been shown that already established motor responses can be evoked in all stages of sleep, but it has proved much more difficult to demonstrate that new responses can be acquired during sleep. When EEG criteria of sleep are employed, it appears that "sleep learning" of verbal material takes place only to the degree that the person being tested is partially awake during the presentation of the stimuli. Another line of behavioral study is the observation of spontaneously occurring integrated behaviour patterns, such as walking and talking during sleep. In keeping with the idea of a heightened tonic (continuous) motor inhibition during REM sleep, but contrary to the idea that such behaviour is an acting out of especially vivid dream experiences or a substitute for them, sleep talking occurs primarily in NREM sleep and sleepwalking exclusively in NREM sleep. Talking in one's sleep is particularly characteristic of lighter NREM sleep (stage 2), while sleepwalking is initiated from deeper NREM sleep (stage 4). Episodes of NREM sleepwalking generally do not seem to be associated with any remembered dreams, nor is NREM sleep talking consistently associated with reported dreams of appropriate content.

Dreaming. Aserinsky and Kleitman suggested that REMs are related to the visual imagery of ongoing dream experiences. They found that persons awakened during REM periods were able to recall vivid visual dreams, while NREM awakenings were associated with little or no dream recall. Subsequent research has established that rapid eye movements in sleep are indeed associated with vivid visual dreaming (85 percent or so of REM-sleep arousals in young adults producing reported dreams) but also has demonstrated that NREM sleep also can be associated with memorable mental activity. While NREM mental activity generally is not as dreamlike (*i.e.*, visual, dramatic, bizarre, emotional) as is typical REM-sleep dreaming, it has at least some features in common with REM dreams, particularly mental activity during NREM stage 1 at the onset of sleep. Some reports from this latter stage are of vivid, visual, hallucinated dramatic episodes indistinguishable from typical REM reports. Thus the physiological distinction between REM and NREM sleep is not always paralleled by accompanying differences in mental activity during sleep, and REM sleep is not the only stage of sleep capable of supporting vivid dream activity. The dreams associated with REM sleep, however, seem most likely to be spontaneously recalled, and it is probably REM dreams that have given rise to dream theories and that are most widely employed today in psychotherapeutic practice. It once was believed that the REMs of this stage are in point-for-point correspondence with visual

Sleep learning; sleep-walking, sleep talking

Recall of REM sleep dreams

imagery, with a dream of watching a tennis match, for instance, associated with a REM sequence of right–left–right–left. The evidence for such a correspondence now seems equivocal. An alternative proposal is that the REMs are not specific responses of the visual system to ongoing mental activity but rather are part of a much more diffusely organized system of intermittent activation that also happens to include vivid moments of dreaming. The most important contributions to studies on dreams that psychophysiological research on sleep has made have been the demonstrations of much more dreaming (four or five separate, lengthy periods of REM sleep, totalling as much as two hours), and of many more different kinds of dreaming (*e.g.,* reports of everyday thinking sometimes elicited on awakenings from NREM) during sleep than previously had been recognized. As yet, psychophysiological dream studies have not had a marked impact on either clinical dream theory or clinical dream practice, perhaps because they have focussed on physiological concomitants of manifest dream content rather than on unconscious determinants of such content.

EFFECTS OF SLEEP DEPRIVATION

Types of sleep deprivation

One time-honoured approach to determining the function of an organ or process is to deprive an organism of the organ or process. In the case of sleep, the deprivation approach to function has been applied, both experimentally and naturalistically, to sleep as a unitary state (general sleep deprivation), and, experimentally only, to particular kinds of sleep (selective sleep deprivation). General sleep deprivation may be either total (*e.g.,* a person has had no sleep at all for a period of days) or partial (*e.g.,* over a period a person obtains only three or four hours of sleep per night). The method of general deprivation studies is enforced wakefulness. Selective sleep deprivation has been reported for two stages of sleep: stage 4 of NREM sleep and REM sleep. Both typically occur after the appearance of other sleep stages, REM sleep after all four NREM stages and stage 4 after the lighter NREM stages. The general idea of selective deprivation studies is to allow the sleeper to have natural sleep until the point at which he enters the stage to be deprived and then to prevent the stage, either by experimental awakening or by other manipulations such as application of a mildly noxious stimulus or prior administration of a drug known to suppress it. The hope is that total sleep time will not be altered but that increased occurrence of some other stage will substitute for the loss of the one selectively eliminated.

General sleep deprivation. On a three-hour sleep schedule, partial deprivation does not reproduce, in miniaturized form, the same relative distribution of sleep patterns achieved in a seven- or eight-hour sleep period. Some increase is observed in absolute amounts of REM sleep during the three-hour sleep period as compared to the first three hours of normal sleep, and there also is a significant increase in the amount of stage 4 of NREM sleep. Lighter NREM sleep (*e.g.,* stage 2) seems to have a particularly low priority under partial sleep deprivation. Although the REM sleep percentage increases somewhat under partial deprivation, the person is still far from achieving his usual quota in absolute minutes of sleep time. On uninterrupted recovery nights following the termination of the deprivation, there is more REM sleep than there was before the deprivation. This change is viewed as a compensatory "rebound" of REM sleep such that at least some of the quota is made up. Most if not all of the nightly quota of stage 4 of NREM sleep can be achieved on a three-hour nightly schedule. Because partial deprivation on a three-hour nightly regimen also tends to be selective deprivation (the person receives most of his quota of stage 4 NREM sleep but relatively little of his quota of stage REM), the behavioral effects of such deprivation may be relevant to the question of the adaptive functions served by REM sleep. One study has reported no effects from deprivation of REM sleep on the capacity for performance on a perceptual discrimination task but decreased motivation. When a schedule of partial deprivation began to interfere with the routine accumulation of stage 4 (*i.e.,* less than three hours of sleep per night), on

the other hand, the capacity for performance seemed to be adversely affected.

Effects of total sleep deprivation

In view of several obvious practical considerations, many general deprivation studies have used animals rather than human beings as experimental subjects. Waking effects routinely observed in these studies have been of deteriorated physiological functioning, sometimes including actual tissue damage. The pattern of findings, however, has been variable from study to study and even from animal to animal within a given study, so that it is difficult to draw any clear conclusions. There is some suggestion that age is related to sensitivity to the effects of deprivation, younger organisms proving more capable of withstanding the stress than mature ones.

Among human subjects, the champion nonsleeper apparently was a 17-year-old student who voluntarily undertook a 264-hour sleep deprivation experiment. Effects noted during the deprivation period included irritability, blurred vision, slurring of speech, memory lapses, and confusion concerning his identity. No long-term (*i.e.,* postrecovery) effects were observed on either his personality or his intellect. More generally, although brief hallucinations and easily controlled episodes of bizarre behaviour have been observed after five to ten days of continuous sleep deprivation, these symptoms do not occur in most subjects and thus offer little support to the hypothesis that sleep loss induces psychosis. In any event, these symptoms rarely persist beyond the period of sleep that follows the period of deprivation. When inappropriate behaviour does persist, it generally seems to be in persons known to have a tendency toward such behaviour. Generally, upon investigation, injury to the nervous system has not been discovered in persons who have been deprived of sleep for many days. This negative result must be understood in the context of the limited duration of these studies and should not be interpreted as indicating that sleep loss is either safe or desirable. The short-term effects observed with the student mentioned are typical and are of the sort that, in the absence of the continuous monitoring his vigil received, might well have endangered his health and safety.

Other commonly observed behavioural effects during total sleep deprivation include fatigue, inability to concentrate, and visual or tactile illusions and hallucinations. These effects generally become intensified with increased loss of sleep, but they also wax and wane in a cyclic fashion in line with 24-hour fluctuations in EEG alpha-wave (8–12 hertz) phenomena and with body temperature, becoming most acute in the early morning hours. Changes in intellectual performance during moderate sleep loss can, to a certain extent, be compensated for by increased effort and motivation. In general, tasks that are work paced (the subject must respond at a particular instant of time not of his own choice) tend to be affected more adversely than tasks that are self-paced. Errors of omission are common with the former kind of task and are thought to be associated with "microsleep"—momentary lapses into sleep. Changes in body chemistry and in workings of the autonomic nervous system sometimes have been noted during deprivation, but it has proved difficult to establish either consistent patterning in such effects or whether they should be attributed to sleep loss per se or to the stress or other incidental features of the deprivation manipulation. In general, involuntary bodily functions seem relatively more impervious to effects of short-term deprivation than are adaptive, or voluntary, ones. The length of the first recovery sleep session for the student mentioned above, following his 264 hours of wakefulness, was slightly less than 15 hours. His sleep demonstrated increased amounts of both stage 4 NREM and stage REM sleep. After shorter periods of sleep loss, the tendency is for stage 4 compensation to occur first (during the first recovery session), and REM-sleep compensation later (during the second recovery session).

Selective sleep deprivation. Studies of selective sleep deprivation have confirmed the attribution of need for both stage 4 NREM and REM sleep, because an increasing number of experimental arousals is required each night to suppress both stage 4 and REM sleep on successive nights

Effects of selective sleep deprivation

of deprivation, and because both show a clear rebound effect following deprivation. Rebound from stage 4 NREM-sleep deprivation occurs only on the night following termination of the deprivation regardless of the length of the deprivation, whereas the duration of the rebound effect following REM-sleep deprivation is related to the length of the prior deprivation. Little is known as yet of the consequences of stage 4 deprivation.

Particular interest has attached to the selective deprivation of REM sleep, partly because of its unique and somewhat puzzling properties as an activated state of sleep and partly because of the association of this stage with vivid dreaming. REM-sleep-deprivation studies once were considered also to be "dream-deprivation" studies. This psychological view of REM sleep deprivation has become less pervasive since the experimental demonstration of the occurrence of dreaming during NREM sleep stages, and because, contrary to the Freudian position that the dream is an essential safety valve for the release of emotional tensions, it has become evident that REM-sleep deprivation is not psychologically disruptive. REM-sleep-deprivation studies have focussed more upon the presumed functions of the REM state than upon those of the vivid dreams that accompany it. The evidence from these studies has proved to be partially supportive of a number of different theoretical positions concerning REM sleep. Some animal studies have reported deleterious effects of REM-sleep deprivation on learning or other cognitive tasks (*i.e.*, tasks concerned with thinking, remembering, perceiving, and the like), in line with the view that cognitive processing may be one function of REM sleep. Other animal studies have shown heightened levels of sexuality and aggressiveness after a period of deprivation, suggesting a drive-regulative function for REM sleep. Other observations suggest increased sensitivity of the central nervous system to auditory stimuli and to electroconvulsive shock following deprivation, as might have been predicted from the theory that REM sleep somehow serves to maintain CNS integrity.

Effects of REM sleep deprivation

Although there is a need for REM sleep, apparently it is not absolute. Animals have been deprived of REM sleep for as long as two months without showing behavioural or physiological evidence of injury. Several problems arise in connection with the methods of most REM-sleep-deprivation studies. Controls for factors such as stress, sleep interruption, and total sleep time are difficult to manage. Thus it is unclear whether observed effects of REM-sleep deprivation are the result of REM-sleep loss or the result of such factors as stress and general sleep loss. It also is unclear whether it is the loss of continuous REM sleep or of the intermittent events that accompany it that is crucial in REM-sleep deprivation. Preliminary research indicates the latter, suggesting that REM-deprivation studies are more relevant to the function of separate intermittent events occurring in sleep than to the function of the continuous REM sleep.

PATHOLOGICAL ASPECTS

It is important, at the outset, to emphasize that, as dramatic and reliable as the various stages of sleep are, their functions or relationships to waking performance, mood, or health still are largely unknown. Thus, association of a sleep abnormality with a certain stage of sleep (either in the sense that an abnormal event occurs during a certain stage or in the sense that an abnormal condition is associated with an increase or decrease in the proportion of total sleep time spent in that stage) is difficult to interpret when the function or necessity of that stage is uncertain. The pathology of sleep includes: (1) primary disturbances of sleep–wakefulness mechanisms, such as seem to characterize encephalitis lethargica ("sleeping sickness"), narcolepsy (irresistible brief episodes of sleep), and hypersomnia (sleep attacks of lesser urgency but greater duration than those of narcolepsy); (2) minor episodes occurring during sleep, such as bedwetting and nightmares; (3) medical disorders such as duodenal ulcer whose symptoms are accentuated during sleep; and (4) sleep symptoms of the major psychiatric disorders.

Primary disturbances. Epidemic lethargic encephalitis is produced by viral infections of sleep–wakefulness mechanisms in the hypothalamus, a structure at the upper end of the brainstem. The disease often passes through several stages: fever and delirium; hyposomnia (loss of sleep); and hypersomnia (excessive sleep), sometimes bordering on a coma. Inversions of 24-hour sleep–wakefulness patterns also are commonly observed, as are disturbances in eye movements.

Narcolepsy, like encephalitis, is thought to involve specific abnormal functioning of subcortical sleep regulatory centres. Some persons who experience attacks of narcolepsy also have one or more of the following auxiliary symptoms: cataplexy, a sudden loss of muscle tone often precipitated by an emotional response such as laughter or startle and sometimes so dramatic as to cause the patient to fall down; hypnagogic (sleep onset) and hypnopompic (awakening) visual hallucinations of a dreamlike sort; and hypnagogic or hypnopompic sleep paralysis, in which the patient is unable to move voluntary muscles (except respiratory muscles) for a period ranging from several seconds to several minutes. When narcolepsy includes one or more of the accessory symptoms, some of the sleep attacks consist of periods of REM at onset of sleep. This precocious triggering of REM sleep (which occurs in adults generally only after 70–90 minutes of NREM sleep) may indicate that the accessory symptoms are dissociated aspects of REM sleep; *i.e.*, the cataplexy and the paralysis represent the active motor inhibition of REM sleep and the hallucinations represent the dream experience of REM sleep. In the narcoleptic patient without the accessory symptoms, the narcoleptic attacks usually consist of NREM sleep. Thus, narcolepsy may involve either REM or NREM sleep, and it is thought that both forms of narcolepsy probably involve a failure of wakefulness mechanisms to inhibit sleep mechanisms.

Hypersomnia;
hyposomnia

Hypersomnia may involve either excessive daytime sleep and drowsiness or a nocturnal sleep period of greater than normal duration, but does not include sleep-onset REM periods. One reported concomitant of hypersomnia, the failure of heart rate to decrease during sleep, suggests that hypersomniac sleep may not be as restful per unit of time as is normal sleep. In its primary form, hypersomnia is probably hereditary in origin (as is also narcolepsy) and is thought to involve some disruption of the functioning of hypothalamic sleep centres. Narcolepsy and hypersomnia are not characterized by grossly abnormal EEG sleep patterns. The abnormality seems to involve a failure in "turn on" and "turn off" mechanisms regulating sleep, rather than in the sleep process itself. Both narcoleptic and hypersomniac symptoms can be managed by administration of drugs. Several forms of hypersomnia are periodic rather than chronic. One very rare disorder of periodically excessive sleep, the Kleine-Levin syndrome, is characterized by periods of two to four weeks of excessive sleep in association with a ravenous appetite and psychotic-like behaviour during the few waking hours. The "Pickwickian syndrome" (in reference to the fat boy, Joe, in Dickens' *Pickwick Papers*), another form of periodically excessive sleep, is associated with obesity and respiratory insufficiency.

Hyposomnia (this word, meaning "too little sleep," is chosen in preference to "insomnia," or "lack of sleep," because some sleep invariably is present) is less clearly understood than the conditions already mentioned. It has been demonstrated that, by physiological criteria, self-described poor sleepers generally sleep much better than they imagine. Their sleep, however, does show signs of disturbance: frequent body movement, enhanced levels of autonomic functioning, and reduced levels of stage REM. Although hyposomnia in a particular situation is common and without pathological import, chronic hyposomnia may be related to psychological disturbance. Hyposomnia conventionally is treated by administration of drugs, but often with substances (*e.g.*, barbiturates) that are potentially addicting and otherwise dangerous when used over long periods.

Minor episodes. Among the minor episodes sometimes considered abnormal in sleep are: somniloquy (sleep talking) and somnambulism (sleepwalking), enuresis (bed-wetting), bruxism (tooth grinding), snoring, and nightmares. Sleep talking seems more often to consist of inarticulate mumblings than of extended, meaningful utterances. It occurs at least occasionally for many people, and at this level cannot be considered pathological. Sleepwalking is not uncommon in children, but its continuity into adulthood is considered suggestive of persistent immaturity of the central nervous system. Enuresis may be a secondary symptom of a variety of organic conditions or, more frequently, a primary disorder in its own right. In the latter case, it seems to involve some immaturity in neural control of bladder muscles. While mainly a disorder of early childhood, enuresis persists into adulthood for a small number of persons. Treatment generally has been directed either toward sensitizing the sleeper to bladder distention, so that he will awaken and urinate according to appropriate social norms, or toward increasing bladder capacity, so that sleep can be sustained without bed-wetting episodes. Primary enuresis does not seem to be an abnormality of sleep, sleep cycles of bedwetting and of normal children being roughly the same. Tooth grinding is not consistently associated with any particular stage of sleep, nor does it appreciably affect overall sleep patterning; it, too, seems to be an abnormality in rather than of sleep. Rhythmic snoring can occur throughout sleep, although it probably is most prevalent in the NREM stages. It indicates the partial muscular relaxation of sleep, and its occasional occurrence is not considered abnormal.

A variety of frightening experiences associated with sleep have, at one time or another, been called nightmares. As not all such phenomena have proved to be identical in their associations with sleep stages or with other variables, several distinctions need to be made among them. Incubus, the classical nightmare of adult years, consists of arousal from stage 4 NREM sleep with a sense of heaviness over the chest, with diffuse anxiety, but with little or no dream recall. Night terrors (*pavor nocturnus*) are disorders of early childhood. Delta-wave NREM sleep suddenly is interrupted with a scream, the child may sit up in apparent terror, and he is incoherent and inconsolable. After a period of minutes, he returns to sleep, often without ever having been fully alert or awake. Dream recall generally is absent, and the entire episode may be forgotten in the morning. Anxiety dreams most often seem associated with spontaneous arousals from REM sleep. There is remembrance of a dream whose content is in keeping with the disturbed awakening. While their persistent recurrence probably indicates waking psychological disturbance or stress caused by a difficult situation, anxiety dreams occur occasionally in many otherwise healthy persons.

Disorders accentuated during sleep. A variety of medical symptoms may be accentuated by the conditions of sleep. Attacks of angina (spasmodic, choking pain), for example, apparently can be augmented by the activation of the autonomic nervous system in REM sleep; the same is true of gastric acid secretions in persons who have duodenal ulcer. NREM sleep, on the other hand, can increase the likelihood of certain kinds of epileptic discharge.

The resemblance of dream consciousness to waking psychotic experience often has been noted, and the psychotic has been considered a "waking dreamer." Thus it has been theorized that waking psychotic symptoms may be generated by a spontaneous, or REM-sleep-deprivation-induced, shift of REM phenomena from sleep to the waking state. Many authorities also have suggested that in depression not caused by external factors, hyposomnia, a prominent feature of the state, may be a causal factor. While these ideas are intriguing, and have received much systematic study, the evidence at present is inconclusive. Symptomatically, schizophrenic persons have shown neither the exacerbation of psychotic symptoms under experimental REM-sleep deprivation nor the consistent or large deviations from normal EEG sleep patterning that would seem to be required by the hypothesis that sleep mechanisms play some critical role in bringing on psychotic episodes. Depressed persons do sleep less and often have a lower percentage of REM sleep than normal persons and do obtain little delta-wave NREM sleep, but it is not clear whether these sleep symptoms indicate a fundamental involvement of sleep mechanisms in the causation of depressive states.

DRUGS AND SLEEP

Various chemical substances long have been employed to induce or prolong sleep, but there have been few controlled, double-blind (neither the physician who evaluates the results nor the patient knows whether the latter has received drug or placebo—an inert substitute) studies of alleged hypnotics (sleep-inducing drugs) in which sleep has been assessed by physiological measurement; and the mechanisms of sleep themselves are only now beginning to be isolated. The little research that has been done makes it clear that the manner in which a drug affects sleep can be extremely complex, with different effects sometimes attributable to different dosages of the same substance and with different effects sometimes observed for short-term and long-term administration of the same substance.

Many pharmacological agents tend to reduce the absolute amount and relative proportion of sleep spent in REM sleep. In this sense, REM sleep has been called a fragile state. Specifically, most effective hypnotics, particularly the barbiturates (*e.g.*, pentobarbital, secobarbital), decrease both total REM time and the proportion of sleep spent in REM sleep, with enhanced amounts of NREM sleep. Amphetamine, an analeptic (stimulant), decreases REM sleep. Many tranquillizers also slightly reduce REM sleep. There is evidence that the withdrawal symptoms of persons taken off addictive drugs of any variety (*e.g.*, barbiturates, amphetamines, narcotics) are accompanied by relatively high percentages of REM sleep. It has been suggested that the drugs in question are REM-sleep deprivers, that the elevated periods spent in REM sleep on withdrawal represent REM-sleep rebound, that the withdrawal syndrome may be functionally related to high pressure for REM sleep, and that the vivid, unpleasant dreams associated with REM-sleep rebound may be responsible for patients' return to the use of the REM-sleep-depriving agents. Caffein seems to have little effect on normal sleep patterning, but the effects of alcohol are variable: the short-term effect is to reduce the time spent in REM sleep, but, with continued administration, there may be a REM-sleep rebound. Not all drug effects are on REM sleep; some of the more recently developed tranquillizers and hypnotics have been found to reduce stage 4 sleep.

Much interest has attached to the search for hypnotic substances that are not REM-sleep deprivers; *i.e.*, that induce or prolong sleep without altering natural sleep patterns. While some such hypnotics have been found, they most often either have adverse side effects or have not been fully evaluated. Theoretically, the most interesting substances are those few that have been found to increase REM sleep. In certain dosage ranges and under certain conditions, such an effect has been noted for reserpine, a tranquillizer, and for D-lysergic acid diethylamide (LSD), a hallucinogen. Both substances have important interactions with neurohumors (serotonin and norepinephrine —substances formed in nerve cells), and their effects may offer clues to the mechanisms underlying REM sleep.

THEORIES OF SLEEP

Two kinds of sleep theory of contemporary interest may be distinguished. One begins with the peripheral physiology of sleep and relates it to underlying neural (nervous-system) or biochemical mechanisms. Such theories most often rely on experiments with animals by means of drugs or surgery. Alternatively, sleep theories may start with behavioral observations of sleep and may attempt to specify the functions of such a state of lethargy and insensitivity from an evolutionary or adaptive point of view. The question here is not so much how we sleep, or even why we sleep, but what good it does.

Mechanistic theories. Historically, mechanistic theories of sleep have focussed on a succession of organs or structures in a manner reflective of the degree of access different civilizations have had to the inner workings of the human body. Thus the relatively perceptible processes of circulation, digestion, and secretion played large roles in the theories of classical antiquity, and modern theories have been concerned with the central nervous system, particularly the brain, although various peripheral factors in the induction of sleep are not ruled out. Proposals that blood composition, metabolic changes, or internal secretions regulate sleep are necessarily incomplete to the extent that they ignore the contributions of environment and intent to the onset of sleep. It also is noted that in two-headed human monsters one "twin" may seem asleep while the other is awake, despite their sharing circulatory system.

Neural theories. Among neural theories of sleep, there are certain issues that each must face. Is the sleep-wakefulness alternation to be considered a property of individual neurons (nerve cells), making unnecessary the postulation of specific regulative centres, or is it to be assumed that there are some aggregations of neurons that play a dominant role in sleep induction and maintenance? The Russian physiologist Ivan Petrovich Pavlov adopted the former position, proposing that sleep is the result of irradiating inhibition among cortical and subcortical neurons (nerve cells in the outer brain layer and in the brain layers beneath the cortex). Micro-electrode studies, on the other hand, have revealed high rates of discharge during sleep from many neurons in the motor and visual areas of the cortex, and thus it seems that, as compared with wakefulness, sleep must consist of a different organization of cortical activity rather than some general, overall decline.

Pavlov's theory

Another issue has been whether there is a waking centre, fluctuations in whose level of functioning are responsible for various degrees of wakefulness and sleep, or whether the induction of sleep requires another centre, actively antagonistic to the waking centre. Early speculation favoured the passive view of sleep. A *cerveau isolé* preparation, an animal in which a surgical incision high in the midbrain has separated the cerebral hemispheres from sensory input, demonstrated chronic somnolence. It has been reasoned that a similar cutting off of sensory input, functional rather than structural, must characterize natural states of sleep. Other supporting observations for the stimulus-deficiency theory of sleep included presleep rituals, such as turning out the lights, regulating stimulus input, and the facilitation of sleep induction by muscular relaxation and fatigue. With the discovery of the ascending reticular activating system (ARAS, a network of nerves in the brainstem), it was found that it is not the sensory nerves themselves that maintain cortical arousal but rather the ARAS, which projects impulses diffusely to the cortex from the brainstem. Presumably sleep would result from interference with the active functioning of the ARAS. Injuries to the ARAS were, in fact, found to produce sleep. Sleep thus seemed passive, in the sense that it was the absence of something (ARAS support of sensory impulses) characteristic of wakefulness.

Theory has tended to depart from this belief and to move toward conceiving of sleep as an actively produced state. Two kinds of observation primarily have been responsible for the shift. First, earlier studies showing that sleep can be induced directly by electrical stimulation of certain areas in the hypothalamus have been confirmed and extended to other areas in the brain. Second, the discovery of REM sleep has been even more significant in leading theorists to consider the possibility of actively produced sleep. REM sleep, by its very active nature, defies description as a passive state. As is noted below, REM sleep can be eliminated in experimental animals by the surgical destruction of a group of nerve cells in the pons, the active function of which appears to be necessary for REM sleep. It thus is difficult to imagine that the various manifestations of REM sleep reflect merely the deactivation of wakefulness mechanisms.

The REM–NREM-sleep dichotomy poses a third issue for the theories of sleep mechanisms, or at least for those that accept the idea of sleep as an active phenomenon. Does one hypnogenic (sleep-causing) system serve both kinds of sleep, or are there two antagonistic sleep systems, one for REM sleep and one for NREM sleep? Opinion is sharply divided. One group of theorists states that there must be two sleep systems. It is noted that NREM sleep is not affected by injuries to the pontine tegmentum (the posterior part of the pons) but that REM sleep is abolished and that NREM sleep is suppressed in animals whose brainstem has been severed at the midpoint of the pons, suggesting that an NREM-sleep centre behind this section no longer is capable of suppressing the effect of the ARAS. It is further observed that the neurohumor serotonin is localized in the brainstem regions presumed to be responsible for NREM sleep; that destruction of serotonin-containing nerve cells in the brainstem may produce insomnia; that, in some species, reductions of serotonin by chemical interference with its production produces an amount of sleep loss correlated with the reduction of serotonin; that administration of a serotonin precursor (a substance from which serotonin is formed) after interference with production of serotonin produces a sleeplike state and that artificially induced increases in brain serotonin increase NREM sleep; that the neurohumor norepinephrine is localized in the brainstem regions presumed to be responsible for REM sleep; and that substances interfering with the synthesis of norepinephrine suppress REM sleep. Other theorists have proposed that REM and NREM sleep are served by a common hypnogenic system. Chemical stimulation of certain brain structures, assumed to constitute a hypnogenic system, has been found capable of inducing both stages of sleep. It also is argued that different varieties of sleep should require different mechanisms no more than do different varieties of wakefulness (*e.g.*, alertness, relaxation).

Functional theories. Functional theories stress the recuperative and adaptive value of sleep. Sleep arises most unequivocally in animals (birds and mammals) that maintain a constant body temperature and that can be active at a wide range of environmental temperatures. In such forms, increased metabolic requirements may find partial compensation in periodic decreases in body temperature and metabolic rate (*i.e.*, during NREM sleep). Thus, the parallel evolution of temperature regulation and NREM sleep has suggested to some authorities that NREM sleep may best be viewed as a regulatory mechanism conserving energy expenditure in species whose metabolic requirements are otherwise high. As a solution to the problem of susceptibility to predation that comes with the torpor of sleep, it has been suggested that the periodic reactivation of the organism during sleep better prepares it for fight or flight, and that the possibility of enhanced processing of significant environmental stimuli during REM sleep may even reduce the need for sudden confrontation with danger. Other functional theorists agree that NREM sleep may be a state of "bodily repair," while suggesting that REM sleep is one of "brain repair" or restitution, a period, for example, of increased cerebral protein synthesis or of "reprogramming" the brain so that information achieved in wakeful functioning is most efficiently assimilated. In their specification of functions and provision of evidence for such functions, such theories are necessarily vague and incomplete. The function of stage 2 NREM sleep is still quite unclear, for example. Such sleep is present in only rudimentary form in subprimate species, yet consumes approximately half of human sleep time. Comparative, physiological, and experimental evidence is yet unavailable to suggest why so much human sleep is spent in this stage.

BIBLIOGRAPHY. The standard reference on the physiology of sleep is N. KLEITMAN, *Sleep and Wakefulness*, rev. ed. (1963). The more recent physiological literature is summarized in A. KALES (ed.), *Sleep: Physiology and Pathology: A Symposium* (1969). The behavioral approach to sleep is exemplified by E.J. MURRAY, *Sleep, Dreams, and Arousal* (1965). Sound, well-written popularizations are G.G. LUCE and J. SEGAL, *Sleep* (1966), and *Insomnia: The Guide for Troubled Sleepers* (1969).

(D.F.)

Slime Mold

Science fiction did not invent the slime molds, but it has borrowed from them in using the idea of sheets of liquid,

Varieties of Myxomycete fruiting bodies.
(Top left) *Arcyria incarnata,* after active life in dead wood, emerges to form fruits. (Top right) *Tubifera ferruginosa,* with individual sporangia crowded together, illustrates transition from solitary fruits to aethalium. (Bottom left) *Badhamia macrocarpa* fruiting on living plant. (Bottom right) Emerging red plasmodium of *Tubifera ferruginosa.*
Arthur L. Cohen

flowing cytoplasm engulfing and dissolving every living thing they touch. What fiction can only imagine, nature has produced, and only their small size and dependence on coolness, moisture, and darkness has kept the slime molds from ordinary observation, for they are common enough.

Coolness, moisture, and darkness are found in the soil and in logs, twigs, and leaves decaying on the forest floor; there also are found the slime molds. An old log turned over—preferably a few days after a warm summer rain —may reveal on its underside a white or yellowish fan of almost liquid consistency, a sheet of slowly flowing living substance. The drier upper side of the log may be covered with what look like pinhead-sized toadstools that, when touched, give off clouds of dust-fine spores. The creeping, feeding fan—the plasmodium, or vegetative phase, of a slime mold—has the characteristics of a primitive animal called an amoeba. The reproductive stage—the fruiting body, or sporangium, with its dusty spores—has the characteristics of a lower plant, a mold.

The preceding account is an abbreviated, general description of one group of slime molds, the Myxomycetes, which includes the largest, most abundant, and best known of the slime molds. The Myxomycetes have a plasmodial stage and definite fruiting bodies—they are the true slime molds. Other slime molds, mostly not all closely related to the Myxomycetes, include the Acrasieae, the Plasmodiophoreae, the Labyrinthulales, and the Protosteliales. The Acrasiales are forms in which individual amoebas aggregate without fusing to form a multicellular fruiting structure—they are the simple slime molds, or cellular slime molds. The Plasmodiophorales, also called the endoparasitic slime molds, are root parasites of higher plants; they have a plasmodial stage but lack definite fruiting bodies. The Labyrinthulales—the

net slime molds—are largely marine organisms consisting of spindle-shaped cells that glide within a network of slime tubes (the net plasmodium). The Protosteliales are near-microscopic organisms that show some affinities with the Myxomycetes.

The economic importance of the Myxomycetes is negligible. The ashy-gray sporangia of *Physarum cinereum* sometimes develop overnight in large patches on well-watered lawns. These grayish crusts with their sooty spores, which appear so dramatically, do no harm, however, and soon disappear.

The vast majority of Plasmodiophorales are rather benign parasites of plants of no economic importance, but *Plasmodiophora brassicae,* clubroot of cabbage, is the single most serious disease of cabbages and other members of the mustard family. *Spongospora subterranea,* a parasite of potatoes, while usually unimportant, may at times have disastrous effects on the crops.

The Acrasiales and Protosteliales have no known economic importance and, unlike true fungi and bacteria, are apparently only minor participants in the great material cycles of nature, such as the decomposition of organic matter into its basic chemicals, carbon dioxide and water.

Economic importance

THE MYXOMYCETES (TRUE SLIME MOLDS)

The Myxomycetes include approximately 60 genera containing about 500 species. They are divided into two subclasses, the Exosporeae and the Endosporeae. In the Exosporeae the spores are apparently borne externally instead of within a sporangium, but studies have indicated that each "spore" is itself a much reduced sporangium, containing the genuine spore within. The Exosporeae contains only one genus, *Ceratiomyxa,* with about three species.

The Endosporeae have the spores obviously borne within a sporangium. The majority of slime molds with surface-crawling plasmodia belong to the Endosporeae in the order Physarales, a group distinguished by dark spores and the presence of calcium carbonate (lime) at least in the sporangium wall (peridium). The most thoroughly studied slime mold genera—*Physarum*, *Didymium*, and *Fuligo*—are all members of the Physarales, which is sometimes also known as the Calcareae.

The sporangium. Although some Myxomycetes (*e.g.*, *Didymium*) form fruiting structures (sporangia) from plasmodia that creep over the surface of wood and leaves, others, such as the common and beautiful *Stemonitis*, form the fruits from plasmodia buried within the decaying wood. There is no indication that a log or tree stump is inhabited until drops of creamy liquid appear on the surface—as if the dead wood were perspiring living protoplasm. This is the first sign that the plasmodium, whose strands are spread throughout the porous wood, is finishing its days as an active, growing, feeding network. These droplets coalesce and grow, expanding to a thick cushion that eventually becomes a column, perhaps half an inch wide and an inch high. A purplish tinge, gradually darkening to black, spreads over the column as it begins to take shape as a bundle of cylinders, each supported by the stalk it has formed. The bundle, now almost black, dries out, and each sporangium, densely filled with dark spores, separates from its neighbours. The tenuous wall enclosing the sporangium, the peridium, disintegrates on drying. A touch of the hand or a puff of wind is all that is required to disperse the spores. Finally, only the delicate skeletons of the sporangia are left; each consists of a stalk with an intricate network of branches, the capillitium, which held the spores. This whole feathery tuft of sporangia, resting on a silvery sheet of dried slime, the hypothallus, forms and fulfills its mission of reproduction within a day.

The startling transformation of a shapeless, ever-changing plasmodium into an intricately organized fruiting structure is the very remarkable feature of the Myxomycetes.

The capillitium

The capillitium of different species is formed variously, but a composite picture of its formation is as follows. Within the mass of cytoplasm enclosed by the peridium, lines appear that later become chains of clear droplets, or vacuoles. The vacuoles coalesce to form hollow tubes whose walls become coated with dense material. Some capillitia are what the name implies, fine hairlike processes. Some have the walls beautifully sculptured with spirals and cogs, as in the genera *Trichia*, *Hemitrichia*, and *Arcyria*, in which, on drying, the capillitium expands into a fluffy mass, scattering the spores as it does so. In others, the capillitium is permeated with lime.

Not all sporangia are stalked. Some plasmodia break up into sessile droplets that invest themselves with a sporangial wall and complete their development without ever rising on a stalk. In those with fruiting structures known as plasmodiocarps, the plasmodium hardly breaks up at all, but the profound interior change of liquid cytoplasm to dusty spores still occurs. The largest sporangia are aethalia, compound sporangia composed of individual sporangia incompletely separated from each other. In the genera *Fuligo* and *Brefeldia*, they form great cushiony masses, those of *B. maxima* sometimes reaching a foot in length. The massed compound sporangia (aethalia) may range from the easily delineated individual

Arthur L. Cohen

Lamproderma fruiting stages.
(Left) Fruiting bodies forming. (Right) Dark mature sporangia.

sporangia of *Tubifera* through the tortuous interwoven structures of *Fuligo* (plasmodiocarps) to the spherical fruit of *Lycogala*, in which individual sporangia are so reduced and mutually joined that the sphere is practically a single entity.

The remarkable genus *Ceratiomyxa* represents another extreme, for each sporangium contains only one spore. Thus the crowded fruiting structures of this genus, which cover well-decayed logs like miniature coral reefs, are not sporangia but the tremendously developed hypothallus. The sporangia are the powdery microscopic structures on the surface, each containing one spore.

Arthur L. Cohen

Ceratiomyxa fruiting structures.
(Top) Two forms of *Ceratiomyxa* growing together: spongelike *C. porioides* and branched *C. fruticulosa*. It has been argued these may be different environmental forms of same species. This photograph does not indicate this since there is no intergrade. (Bottom) Young colonies of *fruticulosa* with young brown fruiting bodies of another Myxomycete among them. The yellow form is uncommon; it turns white upon complete maturity.

Spores and swarm cells. The spores are formed in the sporangium by successive furrowing, or cleavage, of the cytoplasm; the furrows redivide the mass until each unit contains one nucleus. Each block rounds up, becomes surrounded by a dense spore wall, and shrinks away from its fellows as it dries. The spores of Myxomycetes may vary slightly in shape from oval to round and in size from four to 15 microns (0.004 to 0.015 millimetre, or about 0.0002 to 0.0006 inch) in diameter. The colour may be black, gray, brown, brilliant red, yellow, or—rarely—white (except in *Ceratiomyxa*, which usually has white spores). The spore surface is often covered with ridges or spines.

If the spores are placed in water, they swell, and, in a half hour to a week, depending on species and on such factors as the age of the specimen, the spore wall either splits open or a pore forms, from which a minute, naked mass of cytoplasm emerges. This globule, the swarm cell, shoots out a whiplike process, a flagellum, becomes pearshaped and, with the flagellum lashing in front of it, swims away. Two flagella are usually present, but the second flagellum is short, inactive, and rarely seen. The swarm cell may suddenly come to rest on any surface, put forth pseudopods—lobes of living substance—and creep along. In this stage, called a myxamoeba, it can feed as any amoeba does, by engulfing bacteria. If the flagella are entirely retracted, the myxamoeba is practically indistinguishable from any of the many species of small amoebas in the soil. It may put forth its flagella and suddenly take off; the myxamoeba transforms again into a swarmer.

The myx-amoeba

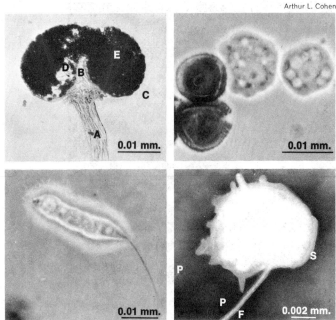

Arthur L. Cohen

Structural details of Didymium iridis.
(Top left) Section of mature sporangium showing (A) stalk, (B) columella (projection of stalk into spore head), (C) peridium, (D) few strands of capillitium in mass of spores, (E) spores. (Top right) Phase photomicrograph of living amoebas and spores showing germination split in empty spore case. (Bottom left) Phase photomicrograph of live swimming swarm cell showing flagellum. (Bottom right) Electron micrograph of swarm cell in transition between amoeboid and flagellate phases showing (F) flagellum, (S) second flagellum, (P) pseudopodia.

The myxamoeba or its transform, the flagellated swarm cell, is a gamete (sex cell). The fusion of two such cells and the fusion of their nuclei is the fundamental sexual act in reproduction of Myxomycetes, as it is in other organisms.

The plasmodium. *Growth and appearance.* The fusion of the two gametes, whether flagellate or amoeboid, and the subsequent fusion of their nuclei, initiates the plasmodial phase. The flagella are permanently retracted and the amoeboid zygote (fertilized cell) begins to grow. Instead of following the pattern found in most other organisms, in which the cell divides after the nucleus has duplicated itself, in the slime molds only the nuclei divide repeatedly, first in complete synchrony and then in synchronous waves, as the ever-growing plasmodium becomes larger. As the plasmodium flows over the damp undersurface of logs or through the rotting wood itself, over leaves, or through the soil, it feeds on bacteria, molds, and sometimes large fungi, leaving the undigested remains behind as dark imprints of its own shape.

On a smooth surface a vigorous plasmodium generally takes the form of a fan with trailing veins, creeping in the direction of the broadly curved front edge. Microscopically, the fan looks like a broad river delta, with a network of channels in which the cytoplasm streams now slowly, now so rapidly that the particles are but blurred streaks. These channels gradually separate into distinct veins from front to rear. The internal streaming is not all in one direction. In any vein or channel, the cytoplasm slows, pauses, and then often reverses direction. Gener-

ally, a little more flows toward the front than flows back, so that the plasmodium moves in a pulsating fashion, advancing steadily like an incoming tide on a beach.

The description above is that of the "classical" or phaneroplasmodium, but other types have been observed. They are the protoplasmodium, a minute, sluggishly amoeboid form, without distinct veins, each plasmodium giving rise to one sporangium (*e.g., Echinostelium minutum*); and the aphanoplasmodium, a colourless mass consisting of fine veins forming a network or sometimes lying parallel to each other, but the whole structure lacking the fan structure described above. Almost invisible, it is, nevertheless, of fairly frequent occurrence (*e.g., Stemonitis, Comatricha, Lamproderma*).

Cytoplasmic movement. If the plasmodium is moved about or cut, flow ceases and the cytoplasm sets, forming a gel. Then hesitantly but with increasing vigour, flow resumes. If a strand of a vigorous plasmodium is cut, a drop of the liquid interior substance oozes out and usually immediately sets to a gel. This droplet, if gently detached and placed on a clean surface, may, in a few hours, become a minute plasmodium.

Although many cells show this streaming of the liquid living substance, only the myxomycete plasmodium shows it on such a grand scale. The theory has long been that the streaming results from contraction of the walls, which squeeze the inner liquid plasm from one part to another. In apparent confirmation of this muscular action of the more solid parts, there has been isolated from the cytoplasm of *Physarum polycephalum* a protein called myxomyosin, which resembles in its properties myosin, the contractile protein of muscle. The myxomycete plasmodium thus resembles in many aspects a primitive muscle but with this difference: the muscle cell has a constant array of longitudinal fibres, but the plasmodium unceasingly dismantles and reconstructs its array of contractile fibres.

Theory of plasmodium movement

Microscopic structure and chemical composition. The cytoplasm of the Myxomycetes resembles that of other cells in having internal structures such as nuclei, mitochondria, and vacuoles (see CELL AND CELL DIVISION), and, in the plasmodium stage, it resembles the cytoplasm of amoebas. The major difference is the giant size—one plasmodial cell membrane encompasses dozens to millions of nuclei and other subcellular structures. Like amoebas, the plasmodium puts forth microscopic extensions, or pseudopods; engulfs food in digestive vacuoles; and discards waste in excretory vacuoles, which burst like blisters at the surface. Also like amoebas, the thin layer of cytoplasm just beneath the cell membrane, particularly at the advancing edge, is colourless and glassy, lacking the innumerable organelles and particles of the interior.

The nuclei are characteristically small and usually have one prominent nucleolus, a small body with the nucleus. Nuclear division in the Myxomycetes is remarkable in being of two types. In the plasmodium and spores, it is of the so-called primitive type, in which the nuclear membrane remains intact during division. In swarm cells and myxamoebas it is of the more common and presumably more advanced type in which the nuclear membrane disintegrates and a new membrane forms around each daughter nucleus.

Characteristic of the plasmodium is an external layer of slime clothing the entire active mass. Being unceasingly secreted, it is unceasingly left behind the creeping plasmodium as a network of collapsed tubules. The slime of several species of *Physarum* is a glycoprotein (a combination of sugars and protein) similar to many other lubricant secretions, such as mucus and saliva. The sugar component in all cases so far investigated is known as galactose.

Plasmodia may be colourless, red, white, buff, maroon; most frequently yellow or orange; and rarely blue, black, or green. Colour may be influenced by age, diet, and growth conditions. The basic colour is often shaded by the colour of the growth medium or particles picked up. The pigment is contained in granules in the colourless ground substance; but on the death of the plasmodium, it

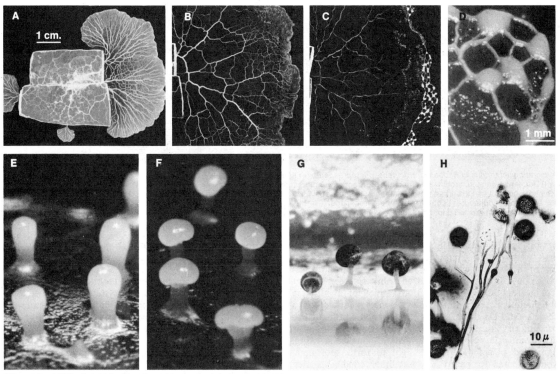

Life cycle of Didymium iridis (duration of approximately twenty hours).
(A) Plasmodial fans creeping off blocks of agar containing yeast food. (B) First visible evidence of fruit forming; protoplasm collecting into broad band along front of fan. (C) Plasmodium separating into droplets. (D) Higher magnification of stage shown in C; droplets still connected by veins. (E) Stalks of young sporangia forming. (F) Sporangia well separated into head and stalk; stalk contracting and protoplasm moving into head. (G) Mature fruit; spore head black. (H) Capillitium, consisting of simple, branched threads among which spores are enmeshed.
Arthur L. Cohen

dissolves in water and stains the surrounding medium—a sure sign in laboratory cultures that at least a portion of the plasmodium has been killed. Numerous studies have not yet determined the chemical nature of the pigments.

Sexual processes.   Over 100 years ago it was thought that plasmodia were formed by several swarm cells or myxamoebas coming together and fusing nonsexually. Fusion between swarmers (flagellated swarm cells or myxamoebas), however, has been shown to be sexual, and the zygote formed initiates the young diploid (having two sets of chromosomes per nucleus) plasmodium. Nevertheless, although nuclear fusion occurs, its location in the life cycle has been placed by various researchers anywhere from the fusion of the swarmers to the transformation of the plasmodium into sporangia. Nuclei in plasmodia of the same species and strain are now known to be haploid (with one chromosome set), diploid, or polyploid (having more than two chromosome sets). All nuclei of one plasmodium have uniform ploidy.

Reduction divisions (gamete formation) occur somewhere in the sporangial phase, either in the formation of the spores or in the spores themselves. There is general agreement, however, that the fully developed spore is a meiospore—its nucleus or nuclei are the immediate products of meiosis, reduction division that produces nuclei with one set of chromosomes each.

Individuality and self-recognition.   The plasmodium is not an individual in the full sense. Although it behaves as a unit, it can be cut into small pieces that may either fuse together again or grow into new plasmodia. The nature of the plasmodium was shown by a classical experiment in the late 19th century. A plasmodium, gorged with debris and food particles, was placed on moist cotton. It strained itself through the fibres, leaving the debris behind, and reconstituted itself, thoroughly scoured, on the other side of the barrier.

The plasmodia of *Fuligo septica*, usually lemon yellow when found in nature, may become white under certain laboratory conditions and remain yellow under others. Yellow and white plasmodia from the same parent no longer fuse when brought into contact, but each can merge with a plasmodium of its own colour. The same interesting phenomenon has been observed in other species. Plasmodia or "incompatible" strains of the same species will not fuse. As in higher forms, fusion or rejection is controlled by "incompatibility genes." Genetic compatibility, however, does not explain the failure of fusion of plasmodia of the same source.

The sclerotium.   If a plasmodium is rapidly dried, it becomes a dull, lifeless, horny mass. But given some time to dry, perhaps 24 hours, it contracts, becomes somewhat waxy, and usually retains its colour, having thereby transformed into a sclerotium. The sclerotium is composed of many cells, each containing a number of nuclei, with each cell separated from its neighbours by very thin walls. If the sclerotium is moistened, the walls dissolve within a few hours, and what earlier resembled a splash of dry, orange paint resumes activity. The sclerotium is a resistant resting stage that ensures survival during times of environmental stress. Plasmodia that form sclerotia, for example, easily may be filed away in envelopes for a year or more and come alive again when dampened.

Habitat and geographical occurrence.   The majority of Myxomycetes are inhabitants of the temperate zones and are typically active—in creeping about as plasmodia or in fruit formation—in warm, moist weather of spring or early summer; nevertheless, active plasmodia of some species may be found any time the temperature has remained above freezing for a few days, and some forms are typically alpine, the new fruits developing on sodden branches and leaves at the snow line.

Surprisingly few forms are exclusively tropical, the best known being *Alwisia bombarda*, although some, such as species of *Didymium*, extend well into the tropics.

Geographically the Myxomycetes recognize no boundaries. Species that are common in one region are generally found in any similar habitat and climate.

Stemonitis, Lycogala, Reticularia, Ceratiomyxa, and a host of other genera are practically always found on wood. Many of the lime-bearing types—such as species of *Physarum, Didymium,* and *Badhamia*—are found on leaves and straw. *Physarum cinereum* typically lives in

Plasmodium fusion

Germinating sclerotium of Badhamia utricularis, photographed over nine-hour period.
(Left) Dormant orange sclerotium on piece of absorbent paper placed in moist petri dish;
within four hours it has absorbed water and begun to show activity. (Centre) One hour later
fully active plasmodium has begun to spread out from paper. (Right) After four more hours
bulk of plasmodium has left paper and formed typical veined plasmodial fan.
Arthur L. Cohen

the soil, and sometimes its gray fruits cover lawns overnight. Only *Fuligo septica* can throw up its formless yellow or brown or white aethalia (massed structureless sporangia) anywhere—on a tree trunk six feet (about two metres) above ground, in the crack of a concrete pavement, on desert sand, and, as once recorded, on a whale's skull set to bleach on the grounds of the British Museum of Natural History.

Environmental responses. In general, surface-growing, pigmented plasmodia require light to form sporangia. Nonpigmented forms do not, but other conditions may be necessary; for example, at least some strains of *Didymium iridis* invariably fruit in the laboratory when they exhaust their food supply. In all forms studied there seems to be a point beyond which the plasmodium is committed to form sporangia, and, although no sign may be visible, the plasmodium—or even a minute fragment too small to form a good sporangium—will attempt to fruit, even if the fragment literally dies in the attempt. Profound and complex changes, particularly in the quantity of enzymes (biological catalysts) concerned with respiration, occur naturally during the fruiting process.

Spore germination

Some myxomycete spores, such as those of *Reticularia lycoperdon*, germinate very readily; any suspension of spores will show swarm cells, sometimes within 30 minutes, and will achieve nearly 100 percent germination in about four hours. Many others take several days, and some, such as those of *Tubifera ferruginosa*, very rarely germinate in the laboratory. An aging phenomenon seems to be effective for some species, since spores that germinate hardly at all when freshly collected produce swarmers or myxamoebas in high percentage after several months of rest or following alternate wetting and drying.

Swarm cells and myxamoebas respond to nonlethal unfavourable conditions, such as drying or a stale growth medium, by forming thin-walled microcysts (sporelike resting bodies) that may germinate again with the return of an appropriate environment.

Plasmodia have approximately the same environmental preferences as do spores during germination—a slightly acid growth medium (pH6) and an optimum temperature of about 27° C (81° F). In general, however, they prefer a film of moisture rather than total immersion in water. Neither plasmodia nor swarm cells can withstand high concentration of decay products or other metabolic substances. Although plasmodia feed on yeasts, molds, and bacteria, they are easily stifled if conditions are such that the food supply outgrows the plasmodium.

Oriented responses are well known in plasmodia. They will, for example, usually creep off a stale growth medium to a fresh one. They will move away from light except when preparing to fruit, in which case they seek the nearest exposed region by moving toward lighted areas. A plasmodium will also creep upstream against gently flowing water.

Nutrition. A number of slime molds can thrive on laboratory media that contain either killed bacteria or yeasts or extracts prepared from them. Such a medium is not completely known chemically. The continuous growth of one strain of *Physarum polycephalum* plasmodia on a completely known growth medium has, however, been accomplished. The medium contained nearly 40

Arthur L. Cohen

Fuligo septica fruiting and plasmodial stages.
(Left) Compound fruiting body (aethalium) on log. (Right) Plasmodium that has crept off rotten
wood chip in a culture dish.

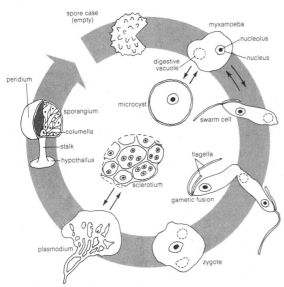

spore case (empty)

myxamoeba

nucleolus

nucleus

digestive vacuole

peridium

microcyst

swarm cell

sporangium

columella

stalk

hypothallus

flagella

sclerotium

gametic fusion

plasmodium

zygote

Life cycle of a true Myxomycete.

constituents including minerals, amino acids, and vitamins. The majority of Myxomycetes, however, have not been successfully cultivated in the laboratory. The cultivation of a few forms is extremely simple, and these have become favourite study and research organisms. *Physarum polycephalum*, the most rapidly growing form known, can be purchased from biological supply houses. It forms gigantic plasmodia in a few days and may be kept on a moist paper towel sprinkled with oatmeal. This species has probably been used more than all other forms for studies involving cytoplasmic streaming, nutrition, and biochemistry. *Didymium iridis* forms smaller plasmodia, but, since it can be reliably carried through its cycle from spore to spore, it is much used for genetic studies and for detailed cytological investigations.

THE PLASMODIOPHORALES (ENDOPARASITIC SLIME MOLDS)

As the only known parasitic group of slime molds, the Plasmodiophorales are also the only economically important ones. The frequently devastating disease, club root of cabbage, caused by *Plasmodiophora brassicae*, has been known since classical times. *Plasmodiophora* causes monstrous deformities of the roots of cabbage and other members of the mustard family. By interference with the functions of the roots, the plants are stunted and frequently die. Because the mustard family includes, besides cabbage, such important vegetables as cauliflower, brussels sprouts, turnips, radishes, and kale, the disease and its causative organism have been extensively studied.

No member of the Plasmodiophoreae has been carried indisputably through its life cycle in the laboratory, and its subterranean habitat makes observation difficult. A generalized life cycle can be constructed by putting together the pieces that have been observed. Upon decay of the parasitized tissue, spores are released into the soil and produce swarm cells with two anterior flagella. Swarm cells may transform into myxamoebas, which penetrate root hairs and there grow into primary plasmodia. The primary plasmodia produce a second crop of swarm cells that now serve as gametes. These fuse and infect the body of the root by growing into a massive plasmodium and stimulating the characteristic tumourlike growth of the parasitized cells. The plasmodia divide into spores, which are released on the death of the host tissues. The spores can survive in fields for many years, so that after an infestation has occurred, it is very difficult to eradicate.

PROTOSTELIALES

If the dead leaves and stems of grasses and weeds are kept damp in a rather cool room for a week or so, their surfaces bear microscopic transparent stalks, each topped by a glassy spore. These minute organisms, barely discernible at about 0.01 inch in height, can be mistaken for any of the innumerable small molds that grow on dead plant tissues. They are, however, members of the order Protosteliales that are like the other slime molds in masquerading as genuine fungi.

In general, a myxamoeba of the genus *Protostelium* transforms into a spore by secreting a stalk on which it is elevated. The spore (or cyst) rapidly reverts to an amoeba again when wetted under favourable conditions. But in *Schizoplasmodium*, another genus in the Protosteliales, a very small plasmodium transforms into a multinucleate spore that germinates to form another plasmodium. In *Cavostelium*, flagellate swarmers are formed bearing one or more anterior flagella. In none of the Protosteliales has true sexual fusion ever been observed. Since no more cells come out of the germinating spore or cyst than went into them, the stalked spore is a resting stage rather than a reproductive one. True reproduction occurs by division of amoebas or plasmodia.

Schizoplasmodium cavostelioides has ballistospores—spores that are shot off by formation and explosion of a gas bubble formed within the outer membrane of the spore. Although several true fungi have ballistospores, such jet propulsion is otherwise unknown among slime molds.

The Protosteliales are literally everywhere, provided there is vegetation and a reasonable amount of moisture. Although a few have been recovered from rotten wood and manure, the favourite location seems to be on the dead stalks, shrivelled flowers, and withered leaves of standing plants. In the laboratory they are rather easily grown on yeasts and bacteria when these in turn are growing on an impoverished medium to prevent excessive growth. Undoubtedly future search will discover more than the present approximately six genera and one dozen species.

Protostelid habitats

THE ACRASIALES (CELLULAR SLIME MOLDS)

The cellular slime molds are remarkable organisms. *Dictyostelium mucoroides*, for example, looks very much like a common mold, a mass of spores set on a slender stalk, but its basic structure and mode of formation are completely different from that of any mold, in fact, different from that of any other group of organisms known.

In a suitable habitat the spore germinates, and from the split spore case emerges a small amoeba. Each amoeba feeds by engulfing bacteria before it divides. The amoebas greatly increase in numbers under proper conditions and then begin to converge. Until this time of aggregation, they are virtually indistinguishable from the many other amoebas that swarm in the soil.

If a plate of growth medium (agar), very dilute in nutrients, is streaked with suitable bacteria, such as the ordinary *Escherichia coli* and a few of the spores of *D. mucoroides* are placed on the plate, the spores germinate, each yielding a very small amoeba. These amoebas feed on the bacteria and divide again until the plate is practically devoid of bacteria, the amoebas forming almost a complete covering. The amoebas then begin to congregate, climbing up on each other as they form a little mound. The centre pile becomes a hemisphere with a nipple, similar in appearance to half a lemon set on end, and, in its interior, a sheath forms around a core of amoebas each of which fills with a fluid, swells, secretes stiff cell walls, and dies, becoming in structure and function a central stalk. This cylinder of sacrificed amoebas forms the stalk on which the remaining amoebas climb. The stalk becomes narrower until finally it is a chain of single cells; the survivors of the ascension transform into oval spores, held in a drop of mucus.

Dictyostelium discoideum has one further stage in the welding of separate living entities into one composite organism. When the myxamoebas have aggregated to the conical stage with the little nipple at the top, the whole pyramid falls over on its side, and, with the nipple raised and leading the way, the "slug" moves over the surface toward the light before continuing further development.

Other cellular slime molds also have a migration stage. After aggregation some species of *Dictyostelium* and *Polysphondylium* form slugs that crawl along the surface, more or less intermittently, forming a horizontal stalk.

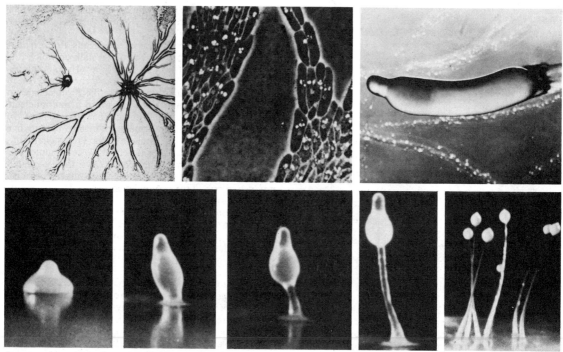

Sequence from aggregation state to fruiting stage in Dictyostelium discoideum.
(Top left) Entire aggregate. (Top centre) Highly magnified section of stream. (Top right) View
from above of slug-shaped, migrating pseudoplasmodium. (Bottom) Culmination stages over
approximately nine hours.
(Top left, centre, right) D.R. Francis, (bottom) J.T. Bonner

Later they culminate by building a vertical single or
branched stalk on which the spore balls form. But in
these forms, stalk formation and migration loosely overlap; only in *Dictyostelium mucoroides* are they sharply
distinct.

Effects of mixing pseudo-plasmodia   There are several different genera and species of Acrasiales, which differ strikingly in colour and shape. If the
amoebas of the different forms are mixed, each sort separates itself and forms its own fruiting structures. If aggregation has started, and the early aggregations, say, of the
purple, branched *Polysphondylium violaceum* and of the
white, single-stalked *Dictyostelium discoideum* are
mixed, the amoebas again sort themselves out and build
their own pure sporangia. But if the aggregations have
continued almost to the point of differentiation, sorting
out no longer occurs; instead, hybrid fruiting structures
are produced. But when the spores from these germinate,
each produces amoebas after its own kind; the "mixed
decks" thus unshuffle themselves.

There has been debate on sexual reproduction in the
Acrasiales. What some biologists called sexual fusion of
amoebas, others called cannibalism. The preponderant
evidence now favours a completely asexual mode of life.

The Acrasiales resemble the Myxomycetes and Protostelida in being phagotrophic; *i.e.*, they feed on small particles by engulfing them. The diet is bacterial, and they
are very easily grown in culture on bacteria washed to
remove injurious metabolic products or on bacteria
growing on a medium so weak that toxic metabolites do
not accumulate significantly.

The Acrasiales, first thought to be inhabitants of dung,
are now known, with a few possible exceptions, to be
inhabitants of the soil. Collection methods indicate that
they are common, being numerous in species and numbers in forest soil, but they also occur in garden, lawn,
and field soils.

Unlike the Myxomycetes, the Acrasiales consist of relatively few forms. The vast majority isolated from soil are
species of either the genus *Dictyostelium* or the closely
related *Polysphondylium*.

There are a few genera, such as *Guttulina* and *Guttulinopsis*, that fruit on the dung of various animals. In these,
separation into stalk and spore head is highly imperfect,
the spore cells and stalk cells shading into each other.

By excluding some doubtful and imperfectly known

forms, the Acrasiales may be divided into two groups or
families containing six genera and about a dozen species
(see below *Annotated classification*).

ORGANISMS RESEMBLING SLIME MOLDS

Since the late 19th century a number of organisms have
been assigned to the slime molds largely on the basis of a
plasmodial or apparently plasmodial stage. Many have
not been seen since the original descriptions. A notable
exception is the genus *Labyrinthula*. Formerly considered
very rare, it is now recognized to be the cause of an
extremely destructive disease of eel grass. *Labyrinthula*
forms a net plasmodium, an open network that can creep
about as a unit. Close examination has shown that this is
not a plasmodium, but a colony consisting of often
closely packed, spindle-shaped individual cells that glide
within tubes of secreted slime. The net plasmodium is
thus more like an elastic subway system than a true plasmodium. While flagellate swarm cells have been reported
for several species and heaps of cysts or spores for another, too little is known of the life cycle to place these
organisms with any certainty. Modern authorities tend
to exclude them from the slime molds.

A unique group of organisms, the Myxobacteria, form   **The Myxo-bacteria**
thin, spreading amoeboid colonies consisting of bacteria-
like cells embedded in a slimy sheet. The whole colony
can act as a unit, very much as does the acrasian aggregation stage in building a fruiting structure, in some
cases forming simple spheres, in other cases complicated
treelike forms. All evidence, however, points to the Myxobacteria being either true bacteria or closely related to
them and, hence, distinct from any slime mold.

CLASSIFICATION

Distinguishing taxonomic features.   The various orders,
families, genera, and species of the Myxomycetes are
distinguished from each other by the characteristics
of the fruiting structures. In rough order of importance
these are spore colour; presence and type of a capillitium
(fibres or tubes, usually hairlike, within the sporangium); presence and location of lime in the sporangium;
and the dimensions and surface structures of the fruits,
capillitium, and spores. Identification to family and sometimes to genus can usually be made by the naked eye,
although separation of many genera requires at least

a hand lens. Specific identification usually requires a high-powered microscope, careful observation, and shrewd guessing.

The other slime-mold groups are not necessarily closely related to the Myxomycetes, but they do resemble them in being primitive amoeba-like colonial organisms at some stage in their life cycle. They also produce fungus-like fruiting structures (except for the Plasmodiophorales), as do the Myxomycetes.

Annotated classification. The slime molds are not presented in the following classification to show relationships, but to emphasize differences between the classes. Botanical nomenclature is used, although zoological nomenclature could be used with equal justification. In the following classification, the portion on the Myxomycetes is based largely on that of Martin and Alexopoulos (1969).

DIVISION MYXOMYCOPHYTA (MYCETOZOA)

Primitive eucaryotic (having true nuclei) organisms resembling both protozoa (one-celled animals) and fungi, having a vegetative (active, growing, feeding) phase consisting of individual amoeboid cells (myxamoebas) or of a multinucleate amoeboid mass or sheet (plasmodium); at length, by transformation of the plasmodium or by congregation and transformation of the myxamoebas, forming usually fungus-like fruiting structures bearing one to many spores. Some have flagellated cells (swarm cells) at one stage of the life cycle. Sexual fusion of myxamoebas or swarm cells known in some.

Class Myxomycetes (True Slime Molds)

Vegetative phase a plasmodium; fruiting structure a sporangium containing 1 to many spores. Each spore on germination producing 1 or more myxamoebas that may transform into flagellated swarm cells, which in turn often revert back to the amoeboid stage. Swarm cells usually with 2 flagella, one longer and projecting anteriorly for swimming, the other usually short, inactive, and folded closely back against the cell surface; hence infrequently observed. Cosmopolitan terrestrial forms, usually found in decaying plant material.

Subclass Ceratiomyxomycetidae (Exosporeae)

Spores borne singly and externally on sporophores (fingers, ridges, or flat sheets of jelly-like material which dries down at maturity). On germination spores produce a 4-nucleate amoeboid body with the nuclei soon dividing, and the mass splitting into 8 swarm cells. Possibly each so-called spore actually a reduced sporangium, the sporangial wall closely adherent to the contained single spore.

Order Ceratiomyxales. The only order, it has the characteristics of the subclass.

Family Ceratiomyxaceae. The only family. One genus (*Ceratiomyxa*) with 3 species.

Subclass Myxogastromycetidae (Endosporae, Myxogastres)

Spores few to many, borne within a definite fruiting structure (sporangium) with a more or less persistent sporangial wall (peridium). A capillitium (system of simple or branching fibres or tubes) may permeate the spore mass. The sporangium may contain a columella (an axis), which, according to species, may range from a spherical mass to a tapering rod, attached to the base of the sporangium; in stalked forms it is an actual or apparent continuation of the stalk. Sporangia may be distinct and sessile (sitting on the substrate) or stalked; or more or less imperfectly distinct from each other in the form of plasmodiocarps (strands of the plasmodia that secrete a peridium, and form spores internally without breaking up into individual sporangia), or aethalia (compound fruiting bodies consisting either of tightly interwoven plasmodiocarps or of closely compacted and more or less fused sporangia with reduced or lost individuality at maturity). Aethalia may have a pseudocapillitium (individual sporangial walls reduced to fibres, shreds, or perforated ragged plates) along with or replacing the true capillitium. Fruiting structures at maturity may rest on a hypothallus (a thin sheet of dried gelatinous material derived from the mucoid covering of the plasmodium). Spores germinate to produce 1 or more myxamoebas, which in some cases immediately divide, and become transitorily to persistently flagellate. Approximately 60 genera and 500 species.

Order Liceales. Spore mass brownish yellow to dark brown or black, or gray to pinkish gray, occasionally (in *Cribraria* and *Dictydium*) dark purple. Capillitium absent, but aethalia may have pseudocapillitium formed from reduced sporangial walls.

Family Liceaceae. Spore mass varying from yellowish brown to black. Fructifications sessile, stalked, or of small plasmodiocarps. One genus (*Licea*) with 19 species.

Family Reticulariaceae. Spore mass light brown (rarely yellow), rust-coloured, olive brown, or dark brown. Individual sporangia closely compacted together or more commonly partly or completely fused into an aethalium. Pseudocapillitium frequently present. Four genera (*Tubifera, Dictydiaethalium, Lycogala,* and *Reticularia*) with about 20 species.

Family Cribrariaceae. Spores tawny to dark brown, in some species of *Cribraria* and *Dictydium* dark purple or brownish-purple. Sporangia usually stalked. Dictydine granules (dense, usually dark microscopic granules) characteristic of the family found in peridium, stalk, and sometimes on the spores. Three genera (*Lindbladia, Cribraria,* and *Dictydium*) with about 30 species.

Order Echinosteliales. Spore mass white, gray-yellow, pink, or brown; spores nearly smooth but with characteristic circular plates on the surface. Sporangia separate, minute, stalked; usually less than 0.5 millimetre in height, light coloured. Capillitium, if present, ranging from few threads to well-developed net, columella present or absent. Sporangia develop from minute protoplasmodia, each giving rise to a single sporangium.

Family Echinosteliaceae. One family with the characteristics of the order. One genus (*Echinostelium*) with 5 species, including the smallest known myxomycete, *E. roseum*.

Order Trichiales. Spore mass usually bright coloured: yellow, orange, various shades of red, maroon, sometimes gray. Sporangia stalked, sessile, plasmodiocarpous or united into aethalia. Capillitium always present, often ornamented with spirals, bands, or spines. Columella never present.

Family Dianemaceae. Capillitium of solid threads, surface smooth or with reduced ornamentation; capillitium never forming a net. Sporangia usually minute, usually sessile or plasmodiocarpous. Four genera (*Listerella, Dianema, Calomyxa,* and *Minakatella*) with 9 species.

Family Trichiaceae. Capillitium obviously tubular (except solid or nearly solid in *Prototrichia*), with often prominent sculpturing or ornamentation in the form of rings, spines, or spirals. Capillitium frequently netlike or consisting of a tangled mass of short threads. Sporangia stalked, sessile, plasmodiocarpous, or occasionally united into aethalia. In the major genera sporangia and spore mass often bright coloured: yellow, orange, red, maroon. Ten genera (the most important and largest are *Arcyria, Trichia, Hemitrichia,* and *Perichaena*) with about 60 species.

Order Stemonitales. Spore mass dark, ranging from dark rust to deep brown, black, and purplish black. Lime absent from peridium and capillitium in all species, but present in hypothallus, and stalk (when present) of *Diachea* and *Leptoderma,* and in columella of *Diachea.* Capillitium often much branched, of dark threads. Peridium usually thin, frequently vanishing at maturity. Sporangia distinct or united into an aethalium. The genus *Stemonitis* includes some of the largest and most beautiful of myxomycete sporangia.

Family Stemonitaceae. With the characteristics of the order. Fifteen genera (the most important are *Stemonitis, Comatricha, Lamproderma,* and *Diachea*) and about 90 species.

Order Physarales. Spore mass dark brown to black or purplish black. Lime always present in peridium, sometimes in capillitium, and usually in stalk if present. Sporangia of all forms; stalked, sessile, plasmodiocarpous, or united into aethalia. These are the most widely distributed of Myxomycetes and occupy the most diverse habitats.

Family Physaraceae. Capillitium in the form of lime-impregnated tubes or collapsed tubes with limy nodes. Lime granules always amorphous. Eight genera (the largest and most common being *Physarum, Badhamia,* and *Fuligo*) with about 140 species. The genus *Physarum,* with over 100 species, accounts for about 20 percent of all known Myxomycetes.

Family Didymiaceae. Capillitium nonlimy, usually of slender threads. Peridium with lime forming an eggshell-like crust, or in distinct pegs, or in needle-like crystals. Six genera (the largest are *Didymium* and *Diderma*) with about 70 species.

Class Plasmodiophoromycetes (Plasmodiophorida) (Endoparasitic Slime Molds)

Vegetative stage a plasmodium living parasitically within the cells and tissues of higher and lower plants; at length forming spores in clusters of defined shape or in amorphous masses, but not within sporangia. Spores liberated on disintegration of host cells. Myxamoebas and anteriorly biflagellate swarm cells formed; thus resembling Myxomycetes, though possibly not related. Sexual cycle not confirmed.

Order Plasmodiophorales. The only order, it has the characteristics of the class.

Family Plasmodiophoraceae. The only family. Nine genera and about 35 species. *Plasmodiophora* and *Spongospora* are the most important genera.

Class Protosteliidae (Protostelia)

Minute stalked forms, each stalk bearing one to few spores,

but apparently without sporangial walls. Myxamoebas known in all, anteriorly biflagellated or monoflagellated swarm cells in some. Vegetative stage a uninucleate amoeba or plurinucleate minute plasmodium. The Protostelia have been recognized as a group only since 1966, and as methods for their isolation, recognition, and study are developed, it may be expected that more genera and species will be added.

Order Protosteliales. The only order, it has the characteristics of the class.

Family Cavosteliaceae. Flagellated cells present. One genus (*Cavostelium*) with 2 species.

Family Protosteliaceae. Flagellated cells absent. Five genera (the best known are *Protostelium* and *Schizoplasmodium*) with about a dozen species.

Class Acrasieae (Cellular Slime Molds)

Vegetative phase consists of individual myxamoebas, which later aggregate into a pseudoplasmodium (plasmodium-like mass but with individual cells retaining their identity), which then forms a fruiting structure, the cells more or less differentiating into stalk and spore cells. Flagellated stage apparently nonexistent; sexual fusion debatable.

Order Acrasiales. The only order, it has the characteristics of the class.

Family Guttulinaceae. Myxamoebas with few, blunt (lobose) pseudopodia. Spore mass on a more or less ill-defined stalk; spores and stalk cells intergrading. Three genera (*Guttulina, Guttulinopsis,* and *Acrasis*) with about 10 species.

Family Dictyosteliaceae. Myxamoebas with numerous fine needle-like (filose) pseudopodia. Stalk sharply distinct from spore mass. Four genera (*Dictyostelium, Polysphondylium, Coenonia,* and *Acytostelium*) with about 10 species.

Groups Resembling Slime Molds

Often included in discussions of slime molds, and at times classified with them, these organisms are now considered unrelated to any of the above groups. They are included here for completeness.

Order Labyrinthulales (Net Slime Molds). Marine, terrestrial, or freshwater parasites or saprobes (organisms obtaining food from dead organic matter) with spindle-shaped cells that congregate in networks of mucous filaments or tubes. Sexual reproduction not confirmed. Fruiting bodies absent. Swarm cells, where known, have 2 flagella inserted at the side, one of which bears fine, lateral, filamentous processes (tinsel flagellum); hence completely unlike swarm cells in the slime molds. The order includes the genus *Labyrinthula,* and 3 other doubtful genera, with about a dozen species.

Order Myxobacteriales (Slime Bacteria). Rod-shaped bacterial cells often held together as a slowly moving pseudoplasmodium in a common mucous sheet. Fruiting structures consist of clumps of aggregated cells forming globular masses, ridges, or branched tree-like structures. Eleven genera with about 60 species. *Myxococcus* and *Chondromyces* are the largest genera.

Critical Appraisal. The slime molds are opsimorphic organisms, which means that they have in common a clear distinction in time between growth in terms of increase in mass or of cell number and development. The active stages are amoeboid, whether as single cells, as in the Acrasiales and some Protosteliales, or as a true plasmodium, as in some Myxomycetes and a few Protosteliales. Otherwise, the active stages are quite different, and the term slime mold is more a convenient, if misleading, designation than a term inferring relationship. In their possession of true plasmodial stages, swarm cells with two flagella at the anterior end, the Myxomycetes and Plasmodiophorales seem to be related. The Plasmodiophorales could be considered Myxomycetes adapted for a parasitic life. The Protosteliales may themselves be a heterogeneous group. Relationships would be easier to define if all of them had plasmodial and flagellate swarm-cell stages. But some form neither, and those that form plasmodia do not have flagellated swarmers.

The Acrasiales were first associated with the Myxomycetes by accident, because it was thought that the aggregation stage was a true plasmodium. But they lack both any flagellated stage and any convincing evidence of sexuality; in addition, the aggregated individuals are distinct. The fruiting structure of the Acrasiales is a cellular stalk on which the spores are borne. The fruiting structure of the Myxomycetes is a secreted noncellular envelope in which the spores are contained. Small soil amoebas closely resembling acrasian myxamoebas are very common, and, in the laboratory, they often form

Comparisons and relationships among slime molds

veritable pavements of closely packed cells and tend to form heaps of cysts. It is not too great a step from these amorphous heaps to the structures of the more differentiated Acrasiales.

Though the myxomycete fruits superficially resemble those of higher fungi, the fact that all structural parts of the fruit are dead secretions rather than the more or less interwoven cellular filaments so characteristic of true molds and mushrooms remove them from the true fungi.

BIBLIOGRAPHY

General works and systematic treatments: C.J. ALEXOPOULOS, *Introductory Mycology,* 2nd ed. (1962), a survey of fungi including a brief discussion on the life histories, classification, and relationships of several groups of slime molds; J.T. BONNER, *The Cellular Slime Molds,* 2nd ed. rev. (1967), a well-written, easily understood book, illustrated with clear diagrams and excellent photographs, containing all important information on the Acrasieae up to the year of publication; A.L. COHEN, "The 'Late Formers'—Changing Concepts of the Opsimorphs (*Myxomycetes, Acrasieae, Myxobacteria*)" *Arch. Mikrobiol.,* 59:59–71 (1967), a review of the slime molds and other organisms in which development comes after increase in size ("opsimorphs"); W. CROWDER, "Marvels of Mycetozoa," *Natn. Geogr. Mag.,* 49:421–443 (1926), a popular account of the Myxomycetes illustrated with coloured plates of unexcelled beauty; M. DWORKIN, "Biology of the Myxobacteria," *A. Rev. Microbiol.,* 20:75–106 (1966), the only complete review of the Myxobacteria, necessarily somewhat technical and condensed; J.F. PETERSON, "The Fruiting Myxobacteria: Their Properties, Distribution, and Isolation," *J. Appl. Bact.,* 32:5–12 (1969), a review of the systematics and distribution of the fruiting Myxobacteria with explicit directions for isolating and cultivating them; W.D. GRAY and C.J. ALEXOPOULOS, *Biology of the Myxomycetes* (1968), a thorough review of the Myxomycetes, treating all aspects except classification; J.S. KARLING, *The Plasmodiophorales,* 2nd rev. ed. (1968), a very thorough but highly technical account of the Plasmodiophorales including doubtful forms; A. LISTER, *A Monograph of the Mycetozoa,* 3rd ed. (1925), an excellent handbook of myxomycete taxonomy, well illustrated in colour and monotone; T.H. MACBRIDE and G.W. MARTIN, *The Myxomycetes* (1934), although particularly stressing the North American forms, this volume covers the Myxomycetes of the world; G.W. MARTIN and C.J. ALEXOPOULOS, *The Myxomycetes* (1969), chiefly a taxonomic survey of the Myxomycetes, including a thorough condensed review of slime mold biology, illustrated with coloured plates; L.S. OLIVE, "The Protostelida: A New Order of the Mycetozoa," *Mycologia,* 59:1–29 (1967), a comprehensive treatment of this small group with a discussion of their affinities; "The Mycetozoa: A Revised Classification," *Bot. Rev.,* 36:59–89 (1970), a critical discussion of the relationships of all the slime molds, with formal keys to the different groups; K.S. POKORNY, "*Labyrinthula,*" *J. Protozool.,* 14:697–708 (1967), a brief and not overly technical survey of the genus *Labyrinthula* and its relatives, treating nutrition, development, and relationships.

Special works: J.T. BONNER, "Differentiation in Social Amoebae," *Scient. Am.,* 201:152–162 (1959), a very lucid semipopular account of cellular differentiation in the Acrasieae as they go through their remarkable life cycle; H.R. HENNEY and T. LYNCH, "Growth of *Physarum flavicomum* and *Physarum rigidum* in Chemically Defined Minimal Media," *J. Bacteriol.,* 99:531–534 (1969), a technical paper containing full references to previous similar work; L.S. OLIVE and C. STOIANOVITCH, "Monograph of the Genus *Protostelium,*" *Am. J. Bot.,* 56:979–988 (1969), a brief, somewhat technical description of all the species of *Protostelium* known up to 1969.

Works on the collection, care, and simple cultivation of slime molds: The following references give directions for the isolation of Acrasieae, the collection of myxomycete fruits and plasmodia, and the cultivation of various slime molds. Methods are those that may be done in the home and with ordinary biology classroom equipment. A.L. COHEN, "The Isolation and Culture of Opsimorphic Organisms. I. Occurrence and Isolation of Opsimorphic Organisms from Soil and Culture of Acrasieae on a Standard Medium," *Ann. N.Y. Acad. Sci.,* 56:938–943 (1953); J.C. SOBELS and A.L. COHEN, "The Isolation and Culture of Opsimorphic Organisms. II. Notes on Isolation, Purification, and Maintenance of Myxomycete Plasmodia," *Ann. N.Y. Acad. Sci.,* 56:944–948 (1953); A.C. LONERT, "How to Cultivate the Slime Molds and Perform Experiments on Them," *Scient. Am.,* 214:116–121 (1966).

(A.L.C.)

Sluter, Claus

The works of Claus Sluter (c. 1340/50–1406), one of the masters of early Netherlandish sculpture, infuse realism with spirituality and monumental grandeur. His influence was extensive among both painters and sculptors of 15th-century northern Europe. Born in the mid-14th century, he is known through his works rather than accounts of his person. He is thought to be the Claes de Slutere van Herlam (Haarlem) listed in the records of the stonemason's guild in Brussels about 1379. The sculptured consoles—brackets that support cornices or ornaments—that projected from Brussels Town Hall, now in the Musée Communal, are thought to show if not his hand at least his guiding spirit. From ducal archives he is known to have entered in 1385 the service of Philip the Bold, at the Burgundian capital of Dijon. Philip, duke of Burgundy, was ruler of the Netherlands and regent of France in the last decades of the century. He founded the Carthusian monastery of Champmol at Dijon in 1383 and made its chapel a dynastic mausoleum adorned with sculpture by Sluter.

Lauros—Giraudon

"Moses" from the "Well of Moses," marble sculpture by Claus Sluter, 1395–1404/5. In Chartreuse de Champmol, Dijon, France. Figures are life-size.

All of the surviving sculpture known to be by Sluter was made for Philip. Two compositions are still at the site of Champmol: the figures, on the central pillar that divided the portal of the chapel, showing the Duke and Duchess presented by their patron saints John the Baptist and Catherine to the Virgin and Child and the famous "Well of Moses" in the cloister, the remains of a wellhead that had been surmounted by a group showing the Calvary of Christ (the head and torso fragment of Christ is in the Archaeological Museum, Dijon). The other extant work is the Duke's own tomb, which once stood in the chapel at Champmol but is now reassembled in the Dijon museum.

Life The archives in Dijon provide some information on Sluter's life and sculptural commissions. In 1389 he succeeded Jean de Marville as chief sculptor to the Duke, replacing Marville's assistants with sculptors from Brussels. In that year he began carving the portal sculptures, which had been planned as early as 1386. He replaced the portal's damaged central canopy and by 1391 had completed the statues of the Virgin and Child and the two saints. By 1393 the statue of the Duchess was completed, and it is presumed that the Duke's statue also was finished by then. In 1392 he bought alabaster in Paris, and in the following year he inspected work at Mehun-sur-Yèvre by André Beauneveu, talented sculptor to the greatest art patron of the period, Philip's extravagant brother, Jean, duc de Berry. In 1395 Sluter travelled in the Low Countries, going to Dinant for marble and to Malines. That same year he began the Calvary group for the cloister and in 1396 brought to Dijon his nephew Claus de Werve and more sculptors from Brussels to assist in his numerous ducal commissions. The architectural portion of the Duke's tomb had been completed by 1389, but only two mourning figures of the sculptural composition were ready when the Duke died in 1404; three weeks earlier, Sluter, to ensure the peace of his soul and body and for shelter and protection in his old age, purchased—in modern terms—a retirement plan at the abbey of Saint-Étienne, Dijon. It seems, however, he never availed himself of that retreat before his own death in 1406. Philip's son, Duke John the Fearless, contracted in 1404 for the completion of his father's tomb within four years; but Sluter's nephew did not finish it until 1410, and he used it as the model for Duke John's own tomb. (Many of the mourning figures around the base are copies of what must be Sluter's work, though the problem of establishing his exact contribution is difficult because the two tombs were disassembled in the French Revolution and extensively restored from 1818 to 1823.)

Sluter, an innovator in art, moved beyond prevailing French taste for graceful figures, delicate and elegant movement, and fluid falls of drapery. In his handling of mass, he also moved beyond the concern with expressive volumes visible in Beauneveu's sculpture. The grandeur of Sluter's monumental, naturalistic forms can only be paralleled in Flemish painting—by the van Eycks and Robert Campin—or in Italian sculpture—by Jacopo della Quercia and Donatello—several decades later.

The portal of the Champmol chapel is now somewhat damaged (the Virgin's sceptre is missing, as are the angels, once the object of the child's gaze, holding symbols of the Passion). This work, though begun by Marville, must have been redesigned by Sluter, who set the figures strongly before an architecture with which they seem intentionally not closely aligned, the doorway becoming a background for the adoring couple of Duke Philip and his wife. This transforms traditional portal design into a pictorial form in which architecture has become a foil, the framework for a figured triptych. Projecting canopies and jutting corbels carved with figures, deep undercuttings and swirling draperies aid Sluter's dynamic naturalism. This is a weighty, massive art of dominantly large, balanced forms.

"Well of Moses" The six-sided "Well of Moses," now lacking its crowning Calvary group, which made the whole a symbol of the "fountain of life," presents six life-sized prophets holding books, scrolls, or both. The figures, beginning with Moses, proceed counterclockwise to David, Jeremiah, Zechariah, Daniel, and Isaiah (the first three were in place by 1402). The French art historian Émile Mâle (1862–1954) popularized the discovery that their scrolls contain the prophetic passages the figures spoke in a medieval mystery play, *The Trial of Christ*, foretelling the death of Christ for the redemption of mankind. Six angels at the corners of the cornice mourn the event at one time depicted above. Moses was placed directly below the face of Christ, and the location of Zechariah, father of John the Baptist, was at Jesus' back, as befits a precursor. Zechariah looks down sadly as youthful Daniel vigorously points to his prophecy. On the other side of Daniel, and serving to balance Daniel's passionate temperament, is the calm reflective Isaiah. This juxtaposition reveals Sluter's use of alternating naturalistic balances. The head and torso fragment of Christ from the Calvary (now at the Musée Archéologique, Dijon) reveal a power and intensity of restrained expression that conveys overwhelming grandeur. Suffering and resignation are mingled, a result of the way the brow is knitted, though the lower part of the face, narrow and emaciated, is calm and without muscular stress. The "Well of Moses" was originally painted in several colours by Jean Malouel, painter to the duke, and gilded by Hermann of Cologne (the figure of Jeremiah even wore copper spectacles for which there exists a payment record of 1403). The figures of the composition dominate the architectural framework but also reinforce the feeling of support the structure provides through their largeness of movement.

Sluter's latest preserved work, the tomb of Philip the Bold, now in the Musée de Dijon, France, was first commissioned from Jean de Marville, who is responsible only for the arcaded gallery below the sepulchral slab of black marble from Dinant. Forty figures, each about 16 inches high and either designed or executed by Sluter, made up the mourning procession. Not all the figures are still in position at the tomb; three are lost, three are in the Cleveland Museum of Art, and one is in a French private collection. They served as models for Sluter's nephew, Claus de Werve, Juan de la Huerta, and other artists for sculptured tombs in France and beyond its borders. Sluter did not invent the mourning procession nor did he design the setting. But he conceived of the figures as *pleurants* (weepers), of whom no two are alike; some are openly expressing their sorrow, others are containing their grief, but all are robed in heavy wool garments that occasionally veil a bowed head and face to convey a hidden mourning. The voluminous draperies continue to suggest the sense of large movement visible in such a figure as the Moses of the wellhead. The figures for the tomb are a culmination of Sluter's awareness of natural forms and individual expression, the supreme realization in sculpture of the volatility of his age that was so quick to respond to opposite moods, to weep as strongly as it laughed, that in one moment contemplated with gloom this sinful world and in the next moment delighted in the variety of nature. Spiritualist and naturalist in one, Sluter epitomized in sculpture the growing awareness of an individualized nature with discoverable laws and an enduring grandeur.

MAJOR WORKS

The known extant works of Sluter were constructed for the Chartreuse de Champmol (Dijon, France), which was destroyed in 1792. The only works of Sluter remaining there are parts of the portal of the Chapel (1385–93), and the remains of the "Puits de Moïse," or "Well of Moses" (1395–1404/5), still in the cloister of the Chartreuse. The Musée des Beaux-Arts in Dijon, in the palace of the dukes of Burgundy, contains the tomb of Philip the Bold (1389–1410), now extensively restored. The Musée Archéologique in Dijon contains fragments of the Calvary group (1395–1400), which was originally the upper part of the "Puits de Moïse," including the head and upper torso of the Christ.   (C.D.Cu.)

BIBLIOGRAPHY. Receipts and accounts by and concerning Sluter and the ducal workshop are located in the Archives de la Côte-d'Or and the Bibliothèque Municipale (Dijon), and are also catalogued by the Musée des Beaux-Arts (Dijon). An important catalogue of that museum, from the exhibition "La Chartreuse de Champmol, foyer d'art au temps des Ducs Valois" 1960), contains plates of Sluter's works and an extensive bibliography.

Comprehensive biographical studies are AENNE LIEBREICH, *Claus Sluter* (1936); HENRI DAVID, *Claus Sluter* (1951); and the article by HENRI PAUWELS in the *Encyclopedia of World Art*, vol. 13, col. 113–119 (1967). An important critical study is D. ROGGEN, *Les pleurants de Klaas Sluter à Dijon* (1936). Important critical studies considering the work of Sluter in the context of his period and his influence on European sculpture include: A. KLEINCLAUSZ, *Claus Sluter et la sculpture bourguignonne au XVe siècle* (1905); GEORG TROESCHER, *Claus Sluter und die burgundische Plastik um die Wende des XIV. Jahrhunderts* (1932); and THEODOR MUELLER, *Sculpture in the Netherlands, Germany, France, and Spain: 1400 to 1500* (1966).

Small Arms, Military

Military small arms are the weapons of infantry soldiers and other troops, including sea and air forces. They include firearms, usually issued in companies and platoons and operated by individuals or by small crews. For primitive, ancient, and shock weapons and larger ordnance, see WEAPONS AND DELIVERY SYSTEMS; GUNNERY. For civilian firearms, see GUNS, SPORTING AND TARGET. For details on propellants and explosive charges, see AMMUNITION.

Development of small arms

HISTORY TO 1890

Shock and missile arms of various types had reached a considerable state of efficiency long before explosives were practical for military use. Small military firearms were used in Europe during the 14th century.

Hand cannon. As soon as artillery became effective, inventors began a crude process of miniaturization. Early hand cannons were small enough to be handled by one man but required him to direct his attention towards two different objectives. The weapon had to be aimed with one hand and fired with the other; both operations required part of the soldier's vision. These weapons were fired by inserting a hand-held, red-hot wire into the powder charge through a touchhole on top of the rear of the barrel. Hitting a moving target was difficult at best.

[margin: Firing by red-hot wire]

An early improvement was to make the weapon larger and to employ a crew of two to handle it: one man aimed while the other fired on command. Firearms of this sort, however, were heavy and usually required a support. Neither type of hand cannon was militarily effective. Two other early improvements helped. A slow-burning match, consisting of a soft cord that had been soaked in nitre and dilute alcohol and then dried, was substituted for the red-hot wire about 1400. The touchhole was moved from the centre of the barrel to the side, and a small pan for priming powder was added.

Matchlock weapons. The first great small-arms invention appears to have been made about 1425. A length of glowing match was secured in the end of an S-shaped lever, or "serpentine," which pivoted on a pin. When the firer pressed on one end of this serpentine, the other carried the glowing end of the match precisely to the priming powder in the pan. A soldier could concentrate on his target and know that positive firing depended only on his pressing the lever.

With a matchlock weapon, individual enemies could be hit even while moving. The new firearms were accepted almost immediately. They were improved by making the lock itself (*i.e.*, the mechanism for igniting the charge) more compact, by enclosing it within the weapon, and by having the serpentine operate by trigger pressure against a spring. A cover for the pan holding the priming powder was introduced, and a fence was installed behind the touchhole and pan to shield the face and eyes of the firer from the flash of the priming powder. The match was improved; loading was made more convenient. A few matchlock handguns or pistols were also used, but this form of ignition was not suitable for horsemen.

For more than a century from around 1425 to 1550 matchlock shoulder weapons in widely varying sizes and shapes were used more or less haphazardly in battle. A curved stock to reduce recoil and facilitate aiming was probably introduced about 1500. A Spanish general produced a semi-standardized weapon and introduced tactics that for the first time made infantry firearms truly effective in battle. Spanish infantry in formation began to use matchlock *mosquetes* ("muskets") that were capable of sending bullets through the best armour that could be worn by a mobile soldier. These weapons weighed as much as 25 pounds (11 kilograms) and usually required a forked staff as a rest to enable a man of normal strength to fire them accurately from the shoulder. They were slow and clumsy to load, so that pikemen had to be included in infantry battalions to protect musketeers from enemy cavalry. Almost overnight, however, firepower from muskets became the dominant force in war.

The matchlock musket and pike were virtually the only armaments of infantry from about 1550 to 1675. The muskets became smaller as more powerful gunpowder was created; fully armoured soldiers almost disappeared from European battlefields toward the end of the 16th century. Armour-piercing capability was no longer required so that lighter weapons used without rests were normal.

Pikemen gradually became less effective and decreased in numbers until another major small-arms invention eliminated them. The long muskets of the 17th century could be converted into tolerable short pikes by mounting knives in or around their muzzles. This improvement began modestly in the French infantry around the middle of the 17th century. The name bayonet probably originated in the town or district of Bayonne in southwest France. Plug bayonets, which fitted into the muzzles of muskets, were used first. Ring and socket bayonets, which attached to the barrel without obstructing the bore, became common early in the 18th century; sword or knife bayonets, which could be used for a variety of purposes, appeared soon thereafter and are still in use.

Firelock muskets. All matchlock muskets required a long piece of match secured in the small vise at the end of the serpentine before the weapons could be fired. In a rainstorm, the match could not be ignited or kept alight. Surprise was nearly impossible for soldiers armed with matchlock muskets because of the smell, glow, and noise of the matches themselves. There was always the danger that a matchlock-armed infantryman would accidentally set off his own or a companion's ammunition.

Two other forms of firearms ignition were known for at least a century before the end of the military matchlock era. Both were called firelocks in most records that survive, though they are now known as wheel locks and flintlocks. They have several advantages over matchlocks. Both can be loaded and primed at leisure and then fired with only a moment of notice. They were not, however, as satisfactory as matchlock muskets in sureness of fire or in the number of rounds that could be fired in a given time on a fine day without cleaning. Both were considerably more expensive and more likely to need repairs.

The wheel lock may have been invented by Johann Kiefuss at Nürnberg, Germany, about 1515. It was never widely employed by infantry. A military wheel lock musket of the earliest successful type is similar to a matchlock, save in its method of ignition. The lock itself is more complicated, bulkier, and composed essentially of a serrated wheel wound under spring tension and a piece of iron pyrites held against it in a doghead vise (not shown). When the trigger (see Figure 1) is pressed a

Use of serrated wheel

er one shot even in a rainstorm. On the other hand, it was slow to load and more complicated. Military wheel-lock weapons were found to be appropriate for cavalry because they could be carried, loaded and ready to fire, in holsters for hours or even days. Long, heavy pistols of this type had a considerable influence on tactics in north Europe.

Flintlock muskets are believed to be not so old as the wheel-lock types but were known by the middle of the 16th century, about a hundred years before they made their appearance in quantity in infantry units. A flintlock musket is similar to a wheel lock except that ignition comes from a blow of flint against serrated steel, with the sparks directed into the priming powder in the pan. This lock was an adaptation of the tinderbox concept used for starting fires.

In the several different types of flintlocks that were produced, the flint was always held in a small vise, called a cock, which described an arc around its pivot to strike the steel (generally called the frizzen) a glancing blow (see

From H. Peterson, *Arms and Armor in Colonial America*

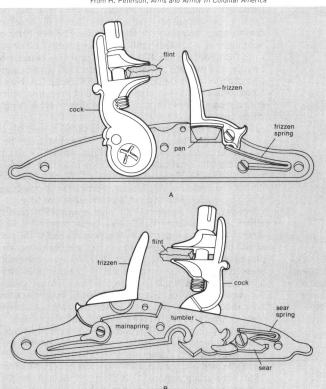

Figure 2: Typical flintlock mechanism (*c.* middle 17th century) with sear in safety position. Phantom view: (A) right side (outer), (B) left side (inner).

Figure 2). A spring inside the lock, similar to that used in most wheel locks, was connected through a tumbler to the cock. The sear, a small piece of metal attached to the trigger, either engaged the tumbler inside the lock, as shown, or protruded through the lock plate to make direct contact with the cock. Locks of the latter sort persisted in Spain and Spanish America until the end of the flintlock era.

Flintlocks were not as surefire as either the matchlock or the wheel lock, but they were cheaper than the latter, contained fewer delicate parts, and were not as difficult to repair in primitive surroundings, a virtue which probably accounts for their popularity in 17th-century America. In common with the wheel locks they have the priceless advantage, for use in the wilderness, of being ready to fire one shot immediately. A flintlock is slightly faster to load than a matchlock, if the flint itself does not require adjustment.

Advantages and disadvantages of the flintlock

Percussion ignition systems. Early in the 19th century, several persons appear to have discovered a firearms ignition system based on the explosive property of potassium chlorate and fulminate of mercury, both of which detonate when struck a small, sharp blow. A Scottish clergy-

From H. Peterson, *Arms and Armor in Colonial America*

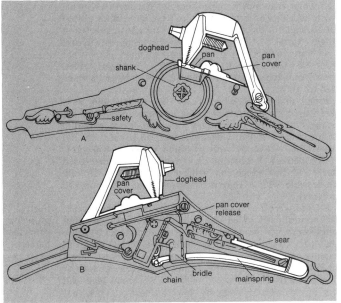

Figure 1: Typical wheel-lock mechanism of the mid-16th century. Phantom view: (A) right side (outer), (B) left side (inner).

stream of sparks is directed, cigarette-lighter fashion, into the priming powder in the pan. A well-made device of this type, properly adjusted, wound, and dry, would almost surely fire if the weapon itself was properly loaded. Since this lock could be waterproof-covered and the trigger pulled without disturbing the covering, it could deliv-

man, Alexander John Forsyth, is credited with this invention in 1805. In the early Forsyth weapons, a small pill of detonating explosive was usually placed below a plunger at the entrance to the touchhole. A hammer, similar to the flintlock cock, struck the plunger when the trigger was pulled. Small tubes containing detonating substances were also used.

The percussion cap was invented about 1815, possibly by Joshua Shaw of Philadelphia. A truncated cone of metal—copper was best—contained a small amount of fulminate of mercury inside its crown, protected by foil and shellac. This cap was shaped to fit tightly over a steel nipple rigidly set in the gun barrel or an extension thereto. When the cap was detonated, a jet of flame passed down an open channel in the nipple into the powder charge. The rest of the lock was similar to that used in flintlock weapons, with a hammer substituted for the cock.

Percussion military muskets were possible before 1820; the advantages of the new system over the flintlocks were obvious both in regard to speed and sureness of fire. The percussion systems were simpler, cheaper, and did not require the special personal attention to small pieces of flint that was necessary for all flintlocks. The new form of ignition was not used regularly in any army, however, until the middle of the 19th century, probably because in Europe and to some extent in America most armies were oversupplied with flintlock muskets following the Napoleonic Wars; there was also the fear that units that relied entirely on the new caps might not always get a supply when needed.

Flintlock weapons predominated in the U.S. and Mexican armies that fought in 1846 and 1848, but many percussion arms were used in the British, French, Russian, and some other national forces which fought in the Crimea in 1854–56. By the American Civil War of 1861–65, flintlock weapons were obsolete. Percussion forms of ignition have been used in most firearms since that time.

Breech-loading weapons.   Another major 19th-century advance in military small arms was breech-loading. Breech-loading weapons (*i.e.*, weapons loaded at the rear of the bore) were not new, and in fact the fieldpieces employed at the Battle of Crécy in 1346 were probably breechloaders. A few breech-loading flintlock rifles were used briefly by a small corps in the British Army during the American Revolution. Breechloaders, both rifles and smoothbores, were made and issued in small numbers to special American units between 1819 and the middle of the century. Percussion ignition, however, greatly simplified breechloading and made it practical for general military use. Literally dozens of new military breechloaders were invented and used in small numbers betwen 1820 and 1865. One group required that the projectile and the propellant, perhaps wrapped in paper, be introduced at the breech but fired by means of a separate percussion cap on a nipple outside the barrel as if it were a normal percussion muzzle-loader. Among the best known of these were the American Sharps and the British Westley Richards. Both are sometimes referred to as cap-and-ball breechloaders.

Another group of breechloaders used paper- or cloth-wrapped cartridges but included inside them a percussion primer. The German Dreyse military rifle, by far the best known of this type, was widely used in the Prussian and allied armies for many years. In the Dreyse paper cartridge, the percussion cap is located in the base of the bullet. A long, slender firing pin pierces the cartridge from the rear, goes entirely through the propellant powder, and strikes the primer. This system worked fairly well as far as sureness of fire went but allowed gas to escape at the breech in the user's face. Dreyse weapons required considerable maintenance and fouled badly with continued firing. The needlelike firing pins had to be replaced frequently. The early French Chassepot rifle also used an internally primed cartridge similar to the Dreyse, but with the primer in a disk to the rear.

There were many percussion systems that combined unburnable cartridge cases with separate percussion caps, but none was militarily important. The American Burnside

carbine may have been the best. It used copper or brass cartridges that contained the propellant and the bullet, but it required a musket cap to be placed on a nipple in the breechlock.

Rim- and centre-fire cartridges.   The first cartridge containing propellant, bullet, and primer to be successfully employed in war was the U.S. Spencer rimfire, in the American Civil War. A ring of fulminate of mercury was deposited all around the entire base of a thin copper cartridge. Force from an external hammer crushed the case rim in one spot and fired the round. Tens of thousands of Spencer carbines and millions of rimfire cartridges for them were used by the U.S. cavalry during the Civil War.

Rimfire cartridges were not satisfactory for infantry use, however, because they had to be made of a metal that would be light and soft enough to crush easily and positively. A powerful cartridge such as was thought necessary for infantrymen would create too much pressure and rupture the rimfire cases. Spencer infantry rifles were unsatisfactory. There were also entirely self-contained pinfire cartridges, fired by means of a small rod that crushed a fulminate cap inside the base, but these were used mostly in pistols.

The concept of centre-fire ammunition, with the percussion cap positioned in the centre of the base of a strong cartridge case, was known before the middle of the 19th century, but practical copper and brass cases of this type were not issued until after 1865. Within a decade they had replaced all other types for military use. A soldier could load his weapon from the breech, fire it, and quickly remove the cartridge case. The closure at the breech was complete; most of the fouling went out in the discarded case. The weapon could be fired many times without cleaning, although accuracy fell off with bore fouling.

Centre-fire metallic cartridges of drawn brass, containing propellant, bullet, and primer, are still essentially the same after more than a century. Bullets are longer, but smaller in diameter; new priming compositions have been introduced from time to time, but fulminate of mercury is still the most positive. Propellant powders are more powerful and burn cleaner and practically without smoke. In aggregate, however, ammunition changes over the past century have been limited.

The early rifles and their disadvantages.   A projectile that spins about its long axis in flight is more accurate than one that moves unpredictably; the feathers in arrows and fins on crossbow bolts were sometimes placed at an angle to the shaft to cause the missile to revolve in flight. Spiral or rifling grooves on the inside of a barrel can cause bullets to spin in the same manner. These were first used as early as the 16th century. Some early rifles, however, have straight grooves, perhaps to inhibit spin or reduce fouling.

Rifled small arms, which make their bullets spin, have been used for accurate shooting at game and targets for some 400 years. Even today, a single bullet carefully loaded into a rifled wheel-lock weapon more than 300 years old will shoot with precision to about 150 yards (140 metres). Every shot can be placed on a man-sized target at this range, an achievement that is virtually impossible with a smoothbore musket at 75 yards (70 metres).

Efforts were made to take advantage of this increase in accuracy of rifled arms in military weapons, but they were not practical because of loading difficulties. In order to spin accurately in flight, a bullet has to fit tightly into the rifling of the barrel, either with direct lead-to-iron contact, or by means of a patch of cloth or leather between the two. Loading a spherical lead ball of the proper size tightly into a clean bore is not difficult. As the bore becomes dirty from repeated firing, however, the loading operation becomes progressively more difficult. For this reason, early rifle-armed military units were not a success. Daniel Morgan's famous battalion of Pennsylvania and Maryland riflemen of the American Revolution were re-equipped with smoothbore muskets before the end of the war, because these weapons were more satisfactory for use in battle.

A special loading procedure was used in British rifle

Breech-
loaders
at Crécy

Few
changes in
ammuni-
tion

Early
problems
with rifled
barrels

units during the Napoleonic Wars, so that the Baker military flintlock rifle could be loaded with patched balls for accurate shooting when the weapon was clean and then with bare balls smoothbore-fashion thereafter. The early rounds were accurate, but those fired later were inferior to bullets from regular Brown Bess muskets—smoothbore shoulder weapons used in the British and other services for about 150 years. Several other flintlock and percussion rifles employing essentially the same system with spherical lead bullets were used around the world, but with limited success. A small increase in accuracy was offset by loading problems. The obvious solution—breech-loading, so that the balls did not have to be forced down clogged bores—encountered another problem: sealing the breech was almost impossible before metallic cartridges. Modern test-firing of such weapons as Ferguson and Hall flintlock breech-loading rifles casts serious doubt on their military efficacy.

The Minié and contemporary systems. Beginning about 1830, a number of men in different countries began to experiment with ways to load a rifle easily from the muzzle and have the bullets take and hold the rifling on the way out. A number of workable systems were invented. Perhaps the simplest arrangement was to abandon spherical bullets in favour of a formed projectile of some sort to fit special riflings. Elongated cylindrical projectiles with two or four ribs cast into them to fit the wide, deep rifling grooves in their barrels showed promise. Another system was to make the inside of the bore in the shape of a regular polygon with rounded corners, and a twist. Whitworth rifles, used briefly in the British army and in the Confederacy during the American Civil War had hexagonal bores and bullets with a relatively quick twist.

Years before the Whitworth system was developed several French officers conducted experiments in which they deformed spherical and elongated projectiles in the breech of their rifles so that the bullets actually filled the grooves in the rifling before they were fired. Accuracy was poor, however, because the deformed bullets had poor ballistic shapes.

The principle of Minié rifling

In 1849 a French captain, Claude-Étienne Minié, developed a better rifling concept. Minié used a cylindrical projectile with a rounded point and a hollow base into which a conical plug was fitted. The bullet's diameter was such that it slid freely down the bore. On being fired, however, the conical plug in the hollow base was driven forward to expand the lead bullet into the rifling grooves. This muzzle-loading Minié system was an immediate success. It did not even require the plug; powder gases alone sufficed to expand the lead bullet. Minié bullets were superior to almost all others not only in accuracy, but also in range. Spherical bullets lost velocity because they were light in proportion to their cross-sectional area. The elongated bullets of the Minié and other similar systems were stable in flight even out to 1,000 yards (900 metres).

Muzzle-loading percussion rifles designed to fire Minié bullets were introduced into several armies in the 1850s and were of extreme importance tactically. Infantry armed with them could be effective with fire up to five times the maximum range of the old muskets, with little or no sacrifice in speed of loading. The old balance between infantry and cavalry was at once upset in favour of the infantry: horsemen received five times as many bullets before they were close enough to use their sabres or lances, essentially their only effective weapons when mounted. The old infantry–artillery balance was also upset. Gunners and their pieces could at one time approach infantry to within 200 yards (180 metres) and fire multiple-projectile charges known as grapeshot and canister, the only really lethal ammunition of that era. The Minié rifles kept enemy artillery so far back, however, that the pieces were nearly useless. They could only reach enemy infantry with solid projectiles or the ineffective shell of that era, which burst into only a few fragments.

Breech-loading small arms. The Minié system, in spite of its great advantages over its predecessors, was short-lived. The breech-loading, metallic-cartridge firearms made all muzzle-loaders obsolete soon after 1865. A bullet loaded at the breech did not need to be expanded at the moment of firing in order for the grooves in the bore to grip it tightly. The early rimfire cartridges were not powerful enough for infantry rifles, but centre-fire cartridge rifles, introduced as early as 1866, were fully equal to the muzzle-loading Minié types.

Most armies changed from muzzle-loaders to breech-loaders without adopting entirely new weapons. In several cases, Minié-type muzzle-loaders were converted to breechloaders by cutting off the rear of the barrel, threading it, and screwing it into a new single-shot action. The British calibre .577 Snider was of this type. (Calibre is a measure of bore diameter; in British and United States firearms, it is expressed as a decimal fraction of an inch.) In the American Allin-Springfield, the conversion was made in this manner, but the old barrel was reduced to calibre .50 by the insertion of a liner. Similar new single-shot, metallic-cartridge, military breechloaders were developed in France by Antoine-Alphonse Chassepot, in Germany by Paul von Mauser, and in the United States by the Remington Arms Company, among others.

Repeating rifles. During the 1880s, new breech-loading rifles gained another dimension by becoming repeaters. Mauser, Chassepot, and others added tubular magazines under the barrels of their rifles. Spencer rifles and carbines had a magazine in the buttstock which contained seven cartridges that were fed by means of a trigger-guard operating lever into the chamber in succession. None of these early repeating systems, however, was entirely satisfactory for military service. Mauser, the Austrian Ferdinand Ritter von Mannlicher, Remington Arms Company, and others gradually developed more practical box magazines which by the late 19th century were almost universal. The basic bolt action Mauser rifle of this sort, first made for Belgium in 1889, was adopted by armies throughout the world with small changes and modifications until it became the most popular type. The U.S. Model 1903 Springfield and the Japanese Arisakas, used in both world wars, are remarkably similar.

The early infantry breechloaders fired bullets similar in diameter and shape to those used by the Minié muzzle-loaders, about 0.5 inch (1.25 centimetre) in diameter. These weapons used essentially the same propellant, black powder, that had been employed for centuries, but in a more efficient manner. Cartridge and bullet diameters were soon reduced slightly, usually to about calibre .45 (11 millimetres).

Nitrocellulose, or guncotton, was invented in 1846 but was not utilized successfully for propellants until smokeless powder (nitrocellulose or nitroglycerin–nitrocellulose) was first used for military purposes by the French about 1885. This powder is much more powerful because it burns more completely; rifle projectiles could be made longer and thinner and be given more energy by a smaller charge because their lighter weight and better shape gave them higher velocities. Bore diameters dropped again to about calibre .30 (eight millimetres), with increases in both range and accuracy.

First use of smokeless powder

These smokeless-powder rifles generally fired jacketed lead bullets that weighed half an ounce or less, travelled at a velocity of between 2,000 and 2,800 feet (600–850 metres) per second leaving the muzzle, and were reasonably accurate up to 1,000 yards (900 metres) under ideal conditions. Their high muzzle energies gave them lethal power at as much as 3,000 yards (2,700 metres). Cartridges were usually made of drawn brass; the lead bullets were normally encased in a harder jacket that contained copper or nickel or both. In emergencies, both cartridge cases and the bullet jackets could be made of soft iron.

The new bolt action had a number of variations. The Mauser, Dreyse, and Chassepot rifles, along with the American Green, were all bolt-action breechloaders, in which the bolt itself turned. In all early bolt actions one or more projections, frequently called lugs, revolved from open space into recesses in the receiver, the rear portion of the weapon. The bolt handle itself often acted as a locking lug, the only one in some early types. In the Mauser actions of 1889 and later, however, locking lugs were at the front end of the bolt, which is still the most common position.

In another type of bolt-action military rifle, the bolt itself does not turn at all, but simply slides backward and forward for extraction, ejection, and reloading. Locking is accomplished when the lugs are thrust out into recesses at the end of each forward stroke. When all goes well and ammunition is clean, straight-pull rifles can probably fire faster than turning bolt types. The Austrian, Swiss, and some other armies found them satisfactory; the Canadian Ross straight-pull rifle was not reliable for combat in World War I.

Military pistols. The early hand cannon and wheel-lock pistols for cavalry were succeeded by flintlock and percussion muzzle-loading handguns and single-shot, metallic-cartridge pistols. All functioned similarly to contemporary shoulder weapons but were far less useful. Mechanical repeating pistols existed toward the end of the 19th century but were too complicated and expensive for general issue. In fact, pistols have rarely been effective in military combat, because of inherent range and accuracy disadvantages in comparison with shoulder weapons. They are essentially personal-defense weapons that may be more important psychologically than for their ability to harm an enemy in battle.

From an early date, however, officers and others in military service wanted repeating handguns. Flintlock revolvers and even mechanical flintlock repeaters were made. So-called pepperbox percussion revolvers, essentially several separate small pistols revolving around a central pivot, saw some service. Heavy and bulky for their power, they were not really practical.

Toward the middle of the 19th century, several inventors separately perfected repeating pistols in which a cylinder could be loaded from the front with five, six, or more rounds with a percussion cap on each chamber. The pistol could then be operated to fire all chambers in succession when the hammer was cocked by hand and the trigger pulled. These cap-and-ball revolvers were popular because several moderately powerful shots could be fired before reloading, and the weapon was of reasonable bulk and weight. They were widely issued in some armies for cavalry service and when satisfactory metallic cartridges were available, revolvers became even more attractive. All handguns continued, however, to have inherent disadvantages in accuracy and range.

DEVELOPMENTS TO 1918

Machine guns. The desire to fire a number of projectiles from a single weapon in a brief time was first satisfied by the simple expedient of charging a weapon with more than one bullet. The results were not very effective, because all projectiles from a single discharge followed roughly the same path, and the propelling charges gave reduced velocity under the heavier weight of projectiles. A similar idea was to load more than one charge into a single barrel and fire them successively through different touchholes. Military weapons of this type survive from an early date, but test firing has not shown them to be satisfactory. Volley shoulder weapons were also tried from time to time; they generally involved a number of barrels loaded separately, but fired together. Dispersion, obtained by making the barrels not quite parallel, was rarely uniform.

The middle years of the 19th century brought dozens of inventions involving larger military weapons that would fire several projectiles either together or serially. The percussion system of ignition helped in regard to these. A number of volley field pieces were designed and made, especially in the United States and France. Less effective than howitzers loaded with grapeshot and canister, they took longer to load because of their many barrels and were more expensive to produce.

Even the concept of the modern machine gun, a number of serial discharges from a single barrel, is of ancient origin. A small revolving cannon that required a manually applied match to fire was patented in England as early as 1718; examples of it survive in museums. Even after percussion ignition was well established, mechanical repeaters not using mass-produced metallic cartridges were not really satisfactory for military use. But as soon as

centre-fire rifle cartridges of satisfactory quality were produced in large numbers, there were dozens of inventions, many of which were produced and tested. The best known were the U.S. Gatling gun and the French mitrailleuse, both developed in part before metallic cartridges were common, but both requiring mass-produced centre-fire ammunition to be militarily effective.

The Gatling gun and the mitrailleuse. Gatling guns had several barrels mounted around a central stem and revolved by means of a hand crank. After a barrel fired a round, it went through successive unlocking, extracting, ejecting, reloading, and relocking. In the most successful Gatling guns, magazines held 400 cartridges, but, by means of a feed device, stacks of rounds could be fed to give continuous fire for long periods. Gatling weapons were made to take a variety of ammunition, up to a full inch (2.5 centimetres) in bullet diameter. Though practical, they never saw extended service in a major war. A few were used by United States forces in Cuba in 1898 and in minor military operations around the world. Gatling guns operated best with ammunition loaded with fulminate of mercury primers and black powder propellants, a combination in which ignition was sure and quick. They were often unsatisfactory with the early smokeless powder propellants because a cartridge that did not go off precisely when its primer was struck—a hangfire—would damage the mechanism.

The French mitrailleuse was also a multibarrelled, serially fired weapon. It used a loading plate that contained a cartridge for each of its 25 barrels. The barrels and the loading plate remained fixed, but a mechanism (operated by a crank) struck individual firing pins in succession. The mitrailleuse issued in the French Army fired standard Chassepot rifle ammunition. The weapon weighed more than 2,000 pounds (900 kilograms). The French forces in the Franco-Prussian War of 1870–71 endeavoured to use them in a manner similar to artillery, but they were no match for Prussian, steel, breech-loading cannon made by Krupp, firing explosive shell. For a time the failure of the mitrailleuse discouraged machine-gun development. Several more manually operated types were made and tried out. Some were put into service in small numbers in various armies and navies, generally chambered for artillery ammunition of small size.

Maxim guns. The first successful automatic machine gun was invented by Sir Hiram Stevens Maxim, an American working in Europe. Beginning about 1883, he produced a number of weapons in which operation was based on recoil energy. In all Maxim guns, the force that opened and closed the action, feeding successive rounds to the chamber and ejecting spent cartridges, came from the cartridge itself as it was fired. The bullet's recoil energy was employed to unlock the bolt (or breechblock) from the barrel, to eject the fired case from the gun, and to store sufficient energy in a main spring to push the bolt forward, pick up a fresh round, load the chamber, and lock the piece. If the trigger was held back, the weapon fired again and continued to fire until it had expended all the rounds in the magazine. Both barrel and action recoiled a short distance to the rear locked together; then the action continued back alone after unlocking. An early feature of Maxim automatic machine guns was a positive control of the rate of fire, from one round in ten seconds, or even slower, to about 13 rounds per second, depending on ammunition. This variable fire control feature, however, was not retained.

Maxim weapons were ideal for firing the new smokeless-powder rifle cartridges. Until the cartridge went off there was no power to operate the weapon; though delayed firing was almost certain to damage a Gatling gun, it did no harm in a Maxim weapon, because the cycle did not begin until the cartridge actually fired. Since it operated by the power of the cartridges, it could be made lighter than the mechanical types. Its light weight made it satisfactory for use by special infantry elements. Since the effectiveness of combat infantry depended on firepower from rifles, weapons delivering several hundred bullets per minute with accuracy considerably increased the combat potential of foot soldiers.

Cylinder
repeating
pistol

Use of
recoil
energy in
Maxim
guns

Maxim guns were first used by the British in a colonial war in 1895 and were employed on a much larger scale in the Russo-Japanese War (1904–05). The Russians used Maxim water-cooled machine guns manufactured in Great Britain. The Japanese used the French Hotchkiss (see below). The Maxim guns sold to most European nations were chambered for the national rifle cartridge. The Russian Model 1910 weighed about 160 pounds (70 kilograms), including mount, water-cooling apparatus, and a steel shield for the gunner. The German Model 1908 with sled mount weighed 100 pounds (45 kilograms). On the eve of World War I, armies differed radically in how to place machine guns in their organizations. In the German infantry, some companies were equipped with machine guns but British rifle battalions —each of which consisted of several companies—had no weapons of this type; they were used throughout the war by Great Britain in a separate machine-gun corps.

Machine guns of the heavy Maxim type were deadly throughout World War I, from 1914 to 1918. Their defensive fire so limited the offensive power of enemy infantry that the entire Western Front, from the Swiss border to the English Channel, became one vast siege operation. A few of these weapons sometimes caused thousands of casualties. On the other hand, because of their bulk and weight, they were only marginally useful for offensive operation by the infantry.

Other machine guns of World War I. Not all the heavy machine guns of World War I were of the water-cooled Maxim type in which recoil pushed both the barrel and the action to the rear for a short distance before unlocking. Gas operation was also employed. A piston located in a cylinder below the barrel was driven to the rear by gas from the barrel through a port to unlock the action and sent the bolt back to extract, eject, and compress the main spring; a new round was picked up, moved into the chamber, and fired on the forward stroke. The best known gas-operated heavy machine gun was the French Hotchkiss. It was air-cooled, but the barrel itself was heavy and provided with metal fins to increase heat radiation. The breech remained open at the end of each burst, a feature possible with any machine gun and used by many of them. Two machine guns of this type are said to have fired 75,000 rounds each in the defense of Verdun, and remained serviceable.

The Austrian Schwarzlose Model 1907/1912 operated on a third principle often called "blowback." In this, the action and barrel are never locked rigidly together; the barrel does not move, nor is there a gas cylinder and piston. To prevent too early opening of the action and case rupture, the block is heavy and the main spring strong. There is usually also a linkage of parts not quite on centre to delay the actual opening. Finally, the barrel is shorter than standard. The Schwarzlose, which was water-cooled and in the Maxim class in weight, was a delayed blowback. The weapon was entirely satisfactory in combat.

Light machine guns and automatic rifles. Heavy machine guns of the Maxim and Hotchkiss types were satisfactory for defensive roles but were not really portable. A number of lighter machine guns that could be carried by one man without great inconvenience began to be used in 1915 and later. These include the British Lewis gun (invented in America but manufactured and improved in Great Britain), the French Chauchat, several German weapons, and the U.S. Browning automatic rifle known as the BAR. All these were light enough to be carried and fired by one man. They could be fired rifle-fashion but were also capable of delivering from a prone position, with bipod, full automatic fire almost as effective as that from the heavy machine guns, restoring some of the offensive power of foot soldiers.

Most, but not all, of these light weapons were gas-operated. Almost all were air-cooled. Generally, a light machine-gunner had an assistant to help him carry ammunition. Toward the end of World War I, one light machine gun was issued per squad or section of six to ten men in most armies. These light machine guns usually fired from magazines rather than belts of ammunition because they

were more convenient and more easily transported. The guns weighed as little as 15 pounds (7 kilograms), giving rise to the idea that a similar infantry rifle could be constructed that would operate semi-automatically. Several such automatic rifles were issued in small numbers by 1918, but none was a military success. Recoil-operated weapons were prohibitively expensive at that time, and the gas-operated types needed too much cleaning to remain reliable. The principle causes of malfunctions in all weapons of this type are the accumulation of powder residue in the gas system and the breakage of small parts.

Automatic pistols and submachine guns. The anticipated success of the automatic machine guns late in the 19th century led to dozens of different so-called automatic pistols, actually semi-automatic; when the trigger is pulled, the cartridge in the chamber is fired producing power to extract and eject the empty case, load another round, and cock the weapon. There is no mechanical problem in making a pistol fully automatic (*i.e.*, causing it to fire continuously until the trigger is released or the weapon is empty), but only the first bullet will be target effective, the rest going high.

The early automatic or self-loading pistols operated by means of recoiling or blowback action. There have been no successful gas-operated military pistols. If the cartridge power is high, recoil operation is preferable. The best known military pistols of this class used in World War I were the German Lugers and Mausers and the U.S. Model 1911. Similar pistols used in other armies included the British Webley, the Austrian Steyr, and the Italian Glisenti. In all of these, the barrel and action move a short distance to the rear before unlocking.

Simple blowback-operated pistols were also widely used, firing relatively weaker cartridges. These have less than half the muzzle energy of the more powerful pistol ammunition. Accuracy and range are both limited compared with that of a shoulder weapon. Early in the history of self-loading pistols, however, the more powerful types were often equipped with a detachable stock that functioned as a holster when the weapon was not in use. Probably the most widely issued weapon of this sort was a special long-barrelled German Luger with a 32-shot drum magazine. It was normally carried as a secondary arm by machine-gunners; it fired only one shot per trigger pull.

This Luger and other similar arms confirmed the belief that a shoulder small arm that fired pistol ammunition could be militarily effective. The result was the submachine gun. The first successful weapon of this type was developed by a German, Louis Schmeisser, who at first used the 32-shot Luger magazines and the nine millimetre Parabellum or Luger cartridge. The Model 1918 Schmeisser was of rifle weight and conformation, but with a barrel only 7.9 inches (20 centimetres) long. It was blowback operated, easily possible with this cartridge and barrel length, because of the relatively heavy bolt and main spring, and was moderately effective in the few months it was used before the end of World War I.

Other fully automatic shoulder weapons firing pistol ammunition in World War I included the Italian Villar Perosa and the Pedersen device, but neither was of much combat importance. The Villar Perosa was used mostly in dual mounts for missions better accomplished by light machine guns. The Pedersen device allowed the standard U.S. Springfield to deliver fully automatic fire with a special, powerful, calibre .30 pistol-type cartridge, but the rifle could be converted back to fire rifle ammunition quickly if the soldier had not lost his bolt. Pedersen devices were in France before the Armistice in 1918; training results with them were encouraging, but they saw no combat service. All were scrapped soon after the war ended, although the cartridge was used later in French semi-automatic pistols and submachine guns.

Infantry support weapons. The widespread use of water-cooled machine guns in field fortifications and other innovations in World War I encouraged the introduction of new weapons into rifle companies. A small, light cannon firing a low-velocity explosive shell about 37 millimetres (1.5 inches) in diameter gave units of this size a

The Hotchkiss gun at Verdun

Pistols of World War I

Combination stock and holster

means of destroying enemy machine-gun nests, although weapons of this type were not totally successful. The advent of tanks led to the development of infantry anti-tank weapons. The Germans produced a single-shot Mauser rifle of about calibre .51 (13 millimetres) capable of penetrating the armour of most 1918 tanks. It gave trouble because of its excessive weight and recoil but was reasonably effective.

The conditions of trench warfare also led to the reintroduction, after about 150 years, of hand grenades. Heavier bombs were projected in a number of ways, but simple muzzle-loading mortars were by far the most common. These trench mortars of about three-inch bore continued in the infantry inventories of the major armies after the war was over but were soon known simply as mortars.

CHANGES AFTER 1918

Research and development in small arms as in the other weapons was virtually suspended in most countries at the end of World War I, partly because of peace, partly because of the vast stocks on hand. With the rise of Hitler in Germany in the 1930s, militarism and military production began to revive.

Rifles and assault rifles. To improve on the bolt-action, box-magazine rifles of 1914–18, every nation having an arms industry sought to produce a semi-automatic or self-loading weapon that would load the next round in the chamber without the necessity of pulling back the bolt. The Soviet army was equipped in part with Tokarev semi-automatic rifles, but in 1941 these were abandoned after a few months of combat. The Germans produced only a small quantity of semi-automatic rifles (FG-42s) chambered for their full power 7.92-millimetre round. The United States armies of 1942 and later were supplied, however, with an ever-increasing flow of the U.S. M1 Garand semi-automatic rifles. The Japanese produced a copy of the Garand, but poor material and execution made it unsatisfactory.

In addition, many fully automatic weapons of infantry weight (eight to ten pounds) were designed. The search for a satisfactory light machine gun before and during World War I led to experimental production of self-loading arms in the rifle-weight class. Several different principles worked well in sporting arms, including both short and long recoil, gas operation, and various forms of delayed blowback operation. The submachine gun, though not used in quantity during World War I, became extremely popular in the next 20 years. These weapons will be discussed below, but their use in the German Army led to what may be called a new infantry weapon, the assault rifle.

The Germans used a number of good submachine guns early in World War II, but all were chambered for the nine-millimetre Luger, which lacked both range and power. The German FG-42, firing a full-power rifle round, recoiled too much for burst-fire accuracy even in a prone position. A round was developed in 1943, the 7.92 Kurz (short), which fired a bullet intermediate in power between the 7.92-millimetre Mauser rifle and the Luger pistol. The German assault rifle finally developed to fire this round is usually called the MP-44. Bursts from it were as accurate as from most submachine guns, but effective out to at least 300 metres (about 1,000 feet).

After World War II the Soviets adopted the German assault rifle in their AK-47 (Kalashnikov Model 1947). This assault rifle (see Figure 3) was more powerful than a submachine gun and more stable in burst fire than weapons chambered for full-power rifle rounds. Later they were equipped with detachable box magazines to facilitate reloading. A Soviet carbine, the SKS or Simonov, had to be recalled because of loading troubles when ammunition was transferred from long clips into an integral box magazine. Both the MP-44 and the AK-47 were gas-operated with cylinders and pistons above the barrel, fired both fully and semi-automatically, and weighed about 12 pounds (five kilograms) loaded with detachable 30-round box magazines. Both fired from closed bolts but differed from each other in minor respects.

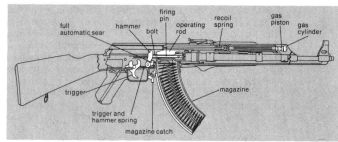

Figure 3: Soviet AK-47 assault rifle.
From W. Smith, *Small Arms of the World*

Communist armies, including the Chinese, adopted the AK-47 and an associated family of small arms firing the same cartridge. Other armies, however, had little success at first with the assault-rifle concept. In the early 1950s, the United States was unwilling to give up full-power rifle ammunition. The North Atlantic Treaty Organization (NATO) armies adopted a new common round, the 7.62-millimetre NATO, in 1952, which is shorter and lighter than most old rifle cartridges but is still of full rifle power. Several new rifles, chambered for this round, have been introduced into various Western armies. The best known are the Belgian FN, the German G3, the U.S. M14, the Japanese Model 1962, and the Italian Beretta.

The NATO common round

In the early 1970s, however, the U.S. Armed Forces were changing from the World War II M1 and the more recent M14 to a new weapon, once called the AR-15, but now known as the M16, which fires a 5.56-millimetre round. The M16 is a true assault rifle, capable of delivering bursts with reasonable accuracy. Its great advantage is lightness of both weapon and ammunition; roughly twice as many rounds can be carried for the same total load, weapon and ammunition combined. But the M16 has a much shorter effective range than the full-power rifles, perhaps 350 yards (320 metres) compared with about 1,000 yards (900 metres). The Soviet 7.62 intermediate-power cartridge is heavier than the 5.56 but probably has more effective range. U.S. allies in Southeast Asia have many M16 rifles and some other weapons firing the same cartridge, and the British Army has about 6,000.

Pistols and submachine guns. Pistols have never been satisfactory for military use because of their lack of accuracy and power. In the 20th century, many major nations have endeavoured to abandon military pistols entirely, but none has succeeded. Some soldiers cannot perform their major duties encumbered by any form of shoulder weapon, yet need something for personal defense. In guerrilla war situations, all war personnel need some kind of weapon, but often the need is for something convenient to carry, especially into and out of vehicles (for example, see Figure 4).

Figure 4: Colt semi-automatic pistol, calibre .45.

Submachine guns, which developed astonishingly after 1918, have distinct advantages. They are shorter than rifles but are much more accurate and have greater magazine capacity than pistols. Submachine guns lack rifle or even assault-rifle power and range, but they can fire reasonably accurate bursts, an enormous psychological advantage.

Hugo Schmeisser of Germany (son of Louis Schmeisser

mentioned above), who produced the best submachine gun of World War I, developed a new model in 1928, which took long, straight magazines, extending out to the left side. This widely copied weapon was blowback-operated. An infantry soldier equipped with a weapon of this sort was thought to be more effective in some combat situations, especially in towns, than if he had a rifle. During the Spanish Civil War of 1936–39, rifles and submachine guns were issued in about equal numbers in some infantry units. The riflemen took care of long-range targets, and the submachine gunners gave close-in firepower.

Both the German and Soviet armies issued submachine guns widely in infantry units during World War II. The Germans used mainly Schmeisser types. The Soviets had two submachine guns: the first, known as the PPSh often used a 71-round drum magazine that gave trouble and fired too fast for accuracy (900 rounds per minute); the second, the PPS, was an outstanding success because it was simple, slow firing, and light. The 7.62 Soviet pistol and submachine gun cartridge had greater range than the German nine-millimetre Parabellum because of its smaller diameter bullets, which had higher velocity. A spare magazine loaded with 35 rounds weighed only 1.5 pounds (less than a kilogram). Many Soviet infantrymen used the PPS in their final successful offensives against the Germans late in 1944 and in 1945.

"Tommy gun"

The first submachine gun issued in the United States armed forces was the well-designed Thompson Model 1928, the "tommy gun" of the American underworld and motion pictures. The early Thompsons were satisfactory, but complicated and expensive, and needed careful cleaning and maintenance. They were not at first straight blowbacks but used a locking system that was not necessary. They were employed in small quantities by American troops in Caribbean actions and by the Western Allies early in World War II. A wartime redesign changed them into the U.S. M1 submachine gun, in which they did become blowbacks. The M1 was replaced by the M3, which fired more slowly and reliably and could be produced for a fifth of the man–machine hours.

The U.S. during World War II had another weapon midway between the rifles and pistols in power, the semiautomatic M1 carbine, which fired a special calibre .30 cartridge. Toward the end of the war, this weapon was issued with a switch to allow fully automatic fire, but results were not satisfactory—the weapon was too light for the rate of fire.

Other individual weapons. Bayonets and knives continue to be carried in most modern infantry units. A few Japanese officers used swords during World War II. Grenades are still widely issued, although their effectiveness when hand thrown is subject to question. Special skill, strength, and coordination are required for range and accuracy in combat. Shotguns have high efficiency when range is short, but they are ineffective beyond about 75 yards (70 metres) and their ammunition is heavy.

The outstanding new individual small arm since World War II is the U.S. M79 grenade launcher, a light, single-shot, shoulder-fired rifle with a large (40-millimetre) bore designed to project small bombs at the remarkably low velocity of 250 fps (foot-pound-second). These little shells weigh slightly less than six ounces, but their segmented wire and powerful explosive give them about the same killing power as World War I hand grenades. Maximum range is said to be 400 metres (about 435 yards).

The concept of discharging bombs from a small arm has also been incorporated into a 2.5-pound attachment for an infantryman's rifle. These were used in combat in small numbers in Vietnam with mixed results. The combination of a rifle and grenade launcher is versatile, but clumsy and heavy. Supplies of ammunition for both are difficult to carry in rough terrain during poor weather.

Machine guns. The heavy, water-cooled machine guns of World War I were widely used during World War II and later, but lighter, air-cooled weapons began to take their place during the 1930s. The most important were the several different models known collectively as the German MG-34, all recoil-operated. Their greatest vir-

The MG-34

tue lay in their effectiveness both as light machine guns fired from bipods and as substitutes for the old heavy machine guns when mounted on tripods for sustained fire. A shift in terms occurred between the wars. In 1918 a heavy machine gun was typically a water-cooled Maxim, firing rifle cartridges. In 1939 the same weapon was considered to be medium; the term heavy now referred to machine guns firing cartridges of several times rifle power.

The MG-34s and the similar MG-42s were reliable and satisfactory in both light and medium roles, especially models with barrels that could be changed quickly. Even with their tripods, they were lighter and more portable than the weapons they replaced. These dual-purpose machine guns used belts for holding their ammunition, but short lengths could be carried in containers like magazines.

Light machine guns. The light machine guns of World War II, usually issued with bipod mounts only, were normally magazine-fed. There is a difference in tactical value between belt-fed and magazine-fed types in regard to firepower. If a weapon fires from a magazine, it is out of action between the time one magazine is exhausted and another is installed. Belt-fed weapons can be in action continuously for short periods at least, because one belt can be attached to another while the first is being fired. Belt-fed weapons on the other hand, are usually longer, heavier, and more troublesome when carried in thick jungle than those that use magazines.

The best-known light machine guns of World War II were the Soviet Degtyarev (DP and DPM), the British Bren, and the already mentioned U.S. BAR. There are different models of each of these, but all are gas-operated and magazine-fed, and weigh from slightly over 20 pounds (nine kilograms) to more than 30 (14 kilograms) loaded. They fire slowly enough to deliver accurate bursts from their bipods, 350–600 rounds per minute. In general, lighter weapons must be fired more slowly to achieve accuracy.

Heavy machine guns. The new heavy machine guns were designed partly to overcome the insufficient power of rifle ammunition for some tactical missions, especially for attacking armoured vehicles. Even before World War I, fully automatic weapons were used with ammunition more powerful than rifle cartridges, but smaller than that for conventional artillery. Such ammunition was not necessary for infantry missions, however, until foot soldiers encountered armoured vehicles. During the 1930s, many higher powered weapons were manufactured and tested. Several were actually adopted, although only two had outstanding success. The U.S. calibre .50 Browning is still widely used throughout the non-Communist world. The cartridge delivers bullets of various weights and types at high muzzle velocities, roughly five to seven times the energy of full, rifle power ammunition. The weapon is essentially the Model 1917 calibre .30 weapon, increased in size. It is recoil-operated and was at first water-cooled, but this refinement was found to be unnecessary for most ground missions. Firing rate is about 450 rounds per minute; the air-cooled M2 weapon with tripod and 500 rounds joined with disintegrating links weighs about 300 pounds (135 kilograms). The Soviet 12.7-millimetre weapon, the DShK, is similar and is almost as widely used in the Communist armies, but is gas-operated. The two bullets are almost identical in diameter, and the cartridge cases and ballistics are similar.

Since 1945, several super-heavy machine guns (above calibre .50) have been developed in several countries, mostly for aircraft and antiaircraft use. The Soviets introduced a 14.5-millimetre weapon into their ground forces especially for use in armoured vehicles. It is recoil-operated and belt-fed and has a barrel that can be changed quickly. Armoured personnel carriers also often carry small automatic cannon, up to even 30 millimetres, but these cannot be considered small arms.

At the other end of the modern machine-gun spectrum, there are weapons firing assault-rifle ammunition of intermediate power. In the early 1970s the Communist nations, their allies, and their weapons customers were using a machine gun chambered for the 7.62 intermediate round. A successful light machine gun firing the same cartridge used in rifles offers advantages at the platoon level, but lack of effective range may more than counterbalance them.

Additional platoon and company support weapons. During World War I, small mortars came to be associated with infantry instead of artillery. Weapons with bores of two to three inches (50 to 75 millimetres) in diameter were issued throughout World War II in most infantry platoons or companies and continue to be used by them to deliver high-angle fire like artillery. Accuracy and range depend, of course, on size, stabilization, mounting, and sighting equipment as well as the skill of the crew. A good crew with the latest in equipment can deliver effective fire out to 4,000 metres (13,000 feet). Larger mortars are usually classified as artillery.

Infantry antitank weapons became extremely important early in World War II. The Germans had a single-shot rifle that delivered an extremely high-velocity 7.92-millimetre rifle bullet with a hardened core that could penetrate the armour of tanks of the 1939–41 era. The British had a calibre .55 "shoulder" rifle similar to the German Mauser of World War I, save that the British weapon had a recoil-absorbing device incorporated in the stock. Tank armour soon became too strong and thick, however, for either of these. Kinetic-energy projectiles (*i.e.*, those that penetrate because of their own weight and velocity) that could defeat tank armour after 1943 required a delivery system too heavy for infantry companies.

On the other hand, a discovery made before World War II led to a highly effective means of attacking armour with light weapons firing low-velocity projectiles. A hollow cone of high explosive, with its open end toward the target, was detonated several inches from the armour to be penetrated. A jet of white-hot gas and molten steel was projected forward and penetrated several inches of the best armour plate. These "shaped-charge" projectiles could be delivered even by means of fin-stabilized rifle grenades discharged from the muzzle of an individual soldier's weapon, though they were more effective in larger sizes. Two new types of infantry-support weapons were introduced to launch larger projectiles: the bazooka, from which a rocket was launched out of an open tube; and a recoilless device such as the German Panzerfaust. The Panzerfaust was held in the hands of a soldier; the thrust is generated as in artillery, but with an exact balance between the energy of the projectile moving forward and gases from the propellant moving to the rear. These weapons resembled rocket launchers but were better in both accuracy and range. The backblast, however, gave away the position of the firer.

Following World War II, both the rocket and recoilless principles of delivery were used in infantry antitank weapons. The weapons themselves were reduced in weight and bulk but increased in effectiveness. Rifle units now have recoilless weapons with bores of 82–90 millimetres that can be carried by one man but will defeat the armour of any known tank at any range at which a hit can be scored, probably a maximum of about 400 metres (1,300 feet). Communist countries throughout the world also possess a lighter weapon for use at squad level, an adaptation of the German Panzerfaust, in which the projectile is launched recoillessly but then given additional velocity and increased range by means of rocket assistance. It is known officially as the RPG-7 antitank weapon but is often called a grenade launcher. In the early 1970s, the United States and her allies used a light 66-millimetre non-reloadable rocket launcher known as the LAW (light antitank weapon) weighing less than four pounds but with a shaped charge capable of destroying any enemy tank it can hit in a vital spot.

Contemporary small arms

Modern mechanical concepts being thoroughly international, military small arms generally vary less from army to army than do uniforms. A no less striking generalization is that nothing radically new has been introduced in small arms in this century.

Shaped charges

Manually operated rifles are still used in many parts of the world. Well-aimed single shots are still effective. Bolt-action arms stand up better to extremes of climate and abuse than more complicated types. Most of those still used are of the turning bolt type.

Pistols are of two main types, revolvers and semi-automatics. The revolving principle of operation was used in firearms before metallic cartridges were available. A cylinder containing several chambers is aligned with the barrel successively so that each metallic cartridge can be fired in turn. The power required for this operation is normally supplied by the pull on the trigger. An automatic revolver in which recoil energy revolved the cylinder one step and cocked the weapon was once issued in small numbers in the British army. Most military revolvers are now of the double-action type; by merely pulling the trigger, the weapon is cocked and fired and the cylinder is rotated. These weapons can also usually be cocked with the thumb and fired single-action, a more accurate procedure because less trigger pressure and travel are required.

Semi-automatic military pistols were being made before the end of the 19th century. Those that fire low-power cartridges, up to and including the nine-millimetre short Browning or .380 ACP, operate on the blowback principle. Recoil pressure causes the cartridge to fly free and stores enough energy in the main spring to close the slide on a new round, which is stripped from a magazine in the butt of the pistol. In a semi-automatic pistol, the trigger must be released and pulled again for each shot.

Military pistols firing more powerful cartridges are generally recoil-operated, the barrel and breechblock, or slide, moving to the rear a short distance locked together. The breechblock then separates and goes all the way back and forward again to complete the cycle. More powerful cartridges require a more complicated action, because if they were fired in a light blowback weapon, they would open before the pressure inside had dropped sufficiently and might rupture the case. In general, pistol actions are designed not to open until the bullet has left the barrel.

Semi-automatic pistols firing powerful cartridges were more popular than either revolvers or blowback automatics through World War II. The Soviets have since adopted a pistol cartridge less powerful than the nine-millimetre Parabellum and two blowback weapons to fire it, and some other armies, including those of Italy and Turkey, use similar pistols.

Full-automatic fire from a weapon held in one hand is ineffective. Holster-stock pistols, which have wooden or metal-and-leather holsters that can be attached to the pistol, allow both hands and the shoulder to be used for greater stability; they have long been equipped with burst-fire switches. A variation of the Mauser pistol Model 1896, one type of Browning Model 1935, and one of the Soviet handguns mentioned above, the APS or Stechkin, are of this type. A pistol with a stock attached is actually a light, or submachine, gun. With the possible exception of the Stechkin, such weapons usually have cyclic rates that are too high for burst-fire accuracy.

Almost all submachine guns are blowback-operated, because the moving parts and the mainspring are substantial enough to keep the breech closed until the bullet has left their short barrels. Perhaps the most modern and effective submachine gun is the Israeli Uzi, which is certainly the most compact when used with a folding metal stock, or without a stock. The Uzi breechblock extends forward around the chamber, telescope-wise, to allow this compactness without sacrificing stability or barrel length. This weapon can also be equipped with a wooden stock, a conformation especially favoured in Israel where the Uzi is often issued instead of a rifle.

Nearly all submachine guns have several features in common. They fire from an open breech, which means that the bolt remains to the rear until the trigger is pulled. The bolt then closes, picking up a loaded round from the top of the magazine and firing it, usually by means of a fixed firing pin. Most weapons of this sort have switches for either single-shot or fully automatic fire.

Pistol types

Mortars are among infantry support weapons that are obsolescent. They are generally muzzle-loading; a round of ammunition that consists of a projectile with a propellant charge in or around its base is dropped down the barrel so that the primer hits on a fixed firing pin at the bottom and fires instantly. Some weapons of this type can be loaded from the muzzle and trigger-fired. A few infantry mortar weapons are loaded from the breech and trigger-fired like a small artillery piece. Accuracy is attained in mortars by rifling inside the barrel, or by means of stabilizing fins during flight.

Rocket launchers of various types are still in use in some armies and in reserve units, but they appear less effective against enemy armour than recoilless weapons. Both rocket launchers and recoilless weapons are lighter than standard artillery pieces of similar projectile size, but their ammunition is heavier. Loading and firing are simple, but rockets are relatively inaccurate and recoilless weapons shorter ranged than conventional cannon. Recoilless devices also have backblast.

NEWER WEAPONS AND OPERATION

Rifles and assault rifles. Modern military rifles are all at least semi-automatic, that is, automatically reload after firing. Many armies now allow a soldier to determine whether he will fire one round per trigger pull or several by changing a lever or switch. Detachable box magazines holding 20–30 rounds have become standard.

Most military rifles of the 1960s and early 1970s were gas-operated; that is, the power for the unloading–reloading cycle came from the propellant gases in the barrel before the bullet left the muzzle. In such a rifle a port in the barrel, usually closer to the muzzle than the breech, is uncovered when the bullet passes; gas enters, forcing a piston to the rear, and compressing a main spring, an operation similar to the early gas-operated machine gun. Both full and intermediate power cartridges can be handled equally well in light gas-operated actions. In assault rifles, the operating cylinder is frequently above, rather than below, the barrel in order to provide for an "in line" stock. Assault rifles generally fire from a closed breech.

The Soviet SKS gas-operated carbine, for a time more popular in the Soviet Army than the AK-47, is still in wide use in China. It is an effective semi-automatic weapon.

The new German G3 family of rifles does not rely on either gas or recoil operation but employs instead a roller principle involving friction; the breech is held closed while the pressure inside the cartridge case is high but opens when pressure has fallen to a safe level. The bolt is securely locked under high pressure but opens easily later. Malfunctions are even less frequent than in gas-operated rifles.

Machine guns. There are no radically new principles of operation for weapons of this sort. Recoil systems still hold their own in the heavier types, though gas operation is also employed. The roller-operated G3 principle is also applicable to machine guns.

The dual-purpose weapon called in the British Army the GPMG (general purpose machine gun) and the U.S. M60 (see Figure 5) are both gas-operated, belt-fed, and cap-

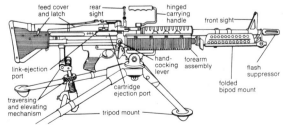

Figure 5: Components of a typical machine gun (U.S. M60).

able of effective fire, either bipod-mounted in a light role, or from a tripod for heavier duty. The West German MG 42-59 is recoil-operated. The GPMG and the MG 42-59 can deliver fire at variable cyclic rates. In the MG 42-59, three different sets of components can be assembled into

the same weapon to allow nine different cyclic rates from below 600 rounds per minute to as high as 1,400. A low cyclic rate is best for ground combat, but the highest possible number of bullets are more useful for firing at aircraft and for use in helicopters against ground targets.

Machine guns and other automatic weapons have successfully used operating principles other than those mentioned above. Blowbacks with heavy blocks and springs work well; delays introduced by various expedients can be both simple and effective. A continuing problem is an acceptable ammunition holder. Belts are not good for use in jungle. A simple practical means of converting a belt-fed weapon to handle magazines is still being sought. The Communist armies have a 7.62-millimetre, full-power, dual-purpose machine gun that can be made either belt- or magazine-fed by changing only three components, requiring only 15 seconds. Ten years after the introduction of this system, however, it was still not widely employed for full-power machine guns, presumably because of its disadvantages. On the other hand, the Soviet gas-operated RPD light machine gun, which handles the intermediate-power (AK-47) rounds, normally fires from belts that are satisfactorily housed in round metal containers attached to the weapon, 100 cartridges in each magazine. This feed arrangement can, of course, be changed easily to accommodate longer belts in boxes. Later weapons of this type sometimes are fitted with an integral adapter to use AK-47 magazines. If intermediate-power cartridges are satisfactory tactically, this weapon is one of the best.

The new heavy machine guns, those of about calibre .50–.60, do not differ in operating principles from those already discussed. Both gas and recoil operation are regularly employed. Barrels can be changed easily in some, but not in others. The Gatling principle of operation has also been reintroduced, with the weapon driven mechanically, usually by means of an electric motor. The modern Gatling weapon, known as the Mini-gun, has a number of barrels and actions employed to deliver extremely high rates of fire; these weapons are chambered for various cartridges, from intermediate rifle power to 20-millimetre cannon rounds. The latter, known as the Vulcan, are useful for firing at both aerial and ground targets; they are not in the small-arms category because they are not used at infantry-company level, though they might be so assigned in special circumstances. In rifle calibres, a single Mini-gun can fire at a rate of 6,000 rounds per minute and even more.

Guided missiles. An entirely new sort of weapon that has appeared, even at platoon level, is the guided missile. A single infantryman can carry and launch one of these unassisted. There are two general types, classified according to the targets they attack. One type is essentially a high-speed rocket with an internal guidance system that can lock onto a heat source, such as the manifold of an enemy aircraft, and then fly along a path to hit it. The other type, which is employed by infantrymen in attacking tanks and similar vehicles, uses one of two systems of guidance, both requiring the attention of skillful operators throughout the projectile flight. In one system, the missile unwinds two thin wires, and the gunner, who watches the projectile through binoculars, controls its motor by means of them. The other guidance system, which is more advanced and effective, does not require wires; it allows the gunner to hold the crosshairs of his sight on his target continuously (see ROCKETS AND MISSILE SYSTEMS).

Small arms of the predictable future. Basic small arms, rifles, submachine guns, and machine guns, at least, operate according to principles worked out in the 19th century. Even rockets are of ancient origin; recoilless weapons are the only newcomers, and they are no longer really new. Most of the small arms used today were developed slowly over the last three-quarters of a century.

This static small-arms situation is not likely to continue indefinitely. The science and engineering that devised nuclear warheads and put men on the moon should also be capable of producing much better individual weapons. Many nations are spending millions of man-hours trying to evolve new and dramatically effective weapons. For a

brief discussion of the more likely possibilities, see
WEAPONS AND DELIVERY SYSTEMS.

BIBLIOGRAPHY. An entire literature composed of hundreds of authors and thousands of volumes and articles has grown up in this field since weapons of all types began to be studied exhaustively in the 19th century. The following books are especially recommended: JOHN G.W. DILLIN, *The Kentucky Rifle* (1946); WILLIAM B. EDWARDS, *The Story of Colt's Revolver: The Biography of Col. Samuel Colt* (1953); T.F. FREMANTLE, *The Book of the Rifle* (1901); CLAUD E. FULLER (comp.), *Springfield Muzzle-Loading Shoulder Arms* (1930); IAN GLENDINNING, *British Pistols and Guns, 1640–1840* (1951); ALDEN HATCH, *Remington Arms in American History* (1956); THOMAS J. HAYES, *Elements of Ordnance: A Textbook for Use of Cadets of the United States Military Academy* (1938); G.S. HUTCHISON, *Machine Guns: Their History and Tactical Employment, Being Also a History of the Machine Gun Corps, 1916–1922* (1938); MELVIN M. JOHNSON, JR., and CHARLES T. HAVEN, *Automatic Weapons of the World* (1945); BERKELEY R. LEWIS, *Small Arms and Ammunition in the United States Service* (1956); W. KEITH NEAL, *Spanish Guns and Pistols* (1955); THOMAS B. NELSON, *The World's Submachine Guns (Machine Pistols)*, vol. 1 (1963); H. OMMUNDSEN and ERNEST H. ROBINSON, *Rifles and Ammunition and Rifle Shooting* (1915); HAROLD L. PETERSON, *Arms and Armor in Colonial America, 1526–1783* (1956); W.H.B. and JOSEPH E. SMITH, *The Book of Rifles*, 3rd ed. (1963); Great Britain, WAR OFFICE, *Textbook of Small Arms* (1929).

(J.We.)

Smith, Adam

After nearly two centuries, Adam Smith remains a towering figure in the history of economic thought. Known primarily for a single work, *An Inquiry into the nature and causes of the Wealth of Nations* (1776), the first comprehensive system of political economy, Smith is more properly regarded as a social philosopher whose economic writings constitute only the capstone to an overarching view of political and social evolution. If his masterwork is viewed in relation to his earlier lectures on moral philosophy and government, as well as to allusions in *The Theory of Moral Sentiments* (1759) to a work he hoped to write on "the general principles of law and government, and of the different revolutions they have undergone in the different ages and periods of society," then *The Wealth of Nations* may be seen not merely as a treatise on economics but as a partial exposition of a much larger scheme of historical evolution.

Early life. Unfortunately, much more is known about Smith's thought than about his life. Though the exact date of his birth is unknown, he was baptized on June 5, 1723, in Kirkcaldy, a small (population 1,500) but thriving fishing village near Edinburgh, the son by second marriage of Adam Smith, comptroller of customs

Adam Smith, paste medallion by James Tassie, 1787. In the Scottish National Portrait Gallery.
By courtesy of the Scottish National Portrait Gallery

at Kirkcaldy, and Margaret Douglas, daughter of a substantial landowner. Of Smith's childhood nothing is known other than that he received his elementary schooling in Kirkcaldy, and that at the age of four years he was said to have been carried off by gypsies. Pursuit was mounted, and young Adam was abandoned by his captors. "He would have made, I fear, a poor gypsy," commented his principal biographer.

At the age of 14, in 1737, Smith entered the University of Glasgow, already remarkable as a centre of what was to become known as the Scottish Enlightenment. There, he was deeply influenced by Francis Hutcheson, a famous professor of moral philosophy from whose economic and philosophic views he was later to diverge, but whose magnetic character seems to have been a main shaping force in Smith's development. Graduating in 1740, Smith won a scholarship (the Snell Exhibition) and travelled on horseback to Oxford, where he stayed at Balliol College. Compared to the stimulating atmosphere of Glasgow, Oxford was an educational desert; one of the few known instances of interference by the University with Smith's intellectual development was its confiscation of his copy of the philosopher David Hume's *Treatise of Human Nature*, a book popularly thought at that time to be heretical and atheistic. Those years were spent largely in self-education, from which Smith obtained a firm grasp of both classical and contemporary philosophy.

Smith's recognition as a philosopher

Returning to his home after an absence of six years, Smith cast about for suitable employment. The connections of his mother's family, together with the support of the jurist and philosopher Lord Henry Kames, resulted in an opportunity to give a series of public lectures in Edinburgh—a form of education then much in vogue in the prevailing spirit of "improvement." The lectures, which ranged over a wide variety of subjects from rhetoric to history and economics, made a deep impression on some of Smith's great contemporaries. They also had a marked influence on Smith's own career, for in 1751, at the age of 27, he was appointed professor of logic at Glasgow, from which post he transferred in April 1752 to the more remunerative professorship of moral philosophy, a subject that embraced the related fields of natural theology, ethics, jurisprudence, and political economy.

Glasgow. Smith then entered upon a period of extraordinary creativity, combined with a social and intellectual life that he afterward described as "by far the happiest, and most honourable period of my life." During the week he lectured daily from 7:30 to 8:30 AM and again thrice weekly from 11 AM to noon, to classes of up to 90 students, aged 14 to 16. (Although his lectures were presented in English, following the precedent of Hutcheson, who had abandoned the earlier practice of discoursing in Latin, the level of sophistication for so young an audience today strikes one as extraordinarily demanding.) Afternoons were occupied with university affairs in which Smith played an active role, being elected dean of faculty in 1758; his evenings were spent in the stimulating company of Glasgow society.

Among his wide circle of acquaintances were not only members of the aristocracy, many connected with the government, but a range of intellectual and scientific figures including Joseph Black, a pioneer in the field of chemistry, James Watt, later of steam-engine fame, Robert Foulis, a distinguished printer and publisher and subsequent founder of the first British Academy of Design, and, not least, David Hume, a lifelong friend whom Smith had met in Edinburgh. Smith was also introduced during these years to the company of the great merchants who were carrying on the colonial trade that had opened to Scotland following its union with England in 1707. One of them, Andrew Cochrane, had been a provost of Glasgow and had founded the famous Political Economy Club. From Cochrane and his fellow merchants Smith undoubtedly acquired the detailed information concerning trade and business that was to give such a sense of the real world to *The Wealth of Nations*.

His friends and acquaintances

"The Theory of Moral Sentiments." In 1759 Smith published his first work, *The Theory of Moral Sentiments*. Didactic, exhortative, and analytic by turn, the

Theory lays the psychological foundation on which *The Wealth of Nations* was later to be built. In it Smith described the principles of "human nature," which, together with Hume and the other leading philosophers of his time, he took as a universal and unchanging datum from which men's social institutions, as well as their social behaviour, could be deduced.

One question in particular interested Smith in *The Theory of Moral Sentiments.* This was a problem that had attracted Smith's teacher Hutcheson and a number of Scottish philosophers before him. The question was the source of man's ability to form moral judgments, including judgments on his own behaviour, in the face of his seemingly over-riding passions for self-preservation and self-interest. Smith's answer, at considerable length, is the presence within each of us of an "inner man" who plays the role of the "impartial spectator," approving or condemning our own and others' actions with a voice impossible to disregard. (The theory may sound less naïve if the term superego is substituted for "the impartial spectator" and if the question is reformulated to ask how instinctual drives are socialized.)

The thesis of the impartial spectator, however, conceals a more important aspect of the book. Smith saw man as a creature *driven* by passions and at the same time *self-regulated* by his ability to reason and—no less important —by his capacity for sympathy. This duality serves both to pit men against one another, and to provide them with the rational and moral faculties to create institutions by which the internecine struggle can be mitigated and even turned to the common good. He wrote in his *Moral Sentiments* the famous observation that he was to repeat later in *The Wealth of Nations:* that self-seeking men are often "led by an invisible hand . . . without knowing it, without intending it, [to] advance the interest of the society."

Travels on the Continent. The *Theory* quickly brought Smith wide esteem and in particular attracted the attention of Charles Townshend, himself something of an amateur economist, a considerable wit, and somewhat less of a statesman, whose fate it was to be the chancellor of the exchequer responsible for the measures of taxation that ultimately provoked the American Revolution. Townshend had recently married and was searching for a tutor for his stepson and ward, the young duke of Buccleuch. Influenced by the strong recommendations of Hume and his own admiration for *The Theory of Moral Sentiments,* he approached Smith to take the charge.

The terms of employment were lucrative (an annual salary of £300 plus travelling expenses and a pension of £300 a year thereafter), considerably more than Smith had earned as a professor. Accordingly, Smith resigned his Glasgow post in 1763 and set off for France the next year as the tutor of the young duke. They stayed mainly in Toulouse, where Smith began working on a book (eventually to be *The Wealth of Nations*) as an antidote to the excruciating boredom of the provinces. After 18 months of ennui he was rewarded with a two-month sojourn in Geneva, where he met Voltaire, for whom he had the profoundest respect, thence to Paris, where Hume, then secretary to the British embassy, introduced Smith to the great literary salons of the French Enlightenment. There he met a group of social reformers and theorists headed by François Quesnay, who called themselves *les économistes,* but are known in history as the physiocrats. There is some controversy as to the precise degree of influence that the physiocrats exerted on Smith, but it is known that he thought sufficiently of Quesnay to have considered dedicating *The Wealth of Nations* to him, had not the French economist died before publication.

The stay in Paris was cut short by a shocking event. The younger brother of the duke of Buccleuch, who had joined them in Toulouse, was assassinated in the street. Smith and his charge immediately returned to London. Smith worked in London until the spring of 1767 with Lord Townshend, a period during which he was elected a fellow of the Royal Society and broadened still further his intellectual circle to include Edmund Burke, Samuel

Johnson, Edward Gibbon, and perhaps Benjamin Franklin. Late that year he returned to Kirkcaldy, where the next six years were spent dictating and reworking *The Wealth of Nations,* followed by another stay of three years in London, where the work was finally completed and published in 1776.

"The Wealth of Nations." Despite its renown as the first great work in political economy, *The Wealth of Nations* is in fact a continuation of the philosophical theme begun in *The Theory of Moral Sentiments.* For the ultimate problem to which Smith addresses himself is how the inner struggle between the passions and the "impartial spectator"—explicated in *Moral Sentiments* in terms of the single individual—works its effects in the larger arena of history itself, both in the long-run evolution of society and in terms of the immediate characteristics of the stage of history characteristic of Smith's own day.

The answer to this problem enters in Book III, in which Smith outlines the four main stages of organization through which society is impelled, unless blocked by deficiencies of resources, wars, or bad policies of government: the original "rude" state of hunters, a second stage of nomadic agriculture, a third stage of feudal or manorial "farming," and a fourth and final stage of commercial interdependence.

It should be noted that each of these stages is accompanied by institutions suited to its needs. For example, in the age of the huntsman, "there is scarce any property . . .; so there is seldom any established magistrate or any regular administration of justice." With the advent of flocks there emerges a more complex form of social organization, comprising not only "formidable" armies, but the central institution of private property with its indispensable buttress of law and order. It is of the very essence of Smith's thought that he recognized this institution, whose social usefulness he never doubted, as an instrument for the protection of privilege, rather than one to be justified in terms of natural law: "Civil government," he writes, "so far as it is instituted for the security of property, is in reality instituted for the defence of the rich against the poor, or of those who have some property against those who have none at all." Finally, Smith describes the evolution through feudalism into a stage of society requiring new institutions such as market-determined rather than guild-determined wages, and free rather than government-constrained enterprise. This later became known as laissez-faire capitalism; Smith called it the system of perfect liberty.

There is an obvious resemblance between this succession of changes in the material basis of production, each bringing its requisite alterations in the superstructure of laws and civil institutions, and the Marxian conception of history. Though the resemblance is indeed remarkable, there is also a crucial difference: in the Marxian scheme the engine of evolution is ultimately the struggle between contending classes, whereas in Smith's philosophical history the primal moving agency is "human nature" driven by the desire for self-betterment and guided (or misguided) by the faculties of reason.

Society and the "invisible hand." The theory of historical evolution, although it is perhaps the binding conception of *The Wealth of Nations,* is subordinated within the work itself to a detailed description of how the "invisible hand" actually operates within the commercial or final stage of society. This becomes the focus of Books I and II, in which Smith undertakes to elucidate two questions. The first is how a system of perfect liberty, operating under the drives and constraints of human nature and intelligently designed institutions, will give rise to an *orderly* society. The question, which had already been considerably elucidated by earlier writers, required both an explanation of the underlying orderliness in the pricing of individual commodities and an explanation of the "laws" that regulated the division of the entire "wealth" of the nation (which Smith saw as its annual production of goods and services) among the three great claimant classes—labourers, landlords, and manufacturers. This orderliness, as would be expected, was produced

Smith's view of human nature

The role of competition

by the interaction of the two aspects of human nature, its response to its passions and its susceptibility to reason and sympathy. But whereas *The Theory of Moral Sentiments* had relied mainly on the presence of the "inner man" to provide the necessary restraints to private action, in *The Wealth of Nations* one finds an *institutional* mechanism that acts to reconcile the disruptive possibilities inherent in a blind obedience to the passions alone. This protective mechanism is *competition*, an arrangement by which men's passionate desire for bettering their condition—"a desire that comes with us from the womb, and never leaves us until we go into the grave"—is turned into a socially beneficial agency by pitting one man's drive for self-betterment against another's.

It is in the unintended outcome of this competitive struggle for self-betterment that the "invisible hand" regulating the economy shows itself, for Smith explains how the mutual vying of men forces the prices of commodities down to their "natural" levels, which correspond to their costs of production. Moreover, by inducing labour and capital to move from less to more profitable occupations or areas, the competitive mechanism constantly restores prices to these "natural" levels despite short-run aberrations. Finally, by explaining that wages and rents and profits (the constituent parts of the costs of production) are themselves subject to this same discipline of self-interest and competition, Smith not only provided an ultimate rationale for these "natural" prices but also revealed an underlying orderliness in the distribution of income itself among workers, whose recompense was their wages; landlords, whose income was their rents; and manufacturers, whose reward was their profits.

Economic growth. Smith's analysis of the market as a self-correcting mechanism was impressive. But his purpose was more ambitious than to demonstrate the self-adjusting properties of the system. Rather, it was to show that, under the impetus of the acquisitive drive, the annual flow of national wealth could be seen steadily to *grow*.

Smith's explanation of economic growth, although not neatly assembled in one part of *The Wealth of Nations,* is quite clear. The core of it lies in his emphasis on the division of labour (itself an outgrowth of man's "natural" propensity to trade) as the source of society's capacity to increase its productivity. *The Wealth of Nations* opens with a famous passage describing a pin factory in which ten persons, by specializing in various tasks, turn out 48,000 pins a day, compared with the few, perhaps only one, that each could have produced alone. But this all-important division of labour does not take place unaided. It can occur only after the prior accumulation of capital (or stock as Smith calls it), which is used to pay the additional workers and to buy tools and machines.

The drive for accumulation, however, brings problems. The manufacturer who accumulates stock needs more labourers (since laboursaving technology has no place in Smith's scheme), and in attempting to hire them he bids up their wages above their "natural" price. Consequently his profits begin to fall, and the process of accumulation is in danger of ceasing. But now enters an ingenious mechanism for continuing the advance. In bidding up the price of labour, the manufacturer inadvertently sets into motion a process that increases the supply of labour, for "the demand for men, like that for any other commodity, necessarily regulates the production of men." Specifically, Smith had in mind the effect of higher wages in lessening child mortality. Under the restraining influence of a larger labour supply, the wage rise is moderated and profits are maintained; the new supply of labourers offers a continuing opportunity for the profit-seeking manufacturer to introduce a further division of labour and thereby add to the system's growth.

The attack on mercantilism

Here then was a "machine" for growth—a machine that operated with all the reliability of the Newtonian system with which Smith was quite familiar. Unlike the Newtonian system, however, Smith's growth machine did not depend for its operation on the laws of nature alone. Human nature drove it, and human nature was a complex rather than a simple force. Thus, the wealth of nations would grow only if men, through their governments, did not inhibit this growth by catering to the pleas for special privilege that would prevent the competitive system from exerting its benign effect. Consequently, much of *The Wealth of Nations*, especially Book IV, is a polemic against the restrictive measures of the "mercantile system" that favoured monopolies at home and abroad. Smith's system of "natural liberty," he is careful to point out, accords with the best interests of all men but will not be put into practice if government is entrusted to, or heeds, "the mean rapacity, the monopolizing spirit of merchants and manufacturers, who neither are, nor ought to be, the rulers of mankind."

The Wealth of Nations is therefore far from the ideological tract it is often supposed to be. Although Smith preached laissez-faire (with important exceptions), his argument was directed as much against monopoly as government; and although he extolled the social results of the acquisitive process, he almost invariably treated the manners and manoeuvres of businessmen with contempt. Nor did he see the commercial system itself as wholly admirable. He wrote with discernment about the intellectual degradation of the worker in a society in which the division of labour has proceeded very far; for by comparison with the alert intelligence of the husbandman, the specialized workman "generally becomes as stupid and ignorant as it is possible for a human being to become."

In all of this, it is notable that Smith was writing in an age of preindustrial capitalism. He seems to have had no presentiment of the gathering Industrial Revolution, harbingers of which were visible in the great iron works only a few miles from Edinburgh. He had nothing to say about large-scale industrial enterprise, and the few remarks in *The Wealth of Nations* concerning the future of joint-stock companies (corporations) are disparaging. Finally, one should bear in mind that if growth is the great theme of *The Wealth of Nations*, it is not unending growth. Here and there in the treatise there are glimpses of a system that has reached its "full complement" of riches, at which point an impoverished stagnation reigns.

The Wealth of Nations was received with admiration by Smith's wide circle of friends and admirers, although it was by no means an immediate popular success. The work finished, Smith went into semi-retirement. The year following its publication he was appointed commissioner both of customs and of salt duties for Scotland, posts that brought him £600 a year. He thereupon informed his former charge that he no longer required his pension, to which Buccleuch replied that his sense of honour would never allow him to stop paying it. Smith was therefore quite well off in the final years of his life, which were spent mainly in Edinburgh with occasional trips to London or Glasgow (which appointed him a rector of the university). The years passed quietly, with several revisions of both major books but with no further publications. On July 17, 1790, at the age of 67, full of honours and recognition, Smith died; he was buried in the churchyard at Canongate with a simple monument stating that Adam Smith, author of *The Wealth of Nations*, was buried there.

Beyond the few facts of his life, which can be embroidered only in detail, exasperatingly little is known about the man. Smith never married, and almost nothing is known of his personal side. Moreover, it was the custom of his time to destroy rather than to preserve the private files of illustrious men, with the unhappy result that much of Smith's unfinished work, as well as personal papers, was destroyed (some as late as 1942). Only one portrait of Smith survives, a profile medallion by Tassie; it gives a glimpse of the older man with his somewhat heavy-lidded eyes, aquiline nose and a hint of a protrusive lower lip. "I am a beau in nothing but my books," Smith once told a friend, to whom he was showing his library of about 3,000 volumes.

From various accounts, he was also a man of many peculiarities that included a stumbling manner of speech (until he had warmed to his subject), a gait described as "vermicular," and above all an extraordinary and even comic absence of mind. On the other hand, contemporaries wrote of a smile of "inexpressible benignity," and of his political tact and dispatch in managing the sometimes acerbic business of the Glasgow faculty.

Certainly he enjoyed a high measure of contemporary fame; even in his early days at Glasgow his reputation attracted students from nations as distant as Russia, and his later years were crowned not only with expressions of admiration from many European thinkers but by a growing recognition among British governing circles that his work provided a rationale of inestimable importance for practical economic policy.

Over the years, Smith's lustre as a social philosopher has escaped much of the weathering that has affected the reputations of other first-rate political economists. Although he was writing for his generation, the breadth of his knowledge, the cutting edge of his generalizations, the boldness of his vision, have never ceased to attract the admiration of all social scientists, and in particular economists. Couched in the spacious, cadenced prose of his period, rich in imagery and crowded with life, *The Wealth of Nations* projects a sanguine but never sentimental image of society. Never so finely analytical as David Ricardo, nor so stern and profound as Karl Marx, Smith is the very epitome of the Enlightenment: hopeful but realistic, speculative but practical, always respectful of the classical past but ultimately dedicated to the great discovery of his age—progress.

BIBLIOGRAPHY

Works: The Theory of Moral Sentiments (1759); *An Inquiry into the nature and causes of the Wealth of Nations* (1776); *Early Writings of Adam Smith* (1795), includes "Essays on Philosophical Subjects" and other writings.

Lecture notes taken by Smith's students: Lectures on Justice, Police, Revenue, and Arms (1763); *Lectures on Rhetoric and Belles Lettres* (1762–63).

Biographical works: JOHN RAE, *Life of Adam Smith*, with an introduction by JACOB VINER (1895, reprinted 1965); W.R. SCOTT, *Adam Smith as Student and Professor*, including "An Early Draft of Part of *The Wealth of Nations*," various documents, and correspondence (1937, reprinted 1965); DUGALD STEWART, "Biographical Memoir of Adam Smith," in *The Collected Works of Dugald Stewart*, vol. 10 (1858).

Other references: ADOLPH LOWE, "The Classical Theory of Economic Growth," *Social Research*, 21:127–158 (1954); NATHAN ROSENBERG, "Adam Smith on the Division of Labour: Two Views or One?" *Economica*, 32:127–139 (1965), "Some Institutional Aspects of the Wealth of Nations," *Journal of Political Economy*, 68:557–570 (1960); JACOB VINER, "Adam Smith," *International Encyclopaedia of the Social Sciences*, 14:323–329 (1968); JOSEPH SPENGLER, "Adam Smith's Theory of Economic Growth," *Southern Economic Journal*, 25:397–415, 26:1–12 (1959); ANDREW SKINNER (ed.) "Introduction," *Wealth of Nations* (1970).

(R.L.He.)

Smith, William

William Smith lived during what has been called the "heroic age of geology" when the foundations of the subject were being laid in Great Britain and Europe. He was the first person to recognize that sedimentary rock layers occur in regular sequences, which are traceable over long distances, and that different strata can be identified by the fossils they contain. These observations revolutionized the practice of geology, especially in Britain. Smith's great geologic map of England and Wales (1815) set the style for modern geologic maps, and many of the colourful names he applied to the strata are still in use today.

Smith was born March 23, 1769, his father an Oxfordshire blacksmith of farming stock. Only seven when his father died, Smith was cared for by a farming uncle. He attended a village school, learned the basic methods of surveying from books he bought himself, and collected the abundant fossils of his native Cotswold hills. In 1787 he became an assistant to Edward Webb, a surveyor in nearby Stow-on-the-Wold, who in 1791 helped Smith become established in the Somersetshire coal district southwest of Bath. The steam locomotive had not yet been invented, and canal-building was at its height, particularly for the transportation of coal. There was also abundant work in the enclosure and drainage of fields.

During preliminary surveys for a proposed Somerset-

Early practical experience

William Smith, oil painting by M. Fourau, 1837. In the collection of the Geological Society of London.
By courtesy of the Geological Society of London

shire Coal Canal in 1793, Smith discovered that the strata outcropping in the northern part of the region dip regularly eastward, like so many "slices of bread and butter." On a long trip in 1794 to examine canals and collieries, he had an opportunity to extend his observations. His suspicion that the strata of Somerset could be traced far northward across England was brilliantly confirmed as the familiar beds were encountered again and again during this journey. Excavation of the new canal began in 1795; and Smith, studying the fresh cuts, found that each stratum contained "fossils peculiar to itself."

His work on the canal continued until 1799, when he was abruptly dismissed, probably over an engineering dispute. But Smith had a good reputation in Bath, at that time a major intellectual and social centre, and quickly built a far-flung business as a geological engineer. In 1804 he moved his business headquarters to a house in London, where his fossil collection and geologic maps were always on display.

In 1799 Smith dictated to an amateur geologist in Bath his now-famous table of strata in the vicinity of Bath, which became a principal means for circulating his revolutionary discoveries. He also exhibited his maps and stratigraphic sections at agricultural fairs, such as the Holkham "Sheepshearings," which he regularly attended. Much of his professional work was for the gentleman farmers who supported these shows, but he also supervised major reclamation projects in Norfolk and Wales, restoration of the hot springs at Bath, and a multitude of canal and colliery projects, sometimes travelling 10,000 miles a year (an incredible total made possible by the inauguration of fast mail coaches in 1784).

Smith's intelligence and practical knowledge of geology and groundwater took him to the front rank of his profession, but he never became wealthy because of his personal objective: mapping the geology of England. He always made copious notes of what he saw on the job and spent all his extra time and money on side trips to fill in blank spaces on his map, often sleeping in the coach on the way to his next appointment. Where exposures were few, he used soil, topography, and vegetation to identify underlying rock. His epochal geologic map of England and Wales appeared in 1815 under the title *A Delineation of the Strata of England and Wales, with part of Scotland*. This was followed by an excellent series of county maps between 1819 and 1824.

During these years, Smith was in financial straits, undoubtedly exacerbated by the agricultural depression that followed the Napoleonic Wars. Failure of a quarry in Somerset lost him the property and forced the sale of his fossil collection to the British Museum in London. When creditors seized his London property after he had spent ten weeks in debtor's prison in 1819, he sold out

The 1815 geologic map of England and Wales

and left for Yorkshire. For some years he had no permanent home but finally settled in Scarborough among a small band of geological enthusiasts, one of whom retained him as a consultant on his nearby estate. Recognition of his achievements came from other sources. In 1822 his work was praised by William D. Conybeare and William Phillips in their textbook on English stratigraphy, *Outlines of the Geology of England and Wales*. In 1831 he received from the Geological Society of London the first Wollaston Medal and in 1832 a yearly pension from the crown. He died August 28, 1839, on his way to a scientific meeting in Birmingham.

Assessment Smith was not only exceptionally observant but possessed the power to integrate his observations. He saw that different rock layers contained different fossils and used this fact to trace strata over hundreds of miles. So great was his ability that geologists still use all of the techniques he introduced, and current geologic maps of England differ from his primarily in detail. Between 1815 and 1817 he published a few thin volumes on his work, but in a sense they were too late. Smith had always talked freely to anyone interested, and his knowledge was already public property being applied by geologists in every part of Britain. The fame Smith achieved in his lifetime remains undimmed to this day, and he is universally admired as the "Founder of Stratigraphy."

BIBLIOGRAPHY. JOHN PHILLIPS, *Memoirs of William Smith* (1844), still definitive, though as rare as Smith's own works. L.R. COX, *William Smith and the Birth of Stratigraphy* (18th International Geological Congress, 1948), an excellent short biography; J.M. EYLES, "William Smith, Some Aspects of His Life and Work," in C.J. SCHNEER (ed.), *Toward a History of Geology* (1969), with an indispensable bibliography.

(R.W.Ma.)

Smollett, Tobias

An outstanding exponent of the early English novel in the mid-18th century, Tobias George Smollett is not the equal of his older contemporaries, the novelists Samuel Richardson and Henry Fielding, but he is unrivalled for the pace and vigour that sustain his comedy. He is especially brilliant in the rendering of comic characters in their externals, thus harking back to the manner of the Jacobean playwright Ben Jonson and looking forward to that of Charles Dickens. By modern criteria, his art as a satirical novelist is defective, his model being the "picaresque" novel, relating loosely linked episodes in the life of a rogue hero. But his panoramic picture of the life of his times is surpassed only by that given by Henry Fielding, while his account of conditions in the Royal Navy is especially valuable.

Smollett was baptized in the parish church of Cardross, Dumbartonshire, on March 19, 1721. He came of a fami-

By courtesy of the National Portrait Gallery, London

Smollett, oil painting by an unknown Italian artist, *c.* 1770. In the National Portrait Gallery, London.

ly of lawyers and soldiers, Whig in politics and Presbyterian in religion. In 1727 or 1728 he entered Dumbarton grammar school, proceeding from there to the University of Glasgow and apprenticeship to William Stirling and John Gordon, surgeons of that city. His first biographer states that he "attended the anatomical and medical lectures," and, if his first novel, *Roderick Random*, may be taken as evidence, he also studied Greek, mathematics, moral and natural philosophy, logic, and belles lettres. He left the university in 1739 without a degree and went to London, taking with him his play *The Regicide*. A year later he was commissioned surgeon's second mate in the Royal Navy and appointed to HMS "Chichester," which reached Port Royal, Jamaica, on January 10, 1741. It is probable that Smollett saw action in the naval bombardment of Carthagena. In Jamaica he met and was betrothed to—and perhaps there married—an heiress, Anne Lassells. He returned to London alone to set up as a surgeon on Downing Street, Westminster, his wife joining him in 1747. He failed to secure a production of *The Regicide*, but in 1746, after the defeat of the Jacobite rebels at Culloden, he wrote his most famous poem, "The Tears of Scotland." He had by now moved to cheaper accommodations in Chapel Street, Mayfair, no doubt because, despite litigation, he had managed to recover only a fraction of his wife's considerable dowry, which was invested in land and slaves. It was in Chapel Street that he wrote *Advice* and *Reproof*, verse satires in the manner of the Roman poet Juvenal.

Education and early literary works

In 1748 Smollett published his novel *The Adventures of Roderick Random*, a graphic account of British naval life at the time, and also translated the great picaresque romance *Gil Blas* from the French of Alain-René Lesage. In 1750 he obtained the degree of M.D. from Marischal College, Aberdeen. Later in the year he was in Paris, searching out material for *The Adventures of Peregrine Pickle* (1751). This work contains a great comic figure in Hawser Trunnion, a retired naval officer who, though living on dry land, insists on behaving as though he were still on the quarterdeck of one of His Majesty's ships at sea.

In 1752 he published "An Essay on the External Use of Water," an attack on the medicinal properties of the waters of a popular English health resort, Bath. The essay made him many enemies and little money. His financial difficulties were intensified by his generosity in lending money to a hack writer called Peter Gordon, who employed legal stratagems to avoid repayment. Smollett came to blows with Gordon and his landlord and was sued by them for £1,000 and £500, respectively, on charges of trespass and assault. In the event, Smollett was required to pay only small damages. He was now living at Monmouth House, Chelsea, where he was host to such leading literary figures as Samuel Johnson and Oliver Goldsmith, the actor David Garrick, and John Hunter, a famous surgeon and anatomist. On Sundays, if one may take a passage in *Peregrine Pickle* as autobiographical, Smollett threw his house open to "unfortunate brothers of the quill," whom he regaled with "beer, pudding, and potatoes, port, punch, and Calvert's entire butt-beer." He himself seems to have been a man irascible, pugnacious, infinitely energetic, courageous, and generous.

The Adventures of Ferdinand Count Fathom (now, with *The History and Adventures of an Atom*, the least regarded of his novels) appeared in 1753. It sold poorly, and Smollett was forced into borrowing from friends and into further hack writing. In June 1753 he visited Scotland for the first time in 15 years; his mother, it is said, recognized him only because of his "roguish smile." Back in London, Smollett set about a commitment to translate *Don Quixote* from the Spanish of Miguel de Cervantes, and this translation was published in 1755. Smollett was already suffering from tuberculosis. Early in 1756 he became editor of *The Critical Review*, a Tory and church paper, at the same time writing his *Complete History of England*, which was financially successful. A year later, his farce *The Reprisal: or, The Tars of Old England* was produced at Drury Lane and brought him a profit of almost £200. In 1758 he became what today might perhaps be called general editor of *Universal History*, a

Career as translator and editor

compilation of 58 volumes; Smollett himself wrote on France, Italy, and Germany. His friendship with the politician John Wilkes enabled him to secure the release of Francis Barber, Dr. Johnson's Negro servant, from the press-gang. But a libel on Adm. Sir Charles Knowles in *The Critical Review* led to Smollett's being sentenced to a fine of £100 and three months' imprisonment in the King's Bench Prison. He seems to have lived there in some comfort and drew on his experiences for his novel *The Adventures of Sir Launcelot Greaves* (1762), which was serialized in *The British Magazine*, of which Smollett became editor in 1760.

Two years later he became editor of *The Briton*, a weekly founded to support the prime minister John Stuart, the 3rd earl of Bute. He was also writing an eight-volume work entitled *The Present State of all Nations*, and he had begun a translation, in 36 volumes, of the varied works of the French writer Voltaire. Smollett was now seriously ill; attempts to secure a post as physician to the army in Portugal and as British consul in Marseilles or Madrid were fruitless. In 1763 the death of his only child, Elizabeth, who was 15 years old, overwhelmed him "with unutterable sorrow." He severed his connection with *The Critical Review* and, as he said, "every other literary system," retiring with his wife to France, where he settled at Nice.

In 1766 Smollett published *Travels Through France and Italy*, his one nonfiction work that is still read. He returned to England in that year, visited Scotland, and at Christmas was again in England (at Bath), where he probably began what is his finest work, *The Expedition of Humphry Clinker*, an epistolary novel that recounts the adventures of a family travelling through Britain. In 1768, steadily weakening in health, he retired to Pisa, Italy. During the autumn of 1770 he seems to have written the bulk of *Humphry Clinker*, which was published on June 15, 1771. He died, probably near Leghorn, on September 17, 1771.

MAJOR WORKS

NOVELS: *The Adventures of Roderick Random*, 2 vol. (1748); *The Adventures of Peregrine Pickle*, 4 vol. (1751); *The Adventures of Ferdinand, Count Fathom*, 2 vol. (1753); *The Adventures of Sir Launcelot Greaves* (serially, 1760–61; 2 vol., 1762); *The Expedition of Humphry Clinker*, 3 vol. (1771).

PERIODICAL JOURNALISM: Contributions to *The Critical Review* (1756–59); *The Briton* (1762–63).

TRANSLATIONS: *The Adventures of Gil Blas of Santillane*, 4 vol. (1748; no known copy); *The History and Adventures of the Renowned Don Quixote*, 2 vol. (1755); *Select Essays on . . . Useful Subjects* (1754); *The Works of Mr. de Voltaire*, 35 vol. (1761–65).

POETRY: "The Tears of Scotland" (*c.* 1746); "Ode to Independence" (1773).

DRAMA: *The Regicide* (1749); *The Reprisal* (1757).

OTHER WORKS: "An Essay on the External Use of Water" (1752); *The History and Adventures of an Atom*, 2 vol. (1769); *A Complete History of England*, 4 vol. (1757–58); *Travels Through France and Italy*, 2 vol. (1766).

BIBLIOGRAPHY. There is no collected edition of all Smollett's works. There is an edition of the novels by GEORGE SAINTSBURY, 12 vol. (1895), and an Oxford edition, 11 vol. (1925–26). Individual novels are readily obtainable, especially in Everyman's Library and World Classics. Smollett's *Letters* were edited by EDWARD S. NOYES (1926, reprinted 1969); this edition was superseded by that of LEWIS M. KNAPP (1970), which also contains details of Smollett manuscripts. The most authoritative biography is LEWIS M. KNAPP, *Tobias Smollett: Doctor of Men and Manners* (1949). The relevant chapters in WALTER SCOTT, *The Lives of the Novelists*, 4 vol. (1821–24), are also recommended, as is the article by THOMAS SECCOMBE in the *Dictionary of National Biography*, vol. 18 (1909). ROBERT ALTER, *Rogue's Progress: Studies in the Picaresque Novel* (1964), is a useful critical work. ROBERT D. SPECTOR, *Tobias George Smollett* (1968), is a study of fundamental techniques in Smollett's minor works, and an analysis of the structure, themes, and fictional devices of the major works. Of more interest to the student than to the nonspecialist reader is GEORGE M. KAHRL, *Tobias Smollett, Traveler-Novelist* (1945), which is valuable for its information on Smollett's sources.

(W.E.A.)

Smuts, Jan

"But my dear lady, I am only a general in my spare time." This was Jan Smuts's reply to an American botanist who wondered why he, a general, should be an authority on grasses. He was, in his spare time, a philosopher, botanist, and lawyer. His full-time occupation was that of a South African and world statesman and, during three wars, a soldier.

EB Inc.

Smuts.

Early life. Jan Christiaan Smuts was born on May 24, 1870, on a farm near Riebeeck West in the Cape Colony. His ancestors were mainly Dutch, with a small admixture of French and German but no English, though he was born a British subject. Until he went to school at the age of 12 Smuts lived the life of a South African farm boy, taking his share in the work of the farm, learning from nature, and developing a life-long love of the land.

At 16 he went to Victoria College (subsequently the University of Stellenbosch) where he studied science and arts and obtained first-class honours in both. At Stellenbosch he fell in love with a fellow student, Isie Krige, whom he later married and who remained a source of strength through the stresses and strains of an eventful life. In 1891 he obtained a scholarship and entered Christ's College, Cambridge, where he read law and was generally recognized as one of the most brilliant law students Cambridge had had. He was the first ever to take both parts of the law tripos examinations in the same year, and in both he came first. From Cambridge he went to London, where he came first in the Inns of Court honours examination and was awarded two prizes. It seemed clear that a distinguished academic career lay ahead of him; nevertheless, Smuts wanted to return to South Africa. *(margin: Achievements at Cambridge)*

Apart from law he read widely in philosophy, poetry, and science, and it was at this time that he first read the poems of Walt Whitman. Many years later he compared the effect that Whitman had on him to St. Paul's experience on the road to Damascus. Whitman's conception of natural man liberated him, he believed, from the sense of sin induced by a strict Calvinist upbringing. Before he left England he wrote a book about Whitman but failed to find a publisher.

Political career. Returning to Cape Town in 1895, Smuts was at once drawn into politics. At first he supported Cecil Rhodes, prime minister of Cape Colony. But the raid of L.S. Jameson on the Transvaal destroyed his confidence in Rhodes and, finding himself without political attachment and with insufficient legal work, Smuts decided to move to Johannesburg. At the end of 1897 he married Isie Krige, moving to Pretoria a year later when he was appointed state attorney by President Paul Kruger. At the age of 28 he was thus at the centre of Transvaal politics and, in effect, at the centre of South African politics. From then until his death he was continuously involved in South African and world affairs.

Role in
the Boer
War

For the first nine months of the South African (Boer) War, which began in October 1899, Smuts was part official and part soldier, moving between Pretoria and the front. When Pretoria was occupied by the British he became a full-time soldier, eventually receiving an independent command. He was an apt pupil in the guerrilla tactics that were so successfully exploited against the overstretched British lines of communication. In April 1902 he invaded the Cape Colony—to within 120 miles (190 kilometres) of Cape Town, but by then his force was too little and too late. When the war ended he had to be recalled, under British escort, to take part in drafting peace terms.

The Boers lost their independent republics, but Smuts remained firm in his belief in the future of a united South Africa. He returned to Pretoria and family life but was inevitably drawn into public affairs. He and Gen. Louis Botha combined to oppose the high commissioner Alfred Milner's narrow interpretation of the peace terms and to insist on Boer rights. It was a remarkable partnership, in which Smuts supplied the intellectual vigour and Botha a deep knowledge of his fellow men and great wisdom in dealing with them. Their first objective was responsible government for the two former republics; after that would come union of the four colonies. Smuts played a major role in the achievement of responsible government for the Transvaal (1906) and the Union of South Africa (1910).

When Smuts went to England at the end of 1905 to urge the cabinet to give the Transvaal self-government he came to know a new English world. At Cambridge he had known few Englishmen, and after his return to South Africa he had to devote his energies to fighting the British. But from 1905 his personal friends in England were the intelligent, liberal-minded people whom he now began to meet. To them he escaped from the exacting and exhaustingly boring official social life of London; with them he found the intellectual and spiritual refreshment that, because of long absences, he too seldom enjoyed at home. He had the reputation of being cold and aloof, but among his friends and in his own family circle he was a different man—relaxed and genial, fond of and easy with children.

Role in
World
War I

Just as Smuts was drawn into the public life of his own country, so, after the outbreak of World War I, he was drawn into international affairs. When he and Botha had suppressed rebellion in South Africa, conquered South West Africa, and launched a campaign in East Africa, he went to England for an imperial conference (March 1917). Prime Minister Lloyd George at once recognized his abilities and made him minister of air. From then on he was used in a variety of tasks. He organized the R.A.F. and was concerned in all major decisions about the war. At the peace conference at Versailles, the English economist J.M. Keynes regarded him as the greatest protagonist of a moderate peace that would not crush Germany, and he may justly be called one of the principal progenitors of the League of Nations.

A few months after their return from Versailles, Botha died, and Smuts became prime minister. Nearly five years later he was defeated by a coalition of the Nationalist and Labour parties and remained in opposition until 1933, when he and J.B.M. Hertzog joined forces against the more extreme nationalists. Smuts was content to serve under Hertzog, but they were in deep disagreement about whether South Africa should go to war if Britain did. When the crisis came in September 1939 Smuts's view prevailed by a narrow majority of 13 in Parliament. Smuts became prime minister, and South Africa declared war on Germany.

During World War II South Africa played a much greater part than in World War I, but Smuts himself was not as important a figure as he had been during 1914–18. He was consulted by Sir Winston Churchill and other Allied leaders, but his main role was to mobilize all his country's resources to prevent Germany and Italy from conquering North Africa. Once that objective was achieved, he and his country became of relatively minor importance. Smuts represented South Africa at the 1945 San Francisco Conference at which the Charter of the United Nations was drafted.

At the general election of 1948 Smuts' party was defeated by the Nationalists. Dr. D.F. Malan became prime minister, and one of his first acts was to offer Smuts an official airplane to go to Cambridge, where he was to be installed as chancellor, an offer that Smuts accepted. Two years later, at his home near Pretoria, he died.

Assessment. Despite his great abilities and achievements, Smuts was not a popular leader—he had a subtle and sophisticated mind, was impatient, could not tolerate mediocrity, was immensely hardworking, and had no time for the sociabilities that make for popularity. For almost half his lifetime—from 1912 to 1950—he was derided, mistrusted, reviled, and even hated by an increasing majority of his fellow Afrikaners. He was called a lackey of the empire and a betrayer of his own people. Before and during the South African War he was staunchly anti-British and in favour of a united Afrikaner people. In 1917 and 1919 he persuaded British statesmen to grant dominion status and (in 1920) to drop the word empire. It was believed by some that Smuts was trying to break up the empire. In fact, he knew that the only way to preserve it was to allow as much independence as possible to its components. Nationalist Afrikaners knew this, too—hence, their detestation of Smuts. He was a great South African; they wanted him to be a great Afrikaner. He wanted an independent South Africa closely linked with the Commonwealth; they wanted an independent republic outside the Commonwealth. Ten years after his death the Nationalists achieved their aim.

BIBLIOGRAPHY. WILLIAM KEITH HANCOCK, *Smuts,* vol. 1, *The Sanguine Years, 1870–1919* (1962), and vol. 2, *The Fields of Force, 1919–1950* (1968), is the definitive biography. See also J.C. SMUTS, *Jan Christiaan Smuts: A Biography* (1952), written by his son; and F.S. CRAFFORD, *Jan Smuts: A Biography* (1943).

(L.Ma.)

Snow and Snowflakes

In the broad sense, snow is the solid crystalline phase of water that forms in the free air of the atmosphere and covers, permanently or temporarily, about 23 percent of the earth's surface. Snow is a common Indo-Germanic word (German *Schnee,* Latin *nix,* French *neige,* Russian *sneg*) that is indiscriminately used for falling and lying snow. The Eskimo, for whom snow is of great importance, distinguishes the two kinds of snow by different words (*qanît*: falling; *aput*: lying snow).

Importance
of snow
cover

Snow cover has a strong influence on climate and on plant, animal, and human life. The small intake of radiative heat by snow and its poor heat conductivity induce a cold climate. The great amounts of heat needed for the removal of a snow cover delay the coming of spring. The low heat conduction protects small plants, wild and cultivated, from the effects of the lowest winter temperatures, but the late disappearance of snow and the cooling of the ground by meltwater delay the growth of summer crops. A snow cover represents a store of moisture that can supply water for irrigation and for shipping in rivers at a time when it is most needed and would not be available from precipitation. Many rivers that are fed to an important degree by the melting of winter snow have their highest runoff in spring and early summer.

Heavy snowfalls hinder or even block traffic on streets, roads, railways, and airports; the cost of snow clearing can be very high. In regions with cold winters the period of snowmelt can make the countryside quite impassable, particularly where permanently frozen ground prevents the infiltration of meltwater. In regions of heavy snowfall roofs have to be strengthened and to be steeply inclined to withstand the additional load and to let the snow glide down. Avalanche tracks determine in mountain regions the location of settlements and necessitate extensive structures for protection. On the other hand, a snow cover allows transport in many otherwise inaccessible areas. In many mountain regions timber is transported on sledges or slides downhill on snow races. The life of many Eskimo tribes would not have been possible without a snow

type	graphic symbol	forms

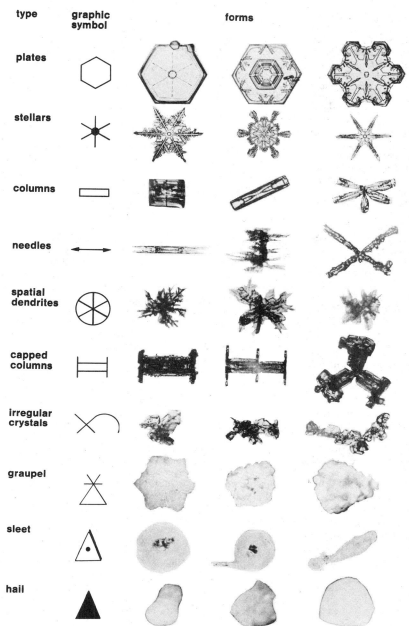

plates

stellars

columns

needles

spatial dendrites

capped columns

irregular crystals

graupel

sleet

hail

Figure 1. Classification of frozen precipitation.
Vincent J. Schaefer

cover for the use of sledges and the building of snowhouses. In recent decades the economy of many mountain regions has been completely changed by the growth of winter sports, particularly of skiing, which depend upon the presence of a snow cover.

This article treats the formation and properties of ice crystals and snowflakes in the atmosphere, the precipitation of snow and its properties, occurrence, and distribution on the ground. For coverage of relevant atmospheric aspects, see PRECIPITATION and CLOUDS; for the ultimate consequences of snowfall, see ICE SHEETS AND GLACIERS; and for an overview of the place of snow in the physical world, see CLIMATE and HYDROLOGIC CYCLE.

Snow in the atmosphere. Snow in the atmosphere can be subdivided into ice crystals and snowflakes. Ice crystals generally form on ice nuclei at temperatures appreciably below the freezing point. Below −40° C (−40° F) water vapour can solidify without the presence of a nucleus. Snowflakes are aggregates of ice crystals that appear in an infinite variety of shapes, mainly at temperatures near the freezing point of water.

From earliest times snow crystals and flakes have attracted attention and admiration. The book of Job (38:22) hints at the beauty of snow. Numerous early Chinese writers have dealt with the hexagonal form. Olaus Magnus depicted the crystals in a book published in 1555 in Rome. Johannes Kepler, in a pamphlet "On the Six-Cornered Snowflake" (1611), was intrigued by the fact that all elements of snow were hexagonal. The invention of the microscope increased the knowledge of the snow structure. The English physicist Robert Hooke published in 1665 illustrations of snow crystals seen through a microscope. Early in the 19th century, William Scoresby Jr., English whaler and explorer, who had made observations in the Arctic regions, provided a classification of snow that was basic for almost 100 years. Photomicrography made documentation of the endlessly varying shapes possible. A wonderfully rich collection of photographs was published by the American farmer W.A. Bentley in 1931. More recently, the conditions of formation of different shapes of snow crystals have been experimentally studied. The forms of these crystals and of snowflakes can be retained in a replica film produced from a dilute (0.5 to 3 percent) solution of polyvinyl formal (Formvar) dissolved in ethylene dichloride and cooled a few degrees below 0° C (32° F).

Physical
properties
and
conditions
of
formation

Snow crystals generally have a hexagonal pattern, often with beautifully intricate shapes. Three- and 12-branched forms occur occasionally. The hexagonal form of the atmospheric ice crystals, their varying size and shape notwithstanding, is an outward manifestation of an internal arrangement in which the oxygen atoms form an open lattice (network) with hexagonally symmetrical structure. According to a recent internationally accepted classification there are seven types of snow crystals: plates; stellars; columns; needles; spatial dendrites; capped columns; and irregular crystals; and three types of other solid precipitation—graupel, sleet, and hail. They are shown in Figure 1. "Graupel" and "sleet" in American terms are "soft hail" and "ice pellets" in British terms. The size and shape of the snow crystals depend mainly upon the temperature of their formation and upon the amount of water vapour that is available for deposition. The two principal influences are not independent; the possible water vapour admixture of the air decreases strongly with decreasing temperature. The vapour pressure in equilibrium with a level surface of pure ice is 50 times greater at $-2°$ C than at $-42°$ C, the likely limits of snow formation in the air. Crystal shape and temperature at formation are related in the Table.

At temperatures above about $-40°$ C the crystals form on nuclei of very small size that float in the air (heterogeneous nucleation). The nuclei consist predominantly of silicate minerals of terrestrial origin, mainly clay minerals and micas. The contribution of meteoritic dust is not definitely established. At still lower temperatures ice may form directly from water vapour (homogeneous nucleation). The influence of the atmospheric water vapour depends mainly upon its degree of supersaturation with respect to ice.

Snow and
ice crystals
in clouds

If the air contains a large excess of water vapour, the snow particles will grow fast and there may be a tendency for dendritic (branching) growth. With low temperature the excess water vapour will be small, and the crystals will remain small. In relatively dry layers the snow particles will have simple forms. Complicated forms of crystals will cling together with others to form snowflakes that consist occasionally of up to 100 crystals; the diameter of such flakes may be as large as one inch. This process will be furthered if the crystals are near freezing point and wet, possibly by collision with undercooled water droplets. If a crystal falls into a cloud with great numbers of

Relation of Crystal Shape and Temperature at Formation

temperature (°C)	form	temperature (°C)	form
0 to −3	thin hexagonal plates	−12 to −16	dendritic crystals
−3 to −5	needles	−16 to −25	hexagonal plates
−5 to −8	hollow, prismatic columns	−25 to −50	hollow prisms
−8 to −12	hexagonal plates		

such drops, it will sweep some of them up. Coming into contact with ice they freeze and form an ice cover around the crystal. Such particles are called soft hail or graupel. Sleet or ice pellets may consist of either frozen raindrops or melted and refrozen snowflakes. Hail consists of layered spheres of ice.

Snow particles constitute the clouds (*q.v.*) of cirrus type, namely cirrus, cirrostratus, and cirrocumulus, and many clouds of alto type. Ice and snow clouds originate normally only at temperatures some degrees below the freezing point; they predominate at $-20°$ C. In temperate and low latitudes these clouds occur in the higher layers of the troposphere. In tropical regions they hardly ever occur below 15,000 feet. On high mountains and particularly in polar regions they can occur near the surface and may appear as ice fogs. If cold air near the ground is overlain by warmer air, a very common occurrence in polar regions, especially in winter, mixture at the border leads to supersaturation in the cold air. Small ice columns and needles, "diamond dust," will be formed and float down, glittering, even from a cloudless sky. In the coldest parts of Antarctica, with temperatures near the surface below $-50°$ C on the average and rarely above $-30°$, the formation of "diamond dust" is a common occurrence. The floating and falling ice crystals produce in the light of the sun and moon the manifold phenomena of atmospheric optics, halos, arcs, circles, mock suns, some coronas, and iridescent clouds. Most of the different optical appearances can be explained by the shapes of the crystals and their position with respect to the light source.

Precipitation from ice clouds

Most of the moderate to heavy rain in temperate latitudes depends upon the presence of ice and snow particles in clouds. In the free atmosphere droplets of fluid water can be quite considerably undercooled; typical ice clouds originate mainly at a temperature near $-20°$ C. At an identical temperature below freezing point the water molecules are kept more firmly in the solid than in the fluid state; the equilibrium pressure of the gaseous phase is smaller in contact with ice than with water. At $-20°$ C, which is the temperature of the formation of typical ice clouds (cirrus), the equilibrium pressure with respect to undercooled water (relative humidity 100 percent) is 22 percent greater than the equilibrium pressure of the water vapour in contact with ice. Hence, with an excess of water vapour beyond the equilibrium state the ice particles tend to incorporate more water vapour and to grow more rapidly than the water droplets.

Being larger and, hence, less retarded by friction, the ice particles will fall more rapidly. In their fall they will sweep up some water droplets, which on contact become frozen. Thus a cloud layer originally consisting mainly of undercooled water with few ice crystals will be transformed into an ice cloud. The development of the anvil shape at the top of a towering cumulonimbus cloud shows this transformation very clearly. The larger ice particles overcome more readily the rising tendency of the air in the cloud. Falling into lower levels they grow, aggregating with other crystals and possibly with water drops, melt, and form raindrops when near-surface temperatures permit.

The ice crystals in clouds, their collisions, their breaking up, and their interaction with undercooled water droplets produce electrical charges that result in radio static and frequently in lightning discharges. St. Elmo's fire, a quiet, brushlike discharge of atmospheric electricity, also is often connected with the action of ice crystals, snowflakes,

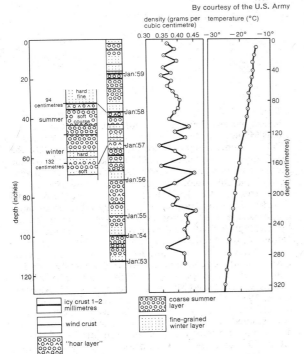

By courtesy of the U.S. Army

Figure 2: Variation of physical properties of snow with depth, measured at Byrd Station, Antarctica, in January 1960.

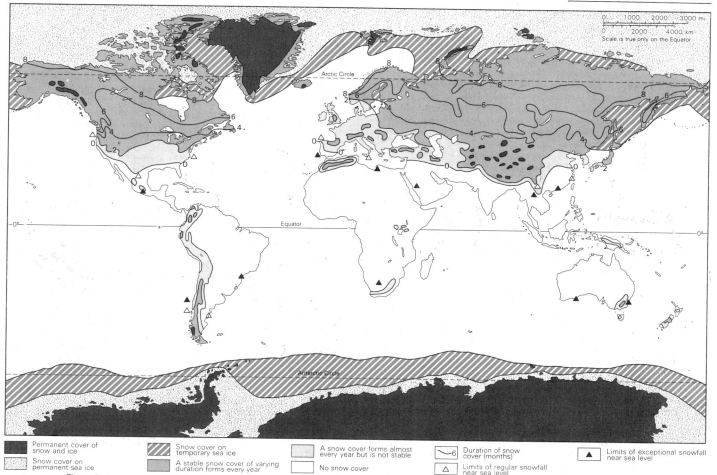

Figure 3: World distribution of snow cover.
Adapted from G.D. Rikhter, *Geografiie Mezhnogo Pokrova*

Legend:
- Permanent cover of snow and ice
- Snow cover on permanent sea ice
- Snow cover on temporary sea ice
- A stable snow cover of varying duration forms every year
- A snow cover forms almost every year but is not stable
- No snow cover
- ～6 Duration of snow cover (months)
- △ Limits of regular snowfall near sea level
- ▲ Limits of exceptional snowfall near sea level

and soft hail. Blowing snow, driven nearly horizontally along the surface by heavy wind, also carries strong electrical charges.

It has been known since 1947 that substances exist that can more readily serve as nuclei for the formation of ice crystals than the naturally occurring and sometimes sparse nuclei. This holds particularly for silver iodide (AgI), which has a crystal structure similar to that of ice and which can be very finely dispersed (10^{15} particles per gram). It is also possible to induce the formation of ice crystals in a supercooled water cloud by the introduction of solid carbon dioxide ("Dry Ice"). This cools a thin sheet of air to about $-70°$ C, far below the limit of homogeneous nucleation. The presence of ice particles fosters the growth of the cloud elements, which then become able to fall out of the cloud. These facts are at the base of the endeavours to induce the precipitation of snow and rain and thus forestall the development of towering clouds, in which thunderstorms and hail might form (see also WEATHER MODIFICATION).

Snow cover. If the temperatures of the air and of the snow are sufficiently low, fallen snow does not melt but forms a cover on the solid ground. The thickness of the snow cover can be measured by stakes. In order to know the deposited mass, the density of the snow must be known. Thickness and density can be established by weighing the content of a coring sampler that has penetrated the whole snow layer. To measure the accumulation in remote places a radioactive source is placed on the surface, and a detector is placed at a fixed distance above. As the accumulating snow covers the source, the intensity of the radiation at the detector diminishes. The information can be telemetered to an inhabited place. Where the snow cover persists for several years, the accumulation can be measured by the seasonal differences in the appearance of the deposited snow or by differences in the

proportion of the stable isotopes deuterium and oxygen-18, which varies with the temperature at which the ice crystals are formed.

A lying snow cover takes up little of the radiative energy from sun and daylight sky. Fresh snow absorbs not more than about one-sixth to one-eighth of it, and even old snow does not absorb more than one-half. Soil and water, however, will absorb about nine-tenths of the energy. The absorption is mainly in the infrared range; in the visible range clean snow reflects nearly all incident radiation because it is almost perfectly white. In the range appropriate to its own temperature, at or below $0°$ C, snow emits almost the maximum possible energy. Hence the radiative economy of a snow cover tends toward a deficit. Because a loose snow cover is a poor conductor of heat, the loss of radiative energy from the surface is poorly replaced from below. The heat conductivity of loose snow is only one-tenth of that of soil. The surface layers of a snow cover get cold. They transmit their low temperature to the adjacent air layer. A low temperature of air near the ground with warmer air above, an inversion of temperature, is typical for snow-covered regions. On the other hand, the poor heat conduction of the snow prevents the cold of the surface from penetrating into the deeper layers. In a snow cover not much more than one foot thick, surface temperatures of less than $-18°$ C can be accompanied by temperatures close to the freezing point at the interface with the underlying rock. Snow and ice have a rather high heat capacity and a very high heat of fusion and sublimation; much heat is needed to melt lying snow and even more to evaporate it.

The texture and density of freshly fallen snow depend largely upon the meteorological conditions. The size of the individual grains of snow varies with temperature and wind. They range from fractions of a millimetre to one or two millimetres. With temperature near freezing point,

Radiation budget of lying snow

Properties and forms of snow

the grains are generally larger than with lower temperature. Strong winds lead to collisions and to fragmentation of the blown snow particles; small rounded grains with a diameter of about 0.10 millimetre result. The density of a freshly deposited snow cover varies from 0.05 grams per cubic centimetre for fluffy snow under calm conditions to 0.45 for the small closely packed particles of blown snow deposited during a gale.

Once deposited, the snow cover undergoes continuous modification. It is diminished by melting and runoff, by percolation into the ground, and by evaporation. It becomes more dense by compaction under its own weight, by pressure of the wind, and by refreezing of meltwater. Strong winds form a hard crust at the surface. Helped by the impact of hard snow particles, the wind transforms the surface into a pattern of ridges and grooves, sastrugi, which stretch in the direction of the wind, and deposits the loose snow in rounded piles termed whaleback dunes. At a smaller scale and with lighter winds the surface becomes pitted and small transverse ripples are formed. Under special conditions of insolation and humidity of the air and of snow structure, the snow cover of tropical mountains can be transformed into bizarre shapes, *nieves penitentes*, several yards high.

Internally, too, a snow cover is subject to incessant changes. Neighbouring snow particles grow bonds and cause the snow cover to become more coherent with time, though this is frequently nullified by other forces. All snow grains are surrounded by a layer of water vapour in equilibrium with the ice surface. The equilibrium pressure of the vapour is higher at strongly convex surfaces than at straight or concave parts. This means that the pressure near the most pointed parts of the ice grain represents supersaturation at other points. The water vapour migrates to and solidifies at the less curved parts. The solid phase at the points tends to re-establish the equilibrium pressure by evaporation. This produces a rounding off of the snow grains. In the same way, a migration of substance occurs from the smaller, more curved grains to the larger grains. For a similar reason, namely a higher equilibrium pressure at the warmer than at the colder parts of the snow cover, there is also a transfer of mass from the warmer to the colder layers. In this respect the heat flux from the unfrozen ground below and the diurnal temperature change at the surface can be of importance. These changes tend to lower the coherence within a snow cover. Layers of loose, rounded particles, called depth hoar, can be formed. The snow may be enabled to overcome the internal friction within the layer and the friction between the snow layer and the ground. On an inclined base the snow will then move down, the speed varying from a slow creep to a rapid slide to snow avalanches that can reach a rapid speed of 200 miles per hour.

World distribution of snow cover

Snow cover is a very widespread feature on earth; 50 percent of the land and 10½ percent of the sea—23 percent of the globe, or 48,000,000 square miles—are permanently or temporarily snow covered. Where a snow cover survives for some years it is transformed into ice, frequently with the aid of melting and refreezing, at permanently low temperatures by mere compression under the growing load. In this way the permanent ice cover of the glaciers is formed. The areas of prevailing accumulation of glaciers on earth, almost 6,000,000 square miles, are always covered by snow.

The thickness and duration of a temporary snow cover depends upon the amounts of solid precipitation, the snow transport by wind, the air temperature, and the strength of the solar radiation. Mountain regions, with lower temperature and generally higher precipitation, tend to have a relatively thick and long-lasting snow cover. Normally the snow cover will last longer in high than in lower latitudes. Three types of temporary snow cover can be distinguished. (1) In some areas snow cover lies without interruption during the colder part of the year. This requires a temperature of the coldest month not higher than −3° C. Most of northern Europe, the Soviet Union, Canada and Alaska, and the northern fringe of the United States belong to this type. There are,

however, regions where even with low winter temperatures no permanent snow cover persists because the precipitation is very small. The region east of the Canadian Rockies and parts of Turkestan and of the Tibetan plateau are examples. (2) Other regions have snow covers that form almost every winter but do not last throughout the winter. They are enclosed roughly between the isotherms of the coldest month of −3° C and 4° C. Europe west of 20° east and most of the United States north of 30° north belong to this type. (3) In still lower latitudes a snow cover of short duration will occasionally form. Jerusalem is such a place. The equatorial border of snowfall, as opposed to snow cover, is at sea level on the average not far from 30° north and 35° south. In southern China, eastern Mexico, and possibly southern Brazil, snowfall near sea level occasionally reaches the tropics.

Generally, the proportion of precipitation falling as snow and the duration of the snow cover increase with height. The level at which more snow is deposited than is removed is called the firn line and is the level above which glaciers form. It is lower in regions of heavy snowfall and higher in drier regions. The firn line descends in high Arctic latitudes to 1,000 feet and in the Antarctic to sea level. At the Equator the firn line is at about 16,000 feet. It rises in the dry tropical regions of Central Asia and South America to well above 20,000 feet.

BIBLIOGRAPHY. C. BELL, *The Wonder of Snow* (1957), a popular account of all aspects of snow; E.R. LA CHAPELLE, *Field Guide to Snow Crystals* (1969).

Falling snow: W.A. BENTLEY and W.J. HUMPHREYS, *Snow Crystals* (1931, reissued 1962), a rich collection of photographs of all kinds of snow flakes; "International Classification of Snow," *Tech. Memo. Ass. Comm. Soil Snow Mech. Can.* 31 (1954), the generally accepted classification; B.J. MASON, *Clouds, Rain and Rainmaking* (1962), a simple introduction to modern ideas on snow; U. NAKAYA, *Snow Crystals, Natural and Artificial* (1954), another beautiful collection of photographs, more scientifically organized than that of Bentley; J. NEEDHAM and LU GWEI-DJEN, "The Earliest Snow Crystal Observations," *Weather*, 16:319–327 (1961), an interesting report on early ideas on snowflakes; V.J. SCHAEFER, "A Method of Making Replicas of Snowflakes, Ice Crystals and Other Shortlived Substances," *Museum News*, 19:11–12 (1941), a frequently used device to perpetuate the elusive forms of snowflakes.

Lying snow: R. GEIGER, *Das Klima der Bodennahen Luftschicht*, 4th ed. (1961; Eng. trans., *The Climate Near the Ground*, 1966), an elementary representation of the conditions and influence of a snow cover; G. SELIGMAN, *Snow Structure and Ski Fields* (1936), a richly illustrated survey; J. BLUTHGEN, *Allgemeine Klimageographie*, rev. ed. (1966); M. MELLOR, *Snow and Ice on the Earth's Surface* (1964); and G.D. RIKHTER, *Snow Cover: Its Formation and Properties* (Eng. trans. 1954), three comprehensive studies of the distribution of snow on earth and its influence upon nature and man.

(F.P.L.)

Soaps and Detergents

Soaps and detergents are substances that, when dissolved in water, give it the ability to remove dirt from surfaces such as the human skin, textiles, and other solids. The seemingly simple process of cleaning a soiled surface is, in fact, complex, and consists of the following physical-chemical steps:

The chemical steps in cleaning

1. Wetting of the surface and, in the case of textiles, penetration of the fibre structure by wash liquor containing the detergent. Detergents (and other surface-active agents) increase the spreading and wetting ability of water by reducing its surface tension, that is, the affinity its molecules have for each other in preference to the molecules of the material to be washed.

2. Absorption of a layer of the soap or detergent at the interfaces between the water and the surface to be washed and between the water and the soil. In the case of ionic surface-active agents (explained below), the layer formed is ionic (electrically polar) in nature.

3. Dispersion of soil from the fibre or other material into the wash water, facilitated by mechanical agitation and high temperature; in the case of toilet soap, soil is dispersed in the foam formed by mechanical action of the hands.

4. Preventing the soil from being deposited again onto the surface cleaned. The soap or detergent accomplishes this by suspending the dirt in a protective colloid, sometimes with the aid of special additives. In a great many soiled surfaces the dirt is bound to the surface by a thin film of oil or grease. The cleaning of such surfaces involves the displacement of this film by the detergent solution, which is in turn washed away by rinse waters. The oil film breaks up and separates into individual droplets under the influence of the detergent solution. Proteinic stains, such as egg, milk, and blood, are difficult to remove by detergent action alone. The proteinic stain is non-soluble in water, adheres strongly to the fibre, and prevents the penetration of the detergent. By using proteolytic enzymes (enzymes able to break down proteins) together with detergents, the proteinic substance can be made water-soluble or at least water-permeable, permitting the detergent to act and the proteinic stain to be dispersed together with the oily dirt. The enzymes may present a toxic hazard to some persons habitually exposed.

Enzymes

If detached oil droplets and dirt particles did not become suspended in the detergent solution in a stable and highly dispersed condition, they would be inclined to flocculate or coalesce into aggregates large enough to be redeposited on the cleansed surface. In the washing of fabrics and similar materials, small oil droplets or fine, deflocculated dirt particles are more easily carried through interstices in the material than are relatively large ones. The action of the detergent in maintaining the dirt in a highly dispersed condition is therefore important in preventing retention of detached dirt by the fabric.

In order to perform as detergents (surface-active agents), soaps and detergents must have certain chemical structures: their molecules must contain a hydrophobic (water-insoluble) part, such as a fatty acid or a rather long chain carbon group, such as fatty alcohols or alkylbenzene. The molecule must also contain a hydrophilic (water-soluble) group, such as $-COONa$, or a sulfo group, such as $-OSO_3Na$ or $-SO_3Na$ (such as in fatty alcohol sulfate or alkylbenzene sulfonate), or a long ethylene oxide chain in non-ionic synthetic detergents. This hydrophilic part makes the molecule soluble in water. In general, the hydrophobic part of the molecule attaches itself to the solid or fibre and onto the soil, and the hydrophilic part attaches itself to the water.

Types of surface-active agents

Four groups of surface-active agents are distinguished:

1. Anionic detergents (including soap and the largest portion of modern synthetic detergents), which produce electrically negative colloidal ions in solution.
2. Cationic detergents, which produce electrically positive ions in solution.
3. Non-ionic detergents, which produce electrically neutral colloidal particles in solution.
4. Ampholythic, or amphoteric, detergents which are capable of acting either as anionic or cationic detergents in solution depending on the pH (acidity or alkalinity) of the solution.

The first detergent (or surface-active agent) was soap. In a strictly chemical sense, any compound formed by the reaction of a water-insoluble fatty acid with an organic base or an alkali metal may be called a soap. Practically, however, the soap industry is concerned mainly with those water-soluble soaps that result from the interaction between fatty acids and alkali metals. In certain cases, however, the salts of fatty acids with ammonia or with triethanolamine are also used, as in shaving preparations, for instance.

HISTORY

Use. Soap has been known for at least 2,300 years. According to Pliny the Elder, the Phoenicians prepared it from goat's tallow and wood ashes in 600 BC and sometimes used it as an article of barter with the Gauls. Soap was widely known in the Roman Empire; whether the Romans learned its use and manufacture from ancient Mediterranean peoples or from the Celts, inhabitants of Britannia, is not known. The Celts, who produced their soap from animal fats and plant ashes, named the product *saipo*, from which the word soap is derived. The importance of soap for washing and cleaning was apparently not recognized until the 2nd century after Christ; the Greek physician Galen mentions it as a medicament and as a means of cleansing the body. Previously soap had been used as medicine. The writings attributed to the 8th-century Arab savant Jābir ibn Hayyān (Geber) repeatedly mention soap as a cleansing agent.

In Europe, soap production in the Middle Ages centred first at Marseilles, later at Genoa, then at Venice. Though some soap manufacture developed in Germany, the substance was so little used in central Europe that a box of soap presented to the Duchess of Juelich in 1549 caused a sensation. As late as 1672, when the German, A. Leo, sent Lady von Schleinitz a parcel containing soap from Italy, he accompanied it with a detailed description of how to use the mysterious product.

The first English soapmakers appeared at the end of the 12th century in Bristol. In the 13th and 14th centuries, a small community of them grew up in the neighbourhood of Cheapside in London. In those days, soapmakers had to pay a duty on all the soap they produced. After the Napoleonic Wars, this tax rose as high as three pence per pound; soap-boiling pans were fitted with lids that could be locked every night by the tax collector in order to prevent production under cover of darkness. Not until 1853 was this high tax finally abolished, at a sacrifice to the state of over £1,000,000. Soap came into such common use in the 19th century that Justus von Liebig, a German chemist, declared the quantity of soap consumed by a nation was an accurate measure of its wealth and civilization.

Early soap production. Early soapmakers probably used ashes and animal fats. Simple wood or plant ashes containing potassium carbonate were dispersed in water, and fat was added to the solution (see Figure 1). This mix-

By courtesy of CIBA Review, Basel, Switzerland

Figure 1: A French soap-boiling plant with the vessels for lye (far left) and the circular boiling pans; engraving published in Paris, 1771.

ture was then boiled; ashes were added again and again as the water evaporated. During this process a slow chemical splitting of the neutral fat took place; the fatty acids could then react with the alkali carbonates of the plant ash to form soap (this reaction is called saponification).

Animal fats containing a percentage of free fatty acids were used by the Celts. The presence of free fatty acids certainly helped to get the process started. This method probably prevailed until the end of the Middle Ages, when slaked lime came to be used to causticize the alkali carbonate. Through this process, chemically neutral fats could be saponified easily with the caustic lye. The production of soap from a handicraft to an industry was helped by the introduction of the Leblanc process for the production of soda ash from brine (around 1790) and by the work of a French chemist, Eugène-Michel Chevreul, who in 1823 showed that the process of saponification is the chemical process of splitting fat into the alkali salt of fatty acids (that is, soap) and glycerin. The method of producing soap by boiling with open steam, introduced at the end of the 19th century, was another step toward industrialization.

Early synthetic detergents.   If turkey-red oil, *i.e.*, sulfated castor oil, still used in textile and leather industries today, is considered as the first synthetic detergent, the industry began in the midst of the last century. The first synthetic detergents for general use, however, were produced by the Germans in the World War I period so that available fats could be utilized for other purposes. These detergents were chemicals of the short-chain alkylnaphthalene-sulfonate type, made by coupling propyl or butyl alcohols with naphthalene and subsequent sulfonation, and appeared under the name of Nekal. These products were only fair detergents, but good wetting agents, and are still being produced in large quantities for use in the textile industry.

In the late 1920s and early '30s, molecules consisting of long chain alcohols were sulfonated and sold as the neutralized sodium salts without any further additions except for sodium sulfate as an extender. In the early '30s molecules consisting of long chain alkylaryl sulfonates (with benzene as the aromatic nucleus and the alkyl portion made from a kerosene fraction) appeared on the market in the United States. Again, these were available as the sodium salts extended with sodium sulfates. Both the alcohol sulfates and the alkylaryl sulfonates were sold as cleaning materials but did not make any appreciable impression on the total market. By the end of World War II the alkylaryl sulfonates had almost completely swamped the sales of alcohol sulfates for the limited uses to which they were applied as general cleaning materials, but the alcohol sulfates were making big inroads into the shampoo and fine detergent fields.

Historically, synthetic detergents began as mainly a substitute for fat-based soap but developed into a sophisticated product, superior in many respects to soap.

Advan-
tages of
synthetic
deter-
gents over
soap Soap forms a scum or precipitate in hard water, leaving a ring around the bathtub, a whitish residue on glassware, and a sticky curd in the rinse water of the laundry tub. Not so easily perceived is the relation of this hard-water scum to a dull, lustreless condition of hair after shampooing, yellow spots on laundry after ironing, and a heavy usage of soap in the household. All these effects point to a serious defect of soaps, namely, their reaction with the calcium and other metal salts present in hard water to give a precipitate that constitutes the hardness of the water. Soaps also react with traces of acidic compounds to form a precipitate. On the other hand, the synthetic detergents generally are unaffected or very little affected by metal salts or acids; although they may react chemically with them, the resulting compounds are either soluble or remain dispersed in colloidal form in the solution. Other useful properties of the synthetics, such as solubility in cold water and flexibility in formulation, also contributed to their rapid replacement of soap products.

SOAP MANUFACTURING PROCESSES AND PRODUCTS

Hot caustic alkali solution, such as caustic soda (sodium hydroxide), acts on natural fats or oils, such as tallow or vegetable oil, to produce sodium fatty acid salt (soap) and glycerol (or glycerin). This reaction, called saponification, is the basis for all soapmaking. If industrially produced fatty acids are used in place of natural fats or oils, the reaction with caustic soda yields soap and water instead of soap and glycerin.

Raw materials and additives.   The major raw materials for soap manufacture are fat and alkali. Other substances, such as optical brighteners, water softeners, and abrasives are often added to obtain specific characteristics.

Alkali.   Sodium hydroxide is employed as the saponification alkali for most soap now produced. Soap may also be manufactured with potassium hydroxide (caustic potash) as the alkali. Potassium soaps are more soluble in water than sodium soaps; in concentrated form, they are called soft soap. Though soft soaps are declining in importance, potassium soap is still produced in various liquid concentrations for use in combination with sodium soaps in shaving products and in the textile industry.

Certain alkaline materials (builders) are almost universally present in laundry soaps, functioning to increase detergency. The most important are sodium silicate (water glass), sodium carbonate (soda ash), sodium perborate, and various phosphates.

Fats and oils.   Fatty raw materials for soap manufacture include animal and vegetable oils and fats or fatty acids, as well as by-products of the cellulose and paper industry, such as rosin and tall oil. Four groups of these raw materials can be distinguished according to the properties of the soap products they yield:

1. Hard fats yielding slow lathering soaps include tallow, garbage greases, hydrogenated high-melting-point marine and vegetable oils, and palm oil. These fats yield soaps that produce little lather in cold water, more in warm water; are mild on the skin; and cleanse well. This is the leading group of fats used in the international soap industry, with tallow the most important member.

2. Hard fats yielding quick-lathering soaps include coconut oil, palm-kernel oil, and babassu oil. (Palm-kernel oil is extracted from the kernel of the fruit of the oil palm, whereas palm oil, listed above in 1, is expressed from the pericarp or outer fleshy portion of the fruit.) These fats are not very sensitive to electrolytes, such as salt; thus, they are suitable for manufacture of marine soap, which must lather in seawater. This is the second most important group of soap fats, with coconut oil the most used.

3. Oils yielding soaps of soft consistency, such as olive oil, soybean oil, and groundnut (peanut) oil are most important here, and linseed and whale oils also belong to the group, as do some semi-drying or drying oils. Because these oils readily undergo changes in air or light or during storage, soaps made from them may become rancid and discoloured.

4. Rosin and tall oil form a group in themselves. Rosin is used in laundry soap, less expensive toilet soaps, and specialty soaps in various industries. Tall oil (a resinous by-product of the manufacture of chemical wood pulp) is mainly used in liquid soap.

Optical brighteners.   Now an integral part of all washing powders, optical brighteners are dyestuffs absorbed by textile fibres from solution but not subsequently removed in rinsing. They convert invisible ultraviolet light into visible light on the blue side of the spectrum, causing the fibre to reflect a greater proportion of visible light and making it appear brighter. Furthermore, since the tone of the extra light reflected is on the blue side of the spectrum, this blue-violet tinge will complement any yellowishness present on the fibre to make it look whiter as well as brighter. The chemical structures of optical brightening agents are complicated; many formulas are trade secrets.

Though the action of optical brighteners resembles old-style laundry blueing in some ways, the two methods must not be confused. In the old method, a blue dye or pigment is adsorbed onto the fibre; this blue tends to absorb yellow light falling on it, reflecting light richer in blue. With blueing, however, the fabric absorbs some of the light falling on it and hence reflects less light than it receives. Thus, the fabric looks whiter, not brighter. Laundry
blueing

Sequestering or chelating agents.   EDTA (ethylenediamine tetraacetic acid) or its sodium salt has the property of combining with certain metal ions to form a molecular complex that locks up or chelates the calcium ion so that it no longer exhibits ionic properties. In hard water, calcium and magnesium ions are thus inactivated, and the water is effectively softened. EDTA can form similar complexes with other metallic ions.

Abrasives.   Water-insoluble minerals such as talc, diatomaceous earth, silica, marble, volcanic ash (pumice), chalk, feldspar, quartz, and sand are often powdered and added to soap or synthetic detergent formulations. Abrasives of an organic nature, such as sawdust, are also used.

Soap production processes.   Several techniques are employed in making soap, most of which involve heat. Processes can be either continuous or on a batch basis.

Boiling process.   Still widely used by small and medium-sized producers is the classical boiling process. Its object is to produce neat soap in purified condition, free from glycerin. Neat soap is the starting material for making bars, flakes, beads, and powders. The boiling process

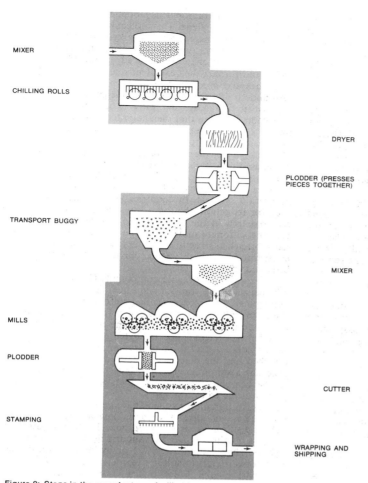

MIXER

CHILLING ROLLS

DRYER

PLODDER (PRESSES
PIECES TOGETHER)

TRANSPORT BUGGY

MIXER

MILLS

PLODDER

CUTTER

STAMPING

WRAPPING AND
SHIPPING

Figure 2: Steps in the manufacture of milled bar soap.
Drawing by D. Meighan based on N. Shreve, *Chemical Process Industries*, 3rd ed. (1967); McGraw-Hill Book Co.

is conducted in a series of steps called changes; these occur in the kettle (called the pan in Great Britain).

In the first step, melted fats are placed in the kettle, and caustic soda solution is added gradually. The whole mass is then boiled with open steam from perforated coils within the kettle. The saponification reaction now takes place; the mass gradually thickens or emulsifies as the caustic soda reacts with the fat to produce both soap and glycerin.

Salting out   To separate the glycerin from the soap, the pasty boiling mass is treated with brine. Contents of the kettle salt out, or separate, into an upper layer that is a curdy mass of impure soap, and a lower layer, that consists of an aqueous salt solution with the glycerin dissolved in it. Thus the basis of glycerin removal is the solubility of glycerin and the insolubility of soap in salt solution. The slightly alkaline salt solution, termed spent lye, is extracted from the bottom of the pan or kettle and subsequently treated for glycerin recovery.

The grainy, curdy mass of soap remaining in the kettle after the spent lye has been removed contains any unsaponified fat (usually traces that escaped reaction during saponification) plus dirt and colouring matter present in the original oils. During the next step, called strong change, strong caustic solution is added to the mass, which is then boiled to remove the last of the free fat.

The final stage, called pitching and settling, transforms the mass into neat soap and removes dirt and colouring matter. After the strong change, the soap may be given one or more salt-water washes to remove free alkali, or it may be pitched directly. Pitching involves boiling the mass with added water until a concentration is attained that causes the kettle contents to separate into two layers. The upper layer is neat soap, sometimes called kettle soap, of almost constant composition for a given fat (about 70% soap, 30% water); the lower, called nigre,

varies in soap content from 15% to 40%. Since colouring matter, dirt, salt, alkali, and metal soaps are soluble in nigre but relatively insoluble in neat soap, and since most of the impurities are dense and tend to settle, the nigre layer takes these from the neat soap.

Continuous soapmaking—the hydrolyzer process. The boiling process is very time consuming; settling takes days. To produce soap in quantity, huge kettles must be used. For this reason, continuous soapmaking has largely replaced the old boiling process. Most continuous processes today employ fatty acids in the saponification reaction in preference to natural fats and oils. These acids do not contain impurities and, as explained at the beginning of this section, produce water instead of glycerin when they react with alkali. Hence, it is not necessary to remove impurities or glycerin from soap produced with fatty acids. Furthermore, control of the entire process is easier and more precise. The fatty acids are proportionally fed into the saponification system either by flowmeter or by metering pump; final adjustment of the mixture is usually made by use of a pH meter (to test acidity and alkalinity) and conductivity-measuring instruments.

The continuous hydrolyzer process begins with natural fat that is split into fatty acids and glycerin by means of water at high temperature and pressure in the presence of a catalyst, zinc soap. The splitting reaction is carried on continuously, usually in a vertical column 50 feet (15 metres) or more in height. Molten fat and water are introduced continuously into opposite ends of the column; fatty acids and glycerin are simultaneously withdrawn. Next, the fatty acids are distilled under vacuum to effect purification. They are then neutralized with an alkali solution such as sodium hydroxide (caustic soda) to yield neat soap. In toilet-soap manufacture, a surplus of free fatty acid, often in combination with such superfatting agents as olive oil or coconut oil, is left or added at the final stage so that there is no danger of too much alkali in the final product. The entire hydrolyzer process, from natural fat to final marketable product, requires a few hours, as compared with the four to 11 days necessary for the old boiling process. The by-product glycerol is purified and concentrated as the fatty acid is being produced.

Cold and semiboiled methods. In the cold method, a fat and oil mixture, often containing a high percentage of coconut or palm-kernel oil, is mixed with the alkali solution. Slightly less alkali is used than theoretically required in order to leave a small amount of unsaponified fat or oil as a superfatting agent in the finished soap. The mass is mixed and agitated in an open pan until it begins to thicken. Then it is poured into frames and left there to saponify and solidify.

In the semiboiled method, the fat is placed in the kettle and alkali solution is added while the mixture is stirred and heated but not boiled. The mass saponifies in the kettle and is poured from there into frames, where it solidifies. Because these methods are technically simple and because they require very little investment for machinery, they are ideal for small factories.

Finishing operations. Finishing operations transform the hot mass coming from the boiling pan or from continuous production equipment into the end product desired. For laundry soap, the soap mass is cooled in frames or cooling presses, cut to size, and stamped. If soap flakes, usually transparent and very thin, are to be the final product, the soap mass is extruded into ribbons, dried, and cut to size. For toilet soap, the mass is treated with perfumes, colours, or superfatting agents, is vacuum dried, then cooled and solidified. The dried solidified soap is homogenized (often by milling or crushing) in stages to produce various degrees of fineness (see Figure 2). Air can be introduced under pressure into the warm soap mass as it leaves the vacuum drier to produce a floating soap. Medicated soaps are usually toilet soaps with special additives, chlorinated phenol, xylenol derivatives, and similar compounds, added to give a deodorant and disinfectant effect. As mentioned above, shaving creams are based on potassium and sodium soap combinations.

Anionic detergents. Among synthetic detergents, commonly referred to as syndets, anionic-active types are the most important. The molecule of an anionic-active synthetic detergent is a long carbon chain to which a sulfo group (–SO₃) is attached, forming the negatively charged (anionic) part. This carbon chain must be so structured that a sulfo group can be attached easily by industrial processes (sulfonation), which may employ sulfuric acid, oleum (fuming sulfuric acid), gaseous sulfur trioxide, or chlorosulfonic acid.

Raw materials. An important group of raw materials for anionic synthetic detergents is that of the fatty alcohols. Development of commercially feasible methods in the 1930s for obtaining these provided a great impetus to synthetic-detergent production. The first fatty alcohols used in production of synthetic detergents were derived from body oil of the sperm or bottle-nosed whale (sperm oil). Efforts soon followed to derive these materials from the less expensive triglycerides (coconut and palm-kernel oils, and tallow). The first such process, the Bouveault-Blanc method of 1903, long used in laboratories, employed metallic sodium; it became commercially feasible in the 1950s when sodium prices fell to acceptable levels. When the chemical processing industry developed high-pressure hydrogenation and oil-hardening processes for natural oils, detergent manufacturers began to adopt these methods for reduction of coconut oil, palm-kernel oil, and other oils into fatty alcohols. Synthetic fatty alcohols have been produced from ethylene; the process, known as the Alfol process, employs diethylaluminum hydride.

Soon after World War II, another raw material, alkylbenzene, became available in huge quantities. Today it is the most important raw material for synthetic detergent production; about 50% of all synthetic detergents produced in the United States and western Europe are based on it. The alkyl molecular group has in the past usually been C₁₂H₂₄ (tetrapropylene) obtained from the petrochemical gas propylene. This molecular group is attached to benzene by a reaction called alkylation, with various catalysts, to form the alkylbenzene. By sulfonation, alkylbenzene sulfonate is produced; marketed in powder and liquid form, it has excellent detergent and cleaning properties and produces high foam.

An undesirable effect of the alkylbenzene sulfonates, in contrast to the soap and fatty-alcohol-based synthetic detergents has been that their high foam is difficult to get rid of. This foam remains on the surface of waste water as it passes from towns through drains to sewers and sewage systems, then to rivers, and finally to the sea. It has caused difficulties with river navigation; and because the foam retards biological degradation of organic material in sewage, it caused problems in sewage-water regeneration systems. In countries where sewage water is used for irrigation, the foam was also a problem. Intensive research in the 1960s led to changes in the alkylbenzene sulfonate molecules. The tetrapropylene, which has a branched structure, was replaced by an alkyl group consisting of a straight carbon chain which is more easily broken down by bacteria.

Processes. The organic compounds (fatty alcohols or alkylbenzene) are transformed into anionic surface-active detergents by the process called sulfonation. Sulfation is the chemically exact term when a fatty alcohol is used and sulfonation when alkylbenzene is used. The difference between them is that the detergent produced from a fatty alcohol has a sulfate molecular group (–OSO₃Na) attached and the detergent produced from an alkylbenzene has a sulfonate group (–SO₃Na) attached directly to the benzene ring. Both products are similarly hydrophilic (attracted to water).

Recent sulfonation methods have revolutionized the industry; gaseous sulfur trioxide is now widely used to attach the sulfonate or sulfate group. The sulfur trioxide may be obtained either by vapourizing sulfuric acid anhydride (liquid stabilized SO₃) or by burning sulfur and thus converting it to sulfur trioxide.

The basic chemical reaction for a fatty alcohol is

$$RCH_2OH + SO_3 \longrightarrow RCH_2OSO_3H,$$

$$\underset{\text{alcohol}}{\text{fatty}} + \underset{\text{trioxide}}{\text{sulfur}} = \underset{\text{hydrogen sulfate}}{\text{fatty alkyl}}$$

and for an alkylbenzene is

R in both reactions represents a hydrocarbon radical.

Following this, caustic soda solution is used to neutralize the acidic products of the reaction. Figure 3 shows the principles of this process.

Research on the part of the petrochemical industry has evolved new anionic synthetic detergents, such as directly sulfonated paraffinic compounds—alpha olefins, for example. Paraffins have been transformed directly into sulfonates by treatment with sulfur dioxide and air using a catalyst of radioactive cobalt.

Non-ionic detergents. The most important non-ionic detergents are obtained by condensing compounds having a hydrophobic molecular group, usually a hydroxyl (OH) group, with ethylene oxide or propylene oxide. The most usual compounds are either alkylphenol or a long chain alcohol having a hydroxyl group at the end of the molecule. During the condensation reaction, the ethylene oxide molecules form a chain which links to the hydroxyl group. The length of this chain and the structure of the alkylphenol or alcohol determine the properties of the detergent.

The reaction may take place continuously or in batches. It is strongly exothermic (heat producing), and both ethylene and propylene oxide are toxic and dangerously explosive. They are liquid only when under pressure. Hence, synthesis of these detergents requires specialized,

Marginal notes:

Alkylbenzene sulfonates and foam

Sulfonation and sulfation

most universally present in laundry soaps. These materials give increased detergent action. The most important are sodium silicate (water glass), sodium carbonate (soda ash), and various phosphates; the latter have contributed to the problem of waste-water pollution by contributing nutrients which sustain undesirable algae and bacteria growth, and much work is being done to find acceptable builders which may replace, at least partially, phosphates. The slurry is atomized in heat to remove practically all the water. The powder thus obtained consists of hollow particles, called beads, that dissolve quickly in water and are practically dust free. Another portion of the syndets is transformed into liquid detergent products and used primarily for hand dishwashing. Though syndet pastes are seldom produced, solid products, manufactured in the same way as toilet or laundry soap, were being sold in greater and greater quantity in the 1970s. Sodium perborate is sometimes added to the spray-dried beads to increase cleaning power by oxidation. Enzymes may be added as well. Many modern washing powders combine synthetic detergents, anionic and non-ionic, with soap, to give maximum efficiency and controlled foam for use in household washing machines.

Applications and economic aspects. Soap and detergents are used mainly for cleaning and washing in the household but also in textile, metal, and paper industries and commercial laundries. Wherever strongly alkaline or acid or inorganic salts are used, synthetic detergents have replaced soap in industry.

Table 1: Annual Per Capita Consumption of Soap and Synthetic Detergents in U.S. and Western Europe, 1966 (kilograms)

U.S.	18.8	France	12.4	Portugal	9.2
Switzerland	14.1	Canada	11.9	Spain	9.0
West Germany	13.1	Italy	11.6	Finland	8.6
Belgium–		The Netherlands	10.7	Greece	6.2
Luxembourg	13.0	Norway	10.7	Ireland	6.2
Sweden	12.9	Austria	10.6		
Denmark	12.5	Iceland	9.8		

Table 1 shows annual per capita consumption of soap and synthetic detergents (1966) in the U.S. and western Europe. The lower figures in some countries are partly explained by their use of laundry soap, which is more concentrated than compounded soap or syndet products and used in smaller quantities by weight. Table 2 shows world soap and synthetic-detergent production (1967).

Table 2: World Soap and Syndet Production, 1967 (000 tons)

Soaps	
Laundry soap	4,464
Toilet soap	1,293
Soap flakes	121
Soap powder	528
Syndets	
Syndet powder	5,174
Liquid syndets	1,280
Scouring powder	686
Other syndet products	971
Total soap and syndet production	14,760

Source: Henkel, *Chemische Industrie*, 1969.

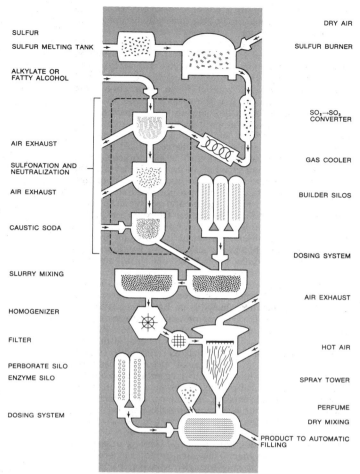

Figure 3: Steps in the manufacture of synthetic detergents.
Drawing by D. Meighan

SULFUR
SULFUR MELTING TANK
ALKYLATE OR FATTY ALCOHOL
AIR EXHAUST
SULFONATION AND NEUTRALIZATION
AIR EXHAUST
CAUSTIC SODA
SLURRY MIXING
HOMOGENIZER
FILTER
PERBORATE SILO
ENZYME SILO
DOSING SYSTEM

DRY AIR
SULFUR BURNER
SO₂→SO₃ CONVERTER
GAS COOLER
BUILDER SILOS
DOSING SYSTEM
AIR EXHAUST
HOT AIR
SPRAY TOWER
PERFUME
DRY MIXING
PRODUCT TO AUTOMATIC FILLING

explosion-proof equipment and careful, skilled supervision and control.

Other non-ionic detergents are condensed from fatty acids and organic amines (alkylol amines). They are important as foam stabilizers in liquid detergent preparations and shampoos.

Some non-ionic synthetic detergents may cause problems with unwanted foam in waste-water systems; the problem is not as serious as with anionic synthetic detergents, however.

Cationic detergents. Cationic detergents contain a long-chain cation that is responsible for their surface-active properties. Marketed in powder form, as paste, or in aqueous solution, they possess important wetting, foaming, and emulsifying properties but are not good detergents. Most applications are in areas in which anionic detergents cannot be used. Cationic-active agents are used as emulsifying agents for asphalt in the surfacing of roads; these emulsions are expected to "break" soon after being applied and to deposit an adhering coat of asphalt on the surface of the stone aggregate. These agents absorb strongly on minerals, particularly on silicates, and therefore make a strong bond between the asphalt and the aggregate. Cationic detergents also possess excellent germicidal properties and are utilized in surgery in dilute form.

Ampholytic detergents. Ampholytic detergents are used for special purposes in shampoos, cosmetics, and in the electroplating industry. They are not consumed in large quantities at present.

Finishing synthetic detergents. The largest quantities of synthetic detergents are consumed in the household in the form of spray-dried powders. They are produced from an aqueous slurry, which is prepared continuously or in batches and which contains all the builder components. Builders, consisting of certain alkaline materials, are al-

BIBLIOGRAPHY. I. DAVIDSOHN et al., *Soap Manufacture*, vol. 1 (1953); A.M. SCHWARTZ, J.W. PERRY, and J. BERCH, *Surface Active Agents and Detergents*, vol. 2 (1958); A. DAVIDSOHN and B.M. MILWIDSKY, *Synthetic Detergents* (1967); J.G. KANE, *Soaps: Their Chemistry and Technology* (1959); W.W. NIVEN (ed.), *Industrial Detergency* (1955); J.L. MOLLIET, B. COLLIE, and W. BLACK, *Surface Activity: The Physical Chemistry, Technical Applications, and Chemical Constitution of Synthetic Surface-Active Agents*, 2nd ed. rev. (1961). Information may also be found in chapters on soaps and detergents in A.E. BAILEY, *Industrial Oil and Fat Products*, 3rd ed. by D. SWERN (1964); and in R.N. SHREVE, *Chemical Process Industries*, 3rd ed. (1967).

(A.S.D.)

Social and Cultural Change

Social and cultural change consists of the modification of society and culture through time—modification in social institutions, ideas, values, technology, and other products of human interaction. The current body of knowledge regarding social and cultural change is neither large nor certain. It began barely two centuries ago to differentiate from the vast accumulation of philosophic and religious commentary on permanence and change. It consists of a heritage of grand theory, often utilizing analogies between organic growth and human progress, deriving from the thought of such philosophers as Comte and Oswald Spengler, continuing into the late 20th century through the contributions of the English historian Arnold Toynbee and the American anthropologist Alfred Louis Kroeber. It is composed also of ideas drawn from the great 19th-century efforts to compare all human societies, past and present and simple and complex, in terms of rationally conceived evolutionary stages from "savagery" to "civilization," as defined by such anthropologists as Sir Edward Burnett Tylor, Lewis Henry Morgan, and Henry Maine (see CIVILIZATION AND CULTURAL EVOLUTION). A third component derives primarily from the ideas and voluminous analyses of processes of industrialization and technological innovation inaugurated by Marx and furthered in different ways by subsequent investigators. A fourth major influence has stemmed from detailed studies of the effects of Western contacts on primitive or peasant societies in the 20th century.

THE CONCEPT OF SOCIAL AND CULTURAL CHANGE

Historical background. The great speculative literature on change, to which men have turned for comfort and inspiration for thousands of years, derives from both East and West and includes the conceptions of cycles in human affairs as offered in the *Upaniṣads* of India and in the great sermon of the preacher in the Jewish book of Ecclesiastes. It includes the concept of the unchanging and eternal as enunciated by Gautama Buddha in his view of Nirvāṇa and the realm of unchanging ideas as defined by Plato. It includes the ancient Greco-Roman conception of the universe as an ever-changing flow and the Confucian conception of an ongoing familial network of mutual obligations among sons and fathers.

The first known questions about the nature of permanence and change were asked in Greece by Heracleitus around 500 BC. What he and philosophers to follow him were concerned with, however, were not social and cultural phenomena but rather the physical elements, fire, water, earth, and air. It required another 2,000 years before the question began to be asked specifically regarding men's social life. In 1748 Montesquieu in *De l'esprit des lois* (*The Spirit of Laws*) encouraged the process of objectifying human institutions by asking about the nature of law and how laws vary. It has been no simple matter for men to develop concepts by means of which they are able to stand outside their customs and analyze them quite apart from making judgments on them. Although beginnings were made by Montesquieu and later by the English jurist Henry Maine with regard to the law and by the English philologist Sir William Jones and later the Brothers Grimm with regard to language, it was not until the 1870s that a general concept came into use that moved men decisively in the direction of the necessary objectification. This was the concept of culture, as presented by the English anthropologist Edward Burnett Tylor, which has ever since been accepted largely in his terms, namely, as having the meaning of "all those habits and capabilities acquired by man as a member of society." The concept has aided immensely in enabling men to stand aside from their own learned behaviour and ways of thought and subject them to the kind of analysis that the sciences require.

"Culture," "social," and "change." Cultural change is now taken generally to mean change in any learned behaviour and beliefs and their products (such as tools, paintings, books, or dwellings). Cultural change deals, then, with changes in technology, in languages, in kinship systems, in political and economic institutions, in the arts, in human value orientations, in ideologies, and in religions, these being some of the generally accepted subdivisions of any culture.

Nevertheless, the concept is regarded by many social scientists as not the most useful for focussing attention on the locus of change in human institutions. For such students culture seems to refer to the inferred products of human interaction. As such it is an abstraction from many interactions, and it is the specific interactions that maintain social relationships and in which changes take place. For such investigators, it seems important that the term social be used for the phenomena under examination in order to keep a focus on the real world in which one observes people in action. The phenomena to be observed are for them social relations. On the surface, the distinction may not seem to be important. There are, however, important contributions to the understanding of cultural change in which a distinction between the social and the cultural has to be made. Clifford Geertz, an American anthropologist, for example, advocates a distinction between observable social interactions and the web of meanings that those actions have for the participants. He has pointed out how the ritual activities of migrants from rural to urban communities in Indonesia change before the meanings of those rituals do. Making a distinction between social interactions and their significance provides a basis for fruitfully analyzing the effects of changing action patterns on the traditional culture. American sociologist Talcott Parsons has made a somewhat different, though related, distinction. Like many others, he sees "social" as referring to role relationships and the maintenance of these as constituting the social system, which exists in turn in an environment that includes a cultural system. Each type of social system depends for its existence on certain controlling cultural orientations or patterns. Changes in the cultural system immediately affect the social system and vice versa.

Although there is considerable agreement on the nature of the social and the cultural, there is less agreement on what constitutes change. This uncertainty is age-old and runs as a constant theme through the questions and answers of the philosophers. The old French saying "The more it changes the more it remains the same thing" expresses the bemusement with the passing scene and the paradox of its apparently ceaseless flow. If all is change, and there is no permanence, then the category cultural change has no utility or significance. Yet, in the face of the unmistakably constant flow of events, one must take the position that there are relatively unchanging features of societies and cultures; otherwise, one must abandon the concept of cultural change. There is a paradox here that must be resolved.

All societies exist by virtue of ceaseless interaction. Every member of a society is different, and consequently every combination of individuals in interaction is unrepeatable. There is indeed constant flow. It is only when one adopts the concept of role that one has a tool for distinguishing permanence and change. A role is that part of the behaviour of individuals in interaction that is traditional, which each expects of the other as a result of his having been socialized in that society. A social structure is maintained through the repetition in the role situations. The persistence of legal codes for decades, centuries, and even millennia with basic principles and even wording merely added to but not replaced, for example, is a phenomenon not so obvious but just as certain as the relatively frequent changes of the personnel who administer the legal codes. The persistence of such "products of interaction" as legal codes exemplifies the kind of permanence that characterizes human society. The ceaseless activities of judges, legislators, policemen, and citizens of the state constitute not change but structural stability.

As the processes of interaction go on, certain necessary functions are performed for the continuing existence of these social institutions. What looks to ordinary people like change, such as putting persons out of political office and putting others in, is actually a process of renewal of personnel enabling the state structure to continue to be the same structure that it has been. Every society has its

Concept of culture

Importance of social roles

renewal processes; these are not change but maintenance. Processes of renewal of personnel, processes of intensification of solidarity of groups, processes of distribution of economic goods and their production, these and many others are maintenance processes. They are not the focus of concern in the effort to understand sociocultural change.

The maintenance of social and cultural systems may be seen to take place in rhythmic cycles; that is to say, in many recurrent series of events. Not only the more obvious sequences, such as recurrent elections characterizing certain kinds of political organizations, but also shorter cycles, such as daily gathering of a family for a meal in the evening with perhaps some group ritual or the seasonal recurrences of planting and harvesting—such cyclic activities are the stuff of which the persistence of groups and their cultures are made. There are, however, other kinds of recurrent sequences that are not clearly part of the maintenance processes of societies. These have been regarded by some students of cultural change as important for understanding the dynamics of societies. They range from cycles in women's dress through recurrent rises and falls in prices and wages to the rise and decline of "civilizations."

Older, related concepts.   In trying to understand the scope of current concepts of sociocultural change, it is necessary to dispense with older views of the subject. For many decades, interest was largely confined to certain kinds of long-term change called cultural or social evolution. Many 19th-century anthropologists, social scientists, and philosophers focussed attention on evolutionary change. Each varying specific conception became a hook on which information about different social systems was hung. The most important of these was probably Herbert Spencer's view, which, influenced by the biology of the time, held that human societies in the long run become more heterogeneous and differentiated as they adapt to different environments. His vast collection of data for demonstration of this long-term trend was not much used by other cultural evolutionists; but his view is essentially that which remains most influential in the interpretation of succession of technologies today. Evolutionary development, however, whether in Spencer's terms or others, does not subsume the subject of cultural change. Evolutionary processes are only one kind of change process among many that exist.

Still less is social and cultural change to be identified with that pervasive and deeply influential conception of long-term change that has been called the idea of progress, a concept that has been a dominating influence for 200 years or more. The idea that societies and cultures move more or less steadily toward better and better conditions for men has affected numerous students of sociocultural change. This assumption was inherent in much of the work of the students of cultural evolution in the 19th century, when it was held that all non-Western societies were moving toward economic, political, and religious conditions comparable to those prevailing in the countries of western Europe. The ethnocentrism of these early investigators has been repudiated long since, even though their works are still read and used. Nevertheless, something very like the 19th-century concept of progress toward west European conditions pushes unsuspected into current comparative studies of "modernization" and industrialization. Not only the idea that change moves inevitably in the direction of west European and North American technology and economy but also the value judgment that this is somehow good creeps in. Progress as defined by members of various societies is an interesting phenomenon and must be studied, but the tendency, long existent and still present, of Westerners to assume that all change or at least change most worthy of study is a progress toward conditions that they value highly runs counter to sound method.

THE PROCESS OF SOCIOCULTURAL CHANGE

The general process of sociocultural change is characterized by three phases: innovation, selection, and integration.

The innovative phase.   Innovation includes any new combination of cultural elements. The key word here is combination, for innovations are made up not out of thin air but of well-known elements of the cultural system. They are new in the sense that, under conditions favourable to innovation, some member of a society or some group puts familiar items into new relationships. Most people are aware of the process of innovation whereby the automobile emerged as a new combination of wheels, steam engine, horse-carriage body, and so on or whereby the clock emerged in the monasteries of medieval Europe as the combination of gears, coiled springs, and escapement, all of which had long been known as separate items but not in combination. People in fact are inclined to associate innovation exclusively with mechanical invention, so well have the records on technological innovations been compiled. But the same sort of recombination of familiar elements into new structures has been documented for social organization, such as the city-manager form of municipal government, and for belief systems, such as the Black Muslim doctrines of the 20th century.

The process of combination itself is understood better than the general sociocultural conditions that encourage or inhibit innovation. The analysis of specific innovations often seems to be based on an assumption that the process is an individual psychological matter. Some writers, for example, have emphasized the importance of what they call dissident, disaffected, and resentful types of individuals in the creation of innovations. Others have not only pointed to the innovation-mindedness of individuals but have also emphasized the kinds of social relations and cultural orientations that tend to encourage the development of such individuals in certain types of societies. It is clear enough that certain societies do put high value on innovative activities. One is familiar with this tendency in industrialized societies, which establish groups of individuals organized specifically, as in modern chemical and automobile industries, to produce new products. Such organized innovation, it should be noted, is nevertheless guided by what have become traditional interests in the industrialized societies. Innovations in technology are sometimes sought as means of maintaining the social or economic status quo. The question indeed may be asked as to whether such planned activity should be classified as true innovation.

If the study of sociocultural change is to avoid bogging down in the analysis of fads and fashions—that is to say, unimportant variations—distinctions among types of innovations might be recognized. No terminology has yet been developed for this purpose, but perhaps one kind of innovation might be designated as novelty. Innumerable new combinations are produced daily in every modern society. Most never go through the third phase of the change process—integration. They remain unimportant with reference to any aspect of the cultural system, are accepted only briefly, and ultimately disappear without leaving any mark.

The selective phase.   The second phase of the general process is selection—also called acceptance, diffusion, and so on. Change in the sociocultural system can come about only if individuals accept the innovations into their stock of behaviour and beliefs. The acceptance is a process of social interactions. It involves a series of choices or decisions by individuals or groups of individuals.

In complex societies it is normal to have a large number of alternatives. Innovations may be created and added to the ranks of the alternatives. This area of alternatives must be understood to be the arena in which competition among elements decisive for the future takes place. A shift in the number of individuals choosing one alternative as opposed to another may begin a trend in a direction leading to extensive reorganization of the whole society and its culture. Choice, or selection among alternatives, may thus be seen as a necessary phase in all sociocultural change.

It should be clear that a given trend toward change may become apparent only in this so-called second phase; the implications of an invention begin to be developed not in terms of its being an alternative but in terms of its becom-

Cultural evolution

Combination in innovation

The question of choice

ing the dominant mode of behaviour or belief. Under such circumstances what happens in the selective phase, rather than in the innovative phase, becomes the significant focus of analysis for understanding change.

The integrative phase.   The third phase, integration, is the process whereby the innovation (or selected alternative) is adapted to all parts of the system into which it enters. Admittedly, the integration begins with the selection phase, and the two phases are not really separable; but for analytical purposes they are better separated. The selection subprocess is best thought of as initial social interactions through which the innovation becomes established as part of the social system; it may then be regarded as extending farther as more and more persons accept the innovation throughout the society. In short, the selection phase focusses directly on the innovation. Then the integration phase might be regarded as the process of modification of the innovation as it is adapted to the beliefs, sentiments, and common understandings of the cultural system. This is a matter of mutual adaptation of both the innovation and the parts of the system.

Mutual adaptation of the innovation and the system

There are a host of rather well-known examples of integration. Following its initial acceptance by politically powerful families, the factory system in Japan, for instance, was adapted to Japanese family and ritual kinship institutions and to the village economies in such a manner as to make it quite different from the factory system developed in England. The whole story of this process of mutual adaptation or integration of the factory into Japanese social life and Japanese culture is very complex. Similarly, the integration of single elements, such as the automobile or the radio, into the sociocultural system of the United States, as traced in several studies, demonstrates very complex mutual adaptations. The continuing process of integration, moreover, seems often to have no end; it is not possible to pinpoint the time when Japanese feudal society became an industrialized society. Human interaction is a continuum, and it must be always arbitrary to say that the effects of the introduction of a certain innovation have come to a conclusion. The criteria for industrial society may be arbitrary, but there can be no question about a decisive difference between the Japan of the 1870s and the Japan of the 1970s.

DIFFERENT CONCEPTIONS OF CHANGE

Various specific processes of change have been identified within the general concept of sociocultural change.

Culture contact.   A variety of change that has attracted anthropologists for some 100 years has been called acculturation, or, more simply, culture contact—defined as all those processes that come into operation when societies with different cultures come into contact. Until recently this study was developed in the colonial areas of the European empires in Africa and Asia and among the "internal colonials" of the American countries. The term acculturation came to be used when contacts involved colonial people being subordinated and required to adjust to the cultures of the Western colonial powers.

Under colonial conditions, there was deemed to be a superordinate and subordinate society. In all such situations, the superordinate society made an effort to change the subordinate society in some way and even to direct that course of change in some degree. This change may occur only in certain specialized areas of contact, such as in employment in factories or plantations, or it may be on a very broad scale, as in the case of the Indians of the United States who experienced directed culture change through schools, jobs, agricultural development, household management, and many other aspects of life under the direction of the Bureau of Indian Affairs. Some writers have made a distinction between directed culture change and processes of change in which choice was free. The implication of the term is not that the management of change is successfully directed by the dominant society (frequently the results are the reverse from what it desires) but simply that the dominant society's cultural values and social sanctions become deeply involved in the subordinate society's life. The selection phase here is affected powerfully by the dominant society's interests.

A second distinctive feature of contact change has been called syncretism, or cultural fusion. The fusion of elements from diverse cultural sources—in religious belief and ritual, in the lexicons of languages, in technologies, and more recently in economic and political organization —testifies to the importance of this kind of ultimate integration of borrowed or imposed cultural elements in the growth of civilizations. Important in situations in which empires were built by conquest, it was also important in connection with the diffusion of the great world religions, and now, with the spread of industry and representative democracy, one finds again the great tendency to fuse and combine cultural elements. Cultural fusion may also take place whenever a receiving society tries to reject the dominant society's impositions, as in the well-studied phenomena of nativistic and nationalistic movements.

Cultural fusion

It is notable that the concept of acculturation, though developed in the study of "primitive" societies under colonial conditions, has larger and more current applications. Complex modern societies are composed of subsocieties often as different in cultural tradition, structure, and orientation as were isolated, simpler societies of the 19th century and the colonial powers that dominated them. Thus, within modern political units of nation-states there are contact situations characterized by phenomena similar to those of the earlier colonial environments.

Conflict and cooperation.   In the work of Marx, there is an explanation for sociocultural change, called dialectic, that has been of great influence. This concept, intended to account for change throughout human history, has been less and less accepted in the Western world and more and more in the Eastern; nevertheless, its influence in conflict theories of the causes of change is important. Change is initiated, according to the theory, by conflict between classes; that is, collectivities of individuals whose interests are determined and limited by their roles in the production process. In various forms, this view of the basic impetus for change is used in modern analysis. Some writers have used ideas regarding tension management and release; certain roles are said to have built into them the means of creating tensions among individuals. Societies may be forced to change their structure in an effort to alleviate tensions, or they may devise techniques that keep the tensions under control.

Marx and the concept of conflict

At present, perhaps equally vigorous as any conflict theory of change are theories of change through cooperation. There is a view, for instance, that, whenever individuals are brought into working relationships, their adaptations result in changes in the system of which they are a part. The change, in other words, is a result of bringing people together on a cooperative working basis. There is a question, however, as to how much, if any, of this represents sociocultural change and how much merely constitutes adjustments toward maintaining given systems.

Environment.   Theories have been offered from time to time regarding environmental influences on societies and cultures, theories sometimes labelled geographical, or environmental, determinism. Although the old ideas that man is somehow at the mercy of his environment have been abandoned, it is nevertheless recognized that the physical environment does set some measure of limitation on the possibilities for change and development in a society. The more isolated a society, as in the case of the Eskimos two centuries ago, the more important the influence of environment. Beginning in the 19th century, however, societies heretofore isolated have been subjected to contacts with the outside world, and relationships between any society and its immediate physical environment have assumed less and less importance. Nevertheless, in the study of change there has appeared a school of cultural ecology that is much concerned with the environmental influences and has focussed, for instance, on what has been called core culture; that is, those elements of a culture most positively and directly related to the environment. The core responds to changes in the environment, and the process of adaptation itself in turn affects the environment. As the ecologists have expanded their interest into modern societies, they have broadened

Cultural ecology

their conception to include the social as well as the physical environment, so that they take into consideration such factors as competition and cultural fusion.

A similar but theoretically much more elaborate approach characterizes the work of the sociologist Parsons, in whose view the social system exists in a complex environment composed of four other systems—namely, the cultural system, the personality system, the organic-life system, and the system of the physical environment. The cultural system is sometimes defined as the set of legitimizing values for the social order or as a network of roles in the social system. The personality system is regarded as the system of human motivations causing participation in the social systems. The organic-life system consists of the human biology out of which personality arises. And the physical environmental system is composed of the interrelated elements of climate, topography, fauna and flora, and so on. Each of these systems has its own requirements, and all are articulated. Changes in one may initiate a sequence of events ultimately reflected in the others. The environment is thus conceived as a number of specialized relationships, and change is conceived as originating in any of them.

Demographic factors. Another set of factors increasingly taken into consideration by students of sociocultural change is the demographic conditions. Population size and density, age, and sex distribution, and birth rates and death rates are dealt with as sources of extensive change. Social relations, whether in family, community, or state, must constantly adapt to the numbers and distributions of the human individuals involved. For instance, the worldwide lowering of the death rate has been accompanied by a whole series of other demographic shifts, and these seem to be correlated with industrialization. It is not that the demographic shifts entail industrialization or vice versa but merely that the demographic shifts and the processes of industrialization are correlated. Each is an indicator of the other, and thus, wherever there is evidence of a declining death rate, changes in the labour supply and other socioeconomic phenomena associated with the processes of industrialization can also be predicted.

Concept of social scale

Another approach involving efforts to understand the train of social and cultural changes accompanying population shifts is that of two British anthropologists, Godfrey and Monica Wilson. They phrase the analysis in terms of social scale, which has to do with the size or scope of a society but is not to be conceived in the simple terms of population rises and falls. Social scale is affected by changes in the number of people in a given area, but what is decisive with regard to the scale of the society is the number of people involved with one another in active social relations and the intensity—that is, the frequency —of those social interactions. Furthermore, social scale is affected by other things, such as the introduction or increase of literacy. Through reading, the scale of the society is increased, because people are in a sense interacting with persons not physically present. It should be clear that scale is no simple concept of population curve but is nevertheless much involved with changes in the population. The Wilsons have related increase in scale, as exemplified in European expansion into Africa, with a large number of correlated changes in the character of African societies, such as a decrease in the use of magic for control of the environment, an increase in contractual as contrasted with personal relations, and a development of social mobility.

The expectation of discovering a unitary theory of sociocultural change in the sense of a master single source of innovation, such as technology or the natural environment, has steadily faded. Instead, the analysis of sequences of events is carried on in terms of many factors that in combination, it is assumed, encourage innovation or the selection of those alternatives that lead decisively to one or another kind of change.

BIBLIOGRAPHY. WILBERT E. MOORE, *Social Change* (1963), is the broadest and most compact summary of our knowledge of sociocultural change. All others, except for a textbook or two like BRYCE F. RYAN, *Social and Cultural Change* (1969); and DON MARTINDALE, *Social Life and Cultural Change* (1962),

are specialized in some direction or reflect only the interests of a single discipline. AMITAI and EVA ETZIONI (eds.), *Social Change: Sources, Patterns, and Consequences* (1964), achieves a broad survey by means of quotations from major thinkers and investigators. Among classics from which ideas are constantly drawn, but which offer special viewpoints rather than broad coverage are: HERBERT SPENCER, *The Principles of Sociology*, 3 vol. (1876–96); FERDINAND TOENNIES, *Gemeinschaft und Gesellschaft* (1887; Eng. trans., *Community and Society*, 1957); MAX WEBER, *Wirtschaft und Gesellschaft*, pt. 1 (1922; Eng. trans., *The Theory of Social and Economic Organization*, 1947); WILLIAM F. OGBURN, *Social Change, with Respect to Culture and Original Nature* (1922; rev. ed., 1950); PITIRIM A. SOROKIN, *Social and Cultural Dynamics*, 4 vol. (1937–41); and A.L. KROEBER, *Configurations of Cultural Growth* (1944). H.G. BARNETT, *Innovation: The Basis of Cultural Change* (1953), is the most comprehensive summary of what has been called the first phase of sociocultural change. Limited largely to contact situations between industrialized and nonindustrialized societies, GEORGE M. FOSTER, *Traditional Cultures: And the Impact of Technological Change* (1962); and CHARLES J. ERASMUS, *Man Takes Control* (1961), nevertheless attempt interesting generalizations about the selection process. CHARLES P. LOOMIS, *Social Systems: Essays on Their Persistence and Change* (1960), discusses all phases of change in a special framework. MELVILLE J. HERSKOVITS, *Cultural Dynamics* (1964); and GODFREY and MONICA WILSON, *The Analysis of Social Change* (1965), are inclusive in their handling of processes, but nevertheless reflect the peculiar (and fruitful) biases of anthropologists. JULIAN H. STEWARD, *Theory of Culture Change* (1955), focusses on multilinear evolution but also summarizes an ecological approach to cultural change. Although outdated in some ways, still one of the most basic discussions of acculturation is RALPH LINTON (ed.), *Acculturation in Seven American Indian Tribes* (1940).

(E.H.S.)

Social and Welfare Services

Terminology

The terms "social service," "social work," and "welfare service," and such related phrases as "social administration" and "social welfare administration" and most of the policies and programs involving these terms are essentially formulations and practices of the 20th century. Admittedly in some form or other, most of the things done today by individuals, charitable societies, or governments as social and welfare services have been done in the past in many societies. The Mosaic Law, the sociopolitical systems of classical Greece and the Roman Empire, the edicts of Aśoka, the simple rules of early Christian communities, and the institutions of family, village, and caste in India, to mention only a few instances, contained the elements of what are today called social and welfare services. The Elizabethan English are known for their pioneering work in some fields of social and welfare services, which they called "relief of the paupers." Closer to current times, the Victorian reformers who were distressed by poverty, child neglect, and other social ills were pioneers in many of today's social and welfare services, although they too had called such services by various other names such as "organized charity," "philanthropic work," or "relief of destitution."

There are no universally valid definitions of such terms as "social services" and "welfare services." Some countries, notably the newly independent and developing countries of the East, have attempted to apply the term social services to those services, such as education and health, that are addressed to the general population and to apply the term welfare services to services rendered to vulnerable groups—groups that are socially, economically, physically, or mentally handicapped or special groups like children, youth, or the aged. Thus welfare services would apply to those persons who because of the misfortunes of circumstances have tended to lag behind or fall by the wayside.

Another classification of social and welfare services focusses on their remedial, preventive, and supportive roles. Remedial services express the basic humanitarian and social responsibility of society toward people in dire need or distress. They seek to meet the special needs of various sections of the population, such as the young, the old, the destitute, and the handicapped. Such aims may be achieved through a variety of needed services on the welfare front and through a redistribution of income in favour of the needy on the economic front. Preventive services seek to lessen the stresses and strains of life resulting from social and technological changes. They try to provide built-in safeguards to meet the problems facing individuals and families, particularly in times of economic growth. If effective, they should reduce the need for more expensive remedial programs. Supportive services deal with educational programs, health services, population policies, manpower planning, employment and training, and community development projects.

Broadly speaking, there have been two rationales for social and welfare services. The "residual" view considered them as a collection of emergency measures to be provided when normal mechanisms—including the market economy, the individual, and the family—failed to meet the needs of the people. This view has been replaced in modern times by the "institutional" view, which accepts social and welfare services as a necessary function of any society, not only to provide for unmet needs but to serve individuals and groups positively so that they may develop and achieve to the fullest extent possible.

The background of social and welfare services

MODERN INFLUENCES

Factors that seem to have affected the status and course of social and welfare services in developed countries have been growth of population, changes in the composition of labour force, the change from agricultural to industrial employment, migration from rural to urban areas, changes in the pattern of family life, and the progress of medical and social sciences leading to a better understanding of human needs, physical, psychological, and social, and the provisions for meeting them.

On the continents of Asia and Africa, where traditional economic and social institutions have been functioning undisturbed for centuries, the dramatic changes trailing technological advances in the industrial and agricultural fields often have led to the breakdown of the built-in systems of caring for the individual and family. The close ties of kinship in India, for example, have provided a measure of economic, emotional, and social security in the past, but they could not function effectively in the changed circumstances of today. The attainment of independence by about 600,000,000 people in Asia following World War II and the wave of rising expectations among them have greatly influenced the course of social and welfare services. In particular, the population explosion in the developing countries, where widespread poverty and scarcity of resources are already limiting the scope of economic and social progress, creates special problems in the provision of social and welfare services. The level of fertility clearly marks off the developing countries from the rest, with the developed countries consistently having a birthrate that is just half of that in the developing countries. This has many implications for social and welfare services, particularly in attempts to lower the birthrate in the developing countries, which can least afford to have the kind of population growth that they are experiencing.

Age distribution also shows much variation. Censuses in the late 1960s show that younger persons (0–19 age group) in more than 16 developing countries comprise from 49 to 55 percent of the population, whereas they represent only between 31 and 42 percent in the developed countries. Thus the problem in the developing countries is that the needs of the young persons will consume a proportionately higher share of the national income for social and welfare programs, and it is significant to note that youth represent largely an economically unproductive group. This would affect savings and investment in other fields.

The proportion of those above 65 years of age was estimated in the late 1960s as only 3 percent of the population in the developing countries, whereas it was about 10 percent for the developed countries of Europe and North America and about 7 percent for Oceania and the Soviet Union. The dependency ratio—the ratio of consumers to producers—reflects the proportion of those under 15 years of age and those above 65 to the rest of the popula-

New population growths

tion. This is highest in the developing areas of Africa, Asia, and Latin America, where it ranges between 79 and 86, whereas it is only 63 to 66 in North America, Oceania, and the Soviet Union, and 59 for Europe. The world average is 72.

The average life expectancy has shown much advancement, particularly in the developed countries. Norwegians, for instance, have an average life expectancy of 71 years for males and 76 for females. The proportion of old and young persons in the populations greatly determines the social and welfare services needed.

One of the major changes in the composition of the labour force that has had a far-reaching impact on social and welfare services is the increase in the proportion of women in the labour force. The increased participation of women, a large proportion of whom are working mothers, both in the developed and developing countries, has created the need for new social and welfare services to deal with the management of home and children. In the United States the total labour force increased from 41,600,000 in 1920 to 82,000,000 in 1970, and the number of women in the labour force increased in the same period from 8,500,000 to 31,000,000. The proportion of women employed in the different branches of the economy in the Soviet Union varies from 46 to 86, women dominating in fields like public health and education. In the Soviet Union, it is a criminal offense to refuse to employ a pregnant woman or a nursing mother.

New female roles

Finally, the rapidly increasing urbanization has thrown up many new challenges. Whereas the total world population increased by 61 percent from 1920 to 1960, the urban population increased by 200 percent. The projections for urban population growth show that by 1980 about one-third of the world population will be living in urban localities, although the increase in the developed countries is expected to be 52 percent, as contrasted with a 24 percent increase in developing countries. These trends call for changes in approach to and emphasis on problems of social and welfare services in the urban areas.

HISTORICAL BACKGROUND

The history of social and welfare services can be traced to the personal charity that has characterized human society from very early times. Either as a natural expression of feelings of compassion or in a pursuit of virtue, individuals have always exercised personal charity, but this seldom has been an adequate answer to problems of need and distress. So from time to time groups of people and governments have sought to meet current need in a variety of ways. Most of these have been attempts at organizing charity and administering it with legal or ecclesiastical sanction. The English Poor Law of 1601 in the reign of the first Elizabeth (popularly known as the Elizabethan Poor Law) is an instance in point. Here the responsibility for poor relief was entrusted to the parish. Poor relief in the United States in the 17th and 18th centuries followed the broad framework of the Elizabethan Poor Law. Paupers received a little relief, but the treatment and punishments that they had to endure for the violation even of the simplest of regulations included severe penalties. It was only in the 18th century that the use of almshouses and workhouses became common. Earlier the poor were "auctioned" and given away to the lowest bidder who "took care" of them on payment of the sum agreed upon. The churches also used to be active in charitable work, but it was generally confined to their own members.

The course of social and welfare services in the 18th and 19th centuries was influenced by certain rigid attitudes that prevailed in the Western world. The most important among these was the belief that the government that governed least was the best and that it should confine itself to protecting its subjects from internal disturbance and external aggression. Basic to this was the assumption that the existing socioeconomic structure was sacrosanct and that the individual's freedom to pursue his best interests as he conceived them was immutable. The individual should find fulfillment in the expression of his free will and conversely should accept personal responsibility for failure. This kind of rugged individualism would admit of

Influence of laissez-faire

little interference with the individual's course of action, even if it were to prevent general poverty or destitution.

The dawn of the 20th century coincided with the first development of the systematic organization of charity and its objects. An attempt was made to delve deeper into the causes of social evils instead of confining one's concern only to external manifestations. A beginning in this direction was made by Charles Booth, who conducted investigations into the lives of the people of London; the publication of his report entitled *Life and Labour of the People in London* (17 volumes, 1892–1903) had far-reaching effect, for it revealed that about one-third of London's population lived in poverty. Seebohm Rowntree's investigations in York in 1900 led to nearly the same conclusions. These studies had a profound influence on the thinking on the subject of poverty and the ways of dealing with it.

Organized charity in the late 19th century

The best instance of institutionalized charity in the late 19th and early 20th centuries was the so-called charity organization movement that began in England in the 1860s and was later adopted in the United States. This represented a basic shift from personal philanthropy to more organized and institutionalized forms of charity. One of the criticisms of personal charity that were widely prevalent until then was that provision of indiscriminate relief, unrelated to needs, perpetuated the problem it sought to remedy. Edward Denison and Octavia Hill had founded the Charity Organization Society (COS) in London in 1869; Charles Loch, who remained its general secretary for four decades, was greatly instrumental in developing the principles and policies on which it worked. The COS was opposed to public relief and believed that charity should be dispensed in such a manner as to enable the recipients to become self-supporting. Basic to this approach was the conviction that the individual, and not the socioeconomic framework, was to be blamed for his failure. State intervention was to be kept to a minimum, implying that the problems of destitution and distress can be and should be dealt with by private charity. The greatest contribution of COS was to pioneer the system of investigation into the conditions of the recipients through its volunteers and, later, paid workers. Material relief on the basis of the assessed needs of the persons was to be given, but more important was to be the moral influence of the visitors in changing the life pattern of the poor.

Reformist developments toward government responsibility. The direction of social welfare in the 20th century was affected by a marked change in the conception of the role of the state in the provision of welfare services. Adherents of the philosophy of rugged individualism gave way increasingly to those advancing the philosophies of socialism and the welfare state and the betterment of the working classes. The existence of pockets of widespread poverty side by side with the prosperity of the few set some people thinking. The leaders of organized labour were the first to see that they had nothing to lose by state intervention. In Germany and England the political influence of the middle and working classes had already begun to assert itself in the area of social and welfare legislation. What was needed to wipe out the destitution of the poor and the insecurity of the working classes was a bold new initiative to deal with their problems—namely, comprehensive programs of social insurance and public assistance. Between 1897 and 1930 most of the western European countries had adopted social security measures, Germany starting them as early as 1883.

Early development of social insurance and public assistance

One of the distinct developments in the present century is the growing consensus that the leadership and intervention of the state is called for in order to provide a comprehensive system of social and welfare services at the national level. In the democratic countries—particularly in the developed countries, where private charity had been most active—a partnership has developed between governmental and voluntary agencies so that each supplements and supports the other. In socialistic countries the state has assumed complete charge of social and welfare services, and these are integrated into the state's overall system of planning for social, economic, and cultural growth and development. Increased expenditure from public funds for social and welfare services is a common trend in most countries of the world. In the developing countries, it is increasingly accepted that there is no alternative to government initiative and leadership for national programs. Confronted by mass socioeconomic problems and the inability of the existing institutions to deal with them, the governments have shown eagerness to participate in social and welfare programs. Often a paucity of resources, however, has prevented such governments from playing a more active role.

Professional social work. Charity workers, as the predecessors of modern social service workers, were a mixed lot but distinguishable by the end of the 19th century. Clergymen of many faiths, volunteer "friendly visitors" from the upper and middle classes, wealthy and influential citizens on agency boards and state boards of charities and correctional institutions, overseers of the poor, and paid charity agents were associated in a common effort. But as yet there was no bond of common education or united purpose to bind them together.

Mary Richmond in the United States was one of the first to proclaim that good intentions and common sense were not enough for charity work. She saw, too, that apprenticeship programs in each of the agencies were expensive, too narrowly focussed, and time consuming. With her successful proposal in 1897 that a training school of applied philanthropy be established, charity work took a giant step in the direction of social service as a profession. The time was ripe for action, for sociological studies of poverty and crime and the experience of charity workers in Europe and the United States had begun to give shape to a body of knowledge. The "scientific approach" to charity had given rise to defined methods of work. In London, as early as 1873, training activities initiated by Octavia Hill had evolved into a joint lecture and training program for both settlement and charity workers.

The New York Charity Organization Society launched a summer school of philanthropic work in 1898. A more significant step was taken in 1899 when an Institute for Social Work Training, the first full-scale school of social work in the world, was established in Amsterdam. That school offered a two-year course combining study of general sociological knowledge, socioeconomic problems, and legislation with supervised practical training in various fields of social work. By 1903 the training activities of the COS in England had led to the development of a two-year program of theory and practice in a formal School of Sociology. In 1904 the short course sponsored by the New York Charity Organization Society was transformed into a full-time one-year program in the New York School of Philanthropy, the first school of social work in the United States, which later became the Columbia University School of Social Work.

Early schools of social work

The success of these early efforts, coupled with the recognized need for trained minds as well as good hearts in charity work, led to widespread development of schools of social work. Boston followed New York in 1904; Chicago and Berlin were next in 1908. The movement spread rapidly within Europe and throughout the United States, and by 1920 it had reached Latin America, where the first school was established in Santiago, Chile. Charitable and philanthropic work had by then become generally known as social work or social service; its personnel were identified and designated as social workers.

In the developed countries, where a generally higher standard of living and programs of social security have tended to meet the material needs of most people, professional social work has been called upon to deal with psychosocial problems largely through casework. The casework method derived from the idea, developed early in the charity organization movement, that each person (or family) represented a unique situation, or constituted an individual case, and that helping individuals or small groups to help themselves was the central goal and purpose of social service. In later years, however, the new challenges arising in complex urban industrial societies have tended to shift the emphasis from individual or group problems to broad social evils. There have arisen several unified efforts to induce social as well as individ-

Casework

ual change, to prevent social problems as well as to alleviate their end results, to affect the destiny of large population groups as well as to help individuals and families and small groups. This transitional situation is also reflected in new attempts to synthesize sociological and psychological knowledge and to undergird professional practice with social work's own developing theory.

The emerging new notion of social service as a force and instrument in the promotion of planned social change enlarges the scope of professional social-work activity, which, traditionally, has been associated with such fields of practice as child and family welfare, medical and psychiatric social work, school social work, corrections, and group services. To these significant tasks, the social-work profession, in the view of practitioners, is now adding newer responsibilities of joining with other disciplines to attack mass poverty at its source, to seek out and prevent the problems that blight the lives of people in affluent as well as struggling new societies, and even, it has been said, to reshape social structures in directions thought to provide new and better opportunities for productive and satisfying living. In developing countries, in particular, the methods of community organization seem to have far more relevance than casework or group work because mass problems are not amenable to individual treatment.

In addition to the basic methods of casework, group work, and community organization (which deal respectively with individuals, groups and communities), there have developed the methods of social research, social administration, and social action. In an earlier day, as already suggested, there tended to be a preoccupation with casework, and aspiring social workers tended to get almost all their training in casework. But more recently the trend in Europe, and to some extent even in the United States and Canada, is toward the "multipurpose" social-work functionary trained and disciplined in the use of all the different social-work methods, so that he can judiciously use appropriate methods as demanded by the circumstances. In some of the developing countries—particularly India—specialization in training and practice has developed not by methods but by fields, such as medical social work, school social work, and family and child welfare. In India, labour welfare and personnel management are taught as one of the fields of social work by most of the training institutions.

Another new trend is the increase in private practice by professional social workers, though this has been confined mostly to the United States. Although controversies centre on the propriety of private practice in social work (largely because it involves fees), the National Association of Social Workers in the United States has declared that private practice comes within the purview of social work practice.

Fields of service: problems and policies

PERSONAL SERVICES

Family welfare. Family welfare services are designed to enable individuals and families to meet their needs, cope with stresses, develop harmonious interpersonal relationships, and improve family functioning. The auspices under which these services are rendered differ from country to country: in some, each program is organized independently, whereas in many others, each program is integrated into larger programs of community centres. In most developed countries nationwide programs of cash assistance are an integral part of family welfare services, but in developing countries mass poverty and lack of resources make such cash assistance generally unavailable, or extremely limited if available. Apart from material help, family welfare agencies provide casework help and other assistance to deal with psychosocial problems.

Marriage counselling. One of the services offered mainly through family-welfare agencies is to assist marital partners in meeting marital responsibilities and to resolve marital conflicts. The urgent need for marriage counselling is indicated by the increasing rate of separations and divorce. Among developed countries, Canada has extensive family counselling services under public auspices. In Japan citizens' counselling services are super-

vised by the Ministry of Social Welfare. In the United States, Great Britain, and other western European countries marriage counselling and social casework services are available on a wide scale as part of family welfare services both public and private. In sharp contrast, there is almost complete absence of any formal system of marriage counselling in the Soviet Union, where the judges of the divorce courts are entrusted with responsibility of bringing about reconciliation between parties, failing which they grant divorce. Among some of the developing countries and some of the more conservative Western countries, family counselling and guidance is a relatively new service confined to urban areas only. In these countries, heads of joint or extended families and religious or community leaders give advisory or counselling help of an informal type. The formal type of family counselling services has been rudimentarily introduced in Malaysia, India, Indonesia, Italy, and South Africa.

Maternal care and family planning. Measures for promoting the mental and physical health of children from the prenatal stage onward and that of mothers, particularly during the gestation period, have been included in maternal care programs. These services are now an integral part of the public-health programs of most countries and are linked with social-insurance and maternity-benefit schemes. High rates of maternal and child mortality in developing countries are an index of the qualitative and quantitative inadequacy of maternal- and child-health programs. The extent of child- and maternal-care services needed in developing countries may be judged by the situation in India, where there are about 75,000,000 infants in the 0–5 age group and about 20,000,000 expectant and nursing mothers. Comprehensive programs for such a large number require enormous resources, which presently are unavailable. This gap between needs and resources is typical of most developing countries.

Among developing nations, India and Pakistan were the first to have launched family planning or birth control as part of the national development program under their Five Year Plans. Other Asian countries—South Korea, Ceylon (now Sri Lanka), Malaysia, and Singapore, for example—adopted family planning as part of governmental programs. Egypt, and Tunisia started family planning programs in 1955, followed by Kenya, Mauritius, Morocco, and Jamaica. In such countries as Chile, Colombia, Hong Kong, Thailand, and Venezuela family planning has been introduced by private agencies. Several Latin-American countries are introducing the family-planning movement primarily to solve the problems of widespread illegal abortions. Japan is the only country where population growth has been drastically cut by the legalization of abortions; with about 13,000,000 registered abortions and 6,000,000 unregistered, abortions in Japan since 1948 have exceeded the total number of births. Most eastern European countries, including the U.S.S.R., have legalized abortions; some western European nations—notably the United Kingdom—have a liberal policy on abortions, as do certain states of the United States (see also BIRTH CONTROL).

Family-life education. One of the services provided by family-welfare agencies, particularly in western Europe and North America, is family-life education. It seeks to develop through discussion, lectures, and radio and television programs healthy family relationships and efficient home economics. Initiated by a group of volunteers in the United States, family-life education has grown into a major movement. In some countries it started as a movement for parent education. In developing countries programs of this nature have been developed through women's clubs and other groups as part of community development programs. In Ghana, women's clubs are taking the lead in community development for "better homes" by demonstrations in home economics and home-making. In Belgium the government subsidizes courses promoting the improvement of family life.

Home-help programs. "Homemaker" service or "home-help" service is provided through public or voluntary welfare agencies to aid families to carry on household responsibilities and enable the family to stay together

Expansion of methods and fields

Birth control

despite chronic illness, handicaps, or other types of family distress. Homemakers, selected for their skills and personalities and supervised by family service or children's agencies, are placed in homes where the mother is temporarily unable to care for the family. Such services have become increasingly important as the number of families without relatives or obliging neighbours attempt to survive in the impersonal atmosphere of large cities. Moreover, the concept is broadening to include services to adults in their own homes who are dependent, physically and emotionally ill, or handicapped. In Scandinavian countries, home-helper service is organized on a large scale, and per capita availability is much higher than in any other country. In 1963 there were 55,000 home-helpers in Great Britain (which offers such services under the National Health Service Act), whereas the United States, with four times the population of Great Britain, had only 4,000, providing only about one homemaker for 50,000 inhabitants.

Old-age care. The care of the aged is assuming greater importance with the general increase in longevity, particularly in the developed countries, where the old are at least measurably protected through social insurance or public assistance schemes and receive institutional care on a very large scale. The developed countries have organized systems that include pension schemes, old-age assistance, institutional care, clubs for senior citizens, homes for the aged, "meals on wheels" (mobile canteens for visiting from house to house), friendly visiting, home helps, adoption of grandparents (securing, in effect, foster homes for the elderly), mail order drugs at reduced cost, patient sitters, and cooperative buying. In developing countries, which are largely agricultural, the pattern of the joint or extended family had traditionally provided a built-in system of care of the aged within the family itself. Where there is no separation of the work place from residence, the aged are still able to retain social functioning in the family and the neighbourhood even after their economic productivity has ceased. This familial situation, however, is changing in developing countries; the old system does not provide sufficient protection to the aged in the changing socioeconomic circumstances but the developing countries lack the funds and resources to meet these new needs.

Child welfare. The field of child welfare is universally accepted as one of the most important. Its services seek to promote the healthy growth and development of children and meet their needs either through direct assistance or through assistance to parents or families. Supplying or supplementing family income so that parents can maintain a home for their children is usually the first such service to be provided. Assistance, usually by means of a public assistance program, may range from the distribution of food, medicine, and clothing to complex systems of social insurance. In addition to programs of general family relief, special assistance to broken families often is provided. In cases where parental care is temporarily or permanently unavailable, the child is given substitute care in the form of foster care, adoption, or institutional care. Although child welfare programs are common in the developed countries, they are inadequate or lacking in the developing countries, where 500,000,000 children represent three-quarters of the world's juvenile population.

Maternal and child health care. Although child welfare increasingly stresses social services, public health and medical services usually are the first to be organized in the newly developed nations. This recognizes the fact that the infant and maternal death rates are the primary indexes of a nation's progress in child welfare. In India, for example, the main programs for child welfare are health services, such as infant health centres, and provision of vaccination and immunization.

In many countries, particularly in Africa and Asia, the first steps were public health attacks on such diseases as yaws, tuberculosis, malaria, and leprosy and efforts to improve child nutrition. This was often followed by instruction of native midwives in the simple principles of hygiene. The assistance of the United Nations Children's Fund (UNICEF) and the World Health Organization

(WHO) was particularly significant in inaugurating three basic programs of infant and maternal welfare. The industrialized countries have gone far beyond this with the provision of professional prenatal, delivery, and postnatal care for mothers without reference to their ability to pay. Infant welfare clinics that provide expert advice on child care are widely available in Great Britain, where, in the 1960s, 80 percent of all babies received care in these clinics, and in the United States. Additional services in the United States under this program include, among others, health services to school-age children, dental care, hearing and vision services, immunizations and diagnostic treatment, and counselling services for mentally retarded children.

Protective services. Not all parents love their children and some are grossly incompetent and neglectful. Children of such parents require special protective services. Societies for the prevention of cruelty to children, organized under voluntary auspices, date from the middle of the 19th century and still exist under various names in some cities, although the trend has been to place responsibility for such services in public child-welfare agencies. In some jurisdictions probation officers of the family court or children's court carry on the work. Protective services are usually invoked on the complaint of neighbours or others aware of cases of parental abuse or neglect. The fact that the services are not sought by and may be resisted by the parents requires that the workers have special skills and that there be some modification of the usual casework practices. Because removal of a child from his own home, even if it is not a very good one, is such a serious matter, all reasonable efforts are made to avoid this drastic step.

Children who have been battered and abused and those whose emaciated bodies give evidence of neglect are not the only ones needing special assistance, although they are the ones most likely to be found in the case loads of protective agencies. Equally serious but less conspicuous are the emotional scars that many children bear. The subtler forms of emotional damage that parents can inflict on their children are only beginning to be recognized. In general, only in extreme cases, where the children are severely exploited by parents or others, are they removed from their homes by legal intervention. This caution of the courts is based on the conviction that the home, in spite of poverty or other disturbing conditions, is still the best place for the child to grow and develop.

Care of unwed mothers and their children. The care and protection of children born out of wedlock poses special problems arising from society's attitude toward premarital conception. From being tolerantly viewed or even expected, as in some tribal communities, some other communities impose extreme strictures, ostracize, or even exhibit violence toward the unwed mother and her child. Nevertheless, most modern societies recognize that the unwed mother should receive some assistance. Typical services for the unwed mother include maintenance, medical care, hospitalization, and above all casework to help her to meet the social crisis and to make a constructive decision for her own and for the child's future. Where family-welfare agencies operate, caseworkers counsel the mothers particularly about the arrangements either for keeping the baby or giving the child up for adoption. The services to the unwed mothers are provided in the developed countries of the West mainly through private agencies, supplemented by cash allowances from public funds, whereas in the Socialist countries of eastern Europe full maintenance is paid by the state; the child, for instance, can be kept in a children's home at state expense as long as the mother likes. In Scandinavian countries the state directly helps unmarried mothers in establishing paternity. Institutions known as *hôtels maternels* in France and working mothers' hotels in Great Britain admit unmarried mothers and look after their children. In developing countries services to unmarried mothers or their children are still in an elementary state and are dealt with by individual charity or private welfare agencies.

Day care. Day-care centres are intended for young children, generally between the ages of two and five, who

Prevention of cruelty to children

are looked after while their mothers are away at work. With more and more women employed either full-time or part-time both in developed and developing countries, the need for day-care services for the children has been universally felt. What was originally meant to provide custodial care for the children, however, has in many countries developed into broader health and educational services in collaboration with other child- and family-welfare agencies. The emphasis in the Soviet Union—unlike that in the United States and Japan—is more on care of children outside the family and in large groups under government supervision, some of the children returning to their homes only for weekends. In the developing countries there is great need for day-care centres, particularly in the urban and industrialized areas. In some countries of Asia, day-care centres must by law be provided by industries; in India, for example, every industrial establishment employing more than 50 women must maintain a crèche.

The various kinds of centres provide supervised indoor and outdoor play, a mid-day meal, and naps, as a minimum. In addition, there may be instructions in crafts, reading, music, and simple hygiene. Some centres are staffed with or have access to psychiatrists, pediatricians, and social workers and are used for the diagnosis and treatment of emotional problems of children and their parents.

Substitutes for parental care. Although most theories of modern child welfare place major emphasis on keeping children in their own homes, the unfortunate group of children who have to be removed from them absorbs more than half the time of all child-welfare personnel, at least in the United States.

There have been marked changes over the years in the reasons children have lost their homes, and corresponding changes in the kinds of care provided for them. Whereas death of parents and destitution used to lead the list, in the second half of the 20th century this was no longer the case. Most so-called orphan asylums have almost no orphans and many of them have acknowledged this fact by dropping the word orphan from their institutional names. Medical science and public health measures have succeeded in various ways in reducing the number of children who lost their parents by death. The most frequent causes for removal of a child from his home more recently have become marital discord, parental irresponsibility and neglect, separation, and illegitimacy. Temporary placement may sometimes be necessary because of behaviour problems of the child or because of family emergencies.

Foster care

Foster-care services are designed for neglected or dependent children who lack the protective atmosphere of home for short or long periods and are hence placed with families or institutions. It is now accepted that a children's agency should be able to make available both types of care since experience has shown that not all children can benefit from foster-family care. For example, children whose experiences with their own parents have been emotionally devastating may not be able to fit into the intimacy of a foster family and may do better in the more impersonal life of an institution. The same is frequently true of emotionally disturbed adolescents.

Modern standards for foster care emphasize careful selection of homes, close supervision of the children placed in them, and payment of board. Clothing, medical and dental care, and allowances for the children are often provided by the placing agency. Particularly important are the counselling services provided by the agency's caseworkers to foster parents. In the absence of such services children may be needlessly uprooted and shifted from one home to another with damaging results. It is open to doubt whether remuneration can be an important factor in the foster parents' decision to take a foster child. The most successful foster parents do it because they like to have children around them, and in Great Britain it was found that women who had had more than one foster child also had children of their own.

Instead of the former austere buildings with rows of beds in dormitories and children sitting silently at long tables in the dining rooms, the modern foster institution is more likely to be of the so-called cottage type. Under the cottage system there are small homelike units with living rooms, and single and double bedrooms, each housing from five to ten children along with a housemother or couple. Meals may be served in a common dining room although many cottages have their own dining rooms and have food delivered from a central kitchen. The purpose is to create a family rather than an institutional atmosphere. It should be noted that the shift from the congregate- to the cottage-type institution has been slower in Europe and in other parts of the world where the institutions are under religious auspices or where funds and resources are very limited.

Many new types of foster care are being devised for dependent, neglected, delinquent, or otherwise handicapped children. New kinds of foster homes have been started—professional foster homes, group foster homes, agency-owned foster homes. New patterns of institutional care are emerging—smaller groups, professional staff, experimental cottages, off-campus cottages. And, somewhere between these two groups of resources, another type of facility referred to as agency-operated group homes is being established. The children live together with a group of mature and responsible young people, usually volunteers, capable of exercising a stabilizing influence. In

Adoption

contrast to foster care, adoption is a social and legal process by which a child is received as a permanent member of the adopting family, with legal rights including that of inheritance. As a child care measure it seeks to take children of deceased or incapacitated natural parents and provide them with substitute parents and a healthy home environment. The procedure connected with adoption differs from country to country, but the general pattern is that legislative provisions seek to ensure that separation from natural parents is resorted to only where absolutely essential and only on the basis of consent if the parents live. Social agencies or departments arranging for adoption conduct social investigations for matching the child against the background of the adopting parents after study of their age, character, and motivation.

Youth welfare. While the basic needs of youth normally are met within their own families, a wide range of cultural, social, recreational, vocational, and counselling programs, whether public or private, may be needed to help youth assume leadership and responsibility. The programs can involve playgrounds, recreation centres, or hostels and can be organized around friendship clubs, classes, athletic teams, or interest or hobby groups. For such groups social services provide a place to meet and a group leader, teacher, or coach, as appropriate.

Youth organizations

Almost all European countries have large youth organizations. Sweden, for instance, has "leisure-time groups" that serve small groups of five to 24 members in the age group of 12 to 24 years old. The popularity of these groups can be judged from the fact that in the period from 1955 to 1965 the number of such groups increased from a little over 9,000 to nearly 100,000. The Soviet Union contains the largest youth organizations in the world, all of them governmentally sponsored and not private or voluntary in the Western sense. Membership is encouraged in the Pioneers (for youth aged eight to 15) and in the Komsomols (for young people aged 14 to 26). Together with various physical culture organizations, such Soviet societies are said to reach membership of some 45,000,000. In most countries, there are Boy Scouts, Girl Guides or Girl Scouts, 4-H Clubs, the Young Men's Christian Association, the Young Women's Christian Association, and a number of national organizations with programs varying with local needs and conditions—for example, the Young Buddhists Association or the Young Men's Indian Association. Some such groups have "permanent" memberships, whereas others offer various programs for temporary get-togethers. Although most have at least some kind of meeting place or places, there are also such programs as Great Britain's Outward Bound, which draws together youth who sign up for various kinds of short-term camping, mountaineering, sea outings, and the like. The international Youth Hostels provide accommodations for youth gaining the experience of travelling either abroad or within their own countries.

Volunteer service organizations

Many programs try to involve youth in nation building and other constructive endeavours, whereby both society and the individual youth profit. One of the new developments in India is that all university students are compelled to engage in cocurricular activities in military training, sports activities, or social service. It is hoped that the use of millions of Indian college students as volunteers in community improvement projects and social-welfare activities will fill a gap that today exists in the availability of educated youth leaders in nation-building activities. Israel is one of the countries that has successfully used its youth volunteers in larger nation-building activities, particularly in the development of new communities in unsettled areas. A well-known overseas program is the U.S. Peace Corps, which, during the 1960s, distributed thousands of young Americans into technical assistance projects around the world. A similar domestic U.S. program, VISTA (Volunteers in Service to America), sent youth to impoverished city slums and depressed rural areas.

Finally, in many countries, particularly such developed Western countries as the United States, there have developed the new "guidance" professions among social workers, who offer youth vocational, educational, and personal-social advice and counselling. Such guidance originally was provided mainly for special categories of youth—for example, school dropouts or leavers looking for jobs, emotionally disturbed children, college-bound youth, slow-learning students, or juvenile delinquents. Many private and public guidance agencies still serve special groups such as these, but more recently guidance has come to be viewed as valuable for all students.

Youth agencies recognize the need to extend services to the "hard to reach" youth and others who do not voluntarily come forward to take advantage of the recreation and other youth welfare programs. It is clear that in some countries youth welfare services must deal with not only the conventional physical handicaps but also social handicapping situations such as very low standard of living and unfavourable social conditions.

Group welfare. *Social settlements and community centres.* Neighbourhood social-welfare agencies—variously called social settlements, settlement houses, community centres, or neighbourhood houses, centres, associations, or guilds—began with the founding of Toynbee Hall in London in 1884. S.A. Barnett, then vicar of St. Jude's parish, invited a number of university students to join him and his wife in "settling" in a deprived area. The movement spread to the United States when Stanton Coit, who was one of the early visitors to Toynbee Hall, established Neighborhood Guild, now University Settlement, on the Lower East Side of New York City in 1886. In 1889 Jane Addams, another Toynbee Hall visitor, and Ellen Gates Starr bought a residence on the Near West Side of Chicago, and started Hull House. In the same year Jane E. Robbins and Jean Fine (Mrs. Charles B. Spahr) opened the College Settlement in New York City. Two years later Robert A. Woods established Andover House, later called South End House, in Boston. The movement spread to other countries—particularly in western Europe, Southeast Asia, and Japan—mainly through the influence of visitors from those countries to settlements in England or the United States.

Settlements seek to develop harmonious relationships among community groups of different cultural, economic, religious, and social characteristics and to help people to act together as an informed citizenry to improve their living conditions and environment. Under the leadership of pioneer workers, social settlements have helped win the enactment of legislation providing for juvenile courts, mothers' pensions, workmen's compensation, and the regulation of child labour; they have promoted playgrounds and recreation centres, maternal, infant, and child health clinics and services, and adult-education programs and have taken part in housing and other reforms.

The difficulty of finding financial support in smaller communities that are less well organized (for purposes of social welfare) has tended to confine settlements to metropolitan areas where such support can be found. Some small agricultural and newer industrial communities,

Settlement houses

however, have been helped—often by religious organizations—to establish and maintain a community centre, similar to a settlement. Dispersion of industry outside of metropolitan areas has brought into being new towns that need this general purpose type of community service. Communities of migratory agricultural labour, particularly where children are involved, have claimed the attention of religious organizations in the United States, with the result that some settlement houses have been established.

Services to migrants, aliens, and transients. One of the largest of social services has been directed toward migrants moving within nations and across international boundaries. The early settlement houses in the U.S. were particularly concerned with helping the foreign born survive the trials of living in a new environment; before this, migrants were generally left almost completely helpless.

Refugees and immigrants

A major problem in the 20th century has been that of involuntary migrants or refugees who have been forced by political circumstances to flee their original houses (see REFUGEES). The partition of India and Pakistan in 1947 and the Arab-Israeli conflict since 1948 have been occasions when millions of people were uprooted from their homes. The intercountry movement of refugees in Europe during and after World War II was on a scale unprecedented in history, requiring services and relief operations for millions of refugees.

In Europe and North America various church denominations and religious orders have been active in providing services to immigrants and transients. In the United States also, services for migratory farm workers and their families have been provided since 1920. Those migrating from European countries to other parts of the world are assisted by the Intergovernmental Committee for European Migration. With the increase of immigrants to Britain from Commonwealth countries in Asia and Africa, local authorities have taken increased interest in the welfare of immigrants; liaison officers who speak the language of the immigrants are employed to help the migrants with problems they face in the initial stage. Similar services are available in many countries.

Policies of assimilation and pluralism

As an example of the growth of such services, in the early part of the 20th century, a U.S. domestic movement called Americanization developed several agencies and centres directed toward the "correction" of what were considered "deficiencies" in the foreign born. The core of the curriculum was the English language, American history, and the governmental structure of the United States, all necessary for naturalization. Soon the offering included courses in such things as millinery, cooking, social amenities, and the care of children, all presented as "essential" and elements of American culture. Occasionally such centres as Hull House did try to preserve a respect for the alien cultures. Eventually, especially after World War II, the term Americanization began to be shunned; instead of the old idea of supplanting all foreign traits by a standard pattern, there grew up the idea of cultural pluralism, the preservation of separate cultures within the national boundaries. Still other critics contended that this pluralism itself would gradually disappear over the years, that the American character was still in the process of formation and that as it gradually emerged, it would be enriched by the blending of the admirable features of the various foreign nationalities. Thus, although special programs of education still exist to help children and adults make their primary adjustment to life in a new land, the quality and emphases of such programs have changed.

Aid to transients has been characteristic of countries that have had to cope with large numbers of mobile individuals. In the United States and Canada, for instance, there are the Travelers Aid societies, which shepherd the aged, the very young, the handicapped, and the foreign visitor through transportation difficulties at airport and railway terminals, offer counsel or aid to runaway youths, the emotionally disturbed, or the physically injured, give technical or legal advice to aliens and other newcomers, and even provide emergency financial help or job assistance.

Services for ethnic and minority groups. Programs designed to improve intergroup relations—that is, relations between races and castes—have become increasingly versatile instead of relying on any one method or technique. The debate as to whether one must first reduce prejudice before embarking on legislation to combat discrimination, or whether the approach should be the other way round, has yielded to the conviction that both procedures should be followed simultaneously. As a result, in many nations there have developed programs of education and information, including the revision of school textbooks, and there have arisen various informational and self-help societies and associations, all designed to improve attitudes toward certain ethnic groups. At the same time there have been efforts to strengthen laws that make racial and caste discrimination a punishable offense.

Services for the handicapped. In an earlier day services for the physically and mentally handicapped hardly went beyond the provision of shelter and food; now the emphasis is on rehabilitation—helping the patient to overcome immediate domestic difficulties and to reconcile himself and his family to his condition. In general, the emphasis throughout is on self-help and productive work, not entirely from financial considerations but because self-help maintains self-respect and affords an outlet for the creative drive, while productive work is more pleasurable for most people than enforced idleness. In Denmark, for example, therapists, job specialists (*e.g.*, engineers), vocational guidance experts, and employment exchanges cooperate to achieve for the disabled employment conditions as near normal as possible. In the U.S.S.R. the Ministry of Social Welfare retrains the handicapped and obliges employers to give them suitable work and conditions, while special medical commissions supervise them and research institutes study their labour problems. Austria, France, West Germany, Great Britain, Greece, and Israel have "quota" arrangements for employment of the handicapped; that is, certain classes of employers are required by law to have in their work force a specific percentage of handicapped.

Services for military veterans. Services for persons who have completed a term of service in the armed forces have been provided from very early times. Down to the 20th century one of the most common solutions for the "veterans' problem" was to grant tracts of land to disbanded soldiers. Land grants were offered to encourage enlistments, reward military service, avoid unrest among veterans, or promote the settlement of frontier territory. By 1945, however, with war veterans more numerous, society more urban and industrial, and farm operation more complex, land settlement for veterans lost its traditional appeal; instead, the governments of the warring powers adopted a variety of plans, including public works programs, job reinstatement, educational aid, counselling services, employment preference, housing programs, and loans for veterans.

Services for disabled veterans

Unlike most other countries, the United States at an early date adopted a policy of granting liberal military pensions. Pensions for war widows and orphans were not common in Europe until World War I, but they existed in the United States from the time of the American Revolution. Pensions also were granted to U.S. veterans with a "service-connected disability," a term that was flexibly interpreted. Demobilization aid to disabled servicemen, however, reached high levels after World War II among all the warring nations. Great progress was made in medical and surgical treatment, in re-education, and in vocational guidance and placement services (even though there have been occasional exposures of inadequate or corruptly governed services). Veterans' preference and the reservation of certain civil service positions for the disabled were practically universal, while training allowances and disability benefits were more liberal than ever before.

There are also many voluntary associations and ex-servicemen's organizations that provide financial and personal services to disabled former servicemen and former servicewomen and their families. One special feature is the close coordination between the work of welfare offices of government departments and the voluntary bodies.

Disaster relief. Disaster relief refers to assistance to persons who are deprived of the essential needs of life because of natural disasters resulting from flood, fire, earthquake, volcanic eruption, cyclones, or similar catastrophes. The term is also extended to assistance to communities and people suffering from the effects of war. During World War II, for instance, a nationwide civil defense program in Great Britain prevented the loss of many lives and helped to reduce some of the suffering following bomb attacks. Plans have since been developed by many countries to provide relief in the event of catastrophe, whether it results from war or natural causes.

Several research studies have been made in order to determine the human and organizational reactions to disaster. During and immediately after World War II several social surveys in the cities of Great Britain, Germany, and Japan that had been subjected to incessant bombing indicated the morale and interpreted the behaviour of those affected by disaster. Such studies revealed that in many cases, far from becoming panicky or hysterical, the people organized themselves with remarkable presence of mind and dedication, maintaining the morale and the tempo of relief operations. Breakdown of law and order and antisocial behaviour such as looting were relatively rare.

Relief operations. Before 1900, disaster relief consisted largely of emergency grants of food, clothing, and medical care, and the provision of mass shelter through hastily organized local committees, often with the aid of voluntary contributions of money or supplies from other communities or countries. In the 20th century disaster relief became one of the chief activities of such organizations as the International Red Cross, which originally had been organized in the 1860s to aid the victims of war. National systems have included nationwide expansion of disaster preparedness in Red Cross chapters, including the training of volunteers to serve in emergencies and the development of plans and programs to be used in case of either natural disaster or enemy attack. Other voluntary organizations that have been especially active in providing supplies and services for relief in cases of natural disasters have been the Cooperative for American Relief to Everywhere (CARE), the Salvation Army, and church groups.

Civil defense and emergency programs

In many countries, cities and regional administrative areas have established some disaster programs and prepared inventories of resources available in case of an emergency and of individuals with knowledge of the location of such resources. Locally, the mayor or some designated official is usually the top authority for directing the services when needed. In most instances the major city department involved is the fire department. (This more or less follows the pattern established in Great Britain during World War II.) Other officials generally represented on a disaster relief authority include the commissioners of police and health departments, officials of public and private welfare agencies, hospital authorities, representatives of the local medical society, and transportation authorities. In many communities the Red Cross and public services are organized to determine the need for food, clothing, and shelter in the event, for example, of a large fire. In case of a disaster affecting a large area, transportation facilities—public or commercial—are drawn into service. Emergency medical services and hospital care are important elements in relief after serious fires, floods, and windstorms. In countries like India, famine relief follows a pattern laid down by the Famine Code, whereby the state assumes control of the supply, distribution, prices, and movement of food grains and also grants exemptions from levies on land holdings. Where health standards are low, efforts to check the spread of epidemic diseases such as typhoid, cholera, dysentery, and smallpox are given special priority.

Warning services. Although it is possible to give warnings about certain kinds of disasters, people tend not to heed the warning. One common reason is the inherent optimism, indifference, or disbelief of the people, who tend to underestimate the seriousness of any impending calamity. But warning and preparedness must go hand in hand. Establishing flood control schemes in areas susceptible to flood, controlling epidemics like plague by preventive health programs, counteracting famine conditions by crash agricultural development programs, building up of buffer stock of food grains, maintaining fleets of transport for men and materials to be rushed to the needed areas, and promoting effective systems of meteorological prediction and warning are steps that, in varying degree, can considerably lessen the adverse impact of many of these disasters. Meteorological departments in different countries, in collaboration with the International Meteorological Organization established in 1878, have been active in giving warnings particularly about cyclonic storms and floods.

COMMUNITY DEVELOPMENT

Self-help in community projects

One of the definitions of community development formulated by the United Nations indicates its areas and objectives by saying that it consists of the "processes by which the efforts of the people are united with those of governmental authorities to improve the economic, social and cultural conditions of communities in the life of the nation and enable them to contribute fully to national progress." Its main rationale is that developmental programs must be initiated with the active support and participation of the local community. The importance of motivation and self-help has been brought out by community development projects in India that seek "to bring about a change in the mental attitude of the people, and to instill in them an ambition for higher standards of life, and the will and determination to work for such standards . . . to arouse enthusiasm in them for new knowledge, and new ways of life, and fill them with the ambition and will to lead a better life." Thus it seeks to effect changes in the attitude of people by engendering a feeling of dissatisfaction with the existing low levels of living and by arousing the enthusiasm for leadership, self-help, and mutual aid.

In such developed countries as the United States, community-development programs have aimed at eliminating the imbalances between highly developed industrial centres on the one hand and backward rural communities on the other—or even backward communities within otherwise affluent metropolitan areas. These programs have been organized by government agencies (such as the U.S. Department of Agriculture) aiming at either agricultural and farm improvement or urban-slum amelioration of various kinds.

In developing countries, community development is usually more intimately geared to the nation's overall development plan. Although the actual content of each program or its emphasis has shown a great deal of variation in different countries, the general trend has been to begin with village improvement projects, focussing on such things as roads, schools, hospitals, community centres, and recreation facilities. These have been attempted first because people are likely to generate general enthusiasm for obtaining these physical amenities. In developing countries that are predominantly agrarian, programs of community development have also focussed on agricultural development and extension work in rural areas; this is so because community development can make headway only if it can make an economic contribution and help improve living standards. In certain countries governmental grants are made available on a matching basis, usually 50–50, the contribution of the community being regarded as an index of the community's recognition of its needs and its willingness to participate to meet its needs. In poorer regions, some local communities have found it difficult, however, to raise matching resources for development programs; some others perceive needs and possess resources but lack leadership. In many such cases the national governments do not have the wherewithal to intervene. But in some Asian and African countries, an effort is being made to use idle manpower by directing the unemployed and underemployed into productive avenues for development purposes, and usually there is some kind of administrative machinery trying to link together the various self-governing units at different levels and to coordinate their programs.

Grants in aid

Various techniques have evolved to cope with local conditions. One special feature in Lebanon is the dependence on existing village institutions such as village councils to get things going. In Egypt there have been established Rural Social Units, which handle not only local community development projects but also social and welfare services generally under the Ministry of Social Affairs. A special feature of community development in Ghana, which started as early as 1945, is the leading role played by women workers and volunteers; one of their projects, Better Homes, aims at the all-round improvement of the home and its environs and the introduction of supplementary income through poultry-keeping and vegetable gardening.

Urban areas have their special problems of community involvement. The special features of urban life such as over-crowding, growing urban anonymity, poor amenities, absence of communication, impersonal relationships, frequent changes of jobs or residences, lack of involvement in the life of the community outside, and the depressing conditions of slums and other blighted spots put severe limitation on the extent of community feeling and involvement in urban community developmental programs.

SERVICES IN THE CONTEXT OF OTHER AGENCIES

Medical social service. The social and psychological conditions of patients can obviously help or hinder their recovery. Some do not recognize that they are ill, whereas others do not want a cure. Some do not want to do anything, whereas others are too upset by the diagnosis to do anything. The course and success of treatment thus may depend on the help of such personnel as medical social workers, who try to (1) give the physician a picture of the social and psychological factors causing or aggravating an illness, (2) help patients to make full use of all available facilities, (3) work with family and community to tap resources in support of the treatment and aftercare of the patient. Areas in which the skills of social workers have greatly benefitted patients have been those in which long-term medication and observance of various precautions are needed—involving such conditions as diabetes, cardiac disorders, handicapping conditions like poliomyelitis, stigmatized diseases like tuberculosis, leprosy, epilepsy, and venereal disease, and various psychosomatic conditions. Particularly in developing countries with low educational levels among the mass of the population, a great deal of the social worker's time is taken up with educating patients and families about the nature of diseases, the course of treatment, and the precautions to be taken.

Medical social workers

The medical social worker also helps to arrange finances or offers counselling on economic situations centering on the job, housing, and family. Whereas in developed countries medical-care programs are often comprehensive enough to make the social worker's duties largely psychological, in developing countries a great deal of attention is additionally paid to financial help and to programs of family planning and health education.

Psychiatric social service. Assisting a clinical team of psychiatrists, psychologists, and other professionals is often a psychiatric social worker, who provides casework and group-work services for patients suffering from mental illness and who helps plan for their rehabilitation and aftercare. He also works with parents and relatives, and he engages in various preventive services in the area of mental health. Psychiatric social services made a beginning in the United States in 1905, when some of the neurological clinics attached to hospitals in Boston and New York started employing psychiatric social workers; specialized training began at the same time. During and after World War II, there was great demand for psychiatric social services, which were provided under military auspices and with the help of the American Red Cross.

In many countries mental patients not requiring active treatment are placed in suitable boarding or foster homes, "halfway houses," and community residences, usually under the guidance of psychiatric social workers. In Great Britain the National Health Service provides a broad range of social services for patients with mental disorders, including job placement and the help of social centres. Psychiatric treatment facilities in most of the developing countries, however, are inadequate. Even the few mental hospitals that exist in these countries are not properly equipped in terms of staff, equipment, or services. For example, with a total of only about 1,500 beds in mental hospitals, India in the early 1970s had 33 beds per 1,000,-000 persons, compared with 3,500 and 2,780 beds per 1,000,000 persons in the United States and Great Britain, respectively.

School social services. School social workers deal with children who, potentially or actually, face problems of adjustment in the family, the school, or the neighbourhood to such an extent as to interfere with their studies. The actual problems faced by school children are different in the developed countries—where schools provide advanced educational facilities and where education is generally compulsory—from those of children in many developing countries, where educational facilities are inadequate. Even these limited facilities often go unutilized because children stay away from school or withdraw from school in order to support the family or to look after younger children. The school social worker tries to see that better use is made of the existing educational facilities. Among the social services available in schools are health services, psychiatric services, vocational guidance and counselling, supplementary diet programs, hobby centres, and other extracurricular programs. One of the trends in school social work is the development of an interprofessional approach involving social workers, educators, and other professionals like doctors and psychiatrists. Teamwork with parents and teachers for the solution of children's problems has been found to be very effective. There is much wider involvement of the parents and community in dealing with the problems of school children. Parents who have children with handicaps need special help; group meetings with parents of children with some handicaps have been found useful in sharing their insights and lightening their burden. School social workers play a crucial role in all of these programs.

Correctional services. Although there obviously are many views on the treatment of criminals and delinquents, the dominant conflict of views is between those who put their faith in severe punishment in the belief that this will prevent the criminal from repeating his crimes and also serve as a deterrent to others and, at the other extreme, those who emphasize the futility of punishment and the evil effects of prison life. The advocates of this latter position often conceive of the criminal as a victim of social and psychological forces outside his control. A compromise position located between the two extremes seems to be the one toward which most nations and most social workers are moving. The evils of prison life are admitted, but it is proposed to mitigate them by imposing shorter sentences, by using probation, fines, and other substitutes for imprisonment, by improving conditions within prisons, and by experimenting with new kinds of prisons and rehabilitative techniques. It is also commonly recognized that some criminals must be incarcerated for long periods of time, not so much for the sake of severity as for the protection of society. The major correctional areas in which social workers are involved are probation, parole, and delinquency control.

Probation. The probation process begins with a presentence investigation of the offender after his guilt has been established. This investigation—usually by a social worker—serves first to help the court determine whether the offender is suitable for probation and second to outline a plan of corrective treatment. It is primarily concerned with the offender as an individual, his personality and background, education and employment, and his Probation family and social environment. When probation is approved by the court, the offender is placed under the supervision of a probation officer or a person appointed by the court—usually a person with a background of social work. The probation officer's fundamental task is to help the probationer become a more responsible and better adjusted person. The essence of probation is good casework, not mere supervision, and its aim is individual rehabilitation, not the relief of crowded institutions. Individual counselling and available social, occupational, educational, and mental-health resources are employed to help the probationer resolve specific problems, conflicts, and attitudes that led to his delinquent behaviour.

Unlike the United Kingdom and the United States,

which have generally established official, salaried probation officers, most continental European countries have delegated the personal supervision of probationers to social welfare organizations dependent on volunteer services. A general trend toward professional probation services has been exemplified in the Belgian, French, Dutch, and Swedish systems. There, trained probation consultants are responsible for indoctrinating volunteer agents, supervising their work, and in many cases giving direct services to probationers. The move toward professionalization has been accompanied by increased central government responsibility for coordination, regulation, or administration of probation services.

Those metropolitan areas in Latin America, Asia, and Africa where the juvenile court philosophy has been embraced offer probation services largely limited to juveniles. Voluntary welfare organizations usually have provided the necessary supervision and treatment services.

Parole. Various forms of parole or conditional release from prison have been adopted in the majority of countries around the world. The responsibilities of a parole board and a parole officer are comparable to those of a court offering probation and a probation officer: parole selection involves the evaluation of emotional, psychological, and social traits of offenders; and parolees are sub- **Parole** ject to field supervision by parole officers (sometimes **officers** identical to probation officers) or, in several European countries, by private social or rehabilitation agencies.

Parole supervision is based on the concept that the individual parolee has the capacity to accept help and to change his behaviour. But the parolee may need counselling on such matters as continued vocational training, employment placement, and adjustment to unexpected marital, economic, or other personal or family problems. The skills of the parole officer when applied through counselling and casework or group-work services can contribute much to the continuing rehabilitation of offenders. Parole supervision varies in quality from little more than perfunctory monthly reporting to skilled individual casework treatment. Given adequate administration and sufficient budgets to command competent staff with reasonable case loads, experience has shown that four out of five parolees will respond to constructive guidance and supervision by satisfactorily completing their paroles.

Delinquency control. Faced with mounting public concern over juvenile delinquency and the apparent failures of various programs of treatment and prevention, many countries and smaller jurisdictions have experimented with methods of control. Notable among these have been attempts to coordinate the work of agencies in local communities, to identify gaps in youth services and fill these gaps with new programs. Several methods of both treatment and prevention have recognized the importance of peer groups for the behaviour of youngsters. Group therapy has been widely practiced in institutions and in the community as an adjunct of probation. Work with "street corner" gangs has taken a variety of forms, usually involving extension of the services of a social agency by assigning personnel as "street workers" rather than primarily within traditional agency programs and facilities. Neighbourhood youngsters and adults have been organized and in many instances hired to aid in coping with delinquency and other community problems related to youth. "Opportunity theory" (*i.e.*, the theory that many young people lack the opportunity to succeed in conventional, accepted ways) has had a notable impact on youth services, especially in the U.S., where federal support has been extended to local communities on a broad scale to improve educational and economic opportunities. Other programs have been based on a variety of intensive clinical services.

Despite rising public concern and widespread experimentation with techniques of rehabilitation and prevention, youth services in most countries still are extremely limited, and the discretion of the juvenile court in most jurisdictions is severely handicapped by the paucity of available alternatives for treatment or protection of children. Supervision within the community (probation from the court, or "aftercare"—parole—following release from

Probation
officers

an institution) is handicapped by staffs that are inadequate in numbers and in training; institutions tend to be primarily custodial in nature, with professional personnel limited to diagnostic rather than treatment functions.

BIBLIOGRAPHY. A.E. FINK, E.E. WILSON, and M.B. CONOVER, *The Field of Social Work*, 3rd ed. (1955); R.A. SKIDMORE and M.G. THACKERAY, *Introduction to Social Work* (1964); K.K. JACOB, *Methods and Fields of Social Work in India*, 2nd rev. ed. (1965); and W.A. FRIEDLANDER, *Introduction to Social Welfare*, 3rd ed. (1968), are the basic introductory volumes to the study of social work and social welfare. A useful survey of the methods of study of social administration and the historical development of social services is presented in A.V.S. LOCHHEAD (ed.), *A Reader in Social Administration* (1968). R.M. TITMUSS, *Commitment to Welfare* (1968), is a collection of essays that attempts to define the principles and models of social policy. A number of critical issues in social welfare and new perspectives in dealing with the organization of welfare services is given in P.E. WEINBERGER (comp.), *Perspectives on Social Welfare* (1969). C. KASIUS (ed.), *New Directions in Social Work* (1954), is a symposium on the present state of social work and the responsibilities of the profession. An invaluable reference work on all aspects of social work methods and programs is the NATIONAL ASSOCIATION OF SOCIAL WORKERS, *Social Work Year Book* (annual).

The following works provide information on the programs and services of individual countries and areas: K. WOODROOFE, *From Charity to Social Work in England and the United States* (1962); B.N. RODGERS et al., *Comparative Social Administration* (1968), a comparative analysis of social policy, planning, and administration in France, Norway, and Canada; GUNNAR MYRDAL, *Asian Drama: An Inquiry into the Poverty of Nations*, 3 vol. (1968); REPUBLIC OF INDIA, PLANNING COMMISSION, *Plans and Prospects of Social Welfare in India, 1951–61* (1963); B.Q. MADISON, *Social Welfare in the Soviet Union* (1968), a history of welfare programs from 1917 to the late 1960s.

Publications of the UNITED NATIONS DEPARTMENT OF ECONOMIC AND SOCIAL AFFAIRS include: *1967 Report on the World Social Situation* (1969); *Assistance to the Needy in Less Developed Areas* (1956); *Proceedings of the International Conference of Ministers Responsible for Social Welfare, 1968* (1969); *Family, Child and Youth Welfare Services* (1965); and *Organization and Administration of Social Welfare Programmes*, a series of country studies on Canada (1967), Jordan (1968), Italy (1969), Norway (1969), Romania (1967), Egypt (1967), the United Kingdom (1967), and the Union of Soviet Socialist Republics (1967).

(K.K.J.)

Social Behaviour, Animal

Humans have long been interested in the societies of other animals. The Paleolithic cave paintings of southern Europe bear witness to the keen attention paid by early man to the social lives of the animals he hunted. Aristotle, in the 4th century BC, noted the dances by which honeybees tell each other the distance and direction of food. Chicken ranchers have now learned that two chickens penned together will eat more food and produce more meat or eggs than if they are kept in separate pens.

Knowledge of the social behaviour of screwworm flies (*Cochliomyia hominivorax*), tsetse flies (*Glossina* species), and desert locusts (*Schistocerca gregaria*) has helped mitigate ancient plagues. Man studies the aggressive kinds of sociality in animals to see how war can be avoided. Finally, humans study animal social behaviour as an avocation as human societies become more crowded. The study of animal social behaviour thus helps to stave off all four horsemen of the Apocalypse—starvation, plague, war, and "death" by malaise.

This article is divided into the following sections:

I. The characteristics of social behaviour

GENERAL FEATURES

Social behaviour among animals takes many forms. The American naturalist and artist John James Audubon observed one of the largest social groups that man has ever known, in the fall of 1813 near Henderson, Kentucky. The species was the passenger pigeon (*Ectopistes migratorius*), once incredibly numerous but hunted to extinction by the end of the 19th century. Audubon wrote:

> The air was literally filled with pigeons; the light of noonday was obscured as by an eclipse; the dung fell in spots not unlike melting flakes of snow . . . . The people were all in arms . . . . For a week or more, the population fed on no other flesh than that of pigeons . . . . The atmosphere, during this time, was strongly impregnated with the peculiar odour which emanates from the species . . . . Let us take a column of one mile in breadth, which is far below the average size, and suppose it passing over us without interruption for three hours, at the rate mentioned above of one mile in the minute. This will give us a parallelogram of 180 miles by 1, covering 180 square miles. Allowing 2 pigeons to the square yard, we have 1,115,136,000 pigeons in one flock.

The largest social organizations ever known are those of desert locusts; the pigeons were second; and present-day China is probably third, although some pelagic fish schools may be next. Persecution by man is reducing all the large social organizations except his own: the bison and the anchovies off California and Peru have fared poorly compared to smaller groups.

Social and nonsocial behaviour

Large numbers or crowding do not in themselves constitute social behaviour. It is usually true, for instance, that a fish that produces a million eggs tosses them out less socially than does a fish that produces a single young and cares for it much more, and that a polygamous bird is less social than a faithfully monogamous one. Overcrowding leads to many social abnormalities. Crowded cats, for instance, develop a "despot" and "pariahs," and there is an almost continuous frenzy of spiteful hissing, growling, or fighting. Crowded rats display, in addition, hypersexuality, homosexuality, and cannibalism.

Animals sometimes are brought together by some localized attraction or scarcity, as are moths around an electric light, animals at a water hole in the dry African savanna, birds and bees at a fruit-bearing tree, or iguanas crowding to nest on islands free of predators. To determine if a grouping is social or not, it is necessary to examine the distribution of the animal within the limits of its needed habitat. Most animals require a certain sort of habitat—woodland for a squirrel, or nearly bare ground for a horned lark. Within the correct habitat, the animal also requires certain resources, such as food and water and nesting or roosting sites. The needed habitats and resources collectively form the "niche" of the animal. If an animal's niche is locally distributed, the animal may be found clumped, even if it is not particularly social. If the niche or habitat is patchily or irregularly distributed and the animal cannot move easily from one patch to another, it is said to live in a "coarse-grain" environment or to have a "coarse-grained" niche. Such animals often seem social when they are not. If the niche or habitat of an animal is rather uniform, so that the animal can move about and find what it needs in many places, it is said to live in a "fine-grain" environment or to have a "fine-grained" niche. Such animals often seem solitary when they actually are reacting to each other and hence are social. They tend to be solitary because they do not need to follow others to get to the right environment.

Within a fine-grain environment, or within one "grain" of a coarse-grain environment, animals may occur in groups even when they are not social. A "random" pattern of distribution, in which animals wander without regard to each other, brings asocial animals together at times. An even distribution is much more common, as in territories of many songbirds in which each pair occupies its own plot of ground; these are actually social animals, in the sense that each interacts with its neighbours so as to keep them at a certain long distance. "Clumped" distribution of animals is also common; this usually is truly social in the sense that each animal interacts with its neighbours so as to keep them at a certain short distance. Regularity of the short or long distance an animal keeps from its neighbours is thus as much an indication of sociality as is grouping; only the theoretical (and probably nonexistent) animal that completely ignores its neighbours is truly nonsocial. Time is also a factor in spacing; truly social animals have a tendency to move to the correct distances from each other and to maintain those positions over specifiable time periods, such as for the morning hours each day.

FACTORS INVOLVED IN SOCIAL INTERACTION

Leadership and dominance Social interaction in time and space is sometimes shown to the ethologist by patterns of following and leadership, although neither of these is necessarily social; following occurs in a dog tracking a rabbit, and leading is seen in an anglerfish luring a smaller fish for dinner by dangling a fleshy protuberance on the snout. In the Eurasian red deer (*Cervus elaphus*), an old female leads the does and fawns about. Spanish merino sheep have been bred to follow each other, while the Scottish highland sheep have been bred to be more independent; following may thus vary within a species according to its needs or to the environmental pressures on it.

Following need not mean there is a leader. The first bird in a migratory "V" of geese or pelicans is not continually the same, and the leaders of a school of fish change every time the school changes direction.

Leadership is sometimes, but not always, associated with a dominance hierarchy or peck order, which may or may not be a sign of social behaviour. Peck order, first noted in bumblebees, means that *A* pecks *B*, *B* pecks *C*, etc., but it does not necessarily mean that *A* leads *C* or *B* or that the three are interacting constructively. The dominant central males of a baboon troop tend to influence the direction taken by the rest of the troop around them; but the bullying dominant stag circling around a herd of red deer has to follow wherever the females decide to go, and his initiative is limited to running straying females back to the herd.

Dominance hierarchies may occur whether or not there is social behaviour in the usual sense. Among several species of birds that follow swarms of army ants in Panama to catch insects flushed by the ants, the big ocellated antbird (*Phaenostictus mcleannani*) is dominant, the medium-sized bicoloured antbird (*Gymnopithys bicolor*) is next, and the small, spotted antbird (*Hylophylax naevioides*) is chased by all the other members of the flock (Figure 1).

Crowding almost any two solitary animals together will produce a dominance hierarchy, in which one animal becomes boss or kills the other. This is a major cause of deaths in zoos and aquariums, but it is not necessarily social behaviour. Some biologists even say that dominance hierarchies are evidence of antisocial rather than social behaviour and are expressions of inadequacy in overcrowded social systems. It is certainly true that most peck orders appear in unnatural situations, such as among chickens in a henyard or animals in a cage. In most animals, the absence of a dominance hierarchy, rather than the presence of such, in a crowded context is a sign of a high development of social behaviour.

Division of labour A further interaction that the ethologist watches for in social animals is division of labour. Any two animals will, of course, divide up food or any other resource between them. Indeed, no two animals in nature ever have precisely the same niche; if two species have similar niches, they will tend to develop different ways of doing things, or one will exterminate the other. Ecologists call this the "competitive exclusion principle." Man attempts to reduce insect competition by various methods of "control." He kills off other animals by cutting down the trees in which they live. Most animals are less destructive and tend to divide up the world rather than to exterminate other species. Evolution, before the advent of man, seems to have produced continuously more kinds of animals and a greater division of niches, except in periods of environmental disaster. The three antbirds mentioned above tend to specialize in large, medium, and small prey; to the degree that these birds take different foods, they are cooperating better with each other.

Division of labour also occurs within a species. Males and females of some woodpecker species forage in different places in the trees, taking different types of food. Some animals use the same resource but do different things to get it. The male huia (*Heterolocha acutirostris*), an extinct bird of New Zealand, apparently used his short straight beak to open logs while the female, with her long curved beak, removed the insect larvae from the long tunnels he exposed. Male and female birds often build nests together, dividing the labour equally in some cases.

Social insects have more elaborate divisions of labour. Animals that cooperate by division of labour tend to use varied resources and to find more uses for them.

Division of labour seems to be a passing phase in the evolution of most animals other than man. It is evidently of little advantage to most animal societies. The honeybee, the leaf-cutter ants, and other animals with division of labour nearly always occur only where there is little competition from more specialized animals. Few of the most advanced insects or other animals show division of labour. In habitats such as the coral reef and the tropical forest, division of labour tends to be among different species rather than within a species.

Social interactions of various types are more important in determining degree of sociality than are most of the above characteristics. The only interactions between animals that are seldom considered social are behaviours

Drawing by Christian D. Olsen

Figure 1: *Feeding positions of six birds in relation to a T-shaped swarm of ants* (stippled).
(A) Gray-headed tanager, *Eucometis penicillata*. (B) Plain-brown woodcreeper, *Dendrocincla fuliginosa*. (C) Barred woodcreeper, *Dendrocolaptes certhia*. (D) Ocellated antbird, *Phaenostictus mcleannani*. (E) Bicoloured antbird, *Gymnopithys bicolor*. (F) Spotted antbird, *Hylophylax naevioides*.

in which animals take something needed by others. The question arises, however, as to how to classify the parasitic relationships of a fetus in the mother and the male anglerfish (*Photocorynus spiniceps*) on his mate, or the fact that killing by predators may help animals to avoid overgrazing their habitats. One could speak of communication of feint and chase in the interaction between moose and wolves. When a bird chases another off its territory, it uses communication and interacts with the other bird very strongly.

Humans often consider chimpanzees or bees as more social than desert locusts, because the locusts have rather simple interactions. Male hummingbirds and birds of paradise, however, have their elaborate plumages and social displays because the females get together with them so seldom that they might not recognize a suitable mate without the displays. It seems generally true that elaborate rituals evolve where social bonds are most fleeting or likely to be disrupted. To determine sociality, one must look at the total spectrum of social interactions as well as at their diversity and productivity, rather than just at a single feature such as complex communicatory rituals.

Communication

Social behaviour commonly includes communication, which may be defined as the sending of a message through a medium to a receiver so as to change the status and perhaps the behaviour of the receiver. Communication need not be overt or frequent or complex; one flick of an eyebrow by a dominant baboon is sometimes enough to send others away. Communication takes many forms. The voluble babble of a group of birds mobbing or attacking an owl is communication. The purveying of falsehoods also occurs in nature: the katydid that mimics or looks like a leaf, or the phasmid insect that looks like a stick, is telling predatory birds that it is inedible. Animals commonly exaggerate their characteristics to impress a mate, a rival, or a predator, puffing themselves out or blustering even if they do not lie outright. It has been well stated that a patch of colour on an animal is almost certain to have communicating functions, to mean something when displayed in exaggerated fashion to its social companions. Some animals also communicate by taste or odour, by voice, by electric impulses, by heat, or by touch; and many animals have more than one of these systems.

Communication between animals of different species becomes of increasing importance as environmental associations grow more complex. In such ecologically advanced habitats as coral reefs and tropical forests there is much interspecific communication.

Altruistic behaviour

Altruistic social behaviour is often found among animals. An altruistic animal is one that expends some of its energy helping another without direct benefit to itself, be it a mother bear protecting her cubs against their hungry father or a bird giving an alarm call that warns its neighbours of a hawk. An alarm call may help the bird itself, of course, by startling the predator or warning it that this alert bird will be hard to catch.

Psychologists have found that a rat or monkey will slow its rate of pressing a lever for food if that lever also gives an electric shock to a nearby rat or monkey. Rats will take turns sitting on a platform so that others can feed without being interrupted by electric shock. Rats or pigeons can be trained to cooperate in getting food.

Since the altruistic animal always loses something by its behaviour, the question arises why altruism exists. One answer is that, as the evolutionist Charles Darwin suggested, when an animal protects its offspring, it helps its kind to survive the process of natural selection. When porpoises help an injured relative to the surface where it can breathe, they seem to be following a pattern of behaviour that can be accounted for by evolution. Their altruism clearly helps the group and therefore becomes part of the genetic endowment. Altruism, significantly enough, is usually limited to an animal's relatives. Most social animals, such as penguins, feed only their own young. When the individual animal loses more than it or its relatives gain, as when female seals nurse young not their own, the question arises whether this serves the

survival of the larger group or the species. Under some conditions, the survival of the group may be more important even than survival of the individual, as when the honeybee dies defending the hive. The worker honeybee, which is not able to reproduce, is in the biological sense not an individual so much as an extra limb of a collective animal.

Reciprocal altruism, in which a benefit is later returned to the benefactor, need not be between related animals and may not even seem altruistic. Alarm calls of birds often alert entirely unrelated kinds of birds, which later may return the favour. An act that seems selfish in the short run is sometimes altruistic in the long run, or vice versa, in the case of maladaptation. Wasps, ants and termites that cannibalize or dominate nestmates at times of food shortage may better keep the colony from starving. Individual ants and bees are often lazy, spending most of their time resting or wandering aimlessly, but these unemployed individuals form an easily mobilized reserve in times of danger.

Individual and group recognition are often important aspects of social structure. Ovenbirds (*Seiurus aurocapillus*) in North America recognize neighbouring males by their songs and react aggressively mainly to songs of strange males. Animals that have long parental bonds often show individual recognition. Herring gulls (*Larus argentatus*), for example, recognize chicks or mates by slight differences in voice or appearance. The larger or more ephemeral the society, the less there can be individual recognition between distant individuals and the more important becomes recognition by group characters, such as the "nest odours" of social insects. Ants, bees, and termites often attack strangers, or even members of their own colony that have been experimentally removed for a few days or washed. Many kinds of parasitic insects (beetles, flies, butterfly caterpillars), however, provide food or scents that gain them entry to a nest, then prey on larvae there.

Other internal characteristics of societies are age structure, birth rates, and death rates. A young wasp or termite colony has few old animals, a mature colony has more, and a declining colony or one that is producing reproductive forms has few young. The old colony has a lower percentage of foraging workers than does the young colony, and has a lower birth rate and higher death rate as a consequence; but only the old colony produces reproductive forms.

Societies also perform movements, such as nomadism and migration. Army ants wander nomadically after prey. Wildebeest and locusts of Africa emigrate to green areas of local rains; flocking or solitary birds migrate back and forth to escape winter or drought; anadromous fishes, such as salmon, move to the sea for food and to rivers to spawn; catadromous ones, such as eels, do the reverse.

Migrants are often placed at a disadvantage compared to residents, for the latter can take the regular food supplies and leave only ephemeral sources for migrants. Migrants that follow army ants for food in Central America are subordinate to residents, and succeed only when residents are absent. The migrant can turn its world from a coarse-grained one to a fine-grained or dependable one by migrating from one patch to the next; and by force of numbers migrants sometimes displace residents.

Societies can make use of seasonal environmental changes by migrating locally, such as sowbugs clustering to estivate in hot weather or ladybugs hibernating in masses. Other societies show food storage; *e.g.*, harvester ants (*Messor*) and wood or pack rats (*Neotoma*). Honey ants (*Myrmecocystus*) have a "replete" caste that bloat their abdomens with stored honey and hang from the roofs of underground chambers until tapped by other workers.

Societies show population fluctuations, from extinction to explosion. Mass emigrations in some, such as lemmings and squirrels, occur mainly after population explosions or periodic extirpations of food supplies. Some populations, such as many protozoans, worms, and insects, normally undergo violent fluctuations, but are resistant to extinction. These are animals in which the adults emigrate or both adults and young emigrate. Animals in which the adults normally occupy a fine-grained habitat and only the young move, such as most higher animals, normally have relatively stable populations, but are easily killed off by a new predator or temporally unpredictable events.

A major external characteristic of the more complex societies is that they construct things, or modify their environments. The elaborate air-conditioned castles of some termites, the path systems of feral house cats, and the patterns of singing at dawn among birds of ephemeral or coarse-grain habitats, all are "structures" created by animals.

Cooperation and competition are major aspects of animal social behaviour. Social facilitation, as when yawning spreads through a pride of lions or chickens eat more rapidly together, shows that cooperative competition can be social. Social animals, which live close together, often interfere and fight more with each other, especially in early stages, than do solitary ones. A fair percentage of the communication between social animals involves "agonistic" or threat-submission behaviour. If this behaviour results in a more adaptive dispersion of the animals, it has been altruistic. Grouped goldfish and other animals survive heat, cold, metallic ions, and other "pollution" better than do isolated animals; but if too many animals aggregate, they pollute each other. Social groups therefore have an optimum size and density, based upon an equilibrium between advantages and disadvantages.

Linking the internal and external characteristics of social systems are flows of energy and materials. Social systems use energy in building structures, or information-rich systems. Physically, one can measure the success of a social system by how efficiently and extensively it uses energy and materials and converts them to physical, biological, or cultural structures. However, success in the short run can lead to disaster in the long run, as when elephants or humans destroy an African forest and then must starve or emigrate. Energy and material flows involve an interspecific web, the ecosystem, and must be measured over the long run and in general as well as locally or in the short run.

Social behaviour, therefore, must include interactions between different kinds of animals. A flock of sandpipers in flight is not less social if it includes two species rather than one. If species cooperate, a flock of two species can even be more social than a flock of one species. At African waterholes, baboons keep the lookout while associated antelope are good at scenting predators. Symbiosis is social, even though the late biologist Traian Savesculu of Romania was half right when he joked "Symbiosis is like marriage—a mutual exploitation." Like all social organizations, it is both cooperative and competitive.

Social behaviour may thus be defined as "more or less diverse and constructive interactions among two or more animals." Social behaviour is usually constructive, productive, and adaptive; but it sometimes persists for a time after the evolutionary basis for it is gone. For instance, many kinds of hawks in the eastern United States have almost disappeared, but the flocks of small birds that were formerly their prey still form as vigilante groups.

II. Types of animal societies

To understand social behaviour more fully, it is necessary to examine it throughout the range of animal life. W.C. Allee, in his classic book *The Social Life of Animals*, distinguishes two major types of animal societies. One is the parental, or familial, society, in which parent and offspring stay together for varying lengths of time. The other is the pair bond, or club, society, composed of individuals that come together from different families. This type was much emphasized by the 19th-century English philosopher Herbert Spencer because it corresponded to his social Darwinist ideas. The social Dar-

Figure 2: (Top) A colony of three species of sponges, approximately life-size. At top of colony is small bread-crumb sponge (*Halichondria*); branching mass at lower right is *Leucosolenia complicata*; tubular sponges on left are *Scypha ciliatum*. (Bottom) Portuguese man-of-war (*Physalia physalis*), one-third life-size.
Douglas P. Wilson

winist does not like to admit that a weak son can win out if he has powerful parents; but recent work with rhesus monkeys shows clearly that the son of a high-ranking mother tends to be protected by his mother and hence gets to the top of the hierarchy even if he himself is a weakling. Parental societies are very common.

PARENTAL SOCIETIES

Parental societies are found at all levels, from the cell to the monkey troupe. All animals provide for their young in some way. In every animal there is a period when the young is part of the parent and receives materials from the parent. Later, the young may partly or completely separate from the parent; in some animals, the more or less separate young is then helped by the parent, or helps it.

Parental behaviour among simple organisms. Even some of the simplest organisms show colonial aggregations of the parental type. Some viruses form inclusion bodies in the cells they attack; these bodies are thought to be colonies of daughter viral strands. Other viruses form ordered arrays.

Bacterial
colonies Bacteria, only a few steps up the evolutionary scale beyond viruses, also show parent–young colonies. Diplococci, which can cause pneumonia, are dot-shaped bacteria that have two daughter cells in each group. Streptococci form chains, and staphylococci arrange themselves in grapelike clusters. In all of these, and in a large number of other colonial bacteria, the offspring that are produced by a dividing parent stay together for some length of time.

Protozoa, a few steps beyond bacteria, also show parental sociality. Many reproduce by simple division and hence give the daughters help only before the split. Under difficult conditions, protozoans commonly form a protec-

By courtesy of the American Museum of Natural History, New York

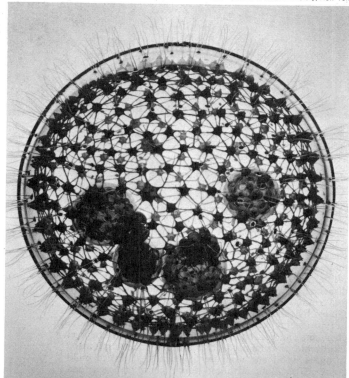

Figure 3: (Top) Glass model of protozoan colony *Volvox* (magnified about 75 X). (Bottom) Colony of coral animals *Astrangia danae* magnified about 3 X).

tive "cyst" and divide within it. In such divided cysts 2, 4, 8, 16, 32, or even more daughter cells may associate until the cyst "hatches."

Some protozoans form definite colonies in addition to or in place of cysts. *Volvox* and many other slow-moving or sedentary colonial protozoans show differentiation or division of labour between cells of a colony. In *Volvox*, the forward cells have large eyespots and a few rear cells take care of reproduction (Figure 3, top).

It is almost certain that sponges evolved from colonial flagellate protozoans. Sponges are integrated networks of cells, some of them amoeboid (amorphous) and some flagellate. It has been shown that if a sponge is strained through cloth so that the cells are separated, they will reunite and form new sponges so long as a flagellate collar cell can rejoin an amoeboid cell. The sponge is thus on the border between colonial organization and integrated multicellular organization (Figure 2, top). One advantage of integrated multicellular organization, with different types of cells performing different functions, was probably that the sponges could become much larger than the largest multinucleate or even colonial protozoans and thus could capture these protozoans. This type of organization also provides strength: some cells can hold on in swift currents, while some can secrete skeletons and others concentrate on food getting. Thus cooperation gave sponges and similar multicellular animals an advantage in competition with even the largest and most aggressive single-celled animals. Sponges
and
coelen-
terates

The colonial organization of cells into protozoan colonies or into multicellular animals will be referred to below as the "colonial-1" stage (Figure 3, top), in contrast to the colonial organization of attached multicellular animals—the "colonial-2" stage. The colonial-2 stage is well developed in successful aquatic animals just above the sponges; the coelenterates (hydroids, jellyfishes or medusae, sea anemones). Coral reefs bear witness to the success of colonial-2 growth in other coelenterates (Figure 3, bottom). Many different types of free-swimming colonies, such as the dangerous fish-killing Portuguese man-of-war (*Physalia*), exhibit huge complexity on the colonial plan (Figure 2, bottom). In corals and other colonies, the original individual is linked to its offspring in a network. Food material and chemicals are often exchanged between individuals over the tubes of this network. Often the different individuals in this network show division of labour. Sometimes, as in *Obelia*, there are only reproductive and feeding individuals. In *Physalia*, there are swimming individuals, stinging ones, and many others, including one that serves as a gas-filled float. The interdependence and communication in such a colony is so extensive that the colony seems almost to be an individual and is sometimes called a superorganism.

Despite the great success of sponges and coelenterates, the main line of evolution goes onward through colonial-1 animals. The link was probably wormlike animals somewhat like present-day flatworms. Most flatworms and higher worms show little association between parents and young.

From flatworms to insects. The main line of evolution leading from flatworms to insects shows little parent–young cooperation or colonial development. The entoproct Bryozoa, or moss animals, form treelike colonies like those of corals and thus show type-2 coloniality; but it is not certain whether the Bryozoa actually belong to the line leading to insects. A few wheel worms or rotifers, such as the free-floating *Conochilus volvox*, form colonies. A few annelid worms, such as sybellid fan worms, bud off chains of individuals in a manner like the flatworm *Catenula*. This is a common method of breeding in some annelids; the special rear "worm," or "epitoke," breaks off and swims to the surface where it releases sperm or eggs and dies, often in huge swarms of epitokes as in the Samoan palolo worm (*Eunice viridis*).

Typically such worms as roundworms and earthworms strew their eggs about or attach them to something as soon as they are fertilized or brood the eggs only briefly. A few nemertine worms are viviparous—*i.e.*, they produce live young. The annelid worm *Ctenodrilus* is said to be truly viviparous, the nutrition of young coming via maternal blood vessels. Most mollusks take little care of their young. One chiton, *Callistochiton viviparus,* gives birth to young that have undergone development in the ovary. In a few bivalves such as the European oyster (*Ostrea edulis*), the eggs develop in the gill filaments. Most squids release single eggs or chains of eggs, but some members of the octopus group stay near their eggs and remove debris from them. The paper nautilus, *Argonauta,* forms a paper nautilus shell and the mother takes care of her eggs in it. At times the male hides in the shell.

Peripatus and its relatives, the onychophorans, are intermediate between annelid worms and arthropods and have well-developed parental systems. Some Australian forms lay eggs, but others keep the eggs inside until young hatch; many of these are viviparous, giving the young secretions from the uterus.

Not until one reaches such jointed-legged animals as crabs and insects (arthropods) does one find much extended association between young and their parents. A few scattered arthropods still have no parental care other than production of eggs. The female walkingstick casually drops eggs as she moves about. Many ostracods and copepods, and many of the edible shrimps, shed eggs into the ocean waters. Most arthropods, however, care for their young briefly.

Parental care among arthropods

Scorpions are all viviparous or ovoviviparous (eggs developing in the mother), and many carry their young about. The female pseudoscorpion of the leaf litter often builds a little nest, and the young get nourishment from her in a belly pouch. The female solifugid, or sun scorpion, makes a burrow for her eggs and then brings prey to the young after they emerge from the burrow. The female whip scorpion attaches eggs to herself and carries them until the young go through several molts; she dies as soon as they leave. Spiders generally weave a silken case for eggs and young. The female wolf spider carries her young on her back. Some young spiders build a family or community web together. The harvestmen and mites mostly lay eggs in the environment, but some mites carry eggs until they hatch. Some ticks deposit egg masses, and hundreds of young seed ticks may stay together, to the dismay of a human when such a mass drops on him and starts to spread. Sea spiders (pycnogonids) are strange, for the male takes the egg mass from the female and cares for the eggs until they hatch, or slightly longer. Most crustaceans briefly brood their eggs, or eggs and young, often in special pouches on the body of the female.

Millipedes often form a nest; the young *Spirobolus* later eat the material of that nest. Some female millipedes coil about the eggs for several weeks. Many centipede females brood eggs, but others do not. In symphylans, often considered a link to insects, the female carries eggs in cheek pouches.

Insect families

Social insects. Insects show the greatest development of family structure among animals. Most so-called insect societies are, strictly speaking, families. Sometimes they are called colonies, but the individuals are not directly attached to each other as in the "colonies-1" of protozoa and multicellular animals or the "colonies-2" of corals. They might be called "colonies-3" because they are "attached" by chemicals as well as by social behaviour. The young stay with both parents or with the mother and form social organizations of high complexity. Social behaviour of this type is known among the thrips (Thysanoptera), Zoraptera, book lice (Psocoptera), web spinners (Embioptera), termites (Isoptera), and roaches (Blattoidea) of the more primitive insects, and in some groups of the higher insects—the aphids and lace bugs of the Heteroptera, and especially, in the ants, bees, and wasps of the Hymenoptera. Some of these groups bear little resemblance to the families of vertebrates. A critical observer might say of insect societies that the parents enslave their first children or their sisters, frequently with "drugs," and thereby ensure better care of their later ones.

Societies of lower insects are simple. The female (or male in the case of mole crickets, *Gryllotalpa*), works hard to build a nest and to protect its first offspring. The

Figure 4: Bivouac of army ants (*Eciton*) between trees, which are about 14 inches apart. Inset is detail of bivouac magnified slightly larger than life.
Carl W. Rettenmeyer

offspring may reciprocate by helping to build a colony web under a stone or leaf or under tree bark, as in the web spinners and book lice. In wood roaches, such as *Cryptocercus punctulatus* of the southeastern United States, the young must stay with the adults, because all have symbiotic protozoans inside them that digest wood cellulose: at every molt the roach loses all its protozoa (because the linings of the fore- and hindgut are also molted) and must eat the feces of another roach or die.

In termites, the male and female lose their wings after a dispersal flight and dig a cavity in which they raise the first young. These young have their sexual growth inhibited by chemical secretions from their parents; instead of reproducing themselves, they work hard to make more chambers and get food for the next young. They often get fecal material from each other full of symbiotic protozoa to digest wood and also use the fecal material to build houses. The more advanced forms chew up wood and grow fungus on it. The young have a division of labour, some being workers and some soldiers; there are also nasutes, which have snoutlike processes that eject a sticky substance used in warfare to protect the colony. Such colonies may become huge and build houses higher than a man's head. The first parents are not so much the leaders of the colony as egg-producing machines cared for by their first offspring. Eventually some of the slaves achieve their freedom when the chemical secretion from their parents runs short; they develop wings, fly off, and start new worlds of their own.

Some beetles show behaviour approaching the social. A British rove beetle defends its eggs and young against intruders. Dung beetles dig burrows and store dung for their larvae. The male and female burying beetle cooperate to dig away the soil underneath small dead animals; the female feeds her larvae on regurgitated food. Bark and ambrosia beetles dig tunnels in wood and grow fungal spores; the female feeds her young on pieces of fungus while the male keeps away other males.

Some moths and butterflies associate in the caterpillar stage. Social caterpillars, such as the tent caterpillars (Lasiocampidae) and the larvae of small ermine moths

(*Yponomeuta padella*), make webs similar to those of colonial spiders but use them only to hide in rather than to catch prey.

Bees and wasps

The origins of social behaviour can be seen in bees and wasps. There are solitary bees and wasps, all of which prepare a protected place for the egg and later the larva. Some "gall wasps"—as in "gall aphids" and some mites—sting plants, which then provide fleshy galls for the young larvae. The parent often provides food for the larva. The tarantula-killer wasp will sting a huge spider and store it in a drugged state by the egg. The "parasitoid" hymenopterans lay an egg on or in a wandering caterpillar to parasitize it. Some bees or wasps return to put a new spider or other food source into the nest after the first food has been eaten, a process called progressive provisioning. From this it is only a short step to having a single female care for several young in a compound nest, as in *Polistes* wasps, and another short step to having sisters or young stay around the nest and help care for the later young. In some insects, such as wasps of the genus *Polistes*, this is done by having the first or strongest female harass or dominate the later or weaker ones. Their sexual growth is repressed and they cannot lay eggs as long as the dominant female is there. Chemical dominance, or drugging, is the next step; in the more social bees and ants, chemicals produced by the queen are actually needed by the workers, and exchange of food and drugs (trophallaxis) is regular.

Division of labour often occurs in ant and bee societies. Ants are often polymorphic, with small individuals working in the nest and medium or medium-large ones working outside; huge-headed individuals become protective soldiers or even use their heads as plugs to stop up the nest entrance to all besides members of the colony. Honeybees have division of labour by age—the youngest bees feeding larvae, older ones building the comb, and still older ones flying out for nectar and pollen and bee glue. Many of the polymorphic differences are apparently determined by food, as when the new queen bee gets royal jelly regularly, while the smaller workers get royal jelly for only a few days. Other differences are genetic, as in the case of the male ant or bee, which comes from an unfertilized egg.

These family societies of insects are diverse and successful. Termites and ants are among the most common tropical insects, bees and wasps among the common subtropical and temperate ones. The houses of termites—earth castles with shingled construction to shed rain and porous outer layers to control carbon dioxide and humidity—are equalled in their intricacy only by those of man. The honeybees communicate with chemicals and dances to tell each other the distance and direction of flowers.

The ferocious defense of the nest by wasps and hornets avails them little, however, against the onslaughts of marauding hordes of army ants (tribe Ecitonini) in the tropical forests of the Western Hemisphere, and of hordes of driver ants (tribe Dorylini) in Africa. The army ants (see Figure 4) do not eat trees or people, as early stories would have it, but they tear apart arthropods. The driver ants, which have scissor-like mandibles that cut flesh, can tear apart humans if given the chance. These are probably the largest of the familial or "colonial-3" societies. It has been estimated that a large colony of the army ant *Eciton burchelli* includes 1,500,000 individuals, and the colonies of the driver ant *Anomma wilverthi* probably contain up to 22,000,000.

The leaf-cutter ants of the Western Hemisphere live in huge underground colonies. They, along with termites and a few beetles and moths, are agriculturalists. The leaf-cutter ants cut strips of green leaves and make a paste of them in which they grow fungus. Their underground chambers may reach several yards. It is hard to realize that such huge colonies are extended families.

From bryozoans to humans. In the other great line of evolution, which leads to man, the social use of the family has taken a different tack. Where the first line began with actively moving, wormlike individuals and ended with drugged, tiny individuals in huge families, the line that leads to humans begins with colonial, attached animals of

Polymorphism and behaviour

the general appearance of corals but of the structure of worms and ends with social animals in which families play an important but relatively small role.

Wormlike animals

Some early wormlike animals evidently settled down on the floors of ancient oceans, and to protect themselves had to develop shells (as in the lamp shells or brachiopods) or colonies with specialized defensive members (as in the moss animals or bryozoans). Brachiopods are solitary and shed their gametes into the seawater. Moss animals form colonies in which there is direct or partially impeded exchange of body fluids. Their societies show more division of labour than do termite colonies. There are feeding individuals, reproductive individuals, special whiplike individuals (vibracula), and bird-head individuals (avicularia) that hit or bite other animals settling on the colony.

It seems incongruous to suggest that active vertebrates developed from tiny wormlike animals living sedentary and colonial lives, but the future does not always belong to the strongest, biggest, or fastest animals of a given age. The moss animals, with their tiny encrustations or filamentous colonies, are internally much advanced over the more abundant corals.

One major side branch of this line of descent does lead to the nonsocial echinoderms—starfish, brittle stars, sea cucumbers. Few of these animals take care of their offspring, and even their gametes tend to be shed broadcast into the seawater. Some sea stars, brittle stars, and sea urchins of the Arctic and Antarctic brood their eggs. In some, as the brittle star *Amphipholis squamata*, the young are attached to the mother and get nourishment from her. Some sea cucumbers, equally divided among cold-water and warm-water forms, brood their eggs externally or, as in *Thyone rubra* of California, inside. A few sea lilies or crinoids brood eggs or young.

There is also little parental care in several of the wormlike side branches of this line of descent. Pogonophoran worms, which even lack a digestive tract, sometimes brood eggs in their tubes in the ocean mud. Arrowworms (Chaetognatha) occasionally carry eggs about, but most release them into the ocean waters where they swim. The arrowworms are successful predators, but the line to vertebrates leads for the most part through the colonial or sedentary filter feeders—the pterobranchs, the acorn worms, and the tunicates or sea squirts.

The pterobranchs are sedentary, colonial wormlike animals, with a central stalk in some colonies but no direct connection in others. The individuals of the latter wander in and out of the colony tubes. Pterobranchs are related to burrowing solitary acorn worms, the hemichordates. All these animals release their eggs and sperm rather casually into the ocean.

The sea squirts (Tunicata) are mostly soft spongelike masses that cling to rocks or pilings in the sea. Most shed eggs into the sea, but some brood eggs or young and release them partly grown. The young are either free-swimming tadpole-like animals or are budded from the adult to form a colony.

The line of descent up to this point is, curiously enough, closely associated with colonial animals, while the line that led to insects produced rather few colonial animals. It has been suggested that advances made during periods of coloniality may produce better free-living individuals and vice versa; the inference is that drastic new changes in a colonial animal can be perpetuated because of feeding by the rest of the colony and later be incorporated in a viable free-living combination.

Some biologists, including Darwin (with his vested interest in competition), have suggested that the sea squirts and all the other colonial animals are unimportant sidelines in evolution. They suggest that the mainline passed through nonsocial, competitive, free-living, wormlike and, later, tadpole-like animals. Wormlike animals led to animals like arrowworms, to the tunicate tadpole, and then to fishlike animals such as *Amphioxus*.

Certainly the next steps were through free-swimming animals with relatively little family life—cephalochordates (lancets) and the jawless fishes. Modern lampreys make a nest for external fertilization, but the hatching larvae make their own way to live as filter feeders in the muddy debris of stream bottoms.

Fish and amphibians Many jawed fishes take little care of their eggs or young, but there are some major exceptions. Many sharks, skates, and rays give birth to live young, and some have placentas to nourish them. Some fishes make nests; the Siamese fighting fish (*Betta splendens*) and others make bubble nests at the surface, while sticklebacks (*Eucalia*) and a mormyrid fish (*Gymnarchus*) make weed nests, and such fishes as salmon dig spawning nests in the bottoms of streams. Stickleback males fan their eggs until the young hatch, making sure there is enough oxygen. Other fish, such as the black-chinned mouthbreeder, fan their eggs by keeping them in their mouths. Other mouthbreeder fish periodically spit out the young fry and take them back in until the young are feeding well. Mouthbreeders include a freshwater catfish (*Loricaria typus*) and some marine catfishes (*Galeichthys felis* and its relatives), plus cardinal fishes (Apogonidae). There are several fish of a dozen different taxonomic assemblages that bear their young alive, among them the surf perches (Embiotocidae) and the mollies (Poeciliidae). Some have a placenta-like arrangement to nourish the young until birth.

While care of young by the male is frequent in fishes, it is rare among invertebrates (where the sea spiders are the only major example). Care by the males frees the female to obtain more food and hence raise more young per unit of time, which may be necessary in the event that food is difficult to find.

Male care of the young is well developed in lungfishes, predecessors of land vertebrates. Most salamanders and frogs, on the other hand, are not very good parents. The male Surinam toad (*Pipa pipa*) presses the eggs into the back of the female, and the young of *Rhinoderma darwinii* go through development in the vocal pouch of the male. The live-bearing frog (*Nectophrynoides*) of Africa, in which the young hatch within the mother and remain with her for protection, is another exception to the general rule that amphibians release their eggs and care for them little.

Higher vertebrates Among reptiles the best parental care is in alligators and some crocodiles, where the female makes a mound of dead leaves or sand and stays around to protect the eggs, to release them when they hatch, and to guard the young for perhaps as long as a year.

Birds are well-known for parental care. Most build nests, incubate eggs, and care for young. The males commonly help the females in this. Often young birds stay with their parents a year or more, and numerous examples are known of the young of one brood helping to feed the young of later broods. Often the young help the parents defend a "group territory," as among Australian bell magpies (*Cracticus*) and Mexican jays (*Aphelocoma ultramarina*).

The most advanced parental society yet recorded among birds is that of the ocellated antbird, which follows swarms of army ants in order to capture insects they flush in the neotropical forests. This bird's young stay with their parents for several months, then go and find mates, but return to their parents periodically for several years. The young bird and its mate are accepted as part of the extended family; they are not chased away as often as are unrelated birds.

An even greater organization of parental care is found in mammals, except that the males seldom help care for the young. The young are usually nourished before birth by the placenta of the mother, except in the egg-laying duck-billed platypus, the spiny echidna, and in marsupials. The young of marsupials are born prematurely and grow in the pouch of the mother for long periods. All mammal young, even the platypus and spiny echidna, must lap or suck milk produced by the mammary glands of the mother. This ensures that there is a strong family association between mother and young (Figure 5).

Commonly, groups develop around a mother, and may be joined by other such groups and by males to form bands, troops, and herds. Troops of monkeys and apes are basically families or grouped families. These and wolf bands include males, which may help to raise young. The "extended families" of humans lead to tribes, states, and nations.

Nationalism as a force in human affairs is commonly related to mother and home and family, as well as to interlocking family relationships even more complex than those of ocellated antbirds or wolf societies.

SOCIETIES WITH SEXUAL BONDS

Nonparental social relationships fall into two categories, sexual bonds and nonsexual bonds. Normally, only the latter can involve members of two or more species. Sexual bonds lead in many animals to parental bonds, of course, but differ in that the bond is normally between offspring of different families. The reason for this is that the main advantage of sexual union is to combine the good genetic features of two different lines. Some young, of course, will have the bad features of both lines and will be eliminated—a wastage tolerated in nature as a necessary expense.

Most animals depend on elaborate behaviour patterns to bring the male and female and their gametes together at the right time, rather than using the seemingly more certain processes of asexual reproduction, virgin birth, hermaphroditic self-fertilization, or male parasitism. Many marine animals shed eggs and sperm into the water or into special nests but do so only when chemically stimulated by the presence of substances from the opposite sex. Others use their "internal clocks" to release gametes only at a certain time of day or year. Samoan palolo worms form special gonadal body sections by budding, then release them to swarm in huge numbers at the surface of the ocean on a schedule set by the moon. The grunion (*Leuresthes tenuis*), a small Pacific fish of the silversides family, is famous for its males and females meeting to fertilize eggs high on the beach at the highest tide each month and at the highest waves of that tide as well. The synchronization of male and female requires them to have an internal lunar clock, such as that known for the colour changes of fiddler crabs.

Courtship must basically ensure two things: that the correct male and female get together at the right time with as little loss as possible; and that the offspring have the best possible chance to survive. Ensuring these two things has led to elaborate courtship patterns in animals. Where different kinds of animals that look, smell, or feel alike coexist, each individual must be especially careful not to hybridize with the wrong species. Otherwise it will **The functions of courtship**

Irven DeVore

Figure 5: Mother olive baboon (*Papio anubis*) and young.

waste its eggs or sperm in a union that will produce no young, or young that are malformed or maladapted for the world into which they emerge. Animals often develop complicated odours, colours, or voices as means of identification. There are many species of fruit flies of the genus *Drosophila*, and to avoid mismatings, each species has its own pattern of waving the wings by the male. The sight and sound of the wrong pattern of waving is enough to cause a female fruit fly to flee. (For further information on this aspect, see REPRODUCTIVE BEHAVIOUR.)

Where there is only a limited breeding area or a patchy environment in which the good areas are restricted, strong male–female differences are advantageous. In these cases the males have to advertise, often with song, to help females locate good areas. Males of species whose courtship displays are performed in groups usually have to compete more directly with each other and thus tend to develop large size or striking colours, overpowering scents or voices, or other exaggerated features. Female domestic chickens, sage grouse, and baboons tend to copulate mainly with the lordliest and most dominant males. This is not so evident in other animals, in which the females tend to mate with the male holding the best territory. The dominant male is likely to be the oldest one, the one that has proved he can survive and hence is "fittest."

Super-masculinity

The success of the "supermasculine" or lordly males in a few species may be advantageous only to those males. A few lordly males often usurp the few suitable places to breed, as in male sea elephants (*Mirounga angustirostris*) on Pacific beaches and in male red-winged blackbirds in North American marshes. If the lordly male blackbirds are eliminated, however, other males come in and the females breed with them just as quickly.

The supermasculine males in these species, full of pomp and strutting, seldom care for their young. Baboon males, it is true, do at times stop fights between lesser animals and drive away leopards or other predators. But usually the female takes care of the young herself. It may even be an advantage if she is "ladylike" and unobtrusive, so that the lordly male may draw predators away from the young. Keeping the male away from the young may also allow the female and her young more food. If environments are limited in food, keeping excess males out of the breeding area clearly is an advantage.

Supermasculinity, as well as being correlated with female care of the young, is also associated with polygamy. The mating of several animals of one sex with a single individual of the other sex tends to be associated in birds and mammals with great differences between the sexes. Serial polygamy, or the mating of an animal of one sex with several of the other sex at different times, may also occur. Promiscuity, or the mating of each female with several males and each male with several females, tends in supermasculine animals to resemble serial polygamy. Monogamy, or the mating of each male with one female, tends to occur mainly in animals with little difference between the sexes.

Having many mates does not necessarily mean that an animal is more social than if it has only one mate. In most cases, the polygamous male spends much time driving away other males and little time courting his females. His females spend little time with him, because they are busy raising many young—with little care for each. Among African weaver birds (*Ploceus*), monogamous species of the forest have smaller clutches than do polygamous ones of the savanna.

The whole system of lordly males, ladylike females, polygamy or serial polygamy, and multiple young, tends to occur mainly in animals with restricted and undependable sources of food and other necessities. One investigator found that males of the long-billed marsh wren (*Cistothorus palustris*) in Washington, where their marshes varied greatly in quality, had several mates; females went to males with good territories and left neighbouring males, with poor territories, mateless. Another investigator found that in Georgia, where the marshes were everywhere about equal in food supply and nesting cover, the long-billed marsh wrens were usually monogamous. The

correlation suggested by many recent studies is this: sexual dimorphism and diethism (behavioral differences) arise in animals in which environmental opportunities are restricted due to undependability or local distribution.

NONFAMILIAL SOCIAL BONDS

Social behaviour also occurs among animals that are not necessarily related by parental or sexual bonds. A "flock" or "band" of animals may be formed of only one family in some cases, but often several families or individuals join together.

Spacing. As previously noted, social organization within a species may be shown not only by the presence of clumping or positive movement of individuals but also by even spacing resulting from negative movements away from each other. Sociality is shown more by the presence of a definite spacing than by nearness.

Absence of spacing among simpler forms

There is little evidence for social spacing in protozoans and simpler beings, such as viruses and bacteria. Most recorded groups of unicellular or lower animals are probably parental or sexual groups. There seem to be few social interactions among micro-organisms, but this apparent dearth of social behaviour may be an artifact introduced by the disturbance of observation.

Most colonies of sponges and coelenterates seem to be parental colonies or aggregations in favourable sites rather than nonfamilial societies. There is little information on nonfamilial social organization among colonial-2 animals, even among those that can move, such as the colonies of Portuguese man-of-wars or the planktonic rotifer or sea-squirt colonies. Most worms and their relatives are not known to react to each other or to form social structures of the "flock" type. Little is known about mollusk organization; but the fact that mollusks do not pile up on top of each other suggests that there are negative social reactions.

Barnacle larvae prefer to attach next to another member of their own species or on a place where one of their species has just been removed. They avoid settling on top of another member of their own species, even though they readily settle on a member of another species. They react in part to chemicals that are specific to their species. Barnacles, then, aggregate in colonies but within a colony space themselves out. If the multicellular animal is a colony-1, the coral colony a colony-2, and the bee society a colony-3, the barnacle society may be called a colony-4. Colonies-4, in which the interactions are between unrelated, unmated, and unattached individuals, are regular in arthropods. In many cases the colony-4 is not obvious or is problematical. Bees form colonies-3 and perhaps also colonies-4, for colonies of bees space themselves out in the environment and avoid getting too close to other active colonies; but there is no evidence that bee colonies avoid getting too far apart, although if they did then mating between bees from different colonies would become difficult.

Colonies-4 are known among other arthropods. Tube-dwelling amphipods form colonies but chase each other and avoid getting too close. They show the phenomenon of "personal space," or "individual distance," as surely as do swallows sitting on a wire, in which a new arrival settling will sometimes cause shifting outward by individuals on both sides. Individual distance or personal space is a space around each individual that can be penetrated by another individual without hostility only after certain overtures.

Territoriality

The amphipod colonies also show the phenomenon of territoriality. Territoriality differs from personal space in that a territory is centered on some object outside the body of the animal itself. The male bitterling (*Rhodeus sericeus*), a European fish that lays its eggs inside a freshwater clam, will chase male intruders away from his clam even if the clam gets up and moves several feet. The male house finch (*Carpodacus mexicanus*) of North America chases other males away from his female, wherever she moves. More often, however, the external reference for territory is a fixed plot of ground, a nest hole, or some immovable set of objects. The animal may chase out intruders or tolerate them in the territory, but in his territory he is in charge. Work with bicoloured antbirds in Panamanian forests suggests that a territory may be defined as "an external referent in which one animal or group dominates others that become dominant elsewhere." A pair of bicoloured antbirds permits others on its territory, but as soon as the pair crosses a boundary line into another territory, it becomes subordinate to the pair of that territory.

Territoriality is known to exist among insects such as dragonflies and ants, some fish, a few frogs, some lizards, most birds, and many mammals. It probably exists, at least in chemical forms, in tube worms of a muddy beach or rocky shore, and perhaps even among sedentary protozoans.

Swarming. Personal space and territoriality are definite negative signs of coloniality-4, but there are also positive signs. Mutual repulsion is only part of sociality, for mutual attraction must also exist. Mutual attraction is found in many arthropods above the barnacles. Some of the best studied examples are the mating swarms of ants, flies, midges, and, especially, fireflies. Another example of mutual attraction is the migratory horde, of which the African migratory locust (*Schistocerca migratoria*) is the best studied example.

Communal
displays The synchronized communal displays of the fireflies of Thailand are among the most impressive exhibitions of the insect world. The gatherings of thousands of males on the mangroves of the coastal swamps have been described as a city of pulsating glitter, every male anticipating the flicker of his neighbours and flashing in unison with them. Communal mating displays of this type are common in birds such as manakins, sage grouse, ruffs, and birds of paradise, and are called lek displays. Presumably, the communal display enables females to find the males more easily. Seldom do bird leks approach the numbers or synchrony of a firefly lek in Thailand, but several male manakins sometimes cooperate in a synchronized cartwheel dance. It is difficult to explain why males competing with each other for mates should help one another, but the phenomenon has been well documented.

The legendary colonies-4 of the migratory locusts are far larger and more impressive than the migratory colonies-3 of the army and driver ants. When food is abundant, the locusts disperse widely and grow up in what is called the "solitaria" phase. As the locusts crowd and encounter each other, they begin to change colour and enter the "gregaria" phase, in which they look so different that they were once considered a separate species. The "gregaria" locusts behave differently too, for they are excitable and social. They begin to march over the ground as food supplies diminish. Finally they take wing in huge hordes and fly downwind to a low-pressure area where rains have recently fallen. Here they descend on crops and other vegetation, eating it to the ground before flying to the next low-pressure area. The extinct migratory hordes of passenger pigeons were apparently similar in their effects on vegetation.

Many other examples of flocks occur in higher animals, especially insects and vertebrates. Most show little internal structure. The migratory hordes of armyworms that devastated midwestern corn fields in the United States before the days of synthetic insecticides, the swarms of male and female palolo worms in the ocean, the feeding swarms of sharks, and the dense schools of herring, are all examples of flocks with little internal structure. The Austrian ethologist Konrad Lorenz calls them "anonymous flocks," because it matters little if individuals change places and bonds are seldom individualized. When the fish school turns, it is like an army platoon turning to the flank, for the former side fishes are now the leaders.

The mating choruses at frog ponds provide an example of an auditory lek. Some salamanders congregate to breed, generally by sight and by odour, in running streams. Snakes form winter dens in which there may be hundreds of individuals rolled up in balls.

Flocks,
herds, and
packs Among birds, pigeons (Columbidae), starlings (Sturnidae), and various blackbirds (Icteridae) form dense flocks that wheel about in the sky or mill along the ground during foraging, the rearmost flying ahead to become briefly the leaders. Shorebirds and gulls gather on mud flats or elsewhere to feed. Such birds as the brown creepers (*Certhia familiaris*) reduce the winter cold by clumping together at night. Flocks of geese are made of many families of geese. Many birds gather into huge roosts, containing thousands or even millions of individuals in the case of the red-winged blackbirds (*Agelaius phoeniceus*) of North America. Tricoloured blackbirds (*A. tricolor*) of California are even more colonial than redwing blackbirds when nesting, and by sheer force of numbers push into colonies of the more dominant redwings and displace them. The nesting colonies of queleas (*Quelea quelea*) in Africa contain millions of nests. There are many such colonies of birds, such as the phenomenal colonies of seabirds that are found on islands throughout the world.

Mammals often form herds or packs. Many herds are more structured than bird societies, simply because many mammal groups are combined families plus males. Huge migratory herds of wildebeest and zebra wander the African plains. Each herd of zebra includes many familial harems that are held together by individual males. The herd of Scottish red deer is a matriarchal group led by an old female and composed of her extended family plus other extended families like hers.

George Porter—National Audubon Society

Figure 6: A herd of American bison (*Bison bison*).

Hunting mammals often have even more structured groups. A male and female wolf (*Canis lupus*) and their offspring form a hunting pack that may fuse with another pack or split apart. African hunting dogs (*Lycaon picta*) and hyenas (*Hyaena* and *Crocuta*) form similarly flexible hunting packs, which are said to be even more effective than lion groups at running down prey.

Primate troops are often as complex as societies of hunting mammals or more so. Superimposed on their parental and sexual bonds is a group organization based on the occupation of a given area. The troop may also accept animals from outside. The society of baboons (Figure 5), as studied on the plains of Kenya, is very highly organized. Around the edge of the troop as it moves are the subadult males, watching carefully for predators and snatching bites of food when they can. Inside, the playful groups of juveniles stay close to the central hierarchy, a cooperating group of two or three big males that keep the subadult males at the periphery. The males of the central hierarchy are replaced, as they get old and toothless, by brash young males moving in from the periphery. With the central hierarchy march the females and their infants, protected both by the big males and by the peripheral younger males. The society is integrated by mutual grooming sessions, in which the big males get most of the grooming, and by domination by the big males.

INTERSPECIFIC ASSOCIATIONS

Individual animal interactions. Associations of animals often include more than one species. These groups may be called colonies-5 or colonies-0, since there is recent evidence that the nucleus and other parts of the cell were originally symbiotic viruses and bacteria. The most intimate form of interspecific association is that known as symbiosis, or mutualism, in which dissimilar organisms live together (see BIOTIC INTERACTIONS).

Multicellular animals often live on or beside other animals. Small fish live in the tentacles of some jellyfish, sea anemones, and even the Portuguese man-of-war, yet are able to evade or inactivate the stinging cells. Some hydroids and worms live on tubes of other worms or on the shells of other invertebrates. The tubes of worms and shrimp often harbour other worms or fish. At times, the animal will live only on one kind of shell and is found nowhere else. Paleontologists have found some evolutionary sequences in which such an animal first lived on rocks and shells of a wide variety of types, then developed larger forms that lived on one type of animal and probably got food from it.

Complex associations. Slave making is a kind of social relation that verges on parasitism. Certain kinds of ants raid colonies of other kinds of ants, carry off their young, and raise them as slaves. The slaves are perfectly socialized members of the colony and probably do not even realize that their social behaviour is misdirected. They exchange food and drugs with their captors as willingly as they would have with their own species, had they been reared by their own workers.

Associations in ant colonies

One of the most complex associations is that of animals around army and driver ants. In the huge colonies of army ants live dozens of other kinds of insects, millipedes, and mites. Some help clean debris below the nests; some have chemicals that allow them to fool the ant security guards and enter the colony. Mites, beetles, and others ride on the ants or march in their columns. Some may help the ants by cleaning them or by giving them chemicals they crave. Others are like wolves in the fold, eating the food of the ants or even their larvae. The swarms of ants are also waited upon by many kinds of flies and birds. The flies lay eggs on insects and spiders fleeing from the ants. The birds capture animals flushed by the ants. In the tropics of the Western Hemisphere, nearly 50 kinds of birds follow the army ants persistently and would probably die without them.

Some of these associations may not be social in any accepted sense of the word. Humans are not social with rats and fleas merely because they live with them. Some interspecific associations, however, are definitely social. These include the mixed flocks of antelope, zebra, and wildebeest on the African plains, for example, and mixed flocks of birds throughout the world.

One can travel for hours across the African plains or through a tropical forest scarcely seeing an animal and suddenly be surrounded by a herd or flock of many kinds of animals. Usually each animal eats a different kind or type of grass or fruit or insect, although sometimes there is overlap in the foods taken or ways of feeding. The flock moves along together, not spending much time at each concentrated food source. Often it includes parental groups (colonies-2 in the case of mothers carrying young, or colonies-3 after the young separate).

The fact that forest flocks are usually of several species rather than one probably reflects the fact that forests have more species of animals, and hence each species has less of a food supply and must not allow competitors of its own species about it, even its own offspring. In less-complex habitats, there are usually very few species, and the animals can tolerate their own young even though these are competitors. They may even use their young—to detect predators (in the case of baboons) or to build a "city" (in the case of bees and ants).

Eco-systems

When a forest is destroyed and begins to grow back, the first animals that come in tend to be kinds that are solitary and very antagonistic or uncommunicative. Later, flocking animals become more common, although they still resist groups of outsiders. Finally, as the mature forest re-establishes itself, one finds mostly paired animals that do not keep their young with them. These paired animals tend to associate with pairs of other species to form mixed flocks. Eventually, every animal links itself with every other animal in the system, forming what ecologists call a complex "food web," "ecosystem," or "web of life." It is gradually being recognized that such a web is socially cooperative as well as socially competitive. The ecosystem eventually approaches a stage of "colony-6," or what the French biologist and philosopher Teilhard de Chardin called the noosphere.

III. Dynamics of social behaviour

COSTS AND GAINS

Social behaviour among humans is often regarded as an end in itself, the expression of a basic drive that has no necessary purpose. Biologists doubt that any animal has social tendencies without some adaptive advantage.

The costs. Social behaviour and communication not only take an animal's substance and energy; they impede feeding, drinking, and other inputs necessary for life. The first cells that associated with other cells to form multicellular filaments lost the ability to absorb on the side by which they were attached. Perhaps the reason most multicellular filaments occur among animals that are attached to the ground or to some other surface is that such animals lose less proportionately than members of free-floating aggregations; attachment on one side to the ground already limits their input. Locomotion is impaired if animals must stay together. The single-celled ciliates could not readily have evolved into higher organisms, because dividing them into many joined cells would have slowed down these fast-moving predators. A speedy golden plover trying to stay with other shorebirds in a mixed flying group near shore constantly turns back to keep with them; it is impeded by its social tendency.

Social behaviour also attracts enemies. Groups of animals have epidemics, while solitary animals seldom do. Many disease-carrying parasites spread much more easily at times when animals are together. Some rabbit fleas are even adapted to the hormonal cycles of the rabbits, so that they reproduce at the times of year the rabbits are reproducing and hence are social.

Predators, like parasites, often have an easier time if animals are crowded together; the animals are often busy reacting to each other and the predator can sneak up without being observed. Their communicatory systems may even attract predators. Tuna prey specifically on fish in schools; a small hawk in tropical America (*Accipiter superciliosus*) mainly on mixed bird flocks.

Social behaviour increases the number of interactions between animals and thus the chances of conflict. The conflicts may be solved by fighting, by patterns of dominance and submission (peck orders), or by mutual avoidance. Mutual fighting and mutual avoidance have the same result—a partitioning of resources for which the animals are competing. Conflict and its avoidance

The gains. Against these disadvantages of being social, it is possible to set a number of clear advantages. They fall into six broad categories, corresponding to the six possible kinds of animal behaviour. By social behaviour animals gain: (1) food and other resources, (2) reproductive advantages, and (3) shelter and space. They are enabled to avoid (4) physical and other small hazards, (5) competitors, and (6) predators or other large dangers. The first and third of these gains are reactions to desirable things of small (1) and medium to large size (3) respectively; the fourth and sixth are reactions to undesirable things of these sizes.

Food. The value of being social in getting food is obvious in the case of hunting bands. Cooperative hunting has been found among wolves and African hunting dogs, hyenas, lions, killer whales, porpoises, cormorants, white pelicans, pairs of eagles and of ravens, tuna when chasing small fish, army ants, primitive and modern men, and many other animals. Animals that hunt cooperatively can trap, chase, and tear apart prey that would otherwise be too fast, strong, or large for them. In African hunting dogs the chase is run by the leader of the pack, but the rest keep the antelope or other prey from dodging left or right and also help fall on it when the leader catches it. Flocks of wattled starlings (*Creatophora ci-* Cooperative hunting *nerea*) fly after African migratory locusts and surround one group after another, eating every trapped locust from each group. In army ants, the individuals are bound to each other by chemical "trail substances" so that no individual gets far from the group; when one finds prey, it grabs it and emits an "alarm" chemical that causes nearby ants to grab, bite, and sting so that the prey is overwhelmed within seconds. They then tear the prey, usually insects or other arthropods, limb from limb and carry it back to the nest.

Interspecific groups of birds are sometimes food-getting societies. Drongos (*Dicrurus* species) of Africa flush much food, and other birds follow them to get it. Honeyguides (*Indicator* species) of Africa lead honey badgers or men to bee nests and eat wax after the mammals break open the nests for honey. Hawks have been known to follow railroad trains for the same reason, and hornbills and hawks follow monkeys. The birds, lizards, flies, and other animals that associate with army ants offer other examples of interspecific food-providing associations. One animal may steal food from another, as American widgeons (*Anas americana*) steal grass from redheads (*Aythya americana*).

In addition to hunting and flushing food cooperatively, animals sometimes lead others to food or teach them to use it. Parents, especially among mammals, often teach their young to hunt or lead them to food. Animals that must migrate or depend upon seasonally available resources often depend on others to show them what foods are good and where. Vultures and jackals flock to carcasses on the African plains. American robins (*Turdus migratorius*) in California have been observed learning to use certain berries after flocks of cedar waxwings (*Bombycilla cedrorum*) came through and started eating the berries. Tests with a tape recorder show that the recorded calls of some birds that follow army ants will attract unrelated kinds of birds that also follow ants. In the laboratory, some animals learn to push a lever for food by watching others get food that way and learn to avoid distasteful foods by watching others cough it up. In studies of Japanese monkeys (*Macaca fuscata*), the habit of washing potatoes before eating spread from the younger to older monkeys of a troupe. In Britain, a few titmice learned to open milk bottles and drink cream; the habit spread much too rapidly to be a genetic change. (Coverage of learned behaviour is found in LEARNING, ANIMAL.)

Mating behaviour

Reproduction. The reproductive advantages of social behaviour have mostly been discussed earlier. It was noted that sex is a way of combining desirable genes from different lines, genes that otherwise might slowly or never get together. In many lines of animals, parental behaviour is clearly useful in protecting or teaching the young. This normally requires the adult to have fewer young. The careful parent loses in time and energy and number of offspring but comes to prevail in evolution if it has more descendants than does a careless parent that lets its young die. The careless parent prevails if it can get more young out by caring for each one less; some parasites are careless parents because each of the young needs little care and a large number must be produced to get to an extremely distant host.

Shelter. Social behaviour is often used in habitat selection and shelter selection, even to the extent of making it possible for the animal to improve the environment it finds. Male birds that later will fight with each other over territorial boundaries gather first at areas where they hear another bird singing, rather than hunting for a more isolated (and probably unsuitable) place. Certain beetles that attack pines put out a scent that attracts other beetles; only as a result of concerted attack by all beetles can the protective pitch of the tree be reduced so that all may enter. Movement to a flock is a good way to find a patch of habitat or a shelter. It has been suggested that flocking increases the accuracy of migration, since the average direction taken by a flock is more correct than the individual directions taken by individual birds. Small flocks of European starlings returning to a California roost were less accurate in their direction than large flocks. Cooperative building of structures is well-known

in humans, prairie dogs, and rats (whose tunnel systems rival the catacombs in complexity), beavers, certain weaver finches, wasps, bees, termites, and many others; symbiotic use of structures occurs in many animals.

Hazards. Social behaviour can also help animals avoid small hazards. This includes avoiding heat or cold and wet or dry situations as well as preening or grooming to keep off dirt, parasites, and other small environmental hazards. A goose cleaving the air for its companions at the front of a V-shaped flock, a parent bird brooding its young or sheltering it from the sun, a group of creepers roosting together to help each other survive the cold winter night, a group of baboons grooming each other to pick off ticks, furnish other examples.

Competitors. Dangers from competition are avoided by agonistic behaviour. The five basic types of agonistic behaviour are aggressive display (threat), submissive display (appeasement), attack, avoidance, and fighting.

Agonistic behaviour

Social aggressive display is not common. Males of a troupe of howler monkeys all yell at a neighbouring troupe to make them keep their distance. Baboon males in the "central hierarchy" cooperate to keep aggressive young males from winning, backing each other up with threats. Social attack occurs in some birds and mammals that keep group territories and may lead to fighting if the other group attacks or threatens.

Highly social submissive display and escape also are not common. A baboon troupe may retreat as another moves in at a water hole. But even when a single animal retreats from a competitor it is a social act. Territoriality is certainly a system in which an animal defends its right to be dominant in part of its home range. The basic feature of territoriality, however, is not aggression in a certain area but submission outside that area. The common idea that strong animals survive and the weak do not is true only in the short run, for in a few generations all reproducing animals are equally strong. Strong animals will begin to lose if they keep on chasing others. An animal that keeps too large a territory will spend more time chasing away intruders than it will in eating or reproducing, unless it can get others to help it. Bees get help by drugging the nonreproductive members of their colony. Most animals limit themselves so that the territory of the most dominant animal or group of animals never exceeds about twice the size of the least dominant animal or group of animals of that species. Most often the young animal has a small territory but defends a larger one as he gains experience, then gradually loses it as he reaches old age.

Predators. The final reason for social behaviour, and one of the most important, is to avoid predators or other large dangers. Just as animals can sometimes overcome large prey by grouping to attack it, so they can sometimes overcome large predators by grouping to defend against them. Cooperative and spirited attacks upon predators occur in most animals that protect their young and are a regular phenomenon in gull and tern colonies, in baboon troupes, in bees and wasps, and many others. "Mobbing" is a similar phenomenon in which the attack is not carried all the way to the predator but so harasses it that it departs or at least is prevented from getting its prey. The massed effect of many mobbing birds is more intimidating to a predator than is mobbing by one or two birds.

Grouping and flocking

Grouping also helps against predators because a predator is distracted by the "confusion effect" of so many shapes, sounds, or smells. Human hunters know that one cannot shoot a duck out of a flock by aiming at the flock; the shot is more likely to pass between the birds than if the hunter aims at one of them. Similarly, hawks have been seen to dive through a flock and miss every bird. Successful predators either dive to break up a flock and then grab a separate animal or pick off an outlying one at the start. Butterflies on tropical trails also swirl up in a confusion effect from a mud puddle. The phenomenon is caused by the difficulty the eye or other sense organ has in analyzing or following very complex motions that cross each other.

Another advantage of the group or flock is that many eyes can see a predator more quickly than can one pair of eyes. Ornithologists have found that social birds are nervous outside of a flock and must spend too much time watching to be able to forage effectively. Certain species that forage by peering in dense vegetation are especially in danger and must associate with other species that look about more actively in open foliage. The peering species often are good at yelling and perhaps help the other birds by scaring or disturbing predators. This suggests that a social organization may have many reasons for being.

DEVELOPMENT FACTORS

Instinct and learning

Behaviour changes somewhat in the course of evolution. Biologists commonly call the genetic determinants of behaviour in a line of organisms "instinct." Every behaviour pattern, however, can be changed somewhat by the individual animal in the course of its experience, a process called "learning." The old view that instinct and learning are two different types of behaviour is seldom accepted now, even though some kinds of behaviour certainly have little learning superimposed.

The real question is how social behaviour develops. It is possible to breed animals for aggressiveness or nonaggressiveness, and by further crosses to study the inheritance of behaviour. Mouse strains that show different degrees of aggressiveness are easy to develop. Biochemical imbalances also affect behaviour: in many animals an oversupply of male hormones causes aggressive and antisocial behaviour. Pituitary hormones, especially luteinizing hormone, have the same effect in other animals, such as starlings.

Stimulation of the brain or removal of part of it gives evidence of a structural basis for behaviour; stimulation of the hypothalamus produces many social behaviour patterns, such as sexual activity and aggression. There are even "pleasure centres" that the animal will stimulate on its own, if given a bar to press that sends a shock to its head. Sexual centres are one of the "pleasure centres" that rats are fond of stimulating.

Another approach is to isolate the animal and see if it still develops a particular behaviour. Young pigeons reared in cardboard tubes will fly soon after release, showing that practice is not necessary. Some young songbirds reared in isolation develop normal songs, and many develop normal calls. Many songbirds must listen to songs of their own species at a particular age, however, to learn them.

An animal may develop social behaviour while still in the egg or mother. Baby ducklings peep to the calling mother from the egg. An animal may develop social behaviour soon after it emerges or at some critical period later. A young duckling follows the first object it sees, be it a duck or a duckling or the hand of the experimenter. Young birds, ants, and some mammals "imprint" on the first object they see to such an extent that they may court it or show agonistic behaviour to it later. A mother goat given a lamb in exchange for her kid soon after birth will adopt the lamb and drive away her own kid when it is returned to her.

Later learning also influences social behaviour. Mice that experience defeat learn to run rather than fight; the opposite holds for mice that win. Most animals, however, start at the bottom of a peck order and take defeats in stride, later becoming the dominant animals if they manage to survive. It has been found that association with other young monkeys helps a monkey to behave properly in sexual activity later, although many learn to copulate properly without this opportunity.

THE EVOLUTION OF SOCIALITY

Social behaviour as an adaptation

The fact that bees and ants form complex societies, more complex in some ways than those of apes, shows that social behaviour occurs in small animals as well as in large ones, in animals with small brains or large ones, and in both major lines of evolution. If bacteria can be rather social and humans rather solitary, there is no reason to suppose sociality is more advanced in evolution than is solitary life.

Social behaviour is instead an adaptation to certain environmental opportunities. The evolution of sociality can be glimpsed in the line that leads from the earwig through wood-eating cockroaches to termites, or in the line from solitary bees to social ones. Communication systems also evolve, as may be seen in the line leading from dully coloured monogamous crows to brightly coloured birds of paradise and plain bowerbirds in New Guinea. In this system, the male bird of paradise is brightly coloured to attract the crowlike female. The bright male also attracts predators. The bowerbirds have lost the bright plumage; instead they make elaborate maypoles or bowers decorated with flowers to attract females. One bowerbird even paints the walls of his bower, using a mashed berry or a straw stained in berry juice. These bowerbirds have become safely coloured, for they have replaced bright plumage with bright objects.

The ecological maturity and regularity of a habitat seem to determine to some extent how social its inhabitants will be. Among African weaver finches, the forest-living ones are solitary and monogamous; birds of savannas and marshes flock and nest polygamously; and those of very dry habitats tend to be relatively solitary. The same phenomenon has been noted for cats; leopards of the forest and cheetahs of very open country tend to be less social than lions of open savanna areas. Antelope, deer, monkeys, and apes show similar differences. The general rule is that, as an environment grows up from the level of bare ground to that of savanna and finally forest, the solitary animals are replaced by social ones and then by solitary ones again. In the forest, however, one-species societies decline in importance and societies of several species form. The same things happen as a marine community goes from bare rock to the complexity of a coral reef.

Societies of the same species, therefore, seem adapted for intermediate habitats that are in transition between bare ground and forest. It may be that the reason for this is that most intermediate habitats are unstable, likely to be limited in space or time.

BIBLIOGRAPHY. W.C. ALLEE, *The Social Life of Animals* (1938), a readable classic, emphasizing peck order and social facilitation at the expense of other aspects of social behaviour; ROBERT ARDREY, *The Territorial Imperative* (1966), a somewhat tendentious discussion of animal territories by a playwright; R.D. BARNES, *Invertebrate Zoology*, 2nd ed. (1968); J.T. BONNER, *Cells and Societies* (1955), a readable account of social life from the howler monkeys down to the cell; T.D. BROCK, *Biology of Microorganisms* (1970); J.H. CROOK (ed.), *Social Behaviour in Birds and Mammals* (1970), several excellent technical summaries of modern research in social behaviour, including a discussion of habitat and society; FRANK FRASER DARLING, *A Herd of Red Deer* (1937), one of the earliest field studies of a wild society, establishing that deer are matriarchal; IRVEN DEVORE (ed.), *Primate Behavior* (1965), the best collection of relatively nontechnical articles on the behaviour of free-living monkeys and apes; S.J. DIMOND, *The Social Behaviour of Animals* (1970), a discussion of recent experiments on learning of social behaviour in domestic and caged animals; JOHN F. EISENBERG, "The Social Organizations of Mammals," *Handb. Zool.* 10:1–92 (1965), a review of mammalian social behaviour that shows it derives mostly from maternal societies; PEGGY E. ELLIS (ed.), *Social Organization of Animal Communities* (1965), a useful set of rather technical articles, concentrating on social behaviour in insects; WILLIAM ETKIN (ed.), *Social Behaviour and Organization Among Vertebrates* (1964), a set of moderately technical articles on social behaviour; E.S.E. HAFEZ (ed.), *The Behaviour of Domestic Animals* (1969), a set of technical articles on animals such as cats, dogs, sheep, and goats, with an excellent discussion of physiology; S. MARK HENRY (ed.), *Symbiosis*, 2 vol. (1966–67), informative summaries of a few of the many symbioses known to occur, from viruses to man; DAVID LACK, *Ecological Adaptations for Breeding in Birds* (1968), a demonstration that the social behaviour of nesting birds depends on their habitats and their foraging; MARTIN LINDAUER, *Communication Among Social Bees* (1961), a fascinating account of evolution in and experiments on social bees; KONRAD LORENZ, *Das sogenannte Böse* (1963; Eng. trans., *On Aggression*, 1966), a discussion by a founder of ethology who maintains that aggression is needed for social bonds, but omits sexual and parental ties; LYNN MARGULIS, *Origin of Eukaryotic Cells* (1970), a discussion of the origin of cells by symbiosis; DESMOND MORRIS, *The Naked Ape* (1967), a witty and somewhat sensationalized examination of social behaviour by an experienced ethologist; HARRIET L. RHEINGOLD (ed.), *Maternal Behaviour in Mammals* (1963), a set of moderately technical articles on the mother-infant relationship in mammals; JOHN PAUL SCOTT and JOHN L. FULLER, *Genetics and the Social Behaviour of the Dog* (1965), a scientific analysis of heredity and learning that shows how they interact; EDWARD C. SIMMEL, RONALD A. HOPPE, and G. ALEXANDER MILTON (eds.), *Social Facilitation and Imitative Behaviour* (1968), scientific articles on imitative learning in animals and men; NIKO TINBERGEN, *Social Behaviour in Animals, with Special Reference to Vertebrates* (1953), a popular account by a founder of ethology, concentrating on birds, fish, and insects; E.O. WILSON, *The Insect Societies* (1971), one of the best surveys of the behaviour of social insects, but omits locusts; V.C. WYNNE-EDWARDS, *Animal Dispersion in Relation to Social Behaviour* (1962), a polemic reviewing much of social behaviour to support the view that animals practice birth control by means of social behaviour—but control is usually by agonistic reactions.

(E.O.W.)

Social Class and Mobility

The term class began to be widely used in the early 19th century, first replacing such other terms as rank and order as descriptions of the major hierarchical groupings in society. The usage reflected changes in the structure of western European societies after the industrial and political revolutions of the 18th century. The feudal distinctions of rank were declining in importance, and the new social groups that were developing—the commercial and industrial capitalists and the urban working class in the new factories—were defined mainly in economic terms, by the ownership of capital, on one side, or dependence upon wages, on the other. This phenomenon was recognized by many writers in the 18th century, even though the older terminology continued to be used. Early examples of the use of the concept are found in the Scottish historian and social philosopher John Millar's *The Origin of the Distinction of Ranks* (1771); and, in North America, where a new type of society without feudal antecedents was being established, in *The Federalist*, in which the significance of the unequal distribution of property in creating different classes and producing antagonistic political interests was emphasized by one of the founding fathers, James Madison. As Marx later observed:

> no credit is due to me for discovering the existence of classes in modern society, nor yet the struggle between them. Long before me bourgeois historians had described the historical development of this struggle of the classes and bourgeois economists the economic anatomy of the classes. (From letter to J. Weydemeyer, March 5, 1852.)

THE CONCEPT OF CLASS

Problems of definition. Although the economic basis of classes has been generally recognized, many disagreements have arisen as a result of attempts to define social class. First, there has been confusion about how widely the concept should be employed. It was used initially to denote the social groups that emerged in postfeudal societies, but it was then applied to the divisions in a wide range of societies. Madison, for example, said:

> Those who hold property and those who are without property have ever formed distinct interests in society. Those who are creditors, and those who are debtors, fall under a like discrimination. A landed interest, a manufacturing interest, grow up of necessity in civilized nations, and divide them into different classes, actuated by different sentiments and views.

Similarly, Marx and Engels in *The Communist Manifesto* spoke of "freeman and slave, patrician and plebeian, lord and serf, guild master and journeyman" as being engaged in class struggles and regarded the distinctive feature of modern societies as being merely that the class antagonisms have been simplified, so that society is more and more splitting up into "two great classes directly facing each other: bourgeoisie and proletariat." In an unfinished chapter on social classes in *Das Kapital*, it seems to have been Marx's intention to confine the use of the term class to the "three great classes of modern society": wage labourers, capitalists, and landowners.

A major problem is that of choosing between a definition of class that would make it possible to apply the concept to all forms of society—ancient city-states, early empires, caste society, and feudal society, as well as to

modern capitalist societies—while taking into account the specific characteristics of each of these forms; and a definition that would confine the concept to the social divisions in modern societies, treating other forms of society as having quite different kinds of stratification, arising from other factors besides the ownership of property. It is difficult, for example, to apply the concept of class to the traditional Indian caste system, which seems to depend, to a large extent, upon occupational differentiation and religious distinctions and which also seems to result in a fragmentation of society that is an obstacle to the formation of broad social classes (see CASTE SYSTEMS).

Class and related concepts. Even when the term class is applied to modern societies differences of view arise about its scope and meaning. Some of these differences result from disagreements concerning the relations between classes and the influence of classes in political life, and they will be more fully considered below. There are also problems, however, in distinguishing classes in a precise way from elites, status groups, or interest groups. The concept of elite, for example, was elaborated by the Italian sociologists Vilfredo Pareto and Gaetano Mosca as an alternative to the Marxist concept of the ruling class, and, although it has not been used consistently in this way, it does still overlap, to some extent, with the notion of class. Among recent writers, an American, C. Wright Mills, used the term power elite instead of ruling class (1956), in order to avoid the assumption that political power is always based upon property ownership; others have made a careful distinction between elites and classes and have been concerned to examine the nature of the connection between them.

The distinction between classes and status groups was made most clearly by the German sociologist Max Weber, who regarded the former as being based upon economic interests, while the latter were constituted by evaluations of the honour or prestige of an occupation, cultural position, or family descent. But this distinction also has not always been observed, with the result that individuals having roughly the same social prestige, such as those in a particular category of occupations, have sometimes been regarded as forming a class (see SOCIAL DIFFERENTIATION AND STRATIFICATION).

It is also necessary to differentiate between social classes and interest groups (see SPECIAL-INTEREST GROUPS), even though classes themselves may be regarded as being, in a very broad sense, interest groups. In modern societies, particularly, interest groups are numerous. They include many occupational associations, as well as cultural, recreational, regional, and other groups that pursue their special interests by a variety of means. The number of social classes is, in the view of all writers on the subject, much more limited, and classes may be seen as pursuing the more general economic and political interests of their members and as being involved, to some extent, in shaping and changing the character of society as a whole.

Another major disagreement in the definition of social class exists between those who regard classes as real social groups, possessing a class consciousness and exhibiting a distinctive culture and style of life, and those who treat "class" as an analytical construct, useful for some purposes in distinguishing categories of individuals on the basis of their income, education, or occupation. The first kind of definition is to be found in Marxist theory, which is concerned particularly with the historical development of classes as social groups having a determining influence upon the course of social events. Marx himself sketched a historical account of the rise of the bourgeoisie and, subsequently, of the proletariat (see especially, *The Poverty of Philosophy*, 1847) and made a distinction between the "class in itself" (that is, a collection of individuals who were placed in similar economic conditions) and the "class for itself" (that is, a more or less organized group, pursuing in a conscious fashion definite economic and political ends). Among later Marxist writers, the Hungarian philosopher and critic György Lukács, in several essays collected in *History and Class Consciousness* (1923), emphasized the importance of class consciousness, while introducing a new element in his account of

Early use of the concept of class

Classes and elites

Marx's two concepts of class

the role of revolutionary intellectuals in the formation of such a consciousness. It is, however, not only in Marxist theory that the idea of class, in Marx's latter sense, has prevailed, since non-Marxist sociologists have made studies of working class, middle class, and upper class as distinct communities; and Weber regarded class as one of the most important bases for communal action.

The concept of class as a collection of individuals sharing similar economic circumstances has been used widely in censuses and in studies of social mobility. Thus, the Office of Population Censuses and Surveys in Britain makes use of five broad categories of social class, based on an occupational classification; and studies of social mobility, examined below, have generally employed categories formed in a similar way by grouping together occupations that are regarded as being at approximately the same level in the social hierarchy. Some other sociological studies have made distinctions between categories of individuals in terms of prestige, without paying much attention to questions concerning the formation and development of classes.

THEORIES OF SOCIAL CLASS

Many disagreements over the definition of class are bound up with differences in theoretical approach, involving divergent conceptions of the importance of classes in the social structure and of the nature of the relationship between classes. Theories of social class were only fully elaborated in the 19th century as the modern social sciences, especially sociology, developed. Earlier writers, although they could not fail to observe the existence of great economic inequalities in their societies, did not attempt to formulate a general theory of the causes and consequences of such inequalities. At the most, they reflected, as did Plato and Aristotle, upon some of the more prominent features of social stratification and proposed ideal systems that would be conducive to political stability and rational government. Plato thus advocated a society divided into three classes—guardians, auxiliaries, and workers—in which the guardians would form a disinterested ruling elite, while Aristotle recognized in society three elements—the very rich, the very poor, and those in the middle—and considered the best political system to be that in which the middle strata had a preponderant influence.

Pre-Marxist approaches. In the 17th and 18th centuries a new discussion of social inequality and stratification began, provoked largely by the challenge to aristocratic rule from the bourgeoisie. In the writings of the English political philosophers Thomas Hobbes and John Locke there was developed an individualistic theory of property, corresponding with the growth of a market economy, which either assumed, in Hobbes' case, an equality among men, a struggle between individuals needing to be regulated by a powerful state, and the absence of cohesive classes; or, in the case of Locke, accepted the existence of a division between property owners and a labouring class. The French political philosopher Jean-Jacques Rousseau, in an essay on the origin of inequality (1755), made a distinction between natural inequalities and those that resulted from social conventions, but he conceived society in terms of the relations between individuals rather than between classes. Madison, writing in a society which had declared the principle of human equality and in which few aristocratic privileges existed, was more aware of the social divisions that might arise from divergent economic interests, and his emphasis upon the distinction between the owners of property and those without property foreshadows one of the important elements in Marx's theory. Madison, however, went on to distinguish a considerable number of interest groups as the basis of political factions, and he was far from conceiving society as a class system in which one class must necessarily dominate others.

Other writers in the later 18th and early 19th century who contributed elements of a theory of social classes include the Scottish philosopher Adam Ferguson and Millar, in whose works a distinction was established between civil society (*i.e.,* the nonpolitical elements in so-

Class relations in the political theory of Plato and Aristotle

ciety, such as the economic system and the family) and the state. The conditions of civil society, especially the property system, were seen as determining, to a large extent, the form of political life. This idea was expounded by the French social theorist Saint-Simon (1817), who argued that government was only a form that corresponded with the character of the underlying system of production and who analyzed the changes in production that led to the decline of the feudal ruling class and the rise of the new class of industrialists. In the writings of Saint-Simon's Socialist followers, a theory of the proletariat was first adumbrated (1824). A later work, by the sociologist and legal theorist Lorenz von Stein (1842), developed a conception of the proletariat as a major political force in modern society. This directly influenced the development of Marx's theory.

Another contribution to the theory of class comes from political economy. In Adam Smith's *Wealth of Nations* (1776) the principal emphasis was upon social differentiation and stratification resulting from the division of labour, but the English economist David Ricardo (1817) treated the main factors of production—land, labour, and capital—as constituting economic interest groups or classes, between which there was a profound clash of interests.

Marx's analysis. These diverse elements were brought together in Marx's theory of class, which has dominated all later discussion. In the passage quoted earlier, Marx disclaimed any credit for having discovered the existence of classes or the conflict between them; what he had accomplished, he claimed, was to show: "(1) that the *existence of classes* is only bound up with *particular historical phases in the development of production*, (2) that the class struggle necessarily leads to the *dictatorship of the proletariat*, (3) that this dictatorship itself constitutes only the transition to the *abolition of all classes* and to a *classless* society." The starting point of his theory was an elaboration of the distinction between civil society and the state. The anatomy of civil society, according to Marx, was to be found in political economy. What distinguishes one type of society from another is its mode of production (that is to say, the nature of its technology and division of labour), and each mode of production engenders a distinctive class system in which one class controls and directs the process of production while another class is, or other classes are, the direct producers and the providers of services to the dominant class. The relations between the classes are antagonistic since the classes are in conflict over the appropriation of what is produced; and, in certain periods, when the mode of production itself is changing as a result of developments in technology and in the utilization of labour, such conflict becomes extreme and a new class challenges the dominance of the existing rulers of society. The dominant class at any time controls not only material production but also the production of ideas; it thus establishes a particular cultural style and a dominant political doctrine, and its control over society is consolidated in a particular type of political system. The subject classes and especially a class that is growing in strength and influence as a consequence of changes in the mode of production generate political doctrines and movements in opposition to the ruling class.

The theory of class is at the centre of Marx's whole social theory, for it is the social classes formed within a particular mode of production that are regarded as establishing a specific form of state, animating political conflicts, and bringing about major changes in the structure of society.

Marx distinguished several historical types of society: "In broad outline we can designate the Asiatic, the ancient, the feudal, and the modern bourgeois modes of production as progressive epochs in the economic formation of society" (1859). But Marx and the Marxists who followed him did not undertake any detailed historical studies of earlier forms of society, and he was not able to set out a convincing empirical account of the development of social classes over the whole span of human history. He restricted his analysis of class structure mainly

Marx's view of the inevitability of class antagonism

to modern capitalist society, and he was concerned above all with the rise of the proletariat, the progress of its struggles against the bourgeoisie, and the conditions arising out of the capitalist system of production that would make possible a successful working class revolution and the inauguration of a new type of society that would be without classes.

Post-Marxist analyses. Later theories of class have been concerned in the main to revise, refute, or provide an alternative to the Marxist theory and, in a similar way, have been concentrated upon the development of classes in modern capitalist societies. In recent years, however, a growing amount of attention has been given to the formation of new classes in the Socialist societies of eastern Europe and in the developing countries. The German sociologist Max Weber was one of the first to undertake a critical revision of the Marxist theory, mainly in his essay on class, status, and party (1922), but, in more general terms, in many of his writings. Weber, in the first place, questioned the importance attributed to social classes in the political development of modern societies and in the causation of major social changes. In his view, capitalism had been brought into existence by the influence of certain ideas and especially by the influence of Protestantism on economic behaviour, as well as by the economic interests of the bourgeoisie. He also argued that the development of the European countries in the late 19th century had been affected by nationalism as much as it had by class ideologies and movements. There was another factor, too, that limited the significance of class as a basis of political action, namely, the existence of social stratification in terms of social honour or prestige, which cut across class divisions and tended to produce a condition of social harmony in which peaceful competition and emulation prevailed, rather than an increasingly intense class struggle. More generally, Weber contested Marx's view of the future development of capitalist society, for, whereas Marx envisaged the successful outcome of the working class struggle as the creation of a liberated classless society, Weber foresaw a continuation of the increasing organization of social life and a monstrous growth of bureaucratic regulation, which would attain its greatest extent in a Socialist society.

From a different aspect, Pareto and, in a more qualified way, Mosca also rejected Marx's division of society into contending classes and propounded instead a theory based upon a distinction between the "governing elite" and the masses. Pareto praised Marx's conception of the class struggle as a major contribution to social theory but then transformed it into the idea of a conflict for the possession of political power between an established elite and a rising elite. This conflict resulted, throughout history, in the substitution of one ruling elite for another, while domination and exploitation of the masses continued; in Pareto's view there is no progressive movement toward a classless society as Marx thought. This notion of the rise and fall of ruling elites is to be found in much modern writing on the class structure; it appears, for example, in the U.S. economist Thorstein Veblen's account (1921) of the rise of the engineers (though, in other respects, Veblen remained closer to the Marxist theory) and in recent discussions of technocracy.

One of the most important issues that has divided social theorists in their analysis of class structure has been, in fact, the assessment of the extent and significance of class conflict. Those who have opposed the Marxist theory most strongly have focussed attention on the functional interdependence of classes and their harmonious collaboration. The sociological theory known as functionalism, which attained its greatest influence in the United States, has developed this theme. Functionalism stands quite clearly in a general opposition to Marxism by virtue of its unhistorical approach, by its emphasis upon the regulation of social life by values that are more or less universally accepted in a given society, and by the importance that it assigns to social integration as against social conflict. Functionalism does not offer, in the strict sense, a theory of class. Its concern is with stratification as it arises from social differentiation and the evaluation and

Views of Max Weber

The extent and significance of class conflict

ranking of mainly occupational roles. The functionalist writers, therefore, take up the problem of social status, in the sense in which Max Weber distinguished this from the problem of social class, and they deal with the placement of individuals in the social hierarchy rather than with the formation of distinctive social groups.

Although the attention given to social status grew considerably in the two decades after 1945, partly under the influence of functionalist ideas, problems of class were far from neglected. Indeed, renewed reflection upon the nature and significance of social classes was stimulated by changes in class structure that seemed to be taking place, especially in Western industrial societies.

The theme of the relation between class and politics has figured prominently in most recent discussions. It is argued that in the new "postindustrial" society, which many believe is now emerging, the ruling class is no longer the property-owning bourgeoisie but the technocrats and bureaucrats who direct the process of technological innovation and economic growth; and the opposition to their rule is led not by the working class but by those groups that feel most keenly their dependent position and their exclusion from genuine political participation. Social conflict has therefore assumed a directly political character, instead of arising from economic antagonism.

The Marxist theory of class has thus been questioned in several respects. First, it has been claimed that classes in capitalist societies have tended to lose their distinctive character, while the antagonism between them has declined to such an extent that it no longer produces serious political conflict. From this point of view it may be argued that the class system has lost much of its social significance and that gradations of social status are now more important in determining the actions of individuals and groups. On the other side, however, it is suggested that although the major social classes of 19th-century capitalism have declined, new social classes are being formed in the advanced industrial societies (both capitalist and Socialist) that are beginning to engage in social struggles of a new kind. Furthermore, there are Marxists who would contend that, despite the uncertainties produced by the economic and social changes of the past few decades, the division between bourgeoisie and proletariat remains the fundamental source of conflict in society and continues to be expressed in the ideologies of vigorous social movements. These theoretical disagreements are far from being resolved, but further light may be shed on the problems that they pose by considering some of the ways in which differences between social classes have been characterized.

CHARACTERISTICS OF DIFFERENT SOCIAL CLASSES

In spite of controversies over the theory of class, there is a large measure of agreement among social scientists on the characteristics of the principal social classes, especially in modern societies. A distinction is habitually made between the upper class, the middle class, and the working class, but this needs to be refined and supplemented in various ways. Some writers have used the term lower class to refer to the working class, but others have distinguished a lower class, or lumpenproletariat, from the main body of the working class. This lower class may comprise particular ethnic groups, such as black and Mexican workers in the United States, and immigrant workers, such as those recruited from former colonial territories and from southern Europe by the industrially advanced European countries, as well as casual and unskilled workers in backward regions and declining industries, all of whom are characterized by exceptionally low levels of living, economic insecurity, and lack of social rights.

It is also necessary to take account of the peasantry as a distinct social class, though it was neglected for a considerable time by Western social scientists. In many European societies there are still a substantial number of peasant cultivators; and in the Socialist countries of eastern Europe, in particular, a description of social classes cannot ignore the development of the peasantry and its relations with other groups in society. The importance of the peas-

Conventional class divisions

antry has also been more fully recognized in recent years because of the role of political movements based largely upon peasant support in the developing countries. Marx's view of the peasantry as a predominantly conservative element in society and as a group that was unlikely to evolve an independent political consciousness or organization has been modified or abandoned by later Marxists. Radical social thinkers are now more inclined to attribute a major revolutionary role to the peasantry, or to large sections of it, in the countries of the Third World.

The delineation of the principal social classes does not imply that these classes have exactly the same character in all modern societies nor that they are entirely homogeneous groups. Nevertheless, there are broad differences between classes and common characteristics within them that make the distinction valid and useful.

The upper class. The upper class in Western capitalist societies is distinguished above all by the possession of largely inherited wealth. In Great Britain, for example, some 40 percent of all personal wealth is concentrated in the hands of the top 1 percent of property owners; in the United States, where the distribution of property is rather less unequal than in most European countries, the top 1 percent still owns about 30 percent of all personal property. Since the beginning of the 20th century, this concentration of wealth has tended to diminish in most countries, but the wider diffusion of property ownership is still mainly confined to the upper percent of the population. The ownership of large amounts of property and the income derived from it confer many advantages upon the members of the upper class. They are able to develop a distinctive style of life based upon expensive cultural pursuits and leisure activities, from which the great majority of the population is excluded, to exert a considerable influence upon economic policy and political decisions, and to procure for their children a superior education and economic opportunities that help to perpetuate family wealth.

Whether these characteristics make the upper class a ruling class in the Marxist sense is still vigorously debated. The question involves considering how far major political and economic decisions are influenced by the general interests of the upper class and how far this class is pre-eminent as a source of recruitment of top decision makers. On one side, it is argued that the upper class of large property owners provides the elites—economic, political, military, and intellectual—that determine the main course of a society's development, while, on the other side, it is claimed by the pluralist political thinkers that decision making results from the activities, often conflicting, of many different groups in society, none of which is clearly or permanently predominant.

The "new class" of Socialist societies

In the Socialist societies of eastern Europe, personal wealth obviously has little significance in the formation of a class, but it has been argued by the Yugoslav writer Milovan Djilas that a new upper class, indeed, a ruling class, has emerged in these societies on the basis of the possession of political and administrative power. The members of this class are not able to accumulate personal property on a large scale but can acquire in other ways all kinds of privileges—in housing, education, travel, and consumption—that enable them to develop an exclusive style of life. One difference from Western capitalist societies is that such advantages are less easy to transmit by inheritance than is private property, and for this reason an upper class in the Socialist societies is likely to be less stable in its membership over time. Nevertheless, some advantages may well be transmitted as a result of the privileged access to higher education and to important jobs that the children of upper class families enjoy.

Although the upper class in most societies shows a considerable degree of continuity in its membership from generation to generation, changes do occur through the rise and fall of individuals and groups as a result of changes in the social structure, the occurrence of exceptional ability or lack of ability in particular individuals, or by sheer chance. Such changes are particularly evident in many developing countries, and there may be considerable variations in the composition of the upper class. In some countries (as, for example, in Latin America or in the Middle East) large landowners may still form an important element in the upper class, though their pre-eminence is being challenged by the rise of a business class. Elsewhere, in Asia and Africa, nationalist political leaders who rose to prominence in the course of struggles against colonial rule and high officials or military leaders may form the nucleus of a new upper class, while in those countries in which revolutions have occurred, as in China, the new elites may be largely recruited from the working class and peasantry. They may tend, as in the countries of eastern Europe, to draw together in the formation of a new upper class, although some aspects of the Chinese cultural revolution seem to have been directed against such a development.

The working class. The principal contrast with the upper class in the industrial societies is provided by the working class, constituted essentially by manual workers in extractive and manufacturing industry. What characterizes the working class as a whole is lack of property and dependence upon wages. With this condition are associated relatively low levels of living and of education, restricted access to secondary and higher education, limited opportunities for leisure and cultural activities, and exclusion, to a large extent, from the spheres of important decision making. There are, of course, considerable differences within the working class, and a distinction has commonly been made between skilled, semiskilled, and unskilled workers, corresponding broadly with differences in income level. More recently, social scientists have emphasized the difference between the relatively prosperous workers in modern expanding industries and the less prosperous workers in some of the older industries.

There have been significant changes in the condition of the working class over the past few decades. Levels of living have risen, although as a consequence of general economic growth rather than any major redistribution of wealth and income; and access to education has improved, though it is still the case, in most countries, that a very small proportion of working class children enter higher education and hence make their way into the occupational and social elites. At the same time, the economic security of most workers has been increased by policies of full employment and by more extensive welfare services. These changes were widely interpreted during the 1950s as the *embourgeoisement* of the working class—that is, as an erosion of its distinctive characteristics and its gradual assimilation into the middle class. Such accounts have, however, been examined more critically in recent years, and the extent to which the working class remains socially, culturally, and politically distinct from other groups in society has been emphasized. The idea that the advanced industrial societies were becoming "middle class societies" and that this condition had already been more or less attained in the United States, which developed from the *embourgeoisement* thesis, was also sustained by the general shift in the economy from manufacturing to service industries, which involved a relative contraction in the numbers of manual workers and an increase in the numbers of clerical, technical, and professional workers. Thus, although there are still disagreements among social scientists about the size of the working class and the general features of its development, it can scarcely be denied that some important changes have occurred that require, at the least, a reconsideration of the Marxist theory of its political role.

The *embourgeoisement* thesis

It is evident that the position of the working class varies quite widely from one country to another. In some European countries, notably in France and Italy, a large part of the working class is strongly influenced by Marxist ideas and supports political parties that aim to bring about revolutionary changes in society, whereas in other countries—in Great Britain, West Germany, and Sweden, for example—the main working class parties are reformist in their policies. In the United States, on the other hand, there has been no major independent political movement of the working class since World War I, and class consciousness has had much less influence in political life than has been the case in Europe. These differences cannot easily be explained in general terms, but it has been observed that working class consciousness was more intense and took a more revolutionary form in those European societies in which the development of capitalism was slower and more backward than elsewhere; and this observation would apply also to Russia before 1917. In the case of the United States, the failure of a political movement of the working class to develop on anything like the European scale has been accounted for in various ways: by the exceptional opportunities for mobility (or at least the strong and pervasive belief that such opportunities existed), by the fragmentation and disruption resulting from massive immigration, by the existence of a large black lumpenproletariat, and by the divisions in the working class movement that were produced by World War I and the Russian Revolution. At all events, it is clear that the working class in different countries has assumed different characteristics and has espoused very diverse ideologies.

The middle class. While the upper class and the working class can be viewed as relatively homogeneous groups quite sharply differentiated from each other, the middle class often has been treated as a more varied, residual category, comprising those groups, mainly defined in terms of occupation, that do not clearly belong to one of the other classes. Marx, for example, referred to the "intermediate and transitional strata" that obscured the boundaries of the principal classes. Generally speaking, the middle class has been taken to include the various levels of clerical workers, those engaged in technical and professional occupations, supervisors and managers, and self-employed workers, such as small shopkeepers, farmers, and (in some societies) the wealthier peasants. At the top—in the case of wealthy professional men or managers in large corporations, for example—the middle class merges into the upper class, while at the bottom—where routine and poorly paid jobs in sales, distribution, and transport are concerned—it merges into the working class. When a contrast is drawn between middle class and working class styles of life it is often based implicitly upon "ideal types": the middle class individual is conceived as a professional or senior clerical worker, the working class individual as a factory worker.

To some extent, these distinctions within the middle class are recognized by references to the upper middle class and lower middle class, but there are other differences that do not coincide exactly with this division. There is, for example, considerable diversity of social and political outlook in the middle class: in Western societies the predominant political attitudes may range between liberal and conservative, but in some conditions a part of the middle class, at least, may adopt extreme right-wing views (as in its support for National Socialism in Germany); and, on the other hand, there is a well-known phenomenon of middle class radicalism, which became more prominent during the 1960s with the development of the largely middle class student movement. Other distinctions arise from longer term historical changes in the composition and social situation of the middle class. The "old" middle class, with which Marx and other 19th-century writers were largely concerned, consisted chiefly of small independent producers and independent professional men; the "new" middle class of the late 20th century is made up primarily of employees in public services and in large business enterprises at various levels of clerical, technical, and professional work. This transformation seems to have produced a greater diversity, fluidity, and uncertainty in the cultural and political character of the middle class, so that to speak of the advent of middle class societies, as the numbers of the new middle class increase, may not provide any clear indication of the form that such societies will eventually take.

The industrial countries resemble each other in their occupational structure, and the development of occupations under the influence of technological innovation and economic growth is also similar, but this does not prevent considerable differences in the class structure. There is, as has been noted, an important distinction to be made between the Western capitalist countries and

Middle class divergencies in social and political outlook

the Socialist countries of eastern Europe in respect to the character of the upper class or elites, and other classes in these two types of society may also show important differences, especially in their social outlook and political involvement.

International comparisons. It is difficult to make rigorous comparisons of the character of different classes in different countries, since comprehensive studies of the class system are lacking, especially in the Socialist countries, though a major study in Czechoslovakia (1969) provides much valuable information. Even within Western societies there is much diversity, and the degree of class consciousness and class conflict, in particular, varies widely from one country to another, as well as fluctuating over time. One observer, for example, wrote in 1914 of the first decade of the 20th century that it was a turning point in American society, when deep class feeling found expression in both political parties and brought to public attention the existence of a profound conflict between great wealth and the lower middle and working classes; but the feeling, and the conflict, subsided again, and in spite of a limited revival of class consciousness in the 1930s the general character of American society has been one of ideological classlessness. In most of the European countries, though, class consciousness has found expression in distinctive parties, and class conflict has been overt.

In the developing countries, modern social classes exist, for the most part, only in embryonic form. It has been observed already that the upper class in these societies may be far from homogeneous or stable and may include such disparate elements as feudal landowners, capitalist entrepreneurs, nationalist or revolutionary leaders, higher castes, and military chiefs. In those countries in which industrialization is not far advanced, the urban working class will be small, and, if the workers have only recently migrated to the towns, as is the case in many African and Asian countries, there may be little development of class consciousness. Similarly, the middle class is likely to be small, although some sections of it may be particularly privileged and influential by virtue of the educational level of their members, who may form part of a Western educated elite. Numerically, the most important class in African and Asian societies is the peasantry, and, even in the more urban and industrial societies of Latin America, this class is still relatively large. Consequently, peasant organizations and movements are of great political significance, and major social conflicts are likely to occur over issues of landholdings, land reform, and agricultural prices, rather than over industrial conditions. As industrialization proceeds, the occupational structure of the developing countries will come to resemble more closely that of the industrial countries, but the class structure may take various forms, depending upon historical traditions and political changes. Many developing countries aim deliberately to bring about a condition of much greater economic and social equality, and it has still to be seen what kind of class system, or classlessness, will emerge from the profound changes that are occurring in such societies as India, China, Tanzania, and Chile.

Classes in the developing countries

SOCIAL MOBILITY

The term social mobility, in its widest sense, refers to any movement of individuals, families, or groups between different sectors of society. Thus movement from one occupation to another, or from one region of a country to another, is a kind of mobility. On an international scale, migration is a very important type of mobility.

Types of mobility. A distinction is usually made between "horizontal" and "vertical" social mobility, the former involving no change in the position of the individual or group in the social hierarchy, while the latter does involve a change of social level. When an industrial worker moves from one factory to another or a manager takes a position in another company, there is no significant change in his social status or class membership. But, if an industrial worker or the child of an industrial worker becomes a wealthy businessman or lawyer, he has changed quite radically his position in the class system. Vertical mobility may, of course, involve either upward or downward movement. A ruined aristocrat, or a member of an upper class dispossessed of his wealth in a revolution and obliged to enter a manual occupation, has experienced a change of social level that may affect his whole life or particular aspects of it. Modern sociologists have concentrated their attention mainly on upward social mobility, because they have been preoccupied with the question of equality of opportunity in the relatively open and democratic industrial societies; but it has been suggested more recently that the degree of downward mobility might be a better indicator of the "openness" of a society, since it would show the extent to which it is relatively easy or difficult for privileged individuals and groups to maintain and transmit to their descendants the advantages that they enjoy.

There has also been a marked preoccupation with the mobility of individuals, although it is evident that whole families, groups, and even classes may at certain times change their position in the social structure. One of the few writers to bring out the diverse aspects of vertical mobility was the economist Joseph Schumpeter (1927), who analyzed and illustrated what he termed the "rise and fall" of individuals, families, and whole classes within the class system. But Pareto, too, in his examination of the "circulation of elites" (1915–19), paid attention both to the movement of individuals into and out of the elites, and to the rise and fall of whole elite groups.

Intra-generational and inter-generational mobility

In studying the movement of individuals, sociologists have distinguished between intragenerational and intergenerational mobility; that is to say, between the mobility of an individual within his own adult lifetime and the mobility represented by a change in social level from the parental to the filial generation (almost always from father to son). Comprehensive national studies of mobility that have been undertaken in recent years have dealt almost entirely with intergenerational mobility, examining changes in occupation between father and son in terms of a scale of occupational prestige. At the same time, such studies have concentrated heavily upon educational opportunity as a major factor influencing upward mobility.

The rise and fall of families, groups, and classes is less easy to study in a quantitative manner, but such changes can be documented in other ways. The emergence of new ruling dynasties is one example of the upward mobility of families, and other examples can be found in the rise and fall of family businesses, of politically influential families, or of intellectual families. The mobility of particular social groups may occur as a result of economic, political, or cultural influences.

There have been important changes in the position of various groups in the modern industrial societies: the prestige and influence of scientists has increased, while that of clergymen has diminished; bureaucrats have become a much more important group, as have the officials of a dominant political party in some societies. Finally, the rise and fall of whole classes is a phenomenon that occurs when there are substantial changes in the whole structure of society. In the Marxist theory, such changes take the form of a social revolution, in which the established ruling class is overthrown by a new class, as in the rise to power of the bourgeoisie with the development of modern capitalism. But a change in the relative position of classes may also occur in a more gradual way, and an example may perhaps be found in the growth of the new middle class in present-day industrial societies.

Vertical social mobility is a feature of all societies, except perhaps the most simple and primitive. In European feudal societies, there were opportunities for upward mobility, one avenue being through the church, and these opportunities increased with the revival of the towns and the growth of trade. One study of the circulation of elites in France between the 11th and 18th centuries gives examples of the rise and fall of particular individuals and families, as well as tracing the fortunes of such groups as lawyers, financiers, and traders.

The problem posed by such historical studies is that they largely provide illustrations and, for lack of data, do not show the degree of mobility; that is to say, the numbers of individuals or families who actually changed their position in the social hierarchy over a given period. Historical comparisons of mobility are thus difficult and largely speculative, and there are many problems even in examining the trends of mobility in the industrial societies in recent times. It is nevertheless generally considered that vertical social mobility (especially of individuals) is greater in modern industrial societies than in earlier societies. Modern studies suggest, however, that, even in industrial societies, mobility is limited and that there are no substantial differences between industrial societies in the amount of mobility, even though, for example, it has been generally believed that social mobility is greater in the United States than in European countries. In particular, the movement of individuals from the working class into the upper class is rare in all societies. Sociologists have, therefore, introduced another distinction between short-range and long-range vertical mobility; and comparisons between industrial societies show that the greater part of mobility is short-range.

Inadequacy of historical studies of mobility

These modern studies suggest a cautious interpretation of historical accounts of social mobility, which may give undue prominence to exceptional cases of upward or downward movement. It is likely that in all societies, at most times, there is a considerable stability of class membership that, even when not maintained by any formal sanctions, is ensured by the inheritance of property, educational advantages, or political influences.

The process of mobility. The nature and degree of vertical mobility in a society is affected by a variety of influences. One universal factor is the occurrence, in any population, of individuals who are exceptionally endowed—with intelligence, physical strength, beauty, skill in warfare or business, or the quality of charisma that enables them to become religious or political leaders. Beautiful women have risen to social eminence as the mistresses of kings and nobles and as film stars, just as men (and to a much lesser extent women) have risen by the accumulation of wealth, the attainment of political or military power, and intellectual or artistic achievement. But the manifestation of such personal qualities and the advantages that they bring are limited and controlled by many social factors.

Social determinants. In the first place, the open or closed nature of the class system has a powerful influence. It is not only that the individual in a closed system will encounter great practical obstacles if he seeks to escape from his situation as a slave, serf, or member of a lower caste; the ideology that upholds such a system and emphasizes the importance of everyone "knowing his place" tends to inhibit the development of personal talent and ambition at the lower levels of society. In the more open class systems of modern societies, on the contrary, there are no formal restrictions upon vertical mobility, and the ideas of equality and reward for merit, which have gradually entered the general social consciousness since they were formulated in the 18th-century revolutions, encourage an individualistic striving for success throughout large sections of society. Even in these societies, however, talented individuals in a lower social class have to surmount many obstacles, arising mainly from poverty and the difficulties of access to education. On the other side, less talented individuals are able to maintain their position in the upper class because of their inherited social advantages.

The extent to which individual talent will result in upward mobility is also limited by the general orientation of a society's activities. A tribal society that lives by hunting or is engaged in continual warfare will place a high value on physical strength and agility; a nation engaged in imperial expansion is likely to rate military qualities highly; and one that is chiefly concerned with industrial development may attach the greatest importance to business ability. The role of science and technology in present-day industrial societies makes certain kinds of intellectual ability (and the selection and training of such ability) particularly important, so that some writers have referred

Mobility
and
changes
in social
structure

to the rise of a "meritocracy" or a "scientific and educational estate" or a "technocratic elite."

One of the most profound influences upon mobility comes from the general changes in social structure. A revolution that dispossesses an existing upper class or a national liberation movement that overthrows foreign rule creates opportunities for other individuals, groups, and whole classes to establish themselves in a dominant position. In the early years of the Socialist regimes in eastern Europe, for example, the universities were opened to young people from working class and peasant families, while restrictions were placed upon the entry of those from the middle class. More gradual changes, especially in the occupational structure, also affect mobility. The expansion of clerical, technical, and professional employment involves a continuing movement out of manual work and accounts for a large part of the upward mobility in Western industrial societies. In earlier periods economic changes had similar effects; the revival of trade and the growth of towns in European feudal societies made it possible for serfs to embark upon new occupations and to escape the constraints of the feudal system. A similar movement from country to town is occurring in the present-day developing countries and involves, in most cases, upward mobility in terms of rewards, opportunities, and social status. There are also movements from poorer to wealthier regions in a particular country. The postwar movement in Italy from the relatively poor agrarian south to the more prosperous industrial north and the movement of black Americans from the South to industrial areas provide examples.

After a revolution a new system of stratification may emerge, and the rate of social mobility may decline again. Similarly, if there is little economic development or the rate of growth slows down, opportunities for mobility will be diminished. In such conditions, the possibilities of upward mobility will depend largely upon the extent of downward mobility. One other factor, however, may influence this situation. If the upper and middle classes practice family limitation to such an extent that they do not reproduce themselves from generation to generation, the vacant places may be filled by individuals who rise from lower classes. Such differential fertility, however, has rarely, if ever, been a major influence, and most analysts believe that it has been declining in the developed industrial societies during the past few decades.

Mobility
and
migration

International movements of population have been important at various times in promoting upward mobility. The colonial expansion of the western European countries from the 16th century on provided opportunities for individuals to enrich themselves as traders or settlers, at the same time as they subjugated and enslaved other peoples in Asia, Africa, and America. Later, with the creation by European settlers of new societies, especially in North America, fresh opportunities for mobility were provided by large-scale immigration. The expansion of U.S. society across the continent during the 19th century brought millions of working class and peasant immigrants from Europe who were leaving conditions of poverty and subordination that seemed unalterable in their own societies.

Consequences of mobility. The determinants of mobility outlined above are difficult to isolate and measure, as are the social consequences of mobility. On one side, it may be said that the movement of large numbers of people up and down the social hierarchy tends to break down the exclusiveness of social classes and to create a more uniform national culture. Presumably, this would also lead to a diminution of class prejudices and class conflicts. It has often been claimed, in fact, that the allegedly lesser degree of class consciousness in U.S. society, as compared with European societies, is due to a higher rate of mobility in the former. Although this may be doubtful in the light of recent studies that show no great differences in overall mobility in the industrial societies, the widespread belief that opportunities for upward mobility are actually greater than in other societies may itself have had an important influence. From another aspect, however, it can be argued that the preoccupation with

vertical mobility reinforces the class system; the individual who is concerned to rise or avoid falling in the social hierarchy accepts and indeed emphasizes the importance of class and status distinctions. It has been suggested that these distinctions might be diminished much more by the attainment of greater economic and social equality than by any amount of individual mobility.

Another consequence of mobility that is seen as beneficial from the point of view of society as a whole is the more effective use of ability. If individuals are confined to the social sphere in which they are born, many useful talents will remain undiscovered and unused. The expansion of education in modern industrial societies has been stimulated by the desire to provide opportunities for the development of all the abilities available in the population, though this is still very imperfectly achieved.

On the other hand, vertical mobility may have some undesirable consequences. Such mobility, whether upward or downward, imposes strains upon the individual striving for success and adapting to new social milieus and may be disruptive of families and local communities. More generally, a high rate of mobility may be regarded as producing in society the condition that the French sociologist Émile Durkheim called "anomie" (normlessness and resultant disorientation and anxiety), in which there is insufficient regulation of behaviour and the individual suffers from the "malady of infinite aspiration." The existence of such strains may lead to a higher incidence of mental illness among highly mobile individuals, but it seems doubtful that mobility is a major factor in mental illness, given that such illness has been increasing rapidly in the industrial societies, while there has been no correspondingly marked increase in mobility. It seems likely that it is the pace of economic and cultural change in general and the conditions of urban-industrial life that impose the greatest strain upon individuals.

Possible
undesirable
conse-
quences
of
mobility

CURRENT TRENDS

The economic development of Western industrial countries after 1945 and changes in social policy that resulted in the provision of more elaborate welfare services seemed to many observers to be generating significant changes in the class system. Diverse interpretations of these changes have been proposed. According to one view, there has been a general diminution in class differences resulting from higher levels of living, greater social mobility, and a limited redistribution of wealth and income. These changes, it is held, are reflected in a decline of class ideologies and class conflict. This interpretation of events could lead to a conception of Western societies as progressing toward a relative classlessness or as becoming predominantly middle class societies.

Other social scientists, however, have argued that new social classes are being formed, notably a new upper class comprising the managers and organizers of production in both the public and the private sector, and that class struggles are developing that are related less to economic questions and more directly to the degree of participation in or exclusion from political decisions that affect the general course of development of a society. This interpretation seemed more plausible with the re-emergence of profound ideological and political conflicts in the industrial countries of Europe and North America during the 1960s, after the relative social peace of the previous decade. It also had the merit of being applicable to the Socialist countries of eastern Europe, in which it may be claimed that a new upper class of economic managers and party officials has developed.

Some Marxist writers continue to uphold the traditional view of the class system in capitalist societies and to assert the fundamental importance of the opposition between bourgeoisie and proletariat, while attaching little significance to the growth of middle class occupations or to changes in the character of ideological and political conflicts. Others, as noted above, have concluded that the opposition between these 19th-century classes no longer has a major political influence. They go on to suggest that the most important division in world society is that between the industrial nations and the developing countries.

Many social scientists, in fact, would regard the gap between rich and poor nations as the principal modern manifestation of inequality, but to treat this as a difference between classes and to refer to "bourgeois" and "proletarian" nations is to use the term class in quite another sense from that which it has had in the social sciences for the past century or more and would require a more elaborate justification than has yet been given.

BIBLIOGRAPHY. Two short introductions to the study of social class are KURT B. MAYER and WALTER BUCKLEY, *Class and Society*, 3rd ed. rev. (1969); and T.B. BOTTOMORE, *Classes in Modern Society*, 2nd ed. (1966). The historical development of ideas and theories of class has not been very fully discussed, but some treatment is given in STANISLAW OS-SOWSKI, *Struktura klasowa w społecznej świadomości* (1957; Eng. trans., *Class Structure in the Social Consciousness*, 1963), which also contains a good account of the Marxist theory. Another exposition and critical examination of Marx's theory is provided by RALF DAHRENDORF, *Soziale Klassen und Klassenkonflikt in der industriellen Gesellschaft* (1957; Eng. trans., *Class and Class Conflict in Industrial Society*, 1959). The ideas of the early American sociologists are discussed in CHARLES H. PAGE, *Class and American Sociology*, new ed. (1969), which contains a long introduction surveying much of the research on social class and mobility over the past 30 years. MAX WEBER's writings on social class and status are to be found mainly in his work *Wirtschaft und Gesellschaft*, 4th ed., 2 vol. (1922; Eng. trans., *Economy and Society*, ed. by GUENTHER ROTH and CLAUS WITTICH, 3 vol., 1968). The theory of elites is expounded by VILFREDO PARETO in *Trattato di sociologia generale*, 2nd ed., 3 vol. (1923; Eng. trans., *The Mind and Society*, 4 vol., 1935); more recent studies include C. WRIGHT MILLS, *The Power Elite* (1956); and T.B. BOTTOMORE, *Elites and Society* (1964). Among the general studies of class are REINHARD BENDIX and S.M. LIPSET (eds.), *Class, Status and Power*, 2nd ed. (1966); and GERHARD E. LENSKI, *Power and Privilege* (1966). Particular social classes are discussed in C. WRIGHT MILLS, *White Collar* (1951); G.A. BRIEFS, *The Proletariat* (1937); J.H. GOLDTHORPE et al., *The Affluent Worker*, 3 vol. (1968–69); and ERIC R. WOLF, *Peasants* (1966).

A pioneer survey of social mobility is P.A. SOROKIN, *Social Mobility* (1927, reprinted with an additional chapter on cultural mobility, 1959). Two major national studies are D.V. GLASS (ed.), *Social Mobility in Britain* (1954); and PETER M. BLAU and OTIS D. DUNCAN, *The American Occupational Structure* (1967). Comparisons between societies are discussed in S.M. LIPSET and REINHARD BENDIX, *Social Mobility in Industrial Society* (1959); and S.M. MILLER, "Comparative Social Mobility," *Current Sociology*, 9:1–89 (1960). Some aspects of the social context in which mobility occurs are examined, with reference to the United States, in ANSELM L. STRAUSS, *The Contexts of Social Mobility* (1971).

There are few studies of the class system as a whole, but reference can be made to C. WRIGHT MILLS, *The Power Elite* (1956); and JOHN PORTER, *The Vertical Mosaic: An Analysis of Social Class and Power in Canada* (1965). The class system and stratification in the U.S.S.R. and other Socialist societies has begun to be studied more fully; an early work was MILOVAN DJILAS, *The New Class* (1957); and more recent studies include DAVID LANE, *Politics and Society in the USSR*, ch. 12 (1970); FRANK PARKIN, "Class Stratification in Socialist Societies," *British Journal of Sociology*, 20:355–374 (1969); and the study of Czechoslovakia by PAVEL MA-CHONIN, *Cesty k beztřídní společnosti* (1961).

Changes in the class system in Western industrial societies are discussed in ALAIN TOURAINE, *La Société post-industrielle* (1969; Eng. trans., 1971); and there are earlier observations on European societies by S.M. LIPSET and RALF DAHRENDORF in S.R. GRAUBARD (ed.), *A New Europe?* (1963). In the case of the developing countries attention has been concentrated mainly on the emergence of new elites; see S.M. LIPSET and ALDO SOLARI (eds.), *Elites in Latin America* (1967), and PETER C. LLOYD, *Classes, Crises and Coups* (1971).

(T.B.B.)

Social Differentiation and Stratification

"Social differentiation" refers to the recognition and establishment in society of differences between groups or categories of individuals. It is evident that not all differences between individuals give rise to social differentiation. On the one hand there are personal qualities or combinations of qualities that distinguish a particular individual from all others; and on the other hand there are some characteristics that may be possessed in similar degree or kind by a number of individuals—for example, height or weight, colour of hair or eyes, temperament—but which never, or very rarely, lead to social differentiation. Many differences between individuals, however, are invested with social significance (or may be said to be created by society), with the result that the individual is seen as belonging to specific groups and categories that define his position in society. Thus he can be described as male or female, middle class or working class, young or old, married or unmarried, or belonging to a particular ethnic, linguistic, or religious group; and these classifications will refer to typical or expected kinds of behaviour, styles of life, and opportunities.

Another way of describing the same phenomena is to say that each individual occupies or performs "social roles." A society is thus regarded as a system of differentiated roles, and the position of an individual in the society is, in some sense, a product of his various roles.

Whether social differentiation is conceived in terms of roles or in terms of the groups and categories to which an individual belongs or is assigned, it has diverse aspects that must be clearly distinguished. In the first place, differentiation is closely associated with stratification; many social differences are invidiously ranked, so that some categories or groups of individuals have higher status or belong to higher classes than others. Second, the social importance of the various recognized differences may be unequal, and it is generally the case that those differences accompanying major social stratification have the greatest prominence. In society as a whole, the distinction between married and unmarried, or between young and old, is usually less significant than the distinction between an aristocrat and a commoner or between an executive of a large corporation and a manual worker. Third, the various positions that an individual occupies may be non-aggregative, incongruous, or conflicting. It does not seem possible, for example, to aggregate the roles of father and corporation executive into an intelligible whole; and from this it follows that differentiation needs to be observed in several distinct spheres of social life and that a distinction has to be made between those roles that fit together in a significant whole and those that do not. Incongruous or conflicting roles appear particularly in connection with stratification; thus, an individual may be highly educated but poor and socially despised, or on the other hand he may be wealthy or powerful but uneducated and lacking the cultural attributes of established members of an upper class. Fourth, it should be noted that social differentiation varies in character from one type of society to another, and even from one society to another within the same type, and that it changes over time. Indeed, one of the principal features to which sociologists have drawn attention is the growth of social differentiation (especially in the form of a more extensive division of labour) in the course of social development.

THE CRITERIA OF DIFFERENTIATION

It will be evident from what has been said that a great many factors enter into the process of differentiation. Initially, a broad distinction may be made between two kinds of factors: those that depend upon biological differences among human beings and those that arise wholly or largely from social or cultural conditions.

Biological factors. *Sex differentiation.* One of the most obvious differences among human beings is that between the sexes. In all societies men and women are treated differently (often unequally) and have different functions, or roles. Many social scientists from the 19th century onward (among them Karl Marx and Herbert Spencer) have suggested that the economic division of labour began with the division of tasks between the sexes; and this, it is generally held, would arise from biological differences—in particular, men's greater physical strength, which equipped them for the activities of hunting and warfare, and women's reproductive function, which tended to confine them to the area of the home or settlement. Many other social and cultural differences between men and women in early societies, and notably

The concept of international class conflict

Definitions of "social differentiation" and "social stratification"

Social differences between men and women

the male dominance in political life, may have followed from this original division of labour; and these differences were perpetuated and developed in later societies. Thus, in spite of considerable variations in the social position of women from one society to another, there has been a general male predominance which has continued up to the present time. In the new industrial societies of the 19th century, women still lacked many of the civil rights (especially property rights) and political rights enjoyed by men, and although they have now gained these rights in most modern societies, considerable differences remain: women workers are concentrated in the less skilled and lower paid occupations; disproportionately few women are in the higher professions; and women usually play little part in politics at the national level. Nevertheless, there have been gradual changes in all these spheres during the present century, and at the same time movements for women's rights—from the woman suffragists to the Women's Liberation Movement—have been a significant element in the more general movements of radicalism and reform.

The social differentiation of the sexes poses an important problem that is relevant to all discussion of the biological factors in social life. Some writers have argued that the physical differences between men and women determine the major psychological differences—of intellect and temperament—that largely account for the differentiation of social roles. Against this view it has been argued that biological elements acquire importance only when they are socially recognized and established; that there are in fact great variations, between societies and between historical periods, in the relative positions of men and women; and that in modern times the differences between the social roles of men and women have tended to diminish. Moreover, the existence of substantial, innate psychological differences between men and women is not securely established, and such differences as do appear can be explained as a consequence of social and cultural influences rather than biological inheritance. In this case, as in many others, the question of the relative importance of nature and nurture is still unsettled. At least, however, it can be said that the differences between men and women need not necessarily lead to economic and social inequality; and it may be claimed further that there is no longer any reason in advanced industrial societies for these differences to produce any large degree of differentiation at all outside the sexual sphere (see also WOMEN, STATUS OF).

Age differentiation. Another biological factor that leads to differentiation is age. In all societies a distinction is made between the young, the mature, and the old; and different roles are assigned to them. A more elaborate classification exists in many societies—for example, according to Hindu doctrine, four stages are to be distinguished in the individual's life (a period of preparation, a period as a householder, a period as a recluse, and a final period of renunciation of the world). In many modern societies it is common to distinguish the periods of childhood, youth (including the transitional stage of adolescence), middle age, and old age. The extent to which these stages are clearly defined or formally recognized, however, varies considerably from one type of society to another, as do the social attitudes toward the members of each category. In some tribal societies there are organized age sets that mark the progress of the individual toward full adult membership of the tribe. On the other hand, in modern industrial societies the points of transition from one age category to another tend to be less well defined, to change over time, and to vary from one sphere of social life to another. Childhood may be regarded as lasting until puberty (or, in social terms, adolescence), and it has corresponded also, to some extent, with the period of formal school education; however, the continuing extension of the period of education has meant that childhood now merges into youth while a condition of dependency continues, without the sharp break that occurred in earlier societies when the individual moved at an earlier age from school or family to adult work. At the same time, there has developed in modern societies in recent decades a more distinctive "teen-age" culture within a broader youth culture. In the legal and political spheres there has been a tendency to recognize earlier maturation by reducing the age of majority and of acquisition of political rights (in Great Britain in 1970, for example, from 21 to 18 years), but there is still not a complete correspondence between the ages at which, in different spheres, individuals assume adult roles.

The evaluation of different age groups varies widely from one kind of society to another. In many tribal societies and traditional societies, the elders have considerable prestige and power as the possessors of a store of valuable knowledge and experience. In modern industrial societies, on the other hand, they may be regarded as old-fashioned and out-of-date, because of the rapid growth and transformation of knowledge.

Differentiation by age is accompanied by inequalities. In most societies economic resources and political power are in the hands of the middle-aged or old, though there are considerable variations and in periods of social upheaval the young may increase their influence or power. The inequalities arising from age differences, like those arising from the differences between the sexes, are in any case less prominent in most societies than those that emerge from property ownership and other directly social elements in stratification (see also YOUTH, SOCIAL ASPECTS OF; OLD AGE, SOCIAL ASPECTS OF).

Racial differentiation. Race differences have been another important source of social differentiation. In the first place, it may be claimed that the various races of mankind have created widely different civilizations. But this assertion raises difficulties of the kind already encountered in discussing the differences between men and women, namely, that it is not possible to establish a strict relation between the physical characteristics and the psychological and cultural features. In this particular case it seems clear that the diverse forms of nations and civilizations are mainly the product of geographical, social, and historical influences, although the actual creation of nations may have owed something to a sense of racial distinctiveness, among many other factors.

Perhaps the most important observation to be made about differences of race is that they may be either emphasized or treated as unimportant in different times and places, according to the prevailing cultural and political circumstances. Race relations in modern times have undoubtedly been most strongly affected by the colonial situation that followed the overseas expansion of the western European countries. Ideas of racial superiority and inferiority accompanied colonization, and these ideas have persisted up to the present time, sustained by the great discrepancies in wealth and power between the nations of western Europe and North America and the countries of the Third World. Not only were race differences and inequalities emphasized on a world scale during the period of modern imperialism, but they also became prominent within particular societies in which, for one reason or another, different racial groups lived together. Thus, in the Republic of South Africa, a white minority which possesses economic and political power maintains, through the institutions of apartheid, a strict separation between white, black, and coloured members of society in order to perpetuate its own supremacy. In the United States, a black minority originating in the African slave trade of the early period of colonialism has enjoyed formal political rights for a century, but it still occupies in practice a situation of economic, cultural, and political inferiority that is increasingly a source of major political conflict. More recently, in Great Britain, the growth of an immigrant population drawn mainly from the West Indies, India, and Pakistan has resulted in more widespread manifestations of racism and, on the other side, attempts by legislation and by other means to prevent racial discrimination.

The principal aspect of race differences in modern times, therefore, is that such differences have taken the form not merely of differentiation but of gross inequality. It is possible to conceive of a state of affairs in which the differences between races, and the cultural differences

Inequalities among age groups

Effects of modern colonialism and imperialism upon race relations

that have become associated with them, would be generally regarded as creating a pleasurable diversity of human life; but this is far from being the case at the present time. The colonial conquests established inequality as a principal element in the relations between races, and the dissolution of the colonial empires is still too recent for their historical consequences to have been eliminated (see also RACISM; MINORITIES AND ETHNIC GROUPS).

Intellectual differentiation. Besides the major biological factors of sex, age, and race, there are other genetic differences between individuals which may lead to social differentiation. One of those most frequently discussed is differences in intelligence. In this case social differentiation is directly linked with stratification; those who are intellectually more able, it is suggested, will attain the leading positions in society. This thesis is clearly most readily applicable to the modern industrial societies, in which social mobility (that is, movement from one level to another in the social hierarchy) is possible and even encouraged and in which, moreover, such mobility occurs to a large extent through the acquisition of educational qualifications. To say this, however, is to recognize that social differentiation and stratification do not by any means correspond with the variations in intellectual ability in all societies. Where there exists a rigid system of stratification (as in a caste system), an individual's position in society is fairly strictly determined by descent, and intellectual or other personal qualities can have little effect upon it. Again, intellectual ability may be more or less highly valued in different types of society; if the principal social activity is hunting or warfare, then physical strength, energy, and courage may be much more important. Even in modern industrial societies, the relation between intelligence and social position is far from straightforward. The inheritance of class position limits the possibility of social differentiation in terms of intelligence; moreover, it is generally acknowledged that there are social, as well as genetic, factors in intelligence itself, so that it may be said that those individuals born into high social positions will display, on average, high intelligence and hence are likely to maintain themselves in these positions, while those born into lower social strata will experience much greater difficulty in developing their intellectual qualities.

This consideration of the biological factors in social differentiation brings to light a question of crucial importance. Although sex, age, race, and individual qualities such as intelligence obviously play some part in social differentiation, they do not have a directly determining influence. Their effect depends upon the way in which they are conceived and treated in each society, and this, in turn, depends upon a great variety of social, cultural, and historical influences.

Social and cultural factors. Among the most obvious forms of social differentiation arising from social and cultural factors are (1) the diversity of nations and civilizations, and (2) the distinctions within societies between classes or status groups. The second of these forms will be considered later in discussing stratification. The distinctions between nations, or more generally between the numerous autonomous communities into which mankind has always been divided, are closely associated with differences of language and of culture. Primitive societies, relatively isolated from one another even in the same geographical region, differed in language, in kinship structure, in religious belief and practice, and in economic system—the latter depending partly upon the nature of the physical environment and partly upon the level of technological development in a particular society. Many of these features persist in present-day tribal societies, although they have been greatly modified by the impact of the industrial countries.

It is impossible now to trace the ways in which this differentiation of early human societies came about; and, even in the case of ancient societies that have left historical records, it is not easy to follow in detail the processes by which distinct political communities were created. War and conquest, associated with migrations, played an important part in creating new and larger scale societies,

but there were also contrary processes of disintegration and further differentiation. At a later stage, the world religions played a large part in forming distinct areas of civilization. The modern nation-states in Europe were formed largely on the basis of language and historical traditions, while in other parts of the world, more recently, new independent nations have been created on the basis of a religious or cultural identity or have established themselves as the successors to somewhat arbitrarily defined colonial territories (and consequently face difficult problems of social integration).

In considering social differentiation on a world scale, social scientists have been concerned not only with the distinctive features of particular societies and civilizations but also with *types* of society as they have appeared in different historical periods. The French sociologist Émile Durkheim in 1893, for example, distinguished between societies characterized by "mechanical solidarity" and those characterized by "organic solidarity." In the former (primitive and early societies) individuals differ little from each other and are uniformly subjected to the authority of the social group; in the latter (especially modern societies) there is great internal differentiation, individualism flourishes, and individuals are bound to each other by mutual dependence, especially through the extensive division of labour. A distinction that is similar in certain respects to that made by the German sociologist Ferdinand Tönnies in 1887 between *Gemeinschaft* (community) and *Gesellschaft* (society); in the former type of social system, men live in small-scale groups and have direct, face-to-face relations with one another, whereas in the latter type they belong to large-scale groups and are related indirectly and impersonally. This distinction, like Durkheim's, is, at least in part, one between primitive and early societies on the one hand and modern societies on the other.

Other writers have established quite different distinctions between types of society, often making use of economic criteria. One of the best known classifications along these lines is that of Karl Marx, who distinguished several types in terms of their mode of production and the class system arising from it: primitive communism, ancient society, Asiatic society, feudal society, modern capitalist society. More recently, another kind of economic distinction has been made, between industrial societies and nonindustrial or preindustrial societies, the latter being referred to quite frequently as the "developing countries." At the same time, a distinction is now increasingly made between socialist and capitalist economic systems and between the societies that develop upon these different economic bases, even though there are important similarities between all the industrial countries as a social type, on one hand, and the developing countries as a contrasting type, on the other, in spite of differences of economic regime within each type.

The consideration of social and cultural differences between whole societies, or types of society, or civilizations, involves treating these units as if they were themselves relatively homogeneous and undifferentiated. The aspect of social differentiation that has attracted most attention, however, is that which occurs within each society. Some kinds of internal differentiation related to biological characteristics, notably those resulting from sex and age differences, have already been mentioned; but the most prevalent types of social differentiation are those arising directly from social and cultural influences. Many social scientists have regarded the division of labour as the most important factor; one of the most obvious differences between individuals and groups in society is to be found in the kind of work that they perform. In the late 18th century the Scottish economist Adam Smith discussed not only the economic consequences of the extending division of labour but also its effects in determining the characteristics and life-styles of individuals. In the late 19th century the English philosopher Herbert Spencer conceived of the division of labour as a primary element in social differentiation and traced its development in the various parts of society. Similarly, Durkheim considered that the division of labour was the source of the individualism to

National or societal differentiation

Differentiation within societies

be found in modern societies and that, although it posed problems of fragmentation and social disintegration, it offered the possibility of a new form of social solidarity based upon the interdependence of individuals and groups.

The great importance of the economic division of labour in producing social differentiation cannot be denied. Moreover, it is closely connected, as will be seen later, with the establishment and modification of social stratification. Nevertheless, it is now generally acknowledged that social differentiation extends beyond the economic division of labour and its effects; as one scholar noted, it "should be thought of as a differentiation of activity of every sort that has significance for the group." Spencer, for example, wrote in terms of the "specialization of functions" which resulted in a clearer distinction between the major parts of society—the governmental, the military, the ecclesiastical, the professional, the industrial—as well as a more intensive division of labour in the productive sphere. But the writer who brought out most plainly the complexity of social differentiation in modern societies was the German sociologist Georg Simmel. In his volume of essays *Über soziale Differenzierung* (1890; "On Social Differentiation") and in other works, he considered the great variety of influences that had contributed to the growth of individualism and the diversification of social groups in the western European countries during the 19th century. The rapid development of a money economy, the growth of cities, the mobility of individuals, the emergence of new social and cultural interests all have tended to produce more varied styles of life. In particular, city life offered the stimulus of diverse and competing intellectual and cultural outlooks, from which new kinds of differentiation could again arise, while the increase in the number of associations of all kinds, concerned with specific interests, permitted the individual to develop particular aspects of his own character and purposes. According to Simmel, in early societies the individual was more or less completely absorbed in the family group, but later he was able to enter into relationships with persons outside his circle on the basis of a similarity in character, tendencies, and activities. Thus new "social circles" arose which intersected the existing "natural groups." In modern societies a vast superstructure of social circles has grown up, and this process has been accompanied by an increase in individual liberty; in Simmel's view, the number of social circles to which the individual belongs is, to some extent, a measure of the development of civilization.

The twin processes of individualism and diversification

Although Simmel attached great significance to social differentiation, he also observed that differentiation was accompanied by a process of integration; and he suggested that human nature shows a fundamental need for both kinds of association—that association which differentiates individuals on the basis of competition and that which brings them together on the basis of cooperation. Thus, he observed that although there is a continual proliferation of more specialized circles because of the appearance of new occupations, new scientific pursuits, and new cultural styles, there is also a continual formation of large circles out of smaller ones—for example, the formation of a working class out of diverse occupational groups. This relationship between differentiation and integration can best be studied by looking at the historical development of social differentiation.

THE DEVELOPMENT OF SOCIAL DIFFERENTIATION

The process of social differentiation has often been taken as one of the principal indexes of social development. Thus, in 1926 the American sociologist Cecil C. North observed that the most significant distinction between a primitive and a highly civilized society was probably the degree to which functional differentiation had taken place. This followed the view of many earlier sociologists. Herbert Spencer for instance, had argued that it is

a character of social bodies, as of living bodies, that while they increase in size they increase in structure. . . . At first the unlikenesses among [society's] groups of units are inconspicuous in number and degree but as population aug-

ments, divisions and subdivisions become numerous and more decided . . . progressive differentiation of structures is accompanied by progressive differentiation of functions.

Spencer's ideas have been revived recently by the American sociologist Talcott Parsons, who has treated social change and development wholly as a process of increasing social differentiation.

It should be recognized, however, that although increasing social differentiation is one important aspect of social development, there are other features that have been regarded by many writers as having equal or greater significance in defining or explaining historical transformations of society. Spencer, for example, saw as one major element in social differentiation the emergence of dominant classes; this, too, was the crucial element in Marx's theory, which—in contrast to the idea of social development through a gradual, progressive differentiation of function—conceived of historical change as proceeding by revolutionary leaps whenever a new ruling class arose as a result of new modes of production. Many recent studies by sociologists and economists have emphasized particularly the distinction between industrial and nonindustrial societies and have considered industrialization, in which social differentiation is only one element, as the major form of social change.

Another important qualification must be applied to the view that social change consists essentially in the process of social differentiation. It is true that in many respects —especially in their occupational structures—modern societies are more differentiated and more heterogeneous than were earlier societies; but forces are also at work making for greater homogeneity. The rise of the European nation-states in the 19th century, the development of national systems of education, the improvement of communications, the increasing size of economic enterprises, and more recently the growth of the mass media have all contributed, in the opinion of many writers, to a greater uniformity of national culture and to the disappearance or attenuation of local and regional diversity. Such developments have been commented upon, from various points of view, in writings on "mass society" and the "consumer society." It has also been argued that increasing social equality in the industrial countries (a diminution of the differences between social strata and greater social mobility) has begun to create a more homogeneous national culture. The factual basis of this argument, however, is disputed, and the most that can be said probably is that the general rise of levels of living, rather than equalization, has had some effect in producing more uniformity in styles of life. The tendencies toward homogeneity are to be seen not only at the national level but also on an international scale, and it has been suggested that all the advanced industrial countries show certain fundamental similarities in their structure and culture— primarily because of industrialism, urbanism, vastly improved communications systems, and the influence of international economic organizations. It would be very difficult, nevertheless, to establish in a precise way the degree to which present-day societies are becoming more or less heterogeneous. What is important is to recognize that the two processes of differentiation and homogenization proceed together, both within and between societies.

Contrasting processes of differentiation and homogenization

The processes of differentiation and stratification. It will be evident from the preceding account that many socially differentiated roles are evaluated as being "higher" or "lower" in some scale of prestige. Social differentiation, that is, overlaps with social stratification, the arrangement of groups and categories of individuals in a hierarchical order. Men and women, different age categories, ethnic groups, religious groups, or occupations may be treated not merely as different but as unequal. Stratification within societies is one of the most important forms of differentiation, but it has been conceived in diverse ways. Most students of the subject would agree that its basis is primarily economic, but economic differentiation itself can be viewed from a variety of aspects. According to Marxist theory, the most important distinction in all societies beyond the most primitive was that between the owners of the means of production and those who supplied their labour power. These two groups constituted the principal classes in every society (though Marx also recognized the existence of intermediate and transitional strata), and the relations between the classes determined the general course of social events in all spheres of life. Depending upon the character of the means of production and, thus, to a large extent, upon the level of technology, different forms of class society have existed. Marx distinguished, in the Western world, ancient society, feudal society, and modern bourgeois (or capitalist) society; and he envisaged the advent of a new form of society, socialism, in the future. In all cases, the rise of new classes and the struggle between classes were the principal causes of major changes in social structure. In the modern capitalist societies, according to Marx, it was the industrial working class, in the various forms of labour movement that are its political expression, that would accomplish such changes and inaugurate a new society.

Marx was not alone in recognizing the importance of social classes; many 19th-century historians, political scientists, and sociologists made similar observations, but they did not all explain the origins and development of classes in the same way, nor did they attach the same political importance to class conflict or envisage the future, as Marx did, in terms of a working class revolution to establish socialism. Spencer drew attention to the role of dominant classes, and Durkheim recognized the pervasiveness of class conflict in the modern European societies, but both considered that classes could coexist harmoniously in the industrial societies, so long as these societies continued to develop their relatively open and democratic character. Other writers, such as the Italian economist Vilfredo Pareto, while adopting the conception of class from Marxist thought, argued that the existence of a governing class or elite was unavoidable and were chiefly concerned, as many later writers have been, with the effectiveness of the dominant class in maintaining a stable social order.

The Marxist scheme has, at various times, been ignored (largely because of its ideological orientation), criticized, and revised. One point of criticism concerns its applicability to all the diverse forms of stratification. It seems most relevant to the 19th-century European societies and to the transition from feudalism to capitalism in western Europe, but much less useful in dealing with such a phenomenon as the Indian caste system. Caste has undoubtedly an economic basis: the major caste categories (the *varnas*) resemble feudal estates, while the effective caste groups (the *jātis*) are closely related to differences of occupation. Nevertheless, the complexities of the caste system and the sanctions maintaining it can hardly be understood without taking account of the influence of religious ideas; and the historical relations between castes seem far removed from those which characterize the conflict between classes.

The interrelations of class, status, and power. A more general criticism of the Marxist theory leads to an alternative conception of social stratification. In writings published posthumously in 1922 the German sociologist Max Weber made a distinction between class, status, and power, arguing that these represented different forms of stratification that coexisted but did not necessarily coincide in modern societies. According to Weber, class situation was mainly determined by the ownership or nonownership of property (more or less along the lines that Marx had described); status situation was determined by the attribution of "social honour" on the basis of consumption or style of life; and the power situation was determined by possession or nonpossession of the means of command. Thus the relative importance of class and status in the stratification system has to be investigated in particular societies and periods; the predominance of one or the other would depend upon economic and cultural conditions that affect the extent to which men become class conscious or status conscious. Moreover, political power is relatively independent of both class and status; it is not regarded, as in Marx's theory, as being merely a consequence or reflection of class position.

Definitions of class, status, and power

The introduction of the notion of social status (which was developed from the feudal idea of legal status) led in due course to the formulation of a distinctive theory of social stratification. In contrast to the Marxist conception —according to which society was divided into major classes engaged in economic, political, and cultural conflict over the basic structure of society itself—the new theory viewed society as a hierarchy of status levels, with each level determined by a social evaluation of the importance or worth of the activities carried on by individuals at that level. The emphasis was upon the placement of individuals in the social hierarchy, not upon the formation of groups and their interrelations. The fact that numbers of individuals occupied the same rank position was considered (if at all) as a secondary phenomenon, and those occupying the same position tended to be treated as forming statistical categories rather than social groups. Thus, in many recent studies of social mobility the various social levels have been defined in terms of occupational prestige, and the scheme of ranking that has been constructed in this way is acknowledged to be a partly arbitrary set of categories, not a system of significant social groups. One researcher in 1954, for instance, distinguished seven occupational prestige categories for the purpose of studying movement between lower and higher social levels in Great Britain, while a pair of researchers in 1967 used a prestige scale of 17 types of occupation for their study of mobility in the United States.

Conceived in this way, stratification is very closely connected with social differentiation in the form of the division of labour, since it is the differentiation of occupations and their evaluation and ranking that are taken to be the source of stratification. It is clear, however, that this does not provide a complete picture of the social hierarchy. Besides the ranking of occupations, and the construction of categories of occupations that are judged to have equal prestige, there is a process of formation of social groups that, through their pursuit of particular interests, play a distinctive part in the system of stratification. Most of what are called the liberal professions, and even the professions as a whole, have generally been regarded as constituting groups of this kind, and it has also been widely recognized that there are various types of elites, not all based upon specific occupations, that have a major influence in shaping the institutions and culture of a society. Furthermore, the various stratified groups and prestige categories are themselves closely connected with social classes, as may be seen from the fact that occupations are thought of, and referred to, as being upper class, middle class, or working class in character. As Simmel observed, the process of occupational specialization is accompanied by an opposite process of incorporation of the occupations into social classes.

There is still another aspect from which the association between status, class, and power should be observed. The prestige of occupations, which is often taken to be the crucial element in establishing a hierarchy of status, at least in modern societies, is determined by social evaluations, but one needs to ask how these evaluations themselves come to be made and accepted. The importance or worth of particular occupations is not something established by nature, and it may be argued that it is those persons who are already wealthy or powerful (that is to say, dominant) in society who decide the scale of prestige. In this sense, therefore, the existence of a status system presupposes the existence of dominant and subordinate classes or of governing elites and subject groups. Nevertheless, other influences upon the prestige of occupations also seem to arise directly from economic and cultural conditions—for example, the changes brought about by the rise of modern science and technology, by the growing secularization of culture, and by the development of mass leisure that has given higher incomes and greater prestige to entertainers of all kinds.

The relations between class, status, and power, as different forms of social stratification, are complex and variable. In some times and places the formation of classes and the struggles between them for political power may be of pre-eminent importance, as was the case in western Europe during the period of the rise of the bourgeoisie in feudal society, and again in the 19th century when the organized working class movement began to develop. Under other conditions, however, though class divisions exist, they may be less significant than differences of status arising from the diversity of occupations, ethnic origins, and styles of life, influenced by a variety of cultural factors including religious doctrines. It has been argued, for instance, that class differences in the Western industrial societies have begun to lose some of their cultural and political importance in recent decades as a consequence of such changes as the more extensive division of labour leading to a greater variety of status positions, greater social mobility, the expansion of education and of middle class occupations based upon educational qualifications, and higher levels of living. It remains a matter of controversy, however, whether or not social classes have yet ceased to be the principal source of political ideologies and conflicts in these societies.

Social mobility. In the earliest human societies, differences of class and status as one of the principal types of social differentiation may have emerged in various ways—partly as a result of the accumulation of property or the monopolization of leadership positions by particular individuals and families and partly by means of conquest and the enslavement of other social groups. Once established, these differences are maintained by inheritance and strengthened by the elaboration of cultural distinctions in dress, education (initially a distinction between literacy and nonliteracy, and, later, differences in quality and duration of education), and style of life as a whole; they are also consolidated by legal and religious codes. Occupations may become hereditary (either in a formal way, as in the Indian caste system, or on a customary basis); property is transmitted through the family; and political power is inherited by the members of royal and noble families. Of course, the inheritance of social position is never complete in the sense that no new men can attain to wealth, prestige, or power. Pareto exaggerated somewhat when he wrote that "history is a graveyard of aristocracies," but it is certainly true that in all societies there has been some circulation of individuals and families between different social levels. Even in the Indian caste system, which was a particularly closed form of social stratification, it was possible for individuals, and especially for caste groups, to rise in the social hierarchy by various means; and in the European feudal societies there were considerable opportunities for mobility, particularly after commerce and the towns began to develop.

It would seem that modern industrial societies are the ones in which social mobility has generally attained its highest degree and in which inheritance of social position has diminished most. But, in truth, it is difficult, and in many cases impossible, to make rigorous comparisons of the degree of social mobility in one society at different times or in different societies; for the judgments that are made about the relative openness of different types of society tend to be based more upon a consideration of formal opportunities and restrictions than upon an examination of actual movement between social levels. Thus there is controversy about whether or not social mobility in industrial societies has increased during the present century; and, moreover, it is quite clear that there is still a very significant inheritance of class position. The distribution of wealth is obviously highly unequal, and it is primarily through the transmission of property that families in the upper strata maintain their social position and exclude those from lower strata.

There are some conditions under which social mobility undoubtedly increases. After a revolution, for example, there is likely to be a general reshuffling of the dominant groups in society; thus, in the U.S.S.R. after November 1917, and in the countries of eastern Europe after 1945, many individuals from subordinate groups in society rose to positions of considerable prestige and power, while others who had previously been dominant fell in the social hierarchy. But at a later stage there may be a new consolidation of status positions. This is particularly noticeable in the sphere of higher education; immediately

after the revolutions in eastern Europe, the universities were thrown open to children of working class and peasant families, but as the new upper and middle strata of the population became established they began to acquire privileges for their children, in education as in other spheres, and the recruitment of university students from the working class and peasantry declined again.

Another, more gradual, process affecting social mobility has been the changing structure of occupations in the advanced industrial countries. There has been a steady decline in the numbers employed in agriculture and extractive industries and, more recently, the beginnings of a decline in the numbers of manual workers in manufacturing industry; whereas there has been a continual expansion of clerical, technical, and professional occupations. This process has gone farthest in the United States, where one-half of the employed population is now engaged in middle class occupations, but it is taking place, also, in the European industrial countries and Japan. Its result is to move a proportion of each new generation from low-status manual occupations to higher status white-collar occupations and, at some point, to create, as has been claimed for the United States, a predominantly middle class society. But this process has further implications for social differentiation; insofar as it establishes, over a large area of society, a middle class style of life, depending upon similarity of income and occupation, it diminishes differentiation and produces a greater uniformity. This is one aspect of the phenomenon mentioned earlier that sociologists have characterized as mass society. The extent of such uniformity is limited, however, even in the most advanced countries. There is still a clear distinction between the small group of wealthy property owners and the rest of the population; and there are many groups—such as certain ethnic groups, workers in backward or declining industries, and retired workers—who live in conditions of relative poverty far below the standards of middle class society.

The individual and society. The phenomenon of social differentiation throws some new light upon the relations between the individual and society. It is not the case that each individual, with his array of personal qualities, confronts the whole society to which he belongs. He is born into particular, differentiated social groups, and his life experiences in these groups do something to form his character and determine his outlook, aims, and achievements. Nevertheless, social differentiation may be regarded as one of the main factors responsible for modern individualism. In broad outline, Durkheim's contrast between early, relatively simple societies, in which the individual is molded to a single pattern of behaviour, and modern complex societies, in which the individual is more differentiated, seems valid if one takes into account not only the increasing division of labour but also the increasing cultural diversity (which arose partly from the criticism of established religious and moral ideas), the development of towns and the consequent opportunities for competition between ideas, and the greater mobility of individuals. Durkheim thought, in fact, that individualism had gone too far in France and was endangering the cohesion of the society. Simmel, on the contrary, writing at about the same time, toward the end of the 19th century in Germany, suggested that modern societies had achieved a better proportion of freedom and restraint than had earlier societies; the individual was freer to choose the social circles to which he would belong, but these numerous and diverse circles were more fully integrated into larger groupings and into the whole society. The proportion between freedom and restraint, between differentiation and individualism, on one side, and the overall regulation of social life, on the other, is clearly not established once and for all in a particular type of society. The industrial societies of the late 20th century seem to many observers to have moved toward greater restraint in many areas of life; the sheer size of organizations, the more powerful means of control in the hands of governments, and the emphasis upon national unity in a century characterized by large-scale international conflicts have all contributed to a loss of individu-

Ways in which stratification develops

Ways in which social mobility develops

Trends toward increasing restraint or permissiveness

ality and widespread sentiments of individual powerlessness. These tendencies seem to have been countered only in a small degree, in limited areas of life outside the economic and political sphere, by the cultural "permissiveness" that has developed during the past two decades. It remains to be seen how a new balance between individualism and the general regulation of social life (which is needed increasingly on a world scale) will be achieved in the rapidly changing conditions of the late 20th century; but there seems no reason to doubt that it will have to take account of the duality that Simmel observed—the human need, on one side, for differentiation, diversity of life, and individual expression and, on the other side, for cooperation with other men within an ordered social framework in which similarities rather than differences are emphasized.

BIBLIOGRAPHY. The principal general studies of social differentiation are GEORG SIMMEL, *Über soziale Differenzierung: Soziologische und psychologische Untersuchungen* (1890); and C.C. NORTH, *Social Differentiation* (1926). Differentiation in terms of social roles is discussed in R. LINTON, *The Study of Man* (1936); H.H. GERTH and C. WRIGHT MILLS, *Character and Social Structure* (1953); and M.P. BANTON, *Roles* (1965).

There is a large literature on sexual differentiation, particularly from the aspect of the position of women in society, ranging from J.S. MILL's classic essay, *The Subjection of Women* (1869), to anthropological studies such as MARGARET MEAD, *Male and Female* (1949); and more polemical works by SIMONE DE BEAUVOIR, *Le Deuxième sexe*, 2 vol. (1949; Eng. trans., *The Second Sex*, 1953); and KATE MILLETT, *Sexual Politics* (1970). Age differentiation is discussed in KARL MANNHEIM, "The Problem of Generations," in *Essays on the Sociology of Knowledge*, 2nd ed. (1952); S.N. EISENSTADT, *From Generation to Generation* (1956); and MARGARET MEAD, *Culture and Commitment: A Study of the Generation Gap* (1970). Racial differentiation has attracted increasing attention and concern; it is discussed from various aspects in OLIVER C. COX, *Caste, Class and Race* (1948); in the series of studies published by UNESCO, *The Race Question in Modern Science* (1951–53); and in PIERRE L. VAN DEN BERGHE, *Race and Racism: A Comparative Perspective* (1967).

The division of labour is treated at length in EMILE DURKHEIM, *De la division du travail social* (1893; Eng. trans., *The Division of Labour in Society*, 1933), which also deals with the differentiation of societies into types. Other classifications of the types of society include FERDINAND TONNIES, *Gemeinschaft und Gesellschaft* (1887; Eng. trans., *Community and Association*, 1955), KARL MARX and FRIEDRICH ENGELS, *Die deutsche Ideologie* (1846; Eng. trans. of pt. 1 and 3, *The German Ideology*, 1938), *Manifest der kommunistischen Partei* (1848; Eng. trans., *The Communist Manifesto*, 1933); RAYMOND ARON, *The Industrial Society* (1967).

The literature on stratification is extensive, but the following works provide a view of the major aspects: S. OSSOWSKI, *Class Structure in the Social Consciousness* (Eng. trans., 1963); MAX WEBER, "Class, Status, Party," in *Wirtschaft und Gesellschaft* (1922), Eng. trans. in H.H. GERTH and C. WRIGHT MILLS (eds.), *From Max Weber* (1946); J.A. SCHUMPETER, "Social Classes in an Ethnically Homogeneous Environment," *Imperialism and Social Classes* (1951); KINGSLEY DAVIS and WILBERT MOORE, "Some Principles of Stratification," in R. BENDIX and S.M. LIPSET (eds.), *Class, Status and Power*, 2nd rev. ed. (1966). On elite groups, see C. WRIGHT MILLS, *The Power Elite* (1956); and T.B. BOTTOMORE, *Elites and Society* (1964). There have been many studies of social mobility; two national inquiries which also deal with wider issues are D.V. GLASS (ed.), *Social Mobility in Britain* (1954); and PETER BLAU and OTIS D. DUNCAN, *The American Occupational Structure* (1967).

(T.B.B.)

Social Groups

A social group can be defined at the most general level as any set of human beings who either are, recently have been, or anticipate being in some kind of interrelation. The term group, or social group, has been used to designate many kinds of aggregations of humans. Aggregations of two members and aggregations that include the total population of a large nation-state have been called groups.

Most applications of the concept of group have been based on definitions more rigorous and limiting than that given above; they tend to identify narrower types of groups by specifying one or another part of the general definition. The term small group, for example, which is treated later in this article, limits the number of members and sometimes the nature and extent of their interdependence. As another example, distinctions such as family or work group represent specifications of the basis for membership as well as of the type or extent of member interdependence.

TYPES OF GROUPS

Contrasting criteria for classifying groups. One of the earliest and best known classifications of groups was the American sociologist C.H. Cooley's distinction between primary and secondary groups, set forth in his *Human Nature and the Social Order* (1902). "Primary group" refers to those personal relations that are direct, face-to-face, relatively permanent, and intimate, such as the relations in a family, a group of close friends, and the like. "Secondary group" (an expression that Cooley himself did not actually use but that emerged later) refers to all other person-to-person relations, but especially to those groups or associations, such as work groups, in which the individual is related to others through formal, often legalistic or contractual ties. Cooley felt that primary groups were the fundamental agencies through which the individual's character or personality was formed. In more recent times, sociologist Talcott Parsons in the United States distinguished five dichotomous characteristics, or pattern variables, that help to distinguish primary groups from secondary groups; relations among members of primary groups, as contrasted with secondary groups, tend to be (1) diffuse, rather than specific or delimited; (2) particularistic, rather than universalistic; (3) ascription based (*i.e.*, who or what you are), rather than achievement based (*i.e.*, what you do or have done); (4) other oriented or group oriented, rather than self-oriented; (5) affective or emotion laden, rather than emotionally neutral. Secondary groups are sometimes viewed as the logical complement—that is, all groups that are not primary are secondary. It is probably more instructive to consider secondary groups as those in which relations between members tend to fit the opposite poles of the five pattern variables.

Historically, many other pairs of terms have been used to classify groups, and there is a great deal of overlap among them and between each of them and the primary-secondary distinction. The German sociologist Ferdinand Tönnies coined the now-famous distinction between *Gemeinschaft* and *Gesellschaft*, which is usually translated as community versus society or association and which for all practical purposes reflects the same distinction as primary versus secondary. The American anthropologist Robert Redfield distinguished between folk society and urban society. The English jurist Sir Henry Maine talked of societies of status and societies of contract. But all of these, too, are virtually coterminous with the primary-group–secondary-group distinction. There is also a close correspondence between these pairs of terms and the distinction between mechanical solidarity and organic solidarity, which was emphasized by the French sociologist Émile Durkheim.

Still other sets of terms are used, not as bases for distinguishing types of groups but as bases for describing the individual's relationship to different groups. Thus, the terms we-group and they-group, as well as the terms ingroup and outgroup, are used to contrast a group of which the referent or focal person is a member (often, a primary-type group) and some other group—not necessarily different in kind—of which the focal person (and other members of his ingroup, or we-group) is not a member and toward which he feels some degree of animosity or negative affect.

Another set of distinctions based on the individual's relationship to the group are the terms membership group and reference group. The former has the obvious meaning of a group of which the individual is a member, here and now, by reason of one characteristic or another (such as being a member of a particular family or a member of the sixth-grade class in Jefferson School). The

Primary and secondary groups

Statistical
groups
and
actual
groups

term reference group has been used in two ways, to mean either a group for which the individual aspires to membership or a group whose values, norms, and attitudes serve as points of reference for the individual. In either case, the crucial feature is that the individual adapts his attitudes and behaviour to model those of the members of the reference group. Obviously, membership groups and reference groups are not mutually exclusive.

The term group, or social group, has been used to refer to very divergent kinds of aggregations of people. Indeed, the term has been used so broadly as to threaten its fruitfulness as a focal concept. For one thing, the word group has sometimes been used to designate the members of a social category based on possession of a common attribute, even when the members have no meaningful degree of interrelation. Thus, it has been used to refer to such collections as persons of a particular age, all persons having similar incomes or occupations, or all persons with similar reading habits. These are what might be called statistical groups, as distinct from actual groups, the latter being characterized by some kind and degree of interrelatedness among the members.

As soon as one differentiates between statistical groups based on possession of a specified attribute and actual groups based on interrelation of members, however, it becomes apparent that there are many forms of human relations that do not fit neatly within this dichotomy. For example, although "all of the residents of the state of Iowa" might be viewed as a statistical group but not an actual group, it is not necessarily clear that the members of that set are not interrelated, at least in regard to certain political decisions and economic events. It might be argued that "residents of Iowa" are not an actual group, because each member does not directly affect every other member, but by that criterion one would have to draw the same conclusion regarding many other aggregations, such as all employees of a particular industrial plant or all members of a certain religious denomination or even all members of some very large families. The same would be the case if one were to argue that "residents of Iowa" are not an actual group because each member is not simultaneously aware of and taking into account the attitudes and behaviour of every other member. Such a criterion would eliminate any but relatively small groups, and this is indeed one of the criteria that has been applied to define the small group.

Classifications of social groups and other social aggregates. Because of some of the problems of definition and classification, sociologists have attempted to distinguish among various kinds of social aggregates, some to be considered groups and others to be identified by other terms—audiences, publics, and the like. There is no generally accepted classification at this time; but the following distinctions, drawn in terms of the bases for membership and the degree of person-to-person influence, seem helpful in clarifying this complex picture.

Artificial aggregations

A statistical group, or social category: Members have one or more properties in common (*e.g.*, age; sex; political-party preference) but otherwise are not necessarily in any kind of interrelation or aware of one another.

Unorganized aggregates

An audience: Members are attending to a common set of stimuli (*e.g.*, a mass-media presentation; an eclipse) but are not necessarily in interaction or aware of the communality of this experience.

A crowd: Members are attending to a common set of stimuli and are in physical proximity with one another, hence interrelated, at least in terms of sensory stimulation.

A public: Members are attending to a common set of issues and are in at least indirect interaction on these issues and thus are aware of the communality of interest, though not necessarily in physical proximity or direct communication.

Units with patterned relationships

A culture: All of the members share a common and patterned set of value orientations and common language, dress, and customs, although with patterned variations. Members are interdependent with respect to these aspects of the culture, though not necessarily explicitly aware of all of these interdependencies.

A subculture: Members share a set of value orientations,

language, etc., common to members of that subculture and in notable contrast to (often a variant of) the surrounding culture. At the same time, members of the subculture share many other features of the surrounding culture.

A kinship group: All of the members are related by birth or marriage. Depending on the surrounding culture, the recognized kinship group may be extensive or limited, and it may or may not function as a crucial basis for other organized social forms.

Structured social units

A society: The structured relations, formal and informal, among the members of a large, more or less autonomous social aggregate; usually within a single culture, in a defined geographical region, and with an integrated political system (*e.g.*, a large nation-state). Relations between members and subsets of members are characterized by a high degree of interdependence.

A community: A geographic or residency-based subdivision of a society in which members reside in close proximity to one another; are highly interdependent; interact frequently, in many relationships and over extended time; and are aware of their mutual interaction and interdependence (*e.g.*, a small town, a neighbourhood).

A family (also the kinship group above): A kin-based or residence-based basic unit of a social system or culture in which members share a dwelling and other resources are highly and pervasively interdependent and are aware of their interdependence.

Deliberately designed social units

An organization: A large aggregate of people and material, explicitly organized to pursue certain goals (*e.g.*, profit for a business organization, education for a school system). Members are recruited, selected, or hired with reference to specific roles or positions in the organization. They are related to one another in ways that specify how each member or subunit is to contribute to pursuit of the organization's goals.

A suborganization: The portion of an organization within which a particular member is located (*e.g.*, a division of a company, an office of an agency, a department of a university). It is the part of the organization that most directly affects that person's behaviour.

A crew (or work team): The small set of persons within a work organization with whom a given person is in continual or frequent face-to-face interaction on the job and with whom he is highly interdependent in terms of task performance, resources, rewards, and the like.

Less deliberately designed social units

An association (or voluntary organization or interest group): Members share and are aware of their common interests in certain issues and deliberately seek interaction dealing with these issues. The relationship among members can remain relatively limited in extent (thus approaching a public); or the interaction among members can become highly frequent, intense, and extensive (thus approaching an organization). For example, membership in a political party may vary from nominal membership to a full-time commitment in the form of a vocation.

A friendship group: Members associate voluntarily, frequently, extensively, on a continuing basis, and with positive affect or emotional relations. Such groups are relatively small in number of members. Their basic goal may be group interaction per se, rather than specific task attainments. A friendship group may overlap in membership with a work crew, a suborganization, a family, a kin group, a community, or an association or interest group.

This list gives an indication of the main kinds of distinctions that have been made about various social aggregates. Various social scientists would probably consider some kind but not all of these to be properly labelled as social groups.

THE STUDY OF SMALL GROUPS

Definitions
of
small
groups

Researchers and theoreticians who have concerned themselves with small groups have used many definitions, differing in detail and emphasis. But the definitions contain certain common features that can be taken as the essential conditions for defining the term:

1. The set of members must be few enough so that each one can directly apprehend and (potentially) communicate with every other member. Many authors have suggested an upper limit of the order of 20 to 30, though ten or fewer members are usual.

2. The members must be engaged in some enterprise or have some objective or goal or be immersed in some situation, such that their outcomes (rewards and costs) are interdependent.

This notion has been expressed in terms of members having a common fate.

3. The members must be aware of their interdependence with the other members; that is, they must perceive the existence of the group at least in terms of the relationship of the outcomes to the membership.

4. The above conditions imply that the members must be at least to some degree in communication or interaction with one another and that this relationship must continue (or has been continuing) for some meaningfully long period of time.

It should be noted that the definitional constraints do not specify that all of the members share the same goals, only that their goals be interdependent. Thus, members of small groups may be related in either competitive or cooperative relations; they may also be involved in a mixture of competition and cooperation.

As with the broader categories of social groups, small groups can and have been classified into types on many bases. For example, groups have been compared on the basis of difference in number of members: dyads (two-person groups), triads (three-person groups), and so forth. Groups have been classified as task-oriented or personally oriented groups. Task-oriented groups are those supposedly engaged in activities instrumental to some specific goal(s). Personally (or emotionally) oriented groups are those supposedly focussed on the personal relations among group members. Many real-life groups, such as the family, do not fit this dichotomy neatly; their members are engaged in both task-oriented and interpersonal behaviour. Indeed, many theorists hold that all groups are continually engaged in both kinds of behaviour.

History of small-group study. Man's interest in group phenomena probably goes back as far as recorded history. Certainly, the roots of issues concerning groups can be traced back to the ancient Greek philosophers, to thinkers of the Renaissance, and to western European scholars of the 16th, 17th, and early 18th centuries. But modern social psychology and sociology and the study of group phenomena within those disciplines really began in the latter years of the 19th century among sociologists in France, Germany, and the United States. In those years, the major effort was spent grappling with basic theoretical issues: the importance of innate instincts and what those basic instincts were; the role of experience or learning or habit on man's social behaviour; the "reality" of social groups and the existence of a "group mind"; principles of human behaviour alleged to be fundamental social forces, such as imitation, suggestion, sympathy. These efforts were largely theoretical—the product of speculative thought, based on personal experience and reading—rather than empirical, or based on systematic observation.

Decline of theory building This theory-oriented period ended in the 1920s, and the field of social psychology and small-group study came under the sway of Positivism, with its emphasis on the collection and interpretation of empirical, or observational, evidence. At first, the social psychologists and small-group researchers brought their problems into the laboratory and borrowed the guidelines and methodology of the physical sciences. By the 1930s, however, social psychology and small-group research shed their laboratory confinement, though not their emphasis on data over theory, and began to grapple with problems in real-life settings. Perhaps this movement was in response to the worldwide economic depression and the social turmoil that accompanied it. Researchers began to study mass movements, prejudice, gangs and delinquency, and the like. But this decade also saw the development of the so-called group-dynamics movement, under the leadership of a German-born social psychologist, Kurt Lewin, and this movement in large part shaped the field of group research for years to come. In its early years, under Lewin's genius, the group-dynamics movement was a balanced blend of concern with theory, with its application to socially significant problems (frustration, leadership styles, attitude change, and so on) but with experimental or laboratory methodology.

In the 1940s small-group research, like everyone else, went off to war, so to speak. The new problems opened up by the early promise of the group-dynamics movement and the "boom" aspects of the wartime setting stimulated large quantities of research. These served to advance the field in two ways: by generating much new evidence on certain substantive problem areas (such as leadership or attitude change in groups) and by producing a marked development and refinement of methods (such as techniques for measuring interpersonal feelings, techniques for constructing experimental groups of desired composition, and the like). But the strong theoretical orientation of Lewin's early work was apparently a casualty, perhaps in part because of the wartime spirit of urgent pragmatism.

Since World War II, although there has been a vast amount of research that has resulted in the piling up of evidence, there have been few significant attempts to formulate comprehensive theories. In the 1970s even the research has seemed to decline. Meanwhile, many persons in related fields have tried to find practical uses for the evidence and methods that have been developed. So-called group methods were introduced into psychotherapy, into teaching, and into business management, in efforts to improve practices in those fields. The efforts went under such names as group therapy, training group or training laboratory, encounter group, and sensitivity training. Many of these movements were and continue to be quite successful, in the sense of widespread adoption and ardent belief in them by their exponents. But remarkably little research has been done to assess the effectiveness of these practices in accomplishing substantial and enduring "improvements" in the groups in question.

Group training movements

Major areas of concern. Because the history of small-group research has been marked by a great deal of evidence gathering and very little theorizing and integration of the findings, it is difficult to put the information together into a coherent pattern. The sections that follow can indicate only the major constellations of evidence in a few problem areas.

The individual in relation to others in a social group. People influence one another in many ways. Such influences occur in many kinds of person-to-person relationships, which are not usually thought of as groups but which are closely related to effects that do occur in groups. It is useful to consider, first, some ways in which the presence and behaviour of other persons affect a given individual in a "one-way" relation and, second, some kinds of two-way relations between people.

The way in which an individual can be influenced may depend on the state of his relationship with others—that is, on the degree of his involvement or interaction with them:

1. The individual can be under observation by an audience. The audience can either be seen by him or unseen but known to him. The audience can be merely passively observing or observing and in some way obviously evaluating (as by applause or laughter).

2. The individual can be observing the behaviour of one or more other persons—either by himself (as an audience of one) or along with other members of an audience. The other person can be said to be modelling certain behaviours for the observer.

3. The individual can be engaged in the performance of some task, in the presence of others also engaged in that task but without the interdependence of his work with theirs. Persons in this relationship are sometimes said to be in a coacting group (as distinguished from an interacting group, below).

4. The individual can be engaged in performance of some task in the presence of or in communication with others also engaged in that task or in complementary tasks, under conditions of mutual influence. Persons in this relationship are sometimes referred to as in an interacting group (as distinguished from a coacting group, above).

There is considerable evidence that individual performance is influenced by the mere presence of others, as, for example, in an unseen (but known to be present) passive audience. The influence is greater for an active (*i.e.*, evaluating) audience, for a model observed by the person, and for other persons in a coacting relation.

Many early studies of individual performance focussed

on the concept of social facilitation, which denoted that the sights and sounds of others somehow stimulated the individual and increased his efforts. The general findings from those studies were that the presence of others led to increased efforts or intensity of performance, yielding increased quantity of productivity and sometimes increased speed but also yielding reduced quality or accuracy. Results of these early coaction studies, however, were not always consistent; some studies showed performance gains, some performance decrements. The differences in results appeared to be attributable to the type of task and were interpreted by some to mean that social facilitation aided motor performance but was detrimental to performance on intellectual tasks.

More recent work has tended to clarify these effects of social facilitation. The presence of others seems to lead to an increase in physiological arousal. It had been shown in earlier work on human and animal learning that increased arousal tends to make the most dominant response (that is, the strongest or best learned habit) even more dominant. It would seem to follow, then, that the presence of others, leading to increased arousal, which in turn leads to an increasing dominance of the best learned response, will facilitate the performance of a well-learned response. But at the same time such arousal will hinder the learning of new responses. Thus, the presence of others helps performance on well-learned tasks (which many of the motor tasks used in the early studies were) but hinders performance on tasks that call for the learning of new responses (which was the case with many of the intellectual tasks used in the earlier studies).

Not only can the presence of other people be a source of arousal, but also their behaviour or their inactivity can function as a source of information for an individual. A person, for instance, is much less likely to respond to an apparent emergency when in the presence of others who do not respond (inactive bystanders) than when faced with the same situation alone. Under some conditions, the presence of other people may offer emotional support; a person anticipating an aversive situation (such as a painful injection or shock) apparently prefers to await the event in the company of others who are in the same predicament. This seems to hold true even if direct communication with the others is impossible, so that their comforting behaviour cannot be a factor. Again, this effect may arise in part because others represent a potential source of information about how to act in the threatening situation.

When an individual is kept in social isolation for an extended time, he apparently suffers more or less from deprivation of social contact. There are wide individual differences in such social deprivation, however; and it is not clear whether the effects of the social deprivation ensue from the lack of arousal (which the presence of others brings) or from the lack of information (which other people provide) that could serve as cues to the meaning and proper behaviour for the situation.

Overall, it is apparent that the presence and behaviour of other persons in any of several kinds of relations can influence the individual in any of several ways. Other persons can increase arousal, hinder learning but facilitate performance of already-learned responses, provide cues to appropriate behaviour and to the consequences of behaviour, and produce both positive and negative emotional effects.

Group composition. One major class of factors potentially influencing group behaviour has to do with the composition of the group. These factors consists of all of the attributes or properties that the individual persons bring with them to the group and that may affect their behaviour while members of the group. These factors may be conveniently divided into five classes: (1) biographical characteristics of members (sex, age, socioeconomic class, etc.), (2) personality characteristics of members, (3) abilities of members (both general abilities such as intelligence and specific abilities pertinent to the group's tasks), (4) attitudes of members (their beliefs and feelings about the task, the situation, and various outside persons, groups, and objects), and (5) position of each member in the group (including aspects of his social position or status and aspects of his task position or physical location).

Though evidence in this area is not very clear-cut, it seems to suggest that personality factors do not affect a group's task performance as much as one might suppose. It may be that group behaviour is more apt to be influenced by the pattern of member traits—personality, biographical, or otherwise—than by the presence of some seemingly beneficial or adverse trait, in any one individual or average of individuals. These patterns of traits may involve many things but are broadly based on similarity of some needs (such as affection) or complementarity for other needs (such as control). In any event, there would seem to be no simple and general prescription for putting together an effective group on the basis of the personal attributes of potential members.

Neither do abilities necessarily predict the performance of the group as a whole (though they may predict the task performance of individual members somewhat). This is not surprising, in that the effective performance of group tasks often requires intricate teamwork or coordination, and such coordination is not directly reflected in the individual abilities of individual members. Indeed there are several ways in which the performances of individuals can be combined to yield a group performance, depending on the nature of the task and the organization of the group. One suggested list of patterns is the following:

1. Additive: the group product is the sum of individual outputs, as when several members each work independently, and their results are combined. Here, group performance should reflect the summation of member abilities.
2. Compensatory: the group product is achieved by a combination of member efforts such that one member's low or inaccurate production can be compensated for by other members' high production. Here, group performance should reflect the average member ability.
3. Disjunctive: the group successfully achieves the task if any one member achieves it successfully. Here, group performance should reflect the ability of the most able member.
4. Conjunctive: the group successfully does the task if and only if each member successfully does his part. This might be exemplified by team performance in a sport such as rowing. Here, group performance is limited by the ability of the least able member.
5. Complementary: the group task requires the blending or coordination of different kinds of performances by team members, simultaneously or in a close sequence. This might be exemplified by various complex routines within team sports, such as a complex play in hockey or football. Here, successful group performance requires not only that all of the requisite skills exist in sufficient degree among the group's members but also that the distribution of those skills among the members fits the distribution of task requirements among them.

In these terms it would seem that the abilities of members, combined according to the model that fits the particular group's task, will represent the upper limit of potential group performance. Actual performance may depart from that upper limit insofar as the group activities require coordination and also insofar as members are less than optimally motivated toward effective task performance.

It is through these processes of coordination and motivation, that many factors other than member abilities come to play a part in affecting group performance: interpersonal relations, authority and influence relations, member attitudes toward the task and one another, and so forth. Again, as with personality and biographical characteristics of members, the abilities of members contribute to but do not solely determine behaviour in groups; their contribution depends not so much on amount as on pattern; and the most effective pattern interacts with factors relating to the group's task and situation.

Power and influence. It is useful to distinguish between power, or the potential for influencing others, and influence, or the actual modification of the behaviour of others. At least five possible bases or sources of power may be listed:

1. Legitimate power: potential for influence that derives from being the incumbent of some position or office.

2. Referent power: potential for influence that derives from being liked or respected, personally.

3. Reward power: potential for influence that derives from being able to bestow or withhold valued objects.

4. Coercive power: potential for influence that derives from being able to impose or withhold punitive actions.

5. Expert power: potential for influence that derives from possessing information or skills necessary or valuable to the other.

The study of power (and influence) relations in groups underlies some of the main topical areas in the study of small groups, such as in the study of leadership and conformity.

Nature of leadership

In recent times the focus of leadership research has shifted away from a concern with identifying the leader (as opposed to the follower) or the effective leader (as opposed to the ineffective one)—all largely out of context. The shift has been toward studying the process of leadership itself—that is, studying influence rather than power. Furthermore, the present conviction is that leader, group, task, and situation must be studied concurrently as interacting elements.

One of the most prominent of current theories holds that the kind of leadership style that is most effective depends on the "favourability" of the group–task–situation complex. A situation is favourable to the extent that the leader is liked by his group (referent power), to the extent that he has a strong formal position in the group (legitimate power and perhaps expert power), and to the extent that the group's task is well structured (hence, amenable to the use of reward and coercive power by the leader). In very favourable situations and in very unfavourable ones, a strong or directive or task-oriented leadership style is most successful. In situations of intermediate favourability, in contrast, a more personal-oriented style of leadership seems to be generally more effective.

There is an important competitive line of thought. Early research on leadership focussed on the leader—and often on a search for the traits that made him a leader or a good leader—and the unsuccessful course of that research led many scholars to make an about-face. There is no inherent reason, they thought, why all of the groups must have a singular leader. Indeed, there is considerable evidence that groups often develop more than one kind of leader role. In any case, it is clear that the leader is dependent on his followers to execute tasks necessary to group success. Thus, they may exercise some influence on him, as well as he on them; that is, influence between people is mutual, even when there is a subordinate–superordinate power relationship between them. From this perspective, every man is a leader, in some degree. Hence, it is not fruitful to use leadership as a focal concept; rather, it is more useful to consider the influence process itself.

Nature of conformity

Also related to power and influence is the concept of conformity, which has long been a central object of group research. It was early shown that, when people are influenced by the judgments of others, the direction of influence is toward a common judgment or norm and that the influence persists, later, when the person is again making judgments alone. It was later shown that such social influence was still considerable even when the others were deliberately making incorrect judgments of unambiguous events. These findings triggered an avalanche of research on the antecedents, limiting conditions, and consequences of conformity.

Some of the more systematic research on conformity developed evidence in support of the following network of relationships: physical proximity and other opportunities for encounter increase the probability that communication will take place between any given pair of people. Increased communication leads to positive personal attraction. Personal attraction leads to pressures for uniformity of attitudes, at least on issues relevant to the relationship (that is, conformity to shared attitudes or norms). Deviation of attitudes leads to increased communication, aimed at persuasion. If persuasion is not suc-

cessful in leading to conformity, there will be a shift toward negative attitudes and rejection and a drastic reduction in communication.

Other studies have tended to clarify the complex interdependence of communication, influence, and attraction among group members. Interdependence, here, implies that a change in any one of these will produce compensatory changes in the other two. Thus, increasing communication will tend to increase attraction and influence; increasing influence (such as by increasing a member's power or status) will tend to increase attraction and communication to him; and increasing attraction will tend to increase communication and influence.

The process presumably underlying these phenomena is a tendency for what has been called cognitive balance, or consonance. To take a hypothetical example, when persons A and B are in potential interaction regarding some issue or person X, there is a tendency for one of several balanced states to exist in their pattern of relations. The major balanced state is mutual positive attraction to each other and agreement on X. If A and B are mutually attracted but discover that they disagree on X, this creates an imbalanced state (or a state of dissonance). Dissonance operates as a force toward change. The major modes of such change are: communication to persuade the other; change in one's own attitude toward X (conformity); change in one's own attitude toward B (change in attraction); misperception of the other's disagreement; or a redefinition of X (such as downgrading the importance of X). These mechanisms operate as alternatives to reduce interpersonal imbalance or dissonances. It seems that any given individual will tend to have a preferred mechanism for reducing dissonance and to employ it predominantly.

The ideas of power and influence and of interpersonal dissonance and conformity further imply the idea of conflict. In the main, conflict between persons and groups has been viewed as something "bad," to be avoided or eliminated or at least resolved or managed, by bargaining, negotiation, compromise, conformity, persuasion, or, if all else fails, by withdrawal or by "conquest." It has been pointed out, however, that there are a number of potentially positive social functions of conflict. Conflict between groups tends to bind each group's members to one another. It can bind two rival groups when they are threatened by a common enemy. It also can "clear the air," providing a safety-valve function. A conflict relation is, itself, a structured relation that allows social processes to continue between the contending parties; that is, conflict binds the antagonists to an ordered relationship to one another. Conflict can create associations and alliances that would not otherwise have a reason for being. Finally, conflict can lead to a search for and the generation of new and creative solutions.

Nature of conflict

Norms and roles. One of the central concepts of social psychology and of small-group research is the concept of norms. The concept has several uses. The term norm is often used simply to mean beliefs, attitudes, or values that are shared by members of a social group. Sometimes, though, the concept of norm carries the further restriction that it be recognizably shared and that the group apply sanctions (rewards and punishments) or at least social pressure to produce conformity to its norms. The idea of a norm, in other words, consists of a shared or common frame of reference, leading to a close agreement in judgments. Many of these judgments are based on social rather than physical reality, which in turn depends on a social consensus as to the meanings of objects, events, and situations. Social norms serve as definitions of social reality for those who share them.

In a sense, a norm is a rule or an agreement or a precedent about behaviour (such as a rule of alternation—"we'll watch your favourite program this week and mine next week"). Once such a rule exists and is recognized, it becomes like a third-party regulator. One can call on adherence to the norm, rather than on informal or personal power, to induce another person to exhibit the indicated behaviour. Moreover, adherence to the norms takes on a moral, or "rightness," quality. When norms have

Regulatory effects of norms

developed in a group containing members of unequal power, they bind the stronger as well as the weaker partners of the relationship; thus, norms serve to control and limit the arbitrary exercise of power.

Another basic concept is role, which might best be approached by considering a person's "place" or "location" or "position" in a group. The idea of position is quite clear in formal organizations. One man is director of a division; another man is president of a company; still another is an assistant sales manager. Each of these positions or offices can exist independently of any particular incumbent; and each entails a more or less explicit set of responsibilities and prerogatives. The same kind of concept of position is applicable to the location or status of an individual in informal groups, although such positions are seldom distinguished by formal titles outside of formal organizations.

The idea of position (or office or status) in a group is related to the idea of role. A role is a set of expectations about how the incumbent of one position should behave toward the incumbent of another position. Thus, a role (or role expectation) is a special kind of norm: a shared rule about behaviour, in this case about behaviour between incumbents of particular positions.

In any group, members develop and depend on expectations about how other group members will behave. When these expectations are not fulfilled in a particular role, persons in related roles generate social pressures directed toward fulfillment of these role expectations. There is pressure, in other words, toward conformity.

Role conflict Many times the incumbent of a role (or of a set of roles) is faced with conditions that produce role conflict. For one thing, different "others" may hold different and conflicting expectations for his role. The classic example of this case is the first-line supervisor in industry. Management, on the one hand, and his men, on the other, are likely to hold incompatible expectations for his behaviour as a supervisor. A second form of role conflict may arise when multiple expectations within a role are internally conflicting—for example, mothers are to be loving but firm with their small children. In still another case, the expectations for a given role may be unclear or ambiguous—as is often the case for a new role. Any of these and other forms of role conflict can present the individual with difficulties in performing his role and can have harmful effects on his relationships with others and on his self-evaluation.

Individual versus group effectiveness. Generally speaking, it was long thought that groups are more effective than individuals in solving problems, apparently because they provide a wider range of relevant knowledge and perform an error-checking function. This belief even led to the technique of brainstorming, which was alleged to increase **Creative** creativity. In brainstorming, a set of people try to think **solutions** of a solution to a stated problem, under rules whereby no **by groups** one is allowed to evaluate any suggested ideas, although **and** they are allowed to build upon a previously voiced idea. **individuals** This technique gained considerable popularity as a problem-solution procedure in work organizations, but careful research has indicated clearly that groups do not develop more or more creative solutions under brainstorming than do the same individuals working alone. Indeed, viewed on a man-hours basis, brainstorming in a group is distinctly inferior to working on the same problem alone. This finding is quite compatible with other findings that indicate the negative effects of the presence of others on tasks requiring new responses.

Although groups may be inferior to individuals in generating creative solutions, groups are in fact advantageous for certain kinds of functions. For problems demanding cross-checking of errors; for problems in which the task can be subdivided; for problems requiring many skills, not likely to be found in a single individual; for problems in which sheer numbers of "units produced" are important—in all of these, a group will be superior to a single individual of the same competence. What matters, here, is the way in which the task is organized, as mentioned earlier with reference to member abilities.

But, beyond these considerations, there are certain situations in which assigning a task to a group rather than an individual is an advantage. For one thing, a group potentially represents a broader pool of knowledge and skills, proportional to its numbers. Often, groups are used as information sources. Moreover, it is almost mandatory that certain kinds of decisions be made by groups, whose membership is in some way representative of conflicting views, because it takes concurrence of such a group (presumably after negotiation and compromise) to lend legitimacy to the resulting decision. Thus, even though group brainstorming is not a guarantee of more and better creative solutions and even though problem solving by groups is partially a waste of man-hours, the performance of tasks by groups, rather than by individuals, is an effective procedure under some conditions and an essential one under others.

As there is considerable difference between individuals and groups, so there is also considerable difference between groups of two members and groups of three or more members. For one thing, a triad, or group of three, is the smallest group in which it is possible for a coalition to form. Furthermore, in triads in which two members hold opposed views, the third member, holding the "balance of power," can exercise considerable influence on group choice. Beyond this, the dyad has only one while the triad has three pair relations, which represent a considerable increase in complexity of group relations and processes.

It is likely that the effects of numbers in a group depend, **Under-** in part, on what level of manpower is called for by the **manning** situation. This involves the question of undermanning **versus** versus overmanning. It seems that in cases of undermanning—that is, when the number of persons in the setting **manning** is insufficient or barely sufficient to handle the task requirements of the setting—group members tend to become more involved in, committed to, and motivated toward group tasks and goals and experience more success, failure, and satisfactions than do persons in overmanned settings.

Current problems in small-group study. These tracings of a few of the elements of the small-group field may suggest some of the problems or dilemmas. It should be noted particularly that experience or environment, rather than innate attributes or heredity, have been virtually the whole concern. There have been some proponents of Freudian views who have focussed on innate unconscious motives, and there have been other theorists who have held that group behaviour reflects built-in personality patterns of members. But their views have gained little support and are backed by scant evidence. Recent major advances in genetics, though, may well lead to new support for the importance of innate characteristics in shaping human behaviour in groups.

Another dilemma of long standing involves the relative emphasis on theory and on empirical evidence. The latter, of course, has been getting most of the attention. Indeed, the very success of that emphasis—the development of a highly efficient and sophisticated data-generating technology—is one major element in the current unsettledness of the small-group field. The other major element in that unsettledness is the other side of the same coin—the virtual total lack of emphasis on development of broad or even middle-range theoretical structures. A rebalance of emphasis is clearly indicated for the future.

BIBLIOGRAPHY. The most comprehensive current review of the entire field of social psychology is G. LINDZEY and E. ARONSON (eds.), *The Handbook of Social Psychology*, 2nd ed., 5 vol. (1968–70). The experimental literature is reviewed in a series of volumes edited by L. BERKOWITZ, *Advances in Experimental Social Psychology* (1964–). For collections of articles on small groups, see D. CARTWRIGHT and A.F. ZANDER (eds.), *Group Dynamics*, 3rd ed. (1968); and A. PAUL HARE, E.K. BORGATTA, and R.F. BALES (eds.), *Small Groups*, rev. ed. (1965). Comprehensive reviews of the small-group research literature appear in A. PAUL HARE, *Handbook of Small Group Research* (1962); J.E. MCGRATH and I. ALTMAN, *Small Group Research* (1966); and B.E. COLLINS and H. GUETZKOW, *A Social Psychology of Group Processes for Decision-Making* (1964).

(J.E.McG.)

Socialism

Socialism refers to both a set of doctrines and the political movements that aspire to put these doctrines into practice. Although doctrinal aspects loomed largest in the early history of socialism, in its later history the movements have predominated over doctrine, so much so that there is no precise canon on which the various adherents of contemporary socialist movements agree. The most that can be said is that socialism is, in the words of C.A.R. Crosland, a British socialist, "a set of values, or aspirations, which socialists wish to see embodied in the organization of society."

Problems of definition Although it is possible to trace adumbrations of modern socialist ideas as far back as Plato's *Republic*, Thomas More's *Utopia*, and the profuse Utopian literature of the 18th-century Enlightenment, realistically, modern socialism had its roots in the reflections of various writers who opposed the social and economic relations and dislocations that the Industrial Revolution brought in its wake. They directed their critical shafts against what they conceived to be the injustice, the inequalities, the suffering brought about by the capitalist mode of production and the free and uncontrolled market on which it rested. To the acquisitive individualism of their age they opposed a vision of a new community of producers bound to each other through fraternal solidarity. They conceived of a future in which the masses would wrest control of the means of production and the levers of government from the capitalists.

Although the great majority of men calling themselves socialists in the 19th and 20th centuries have shared this vision, they have disagreed about its more specific ideas. Some of them have argued that only the complete nationalization of the means of production would suffice to implement their aims. Others have proposed selective nationalization of key industries, with controlled private ownership of the remainder. Some socialists insist that only strong centralized state direction and a command economy will suffice. Others advocate a "market socialism" in which the market economy would be directed and guided by socialist planners.

Socialists have also disagreed as to the best way of running the good society. Some envisage direction by the government. Others advocate as much dispersion and decentralization as possible through the delegation of decision-making authority to public boards, quasi-public trusts, municipalities, or self-governing communities of producers. Some advocate workers' control; others would rely on governmental planning boards. Although all socialists want to bring about a more equal distribution of national income, some hope for an absolute equality of income, whereas others aim only at ensuring an adequate income for all, while allowing different occupations to be paid at different rates.

"To each according to his need" has been a frequent battle cry of socialists, but many of them would in fact settle for a society in which each would be paid in accordance with his contribution to the commonwealth, provided that society would first assure all citizens minimum levels of housing, clothing, and nourishment as well as free access to essential services such as education, health, transportation, and recreation.

Socialists also proclaim the need for more equal political rights for all citizens, and for a levelling of status differences. They disagree, however, on whether difference of status ought to be eradicated entirely, or whether, in practice, some inequality in decision-making powers might not be permitted to persist in a socialist commonwealth.

The uses and abuses of the word socialism are legion. As early as 1845, Friedrich Engels complained that the socialism of many Germans was "vague, undefined, and undefinable." Since Engels' day the term socialism has been the property of anyone who wished to use it. The same Bismarck who as German chancellor in the late 1870s outlawed any organization that advocated socialism in Germany declared a few years later that "the state must introduce even more socialism in our Reich." Mod-

ern sophisticated conservatives, as well as Fascists and various totalitarian dictators, have often claimed that they were engaged in building socialism.

ORIGINS OF THE SOCIALIST IDEA

The term socialism, in its modern sense, made its first appearance around 1830. In France it was applied to the writings of Fourier and the Saint-Simonians and in England to those of Robert Owen. The utopians of the early 19th century

Saint-Simon and Fourier. Comte Henri de Saint-Simon (1760–1825) was an erratic genius with a fertile and yet disorganized mind. His socialist writings revolved around the idea that his age suffered from an unhealthy and unbridled individualism resulting from a breakdown of order and hierarchy. But he held that the age also contained the seeds of its own salvation, which were to be found in the rising level of science and technology and in the industrialists and technicians who had already begun to build a new industrial order. The joining of scientific and technological knowledge to industrialism would inaugurate the rule of experts. The new society could not be equalitarian, Saint-Simon argued, because men were not equally endowed by nature. Yet it would make the maximum use of potential abilities by assuring that everyone would have equal opportunity to rise to a social position commensurate with his talents. By eradicating the sources of public disorder, it would make possible the virtual elimination of the state as a coercive institution. The future society would be run like a gigantic workshop, in which rule over men would be replaced by the administration of things.

Saint-Simon's followers bent the founder's doctrine in a more definitely socialist direction. They came to see private property as incompatible with the new industrial system. The hereditary transmission of power and property, they argued, was inimicable to the rational ordering of society. The rather bizarre attempt of Saint-Simon's followers to create a Saint-Simonian church should not obscure the fact that they were among the first to proclaim that bourgeois-capitalist property was no longer sacrosanct.

François-Marie-Charles Fourier (1772–1837), a lonely and neglected thinker who was more than a little mad, was led to his anticapitalist vision by a loathing for a world of competition and wasteful commerce in which he spent most of his life as a salesman. Possessed by an inordinately wide-ranging imagination, he argued that the regenerated world to come would be characterized not only by social but also by natural and even cosmological transformations. The ocean would be changed into lemonade, and wild animals would turn into anti-lions and anti-tigers serving mankind.

With meticulous and obsessive care, Fourier set forth plans for his model communities, the *phalanstères*, the germ cells of the good society of the future. In these communities men would no longer be forced to perform uncongenial tasks but would work in tune with their temperaments and inclinations. They would cultivate cabbages in the morning and sing in the opera in the evening. Fourier's was an antinomian vision in which human spontaneity made outside regulation unnecessary. Whereas Saint-Simon called for the rule of experts, Fourier was convinced that love and passion would bind men together in a harmonious and noncoercive order.

Owenism. The Englishman Robert Owen (1771–1858) held more sober views. Early in his career he became known as a model employer in his textile works in Scotland, and as an educational and factory reformer. Despairing of his fellow capitalists he later turned to the emergent trade union movement. Acutely conscious of the evils of industrialism by which he had acquired his wealth, he thought that the new productive forces could be turned to the benefit of mankind if competition were eliminated and the effects of bad education were counteracted by rational enlightenment. He advocated cooperative control of industry and the creation of Villages of Unity and Cooperation in which the settlers, in addition to raising crops, would improve their physiques as well as their minds. Owenite communities established in New Harmony and elsewhere in America all failed. His attempts to join the cooperative and the trade union movements in a "great trades union" also proved a failure. Yet he left a lasting imprint on the British socialist tradition; his indictment of the competitive order, his stress on cooperation and education, his optimistic message that men could increase their stature if only the stultifying effects of an unhealthy environment were removed have continued to inform the socialist movement.

Other early socialists. The 1840s saw the rise of a number of other socialist doctrines, particularly in France. Louis-Auguste Blanqui evolved a radical socialist —or, as he called it, communist—doctrine based on a democratic populism and on the belief that capitalism as an inherently unstable order would soon be replaced by cooperative associations. Impatient with theorizing, given to a strong belief in voluntarism and the virtues of revolutionary action, he is remembered for his many attempts at organizing insurrections rather than for his theoretical contributions.

Étienne Cabet, in his influential utopian work *Voyage en Icarie* (1840), carried on the tradition of Thomas More as well as of Fourier. Louis Blanc is best known for *L'Organisation du travail* (1839), in which he advocated the establishment of national workshops with capital advanced by the government. These workshops would remain free from government control, with workers electing their management. The national workshops he organized in Paris after the revolution of 1848 were soon dissolved by a resurgent middle class. His plans for the "organization of labour" and his pleas for the recognition of the "right to work" were nevertheless a foreshadowing of the modern welfare state.

Pierre-Joseph Proudhon (1809–65) is best viewed as one of the founders of the anarchist tradition. But his attacks against private property and the institutions on which it rests, as well as his championing of a system of human relationships in which reciprocity, equity, and justice would replace what he saw to be rapacity, exploitation, and greed, powerfully stimulated the socialist imagination. His anti-statist and federalist vision of producers' communities provided a counterweight to the centralizing and statist impulses in the socialist tradition.

In England, the first half of the 19th century saw the emergence of a number of writers attacking the inequities of capitalism and basing their indictment of wage labour on radical interpretations of the thinking of an eminent economist, David Ricardo. Somewhat later, a Christian socialist movement led by Frederick Denison Maurice and Charles Kingsley attempted to combine radical economic views with political conservatism. The radical Chartist Movement of the 1830s and 1840s is better viewed as a political movement of the working class than as a specifically socialist formation, though anticapitalist ideas played a strong part in it.

MARX AND THE RISE OF SOCIAL DEMOCRACY

The idea of class struggle

In the perspective of intellectual history, all of these pre-Marxist socialist thinkers produced ideas of considerable intrinsic worth. But from the viewpoint of the subsequent development of socialism their ideas seem to be tributaries feeding the mighty stream of the Marxist movement that came to dominate the socialist tradition in the last third of the 19th century.

The Communist Manifesto. Karl Marx (1818–83) had a synthesizing mind. He fused German idealistic philosophy with British political economy and French socialism. Marx's earlier writings are discussed elsewhere (see MARXISM). In this article the focus is on his mature thought as first developed in *The Communist Manifesto* (1848), which he wrote in conjunction with Friedrich Engels, his lifelong companion.

To Marx, society is a moving balance of antithetical forces; strife is the father of all things, and social conflict is the core of the historical process. Men struggle against nature to wrest a livelihood from her. In the process they enter into relations with one another, and these relations differ according to the stage they have reached in their productive activities. As a division of labour emerges in human society, it leads to the formation of antagonistic classes that are the prime actors in the historical drama. In contrast to his predecessors, Marx did not see history as simply a struggle between the rich and the poor, or the powerful and the powerless; he taught that such struggles differ qualitatively depending on what particular historical classes emerge at a given stage in history. A class is defined by Marx as a grouping of men who share a common position in the productive process and develop a common outlook and a realization of their mutual interest.

Marx, like Hegel and Montesquieu, considered societies as structured wholes; all aspects of a society—its legal code, its system of education, its religion, its art—are related with one another and with the mode of economic production. But he differed from other thinkers in emphasizing that the mode of production was, in the last analysis, the decisive factor in the movement of history. The relations of production, he held, constitute the foundation upon which is erected the whole cultural superstructure of society.

Marx distinguished this doctrine, which he called scientific socialism, from that of his predecessors whom he labelled utopian socialists. He asserted that his teachings were based on a scientific examination of the movement of history and the workings of contemporary capitalism rather than simply on idealistic striving for human betterment. He claimed to have provided a guide to past history as well as a scientific prediction of the future. History was shaped by class struggles; the struggle of contemporary proletarians against their capitalist taskmasters would eventuate in a socialist society in which associated producers would mold their collective destinies cooperatively, free from economic and social constraints. The class struggle would thus come to an end.

The First International. *The Communist Manifesto*, which had been written as a program for the Communist League, a group of continental workmen, failed to have an impact on the European revolutions of 1848. For a number of years thereafter Marx and Engels lived in complete isolation from the labour movements developing in England and on the Continent. Socialism in those years was only the creed of isolated sects, often of exiles. In 1864, however, after a gathering in London of continental and English workers' representatives and associated intellectuals, there emerged the International Working Men's Association, commonly known as the First International. Although it encompassed various tendencies ranging from simple trade unionism to anarchism, Marx dominated it from its inception and made it an instrument for the diffusion of his message. Its headquarters were in London, but it never exerted much influence in England, where the labour movement remained impervious to Marxist revolutionary ideology. On the Continent, particularly in Germany, Marxism spread rapidly and soon became the major doctrine of the emerging labour movement.

German Social Democracy. In Germany, Ferdinand Lassalle (1825–64), the architect of the German labour movement, agreed with Marx on the need for autonomous organization of the working class but differed from him in wanting the government to provide the necessary capital for the establishment of producers' cooperatives that would emancipate labour from capitalist domination. To Marx, any appeal to the bourgeois state was out of the question, and he proceeded to organize followers in Germany against Lassalle. In 1869 they created the Social Democratic Party. The division between the followers of Lassalle and those of Marx persisted until 1875, when the two parties united on the basis of a compromise program (which Marx sharply criticized for its Lassallean vestiges).

The German Social Democratic movement grew rapidly, despite Chancellor Otto von Bismarck's attempts to suppress it through anti-socialist legislation and to undercut its appeal by social reforms. In 1877 the Socialists obtained half a million votes and a dozen members in the Reichstag. In 1881 the party claimed 312,000 members, and, by 1890, 1,427,000. After the repeal of the anti-Socialist laws the party adopted the so-called Erfurt Pro-

The growth of organized parties

gram of 1891, eliminating all demands for Lassallean state-aided enterprises and pledging itself to the orthodox Marxian goal of "the abolition of class rule and of classes themselves."

Revisionism. It soon became apparent that Marx's own thought had gone through a process of evolution so that different disciples could quote chapter and verse in support of fairly divergent political views. In particular, whereas Marx in the late 1840s and early 1850s had asserted that only a violent revolutionary overthrow of bourgeois rule and the emergence of the "dictatorship of the proletariat" would lead to the emancipation of the working class, by the late 1860s his views had considerably mellowed. Writing in England after the second Reform Bill (1867), which had given the vote to the upper strata of the workers, Marx suggested the possibility of a peaceful British evolution toward socialism. He also thought that such a peaceful road might be possible in the United States and in a number of other countries.

Although the leaders of German Social Democracy liked to speak in revolutionary Marxist rhetoric, they had in daily life become increasingly absorbed in parliamentary activities. Under the intellectual guidance of their theoretician Karl Kautsky (1854–1938) they developed a brand of economic determinism according to which the inevitable development of economic forces would necessarily lead to the emergence of socialism. The official Social Democratic platform remained ideologically intransigent, while the party's activities became increasingly pragmatic.

Eduard Bernstein (1850–1932), once a close companion of Engels, challenging prevailing orthodoxy in his famous *Die Voraussetzungen des Sozialismus und die Aufgaben der Sozialdemokratie* (1899; Eng. trans., *Evolutionary Socialism*, 1909), appealed to the party to drop its revolutionary baggage and recognize theoretically what it had already accepted in practice; namely, that Germany would not have to go through revolutionary convulsions in order to reach socialist goals. Ignoring the differences between political conditions in Germany and England, Bernstein urged the party to travel along the English road in hope of gradually transforming capitalism through socialist reforms brought about by parliamentary pressure.

The struggle between Kautsky's orthodoxy and Bernstein's revisionism shook the German party. Bernsteinian doctrine was officially defeated in 1903, but revisionism in fact permeated the party, especially its parliamentary and trade union leaders. At the outbreak of World War I practically all the leaders supported the government and the war, thus ending the party's revolutionary pretensions.

Other Social Democratic parties on the Continent. In France, the Marxists had to contend with rival socialist traditions that had profound roots in French working-class history. The followers of Blanqui and Proudhon played leading roles in the Paris Commune of 1871. In the years that followed, French socialism was torn by conflicting tendencies. The Parti Ouvrier founded by Jules Guesde in 1875–76 represented Marxist orthodoxy, but there were other socialist parties that reflected the influence of Blanqui, Blanc, and Proudhon, as well as the 18th-century revolutionary heritage. Even after the various parties amalgamated in 1905, the movement continued to be torn by dissension between its revolutionary and reformist wings. None the less, it continued to grow. At its first congress the unified party claimed 35,000 members, and in the elections of 1906 it won 54 seats in Parliament. By 1914 it had more than 100 members in the Chamber of Deputies. As in Germany, however, revolutionary rhetoric usually went hand in hand with pragmatic action, and the party became in fact a skillful participant in the parliamentary games of the Third Republic. After Jean Jaurès, the great Socialist orator and a principled leader of the peace elements, was assassinated on the eve of World War I, most of the Socialists supported the French war effort.

In the last part of the 19th century, Social Democratic parties generally beholden to Marxist doctrine sprang up in most of the countries of continental Europe. A Danish Social Democratic Party was founded in the 1870s; the Swedish Socialist movement in 1889. The Norwegian Labour Party (first called the Social Democratic Party) was formed in 1887 but became a major political force only in the early 20th century. In central Europe, Social Democratic parties fairly rapidly assumed a major place on the political horizon. An Austrian Social Democratic Party was founded in 1888. By 1908 it had gained about one-third of the vote cast in the parliamentary elections, to become the strongest Socialist party outside Germany. The Belgian Labour Party, formed in 1885 as an amalgamation of trade union, cooperative, and other groups, rapidly organized thousands of mutual aid societies, built a very strong trade union movement, and led a number of general strikes on behalf of the more liberal suffrage laws. The Dutch Socialist-Democratic Workers Party, founded in 1894, became a significant force only in the years immediately preceding World War I. It held 20 percent of the seats in the lower house of Parliament in 1912.

All of the continental parties were torn by internal tensions. Proposals to enter liberal coalition governments often were defeated by only narrow margins; Marxist orthodoxy prevailed only after sharp struggles. In The Netherlands, for example, a proposal to enter a coalition government was rejected by the close vote of 375 to 320 at the party congress of 1913.

Anarchist tendencies. In the less industrialized parts of Europe, particularly in Italy and Spain, Marxism had to contend with anarchist tendencies mainly rooted in the precapitalist and peasant strata. European anarchism as a political force was created by Mikhail Bakunin, the highly influential Russian libertarian thinker. His Anarchist Federation had belonged to the First International, but quarrels with Marx led to the expulsion of Bakunin and his followers in 1872.

Bakuninist and other anarchist strains of thought remained powerful in Spain, despite the founding of the Social Labour Party in 1879. The Spanish socialist movement suffered from the competition of the anarchists throughout its subsequent history, and only after World War I did it become a political force to be reckoned with.

In Italy anarchist tendencies also impeded the growth of a socialist movement. The Italian representatives to the First International followed Bakunin's lead. Not until 1892 was a distinctly Socialist party formed under the leadership of Filippo Turati. In 1913, after the electoral franchise was broadened, the official Socialist Party secured 51 seats in Parliament, and two other Socialist parties that had split from its ranks gained 31 seats. Although it continued to suffer from internal dissension and from anarchist tendencies in the more backward areas of the country, by World War I the Italian Socialist Party had become one of the strongest Marxist organizations in Europe.

The Second International. The First International had brought into being a variety of Socialist movements throughout Europe. When these began to grow roots in their respective political systems, it became apparent that the international movement could no longer be controlled by a single directing centre. After the dissolution of the First International in 1876, Marx and Engels remained father figures whose counsel the movement eagerly sought; but they could no longer direct it. The history of socialism now became largely the history of separate national movements that, for all their ceremonial acknowledgment of Marxist orthodoxy, increasingly tended toward a revisionist and nonrevolutionary line. By the early years of the 20th century socialism had become a powerful parliamentary force in most European countries. Except in Russia, where autocracy still held sway, the Socialists were reformers seeking a transformation of the existing system rather than its violent overthrow. Only left-wing minorities within the various parties still stood for revolutionary orthodoxy.

The Second International, founded in 1889, reflected the changed character of the movement. It was a kind of international parliament of socialist movements rather than the unified and doctrinally pure organization that the First International had attempted to be. It was dominated by the German party. With traditional Marxist rhetoric, the German delegates stood adamant against proposals to sanction socialist participation in bourgeois governments, and thus appeared to favour a "left" course. But socialist participation in government was not a realistic option in Kaiser William's Germany, and so the German delegates could be intransigent at no cost to themselves. When the issue was put to a vote at the Amsterdam congress in 1904, the Germans sided with those who opposed participation, against Jaurès, and those who condoned it. But Jaurès had the better of it when he pointed out that "behind the inflexibility of theoretical formulas which your excellent comrade Kautsky will supply you with till the end of his days, you concealed . . . your inability to act." As with the issue of government participation, so with the issue of war. The Second International, under its German leadership, issued many moving and stirring manifestoes against war, but when war broke out it disclosed its paralysis. Most of its national components sided with their own governments and abandoned the idea of international working-class solidarity. Almost all of them recognized what they may secretly have believed for a long time: the workers, after all, had a fatherland.

OTHER SOCIALIST TENDENCIES BEFORE WORLD WAR I

The non-Marxists

British Fabianism. Although Marxism triumphed in the continental Socialist movement, it did not do so in Great Britain. Henry Hyndman, a radical journalist, founded the Social Democratic Federation on strictly Marxist principles in the 1880s, but it ever remained marginal to the British socialist movement. The Socialist League, founded by the poet William Morris, propounded libertarian-syndicalist ideas and likewise failed to make headway. Fabian socialism, on the other hand, based on non-Marxist ideas, was to have an enduring influence in Britain.

The Fabian Society was organized in the 1880s by a number of young radical intellectuals among whom Sidney and Beatrice Webb, Graham Wallas, Sidney Olivier, and George Bernard Shaw were the most outstanding. It developed an evolutionary and moderate form of socialism. Convinced of "the inevitability of gradualness," the Fabians never endeavoured to become a mass organization but preferred to be a ginger group of intellectuals working to transform society through practical and unobtrusive advice to the men of power. The extremely influential *Fabian Essays* (begun in 1889) contained detailed blueprints for social legislation and reform that influenced policy makers whether they were socialists or not. Through "permeation," which Shaw defined as "wire-pulling the government in order to get socialist measures passed," the Fabians attempted to convince key politicians, civil servants, trade union officials, and local decision makers of the need for planned and constructive reform legislation. Basing their doctrine at least as much on non-Marxist economics as on the continental socialist tradition, they worked for a new order "without breach of continuity or abrupt change of the entire social tissue."

Syndicalism. The syndicalist movement grew out of French trade unionism when it was reconstituted after the bloodletting of the Paris Commune (1871). Convinced of the futility of parliamentary and political activity, the syndicalists stressed that only direct action by workers organized in their unions would bring about the desired socialist transformation. Under the leadership of Fernand Pelloutier the Fédération des Bourses du Travail (founded in 1892), which was later amalgamated with the Confédération Générale du Travail (1902), was built on the idea that the emancipation of labour would come through a "general strike" that would paralyze the country and deliver power into the hands of organized workers. The unions would become the directing and administering nuclear cells of production.

The syndicalists attracted a number of intellectuals to their ranks, who attempted to provide a philosophical basis for syndicalism and its rejection of the political road to socialism. The most important of their writings, Georges Sorel's *Réflexions sur la violence* (1908; Eng.

trans., *Reflections on Violence*, 1916), has continued to exercise considerable influence on the thinking of revolutionary militants, even though Sorel himself soon shifted his allegiance to the extreme right.

Guild socialism. The guild socialist tradition developed in Britain in the years before World War I. Sharing the general socialist hostility to the wage system and production for profit, guild socialists took from the syndicalists their distrust of the state and their emphasis on producers' control. They looked back to the Middle Ages when independent producers, organized in guilds, controlled the conditions of their employment and took pride in creative work. Aiming at self-government in industry, guild socialists urged that industrial organizations, churches, trade unions, cooperative societies, and municipalities be granted autonomy. They argued that every group in society should carry out its particular functions without control from above, and that individuals should have a say in the direction of all those functional units in which they happened to be interested. Cooperation between functional units would replace direction by the state, which would be restricted to providing needed national services such as police protection. The state would be a functional unit among many others, rather than an all-encompassing sovereign.

Although guild socialism owes its origin to several thinkers, it grew into a mature doctrine only when in 1913 it recruited G.D.H. Cole, a brilliant Oxford don, two of whose early books, *The World of Labour* (1913) and *Self-Government in Industry* (1917), contain the best exposition of guild socialist doctrine. The movement never attained wide popular appeal but has continued to be a source of ideas in the British labour movement, if only as a counterpoint to the bureaucratic and centralizing tendencies of Fabianism.

Socialism in the United States. Socialism never became as influential in the United States as it did in Europe. When the Socialist Party was formed in 1901 it claimed a membership of 10,000 that grew to 150,000 in 1912, in which year the party polled a presidential vote of 897,000, or 6 percent of the national total. Although its strongest roots were among recent immigrants from Europe, it also drew its inspiration from the utopian colonies of the 19th century, from the slavery abolitionists, trade unionists, and agrarian reformers, and from isolated socialist groups of the 1880s and 1890s.

The Socialist Labor Party, a predecessor of the Socialist Party, was formed in 1877 but acquired a distinct outlook only when the journalist and polemicist Daniel De Leon joined it in 1890. De Leon attempted to marry a doctrinaire brand of Marxism to a "labourism" nourished in part on French syndicalist doctrine. He and his followers wished to raise the membership of the unions above "paltry routine business" and prepare them for a successful contest with the power of capital, both at the ballot box and in industrial combat.

The Socialist Labor Party remained a sect. But the Socialist Party developed into a mass movement under the leadership of Eugene Debs, a former union official who had been converted to socialism by reading the works of various socialist writers while in jail. The Socialist Party of Debs was neither centralized nor politically homogeneous. In its ranks it harboured reformists and revolutionaries, orthodox Marxists, Christian ministers, municipal reformers, populists who hated the railroads and the trusts, and Jewish garment workers dreaming of fraternity in the sweatshops. It produced no major theoretical works, but it managed in its undoctrinaire way to be an effective voice for the idea of socialism in America. It declined after World War I, its last well-known leader being Norman Thomas.

THE RISE OF RUSSIAN SOCIALISM

The populist tradition. The dominant radical tendency in 19th-century Russia was populism, a doctrine first developed by the author and editor Aleksandr Herzen, who saw in the peasant communes the embryo of a future socialist society and argued that Russian socialism might skip the stage of capitalism and build a cooperative commonwealth based on ancient peasant tradition. Herzen idealized the peasantry. His disciples inspired many students and intellectuals to "go to the people" in order to stir them into revolutionary action.

In the 1860s and 1870s, the more radical populists lost their faith in a peasant revolt and turned instead to terrorism. Small groups of student revolutionaries sought to bring down tsarism through terroristic action; their efforts culminated in the assassination of Alexander II in 1881. Sergey Nechayev's *Revolutionary Catechism*, in the writing of which Bakunin had a hand, stressed that the sole aim of the revolutionary is to destroy "every established object root and branch, [to] annihilate all state traditions, orders and classes in Russia." It is one of the ironies of history that Bakunin helped create in Russia an elitist and terrorist movement composed almost exclusively of alienated intellectuals, while in western Europe he appealed to skilled craftsmen and peasants and appeared to be the heir of Proudhon.

Within the broad stream of populism, terrorism was opposed by an evolutionary socialism that put its faith in peaceful propaganda and the education of the masses. While the elitists pursued their campaign of terror, the gradualists stuck to propaganda among the people.

Marxism in prerevolutionary Russia. The father of Russian Marxism was Georgy Plekhanov, who began his socialist career as a populist and was converted to Marxism when he settled in Geneva in 1880; in 1883 he founded the first Russian Marxist organization, the Osvobozhdenie Truda (Liberation of Labour Group). Plekhanov thought Russian socialism ought to be based primarily on the growing factory proletariat. Rejecting Herzen's idea that Russia was exceptional, he held that the revolution would be European in character and that Russia's place in it would be determined by its own labour movement. In a variety of books and pamphlets in the 1880s and 1890s, Plekhanov attacked the populists and argued that Marx had shown the objective historical necessity of socialism. The laws of social evolution could not be flouted. A bourgeois revolution in Russia was inevitable in the course of industrial development. The organized working class would know how to take advantage of the bourgeois revolution and push it forward.

The Leninists

Against this German brand of Marxism, Vladimir Ilich Ulyanov (1870–1924), later to be known by his party name of Lenin, argued for a more militant approach to revolution. In *What Is To Be Done?* (1902) he formulated his characteristic doctrine. Socialism would be achieved only when professional revolutionaries succeeded in mobilizing and energizing the masses of workers and peasants. Left to themselves, the workers would get no farther than a trade union consciousness. A militant, disciplined, uncompromising organization of revolutionaries was needed to propel the masses into action.

Lenin's followers parted company with the other Russian Marxists at the second congress of the (illegal) Russian Social Democratic Workers Party held in London in 1903. The anti-Leninist position was formulated by the leader of the more orthodox Marxists, L. Martov, when he declared, "In our eyes, the labour party is not limited to an organization of professional revolutionaries. It consists of them, plus the entire combination of the active, leading elements of the proletariat. . . ."

The two factions within the Russian Social Democratic movement at first cooperated and even held joint meetings; the final split came only in 1912. Individual leaders switched from one faction to another (Plekhanov, who originally sided with Lenin, joined his opponents in 1904). Others, such as Leon Trotsky, attempted for a time to stay free from factional alignments. These disputes were fought out in the West, where most of the leaders of both sides lived as émigrés. Within Russia itself, however, Lenin's opponents (the Mensheviks) mainly attracted the better educated and skilled workers, as well as the Jewish intelligentsia, while his Bolsheviks tended to be most successful among the more backward strata of the working class.

After the February Revolution of 1917 toppled the tsarist regime and installed a liberal and vaguely socialistic leadership, the Bolsheviks managed to extend their organization among the urban masses. When Lenin returned from exile in April 1917, he startled his followers by calling for an entirely new strategy. Previously they had believed that their immediate task was to work within the limits of a democratic republic while preparing for future revolutionary opportunities. Lenin argued instead that they must seek power at once. The desire of the masses for an immediate end to the war, the land hunger of the peasantry, the feebleness of the new regime, he urged, made possible what had not been possible in the abortive revolution of 1905: a socialist revolution led by Bolshevik cadres. Moreover, Lenin argued, a Russian revolution would not be isolated for it would soon be followed by a German revolution.

The soviets (workers' and peasants' councils), which had sprung up spontaneously when the tsarist power collapsed, were the main organizational bases from which the Bolsheviks mounted their assault on the established order. Lenin's slogan "All power to the soviets" found a ready response in the major urban centres. In September 1917 the Bolsheviks won elections for the Moscow and St. Petersburg soviets. These now became centres of "dual power" challenging the official government. It was the St. Petersburg soviet that in October 1917 gave Trotsky the military instrument with which he was able to topple the provisional government and install a revolutionary regime headed by Lenin.

Lenin and the Third International. The Bolshevik seizure of power had been undertaken in the belief that the revolution would soon spread to the rest of Europe. Lenin's perspective had always been internationalist. When most of the socialist leaders of the Second International rallied to their national governments in 1914, Lenin denounced them as traitors to the cause and sought to lay the groundwork for a new organization of revolutionary Socialists. After their seizure of power, the Bolsheviks resolved to create a Third International. By the time the delegates had assembled in Moscow in 1919, a revolutionary uprising in Berlin had been crushed and its leaders murdered. The great majority of the German working class was evidently willing to give the Social Democratic leadership of the new German republic a chance. But to the Russian leaders world revolution still seemed near. Soon after the first congress of the Third International a short-lived soviet republic was proclaimed in Hungary and another in the German state of Bavaria. Communist parties began to be organized in all the major countries of Europe.

When the so-called Communist International (Comintern) met for its second world congress in July 1920, it was no longer a small gathering of individuals or representatives of small sects but a union of delegations from a dozen major Communist parties. The outcome of this meeting was to give the Russian leaders control of the new International, now broken away sharply from the Socialist movement. It adopted 21 conditions for membership in the Comintern, demanding that its adherents reject not only those Socialist leaders who had been "social patriots" in the war but also those who had taken a middle position. It aimed at creating a disciplined and militantly revolutionary world organization patterned after the Russian model, which would accept willingly the direction and unquestioned authority of the Russian leadership.

By 1923 the hoped-for revolutionary tide in Europe had not developed. New uprisings in parts of Germany failed completely in 1923. The Red Army's attempted invasion of Poland had been thrown back. Many Socialists who had for a time joined the Comintern, including the leadership of the Norwegian Labour Party, left-wing Communists in Germany, and Syndicalists in France and Spain, now turned away, rejecting its policy of centralized dictation.

Europe achieved a measure of economic and social stabilization. By the time of Lenin's death in 1924, Moscow was beginning to use the parties over which it still held command as instrumentalities of Russian foreign policy. Although some Comintern leaders like Trotsky still believed that world revolution was on the agenda, their faith was no longer shared by the majority of the Russian leadership.

SOCIALISM BETWEEN THE WARS

Socialists
and
Com-
munists

The split with the Communists. Communists throughout the world denounced the leaders of the reconstructed Socialist parties as "social traitors" who "objectively" fostered the maintenance of capitalism. They accused them of having repudiated Marxism and betrayed international socialism by collaborating during the war with the bourgeoisie in the defense of their national states. The Socialist leaders retorted by pointing to the dictatorial features of the Soviet state and accusing the Communists of having betrayed the democratic socialist tradition.

The European Socialist movement was irremediably split. In Germany, the Social Democrats united again and succeeded in enrolling the bulk of the working class under their banner; the Communists were reduced to a minority position in the German labour movement. In France, where the Communists at first succeeded in attracting the majority of the Socialist Party, their opponents soon regained ascendancy and the Communists became a minority on the French left. Italian socialism split into Communists and left-wing and right-wing Socialists and thus greatly facilitated Mussolini's march to power. In Great Britain the Communists hardly made a dent in the Labour Party and never became more than a radical sect. European socialism as a whole, as well as socialist movements on other continents, was sharply split between adherents of the Second International and the Communists organized in the Third.

The Comintern followed an erratic course, sometimes veering toward a revolutionary line and sometimes making attempts to collaborate with the more militant strata of the socialists. After the onset of the economic depression in 1929 the Comintern took a sharp leftist turn, expecting the "final crisis" of capitalism to bring proletarian revolution everywhere. It denounced Social Democratic leaders as "social Fascists" and enemies of the working class. In the Prussian Landtag the Communists actually voted with the Nazis to bring down a Social Democratic government, on the theory that the Nazi movement was a passing phenomenon.

At the same time the Socialists gave up in practice, though not always in theory, their commitment to revolutionary doctrine. They became in effect pressure groups trying to extract maximum advantages for the working classes from their respective national regimes. In Germany, in Britain, and in the Scandinavian countries they participated at times in the government. Elsewhere, as in France, they tended to support congenial left-bourgeois regimes. But they lacked, on the whole, a concrete plan of social and economic action, and consequently were ineffective when the world depression unsettled the economies and political regimes of western and central Europe.

Response to the world economic crisis. Nowhere, except in Sweden and Belgium, did the socialists press for comprehensive socialist planning during the depression. Where they were in power they followed orthodox policies of budgetary management and public finance. When they were out of power they contented themselves with a defense of the immediate interests of the workers by demanding more unemployment insurance and opposing reductions in wages.

As the crisis deepened, the Communists gained influence, particularly among the unemployed and those unskilled workers hit most severely by the depression. They did not make deep inroads among other workers.

The rise of Fascism. Hitler's rise in Germany led to the destruction of both the Communists and the Socialists in that country. The Communists had hoped that a Nazi victory would be only temporary, and that afterward they would be called upon to lead the masses of Germany to victory. Their battle cry was, "After the Nazis—We." The Socialists played politics as usual, expecting that the depression would run its "natural" course and that a gradual decline of the Nazi fever would follow. A disunited labour movement proved unable to stay the Nazi

march to power. This disaster led both Communists and Socialists to reconsider their previous policies and to revise their strategy and tactics.

Austrian Socialists, threatened with destruction by the reactionary regime of Chancellor Engelbert Dollfuss, resolved to offer armed resistance in February 1934. The Austrian party had long been regarded as a model for both its theoretical contributions and its concrete accomplishments. It enjoyed the nearly total support of the workers; 500,000 of Vienna's 2,000,000 inhabitants were dues-paying members. But the party was almost completely metropolitan and urban. Consequently the bloody battles of February 1934 remained localized in Vienna. The uprising was suppressed after four days, and the party had to go underground.

Socialists
in office

Experience in government. *Germany.* The end of World War I had seen a somewhat reluctant Social Democratic Party installed in the seat of German government. Friedrich Ebert, the head of the party, became the first president of the new republic. But the Socialists were split internally. The "majority Socialists," the right wing of the party, wished to proceed in a cautious and pragmatic manner. The "independent Socialists," led by Kautsky and his former antagonist Bernstein, pressed for fundamental structural reforms. The extreme left, led by Rosa Luxemburg and Karl Liebknecht, wished to organize a revolutionary party and founded the Communist Party of Germany. When younger extremists, overruling Luxemburg and Liebknecht, organized a left-wing *Putsch* early in 1919, they were isolated and easily defeated by the government of the majority Socialists and its allies among right-wing officers. Luxemburg and Liebknecht were assassinated, and the remaining leaders took the group into the Comintern. Another left-wing and Communist putsch in Bavaria a few months later was also unsuccessful. In the early 1920s, the independents reunited with the majority Socialists.

In the first election to the new National Assembly in 1919 the majority Socialists obtained a plurality of the votes cast (39.3 percent), and the independent Socialists won another 8 percent. The Socialist government proclaimed the need for socialization of monopolistic industries and other radical measures. But after the elections of June 1920, a non-Socialist cabinet took office. In subsequent years the cabinets were largely non-Socialist in character, though Socialists participated in some of them. The middle classes were again in the saddle, and when President Ebert died in 1925 the conservative nationalist Hindenburg succeeded him. Throughout the turmoil of the first years of the Weimar Republic, the Social Democrats remained a bulwark of republican legality against both the extreme right and the extreme left. In the *Länder* (states), Prussia in particular, they held positions of governmental power and managed to institute a number of reformist welfare measures. But they failed to gain a controlling voice in national politics.

In the May 1928 elections, the Social Democrats emerged as the strongest party in the Reichstag. Although they lacked a majority, their leader Hermann Mueller became chancellor, and their financial expert was named minister of finance. This largely Socialist government, however, proved unable to deal with the economic depression that soon afflicted Germany along with the rest of the world. The government followed an orthodox deflationary policy, pressed for the reduction of unemployment benefits in order to save taxes, and attempted to reduce budget deficits. Unable to stem the tide of depression, it resigned in 1930. This was the last government of the Weimar Republic in which Social Democrats participated. Soon afterward, the Nazis started on their way to power.

England. In the British elections of 1923, the Labour Party, which had adopted a Socialist program only five years earlier, won a plurality; with the support of the Liberals it formed the first Labour government under Ramsay MacDonald in January 1924. Its tenure proved short. After implementing a few modest reform measures, it was ousted by an electorate which, partly because of manufactured fears of a "Bolshevist menace," turned sharply to the right in the elections of October 1924.

In June 1929 the Labour Party had its second chance. It won 288 out of 615 seats in the House of Commons and, with the support of the Liberals, formed the second Labour government, again under Ramsay MacDonald. But Labour, like the German Social Democrats, proved unable to deal with the depression, particularly with mounting unemployment. It was pledged to far-reaching social reforms that it was not prepared to carry out. The flight of capital from London assumed catastrophic proportions; business circles demanded a balanced budget and lower unemployment benefits. When MacDonald proposed to accede to some of these demands, the trade unions sharply opposed him. He then split the Labour government and formed a national coalition with the Conservatives and the Liberals. For the remainder of the 1930s the Labour Party was out of power.

Italy. In the Italian elections of 1919, the Socialists won 2,000,000 votes out of a total of 5,500,000. Italy seemed on the verge of revolution; large-scale strikes, mass demonstrations, factory occupations, and spontaneous expropriations of landed estates spread throughout the country. In August 1920, a revolutionary situation developed in the industrial north after a breakdown in wage negotiations; 500,000 workers occupied the factories, kept production going, and prepared for armed resistance. The far left called for an extension of the strike, but a divided Socialist leadership hesitated. The discouraged workers retreated. Mussolini's Blackshirts began breaking up working-class meetings. In 1921, the right-wing Socialists proposed that the party form a coalition government with the Liberals, but the left vetoed the idea. Mussolini's terror squads made further inroads in the large industrial centres. A general strike called by the trade unions proved a dismal failure. Soon afterward Mussolini made his March on Rome (October 1922) and was installed as premier. By 1926 parliamentary government had completely ended in Italy. The Socialists were driven underground.

France. None of the French governments from the end of World War I until the middle 1930s included Socialists. Although the Socialist Party was in fact deeply committed to gradualism, it still clung to its prewar policy of not participating in "bourgeois" governments. Only in the mid-1930s, when militant right-wing groups threatened the Third Republic, did the Socialists change their policy. In June 1936, a government took office representing a Popular Front, ranging from the Communists on the left to Radical Socialists in the centre, and headed by the Socialist leader Léon Blum. The Communists had at last abandoned their doctrine of "social Fascism" and were now willing to enter coalitions with other parties of the centre and left.

The victory of the Popular Front in June 1936 was accompanied by sit-down strikes in the factories; these helped push the government, headed by Léon Blum, in a radical direction. Collective bargaining rights, never recognized before by French employers, were now protected by law; social security and general working conditions were significantly improved; the 40-hour week was made mandatory. The Blum government attempted to institute a French version of the U.S. New Deal. But after the initial enthusiasm had waned, French employers took courage and pressed the government to return to traditional fiscal and budgetary policies. When in June 1937 his middle-of-the-road partners in the coalition refused his demands for emergency fiscal powers, Blum resigned. The Socialists participated in the next government headed by a Radical Socialist, and Léon Blum later formed another Popular Front government that held office for about a month in 1938. When France went to war against Germany in 1939 the Communist Party, which opposed the war, was banned. After France's collapse in 1940, the Socialist Party was dissolved by the Vichy government.

Sweden. Only in Sweden were Socialists successful in their governmental policies. A Swedish Labour government was formed for the first time in 1932. Unlike the other European Socialist parties, the Swedes broke with orthodox budgetary and financial policies and stressed large-scale intervention by the government in the planning of economic affairs. Extensive public works, financed by borrowing from idle capital resources, helped to reduce unemployment and stimulated the economy; public investment was used methodically to offset the effects of reduced private spending. Unemployment, which had reached 164,000 in 1933, was eliminated by 1938 through a policy of steady economic expansion. The Swedish innovations helped lead the way to the economic policies practiced by almost all Western countries after World War II.

SOCIALISM SINCE WORLD WAR II

The worldwide spread of "socialist" parties. Orthodox Marxists had always assumed that socialism would emerge first in the industrial countries of the world. But a new kind of "socialism" spread rapidly in agrarian societies and backward countries after World War II. In many of these countries Marxism became, despite the intention of its founders, the ideology of industrialization. In the struggle against colonialism the liberation movements, especially the intellectuals and semi-intellectuals who led them, adopted what they conceived to be socialist ideas. It seemed to them that meaningful national independence could be attained only through state direction of the economy. Rapid economic growth, they believed, could be fostered only by restricting consumption and channelling national resources into the building up of productive facilities. In one degree or another the new countries took the Soviet Union as their model for rapid industrialization. All manner of regimes, from totalitarian one-party states to military dictatorships, proclaimed that they were socialist. Only in India and a very few other countries did the ruling party retain the traditional Western socialist vision of social justice, equality, and democracy.

New concepts of socialism

In the meantime, ironically, the Socialists of western Europe were giving up their Marxist views and turning toward the welfare state. During World War II almost all of the Socialist parties had joined governments of national unity. Afterward they sought to become popular parties following the parliamentary road to power and ready to participate in coalition governments with Liberal or Christian Democratic partners. Surrendering the idea that only full state ownership would bring the good society, they aimed at a mixed economy in which public control and a certain amount of planning would bring social benefits for all. This was, in essence, the idea of "the inevitability of gradualism" that the English Fabians and the German revisionists had preached around the turn of the century.

The transformation of western European socialism. *West Germany.* The changed orientation of the postwar German Social Democratic Party was expressed in its Frankfurt declaration of 1951, which made no mention of the class struggle and other traditional Marxist doctrine, stating instead that the party "aims to put economic power in the hands of the people as a whole and to create a community in which free men work together as equals." It advocated public control of the economy but rejected comprehensive state ownership. It accepted planning, but stressed that democratic socialist planning had nothing in common with the Communist and totalitarian kind.

From socialism to welfare

A few years later, in its program of principles adopted in Bad Godesberg in 1959, the party shed the last remnants of Marxism. The name of Marx and the words "class" and "class struggle" are not to be found in that program, which even advocates private property in the means of production. It rejects overall central planning and endorses the idea of a competitive free market. The party stands for "as much competition as possible—as much planning as necessary." A "mixed economy" is seen as the ideal. The party no longer claims to possess a universally valid doctrine, but stands for a pluralistic society in which no party seeks to impose its particular philosophy on society as a whole. Thus to all intents and purposes the Social Democratic Party of Germany, which in 1969 formed a government under the leadership of Willy Brandt, has become a reformist party striving for an extension of the welfare state.

British Labour. The British Labour Party was never committed to Marxism, and hence found it easier to adjust to the political realities of the postwar world. In 1945 it won a majority in Parliament for the first time. The government of Prime Minister Clement Attlee, during its six years of power, laid the foundations of the British welfare state. A number of basic industries such as coal, railways, road transport, and steel were nationalized. A comprehensive system of nationalized medical care was established. Social services were extended. Full employment was maintained. Although Labour was voted out of office in 1951, its main achievements remained. The steel industry again reverted to private control, but the Conservatives made no effort to undo the other features of the welfare state.

Hugh Gaitskell, who succeeded Attlee in the leadership of the party, wanted to revamp its program by eliminating earlier pledges that the party seek large-scale nationalization of industry. He was not successful, but in practice the party became married to a reformist course aiming at the extension of the welfare state and of pragmatic planning. When the party returned to power in 1965, its leader, Harold Wilson, prime minister until the elections of 1970, pursued a cautiously reformist policy. Harrassed by economic difficulties and forced to pay more attention to the balance of payments than to internal reforms, the Labour government made few policy decisions of a distinctively socialist character.

Trends in French and Italian socialism. The French Socialist Party, reconstituted after World War II, participated in leading positions in the first few postwar French governments. It supported nationalization of parts of French industry, especially public utilities, mining, and much of banking and insurance, as well as wide-ranging measures of public control over the economy and structural reforms in the field of social security. But the party had lost much of its prewar support among the workers to the Communists. The Socialists increasingly became a party of civil servants, middle-class professionals, and other white-collar employees. While they made no attempt to recast their program as the German Social Democrats did, their actual orientation was equally moderate.

The Italian Socialist movement split into a number of parties. The largest organization, the Italian Socialist Party under Pietro Nenni, attempted to revive the pre-Mussolini left-wing socialist tradition. It contended that the interests of the working class could best be served by cooperation with the Communists. Of all the Socialist parties of Europe it stood closest to the prewar Marxist tradition of class conflict and "orthodox" Marxism. After the Hungarian revolution of 1956, however, the party increasingly drew away from collaboration with the Communists, finally entering a centre-left coalition government with the Christian Democrats in 1963. Since then it has in practice become indistinguishable from other western European Socialist parties.

The second largest Socialist party of Italy during the post-World War II period has been the Democratic Socialist Party formed under the leadership of Giuseppe Saragat. It was committed to moderate social reforms, and participated in almost every Italian coalition government after 1947. In 1966 the two major Socialist parties merged, but they separated again in the late 1960s.

The welfare state. All the western European Socialist parties have become committed to the welfare state, though they vary in the extent to which they have formally abandoned their Marxist orientation. Some of their theoreticians still cling to the hope that socialism will eventually go beyond the welfare state toward a society in which class distinctions will have been erased and wealth will be more equitably distributed. But while this may be their dream, it no longer informs their political actions.

African socialism. Socialist ideas were carried to North Africa mainly by French-educated African intellectuals; in addition, many French settlers, especially schoolteachers and civil servants, were Socialists or Communists. The various national liberation movements, especially in Tunisia and Algeria, linked the struggle against colonial domination with socialist ideas. When Algeria became independent its first leader, Ahmed Ben Bella, surrounded himself with French advisers from various Marxist groups.

Collectivization of agriculture and self-management in industry stood high on the agenda of the Algerian national government. When these programs failed, Ben Bella was replaced by Col. Houari Boumedienne, who was pledged to continue "Algerian socialism" but settled in fact for an economy based on state-directed enterprises and private landholdings. The country was, in fact, run by a military dictatorship.

In Tunisia a one-party regime was installed after the liberation of 1956; under its leader, Habib Bourguiba, it proceeded to nationalize the major enterprises. The ruling party, the Destour Socialist Party, permitted no rival political organization; it was committed to modernization through planned development of the economy.

Elsewhere in Africa a variety of "African socialisms" sprang up in the 1950s and 1960s. Pres. Léopold-Sédar Senghor of Senegal advocated a socialist "humanism" based only partly on Marx. Pres. Sékou Touré of Guinea sought to combine Marxist-Leninist ideas with the communal values of precolonial Africa—to "Africanize" Marxism. Pres. Kwame Nkrumah of Ghana proclaimed "consciencism" as the basis for his regime and stated that "only totalitarian measures can preserve liberty"; he was overthrown in 1966.

In Kenya, Tanzania, and other African countries, the ruling elites proclaimed their adherence to one or another version of "African socialism" while in fact being committed above all to rapid industrialization and modernization. Many African socialist writers stressed the need to build their socialism upon African traditions such as communal land ownership, the egalitarian practices of some tribal societies, and the network of reciprocities and obligations that once existed in tribal societies.

Throughout Africa the commitment to socialism was hardly more than lip-service to an ideal. The pressing need was to move from a subsistence to a market economy, to industrialize, and to organize health services, education, housing, and public administration. Autonomous institutions in which men might strive for concerted political and social goals independent of government control scarcely existed in Africa. Hence the prospect for democratic, as distinct from imposed, socialism was remote.

Arab socialism. The "socialist" movements of the Middle East have been led by European-educated intellectuals belonging to a new middle class of civil servants, army officers, and schoolteachers. Trying to appeal to the Arab people as a whole, and without distinction as to class, they have stood for modernization and for the brotherhood of all Arabs.

The major socialist movement has been the Arab Socialist Party, usually called the Ba'ath Party. Founded in Syria, it has rejected tribal or regional loyalties. Ba'ath factions have held power in Iraq and Syria but have not promoted specifically socialist measures or made concrete reforms.

When Gamal Abdel Nasser came to power in Egypt in 1952, his group of young army officers of lower middle class origin had little if any interest in socialism. Nasser was led to socialist ideas in his struggle against the domination of foreign business. By the middle of the 1960s Egypt had nationalized all large industrial and financial enterprises, whether domestic or foreign; it had expropriated large-scale landowners; and it had placed all important sectors of the economy under the control of state planners. But the structure of power remained that of a military dictatorship.

Asian socialism. Representatives of a dozen Asian Socialist parties met in Rangoon in January 1953 for the first Asian Socialist Conference. Some of the delegates had international reputations. The governments of several Asian countries—India, Burma, Ceylon, Indonesia, and Singapore—called themselves Socialist. Yet the Socialist parties soon thereafter lost even the semblance of power and influence. In India, where several Socialist organizations competed, the ruling Congress Party was in fact a national party striving to unite within its ranks

Failure of socialism to take root in Asia

many divergent political and social tendencies. The Burmese Socialist Party was for many years part of a coalition that ruled the country, but it was outlawed in 1962 when Gen. Ne Win seized power. The Indonesian Socialist Party was abolished by President Sukarno in 1960. Except in Singapore, the postwar Socialist parties in Southeast Asia played no major role in the 1960s.

As the influence of the European-style Socialist parties waned, a variety of authoritarian regimes arose speaking in socialist accents. Indonesia's President Sukarno proclaimed Resopim (Revolution, Indonesian Socialism, and National Guidance) his official ideology. The Burmese military dictatorship proclaimed Burma a socialist state. North Vietnam was ruled by a Communist party; in the rest of Indochina, revolutionary movements inspired by Communist ideology battled traditionalist forces supported by the United States. In China, the Communist People's Republic has been in power since 1949.

The Socialist parties of Southeast Asia, after playing a brief role in the struggle for independence, failed to take root in national politics. They were led by European-educated intellectuals, who attempted to emulate European models and were committed to the idea of a democratic road to socialism. But the countries of Southeast Asia were not prepared to follow them; they turned instead to authoritarian regimes that pursued industrial development. Only in Singapore and India were attempts made to combine democracy and socialist planning. In most of Asia, as in Africa, "socialism" has become the ideology of new elites seeking modernization and rapid industrialization.

Japan. Only in Japan, by far the most developed of Asian countries, have traditional socialist organizations become firmly established. The first Socialist Party of Japan, formed in 1901, was soon dissolved and forced to go underground. During and after World War I socialist organizations again sprang up. In 1936 the Social Mass Party elected 18 members to the Parliament and received more than half a million votes. After World War II, socialist organizations that had been suppressed since 1940 appeared again. In 1946 the Socialist Party won over 90 seats to become the third strongest party. A year later, it gained the largest number of seats in Parliament, and its leader Katayama Tetsu became prime minister in a coalition government. In October 1948, however, the conservatives took office. The Socialists were deeply split between gradualists and revolutionaries. The left wing tended to be sharply anti-American and leaned toward the Soviet Union; the right wing favoured a gradual relaxation of close military and political ties with the United States. The two wings broke apart in the 1950s to form the (left) Socialist Party of Japan and the (right) Democratic Socialist Party. Together they controlled about one-third of the seats in Parliament, but seemed condemned to a permanent minority status. Japanese socialism still awaits a transformation similar to that undergone by western European Socialism in the postwar era.

Other areas and countries. *Australia.* Socialism has deep roots in the British Commonwealth countries of Australia, New Zealand, and Canada. The Australian Labor Party was formed in 1901, when the Australian Commonwealth came into existence. Only three years later its leader, J.C. Watson, became the world's first Labor prime minister. In 1908, and again from May 1910 to June 1913, Labor headed the government. In subsequent years the Labor Party has been frequently in office. It held power throughout most of the 1940s, and again achieved power in the early 1970s.

New Zealand. A loose Liberal-Labour alliance dominated New Zealand politics between 1893 and 1906, but the New Zealand Labour Party, as a social-democratic party committed to the socialization of the means of production, did not emerge until 1913. It grew steadily, coming to power for the first time in 1935. Labour cabinets headed the government from 1935 until 1949, from 1957 until 1960, and from 1972.

The Australian and New Zealand labour movements have been committed to a gradualist and reformist course since their inception. They are strongly tied to the unions,

Success in Australia, New Zealand, Canada

and though in principle pledged to a Socialist program they are in fact mainly concerned with using governmental control as a means of dealing with immediate problems and expanding social services. The various social security acts that they introduced helped to make Australia and New Zealand modern welfare states, and relatively equalitarian societies, even before World War II.

Canada. Canadian socialism had a slower beginning than its Australian and New Zealand counterparts. Prior to World War I, the Canadian Socialist movement was split between two parties, neither of which managed to win seats in the federal Parliament. During the 1920s various Socialist and Labour parties flourished in different parts of Canada, but only rarely did they send a representative to the federal Parliament. Only with the organization of the Co-operative Commonwealth Federation (CCF) in 1932 did the Socialist movement begin to achieve national importance. Basing its campaigns on the need for "social and economic planning on a bold and comprehensive scale," it gained support in most provincial elections and in June 1944 was able to form a government in the province of Saskatchewan, where it remained in power for 20 years. In 1961 progressive union leaders of the labour congress met with the CCF leadership and formed the New Democratic Party. Whereas the CCF had been largely agrarian in character, the new party had a following in the industrialized parts of the country. In the 1960s it commanded around 18 percent of the vote in elections to the federal Parliament, and played a major role in the politics of such provinces as Saskatchewan, British Columbia, and Ontario. Advocating a planned economy, it stood for increased social security, government employment guarantees, large-scale construction of low-rent housing, and the like. Its policies were similar to those of postwar western European socialism.

Latin America. The historical roots of Latin American socialism are fairly old. Several branches of the First International were established in Argentina in the early 1870s. In Chile and Argentina, and to a lesser extent in other Latin American countries, socialists at times played leading roles, but they were hampered by a variety of splits and by the fact that their following consisted mainly of immigrant industrial workers. They failed to make an impact in rural areas. In Chile, however, they participated in various coalition and popular front governments in the 1920s, 1930s, and 1940s. In the elections of 1958, Chilean socialists supported the Popular Action Front (FRAP) candidate, Salvador Allende. He was narrowly defeated, and defeated again in 1964. In 1970, however, he won by a narrow plurality in a three-way presidential election and became head of a government supported by a popular front ranging from Communists to democratic reformers. His government was pledged to the nationalization of foreign-owned industry and to the planned reconstruction of the country.

Millions of persons throughout the world cling to the socialist vision of an equalitarian, democratic, fraternal society based on comprehensive planning and public control of the means of production. But the political movement which embodied that vision is fragmented and has lost much of its earlier elan. The socialist spirit was sapped when the Russian Revolution brought forth a totalitarian dictatorship, and further weakened when a variety of authoritarian movements usurped the socialist name. In western Europe and the United States, socialism has come to be equated with the extension of social security and other elements of the welfare state. Few socialist theoreticians ask, "After the Welfare State—What?" Whether socialism will get a second chance is hard to say.

BIBLIOGRAPHY

General works: DANIEL BELL, "Socialism," in *International Encyclopedia of the Social Sciences,* 14:506–534 (1968), one of the best short surveys of socialism from its origins to the present day; G.D.H. COLE, *A History of Socialist Thought,* 5 vol. (1953–60), the most complete and detailed general study; H.W. LAIDLER, *History of Socialism,* rev. and enl. ed.

(1968), and CARL LANDAUER, *European Socialism*, 2 vol. (1959), two histories written from a social democratic perspective; IRVING HOWE (ed.), *Essential Works of Socialism* (1970), a collection of readings in many varieties of Marxist thought.

Other works: C.A.R. CROSLAND, *The Future of Socialism* (1957), an assessment of the prospects for socialism by a leading member of the British Labour Party; MICHAEL HARRINGTON, "Why We Need Socialism in America," *Dissent*, 17:240–303 (1970), a defense of the relevance of socialism in the United States by a leading American socialist; JAMES JOLL, *The Second International 1889–1914* (1966), a standard but very readable history of 19th-century social democracy; GEORGE LICHTHEIM, *Marxism* (1961), a sophisticated and searching work dealing with the transformation of Marxism from the time of its founders to that of Lenin and Stalin; *A Short History of Socialism* (1970) and *The Origins of Socialism* (1969), idiosyncratic but stimulating reading; A.F. STURMTHAL, *The Tragedy of European Labor* (1943), a study of the failures of social democratic policies during the depression of the 1930s, by a sympathetic observer.

(L.A.C.)

Social Movements

The term social movement is familiar to readers of the popular press and even the most casual students of history. Reform movements, religious movements, revolutions, and the multiplicity of "-isms" loom large in the story of mankind. When the layman speaks of a social movement he usually implies a program or a sequence of actions by a large number of individuals directed toward some social change. Sometimes he may use the term to denote the groups who engage in these actions, saying that someone "joins a movement."

The term signifies also a conceptual tool of social thinkers. The study of social movements is conventionally included in the field of collective behaviour. The subject matter of collective behaviour includes special types of human groupings, referred to in this sense as "collectivities," whose activities and behaviour, emerging from less defined and more problematic situations, are governed by novel or emergent norms rather than by preexisting, conventional customs and rules. Some scholars seek to explain the novel, spontaneous character of collective behaviour through a theory of emergent norms. Others emphasize psychological mechanisms such as contagion, a form of imitation, or convergence, the simultaneous release of latent predispositions among a number of people. Collective behaviour also includes the study of crowds, large publics, fads and fashions, and mass communication.

CHARACTERISTICS OF SOCIAL MOVEMENTS

Scholarly definitions correspond closely to popular usages. These definitions vary according to their emphasis on the activities of a social movement or the people who engage in these activities. Those that emphasize the nature of the activities tend to focus attention on the conditions that produce movements and the individual motives that prompt large numbers of people to participate in them. Those who view social movements primarily as collectivities tend to shift the emphasis to the structural properties of social movements, the influence of these properties on the behaviour of members, and the interaction between members.

Social movements and social change. All definitions reflect the notion that social movements are intrinsically related to social change. They do not encompass the activities of people as members of stable social groups with established, unquestioned structures, norms, and values. The behaviour of members of social movements does not reflect the assumption that the social order will continue essentially as it is, with individuals being born into a stable society, passing through their own life cycles, and being replaced at death by succeeding generations who will live much the same type of life. It reflects, instead, the assumption that men can change the social order and affect the course of history. It is behaviour based on the faith that men collectively can bring about or prevent social change if they will dedicate themselves to the pursuit of a goal. Uncommitted observers may regard these

goals as illusions, but to the members they are hopes that are quite possible of realization. Asked about his activities, the member of a social movement would not reply, "I do this because it has always been done" or "It's just the custom." He is aware that his behaviour is influenced by the goal of the movement: to bring about a change in the way things have "always" been done or sometimes to prevent such a change from coming about.

The membership. The quixotic efforts of bold, imaginative individuals do not constitute social movements. A social movement is a collectivity or a collective enterprise. The individual member experiences a sense of membership in an alliance of people who share his dissatisfaction with the present state of affairs and his vision of a better order. Like a group, a social movement is a collectivity with a common goal and shared values. Each member is aware that there are other people who share his perception of what is desirable and what is undesirable, what is good and what is bad. While a larger number of people in his society or group may disagree with his definitions, he knows that he is not isolated. The social movement constitutes a new reference group for him.

The individual in the social movement

This sense of membership suggests that the individual is subject to some discipline. In addition to shared values, a social movement possesses norms. These are shared expectations as to how an individual who considers himself a member will behave toward other members and toward members of outgroups. These norms prescribe behaviour that will symbolize the member's loyalty to the social movement, strengthen his commitment to it, and set him apart from nonmembers. The norms prohibit behaviour that may cause embarrassment to the movement or provide excuses for attacks by opponents. Loyalty to a movement may be symbolized by the wearing of badges, by style of dress, or by financial contributions. Commitment is strengthened by participation in group activities with other members and by engaging in actions, individual or collective, that publicly define the individual as a committed member. Engaging in illegal or socially reprehensible activities in response to the demands of the movement may bring the individual to a "point of no return," so that his fate is irrevocably tied to the movement unless he is willing to defect and accept the penalties that will be imposed both by the larger society and by the movement.

A social movement also provides guidelines as to how members should think. Norms of this kind constitute something resembling a "party line"—a definition of the "correct" position for members to take with regard to specific issues. There is subtle pressure on the individual to espouse this position even in the absence of personal knowledge of the arguments for it. At the same time, the movement, through its ideology, provides a justification for the values shared by the members. The ideology is a collective product, produced by the intellectuals of the movement and accepted and shared by the membership. Not every member can be expected to study and think through the philosophy that justified the movement and its values. The ideology provides him with a ready-made presumably authoritative set of arguments. One of the defining characteristics of a social movement is that it is relatively long lasting; the activity of the membership is sustained over a period of weeks, months, or even years, rather than flaring up for a few hours or a few days and then disappearing. A social movement is usually large but, like duration, largeness is only relative. Some social movements, extending over a span of many decades, may enlist hundreds of thousands of members. Some movements take place within the boundaries of a specific secondary group, such as a religious association or a local community, and may include only a few score or a few hundred members. Thus, while a social movement is typically large, long lasting, and widespread, some marginal social movements are relatively limited in scope; but all social movements take place within groups that are large enough to be classified by the sociologist as secondary groups. Furthermore, the exact size of a social movement is impossible to determine exactly, for membership is not formally defined.

The lack of formal structure

Indeed, one of the salient characteristics of a social movement is the semiformal character of its structure. It is not informal in the sense that a small, primary group is. At the same time it lacks the fully developed, formal structure of a stable association, such as a club, a corporation, or a political party. The leaders do not possess authority in the sense of legitimatized power, and membership is not formal. Even though some of the inner circle of members may go through a ceremony that signifies the act of joining, many members ally themselves to the movement simply by supporting it and "resign" by withdrawing their support. Because of its emergent and developing character, a social movement lacks defined procedures for selecting and identifying members. While it acts collectively in pursuit of some shared goal, it lacks formal procedures for arriving at decisions.

While a social movement does develop some regularities in its modes of activities, these do not constitute a relatively inflexible "standing operating procedure" of the sort that marks a bureaucracy. The movement is not stable and secure in its existence. There is always a state of tension and often one of conflict between it and the larger group or society of which it is a part. Hence its modes of activity are frequently described as strategy and tactics, terms borrowed from military thought. Strategy implies long-range planning for the utilization of all resources available for the attainment of the ultimate goal of the movement. Tactics are procedures for utilizing specific resources to deal with short-term problems or opportunities in a manner that will contribute to the overall goal. Both strategy and tactics must be amenable to change if the course of the struggle indicates that they are not effective. The informal, noncontractual quality of membership, the absence of formal decision-making procedures, and the requirement for flexibility in strategy and tactics place a premium on blind faith and fanatical loyalty on the part of members. While not all members display these traits, the ideal member gives his total, unselfish loyalty to the movement. Since no legal obligation is assumed on becoming a member, either to conform to the movement's norms or to remain a member, commitment to the movement and its values becomes one of the most important sources of member control. The deeply committed member, accepting without question the decisions and orders conveyed by the leaders, sacrificing self, family, and friends if required to do so, is likely to be regarded by outsiders as a fanatic. Some students of social movements, particularly those whose analysis has a psychoanalytic orientation, have suggested that the fanaticism of dedicated members results from individual psychopathological states. An alternative explanation is that the social movement becomes a reference group that provides the member with a new and deviant view of social reality. His basic assumptions about the nature of the social order become so divergent from those of the "normal" members of society that his logic and conclusions are incomprehensible to them. Like them, he is responding to social definitions of reality; but these definitions are derived from a different universe of discourse.

RELATIONSHIPS TO OTHER CONCEPTS

Social movements are intrinsically related to social change; but social change is continuous and not all of it involves social movements. The student of social change may identify social trends that arise out of the uncoordinated actions of many individuals who have no sense of being part of a collective movement but who, nevertheless, modify their culture. In other instances social change is deliberately planned and fostered by agents of change who are assigned the functions of research, development, and planning in stable associations. Social change, whether it results from cultural drift or planned development, generates new problems and new aspirations for members of the society. As a result social movements may arise with the goal of speeding up, redirecting, or blocking ongoing changes in culture.

Comparison with associations, crowds, and publics. The social movement, as a collectivity with a semiformal structure and acting on the basis of emergent norms, stands in contrast to formal associations with codified norms and established traditions. Yet many of the persons who become members of social movements are, at the same time, members of such associations. Some movements arise within the boundaries of large associations, as when the Protestant Reformation started within the Roman Catholic Church. A movement cuts across the boundaries of associations when segments of the membership of several associations, such as religious denominations, unite in a joint effort such as a peace movement. A movement may include within it entire associations whose members become part of the movement by virtue of their preexisting group memberships. Finally, a social movement that succeeds in having its values accepted and legitimatized by the larger society may itself become an association in the formal sense.

Like a social movement, a crowd is a collectivity but more limited in size and duration. The members of a compact crowd are physically together, in sight and hearing of one another. A diffuse crowd includes persons whose communication is indirect; but it is of relatively short duration, for the objectives of a crowd are limited and short-range. Out of the excitement, the imagery, and the sense of unity that exist for a short time in a crowd may grow a more enduring social movement. On the other hand, the tactics employed by a social movement may, with or without design, foster episodes of crowd behaviour by partisans or opponents of the movement.

Publics and social movements

The public is also a collectivity and one that, like a social movement, is usually diffuse and widespread. It may be distinguished from a social movement by the fact that the public assumes that differences of opinion about an issue legitimately exist and will be debated. The social movement exhibits no such tolerance of divergent opinions. When some members of a public become so persuaded of the righteousness of their cause that they regard disagreement as immoral, they may be transformed into a social movement. Publics also arise in relation to social movements. In such cases the movement itself and its right to exist, rather than the values with which it is concerned, may become the issue for a public. Influencing opinion within such a public may become a matter of great concern to the movement.

Comparison with interest groups and political parties. Interest groups are related both to publics and to social movements. An interest group is a number of people with a deep and continuing interest in a particular issue, who evaluate other current issues on the basis of their implications for this central interest. Thus black Americans, as an interest group, have evaluated American participation in international wars in terms of the significance for Negro rights. An interest group may participate in various publics, or its members may be attracted to a social movement that seems to serve their interests.

Social movements may be regarded as a form of pressure group, though other pressure groups do not act as social movements. The term itself comes primarily from a political context; and the lobby is an example of an institutionalized pressure group, legitimatized and regulated by government and supported by an association that it serves.

Some confusion arises in the identification of certain political parties as social movements. In a stable, democratic political system the major parties constitute associations with bureaucratic structures and rules of procedure that function between elections. "New" parties, exemplified in the United States by the term third parties, constitute social movements in their struggle for recognition as regular participants in electoral contests. These new parties have a tentative nature, tend to be concerned with a single issue, and are typically identified with a charismatic leader. Social movements may arise within established parties when a dissident element seeks to displace the "regular" bureaucracy. If a third party succeeds in winning a major election, it is likely to become stabilized as an independent association. Sometimes, however, unsuccessful third parties survive for a long time as movements in which participation, rather than winning elections, is the dominant theme.

TYPES OF SOCIAL MOVEMENTS

There is no single, standard typology of social movements. As various scholars focus on different aspects of movements, different schemes of classification emerge. Hence any social movement may be described in terms of several dimensions.

Herbert Blumer proposed a broad distinction between *general* and *specific* social movements, based on differences in structure and goals. A general social movement develops out of a cultural drift and is characterized by vagueness and generality of goals. It lacks organization, and its activities consist of the parallel but uncoordinated behaviour of many individuals. It is not truly a social movement in the sense that a specific social movement is, for the latter has an emergent organization and collectively defined values and norms.

Dimensions of social movements　Many attempts at categorization direct attention to the objective of the movement. The social institution in or through which social change is to be brought about provides one basis for categorizing social movements as political, religious, economic, educational, and the like. It may be argued that all movements tend to be either political or religious in character, depending upon whether their strategy aims at changing political structures or the moral values of individuals.

Neil J. Smelser suggests two inclusive types of social movements differentiated according to the level of objective. The norm-oriented movement seeks to bring about changes in the accepted procedures for attaining the values of the society but does not challenge these values themselves. A value-oriented movement stems from a generalized belief that changes should and can be brought about in one or more of the values of the society, as well as in the norms necessary for the implementation of these values.

A commonly used but highly subjective distinction is that between "reform" and "revolutionary" movements. Such a distinction implies that a reform movement advocates a change that will preserve the existing values but will provide improved means of implementing them. The revolutionary movement, on the other hand, is regarded as advocating replacement of existing values. Almost invariably, however, the members of a so-called revolutionary movement insist that it is they who cherish the true values of the society and that it is the opponents who define the movement as revolutionary and subversive of basic, traditional values.

Ralph H. Turner and Lewis M. Killian suggest that social movements may be categorized in terms of what constitutes success for the movement. There are three basic criteria, and every movement incorporates all three to some degree. A value-oriented movement emphasizes the implementation of its program of social change as the measure of its success. A power-oriented movement places greater emphasis on the achievement of power. A participation-oriented movement places the greatest weight on the gratifications that the members gain from participating in the movement, such as a conviction of being "saved."

Some attempts to characterize movements involve the direction and the rate of change advocated. Adjectives such as "radical," "reactionary," "moderate," "liberal," and "conservative" are often used for such purposes. In this context the designations "revolutionary" and "reform" are often employed in a somewhat different sense than that described above, with the implication that a revolutionary movement advocates rapid, precipitous change while a reform movement works for slow, evolutionary change.

Killian advances still another typology based on the direction of the change advocated or opposed. A reactionary movement advocates the restoration of a previous state of social affairs, while a progressive movement argues for a new social arrangement. A conservative movement opposes the changes proposed by other movements, or seeming to develop through cultural drift, and advocates preservation of existing values and norms.

Turner and Killian argue that it is useful at times to categorize social movements on the basis of their public definition, the character of the opposition evoked, and the means of action available to the movement. This scheme is designed to eliminate the subjective evaluation of goals inherent in such categories as reform and revolutionary. A movement that does not appear to threaten the values or interests of any significant segment of society is publicly defined as respectable. If there is no competing movement advocating the same objective, it is also nonfactional. The respectable nonfactional movement must contend primarily with the problems of disinterest and token support, but it has access to legitimate means of promoting its values. A respectable factional movement must contend with competing movements advocating the same general objective, but also has access to legitimate means of extending its influence. A movement that appears to threaten the values of powerful and significant interest groups within the society is publicly defined as revolutionary and encounters violent suppression. As a result, it is denied access to legitimate means of promoting its program. A fourth type of movement is defined as neither respectable nor dangerous but as peculiar; this type, seen as odd but harmless, encounters ridicule and has limited access to legitimate means.

Social movements may also be categorized on the basis of the general character of their strategy and tactics; for instance, whether they are legitimate or underground. The popular distinction between radical and moderate movements reflects this sort of categorization. An obvious difference between types of movements depends upon their reliance on violent or nonviolent tactics. But a nonviolent movement may also be defined as revolutionary or radical because it accepts civil disobedience, rather than legal or parliamentary manoeuvring, as a major feature of its strategy.

There are many other dimensions in which social movements may vary. Some are obviously smaller than others and may be described as cabalistic, reflecting both their limited size and their secrecy. While all movements develop some degree of semiformal organization, they vary in the degree of organization. Some remain loosely organized, others develop a highly structured central leadership group that resembles an association in its continuity and stability.

PROMINENT SOCIAL MOVEMENTS OF RECENT CENTURIES

Historical and scientific accounts make possible the analysis of a formidable number of movements that have arisen during the 18th, 19th, and 20th centuries. Historians such as George Rudé and Eric Hobsbawm have made analyses of the French Revolution, the Chartist and Luddite movements, and various peasant revolts of the 19th and 20th centuries.

The 18th and 19th centuries. The 18th century was marked by two of the great political movements of history: the French and American revolutions. During the same century one of the great religious movements, Methodism, arose in England and spread to the American colonies. Less well known are the peasant revolts that occurred in Italy and Spain.

The great age of social movements　The 19th century was also an age of revolutions. Political movements swept many European countries in the wake of the French Revolution, signifying the rise of bourgeois nationalism, and across the Atlantic Ocean independence movements arose in several South American countries. In the United States a wide variety of movements emerged. The Abolition movement was countered by the Southern Proslavery and Secessionist movements. The Temperance and the Women's Rights movements were begun, as was Christian Science. Near the end of the century, the ideology of populism supported one of the great third-party movements in U.S. history. The labour movements that extended into the next century in both Europe and America had their inception in the 19th century, which saw the beginnings of the industrial workers' dissatisfaction with bourgeois dominance of economic and political institutions. At the same time, there was an important peasant movement in semifeudalistic Russia. More significantly, the world socialist movement, including Communism, achieved its initial organization and developed its basic ideology. Japan underwent a political movement that resulted in the overthrow of the Tokugawas and the modernization of the nation.

The 20th century. Many social movements that had their greatest impact in the 20th century had their beginnings shortly before the turn of the century. The Communist movement achieved its greatest triumph in the Russian Revolution, but it continued to challenge and sometimes overthrow established regimes in China and in smaller nations around the world. Zionism, the Women's Rights movement, and the Temperance movement all began in the 19th century but achieved their most notable successes in the 20th.

Fascist movements in Italy, Germany, and many smaller European nations, as well as in the United States, rose and fell within the first half of the 20th century, but remnants still exist. The latter part of the century saw the rise of a many-faceted "far right" movement in the United States, which included the revival of the Ku Klux Klan.

The 20th century has seen a new wave of nationalist movements. Colonized peoples in Africa and Asia revolted against European domination in such movements as the Algerian Revolution. In other areas where European or United States influence was subtle and indirect rather than explicit and formal, movements, which combined nationalistic and socialistic themes, developed to challenge existing regimes alleged to be agents of imperialism. The Cuban Revolution overthrew the Batista government and then expropriated United States properties. Arab nationalism developed partly as a response to Zionism, partly as a response to Western economic influence. Other significant nationalist movements arose in Turkey, India, and Iran. Afrikaner nationalism in South Africa and French nationalism in Canada were movements in which people of European ancestry sought political dominance or independence in pluralistic societies.

The Negro protest movement in the United States passed through many phases during the 20th century. The civil rights movement, beginning shortly after the turn of the century under the leadership of the National Association for the Advancement of Colored People, competed with the Marcus Garvey "Back-to-Africa" movement. It was transformed by the strategy of nonviolent direct action inspired by Martin Luther King, Jr., and was subsequently diminished by the Black Power movement and black nationalism. It evoked a countermovement, the resistance movement in the South, and was one of the stimuli for the rise of George Wallace's third-party movement. Movements for self-determination and economic welfare also arose among American Indians and Mexican Americans.

The threat of nuclear war and the involvement of the United States in Viet Nam were met by a peace movement in the United States and were reflected in similar movements in many European countries. Intersecting with the peace movement in the United States was the student movement, which also had counterparts in other nations.

The 20th century has been marked by no great religious movements like those of earlier centuries, but both Protestant and Catholic Christianity have been torn by conflicts between "modernist" and "fundamentalist" movements.

THE DYNAMICS OF SOCIAL MOVEMENTS

As an enduring, sustained collectivity a social movement undergoes significant changes during its existence. This characteristic has led to attempts to formulate a theory of the "life cycle" or "natural history" of social movements. Several scholars, including Rex D. Hopper, have undertaken to identify patterns of developmental change in revolutions. Hopper postulates a preliminary stage of mass excitement and unrest, a popular stage of crowd excitement, a formal stage of formulation of issues and publics, and an institutional stage of legalization and societal organization.

Other scholars question the value of the life-cycle approach to social movements, arguing that empirical studies of numerous movements fail to support the notion of invariant stages of development. Smelser suggests as an alternative a value-added theory, which postulates that while a number of necessary determinants for the occur-

rence of a social movement may be isolated, they need not be added to the situation in any particular order. Some may be present for some time without effect only to be activated later by the addition of another determinant. At most it can be said that the idea of the life cycle permits the discovery of conditions that must be present if any movement is to proceed from one stage to another. It may also help identify the conditions that cause a movement to take one direction rather than another. Still, it can be said that a social movement has a career; for as it endures it always undergoes changes in many of its characteristics, though the sequence of these changes may vary from movement to movement.

Progressive changes in leadership and membership. One of the most apparent changes is a shift in leadership. While social movements are often identified with one outstanding symbolic leader, there is usually a leadership group that includes different types of leaders. In its earliest stages the strongest influence on a movement is likely to be the charismatic leader who personally symbolizes its values. At some point intellectuals play a leadership role by contributing to the developing ideology of the movement. And if a movement endures and grows for any length of time, administrative leaders arise who are concerned with the practical matters of organization and strategy. Influence in the movement may shift between these types. Furthermore, new charismatic leaders may arise to challenge the earlier leaders, suggesting changes in values and strategy and giving rise to factional struggles.

Usually the membership of a movement grows during its career, which introduces an element of greater heterogeneity. In the early stages the followers typically are deeply committed with an almost fanatical dedication to the values. Later, a movement attracts a greater number of other types of members. These include persons disaffected with the social order who need to identify with some unconventional cause. The particular values of the movement are not as important to them as the psychological rewards of participation. Another type, who may be called the "exploiters," see in the movement an opportunity to serve certain private goals. If the movement gains a measure of respectability in some segment of society, members may be acquired who are not deeply committed. They are likely to have significant reservations about the movement and their participation is sporadic. On the other hand, if a movement is publicly defined as revolutionary and subjected to harsh oppression, the membership is likely to be reduced mainly to deeply committed converts or to fanatics who derive some satisfaction from the feeling of being persecuted.

Progressive changes in goals and strategies. The goals rarely remain unchanged. As the movement endures and grows, they are likely to become broader and vaguer than they were at the beginning. Proposals for limited, specific reforms become embedded within programs of general social reform. As the leaders and members begin to acquire a sense of power through early victories, the power orientations of the movement may increase. Acquisition of greater power by the population segment that the movement purportedly represents, rather than the implementation of the values of the movement, then becomes a goal. At the same time, the statement of the movement's aim in acquiring power becomes vaguer and more utopian.

Changes also occur in the strategy, which may tend in either of two general directions. It may emphasize *personal transformation*, bringing about social change by converting a majority of society to implement the values by their actions. Or it may emphasize a strategy of *societal manipulation*, changing social institutions so that the program may be implemented without regard to the number of people favouring the new order. Failure of a movement to gain a large number of converts, combined with indications that it has at its disposal effective means of coercion, leads to a shift to this type of strategy.

Strategy and changes in strategy are strongly influenced by the relationship of the social movement to the larger society and to other social movements. The social struc-

The pattern of social movements

ture and the prevailing belief system may suggest either that change can be brought about by changing the hearts and minds of the individual members or that individuals have little effect on the social order. A public definition of the movement as dangerous and subversive may force it to rely increasingly on a strategy of societal manipulation, including violent tactics. The opposition posed by a countermovement may have the same effect, making attempts at persuasion difficult and dangerous and pushing a nonviolent, noncoercive movement to meet force with force.

RELATIONSHIPS BETWEEN STRUCTURAL ELEMENTS

As a collectivity, a social movement is characterized by an emergent social structure and a culture. The social structure is reflected in the relationship between leaders and followers, the culture in the values and norms.

Unlike an association, a social movement does not possess legitimate leaders in the sense of being endowed with authority through some formal process. Leaders must constantly substantiate their claims to leadership by demonstrating the effectiveness of their influence on the followers. There is a relationship of reciprocal influence. The followers, for their part, lack institutionalized means of making their influence felt, such as referendums, legislatures, or periodic elections of leaders. They have no way of arriving at collective decisions except in occasional crowd situations. It falls to the leaders, therefore, to formulate policies and decisions that will strike a responsive note in their following. Having advanced such proposals, they must rely on either persuasion or coercion to create the illusion that these are collective decisions made by the entire movement. Propaganda thus becomes an important tool of leadership. Occasionally, a leadership group will employ coercion to prevent dissident elements from destroying the illusion that the leaders' decisions are merely statements of what the followers had already decided. The successful leader must, of course, be able to judge the mood and the attitudes of his potential followers in order to evoke a favourable response.

Interior structures   Propaganda is also important for maintaining morale and unity. A social movement lacks both the intimacy of a primary group and the formal boundaries of an association. The speeches and writings of leaders serve, in part, to assure the followers of the size, the strength, and the potential for success of the movement—matters difficult for the followers to observe directly. Movements do utilize interpersonal relations to enhance their unity, encouraging small groups of members to meet frequently in circumstances in which they can form personal ties. Mass meetings and parades, with the accompanying ritual, reduce the feelings of isolation that scattered members may experience. Demanding of members acts that constitute public declarations of allegiance serves as a commitment mechanism, making it difficult for the member to disassociate himself. Of extraordinary value to a movement is the example of martyrs whose fate arouses indignation in the members, symbolizes unreserved commitment, and lightens the burden of sacrifices.

The culture of a movement encompasses norms and values. Norms are standardized expectations of behaviour developed by members. Values include the program and the ideology. The program is the scheme of change, the new social order that the movement proposes to bring about. The ideology is a body of ideas justifying the program and the strategy of the movement. It usually includes a reinterpretation of history, a projection of the utopia that the success of the movement will introduce, a projection of the disastrous consequences of failure, and a reevaluation of population segments in terms of their relationship to the movement.

THE CAUSES OF SOCIAL MOVEMENTS

Both individual psychological states and the characteristics of a society at a particular time may be considered as causes of social movements.

Psychological factors. Individual factors are psychological states that either convince a person to join a movement or so weaken his commitment to conventional groups that he is willing to risk their disapproval because of his belief in an unpopular cause. Failure to achieve a satisfying status and identity within normal membership groups may be such a factor. The prestige and sense of belonging, which such a person may gain as a member of a social movement, may be even more important to him than the values of the movement. Marginality may be a source of spoiled identity. The marginal man, fitting satisfactorily into no group, may possess a sense of detachment that enables him to be unusually critical of the social order.

Alienation, feelings of powerlessness, hopelessness, and estrangement from society may predispose an individual to participation. Some scholars argue, however, that there are different kinds of alienation. One type leads merely to apathy and resignation. Political alienation, however, reflects a loss of faith in the political community and predisposes the individual to join a movement that challenges it.

Closely akin to these ideas is the theory of Hadley Cantril that participation represents a search for meaning. The need to find meaning in a world that does not seem to make sense might be interpreted as a variation of spoiled identity or alienation.

Deprivation, discontent, and frustration are frequently assumed to be sufficient causes for initiating or joining a social movement. The relationship is not a simple one, however. There is little evidence that the most deprived segments of a population are the most likely to participate in social movements. The concept of relative deprivation has been utilized to explain the fact that persons who could be much worse off than they are but still feel deprived in comparison with even more fortunate groups often play a prominent part in social movements.

Given that discontent and frustration are always present to some degree in every person's life, there must be some basis for the belief that it is possible to change the underlying conditions for a person to cast his lot with a social movement. In addition, there must be a sense that other people share his discontents and his belief in the possibility of change.

Social factors. An important task of the student of social movements is to identify those conditions under which social movements are most likely to arise. While the existence of widespread poverty and suffering might seem sufficient to give rise to efforts at reform, it must be emphasized again that some basis for hope must also exist to stir people to make the effort. Paradoxically, partial alleviation of conditions of deprivation may provide such a basis, serving as the impetus for the formation of a social movement just as things seem to be getting better. The success of other people similarly situated, such as victorious revolutionaries in a neighbouring nation, may be another source of hope.

Social movements and discontent   More general theories of the origin of social movements, such as those of Smelser, Turner, and Killian, suggest that social change may result in strains or conflicts in one or more crucial aspects of the social order. Normative strain arises when changing conditions create a situation in which the established norms no longer lead to the attainment of important, accepted values. Strain in values arises when the values themselves seem to interfere with the satisfaction of important needs of a segment of the society. This sort of strain often arises when different groups, such as immigrants, minorities, or the younger generation, develop values that conflict with those of more established groups. Even with little change in norms and values, changes in social structure reflected in the failure of important functionaries to play their roles adequately may lead to discontent.

Another type of change is a shift in the balance of power within a society. Strain and individual discontent may exist within a social system without leading to a social movement because the distribution of power seems to preclude effective action. A state of accommodation exists; but signs of weakening on the part of the powerful or the acquisition of new resources by the powerless changes the balance of power and gives rise to the hope that, combined with discontent, leads to a social movement.

Changes in the communications system of a society are of particular importance in facilitating the rise of social movements. A breakdown in communication, blocking the transmission of grievances to functionaries who can act on them, may lead to discontent and political alienation. An increase in the flow of messages between scattered members of a society leads to the socialization of unrest. The growth of mass-communication media, which allows people in many parts of a large society to know what others are thinking and doing, is especially conducive to the development of social movements. By the same token, restrictions on communications, such as censorship, are important techniques for preventing the mobilization of the discontented in social movements.

The general nature of the belief system existing in the culture of a society affects the likelihood that social movements will arise and defines the type that will occur. For example, a system that is essentially fatalistic is less conducive to social movements, particularly those with a strategy of societal manipulation, than one that emphasizes the perfectibility of man and his control over his own fate.

THE FUNCTIONS OF SOCIAL MOVEMENTS

Whatever the specific social factors that give rise to them and the individual factors that cause people to join, social movements have significant personal and social consequences.

Effects on members' lives

Wholehearted commitment to a social movement may produce temporary or even enduring changes in the personality of a member. This may go so far that to his friends and to himself he often seems to have become a quite different person. The mere fact of his belonging may give him a sense of security and importance. Since he is likely to form strong ties with the few with whom he works closely, he receives not only esteem but affection. He also derives a sense of security from the oversimplified version of reality often presented in the ideology; previous doubts and ambivalence are eliminated; he feels that he has found the truth. This fanaticism and single-mindedness makes life simpler for him. Other reference groups decrease in importance, and the difficult decisions required when a person has conflicting group loyalties are minimized. In addition, those who have felt insignificant in the past may find in a social movement opportunities for some degree of leadership. To the extent that a person makes a social movement his most important reference group, he gains a new identity.

In the process, society gains future leaders for whom the social movement has been a training school. Some men who have had their first experience of leadership in a labour movement or a civil rights movement have gone on to become important government officials.

Even when a movement is publicly defined as revolutionary, it has significant effects on public opinion. The socialization and focussing of the discontent of people whose grievances previously have been ignored formulates new issues around which publics develop. Politicians may be forced to take positions on issues that they prefer to avoid. The confrontations that a social movement often precipitates serve to sharpen an issue and lead to the process of polarization. The conflict between a movement and a countermovement may be paralleled by a raging debate in a public consisting of members who are not fully committed to either. In the long run, a social movement may introduce new values into a social order and, even though unrealized, the utopia that it promises may suggest new rights and goals that are cherished long after the movement is ended.

THE CONSEQUENCES OF SOCIAL MOVEMENTS

It has been suggested that the committed participant in a social movement undergoes a psychological reorganization. It is clear that his new sense of security and importance is acquired at the sacrifice of autonomy. As a loyal member he tends to let the leaders do his thinking for him, suppressing doubts as to the validity of the ideology and the wisdom of the leader's decision. He repeats their arguments in a dogmatic fashion; persons who are not in the movement find it difficult to debate with him since they start from different premises. His perception is selective in a different way from theirs. The ideology, for example, may lead him to view all governmental authorities as villains, while the ordinary citizen views them as legitimate leaders, some good, some bad. The end product of this surrender of autonomy may be an altered world view. Some things taken for granted before becoming part of the movement will never seem the same again, even after leaving the discipline of the movement.

The end products of social movements as collectivities attempting to change the social order cannot be analyzed simply in terms of victory or defeat. Defeat may come as a result of ruthless suppression of the movement or through widespread apathy. A movement may wither away because too few take it seriously and it does not develop enough power to force its program on society. Sometimes the remnants may linger for a long time as a cult, oriented inward toward the gratifications that the members obtain from participation but making no serious effort to change the social order.

Consequences of success

Success is most apparent when a movement manages to have its power legitimized as authority. In a successful revolution, the social movement becomes the new source of authority and respectability, and opposition to its values is defined as counterrevolutionary. In other instances, the movement achieves power through secession. Failing to compel acceptance of its values in the larger group or society, the members withdraw into a new social system in which they can attempt to implement the values.

A less obvious form of success is the institutionalization of the values or some important part of them. Accepting the legitimacy of the movement's values, the traditional associations in the society incorporate them into their own values and implement them without a transfer of authority to the social movement. Thus the Socialist Party has seen many of its proposals adopted by the two major political parties and the government of the United States without winning a major election or overthrowing the government. Sometimes, however, the social movement itself is institutionalized by being accorded authority as the legitimate custodian of the new values. The movement is then transformed into a bureaucratic association, as happened with the American labour movement of the early part of the 20th century or the Congress Party of India after the end of British rule.

THE FUTURE OF SOCIAL MOVEMENTS

The rapidity and complexity of social change throughout the world during the 19th and 20th centuries suggest that conditions will be conducive to the multiplication of social movements. The development and diffusion of technology, particularly automation, has made possible the industrialization of an ever-growing portion of the world, changing the living conditions of millions of people. This trend has been accompanied by the urbanization of a growing portion of the world's population. Some become more affluent and find life easier although more impersonal. Others find themselves displaced, poorer than before, and forced to live in the crowded slums of cities so large that they seem to defy efficient management. City governments as well as national governments appear to many people as increasingly bureaucratic, remote and unresponsive to the problems of the ordinary citizen. This may lead to a growth in political alienation and a decline of faith in the efficacy of political systems that purport to be democratic. At the same time, the expansion of radio and television makes possible more rapid and graphic diffusion of the discontent of "the wretched of the earth," to use the phrase of Frantz Fanon.

What are often identified as the two greatest threats to the survival of humanity must be considered in assessing the likelihood of an increase in the number of social movements. One is the population explosion, which leads to physical deprivation among an increasing number of people and presents a growing challenge to prevailing economic systems of distribution. The second is the threat of nuclear holocaust. Some observers of the worldwide youth movement suggest that young people who have grown up in a world capable of self-destruction have acquired a different world view from that of earlier generations.

A single major factor must be considered capable of limiting the increase of social movements and leading to the rapid suppression of those that do arise. This is the highly efficient means of social control, physical and psychological, now at the disposal of established political regimes. The totalitarian control of populations, which such means make possible, is not conducive to the rise of social movements.

BIBLIOGRAPHY. H. BLUMER, "Collective Behavior," in A.M. LEE (ed.), *Principles of Sociology*, 2nd ed. (1951), presents a widely accepted definition of the social movement as a form of collective behaviour. R.H. TURNER and L.M. KILLIAN, *Collective Behavior* (1957); L.M. KILLIAN, "Social Movements," in R.E.L. FARIS (ed.), *Handbook of Modern Sociology* (1964); K. and G. LANG, *Collective Dynamics* (1961); and N.J. SMELSER, *Theory of Collective Behavior* (1963), offer general sociological theories of types of social movements and the dynamics of their development. R. HEBERLE, *Social Movements* (1951), develops general sociological theories but focuses on the relationship between social movements and political parties. C.W. KING, *Social Movements in the United States* (1956), develops general principles from the sociological analysis of selected social movements. H. CANTRIL, *Psychology of Social Movements* (1941); H.H. TOCH, *The Social Psychology of Social Movements* (1965); S. MILGRAM and H.H. TOCH, "Social Movements," in G. LINDZEY and E. ARONSON (eds.), *Handbook of Social Psychology*, 2nd ed. (1968); and M. and W.C. SHERIF, *Social Psychology* (1969), represent theoretical approaches, placing greater emphasis on individual motivational and perceptual processes. L.P. EDWARDS, *The Natural History of Revolution* (1927); C. BRINTON, *The Anatomy of Revolution* (1938); and G.S. PETTEE, *The Process of Revolution* (1938), represent attempts to develop general theories of revolution as a type of social movement through the analyses of American and European revolutions. A similar effort based on studies of more recent revolutions in Latin America and the Middle East is found in C. LEIDEN and K.M. SCHMITT, *The Politics of Violence* (1968). There are numerous studies of particular social movements. Representative of those that include theoretical propositions, as well as historical descriptions are E.J. HOBSBAWN, *Primitive Rebels* (1959; U.S. title, *Social Bandits and Primitive Rebels*, 1960), a study of archaic forms of social movements in the 19th and 20th centuries; and G.F.E. RUDE, *The Crowd in History: A Study of Popular Disturbances in France and England, 1730–1848* (1964), an analysis of crowds in pre-industrial social movements in England and France; C.A. DUBOIS, *The 1870 Ghost Dance* (1939); and K.L.M. BURRIDGE, *Mambu: A Melanesian Millennium* (1960), studies of nativistic movements; sociological analyses of Communism and Nazism in P. SELZNICK, *The Organizational Weapon: A Study of Bolshevik Strategy and Tactics* (1952); and T.F. ABEL, *Why Hitler Came into Power* (1938); essays on the Algerian revolution in F. FANON, *L'an V de la révolution algérienne* (1963; Eng. trans., *Studies in a Dying Colonialism*, 1965); and sociological analyses of social movements in the U.S. in T.H. GREER, *American Social Reform Movements: Their Pattern Since 1865* (1949); L.M. KILLIAN, *The Impossible Revolution? Black Power and the American Dream* (1968); and J.H. SKOLNICK, *The Politics of Protest* (1969).

(L.M.K.)

Social Sciences, History of

Scope of the social or behavioral sciences

The social sciences, which deal with human behaviour in its social and cultural aspects, include the following disciplines: economics, political science, and sociology; social and cultural anthropology, social psychology, and social and economic geography; and those areas of education that deal with the social contexts of learning and the relation of the school to the social order. History is regarded by many of its practitioners as a social science, and certain areas of historical study today are almost indistinguishable from work done in the social sciences. Most historians, however, still consider history as one of the humanities. It is generally thought best, in any case, to consider history as marginal to the humanities and social sciences, since its distinctive insights and techniques pervade both spheres.

During the past quarter of a century, the term behavioral sciences has become more and more commonly used for the disciplines mentioned above. Those who favour this term do so in part because these disciplines are thus brought closer to some of the sciences, such as physical anthropology, linguistics, law, demography, and physiological psychology, which also deal with the behaviour of man but which do not properly fall among the social sciences. The term is also favoured by many because it carries with it implications of greater methodological rigour, a more definite empirical and behavioral base, and a freedom from moral presuppositions than is the case with the "social sciences," all of which arose in the 19th century when, despite the fashionable quest for scientific character, they were still heavily freighted with traditional philosophical and humanitarian interests. Whether the term behavioral sciences will in time supplant "social sciences" or whether it will, as neologisms so often have before, disappear without trace in a few years is impossible to say. For the purposes of this article, the two terms may be considered synonymous, though the preference throughout will be given to the older and still more universal "social sciences."

The concern in this article is much less with the conclusions and results of the individual social sciences than with their disciplinary identity in modern society. The concern is with the social sciences as vital elements in the aftermath of the two great revolutions, the political and industrial, which opened the 19th century, with the pattern the social sciences assumed in that century, and their extraordinary development in the 20th century. The concern will also be with the intellectual roots of the social sciences and their relation to other areas of thought.

The article is divided into the following sections:

I. The origins of the social sciences

Although, strictly speaking, the social sciences do not precede the 19th century—that is, as distinct and recognized disciplines of thought—one must go back farther in time for the origins of some of their fundamental ideas and objectives. In the largest sense, the origins go all the way back to the ancient Greeks and their rationalist inquiries into the nature of man, state, and morality. The heritage of both Greece and Rome is a powerful one in the history of social thought as it is in so many other areas of Western society. Very probably, apart from the initial Greek determination to study all things in the spirit of dispassionate and rational inquiry, there would be no social sciences today. True, there have been long periods of time, as during the Western Middle Ages, when the Greek rationalist temper was lacking. But the recovery of this temper, through texts of the great classical philosophers, is the very essence of the Renaissance and the Age of Reason in modern European history. With the Age of Reason, in the 17th and 18th centuries, one may begin.

HERITAGE OF THE MIDDLE AGES AND THE RENAISSANCE

The same impulses that led men in that age to explore the earth, the stellar regions, and the nature of matter led them also to explore the institutions around them: state, economy, religion, morality; above all, the nature of man himself. It was the fragmentation of medieval philosophy and theory, and, with this, the shattering of the medieval world view that had lain deep in thought until about the 16th century, that was the immediate basis of the rise of the several strands of specialized thought that were to become in time the social sciences.

Adverse effects of medieval theology Medieval theology, especially as it appears in St. Thomas Aquinas' *Summa theologiae*, contained and fashioned syntheses from ideas about man and society—ideas indeed that may be seen to be political, social, economic, anthropological, and geographical in their substance. But it was partly this close relation between medieval theology and ideas of the social sciences that accounts for the longer time it took these ideas—by comparison with the ideas of the physical sciences—to achieve what one would today call scientific character. From the time of the great Roger Bacon in the 13th century, there were at least some rudiments of physical science that were largely independent of medieval theology and philosophy. Historians of physical science have no difficulty in tracing the continuation of this experimental tradition, primitive and irregular though it was by later standards, throughout the Middle Ages. Side by side with the kinds of experiment made notable by Roger Bacon were impressive changes in technology through the medieval period and then, in striking degree, in the Renaissance. Efforts to improve agricultural productivity; the rising utilization of gunpowder, with consequent development of guns and the problems that they presented in ballistics; growing trade, leading to increased use of ships and improvements in the arts of navigation, including use of telescopes; and the whole range of such mechanical arts in the Middle Ages and Renaissance as architecture, engineering, optics, and the construction of watches and clocks—all of this put a high premium on a pragmatic and operational understanding of at least the simpler principles of mechanics, physics, astronomy, and, in time, chemistry.

In short, by the time of Copernicus and Galileo in the 16th century, a fairly broad substratum of physical science existed, largely empirical but not without theoretical implications on which the edifice of modern physical science could be built. It is notable that the empirical foundations of physiology were being established in the studies of the human body being conducted in medieval schools of medicine and, as the career of Leonardo Da Vinci so resplendently illustrates, among artists of the Renaissance, whose interest in accuracy and detail of painting and sculpture led to their careful studies of human anatomy.

Very different was the beginning of the social sciences. In the first place, the church, throughout the Middle Ages and even into the Renaissance and Reformation, was much more attentive to what scholars wrote and thought about man's mind and his behaviour in society than it was toward what was being studied and written in the physical sciences. From the church's point of view, while it might be important to see to it that thought on the physical world corresponded as far as possible to what Scripture said—witnessed, for example, in the famous questioning of Galileo—it was far more important that such correspondence exist in matters affecting the nature of man, his mind, spirit, and soul. Nearly all the subjects and questions that would form the bases of the social sciences in later centuries were tightly woven into the fabric of medieval scholasticism, and it was not easy for even the boldest minds to break this fabric.

Adverse effects of reverence for classics and Cartesianism Then, when the hold of scholasticism did begin to wane, two fresh influences, equally powerful, came on the scene to prevent anything comparable to the pragmatic and empirical foundations of the physical sciences from forming in the study of man and society. The first was the immense appeal of the Greek classics during the Renaissance, especially those of the philosophers Plato and Aristotle. A great deal of social thought during the Renaissance was little more than gloss or commentary on the Greek classics. One sees this throughout the 15th and 16th centuries.

Second, in the 17th century appeared the powerful influence of the philosopher René Descartes. Cartesianism, as his philosophy was called, declared that the proper approach to understanding of the world, including man and society, was through a few simple, fundamental ideas of reality and, then, rigorous, almost geometrical deduction of more complex ideas and eventually of large, encompassing theories, from these simple ideas, all of which, Descartes insisted, were the stock of common sense—the mind that is common to all human beings at birth. It would be hard to exaggerate the impact of Cartesianism on social and political and moral thought during the century and a half following publication of his *Discourse on Method* and his *Meditations*. Through the Age of Reason and down through the Enlightenment in the later 18th century, the spell of Cartesianism was cast on nearly all those who were concerned with the problems of the nature of man and society.

Both of these great influences, reverence for the classics and fascination with the geometrical–deductive procedures advocated by Descartes must be seen from today's vantage point as among the major influences retarding the development of a science of society comparable to the science of the physical world. It is not as though data were not available in the 17th and 18th centuries. The emergence of the national state carried with it evergrowing bureaucracies concerned with gathering information, chiefly for taxation, census, and trade purposes, which might have been employed in much the same way that physical scientists employed their data. The voluminous and widely published accounts of the great voyages that had begun in the 15th century, the records of soldiers, explorers, and missionaries who perforce had been brought into often long and close contact with primitive and other non-Western peoples, provided still another great reservoir of data, all of which might have been utilized in scientific ways as such data were to be utilized a century or two later in the social sciences. Such, however, was the continuing spell cast by the texts of the classics and by the strictly rationalistic, overwhelmingly deductive procedures of the Cartesians that, down until the beginning of the 19th century, these and other empirical materials were used, if at all, solely for illustrative purposes in the writings of the social philosophers.

HERITAGE OF THE ENLIGHTENMENT

There is also the fact that, especially in the 18th century, reform and even revolution were often in the air. The purpose of a great many social philosophers was by no means restricted to philosophic, much less scientific, understanding of man and society. The dead hand of the Middle Ages seemed to many vigorous minds in western Europe the principal force to be combatted, through critical reason, enlightenment, and, where necessary, major reform or revolution. One may properly account a great deal of this new spirit to the rise of humanitarianism in modern Europe and in other parts of the world and to the spread of literacy, the rise in the standard of living, and the recognition that poverty and oppression need not be the fate of the masses. The fact remains, however, that social reform and social science have different organizing principles, and the very fact that for a long time, down indeed through a good part of the 19th century, social reform and social science were regarded as pretty much the same thing could not have helped but retard the development of the latter.

Nevertheless, it would be wrong to discount the significant contributions to the social sciences that were made during the 17th and 18th centuries. The first and greatest of these was the spreading ideal of a science of society, an ideal fully as widespread by the 18th century as the ideal of a physical science. Second was the rising awareness of the multiplicity and variety of human experience in the world. Ethnocentrism and parochialism, as states of mind, were more and more difficult for educated people to maintain given the immense amount of information about—or, more important, interest in—non-Western peoples, the results of trade and exploration. Third was the spreading sense of the social or cultural character of human behaviour in society—that is, its purely historical or conventional, rather than biological, basis. A science of society, in short, was no mere appendage of biology but was instead a distinct discipline, or set of disciplines, with its own distinctive subject matter.

Ideas of structure and developmental change

To these may be added two other very important contributions of the 17th and 18th centuries, each of great theoretical importance. The first was the idea of structure. First seen in the writings of such philosophers as Hobbes, Locke, and Rousseau with reference to the political structure of the state, it had spread by the mid-18th century to highlight the economic writings of the Physiocrats and Adam Smith. The idea of structure can also be seen in certain works relating to man's psychology and, at opposite reach, to the whole of civil society. The ideas of structure that were borrowed from both the physical and biological sciences were fundamental to the conceptions of political, economic, and social structure that took shape in the 17th and 18th centuries. And these conceptions of structure have in many instances, subject only to minor changes, come down to 20th-century social science.

The second major theoretical idea was that of developmental change. Its ultimate roots in Western thought, like those indeed of the whole idea of structure, go back to the Greeks, if not earlier. But it is in the 18th century, above all others, that the philosophy of developmentalism took shape, forming a preview, so to speak, of the social evolutionism of the next century. What was said by such writers as Condorcet, Rousseau, and Adam Smith was that the present is an outgrowth of the past, the result of a long line of development in time, and, furthermore, a line of development that has been caused, not by God or fortuitous factors, but by conditions and causes immanent in human society. Despite a fairly widespread belief that the idea of social development is a product of prior discovery of biological evolution, the facts are the reverse. Well before any clear idea of genetic speciation existed in European biology, there was a very clear idea of what might be called social speciation—that is, the emergence of one institution from another in time and of the whole differentiation of function and structure that goes with this emergence.

As has been suggested, these and other seminal ideas were contained for the most part in writings, the primary function of which was attack on the existing order of government and society in western Europe. Another way of putting the matter is to say that they were clear and acknowledged parts of political and social idealism—using that word in its largest sense. Hobbes, Locke, Rousseau, Montesquieu, Adam Smith, and other major philosophers had as vivid and energizing sense of the ideal—ideal state, ideal economy, ideal civil society—as any earlier utopian writer. These men were, without exception, committed to visions of the good or ideal society. Their interest in the "natural"—that is, natural morality, religion, economy, or education, in contrast to the merely conventional and historically derived—sprang as much from the desire to hold a glass up to a surrounding society that they disliked as from any dispassionate urge simply to find out what man and society are made of. The fact remains, however, that the ideas that were to prove decisive in the 19th century, so far as the social sciences were concerned, arose during the two centuries preceding.

II. The 19th century

Effects of the democratic and industrial revolutions

The fundamental ideas, themes, and problems of the social sciences in the 19th century are best understood as responses to the problem of order that was created in men's minds by the weakening of the old order, or European society, under the twin blows of the French Revolution and the Industrial Revolution. The breakup of the old order—an order that had rested on kinship, land, social class, religion, local community, and monarchy—set free, as it were, the complex elements of status, authority, and wealth that had been for so long consolidated. In the same way that the history of 19th-century politics, industry, and trade is basically about the practical efforts of human beings to reconsolidate these elements, so the history of 19th-century social thought is

about theoretical efforts to reconsolidate them—that is, to give them new contexts of meaning.

In terms of the immediacy and sheer massiveness of impact on human thought and values, it would be difficult to find revolutions of comparable magnitude in human history. The political, social, and cultural changes that began in France and England at the very end of the 18th century spread almost immediately through Europe and the Americas in the 19th century and then on to Asia, Africa, and Oceania in the 20th. The effects of the two revolutions, the one overwhelmingly democratic in thrust, the other industrial–capitalist, have been to undermine, shake, or topple institutions that had endured for centuries, even millennia, and with them systems of authority, status, belief, and community.

It is easy today to deprecate the suddenness, the cataclysmic nature, the overall revolutionary effect of these two changes and to seek to subordinate results to longer, deeper tendencies of more gradual change in western Europe. But as many recent historians have pointed out, there was to be seen, and seen by a great many sensitive minds of that day, a dramatic and convulsive quality to the changes that cannot properly be subsumed to the slower processes of continuous evolutionary change. What is crucial, in any event, from the point of view of the history of the social thought of the period, is how the changes were actually envisaged at the time. By a large number of social philosophers and social scientists, in all spheres, those changes were regarded as nothing less than of earthquake intensity.

The coining or redefining of words is an excellent indication of men's perceptions of change in a given historical period. A large number of words taken for granted today came into being in the period marked by the final decade or two of the 18th century and the first quarter of the 19th. Among these are: industry, industrialist, democracy, class, middle class, ideology, intellectual, rationalism, humanitarian, atomistic, masses, commercialism, proletariat, collectivism, equalitarian, liberal, conservative, scientist, utilitarian, bureaucracy, capitalism, and crisis. Some of these words were invented; others reflect new and very different meanings given to old ones. All alike bear witness to the transformed character of the European social landscape as this landscape loomed up to the leading minds of the age. And all these words bear witness too to the emergence of new social philosophies and, most pertinent to the subject of this article, the social sciences as they are known today.

THEMES EMANATING FROM THE SOCIAL REVOLUTIONS

It is illuminating to mention a few of the major themes in social thought in the 19th century that were almost the direct results of the democratic and industrial revolutions. It should be borne in mind that these themes are to be seen in the philosophical and literary writing of the age as well as in social thought.

Effects of population growth

First, there was the great increase in population. Between 1750 and 1850 the population of Europe went from 140,000,000 to 266,000,000; in the world from 728,000,000 to well over 1,000,000,000. It was an English clergyman-economist, Thomas Malthus, who, in his famous *Essay on Population*, first marked the enormous significance to human welfare of this increase. With the diminution of historic checks on population growth, chiefly those of high mortality rates—a diminution that was, as Malthus realized, one of the rewards of technical progress—there were no easily foreseeable limits to growth of population. And such growth, he stressed, could only upset the traditional balance between population, which Malthus described as growing at geometrical rate, and food supply, which he declared could grow only at arithmetical rate. Not all social scientists in the century took the pessimistic view of the matter that Malthus did but few if any were indifferent to the impact of explosive increase in population on economy, government, and society.

Second, there was the condition of labour. It may be possible to see this condition in the early 19th century as in fact better than the condition of the rural masses at earlier times. But the important point is that to a large number of writers in the 19th century it seemed worse and was defined as worse. The wrenching of large numbers of people from the older and protective contexts of village, guild, parish, and family, and their massing in the new centres of industry, forming slums, living in common squalor and wretchedness, their wages generally behind cost of living, their families growing larger, their standard of living becoming lower, as it seemed—all of this is a frequent theme in the social thought of the century. Economics indeed became known as the "dismal science," because economists, from David Ricardo to Karl Marx, could see little likelihood of the condition of labour improving under capitalism.

Third, there was the transformation of property. Not only was more and more property to be seen as industrial —manifest in the factories, business houses, and workshops of the period—but also the very nature of property was changing. Whereas for most of the history of mankind property had been "hard," visible only in concrete possessions—land and money—now the more intangible kinds of property such as shares of stock, negotiable equities of all kinds, and bonds were assuming ever greater influence in the economy. This led, as was early realized, to the dominance of financial interests, to speculation, and to a general widening of the gulf between the propertied and the masses. The change in the character of property made easier the concentration of property, the accumulation of immense wealth in the hands of a relative few, and, not least, the possibility of economic domination of politics and culture. It should not be thought that only socialists saw property in this light. From Edmund Burke through Auguste Comte, Frédéric Le Play, and John Stuart Mill down to Karl Marx, Max Weber, and Émile Durkheim, one finds conservatives and liberals looking at the impact of this change in analogous ways.

Effects of urbanization and technological change

Fourth, there was urbanization—the sudden increase in the number of towns and cities in western Europe and the increase in number of persons living in the historic towns and cities. Whereas in earlier centuries, the city had been regarded almost uniformly as a setting of civilization, culture, and freedom of mind, now one found more and more writers aware of the other side of cities: the atomization of human relationships, broken families, the sense of the mass, of anonymity, alienation, and disrupted values. Sociology particularly among the social sciences turned its attention to the problems of urbanization. The contrast between the more organic type of community found in rural areas and the more mechanical and individualistic society of the cities is a basic contrast in sociology, one that was given much attention by such pioneers in Europe as the French sociologists Frédéric Le Play and Émile Durkheim; the German sociologists Ferdinand Tönnies, Georg Simmel, and Max Weber; the Belgian statistician Adolphe Quetelet; and, in America, by the sociologists Charles H. Cooley and Robert E. Park.

Fifth, there was technology. With the spread of mechanization, first in the factories, then in agriculture, social thinkers could see possibilities of a rupture of the historic relation between man and nature, between man and man, even between man and God. To thinkers as politically different as Thomas Carlyle and Karl Marx, technology seemed to lead to dehumanization of the worker and to exercise of a new kind of tyranny over human life. Marx, though, far from despising technology, thought the advent of socialism would counteract all this. Alexis de Tocqueville declared that technology, and especially technical specialization of work, was more degrading to man's mind and spirit than even political tyranny. It was thus in the 19th century that the opposition to technology on moral, psychological, and aesthetic grounds first made its appearance in Western thought.

Sixth, there was the factory system. The importance of this to 19th-century thought has been intimated above. Suffice it to add that along with urbanization and spreading mechanization, the system of work whereby masses of workers left home and family to work long hours in the factories became a major theme of social thought as well as of social reform.

Seventh, and finally, mention is to be made of the development of political masses—that is, the slow but inexorable widening of franchise and electorate through which ever larger numbers of persons became aware of themselves as voters and participants in the political process. This too is a major theme in social thought, to be seen most luminously perhaps in Tocqueville's *Democracy in America*, a classic written in the 1830s that took not merely America but democracy everywhere as its subject. Tocqueville saw the rise of the political masses, more especially the immense power that could be wielded by the masses, as the single greatest threat to individual freedom and cultural diversity in the ages ahead. Effects of the rise of the masses

These, then, are the principal themes in the 19th-century writing that may be seen as direct results of the two great revolutions. As themes, they are to be found not only in the social sciences but, as noted above, in a great deal of the philosophical and literary writing of the century. In their respective ways, the philosophers Hegel, Coleridge, and Emerson were as struck by the consequences of the revolutions as were any social scientists. So too were such novelists as Balzac and Dickens.

THE NEW IDEOLOGIES AND PHILOSOPHIES

One other point must be emphasized about these themes. They became, almost immediately in the 19th century, the bases of new ideologies. How men reacted to the currents of democracy and industrialism stamped them conservative, liberal, or radical. On the whole, with rarest exceptions, liberals welcomed the two revolutions, seeing in their forces opportunity for freedom and welfare never before known to mankind. The liberal view of society was overwhelmingly democratic, capitalist, industrial, and, of course, individualistic. The case is somewhat different with conservatism and radicalism in the century. Conservatives, beginning with Edmund Burke, continuing through Hegel and Matthew Arnold down to such minds as John Ruskin later in the century, disliked both democracy and industrialism, preferring the kind of tradition, authority, and civility that had been, in their minds, displaced by the two revolutions. Theirs was a retrospective view, but it was a nonetheless influential one, affecting a number of the central social scientists of the century, among them Auguste Comte and Tocqueville and later Max Weber and Émile Durkheim. The radicals accepted democracy but only in terms of its extension to all areas of society and its eventual annihilation of any form of authority that did not spring directly from the people as a whole. And although the radicals, for the most part, accepted the phenomenon of industrialism, especially technology, they were uniformly antagonistic to capitalism.

These ideological consequences of the two revolutions proved extremely important to the social sciences, for it would be difficult to identify a social scientist in the century—as it would a philosopher or a humanist—who was not, in some degree at least, caught up in ideological currents. In referring to such minds as Saint-Simon, Comte, Le Play among sociologists, to Ricardo, the Frenchman Jean-Baptiste Say, and Marx among economists, to Jeremy Bentham and John Austin among political scientists, even to anthropologists like the Englishman Edward B. Tylor and the American Lewis Henry Morgan, one has before one men who were engaged not merely in the study of society but also in often strongly partisan ideology. Some were liberals, some conservatives, others radicals. All drew from the currents of ideology that had been generated by the two great revolutions.

It is important also to identify three other powerful tendencies of thought that influenced all of the social sciences. The first is a positivism that was not merely an appeal to science but almost reverence for science; the second, humanitarianism; the third, the philosophy of evolution.

The Positivist appeal of science was to be seen everywhere. The rise of the ideal of science in the Age of Reason was noted above. The 19th century saw the virtual institutionalization of this ideal—possibly even canonization. The great aim was that of dealing with moral values, institutions, and all social phenomena through the same fundamental methods that could be seen so lumi- Effects of Positivism nously in such areas as physics and biology. Prior to the 19th century, no very clear distinction had been made between philosophy and science, and the term philosophy was even preferred by those working directly with physical materials, seeking laws and principles in the fashion of a Newton or Harvey—that is, by persons whom one would now call scientists.

In the 19th century, in contrast, the distinction between philosophy and science became an overwhelming one. Virtually every area of man's thought and behaviour was thought by a rising number of persons to be amenable to scientific investigation in precisely the same degree that physical data were. More than anyone else, it was Comte who heralded the idea of the scientific treatment of social behaviour. His *Cours de philosophie positive,* published in six volumes between 1830 and 1842, sought to demonstrate irrefutably not merely the possibility but the inevitability of a science of man, one for which Comte coined the word "sociology" and that would do for man the social being exactly what biology had already done for man the biological animal. But Comte was far from alone. There were many in the century to join in his celebration of science for the study of society.

Humanitarianism, though a very distinguishable current of thought in the century, was closely related to the idea of a science of society. For the ultimate purpose of social science was thought by almost everyone to be the welfare of society, the improvement of its moral and social condition. Humanitarianism, strictly defined, is the institutionalization of compassion; it is the extension of welfare and succour from the limited areas in which these had historically been found, chiefly family and village, to society at large. One of the most notable and also distinctive aspects of the 19th century was the constantly rising number of persons, almost wholly from the middle class, who worked directly for the betterment of society. In the many projects and proposals for relief of the destitute, improvement of slums, amelioration of the plight of the insane, the indigent, and imprisoned, and other afflicted minorities could be seen the spirit of humanitarianism at work. All kinds of associations were formed, including temperance associations, groups and societies for the abolition of slavery and of poverty and for the improvement of literacy, among other objectives. Nothing like the 19th-century spirit of humanitarianism had ever been seen before in western Europe—not even in France during the Enlightenment, where interest in mankind's salvation tended to be more intellectual than humanitarian in the strict sense. Humanitarianism and social science were reciprocally related in their purposes. All that helped the cause of the one could be seen as helpful to the other.

Effects of evolutionary theory

The third of the intellectual influences is that of evolution. It affected every one of the social sciences, each of which was as much concerned with the development of things as with their structures. An interest in development was to be found in the 18th century, as noted earlier. But this interest was small and specialized compared with 19th-century theories of social evolution. The impact of Charles Darwin's *Origin of Species,* published in 1859, was of course great and further enhanced the appeal of the evolutionary view of things. But it is very important to recognize that ideas of social evolution had their own origins and contexts. The evolutionary works of such social scientists as Comte, Herbert Spencer, and Marx had been completed, or well begun, before publication of Darwin's work. The important point, in any event, is that the idea or the philosophy of evolution was in the air throughout the century, as profoundly contributory to the establishment of sociology as a systematic discipline in the 1830s as to such fields as geology, astronomy, and biology. Evolution was as permeative an idea as the Trinity had been in medieval Europe.

THE DEVELOPMENT OF THE SEPARATE DISCIPLINES

Unification versus specialization

Among the disciplines that formed the social sciences, two contrary, for a time equally powerful, tendencies at first dominated them. The first was the drive toward unification, toward a single, master social science, whatever it might be called. The second tendency was toward special-

ization of the individual social sciences. If, clearly, it is the second that has triumphed, with the results to be seen in the disparate, sometimes jealous, highly specialized disciplines seen today, the first was not without great importance and must also be examined.

What emerges from the critical rationalism of the 18th century is not, in the first instance, a conception of need for a plurality of social sciences, but rather for a single science of society that would take its place in the hierarchy of the sciences that included the fields of astronomy, physics, chemistry, and biology. When, in the 1820s, Comte wrote calling for a new science, one with man the social animal as the subject, he assuredly had but a single, encompassing science of society in mind—not a congeries of disciplines, each concerned with some single aspect of man's behaviour in society. The same was true of Bentham, Marx, and Spencer. All these minds, and there were many others to join them, saw the study of society as a unified enterprise. They would have scoffed, and on occasion did, at any notion of a separate economics, political science, sociology, and so on. Society is an indivisible thing, they would have argued; so, too, must be the study of society.

It was, however, the opposite tendency of specialization or differentiation that won out. No matter how the century began, or what were the dreams of a Comte, Spencer, or Marx, when the 19th century ended, not one but several distinct, competitive social sciences were to be found. Aiding this process was the development of the colleges and universities. With hindsight it might be said that the cause of universities in the future would have been strengthened, as would the cause of the social sciences, had there come into existence, successfully, a single curriculum, undifferentiated by field, for the study of society. What in fact happened, however, was the opposite. The growing desire for an elective system, for a substantial number of academic specializations, and for differentiation of academic degrees, contributed strongly to the differentiation of the social sciences. This was first and most strongly to be seen in Germany, where, from about 1815 on, all scholarship and science were based in the universities and where competition for status among the several disciplines was keen. But by the end of the century the same phenomenon of specialization was to be found in the United States (where admiration for the German system was very great in academic circles) and, in somewhat less degree, in France and England. Admittedly, the differentiation of the social sciences in the 19th century was but one aspect of a larger process that was to be seen as vividly in the physical sciences and the humanities. No major field escaped the lure of specialization of investigation, and clearly, a great deal of the sheer bulk of learning that passed from the 19th to the 20th century was the direct consequence of this specialization.

Economics. It was economics that first attained the status of a single and separate science, in ideal at least, among the social sciences. That autonomy and self-regulation that the Physiocrats and Adam Smith had found, or thought they had found, in the processes of wealth, in the operation of prices, rents, interest, and wages during the 18th century became the basis of a separate and distinctive economics—or, as it was often called, "political economy"—in the 19th. Hence the emphasis upon what came to be widely called laissez-faire. If, as it was argued, the processes of wealth operate naturally in terms of their own built-in mechanisms, then not only should these be studied separately but they should, in any wise polity, be left alone by government and society. This was, in general, the overriding emphasis of such thinkers as David Ricardo, John Stuart Mill, and Nassau William Senior in England, of Frédéric Bastiat and Jean-Baptiste Say in France, and, somewhat later, the Austrian school of Karl Menger. This emphasis is today called "classical" in economics, and it is even now, though with substantial modifications, a strong position in the field.

Classical economists and socialists

There were almost from the beginning, however, economists who diverged sharply from this laissez-faire, classical view. In Germany especially there were the so-called historical economists. They proceeded less from the discipline of historiography than from the presuppositions of social evolution, referred to above. Such men as Wilhelm Roscher and Karl Knies in Germany tended to dismiss the assumptions of timelessness and universality regarding economic behaviour that were almost axiomatic among the followers of Adam Smith, and they strongly insisted upon the developmental character of capitalism, evolving in a long series of stages from other types of economy.

Also prominent throughout the century were those who came to be called the Socialists. They too repudiated any notion of timelessness and universality in capitalism and its elements of private property, competition, and profit. Not only was this system but a passing stage of economic developments; it could be—and, as Marx was to emphasize, would be—shortly supplanted by a more humane and also realistic economic system based upon cooperation, the people's ownership of the means of production, and planning that would eradicate the vices of competition and conflict.

Political science. Rivalling economics as a discipline during the century was political science. The line of systematic interest in the state that had begun in modern Europe with Machiavelli, Hobbes, Locke, and Rousseau, among others, widened and lengthened in the 19th century, the consequence of the two revolutions. If the Industrial Revolution seemed to supply all the problems frustrating the existence of a stable and humane society, the political-democratic revolution could be seen as containing many of the answers to these problems. It was the democratic revolution, especially in France, that created the vision of a political government responsible for all aspects of human society and, most important, possessed the power to wield this responsibility. This power, known as sovereignty, could be seen as holding the same relation to political science in the 19th century that capital held to economics. To a very large number of political scientists, the aim of the discipline was essentially that of analyzing the varied properties of sovereignty. There was a strong tendency on the part of such political scientists as Bentham, Austin, and Mill in England and Francis Lieber and Woodrow Wilson in the United States to see the state and its claimed sovereignty over human lives in much the same terms in which classical economists saw capitalism.

Among political scientists there was the same historical-evolutionary dissent from this view, however, that existed in economics. Such writers as Sir Henry Maine in England, Numa Fustel de Coulanges in France, and Otto von Gierke in Germany declared that state and sovereignty were not timeless and universal nor the results of some "social contract" envisaged by such philosophers as Locke and Rousseau but, rather, structures formed slowly through developmental or historical processes. Hence the strong interest, especially in the late 19th century, in the origins of political institutions in kinship, village, and caste, and in the successive stages of development that have characterized these institutions. In political science, as in economics, in short, the classical analytical approach was strongly rivalled by the evolutionary. Both approaches go back to the 18th century in their fundamental elements, but what is seen in the 19th century is the greater systematization and the much wider range of data employed.

Anthropology. In the 19th century, anthropology also attained clear identity as a discipline. Strictly defined as "the science of man," it could be seen as superseding other specialized disciplines such as economics and political science. In practice and from the beginning, however, anthropology concerned itself overwhelmingly with primitive man. On the one hand was physical anthropology, concerned chiefly with the evolution of man as a biological species, with the successive forms and protoforms of the species, and with genetic systems such as stocks and races in the world. On the other hand was social and cultural anthropology: here the interest was in the full range of man's institutions but confined to those found in fact among existing preliterate or "primitive" peoples in Africa, Oceania, Asia, and the Americas. Above all other concepts, "culture" was the central element of this great area of anthropology, or ethnology, as it was often called

Concern with sovereignty

Anthropological focus on primitive man and evolutionism

to distinguish it from physical anthropology. Culture, as a concept, called attention to the nonbiological, nonracial, noninstinctual basis of the greater part of what one calls civilization: its values, techniques, ideas in all spheres. Culture, as defined in Tylor's landmark work of 1871, *Primitive Culture*, is the part of man's behaviour that is learned. From anthropology more than from any other single social science has come the emphasis on the cultural foundations of man's behaviour and thought in society.

Scarcely less than political science or economics, anthropology shared in the themes of the two revolutions and their impact on the world. If the data that anthropologists actually worked with were generally in the remote areas of the world, it was the effects of the two revolutions that, in a sense, kept opening up these parts of the world to more and more systematic inquiry. And, as was true of the other social sciences, the cultural anthropologists were immersed in problems of economics, polity, social class, and community, albeit among preliterate rather than "modern" peoples.

Overwhelmingly, without major exception indeed, the science of anthropology was evolutionary in thrust in the 19th century. Edward B. Tylor and Sir John Lubbock in England, Lewis Henry Morgan in the United States, Adolf Bastian and Theodor Waitz in Germany, and all others in the main line of the study of primitive culture saw existing native societies in the world as prototypes of their own "primitive ancestors," fossilized remains, so to speak, of stages of development that western Europe had once gone through. Despite the vast array of data compiled on non-Western cultures, the same basic European-centred objectives are to be found among anthropologists as among other social scientists in the century. Almost universally, then, the modern West was regarded as the latest point in a line of progress that was single and unilinear and on which all other peoples in the world could be fitted as illustrations, as it were, of Western man's own past.

Sociology. Sociology came into being in precisely these terms, and during much of the century it was not easy to distinguish between a great deal of so-called sociology and social or cultural anthropology. Even if almost no sociologists in the century made empirical studies of primitive peoples, as did the anthropologists, their interest in the origin, development, and probable future of mankind was not less great than what could be found in the writings of the anthropologists. It was Auguste Comte who coined the word sociology, and he used it to refer to what he imagined would be a single, all-encompassing, science of society that would take its place at the top of the hierarchy of sciences—a hierarchy that Comte saw as including astronomy (the oldest of the sciences historically) at the bottom and with physics, chemistry, and biology rising in that order to sociology, the latest and grandest of the sciences. There was no thought in Comte's mind —nor was there in the mind of Herbert Spencer, whose general view of sociology was very much like Comte's— of there being other, competing social sciences. Sociology would be to the whole of the social world what each of the other great sciences was to its appropriate sphere of reality.

Both Comte and Spencer believed that civilization as a whole was the proper subject of sociology. Their works were concerned, for the most part, with describing the origins and development of civilization and also of each of its major institutions. Both declared sociology's main divisions to be "statics" and "dynamics," the former concerned with processes of order in society, the latter with processes of evolutionary change in society. Both men also saw all existing societies in the world as reflective of the successive stages through which Western society had advanced in time over a period of tens of thousands of years.

Not all sociologists in the 19th century conceived their discipline in this light, however. Side by side with the "grand" view represented by Comte and Spencer were those in the century who were primarily interested in the social problems that they saw around them—conse-

The "grand" view of sociology

The
"problems"
view of
sociology

quences, as they interpreted them, of the two revolutions, the industrial and democratic. Thus in France just after midcentury, Frédéric Le Play published a monumental study of the social aspects of the working classes in Europe, *Les Ouvriers européens*, which compared families and communities in all parts of Europe and even other parts of the world. Alexis de Tocqueville, especially in the second volume of his *Democracy in America* (1835), provided an account of the customs, social structures, and institutions in America, dealing with these—and also with the social and psychological problems of Americans in that day—as aspects of the impact of the democratic and industrial revolutions upon traditional society.

At the very end of the 19th century, in both France and Germany, there appeared some of the works in sociology that were to prove most lasting in their effects upon 20th-century sociology. Ferdinand Tönnies, in his *Gemeinschaft und Gesellschaft* (1887; translated as *Community and Society*), sought to explain all major social problems in the West as the consequence of the West's historical transition from the communal, status-based, concentric society of the Middle Ages to the more individualistic, impersonal, and large-scale society of the democratic–industrial period. In general terms, allowing for individual variations of theme, these were the views of Max Weber, Georg Simmel, and Émile Durkheim (all of whom also wrote in the late 19th and early 20th century). These were the men who, starting from the problems of Western society that could be traced to the effects of the two revolutions, did the most to establish the discipline of sociology as it is found for the most part in the 20th century.

Social psychology. Social psychology as a distinct discipline also originated in the 19th century, although its outlines were perhaps somewhat less clear than was true of the other social sciences. The close relation of the human mind to the social order, its dependence upon education and other forms of socialization, was well-known in the 18th century. In the 19th century, however, an ever more systematic discipline came into being to uncover the social and cultural roots of human psychology and also the several types of "collective mind" that analysis of different cultures and societies in the world might reveal. In Germany, Moritz Lazarus and Wilhelm Wundt sought to fuse the study of psychological phenomena with analyses of whole cultures. Folk psychology, as it was called, did not, however, last very long in scientific esteem.

Early
group
studies

Much more esteemed, and closer to 20th-century conceptions of social psychology, were the works of such men as Gabriel Tarde, Gustave Le Bon, Lucien Lévy-Bruhl, and Émile Durkheim in France and Georg Simmel in Germany (all of whom also wrote in the early 20th century). Here, in concrete, often highly empirical studies of small groups, associations, crowds, and other aggregates (rather than in the main line of psychology during the century, which tended to be sheer philosophy at one extreme and a variant of physiology at the other) are to be found the real beginnings of social psychology. Although the point of departure in each of the studies was the nature of association, they dealt, in one degree or other, with the internal processes of psychosocial interaction, the operation of attitudes and judgments, and the social basis of personality and thought—in short, with those phenomena that would, in the 20th century, be the substance of social psychology as a formal discipline.

Social statistics and social geography. Two final manifestations of the social sciences in the 19th century are social statistics and social (or human) geography. At that time, neither achieved the notability and acceptance in colleges and universities that such fields as political science and economics did. Both, however, were as clearly visible by the latter part of the century as any of the other social sciences. And both were to exert a great deal of influence on the other social sciences by the beginning of the 20th century: social statistics on sociology and social psychology pre-eminently; social geography on political science, economics, history, and certain areas of anthropology, especially those areas dealing with the dispersion

of races and the diffusion of cultural elements. In social statistics the key figure of the century was a Belgian, Adolphe Quetelet, who was the first, on any systematic basis, to call attention to the kinds of structured behaviour that could be observed and identified only through statistical means. It was Quetelet who brought into prominence the momentous concept of "the average man" and his behaviour. The two major figures in social or human geography in the century were Friedrich Ratzel in Germany and Paul Vidal de la Blache in France. Both broke completely with the crude environmentalism of earlier centuries, which had sought to show how topography and climate actually determine human behaviour, and they substituted the more subtle and sophisticated insights into the relationships of land, sea, and climate on the one hand and, on the other, the varied types of culture and human association that are to be found on earth.

In summary, by the end of the 19th century all the major social sciences had achieved a distinctiveness, an importance widely recognized, and were, especially in the cases of economics and political science, fully accepted as disciplines in the universities. Most important, they were generally accepted as sciences in their own right rather than as minions of philosophy.

III. The 20th century

What is seen in the 20th century is not only an intensification and spread of earlier tendencies in the social sciences but also the development of many new tendencies that, in the aggregate, make the 19th century seem by comparison one of quiet unity and simplicity in the social sciences.

In the 20th century, the processes first generated by the democratic and industrial revolutions have gone on virtually unchecked in Western society, penetrating more and more spheres of once traditional morality and culture, leaving their impress on more and more nations, regions, and localities. Equally important, perhaps in the long run far more so, is the spread of these revolutionary processes to the non-Western areas of the world. The impact of industrialism, technology, secularism, and individualism upon peoples long accustomed to the ancient unities of tribe, local community, agriculture, and religion was first to be seen in the context of colonialism, an outgrowth of nationalism and capitalism in the West. The relations of the West to non-Western parts of the world, the whole phenomenon of the "new nations," are vital aspects of the social sciences.

So too are certain other consequences, or lineal episodes, of the two revolutions. The 20th century is the century of nationalism, mass democracy, and large-scale industrialism beyond reach of any 19th-century imagination so far as magnitude is concerned. It is the century of mass warfare, of two world wars with toll in lives and property greater perhaps than the sum total of all preceding wars in history. It is the century too of totalitarianism: Communist, Fascist, and Nazi; and of techniques of terrorism that, if not novel, are to be seen on a scale and with an intensity of scientific application that could scarcely have been predicted by those who considered science and technology as unqualifiedly humane in possibility. It is a century of affluence in the West, without precedent for the masses of people, to be seen in a constantly rising standard of living and a constantly rising level of expectations.

The last is important. A great deal of the turbulence in the 20th century—political, economic, and social—is the result of desires and aspirations that have been constantly escalating and that have been passing from the white people in the West to ethnic and racial minorities among them and, then, to whole continents elsewhere. Of all manifestations of revolution, the revolution of rising expectations is perhaps the most powerful in its consequences. For, once this revolution gets under way, each fresh victory in the struggle for rights, freedom, and security tends to magnify the importance of what has not been won.

Once it was thought that by solving the fundamental problems of production and large-scale organization, man could ameliorate other problems, those of a social, moral, and psychological nature. What in fact occurred, on the testimony of a great deal of the most notable thought and writing, was a heightening of such problems. It would appear that as man satisfies, relatively at least, the lower order needs of food and shelter, his higher order needs for purpose and meaning in life become ever more imperious. Thus such philosophers of history as Arnold Toynbee, Pitirim Sorokin, and Oswald Spengler have dealt with problems of purpose and meaning in history with a degree of learning and intensity of spirit not seen since perhaps St. Augustine wrote his monumental *The City of God* in the early 5th century when signs of the disintegration of Roman civilization were becoming overwhelming in their message to so many of that day. In the 20th century, though the idea of progress has certainly not disappeared, it has been rivalled by ideas of cyclical change and of degeneration of society. It is hard to miss the currency of ideas in modern times—status, community, purpose, moral integration, on the one hand, and alienation, anomie, disintegration, **breakdown** on the other—that reveal only too clearly the divided nature of man's spirit, the unease of his mind.

There is to be seen too, especially during later decades of the century, a questioning of the role of reason in human affairs—a questioning that stands in stark contrast with the ascendancy of rationalism in the two or three centuries preceding. Doctrines and philosophies stressing the inadequacy of reason, the subjective character of human commitment, and the primacy of faith have rivalled —some would say conquered—doctrines and philosophies descended from the Age of Reason. Existentialism, with its emphasis on the basic loneliness of the individual, on the impossibility of finding truth through intellectual decision, and on the irredeemably personal, subjective character of man's life, has proved to be a very influential philosophy in the writings of the 20th century. Freedom, far from being the essence of hope and joy, is the source of man's dread of the universe and of his anxiety for himself. Sören Kierkegaard's 19th-century intimations of anguished isolation as the perennial lot of the individual have had rich expression in the philosophy and literature of the 20th century.

It might be thought that such intimations and presentiments as these have little to do with the social sciences. This is true in the direct sense perhaps but not true when one examines the matter in terms of contexts and ambiences. The "lost individual" has been of as much concern to the social sciences as to philosophy and literature. Ideas of alienation, anomie, identity crisis, and estrangement from norms are rife among the social sciences, particularly, of course, those most directly concerned with the nature of the social bond, such as sociology, social psychology, and political science. In countless ways, philosophical, literary, and popular interest in the loss of community, in the search for community, and in the individual's relation to society and morality have had expression in the work of the social sciences. Between the larger interests of a culture and the social sciences there is never a wide gulf—only different ways of defining and approaching these interests.

MARXIST INFLUENCES

The influence of Marxism in the 20th century must not be missed. Currently the works of Lenin have outstripped the Bible in distribution in the world. For hundreds of millions of persons today the ideas of Marx, as communicated by Lenin, have profound moral, even religious significance. But even in those parts of the world, the West foremost, where Communism has exerted little direct political impact, Marxism remains a potent source of ideas. Not a few of the central concepts of social stratification and the location and diffusion of power in the social sciences come straight from Marx's insights. Far more is this the case in the Communist countries—the Soviet Union, other eastern European countries, China, and even Asian countries in which no Communist domination exists. In all these countries, Marx's name is virtually sacrosanct. There is not the same degree of differentiation of social sciences in

these countries that is found in the West. As an example, sociology hardly exists as a recognized discipline in these countries, and by the standards of the West, the other social sciences have little more than a rather rudimentary existence. Economics alone tends to be favoured, and this is, of course, largely Marxian economics—the economics of Marx's *Das Kapital*.

But even though Marxism has had relatively little direct impact on the social sciences as disciplines in the West, it has had enormous influence on states of mind that are closely associated with the social sciences. Especially was this true during the 1930s, the decade of the Great Depression. Today signs are not lacking of a strong revival of interest in Marx that could very well, through sheer numbers of its adherents, affect the nature of the social sciences in the years ahead. Socialism remains for a great many persons an evocative symbol and creed. Marx remains a formidable name among intellectuals and is still, without any question, the principal intellectual source of radical movements in politics. Such a position cannot help but influence the contexts of even the most abstract of the social sciences.

What Marx's ideas have suggested above all else in a positive way is the possibility of a society directed, not by blind forces of competition and struggle among economic elements, but instead by directed planning. This hope, and this image, has proved a dominant one in the 20th century even where the influence of Marx and of Socialism has been at best small and indirect. It is this profound interest in central planning and governance that has given almost historic significance to the ideas of the English economist J.M. Keynes. What is called Keynesianism has as its intellectual base a very complex modification of the classical doctrines of economics—one set forth in Keynes's famous *The General Theory of Employment, Interest and Money*, published in 1936. Of greater influence today, however, than the strictly theoretical content of this general theory is the political impact that Keynesian ideas have had on Western democracies. For out of these ideas came the clear policy of governments dealing directly with the business cycle, of pumping money and credit into an economic system when the cycle threatens to turn downward, and of then lessening this infusion when the cycle moves upward. Above all other names in the West, that of Keynes has become identified with such policy in the democracies and with the general movement of central governments toward ever more active and constant regulation of processes once thought best left to what the classical economists thought of as natural laws. True, the root ideas of the classical economists are found in modified form even today in the works of such economists as the American Milton Friedman. But it would not be unfair to say that Keynes's name has become associated with democratic economic planning and direction in much the way that Marx's name is associated with Communist economic policies.

FREUDIAN INFLUENCES

In the general area of personality, mind, and character, the writings of Sigmund Freud have had influence on 20th-century culture and thought scarcely less than Marx's. His basic theories of the role of the unconscious mind, of the lasting effects of infantile sexuality, and of the Oedipus complex have gone beyond the discipline of psychoanalysis and even the larger area of psychiatry to areas of several of the social sciences. Anthropologists have applied Freudian concepts to their studies of primitive cultures, seeking to assess comparatively the universality of states of the unconscious that Freud and his followers held to lie in the whole human race. Some political scientists have used Freudian ideas to illuminate the nature of authority generally, and political power specifically, seeing in totalitarianism, for example, the thrust of a craving for the security that total power can give. Sociology and social psychology have been influenced by Freudian ideas in their studies of social interaction and motivation. From Freud came the fruitful perspective that sees social behaviour and attitudes as generated not merely by the external situation but also by internal emotional needs springing from child-

Effects of alienation and social isolation

Triumph of social planning and Keynesianism

Freudian emphases on the unconscious and the unrational

hood—needs for recognition, authority, self-expression. Whatever may be the place directly occupied by Freud's ideas in the social sciences today, his influence upon 20th-century thought and culture generally, not excluding the social sciences, has been hardly less than Marx's.

THE CHANGING CHARACTER OF THE DISCIPLINES

It is appropriate to turn next to some of the trends and developments that may be seen against these backgrounds.

Specialization and cross-disciplinary approaches. The first point to make about the social sciences of the 20th century is the vast increase in the number of social scientists involved, in the number of academic and other centres of teaching and research in the social sciences, and in their degree of both comprehensiveness and specialization. The explosion of the sciences generally in the 20th century—an explosion responsible for the fact that a majority of all scientists who have ever lived in human history are now alive—has had, as one of its signal elements, the explosion of the social sciences. Not only has there been development and proliferation but there has

Diffusion of the social sciences

also been a spectacular diffusion of the social sciences. Beginning in a few places in western Europe and the United States in the 19th century, the social sciences, as bodies of ongoing research and centres of teaching, are today to be found almost everywhere in the world. In considerable part this has followed the spread of universities from the West to other parts of the world and, within universities, the very definite shift away from the hegemony once held by humanities alone to the near-hegemony held today by the sciences, physical and social.

Specialization has been as notable a tendency in the social sciences as in the biological and physical sciences. This is reflected not only in varieties of research but also in course offerings in academic departments. Whereas not very many years ago, a couple of dozen advanced courses in a social science reflected the specialization and diversity of the discipline even in major universities with graduate schools, today a hundred such courses are found to be not enough.

Side by side with this strong trend toward specialization, however, is another, countering trend: that of cross-fertilization and interdisciplinary cooperation. At the beginning of the century, down in fact until World War II, the several disciplines existed each in a kind of splendid isolation from the others. That historians and sociologists, for example, might ever work together in curricula and research projects would have been scarcely conceivable prior to about 1945. Each social science tended to follow the course that emerged in the 19th century: to be confined to a single, distinguishable, if artificial, area of social reality. Today, evidences are all around of cross-disciplinary work and of fusion within a single social science of elements drawn from other social sciences. Thus there are such vital areas of work as political sociology, economic anthropology, psychology of voting, and industrial sociology. Single concepts such as "structure," "function," "alienation," and "motivation" can be seen employed variously to useful effect in several social sciences. The techniques of one social science can be seen consciously incorporated into another or into several social sciences. If history has provided much in the way of perspective to sociology or anthropology, each of these two has provided perspective, and also whole techniques, such as statistics and survey, to history. In short, specialization is by no means without some degree at least of countertendencies such as fusion and synthesis.

Professionalization

Another outstanding characteristic of each of the social sciences in the 20th century is its professionalization. Without exception, the social sciences have become bodies of not merely research and teaching but also practice, in the sense that this word has in medicine or engineering. Down until about World War II, it was a rare sociologist or political scientist or anthropologist who was not a holder of academic position. There were economists and psychologists to be found in banks, industries, government, even in private consultantship, but the numbers were relatively tiny. Overwhelmingly the social sciences had visibility alone as academic disciplines, con-

cerned essentially with teaching and with more or less basic, individual research. All this has changed profoundly, and on a vast scale, during the past three decades. Today there are as many economists and psychologists outside academic departments as within, if not more. The number of sociologists, political scientists, and demographers to be found in government, industry, and private practice rises constantly. Equally important is the changed conception or image of the social sciences. Today, to a degree unknown before World War II, the social sciences are conceived as policy-making disciplines, concerned with matters of national welfare in their professional capacities in just as sure a sense as any of the physical sciences. Inevitably, tensions have arisen within the social sciences as the result of processes of professionalization. Those persons who are primarily academic can all too easily feel that those who are primarily professional have different and competing identifications of themselves and their disciplines.

Nature of the research. The emphasis upon research in the social sciences has become almost transcending within recent decades. This situation is not at all different from that which prevails in the physical sciences and the professions in this age. Prior to about 1945, the functions of teaching and research had approximately equal value in many universities and colleges. The idea of a social (or physical) scientist appointed to an academic institution for research alone, or with research preponderant, was scarcely known. Research bureaus and institutes in the social sciences were very few and did not rival traditional academic departments and colleges as prestige-bearing entities. All of that was changed decisively beginning with the period just after World War II. From governments and foundations, large sums of money passed into the universities—usually not to the universities as such, but rather to individuals or small groups of individuals, each eminent for research. Research became the uppermost value in the social sciences (as in the physical) and hence, of course, in the universities themselves.

Use of mathematics and computers

Probably the greatest single change in the social sciences during the past generation has been the widespread introduction of mathematical and other quantitative methods. Without question, economics is the discipline in which the most spectacular changes of this kind have taken place. So great is the dominance of mathematical techniques here—resulting in the eruption of what is called econometrics to a commanding position in the discipline—that, to the outsider, economics today almost appears to be a branch of mathematics. But in sociology, political science, social psychology, and anthropology, the impact of quantitative methods, above all, of statistics, has also been notable. No longer does statistics stand alone, a separate discipline, as it did in effect during the 19th century. This area today is inseparable from each of the social sciences, though, in the field of mathematics, statistics still remains eminently distinguishable, the focus of highly specialized research and theory.

Within the past decade or two, the use of computers and of all the complex techniques associated with computers has become a staple of social-science research and teaching. Through the data storage and data retrieval of electronic computers, working with amounts and diversity of data that would call for the combined efforts of hundreds, even thousands of technicians, the social sciences have been able to deal with both the extensive and intensive aspects of human behaviour in ways that would once have been inconceivable. The so-called computer revolution in modern thought has been, in short, as vivid a phase of the social as the physical sciences, not to mention other areas of modern life. The problem as it is stated by mature social scientists is to use computers in ways in which they are best fitted but without falling into the fallacy that they can alone guide, direct, and supply vital perspective in the study of man.

Closely related to mathematical, computer, and other quantitative aspects of the social sciences is the vast increase in the empiricism of modern social science. Never in history has so much in the way of data been collected, examined, classified, and brought to the uses of social theory and social policy alike. What has been called the triumph of the fact is nowhere more visible than in the social sciences. Without question, this massive empiricism has been valuable, indispensable indeed, to those seeking explanations of social structures and processes. Empiricism, however, like quantitative method, is not enough in itself. Unless related to hypothesis, theory, or conclusion, it is sterile, and most of the leading social scientists of today reflect this view in their works. Too many, however, deal with the gathering and classifying of data as though these were themselves sufficient.

Emphasis on empirical evidence and data gathering

It is the quest for data, for detailed, factual knowledge of human beliefs, opinions, and attitudes, as well as patterns and styles of life—familial, occupational, political, religious, and so on—that has made the use of surveys and polls another of the major tendencies in the social sciences of this century. The poll data one sees in his newspaper are hardly more than the exposed portion of an iceberg. Literally thousands of polls, questionnaires, and surveys are going on at any given moment today in the social sciences. The survey or polling method ranks with the quantitative indeed in popularity in the social sciences, both being, obviously, indispensable tools of the empiricism just mentioned.

THEORETICAL MODES

It is not the case, however, that interest in theory is a casualty of the 20th-century fascination with method and fact. Though there is a great deal less of that grand or comprehensive theory that was a hallmark of 19th-century social philosophy and social science, there are still those persons occasionally to be found today who are engrossed in search for master principles, for general and unified theory that will assimilate all the lesser and more specialized types of theory. But their efforts and results are not regarded as successful by the vast majority of social scientists. Theory, at its best, today tends to be specific theory—related to one or other of the major divisions of research within each of the social sciences. The theory of the firm in economics, of deviance in sociology, of communication in political science, of attitude formation in social psychology, of divergent development in cultural anthropology are all examples of theory in every proper sense of the word. But each is, clearly, specific. If there is a single social science in which a more or less unified theory exists, with reference to the whole of the discipline, it is economics. Even here, however, unified, general theory does not have the sovereign sweep it had in the classical tradition of Ricardo and his followers before the true complexities of economic behaviour had become revealed.

Specific versus grand theory

Developmentalism. Developmentalism is another overall influence upon the work of the social sciences, especially within the past three decades. As noted above, an interest in social evolution was one of the major aspects of the social sciences throughout the 19th century in western Europe. In the early 20th century, however, this interest, in its larger and more visible manifestations, seemed to terminate. There was a widespread reaction against the idea of unilinear sequences of stages, deemed by the 19th-century social evolutionists to be universal for all mankind in all places. Criticism of social evolution in this broad sense was a marked element of all the social sciences, pre-eminently in anthropology but in the others as well. There were numerous demonstrations of the inadequacy of unilinear descriptions of change when it came to accounting for what actually happened, so far as records and other evidences suggested, in the different areas and cultures of the world.

Influences of national growth and development

Beginning in the late 1940s and the 1950s, however, there was a resurgence of developmental ideas in all the social sciences—particularly with respect to studies of the new nations and cultures that were coming into existence in considerable numbers. Studies of economic growth and of political and social development have become more and more numerous. Although it would be erroneous to see these developmental studies as simple repetitions of those of the 19th-century social evolutionists, there are, nevertheless, common elements of thought, including the idea of stages of growth and of change conceived as continuous and cumulative and even as moving toward some more or less common end. At their best, these studies of growth and development in the new nations, by their counterposing of traditional and modern ways, tell a good deal about specific mechanisms of change, the result of the impact of the West upon outlying parts of the world. But as more and more social scientists have recently become aware, efforts to place these concrete mechanisms of change into larger, more systematic models of development all too commonly succumb to the same faults of unilinearity and specious universalism that early-20th-century critics found in 19th-century social evolution.

Social-systems approach. Still another major tendency in all of the social sciences since World War II has been the interest in "social systems." The behaviour of individuals and groups is seen as falling into multiple interdependencies, and these interdependencies are considered sufficiently unified to warrant use of the word "system." Although there are clear uses of biological models and concepts in social-systems work, it may be fair to say that the greatest single impetus to development of this area was widening interest after World War II in cybernetics —the study of human control functions and of the electrical and mechanical systems that could be devised to replace or reinforce them. Concepts drawn from mechanical and electrical engineering have been rather widespread in the study of social systems.

In social-systems studies, the actions and reactions of individuals, or even of groups as large as nations, are seen as falling within certain definable, more or less universal patterns of equilibrium and disequilibrium. The interdependence of roles, norms, and functions is regarded as fundamental in all types of group behaviour, large and small. Each social system, as encountered in social-science studies, is a kind of "ideal type," not identical to any specific "real" condition but sufficiently universal in terms of its central elements to permit useful generalization.

Structuralism and functionalism. Structuralism in the social sciences is closely related to the theory of the social system. Although there is nothing new about the root concepts of structuralism—they may be seen in one form or other throughout Western thought—there is no question but that in the present century this view of behaviour has become a dominant one in many fields. At bottom it is a reaction against all tendencies to deal with human thought and behaviour atomistically—that is, in terms of simple, discrete units of either thought, perception, or overt behaviour. In psychology, structuralism in its oldest sense simply declares that perception occurs, with learning following, in terms of experiences or sensations in various combinations, in discernible patterns or gestalten. In sociology, political science, and anthropology, the idea of structure similarly refers to the repetitive patternings that are found in the study of social, economic, political, and cultural existence. The structuralist contends that no element can be examined or explained outside its context or the pattern or structure of which it is a part. Indeed, it is the patterns, not the elements, that are the only valid objects of study.

Emphasis on pattern and interdependence

What is called functionalism in the social sciences today is closely related to structuralism, with the term structural–functional a common one, especially in sociology and anthropology. Function refers to the way in which behaviour takes on significance, not as a discrete act but as the dynamic aspect of some structure. Biological analogies are common in theories of structure and function in the social sciences. Very common is the image of the biological organ, with its close interdependence to other organs (as the heart to the lung) and the interdependence of activities (as circulation to respiration).

Interactionism. Interaction is still another concept that has had wide currency in the social sciences of the 20th century. Social interaction—or, as it is sometimes called, symbolic interaction—refers to the fact that the relationships among two or more groups or human beings are never one-sided, purely physical, or direct. Always there is reciprocal influence, a mutual sense of "otherness." And always the presence of the "other" has crucial effect in one's definition of not merely what is external but what is internal. One acquires one's individual sense of identity from interactions with others beginning in infancy. It is the initial sense of the other person —mother, for example—that in time gives the child its sense of self, a sense that requires continuous development through later interactions with others. From the point of view of interactionist theory, all one's perceptions of and reactions to the external world are mediated or influenced by prior ideas, valuations, and assessments. Always one is engaged in socialization or the modification of one's mind, role, and behaviour through contact with others.

FUTURE OF THE SOCIAL SCIENCES

What has been covered in the preceding paragraphs may be the most that can be said within restricted compass about the social sciences of the 20th century without turning to the articles on the individual social sciences themselves and on related disciplines (see ANTHROPOLOGY; SOCIOLOGY; ECONOMICS; POLITICAL SCIENCE; PSYCHOLOGY, SOCIAL; GEOGRAPHY; and STATISTICS). The concern here has been with only those major contextual influences, tendencies of overall character, and dominant ideas or theories that the social sciences taken as a whole manifest in one degree or other.

Relation of social sciences to society — There is one final aspect of the subject that must be considered briefly, for how it is resolved will have much effect upon the future of the social sciences in the West. This is the relation of the social sciences to organized society, to government and industry, and other institutional centres of authority. At the present time, there is a significant and undoubtedly growing feeling among social scientists, especially younger ones, that the relationship has become altogether too close. The social sciences, it is said, must maintain their distance, their freedom, from bureaucratized government and industry. Otherwise they will lose their inherent powers of honest and dispassionate criticism of the ineffective or evil in society. Although there may be a certain amount of feeling ranging from the naïve to the politically revolutionary in such sentiments, they cannot be taken lightly, as is apparent from the serious consideration that is being given on a steadily rising scale to the whole problem of social science and social policy.

Since the inception of the social sciences—since, indeed, the time when the universities in the West came into being for the express purpose of training professional men in law, theology, and medicine—man has properly sought, through knowledge, to influence social policy, taking this latter term in the widest sense to include not merely national government but local government, business, professions, and so on. What else, it may be asked, are the social sciences all about if it is not to use knowledge to improve social life; and how else but through influencing of the major institutions can such improvement take place?

So much is true, comes the answering response. But in the process of seeking to influence the great agencies of modern power and function—of what is loosely called the Establishment—the social sciences may themselves become influenced adversely by the values of power and affluence to be found in these great agencies. They themselves may become identified with the status quo. What the social sciences should give, say the partisans of this view, is a continuation of the revolutionary or at least profoundly reformist tradition that was begun in the 18th century by the philosophers of reason who, detesting the official establishment of their day, sought on their own to transform it. What is today called objectivity or methodological rigour turns out to be, say these same partisans, acceptance of the basic values of reigning government and industry.

It is this essential conflict regarding the purposes of the social sciences, the relation of the social sciences to government and society, and the role of the individual social scientist in the society of the 20th century that bids fair at this moment to be the major conflict of the years ahead.

How it is resolved may very well determine the fate of the social sciences, now less than two centuries old.

BIBLIOGRAPHY. The most comprehensive and detailed bibliographical background for the history of the social sciences is to be found in the *Encyclopaedia of the Social Sciences*, 15 vol. (1930–35), still valuable, especially in its historical sections, despite the many years that have passed since its publication; and in the *International Encyclopedia of the Social Sciences*, 17 vol. (1968). The latter is indispensable for its coverage of recent developments in the social sciences. The best individual work, by now a classic in the history of ideas, on the period leading up to the emergence of the individual social sciences, is PRESERVED SMITH, *A History of Modern Culture*, 2 vol. (1930–34, reprinted 1962), it is especially good in its treatment of the circumstances attending the rise of natural science and modern social philosophy. JAMES WESTFALL THOMPSON, *A History of Historical Writing*, 2 vol. (1942), is useful in this respect also; its stress on historians does not prevent its covering areas adjacent to history and closely involved in the roots of the social sciences. On the Enlightenment in France, the age immediately preceding the rise of the social sciences, the best study by far is LESTER G. CROCKER, *Nature and Culture: Ethical Thought in the French Enlightenment* (1963), and *An Age of Crisis: Man and World in Eighteenth Century French Thought* (1959), here recommended to be read or consulted in that order. The best general work on the history of the social sciences and the history of social philosophy back to earliest times in the West is HARRY ELMER BARNES and HOWARD BECKER, *Social Thought from Lore to Science*, 2nd ed., 2 vol. (1952). The first volume deals with the issues and problems of all the social sciences, with major emphasis on the period following the breakup of the Middle Ages; the second volume is primarily concerned with sociology in the 20th century.

Nineteenth century: ERIC J. HOBSBAWM, *The Age of Revolution: 1789–1848* (1962), is an important and fascinating treatment of the social, cultural, and intellectual aspects of the age in which the individual social sciences emerged in western Europe. Its treatment of both the democratic and industrial revolutions, and the problems that they presented to intellectuals and scholars, is incisive and authoritative. ROBERT A. NISBET, *The Sociological Tradition* (1966), although concerned primarily with sociology, deals with the specific ways in which the ideologies and themes of the two revolutions became translated into social theory. The same author's *Social Change and History* (1969), deals in detail with the incorporation of the theory of social evolution into the social sciences of the 19th century and shows the relation of this theory to the earlier idea of progress and its antecedents in Western thought. For the rise and development of the individual social sciences in the 19th and 20th centuries, the following works are recommended: (*Anthropology*): ROBERT H. LOWIE, *The History of Ethnological Theory* (1937); and MARVIN HARRIS, *The Rise of Anthropological Theory: A History of Theories of Culture* (1968). (*Economics*): ERICH ROLL, *A History of Economic Thought*, 3rd ed. rev. (1954); and the extremely readable ROBERT HEILBRONER, *The Worldly Philosophers: The Lives, Times, and Ideas of the Great Economic Thinkers*, 3rd ed. (1967). (*Political Science*): GEORGE SABINE, *A History of Political Theory*, 3rd ed. (1959), has become deservedly a classic. It is best on the three centuries preceding the 20th. FRANCIS W. COKER, *Recent Political Thought* (1934), is excellent for the early 20th century. LEO STRAUSS and JOSEPH CROPSEY (eds.), *History of Political Philosophy* (1963), deals learnedly and penetratingly with aspects of the discipline not ordinarily found in general histories. (*Sociology*): Barnes and Becker, referred to above, supplies the greatest amount of detailed information on the history of sociology in the 19th and early 20th centuries. Nisbet, also referred to above, deals with the relation between political ideologies and the currents of sociological thought in the late 19th century. LEWIS A. COSER, *Masters of Sociological Thought* (1971), is undoubtedly the best recent general history of sociology in 19th and 20th century Europe and America. (*Social Psychology*): The best, indeed almost only, account of social psychology in the 19th and early 20th century is FAY BERGER KARPF, *American Social Psychology: Its Origins, Development and European Background* (1932).

Twentieth century: For authoritative and easily available accounts of very recent developments in the social sciences and their contexts, no single work, not even any few works, will suffice. The reader is advised to turn to the articles in this encyclopaedia on the individual social sciences both for content and for bibliographical sources. The *International Encyclopedia of the Social Sciences*, already referred to above, is indispensable in this respect.

(R.A.N.)

Social Structure and Organization

The terms social structure and social organization are metaphors or analogies, applying to human social relations or conditions certain descriptions that ordinarily would be applied to such things as machines, buildings, or the body organism. The term structure, in particular, was borrowed by social scientists from physics and anatomy. The basic assumption is that there exists in a society—as there presumably exists in a machine or an organism—a functional interdependence of the parts of the whole, all seeking or maintaining an equilibrium. According to the context or the writer, the parts might be social institutions, social groups, obligatory relations, statuses and roles, or other social components. It should be remembered, however, that metaphors or analogies are useful only in their illustration of particular principles. They are intellectual tools, not properties of empirical reality. If pressed in their empirical reality they can become useless and misleading.

Structure and organization as purely intellectual tools

In groupings ranging from the state to the mother bearing her child, human beings congregate and disperse, associate and disassociate themselves for a variety of purposes and ends that are to a large extent routinized or institutionalized. They enter into a variety of roles and statuses, more or less hierarchically arranged, and they take up a variety of positions in relation to one another and the offices and institutions of their society. They interact, play their parts, and bring more or less to their parts than they or others had thought possible or usual. In reality, people do not behave or play their parts precisely as the ideal prescribes or even as an observer may state they do. Categories of age, sex, kinship, allegiance, association, class, cooperation, competition, work, play, obligation, and ordination all involve particular kinds of relations between individuals that are ever-changing and subject to a variety of levels of understanding and interpretation. Still, in all this there appears to be more order than muddle and confusion. Activities, rationalizations on those activities, ideas, and statements all seem to have such correspondence that even in strife and discrepancy the human mind can perceive some sort of ordering or pattern in social affairs. The problem is how to realize this pattern—this ordering of concrete activities and rationalizations, or categories of understanding—in some sort of scientific or intellectual mode.

There are various ways of doing this or attempting to do this. Not all the approaches involve use of the term structure or organization per se, but, whatever terms are used, they are used more or less synonymously within the overreaching idea of structure or organization. The remainder of this article considers one by one the major models or approaches.

Culture-pattern model. Three convergent circumstances may be adduced as greatly influencing the development of the culture-pattern model, which was most influential from the 1920s to the 1950s. First, the end of World War I found anthropology at a crossroads. The war had brought to light the fact that while prewar (and especially 19th-century) scholars had been preoccupied with global theories of human social development, very little was known in a scientific way of the ways in which people actually lived, quarreled, and somehow got on together. There was a need for new ideas, ideas that would both stimulate research and discover the determinants of living together in harmony. Second, Sigmund Freud and other psychologists were in their ascendant. It was thought that if anything could rebuild a world shattered and changed out of all recognition by the war, psychology would surely provide the key. Anthropologists began to look to psychology to lead them through and out of their theoretical dearth, and they developed culture-pattern theory as a consequence. Third, the people who advanced culture-pattern theory were mostly Americans, and they were in a rather unique position. Unlike the situation in many other parts of the world, the lives and times of North American native peoples were relatively well documented. They had a discoverable history. Moreover, their geographical circumstances were relatively unusual; the various Indian societies tended to inhabit distinct ecological zones and form mutually exclusive groups; although they interacted with one another, they were nonetheless physically discernible and bounded groups, each with its own peculiar style of making and doing. The idea of culture as a patterned functioning whole fell in naturally with the circumstances: groups were cultures.

The method used in the culture-pattern approach was essentially to derive a people's culture from an examination of individual people and their personalities. Thus, Ruth Benedict characterized certain cultures on the basis of patterns of institutionalized purposes, motives, emotions and values. Indeed, so direct was the derivation of "culture" from "individual" that a culture, it was thought, could be spun out of the psychoanalysis of a single individual representative.

Culture and personality

The model took predominant or basic personality types as the given data, and events in the culture were construed through the lens of such personality types. Clyde Kluckhohn could thus "explain" witchcraft and sorcery as resulting from the interaction between particular events and the given personality type. Furthermore, since culture was derived from the personalities of individuals and since the significance of events depended on predominant types of personality, it was important to find out how this personality was formed—hence the concentration on sexual mores and on the conception, birth, nurture, and upbringing of children. If these practices, taken to be formative of the basic personality, could be changed, then the basic personality would be changed; and this genetic approach could be made to seem historically relevant. Indeed, the shape of history could be made to seem dependent on modes of child nurture. Later developments took status, role, group memberships, and situational determinants into account. Aggression, frustration, conflict, competition, cooperation, motivation, national character, socialization, and character formation were terms frequently encountered in culture-pattern models. Developing a culture pattern for a people was achieved by interrelating some or all of these features. It is a resultant, rather than a predicative, mode of operation.

There is no doubt that culture-pattern studies have made an enormous and valuable contribution to social science, particularly in their close observation and recording of the processes in culture. The mutual mirror image of individual personality and culture, however, has tended to obscure the institutional matrix that individuals with specific economic and political interests have to manipulate to gain their ends. Man's highest cultural achievement, his articulate thought, tends to be lost in a mass of nonverbal behaviour. Changes in economic resources go unnoticed. The conflicts of political and economic interests, whether within the culture or imposed from outside, tend to be subsumed in personality differences.

The structure-function model. The structure-function model, typified in British anthropology, although derived from the French, is the precise opposite of the culture-pattern model. The individual is seen as subordinate not so much to the group as to the categories of collective representation. The collective categories exist and persist; an individual is born into them, manipulates them, and changes them perhaps. But when he dies the collective categories live on. Individuals are not so much personalities in themselves as actors with parts to play. Consequently, role, status, and positional relationships are of paramount importance; so are economic and political interest.

The French sociologist Émile Durkheim was the prime sponsor of this approach. For Durkheim the basic units were the "social facts"—the roles, offices, institutions, or whatever that went on existing independently of the particular individuals who might transiently be occupied with them. These units were thought of as fundamentally centripetal: like an organism, society maintained itself in virtue of the integrationist nature of the relations between various parts of the whole. Conformity was necessary to the maintenance of the social order. If there were acts or activities that tended to break down the solidarity

Continuity and permanence of the social fact

and produce mutually exclusive unities, somehow these unities came to be rebuilt into a larger whole or brought together into necessary mutual alliances immediately or concurrently. The British anthropologist A.R. Radcliffe-Brown asserted that,

the continuity of social structure . . . is not static like that of a building, but a dynamic continuity, like that of the organic structure of a living body. Throughout the life of an organism its structure is being constantly renewed; and similarly the social life constantly renews the structure. (From *Structure and Function in Primitive Society,* 1952.)

The structure-function model seems to have been most successful in application to small-scale societies, in which kinship categories could be made the main components of structure. The kinship categories defined who in a society should be thought of as consanguines and affines; evoked role, status, and positional relationships; generated mutual obligations and expectations of behaviour and attitude; and, further, in small-scale societies could be used to classify the total environment.

Study of small-scale societies

The chief British exponents of the structure-function approach, the anthropologists Bronisław Malinowski and Radcliffe-Brown, emphasized the importance of searching for "laws" of social life and society. Only within such laws (or regularities) was social change considered admissible. Critics of the British school have charged that the neglect of change and of history left the model incomplete. But such a charge can hardly be sustained. Much more weighty is the criticism that, being integrationist and wedded to what is permanent, the structure-function model might be able to include minor rebellion and conflict but could not contain revolution, innovative changes, or deep-seated centrifugal or disintegrative tendencies. Furthermore, being normative, it seemed to have few predictive properties.

These criticisms were well founded. Again, it is often said that the model was too intellectualized, too depersonalized. Where are the people in all this manipulation of the categories? Certainly the model is politically conservative and even emasculating: it serves to discover and interpret an unknown but has little or no potential within itself of generating new policies or ideas. It is itself a closed system and can only be adumbrated, developed, and readumbrated in relation to more and more detailed field material.

There was also an American branch of the structure-function proponents, led by such sociologists as Robert K. Merton and Talcott Parsons. It laid less emphasis on kinship patterns and more on various aspects of stratification—role, status, and positional relationships determined by personal qualities, possessions, authority and power, and the like. The shift in emphasis was necessary because there was a shift in the object of study from small-scale to large-scale modern societies. Perhaps, in this, too much was attempted. A model born of and devised for the study of simple and small-scale communities was adapted to the complex organizations of modern civilized society, and in the process the simple coherence of the model was lost in a jumble of jargon, an esoteric maze of words.

The conflict model. The conflict model is grounded in political theory and in attempts to explain the historical process. It generally attempts to predict or, in the words of one of its chief current advocates, the German theorist Ralf Dahrendorf, to "account for the rate and direction of change" (*Conflict After Class,* 1967). It is actually a model that has preoccupied thinkers from earliest times. It involves whole philosophies as to the nature, being, and purpose of man. From Plato and Aristotle through Saint Paul the Apostle, Saint Augustine of Hippo, and numerous Medieval and Renaissance thinkers to men such as John Locke, Thomas Hobbes, Jean-Jacques Rousseau, G.W.F. Hegel, Herbert Spencer, Charles Darwin, Karl Marx, and, indeed, every politician, some model of the locus of conflict and its probable consequences has been essential.

Emphasis on change in large-scale societies

Two major but not necessarily mutually exclusive themes may be identified. First the locus of conflict may be placed squarely in the nature of man; second, it may be placed in the nature of his social order. Most often the two themes are combined in either of two general ways: (1) In the nature and consciousness of man there is a variety of things (original sin, frustrated sexual drives, the will to dominance or power, competitiveness, territoriality, control of wealth, etc.) that give rise to conflict; these things, or agitants, can be contained, controlled, and rendered nugatory by a particular kind of social order. Nearly all Utopian thought—political, philosophical, or sociological—conforms to this formula. And since the locus (whatever it may be) is inherent in man, few such models can avoid Plato's solution (in *The Republic*) of a dominant corps of guardians to enforce and maintain the harmony. (2) Since the nature and consciousness of man is a product of his social order, conflict results from the contradictions in the social order: the solution to conflict must reside in rearrangements of the social order.

Such models belong mainly to political theory that seeks to promote and bring about certain kinds of change. Hence, both structure and organization are loosely described and subordinated to whatever is deemed the impetus for conflict.

Dahrendorf does present a theory of integration in society, whose social structure is held in equilibrium by certain patterned and recurrent processes; but he joins it to a theory of coercion in which the social structure is held together by force and constraint and contains within itself forces causing an unending process of change. Thus the model becomes a dialectic between stability and change, integration and conflict, consensus and coercion. The model is furthermore focussed on large-scale and complex societies and on class conflict. Unlike Marx, however, he does not identify entities in conflict (such as capital and labour), but identifies conflict in terms of groups and individuals occupying particular roles and exercising power vis-à-vis one another. The roles reflect structure or stasis; the exercise of power and the response to it cause change.

Integration and coercion

In the model devised by the American sociologist Lewis Alfred Coser, the essential equilibrium is the equilibrium maintained by conflict. What emerges is less a model of structure than a series of propositions about the functions of conflict or what conflict does: it maintains or disrupts cohesion depending upon circumstances; it forms groups and associations, and also destroys them; it is the locus of social dynamics and change, but it also maintains a balance of powers.

In the sense that all conflicts take place within a framework of rules, they do have a structure. The critical situation arises when the parties to a conflict operate under different frameworks of rules—as do members of revolutionary social movements vis-à-vis defenders of the status quo. Here the sociologist should turn historian and attempt to subsume the two sets of rules and relations into an overarching framework. A sociology of revolution, the transformation of one structure into another, however, has so far been elusive. It is not simply a matter of changing the meaning of structure or organization. There are very real conceptual difficulties involved in creating a model capable of transforming itself into another. Adaptations of the Hegelian formula (thesis–antithesis–synthesis) must still suffice.

Physical-science models. Most of the difficulties inherent in physical-science models stem from (1) the nature of social material, (2) basic assumptions and purposes, and (3) language. The empirical realities of physical science may be subjected to innumerable experiments by large numbers of scientists supported and funded by a large proportion of the gross national product. It is questionable whether a comparable effort and investment in social science would obtain comparable results. But since the empirical realities of social life can only be obtained ad hoc, under the artificial conditions of a small group laboratory, or by maintaining an institution very like a concentration camp, it is doubtful whether social scientists would ever have access to the same range of experimental data as do physical scientists. Moreover, in social science there is a moral relationship between investigator and investigated that inhibits an objective analysis and

Difficulties in experimenting and securing data

explanation of social behaviour in physical-science terms. When one of the chief proponents of the physical-science model, the American sociologist George A. Lundberg, states that "human sociology deals with the communicable adjustment technique which human groups have developed in their long struggle to come to terms with each other and the rest of their environment" (*Foundations of Sociology*, 1964, p. 1), he asserts an assumption about human existence with which not everyone would be able to agree.

Moreover, if there could be agreement on the nature of human existence and purpose, there is the additional question of the nature and purposes of sociology, namely, whether it merely analyzes, whether it explains, or both. It is a truism, for instance, that in any interplay of human activities, more energy is expended to reach some goal or conclusion than a rigid physical-science measurement would indicate; that is, most of the empirical reality of social life is totally unnecessary. If the sociologists must explain that all this transparently unnecessary activity appears to be necessary, he raises questions of what is rational and draws in the opinions of his own conscience; as a result, he manipulates more than he observes.

The problem of talking about values and beliefs raises the question of a language that is "value free." The problem is not solved by the invention of new terms and phrases, the creation of new jargon. Such metalanguages, however, are not wholly without value. Hence the present emphasis on using various kinds of computer languages.

Mathematical or logical models. Mathematical and logical models are based on the use of a metalanguage: analyses of empirical realities or rationalizations or categories in terms of the relations of mathematics or logic. From Plato through the Enlightenment until the rise of humanism and the Romantic movement, it had always been an axiom that the cosmos had an underlying harmony that could be expressed in mathematical terms. This was most obvious in the behaviour of celestial bodies, and least obvious in the behaviour of men and women; but, if human behaviour could be expressed in mathematical terms and realized in the forms of social organization or the state, man had perfection in his grasp. Such indeed was the purpose of Plato's *Republic*. Eighteenth-century Humanism and the Romantic movement obscured this ideal. Now, however, it is in process of realization. Primitive as yet, long-winded, and not wholly convincing as explanatory modes, mathematical and a priori logical models are not so much models of structure or organization—though they *can* be—as analytical modes directed toward the building of a variety of models of structure and organization.

While physical and natural sciences are concerned with the extraction of systematic relationships between sets of empirical data, and social science is mainly concerned with systematic relationships between rationalizations on the empirical data, mathematics and logic are concerned with abstract relations that have no empirical content. They are, like languages, tools whose relational content can be used to bring order to the variety of semantic fields generated by a consideration of data obtained by field research. Myth, kinship, and the decision-making process have been found particularly susceptible to analysis with these tools.

Although there is little doubt that the wedding of mathematics and social science will be fruitful, criticism of such work stems from the fact that sociology was born of, and still carries, a desire to improve society. It is all very well to perform mathematical and logical exercises with ethnographic material, but questions arise over the kinds of policy that will result from them. A first answer resides in the example of physical and natural science: not only do mathematical and logical techniques create a rigour of discipline in the kinds of things that can be said about the data, but the data itself may open further avenues of relations in the abstract terms characteristic of mathematics and logic.

In view of some of the claims of sociology, this would be no small gift. A second answer resides in the work that has already been done. Given the initial intuitive and intellectual perception of harmony in social affairs, mathematical and logical harmonies may be spun out. And the feedback from such operations will correct the initial perceptions. But at this point one is returned to Plato's problem: what if social relations are basically inharmonious?

General conclusion. Such concepts as social structure and social organization have been guiding notions, basic to the development of sociology as well as social and cultural anthropology. What was once a general term connoting some idea of wholeness, "structure" had attained a certain specificity by the 1940s, mainly because of the work of the British proponents of the structure-function model. But in the course of the subsequent decades it became a general term used to refer to the rules, explicit or implicit, within which any kind of behavioral sequence—verbal, ideational, or physical—could be said to operate. And because structure is a property of any behavioral sequence, the notion of structure is definitely no longer static. It has come to encompass the dynamic aspect, change.

From the 18th century to the present there has been a generalized movement from macromodels to micromodels, from global theories about the nature of human society to micromodels about the nature of specific kinds of situations in particular environments. It is at this point that psychology and sociology or social and cultural anthropology begin to mesh. It is at this point, too, that mathematical and logical models, as well as a variety of investigatory and measuring techniques, are proving to be most useful, both experimentally and when considering the interrelations of small-scale societies. Here lies a growing point whose virtues are only slowly beginning to dawn.

BIBLIOGRAPHY. An early and succinct statement of the notion of system may be found in PERE LAFITAU, *Moeurs des sauvages amériquains comparées aux moeurs des premiers temps*, 2 vol. (1724), though not further developed at the time. Evolutionary theory, particularly in HERBERT SPENCER, *Social Statics* (1850) and *Principles of Sociology*, 3 vol. (1876–96), used the concept, as did Marxist writing. W.H.R. RIVERS, *The Todas* (1906) and *Kinship and Social Organisation* (1914); A.R. RADCLIFFE-BROWN, *The Andaman Islanders* (1922); and BRONISLAW MALINOWSKI, *Argonauts of the Western Pacific* (1922), brought the concept of social structure to the forefront. RUTH BENEDICT, *Patterns of Culture* (1934); A. KARDINER (ed.), *The Individual and His Society* (1939); FELIX KEESING, *Cultural Anthropology* (1958); and A.F.C. WALLACE, *Culture and Personality* (1961), show the development of the culture-pattern school. The structure-functionalists are well represented by A.R. RADCLIFFE-BROWN, *Structure and Function in Primitive Society* (1952); E.E. EVANS-PRITCHARD, *Witchcraft, Oracles and Magic Among the Azande* (1937), *The Nuer* (1940), and *Nuer Religion* (1956); TALCOTT PARSONS, *The Structure of Social Action* (1937); MEYER FORTES, *The Dynamics of Clanship Among the Tallensi* (1945); R.K. MERTON, *Social Theory and Social Structure* (1949); G.P. MURDOCK, *Social Structure* (1949); and E.R. LEACH, *Political Systems of Highland Burma* (1954). RAYMOND W. FIRTH, *Elements of Social Organization* (1951); and FREDRIK BARTH, *Models of Social Organization* (1966), offer some of the most influential analyses of organization and structure; and CLAUDE LEVI-STRAUSS, *Anthropologie Structurale* (1958; Eng. trans., 1963); and PIERRE and ELLI KONGAS MARANDA (eds.), *Structural Analysis of Oral Tradition* (1971), reveal the growing distinction between functionalism and structuralism. Conflict models are based on KARL MARX, *Capital*, 3 vol. (1867–79); GEORG SIMMEL, *Soziologie* (1908; 3rd ed., 1923); and MAX WEBER, *Wirtschaft und Gesellschaft*, 2nd ed., 2 vol. (1925; Eng. trans. of pt. 1, *The Theory of Social and Economic Organization*, 1947); for further developments of the conflict model, see GEORGE A. LUNDBERG, *Foundations of Sociology* (1964); LEWIS A COSER, *The Functions of Social Conflict* (1956); and C. WRIGHT MILLS, *Power, Politics and People* (1963). Mathematical models are illustrated in GEORGE KINGSLEY ZIPF, *Human Behavior and the Principle of Least Effort* (1949); and in IRA R. BUCHLER and HENRY A. SELBY, *Kinship and Social Organization* (1968). General, if necessarily tendentious, reviews are contained in ROBERT H. LOWIE, *The History of Ethnological Theory* (1937); A.L. KROEBER, *Configurations of Culture Growth* (1944); and MARVIN HARRIS, *The Rise of Anthropological Theory* (1968).

Sociology

Sociology is a branch of the science of human behaviour that seeks to discover the causes and effects that arise in social relations among persons and in the intercommunication and interaction among persons and groups. It includes the study of the customs, structures, and institutions that emerge from interaction, of the forces that hold together and weaken them, and of the effects that participation in groups and organizations have on the behaviour and character of persons. Sociology is also concerned with the basic nature of human society, locally and universally, and with the various processes that preserve continuity and produce change.

It is social life that is distinctive in the regulation of behaviour in human beings; the human animal does not have such instincts as serve to guide the behaviour of lower animals, and he is therefore more dependent on social organization than is any other species. Institutionalized social forms therefore are assumed to play the major part in influencing human actions, and it is the task of sociology to discover how these forms operate on the person, as well as how they are established, develop, elaborate, interact with one another, and decay and disappear. Among the most important of such structures is the family, the subject of an important field of sociology. The peer group, the community, the economic and political orders, various voluntary associations, and special organizations such as the church and the military are of particular importance in this inquiry.

Relation of sociology to other disciplines

Though sociology can be considered as a part of the Western tradition of rational inquiry inaugurated by the ancient Greeks, it is specifically the offspring of 18th- and 19th-century philosophy and has been viewed as a reaction against the frequently nonscientific approaches of classical philosophy and folklore to social phenomena. It was for a time presented as a part of moral philosophy, which covered the subject matter that eventually also became the concern of the various social sciences that are now separate from moral philosophy. Some aspects of other fields remain of interest to the sociologist. Although psychology has traditionally centred its interest on the individual and his internal mental mechanisms, and although sociology has given its major attention to collective aspects of human behaviour, the two disciplines share the subfield of social psychology. The relation of sociology to social anthropology is even closer, and until about the first quarter of the 20th century the two subjects were usually combined in one department, differentiated mainly by the emphasis of the anthropologists on the sociology of preliterate peoples. Recently even this distinction has been fading, as social anthropologists have increasingly added studies of various aspects of modern society to their field of interest. Political science and economics had much of their early development in the practical interests of nations and for a time evolved separately from basic sociology; but recently in both fields an awareness of the potential utility of some infusion of sociological concepts and methods has brought relations closer. A somewhat similar situation has also been developing in respect to law, education, and religion and to a lesser extent in such contrasting fields as engineering and architecture.

Nineteenth-century sociology, influenced by the successes of biology and evolutionary theory, took an interest in resemblances between men and lower animals—in their having, for example, similar instincts—and also in the parallels between biological and social evolution. These interests have declined, but sociology continues to share with the other sciences some interest in ecology, behavioral genetics, and questions of fertility and mortality as they relate to population studies. There is also a conviction among sociologists that contact between physiology and sociology is necessary to avoid errors of ignorance in both fields.

THE BACKGROUNDS OF CONTEMPORARY SOCIOLOGY

Early major schools of thought. The founders of sociology spent decades almost exclusively in the process of finding a direction for their new discipline. In the course of this groping effort they tried several highly divergent pathways, some suggested by methods and contents of other sciences, others invented outright by the imagination of the scholar.

Social Darwinism and evolutionism. Darwinian evolutionary theory doubtlessly suggested a way in which a science of human behaviour could become academically respectable, and a line of creative thinkers, including Herbert Spencer, Benjamin Kidd, Lewis H. Morgan, E.B. Tylor, L.T. Hobhouse, and others, developed analogies between human society and the biological organism and introduced into sociological theory such biological concepts as variation, natural selection, and inheritance—evolutionary factors resulting in the progress of societies through stages of savagery and barbarism to civilization, by virtue of the survival of the fittest. Some writers also perceived in the growth stages of each individual a recapitulation of these stages of society. Strange customs were thus accounted for on the assumption that they were throwbacks to an earlier useful practice; an example offered was the make-believe struggle sometimes enacted at marriage ceremonies between the bridegroom and the relatives of the bride, reflecting an earlier bride-capture custom.

The notion of stages of evolution

Social Darwinism waned in the 20th century, but in its popular period it was used to justify unrestricted competition and a laissez-faire doctrine in order that the "fittest" would survive and that civilization would continue to advance.

Determinism: economic, environmental, biological. Except in the philosophy of Karl Marx (whose writings ranged over all the social science fields rather than specifically in sociology), the doctrine of economic determinism never gained a strong foothold in sociology. This was not a consequence of scholarly ignorance; sociologists of all periods have read Marx and have usually read such writers as the historian Charles A. Beard, who emphasized economic self-interest, and Werner Sombart, the German sociologist who had been a convinced Marxist in his early career. But there have been only some adapted reflections of these economic views in the writings of such sociologists as Franklin H. Giddings or Frank H. Hankins who viewed some political and religious doctrines as rationalizations of economic and social interests.

The human geographers—Ellsworth Huntington, Ellen Semple, Friedrich Ratzel, Paul Vidal de La Blache, Jean Brunhes, and others—were also read critically by sociologists but did not make a lasting major contribution to the mainstream of sociological thought, even though there are some who believe that the social morphology of Émile Durkheim, Maurice Halbwachs, and others—that is, their theories about the roles of individuals interacting in a social system—grew in part from this interest.

Aside from the interest in evolution, organismic analogies, and the instinct concept, sociologists have not found biological determination of value to them and have spent more energy in refuting it than in making use of it.

Early functionalism. Following the achievement of a consensus that there should be a place for a science of sociology, there emerged an international effort to define the distinctive character of the subject and especially to clarify its differences from psychology and biology, fields that had also begun to generalize about human behaviour. A Frenchman, Émile Durkheim (1858–1917), was prominent among scholars who considered this question; he argued that there can arise from various kinds of interaction among individuals certain new properties (*sui generis*) not found in separate individuals. These "social facts" as he called them—collective sentiments, customs, institutions, nations—call for study and explanation on a distinctly sociological level rather than on the level of individual psychology. Furthermore, the interrelations of the parts of a society were perceived as cohering into a unity, an integrated system with a life character of its own, exterior to the individual, and exercising constraint over his behaviour. This direction of causation, from group to individual (rather than the reverse as conceived by most biologists of the time) gave encouragement to the scholar of the new science. Some writers have designated such a view "functionalism," although the term has in recent years acquired some broader variations of meaning.

Durkheim also pointed out that groups could be held together on two contrasting bases: the sentimental attraction of similarities (mechanical solidarity), such as occurs in friendship groups and among relatives and neighbours, and the organization of complementary differences (organic solidarity), such as occurs in industrial, military, governmental, and other organizations that exist because they have tasks to perform. Other theorists of Durkheim's period, notably Henry Maine and Ferdinand Tönnies, made similar distinctions in different terms—*status* and *contract* (Maine) and *Gemeinschaft* and *Gesellschaft* (Tönnies)—and conceived of the major trend of civilization as an expansion of the latter and a relative decline of the former.

Some later anthropologists, especially Bronisław Malinowski and A.R. Radcliffe-Brown, developed a doctrine also called functionalism, based on the recognition of the interrelatedness of the parts of a society, in bonds so thoroughly interpenetrating that a change in any single element would tend to produce a general disturbance in the whole. This concept gained a following for a time among many social anthropologists, leading some to advocate a policy of complete noninterference with even the most objectionable practices in a preliterate society (such as headhunting) for fear that control might produce far-reaching disorganization.

William G. Sumner, in his *Folkways*, defined an institution as a "concept and a structure," meaning a purpose or function that is carried out by some systematic organization of persons. Much of the sociology of Max Weber consists of the analysis of societies in such terms. Georg Simmel, sometimes called the founder of the "formal school" of sociology, viewed society as a process ("something functional") that is real and not merely an abstraction, and he built on this idea a statement of sociology consisting of a systematic analysis of social forms.

Modern major directions of interest.   The early schools of thought—each presenting a systematic formulation of sociology that implied possession of exclusive truth and that involved a conviction of the need to destroy rival systems—in time gave way to distinguishable directions of interest and emphasis that did not have to be considered inharmonious. These new directions have no dominant leaders and no clearly defined borderlines.

Functionalism and structuralism.   Following the main contributions in the earlier theoretical formulations of Charles H. Cooley, such later authors as Pitirim A. Sorokin, Talcott Parsons, Robert Merton, Everett C. Hughes, and others have elaborated on the nature of organizations and their relation to the behaviour of persons and have attempted to build workable conceptualizations of very large social systems, nations, and societies. Sorokin designated his viewpoint as "integralist" and wrote at length about the civilization-cultures that in their balance of values and conditions could be viewed as entities that had distinguishable life cycles, with "ideational," "idealistic," and "sensate" stages marking their growth and decline, thus following a philosophy-of-history tradition shared by Edward Gibbon, Oswald Spengler, and Arnold Toynbee.

Talcott Parsons has given attention to social systems in a more analytical way, inquiring into the conditions that each system must meet in order to survive (the "functional prerequisites"), the character of the standardized and stable interpersonal arrangements (structures) needed to make each system work, the relations to environmental conditions, problems of boundaries, the recruitment and control of members, and the like. Along with Robert Merton and others, he also worked on the classifications of such structures and on distinctions of function.

The subject matter and methods involved in such structural-functional analysis have indeed become so broad that some authors (such as Marion Levy) have held that it becomes synonymous with scientific analysis in general, or at least with scientific study of the nature of organization.

On a smaller scale, Kurt Lewin and his co-workers pursued somewhat parallel questions, investigating the nature of small groups, families, professional and military units, looking for arrangements and relationships of the parts of each person's "psychological life space" and of the interrelations of these to a "social space" or society's total range of action. The choice of such relatively small units for research made fruitful experimentation possible, and from Lewin's leadership grew the influential research movement that became known as group dynamics. Some writers have also applied the descriptive term *microfunctionalist* to this tradition.

Symbolic interactionism.   Sociologists did not for long find the 19th-century instinctivist psychology congenial, and most of them also failed to appreciate the doctrines of classical or Watsonian behaviourism, which sought to be totally objective and experimental. One influential movement in social psychology, however, did take early root and eventually became the largest and most influential field in modern American sociology. In recent years it has become known as "symbolic interactionism," but it was under development for decades before it acquired a name.

Out of early ideas expressed by J. Mark Baldwin and William James, a group of three scholars, John Dewey, George H. Mead, and Charles H. Cooley, built the foundations of a psychology that was to become most useful to sociology. In brief, their contribution was to advance the theory that mind and self are not part of the innate equipment of the human organism but arise in experience and are constructed in a social process—that is, in a process of interaction among persons in intimate, personal communication with one another. The self, or self-concept, as developed by Mead and others, is thus essentially an internalization of aspects of an interpersonal or social process. It exists in imagery and symbolization and is internalized and organized for each person out of his perception of how other persons conceive him. This self-concept, however inexact, fluctuating, and uncertain, nevertheless functions as a guide in social behaviour—that is, persons tend to act in order to preserve the existing or desired image of their self.

The concept of self

William I. Thomas, a sociologist and colleague of the philosopher Mead at the University of Chicago in the early years of the 20th century, regularly taught a course in social psychology based on Mead's conceptions. Thomas was succeeded in 1919 by Ellsworth Faris, himself a psychologist but later a member of the department of sociology, and through his work the tradition was further developed and brought into closer relation to the sociological tradition of Robert E. Park and Ernest W. Burgess, also at Chicago. In this tradition an interest in an appropriate methodology accompanied the growth of substantive knowledge; Thomas particularly emphasized the value of extensive use of personal documents, life histories, and autobiographies. In recent years interest in research on the self and self-conscious behaviour has spread widely, and is now participated in by psychologists, philosophers, and essayists, as well as by a movement within sociology called "ethnomethodology," which investigates areas of symbolic interaction by informal observation, reflection, and skilled interpretation, methods sometimes called *Verstehen* (understanding).

Modern determinism.   Economic determinism reflects the interest that a few early sociologists took in views of Karl Marx, such as the idea that differentiation into social classes and conflict between these classes derive from economic factors and the belief that the political system is in large part a product of such social stratification. A residue of this kind of determinism is found among the self-proclaimed "Marxian sociologists." Perhaps the most widely read of these was C. Wright Mills, whose concept of a "power elite" has been extensively and critically examined, with varying resulting judgments on its utility. As Mills saw it, this elite constitutes an integrated ruling group of a capitalistic economic and military system, sometimes called the military-industrial complex, exercising arbitrary power in its own interests. This particular determinism is not supported by most existing objective research, which generally finds a far more pluralistic distribution of political power.

A contrasting view of class conflicts was advocated by Karl Mannheim, who saw the cleavages as ideologically produced, as divergences in modes of thought rather than as rational perception of economic interests. Since Mannheim hoped that such conflicts could be resolved, his doctrine should not be considered fully deterministic, but it did stimulate an effort to interpret the relations between ideas and actions that came to be known as the "sociology of knowledge."

Mathematical modelism. A variety of efforts has been made to describe and investigate behaviour mathematically, through measurement and counting and the use of mathematical models. This approach in part characterized the early "sociometry" of J.L. Moreno (although its meaning has greatly drifted and broadened in recent years), the "field theory" of Kurt Lewin, and the investigations by George K. Zipf, John Q. Stewart, and others into the relations of rank and size of political units, the frequency of word use in language, and other simple arithmetic relations. Some of the concepts of game theory, first introduced into economics by its inventors, John von Neumann and Oskar Morgenstern, have also penetrated into sociology. Also the rapidly expanding use of computers has in recent times encouraged the development of various kinds of simulation of behaviour. Some investigations of complex interaction patterns have been carried out by devising games with rules to fit the problem and persons to execute the roles. When specified rules become highly detailed and complex, the outcome may be sought through the use of a computer; thus the game is converted into a simulation. Sociologists have participated, along with other social scientists, in the creation of such simulations of various political and military processes. Extension of these techniques into a variety of interaction processes is to be expected.

METHODOLOGICAL CONSIDERATIONS IN CONTEMPORARY SOCIOLOGY

Much of 19th-century sociology was devoid of systematic method, but late in the period the proliferation of schools of thought, based on speculative sociologies, made evident the need for ways of obtaining verifiable knowledge. Early attempts were crude and unfruitful; such broad surveyors as Charles Booth, who produced a monumental series on London, relied mainly on the gathering of masses of facts. Frédéric Le Play in France made extensive studies of family budgets. Herbert Spencer and others assembled vast stores of observations made by other persons, using these to illustrate and support generalizations already formulated.

Early exploitation of statistical materials, such as officially recorded rates of births, deaths, crimes, and suicides, provided only a moderate advance in knowledge, because this approach was too capable of supporting preconceived ideas. Among the most successful of this type of study was research on suicide by Émile Durkheim, whose successors in France and elsewhere developed the methodology a considerable way toward scientific adequacy.

After the turn of the century, interest in, and the determination to achieve, a sociological methodology grew steadily. The *Methodological Note*, constituting the greater part of a volume in W.I. Thomas and Florian Znaniecki's *Polish Peasant in Europe and America* (5 vol., 1918–20), has been recognized as an important advance, not so much in methodology as in committing sociologists to the task of achieving it.

Park and Burgess studies. Significant advances toward scientific effectiveness occurred at the University of Chicago in the 1920s. Under the stimulation of Robert E. Park, Burgess, and their colleagues a series of studies of the metropolis was conducted. The spirit was inductive, and hypotheses were discovered in rather than imposed on gathered information. Large numbers of students took part in the effort and contributed to both methods and findings. A conspicuous part of the effort consisted of mapping locations of various phenomena: land uses, residences of population categories (racial, ethnic, and occupational), residences of persons who commit various types of crimes or suicide, families becoming divorced or bro-

Inductive research

ken through desertion, and so forth. But along with such information on spatial distributions, data were sought by other means, including participant observation in groups and communities, gathering of life histories and case studies, assembly of relevant historical information, study of the life cycles of social movements and sects, and the like. Attention was explicitly given to the improvement of methodology in all of these efforts, to an extent approximately equal to the attention given to substantive findings. Here for the first time was developed a large-scale cooperative effort in which theory, methodology, and findings evolved together in an inductive process. The influence of this development at Chicago spread rapidly about the United States and in time influenced sociology almost everywhere it was studied in the world.

Statistics. Statistical methods were introduced into sociology from other sciences, and virtually from the start, sociologists have found statistical measures of relationship of great value. Karl Pearson's "coefficient of correlation," for example, has been a popular as well as important statistical concept for the measurement of cause-and-effect relationships among continuous variables. This method reveals the *degree* of causal connection between two variables, though not necessarily the *nature* of the connection. In sociology there are types of data that are relevant to causal inquiry but do not have the characteristics that qualify for the Pearsonian coefficient. Thus, much development work has been done to provide other measures of association involving, for example, rankings of groups or individuals or qualitative comparisons (such as whether males and females differ systematically in specified qualities).

Factor analysis, also based on an elaboration of Pearsonian correlation, performs another valuable service to sociology. If there are a large number of variables causally intertwined in a complex way, it is possible that these variables can be reduced to a small number of factors. Fifty different tests of mental ability, for instance, may be in fact fifty different mixtures of only seven or eight dimensions of mental ability. Factor analysis involves reducing such variables to a more limited number of common factors and determining the relative importance of each factor in the original variables. The process has its imperfections and the computations are laborious, but the availability of computers has overcome the latter disadvantage, and in recent years the technique has increased in use.

These statistical methods and many others are applicable to all branches of sociology and are increasingly fruitful in transforming sociology into science (see also STATISTICS). In general, the growth of statistical methods has been so rapid that the invention of new techniques has outstripped the ability of scholars to find data worthy of the devices. Thus the rate of progress in the near future may depend to a large extent on improvement in satisfactory data gathering and measurement. Methodologies of data gathering are in fact of major interest in sociology. Techniques of observation—of persons, groups, organizations, communities—have been extensively developed. Important for the same purpose are the various means of quantifying these observations, including scales of various kinds, sociometric techniques that make interrelations subject to statistical analysis, content analysis of written materials, and classification of cross-cultural information.

Experiments. Experimental methods, once believed to be inapplicable to sociological research, were extensively applied by psychologists, first on individuals and later on groups. By the 1930s some psychologists—notably Kurt Lewin and his colleagues and also Muzafer Sherif—found means of conducting experiments on social interaction. Sociologists soon followed their example and in time a number of laboratories for such research were established; Robert F. Bales, at Harvard, has made systematic observations on interaction in small, artificial groups and has produced clear and useful results, confirmed in other laboratories. Experiments are also conducted in classrooms, in summer camps, in formal organizations, and elsewhere. In general the success of experimentation has been greatest in simple situations in which the number of

Harvard interaction studies

variables is limited. Complex experiments, however, are possible in some circumstances, and the design of complex formal experiments is becoming a developed art in a variety of fields, including sociology.

Data collection. Within the main categories of research methods there are many special problems for which techniques have been devised. Data collection, for example, is effected in many different ways, from unstructured observation, essentially methodless, to sophisticated measurement through special instruments. Some of the basic problems of data collection concern such matters as the most efficient use of terminology, the definitions of units to be measured, and the classifications to be used. In general it is necessary to consider the nature of a specific problem in order to choose the most appropriate unit. For example, in a study of the relation of the size of a city to the cost of operating its local government, the proper unit might well be the population residing within its political boundaries. If the research question, however, is the relation of city size to any of a number of forms of social disorganization, it may be more fruitful to recognize that sociologically the significant unit would include much or all of the settled areas outside the city limits.

In the fields of social differentiation and occupational mobility the matter of definition of specific occupations is critical. If persons are asked in a questionnaire to state their occupation, the usual response is to give only one occupation, and this one is sometimes vaguely defined and made obscure by the tendency to give a euphemistic answer. Persons change occupations; some have more than one; some might claim an occupation that they merely aspire to. The art of obtaining useful answers to such important questions involves carefully designed questions adapted to the specific purposes of the study. General classifications, intended for a variety of studies, have limited utility.

In the process of gathering research data for sociology there are occasional obstacles to direct observation. In such cases indirect indicators may provide crude but useful substitutes. For example, alcoholic consumption in a small village in which the beverage is supposed to be prohibited may be estimated by a count of empty bottles in trash receptacles, or perhaps in the town dump. Library book circulation has been used to estimate the use of television in a community in which withdrawals of books of fiction declined, while nonfiction withdrawals remained as before.

Questionnaires are convenient for obtaining information from large numbers of respondents but involve many methodological problems. Wording of questions must of course be intelligible to uneducated and uninterested persons, must have standard meanings to persons of varying backgrounds, must avoid topics that arouse resistance and refusal to complete the questionnaire, and must avoid being too complex or difficult so that returns are insufficient or constitute a biased sample. Since it is known that slight alterations in the wording of questionnaire items may produce considerable variations in the pattern of responses, the precise wording becomes a matter of some art as well as science. A similar effect occurs in the order of items, since some may suggest or influence responses on later ones.

Similar issues are involved in data gathering through interviewing. It is necessary to control such variables as the appearance, manner, and approach of the interviewer, the specific manner in which questions are asked, ways of avoiding interviewer influence on the responses, and the tendency of some respondents to refuse to answer questions or to discontinue the interview. To meet the problems of resistance on sensitive subjects and inarticulateness about some feelings, various indirect or projective devices may be employed so that a respondent in answering one question provides information he may not realize he is giving about other questions.

Questionnaires and interviews may be so arranged that the patterns of responses form a scale, converting qualitative variations into measures available for statistical treatment. An early scaling method, devised in the late 1920s by a psychologist, L.L. Thurstone, is still widely used in sociology. It is formed in the following way: a list of questionnaire items is presented to a number of judges who independently relist the items in the order in which they consider them important or of interest. From their decisions are selected items on which there is satisfactory agreement of scale value.

Scaling may also be provided by statements to which a respondent is asked whether he "strongly approves," "approves," is "undecided," "disapproves," or "strongly disapproves." Or the quantitative differences may be introduced through a logical sequence of preference answers —for example, whether the respondent would admit a particular category of person (a) to close kinship by marriage, (b) to his club as a personal chum, (c) to employment in his occupation, (d) to citizenship in his country. Here it is assumed that the later answers imply more desired social distance.

A method or class of methods called sociometry has been under development since its introduction in the middle 1930s by J.L. Moreno. The essence of the method is the collection and tabulation of information about various types of interaction among members of groups of small or moderate size. The interaction may be either actual behaviour or merely anticipated or desired behaviour, and it may consist of preferences for various kinds of association with other persons, such as having them as friends, sitting with them, working with them, and the like. The information may be collected by observation of real behaviour or by interviews or questionnaires with specific items regarding personal choices. After the information is gathered, it is sometimes put in the form of a sociogram, consisting of names of persons enclosed in circles or squares distributed over an area and connected with lines and arrows that indicate both detail of choices and general patterns of relationships. A person receiving many choices is readily seen as the target end of many lines and is sometimes referred to as a "star." A person completely unchosen has no lines pointing toward his name and is called an isolate. Further investigation of persons typed in this fashion may be made by statistical methods, case studies, or otherwise. Overall, it can be said that various improvements and elaborations of the basic sociometric approach have been made, and the method is now less distinctively separate from other social psychology research than it was originally.

Ecological patterning. Ecological methods in sociology were first developed in connection with research on the characteristics of the metropolis, especially in regard to features of a nonsocial character, such as the patterns resulting from the distribution and movements of populations and institutions in the general process of struggling for advantage. A conspicuous part of most early urban studies consisted of mapping such distributions. The patterns of land values, of locations of various types of businesses and industries, of ethnic categories of the population, and of types of behaviour (delinquency and crime, vice, family disorganization, mental disorders, etc.) were all shown to be interrelated in a general urban ecology. This fact was then shown to be related to many aspects of behaviour of city people, and valuable contributions were made to such general sociological topics as social differentiation, migration and vertical mobility, and social disorganization.

In recent years sociological ecology has broadened in meaning and in the elaboration of methods. One modern approach, known as ecosystem theory, consists of tracing general patterns of flow of materials, energy, and information into a system and their transformation during the flow through the system, among other things.

Problems of bias. Since most sociological knowledge is based on the study of samples from some larger universe of items, the possibilities of major errors from sampling bias constitute a methodological issue. Where biases cannot be controlled, the direction and extent may sometimes be estimated, but elimination of biases through use of quotas—or, when possible, random methods—yields the best results. This can be done, for example, by first randomly selecting a number of definable regions and metropolitan areas, then selecting randomly from each such

Questionnaires

Interviewing

Sociometry

area certain urban blocks and rural segments, then further selecting from these segments certain dwelling units, and finally selecting from the dwelling units the specific persons to constitute the sample.

In every stage of the process of discovery in sociology there are possibilities of error, and recognition of these is a part of the progress of sociological methodology. There is continuous creation of technical devices to reduce such errors and to estimate the amount of error that has not been eliminated.

National methodological preferences. All the methods described above are widely used, but their relative popularity in various nations is somewhat related to both the nature of the financial support of research and the field of national interest. Where agricultural problems are of major interest, rural sociology and community studies that can be conducted inexpensively by one or a few investigators are popular. In France, Italy, and several other European nations, industrial sociology is understandably important, much of it based on case studies of industries and the experiences of workers. Sociology in Great Britain, the Scandinavian countries, and Japan covers most of the fields mentioned above.

The broad methodological concepts have varied somewhat according to the country and according to the subfield of sociology. Early in the century there was presumed to be a general difference between the sociologies of European countries and the sociologies of the United States—the former appearing to prefer broad sociological theory based on philosophical methods and the latter showing more inclination toward induction and empiricism. Such differences have declined steadily in recent times, and what differences remain may be in part a result of the differential financing of expensive research.

In the U.S.S.R. and nations under its influence there is much emphasis on the concepts and methods of Marxist sociology, which has only a small following elsewhere. A more important methodological issue divides basic scientific sociology from applied sociology; scholars interested in applied sociology tend to deprecate the methods and findings of the scientific sociologists as being either irrelevant or supportive of an objectionable status quo. Issues of ethics have also in recent years been raised, particularly in regard to observations and experiments in which the privacy of subjects may be felt to be invaded.

STATUS OF CONTEMPORARY SOCIOLOGY

Professional status. The Greek philosophers and the line of European philosophers in the succeeding centuries throughout Western civilization discussed much of the subject matter of sociology without thinking of it as a distinct subject. In the early 19th century all the subject matter of the social sciences was discussed under the heading of moral philosophy. Even after Auguste Comte introduced the word *sociologie* in 1838, the matter was combined with other subjects for some sixty years. Not until the universities undertook a commitment to the subject could a person make a living as a full-time sociologist. This commitment had first to be made by scholars of other fields, of which history was a principal early sponsor.

As early as 1876, at the new Johns Hopkins University, some of the content of sociology was taught in the department of history and politics. In 1889 at the University of Kansas, the word appeared in the title of the department of history and sociology. In 1890 at Colby College, a historian, Albion Small, taught a course called sociology, as did Franklin H. Giddings in the same year at Bryn Mawr College. But the first real commitment to the creation of a field of sociology took place in 1892 at the new University of Chicago, where newly arrived Albion Small asked for and received permission to create a department called sociology—the first such in the world. In the following year or two, departments in the subject were founded at Columbia, Kansas, and Michigan and very soon afterward at Yale, Brown, and many other universities. By the late 1890s nearly all of the educational institutions in the United States either had departments of sociology or offered courses in the subject.

In 1895 the *American Journal of Sociology* began publication at the University of Chicago, in time to be followed by a large number of journals in many other countries. Ten years later the *American Sociological Society* was organized, also to be followed in time by a large number of national, regional, international, and special sociological organizations. These quickly institutionalized the subject and have continuously served to guide its directions and to establish, very roughly, its boundaries. Eventually in 1949 the International Sociological Association was established under the sponsorship of UNESCO, and Louis Wirth (1897–1952) of the University of Chicago was elected its first president.

The rapid growth in numbers of full-time sociologists, along with growth of publications, allowed the content of the discipline to expand rapidly. By 1970 there were more than a dozen important sociological journals and an indefinite number of minor journals in the U.S., as well as a considerable number in other nations. Research grew throughout the 20th century at an accelerated pace, especially since the 1920s, partly as a consequence of strong financial support from foundations, government, commercial sources, and private gifts. Along with this there came a flourishing of research institutes, some affiliated with university departments and some independent. A small but increasing number of full-time sociologists gain their livelihood through full-time research independent of universities.

Similar developments have occurred in various other parts of the world, with variations resulting from special conditions in each case. In France, where Auguste Comte and later Émile Durkheim gave early impetus to sociology, there was early development in many fields of the subject. The two World Wars slowed the development, but after 1945 a strong revival of interest in sociology took place, during which the French government established a number of institutes in the social sciences at the level of institutes in the natural sciences, including several in Paris for sociological research—notably the Centre d'Études Sociologiques, the Institut National d'Études Démographiques, and the Maison des Sciences de l'Homme. These institutes receive government funds and employ many full-time sociologists, some of them among the prominent scholars in the nation. French universities have been somewhat more conservative; the Sorbonne, for example, had in 1970 only one chair officially assigned to sociology. The new University of Nanterre, however, established a department with four professorships. A rich amount of research publication has been produced in France since World War II, particularly in general sociology, theory, methodology, social psychology, industrial sociology, and the sociology of work.

German sociology had a strong base in the late 19th century and afterward, and the writings of Ferdinand Tönnies, Max Weber, Georg Simmel, and others were influential in all parts of the world. By the early 1930s, however, official Nazi hostility had impeded its development and by the time of the Second World War had destroyed it as an academic subject in Germany. Immediately after the war a new generation of scholars, aided by visiting sociologists, imported the new empirical research methods and began the development of a style of German sociology much different from the earlier theoretical and philosophical traditions. At the University of Frankfurt the Institut für Sozialforschung (social research), established by private financing before the war, was revived and has stimulated much research production. West German universities remained conservative for a time, but two newly created universities—the Free University of Berlin and the University of Constance—made sociology one of their major subjects. By 1970 most West German universities had at least one chair in sociology. National needs received special emphasis, including administrative research of use to planning, studies of unemployment, youth problems, and delinquency. A significant amount of research is also published in such fields as rural sociology, political sociology, and the family.

In Great Britain, despite the early prominence of Herbert Spencer and L.T. Hobhouse, sociology was little regarded by leading universities until recent years. Before World War II Britain excelled in anthropology, especially in the study of nonwhite societies of the empire. Sociology concentrated on studies of the poor, and much of it was undertaken by persons whose affiliation was similar to that of social workers in the U.S. The major prewar sociology department, at the London School of Economics, had the objective more of social reform than scientific objective research. In the postwar period, however, a considerable revival of sociology took place; Oxford and Cambridge recognized the subject by creating positions for sociologists, and various new universities established chairs and departments. Significant work in Britain has been done in such fields as population and demography, sociology of organization, and general sociology. The Tavistock Institute of Human Relations in London has become world famous and concentrates on human relations in the family, the work group, and organizations.

A parallel growth took place in Canada, Australia, and New Zealand. Canada, with some apparent reluctance, allowed itself to be much influenced by American sociology and has recently built many new departments with sociologists trained in the U.S.

The Scandinavian countries have also to a considerable extent adopted the methods and some of the content of American sociology, and the subject has had rapid development in many of the universities and in research institutes, some of which are connected with universities. There is also a considerable amount of interchange between sociologists in these countries.

Japan has a record of much sociological activity dating back to the 1870s. The Japanese Sociological Society (Nippon Shakai Gakkai), headquartered at the University of Tokyo, was founded in 1923; and by 1960 there were about 150 universities and colleges with courses in the subject. In the early period sociology was nearly all imported; Comte and Spencer, and later Giddings and Gabriel Tarde, were their important theorists. After the Second World War there were rapid changes in sociology in Japan, with empirical research methods largely replacing the earlier philosophical style. Importations from American sociology became abundant. Popular among these were industrial sociology, educational sociology, public opinion research, and the study of mass communications.

Sociology in the Soviet Union was long held back by the perceived incompatibility of the subject with Marxist theory. In recent years, however, it has been permitted to develop, and sociological institutes and chairs of sociology are increasing. By 1970 the Soviet Sociological Association had more than a thousand members. Leading research interests have been such subjects as labour productivity, education, crime, and alcoholism. There remains an apparent tendency to avoid issues that might imply conflict with Marxist thought.

Nations under the influence of the Soviet Union have also from time to time been inhospitable to sociology, but the strong interest of younger scholars has made possible some relaxation of this opposition, and in recent years there has been considerable progress of sociology in Yugoslavia, Czechoslovakia, Hungary, and Poland, with occasional setbacks in some areas, such as Czechoslovakia.

In Israel the dominant department of sociology is at the Hebrew University in Jerusalem, where there are also several research institutes. Israeli sociology maintains continuous close contacts with American sociology, and many of the leading Israeli sociologists have had training or teaching experience in the U.S. Among the specialties in Israel are research in methodology, communication, criminology, and the collective settlements (*kibbutzim*) in which new forms of custom and social organization are observed while under development.

The passing of the Fascist regime in Italy and the relative liberalization in Spain have opened the door to sociology, and academic chairs and research institutes are gradually increasing in these countries. Of particular interest are studies of industrial efficiency and social mobility. The general conservatism of universities, however, may constitute a retarding influence for some time to come.

In Latin America objective sociology has been much resisted, partly because it has been viewed as a threat to the political and social order, but also because of meagre financial support of research and the low salary level of professors, many of whom must supplement their earnings in the practice of law, in civil service, and other occupations. In the 1960s, however, the number of full-time chairs increased and a number of research institutes, some financed by U.S. funds, were established. Political instability in some countries remains a major hindrance, and in such countries able scholars continue to be forced from their university positions from time to time.

Little by little sociology is penetrating into some of the developing nations. A number of African universities have formed departments, and the subject is gaining in importance in the Philippines, India, Indonesia, and Pakistan.

Scientific status. It is evident that sociology has not achieved triumphs comparable to those of the several older and more heavily supported sciences. A variety of interpretations have been offered to explain the difference—most frequently, that the growth of knowledge in the science of sociology is more random than cumulative. The true situation appears to be that in some parts of the discipline—such as methodology, ecology, demography, the study of social differentiation and mobility, attitude research, and the study of small-group interaction processes, public opinion, and mass communication—there has in fact taken place a slow but accelerating accumulation of organized and tested knowledge. In some other fields the expansion of the volume of literature has not appeared to have had this property. Critics have attributed the slow pace to a variety of factors—the appetite of sociologists for neologisms and jargon, a disposition for pseudo-quantification, and excessive concern with imitation of the methods of natural sciences, overdependence on data from interviews, questionnaires, and informal observations. All these shortcomings can be found in contemporary sociology, but none is characteristic of all areas. In general there has been progress toward efficient terminology and methods and toward more satisfactory data, and conclusions are increasingly based on the harmonious mixture of research methods applied to varied and repeated studies, and therefore are less dependent on the strength of one particular methodological device.

Bias, in more than one direction, is sometimes presumed to be a chronic affliction of sociology. This may arise in part from the fact that the subject matter of sociology is familiar and important in the daily life of everyone, so that there exist many opportunities for the abundant variations in philosophical outlook and individual preferences to appear as irrational bias. Thus critics have expressed disapproval of the sociologists' skepticism on various matters of faith, of their amoral relativism concerning customs, of their apparent oversimplifications of some principles, and of their particular fashions in categorization and abstraction. But skepticism toward much of the content of folk knowledge is a characteristic of all science, and relativism can be interpreted as merely an avoidance of antiscientific ethnocentrism. Furthermore, abstraction, categorization, and simplification are necessary to the advancement of knowledge, and no one system satisfies everyone.

Polarization of views. The dispute about the main purpose of sociology, whether it works to understand behaviour, or to cause social change, is a dispute found in every pursuit of scientific knowledge, and such polarization is far from absolute. Persons differ in the degree to which they regard the value of science as an intellectual understanding of the cosmos or as an instrument for immediate improvement of the human lot. Since even the "purest" scientist conceives of his work as benefiting mankind, the issue narrows to a difference in preference between an *ad hoc* attack on immediate human problems and a long-run trust that basic knowledge, gathered without reference to present urgencies, is even more valuable. Sociologists differ on this issue; in some countries there is much pressure toward early practicality of results; in others, including the United States, the larger number of scholars and the principal sociological associations have shown

Criticisms of sociology

preference for "basic science." In very recent times, however, there has emerged a radical movement among students in various countries involving advocacy of complete commitment to action on current political and social problems.

A degree of polarization has also arisen over the proper strategy for research—whether research should take its directions from the needs of society and mankind or from the evolving theoretical corpus of sociology. In nations that allow academic freedom such disputes are usually of low intensity, because each scholar selects his research interests on any basis he prefers, including that of personal taste. In this way presumably the motivation of the investigator is maximized.

The place of values in sociology. Sociologists most interested in action express impatience at the claims of others who prefer to separate their research from personal values. Much of the dispute prevails only because the two sides argue past each other. There can be wide agreement that no human being is without personal values, that research forced to confirm a particular set of values is not good science, and that there can be scientific issues toward which a particular investigator is value-neutral. In research that is susceptible to contamination by the values of the worker, it is generally possible to minimize the damage by employing methodological devices that help to insulate the scientist from his wishes for a particular outcome—such devices as objective observational techniques and measurement methods, independent and blind analysis of results, and so forth.

THE FUTURE OF SOCIOLOGY

Forces that may influence sociology. It would appear that the growth of sociology will accelerate in the visible future. Among present trends suggesting this likelihood are the increase in public appreciation of the subject, the expansion of available funds for both teaching and research, the steady reduction of sectarian opposition to inquiry into social institutions, the improvement in research methods and methods for gathering data that qualify for modern statistical treatment, and the growth of acceptance and support from scientists in other fields. There are possible factors that could inhibit such growth, such as some forms of extreme nationalism and internal conflict, but such conditions so far have impeded development only locally and temporarily.

Furthermore, it appears likely that public interest in the development of sociological knowledge will increase as a consequence of rising awareness of its promise for human safety and welfare. As the expansion of civilization, with its advanced science and technology, progressively conquers the natural hazards that afflict preliterate and preindustrial peoples and diminishes such threats as natural catastrophes, famine, and disease, a wide range of new problems emerges. These are not the menaces of an impersonal nature, but dangers that arise from imperfection in human behaviour, particularly in organized human relations. Wars have shown a tendency to become larger and ever more destructive, and the causes, though far from being understood, clearly lie, in large measure, in the complexities of social organization, in the interaction of great corporate national bodies. There appears to be little hope that politics, unaided by social science among other disciplines, could reverse this trend.

Domestic problems within nations, regions, cities, and towns appear also to become increasing sources of human troubles. There is a general rise in the severity of ethnic hostilities, and of internal conflicts between generations, political factions, and other divisions of the populations. There are also threats to human welfare from various forms of general social disorganization, reflected in the spread of pockets of poverty, crime, vice, political corruption, and family disorganization. In recent times the threats of overpopulation and potential destruction of the ecological environment have added a further reason for public alarm. Contemporary sociology obviously does not yet provide the solutions, but what prospects of human survival there are depend a great deal on the increase of the applicable knowledge of various social sciences, including sociology.

Emerging subfields. Because human behaviour observes no limits in its directions, it is possible for sociologists to extend their inquiries accordingly. The expansion of sociological interests thus has involved some penetration of adjacent traditional academic fields, such as political science, economics, anthropology, psychology, communications, speech, and to some extent even physiology and zoology. Fields within traditional sociology have also broadened their content, producing such expanded subjects as ecology and comparative sociology. Not all this extension is new, however, since much of the 19th century sociology was also very broad, especially the cosmic sociology of one worker, Lester F. Ward, who conceived sociology as the science of sciences, properly covering and organizing all knowledge.

Applications of sociology also appear to be spreading in a variety of directions, and here the possibilities seem unlimited. Sociologists aid industries in obtaining more efficient production; they help unions to increase their power; they organize rebellions of young persons, reform disorganized villages, counsel persons and families, and give or sell services to a wide variety of consumers. To what extent these applied activities will continue to spread will doubtless depend on their effectiveness relative to other means of gaining the same effects. *Applications of sociology*

There is also an expansion of sociology into other than practical applications; for example, there is mathematical sociology, in which mathematical models of social behaviour are developed without systematic observations of behaviour. These efforts are not directed toward immediate human use, but may have value as bases for comparison with real behaviour and thus aid explanation of behavioral causes. A mathematical model of a completely just theoretical process of social mobility, for example, could be useful as a standard for comparing actual mobility at different times and in different nations.

Emerging methodologies. After the easiest sociological questions have been answered, the further progress of research requires ever greater effort and cost, and the proportion of discoveries by individual investigators declines as the necessity for larger teamwork research expands. This foreshadows increasing complexity of the organization of research, as has already taken place in older sciences. Large-scale research in sociology is made possible, and perhaps inevitable, by the availability of expensive computers, elaborate techniques of multivariate analysis, and the storage of information in the form of data banks and the like.

The strongest methodological emphasis in the near future is likely to be on the processes of rigorous testing of generalizations that now appear to be of strategic value in the general structure of sociological knowledge. Complete surprises in the field of human behaviour are less likely than in other sciences, since most of the possible human situations have been familiar in folk knowledge as well as in academic sociology. But the subject contains many inconsistent principles, and few of these have been put to a definitive test, partly from lack of adequate methodology and to some extent from shortage of funds and scientific manpower.

Emerging roles for sociologists. In general the principal employment of sociologists has been in educational institutions, but recently, in various countries, there has been an increasing penetration into other fields of activity. Sociologists, particularly in earlier decades, have been involved in various organized agencies devoted to social work. They have also participated in government work at various levels, from the lower bureaucratic ranks all the way to high administrative responsibility, and in the case of Thomáš Masaryk, former president of Czechoslovakia, to the highest office of a nation. In the United States sociologists have been extensively employed in the Bureau of the Census; the Bureau of the Budget; the Institutes of Health; various other sections of the Department of Health, Education, and Welfare; and the office of the president, where they have made contributions to policy.

Other directions of sociological activity include the roles of consultant, social critic, and social activists and even revolutionaries. When the activity diverges far enough from traditional academic sociology, it may cease to be regarded as sociological, but it appears likely that sociologists will continue to spread their activities over the ever-widening region of national or global concern, in the name of their science or otherwise.

BIBLIOGRAPHY. Among older titles of major significance, generally considered classics and still of value today, are: W.G. SUMNER, *The Folkways* (1907, reissued 1940); C.H. COOLEY, *Human Nature and the Social Order* (1902, reissued 1967); G.H. MEAD, *Mind, Self, and Society* ed. by C.W. MORRIS (1934); E. FARIS, *The Nature of Human Nature* (1937); R.E. PARK and E.W. BURGESS, *Introduction to the Science of Sociology* (1921, reissued 1969); and W.F. OGBURN, *Social Change with Respect to Culture and Original Nature*, new ed. (1950; suppl. ch., 1964). A comprehensive summary of early sociological theory is available in H.E. BARNES (ed.), *An Introduction to the History of Sociology* (1948).

The following titles provide excellent coverage of the main directions and subfields of recent and contemporary sociology: R.E.L. FARIS (ed.), *Handbook of Modern Sociology* (1964); R.K. MERTON, L. BROOM, and L.S. COTTRELL (eds.), *Sociology Today*, 2 vol. (1959, reissued 1965); G.D. GURVITCH and W.E. MOORE (eds.), *Twentieth Century Sociology* (1945); J.G. MARCH (ed.), *Handbook of Organizations* (1965); and N.J. SMELSER and J.A. DAVIS (eds.), *Sociology* (1969). Two modern and influential general texts are L. BROOM and P. SELZNICK, *Sociology*, 4th ed. (1968); and G.A. LUNDBERG *et al.*, *Sociology*, 4th ed. (1968).

Leading books treating communities and societies as wholes, as well as the general theory of society and social systems are these: TALCOTT PARSONS, *Societies: Evolutionary and Comparative Perspectives* (1966); I.T. SANDERS, *The Community*, 2nd ed. (1966); R.K. MERTON, *Social Theory and Social Structure*, rev. ed. (1957); G.C. HOMANS, *Social Behaviour: Its Elementary Forms* (1961); G.E. LENSKI, *Human Societies: A Macrolevel Introduction to Sociology* (1970); and A.L. STINCH-COMBE, *Constructing Social Theories* (1968).

The following symposia provide useful coverage of sociological activity in the field of social psychology: E.F. BORGATTA (ed.), *Social Psychology: Readings and Perspective* (1969); C. GORDON and K.J. GERGEN (eds.), *The Self in Social Interaction*, vol. 1, *Classic and Contemporary Perspectives* (1968); and J.G. MANIS and B.N. MELTZER (eds.), *Symbolic Interaction: A Reader in Social Psychology* (1967). Modern technical and statistical methods used in sociology are presented in E.F. BORGATTA (ed.), *Sociological Methodology* (1968); and J.H. MUELLER, K.F. SCHUESSLER, and H.L. COSTNER, *Statistical Reasoning in Sociology*, 2nd ed. (1970).

For special topics and for definitions of sociological terms, consult the *International Encyclopedia of the Social Sciences*, 17 vol. (1968); and J. GOULD and W.L. KOLB (eds.), *A Dictionary of the Social Sciences* (1964).

(R.E.L.F.)

Socrates

Socrates of Athens, who flourished in the last half of the 5th century BC, was the first of the great trio of ancient Greeks—Socrates, Plato, and Aristotle—who laid the philosophical foundations of Western culture. As Cicero said, Socrates "brought down philosophy from heaven to earth"—*i.e.*, from the nature speculation of the Ionian and Italian cosmologists to analyses of the character and conduct of human life, which he assessed in terms of an original theory of the soul. Living during the chaos of the Peloponnesian War, with its erosion of moral values, Socrates felt called to shore up the ethical dimensions of life by the admonition to "know thyself" and by the effort to explore the connotations of moral and humanistic terms.

LIFE

Socrates was born in or about 470 BC, ten years after the Battle of Salamis. His father, Sophroniscus, was a friend of the family of Aristides the Just, founder of the Delian League, from which the empire arose. The tale that his father was a sculptor rests on Plato's reference to the mythical sculptor Daedalus as the ancestor, or work-lineage, of Socrates. Although the philosopher's mother, Phaenarete, acted as a "midwife," this fact implies nothing about her social status.

The memoir writer Ion of Chios mentioned meeting Socrates at Samos in the company of the philosopher Archelaus, a pupil of Anaxagoras (Athens' first philoso-

Socrates, herm with a restored nose probably copied from the Greek original by Lysippus, *c.* 350 BC. In the Museo Archeologico Nazionale, Naples.
By courtesy of the Soprintendenza alle Antichità della Campania, Naples

pher), presumably during the military operations of 441–439. The connection between the two men is also asserted by the musicologist Aristoxenus, whereas the tradition of commentaries based on Theophrastus, Aristotle's successor, calls Socrates the "disciple" of Archelaus.

Early life and connections

Plato and Aeschines the Socratic, both writers of Socratic dialogues, agree with the military historian Xenophon in depicting him as intimate with the leading figures of the Periclean circle (Aspasia, Alcibiades, Axiochus, Callias), then dominant in Athens. Xenophon concurs with Plato in saying that he was well versed in geometry and astronomy, and this representation agrees with the narrative of Plato's *Phaedo* as well as the burlesque *The Clouds*, which was written by the playwright Aristophanes.

Socrates must already have been a conspicuous figure at Athens when Aristophanes and Ameipsias both made him the subject of their comedies in 423, and, because they made a special point of his neediness, he had probably suffered recent losses. (The marked poverty of his old age is said in Plato's *Apology* to have been caused by his preoccupation with his mission to mankind.)

Socrates was married, apparently late in life, to Xanthippe, by whom he left three sons, one an infant. Xenophon speaks of her high temper; there is no evidence, however, that she was a "shrew"; the sons, according to Aristotle, proved insignificant.

Socrates' record for endurance was distinguished. He served as a hoplite, perhaps at Samos (440), and at several stations during the Peloponnesian War. (At Potidaea he saved the life of Alcibiades.) In politics he took no part, knowing, as he told his judges, that office would mean compromise with his principles. Once at least, in 406–405, he was a member of the Boule, or legislative council, of 500; and at the trial of the victors of Arginusae, he resisted, at first with the support of his colleagues, afterward alone, the unconstitutional condemnation of the generals by a collective verdict. He showed the same courage in 404, when the oligarchy of the Thirty Tyrants in Athens, wishing to implicate honourable men in their proceedings, instructed him and four others to arrest Leon, one of their victims. Socrates disobeyed, and he says in Plato's *Apology* that this might have cost him his life but for the counterrevolution of the next year. (For the background to these events see GREEK CIVILIZATION, ANCIENT.)

In 399 Socrates was indicted for "impiety." The author of the proceedings was the influential Anytus, one of the two chiefs of the democrats restored by the counterrevolution of 403; but the nominal prosecutor was the obscure and insignificant Meletus. There were two counts

Indictment, trial, and death

in the accusation, "corruption of the young" and "neglect of the gods whom the city worships and the practice of religious novelties," Socrates, who treated the charge with contempt and made a "defense" that amounts to avowal and justification, was convicted, probably by 280 votes against 220. The prosecutors had asked for the penalty of death; it now rested with the accused to make a counterproposition. Though a smaller, but substantial, penalty would have been accepted, Socrates took the high line that he really merited the treatment of an eminent benefactor: maintenance at the public table. He consented only for form's sake to suggest the small fine of one mina, raised at the entreaty of his friends to 30.

The claim to be a public benefactor incensed the court, and death was voted by an increased majority, a result with which Socrates declared himself well content. As a rule at Athens, the condemned man "drank the hemlock" within 24 hours but, in the case of Socrates, the fact that no execution could take place during the absence of the sacred ship sent yearly to Delos caused an unexpected delay of a month, during which Socrates remained in prison, receiving his friends daily and conversing with them in his usual manner. An escape was planned by his friend Crito, but Socrates refused to hear of it, on the grounds that the verdict, though contrary to fact, was that of a legitimate court and must therefore be obeyed. The story of his last day, with his drinking of the hemlock, has been perfectly told in the *Phaedo* of Plato, who, though not himself an eyewitness, was in close touch with many of those who were present.

Main sources of information.   Socrates wrote nothing; therefore, information about his personality and doctrine has to be sought chiefly in the dialogues of Plato and in the *Memorabilia* of Xenophon. As both men were nearly 45 years younger than Socrates, they could speak from firsthand knowledge about only the last ten to 12 years of his life.

Xenophon, whose relations with Socrates seem not to have been close, has even been suspected of drawing from Plato. His admitted deficiencies in imagination and capacity for thinking do not make him the more faithful exponent of a philosophical genius. Moreover, Xenophon's apologetic purpose calls for some discounting. His most valuable statements are those that appear to be most at variance with his main thesis, viz., that the prosecutors of Socrates were mistaken even from their own point of view.

Plato's depiction of Socrates

Plato's more vivid picture has been suspected on the grounds that he used Socrates as a "mouthpiece" for speculations of his own: the theory of "Ideas" or doctrine of "Forms" is thus held to have been originated by Plato. There are serious reasons for denying this assumption, though they have not yet convinced many scholars; in any case, to employ it, without investigation, to discredit Plato's testimony begs the question.

In some important respects, Plato's testimony is confirmed by the extant writings of Aeschines Socraticus. *The Clouds* of Aristophanes yields valuable information about Socrates in his middle 40s, though allowance must be made for the work's character as a burlesque. It should be compared carefully with the autobiographical statements put into the mouth of Socrates in the *Phaedo*, which, though not "contemporary evidence," are clearly meant to express Plato's bona fide belief about his master's intellectual history. Whichever way the evidence is interpreted, however, a Platonic view of Socrates is available in the *Dialogues* that is valuable in its own right; hence the following discussion will draw heavily upon the *Dialogues* as the primary source for the portrait of Socrates.

Personal characteristics.   Though Socrates was a good fighting man, his outward appearance was grotesque. Stout and not tall, with prominent eyes, snub nose, broad nostrils, and wide mouth, he seemed a very Silenus. But, as his friends knew, he was "all glorious within," "the most upright man of that day" (Plato, *The Seventh Letter* [324*e*]). His self-control and powers of endurance were exemplary; "he had so schooled himself to moderation that his scanty means satisfied all his wants."

But Socrates was no self-tormenting ascetic: he "knew both how to want and how to abound" and could be the soul of the merriment at a gay party. He had no sympathy with the slatternliness of his friend Antisthenes nor with the godly dirtiness often affected by the followers of Pythagoras (the philosopher of number). There was nothing of the complacent self-righteousness of the Pharisee nor of the angry bitterness of the satirist in his attitude toward the follies or even the crimes of his fellowmen. It was his deep and lifelong conviction that the improvement not only of himself but also of his countrymen was a task laid upon him "by God," not to be executed, however, with a scowling face and an upbraiding voice. Like St. Francis Xavier, he understood that to win men's souls one must be "good company." Conscious of his own infirmities, he felt a profound sympathy for the intemperate.

Socrates was a true patriot who felt that he could best prove his devotion to Athens by setting his face resolutely against the attractions of specious, and popular but deadly, false theories of public and private morality. When the city brought him to trial and threatened him with death, his sense of civic duty forbade him to escape into exile either before or after the trial. It was his very patriotism that made him an unsparing critic of the Athenian "democracy" and so led to his being condemned to death.

The Socratic irony

Nothing was more marked in his character than an unusually keen appreciation of the comic in human nature and conduct that protected him at once against sentimentality and against cynicism. This is what his opponents in Plato call his "irony" and treat as an irritating affectation. "Intellectually the acutest man of his age, he represents himself in all companies as the dullest person present. Morally the purest, he affects to be the slave of passion" (W.H. Thompson). No doubt, in part, this irony was "calculated"; it "disarmed ridicule by anticipating it." But its true sense is the spontaneous sense of fun that makes its possessor the enemy of all pretentiousness, moral or intellectual. And it is certain that, though the purity of Socrates is beyond question, he really had an ardent and amorous temperament.

Religious beliefs.   Socrates was clearly a man of deep piety with the temperament of a mystic. He regarded mythology, with its foolish or immoral tales about gods, as a mere invention of the poets. But he found it easy to combine his own strong belief in God as ruler of the world with the view that, in practice, one could worship God in the way prescribed by "the usage of the city." God's existence is shown, he held, not only by the providential order of nature and the universality of the belief in him but also by warnings and revelations given in dreams, signs, and oracles. The soul of man partakes of the Divine; and, as Plato argued in the *Phaedo*, Socrates believed in the soul's immortality. Aristophanes makes Socrates combine the parts of "infidel" physicist and hierophant of a mysterious private faith and, in *The Birds*, presents him as presiding at a fraudulent séance. He was regular, says Xenophon, in prayer and sacrifice, though he held that, because only the gods know what is good for a man, his prayer should simply be "give me what is good." It is clear from Plato that Socrates was quite familiar with Pythagorean and Orphic religious ideas—with the doctrine of the divine origin and destiny of the soul, for example—though he regarded the ordinary Orphic mystery monger with healthy contempt.

The evidence that Socrates had a markedly "mystical" temperament is abundant. Plato tells of his curious "rapts," in one of which he stood spellbound for 24 hours in the trenches. The accounts of the philosopher's "divine sign" tell the same story. This, according to Plato, was a "voice" often heard by Socrates from childhood. It forbade him to do things but never gave positive encouragement. According to Plato, it merely gave prognostications of good or bad luck, and the occasions of its occurrence were often "very trivial." Thus, it was neither an intuitive conscience nor a symptom of mental disorder but an interior psychic audition.

Mode of life.   Socrates seemed to spend all his time in the streets, the marketplace, and, more particularly, the *gymnasia.* He cared little for the country. Though he frequented by choice the society of young men of promise, he also talked freely to politicians, poets, and artisans about their various callings, their notions of right and wrong, the familiar matters of interest to them. The object of all this dialogue was to test the famous oracle of Apollo at Delphi, which had pronounced him the wisest of men. This pronouncement was made before Socrates had become conscious of his mission to his fellowmen: even at that early date, it is implied, he had the highest of reputations in circles interested in wisdom. (This early date is attested by the fact that the Eleatics from Megara and the young pupils of the Pythagoreans from Thebes and Phlious who were attached to Socrates must have formed their connection with him before the Peloponnesian War.)

The test of the Delphic oracle

Socrates set himself to convict "the god" of falsehood. But finding that those who thought themselves wise were unable to give any coherent account of their wisdom, Socrates had to admit that he was wiser than others, just because he alone was aware of his own ignorance. This account is plainly tinged with the usual "irony." Socrates took the Delphic oracle seriously enough to probe into its real import. He believed himself charged with a mission from God to make his fellowmen aware of their ignorance and of the supreme importance of knowledge of what is for the soul's good. This is proved by his declaration that he was more than ready to face instant death rather than to neglect his commission.

The poverty in which this mission had involved him and the austerity of the rule of life that it entailed were notorious. Summer and winter, Socrates' coat was the same; he had neither shoes nor shirt. "A slave who was made to live so," the Sophist Antiphon said, "would run away." This self-imposed life of hardships was the price of his spiritual independence.

His message, however, was variously received. Some of those whose false pretensions were exposed by his trenchant criticizing regarded him with ill will; many thought him an officious busybody. Among the younger men, many merely thought it good sport to see their elders silenced. Others, such as Alcibiades and Critias, deliberately attached themselves to him for a time "for private ends," believing that to learn the secret of so acute a reasoner would be the best preparation for success in the law courts, the council, and the assembly. Others sincerely hoped by associating with him to become good men and true, capable of doing their duty by house and household, by relations and friends, by city and fellow citizens. Finally, there was an inner circle that entered more deeply into Socrates' principles and transmitted them to the next generation. But these were not "disciples" united by a common doctrine. The bond of union was a common reverence for a great man's intellect and character. It was, in the main, this group—many from states that had been enemies of Athens in the recent war—that collected around Socrates on the day of his death.

The accusation and its causes. The explanation of the attack made on Socrates is simple. He had been on terms of close friendship with the two men whose memories were most obnoxious to the democrats: Critias, the fiercest spirit among the extremists of the "terror" of 404; and Alcibiades, whose self-will had done so much to bring about the downfall of the Athenian empire. The charge of "educating Alcibiades" was made prominent in the pamphlet written a few years after the trial by the Sophist Polycrates, in justification of the verdict. More than half a century later, the orator Aeschines reminds his audience that Socrates had been put to death because he was believed to have educated Critias. In point of fact, it was absurd to make Socrates responsible for the ambitions of Alcibiades, and, as he reminded his judges, he had disobeyed an illegal order from Critias and his colleagues at the risk of his life. But it is natural that he should have had to suffer for the crimes of both men, the more so because he had been an unsparing critic of democracy and of the famous democratic leaders and, furthermore, had not, like the advanced democrats, withdrawn from Athens during the "terror."

His association with political enemies

Socrates was, in fact, suspected of using his great abilities and gifts to pervert his younger associates from loyalty to the principles of democracy, and the convinced democrats who had recovered the city in 403 were unwilling, as J. Burnet has said, "to leave their work at the mercy of reaction." The motives of Anytus, an upright, unintelligent democrat, are thus quite explicable: from his point of view, Socrates would be at the best a moderate oligarch, and democrats who remembered the career of the statesman Theramenes, who had tried to mix oligarchy and democracy, could not be expected to make a fine distinction between the moderate oligarch and the traitor.

The real grounds for the attack could not be disclosed in the indictment because of the amnesty that had terminated the struggle, of which Anytus himself had been a main promoter. Hence, the charge took the form of a vague accusation of "corruption of the young." Probably for the same reasons, Anytus was ashamed to appear as the principal in the matter and put forward the obscure Meletus, who might venture on "indiscretions" more openly. If this was the same Meletus who prosecuted Andocides on the same charge of "impiety," he must have been a half-witted fanatic—and this may explain why the charge of irreligion was added. Xenophon suggests that the allusion was to the "divine sign," but this cannot be correct. Meletus said nothing about the "sign" at the prosecution, and Socrates is speaking with his "usual irony" when he pretends to guess that the mention of "religious novelties" in the indictment referred to the "sign." In the *Apology*, Socrates says that the prosecution is, no doubt, relying on memories of Aristophanes' *The Clouds*, where he had been made to talk "atheism" as part of the burlesque on men of science.

But there must have been more behind the charge. It seems likely that the prosecution of Andocides revived the old scandal of the "profanation of the mysteries" that had thrown Athens into a ferment on the eve, in 415, of the Sicilian expedition. The two chief victims, Alcibiades and his uncle Axiochus, had both been among the intimates of Socrates, and there is reason to think that others of his friends were affected. If this is what lay behind the charge, it can be understood why its real meaning seems never to have been explained: for in view of the terms of the amnesty, the matters in question were not within the competence of the court.

Meaning of the charge against him and his conviction

Socrates himself treats the whole matter with contempt. His defense consists in narrating the facts of his past life, which had proved that he was equally ready to defy the populace and the Thirty in the cause of right and law, and in insisting on the reality of his mission from God and his determination to discharge it, even at the cost of life. The prosecutors had no desire for blood. They counted on a voluntary withdrawal of the accused from the jurisdiction before trial; the death penalty was proposed to make such a withdrawal certain. Socrates himself forced the issue by refusing at any stage to do anything involving the least shade of compromise. The prosecution had raised the question whether he was a traitor or, as he held himself to be, an envoy from God; Socrates was determined that the judges should give a direct verdict on the issue without evasion. This is not only what makes him a martyr but also what forbids us to call Anytus a murderer.

DOCTRINE AND METHOD

Socrates was a man of the Periclean age, which witnessed one of the periodic "bankruptcies of science." Cosmological speculation, which had been boldly pursued from the beginning of the 6th century, seemed to have led to a chaos of conflicting systems of thought. The Rationalist Parmenides of Elea had apparently cut away the ground from science by showing that the real world must be quite unlike anything that the senses reveal and that, consequently, the interpretation of the world by familiar analogies is inherently fallacious; and his pupil Zeno of Elea seemed to have shown that even the postulates of mathematics are mutually contradictory. Thus, the ablest men, such as the Sophists Protagoras and Gorgias, had turned away from the pursuit of science and concerned them-

**Socrates'
early
interest in
"natural
science"**

selves not with truth but with making a success of human life.

Socrates, as a young man, was enthusiastically interested in "natural science" and familiarized himself with the various current systems—with the Milesian cosmology with its flat Earth and the Italian with its spherical Earth and with the mathematical puzzles raised by Zeno about "the unit" (*i.e.*, the problem of continuity). There was a complete lack of critical method. For a moment, Socrates hoped to find salvation in the doctrine of Anaxagoras that "Mind" is the source of all cosmic order because this seemed to mean that "everything is ordered as it is best that it should be," that the universe is a rational teleological system. But on reading the book of Anaxagoras, he found that the philosopher made no effective use of his principle; the details of his scheme were as arbitrary as those of any other.

The Socratic "hypothesis." After this disappointment, Socrates resolved from then on to consider primarily not "facts" but *logoi*, the "statements" or "propositions" that one makes about "facts." His method would be to start with whatever seemed the most satisfactory "hypothesis," or postulate, about a given subject and then consider the consequences that follow from it. So far as these consequences proved to be true and consistent, the "hypothesis" might be regarded as provisionally confirmed. But one should not confuse inquiry into the consequences of the "hypothesis" with proof of its truth. The question of truth could be settled only by deducing the initial "hypothesis" as a consequence from some more ultimate, accepted "hypothesis."

The doctrine of Forms. According to Plato, Socrates next proceeded to take it as his own fundamental "hypothesis" that every term (such as "good," "beautiful," "man") that has an unequivocal denotation directly names a selfsame object of a kind inaccessible to sense perception and apprehensible only by thought. Such an object Socrates calls an *Idea* or *Eidos*; *i.e.*, a Form. The sensible things on which a man predicates beauty, goodness, humanity, have only a secondary and derivative reality; they *become* this or that for a time, in virtue of their "participation" in the Form.

**Whether
the
Forms
are
Socratic**

Scholars in the 19th century usually assumed that this doctrine of Forms was consciously devised by Plato after the death of Socrates. The chief argument for this view is based upon the observation of Aristotle that Socrates rightly "did not separate" the universal from the particular as, it is apparently implied, Plato did. He might equally have meant, however, that the doctrine of the *Phaedo* does not itself involve the kind of "separation" to which he objects in the Platonic theory. On the other side, the doctrine is expressly said in the *Phaedo* to be a familiar one, which Socrates "was always" repeating; and, if untrue, it is hard to see what could be the point of such a mystification and harder to understand how Plato could have expected it to be successful, especially as most of the personages of the *Phaedo* were certainly still alive. If true, however, one must be prepared to admit the possibility that he is also reproducing the thought of Socrates in the *Symposium* and *Republic*, in which he speaks of a supreme Form, that of Beauty, or Good, the vision of which is the far-off goal of all intellectual contemplation. Unfortunately, no complete separation of the Socratic and the Platonic is possible.

Logical methods. On the logical side, both Plato and Xenophon bear out the remark of Aristotle that Socrates may fairly be credited with two things: "inductive arguments" and "universal definitions." The "universal definition" is an attempt to formulate precisely the meaning of a universally significant predicate—*i.e.*, to apprehend what the *Phaedo* calls a Form. And it is from the practice of Socrates, who aimed at the clarification of thought about the meaning of moral predicates as the first indispensable step toward the improvement of practice, that the theory of logical division and definition, as worked out by Plato and Aristotle, has arisen.

The "inductive arguments" mean the characteristic attempts to arrive at such formulations by the consideration of simple and striking concrete illustrations, the per-

petual arguments about "shoemakers and carpenters and fullers," which the fashionable speakers in Plato profess to think vulgar. Induction, on this view of it, is not regarded as a method of proof; its function is that of suggestion: it puts the meaning of a proposed "definition" forcibly and clearly before the mind. The justification of the definition, then, has to be sought in a consideration of the satisfactoriness of the "consequences" that would follow from its adoption. Socrates himself sought for his "definitions" principally in the sphere in which he was most interested: as Aristotle says, he concerned himself with the "ethical," character and conduct, both private and public, not with "nature" at large.

Ethics and politics. With Socrates the central problem of philosophy shifted from cosmology to the formulation of a rule of life, to the "practical use of reason." As the *Apology* relates, the specific message from God that Socrates brought to his fellowmen was that of the "care" or "tending" of one's "soul," to "make one's soul as good as possible"—"making it like God," in fact—and not to ruin one's life, as most men do, by putting care for the body or for "possessions" before care for the "soul"; for the "soul" or *psychē* is that which is most truly a man's self.

**His
original
view
of the
soul**

Socrates' view of the soul stands in sharp contrast with the Homeric and Ionian view of the *psychē* as "the breath of life," which is given up when the man "himself," his body, has perished, and also with the view prevalent in circles influenced by Orphic-type religions, according to which the soul is a sort of stranger loosely inhabiting the body, which "sleeps while the body is active, but wakes when the body sleeps"; instead, the soul came in the 4th century to be viewed as the normal walking personality, the seat of character and intelligence, "that," as Socrates says in Plato, "in virtue of which we are called wise or foolish, good or bad." And as this usage of the word first appears in writers who are known to have been influenced by Socrates (Isocrates, Plato, and Xenophon), it may fairly be ascribed to his influence. Thus the soul *is* the man.

A man's happiness or well-being, in Socrates' view, depends directly on the goodness or badness of his soul. No one ever wishes for anything but true good—*i.e.*, true happiness. But men miss their happiness because they do not *know* what it is. For real good they mistake things that are not really good (*e.g.*, unlimited wealth or power). In this sense, "all wrong-doing is involuntary." Men need to *know* true good and not confuse it with anything else, so as to keep from *using* strength, health, wealth, or opportunity wrongly. If a man has this knowledge, he will always act on it, since to do otherwise would be to prefer known misery to known happiness. If a man really knew, for instance, that to commit a crime is worse than to suffer loss or pain or death, no fear of these things would lead him to commit the crime. To the professional Sophist, "goodness" is a neutral "accomplishment" that can always be put to either of two uses, a good one or a bad one. To Socrates, in contrast, knowledge of good is the one knowledge of which it is impossible to make an ill use; the possession of it is a guarantee that it will always be used properly. Thus, Socrates becomes—as against the relativism of Protagoras—the founder of the doctrine of an absolute morality based on the conception of a felicity that is the good not of Athenians or Spartans or even of Greeks but of man as man, as part of universal humanity.

**His
political
philosophy**

Politics, from this point of view, is the task of "tending" the souls of all his fellow citizens and making them "as good as possible." The knowledge of good is also the foundation of all statesmanship. The radical vice of ancient democracy, according to Socrates, is that of putting society in the hands of men without true insight and with no adequate expert knowledge. His main criticism, however, is that, though in some departments democracy takes the advice only of a qualified expert, on questions of morality and justice it treats any one citizen's opinion as of equal value with another's.

Even a Themistocles or a Pericles plainly had no knowledge of true statesmanship: they gave the populace the things that tickled its taste, such as a navy and a commerce; but they were no "physicians of the body politic," for they did not promote "righteousness and temperance," the spiritual health of the community. Socrates maintained that he alone deserved the name of statesman, because he understood, as the men of action did not, that knowledge of the absolutely good is the necessary and sufficient condition of national well-being and felicity. Indeed, Plato's *Republic* may fairly be viewed as a picture of life in a society governed by this Socratic conviction. How far any of the special regulations of the *Republic* embody actual convictions of Socrates is more than can be said, though it is significant that the *Aspasia* of Aeschines represents Socrates as maintaining one of Plato's "paradoxes," the capacity of women for war and for politics.

Socrates exerted a temporary influence on a group of men who have come to be known as "the minor Socratics," among whom the most important were Antisthenes of Athens and Eucleides of Megara, with whom the Cynics and the Megarian school were connected. It was mainly through his influence on Plato, however, who took up the thought of Socrates and continued it in his own life's work, that Socrates' efforts bore their full fruit for subsequent ages (see PLATO and PLATONISM AND NEOPLATONISM).

BIBLIOGRAPHY

General studies: The most thorough and balanced introduction to Socrates and recent scholarly discussion is W.K.C. GUTHRIE, *A History of Greek Philosophy,* vol. 3, *The Fifth-Century Enlightenment,* pp. 323–507 (1969). Socrates' cultural and philosophical context is concisely described in F.M. CORNFORD, *Before and After Socrates* (1932; paperback ed., 1960); and in W.K.C. GUTHRIE, *The Greek Philosophers: From Thales to Aristotle,* ch. 4 (1950), on the reaction toward humanism. Older classical accounts by JOHN BURNET, *Early Greek Philosophy,* 4th ed. (1930); A.E. TAYLOR, *Socrates* (1932); and CONSTANTIN RITTER, *Sokrates* (1931, in German), ascribe to Socrates himself much of Plato's formal theory of Ideas while also giving sympathetic portraits of his personality and thought.

The historical Socrates: Many studies centre on the historical value of the principal informants about Socrates: Plato and Xenophon, Aristotle and Aristophanes. The main source materials and problems are presented by R.L. LEVIN and JOHN BREMER, *The Question of Socrates* (1961); a brief informative survey of positions comes from C.J. DE VOGEL, *Philosophia,* pt. 1, *Studies in Greek Philosophy,* ch. 5 (1970); and some useful principles for understanding and using the Socratic sources are furnished by EMILE DE STRYCKER, "Les Témoinages historiques sur Socrate," *Mélanges Henri Grégoire* (1950). Reliable accounts are given of the Socrates–Plato relationship by G.C. FIELD, *Plato and His Contemporaries,* 3rd ed. (1967); and of Socrates' last days by COLEMAN PHILLIPSON, *The Trial of Socrates* (1928). Historical facts are skeptically regarded and the functions of myth and political polemic on the part of the sources are stressed by O. GIGON, *Sokrates: Sein Bild in Dichtung und Geschichte* (1947); A.H. CHROUST, *Socrates, Man and Myth: The Two Socratic Apologies of Xenophon* (1957), with special criticism of Xenophon and Antisthenes; and the two reporting dissertations by V. DE MAGALHAES-VILHENA: *Le Problème de Socrate* (1952) and *Socrate et la légende platonicienne* (1952). There are some scholarly defenses and methodological interpretations of the historicity of the major Socratic sources: AUGUSTE DIES, *Autour de Platon,* 2 vol. (1927); T. DEMAN, *Le Témoinage d'Aristote sur Socrate* (1942); K.J. DOVER's introduction and commentary to his edition of Aristophanes, *Clouds* (1968); and HUGH TREDENNICK's introduction to his translation of Xenophon, *Memoirs of Socrates and the Symposium (The Dinner Party)* (1970).

Socrates in history: The personality, ideals, and examples of Socrates are a perennial inspiration for subsequent thinkers and traditions. His influence is visually manifested in the many illustrations and texts of MICHELINE SAUVAGE, *Socrate et la conscience de l'homme* (1956; Eng. trans., *Socrates and the Human Conscience,* 1960); as well as in the collection of testimonies gathered by HERBERT SPIEGELBERG in *The Socratic Enigma* (1964). His educational impact is measured by W.K. RICHMOND, *Socrates and the Western World* (1954), while his deep impress upon Christian religious awareness and Existential thinking is affirmed in ROMANO GUARDINI, *Der Tod des Socrates* (1943; Eng. trans., *The Death of Socrates,* 1948 and 1962). Three samples of Socrates' relationships with modern philosophy are: SOREN KIERKEGAARD, *Om*

Begrebet Ironi med stadigt Hensymtil Socrates (1841; Eng. trans., *The Concept of Irony, with Constant Reference to Socrates,* 1968), reformulating his view of irony in terms of Romanticism and Hegel; LEONARD NELSON, *Socratic Method and Critical Philosophy* (1949, reprinted 1965), giving a Neo-Kantian interpretation of his maieutic method; and LASZLO VERSENYI, *Socratic Humanism* (1963), showing Socrates' implications for reflective and Existential humanisms today.

(A.E.Ta.)

Sodium and Potassium Products and Production

Sodium and potassium are both soft, silvery-white metals. When freshly cut they have a brilliant lustre, but since they are among the most reactive of the metallic elements, they tarnish in contact with air, turning a dull, gray colour. They also react vigorously with water, decomposing it and forming sodium hydroxide or potassium hydroxide and liberating hydrogen. The hydrogen may ignite, and sometimes the reaction is slightly explosive. Potassium is more reactive than sodium and is likely to flame spontaneously in moist air. Both must be kept under a liquid containing no oxygen and handled very carefully because they are extremely caustic to all tissues. (For further information on the physical and chemical properties of these two elements, see ALKALI METALS AND THEIR COMPOUNDS.)

Because they are extremely reactive chemical elements, sodium and potassium are not found in nature in the free state (as metals) but are widely distributed in combined form as compounds. The most familiar compound is sodium chloride—ordinary salt. Other salts of sodium and potassium are found in nearly all soils and terrestrial waters and in many rocks. The rocks and soil are richer in potassium, but the oceans contain only about $\frac{1}{30}$ as much potassium as sodium. Sodium and potassium are the sixth and seventh most abundant elements in the Earth's crust, of which they constitute 2.8 percent and 2.6 percent, respectively. Both elements are important in nutrition; their compounds are contained in most plant and animal tissues, and potassium compounds are important fertilizers.

History. The histories of sodium and potassium are as closely related as their chemical natures. Some of the earliest civilizations knew and used materials containing compounds of both sodium and potassium, and as these compounds were similar, they did not distinguish between them. Records originating in lower Mesopotamia and dating from the 17th century BC mention saltpetre (potassium nitrate) for making glazes. The Egyptians used native sodium carbonate as early as the 16th century BC for making glass.

Both sodium carbonate and potassium carbonate were termed alkali and were prepared from early times by passing water through the ashes of burned plants and evaporating the water from the solution. The term soda was applied at first to either alkali and later only to the ashes of sea plants; the term potash, however, was restricted to the ashes of land vegetation, and the term originated from the use of large pots from which the solutions were evaporated. The two alkalies, soda and potash, were successively designated as natural and artificial and as mineral and vegetable; but finally, in the 18th century, it was found that the so-called mineral alkali occurred in the ashes of sea plants and the so-called vegetable alkali occurred in a number of minerals; then the terms soda and potash were assigned to specific substances.

Early methods of preparation

In 1807 the brilliant English chemist Sir Humphry Davy decomposed both alkalies, obtaining first the metallic potassium and then sodium. He coined the names potassium and sodium, latinized versions of potash and soda. Among the strongest reducing agents known, sodium and potassium cannot be isolated by ordinary chemical reduction, so it is not surprising that they were only prepared after electric current was discovered in 1800 and electrolytic methods were developed.

Sources. *Sodium.* Sodium occurs in the form of halides, silicates, carbonates, sulfates, and nitrates. The principal source of sodium, of such importance that it outweighs all others, is sodium chloride, particularly rock salt deposits, but also salt evaporated from brine from underground salt deposits and salt obtained from seawater by solar evaporation. (For mining and recovery, see SALT AND SALT PRODUCTION.)

Sodium is disseminated throughout the rocky crust of the Earth in the form of soda feldspar (*i.e.*, as silicate of sodium) and in other sodium-containing rocks. Sodium carbonate is also widely dispersed in nature, forming constituents of many mineral waters and occurring as the principal saline component in natron or trona (hydrated sodium carbonate, sodium bicarbonate) lakes, as efflorescences, and as solid crusts found at the bottom of certain salt lakes. Gaylussite is a double salt, $Na_2CO_3 \cdot CaCO_3 \cdot 5H_2O$, occurring in Colombia.

Sodium sulfate occurs in an anhydrous condition as thenardite and in a hydrated condition, Glauber's salt. Glauberite is a double sulfate of sodium and calcium. Cryolite is a fluoride of aluminum and sodium, mined extensively for industrial purposes.

Potassium. Potassium occurs in many silicate rocks and minerals. The most important source is salt deposits, but a small percentage is obtained from plant and animal sources. Only a small fraction of the forms of potassium are economical to recover, those compounds that are water-soluble, viz., potassium chloride and potassium sulfate; they are frequently found in mixtures with magnesium salts, both as dry mineral deposits and in brines. Their solubility allows them to be easily extracted, and they are readily amenable to chemical operations. Although nearly as abundant as sodium, potassium is less accessible; the relatively few workable deposits contain saline residues formed by the evaporation of inland seas of past geological eras.

Plants as potassium sources

All plants are potential sources of potassium compounds. The proportion of potassium present in organisms varies widely; but in higher animals and most vegetation, except some marine plants, the potassium content is greater than that of sodium. Sugarcane and sugar beets contain significant quantities of potassium salts, 90 percent of which is extracted with the sugar. Soluble potassium salts are drawn into the roots of plants from fertile soil and accumulate in the plant structure, where some of them are metabolized into organic salts, such as tartrates and oxalates. If, however, the plants are burned, the organic potassium salts are converted into potassium carbonate.

Recovery of the metals. When Davy first isolated potassium and sodium in 1807, he did it by electrolysis of the fused hydroxides. A modification of his method, called the Castner process, was long used commercially to prepare sodium, but it was not entirely satisfactory for the more difficult potassium reduction. Most sodium is now prepared by the Downs process, in which a fused mixture of sodium chloride and either calcium chloride or sodium carbonate is electrolyzed to yield chlorine as well as the metal. Pure molten sodium chloride is not used because at the high temperature required to melt it (801° C, or 1,474° F) the vapour pressure of sodium metal is dangerously high, and sodium is appreciably soluble in the molten salt. With the fused mixture, a lower temperature (in the vicinity of 600° C, or 1,100° F) may be used.

Potassium metal was obtained in 1808 by chemists Joseph-Louis Gay-Lussac and Louis-Jacques Thenard of France by reduction of the hydroxide with iron; they packed the hydroxide and iron wire or turnings into a gun barrel, which was coated with clay and heated to white heat. During the same year, François-René Curaudeau prepared potassium by reducing potassium carbonate with carbon. During the following 50 years, various chemists studied this reaction to devise methods of separation and rapid cooling of the products; such methods were necessary to prevent the explosive compound $K_6C_6O_6$ from forming.

Reduction methods using metals

The processes that evolved were the forerunners of reduction methods using metals, such as magnesium and aluminum, or using compounds, such as calcium carbide, hydride, or silicide. After high-vacuum techniques were developed, calcium could be used to reduce potassium to the pure metal in a vacuum; sodium vapour has been used similarly as a fairly successful reducing agent for potassium.

Electrolytic methods of preparing potassium entail decomposing the fused hydroxide, the cyanide, or a potassium oxysalt dissolved in a fused potassium halide.

Uses of the metals and their alloys. *Sodium.* Metallic sodium is used to manufacture sodium chemicals of technical importance, particularly sodium peroxide, sodium cyanide, sodium amide, sodium hydride, sodium azide, and sodium borohydride. Sodium is also used extensively in synthetic chemistry; *e.g.*, as a reducing agent and a drying agent.

Because sodium exhibits the photoelectric effect to a marked degree, emitting electrons when exposed to light, it has been used in the manufacture of photoelectric cells. Because of its relatively high heat capacity and high heat conductivity, sodium is used as a heat-transfer medium. In some types of nuclear reactors, molten sodium carries heat from the core of the reactor to a boiler for generation of steam. Metallic sodium is also being investigated as an electrical conductor, when properly protected from air and moisture.

Sodium-vapour lamps, in which gaseous sodium is made to glow inside a tube by an applied voltage, give a yellow-coloured light of good illumination characteristics and are extensively used for street and road lighting.

Potassium. Metallic potassium has few uses, the most important being the synthesizing of potassium compounds, such as potassium superoxide, KO_2, used in protective breathing equipment. In the rebreather gas mask, the superoxide reacts with exhaled air to liberate oxygen and remove carbon dioxide and water vapour.

During the first half of the 19th century, metallic potassium was used to produce aluminum by the reduction of the chloride; magnesium, boron, and silicon were produced by a similar method. In 1854 it was found that sodium, which is cheaper, serves as well as potassium, and sodium was used for these purposes until electrolytic processes were developed. Sodium also replaced potassium in many other industrial processes. Potassium, however, still plays a role in certain organic syntheses.

A radioactive isotope of potassium, K-40, has been used to estimate the age of the Earth and some of the Moon rocks.

Alloys. Alloys of sodium and potassium serve as heat-transfer media, such as are described above for sodium alone. An alloy of 77.2 percent potassium and 22.8 percent sodium has been suggested as a liquid coolant for nuclear reactors. A potassium–sodium alloy takes part in the reduction of titanium tetrachloride to the metal.

Sodium–lead alloy often is substituted for metallic sodium as a reducing agent or a drying agent and is also employed in the manufacture of tetraethyllead, a common constituent of antiknock gasoline.

Compounds and their uses. *Sodium compounds.* Sodium chloride (common salt) is the most abundant form and the most important source of sodium. It is the main salt present in seawater, of which it comprises about 80 percent of the dissolved matter. Throughout the world there are extensive deposits of sodium chloride, which probably originated when prehistoric seas evaporated. It is a white, cubic crystalline salt, very soluble in water; the large crystals are transparent. Present in all body fluids, sodium chloride is essential to human and animal nutrition, and it is a food preservative and seasoning. Sodium chloride is important in the manufacture of soaps, dyes, ceramic glazes, leather, and other sodium-containing chemicals. (See also SALT AND SALT PRODUCTION.)

Abundance of sodium chloride

Sodium hydroxide, or caustic soda, the most important industrial caustic, is a white, deliquescent (moisture-attracting) solid that may be obtained from a solution of sodium chloride by electrolysis. It is highly corrosive to animal and vegetable tissue. The alkaline solutions it forms when dissolved in water neutralize acids in various commercial processes: in petroleum refining, it removes sulfuric and organic acids; in soapmaking, it reacts with fatty acids. In the making of cellophane, paper, viscose rayon, and other products, its alkaline solutions enter into the treatment of cellulose and into the manufacture of many chemicals.

Sodium carbonate is a crystalline white salt soluble in water; in the technical grade, the anhydrous form is known as soda ash, and the decahydrate is known as washing soda. Its first industrial-scale manufacture was by the historic Leblanc process, which has since been supplanted by the Solvay process, or by electrolysis. (For descriptions of these processes, see CHEMICAL INDUSTRY.) A general cleaner, sodium carbonate has many industrial applications, and in medicine it is used to treat skin inflammations and to cleanse body orifices.

Sodium bicarbonate (sodium hydrogen carbonate), household baking soda, is a white crystalline powder or granular salt soluble in water; it is prepared principally from sodium carbonate. A source of carbon dioxide gas, sodium bicarbonate goes into the manufacture of effervescent beverages and baking powder and is a component of fire extinguishers. Medically, it counteracts urinary and stomach acidity, cleanses mucous membranes, and dresses burns.

Sodium sulfate, in water-soluble white powder or crystalline form is usually called mirabilite or thenardite when obtained from deposits or brines; the name Glauber's salt refers to the decahydrate $Na_2SO_4 \cdot 10H_2O$. Its uses include the dyeing and printing of textiles and the manufacture of glass and paper.

Sodium
nitrate's
wide
range
of uses

Sodium nitrate, a soluble crystalline white salt, occurs naturally in the impure form of Chile saltpetre (caliche) or is manufactured from sodium carbonate and nitric acid. It goes into the manufacture of chemicals, fertilizer, glass, pottery, enamels, matches, explosives, and dyes. It also serves as a meat-pickling agent.

Sodium peroxide, a yellowish-white powder made by heating metallic sodium in dry air, is an oxidizing agent for bleaching paper, cloth, wood, ivory, and sponges, and for purifying air in confined spaces, such as submarines and airplanes. Although not explosive in itself, sodium peroxide is dangerous and may react explosively with combustible substances, particularly if moisture is present.

Sodium sulfide, prepared by heating sodium sulfate with coal, is important in the manufacture of sulfur dyes and rubber. It is an intermediate compound in the production of other chemicals and a laboratory reagent.

Sodium fluoride is made from sodium carbonate and hydrofluoric acid. An insecticide and pesticide, it is poisonous and may be fatal to human beings if ingested; but when added in minute amounts to municipal water supplies, sodium fluoride reduces the incidence of dental caries.

Sodium alkyl sulfates are important intermediate chemicals that may be derived from petroleum; they are essential in the synthetic-detergent industry, in the dye industry, and in the processing of a number of different oils.

Sodium thiosulfate (sodium hyposulfite) is in the "hypo" solution with which photographers fix developed negatives and prints; it acts by dissolving the unchanged silver salts. It is also used to remove traces of chlorine from bleached paper and textiles.

Water glass is sodium silicate of varying composition; it may be in the form of dry powder, an amorphous mass, or a syrupy liquid. It is a binder in the manufacture of abrasive wheels, grindstones, glass, and porcelain. As a water solution, it was formerly used to preserve shell eggs. In the paper and textiles industries, water glass is used as a protective coating and fireproofing agent.

Sodium amide (sodamide) is a reagent used in the chemical industry to introduce amino groups into molecules, particularly in dye production. Made directly from sodium and ammonia, sodium amide is used in turn along with carbon at red heat to prepare sodium cyanide.

Uses of
sodium
cyanide

Sodium cyanide solution readily dissolves gold and silver metals in the presence of air and is used to extract these metals from their ores. A violent poison, it is also used as an insecticide and as a source of the fumigant hydrogen cyanide. Sodium cyanide is an intermediate compound in the preparation of other useful chemicals, particularly for the manufacture of dyes, pigments, and nylon.

Sodium hypochlorite is a salt that is unstable, except when it is mixed with sodium hydroxide. Used in solution, it is a bleach, being used in the manufacture of paper, textiles, and other products, as well as in the household.

Potassium compounds. Potassium chloride, a white crystalline solid or powder, is the most abundant of the naturally occurring salts of potassium and closely resembles sodium chloride. Potassium chloride is used in various pharmaceutical preparations, as a fertilizer, and as a starting material in the manufacture of many important potassium compounds, including the hydroxide and the carbonate.

Potassium hydroxide, the caustic potash of commerce, is a white solid that can cause severe burns to human tissue. It dissolves in water to give a strongly alkaline solution. Deliquescent (moisture-attracting), it sometimes serves as a drying agent. Potassium hydroxide may be produced from a solution of potassium chloride by electrolysis. Formerly, it was prepared by reacting wood ashes (potassium carbonate) with slaked lime (calcium hydroxide), and from this primitive alkali, soap was made. Essentially, this was also the standard industrial method for manufacturing potassium hydroxide until the end of the 19th century, when it was superseded by the electrolytic process. Because it is more expensive than sodium hydroxide, the use of potassium hydroxide is somewhat limited, but it does go into the manufacture of soap, particularly liquid soap, and chemicals.

Potassium carbonate (potash) is essential to the production of Bohemian glass, soft soaps, fertilizers, and many inorganic chemicals. The first industrial-scale process for manufacturing this salt was an adaptation of the Leblanc sodium carbonate process, since replaced by a number of modern processes.

Potassium bicarbonate (potassium hydrogen carbonate), a white soluble salt, like sodium bicarbonate, is a source of carbon dioxide gas. It is used in baking powders and fire extinguishers and medically as a buffer for stomach and urinary acid.

Potassium sulfate is a constituent of a number of saline minerals. The colourless or white, hard rhombic crystals are used in fertilizers, in the manufacture of glass and alums, and as a laboratory reagent.

Potassium nitrate, also called nitre, or saltpetre, is a soluble crystalline white salt. As the quantity obtained from natural deposits is limited, it is prepared either from synthetic nitric acid and potassium hydroxide or from naturally occurring potassium chloride and sodium nitrate. It is a valuable fertilizer and has many other uses: in the manufacture of fireworks, matches, blasting powders, explosives, fluxes, and glass, and in the food industry for curing meats and pickling.

Methods of
preparing
saltpetre

Potassium bromide, a white crystalline salt, is used in photography to make gelatin papers and plates, and in medicine as a sedative and an antiepileptic.

Potassium dichromate is a soluble, bright orange-red crystalline salt prepared from chrome iron ore. It is an important oxidizing agent in leather tanning, and in the chemical, paint, and dye industries. A corrosive poison internally, its dust is caustic to human tissue.

Potassium permanganate, a deep purple crystalline salt, dissolves in water to give beautiful purple oxidizing solutions, that are used as bleaches, deodorizers, dyes, and reagents in laboratory analyses. Medically, it is used as a topical astringent, antiseptic, and antidote for some poisons.

BIBLIOGRAPHY. The *Kirk-Othmer Encyclopedia of Chemical Technology*, 2nd ed. rev., vol. 16, pp. 361–400 (1968) and vol. 18, pp. 432–515 (1969), is an extensive, authoritative, and modern treatise of elements and compounds that includes some theory, ample properties, and rather complete industrial processes. Each section contains an excellent bibliography affording a wide selection of papers for the reader. PAUL G. STECHER (ed.), *The Merck Index: An Encyclopedia of Chemicals and Drugs*, 8th ed. (1968), providing a brief and concise treatment of each element and its important compounds, including some significant properties together with the industrial and medical uses, is the most complete work of its kind in the English language. The bibliography is extensive. F.A. COTTON and GEOFFREY WILKINSON, *Advanced Inorganic Chemistry*, 2nd rev. ed. (1966), contains a brief chapter in which a few of the more esoteric properties are mentioned. *Mellor's Comprehensive Treatise on Inorganic and Theoretical Chemistry*, vol. 2, suppl. 2–3 (1961–63), contains exhaustive discussions of the preparation, physical properties, chemical properties, and compounds of the alkali metals, with each alkali metal constituting a separate chapter. Other works recommended include: AMERICAN CHEMICAL SOCIETY, *Handling and Uses of Alkali Metals* (1957), a collection of papers comprising a symposium on industrial problems in the handling and application of the alkali metals; IRVING FATT and MARIE TASHIMA, *Alkali Metal Dispersions* (1961), a rather extensive work with details of the methods of preparation; D.W. KAUFMANN (ed.), *Sodium Chloride* (1960), an exceedingly thorough treatise on salt; and MARSHALL SITTIG, *Sodium: Its Manufacture, Properties and Uses* (1956), a thorough account of the manufacture, handling, uses, and reactions of sodium metal.

(W.L.J./J.B.Pa.)

Sofia

The capital and the dominant political, economic, and cultural centre of the People's Republic of Bulgaria, Sofia owes much to its crossroads location, a favourable site, good economic conditions, and famous mineral springs. Though it had an ancient foundation, centuries of Ottoman domination impeded its full exploitation until 1878, when the town began to flourish following liberation from foreign rule. A major transformation occurred following World War II and the advent of a Socialist government. The city and immediate region had become the home of some 1,000,000 people by the early 1970s. New housing projects and parks have added a modern flavour to a city once dominated by minarets, and Sofia has become one of the most attractive of Balkan cities.

The city lies in the southern portion of the Sofia Basin of the mountainous central western portion of Bulgaria and commands the geographical centre of the whole Balkan region. To the north lies the Balkan Mountains (Stara Planina Range). Mt. Lyulin rises to the immediate west; Mt. Lozen to the southeast; and Mt. Vitosha, intimately linked with the territorial growth of the town, to the south. Although situated in a basin the scenery of which adds much to its charm, Sofia is not isolated: convenient passes in the mountains encircling the basin, together with the deeply sunk gorges of the Iskŭr and Pancharevo rivers, facilitate communications with the rest of the country. Important routes connecting the Adriatic and central Europe with the Danube, the Black Sea, and the Aegean are cut through the mountain passes.

History. Traces of Neolithic settlements of the 4th millennium BC have been unearthed within the modern city limits, and in this respect Sofia is one of the oldest of European urban communities. The Serdi, a Thracian tribe, established a settlement near the hot mineral springs as early as the 8th century BC. This community was conquered soon after 29 BC by the Romans, who named it Serdica. During the reign of the emperor Trajan (98–117) it became the administratively autonomous town of Ulpia Serdica, and in the late 2nd century the community was strengthened by fortress walls and towers.

Inside the walls, its streets ran according to a grid pattern running south–north and east–west and were paved with stone concealing a complex drainage and water supply system; in the centre of the community, monumental public and richly ornamented buildings arose. From the 3rd century, the town was the main centre of the Roman province of Inner Dacia and possessed the important privilege of issuing its own coins. Parts of the surviving Church of St. George date from the 4th century.

The community reached its greatest height under the emperor Constantine the Great; from the later 4th century it was part of the Eastern Roman Empire centred on Byzantium, and it was plundered by Attila the Hun in 441–447. During the 6th century, Byzantine influence increased under the emperor Justinian, and the restored Church of St. Sofia, which later gave the town its name, survives from this period. In 809 the Bulgarian khan Krum seized the town and incorporated it in the Bulgarian state: it was given the Slav name Sredets (meaning "middle" or "centre"), and Byzantine authors began to refer to it as Triaditsa, the Greek equivalent. The community became a strong Bulgarian fortress and an important strategic and administrative centre. From 986 onward its walls were unsuccessfully besieged by Byzantine troops, but from 1018 to 1194 it succumbed to Byzantine rule.

From the 12th to the 14th centuries, Sredets was a developed handicrafts centre, with a brisk trade in goldsmiths' and ironsmiths' products, arms, and ornamental table pottery; toward the end of this period the town acquired the name of Sofia, from its reconstructed church. Sofia fell to the Turks in 1382; the *beylerbeyi* of Rumelia, a Turkish potentate, took up residence there; its appearance gradually took on a distinctive Oriental cast; and, by the time of the Crimean War, in the mid-19th century, it declined to the status of a minor provincial community. The population nevertheless took an active part in the long national struggle for liberation and an independent Bulgarian church. Finally, in 1870 the Bulgarian revolutionary Vasil Levsky founded a revolutionary committee in the city. Sofia was liberated from Ottoman rule by Russian troops on January 4, 1878. Designated the Bulgarian capital on April 3, 1879, the town subsequently grew in both area and population, and its citizens headed the political and economic struggles of the emergent working class. The capital later played a leading role in the anti-Fascist movements of World War II; it was the headquarters of all the main resistance organizations, became the centre of the first zone liberated by the resistance forces, and became the seat of the coalition government set up in 1944. Massive reconstruction followed in the 1940s and 1950s, and renewed expansion and development followed the adoption of a general urban plan in 1961.

The contemporary city. *Site and administration.* The modern city extends across the terraces of the Iskŭr River and its tributaries, the Vladayska, Perlovska, and Erma, and at the foot of Mt. Vitosha and the Lyulin Mountains. The average altitude of this setting is 1,800 feet, but it reaches almost 2,300 feet in the Vitosha foothills.

Sofia has a moderate continental climate, with a warm summer, a dry and pleasant autumn, a cold winter with frequent snowfall, and a cool, rainy spring. Fog occurs in the colder half of the year.

The city occupies the 65-square-mile (167-square-kilometre) area of the Sofia *gradska obshtina* (city municipality), divided administratively into seven sections. It is also the centre of the *okrug* (district) of Sofia and, in its function as administrative centre of the municipality, an *okrug* in its own right. The Municipal People's Council (315 members) and its executive and administrative organ, the Executive Committee (17 members), headed by a president, direct the affairs of the city community. The council and the committee are re-elected every two and a half years. The city proper population was almost 890,000 by the early 1970s, and people living in contiguous suburban regions took the figure to over 1,000,000.

Economic life. The new socialist content that has been introduced into the social, economic, and cultural life of the city since World War II, transforming its physical appearance, is particularly noticeable in the economic sphere. More than half the working population are engaged in industry, the building trade, and transportation, while about 20 percent of Bulgaria's workers and almost the same percentage of the country's large industrial enterprises are found in the city, which accounts for 18 percent of the Bulgarian industrial output. The engineering and metalworking industries, with products ranging from locomotives to medical instruments, are the most

(margin notes)
Ottoman rule

Foundation and early settlement

Major industries

Bujuk Dzhamija (mosque) and modern buildings, Sofia, Bulgaria.
Paul Almasy

developed, followed by ferrous and nonferrous engineering, including the massive Kremikovski metallurgical combine, and plants producing electronic materials. The food industry (processing meat, flour, sugar confectionary, cigarettes, and wine) is next in importance, together with the textile and clothing industries, which have ancient roots. Rubber, footwear, furniture and woodworking, paper, and chemical industries are also well developed. About three-quarters of the national printing industry is located in the city, including a modern plant, in which practically all the Bulgarian dailies are printed. There are television and several broadcasting centres. Several large hydroelectric and thermoelectric power stations supply the city with power.

Around the town there is a well-developed agricultural zone, characterized by fruit and vegetable production and dairy farming, while a dense radial and circular road network links Sofia with neighbouring settlements. The airport, largest in the country, has scheduled flights to some 35 countries, while the city's railway stations handle over 5,000,000 tons of goods and over 25,000,000 passengers annually. Internal transport needs are served by tramways, trolleybuses, and buses, while several cable lifts connect the city with neighbouring Mt. Vitosha.

Sofia is also a growing commercial and consumer centre, with many specialized shops, hotels, and restaurants catering to local needs and to the growing number of tourists visiting the city. Most commercial, administrative, and cultural life is carried on in the historic central core of the city, while new multistoried housing estates and industrial plants rise up on the periphery.

Cultural life; recreation and health facilities. The cultural life of the city has very deep roots; Sofia contains the Bulgarian Academy of Sciences, the Academy of Agricultural Sciences, the Sofiiski Universitet "Kliment Ohridsky" (University of Sofia)—the oldest establishment of higher learning in Bulgaria, founded 1888—and a number of other institutions of higher learning, serving, in all, some 30,000 students. The city also contains the Cyril and Methodius National Library, the National Art Gallery, the Ivan Vasov National Theatre and Opera House, an astronomical observatory, and a number of museums. In addition to the restored St. George, Boyana, and St. Sofia

Historical monuments

churches, historical monuments include two mosques, one housing a fine archaeological collection, and the Alexander Nevsky Cathedral, the domed structure of which was erected to commemorate the gratitude of the Bulgarian people to the Russian liberators of 1878. The massive headquarters of the Bulgarian Communist Party, and the mausoleum of the statesman Georgi Dimitrov are also noteworthy.

Recreational and health facilities, much developed in recent years, include modern sports grounds and well-equipped mineral baths and sanatoriums. The nearby beauty spots of the Pancharevo and Iskur gorges are popular tourist attractions, whether for weekend trips or summer vacations, and settlement has been spreading in recent years to the foothills of equally scenic Mt. Vitosha and Lyulin Mountains. In the city itself, the parks add touches of greenery to the clean lines of the modern thoroughfares and buildings.

BIBLIOGRAPHY. Additional information may be found in DIMITUR MIHAILOV, *Guide to Sofia* (1971); and STOIKO KOZHUKHAROV, *Sofia* (1969).

(D.Ko.)

Soft Drinks

Soft drinks are a class of nonalcoholic beverage, usually but not necessarily carbonated, containing a sweetening agent, edible acids, and natural or artificial flavours. Natural flavours are derived from fruits, nuts, berries, roots, herbs, and other plant sources. Coffee, tea, milk, cocoa, and undiluted fruit and vegetable juices are not considered soft drinks.

The term obviously was originated to distinguish the flavoured refreshment from hard liquor, or "spirits." Soft drinks were recommended as a substitute in the effort to change the hard-drinking habits of early Americans.

The cola beverages, lemon, lime, orange, grape, and other fruit flavours, as well as ginger ale and root beer, are popular in most countries. Carbonated beverages without flavouring or sweetening are known as soda water, club soda, sparkling water, etc.; these may contain mineral salts.

There are many specialty soft drinks. Kava, made from roots of a bushy shrub, *Piper methysticum*, is consumed by the people of Fiji and other Pacific islands. In Cuba people enjoy a carbonated cane juice; its flavour comes from the unrefined syrup. In tropical areas, where diets frequently lack sufficient protein, soft drinks containing soybean flour have been marketed. These provide a pleasant, inexpensive way to add protein to one's diet. In Egypt, carob or locust bean extract is used. In Brazil a soft drink is made using maté as a base. The whey obtained from making buffalo cheese is carbonated and consumed as a soft drink in North Africa. Some eastern Europeans enjoy a drink prepared from fermented stale bread. Honey and orange juice go into a popular drink of Israel.

HISTORY

Carbonated beverages and waters were developed from European attempts to imitate the popular and naturally effervescent waters of famous springs, with primary interest in their reputed therapeutic values. The effervescent feature of the waters was recognized early as most important. Jan Baptista van Helmont (1577–1644) first used the term gas in his reference to the carbon dioxide content. Gabriel Venel referred to aerated water, confusing the gas with ordinary air. Joseph Black named the gaseous constituent fixed air.

Numerous reports of such experiments and investigations were included in the *Philosophical Transactions* of the Royal Society of London in the late 1700s, including the studies of Stephen Hales, Joseph Black, David Macbride, William Brownrigg, Henry Cavendish, Thomas Lane, Joseph Priestley, and others. Duplication of the waters of Bad Pyrmont, a spa in Germany near the city of Hameln, was one of the major objectives, probably because of the popularity of the spa and because of the relatively simple nature of the mineral content of the waters there.

Priestley's contribution In 1772 Joseph Priestley published *Directions for Impregnating Water with Fixed Air*. He had obtained fixed air for his experiments from a brewery near his house. In 1773 Priestley received the Copley Medal from the Royal Society of London for his reports concerning fixed air and mixture of waters with it. His reports emphasized the alleged medicinal value of artificially carbonated water.

Meanwhile, other European scientists were active in the field. Studies by Torbern Bergman, a Swedish chemist, were published in the reports of the Royal Swedish Academy of Sciences in 1775. Carl Wilhelm Scheele of Sweden was similarly engaged. Antoine Lavoisier, in France, identified the fixed air of Priestley as a combination of carbon and oxygen, which he called *gaz acide carbonique*. In England John Mervin Nooth developed special apparatus for preparing small quantities of effervescent waters. His report appeared in 1775 in the *Philosophical Transactions* of the Royal Society.

Improvements in the Nooth device were made by João Jacinto de Magalhães in 1777. In 1781–83 the English chemist Thomas Henry described apparatus for the production of carbonated waters on a commercial scale. Many others followed, and factories and bottling plants opened in Geneva, Paris, London, Dublin, Dresden, and several other European cities during the period 1789–1821.

U.S. investigators also were interested in carbonated water and its health values. As early as the summer of 1807, in New Haven, Connecticut, Benjamin Silliman of Yale College began producing bottled soda water on a commercial scale and opened a public establishment for dispensing it. In Philadelphia artificially carbonated waters were bottled and sold commercially by Joseph Hawkins, with machinery of his own invention. The firm was known as Shaw and Hawkins. Hawkins received a U.S. patent for preparation of imitation mineral waters in 1809, the first of record in this field.

PRODUCTION

All ingredients used in soft drinks must be of high purity to obtain a quality beverage. These include the water, carbon dioxide, sugar, acids, and flavours.

Water. Although water is most often taken from a safe municipal supply, it usually is processed further to ensure uniformity of the finished product; the amount of impurities in the municipal supply may vary from time to time. In some bottling plants the water-treatment equipment may simply consist of a sand filter to remove minute solid matter and activated carbon purifier to remove colour, chlorine, and other tastes or odours. In most plants, however, water is treated by a process known as superchlorination and coagulation. Here, the water is exposed for two hours to a high concentration of chlorine and to a flocculant, which removes such organisms as plankton (minute plants and animals); it then passes through a sand filter and activated-carbon purifier.

Superchlorination and coagulation

Carbon dioxide and carbonation. Carbon dioxide gas gives the beverage its sparkle and tangy taste and prevents spoilage. While it has not been conclusively proved that carbonation offers a direct medical benefit, carbonated beverages are used to alleviate postoperative nausea when no other food can be tolerated, as well as to ensure adequate liquid intake.

Carbon dioxide is supplied to the soft drink manufacturer in either solid (Dry Ice) or liquid form maintained under approximately 1,200 pounds per square inch pressure in heavy steel containers. Lightweight steel containers are used when the liquid carbon dioxide is held under refrigeration. Here, the internal pressure is about 325 pounds per square inch. As the carbon dioxide is used the liquid changes into a gas in which form it can be dissolved in water.

Carbonation (of either the water or the finished beverage mixture) is effected by chilling the liquid and cascading it in thin layers over a series of plates in an enclosure containing carbon dioxide gas under pressure. The amount of gas the water will absorb increases as the pressure is increased and the temperature is decreased.

Flavouring syrup. Flavouring syrup is made from sugar, either granulated or as a 67 or 76 percent solution known as liquid sugar. The sugar is dissolved or diluted with processed water. Desired flavouring substances are then added, along with edible acids and colouring. In some cases preservatives protect the beverage from rancidity or microbiological spoilage.

Finishing. There are two methods for producing a finished beverage. In the first, the syrup is diluted with water and the product then cooled, carbonated, and bottled. In the second, the maker measures a precise amount of syrup into each bottle, then fills it with carbonated water. In either case, the sugar content (51–60 percent in the syrup) is reduced to 8–13 percent in the finished beverage.

The blending of syrups and mixing with plain or carbonated water, the container washing, and container filling are all done almost entirely by automatic machinery. Returnable bottles are washed in hot alkali solutions for a minimum of five minutes, then rinsed thoroughly. Single-service or "one-trip" containers are generally air- or water-rinsed before filling. Automatic fillers service from 30 to over 1,000 containers per minute.

Pasteurizing noncarbonated beverages. Noncarbonated beverages require ingredients and techniques similar to those for carbonated beverages. However, since they lack the protection against spoilage afforded by carbonation, these are usually pasteurized, either in bulk or by continuous flash pasteurization prior to filling, or in the bottle.

Powdered soft drinks. These are made by blending the flavouring material with dry acids, gums, artificial colour, etc. If the sweetener has been included, the consumer need only add the proper amount of plain or carbonated water.

Iced soft drinks. The first iced soft drink consisted of a cup of ice covered with a flavoured syrup. Today's sophisticated dispensing machines blend measured quantities of syrup with carbonated or plain water to make the finished beverage. To obtain the soft ice, or slush, the machine reduces the beverage temperature to between 22° and 28° F (−5° and −2° C).

PACKAGING AND VENDING

Soft drinks are packaged in glass bottles, tin or aluminum cans, plastic bottles, treated cardboard cartons, or in large stainless steel containers.

Vending of soft drinks had its modest beginning with the use of ice coolers over a half-century ago. Nowadays, most drinks are cooled by electric refrigeration for consumption on the premises. Vending machines dispense soft drinks in cups, cans, or bottles. There are two methods of vending soft drinks in cups. In the "pre-mix" system, the finished beverage is prepared by the soft drink manufacturer and filled into five- or ten-gallon stainless steel tanks. The tanks of beverage are attached to the vending machine where the beverage is cooled and dispensed. In the "post-mix" system the vending machine has its own water and carbon dioxide supply. The water is carbonated as required and is mixed with flavoured syrup as it is dispensed into the cup.

ECONOMIC IMPORTANCE

The soft drink consumption pattern throughout the world is unknown. However, it is believed that the United States and Canada are the leaders in consumption of this type of beverage. In the U.S. some 2,970 (1970) soft drink plants produce in excess of 72,000,000,000 carbonated soft drinks on an eight-ounce size basis per year. This amounts to more than 355 per person per year. Currently in the United States 55 percent of carbonated soft drinks are sold in returnable bottles, 30 percent in one-trip containers, and 15 percent through cup vending machines and fountains. In other parts of the world soft drinks are sold mainly in returnable bottles. Canned soft drinks are becoming popular in countries such as Australia, Canada, the Philippines, and England.

BIBLIOGRAPHY. J.J. RILEY, *A History of the American Soft Drink Industry* (1958), a comprehensive text on the evolution of the American flavoured soft drink, European development of simulated effervescent waters during the early 1800s, and early development of the flavoured carbonated beverage in the U.S. from 1807 to 1957; M.B. JACOBS, *Manufacture and Analysis of Carbonated Beverages* (1959), a detailed discussion of various aspects of carbonated beverages, including sugars, acids, water treatment, flavours, colouring, carbonation, spoilage, and packaging; D.K. TRESSLER and M.A. JOSLYN, *Fruit and Vegetable Juice Processing Technology* (1961), a modern text on the chemistry and technology of fruit and vegetable juice production; and J. MERORY, *Food Flavorings: Composition, Manufacture and Use*, 2nd ed. (1968), a useful manual on flavour technology, natural and imitation food flavourings, and their uses.

(H.E.K.)

Soil Mechanics, Applications of

Soil mechanics is concerned with the use of the laws of mechanics and hydraulics in engineering problems related to soils. Soil is a natural aggregate of mineral grains, with or without organic constituents, formed by the chemical and mechanical weathering of rock. It consists of three phases: solid mineral matter, water, and air or other gas. Soils are extremely variable in composition, and it was this heterogeneity that long discouraged scientific studies of these deposits. Gradually, the investigation of failures of retaining walls, foundations, embankments, pavements, and other structures resulted in a body of knowledge concerning the nature of soils and their behaviour sufficient to give rise to soil mechanics as a branch of engineering science.

History. Little progress was made in dealing with soil problems on a scientific basis until the latter half of the 18th century, when the French physicist Charles-Augustin de Coulomb published his theory of earth pressure (1773). In 1857 the Scottish engineer William Rankine developed a theory of equilibrium of earth masses and applied it to some elementary problems of foundation engineering. These two classical theories still form the basis of current methods of estimating earth pressure, even though they were based on the misconception that all soils lack cohesion, as does dry sand. Twentieth-century advances have been in the direction of taking cohesion into account; understanding the basic physical properties of soils in general and of the plasticity of clay in particular; and systematically studying the shearing characteristics of soils—that is, their performance under conditions of sliding.

Both Coulomb's and Rankine's theories assumed that the surface of rupture of soil subjected to a shearing force is a plane. While this is a reasonable approximation for sand, cohesive soils tend to slip along a curved surface. In the early 20th century, Swedish engineers proposed a circular arc as the surface of slip. During the last half century considerable progress has been made in the scientific study of soils and in the application of theory and experimental data to engineering design.

A significant advance was made by the German engineer Karl Terzaghi, who in 1925 published a mathematical investigation of the rate of consolidation of clays under applied pressures. His analysis, which was confirmed experimentally, explained the time lag of settlements on fully waterlogged clay deposits. Terzaghi coined the term soil mechanics in 1925 when he published the book *Erdbaumechanik* ("Earth-Building Mechanics").

Research on subgrade materials, the natural foundation under pavements, was begun about 1920 by the U.S. Bureau of Public Roads. Several simple tests were correlated with the properties of natural soils in relation to pavement design. In England, the Road Research Board was set up in 1933. In 1936 the first international conference on soils was held at Harvard University.

Today, the civil engineer relies heavily on the numerical results of tests to reinforce experience and correlate new problems with established solutions. Obtaining truly representative samples of soils for such tests, however, is extremely difficult; hence there is a trend toward testing on the site instead of in the laboratory, and many important properties are now evaluated in this way.

Engineering properties of soils. The properties of soils that determine their suitability for engineering use include internal friction, cohesion, compressibility, elasticity, permeability, and capillarity.

Internal friction is the resistance to sliding offered by the soil mass. Sand and gravel have higher internal friction than clays; in the latter an increase in moisture lowers the internal friction. The tendency of a soil to slide under the weight of a structure may be translated into shear; that is, a movement of a mass of soil in a plane, either horizontal, vertical, or other. Such a shearing movement involves a danger of building failure.

Also resisting the danger of shear is the property of cohesion, which is the mutual attraction of soil particles due to molecular forces and the existence of moisture between them. Cohesive forces are markedly affected by the amount of moisture present. Cohesion is generally very high in clays but almost nonexistent in sands or silts. Cohesion values range from zero for dry sand to 2,000 pounds per square foot for very stiff clays.

Compressibility is an important soil characteristic because of the possibility of compacting the soil by rolling, tamping, vibration, or other means, thus increasing its density and load-bearing strength.

An elastic soil tends to resume its original condition after compaction. Elastic (expansible) soils are unsuitable as subgrades for flexible pavements since they compact and expand as a vehicle passes over them, causing failure of the pavement.

Permeability is the property of a soil that permits the flow of water through it. Freezing–thawing cycles in winter and wetting–drying cycles in summer alter the packing density of soil grains. Permeability can be reduced by compaction.

Capillarity causes water to rise through the soil above the normal horizontal plane of free water. In most soils numerous channels for capillary action exist; in clays, moisture may be raised as much as 30 feet by capillarity.

Density can be determined by weight and volume measurements or by special measuring devices. Stability of soils is measured by an instrument called a stabilometer, which specifically measures the horizontal pressure transmitted by a vertical load. Consolidation is the compaction or pressing together of soil that occurs under a specific load condition; this property is also tested.

Site investigation. Soil surveys are conducted to gather data on the nature and extent of the soil expected to be encountered on a project. The amount of effort spent on site investigation depends on the size and importance of the project; it may range from visual inspection to elaborate subsurface exploration by boring and laboratory testing. Collection of representative samples is essential for proper identification and classification of soils. The number of samples taken depends on previously available data, variation in soil types, and the size of the project. Generally, in the natural profile at a location, there is more variation in soil characteristics with depth than with horizontal distance. It is not good practice to collect composite samples for any given horizon (layer), since this does not truly represent any one location and could prove misleading. Even slight variations in soil characteristics in a horizon should be duly noted. Classification of the soil in terms of grain size and the liquid and plastic limits are particularly important steps.

An understanding of the eventual use of the data obtained during site investigation is important. Advance information on site conditions is helpful in planning any survey program. Information on topography, geological features (outcrops, road and stream cuts, lake beds, weathered remnants, etc.), paleontological maps, aerial photographs, well logs, and excavations can prove invaluable. Geophysical exploration methods yield useful corroboratory data. Measurement of the electrical resistivity of soils provides an insight into several soil characteristics. Seismic techniques often are used to determine the characteristics of various subsurface strata by measuring the velocity of propagation of explosively generated shock waves through the strata. The propagation velocity varies widely for different types of soils. Shock waves also are utilized to determine the depth of bedrock by measuring the time required for the shock wave to travel to the bedrock and return to the surface as a reflected wave.

Dependable subsurface information can only be obtained by excavation. A probe rod pushed into the ground indicates the penetration resistance. Water jets or augers are used to bring subsurface materials to the surface for examination. Colour change is one of the significant elements such an examination can reveal. Various drilling methods are employed to obtain chips from depth. Trenches or pits provide more complete information for shallow depths. Pneumatic or diamond drilling may be required if hard rock is encountered. At least a few of the boreholes should exceed the depth of significant stress that is established for the structure.

Avoidance of structural disturbance of the samples is not critical for some tests but is very important for in-place density or shearing strength measurements.

Complete and accurate records, such as borehole logs, must be prepared and maintained, and the samples themselves must be retained for future inspection.

Foundations. A foundation distributes the loads due to its own weight, the weight of the superstructure, and any forces acting upon them. The loads are distributed over the soil surface in such a manner as to avoid excessive stresses in the soil. Such stresses could induce rupture of the supporting soil, causing differential settlement and cracking of the structure.

Structural foundations may be divided into two categories: spread and deep. Each of these may be classified in various ways. Spread foundations include: spread footings, mats, and floating foundations. Deep foundations are of two main types: piles and caissons.

Spread foundations. Spread footings are small compared with the total area of the structure and are used to support individual columns or bearing walls. Factors governing their settlement include load size, depth below original grade, and groundwater level. A mat foundation generally consists of a thick reinforced concrete slab beneath all, or a major portion, of the structure. It provides support for structures containing heavy, widely distributed loads, as would be the case in bins or silos. Mats are not suited to buildings with large, open floor spaces owing to the unfavourable bending effects produced. A true
floating foundation is boxlike in construction and extends to a depth below the ground surface such that the weight of the excavated earth equals the gross weight of the structure; thus, the contact pressures approximate the intensity and distribution of pressures exerted by the soil mass prior to excavation. Floating foundations are generally quite rigid, with the exterior foundation walls, and often the interior cross walls, integrated with the base slab. This entire substructure constitutes the floating foundation. Such foundations are normally employed when the soil has negligible bearing capacity or shearing strength.

Deep foundations. Piles, which are driven into the ground, are of two types: end bearing and friction. End-bearing piles are driven to the load-bearing stratum—*e.g.*, bedrock. They are assumed to derive all their vertical support from the strong formation in which the lower end is embedded and none from the overlying material by which they are surrounded. In friction piles, on the other hand, the load is transmitted to the adjacent soil along the full length of the pile through friction and surface adhesion. Hence, the compressive stress in the pile itself decreases with depth, permitting the use of tapered piles, whose configuration helps transmit the loading to the soil. To support concentrated loads, a group of piles with a cap is often used, since it is impractical to locate and drive a pile precisely as required. Piles are commonly made of timber, concrete, or steel.

Caissons, being larger than piles, are constructed in excavations. A belled caisson is essentially a concrete pile cast in place in an excavation. It has an enlarged section or bell at the bottom of the shaft. Caissons of this type transmit the load to the bottom stratum, in the same way as a footing. Socketed or drilled-in caissons extend for a short distance into the rock formation, which has been excavated to form a socket. When excavating in soft or flowing formations, a casing may be used that later can be retrieved.

Sometimes it is necessary to add permanent support to an existing foundation, either to provide additional load-bearing capacity or greater depth. This is termed underpinning, and is most prevalent in urban areas. When the excavation for a new building is deeper than the adjoining structures, underpinning of those structures usually is required. It may also be necessary because of increased floor capacity in a building or addition of more stories, changes in subsurface stability (due to such factors as vibration or lowering of water level), or inadequate footing capacity during initial construction. Settlement invariably accompanies underpinning, but usually it is within tolerable limits. Precautions need to be taken to ensure that settlement is uniform throughout the building. During the operation, the bracing of both the underpinning and the building against lateral movement is of the utmost importance. Underpinning designs are similar to those for other foundations.

Slopes, embankments, and dams. Any ground surface that is inclined to the horizontal constitutes an unretained earth slope. Crustal movements or the processes of weathering, erosion, sedimentation, and transportation create natural slopes, whereas man-made slopes are formed by excavation or filling. Slopes used for engineering purposes include highway or railroad cuts, canal banks, open-pit mines, trenches, mill-tailing piles, levees, earth dams, and embankments for highways, railroads, and airfields.

All slopes are continually being degraded or flattened. This may occur imperceptibly by creep or erosion, or it may occur catastrophically as in a landslide. Surface soil particles are maintained in static equilibrium by the downward pull of gravity and by friction, cohesion, and other passive restraining forces. This equilibrium is readily disturbed by any increase in the downslope forces or decrease in resistance to sliding. Both may be accelerated by water. When the mass that has broken away from the main slope remains relatively intact, it is termed a mass slide. Some soils, especially clays, suddenly change from a relatively firm consistency to a nearly liquid state, causing flow slides. This change is generally induced by the presence of a critical amount of water. In granular soils, flows may occur due to liquefaction induced by vibratory motion.

Stability analyses are performed to determine the factor of safety of slopes. A factor of safety of 1.0 is assigned to a slope on the brink of failure. It is defined as the ratio of the restraining forces to the forces inducing motion; 1.0 indicates exact equilibrium. Generally, safety factors of 1.5 to 2.0 are employed, although values of 1.1 are acceptable for highway and railroad cuts, where failure would not present major hazards. For rotational slides—*i.e.*, slides along a curved surface—the trace of the failure surface may be approximated by a circular arc. Translatory slides—*i.e.*, slides along a flat or nearly flat plane—occur along a weak layer in the strata. The slope is considered as consisting of a block and wedges subjected to appropriate gravitational and resistance forces.

Improving drainage is often the first step in enhancing the stability of slopes. Although gravity flow is preferable, pumping occasionally is used. To protect against potential mud flows, it is essential to prevent entry of water into both surface and subsurface strata. Plant growth on a clay surface improves stability. Proper grading helps to provide positive runoff. Flattening of the slope increases slope stability but this may not be adequate protection in itself, especially against translatory slides.

Stability procedures used for slopes are generally applicable to embankments; however, an embankment induces a considerable loading on the existing soil. If the load distribution due to an embankment is known, it is possible to make an analysis of the stress conditions in the foundation so that the magnitude and direction of the principal stresses can be determined at strategic locations. Traditional photoelastic stress analysis techniques may also be employed. On the basis of these studies, the embankment design can be altered to reduce the undesirable stresses. Foundations of embankments may be stabilized by slope flattening, water drainage, compaction, grouting (injection of stabilizing substances, such as cement), or excavation and replacement by a selected material. It is imperative that the nature and magnitude of settlement be determined prior to initiation of construction, since these may affect the shape of the embankment and increase the cost of stabilization.

Embankments constructed for the purpose of creating reservoirs or diverting streams are referred to as earth dams or levees. The watertightness requirements for dams vary considerably with the purpose for which they are built, but in no case should the seepage be allowed to threaten the stability of the structure. Instability can result from seepage through the dam or from rapid drawdown (lowering of the water level on the upstream side of the dam).

Dams generally are designed with several distinct components. The central core consists of impervious material to minimize seepage. Sometimes a cutoff trench filled with impervious material is also located in the foundation. Occasionally, a concrete cutoff wall is provided in the core, and either this or sheet piling may extend into the foundation. The slopes of the dam are formed with pervious material; these are called shell sections. On the upstream side, the shell protects against the effects of rapid drawdown, while downstream it prevents deterioration due to seepage. Between the core and shell, transition sections of an intermediate grade material are placed. This material acts as a filter, preventing desilting or lateral movement of the fines (fine soil particles) from the core. Rock is often placed at the downstream slope and is covered with riprap (irregular rock fragments) to prevent damage by wave wash (see also DAM).

Pavements. Pavements are required for roads, highways, and airfield runways and taxiways. They are generally constructed on natural soil formations or fills. The load-carrying capacity and service life of such structures are governed both by pavement construction and the nature of the underlying soil. Many special methods of evaluating subgrade soils and selecting pavement materials have been developed.

Pavement construction generally begins with the preparation of the subgrade, which is accomplished by grading the ground to obtain the desired cross section and profile. Since the subgrade is the local material on which the pavement is built, no selection of material is possible. Limited modification takes the form of compaction and drainage. Subgrades have inadequate bearing capacity for

modern vehicles, and the capacity deteriorates due to weather, hence, the need for paving. Pavements may be classed as rigid or flexible, depending on the manner in which they distribute loads. A rigid pavement has sufficient strength in flexure to distribute a concentrated load over a considerable supporting area. Portland cement concrete pavements are considered to function in this manner. Such pavements may rest directly on the subgrade, but generally they rest on a base course of sand, gravel, or stone. Flexible pavements are flexurally weak but are designed with sufficient thickness so that the stresses on the subgrade are relatively low. These pavements have two components: a base course of granular material and a specially treated wearing course. The lowermost layer may be referred to as the subbase. The wearing course, which is abrasion resistant and provides weatherproofing, may consist of crushed stone bound with asphalt. The nature of the subgrade, pavement loading, traffic volume, and climate determine pavement thickness (see also ROADS AND HIGHWAYS).

Underground excavations. The methods used to make underground excavations or tunnels depend on the nature of the soil or rock in which the facility is to be located and its intended purpose. Excavation methods may be classified as hard rock, soft ground, immersed tube, and cut-and-cover.

Hard rock. Although some hard rock tunnels are now driven with tunnelling machines or "moles," most of them are still excavated using drilling and blasting techniques. Machine tunnelling results in a smoother wall surface, which, since it has fewer stress concentrations, makes possible the use of a thinner lining. When blasting is employed for large tunnels, often a small pilot heading or "monkey drift" is driven ahead of the main excavation. In addition to providing an extra free face for rock breakage, it permits accurate geological studies.

Soft ground. In soft ground tunnelling, machines are used more commonly. The drilling and blasting method, however, is also employed. When tunnelling through a stiff clay, for instance, a method known as the liner-plate method may be used. Light liner plates, strengthened by steel ribs, are installed to support the clay before the concrete lining is placed. The shearing strength of the clay and the width of the tunnel are important considerations when using this method. The unit pressure on the footing for the temporary lining is dependent on tunnel width, and if it exceeds the shear strength, intolerable settlement or even failure may occur. Compressed air may be used during construction to reduce the pressure on the clay until a permanent lining is installed. This technique is also very useful in restricting the flow of water into the tunnel, but is most successful only in the smaller diameter tunnels. In tunnels of larger section it is preferable to employ the shield.

In the shield tunnelling method, a metal shield is forced forward into the ground by means of a set of hydraulic jacks located around the periphery of the shield. The stroke of the jacks is made equal to the width of each ring of lining. After the shield has been thrust forward, the jacks may be relieved of pressure and the lining segments positioned. These then serve as the reaction frame for the next thrust forward. The shield prevents loss of ground radially, and the face soil is allowed into the shield through openings in the face of the machine.

Immersed tube. Immersed tube techniques are best for underwater tunnelling. A trench is dredged, with slopes depending on soil characteristics and prevalent current velocities. Then a series of tunnel shells, built of steel or reinforced concrete, with ends closed by temporary bulkheads to permit flotation, are towed into position and sunk. The shell sections are then joined.

Cut-and-cover. In the cut-and-cover method of excavation, frequently used in subway construction, a long trench is dug, the tunnel lining is put in place, and the tunnel is covered over. It is an economical method, especially for shallow tunnels. Sheet piling and other appropriate measures need to be taken to prevent flow of material into the trench, which could cause settlement of adjoining ground and buildings.

Since the full weight of the overburden comes to bear on the tunnel lining only some time after construction, the permanent lining must be designed to support this full weight (see also TUNNELLING AND UNDERGROUND EXCAVATION).

BIBLIOGRAPHY. General works on this subject include: T.W. LAMBE and R.V. WHITMAN, *Soil Mechanics* (1969); and K. TERZAGHI and R.B. PECK, *Soil Mechanics in Engineering Practice*, 2nd ed. (1967). Specialized aspects are treated in: F.D.C. HENRY, *The Design and Construction of Engineering Foundations* (1956); J.L. SHERARD *et al.*, *Earth and Earth-Rocks Dams: Engineering Problems of Design and Construction* (1963); C.H. OGLESBY and L.I. HEWES, *Highway Engineering*, 2nd ed. (1963); and C.A. PEQUIGNOT (ed.), *Tunnels and Tunneling* (1963).

(M.M.S.)

Soil Organism

The soil, often considered to be lifeless and inert, contains vast numbers of living organisms, which range in size from microscopic single cells to small mammals. One square metre of rich soil may contain more than 1,000,000-000 organisms.

IMPORTANCE OF SOIL ORGANISMS

As decomposers. Soil organisms are important because they improve soil fertility by breaking down plant and animal tissues; during this process, the nutrients that are released and the minerals that are fixed are incorporated into the soil. Soil flora and fauna break down dead plant material into a finely divided organic complex called humus; the exact composition of humus is unknown, but it probably contains a small proportion of water-soluble organic substances, many phenolic compounds, some organic phosphates, and a polyuronoid substance containing complex sugars. It consists of about 60 percent carbon; the ratio of carbon to nitrogen is about 10 to 1 (*i.e.*, the nitrogen content is about 6 percent). Soil animals incorporate the humus into soil, where it is gradually broken down by micro-organisms that release its constituents for plant nutrition.

As pests. Some soil organisms are pests of crops or animals. Growth of a single crop favours the proliferation of specific soil animals that feed on roots; these organisms then become pests and may kill the plants or cause decreased crop yields. Among the soil animals that feed on, or in, roots are nematodes, slugs and snails, symphylids, beetle larvae, fly larvae, caterpillars, and root aphids. Millipedes and springtails may occasionally attack growing roots, although normally they feed on decaying matter. Some soil organisms cause rots such as those in potato wart disease and potato blight (see DISEASES OF PLANTS). Some soil micro-organisms release substances that inhibit the growth of higher plants, and some soil animals are intermediate hosts for organisms that cause animal diseases, particularly those caused by nematode or helminth parasites.

Pesticides and other soil pollutants affect the populations of many soil organisms. Some soil invertebrates are susceptible to pesticides. The active predatory species often are killed first, allowing the numbers of their prey to increase; for example, populations of springtails increase when their mite predators are killed by DDT. Other agricultural practices decrease the populations of soil organisms. Although the ecological balance of the soil is changed by pesticides, the total numbers or weight of soil organisms is not always decreased. Persistent pesticides affect the fauna over long periods of time. Herbicides, which may kill the soil microflora, often affect the soil fauna indirectly by killing some of their plant foods.

GENERAL FEATURES OF SOIL ORGANISMS

Types of soil organisms. *Protists.* Many of the micro-organisms in the soil participate in breaking down organic matter, in soil formation and fertility, and in returning mineral elements to the soil. The smallest and most numerous soil micro-organisms are bacteria; these spherical, rod-shaped, or spiral cells usually reproduce by simple division and survive unfavourable periods as resistant spores; they are more numerous in alkaline than in acid soils. The actinomycetes resemble both bacteria and fungi; actinomycete spores, although similar to those of bacteria, germinate into very fine colourless mycelia (or threads) that resemble those of fungi. Such fungi as molds, mildews, or mushrooms are usually larger and more variable in form than either bacteria or actinomycetes; they prefer acid soils. They also have resting spores, which germinate into actively growing, straight or branched, white or colourless mycelia (threads) that produce fruiting bodies on which spores develop. There are also algae, which are found as motile single cells or non-motile filaments and contain pigments (*e.g.*, chlorophyll); they are most abundant near the soil surface (see Figure 1).

Microfauna. The soil microfauna, which are usually defined as animals less than 100 microns long, include single-celled protozoans, some smaller nematodes, small flatworms, rotifers, and tardigrades (eight-legged arthropods); the microfauna feed on micro-organisms. The abundant soil protozoans range from the shapeless amoeba to forms with whiplike flagella or tiny hairlike cilia; all protozoans have a nucleus, multiply by cell division, and form resting cysts. Much of the microfauna is confined to water films in litter and soil.

Mesofauna (Meiofauna). Other soil animals, somewhat larger than microfauna, have been placed in a heterogeneous group called the mesofauna. Many of them are nematodes, which are bisexual, survive unfavourable conditions as eggs in resistant cysts, and feed on micro-organisms, other soil animals, decaying organic matter, or living plants. The mites (Acarina), which are the most numerous arthropods in soil, have eight legs when adult and feed on plant or animal material; some are important in breaking down organic matter. Springtails (Collembola), which are wingless insects commonly found in soil, feed on decaying organic matter and micro-organisms; collembolans that live near the soil surface have a springing organ, which enables them to leap. Small, wingless, insect-like organisms called proturans lack antennae and eyes and probably feed on fungi; members of another arthropod group, the pauropods, have nine pairs of legs when mature and feed on decaying plant material.

Macrofauna. The most common soil animals in the group known as the macrofauna are potworms (Enchytraeidae), small, white, segmented worms that feed on fungi, bacteria, and decaying plant material. The myriapods include the small white symphylids, which have 12 pairs of legs and feed on plant roots or decaying material; the centipedes (Chilopoda), which are many-legged, long, slender arthropods that prey on other soil animals; and the millipedes (Diplopoda), which have many legs arranged in pairs and feed principally on decaying plant material. Among the other macrofauna are slugs and snails, which eat mostly plant tissues and organic debris. Among the soil-inhabiting insects are fly larvae, and beetles and their larvae; some of these are predatory but most feed on decaying matter.

Megafauna. The megafauna are the largest soil organisms and include the larger earthworms, which pass both soil and organic matter through their guts, and several vertebrates (*e.g.*, moles, mice, hares, rabbits, badgers, gophers, snakes, lizards), whose food habits vary. The earthworm is important in maintaining soil fertility.

Vertical distribution of soil organisms. The vertical distribution of soil organisms is not uniform; most of them are concentrated in the litter layer and the top two inches of soil in woodlands. It has been calculated that as much as 90 percent of the soil fauna may be in this upper stratum. Many soil invertebrates move up and down through the soil either daily, seasonally, or in response to changes in temperature or moisture in the upper soil. Some invertebrates penetrate deep into the subsoil, usually moving through cracks and fissures. The vertical distribution of micro-organisms follows that of organic matter; as a result, much of the soil microflora is concentrated close to the soil surface.

THE ROLE OF MICRO-ORGANISMS IN SOIL

The most important functions of soil micro-organisms are to break down plant and animal organic matter and to

Humus [marginal note]

Effects of pesticides [marginal note]

Movement through soil [marginal note]

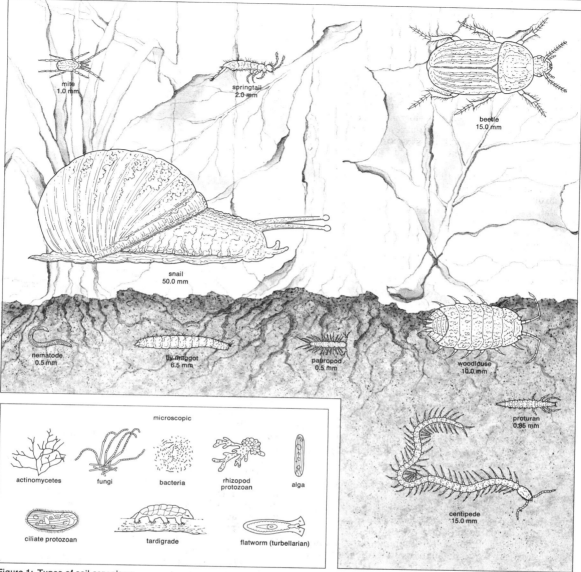

Figure 1: Types of soil organisms

help convert it into a form usable by plants. Heterotrophic soil micro-organisms, which derive their carbon and energy from organic materials, are concerned mainly with the breakdown of organic matter, the carbon cycle, and nitrogen fixation. Autotrophic micro-organisms, which obtain carbon from carbon dioxide and energy from the oxidation of simple organic compounds, form nitrites and nitrates and oxidize sulfur and iron compounds. Most micro-organisms produce carbon dioxide, which dissolves in water to form a weak acid (carbonic acid); this carbonic acid dissolves relatively insoluble soil minerals, which thereby makes these minerals available to plants as nutrients.

Since most functions of soil micro-organisms are beneficial, soils with large populations are usually naturally fertile. Micro-organisms are more numerous and more active in woodland soils than they are in pasture soils; these in turn have a greater microbial activity than fallow or cultivated soils.

The carbon cycle. One of the most important functions of soil micro-organisms is to recycle the carbon that is bound as complex substances in decaying plant and animal matter. Green plants convert carbon dioxide and water into organic plant substances. Animals eat these plants and convert their constituents into animal tissues. When plants and animals die, micro-organisms begin the decay process and complete the carbon cycle by liberating carbon dioxide to the atmosphere. They also liberate minerals (for example, nitrogen and sulfur) and such complex molecules as proteins, polysaccharides, and nucleic acids into the soil.

The nitrogen cycle. Nitrogen, because it is an important component of proteins, is an indispensable element for the growth of micro-organisms, plants, and animals. The availability of nitrogen in soil, in a form that is useful to plants, quite often influences natural vegetation and crop yields.

One essential role of soil micro-organisms in the nitrogen cycle is to break down complex nitrogenous compounds (*e.g.*, proteins, polypeptides, nucleic acids) in soil and humus to simple inorganic compounds (ammonium ions, nitrite, and nitrate) that can be used by plants. Proteins can be decomposed by certain bacteria and fungi. Bacteria usually are most active in alkaline soils, whereas fungi are more active in acid ones. Micro-organisms may release nitrogen in the form of ammonium ions (ammonification); these ions may be oxidized to nitrates by other micro-organisms in a process that is known as nitrification.

Some micro-organisms (*e.g.*, *Nitrosomonas* species) reduce nitrates to nitrites; others (*e.g.*, *Nitrobacter* species) convert nitrites to ammonium ions; still others convert nitrites or ammonium ions back to gaseous nitrogen (denitrification). Soils may be depleted of their nitrogen in this way if no organisms are present to convert the nitrogen back into compounds useful to plants.

Nitrogen fixation

Another essential role of soil micro-organisms in the nitrogen cycle is to return (or fix) nitrogen from the atmosphere; this can occur either by the activity of free-living micro-organisms or as a result of a symbiotic association between plants and micro-organisms.

Free-living micro-organisms capable of utilizing atmospheric nitrogen include bacteria (*e.g.*, *Azotobacter*, *Clostridium*) and blue-green algae (*e.g.*, *Anabaena*). Since many of these bacteria also can use ammonium ions and other nitrogenous compounds as nitrogen sources, they fix nitrogen only when alternative sources are not available. Their transformations are not as important as the symbiotic associations between plants and bacteria described below.

The genus *Rhizobium* causes the formation of root nodules on suitable leguminous plants as well as some trees and shrubs. The roots of the plants secrete substances that stimulate growth and multiplication of *Rhizobium* in the soil around the roots. During nodule formation, atmospheric nitrogen is fixed by these bacteria.

The sulfur cycle. Sulfur is an essential component of plant and animal tissues. Although abundant in nature, as much as three-fourths of soil sulfur may be bound in a form that is unavailable to plants. The most important forms of sulfur for plant nutrition are sulfate salts, although some sulfur in the atmosphere may be taken into plants through the leaves as sulfur dioxide gas. Soil micro-organisms release sulfur from organic compounds and form inorganic compounds; hydrogen sulfide, for example, is released into the atmosphere. Some autotrophic micro-organisms oxidize inorganic forms of sulfur into elemental sulfur, then to sulfurous acid, and, finally, to sulfuric acid.

Sulfates formed by the combination of sulfuric acid and calcium, magnesium, sodium, and potassium provide food for plants. Sulfates may be reduced to sulfites by specific bacteria in transformations that are similar to those that occur in the nitrogen cycle. In well-aerated soil, sulfates are formed readily; in oxygen-depleted soils, however, as are often common in swamps, hydrogen sulfide is produced.

(For additional information about biogeochemical cycles, see BIOSPHERE.)

Adverse effects of soil micro-organisms. Although most soil micro-organisms are beneficial, some are harmful. There are pathogens that cause root rots of higher plants; in greenhouses, for example, "soil sickness" may result from large populations of pathogenic organisms.

Micro-organisms sometimes compete with higher plants for available nutrients, particularly nitrogen and phosphorus. The addition of carbon-rich organic matter to soil often causes significant increases in the numbers of micro-organisms, which utilize the nitrates available in the soil, thus depriving higher plants of nitrogen.

Toxins

Another harmful effect of soil micro-organisms is their production, particularly under oxygen-poor conditions, of substances that inhibit or prevent the growth of higher plants and other micro-organisms. These toxic substances (*e.g.*, methane, hydrogen sulfide, phosphine, skatole, indole, various organic acids) are found most commonly in woodland soils and in lesser amounts in pastures and plowed and cultivated soils.

Their concentrations are highest in summer and autumn and lowest in the spring. Soil can be detoxified by washing or flooding, by adding lime, by using fertilizers, and by cultivating frequently.

THE ROLE OF ANIMALS IN SOIL

Animals are usually not important in maintaining the fertility of agricultural soils. In woodlands, however, soil animals are essential; they maintain the cyclic breakdown of organic material, return organic matter to the soil, and improve soil structure. Soil animals feed on decaying organic matter, living plants, animal excreta, or other animals. The number of animals in a given area of soil is dependent on the availability of food, temperature, moisture, and the degree of aeration and drainage; several hundred million animals (with a fresh weight of as much

as a ton) are probably a valid estimate for the number of animals in an acre of soil (see Figure 2).

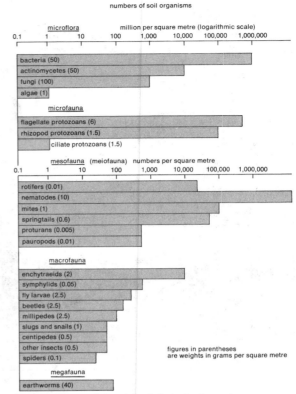

Figure 2: Characteristics of populations of soil organisms.

Formation of humus. Although they contain micro-organisms when they fall, leaves usually are unpalatable to soil animals until they have weathered for several weeks in a litter layer. During this period, after water-soluble materials (*e.g.*, polyphenols) are leached out of the leaves, they are invaded by fungi and other microflora (called primary micro-organisms) and become damp and soft in texture. These changes render the leaf tissues palatable to various soil animals.

A period of intense invertebrate activity occurs; the invertebrates that attack litter at this early stage have been called primary soil animals (see Figure 3). They include millipedes, wood lice, fly larvae, springtails, oribatid mites, enchytraeid worms, and earthworms. Earthworms are important; the burrowing species, such as the "night crawler" (*Lumbricus terrestris*), break up large quantities of leaves before pulling them down into their burrows as food. During this fragmentation of the litter, the invertebrates initiate the conversion of leaf material into a medium suitable for the growth of microflora; for example, invertebrates increase the surface area of leaf tissues by feeding on them. The organic constituents of leaf tissues do not undergo much change, however, as they pass through the invertebrate intestines.

Some chemical changes occur during fragmentation of the litter by soil animals. A few complex molecules are broken down into simpler molecules; for example, certain invertebrates, with the help of symbiotic organisms in their guts, can break down complex substances such as cellulose, keratin, and chitin. The leaf litter and the feces of the animals are now suitable substrates for the growth of other micro-organisms, and a second wave of microbial activity occurs. These micro-organisms act on the organic matter to make it palatable to other soil animals (the secondary decomposers), which flourish only on pre-digested material.

The secondary animals, which feed on this and also on micro-organisms, include springtails, oribatid mites, and enchytraeid worms. Some secondary animals may also be primary decomposers, but different species usually are

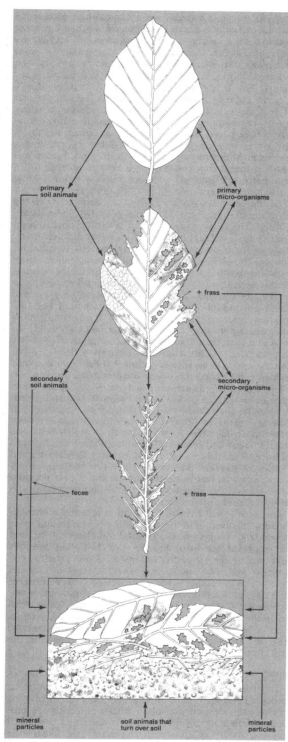

Figure 3: Formation of humus.

stances in the litter increases and mixes thoroughly with other materials.

The soil fauna ultimately destroy the mesophyllic tissues of the leaves, leaving only veins and toughened leaf margins. The rate at which destruction of the mesophyll continues is dependent on the moisture and temperature of the litter layer; destruction is rapid when the litter is moist and temperatures are high.

The organic matter of leaves, therefore, is continuously eaten and excreted by soil animals, acted upon by micro-organisms, and mixed with other soil materials. As this process proceeds, the cellulose, protein, and sugar content of the humus diminishes; the ratio of carbon to nitrogen decreases as starches and sugars in the litter are broken down to carbon dioxide and water. Mineral elements such as sodium, potassium, and magnesium are leached away gradually; eventually the humic substances that remain may represent as little as one-fourth of the organic matter in the original leaf tissues. The remainder of the content of the humus at this stage is lignin (a substance related to cellulose) and protein; fats, waxes, and other residual materials also are present.

Humus increases the porosity and the water holding capacity of soil and also acts as a reservoir for essential plant nutrients; these substances, released gradually, are made available to plants by the action of soil micro-organisms.

Soil fertility and structure. After the formation of humus, soil animals play an important role in soil fertility and structure. The incorporation of humus from litter into soil is a gradual process dependent on the activities of soil animals. In soil that contains small animals and a few micro-organisms, most of the leaves and wood fragments are not decomposed and lie on the soil surface; below the surface is a distinct humus layer, and soil horizons are defined; such a soil is said to be in a mor, or raw humus, condition.

When the soil flora and fauna are abundant, however, decomposition of plant material is rapid, and the humus is mixed into the soil so that layers or horizons are hard to define; such a soil is classified as a mull humus form.

The earthworms are important soil animals in temperate soils; they create the mull condition by turning over the soil—*i.e.*, taking organic matter deep into the soil and bringing subsoil to the surface as "casts" (*i.e.*, excrement). Estimates as to the amount of soil turned over in this way by earthworms vary from 3 to 24 tons per acre per year, with an average of 11 tons. This is equivalent to completely turning over all the soil on the earth to a depth of one inch every ten years. *Turnover of soil*

Soil also is turned over by earthworm species that do not burrow or cast soil to the surface. Moles, which feed mainly on earthworms, also turn over large quantities of soil as they tunnel. In tropical soils, termites, as they construct mounds or gallery systems, are more important than earthworms in turning over soil. Many other animals distribute soil by tunnelling; in particular millipedes, wood lice, ants, and mollusks can turn over large amounts. An important aspect of soil turnover by animals is that it distributes micro-organisms to suitable substrates.

Soil animals also aerate and drain the soil as they dig their tunnels or burrows. Earthworms, termites, ants, wood lice, millipedes, centipedes, and mites break open soil that has been compacted and improve its aeration as they move through it.

Soil without animals lacks "aggregates." Mineral soil particles (particularly clay and lime) and organic matter are cemented together as they pass through the intestines of soil animals; when these substances are excreted they are in the form of water-soluble aggregates; millipedes, wood lice, and earthworms are particularly valuable in forming such aggregates.

Soil animals contribute to the turnover of soil nitrogen; their feces contain nitrogen in forms such as ammonia, urea, uric acid, and other compounds that are readily converted to substances that plants can utilize. It has been calculated that the amount of nitrogen excreted by an

involved. The arthropods produce distinctive feces in the form of fine pellets, and enchytraeid worms produce amorphous black feces. During this stage algae, protozoans, nematodes, and rotifers invade the fine water films that form on the surfaces of leaf fragments and animal feces. (Many activities of the soil fauna and flora are dependent on moisture; if the litter layer dries, many soil organisms encyst or enter a resting stage.)

The roles of the soil fauna and microflora in decomposing organic matter are complementary and interrelated. If soil animals are numerous, bacteria also are abundant. Consumption, digestion, and excretion of leaf litter by soil animals alternates with increases in the population of micro-organisms; as a result the proportion of humic sub- *Complementary roles of organisms*

average earthworm population is about equal to the amount removed by an average crop of hay—*i.e.*, about 50 pounds of nitrogen per acre; however, soil micro-organisms contribute much greater quantities of nitrogen. Organic matter bound in the tissues of soil animals is perhaps as much as a ton per acre, expressed as fresh weight. This is a reservoir of nutrients that is released gradually to the soil as the animals die.

BIBLIOGRAPHY. M. ALEXANDER, *Introduction to Soil Microbiology* (1961), a good introductory text that emphasizes soil transformations by microflora; A. BRAUNS, *Praktische Bodenbiologie* (1968), an up-to-date, well-illustrated account in German of practical soil biology and ecology; N.A. BURGES and F. RAW, *Soil Biology* (1967), a comprehensive text on the biology of soil invertebrates and microflora; J. DOEKSEN and J. VAN DER DRIFT (eds.), *Soil Organisms* (1963), a collection of original papers that emphasize the interrelationships between the soil fauna and microflora; C.A. EDWARDS *et al.*, "The Role of Soil Invertebrates in Turnover of Organic Matter and Nutrients," in *Studies in Ecology*, vol. 1, ed. by D.E. REICHLE (1970), a recent article emphasizing energy changes during litter breakdown; T.R.G. GRAY and D. PARKINSON (eds.), *The Ecology of Soil Bacteria: An International Symposium* (1967), a collection of important papers on soil bacteria; D.K.M. KEVAN, *Soil Animals* (1962), an introductory text; G. MULLER, *Bodenbiologie* (1965), good summaries in German of the various elemental cycles; E.J. RUSSELL, *The World of the Soil* (1957), a popular, readable account that emphasizes the importance of soil organisms.

(C.A.E.)

Soils

Soil may be defined as the fine earth covering land surfaces that has the important function of serving as a substratum of plant, animal, and human life. Soil acts as a reservoir of nutrients and water, and absorbs and oxidizes the injurious waste substances that plant growth accumulates in the rhizosphere (*i.e.*, the root zone). These functions of soil are possible because it contains clay minerals and organic substances (clay and humus form the finer part of soil) that absorb both ions (electrically charged atoms) and water.

Soil usually consists of a sequence of chemically and biologically differentiated layers, called horizons, that have been formed by the action of natural forces on the unconsolidated residue (regolith) of rocks and minerals on the Earth's surface. The regolith itself is the result of weathering of the original massive rocks at the surface and may be considered to be incipient soil. In the process of weathering, fracturing occurs along planes of weakness in the rocks and their mineral components react chemically with water, oxygen, and organic, carbonic, nitric, and sulfuric acids that are derived from the atmosphere and living organisms. Through the continuation of these chemical, physical, and biological actions and reactions, the regolith material is transformed into soil that exhibits one to four master horizons called, from the surface downward A, B, and C horizons (the soil profile), and the underlying consolidated rock, R.

Surface and subsurface horizons are distinguished by the differences in conditions at various depths. Some materials accumulate in the soil and some substances decompose or are dissociated to release compounds that may be dispersed, dissolved, or transported from one horizon to another; they may even be carried away from the immediate locality. Solutions are present in the soil layers, and these vary in composition and concentrations, and thus in the chemical changes they effect. These several conditions determine the abundance and variety of living organisms, from microscopic ones to vertebrates, which in turn influence the further development and the properties of the soil. In the soil profile that results, the horizons differ from each other in characteristics such as colour, chemical composition, particle sizes and distribution, and structure (*i.e.*, arrangement of the particles in groups, aggregates, or independent units).

The A horizon extends from the ground surface to the unmodified regolith or consolidated rock. It is the horizon in which weathering is most intense, with partial removal of the resulting products and a zone of accumulation of organic material. In a typical high-productive soil, the A horizon is rich in humus (more than 1 percent carbon) to a depth of 15 centimetres (6 inches) or more; it contains the greater part of immediately available plant nutrients. Soils of low productive capacity tend to have A horizons that are poor in humus and plant nutrients. The B horizon lies immediately beneath the A horizon and may reach a depth of 25 to 36 inches (64 to 91 centimetres). It is a zone of more moderate weathering in which there is an accumulation of many of the products removed from the A horizon. Sometimes the B horizon is very clayey and impermeable, constituting a serious impediment to plant growth. In a productive soil water, air, and root penetration is easy to a depth of 75 centimetres (30 inches) or more and the water-holding capacity of the entire layer is 15 centimetres (6 inches) of available water, or more. The C horizon contains the parent materials, from which the A and B horizons are formed. The R layer is not part of the soil proper; it is an underlying layer that has properties much different from those of the C horizon immediately above it and that influences the soil by its position. Because of soil development factors that will be discussed in following sections of this article, some master horizons can be missing in certain soil profiles. For example, erosion may remove the A horizon; shortness of time or absence of key factors may preclude development of a B horizon; a shallow, weathered layer may be transformed completely into A and B horizons, so that no parent materials are left to constitute a C horizon; or conversely a deep regolith can screen the A layer to the point that the latter does not influence the properties of the overlying soil horizon.

There are many functions provided by soil that are important to man. Agriculture and animal husbandry produce more than 90 percent of man's food; together with forestry these soil-connected activities produce many other materials needed by man, such as wood, cellulose, textile fibres, and leather. The utilization of soil by agriculture, animal husbandry, and forestry is often termed "soil exploitation." Soil is necessary for dwellings, highways, airports, and recreation areas, and it also provides road fill and material for water retention structures and many other essential functions.

This article will treat soil formation and the influential factors involved, soil profiles, soil properties and their dependence on geographic factors, soil classification, and the geographical distribution of soil. Soil-plant relations and engineering properties are treated in the articles ECOSYSTEM and SOIL MECHANICS, APPLICATIONS OF, respectively. For coverage of the processes of rock weathering and the products involved, see WEATHERING and CLAY MINERALS. Certain special soil types are principally treated in the articles LOESS and DURICRUSTS, and the interaction of soils and climate is discussed in MICROCLIMATES. (See also HYDROLOGIC CYCLE for the role of soils in the world's water system.)

PROCESSES OF SOIL FORMATION

Clay formation. The most fundamental soil forming process is weathering. During the weathering process the crystals of feldspars and other silicate minerals are broken up, releasing chemical compounds such as bases, silica, and oxides of iron and aluminum (specifically the sesquioxides: Fe_2O_3 and Al_2O_3). Leaching (*i.e.*, washing or draining away by percolation of water through the soil) removes most of the bases and some of the silica, and the remaining silica combines with alumina and forms crystalline clays.

The kind of crystalline clay produced depends on leaching intensity. Rapid leaching leaves little silica to combine with alumina and results in what are known as 1:1 clays consisting of a tetrahedral (silica) and octahedral (alumina) layer; slow leaching leads to the formation of 2:1 clays, consisting of one octahedral (alumina) layer sandwiched between two tetrahedral (silica) layers. In neither case is the result solely one of the two types, but 1:1 clay is predominant after rapid leaching, and 2:1 clay more abundant when leaching is slow (see Figure 1).

Ions are atoms or groups of atoms that have become

The weathering process

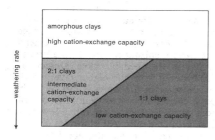

Figure 1: Influence of weathering and leaching rates on clay mineralogy and cation-exchange capacity; rates increase in the direction shown by the arrows (see text).

electrically charged through the loss or gain of electrons; ions of positive charge are cations and those of negative charge, anions. The phenomenon known as cation exchange is the result of the differences in the force with which clay holds different cations. The surfaces of clay minerals contain many negative charges, which are balanced electrically by the adsorption (i.e., taking up on the surface, as opposed to taking up and distributing throughout the body of an absorbent) of cations. The tightness with which the soil holds cations varies; it is greatest for hydrogen cations and decreases for other cations in the following order: calcium, magnesium, potassium, sodium. Because of the differences in attractive forces, adsorbed cations may be removed and replaced by other cations. Because clay formation is very slow, for long time periods the silica and alumina constitute an amorphous (structureless) clay that has a cation-exchange capacity several times greater than that of crystalline clays. Alumina-rich 1:1 clays have low cation-exchange capacity. Silica-rich 2:1 clays have higher cation-exchange capacity, but lower than that of amorphous clays. Thus young soils and lower horizons that have undergone little weathering have high cation-exchange capacities per unit of clay, as do volcanic soils, because their weathering has been so rapid that clay formation has not had time to take place. Such capacity is lower in old soils in dry or cold climates, and it is lowest in tropical soils.

The most significant aspect of weathering is its relationship to clay crystallization or leaching, rather than its rapidity. Minerals differ greatly in their weatherability, and they have been classified in this respect. Clay crystallization seems to be accelerated by a basic medium, especially magnesium. Leaching is an irreversible process (see Figure 2), and thus the effect of a humid season cannot be undone by a dry season. What is important is leaching rainfall, Ln., which is the difference between rainfall and potential evapotranspiration (i.e., return to the air by direct evaporation or by transpiration of vegetation, or both) during the humid season. Leaching rainfall is low in temperate countries, even when they are humid (as in London and Moscow), and high in tropical countries, even when they have a long dry season (as in Kano, Nigeria). The prevalence of 1:1 clays in tropical countries is more directly the result of leaching rainfall (see Table 1) than of the great age of the rocks.

The character of clay

Rocks subjected to weathering, young soils, and soils formed from easily weatherable materials (e.g., volcanic ashes, lava, or basalt) are rich in amorphous clays of high cation-exchange capacity. Such amorphous clays are mixed with 1:1 clays or 2:1 clays, depending on leaching intensity. Old soils and soils formed from materials that weather with difficulty are poor in amorphous clays and rich in 1:1 clays or 2:1 clays according to whether leaching is rapid or slow. Soil usually contains a great variety of clays that differ in their relative proportions.

In addition to the absorbing capacity for water and ions, which is the most important soil property, clay mineralogy affects such physical properties of soil as its structure and permeability to air and water. A soil rich in amorphous clays has a low apparent density and is very permeable to air and water; decay of organic matter is slow and humus content is unusually high. Soils rich in

1:1 clays usually have a stable structure and swell very little when moistened; on the other hand, a soil rich in 2:1 clays, more especially montmorillonite, has a weak structure, low permeability, and swells easily when moistened.

Tropical soils are usually dominated by 1:1 clays, whereas those of temperate countries contain chiefly 2:1 clays. But pedology, the study of soils, began in temperate countries and is consequently based on what is observed in soils with 2:1 clays; it was some time before the fundamental difference between tropical and temperate soils was realized and understood. For analogous reasons, and because amorphous clays were lost when preparing clay sample for analysis, understanding of volcanic soils has been much delayed. It is only recently that they have been recognized as a special group. Even now the volcanic soils of dry climates are little known.

Mica is a platy silicate mineral that is directly altered (i.e., changed in mineralogical composition) to clays. The first clays formed have high cation-exchange capacity; later 2:1 or 1:1 clays dominate, so that the foregoing outline of the weathering process is applicable to soils formed from materials rich in mica.

Experiments show that weathering is more rapid in a medium containing organic acids. Hence, when soil is covered by raw humus, as in podsolic regions, amorphous clays are formed as a result of the rapid weathering.

By eluviation (the transposition of soil material from one horizon to another) an illuvial horizon is formed by the deposition of materials leached out of an overlaying layer. The illuvial horizon of podsols, called

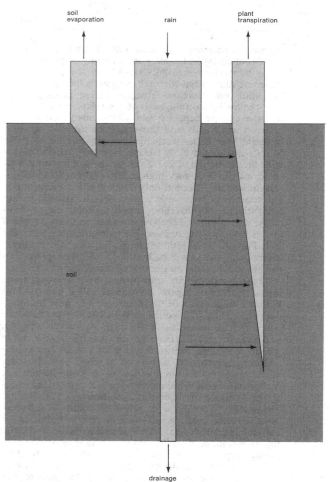

Figure 2: Water movement in the soil.
In general, water moves in the soil in only one direction—it descends. While descending it is absorbed by plant roots, and the substances it contains precipitate; in this way various substances are transported from the higher layers (horizons) to the lower ones. Under moderate rainfall, the quantity of water that is lost by drainage is little, if any, and only very soluble substances are eliminated.

Table 1: Leaching Rainfall
(in millimetres)

	Ln		Ln
Bahía Blanca, Argentina	0	Budapest	140
Damascus	10	London	160
Tobolsk, R.S.F.S.R.	10	Berlin	170
Reno	10	Moscow	220
Eureka, Northwest Territories, Canada	20	Jerusalem	230
		Cienfuegos, Cuba	240
Tehrān	20	Stockholm	240
Irkutsk, R.S.F.S.R.	20	Oslo	260
Barrow, Alaska	30	Mexico City	270
Saskatoon, Saskatchewan, Canada	40	Chicago	270
		Rio de Janeiro	280
Baker Lake, Northwest Territories, Canada	40	Amsterdam	310
		Naples	320
Prague, Czechoslovakia	40	Kano, Nigeria	362
Harbin, China	40	Kiel, West Germany	410
Salt Lake City	40	New Orleans	460
Anadyr, R.S.F.S.R.	40	New York	470
Rosario, Argentina	50	Nāgpur, India	517
Nizhnekolymsk, R.S.F.S.R.	50	Bamako, Mali	520
Ankara	50	Kinshasa, Zaire (Congo, Dem. Rep. of the)	640
Omsk, R.S.F.S.R.	50		
Resolute, Northwest Territories, Canada	60	Yaoundé, Cameroon	690
Madrid	60	Djakarta	690
Lincoln, Nebraska	60	Wellington, New Zealand	690
Santiago, Chile	70		
Corrientes, Argentina	80	Canton	820
Athens	80	Tokyo	870
Tripoli, Libya	80	New Delhi	1,040
Tientsin	90	Valencia, Ireland	1,150
Rabat, Morocco	90	Bombay	1,679
Niamey, Niger	100	Rangoon	2,000
Bucharest	100	Valdivia, Chile	2,120
Kiev	110	Cochin, India	2,462
Des Moines, Iowa	120	Conakry, Guinea	3,740
Paris	130	Monrovia, Liberia	3,860
Warsaw	130	Cherrapunji, India	10,922

the spodic horizon, is rich in amorphous clays and resembles ando (volcanic ash) soil in many respects.

Clay mineralogy is usually studied by X-rays and techniques of differential thermal analysis, which provide information on structural changes during heating. Soils may be classified on the basis of the relationship between cation-exchange capacity and clay content. Gradations between ando soils and those rich in the clay mineral kaolinite have cation-exchange capacity similar to those of soils dominated by 2:1 clays, but when conditions favour the formation of 2:1 clays, or the soil is young, volcanic soils exhibit very high cation-exchange capacities.

Humification. Second only to clay in importance as a soil constituent is organic matter, which contributes significantly to soil absorbing capacity. Roots die continuously, vegetation and crop residues fall on the soil surface and decay, and the organic leaching products enter the soil. Part of these residues is mixed with soil by organisms living in the soil or by tillage operations; some algae produce organic matter that also is added to soil.

Types of humus
All these residues are transformed by micro-organisms into a mixture of organic substances called humus. Two kinds of humus may be distinguished: (1) mild humus is dark in colour, well saturated with bases, especially calcium, rich in humic acids (of high molecular weight), and serves to stabilize clay; (2) raw humus is more red in colour, less basic, rich in fulvic acids (of low molecular weight), and favours dispersion of clay. Soil also contains organic matter that has not yet been humified and in certain cases peat, which is more or less carbonized material that still retains its original structure.

Vegetation determines the kind of humus a soil contains. Grasses produce mild humus rich in humic acids, and conifers produce raw humus rich in fulvic acids. But the base content of soils is also important in determining humus type; for example, calcium-rich soils produce milder humus than do hydrogen-saturated soils. Waterlogging also has an effect, favouring production of raw humus. Root growth is more abundant near the soil surface, and aerial residues accumulate on the surface; thus, organic-matter content decreases with depth.

The effects of leaching. Except for the amount that is immediately evaporated from the surface, rainwater moves through the soil in only the downward direction, and

while descending it is absorbed by plant roots. Excess water may be eliminated by drainage, so that even in dry climates the upper layers of soil are somewhat leached. Leaching decreases with depth (see Figure 2). Descending water dissolves various substances, which are precipitated when the water is absorbed by roots. Descending water transports substances from the higher layers to the lower ones, and when some of the water is lost by drainage, the substances it carries are lost as well. More soluble substances are more easily leached away from a layer and are accumulated at greater depth. All chlorides and sodium, potassium, and magnesium sulfates are more soluble than gypsum, which is in turn more soluble than calcium and magnesium bicarbonates.

When there is no drainage, all substances remain in the profile, stratified according to their solubility (see Figure 3)—chlorides and sulfates at the lowest part of the rhizo-

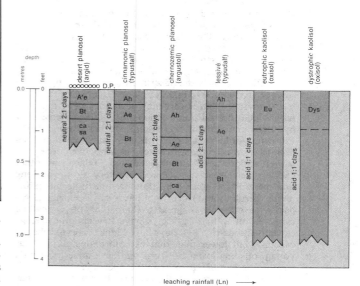

Figure 3: *Influence of leaching rainfall (Ln) on soil formation.*
Leaching rainfall increases from left to right, as shown by the arrow. D.P., desert pavement; A'e, surface horizon poor in humus and eluvial; Bt, textural B; ca, lime accumulation; sa, salts accumulation; Ah, surface horizon rich in humus; Ae, eluvial surface horizon; Eu, eutrophic upper soil; Dys, dystrophic upper soil (see text).

sphere (root zone of plants), gypsum above them, and calcium carbonate at a higher level. With more leaching the profile deepens, salts are leached away, gypsum accumulates in the lowest part of the rhizosphere, and lime above it. Still further leaching removes first the gypsum, while the lime accumulates in the lower part of the rhizosphere; then it removes the lime, and the soil becomes acidified. Because silica is less soluble than lime, 1:1 clays are usually formed in an acid medium, and are usually acid. But an acid soil may later be basified, and 1:1 clays are sometimes inherited from parent material, as in the case of allochthonous soils (*i.e.*, those transported from other environments).

Dispersion mechanisms of soil constituents. *Biological transport of elements.* Plants absorb various elements from the profile and deposit them, with their residues, on the soil surface, a process that counteracts leaching. In soils rich in bases leaching is more important. This accounts for the fact that base saturation and pH (the standard measure of acidity, related to the concentration of hydrogen ions; a pH value of 7.0 is neutral, whereas that from 1.0 to 7.0 is acid and that from 7.0 to 14.0 is alkaline) usually increase with depth. In acid soils, leaching is difficult because cations are firmly retained by soil colloids, and biological transport to the surface prevails; base saturation decreases with depth. In the kaolisols of the humid tropics, the upper 25 centimetres (ten inches) of soil often contain more bases than the rest of the profile to a depth of 150 centimetres (five feet). The process is selective, however; *e.g.*, sodium and magnesium are less absorbed by plants than are potassium and calcium.

Base saturation acidity

Addition of constituents by running water and wind. Floodwaters always contain salt, and soil, when flooded, may become saline (*i.e.*, high in chlorides and sulfates of sodium, potassium, calcium, and magnesium) unless some of the water is lost by drainage. Floods sometimes deposit fine earth or coarse materials on the soil surface. Sea winds often bring salts, and some soils, such as those of New Zealand and the Falkland Islands (Islas Malvinas), have probably been salinized in this way. In other cases winds bring dust or volcanic ash, additions that may counteract leaching and modify the soil profile.

Subirrigation. In some soils there is a water table one to two metres below the rhizosphere. During the dry season water rises by capillary action from this water table to the rhizosphere, where it is absorbed by plant roots, and the substances it contains accumulate. In this way a horizon of salts, gypsum, lime, silica, or iron accumulation is formed, depending upon the substances that are contained in subirrigation water. When the accumulation takes place in a layer poor in clay, the lime, silica, or iron are deposited on the surface of sand or gravel and may cement them, forming a hardpan (cemented layer impenetrable by roots). Many calcareous horizons, duripans, fragipans, and iron pans have this origin, but they also may be cemented by substances that descend in the profile. When the water table is shallow, the hardpan may reach the soil surface.

Solonization. Sodium clay is easily dispersible, and in sodium soils it is transported from the surface to some depth. Sodium soils swell when moistened, however, which impedes clay movement, so that clay illuviation takes place near the surface rather than at depth. This process is called solonization, or solonetization, and results in sodium-saturated soils (solonetz) that have a richer clay horizon at depth than at the surface.

Transport of chemicals in soils

Leaching activated by vegetation, however, produces organic acids and transports calcium from the lower layers to the surface. Sodium then is replaced by calcium or hydrogen in the eluvial layer and the upper part of the illuvial one. Clay illuviation thus takes place at a greater depth, and soil becomes planosol or solod (calcium- or hydrogen-saturated soils with considerable difference in clay content between the eluviated surface and the clay illuvial horizon).

Planosols can also be formed directly from a slightly sodium-saturated soil; low sodium saturation is sufficient to facilitate clay dispersion and permits clay movement to greater depth. Solonetz are often formed from sodium-saline soils, and planosols from easily weatherable materials, such as volcanic ash, under conditions that impede leaching (*e.g.*, dry climate or poor drainage or both).

Iron and clay illuviation. Fulvic acids react with iron and may cause its eluviation and that of clay. For that reason, soils formed under forest vegetation, which produces humus rich in fulvic acids, are often leached; there is a difference in clay content between the surface horizon and the B horizon in which the clay is illuviated. Moreover, such soils are relatively rich in free iron, and a difference in free iron content is often observed between the surface horizon, which is poorer, and a lower enriched horizon. Because dispersed iron is easily precipitated by bases or concentration of soil solution, soils developed under conditions that favour the formation of fulvic acid-rich humus are usually rich in iron that is finely precipitated with organic matter, which gives them a brown colour (brunisolic soils).

Podsolization. Weathering in a strongly acid medium produces an eluviation of the sesquioxides (Fe_2O_3 and Al_2O_3) released by weathering. Because weathering is very rapid amorphous clays of high cation-exchange capacity are formed. The soil formed has an upper horizon rich in unweathered minerals (sand), and an illuvial one rich in amorphous clays ("spodic" horizon). Such soils are called podsols. Although vegetation and other conditions may favour the accumulation of raw humus, its acidity is neutralized when soil contains lime or when weathering releases bases in sufficient quantity. Podsolic weathering is therefore observed in sandy materials rich in quartz and other minerals of low weatherability. The

organic matter that produces eluviation of clay or sesquioxides decays and cannot accumulate in the illuvial horizon; but when this horizon is waterlogged or when its temperature is very low, an accumulation of organic matter takes place and a humus illuvial horizon is formed. Such soils are called humus podsols.

Rubification. When soil is thoroughly dried from time to time, precipitates of iron and organic matter cannot accumulate and the organic matter disappears by decay, causing irreversibly dehydrated iron sesquioxides to form. This process is known as rubification, and the resulting soils, called cinnamonic, are rich in fine crystallites of dehydrated iron sesquioxides.

Ferrugination. Iron sesquioxides adhere firmly to sand grains and gravel, give them a red colour, and may cement them to form an iron pan. This process is most common in soils that have been formed from materials that release much iron upon weathering and leave much sand, whereas humic horizons are seldom ferruginized, probably because organic acids and reductive processes remove the iron coating from sand grains. Fulvic acids favour iron eluviation and the formation of ferruginized horizons at some depth; thus, fragipans and other iron-cemented pans are common in podsols and brunisolic soils. The ferruginous horizons of tropical soils are formed similarly, fulvic acids contributing to their formation, but reductive processes can also be responsible for iron eluviation. Periodic soil drying may consolidate iron coatings, especially in climates in which a humid and a dry season alternate. It seems that iron coatings protect sand and gravel grains from weathering, and they are the cause of many "stone lines" parallel to soil surface.

Formation of cemented pans

Segregation of iron. In soil that is rich in iron and poor in 2:1 clays that retain it, iron tends to segregate, forming irregular concretions and nodules. After repeated moistenings and dryings, the nodules become as hard as stone and may form a pan cemented with iron and gravel (laterite). Waterlogging seems to further iron segregation, and alternative moistenings and dryings harden the nodules or pan. This process resembles ferrugination, the difference being in degree of segregation.

Gleization. Under waterlogging conditions, iron becomes ferrous and has a valence of 2+. (Valence is an expression of the combining power of an element, which is determined by the number of electrons in its outer or valence shell of electrons; valence is represented by a number that corresponds to the number of electrons an atom of the element can accept [if the number is positive] or donate [if the number is negative]). Ferrous soil has gray-blue colours, is called gley, and the process is called gleization. When waterlogging is less severe and transitory, ferrous iron is oxidized (*i.e.*, loses an electron, with a resulting change in valence to 3+, which is that of ferric iron, F^{3+}), and ruggy mottles (spots) are produced in the soil. Because ferrous iron is more mobile than ferric iron, gleization favours iron eluviation, resulting in a leached upper horizon; iron accumulates at a lower depth or is leached away. Or the iron may ascend by capillarity from the water table to the lower part of the rhizosphere.

Development of soil characteristics. *Soil profile and horizons.* Humification, leaching, clay eluviation, and other soil-forming processes all create differences between soil horizons. Soil profiles vary considerably in horizon types and their thicknesses.

Soil properties. Both water-holding capacity and cation exchange depend on clay content, clay mineralogy, humus content, kind of humus, and nature of absorbed ions. Mineral constituents larger than clay also have some water-holding capacity, and in some cases silt exhibits considerable ion exchange capacity. This may be attributed to its formation by aggregates of amorphous clays or by amorphous clay that adheres to silt particles.

Soil texture (*i.e.*, the relative proportion of mineral constituents classified according to their size) determines to a considerable extent soil porosity and, consequently, permeability to air and water, which are essential for root life and many processes that take place in soil. A high content of coarse constituents usually increases porosity.

Nature of soil texture and structure

But clay and humus bind single soil grains together in increasingly larger aggregates.

Soil has a "structure" on which its porosity-permeability depends greatly. Soil structure is built up by alternate moistening and drying, and plant roots contribute greatly by opening pores between soil aggregates; it is undone by waterlogging. The stability of aggregates increases with humus content, especially humus that originates from grass vegetation (forest humus is less effective).

Calcium and hydrogen soils have structural stability, whereas sodium soils lose stability easily. Soils rich in amorphous clays are very porous and permeable, and their apparent density is exceptionally low. Soils rich in 1:1 clays are also permeable. High content of 2:1 clays, however, is usually associated with low permeability because the soil swells when moistened and the pores close. The clay type is very important; montmorillonite is the worst in this respect. Water movement in 2:1 clayey soils is chiefly through cracks produced when soil dries, and water movement in pores between small aggregates is very slow. Soils rich in coarse constituents are usually permeable. Soils with a high fine-sand content, however, have low permeability, poor aggregation, and small pores between single grains of fine sand; moreover, they are not extensible, and they resist root penetration.

Texture variations in horizons

Because soil horizons vary in texture, humus content, and absorbed ions, soil properties vary from horizon to horizon. This fact should be taken into consideration in evaluating the soil as a whole. Distinction must be made between intrinsic qualities—such as texture, clay mineralogy, the nature of absorbed cations, and their variation along the profile—and the secondary qualities that are consequences of the first and are more or less transitory—such as structure and permeability. Humus content and soluble salts are intermediary; they can be modified by management, added, or leached away.

From an agricultural point of view, the most important soil qualities are cation-exchange and water-holding capacities, the nature of absorbed cations, richness in assimilable plant nutrients and certain other substances (e.g., lime, free aluminum), permeability, structure, humus content, and waterlogging. For engineering uses, texture, clay mineralogy, humus content, swelling capacity, capacity to corrode metals, structure (which can be modified), permeability, and waterlogging (chiefly extrinsic), are important.

Horizon nomenclature. Usually the upper horizon, which is generally richer in humus and may be eluvial, is called A; it may be "humic" (Ah), eluvial (Ae), or "bleached" (A$_2$). The horizon in which clay has been illuviated is called Bt; that of amorphous clays produced by podsolization ("spodic" horizon) Bir (from iron, which was considered the most important illuvial substance); and that of humus illuviation Bh. Weathered material that has not been sufficiently enriched in humus to be humic and has not had important illuviation of clay or humus is called C. Underlying consolidated rock is called an R horizon.

A horizon of lime accumulation is usually called ca, but the term can be extended to all horizons that give effervescence with an acid. An accumulation of gypsum is indicated as cs; a horizon unusually rich in easily soluble salts by sa; cn designates an accumulation of ferruginous concretions and nodules; mf a ferruginous hardpan; mc a calcic hardpan; x a fragipan (fragil hardpan cemented with iron); G denotes strong gleying; g moderate gleying.

According to clay mineralogy a horizon may be allophanic, illitic, kaolinitic, or superkaolinitic, the diagnosis being chiefly based on the relation between cation-exchange capability (CEC) and clay content. According to base saturation, a horizon may be acid, neutral, natric, magnesic, or calcic. Fifteen percent sodium saturation is sufficient to make a horizon "natric." The terms acid and neutral are replaced by dystrophic and eutrophic (poor or rich in nutrients) in the case of kaolinitic and organic soils in which the relation of absorbed cations to clay content is a better diagnostic indicator than base saturation. Many of these terms are poorly defined in the literature, and definitions vary from author to author.

Rates of soil formation. Rates of soil formation vary enormously according to the process involved, and for the same process according to conditions. Weathering varies according to the weatherability of the material, and minerals may be classified in this respect. Weathering of a consolidated rock is usually slow at the beginning, accelerates as the rock breaks up and more surface area is exposed to attack, and then becomes increasingly slower as weatherable minerals disappear. It is accelerated by plant roots and by the accumulation of raw humus, and also by a rapid removal of the bases by leaching.

Mineral composition and rock weathering

Weathering is more rapid than is usually thought. In experimental leaching of coarse gravel of basalt with pure water at 20° C (68° F), 0.45 percent of the silica was eliminated in 11 months. Leaching with water containing acetic acid (pH 2.5, which is a common acidity value in the vicinity of roots and decaying organic matter) accelerated the process by a factor of 21. Volcanic ashes weather sufficiently to support vigorous vegetation in a few decades.

Tombstones and other man-made structures weather more slowly because they are not in contact with plant roots or decaying organic matter, and, moreover, the surface of attack is very small.

Humification is a very rapid process. Experiments and agricultural practice all over the world have shown that soil organic matter can be doubled or reduced to half in 5–50 years. Podsolization is also rapid, and it has been reported that soils planted with conifers have been podsolized in a century. Salinization and desalination are also rapid because of the higher solubility of salts less soluble than gypsum. Decalcification and acidification with water containing carbon dioxide are intrinsically slower but may be accelerated when produced by water containing organic acids, which is usually the case.

There is less information concerning clay eluviation, but experiments show that this is a relatively rapid process because water often moves through soil cracks, carrying much clay per unit of water. The formation of argillic (clay illuvial) horizons has been estimated to require between 550 and 5,250 years. In many cases the age of soil that has been formed in previously glaciated areas, newly formed terraces, or from recent volcanic material, is known; but it is not always possible to ascertain whether clay eluviation required all this time. In any case, existing evidence and the fact that soils correspond well to present climatic conditions indicate that soil formation processes are relatively rapid.

FACTORS INVOLVED IN SOIL FORMATION

Basic types of factors. *Climate.* The amount and kind of clay that is formed, soil depth, base saturation, and the formation and depth of saline, gypsic, or calcic horizons all depend on leaching intensity. Consequently, the significant factor is leaching rainfall (see Figure 3). The soils of temperate climates are rich in 2:1 clays, whereas those of tropical countries are rich in 1:1 clays. But in both cases when the soil is young, or has been formed from volcanic ashes, it contains considerable amorphous clays, which increase its cation-exchange capacity.

Temperature is another influence in soil formation. Because the solubility of silica increases with temperature, high temperatures favour the formation of 1:1 clays, which is another reason for the abundance of such clays in tropical soils. Water penetration and root penetration depend on leaching rainfall, so that the depth of weathering and of soil increase with Ln. Soils of tropical countries are usually very deep; those of cold or dry climates, or of both, shallower. Temperature is also important. At high latitudes and altitudes the lower layers of soil are very cold, even in summer; consequently, weathering and soil depth are limited, which is important in the case of autochthonous soils (*i.e.*, formed in the original location) developed from consolidated rocks. Permafrost limits both soil depth and drainage. In very dry climates no water is lost by drainage. In dry climates substances formed by weathering accumulate in the profile, stratified according to their solubility, and as leaching increases the lower horizons disappear, and the profile becomes deep-

Effects of Ln on weathering depth

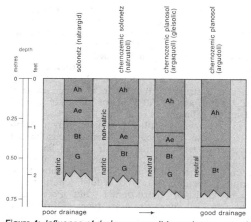

Figure 4: *Influence of drainage on soil formation.*
Ah, rich in humus surface horizon (layer); Ae, eluvial surface
horizon; Bt, textural B (clay illuviation); G, gley.

er. Finally, there are insufficient bases in the soil to neutralize the organic acids produced by decay of roots and
organic matter. Solution in the soil then tends toward
acidity, the soil is leached with acid water, and hydrogen
ions replace other ions. The result of this cycle is an
increasingly more acid soil. Acidification, however, also
depends greatly on vegetation type, temperature, and
waterlogging. In addition to the above direct influences,
climate greatly affects vegetation, which is one of the
most important factors in soil formation.

Drainage and topography. Leaching is impossible without drainage; thus, impeded drainage has to some extent the same effect as drought. Impeded drainage may
result in the formation of soils with 2:1 clays, well saturated with bases, saline, gypsic, or calcareous horizons. It
also causes gleization and may result in the formation of
a water table, which has various influences, especially
salinization and formation of various pans—petrocalcic
horizons, duripan, ironstone, fragipan, laterite, etc. (see
Figure 4). Topography greatly influences erosion, drainage, flooding, and subirrigation, which have a profound
influence on soil formation, as has been discussed. Soils
on slopes are usually shallow and stony (lithosols), and
those in the valleys are alluvial.

**Variation
in humus**

Vegetation and living organisms. Vegetation largely determines the kind of humus that is formed. Some trees,
especially conifers, usually produce raw humus that may
cause podsolization. Other trees produce weakly acid humus capable only of producing iron mobilization and
clay illuviation. Such soils are brown (brunisolic) and
more or less leached. Grasses produce mild humus rich in
acids that stabilize clay. The distribution of humus along
the profile also depends on the type of vegetation. Grasses
have numerous roots that decay rapidly and enrich soil in

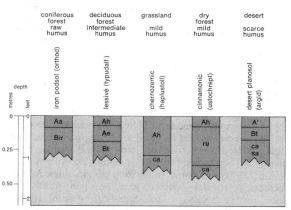

Figure 5: *Influence of vegetation and humus on soil formation.*
Aa, albic (ashy) surface horizon (layer); Bir, iron podsolic B
(spodic horizon); Ah, humus rich surface horizon; Ae, eluvial
surface horizon; Bt, textural B (clay illuvial); ca, lime
accumulation; ru, rubified, A', poor in humus surface
horizon; sa, salts accumulation.

humus to considerable depth. Tree roots contribute little
to soil humus; thus, the humic horizon of forest soils is
usually shallow (see Figure 5).

Vegetation protects soil from the sun's rays and retards
organic matter decay; it absorbs calcium, potassium, and
phosphorus from the lower soil layers and counteracts
their leaching; and it protects soil against erosion. Erosion, even hydraulic, is severe in deserts because there is
no vegetation to protect the soil. Living creatures within
the soil such as earthworms and termites mix the various
soil horizons and counteract their differentiation; they
also mix soil plant residues on the soil surface and contribute to organic matter decay and humus formation. A
certain mixing also occurs when old trees are uprooted by
wind.

Parent material. Soil is parent material that has been
altered by various processes, and its ultimate nature depends upon its original composition. In soils formed from
unconsolidated sedimentary rocks, much of the clay is
inherited from parent material. Materials rich in lime are
difficult to decalcify, acidify, or podsolize. Materials rich
in iron usually give red soils.

Time. Although in geological terms soil formation is
rapid, in human terms it requires many decades or centuries. Soil age has a great influence on soil properties.
The age of a soil usually is measured from the time the
rock was first exposed to the surface or from the time the
alluvial material was deposited. The time factor is not
always clear because erosion and deposition are continual
processes. Moreover, clay is often much older than the
deposition, having been formed in one place and transported to another.

Young soils commonly have an undifferentiated profile.
Saline, gypsic, and calcic horizons are formed more rapidly than those of clay accumulation, whereas a humic
horizon may be formed in a few decades. Young soils are
richer in amorphous clays and, under conditions that
favour acidification, are less acid than old ones; pH increases with depth in young soils, and it decreases with
depth in old ones.

Interaction of factors and processes. Any effect that
each factor has on soil formation depends on the other
factors; for example, the effect of climate depends on
drainage, parent material, time, etc., and the other factors
are similarly interdependent. Different soils are formed
under the same climatic conditions according to drainage,
parent material, time, vegetation, and other relevant influences; in like manner, different soils may be formed
from the same parent material. Because soil is the result
of various processes and each factor acts on several of
them, it is better to relate soils to processes, and through
processes to factors. The environment under which a soil
is formed may vary during its formation: drainage may
improve or deteriorate; exposure to such factors as erosion, flooding, or subirrigation may be ended or initiated;
or there could be a change in vegetation. Thus soil does
not always reflect the conditions under which it is encountered.

The
poly-
genesis
of soils

Climatic changes are very slow, and to affect soil formation appreciably they must be radical. A change in drainage will impede leaching, just as will a very drastic reduction of leaching rainfall; waterlogging may cause the formation of raw humus that produces podsolization in a
warm climate, that otherwise favours organic matter decay and excludes podsolization, when drainage is normal. Little leaching rainfall is needed to leach a coarse
soil; a great deal of rainfall is needed to leach a
clayey soil. Acidification is faster and more extensive
when parent material is poor in bases. For all these reasons, caution should be used when attributing the properties of a soil to climatic changes or, still more, when
explaining climatic changes on the basis of pedologic
evidence.

There are cases, however, in which such evidence is
convincing. In Australia and Africa, soils rich in 1:1
clays are found in the desert; they have certainly been
formed under a considerably more rainy climate. Because
allitic weathering (that producing chiefly 1:1 clays) is
deep, subsequent erosion and deposition merely transport

such soils from one place to another. In some cases 1:1 clays have been transported great distances from where they were formed: in the delta of the Paraná, near Buenos Aires, there are soils with clays that came from the centre of Brazil, and many soils of northern India have 2:1 clays that have been formed in the Himalayas.

The frequent variation in conditions during soil formation, resulting in polygenetic soils, usually is more closely related to topography than to climate; also, the clay found in a soil may have been formed in past time or at a distant site.

SOIL GROUP CLASSIFICATION AND NOMENCLATURE

Observation of natural categories. The question of soil classification is a controversial one, but there is no doubt that classification should be based on categories that exist in nature, rather than on arbitrary creations of a classification system.

Rationale of group selection In a natural classification, groups are recognized and subsequently arranged in a system; the system may change, but the groups will pass almost unchanged from one system to another. Pedologists have approached soil classification in such a manner. Observing that some soils have an ashy surface horizon, resting on another darker in colour and richer in fine earth, pedologists called them podsols (ashy soils). Other soils with a deep, dark horizon rich in organic matter and well saturated with calcium were termed chernozems (black soils). Soils of rather undifferentiated profile and of red colour were named krasnozems (red soils). In this way, groups of soils have been recognized and arranged in classification systems; although opinions differ as to how these groups should be arranged within a classification system, essentially the same groups exist for all pedologists.

The soil continuum. Because soils form a continuum, it has been difficult to follow the example of other scientists in categorizing on the basis of clear distinctions between groups. The same processes are involved in the formation of various soils, with the result that a soil may have the essential features of ando soils (amorphous clays) and those of chernozemic soils (deep humic horizon, dark and well saturated with bases) and thus be both ando and chernozemic. Soils may reflect many such heterogeneous conditions—for example, chernozemic (mollic) and gleisolic, gleisolic and podsol, and the like. Accordingly, soil classification must be manifold, recognizing that the same soil may belong to various groups. When this necessity is understood, the problem of soil classification is simplified, and the major categories shown in Table 2 may be recognized (see Figure 6).

Fundamental classes of soil

Supplementary descriptions. Various other terms, denoting special features, also may be precisely and simply defined and included in soil nomenclature. For example: clay, loam, sand (referring to soil texture); lithosol (stony, gravelly); regosol (sandy); aeolian (formed by wind, dune); hammada (stony desert); and rock outcrop. Acid (H s.), natric (Na s.), magnesic (Mg s.), Ca soil, eutrophic, and dystrophic all refer to absorbed cations. Takyr and lunettes are special kinds of saline soils. Roof clays and sulfate saline clays (cat clays) are special kinds of clays. Gray-brown podsolic, noncalcic brown, gray-wooded, red-yellow podsolic, and lateritic podsolic are different kinds of lessivé soils; the first three have 2:1 clays, the later two are kaolinitic. Sod and humic are used for soils unusually rich in humus for their groups. Prairie, chestnut (kastanozems), and reddish chernozemic are different kinds of chernozemic soils. Podsolized, leached, or degraded chernozems are types of brunisolic or leached soils or both. Claypan planosols are planosolic clays. Serozems are rendzinas lacking humic horizon. Rubrozems are kaolisols with a deep humic horizon. Red desert are mini-planosols (thin horizons). Mini-planosols, mini-solonetz, and mini-podsols are planosols, solonetz, or podsols with thin horizons. Arctic browns are brunisolic permafrost rankers. Terra rossa is a cinnamonic soil from hard limestone. Terra roxa is an ando-kaolisol intergrade soil. Terre de barre is a eutrophic latosolic kaolisol. Low humic gley is an acid gleisolic soil. Humic gley is a gleisolic chernozemic soil. Desert crust is an accumulation of products of weathering in virtual absence of leaching. Alluvial, desert, forest, forest-steppe, grassland, groundwater, lowland, mangrove, meadow, mountain, paddy, paramo, prairie, tropical, and tundra are environmental, nontaxonomic terms often used in soil nomenclature.

Seventh Approximation System. A system based on measurable soil properties rather than on theories of soil formation, the 7th American Approximation System, was introduced in 1960 and has expanded continuously by supplements. It is the first approach to precise definition of soil groups and pedologic terms, and, moreover, it has implicitly adopted manifold classification: adjectives (mollic, spodic, andic, etc.) are used to show relationships with other groups; names are formed by aggregation of formative elements that denote special characteristics, and consequently groups. Many of the groups named in the preceding section correspond in 7th Approximation to several taxa the nomenclature of which includes the corresponding formative element. For example, andepts and andic correspond to ando; histosols to organic; spodosols to podsols; vertisols to dark clays. The formative element aqu denotes gleisolic; natrarg, solonetz; rend, rendzina; sal, saline.

Precise definition of soil properties

Indication of soil properties. Some formative elements show soil properties: acr denotes extreme weathering; allic, free aluminum; anthr, man-made soil; arenic, sandy; calci, calcic; chrom, high chroma (red colours); dys or dystr, dystrophic; eu or eutr, eutrophic; gibbs, presence of gibbsite; hydr, saturated with water; lithic, stony; pale, old (soil); pell, dusky colour; psam, sandy; rhod, red; sal, saline; sider, rich in free iron; sombri, dark colour; thapto, a buried soil is included in the profile; vermi, wormholes, worm casts, or filled animal burrows; vitr, ando rich in unweathered volcanic glass.

Identification of horizons. Other formative elements denote presence of certain horizons: abruptic, abrupt textural change; alb, albic horizon; cumulic, thickened humic horizon; dur, duripan; ferr, B horizon rich in free iron, or iron concretions or nodules; frag, fragipan; glossic or gloss, horizon A_2 is tongued; hapl, typical profile; hum, unusually deep humic horizon, or humus podsolic B horizon; ochr, light-coloured A horizon; pachic, thick A; petrocalcic, petrocalcic horizon; plac, thin pan; plinth, laterite; ruptic, broken (discontinuous) horizon; stratic, stratified horizon; superic, laterite in the surface; umbr, deep nonchernozemic humic horizon. Other formative elements of the nomenclature indicate the manner in which the material has been deposited: fluv; alluvial; limnic, lacustrine.

Table 2: Major Soil Types	
Ando rich in amorphous clays	**Organic** extremely rich in organic matter; may have peaty and/or organic horizon
Brunisolic 2:1 clays; braunified or acid horizons	**Podsols** eluviation of alumina and iron, usually producing ashy sandy surface horizon and illuvial horizon rich in amorphous clays
Chernozemic 2:1 clays; deep neutral dark humic horizons	
Cinnamonic 2:1 clays; reddish colour; rich in dehydrated iron oxides	**Planosols** clay eluviation produced by sodium; illuvial horizon not natric
Dark clays 2:1 clays; rich in expanding clays; well saturated with bases	**Rankers** 2:1 clays; humic horizon resting on rock or permafrost
Gleisolic gray-blue colours or mottles due to waterlogging	**Raw** 2:1 clays; undifferentiated soil profile
Kaolinitic tropical; rich in 1:1 clays; may have undifferentiated profile, or horizons rich in iron concretions or laterite	**Rendzinas** high lime content
	Solonchaks rich in salts such as chlorides, sulfate, etc.; related to gypsisols, rich in gypsum
Lessivé clay illuviation produced by organic matter	**Solonetz** clay illuviation produced by sodium; natric illuvial horizon

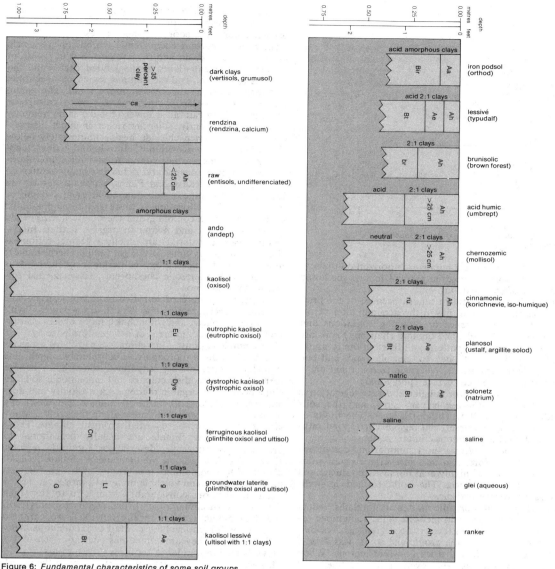

Figure 6: *Fundamental characteristics of some soil groups.*
Specifications referring to reaction (acid, neutral) and to type of clay refer to the whole profile. Aa, albic (ashy) surface; Bir, iron podsolic B (spodic); Ah, humus rich surface h.; Ae, eluvial surface h.; Bt, textural (clay illuvial) B; br, braunified; ru, rubified; G, gley; R, rockbed; Eu, eutrophic (rather well provided with bases) soil; Cn, ferruginous concretions and nodules; Lt, laterite; Dys, dystrophic (poor in bases) upper soil.

Climatic elements of the system. Although soil temperature and moisture are not intrinsic soil properties, they are used as diagnostic features in the 7th Approximation; *i.e.*, soils are classified according to the climate in which they are encountered. Such formative elements include: bor, boreal; cryo, very cold; pergelic, permafrost; torri, torrid (usually dry); trop, small annual range of temperature; ud, usually humid; ust, dry but not long dry seasons; xer, long dry seasons.

The 7th Approximation System demonstrates that soil description, classification, and nomenclature may be achieved with few symbols that, in combination, can represent the enormous variety of soils existing in nature.

GEOGRAPHIC DISTRIBUTION OF SOILS

Because soil formation depends so much on climate, topography, vegetation, and parent material, soils vary in association with other geographic features, and soil regions may be distinguished in the same manner as climatic and vegetation regions. Such soil regions lend themselves to being further subdivided or combined into higher groups. Each region contains a variety of soils, many of which are also encountered in other regions, but the distribution of soils follows a definite pattern.

The concept of soil region is important from both a theoretical and a practical point of view. Theoretically, soil distribution is often the key to answering many questions about soils. From a practical viewpoint, it is difficult and costly to prepare detailed maps of soil locations, which can vary in short distances—sometimes within a few metres.

Polar regions. *Tundra.* Vegetation is scarce in tundra regions (see Figure 7) and consists of herbs and grasses that do not produce very acid humus. Rainfall in the tundra is low and leaching rainfall (Ln) is still lower: 40 millimetres (one in. equals 25mm) in Baker Lake, Northwest Territories; 20 in Eureka, Alaska; 60 in Resolute, Northwest Territories, Canada; 30 in Barrow, Alaska; 40 in Anadyr, 70 in Bulun, 50 in Nizhnekolymsk, and 40 in Russkoye Ustye, Siberia. The bases leached from the surface accumulate in the lower part of the profile and circulate in it through plants and by capillarity (soil surface is often humid and soils are shallow); moreover, drainage is often impeded by permafrost. Acidity is not sufficient to produce podsolization, but it reacts with iron to produce complexes that result in brunisolic soils. The soils formed, arctic brown, are relatively shallow; the pH increase with depth is more rapid than usual; and there is a tendency

The
function
of soil
maps

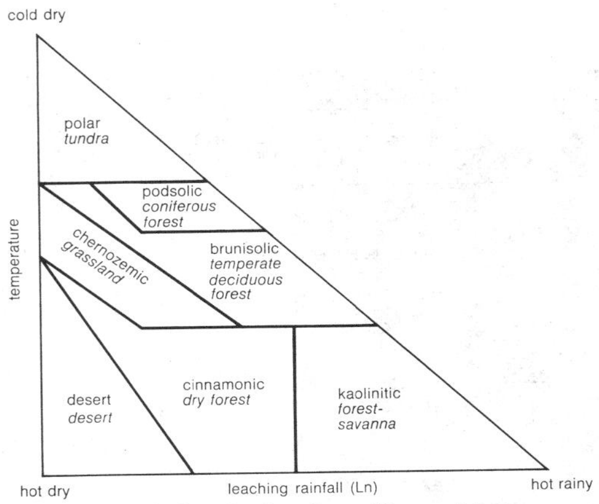

Figure 7: Distribution of soil regions with associated vegetation according to temperature and leaching rainfall (see text).

toward the formation of a humus-rich horizon on the surface of permafrost. In the drier parts of tundra, the lower horizons are often calcareous.

Waterlogging is frequent in tundra because of the presence of permafrost, resulting in the accumulation of organic matter, a prevalence of reducing conditions and peat formation. Gleisolic and organic (half bog) soils are frequent. The general pattern of distribution is arctic brown in well-drained sites to gleisolic and half-bog mini-podzols in depressions. Alternate freezing and thawing results in a patterned surface (polygonal).

Subglacial desert. In the subglacial desert vegetation is almost absent, weathering is very slow, and the soils formed are very shallow (lithosols, etc.). The limits of tundra and subglacial desert soil regions correspond rather well with the homonymous climatic regions.

Podsolic regions. With a short summer and conditions not too frosty for forest, so that an evergreen coniferous forest prevails, a raw, highly acid humus is produced and podsolization takes place. The soils formed in well-drained sites are iron podsols.

Drained and waterlogged conditions

In waterlogged sites organic matter accumulates, reducing conditions prevail, and gleisolic soils, sometimes organic, are formed. When there is no drainage, bases cannot be eliminated from the profile and soil is less acid, a condition common in the drier podsolic regions. When there is a slow drainage, however, soil is acidified and becomes humus podsol, somewhat gleisolic and peaty. Such soils usually have heath or sphagnum vegetation.

Humus podsols are more common in atlantic regions because of their higher rainfall, than in continental regions. Hardpans are more common in atlantic regions. Some regions of Central Siberia have permafrost that interferes with drainage; moreover leaching rainfall is low, with the result that iron leaching is incomplete and the eluvial horizon is yellow rather than ashy. The yellow podsols may be considered as intergrades to arctic brown.

Brunisolic regions. With a longer summer, deciduous forest prevails, which produces milder, less acid humus that forms brunisolic soil, more or less leached. Where leaching rainfall is low and parent materials are calcareous or basalt, soils are neutral (braun erde); in the opposite rainy condition, soil is acid (brun acide).

The most important brunisolic regions are in western Europe, the eastern United States, the state of Washington, and the adjacent Canadian coast. In western Europe, there are many small regions with calcareous materials, basalt, or loess, and low leaching rainfall. Braun erde abound; some of them are chernozemic or have a calcareous horizon at some depth or both. In the transition zone to the chernozemic region of North America, chernozemic braun erde (brown earth) and chernozemic lessivé (prairie) are common, and in the Appalachian Mountains, brun acide.

Chernozemic regions. A grassland vegetation with chernozemic soils occurs when spring is not dry, winter is relatively cold, and leaching rainfall is low. Calcareous,

gypsic, or salic horizons are frequent. Solonchaks, solonetz, and planosols—more or less gleisolic and chernozemic—are common in poorly drained depressions.

The most important chernozemic regions of the world are the Danube Basin and the southern Soviet Union in Eurasia, the Great Plains of the United States and the prairies of Canada, and the Pampas region of Argentina. But there are some differences among them. The parent materials of Russian chernozems are more calcareous and the leaching rainfall is lower (for the same humidity index). Consequently, soils are richer in lime; effervescence with hydrogen chloride begins immediately below the humic horizon or within it; clay eluviation and planosolic chernozems are not common; and the humic horizon is, in general, deeper and richer in organic matter. In the North American Great Plains, parent materials are less calcareous, lime is encountered at greater depth or not at all, clay eluviation is more frequent, planosolic chernozems more common, and the humic horizon is in general shallower and poorer in organic matter. In Argentina, parent materials are chiefly volcanic; cation-exchange capacity is unusually high (andic chernozemic); much sodium is released by weathering; clay eluviation is frequent; and planosolic chernozems, solonetz, and solonchaks are common.

The three chernozemic regions

The general pattern of soil distribution in chernozemic regions, is chernozemic soils in well-drained areas, with planosols, solonetz, and solonchaks, more or less chernozemic and gleisolic, in areas of deficient drainage.

Cinnamonic regions. In climates with dry seasons where soil is dried thoroughly to considerable depth, fine crystallites or irreversibly dehydrated iron sesquioxides are formed, giving reddish colours and cinnamonic soils. In cinnamonic soils organic matter decays rapidly and does not accumulate on soil surface. Humus originates chiefly in roots and it is well distributed along the profile. Many cinnamonic regions have a Mediterranean climate. Those with a monsoon climate are usually transitional to brunisolic, chernozemic, desertic, or kaolinitic regions. Except for Australia, a Mediterranean climate is associated with mountainous topography and high frequency of limestones and volcanic materials; moreover, leaching rainfall varies considerably from zero to very high figures. Brown cinnamonic (bruns mediterraneans) and red cinnamonic (rouges mediterraneans) are common in areas with high leaching rainfall or ferruginous materials or both. They are sometimes acid and rich in 1:1 clays, being intergrades to kaolisols (krasnozems).

Desert regions. Vegetation is very scarce in the desert, and soil erosion is very severe from wind and occasional rains; weathering is slow and shallow, and leaching is almost absent. Soils are very poor in organic matter and do not have a humic horizon.

Because sodium elimination is difficult, autochthonous soils are usually planosols and solonetz with very thin horizons (mini-planosols and mini-solonetz); a calcareous horizon usually underlies the B horizon. Soil is often covered by coarse material (desert pavement), which partly results from wind erosion and protects the soil. In such absolute deserts as the Chilean desert, however, products of weathering remain in the place of their formation and a loosely cemented desert crust is formed. Materials eroded from higher land accumulate in depressions, forming dunes and alluvial soils. Where waters accumulate, planosolic, solonetzic, and saline soils abound, and "salares" also are frequent. There are many good alluvial soils, however (rendzinas, chernozemic, etc.), and some of them are gleisolic.

Occurrence of mini-horizons

The general pattern of soil distribution may be summarized as follows: high plateaus and plains areas exhibit autochthonous soils, mini-planosols, mini-solonetz, and solonchaks with salares (salt accumulations); slopes exhibit lithosols; and depressions exhibit dunes and alluvial soils, with many solonetz, solonchaks, serozems, and gleisolic soils with salares.

A distinction may be made between American (North and South), Asian, and African deserts. American deserts received much volcanic ash from active volcanoes, and mini-solonetz, mini-planosols, and duripans are plentiful.

In Asia, calcareous materials abound, and raw (undifferentiated) soils that produce effervescence with hydrogen chloride are common. In Africa and Australia, palaeosols formed from kaolinitic materials are frequent.

Kaolinitic regions. The high leaching rainfall of tropical countries, even though there may be a long dry season, results in formation of 1:1 clays. Soils are usually acid in the lower horizons, whereas the upper horizon may be eutrophic. The difference between eutrophic and dystrophic soils, which is important from an agricultural point of view, seems well associated with the presence or absence of a dry season. A dry season, even a short one, activates decay of organic matter, favours fires, and interferes with the production of acid humus, which is the principal factor of acidification, several times more effective than water mixed with carbon dioxide.

Water-
logging
and iron
concre-
tions

In soils rich in 1:1 clays, waterlogging produces segregation of iron in the form of concretions or nodules. For that reason laterite is common in waterlogged areas, and, because it is impermeable, aggravates waterlogging and may reach the surface. In granite, gneiss, and similar materials, very common in Africa, the iron released by weathering may adhere to sand or gravel surfaces and cover them with a red coating. When soil is thoroughly dried periodically, such coatings become irreversibly dehydrated, protect the particle or gravel from further weathering, and a ferruginous horizon is formed. Such protection is insufficient in the upper horizon, where organic acids abound, and also in the lower horizons, which are waterlogged continuously; as a result, the ferruginous horizon is encountered at some depth. Some of the iron may come from the waterlogged horizons.

It is of interest that concretions of gravel and laterite contain unweathered material imprisoned in iron sesquioxides. Such material is virtually absent in the overlying and underlying horizons, indicating that both ferruginous horizons and laterite are formed at an early stage of weathering. This also indicates that stone lines of geologic origin may contribute to the formation of ferruginous horizons. It is, however, difficult to believe that there was a stone line parallel to soil surface each time a ferruginous horizon was formed. Ferruginous horizons and laterite are seldom found in soils formed from easily weatherable materials such as basalt, fine sand, and in continuously humid climates.

Young soils from volcanic ash are naturally ando in type. With time amorphous clays crystallize, cation-exchange capacity decreases, and soil becomes first terra roxa (intergrade ando-kaolinitic) and then kaolinitic. Terra roxa, however, is often made up of young soils formed from basalt and abound in basaltic slopes, where erosion does not permit soil to become old (Misiones, Argentina; coffee region, Brazil).

Mountainous regions. Erosion is the main characteristic of mountainous regions. The soils are usually young, consisting of lithosols and rankers in slopes and alluvial soils in the valleys and surrounding the mountain plains.

Three kinds of mountainous regions may be distinguished: humid-temperate, dry, and humid-tropical. In humid-temperate climates organic matter accumulates and there is an abundance of brunisolic soils (braun erde, brun acide). There are also lessivé and podsols, but many podsols do not have an ashy horizon. The spodic horizon, rich in amorphous clays, is overlain by a gray-brown horizon (brown podsols), and limestones often form lithosolic rendzinas. Acid humus and peaty soils, more or less gleisolic, are common in depressions.

In dry but not desertic mountains, grassland vegetation, sometimes scattered with woody plants, is common. Lithosols and other raw soils and rendzinas, basically cinnamonic and chernozemic, are widespread, with saline, solonetzic, planosolic, and organic, relatively gleisolic soils in depressions.

In humid-tropical mountains the growing season is longer and the growth index much higher; soils are deeper and richer in organic matter (some giant podsols have been found); otherwise they resemble those of humid-temperate climate of the same summer type. At lower altitudes kaolinitic weathering begins and forms kaolini-

tic soils; erosion, however, results in soils remaining younger than in the lowlands, eutrophic soils and terra roxa are more frequent, and soils are also richer in organic matter. These characteristics partly account for the higher density of population in mountainous regions.

Intermediate and modified regions. Passage from one type of soil region to another is gradual, and intermediate regions can be recognized. Moreover, preponderance of allochthonous alluvial soils, waterlogging, or presence of a particular material justify separation of some regions from the main type.

Nature of
transition
belts

In the transition belt from podsolic to brunisolic regions, the prevailing soils are podsols and lessivé (gray-brown podsolic), and the distribution is chiefly determined by parent material. In the transition between podsolic and chernozemic regions, Soviet authors recognize a forest-steppe zone with gray-wooded soils (lessivé with somewhat ashy horizon, better saturated with bases, and sometimes calcareous at some depth). Near this forest-steppe region are many sod-podsols (podsols with rather well developed humic horizon), attributed to cropping. An analogous transitional region in Canada occurs between the podsolic and chernozemic region.

The prairie soils in the United States are characteristic of the transition between chernozemic and brunisolic regions and may be considered as chernozemic lessivé or chernozemic braun erde. They are also found in the Danube Basin and other parts of Europe, and combine characteristics of both the chernozemic and brunisolic, or lessivé groups. The region of red-yellow podsolic soils of the southeastern United States may be considered as a transitional kaolinitic-brunisolic region with soils usually lessivé and very acid, usually low in cation-exchange capacity in comparison to their clay content. In other parts of the world, the transition between brunisolic and kaolinitic coincides with mountainous topography or special parent materials. The transition between brunisolic and cinnamonic regions in Europe is marked by cinnamonic-brunisolic intergrades (brun mediterraneans, southern braun erde, etc.); that between chernozemic and cinnamonic regions in the United States by reddish chernozems. The transition between cinnamonic and desertic regions in the United States is marked by reddish brown soils. Comparable soils are encountered in many parts of Asia, Africa, and Australia. Planosolic, solonetzic, and saline soils are common in these transitional regions.

In the transition between cinnamonic and kaolinitic regions, materials rich in easily weatherable minerals give soils with 2:1 clays, whereas 1:1 clays predominate in the opposite case, a condition that prevails in many parts of the Mediterranean Basin with high leaching rainfall and mild winters (e.g., Portugal). In Africa and Australia, however, many kaolisols of such a transitional region are palaeokaolisols.

Volcanic regions. Volcanic ashes have such great influence on soil formation that volcanic regions constitute a special group. Ando soils are frequent in volcanic regions. A distinction may be made between humid volcanic regions with acid ando, often deficient in phosphorus, and dry volcanic regions with soils well provided with bases, often chernozemic. Planosolic, solonetzic, and saline soils, and duripans or calcareous horizons, are frequent in dry volcanic regions and still more so in desertic ones, where planosols and solonetz become mini-planosols and mini-solonetz. Ando soils are usually fertile, and as a result settlements grow around volcanoes in spite of dangers. The most important volcanic soil regions of the world are: The Cordillera (mountain ranges) of North, Central, and South America; the entire Pacific Coast of these regions; the Great Basin of North America between the Cordillera and the Rocky Mountains, Mexico, and Central America; all the Cordillera of South America, the plains to the north and west, and many lands to the east; all of Patagonia, the Pampas region of Argentina, and to a certain extent the Chaco; many parts of the Mediterranean Basin, especially in Italy; Indonesia, the Philippines, Japan, and Kamachatka; and some parts of Ethiopia, Kenya, Uganda, Rwanda, Burundi, and Cameroon.

Humid and
dry
volcanic
soils

Alluvial and waterlogged regions. Some regions have alluvial soils of materials that came from regions of different climate. The most conspicuous examples are the alluvial region of northern Italy, one of the better agricultural regions of the world, and those of northern India and Indochina, which nourish a dense population or export much food. In Australia, and to a certain extent in Africa, are regions in which the soils have been formed from kaolinitic materials developed under different conditions; these regions may be called palaeokaolinitic.

In some regions waterlogging is so common that the soils may be called gleisolic. Some of them are podsolic, for example the southwestern coast of Hudson Bay in Canada, most of Finland, and most of northern Soviet Union.. Others are chernozemic, as the "Pampa Deprimida" of Buenos Aires, Argentina. Still others are found in the transition region between chernozemic and kaolinitic soils of southern Brazil, Uruguay, and Corrientes, Argentina. Soils vary as a consequence: gleisolic humus podsols and peat in the first case; gleisolic chernozemic planosols and solonetz in the second; chernozemic lessivé (prairie), chernozemic gleisolic (humic gley), dark clays (vertisols), planosols, acid gleisolic (low humic gley), kaolinitic podsolic (red-yellow podsolic), with krasnozems and terra roxa on basaltic hills in the third.

Some tropical regions have relatively young soils, many of which have been formed from calcareous materials. This is the case in the Yucatán Peninsula of Mexico, in the West Indies, and on the coral islands of Oceania. Their soils are predominantly brunisolic-kaolinitic.

BIBLIOGRAPHY. Some classic and general works include v.v. DOKUCHAIEV, "Abridged Historical Account and Critical Examination of the Principal Soil Classifications Existing," *Trans. St. Petersburg Soc. Nat.*, 10:64–67 (1879), in Russian; K.D. GLINKA, *The Great Soil Groups of the World and Their Development*, 2nd ed. (1937, Eng. trans. from the German edition of 1914); EMIL RAMANN, *Bodenbildung und Bodeneinteilung* (1918; Eng. trans., *The Evolution and Classification of Soils*, 1928); C.F. MARBUT, "A Scheme for Soil Classification," in the *Proceedings and Papers of the First International Congress of Soil Science, June 13–22, 1927*, vol. 4, pp. 1–31 (1928); W.L. KUBIENA, *Bestimmungsbuch und Systematik der Böden Europas* (1953; Eng. trans., *The Soils of Europe*, 1953), important for brunisolic, podsolic, and gleisolic soils; A.A. RODE, *Soil Science* (Eng. trans. 1962), an excellent account of Russian pedology; and J. PAPADAKIS, *Soils of the World* (1964), a discussion of their formation, diagnostics, classification, geographic distribution, and agricultural potentialities. Soil genesis is covered in the following works: H. JENNY, *Factors of Soil Formation* (1941); M.L. JACKSON and G.D. SHERMAN, "Chemical Weathering of Minerals in Soils," *Adv. Agron.*, 5:219–318 (1953), excellent account of weathering, especially differences in weatherability between minerals; B.B. POLYNOV, *The Cycle of Weathering* (1937; orig. pub. in Russian, 1934), points out the consequences of differences in solubility between the principal soil constituents; B. BARSHAD, "Chemistry of Soil Development," in F.E. BEAR, (ed.), *Chemistry of the Soil*, 2nd ed., pp. 1–70 (1964); and J. PAPADAKIS, *Geografía agrícola mundial* (1960), introduced the concept of "leaching rainfall" (Ln), and gives a formula for its calculation. Basic works on soil classification include the following: J. THORP and G.D. SMITH, "Higher Categories of Soil Classification: Order, Suborder, and Great Soil Groups," *Soil Sci.*, 67:117–126 (1949), a fundamental work on the subject; UNITED STATES SOIL CONSERVATION SERVICE, *Soil Classification: A Comprehensive System, 7th Approximation* (1960 and suppl.), a classic contribution to soil classification, although it needs to be improved; A. LEAHEY, "The Canadian System of Soil Classification and the Seventh Approximation," *Soil Sci. Soc. Am. Proc.*, 27:224–225 (1963); and J. PAPADAKIS, "Some Considerations on Soil Classification: The 7th Approximation," *Soil Sci.*, 94:115–119 (1962). Basic works on experimental pedology include GEORGES PEDRO, *Contribution à l'étude d'expérimentale de l'altération géochimique des roches cristallines* (1964); E.G. HALLSWORTH, "An Examination of Some Factors Affecting the Movement of Clay in an Artificial Soil," *J. Soil Sci.*, 14:360–371 (1963); and C. BLOOMFIELD, "A Study of Podzolization," 6 pt., *J. Soil Sci.*, vol. 4–6 (1953–55).

(J.Pa.)

Solar System

The solar system consists of the Sun and the complex assemblage of bodies, gas, and dust particles revolving around it in closed orbits under the dominating influence of its gravitational attraction. For a detailed treatment of the various members of the solar system see SUN; INTERPLANETARY MEDIUM; PLANET, MINOR; COMET; METEOR; METEORITE; MOON; and articles about the planets under their individual names. Apart from the Sun, the known constituents of the solar system are the major planets; the planetary satellites (number for each planet shown in Figure 1); thousands of minor planets, mostly between Mars and Jupiter, of kilometre size and smaller; thousands or perhaps millions of comets with smaller mass still, most of them in elongated orbits; meteorites; and very tenuous dust and gas. A brief survey of the solar system as a whole is given here.

The solar system is usually defined as extending to the orbit of the outermost known planet, Pluto, about 40 astronomical units from the Sun. (The astronomical unit is equal to the semi-major axis of Earth's orbit, 93,000,000 miles, or 150,000,000 kilometres; see also below.) The solar system is sometimes considered to extend to the aphelia (the points of their orbits most distant from the Sun) of the comets with nearly parabolic (open) orbits, however, or to the edge of the roughly spherical region known as the solar cavity (the solar cavity is the volume of space, centred on the Sun, that contains the extremely tenuous interplanetary dust and gas). Then, the extent of the solar system is much larger, perhaps hundreds of astronomical units.

The Sun comprises more than 99 percent of the mass of the solar system. The rest consists of almost empty space traversed at wide intervals by bodies of relatively insignificant mass. These bodies may be grouped into two solar families: (1) the nine major planets (possibly ten, if the existence of a suspected planet beyond Pluto is confirmed), with 32 satellites attending six of them, and almost 1,700 known bodies of kilometre size called minor planets (formerly asteroids); and (2) several thousand or more comets, a horde of meteors and meteorites, and a thin cloud of interplanetary dust and gas. It has been estimated that there are 40,000 minor planets bright enough to be photographed with a 100-inch telescope. A long search with a large telescope might reveal still more satellites, especially of Jupiter and Saturn. New comets are discovered at the rate of several per year on the average. But it is very doubtful if any unknown distant major planets brighter than the 16th magnitude exist.

The two solar families

The solar system was thought for centuries to be the centre of the universe. Up to the 16th century, two conflicting theories were held. Some early Greek philosophers reasoned that the then known five inner planets revolved around the Sun, but this idea was later supplanted by the geocentric theory in which the Earth, not the Sun, was placed at the centre. As observations improved in accuracy, more complicated schemes became necessary to account for the motion of the planets. These in turn became inadequate; and, by the 16th century, the foundations of the theory of gravitation were laid.

Gravity controls the solar system, the motions of all bodies being consistent to a high degree of accuracy with the effects of gravitational attraction of the Sun and the other bodies. The planets are the only bodies massive enough for their effects to be appreciable, and their presence complicates the calculations; in practice the effects are comparatively small and are only included in computing the orbits of bodies that approach a planet closely. Usually only comets or minor planets in highly elongated orbits are affected, but a celebrated 19th-century case of investigation of the perturbation of one planet, Uranus, by another, then unknown, led to the discovery of the latter planet, Neptune.

The Sun. The Sun is the only star close enough so that its surface details can be viewed from Earth. All other stars are so distant that they appear merely as points of light even in the largest telescopes. In a sense Earth is in actual contact with the Sun since the solar wind, a stream of electrons and ionized atoms from the Sun (see below), passes through the Earth's orbit. Compared with the average star, the Sun is slightly more luminous, slightly larger and more massive, and slightly less dense. Its diam-

Relative sizes of the planets, arranged in order of distance from the Sun (but not according to their respective distances from each other), and the numbers of their satellites.

eter is 109 times the diameter of the Earth, and it is 333,000 times as massive. The temperature at the surface of the Sun is about 6,000° K and is believed to increase to perhaps 20,000,000° K at the centre. Although the density of material near the centre of the Sun is eight times the density of lead, it is gaseous throughout.

The Sun radiates at the rate of about 9×10^{25} calories per second, emitting enough energy to melt a 3,000-foot layer of ice surrounding it in 90 minutes. It heats the planets and other bodies that have only small or no internal heat sources of their own. This energy is derived from thermonuclear processes involving the transformation of hydrogen into helium. Although the Sun loses 4,000,000 tons of hydrogen per second in this process, it is believed that the Sun will continue to radiate at essentially its present rate for hundreds of millions of years.

The solar wind The material lost by the Sun streams outward continuously (the quiet component) with additions (active component) from bursts of activity on the Sun's surface. This streaming, called the solar wind, can be detected in several ways well beyond the Earth's orbit. The outgoing radiation affects the direction of the gaseous tails of comets so that they turn away from the Sun. The magnetic lines of force around the Earth and Jupiter are also affected, being compressed on the side nearest the Sun and greatly elongated on the side away from it; this effect was first predicted by theory and later confirmed by direct measurements from space probes.

The active component of the solar wind comprises plasma (ionized gas) clouds that move out from flare regions on the Sun's surface at speeds reaching 2,000 kilometres (about 1,000 miles) per second. The material reaches the Earth a day or so later. Interactions with the particles and magnetic fields in the upper atmosphere produce aurorae and geomagnetic storms. Cosmic ray particles from very large flares have been detected also at ground level.

Size of the solar system. Distances within the solar system are measured in several units, usually in miles or kilometres or in astronomical units. Distances to the stars are much larger and are measured usually in light-years (the distance travelled by light in one year) or in parsecs (the distance at which half the difference in the direction of a star seen against the background of faint stars changes by one second of arc in six months). The six-month baseline for the measure of the direction of the star is the distance across the Earth's orbit—i.e., two astronomical units. Simple geometry relates the astronomical unit and the parsec. The astronomical unit serves as the link between the large stellar distances and the distances measurable on the Earth; knowledge of the scale

of the solar system is essential for connecting the larger and smaller units (see PARALLAX, ASTRONOMICAL).

The distance from the Sun to the outermost known planet, Pluto, is 39.4 astronomical units, whereas the distance to the nearest star is 1.33 parsecs (4.35 light-years). Highly elongated cometary orbits may extend to hundreds or thousands of astronomical units; but beyond Pluto there are vast volumes of almost empty space, so that the sparsely populated solar system is surrounded by even emptier space. Compared to the size of the Galaxy, of which it is part, it is an insignificant point; and it would be difficult, even from the nearest star, to detect the presence of any part of it except for the Sun itself.

The solar system is located just outside the galactic plane, or Milky Way, about two-thirds of the way out from the centre of the Galaxy. Its distance from the centre is about ten kiloparsecs. For comparison, one kiloparsec is 1,000 parsecs; one parsec is 3.26 light-years, or 206,265 astronomical units. The astronomical unit is equivalent to 150,000,000 kilometres.

The major planets and their satellites. *Basic properties.* The known major planets in order of increasing distance from the Sun are Mercury, Venus, Earth, Mars, Jupiter, Saturn, Uranus, Neptune, and Pluto. The terrestrial planets are Mercury, Venus, Earth, and Mars; the giant planets are Jupiter, Saturn, Uranus, and Neptune. Pluto, the outermost, is believed to be about 0.45 times the size of Earth, and its orbit crosses the orbit of Neptune. There are reasons for believing that Pluto may once have been a satellite of Neptune that escaped from its gravitational control. The terrestrial planets are of about the same size and mass as the Earth and are of high density, between about three and six times that of water. The giant planets have from 15 to 318 times the volume of Earth but have only about 20 percent the density of the terrestrial planets. Saturn is so light that an average piece of it, if available, would float in water. The high density of the terrestrial planets is attributed to their large metallic content. The giant planets are believed to consist mostly of the lightest elements, hydrogen and helium, which, deep in the interior, are probably in a solid or even metallic state.

Comparisons among the planets. A separate article on each planet describes individual characteristics. The following section deals with comparisons among them.

The Earth and Venus have been described as sister planets because their sizes, masses, and densities are roughly the same. Both have extensive atmospheres, but the composition of these are not the same. Venus has no moon. It is difficult to take the comparison further owing to observational difficulties caused by the extensive cloud cover The inner or terrestrial planets

on Venus. Surface relief and the existence of at least one probable mountain range have been discovered by radar. Oceans cannot exist on Venus because of the high surface temperature of about 700° K, and evidence is still poor regarding the existence of other features similar to geological ones on Earth.

Mars, though smaller than Earth, has some similarities, and more extensive photographic coverage in the 1970s is beginning to show the presence of many features on Mars that may have similar origins to those of their counterparts on Earth. Results from space probes sent to Mars and from radar studies in the early 1970s have allowed some direct comparisons between planetary details. Many Martian features suggest glaciation and erosion, possibly in long-past ages; they also suggest possibly still-active volcanism. Large areas resembling groups of calderas and craters have been photographed. Further, rifts and cracks in long double and single nearly straight lines and areas of intersecting sets of parallel rift systems have been found on Mars. All these can be matched on Earth. Many large height differences (up to several kilometres) have been found to exist on Mars.

Many Martian craters have counterparts on the Moon, which also shows large-scale systems of apparently tectonic lineaments (rills, raised ridges in intersecting sets of parallel systems).

The giant planets

Detailed knowledge of the outer planets and cross comparisons of the data may become possible during the 1980s. Pioneer 10, launched on March 2, 1972, is expected to pass close to Jupiter in December 1973. Jupiter is the only planet other than Earth that is known to have an appreciable overall magnetic field. Like Earth, it also has a surrounding magnetosphere.

The natural satellites. A satellite is defined as a body that revolves around a planet. It is thus distinguished from a planet by its motion rather than by any physical property. Mercury, Venus, and Pluto have no known satellites; Earth has one, Mars two, Jupiter 12, Saturn ten, Uranus five, and Neptune two. Some satellites are only a few miles in diameter, as in the case of the two tiny moons of Mars and the outer satellites of Jupiter. A few satellites are about the size of Mercury and Mars, as in the case of satellites Ganymede and Callisto of Jupiter, Titan of Saturn, and Triton of Neptune, each of which is about 3,500 miles in diameter.

Other constituents of the solar system. *Minor planets or asteroids.* The orbits of more than 1,600 asteroids have been computed since the discovery of the first asteroid in 1801. The size of these minor planets ranges from approximately 500 miles (800 kilometres) in diameter to one mile or less. Their total mass is estimated at only $\frac{1}{3,000}$ that of Earth. Almost all of the asteroids revolve around the Sun between the orbits of Mars and Jupiter; but a few exceptional ones have elongated orbits that extend from Mercury to Mars, in the case of the minor planet Icarus, and from Mars to Saturn, in the case of the minor planet Hidalgo. Some of the exceptional asteroids, such as Hermes and Eros, have come within a few million miles of Earth.

Comets. Comets are bodies of great size but small mass. They are popularly pictured as bright stars flashing erratically across the sky, followed by long luminous tails. But few comets become bright enough to be seen without a telescope. Only those that approach the Sun closely enough have tails, and their motions are not erratic but, as with the planets, are in accordance with the law of gravitation. Apparent slight deviations from gravitational motion observed in a few comets, such as Encke's, may be caused by the action of forces within the comet's nucleus. The extremely tenuous material in the tails is deflected away from the Sun by repulsive forces stronger than gravity; such forces are caused by the solar wind and radiation pressure from the Sun.

In contrast to the nearly circular orbits in which the planets and most of the asteroids move, most comets revolve in greatly elongated orbits. Cometary orbits may also be inclined at any angle to the ecliptic (the plane of the Earth's orbit). The comets of short period, less than 100 years, move in orbits of moderate inclination. Halley's Comet is the only periodic comet that moves in a retrograde direction. A few comets revolve in nearly circular orbits.

Meteors and meteorites. A meteor, or "shooting star," refers both to the flashes of light occasionally seen darting across the night sky and to the objects that produce the light. Meteors may be solid objects no larger than a grain of sand or a pea. The glow is produced by collisions between the atoms of the meteor and the molecules of the air. Such meteors are consumed in the atmosphere of Earth at altitudes of about 60 miles (95 kilometres). Some solid bodies, having a mass of a few ounces to many tons, reach Earth. They are called meteorites. Micrometeorites a few microns in diameter sift through the atmosphere and reach Earth as dust particles.

When the Earth encounters a swarm of meteors moving in an orbit around the Sun, there occurs a meteor "shower," during which the number of meteors counted per hour may amount to several dozen or more. Very seldom does a display resembling a real shower occur. But there have been a few times when meteors appeared to stream from the sky as thickly as snowflakes. The orbital elements of some meteor swarms are so similar to those of certain comets that there can be no doubt that the comets and meteor showers are related. The meteoric material evidently originates from debris left behind by the disintegration of some comets.

Meteor "showers"

Interplanetary material. Under favourable conditions a wedge-shaped glow may sometimes be seen along the ecliptic extending upward from the western horizon after sunset or from the eastern horizon before sunrise. This is the zodiacal light, which apparently originates from a swarm of dust particles surrounding the Sun in the plane of the Earth's orbit, or ecliptic, and extends out beyond the orbit of the Earth. The total quantity of dust must be very small, as it does not noticeably interfere with the motion of the inner planets.

Another phenomenon attributed to dust or meteorites is the gegenschein, or "counterglow," which may sometimes be seen as a faint hazy patch of light in the night sky always directly opposite the Sun. It is variously attributed to light reflected from meteorites or dust trapped by magnetic or electrical forces in the tail of the magnetosphere around the Earth in the direction away from the Sun.

Regularities in the solar system. So far as can be ascertained, there is not only a regular progression of diminishing surface temperature outward with distance from the Sun but also a change of chemical composition. The number of known satellites also varies in a possibly significant way (see the Table). The greatest number of satellites is found around planets near the minor-planet belt. Some of Jupiter's outer satellites may be captured minor planets; more than 40 of these little bodies, the Trojan planets, share Jupiter's orbit but are at some distance from the planet in two groups. The groups lie near one corner of two equilateral triangles, each of which has Jupiter and the Sun at the other corners.

The sizes of the planetary orbits, including the mean path of the minor planets as one, follow a curious rule, the Titius-Bode law, which has sometimes been considered to have evolutionary significance. This rule is as follows: If a series of fours be written down and three added to the second, 3×2 to the third, 3×2^2 to the fourth and so on, the sums are 4, 7, 10, 16, 28, 52, 100, 196, 338, 772, and so on. These numbers divided by 10 give a fair approximation to the planetary distances expressed in terms of the Earth's distance (one astronomical unit) up to the distance of Uranus, if the average size of the minor planet belt is taken as 2.8 astronomical units. It can be seen that five quantities called parameters are needed for the rule: the numbers 4, 3, and 2, the device of dropping the second term for Mercury (equivalent to making the power of 2 to be minus infinity for this planet), and the device of starting the series proper at Venus. Nevertheless, eight planets (counting the minor-planet belt as one) fit the rule, and it received much acclaim in the early 19th century when it led to the discovery of Ceres.

The relative sizes of the planetary orbits may have been determined largely by the local density of the primordial

Comparative Data for Solar System Bodies

	mass (unit: Earth's mass)	equatorial radius (unit: Earth's equatorial radius)	mean density (gm/cm³)	number of satellites	distance from Sun (astronomical units)		surface temperature (° K)
					actual	Bode's law	
Sun	332,945.6	109.2	1.4	—	—	—	4,700–6,000
Mercury	0.056	0.382	5.50	0	0.3871	0.4	900?
Venus	0.815	0.9489	5.25	0	0.7233	0.7	725
Earth	1.000	1.000	5.52	1	1.0000	1.0	290
Mars	0.1074	0.5327	3.94	2	1.5237	1.6	230
Minor planets (mean)	<0.0003	<0.060	<7.9	—	2.7	2.8	—
Jupiter	317.881	11.20	1.33	12	5.2028	5.2	150?
Saturn	95.168	9.38	0.72	10	9.5388	10.0	95?
Uranus	14.602	4.23	1.10	5	19.182	19.6	90?
Neptune	17.251	3.95	1.57	2	30.058	(38.8)	80?
Pluto	0.095–0.1*	0.5?	?	0	39.4	(77.2)	60?
Halley's Comet (largest)	<10^{-9}	<0.003	—	—	17.95†	—	—

*Determined 1970 from orbital characteristics; but for reasonable density (about 5.5), the mass must be only about 0.03 of the Earth's mass.   †Average.

material from which the planets formed. What is equally difficult to explain is why only one planet formed in each orbit. It may be that this was due to a local increase in density that served as a gravitational nucleus.

Movements of the planets The nine major planets from Mercury to Pluto revolve around the Sun in the direction customarily referred to as direct. They move in elliptic orbits that depart only slightly from circles. The orbits lie nearly in the plane of Earth's orbit, which is used as a reference plane. Except for the orbit of Pluto, which has a tilt of 17°, no other planet has a tilt to this plane greater than 7°. The Sun also rotates on its axis in the direction in which the planets revolve around it. Most of the planets also spin about their own axes in the same direction as they rotate about the Sun. The exceptions are Uranus, the axis of which, nearly in the plane of the ecliptic, is tilted over so far that it revolves in a retrograde, or reversed, manner, and Venus, the retrograde motion of which is extremely slow. The direction of spin, if any, of the belt of minor planets between the terrestrial and giant planets is not known. Earth's Moon, the two satellites of Mars, eight of the 12 satellites of Jupiter, and nine of the ten satellites of Saturn revolve in this same direction. But four of the small satellites of Jupiter and the outermost satellite of Saturn revolve in a retrograde direction. These tiny bodies may be captured asteroids. This explanation is not so plausible, however, in the case of a large satellite of Neptune that also revolves in the retrograde direction.

All of the 1,700 asteroids for which orbits are known revolve around the Sun in the same direction as the planets and in about the same plane. Most of the asteroids also move in nearly circular orbits. As already noted, there are a few exceptional asteroids that move in elongated orbits, as do most of the comets. But there are also several comets that move in nearly circular orbits, like the majority of the asteroids.

Interactions among various bodies.   Direct interaction among the planets does not now seem possible; but the paths of some of the smaller bodies, such as the minor planets, are easily perturbed, and comets are even more easily influenced by a close approach to one of the larger planets, particularly Jupiter. In this way, a small body could be deflected into a new path bringing it close to a large planet. Several of the minor planets, such as those named Icarus, Eros, and Geographos, have very elongated paths that bring them inside the Earth's orbit. Many comets have made close approaches, and in 1910 Earth passed (unnoticeably for most people) through the enormous but very diffuse tail of Halley's Comet. The chances of a direct hit are very low indeed, perhaps once or twice in the history of the solar system. Two unusual events in Siberia, however, at Sikhote Alin in 1947 and at Tunguska in 1908, have been attributed to the fall of a minor planet and of a comet, respectively. In each case, great explosions of unknown origin that devastated large, forested areas occurred. The arrival of meteors and meteorites is less rare, but a few records of damage to houses or persons due to the fall of meteorites are known.

Theories of the origin of the solar system.   The orderly arrangement and motion of the planets and asteroids are impressive evidence that they form a true solar system. It seems impossible that such a system could have resulted from chance encounters between these hundreds of bodies. Another significant factor is the extreme isolation of the solar system. The nearest star is 60,000 times as far away as Pluto. The evidence is thus overwhelming that the members of the solar system had a common origin. Theories of the origin of the solar system have been of two general types: (1) origin by an orderly process of evolution, and (2) origin by catastrophe.

Laplace's nebular hypothesis The classic example of the first type is the nebular hypothesis advanced by the French mathematician Pierre-Simon Laplace in 1796. He postulated a vast disc-shaped mass of cold gas in slow rotation, extending beyond the orbit of the farthest planet. As this nebula contracted under the mutual gravitation of its parts, its rate of rotation necessarily increased to conserve angular momentum. The angular momentum of a body rotating around a centre is the product of its mass, velocity, and the radius connecting it with the centre. It can be proved that the angular momentum of a closed system cannot change. If, for example, the radius decreases, the velocity increases proportionately so that the product remains the same. Eventually the rate of rotation increased so much that the centrifugal force at the periphery of the nebula exceeded gravitation, causing a ring of material to separate from the main mass. As contraction continued, other rings broke off at successively smaller distances from the centre.

These rings were not of uniform width all the way around. The densest portion gradually drew material to it and condensed into a planet. The satellites were formed by condensation from the contracting planets. The comets and meteors were presumably formed from material left over between the planets. Today the Sun is all that remains of the primeval nebular mass.

Laplace's nebular hypothesis was one of the most successful theories in the history of science. For a century it was practically unchallenged. About 1900, however, it encountered criticism that caused it to be discarded. The chief objection to the nebular hypothesis is the peculiar distribution of angular momentum found in the solar system. The planets, which possess less than 1 percent of the mass of the solar system, by some means have been able to acquire 98 percent of its angular momentum. Scientists cannot conceive of a natural physical process during which the angular momentum of a system could have been so unequally distributed. It is also more likely that matter would have separated from the nebula particle by particle rather than in the form of a ring.

One way to get a large amount of angular momentum into the planets is to put it there. This could be done by having the necessary energy forcibly injected from outside the system. A theory of catastrophe supplies the needed omission. Accordingly, the theory assumes that the Sun suffered a collision or near-collision with a passing star.

As the star approached, great tides were raised on the Sun. If the star came close enough, there was not merely a tidal bulge but an ejection of matter from the Sun in the form of a long filament. The end of the filament tended to follow the star into space, causing it to move in a curved direction around the Sun. Some of the material also fell back on the Sun and started it rotating in the same direction as the revolution of the filament around it. According to this theory, the filament broke into separate parts that ultimately condensed into the planets. Again the asteroids, comets, and meteorites consist of debris left over between the planets.

Objections to the catastrophe theory

This theory sounds fairly plausible, but the calculations indicate that the ejected filament, instead of revolving around the Sun, would probably have followed along behind the passing star into outer space. To meet this objection the theory has been modified by assuming that the Sun was originally a double star and that the collision was with the Sun's companion. The colliding stars could have gone off in different directions, leaving the central part of the filament torn from them nearly motionless near the Sun. But highly heated material dragged from the interior of a star would be more likely to explode and form a thin atmosphere around the Sun, rather than condense into planets. However, the most serious objection to any encounter theory is the great distance between the stars, which makes the probability of two stars colliding practically nil. In an attempt to circumvent this difficulty it has been assumed that the filament was formed when a companion of the Sun exploded, becoming a nova.

Modern theories of the origin of the solar system generally reject catastrophic processes and prefer as their starting point a primeval mass of cold gas, as in the old nebular hypothesis. There would be considerable turbulence in such a large mass, with currents forming and dying down and forming again. Eventually this mass would break up into gas clouds or protoplanets. The material at this time would have been cold; but eventually, with contraction, the central mass would have become hot enough to radiate. The radiation would have caused the planets to lose much of their mass into space by evaporation. In this way the difficulty in connection with angular momentum is avoided.

It should be emphasized that no theory of the origin of the solar system has as yet won general acceptance. All involve highly improbable assumptions. But the difficulty is in trying to find a theory with any degree of probability at all.

Possible uniqueness of the solar system. With the largest telescopes a planet even as large as Jupiter cannot be detected revolving around the nearest stars. Hence there is no direct knowledge of any stellar planetary systems involving small planets. Stellar associations are common in the Milky Way. Probably more than half of the "stars" are actually binaries or systems of higher multiplicity. At least one star exists with a companion only 0.016 as massive as the Sun, or 17 times the mass of Jupiter. It seems reasonable to suppose, therefore, that many stars are accompanied by bodies of planetary dimensions.

BIBLIOGRAPHY. GEORGE ABELL, *Exploration of the Universe*, 2nd ed. (1969), contains chapters on the solar system at an elementary level. Two popular accounts are F.L. WHIPPLE, *Earth, Moon, and Planets*, 3rd ed. (1968); and JONATHAN LEONARD and CARL SAGAN, *Planets* (1966). V.I. MOROZ, *Physics of Planets* (NASA TT F–515, 1968; orig. pub. in Russian, 1967), deals mainly with planetary atmospheres; and W.M. KAULA, *An Introduction to Planetary Physics* (1968), deals with orbits and the solid bodies of the inner planets. *The Solar System*, ed. by G.P. KUIPER and B.M. MIDDLEHURST, 4 vol. (1953–63), contains much still valid data; reviews of recent work are given in the *Annual Review of Astronomy and Astrophysics*.

(D.G.R.)

Solid State of Matter

Matter in bulk may have several states or phases; the most familiar of these being the gas, liquid, and solid states. Each of these general types of phases can be further subdivided into groups based on particular types of properties. Thus, solids may be divided into crystalline (*e.g.*, sodium chloride) or non-crystalline (*e.g.*, glass), into metallic (*e.g.*, copper), ionic (*e.g.*, sodium chloride), covalent (*e.g.*, germanium), or molecular (*e.g.*, solid argon), etc. These classifications are not exact. The properties of the solids depend on the properties of the atoms that form the solid, on the arrangement of atoms in the solid, and on the conditions (temperature, pressure, etc.) under which the solid is examined.

The wide variety of behaviour exhibited by solids is a direct result of the type of bonding that holds the atoms of the solid together and of the structural arrangement of the atoms. Classification of solids based on their structures can be developed at various levels of magnification, ranging from the scale of centimetres to angstroms (10^{-8} centimetre). As might be expected, the earliest structural studies were based on features that could be seen by the unaided eye. Thus, speculations on atomism by the ancient Greeks (*e.g.*, Democritus, at about 400 BC) were based on observations of the textures of ceramic materials and visual observations of the fractured surfaces of ceramics and bronzes. In the 19th century the etching of metals with acids and their subsequent examination with low-magnification optical microscopes was extensively carried out and revealed microstructural features of solids on the scale of what is presently known as the grain structure (about 10^{-3} centimetre). This work was part of a progression of much earlier work by metalsmiths in many parts of the world, who revealed the macrostructure of objects such as swords and armour by differentially polishing, scraping, or etching with naturally acidic liquids. These processes revealed the distribution of hard and soft constituents of the metals and gave rise to the beautiful and remarkable patterns on the Japanese and Damascus swords.

Early recognition of solid structure

Parallel to the developing understanding of the microstructure of solids, mineralogists had been examining and classifying crystals of naturally occurring minerals. By the 19th century many of the crystallographic features of crystals and their symmetry properties were known as a result of such studies, since the shapes of natural crystals often reflect the atomic arrangements. It was not, however, until the discovery of X-ray diffraction from crystalline solids in 1912, following a suggestion by Max Theodor von Laue, a German physicist, that the atomic structure of crystals began to be understood. By this date the atomic nature of matter was accepted, and it was the patterns produced by the diffraction of X-rays from the regular arrangement of atoms in crystals that resulted in an understanding of the structure of solids on an atomic scale (about 10^{-8} centimetre). Resolution by different methods of examination has improved, until today, with the use of the electron microscope and the field ion microscope, individual atoms in a solid can be resolved and studied. As understanding of the structure of solids has progressed, it has become clear that imperfections in the arrangements of atoms in solids have a major effect on the properties of solids, and a wide variety of these imperfections have been studied.

The solid state of matter cannot be understood without knowledge of the atomic structure of matter, details of which are treated fully in the articles ATOMIC STRUCTURE, MOLECULAR STRUCTURE, and others that are referred to below. Here, only a brief summary of this knowledge can be made.

General view of atomic structure

In most general terms, each of the chemical elements consists of a characteristic type of atom that is composed of subatomic particles arranged in a specific fashion. The nucleus of every atom consists of neutrons, particles with no electrical charge, and protons, particles with a single positive charge; this positively charged nucleus is surrounded by electrons, particles with a single negative charge, arranged in a structure according to the force of attraction between opposite charges and the force of repulsion between similar charges. The lightest element, hydrogen, has only one proton in the nucleus and a single electron; the heaviest naturally occurring element, uranium, has 92 protons and 92 electrons; between these are 90 other elements. The number of neutrons also increases, but not in such an orderly manner. The electrons around a nucleus may be thought of as occupying positions in a series of concentric shells. Some of these configurations are less stable than others, and the distribution of energy is such that the electrons tend to arrange their positions to attain the most stable arrangements. Thus, some atoms tend to donate electrons and others to accept them in chemical reactions; frequently, an exchange produces charged atoms, or ions, which may then form one of the chemical bonds that hold together compounds. Some atoms may share electrons in a chemical reaction, a bonding process in the formation of compounds. The electrons involved in chemical reactions are called the valence electrons, and they may occupy one or more of the outer shells. Changes in the states of matter (gas, liquid, solid) also involve bonds among atoms through their electron structures.

Many topics in this article are treated elsewhere in much greater detail, specifically the articles CHEMICAL BONDING; CRYSTALLIZATION AND CRYSTAL GROWTH; IONIC CRYSTALS; METALS, THEORY OF; MOLECULAR STRUCTURE; POLYMERS; SEMICONDUCTORS AND INSULATORS, THEORY OF; MAGNETISM; ELECTRICITY; DEFORMATION AND FLOW; ELASTICITY. The solid state has been most important in focussing scientific attention on properties of matter.

This article is divided into the following sections:

I. General structure and properties of solids
   Classification of solids based on the type of bonding
      Ionic solids
      Covalent solids
      Metallic solids
      Molecular solids
      Hydrogen-bonded solids
   Crystal structures
   Mechanical properties of solids
      Elastic and plastic properties
      Thermal properties
II. Electrical and magnetic characteristics
   Electronic structure and properties of solids
      Conductors
      Insulators
      Semiconductors
      Thermoelectricity
      Electron emission
      Liquids and amorphous solids
   Magnetism in solids
      Paramagnetism and diamagnetism
      Ferromagnetism
      Soft magnetic materials
      Hard magnetic materials
III. Interaction of radiation with matter
      Behaviour of solids illuminated with radiation
      Generation of electromagnetic radiation

I. General structure and properties of solids

CLASSIFICATION OF SOLIDS
BASED ON THE TYPE OF BONDING

Role of energy in formation of solids

Solids form from either the liquid or the vapour state, because the energy of the atoms (more properly, the thermodynamic variable called free energy) decreases when the atoms take up a relatively ordered, three-dimensional structure. The decrease in energy on forming the solid from the vapour phase is termed the cohesive energy and results from two types of interactions: a repulsive action (or term) that prevents the atoms from moving too close together and an attractive, or bonding, term that stabilizes the crystal against separation of the atoms. The origin of these energy terms serves as one basis for classifying solids into five groups: ionic, covalent, metallic, molecular, and hydrogen-bonded solids. In discussing real materials, it is important to realize that many cases occur in which the type of bonding falls into two or more of the above ideal classes. Thus, the compounds gallium arsenide, indium antimonide, and aluminum phosphide are examples of materials that have both covalent and ionic contributions to the atomic bonding, and the elements bismuth and antimony are examples of materials that have a partially metallic and partially covalent type of atomic bonding.

Ionic solids. Ionic bonding occurs between strongly electropositive (with weak affinity for electrons) elements, such as the alkali metals (lithium, sodium, etc.),

which form positive ions, and strongly electronegative (with strong affinity for electrons) elements, such as the halogens (fluorine, chlorine, etc.), which form negative ions. In this type of solid, electron transfer occurs between atoms, from electropositive to electronegative, and the solid consists of the resulting positively and negatively charged atoms or ions. For simple ionic solids such as sodium chloride, lithium fluoride, and cesium chloride, this electron transfer results in each ion having a closed electronic shell. The charged ions arrange themselves in space so that the coulombic attraction (a term for the attraction or repulsion between charges) between unlike charged ions equals the coulombic repulsion of similarly charged ions. While many different crystal structures can result from ionic bonding, three commonly occurring crystal structures are cesium chloride, sodium chloride, diamond, and zinc sulfide, types shown in Figure 1. It should be noted that in these crystal structures each ion has oppositely charged ions as its nearest neighbours, as a result of the coulombic forces acting between the ions.

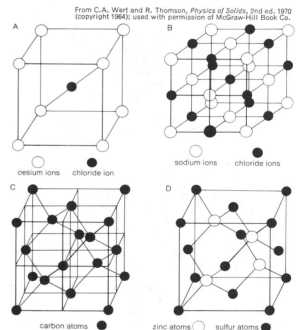

From C.A. Wert and R. Thomson, *Physics of Solids*, 2nd ed. 1970 (copyright 1964); used with permission of McGraw-Hill Book Co.

Figure 1: *Examples of crystal structures.*
(A) Cesium chloride; (B) sodium chloride; (C) diamond; (D) zincblende.

Calculating electrostatic interaction

The major contributions to the cohesive energy are electrostatic in origin and are called the Madelung energy. In calculating this energy, coulombic interactions between all the charged ions are summed. For a stable atomic arrangement, this energy must be attractive. The electrostatic, or coulomb-interaction, energy is calculated as the product of the charges on each ion, $\pm q$, divided by r, the distance between the ions, this quantity having the form q^2/r. Thus, as the separation becomes less, the interaction increases, and the closely packed crystal structures in which each ion is surrounded by nearest neighbours having opposite charges lead to a total electrostatic energy that is negative; *i.e.*, energy decreases on forming the crystal from dissociated ions. As the spacing between ions decreases, the crystal energy becomes increasingly negative, due to the $1/r$ dependence of the coulomb interaction. At small ionic separations, however, the closed electron shells of the adjacent ions begin to overlap in space, resulting in a rapid increase in energy as the ionic separation decreases. (The basic cause of this repulsion is accounted for by the Pauli exclusion principle, which states that no two electrons can have the same quantum numbers.) Equilibrium separation of ions of the crystal corresponds to the minimum energy position and is equal to about three angstroms (3×10^{-8} centimetre). The properties of ionic crystals are largely determined by the charge transfer that takes place. For example, when an electric field is applied, the current is carried by the motion of the charged ions and therefore depends on the diffusion of negatively charged ions toward the electrode carrying a positive charge or the positive ions toward a negative electrode or both. The electrical conductivity of a crystal therefore increases exponentially with temperature (since the increased thermal energy causes an increased rate of atomic jumping) at a rate that reflects the rate of diffusion of the ions.

Covalent solids. Covalent bonding (also known as homopolar bonding in organic chemistry) occurs when the valence (or outer) electrons of neutral atoms are shared between nearest neighbours in the crystal. This atomic arrangement allows each of the atoms to achieve a closed outer electron shell by sharing electrons with its neighbours. Covalent bonds generally contain two electrons, one from each neighbouring atom, and, since eight electrons are required for a closed electron shell, the arrangement of the atoms is such that each has four nearest neighbours. This results in a tetrahedral (having four faces) arrangement of atoms in space, and covalently bonded solids often have the diamond structure shown in Figure 1. The covalent bonds are highly directional, with the bonding electrons being predominantly located along the directions between nearest neighbour atoms; *i.e.*, the atoms that provide the two electrons forming the bond.

The role of electron spin

One of the parameters describing the energy state of the electron is the direction of its own spin, and, when the electrons of the bonding pair have opposite spin, the interaction between them is attractive. The energy of the associated atoms of the solid system is decreased from the energy of the atoms when they are free by the sharing of electrons between nearest neighbours (to allow a completed electron shell for each atom), and the decrease provides the cohesive energy for the system.

This ideal picture of the covalent solid is applicable to the bonding of the Group IV elements in the periodic table, such as carbon (when it occurs in the form of diamond), silicon, and germanium. Each of these has four valence electrons, which are shared in four tetrahedral covalent bonds. Other elements, however, also can exhibit covalent bonding. The two atoms of molecular hydrogen (H_2) are covalently bonded. Compounds of Group III and Group V elements such as gallium arsenide (GaAs) or indium antimonide (InSb) have at least partial covalent bonding, with the Group III element, gallium or indium (Ga, In), contributing three and the Group V element, arsenic or antimony (As, Sb), contributing five valence electrons to the covalent bonds. In these compounds the atomic structure is termed the zinc-blende structure, which differs from the diamond structure only in that each atom (*e.g.*, gallium) is surrounded by nearest neighbours of unlike atoms (*e.g.*, arsenic). Some of the elements of Groups V, VI, VII of the periodic table (such as arsenic, antimony, tellurium, iodine, and bromine) form complex crystal structures in which the bonding is at least partially covalent. In these less simple solids, covalent bonding occurs between atoms with fewer than four nearest neighbours arranged in sheets, chains, or molecules. The bonding between these sheets, etc., is the result of the induced displacement of the electrons and nuclei of neighbouring atoms and is called the van der Waals force; it is much weaker than covalent bonding.

The properties of crystals in which the bonding is predominantly covalent are determined largely by the localized nature of the electrons forming the bonds. These materials include electrical insulators such as diamond (room-temperature conductivity of about 10^{-14} [ohm-centimetre]$^{-1}$) and semiconductors such as germanium (room-temperature conductivity of about 40 [ohm-centimetre]$^{-1}$). In both cases, the electric current is carried by electrons that have been thermally excited (*i.e.*, their energies have been raised by heat) from their localized configuration (*i.e.*, basic position in the normal atom) to a more energetic state, or state of higher energy, in which they are nonlocalized and can move in response to an outside electric field. This excitation of electrons from the valence band (*i.e.*, electrons involved with bonding forces) to the conduction band (*i.e.*, electrons with enough energy to overcome local bonds and move through the spaces among the atoms if an electrical force is applied) leads to an electrical conductivity that increases exponentially with temperature. The various covalently bonded crystals differ in the amount of energy required to excite an electron to the conduction band, the value being about 160,000 calories per mole (*i.e.*, per 6.02×10^{23} electrons) in diamond and 28,000 calories per mole in silicon.

Valence and conduction bonds

Metallic solids. Bonding of solids formed from elements such as copper, aluminum, beryllium, sodium, and the many others classified as metals arises from the non-localized nature of the valence electrons in these solids. When an atom is brought into a metallic crystal, those properties of the valence electrons that are called its wave functions are altered because of the proximity of the valence electrons and the positively charged ionic cores (*i.e.*, the electrons that do not function in the chemical bond because they are held so firmly by the nucleus) of the other atoms in the structure. The resulting valence-electron wave functions are associated with the entire volume of the metal, and therefore each valence electron can no longer be associated with a particular ion core. The average energy of these nonlocalized valence electrons, which is partly kinetic energy of motion through the solid and partially potential energy due to interactions with the ionic cores and the other valence electrons, is reduced on forming the solid, thus providing the cohesive energy. It is the nonlocalized or free-electron nature of the valence electrons in metals that results in their characteristic properties. In some cases, however, the electrons can still retain much of their localized nature. Thus, many of the properties of the transition elements in the periodic table (*i.e.*, those with unfilled *d* shells in the structure of orbitals arranged according to energy distribution among the electrons; *e.g.*, iron, vanadium, chromium, zirconium, molybdenum) are determined by the behaviour of these *d* electrons in the solid. The *d* electrons remain largely localized around the ionic core; *i.e.*, they are not free to move through the solid but still contribute to properties such as the cohesive energy and magnetic properties.

Metallic crystals have characteristically high electrical conductivity (about 10^6 [ohm-centimetre]$^{-1}$ for a metal such as copper) due to the free-electron character of the valence electrons. They can move away when an electrical field is applied without requiring any thermal activation; *i.e.*, without having to be thermally excited (heated) into a conduction band, as in covalent crystals. In these cases, however, the motion of the electrons is limited; they are scattered when they meet imperfections in the crystal and when they approach atoms that are vibrating due to heat energy. The electrical conductivity, therefore, decreases as the temperature is increased, because an increase in the magnitude of thermal vibrations of the atoms obstructs the movement of free electrons.

Heat and metallic conductivity

Molecular solids. Rare-gas solids (such as argon, krypton, and xenon) and some molecular solids (*e.g.*, methane, CH_4; hydrogen, H_2; chlorine, Cl_2) exhibit weak van der Waals or molecular bonding in the solid state. Since the bonding occurs between atoms that have completely filled outer electron shells or non-ionized molecules, the crystals are only weakly bonded and are stable only at low temperatures. The van der Waals bonding results from the displacement of the atomic nuclei from the centres of the electron charge distribution in each atom, the displacement resulting when neutral atoms or molecules are brought close to each other. This induced charge displacement creates an electric dipole (*i.e.*, a body with two poles oppositely charged) that interacts with the adjacent induced dipoles to reduce the energy of the crystal and provide a small cohesive energy. The attractive interaction energy between the induced electric dipoles is of very short range and varies as the distance between atoms to the -6 power (or 1/distance^6). It is balanced by the repulsive interaction that occurs as the filled electron shells of the atoms begin to overlap on bringing the atoms closer together, a consequence of the increase in energy due to electrons having the same energy; *i.e.*, the same four quantum numbers, which account for all the energy of an electron relevant to that electronic structure, occupying the same volume. (According to the Pauli exclusion principle, no two electrons of an atom may have the same four quantum numbers.) The nature of this type of molecular bonding leads to electrons that are localized at each atom and therefore to molecular solids that do not conduct electricity. They are insulators. Very large amounts of energy are required to excite an electron in such a solid from a localized state to a nonlocalized one. Due to the low cohesive energy of these crystals, significant electron excitation does not occur in the temperature range in which they are solid.

Hydrogen-bonded solids. Hydrogen bonding is of great significance in organic solids and in certain molecular solids such as ice, hydrogen fluoride, and potassium hydrogen phosphate. The single valence electron of hydrogen allows it to form a covalent bond with only one other atom, as with another hydrogen atom in the hydrogen molecule, H_2. In some solids containing strongly electronegative atoms, such as nitrogen, oxygen, or fluorine, hydrogen can form a bond between two of the electronegative atoms. In these cases, the hydrogen is at least partially positively ionized (*i.e.*, its electron has been partially removed) and serves to bond two negatively charged ions. Such bonding is of significance in many polymeric materials and in organic solids such as DNA (deoxyribonucleic acid), where it acts to bond the strands of the DNA molecule.

Comparison of bond strengths

As was previously stated, solids rarely exhibit a single idealized type of atomic bonding. In general, ionic and covalent bonding is very strong, leading to high heats of vaporization and melting points; molecular bonding is very weak; and metallic bonding occupies an intermediate position. The type of bonding also places some constraints on the structures in which the solids crystallize; however, the variety of crystal structures observed is much greater than might be suspected from the few simple types of atomic bonding described above.

CRYSTAL STRUCTURES

While it has been recognized since about the 17th century that crystalline solids consist of a regular array of repetitive units, the three-dimensional periodic arrangement of atoms that form crystals was first established in the early 20th century. In 1912 M. Laue developed the theory of diffraction of X-rays from a periodic arrangement of atoms, and in 1913 W.L. Bragg used X-ray diffraction to establish the structures of some ionic crystals, such as sodium chloride and potassium bromide, potassium chloride, and potassium iodide. Since then, the diffraction of X-rays, electrons, and neutrons has been used to determine the structure of a myriad of simple and extraordinarily complex structures, ranging from the relatively simple structures of the elements to the structures of proteins and DNA. While the nature of the atomic bond may place certain constraints on the structure of the solid, it does not determine it, and, as shall be indicated below, a wide variety of crystals is formed from materials of the same class of atomic bonding.

Atoms in a crystalline solid are arranged in a repetitive three-dimensional arrangement termed a lattice, and the position of any point in the lattice is determined relative to a set of crystal axes. Both the lattice and the axis system are mathematical fictions used to describe the actual atomic positions in space. Nonetheless, they facilitate the description of many crystalline properties, and a standard set of axes and lattices has been developed. (The details of crystal structure are fully treated in the articles CRYSTALLOGRAPHY and CRYSTALLIZATION AND CRYSTAL GROWTH.) The arrangement of points forming these unit cells is the basic repetitive unit of the lattice that is formed by translation of the unit cells along each of the three crystal axes. The magnitude of the basic translation distance in the unit cell is about three to eight angstroms (3 to 8 × 10⁻⁸ centimetre). It has been conventional to describe the crystal structures using seven crystal axes

(triclinic; monoclinic; orthorhombic; tetragonal; cubic; trigonal, or rhombohedral; and hexagonal) and 14 unit cells. While those choices are not unique, all possible repetitive arrangements of points in space (*i.e.*, all lattices) can be described by one of these 14 conventional unit cells, which are called Bravais lattices.

Bravais lattices

A description of the crystal structure requires that the positions of all atoms be established relative to the Bravais lattice. In the simple cases there is one atom per lattice point; *e.g.*, the structure of copper is face-centred cubic, with one copper atom at each point, while iron (at room temperature) has a body-centred cubic unit cell with one atom per lattice point. Most crystals have a rather more complex structure, with several atoms per lattice point. Thus, the diamond structure, which is characteristic of many covalently bonded elements (shown in Figure 1), has two atoms per lattice point in the face-centred cubic lattice; and the sodium chloride structure (shown in Figure 1), which is characteristic of many ionic crystals, has two ions, Na^+ and Cl^-, associated with each lattice point of a face-centred cubic lattice. Many more complex structures are known where the number of atoms per lattice point is large. For example, the element manganese has a crystal structure below 742° C (1,368° F) that is simple cubic with 58 atoms per unit cell, another structure from 742° C to 1,095° C (1,368° to 2,003° F) that is simple cubic with 20 atoms per unit cell, a third structure between 1,095° C and 1,133° C (2,003° to 2,071° F) that is face-centred cubic with four atoms per unit cell, and a fourth structure from 1,133° C (2,071° F) to the melting point that is body-centred cubic with two atoms per unit cell.

Crystal symmetry determines the dependence of many of the macroscopic properties on direction in the crystal. Thus, properties such as electrical conductivity, magnetic susceptibility, elastic constants, and dielectric constants reflect the symmetry of the crystal structure. As a result, cubic crystal structures such as sodium chloride are isotropic (*i.e.*, their properties, such as dielectric constant, are independent of the direction in which they are measured) while quartz, having a trigonal crystal structure, has two independent dielectric constants, and the experimentally measured value depends on the direction of measurement. As a consequence of these crystal symmetry elements, a cubic crystal (copper, germanium, sodium chloride, etc.) has three independent elastic constants, while for a hexagonal crystal (zinc, cadmium, magnesium, etc.) there are five independent elastic constants.

Atomic bonding limits the variety of crystal structures possible in the case of covalent, ionic, and hydrogen bonding. For example, as a result of the nature of the coulombic interaction, ionic crystal structures are limited to those in which each ion has oppositely charged ions as nearest neighbours. Simple monovalent ionic solids in which positive ions have small radii crystallize in the sodium chloride structure, and the same crystal structure is characteristic of some simple divalent ionic solids. The cesium chloride structure is characteristic of monovalent ionic structures in which the positive ionic radius is relatively large. A variety of ionic crystals crystallize in the zinc sulfide structure, in which the positive and negative ions are tetrahedrally coordinated and the structure is similar to the diamond structure. Much more complicated crystal structures are formed when the atoms in the molecule are ionically bound and the molecules themselves are arranged in layered structures with bonding between layers arising through van der Waals forces.

Limitation on the variety of structures

The covalently bonded elements form in the diamond structure, which allows tetrahedral coordination of the atoms. In covalently bonded compounds, which generally also exhibit at least partial ionic nature, the structure formed is the zinc sulfide structure. Hydrogen bonding places severe restrictions on the structures of organic crystals such as proteins and DNA. These crystalline constraints are of great importance in molecular genetics. Metallic bonding places relatively few constraints on the crystal structure, and consequently a wide variety is observed.

While some of the polymeric materials crystallize in

regular three-dimensional structures, these are not nearly as perfect as more normal crystalline solids. The basic polymeric unit (or mer) consists of covalently bonded carbon and hydrogen atoms (with the possibility of other atoms, such as oxygen, fluorine, or other covalently bonded groups of atoms, added in particular polymers). These basic units, or monomers, are covalently bonded into long chains that may consist of thousands of repeating units. The angles between the covalent bonds along this chain are limited to discrete values by the nature of the covalent bonding. Polyethylene is an example of a simple polymer: the basic mer is a three-atom group linked by single bonds—hydrogen–carbon–hydrogen, or H—C—H, which is repeated in a sequence by single bonds between the carbon atoms:

$$
\begin{array}{ccc}
H & H & H \\
| & | & | \\
-C- & C- & C- \\
| & | & | \\
H & H & H
\end{array} \; .
$$

These chains may be thousands of units long (for details see POLYMERS).

Crystalline defects   Macroscopic solids are far from being perfect crystals, in general. They usually contain a variety of crystalline defects, some of which are shown in Figure 2. Solids usually consist of a set of smaller three-dimensional volumes called grains, in each of which the crystal axes have a constant orientation but between which the crystal axis orientation varies. The surfaces separating the grains are termed grain boundaries. Inside each grain the perfection of the crystalline lattice is perturbed by line imperfections termed dislocations, which correspond to a local change in the atomic arrangement. The simplest of these, the edge dislocation, corresponds to the insertion of a partial atomic plane into the lattice. A number of crystal defects exist at individual points in the lattice. Some of the atomic positions may be occupied by foreign atoms; these atoms may either substitute for host atoms on the regular crystal sites or occupy small interstices between the normal atomic positions. Vacancies (called Schottky defects) and small clusters of vacancies are formed by removal of atoms from their normal lattice positions, leaving them vacant, and self interstitials can be formed by inserting the atoms in between the normal sites. In ionic crystals these point defects are often charged and tend to occur in small clusters in order to preserve electrical neutrality. Such ionic point defects are often associated with "colour centres," or defects that absorb light causing a colouring of the crystal.

A number of other primary imperfections can be described in addition to these crystalline defects. One of these is the phonon, a quantum of lattice vibrational energy. In analogy to a photon, the phonon can be treated as a wave or a particle. Its characteristics determine certain properties of solids such as heat capacity, thermal conductivity, and optical absorption. In insulators and covalent crystals, free electrons and holes (regions of positive electrical charge) can be introduced by ionizing radiation, thermal excitation by phonons, or high electric fields. A bound electron-hole pair can form and is termed an exciton.

MECHANICAL PROPERTIES OF SOLIDS

Elastic and plastic properties.   Many of the uses of solids depend on their ability to support stresses (applied load divided by the area of application); indeed, the ability of a solid to support normal loads (loads applied perpendicular to a surface) and shear loads (loads applied parallel to the surface) distinguishes a solid from a gas or liquid. The deformation (change of shape of the solid) **Types of deformation** that results from the application of a stress may be divided into three general types: elastic, plastic, and anelastic. These may be best defined with reference to the dependence on the rate at which the stress is applied and the permanence of the deformation when the stress is removed.

Elastic deformation is an instantaneous shape change in response to an applied stress and is completely and immediately recovered when the stress is removed; i.e., there is

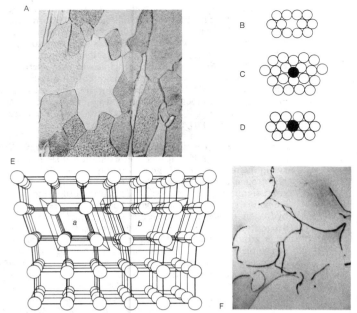

Figure 2: *Crystalline lattice defects.*
(A) Grain structure in polycrystalline iron. The orientation of the grains changes across the grain boundaries (magnified 100 ×). (B) Lattice vacancy. (C) Interstitial atom. (D) Substitutional solute atom. (E) Edge dislocation in simple cubic lattice. The extra half plane is shown at position *b*, which indicates the distortion and disruption of bonding at the dislocation. At position *a* the lattice is perfect except for elastic distortions. (F) Electron microscope photograph of dislocations in vanadium (magnified 100,000 ×).
From (B—D) C.A. Wert and R. Thomson, *Physics of Solids*, 2nd ed. 1970 (copyright 1964); used with permission of McGraw-Hill Book Co., (E) J. Ziman, "The Thermal Properties of Materials." Copyright © 1967 by Scientific American, Inc. All rights reserved.

no permanent "set." In contrast to this, plastic deformation results in a permanent shape change that depends on the rate at which a stress is applied and that is not recovered on removal of the stress. Anelastic deformation, occupying a middle ground between these two extremes, is a recoverable deformation that depends on the rate of application of the stress and on the time during which it remains applied. These three types of deformation have been commonly experienced in the stretching of a steel spring or of a rubber band (elastic deformation), the bending of a paper clip (plastic deformation), and the decreasing amplitude of vibration of a plucked violin string (caused by anelastic deformation). Unfortunately for the investigators of these phenomena, it is not easy to separate these three classical types of behaviour, and the overall result of the application of a stress is a combination of all these types.

Thermal properties.   The excitation of lattice vibrations and electrons on increasing the temperature of a solid has a major effect on many properties of solids. Attempts at understanding these thermal effects have played a central role in the development of solid-state physics. The early quantitative experiments on the specific heat of solids in the 18th century were interpreted as **Early theory of heat** the introduction of heat as a "caloric fluid" that had properties such as weightlessness and transparency and that seeped from hot to cold. It was not until 19th-century work on the behaviour of gases that heat was interpreted as the motion of molecules and that the kinetic molecular theory stating this in specific terms became accepted. The application of principles that had been developed for gases to an understanding of the thermal properties of solids was not possible in the context of classical physics, and the attempt provided some motivation for the development of quantum mechanics early in the 1900s.

The two major thermal phenomena in solids are the specific heat (or heat capacity: the quantity of heat that will raise the temperature of a unit mass 1°) and the conduction of heat. Based on the understanding of gases, it was realized that each atom stored energy in its vibrational modes (frequency and amplitude) as kinetic energy (energy of motion) of the atom and as potential energy of the distorted bonds that join the atom to its nearest neighbours. The amount of energy per mode in the temperature range where the solid behaved classically —i.e., where the atomic motion can be described without the use of quantum mechanics—was one-half of the product of Boltzmann's constant, k (3.3×10^{-24} calorie per degree Kelvin) and the absolute temperature, T (degrees Kelvin): $\frac{1}{2} kT$. Since the vibration of each atom in a solid can be described as motion in three independent directions (i.e., three kinetic and three potential energy modes), the classical energy of a mole of atoms in a solid is three times the product of Boltzmann's constant, k, the temperature, T, and Avogadro's number, N, 6×10^{23} (the number of atoms in the atomic weight in grams of an element): $3 NkT$. The heat capacity, the rate of change of energy with temperature, is $3 Nk$ (or about six calories per mole). In addition to energy stored as lattice vibrations (phonons), excitation of electrons to higher energy states may also occur. In metals this electronic specific heat increases linearly with temperatures and is small compared to the lattice vibration term.

Conduction of heat along a temperature gradient in a solid can involve the transport of energy by electrons, by phonons, or by both. Transport of heat by electrons accounts for the majority of the thermal conductivity in metals at room temperature and above. The thermal currents due to electron and phonon transport, however, are additive and at low temperatures the heat conductivity is due solely to phonons. Motion of phonons and electrons through the lattice is limited by scattering from crystalline defects such as impurities, grain boundaries, external surfaces, dislocations, etc. and from other phonons and electrons. These scattering processes determine the thermal conductivity of the solid.

II. Electrical and magnetic characteristics

Variation in metal conductivity

Materials display a wide range of electrical behaviour, typified by the electrical conductivity of such elements as aluminum, silicon, and phosphorus, which are neighbours in the periodic table of elements. Wires made of each of these materials about the size and length of wires in a lamp cord and connected across the terminals of a 12-volt auto battery would conduct greatly different currents. Through the aluminum wire a current of about 100 amperes would flow, through the silicon wire a current many times smaller would flow, about 10^{-6} ampere, and through the phosphorus wire a current of only about 10^{-15} ampere would flow.

This wide range of electrical behaviour among aluminum, a useful metal, silicon, a widely used semiconductor, and phosphorus, a good insulator, typifies the enormous variety of electrical applications of materials now possible. Why should the adjacent elements, aluminum with 13 electrons, valence 3, silicon with 14 electrons, valence 4, and phosphorus with 15 electrons, valence 5, behave so differently? The answer requires understanding of the basic characteristics of electrons in solids.

ELECTRONIC STRUCTURE AND PROPERTIES OF SOLIDS

The general structure of matter has occupied the attention of scientists for centuries, but the present view of the electronic structure has been developed rather recently. The discovery of the electron and its properties in the early part of the 20th century and the invention of quantum mechanics in the 1920s led to development of a detailed theory of the electronic structure of solids in the 1930s. The theory is rather good, overall, even though some fine details are not yet clear. This lack has not prevented technical application of knowledge of the electronic structure of solids; indeed, the rapid development of solid-state devices has its basis in the close interplay among the developing theory, basic experiments, and practical applications.

Conductors. Wide variability of electrical behaviour is not limited to the three examples just described; rather, this variability is common as is illustrated for a number of materials in Figure 3. The group of materials at the bottom, the metals, are good conductors. The individ-

ual atoms in the metals are assumed to have lost electrons (the valence electrons) to the entire solid. These free electrons move as a group in an electric field and hence conduct current. Indeed, early in the 20th century a quantitative theory of conductivity was developed to explain electrical conductivity in terms of the number of free electrons, their charge, and their degree of mobility. Later refinements were added by application of quantum mechanics, but the basic principles still apply.

Free electrons in metal. Description of the free electrons in a metal can be made by application of fundamental features of quantum theory. First, only the valence electrons of the atoms of the metal can become free. The inner electrons remain bound to the nucleus of the individual atoms and form with the nucleus a charged entity called the ion core. Second, the free electrons are subject to the constraints of the fundamental precepts of quantum mechanics—the Pauli exclusion principle and the Heisenberg uncertainty principle. The first of these requires that no two electrons may move in the same direction in the crystal with the same speed. The second defines the words "the same"; i.e., it fixes the direction and velocity intervals permitted the various electrons. Consideration must also be given to electron spin; this feature and a more precise statement of the two principles are given in the article METALS, THEORY OF.

Detailed application of these principles of quantum mechanics yields the following picture of the free electrons: the electrons indeed have access to all parts of the metal. Their speed of movement through the crystal ranges from near zero to a few million metres per second, about 1 percent of the velocity of light. Their wavelength (i.e., their de Broglie wavelength; see ELECTRON) ranges between the actual size of ordinary solids (a few feet, say) to a lower limit of about five to ten angstroms. They have a mass about the same as that of an electron in a vacuum (i.e., what is called the rest mass) but not precisely this

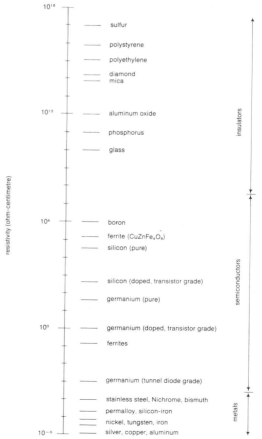

Figure 3: The electrical resistivity of various materials at room temperature. The unit, ohm-centimetre, is the resistivity across a one-centimetre cube of the material.

mass, and interactions with the lattice ions can cause variation.

The range in velocity is not the most convenient way of describing the motion of the electrons. A more useful description is their range in energy—the sum of their kinetic energy of translation or displacement through the crystal and their residual energy of association with the ion cores, an association that is not completely lost even when the electrons become free. For example, when sodium atoms condense to form solid sodium, not much change occurs in the inner states (those electron orbitals designated as 1s, 2s, and 2p) of the ion core. But the outermost state (the 3s orbital) is broadened into a band of closely spaced energy levels, some occupied by electrons, some empty (see Figure 4). The energy of the highest occupied states, called the Fermi energy, lies about 2.5 electron volts (or eV; defined below) above the bottom of the band for sodium. The spacing of the levels at the Fermi energy is exceedingly small; adjacent levels are only about 10^{-8} electron volt apart for a few cubic centimetres of sodium. Electrons can easily be excited into these empty levels by electric fields, by heat energy, and by light. It is this easy excitation of electrons into empty levels that makes metals good conductors of electricity and heat, makes metals opaque to visible light, and gives them their characteristic lustre.

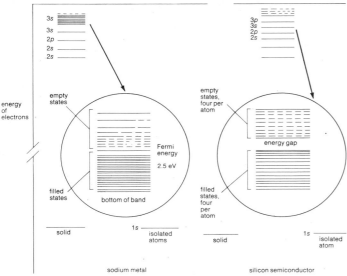

Figure 4: The energy levels of sodium and silicon for both isolated atoms and the solid material. The energy levels are not to scale; the 1s level, in particular, should lie much deeper than is shown (see text).

The electron volt

The unit of energy universally used in consideration of electrons is the electron volt. It is the energy acquired by an electron when it moves through a potential difference of one volt. The electron striking the screen of a television tube has a kinetic energy of about 20,000 electron volts. It is a very small unit; a mosquito buzzing about may have a kinetic energy of perhaps 100,000,000,000 electron volts. Even so, a few electron volts is a great deal of energy in terms of events that happen in solids.

No net electric current flows in a metal if no electric field exists; an electron moving in one direction with a certain speed is paired off with one moving in the opposite direction with that speed. This pairing off is altered slightly when an electric field is applied, however. All electrons experience a force in the same direction because of the field and are accelerated to higher velocities (i.e., they go into some of the higher energy states). Since all are accelerated in the same direction, they provide a net flow of electric charge—i.e., an electric current. The current does not become infinitely large, however, because the increase in velocity of the electrons is limited by collisions with the ion cores; the electrons must pick their way through a dense cloud of ions whose electric fields deflect and scatter them. A steady-state condition is

established when the extra energy gained from acceleration in the field is just balanced by the loss of energy in the collisions. Detailed analysis of this situation yields the equation known as Ohm's law (see ELECTRICITY).

The excess velocity the electrons gain in fields of ordinary size is not very large compared to their intrinsic velocity of a few million metres per second. In the lamp filament of a flashlight, for example, the electrons drift along only a few centimetres per second under the influence of the electric field produced by the battery.

Effect of alloying on conductivity. Metals tend to heat up when they carry an electric current. The electrons gain kinetic energy in the electric field. This kinetic energy is transferred to the metal ions by the collisions, increasing the vibrational energy of the atoms of the metal and hence increasing the temperature of the metal. In fact, an extension of the mathematical treatment which gives Ohm's law yields Joule's law, which relates the heat generated to the number of conduction electrons and to their mobility in the metal and to the electric field imposed.

The resistivity of metals and alloys has a range of about 100 times from that of silver to that of the stainless steels. This range is certainly not caused principally by differences in the number of conduction electrons. Rather, it is caused mainly by differences in mobility. Consider the example of nickel and Nichrome (i.e., the heating element in an electric stove, 80 percent nickel and 20 percent chromium): Nichrome has a resistivity about 20 times greater than that of pure nickel, even though the two materials have nearly the same number of free electrons. The difference in resistivity must be caused by a greater probability of collisions of electrons in the Nichrome, hence a lower mobility of the electrons. Alloying nickel with chromium atoms increases the lattice irregularities, making collisions of electrons with the lattice atoms more likely.

Effect of heat on conductivity. Increasing the temperature of a metal also increases the probability of collisions and thus increases the resistivity. For example, the resistivity of the tungsten filament of a 100-watt incandescent lamp increases by about 20 times when the lamp is heated from room temperature to its operating temperature of about 2,500° C (4,500° F). The ions in the solid oscillate more vigorously at higher temperatures, increasing the chance that collisions with electrons will occur. These two examples, one the effect of alloying and the other the effect of temperature, are a general feature of metallic conductors; theory, in fact, predicts and experiments show that atoms in a pure, perfect crystal should not impede the motion of the electrons at all. The resistivity of a metal should disappear completely if collisions of the electrons with the ions of the crystal could be eliminated. Thus, the resistivity of the pure metals tends toward zero near the temperature of absolute zero (−273° C [−460° F]). But, even more, below a certain temperature (called the critical temperature) the electrical resistivity of a certain group of materials called superconductors is actually zero; they become infinitely good conductors of electricity. Thousands of metals and alloys are known to show superconductivity; all must be cooled to extremely low temperatures to show the effect. This limits their practical use, of course, but they are beginning to be technologically important. Since they can carry immense currents without loss, they are useful in generating high magnetic fields and have tremendous potential in electrical-power transmission (see the article SUPERCONDUCTIVITY).

Insulators. The electrical insulators are at the other extreme of the electrical-resistance scale; they conduct poorly (see Figure 3). A number of the pure elements are good insulators, among them phosphorus, sulfur, boron, and carbon (in the form of diamond); however, an immense number of compounds are insulators, among them many oxides and salts, a wide variety of glasses and other ceramic materials, and most plastics. They are useful mainly for two reasons. Their poor conductivity makes them useful as electrical insulators for conducting metals and semiconductors, and they can be used to increase the storage capacity of electrical condensers.

Variations in resistivity

Types of insulators

The valence electrons of these solids are tightly bound to the ion cores; thus, they do not readily become free, as do the valence electrons in a metal. This in turn means that they cannot conduct much current in an electric field; that is, these solids are electrical insulators. As an example, consider a crystal of diamond. An energy of about five electron volts is required to free a valence electron; at room temperature virtually none of these electrons is free, fewer than one in 10^{40} (*i.e.*, a sphere of diamond about 100 miles in diameter would have only a single free electron from thermal excitation). Thus, the capability of diamond or of the other good insulators to conduct current by free electrons is exceedingly small. It is so small, in fact, that most of the conduction of electricity at ordinary temperatures is caused by migration of the ions themselves.

Though good insulators have very few free electrons, they cannot remain insulators if the electric field is made indefinitely large. Eventually, breakdown occurs and a spark jumps, oftentimes destroying the dielectric. Most solid insulators break down at about 500,000 volts per inch (air and gas mixtures at somewhat lower fields).

Electrons in insulators are bound to the ions rather firmly, but they are indeed influenced by an electric field. They and the ions (which are charged positively) are displaced relative to each other a small amount by the presence of a field and hence form a minus–plus, or $-+$, pair, called an electric dipole. Since all electron–ion pairs are aligned parallel to each other, the entire solid possesses an overall dipole that is simply the vector sum of all the individual dipoles. Though the strength of each little dipole is so small that it is measurable only by the most special and sensitive techniques, a piece of solid—*e.g.*, a cubic centimetre—contains so many dipoles that the dipole strength of the overall solid can be appreciable. This, combined with the higher breakdown strength of solid insulators relative to that of air, has important practical application. For example, the capacitor in the power supply of an alternating-current radio is about a centimetre in diameter and a few centimetres long. If the metal oxide that serves as the heart of that capacitor were to be replaced by air, reasonable manufacturing tolerances would require that the air capacitor be a volume many metres in each direction.

Dielectric materials

This phenomenon, which produces these dipoles, called the dielectric effect, is actually possessed by all solids, but the only materials for which it is significant are the insulators. Mica and quartz have long been important practically. The oxide of aluminum, Al_2O_3, and more recently that of tantalum, Ta_2O_5, are important in high-capacitance condensers of small physical size of miniature electronic circuits. Oil, waxed paper, glass, and plastic and films are also dielectric materials of great importance.

Semiconductors. The semiconductors are partway between the insulators and the metals in terms of electrical conductivity (see Figure 3). They possess more free electrons than the insulators but not as many as the metals; whereas the best insulators have fewer than one free electron per cubic centimetre at room temperature, and metals have 10^{22}, germanium, a widely used semiconductor, has about 10^{14}, and silicon has about 10^{10}. The mobility of the free electrons in these semiconductors is about the same as that for electrons in the metals; in fact, it is a little larger, so the lower conductivity of semiconductors (compared to the metals) is directly a result of the smaller number of free electrons. The practical value of semiconductors lies not in the precise number of free electrons for pure materials, however, but in the easy control of the number of free electrons made possible by alloying. Thus, the conductivity of semiconductor alloys can be rather completely controlled (see SEMICONDUCTORS AND INSULATORS, THEORY OF).

Experiments that measure not only the number of free charges responsible for current flow but also the sign of the charges show an additional curious feature. Current in some semiconductors is carried by motion of negative charges—*i.e.*, electrons—but in some others by motions of positive charges. The explanation is based on detailed examination of the electronic structure of semiconductors and the process of electron excitation.

Atoms of a semiconductor such as silicon are bound together in the solid in a covalent-bonding arrangement of the valence electrons, of which there are four per atom. All of the valence electrons are required to fill these bonding states, and no electrons are left over in this valence band to be free (see Figure 4). Thus, without electron excitation, the number of free electrons is zero, and the conductivity is low; in fact, it would be zero. When excitation of an electron does occur—say, by a thermal fluctuation—not only does the electron become free, but an empty state is left in the covalent group of bonding electrons. This empty state, called a hole, can itself move through the crystal. It acts like a free positive charge.

Some semiconductors have equal numbers of free electrons and holes; *e.g.*, pure silicon and pure germanium. These materials are called intrinsic; their properties are determined by the inherent character of the pure, perfect material. Other semiconductors have an excess of electrons and are called *n*-type; examples are pure silicon alloyed with a little phosphorus and pure germanium alloyed with a little antimony or arsenic. Still others have an excess of holes, and these are called *p*-type; examples are silicon alloyed with a little boron or aluminum and germanium with a little indium or gallium. The examples illustrate the principle that *n*-type material is formed from silicon or germanium (valence 4) alloyed with an element of valence 5, which provides an extra free electron per alloying atom. Material of *p*-type is formed by alloying with elements of valence 3, which provides an extra hole per alloying atom.

The use of semiconductor materials in devices is based on two technological capabilities: (1) Through alloying chemistry, the material can be made either *n*-type or *p*-type. This control of the amount of alloying element extends to control of the number of charge carriers, thus to control of the level of conductivity. (2) Layered arrangements can be made in which *p*-type and *n*-type material butt against each other in the same chip of semiconductor crystal. It is these multilayered sandwiches of alternate *p*-type and *n*-type material, the layers having carefully controlled chemistry and thickness, that make possible devices such as rectifiers, transistors, integrated circuits, junction lasers, and switches.

Uses of semiconductors

Thermoelectricity. The article to this point has described both the fundamental nature of electrons in solids and the effects produced by an electric field applied externally; *i.e.*, a gradient, or change, in the voltage from one point to another. Other kinds of external fields can be introduced, however, an important one being a temperature difference or a gradient in temperature along a solid. Such a gradient leads to an effect called thermoelectricity. This effect has long been known and has several practical applications.

The maximum energy of electrons in solids, the Fermi energy, varies from material to material. Therefore electrons on the two sides of an interface formed when two materials are in contact will not be at the same energy, and electrons will flow across the interface in one direction or the other to occupy empty states of lower energy. For differences of Fermi energy of sizable amounts—*e.g.*, an electron volt—the expectation would be that large fractions of the electrons in one solid would transfer to the other, but that is not the case. Another phenomenon enters when charge is transferred; a potential difference—that is, a voltage—is set up because of a growing unbalance of total charge (ions plus electrons) in each piece of the solid. This potential difference opposes the transfer of electrons beyond a certain point. At the point of equilibrium the potential difference is called the contact potential difference. It can be a sizable effect; for example, between gold and aluminum, 0.6 volt, and between copper oxide and cadmium sulfide, 0.4 volt.

This contact potential difference cannot easily be measured, as with a voltmeter. In a series of interfaces—*e.g.*, copper to nickel to iron and back to copper—all contact voltages cancel out. The laws of thermodynamics require it; that is, if the temperature of the entire circuit is constant. If two junctions are not at the same temperature (*e.g.*, the copper–nickel and the nickel–iron in the example just described), then a voltage may indeed be developed around the circuit, a thermoelectric voltage. It develops because the Fermi energy of different materials varies differently as temperature is changed; hence, the contact potential difference of a given type of junction varies with temperature.

The thermoelectric voltage developed at junctions in circuits consisting of a series of dissimilar metals, when the junctions are held at different temperatures, is small. For example, the thermoelectric voltage developed between one junction of iron and copper at 0° C (32° F) and another at 100° C (212° F) is only about 0.001 volt. Certain combinations of alloys give somewhat higher voltages, up to 0.010 volt for the same temperature range, and some combinations of materials partway between the metals and semiconductors, the semimetals, yield even higher values. Even so, the effect is a small one, though a cascade of junctions, called a thermopile, can be used to produce higher voltages.

Two chief uses are made of thermoelectric circuit voltages: (1) to measure temperature; (2) to convert heat to electric power with no moving parts other than the electrons. Unfortunately, the efficiency is low, at most around 10 percent (compared to an efficiency of about 45 percent for a steam-turbine generating plant), and therefore they are not widely used for generation of electric power.

A related effect occurs in a circuit containing a thermoelectric junction when a current is passed through the circuit, as from a battery. Depending on the nature of the junction and the direction of current flow, heat is absorbed or liberated at the junction. This phenomenon, *The Peltier effect* called the Peltier effect, again is not large, but it does have one practical application: such a junction can be used as a refrigerator whose only moving parts again are the electric charges themselves. Because of the high cost of suitable materials and low efficiency, it is not now a practical substitute for the conventional rotary-compressor-type of refrigerator.

Electron emission. The free electrons in a metal have kinetic energy ranging from near zero to several electron volts. Nevertheless, their interaction with the ion cores is still sufficiently large so that they must have appreciably more energy before they can leave the solid. That is, an energy barrier a few electron volts in size exists at the surface of a solid. Electrons are indeed emitted from solids, and this additional energy is available from several sources.

Thermionic emission. Electrons may gain the required energy from lattice phonons—emission resulting from this source is called thermionic emission. It occurs because electrons are occasionally excited to higher energy states by collisions with the lattice ions. Although the chance of an excitation large enough to overcome the surface barrier is small, it is not zero at any temperature. Furthermore, the chances increase as the temperature is raised. For example, cathodes in television tubes emit about 10^{15} times more electrons per second at their operating temperature than they do at room temperature. The current is large enough to be useful.

Photoelectric emission. Electrons can also be emitted from a solid by the action of electromagnetic radiation, a phenomenon called the photoelectric effect. Photons (the quanta of energy associated with electromagnetic waves) of visible light have ample energy to cause this emission from most solids, but radiation of a wavelength longer than infrared is insufficient to cause emission of electrons.

Field emission. Finally, emission can occur even at room temperature if an applied electric field is high enough. This phenomenon, called field emission, is caused by a purely quantum-mechanical effect called tunnelling. A strong electric field of at least 1,000,000 volts per centimetre is applied to a metal surface. This field causes the surface barrier to become exceedingly thin (like a semitransparent sieve), so that the electrons can penetrate through the barrier without need of enough energy to surmount it, hence the term tunnelling. Fields of this size are conveniently formed by sharpening a metal electrode to a fine tip, just as a high electric field is formed at the point of a lightning rod.

Currents produced off sharp tips can be very large, as much as millions of amperes per square centimetre. Even though the tip is commonly much sharper than the point of a pin, the power produced by the electron stream can be hundreds of watts. Thus, it can act as the source of electrons for a high-power "flash" X-ray tube. It can also serve as the source for a high-magnification microscope, a device with magnification so large that it can resolve the individual atoms themselves.

Liquids and amorphous solids. Continued reference to *Liquids as conductors* the motion of electrons in crystals does not mean that liquids do not conduct electricity. Liquid mercury, for example, is widely used in electrical switches. The wonder is that liquid metals are as good conductors as they are; their conductivity at the melting point differs little from that of metals at room temperature. Somehow the electrons are able to pick their way through the helter-skelter collection of disordered ions that form the liquid without being continuously scattered.

A related kind of material, amorphous solids, may also conduct electricity well. Amorphous, meaning noncrystalline, metals and semiconductors are something of a laboratory curiosity at this time, but they may become important technically. Most promising, perhaps, is the prospect that amorphous semiconductors may be important in devices. Many elements, among them silicon, germanium, arsenic, antimony, selenium, tellurium, and some mixtures of them, can readily be solidified in an amorphous state. They are usually semiconductors in this amorphous, glassy state, but little filamentary islands of crystalline material of good conductivity can be made to form under certain circumstances. The entire phenomenon is not well understood nor are its applications fully evident (see GLASSY STATE).

MAGNETISM IN SOLIDS

Few subjects in science are more difficult to understand than magnetism. A magnetic field is invisible, it can be detected only by its effect on moving charges or on other magnetic fields, and the state of magnetization of a particular piece of material is not easy to measure. Yet magnetism is important technologically for such devices as motors, relay armatures, electrical transformers, and speakers for communications systems, and many natural phenomena are a result of magnetism, such as sunspots, the Van Allen radiation belts, and the Northern Lights (see EARTH, MAGNETIC FIELD OF).

One of the obstacles to understanding magnetic solids is *Observing the* difficulty of making measurements on them. Since *the* lines of magnetic force cannot be seen and in fact are *magnetic* simply a convenient way of thinking about magnetic in- *field* teraction, indirect methods of observing magnetic fields must be used; for example, the torsional, or twisting, effect on a permanent magnet. A magnetic field is produced by a coil of wire when a current flows through the coil. If the coil has 50 turns per metre and carries a current of one ampere, the magnetic field at the centre of the coil is said to be 50 ampere-turns per metre. This is about the average size of the Earth's magnetic field and is rather small. If an iron rod is inserted inside the coil, though, a much higher field results, perhaps 10,000 times as much. Such a field, 500,000 ampere-turns per metre, is large enough to be extremely useful. A field of this size is large enough to drive an electric motor, to activate an electric-power generator, or to power a loudspeaker.

Paramagnetism and diamagnetism. Not all materials inserted into the coil would increase the magnetic field by such a large amount. Some, called paramagnetic solids, would increase the field only slightly. Such solids include aluminum, sodium, manganese, chromium, magnesium, potassium, titanium, and many others. Another large group would actually decrease the strength of the field but again only slightly; they are called diamagnetic. They include copper, zinc, germanium, silver, gold, and bismuth. Neither the paramagnetic nor the diamagnetic materials are technically important, but it is instructive to examine the reason for their behaviour.

Paramagnetism occurs in matter because small magnetic dipoles on the individual atom are slightly aligned by a magnetic field. (A magnetic dipole of an atom can be considered to be a tiny permanent magnet.) The effect is small; the increase in magnetic field produced by paramagnetic materials is commonly only about one part in 100,000, at the greatest.

Diamagnetism is caused by a change in the orbital motion of electrons that occurs upon application of a magnetic field. The change causes formation of induced dipoles that are aligned opposite to the applied field; hence, they reduce the overall strength of the field. All materials possess some diamagnetic characteristics, even those that are paramagnetic or ferromagnetic; in these last cases, the positive effects overwhelm the negative diamagnetic features. Even at its strongest, the diamagnetism of most materials is very weak; for copper, silver, and gold the influence is only a few millionths of the external field.

Ferromagnetism. The strong magnetic effect that is called ferromagnetism is by far the most interesting. It exists in a number of metals and alloys, but by far the most important are the elements iron, cobalt, nickel, and their alloys. The first magnetic materials known to man were not these pure metals and alloys, however, but lodestone, a type of iron oxide. This material, which occurs in nature in great quantity, was known for its magnetic qualities at least as early as 600 BC. Modern alloys of this same kind, called ferrites, are exceedingly important.

Just as the conduction of electric current is a property of the electrons (*i.e.*, their charge), so is magnetism a basic property of the electrons. Each electron behaves like a small permanent magnet of a certain size, a fundamental unit given the name Bohr magneton. This tiny dipole is an inherent characteristic of the electron, and no magnetic field is required to produce it. Whereas the electrical conductivity of solids is caused by the motion of the free electrons, the electrons important to ferromagnetism in solids are the ion-core electrons. In fact, not all of them contribute, since they partly cancel each other. The ferromagnetic materials (*e.g.*, iron, cobalt, and nickel) are those for which the cancellation is not complete and the effects of some of the inherent dipoles add. Furthermore, dipoles interact so as to align themselves parallel to each other in certain directions, even in the absence of a field. Since different materials have different numbers of uncompensated dipoles, the strength of magnetic materials differs. For example, cobalt and iron have about the same strength, nickel only about one-third as much.

Notions about the origins and details of magnetism developed gradually, culminating about 1910 in a theory by the French physicist Pierre-Ernest Weiss. His theory of magnetization and demagnetization utilizes the concept of domains, small regions in which dipoles on adjacent ions spontaneously align themselves parallel. Direct observation of domains required another two decades of work, but they were observed in the 1930s by Francis Bitter, an American physicist. By now, a great deal is known about the structure of domains and the details of the magnetization process.

Ferromagnetism disappears above a certain temperature, called the Curie temperature. The self-alignment capability of the dipoles gradually disappears as the temperature goes up, because the increasing energy of the thermal vibrations misaligns the dipoles. Finally, the dipoles lose their self-aligning capability completely, and the solid is no longer ferromagnetic. The Curie temperature of nickel is 358° C (676° F), of iron, 770° C (1,418° F), and of cobalt, 1,131° C (2,068° F). Alloys of these elements have intermediate Curie temperature in general; obviously, a ferromagnetic material must have a Curie temperature higher than any temperature at which it is actually used.

Soft magnetic materials. Soft ferromagnetic materials become demagnetized easily when the external field is removed. Hard magnetic materials become magnetized and demagnetized with great difficulty. The most widely used soft magnetic material is transformer steel, an alloy of iron with a few percent of silicon. Another group consists of

iron–nickel alloys, one of 50–50, the other around 20–80, both being called Permalloys. A third alloy, with certain characteristics superior to either of these groups, has a composition of around 78% nickel, 18% iron, and 4% molybdenum; appropriately, it is called Supermalloy.

Magnetic materials made from metals become useless at high frequencies, because energy losses caused by eddy currents are too high to be tolerated. The problem is solved through use of magnetic insulators, mainly oxides of iron. One important group of these oxides (called ferrites) is based on the iron oxide compound Fe_3O_4. This is the natural magnetic material that constitutes lodestone.

An interesting and promising material is a special group of magnetic iron oxides having the garnet structure. A typical example is yttrium iron oxide, $Y_3Fe_5O_{12}$. Tiny cylindrical domains can be formed across thin strips of this material, the direction of magnetization in a domain being opposite to that of the material surrounding it. These little cylinders behave like tiny magnetic "bubbles"; they are stable in size and can be moved about very rapidly by a small magnetic field. The bubbles are so small, about 0.001 millimetre in diameter, that their density in a sheet can be very high, perhaps 1,000,000 per square inch. They can also be made to step from site to site about 1,000,000 times per second with expenditure of very small energy. They have potential use as high-density, rapid access memory systems for computers.

Hard magnetic materials. Striking as are the advances that have been made in soft magnetic materials, advances in the hard magnetic materials for permanent magnets are just as startling. Three periods characterize the development of permanent magnets in the last century. The first, from about 1880 to 1930, saw a development of special steels; the magneto of the early automobiles and the old telephone receiver got their size and shape from the quality of these steels. In the second period, from 1930 to 1960, the Alnicos (*i.e.*, alloys of iron with copper, titanium, aluminum, nickel, and cobalt) were supreme, yielding smaller, stronger magnets, though so brittle and hard that they could not be fashioned by machine. Finally, after 1960, the ceramic magnets and alloys of the rare earths have been developed. The successes achieved in these three periods depend on a particular characteristic of magnetic materials.

The word permanent applied to magnets means "not easily demagnetized." This characteristic is measured by the size of field necessary to reduce the magnetization of a permanent magnet to zero, called the coercive field. Good permanent magnets must have coercive fields of 50,000 ampere-turns per metre or more. Such quality was first achieved by use of physically hard tool steels (a typical alloy had 71% iron, 17% molybdenum, 12% cobalt), which produced large magnetic fields because they contained large amounts of iron and cobalt. They also contained many finely dispersed carbides that impede motion of the domain walls. Thus, they were not easily demagnetized; domain walls separating domains of opposite polarity could not easily move through the material.

The permanent-magnet tool steels were replaced by materials whose high coercive force comes from the actual shape of magnetized regions in the alloys. The alloy Alnico is typical. It consists of extremely fine needlelike particles of magnetic material imbedded in a nonmagnetic binder. When solidified and heat-treated in a magnetic field, the long particles tend to line up with the field, yielding a strong magnet. If the particles are fine enough, domain walls cannot form in them, and the individual particles cannot be readily demagnetized.

Small-particle theory in the 1950s led to attempts to produce permanent magnets by dispersing fine suspensions of iron in plastic or a metallic binder. Several products were made and sold, but manufacturing problems are difficult, and these magnets are not of great commercial importance.

The third phase of permanent-magnet development has used a property known as crystalline anisotropy. Simply put, certain directions in a crystal are magnetically pre-

Electrons and magnetism

The ferrites

Anisotropy

ferred over others. For iron, the cube edge is preferred; for nickel, the cube diagonal; and, for cobalt, the axis normal to the hexagonal plane. In switching the direction of magnetization from one preferred direction to another, parts of the crystal will be at one time or another in a higher energy state—hence, a large coercive force is required to change the direction of magnetization.

Attempts have been made for many years to find alloys that would utilize this strong directional preference. Until recently, they were largely unsuccessful. Work on ferrites, though, led to discovery of a hexagonal oxide of iron, $BaFe_{12}O_{19}$, that has high coercive force. Like the cubic ferrites based on the Fe_3O_4 structure, however, it does not produce the highest magnetic fields, since much of its volume is taken up by nonmagnetic ions. Even so, many ceramic magnets are made from this material.

Strenuous attempts were made in the 1960s to find a metallic alloy with hexagonal structure, large anisotropy, and large density of a high-moment ion. Thus, it would be a strong magnet to give high field and a hard magnet to resist demagnetization. Such a group of materials has been found, a hexagonal compound of cobalt with some of the rare-earth metals. A compound of cobalt with samarium, Co_5Sm, makes a permanent magnet more than ten times as strong as the best Alnico.

III. Interaction of radiation with matter

The electromagnetic spectrum covers an immense range of frequencies. That part most commonly used, visible light, is but a tiny part of the known range. Even so, this discussion is concentrated on the interaction of the visible spectrum with matter (see also the articles RADIATION EFFECTS ON MATTER; ELECTROMAGNETIC RADIATION).

Electromagnetic waves are pulsations of electric and magnetic fields. In a vacuum they travel with a velocity of 300,000 kilometres per second (186,000 miles per second). Their frequency, v, and wavelength, λ, are related to their velocity, c, by a simple equation in which the velocity equals the product of wavelength and frequency: $v\lambda = c$. A stationary observer who could detect the electric field of the waves as it passed by would find that its strength, E, would have some maximum amplitude, A, and would vary with time in a very regular fashion. Furthermore, the electric field is maximum at right angles to the direction of motion of the wave.

The energy of electromagnetic waves is quantized; that is, the energy comes in discrete, well-defined units called photons, the size of which is given by the product, hv, of a universal number called Planck's constant, h, and the frequency, v, of the wave. Strong radiation fields contain more photons than weak ones, but all photons of a given frequency have the same energy.

Essential features of electromagnetic waves

Thus, electromagnetic waves have four essential features: (1) they travel with a certain speed, 186,000 miles per second in vacuum but less in solids, liquids, or gases; (2) each wave has a particular frequency that is determined by the manner in which it is excited; (3) the wave consists of electric and magnetic fields at right angles to the direction of propagation, and these fields vary sinusoidally (i.e., their values when charted follow a sine curve) with time as observed by a stationary observer; (4) the energy of the wave is packaged into individual units, called photons, whose energy has magnitude hv.

For all the value of materials as building materials, for all their value in electrical and magnetic uses, nothing about materials is more important to mankind than this relationship to electromagnetic radiation. The infrared in the sun's rays provides warmth; more detailed information is provided by sight than by any other sense; food and clothing come ultimately from chemical interactions of plants with radiation. The sections that follow deal with the way materials behave when they are illuminated with radiation, the changes in the internal structure induced by the energy of incoming waves, and the way radiation is generated in materials.

BEHAVIOUR OF SOLIDS ILLUMINATED WITH RADIATION

Most materials do not emit light of their own; mostly, they simply reflect light, transmit it, or absorb it. How matter behaves when illuminated depends on what the electrons do. If the light photon has a frequency such that its energy matches the energy needed to excite an electron to a higher state, then the photon may be absorbed. The electron, which may be an ion-core electron or one of the free electrons in a solid, may return to its initial state from this higher energy excited state by re-emission of the photon of the same frequency v. Detection of this photon permits viewing of an object by reflected (that is, by re-emitted) light. The process of absorption and re-emission of photons is very selective. If the energy of the incoming photon does not closely match the required excitation energy, no excitation occurs. The sharpness of absorption lines for gas atoms can be noted by observation of the dark lines observed in spectra of nebulae and stars, including the sun (see ASTRONOMICAL SPECTROSCOPY, PRINCIPLES OF). Radiation falling on solids and liquids must meet this same requirement of energy matching, called resonance, but solids have such an abundance of frequencies of excitation possible that excitations may exist in broad ranges of frequency.

Transparency of ice

Ice is transparent to visible light because no excitations exist whose energy matches photons in the visible part of the spectrum. Excitation levels do exist in the ultraviolet, so ice is opaque to ultraviolet. Radiation in this part of the spectrum has wavelengths shorter than 4,000 angstrom units; i.e., frequencies greater than 10^{15} hertz (or cycles per second). Photons of this frequency have energies of about 1.6×10^{-19} calorie; i.e., about four electron volts. This is the energy required to free a valence electron in the ice crystal. Ice (liquid water as well) also absorbs photons with frequencies in the infrared; were it not so, all lakes and rivers might be frozen permanently.

The warming of ice and water by infrared radiation shows another feature of excitation of electrons by photons. Energy of excitation in solids and liquids need not be re-emitted as the same type of photons—the energy may be transferred to thermal vibrations (that is, into heat), or it may produce other physical or chemical changes in matter.

Transparency of insulators

Insulators such as glass, quartz, diamond, and rocksalt crystals are transparent to visible light for the same reason as ice. No excitation resonances exist in the visible spectrum, because the valence electrons are so tightly bound that photons with energy in the ultraviolet are required to free them. Addition of impurities with resonances in the visible range, however, reduces the transparency and may give the crystal a colour. Crystalline aluminum oxide, corundum, is transparent to visible light; addition of a little chromium gives it a red colour to produce the gemstone ruby; addition of titanium and iron produces the blue sapphire (see GEMSTONES).

Metals are opaque to visible light; they also reflect light with little loss. This reflection comes entirely from the free electrons. These electrons are able to move so freely that no electric field may be propagated in the solid, and light penetrates only a few hundred angstroms. The motion of the electrons, in fact, causes the light to be re-emitted; indeed, if the surface of the metal is smooth, the re-emitted radiation from all parts of the surface is in phase, and the surface acts like a mirror.

Metals are excellent reflectors of radiation not only in the visible part of the spectrum but also for radiation of longer wavelength, far into the infrared ($\lambda = 1$ to 500 microns). Gradually, the depth of penetration of the wave increases, and transformation of the incident energy to heat increases. Power lines conducting electric current alternating at 60 cycles per second to heat a lamp filament are supplying radiation of wavelength 5,000,000 metres to the metal. All of this energy is absorbed in the filament; none is reflected (neglecting inductive effects of the tiny coil). Waves with even lower frequency have been detected in nature by geophysicists using sensitive magnetometers. These waves (of wavelength up to 10,-000,000,000 metres) are thought to penetrate deeply into the earth—far down into the molten metallic core.

Optical properties of semiconductors lie between those of metals and those of insulators. They are commonly transparent at radio frequencies and down into the infrared. In the visible region they are opaque like metals; incident photons are absorbed by the excitation of valence electrons into higher energy states. For germanium the crossover wavelength is about 15,000 angstroms, for silicon about 12,000.

The most useful radiations in the other direction (*i.e.*, to shorter wavelengths) occur in the X-ray region (from one to 1,000 angstroms). These waves have energy sufficiently large to excite the ion-core electrons in all materials, whether metals, semiconductors, or insulators. Thus, discrete line absorption occurs at well-defined frequencies. Furthermore, at wavelengths in the range of one to five angstroms, diffraction effects occur, permitting crystal-structure determination to be made (see X-RAYS; CRYSTALLOGRAPHY).

Photochemical reactions, such as photosynthesis, photography, and the physics and chemistry of vision, constitute a fascinating field of study, the details of which are treated in the articles PHOTOCHEMICAL REACTIONS; PHOTOGRAPHY, TECHNOLOGY OF; and EYE AND VISION, HUMAN.

GENERATION OF ELECTROMAGNETIC RADIATION

The immediate re-emission of incident radiation associated with reflection or transmission of incident photons is not really generation of radiation. Solids (and liquids and gases), however, can be self-luminous; they may generate photons from energy supplied to the solid in some other form. The photons emitted may have a sharp, well-defined frequency, or they may cover a broad range of frequencies.

Conversion of energy into photons

Energy can be converted into photons in a variety of ways. The most important is the conversion of heat into light—thermoluminescence. Another way, electron bombardment, is important in luminescence of both solids and gases. Fission and fusion reactions produce high-energy photons as well as ions and elementary particles of high kinetic energy. Some solids have the capability of converting photons of incoming radiation into photons of another frequency, photoluminescence. Others produce light by mechanical means, by rupture of materials, a phenomenon called triboluminescence; still others convert chemical energy into light, chemiluminescence; finally, some solids convert electrical energy into photons directly, electroluminescence.

The variety of ways in which these phenomena can occur is vast, almost beyond counting if one considers that they can occur in combination. Therefore, the discussion below is limited to a few examples that are important because of practical value or because of insight they give into basic features of the emission processes.

Monochromatic radiation. Photons of a single frequency—*i.e.*, monochromatic radiation—are produced when atoms or molecules in some excited state revert to a lower state. These photons may be of high energy, such as X-rays or gamma rays, if the states are of widely different energy; that is, different by more than 1,000 electron volts. Photons are in the visible spectrum if the energy difference is from 1.5 to three electron volts. The radiation is in the infrared or even radio wavelengths if the transitions involve energy differences of fractions of an electron volt.

Excitation of electrons to the higher states can be provided by several means. An electric discharge—a spark —can eject electrons from low levels into higher levels in the atom. A continuous electric arc, as in a neon tube or a sodium-vapour lamp, may produce excited states. Incident photons or high-energy electrons may provide energy for excitation.

Monochromatic light from isolated atoms (as in a gas) is of immense value. By its use the electronic structure of atoms has been deduced and many practical light sources have been developed: neon, sodium-vapour and mercury-vapour lamps, fluorescent lamps, and X-ray tubes. And an additional important feature, laser action, has recently been discovered and is now being exploited.

Laser emission

Laser emission results from a special type of interaction of light with atoms. Not only can radiation be absorbed if the photon energy matches an excitation energy of an atom, but an additional photon (of the same energy) can be emitted if the atom is already in the excited state. This emission process, called stimulated emission, results in amplification of light, in contrast to dimunition caused by absorption. Amplification will predominate if more atoms are in the excited state than in the lower state and, in fact, sufficiently more to compensate for loss of photons that escape without participating in the process. Many materials are suitable for holding the excited atoms: gases (carbon dioxide is an example), liquids (such as organic molecules in alcohol), or solids (ruby or glass containing atoms of the rare-earth metal neodymium).

Band of radiation. Every photon has a certain frequency, but photons within a band of frequencies will be emitted if the allowed electron transitions form a continuous range. Much of the radiation of use is of this type; three examples are described in the following paragraphs.

1. Excitation of free electrons in metals by varying electric fields can be used to excite radio waves. By means of the electric field generated by an oscillator, the free electrons in an antenna are accelerated and decelerated. These electrons oscillating in phase in the antenna radiate photons whose frequency is that of the oscillator. The electrons themselves do not possess an inherent resonant frequency; rather, the frequency is set by the oscillator and the antenna. Enormous amounts of power, hundreds of thousands of watts (corresponding to myriads of individual photons), can be radiated in the radio and television frequencies.

2. Radiation from solids by thermally induced motion of atoms is by far the most important scheme of energy conversion. The allowed frequencies of vibration of atoms and groups of atoms in solids form a continuous band; hence, the radiation itself covers a wide range of frequencies. The greatest amount of light comes in the infrared and the visible parts of the electromagnetic spectrum; thus, hot objects can be used as sources of both heat and visible light.

Metals, semiconductors, and insulators, both solid and liquid, produce such radiation. The efficiency of production of light depends partly on the temperature of the material; the maximum energy in the spectrum comes at shorter wavelengths as the temperature of the solid is increased. Thus, a heat lamp may operate at 800° C (1,500° F), an incandescent lamp at 2,500° C (4,500° F). The energy radiated in the visible part of the spectrum from a lamp filament—*e.g.*, a 100-watt lamp—is only a few percent of the electrical energy supplied to the lamp. Even so, a 100-watt lamp filament radiates about 10^{19} photons per second in the visible range.

3. The abrupt deceleration of high-energy electrons when they strike solids also produces radiation in a broad band. This effect is most widely used to produce X-rays. With operating voltages of 10,000 to 50,000 volts, X-rays of wavelengths near one angstrom are generated when the incident electrons are slowed by collision with lattice ions of the target. Of course, the incident electrons may also cause generation of line spectra characteristic of the target ions, typically tungsten or molybdenum. The overall emission spectrum thus consists of sharp line spectra superimposed on broad-band (so-called white) radiation.

Production of X-rays

Photoluminescence. Materials may emit radiation of one wavelength when they are irradiated with photons of another wavelength. This event, photoluminescence, is most widely used to produce visible light, but it also occurs in the X-ray region and in other regions of the electromagnetic spectrum. Radiation emitted immediately upon absorption of the incident light is called fluorescent radiation; such radiation in the visible spectrum is frequently produced when ultraviolet light, often the characteristic lines of mercury, is absorbed by an inorganic compound, often a metal oxide, a phosphide, or a sulfide, or by an organic material such as motor oil. The absorption of the incident photons is accompanied by excitation of valence electrons into some excited state. Recovery to the original state does not occur by a single-step process involving re-emission of a photon of the original wavelength; rather, the excited state decays in two or more steps to the original state; hence, the re-emitted photons are of less energy (*i.e.*, of longer wavelength) than the original photons.

Practical use of fluorescence in lighting uses the mercury lines excited by electrons streaming through mercury vapour. These ultraviolet lines are absorbed by a mixture of compounds (called phosphors) coated on the inside of the glass envelope. These phosphors, blended to give the desired colour, produce visible light.

Visible light can also be produced by these same phosphors if the incident "radiation" is electrons. This process —cathodoluminescence—is widely used in cathode-ray tubes. Television display tubes and their predecessor— tubes for cathode-ray oscilloscopes—use this mode of light excitation.

Many other types of interactions of radiation with matter exist, some of which have practical application while others have only scientific interest; for details of these, see LIGHT; SPECTROSCOPY, PRINCIPLES OF; MOSSBAUER EFFECT; LUMINESCENCE.

BIBLIOGRAPHY. Among the most useful sources for the general reader are the magazine *Scientific American*, especially the September 1967 issue on "Materials" and the September 1968 issue on "Light"; issues of *Science* (weekly), the journal of the American Association for the Advancement of Science; and *Physics Today* (monthly), of the American Physical Society. General reference books include: HENRY HODGES, *Technology of the Ancient World* (1970), a readable history of man's development of materials usage; C.S. SMITH, *A History of Metallography* (1960); LAWRENCE VAN VLACK, *Elements of Materials Science* (1964), an elementary modern textbook; CHARLES A. WERT and ROBB M. THOMSON, *The Physics of Solids*, 2nd ed. (1970), an intermediate level text; CHARLES KITTEL, *Introduction to Solid State Physics*, 4th ed. (1971), an advanced level text; and JOHN ZIMAN, *Electrons and Phonons* (1960), a treatise. See also the series FREDERICK SEITZ and DAVID TURNBULL, *Solid State Physics*, 22 vol. (1956–71), written for the expert.

The classic reference work on bonding is LINUS PAULING, *Nature of the Chemical Bond and the Structure of Molecules and Crystals*, 3rd ed. (1960). A readable treatment of crystal structure is C.S. BARRETT and T.B. MASSALSKI, *Structure of Metals*, 3rd ed. (1966).

References on mechanical properties are many; among the most useful at an intermediate level are A.H. COTTRELL, *The Mechanical Properties of Matter* (1964); and GEORGE E. DIETER, JR., *Mechanical Metallurgy* (1961). Interaction of radiation with matter may be found in many books, among them: EARLE B. BROWN, *Modern Optics* (1965); and GRANT R. FOWLES, *Introduction to Modern Optics* (1968); RALPH S. BECKER, *Theory and Interpretation of Fluorescence and Phosphorescence* (1969); and P.R. THORNTON, *The Physics of Electroluminescent Devices* (1967). General books on magnetism and magnetic materials are: JAN SMIT (ed.), *Magnetic Properties of Materials* (1971); JOHN E. THOMPSON, *The Magnetic Properties of Materials* (1968); and ROY CAREY and EVAN D. ISAAC, *Magnetic Domains and Techniques for Their Observation* (1966). The classic book on materials of ferromagnetism for many years has been RICHARD M. BOZORTH, *Ferromagnetism* (1956).

(C.A.W./H.K.B.)

Solomon

Solomon, the son and successor of David, has traditionally been remembered as the greatest king of Israel, although some modern historians have been less favourable in their judgment of him. The dates of his reign are not known with certainty, but it was a long reign of about 40 years that occurred in the middle of the 10th century BC. Nearly all that is factually known of him comes from the Bible (especially I Kings 1–11 and II Chron. 1–9). While the latter already contains some legendary material, it is, in the main, a wealth of historical facts of the most prosaic and reliable nature.

Background. Solomon's background is both well-known and colourful. His father, David, was a self-made king, who, against great odds, founded the Judean dynasty and carved out an empire from the border of Egypt to the Euphrates River. His first and greatest enemies were the Philistines, who controlled Palestine and kept the Tyrians and Sidonians from prospering on the sea. By training the Israelite infantry, especially the bowmen, he proved more than a match for Philistine and other foes who employed horses and chariots. In addition, David made common cause with King Hiram of Tyre, forming a land and sea alliance that endured into Solomon's reign. Solomon, accordingly, inherited a considerable empire, along with a Phoenician ally of prime importance for naval and merchant marine operations.

Solomon's mother was Bathsheba, formerly the wife of David's Hittite general, Uriah. Bathsheba proved to be adept at court intrigue, and it is possible that she had exposed herself to David's susceptible eye with a view to rising from general's wife to queen.

David seems to have been senile toward the close of his reign, and one of his wives, Haggith, tried to execute a plot in which her son, Adonijah, would be appointed as David's successor. Adonijah enlisted the aid of powerful allies: David's senior general, Joab, Abiathar the priest, and several other court figures. It was only through the efforts of Bathsheba, in concert with the prophet Nathan, that Solomon, who was younger than several of his brothers, was anointed king while David was still alive.

Empire builder. As soon as he acceded to the throne, Solomon consolidated his position by liquidating his opponents ruthlessly, one by one. Once rid of his foes, he established his friends in the key posts of the military, governmental, and religious institutions. In an ancient Near Eastern empire, this was almost the only means of establishing stable government.

Solomon also strengthened his position through marital alliances. Although the astonishing harem of Solomon— 700 wives and 300 concubines—recorded in I Kings is no doubt an exaggeration of popular tradition, the figures do indicate his position as a grand monarch. Such a ménage brought prestige as well as pleasure, and the marriages were a form of diplomacy. He wed the sisters and daughters of kings from far and wide, cementing alliances of arms and trade to facilitate his establishment of a huge commercial empire. One of his brides was the daughter of an Egyptian pharaoh; the pharaoh captured and burned down the Canaanite city of Gezer and gave it to his son-in-law Solomon.

Marital alliances

Like all empire builders, Solomon maintained his dominions with military strength. In addition to infantry, he had at his disposal impressive chariotry and cavalry. II Chron. 8 recounts Solomon's successful military operations in Syria, where his targets included Tadmor-Palmyra, a caravan oasis city in the desert, midway between Syria and Mesopotamia. His aim was the control of a great overland trading route. To consolidate his interests in the province, he planted Israelite colonies to look after military, administrative, and commercial matters. Such colonies, often including cities in which chariots and provisions were kept, were in the long tradition of combining mercantile and military personnel to take care of their sovereign's trading interests far from home. Megiddo, a town located at the pass through the Carmel range connecting the coastal plain with the Plain of Esdraelon, is the best preserved example of one of Solomon's cities. The remains of stalls for 450 horses discovered in Megiddo show that the figures of 1,400 chariots and 12,000 horses given for Solomon's forces in I Kings are scarcely exaggerated. (Some scholars question whether these are horse stalls or shop stalls.) The network of Solomon's far-flung trading posts eventually formed the nucleus of the first great Jewish Diaspora.

Palestine was destined to be an important centre because of its strategic location for trade by land and sea. By land, it alone connects Asia and Africa; and, along with Egypt, it is the only area with ports on the Atlantic–Mediterranean and Red Sea–Indian Ocean waterways. It was Solomon who fulfilled the commercial destiny of Palestine and brought it to its greatest heights.

The nature of his empire was predominantly commercial—it served him and friendly rulers to increase trade by land and sea. Hiram of Tyre, for example, needed the port of Ezion-geber, near Elath on the Gulf of Aqaba, which leads into the Red Sea and thence into the Indian Ocean. The joint merchant marine expeditions of Hiram and Solomon sailed practically to the ends of the known world. Some of the scheduled voyages took three years for the round trip.

Relations with the Queen of Sheba

A celebrated episode in the reign of Solomon is the visit of the Queen of Sheba. Her south Arabian kingdom lay along the Red Sea route into the Indian Ocean, and her terrain was rich in gold, frankincense, and myrrh. Solomon needed her products and her trade routes for maintaining his commercial network; she needed Solomon's cooperation for marketing her goods in the Mediterranean via his Palestinian ports. Legend makes much of a romance between the Queen of Sheba and Solomon, for his granting her "all that she desired, whatever she asked" (I Kings 10:13) has been interpreted to include an offspring.

Builder, administrator, and sage. The demand for fortresses and garrison cities throughout his homeland and empire made it necessary for Solomon to embark on a vast building program; the prosperity of the nation made such a program possible. He was especially lavish with his capital, Jerusalem, where he erected a city wall, a construction called the Millo, the royal palace, and the famous Temple. Around Jerusalem (but not in the Holy City itself), he built facilities, including shrines, for the main groups of foreigners on trading missions in Israel. Later generations, in less secure and less prosperous times, destroyed those shrines around Jerusalem in a parochial spirit that could not accommodate itself to Solomon's ecumenical outlook. Solomon's Temple was to assume an importance far beyond what its dimensions might suggest, for its site became the only central shrine for Judaism and early Christianity.

The prayer ascribed to Solomon in I Kings 8 when he dedicated the Temple is of far-reaching significance. In it the God of Jerusalem is the one and only God of the universe. In addition to invoking blessings on God's people Israel, Solomon begs God to heed also the prayers of aliens who come from the ends of the earth, having heard of the fame of Jerusalem and the great God who dwells there; and he reminds God that helping such aliens will further enhance the reputation of God and his Temple in

Effects of Solomon's trade policy

every land. Solomon's involvement in international trade brought in its train intellectual and spiritual universalism, but it took a few centuries of maturation for the universality of the Solomonic age to find its classical expression in the words of Israel's prophets. Practical universality gave rise to universal religion, and not vice versa. Furthermore, international trade taught men the lesson that international peace is necessary for prosperity. The requirements of the Solomonic age led to the first known formulation of international peace; i.e., "nation shall not lift up sword against nation, neither shall they learn war anymore" (Isaiah 2, Micah 4).

The vigour of Solomon's building program made it oppressive. For example, men had to put in one month out of every three in forced labour. In theory, such labour was to be performed by the Canaanites—not by the noble Hebrew tribesmen, who were supposed to be the administrators, priests, and fighters. But Solomon's demands were such that there were not enough Canaanites to go around, so that Israelites were forced to do menial labour for the crown.

Solomon was a vigorous administrator, and he realized that the old division of the nation into 12 tribes posed a threat to the unity of the realm because the tribal feeling that was retained was not for the good of the state. Accordingly, he redivided the realm into 12 administrative districts, deviating, for the most part, from the tribal boundaries. The figure of 12 was retained because each district was to "support the palace" (i.e., shoulder federal obligations) for one of the 12 months in the year. Each district had its royally appointed governor, and a chief ruled over the 12 governors. Another important but unpopular appointee of the king was the chief of taxation; taxes were exacted most commonly in the form of forced labour and in kind.

Reputation

Solomon also became famous as a sage. When two harlots each claimed to be the mother of the same baby, he determined the real mother by each woman's reaction to the prospect of dividing the child into two halves. Solo-

mon was deemed wiser than all the sages of Egypt and the Near East—even wiser than some ancient paragons of wisdom. The book of Proverbs contains collections of aphorisms and other wise teachings attributed to him. Solomon was also famed as a poet who composed 1,005 songs. The biblical Song of Solomon is attributed to him in the opening verse. His reputation as a great lover, reflected in the size of his harem, is appropriately a major theme in the Song of Solomon. Post-biblical tradition attributed later works to him: the apocryphal Wisdom of Solomon, on the one hand, and the *Odes of Solomon* and *Psalms of Solomon*, on the other, are tributes to his stature as a sage and poet.

Solomon's legend also stresses another dimension of his prowess: his power over all creatures, natural and supernatural. It was he, according to *The Arabian Nights*, who imprisoned jinn (supernatural beings below the level of angels and demons) in sealed jars and cast them into the sea. Magic texts, such as the Aramaic *Incantation Bowls*, invoke the potent seal of Solomon son of David. When Jesus is called "the Son of David," it does not mean simply that he was of the royal Davidic line but that the wonder-working Christ, against whom no demon could stand, was a veritable "Solomon son of David," that master over men and jinn.

Division of the nation. Solomon's personal prestige and genius were required to perpetuate the powerful nation he had acquired from his father and then further strengthened. It is suspected that the increase in Israel's wealth was matched by an increase in extravagance and that the wealth was not diffused to the people. It is also considered possible that Solomon's treatment of the northern tribes showed favouritism to his own tribe of Judah. When his son Rehoboam succeeded him, the northern tribes wanted to know his policy concerning the burdens borne by the people. Rehoboam ill-advisedly announced a harsher course, whereupon the northern tribes seceded and formed their own Kingdom of Israel, leaving the descendants of Solomon with the southern Kingdom of Judah. Thus Solomon's empire was lost beyond recall, and even the homeland was split into two, often hostile, kingdoms.

BIBLIOGRAPHY. EDOUARD MEYER, *Geschichte des Altertums*, 2nd ed., vol. 2 (1931), provides a succinct but masterful account of Solomon in ancient Near Eastern context. A history of Solomon's reign with extensive bibliography is provided by O. EISSFELDT, "The Hebrew Kingdoms," in *Cambridge Ancient History*, rev. ed., vol. 2, ch. 34 (1965). CYRUS H. GORDON, *The Ancient Near East*, pp. 180–189 (1965), offers an account of Solomon, in keeping with the Bible sources but within the framework of extra-biblical materials. For a detailed analysis of the subject, see JAMES A. MONTGOMERY, *The Books of Kings* (1951). CYRUS H. GORDON, *Before Columbus*, pp. 113–135 (1971), outlines Solomon's maritime activities in a global setting. MARTIN NOTH, *Geschichte Israels* (1958; Eng. trans., *The History of Israel*, 2nd ed. rev., 1960), gives an account of Solomon within a recent standard history.

(C.H.G.)

Solon

Solon, Athenian statesman and poet, embodied the cardinal Greek virtue of moderation. He put an end to the worst evils of poverty in Attica (the territory of the city-state of Athens) and provided his fellow countrymen with a balanced constitution and a humane code of laws. Standing, in time, midway between the epic poets Homer and Hesiod (fl c. 800) and the 5th-century classical tragedians Aeschylus, Sophocles, and Euripides, Solon was also Athens' first poet—and a poet who truly belonged to Athens. As the medium through which he warned, challenged, counselled the people, and urged them to action, his poetry was the instrument of his statesmanship.

In Solon's lifetime (c. 630–c. 560 BC), the Greeks had not yet begun to write history or biography. It was not until the 5th century that accounts of his life and works began to be put together, on the evidence of his poems (of which the 300 or so lines preserved by quotation probably represent only a small proportion), his law code, oral tradition, and inference from existing institutions. Although certain details have a legendary ring, the main features of the story seem to be reliable.

Solon was of noble descent but moderate means. As the tradition states and his travels and economic measures suggest, he may have been a merchant. He first became prominent about 600 BC, when the Athenians were disheartened by ill success in a war with their neighbours of Megara for possession of the island of Salamis. By publicly reciting a poem that made the issue a matter of national honour and that called on the Athenians to "arise and come to Salamis, to win that fair island and undo our shame," Solon induced them to resume the war, which they eventually won.

Social and
political
conditions
of
6th-century
Greece

The early 6th century was a troubled time for the Athenians in other ways as well. Society was dominated by an aristocracy of birth, the eupatridae, who owned the best land, monopolized the government, and were themselves split into rival factions. The poorer farmers were easily driven into debt by them and when unable to pay were reduced to the condition of serfs on their own land and, in extreme cases, sold into slavery. The intermediate classes of middling farmers, craftsmen, and merchants resented their exclusion from the government. As Solon described it, no Athenian could escape these social, economic, and political evils:

The public evil enters the house of each man, the gates of his courtyard cannot keep it out, it leaps over the high wall; let him flee to a corner of his bedchamber, it will certainly find him out.

The public evil might well have culminated in a revolution and subsequent tyranny (dictatorship), as it had in other Greek states, had it not been for Solon, to whom Athenians of all classes turned in the hope of a generally satisfactory solution of their problems. Because he believed in moderation and in an ordered society in which each class had its proper place and function, his solution was not revolution but reform.

Economic reforms. Solon had already held office as archon (annual chief ruler) c. 594 BC. It was probably about 20 years later that he was given full powers as reformer and legislator. His first concern was to relieve the immediate distress caused by debt. He redeemed all the forfeited land and freed all the enslaved citizens, probably by fiat. This measure, known popularly as the "shaking off of burdens," was described by Solon in one of his poems:

Relief for
debtors

These things the black earth . . . could best witness for the judgement of posterity; from whose surface I plucked up the marking-stones [probably signs of the farmers' indebtedness] planted all about, so that she who was enslaved is now free. And I brought back to Athens . . . many who had been sold, justly or unjustly, or who had fled under the constraint of debt, wandering far afield and no longer speaking the Attic tongue; and I freed those who suffered shameful slavery here and trembled at their masters' whims.

He also prohibited for the future all loans secured on the borrower's person. But he refused to go to the length demanded by the poor, which was to redistribute the land. Instead, he passed measures designed to increase the general prosperity and to provide alternative occupations for those unable to live by farming: *e.g.*, trades and professions were encouraged; the export of produce other than olive oil was forbidden (so much grain had been exported that not enough remained to feed the population of Attica); the circulation of coined money (invented in Solon's lifetime) was stimulated by the minting of a native Athenian coinage on a more suitable standard than that of the coins of neighbours, which had been used hitherto; and new weights and measures were introduced. The rapid spread of the new coinage and of Athenian products, particularly olive oil and pottery, throughout the commercial world of the times, attested by archaeology, shows that these measures were effective. Poverty, though not eliminated, was never again in Attica the crying evil that it had been before Solon's reforms.

Political reforms. Solon's new political constitution abolished the monopoly of the eupatridae and substituted for it government by the wealthy citizens. He instituted a census of annual income, reckoned primarily in measures

of grain, oil, and wine, the principal products of the soil, and divided the citizens into four income groups, accordingly. (Those whose income was in other forms, including money, must have been rated on a system of equivalents.) Henceforth, political privilege was allotted on the basis of these divisions, without regard to birth. All citizens were entitled to attend the general Assembly (Ecclesia), which became, at least potentially, the sovereign body, entitled to pass laws and decrees, elect officials, and hear appeals from the most important decisions of the courts. All but those in the poorest group might serve, a year at a time, on a new Council of Four Hundred, which was to prepare business for the Assembly. The higher governmental posts were reserved for citizens of the top two income groups. Thus, the foundations of the future democracy were laid. But a strong conservative element remained in the ancient Council of the Hill of Ares (Areopagus), and the people themselves for a long time preferred to entrust the most important positions to members of the old aristocratic families.

Code of laws. Solon's third great contribution to the future good of Athens was his new code of laws. The first written code at Athens, that of Draco (c. 624 BC), was still in force. Draco's laws were shockingly severe (hence the term draconian)—so severe that they were said to have been written not in ink but in blood. On the civil side they permitted enslavement for debt; and death seems to have been the penalty for almost all criminal offenses. Solon revised every statute except that on homicide and made Athenian law altogether more humane. His code, though supplemented and modified, remained the foundation of Athenian statute law until the end of the 5th century, and parts of it were embodied in the new codification made at that time.

Response to Solon's reforms. When Solon had completed his task, complaints came in from all sides. In attempting to satisfy all, he had satisfied none. The nobles had hoped that he would make only marginal changes; the poor, that he would distribute all the land in equal shares and, if necessary, make himself tyrant in order to enforce the redistribution. But Solon, although concerned for freedom, justice, and humanity, was no egalitarian, nor had he any ambition for autocratic power. His poems make this clear:

Solon and
tyranny

I gave the people as much privilege as sufficed, . . . and I took care that the rich and powerful should suffer nothing amiss; I stood holding a strong shield over both parties, and let neither side prevail unjustly.

It does not please me to achieve anything by force as a tyrant, or to let the nobles and the meaner sort share equally in the rich land.

Though discontented, the Athenians stood by their promise to accept Solon's dispositions; they were given validity for 100 years and posted for all to see on revolving wooden tablets. To avoid having to defend and explain them further, he set off on a series of travels, undertaking not to return for ten years.

Later years. Among the places he visited were Egypt and Cyprus. These visits are attested by his poems. Less credible (because of chronological difficulties) is the famous encounter with the fabulously rich Croesus, king of Lydia, who, so the story goes, learned from Solon that wealth and power were not happiness and that, so long as he was alive, no man could be counted happy.

When Solon returned, he found the citizens divided into regional factions headed by prominent nobles. Of these, his friend Peisistratus, general in the final war for Salamis and leader of northeastern Attica, seemed to Solon to be planning to become tyrant. The old statesman's urgent warnings were disregarded, even dismissed as the ravings of a madman. His reply was that "A little time will show the citizens my madness, /Yes, will show, when truth comes in our midst." It was not long before he was proved right: Peisistratus did become tyrant (560 BC). Although on this occasion he was soon ejected, it seems that Solon did not live to see it.

Reputation. It was probably before the end of the 5th century that the Greeks first drew up a list of the Seven

Wise Men who had been prominent intellectually and politically in the 6th century. The earliest list, accepted by the Greek philosopher Plato, did not satisfy later writers, who expanded it to ten and even 17 to accommodate rival claimants. Every version, however, contained four names that were not challenged. One of them was that of Solon of Athens, a testimony to the abiding respect in which his memory was held.

BIBLIOGRAPHY. The principal ancient evidence for the life and work of Solon consists of the surviving fragments of his laws, edited, without translation, by E. RUSCHENBUSCH, Σόλωνος νόμοι (1966); poems (discussion, text, translation, and commentary) in I.M. LINFORTH, *Solon the Athenian*, pp. 103–245 (1919); the discussion of his reforms in the Aristotelian *Constitution of Athens*, trans. by K. VON FRITZ and E. KAPP, pp. 72–82 (1950); and the biography by PLUTARCH, written in the early 2nd century AD (translations in Everyman edition of the *Lives*, vol. 1, pp. 120–144; and by B. PERRIN in the Loeb edition, vol. 1, pp. 405–499). There are separate modern accounts of Solon in English by Linforth (cited above); by K. FREEMAN, *The Work and Life of Solon* (1926); and by W.J. WOODHOUSE, *Solon the Liberator* (1938), dealing mainly with the agrarian reforms. Although the main lines of Solon's life and work are clear, there are numerous unresolved controversies, and none of these three books, and little else on Solon, can be regarded as definitive. There is an excellent short account by A. ANDREWES in *The Greek Tyrants*, ch. 7 (1956). The constitutional problems raised by the ancient accounts of the reforms, and also their date, are fully discussed by C. HIGNETT in *History of the Athenian Constitution to the End of the Fifth Century B.C.* (1952); the economic background is given by A. FRENCH in *Growth of the Athenian Economy*, ch. 2 (1964). The most up-to-date treatment is by V. EHRENBERG in *From Solon to Socrates*, ch. 3 (1968).

(T.J.C.)

Solutions and Solubilities

The ability of liquids to dissolve solids, other liquids, or gases has long been recognized as one of the fundamental phenomena of nature encountered in daily life. The practical importance of solutions and the need to understand their properties have challenged numerous writers since the Ionian philosophers and Aristotle. From the Middle Ages to the Enlightenment, alchemists sought a universal solvent that would dissolve everything, seeing therein a physical counterpart to attainment of salvation. About a century ago, the beginnings of physical chemistry were motivated largely by fascination with liquid mixtures. Though many physicists and chemists have devoted themselves to a study of solutions, this is today still an incompletely understood subject under active investigation.

A solution is a mixture of two or more chemically distinct substances, a mixture that is said to be homogeneous on the molecular scale—the composition at any one point in the mixture is the same as that at any other point. This is in contrast to a suspension (or slurry), in which small discontinuous particles are surrounded by a continuous fluid. Although the word solution is commonly applied to the liquid state of matter, solutions of solids and gases are also possible; brass, for example, is a solution of copper and zinc, and air is a solution primarily of oxygen and nitrogen with a few other gases present in relatively small amounts.

The ability of one substance to dissolve another depends always on the chemical nature of the substances, frequently on the temperature, and occasionally on the pressure. Water, for example, readily dissolves methyl alcohol but does not dissolve mercury; it barely dissolves benzene at room temperature but does so increasingly as the temperature rises. While the solubility in water of the gases present in air is extremely small at atmospheric pressure, it becomes appreciable at high pressures where, in many cases, the solubility of a gas is (approximately) proportional to its pressure. Thus, a diver must breathe air (four-fifths nitrogen) at a pressure corresponding to the pressure around him, and, as he goes deeper, more air dissolves in his blood. When he ascends, the solubility of the gases decreases so that they leave his blood, forming bubbles in the blood vessels. This condition (known as

the bends) is extremely painful and may cause death; it can be alleviated by breathing, instead of air, a mixture of helium and oxygen because the solubility of helium in blood is much lower than that of nitrogen.

The solubility of one fluid in another may be complete or partial; thus, at room temperature, water and methyl alcohol mix in all proportions, but 100 grams of water dissolve only 0.07 gram of benzene. Though it is generally supposed that all gases are completely miscible—*i.e.*, mutually soluble in all proportions—this is true only at normal pressures (pressure is usually expressed in atmospheres, one atmosphere being the pressure exerted by a column of mercury 760 millimetres high, or about 14.7 pounds per square inch). At high pressures, pairs of chemically unlike gases may exhibit only limited miscibility; for example, at 20° C (68° F) helium and xenon are completely miscible at pressures below 200 atmospheres but become increasingly immiscible as the pressure rises.

The ability of a liquid to dissolve selectively forms the basis of common separation operations in chemical and related industries. A mixture of two gases, carbon dioxide and nitrogen, can be separated by bringing it into contact with ethanolamine, a liquid solvent that readily dissolves carbon dioxide but hardly dissolves nitrogen. In this process, called absorption, the dissolved carbon dioxide is later recovered, and the solvent made usable again by heating the carbon dioxide-rich solvent, since the solubility of a gas in a liquid usually (but not always) decreases with rising temperature. A similar absorption operation can remove a pollutant such as sulfur dioxide from smokestack gases in a plant using sulfur-containing coal or petroleum as fuel.

The process wherein a dissolved substance is transferred from one liquid to another is called extraction. As an example, phenolic pollutants (organic compounds of the types known as phenol, cresol, and resorcinol) are frequently found in industrial aqueous waste streams, and, since these phenolics are damaging to marine life, it is important to remove them before dumping the waste stream into a lake or river. One way to do so is to bring the waste stream into contact with a water-insoluble solvent (*e.g.*, an organic liquid such as a high-boiling hydrocarbon) that has a strong affinity for the phenolic pollutant. The solubility of the phenolic in the solvent divided by that in water is called the distribution coefficient, and it is clear that for an efficient extraction process it is desirable to have as large a distribution coefficient as possible.

For an understanding of solutions, it is desirable to have knowledge of the subjects treated in detail in the articles MOLECULAR STRUCTURE; CHEMICAL REACTIONS, MECHANISMS OF; CHEMICAL BONDING; PHASE CHANGES AND EQUILIBRIA; LIQUID STATE; GASEOUS STATE; SOLID STATE OF MATTER. Only the briefest reference to this information can be given here.

All matter is composed of elements consisting of atoms made up of a positively charged nucleus surrounded by negatively charged electrons. The nucleus, in turn, consists of tightly packed protons, each with a positive charge, and neutrons, which have no charge. The number of protons is the same for all atoms of an element and is called the atomic number, but the number of neutrons varies, thus producing atoms of the same element with different masses; these are called isotopes. The electrons around the nucleus determine the chemical and most of the physical properties of an atom. In a neutral atom, the positive charges of the protons are balanced by an equal number of electrons arranged according to a periodic system that makes the electron structure characteristic for each element. The main difference between the atoms of different elements is the affinity with which a nucleus holds its electrons. Some atoms have structures that are exceedingly stable, some tend to give up electrons easily, and others tend to add electrons to their normal complement. This potential for rearranging electron structures is the basis of chemical reaction and of bonding that takes place between atoms when they form the different molecules of the millions of known compounds. Compounds can be classified according to the type of bond holding

Effects of temperature and pressure

Bonds
between
atoms

the atoms together. In one class, called covalent, the bond consists of pairs of electrons shared mutually by the component nuclei. In another class, called ionic, one atom's affinity for electrons is so much greater than that of another that electrons are transferred, leaving the donor positively charged and the acceptor negatively charged. The charged atoms, called ions, then may associate (opposite charges attract) to form ionic, or electrovalent, bonds. In the third type of bonding, called metallic, the bonds between atoms free some electrons to move about and, thereby, form the basis for electrical conduction. Various other kinds of bonds are important to the phenomena of solutions. For example, an unsymmetrical distribution of charges on a molecule causes it to be attracted toward other unsymmetrically charged molecules, including its own kind, with the positive end of one toward the negative end of the other. Such polar molecules behave differently in solution from nonpolar molecules. When a hydrogen atom is bonded covalently to a molecule at a position at which the hydrogen nucleus (a single proton) is exposed, it will attach itself (and thus its molecule) to the dense electron structures surrounding atoms of certain elements in other molecules. The two molecules are thus linked by what is called a hydrogen bond, which, though not as strong as the usual chemical bonds, tends to be extremely influential in the behaviour of large, complex molecules, such as those found in the fluids of living organisms, as well as in the behaviour of such simple molecules as water. Groups of atoms, covalently bonded, may have a negative or positive charge, in which case they are also called ions or radicals, and their behaviour, too, is drastically different because of the attachments they make with other particles of opposite charge and because of the repulsion that they exert on particles with the same kind of charge.

An atom is represented by the symbol of the element, and molecules, or compounds, are represented by the symbols of their component atoms, with the number of atoms indicated in subscripts; thus, one molecule of water consists of two atoms of hydrogen (H) and one atom of oxygen (O), and the formula for water is written H_2O. Ions are represented by the symbols with the charge indicated in superscripts; thus, hydrogen ion, (H^+); hydroxide ion, (OH^-).

The properties of mixtures and solutions are, therefore, not merely the sum of the properties of their components; they usually have properties characteristic of themselves because molecules and atoms are not indifferent to one another's presence.

CLASSES OF SOLUTIONS

Electrolytes and nonelectrolytes. Broadly speaking, liquid mixtures can be classified as either solutions of electrolytes or solutions of nonelectrolytes. Electrolytes are substances that can dissociate into electrically charged particles called ions, while nonelectrolytes consist of molecules that bear no net electric charge. Thus when ordinary salt (sodium chloride, formula NaCl) is dissolved in water, it forms an electrolytic solution, dissociating into positive sodium ions (Na^+) and negative chloride ions (Cl^-), whereas sugar dissolved in water maintains its molecular integrity and does not dissociate. Because of its omnipresence, water is the most common solvent for electrolytes; the ocean is a solution of electrolytes. Electrolyte solutions, however, are also formed by other solvents (such as ammonia and sulfur dioxide) that have a large dielectric constant (a measure of the ability of a fluid to decrease the forces of attraction and repulsion between charged particles). The energy required to separate an ion pair (i.e., one ion of positive charge and one ion of negative charge) varies inversely with the dielectric constant, and, therefore, appreciable dissociation into separate ions occurs only in solvents with large dielectric constants.

Ion pairs

Most electrolytes (for example, salts) are nonvolatile, which means that they have essentially no tendency to enter the vapour phase. There are, however, some notable exceptions, such as hydrogen chloride (HCl), which is readily soluble in water, where it forms hydrogen ions (H^+) and chloride ions (Cl^-). At normal temperature and pressure, pure hydrogen chloride is a gas, and, in the absence of water or some other ionizing solvent, hydrogen chloride exists in molecular, rather than ionic, form.

Solutions of electrolytes readily conduct electricity, whereas nonelectrolyte solutions do not. A dilute solution of hydrogen chloride in water is a good electrical conductor, but a dilute solution of hydrogen chloride in a hydrocarbon is a good insulator. Because of the large difference in dielectric constants, hydrogen chloride is ionized in water but not in hydrocarbons.

Weak electrolytes. While classification under electrolyte-solution or nonelectrolyte-solution headings is often useful, some solutions have properties near the boundary between these two broad classes. Although such substances as ordinary salt and hydrogen chloride are strong electrolytes—i.e., they dissociate completely in an ionizing solvent—there are many substances, called weak electrolytes, that dissociate to only a small extent in ionizing solvents. For example, in aqueous solution, acetic acid can dissociate into a positive hydrogen ion (H^+) and a negative acetate ion (CH_3COO^-), but it does so to a very limited extent; in an aqueous solution containing 50 grams acetic acid and 1,000 grams water, less than 1 percent of the acetic acid molecules are dissociated into ions. Therefore, a solution of acetic acid in water exhibits some properties associated with electrolyte solutions (e.g., it is a fair conductor of electricity), but in general terms it is more properly classified as a nonelectrolyte solution. By similar reasoning, an aqueous solution of carbon dioxide is also considered a nonelectrolyte solution even though carbon dioxide and water have a slight tendency to form carbonic acid, which, in turn, dissociates to a small extent to hydrogen ions and bicarbonate ions (HCO_3^-).

Endothermic and exothermic solutions. When two substances mix to form a solution, heat is either evolved (an exothermic process) or absorbed (an endothermic process); only in the special case of an ideal solution do substances mix without any heat effect. Most simple molecules mix with a small endothermic heat of solution, while exothermic heats of solution are observed when the components interact strongly with one another. An extreme example of an exothermic heat of mixing is provided by adding an aqueous solution of sodium hydroxide, a powerful base, to an aqueous solution of hydrogen chloride, a powerful acid; the hydroxide ions (OH^-) of the base combine with the hydrogen ions (H^+) of the acid to form water, a highly exothermic reaction that yields 75,300 calories per 100 grams of water formed. In nonelectrolyte solutions, heat effects are usually endothermic and much smaller, often about 100 calories, when roughly equal parts are mixed to form 100 grams of mixture.

Formation of a solution usually is accompanied by a small change in volume. If equal parts of benzene and stannic chloride are mixed, the temperature drops; if the mixture is then heated slightly to bring its temperature back to that of the unmixed liquids, the volume increases by about 2 percent. On the other hand, mixing roughly equal parts of acetone and chloroform produces a small decrease in volume, about 0.2 percent. It frequently happens that mixtures with endothermic heats of mixing expand—i.e., show small increases in volume—while mixtures with exothermic heats of mixing tend to contract.

A large decrease in volume occurs when a gas is dissolved in a liquid. For example, at 0° C (32° F) and atmospheric pressure, the volume of 28 grams of nitrogen is 22,400 cubic centimetres. When these 28 grams of nitrogen are dissolved in an excess of water, the volume of the water increases only 40 cubic centimetres; the decrease in volume accompanying the dissolution of 28 grams of nitrogen in water is therefore 22,360 cubic centimetres. In this case, it is said that the nitrogen gas has been condensed into a liquid, the word condense meaning "to make dense"—i.e., to decrease the volume.

Volume
changes
caused by
the
formation
of a
solution

PROPERTIES OF SOLUTIONS

Composition ratios. The composition of a liquid solution means the composition of that solution in the bulk

—that is, of that part that is not near the surface. The interface (the surface separating them) between the liquid solution and some other phase (for example, a gas such as air) has a composition that differs from that of the bulk, sometimes very much so. The environment at an interface is significantly different from that in the bulk of the liquid, and in a solution the molecules of a particular component may prefer one environment over the other. If the molecules of one component in the solution prefer to be at the interface as opposed to the bulk, it is said that this component is positively adsorbed at the interface. In aqueous solutions of organic liquids, the organic component is usually positively adsorbed at the solution–air interface; as a result, it is often possible to separate a mixture of an organic solute from water by a process called froth separation. Air is bubbled vigorously into the solution, and a froth is formed. The composition of the froth differs from that of the bulk because the organic solute concentrates at the interfacial region. The froth is mechanically removed and collapsed, and, if further separation is desired, a new froth is generated. The tendency of some dissolved molecules to congregate at the surface has been utilized in water conservation. A certain type of alcohol, when added to water, concentrates at the surface to form a barrier to evaporating water molecules. In warm climates, therefore, water loss by evaporation from lakes can be significantly reduced by introducing a solute that adsorbs positively at the lake–air interface.

The composition of a solution can be expressed in a variety of ways, the simplest of which is to use weight fraction, or weight percent; for example, the salt content of seawater is about 3.5 weight percent; *i.e.*, of 100 grams of seawater, 3.5 grams is salt. For a fundamental understanding of solution properties, however, it is often useful to express composition in terms of molecular units such as molecular concentration, molality, or mole fraction. To understand these terms, it is necessary to define atomic and molecular weights. The atomic weight of elements

Role of atomic weight

is a relative figure, with one atom of the carbon-12 isotope being assigned the atomic weight of 12; the atomic weight of hydrogen is then approximately 1, of oxygen approximately 16, and the molecular weight of water (H_2O) 18. The atomic and molecular theory of matter asserts that the atomic weight of any element in grams must contain the same number of atoms as the atomic weight in grams (the gram-atomic weight) of any other element. Thus, two grams of molecular hydrogen (H_2)—its gram-molecular weight—contain the same number of molecules as 18 grams of water or as 32 grams of oxygen molecules (O_2). Further, a specified volume of any gas (at low pressure) contains the same number of molecules as the same volume of any other gas, at the same temperature and pressure. At standard temperature and pressure (O° C and 1 atmosphere) the volume of one gram-molecular weight of any gas has been determined experimentally to be approximately 22.4 litres. The number of molecules in this volume of gas, or in the gram-molecular weight of any compound, is called Avogadro's number.

Molarity. By molecular concentration is meant the number of molecules of a particular component per unit volume. Since the number of molecules in a litre or even a cubic centimetre is enormous, it has become common practice to use what are called molar, rather than molecular, quantities. A mole is the gram-molecular weight of a substance and, therefore, also Avogadro's number of molecules (6.02×10^{23}). Thus, the number of moles in a sample is the weight of the sample divided by the molecular weight of the substance; and it is also the number of molecules in the sample divided by Avogadro's number. Instead of using molecular concentration, it is more convenient to use molar concentration; instead of saying, for example, that the concentration is 12.04×10^{23} molecules per litre, it is simpler to say that it is two moles per litre. Concentration in moles per litre (*i.e.*, molarity) is usually designated by the letter M.

Molality. In electrolyte solutions it is common to distinguish between the solvent (usually water) and the dissolved substance, or solute, which dissociates into

ions. For these solutions it is useful to express composition in terms of molality, designated as *m*, a unit proportional to the number of undissociated solute molecules (or, alternatively, to the number of ions) per 1,000 grams of solvent. The number of molecules or ions in 1,000 grams of solvent usually is very large, so molality is defined as the number of moles per 1,000 grams of solvent.

Formality. Many compounds do not exist in the form of molecules, either in the pure substances or in their solutions. The particles that make up sodium chloride (NaCl), for example, are sodium ions (Na^+) and chloride ions (Cl^-), and although equal numbers of these two ions are present in any sample of sodium chloride, no Na^+ ion is associated with a particular Cl^- ion to form a neutral molecule having the composition implied by the formula. Therefore, even though the compositions of such compounds are well defined, it would be erroneous to express concentrations of their solutions in terms of molecular weights. A useful concept in cases of this kind is that of the formula weight, defined as the sum of the weights of the atoms in the formula of the compound; thus, the formula weight of sodium chloride is the sum of the atomic weights of sodium and chlorine, 23 plus 35.5, or 58.5, and a solution containing 58.5 grams of sodium chloride per litre is said to have a concentration of one formal, of 1 *f*.

Mole fraction and mole percentage. It often is useful to express the composition of nonelectrolyte solutions in terms of mole fraction or mole percentage. In a binary mixture—*i.e.*, a mixture of two components, 1 and 2—there are two mole fractions, x_1 and x_2, which must obey the relation $x_1 + x_2 = 1$. The mole fraction x_1 means the fraction of molecules of species 1 in the solution, and x_2 means the fraction of molecules of species 2 in the solution. (Mole percentage is the mole fraction multiplied by 100.)

Volume fraction. The composition of a nonelectrolyte solution containing very large molecules, known as polymers, is most conveniently expressed by the volume fraction (Φ)—*i.e.*, the volume of polymer used to prepare the solution divided by the sum of that volume of polymer and the volume of the solvent.

Equilibrium properties. A quantitative description of liquid-solution properties when the system is in equilibrium is provided by relating the vapour pressure of the solution to its composition. The vapour pressure of a liquid, pure or mixed, is the pressure exerted by those molecules that escape from the liquid to form a separate vapour phase above the liquid. If a quantity of liquid is placed in an evacuated, closed container the volume of which is slightly larger than that of the liquid, most of the container is filled with the liquid, but, immediately above the liquid surface, a vapour phase forms consisting of molecules that have passed through the liquid surface from liquid to gas; the pressure exerted by that vapour phase is called the vapour (or saturation) pressure. For a pure liquid, this pressure depends only on the temperature, the best known example being the normal boiling point, which is that temperature at which the vapour pressure is equal to the pressure of the atmosphere. (The standard atmosphere is equal to the pressure exerted by a column of mercury 760 millimetres high, or about 14.7 pounds per square inch.) Figure 1 shows vapour pressures for a few common liquids. The vapour pressure is one atmosphere at 100° C for water, at 78.5° C for ethyl alcohol, and at 125.7° C for octane. In a liquid solution the component with the higher vapour pressure is called the light component, and that with the lower vapour pressure is called the heavy component.

In a liquid mixture, the vapour pressure depends not only on the temperature but also on the composition, and the key problem in understanding the properties of solutions lies in determining this composition dependence. The simplest approximation is to assume that, at constant temperature, the vapour pressure of a solution is a linear function of its composition (*i.e.*, as one increases, so does the other in such proportion that, when the values are plotted, the resulting graph is a straight line). A mixture following this approximation is called an ideal solution.

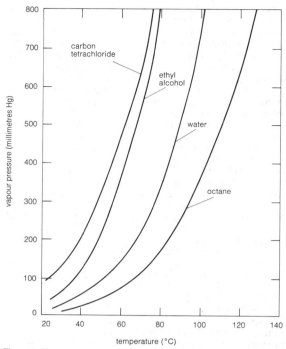

Figure 1: Vapour pressures of several pure liquids.

Fugacity. In a pure liquid, the vapour generated by its escaping molecules necessarily has the same composition as that of the liquid. In a mixture, however, the composition of the vapour is not the same as that of the liquid; the vapour is richer in that component whose molecules have greater tendency to escape from the liquid phase. This tendency is measured by fugacity, a term derived from the Latin *fugere* ("to escape, to fly away"), which is also the root of the word fugitive. The fugacity of a component in a mixture is (essentially) the pressure that the component exerts in the vapour phase when the vapour is in equilibrium with the liquid mixture. (A state of equilibrium is attained when all the properties remain constant in time and there is no net transfer of energy or matter between the vapour and the liquid.) If the vapour phase can be considered to be an ideal gas (*i.e.*, the molecules in the gas phase are assumed to act independently and without any influence on each other), then the fugacity of a component, *i*, is equal to its partial pressure, which is defined as the product of the total vapour pressure, P, and the vapour-phase mole fraction, y_i. Assuming ideal gas behaviour for the vapour phase, the fugacity (y_iP) equals the product of the liquid-phase mole fraction, x_i, the vapour pressure of pure liquid at the same temperature as that of the mixture, $P_i°$, and the activity coefficient, γ_i. The real concentration of a substance may not be an accurate measure of its effectiveness because of physical and chemical interactions, in which case an effective concentration must be used, called the activity. The activity is given by the product of the mole fraction x_i and the activity coefficient γ_i. The equation is:

$$y_iP = \gamma_ix_iP_i°.$$

Raoult's law. In a real solution, the activity coefficient, γ_i, depends on both temperature and composition, but, in an ideal solution, γ_i equals 1 for all components in the mixture. For an ideal binary mixture then, the above equation becomes, for components 1 and 2, $y_1P = x_1P_1°$, and $y_2P = x_2P_2°$, respectively. Upon adding these equations—remembering that $x_1 + x_2 = 1$, and $y_1 + y_2 = 1$ —total pressure, P, is shown to be expressed by the equation $P = x_1P_1° + x_2P_2° = x_1[P_1° - P_2°] + P_2°$, which is a linear function of x_1.

Assuming $\gamma_1 = \gamma_2 = 1$, equations for y_1P and y_2P express what is commonly known as Raoult's law, which states that at constant temperature the partial pressure of a component in a liquid mixture is proportional to its mole fraction in that mixture (*i.e.*, each component exerts a pressure that depends directly on the number of its molecules present). It is unfortunate that the word law is associated with this relation, because only very few mixtures behave according to the equations for ideal binary mixtures. In most cases the activity coefficient, γ_i, is not equal to unity. When γ_i is greater than 1, there are positive deviations from Raoult's law; when γ_i is less than 1, there are negative deviations from Raoult's law.

An example of a binary system that exhibits positive deviations from Raoult's law is represented in Figure 2, the partial pressures and the total pressure being related to the liquid-phase composition; if Raoult's law were valid, all the lines would be straight, as indicated. As a practical result of these relationships, it is often possible by a series of repeated vaporizations and condensations to separate a liquid mixture into its components, a sequence of steps called fractional distillation.

When the vapour in equilibrium with a liquid mixture has a composition identical to that of the liquid, the mixture is called an azeotrope. It is not possible to separate an azeotropic mixture by fractional distillation because no change in composition is achieved by a series of vaporizations and condensations. Azeotropic mixtures are common. At the azeotropic composition, the total pressure (at constant temperature) is always either a maximum or a minimum, and the boiling temperature (at constant pressure) is always either a minimum or a maximum.

Azeotropic mixtures

Partial miscibility. Only pairs of liquids that are completely miscible have been considered so far. Many pairs of liquid mixtures, however, are only partially miscible in one another, the degree of miscibility often depending strongly on temperature. In most cases, rising temperature produces enhanced solubility, but this is not always so. For example, at 50° C (122° F) the solubility (weight percent) of *n*-butyl alcohol in water is 6.5 percent, whereas that of water in *n*-butyl alcohol is 22.4 percent. At 127° C (261° F), the upper consolute temperature, complete miscibility is attained: above 127° C the two liquids mix in all proportions, but below 127° C they show a

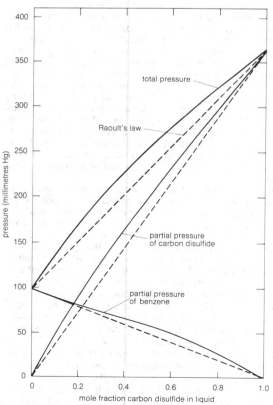

Figure 2: Total pressure and partial pressures for the system benzene–carbon disulfide at 25° C (see text).

miscibility gap. Thus, if *n*-butyl alcohol is added to water at 50° C, there is only one liquid phase until 6.5 weight percent of the mixture is alcohol; when more alcohol is added, a second liquid phase appears the composition of which is 22.4 weight percent water. When sufficient alcohol is present to make the overall composition 77.6 weight percent alcohol, the first phase disappears, and only one liquid phase remains. A qualitatively different example is the system water–triethylamine, which has a lower consolute temperature at 17° C (63° F). Below 17° C, the two liquids are completely miscible, but at higher temperatures they are only partially miscible. Finally, it is possible, although rare, for a binary system to exhibit both upper and lower consolute temperatures. Above 128° C (262° F) and below 49° C (120° F), butyl glycol and water are completely miscible, but between these temperatures they do not mix in all proportions.

Colligative properties. Colligative properties depend only on the concentration of the solute, not on the specific properties of the solute molecules. The concept of an ideal solution, as expressed by Raoult's law (at constant temperature the partial pressure of a component in a liquid mixture is proportional to its mole fraction in the mixture), was already well-known during the last quarter of the 19th century, and it provided the early physical chemists with a powerful technique for measuring molecular weights. (Reliable measurements of molecular weights, in turn, provided important evidence for the modern atomic and molecular theory of matter.)

Rise in boiling point. It was observed that, whenever one component in a binary solution is present in large excess, the partial pressure of that component is correctly predicted by Raoult's law, even though the solution may exhibit departures from ideal behaviour in other respects. When Raoult's law is applied to the solvent of a very dilute solution containing a nonvolatile solute, it is possible to calculate the mole fraction of the solute from an experimental determination of the rise in boiling point that results when the solute is dissolved in the solvent. Since the separate weights of solute and solvent are readily measured, the procedure provides a simple experimental method for the determination of molecular weight. If a weighed amount of a nonvolatile substance, w_2, is dissolved in a weighed amount of a solvent, w_1, at constant pressure, the increase in the boiling temperature, ΔT_{b_1}, the gas constant, R (derived from the gas laws), the heat of vaporization of the pure solvent per unit weight, l_1^{vap}, the boiling temperature of pure solvent, T_{b_1}, are related in a simple product of ratios to equal the molecular weight of the solute, M_2. The equation is:

$$M_2 = \left(\frac{RT_{b_1}^2}{l_1^{\text{vap}}}\right)\left(\frac{w_2}{w_1}\right)\left(\frac{1}{\Delta T_{b_1}}\right).$$

The essence of this technique follows from the observation that, in a dilute solution of a nonvolatile solute, the rise in boiling point is proportional to the number of solute molecules, regardless of their size and mass.

Decrease in freezing point. Another colligative property of solutions is the decrease in the freezing temperature of a solvent that is observed when a small amount of solute is dissolved in that solvent. By reasoning similar to that leading to the equation above, the freezing-point depression, ΔT_f, the freezing temperature of pure solvent, T_{f_1}, the heat of fusion (also called the heat of melting) of pure solvent per unit weight, l_1^{fusion}, and the weights of solute and solvent in the solution, w_2 and w_1, respectively, are so related as to equal the molecular weight of solute, M_2, in the equation

$$M_2 = \left(\frac{RT_{f_1}^2}{l_1^{\text{fusion}}}\right)\left(\frac{w_2}{w_1}\right)\left(\frac{1}{\Delta T_f}\right).$$

A well-known practical application of freezing-point depression is provided by adding antifreeze to the cooling water in an automobile's radiator. Water alone freezes at 0° C (32° F), but the freezing temperature decreases appreciably when ethylene glycol is mixed with water.

Osmotic pressure. A third colligative property, osmotic pressure, helped to establish the fundamentals of mod-

ern physical chemistry and played a particularly important role in the early days of solution theory. Osmosis is especially important in medicine and biology, but in recent years it has also been applied industrially to problems such as the concentration of fruit juices, the desalting of seawater, and the purification of municipal sewage. Osmosis occurs whenever a liquid solution is in contact with a semipermeable membrane—*i.e.*, a thin, porous wall whose porosity is such that some, but not all, of the components in the liquid mixture can pass through the wall. A semipermeable membrane is a selective barrier, and many such barriers are found in plants and animals. Osmosis gives rise to what is known as osmotic pressure, as illustrated in Figure 3, which shows a container at

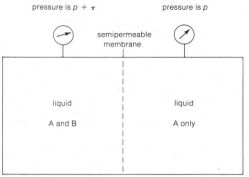

Figure 3: Osmotic pressure π caused by a membrane that allows A to pass, but not B.

uniform temperature divided into two parts by a semipermeable membrane that allows only molecules of component A to pass from the left to the right side; the selective membrane does not allow molecules of component B to pass. Molecules of component A are free to pass back and forth through the membrane, but, at equilibrium, when the fugacity (escaping tendency) of A in the right-hand side is the same as that in the left-hand side, there is no net transfer of A from one side to the other. On the left side, the presence of B molecules lowers the fugacity of A, and, therefore, to achieve equal fugacities for A on both sides, some compensating effect is needed on the left side. This compensating effect is an enhanced pressure, designated by π and called osmotic pressure. At equilibrium, the pressure in the left side of the container is larger than that in the right side; the difference in pressure is π. In the simplest case, when the concentration of B is small (*i.e.*, A is in excess), the osmotic pressure is the product of the gas constant (R), the absolute temperature (T), and the concentration of B (c_B) in the solution expressed in moles of B per unit volume: $\pi = RTc_B$. Since the osmotic pressure for a dilute solution is proportional to the number of solute molecules, it is a colligative property, and, as a result, osmotic-pressure measurements are often used to determine molecular weights, especially for large molecules such as polymers. When w_B grams of solute B are added to a large amount of solvent A at temperature T, and V is the volume of liquid solvent A in the left side of the container, then the molecular weight of B, M_B, is given by

$$M_B = \frac{w_B RT}{\pi V}.$$

Transport properties in solutions. Pure fluids have two transport properties that are of primary importance: viscosity and thermal conductivity. (Transport properties are not equilibrium properties because they reflect not what happens at equilibrium but the speed at which equilibrium is attained.) In solutions these two transport properties are also important. In addition, there is a third one, called diffusivity.

Viscosity. The viscosity of a fluid (pure or not) is a measure of its ability to resist deformation. If water is poured into a thin vertical tube with a funnel at the top, it flows easily through the tube, but salad oil is difficult

Osmotic
equilibrium

to force into the tube. If the oil is heated, however, its flow through the tube is much facilitated. The intrinsic property that is responsible for these phenomena is the viscosity (the "thickness") of the fluid, a property which is often strongly affected by temperature. All fluids (liquid or gas) exhibit viscous behaviour (i.e., all fluids resist deformation), but the range of viscosity is enormous: the viscosity of air is extremely small, while that of glass is essentially infinite. The viscosity of a solution depends not only on temperature but also on its composition. By varying the composition of a petroleum mixture, it is possible to attain a desired viscosity at a particular temperature. This is precisely what the oil companies do when they sell oil to a motorist: in winter, they recommend an oil with lower viscosity than that used in summer, because otherwise, on a cold morning, the viscosity of the lubricating oil may be so high that the car's battery will not be powerful enough to move the lubricated piston.

Thermal conductivity. The thermal conductivity of a material reflects its ability to transfer heat by conduction. If one end of a rod of copper is held in a pot of boiling water, the other end soon burns the hand. If the same is done with a stick of wood, no discomfort is felt; the thermal conductivity of copper is much greater than that of wood. Gases and liquids also can transfer heat by conduction.

In practical situations both viscosity and thermal conductivity are important, as is illustrated by the contrast between an air mattress and a water bed. Because of its low viscosity, air yields rapidly to an imposed load, and thus the air mattress responds quickly when someone lying on it changes position. Water, because of its higher viscosity, noticeably resists deformation, and someone lying on a water bed experiences a caressing response whenever position is changed. At the same time, since the thermal conductivity as well as the viscosity of water are larger than those of air, the user of a water bed rapidly gets cold unless a heater keeps the water warm. No heater is required by the user of an air mattress because stagnant air is inefficient in removing heat from a warm body.

Composition and temperature affect the thermal conductivity of a solution but, in typical liquid mixtures, the effect on viscosity is much larger than that on thermal conductivity.

Comparison of viscosity and diffusivity *Diffusivity.* While viscosity is concerned with the transfer of momentum and thermal conductivity with the transfer of heat, diffusivity is concerned with the transport of molecules in a mixture. If a lump of sugar is put into a cup of coffee, the sugar molecules travel from the surface of the lump into the coffee at a speed determined by the temperature and by the pertinent intermolecular forces. The characteristic property that determines this speed is called diffusivity—i.e., the ability of a molecule to diffuse through a sea of other molecules. Diffusivities in solids are extremely small, and those in liquids are much smaller than those in gases. As a result, a spoon is used to stir the coffee to speed up the motion of the sugar molecules; but if a room smells foul from cigarette smoke, no effort is needed to obtain significant relief—opening the windows for a few minutes is sufficient.

In order to define diffusivity, it is necessary to consider a binary fluid mixture in which the concentration of solute molecules is c_1 at position 1 and c_2 at position 2, l centimetres from position 1; if c_1 is larger than c_2, then the concentration gradient (change with respect to distance), or $(c_2 - c_1)/l$, is a negative number, indicating that molecules of solute spontaneously diffuse from position 1 to position 2; the number of solute molecules that pass through an area of one square centimetre perpendicular to l, per second, is called the flux J (expressed in molecules per second per square centimetre). The diffusivity D is given by the ratio of the flux to the gradient multiplied by minus one:

$$D = -\frac{J}{\left(\dfrac{c_2 - c_1}{l}\right)}.$$

The minus sign is introduced because, when the gradient is positive, J is negative, and, by convention, D is a positive number. In binary gaseous mixtures, diffusivity depends only weakly on the composition, and, therefore, to a good approximation, the diffusivity of gas A in gas B is the same as that of gas B in gas A. In liquid systems, however, the diffusivity of solute A in solvent B may be significantly different from that of solute B in solvent A. In a very viscous fluid, molecules cannot rapidly move from one place to another. Therefore, in liquid systems, the diffusivity of solute A depends strongly on the viscosity of solvent B and vice versa. While the letter D is always used for diffusivity, viscosity is commonly given the symbol η (Greek eta); in many liquid solutions it is observed that, as the composition changes (as long as the temperature remains constant), the product $D\eta$ remains nearly the same.

THERMODYNAMICS AND INTERMOLECULAR FORCES IN SOLUTIONS

The properties of solutions depend, essentially, on two characteristics: first, the manner in which the molecules arrange themselves (that is, the geometrical array in which the molecules occupy space) and, second, the nature and strength of the forces operating between the molecules.

Energy considerations. The first characteristic is reflected primarily in the thermodynamic quantity S, called entropy, which is a measure of disorder, and the second characteristic is reflected in the thermodynamic quantity H, called enthalpy, which is a measure of potential energy—i.e., the energy that must be supplied to separate all the molecules from one another. Enthalpy minus the product of the absolute temperature T and entropy equals a thermodynamic quantity G, called Gibbs energy (also called free energy): Enthalpy

$$G = H - TS.$$

From the second law of thermodynamics, it can be shown that, at constant temperature and pressure, any spontaneous process is accompanied by a decrease in Gibbs energy. The change in G that results from mixing is designated by ΔG, which, in turn, is related to changes in H and S at constant temperature by the equation

$$\Delta G = \Delta H - T\Delta S.$$

At a fixed temperature and pressure, two substances mix spontaneously whenever ΔG is negative; that is, mixing (either partial or complete) occurs whenever the Gibbs energy of the substances after mixing is less than that before mixing.

The two characteristics that determine solution behaviour, structure and intermolecular forces, are, unfortunately, not independent, because the structure is influenced by the intermolecular forces and because the potential energy of the mixture depends on the structure. Only in limiting cases is it possible, on the one hand, to calculate ΔS (the entropy change upon mixing) from structural considerations alone and, on the other, to calculate ΔH (the enthalpy change of mixing) exclusively from relations describing intermolecular forces. Nevertheless, such calculations have proved to be useful for establishing models that approximate solution behaviour and that serve as guides in interpreting experimental measurements. Solutions for which structural considerations are dominant are called athermal solutions, and those for which the effects of intermolecular forces are more important than those of structure are called regular solutions (see below *Regular solutions* and *Athermal solutions*).

Effects of molecular structure. A variety of forces operate between molecules, and there is a qualitative relation between the properties of a solution and the types of intermolecular forces that operate within it. The volume occupied by a solution is determined primarily by repulsive forces. When two molecules are extremely close to one another, they must necessarily exert a repulsive force on each other since two molecules of finite dimensions cannot occupy the same space; two molecules in very close proximity resist attempts to shorten the distance between them just as passengers in a crowded subway car resist entry of an additional passenger.

At larger distances of separation, molecules may attract or repel each other depending on the sign (plus or minus) and distribution of their electrical charge. Two ions (atoms or molecules with net positive or negative electric charges) attract one another if the charge on one is positive and that on the other is negative; they repel when both carry charges of the same sign. Forces between ions are called Coulomb forces and are characterized by their long range; the force (F) between two ions is inversely proportional to the square of the distance between them—i.e., F varies as $1/r^2$. Noncoulombic physical forces between molecules decay more rapidly with distance; i.e., in general F varies as $1/r^n$, n being larger than 2 for intermolecular forces other than those between ions.

The Coulomb force (F) equals the product of the magnitude of the charge on one ion (e_1) and that on the other (e_2) divided by the product of the distance squared (r^2) and the dielectric constant (ε):

$$F = \frac{e_1 e_2}{r^2 \varepsilon}.$$

If both e_1 and e_2 are positive, F is positive and the force is repulsive. If either e_1 or e_2 is positive, while the other is negative, F is negative and the force is attractive. Coulomb forces are dominant in electrolyte solutions.

Molecular structure and charge distribution. If a molecule has no net electrical charge, its negative charge is equal to its positive charge. The forces experienced by such molecules depend on how the positive and negative charges are arranged in space. If the arrangement is spherically symmetric, the molecule is said to be nonpolar; if there is an excess of positive charge on one end of the molecule and an excess of negative charge on the other, the molecule has a dipole moment (i.e., a measurable tendency to rotate in an electric or magnetic field) and is therefore called polar. The dipole moment (μ) is defined as the product of the magnitude of the charge, e, and the distance separating the positive and negative charges, l: $\mu = el$. Electric charge is measured in electrostatic units (esu), and the typical charge at one end of a molecule is of the order of 10^{-10} esu; the distance between charges is of the order of 10^{-8} centimetres. Dipole moments, therefore, usually are measured in debyes (one debye is 10^{-18} esu-cm). For nonpolar molecules $\mu = 0$.

Polar molecules. The force F between two polar molecules is directly proportional to the product of the two dipole moments (μ_1 and μ_2) and inversely proportional to the fourth power of the distance between them (r^4): F varies as $\mu_1 \mu_2 / r^4$. The equation for this relationship contains a constant of proportionality ($F = k \mu_1 \mu_2 / r^4$) the sign and magnitude of which depend on the mutual orientation of the two dipoles; if the positive end of one faces the negative end of the other, the constant of proportionality is negative (meaning that an attractive force exists), while it is positive (meaning that a repulsive force exists) when the positive end of one faces the positive end of the other. When polar molecules are free to rotate, they tend to favour orientations that led to attractive forces. To a first approximation, the force (averaged over all orientations) is inversely proportional to the temperature and to the seventh power of the distance of separation. Mixtures of polar molecules often exhibit only mild deviations from ideality, but mixtures containing polar and nonpolar molecules are frequently strongly nonideal. Because of the qualitative and quantitative differences in intermolecular forces, the molecules segregate: the polar molecules prefer to be with each other, and so do the nonpolar ones. Only at higher temperatures, such that the thermal energy of the molecules offsets the cohesion between identical molecules, do the two liquids mix in all proportions. In mixtures containing polar and nonpolar components, deviations from Raoult's law diminish as temperature rises.

Nonpolar molecules. A nonpolar molecule is one whose charge distribution is spherically symmetric when averaged over time; since the charges oscillate, a tempo-

rary dipole moment exists at any given instant in a so-called nonpolar molecule. These temporary dipole moments fluctuate rapidly in magnitude and direction, giving rise to intermolecular forces of attraction called London (or dispersion) forces. All molecules, charged or not, polar or not, interact by London forces. To a first approximation, the London force between two molecules is inversely proportional to the seventh power of the distance of separation; it is therefore short-range, decreasing rapidly as one molecule moves away from the other. The London theory indicates that for simple molecules positive deviations from Raoult's law may be expected (i.e., the activity coefficient γ_i is greater than 1, as explained previously). Since the London theory suggests that the attractive forces between unlike simple molecules are smaller than those corresponding to an ideal solution, the escaping tendency of the molecules in solution is larger than that calculated by Raoult's law. As a result, mixing of small nonpolar molecules is endothermic (absorbing heat from the surroundings) and the volume occupied by the liquid solution often exceeds that of the unmixed components (the components expand on mixing).

In addition to the forces listed above, there are so-called induction forces set up when a charged or polar molecule induces a dipole in another molecule: the electric field of the inducing molecule distorts the charge distribution in the other. When a charged molecule induces a dipole in another, the force is always attractive and is inversely proportional to the fifth power of the distance of separation. When a polar molecule induces a dipole in another molecule, the force is also attractive and is inversely proportional to the seventh power of separation. Induction forces are usually small but may make a significant contribution to the energy of a mixture of molecules that are strongly dissimilar.

Effects of chemical interactions. In many cases the properties of a mixture are determined primarily by forces that are more properly classified as chemical rather than physical. For example, when dinitrogen pentoxide is dissolved in water, a new substance, nitric acid, is formed; and it is necessary to interpret the behaviour of such a solution in terms of its chemical properties, which, in this case, are more important than its physical properties. This example is extreme, and there are many solutions for which the chemical effect is less severe but nevertheless dominant.

Hydrogen bonding: association. This dominance is especially important in those solutions that involve hydrogen bonding. Whenever a solution contains molecules with an electropositive hydrogen atom and with an electronegative atom (such as nitrogen, oxygen, sulfur, or fluorine), hydrogen bonding may occur and, when it does, the properties of the solution are affected profoundly. Hydrogen bonds may form between identical molecules or between dissimilar molecules; for example, methanol (CH_3OH) has an electropositive (electron-attracting) hydrogen atom and also an electronegative (electron-donating) oxygen atom, and therefore two methanol molecules may hydrogen-bond singly to form the structure

or in chains to form

Hydrogen bonding between identical molecules is often called association.

Dipole moment

Hydrogen bonding: solvation. In a mixture of methanol and, say, pyridine (C_5H_5N), hydrogen bonds can also form between the electropositive hydrogen atom in methanol and the electronegative nitrogen atom in pyridine. Hydrogen bonding between dissimilar molecules is often called solvation. Since the extent of association or solvation or both depends on the concentrations of the solution's components, the partial pressure of a component is not even approximately proportional to its mole fraction as given by Raoult's law; therefore, large deviations from Raoult's law are commonly observed in solutions in which hydrogen bonding is extensive. Broadly speaking, association of one component, but not the other, tends to produce positive deviations from Raoult's law, because the associating component associates to a smaller extent when it is surrounded by other molecules than it does in the pure state. On the other hand, solvation between dissimilar molecules tends to produce negative deviations from Raoult's law.

THEORIES OF SOLUTIONS

Solutions of nonelectrolytes. *Activity coefficients and excess functions.* As has been explained previously, when actual concentrations do not give simple linear relations for the behaviour of a solution, activity coefficients, symbolized by γ, are used in expressing deviations from Raoult's law. Activity coefficients are directly related to excess functions, and, in attempting to understand solution behaviour, it is convenient to characterize nonelectrolyte solutions in terms of these functions. In particular, it is useful to distinguish between two types of limiting behaviour: one corresponds to that of a regular solution; the other, to that of an athermal solution (*i.e.*, when components are mixed, no heat is generated or absorbed).

In a binary mixture with mole fractions x_1 and x_2 and activity coefficients γ_1 and γ_2, these quantities can be related to a thermodynamic function designated by G^E, called the excess Gibbs (or free) energy. The significance of the word excess lies in the fact that G^E is the Gibbs energy of a solution in excess of what it would be if it were ideal.

In a binary solution the two activity coefficients are not independent but are related by an exact differential equation called the Gibbs-Duhem relation. Thanks to this equation, if experimental data at constant temperature are available for γ_1 and γ_2 as a function of composition, it is possible to check the data for thermodynamic consistency: the data are said to be consistent only if they satisfy the Gibbs-Duhem relation. Experimental data that do not satisfy this relation are thermodynamically inconsistent and therefore must be erroneous.

To establish a theory of solutions, it is necessary to construct a theoretical (or semitheoretical) equation for the excess Gibbs energy as a function of absolute temperature (T) and the mole fractions x_1 and x_2. After such an equation has been established, the individual activity coefficients can readily be calculated.

Gibbs energy, by definition, consists of two parts: one part is the enthalpy, which reflects the intermolecular forces between the molecules, which, in turn, are responsible for the heat effects that accompany the mixing process (enthalpy is, in a general sense, a measure of the heat content of a substance); and the other part is the entropy, which reflects the state of disorder (mixed-upness, or a measure of the random behaviour of particles) in the mixture. The excess Gibbs energy G^E is equal to the excess enthalpy H^E minus the excess entropy S^E times the absolute temperature T:

$$G^E = H^E - TS^E.$$

The word excess means in excess of that which would prevail if the solution were ideal. In the simplest case, both H^E and S^E are zero; in that case the solution is ideal and $\gamma_1 = \gamma_2 = 1$. In the general case, neither H^E nor S^E is zero, but two types of semi-ideal solutions can be designated: in the first, S^E is zero but H^E is not; this is called a regular solution. In the second, H^E is zero but S^E is not; this is called an athermal solution. An ideal solution is both regular and athermal.

Regular solutions. The word regular implies that the molecules mix in a completely random manner, which means that there is no segregation or preference; a given molecule chooses its neighbours with no regard for chemical identity (species 1 or 2). In a regular solution of composition x_1 and x_2, the probability that the neighbour of a given molecule is of species 1 is given by x_1, and the probability that it is of species 2 is given by x_2.

Two liquids form a solution that is approximately regular when the molecules of the two liquids do not differ appreciably in size and there are no strong orienting forces caused by dipoles or hydrogen bonding. In that event, the mixing process can be represented by the lattice model shown in Figure 4; the left half of the diagram

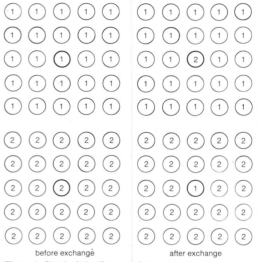

Figure 4: Physical significance of interchange energy. The energy absorbed in the process above is 2ω (see text).

shows pure liquids 1 and 2, and the right half shows the mixture obtained when the central molecule of liquid 1 is interchanged with the central molecule of liquid 2. Before interchange, the potential energy between central molecule 1 and one of its immediate neighbours is Γ_{11} and that between central molecule 2 and one of its immediate neighbours is Γ_{22}. After interchange, the potential energy between molecule 1 and one of its immediate neighbours is Γ_{12}, and that between molecule 2 and one of its immediate neighbours is also Γ_{12}. The change in energy that accompanies this mixing process is equal to twice the interchange energy (ω), which is equal to the potential energy after mixing less one-half the sum of the potential energies before mixing, the whole multiplied by the number of immediate neighbours, called the coordination number (z), surrounding the two shifted molecules:

$$\omega = z[\Gamma_{12} - \tfrac{1}{2}(\Gamma_{11} + \Gamma_{22})].$$

In the two-dimensional representation (Figure 4), z equals 4; but, in three dimensions, z varies between 6 and 12, depending on the lattice geometry. In this simple lattice model, the interchange process occurs without change of volume, and therefore, in this particular case, the excess enthalpy is the same as the energy change upon mixing. Assuming regular-solution behaviour (*i.e.*, $S^E = 0$), an equation may be derived relating Gibbs energy, Avogadro's number, interchange energy, and mole fractions. In principle, the interchange energy (ω) may be positive or negative, but, for simple molecules, for which only London forces of attraction are important, ω is positive. The equation obtained from the simple lattice model can be extended semi-empirically to apply to mixtures of molecules whose sizes are not nearly the same by using volume fractions, rather than mole fractions, to express the effect of composition and by introducing the concept of cohesive energy density, which is defined as the potential energy of a liquid divided by its volume. The adjective cohesive is well chosen because it correctly indi-

Deviations from Raoult's law

Types of semi-ideal solutions

cates that this energy is associated with the forces that keep the molecules close together in a condensed state. Again restricting attention to nonpolar molecules and again assuming a completely random mixture ($S^E = 0$), an equation may be derived that requires only pure-component properties to predict the excess Gibbs energy (and hence the activity coefficients) of binary mixtures. Because of many simplifying assumptions, this equation does not give consistently accurate results, but in many cases it provides good semiquantitative estimates. The form of the equation is such that the excess Gibbs energy is larger than zero; hence, the equation is not applicable to mixtures that have negative deviations from Raoult's law.

Athermal solutions. In a solution in which the molecules of one component are much larger than those of the other, the assumption that the solution is regular (*i.e.*, that $S^E = 0$) no longer provides a reasonable approximation even if the effect of intermolecular forces is neglected. A large flexible molecule (*e.g.*, a chain molecule such as polyethylene) can attain many more configurations when it is surrounded by small molecules than it can when surrounded by other large flexible molecules; the state of disorder in such a solution is therefore much larger than that of a regular solution in which $S^E = 0$. A solution of very large molecules (*i.e.*, polymers) in an ordinary liquid solvent is similar to a mixture of cooked spaghetti (the polymers) and tomato sauce. When there is a lot of sauce and little spaghetti, each piece of spaghetti is free to exist in many different shapes; this freedom, however, becomes restricted as the number of spaghetti pieces rises and the amount of sauce available for each strand declines. The excess entropy then is determined primarily by the freedom that the spaghetti has in the tomato sauce mixture relative to the freedom it has in the absence of sauce.

Regular solutions and athermal solutions represent limiting cases; real solutions are neither regular nor athermal. For real solutions it has been proposed to calculate G^E by combining the equations derived separately for regular solutions and for athermal solutions, but, in view of the restrictive and mutually inconsistent assumptions that were made in deriving these two equations, the proposal has met with only limited success.

Associated and solvated solutions. For those solutions in which there are strong intermolecular forces due to large dipole moments, hydrogen bonding, or complex formation, equations based on fundamental molecular theory cannot be applied, but it is frequently useful to apply a chemical treatment—*i.e.*, to describe the liquid mixture in terms of association and solvation, by assuming the existence of a variety of distinct chemical species in chemical equilibrium with one another. For example, there is much experimental evidence for association in acetic acid, in which most of the molecules dimerize; *i.e.*, two single acetic acid molecules, called monomers, combine to form a new molecule, called a dimer, through hydrogen bonding. When acetic acid is dissolved in a solvent such as benzene, the extent of dimerization of acetic acid depends on the temperature and on the total concentration of acetic acid in the solution. The escaping tendency (vapour pressure) of a monomer is much greater than that of a dimer, and it is thus possible to explain the variation of activity coefficient with composition for acetic acid in benzene; the activity coefficient of acetic acid in an excess of benzene is large because, under these conditions, acetic acid is primarily in the monomeric state, whereas pure acetic acid is almost completely dimerized. In the acetic acid–benzene system, association of acetic acid molecules produces positive deviations from Raoult's law.

Solvation When a solvent and a solute molecule link together with weak bonds, the process is called solvation. For example, in the system acetone–chloroform, a hydrogen bond is formed between the hydrogen atom in chloroform and the oxygen atom in acetone. In this case, hydrogen bonding depresses the escaping tendencies of both components, producing negative deviations from Raoult's law.

While hydrogen bonding is frequently encountered in solutions, there are many other examples of weak chemi-cal bond-formation between dissimilar molecules. The formation of such weak bonds is called complex formation—that is, formation of a new chemical species, called a complex, which is held together by weak forces that are chemical in nature rather than physical. Such complexes usually exist only in solution; because of their low stability, they cannot, in general, be isolated. The ability of different molecules to form complexes has a strong effect on solution behaviour. For example, the solubility of a sparingly soluble solute can be very much increased by complex formation: the solubility of silver chloride in water is extremely small since silver chloride dissociates only slightly to silver ion and chloride ion; however, when a small quantity of ammonia is added, solubility rises dramatically because of the reaction of six molecules of ammonia with one silver ion to form the complex ion $Ag(NH_3)_6{}^+$. By tying up silver ions and thereby forcing extensive dissociation of molecular silver chloride, the ammonia pulls silver chloride into aqueous solution.

In recent years there has been much interest in the use of computers to generate theoretical expressions for the activity coefficients of solutions. In many cases the calculations have been restricted to model systems, in particular to mixtures of hard-sphere (envisioned as billiard balls) molecules—*i.e.*, idealized molecules that have finite size but no forces of attraction. These calculations have produced a better understanding of the structure of simple liquid solutions since the manner in which nonpolar and non-hydrogen-bonding molecules arrange themselves in space is determined primarily by their size and shape and only secondarily by their attractive intermolecular forces. The results obtained for hard-sphere molecules can be extended to real molecules by applying corrections required for attractive forces and for the "softness" of the molecules—*i.e.*, the ability of molecules to interpenetrate (overlap) at high temperatures. While practical results are still severely limited and while the amount of required computer calculation is large even for simple binary systems, there is good reason to believe that advances in the theory of solution will increasingly depend on computerized, as opposed to analytical, models.

Solutions of electrolytes. Near the end of the 19th century, the properties of electrolyte solutions were investigated extensively by the early workers in physical chemistry. A suggestion of Svante August Arrhenius, a Swedish chemist, that salts of strong acids and bases (for example, sodium chloride) are completely dissociated into ions when in aqueous solution received strong support from electrical-conductivity measurements and from molecular-weight studies (freezing-point depression, boiling-point elevation, and osmotic pressure). These studies showed that the number of solute particles was larger than it would be if no dissociation occurred. For example, a 0.001 molal solution of a uni-univalent electrolyte (each ion has a valence, or charge, of 1, and, when dissociated, two ions are produced) such as sodium chloride, Na^+Cl^-, exhibits colligative properties (dependent only on the concentration) corresponding to a nonelectrolyte solution whose molality is 0.002; the colligative properties of a 0.001 molal solution of a univalent–divalent electrolyte (yielding three ions) such as magnesium bromide, $Mg^{2+}Br_2{}^-$, correspond to those of a nonelectrolyte solution with a molality of 0.003. At somewhat higher concentrations the experimental data showed some inconsistencies with Arrhenius' dissociation theory, and initially these were ascribed to incomplete, or partial, dissociation. In the years 1920–30, however, it was shown that these inconsistencies could be explained by electrostatic interactions (called Coulomb forces) of the ions in solution. The current view of electrolyte solutions is that, in water at normal temperatures, the salts of strong acids and strong bases are completely dissociated into ions at all concentrations up to the solubility limit. At high concentrations Coulombic interactions may cause the formation of ion pairs, which implies that the ions are not dispersed uniformly in the solution but have a tendency to form two-ion aggregates in which a positive ion seeks the close proximity of a negative ion and vice

Arrhenius' theory of salts

Current theory of salts

versa. While the theory of dilute electrolyte solutions is well advanced, no adequate theory exists for concentrated electrolyte solutions primarily because of the long-range Coulomb forces that dominate in ionic solutions.

The equilibrium properties of electrolyte solutions can be studied experimentally by electrochemical measurements, freezing point depressions, solubility determinations, osmotic pressures, or measurements of vapour pressure. Most electrolytes, such as salts, are nonvolatile at ordinary temperature, and, in that event, the vapour pressure exerted by the solution is the same as the partial pressure of the solvent. The activity coefficient of the solvent can, therefore, be found from total-pressure measurements, and, using the Gibbs-Duhem equation, it is then possible to calculate the activity coefficient of the electrolyte solute. This activity coefficient is designated by $\gamma_\pm$ to indicate that it is a mean activity coefficient for the positive and negative ions; since it is impossible to isolate positive ions and negative ions into separate containers, it is not possible to determine individual activity coefficients for the positive ions and for the negative ions. The mean activity coefficient $\gamma_\pm$ is so defined that it approaches a value of unity at very low molality where the ions are so far apart that they exert negligible influence on one another. For small concentrations of electrolyte, the theory of Peter Debye, a Dutch-born U.S. physical chemist, and Erick Hückel, a German chemist, relates $\gamma_\pm$ to the ionic strength, which is the sum of the products of the concentration of each ion (in moles per litre) and the square of its charge; the equation predicts that $\gamma_\pm$ decreases with rising ionic strength in agreement with experiment at very low ionic strength; at higher ionic strength, however, $\gamma_\pm$ rises, and in some cases $\gamma_\pm$ is greater than 1. The derivation of the Debye-Hückel theory clearly shows that it is limited to low concentrations. Many attempts have been made to extend the Debye-Hückel equation to higher electrolyte concentrations. One of the more successful attempts is based on the idea that the ions are solvated, which means that every ion is surrounded by a tight-fitting shell of solvent molecules.

The concept of solvation is often used to explain properties of aqueous solutions; one well-known property is the salting-out effect, in which the solubility of a nonelectrolyte in water is decreased when electrolyte is added. For example, the solubility of ethyl ether in water at 25° C (77° F) is 0.91 mole percent, but, in an aqueous solution containing 15 weight percent sodium chloride, it is only 0.13 mole percent. This decrease in solubility can be explained by postulating that some of the water molecules cannot participate in the dissolution of the ether because they are tightly held (solvated) by sodium and chloride ions.

Electrolyte solutions have long been of interest in industry since many common inorganic chemicals are directly obtained, or else separated, by crystallization from aqueous solution. Further, many important chemical and metallurgical products (*e.g.*, aluminum) are obtained or refined by electrochemical processes that occur in liquid solution. In recent years there has been renewed interest in electrolyte solutions because of their relevance to fuel cells as a possible source of power for automobiles.

Electro-lytes in physiology

The properties of electrolyte solutions also have large importance in physiology. Many molecules that occur in biological systems bear electric charges; a large molecule that has a positive electric charge at one end and a negative charge at the other is called a zwitterion. Very large molecules, such as those of proteins, may have numerous positive and negative charges; such molecules are called polyelectrolytes. In solution, the conformation (that is, the three-dimensional structure) of a large, charged molecule is strongly dependent on the ionic strength of the dissolving medium; for example, depending on the nature and concentration of salts present in the solvent, a polyelectrolyte molecule may coagulate into a ball, it may stretch out like a rod, or it may form a coil or helix. The conformation, in turn, is closely related to the molecule's physiological function. As a result, improved understanding of the properties of electrolyte solutions has direct consequences in molecular biology and medicine.

SOLUBILITY OF SOLIDS AND GASES

Since the dissolution of one substance in another can occur only if there is a decrease in the Gibbs energy, it follows that, generally speaking, gases and solids do not dissolve in liquids as readily as do other liquids. To understand this, the dissolution of a solid can be visualized as occurring in two steps: in the first, the pure solid is melted at constant temperature to a pure liquid, and, in the second, that liquid is dissolved at constant temperature in the solvent. Similarly, the dissolution of a gas can be divided at some fixed pressure into two parts, the first corresponding to constant-temperature condensation of the pure gas to a liquid and the second to constant-temperature mixing of that liquid with solvent. In many cases, the pure liquids (obtained by melting or by condensation) may be hypothetical (*i.e.*, unstable and, therefore, physically unobtainable), but usually their properties can be estimated by reasonable extrapolations. It is found that the change in Gibbs energy corresponding to the first step is positive and, hence, in opposition to the change needed for dissolution. For example, at −10° C (14° F), ice is more stable than water, and, at 110° C (230° F) and one atmosphere, steam is more stable than water. Therefore, the Gibbs energy of melting ice at −10° C is positive, and the Gibbs energy of condensing steam at one atmosphere and 110° C is also positive. For the second step, however, the change in Gibbs energy is negative; its magnitude depends on the equilibrium composition of the mixture. Because of the positive Gibbs energy change that accompanies the first step, there is a barrier that makes it more difficult to dissolve solids and gases as compared with liquids.

For gases at normal pressures, the positive Gibbs energy of condensation increases with rising temperature, but, for solids, the positive Gibbs energy of melting decreases with rising temperature. For example, the change in energy, ΔG, of condensing steam at one atmosphere is larger at 120° C (248° F) than it is at 110° C (230° F), while the change in energy of melting ice at −5° C (23° F) is smaller than it is at −10° C (14° F). Thus, as temperature rises, the barrier becomes larger for gases but lower for solids, and therefore, with few exceptions, the solubility of a solid rises while the solubility of a gas falls as the temperature is raised.

For solids, the positive Gibbs energy "barrier" depends on the melting temperature. If the melting temperature is much higher than the temperature of the solution, the barrier is large, shrinking to zero when the melting temperature and solution temperature become identical.

Table 1 gives the solubilities of some common gases,

Table 1: Solubilities of Some Gases*
(mole percent)

	heptane	benzene	water
Hydrogen	0.069	0.026	0.0015
Nitrogen	0.12	0.45	0.0012
Methane	0.47	0.21	0.0024
Carbon dioxide	0.77	0.97	0.0608

*At one atmosphere partial pressure, 25° C.

and Table 2 the solubility of (solid) naphthalene in a few typical solvents. These solubilities illustrate the qualitative rule that "like dissolves like"; thus naphthalene, an aromatic hydrocarbon, dissolves more readily in another aromatic hydrocarbon such as benzene than it does in a chlorinated solvent such as carbon tetrachloride or in a hydrogen-bonded solvent such as methyl alcohol. By similar reasoning, the gas methane, a paraffinic hydrocarbon, dissolves more readily in another paraffin such as hexane than it does in water. In all three solvents, the gas hydrogen (which boils at −252.5° C, or −422.5° F) is less soluble than nitrogen (which boils at a higher temperature, −195.8° C, or −320.4° F).

While exceptions may occur at very high pressures, the solubility of a gas in a liquid generally rises as the pressure of that gas increases. When the pressure of the gas is much larger than the vapour pressure of the solvent, the

Table 2: Solubility of Naphthalene in Various Solvents*	
solvent	mole percent naphthalene
Benzene	24.1
Carbon tetrachloride	20.5
Hexane	9.0
Methyl alcohol	1.8
Water	0.0004
*At 20° C.	

solubility is often proportional to the pressure; this proportionality is consistent with Henry's law, which states that, if the gas phase is ideal, the solubility x_2 of gas 2 in solvent 1 is equal to the partial pressure (the vapour-phase mole fraction y_2 times the total pressure P—i.e., y_2P) divided by a temperature-dependent constant, $H_{2,1}$ (called Henry's constant), which is determined to a large extent by the intermolecular forces between solute 2 and solvent 1; then

$$x_2 = \frac{y_2P}{H_{2,1}}.$$

When the vapour pressure of solvent 1 is small compared with the total pressure, then the vapour-phase mole fraction of gas 2 is approximately one, and the solubility of the gas is proportional to the total pressure.

BIBLIOGRAPHY. An introductory but quantitative discussion of liquid solutions is given by A.G. WILLIAMSON in *An Introduction to Non-Electrolyte Solutions* (1967); and E.A. MOELWYN-HUGHES in *States of Matter* (1961). A comprehensive view is presented by J.H. HILDEBRAND and R.L. SCOTT in *Solubility of Non-Electrolytes*, 3rd ed. (1950); more recent work is reviewed in J.H. HILDEBRAND, J.M. PRAUSNITZ, and R.L. SCOTT, *Regular and Related Solutions* (1970). An advanced study of solutions of non-electrolytes J.S. ROWLINSON, *Liquids and Liquid Mixtures*, 2nd ed. (1969); and I. PRIGOGINE, *Molecular Theory of Solutions* (1957). Hildebrand's books tend to stress phenomena while those of Rowlinson and Prigogine emphasize solution theory based on statistical mechanics. The more practical engineering aspects of solutions are presented by J.M. PRAUSNITZ in *Molecular Thermodynamics of Fluid-Phase Equilibria* (1969); and by M.B. KING in *Phase Equilibrium in Mixtures* (1969). A thorough discussion of solutions of electrolytes is R.A. ROBINSON and R.H. STOKES, *Electrolyte Solutions*, 2nd ed. (1959, reprinted 1965); the properties of solutions of large molecules (polymers) are discussed by H. TOMPA in *Polymer Solutions* (1956); and by H. MORAWETZ in *Macromolecules in Solution* (1965).

(J.M.P.)

Somalia

The Somali Democratic Republic, popularly known as Somalia, a state in northeast Africa stretching from the Equator to the Red Sea, occupies most of the Horn of Africa, the most easterly projection of the continent. With an area of about 246,000 square miles (637,500 square kilometres), it is bounded on the north by the Gulf of Aden and on the east by the Indian Ocean; from its southern point, its western border is bounded by Kenya and Ethiopia and, to the northwest, by the French-administered Territory of the Afars and Issas (formerly French Somaliland). The capital is Mogadiscio (Mogadishu). Somalia was known to the early Egyptians as the Land of Punt.

Living in a hot climate and on an unforgiving terrain, much of which is desert, the Somali inhabitants of the country, numbering almost 2,900,000, the majority of whom are nomadic, are Muslim by religion and fiercely independent by nature. Due to the existence of Somali communities in Kenya, Ethiopia, and the French Territory of the Afars and Issas (the Issas being Somalis) and the nomadic way of life that is virtually a national characteristic, most of the western boundary of the country is in dispute. When, on July 1, 1960, the former British Somaliland Protectorate joined with the former Italian-administered United Nations Trust Territory of Somalia to form the independent Somali Republic, efforts to reach international agreement on the bound-

aries of the new state were unsuccessful. The disputed frontier, particularly that shared with Ethiopia, and the need for economic development constitute the two most important problems facing Somalia today.

Somalia's geopolitical position is one of strategic significance, potentially affecting developments of the African hinterland, the Gulf of Aden, the Arabian Peninsula, and the Indian Ocean. Somalia receives budgetary assistance from Italy and has also received aid from the Soviet Union, which has modernized the port of Berbera on the Gulf of Aden, and from the United States, which has financed the building of a new port at Kismayu (Chisimaio) near the Equator. For coverage of historical aspects, see EAST AFRICA, HISTORY OF.

Importance of its geopolitical position

THE LANDSCAPE

In the north and northeast, some of the land is mountainous, but most of the remainder of the country is a flat, low plateau. In the south, there are two permanent rivers, the Giuba (Juba) and the Shebelle, both originating in the highlands of Ethiopia.

In the north, extending along the whole coastal area, is a barren coastal plain called the Guban ("burned"), characterized by hot, humid weather, low rainfall, and sparse vegetation. Inland, this gives way to maritime ranges forming the Ogo Highlands. To the west this begins with the Golis Range, which rises in the Eritrean Highland and continues intermittently up to the end of Migiurtinia (Mijurtein), which forms the tip of the Horn of Africa. Along this range occur the highest altitudes in the country, the Surud Ad, near Erigavo, reaching a height of 7,900 feet (2,408 metres). To the south the mountains give way to the Haud Plateau and to the Nogal (Nugal) Valley. The Haud Plateau is flat land with soil containing gypsum. It has slightly more rainfall than the Guban and is cooler and drier. In recent years, the lack of adequate rain has been overcome by the construction of *barkado*, or artificial water reservoirs, throughout the Haud area to supply the needs of the people and their livestock. The Nogal Valley, running from northwest to southeast, is a low depression that, despite the sparse rainfall, is relatively well watered. Its name means "the fertile land," as it was once noted for fertility. In recent years, however, erosion has wrought so much havoc that it is rapidly losing its rich soil and thick vegetation. The extreme south of the country consists mainly of flat plains; there are no mountains, and the highest altitudes are no more than 300 to 400 feet. Because of the two rivers and better rainfall, the southern plains are generally less arid.

Climate. Somalia extends from about latitude 2° S to 12° N, and so lies within the tropical and subtropical zones. The climate is monotonously uniform throughout the year, although slight changes occur at altitudes of 5,000 feet and above at certain times of year. Borama, Hargeisa, Sheikh, and Erigavo usually experience somewhat cooler and more pleasant temperatures from October to February. At Sheikh and Erigavo, temperatures sometimes drop to the freezing point, and frost appears on the ground. The coastal areas, on the other hand, experience weather that is hotter, more humid, and enervating; in such places as Berbera and Bosaso, temperatures rise as high as 108° F (42° C) from June to September. In the south, the weather is generally more uniform, being hot and humid in the coastal areas and hot and dry in the hinterland. Rainfall is usually higher in the south, varying from 13 inches to 20 inches a year. The Ogo Highlands in the north also receive as much as 20 inches a year, especially in the west.

The year is divided into several distinct seasons. There are two rainy seasons, each of which is followed by a dry season. The first rainy season, which generally lasts from March to June, is called *gu*; the second, which usually begins in September and ends in about December, is called *dayr*. Seasonal changes are not, however, entirely regular. Sometimes the rain fails to come when expected, and the much dreaded drought occurs, destroying plants and animals and impoverishing the land.

Climatic seasons

Vegetation and animal life. Vegetation consists primarily of shrub bush and grass. In some areas—for example, in some parts of Migiurtinia—the land is practically denuded of trees. In most parts of the country, however, plants and grass are plentiful, and in the Haud and the extreme south vegetation is thick. The shrubs, which have adapted to the harsh environment, with its low rainfall and hot sun, are nutritious, sustaining the country's abundant livestock as well as its wild animals. Erosion and overgrazing in recent times, however, have damaged the fertility of the land, and conservation measures are now required. The most useful economic vegetation consists of dosok (a species of box tree); galol (a species of acacia, of which the roots are used as a framework for huts, the bark is used for making ropes and mats, the ripe fruit is eaten, and the leaves are fed to livestock); and the *Boswellia*, which produce frankincense, and other gum trees. In higher regions of the Ogo Highlands—for example, on Surud Ad Mountain, near Erigavo—small forests grow. At present the greatest single resource of the country consists of its livestock, chiefly cattle, camels, sheep, and goats. There are also many wild animals, such as lions, elephants, hyenas, foxes, leopards (the skin of the Somali leopard is the most valuable on the world market), and hippopotamuses, such game as giraffes, zebras, antelope, and many species of birds. The Basso Giuba (Lower Juba) Region is the most abundant in wild animals and game.

Traditional regions. Somalia is perhaps the most homogeneous of the nations of Africa. The country may, nevertheless, be divided into several traditional regions, although these cannot be sharply delineated. These are the following.

The Northern Region. This consists of the former British Somaliland Protectorate and the districts of Mudugh and Migiurtinia. Nomadic habits and customs predominate here, although seafarers and fishermen live in the coastal towns, while agriculture is also pursued in some parts of the west. The character of the nomadic people is martial, individualistic, egalitarian, and inimical to authority.

Benadir, including Hiran. The Benadir Region, extending for almost 400 miles (650 kilometres) along the coast, and the Hiran Region inland together comprise most of the Shebelle River Valley. These regions have a wide diversity in habits and customs. While agriculture remains the mainstay of the regional economy, the region is the most developed in the country, because Mogadiscio, the capital, is located in it.

Alto Giuba (Upper Juba). In this southern region, traversed by the Giuba River, the Somali dialect spoken differs from the standard Somali to such an extent that other Somalis rarely understand it at first. Dry farming (tilling the soil so as to conserve moisture and using

---

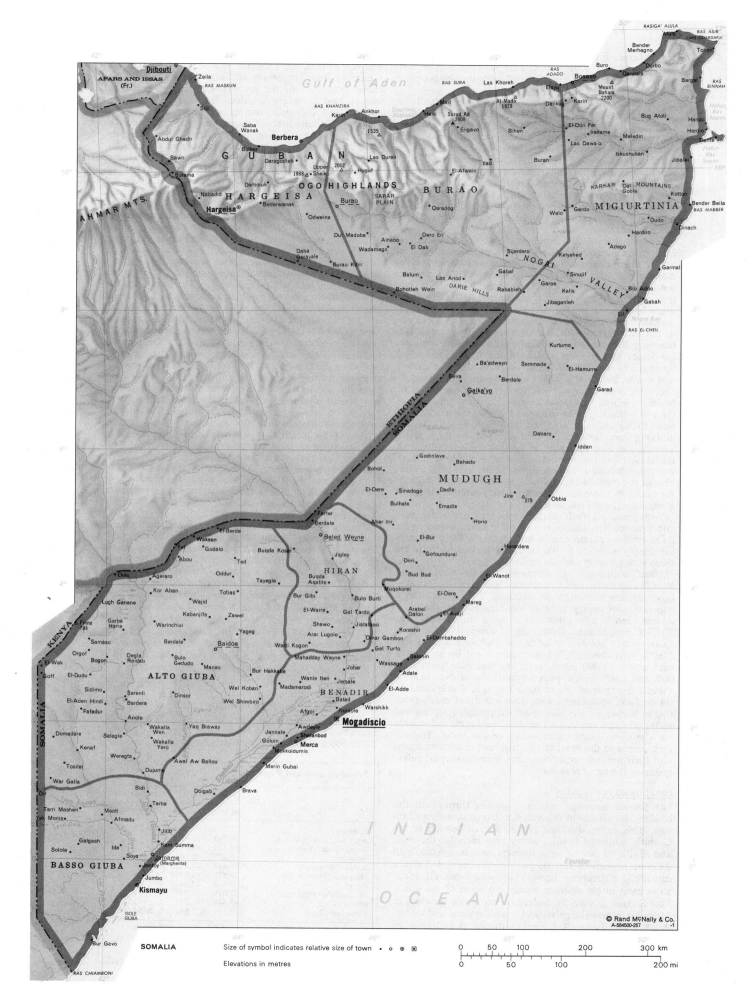

SOMALIA

Size of symbol indicates relative size of town • ○ ⊙ ▣

Elevations in metres

0   50   100   200   300 km

0   50   100   200 mi

© Rand McNally & Co.
A-584500-257   -1

drought-resistant crops) is pursued, and the region is particularly rich in livestock. The people are generally placid, but tend to be suspicious of intrusions by Somalis from other regions.

Basso Giuba (*Lower Juba*). This region is potentially the richest region of the land. In the districts of Gelib and Giamama, the inhabitants are settled farmers. The potential, consisting of the fertile, arable land and the availability of the water of the Giuba River, still remains relatively untapped. Livestock raising is the most vital economic activity pursued in the districts of Kismayu and Afmedou. In Kismayu, the largest meat-packing factory in the country has been established. Kismayu is also the name of a coastal town possessing a recently built modern port, which facilitates the export of bananas, livestock, and canned meat.

Modes of life. In the country as a whole, as mentioned earlier, the nomadic mode of living predominates. The coastal towns once maintained contacts with ancient civilizations, but there were hardly any towns in the interior until the beginning of the 20th century. Nomadism consists essentially of a restless movement of people from place to place in search of water and grazing for their animals. This movement is governed by the incidence of the rainy seasons. A characteristic of the nomad is a tendency to engage in feuds that arise from competition for water and grazing lands. In the hinterland, tribal fighting and the theft of livestock, particularly of camels and cattle, frequently occurred. Feuding has been reduced by three factors. These are (1) the construction of *barkado*, which make water available for payment; (2) the more effective enforcement of law by the authorities; and (3) the growing spirit of nationalism, which acts as a unifying force among the nomadic peoples themselves. Villages are also springing up around the *barkado*, with the result that the nomads are now entering a money economy, selling livestock, hides, skins, and ghee in exchange for manufactured goods. In the Northern Region, for example, nomads now use transistor radios to listen to Somali-language broadcasts.

Cultivators, for their part, live in settled communities and practice agriculture, mostly of the subsistence type, using traditional implements and methods. These farmers are deeply attached to the land, but it does not provide them with an adequate standard of living.

Urban settlement has increased rapidly since World War II and is expected to continue. The cities of Somalia, however, are not large. Mogadiscio, the capital, had a population of nearly 173,000 inhabitants as of the 1967 estimate but is now estimated to have from 250,000 to 300,000 inhabitants. Other major towns include Hargeisa, with a population of about 50,000; Kismayu and Merca, with about 18,000 each; Burao and Berbera, each with about 12,000 inhabitants; Baidoa, with about 15,000; and Belet-Weine, with a population of over 11,000.

While the style of life in these towns is westernized on the surface, social behaviour does not differ much from that in Somali society elsewhere. Language, religion, and social customs are so similar that observable differences are viewed as slight modifications of the norm. The nomad comes to the town frequently, and many townsmen visit their nomadic relatives in the hinterland, particularly during the rainy seasons.

PEOPLE AND POPULATION

The Somali language, which is spoken throughout the country, forms one of the nation's strongest unifying factors. Rich, expressive, and poetic, Somali belongs to the Cushitic language family, which also includes the Afar and Galla. It has several dialects and is spoken with different accents in various parts of the country. Despite superficial differences, however, standard Somali dominates most of the country, except for parts of the south. This Somali is used by Somalia's two radio stations, in Mogadiscio and Hargeisa, and is also spoken and understood in the French Territory of the Afars and Issas, in the Somali-inhabited part of Ethiopia (referred to as Western Somalia by the Somalis), and in Wajir (Northern Frontier) District of Kenya, where there is also a

The nomadic way of life (margin)

The Somali language (margin)

Somali community. Since, prior to 1973, the language was not written, the adoption of a script for Somali was a burning issue for nearly 20 years, and one of the declared objectives of the revolution proclaimed in 1969 was to find a speedy solution to the problem. Latin, Arabic, and Osmanian scripts were all suggested. Osmanian is a Somali script, named after its inventor, Osman Yusuf Kenadid, who, early in the 20th century, devised an alphabetic system for representing the peculiar sounds of the Somali language. In January 1973, a Latin script for the Somali language was adopted, and simultaneously made the sole official language. In the absence of a written Somali language, three foreign tongues, Arabic, English, and Italian, had been used as official languages. Arabic was the language of instruction in primary schools; English was used at higher levels.

Ethnically, the Somali are a Cushitic people, being closely related to the Gallas and the Afars. The typical Somali is tall and slender, with a long, oval face, a straight nose, and delicate features, and with a skin colour varying from jet black to light brown. The Somalis subdivide themselves into several major tribes, each of which traces its genealogical line to a single father. These tribes are the Ishaak, the Hawiya, the West Somali (Dir), the Geri (Darod), the Sab (Dighil), and the Mijurtein (Mirifle). Numerous subtribes branch off from these groups until, at its ultimate level, social organization is represented by the family unit. Because language, customs, and physical features remain so similar, tribalism does not have the connotation it often does elsewhere in Africa, nor does it represent a disintegrative force in the nation. Basically a homogeneous people, the Somalis had achieved nationhood long before the arrival of Europeans in Africa. Tribalism today is slowly being superseded by the growth of nationalism. Several small but distinct minorities nevertheless exist in Somalia, such as the riverine Bantus, who live along the banks of the Shebelle and Giuba rivers; the Bajun of Kismayu; the Brava town dwellers, who claim descent from Portuguese settlers; and some of the Rer Hamar and Merca people, who are of Arab if not of Persian origin.

Islām is the official religion of the Somali nation, and the vast majority of the people profess the Islāmic faith. There are extremely few Christian Somalis. Islām in Somalia is primarily of the strict Shāfi'ī rite of the Sunni denomination. Şūfism also exists in the country in several forms. The two largest Şūfī orders are the Şaliḥiyah order, named after its founder, Shaykh Muḥammad Şaliḥ of Mecca, which has a large following in the north, and the Qādirīyah order, also named after its founder, Shaykh 'Abd, al-Qādir al-Jīlānī of Baghdad, which has many adherents in the south. The veil for women is a foreign importation, and those who wear it are largely of Arab or Indo-Pakistan origin. Animism is virtually nonexistent, although superstitious beliefs in demons and witchcraft sometimes still persist.

Religious groups (margin)

Due to the absence of an adequate census, reliable information about the demographic situation in Somalia is not available. The population is estimated to number between 2,500,000 and 3,000,000, and the annual rate of growth is

Somalia, Area and Population*			
	area		population
	sq mi	sq km	1971 estimate
Regions			
Alto Giuba (Upper Juba)	50,769	131,492	...
Basso Giuba (Lower Juba)	19,273	49,917	...
Benadir	17,376	45,004	...
Burro (Northeast)	49,421	128,000†	...
Hargeisa (Northwest)	18,533	48,000†	...
Hiran	9,902	25,647	...
Migiurtinia (Mijurtein)	35,036	90,744	...
Mudugh	45,844	118,737	...
Total Somalia	246,154	637,541	2,864,000

*Last census in the Italian Trusteeship Territory of Somalia was taken in 1953. No census was ever taken in British Somaliland.   †Approximate.
Source: Official government figures; UN.

said to be about 2 percent. Immigration and emigration are negligible. Because of growing urbanization, the settlement of some nomads, and the improved medical services in the towns, a higher rate of population growth is anticipated.

THE NATIONAL ECONOMY

Somalia is an underdeveloped country. Its economy is based upon livestock and agriculture, which are dominated by traditional modes of production. Industrialization is not yet even a dream, since trained manpower, easily available raw materials, and a cheap source of power are all lacking. Average per-capita income is among the lowest in the world, amounting to about $50 or $60 U.S. a year. Despite this situation, a potential for economic growth exists. While no complete evaluation of the country's mineral resources has been undertaken, mineral reserves of iron ore, gypsum and other minerals, and uranium ore, have been located.

Mineral resources. In the Alto Giuba region, iron ore deposits with an iron content of 40 percent are estimated at about 300,000,000 tons. Reserves at Dagareh are estimated at 40,000,000 tons, while those at el-Garas are in the vicinity of 30,000,000 tons. Altogether, iron ore deposits are estimated to total about 440,000,000 tons. Gypsum sepiolite (a clay mineral) and manganese also have been discovered. It is upon uranium, however, that the country has pinned its hopes for rapid economic growth. Prospecting has revealed that about 250,000 tons of exploitable ore are deposited in the Bur Hacaba area in the Upper Juba region. A United Nations Development Programme project operating in the Mudugh Region has also reported the existence of uranium there, but no estimates have yet been made. Exploration for oil has been proceeding for many years but so far without success.

Livestock: the economic mainstay

Raising livestock is at present the principal economic activity of the country. Estimates of the animal wealth of Somalia range from 12,000,000 to 15,000,000 head, composed of sheep, goats, cattle, and camels. The economic importance of stock raising is evident from the fact that about 75 percent of the people make their living from it, while, at the same time, livestock is the chief export commodity and the principal earner of foreign exchange. Sheep, cattle, and camels are exported to Arab lands, especially to Egypt, Saudi Arabia, and Yemen (Aden). The livestock in Somalia are relatively free from serious diseases, so that the two perennial problems of animal husbandry remain the availability of water and of grazing. A serious program of *barkado* construction in all parts of the country is helping to remedy the water shortage, but grazing is being badly damaged by erosion, as well as by overgrazing in certain areas.

Agriculture, the second most important economic activity, suffers from an extremely low productivity, owing to the use of traditional methods. Arable land is nevertheless, plentiful. Of an estimated 20,000,000 acres (8,000,000 hectares) of arable land, only about 1,000,000 acres (400,000 hectares) are now under cultivation. Sugarcane and bananas are the two principal crops. Sugarcane is produced solely for domestic consumption, but bananas are the second most important export commodity. Other agricultural products are maize, sorghum, cotton, groundnuts (peanuts), and sesame oil.

Power supplies are scarce; electricity is generated by diesel engines for limited domestic and industrial use. Only the major towns have power stations, and rural settlements are practically without light or electricity.

Trade and finance. Livestock and agriculture represent the largest source of revenue. Animals, animal products, and agricultural crops constitute about 80 percent of the national income. Manufacturing is embryonic. Apart from the sugar factory at Giohar, the various small factories are no more than fledgling enterprises struggling to survive. The two principal banks, which were recently nationalized, are the Somali National Bank, which carries out central-banking and commercial-banking functions, and the Somali Development Bank, which provides loans for development projects. Foreign trade yields

much of the national income; exports earn foreign exchange, while import duties form the largest source of government revenue.

The budget suffers from chronic deficit that, although progressively decreasing, still presents financial problems. In 1963, the deficit was more than 50,000,000 Somali shillings (So. sh.), while by 1970 it had dropped to less than 14,000,000 So. sh. (The So. sh., which is the official unit of currency, is divided into 100 centesimis; 7.14 So. sh. = $1 U.S., and 17.14 So. sh. = £1 sterling in 1971.) The deficit has hitherto always been met by the financial aid from the Italian government. Tax revenues are obtained from import duties (which amount to over half of the total), export duties, administrative taxes, production and consumption taxes, and taxes on income and property. The economic policy of the revolutionary government that came to power in 1969 is to reduce government expenditures and to increase revenue through investment in productive public enterprises.

TRANSPORT

Port improvements

There is no railroad in the country. Good asphalted roads are scarce, amounting to only about 600 miles (900 kilometres) out of 8,000 miles (14,000 kilometres) of roads. Large trucks are used for the transport of goods, materials, and people to distant areas. Minibuses operate where good roads are available, particularly in the Afgoi, Merca, Giohar, and Baidoa areas. Sea transport is used for overseas trade. Mogadiscio, Kismayu, Berbera, and Merca are the major ports. Kismayu is a modern port built recently with U.S. financing, while the port of Berbera has been vastly improved with Soviet assistance. The improvement of facilities at the port of Mogadiscio with a financial loan from the World Bank is also planned. From many smaller ports, dhows move people and goods from one part of the coast to another. Air transport is increasing; Somali Airlines has weekly flights to all major towns, particularly regional capitals such as Hargeisa (the second largest city), Kismayu, Burao, Galcaio, Bosaso, and Candala. Mogadiscio has an international airport, from which Alitalia flights leave for Rome and Egypt; East African Airways flies to East Africa; and Aeroflot flies to the Soviet Union. Somali Airlines has weekly flights to Aden, Djibouti, Nairobi, and Dar es Salaam.

ADMINISTRATION AND SOCIAL CONDITIONS

After nine years of parliamentary rule, a revolution occurred October 21, 1969, resulting in the accession to power of a military government. The administrative system has two organs. The first is the Supreme Revolutionary Council, presided over by Major General Mohammed Siad Barre, the former commander of the national army. It has 23 members, all of whom are military officers. The functions of this body are (1) to enact laws for the country; (2) to appoint secretaries of state; and (3) to approve the laws, decisions, and appointments made by the second organ, the Council of Secretaries. Some members of the Supreme Revolutionary Council also are secretaries of state and, therefore, have membership in both councils. The functions of the second organ, the Council of Secretaries, are (1) to prepare draft laws for the approval of the Supreme Revolutionary Council; (2) to make appointments to senior administrative posts, subject to the approval of the Supreme Revolutionary Council; and (3) to run the ministries. There are 8 regional revolutionary councils and over 40 district revolutionary councils, all charged with the responsibility of executing the laws, decisions, and policies of the Supreme Revolutionary Council. These administrative bodies also are entrusted with the task of generating development through self-help schemes. Each region has a governor, who is chairman of the regional revolutionary council and who is appointed by the Supreme Revolutionary Council.

Justice. The Supreme Revolutionary Council also is responsible for the administration of justice, having assumed the powers and functions of the former Higher Judicial Council, which regulated the appointments, promotions, transfers, and disciplinary proceedings of the judiciary. The Supreme Revolutionary Council has created a new court, the National Security Court, which has jurisdiction over such crimes as treason, embezzlement of public funds, and antirevolutionary activities. Apart from these changes, the judiciary remains intact. At the lower level, there are district courts, above which there are regional courts, above which there are regional courts of appeal. At the apex of the judicial system is the Supreme Court. The legal system in use is a mixture of the Italian and British systems of law, modified by local factors. Islāmic law is also applied, particularly in civil cases.

Education. Education is little developed. Traditionally, Somali education consisted primarily of the teaching of the holy Qur'ān and of other aspects of the Islāmic religion. In the earlier colonial period, the Somalis vehemently resisted the introduction of Western education, fearing that it might be used to convert the Somali people to Christianity. Only after World War II did the Somalis permit the colonial powers to open modern schools. Since then, the educational system has been expanding slowly, while the demand for education has increased beyond the capacity of the state to satisfy it. The student population in all schools is about 60,000, out of which more than 40,000 are in government schools and the remainder in private schools. Schooling is divided into the elementary, intermediate, and secondary stages, each of which lasts for four years. University education does not yet exist in Somalia, although there is a National University (formerly the University Institute of Somalia) which is planning to expand its academic program in order to enable it, following the Italian pattern, to award a doctoral degree after the successful completion of four years of study. Most Somalis, however, still go abroad for higher education. In the academic year 1969–70, Somali students abroad numbered about 1,300, following courses in the Soviet Union, Italy, Egypt, West Germany, the United States, and elsewhere. The illiteracy rate in the country is probably about 85 percent. As, until 1973, Somali was unwritten, instruction in the schools has been in Arabic, English, and Italian. The educational system is beset by a lack of textbooks, qualified teachers, instructional materials, and classrooms.

Health. The health service in Somalia is insufficient. Hospitals exist only in major towns and, even when available, do not have the capacity to provide efficient medical service. Small towns and villages have only dispensaries. Doctors are few, specialists fewer, medical supplies scarce, instruments and techniques out of date, and nurses and laboratory technicians virtually unavailable.

Social conditions. Social conditions are poor. Wages and salaries are virtually at the subsistence level. There is an acute housing shortage in the towns, rents are high, and the cost of living has been rising faster than incomes. The Supreme Revolutionary Council has sought to combat these conditions by reducing salaries and wages as well as house rents.

CULTURAL LIFE AND INSTITUTIONS

Cultural activities consist primarily of poetry, folk dancing, the performance of plays, and singing. Somalis love poetry and accord recognition to poetic merit. The principal Somali poetic themes are war, peace, women, horses, and camels. Poetry recitals form a popular pastime. Folk

(margin note) Lack of higher education facilities

dancing is a popular art. The theatre, introduced only in 1950, is increasingly popular. Several theatre groups are in existence and tour the country regularly, performing plays with nationalistic or social themes or satires on contemporary politics, manners, and morals. The two principal cultural institutions in the country are the Garesa Museum and the National Theatre.

Because the Somali language was unwritten, the press in Somalia has been printed in Arabic, Italian, or English—a circumstance which restricts readership to a small, educated elite. The newspapers include the *October Star*, published daily in Arabic and Italian; the *Dawn*, which appears weekly in English; and the *New Era*, published periodically as occasion demands. All newspapers are government owned, and the publication of private newspapers is forbidden. Radio Mogadiscio and Radio Somali in Hargeisa broadcast daily in the Somali language. Broadcasts to the outside world are made in English, Arabic, Amharic, Swahili, and Italian. Daily Somali broadcasts also are made by several foreign stations, including the BBC, Moscow, Rome, Addis Ababa, and Cairo.

CONCLUSION

Stagnation, rather than development, is the present characteristic of the Somali economy. After a decade of independence, every major national enterprise—in finance, education, health, or development—presents serious problems. The attainment of a faster pace of economic development is a vital national objective. To achieve this, the first necessity is to build an administrative machinery capable of planning and implementing development programs. The second necessity is to utilize available resources to reach developmental goals, instead of squandering them on uneconomic but prestigious projects. The third necessity is to mobilize and harness the energies of the people themselves to forward development.

BIBLIOGRAPHY. B.W. ANDRZEJEWSKI and I.M. LEWIS (comps.), *Somali Poetry: An Introduction* (1964), a translation of representative samples of classical Somali poetry by two British scholars; L.W. DOOB, *Resolving Conflict in Africa* (1970), a report on the territorial dispute in the Horn of Africa by a social psychologist, containing representative Somali, Ethiopian, and Kenyan views; J.A. HUNT, *A General Survey of the Somaliland Protectorate, 1944–1950* (1951), a standard work containing geological and climatic information on the northern regions (formerly British Somaliland); U.S. INTERNATIONAL COOPERATION ADMINISTRATION, *Inter-River Economic Exploration: The Somali Republic* (1961), data on the agricultural potential of the inter-river area; I.M. LEWIS, *A Pastoral Democracy* (1961), an anthropological investigation into the Somali way of life, particularly in its nomadic form, *The Modern History of Somaliland, From Nation to State* (1965), a discussion of the rise and formation of the modern Somali state, from the advent of colonial rule to independence; SOMALI DEVELOPMENT BANK, *Information About Somalia: The Bank and Investment Opportunities* (1969), a guide for the visitor and for the potential investor; SOMALIA MINISTRY OF FOREIGN AFFAIRS, *The Somali Republic and the Organization of African Unity* (n.d.), a booklet presenting the view of the Somali government on territorial disputes with neighbouring states; UNITED NATIONS DEVELOPMENT PROGRAMME, FAO, *Agricultural and Water Survey: Somalia*, vol. 6, *Social and Economic Aspects of Development* (1968), a report on the sociological considerations affecting the developmental agriculture.

(H.A.Mi.)